D1830257

A

DICTIONARY,

PERSIAN, ARABIC, AND ENGLISH

Owing to the antiquity and rarity of this book, certain pages are regrettably absent, and readability is compromised due to the blurring of the original text. If you possess any insights regarding the availability of these missing sections, kindly inform us. Your assistance is crucial in ensuring the completion of this significant work for the benefit of future generations.

A

DICTIONARY,

PERSIAN, ARABIC, AND ENGLISH.

BY

FRANCIS JOHNSON.

GYAN

Published by

Gyan Publishing House
5, Ansari Road
Daryaganj, New Delhi-110002
Phone: 011-47034999, 9811692060
E-mail: books@gyanbooks.com

Distribution Network
gyanbooks.com
India, USA, Canada, UK, Australia

© Publisher

All rights reserved. No part of this work may be reproduced, stored, adapted, or transmitted in any form or by any means, electronic, mechanical, photocopying, micro-filming, recording or otherwise, or translated in any language, without the prior written permission of the copyright owner and the publisher.

ISBN: 978-81-212-0716-4 (HB)
First Published, 1852

2nd Impression 2024

Printed at: Gyan Press, Delhi.

The book is sold subject to the condition that it shall not, by way of trade or otherwise, be lent, resold, hired out, or otherwise circulated without the prior publisher's written consent.

A DICTIONARY, PERSIAN, ARABIC, AND ENGLISH
Author: FRANCIS JOHNSON

DICTIONARY,

PERSIAN, ARABIC, AND ENGLISH.

BY

FRANCIS JOHNSON.

PUBLISHED UNDER THE PATRONAGE

OF THE

HONOURABLE EAST-INDIA COMPANY.

LONDON:

Wm. H. ALLEN AND CO.,

7, LEADENHALL-STREET.

1852.

TO

SIR JAMES WEIR HOGG, BART., M.P., *Chairman*,

RUSSELL ELLICE, ESQ. *Deputy Chairman*,

WILLIAM WIGRAM, ESQ.,
SIR ROBERT CAMPBELL, BART.,
JOHN LOCH, ESQ.,
CHARLES MILLS, ESQ.,
JOHN MASTERMAN, ESQ., M.P.,
JOHN PETTY MUSPRATT, ESQ.,
LIEUT.-GEN. SIR JAMES L. LUSHINGTON, G.C.B.,
HENRY SHANK, ESQ.,
SIR RICHARD JENKINS, G.C.B.,
JOHN COTTON, ESQ.,
WILLIAM BUTTERWORTH BAYLEY, ESQ.,
SIR HENRY WILLOCK, K.L.S.,
MARTIN TUCKER SMITH, ESQ., M.P.,
LIEUT.-COL. WILLIAM HENRY SYKES,
W. H. CHICHELEY PLOWDEN, ESQ., M.P.,
ELLIOT MACNAGHTEN, ESQ.,
JOHN CLARMONT WHITEMAN, ESQ.,
ROSS DONNELLY MANGLES, ESQ., M.P.,
WILLIAM JOSEPH EASTWICK, ESQ.,
WILLIAM DENT, ESQ.,
MAJOR JOHN ARTHUR MOORE,
JOHN HARVEY ASTELL, ESQ.,

DIRECTORS

FOR

MANAGING THE AFFAIRS

OF THE

HONOURABLE EAST-INDIA COMPANY,

THIS DICTIONARY

IS,

WITH MUCH RESPECT,

DEDICATED,

BY THEIR VERY OBEDIENT SERVANT,

FRANCIS JOHNSON.

PREFACE.

The acknowledged usefulness of the Dictionary to which prescription has inappropriately assigned the title of RICHARDSON's Persian, Arabic, and English Dictionary, and the probability that at no very distant period a reprint of it would be required, induced the editor of the last edition, shortly after it had issued from the press, to commence a careful revision of the work, in order to supply such deficiencies as might still be detected. The period he looked forward to has arrived: the exhaustion of the edition has been simultaneous with the completion of his labours; and he now responds to the call for a new edition, or, to speak more accurately, for a new Dictionary, by the present publication.

The Dictionary of RICHARDSON, as published in 1777, however well suited to the style and wants of that day, was open to obvious objections. It was inconvenient in size, being printed in folio, with an ungraceful oriental type, and it was very defective in its stock and choice of words. It was little else than an abridgement of the Oriental Thesaurus of MENINSKI, printed in four folio volumes at Vienna in 1680, effected by omitting the Turkish words incorporated in that collection, and by putting together words of similar sound, but of different significations, and sometimes of different etymology, which the original had more consistently kept distinct. RICHARDSON made some additions to his text, chiefly from the lexicons of GOLIUS and CASTELLUS. He also published in a second volume a reversed dictionary, English and Persian: but the unidiomatic character of his equivalents has led to this being rarely consulted.

The first volume of RICHARDSON's Dictionary was reprinted in 1806, and the second volume in 1810, by the late distinguished oriental scholar, Sir CHARLES WILKINS, who on that occasion compared the English version of MENINSKI with the original. In doing this, many alterations and numerous additions were made, and many mistakes corrected. He also reformed the mode of representing the Oriental by Roman characters—reduced the size to the more convenient dimensions of a quarto —printed the oriental words with a new and greatly-improved Arabic type, and made additions both of words and meanings, which, to use his own expression, "might be counted by thousands."

The work assumed, therefore, an entirely new aspect; and was mainly indebted to the learning and industry of Sir CHARLES WILKINS for its standard reputation as an Arabico-Persian Lexicon.

In 1829, although not withholding his aid or interest from a new edition of the Dictionary, Sir C. WILKINS consigned the task of preparing it for publication and conducting it through the press to the compiler of the present work. On that occasion also voluminous additions were made. A great body of Arabic words, which RICHARDSON had omitted, were supplied from MENINSKI, WILLMET, DE SACY, GLADWIN, the Kāmūs (قاموس), and other sources; at the same time the Persian division of the Dictionary was enriched by numerous and useful contributions from the Burhāni Kātiʿ (برهان قاطع) and the voluminous Persian Dictionary, Haft Kulzum (هفت قلزم), compiled under the orders of the King of Oude, and printed at Lucknow; but chiefly from a manuscript collection of words, consisting of about five and twenty thousand, taken from the works of twenty-four of the most celebrated Persian writers, which had been compiled in India under the directions of the late Sir GRAVES CHAMNEY HAUGHTON. This valuable compilation was most liberally placed by that eminent scholar and zealous colleague at the Editor's disposal. About thirty-eight thousand new words were inserted, and many new meanings that had been previously overlooked or omitted, were introduced under their respective terms.

It is not possible that a Lexicon, however carefully and laboriously compiled, should embrace all the words of a copious form of speech and an extensively-cultivated literature. If such be the case with one language, it is still more applicable to a work which in fact comprehends to a certain extent the two classical languages of the Muhammadan world, Arabic and Persian. To embody all the words of both these languages without any omission, would require an amount of knowledge and an extent of research to which the compiler of the present work makes no pretension. All that he has attempted on the present, as well as on the former occasion, has been to supply such defects as could be supplied from sources within his reach. With this purpose, he has gone over, with all the care he could bestow, the Surāh (صراح) a Dictionary of Arabic words explained in Persian, in two volumes quarto, printed at Calcutta in 1812; also the great Arabic Lexicon, Kāmūs (قاموس), in two volumes folio, printed at Calcutta in 1817; and the Persian translation of the same, including the Sahāhu 'l lughāt (صحاح اللغات), Shamsu 'l ʿulūm (شمس العلوم), and other Vocabularies, printed in four quarto volumes at Calcutta in the year of the Hijra 1257 (A.D. 1841), under the title of Muntaha 'l arab fī lughāti 'l ʿarab (منتهي الارب في لغات العرب) by Munshi Abdu 'r rahīm (عبد الرحيم بن عبد الكريم صفي پوري). The author has also carefully perused, with reference to the present compilation, several standard Persian writings, as the Anvári Suhayli (انوار سهيلي), Akhlāki Muhsinī (اخلاق محسني), the Tuhfatu 'l ahrār (تحفة الاحرار), and Salāmān u Absāl (سلامان و ابسال) of Jāmī (جامي) which two last-named works have been most accurately edited by Mr. Falconer; and L'histoire des Mongols, translated by M. Quatremère and forming one volume of that splendid series the Collection Orientale.

From these and a few other sources, more than thirty thousand words that had no place in the third edition of RICHARDSON, will be found in the present work. It is hoped therefore, that the Dictionary will now rarely leave a Persian student at a loss for the meaning of any term, whether of Persian or Arabic origin, which he may meet with in a Persian author.

With respect to Arabic, the case is different. Although containing a very large proportion of Arabic words, the compilation is intended to be an Arabic Lexicon chiefly in relation to the indefinite extent to which the best Persian writers avail themselves of the Arabic language, either to enrich their style or to display their erudition. The words that are thus embodied, are substantives, adjectives, verbal nouns, participles, nouns of agency, and particles — not verbs: and, accordingly, the latter, either in their primitive or derivative forms as verbal roots, constitute no part of the collection. It is only to this extent that the Dictionary is a Dictionary of Arabic; and although it is, no doubt, true that it contains very many words for which it might be difficult to produce the authority of a Persian author; yet so long as the best Persian writers may, and do employ Arabic words at their own discretion, without limit or reserve, it would scarcely be safe to predicate of any Arabic word that it never occurs in a Persian composition. On this account, it has been thought advisable, not only to retain a large number of Arabic words of very questionable usefulness, merely because they had found a place in the former editions, but to add many others which may possibly be foreign to Persian literature, but which may also be found in it, and of an explanation of which the student may occasionally stand in need. Superfluity has appeared to the author preferable to deficiency, although he is by no means disposed to question the justness of the objections which have been made to the Arabic portion of his labours, by scholars for whose opinion he entertains the greatest respect and deference.

It might, indeed, have been a preferable course to have compiled the Dictionary in the first instance from a careful collation of the standard literature of Persia, rather than from the existing lexicons: but there can be no doubt that native lexicographers are, for the most part, more conversant with their own literary compositions than European scholars can hope to be. A wider field is open to them whence to accumulate their gleanings. To have recourse to them is therefore a natural and obvious procedure: to discard their aid would be recklessly to cast away valuable materials. In the present instance, however, the author has had no choice. The original compilation of Meninski, based upon native Lexicons, and amplified and corrected from the same by Mr. Richardson and Sir Charles Wilkins, is the acknowledged groundwork of his own labours: and he holds himself accountable only for the fuller development of their plan, and the compilation of a Dictionary which, while it may be not wholly useless to the student of Arabic, will furnish the student of Persian with an explanation of every word he is likely to meet with, whether it be of Persian or Arabic extraction.

With a hope of rendering the work more serviceable to the student of Arabic, the irregular plurals of nouns and adjectives will not only be found in their places alphabetically arranged, but have also been given along with their respective singulars after the manner observed by Arabian lexicographers. In many of the commonest terms these irregular plurals are very numerous, as may be seen by a reference to the words عبد *ʻabd*, a servant; شيخ *shaykh*, an old man; دار *dār*, a house; اسد *asad*, a lion; حظّ *hazz*, good fortune; حمار *himār*, an ass; ارض *arz*, the earth; كلب *kalb*, a dog; شجيع *shajīʻ*, bold, brave; كبير *kabīr*, great, &c. &c. But notwithstanding the large space occupied by these repetitions, the addition of more than thirty thousand words, and the insertion of the tashdīd ـّ (sign of reduplication), the typographical arrangements that have been adopted have diminished the bulk of the volume by three hundred pages, without, it is believed, impairing the merits of its execution, the elegance of the type, or the distinctness of the impression.

A still more important result is the reduction of the price, which barely exceeds a third of the former charge, and furnishes a precedent of economy in oriental printing hitherto unparalleled, for which oriental students cannot be too thankful. This is partly owing to the improved facilities which practice has given to the printers of oriental books: and in particular, to the oriental press of Mr. Watts, which has earned a just reputation above all others in this country for the immense variety of its resources in oriental typography, and the skill and cheapness with which they are employed.

It is further owing to the liberality of the Court of Directors of the East-India Company, by whom the entire cost of the publication has been defrayed: and who have in this, as on various other occasions, manifested their desire to facilitate the acquirement of every oriental language, a knowledge of which is subservient to an acquaintance with the speech, the institutions, or the sentiments of the people of India.

East-India College, Haileybury, Herts,
October 1, 1852.

A

DICTIONARY,

PERSIAN, ARABIC, AND ENGLISH.

ا *ALIF*, the first letter of the Arabic and Persian alphabets, in arithmetic represents the number one, and in almanacks and astronomical books, Sunday and Taurus. It also denotes an unmarried man. Like its sisters و *wāw* and ي *yā*, this letter is sometimes a vowel, and at other times a consonant. As a vowel, it is called الف ساكنه *alif sākina*, Quiescent alif, الف لينه *alif layyina*, Soft alif, or الف المدّ *alifu'l madd*, Alif of extension or prolongation. Being invariably preceded by a consonant inflected with the vowel *a*, called فتحه *fatha*, which is akin to ا *alif*, it merely prolongs the sound, so as to form the simple long vowel *ā* of "far" or "father": as, مال *māl*, Wealth. In Persian, however, a broader sound is given to it, more nearly allied to the *a* in "water" or "war": as, حال *hāl*, (pronounced haul) State, جا *jā*, (pronounced jaw) A place. When, in Arabic words, ا *alif*, occurs at the end of a word, or at least is followed only by ء *hamza*, then the sound of مدّه *madda*, which means "extension or prolongation," is given to it, whether the sign ˜ be written or not: as, حمرآء or indifferently حمراء *hamrā*, fem. Red, (to be sounded like the *a* in "huzzà"). In this case it is called الف ممدوده *alif mamdūda*, Extended alif, in contradistinction to الف مقصوره *alif maksūra*, Short alif. This latter ا *alif* is not unfrequently met with at the end of Arabic words: as, عصا *ʻasa'*, (originally عصو *ʻasaw*) A staff; دنيا *dunya'*, The world. But الف مقصوره *alif maksūra* appears more frequently in the form of ي *yā*, with a small ا *alif* placed above: as in بشري *bushra'*, Glad tidings; مصطفي *mustafa'*, Elect; حبلي *hubla'*, Pregnant; فضلي *fuzla'*, fem. Excellent.

In Arabic, ا *alif* may be substituted for و *wāw* or ي *yā*: as, قال *kāla* (originally قول *kawala*) He spake; باع *bāʻa*, (originally بيع *bayaʻa*) He sold. It is employed to form the dual in verbs and nouns: as, كتبا *katabā*, They two wrote; يكتبان *yaktubāni*, They both will write; رجلان *rajulāni*, Two men. It also forms the noun of agency: as, ضارب *zārib*, A striker. Likewise, adjectives: as, سكران *sakrān*, Drunk; كبري *kubra'*, fem. Greater. It is used in the formation of plurals, both regular and irregular: also of several of the مصدر *masdars*, or verbal nouns, &c., for all of which see Grammar.

In a few instances, ا *alif*, though written, is not pronounced. This is the case after و *wāw* of the plural of the verb: as, نصروا *nasarū*, They assisted; and seems to have been introduced in order that this و *wāw* may not be taken for the conjunction و *wāw*. Some grammarians extend the use of this silent ا *alif* to other words: as, بنون *banūn*, Sons; بنوا زيد *banū* (for بنو *banū*) *Zayd*, Sons of Zayd; شاربوا الماء *shāribū'l māʼ*, (for شاربو الماء) Drinkers of water. After تنوين *tanwīn* preceded by فتحه *fatha*, ا *alif* is written, but not sounded: as, ضربت زيدًا *zarabtu zaydan*, I smote Zayd. Also, when it is the substitute of the light ن *nūn* in such a phrase as لنسفعًا بالناصية *la nasfaʻan* (originally لنسفعن) *bi'n nāsiyat*, Verily we will drag by the forelocks. Neither is it pronounced when following the رويّ *rawīy*, or last letter of a verse: as when التعاب *iltiʻāba*, اصاب *asāba*, are written التعابا *iltiʻābā*, اصابا *asābā*.

Then there is the ا *alif* of lamentation (ندبه *nadba*): as, وا زيداه *wā zaydāh*, Alas! Zayd: and of imploring aid (استغاثه *istighāsa*): as, يا زيداه *yā zaydāh*, Ho! help, Zayd.

In Persian, ا *alif* is of two kinds.—1. Prefixed to certain particles: as, ابا *abā* (for با *bā*), With; also to words of three or more letters, when it takes the vowel originally belonging to the first letter, which then becomes quiescent: as, اشكم *ishkam*, (originally شكم *shikam*), The belly.—2. To denote privation: as, اجنبان *aumbān*, Motionless; اخواستي *akhwāstī*, Unwillingness.

ا *alif* in the middle of a word is of five kinds.—1. When employed to convert the third person singular of the aorist into the precative: as, ميراد *mīrād*, May he die! (from ميرد *mīrad*); بواد *buvād*, May he be! (from بود *buvad*); مرواد *maravād*, May he not go! (from رود *ravad*). Or when it stands in the place of the prefix ب *bi*: as, ميرام *mīrām*, I will die (for بميرم *bimīram*).—2. Pleonastic, for ornament, or by poetic licence: as, سبكسار *sabuk-sār* (for سبك سر *sabuk-sar*), Light-headed; ستمگار *sitamgār* (originally ستمگر *sitamgar*), Tyrannical; خوار *khwār* (for خور *khwur*), Contemptible.—3. To denote continuation or proximity: as, خنداخند *khandākhand*, Incessant laughter; دمادم *damādam*, Moment to moment, every moment; دوشادوش *doshādosh*, Shoulder to shoulder, arm in arm.—4. To denote totality, or completeness: as, سراسر *sarāsar*, From beginning to end; سراپا *sarāpā*, From head to foot.—5. In lieu of the conjunction و *vāv*: as, تكاپوي *takāpūy* (for تك و پوي *tak u pūy*), A running to and fro, search. In some parts of Persia a medial ا *alif*, when followed by ن *nūn*, is sounded like *ū*: as, باران *bārān* (pronounced as if written بارون *bārūn*), Rain.

ا *alif* at the end of words is of seven kinds.—1. Used in calling: as, شها *shahā*, O King! شهريارا *shahr-yārā*, O friend of the city!—2. To denote prayer: as, ننشينادا *na nishīnadā*, May he not sit! بينادا *bīnadā*, May he see! Sometimes two ا *alifs* occur in one word for emphasis; the one being placed before, and the other after, the final letter: as, شوادا *shavādā*, May he become!—3. To denote the agent: as, دانا *dānā*, Knowing, learned; بينا *bīnā*, Seeing, or a seer; گويا *goyā*, Speaking, or a speaker; شنوا *shinavā*, Hearing, or a hearer; روا *ravā*, Current.—4. For filling up (اشباع *ishbāʿ*), borrowed from the Arabians; as, when poetic metre requires it, كمال *kamāl* is written كمالا *kamālā*. In strict parlance, the final consonant of every Persian word is silent, that is, not followed by a vowel. When, therefore, it is required to inflect such a consonant with a vowel, an ا *alif* must be subjoined: as, دانيا *dāniyā*, رايگانيا *rāygāniyā*, from داني *dāniy*, رايگاني *rāygāniy*.—5. To form abstract nouns: as, درازا *darāzā*, Length, from دراز *darāz*, Long; فراخا *firākhā*, Width, from فراخ *firākh*, Wide.—6. Pleonastic: as, گفتا *guftā* (for گفت *guft*,) He spoke.—7. To form a kind of intensive superlative: as, خوشا *khwushā*, Very happy, from خوش *khwush*, Happy; بسا *basā*, Very much, from بس *bas*, Much. ا *alif* is sometimes sounded like ū: as when فرماي *farmāy*, Command thou, is made to rhyme with روي *rūy*. ا *alif* may be changed to دال *dāl* or ي *ye*: as for بان *ba ān*, باين *ba īn*, they write بدان *ba dān*, بدين *ba dīn*. For اكدش *akdish* and ارمغان *armaghān* they say يكدش *yakdish*, يرمغان *yarmaghān*. The initial ا *alif* of a verb, when preceded by the particle ب *bi*, the prohibitive م *ma*, or negative ن *na*, is changed to ي *ye*: as, افراختن *afrākhtan*, To exalt; بيفراخت *biyafrākht*, He exalted; بيفراز *biyafrāz*, Exalt thou; ميفراز *miyafrāz*, Exalt not thou; نيفراخت *nayafrākht*, He exalted not.

OF HAMZA.

When ا *alif* is regarded as a consonant, it is called hamza, the orthographical sign of which ء it ought, in strictness, always to bear; although, at the beginning of a word, it seldom is written. In shape, hamza resembles the upper part of ع *ʿayn*; and, like that letter, is uttered by a compression of the muscles of the throat. Hamza, however, is neither so deep nor so strong a guttural as ع *ʿayn*. In representing a word which contains a hamza in the Roman character, the peculiar symbol of this letter will be retained, according to the mode followed with regard to ع *ʿayn*.

At the beginning of a word, hamza invariably assumes the form of ا *alif*; and may take either of the three vowels, *a*, *i*, or *u*: as, أمير *ʾamīr*, A prince or commander; إمام *ʾimām*, A chief or leader; أمراء *ʾumarāʾ*, Princes. In that situation, however, the sign hamza is seldom written, as it cannot there be mistaken for quiescent ا *alif* or alif of prolongation; the latter, as we have already observed, being never found but when preceded by a consonant marked with its own vowel فتحه *fatha*. These words, then, will commonly appear written امير, امام, امراء; and will be spelt accordingly in English, *amīr*, *imām*, *umarāʾ*, without the orthographical sign hamza.

In the middle of a word, hamza is changed to و *wāw* when inflected by ضمه *zamma*, and to ي *yā* without the diacritical points when inflected by كسره *kasra*: as, رؤف *raʾufa* (originally رأف), He was kind; سئم *saʾima* (originally سأم), He was sick. But when moved by فتحه *fatha*, it generally assumes the form of that letter which is homogeneous with the vowel of its own prepositive: as, سأل *saʾala*, He asked; جؤن *juʾan*, The pots of a druggist; سأة *saʾat*, سئة *siʾat*, or سؤة *suʾat*, The horn of a bow. As a quiescent medial, it remains when preceded by fatha: as, رأس *raʾs*, Head: becomes و *wāw* if preceded by zamma: as, بؤس *buʾs*, Calamity, and ي *yā* without the diacritical points if preceded by كسره *kasra*: as, بئر *biʾr*, A well.

At the end of a word, after فتحه *fatha*, it assumes the form of ا *alif*: as, قرأ *qaraʾa*, He read. After كسره *kasra*, it assumes the form of ي *yā*: as, دفئ *dafiʾa*, He was warm; and after ضمه *zamma*, the form of و *wāw*: as, جرؤ *jaruʾa*, He was bold. After a silent letter, it retains its own shape: as, خبء *khabʾ*, Concealment; جزء *juzʾ*, A portion (though sometimes it is found with a و *wāw*, as, بدؤ *badʾ*, Commencement): ابتداء *ibtidāʾ*, or with تنوين *tanwīn*, ابتداءٌ *ibtidāʾun*, A beginning. In this situation it is commonly omitted by the Persians, who would write it ابتدا *ibtidā*.

In Arabic, *hamza* ء may be substituted for a radical و *wāw* or ي *yā*: as, قائل *kāʾil* (for قاول *kāwil*), A speaker; بائع *bāʾiʿ* (for بايع *bāyiʿ*), A seller; احد *ahad* (for وحد *wahad*), One. Hamza, like alif, is one of the letters of increase (حروف الزيادة *hurūfu'z ziyādat*); and is therefore used extensively in forming several of the augmented conjugations which branch out from the simple triliteral or quadriliteral root. It is also employed in the formation of some of the irregular plurals: as, اطعمة *atʿimat*, Viands; الوان *alwān*, Colours; احرف *ahruf*, Letters; صحائف *sahāʾif* (originally صحايف) Volumes:—also of adjectives descriptive of colour: as, احمر *ahmar*, Red; اسود *aswad*, Black; and of comparatives: as, اشرف *ashraf*, More noble, &c.

As a native of Arabia is able to articulate with facility sounds which are wholly unfamiliar to a European ear; so, on the other hand, in the languages of Europe are found combinations of letters, the correct pronunciation of which, to a native of the East, is a matter of difficulty. This is more especially the case, when, at the beginning of a word, two consonants occur without an intervening vowel, as in Fraud, Slow, Spear, &c. Accordingly, when any foreign word of this kind is adopted into Arabic, it usually appears with one of the vowels *a*, *i*, *u*, prefixed to it. Thus the words Plato, Stabulum, Stater, become severally افلاطون *aflātūn*, اصطبل *istabl*, اصطر *ustur*. Nor is it in words only of foreign origin that ا *alif* is thus employed. In the structure of words in their own language the Arabians have recourse to the same expedient. In Arabic, the imperative is formed by dropping the initial letter which is the sign of the aorist: consequently, in a large proportion of simple triliteral verbs, the imperative would be found commencing with a silent consonant. For instance, the root كتب *kataba*, He wrote, makes in the aorist يكتب *yaktubu*; and hence the imperative would be كتب *ktub*. To remedy the inconvenience of an initial double consonant, an ا *alif* is prefixed, and the word is therefore اكتب *uktub*, Write thou. But as often as the imperative follows any word whose final is inflected with a vowel, then this ا *alif*, characteristic of the imperative, and called indifferently الف الوصل *alifu'l wasl*, Alif of union, همزة الوصل *hamzatu'l wasl*, Hamza of union, or همزة وصليّه *hamzat wasliya*, Conjunctive hamza, though retained in writing, loses its vowel in pronunciation, and the two words coalesce. This coalescence is indicated by the sign ٓ وصله *wasla*, Union: as in وٱكتب *waktub* (and without wasla وَاكتب), And write thou; which must be pronounced as if written وكتب, and not *wa uktub*. The conjunctive hamza is not confined to the imperative of the major part of triliteral verbs; but is employed in the preterite, imperative, and verbal nouns of the increased conjugations of the forms انفعل *infaʿala*, افتعل *iftaʿala*, افعلّ *ifʿalla*, استفعل *istafʿala*, افعالّ *ifʿālla*, افعوعل *ifʿawʿala*, and افعوّل *ifʿawwala*; and in the forms افعنلل *ifʿanlala*, افعللّ *ifʿalalla*, derived from the quadriliteral فعلل *faʿlala*. The hamza of the article ال *al* is also conjunctive: as, امير المؤمنين *amīru 'l muʾminīn* (not *amīru al muʾminīn*) Commander of the faithful; and so is the initial ا *alif* of the following ten nouns substantive: ابن *ibn*, ابنم *ibnam*, ابنة *ibnat*, اسم *ism*, است *ist*, اثنان *isnāni*, اثنتان *isnatāni*, امرء *imraʾ*, امراة *imraʾat*, ايمن *aymun*.—Except in the above-mentioned instances, every initial hamza is termed قطعيّة *katʿīya*, Disjunctive. The fourth conjugation (افعل *afʿala*) is not included in the foregoing list: its hamza, therefore, being disjunctive, retains its vowel, and allows no coalition: it is necessary, therefore, to read وأكتب *wa ʾaktaba* (or indifferently واكتب *wa aktaba*, never *waktaba*,) And he made (him) write.

As forming a distinct word of itself, أ *hamza* ...

A P آبدة *ābidat*, (pl. ابّد *ubbad*, and اوابد *awābid*) A timorous untamed animal. A wild beast. A fable, apologue, parable; a history, romance. Any word difficult to pronounce. A poem not generally known. Any thing strange or uncommon. An idle talker, a babbler. A great and memorable calamity to be remembered for ages.

A ابدة *ibidat*, Prolific (camel).

A ابّدة *ubbadat*, Name of a town in Spain.

A ابدّة *abiddat*, (pl. of بداد *bidād*) Stuffings under wooden saddles, to prevent the galling of camels' backs.

A ابدح *abdah*, An extensive plain, a wide area. Tall (man). Broad-sided (horse). اكل ماله بابدح و دبيدح *akala mālahu bi abdaha wa dubaydaha*, He consumed his substance in vanities.

P ابدرم *ibdaram*, Name of the book of Sākya muni or Buddha.

P آب دزدك *āb-duzdak*, A syringe, a squirt.

P آبدست *āb-dast*, The ablution or washing of the hands, face, and other parts, with certain ceremonies used by the Muhammadans before prayer. Devotion. A devout man. Dexterous, clever-handed, skilful. Prosperous.

P آبدستان *āb-dastān*, (آبدستدان *āb-dastdān*, or آبدسدان *āb-dasdān*) An ewer, any vessel from which water is poured upon the hands. A wash-hand bason. Purification. Custom. Fraud.

P آبدستاندار *āb-dastān-dār*, An ewer-holder.

P آبدست جاي *ābdast-jāy*, A privy.

P ابد شهر *abad-shahr*, The eternal city, the future world. Name of a river. Name of a city.

P آبدن *ābdan*, (for آبدان *ābdān*) A pond, lake, conflux of water. A drinking-vessel. A cucumber, a water-melon.

A ابدن *abdun*, (pl. of بدن *badan*) Aged mountain-goats.

P آبدندان *ābdandān*, Weak. Strong, firm. Fit, congruous. Base, mean. Rude, raw, ignorant, inexperienced. A gambler who is always unsuccessful. A species of pomegranate. A kind of a pear. A tree. Herbage. Any fruit that soon dissolves in the mouth. A kind of sweetmeat.

P ابدوج *ubdūj*, A saddle-cloth, a felt-cloth.

P آب ده *āb-dih*, Splendour-giving. آبده دست *ābdihi dast*, One who graces the chief seat. Muhammad.

A ابديّ *abadīy*, Eternal. For ever and ever.

A ابديّة *abadīyat*, Eternity.

P آب ديد جام *āb-dīdi jām*, Wine, or a draught.

P آبديدة *āb-dīda*, In tears, weeping.

A ابذاء *ibzāʼ*, (v. n. 4 of بذا for بذو) Being obscene in conversation.

A ابذاع *ibzāʻ*, (v. n. 4 of بذع) Terrifying.

P آبذان *ābzān*, Worthy. A household, family.

A ابذعرار *ibziʻrār*, (v. n. 4 of بذعر Q not used) Being divided, scattered, put to flight. Stretching out the legs when galloping in pursuit (a horse).

A ابذقرار *ibziḳrār*, (v. n. 4 of بذقر Q not used) Being dispersed, scattered in every direction. Being blended, amalgamated (blood and water).

A آبر *ābir*, One who fecundates palm-trees. *Ābur*, (pl. of بئر *biʼr*) Wells. Name of a village in Sijistan.

P ابر *abr*, A cloud. A man. ابر آذر *abri āzur*, November-clouds. ابر رگالي *abri rugālī*, A swift-flying cloud. ابر سحري *abri saharī*, Morning-clouds. ابر سنبل گون *abri sumbul-gūn*, A black cloud. ابر سير *abri ser*, (or ابر سيراب *abri ser-āb*) A cloud full of water. ابر طوروش *abri tūrvash*, (A Sinai-resembling cloud) A strong and large-bodied horse. ابر كهن *abri kuhan*, or ابر مردة *abri murda*, A sponge. ابر نيسان *abri naysan*, Vernal-clouds. Cold rain. *Abar*, (for بر *bar*) On, upon, above. According to. The bosom. A kind of lute. Confections, preserved fruits. The curved part of a bow. An artery. (in zand and pāzand) Penis.

A أبر *abara*, (fut. يأبر *yaʼbiru*) He pricked.

A ابر *abr*, (v. n. of ابر) Pricking with the point of the tail (a scorpion). Giving (a dog) a needle in (his) food. Destroying, ruining. Defaming, reproaching. Fructifying the female palm-tree by the sprinkling of the flowers of the male. Dressing, fertilizing a sown field. Being good, excellent. A puncture, sting, point or prominent part of any thing. *Ibar*, (pl. of ابرة *ibrat*) Needles. Points, prickles. Stings. Tips of elbows, or hough-bones. Shoots of dwarf palm-trees.

A ابرّ *abarr*, More or most just, juster, justest. More or most exemplary in duty to parents. Furthest removed into the desert. اصلح العرب ابرّهم *aslahu 'l ʻarab abarruhum*, The best of the Arabs are those who live furthest in the desert.

A ابراء *abrāʼ*, (pl. of بريء *bariʼ*) Free, discharged, absolved. *Ibrāʼ*, (v. n. 4 of برأ) Liberating, discharging, remitting, releasing, delivering from danger. Healing, restoring to health. Entering upon the first or last day or night of the month. ابراء ذمّة *ibrāʼi zimma*, Release from responsibility, quittance from obligation. A safe conduct.

A ابراء *ibrāʼ*, (v. n. 4 of برا for برو), Putting a ring through a camel's nose. (v. n. 4 of بري) Arriving at, reaching (soil or sugar-cane).

A ابرات *abrāt*, (pl. of برت *burt*, *bart*, or *birt*) Guides. *Ibrāt*, Acuteness, shrewdness, cleverness.

A ابراث *abrās*, (pl. of برث *bars*) Plain, level, soft grounds.

A ابراج *abrāj*, (pl. of برج *burj*) Towers. Signs of the zodiac. (pl. of برج *baraj*) Beautiful, clear, shining. *Ibrāj*, (v. n. 4 of برج) Building a tower.

A ابراح *ibrāh*, (v. n. 4 of برح) Honouring, magnifying. Causing surprise. Giving pleasure.

A ابراد *abrād*, Stages, posts, halting-places. (pl. of برد *burd*) Striped stuffs. *Ibrād*, (v. n. 4 of برد) Bringing (any thing) cold. Presenting cooled liquor. Experiencing cold weather. Sending a Berid or courier. Entering on the close of the day. Weakening.

A ابرار *abrār*, (pl. of برّ *burr*) Wheats. (pl. of بارّ *bārr*) Just, holy, pious, dutiful. *Ibrār*, (v. n. 4 of برّ) Accepting, justifying. Departing for the desert, and continuing there. Swearing an oath according to truth. Increasing (offspring), multiplying (people). Overcoming, conquering. Leading (sheep) home from water.

A ابراز *ibrāz*, (v. n. 4 of برز) Producing, publishing, bringing out. Undertaking. Setting out on a journey. Taking the pure gold, ابريز *ibrīz*. Proof, document. An edition. P احتجاج و ابراز آوردن *ihtijāj u ibrāz āwardan*, To adduce proofs and documents.

A ابراص *ibrās*, (v. n. 4 of برص) Afflicting with leprosy. Bringing forth a leprous child.

A ابراض *abrāz*, (pl. of برض *barz*) Few. *Ibrāz*, (v. n. 4 of برض) Producing young grass, just sprouting above ground.

A ابراق *abrāk*, (pl. of برق *barak*) Lambs. *Ibrāk*, (v. n. 4 of برق) Casting forth lightning (the sky). Being visited or terrified by lightning. Menacing, threatening. Giving false signs of pregnancy (a camel). Making (a sword) gleam. Mixing water with oil. Shewing (her) face (a woman). Starting (game). Sacrificing (a pie-bald sheep). Quitting, abandoning. Flash, glitter, coruscation. Pouring a little oil on water.

A ابراك *abrāk*, (pl. of بركة *burkat*) Certain aquatic birds, white and small. *Ibrāk*, (v. n. 4 of برك) Making (a she-camel) kneel down. Raining incessantly.

A ابرام *abrām*, (pl. of برم *baram*) Those who refuse to go partners with gamesters. *Ibrām*, (v. n. 4 of برم), Twisting (a rope) tight. Doing business well. Observing strictly (a treaty). Wearying, disgusting. Urgency, importunity. Producing berries (a thorn), and unripe grapes (a vine).

P آبرانه *āb-rāna*, Travelling by water.

P آبراه *āb-rāh*, A canal, conduit, pipe, aqueduct, water-course, channel of a river; any place through which water flows.

A ابراه *ibrāh*, (v. n. 4 of بره) Adducing indisputable proofs or miracles. Overcoming.

A ابراهام *ibrāhām*, Abraham.

A ابراهم *ibrāhim*, *ibrāhum*, or *ibrāham*, Abraham.

A ابراهوم *ibrāhūm*, Abraham.

P آبراهه *āb-rāha*, A water-course. A lachrymal duct.

A ابراهيم *ibrāhīm*, The patriarch Abraham, surnamed النبيّ *an nabīy*, The prophet, or خليل الله *khalīlu'llāh*, The friend of God. Zoroaster. Name of a mountain in Karamania.

A ابراهيمي *ibrāhīmiy*, Name of a black fruit. الابراهيميون *al ibrāhīmiyūna*, Certain companions of Muhammad, twelve in number.

A ابرة *ibrat*, (pl. ابرات *ibarāt*, ابر *ibar*, and ابار *ibār*) A needle. The sting of a scorpion. The point of any thing. Tip of the elbow, or of the hough of a horse. A shoot or sucker of the tree مقل *mukl*. Detraction, slander. A kind of tree resembling the fig. ابرة الراعي *ibratu'r rāʻī*, Crane's bill (a plant).

A ابرج *abraj*, One who has fine handsome eyes.

P ابرجن *abrajan*, A bracelet. An anklet.

A ابرح *abrah*, More or most heavy, or grievous.

A ابرخ *abrakh*, One whose back bends inwardly.

A ابرد *abrad*, Colder. A cloud showering hailstones. Speckled white and black (a bull). (pl. ابارد *abārid*) A male leopard. ابو الابرد *abū'l abrad*, Name of a follower of Muhammad. حمى ابرد *humma' abrad*, The cold fit of an ague. *Abrud*, (pl. of برد *burd*) Striped stuffs. Upper garments.

A الابردان *al abradāni* (dual), The two colds, *i.e.* the morning and the evening. The shades of morning and evening.

A ابردة *abradat*, A leopardess. *Ibradat*, Cold, chill in the belly. *Ibridat*, Chilliness.

A ابرزي *ibriziy*, Pure (gold).

A ابرساء *abrasāʼ*, A kind of lily.

P ابرش *abrash*, Spotted red and white.

A ابرش *abrash*, Dapple-gray, pie-bald (horse). (A spot) variegated with herbage of different kinds. Marked with white or coloured spots or points.

A ابرشاش *ibrishāsh*, (v. n. 9 of برش) Being pie-bald (a horse).

P ابرش خورشيد *abrash-khwurshed*, The sky.

P ابرشم *abrasham*, Silk, sewing silk.

P ابرشمي *abrashamī*, A silk-merchant. A silk-worm. Silken.

P ابر شهر *abr-shahr*, (High town) the old name for Nishābūr, one of the four cities in Khurāsān.

A ابرص *abras*, Leprous. Spotted (animal) from bites of insects. الابرص *al abras*, The moon. سامّ ابرص *sāmm abras*, (pl. سوامّ ابرص *sawāmm abras*, or سوامّ *sawāmm*, برصة *birasat*, or ابارص *abāris*) A species of large lizard.

A ابرع *abraʻ*, Bigger, bulkier, thicker.

A ابرغشاش *ibrighshāsh*, (v. n. 4 of برغش Q not used) Recovering from a disease being healed, and rising up and walking.

P آبرفت *āb-raft*, Any thing carried down by the current. Water spilled or dried up. A stone which imbibes water. *Āb-ruft*, A stone worn smooth by water flowing over it. A sprinkling of water previous to sweeping.

A ابرق *abrak*, Conspicuous. Pie-bald, black and white. Of different coloured hairs (rope). Any thing varied, black and white, having also a shining appearance (as the eye). Name of a bird. (pl. ابارق *abārik*) A coarse, stony, sandy, soil. Lapis specularis, talc. A certain medicine.

P ابر قباد *abar-kubād*, Name of a country.

A ابرقوه *abarkūh*, Name of a city in Persia; also of a village near Nishāpūr.

P ابرك *abrak*, A little cloud. A sponge.

A ابرك *abrak*, More or most blessed.

P ابركار *abrkār*, Astonished, confounded, stupefied, amazed.

P ابركاكيا *abarkākiyā*, (or ابركاكياب *abarkākiyāb*) A cobweb.

A ابركوباد *abarkūbād*, Name of a city in the province of Arrajān, lying between the districts of Fars and Ahwāz.

P ابركوه *abar-koh*, Name of a town in Chaldea, or the Arabian Irāk. Also of another in the Persian Irāk, which is commonly supposed to be the ancient Persepolis, distant 20 parasangs or 80,000 paces from Ispahān. It is situated on the summit of a mountain, as the name implies.

A ابرم *abram*, Name of a place. A sort of plant. A sort of disease.

P ابرمادران *abarmādarān*, A kind of sweetmeat.

A ابرمة *abrimat*, (pl. of برام *burām*) Tikes.

P ابرناك *abrnāk*, Cloudy.

A ابرنتاء *ibrintāʼ*, A preparing of one's self.

P ابرنجين *abranjīn*, (or ابرنجن *abranjan*) A bracelet. An ankle-ornament (of gold or silver).

A ابرنذاع *ibrinzāʻ*, (v. n. 3 of برذع Q) Preparing, making ready for.

A ابرنشاق *ibrinshāk*, (v. n. 3 of برشق Q) Being joyful. Flourishing (a tree), expanding (a flower).

P آبرو *āb-rū*, (or آبروي *āb-rūy*) (Water of the face) Dignity, honour, renown, glory, reputation. Rank, office. Elegance, gracefulness. Sweat. Held in estimation by the great. آبرو دادن *āb-rū dādan*, To pay respect. آبرو ريختن *āb-rū rekhtan*, To disgrace. آبرو كردن *āb-rū kardan*, To honour. آبروي شهر *āb-rūyi shahr*, The chief magistrate of a city. آبروي عسكر *āb-rūyi ʻaskar*, The commander of an army.

P ابرو *abrū*, The eye-brow. ابرو چيدن *abrū chīdan*, To knit the brow. ابرو زدن *abrū zadan*, To nod, wink, beckon, approve by motion of the eye. ابروي زال زر *abrūwi zāl-zar*, The new moon. ابروي صنم *abrūwi sanam* The mandrake.

P ابروان *abruwān*, The eye-brows. Morning and evening.

P آبرود *āb-rūd*, A hyacinth. A water-lily.

P ابروز *abrūz*, (or corruptly Alborz) Name of a mountain near Hamadān in Persia.

P ابروصنم *abrū-sanam*, The mandrake.

P ابرو فراخي *abrū-firākhī*, Cheerfulness.

P ابروكن *abrū-kan*, Tweezers.

P آبرون *ābrūn*, Houseleek, sempervivum.

P ابرونتن *abrūnitan*, (in zand and Pāz.) To die.

P آبروي *āb-ravī*, A going through water: an oar.

A ابرويز *abrawayz*, (or ابرواز *abrawāz*) Name of a Persian king.

P ابرة *abra*, The outside of a garment or cap. *Ibara*, First fruits; early fruit. *Ubara*, A bustard.

A ابرة *abrah*, White, fair, and ruddy.

P ابرهام *abarhām*, Nature, essence. Name of an angel. Abraham.

A ابرهة *abrahat*, A name proper to three kings of Yaman. 1. ابرهة بن الحارث *abrahat binu'l hārith*, called also ذو المنار *zū'l manār*. 2. ابرهة بن الصبّاح *abrahat binu's sabbāh*, celebrated for his learning and generosity. 3. ابرهة الاشرم الحبشيّ *abrahat al ashram al habashiy*, (called also ابو يكسوم *abū yaksūm*). In the Kur'ān the latter is styled Lord of the elephant.

P ابرهه *abraha*, A kind of bird. Name of a general, called also ذو الفيل *zū'l fīl*, who made an unsuccessful attempt to take Mecca.

P ابرهيمية *ibrahīmīya*, A kind of broth.

P ابري *abrī*, Clouded, variegated. ابري كاغذ *abrī kāghiz*, A kind of thick and shining paper (clouded from Kashmīr).

A ابريّ *ibriy*, Sharp, aculeate. A needle-dealer.

A ابرئاء *abriʼāʼ*, (pl. of بريء *bariʼ*,) Free, clear, discharged, absolved. (pl. of بريء *bariʼ*) Pure.

A ابرية *ibriyat*, Scurf on the head, dandruff.

A ابريج *ibrīj*, A churn.

P آبريز *āb-rez*, A vessel used in baths for pouring water over the head and body. A bucket. A water-pipe, a spout. A drain, a ditch. A water-closet, privy. A spade.

A ابريز *ibrīz*, Pure gold.

P آب ريزان *āb-rezān*, Name of an ancient Persian festival, in which each person sprinkles rose-water on his neighbours.

P آبريزگان *ābrezgān*, A festival among the Armenians, Chaldeans, or Persians, during which the people in their visits sprinkle one another with orange-flower, rose, or pure water. It falls upon the thirteenth day of the month Tir, corresponding nearly to our September. A sort of food.

A ابريسم *ibrīsam*, or *abrīsam*, Silk.

P ابريشم *abrīsham* or *abrīshum*, Silk. The string of a musical instrument. ابريشم سطبر *abrīshami sitabr*, The bass string of a musical instrument.

P ابريشمي *abrīshamī*, Silken.

P ابريشيم *abreshīm*, Silk.

P ابريشمين *abreshīmīn*, Silken.

A ابريق *ibrīk*, A bright, shining sword. Bright-streaked (bow). Handsome and beautiful (woman). (pl. اباريق *abārīk*) An ewer, a water-pot with a spout, a jug.

A ابرئلال *ibriʼlāl*, (v. n. 4 of برأل Q) Ruffling up his feathers when preparing to fight (a bird).

A ابرين *abrīn*, Name of a sandy tract in Arabia.

A ابز *abaza*, (fut. يأبز *yaʼbazu*) He leaped.

A ابز *abz*, (v. n. of ابز) Leaping, bounding. Stopping suddenly, and then rushing forward with velocity. Assaulting, insulting, injuring. Dying suddenly. *Abiz*, Leaping, springing, bounding (deer).

A ابزاء *ibzā*, (v. n. 4 of بزا for بزو) Suckling, giving suck. Overpowering, seizing, carrying off by force. Raising the hips in walking.

P ابزار *abzār*, A kind of carrot or parsnip.

A ابزار *abzār*, (pl. of بزر *bazr*) Pot-herbs. (pl. ابازير *abāzīr*) Pot-herbs, or spiceries for seasoning.

P ابزاردان *abzārdān*, A spice-box, a pepper-box.

A ابزاريّ *abzāriy*, A seedsman. ابزاريون *abzāriyūn*, Certain reporters of Muhammadan traditions.

A ابزال *ibzāl*, (v. n. 4 of بزل) Breeding the tooth called ناب *nāb* in his ninth year (a camel).

A ابزام *ibzām*, (v. n. 4 of بزم) Giving (a thousand). (pl. ابازيم *abāzīm*) A buckle.

A ابزخ *abzakh*, One who has a protuberance on the breast and hollowness in the back.

P ابزر *abzar*, Name of a mountain near Hamadān in Persia, about 150 leagues west of Ispahān.

P آبزرفت *āb-zuruft*, A cucumber, water-melon. An isle.

P آبزن *āb-zan*, (Casting water) A particular kind of bathing-vessel made of copper or iron, the full length of the human body, filled with warm water medicinally prepared, in which the patient sits or lies down. The bason of a fountain. Imparting tranquillity of mind, consoling, consolatory. (imperative) Console, appease.

A ابزن *abzan*, *ibzan*, or *ubzan*, A bath, a laver, sometimes made of brass.

P آبزندرود *āb-zand-rūd*, Name of a river which runs through Ispahān. Our travellers call it Senderut. The name implies, The river of living water, being formed from a collection of several springs into one channel.

P آبزه *āb-zih*, Water flowing from a fountain, or a corner of the eye. Liquid pressed through a cullender or strainer. Pincers.

A ابزي *abza'*, One who has a protuberance of the breast and the back bent. *Abaza'*, (v. n. of ابز) Leaping, springing, bounding.

P ابزيدن *abzīdan*, To fill.

P آبزيركاه *āb-zīr-kāh*, (Water under straw) A splinter, thorn in the flesh. A hypocrite, dissembler. A secret fomenter of mischief. One whose merit lies concealed.

A ابزيم *ibzīm*, (pl. ابازيم *abāzīm*) A buckle.

A ابزين *ibzīn*, (pl. ابازين *abāzīn*) A buckle.

P آبژ *ābaj*, Sparks of fire. A kind of grass.

P آبس *ābas*, Name of a city.

A أبس *abasa*, (fut. يأبس *ya-bisu*) He rebuked.

A ابس *abs*, (v. n. of ابس) Rebuking, reproving, reproaching. Frightening. Throwing in one's teeth whatever is disagreeable; treating unkindly. Subjecting, mastering, bringing under subjection, conquering, overcoming. Incarcerating. Contemning, disdaining, scorning. Rough unequal ground. A male tortoise. Sterility. A barren spot. *Ibs*, Rough ground. A bad origin.

A ابساء *ibsā*, (v. n. 4 of بسأ) Making (any one) familiar or accustomed to.

P ابسار *absār*, A whetstone.

A ابسار *ibsār*, (v. n. 4 of بسر) Doing or asking any thing prematurely or unseasonably. Bearing dates in the stage called بسر *busr* (a palm-tree). Taking the scab off a sore before it is healed. Mixing unripe with ripe dates in order to press the juice from them. Being out at sea (a ship). Digging in ground seized by force.

A ابساس *ibsās*, (v. n. 4 of بسّ) Calling to camels in a coaxing way to drink or to be milked.

A ابساط *absāt*, (pl of بسط *bist*, *bust*, or *busut*) She-camels left at liberty with their colts. *Ibsāt*, (v. n. 4 of بسط) Being left at liberty with her colt (a camel). Leaving (a camel) thus at liberty.

A ابساق *ibsāk*, (v. n. 4 of بسق) Having beestings in her udder, just before foaling (a camel).

P آبسال *ābsāl*, (or آبسالان *ābsālān*), A garden.

A ابسال *ibsāl*, (v. n. 4 of بسل) Forbidding, prohibiting, making unlawful. Betraying, abandoning, consigning to destruction. Exposing. Pledging, pawning. Familiarising the mind with death. Cooking or drying (an unripe date). Appointing a lieutenant, deputy, factor or agent.

P آبسان *ābsān*, A bracelet.

A ابسان *ibsān*, (v. n. 4 of بسن) Being beautiful.

P آب سبك *āb-sabuk*, Easy of digestion.

P آبست *ābast*, Orange-pulp. *Ābist*, Pregnant.

P ابست *abist*, or *ibast*, Orange-pulp.

P ابستا *abistā*, Name of a book which the Magi of Persia attribute to the Patriarch Abraham, whom they suppose to be the same with *Zarādasht* or Zoroaster. It is an explanation of the two books called the *Zand* and *Pāzand*; comprehending, with these volumes, the whole religious system of the Magi or adorers of fire; who have a tradition that Abraham repeated them in the midst of a furnace, into which he had been thrown by order of Nimrod.

P آبستان *ābistān*, Pregnant.

P آبستانه *ābistāna*, A caldron, pot, kettle, vat.

P آبستگي *ābistagī*, Pregnancy.

P آبستن *ābistan*, Pregnant. Concealed. آبستن شدن *ābistan shudan*, To be with young. آبستن فرياد *ābistani faryād*, or آبستن فرياد خوان *ābistani faryād-khwān*, A kind of harp or lute.

P آبستنگاه *ābistan-gāh*, A lying-in chamber. A privy.

P آبستني *ābistanī*, Pregnancy, conception. Pregnant. A kind of lute.

P آبسته *ābasta*, Ground prepared for sowing. A spy. A flatterer. *Ābista*, Pregnant. An animal with young. The womb.

P ابسته *abista*, A spy. A flatterer.

P آبسرد *āb-sard*, Jelly.

P آبسردن *āb-sardan*, A gonorrhœa.

P آبسردي *āb-sardī*, Water cooled by the wind.

P آبسفيد *āb-safed*, A pearl on the eye.

P آبسگون *ābisgūn*, (or ابسگون *abisgūn*) Name of an island formerly existing in the Caspian sea at three parasangs distance from Astarābād.

P آبسوار *āb-suwār*, (Floating on water) A bubble.

P آبسيان *āb-siyān*, Tears.

P آبسياه *āb-siyāh*, (or آب سياه *ābi siyāh*) Tears.

P آبسير *āb-sayr*, Easy-paced (horse).

A آبش *ābish*, (or ابشّ *abashsh*) One who decorates the court or vestibule of another's house, and places in it meat and drink (a custom which prevails in Arabia, especially on the arrival of strangers, when every friendly neighbour brings his ornaments, his victuals, and liquor, to the house where they reside, in order to assist in their entertainment).

P آبش *ābish*, Abyssinia.

A ابش *absh*, (v. n. of ابش) Collecting.

A ابشّ *abashsh*, Smiling-faced.

P آب شار *āb-shār*, A waterfall, a cataract.

A ابشار *abshār*, (pl. of بشر *bashar*) Men, mortals. Skins, outer cuticles, epidermes, scarfskins. *Ibshār*, (v. n. 4 of بشر) Rejoicing at good news. Announcing good news. Putting forth its verdure or gay clothing (the earth). Doing well or handsomely. Blessing with beauty and every ornamental excellence. Shaving, scraping, peeling.

A ابشاش *ibshāsh*, (v. n. 4 of بشّ) Having luxuriant, entangled herbage (ground). Putting forth its early grass.

A ابشاط *ibshāt*, (v. n. 4 of بشط) Making haste. Hastening another.

A ابشاغ *ibshāgh*, (v. n. 4 of بشغ) Moistening with a slight shower.

A ابشام *ibshām*, (v. n. 4 of بشم) Disagreeing with any one (indigestible food).

P آبشت *ābasht*, Concealed, hidden, covered up.

P آبشتگاه *ābashta-gāh*, *ābishta-gāh*, (آبشتگه *ābashta-gah*, *ābishta-gah*, آبشتنگاه *ābishtan-gāh* or ابشتنگه *abishtan-gah*,) A place of concealment. A back yard where rubbish is thrown; a privy.

P آبشتن *ābishtan* (or *ābashtan*), To hide, cover.

P ابشتن *abishtan*, To conceal.

P آبشخور *ābish-khwur*, A cistern, a watering-place, reservoir. The bed of a river. A fountain-head. A drinking-vessel. Fortune, chance, lot, portion. A dwelling, residence, halt, stay.

A ابشر *abshar*, Handsomer, fairer, fatter.

P آبشم *ābsham*, The cone of silk in which the worm encloses itself, the cocoon. A coarse kind, or refuse, of silk.

P آبشن *ābishan*, A bridegroom's shirt.

P آبشناس *āb-shinās*, Skilful in discovering springs, or conveying water by aqueducts. A pilot. The man who keeps a look out for shoals from the mast-head. Intelligent, expert, familiar with fundamental truths.

P آبشنگ *āb-shang,* The bathing vessel described under آبزن *āb-zan.*

P آبشوره *āb-shora,* Water cooled with saltpetre.

P آبشيب *āb-shīb,* A channel for water flowing from high grounds.

A ابس *abs,* (v. n. of ابس) Being nimble, brisk, sprightly. *Abis,* Sweet, fleet.

A ابصار *absār,* (pl. of بصر *basar*) Eyes, looks. Perceptions by the eye. *Ibsār,* (v. n. 4 of بصر) Looking at, seeing. Judging, thinking. Going to Basra. Causing to see.

A ابصاص *ibsās,* (v. n. 4 of بصّ) Flowing, distilling, trickling (water). Producing its earliest crop (the ground).

A ابصاق *ibsāk,* (v. n. 4 of بصق) Letting her milk flow (a ewe).

A ابصر *absar,* More or most clear-sighted.

A ابصع *absaʿ,* All, universal. Foolish.

A ابصنة *absinat,* (pl. of بصان *busān*) Months of Rabi the Second.

A ابض *abz,* (v. n. of ابض) Binding the fore foot of a camel with a rope (the knees being bent) to the shoulder. Hurting the nerves or tendons by such ligature. A widening, an unloosing. Motion. Rest. *Ubz,* The inside of the knee of a man, or of the elbow of a camel. (pl. آباض *ābāz,* An age. *Abaz,* (v. n. of ابض) Contracting, shrinking (the hip-nerve). *Ubuz,* (pl. of اباض *ibāz*) Ropes with which they fasten the feet of camels, as above.

A ابضاض *ibzāz,* (v. n. 4 of بضّ) Giving little.

A ابضاع *ibzāʿ,* (v. n. 4 of بضع) Sorting goods for sale. Sending a lot or sample. Declaring, making clear. Answering categorically. Quenching one's thirst (water). Satisfying any one with regard to what he asks. Giving in marriage.

A ابضع *abzaʿ,* Lean, emaciated.

A ابط *abt,* (v. n. of ابط) Humbling, abasing (God). *Ibt,* or *ibit,* (pl. آباط *ābāt*) The arm-pit. *Ibt,* The smaller particles of sand. The extremity of a sandhill. Name of a place in Arabia.

A ابطاء *ibtāʾ,* (v. n. 4 of بطؤ) Delaying, proceeding slowly, tarrying, lingering. Having a sluggish horse or other beast of burden, that lags behind the rest. Retarding, hindering.

A ابطاخ *ibtākh,* (v. n. 4 of بطخ) Having melons in abundance.

A ابطار *ibtār,* (v. n. 4 of بطر) Astounding, terrifying. Making petulant and saucy. Overloading. Lessening, diminishing the means of support, and enfeebling the body.

A ابطاش *ibtāsh,* (v. n. 4 of بطش) Seizing or carrying away by force.

A ابطاط *ibtāt,* (v. n. 4 of بطّ) Purchasing a jar of butter.

A ابطال *abtāl,* (pl. of بطل *batal*) Brave warriors, heroes. *Ibtāl,* (v. n. 4 of بطل) Making void, abolishing, rendering fruitless and abortive. Talking idly, jesting. Dealing in trifles and vanities. Negation, repeal.

A ابطالة *ibtālat,* A false, vain, trifling thing. Vanity, falsehood.

A ابطان *ibtān,* (v. n. 4 of بطن) Girthing a beast. Girding on a sword. Lining a garment. Admitting one to intimate friendship.

A ابطح *abtah,* (pl. اباطح *abātih*) Low-lying, gravelly ground.

A ابطر *abtar,* Thick and prominent-lipped.

A ابطع *abtaʿ,* One who has the inner part of the lips whitish, as among the Ethiopians. Toothless, particularly in the lower jaw.

A ابطل *abtal,* More or most vain, or fruitless.

A ابطن *abtan,* A vein in the lower part of the fore-leg of a horse. *Abtun,* (pl. of بطن *batn*) Bellies. The inner parts of any thing. Small sections of a tribe. عشرة ابطن *ʿasharatu abtunin,* Ten bellies or colts. ولدت عشرة ابطن *waladat ʿasharata abtunin,* She brought forth a tenth child.

A ابطنة *abtinat,* (pl. of باطن *bātin*) Inward parts. Low grounds. (pl. of بطان *bitān*) Girths.

A ابطولة *ubtūlat,* A false, vain, trifling thing. Vanity, falsehood.

A ابطيّ *ibtīy,* Axillary. الابطيّ *al ibtīy,* The axillary vein.

A ابظاظ *ibzāz,* (v. n. 4 of بظّ) Becoming fat.

A ابظر *abzar,* Uncircumcised. One who has a protuberance in the middle of the upper lip.

A ابعاء *ibʿāʾ,* (v. n. 4 of بعا for بعو) Lending. Exciting to the commission of sin. Impregnating.

A ابعاد *abʿād,* (pl. of بعد *buʿd*) Distances. ابعاد ثلاثه *abʿādi salāsa,* The three distances, *i.e.* Length, depth, and breadth. *Ibʿād,* (v. n. 4 of بعد) Going to a distance. Placing at or drawing to a distance. Alienating.

A ابعار *abʿār,* (pl. of بعر) *baʿr*) Excrements of camels or sheep. *Ibʿār,* (v. n. 4 of بعر) Purging the intestines.

A ابعاض *abʿāz,* (pl. of بعض *baʿz*) Parts of a thing. *Ibʿāz,* (v. n. 4 of بعض) Abounding in gnats.

A ابعاط *ibʿāt,* (v. n. 4 of بعط) Placing at a distance. Removing to a distance (particularly with cattle for the benefit of pasture). Exceeding bounds in ignorance or turpitude. Going beyond one's power. Being made to undertake what is beyond one's power. Fleeing, running away. Pride. Ignorance. An indecent word, a shameful act.

A ابعد *abʿad,* (pl. اباعد *abāʿid*) Very remote. Profit, advantage. A traitor. غير ابعد *ghayr abʿadin,* Worthless.

A ابعرة *abʿirat,* (pl. of بعير *baʿīr*) Camels four years old, or nine years old.

A ابغاء *ibghāʾ,* (v. n. 4 of بغي) Seeking, enquiring for another. Assisting another in searching for any thing. Rendering one insolent and rebellious (prosperity).

A ابغاش *ibghāsh,* (v. n. 4 of بغش) Moistening with a slight shower.

A ابغاض *abghāz,* (pl. of بغض *bughz*) Hatreds. *Ibghāz,* (v. n. 4 of بغض) Bearing hatred, hating. Provoking, making hate. Holding (one) as an enemy.

A ابغث *abghas,* Dusty, inclining to a brown or dusky colour. A dusty place. A variegated ram. A lion. الابغث *al abghas,* A lion. A sort of bird.

A ابغثة *abghisat,* (pl. of بغاث *baghās, bughās,* or *bighās*) Kites or birds of prey, of the inferior kind of the hawk-species.

A ابغض *abghaz,* A great hater. Most odious.

P آبفت *ābaft,* A kind of coarse cloth.

P ابفره *abfara,* A stallion.

A ابفون *abfūn,* Berries of the wild olive.

P آبق *ābak,* Quicksilver.

A آبق *ābik,* (pl. اُبّاق *ubbāk*) Runaway (slave).

A أبق *abaka,* (fut. يأبق *yaʾbuku,* or *yaʾbiku*) (The slave) absconded.

A ابق *abk* or *abak,* (v. n. of ابق) Running away (a slave). *Abak,* A kind of bark of which they make ropes. Hemp, or the bark of it.

A ابقاء *ibkāʾ,* (v. n. 4 of بقي) Confirming, establishing. Keeping, preserving, hoarding, laying by. Pitying, regarding with compassion, sparing.

A ابقاق *ibkāk,* (v. n. 4 of بقّ) Being loquacious and talkative. Doing on a large scale (good or evil). Bringing forth many children. Yeaning in a time of scarcity and being lean (a sheep). Going out (the sticks, straws, and rubbish of a valley).

A ابقال *ibkāl,* (v. n. 4 of بقل) Being fruitful in pot-herbs or herbage in general. Having cattle feeding on pot-herbs. Sprouting (the beard of a youth). Making (the beard) sprout. Becoming green and flourishing (the plant رمث *rims*).

A ابقان *ibkān,* (v. n. 4 of بقن) Being fruitful, abounding in produce.

P A ابقر *abkar,* Nitre, saltpetre.

A ابقع *abkaʿ,* (A pye) variegated, black and white. Clad in patched raiment.

A ابقور *ubkūr,* (pl. of بقرة *bakarat*) Cows, oxen.

A ابقيٰ *abka',* More or most lasting.

P آبك *ābak,* Quicksilver. Measles, pimples, blotches. *Ābuk,* Any thing watery.

A آبك *ābaka,* (or آب لك *āba laka*) Woe to thee! Name of a place.

A ابك *abak,* (v. n. of ابك) Being very fleshy. لا ابك *lā abaka,* There is no escape for thee. *Abik,* Dull, stupid, unskilful.

A ابكّ *abakk,* (pl. بكّان *bukkān*) A severe season (for cattle). One who takes care of the property of his relations. One who drives (asses, &c.) into a thronged compact body. One whose hand has been cut off. Very wise. Name of a place.

A ابكاء *ibkā*, (v. n. 4 of بكي) Making one weep.

P آبكار *āb-kār*, A water-carrier. A cup-bearer. A wine-merchant. A drinker of wine. A jeweller, polisher of gems. A distillery.

P ابكار *abkār*, Agriculture.

A ابكار *abkār*, (pl. of بكر *bikr*) Virgins, maidens. *Ibkār*, (v. n. 4 of بكر) Performing any thing in the morning. Making haste, taking time by the forelock. Coming to drink early in the morning (camels). Causing (one) to rise betimes. Preceding, going before. The morning.

P آبكاري *āb-kārī*, A tax on the manufacture and sale of spirituous liquors, and intoxicating drugs. A distillery.

A ابكام *ibkām*, (v. n. 4 of بكم) Silencing, striking dumb. Abstaining from cohabitation with a wife.

P آبكامه *āb-kāma*, A kind of sour and bitter gruel or drink, prepared in different ways, for creating appetite or aiding digestion. Sauce, condiment.

P آبكبود *āb-kabūd*, The China sea. An excellent sword.

A ابكر *abkur*, (pl. of بكر *bakr*) Young camels.

P آبكش *āb-kash*, A water-carrier, or drawer.

P آب كشي *āb-kashī*, The drawing of water. آب كشي كردن *āb-kashī kardan*, To draw water. گاو آبكشي *gāvi āb-kashī*, An ox for drawing water.

P آبكشين *ābkashīn*, A bracelet.

P آبكم *ābkam*, A kind of serpent.

A ابكم *abkam*, (pl. بكم *bukm*) Dumb.

P آبكمه *āb-kuma*, A dark-coloured and fetid water found in certain fish, applied in cases of fracture.

P آبكند *āb-kand*, Any hollow channel excavated by the rushing of a torrent; a place where water collects and stagnates. A pond. Name of a city.

P آبكور *āb-kūr*, Miserly, churlish.

A ابكي *abka'*, More or most of a weeper.

P ابگ *abag*, Name of a town near Shirāz.

P آبگانه *ābgāna*, An abortion.

P آبگاه *āb-gāh*, The back and sides under the short ribs. A pond, a cistern.

P آبگذار *āb-guzār*, A ford, a ferry. An express.

P آبگذر *āb-guzar*, A canal, a channel for water.

P آب گردان *āb-gardān*, A ladle.

P آبگردش *āb-gardish*, A whirlpool, an eddy. A fleet horse. Vertigo. Crop sickness.

P آبگور *āb-gūr*, A horse-trough, an aqueduct.

P آبگورکش *āb-gūr-kash*, A worthless fellow.

P آبگون *āb-gūn*, Water-coloured, azure, liquid blue. The heavens. Glass. Ice. A bright sword. A kind of knife. A river. Starch mixed with blue. Name of a river flowing from Khwārazm, and falling into the Caspian sea. آبگون پل *āb-gūn pul*, The heavens. P آبگون صدف *āb-gūn sadaf*, (or آبگون قفس *āb-gūn kafas*) The heavens. The sun and moon. آبگون طارم *āb-gūn-tāram*, The heavens.

P آبگه *āb-gah*, A watering-place, cistern, reservoir.

P آبگي *ābagī*, Watery.

P آبگير *āb-gīr*, Any hollow place where water collects and stagnates; a pool, pond, ditch. A weaver's brush for sprinkling yarn in the loom.

P آبگيرناك *āb-gīrnāk*, Full of pools and ditches.

P آبگينه *āb-gīna*, Glass. A drinking-glass. A foil set under gems. A diamond. Wine. A lover's tears. آبگينهٔ شامي *ābgīnaï shāmī*, A name for the most transparent glass. آبگينهٔ طارم *ābgīnaï tāram*, The heavens.

P آبگينه خانه *ābgīna-khāna*, A glazed house. A room hung with mirrors. The first heaven.

P آبگينه گر *ābgīnagar*, A glass-maker.

A آبل *ābal*, More or most expert in the tending and management of camels. *Ābil*, (pl. ابّال *ubbāl*) (A camel) which supplies the absence of water by fresh grass. A possessor of camels. Expert in the management of camels or sheep.

A ابل *abl*, (v. n. of ابل) Possessing many camels; being skilful and careful in the management of them. Being numerous (camels). Making camels graze for any one. Supplying by green herbage the absence of water (cattle). Wandering and pasturing without a keeper (camels), straying, running away. Abstaining, refraining. Being religious, devout. Overcoming, conquering. Striking with a stick. Constructing a parapet round a well. *Abl*, or *ubl*, A date, fresh or dry. *Ibl*, or *ibil*, (pl. آبال *ābāl*) A camel, the camel species. Clouds fraught with rain. *Ubl*, (pl. of ابيل *abīl*) Christian monks. *Abal*, (v. n. of ابل) Being skilful in the management of camels or sheep. Becoming numerous (camels). Depression of spirits, oppression of the stomach (from bad air or indigestion). *Abil*, Skilful in the management of camels or sheep. A possessor of camels. A corpulent camel. *Ubul*, Grass or stubble remaining after reaping or mowing, or left uncropped by cattle. ابل ابل *ibl ubbal*, Camels straying without a keeper.

P ابل *abil*, The lesser cardamom. *Abul*, Name of a stringent medicinal plant.

A ابلّ *aball*, More or most humid, moist. A perjured man, a wicked wretch. A fornicator. Shameless. Inaccessible. Close-fisted, covetous. One who delays payment of a debt. Quarrelsome, contentious. Cruel, tyrannical. Smooth, bare.

A ابلاء *ablā'*, (pl. of بلي *baly*, or بلو *balw*) Fatigued, emaciated (camels). Worn out with cares and misfortunes. Managers of money or other estates. *Iblā'*, (v. n. 4 of بلي) Wearing out a garment. Trying, proving. Making one a partaker of any benefit. Swearing. Tendering an excuse or apology which is accepted. Requiring one to swear. Tying a camel to the grave of her deceased master. Having enough, being content.

A ابلات *iblāt*, (v. n. 4 of بلت) Causing to swear, adjuring. Progeny, breed.

A ابلاج *iblāj*, (v. n. 4 of بلج) Shining forth, appearing (the dawn). Making clear. Exhilarating.

A ابلاح *iblāh*, (v. n. 4 of بلح) Bearing unripe dates called بلح *balah*, (a palm-tree). Fatiguing, tiring any one (travel).

A ابلاد *ablād*, (pl. of بلد *balad*) Signs, marks. *Iblād*, (v. n. 4 of بلد) Cleaving to the earth; being poor. Having a sluggish beast. Compelling to dwell in a place.

A ابلاس *iblās*, (v. n. 4 of بلس) Being astonied, confounded, broken-spirited, and silent from grief or eager desire.

A ابلاط *iblāt*, (v. n. 4 of بلط) Sticking close to the ground. Becoming poor. Poverty. Importuning, troubling. Stripping one of all his possessions. Paving with stones. Wetting the pavement.

A ابلاع *iblā'*, (v. n. 4 of بلع) Causing, allowing, or giving time to swallow.

A ابلاغ *iblāgh*, (v. n. 4 of بلغ) Causing to arrive.

A ابلاق *iblāk*, (v. n. 4 of بلق) Opening wide a door. Shutting a door. Begetting pie-bald stock.

A ابلال *iblāl*, (v. n. 4 of بلّ) Recovering from sickness. Escaping. Bearing fruit. Travelling. Becoming strait and narrow. Being weak (through mischief and wickedness). Straying, being lost (cattle). Becoming full of sap (a branch). Prevailing against, overcoming.

A ابلام *iblām*, (v. n. 4 of بلم) Being swollen (a man's lip). Wanting the male. Keeping silence. Exposing a foul deed.

A ابلان *ibilāni*, Two troops of camels (as two flocks of sheep are called غنمان *ghanamāni*).

A ابلاه *iblāh*, (v. n. 4 of بله) Discovering one to be simple and ignorant.

A ابلة *ablat* or *abalat*, Heaviness or oppression of spirits (from indigestion). A fault, crime. كلّ مال اديت زكوته فقد ذهبت ابلته *kullu mālin uddiyat zakātuhu, fa kad zahābat abalatuhu*, All cattle on which tithe has been paid are secure from disease. *Iblat*, Hostility, enmity. *Ublat*, A murrain, blight. A tribe. *Abilat*, A petition. Any thing wanted. Necessity, indigence. Prolificness.

A ابلّة *ibillat*, Progeny, tribe. *Ubullat*, Companions, tribes. Progeny. Dates bruised between two stones, and then milked upon. A lump of dates. Name of a very pleasant place near Basra. هو من ابلة سوء *huwa min ubullati saw'in*, He is of a bad stock.

A ابلج *ablaj*, One whose eye-brows are wide apart (in opposition to those which meet at the nose). Clear, bright, resplendent, evident.

A ابلجاج *iblijāj*, (v. n. 9 of بلج) Being clear.

A ابلح *ablah*, The myrobalan-nut.

A ابلخ *ablakh*, Proud (man).

A ابلد *ablad*, One whose eye-brows are distant. Corpulent. Dull, stupid.

A ابلغ *ablagh*, More or most perfect, most effectual. More or most emphatic. ابلغ وجوه *ablaghu wujūhin*, The most effectual of modes.

A ابلق *ablak*, Pie-bald, black and white, party-coloured. The animal براق *burāk*. A lute, harp. Name of a tribe. الابلق الفرد *al ablaku'l fard*, Name of the fortress of سموءل بن عاديا *samawɛal bin ɛādiyā*, said to have been built by Solomon, and considered impregnable. الابلق العقوق *al ablaku'l ɛakūk*, The dawn. An impossibility. ابلق ايام *ablaki ayyām*, The world. P ابلق چرخ *ablaki charkh*, (or ابلق فلك *ablaki falak*) Night and day. Time. The world.

A ابلقاق *iblikāk*, (v. n. 9 of بلق) Being pie-bald.

P ابلگ *ablag*, Pie-bald. *Abalag* or *abilg*, A spark of fire.

A ابلم *ablam*, One who has swelled lips. Swollen-lipped (man). A kind of pot-herb like a bean. *Ablam*, *iblam*, or *ublam*, The leaf of the bdellium.

A ابلمة *ablamat*, *iblamat*, or *ublamat*, The leaf of the bdellium-tree. شقّ الابلمة *shakku'l ablamat*, In equal halves.

A ابلنداح *iblindāh*, (v. n. 3 of بلدح Q) Being spacious. Being broken down (a cistern).

A ابلنداك *iblindāk*, (v. n. 3 of بلدك Q) Being spacious (a place). Being broken down even with the ground (a cistern).

A ابلنصاء *iblinsāɛ*, (v. n. 3 of بلصيٰ Q) Going. Coming out of.

A ابلنقاع *iblinkāɛ*, (v. n. 3 of بلقع Q) Being dispelled (grief). Shining forth (the dawn).

A ابلنقاق *iblinkāk*, (v. n. 3 of بلقق Q) Being very clear and distinct from others (a road).

P آبلوج *āblūj*, (ابلوج *ablūj*, or ابلوچ *ablūch*) White sugar-candy. A ابلوج السكر *ublūju's sukkar*, Sugar-candy.

P ابلوك *ablūk*, A double-faced man, a hypocrite.

P آبله *ābila*, A blister, pimple. Small-pox. A bubble floating on the water. آبلهٔ چشم *ābilaɛi chashm*, A pearl or white speck upon the eye. آبلهٔ رخ فلك *ābilaɛi rukhi falak*, The stars. آبلهٔ روز *ābilaɛi roz*, The sun. آبلهٔ فرنگ *ābilaɛi firing*, The French or European pox, venereal disease.

A ابله *ablah*, (pl. بله *bulh*) Foolish, simple, ignorant, stupid, oafish. One whose evil is dead or dormant; good-natured, amiable. ابله عقول *ablah ɛakūl*, Simple (from bashfulness) yet intelligent. عيش ابله *ɛayshun ablahu*, An easy life, free from care. شباب ابله *shabāb ablah*, Thoughtless, blundering youth: happy youth, unacquainted with care.

P آبله رسيده *ābila-rasīda*, Blistered (hand).

P آبله زده *ābila-zada*, Pock-marked. Measled.

A ابلهي *ablahī*, Silliness, simpleness, ignorance.

A ابليّ *abuliy*, A Christian monk. *Ibiliy*, *abaliy*, or *ibaliy*, Possessed of, rich in camels.

A ابلئجاج *ibliɛjāj*, (v. n. 12 of بلج) Being clear.

U طين الابليز *tīnu'l ibliz*, Egyptian earth.

A ابليس *iblīs*, The devil. P ابليس پرتلبيس *iblīs pur-talbīs*, The deceitful devil.

P ابليسانه *iblīsāna*, Diabolically, like the devil.

P آبليسه *āblīsa*, A sower, a husbandman.

A ابليقاق *iblīkāk*, (v. n. 11 of بلق) Being very piebald (a horse).

A ابليلاج *iblīlāj*, Clearness, lustre.

A ابليم *iblīm*, Ambergris. Honey.

A ابمّ *abamm*, The bass string of an instrument.

P ابميق *ibmīk*, A coulter. A yoke of oxen.

A ابن *abn*, (v. n. of ابن) Suspecting, rendering suspected. Disgracing any one before his face. Becoming black (blood in a wound). Coagulation, clot, blackness (as of blood in a wound). *Abin*, Thick (soup). Dried (meats). *Uban*, (pl. of ابنة *ubnat*) Enmities, secret grudges. Knots in wood.

A ابن *ibn*, (pl. ابناء *abnāɛ* and بنون *banūn*) A son. It is written بن *bin* when preceded by a proper name and followed by the name of the father: as, حسن بن محمّد *hasan bin muhammad*, Hasan son of Muhammad. ابو عليّ بن سينا *abū ɛaliy bin sīnā*, Father Aliy, son of Sīnā. Name of a celebrated philosopher and physician, known in Europe by the name of Avicenna. ابن الارض *ibnu'l arz*, (Son of the earth) A vegetable. ابن آصيٰ *ibnu āsa'*, A kind of bird. ابن البوح *ibnu'l būh*, A son. ابن بقيع *ibnu bukayɛ*, A dog. ابن البراء *ibnu'l barāɛ*, The first or last day or night of the month. ابن السبيل *ibnu's sabīl*, (Son of the way) A traveller. ابن السحاب *ibnu's sahāb*, (Son of the cloud) Rain. ابن الصبح *ibnu's subh*, (Son of the morning) The sun. A bastard. ابن عشرين *ibnu ɛishrīna*, A youth of twenty. ابن العنب *ibnu'l ɛinab*, (Son of the grape) Wine. ابن الغمام *ibnu'l ghamām*, Hail. ابن الله *ibnu' llāh*, The son of God. Unfortunate, unhappy. ابن الماء *ibnu'l māɛ*, Any water-fowl. ابن مزنة *ibnu muznat*, The moon. ابن مقلة *ibnu muklat*, Name of the inventor of the present Arabic character. ابن الواحد *ibnu'l wāhid*, An only son. ابن الوقت *ibnu'l waht*, A time-server, a sycophant. ابن آوي *ibnu āwa'*, (pl. بنات آوي *banāt āwa'*) A jackal. ابن حبّة *ibnu habbat*, Bread. ابن ذكاء *ibn zukāɛ*, (Child of the sun) The morning.

A ابناء *abnāɛ*, (pl. of ابن *ibn*) Sons. Barbarians, foreigners dwelling in Arabia Felix. ابناي انس و جان *abnāɛi ins u jān*, Men and genii. ابناء جنس *abnāɛi jins*, Persons of rank or condition. ابناء درزه *abnāɛi darza*, Mean, ignoble men. ابناي جهان *abnāɛi jahān*, Men, animals, or plants. ابناي دهر *abnāɛi dahr*, (ابناي زمان *abnāɛi zamān*, ابناي عصر *abnāɛi ɛasr*, or ابناي روزگار *abnāɛi rozgār*) Sons of the age, cotemporaries. *Ibnāɛ*, (v. n. 4 of بني) Ordering a building to be erected. Giving one a building or the means of erecting a building. Fattening.

A ابناج *ibnāj*, (v. n. 4 of بنج) Professing to be allied to a great family.

P ابناخون *abnākhon*, A fortress.

A ابناس *ibnās*, (v. n. 4 of بنس not in use) Fleeing from, shunning (evil).

A ابناق *ibnāk*, (v. n. 4 of بنق) Planting a single palm-shoot.

P آبناك *ābnāk*, Moist, watery, succulent, juicy.

A ابنان *ibnān*, (v. n. 4 of بنّ) Staying, stopping or being confined in a place.

A ابناويّ *abnāwiy*, Barbarous, applied to strangers resident in Arabia.

A ابنبم *abambam*, Name of a place near Taslīs.

A ابنة *ibnat*, (pl. بنات *banāt*) A daughter. ابنة اقعدي و قومي *ibnatu ukɛudī wa kūmī*, (Daughter of sit and rise) A handmaid. ابنة الجبل *ibnatu'l jabal*, (Daughter of the mountain) Echo. *Ubnat*, (pl. ابن *uban*) A vice, stain, spot, blemish. An unnatural propensity. An itching disease in the fundament. A man of sound judgment. Fraud, dissimulation. Secret hatred. A knot in wood, a gnur; a spur. The throat of a camel, the head of the asper artery.

P ابنت زده *ubnat-zada*, Infamous, suspected. A wretch held in abhorrence.

P آبنقره *āb-nukra*, Quicksilver, liquid silver.

A ابنم *ibnum*, (acc. *ibnam*, obliq. *ibnim*) A son.

P آبنوس *ābnūs*, Ebony. A kind of fish.

P آبنوسي *ābnūsī*, Made of ebony. آبنوسي شاخ *ābnūsi-shākh*, An ebony pipe. A pipe played on any festivity.

P آبنوشيدن *āb noshīdan*, To drink water. To be stupefied, astonished, or benumbed.

P ابنه زده *ubna-zada*, Suspected of infamous practices, branded with infamy.

A ابنيٰ *ubna'*, Name of a place in Syria.

A ابنيّ *ibniy*, Filial.

A ابنيات *abniyāt*, (pl. of ابنية *abniyat*) Edifices.

A ابنية *abniyat*, (pl. of بنيّ *baniy*) Edifices, buildings, structures. كتاب الابنية *kitābu'l abniyat*, Name of a grammar by سيبويه *sībawayh*.

P آبو *ābū*, A water-lily.

A ابو *abw*, (v. n. of ابو) Becoming a father. Educating. Paternity.

A ابو *abū*, A father. This word has often the sense of ذو *zū*, Having, endowed with, possessed of: as, ابو الحسن *abū'l husn*, Possessed of beauty. ابو بنات *abū banāt*, Having daughters. ابو شوارب *abū shawārib*, Wearing whiskers. It frequently forms the figure called metonymy: as, ابو اطلاب *abū atlāb*, The father of desires, *i. e.* a lover. ابو الاجساد *abū'l ajsād*, Sulphur. ابو الاخطل *abū'l akhtal*, A horse. ابو الادهم *abū'l adham*, A kettle in which an entire sheep may be dressed. ابو الارواح *abū'l arwāh*, (Father of spirits) Quicksilver. ابو الاضياف *abū'l azyāf*, Father of the guests, *i. e.* a host. ابو اياس *abū iyās*, Any thing used in washing, as marsh-mallows, &c. ابو ايّوب *abū ayyūb*, (Father Job) A camel. ابو

البريص *abū'l burays,* Name of a certain speckled bird. ابو البشر *abū'l bashar,* Adam, the father of man. ابو ثقيف *abū sakif,* Vinegar. ابو حبيب *abū habīb,* Roast kid. ابو حذر *abū hazar,* (Father timidity) A chameleon. ابو الحصين *abū'l husayn,* Father of the little fortress, *i. e.* a fox. ابو الحول *abū'l hiwal,* (Father of prodigies) The sphynx. ابو الحيا *abū'l hayā,* (Father of modesty) Name of Othmān the third Khalīf. ابو الحياة *abū'l hayāt,* (Father of life) Rain. ابو الحيل *abū'l hiyal,* (Father of stratagems) A fox. ابو سرحان *abū sirhān,* A wolf. ابو سريع *abū sarīʿ,* (Father swift) Touchwood. ابو رزين *abū razīn,* A kind of sweetmeat. ابو السرو *abū's sarv,* Incense. ابو سعد *abū saʿd,* Locman the sage. Old age. ابو الشفا *abū'sh shifā,* (Father of health) Sugar. ابو العباب *abū'l ʿubāb,* Water. The first chapter of the Kur'ān. ابو العلاء *abū'l ʿalāʾ,* A dish made of starch, honey, and water. ابو العلا *abū'l ʿula',* Name of a celebrated poet. ابو العمر *abū'l ʿumr,* A vulture which, they say, lives 1000 years. ابو العيزار *abū'l ʿayzār,* A heron. ابو الغياث *abū'l ghiyās,* (Father of relief) Water. ابو الفرج *abū'l faraj,* Name of the author of a Universal History called مختصر الدول *mukhtasaru'd dawal,* (Compendium of the Dynasties), published with a Latin translation by the learned Pocock. ابو الفضل *abū'l fazl,* (Father of excellence) A very learned and accomplished man, secretary to the great Sultān Akbar, Emperor of Hindūstān, and author of the elegant history of the Mogul Emperors (in Persian) called اكبر نامه *akbar nāma.* ابو الفوارس *abū'l fawāris,* Name of a famous orator. ابو القعقاع *abū'l kaʿkāʿ,* (Father of croaking) A crow. ابو قلمون *abū kalamūn,* A kind of changing-coloured silk. A chameleon. A variable, capricious man. The world. A tortoise. A turkey. ابو الكمال *abū'l kamāl,* Father of accomplishments, *i.e.* a drinker of healths. ابو الكنجك *abū'l kunjak,* Any thing new, rare, or agreeable. A facetious, witty, or well-bred man. A buffoon, jester, mimic. ابو مالك *abū mālik,* Hunger. ابو مثوي *abū maswa',* or ابو المنزل *abū'l manzil,* A host. ابو المختار *abū'l mukhtār,* A mule. ابو المرأة *abū'l marʾat,* Father of the wife, *i. e.* a husband. ابو مريم *abū maryam,* A bailiff, a catch-poll. ابو المسافر *abū'l musāfir,* A cheese. ابو المليح *abū'l malīh,* (Father pretty) A lark. ابو مونس *abū mūnis,* (Father sociable) A wax-taper. ابو المهنا *abū'l mahnā,* Wine. ابو نعيم *abū nuʿaym,* White bread. ابو الوثاب *abū'l wassāb,* (Father jump) A flea. ابو الهيجا *abū'l hayjā,* (Father of impetuosity) Name of Alīy, son-in-law of Muhammad. ابو اليقظان *abū'l yakzān,* (Father of the watch) A cock. ابو براقش *abū barākish,* Name of a speckled bird. ابو بكر *abū bakr,* The father-in-law, and first Khalīf, or successor to Muhammad. ابو تراب *abū turāb,* Name of Alīy, son-in-law to Muhammad. ابو جامع *abū jāmiʿ,* (Father collector) A tray. ابو جابر *abū jābir,* (Father restorative) Bread. ابو جعد *abū jaʿd,* (Father of the curled hair) A wolf. ابو جعفر *abū jaʿfar,* A fly. ابو جميل *abū jamīl,* Pot-herbs. ابو جهل *abū jahl,* (Father of ignorance) Name of an uncle of Muhammad. ابو حارث *abū hāris,* A lion. ابو حنيفه *abū hanīfa,* Name of the first great Muhammadan lawyer. ابو خالد *abū khālid,* A dog. ابو خراش *abū khirāsh,* (Father scratch) A cat. ابو خصب *abū khisb,* Flesh. ابو خلسا *abū khalsā,* Melilot, bugloss-plant. ابو ذيال *abū zayyāl,* (Father long-tail) A bull. ابو زيد *abū zayd,* Name of a person mentioned in the *Makāmāti Harīriy.* ابو سليمان *abū sulaymān,* A cock. ابو سيف *abū sayf,* Father of the sword, a name of Nādir Shāh. ابو صفوان *abū safwān,* Milk. ابو طالب *abū tālib,* Name of the Father of Alīy. ابو طامون *abū tāmūn,* Jews' pitch. ابو طيب *abū tīb,* A druggist. ابو عامر *abū ʿāmir,* A hyæna. ابو عكرمة *abū ʿikrimat,* A pigeon. ابو علس *abū ʿals,* A species of violet. ابو عمرة *abū ʿamrat,* Hunger. ابو عون *abū ʿawn,* A date. Salt. ابو فراس *abū farrās,* A tiger. ابو قابوس *abū kābūs,* Name of Nuʿmān king of Arabia. ابو قانيس *abū kānis,* A herb used in dying. ابو قيس *abū kays,* An ape. ابو كلب *abū kalb,* A Dutch coin current in Egypt, something inferior in value to a Spanish piastre (4*s*. 8*d*.). It bears the impression of a lion, which, however, the Arabians have changed to كلب *kalb,* a dog, perhaps to show their contempt for Christians, or on account of its base alloy. ابو كير *abū kīr,* Name of an island near Alexandria. ابو لهو *abū lahw,* A drum. ابو مرّة *abū murrat,* Father of bitterness or sorrow, *i.e.* the devil. ابو مزاحم *abū muzāhim,* A bull. ابو مضا *abū mazā,* A horse. ابو معاشر *abū maʿāshir,* (Father of conversation) The famous astronomer and astrologer, known in Europe by the name of Albumazar. He died an. 885. ابو منصور *abū mansūr,* Father of defence, *i.e.* a city. ابو ناجع *abū nājiʿ,* (Father wholesome) Confection. ابو نافع *abū nāfiʿ,* (Father wholesome) Vinegar. ابو هريرة *abū hurayra,* Father of the kitten; name of one of Muhammad's companions. ابو يحيي *abū yahya',* Name of the angel of death, whom the Arabians call likewise عزرائل *ʿizrāʾil,* and the Persians مرداد *murdād;* whose office it is, according to Muhammadan belief, to separate the soul from the body. لله ابوك *li'llāh abūka,* God has dealt bountifully with thy father (in giving him such a son).

A ابواء *abwāʾ,* The parental relation. A she-goat indisposed from the smell of urine.

A ابواب *abwāb,* (pl. of باب *bāb*) Gates, doors. Chapters. Conjugations. Dues, fees, taxes. Points, principles. (In India) An assessment on lands over and above the original rent. باب الابواب *bābu'l abwāb,* (Port of ports) The fortress of Darband on the Caspian sea. ابواب التحويل *abwābu't tahwīl,* A register of receipts and disbursements of the household and revenue. ابواب السعادة *abwābu's saʿādat,* (The ports of felicity) Title of a book. ابواب المال *abwābu'l māl,* A register containing the amount of revenue, with the increase or deficiency. P ابواب تهانه داري *abwābi thāna-dārī,* Taxes levied on the retailers of liquors and other articles in bazars attached to the garrisons. ابواب حالي *abwābi hālī,* New taxes, arbitrary impositions. ابواب سابق *abwābi sābik,* Old, established taxes. ابواب شادي *abwābi shādī,* An imposition levied to defray the marriage-expenses of a Rājā, chief, or great landholder. ابواب فوجداري *abwābi fawjdārī,* Charges and fines in criminal courts. N.B. There are many other taxes designated by the word ابواب *abwāb,* joined to another. بهمه ابواب *ba hama abwāb,* By all means, in every way.

A ابواز *abwāz,* (pl. of باز *bāz*) Falcons, hawks.

A ابواص *abwās,* (pl. of بوص *baws*) Kinds.

A ابواع *abwāʿ,* A species of sheep (as taking long steps). This word is used also in calling her to be milked. (pl. of باع *bāʿ* or بوع *bawʿ*) Fathoms.

A ابواق *abwāk,* (pl. of بوق *būk*) Trumpets, horns.

A ابوال *abwāl,* (pl. of بول *bawl*) Urines. ابوال البغال *abwālu'l bighāl,* (Mules' urine) Wine, (according to some) the vapour سراب *sarāb.*

A ابوان *abawāni* Parents, father and mother.

A ابوب *ubūb,* (v. n. of ابّ) Blowing (wind).

P ابوبان *abūbān,* Repentance.

A ابوبة *abwibat,* (pl. of باب) Doors. Chapters.

A ابوّة *ubūwat,* Paternity. Fathers.

A ابوت *ubūt,* (v. n. of ابت) Being hot and sultry (a day). Tumour from drinking.

A ابود *ubūd,* (v. n. of ابد) Abiding, remaining permanently. Introducing in a poem words uncommon and hard to understand. Being unsociable, and running away. (pl. of ابد *abad*) Ages.

A ابودردا *abūdardā,* (by some *abūdurdā*) Name of a companion of Muhammad.

A ابؤر *abʾur,* (pl. of بئر *biʾr*) Wells.

P آبورز *āb-warz,* A swimmer.

P آب ورزي *āb-warzī,* Swimming, natation.

A ابؤز *abʾuz,* (pl. of بأز *baʾz*) Falcons.

A ابوز *abūz,* Springing, bounding (deer). *Ubūz,* (v. n. of ابز) Springing, bounding, leaping.

A ابؤس *abʾus,* (pl. of بؤس *buʾs*) Misfortunes.

A ابوص *abūs,* Swift, fleet (horse).

A ابوض *abūz,* Very swift (horse).

A ابوق *abūk,* (pl. ابّق *ubbak*) Runaway (slave).

A ابول *abūl,* A troop of camels, herd or flock of cattle, horses, or birds; a series or string of them following one another. *Ubūl,* (v. n. of ابل Supplying by green herbage the place of water (cattle). Abstaining from venery. Wandering in the night and pasturing without a keeper; straying, running away (camels). Growing long and capable of being cropped by camels (grass). Stopping, or remaining in a place (with camels).

P ابومان *abūmān*, Repentance.

P ابون *abūn*, Elecampane, ginger.

A ابون *abūn*, (pl. of اب *ab*) Fathers. P. دير ابّون *dayr abbūn*, Name of a monastery in Mesopotamia, near which is a large barrow.

A ابونة *abwinat*, (pl. of بوان *biwān* or *buwān*) Tent-posts.

P آبوند *ābwand*, A vessel in which water is kept.

A ابويّ *abawīy*, Paternal.

P ابويان *abūyān*, Repentance.

A ابوين *abawayni*, (oblique dual) The parents.

A آبه الله *ābahu allāh*, May God remove him to a distance!

A ابه *abh*, (v. n. of ابه) Calling one's attention. Suspecting. *Abh* or *abah*, (v. n. of ابه) Attending to, recollecting, remembering. Recalling to mind a thing forgotten. يا ابه *yā abah*, O father!

A ابّة *abahh*, Hoarse.

A ابهاء *abhāʼ*, (pl. of بهو *bahw*) Projecting tents. Extensive countries. Cavities of breasts. Wombs. Lairs of wild oxen. *Ibhāʼ*, (v. n. 4 of بهأ) Tearing (a garment). Emptying (a house). (v. n. 4 of بها for بهو) Demolishing a house or tent. Rending a garment. Emptying (a vessel). Emptying, deserting (a house). Keeping (a war-horse) unemployed. Having a handsome face.

A ابهاج *ibhāj*, (v. n. 4 of بهج) Exhilarating. Being verdant and luxuriant (ground).

A ابهار *ibhār*, (v. n. 4 of بهر) Producing something wonderful. Becoming rich after having been poor. Being scorched by the noon-day sun. Being changeable, versatile, at one time easy and mild, at another cross-grained and perverse. Marrying a lady, slender, beautiful, and delicate.

A ابهاس *ibhās*, (v. n. 4 of بهس not used) Hindering, preventing.

A ابهاض *ibhāz*, (v. n. 4 of بهض) Oppressing, vexing, afflicting.

A ابهال *ibhāl*, (v. n. 4 of بهل) Irrigating a sown field. Giving one liberty to do what he pleases. Leaving, letting alone. Allowing (a camel) to pasture without a keeper, and to be sucked by her colt.

A ابهام *ibhām*, (v. n. 4 of بهم) Shutting, closing (a door). Making obscure and unintelligible. Talking obscurely. Being doubtful and uncertain. Turning (any one) away from a design. Producing abundantly the plant بهمي *buhma'* (the ground). (pl. اباهم *abāhim* or اباهيم *abāhīm*) The thumb. The great toe.

A ابّهة *ubbahat*, Magnificence, grandeur, glory; beauty, grace, elegance.

A ابهج *abhaj*, More or most beautiful.

P ابهر *abhar*, A watermill.

A ابهر *abhar*, The back. A vein in the back. The jugular vein. The middle vein of the arm. (pl. اباهر *abāhir*) The narrower edge of a pen or feather. The back of a bow; also that curved part from the handle to the extremities or horns of a bow. Good ground, but not overflowed. A dry thorn or thistle. Name of a city.

A ابهل *abhal*, The produce of a tree whose leaf is like the tamarisk, and fruit like the نبق *nabk*. It is not the عرعر *ʻarʻar*, as some have imagined.

P ابهل *ubhul*, Seed of the mountain-cypress, or juniper. Juniper-berries.

A ابهم *abham*, (pl. بهم *buhm* and *buhum*) Silent. A stammerer, stutterer, barbarian. Dumb. A woman whom by the laws of consanguinity a man is forbidden to marry.

P ابهول *ubhūl*, Liquorice-root.

P آبهي *ābihī*, Name of the river آهو *āhū*.

A ابهي *abha'*, More or most beautiful. *Abhī*, (and with tanwīn, ابه *abhin*) (pl. of بهو *bahw*) Extensive countries. Cavities of breasts. Wombs.

A ابهيرار *ibhīrār*, (v. n. 11 of بهر) Being half-spent, having reached the middle (the night). Being thick (the darkness). Being gone the greater part of the night, one-third remaining.

A آبي *āba'*, Distempered by the smell of urine (a he-goat). *Ābī*, (pl. آبين *ābīn*, اباة *ubāt*, ابيّ *ubayy*, and اباء *ubāʼ*) One who refuses, rejects, or loathes. آبي اللحم *ābi'l lahm*, (A loather of flesh) Name of one of Muhammad's companions.

P آبي *ābī*, Watery. Blue. A quince. A kind of grape. برج آبي *burji ābī*, A reservoir. A building in the water. The constellation Aquarius. مرغ آبي *murgh-ābī*, A water-fowl, a duck.

A ابي *aba'*, (fut. يأبي *yaʼba'* or *yaʼbī*) He refused.

A ابي *aba'*, (v. n. of ابي) Having the stomach overloaded with milk (a camel's colt), and therefore loathing it. Contracting a disease from the smell of urine (a goat).

P ابي *abī*, Without.

A ابّي *abba'*, Name of a man, of a well in Madīna, of a river near Kūfa, and of another in the marshes of Wāsit.

A ابيّ *abīy*, A refuser, rejecter, loather. Averse, refractory, untractable, difficult, inaccessible. الابيّ *al abīy*, The lion (as untractable). A proper name. (for ابويّ *abawīy*) Paternal. *Ubayy*, (for ابيو *ubayw*, dim. of اب *ab*) A little father. (pl. of آبي *ābī*) Refusers, rejecters, loathers.

A ابيات *abyāt*, (pl. of بيت *bayt*) Verses.

P آبيار *āb-yār*, A waterer, sprinkler, irrigator.

P آبياري *āb-yārī*, Irrigation. آبياري كردن *āb-yārī kardan*, To irrigate, to water (fields).

P ابياري *abyārī*, A kind of stuff of a thin texture. A species of dove.

P آبيان *ābyān*, Penitent.

A ابيان *abyān*, (pl. of بيّن *bayyin*, Eloquent. *Abayān*, (pl. ابيان *ibyān*) A loather of food or vice.

A ابياوات *abyāwāt*, (pl. of بيوت *buyūt*, Houses, pl. of بيت *bayt*, A house) Many houses.

A ابيب *abīb*, Preparation for a journey.

A ابية *ibyat*, A stoppage of milk in the breast. *Ubyat*, Pride, ostentation, greatness.

A ابيّة *abīyat*, A camel taking the male, but not conceiving. A camel refusing water, and not returning home in the evening. A woman who has no taste for supper.

A ابيحر *ubayhir*, (irreg. dim. of بحر *bahr*) A mere.

P آبيد *ābīd*, A spark of fire.

A ابيد *abīd*, Eternal. ابيد الابيد *abīda'l abīd*, For ever, to all eternity. الابيد *al abīd*, An evergreen.

P ابيداد *abīdād*, Tyranny, injustice.

P ابير *abīr*, A bucket. A spark. Tears. A shirt.

A ابير *ubayr*, (dim. of ابرة *ibrat*) A small needle. Name of a mountain, of a well, and of a man.

A ابيرق *ubayrik*, (dim. of استبرق *istabrak*) A vesture of coarse silk.

A ابيره *ubayrih*, (dim. of ابراهيم *ibrāhīm*) Little Abraham.

P ابيز *abīz*, A spark of fire. An urn.

P ابيستن *abestan*, To adorn, embellish, decorate.

A ابيش *abīsh*, A bridegroom's shirt.

P ابيشم *abīsham*, Flue of raw silk; the cocoon.

P ابي شمار *abī shumār*, Innumerable.

A ابيض *abyaz*, (pl. بيض *bīz*) White. A sword (as being bright). Silver. A man of unsullied character. Certain stars in the milky way. Whiter (but expressed more accurately by اشدّ بياضا *ashaddu bayāzan*). ابو الابيض *abū'l abyaz*, Milk. الموت الابيض *al mawtu'l abyaz*, Sudden death.

A ابيّض *ubayyiz*, (dim. of اباض *ibāz*) A small rope for tying a camel's leg.

A ابيضاض *ibyizāz*, (v. n. 9 of باض for بيض) Being white. Whiteness.

A ابيضان *abyazāni*, Two days, or two months. Two veins in a camel's udder. الابيضان *al abyazāni*, Milk and water; wheat and water; fat and young (the two whites).

A ابيعاء *abyiʻāʼ*, (pl. of بيّع) Buyers. Sellers.

P ابيق *abīk*, A bright colour. A depilatory drug.

A ابيقر *ubaykir*, Worthless, good for nothing.

A ابيقع *ubaykiʻ*, A year of little rain.

A ابيكر *ubaykir*, (dim. of بكر *bakar*) Morning.

A ابيل *abīl*, Sad, melancholy. (pl. آبال *ābāl* and ابل *ubl*) An austere Christian monk. The chief of those monks in the East. A bundle of grass or hay. A thick baton, a truncheon. ابيل الابيلين *abīlu'l abīlīn*, (or ابيل الابيليين *abīlu'l abīlīyīn*) (Weeper of weepers) Jesus Christ.

A ابّيل *ibbīl*, A herd or flock of horses, camels, or birds; a string of them following each other.

A ابيلة *abīlat*, A bundle of grass or hay.

A ابيلة *ubaylat*, (dim. of ابل *ibl*) A little camel.

A ابيلى *ubayla'*, Name of a woman.

A ابيلىّ *ubaylīy*, An austere Christian monk, weeping over the sins of the age.

A آبين *ābīn*, Name of a village in the vicinity of which is a cave, whence the substance called موميا *mūmiyā* is procured.

A ابين *abyan*, More or most eloquent. More or most clear, distinct, evident, obvious. *Ubayn*, Name of a reporter of traditions.

A ابيناء *abyināʼ*, (pl. of بيّن *bayyin*) Evident. Eloquent. *Ubaynāʼ*, or ابينون *ubaynūn*, (dim. of ابناء *abnāʼ*) Little sons.

P ابيو *abev*, Blue-coloured.

P ابيورد *abīward*, Name of a city in Khurāsān.

P ابيون *abyūn*, Opium, poppy-juice. Treacle.

A ابييضاض *ibyīẓāẓ*, (v. n. 11 of باض for بيض) Being exceedingly white. Intense whiteness.

G ابي يهميا *abī yahmiyā*, A cramp, a spasm.

P اپار *ipār*, Thyme, sweet marjoram.

P اپاره *apāra*, Extended, level. Simple.

P اپدر *apidar*, Here, behold!

P اپرا *aprā*, (in zand and Pāz.) Soil, earth, mould.

P اپراهام *iprāhām*, (in zand and Pāzand) Abraham, now called in Arabic Ibrāhīm.

P اپرخيده *aparkhīda*, Clear, pure, without alloy.

P اپرناك *apurnāk*, (in zand and Pāzand) A youth. Turks.

P اپرنداخ *aprandākh*, Goat's skin drest.

P اپرواز *aparwāz*, Flight.

P اپرويز *aparwez*, Victorious, glorious. Name of a king. A sieve. A guide. A sugar-refinery.

P اپسان *apsān*, A whetstone.

P اپشك *apshak*, Dew.

P اپغده *ipghada*, Vain, foolish, light-headed.

P اپگانه *apgāna*, An abortion.

P آپوق *āpūk*, Making a noise by filling the mouth with wind, and then striking it.

P اپيرش *apīrash*, A stadium, a race-ground.

P اپيرك *ipayrak*, Of a lead-colour. Name of an island.

P اپيرنداخ *apīrandākh*, Goat's skin drest.

P اپيز *apīz*, (or اپيزه *apīza*) An urn, a pitcher. A crooked billet with which they draw water.

P اپيون *apyūn*, Opium, poppy-juice. Treacle.

P ات *at*, The affix pronoun of the second person singular to a word ending in mute ه *he*: as خانه ات *khāna at*, Thy house.

A اتّ *att*, (v. n. of اتّ) Overcoming in an argument, convincing by proof, gaining a cause. Breaking the skull.

P اتا *atā*, (or *itā*) A father.

A اتاء *itāʼ*, (v. n. of اتا for اتو) Producing, bringing forth copiously, shooting out buds, yielding fruit. Bringing forth young. Any thing produced by a tree (as blossoms or fruit). (pl. of اتيّ *ita'*) Things fallen into and floating on the water (as wood or leaves). *Itāʼ* or *atāʼ*, Thirst. The fruit of the palm-tree. Produce of any kind (whether from land or cattle).

A اتّاء *ittiʼāʼ*, (v. n. 8 of وأي) Taking warning. Receiving a promise.

A آتاب *ātāb*, (pl. of اتب *itb*) Short breeches, drawers. Shifts.

A اتاب *itʼāb*, (v. n. 4 of وأب irreg.) Provoking, enraging. Outraging decency and putting to the blush. Hindering shamefully. Blushing, being ashamed. Averting.

A اتاب *itāb*, (pl. of اتب *itb*) Drawers. Sleeveless shifts.

P اتابك *atābak*, (from اتا *atā*, A father, and بك *bak*, A prince) The lord father (a title given to the governors of Shīrāz. A guardian, preceptor, teacher. اتابك اعظم *atābuki aʼzam*, The prime minister, or vizir; and sometimes the king himself.

A اتأة *atʼat*, Name of a woman and of a mountain.

A T اتات *atāt*, Pomp, grandeur.

A اتاحة *itāhat*, (v. n. 4 of تاح for تيح) Determining, decreeing.

A اتاد *itād*, A rope with which they tie together the legs of a cow whilst milking.

P اتاده *itā-dih*, Tributary. A briber.

A اتأرة *itʼārat*, (v. n. 4 of تأر) Fixing the eye intently upon, following with the eye. Bastinading.

A اتارة *itārat*, (v. n. 4 of تار for تور) Reiterating, repeating. Fixing the eye intently upon.

A اتاسة *itāsat*, (v. n. 4 of تيس) Rendering void.

A اتاعة *itāʼat*, (v. n. 4 of تاع for تيع) Vomiting repeatedly.

A اتاق *itʼāk*, (v. n. 4 of تئق) Filling (a leathern bottle or cistern).

A اتاقة *itākat*, (v. n. 4 of تاق for توق) Bending a bow very much, drawing the arrow to the head.

A اتاكة *itākat*, (v. n. 4 of تاك for تيك) Plucking out (hairs, feathers, &c.).

P اتاله *atāla*, Pottage, gruel.

A اتاليق *atālīk*, A guardian, a tutor.

A اتآم *itʼām*, (v. n. 4 of تأم) Slaughtering a milch ewe in a scarce season.

A اتّآم *ittiʼām*, (v. n. 8 of وأم) Bearing twins.

A اتآمة *itʼāmat*, (v. n. 4 of تأم) Bringing forth twins. Lying with (a woman). Bursting (a woman), making both passages into one.

P اتان *atān* or *utān*, A she-ass.

A اتان *atān*, (or *itān*) (pl. آتن *ātun*, اتن *utn*, *utun*, and مأتوناء *maʼtūnāʼ*) A she-ass. The place at the mouth of a well where they stand to draw water. *Atān*, (pl. اتن *utun*) The seat of a camel's saddle, or the cushion in litters carried by camels on which travellers recline. اتان الضحل *atānu'z zahl*, A stone in the water, the upper part appearing above. A hard round stone placed near a well, green and slippery.

A اتانة *atānat*, (rarely used) A she-ass.

A اتانين *atānīn*, (pl. of اتّون) Furnaces. Ovens.

A اتاوة *itāwat*, (v. n. of اتا for اتو) Bribing. Paying tribute. (pl. اتاويّ *atāwīy*, اتاوي *atāwa'*, اتاوات *itāwāt*, اتا *ata'*, or اتيّ *atīy*) Tribute. Corruption, bribery, a present to a judge with the view to gain a cause. A gift.

A اتاويّ *atāwīy*, (pl. of اتاوة *itāwat*) Tributes. Bribes. *Atāwīy*, *itāwīy*, or *utāwīy*, A guest, stranger, foreigner, traveller. Water brought to a piece of ground. An unexpected overflow of water.

A اتاويات *atāwīyāt*, Strange, foreign (women). Travelling (women) far from home.

A اتاوه *atāwih*, (pl. of توه *tuwah*) Astonished, bewildered. (pl of تيه *tīh*) Deserts.

A اتب *itb*, (pl. آتاب *ātāb*, اتاب *itāb*, and اتوب *utūb*) A kind of short shift or inner garment, slit, and without sleeves, worn by women in Arabia. A kind of drawers. The husk of barley.

P اتبا *atbā*, (in zand and Pāz.) An arrow.

A اتباب *atbāb*, (pl. of تابّ *tābb*) Tall and weak (men). Sore-backed (camels or asses). *Itbāb*, (v. n. 4 of تبّ) Debilitating, enervating.

A اتبار *itbār*, (v. n. 4 of تبر) Ceasing, refraining.

A اتّبار *ittibār*, (v. n. 8 of تبر) Being broken off.

A اتّباس *ittibās*, (v. n. 8 of يبس) Being dried.

A اتباع *atbāʼ*, (pl. of تبع *tabaʼ*) Followers, dependents, servants. اتباع التّابعين *atbāʼu't tābiʼīna*, Followers of the followers (of Muhammad). *Itbāʼ*, (v. n. 4 of تبع) Following, overtaking. Causing to follow, joining one to another. Rendering a generous act complete, as giving the saddle and bridle along with a horse. (In gram.) When one word follows another without altering the sense, answering to the words *hurly burly*: as حسن بسن *hasan basan*, Handsome, شغب جغب *shaghib jaghib*, Exciting a tumult, tumultuous, noisy, riotous.

A اتّباع *ittibāʼ*, (v. n. 8 of تبع) Following, pursuing. Obedience. P فرمان واجب الاتّباع *farmāni wājibi'l ittibāʼ*, A command necessary to be obeyed.

A اتبال *atbāl*, (pl. of تبل *tabl*) Sicknesses. *Itbāl*, (v. n. 4 of تبل) Making weak, sick or insane (love). Ruining, destroying (misfortune).

A اتّبان *ittibān*, (v. n. 8 of تبن) Putting on the short sailors' breeches called تبّان *tubbān*.

P آتبين *ātbīn*, Eloquent. A skilful performer. Most felicitous. Name of Farīdūn's father.

A اتّجاء *ittijāʼ*, (v. n. 8 of وجأ) Being closely packed, or close and full (dates).

A اتّجار *ittijār*, (v. n. 8 of تجر) Trading. Commerce. (v. n. 8 of وجر) Taking or giving medicine.

A اتّجاه *ittijāh*, (v. n. 8 of وجه) Entering (a thought into the mind). Paying attention. Attention, assiduity.

A اتّحاد *ittihād*, (v. n. 8 of وحد) Being single. Union, concord, intimate friendship.

A اتحاف *it-hāf*, (v. n. 4 of تحف not used) Giving a gift, making a present.

A اتّحال *ittihāl*, (v. n. 8 of وحل) Making an

exception, excepting.

A اتحام *ittihām*, (v. n. 8 of تحم) Being black.

A اتحم *at-ham*, Black.

A اتحمي *athamīy*, (or اتحمية *athamīyat*) A kind of striped cloth, manufactured in Arabia Felix.

A اتخاخ *itkhākh*, (v. n. 4 of تخ) Leaving dough to become sour.

A اتخاذ *ittikhāz*, (v. n. 8 of اخذ) Taking to one's self. Making. Placing. Being used, adopted. Assumption, choice, election.

A اتخاف *ittikhāf*, (v. n. 8 of وخف) Slipping.

A اتخام *itkhām*, (v. n. 4 of تخم) Producing indigestion (food).

A اتخام *ittikhām*, (v. n. 8 of وخم) Being oppressed (the stomach). Indigestion.

A اتداء *ittidās*, (v. n. 8 of ودي) Receiving a fine for manslaughter.

A اتداع *ittidāʻ*, (v. n. 8 of ودع) Being quiet, mild, and placid. Complaining of one limb, whilst the rest of the body is in good health. Resting.

A اتدان *ittidān*, (v. n. 8 of ودن) Being steeped. Steeping.

A اتذاء *ittizās*, (v. n. 8 of وذأ) Being chidden.

A اتراء *itrās*, (v. n. 4 of تري) Doing things in a train, with intermitting intervals between each.

A اتراب *atrāb*, (pl. of ترب *tirb*) Companions, equals in age, peers, cotemporaries. *Itrāb*, (v. n. 4 of ترب) Having little wealth. Having much. Becoming the owner of a slave who has already had three masters. Strewing with earth.

A اتراح *atrāh*, (pl. of ترح *turah*) Troubles, cares.

A اتراد *ittirād*, (v. n. 8 of ترد) Crumbling into small pieces.

P اترار *atrār*, Barberries.

A اترار *itrār*, (v. n. 4 of تر) Cutting off, throwing away. Playing at trap and ball, striking the gnur with the bat. Banishing, driving into exile. *Utrār*, Name of a town in Turkistān.

A اتراز *itrāz*, (v. n. 4 of ترز) Hardening. Drying, causing to wither or shrivel. Twisting tight.

A اتراس *atrās*, (pl. of ترس *turs*) Shields.

A اتراص *itrās*, (v. n. 4 of ترص) Making firm, strong, even, straight, just, or equal.

A اتراع *itrāʻ*, (v. n. 4 of ترع) Filling.

A اتراع *ittirāʻ*, (v. n. 8 of ترع) Being filled.

A اتراف *itrāf*, (v. n. 4 of ترف) Bestowing the luxuries of life, bringing up luxuriously. Seducing, corrupting; rendering effeminate and dissolute (affluence). Persevering in disobedience.

A اتراك *atrāk*, (pl. of ترك *turk*) Turks.

A اتراك *ittirāk*, (v. n. 8 of ترك) Leaving, abandoning.

A اتربة *atribat*, (pl. of تراب *turāb*) Grounds, earths, sands.

P اترت *utrut*, Name of a certain king.

P اترج *utruj*, An orange.

A اترج *utrujj*, An orange.

A اترجة *utrujjat*, One single orange.

A اترع *atraʻ*, A torrent that fills its bed.

A اترف *atraf*, One who has a protuberance on the middle of the upper lip.

A اترنج *utrunj*, An orange.

P اتروب *atrūb*, A kind of disease which renders the skin loose and flabby.

A اترور *utrūr*, The servant of a magistrate. A bailiff, a catchpoll. A serjeant or a serjeant's son. An unpaid attendant on a prince. A lad.

A اترهوة *itrahwat*, Pride, self-conceit.

A اتزار *ittizār*, (v. n. 8 of وزر) Sinning.

A اتزاع *ittizāʻ*, (v. n. 8 of وزع) Refraining.

A اتزان *ittizān*, (v. n. 8 of وزن) Receiving money by weight. Being equal in weight. Being equal, just, equitable. Being accurate (the measure in a poem).

A اتساخ *ittisākh*, (v. n. 8 of وسخ) Being dirty. Filthiness, nastiness.

A اتسار *ittisār*, (v. n. 8 of يسر) Distributing by lot the limbs of a slaughtered camel. Playing at dice, casting lots.

A اتساع *itsāʻ*, (v. n. 4 of تسع) Completing the number nine. Having camels which are watered on the ninth day.

A اتساع *ittisāʻ*, (v. n. 8 of وسع) Being wide, ample, extended, diffused. Being comprehended, contained. Being large enough, able to contain.

A اتساق *ittisāk*, (v. n. 8 of وسق) Being joined, connected, arranged, set in order. Setting in order.

A اتسام *ittisām*, (v. n. 8 of وسم) Being branded with a hot iron. Placing a mark upon one's self whereby one may be known.

P اتست *utsat*, A plant (Boerhavia diffusa).

P اتسيز *atsiz* or *itsiz*, Name of a king of Khārazm.

P آتش *ātish*, Fire. Sulphur. Digestive heat. Rage. Desire, appetite, love. Joviality, mirthfulness. A courageous man. The devil. A lover. Light, lustre, beauty. Rank, dignity, value. Dearness, scarcity. آتش آب پرور *ātishi āb-parwar*, A sword of good temper. آتش اژدها *ātishi ajdahā*, The seven planets. آتش آسمان *ātishi āsmān*, A thunderbolt. آتش افرازه *ātishi afrāza*, A rocket. آتش بجان *ātish ba jān*, Sorrow, grief: desire, love. آتش بسته *ātishi basta*, Red gold. آتش بهار *ātishi bahār*, A rose. A tulip. The beauty of spring. آتش بي باد *ātishi bī bād*, Wine. The bustle of a market. Injustice, oppression. آتش بي داد *ātishi bī dād*, Wine. Injustice, oppression. آتش بي دود *ātishi bī dūd*, The sun. Rage, fury. Wine. A ruby. آتش بي زبانه *ātishi bī zabāna*, Wine. A ruby, a cornelian. آتش پارسي *ātishi pārsī*, The Persian fire. The disease called St. Anthony's fire. Pustules breaking out on the lips after a fever. آتش پاشيدن *ātish pāshīdan*, To be hasty, or unsteady. To oppress. آتش پر آب *ātishi pur āb*, Wine. Tears of grief. A goblet of wine. آتش تابنده *ātishi tābinda*, The burning sun. Human nature. آتش تر *ātishi tar*, Liquid fire. Wine. The lip of a mistress. آتش تزوير *ātishi tazwīr*, Soup for the sick. آتش توبه سوز *ātishi toba-soz*, Wine. آتش جام زيبقي *ātishi jāmi zībakī*, Red wine in a goblet of crystal or silver. آتش جهان سوز *ātishi jahān-soz*, A fire consuming the world. آتش حجر *ātishi hajar*, Fire struck from a flint. A ruby, a cornelian. آتش خورشيد *ātishi khwurshed*, The light of the sun. Love. Grief. آتش دادن *ātish dādan*, To fire. To shoot. To provoke. To unsettle the mind. To abandon. آتش دهقان *ātishi dihkān*, A burning up of stubble, to fertilize the land. آتش رز *ātishi raz*, Wine made from grapes. آتش روحانيان *ātishi rūhāniyān*, Angelic bodies. آتش روز *ātishi roz*, The sun. Light and heat. آتش زدن *ātish zadan*, To set on fire. آتش زر *ātishi zar*, Lustre, elegance, beauty. آتش زمزم *ātishi zamzam*, The sun. آتش سرد *ātishi sard*, Red wine. The lip of a mistress. Gold. آتش سگ *ātishi sag*, The dog-violet. آتش سم *ātishi sum*, Fire struck from a stone by the hoof of a horse. آتش سودا *ātishi saudā*, Love. Pensiveness, melancholy. آتش سيّال *ātishi sayyāl*, Red wine. آتش سيماب سان *ātishi simābsān*, The world-adorning sun. آتش شجر *ātishi shajar*, Wine. A pomegranate. آتش صبح *ātishi subh*, (or آتش صليب *ātishi salīb*) The sun. آتش طبع *ātishi tabʻ*, Moroseness, harshness. آتش فرازه *ātishi farāza*, A rocket. آتش فسرده *ātishi fusurda*, Congealed fire, *i. e.* gold. آتش كاروان *ātishi kārwān*, A fire lighted by the caravans at night, to direct those who have remained behind. آتش مجسّم *ātishi mujassam*, (Imbodied fire) A well-tempered sword. آتش معده *ātishi miʻda*, (Fire of the stomach) Hunger. آتش موسي *ātishi mūsaʼ*, The fiery pillar which served as a guide to the Israelites. آتش نشاندن *ātish nishāndan*, To appease anger. To quell a riot. آتش نيستان *ātishi naystān*, The beauty of the spring. آتش هفت مجمرة *ātishi haft mijmara*, The seven planets. آتش هندي *ātishi hindī*, A sword with an Indian blade. آتش و آب *ātish u āb*, A sword. A goblet of wine.

A اتشاح *ittishāh*, (v. n. 8 of وشح) Putting on the belt وشاح *wishāh*.

A اتشار *ittishār*, (v. n. 8 of وشر) Requesting any person to make one's teeth thin and sharp.

P آتش افرازه *ātish-afrāza*, A rocket.

P آتش افروز *ātish-afroz*, (Kindling a flame) Any thing for lighting a fire. Tinder. An colipile. A phœnix. The eleventh month of the era of Yazdagird.

P آتش افروزنه *ātish-afrozana*, Chips, shavings. A tinder-box.

A اتشاق *ittishāk*, (v. n. 8 of وشق) Drying oblong slips of meat.

P آتش انداز *ātish-andāz*, Casting out fire.

P آتش انگیز *ātish-angez*, Kindling of fire. An incendiary.

P آتش بار *ātish-bār*, Raining fire, flaming. A fire-lock. A tinder-box. تیغ آتشبار *teghi ātish-bār*, A flaming sword.

P آتش باز *ātish-bāz*, Playing with fire. A maker of fire-works. Pyrotechnical. An engineer. Lightning.

P آتش بازي *ātish-bāzī*, Fire-works, pyrotechnics. A bonfire.

P آتش بان *ātishbān*, A devil, a demon.

P آتش برگ *ātish-barg*, A tinder-box.

P آتش پاره *ātish-pāra*, A spark of fire, lighted coal, match. A candle. The moon. A glow-worm. Litigious, quarrelsome, choleric.

P آتش پاي *ātish-pāy*, Restless; mettlesome.

P آتش پرست *ātish-parast*, A fire-worshipper. A moth.

P آتش پرستي *ātish-parastī*, Fire-worship.

P آتش پرور *ātish-parwar*, A shining sword.

P آتش پیکر *ātish-paykar*, The sun. A spirit. A demon.

P آتش تاب *ātish-tāb*, A furnace, stove, grate. One who superintends a furnace.

P آتش تابه *ātish-tāba*, A furnace, stove, grate.

P آتش تاو *ātish-tāv*, (or آتش تو *ātish-tav*) Warmth, heat. A furnace.

A اتشح *atshah*, Impetuous; an enthusiast.

P آتش خاطر *ātish-khātir*, In love. One of a quick understanding, or of an enlightened mind.

P آتش خانه *ātish-khāna*, A fire-temple. A park of artillery.

P آتش خوار *ātish-khwār*, (آتش خور *ātish-khwur*, or آتش خواره *ātish-khwāra*) An eater of unlawful food. A receiver of bribes. A phœnix. A salamander. A tyrant.

P آتش داغ *ātish-dāgh*, A burn, a scar.

P آتشدان *ātishdān*, A hearth, a fire-place. A chafing dish, or portable grate for coals.

P آتش دست *ātish-dast*, Dexterous, clever.

P آتش ریز *ātish-rez*, Pouring out fire, incendious.

P آتش زبان *ātish-zabān*, Eloquent, rhetorical.

P آتش زدگي *ātish-zadagī*, Conflagration, arson.

P آتش زنه *ātish-zana*, (or آتش زن *ātish-zan*) A fire-steel, a tinder-box. A flint. Tinder, touch-wood; combustibles.

P آتشستان *ātishistān*, A region of fire; hence applied to a hot fire of cannon or small-arms in battle. A funeral-pile.

P آتش سخن *ātish-sukhun*, A reviler, rebuker, who uses inflammatory language. A usurper.

P آتش فروز *ātish-furoz*, An eolipile. A phœnix. The eleventh month of the æra of Yazdagird.

P آتش فشان *ātish-fishān*, Scattering fire; a volcano. اژدر آتش فشان *ajdari ātish-fishān*, A fiery dragon.

P آتش فعل *ātish-fiʿl*, Fiery, fleet, mettlesome.

P آتشك *ātishak*, A small fire. Lightning. A fire-fly. The venereal disease.

P آتشكار *ātish-kār*, Angry, hasty, tyrannical. A fire-place, a kitchen. A blacksmith.

P آتشكاو *ātish-kāv*, (Fire-stirring) A poker.

P آتشكده *ātish-kada*, A fire-temple. آتشكدهء بهرام *ātish-kadaʾi bahrām*, The sign Aries.

P آتشگاه *ātish-gāh*, A temple of the Magi or worshippers of fire. A furnace, grate, chimney.

P آتشگون *ātish-gūn*, Fiery-coloured. A kind of flower.

P آتش گیر *ātish-gīr*, Whatever catches fire.

P آتشگیره *ātish-gīra*, A fire-shovel: fuel: tinder.

P آتشلاخ *ātishlākh*, A place abounding in fire.

P آتش لباس *ātish-libās*, Clothed in scarlet.

P آتش مزاج *ātish-mizāj*, Fiery-tempered.

P آتشناك *ātishnāk*, Fiery, hot.

P آتش نثار *ātish-nisār*, Weeping, sad, sorrowful.

P آتشنهال *ātish-nihāl*, A fire of faggots.

P آتشواديء ايمن *ātish-wādīʾi ayman*, Divine glory, or the pillar of fire.

P آتشوا هندي *ātishwā-hindī*, An Indian sword.

P آتشي *ātishī*, Belonging to fire, fiery, burning hot. Fired with rage, irascible, choleric.

P اتشي *atishī*, A porcupine.

P آتشيان *ātishiyān*, Demons, infidels. Eloquent.

P آتشيزه *ātishīza*, A glow-worm.

P آتشين *ātishīn*, Fiery.

P آتشين آب *ātishīn-āb*, Red wine. Hot tears.

P آتشين اژدها *ātishīn-ajdahā*, A planet.

P آتشين پنجه *ātishīn-panja*, Skilful, adroit.

P آتشين پيكر *ātishīn-paykar*, The sun. Genii. Devils.

P آتشين پيل *ātishīn-pīl*, The sun.

P آتشين داغ *ātishīn-dāgh*, A burnt mark, a brand.

P آتشين دواج *ātishīn-dawāj*, The sun. A ruddiness in the sky. Wine.

P آتشين زبان *ātishīn-zabān*, A fluent speaker.

P آتشين صدف *ātishīn-sadaf*, (or صليب *salīb*) The sun.

P آتشين كاسه *ātishīn-kāsa*, The sun.

P آتشين لباس *ātishīn-libās*, Clothed in scarlet. Scarlet clothing.

P آتشين مار *ātishīn-mār*, A heart-burning sigh. A flame. A rocket.

P آتشين هفت اژدها *ātishīn haft ajdahā*, The seven planets.

A اتّصاف *ittisāf*, (v. n. 8 of وصف) Being described. Being praised. Praising any thing together. Description, qualification: as, خلوص اتّصاف *khulūs-ittisāf*, Characterized by sincerity. سعادت اتّصاف *saʿādat-ittisāf*, Possessed of happiness, glorious, august.

A اتّصال *ittisāl*, (v. n. 8 of وصل) Being closely united. Arriving. Arrival. Conjunction, contiguity, communication.

A اتّضاح *ittizāh*, (v. n. 8 of وضح) Being clear, evident, manifest.

A اتّضاع *ittizāʿ*, (v. n. 8 of وضع) Pressing down a camel's neck in order to mount on his back. Lowering, beating down (price). Being lowered, let down. Humiliation, abasement, abjectness.

A اتّضان *ittizān*, (v. n. 8 of وضن) Being united.

A اتّطاء *ittitāʾ*, (v. n. 8 of وطا) Being arranged, made smooth and easy (a bed). Standing erect. Hitting the mark, gaining one's end. Preparing for any thing.

A اتّطان *ittitān*, (v. n. 8 of وطن) Fixing one's residence.

A اتعاب *itʿāb*, (v. n. 4 of تعب) Wearying, fatiguing, exhausting. Filling a vessel. Dislocating (a bone) after having had (it) set. Having jaded cattle. مرض موجب الاتعاب *marazi mūjibi'l itʿāb*, A disease producing lassitude.

A اتّعاد *ittiʿād*, (v. n. 8 of وعد) Receiving, or being gratified by, a promise. Promising, or rather threatening, mutually.

A اتعاس *itʿās*, (v. n. 4 of تعس) Destroying.

A اتّعاظ *ittiʿāz*, (v. n. 8 of وعظ) Being admonished. Improving from advice or correction. Deriving profitable instruction or warning.

A اتعب *atʿab*, More or most fatiguing.

A اتغاب *itghāb*, (v. n. 4 of تغب) Ruining.

A اتغام *itghām*, (v. n. 4 of تغم) Causing indigestion (food).

A اتفار *itfār*, (v. n. 4 of تفر not used) Having the hairs of the nostrils growing as low as the groove of the upper lip. Coming forth (the early bud).

A اتّفار *ittifār*, (v. n. 8 of وفر) Being full, complete, abundant.

A اتفاف *atfāf*, (pl. of تفّ *tuff*) Shreds of meat sticking between the teeth.

A اتّفاق *ittifāk*, (v. n. 8 of وفق) Agreeing, consenting. Approaching one another. Happening, coming to pass. Concord, consent, harmony, league. Chance, accident. P اتّفاق حسنه *ittifāki hasana*, Unexpected good fortune; agreeable accidents.

A اتّفاقاً *ittifākan*, Unanimously, in concert, with one accord. Perchance, accidentally. Successfully.

A اتّفاقات *ittifākāt*, (pl. of اتّفاق *ittifāk*) Accidents. Successes.

A اتّفاقي *ittifākī*, Casual, fortuitous. Consenting, agreeing.

A اتفال *itfāl*, (v. n. 4 of تفل) Rendering inodorous, causing to smell offensively.

A اتّقاء *ittikāʾ*, (v. n. 8 of وقي) Being timid and wary. Fearing (God). Heed, caution. Piety.

A اتّقاد *ittikād*, (v. n. 8 of وقد) Being lighted, blazing (a fire).

A اتّقار *ittikār*, (v. n. 8 of وقر) Being quiet, modest, grave, and sedate.

A اتقان *itkān*, (v. n. 4 of تقن) Doing any thing firmly, properly, and well. Strength, stability.

A ما اتقاه لله *mā atkāhu li 'llāh*, How greatly

he fears God!

A اتقاه *ittikāh*, (v. n. 8 of وقه) Obeying. Coming to an end.

A اتقياء *atkiyā,* (pl. of تقي *takiy*) Religious, God-fearing, devout (men).

P اتك *atak*, Attock, a town on the Indus.

A اتكاء *itkā,* (v. n. 4 of تكا) Making recline. Throwing down.

A اتّكاء *ittikā,* (v. n. 8 of تكا) Leaning against; reclining upon one side. Squatting, especially on one's heels. Making a couch for one's self.

A اتّكار *ittikār*, (v. n. 8 of وكر) Building a nest.

A اتّكاع *ittikāʿ*, (v. n. 8 of وكع) Being confirmed, strengthened.

A اتّكال *ittikāl*, (v. n. 8 of وكل) Trusting, relying upon, confiding in God. Reliance.

P آتل *ātil*, Name of a river, now the Volga.

A اتل *atl*, (v. n. of اتل) Walking slowly with short steps (an angry man). Being filled with food. *Utul*, Full, satiated (persons).

A اتلاء *atlā,* (pl. of تلو *tilw*) Following one another; the young of an animal following the mother. *Itlā,* (v. n. 4 of تلا for تلو) Ordering or causing to follow. Proceeding, going or running before, outstripping. Having a colt following (a camel). Entrusting something to another. Giving security for life and property. Forgiving a debt. Allowing part of a debt to remain unpaid. Sending to demand payment.

A اتلاج *itlāj*, (v. n. 4 of تلج not used) Causing to enter, inserting.

A اتّلاج *ittilāj*, (v. n. 8 of ولج) Entering. Causing to enter, inserting.

A اتلاد *atlād*, Riches, hereditary wealth, slaves or cattle brought forth in the family, and descending by way of heritage. *Itlād*, (v. n. 4 of تلد) Possessing the wealth described above.

A اتلاع *itlāʿ*, (v. n. 4 of تلع) Stretching the neck to see or hear; or doing so from pride.

A اتّلاع *ittilāʿ*, (v. n. 8 of ولع) Being concealed from one's knowledge.

A اتلاف *itlāf*, (v. n. 4 of تلف) Consuming, ruining, destroying.

A اتلال *atlāl*, (pl. of تلّ *tall*) Cushions. Kinds of garments. *Itlāl*, (v. n. 4 of تلّ) Causing (liquor or a melted substance) to drip. Tying. Leading.

A اتلام *atlām*, (pl. of تلم *talam*) Furrows in the ground for sowing, draining, or making boundaries.

A اتلان *atalān*, (or اتلال *atalāl*) (v. n. of اتل) Walking with short steps (an angry man). Being filled with food.

A اتلاه *itlāh*, (v. n. 4 of تله) Destroying, ruining, consuming. Making mad with vexation, stupefying, putting in a phrenzy.

A اتّلاه *ittilāh*, (v. n. 8 of وله) Being amazed, stupefied, distracted. Stupifying (wine).

A اتلّة *atillat*, (pl. of تليل *talīl*) Necks.

A اتلع *atlaʿ*, Long-necked.

A اتلئباب *itlisbāb*, (v. n. 4 of تلأب Q) Being well directed and conducted (business). Being extended and level (a road). Standing erect (an ass).

A اتم *atm*, (v. n. of اتم) Tearing, ripping up, bursting two holes into one. Cutting. Abiding in one place. *Atam*, (v. n. of اتم) Being slow and dilatory. Delay, slowness, sloth, sluggishness, laziness, indolence. *Utum*, The wild olive.

A اتمّ *atamm*, More or most perfect or complete.

A آتمات *ātimāt*, Tired and jaded (camels).

A اتمار *itmār*, (v. n. 4 of تمر) Bearing ripe dates (a palm-tree). Becoming تمر *tamr* (the moist date رطب *rutab*). Becoming رطب *rutab* (dates in an earlier stage). Abounding in dates.

A اتماك *itmāk*, (v. n. 4 of تمك) Making fat.

A اتمام *itmām*, (v. n. 4 of تمّ) Completing, bringing to perfection. Granting any one his desire (God). Furnishing with a hoe or mattock. Being near her confinement, having gone her full time (a woman). Being come to the full (the moon). Attaining to its full growth (a plant). P اتمام مصلحت كردن *itmāmi maslahat kardan*, To conclude any business.

A اتمهلال *itmihlāl*, (v. n. 4 of تمهل Q) Being long, strong, and well-proportioned.

P اتميد *itmīd*, A coulter, plough-share. A yoke.

A اتمئرار *itmisrār*, (v. n. 4 of تمأر Q) Being hard (a lance), stiff (a yard).

A اتمئلال *itmislāl*, (v. n. 4 of تمأل Q) Being tall and strong.

A آتن *ātun*, (pl. of اتان *atān*) She-asses.

A اتن *atn*, (v. n. of اتن) Standing, stopping, tarrying. Bringing forth a child with the feet foremost (a woman). Coming forth in that manner (a child). *Utn*, or *utun*, (pl. of اتان *atān*) She-asses. *Utun*, High ground. (pl. of اتان *atān*) Seats in camel-litters. (pl. of اتون *atūn*) Furnaces.

A اتناخ *itnākh*, (v. n. 4 of تنخ) Oppressing with indigestion.

A اتناميس *atnāmīs*, Wild camomile.

A اتنان *atnān*, (pl. of تنّ *tinn*) Alike, resembling. Peers, equals. *Itnān*, (v. n. 4 of تنّ) Being distant. Weakening a boy, and preventing his growth (disease). *Atanān*, Contraction of step, a shortening of pace.

A اتو *atw*, (v. n. of اتا for اتو) Coming. Coming suddenly, surprising. Travelling quick (a camel). Producing, bringing forth copiously, shooting forth buds, producing fruit, bringing forth young. Giving liberally with a view to a return. Bribing a judge or great man to obtain any thing contrary to justice. Watering ground plentifully, in order to have a large crop. Paying tribute. A gift. An arrow. Tribute. Butter forming by the agitation or churning of milk. The motion of a horse's fore-legs in running. Velocity, celerity. An inveterate distemper, calamity, death. Right way, straight path. Manner, way, sect. Any thing erect, upright in walking. A great personage. P اتو كشيدن *atw kashīdan*, To plait linen.

A اتواء *atwā,* (pl. of توّ *taww*) Ropes of single twists. *Itwā,* (v. n. 4 of توي) Destroying, wasting.

A اتّواء *ittiwā,* (v. n. 8 of اوي) Repairing to a place for a temporary or permanent residence.

A اتواق *atwāk*, (pl. of توق *tawk*) Desires.

A اتواه *atwāh*, (pl. of توه *tuwah*) Bewildered.

A اتوب *utūb*, (pl. of اتب *itb*) Sleeveless shirts, tunics. Short breeches or drawers.

A اتوة *atwat*, (v. n. of اتا for اتو) Arriving.

P اتوت *atūt*, (in zand and Pāz.) Roughness, sharpness, pungency.

P آتوربان *ātūrbān*, A monk, a devotee.

A اتوز *atwaz*, Of noble origin.

P اتوشه *atūsha*, Name of king Shāpūr's aunt.

A اتوم *atūm*, Broken, ripped open, two holes burst into one. A woman to whom such a disaster has occurred. Small about the privities (woman).

P آتون *ātūn*, A schoolmistress who teaches reading, writing, and embroidery. The secundine or membrane which encloses the fœtus.

A اتون *atūn*, (pl. اتن *utun*) An oven, furnace. A lime-kiln. *Utūn*, (v. n. of اتن) Residing, staying, tarrying.

A اتّون *attūn*, (pl. اتانين *atānīn*) An oven. A furnace. A lime-kiln.

A اتونات *atūnāt*, (pl. of اتونة *atūnat*) Furnaces.

A اتّوني *attūniy*, One who lights the fires in a bath, furnace, or kiln.

A ما اتوهه *mā atwahahu*, How bewildered he is! How proud he is!

A اتّهاب *ittihāb*, (v. n. 8 of وهب) Accepting a gift.

A اتّهال *ittihāl*, (v. n. 8 of اهل) Marrying a wife. Founding a family.

A اتهام *it-hām*, (v. n. 4 of تهم) Travelling to Tihāmah. Discovering a country to be unhealthy. Suspecting, doubting.

A اتّهام *ittihām*, (v. n. 8 of وهم) Suspecting something bad. Being suspected.

A آتي *āti*, Coming. Subsequent, future. The second letter of a word. آتي البيان *āti'l bayān*, About to be explained.

A أتي *ata'*, (fut. يأتي *yasti*) He came.

A اتي *aty*, (v. n. of اتي) Coming, arriving: coming unawares, surprising. Destroying. Coming together, copulating, knowing carnally. Doing, effecting. The motion of (a horse's) fore-feet in running. *Ita'*, (pl. اتاء *itā,* and اتيّ *utiy*) Any thing flowing on the water (as leaves). من هٰهنا اتيت *min hāhuna utīta*, From this quarter thou hast been troubled.

A اتّي *atta'*, (for حتّي *hatta'*) Unto, until.

A اتيّ *atiy*, Foreign, outlandish, unlooked-for.

An unexpected overflow of water. (pl. of اتاوة *itāwat*) Bribes. *Atīy, itīy,* and *utīy,* Water brought into a field, particularly from another's ground. *Utīy* or *itīy,* (v. n. of اتي) Coming.

A اتّثاء *ittiṡā*, (v. n. 8 of وأي) Receiving, or being gratified by, a promise.

A اتّئاب *ittiṡāb,* (v. n. 8 of وأب) Being ashamed, disgraced, put to the blush.

A اتّئاد *ittiṡād,* (v. n. 8 of وأد) Proceeding gently.

A اتياس *atyās,* (pl. of تيس *tays*) He-goats.

A اتّئاس *ittiṡās,* (v. n. 8 of يئس) Despairing.

A اتيام *ittiyām,* (v. n. 8 of تيم) Slaughtering a sheep or camel which had been kept for milking.

A اتيان *ityān,* (or اتيانة *ityānat*) (v. n. of اتي) Coming. Arrival, accession, meeting. Coition.

A اتياه *atyāh,* (pl. of تيه *tīh*) Deserts.

A آتية *ātiyat,* (fem.) Coming, future. Futurity. آتية الجرح *ātiyat* (or اتية *atyatu*)*'l jurhi,* The pus or matter of a sore.

A اتيشة *utayshat,* A knave, a low fellow. Weak-headed, unable to fight.

A اتيع *atyaɛ,* One who commits repeated acts of folly. A place over whose surface vapour floats.

A آتين *ātin,* (in zand and Pāz.) Manifest, disclosed. Collected together.

A اتيه *atyah,* A wanderer about in astonishment. Proud, arrogant, haughty. ما اتيهه *mā atyahahu,* How bewildered he is! How proud he is!

A اثّ *ass,* Luxuriant, involved, entangled (hair or shrubs). Fleshy and plump (woman).

A اثاء *isṡā,* (v. n. 4 of ثأي) Wounding and killing. Breaking, bursting (the stitches of a leathern bottle). Sewing large holes with a fine thread.

A اثاء *isā,* Stones.

A اثاءة *isāṡat,* (v. n. 4 of ثأ) Hitting with an arrow. (v. n. 4 of ثاء for ثوأ) Shooting, striking one with an arrow.

A اثاب *asāb,* (or اثأب *asṡab*) Name of a tree.

A اثابة *isābat,* (v. n. 4 of ثاب for ثوب) Rewarding. Filling (a well or cistern). Recovering health. Making haste. Doing over again.

A اثابيّ *asābīy,* (pl. of اثبيّة *usbīyat*) Bodies, troops of men.

A اثاث *asās,* (v. n. of اثّ) Growing luxuriantly (herbage); being thick, entangled, involved (shrubs or hair). Having large plump hips and thighs (a woman). (pl. ائثّة *aṡissat* or اثث *usus*) Household furniture, baggage. Wealth of any kind in money, land, or slaves. *Isās,* (pl. of اثيث *asīs*) Luxuriant, entangled (trees or grass). Fleshy.

A اثاثة *asāsat,* (v. n. of اثّ) Growing luxuriantly (herbage), being thick, entangled, involved (shrubs or hair). Being plump and fleshy (a woman). Any one particular species of wealth.

A اثاثيّ *asāsīy,* Wealthy. Wealth. Trivets.

A آثار *āsār,* (pl. of اثر *asar*) Impressions, indications, signs, vestiges. Traditions, annals of memorable sayings or events. الآثار *al āsār,* The traditions of Muhammad. ذو الآثار *zū'l āsār,* Name of Aswad, a satirical poet. آثار سنويه *āsāri sanawīya,* Chronicles. آثار علويه *āsāri ɛulwīya,* Sublime impressions, *i. e.* meteors. اخبار معجز آثار *akhbāri muɛjiz-āsār,* Wonderful narrations. Several books relative to traditions, history, geography, the planets, &c., bear the name of آثار *āsār.* *Āsār,* (or اثآر *asṡār*) (pl. of ثأر *saṡr*) Retaliations. Homicides.

A اثآر *isṡār,* (v. n. 4 of ثأر) Obtaining revenge.

A اثارب *asārib,* (pl. of اثرب *asrub,* pl. of ثرب *sarb*) Thin cauls of fat covering the intestines.

A اثارة *asārat,* The commemoration of traditions, sayings, or actions of any one, particularly of Muhammad. The remains of any thing. على اثارة شيء *ɛala' asārati shayṡin,* Upon the traces of any thing; as if something already existing were followed by its like (as when anger is excited in the mind of an angry man, or when an accession of fat is made to any thing already fat). *Isārat,* (v. n. 4 of ثار for ثور) Raising dust, forcing it into a more impetuous motion; ploughing. Exciting sedition, raising a mob. Starting (game). Studying deeply (the Kur'ān).

A اثافيّ *asāfīy,* (or اثافي *asāfī*) (pl. of اثفيّة *usfīyat* or *isfīyat*) Trivets. Certain stars lying near the constellation called رأس القدر *raṡsu'l kidr.* ثالثة الاثافي *sālisatu'l asāfī,* The third trivet; the projecting part of a mountain, which, together with two stones, is employed by the Badawīn Arabs to support a kettle. A ringleader in mischief. مرجوم بثالثة الاثافي *marjūmun bi sālisati'l asāfī,* Overwhelmed by the last and sorest misfortune.

A اثاكيل *asākīl,* (pl. of اثكول *uskūl*) Clusters of dates.

A اثال *asāl,* or *usāl,* Glory, nobility. *Isāl,* (pl. of اثلة *aslat*) Roots, origins. Stocks, substances. *Usāl,* Surname of one of Muhammad's companions. Name of several places in Arabia.

A آثام *āsām,* (pl. of اثم *ism*) Crimes, sins.

A اثام *asām,* (v. n. of اثم) Convicting of guilt. Punishing for crimes. A criminal. Name of an infernal river, the Styx. *Asām,* or *isām,* A mulct, fine, punishment for crimes.

A اثّام *assām,* A criminal.

A اثامي *asāmī,* A defendant in a law-suit.

A اثانين *asānīn,* (pl. of اثنان *isnāni*) Mondays.

A اثاوة *isāwat,* (v. n. of اثا for اثو) Carrying or citing before a judge; informing against, calumniating, whispering.

A اثاولة *asāwilat,* Tedious old men.

A اثاية *isāyat,* (v. n. of اثي) Citing before a judge. Whispering. *Usāyat, asāyat,* or *isāyat,* Name of a well between Mecca and Madīna.

A اثائث *asāṡis,* (pl. of اثيث *asīs*) Plump, jolly, handsome, tall and full grown (women).

A اثب *asab,* Name of a tree.

A اثبات *asbāt,* (pl. of ثبت *sabt*) Trusty friends. *Isbāt,* (v. n. 4 of ثبت) Confirming, corroborating. Fixing, recording, registering. Knowing for a certainty. Affirmation, proof.

A اثباج *asbāj,* (pl. of ثبج *sabaj*) Middles (of shoulder-blades, or of seas).

A اثبار *isbār,* (v. n. 4 of ثبر) Ruining, destroying.

A اثباط *asbāt,* (pl. of ثبط *sabit*) Fools, sluggards. *Isbāt,* (v. n. 4 of ثبط) Hardly quitting one (disease).

A اثبان *isbān,* (v. n. 4 of ثبن) Carrying (dates) in the skirt of one's garment.

A الاثبة *al asabat,* Name of a country in Arabia abounding in palm-trees.

A اثبج *asbaj,* One who has the middle of the back prominent. Big-bellied. Broad-backed.

A اثبجرار *isbijrār,* (v. n. 4 of ثبجر Q.) Trembling with fear. Being overwhelmed with consternation. Retreating, fleeing away. Being weak and incompetent to achieve (a business), and returning from it. Flowing (water).

A اثبيّة *usbiyat,* (pl. of اثابيّ *asābiy*) A crowd, troop, body.

A اثبيجاج *isbījāj,* (v. n. 11 of ثبج) Being full, thick, large, corpulent, and flabby.

A اثبيرار *isbīrār,* (v. n. 11 of ثبر) Being loth to perform, abstaining from, hanging back.

A اثّماد *istimād,* (v. n. 8 of ثمد) Going to drink at ثمد *samad.*

A اثجاء *isjāṡ,* (v. n. 4 of ثجا for ثجو) Putting to silence. Throwing furniture into confusion.

A اثجام *isjām,* (v. n. 4 of ثجم) Raining heavily. Continuing, acquiring perpetuity.

A اثجر *asjar,* Thick and broad. A short and broad-headed arrow.

A اثجل *asjal,* Large-bellied (man), and fat under the short ribs. A spacious wallet. The widest part of a valley. طعنه الاثجلين *taɛanahu'l asjalayn,* He addressed him in abusive language.

A احاف *as-hāf,* (pl. of ثحف *sihf* or *sahif*) Certain parts of the intestines of cattle.

A اثخان *iskhān,* (v. n. 4 of ثخن) Enfeebling (a wound). Inflicting wounds. Slaying with carnage. Conquering. Striving, straining every nerve.

A اثدي *asdī,* (with tanwin اثد *asdin,* pl. of ثدي *sady* or *sidy*) Breasts, either of man or woman.

A آثر *āsar,* More or most impressive. *Āsir,* Who or what joins. A relater, a recorder. A recorder of traditions. One who marks a camel in the foot. آثر ذات يدين *āsira zāti yadayn,* (or ذي يدين *zī yadayn*) Before all things, in the first place. آثرا ما *āsiram mā,* (or آثر ذي اثير *āsira zī asīrin*) In the first place.

A أثر *asara,* (fut. يأثر *yaṡsuru*) He made to follow.

A اثر *asr,* (v. n. of اثر) Relating, alleging, handing down by tradition. *Asr, isr,* or *usur,* (pl. اثور

usūr) The glittering surface of a bright sword. يطلب اثرا بعد عين *yatlubu asran baɛda ɛaynin*. He seeks for any vestiges of something he has lost. *Isr*, After, subsequent to. Fresh, the best part of butter. علي اثره *ɛala' isrihi*, At his heels. Immediately after. *Isra* (or *asara*) ذي اثيرين *zi asīrayn*, Before all things. *Usr*, The scar of a healed wound. The purest part of butter. Gracefulness or comeliness of countenance. A mark made on the soles of the feet of camels by the impression of which upon the ground they can be traced when straying in the deserts. *Asar* (v. n. of اثر) Commencing, setting about. Resolving, purposing, giving one's whole attention to. Doing a good work, any thing pious, memorable, or illustrious. (pl. آثار *āsār* and اثور *usūr*) A mark, sign, impression, vestige, track, remains. A history, memorial, relation, tradition; a collection of traditions relative to the actions and sayings of Muhammad, the Sunna, or unwritten law, with regard to which the Muhammadans are divided into two great sects, one called Sunnites, who believe in these traditions, the other the Shiites, or followers of Aliy, who reject them.—The Turks are of the first sect, the Persians of the latter. علي اثره *ɛala' asarihi*, Immediately after him, at his heels. اثر البلاد *asaru'l bilād*, The history of countries. P خورشيد اثر *khwurshed-asar*, Resplendent, bright like the sun. تحسين اثر *tahsīn-asar*, Worthy of approbation. عسكر نصرت اثر *ɛaskari nusrat-asar*, An army celebrated for victory, a victorious army. A *Asir*, Studious of excelling. *Asur*, Excellent. Studious of excelling. *Usur*, The scar of a healed wound. The gracefulness of the countenance.

A اثراء *asrās*, (pl. of ثري *sara'*) Moistures. Dusts, earths. *Isrās*, (v. n. 4 of ثرا for ثرو) Being rich. (v. n. 4 of ثري) Being very moist (the ground). Wetting the ground (rain).

A اثراب *isrāb*, (v. n. 4 of ثرب) Blaming, chiding. Being very fat (a wether).

A اثراد *issirād*, (v. n. 8 of ثرد) Crumbling small.

P اثرار *asrār*, Barberries.

A اثرارة *isrārat*, Barberries.

A اثرام *isrām*, (v. n. 4 of ثرم) Causing the teeth to fall out.

A اثرب *asrib*, Name of Madīna. *Asrub*, (pl. of ثرب *sarb*) Thin cauls of fat coating the intestines.

A اثربيّ *asribīy*, Of the city of Madīna.

A اثرة *asrat*, (v. n. of اثر) Making a particular mark on the sole of a camel's foot. *Usrat*, *israt*, or *asarat*, (v. n. of اثر) Being studious of excelling. A desire to excel. *Israt*, A great, noble, memorable work. *Usrat*, or *asarat*, Whatever remains of any science. *Usrat*, The commemoration of traditions, sayings, or acts of any one, and particularly of Muhammad. A barren year. A disagreeable condition. A great, noble, magnificent work, any thing that procures reputation, worthy of remembrance. Hereditary honour, virtue. A mark made on the sole of a camel's foot. اثرة ذي اثير *usrata zi asīrin*, In the first place. *Asarat*, Excellence, pre-eminence.

P اثردار *asar-dār*, Informed, conversant with.

A اثردان *usrudān*, Bread crumbled, grated, or sliced, for putting into milk or broth.

P اثر طراز *asar-tirāz*, A historian, a writer. اثر طرازان اجتهاد *asar-tirāzāni ijtihād*, Sacred writers.

A اثرم *asram*, One whose teeth (the front ones particularly) are falling or knocked out. (In pros.) Cut off (as when فعول *faɛūl* is shortened into عول *ɛūl*). الاثرمان *al asramāni*, (Night and day) as interrupting each other.

A اثرمّاط *isrimmāt*, (v. n. 3 of ثرمط Q) Being swollen (a leathern bottle). Swelling with rage (a man). Prevailing over one (anger).

A اثرنباج *isrimbāj*, (v. n. 3 of ثربج Q not used) Being thoroughly roasted (the skin of a camel).

A اثرنتاء *isrintās*, Fleshiness about the breast.

A اثرنداء *isrindās*, (v. n. 15 of ثرد) Being fleshy.

A اثري *asra'*, Wealthy (man). *Usra'*, (v. n. of اثر) Being studious of excelling. A desire to excel, ambition of excelling.

A اثريّ *asarīy*, One who relates traditions, particularly those of Muhammad.

A اثطّ *asatt*, Thin-bearded, thin of hair.

A اثطاط *astāt*, (pl. of ثطّ *satt*) Thin-bearded men.

A اثّعار *issiɛār*, (v. n. 8 of ثعر) Examining carefully, scrutinizing uncertain rumours.

A اثعال *isɛāl*, (v. n. 4 of ثعل) Being very numerous (guests). Being extensive and intricate (business). Thronging, crowding round a drinking-place. Being high (wages). Opposing, resisting. Abounding in foxes (a country).

A اثعبان *usɛubān*, Flowing water. *Usɛubān*, or اثعباني *usɛubānīy*, Large, fair, handsome face.

A اثعبي *asɛabīy*, A large, fair, and handsome face.

A اثعل *asɛal*, One whose teeth grow out from the side of the gum. A corpulent man. A man of distinction.

A اثعنجاج *isɛinjāh*, (v. n. 3 of ثعجج Q) Raining much and without ceasing.

A اثعنجار *isɛinjār*, (v. n. 3 ثعجر Q) Being poured.

A اثعوب *usɛūb*, Flowing water.

A اثغاء *isghās*, (v. n. 4 of ثغا for ثغو) Giving. Forcing (a sheep) to bleat. Giving away a sheep.

A اثغاب *asghāb*, (pl. of ثغب *saghb*) Springs or reservoirs in glens or groves never visited by the rays of the sun.

A اثغار *isghār*, (v. n. 4 of ثغر) Losing the front teeth. Cutting one's teeth. Striking on the mouth.

A اثّغار *issighār*, (v. n. 8 of ثغر) Cutting the front teeth. Losing the front teeth.

A اثغام *isghām*, (v. n. 4 of ثغم) Producing the plant ثغام *saghām*. Becoming white as this plant (the head). Filling. Irritating. Delighting.

A اثغماء *asghimās*, (pl. of ثغام *saghām*) Mountain-plants of the wormwood species.

A آثف *āsif*, Following. A sectary, a follower.

A أثف *asafa*, (fut. يأثف *yassifu*) He followed.

A اثف *asf*, (v. n. of اثف) Driving away. Following: seeking, pursuing. Placing (a pot) on a trivet. *Asif*, Firm, steady, immoveable. A follower.

A اثفاء *isfas*, (v. n. 4 of ثفا for ثفو) Making a trivet for a pot. Placing (a pot) on a trivet. Having had three wives.

A اثفار *asfār*, (pl. of ثفر *safar*) Cruppers. *Isfār*, (v. n. 4 of ثفر) Making or putting on a crupper. Tying on to the tail. Striking on the backside. Driving forward. Bringing forth (a goat).

A اثفال *isfāl*, (v. n. 4 of ثفل) Depositing sediment (liquor).

A اثفان *isfān*, (v. n. 4 of ثفن) Hardening the hands (labour).

A اثفيّة *usfiyat* or *isfiyat*, (pl. اثافيّ *asāfīy* or اثافي *asāfī*) A stone used to prop a pot, a trivet. A great number. A multitude of men.

A اثقاب *iskāb*, (v. n. 4 of ثقب) Kindling.

A اثقاف *iskāf*, (v. n. 4 of ثقف) Being made equal and like.

A اثقال *askāl*, (pl. of ثقل *sikl*) Burdens, loads, incumbrances, impediments, baggage, equipage, train, suite. اثقال الارض *askālu'l arz*, The treasures of the earth. Men buried in it. Faults. *Iskāl*, (v. n. 4 of ثقل) Bearing heavily (a load). Overcoming (as sleep). Putting in pain (as disease or guilt). Loading heavily. Oppressing, afflicting. Being pregnant (a woman).

A اثقب *askub*, (pl. of ثقب *sakb*) Holes.

A اثقف *askaf*, Sour, sourest.

A اثقل *askal*, More or most heavy, heavier.

A اثقوب *uskūb*, One who meddles much with business, penetrating.

A اثكال *iskāl*, (for عثكال *ɛiskāl*) (pl. اثاكل *asākil*) A branch of a palm-tree bearing unripe dates. *Iskāl*, (v. n. 4 of ثكل) Bereaving a woman of her children. Being bereaved of her children (a mother).

A اثكول *uskūl*, (pl. اثاكيل *asākīl*) A palm-branch bearing unripe dates. A cluster of dates.

A اثكون *uskūn*, A palm-branch; the stalk of a bunch of dates.

A أثل *asala*, (fut. يأثل *yassilu*) It was well rooted.

A اثل *asl*, (pl. اثول *usūl*) A tamarisk-shrub.

A اثلّ *asall*, Rich in sheep and wool.

A اثلاب *aslāb*, (pl. of ثلب *silb*) Worn-out camels. Old men.

A اثلات *aslāt*, Large prickly tamarisks.

A اثلاث *aslās*, (pl. of ثلث *suls*) Thirds. *Islās*, (v. n. 4 of ثلث) Becoming three in number.

A اثلاج *islāj*, (v. n. 4 of ثلج) Snowing. Being snowy (the day). Entering in, being overtaken by the snow. Digging till mud is reached. Being peaceful and joyful. Rendering joyful. Failing (water in a well). (for افلاج *iflāj*) Good fortune, victory, success.

A اثلال *islāl*, (v. n. 4 of ثلّ) Causing to be restored (what had fallen down). Abounding in a species of wool called ثلّة *sallat*, or in flocks.

A اثلب *islab* or *aslab*, Earth or stones, or small fragments of either.

A اثلة *aslat*, (pl. اثال *isāl*) Root, stock, origin. Honour, glory, character, dignity. A fund, substance, provision for an undertaking. The tamarisk species. هو يحت في اثلتنا *huwa yanhatu fī aslatinā*, He vilifies our character. *Aslat* or *asalat*, Household furniture.

A اثلغيّ *aslaghīy*, Penis.

A اثلق *aslak*, Seed of the agnus castus.

A اثلم *aslam*, Broken-edged, notched (sword), pierced, broken, or cracked (wall). Cut off (prosodial foot, as when فعول *faʿūl* becomes عول *ʿūl*).

A آثم *āsim*, A sinner, culprit. Slow. Fatigued.

A أثم *asima*, (fut. يأثم *yaʾsamu*) He was a sinner.

A اثم *asm*, (v. n. of اثم) Convicting of guilt. *Ism*, (v. n. of اثم) Sinning, doing any thing forbidden. A sin, crime, offence; any thing forbidden, as wine, dice, &c. *Asim*, A sinner.

A اثماد *ismād*, (v. n. 4 of ثمد) Draining dry.

A اثّماد *issimād*, (v. n. 8 of ثمد) Going to drink at ثمد *samad*.

A اثمار *asmār*, (pl. of ثمر *samar*) Fruits. *Ismār*, (v. n. 4 of ثمر) Bearing fruit. Having particles of butter adhering to its sides (a churn). Multiplying, increasing.

A اثمال *ismāl*, (v. n. 4 of ثمل) Causing aught to settle at the bottom of a cistern. Being very frothy.

A اثمان *asmān*, (pl. of ثمن *saman*) Prices. (pl. of ثمن *sumun*) Eighths. (pl. of ثمين *samīn*) Eighths. Precious. *Ismān*, (v. n. 4 of ثمن) Completing the number eight. Watering (camels) on the eighth day. Paying a just price.

A آثمة *āsimat*, (fem. of آثم *āsim*) Slow-paced. Tired. نوق آثمات *nūk āsimāt*, Jaded she-camels.

A اثمد *asmad*, Name of a place. *Ismid*, (or *usmud*) A stone from which antimony is prepared.

A اثمن *asman*, More or most valuable, precious. *Asmun*, (or اثمنة *asminat*) (pl. of ثمن *saman*) Prices.

A اثميدار *ismīdād*, (v. n. 11 of ثمد) Being fat.

A اثن *usn*, (pl. of اثنة *usnat*) Thick groves of thorny trees. *Usun*, Statues, figures, idols.

A اثناء *asnāʾ*, (pl. of ثني *siny*) Plaits, foldings. Windings of rivers. (pl. of اثنان *isnāni*) Second days, Mondays. In Persian this word often occurs in the sense of Middle, interval, included space; whilst, during: as, P در اثناي راه *dar asnāʾi rāh*, In the middle of the road, whilst travelling. A *Isnāʾ*, (v. n. 4 of ثني) Losing the front teeth. Rising six years old (a camel). Praising, panegyrizing. Disparaging, defaming.

A اثّناء *issināʾ*, (v. n. 8 of ثني) Being bent, folded. Turning back, returning. Walking pompously.

A اثنا عشر *isnā ʿashara*, (mas.) Twelve.

اثنان *isnān*, (v. n. 4 of ثنّ) Becoming worn out (an old man). *Isnāni*, Two. (pl. اثناء *asnāʾ* and ثانين *asānīn*) Monday. اثنان اثنان *isnāni isnāni*, Two and two.

A اثنة *usnat*, (pl. اثن *usn*) A thick, thorny grove.

A اثنتان *isnatāni*, (fem.) Two.

A اثنويّ *isnawīy*, One who keeps every Monday a private fast.

A اثنيّ *isnīy*, Relating to two.

A اثنية *asniyat*, (pl. of ثناء *sanāʾ*) Praises, encomiums, prayers.

A اثني عشريّة *isnay ʿashariyat*, Name of a sect of Muhammadans who follow the twelve Imāms.

A اثنين اثنين *isnayni isnayni*, Two and two (they came). يوم الاثنين *yawmu'l isnayn*, Monday.

A اثنيناء *isnīnāʾ*, (v. n. 12 of ثني) Being bent, doubled, folded. Retreating.

A اثو *isw*, (v. n. of اثا for اثو) Informing, impeaching. Slander.

A اثواء *iswāʾ*, (v. n. 4 of ثوي) Continuing in any abode. Causing to tarry. Receiving hospitably.

A اثواب *aswāb*, (pl. of ثوب *sawb*) Vestments, clothes, garments. *Iswāb*, (v. n. 4 of ثاب for ثوب) Rewarding, recompensing.

A اثوار *aswār*, (pl. of ثور *sawr*) Bulls. Large pieces of sour curd, quite dry.

A اثوب *aswub* or اثؤب *asʾub*, (pl. of ثوب *sawb*) Garments (implying a small quantity).

A اثوث *usūs*, (v. n. of اثّ) Growing luxuriantly (herbage), being thick and entangled. Having fleshy hips (a woman).

A اثور *usūr*, (pl. of اثر *asr*) The dazzling refulgencies of a bright sword when flourished in the sun. (pl. of اثر *asar*) Vestiges.

A اثول *aswal*, (pl. ثول *sūl*) Foolish, insane, lazy, slow. Affected by a torpor or vertigo (a disease peculiar to sheep or goats). *Usūl*, (v. n. of اثل) Being firmly rooted. (pl. of اثل *asl*) Tamarisk-trees.

A اثولال *iswilāl*, (v. n. 9 of ثال for ثول) Having the staggers (a sheep).

A اثوم *asūm*, A sinner. A liar.

A اثّون *assūn*, (or اتّون *attūn*) A furnace.

A اثوياء *aswiyāʾ*, (pl. of ثويّ *sawīy*) Guests.

A أثى *asaʾ*, (fut. يأثي *yaʾsī*) He falsely accused.

A أثيّ *asīy*, An informer, slanderer, whisperer.

A اثّثار *issiʾār*, (for اثتئار *istiʾār*) (v. n. 8 of ثأر) Taking revenge.

A اثيبج *usaybij*, (dim. of اثبج *asbaj*) One who has a little prominence in the middle of the back.

A اثيث *asīs*, (pl. اثاث *isās*) Luxuriant, involved, entangled (as shrubs or hair). Large, big. Fleshy, full of flesh and blood, large about the hips.

A اثيثة *asīsat*, (pl. اثائث *asāʾis*) Plump, jolly, handsome, tall, full-grown (woman).

A اثيداء *usaydāʾ*, Name of a part of the market-place of عكاظ *ʿukāz*.

P اثير *asīr*, Tears of grief. A ball of fire; the sun.

A اثير *asīr*, Excellent, chosen, selected. An intimate friend. The glittering surface of a bright sword. Sky, æther. اوّل ذي اثير *awwala zī asīrin*, In the first place. كثير اثير *kasīr asīr*, Much. *Usayr*, (dim. of اثر *asar*) A little sign. Name of a physician.

A اثيرة *asīrat*, A beast of burden, whose foot makes a deep impression in the ground. اثيرة ذي اثير *asīrata zī asīrin*, At first, in the first place; above all things.

P اثيژ *asīj*, Southernwood. A spark of fire.

A اثيل *asyal*, (pl. ثيل *sīl*) Large-sheathed (camel). *Asīl*, Radical, firm. Noble, illustrious. مجد اثيل *majd asīl*, Firmly-established glory. *Usayl*, Name of a valley near Madīna, fruitful in dates. ذات الاثيلة *zātu'l usaylat*, Name of a place.

A اثيم *asīm*, A sinner, criminal. A liar. Frequent in sinning. A name of ابو جهل *abū jahl*.

A اثيمة *asīmat*, Frequent in sinning.

A اثين *asīn*, Radical, firm. Illustrious.

A اثيّنية *usaynīyat*, A crowd, multitude, congregation.

P آج *āj*, Desire, avidity.

P اج *aj*, A little. A tamarisk. A gourd. *Uj*, A wager, a stake at play.

A اجّ *ajj*, (v. n. of اجّ) Running, hastening one's pace, running as the ostrich, partly running, partly flying, whose motion makes a certain noise. Attacking. Instigating, exciting, inflaming.

A أجأ *ajaʾa*, (fut. يجأ *yaʾjaʾu*) He ran away.

A اجأ *ajaʾ*, Name of a mountain in Arabia, and of a town in Egypt.

A اجاء *ijāʾ*, (v. n. 4 of جئي) Being of a dark bay colour (a horse).

A اجاءة *ajāʾat*, Name of a place. *Ijāʾat*, (v. n. 4 of جاء for جيأ) Bringing. Compelling, constraining, forcing. Sewing a patch upon a shoe.

A اجاب *ijāb*, An answer.

A اجابة *ijābat*, (v. n. 4 of جاب for جوب) Answering, consenting, admitting, complying with, humouring, listening to. An answer.

A اجاث *ijʾās*, (v. n. 4 of جئث) Weighing down, causing to move slowly (a burden).

A اجاج *ijāj*, (pl. of اجّة *ajjat*) Heats. *Ujāj*, Brackish water.

A اجّاج *ajjāj*, Burning, scorching. The sun.

A اجاجرة *ajājirat*, (or اجاجير *ajājīr*) (pl. of اجّار *ijjār*) Platforms on tops of houses for air.

A اجاجين *ajājīn*, (pl. of اجّانة *ijjānat*, q. v.).

A اجاح *ajāh*, *ijāh*, or *ujāh*, A veil, a curtain.

A اجاحة *ijāhat*, (v. n. 4 of جاح for جوح) Ruining, destroying, eradicating.

A اجاد *ijād*, Any thing resembling a small arch.

A اجادة *ijādat*, (v. n. 4 of جاد for جود) Saying or doing any thing good. Proclaiming any thing good. Possessing a generous horse. Paying in good ready money. Giving money. Being irrigated copiously (a field). Begetting a generous son.

A اجادب *ajādib*, (pl. of اجدب *ajdub*, pl. of جدب *jadb*) Scarcities, dearths. Barren places.

A اجادل *ajādil*, (pl. of اجدل *ajdal*) Hawks of a certain kind.

A آجار *ājār*, (pl. of اجر *ajr*) Prices, rents, hires, wages. Women's marriage portions.

A اجأر *ajʼar*, More robust or corpulent.

A اجار *ijār*, (v. n. of اجر) Being healed (a broken or dislocated bone).

A اجّار *ijjār*, (pl. اجاجير *ajājīr* or اجاجرة *ajājirat*) A platform on the house-top, very common in the East for the benefit of air.

A اجارب *ajārib*, (pl. of اجرب *ajrab*) Scabby.

A اجارة *ijārat*, (v. n. 4 of جار for جور) Protecting, rescuing, delivering, shielding from oppression. Turning (any one) out of the road. Putting (household utensils) into a case or cupboard. Becoming a guide or escort. *Ijārat*, *ajārat*, or *ujārat*, Price, hire, wages, rent, profit, emolument. A privilege, or income of variable amount, sold or let for a fixed sum. P اجاره كردن *ijāra kardan*, To let to a tenant.

A اجارد *ajārid*, (pl. of اجرد *ajrad*) Open countries bare of vegetation.

P اجاره دار *ijāra-dār*, A farmer or renter of land or of revenue. A lease-holder. A monopolist.

A اجازة *ijāzat*, (v. n. 4 of جاز for جوز) Causing (an opinion) to pass, penetrate, or be received. Causing to pass by, sending, despatching. Giving leave. Permission, dispensation; sanction, approval; discharge, dismissal. Leaving behind. Confirming, ratifying. Giving to drink. Giving water for the purposes of irrigation. Conferring a favour. Making an assault upon a wounded man with intent to kill. Terminating the hemistich of another's poem. Finishing the verses of a poem with the letters ط and د alternately. P اجازت دادن *ijāzat dādan*, To give leave. اجازت گرفتن *ijāzat giriftan*, To take leave.

P اجازت خواه *ijāzat-khwāh*, Asking leave.

P اجاس *ijās*, A species of Damasc plum, a prune.

A اجاش *ujāsh*, A mixed crowd.

A اجّاص *ijjāṣ*, (A foreign word introduced into Arabic) A plum. An apricot. A pear.

A اجّاصيّة *ijjāṣiyat*, Prune-soup.

A اجاعة *ijāʻat*, (v. n. 4 of جاع for جوع) Starving, famishing one.

A اجافة *ijāfat*, (v. n. 4 of جاف for جوف) Shutting the door. Penetrating into the heart of any thing. Spearing into the inside of the belly. (v. n. 4 of جاف for جيف) Stinking (a dead body).

P آجاك *ājāk*, Earth, dust.

A آجال *ājāl*, (pl. of اجل *ijl*) Herds of wild oxen. (pl. of اجل *ajal*) Fates. Fixed periods, appointed terms. Deaths.

A اجالة *ijālat*, (v. n. 4 of جال for جول) Causing to turn round. Rounding.

A اجالد *ajālid*, (pl. of اجلد *ajlad*) Hard, solid places. (pl. of اجلاد *ajlād*) Bodies, persons.

A اجاليد *ajālīd*, (pl. of اجلاد *ajlād*) Hard (places).

A آجام *ājām*, Frogs. (pl. of اجم *ajm* or *ujum*) A kind of quadrangular structures on the tops of houses. Fortifications, castles. (pl. of اجمة *ajamat*) Thickets.

A اجام *ijām*, (pl. of اجمة *ajamat*) Forests. Lions' haunts or dens, the retreats of any animals. Reed-beds, cane-plantations. Frogs.

A اجامل *ajāmil*, (pl. of جمل) Full-grown camels.

A اجانب *ajānib*, (pl. of اجنبيّ *ajnabīy*) Aliens.

A اجّانة *ijjānat*, (pl. اجاجين *ajājīn*) A stone bottle, phial, cup, pitcher, or drinking-glass. A circle round the foot of a tree for irrigation.

A اجاود *ajāwid*, or اجاويد *ajāwīd*, (pl. of جواد *jawād*) Liberal, munificent, beneficent.

A اجأي *ajʼaʼ*, Dark bay (horse).

A اجبّ *ajabb*, Bunchless (camel). The privities.

A اجباء *ajbāʼ*, (pl. of جبا *jabaʼ*) Cisterns. Places where drawers of water stand. *Ijbāʼ*, (v. n. 4 of جبأ) Producing mushrooms in great abundance (the earth). Overhanging, jutting out, being in a situation commanding a view. Selling standing corn before it is come to maturity, *i. e.* whilst in the blade. Hiding, concealing. (v. n. 4 of جبا for جبو) Selling standing corn before it is ripe. Hiding one's camels from the tithe-collector.

A اجباب *ajbāb*, (pl. of جبّ *jubb*) Wells (especially deep). *Ijbāb*, (v. n. 4 of جبّ) Having a substance resembling froth (a camel's milk).

A اجباخ *ajbākh*, Places abounding in palm-trees or stones.

A اجبار *ijbār*, (v. n. 4 of جبر) Compelling, constraining. Forcing against one's will. Setting a broken bone. Considering one as a fatalist or predestinarian. Opposition. Constraint.

A اجباس *ajbās*, (pl. of جبس *jibs*) Cowards, knaves, worthless, base fellows. Bears' cubs.

A اجبال *ajbāl*, (pl. of جبل *jabal*) Mountains. *Ijbāl*, (v. n. 4 of جبل) Digging until hard ground appears. Going towards a mountain. Creating, forming, moulding, firmly setting. Having arrow-heads of soft iron. Discovering (any one) to be a miser. Reciting with difficulty (a poet). Striking something hard (a hoof).

A اجبان *ijbān*, (v. n. 4 of جبن) Discovering or reputing one to be a coward.

A اجبح *ajbuh*, (or اجباح *ajbāh*) (pl. of جبح *jabh*, *jibh*, or *jubh*) Beehives.

A اجبس *ajbas*, Weak, feeble.

A اجبل *ajbul*, (pl. of جبل *jabal*) Mountains.

A اجبن *ajban*, More or most cowardly. *Ajbun*, (and اجبنة *ajbinat*) (pl. of جبين *jabīn*) Temples. Foreheads.

A اجبؤ *ajbuʼ*, (pl. of جبء *jabʼ*) Rising grounds of a reddish dusky colour. Mushrooms. Hollows wherein water collects.

A اجبه *ajbah*, One who has a large or prominent forehead. A lion.

A اجّة *ajjat*, (pl. اجاج *ijāj*) Warmth, intense heat. Confusion, commotion, tumult. القوم في الاجّة *al kawm fiʼl ajjat*, The people (are) in a ferment.

A اجتباء *ijtibāʼ*, (v. n. 8 of جبي) Choosing, electing, selecting. Collecting money from different places.

A اجتباب *ijtibāb*, (v. n. 8 of جبّ) Castrating.

A اجتباذ *ijtibāz*, (v. n. 8 of جبذ) Stretching.

A اجتبار *ijtibār*, (v. n. 8 of جبر) Having one's broken fortunes repaired. Repairing the broken fortune of a friend.

A اجتبان *ijtibān*, (v. n. 8 جبن) Discovering or reputing one a coward. Making (milk) into cheese.

A اجتباه *ijtibāh*, (v. n. 8 of جبه) Finding (water) disagreeable and unwholesome.

A اجتثاث *ijtisās*, (v. n. 8 of جثّ) Cutting, plucking up, extirpating.

A اجتحاء *ijtihāʼ*, (v. n. 8 of جحا for جحو) Extirpating, eradicating.

A اجتحار *ijtihār*, (v. n. 8 of جحر) Making a burrow or den.

A اجتحاف *ijtihāf*, (v. n. 8 of جحف) Pillaging, plundering. Exhausting (a well) entirely of water. Taking up hasty pudding with three fingers. Sweeping, snatching away.

A اجتداء *ijtidāʼ*, (v. n. 8 of جدا for جدو) Asking for what one has need of.

A اجتداث *ijtidās*, (v. n. 8 جدث) Preparing a tomb. Making a grave.

A اجتداح *ijtidāh*, (v. n. 8 of جدح) Mixing up a ptisan.

A اجتدار *ijtidār*, (v. n. 8 of جدر) Building a wall.

A اجتذاب *ijtizāb*, (v. n. 8 of جذب) Stretching, extending. Seizing, snatching, pulling, drawing, dragging.

A اجتذال *ijtizāl*, (v. n. 8 of جذل) Being cheerful and merry.

A اجتراء *ijtirāʼ*, (v. n. 8 of جرؤ) Being bold, brave, intrepid. Courageously enduring or bearing up against.

A اجتراح *ijtirāh*, (v. n. 8 of جرح) Purchasing. Acquiring.

A اجترار *ijtirār*, (v. n. 8 of جرّ) Drawing, dragging, pulling. Ruminating, chewing the cud.

A اجتراس *ijtirās*, (v. n. 8 of جرس) Gaining, acquiring. Striving, endeavouring.

A اجتراش *ijtirāsh*, (v. n. 8 of جرش) Earning a living for a family. Seizing forcibly, snatching.

A اجتراع *ijtirāʻ*, (v. n. 8 of جرع) Taking at one draught. Breaking (a stick).

A اجتراف *ijtirāf*, (v. n. 8 of جرف) Sweeping

away in great numbers, depopulating.

A اجترام *ijtirām*, (v. n. 8 of جرم) Committing a crime. Cutting off clusters of dates. Guessing at the produce of a palm-tree. Earning a living for a family.

A اجتران *ijtirān*, (v. n. 8 of جرن) Constructing a bin or place in which to store up dates.

A اجتزاء *ijtizā*, (v. n. 8 of جزأ) Being satisfied. (v. n. 8 of جزي) Requesting, asking recompense.

A اجتزار *ijtizār*, (v. n. 8 of جزر) Killing (a camel). Taking (a sheep, &c.) to be slaughtered. Leaving (corpses) a prey for wild beasts.

A اجتزاز *ijtizāz*, (v. n. 8 of جزّ) Reaping, cutting, mowing. Shearing sheep. Cutting hair.

A اجتزاع *ijtizā'*, (v. n. 8 of جزع) Lopping, severing.

A اجتزاف *ijtizāf*, (v. n. 8 of جزف) Buying at random.

A اجتزام *ijtizām* (v. n. 8 of جزم) Estimating by guess the produce of a palm-tree. Taking part and leaving part. Purchasing a sheep-fold.

A اجتسار *ijtisār*, (v. n. 8 of جسر) Crossing a desert. Sailing across the ocean (a ship).

A اجتساس *ijtisās*, (v. n. 8 of جسّ) Touching, feeling. Eating grass with their jaws (camels).

A اجتساع *ijtisā'*, (v. n. 8 of جسع) Throwing up (as a camel chewing the cud).

A اجتشاء *ijtishā*, (v. n. 8 of جشأ) Disagreeing with any one (a climate). Finding a country disagree with one's self.

A اجتشاش *ijtishāsh*, (v. n. 8 of جشّ) Being luxuriant in vegetation.

A اجتصاص *ijtisās*, (v. n. 8 of جصّ) Taking mortar or plaster. Approaching, coming near each other (a company of persons).

A اجتعاف *ijtiāf*, (v. n. 8 of جعف) Uprooting.

A اجتعال *ijtiāl*, (v. n. 8 of جعل) Taking. Receiving wages. Doing, making.

A اجتفاء *ijtifā*, (v. n. 8 of جفأ) Plucking up (a pot-herb by the root), throwing (it) away. (v. n. 8 of جفا for جفو) Displacing.

A اجتفات *ijtifāt*, (v. n. 8 of جفت not used) Carrying off the whole.

A اجتفار *ijtifār*, (v. n. 8 of جفر) Becoming languid (a stallion).

A اجتفاف *ijtifāf*, (v. n. 8 of جفّ) Eating up the entire contents of a dish.

A اجتلاء *ijtilā*, (v. n. 8 of جلا for جلو) Presenting to the husband a bride unveiled and elegantly attired. Unbinding a turban from off one's head. Looking upon. Forcing to emigrate.

A اجتلاب *ijtilāb*, (v. n. 8 of جلب) Driving from place to place.

A اجتلات *ijtilāt*, (v. n. 8 of جلت) Striking. Eating or drinking all.

A اجتلاد *ijtilād*, (v. n. 8 of جلد) Duelling. Striking one another with whips. Drinking the entire contents of a cup.

A اجتلاط *ijtilāt*, (v. n. 8 of جلط) Snatching, seizing, carrying off. Drinking the entire contents of a vessel.

A اجتلاف *ijtilāf*, (v. n. 8 of جلف) Uprooting.

A اجتلال *ijtilāl*, (v. n. 8 of جلّ) Collecting camels' dung for fuel. Taking the best of any thing.

A اجتلام *ijtilām*, (v. n. 8 of جلم) Cutting flesh from off the bones.

A اجتمار *ijtimār*, (v. n. 8 of جمر) Being perfumed with incense. Burning aloe-wood in a censer.

A اجتماع *ijtimā'*, (v. n. 8 of جمع) Assembling, flocking together. Meeting together. Being admitted, received. Arriving at manhood, and having a full grown beard. A concourse, congress. A heap. Unanimity. Conjunction. Concurrence.

A اجتمال *ijtimāl*, (v. n. 8 of جمل) Melting fat: rubbing it on one's self. Eating of a camel.

A اجتناء *ijtinā*, (v. n. 8 of جني) Gathering, plucking. Coming on rain-water and drinking it.

A اجتناب *ijtinab*, (v. n. 8 of جنب) Shunning, avoiding, declining, flying, abstaining from, retiring; removing to a distance. Being polluted.

A اجتناح *ijtināh*, (v. n. 8 of جنح) Leaning on the palms of the hands in adoration. Inclining to one side. Throwing all her weight forwards when running at full speed (a camel).

A اجتنان *ijtinān*, (v. n. 8 of جنّ) Being concealed. Being conceived in the womb.

A اجتواء *ijtiwā*, (v. n. 8 of جوي) Finding a climate unhealthy. Loathing, nauseating.

A اجتوار *ijtiwār*, (v. n. 8 of جار for جور) Being neighbours.

A اجتهاد *ijtihād*, (v. n. 8 of جهد) Waging a religious war. Striving to accomplish any thing. Labouring hard or studying intensely to arrive at a correct and sound opinion or judgment. Care, effort, study, diligence.

A اجتهاديّ *ijtihādiy*, Relating to a religious war.

A اجتهار *ijtihār*, (v. n. 8 of جهر) Cleaning out or exhausting a well. Being large, and easy to be seen. Regarding (an army) as numerous. Beholding without a veil. Looking at one whose figure and mien are striking and dazzling.

A اجتهاف *ijtihāf*, (v. n. 8 of جهف not used) Taking off a thing by wholesale.

A اجتهام *ijtihām*, (v. n. 8 of جهم) Entering on the last part of the night.

A اجتياب *ijtiyāb* (v. n. 8 of جاب for جوب) Putting on a shift. Digging a well. Traversing a country. Cleaving asunder.

A اجتياح *ijtiyāh*, (v. n. 8 of جاح for جوح) Ruining, destroying. Uprooting.

A اجتياز *ijtiyāz*, (v. n. 8 of جاز for جوز) Passing by or along.

A اجتياس *ijtiyās*, (v. n. 8 of جاس for جوس) Searching, scrutinizing. Patroling in the night. Prowling about for plunder.

A اجتياف *ijtiyāf*, (v. n. 8 of جاف for جوف) Penetrating into any thing hollow, creeping into the middle of any thing. (v. n. 8 of جاف for جيف) Becoming putrid (a carcase).

A اجتيال *ijtiyāl*, (v. n. 8 of جال for جول) Electing, choosing. Circumambulating. Diverting any one from his purpose.

A اجثأ *ajsa*, Hunch-backed, crook-backed.

A اجثاء *ijsā*, (v. n. 4 of جثا for جثو) Causing to kneel, or to stand on tip-toe.

A اجثاث *ijsās*, (v. n. 4 of جثّ) Extirpating.

A اجثئلال *ijsi·lāl*, (v. n. 4 of جثال Q) Plucking out its feathers (a bird). Rushing forth in great anger with intent to kill. Sticking up, becoming erect (feathers). Becoming long and waving, and affording a good bite (grass).

A اجحاح *ijhāh*, (v. n. 4 of جحّ) Being pregnant and near delivery.

A اجحاد *ijhād*, (v. n. 4 of جحد) Being of little value. Being needy. Being stunted (a plant).

A اجحار *ajhār*, (pl. of جحر *juhr*) The dens, holes, or retreats of any beasts or reptiles. *Ijhār*, (v. n. 4 of جحر) Driving (a lizard) into (its) hole. Failing to stir up rain (the stars). Experiencing a barren year. Compelling, forcing one to take refuge.

A اجحاف *ijhāf*, (v. n. 4 of جحف) Carrying away. Attacking, oppressing, pinching (poverty or want). Moving towards. Being near. اجحافات *ijhāfāt*, Oppressions, afflictions.

A اجحام *ijhām*, (v. n. 4 of جحم) Forbearing, drawing back. Being near destroying.

A اجحان *ijhān*, (v. n. 4 of جحن) Stunting the growth of a child by feeding it badly. Stinting one's family through poverty or avarice.

A اجحد *ajhud*, Scanty in acts of charity.

A اجحم *ajham*, One who has large red eyes.

A احجنشاش *ijhinshāsh*, (v. n. 3 of جحنش Q) Becoming large (a boy's belly).

A اجخار *ijkhār*, (v. n. 4 of جخر) Widening (a well's mouth). Causing water to flow copiously, but not from a well. Washing the posteriors partially, so as to leave a bad smell. Marrying a woman جخراء *jakhrā*.

A اجخي *ajkha'*, Lean, meagre, lank-thighed.

A اجد *ijid*, A prohibitory word used to camels. *Ujud*, Robust or compact of body; strong or firm in the back-bone and bunch (applied to a she-camel).

A اجدّ *ajadd*, Small-breasted (man).

A اجداء *ijdā*, (v. n. 4 of جدي) Giving liberally, accommodating, assisting. Bleeding profusely (a wound). Receiving a gift. Supplying the place of another.

A اجداب *ijdāb*, (v. n. 4 of جدب) Suffering distress from dearth. Finding (a land) barren. Yielding no increase (the earth).

A اجداث *ajdās*, (pl. of جدث *jadas*) Tombs.

A اجداح *ijdāh,* (v. n. 4 of جدح) Impressing a mark on the thigh of a camel. Mixing a ptisan.

A اجداد *ajdād,* (pl. of جدّ *jadd*) Grandsires. *Ijdād,* (v. n. 4 of جدّ) Striving, exerting one's self. Renewing, making new. Travelling over hard even ground. Having dates ripe, ready for cutting (a palm-tree). Becoming hard and even (a road). اجدّت قروني منه *ajaddat karūnī minhu,* I left him.

A اجدار *ajdār,* (pl. of جدر *jadar*) Scars. Unnatural excrescences on the body, wens. *Ijdār,* (v. n. 4 of جدر) Producing the herb جدر *jadr.* Putting forth the rudiments of fruit (a tree), as if they were tubercles. Coming out like pimples (the heads of a plant). Swelling.

A اجداش *ajdāsh,* (pl. of جدش *jadash*) Coarse, rough, rugged grounds.

A اجداع *ijdāع,* (v. n. 4 of جدع) Giving unwholesome food to a child. Keeping back, restraining.

A اجداف *ijdāf,* (v. n. 4 of جدف) Crying out, raising a clamour. Being ungrateful for the blessings of Providence, murmuring and blaspheming whilst enjoying them.

A اجدال *ajdāl,* (pl. of جدل *jadl* or *jidl*) Limbs of animals. *Ijdāl,* (v. n. 4 of جدل) Being accompanied by her fawn (a doe).

A اجدام *ijdām,* (v. n. 4 of جدم) Crying out اجدم *ijdam* to a horse.

A اجدان *ijdān,* (v. n. of وجد) Discovering, finding, recovering (any thing lost or sought for). (v. n. 4 of جدن) Becoming rich after being poor.

A اجدّان *ajaddāni,* (dual) Night and day.

A اجدب *ajdab,* Barren (season). Desert, desolate. *Ajdub,* (pl. of جدب *jadb*) Scarcities, dearths. Barren places.

A اجدث *ajdus,* (pl. of جدث *jadas*) Tombs.

P اجدر *ajdar,* (for اژدر *ajdar*), A dragon.

A اجدر *ajdar,* More or most worthy.

A اجدرار *ijdirār,* (v. n. 8 of جرّ) Dragging.

P اجدرونتن *ajdarūnitan,* (in zand and Pāzand) To reap, to mow.

A اجدزاز *ijdizāz,* (v. n. 8 of جزّ) Cutting, clipping, mowing, shearing.

A اجدع *ajdaع,* Mutilated (in the hand, nose, ear, or lips). The devil. A man's name.

A اجدف *ajdaf,* Short, dwarfish.

A اجدل *ajdal,* (pl. اجادل *ajādil*) A species of hawk. Slender (arm).

A اجدليّ *ajdalīy,* A hawk of a particular species.

A اجدماع *ijdimāع,* (v. n. 8 of جمع) Assembling, flocking together, becoming assembled.

P آجده *ājada,* Coloured, dyed. Stitched.

A اجدي *ajda',* More or most serviceable. *Ajdī,* (pl. of جدي *jady*) Kids.

A اجذاء *ijzās,* (v. n. 4 of جذا for جذو) Standing erect. Having a fat bunch (a young camel). Lifting (a stone). (v. n. 4 of جذي) Hindering.

A اجذاذ *ajzāz,* (pl. of جذّ *jazz*) Pieces, bits.

A اجذار *ijzār,* (v. n. 4 of جذر) Rooting up.

A اجذاع *ijzāع,* (v. n. 4 of جذع) Imprisoning, arresting. Becoming جذع *jazaع* (a camel).

A اجذاف *ijzāf,* (v. n. 4 of جذف) Flying fast. Taking short and quick steps.

A اجذال *ajzāl,* (pl. of جذل *jizl*) The roots of great trees; lopped trunks of trees. The summits or projecting parts of mountains. *Ijzāl,* (v. n. 4 of جذل) Rendering cheerful, gladdening.

A اجذام *ajzām,* (pl. of جذم *jazm*) Roots. *Ijzām,* (v. n. 4 of جذم) Amputating, mutilating. Walking fast (a camel). Urging forward. Abstaining, controlling one's self. Proposing, intending.

A اجذع *ajzaع,* Rising three years old (the horse, ass, or ox); five years (camel); two years (sheep).

A اجذم *ajzam,* (pl. جذاميٰ *jazāma'*) Mutilated in the hand, having it cut off. One who having committed to memory the Kur'ān, forgets it afterwards. Leprous. Afflicted with elephantiasis. One who has lost the tips of his fingers.

A اجذئرار *ijzisrār,* (v. n. 4 of جذأر Q) Assuming an erect posture when going to revile. Growing without becoming tall (a plant).

A آجر *ājar,* Hagar the mother of Ishmael, from whom the Arabians claim descent. *Ājir,* or *ājur,* A brick, a tile.

A اجر *ajara,* (fut. يأجر *yasjuru* or *yasjiru*) He rewarded.

A اجر *ajr,* (v. n. of اجر) Letting out on hire. Becoming a hireling. Restoring, healing (a broken or dislocated joint). Being thus restored. Honourable mention. (pl. اجور *ujūr* and آجار *ājār*) Reward, premium, recompense, wages, hire. A marriage-portion or gift. *Ajur* or *ujur,* A brick or tile.

A اجر *ajrin,* (without tanwin اجري *ajrī*) (pl. of جرو *jarw*) Whelps.

A آجرّ *ājurr,* A brick or tile.

A اجرا *ajras,* Bolder, boldest.

A اجرء *ajrus,* (pl. of جرو *jarw, jirw,* or *jurw*) The young ones of any thing animate or inanimate.

P اجرا *ijrā,* Sufficiency of cloth to make a dress.

A اجراء *ajrās,* (pl. of جرو *jarw, jirw,* or *jurw*) Whelps. (pl. of جريء *jariس*) Bold, brave. Leaders of the van in battle. *Ijrās,* (v. n. 4 of جرا for جرو) Going with its whelp (a beast). (v. n. 4 of جري) Making (any thing) to flow, or run, giving currency. Bringing forward, producing: paying; executing, performing. Corning, forming the grain (a plant). Declining, inflecting, conjugating. Appointing an attorney, sending a deputy. P اجراي حق كردن *ijrāsi hak kardan,* (or اجراي شرع كردن *ijrāsi sharع kardan*) To administer or to do justice, promote equity, put the laws into execution. اجراي فرمان كردگار كردن *ijrāsi farmāni kirdigār kardan,* To obey the commands of God. اجراي حدود كردن *ijrāsi hudūd kardan,* To punish legally, to put in execution the penal laws.

A اجراب *ijrāb,* (v. n. 4 of جرب) Having scabby camels or sheep.

A اجراح *ajrāh,* (pl. of جرح *jurh*) Wounds.

A اجراد *ajrād,* (pl. of جرد *jard*) Old threadbare garments.

A اجراذ *ijrāz,* (v. n. 4 of جرذ) Drawing out, bringing forth. Removing, deposing. Compelling, forcing.

A اجرار *ijrār,* (v. n. 4 of جرّ) Granting a delay (for payment of a debt). Leaving any one to his own choice. Slitting a young camel's tongue to prevent him from sucking. Chewing the cud. Piercing with a spear, and leaving it sticking in the body. Following, imitating another (in singing).

A اجراز *ajrāz,* Bare, barren (land). The body (of a serpent). (pl. of جرز *jarz*) Sterile (grounds) having no rain. (pl. of جرز *jirz*) Female garments made of fur. (pl. of جرز *jurz*) Maces, sceptres. (pl. of جرز *jaraz*) Unfruitful seasons. Bodies or breasts of men. *Ijrāz,* (v. n. 4 of جرز) Having ground scantily watered, and producing but little. Suffering from barrenness. Being lean (a camel).

A اجراس *ajrās,* (pl. of جرس *jaras*) Bells. *Ijrās,* (v. n. 4 of جرس) Making a gentle noise (the wing of a bird in flying, or female ornaments). Overhearing a man's talk (a wild beast). Singing aloud (a camel-driver).

A اجراض *ijrāz,* (v. n. 4 of جرض) Causing to be choked.

A اجراف *ajrāf,* (pl. of جرف *jurf*) Particles eaten and carried down by the stream. Banks eaten into by the stream. *Ijrāf,* (v. n. 4 of جرف) Turning (camels) into a luxuriant pasture. Suffering from a sweeping torrent (a place).

A اجرال *ajrāl,* (pl. of جرل *jaral* or *jaril*) Rough and stony places. *Ijrāl,* (v. n. 4 of جرل) Digging to stony stratas.

A اجرام *ajrām,* The utensils of a shepherd. (pl. of جرم *jirm*) Bodies. (pl. of جرم *jurm*) Crimes, trespasses. اوضاع اجرام سما *awzāع ajrāmi samā,* The motions of the heavenly bodies. P اجرام چرخ *ajrāmi charkh,* (or اجرام فلك *ajrāmi falak*) The heavenly bodies. اجرام عنصري *ajrāmi عunsurī,* Elemental bodies. A *Ijrām,* (v. n. 4 of جرم) Committing a crime. Being great. Being clear (colour or voice). Adhering (blood). Charging with a crime.

A اجران *ijrān,* (v. n. 4 of جرن) Housing dates.

A اجرّان *ajarrāni,* (dual) Man and genii.

A اجرب *ajrab,* (pl. جرب *jurb,* also اجارب *ajārib*) Scabby, mangy.

A اجربة *ajribat,* (pl. of جريب *jarīb*) Certain measures of grain containing 384 *mudds,* or about 768 lbs. Spaces of ground where such quantities may be sown. (pl. of جراب *jirāb*) Leathern bags in which travellers carry their provisions. Spaces or areas in wells, from the mouth to the surface of the water.

A آجرة *ājirat*, A brick.

A اجرة *ujrat*, Recompense, hire, rent, wages.

A اجرّة *ajirrat*, (pl. of جرّة *jirrat*) Cuds. (pl. of جرير *jarīr*) Camel-halters or reins.

A اجرد *ajrad*, Bald, hairless (man), bare. (pl. اجارد *ajārid*) A barren field. The yard of any solid-hoofed animal. The back. A horse with very short hair. One who takes the lead and gets far ahead. Entire (day). الاجرد *al ajrad*, Name of a mountain in Arabia.

A اجردّ *ijridd*, (or اجرد *ijrid*) A certain plant which indicates the existence of mushrooms.

A اجردان *ajradāni*, (dual of اجرد *ajrad*) Two branches of a palm-tree. Two trees stript of their bark. Two months or two days.

A اجرز *ajraz*, Bow-legged.

A اجرش *ajrash*, Half-pounded, coarse.

A اجرع *ajraʻ*, A sand-hill where vegetation thrives, or one which yields no herbage.

A اجرعباب *ijriʻbāb*, (v. n. 4 of جرعب Q) Being thrown prostrate.

A اجرعنان *ijriʻnān*, (v. n. 4 of جرعن Q) Inclining. Shaking. Falling down at once.

A اجرمزاز *ijrimzāz*, (v. n. 4 of جرمز Q) Being drawn together. Retiring through fear, fleeing away. Passing by (as the night).

A اجرنباء *ijrimbāʼ*, A sleep without a bolster.

A اجرنثام *ijrinsām*, (v. n. 3 of جرثم Q) Being collected together. Remaining close in one place. Falling from top to bottom.

A اجرنماز *ijrinmāz*, (v. n. 3 of جرمز Q) Drawing one's self together. Being collected together.

A آجرون *ājurūn* or *ājirūn*, A brick, a tile.

A اجرهداد *ijrihdād*, (v. n. 4 of جرهد Q) Making haste. Being extended. Being long. Persevering. Being destitute of vegetation. Being scarce (a year).

A اجري *ajra'*, May (he) make flow or proceed.

A اجريّ *ijriy*, Course, custom. A deputy, agent.

A اجرياء *ajriyāʼ*, (pl. of جريء *jariʼ*) Strong, bold, brave. (pl. of جريّ *jariy*) Agents, deputies, attorneys. *Ijriyāʼ*, (or اجريا *ijriya'*) Custom, course. Nature. Line of pursuit.

A اجريباب *ijribāb*, (v. n. 11 of جرب) Looking with outstretched neck.

A اجرية *ajriyat*, (pl. of جرو *jarw*) Whelps. Small cucumbers. Slices of a colocynth.

A اجريّة *ijriyat*, Nature, custom, course.

A اجرئشاش *ijriʼshāsh*, (v. n. 4 of جرأش Q) Becoming fat and well-liking after having been lean (the body). Waxing fat (camels).

A اجزاء *ajzāʼ*, (pl. of جزء *juzʼ*) Parts, portions, parcels. Ingredients. Materials. Drugs. Minerals. *Ijzāʼ*, (v. n. 4 of جزأ) Satisfying, contenting. Satisfying (a camel) with fresh grass, and enabling (him) to do without water. Growing luxuriantly, being entangled (grass). Bringing forth female children (a woman). Putting a handle to a knife. Putting a ring on the finger. (v. n. 4 of جزي) Supplying the place of another. Being able or enabling to do without. Not sufficing. Paying tribute.

A اجزار *ijzār*, (v. n. 4 of جزر) Having fruit ready for gathering (a palm-tree). Giving a sheep to be slaughtered. Being fit for the butcher (a young camel). Growing old and approaching the period of dissolution.

A اجزاز *ijzāz*, (v. n. 4 of جزّ) Being fit for reaping (wheat). Having dates fit to cut (a palm-tree). Having sheep fit for shearing. Giving (any one) the wool of a sheep. Becoming dry (dates). Being time for (an old man) to die.

A اجزاع *ajzāʻ*, (pl. of جزع *jizʻ*) The windings or branchings off of a valley. Beehives. *Ijzāʻ*, (v. n. 4 of جزع) Rendering impatient and querulous. Leaving a remainder.

A اجزال *ijzāl*, (v. n. 4 of جزل) Exercising liberality. Galling a camel's hunch (a wooden saddle).

A اجزل *ajzal*, (A camel) galled on the back.

A اجزم *ajzam*, One whose nose has been cut off.

A اجزن *ajzun*, (pl. of جزن *jazn*) Huge logs.

A اجساد *ajsād*, (pl. of جسد *jasad*) Bodies, trunks, carcases. ذوات الاجساد *zawātu'l ajsād*, The signs Sagittarius, Pisces, Gemini, and Virgo. *Ijsād*, (v. n. 4 of جسد) Dyeing with saffron. Making a garment stick to the body.

A اجسام *ajsām*, (pl. of جسم *jism*) Solid bodies. *Ijsām*, (v. n. 4 of جسم) Being important and arduous (an enterprise).

P آجستن *ājastan*, or *ājistan*, To plant a tree. To fix a pale or fence, erect a stone. نو آجسته *naw-ājasta*, Newly planted.

A اجسر *ajsur*, (pl. of جسر *jasr* or *jisr*) Bridges.

A اجسم *ajsam*, Large-bodied, corpulent.

A اجسئنان *ijsiʼnān*, A being hard, hardness.

A اجشّ *ajashsh*, One who has a harsh and sonorous voice (man, horse, or thunder). A nasal twang, loud and harsh.

A اجشاء *ajshāʼ*, (pl. of جشء *jashʼ*) Light bows. Branches of trees of which such bows are made.

A اجشاش *ijshāsh*, (v. n. 4 of جشّ) Breaking, pounding. Grinding coarsely.

A اجشام *ijshām*, (v. n. 4 of جشم) Causing one to toil hard at drudgery.

A اجشر *ajshar*, Troubled with a hoarseness and roughness in the breast.

A اجشرة *ajshirat*, (pl. of جشير *jashīr*) Corn-sacks. Leathern quivers.

A اجط *ijt*, A word made use of in driving sheep.

A اجظاظ *ijzāz*, (v. n. 4 of جظّ) Exceeding bounds in insolence, wickedness, or pride.

A اجعاظ *ijʻāz*, (v. n. 4 of جعظ) Pushing, thrusting, driving away. Running away.

A اجعاف *ijʻāf*, (v. n. 4 of جعف) Prostrating.

A اجعال *ijʻāl*, (v. n. 4 of جعل) Promising a price (for labour) and performing it. Being in heat (a bitch). Taking a boiling pot from off the fire with a cloth called جعال *jiʻāl*. Being infected by an immense number of dead beetles (water).

A اجعام *ijʻām*, (v. n. 4 of جعم) Being visited by a large and hungry foraging party. Eradicating.

A اجعان *ijʻān*, (v. n. 4 of جعن) Being coarse, thick, and rough (flesh).

A اجعب *ajʻab*, Large, gor-bellied. Weak, inactive. Astonished, amazed. Dead.

A اجعم *ajʻam*, Greedy, craving.

A اجفاء *ijfāʼ*, (v. n. 4 of جفأ) Shutting a door. Fatiguing (one's cattle) with travelling, and not allowing them to graze. Casting up scum (a river or boiling pot). Throwing, casting. Laying, placing. Departing, going off (a nation's weal). (v. n. 4 of جفا for جفو) Unsaddling a horse. Following sheep so as not to let them graze.

A اجفار *ajfār*, (pl. of جفر *jafr*) Lambs four months old. *Ijfār*, (v. n. 4 of جفر) Being absent, hidden, lying hid. Refraining from venery. Cutting an acquaintance, ceasing to visit him. Smelling disagreeably. Becoming languid (a stallion).

A اجفال *ajfāl*, (pl. of جفل *jifl* or *jafl*) Dungs of elephants. *Ijfāl*, (v. n. 4 of جفل) Running very fast (an ostrich). Causing (an ostrich) to run very fast. Blowing hard and raising the dust (wind). Voiding excrement (an elephant). Moving off from any place (people).

A اجفان *ajfān*, (pl. of جفن *jafn*) Eye-lids. *Ijfān*, (v. n. 4 of جفن) Indulging freely in venery.

A اجفلة *ajfalat*, A flock. *Ajfalatan*, In herds.

A اجفلي *ajfala'*, A crowd. A promiscuous entertainment. Promiscuously, indiscriminately.

A اجفن *ajfun*, (pl. of جفن *jafn*) Eye-lids.

A اجفئظاظ *ijfiʼzāz*, (v. n. 4 of جفأظ Q or اجفيظاظ *ijfīzāz*, 11 of جفظ) Swelling (a carcase).

A اجفيل *ijfīl*, Pusillanimous, timid. A timid ostrich. Far-shooting (bow). Aged (woman).

A اجكار *ijkār*, (v. n. 4 of جكر) Importuning, urging, pressing (a sale).

A آجل *ājil*, One who procrastinates, delays, protracts, grants time, or fixes a term. A hinderer, prohibitor, detainer, retainer, concluder. An exciter, provoker. Future, belonging to the next world, or life to come.

A آجلاً *ājilan*, In regard to the next life.

P آجل *ājul*, (or *ājal*) Eructation. Flatulency.

A اجل *ajl*, (v. n. of اجل) Acquiring, gaining, collecting. Hindering, detaining, preventing. Drawing. Exciting, stirring up mischief. Laying snares. Having a pain in the neck. Curing or applying a remedy for a crick in the neck. *Ajl* or *ijl*, Cause, occasion, reason. من اجل ان *min ajl an*, Because that. من اجل ذلك *min ajli zālika*, For that reason. من اجلك *min ajlika*, On thy account. *Ijl*, (pl. آجال *ājāl*) A kind of wild oxen, a herd of camels or of deer. A pain in the neck, contracted by lying awry. *Ujl*, (pl. of اجيل *ajīl*) Procrastinators. Clays heaped up round palm-trees. *Ajal*, (v. n. of اجل) Delaying. (pl. آجال *ājāl*) A term, an appointed time, the end of a fixed time, a period. The duration of any given space of time. الاجل *al ajal*, The period or end of life, the predestined moment, death. P اجل گرفته *ajal-girifta*, On the point of death, in a situation which precludes all hopes of life. اجل گيا *ajal giyā*, Name of a poisonous root. A اجل مسمّى *ajal musamma'*, The day of judgment. *Ajal*, Yes, synonymous with نعم *naɛam*, but a stronger affirmative. The latter is used when an interrogation precedes, the former when it follows the imperative, &c.: as, سر *sir*, Go, اجل *ajal*, Yes; تسير *tasīr*, Dost thou go? نعم *naɛam*, Yes.

A اجّل *ijjal*, or *ujjal*, A wild goat.

A اجلّ *ajall*, Greater, more excellent, glorious.

A اجلاء *ijlāɛ*, (v. n. 4 of جلا for جلو) Going into exile. Banishing, compelling to migrate. Being dispersed. Being distant. Making haste.

A اجلاب *ajlāb*, (pl. of جلب *jalab*) Things brought or driven for sale from country to country. *Ijlāb*, (v. n. 4 of جلب) Making an uproar. Scheming, practising fraud. Shouting to a horse. Drying up (blood). Threatening mischief. Collecting, convoking. Covering (a camel's saddle) with moist leather in order that it may dry. Assisting. Assembling together. Putting an amulet into a leathern case. Having camels that bring forth males.

A اجلاد *ajlād*, (pl. اجالد *ajālid*) The body, person. (pl. of جلد *jald*) Light, active, brisk. (pl. of جلد *jild*) Skins, hides, parchments. Books. (pl. of جليد *jalīd*) Strong. *Ijlād*, (v. n. 4 of جلد) Being covered with hoar-frost. Forcing, compelling.

A اجلاس *ijlās*, (v. n. 4 of جلس) Causing, requesting, desiring, or ordering one to sit. A session for judicial proceedings.

A اجلاف *ajlāf*, A carcase of mutton, without skin, head, or feet. (pl. of جلف *jilf*) Mean, ignoble: wretches, tyrants. *Ijlāf*, (v. n. 4 of جلف) Removing the crust of clay from the top of a vessel in which corn is kept. Sweeping away, destroying.

A من اجلاك *min ajlāka* or *ijlāka*, For thy sake.

A اجلال *ajlāl*, (pl. of جلّ *jull*) Housings, or any kind of horse-covering. *Ijlāl*, (v. n. 4 of جلّ) Reverencing, honouring. Giving much. Being strong. Being weak. Reverence. من اجلالك *min ijlālika*, From respect to thee, on thy account.

A آجلة *ājilat*, Eternity. Any thing that relates or has reference to a future life.

A اجلة *ijlat*, Name of a village in Yamāma.

A اجلّة *ajillat*, (pl. of جلال *jilāl*) Horse-cloths. (pl. of جليل *jalīl*) Old. Glorious.

A اجلح *ajlah*, Bald on the temples. One whose hair flows down the sides of the head. A camel-litter with a low awning.

A اجلحمام *ijlihmām*, An assembling together.

A اجلخاخ *ijlikhākh*, (v. n. 9 of جلخ) Being weak and languid (bones). Spreading wide the arms in adoration.

A اجلخباب *ijlikhbāb*, A falling down.

A اجلخمام *ijlikhmām*, (v. n. 4 of جلخم Q) Assembling together. Being haughty. Wishing or asking for much.

A اجلد *ajlad*, Hard (ground).

A اجلع *ajlaɛ*, One whose lips are open, so that the teeth appear. One whose privities are exposed.

A اجلعباب *ijliɛbāb*, (v. n. 4 of جلعب Q) Lying in a recumbent posture. Being extended. Departing. Walking earnestly. Being numerous.

A اجلعداد *ijliɛdād*, (v. n. 4 of جلعد Q) Being outstretched prostrate on the ground.

A اجلنخاء *ijlinkhāɛ*, (v. n. 3 of جلخي Q) Being disjointed, falling to pieces. Kneeling down.

A اجلنظاء *ijlinzāɛ*, (v. n. 4 of جلظي Q) Bursting with rage. Lying on the back and lifting up the legs. Reclining, stretched out on one side.

A اجلنفاع *ijlinfāɛ*, A being thick, thickness.

A اجلوّاذ *ijliwwāz*, (v. n. 13 of جلذ) Travelling rapidly (a camel). Going off (rain).

A اجلوّاظ *ijliwwāz*, (v. n. 13 of جلظ) Remaining, persevering, persisting.

A اجله *ajlah*, Bald on the forehead. (A bull) without horns, dodded. Full, broad, plump in the face and temples.

A اجلى *ajla'*, More splendid, bright, or resplendent. Handsome-faced and bald about the temples. Bald on the forehead. ابن اجلي *ibn ajla'*, One whose business is plain and open.

A اجليلاء *ijlīlāɛ*, (v. n. 12 of جلا for جلو) Migrating from country to country.

A آجم *ajim*, Tired, loathing, disgusted, sated (with the same food).

A أجم *ajama*, (fut. يأجم *yaɛjumu*) Fire burned.

A أجم *ajima*, (fut. يأجم *yaɛjimu*) He nauseated.

A اجم *ajm*, (v. n. of اجم) Loathing, nauseating (food). Turning, stinking (water). Forcing one against his will. (pl. آجام *ājām*) Any building with a lofty roof, quadrangular and flat. *Ujm*, *ujum*, or *ajam*, (pl. of اجمة *ajamat*) Red-beds, brakes. *Ajam*, (v. n. of اجم) Loathing, nauseating, being tired of one sort of food. P اجم كردن *ajam kardan*, To loathe. A *Ujum* or *ujm*, (pl. آجام *ājām*) A fort, castle.

A اجمّ *ajamm*, Destitute of battlements (building). Unarmed (man). Hornless, dodded (ram). (A horse) between whose ears the cavalier does not point his lance. Fleshy (bone). A cup, a goblet. Privities (of a woman). (in pros.) The foot مفاعلتن *mufāɛalatun* cut down to فاعلن *fāɛilun*.

A اجمأ *ajmaɛ*, Marked with a plain white star on the forehead (a horse).

A اجماء *ijmāɛ*, A plain white star on the forehead of a horse.

A اجمّاء *ajimmāɛ*, (pl. of جميم *jamīm*) Plants thick and wide-spreading.

P اجماج *ujmāj*, Paradise.

A اجماد *ajmād*, (pl. of جمد *jumd*) High places, eminences. *Ijmād*, (v. n. 4 of جمد) Rendering necessary. Entering on the month Jumāda. Being stingy and good for nothing.

A اجمار *ijmār*, (v. n. 4 of جمر) Laying fragrant wood on the fire. Perfuming (a garment). Being assembled and crowding together. Going fast. Galloping in fetters (a horse). Gathering (her) hair together and fastening it on the crown of (her head). Guessing by the eye the produce of a palm-tree, and afterwards reckoning and collecting the estimated produce. Concealing the new moon (night). Being common to a people (an affair). Exercising (a horse). Collecting, bringing together. Being level (a camel's foot), having no line visible between the soles. Keeping (an army) in an enemy's territory, without allowing (it) to return home.

A اجماع *ajmāɛ*, (pl. of جمع *jumɛ*) Clenched fists. *Ijmāɛ*, (v. n. 4 of جمع) Collecting, putting together, convoking. Consenting, agreeing. Covering the surface of the ground, whether hard or soft (rain). Milking all a camel's teats. Driving (camels) altogether. Applying the mind to an undertaking. Making light. Making ready. Tying a camel's teats together. Rendering familiar or sociable. A senate, council, court, crowd. Union. اجماع امّت *ijmāɛi ummat*, An assembling of the people.

A اجمال *ajmāl*, (pl. of جمل *jamal*) Full-grown camels. *Ijmāl*, (v. n. 4 of جمل) Doing any thing well; multiplying benefits. Casting up an account. Collecting, bringing together (dispersed objects). Proceeding gently and moderately (in a search). Melting fat. Being numerous (camels). An abridgment, summary, compendium, epitome, synopsis.

A اجمالاً *ijmālan*, Briefly, compendiously, summarily.

A اجمالى *ijmālī*, Brief, summary, compendious.

A اجمام *ijmām*, (v. n. 4 of جمّ) Filling a measure so that the grain runs over. Allowing (water) to collect. Letting (a field) lie fallow. Giving rest. Turning loose (a horse). Resting, recruiting strength (jaded horse). Approaching. Being ready.

A اجمة *ajamat*, (pl. اجم *ujm*, *ujum*, *ajam*, آجام *ājām*, اجام *ijām*, and اجمات *ajamāt*) A reed-bed; a low-lying place to which waters flow, a marsh. A forest, haunt, den. A subterraneous granary.

A اجمع *ajmaɛ* or *ajmuɛ*, (اجمعون *ajmaɛūna* or اجمعين *ajmaɛīna*) All, the whole.

A اجمل *ajmal*, More or most beautiful, fairest.

P اجمود *ajmūd*, (or اجموده *ajmūda*) Parsley.

P اجمير *ajmīr*, Name of a province of Hindūstān.

A آجن *ājin*, Altered, corrupted, fetid: tending to corruption (water).

A اجن *ajn*, (v. n. of اجن) Beating cloths (as they do at the fulling-mills, bleaching-greens, &c.). *Ajn* or *ajan*, (v. n. of اجن) Undergoing a change in taste and colour; becoming fetid (water). *Ajin*, Fetid (water).

A اجنّ *ajann*, More or most insane.

A اجنا *ajna'*, Hump-backed (man).

A اجنأ *ajnaʼ*, Hump-backed (man).

A اجناء *ajnāʼ*, (pl. of جاني *jānī*) Gatherers, pluckers. Sinners. (pl. of جنا *jana'*) Golds. Shells, conchæ veneris. Fresh dates. Honeys. *Ijnāʼ*, (v. n. 4 of جنأ) Falling flat upon. (v. n. 4 of جني) Having fruit fit to be gathered (a tree). Being very fertile in produce (land).

A اجناب *ajnāb*, (pl. of جنب *jamb*) Sides, parts. (pl. of جنب *junub*) Polluted. *Ijnāb*, (v. n. 4 of جنب) Causing any one to retire, avoid, or shun. Being in a state of ceremonial uncleanness. Being exposed to the south wind.

A اجناح *ijnāh*, (v. n. 4 of جنح) Rendering inclined. Inclining, leaning.

A اجناد *ajnād*, (pl. of جند *jund*) Soldiers, troops.

A اجناس *ajnās*, (pl. of جنس *jins*) Kinds, sorts, genera, goods, wares. اجناس اموال *ajnāsi amwāl*, Various kinds of riches. اجناس مختلفه *ajnāsi mukhtalifa*, Various sorts, different kinds.

P اجناس لعب بازي *ajnāsi laʻb-bāzī*, Playthings.

A اجناف *ijnāf*, (v. n. 4 of جنف) Declining from the right way, deviating, swerving in a matter of precept, command, will, or testament. Injustice. Discovering any one to be unjust.

A اجنان *ajnān*, (pl. of جنن *janan*) Graves. Corpses. Winding-sheets. (pl. of جنان *janān*) Dark nights. Hearts. Spiders. *Ijnān*, (v. n. 4 of جنّ) Rolling a winding-sheet round a corpse. Burying. Concealing one's self, lying hid. Coming on, concealing a thing (the darkness of night). Hiding, concealing in the heart. Casting forth an embryo. Making mad.

A اجنب *ajnab*, Foreign. A foreigner, a stranger. Inclined or going to one side; obstinate, refractory.

P اجنبان *ajumbān*, (In the language of the *Dasātīr*) Motionless, fixed.

A اجنبة *ajnibat*, (pl. of جناب *janāb*) Sides, parts, margins. Corners. Thresholds, courts.

A اجنبيّ *ajnabīy*, A foreigner, a stranger.

A اجنبية *ajnabīyat*, State of a stranger or alien.

A اجنة *ajnat, ijnat, ujnat*, (for وجنة *wajnat, wijnat, wujnat*,) The cheek, particularly the upper and protuberant part.

A اجنّة *ajinnat*, (pl. of جنين *janīn*) Embrios.

A اجنحة *ajnihat*, (or اجنح *ajnuh*) (pl. of جناح *janāh*) Wings. Hands. Fins. Pinnacles. Projections of any kind.

P اجند *ujand*, Obsequious, obedient.

A اجنف *ajnaf*, One deviating from that which is just; iniquitous in not obeying the commands, or fulfilling the intentions of a will. Crook-backed.

A اجنّك *ajinnaka*, (or من اجنّك *min ajinnaka*) (for من اجل انك *min ajli annaka*) Because that thou.

P آجنگان *ājangān*, Name of a fort in Khurāsān.

A اجنن *ajnun*, (pl. of جنين *janīn*) Embrios.

A اجني *ajna'*, Hump-backed.

A اجنيص *ijnīs*, A stupid, dull, indolent man, who moves not from his place, and who does neither good nor harm. Timid, slow.

A اجواء *ajwāʼ*, (pl. of جوّ *jaww*) Skies, firmaments. *Ijwāʼ*, (v. n. 4 of جوي) Hanging (a kettle). Putting (a kettle) into (its) case.

A اجواب *ajwāb*, (pl. of جوب *jawb*) Large buckets. Women's shifts. Shields. Fire-places.

A اجواد *ajwād*, (pl. of جواد *jawād*) Liberal, bountiful. *Ijwād*, (v. n. 4 of جاد for جود) Saying or doing any thing good. Running swiftly (a horse). Possessing a fleet horse.

A اجوار *ajwār*, (pl. of جار *jār*) Neighbours.

A اجواز *ajwāz*, (pl. of جوز *jawz*) Middles, centres.

A اجواف *ajwāf*, (pl. of جوف *jawf*) Bellies.

A اجوال *ajwāl*, (pl. of جول) Parapets of wells.

A اجوام *ajwām*, (pl. of جام) Cups, bowls, goblets.

A اجواني *ajwānī*, A sort of spice.

A اجواين *ajwāyin*, A species of aniseed. اجواين خراساني *ajwāyini khurāsānī*, Henbane-seed.

A اجوب *ajwab*, Prevailing, efficacious, more or most speedy in bringing an answer (prayer).

A اجوبة *ajwibat*, (pl. of جواب *jawāb*) Answers, replies. اجوبهٔ مسكته *ajwibaʼi muskita*, Answers which put to silence.

A اجوث *ajwas*, One whose belly is prominent above, and lank below.

A آجوج *ājūj*, Gog.

A اجوج *ajūj*, Greatly inflamed, red, resplendent. *Ujūj*, (v. n. of اجّ) Being salt, bitter, or brackish (water).

A اجوح *ajwah*, (pl. جوح *jūh*) Ample, spacious.

A اجود *ajwad*, Better, best.

A آجور *ājūr*, (or اجور *ajūr*) A brick, bricks. An odoriferous apple, or thing held in the hand on account of its pleasant smell.

A اجور *ujūr*, (v. n. of اجر) Being set or healed (a broken or sprained limb). (pl. of اجر *ajr*) Wages. Rewards, premiums. Marriage-portions.

A اجورة *ajūra*, A reward, hire, fare, wages.

P اجوره دار *ajūra-dār*, A labourer for hire.

A اجوز *ajwuz*, (pl. of جائز *jāʼiz*) Beams.

A اجوزة *ajwizat*, (pl. of جائز *jāʼiz*) Beams.

A اجوع *ajwaʻ*, More or most famished.

A اجوف *ajwaf*, Hollow. Ample, large, capacious. Large-bellied (lion). (In gram.) A concave verb, one whose medial radical is either a و or a ي.

A الاجوفان *al ajwafāni*, (dual of اجوف *ajwaf*) (The two hollows) The belly and the matrix.

A اجوق *ajwak*, One of a downcast, distorted countenance. Distorted (face). Thick-necked.

A اجول *ajwal*, Dusty: a dusty day. *Ujūl*, (v. n. of اجل) Delaying, procrastinating.

A اجوليّ *ajwalīy*, Swift (horse).

A اجؤم *ajʼum*, (pl. of جام) Silver cups, chalices.

A اجوم *ajūm*, Disagreeable: loathed, disdained.

A اجون *ujūn*, (v. n. of اجن) Becoming fetid.

A اجوه *ujūh*, (pl. of وجه *wajh*) Faces.

A اجوي *ajwa'*, Dark bay (horse).

A اجوية *ajwiyat*, (pl. of جواء *jiwāʼ*) Spaces between houses. Shepherds' wallets.

A اجهاء *ijhāʼ*, (v. n. 4 of جها for جهو) Lying open and disencumbered (a road). Being clear and serene (the sky). Finding (the sky) so. Giving little; being stingy. Not conceiving.

A اجهاد *ijhād*, (v. n. 4 of جهد) Overloading a beast of burden. Wasting, consuming (one's property). Being fierce in hostility. Being possible, in one's power. Being above, on an eminence. Increasing (gray hair). Becoming clear, evident, apparent. Coming near, being in sight. Using circumspection. Craving food. Growing gray. Being intricate and doubtful. Walking fast.

A اجهار *ijhār*, (v. n. 4 of جهر) Speaking clearly, publishing. Begetting a son who has a slight squint, or sons with comely faces and handsome figures.

A اجهاز *ijhāz*, (v. n. 4 of جهز) Making an assault upon a wounded person with intent to kill, giving him the coup de grace, despatching him.

A اجهاش *ijhāsh*, (v. n. 4 of جهش) Being about to cry, preparing to weep. Stimulating to activity. Running to its mother (a frightened child).

A اجهاض *ijhāz*, (v. n. 4 of جهض) Overcoming, snatching the prey from another. Casting her young (a camel). Causing to depart with haste; removing, putting away. Making haste.

A اجهال *ajhāl*, (pl. of جاهل *jāhil*) Ignorant. *Ijhāl*, (v. n. 4 of جهل) Discovering (any one) to be ignorant.

A اجهام *ijhām*, (v. n. 4 of جهم) Pouring out water (clouds).

A اجهر *ajhar*, One that cannot bear the glare of the sun. Of a beautiful countenance and perfectly-formed body. One who has a slight and delicate cast of the eye, inclining to a squint. A horse whose star covers the whole of his face.

P اجهره *ajhara*, A kind of prickly shrub.

A اجهزة *ajhizat*, (pl. of جهاز *jahāz*) Marriage-portions. Wedding apparel, paraphernalia of brides. Travelling equipages.

A اجهل *ajhal*, More or most ignorant.

A اجهي *ajha'*, Bald. Roofless (house).

A اجهيزاز *ijhīzāz*, A preparing for any thing.

A اجياد *ajyād*, (pl. of جيد *jīd*) Necks, particularly such as are long and taper. Short shirts or shifts. Name of a place in the flat marshy ground of Mecca. Name of a sheep.

A اجياف *ajyāf*, (pl. of جيفة) Stinking carcases.

A اجيال *ajyāl*, (pl. of جيل *jīl*) Peoples, races, nations, tribes.

A اجيج *ajīj*, (v. n. of اجّ) Burning, flaming.

A اجيد *ajyad*, Long and beautiful-necked.

P آجيدن *ājīdan*, To stitch, to sew.

A اجير *ajīr*, A mercenary, hired labourer, hireling.

P اجيرانه *ajīrāna*, In a mercenary manner.

A اجيري *ajīrī*, Servitude, labour, hire.

A اِجِّيرى *ijjīrá'*, Habit, usage, custom.

A اجيل *ajīl*, (pl. اجل *ujl*) Procrastinating, deferring; slow. Collected (water). Heaped up about a palm-tree (mud).

A اجثلال *ijṡilāl*, Terror.

A اجيم *ajīm*, Heat. A flame of fire.

P اجين *ujayn*, Name of a city in Hindūstān.

A اجنواء *ijṡiwāṡ*, (v. n. 9 of جثي) Being of a dark chesnut colour (a horse).

A اجئيون *ajaṡiyūn*, Natives of اجا *ajaṡ* in Arabia.

P آچار *āchār*, Powdered or salted meats, pickles, or fruits, preserved in salt, vinegar, honey, or syrup; particularly onions preserved in vinegar; also the pickle or liquor in which these meats or fruits are preserved. Mixed, collected, assembled together. Uneven rugged ground, full of risings and hollows. Immemorial custom, conformity to religious institutions. (This last is a Sanskrit meaning).

P اچاق *achāk*, A frying-pan.

P آچاك *āchāk*, Earth, dust.

P اچكّه *uchakka*, A pick-pocket.

P اچي *ichī*, A kind of hawk. A vizir.

A آح *āh*, The white of an egg. The noise made in coughing. An exclamation of disgust.

A اح *ahh*, (v. n. of اح) Coughing; repeating often *ah ah* in coughing.

A احابش *ahābish*, (pl. of احبش) Ethiopians.

A احابيش *ahābīsh*, Name of the tribe of Kuraysh.

A احاثة *ihāsat*, (v. n. 4 of حاث for حوث) Digging up the earth, sifting it in order to find any thing. Separating, scattering, shaking.

A احاجة *ihājat*, (v. n. 4 of حاج for حيج) Producing the thorny plant حاج *hāj*.

A احاجي *ahājī*, (pl. of أحجوّة *uhjūwat* and اجيّة *uhjiyat*) Enigmas.

A احاح *uhāh*, Thirst. Rage, indignation, anguish, grief, passion, heat, inflammation, proceeding from agitation of mind.

A احاحة *ahṡahat*, (v. n. of أحاح Q) Saying frequently يا احاح *yā uhāh*.

A آحاد *āhād*, (pl. of احد *ahad*) Units. Sundays. واحد الآحاد *wāhidu'l āhād*, Incomparable man; the one of ones; a phœnix.

A احاد *uhāda*, as جاؤا احاد *jāṡū uhāda*, They came singly. احاد احاد *uhāda uhāda*, One by one.

A احادي *ahādī*, Independent pride.

A احاديث *ahādīṡ*, (pl. of احدوثة *uhdūsat*) Stories, tales. (pl. of حديث *hadīs*) News, things which have recently happened. Sayings or traditions concerning Muhammad, handed down by the Musulmān doctors, to the number of 5266. احاديث قرآن *ahādīsi kur'ān*, The tenets of the Kur'ān.

A احارة *ihārat*, (v. n. 4 of حار for حور) Receiving back produce (especially flour when grinding). Answering, replying. Having a colt called حوار *huwār* (a camel).

A احارر *ahārir*, (pl. of حرّ *harr*) Heats.

A احاسن *ahāsin*, The good, the excellent. Fair, handsome, goodly (persons).

A احاسي *ahāsī*, (pl. of احسية *ahsiyat*) Many broths. Many sips.

A احاشة *ihāshat*, (v. n. 4 of حاش for حوش) Surrounding (game) on all sides, and driving (it) into the net.

A احاطة *ihātat*, (v. n. 4 of حاط for حوط) Surrounding, enclosing, including, embracing, comprehending, understanding. Comprehension.

A احاظي *ahāẓī*, (irreg. pl. of حظّ *hazz*) Fortunes, successes.

A احافير *ahāfīr*, (pl. of حفر *hafar*) Ditches, pits, places hollowed out, excavations.

A احاقة *ihākat*, (v. n. 4 of حاق for حوق) Surrounding. Causing to alight or descend upon.

A احاكة *ihākat*, (v. n. 4 of حاك for حيك) Making an impression (sword or speech): cutting.

A احالة *ihālat*, (v. n. 4 of حال for حول) Revolving (a year). Changing, turning. Being one year old. Remaining in a place by the year. Causing (the year) to revolve. Remaining a year in a place. Completing a year. Leaping on horseback. Relating any thing incredible, impossible, or absurd. Having barren camels. Beginning. Not conceiving, though covered (a camel). Turning Musulmān. Rushing upon any one and striking him (with a whip). Pouring out water, by inclining the vessel in which it is contained. Regarding as weak. Empowering or sending one to demand or exact a debt from another. Being extended over the earth (night). Causing to squint.

A احاليل *ahālīl*, (pl. of احليل) Orifices of teats.

A احامر *ahāmir*, (pl. of احمر *ahmar*) Red (men). Barbarians, persons not natives of Arabia.

A احامرة *ahāmirat*, Name of a people of Persian origin settled in Basra. Flesh. Wine. The aromatic called خلوق *khalūk*. *Uhāmirat*, A hole in a stone wherein water collects.

A احامس *ahāmis*, (pl. of احمس *ahmas*) Barren (years or lands). وقع في مهيد الاحامس *wakaṡa fī muhaydi'l ahāmis*, He fell into misfortune or died.

A احانة *ihānat*, (v. n. 4 of حان for حين) Destroying, putting to death.

A احايين *ahāyīn*, (pl. of احيان *ahyān*, pl. of حين *hīn*) Times, periods, ages.

A احبّ *ahabb*, More or most lovely, dearer. احبّ اليّ *ahabbu ilayya'*, More agreeable to me.

A احباء *ahbāṡ*, (pl. of حبا *habaṡ*) Favourites of a king. *Ihbāṡ*, (v. n. 4 of حبا for حبو) Shooting short of the mark.

A احبّاء *ahibbāṡ*, (pl. of حبيب) Dear friends.

A احباب *ahbāb*, (pl. of حبّ *hibb*) Lovers, friends. (pl. of حبّ *hubb*) Jars. *Ihbāb*, (v. n. 4 of حبّ) Loving, liking, choosing, preferring. Coming into grain (corn). Receiving a hurt, and not stirring from the place until killed or cured. Kneeling down (a camel). Being stubborn and refractory (a camel). Recovering from sickness.

A احباج *ihbāj*, (v. n. 4 of حبج) Appearing suddenly. Approaching, coming in sight. Being elevated, conspicuous. Standing out and flowing copiously (veins).

A احبار *ahbār*, (pl. of حبر *hibr* or *habr*) Learned men. Men of probity and honour. سورة الاحبار *sūratu'l ahbār*, The chapter of the Kur'ān مائدة *māṡida*. *Ihbār*, (v. n. 4 of حبر) Making joyful. Abounding in herbage. Marking, impressing.

A احباس *ahbās*, (pl. of حبس *hibs*) Locks, dams: pent waters. *Ihbās*, (v. n. 4 of حبس) Dedicating to pious uses, prohibiting alienation: mortmain.

A احباش *ihbāsh*, (v. n. 4 of حبش) Producing a child swarthy as an Ethiop or Abysinian.

A احباض *ihbāz*, (v. n. 4 of حبض) Purposing, striving, attempting. Letting an arrow fall carelessly without reaching the mark. Exhausting a well. Excluding (any one) from (his) rights.

A احباط *ihbāt*, (v. n. 4 of حبط) Rendering void, frustrating, marring. Changing a course, going away and not returning. Averting the face.

A احباق *ihbāk*, (v. n. 4 of حبق) Submitting.

A احبال *ahbāl*, (pl. of حبل *habl*) Ropes, cords. Angers. Fruits of the wombs. *Ihbāl*, (v. n. 4 of حبل) Impregnating, getting with child. Losing its blossoms, and setting (the thorny plant عضاه *ṡizāh*).

A احبّة *ahibbat*, (pl. of حبيب *habīb*) Beloved.

A احبجرار *ihbijrār*, (v. n. 4 of حبجر Q) Swelling with rage. Being thick.

A احبش *ahbush*, (pl. احابش) An Ethiopian.

A احبل *ahbul*, (pl. of حبل *habl*) Ropes, cords. *Ihbil* and *ahbal*, A sort of French bean.

A احبن *ahban*, Dropsical.

A احبنجار *ihbinjār*, A swelling with rage.

A احبنطاء *ihbintāṡ*, (v. n. 3 of حبطا Q, or 15 of حبط) Swelling (the belly), being filled with rage.

A احبوش *uhbūsh*, (pl. احابيش *ahābīsh*) A mixed multitude of every tribe. An Ethiopian.

A احبوشة *uhbūshat*, A mixed multitude of men of every tribe.

A احبول *uhbūl*, (or احبولة) A hunter's net.

A نار احبير *nāru ihbīr*, The fire in the tail of the glow-worm.

A احتاء *ihtāṡ*, (v. n. 4 of حتا) Sewing (a garment). Plaiting, twisting, puckering (the edge of a garment). Tying (a knot). Shoring up, strengthening (a wall).

A احتات ahtāt, (pl. of حتّ hatt) (Horses) going with a quick and long step. Swift (camels). Male (ostriches). Generous, noble persons. Dead locusts. Ihtāt, (v. n. 4 of حتّ) Withering (the tree ارطى artu').

A احتار ahtār, (pl. of حترة hutrat) Trifles, small matters. Things sewed to the lower parts of tents to keep them to the ground. Ihtār, (v. n. 4 of حتر) Tying tight, making fast. Providing a feast for builders after finishing a house.

A احتان ahtān, (pl. of حتن hatn) Equal, alike. Ihtān, (v. n. 4 of حتن) Having one's arrows falling in one place.

A احتباء ihtibās, (v. n. 8 of حبا for حبو) Drawing up the legs by means of a bandage passing round the loins (as people do who are weary).

A احتباس ihtibās, (v. n. 8 of حبس) Retaining, containing, confining, imprisoning. Being shut up, besieged, imprisoned, or contained. احتباس بول ihtibāsi bawl, Suppression of urine.

A احتباك ihtibāk, (v. n. 8 of حبك) Drawing the back and the legs together with a bandage. Doing any thing well.

A احتبال ihtibāl, (v. n. 8 of حبل) Taking game with a net, or setting a net for game.

A احتتاش ihtitāsh, (v. n. 8 of حتش) Being hot and fierce in contention.

A احتثاث ihtisās, (v. n. 8 of حثّ) Exciting, instigating. Being stimulated or excited.

A احتجاب ihtijāb, (v. n. 8 of حجب) Being veiled; secluding one's self. Seclusion.

A احتجاج ihtijāj, (v. n. 8 of حجّ) Proving. Pleading. Litigating.

A احتجار ihtijār, (v. n. 8 of حجر) Constructing for one's self a cell. Choosing (a spot) for one's residence, and erecting a tower there that no one else might claim it. Laying or folding to one's bosom. Taking refuge. Becoming obstructed (the belly).

A احتجاز ihtijāz, (v. n. 8 of حجز) Drawing, girding one's breeches round one's waist. Carrying (any thing) in the waistband of one's breeches. Assembling, flocking together. Arriving in Hijāz.

A احتجاف ihtijāf, (v. n. 8 of حجف) Calling off one's attention, renouncing. Claiming and taking entire possession of. Collecting, accumulating, acquiring. Overcoming. Restraining, checking.

A احتجام ihtijām, (v. n. 8 of حجم) Cupping, scarifying. Being turgid from a fulness of blood, requiring to be cupped.

A احتجان ihtijān, (v. n. 8 of حجن) Drawing any thing to one's self with a curved stick, and keeping it. Collecting, accumulating wealth.

A احتداء ihtidās, (v. n. 8 of حدا for حدو) Following (as night does the day).

A احتداد ihtidād, (v. n. 8 of حدّ) Waxing angry. Taking an edge, becoming sharp.

A احتداف ihtidāf, (v. n. 8 of حدف) Seizing, snatching. Cutting (a garment).

A احتدام ihtidām, (v. n. 8 of حدم) Burning. Burning with rage. Being red, inclining to black.

A احتذاء ihtizās, (v. n. 8 of حذي) Putting on shoes. Imitating, following.

A احتذار ihtizār, (v. n. 8 of حذر) Avoiding, taking care, being cautious and wary.

A احتراب ihtirāb, (v. n. 8 of حرب) Fighting, duelling. Plundering one another.

A احتراث ihtirās, (v. n. 8 of حرث) Tilling the ground. Hurting a horse by over work. Gaining.

A احتراز ihtirāz, (v. n. 8 of حرز) Taking care. Being cautious, avoiding. Being on one's guard.

A احتراس ihtirās, (v. n. 8 of حرس) Preserving one's self. Stealing sheep in the night.

A احتراش ihtirāsh, (v. n. 8 of حرش) Hunting the Lybian lizard. Earning, gaining, getting for one's family.

A احتراص ihtirās, (v. n. 8 of حرص) Coveting. Being in earnest, striving.

A احتراف ihtirāf, (v. n. 8 of حرف) Being skilful in any art, trade, or craft.

A احتراق ihtirāk, (v. n. 8 of حرق) Being burnt. Putting forth all his strength in running (a horse). The disappearance or immersion of a planet on account of its nearness to the sun.

A احترام ihtirām, (v. n. 8 of حرم) Honouring, revering. Veneration, honour, reverence, respect. حكّام ذوي احترام hukkāmi zawī ihtirām, Princes (judges, or any great men) worthy of reverence, entitled to respect, honourable.

A احتزاز ihtizāz, (v. n. 8 of حزّ) Cutting, notching.

A احتزاك ihtizāk, (v. n. 8 of حزك) Putting on a girdle, or clothes, wrapping them about one.

A احتزام ihtizām, (v. n. 8 of حزم) Girding one's self with a rope. Putting on clothes or armour.

A احتزان ihtizān, (v. n. 8 of حزن) Being sad.

A احتساء ihtisās, (v. n. 8 of حسا for حسو) Sipping. Causing to sip. Digging to water on a hard stratum. (v. n. 8 of حسي) Perceiving, discovering what is in the mind of any one, and proving it.

A احتساب ihtisāb, (v. n. 8 of حسب) Computing, calculating. Enumerating. Examining, proving. Expecting a reward. Losing (a son) arrived at manhood (when under age it is called افتراط iftirāt). Coming to an end, being finished. Forbidding disorderly conduct, acting as محتسب muhtasib. Imputing. Examination of weights and measures. The police.

A احتسال ihtisāl, (v. n. 8 of حسل) Hunting young Lybian lizards just out of the shell.

A احتشاء ihtishās, (v. n. 8 of حشا for حشو) Wearing a محشى misha' (a woman). Being filled.

A احتشاب ihtishāb, (v. n. 8 of حشب) Being assembled from every quarter.

A احتشاد ihtishād, (v. n. 8 of حشد) Congregating, flocking together for mutual assistance. Assembling for one object.

A احتشار ihtishār, A being large-headed.

A احتشاش ihtishāsh, (v. n. 8 of حشّ) Seeking forage. Stacking hay.

A احتشام ihtishām, (v. n. 8 of حشم) Being ashamed. Putting in a rage. Having many dependants, followers, or domestics. Magnificence, grandeur, state. مجد و احتشام majd u ihtishām, honour and glory.

A احتصاد ihtisād, (v. n. 8 of حصد) Reaping.

A احتصار ihtisār, (v. n. 8 of حصر) Putting a small saddle or cushion on a camel.

A احتصان ihtisān, (v. n. 8 of حصن) Taking refuge; being sheltered, defended.

A احتضاء ihtizās, A stirring of a fire.

A احتضار ihtizār, (v. n. 8 of حضر) Coming into one's presence. Cleaving to one (care and sorrow). Approaching (death).

A احتضاض ihtizāz, (v. n. 8 of حضّ) Regarding (one's self) as deficient and unequal to.

A احتضان ihtizān, (v. n. 8 of حضن) Taking in one's arms, embracing. Sitting, brooding. Keeping back, hindering.

A احتطاب ihtitāb, (v. n. 8 of حطب) Collecting fire-wood. Feeding on dry thorns (a camel). Rooting up trees (rain). See احتقاب ihtikāb.

A احتطاط ihtitāt, (v. n. 8 of حطّ) Bringing down, throwing down, pulling down. Diminishing.

A احتظاء ihtizās, (v. n. 8 of حظي) Being highly honoured, and amply provided for (as a wife by her lord). Acquiring authority and influence.

A احتظار ihtizār, (v. n. 8 of حظر) Constructing the sheepcote حظيرة hazīrat.

A احتفاء ihtifās, (v. n. 8 of حفأ) Pulling up by the roots the papyrus plant حفأ hafa. (v. n. 8 of حفا for حفو) Walking barefoot. Eradicating (a pot-herb). Inquiring minutely into people's concerns. Behaving kindly. Exulting, rejoicing.

A احتفاد ihtifād, (v. n. 8 of حفد) Making haste. Serving or obeying with promptitude.

A احتفار ihtifār, (v. n. 8 of حفر) Digging, excavating. Cleaning out.

A احتفاز ihtifāz, (v. n. 8 of حفز) Sitting down on the point of the foot and preparing to rise. Being urged forward in walking. Striving, using exertion. Drawing one's self together in sitting.

A احتفاظ ihtifāz, (v. n. 8 of حفظ) Being cautious, careful. Guarding, preserving. Being provoked. Keeping one's self from evil. Making special or peculiar. Appropriating.

A احتفاف ihtifāf, (v. n. 8 of حفّ) Eating up all that is in the pot. Cutting up herbage. Plucking, or commanding to be plucked, the hairs from off her face (a woman). Giving orders that her hair be tied up at the back of her head (a woman).

A احتفال *ihtifāl*, (v. n. 8 of حفل) Assembling together. Collecting, bringing together. A concourse, procession. Being plain and open (a road). Pretending to put forth all his speed (a horse). Filling its bed (a river). Caring for, heeding, minding. Giving due attention. Exerting one's self. Straining every nerve. Polishing. Being clear, evident, manifest. Being adorned and decorated. Fearing, being afraid of.

A احتفان *ihtifān*, (v. n. 8 of حفن) Appropriating to one's self. Extirpating, uprooting. Laying hold below the knees, lifting up and carrying.

A احتقاب *ihtikāb*, (v. n. 8 of حقب) Taking a load on one's back. Making up into a parcel, and fastening it to the hinder part of one's saddle. Perpetrating a crime. Being tied behind a saddle (a pad or cloak-bag).

A احتقاد *ihtikād*, (v. n. 8 of حقد) Being withheld (rain). Hating.

A احتقار *ihtikār*, (v. n. 8 of حقر) Despising.

A احتقاق *ihtikāk*, (v. n. 8 of حقّ) Disputing, contending. Killing one (a stab). Being lank (a horse). Being fat (cattle). Striking the socket of the hip. Taking a sure aim, and hitting (a bird).

A احتقان *ihtikān*, (v. n. 8 of حقن) Giving or taking a clyster. Labouring under a suppression of urine. Retaining, confining. Having the sides higher than the middle (a garden).

A احتكاء *ihtikā,*, (v. n. 8 of حكأ) Tying tight. (v. n. 8 of حكي) Being done firmly and effectually.

A احتكار *ihtikār*, (v. n. 8 of حكر) Accumulating, or hoarding up grain against a scarcity; regrating.

A احتكاك *ihtikāk*, (v. n. 8 of حكّ) Rubbing the body against a post. Itching, requiring to be scratched (the head). Occurring to the mind.

A احتكال *ihtikāl*, (v. n. 8 of حكل) Being obscure and ambiguous. Learning Persic after Arabic.

A احتكام *ihtikām*, (v. n. 8 of حكم) Commanding, lording over. Going together before a judge.

A احتلاب *ihtilāb*, (v. n. 8 of حلب) Milking. Flowing (sweat from the body, spittle from the mouth, or tears from the eyes).

A احتلاج *ihtilāj*, A taking of one's right.

A احتلاز *ihtilāz*, A taking or seizing (one's due).

A احتلاس *ihtilās*, (v. n. 8 of حلس) Covering the ground (plants).

A احتلاط *ihtilāt*, (v. n. 8 of حلط) Swearing. Contending obstinately. Being angry. Being hasty, expeditious.

A احتلاق *ihtilāk*, A shaving of (the head).

A احتلال *ihtilāl*, (v. n. 8 of حلّ) Descending, alighting.

A احتلام *ihtilām*, (v. n. 8 of حلم) Dreaming. Reaching the age of puberty. Nocturnal pollution.

A احتم *ahtam*, Black.

A احتماء *ihtimā,*, (v. n. 8 of حمي) Abstaining, avoiding, shunning. Care, caution, forbearance.

A احتماد *ihtimād*, (v. n. 8 of حمد) Being intense (heat). Praising one's self. Self-commendation.

A احتماس *ihtimās*, (v. n. 8 of حمس) Being fired with rage, and attacking each other (two cocks).

A احتماش *ihtimāsh*, (v. n. 8 of حمش) Being fired with rage, rushing to battle (fighting cocks).

A احتمال *ihtimāl*, (v. n. 8 of حمل) Taking up a load. Taking up one's goods, and quitting one's abode. Bearing, carrying, sustaining. Bearing patiently. Receiving and gratefully acknowledging a kindness. Purchasing a captive brought from another country. Changing colour through rage. Being possible, being allowed. Patience. Possibility, probability.

A احتمام *ihtimām*, (v. n. 8 of حمّ) Being restless and sleepless in the night. (for اهتمام *ihtimām*) Anxiety, sleeplessness.

A احتناج *ihtināj*, (v. n. 8 of حنج) Inclining.

A احتناك *ihtināk*, (v. n. 8 of حنك) Putting barnacles or a twitch (on a horse). Seizing another's property. Devouring every green herb (locusts). Teaching a man wisdom (age or trials). Subduing, overcoming. Being firm, steady, tried, and experienced. Strength, firmness.

A احتواء *ihtiwā,*, (v. n. 8 of حوي) Comprehending, containing, collecting. Protecting, guarding. Occupation, enjoyment, possession.

A احتواش *ihtiwāsh*, (v. n. 8 of حاش for حوش) Starting game. Intercepting, surrounding (any one).

A احتوال *ihtiwāl*, (v. n. 8 of حال for حول) Surrounding, encircling, encompassing, getting (one) into the middle.

A احتياج *ihtiyāj*, (v. n. 8 of حاج for حوج) Feeling an inclination for another. Being indigent and necessitous: needing. Returning. Indigence, want, necessity, need, occasion. اصحاب احتياج *as-hābi ihtiyāj*, The necessitous, the poor. احتياجات *ihtiyājāt*, Wants, necessities, things requisite.

A احتياز *ihtiyāz*, (v. n. 8 of حاز for حوز) Collecting together. Surrounding, encircling.

A احتياص *ihtiyās*, (v. n. 8 of حاص for حوص) Being vigilant and cautious; taking care of one's self. Being close, impervious (a she-camel).

A احتياط *ihtiyāt*, (v. n. 8 of حاط for حوط) Surrounding, comprehending, encompassing, enclosing. Looking carefully. Taking care. Caution, circumspection, foresight, scrupulousness. Careful examination.

A احتياطاً *ihtiyātan*, Cautiously, warily.

A احتياك *ihtiyāk*, (v. n. 8 of حاك for حيك) Drawing up the legs by means of a bandage passing round the loins (as weary persons do).

A احتيال *ihtiyāl*, (v. n. 8 of حال for حول) Being one year old. Empowering one to receive a debt. Using fraud and cunning. Fraud, deceit, magical illusion, machination. (v. n. 8 of حال for حيل) Empowering one to receive a debt.

A احتشام *ihtishām*, (v. n. 4 of حتشم Q) Cutting.

A احثّ *ahass*, More or most stimulating.

A احثاء *ihsā,*, (v. n. 4 of حثا for حثو) Trampling down (cities) with their hoofs (horses).

A احثاث *ihsās*, (v. n. 4 of حثّ) Instigating, urging, egging on.

A احثار *ihsār*, (v. n. 4 of حثر) Bursting out of the pod in the first stage of formation (a date).

A احثال *ihsāl*, (v. n. 4 of حثل) Giving unwholesome food to a child. Injuring, afflicting.

A احجّ *ahajj*, Hard (head). A horse that places his hind-foot in the track of his fore-foot.

A احجاء *ahjā,*, (pl. of حجاة *hajāt*) Sides, tracts. (pl. of حجي *hija'*) Dispositions. Wits, geniuses. Quantities.

A احجاب *ahjāb*, (pl. of حجاب *hijāb*) Veils.

A احجاج *ihjāj*, (v. n. 4 of حجّ) Sending (one) on a pilgrimage to Mecca. Exciting to disputation.

A احجار *ahjār*, (pl. of حجر *hijr*) Mares. احجار الخيل *ahjāru'l khayl*, Brood-mares. (pl. of حجر *hajar*) Stones.

A احجاز *ihjāz*, (v. n. 4 of حجز) Reaching Hijāz.

A احجال *ahjāl*, (pl. of حجل *hijl, hajl, hijil*, or حجلّ *hijill*,) Ornaments for the ankles. (pl. of حجل *hijl*) Witnesses. *Ihjāl*, (v. n. 4 of حجل) Unloosing the left and tying up the right foot.

A احجام *ihjām*, (v. n. 4 of حجم) Retiring, desisting from a purpose. Rising, being protuberant (a breast). Suckling an infant for the first time.

A احجان *ihjān*, (v. n. 4 of حجن) Flowering (the herb ثمام *sumām*).

A ما احجاه *mā ahjāhu*, How worthy, fit he is!

A احجّة *ahijjat*, (pl. of حجاج *hajāj* or *hijāj*) Bones that surround the eyes, those on which the eye-brows grow. Sides. Margins of sun's disks.

A احجر *ahjur*, (pl. of حجر *hajar*) Stones.

A احجرّ *uhjurr*, A stone.

A احجن *ahjan*, Crooked, curved. Straight-hanging (hair).

A احجوّة *uhjūwat*, (or احجيّة *uhjīyat*) (pl. احاجي *ahāji*) An enigma; any question put to try the genius.

A احد *ahd*, (v. n. of احد) Making a covenant. *Ahad*, (pl. آحاد *āhād* and احدان *uhdān*) One, any one, sole, alone, separated. الاحد *al ahad*, God. يوم الاحد *yawmu'l ahad*, Sunday. احد عشر *ahad ʼashara*, Eleven. احدكم *ahadukum*, One of you. احد الاحدين *ahadu'l ahadin*, The one of ones; an incomparable man. كلّ احد *kullu ahadin*, Every one, all. ما من احد *mā min ahad*, No one, not one. *Uhud*, Name of a mountain near Madīna.

A احدّ *ahadd*, More or most acute, sharp, or fierce.

A احدًا *ahadan*, One by one, singly.

A احداء *ihdā,*, (v. n. 4 of حدي) Giving serious attention to.

A احدّاء *ahiddā,*, (and احدّة *ahiddat*) (pl. of

حداد *hudād*) Sharp, acute. Fluent, glib. Severe.

A احداب *ihdāb*, (v. n. 4 of حدب) Making hump-backed. Giving an inclination. Rendering favorably inclined or benevolent.

A احداث *ahdās*, (pl. of حدث *hadas*) Pollutions, impurities. Youths. Novelties, accidents, chances. Rains falling at the beginning of the year. *Ihdās*, (v. n. 4 of حدث) Producing, inventing, bringing into existence. Voiding fæces. Fornicating. A seminal effusion. Polishing, furbishing.

A احداج *ahdāj*, (pl. of حدج *hidj*) Loads, burdens. Litters. *Ihdāj*, (v. n. 4 of حدج) Putting a litter on a camel's back. Bearing fruit (wild gourd).

A احداد *ihdād*, (v. n. 4 of حدّ) Mourning the loss of her husband (a woman), and laying aside all ornamental attire. Giving an edge, sharpening. Regarding very attentively, fixing (the eye) steadily.

A احدار *ihdār*, (v. n. 4 of حدر) Swelling from a blow (the skin). Causing to swell. Hemming, or adorning with a fringe (a garment). Twisting and tying in knots the ends of a piece of linen.

A احداق *ahdāk*, (pl. of حدقة *hadakat*) The pupils of the eyes. احداق المرضي *ahdāku'l marza'*, Camomile-flowers. *Ihdāk*, (v. n. 4 of حدق) Encompassing. Becoming enclosed (a garden).

A احدام *ihdām*, (v. n. 4 of حدم) Blazing. Being intense (heat).

A احدان *uhdān*, (pl. of احد *ahad*) Ones; only ones. Sundays. (pl. of واحد *wāhid*) Pre-eminent.

A ابن احداها *ibnu ihdāhā*, Noble on the side of father and mother.

A احدب *ahdab*, Gibbous. A vein in the arm.

A احدباب *ihdibāb*, The being hump-backed.

A احدث *ahdas*, Younger, youngest. Newest.

A احدر *ahdar*, Squint-eyed. Full and fleshy about the thighs, but lank upwards.

A احدل *ahdal*, Partial, inclined to one side, acting unfairly. Left-handed. Having one shoulder higher than the other. Wry-necked. Inclining when walking. One-testicled; a ridgling.

A احدوثة *uhdūsat*, (pl. احاديث *ahādīs*) A parable, narrative, story, tale.

A احدور *uhdūr*, A descent, a declivity.

A احدون *ahadūn*, (pl. of احد *ahad*) Ones.

A احدي *ihda'*, (fem. of احد *ahad*) One. احدي الاحد *ihda'l ahadi*, A direful affair. One of one, any thing wonderful, unequalled. احدي عشرة *ihda' ʿashirat* or *ihda' ʿashrat*, Ten (females). احدي السبع *ihda's sabʿ*, One of the seven, *i.e.* the seven years of famine in the time of Joseph; or one of the nights of misery of the people of عاد *ʿād* (an expression employed to indicate any sore calamity).

P احدي *ahadī*, A kind of Indian military corps.

A احديّ الاحد *ahadīyu'l ahadi*, The one of ones, the incomparable one.

A احديّة *ahadīyat*, Unity. Concord, alliance.

A احديداب *ihdīdāb*, A being hump-backed.

A احديداق *ihdīdāk*, The act of surrounding.

A احذّ *ahazz*, (pl. حذّ *huzz*) Slender-bodied, small-handed (man). Difficult, arduous, ungrateful business. Swift (camel) that drinks on the fifth day. Verse in which حذذ *hazaz* prevails.

A احذاء *ihzā*, (v. n. 4 of حذا for حذو) Putting a shoe on any one. Giving. (v. n. 4 of حذي) Giving a shoe, or share of spoil.

A احذار *ahzār*, Care, caution. ابن احذار *ibn ahzār*, Provident, prudent, cautious.

A احذال *ihzāl*, (v. n. 4 of حذل) Rendering the eyes red and bare of eyelashes (weeping).

A احذاق *ahzāk*, (pl. of حذقة *hizkat*) Parts, segments, sections. (A rope) all to pieces.

A احذر *ahzar*, More or most wary.

A احذيرار *ihzīrār*, A being angry and furious.

A احرّ *aharr*, More or most hot, hotter, hottest. More delicate, finer.

A احراء *ahrā*, (pl. of حرا *hara'*) Sides, quarters. Noises. Lairs, nests. (pl. of حري *harī*) Worthy, fit, proper. *Ihrā*, (v. n. 4 of حري) Diminishing, causing to wane, injuring, impairing.

A احراب *ahrāb*, Name of a place. *Ihrāb*, (v. n. 4 of حرب) Pointing out a road whereby a hostile incursion may be made. Exciting war. Producing dates (a palm-tree).

A احراث *ihrās*, (v. n. 4 of حرث) Making (a beast) lean by overworking (him).

A احراج *ahrāj*, (pl. of حرج *hirj*) Shells of a small white shell-fish. Those parts of the hare or deer which are given to the hounds, their reward. Dogs' collars. *Ihrāj*, (v. n. 4 of حرج) Leading into sin. Making miserable. Prohibiting, interdicting. Compelling, forcing.

A احراح *ahrāh*, (pl. of حرح *hirh*) Vulvæ.

A احراد *ihrād*, (v. n. 4 of حرد) Travelling fast. Making solitary or alone.

A احرار *ahrār*, (pl. of حرّ *hurr*) Free, free-born, noble, free men. Herbs, greens, or any kinds of garden-stuff which are eaten raw. *Ihrār*, (v. n. 4 of حرّ) Being hot. Having thirsty camels.

A احراز *ahrāz*, (pl. of حرز *hirz*) Fortifications. (pl. of حرز *haraz*) Cobnuts, smooth nuts used as counters at play. *Ihrāz*, (v. n. 4 of حرز) Obtaining a reward, and enjoying the benefit of it, getting wages. Hoarding. Affording security, protecting, sheltering. Abstaining. Avoiding. Keeping inviolate her chastity (a woman). P احراز كردن *ihrāz kardan*, To defend.

A احراس *ahrās*, (pl. of حارس *hāris*) Guards. *Ihrās*, (v. n. 4 of حرس) Remaining in a place for a long time.

A احراش *ihrāsh*, (v. n. 4 of حرش) Blistering a (camel's) skin (liquid anointing pitch).

A احراض *ahrāz*, (pl. of حرض *haraz*) Those from whom nothing is to be dreaded or hoped for. *Ihrāz*, (v. n. 4 of حرض) Emaciating (as love or sickness). Begetting bad stock. Corrupting, spoiling.

A احراف *ihrāf*, (v. n. 4 of حرف) Making lean. Being prosperous, increasing in wealth. Labouring for one's family. Requiting, recompensing.

A احراق *ihrāk*, (v. n. 4 of حرق) Setting on fire. Making gruel. Injuring.

A احرام *ahrām*, (pl. of حرم *haram* and حريم *harīm*) Sacred places, sanctuaries, asylums. *Ihrām*, (v. n. 4 of حرم) Being unlawful. Making illegal, prohibiting. Preventing, hindering, keeping back. Depriving of hope, disappointing. Entering the sacred precincts of Mecca, or into an inviolable sanctuary. Engaging in a work, by virtue of which what was lawful becomes unlawful for him (a pilgrim). Being menstruous (a woman). Winning, beating at dice. Beginning the holy month called محرّم *Muharram*, during which it is unlawful with the Muhammadans to fight, hunt, or indulge in any sensual gratification. Putting on a mean garb, in which the pilgrims enter Mecca, in order to celebrate the festival of the 10th day of the last month but one of the Muhammadan year. The cloak or mantle above alluded to, generally made of two long pieces of Indian cambric.

A ما احراه *mā ahrāhu*, How worthy he is!

A احرثة *ahrisat*, (pl. of حراث *hirās*) Unfinished arrows. Lower parts of spear-heads.

A احرد *ahrad*, (A camel) lamed by a hurt in the tendon of the fore-foot. Mean, base, avaricious.

A احرس *ahras*, Ancient, aged. *Ahrus*, (pl. of حرس *hars*) Ages.

A احرش *ahrash*, Rough on account of its newness (coin). The mange, murrain. Scabby, mangy (camel). A land-crocodile (as being rough-scaled).

A احرض *ahraz*, One, the edge of whose eyelids are worn away.

A احرف *ahruf*, (pl. of حرف *harf*) Letters. Particles. Dialects.

A احرمّاز *ihrimmāz*, The being acute, intelligent.

A احرنباء *ihrimbā*, (v. n. 15 of حرب) Growing (hair or grass). (v. n. 3 of حربا Q) Being ready to fly in a passion, preparing for mischief.

A احرنجام *ihrinjām*, (v. n. 3 of حرجم Q) Thronging, crowding together, tumbling over one another. Wishing for a thing, and afterwards retracting.

A احرنفاز *ihrinfāz*, An assembling together.

A احرنفاش *ihrinfāsh*, A swelling with rage.

A احرّون *ahirrūn*, (pl. of حرّة) Stony countries.

A احري *ahra'*, Better, best.

A احرياء *ahriyā*, (pl. of حريّ *harīy*) Suitable.

A احريراف *ihrīrāf*, (v. n. 12 of حرف) Changing, being turned, inclining, deviating.

A احريض *ihrīz*, A species of saffron. Unable to rise; at the point of death.

A احرّين *aharrīn*, (pl. of حرّة) Stony places.

A احزاء *ihzā*, (v. n. 4 of حزي) Fearing, standing in awe of. Being hard and difficult to deal with. Knowing. Being high.

A احزاب *ahzāb*, (pl. of حزب *hizb*) Troops, bands, cohorts. Auxiliaries, allies. Confederate companies of infidels. الشيطان واحزابه *ash' shaytān wa ahzābuhu*, The devil and his crew.

A احزاز *ihzāz*, (v. n. 4 of حزّ) Excelling in nobility and generosity. Chattering from cold (teeth).

A احزاق *ihzāk*, (v. n. 4 of حزق) Hindering.

A احزام *ahzām*, Cohorts, bands. *Ihzām*, (v. n. 4 of حزم) Girthing. Making a girth for a horse.

A احزان *ahzān*, (pl. of حزن *huzn* and *hazan*) Griefs, sorrows. *Ihzān*, (v. n. 4 of حزن) Being rough. Making sorrowful, vexing, grieving. Travelling over rough grounds.

A احزّة *ahizzat*, (pl. of حزيز) Rugged places.

A احزقّة *'uhzukkat*, Narrow. Big-bellied. Short, and who moves the hips in walking.

A احزم *ahzam*, Thick and bulky in the waist. High and rugged ground. More or most prudent.

A احزمة *ahzimat*, (pl. of حزيم *hazīm*) Breasts.

A احزيزاء *ihzīzā*, (v. n. 12 of حزأ) Assembling, coming together. Drawing together her wings (a bird), and sitting off her eggs.

A احزيزام *ihzīzām*, (v. n. 12 of حزم) Being full and compact. Being rugged (a place). Being big-bellied and not filled.

A احزئلال *ihzi,lāl*, (v. n. 4 of حزأل Q) Rising from the ground (a camel). Appearing lofty through a mist (a mountain). Shrinking through fear. Being collected together.

A احساء *ahsā*, (pl. of حسي *hasy*, *hisy*, and *hisa'*) Waters subsiding through any sandy ground, and collecting on a solid stratum. The strata of stone or clay on which waters which have filtered through sand stagnate. *Ihsā*, (v. n. 4 of حسا for حسو) Giving (one) to sip. Perceiving. Knowing.

A احساب *ahsāb*, (pl. of حسب *hasab*) Dignities, honours. *Ihsāb*, (v. n. 4 of حسب) Being sufficient, sufficing. Contenting, gratifying. Causing to eat or drink to the full. Making (one) sit down on a cushion. Giving often.

A احسار *ihsār*, (v. n. 4 of حسر) Overdriving.

A احساس *ihsās*, (v. n. 4 of حسّ) Feeling, perceiving, seeing, finding, knowing, understanding.

A احساف *ihsāf*, (v. n. 4 of حسف) Mixing (dates) with the refuse of rotten ones.

A احساك *ihsāk*, (v. n. 4 of حسك) Giving corn to a horse in a nose-bag fastened round his head.

A احسال *ahsāl*, Newly-hatched crocodiles.

A احسان *ihsān*, (v. n. 4 of حسن) Doing good, conferring an obligation. Making good. Knowing well. Sitting on a high sand-hill. Beneficence, courtesy. Kindness.

P احسان ديده *ihsān-dīda*, Benefited, served, obliged; any one who receives favours.

A احساني *ihsānī*, Beneficent.

A احسب *ahsab*, Better or best arithmetician. (A camel) white and red. Red-haired (man). White, leprous. Bald through disease.

A احسباب *ihsibāb*, (v. n. 9 of حسب) Being of a whitish red colour (a camel). Being white and leprous (a man).

A احسن *ahsan*, More or most beautiful, excellent, or agreeable. *Ahsana*, (in prayer) May (God) be gracious. *Ahsin*, (imperative of احسن *ahsana*, 4th conj.) Do good.

P احسنتا *ihsintā*, Inheritance, possession.

P احسند *ahsand*, (a corruption of A احسنت *ahsanta*) Well done! bravo!

A احسوة *ahsuwat*, (pl. of حسو *hasw*) Broths.

A احسية *ahsiyat*, (pl. of حسو *hasw*) Broths.

A احشاء *ahshā*, (pl. of حشا *hasha'*) Bowels.

A احشاب *ihshāb*, (v. n. 4 of حشب) Enraging.

A احشاد *ihshād*, (v. n. 4 of حشد) Congregating, flocking together for mutual assistance. Assembling for one object.

A احشاش *ihshāsh*, (v. n. 4 of حشّ) Foraging, foddering, collecting fodder. Assisting (one) in cutting and getting in hay. Being easy to be gathered (fodder). Having a dried-up fœtus in the womb (a woman). Keeping back, withholding. Making the shank thin (fat). Withering (a hand).

A احشاف *ihshāf*, (v. n. 4 of حشف) Bearing bad dates (a palm-tree).

A احشاك *ihshāk*, (v. n. 4 of حشك) Giving barley to a horse in the nose-bag.

A احشام *ahshām*, (pl. of حشم *hasham*) Servants, domestics, followers, attendants. Troops, train, matchlock-men. *Ihshām*, (v. n. 4 of حشم) Provoking, annoying. Making ashamed.

A احشان *ihshān*, (v. n. 4 of حشن) Using a milk-bottle till it becomes greasy and stinks.

A احصّ *ahass*, (A man) thin of hair. (A bird) having few feathers on the wing. Serene, sunny (day). Barren (year). Unfortunate. (A sword) not having a glittering surface.

A احصاء *ihsā*, (v. n. 4 of حصأ) Giving plentifully to drink. (v. n. 4 of حصي) Numbering, computing. Comprehending, knowing. Preserving, guarding. Power, ability. لا احصا *lā ihsā*, Inexpressible, beyond computation.

A احصاب *ihsāb*, (v. n. 4 of حصب) Scattering gravel about whilst running (a horse). Turning one's back upon, retiring.

A احصاد *ihsād*, (v. n. 4 of حصد) Coming to maturity, being fit to cut (corn). Twisting tight.

A احصار *ihsār*, (v. n. 4 of حصر) Restraining, prohibiting, hindering, preventing. Keeping one back from travelling (disease). Having the orifice of the teats very small. Costiveness: stricture.

A احصاص *ihsās*, (v. n. 4 of حصّ) Giving any one his share. Removing from office, deposing.

A احصاف *ihsāf*, (v. n. 4 of حصف) Conducting (business) in a steady and judicious manner. Twisting (a rope) tight. Going quickly with short steps. Putting to a distance. Bringing to an end.

A احصال *ihsāl*, (v. n. 4 of حصل) Bearing green unripe dates (a palm): also yellow flowers.

A احصان *ahsān*, (pl. of حصن *hisn*) Fortresses. *Ihsān*, (v. n. 4 of حصن) Taking a wife. Being married, having a husband. Being chaste and virtuous. Keeping one chaste (matrimony). Keeping a wife very much secluded. Fortifying, defending. Being pregnant. Continence, chastity. Besieging. Strength, firmness.

A احصّان *ahassāni*, (dual of احصّ *ahass*) The two unfortunates) A slave and an ass.

A احصد *ahsad*, Firmly twisted (rope).

A احصرة *ahsirat*, (pl. of حصير *hasīr*) Mats. Narrow, tight-chested. Assemblies. Prisons. Kings. Roads. Surfaces of the ground. Rows, ranks. Sides.

A احصنة *ahsinat*, Spear-heads.

A احضاب *ahzāb*, (pl. of حضب *hizb* and *huzb*) The twangs of a bowstring. *Ihzāb*, (v. n. 4 of حضب) Raising a fire or throwing fuel on it. Replacing a rope on the pulley.

A احضاج *ahzāj*, (pl. of حضج *hizj* or *hazj*) Remains of water in a cistern.

A احضار *ihzār*, (v. n. 4 of حضر) Producing, presenting, making appear, bringing: summoning, citing, calling before, causing or ordering to bring or be brought into one's presence. Running. Lifting up his feet high in running (a horse).

A احضان *ahzān*, (pl. of حضن *hizn*) Sides, parts, tracts. Dens of hyænas. *Ihzān*, (v. n. 4 of حضن) Despising, disgracing. Defrauding.

A احضّة *ahizzat*, (pl. of حضيض *hazīz*) Low grounds at the foot of a mountain. Stones.

A احطّ *ahatt*, Smooth on either side of the back.

A احطاب *ahtāb*, (pl. of حطب *hatab*) Firewood. *Ihtāb*, (v. n. 4 of حطب) Being fit for, requiring pruning (a tree). Abounding in small wood.

A احطاط *ihtāt*, (v. n. 4 of حطّ) Being fat, swollen, or covered with pimples (the face).

A احطال *ahtāl*, (pl. of حطل *hitl*) Wolves.

A احطب *ahtab*, Very lean and slender (like a stick). Unfortunate.

A احطيطاء *ihtītā*, (v. n. 12 of حطو) Swelling.

A احظّ *ahazz*, More or most fortunate or happy. *Ahuzz*, (pl. of حظّ *hazz*) Felicities, good fortunes.

A احظاء *ihzā*, (v. n. 4 of حظي) Preferring one to another.

A احظاظ *ihzāz*, (v. n. 4 of حظّ) Becoming prosperous and happy.

A احظي *ahzi*, (pl. of حظي *hiza'*) Good fortunes.

A احفاء *ihfā*, (v. n. 4 of حفي) Walking barefoot. Causing to go unshod. Shaving or trimming one's whiskers. Having a horse whose hoofs are worn. Being very inquisitive and disagreeably importunate. Urging one to enquire and investigate. Despising, slighting.

A احفاث *ahfās*, (pl. of حفث) Tripes, bellies.

A احفاد *ahfād*, (pl. of حافد *hāfid*) Friends, companions. Families, grand-children, sons-in-law, relations. *Ihfād*, (v. n. 4 of حفد) Going fast (but below the pace called خبب *khabab*). Ordering or compelling to travel quick.

A احفار *ahfār*, (pl. of حفر *hafar*) Wide pits, excavations. *Ihfār*, (v. n. 4 of حفر) Changing his teeth (a colt). Assisting one to excavate a well. Changing the two upper and lower front teeth.

A احفاش *ahfāsh*, (pl. of حفش *hifsh*) Cases in which women put their spindles. Small boxes. Small houses, closets, &c. Camels' bunches. Pudenda. Articles of small value, as faded furniture, old vessels or sacks. The worst part of household furniture. The refuse of the earth (as lizards and hedgehogs). *Ihfāsh*, (v. n. 4 of حفش) Making haste, using despatch.

A احفاص *ahfās*, (pl. of حفص *hafs*) Leathern sacks with which they empty out wells.

A احفاض *ahfāz*, (pl. of حفض *hafaz*) Household goods, furniture, utensils. Camels which carry them. Hair tents with columns and ropes. Weak camels.

A احفاظ *ihfāz*, (v. n. 4 of حفظ) Angering.

A احفاف *ihfāf*, (v. n. 4 of حف) Allowing the hair to become matted from neglecting to oil it (a woman). Mentioning any one in a shameful manner. Weaving (a garment) with the instrument called حف *haff*. Causing (a horse) to make the noise called حفيف *hafif*.

A احفة *ahiffat*, (pl. of حفاف *hifāf*) Curls, locks, or braids of hair. Parts, sides.

A احفش *ahfash*, (A camel) the front of whose bunch is ulcerated and eaten away, the back part remaining sound.

A احفلى *ahfala'*, Promiscuously.

A احفيظاظ *ihfīzāz*, (v. n. 11 of حفظ) Swelling, becoming inflated (a serpent).

A احق *ahakk*, More or most worthy, deserving. Legitimate. A horse that does not sweat A horse that places his hind-foot in the footstep of the fore-foot (which is considered a blemish).

A احقاء *ahkās*, (pl. of حقو *hakw*) Waists. Breeches. Waistbands.

A احقاء *ahikkās*, (pl. of حقيق *hakīk*) Worthy.

A احقاب *ahkāb*, (pl. of حقب *hukub*) Periods of 80 years, ages. *Ihkāb*, (v. n. 4 of حقب) Being destitute of minerals (a mine). Putting something into the portmanteau حقيبة *hakibat*, and strapping it behind the saddle. Allowing one to ride behind one's self. Being barren from want of rain.

A احقاد *ahkād*, (pl. of حقد *hikd*) Hatreds, animosities. *Ihkād*, (v. n. 4 of حقد) Stirring up hatred. Making a fruitless search for ore.

A احقاف *ahkāf*, (pl. of حقف *hikf*) Hills of sand. Sands extending a great way, and sloping from trees. Name of a large district of country in Arabia, extending from Hazramawt (to the eastward of the straits of Bābi'lmandib (gate of tears) at the entrance into the Red Sea), to Omān, on the gulf of Persia, and Ormūz. It is covered with little hills of moving sand, which, when the south wind blows, often prove fatal to the caravans.

A احقاق *ahkāk*, (pl. of حقة *hukkat*) Boxes, caskets. *Ihkāk*, (v. n. 4 of حق) Speaking truth, overcoming by truth. Knowing for certain. Rendering necessary. Completing her third and entering on her fourth year (a camel). Coming to. Killing game. P احقاق حق كردن *ihkāki hak kardan*, To administer justice.

A احقال *ahkāl*, (pl. of حقلة *haklat*) Gripes (in camels from eating certain herbs). *Ihkāl*, (v. n. 4 of حقل) Putting forth the blade (corn).

A احقان *ahkān*, (pl. of حقنة *haknat*) Cholics.

A احقب *ahkab*, Name of a demon, genie, or spirit. A wild ass marked with white about the girths. *Ahkub*, (pl. of حقب *hukb* or *hukub*) Periods of 80 years, ages.

A احقد *ahkad*, More or most vindictive, rancorous, or spiteful.

A احقر *ahkar*, More or most vile or contemptible. (Used for I or me.) احقر العباد *ahkaru'l ʿibād*, The meanest of (your) servants.

A احقف *ahkaf*, Lank-bellied (camel).

A احقى *ahkī*, (pl. of حقو *hakw*) Waists, sides, hypochondrias. Waistbands. Breeches.

A احقيقاف *ihkīkāf*, (v. n. 12 of حقف) Being long and crooked (sand, the back, or new moon).

A احك *ahakk*, Rubbed, worn. Toothless.

A احكاء *ihkās*, (v. n. 4 of حكأ) Tying firm, tightening. ما احكاني صدري *mā ahkasanī sadrī*, It never entered my thoughts. (v. n. 4 of حكي) Tying tight. Prevailing against, overcoming, conquering.

A احكاد *ihkād*, (v. n. 4 of حكد) Receding, hanging back. Leaning upon, confiding.

A احكال *ihkāl*, (v. n. 4 of حكل) Being obscure and doubtful. Stirring up mischief.

A احكاك *ahkāk*, Men, people. *Ihkāk*, (v. n. 4 of حك) Rubbing, triturating. Occurring to the mind. Itching, requiring scratching (the head).

A احكام *ahkām*, (pl. of حكم *hukm*) Orders, decrees, mandates. Precepts of law, judgments, sentences. Letters-patent. Mysteries. Predictions, presages. احكام الدين *ahkāmu'd dīn*, The ordinances of religion. احكام الرمي والسيف *ahkāmu'r ramy wa's sayf*, The sciences of the javelin (or the arrow) and the sword. احكام النجوم *ahkāmu'n nujūm*, The judgments of the stars (a book treating of judicial astrology). *Ihkām*, (v. n. 4 of حكم) Doing (any thing) well, firmly, and effectually. Restraining (a fool), restraining from mischief. Curbing (a horse). Causing to recede.

A احكم الحاكمين *ahkamu'l hākimīn*, The judge of judges, lord chief justice: also a title given to governors of provinces.

A احكومة *uhkūmat*, Dominion, sovereignty.

A احل *ahall*, Lank about the buttocks and thighs. Pained in the buttocks and knees. Feeble in the legs, weak in the feet.

A احلاء *ihlās*, (v. n. 4 of حلأ) Applying a collyrium to the eyes. (v. n. 4 of حلا for حلو) Sweetening. Discovering to be sweet. Speaking sweetly.

A احلاب *ihlāb*, (v. n. 4 of حلب) Assisting in milking: milking cattle in the fields, sending the milk to different quarters. Allowing another to milk one's cattle. Having a camel bringing forth females (when males, it is called اجلاب *ijlāb*).

A احلابة *ihlābat*, A milking cattle in the fields and sending the milk to different quarters. Milk. Milk overflowing the bottle.

A احلاس *ahlās*, (pl. of حلس *hils*) Saddle-cloths, or any thing put upon a camel's back to prevent galling. Carpets, or any thing similar laid under rich garments or furniture. *Ihlās*, (v. n. 4 of حلس) Covering the ground (grass). Covering (a camel) with the saddle-cloth حلس *hils*. Pouring down a continued and gentle rain (the sky). Fraud, cheating in a sale. Insolvency.

A احلاط *ihlāt*, (v. n. 4 of حلط) Swearing. Being pertinacious in one's oath. Contending obstinately. Being angry. Exasperating. Making haste, being expeditious. Entering the seat of destruction. Abiding, stopping. Helping (a camel) to cover.

A احلاف *ahlāf*, (pl. of حلف *hilf*) Treaties, agreements, compacts. Confederates, companions swearing mutual fidelity. Faithful observances of agreements. Name given to the tribes اسد *asad* and غطفان *ghatafān*. Name of the tribe of ثقيف *sakīf*; also of six families of قريش *kuraysh*. *Ihlāf*, (v. n. 4 of حلف) Administering an oath. Arriving at manhood or womanhood. Coming to maturity (the plant حلفاء *halfās*).

A احلافي *ahlāfiy*, Name of عمر بن الخطاب *ʿumar bini'l khattāb* the عدوي *ʿadawiy*, one of the six families of Kuraysh who confederated together, and were called احلاف *ahlāf*.

A احلاق *ahlāk*, (pl. of حلق *halk*) Throats, gullets. *Ihlāk*, (v. n. 4 of حلق) Filling a cistern.

A احلاك *ahlāk*, (pl. of حلك) Blacknesses.

A احلال *ihlāl*, (v. n. 4 of حل) Causing one to alight and sojourn (in a place). Sending down, causing (anger) to light. Rendering lawful. Renewing hostilities at the expiration of the sacred months during which war is interdicted. Laying aside a Nazarite's vow. Being released from any engagement by which one was bound. Putting off mourning (a widow). Deserving punishment. Having milk in the udder previous to yeaning (a sheep). Having little milk (a ewe), and abounding in milk after eating spring-grass.

A احلام *ahlām*, (pl. of حلم *hilm*) Intellects. Meeknesses. (pl. of حلم *hulm*) Dreams. Bodies. (pl. of حليم *halīm*) Mild, gentle, clement. *Ihlām*, (v. n. 4 of حلم) Dreaming. Bringing forth meek children.

P احلب دياي رومي *ahlab diyāi rūmī*, A kind of spurge.

A احلس *ahlas*, (A ram) black-bodied with a mixture of red. Of a dark bay colour.

A احلساس *ihlisas*, (v. n. 9 of حلس) Being of a colour between black and red.

A ما احلف لسانه *mā ahlafa lisānuhu*, How sharp and glib his tongue is!

A احلنقام *ihlinkām*, A refusing of food.

A احلوفة *uhlūfat*, A word by which any one is made to swear, a form of adjuration.

A احلى *ahla'*, More or most sweet, sweeter.

A احلية *ahliyat*, Strong withered grasses.

A احليل *ihlīl*, (pl. احاليل *ahālīl*) The orifice of the teat or penis. The penis. Name of a valley.

A احليلاء *ihlīlā*, (v. n. 12 of حلا for حلو) Being sweet. Sweetening. Discovering, finding sweet.

A احليلاك *ihlīlāk*, The being exceedingly black.

A احمّ *ahamm*, Black (horse). White. Headless or wingless (arrow).

A احماء *ahmā*, (pl. of حم *ham*) Fathers or brothers-in-law. A wife's relatives. A husband's relatives. (pl. of حمي *hima'*) Inaccessible, forbidden, guarded (places). *Ihmā*, (v. n. 4 of حما) Befouling (a well) by casting black mud into (it). (v. n. 4 of حمي) Exciting, stirring up. Guarding, preventing. Rendering inaccessible. Finding (a place) to be inaccessible. Heating (iron). Making (a day or fire) hot (God).

A احمّاء *ahimmā*, (pl. of حميم *hamīm*) Relatives.

A احماد *ihmād*, (v. n. 4 of حمد) Receiving, or deserving to receive, praise. Finding a laudable country. Accepting, receiving favourably. Approving of any one's opinions without divulging them. Being praiseworthy.

A احمار *ihmār*, (v. n. 4 of حمر) Having a red son born to one. Feeding (a horse) too plentifully with barley, till his mouth smells offensively.

A احماس *ihmās*, (v. n. 4 of حمس) Enraging.

A احماش *ihmāsh*, (v. n. 4 of حمش) Putting in a rage, exciting, provoking. Kindling (anger). Adding fuel to the fire, making (the kettle) boil.

A احماض *ihmāz*, (v. n. 4 of حمض) Making acid. Being acid and bitter. Producing salt and bitter plants (the earth). Feeding (a camel) with such plants. Feeding on such plants (a camel). Jesting. Keeping (any one) back from doing a thing.

A احماق *ihmāk*, (v. n. 4 of حمق) Bearing a foolish son. Esteeming or discovering one to be a fool.

A احمال *ahmāl*, (pl. of حمل *haml*) Fetuses in the womb. (pl. of حمل *haml* or *himl*) Fruits of trees. (pl. of حمل *himl*) Burdens. Loads. (pl. of حمل *hamal*) Full-grown lambs. احمال رجال *ahmāli rijāl*, The accoutrements or baggage of foot soldiers; any thing carried by foot-travellers; traps. *Ihmāl*, (v. n. 4 of حمل) Loading. Assisting in taking up a load. Emitting milk without conceiving.

A احمام *ihmām*, (v. n. 4 of حمّ) Determining, decreeing. Measuring. Warming water. Washing with cold and hot water. Being feverish and love-sick. Being feverish (a country). Throwing into a fever. Keeping in anxious suspense. Blackening. Approaching, becoming present.

A احمد *ahmad*, More or most laudable. One of the names of Muhammad. P احمد آباد *ahmad-ābād*, (City of Ahmad) the capital of Guzerat. احمد حسن *ahmad hasan*, Name of Mahmūd Sabaktagīn's vizier.

H احمدنگر *ahmad-nagar*, (City of Ahmad) Name of a city of the Dakhan, where Aurangzīb died.

A احمديّ *ahmadiy*, Belonging to Ahmad.

A احمر *ahmar*, (pl. حمر *humr* and حمران *humrān*) Red. Unarmed. Barbarous (not Arabian). Gold. Saffron. Flesh. Wine. A kind of aromatic. A sort of date. White. موت احمر *mawt ahmar*, A violent death.

A احمرار *ihmirār*, (v. n. 9 of حمر) Being very red. Being intensely severe (misfortune). Redness.

A الاحمران *al ahmarāni*, Wine and flesh.

A احمرة *ahmirat*, (pl. of حمار *himār*) Asses.

A احمريّ *ahmariy*, Very red.

A احمريّة *ahmariyat*, Great redness.

A احمز *ahmaz*, Stronger, strongest. Tart (wine).

A احمس *ahmas*, Strong, bold, unwavering. Intrepid, warlike. Hard (place). (pl. احامس *ahāmis*) Barren (year).

A احمش *ahmash*, Spindle-shanked.

A احمص *ahmas*, A sheep-stealer.

A احمق *ahmak*, Foolish, stupid, awkward. A greater or greatest fool. (pl. حماقي *hamāka'*) A fool.

P احمقانه *ahmakāna*, Foolishly. like a fool.

A احمقي *ahmakī*, Folly, stupidity.

A احمل *ahmal*, More or most capable of bearing.

A احموقة *uhmūkat*, An arrant or egregious fool.

A احمي *ahma'*, More or most modest or ashamed. احمي انفا من *ahma' anafan min . . .*, Possessed of a nicer sense of honour than . . . .

A احميرار *ihmīrār*, The being extremely red.

A احميماء *ihmīmā*, (v. n. 12 of حمي) Becoming black (night or a cloud).

A احميماس *ihmīmās*, A waxing wrathful.

A احن *ihan*, (pl. of احنة *ihnat*) Hatreds. Angers.

A احناء *ahnā*, Allegories, metaphors. Intricacies. (pl. of حنو *hinw*) Sides. Curves. Crooked timbers of saddles. *Ihnā*, (v. n. 4 of حنا for حنو) Being loving, affectionate (a mother).

A احناث *ihnās*, (v. n. 4 of حنث) Making (one) swear falsely. Biassing to right or wrong.

A احناج *ihnāj*, (v. n. 4 of حنج) Inclining. Causing to incline, giving a bias. Resting, reposing. Concealing, suppressing. Making haste. Wresting (a person's words).

A احناذ *ihnāz*, (v. n. 4 of حنذ) Diluting (wine) with a little, (according to some) with much water.

A احناش *ahnāsh*, (pl. of حنش *hanash*) Reptiles, serpents, vipers. Flies. Birds or animals which are hunted. Those whose heads are shaped like serpents' heads. *Ihnāsh*, (v. n. 4 of حنش) Driving off, averting. Accelerating, urging on.

A احناط *ihnāt*, (v. n. 4 of حنط) Being fit for reaping (wheat). Being ripe (the plant رمث *rims*). Burying (the dead) with sweet herbs.

A احناق *ihnāk*, (v. n. 4 of حنق) Irritating, exasperating. Hating with unmitigated rancour. Being thin (a camel's bunch). Being lank from much covering (an ass). Touching the belly (the back). Coming out into ear (corn).

A احناك *ahnāk*, (pl. of حنك *hanak*) Palates, or under parts of the mouth opposite them. *Ihnāk*, (v. n. 4 of حنك) Rendering expert. Driving back.

A احنان *ihnān*, (v. n. 4 of حنّ) Mistaking, blundering. Making (a bowstring) twang.

A احنة *ihnat*, (v. n. of احن) Bearing extreme hatred, holding in utter aversion. Hatred: anger.

A احنّة *ahinnat*, (pl. of حنين *hanīn*) Months of Jamādi.

A احنط *ahnat*, One who has a large thick beard.

A احنف *ahnaf*, Bow-legged. A man's name.

A احنك *ahnak*, A camel that eats much, that makes more use of his jaws than others.

A احني *ahna'*, Crook-backed. احني ضلوعا *ahna' zulūan*, More or most benevolent.

A احواب *ihwāb*, (v. n. 4 of حاب for حوب) Turning, becoming inclined to iniquity.

A احوات *ahwāt*, (pl. of حوت *hūt*) Fishes.

A احواج *ihwāj*, (v. n. 4 of حاج for حوج) Wanting. Making want, necessitating, constraining.

A احوار *ahwār*, (pl. of حور *hawar*) Black cattle (as bulls, oxen, or cows).

A احواذ *ihwāz*, (v. n. 4 of حاذ for حوذ) Driving (camels) fast. Drawing together that nothing might escape. Drawing together (a garment). Making (a goblet) light.

A احواز *ahwāz*, Name of the country called by the moderns Khūzistān, and the ancients Susiana: also the capital city.

A احواش *ihwāsh*, (v. n. 4 of حاش for حوش) Surrounding (game), and driving (it) into the net.

A احواض *ahwāz*, (pl. of حوض) Reservoirs.

A احوال *ahwāl*, (pl. of حال *hāl*) States, conditions, situations, affairs, accidents, circumstances, accounts, relations, events (either past or present). Changes, vicissitudes. (pl. of حول *hawl*) Years.

P احوال جنگي *ahwāli jangī*, Military affairs. احوال خير مآل *ahwāli khayr-maāl*, Prosperity, good situations. نوّاب صاحب بسيار احوال پرسيدند *nūwab ṣāḥib bisyār aḥwāl pursīdand*, The nabob enquired about many circumstances. A *Aḥwāla*, Round about. *Iḥwāl*, (v. n. 4 of حال for حول) Remaining a year in a place. Having years pass over. Being a year old (a boy). Causing to squint.

P احوال پرسي *aḥwāl-pursī*, Enquiry after state, health, or affairs.

A احوب *aḥwab*, Guilty. Undutiful to parents.

A احوج *aḥwaj*, More or most needed or necessitous.

A احوذ *aḥwaz*, A quick pace. Quick-paced.

A احوذيّ *aḥwaziy*, Active, ready. Nimble. Clever, intelligent. Despatchful.

A احور *aḥwar*, (fem. حوراء *ḥawrā*, pl. حور *ḥūr*) One who has beautiful eyes. Understanding, intellect, intelligence. The planet Jupiter.

A احورار *iḥwirār*, (v. n. 9 of حار for حور) Being white and fair. Being exceedingly white (the white of the eye). Being very black (the pupil of the eye). Having beautiful eyes.

A احورة *aḥwirat*, Sucking camels' colts.

A احوريّ *aḥwariy*, White, fair, soft, and sleek. *Iḥwariy*, One who has a soft and shining skin.

A احوز *aḥwaz*, Active, nimble, clever, ready.

A احوزيّ *aḥwaziy*, Nimble, swift, despatchful. Intelligent. Black. Clever in driving.

A احوس *aḥwas*, (pl. حوس *ḥūs*) Bold, undaunted, intrepid, fearless. A wolf.

A احوص *aḥwaṣ*, One who has the outer angle of the eye very acute.

A احوط *aḥwaṭ*, Safest. Most comprehensive.

A احوق *aḥwaḳ*, Large-glanded (man).

A احول *aḥwal*, Squinting, squint-eyed (man). Crafty, sly. More or most crafty. ما احوله *mā aḥwalahu*, How sly he is!

A احولال *iḥwilāl*, (v. n. 9 of حول) Squinting. Being verdant (ground).

A احولة *aḥwilat*, (pl. of حال) States, conditions.

A احولى *aḥwalī*, Strabism, squint.

A احوليّة *aḥwaliyat*, Strabism, squint.

A احونصال *iḥwinṣāl*, (v. n. 3 of حوصل Q) Bending the neck and thrusting forward the crop.

A احوواء *iḥwiwā*, (v. n. 9 of حوي) Being black inclining to red or green, or red inclined to black. Being green (the earth).

A احوي *aḥwa'*, (fem. حوّاء *ḥawwā*, pl. حوّ *ḥūw*) Black, dusky (in the lips). Black inclined to green; or red inclined to black.

A احوية *aḥwiyat*, (pl. of حواء *ḥiwā*) Arabian tents made of woollen or goats' hair.

A احويلال *iḥwīlāl*, (v. n. 11 of حول) Squinting. Being verdant (the ground). Being even (plants).

A احوِيواء *iḥwīwā*, (v. n. 11 of حوي) Being green (the earth). Being black and inclining to green; or red inclined to black.

A احيّ *uḥayy*, (dim. of احوي) Blackish-lipped.

A احياء *aḥyā*, (pl. of حيّ *ḥayy*) The living. Tribes, families. (pl. of حياء *ḥayā*) Pudenda fœminum. الاحياء والاموات *al aḥyā wa'l amwāt*, The quick and the dead. *Iḥyā*, (v. n. 4 of حيي) Recalling to life, reviving. Resuscitating (a fire) by blowing. Having healthy, thriving flocks. Having a living colt (a camel). Discovering a place to be fruitful. Migrating to a region abounding with herbs. احيا الموت *iḥyā'l mawt*, A term used (in India) to denote any piece of ground incapable of yielding advantage, either from want of water, from inundation, or any other cause.

A احياج *iḥyāj*, (v. n. 4 of حاج for حيج) Producing the thorny plant حاج *ḥāj*.

A احياد *aḥyād*, (pl. of حيد *ḥayd*) Eminences, or prominent parts of a mountain. Knots on the horns of the ibex or mountain-goat.

A احياز *aḥyāz*, (pl. of حيّز *ḥayyiz*) Places, environs. The courts or avenues leading to a house.

A احيال *aḥyāl*, (pl. of حيل *ḥayl*) Stagnant waters in a river's bed.

A احيان *aḥyān*, (pl. of حين *ḥīn*) Times, ages. *Iḥyān*, (v. n. 4 of حان for حين) Living, passing some time in a place. Gaining one's wishes. Being (time) for camels to be milked or marked.

A احياناً *aḥyānan*, Sometimes, from time to time, now and then, ever and anon. Accidentally.

A احيحة *aḥīḥat*, (or احيح) Great anger or grief.

A احيسن *uḥaysin*, (as ما احيسنه *mā uḥaysinahu*) How pretty and genteel he is!

A احيف *aḥyaf*, Land on which no rain falls.

A احيل *aḥyal*, More or most sagacious, wily, sly, fertile in schemes, prolific in stratagems. ما احيله *mā aḥyalahu*, How wily he is!

A احيمر *uḥaymir* (pl. احيمرون) Reddish.

A احيوي *uḥaywī*, Reddish-lipped (man).

A احيية *aḥyiyat*, (pl. of حياء *ḥayā*) Vulvæ.

P اخ *ākh*, Bravo! courage!

P اخ *aḳh*, Ah! Bravo! well done!

A اخ *aḳh*, (pl. اخون *aḳhūn*, آخاء *āḳhā*, اخوان *iḳhwān*, *uḳhwān*, اخوة *iḳhwat*, *uḳhwat*, اخوّة *uḳhūwat*, and اخوّ *uḳhūw*) A brother, friend, or companion. Like, resembling. The opposite, contrary. اخ الخير *aḳhu'l ḳhayr*, (The opposite of good) Evil. لا اخا لك بفلان *lā aḳhā laka bi fulānin*, Such an one is no brother to you. *Iḳh* or *aḳh*, A word used to make camels bend the knee.

A اخّ *aḳhḳh*, A brother. Fye! ah! alas! *Aḳhḳh* or *iḳhḳh*, Dirt, filth.

A اخا *aḳhā'*, A word for calling sheep.

A آخاء *āḳhā*, (pl. of اخ *aḳh*) Brothers.

A اخاء *iḳhā*, (v. n. 3 of اخا for اخو) Acting like a brother; contracting a most intimate friendship.

A اخابير *aḳhābīr*, (pl. of اخبار *aḳhbār*) News.

P اخ اخ *aḳh aḳh*, Good! good! Ah! alas! *Ukh ukh*, Excellent!

A اخاخة *iḳhāḳhat*, (v. n. 4 of خاخ for خوخ)

Being scanty and lying hid (grass).

A اخادع *aḳhādiʻ*, (pl. of اخدع *aḳhdaʻ*) Veins in the neck to which the cupping-glass is applied.

A اخاديد *aḳhādīd*, (pl. of اخدود *uḳhdūd*) Furrows, clefts in the ground. Lash-marks, wheals.

A اخادير *aḳhādīr*, (pl. of اخدار *aḳhdār*) Curtains.

A اخاذ *iḳhāz*, (pl. اخذ *uḳhuz*) Stagnant water; a pool, ditch, or place where water stagnates. Land of which any one takes possession for himself.

A اخّاذ *aḳhḳhāz*, An extortioner.

A اخّاذات *aḳhḳhāzāt*, Holes, ditches.

A اخاذة *iḳhāzat*, (pl. اخذ *uḳhuz*) A pond. Land of which any one may take possession for himself. Land granted by a prince on feudal or copyhold tenure. A handle. The handle of a leathern shield.

A اخاذي *iḳhāzī*, An acceptance, a receipt.

P آخار *āḳhār*, Any thing thrown away for its insignificance.

A اخارة *iḳhārat*, (v. n. 4 of خار for خور) Bending, turning (an animal from one road to another).

A اخاريج *aḳhārīj*, (pl. of خرج *ḳharj*) Tributes, imposts, revenues.

P آخاز *āḳhāz*, Things of small value.

A اخاسف *aḳhāsif*, Soft grounds.

A اخاسي *aḳhāsī*, (pl. of خسا) Unequal, odd.

A اخاشف *aḳhāshif*, Hard ground.

A اخاضة *iḳhāẓat*, (v. n. 4 of خاض for خوض) Entering into and fording (a river). Making one ford (a river). Inducing (one) to plunge into.

A اخاضر *aḳhāẓir*, Gold, flesh, and wine.

A اخافة *iḳhāfat*, (v. n. 4 of خاف for خوف) Terrifying, intimidating. (v. n. 4 of خاف for خيف) Visiting the temple خيف *ḳhayf* on mount Mina. Forcing (people) to betake (themselves) to higher ground (an inundation).

A اخافش *aḳhāfish*, Name of three grammarians.

A اخاقة *iḳhāḳat*, (v. n. 4 of خاق for خوق) Travelling over a country.

A اخاقيق *aḳhāḳīḳ*, (pl. of اخقوق *uḳhḳūḳ*) Clefts.

P آخال *āḳhāl*, Any kind of rubbish (as husks, fruit-parings, wood-shavings). Name of a city.

A اخالة *iḳhālat*, (v. n. 4 of خال for خيل) Appearing doubtful. Portending rain (a cloud). Considering the appearance of any thing, especially of a cloud disposed to rain. Imagining, fancying. Prognosticating. Putting an image resembling a man near a young camel to scare the wolf. Having milk in the udder. Being fruitful in grass.

A اخامة *iḳhāmat*, (v. n. 4 of خام for خوم) Standing on three feet (a horse), the tip only of the other hoof touching the ground. (v. n. 4 of خام for خيم) Erecting or pitching a tent. Standing on three feet, the tip of the fourth touching the ground.

A اخامص *aḳhāmiṣ*, (pl. of اخمص) The hollow parts of the soles of the feet. Slender in the middle.

A اخاني *aḳhānī*, (for اخوان) Two brothers.

P آخانيدن *āḳhānīdan*, (from آختن *āḳhtan*) To

make come forth. To cause to draw (a sword).

A اخاوة *ikhāwat*, (v. n. of اخا for اخو) Acting as a brother or a friend.

A اخاوين *akhāwīn*, (pl. of خوان *khuwān* or *khiwān*) Trays, dinner-tables.

A اخايا *akhāya'*, (pl. of اخيّة *akhīyat*) Stakes or ropes to which cattle are fastened or tethered.

A اخائل *ukhāʻil*, Vain, proud.

A اخباء *ikhbāʻ*, (v. n. 4 of خبا for خبو) Extinguishing. (v. n. 4 of خبي) Making or pitching a tent.

A اخباب *akhbāb*, A torn garment. (pl. of خبّ *khubb*) Barks of trees. Low grounds. اخباب الفحث *akhbābu'l fahis*, The intestines. *Ikhbāb*, (v. n. 4 of خبّ) Trotting or making a horse amble.

A اخبات *akhbāt*, (pl. of خبت *khabt*) Plains, extensive, level and soft grounds. Unequal and sandy grounds. *Ikhbāt*, (v. n. 4 of خبت) Abasing one's self.

A اخباث *ikhbās*, (v. n. 4 of خبث) Corrupting, teaching what is evil. Keeping bad company. Begetting wicked children. Using nasty discourse.

A اخبار *akhbār*, (pl. of خبر *khabar*) Histories, tales, annals, gazettes, news, relations, advices, chronicles, traditions. A newspaper. P اخبار دربار *akhbāri durar-bār*, Precious advices, happy news, agreeable intelligence. اخبار وحشت مدار *akhbāri wahshat-madār*, Dreadful news, unfortunate advices. اخبار *akhbār* is the title of many books of history: as, اخبار الخلفاء *akhbāru'l khulafāʻ*, History of the Khalifs; اخبار الشعراء *akhbāru'sh shuʻarāʻ*, History of the poets; اخبار العالم *akhbāru'l ʻālam*, History of the world; اخبار البلاد و آثار الكشورات *akhbāru'l bilād wa āsāru'l kishwarāt*, History of countries and description of cities. *Ikhbār*, (v. n. 4 of خبر) Advising, informing, relating, certifying, giving intelligence, telling. Finding (a milch-camel) to abound in milk.

P اخبارنويس *akhbār-navis*, A news-writer.

A اخباريّ *akhbāriy*, A chronicler. *Ikhbāriy*, Declarative, enunciative, expressive.

A اخباط *ikhbāt*, (v. n. 4 of خبط) Being troubled with a cold.

A اخبال *ikhbāl*, (v. n. 4 of خبل) Giving another the benefit of a sheep's milk, or of a camel's hair. Lending a horse to go on a military expedition. Dividing (camels) into two bands, of which one half shall breed every year. Tiring, weakening.

A اخبان *ikhbān*, (v. n. 4 of خبن) Concealing something in the خبنة *khubnat* of one's trowsers.

A اخبث *akhbas*, More or most impure, noxious or unwholesome. More or most malicious.

A الاخبثان *al akhbasāni*, (The two impurities) Excrement and urine. Fetid breath and sleeplessness. Sleeplessness and fidgetiness.

A اخبر *akhbar*, Better or best informed.

A اخبط *akhbat*, A striker with his feet.

A اخبعثاث *ikhbiʻsās*, A walking like a lion.

A اخبل *akhbal*, Mad, crazy.

A اخبنداء *ikhbindāʻ*, (v. n. 15 of خبد) Being large and hard (a camel). Being full-grown, finely made (a man).

A اخبية *akhbiyat*, (pl. of خباء *khibāʻ*) Tents, tabernacles. Private marks impressed on she-camels of a noble breed. سعد الاخبية *saʻdu'l akhbiyat*, Name of the twenty-fifth lunar mansion.

P اخپج *akhpakh*, Understanding, wisdom.

A اخت *ukht*, (pl. اخوات *akhawāt*) A sister. Similar, equal, alike, congenial. اختا سهيل *ukhtā suhayl*, Sisters of Canopus, name of two stars of the second magnitude.

A اختاء *ikhtāʻ*, (v. n. 4 of ختا for ختو) Selling wares piece by piece.

A اختات *ikhtāt*, (v. n. 4 of ختّ) Blushing, being ashamed. Degrading, rendering vile.

P اختاج *akhtāj*, A feudatory vassal to another sovereign.

A اختان *akhtān*, (pl. of ختن *khatan*) A bride's nearest kindred, as father or brother. Sons-in-law.

A اختباء *ikhtibāʻ*, (v. n. 8 of خبا) Hiding, concealing. Being concealed, lying hid. Rendering obscure and enigmatical (a sentence or verse) to any one, and then questioning him about (it).

A اختباب *ikhtibāb*, (v. n. 8 of خبّ) Cutting or tearing a strip from a piece of cloth. Ambling. Lifting up the right and left legs together (a horse). Standing first on one foot, and then on the other.

A اختبار *ikhtibār*, (v. n. 8 of خبر) Trying, proving. Being acquainted or conversant with. Experience, skill, conversancy.

A اختباز *ikhtibāz*, (v. n. 8 of خبز) Baking bread for one's self.

A اختباس *ikhtibās*, (v. n. 8 of خبس) Overcoming one and depriving him of his property.

A اختباص *ikhtibās*, (v. n. 8 of خبص) Cooking the dish خبيص *khabīs*.

A اختباط *ikhtibāt*, (v. n. 8 of خبط) Importunately asking a favour without claim or previous acquaintance. Striking hard. Pawing the ground.

A اختبال *ikhtibāl*, (v. n. 8 of خبل) Depriving any one of his reason, or of the use of his limbs. Being restless and unsteady (a quadruped).

A اختتاء *ikhtitāʻ*, (v. n. 8 of ختأ) Concealing one's self from fear or shame. Turning pale, changing colour (through dread of a king or magistrate). Seizing, snatching off by force. Deceiving. (v. n. 8 of ختا for ختو) Being broken and subdued by grief, fear, or disease. Selling one's goods one by one. (v. n. 8 of ختي) Changing colour (from dread of the magistrate).

A اختتال *ikhtitāl*, (v. n. 8 of ختل) Listening to private conversation, playing the eaves-dropper.

A اختتام *ikhtitām*, (v. n. 8 of ختم) Finishing, completing. End, conclusion, fulfilment. مودّت اختتام *mawaddat-ikhtitām*, Affectionately, friendly, loving, whose end or tendency is love or friendship.

A اختتان *ikhtitān*, (v. n. 8 of ختن) Being circumcised. Circumcising one's self.

A اختثاث *ikhtisās*, (v. n. 8 of خثّ) Being ashamed. Magnificence, grandeur.

A اختداع *ikhtidāʻ*, (v. n. 8 of خدع) Deceiving, cheating, circumventing, insidiously injuring.

A اختدار *ikhtidār*, (v. n. 8 of خدر) Lying hid, concealing one's self.

A اختداف *ikhtidāf*, (v. n. 8 of خدف) Seizing, carrying off by force. Cutting out (a garment).

A اختدام *ikhtidām*, (v. n. 8 of خدم) Serving one's self. Seeking a servant, taking into service.

P اختر *akhtar*, A star. Horoscope, predominant star at any one's nativity. Name of a lunar mansion. An omen, augury. An ensign, standard. Name of an angel. نيك اختر *nek-akhtar*, Born under a lucky planet: fortunate, virtuous. دختر سعد اختر *dukhtari saʻd-akhtar*, A daughter of fortunate stars. اختر پنجم *akhtari panjum*, The fifth constellation, *i.e.* the planet Mars. اختر دانش *akhtari dānish*, The planets of wisdom, *i.e.* Jupiter and Mercury. اختر سر سبز *akhtari sar sabz*, A happy constellation. اختر شمردن *akhtar shumurdan*, To count the stars, *i.e.* to keep awake. اختر كاويان *akhtari kāviyān* (or كاوان *kāvān*), The standard of Kāw or of Farīdūn. اختران تب زده *akhtarāni tab-zada*, Stars appearing in the water.

A اختراب *ikhtirāb*, (v. n. 8 of خرب) Robbing.

A اختراج *ikhtirāj*, (v. n. 8 of خرج) Extracting, drawing out. Selecting, choosing.

A اختراش *ikhtirāsh*, (v. n. 8 of خرش) Scratching. Providing, seeking provision for a family.

A اختراص *ikhtirās*, (v. n. 8 of خرص) Inventing a lie. Putting into a wallet.

A اختراط *ikhtirāt*, (v. n. 8 of خرط) Stripping the leaves off a branch, or grapes off a bunch. Unsheathing (a sword).

A اختراع *ikhtirāʻ*, (v. n. 8 of خرع) Cleaving. Commencing. Inventing, producing something new, contriving. Lending (a horse) for a few days and then taking (him) back. Defrauding. Ruining, or seeking to ruin. Invention.

A اختراف *ikhtirāf*, (v. n. 8 of خرف) Gathering fruit in autumn.

A اختراق *ikhtirāk*, (v. n. 8 of خرق) Pervading, blowing with violence (as the wind). Passing by or through, threading. Making up a false story.

A اخترام *ikhtirām*, (v. n. 8 of خرم) Destroying, extirpating. Cutting off.

P اخترستان *akhtaristān*, Name of a treatise on astronomy.

P اختر شمر *akhtar-shumur*, (or اختر شناس *akhtar-shinās*) An astronomer.

P اخترگو *akhtar-go*, (or *gū*) An astrologer.

A اختزاز *ikhtizāz*, (v. n. 8 of خزّ) Selecting, picking out. Piercing, transfixing with a dart.

A اختزاع *ikhtizāʻ*, (v. n. 8 of خزع) Tearing away, alienating (one) from his kindred.

A اختزاق *ikhtizāḳ*, (v. n. 8 of خزق) Being drawn (a sword), slipping out of the sheath.

A اختزال *ikhtizāl*, (v. n. 8 of خزل) Being alone. Eliding, cutting off. Tearing away, alienating from kindred.

A اختزان *ikhtizān*, (v. n. 8 of خزن) Hoarding. Keeping a secret. Taking the nearest road.

A اختشاب *ikhtishāb*, (v. n. 8 of خشب) Writing a poem off hand.

A اختشاش *ikhtishāsh*, (v. n. 8 of خشّ) Eating creeping things.

A اختشاع *ikhtishāʻ*, (v. n. 8 of خشع) Being humble. Humbling one's self.

A اختصاء *ikhtiṣāʼ*, (v. n. 8 of خصي) Castrating one's self.

A اختصار *ikhtiṣār*, (v. n. 8 of خصر) Abridging, abbreviating, contracting. Placing the hand upon the waist. Laying hold of the waist. Taking (a switch) in the hand. Reading a verse or two at the close of a chapter. Cutting off any exuberance, docking. Taking the nearest road. Cutting up by the roots. An abridgement. بالاختصار *bi'l ikhtiṣār*, In short, briefly. P اختصار كردن *ikhtiṣār kardan*, To cut short (a story), to sum up briefly.

A اختصاص *ikhtiṣāṣ*, (v. n. 8 of خصّ) Distinguishing. Being peculiar, particular, special. Being distinguished. Appropriation.

A اختصاف *ikhtiṣāf*, (v. n. 8 of خصف) Sewing, stitching one sole, fold, or layer upon another. Covering the body with leaves.

A اختصام *ikhtiṣām*, (v. n. 8 of خصم) Disputing, litigating, being at variance. Eating away the scabbard (a sharp sword). Enmity, altercation, dispute.

A اختضاب *ikhtiẓāb*, (v. n. 8 of خضب) Tinging the nails or the hair with cypress. Colouring or dyeing one's self.

A اختضاد *ikhtiẓād*, (v. n. 8 of خضد) Putting a halter on a camel and mounting him.

A اختضار *ikhtiẓār*, (v. n. 8 of خضر) Mowing, reaping, cutting down any thing green. Being cut or broken off. Dying in the flower of youth. Taking up and carrying a load. Deflowering an immature virgin.

A اختضاع *ikhtiẓāʻ*, (v. n. 8 of خضع) Humbling one's self. Passing quickly by. Inclining to set (a star). Following the female (a stallion). Self-abasement.

A اختضام *ikhtiẓām*, (v. n. 8 of خضم) Cutting. Infesting a road.

A اختطاء *ikhtiṭāʼ*, (v. n. 8 of خطا for خطو) Stepping. Over-stepping, passing beyond. Passing quickly and at once.

A اختطاب *ikhtiṭāb*, (v. n. 8 of خطب) Betrothing a wife. Inducing any one to marry. Accepting proposals of marriage.

A اختطاط *ikhtiṭāṭ*, (v. n. 8 of خطّ) Laying out in right lines (the streets of a city). Beginning to have a beard. Taking possession (of land) for one's self. Having lines (the face).

A اختطاف *ikhtiṭāf*, (v. n. 8 of خطف) Seizing, carrying off by force, catching, snatching rapidly. Leaving (as a fever). اختطافا *ikhtiṭāfan*, Forcibly.

A اختفاء *ikhtifāʼ*, (v. n. 8 of خفي) Withdrawing, hiding, concealing one's self. Lying hid. Drawing forth, causing to come out. Committing murder without being detected. P اختفا كردۀ پردۀ ذهول *ikhtifā-kardaʼi pardaʼi zuhūl*, Lurking behind the veil of oblivion, *i.e.* indolent, lazy, obscure.

A اختفاض *ikhtifāẓ*, (v. n. 8 of خفض) Circumcising herself (a girl). Being lowered; sinking.

A اختفاق *ikhtifāḳ*, (v. n. 8 of خفق) Floating, quivering (the vapour called mirage).

P اخ تفو *akh tufū*, Hawking and spitting.

A اختلاء *ikhtilāʼ*, (v. n. 8 of خلي) Retiring with another to a solitary place. Penetrating and cutting (a sword). Cutting, mowing. Pulling up.

A اختلاب *ikhtilāb*, (v. n. 8 of خلب) Cheating, cajoling.

A اختلاج *ikhtilāj*, (v. n. 8 of خلج) Dragging away. Being forcibly separated, being weaned. Trembling. Beating, throbbing (the eye or limbs).

A اختلاس *ikhtilās*, (v. n. 8 of خلس) Seizing, snatching, carrying off. اختلاسا *ikhtilāsan*, Hastily, violently, forcibly.

A اختلاط *ikhtilāṭ*, (v. n. 8 of خلط) Being mixed. Losing one's wits. Growing fat (a camel). Breaking down in running (a horse). Mixture, confusion, perplexity. Insanity. Intercourse, conversation, commerce, association, friendship.

A اختلاع *ikhtilāʻ*, (v. n. 8 of خلع) Being divorced. Sueing for, and taking a divorce. Robbing, plundering.

A اختلاف *ikhtilāf*, (v. n. 8 of خلف) Becoming a substitute. Disagreeing, differing. Watching (any one) away from (his house, and then visiting his wife). Going to and fro. Suffering from a diarrhœa. Disagreement, diversity of opinion. Vicissitude. P اختلاف كردن *ikhtilāf kardan*, To contradict. To disagree.

A اختلافات *ikhtilāfāt*, (pl.) Dissensions.

A اختلاق *ikhtilāḳ*, (v. n. 8 of خلق) Inventing a lie. Adopting foreign habits. Being fragrant.

A اختلال *ikhtilāl*, (v. n. 8 of خلّ) Being lean, emaciated. Standing in need. Sewing, stitching. Piercing through with a spear, spitting. Being confined to the sweet herbage خلّة *khullat* (camels). Turning sour, becoming vinegar. Making vinegar. اختلال حال *ikhtilāli ḥāl*, A state of confusion; disorder, tumult. اختلال مزاج *ikhtilāli mizāj*, An alteration of health or constitution (for the worse, illness, indisposition).

A اختلام *ikhtilām*, (v. n. 8 of خلم) Choosing.

A اختمار *ikhtimār*, (v. n. 8 of خمر) Putting on a veil or coif called خمار *khimār*. Fermenting, rising (as wine or dough). Lying hid.

A اختمال *ikhtimāl*, (v. n. 8 of خمل) Grazing low-lying grounds rich in vegetation.

A اختمام *ikhtimām*, (v. n. 8 of خمّ) Sweeping a house. Cleaning out a well. Cutting.

P آختن *ākhtan*, To draw out, to unsheath (a sword). To castrate, geld. To hang, suspend. To lead, bring. To go forth. To overtake, reach. To play. To accustom. To weave, knit. To fear.

A اختناث *ikhtināṡ*, (v. n. 8 of خنث) Bending outwards the brim of a leathern bottle, so as to be able to drink.

A اختناق *ikhtināḳ*, (v. n. 8 of خنق) Being strangled, choked, throttled. Strangulation.

A اختواء *ikhtiwāʼ*, (v. n. 8 of خوي) Cutting off a part. Piercing (a horse) between the fore and hind-legs. Losing one's wits. Taking all one's property. Carrying off, devouring (a wild beast a calf).

P آخته *ākhta*, Drawn. Castrated. A gelding.

P اخته *akhta*, Castrated. A gelding.

A اختيّ *ukhtiy*, Sisterly, belonging to a sister.

A اختيات *ikhtiyāt*, (v. n. 8 of خات for خوت) Pouncing on his prey (a falcon). Seizing and carrying off (a sheep). Receiving (a tradition) and committing (it) to memory. Travelling by night.

A اختيار *ikhtiyār*, (v. n. 8 of خار for خير) Choosing, preferring, selecting, picking out. Election, choice. Option. Self-controul. P اختيار كردن *ikhtiyār kardan*, To make choice, choose, will.

T اختيار *ikhtiyār*, A man in years.

A اختيارا *ikhtiyāran*, Voluntarily, spontaneously.

A اختياري *ikhtiyārī*, Choice, approbation, power, authority. In one's own power, or disposal.

T اختياريه *ikhtiyārīya*, Old men.

A اختياض *ikhtiyāẓ*, (v. n. 8 of خاض for خوض) Entering or fording (a river).

A اختياط *ikhtiyāṭ*, (v. n. 8 of خاط for خيط) Passing quickly and at once (like a needle).

A اختياف *ikhtiyāf*, (v. n. 8 of خاف for خيف) Visiting the temple خيف *khayf* on Mount Mina.

A اختيال *ikhtiyāl*, (v. n. 8 of خال for خيل) Strutting, walking with dignity: pride, pomp.

A اختيان *ikhtiyān*, (v. n. 8 of خان for خون) Betraying. Deceit, perfidy.

A اخثاء *akhṡāʼ*, (pl. of خثي *khiṡy*) Ox-dungs. Elephant-dungs. *Ikhṡāʼ*, (v. n. 4 of خثي) Setting fire to ox-dung. Selling ox-dung.

A اخثار *ikhṡār*, (v. n. 4 of خثر) Leaving butter to condense. Allowing milk to thicken.

A اخثم *akhṡam*, Flat-nosed; broad-nosed, round-nosed, insensible of smell (as a lion). A broad-sword. A lion.

A اخشيكث *akhsīkaṡ*, A town in Turkistān.

A اخجاء *ikhjāʼ*, (v. n. 4 of خجا) Teasing, importuning. (v. n. 4 of خجي) Copulating much.

A اخجال ikhjāl, (v. n. 4 of خجل) Confounding, putting to shame. Being long and luxuriant (plants).

P اخجسته akhjasta, The threshold of a door.

A اخجي akhja', A woman who makes much water, whose womb lies very deep. One whose toes turn in and whose heels turn out.

P اخچه akhcha, Gold. Silver. A die for coining. A copper-seal.

A اخداء ikhdās, (v. n. 4 of خدي) Walking softly.

A اخداج ikhdāj, (v. n. 4 of خدج) Bringing forth an imperfect colt. Being without rain (the summer). Performing incompletely one's devotions. Failing to emit fire (a fire-steel).

A اخدار akhdār, (pl. of خدر khidr) Curtains. Ikhdār, (v. n. 4 of خدر) Being overcast with clouds or rain. Sitting behind the veil or curtain (as women do in the East, concealed from the view of men). Entering on a rainy, foggy, or windy day. Remaining fixed in a thicket (a lion). Concealing a lion (a thicket or brake). Abiding in a place. Benumbing, deadening.

A اخداع ikhdāع, (v. n. 4 of خدع) Concealing, laying by. Binding, tying fast. Stirring up to the practice of deception.

A اخدال akhdāl, (pl. of خدلة khadlat and khidlat) Plump in the arms and legs (women).

A اخدام ikhdām, (v. n. 4 of خدم) Giving a servant. Seeking a servant, taken one into service.

A اخدان akhdān, (pl. of خدن khidn) Friends. Lovers. Beloved objects.

A اخدب akhdab, A tall, slim fellow. Hasty, precipitate. A fool, an idiot. Self-opiniated.

A اخدّة akhiddat, (pl. of خدّ khadd) Furrows.

P اخدر akhdar, A whole brother or sister.

A اخدر akhdar, Dark (night). Name of a certain celebrated stallion.

A اخدريّ akhdariy, A wild ass.

A الاخدريّة al akhdariyat, Stock descended from a famous sire named اخدر akhdar.

A اخدع akhdaع, More or most fallacious, crafty, artful, wily, cunning. اخدع من الضبّ akhdaع mini'z zabb, More sly than a lizard. (pl. اخادع akhādiع) A vein in the neck to which the cupping-glass is applied.

A اخدم akhdam, (A horse or sheep) having the lower part of the hind-legs of a whitish colour (if on one foot only he is called ارجل arjal).

A اخدود ukhdūd, (pl. اخاديد akhādīd) An oblong fissure in the ground, a furrow. (A blow) cutting the skin, a stripe, a lash. A cleft.

A اخدور ukhdūr, A curtain behind which a woman sits.

A آخذ ākhiz, A taker, receiver, seizer or apprehender. (A camel) beginning to become fat; also to breed teeth. (Milk) beginning to turn sour.

A أخذ akhaza, (fut. يأخذ yaکkhuzu) He took.

A اخذ akhz, (v. n. of اخذ) Taking, seizing, apprehending, procuring. Intercepting. Assailing, taking prisoner. Clipping, trimming, paring. Beginning. A manœuvre or mode of seizing (in wrestling). Way of life, manner, disposition, habit. Punishment, retribution. Rigidity (when the body from any cause becomes stiff, and is thereby deprived of motion). اخذ انتقام akhzi intikām, Taking vengeance. اخذ و جرّ akhz u jarr, Taking and seizing; fraudulent dealing. اخذ و قبض akhz u kabz, A receipt. نجوم الاخذ nujūmu'l akhz, The mansions of the moon. P اخذ كردن akhz kardan, To take, receive. To examine. A اخذت على يد فلان akhaztu ع ala' yadi fulānin, I withheld him from what he wished to do. من اخذ اخذهم man akhaza akhzuhum or akhzahum, or من اخذه اخذهم man akhazahu akhzuhum, Whoever adopted their mode of life. Ikhz, A cautery applied to a camel's side to prevent a threatened distemper. Custom, mode of living. Akhaz, (v. n. of اخذ) (A camel's colt) having the stomach oppressed by too great a quantity of milk, or from its acid quality. Fury, phrenzy of a male camel. Opthalmia. Ukhuz, Opthalmia. (pl. of اخاذ) Pools, stagnant waters.

A اخذاء ikhzās, (v. n. 4 of خذأ) Humbling, making tractable.

A اخذال ikhzāl, (v. n. 4 of خذل) Staying with her young (a doe). Finding the mother disposed to stay with him (the young of a wild beast).

A اخذام ikhzām, (v. n. 4 of خذم) Confessing, acknowledging with submission. Being still and quiet. Making drunk (liquor).

A آخذة ākhizat, Rigidity, stiffness: a disease occasioning a stiffness in the joints.

A اخذة ukhzat, A philtre, fascination, any thing by which the Arabian women seek to keep the men faithful to them. An amulet, charm. اخذة النار ukhzatu'n nār, A little while after sun-set, when candles are lighted. اخذة اسف ukhzatu asafin, A doleful seizure.

P آخر ākhar, A bason, bathing-tub. Yes, surely. For example. Ākhur, A stall for horses. The collar-bone. Name of a city in Dahistan. آخر چرب ākhuri charb, (A fat stall) Plenty, abundance. آخر سنگين ākhuri sangīn, (An empty, or rather, stony cratch) An unprofitable situation.

A آخر ākhar, (pl. آخرون ākharūna, and اخر ukhr) Another, different, second. آخر ديار ākhar diyār, Another, or a foreign country. سمت آخر samti ākhar, Another way, otherwise. P شكل آخر شدن shakli ākhar shudan, To be altered. Ākhir, (pl. اواخر awākhir) Last, posterior, ultimate, final. A name of God. Absent. The end, issue, extremity. The hinder part of a saddle. Finally, at last, afterwards. آخر الامر ākhiru'l amr, At length, finally. آخر زمان ākhiri zamān, The end of time, the last day. اتيتك آخر مرّتين ataytuka ākhira marratayni, I came to thee a second time. اوّل و آخر awwal u ākhir, First and last. P آخر شب ākhiri shab, The latter part of the night. آخر شدن ākhir shudan, To be finished. آخر كار ākhiri kār, A catastrophe. At length. آخر كردن ākhir kardan, To finish.

A اخر akhir, End, extremity. Rejected, removed from good. Ukhar, (pl. of اخرى ukhra', fem.) Others, different. Ukhur, The latter or hinder part. شقّه اخرا shakkahu ukhuran, (or من اخر min ukhurin) He tore it behind, or from behind.

A آخرا ākhiran, (or اخرا ukhuran) Finally.

A اخراب akhrāb, (pl. of خرب kharab) Male bustards. The hairs on the flank of a horse, or on the crown of the head. (pl. of خربة khurbat) Wallet-handles. Ikhrāb, (v. n. 4 of خرب) Laying waste, depopulating, razing, demolishing.

A اخراة ukhrāt, (fem.) (pl. اخر ukhar) Other.

A اخرات akhrāt, (pl. of خرب khurt) Buttons, buckles, or clasps, for fastening breast-harness.

A اخراج akhrāj, (pl. of خرج kharj) Tributes, revenues, produces. Ikhrāj, (v. n. 4 of خرج) Producing, drawing forth, bringing out. Expelling. Expending. Paying tribute. Experiencing a year partly fruitful and partly barren. Grazing one part of a field and leaving the other part untouched. Being variegated with black and white (a ram or ostrich). Hunting black and white ostriches. Marrying a mulatto. P اخراج كردن ikhrāj kardan, To expel, banish. To bring out.

A اخراجات ikhrājāt, (pl. of اخراج) Expenses.

A اخراد ikhrād, (v. n. 4 of خرد) Blushing. Inclining to play. Keeping silence from baseness, not from modesty.

A اخرار ikhrār, (v. n. 4 of خرّ) Causing to fall, throwing down. Cutting off the hand, causing it to fall off.

A اخراس ikhrās (v. n. 4 of خرس) Making dumb. Not allowing the anklet called خلخال khalkhāl to ring (a fat, fleshy leg).

A اخراص akhrās, (pl. of خرص khuras, khurus, and khurs) Sticks with which honey is gathered.

A اخراط ikhrāt, (v. n. 4 of خرط) Suffering under the complaint called خرط kharat (a camel). Closing a wallet, drawing the strings of a purse.

A اخراف ikhrāf, (v. n. 4 of خرف) Yeaning, foaling in autumn (a sheep or camel). Entering upon the autumn. Making a dotard. Corrupting, spoiling, damaging. Growing very tall (millet). Having fruit fit for gathering (a palm-tree). Granting one leave to gather dates. Bringing forth at the same season she conceived (a camel).

A اخراق akhrāk, (pl. of خرق khirk) Very liberal. Handsome youths of generous dispositions. Ikhrāk, (v. n. 4 of خرق) Astonishing, confounding, discouraging, deterring.

A اخرب akhrab, More or most ruinous. Bored in the ear. A hole in the ear. Verse in which the measure مفاعيل mafāʻīl becomes مفعول mafʻūl.

A اخربة akhribat, (pl. of خراب kharāb) Ruins.

P آخربين ākhir-bīn, Far-sighted; prudent.

A آخرة ākhirat, Posterior, last. The extremity. The hinder part of a saddle. Life eternal; the other world. آخرة ākhirat, is always opposed by the Arabians to دنيا dunya', which signifies, The world, or the present life; synonymous to which the Persians make use also of اين جهان in jahān, This world, and آن جهان ān jahān, That world; and likewise figuratively خانهٔ امشب khāna-i imshab, The lodging of to-night, and خانهٔ فردا khāna-i fardā, The habitation of to-morrow. آخرة العين ākhiratu'l ʻayn, The outer angle of the eye. اتيتك آخرة مرّتين ataytuka ākhirata marratayni, I came to thee a second time. الملّة الآخرة al millatu'l ākhirat, The last dispensation, Christianity.

A اخرة akharatan, ukharatan, باخرة bi akharatin or bi ukharatin, In fine, at length. جاء اخرة jāʻa akharatan, He came at last. باع باخرة bāʻa bi akhiratin, He sold upon futurity, i.e. on credit.

A اخرّة akhirrat, (pl. of خرير kharīr) Beaten tracks between two hills.

A اخرج akhraj, Variegated with black and white (ram or ostrich). (A mountain) covered with black and white sand or stones. A kind of bird called مكّاء mukkāʻ.

A اخرجاج ikhrijāj, (v. n. 9 of خرج) Being variegated with black and white (an ostrich or ram).

A اخرجة akhrajat, A well at the foot of a mountain. Akhrijat, (pl. of خراج kharāj) Revenues.

P آخردست ākhar-dast, The occupant of the lowest seat. The last throw of the dice. The end of an affair. A shoe-maker.

A اخرس akhras, (pl. خرس khurs and خرسان khursān) Dumb. (A mountain or road-side column) having no echo. Silent (army). Thick (milk) the sound not being heard (when the vessel which contains it is shaken).

P آخرسالار ākhur-sālār, Master of the horse.

A P آخرش ākhirash, At last, finally, after all.

A اخرفة akhrifat, (pl. of خروف kharūf) Lambs.

A اخرق akhrak, (pl. خرق khurk) Dull, unskilful. A camel, the sole of whose foot touches the ground before the hoof.

P آخرك ākhurak, A small stable. Collar-bone.

A اخرم akhram, Pierced in the ear, nose, &c. Verse of the measure فعولن faʻūlun reduced to عولن ʻūlun, and مفاعلتن mufāʻalatun to فاعلتن.

A اخرمان akhramāni, Two bones at the end of the upper jaw. Two bones in the shoulders.

A اخرمّاس ikhrimmās, (v. n. 4 of خرمس Q not used) Being humble, submissive.

A اخرنباق ikhrimbāk, (v. n. 3 of خربق Q) Skulking, creeping along with mischievous intent.

A اخرنطام ikhrintām, (v. n. 3 of خرطم Q) Tossing the nose, being proud. Being angry.

A اخرنفاق ikhrinfāk, (v. n. 3 of خرفق Q) Skulking. Cleaving to the ground.

A اخرنماس ikhrinmās, (or اخرمّاص) Silence.

A اخروّاط ikhriwwāt, (v. n. 13 of خرط) Being long and tedious (a journey). Being long (the beard). Holding fast the foot of a bird (a springe). Travelling quickly.

P اخروش akhrosh, A clamour, noise.

H آخروط ākhrūt, A walnut.

A آخرون ākharūn, (pl. of آخر ākhar) Others. Posterity. Those of modern times.

A اخرويّ ukhrawīy, Relating to the other world.

A اخري ukhra', (or اخرا ukhra') (fem. of آخر ākhar) (pl. اخريات ukhrayāt) Another, the last. Life eternal, the other world. اخري القوم ukhra'l kawm, The last, the hindmost of the people. في اخري الليالي fī ukhra'l layālī, (or اخري المنون ukhra'l manūn) Ever, at any time.

A اخريًّا ikhrīyan, ukhrīyan, ikhiriyan or آخريًّا ākhiriyan, At length, in the end.

A اخريات ukhrayāt, (pl. of اخري ukhra') The last parts. جاء في اخرياتهم jāʻa fī ukhrayātihim, He came amongst the last of them.

P آخريان ākhriyān, (or اخريان akhriyān) Household furniture, goods and chattels, wearing apparel. Ākhiriyān, The moderns.

T P اخريان akhriyān, An ignorant, stupid oaf.

A اخريجاج ikhrījāj, (v. n. 11 of خرج) Being of a mixed white and black (an ostrich or ram).

A اخريراق ikhrīrāk, The being much torn.

A اخريط ikhrīt, Wild leek.

A آخرين ākhirīn, (oblique pl. of آخر ākhir) Last, latest comers; posterity. آخرين حرف ākhirīn harf, Decree of fate. Termination of an affair. آخرين راعي ākhirīn rāʻī, Muhammad.

A اخزاء ikhzāʻ, (v. n. 4 of خزي) Exposing to shame or infamy.

A اخزان ikhzān, (v. n. 4 of خزن) From being poor, becoming rich. Hoarding, treasuring up.

A اخزّة akhizzat, (pl. of خزز khuzaz) Male hares.

A اخزر akhzar, Small, twinkling-eyed, purblind.

A اخزريّ akhzarīy, A turban made of silk pulled to pieces and re-woven: a shoddy turban.

A اخزل akhzal, Broken-backed. A camel that has entirely lost his bunch.

A اخزم akhzam, A male serpent. Name of the grandfather of Hātim Tayy. Short-frænumed.

A اخزواء ikhziwāʻ, (v. n. 9 of خزي) Falling into misfortune, ignominy and contempt.

A اخزي akhza', More or most ignominious.

A اخسّ akhass, More or most base, avaricious.

A اخساء ikhsāʻ, (v. n. 4 of خسو not used) Playing at odd and even with nuts.

A اخسار ikhsār, (v. n. 4 of خسر) Diminishing. Causing loss. Suffering loss. Damage, loss.

A اخساس ikhsās, (v. n. 4 of خسّ) Acting basely. Discovering one to be vile and contemptible. Diminishing, making small.

A اخساف ikhsāf, (v. n. 4 of خسف) Digging and finding a well overflowing with water. Being put out (the eye).

A اخسان ikhsān, (v. n. 4 of خسن not used) Being depressed after being exalted.

P آخسته ākhasta, The lower lintel, threshold.

A اخسر akhsar, A sufferer of loss or injury.

A اخسفة akhsifat, (pl. of خسوف khasūf) Wells dug in rocks.

P آخسمه ākhsuma, ākhsama, (or اخسمه akhsuma) A liquor made from barley, rice, or millet.

A اخسوم ukhsūm, The ear of a big corn-sack.

P اخسي akhsī, Name of a town in Transoxania.

P اخسيسك akhsīsak, (or اخسيكت akhsīkat) Name of a city in Turkistan.

P آخش ākhsh, Name of a certain Persian Mubid. Ākhash, (or اخش akhsh) Price, worth, value. آخش دادن ākhash dādan, To give a price.

A اخشاب akhshāb, (pl. of خشب) Timbers.

A اخشاش ikhshash, (v. n. 4 of خشّ) Passing a wooden ring through (a camel's) nose.

A اخشام ikhshām, (v. n. 4 of خشم) Stinking.

A اخشب akhshab, Wooden. Wooden-fronted, impudent. Harsh, hard, thick. Coarse (fare). Rough, rugged. Rugged (mountain).

A الاخشبان al akhshabāni, Name of two mountains near Mecca, and of two at Mina.

A اخشف akhshaf, (pl. خشف khushf) One who walks badly by reason of the mange.

A اخشم akhsham, Defective in the sense of smelling. Wide-nosed.

P آخشمه ākhshuma, Barley or rice-water.

A اخشن akhshan, Rugged, extremely rough. Rougher. Contemptible, blameable. A mountain. In evil case, in a bad plight. اخشن الجانب akhshanu'l jānib, Rough and unpolished in manners.

P آخشنج ākhshanj, Adverse, contrary.

P اخشنده akhshanda, A child's rattle.

A اخشي akhsha', Very fearful (place).

P آخشيج ākhshīj, (or اخشيج) Opposite, contrary.

P آخشيجان ākhshījān, (or اخشيجان akhshījān) (pl. of آخشيج ākhshīj or اخشيج akhshīj) The (four) opposites, i.e. the elements.

A اخشيشاب ikhshīshāb, (v. n. 12 of خشب) Being thick, hard, and raw-boned. Putting up with hardships, accustoming one's self to rough it.

A اخشيشان ikhshīshān, (v. n. 12 of خشن) Being extremely rough. Being clad in coarse raiment. Faring coarsely. Talking roughly.

P اخشيك akhshīk, Opposite, contrary.

P آخشيگ ākhshīg, Opposite, contrary.

P آخشيگان ākhshīgān, The elements.

A اخصّ akhass, More or most peculiar, special, particular. اخصّ الخواصّ akhassu'l khawāss, Most excellent of nobles.

A اخصاب *akhsāb*, A kind of garment. Fruitful (country). (pl. of خصب *khusb*) Sides. White mountain snakes. *Ikhsāb*, (v. n. 4 of خصب) Abounding in produce (a place), being fruitful. Going to such a place. Fattening. Flowing (sap).

A اخصاص *akhsās*, (pl. of خص *khuss*) Houses of reeds. Taverns. *Ikhsās*, (v. n. 4 of خص) Despising. Reproaching. Negligence, carelessness.

A اخصاف *ikhsāf*, (v. n. 4 of خصف) Running swiftly. Covering (the body) with leaves.

A اخصال *ikhsāl*, (v. n. 4 of خصل) Striking the mark, or shooting an arrow to fall by the side of it.

A اخصام *akhsām*, (pl. of خصم *khusm*) Corners of wallets or portmanteaus. Those parts of the eye which are covered by the edges of the eye-lids.

A اخصف *akhsaf*, Variegated, party-coloured, black and white (cattle). Ash-coloured.

A اخصن *akhsun*, (pl. of خصين) Small axes.

A اخصوم *ukhsūm*, The ear of a big corn-sack.

A اخضاب *ikhzāb*, (v. n. 4 of خضب) Budding.

A اخضاج *ikhzāj*, (v. n. 4 of خضج) Breaking up.

A اخضاد *ikhzād*, (v. n. 4 of خضد) Pulling the traveller's wallet in playfulness (a horse's colt).

A اخضار *ikhzār*, (v. n. 4 of خضر) Making green.

A اخضاع *ikhzāʿ*, (v. n. 4 of خضع) Humbling, rendering submissive (poverty or necessity). Causing to stoop (age). Speaking politely, amorously.

A اخضال *ikhzāl*, (v. n. 4 of خضل) Moistening.

A اخضد *akhzad*, Bent double.

A اخضر *akhzar*, Green. Dusky brown. Black. بحر الاخضر *bahru'l akhzar*, The green sea: under this name the Arabians comprehend all that ocean which extends from the coasts of Arabia and Ethiopia to India, and even to China. خليج الاخضر *khalīju'l akhzar*, The Persian gulf. طاوس اخضر *tāūs akhzar*, The peacock of paradise.

A اخضرار *ikhzirār*, (v. n. 9 of خضر) Being green. Assuming a green or livid hue. Being dark (the night). Being cut or broken off.

A اخضع *akhzaʿ*, One who hangs his head naturally. Buck-necked (horse or ostrich). Humble, submissive, contented in a lowly station.

A اخضف *akhzaf*, A serpent.

A اخضلال *ikhzilāl*, (v. n. 9 of خضل) Being moist. Being dark (the night).

A اخضيضاب *ikhzīzāb*, Extreme greenness.

A اخضيضار *ikhzīzār*, Extreme greenness.

A اخضيضاع *ikhzīzāʿ*, Excessive humility.

A اخضيضال *ikhzīzāl*, Exceeding moistness.

A اخضيلال *ikhzīlāl*, (v. n. 11 of خضل) Being full of branches and leaves. Being very moist.

A اخطاء *ikhtāʾ*, (v. n. 4 of خطئ) Erring, sinning involuntarily, committing a blunder, making a mistake. Missing. Imputing sin. (v. n. 4 of خطا for خطو) Causing to step.

A اخطاب *akhtāb*, Betrothed (men and women). *Ikhtāb*, (v. n. 4 of خطب) Coming within reach of the hunter (game). Ripening (grapes, gourds, &c.). Being streaked with green (a gourd).

A اخطار *akhtār*, (pl. of خطر *khitr*) Herds of camels, from 40 to 1000. *Ikhtār*, (v. n. 4 of خطر) Causing a thing to recur to the mind after having been forgotten. Recalling to mind. Exposing to danger. Staking one's property. Risking one's life in an engagement. Being equal in rank. Raising to rank and dignity.

A اخطاط *akhtāt*, (pl. of خط *khatt*) Lines. *Ikhtāt*, (v. n. 4 of خط) Having lines (the face). Beginning to have a beard (a youth). Taking possession of a place, marking it out, becoming the first occupant. Marking with lines or stripes.

A اخطاف *ikhtāf*, (v. n. 4 of خطف) Missing the mark. Being folded. Lankness of belly.

A اخطال *ikhtāl*, Obscenity in conversation.

A اخطب *akhtab*, A green magpye. A species of hawk or bird of prey which hunts sparrows. Any thing in which the russet-brown colour prevails. An ass marked with a black stripe along the back. One who repeats best the prayer called خطبة *khutba*. A colocynth marked with green stripes.

A اخطبان *akhtabān*, A kind of bird.

A اخطف *akhtaf*, Lank-bellied.

A اخطل *akhtal*, Flap-eared. Foolishly talkative. Name of several poets. ابو الاخطل *abū'l akhtal*, (Father Flap-ear) A horse. A mule.

A اخطم *akhtam*, Long-nosed. Black.

A اخطياط *ikhtiyāt*, (for اختطاء *ikhtitāʾ*) (v. n. 8 of خطا for خطو) Stepping.

A اخظاء *ikhzāʾ*, (v. n. 4 of خظا for خظو) Making stout, bulky, and fleshy. (v. n. 4 of خظي) Becoming or making fat.

A اخف *akhaff*, Lighter, lightest.

A اخفاء *ikhfāʾ*, (v. n. 4 of خفي) Concealing, hiding, suppressing. Manifesting. علم اخفا *ʿilmi ikhfā*, The art of rendering one's self invisible.

A اخفاء *akhiffāʾ*, (pl. of خفيف *khafīf*) Light.

A اخفات *ikhfāt*, (v. n. 4 of خفت) Bringing forth to the very day (a camel).

A اخفاد *ikhfād*, (v. n. 4 of خفد) Appearing pregnant (a camel). Bringing forth an imperfect colt.

A اخفار *ikhfār*, (v. n. 4 of خفر) Failing to afford protection, betraying. Breaking an engagement. Giving one a protector or guide.

A اخفاس *ikhfās*, (v. n. 4 of خفس) Talking indecently. Inebriating very soon (wine). Putting much or little water into wine.

A اخفاض *ikhfāz*, (v. n. 4 of خفض) Circumcising a girl.

A اخفاع *ikhfāʿ*, (v. n. 4 of خفع) Prostrating any one (hunger).

A اخفاف *akhfāf*, (pl. of خف *khuff*) The hoofs of a camel, feet of an ostrich. Quadrupeds which part not the hoof. (pl. of خفيف *khafīf*) Light. *Ikhfāf*, (v. n. 4 of خف) Loading lightly. Having light, nimble horses. Being in easy circumstances. Causing one to lay aside his gravity.

A اخفاق *ikhfāk*, (v. n. 4 of خفق) Dozing, nodding. Setting (a star). Flapping the wings (a bird). Returning without spoil (a warrior or hunter). Seeking and not obtaining. Being gaily dressed, or clad in shining apparel. Prostrating.

A اخفج *akhfaj*, (A camel) trembling in the limbs. One whose feet are distorted. Bow-legged.

A اخفش *akhfash*, One who has small weak eyes, seeing better at night than in the day-time. A camel whose bunch is small in front, compact, and not elongated. Name of three grammarians.

A اخفض *akhfaz*, Most depressed, lower, lowest.

A اخفى *akhfaʾ*, More or most concealed.

A اخفية *akhfiyat*, (pl. of خفاء *khifāʾ*) Veils, coverings. اخفية الكرى *akhfiyatu'l karaʾ*, The coverings of sleep, *i.e.* the eyes. اخفية النور *akhfiyatu'n nawr*, The follicles or pods which contain the young leaves of flowers.

A اخقاق *akhkāk*, (pl. of خق *khakk*) Fissures, furrows. *Ikhkāk*, (v. n. 4 of خق) Becoming wide (hole of a pulley or notch wherein a pin revolves).

A اخقوق *ukhkūk*, (or اخقيق *ikhkīk*) (pl. اخاقيق *akhākīk*) A fissure in the ground in which one may hide himself.

P اخكار *akhkār*, A fire-brand, burning coal: ashes.

P آخككند *ākhkakand*, (اخكلند *akhkaland*, or اخكلندو *akhkalandū*) A child's rattle.

P اخكل *akhkul*, Long-headed. Chaff.

P اخكلنده *akhkalanda*, A curry-comb.

P اخكم *akhkam*, Rim of a drum or sieve: a fillet.

P اخكمر *akhkamr*, The crupper of a horse.

P اخكوبه *akhkūba*, A button-hole, a loop.

P اخكور *akhkūr*, A wild pear. Unripe, sour fruit. A button-hole.

P اخكوزه *akhkūza*, (or اخكوژه *akhkūja*) A button.

P اخكوژنه *akhkūjāna*, A button.

P اخكوش *akhkūsh*, Unripe fruit.

P اخكوك *akhkūk*, An unripe apricot.

P اخكون *akhkūn*, A button-hole. A button.

P اخگر *akhgar*, Charcoal. A live coal. اخگر تفته *akhgari tafta*, Live embers. اخگر كشته *akhgari kushta*, Extinguished charcoal.

P اخگل *akhgul*, A beard of corn, a pile of barley.

A اخل *akhall*, More or most indigent. Poor, needy. *Akhull*, (pl. of خل *khull*) Vinegars.

A اخلاء *akhlāʾ*, (pl. of خلو *khilw*) Empty, vacant, idle. (pl. of خلى *khalaʾ*) Fresh and tender plants. Potherbs gathered. (pl. of خالي *khālī*) Unmarried (men or women). *Ikhlāʾ*, (v. n. 4 of خلا for خلو) Being empty, void, solitary. Being empty of food (the belly). Courting retirement. Allowing a private audience, retiring to consult together in private. Lighting upon a solitary place. Finding (a place) empty, or (a person) unemployed. Vacating, emptying. Laying waste, depopulating. Bitting (a horse). Adding fuel to the fire. (v. n. 4 of خلي) Supplying (flocks) with herbage (God). Abounding in herbage (ground).

A اخلاء *akhillāʼ*, (pl. of خليل *khalīl*) Friends (intimate and sincere).

A اخلاب النساء *akhlābu'n nisāʼ*, Beloved by women. *Ikhlāb*, (v. n. 4 of خلب) Being thick and muddy (water). Putting forth leaves (a vine).

A اخلاد *ikhlād*, (v. n. 4 of خلد) Rendering eternal. Remaining stationary in a place. Continuing steady in one's attachment. Growing old by slow degrees. Leaning, inclining.

A اخلاس *ikhlās*, (v. n. 4 of خلس) Being partly dry and partly green (herbage). Being intermingled (black and white hairs).

A اخلاص *ikhlāṣ*, (v. n. 4 of خلص) Purifying, correcting. Refining. Demonstrating sincere friendship. Yielding unfeigned obedience. Taking the purest and best part of butter. Becoming very rich (the marrow of a camel). Sincerity, piety, friendship, affection, probity, candour.

A اخلاصا *ikhlāṣan*, Sincerely, unfeignedly.

A P اخلاصمند *ikhlāṣmand*, Sincere, friendly.

A اخلاط *akhlāṭ*, A mixed crowd. (pl. of خلط *khilṭ*) Mixtures, miscellanies. Humours of the body. Seasonings. اخلاط رديه *akhlāṭi radīya*, Corrupted humours. اخلاط اربعه *akhlāṭi arbaʻa*, The four humours, elementary qualities, or complexions in man. *Ikhlāṭ* (v. n. 4 of خلط) Helping to cover. Covering. Breaking down in running (a horse).

A اخلاع *ikhlāʻ*, (v. n. 4 of خلع) Putting forth leaves, flourishing (the عضاه *ʻizāh*). Coming into ear. Finding an evergreen عضاه *ʻizāh*.

A اخلاف *akhlāf*, The teats of a camel. Successors, descendants, posterity. (pl. of خلفة *khilfat*) Opposed, contrary (as black and white, long or short). *Ikhlāf*, (v. n. 4 of خلف) Breaking a promise, disappointing. Discovering one to be a promise-breaker. Giving no rain (clouds). Repairing a garment. Restoring. Repaying, re-imbursing, making amends, compensating. Germinating afresh (a withering plant). Removing a girth from before the sheath of a camel. Drawing water. Putting the hand to the sword. Becoming offensive from long fasting (the breath). Turning (as milk or wine). Being a year under full age (a camel). Getting new feathers after moulting (a bird). Approaching the age of puberty (a lad). Weakening any one (medicine). Leading (a stallion) a second time to cover. Driving or casting back. Following.

A اخلاق *akhlāḳ*, Worn-out clothes. (pl. of خلق *khulḳ*, or *khuluḳ*) Natures, dispositions, habits, manners. اخلاق حسنه *akhlāḳi ḥasana*, Amiable manners. اخلاق جميله *akhlāḳi jamīla*, Laudable qualities. *Akhlāḳ* is a general name for books on morality: as, اخلاق العلماء *akhlāḳu'l ʻulamāʼ*, The morals of learned men; اخلاق الملوك *akhlāḳu'l mulūk*, The manners of kings; اخلاق محسني *akhlāḳi muḥsinī*, Name of a dissertation on ethics. *Ikhlāḳ*, (v. n. 4 of خلق) Wearing out, or being worn out (a garment). Putting on another a worn-out garment.

A اخلال *akhlāl*, (pl. of خلّ *khill* or *khull*) Intimate friends. *Ikhlāl*, (v. n. 4 of خلّ) Causing to want. Necessitating, constraining. Exhausting, impoverishing. Frustrating, disappointing. Deserting, abandoning. Carrying away. Keeping a fort thinly garrisoned. Bearing unripe dates (a palm). Feeding (camels) on the herb خلة *khullat*.

A اخلام *akhlām*, (pl. of خلم *khilm*) Friends.

A اخلّة *akhillat*, (pl. of خلال *khilāl*) Tooth-picks. Small needles. The coverings of sheaths or scabbards. Skewers. Rich sword-sheaths.

A اخلج *akhlaj*, A rope.

A اخلص *akhlaṣ*, More or most pure, sincere. اخلص العباد *akhlaṣu'l ʻibād*, Most faithful of servants. اخلص الفؤاد *akhlaṣu'l fuʼād*, Cordial.

A اخلف *akhlaf*, Foolish, dement, weak in intellect. (A camel) inclining to one side through a distorted shoulder. A male serpent. A current. Squint-eyed. Left-handed. Difficult, disastrous.

A اخلق *akhlaḳ*, More or most apt, fit, proper. (A stone) smooth, even, free from flaw. Poor.

P اخلور *akhlūr*, The fruit of the carob-tree.

A اخلياء *akhliyāʼ*, (pl. of خلي *khalīy*) Free from grief, pain, or care. Idle. Unmarried.

A اخليج *ikhlīj*, A swift horse. A sort of plant.

A اخليلاء *ikhlīlāʼ*, (v. n. 12 of خلي) Persevering in the habit of drinking milk.

A اخليلاق *ikhlīlāḳ*, (v. n. 12 of خلق) Being overcast (the sky), seeming disposed to rain. Being smooth (the loins of a horse). Being level with the ground (the vestiges of a house).

A اخماد *ikhmād*, (v. n. 4 of خمد) Extinguishing a fire. Being quiet. Allowing a fire to become low without being extinguished.

A اخمار *ikhmār*, (v. n. 4 of خمر) Covering, concealing, suppressing. Hiding, concealing from the sight (ground). Leavening (dough). Revolving in the mind. Giving, bestowing, putting in possession of. Entering. Lying hid. Hating. Neglecting. Abounding in wine. Hatred, rancour.

A اخماس *akhmās*, (pl. of خمس *khums* or *khumus*) Fifth parts. يضرب اخماسا لاسداس *yazribu akhmāsan li asdāsin*, He tries to accomplish his object by fraud and deceit. هما في بردة اخماس *humā fī burdati akhmāsin*, They are both very near, have united, made peace, or done a similar act, as though they were in one garment. *Ikhmās*, (v. n. 4 of خمس) Being or becoming five in number. Watering camels, or being the owner of such camels as are watered on the fifth day.

A اخماع *akhmāʻ*, (pl. of خمع) Wolves: robbers.

A اخمال *ikhmāl*, (v. n. 4 of خمل) Rendering obscure or mean. Making (velvet) plushy, or shaggy.

A اخمام *ikhmām*, (v. n. 4 of خمّ) Stinking (meat). Turning sour (milk). Sweeping (a house).

A اخمر *akhmar*, Drunk, intoxicated, crop-sick.

A اخمرة *akhmirat*, (pl. of خمار *khimār*) Veils, coifs.

A اخمساء *akhmisāʼ*, (or اخمسة *akhmisat*) (pl. of خميس *khamīs*) Thursdays, as being fifth days.

P آخمسه *ākhmusa*, (or اخمسه *akhmusa*) Barley, millet, or rice-water.

A اخمص *akhmaṣ*, The hollow part of the sole of the foot which does not touch the ground. Slender-waisted. خمصان الاخمصين *khumṣānu'l akhmaṣayn*, One who has the hollow of his feet slender.

A اخنّ *akhann*, (pl. خنّ *khunn*) One who speaks or makes a twanging noise through the nose.

A اخناء *ikhnāʼ*, (v. n. 4 of خني) Bearing hard upon any one (fortune). Traducing, defaming, talking obscenely or improperly. Ruining, destroying. Abounding with herbage (a place). Being full of eggs (a locust).

A اخناب *akhnāb*, (pl. of خنب *khinb*) The back parts of the knee-joints, the hams. Interstices of the ribs, and fingers. *Ikhnāb*, (v. n. 4 of خنب) Perishing. Destroying. Dislocating the foot. Amputating, cutting. Weakening. Being lame.

A اخناث *akhnāṡ*, (pl. of خنث *khunṡ*) Folds, plaits, wrinkles. The parts of a bucket from which the water is poured out.

A اخناس *ikhnās*, (v. n. 4 of خنس) Keeping back, hindering.

A اخناع *ikhnāʻ*, (v. n. 4 of خنع) Humbling.

A اخنان *ikhnān*, (v. n. 4 of خنّ) Making mad.

A اخنث *akhnaṡ*, More or most flexible, limber, or weak. More or most of a catamite.

A اخنجاج *ikhinjājj*, (v. n. 14 of خجّ) Going awry.

A اخنس *akhnas*, Snub-nosed. A lion. A tike.

A اخنع *akhnaʻ*, The meanest.

A اخنف *akhnaf*, Contracted on one side.

P اخنگل *akhangal*, A sword.

A اخنوخ *akhnūkh*, (or *ukhnūkh*) Enoch. Noah.

A آخنيّ *ākhinīy*, A striped garment. A coarse linen cloth.

A آخنيّة *ākhinīyat*, Bows.

A اخو *akhw*, or *akhū*, A brother. اخو الموت *akhū'l mawt*, (Brother of death) Sleep.

A اخوّ *ukhūw*, (pl. of اخ *akh*) Brothers.

A اخواء *ikhwāʼ*, (v. n. 4 of خوي) Emitting no fire (a flint). Setting (a star) without being followed by rain. Taking away the whole of one's property. Becoming exceedingly fat. Hungering.

A اخوات *akhawāt*, (pl. of اخت *ukht* originally اخوة *akhawat*) Sisters. Of the same class (as the letters و *wāw* and ي *ye* are called sisters).

P اخواستي *akhwāstī*, Unwillingness.

A اخواص *ikhwāṣ*, (v. n. 4 of خاص for خوص)

Putting forth leaves (a palm or plant عرفج ɛarfaj).

A اخواط akhwāt, (pl. of خوط khūt) Limber twigs.

A اخوال akhwāl, (pl. of خال khāl) Maternal uncles. *Ikhwāl*, (v. n. 4 of خال for خول) Possessing maternal uncles.

A اخوان ikhwān, A dinner-table, a tray. *Ikhwān* or *ukhwān*, (pl. of اخ akh) Brethren, friends, companions. اخوان الزمان *ikhwānu'z zamān*, Cotemporaries. *Akhawāni*, (dual) Two brothers.

A اخوة ikhwat or *ukhwat*, (pl. of اخ akh) Brothers. اخوته *ikhwatuhu*, His brothers.

A اخوّة ukhūwat, (v. n. of اخا for اخو) Becoming a brother. Fraternity. (pl. of اخ akh) Brothers.

A اخوث akhwas, Swag-bellied (man).

A اخوذة ukhūzat, (v. n. of اخذ) Growing sour.

P آخور ākhwur, A stable, stall. Litter or straw laid under cattle. The collar-bone. آخور خشك *ākhwuri khushk*, An empty cratch. امير آخور *amīri* (or *amīr*) *ākhwur*, The master of the horse.

P آخورسالار ākhwur-sālār, Master of the horse.

P آخورك ākhwurak, The collar-bone.

A اخوص akhwas, One whose eyes are sunk.

A اخوف akhwaf, Very alarming.

A اخوق akhwak, One-eyed. Deep. Ample, roomy. Wide extended (desert.) Scabby, mangy.

A اخول اخول akhwala akhwala, (Sparks of fire) flying about, (men) dispersed here and there.

A اخولة akhwilat, (pl. of خال) Maternal uncles.

P آخون ākwun, A theologian, preacher, orator.

A اخون akhūn, (pl. of اخ) Brothers, companions.

A اخونة akhwinat, (pl. of خوان khiwān) Tables. (pl. of خوان khawwān or *khūwān*) Third months.

P آخوند ākhwund, A tutor.

A اخويّ akhawīy, Brotherly. Sisterly.

A دم الاخوين damu'lakhawayn, Dragon's blood.

P اخي akhī, A good work. Manly, generous.

A اخي akhī, My brother.

A اخيار akhyār, (pl. of خير khayr) Those who abound in good things. (pl. of خيّر khayyir) Good, religious men. P گزيدهء اخيار *guzīda-i akhyār*, Chosen from the best; most excellent.

A اخياس akhyās, (pl. of خيس khīs) Thickets, dark groves. Haunts of lions. Places full of reeds, where animals shelter. Rays of milk streaming from the teats when milking.

A اخياش akhyāsh, (pl. of خيش khaysh) Linen cloths of a coarse and flimsy texture.

A اخياط akhyāt, (pl. of خيط khayt) Threads, strings, twines.

A اخياف akhyāf, Different kinds of men. Brothers by the same mother, but different fathers. *Ikhyāf*, (v. n. 4 of خيف not used) Visiting the temple Khayf on mount Mina.

A اخيال akhyāl, (pl. of خيل khayl) Horses. Horsemen, cavalry. *Ikhyāl*, (v. n. 4 of خال for خيل) Portending rain. Watching a cloud to see if it will rain. Putting an image resembling the human figure near a young camel to scare the wolf. Lagging behind, being timid and cowardly.

A اخيام ikhyām, (v. n. 4 of خام for خيم) Constructing, erecting, or pitching a tent or pavilion.

A اخيّان ukhayyān, Name of two mountains.

A آخية ākhiyat, or اخيّة akhīyat, (pl. اخايا akhāya' and اواخيّ awākhīy) A stake, peg, or ring with which cattle are fastened; a tether.

A اخيّة akhīyat, Protection, tutelar authority. Clientage. A tent-rope.

A اخيخة akhīkhat, A kind of pottage made of flour, with butter or oil.

P اخيدن akhīdan, To arrive, reach, overtake.

A اخيذ akhīz, Taken. A captive. An aged foreigner.

P آخير ākhīr, The foundation of a house. Cement, plaster. The incrustation of a wall. An unburnt brick. A land-mark.

A اخير akhyar, Better, best. *Akhīr*, Posterior, last. Last mentioned. Absent.

A اخيرًا akhīran, At length, in fine.

G اخيروس akhīros, (or اخيروسه) Wild wheat.

A اخيري ukhayra', (dim. of اخري) Another.

P اخيريدن akhīrīdan, To draw a sword.

P آخيز ākhīz, Cement, plaster of a wall.

P آخيزگر ākhīzgar, A plasterer.

A اخيس akhyas, (عدد اخيس) A great number.

P آخيسه ākhīsa, A ram leading the flock. A march-stone, a land-mark. Defective, imperfect.

A اخيشن ukhayshin, (dim. of اخشن) Roughish.

A اخيص akhyas, (A ram) which has one horn broken. One who has one eye larger than the other.

A اخيضر ukhayzir, A kind of fly. Ophthalmia.

A اخيف akhyaf, Wall-eyed (man or horse).

A اخيل akhyal, Vainer, vainest, prouder, proudest. One who has many moles (on the face). (pl. خيل khīl) A green magpye. A black and white bird called صرد surad. Name of a tribe. Arrogance, pride. بنو الاخيل *banū'l akhyal*, Name of the tribe whence sprang Layla.

A اخيلة akhyilat, (pl. of خيال khayāl) Phantoms, spectres, apparitions.

G اخينوس akhīnos, Wild wheat.

G اخيون akhyūn, Snake's-head (a plant).

P آخيه ākhya, A ram, the leader of the flock. Praise. Spittle. Limit, boundary, hedge, inclosure.

A آد ād, Strength, power, vigour. Victory.

P آداد ād, as آد گردانا ād gardānād, May he make become.

A ادّ add, (v. n. of ادّ) Yearning towards her foal in a plaintive tone (a camel). Stretching, extending. Taking by surprise, overpowering (as an unexpected misfortune). Making a noise in his belly (a camel). Wandering, straying. Power, strength, victory. An unlawful action. *Idd*, (pl. آداد *adād*) Misfortune, sorrow, great danger. An arduous, difficult affair; any great and momentous business. A marvellous thing. A profane or unlawful action. Power, strength, vigour, victory. *Udd*, Name of the father of an ancient Arabian tribe.

A ادا adā', (for أدو adawa) (fut. يأدو ya-dū) He assisted, he strengthened. He became strong. (The fruit) ripened. He armed himself well. He prepared for a journey. He lay in ambush.

P ادا adā, Blandishment. Eloquence, voice, expression, song, music, odes. بلبل نازك ادا *bulbuli nazik-adā*, The nightingale with the melodious voice. نواي مرغان خوش ادا *nawā-i murghāni khwush-adā*, The melody of birds with sweet notes. حسن ادا *hasan-adā*, Just expression or pronunciation. تعبيرات سنجيدهء ادا *taɛbīrāti sanjīda-adā*, Well-weighed, judicious interpretations. ادا كردن *adā kardan*, To pronounce, express, sing, warble.

A اداء adā-, Payment, satisfaction, performance.

P ادا كردن adā kardan, To pay, satisfy, liquidate, discharge. To perform, execute, accomplish. To assist. To bring to perfection. To prepare for a journey. To lie in wait. اداي دين كردن *adā-i dayn kardan*, To make payment of debts. اداي سفر كردن *adā-i safar kardan*, To perform military duty, to make a campaign, to discharge that vassalage which a military tenant owes to his lord. A *Idā-*, The stopple of a leathern bottle.

A ادارة idā-at, (v. n. 4 of دأّ for دوأ) Falling sick. Afflicting with sickness. Suspecting, doubting.

A آداب ādāb, (pl. of ادب adab) Civilities, good manners, devoirs, ceremonies, politeness. Forms of address in writing and speaking, salutations, respects. Many books, particularly of morality and science, have the title of آداب *ādāb*: as, آداب العرب و الفرس *ādābu'l ɛarab wa'l fars*, The manners of the Arabians and Persians; آداب الغرباء *ādābu'l ghurabā-*, The duties of travellers, or the manner in which those who travel to, or reside in, foreign countries ought to conduct themselves; آداب القاضي *ādābu'l kāzī*, The duties of a judge; آداب الكاتب *ādābu'l kātib*, The duties of a secretary; آداب الملوك *ādābu'l mulūk*, The manners of princes, &c.; آداب فضلا في لغات *ādābi fuzalā fī lughāt*, Name of a Persian Dictionary, explained in Arabic and Hindi, by Kāzī Mahmūd bin dahlawīy, a native of Delhi, who died ann. 1420. اصحاب آداب *as-hābi ādāb*, Well-bred, learned men. آداب سنّت *ādābi sunnat*, The minor duties of life. P آدابگاه *ādāb-gāh*, The place of obeisance in the palace of a chief.

A ادآب id-āb, (v. n. 4 of دأب) Causing to toil.

A ادابة adābat, (v. n. of ادب) Being courteous, well-bred, polite or learned.

A ادابر udābir, One who turns his back upon his kindred, who listens to, or cares for nobody.

P ادابند adā-band, A describer of blandishments.

P ادابندي adā-bandī, Description of blandishments. The fixing a period for the performance of a contract, or payment of instalments.

A اداة *adāt*, (pl. ادوات *adawāt*,) An instrument, tool, utensil, apparatus; whatever is necessary in the forming or completing of any thing. (In gram.) An accessory particle: as, اداة التعريف *adātu't taȩrīf*, The definite article (ال *al*). اداة الجزا *adātu'l jazā*, An illative or conclusive particle, prefixed to nouns or verbs: as, فـ *fe*, Then, therefore; ادات توصّل *adāti tawassul*, A conjunctive particle; ادات جمع *adāti jamȩ*, A particle added to form the plural from the singular number; ادات فاعل *adāti fāȩil*, A particle supplementary to nouns or participles in forming names of agents, similar to *er* in English: as, كارگر *kārgar*, A labourer, from كار *kār*, Labour; ادات ندا *adāti nidā*, A vocative particle; ادات نسبت *adāti nisbat*, A particle of relation or possession, which, when added to a substantive, implies the being endowed with any quality: as, آرزومند *ārzūmand*, Desirous, from آرزو *ārzū*, Desire.

A آداد *ādād*, (pl. of ادّ *idd*) Misfortunes, dangers.

A ادادا *adādā*, A species of mezereon.

A ادادة *idādat*, (v. n. 4 of داد for دود) Breeding worms (meat or bread).

A ادار *adār*, The Syrian month of March.

G اداراقي *adārāki*, A kind of Indian medicine, of an acrid and poisonous quality, dog's bane.

A ادارة *idārat*, (v. n. 4 of دار for دور) Turning round, going in a circle. Being subject to a giddiness in the head. Causing to revolve. Turning (one) towards, or turning (him) off from. P ادارۂ جام حمام *idārasi jāmi himām*, A handing round, or pushing about, of the deathful cup.

P ادارين *adārīn*, (in zand and Pāzand) Hideous. Wicked, bad.

P آداش *ādāsh*, Of the same name as another.

A اداف *udāf*, Membrum virile. The ear.

P ادا فهم *adā-fahm*, Understanding by signs.

A اداقة *idākat*, (v. n. 4 of داق for دوق) Surrounding, enclosing.

P اداك *adāk*, (or آداك) An island. A ford.

A ادالة *idālat*, (v. n. 4 of دال for دول) Aiding, making superior, giving the victory. Superiority.

A آدام *ādām*, (pl. of ادام *idām*, and of اديم *adīm*, q. v.) (pl. of ادم *udm*) Condiments eaten with bread.

P ادام *adām*, The celestial globe.

A ادام *idām*, (pl. آدمة *ādimat* and آدام *ādām*) Whatever is eaten with bread. Conformable, congruous. A chief, leader, model. Name of a woman; and of a well a day's journey from Mecca. *Adāma*, (in prayer) May (God) prolong.

A ادّام *addām*, A tanner, currier. A vender of Morocco leather.

A ادامة *idāmat*, (v. n. 4 of دام for دوم) Perpetuating. Keeping (a pot) on the trivet. Filling (a bucket). Trying (an arrow) upon the thumb. Stilling a boiling kettle.

A ادانة *idānat*, (v. n. 4 of دان for دون) Being weak, infirm, base, and despicable. (v. n. 4 of دان for دين) Lending, giving credit to a fixed period. Buying or selling on credit. Running in debt. Compensating.

P ادانوش *adānosh*, Name of a messenger whose eyes were torn out by عذرا *ȩazrā*.

A اداني *adānī*, (pl. of ادنى *adna'*) Nearer, nearest.

A اداوات *adāwāt*, (pl. of اداة *adāt*) Instruments, implements, utensils.

A اداوة *idāwat*, (pl. اداوي *adāwa'*) An ewer or vessel, from which the Muhammadans pour water, for washing the hands, &c.

A اداوي *adāwa'*, (pl. of اداوة *idāwat*) Ewers.

A اداهم *adāhim*, (pl. of ادهم *adham*) Fetters. Black horses.

A آدب *ādib*, (pl. ادبة *adabat*) One who invites to an entertainment. The master of a feast.

A ادب *adb*, (v. n. of ادب) Inviting to an entertainment. Any thing stupendous or wonderful. Wonder, astonishment. *Adab*, (v. n. of ادب) Being courteous, polite, well-bred. Making a feast. Being abundant (water in the sea). Courtesy, politeness, urbanity, good-breeding, respect, reverence. Propriety of conduct. Learning, morality, sound doctrine. The science of polite learning, classed under twelve heads: 1. لغة *lughat*, Words; 2. صرف *sarf*, Declension; 3. اشتقاق *ishtikāk*, Derivation; 4. نحو *nahw*, Grammar; 5. معاني *maȩānī*, Sense, meaning; 6. بيان *bayān*, Eloquence; 7. عروض *ȩarūz*, Prosody; 8. قافية *kāfiyat*, Rhyme; 9. رسم الخط *rasmu'l khatt*, Calligraphy; 10. قرض الشعر *karzu'sh shiȩr*, Versification; 11. انشاي نثر از خطب و رسائل *inshāi nasr az khatb u rasāil*, Epistolary composition; 12. محاضرات *muhāzarāt*, Dialectics. ادب البحر *adabu'l bahr*, Abundance of water in the sea. P ادب دادن *adab dādan*, To correct, civilize, teach. To chastise, correct. ادب كردن *adab kardan*, To behave modestly, properly, or honestly. ترك ادب *tarki adab*, Rudeness, incivility. ترك ادب كردن *tarki adab kardan*, To offend against good manners; to be boorish, rude, unpolished.

A ادبّ *adabb*, One who has little hair on the face. Hairy (camel).

A ادباء *idbāȩ*, (v. n. 4 of دبي) Putting forth buds resembling locusts (the plant عرفج *ȩarfaj*). *Udabāȩ*, (pl. of اديب) Well-bred, polite, learned.

A ادباب *adbāb*, (pl. of دبّ *dubb*) Bears. *Idbāb*, (v. n. 4 of دبّ) Causing to creep. Administering justice in a province.

A ادبار *adbār*, (pl. of دبر *dubr*) The hinder or latter parts of any thing, of the back, neck, &c. Those who come last, the rear. (pl. of دبرة *dabarat*) Ulcers, galled places on the backs of cattle. في ادبار الشهر *fī adbāri'sh shahr*, At the close of the month. *Idbār*, (v. n. 4 of دبر) Turning back. Committing sodomy. Neglecting, slighting the interests of a friend. Waxing rich. Dying. Drawing out a thread in spinning. Turning back (the part of the ear called فتلة *fatlat*). Travelling on Wednesday. Going off, diminishing (the milk of a camel). Galling a horse's back (a saddle). Having a galled back (a horse or camel). Exposing to the west wind. Blowing from the west (wind). Understanding, discriminating. Reverse of fortune.

A ادبارًا *idbāran*, Finally, in the end.

A ادبارة *idbārat*, The slit part of the ears turned towards the hinder part of the head. A bit of leather tied to a sheep's ear.

A ادباس *idbās*, (v. n. 4 of دبس) Putting forth grass (the ground.)

A ادباق *idbāk*, (v. n. 4 of دبق) Glueing together, causing to stick close. Bird-liming.

P ادب آموز كردن *adab-āmoz kardan*, To exalt to high rank. To render illustrious.

P ادبانه *adabāna*, With reverence, with respect; civilly, politely, courteously. Wisely, learnedly.

P ادب آوازه *adab-āwāza*, Loud, clear-voiced.

A ادبب *adbab*, Hairy (camel).

A ادبة *udbat*, An entertainment to which one is invited. Wonder, astonishment. Any thing wonderful. *Adabat*, (pl. of آدب *ādib*) Those who invite to entertainments, masters of feasts.

P ادبخانه *adab-khāna*, A water-closet. A school.

A ادبر *adbar*, Ulcerated, galled in the back. *Adbur*, (pl. of دبر *dibr*) Swarms of bees or hornets.

A ادبس *adbas*, Chesnut-coloured (horse). (A bird) of a blackish red.

A ادبساس *idbisās*, (v. n. 9 of دبس) Being of a dark colour (a horse).

A ادبيّ *adabīy*, Polite. Learned.

A ادبيّات *adabīyāt*, (fem. pl.) Relating to humanity, politeness, or learning. Accomplishments.

A ادبير *adbīr*, A species of serpent.

A ادّة *iddat*, (pl. ادد *idad*) Adversity. Grief. Astonishment. A wonderful, difficult, wicked thing. داهية ادّة *dāhiyat iddat*, A great misfortune.

A ادّثار *iddisār*, (v. n. 8 of دثر) Acquiring influence. Acquiring much property.

A ادثر *adsar*, Perishing. Careless, forgetful.

A ادجاء *idjāȩ*, Darkness (of the night).

A ادجان *adjān*, (pl. of دجن *dajn*) Cloudy, rainy (nights or days). *Idjān*, (v. n. 4 of دجن) Continuing, remaining (rain or fever). Being dark and cloudy (day). Entering into clouds and darkness. Raining incessantly. Abiding in one place.

A ادجن *adjan*, Of an ugly black colour.

A ادجيجاء *idjījāȩ*, (v. n. 12 of دجي) Being dark and cloudy (the day).

A ادجيجان *idjījān*, (v. n. 12 of دجن) Being dark and cloudy (the day).

A ادحاض *idhāz*, (v. n. 4 of دحض) Dismissing a suit. Abolishing.

A ادحاق *idhāk*, (v. n. 4 of دحق) Driving away.

A ادحال adhāl, (or ادحل adhul) (pl. of دحل dahl) Caverns in the earth, narrow at top and wide at bottom, where people may walk. Cavities in the channels of rivers, or the bottoms of wells. Openings in the sides of the Arabian tents, through which the women retire when any man enters. Idhāl, (v. n. 4 of دحل) Descending into a cavern as described above, and remaining concealed there.

A ادحواء idhiwāʼ, A being spread out.

A ادحوّة udhūvat, (ادحيّة udhīyat, ادحيّ udhiy or idhīy) (pl. ادحية adhiyat) The place where the ostrich lays her eggs.

A ادحيّ udhiy or idhiy, Name of a lunar mansion.

P آدخ ādakh, Good, elegant. Auspicious, happy. Height, exaltation.

A ادخار idkhār, (v. n. 4 of دخر) Rendering vile, pitiful, or contemptible.

A ادّخار iddikhār, (v. n. 8 of ذخر) Hoarding.

A ادخال idkhāl, (v. n. 4 of دخل) Causing to enter. Introducing, inserting, thrusting or putting in.

A ادّخال iddikhāl, (v. n. 8 of دخل) Entering.

A ادخان idkhān, (v. n. 4 of دخن) Emitting smoke. Becoming hard (grain).

A ادّخان iddikhān, (v. n. 8 of دخن) Smoking.

A ادخل adkhal, More or most inner or intimate.

A ادخن adkhan, Dirty, smoky coloured (sheep).

A ادخنة adkhinat, (pl. of دخان) Smokes.

A ادد idad, (pl. of ادّة iddat) Adversities, misfortunes. Wonderful things. Udad and udud, Name of the father of a tribe in Arabia Felix.

A اددّيّ udadiy, Belonging to the tribe of ادد.

P آدر ādar, Fire. Ādir, A lancet, a fleam.

A آدر ādar, (pl. ادر udr) Afflicted with rupture, or swelled testicle. Ādur, (pl. of دار) Houses.

A أدر adira, (fut. يأدر yaʼdiru) He was ruptured.

A ادر udr, (pl. of آدر ādar) Ruptured. Adar, (v. n. of ادر) Being ruptured. Rupture.

A ادرّ adarr, One who has oblong, ruptured, or swelled testicles.

A ادراء adrāʼ, Swelled (testicle). Idrāʼ, (v. n. 4 of درأ) Letting her milk flow after colting (a camel). (v. n. 4 of دري) Teaching, instructing. Decoying, lying in wait for game. Scratching the head with a pin or comb called مدري midraʼ.

A ادّراء iddirāʼ, (v. n. 8 of درأ) Lying in wait for game (a hunter). (v. n. 8 of دري) Combing, parting the hair. Attacking, assaulting. Deceiving.

A ادّراب iddirāb, (v. n. 8 of درب) Advancing into an enemy's country from روم rūm.

A ادراج adrāj, (pl. of درج durj) Spindle-cases. رجع ادراجه rajaʻa adrājahu or idrājahu, He returned by the way he came. ذهب دمه ادراج الرياح zahaba damuhu adrājaʼr riyāh, His blood was shed with impunity. Idrāj, (v. n. 4 of درج) Exceeding a year and not bringing forth (a camel). Folding (a letter). Tying a camel's teats. Drawing up a bucket easily.

P ادرار idrār, A pension, a stipend.

A ادرار idrār, (v. n. 4 of درّ) Agitating, moving, whirling round (a spindle), giving it a rotatory motion so rapid that it appears stationary. Turning (an arrow) on the nail to try its goodness. Provoking urine. Sending forth (milk) copiously. Putting in motion. Driving, propelling (as the wind does a cloud). Giving liberally and continually.

A ادرارات idrārāt, Pensions.

P ادراري idrārī, A pension. A dishful.

A ادراس adrās, (pl. of درس dirs) Tattered garments. ابو ادراس abū adrās, Vulva. Idrās, (v. n. 4 of درس) Studying. Saying a lesson.

A ادّراس iddirās, (v. n. 8 of درس) Studying.

A ادراص adrās, (pl. of درص dirs) The fœtuses of mice, moles, hares, or cats. ابو ادراص abū adrās, A fool. امّ ادراص umm adrās, A misfortune.

A ادراع adrāʻ, (pl. of درع dirʻ) Coats of mail. Cuirasses of iron or leather. Women's shifts. Idrāʻ, (v. n. 4 of درع) Having the pasturage round a watering-place eaten bare. Passing over, getting through (half a month). Inserting one thing into another. Running (a shoe-latchet) into the hand.

A ادّراع iddirāʻ, (v. n. 8 of درع) Putting on a cuirass, shift, or smicket. Travelling in the dark.

G ادرافيس idrāfīs, Froth of the sea.

A ادراق adrāk, (pl. of درقة) Shields of leather.

A ادراك adrāk, (pl. of درك dark) Punishments. Lowest pits of hell. Idrāk, (v. n. 4 of درك) Overtaking, attaining, reaching. Living long enough to be contemporary with. Arriving at manhood. Coming to maturity. Coming to an end, being finished, or reduced to nothing, vanishing. Comprehension, apprehension, understanding, perception, intelligence, intellect, capacity, genius. Attainment. Maturity. ادراكات صادقة idrākāti sādika, True, just conceptions.

P ادرام adrām, (or اذرام) A packing-needle.

A ادرام idrām, (v. n. 4 of درم) Changing the teeth. Losing his milk-teeth and breeding others (a boy). Producing a red-leafed plant (the earth).

A ادران idrān, (v. n. 4 of درن) Being dirty (a garment). Dirtying. Eating withered herbs.

A ادرة adarat or udrat, Rupture: swelled testicle.

A ادرجّة udrujjat, The step of a ladder.

P آدرخش ādrakhsh, Lightning, thunder. Cold.

A ادرد adrad, Toothless, or whose teeth are worn to the stump.

P آدرشاخ ādarshākh, A pickle.

A ادرص adrus, (pl. of درص dars or dirs) Young mice, moles, hares, or porcupines.

A ادرع adraʻ, Black-headed and white-bodied (animal). (A horse) of a bad breed. Adruʻ, (pl. of درع dirʻ) Coats of mail.

A ادرعباب idriʻbāb, See ادرعفاف idriʻfāf.

A ادرعشاش idriʻshāsh, (v. n. 4 of درعش Q) Recovering from sickness, being convalescent.

A ادرعفاف idriʻfāf, (v. n. 4 of درعف Q) Going fast with their faces near the ground (camels). Quitting the ranks before a battle.

P ادرفن adarfan, Itch, scab, ringworm.

P ادرك adark, A swinging cot; swing for children. Adrak, Moist ginger. Idrik, A small plum.

P آدرم ādram, A saddle-cloth. Arms, such as swords, daggers, bows and arrows. A large needle.

P ادرم adram, A saddle-cloth.

A ادرم adram, Fleshy on arms, ancles, or thighs. Even, level. Thick, large (hough). Toothless.

A ادرمجاج idrimjāj, (v. n. 4 of درمج Q) Entering without leave. Creeping in clandestinely. Entering and sticking fast.

P ادرمكش adram-kash, A packing-needle.

P ادرمه adrama, A saddle-cloth of coarse wool.

A ادرنفاق idrinfāk, (v. n. 3 of درفق Q) Walking quickly. Going before.

A ادرنقاع idrinkāʻ, (v. n. 3 of درقع Q) Fleeing, escaping from difficulties.

P آدرنگ ādrang, (or ادرنگ adrang) Grief, sorrow, distress, ennui. A heavy calamity.

T ادرنه adrana, Adrianople.

A ادرون idrawn, A manger, crib, stall.

P ادره udra, The crest of a helmet.

A ادرهمام idrihmām, (v. n. 4 of درهم Q) Being aged. Failing (the sight).

A ادري adraʼ, More knowing, better informed.

A ادريس idrīs, The Arabian name for اخنوخ akhnūkh, Enoch. ابو ادريس abū idrīs, Penis.

P ادريس خانه idrīs-khāna, Heaven.

A ادريون adriyūn, Name of a flower.

P ادس adas, Name of a grain.

A ادساف idsāf, (v. n. 4 of دسف not used) Living by panderism, pimping.

A ادساق idsāk, (v. n. 4 of دسق) Filling.

A ادسام idsām, (v. n. 4 of دسم) Corking.

A ادسق adsak, Large-mouthed.

A ادسم adsam, Ash-coloured.

P آدش ādish, Fire.

A ادّعاء iddiʻāʼ, (v. n. 8 of دعا for دعو) Demanding one's right. Assuming, boasting (of family or courage). Pretending to, claiming (whether falsely or truly). Causing one to be called after one who is not his own father. Announcing one's self before a rival in battle. Race, stock, lineage.

A ادعاث adʻās, (pl. of دعث diʻs) Hatreds. Idʻās, (v. n. 4 of دعث) Being far advanced on a journey. Confirming, perpetuating. Stealing. Leaving a remnant. Choosing.

A ادعاص adʻās, (pl. of دعص diʻs, or daʻs) Sand-hillocks. Idʻās, (v. n. 4 of دعص) Killing.

A ادعاق idʻāk, (v. n. 4 of دعق) Urging (a horse) to his full speed. A mode of running.

A ادّعام iddiʻām, (v. n. 8 of دعم) Leaning on a prop, reclining, supporting one's self.

A ادعب adʻab, Foolish. A fool.

A ادعج *adʿaj*, Black. Black-eyed (man).

A ادعر *adʿar*, A steel (literally زند *zand*, A kind of wood) which emits no fire when rubbed.

A ادعم *adʿam*, White on the breast (a horse).

A ما ادعنه *mā adʿanahu*, How impudent he is!

A ادعنة *idʿannat*, A pudendum large and thick.

A ادعنكار *idʿinkār*, (v. n. 3 of دعكر Q) Acting shamefully and oppressively. Rushing on rapidly.

A ادعوة *udʿūwat*, (or ادعية *udʿiyat*) An enigma, riddle, any thing that one strives hard to know.

A ادعياء *adʿiyāʾ*, Adopted sons. Bastards.

A ادعية *adʿiyat*, (pl. of دعاء *duʿāʾ*) Salutations, congratulations, compliments, wishes, prayers, blessings. Invitations.

A ادعية *udʿiyat*, A riddle, an enigma.

A ادّغار *iddighār*, A cutting of the front teeth.

A ادغاش *idghāsh*, (v. n. 4 of دغش) Entering into the darkness of night.

A ادغاص *idghāṣ*, (v. n. 4 of دغص) Filling, inflaming with rage. Preparing for battle, descending into the arena.

A ادغال *adghāl*, (pl. of دغل *daghal*) Corruptions, taints, blemishes. Thick forests, trees, or luxuriant herbage, where the branches and fibres are interwoven and entangled. Ambushes. *Idghāl*, (v. n. 4 of دغل) Lying in ambush, deceiving. Laying an information. Marring, spoiling. Producing trees thickly entangled together (the earth). Assaulting, attacking suddenly.

A ادغام *idghām*, (v. n. 4 of دغم) Making black in the face. Enfeebling, benumbing (heat or cold). Swallowing (food) unmasticated, eating in a hurry lest others should get the start. Putting the bit in a horse's mouth. Inserting one letter into another: coalescence: as, عدّان *ʿiddān*, for عتدان *ʿitdān*.

A ادّغام *iddighām*, Coalescence of two letters.

P آدغر *ādghar*, A summer-house.

P ادغر *adghar*, A vent-hole.

A ادغم *adgham*, (Horse or sheep) black about the head and lips. Ash-coloured. Black-muzzled. Black-nosed. One who speaks through his nose.

A ادغيمام *idghīmām*, (v. n. 11 of دغم) Having the face and lips blackish, the rest white (a horse).

P ادف *adaf*, (or ادفر) A nephew by the brother.

A ادفأ *adfaʾ*, Clad in warm raiment (a man). Warmer. One who lives in a warm tent.

A ادفاء *adfāʾ*, (pl. of دفأ *difʾ*) Warm clothings of wool or camel's hair. *Idfāʾ*, (v. n. 4 of دفئ) Warming. Clothing in warm raiment. Giving bountifully. Coming together. (v. n. 4 of دفي) Despatching (a wounded man). Having long horns.

A ادّفاء *iddifāʾ*, (v. n. 8 of دفئ) Putting on warm clothing. Drawing near the fire.

A ادفاع *idfāʿ*, (v. n. 4 of دفع) Driving violently, pushing hard, thrusting away.

A ادفاف *idfāf*, (v. n. 4 of دفّ) Following in succession. Fluttering, moving the wings and feet.

A ادفاق *idfāk*, (v. n. 4 of دفق) Shedding at once (the contents of a jug).

A ادفان *adfān*, (pl. of دفين) Covered, buried.

A ادّفان *iddifān*, (v. n. 8 of دفن) Running away and hiding himself (a slave), lest he should be sold. Being buried. Hiding under ground, burying.

A ادفر *adfar*, Stinking, filthy, rusty (arms).

A ادفساس *idfisās*, (v. n. 9 of دفس not used) Having a black face.

A ادفع *adfaʿ*, More or most repellent, most skilful in parrying, removing, or carrying off.

A ادفق *adfak*, Swift. Crooked. Bent double with age or grief. (A camel) whose teeth project; also one whose elbows are wide apart from his sides. Clear and upright, not inclined either way (new moon). Swift (march).

A ادفوة *udfuwat*, or *adfuwat*, Name of a village near Alexandria; also of a place in Upper Egypt.

A ادفوي *udfawīy*, Native of Udfuwat.

A ادفي *adfaʾ*, Long-horned (goat). Long-winged (bird). Crooked, decrepit.

A ادفية *udfiyat*, Name of a mountain in Arabia.

A ادقّ *adakk*, More or most subtile, minute, slender, thin, abstruse.

A ادقاق *idkāk*, (v. n. 4 of دقّ) Pounding, pulverizing: attenuating: making thin, slender and fine. Speaking abstrusely. Giving little. Giving a sheep.

A ادقال *idkāl*, (v. n. 4 of دقل) Bearing dates of a bad kind (a palm). Being lean and small-boned (a sheep).

P ادقچه *adakcha*, A cover, wrapper.

A ادقع *adkaʿ*, Keen (hunger). Earth, dust.

A ادقم *adkam*, One who has three teeth broken.

P آدك *ādak*, An island.

P ادك *aduk*, Pudenda fœminæ.

A ادكّ *adakk*, (pl. دكّ *dukk*) Broad-backed (horse). Bunchless (camel).

A ادكاس *idkās*, (v. n. 4 of دكس) Producing herbage (ground).

A ادكل *adkal*, Blackish (stone).

A ادكن *adkan*, Inclining to black.

P ادگر *adgar*, Measure. Comparison. Conjecture.

A ادل *adl*, (v. n. of ادل) Becoming healed (a wound). Churning (milk), stirring (it) up. Going with short steps (one over-loaded). *Idl*, A pain in the neck. Milk thick and sourish (proper for making butter). Any thing heavy and oppressive.

A ادلاء *idlāʾ*, (v. n. 4 of دلا for دلو) Throwing, sending, or letting down, dropping. Letting a bucket into a well. Preparing either to stale or cover (a horse). Forming or seeking an intimate alliance on the score of relationship. Offering a bribe to a judge. Giving money. Pleading in a court of justice. Adducing proof or argument. Speaking evil of another.

A ادلاث *idlās*, (v. n. 4 of دلث) Covering.

A ادلاج *idlāj*, A departing at nightfall.

A ادّلاج *iddilāj*, (v. n. 8 of دلج) Travelling during the last watch of the night.

A ادلاس *adlās*, (pl. of دلس *dalas*) Grass growing at the end of summer. *Idlās*, (v. n. 4 of دلس) Finding such grass. Being green with such grass.

A ادلاع *idlāʿ*, (v. n. 4 of دلع) Lolling the tongue. Sticking out the belly.

A ادّلاع *iddilāʿ* (v. n. 8 of دلع) Dangling, being lolled (the tongue).

A ادلاف *idlāf*, Speaking harshly.

A ادلاق *idlāk*, (v. n. 4 of دلق) Drawing (a sword), bringing out. Chattering with cold (teeth).

A ادّلاك *iddilāk*, A rubbing between the fingers.

A ادلال *idlāl*, (v. n. 4 of دلّ) Looking askance as lovers. Confiding, relying. Being mangy and lean (a wolf). Being bold, impudent, free and easy. Going beyond bounds (in love). Coming down (on an enemy): pouncing on his prey (a hawk.

A ادلة *idlat*, Milk thick and sourish.

A ادلّة *adillat*, (pl. of دليل *dalīl*) Arguments, reasons, proofs, evidences, indications. Guides. Road-guides. ادلّة واضحة *adillat wāzihat*, Clear proofs. ادلّة شرعيّة *adillat sharʿiyat*, Legal, judicial proofs; evidences before a court of justice.

A ادلص *adlas*, (An ass) getting a new coat. Bald. A man who stumbles much.

A ادلصيّ *adlasīy*, An ass getting a new coat.

A ادلعيّ *adlaʿīy*, Penis crassus et longus.

A ادلغفاف *idlighfāf*, (v. n. 4 of دلغف Q not in use) Sneaking with intent to steal.

A ادلم *adlam*, Swarthy (man, mountain, or ass). Black leather. Dusky. A lion.

A ادلمساس *idlimsās*, (v. n. 4 of دلمس Q) Being very dark (night).

A ادلنظاء *idlinzāʾ*, (v. n. 3 of دلظي Q) Passing rapidly by. Being fat.

A ادلهمام *idlihmām* (v. n. 4 of دلهم Q) Being very dark. Becoming aged.

A ادلهنان *idlihnān*, Becoming aged.

A ادلي *adlī*, (pl. of دلو *dalw*) Buckets, urns.

A ادليساس *idlīsās*, (v. n. 11 of دلس) Getting little grass off the land (camels).

A ادليلاء *idlīlāʾ*, (v. n. 12 of دلي) Going quickly.

A ادليمام *idlīmām*, (v. n. 11 of دلم) Being black. Being very dark (the night).

A آدم *ādam*, (pl. ادم *udm*, ادمان *udmān*, and اوادم *awādim*) Brown, dusky, tawny, mulatto. Adam, the father of the human race. White and at the same time hairy (camel). One who has the pupils of the eyes varied, black and white. Name of a reporter of traditions. بني آدم *banī ādam*, The sons of Adam, *i.e.* mankind. آدم الثاني *ādamu's sānī*, The second Adam, *i.e.* Noah.

A ادم *adm*, (v. n. of ادم) Adding one thing to another (as bread to meat); uniting in love or friendship. Becoming a chief, leader, or pattern. An example, model, chief, leader. *Udm*, (pl. آدام

ādam) Any thing eaten with bread (as meat, fish, salt, or vinegar). (pl. of آدم *ādam*) Brown, dusky. White with ash-coloured stripes. Skins. *Adam*, Man, mankind, Adam and his posterity. A tomb. A kind of date. Names of several places in Arabia, and often put for Yaman itself. *Adam* or *udum*, (pl. of اديم *adīm*) Dressed skins (of goats).

P ادم *adam*, A ruby.

A ادماء *admā*, (fem. of آدم *ādam*) Brown. White with ash-coloured stripes (a doe). White (she-camel). *Idmā*, (v. n. 4 of دمي) Making bleed.

A ادمات *adamāt*, (pl. of ادمة *adamat*) Skins.

A ادماج *idmāj*, (v. n. 4 of دمج) Wrapping one's self in a garment.

A ادّماج *iddimāj*, The being firmly inserted.

A ادماع *idmāꜥ*, (v. n. 4 of دمع) Filling (a cup) to overflowing, causing (it) as it were to shed tears.

A ادماغ *idmāgh*, (v. n. 4 of دمغ) Necessitating.

A ادماق *idmāk*, (v. n. 4 of دمق) Inserting.

A ادمال *idmāl*, (v. n. 4 of دمل) Cicatrizing.

A ادمام *idmām*, (v. n. 4 of دمّ) Acting shamefully. Begetting ugly children.

A آدمان *ādamān*, (Pers. pl. of آدم *ādam*) Men.

A ادمان *admān*, A tree which becomes green after having withered in the summer. A disease in a palm-tree. *Idmān*, (v. n. 4 of دمن) Persevering in, keeping long at, constantly doing. Keeping up a continual practice. Perpetuating. *Udmān*, (A buck or doe) of a white colour. (pl. of آدم *ādam*) Brown, dusky. *Adamān*, Rottenness and blackness of a palm-tree. The corruption of the palm-tree. Name of a tree in Paradise.

A ادمانة *admānat*, Brown, dusky (woman).

P آدم پيرا *ādam-perā*, Creator of man, *i. e.* God.

A آدمة *ādimat*, (pl. of ادام *idām*) Meats, seasonings. (pl. of اديم *adīm*) Skins, goats' leathers.

A ادمة *admat* or *adamat*, A chief, a general, a leader, model, exemplar, pattern. *Udmat*, (v. n. of ادم) Being of a brown colour. Brownness, duskiness. A clear shining white with blackness of the eye (in camels). White mixed with black, or any other colour (in deer). *Udmat* or *adamat*, Conjunction, or that which causes it, that which passes between, and unites two bodies; union, mixture, propinquity, affinity. *Adamat*, The inner skin, thin skin, cuticle, or membrane, which covers the flesh or intestines. The outside of the skin. The skin of the head. The inside of the ground.

P آدم خور *ādam-khwur*, A man-eater, a cannibal.

P آدم سر *ādam-sar*, Bald.

P آدم شناس *ādam-shinās*, Knowing mankind.

A ادمص *admaṣ*, One whose eye-brows are thin at the outer and thick at the inner extremity.

A ادمع *admuꜥ*, (pl. of دمع *damꜥ*) Tears.

A ادمغة *admighat*, (pl. of دماغ *dimāgh*) Brains.

P آدم گري *ādamgarī*, Humanity. Valour.

P ادمن *adman*, Pure, fragrant (musk).

A ادموث *udmūs*, A pit under ashes in which they bake bread.

A ادموس *udmūs*, Dark (night).

A آدميّ *ādamiy*, Human. A man. Brown.

P آدميان *ādamiyān*, Men, mortals.

P آدميانه *ādamiyāna*, Humanly, like a man.

P آدمي بچه *ādamī-bacha*, An infant.

A آدميّة *ādamīyat*, Humanity.

P آدمي زاد *ādamī-zād*, A son of man, man.

A ادميماء *idmīmāh*, (v. n. 12 of دمه) Being almost broiled by the heat. Fainting, swooning.

A ادنّ *adann*, Crook-backed (man). Short-necked. Short in the fore-feet (horse). Hollow in the middle of the floor (a chamber).

A ادنا *adna'*, Nearer. Lower. Last. Least. Basest.

A ادنأ *adna*, Crooked, hump-backed (man).

A ادناء *adnā*, (pl. of دنيء *danī*) Mean, small, trifling. Vicious, licentious, careless of reputation. *Idnā*, (v. n. 4 of دنأ) Perpetrating enormities, doing a mean, base thing. (v. n. 4 of دنا for دنو) Bringing near. Being near her time (a camel). Living on spare diet. Approaching, drawing near.

A ادّناء *iddinā*, (v. n. 8 of دنا for دنو) Approaching, becoming near.

A ادناس *adnās*, (pl. of دنس *danis*) Dirty (fellows), nasty (rascals), sorry (dogs).

A ادناف *idnāf*, (v. n. 4 of دنف) Suffering from severe and continued illness. Afflicting sorely for a long time (sickness). Going down (as the sun). Bringing near. Being yellow.

A ادنان *idnān*, (v. n. 4 of دنّ) Staying.

P ادند *adand*, How? See ادنك *adank*.

P ادنك *adank*, How? At what rate? An uncertain, unknown number, conjectural computation. One truss, hamper, &c. One half of a horse's load, as much as a beast carries upon one side. One side of a piece of money.

A ادنيٰ *adna'*, Lower, lowest. Smaller, smallest, least, most trifling. (pl. اداني *adānī*) Nearer, nearest.

A ادنيان *adaniyān*, Name of two valleys.

A ادو *adw*, (v. n. of ادا for ادو) Deceiving, lying in wait for (as a wolf does for a fawn).

A ادوّ *udūw*, The coming to maturity (of fruit).

A ادواء *adwā*, (pl. of داء *dā*) Diseases, sicknesses. *Idwā*, (v. n. 4 of داء for دوأ) Afflicting with disease. Being sick. Suspecting. (v. n. 4 of دوي) Making sick. Keeping company with the sick. Eating a thin skin formed on the surface of milk.

ادّواء *iddiwā*, (v. n. 8 of دوي) Eating the thin skin on the surface of milk.

A ادوات *adawāt*, (pl. of اداة *adāt*) Instruments, tools, utensils. (in gram.) Accessory particles. P ادوات جنگ *adawāti jang*, Arms, warlike apparatus, weapons of war, artillery.

A ادوار *adwār*, (pl. of دار *dār*) Houses, mansions. (pl. of دور *dawr*) Orbs, orbits, revolutions, circles. Periods, ages. Musical periods, cadences. علم الادوار *ꜥilmu'l adwār*, Music. ادوار ملكوت *adwāri malakūt*, The harmony of the heavenly bodies, the music of the spheres, the intelligence which moves them. ادوار و اكرار *adwār u akrār*, The cycles or revolutions of years, according to which the astrologers pretend to prognosticate the accidents of human life. Every *adwār* consists of 360 solar years, and the *akrār* of 120 lunar years; the whole art consisting in finding the combinations of these years, and their respective relations.

P ادواي *adwāy*, (in zand and Pāz.) Voice, echo.

A ادوب *adūb*, Polite, well-behaved.

A ادؤر *adūr*, (ادور *adwur* or ادورة *adwirat*, pl. of دار *dār*) Houses, mansions. Towns.

P ادوس *adūs*, Dim-sighted, purblind.

A ادوش *adwash*, Dim-sighted, squinting, or injured in the eye by disease.

A ادون *adwan*, More or most mean, or base.

A ادويٰ *adwa'*, A viper.

P ادوي *adwe*, Sweet-scented flag. Aloes.

A ادوية *adwiyat*, (pl. of دواء *dawā*, *diwā*, or *duwā*) Medicines. P ادويهٔ گرم *adwiyaï garm*, Hot condiments, as pepper, cloves, cinnamon, &c.

P آده *āda*, A hen-roost. A perch for pigeons.

A اده *adah*, Diligent application and persevering attention to business.

A ادهاس *idhās*, (v. n. 4 of دهس not used) Travelling over soft soil without sand, dust, or clay.

A ادهاش *idhāsh*, (v. n. 4 of دهش) Astounding, striking with amazement, terrifying.

A ادهاض *idhāz*, (v. n. 4 of دهض not used) Bringing forth a hairy foal fully formed (a camel).

A ادهاق *idhāk*, (v. n. 4 of دهق) Filling a cup. Emptying a vessel with violence. Commanding to make haste.

A ادّهاق *iddihāk*, (v. n. 8 of دهق) Entering (one within another), joining (as a row of stones).

A ادهام *idhām*, (v. n. 4 of دهم) Hurting, injuring. Rendering sad.

A ادهان *adhān*, (pl. of دهن *duhn*) Oils, ointments, unguents. *Idhān*, (v. n. 4 of دهن) Anointing. Concealing. Deceiving, dissembling. Making clean. Imposture, deceit, falsehood.

A ادّهان *iddihān*, The anointing of one's self.

A ادهج *adhaj*, A word used in calling a sheep to be milked. A name for a sheep.

P ادهجا *adhijā*, (or ادهجاره) A kind of thorn.

A ادهر *adhur*, (pl. of دهر *dahr*) Times, ages.

A ادهس *adhas*, Reddish, inclining to black.

P ادهلي *adhalī*, Half a gold mohur, in value eight rupees.

A ادهم *adham*, (pl. اداهم *adāhim*) (A horse) of a black colour, inclining to a dusky green. Black. Old, ancient, blackish, much trodden upon. Recent. A fetter. ادهم لجّ *adham lujj*, Very black (camel). ابو الادهم *abū'l adham*, A large cauldron, in which they dress a sheep whole.

A ادهمام *idhimām*, (v. n. 9 of دهم) Being of a black colour with a slight mixture of dark green.

A ادهى *adha'*, More or most subtle or astute.

A ادهية *adhiyat*, (pl. of دهيّ *dahīy*) Shrewd.

A ادهيساس *idhīsās*, (v. n. 11 of دهس) Becoming of a reddish black (ground).

A ادهمام *idhimām*, The being very black.

A آدى *āda'*, More or most exact and punctual in his payments, better or best paymaster.

A اديّ *adīy*, Apparatus (especially of a military kind). Small or middle-sized (vessel or churn). Light, active, quick at work. Little (property). Wide (garment). Readiness, preparation. *Udīy*, (v. n. of ادي) Becoming thick (as milk). Having butter nearly formed (a churn). Being abundant. Deceiving, lying in wait for.

A ايار *adyār*, (pl. of دير *dayr*) Monasteries.

A ادياك *adyāk*, (pl. of ديك *dīk*) Cocks.

P اديان *adyān*, Fat cattle (in motion).

A اديان *adyān*, (pl. of دين *dīn*) Religions.

A ادّيان *iddiyān*, (v. n. 8 of دان for دين) Running in debt. Buying or selling on credit.

A اديب *adīb*, (pl. ادباء *udabāʼ*) Courteous, polite, well-bred. Learned. A professor, tutor.

A اديبر *udaybir*, A species of serpent.

A اديّة *adiyat*, Little, few (sheep).

P اديچاره *adichāra*, The inverted thorn.

P ادید *adīd*, Consequence, A spring of water.

P آدیش *ādīsh*, Fire.

P اديم *adīm*, The face. Perfumed leather, in the East called بلغار *bulghār*, but by us, Morocco.

A اديم *adīm*, (pl. آدمة *ādimat*, ادم *udum*, آدام *ādām*, and ادم *adam*) Goat's leather, perfumed, which they bring from Arabia Felix. Bread when eaten or baked with meat. The surface of the earth. Name of a horse. اديم السماء *adīmu's samāʼ*, The expanse of heaven. اديم النهار *adīmu'n nahār*, The diffusion of light or day. اديم الضحي *adīmu'z zuha'*, Half way between sun-rise and mid-day.

A اديّم *udayyim*, Name of a tract of country in Arabia. Name of a place.

A ادين *adyan*, More or most religious. *Adyun*, (pl. of دين *dayn*) Debts.

P آدیندة *ādyanda*, The rainbow.

P آدینه *ādīna*, Friday.

P اديون *adyūn*, A rapacious animal. Fat cattle.

A قطع الله اديه *kataʻa' llāh adayhi*, (for يديه *yadayhi*) May God cut off both his hands!

A اذ *iz*, When (in a past sense). Indeed. If, it so be. Forasmuch as, because. Already. Behold! lo! اذ *izin*, (حينئذ *hinaʻizin* or اذاك *izzāka*) Then, at that time. يومئذ *yawmaʻizin*, On that day, on the day when. ليلتئذ *laylataʻizin*, On that night. اذ ما *iz mā*, When, if at any time.

A اذّ *azz*, Amputation, a cutting off.

A اذا *izā*, When (in the present or future sense). Behold! lo! It is sometimes redundant, as حتّي اذا اتوا *hatta' izā ataw*, Until they arrived.

A اذاء *azāʼ*, (v. n. of اذي) Being injured, receiving damage.

A اذآب *izʼāb*, (v. n. 4 of ذأب) Being terrified (by a wolf). Adorning with forelocks.

A اذابة *izābat*, (v. n. 4 of ذاب for ذوب) Dissolving, causing to melt. Invading, plundering. Adjusting, correcting.

A اذاة *azāt* (v. n. of اذي) Hurting. Trouble. Damage, loss, injury. Tyranny, oppression.

A اذاخة *izākhat*, (v. n. 4 of ذاخ for ذيخ not used) Going round, moving in a circle.

A اذاخر *azākhir*, Name of a pass between Mecca and Madīna. (pl. of اذخر *izkhir*) Bog-rushes.

A اذادة *izādat*, (v. n. 4 of ذاد for ذود) Helping (one) to drive camels.

A اذآر *izʼār*, (v. n. 4 of ذئر) Putting in a rage. Inspiring with boldness. Instigating. Compelling, forcing.

A اذار *azār*, The Syriac month of March.

P آذارافيون *āzārāfyūn*, Foam of the sea.

U اذاراقي *azārākī*, A plant called dog's bane.

A اذارة *izārat*, (v. n. 4 of ذار for ذور) Frightening.

P آذارطرس *āzārtūs*, A proper name.

A اذاعة *izāʻat*, (v. n. 4 of ذاع for ذيع) Publishing, divulging, blazing. Draining, exhausting. Squandering, lavishing.

A اذاف *uzāf*, Membrum genitale maris.

A اذاقة *izākat*, (v. n. 4 of ذاق for ذوق) Giving one to drink or taste. Tasting, experiencing a taste. اذاق زيد بعدك كرمًا *azāka zaydun baʻdaka karaman*, Zayd became generous and liberal.

A اذالة *izālat*, (v. n. 4 of ذال for ذيل) Letting down a veil. Abusing, over-working and making thin (a slave or a horse). Despising. Appendage.

A اذآم *izʼām* (v. n. 4 of ذأم) Forcing, compelling. Terrifying.

A آذان *āzān*, or اذان *azān*, (v. n. of اذن) Signifying, announcing, giving notice; the signal for summoning to prayers, by the Mu'ezzin or crier, from the minarets or towers of the mosques. *Āzān*, (pl. of اذن *uzn* or *uzun*) Ears, lobes of the ears. Handles. آذان الارنب *āzānu'l arnab*, (Hare's ears) Bupleurum. آذان الثور *āzānu's sawr*, Bugloss. آذان الجدي *āzānu'l jady*, (Kid's ears) Ribwort. آذان الدبّ *āzānu'd dubb*, (Bear's ears) Mullein. آذان الشاة *āzānu'sh shāt*, (Sheep's ears) Hound's tongue. آذان العبد *āzānu'l ʻabd*, (Slave's ears) Shepherd's staff. آذان الغزال *āzānu'l ghazāl*, (Doe's ears) Hound's tongue. آذان الفار *āzānu'l fār*, (Mouse's ears) Chickweed. آذان الفيل *āzānu'l fīl*, (Elephant's ears) The Egyptian bean. آذان القسّيس *āzānu'l kissīs*, (Presbyter's ears) or آذان القاضي *āzānu'l kāzī*, (Judge's ears) Venus's navel-wort.

A اذان *azān*, A stopping, staying, standing. *Azān*, (or اذانة *azānat*) (v. n. of اذن) Knowing. Permitting.

A اذانيّ *uzānīy*, Large-eared (applied to men).

A اذاهيب *azāhīb*, (or اذاهب *azāhib*) (pl. of اذهاب *azhāb*) Yolks of eggs. Certain dry measures in Yaman.

A اذبّ *azabb*, A wild bull. Long. A long tooth projecting from the side of a camel's mouth.

A اذّباح *izzibāh*, (v. n. 8 of ذبح) Preparing a victim for sacrifice.

A اذبال *izbāl*, (v. n. 4 of ذبل) Causing to wither. Debilitating.

A اذبّة *azibbat*, (pl. of ذباب *zubāb*) Flies. Bees.

P اذبك *uzbak*, Usback Tartar.

A اذحاج *izhāj*, (v. n. 4 of ذحج) Stopping, staying, standing still.

A اذحال *azhāl*, (pl. of ذحل *zahl*) Enmities, hatreds. Retaliations, desires of revenge.

A اذخار *azkhār*, (pl. of ذخر *zukr*) Provisions or treasures acquired for future use.

A اذّخار *izzikhār*, (v. n. 8 of ذخر) Storing up.

A اذخر *izkhir*, (pl. اذاخر *azākhir*) The bog-rush.

A اذدكار *izdikār*, (v. n. 8 of ذكر) Recollecting, recalling to mind.

A اذذاك *iz zāka*, Then, at that time.

P آذر *āzar*, (More correctly *āzur*) Fire. Name of the angel presiding over fire, and the affairs of the day آذر *āzar*. Name of seven celebrated fire-temples formerly standing in Persia, and dedicated to the seven planets. Name of Abraham's father. The ninth solar month, when the sun is in Sagittarius. Name of the last lunar winter month. Name of the ninth day in any month, but particularly in the 4th month Tīr-māh.

A اذرأ *azraʼ*, Gray about the forehead. (A ram) white-headed, black-bodied, dapple-eared.

A اذراء *izrāʼ*, (v. n. 4 of ذرأ) Provoking, enraging. Terrifying. Exciting, inspiring with desire. Compelling, forcing. Causing to flow. Allowing her milk to flow (a camel). (v. n. 4 of ذري) Sowing. Winnowing. Sifting. Spearing and unhorsing a cavalier. Sweeping away (wind).

A اذراب *azrāb*, (pl. of ذرب) Obscenities.

P آذر آباد *āzar-ābād*, (or آذر آبادگان *āzar-ābād-gān*) Name of a fire-temple in Tabrīz; also the ancient name of Tabrīz itself.

P اذر آبادگون *āzar-ābād-gūn*, A stove: a forge.

A اذراع *izrāʻ*, (v. n. 4 of ذرع) Seizing by the arm. Putting out the arms from beneath the vest. Bringing forth (the wild cow). Being very talkative.

A اذّراع *izzirāʻ*, (v. n. 8 of ذرع) Putting out the arms from beneath the vest.

P آذر افروز *āzar-afroz*, An eolipile. A phœnix.

P آذر افزا *āzar-afzā*, An eolipile.

A اذراق *izrāk*, (v. n. 4 of ذرق) Muting (a bird). Causing to mute. Producing the lote-plant. Producing clover or trefoil.

A اذّراق *izzirāk*, (v. n. 8 of ذرق) Bathing the

eyes with milk and water. Anointing the eyes with antimony mixed with the expressed juice of trefoil.

P آذر آيين *āzar-āyin*, Name of the fourth temple of the seven called after the planets.

P آذرباد *āzar-bād*, Name of a priest of the Magi.

P آذربادگان *āzar-bād-gān*, (or آذربايگان *āzar-bāy-gān*) Name of a fire-temple in Tabrīz. (It signifies, Conservator of fire.)

P آذربرزين *āzar-barzīn*, Name of the sixth fire-temple of those named after the seven planets.

P آذربو *āzar-bo*, (or *bu*, آذربويه *āzar-boya* or *būya*) Name of a yellow flowering shrub, from whose root pearl-ashes are made.

P آذربهرام *āzari bahrām*, Name of the third fire-temple, called after the seven planets.

A اذربيّ *azrabiy*, A native of Azarbayjān.

P آذربيجان *āzar-bayjān*, (The region of fire), A province of Persia, which corresponds nearly with the ancient Media, though it comprehends also a part of Syria and Armenia Major.

P آذرپرست *āzar-parast*, A fire-worshipper.

P آذرپيرا *āzar-payrā*, (or *perā*) One who attends on a fire-temple.

A اذرّة *azirrat*, (pl. of ذرور *zarūr* and ذريرة *zarīrat*) Drugs pounded and sprinkled.

P آذرتش *āzartush*, A salamander.

A اذرح *azruh*, Name of a town in Syria.

P آذر خرداد *āzar-khurdār*, (or آذر خورداد *āzar-khwurdād*,) Name of a priest of the Magi; also of the angel who presides over fire: also of the fire-temple at Shīrāz: also of the fifth fire-temple.

P آذرخرين *āzar-khurīn*, Name of the fifth fire-temple, called after the seven planets by the ancient Persians.

P آذرخش *āzarkhush*, Name of the ninth day of the month *Āzar*.

P آذرخشا *āzirkhushā*, Intense cold fatal to man and beast. Lightning.

P آذررنگ *āzar-rang*, Bright, shining, red, flame-coloured. Confused, dispersed. Difficult. Trouble, misfortune, calamity, ruin, slaughter.

P آذرزردهشت *āzar-zardahasht*, Name of the seventh fire-temple, named after the seven planets.

P آذرس *āzaras*, A salamander.

P آذرشپ *āzarshap*, (آذرگشسپ *āzar-gushasp*, آذرشسپ *āzarshasp*, or آذر گشپ *āzar-gushp*) Name of the angel or demon of fire. Fire, flame, lightning. Name of one of the temples in the city of Balkh. A salamander.

P آذرشين *āzar-shīn*, A salamander.

P آذرطوس *āzartūs*, Name of the father-in-law of عذرا *ʿazrā*.

A اذرع *azraʿ*, One whose mother is of higher rank than his father. Very eloquent. (A horse) of a bad breed. Quick, sudden (death). *Azruʿ*, (pl. of ذراع *zirāʿ*) Arms.

A اذرعات *azriʿāt*, Name of a town in Syria.

A اذرعفاف *izriʿfāf*, (v. n. 4 of ذرعف Q) Going fast. Advancing from the ranks of battle.

A اذرع قتل *azraʿ katlin*, By a speedy death.

A اذرعيّ *azraʿiy*, Wine produced at *Azriʿāt*.

P آذر فراز *āzar-farāz*, Kindling fire.

P آذرفروز *āzar-furoz*, (or فزا *fazā*) An eolipile.

P آذر كده *āzar-kada*, A fire-temple.

P آذر كو *āzar-kū*, The leaves of the camomile.

P آذر كيش *āzar-kesh*, A fire-worshipper.

P آذرگشپ *āzar-gashp*, Name of an angel presiding over, and living in, fire.

P آذرگشسپ *āzar-gushasp*, Name of a fire-temple erected by Gushtasp in Balkh, in which he kept his treasures. It was destroyed by Alexander. A fire-temple. Lightning. Fire. A fire-worshipper. The angel presiding over and living in fire.

P آذرگل *āzar-gul*, A flower like the anemone.

P آذرگون *āzar-gūn*, Flame-coloured, fiery-red, bright. The anemone, marigold, marsh-mallows. A salamander. A horse.

P آذرم *āzram*, A saddle-cloth. A saddle whose cloth is in two pieces.

P آذرماه *āzar-māh*, Name of the ninth month of the solar year.

P آذرمهر *āzar-mihr*, Name of the first fire-temple called after the planets.

P آذرنگ *āzrang*, Light, luminous, bright, dazzling. Fire. Distress, misery, ruin.

P آذرنوش *āzar-nosh*, Name of the second fire-temple named after the seven planets.

P آذرهمايون *āzar-humāyūn*, Name of a witch.

P آذر هوشنگ *āzar hoshang*, Name of the earliest apostle sent to Persia.

P آذري *āzarī*, A native of Azarbayjān. Name of a poet. A follower of آذرهوشنگ *āzar koshang*.

P آذرياس *āzriyās*, Gum of wild rue.

G اذريطوس *azrītūs*, Name of a medicine.

P آذرين *āzarīn*, Camomile-flower. Ox-eye.

P آذريون *āzar-yūn*, Red, flame-coloured. Any flower of such a colour: anemone. The sun-flower.

A اذطّ *azatt*, Wry-jawed.

A اذعار *izʿār*, (v. n. 4 of ذعر) Terrifying.

A اذعاف *izʿāf*, The act of killing instantly.

A اذعان *izʿān*, (v. n. 4 of ذعن) Obeying, submitting, rendering swift obedience. Abasing one's self. Confessing, acknowledging. Obedience, submission. واجب الاذعان *wājibu'l izʿān*, Necessary to be obeyed.

A اذفاف *izfāf*, (v. n. 4 of ذفّ) Making haste to despatch a wounded man.

A اذفر *azfar*, Fragrant, pungent. Strong, rank. مسك اذفر *miski azfar*, The most fragrant musk.

A اذقان *azkān*, (pl. of ذقن *zakan*) Chins, beards.

A اذقن *azkan*, Long-chinned (man).

A اذقي *azka'*, Flaccid-eared and nosed (horse).

A اذكاء *izkāʾ*, (v. n. 4 of ذكا for ذكو) Making fire burn, or lamp shine clearly. Sending spies.

A اذكار *azkār*, (pl. of ذكر *zikr*) Praises of God, continual prayers or repetitions of the names and attributes of the Supreme Being. *Izkār*, (v. n. 4 of ذكر) Bringing forth a male child. Reminding.

A اذّكار *izzikār*, (v. n. 8 of ذكر) Recalling to one's memory what had been long forgotten.

A اذكر *azkar*, More or most acute, or sharp.

A اذكى *azka'*, Sharper, more or most pungent.

A اذكياء *azkiyāʾ*, (pl. of ذكيّ) Acute, witty.

A اذلّ *azall*, Most vile, abject, or submissive.

A اذلّاء *azillāʾ*, (pl. of ذليل *zalīl*) Abject, vile, mean, contemptible, slavish. Submissive.

A اذلاق *izlāk*, (v. n. 4 of ذلق) Disturbing, troubling. Pouring water into the hole of a lizard. Lighting (a lamp), making (it) burn. Whetting. Muting (a bird). Weakening (poison or fasting).

A اذلال *azlāl*, A state, mode, manner, condition. (pl. of ذلّ *zill*) Courses, currents. The meanest of men. *Izlāl*, (v. n. 4 of ذلّ) Associating with base people. Holding in contempt. Discovering one to be base. Soothing and coaxing (refractory camels) by picking the tikes off them. Contempt, depression. Dishonour.

A اذلّة *azillat*, (pl. of ذلول *zalūl*) Gentle, easily managed, submissive, tractable.

A اذلعباب *izliʿbāb*, (v. n. 4 of ذلعب Q) Walking fast. A kind of camel's pace.

A اذلعيّ *azlaʿiy*, Long and thick (penis).

A اذلغ *azlagh*, (or اذلغيّ *azlaghiy*) Penis.

A اذلف *azlaf*, Small-nosed; ape-nosed.

A اذلق *azlak*, Eloquent, ready, voluble, glib.

A اذليلاء *izlīlāʾ*, (v. n. 12 of ذلي) Escaping clandestinely. Making haste. Submitting. Being broken-hearted. Standing, but not stiff.

A اذما *izmā*, When, the time when, whenever.

A اذماء *izmāʾ*, (v. n. 4 of ذمي) Beating with violence almost to death.

A اذمار *azmār*, Intrepid men. Protectors.

A اذمام *izmām*, (v. n. 4 of ذمّ) Becoming vile and contemptible. Discovering any one to be so, and despising accordingly. Committing an act fraught with turpitude. Protecting, shielding from oppression. Receiving under one's protection. Lagging behind from fatigue.

A اذمّة *azimmat*, Safe-guards. Rights, dues.

A اذمقرار *izmikrār*, (v. n. 4 of ذمقر Q) Being divided into minute particles (milk).

A آذن *āzan*, Long-eared (animal). *Āzin*, A sponsor, a surety. A porter. A chamberlain.

A أذن *azina*, (fut. of يأذن *yaʾzanu*) He listened. He knew.

A اذن *azn*, (v. n. of اذن) Certifying, informing. Striking on the ear. Beginning to dry partially (herbage). *Izn*, (v. n. of اذن) Permitting. Leave, licence. Knowledge, permission. *Izn* or *azan*, (v. n. of اذن) Knowing. *Uzn*, (pl. آذان *āzān*) The ear. A handle. اذن الحمار *uznu'l hi-*

mār, (Ass's ears) A parsnip. اذن السهم *uznu's sahm*, The wing of an arrow. اذن العبد *uznu'l ɛabd*, (Ear of the slave) The water-plaintain. لبست اذنيّ له *labistu uznayya lahu*, I turned my deaf ears to him. *Uzn* or *uzun*, Attentive to what is spoken (man or men). *Azan*, (v. n. of اذن) Giving ear, listening to with pleasure, attending to, obeying. Liking the scent of meat. *Izan*, Well, very well then. Come on. Now. Surely, verily. *Uzun*, (pl. آذان *āzān*) The ear. A handle. (pl. of اذنة *azanat*) Small camels or sheep. Leaves of corn, straws. اذنا القلب *uzunā'l kalb*, The two lobes of the heart.

A اذنّ *azann*, Snotty, snivelly.

A اذناء *aznāʾ*, (fem. of آذن *āzan*) Long-eared.

A اذناب *aznāb*, (pl. of ذنب *zanab*) Tails, rumps, posteriors. The rabble. اذناب الخيل *aznābu'l khayl*, Horse-tails (a plant). اذناب الناس *aznābu'n nās*, Men of low degree; servants, menials, followers, dependants. *Iznāb*, (v. n. 4 of ذنب) Committing a crime or trespass.

A اذنان *uznān*, Name of a man.

A اذنب *aznab*, More or most sinful or criminal.

A اذنبة *aznibat*, (pl. of ذنوب *zanūb*) Long-tailed (horses). Portions, lots of good or evil. Long days of evil. Buckets full or not full of water.

A اذنة *azanat*, (pl. اذن *uzun*) A leaf or blade of corn. The small kind of the camel species; also of sheep, &c. A single straw. Adana, a city of Cilicia near Tarsus. An appetite for the smell of meat. Name of a mountain near Mecca. *Uzanat*, One who believes all he hears.

P اذنك *uznak*, An ear-trumpet.

A اذواء *azwāʾ*, (pl. of ذو *zū*) Kings of Yaman, whose names all begin with ذو *zū*. *Izwāʾ*, (v. n. 4 of ذوي) Causing to wither.

A اذواب *izwāb*, Thick milk, cream.

A اذوابة *izwābat*, The melting of any thing. The choicest or purest part. Thick milk, cream.

A اذواد *azwād*, Troops of camels from 3 to 10.

A اذواط *azwāt*, Spiders with yellow backs.

A اذواق *azwāk*, (pl. of ذوق) Tastes, flavours.

A اذؤب *azʾub*, (pl. of ذئب) Wolves. Wild dogs.

A اذوذ *azūz*, Keen, sharp (knife).

A اذوط *azwat*, Short-chinned, overhung (man).

P آذوقه *āzūka*, Provisions.

A اذوم *izūm*, Idumea.

P آذون *āzūn*, Thus, in that manner.

A اذويّ *izawiy*, Relating to اذا *izā*, Whenever.

A اذهاب *azhāb*, (pl. of ذهب *zahab*) Particles of gold. *Izhāb*, (v. n. 4 of ذهب) Ordering or permitting to go. Removing, driving away, carrying off. Destroying. Gilding.

A اذهال *izhāl*, (v. n. 4 of ذهل) Causing to forget.

A اذهان *azhān*, (pl. of ذهن *zihn*) Geniuses. Memories. *Izhān*, (v. n. 4 of ذهن) Causing to forget. Occupying, drawing off the attention.

A اذيٰ *azaʾ*, (v. n. of اذي) Being injured, receiving damage. Injury, harm, annoyance, impediment, inconvenience. Dirt, nastiness. Hair and filth on the head of a new-born infant, which is shaved on the seventh day. Rubbish. *Azi*, Injured, vexed, hurt, offended. Hurtful, injurious. (A camel) untractable, skittish, restless, impatient.

A آذيّ *āziy*, (pl. اواذيّ *awāziy*) A wave.

A اذيّ *aziy*, Injured, hurt, vexed. Offended. Hurtful, injurious, oppressive.

A اذياخ *azyākh*, (pl. of ذيخ *zīkh*) Male hyenas (especially very hairy). Wolves. Stallions. Certain reddish stars. Prides.

A اذيال *azyāl*, (pl. of ذيل *zayl*) Skirts, tails, ends, borders of a garment. The lower parts of any thing. Appendices. The long tails of animals (as of lions or oxen). The meanest of men. Tracks made in sand by trailing skirts. *Izyāl*, (v. n. 4 of ذال for ذيل) Having a long tail, skirt, or train.

A اذيب *azyab*, Abundant (water). Fright. Cheerfulness, joyousness.

A اذية *aziyat*, (fem.) Skittish, untractable.

A اذيّة *aziyat*, (v. n. of اذي) Injuring, hurting. Injury, harm, damage, nuisance, hurt, wrong, loss.

P اذيت كاران *aziyat-kārān*, Oppressors, tyrants.

P آذيش *āzish*, A door-sill. Chips, rubbish.

A اذيل *azyul*, (pl. of ذيل *zayl*) Trains.

P آذين *āzin*, Custom, common usage, institution, rite, ceremony. Decoration. A churn.

A اذين *azin*, (v. n. of اذن) Permitting. A crier. Summons to prayer. The place to which such summons extends (as a street, or a parish). A sponsor, surety. Permission. The ear. *Uzayn*, (dim. of اذن *uzn*) A little handle or ear. A slight perception, a little knowledge; intimation, inkling.

P آر *ār*, If. (Imperative of آوردن *āwardan*) Bring thou. (In comp.) Bringing; a bringer. Imperative of آرستن *ārastan*, To be able.

A آر *ār*, Reproach, disgrace, shame.

P ار *ār*, without *madda*, when added to the 3d pers. sing. pret. of certain verbs forms abstract nouns: as, رفتار *raftār*, Going, gait, walking, from رفت *raft*, He went; گفتار *guftār*, Speech, from گفت *guft*, He said. Also, nouns of agency or adjectives: as, خريدار *kharīdār*, A purchaser; پديدار *padīdār*, Manifest.

P ار *ar* (for اگر *agar*) If. A saw. Dregs of oil.

A ارّ *arr*, (v. n. of ارّ) Driving on, stimulating, impelling, urging; driving off. Voiding thin excrement. Dropping, falling (dung). Kindling, lighting fire. Resounding, shouting in triumph (particularly an insolent fellow at the gaming-board). Thrusting in the branch mentioned below. A twig rubbed with salt and thrust into the matrix of a she-camel to excite a desire for the male. Coitus.

P آرا *ārā*, (in comp. from آراستن *ārāstan*) Embellishing, adorning. Ornament. مجلس آرا *majlis-ārā*, Gracing the banquet. جهان آرا *jahān-ārā*, (or عالم آرا *ɛālam-ara*) Adorning the world, ornament of the universe, the most noble, excellent, eminent, renowned.

A آراء *ārāʾ* or ارآء *arʾāʾ*, (pl. of رأي *raʾy*) Opinions, counsels, doctrines, views.

A ارآء *irʾāʾ*, (v. n. 4 of رأي) Shewing, exhibiting. Doing any thing to be seen and heard. Becoming intelligent. Being evident and apparent in a person's face (stupidity). Looking in a glass. Moving the eye-lids in looking. Being remarkable (the comeliness of one's appearance). Making an awful example of. Planting a standard. Giving signs of pregnancy by having a large udder (a camel or ewe). Being possessed by a demon. Being hurt in the lungs. Following the opinions of certain theologians or lawyers. Turning the tip of his nose towards his throat (a camel).

A اراءة *irāʾat*, (v. n. 4 of رأي) Showing, exhibiting. P اراءت روي كردن *irāʾati rūy kardan*, To show the face.

A آراب *ārāb*, (pl. of ارب *irb*) The members, hands, feet, &c. Blisters, pimples. السجود علي سبعة آراب *as sujūd ɛala' sabɛat ārābin*, Adoration on seven members, a mode of worship customary among the Muhammadans, the hands, knees, feet, and forehead touching the ground.

A ارآب *irʾāb*, (v. n. 4 of رأب) Closing, filling.

A ارابة *arābat*, (v. n. of ارب) Becoming shrewd, acute. *Irābat*, (v. n. 4 of راب for روب) Thickening (milk). (v. n. 4 of راب for ريب) Becoming doubtful. Doubting, suspecting. Causing to doubt and suspect. Attributing suspicion to any one. Observing something scandalous and suspicious in the behaviour of any one. Doubt. Suspicion.

P ارابچي *arābchi*, (or ارابه كش *arāba-kash*) A carter, a waggoner.

P ارابه *arāba*, A waggon, a cart. A wheel.

A اراث *irās*, Fire. Fuel.

A ارّاج *arrāj*, A liar, tale-bearer, breed-bate.

A اراجل *arājil*, (pl. of رجل) Foot-men. Men.

A اراجيح *arājīh*, Deserts, plains. The swinging motion of camels when they travel with a short step.

A اراجيز *arājīz*, (pl. of ارجوزة *urjūzat*,) Poems consisting of verses called رجز *rajaz*.

A اراجيف *arājīf*, False rumours.

A اراجيل *arājīl*, (pl. of رجل *rajil*) Persons on foot; infantry. Hunters, fowlers.

A اراحة *irāhat*, (v. n. 4 of راح for روح) Giving rest. Bringing cattle home in the evening. Paying a debt. Breathing. Smelling. Discovering the odour of a man (game). Smelling an agreeable odour. Stinking (flesh or water). Taking the air. Being refreshed, reviving after toil. Dying. Entering into the wind. Receiving a kindness.

A اراخ *irākh*, A wild ox. A deer.

A اراخنة *arākhinat*, (pl. of ارخون) Archons.

P آراخيدن *ārākhīdan*, To rest.

P آراد *ārād*, Name of an angel presiding over the twenty-fifth day of each month; also the twenty-fifth day of each month.

A ارادة *irādat*, (v. n. 4 of راد for رود) Wishing, willing, purposing: desire, will, inclination, intention, purpose, design. Discipleship. P ارادت خدا *irādati khudā*, The will of God. ارادت كردن *irādat kardan*, To wish, desire, will, intend.

P ارادتانه *irādatāna*, Voluntarily, cheerfully.

P ارادت بنده *irādat-banda*, A free servant.

P ارادت گذين *irādat-guzīn*, Devoted: a scholar.

A ارادي *irādī*, Willingness.

A اراذل *arāzil*, (pl. of ارذل *arzal*) Low, mean.

A ارار *arʼar*, A sound used to call cattle.

A ارارة *irārat*, (v. n. 4 of رير) Causing marrow to be thin and to stink.

A ارارس *arāris*, (or ارارسة *arārisat*) (pl. of ارّيس *irrīs*) Farmers, husbandmen.

A اراريس *arārīs*, (pl. of ارّيس) Farmers.

P ارارين *arārīn*, (in zand and Pāz.) Ugly, bad.

P آرازش *ārāzish*, Bounty, charity, alms.

A ارأس *arʼas*, Large-headed (sheep). *Arʼus*, (pl. of رأس *raʼs*) Heads. Chiefs, princes.

P آراستك *ārāstak*, A swallow.

P آراستگي *ārāstagī*, Ornament, embellishment, decoration. Order, arrangement.

P آراستن *ārāstan*, To adorn, decorate, embellish. To set in order.

P آراسته *ārāsta*, Adorned, decorated, embellished. Arranged. An idol temple.

A ارأش *arʼash*, Hairy about the face and ears (a camel). Weak.

A آراض *ārāz*, (pl. of ارض *arz*) Earths, grounds.

A اراض *irāz*, A carpet of coarse wool or hair. Broad, wide, spacious.

A اراضة *arāzat*, (v. n. of ارض) Being clean, pleasant, and agreeable to the eye (land). *Irāzat*, (v. n. 4 of راض for روض) Abounding in gardens. Being full of water (a cistern or river). Supplying plentifully with water, soaking, saturating. Collecting, flowing together on account of the moisture of a place (water). Pouring milk upon milk. Drinking a second time.

A اراضي *arāzī*, (pl. of ارض *arz*) Lands.

A اراطى *arāṭaʼ* or *arāṭī*, (pl. of ارطي *arṭaʼ*) Trees of a particular species which grow in sandy soils, with the fruit of which they feed camels, and, with the bark, tan hides. ذو اراط *zū arāṭin*, Name of a place, where numbers of such trees grow. *Urāṭaʼ*, Name of a town.

A اراعة *irāʻat*, (v. n. 4 of راع for ريع) Being redundant. Having food in abundance. Growing strong (corn). Increasing, multiplying (camels).

A اراعيل *arāʻīl*, (pl. of رعلة *raʻlat*) Troops or herds (of horse or oxen) from 20 to 25, or the vans of such herds. Female ostriches Those parts of the ears of sheep or camels, which, being slit, hang flagging down. Tall palm-trees. Palm-trees bearing spoilt dates. Families, domestics, especially when numerous. Prepuces.

A اراغة *irāghat*, (v. n. 4 of راغ for روغ) Petitioning, requesting, desiring, wishing.

A ارافة *irāfat*, (v. n. 4 of راف for ريف) Abounding in pasturage.

A اراق *urāk*, Jaundice.

A اراقة *irākat*, (v. n. 4 of راق for روق or ريق) Spilling, shedding, pouring forth.

A اراقم *arākim*, Persons belonging to the tribe of Arkam. (pl. of ارقم *arkam*) Speckled serpents.

G اراقو *arākū*, A species of wild pulse.

P آراك *ārāk*, An island.

A اراك *arāk*, (pl. ارك *uruk* and ارائك *arāʼik*) A kind of salt and bitter tree, with the fruit and leaves of which they feed camels, and with the roots and branches they make dentifrices. A piece of ground.

G اراكا *arākā*, A kind of nut, which, when chewed with betel-leaves and fine lime, strengthens the stomach, and gives an agreeable flavour to the breath.

A اراكى *arākaʼ*, (pl. of اركة *arikat*) (She camels) griped from eating too much of the tree اراك *arāk*.

A اراكيب *arākīb*, Female privities.

A اراكية *arākiyat*, Camels feeding on اراك.

A اراكين *arākīn*, (pl. of اركان *arkān*, which is pl. of ركن *rukn*) Columns. Chief personages.

A ارال *arʼul*, (pl. of ورل *waral*) Lybian lizards.

P آرام *ārām*, Rest, tranquillity, peace, quiet, repose, cessation, inaction. Power. Obedience, subjection. A garden (especially in a city). A dwelling-place. آرام دادن *ārām dādan*, To give rest, pacify, make easy, calm. آرام گرفتن *ārām giriftan*, To take rest. To be patient. بي آرام *bī ārām*, Restless, uneasy. (In compos.) Tranquillizing: as, دل آرام *dil-ārām*, Heart-easing.

A آرام *ārām*, (pl. of ارم *iram* and *arim*) Stones erected in the desert for the direction of travellers. (pl. of رئم *riʼm*) White deer. ذو آرام *zū rāmā*, Name of a spot where are stones piled by عاد *ʻād*.

A ارآم *arʼām*, (pl. of رئم *riʼm*) White deer. Unicorns? *Irʼām*, (v. n. 4 of رأم) Rendering inclined, moving the affections. Disgusting. Closing up (a wound). Twisting tight (a rope).

A ارأم *arʼam*, Fonder, fondest of one's young.

A ارام *arām*, Name of the father of the first or last عاد *ʻād*, or name of their city, or name of their mother, or name of their tribe. A proper name. The part where the sides of the head meet before.

P آرامانيدن *ārāmānīdan*, To cause to be quiet.

P آرام بانو *ārām-bānū*, (Calm princess) A name.

P آرامبن *ārāmban*, A garden within a city.

P آرامدن *ārāmdan*, To rest, repose.

P آرام دوست *ārām-dost*, Loving ease; indolent.

P آرامش *ārāmish*, Quiet, repose, rest. آرامش باد *ārāmishi bād*, A calm.

P آرام شاه *ārām-shāh*, (Peace-king) Name of a Mogul emperor.

P آرام طلب *ārām-talab*, Seeking ease; idle.

P آرامكار *ārām-kār*, A lazy person, one who does not work unless ordered. One who does a thing slowly. Tedious, patient. Sedate. A sluggard.

P آرامگاه *ārām-gāh*, (or آرامگه *ārām-gah*) The time or place of rest. A calm, peaceable, secure dwelling. A bed-chamber. فردوس آرامگاه *firdaws-ārāmgāh*, (Resting in Paradise) An epithet of Muhammad Shāh.

A ارامل *arāmil*, (or اراملة *arāmilat*) (pl. of ارمل *armal*) Widowed. Distressed, poor, in want of victuals. (pl. of ارمولة *urmūlat*) Pieces of the thorny plant عرفج *ʻarfaj*.

A ارامنة *arāminat*, (pl. of ارمنيّ) Armenians.

G اراموني *arāmūnī*, The anemone.

P آرامي *ārāmī*, Peace, calmness, repose, rest.

P آراميد *ārāmīd*, He rested. Thanksgiving.

P آراميدن *ārāmīdan*, To rest, repose, cease, desist, settle, sleep. To cause to revolve. To give.

P آراميده *ārāmīda*, Quieted, calmed, rested.

A اراميل *arāmīl*, (pl. of ارمل *armal* and ارملة *armalat*) Widowers. Widows. (pl. of ارمولة *urmūlat*) Stumps of the shrub عرفج *ʻarfaj* after the branches have been lopped off.

P آران *ārān*, Name of a city. The elbow.

A اران *irān*, (v. n. of ارن) Being lively, joyous, vivacious. (v. n. 3 of ارن) Exulting against. Longing for the cow (a bull). A bier. (pl. ارن *urun*) The den of a wild beast. A sword. شاة اران *shātu irānin*, A bull.

P ارّان *arrān*, Privet.

A ارّان *arrān* or اران *arān*, Name of a small district, by some comprehended in Armenia, by others made a distinct province, between Āzarbayjān (Media) and Gūrjistān (Georgia). Name of a castle in Kazwin. (for حرّان *harrān*) Name of a town in Mesopotamia.

A ارانب *arānib*, (pl. of ارنب *arnab*) Hares.

A ارانة *irānat*, (v. n. 4 of ران for رين) Losing many sheep by a murrain.

A اراني *arānī*, (pl. of ارنب *arnab*) Hares. *Urānaʼ*, A grain used for curdling milk.

A ارانية *arāniyat*, A plant of the species حمض *hamz* having a tall trunk.

P اراوند *arāwand*, Grief, regret. Desire, wish. The Tigris. Splendour, pomp, grandeur. Name of a mountain in Hamadān.

A اراويّ *arāwiy*, (pl. of ارويّة *urwīyat*) She mountain-goats (from 3 to 10).

A اراويح *arāwīh*, (pl. of ريح *rīh*) Winds.

G اراه *arāh*, Mastic.

A اراهط *arāhiṭ*, (or اراهيط *arāhīṭ*) (pl. of رهط *raht*) Any number of men below ten living together without women. Enemies.

P آراي *ārāy*, Adorn. (in comp.) Adorning. Ornament.

A اراي *arʼa'*, More or most apt, proper, worthy.

P آرايانيدن *ārāyānīdan*, To cause to adorn.

P آرايش *ārāyish*, Ornament, embellishment. Custom, law, institute. Name of a note in music. آرايش خورشيد *ārāyishi khwurshed*, Name of a note in music. A mole on the face. آرايش كردن *ārāyish kardan*, To adorn. آرايش مجلس *ārāyishi majlis*, The ornament of the assembly.

A ارائك *arāʼik*, (pl. of اراك *arāk*) Certain trees on which they feed camels. (pl. of اريكة *arīkat*) Thrones, sofas.

P آرايندة *ārāyinda*, Ornamenting: a decorator.

A ارايح *arāyih*, (pl. of ريح *rīh*) Winds.

P آرائيدن *ārāʼīdan*, To adorn, decorate.

P آرائيدة *ārāʼīda*, Ornamented, adorned.

A أرب *araba*, (fut. يأرب *yaʼribu*) He tied.

A أرب *ariba*, (fut. يأرب *yaʼribu*) He had need.

A ارب *arb*, (v. n. of ارب) Tying a knot. Striking on a limb. The space between the index and the second finger. *Irb*, (pl. آراب *ārāb* or ارآب *arʼāb*) Skill, knowledge, industry, prudence, sagacity, wisdom. Religion. Want, need. Wickedness, dishonesty, disingenuousness, fallacy, perfidy. A member, limb. Membrum genitale. *Urb*, The small-sized young of any animal as soon as it is born. Shrewdness, sagacity. *Arab*, (v. n. of ارب) Being accustomed, exercised. Falling down, being languid and useless (the limbs). Being amputated (the hand). Oppressing, being severe (fortune). Being foul and corrupt (the stomach). Need, necessity. Wanting, needing, asking or searching for any thing necessary. Skill, knowledge, intellect. اربت من يديك *aribta min yadayka* or اربت عن ذي يديك *aribta ɛan zī yadayka*, May thy hands fall dead. *Arib*, Expert, skilled, sagacious, sly, cunning, shrewd, wise, intelligent. *Irab*, (v. n. of ارب) Being shrewd, intelligent, and clever. *Urab*, (pl. of اربة *urbat*) Knots. Necessary affairs.

A ارباء *arbāʼ*, (pl. of ربو *rabw*) Crowds, multitudes. *Irbāʼ*, (v. n. 4 of ربا for ربو) Taking interest. Augmenting, multiplying. Exceeding.

A ارباب *arbāb*, (pl. of ربّ *rabb*) Lords, masters, possessors. ارباب تغلب *arbābi taghallub*, Superiors, conquerors. ارباب تميز *arbābi tamyīz*, Judicious, discerning, prudent. ارباب تيار *arbābi tīmār*, Pensioners. ارباب جاه و تمكين *arbābi jāh u tamkīn*, Possessed of dignity and power. ارباب خرد *arbābi khirad*, Sage, intelligent. ارباب ديوان *arbābi dīwān*, Counsellors. ارباب سخن *arbābi sukhan*, Eloquent orators. ارباب سلوك *arbābi sulūk*, Devout, observers of religious precepts. ارباب صفاي باطن *arbābi safāʼi bātin*, Endowed with purity, of a contemplative and holy life. ارباب صنعت *arbābi sanɛat*, Artificers, artisans. ارباب فضل و افضال و اصحاب علم و كمال *arbābi fazl u afzāl, wa as-hābi ɛilm u kamāl*, Persons of merit and learning. ارباب معالي *arbābi maɛālī*, Grandees, eminent men. ارباب معني *arbābi maɛnā'*, Spiritual persons. ارباب مكرمت *arbābi makrumat*, Most clement lords. ارباب نشاط *arbābi nashāt*, Dancers and singers. ارباب همت *arbābi himmat*, High-minded, liberal (persons). *Irbāb*, (v. n. 4 of ربّ) Coming near unto. Remaining in one place. Keeping close to the male. Blowing without interruption (the south wind).

A ارباج *irbāj*, A begetting dwarfish children.

A ارباح *irbāh*, (v. n. 4 of ربح) Rendering profitable and gainful. Killing a young camel to provide an entertainment for one's guests. Milking (a camel) at morn and noon.

A ارباخ *irbākh*, (v. n. 4 of ربخ) Purchasing a female slave who is subject to fainting fits in coitu. Being heaped up (sand). Falling into misfortune.

A ارباذ *irbāz*, (v. n. 4 of ربذ) Amputating. Making a scourge.

A ارباز *irbāz*, (v. n. 4 of ربز) Rendering sharp and clever. Appearing fat (a ram).

A ارباش *irbāsh*, (v. n. 4 of ربش) Budding, bursting forth into leaf (a tree).

A ارباض *arbāz*, (pl. of ربض *rabaz*) Wives. Houses or places where the people reside. *Irbāz*, (v. n. 4 of ربض) Folding (sheep). Furnishing with necessaries. Satisfying people (a vessel) until they become heavy and lie down to sleep. Shining in his full strength (the sun).

A ارباع *arbāɛ*, (pl. of ربع *rabɛ*) Houses, mansions (particularly for the spring-season). (pl. of ربع *rubɛ*) Fourth parts. (pl. of ربع *rubaɛ*) Camels' colts dropped in the spring. (pl. of رباعي *rabāɛī*) Animals that have shed the tooth رباعية *rabāɛiyat*. *Irbāɛ*, (v. n. 4 of ربع) Having camels which drink on the fourth day. Being four in number. Attacking (as a quartan fever). Suffering from a quartan fever. Asking; then going off and coming again. Allowing a camel to drink his fill. Rising four (a sheep), five (a cow and horse), and seven (a camel). Indulging much in venery. Rushing impetuously to a watering-place (a large multitude of men and camels). Being close, impervious (a she-camel). Entering upon the vernal season. Turning (cattle) out to spring-pasture. Dwelling in a spring-habitation. Begetting children in the decline of life. Breeding the teeth called رباعية *rabāɛiyat*.

A ارباغ *irbāgh*, A letting camels drink their fill.

A ارباق *arbāk*, (pl. of ربقة) Halters with nooses.

A اربال *irbāl*, (v. n. 4 of ربل) Producing trees in leaf, or verdant grass in autumn.

A اربان *irbān*, (v. n. 4 of ربن) Giving earnest money. *Urbān*, Arabians. Earnest-money.

A اربة *irbat*, Want, indigence. Skill, knowledge, sagacity, cunning, stratagem. The privities. *Urbat*, A hard knot. Want, need. Any thing necessary to be done, indispensable business. Skill, sagacity. A collar, whatever is round the neck by way of ornament. The eye of the fetter or stake, with, or to which, they fasten the feet of cattle.

A اربّة *aribbat*, (pl. of رباب *ribāb*) Confederate tribes. (pl. of ربّة *ribbat* or *rubbat*) Great multitudes, myriads.

A ارثاث *irbisās*, A being divided, or scattered.

A اربجان *irbijān*, Name of a plant.

A اربد *arbad*, A deadly kind of serpent. A lion.

A ارىداد *irbidād*, (v. n. 9 of ربد) Being of a dusty colour. Shining with a black and white colour.

A ارساس *irbisās*, (v. n. 9 of ربس) Travelling over the earth. Being weak (any business) so that the parties concerned separate and disperse. Being angry with each other. Having power, exercising controul. Delaying, lagging behind.

A اربش *arbash*, Various or changing coloured.

A اربع *arbaɛ*, (fem.) Four. جاء يمشي علي اربع *jāʼa yamshī ɛala' arbaɛin*, He came walking on all fours. *Arbuɛ*, (pl. of ربع *rabɛ*) Houses, vernal mansions.

A اربعاء *arbaɛāʼ*, *arbiɛāʼ*, or *arbuɛāʼ*, Wednesday. *Arbiɛāʼ*, (pl. of ربيع *rabīɛ*) Spring-seasons. Vernal months called ربيع *rabīɛ*. Rivulets. *Urbuɛāʼ*, Sitting square. A tent-pole. قعد الاربعاء *kaɛada'l arbaɛāʼ*, (or *urbuɛāʼ*) He sat four square. بيت اربعاواء *baytun urbuɛāwāʼ*, A tent supported by one, two, three, or four poles; a house having so many columns.

A اربعاءات *arbaɛāʼāt*, Wednesdays.

A اربعاءان *arbaɛāʼāni*, Two Wednesdays.

A اربعاوي *urbuɛāwa'*, A sitting square.

A اربعة *arbaɛat*, (mas.) Four. Both hands and feet. The four legs of a quadruped. *Arbiɛat*, (pl. of ربيع *rabīɛ*) Spring-seasons or harvests.

A اربعة عشر *arbaɛat ɛashara*, (mas.) Fourteen.

A اربعون *arbaɛūna*, (obl. اربعين *arbaɛīna*) Forty.

A اربغ *arbagh*, Much, many, abundant.

A اربك *arbak*, (pl. ربك *rubk*) (A camel) dark-coloured, or very black about the ears and sides, and darkish elsewhere.

A اربل *arbal*, Clothed afresh in autumn (a tree). *Irbil*, Arbela in Mesopotamia, famous for the defeat of Darius by Alexander the Great. Sidon.

P اربو *arbū*, A pear.

P اربوجينا *arbūjīnā*, (in zand and Pāzand) A water-melon. An island.

P اربودار *arbū-dār*, A pear-tree.

A اربون *urbūn*, Earnest-money. A price.

A اربونا *arbūnā*, The town of Narbonne in France.

A اربي *urba'*, Misfortune, vexatious affair, evil.

G ارباسيوس *arbiyāsayūs*, Name of a doctor.

A اربيان *irbiyān*, A little white fish common at Basra: a prawn, shrimp, lobster. A sort of pot-herb.

A اربيّة *urbiyat*, The top of the thigh which joins the hip, the groin. A family of relations, as cousins-german, &c.

P اربيتا *arbītā*, (in zand and Pāzand) A roof.

A اربيثاث *irbisās*, (v. n. 11 of ربث) Being weak and dilatory. Being impeded and restrained.

A اربيداد *irbīdād*, (v. n. 11 of ربد) Being of a dusty, ashy colour. Shining with black and white.

A اربيكاك *irbīkāk*, (v. n. 11 of ربك) Retiring, desisting. Being puzzled, confused (the wits).

A آرة *ārat*, Name of a mountain in Arabia. وادي آرة *wādi ārat*, Name of a river in Spain.

A ارة *irat*, (pl. ارات *irāt*, ارون *irūna* or *urūna*) A fire-place, a hearth. Fire, heat. Dried flesh. Meat cooked in rough tripe, a haggess. Meat steeped in vinegar, and carried on a journey.

A ارّة *irrat*, Fire.

P آرت *ārat*, A cubit. The elbow.

A ارتّ *aratt*, Stammering. A stammerer.

P ارتا *artā*, (in zand and Pāzand) A country.

A ارتاء *irtāء*, (v. n. 4 of رتأ) Smiling, laughing.

A ارتاب *irtāb*, (v. n. 4 of رتب) Begging after having been rich. Being poured out.

A ارتات *irtāt*, A causing to stammer.

A ارتاج *irtāj*, (v. n. 4 of رتج) Shutting (a door). Being shut (a door, the womb). Having an egg completely formed (a hen). Being in foal (an ass). Stammering. Rolling with a heavy swell (the sea). Being very barren (a year). Being abundant (a year). Snowing continually.

A ارتاحاشت *artāhāsht*, Artaxerxes.

A ارتاع *artāع*, A multitude. *Irtāع*, (v. n. 4 of رتع) Turning into a good pasture. Producing abundance of grass (rain).

P ارتاق *urtāk*, (in Khwārazm) A merchant.

A ارتاك *irtāk*, A causing to run. A smiling.

A ارتام *irtām*, (v. n. 4 of رتم) Tying a thread round the finger, in order to be reminded by it of something. Having a fat bunch (a young camel).

A ارتباء *irtibāء*, (v. n. 8 of ربأ) Keeping watch, looking out. Ascending a watch-tower. Appearing from a height, impending, overhanging.

A ارتباب *irtibāb*, (v. n. 8 of ربّ) Educating.

A ارتباث *irtibās*, A being divided or scattered.

A ارتباز *irtibāz*, (v. n. 8 of ربز) Being full, complete, perfect.

A ارتباس *irtibās*, (v. n. 8 of ربس) Being mixed. Being close and compact (flesh, or bunch of grapes).

A ارتباط *irtibāt*, (v. n. 8 of ربط) Binding. Being tied. Equipping a horse for battle. P ارتباط كردن *irtibāt kardan*, To form a connexion or alliance.

A ارتباع *irtibāع*, (v. n. 8 of ربع) Growing fat on spring grass. Passing the vernal season. Lifting up a stone to try one's strength. Sitting four square. Being arrived (the season for gathering dates). Running violently (a camel).

A ارتباق *irtibāk*, (v. n. 8 of ربق) Being held fast in a noose (a doe). Being entangled in an intricate business.

A ارتباك *irtibāk*, (v. n. 8 of ربك) Being mixed, confused, thrown into the mire. Stammering. Endeavouring to get loose from the toils of a hunter. Finding (an affair) intricate and embarrassing.

A ارتبال *irtibāl*, (v. n. 8 of ربل) Being abundant (riches), being numerous (camels).

A ارتة *urtat*, The crest of a chameleon.

A ارتتاج *irtitāj*, A pronouncing with difficulty.

A ارتتاق *irtitāk*, (v. n. 8 of رتق) Being stitched, or closed up. Being impervious (a female).

A ارتتام *irtitām*, (v. n. 8 of رتم) Having a string tied round the finger to remind one of any thing.

A ارتثاء *irtisāء*, (v. n. 8 of رثي) Being thick and somewhat acid (milk). Drinking the coagulated milk رثيئة *rasīءat*. Perplexing, confusing, embroiling (a business).

A ارتثاث *irtisās*, (v. n. 8 of رثّ) Being carried off the field of battle half-dead.

A ارتثاد *irtisād*, (v. n. 8 of رثد) Laying or piling (wares or furniture) side by side.

A ارتجاء *irtijāء*, A hoping. A fearing.

A ارتجاج *irtijāj*, (v. n. 8 of رجّ) Shaking. Dashing (the waves of the sea). Agitation, tremor.

A ارتجاح *irtijāh*, (v. n. 8 of رجح) Being moved to and fro (a swing). Travelling with a swinging motion (a camel). Shaking (fat buttocks).

A ارتجاز *irtijāz*, (v. n. 8 of رجز) Composing or reciting a poem with the metre called رجز *rajaz*. Rumbling (thunder).

A ارتجاس *irtijās*, (v. n. 8 of رجس) Being shaken. Thundering. Braying (a camel).

A ارتجاع *irtijāع*, (v. n. 8 of رجع) Carrying back. Receiving back. Selling (a camel) and buying another with the proceeds of the sale.

A ارتجال *irtijāl*, (v. n. 8 of رجل) Placing under one's feet. Holding (the wood زند *zand*) between one's hands and feet. Suspending by one or both feet. Speaking extempore. Being alone in any business. Ambling (a horse). Collecting many locusts to roast. Cooking in a large copper. Being singular in one's opinion. ارتجل رجلك *irtajil rijlaka*, Mind your business.

A ارتجالاً *irtijālan*, Extempore, unpremeditatedly.

A ارتجام *irtijām*, A being heaped together.

A ارتجان *irtijān*, (v. n. 8 of رجن) Being confused and difficult to arrange. Not coagulating, but turning sour (milk). Accumulating, being closely packed. Abiding.

P ارتجك *irtajak* or *irtajik*, Lightning.

A ارتحاض *irtihāz*, The being much ashamed.

A ارتحال *irtihāl*, (v. n. 8 of رحل) Departing. Travelling. Saddling (a camel). Migration.

A ارتخ *artakh*, Dry, parched, unmoist (skin).

A ارتخاخ *irtikhākh*, (v. n. 8 of رخّ) Being loose, lax, languid. Being distracted, perplexed (counsel).

A ارتخاش *irtikhāsh*, (v. n. 8 of رخش) Being agitated, disturbed, confused.

A ارتخاص *irtikhās*, (v. n. 8 of رخص) Buying cheap. Reckoning cheap, regarding as such.

A ارتداء *irtidāء*, (v. n 8 of ردي) Putting on a cloak or mantle. Putting on a leathern girdle.

A ارتداد *irtidād*, (v. n. 8 of ردّ) Turning back, Apostatizing, becoming a renegado. Refusing, Opposing. Apostacy. P ارتداد آوردن *irtidād āwardan*, (كردن *kardan* or نمودن *namūdan*) To apostatize.

A ارتداع *irtidāع*, (v. n. 8 of ردع) Abstaining. Being driven back. Being defiled, tinged, stained.

A ارتداغ *irtidāgh*, A falling into the mire.

A ارتداف *irtidāf*, (v. n. 8 of ردف) Riding behind another on the same beast. Following. Pursuing. Taking one up to ride behind one's self.

A ارتدان *irtidān*, A making of a spindle.

A ارتزاء *irtizāء*, (v. n. 8 of رزأ) Overtaking (as a calamity), diminishing, impairing (a man's property). Experiencing a diminution. Diminution, decrease, detriment.

A ارتزاز *irtizāz*, (v. n. 8 of رزّ) Sticking (as an arrow in the mark). Being close-fisted, refusing to give. Being contracted, shrivelled, or puckered. Being penitent. Stinginess.

A ارتزاق *irtizāk*, (v. n. 8 of رزق) Gaining a livelihood. Receiving a stipend, or ration.

A ارتساس *irtisās*, (v. n. 8 of رسّ) Being divulged, circulated, spread abroad (news).

A ارتساغ *irtisāgh*, (v. n. 8 of رسغ) Enlarging one's expenses, being liberal to one's household.

A ارتساف *irtisāf*, A being raised or elevated.

A ارتسام *irtisām*, (v. n. 8 of رسم) Fleeing (to God) for refuge. Being proud and haughty. Yielding obedience to an order. Wishing or requesting to withhold. Reciting the praises of God. Prayer, invocation. A distinguishing mark, whatever is eminent or remarkable. نصرت ارتسام *nusrat-irtisām*, Victorious, famous for victory. مودّت ارتسام *mawaddat-irtisām*, Affectionate, benevolent, friendly.

A ارتسفاف *irtisfāf*, A being raised or elevated.

A ارتشاء *irtishāء*, (v. n. 8 of رشا for رشو) Receiving a bribe (a judge).

A ارتشاف *irtishāf*, A sipping, a sucking.

A ارتصاع *irtisāع*, (v. n. 8 of رصع) Being closely set (the teeth). Bruising between two stones. Sticking fast.

A ارتصاق *irtisāk*, An adhering firmly.

A ارتضاء *irtizāء*, (v. n. 8 of رضي) Approving. Choosing, consenting, accepting.

A ارتضاح *irtizāh*, (v. n. 8 of رضح) Apologizing.

A ارتضاخ *irtizākh*, A speaking inelegantly.

A ارتضاد *irtizād*, (v. n. 8 of رضد) Being arranged, placed side by side (wares).

A ارتضاع *irtizāع*, (v. n. 8 of رضع) Sucking herself (a she-goat).

A ارتطام *irtiṭām*, (v. n. 8 of رطم) Being troublesome, perplexing, intricate (business). Being pressed closely together. Sinking and sticking fast in clay (feet of a quadruped). Being inextricably entangled, sticking fast. Keeping in dung.

A ارتعاء *irtiʿāʾ*, (v. n. 8 of رعي) Going to pasture.

A ارتعاب *irtiʿāb*, (v. n. 8 of رعب) Being frightened. Alarm.

A ارتعاث *irtiʿās*, The putting on of ear-rings.

A ارتعاج *irtiʿāj*, (v. n. 8 of رعج) Being abundant (riches, flocks, or children). Being full (the bed of a river). Tremor, trepidation.

A ارتعاد *irtiʿād*, (v. n. 8 of رعد) Trembling, quaking with fear. Trepidation.

A ارتعاس *irtiʿās*, (v. n. 8 of رعس) Trembling.

A ارتعاش *irtiʿāsh*, (v. n. 8 of رعش) Trembling; trepidation.

A ارتعاص *irtiʿāṣ*, (v. n. 8. of رعص) Twisting himself, writhing (a scotched snake). Being beaten (clothes). Being frisky (a kid). Vibrating greatly (a lance). Flashing (lightning). Becoming dear (provisions).

A ارتعاف *irtiʿāf*, (v. n. 8 of رعف) Running fast, taking the lead. Being strong and powerful.

A ارتغاء *irtighāʾ*, (v. n. 8 of رغا for رغو) Drinking the froth of milk.

A ارتغاب *irtighāb* A desiring, a wishing.

A ارتغاث *irtighās*, A sucking of the mother.

A ارتفاد *irtifād*, (v. n. 8 of رفد) Gaining. Gain.

A ارتفاص *irtifāṣ*, (v. n. 8 of رفص) Being scarce and dear (provisions).

A ارتفاع *irtifāʿ*, (v. n. 8 of رفع) Raising, elevating. Being raised, elevated. Culminating. Being at high noon (the day). Ceasing, being suspended. Citing or going together before a judge. Elevation, height. P ارتفاع فر و شوكت *irtifāʿi far u shawkat*, The height of glory and magnificence. قلاع فلك ارتفاع *kilāʿi falak-irtifāʿ*, Castles high as the heavens. ارتفاع گرفتن *irtifāʿ giriftan*, To take the altitude (of the sun).

A ارتفاف *irtifāf*, (v. n. 8 of رفّ) Shining, glittering (a colour).

A ارتفاق *irtifāk*, (v. n. 8 of رفق) Leaning on the elbow, or on a cushion. Associating with, becoming a companion. Being filled (a cistern).

A ارتقاء *irtikāʾ*, (v. n. 8 of رقى) Climbing, ascending. Addition, accession, augmentation. Ascent, exaltation. Advancement, promotion.

A ارتقاب *irtikāb*, (v. n. 8 of رقب) Expecting, waiting, watching, observing, contemplating. Looking down from an eminence.

A ارتقاش *irtikāsh*, A mixing in battle.

A ارتقاع *irtikāʿ*, (v. n. 8 of رقع) Regarding, attending to, minding, caring for. Fearing.

A ارتقان *irtikān*, The being anointed with saffron.

A ارتكاء *irtikāʾ*, (v. n. 8 of ركا for ركو) Confiding, relying, depending upon.

A ارتكاب *irtikāb*, (v. n. 8 of ركب) Mounting, riding. Attempting, committing. Commission or perpetration (of a crime). Undergoing, enduring. ارتكاب معاصي *irtikābi maʿāṣī*, Commission of sins, perpetation of crimes. ارتكاب زنا *irtikābi zinā*, Commission of adultery.

A ارتكاح *irtikāh*, (v. n. 8 of ركح) Leaning against.

A ارتكاز *irtikāz*, (v. n. 8 of ركز) Throbbing (as an artery). Leaning on a bow. Being firm, stable.

A ارتكاس *irtikās*, (v. n. 8 of ركس) Being inverted, thrown down. Being squeezed into a narrow compass. Falling. Relapsing, backsliding. Standing still on the thrashing-floor (an ox). Going round and round a centre.

A ارتكاض *irtikāz*, (v. n. 8 of ركض) Stirring in the womb (a fœtus). Being in a flurry and flutter at one's work. Agitation, disquietude, amazement.

A ارتكاف *irtikāf*, (v. n. 8 of ركف) Falling and lying on the ground (snow).

A ارتكاك *irtikāk*, (v. n. 8 of ركّ) Shaking, trembling. Being dubious, uncertain. Stammering in altercation, though speaking plainly before.

A ارتكام *irtikām*, (v. n. 8 of ركم) Being closely packed, heaped, or accumulated.

A ارتكان *irtikān*, (v. n. 8 of ركن) Reclining.

A ارتل *artal*, A stammerer, a stutterer.

A ارتم *artam*, A stammerer, a stutterer.

A ارتماء *irtimāʾ*, (v. n. 8 of رمي) Darting forth. Shooting (at game). Being thrown. Throwing (stones) at one another. Reviling mutually. Casting one's self headlong.

A ارتماز *irtimāz*, (v. n. 8 of رمز) Trembling from a severe blow. Moving to and fro, fluctuating, being in commotion in an assembly.

A ارتماس *irtimās*, A plunging, a diving.

A ارتماض *irtimāz*, (v. n. 8 of رمض) Being diseased (the liver). Jumping, leaping, springing. Prevailing against, triumphing over, carrying off. Grieving, disturbing, disquieting.

A ارتمال *irtimāl*, (v. n. 8 of رمل) Being smeared (with blood). Being base and contemptible.

A ارتمام *irtimām*, (v. n. 8 of رمّ) Cropping the shoots of trees (a cow). Beginning to have a bunch (a young camel).

A ارتناح *irtināh*, A staggering from intoxication.

P ارتنگ *artang*, The house of the famous Persian painter and religious impostor, named Mānī; also his book of drawings, which he shewed to his followers as a work given to him by angels. Mānī himself. A Chinese idol-temple or joss-house.

A ارتواء *irtiwāʾ*, (v. n. 8 of روي) Quenching one's thirst. Fetching water. Being filled with moisture. Being twisted thick. Being thick (joint).

A ارتواح *irtiwāh*, (v. n. 8 of راح for روح) Doing any work succeeding each other.

A ارتهاء *irtihāʾ*, (v. n. 8 of رها for رهو) Being mixed, confused.

A ارتهاز *irtihāz*, (v. n. 8 of رهز) Wriggling.

A ارتهاس *irtihās*, (v. n. 8 of رهس) Cutting one foot with the other (a horse). Being filled with water (a valley). Thronging, crowding. Mounting one upon another (locusts). Being shaken and agitated.

A ارتهاش *irtihāsh*, (v. n. 8 of رهش) Cutting one foot with the other (a horse). Fighting. Extirpating, eradicating. Being slender and weak (a bow), the string striking against the belly when shooting. A spear-wound inflicted crosswise. Tremor, trepidation.

A ذووا ارتهاط *zawū irtihāt*, Assembled together.

A ارتهاك *irtihāk*, A weakness or looseness in the joints in walking.

A ارتهان *irtihān*, (v. n. 8 of رهن) Receiving a pledge or hostage.

A ارتئاء *irtiʾāʾ*, (v. n. 8 of رأي) Seeing, looking into, knowing. Deliberation.

A ارتئاب *irtiʾāb*, (v. n. 8 of رأب) Joining, closing up (chinks).

A ارتياب *irtiyāb*, (v. n. 8 of راب for ريب) Doubting, suspecting. Doubt, uncertainty.

P ارتيابانه *irtiyābāna*, Doubtfully.

A ارتياح *irtiyāh*, (v. n. 8 of راح for روح) Rejoicing; being glad, leaping for joy. Setting at liberty, giving rest from trouble. Compassion, mercy. Wine. صباح باهر الارتياح *sabāh bāhiru'l irtiyāh*, A fine or cheerful morning.

A ارتئاد *irtiʾād*, (v. n. 8 of رأد) Exulting, rejoicing (in riches).

A ارتياد *irtiyād*, (v. n. 8 of راد for رود) Looking for a place where to urine (soft and sloping, in order not to make a splash and contract defilement). Seeking, searching (for fodder).

A ارتئاس *irtiʾās*, (v. n. 8 of رأس) Becoming head or chief. Keeping employed.

A ارتياش *irtiyāsh*, (v. n. 8 of راش for ريش) Being in easy circumstances, feathering a nest.

A ارتياض *irtiyāz*, (v. n. 8 of راض for روض) Being broke in (a colt).

A ارتياع *irtiyāʿ*, (v. n. 8 of راع for روع) Fearing, dreading. Terror.

A ارتياغ *irtiyāgh*, (v. n. 8 of راغ for روغ) Asking for. Wishing, desiring, hankering after.

P ارتيشدار *arteshdār*, A company of horsemen. Name of a river.

A آرث *āras*, Black with white spots (a ram).

A ارث *ars*, (v. n. of ارث) Exciting, stirring up (one against another). Kindling (a fire). *Irs*, (v. n. of ورث) Succeeding to as heir, inheriting. Inheritance, heritage, hereditary right. A root. An affair of ancient hereditary custom. Ashes. Remains, residue. *Urs*, A kind of thorn. *Aris*, Black with white spots (cattle). *Uras*, Land-marks, boundaries. Knots.

A ارثّ *arass*, Worn out, falling in pieces.

A ارثاء *arsaʾ*, Spotted black and white (a ram).

A ارثاء *arsā,* Black with white spots (a ewe). *Irsā,* (v. n. 4 of رثا) Becoming thick and clotted.

A ارثاث *irsās,* (v. n. 4 of رث) Being worn out. Being tarnished, disfigured by filth. Wearing, impairing, consuming.

A ارثاد *irsād,* (v. n. 4 of رثد) Being turbid. Digging to a spring. Standing still side by side.

A ارثاط *irsāt,* A remaining fixed to one's seat.

P ارثانه *irsāna,* Hereditary, by hereditary right.

A ارثة *ursat,* (pl. ارث *uras*) A limit, landmark, boundary, confine, border. Plain, level ground. Land bumping out into hillocks of a reddish colour. Dung mixed with ashes for fuel. Black colour mixed with white spots.

P ارثد *arsad,* Root of the wild pepper-tree.

A ارثعنان *irsiɛnān,* (v. n. 4 of رثعن Q) Falling in abundance (rain). Hanging down (hair). Being weak and relaxed.

A ارثم *arsam,* (A horse) white in the upper lip (when in the lower, he is called املظ *almaz*).

A ارثمام *irsimām,* (v. n. 9 of رثم) Having white on the upper lip (a horse).

A ارثى *arsa',* Unskilful in managing business.

P آرج *āraj,* A kind of bird. The elbow.

P ارج *arj,* Price, worth, value, esteem, honour. Extraction. Separating. A rhinoceros. A swan. A bird with soft plumage. Limit, bound, measure.

A ارج *arj,* The stirring up of dissensions, seditions, or quarrels. An æra. *Araj,* (v. n. of ارج) Sending forth an agreeable perfume. Making a great noise. A sweet smell.

A ارجاء *arjā,* (pl. of رجا *raja'*) Sides, parts, margins, coasts. *Irjā,* (v. n. 4 of رجا not in use) Deferring, putting off (any business). Being about to bring forth. Being unsuccessful (a hunter). (v. n. 4 of رجا for رجو) Being near bringing forth. Strengthening the sides of a well with bricks.

A ارجاب *arjāb,* The intestines. (pl. of رجب *rajab*) The months of Rajab. *Irjāb,* (v. n. 4 of رجب) Revering, honouring.

A ارجاج *irjāj,* (v. n. 4 of رج) Being near foaling (a mare).

A ارجاح *irjāh,* (v. n. 4 of رجح) Giving overweight, or the turn of the scale.

A ارجاد *irjād,* (v. n. 4 of رجد) Terrifying. Causing to tremble.

A ارجاس *irjās,* A sounding the depth of water.

P ارجاسپ *arjāsp,* The grandson of Afrasyāb.

A ارجاع *irjāɛ,* (v. n. 4 of رجع) Causing to return. Stretching forth the hand behind the back to receive something. Being ill for two days (an old man), and not recovering strength for a month. Becoming lean and afterwards growing fat (camels). Easing nature. Making one take back a thing purchased. Changing, turning, restoring. Rendering profitable and gainful. Uttering the sentence انا لله و انا اليه راجعون *innā li' llāh wa innā ilayhi rājiɛūna,* Verily we belong to God, and verily to him we are returning.

A ارجاف *arjāf,* (pl. اراجيف *arājīf*) An uncertain or false rumour, a fiction. *Irjāf,* (v. n. 4 of رجف) Engaging in business. Mixing in debates, propagating seditious rumours. Trembling (the earth). Coming along jaded and with the ears flabby and pendulous (a camel). Forcing, compelling. Heat. Restlessness, disturbance.

A ارجال *arjāl,* Beasts turned loose with their young ones. (pl. of رجل *rajul, rajil,* and *rajal*) Men whose hair is partly curled and partly lank. (pl. of رجل *rijl*) Portions of any thing. Large flights of locusts. Sleepy (men). White papers. Calamities. Misanthropes. Armies. Precedencies. *Irjāl,* (v. n. 4 of رجل) Making one go on foot. Leaving a camel at liberty with her foal. Prolonging, granting a delay.

P ارجالون *arjālūn,* A wild vine.

P ارجان *arjān,* A kind of fir. A kind of mountain-almond.

A ارجان *arjān,* A species of wild olive common in Morocco. *Irjān,* (v. n. 4 of رجن) Feeding a camel on hay in the stable. *Arajān,* An attempt to sow dissension.

A ارّجان *arrajān,* Name of a town in Susiana.

A ارجاه *irjāh,* (v. n. 4 of رجه) Deferring beyond the proper time.

A ارجح *arjah,* Heavier, more or most preponderating, better, best.

A ارجحنان *irjihnān,* (v. n. 4 of رجحن Q) Inclining, leaning. Being shaken, agitated. Falling at once. Rising (as a vapour above the plain).

A ارجز *arjaz,* A camel troubled with the disease رجز *rajaz.*

A ارجعة *arjiɛat,* (pl. of رجاع) Camels' halters.

A ارجعنان *irjiɛnān,* (v. n. 4 of رجعن Q not used) Inclining. Shaking. Falling down at once.

A ارجل *arjal,* (Cattle) marked with white on one foot. Large-footed (man). More or most of a man, stronger. *Arjul,* (pl. of رجل *rijl*) Feet.

A ارجلة *arjilat,* (pl. of رجل) Men on foot. Infantry.

P ارجمند *arjmand,* Rare, excellent, worthy of great price, valuable, exquisite, beloved, dear, brave, generous, noble, distinguished. Wise. ارجمند بانو *arjmand-bānū,* (Noble princess) A proper name.

P ارجمندي *arjmandī,* Excellence, preciousness.

P ارجن *arjan,* The bitter-almond tree.

P ارجند *arjand,* Name of a town.

P ارجنگ *arjang,* The house of the celebrated painter and impostor Mānī.

P ارجنه *arjana,* Name of a desert in Persia. Name of a note in music.

P ارجوان *arjawān,* (A *urjuwān*) Purple, deep red. A purple dye. A purple robe or carpet. Redness. Starch. آب ارجوان *ābi arjawān,* (Red water) Wine. روي صفرا و چشم ارجوان *rūyi safrā u chashmi arjawān,* Faces of saffron and eyes of Arjawān are common expressions, to imply passionate lovers, in whose countenances a yellow melancholy is painted, and whose eyes are inflamed with shedding of tears.

P ارجواني *arjawānī,* Very red, purple.

A ارجوانيّ *urjuwānīy,* Very red, purple

A ارجوحة *urjūhat,* A swing, a see-saw.

A ارجوزة *urjūzat* (pl. اراجيز *arājīz*) A poem in the measure called رجز *rajaz.*

A ارجيّة *urjīyat,* Any thing hoped for.

A ارجيس *arjīs,* Name of a fort in Mesopotamia.

P ارچه *archi,* (or ارچند *archand*) Although.

P ارچين *archīn,* A ladder. A staircase.

P ارچيني *archīnī,* Name of a mountain.

A ارح *arahh* Broad or large-footed, and without any hollow beneath.

A ارحاء *arhā,* (pl. of رحي *raha'*) Mills. Breasts, or the callous parts of them on which camels recline. Hoofs of camels and elephants. Grinders, back teeth. Independent tribes, living by themselves. Numbers of domestics. Chiefs of the people. Fields of battle. Crowds of camels pressing upon one another.

A ارحاب *irhāb,* (v. n. 4 of رحب) Being wide, roomy, and spacious. Enlarging, making spacious.

A ارحاض *irhāz,* (v. n. 4 of رحض) Washing.

A ارحاف *irhāf,* (v. n. 4 of رحف not used) Whetting, sharpening (a sword).

A ارحال *irhāl,* (v. n. 4 of رحل) Breaking in a camel. Making a present of a strong camel. Becoming strong after being weak (a camel's back). Becoming fat after having been lean (a camel). Becoming fit for the saddle (a camel). Having many camels fit for the saddle.

A ارحام *arhām,* (pl. of رحم *rihm* or *rahim*) Wombs. Relations by the mother, uterine kindred.

A ارحب *arhab,* The name of a tribe. نجائب ارحبيّات *najāɛib arhabīyāt,* Excellent camels found in that tribe. *Arhib,* (and ارحبي *arhibī*) (imp. of 4) Give way, retire (used chiefly to horses when they want them to back).

A ارحل *arhal,* (A horse) white on the back. (A sheep or goat) black on the back. *Arhul,* (pl. of رحل *rahl*) Small saddles for camels.

A ارحم *arham,* More or most merciful. ارحم الراحمين *arhamu'r rāhimīn,* The most merciful of the merciful (God).

A ارحي *arhī,* (ارحيّ *urhīy,* or ارحية *arhiyat*) (pl. of رحي *raha'*) Mills.

G ارحيقنه *arhīkana,* Name of a dyeing herb.

A ارخ *arkh,* (v. n. of ارخ) Dating (a letter). *Arkh* or *irkh,* A bullock. *Arakh,* Name of a town.

A ارخاء *irkhā,* (v. n. 4 of رخا for رخو) Giving the reins, relaxing. Unfurling a sail. Letting drop a veil or curtain. Running in a straggling manner. Making (a horse) run so. Having soft buttocks (a horse). Making soft, loose, and relaxed. ارخى عمامته arkha' ʻimāmatahu, He let fall his turban-sash, he felt quiet and secure.

A ارخاخ irkhākh, (v. n. 4 of رخّ) Using diligence, straining every nerve. Excess, hyperbole.

A ارخاس irkhās. See ارخاص irkhās.

A ارخاص irkhās, (v. n. 4 of رخص) Finding or purchasing cheap. Making cheap.

A ارخاف irkhāf, (v. n. 4 of رخف) Making (dough) thin and watery.

A ارخام irkhām, (v.n.4 of رخم) Sitting, brooding.

A ارخة arkhat, A wild heifer. *Urkhat*, An epoch, æra, period, date.

A ارخل arkhul, (pl. of رخل rikhl, rakhil, or رخلة rikhlat) Ewe-lambs.

A ارخم arkham, (A horse) with a white head and black body. More or most tender (voice).

P ارخنده arkhanda, A tincture-powder, with which they tinge the nails and other parts of the body of a beautiful red; some nations, mixing it with vinegar, dye the manes and tails of their horses. A kind of tree from which they make a fine oil.

E ارخنگ arakhang, Arracan.

G ارخون arkhūn, A prince, chief, archon. A high-priest, patriarch (among eastern Christians).

A ارخى arkha', Softer, softest; more or most flabby.

A ارخىّ urkhīy, A steer.

A ارخيّة urkhīyat, The loose or pendulous part of any thing. The young of the mountain-goat.

P آرد ārd, Flour, meal. A defect, blemish, deficiency, imperfection. آرد كردن ārd kardan, To grind. آرد جو ārdi jaw, Barley-meal. آرد گندم ārdi gandum, Wheaten flour. آرد و روغن ārd u rawghan, (Flour and oil) A kind of sweetmeat.

P آرد ārad, The twenty-fifth day of every month. Name of the angel presiding over that day.

P ارد ard, The twenty-fifth day of the Persian month. Anger. Flour. *Urd*, Like, similar. Name of a city in Persia.

A اردّ aradd, More or most useful, or profitable, bringing a better return.

A اردأ ardaʼ, More or most wicked, bad, naught.

P اردا ardā, Name of a priest of the Magi.

A ارداء ardāʼ, (pl. of ردئ radiʼ) Bad, naught, corrupt. *Irdāʼ*, (v. n. 4 of ردأ) Assisting. Sustaining. Propping. Quieting. Establishing. Doing evil, marring. Letting down (a veil). Overtaking, reaching, hitting. Exceeding (one hundred) in number. (v. n. 4 of ردي) Increasing, becoming numerous. Travelling. Making (a horse) scamper or strike the ground hard with (his) feet. Throwing down. Destroying.

A اردئاء ardiʼāʼ, (pl. of ردئ radiʼ) Bad, naught.

P آردابه ārd-āba, Pottage, porridge.

A ارداج ardāj, Black leather.

A ارداح irdāh, (v. n. 4 of ردح) Enlarging a tent. Plastering a wall.

P آرداد ārdād, (or ارداد) A deceiver. A satyr.

P ارداد ardād, Name of a priest of the Magi.

A ارداد irdād, (v. n. 4 of ردّ) Having the udder large before yeaning (a ewe).

A ارداغ irdāgh, (v. n. 4 of ردغ) Being very slimy (the ground).

A ارداف ardāf, (pl. of ردف ridf) Buttocks, posteriors. *Irdāf*, (v. n. 4 of ردف) Following, succeeding to. Rising in succession (stars). Causing one to ride behind on the crupper. Carrying double (a horse).

A اردام irdām, (v. n. 4 of ردم) Continuing without intermission (rain, fever). Becoming green again (a tree). Being still and stationary (a cloud). Spurring a camel to quicken his pace. Being fixed and still in a place.

A اردان ardān, (pl. of ردن rudn) Gussets or armholes in sleeves. *Irdān*, (v. n. 4 of ردن) Putting gussets or armholes to the sleeves of a garment. Continuing (a fever). Being dark.

P اردانه ardāna, A species of violet.

P آرداو ārdāv, A demon, evil genius, magician.

P ارداويراف ardāvīrāf, Name of a Persian legislator who flourished about the year 200 of the Christian æra.

P اردب ardab, War, quarrel, altercation.

A اردبّ irdabb, An Egyptian measure equal to 24 صاع sāʻ. An aqueduct of earthen pipes.

P آردبا ārd-bā, A kind of pottage or gruel.

A اردبّة irdabbat, A large sewer made of earthen pipes. A large tile.

P اردبور ardabūr, A beautiful green colour.

P آردبيز ārd-bez, A sieve, searce, boulter.

P اردبيل ardabīl, Name of a city in Media.

P آردتوله ārd-tūla, Pottage, stir-about, gruel.

P اردج ardij, Juniper. اردج آب ardij-āb, Gin.

P اردجان ardajān, Certain figures and mysteries in astrology.

P آردحاله ārdahāla, A kind of milk-pottage.

A اردخل irdakhl or ardakhil, Fat, full of flesh.

P آرددوله ārd-dūla, Gruel. A fine green colour.

P آردزده ārd-zada, A sieve. A fine green colour.

P آردستان ārdistān, (اردستان ardistān or irdistān) Name of a district in Persia.

P اردش aradush, A certain number of crimes.

P آردشير ārd-shīr, Milk and flour pottage.

P اردشير ardshīr, Intrepid, courageous. Name of Bahman son of Isfandyār and father of Dārāb. The Artaxerxes of the Greeks.

P اردشيران ardshīrān, Name of a bitter plant.

P اردشيرخره ardshīr-khurra, Name of a country in Persia.

P اردشيردارو ardshīr-dārū, A bitter medicine.

A اردع ardaʻ, Black-breasted, and white-bodied (ram).

G اردفناني aridfanānī, Wild cucumber.

P اردكان ardakān, Name of a town in the district of Shīrāz; also of a village near Yazd.

P اردگان ardagān, Certain figures in astrology.

A اردل ardal, Transylvania.

P آردم ārdam, The anemone.

P اردم ardam, A section of the book of Zardusht. Dexterity, skill. The anemone.

A اردم ardam, (pl. اردمون) A skilful seaman.

P اردمي ardamī, Name of an animal.

P آردن ārdan, A colander, a strainer.

P اردن ardan, Name of a country. The river Jordan. *Ardan* or *urdan*, A colander. *Irdan*, The oxycanth-fruit. A species of eagle.

A اردن ardan, A kind of raw silk.

A اردنّ urdunn, Doziness, drowsiness. The Jordan and districts adjacent, comprising all Palestine and Samaria. Name of a city in Syria.

A اردنج ardanj, Black leather. Vitriol.

P اردو urdū, A camp, an army. A name for the Hindustani language, made up of Hindi, Persian, and Arabic. (اردو همايون urduwi humāyūn, or اردو معلاّ urduwi muʻallā) The royal camp.

P اردوان ardawān, (or اردبان ardbān) (Strong guard) Name of several princes of ancient Persia, Media, and India. This is supposed to be the Artabanus of the Greeks. Name of a country.

P اردوكند ardūkind, The ancient name of the city of Kāshghār in Turkistān or Tūrān (Scythia).

P اردوله ardūla, Milk-pottage, pap, gruel.

P اردون ardūn, Name of a king of Persia.

P آرده ārda, Flour, meal, flour-bread. A kind of porridge. آردهٔ خرما ārdaʼi khurmā, A dish made of dates with hot bread, butter, &c. آردهٔ كنجد ārdaʼi kunjud, A dish of fresh dates and syrup.

P آردهاله ārdhāla, A kind of pottage or gruel.

P اردهي ardahi, Name of an animal.

P اردي urdī, The second month of the solar year.

A اردئاء ardiʼāʼ, (pl. of ردئ) Bad, naught.

P اردي بهشت urdī bihisht, (Like Paradise) The second Persian month, midspring, April. The third day of every month, especially of that which the old Persians celebrated by a festival.

A اردية ardiyat, (pl. of رداء ridāʼ) Cloaks.

P آردينه ārdīna, A kind of gruel or pottage.

A ارذاء irzāʼ, (v. n. 4 of رذي) Weakening, exhausting. Giving any thing worn out. Having jaded horses. Throwing away.

A ارذاذ irzāz, (v. n. 4 of رذّ) Raining gently. Exuding. Perspiring. Running (a wound).

A ارذال arzāl, (pl. of رذل razl) Vile, ignoble. *Irzāl*, (v. n. 4 of رذل) Despising, treating with scorn. Associating with the base.

A ارذام irzām, (v. n. 4 of رذم) Overflowing. Exceeding (the number fifty).

A ارذل arzal, Mean, base. More or most mean, base, ignoble, or vile. ارذل العمر arzalu'l ʻumr, The end of life, when memory and faculties fail.

A ارذلة *arzilat*, (pl. of رذال *ruzāl*) Vile, bad.

A آرز *āriz*, Firm, steady, rooted, fixed. Drawn together. *Āruz*, Rice.

P ارز *arz*, Price, value. Quantity. Esteem, veneration. ارز بازار *arzi bāzār*, Market-price.

A ارز *arz*, (v. n. of ارز) Being gathered together. Contracting one's self, drawing back through avarice. Being firmly rooted, steady, fixed. Taking refuge in her hole, returning to it, and abiding there (a serpent). Being cold (the night). ارز الكلام *arzu'l kalām*, The connexion, truth, and straight-forwardness of conversation. *Arz* or *urz*, The pine, cedar, pitch, juniper, or any cone-bearing tree. *Urz*, *uruz*, or *aruz*, Rice. *Araz*, A tree (called also ارزن *arzan*) whose timber is very hard.

A ارزّ *aruzz* or *uruzz*, Rice.

A ارزاء *arzāʼ*, (pl. of رزء *ruzʼ*) Afflictions, calamities, disasters. *Irzāʼ*, (v. n. 4 of رزي) Leaning against, supporting one's self by. Fleeing for refuge.

A ارزاز *irzāz*, (v. n. 4 of رزّ) Fixing her tail in the ground to lay her eggs (a locust).

A ارزاغ *irzāgh*, (v. n. 4 of رزغ) Moistening the ground but not flowing (rain), making it muddy. Digging to a moist soil. Abounding in clay (ground). Being scanty (water). Injuring, vexing materially. Despising. Accusing, reproaching, taunting. Coveting. Esteeming or finding weak. Bringing a dew (ground).

A ارزاف *irzāf*, (v. n. 4 of رزف) Going before. Advancing, approaching. Rendering greedy. Egging on, instigating. Being filled with care, grief, or terror. Running away in a fright. Braying inwardly (a camel). Forcing, compelling.

A ارزاق *arzāk*, (pl. of رزق *rizk*) Riches, possessions, goods, commodities, effects, apparel, moveables, provisions. Soldiers' rations.

A ارزام *irzām*, (v. n. 4 of رزم) Murmuring, roaring, rumbling (thunder, or wind in the belly). Yearning towards her colt (a camel). A rattle, a noise, a crash, a clap, a peal (of thunder).

P ارزان *arzān*, Of small value, cheap, low-priced. Worthy. ارزان شدن *arzān shudan*, To be cheap. To be worthy. ارزان كردن *arzān kardan*, To make cheap. *Arzān*, (for اگر زان *agar z'ān*) If from that.

P ارزانش *arzānish*, Charity, good works.

P ارزاني *arzānī*, Cheapness. Abundance. Any thing safe and sure. Any thing given in charge. A worthy object of charity. ارزاني كردن *arzānī kardan*, ارزاني داشتن *arzānī dāshtan*, or ارزاني فرمودن *arzānī farmūdan*, To give, bestow, confer.

P ارزانيدن *arzānīdan*, To be esteemed. To be bought cheap.

P ارزايانيدن *arzāyānīdan*, To render valuable. To make cheap.

A ارزب *irzab*, (or ارزبّ *irzabb*) Short, compressed. Thick, large. Strong. Muliebria crassa.

A ارزبّة *irzabbat*, A large mallet with which they break clods, or make bricks. An iron rod.

A آرزة *ārizat*, (fem.) Firmly-rooted (tree). Strong (she-camel). Cold (night).

A ارزة *arzat*, A single pine.

P ارزرود *arzrūd*, Name of a country in Turkistān.

P ارزش *arzish*, Price, value, worth.

A ارزع *arzaʻ*, More or most cowardly.

A ارزق *arzak*, (for ازرق *azrak*) Azure, cerulean.

P ارزن *arzan*, Millet. ارزن زرّين *arzani zarrīn*, Stars. Sparks of fire. A draught of wine. Bubbles. دشت ارزن *dashti arzan*, Name of a place three leagues distant from Shīrāz.

A ارزن *arzan*, Heavier. A hard kind of tree from which they make walking-sticks. A city in Armenia called Erzeroom (ارزن الروم *arzanu'r rūm*).

P ارزنگان *arzangān*, Name of a city in Armenia.

P ارزنين *arzanīn*, (Bread) made of millet.

P آرزو *ārzū*, Desire, wish, will, resolution, intention, inclination, affection, love, appetite, concupiscence, hope, want. آرزو كردن *ārzū kardan*, To desire. آرزوي نفس *ārzūyi nafs*, Sensuality.

P آرزوانه *ārzuwāna*, Any object of desire. Wistfully. آرزوانهٔ زن باردار *ārzuwāna-i zani bār-dār*, The longing of a pregnant woman.

P آرزودن *ārzūdan*, To desire, wish, hanker.

P آرزو شكست *ārzū-shikast*, The breach of a resolution, change of mind.

P آرزو شكن *ārzū-shikan*, Breaking a resolution, preventing the execution of any design.

P آرزومند *ārzūmand*, Desirous, eager, fond, wishful, covetous, avaricious, greedy. آرزومند احسانم *ārzūmandi ihsānam*, I am desirous, solicitous, or ambitious of favour. آرزومند عطيه *ārzūmandi ʻatiya*, Greedy of gifts.

P آرزومندي *ārzūmandī*, Desire, wish, appetite.

P آرزون *ārzūn*, Amiable qualities, virtues.

P آرزه *ārza*, Clay mixed with straw for plaster.

P ارزه *arza*, Liquid pitch. Clay mixed with straw for plastering walls. The cypress. The pine. The first climate of the earth.

P آرزه‌گر *ārzagar*, (or ارزه‌گر) A plasterer.

A ارزّي *aruzzīy*, A seller of rice.

P ارزيتون *arzaytūn*, Name of a certain princess.

P ارزيدن *arzīdan*, To suit, become: to be worth.

P ارزيز *arzīz*, Lead.

A ارزيز *irzīz*, A trembling, tremor. A thrust with a spear. Small hail, sleet. Loud-voiced (man).

P ارزيش *arzīsh*, Price, value. Dignity.

A ارزيمام *irzīmām*, A becoming enraged.

P ارژن *arjan*, A species of bitter almond.

P ارژنگ *arjang*, The house of the painter Mānī.

P ارژنه *arjana*, Name of a desert in Persia.

P ارس *ars*, A tear. ارس بزان *arsi buzān*, A rheum issuing from the eyes of the mountain-goat from which they prepare an antidote against poison. *Urs*, The larch, plane, or cypress-tree. *Aras*, Name of a river near the Euphrates and Tigris: this is the Araxes of the ancients.

A ارس *ars*, (v. n. of ارس) Practising agriculture. *Irs*, A noble race or stock.

A ارساء *irsāʼ*, (v. n. 4 of رسا for رسو) Being firm, immoveable. Resolving firmly on any thing. Casting anchor. Anchoring.

A ارساب *irsāb*, (v. n. 4 of رسب) Having the eyes sunk in the head from famine. Dragging under, causing to sink to the bottom, precipitating.

A ارساخ *irsākh*, (v. n. 4 of رسخ) Establishing, strengthening, rendering firm, solid, immoveable.

A ارساغ *arsāgh*, (pl. of رسغ *rusgh*) The joints which connect the fetlocks with the hoofs (in animals), pasterns. The wrists or ankles (in man).

A ارساف *irsāf*, A driving of camels in fetters.

A ارسال *arsāl*, (pl. of رسل *rasal*) Flocks (of sheep), herds (of camels). *Irsāl*, (v. n. 4 of رسل) Sending, despatching. Dismissing, discharging. Loosing, letting go. Letting (a curtain) fall. Possessing flocks and herds. Giving absolute authority. Getting abundance of milk from one's sheep. An embassy, mission, legation. Remittance.

P ارسال نامه *irsāl-nāma*, A list of remittances.

A ارسام *irsām*, (v. n. 4 of رسم) Causing (a camel) to leave impressions on the ground.

A ارسان *arsān*, Rugged ground. (pl. of رسن *rasan*) Halters. *Irsān*, (v. n. 4 of رسن) Binding fast with a halter, haltering. Making a halter.

G ارسانيقون *arsānīkūn*, Yellow orpiment.

P آرست *ārast*, Ability, power. Decoration.

P ارست *arast*, The upper or higher part of pack-saddles. Plumpness in the hips (of animals).

P ارستدن *arastdan*, To adorn. To be able.

P آرستن *ārastan*, To adorn. To be able.

P ارستن *arastan*, To adorn. To be able.

P ارستو *arastū*, A swallow. Swallow-wort.

P آرسته *ārasta*, Adorned.

A ارسح *arsah*, Meagre-hipped (wolf).

G ارسط *arast*, (or ارسطا *arastā*) Aristotle.

P آرسطا *āristā*, Henbane.

G ارسطاطلس *arastātalis*, (or ارسطاطاليس *arastātālīs*) Aristotle.

G ارسطلوخيا *aristulūkhiyā*, Long birth-wort.

G ارسطو *aristo*, Aristotle. The herb birth-wort.

A ارسع *arsaʻ*, Distempered in the eyelid.

A ارسغ *arsugh*, (pl. of رسغ *rusgh* and *rusugh*) Pasterns of animals. Wrists or ankles of men.

A ارسل *arsul*, (pl. of رسول *rasūl*) Messengers, ambassadors, apostles.

P ارسلان *arslān*, A lion. This surname has been adopted by several kings of Persia.

A ارسم *arsum*, (pl. of رسم *rasm*) Traces, vestiges of a habitation.

P ارسن *arsan*, An assembly, meeting, congress.

A ارسن *arsun*, (pl. of رسن *rasan*) Halters.

P ارسنگ *arsang*, Mānī the impostor's shop.

A ارسوسة *ursūsat,* A cap, hat, bonnet.

A ارسوف *ursūf,* Name of a town in Syria.

A ارسي *arsa',* May (God) confirm.

P آرش *ārash,* Name of a celebrated archer. Name of the second son of Kay Kubād. Peace having been established between Minuchihr, and Afrāsyāb, on condition that the latter should cede as much of his territory as an arrow could fly across; an arrow was accordingly prepared on some scientific principle, and being discharged by Ārash from a mountain in Tabaristan, dropped not till it had reached the bank of the Oxus. *Ārish,* Signification, meaning.

A آرش *ārish,* Name of a mountain.

P ارش *arsh,* A cubit. An assembly. *Arash,* A cubit, a fathom. Name of a city. *Arish,* Wise, prudent. An assembly.

A ارش *arsh,* (pl. اروش *urūsh*) A gift. Compensation, equivalent. Disagreement, quarrel, dissension, law-suit, discord, altercation, squabble. Provocation, instigation, stimulation to discord. A defect. A scratch. A mulct, fine, particularly that which is paid for the shedding of blood. A demand of the expiatory fine. A gift for conciliating the favour of a judge, a bribe. Whatever a purchaser receives from a seller after discovering a fault in the article bought. A created being.

A ارشاء *arshā,* (pl. of رشأ *rasha,*) Young fawns. *Irshā,* (v. n. 4 of رشا for رشو) Tying on a rope to a bucket. Putting forth long stalks (a colocynth). Being partner in the blood of any one. Putting a young one to suck. Pointing (arms) at any one. Bribing.

A ارشاح *irshāh,* (v. n. 4 of رشح) Perspiring.

A ارشاد *irshād,* (v. n. 4 of رشد) Directing, shewing the right way. P ارشاد انگيز *irshād-angez,* Producing safety.

A ارشاش *irshāsh,* (v. n. 4 of رش) Gently misling. Making a horse prance until he sweats. Being wide (a wound), and bleeding profusely. Sucking the dam with outstretched neck (a camel's colt whose tail is scratched for that purpose).

A ارشاف *irshāf,* (v. n. 4 of رشف) Sipping.

A ارشاق *irshāk,* (v. n. 4 of رشق) Stretching forth the neck. Fixing the eye steadily. Shooting in a certain mode.

A ارشام *irshām,* (v. n. 4 of رشم) Shining, flashing (lightning). Sealing (wheat in a granary). Discovering young herbage peeping above the ground, and grazing it. Putting forth leaves.

A ارشح *arshah,* More or most acute, ingenious, quick. Ingenious, quick, clever.

P ارشد *arshad,* The marcasite-stone.

A ارشد *arshad,* Most upright, most tenacious of the right way. P پسر ارشد *pisari arshad,* The eldest son or heir apparent.

P ارشسنگ *arshasang,* The 25th of the month.

A ارشق *arshak,* Name of a place in Āzarbayjān. ما ارشقها *mā arshakahā,* How rapid in discharging an arrow (a bow)!

P ارشك *arshak,* A poppy. Fault. *Arashk,* Envy.

A ارشم *arsham,* One who gets an appetite by smelling the flavour of meat. Marked on the face or body with lines and spots. Little (rain). A dog.

G ارشيميدس *arshimīdus,* Archimedes.

P ارشن *arshan,* (in Kipjāk) A cloud.

P آرشي *ārishī,* True, real, significant.

P ارشيا *arshyā,* (in zand and Pāz.) A throne.

A ارشية *arshiyat,* (pl. of رشاء *rishā,*) Ropes, or similar things, as trains of snakes, gourd-stalks.

A ارص *arass,* One whose thighs are close together. One whose teeth are closely set.

A ارصاء *irsā,* An abiding in one place.

A ارصاد *arsād,* (pl. of رصد *rasad*) Observations of the stars, or of roads (through deserts). Gentle rains. *Irsād,* (v. n. 4 of رصد) Preparing, making ready for. Recompensing, requiting.

A ارصاع *irsāع,* (v. n. 4 of رصع) Spearing deeply. Having a young one (a palm-tree).

A ارصاف *irsāf,* (v. n. 4 of رصف) Mixing (wine) with the water of a running stream.

A ارصان *irsān,* (v. n. 4 of رصن) Making fast.

A ارصح *arsah,* Close-hipped (man).

A ارصع *arsaع,* Lean, meagre about the thighs or hips. Deep (wound) made with a spear's point.

A ارصوصة *arsūsat,* A cap in the form of a melon.

A آرض *āraz,* More or most worthy.

A ارض *arz,* (v. n. of ارض) Abounding in herbage (ground). Discovering such ground. (pl. ارضات *arazāt,* اروض *urūz,* ارضون *arazūn,* آراض *ārāz,* and اراضي *arāzī*) The earth, ground, soil, country, region. The grave. Any thing low, depressed. Rheum, defluxion from the nose. The lower part of the legs of a quadruped. Tremor, particularly of the limbs in the paroxysm of a fever. ابن الارض *ibnu'l arz,* (Son of the earth) A certain esculent. كرة الارض *kuratu'l arz,* The terrestrial globe. ارض الذئب *arzu'z zisb,* Name of an island near the Equator. ارض الفرس *arzu'l faras,* The feet of a horse, or what is under them. ارض خالي *arzi khālī,* Uncultivated ground. ارض روم *arzi rūm,* (Country of the Romans) Name of a city on the confines of Armenia and Cappadocia. ارض ممالك *arzi mamālik,* A prime minister. ارض نوح *arzi nūh,* The land of Noah, a place so called in the Eastern Arabia. ابن ارض *ibn arz,* A stranger, foreigner, son of the earth. A kind of ginger. اهل الارض *ahlu'l arz,* Demons. كلاب الارض *kilābu'l arz,* Strange dogs. أ زلزلت الارض ام بي ارض *a zalzalat al arz am bī arz,* Was it the earth that trembled, or is there a tremor on me? ان ضرب فارض *in zaraba fa arz,* If you beat the earth—(a proverbial saying, implying, beat the earth, it is immoveable; it cares not). لا ارض لك *lā arza laka,* A form of compliment among the Arabians, implying, You have no occasion for any recommendation of country, ancestry, wealth, &c., you have merit enough in yourself. من اطاعني كنت له ارض *man atāعanī kuntu lahu arz,* Whoever obeys me, I will submit to him. *Araz,* (v. n. of ارض) Becoming raw (a sore). Being clean and pleasant to the eye (ground).

A ارض *arazz,* Sedentary, motionless.

A ارضاء *irzā,* (v. n. 4 of رضي) Gratifying, satisfying, contenting.

A ارضات *arazāt,* (pl. of ارض *arz*) Earths.

A ارضاض *irzāz,* (v. n. 4 of رض) Becoming sluggish and indolent. Thickening (as sour milk). Running violently. Flowing (sweat). Being cut off (milk).

A ارضاع *irzāع,* (v. n. 4 of رضع) Giving suck.

A ارضاك *irzāk,* (v. n. 4 of رضك not used) Half-closing and opening the eyes.

A ارضة *irzat, urzat,* or *irazat,* Luxuriant herbage or grass. *Arazat,* A worm which eats into ships, the white ant. افسد من الارضة *afsad mini'l arazat,* More destructive than the white ant.

A ارضون *arazūn,* (pl. of ارض *arz*) Earths, soils.

A ارضوي *arzuwīy,* Surname of a man.

A ارضي *arzīy,* Terrestrial, earthly, earthy.

A ارضياء *arziyā,* (pl. of رضي *raziy*) Content, pleased, satisfied.

A ارضين *arazīn,* (obliq. of ارضون *arazūn,* pl. of ارض *arz*) Earths.

A ارط *arit,* A reddish colour, like to the fruit and roots of the tree ارطي *arta'.*

A ارطاء *irtā,* (v. n. 4 of رطأ) Becoming marriageable (a maid).

A ارطاب *artāb,* (pl. of رطب *rutab*) Fresh ripe dates. *Irtāb,* (v. n. 4 of رطب) Being fresh and succulent, arriving at the state رطب *rutab,* (dates). Bearing such dates (a palm). Steeping (a vest).

A ارطاة *artāt,* A single tree of the ارطي *arta'.*

A ارطاس *irtās,* (v. n. 4 of رطس not used) Sitting even (one stone upon another).

A ارطاط *irtāt,* (v. n. 4 of رط) Raving, being a fool. Keeping one's seat without stirring.

A ارطال *artāl,* (pl. of رطل *ratl* or *ritl*) Pounds of twelve ounces. *Irtāl,* (v. n. 4 of رطل) Having a soft, delicate son. Hanging down (the ears).

A ارطام *irtām,* (v. n. 4 of رطم) Shutting up, closely confining. Keeping silence.

G ارطاماسيا *artāmāsiyā,* Artemisia, mugwort.

P ارطاميدوس *artāmīdūs,* Name of a prophet.

A ارطاوي *artāwīy,* (A camel) very fond of, or griped by eating too freely of, the tree ارطي *arta'.*

G ارطميس *artamīs,* Artemisia. Diana.

G ارطميسا *artamīsā,* Southernwood.

G ارطنيثا *artanīsā,* Sow-bread.

A ارطوي *artawīy,* (A camel) fond of, or griped by eating too much of, the fruit of the ارطي *arta'.*

A ارطى *artá'*, (pl. ارطيات *artayāt*, اراطى *arāta'*, and *arāti*) The above-mentioned tree, which grows in the sand, bearing flowers of a willow-colour and a bitter fruit, with red roots and branches; with the fruit and leaves of which they feed camels, and with the bark they tan leather.

A ارطيّ *artiy*, (A camel) feeding on the fruit, &c.

P ارطيون *artayūn*, Intelligent, acute, cunning.

A ارعاء *arʻāʼ*, (pl. of رعي *riʻy*) Pastures. *Irʻāʼ*, (v. n. 4 of رعي) Tending (a flock). Giving for pasture. Abounding in pasture. Giving ear. Causing grass to grow as pasture. Sparing, pitying.

A ارعاج *irʻāj*, A becoming strong. An incessant flashing of lightning.

A ارعاد *irʻād*, (v. n. 4 of رعد) Thundering. Being visited or terrified by thunder. Threatening. Inspiring terror. Trembling, being agitated.

A ارعاس *irʻās*, (v. n. 4 of رعس) Terrifying, causing to tremble.

A ارعاش *irʻāsh*, A causing to tremble.

A ارعاص *irʻāṣ*, (v. n. 4 of رعص) Agitating, disturbing, putting in motion.

A ارعاظ *arʻāẓ*, (pl. of رعظ *ruʻẓ*) Holes in the tops of the shafts of arrows or javelins, into which they screw on the heads. *Irʻāẓ*, (v. n. 4 of رعظ) Making in the top of an arrow a hole wherein to fix the point.

A ارعاف *irʻāf*, (v. n. 4 of رعف) Causing (the nose) to bleed, producing hemorrhage. Impelling, causing to make haste. Filling a bottle.

A ارعال *arʻāl*, (pl. of رعلة *raʻlat*) Bodies from 20 to 25 (horse, &c.), the vans of such bodies. Tall palm-trees, palm-trees bearing bad fruit. Heifers. Female ostriches. Prepuces. Those parts of the ears of sheep or camels, which, being slit, hang flagging down. Domestics, or families (especially when numerous). *Irʻāl*, (v. n. 4 of رعل) Stabbing repeatedly. Dangling, trailing (a plant). Shooting forth (a bramble).

A ارعام *irʻām*, (v. n. 4 of رعم) Running at the nose (a sheep).

A ارعاوية *arʻāwiyat*, A herd, a troop of camels marked with the king's signet.

A ارعل *arʻal*, Foolish. A withered, weak, tender plant. A plant growing long and hanging down.

A ارعمة *arʻimat*, (pl. of رعام *ruʻām*) Snots.

A ارعن *arʻan*, Loose, lax, flabby, weak, languid. One who foolishly adorns, sets forth, shews, commends, or thinks much of himself. One who talks quick. Multitudinous, numerous (army). ما ارعنه *mā arʻanahu*, What a coxcomb he is!

A ارعواء *irʻiwāʼ*, (v. n. 9 of رعا for رعو) Abstaining (from evil). Repenting.

A ارعوة *urʻūwat*, The yoke of a ploughing ox.

A ارعوفة *urʻūfat*, (or ارعوسة *urʻūsat*) A stone placed near a well, upon which those who drink sit down. A stone left at the bottom of a well, on which they sit when cleaning it out.

P آرغ *ārugh*, A belch, ructation.

P ارغ *urgh*, Hot and bitter (walnut or almond).

A ارغاء *irghāʼ*, (v. n. 4 of رغا for رغو) Being frothy (milk). Voiding frothy urine. Foaming at the mouth. Making a camel bray.

P ارغاب *arghāb*, (or ارغاو *arghāv*) A river.

A ارغاب *irghāb*, (v. n. 4 of رغب) Stimulating, making one wish for.

A ارغاث *irghās*, (v. n. 4 of رغث) Stabbing repeatedly. Stabbing in the root of the breast. Suckling, giving suck.

P ارغاج *arghāj*, (or ارغاج) Yarn. The weft.

A ارغاد *irghād*, (v. n. 4 of رغد) Having the good things of this life in abundance. Leaving sheep to graze where they list.

P آرغاده *ārghāda*, Name of a river.

A ارغاس *arghās*, (pl. of رغس *raghs*) Benefits, boons, blessings, favours. *Irghās*, (v. n. 4 of رغس) Enriching, bestowing plenteously the good things of this life (God).

A ارغاف *irghāf*, (v. n. 4 of رغف) Looking intently. Walking fast.

P ارغاف *urghāf*, A stream of water.

A ارغال *arghāl*, (pl. of رغل *rughl*) Orachs. *Irghāl*, (v. n. 4 of رغل) Giving suck (applied to animals). Abounding in the plant رغل *rughl*. Straying from pasture (a camel). Inclining. Coming into ear (corn). Erring, blundering, missing. Misplacing (a thing).

A ارغام *irghām*, (v. n. 4 of رغم) Rubbing (a man's nose) in the dirt. Exasperating, enraging. Blackening. Being angry against.

G ارغامن *arghāmun*, A web in the eye, which in the extreme parts of the iris looks red, in the interior white.

G ارغاموني *arghāmūnī*, Wild tansy.

A ارغان *irghān*, (v. n. 4 of رغن) Listening with satisfaction. Exciting desire. Rendering inclined. Causing to eat or drink. Despising, deeming trivial. Rendering (an affair) light and easy.

A ارغب *arghab*, More covetous or longed for.

P ارغج *arghich*, (or ارغژ *arghij*) Ivy.

P ارغچي *arghachī*, A long rope or thread.

A ارغد *arghad*, More or most commodious, pleasant, affluent. *Arghada*, May (God) grant the comforts of life!

A ارغدّاد *irghiddād*, (v. n. 4 of رغدد Q) Being easy, affluent, comfortable.

P آرغده *āraghda*, Covetous, greedy.

P ارغده *arghuda*, Covetous, greedy. Angry, passionate. *Arughda*, Passionate, angry, testy.

P ارغشتك *arghushtak*, A kind of child's game.

A ارغفة *arghifat*, (pl. of رغيف *raghīf*) Round flat cakes, cracknels.

P ارغك *arghak*, Ivy.

A ارغل *arghal*, An easy, agreeable life. Uncircumcised. One who has long testicles.

A ارغلداد *irghildād*, (v. n. 4 of رغلد Q) Being easy, affluent, comfortable.

P ارغمج *arghamj*, A long thread.

P ارغمچي *arghamchī*, A long robe. A thread twenty cubits long, fit for weaving.

G ارغن *arghan*, An organ.

P ارغنج *arghanj*, A long thread.

P ارغند *arghand*, (or ارغنده *arghanda*) Covetous, desirous, wishful. Intrepid. Passionate, angry, testy. A tippler.

P ارغند آب *arghand-āb*, Name of a river.

P ارغنگ *arghang*, The shop of the painter Mānī.

G ارغنن *arghanun*, An organ.

P ارغنون *arghanūn*, An organ.

P ارغوان *arghawān*, Name of a tree whose fruit and flower are of a beautiful red.

P ارغوان تن *arghawān-tan*, (Red-body) Name of the planet Mars.

P ارغواني *arghawānī*, Red, purple. بادهٔ ارغواني *bādaʼi arghawānī*, Red wine.

P ارغون *arghūn*, An organ. A wild horse.

P ارغيان *irghayān*, A village near Nishābūr.

A ارغيداد *irghīdād*, (v. n. 11 of رغد) Being partially thickened (milk). Being confused, perplexed, uncertain how to act.

P ارغيدن *arghīdan*, To quarrel, dispute, scold, brawl, contend. To become hard, to wax dry.

P ارغيده *arghīda*, Angry, passionate.

P آرغيش *ārghesh*, The bark of the box-thorn.

A ارف *uraf*, (pl. of ارفة) Land-marks, bounds.

A ارفاء *irfāʼ*, (v. n. 4 of رفا) Bringing, drawing near. Pressing hard upon, being close in one's dealings. Fleeing for refuge. Combing. Hauling close to shore. Approaching. Inclining, leaning. Shewing respect, conniving. Treating kindly.

A ارفات *irfāt*, A being broken or pounded small.

A ارفاث *irfās*, A talking obscenely.

A ارفاد *irfād*, (v. n. 4 of رفد) Assisting. Giving. Putting on a horse a cushion or pad for the saddle. Bandaging a wound.

A ارفاش *irfāsh*, (v. n. 4 of رفش) Falling into luxury in eating and venery. Remaining fixed and stationary in one place.

A ارفاض *arfāẓ*, (pl. of رفض *rafẓ*), (Camels) straggling and pasturing at discretion. *Irfāẓ*, (v. n. 4 of رفض) Turning (camels) loose to pasture. Being wide (a valley or river).

A ارفاغ *arfāgh*, (pl. of رفغ *rafgh*) Arm-pits, groins (where filth collects). Commonalty, rabble.

A ارفاف *irfāf*, (v. n. 4 of رف) Brooding, covering (her) eggs with (her) wings (a hen).

A ارفاق *arfāk*, (pl. of رفقة *rafkat*, *rifkat*, or *rufkat*) Companies, societies, committees, assemblies. *Irfāk*, (v. n. 4 of رفق) Helping, benefiting. Treating kindly or gently.

A ارفال *irfāl*, (v. n. 4 of رفل) Wearing clothes

that sweep the ground. Walking swingingly.

A ارفاه *irfāh*, (v. n. 4 of رفه) Bestowing affluence, comforting, cherishing. Enjoying peace and the pleasures of life. Anointing the body, and combing the head, daily. Remaining near water (flocks). Having camels feeding near water, and drinking as much as they like.

A ارفة *urfat*, (pl. ارف *uraf*) A boundary, limit, land-mark, or balk. A knot.

A ارفتات *irfitāt*, (v. n. 9 of رفت) Being broken, pounded, or bruised. Being cut off.

A ارفح *arfah*, An animal whose horns project sideways, in the direction of his ears.

A ارفدة *arfidat*, Name of a people in Ethiopia.

P ارفش *arfash*, A caravan.

A ارفش *arfash*, Large-eared (man).

A ارفض *arfaz*, A refuser. An obstinate heretic.

A ارفضاض *irfizāz*, (v. n. 9 of رفض) Flowing (tears): flowing, running. Being divided, scattered.

A ارفع *arfaꜥ*, Higher, highest.

A ارفغ *arfagh*, One who enjoys the comforts of life. *Arfugh*, (pl. of رفغ *rafgh*) Tracts, districts. Worst parts of valleys.

A ارفق *arfak*, (A camel) distorted in the elbow, having it standing out from his side.

A ارفل *arfal*, Awkward, slovenly in dressing or in doing any thing.

A ارفى *arfa'*, One who has large drooping ears.

A ارفى *urfiy*, Milk of a doe. Good, unadulterated milk. A land-measurer.

A ارفئنان *irfiꜥnān*, (v. n. 4 of رفأن Q) Fleeing, and then sitting still. Being appeased (anger). Languor, feebleness.

A آرق *ārik*, Sleepless.

P ارق *ark*, A canal.

A ارق *arak*, (v. n. of ارق) Being watchful, sleepless. *Arik*, Sleepless. *Irik, aruk,* or *ark*, Jaundice.

A ارق *arakk*, More or most slender, or transparent. Thinner, thinnest. Tenderer, tenderest.

A ارقاء *irkāꜥ*, (v. n. 4 of رقأ) Wiping off perspiration. Making (tears) dry (God). Stanching.

A ارقاب *irkāb*, (v. n. 4 of رقب) Giving away (property) on condition that it shall ultimately revert to the survivor. A tontine.

A ارقاد *irkād*, (v. n. 4 of رقد) Putting to sleep, getting one to sleep. Abiding in a place.

A ارقاص *irkās*, (v. n. 4 of رقص) Making (a camel) dance, caper, or trot. Dandling (an infant).

A ارقاع *irkāꜥ*, (v. n. 4 of رقع) Being foolish, idiotic. Wanting repair (clothes).

A ارقاف *irkāf*, (v. n. 4 of رقف) Trembling.

A ارقاق *irkāk*, (v. n. 4 of رق) Making thin or slender. Using polished language. Reducing into a state of servitude, possessing a slave. Being badly off. Becoming quite ripe (a white grape).

A ارقال *irkāl*, (v. n. 4 of رقل) Making haste. Skipping on tip-toe. Skimming (over the plain).

A ارقام *arkām*, (pl. of رقم *rakam*) Writings, notations. ارقام هندي *arkāmi hindī*, Arithmetic, numbers, properly Indian tables, arithmetic being generally supposed to be borrowed from them.

A ارقان *arkān*, Jaundice. *Arakān*, Mildew. Jaundice. *Irkān*, (v. n. 4 of رقن) Moistening with dripping. Tinging with privet or saffron. Privet. Saffron. A certain red tree. Dragon's blood. Mildew. Jaundice.

G ارقان *arkān*, Privet. (In the language of Morocco) The mountain-almond.

A ارقب *arkab*, Thick-necked (man). A lion. *Arkub*, (pl. of رقبة *rakabat*) Necks, especially the lower parts. Slaves, purchased servants.

A ارقداد *irkidād*, (v. n. 9 of رقد) Going very fast.

A ارقش *arkash*, (A serpent) spotted with black and white.

P ارقش *arkish*, Intelligent, skilful. An adept.

A ارقط *arkat*, Variegated with black and white spots. A panther. Dusky (sheep). The tree عرفج *ꜥarfaj* when it presents a spotted appearance.

A ارقطاط *irkitāt*, (v. n. 9 of رقط) Being speckled with black and white.

A ارقعة *arkiꜥat*, (pl. of رقيع *rakīꜥ*) Firmaments.

A ارقم *arkam*, (pl. اراقم *arākim*) (A serpent) speckled with black and white (of a very dangerous species). Name of an Arabian tribe.

P ارقند *arkand*, Name of a mountain in the west.

A ارقيطاط *irkītāt*, (v. n. 11 of رقط) Being speckled (black and white). Putting forth buds (a plant).

A آرك *ārak*, More or most worthy, fit for, apt. *Ārik*, Thick, luxuriant, entangled tree اراك *arāk*.

A ارك *ark*, (v. n. of ارك) Causing a camel to feed on the tree اراك *arāk*. Quarrelling. Persevering in any dilatory business. Going down, subsiding (a swelling). Fastening (a business) upon any one. Abiding in one place. *Irk*, Excellence (of herbage) such as induces (camels) to continue in it. A certain salt and bitter plant on which camels feed. *Arak*, (v. n. of ارك) (Camels) having the gripes from eating too freely of the fruit of the tree اراك *arāk*. Abiding in one place. *Arik*, (A tract of land) over-run with the tree اراك *arāk*. *Uruk*, (pl. of اراك *arāk*) Certain trees on which they feed camels.

A ارك *arakh*, Weak, silly. Worthless. One who neglects his wife and friends, and is despised by them in return.

A ارکاء *irkāꜥ*, (v. n. 4 of رکو for رکا) Granting a delay, putting off. Taking refuge. Preparing, levying an army. Falsely accusing. Disparaging.

A ارکاب *arkāb*, (pl. of رکب *rakab*) Pubes. Muliebria. *Irkāb*, (v. n. 4 of رکب) Being fit for mounting (a camel). Giving any one a camel fit for the saddle.

A ارکات *arkāt*, Arcot, a country on the Coromandel coast, near Madras; also the capital city.

A ارکاح *arkāh*, (pl. of رکح *ruk-h*) Narrow passes through mountains, also the sides, extremities, or promontories of mountains. Foundations. Monastic cells. Areas, quadrangles. *Irkāh*, (v. n. 4 of رکح) Leaning. Causing to recline. Compelling, forcing.

A ارکاز *irkāz*, (v. n. 4 of رکز) Discovering minerals or hidden treasures. Containing gold or silver (a mine). Being the owner of a gold or silver mine.

A ارکاس *irkās*, (v. n. 4 of رکس) Turning upside down. Driving back into infidelity. Beginning to appear (a girl's breasts).

A ارکاض *irkāz*, (v. n. 4 of رکض) (A woman) being pregnant with a fœtus nearly full-grown and stirring in the womb. Becoming large and stirring in the womb (a fœtus).

A ارکاك *arkāk*, (pl. of رك *rakk* or *rikk*) Small rains. *Irkāk*, (v. n. 4 of رك) Raining gently.

P ارکاك *irkāk*, Dew, misling rain.

A ارکان *arkān*, (pl. of رکن *rukn*) Columns, pillars, supports, props, posts, angles. P ارکان دولت *arkāni dawlat*, Nobles (pillars of the state).

A ارکب *arkab*, Large-kneed. (A camel) having one knee larger than the other. *Arkub*, (pl. of رکب *rakb*) Small parties of men riding on camels.

A آرکة *ārikat*, (fem.) Abounding in the tree اراك *arāk*. (pl. اوارك *awārik*) A camel feeding on the tree اراك *arāk*.

A ارکة *arikat*, (pl. اراکى *arāka'*) Griped (she-camel) from eating too freely of the tree اراك *arāk*.

A ارکد *arkad*, Speckled, spotted.

A ارکوب *urkūb*, A troop riding upon camels (more than رکب *rakb*).

G ارکون *arkūn*, A chief, a governor.

A ارکون *urkūn*, The head man of a village.

P ارکونتن *arkūnitan*, (in zand and Pāzand) To give, to bestow. A gift.

A ارکى *arka'*, More or most weak, despicable.

P ارکيا *arkiyā*, (in zand and Pāzand) A river.

P ارگ *arg*, A small citadel within a larger one. Name of a fortress in Sistān. *Arag*, A swing. *Arag* or *urug*, A tether.

P ارگلى *argalī*, A wild sheep.

P ارگنج *urganj*, Name of a city in Khurāsān.

G ارگوس *argūs*, Name of one of Alexander's successors, Lagos?

A ارل *urul*, Name of a mountain, and of two places in Arabia. Name of a fortress in Spain.

A ارلة *urlat*, The foreskin.

A آرم *āram*, Name of a place. *Ārim*, (A severe year) consuming, destroying (provisions or cattle). Name of a town in Māzandarān; also of a village near دهستان *dahistān*.

A أرم *arama*, (fut. يأرم *yaꜥrimu*) He bit.

P ارم *arm*, The arm from the elbow to the shoulder. *Iram*, Name of the inventor of instruments of war. Celebrated but fabulous gardens, said to have been anciently made in Arabia Felix by a king named Shaddād bin Aad, or Iram bin Omad.—Frequent mention is made of these gardens by the Eastern poets, who describe them as a perfect model of that voluptuous paradise which the Muhammadans are promised by their prophet.

A ارم *arm*, (v. n. of ارم) Twisting hard (a rope). Straining. Pulling tight. Biting. Cutting off people (a severe year). Eating up all on the table. Soothing, cajoling. Being spent, consumed (property). The shape of the body, the jointing of the limbs. حسنة الارم *hasanatu'l arm*, (A girl) well formed, of a beautiful shape. ارم و الله *arma wa 'llāh*, (or ارما و الله *armā wa 'llāh*) Truly as God liveth. *Iram*, Name of the first, or of the last عاد *ʻād*: also the name of their city; or the name of their mother, or the name of their tribe. Name of a place given by Muhammad to جعال *jiʻāl*. ارم ذات العماد *iram zātu'l ʻimād*, Damascus. Alexandria. Name of a place in Persia. ارم الكلبة *iramu'l kalbat*, (or ارمي الكلبة *iramīyu'l kalbat*) Name of a place between Basrah and Mecca. *Aram*, One, any one: as, لا بالدار ارم *lā bi'd dār aram*, There is nobody in the house. *Iram*, A mark or butt to shoot at. (pl. آرام *ārām* and اروم *urūm*) A stone or post erected in the desert to direct travellers.

A ارّم *urram*, Cheek-teeth, the grinders. The tips of the fingers. Stones. Gravel. فلان يحرق عليه الارّم *fulān yuharriku ʻalayhi'l urrama*, Such an one gnashes his teeth at him.

A ارماء *armā'*, Desert, desolate, empty (region). (pl. of رميّ *ramīy*) Small parts of clouds. Clouds raining large drops. *Irmā'*, (v. n. 4 of رما) Remaining, dwelling. Increasing (upwards of a hundred). Approaching, drawing near. (v. n. 4 of رمي) Throwing away, hurling, casting, flinging. Ejecting. Unhorsing. Exceeding, increasing. Giving usury. Lending or borrowing on interest.

A ارمات *armās*, Old, worn-out ropes. *Irmās*, (v. n. 4 of رمث) Leaving milk in the udder. Establishing, confirming in the possession of property. Taking interest. Softening, smoothing.

A ارماح *armāh*, (pl. of رمح *rumh*) Spears, lances.

A ارماخ *irmākh*, (v. n. 4 of رمخ) Bearing unripe dates (a palm). Becoming lenient and submissive. Waxing old and fat (a quadruped).

A ارماد *irmād*, (v. n. 4 of رمد) Giving milk (a sheep or a cow). Being reduced to poverty by the loss of one's cattle. Visiting with ophthalmia (God).

A ارماس *armās* (pl. of رمس *rams*) Sepulchres, burying-grounds.

A ارماش *irmāsh*, (v. n. 4 of رمش) Coming into leaf and bursting forth (a tree). Weeping profusely from weak, closed eyelids. Shedding tears scantily.

A ارماض *irmāz*, (v. n. 4 of رمض) Being hot. Grazing under a scorching sun, or on a burning plain. Hurting with heat, scorching the feet (hot ground). Grieving, afflicting, paining.

A ارماط *armāt*, Name of a tree called كادي *kādī*, bearing a yellow flower.

A ارماطس *armātus*, Name of a Grecian king in whose reign sealing clay was discovered.

A ارماق *armāk*, An old rope. (pl. of رمق *ramak*) Last breaths of a dying person.

P ارماك *armāk*, A substance like cinnamon.

A ارماك *armāk*, (pl. of رمكة *ramakat*) Mares. Jades. *Irmāk*, (v. n. 4 of رمك) Making one stay in one place.

A ارمال *armāl*, (or ارماك *armāk*) A species of cinnamon brought from Arabia, Persia, and India. *Armāl*, (pl. of رملة *rumlat*) Black lines (upon white or other-coloured cattle). (pl. of رمل *ramal*) Gentle, small rains. *Irmāl*, (v. n. 4 of رمل) Weaving (a mat) of a flimsy texture. Covering a sofa with a texture of palm-leaves. Being smeared with gore (an arrow). Lengthening (a rope). Becoming a widow. Eating up, and being short of, provisions.

A ارمام *armām*, Old, rotten (rope). *Irmām*, (v. n. 4 of رمّ) Becoming dried up and carious (bones). Being full of marrow. Being silent. Having a propensity to jest.

P آرمان *ārmān*, Desire. A sigh. Remorse.

P ارمان *armān*, Desire. A sigh, regret, vexation, grief, sorrow. The anguish of repentance. A kind of drug which hardens the gums. Oh! alas! *Irmān*, Any thing borrowed. Name of a city.

P ارمان خوار *armān-khwār*, Wishful. Vexed.

P ارمان خور *armān-khwur*, Grieved, vexed.

P ارمان سراي *armān-sarāy*, The house of mourning, *i. e.* the present world.

P ارمانيدن *armānīdan*, To sigh. To be afflicted. To repent, to feel the anguish of repentance.

P ارمائيل *irmā'īl* Name of one of Zahhāk's cooks.

A آرمة *ārimat*, A tooth. A year of scarcity.

A ارمة *arimat*, Destructive (year).

A ارمد *armad*, Of an ash colour. Pernicious, destructive. Blear-eyed, suffering from ophthalmia. Impalpable (ashes).

A ارمداء *armidā'*, Ashes.

A ارمداد *irmidād*, (v. n. 9 of رمد) Suffering from ophthalmia. Being ash-coloured.

P آرمده *āramda*, Vexation, grief, sorrow. Repentance, remorse. *Āramida*, Reposed, rested.

P ارمز *urmuz* or ارمزد *urmuzd*, The first day of the month. Name of the angel who presides over the first day of the month. The planet Jupiter. Name of the son of Isfandyār.

P ارمس *urmus*, The prophet Enoch. Hermes.

P آرمش *ārmish*, (for آرامش) Quiet, repose.

A ارمش *armash*, Various or changed-coloured. Red about the eyelids with a running humour.

A ارمص *armas*, One in the inner corner of whose eye filth is collected.

A ارمض *armuz*, (ارمضاء *armizā'* or ارمضة *armizat*) (pl. of رمضان *ramazān*) Ramazans.

A ارمعلال *irmiʻlāl*, (v. n. 4 of رمعل, Q not used) Slavering (an infant). Being steeped (linen). Being damp (a hide). Dripping (as fat from roasted meat). Flowing apace (tears). Crying aloud. Being dispersed (camels). Making haste.

A ارمعنان *irmiʻnān*, (v. n. 4 of رمعن, Q) Flowing.

P ارمغان *armaghān* or *armughān*, A present, an offering. A piece of money.

P ارمغاني *armaghānī*, A present from a distance.

A ارمغلال *irmighlal*, The flowing apace of tears.

A ارمقاق *irmikāk*, (v. n. 9 of رمق) Being thin (a raw hide). Being weak. Being slender, weak (a rope). Being cut off (flocks, herds). Feebleness.

A ارمك *armak*, Ash-coloured (camel). *Armuk*, Name of an island in the sea of Yaman.

P ارمك *urmuk*, A woollen garment.

A ارمكاك *irmikāk*, (v. n. 9 of رمك) Being small, delicate. Being slender-waisted. Colour of ashes.

P ارمگان *irmagān*, A tutor. Happiness, felicity.

P آرمگاه *āram-gāh*, A place of rest. Delight.

A ارمل *armal*, (pl. ارامل *arāmil*, اراميل *arāmīl*, and اراملة *arāmilat*) Widowed, in a state of celibacy. Poor, indigent, helpless, wanting victuals. (A year) barren, without rain or produce. (A sheep) with black feet. *Armul*, (pl. of رمل *raml*) Sands.

A ارملة *armalat*, A widow. (pl. ارامل *arāmil* and ارامله *arāmilat*) Poor, needy (woman). Indigent, poor, feeble men or women.

P ارمن *arman*, (for اگر من *agar man*) If I. *Arman* or *irman*, Name of a part of the mountainous district of Āzarbayjān, and the birth-place of Shīrīn, famous for the production of silk.

P ارمند *armand*, At rest, reposed.

P ارمنده *armanda*, Tranquil, quiet.

A ارمنيّ *armanīy*, A native of ارمينيّة *irmīnīyat*. *Irmanīy*, (pl. ارامنة *arāminat*) An Armenian.

G ارمنين *armanīn*, The wild pomegranate.

P ارمنيه *irmaniya*, Name of a city where formerly stood a fire-temple called درخش *durukhsh*.

A ارمنيّة *armanīya*, Armenia. This district, according to Eastern geographers, is much more extensive than the country so called by Europeans, being in general considered as nearly the same with the ancient Parthia. It is divided into Greater and Lesser Armenia.

P ارمود *armūd*, (for امرود *amrūd*) A pear.

P ارمولة *urmūlat*, (pl. ارامل *arāmil* and اراميل *arāmīl*) The stump left on the trunk of the plant عرفج *ʻarfaj* after lopping off a branch. Widowed, poor, indigent (youth).

P آرمون *ārmūn*, Earnest-money.

P ارمون *armūn*, Earnest, pledge, stipulation, any thing by which a promise or bargain is confirmed.

P ارمونتن *armūnitan*, (in zand and Pāz.) To sleep, repose.

A ارمهزاز *irmihzāz*, A giving, a bestowing.

A ارمي *arma'*, More or most expert at hurling a

javelin or shooting an arrow, better or best shot.

A ارمي iramīy or aramīy, Any one. A stone set up in a desert to direct travellers. Sign, vestige.

A ارميا armiya', urmiya', or irmiya', Jeremiah. Elias. Aliy. Jerusalem. Name of Bilyān.

A ارمية urmiyat, Name of a city in Āzarbayjān.

P آرميدگي āramidagī, Rest, quiet. Modesty.

P آرميدن āramīdan, To rest, repose.

P آرميده āramīda, Quiet, rested, reposed.

P ارميده armīda, Rested, reposed, quiescent.

A ارميزاز irmīzāz, (v. n. 11 of رمز) Departing, declining. Abiding, cleaving to. Moving (a large army). Being contracted, drawn together.

P ارميس armīs, A kind of thorn.

A ارميقاق irmīkāk, (v. n. 11 of رمق) Being slender and weak (a rope). Perishing with leanness.

P ارمين armīn, The fourth son of king Kaykubād.

A ارمينا arminā, Sal-ammoniac.

A ارمينية arminīyat, or irminīyat, Name of a district in Natolia. A name of four countries.

P ارميون armayūn, Name of a Greek philosopher. Ingenious, intelligent. A sort of stone which breaks in a pentangular shape.

P آرن āran, (for آرنج) The elbow. The arm.

A ارن arn, (v. n. of ارن) Biting. Aran, (v. n. of ارن) Being brisk and lively. Arin, Brisk, lively, joyous, spirited. Urun, (pl. of اران irān) The dens of wild beasts. (pl. of ارون arūn) Poisons. The brains of elephants.

P آرّن arran, (in zand and Pāzand) A ewe.

A ارناء irnās, (v. n. 4 of رنا for رنو) Causing to look, or listen attentively.

A ارناف irnāf, (v. n. 4 of رنف) Drooping (his) ears from fatigue (a camel); also making a peculiar motion with (his) head when travelling. Travelling with expedition (a man).

A ارناق irnāk, (v. n. 4 of رنق) Waving a banner when about to charge an enemy. Being shaken (a flag). Muddying (water). Clearing the eye of motes. Abiding in one place. Being perplexed, non-plused, coming to a stand-still. Fluttering the wings and remaining stationary in the air (a bird). Stealing over the eye-lids (sleep).

A ارنان irnān, (v. n. 4 of رنّ) Resounding, twanging (a bow). Groaning, crying out. Listening unto.

A ارنب arnab, (pl. ارانب arānib and اراني arānī) A hare. A kind of ornament. A kind of field-mouse with a short tail. A woman's name. ارنب بحري arnabi bahrī, A kind of poisonous fish.

A ارنباني arnabānīy, Sombre (silk or beaver).

A ارنبة arnabat, The tip or ridge of the nose. A female hare.

A ارنبية arnabīyat, A species of white thistle.

P ارنبيز arnabīz, A kind of herb, dragon-wort.

A ارنة urnat, New cheese. Any thing drinkable. A grain with which they curdle milk. A lizard's nest.

P آرنج āranj, The elbow. The arm from the shoulder to the elbow.

P ارنج aranj, The elbow.

S ارند arand, The castor-oil plant.

P ارندان arandān, Denial, refusal, prohibition. Heaven forbid! Let it not be!

A ارندج arandaj, or irandaj, (from P رنده randa, Shaved, scraped, curried) Black leather.

P آرنده āranda, A bringer. A porter, carrier.

P آرنگ ārang, Colour. Mode, form, manner. Thought, doubt, suspicion. Grief, trouble, affliction. Craft, deceit, stratagem. A kind of fruit. Like, resembling, in form of. A viceroy. A governor. The elbow. Apparently. Never. A manufactory.

P ارنواز arnawāz, Name of the sister of Jamshed.

A ارنودي arnawdīy, An Albanian or Epirot.

P ار نه ar na, (for اگرنه agar na) If not.

A ارني urna', A grain used for curdling milk.

P ارنيبز aranyabaj, aranyabij, (or ارن بيژ aran bīj) Brazilian wood.

A ارواء irwās, (v. n. 4 of رواء) Abounding in any place (the plant راء rās, or Palma Christi). (v. n. 4 of روي) Giving to drink. Inducing one to repeat the words of another. Taking thought for, considering attentively. The eighth day of Zū'l hijjat.

A ارواث arwās, (pl. of روثة rawsat) Horse-dungs. Tips of noses.

A ارواح arwāh, The afternoon. (pl. of روح rūh) Spirits, souls, minds. (pl. of ريح rīh) Winds. Irwāh, (v. n. 4 of راح for روح) Repaying a debt. Giving repose. Smelling an (agreeable) odour. Snuffing the odour of a man (game). Stinking.

A ارواد irwād, (v. n. 4 of راد for رود) Walking leisurely and comfortably. Driving gently. Assisting, favouring. Being benevolent, kind, and easy.

A ارواض irwāz, (v. n. 4 of راض for روض) Abounding in gardens or lawns (a palace).

A ارواع arwāɛ, (pl. of رائع rāsiɛ) Handsome, winning, engaging.

A ارواق arwāk, (pl. of روق rawk) Tents. Horns. Clear waters. Sides of eyes. Tears. القي ارواقه alkā' arwākahu, He ran violently. He remained quiet in one place. رمي بارواقه علي الدابّة rama' bi arwākihi ɛala'd dābbat, He mounted his beast. He dismounted. القي عليك ارواقه alkā' ɛalayka arwākahu, You like him much. القت السحابة ارواقها alkati's sahābatu arwākahā, The cloud poured down its pure waters. ارواق الليل arwāku'l layl, The middle of the darkness of night.

A اروام arwām, (pl. of روم rūm) Greeks, Romans, especially of the Eastern empire. Turks.

A اروان ariwān, Name of a city in Armenia.

P اروانه arwāna, A wild violet. A kind of camel.

A اروب arwab, Turgid, torpid from satiety or too much sleep. Disturbed in mind.

P اروبك arūbak, Remote, distant. Old.

P اروج arwj, The juniper-tree.

A اروح arwah, More or most refreshing or conducive to repose. Spacious (camel-litter). One whose toes turn in.

A اروخ urūkh, (pl. of ارخ arkh or irkh) Bulls.

A ارود arwad, One who accomplishes his work quietly and easily.

P ارور urwar, (in zand and Pāz.) Vegetables.

A اروز arūz, Firm, steady, rooted, fixed. Collected, drawn together, contracted. Avaricious, covetous, tenacious. Urūz, (v. n. of ارز) Being gathered together. Contracting one's self, drawing back through avarice. Being firm, steady, rooted, fixed. Taking refuge in her hole, returning to it, and abiding there (a serpent). Being cold (night).

A اروس arsus, (pl. of رأس rass) Heads. Chiefs.

P اروس arūs, Furniture. Clothes.

P اروسا arūsā, Name of an Indian plant.

A اروش urūsh, (pl. of ارش arsh) Fines, mulcts for the shedding of blood.

A اروض urūz, (pl. of ارض arz) Earths, grounds.

A اروع arwaɛ, (pl. روع rūɛ and ارواع arwāɛ) Handsome, winning, engaging (either by comeliness or courage).

P آروغ ārūgh, A belch. آروغ دادن To belch.

A اروغ arwagh, More or most subtle or crafty.

P اروغ arūgh, A stem, stalk, family. Urūgh, An ox-hide. A large owl. A day. A mountain (according to Eastern tradition) forty leagues in height, from whose summit flow 1000 fountains each as large as the river Oxus. اروغ كردن urūgh kardan, To dress leather. To clean.

P آروغيدن ārūghīdan, To belch.

P آروق ārūk, A belch.

A اروق arwak, (A man) whose front upper teeth project over the lower. (A horse) between whose ears the cavalier points his lance. رأي الغول علي جمل اروق rasa'l ghūl ɛala' jamal arwak, He saw a dragon mounted on a black and white camel (an Arabian proverb, applied to those who are apprehensive of imaginary dangers, or fancy they see monstrous appearances).

A اروقة arwikat, (pl. of روق rawk) Curtains before doors. (pl. of رواق riwāk or ruwāk) Tents of goats' hair. Porticoes.

A اروك urūk, (v. n. of ارك) Feeding upon the tree اراك arāk. Abiding in the same place. Going down (a swelling). Persevering in any dilatory business. Inclining from side to side. Fastening (a business) upon any one.

A اروُل arsul, (pl. of رأل rasl) Young ostriches.

A اروم arūm, Origin, stock, root (of a tree or horn). Urūm, (pl. of ارم iram) Signs, marks, direction-posts or mile-stones. Sepulchral monuments, grave-stones of عاد ɛād. The part where the sides of the head meet before. (pl. of ارومة arūmat or urūmat) Roots, stocks, origins.

A ارومة arūmat or urūmat, (pl. اروم urūm) A

root, stock, origin. نفس من اطيب الارومة *nafs min atyabi'l arūmat*, A well-disposed mind.

P ارومه *arūma*, A plant whence potash is made.

P آرون *ārūn*, (or ارون *arūn*), Amiable, attractive, winning qualities.

A ارون *arūn*, Cheerful, lively, brisk. (pl. ارن *urun*) Poison, venom. The brain of an elephant. *Irūn* or *urūn*, (pl. of ارة *irat*) Fire-places, hearths.

A اروتان *arwanān*, Sound. Severe, painful (day). (A day) of extreme transport, or excessive sorrow.

P اروننن *arūnitan*, (in zand and Pāz.) To wash.

P آروند *ārwand*, Majesty, grandeur, pomp.

P اروند *arwand*, Experience, proof. The best part of any thing. Majesty, grandeur, pomp. Elegance, beauty, gracefulness. Wish, desire. A sigh of regret. The ocean. The Tigris. Name of a mountain in Hamadān. Name of the father of Lohorasb. Name of a fountain in Sistān.

P اروانداب *arwandāb*, Name of Zahhāk's father.

P اروندیدن *arwandīdan*, To be lazy. To louse.

G ارونس *arūnis*, Valerian.

A اروي *arwa'*, She mountain-goats.

A اروية *arwiyat*, (pl. of رواء *riwā'*) Ropes with which they fasten loads on beasts of burden.

A اروّية *urwīyat*, (or *irwīyat*) (pl. اراويّ *arāwīy* or اروي *arwa'*) A she mountain-goat.

P اروِيس *arwīs*, (or اروِيش *arwīsh*) A board whereon the Parsis place the vessels used in their religious ceremonies. A hair-rope.

P آروين *ārwīn*, (or اروين) Experiment, trial.

P آره *āra*, Root or lower part of teeth, gums.

P ارّه *arra*, A saw. ارّه كشيدن *arra kashīdan*, To saw. ارّهٔ مار دندان *arra-i mār-dandān*, A saw of serpents' teeth.

A ارهاء *irhā'*, (v. n. 4 of رها for رهو) Supplying constantly with meat and drink. Persevering in eating the same kind of victuals. Coming into a spacious district. Marrying a wide woman.

A ارهاب *arhāb*, Timid birds, not rapacious (in opposition to hawks and other birds of prey). *Irhāb*, (v. n. 4 of رهب) Intimidating. Driving away (a camel) from a cistern. Riding on a lean or a tall camel. Having long sleeves.

A ارهاج *irhāj*, (v. n. 4 of رهج obsolete) Raising (dust). Raining plentifully. Having (a house) full of vapours or smoke.

A ارهاص *irhās*, (v. n. 4 of رهص) Laying a foundation of large stones in a wall. Building (a wall) with clay. Laming a horse by means of a stone sticking in the hoof. Bestowing abundantly the goods of this world (God). Persevering in any bad habit. Obstinacy, perverseness.

A ارهاط *arhāt*, (or ارهط *arhut*) (pl. of رهط *raht*) Families or tribes of men, from two to ten, living together without women.

A ارهاف *irhāf*, (v. n. 4 of رهف) Whetting, sharpening (a sword).

A ارهاق *irhāk*, (v. n. 4 of رهق) Bringing near, causing to approach. Obliging, forcing, compelling, imposing a heavy, oppressive burden. Being hard upon. Being dilatory in saying prayers; deferring those prayers which, among the Muhammadans, ought to be said at one hour, till the next hour of prayer arrives. Causing one to hasten away from prayer. Exciting to rebellion. Attaching rebellion to any one.

A ارهام *irhām*, A raining gently.

A ارهان *irhān*, (v. n. 4 of رهن) Pledging, pawning (a garment). Giving (a son) as a hostage. Exposing to danger. Establishing, fixing, rendering perpetual. Buying dear. Making high (a price). Paying a part of the price (by way of securing a purchase). Doubling. Burying (the dead). Making weak.

P ارّه جان *arrajān*, (called also ارّه غان *arraghān*) Name of a city 60 leagues from Shīrāz.

P ارهد *arhad*, A species of grain.

P ارّه زبان *arra-zabān*, A backbiter, slanderer.

A ارهطة *arhitat* (pl. of رهاط *rihāt*) Skins whence thongs are cut.

P ارهفت *arhaft*, Name of a Hindū prophet.

P ارّه كش *arra-kash*, A sawyer.

A ارهم *arham*, Well watered. More fruitful.

P ارهنگ *arhang*, Name of a town in Badakhshān, and a place of pilgrimage, called also ارهنگ حسين *arhang husayn*, because the head of Alī's son Husayn was buried there. The shop of Mānī.

A ارهـون *urhūn*, Menstruous (girl).

P آري *ārī*, Yes, very well, indeed, truly. No.

A آريّ *āriy*, آري *ārī*, or آريّة *āriyat*, (pl. اواريّ *awāriy* or اواري *awārī*) A tethering-post. A manger.

A اري *ary*, (v. n. of اري) Making honey (a bee). Driving the clouds (wind). Pouring forth rain (a cloud). Being burnt at the bottom (a kettle), and leaving something sticking there. Remaining in the stall (cattle). Feeding in the same stall and being familiar (cattle). Bearing malice. Honey. Whatever adheres to the sides of the hive. A copious fall of rain. Whatever sticks to the bottom of the pot. Whatever falls from the hand or mouth when eating. A viscous kind of dew. (pl. of رأي *ra'y*) Opinions, views, doctrines. *Arī*, (or اريّ *ariy*) (pl. اواريّ *awāriy*) A stable, stall. A post, a tether. A hay or corn-bin.

A ارياح *aryāh*, (pl. of ريح *rīh*) Winds.

A ارياش *aryāsh*, (pl. of ريش *rish*) Feathers.

A ارياع *aryā'*, (pl. of ريع *rī'*) Rising grounds, hills. Paths over, or through mountains.

A ارياف *aryāf*, (pl. of ريف *rīf*) Well cultivated, planted, improved (grounds), rich in corn and pasture. *Iryāf*, (v. n. 4 of راف for ريف) Coming into that kind of country which is called ريف *rīf*. Abounding in pasturage.

A ارياق *aryāk*, (pl. of ريق *rīk*) Spittles.

A اريب *arīb*, Sagacious, cunning, shrewd, sly.

P اريب *ureb*, Crooked, inverted.

A اريبة *arībat*, Large, capacious (cauldron).

A اريث *arīs*, Fire.

A اريج *arīj*, (or اريجة *arījat*) (v. n. of ارج) Sending forth an agreeable perfume. A sweet smell.

A اريح *aryah*, Wide, roomy, spacious (camel-litter). Easier, happier.

A اريحا *arīhā*, Jericho in Palestine.

A اريحيّ *aryahiy*, Liberal-minded. Of an open, generous disposition.

A اريحيّة *aryahiyat*, Cheerfulness, alacrity in bestowing a gift.

P آريد بريد *ārīd barīd*, (or اريد بريد *irīd birīd*) A kind of medicine brought from Sijistān, resembling in shape an onion cut through the middle.

P آريدن *ārīdan*, To adorn.

P آرير *ārīr*, Sagacious, shrewd. Sober, chaste.

A ارير *arīr*, The shout of triumph of a loose fellow at a gaming-table. Victory, conquest. Noise.

A اريز *arīz*, Frost, hoar-frost, rime. A cold day. A chief, a leader.

P اريس *ares*, Quick-sighted, acute.

A اريس *arīs*, (pl. اريسون *arīsūn*) A husbandman. Name of a well in Madīna.

A اريّس *irrīs*, (pl. اريّسون *irrīsūn*, ارارسة *arārisat*, اراريس *arārīs*, and ارارس *arāris*) A ploughman, husbandman, farmer. A prince, a headman.

A اريسون *arīsūn*, (pl. of اريس *arīs*) Ploughmen.

A اريّسون *irrīsūn*, (pl. of اريّس *irrīs*) Ploughmen.

P اريسه *urīsa*, The district of Orissa (in India).

A اريسيّ *arīsiy*, A ploughman, a farmer.

P اريش *arīsh*, Ingenious, clever.

A اريش *aryash*, Hairy-eared and faced. Weak.

A اريض *arīz*, Broad, wide, large. Abounding in vegetation. Worthy, suitable. Pure, clean. Humble, modest. Fat (kid).

A اريضة *arīzat*, (Land) clean, pleasant to the eye.

A اريط *arīt*, Unfruitful, childless (man).

P آريغ *ārīgh*, Aversion, abhorrence. Hatred.

A اريق *urayk*, (dim. of اورق *awrak*) A little tawny coloured (camel).

A اريقش *uraykish*, (dim. of ارقش) Speckled.

A اريقط *uraykit*, (dim. of ارقط *arkat*) A surname.

P اريك *arīk*, (in zand and Pāz.) Distant, remote.

A اريك *arīk*, (pl. of اريكة) Thrones, couches.

A اريكة *arīkat*, (pl. اريك *arīk* and ارائك *arā'ik*) The soundness and wholesome flesh of a healed wound. An ornamented sofa or couch in a state apartment. Any place raised above the ground for reclining upon.

P اريكه نشين *arīka-nishīn*, Sitting on a throne.

A اريل *urayl*, Name of a man.

A اريلية *arīliyat*, Name of a fortress in Spain.

A اريم *arīm*, One, any one. A sign or trace.

A اريمة *uraymat*, Name of a place.

P آرين *ārin*, A cubit.

A ارين *arin*, (v. n. of ارن) Being lively and joyous. Blood allowed to be shed with impunity. A place. *Urayn*, A grain used for curdling milk.

A ارينبة *uraynibat*, A species of white thistle.

P آز *āz*, Desire, love, passion, lust. Avidity, avarice, covetousness. Greedy. Name of a city.

P از *az*, From. Of. For. By. Out of. With. Belonging to. By means of. In exchange. On. Than. Through. Off. After. از آتشها دودي نديده *az ātishhā dūde na dīda*, Inexperienced in the vicissitudes of fortune. از الف آدم تا ميم مسيح *az alifi ādam tā mimi masīh*, From Adam to Christ. از آن او *az ān u*, or از آنو *az ānu*, His, her, or hers. از آن ايشان *az ān eshān*, Their, theirs. از آن باز *az ān bāz*, From thence, from that time. از آن تو *az āni tu*, Thy, thine. از آن جا *az ānjā*, Thence, from that place. از آن شما *az āni shumā*, Your, yours. از آن كه *az āni ki*, Whose? از آن ما *az āni mā*, Our, ours. از آن من *az āni man*, My, mine. از او آزادي كرد *az u āzādi kard*, He declared him free. از اين جا *az īn jā*, Hence, from this place. از اين جا *az īn jā*, (از اين دست *az īn dast*, or از اين سبب *az īn sabab*) On this account. از اين جانب *az īn jānib*, From this side or part. از اين جمله *az īn jumla*, From all this. از اين سپس *az īn sipas*, Henceforth. از بالا *az bālā*, From above. از براي *az birāy*, For, because of. از براي آنكه *az birāyi ānki*, On account that. از بن دندان *az buni dandān*, (از بن سي و دو *az buni sī u du*, از بن گوش *az buni gosh*, or از بن ناخن *az buni nākhun*) Obedience, hearty service. Cheerful. Accumulated, treasured up. از بهر ايشان *az bahri eshān*, On their account. از بهر چه *az bahri chi*, On what account? از بهر خدا *az bahri khudā*, For God's sake. از بهر ديدن *az bahri dīdan*, In order to see. از بهر سود *az bahri sūd*, On account of gain. از بهر نماز *az bahri namāz*, In order for prayer. از پاي افتادن *az pāy uftādan*, To fall into disgrace, misery, want. To slip, to fall. To die. To retain no trace of former splendour. از پا در آوردن *az pā dar āwardan*, To throw down, enfeeble, or destroy. از پرگار شدن *az pargār shudan*, To be in an ectasy, beside one's self. از پرده برون شدن *az parda birūn shudan*, To exceed bounds. از پس *az pas*, From behind. از پوست بر آمدن *az post bar āmadan*, To disclose one's secrets. To renounce the world, one's selfishness, or carnality. To laugh. To attain one's object. از پيش *az pesh*, From before. از جان سير آمدن *az jān ser āmadan*, To be weary of life. To be wide awake. از جهت *az jihat*, On account of, because. از چند روز *az chand roz*, How long since? How many days? از خاك بر گرفته او *az khāk bar giriftasi u*, (He is) his client and dependant. از خر افتادن *az khar uftādan*, To fall from the ass (met.). To die. از خود *az khwud*, Voluntarily. از خود غائب شدن *az khwud ghāsib shudan*, To be absent, inattentive. از دست *az dast*, Weak. A subject, a vassal. از دست بر گرفتن *az dast bar giriftan*, To exterminate, to destroy. از دست دهر جستن *az dasti dahr jastan*, To escape from the world; to die. از دست رفته *az dast rafta*, (or از دست شده *az dast shuda*) In an ecstacy, beside one's self. از دل آمد *az dil āmad*, It came into his mind, it occurred to him, he recollected. He did not succeed. از دور *az dūr*, From afar. از دو طرف *az du taraf*, Mutual, reciprocal, from both sides. از راه بردن *az rāh burdan*, To carry or lead out of the road, to seduce, deceive, ruin. از رگ انديشه چكيدن *az ragi andesha chakīdan*, To consider attentively. از زبان جستن *az zabān jastan*, To commit a blunder in speaking. از زبان در آمدن *az zabān dar āmadan*, To be guilty of a slip of the tongue. از سر افگندن *az sar afgandan*, To dethrone. از سر گذشتن *az sar guzashtan*, To desist, withdraw one's hand. To resign one's life. از سر انگشت *az sar angusht*, Rashly, inconsiderately. از سر پا روان شدن *az sari pāravān shudan*, To go quickly. از سر خواستن *az sar khwāstan*, To risk one's life. از سر دست *az sar dast*, Off-hand, without reflection. از سر كردن *az sar kardan*, To seduce. To contradict, to give the lie. از سر نهادن *az sar nihādan*, To turn upside down. از سر وا كرد *az sar vā kard*, It dropped from his memory, he neglected. ازش *azash*, From that time; from him; from them. از شاه خوب اتّفاق است *az shāh khūb ittifāk ast*, Is he on good terms with the king? از شكم افتادن *az shikam uftādan*, To die. از صاحب يك سخن ميدارم *az sāhib yak sukhan mī dāram*, Sir, I want to have a word with you. از طاق دل افتادن *az tāki dil uftādan*, To fail in one's schemes. از فرود *az firod*, From below. از قحط مردن *az kaht murdan*, To perish by famine. از كار دست كشيدن *az kār dast kashīdan*, To give over an enterprise. از كجا *az kujā*, Whence? از كجاست *az kujāst*, Whence is it? از گره رفتن *az girih raftan*, To be squandered, lavished away. از گلها چه گل *az gilhā chi gil*, From what stock (art thou)? از ما *az mā*, From us. از من در گذر *az man dar guzar*, Pardon my fault. از ميان *az miyān*, From among. از نو *az naw*, Anew, afresh, again. از و بار خورد *az u bār khwurd*, He is offended at him. از و بر بست *az u bar bast*, He reaped the fruit of it. از و پهلو كرد *az u pahlū kard*, He retired far from him. از و پهلو تهي كرد *az u pahlū tihi kard*, and از و كناره كرد *az u kanāra kard*, The same. از و دگر كرد *az u digar kard*, He turned from him. از و دل برداشت *az u dil bar dāsht*, He was enraged at him. از و دندان بركن *az u dandān bar kan*, or از و دندان اميد بركن *az u dandāni umed bar kan*, Draw out the tooth of hope, give up all hopes of it. از و زاغ گرفت *az u zāgh girift*, He took the crow from him, *i.e.* he over-reached him. از و گوي برد *az u gūy burd*, He seized the ball from him, he wrested the victory from him. از و طوق برد *az u tawk burd*, The same. از و غائب مشو *az u ghāsib ma shar*, Be not absent from that, *i.e.* Neglect it not. ازوي *az way*, From him. از وي دامن افشاندن *az way dāman afshāndan*, To give a thing up. از هم بر آمدن *az ham bar āmadan*, To be disturbed, sad, and melancholy. از هم شدن *az ham shudan*, To be separated. To expand, open, blossom. از ياد بردن *az yād burdan*, To forget. از اين بيش *az īn besh*, Henceforth.

A ازّ *azz*, (v. n. of ازّ) Moving, removing, shaking, agitating. Kindling, lighting (a fire). Bubbling, boiling (a cauldron). Rumbling at a distance (clouds). Exciting, stimulating, impelling. Accumulating, collecting. The motion or beating of the pulse. Pain from pimples or prickly heat. The boiling, ebullition, or pouring out of water. The over-milking a camel. Coitus.

P آزا *āzā*, Mastic. Over against, opposite.

A ازأ *azasa*, (fut. يازأ *yassazasu*) He satisfied (the cattle), he filled (them) with food. He dared not, he desisted (from any thing) through timidity.

A ازآء *izsās*, (v. n. 4 of زأي) Incommoding and preventing from walking (a full belly).

A ازاء *izās*, Whatever tends to support life; its comforts and luxuries. Situation, place. Whatever is opposite to and corresponding with it, as a fountain-head to the well or reservoir into which the water flows. A canal, conduit, or pipe of lead, wood, stone, or leather, which conveys water from the spring to the reservoir; also the mouth of the urn, water-course, or conduit, from whence the water flows into a cistern or pond. A cause. A prop, support, stay. The manager of an estate. بازائه *bi izāsihi*, Over against him. ازاؤهم *izāsuhum*, Their peers or equals. ازاء العيش *izāsu'l ʿaysh*, The conveniences of life. ازاء الحرب *izāsu'l harb*, He who begins or supports a war. ازاء الامر *izāsu'l amr*, One who presides over, or attends to, a business. ازاء المال *izāsu'l māl*, A steward, manager of property.

P آزاب *āzāb*, An unmarried man. A recruit.

P آزابستان *āzābistān*, New levies, in which none but unmarried men are enrolled.

A ازابيّ *azābīy*, (pl. of ازبيّ *uzbīy*) Ways of walking. Evils, difficult affairs. Velocities.

A ازاتة *izātat*, (v. n. 4 of زات for زيت) Having abundance of oil.

A آزاج *āzāj*, (pl. of ازج *azaj*) Oblong edifices with arched roofs, corridors, arched galleries.

A ازاحة *izāhat*, (v. n. 4 of زاح for زيح) Performing, completing, bringing to a conclusion. Driving away. Removing (any thing from its place). Rendering inclined.

A ازاخة *izākhat*, A driving off, a putting away.

P آزاد *āzād*, Free, independent, liberated, delivered, manumitted, exempted. A lily. A cypress. A fresh date. An evergreen. A delicious kind of fish. The upas-tree. The mountain Alwand. Name of a hamlet in the district of Nakhchuwān. Faultless. Solitary, lonely. A kind of fakeer, or devotee. آزاد ازكاري *āzād az kāre*, Free from care, disengaged from business. آزاد فروختن *āzād firūkhtan*, To sell out and out, and unconditionally. آزاد كردن *āzād kardan*, To set at liberty, absolve, dismiss, allow to go away. آزاد شدن *āzād shudan*, To be liberated, dismissed, permitted to depart. سرو آزاد *sarvi āzād*, The cedar, the tall cypress.

P آزاد آوا *āzād-āwā*, (Free voice) A manner of reciting the praises of God.

A ازادة *izādat*, (v. n. 4 of زاد for زود) Providing with travelling necessaries.

P آزاد خلق *āzād-khalk*, Mankind at large. *Āzād-khulk*, Free (men), unblemished in body or mind.

P آزاد دارو *āzād-dārū*, A species of beet-root.

P آزاد درخت *āzād-dirakht*, (The free tree) A kind of tree which abounds in Georgia, and called there زهر زمين *zahri zamīn*, Poison of the earth. In Persia it is called طاق *tāk* or طغك *taghak*.

T آزاد كاغذي *āzād-kāghizī*, A letter of liberty, a charter.

P آزادگي *āzādagī*, Freedom, independence.

P آزاد مردي *āzād-mardī*, Liberty, freedom.

P آزاد ميوه *āzād-mīva*, A confectionery made of sugar-candy and almonds.

P آزادوار *āzādwār*, Name of a note in music. Name of a village famous for fruit, especially grapes.

P آزاده *āzāda*, Free. Perfect, intact, pure. Excellent, noble. Venerable. The lily. The cypress. مرد آزاده *mardi āzāda*, A noble, liberal, frank, distinguished man. آسوده و آزاده *āsūda u āzāda*, Easy and free. آزادهٔ قيد عشق *āzādasi kaydi ɛishk*, Free from the fetters of love.

P آزاده خرام *āzāda-khirām*, Graceful in walking.

P آزاده خو *āzāda-kho*, Name of the wife of Tūr.

P آزاده دار *āzāda-dār*, A boaster.

P آزاده گاه جامه *āzāda-gāhi jāma*, The place where a piece of cloth is cut from the loom.

P آزادي *āzādī*, Liberty. Freedom from worldly cares. Praise, thanksgiving. آزادي كردن To praise.

A ازاذ *azāz*, A sort of date.

P آزار *āzār*, Trouble, disorder, affliction, sickness, disease, grief, vexation, molestation, injury, outrage. Importunity. Money, a drachma. (in composition) Chiding, reproaching, teasing, affronting; as جان آزار *jān-āzār*, Tormenting the soul; cruel, brutal. آزار كردن *āzār kardan*, (or آزار دادن *āzār dādan*) To molest, vex, rebuke, revile, censure, quarrel, plague, torment, importune. اضرار و آزار *azrār u āzār*, Injury and reproof. آزار يافتن *āzār yāftan*, To be in trouble, to be sick. آزار تلخه *āzāri talkha*, The jaundice.

A ازآر *izɛār*, (v. n. 4 of زأر) Growling inwardly.

P ازار *izār*, A sash of fine muslin wrapt round the turban. Trowsers, drawers reaching to the feet. A cloth worn round the loins and passed between the legs. See also بن رنگ آب *buni rang-āb*. ازار كشتي بان *izāri kishtībān*, Sailors' breeches.

A ازار *izār*, (pl. آزرة *āzirat* and ازر *uzur* or *uzr*) A veil of fine linen or muslin, which, in the East, flows from the ladies' heads below the middle of the leg. Any thing, in general, which covers the naked body. Trowsers, breeches, drawers. The skirts of a tent. Chastity. A woman. A sheep. The sound by which sheep are called to be milked.

P ازار بند *izār-band*, The string of the drawers.

P ازار بندي رشته *izār-bandī rishta*, Connexion through a wife; petticoat-interest.

P ازار پا *izār-pā*, Breeches. Inner breeches, drawers reaching to the feet.

P ازارة *izārat*, (v. n. 4 of زار for زور) Inducing, inciting one to visit. Breeches, trowsers.

P ازاردم *azārdam*, A kind of pulse, French bean.

P آزاردن *āzārdan*, To injure, oppress, revile.

P آزار ده *āzār-dih*, Troublesome, injurious.

P آزار ديده *āzār-dīda*, One who has seen trouble.

P آزار رسان *āzār-rasān*, Troublesome, riotous; hurtful, injurious. An incendiary.

P آزار رسيده *āzār-rasīda*, Vexed, distressed.

P آزارش *āzārish*, Molestation, trouble, annoyance, uneasiness.

A ازارقة *azārikat*, Name of a sect of heretics in the East, declared and powerful enemies of the Muhammadan religion. They trace their origin to نافع بن الازرق *nāfiɛ bini'l azrak*.

P آزارمند *āzārmand*, Sick, infirm, afflicted.

P آزارنده *āzāranda*, Troublesome, injurious, seditious. A hurter, a tormentor.

P ازارود *izārūd* or *azārūd*, Transoxania.

P ازاره *izāra*, A low wall in front of a house.

P آزاري *āzārī*, Trouble, affliction. Sick. A patient. Insolent.

P آزاريدن *āzārīdan*, To molest, afflict, harass, vex.

A ازاز *azāz*, (v. n. of ازّ) Bubbling (a boiling pot or purling stream).

P آزاغ *āzāgh*, Any thing whose inside is black and viscous.

A الازاغب *al azāghib*, Name of a place in Arabia.

A ازاغة *izāghat*, (v. n. 4 of زاغ for زوغ) Moving (any thing) from side to side in order to tear (it) up. (v. n. 4 of زاغ for زيغ) Causing to incline.

A ازآف *izɛāf*, (v. n. 4 of زأف) Hasting to despatch (a wounded man). Oppressing any one (the belly) so that he cannot move.

A ازاق *azāk*, The city of Azof on the Palus Meotis.

A آزال *āzāl*, (pl. of ازل *azal*) Eternities.

A ازال *azāl*, Name of the metropolis of Arabia Felix, otherwise called Sanaa; also of its founder. *Izāl*, A removing of a thing from its place.

A ازالة *izālat*, (v. n. 4 of زال for زول) Removing, driving away, carrying off, ejecting. Erasing, obliterating, cutting off. Causing to decline. (In gram.) The elision of a letter or vowel point from a word. Removal.

A ازآم *izɛām*, (v. n. 4 of زأم) Forcing against one's will. Dabbing (a wound) with blood that (it) may stanch and heal. Dressing (a wound).

A ازام *azām*, A barren, scarce, severe year. *Uzām*, One who sticks close to a thing.

A ازامع *azāmiɛ*, (pl. of ازمع *azmaɛ*) Calamities. Disagreeable or iniquitous things.

A ازامل *azāmil*, (or ازاميل *azāmīl*) (pl. of ازمل *azmal*) Sounds, noises.

P آزامند *āzāmand*, A miser, a covetous person.

P از آن *az ān*, From him, it, thence, or that.

A ازانة *izānat*, (v. n. 4 of زان for زين) Adorning, dressing, decorating.

P از آنجا كه *az ān jā ki*, Since, by reason that, on the ground that.

A ازأنيّ *azɛaniy*, A kind of spear (so named from يزن *yazan*, a certain valley or tribe of Himyar.

A ازانيّ *azāniy*, A kind of spear named after ذو يزن *zū yazan*, A Himyaritic king.

A ازاهير *azāhīr*, (pl. of زهرة *zahrat*) Flowers.

A ازاهيق *azāhīk*, Swiftness, fleetness.

P از ايرا *az īrā*, Because.

A ازب *azb*, (v. n. of ازب) Not ruminating (a camel). Being hard. *Izb*, Short and mean of stature, dwarfish, squat, contemptible. Small-boned and at the same time corpulent. A dwarf. Any thing horrible or monstrous. *Azib*, Tall, long. ازب حزب *azib hazib*, A frightful, monstrous man. ابل ازبة *ibil azibat*, A lean camel.

A ازبّ *azabb*, Hairy. Luxuriant, abundant (in grain, herbage, &c.). Name of a demon. *Azubb*, (pl. of زبّ *zubb*) Membra virilia.

A ازباء *izbāɛ*, (v. n. 4 of زبي) Carrying.

A ازباب *azbāb*, (pl. of زبّ *zubb*) Membra virilia. *Izbāb*, (v. n. 4 of زبّ) Being about to set (the sun). Drying grapes or figs in the sun.

A ازباد *izbād*, (v. n. 4 of زبد) Foaming at the mouth. Foaming (the sea). Frothing (liquor). Flowering (the date-tree).

A ازبار *izbār*, (v. n. 4 of زبر) Being robust, valiant.

A ازبة *azbat*, Calamity. Penury. Barrenness.

P از بر *az bar*, (or از برم *az barm*) By heart. از بر كردن *az bar kardan*, To learn by heart.

A ازبر *azbar*, Broad-shouldered. Injurious.

A ازبيّ *uzbīy*, (pl. ازابيّ *azābīy*) An evil, a great and difficult affair. A manner of walking. Briskness, cheerfulness. Swiftness.

P از بير *az bīr*, By heart, by rote, by memory.

A ازبيرار *izbīrār*, (v. n. 11 of زبر) Standing on end (hair). Bristling up (a dog). Shooting forth (grass or hair). Preparing to commit mischief.

P از پي *az pay*, On account of.

A آزج *āzuj*, (pl. of ازج) Oblong arched edifices.

A ازج *azaja* (fut. يازج *yaɛzuju*) or *azija*, fut. *yaɛzaju*, He hastened. He was dilatory, he failed.

A ازج *azaj*, (pl. آزج *āzuj*, آزاج *āzāj*, and ازجة *izajat*) A kind of oblong arched edifice, or corridor with an arched roof. باب الازج *bābu'l azaj*, Name of a street in Baghdād. *Azij*, Insolent, exceeding the bounds of mirth, petulant, impertinent.

A ازجّ *azajj*, (pl. زجّ *zujj*) (A man) whose eye-brows are long and narrow. Long-striding (ostrich).

A ازجاء *izjā*, (v. n. 4 of زجا for زجو) Driving, propelling. Carrying forward.

A ازجاج *izjāj*, (v. n. 4 of زجّ) Putting a ferrule of iron on the lower part of a spear.

A ازجة *izajat*, (pl. of ازج *azaj*) Arched corridors, long buildings with vaulted roofs.

A ازجر *azjar*, A camel, the vertebræ of whose back are injured by disease or overloading.

A ازجم *azjam*, (A camel) that brays but little.

A ازجي *azja'*, More, most ready, skilful, expert.

A ازحاف *izhāf*, (v. n. 4 of زحف) Being fatigued (a beast of burden). Possessing such a beast. Dragging one leg after the other. Attaining, completing one's object. Proceeding against.

A ازحاك *izhāk*, (v. n. 4 of زحك) Having a jaded beast.

A ازحال *izhāl*, (v. n. 4 of زحل) Compelling, forcing. Driving to a distance.

A ازحلفاف *izhilfāf*, (v. n. 4 of زحلف Q) Being removed; retiring, receding.

P آزخ *āzakh*, A wart. A twig.

A ازخ *azkh*, A bullock. *Azakh*, A wart.

A ازخاف *izkhāf*, (v. n. 4 of زخف) Being proud.

A ازخام *izkhām*, (v. n. 4 of زخم) Stinking (the flesh of wild beasts).

A ازد *azd*, Name of the father of an Arabian tribe.

A ازداء *izdā*, (v. n. 4 of زدا for زدو) Acting equitably, shewing kindness and good will.

A ازداب *azdāb*, (pl. of زدب) Portions, lots.

A ازدار *izdār*, A producing, a making to appear.

A ازداف *izdāf*, (v. n. 4 of زدف not used) Growing dark (night).

P ازدب *azdab*, Beware! Seize! Lay hold!

A ازدباء *izdibā*, (v. n. 8 of زبي) Taking up, carrying off. Driving forward.

A ازدباب *izdibāb*, (v. n. 8 of زبّ) Being filled.

P ازدپ *azdup*, Take! Seize! lay hold!

A ازدجاج *izdijāj*, (v. n. 8 of زجّ) Reaching to the extremities of the eye (the eye-brow).

A ازدجار *izdijār*, (v. n. 8 of زجر) Driving away. Hindering. Rebuking. Being driven away, beaten off, prevented, hindered. Refraining, holding back. Divining, auguring from birds.

A ازدحاف *izdihāf*, (v. n. 8 of زحف) Advancing.

A ازدحام *izdihām*, (v. n. 8 of زحم) Thronging, crowding, pushing on one another. A concourse, press, throng, pressure of a crowd or mob.

A ازدخام *izdikhām*, A taking up and bearing.

P ازدر *azdar*, Worthy, proper, suitable. Beautiful.

A ازدراء *izdirā*, (v. n. 8 of زري) Despising, scorning. Scorn, contempt, disdain.

A ازدراد *izdirād*, (v. n. 8 of زرد) Swallowing.

A ازدراع *izdirā'*, (v. n. 8 of زرع) Sowing seed.

A ازدرام *izdirām*, (v. n. 8 of زرم) Swallowing.

A ازدران *azdarāni*, (dual) Shoulders, or arms. جاء يضرب بازدريه *jā'a yazribu bi azdarayhi*, He came striking his shoulders, *i.e.* empty.

P از دست *az dast*, Obedient. A subject.

P از دست فزا *az dast fazā*, (or از دست پزا *az dast pazā*) Unleavened bread, baked in thin cakes on lamina of iron or earth, placed in a frying-pan. Letters patent conferring immunity from taxation.

A ازدعاب *izdi'āb*, (v. n. 8 of زعب) Lifting, carrying. Filling (a vase). Cutting. Repelling. Rushing with impetuosity (a torrent). Moving heavily (a loaded camel).

A ازدعاف *izdi'āf*, A killing on the spot.

A ازدغاف *izdighāf*, A taking much.

P ازدف *azduf*, (or *izdaf*) A species of small medlar-tree and fruit.

A ازدفات *izdifāt*, A taking of the whole.

A ازدفار *izdifār*, A lifting and carrying of a load.

A ازدفاف *izdifāf*, (v. n. 8 of زفّ) Conducting or sending a bride to the house of her husband. Taking up (a burden).

A ازدق *azdak*, More or most sincere or true.

A ازدقاف *izdikāf*, (v. n. 8 of زقف) Taking with the hand, snatching greedily, and devouring.

A ازدقام *izdikām*, (v. n. 8 of زقم) Ingulphing.

A ازدكاء *izdikā*, (v. n. 8 of زكا) Receiving from another one's due.

A ازدكاك *izdikāk*, (v. n. 8 of زكّ) Being saturated with moisture (tillage).

P آزدگي *āzadagī*, A stitching, a sewing up.

A ازدلاب *izdilāb*, A seizing, a plundering.

A ازدلاع *izdilā'*, (v. n. 8 of زلع) Seizing by stratagem. Cutting off a part of one's due.

A ازدلاغ *izdilāgh*, (v. n. 8 of زلغ) Being scorched.

A ازدلاف *izdilāf*, (v. n. 8 of زلف) Approaching, advancing. Becoming near, or seeking nearness. Nearness. Being dispersed.

A ازدلام *izdilām*, (v. n. 8 of زلم) Eradicating, cutting the nose clean off. Beheading.

A ازدمال *izdimāl*, A lifting, or carrying at once.

A ازدمام *izdimām*, (v. n. 8 of زمّ) Carrying off a lamb with his head erect (a wolf). Being proud.

P ازدمي *azdamī*, Name of a doubtful animal.

P آزدن *āzadan*, (or ازدن *azadan*) To sew. To prick with a needle. To dye.

P ازدو *uzdū*, The sweet gum of a tree, of a reddish colour, with which confections are made. ازدوي تازي *uzdūyi tāzī*, Gum Arabic.

A ازدواج *izdiwāj*, (v. n. 8 of زاج for زوج) Coupling, marrying. Union.

A ازدوار *izdiwār*, (v. n. 8 of زار for زور) Visiting.

P ازدودن *azdūdan*, To polish, to free from rust.

P آزدة *āzada*, Pierced full of holes. Dyed, coloured. Written in letters of gold. Empty.

P ازدة *azada*, Dyed, coloured. Sewed.

A ازدهاء *izdihā*, (v. n. 8 of زها for زهو) Despising. Being proud.

A ازدهاب *izdihāb*, A bearing, a sustaining.

A ازدهاد *izdihād*, (v. n. 8 of زهد) Despising, esteeming lightly.

A ازدهار *izdihār*, (v. n. 8 of زهر) Keeping (any thing) with care; taking a pleasure (in it). Commending diligently to the care of any one. Shining (a lamp, fire, face, or the moon).

A ازدهاف *izdihāf*, (v. n. 8 of زهف) Carrying off. Bearing, sustaining. Destroying. Being near death. Telling a lie. Adding to a narrative. Rushing headlong. Throwing his rider (a horse). Hastening, despatching. Breaking, making void one's word. Talking loud. Prohibiting, checking. Despising, holding light. Incurring enmity. Changing, turning away.

A ازدئاب *izdi'āb*, (v. n. 8 of زأب) Lifting up (a water-pot) and going off with (it).

A ازديات *izdiyāt*, (v. n. 8 of زات for زيت) Anointing one's self with oil.

A ازدياد *izdiyād*, (v. n. 8 of زاد for زيد) Increasing. Increase, accession, profit.

A ازديال *izdiyāl*, (v. n. 8 of زال for زول) Removing, causing to cease.

A ازديان *izdiyān*, The being decked out.

A ازدئام *izdi'ām*, A being exceedingly terrified.

P آزر *āzar*, Cross-tempered. Trouble, grief, vexation. (in comp.) Troubling, grieving, vexing.

A آزر *āzar*, Name of Abraham's uncle. Name of a tract of country in Kūhistān (Susiana). Name of an idol. (A horse) having white thighs with feet of a different colour. Fy!

A ازر *azr*, Strength, power. Debility, weakness. The back. Corroboration, confirmation, strengthening. The encircling, comprehending, embracing, or girding (of a thing). *Izr*, Root, origin. A veil. *Uzr*, The middle, waist, the waistband. Breeches, trowsers. *Uzur*, (pl. of ازار *izār*), Breeches, trowsers, garments which cover the naked body.

A ازراء *izrā*, (v. n. 4 of زري) Despising. Accusing, reproaching, defaming, disparaging, misrepresenting. Negligence, carelessness.

A ازراد *azrād*, (pl. of زرد *zarad*) Coats of mail.

A ازرار *azrār*, (pl. of زرّ *zirr*) Buttons. *Izrār*, (v. n. 4 of زرّ) Putting buttons to a garment. Thrusting its tail into the ground to lay its eggs (a locust).

A ازراع *izrā'*, (v. n. 4 of زرع) Getting possession of a spot for sowing. Growing high (sown corn).

A ازراف *izrāf*, (v. n. 4 of زرف) Purchasing a cameleopard. Going fast. Driving, urging forward. Going before, preceding. Advancing.

A ازراق *izrāk*, (v. n. 4 of زرق) Being turned up (the eye-ball) so as only to leave the white appearing. Throwing her load backwards (a she-camel).

Being a long time pregnant (a camel).

A ازرام *izrām*, (v. n. 4 of زرم) Interrupting the flow of urine, causing a strangury. Cutting short, suspending conversation.

A ازرباب *izribāb*, (v. n. 9 of زرب) Being yellow or brown (a plant).

P آزرباد *āzarbād*, Name of a philosopher.

A آزرة *āzirat*, (pl. of ازار *izār*) Breeches, trowsers.

A ازرة *izrat*, The mode of putting on trowsers.

P آزرخش *āzrakhsh*, Thunder, lightning, storm.

P آزرد *āzard*, Colour. Paint, dye.

P آزرد آلو *āzard-ālū*, An apricot.

P آزردانيدن *āzardānīdan*, To make one injure.

P آزردگان *āzardagān*, (pl. of آزرده) Injured.

P آزردگي *āzardagī*, Grief, pain, uneasiness.

P آزردن *āzardan*, To injure, molest, harass, disturb, vex, trouble, offend, rebuke, reprove, reproach, disgust, afflict.

P آزرده *āzarda*, Afflicted, vexed. Displeased, dispirited, rebuked. Sad, sorrowful, weary. آزرده كردن *āzarda kardan*, To injure.

P آزرده پشت *āzarda-pusht*, Galled in the back. Decrepit.

P آزرده خاطر *āzarda-khātir*, Vexed, disgusted.

P ازرق *azrak*, The fourth line on Jamshed's cup.

A ازرق *azrak*, Blue. Blue-eyed. Extremely bright (spear-head).

A ازرقاق *izrikāk*, (v. n. 9 of زرق) Being of a blue colour. Being upturned (the eye) so that only the white is seen. Being bright and shining (the point of a spear).

P ازرق پوش *azrak-posh*, Clothed in blue.

P ازرك *azarik*, A goat.

P آزرگون *āzar-gūn*, Flame-coloured, yellow, bright, shining, ruddy. The leaves of the myrtle.

P آزرم *āzarm*, Modesty, bashfulness, shame. Courtesy, respect, honour, civility, politeness. Dignity, glory. Equity, justice. Conversion to the Muhammadan faith. Error, sin. Greatness. Unanimity. Commiseration, pity. Ease, security. Custody, guardianship. Power, strength. Clear, evident, manifest. A giving up to contempt and disgrace. Anger, wrath, violence. Pain, sorrow, grief. Name of the daughter of Khusraw Parvez.

P ازرم *azarm*, Shame. Justice. *Azram*, A kind of saddle-cloth.

A ازرم *azram*, A cat.

P آزرماه *āzar-māh*, Name of a month.

P آزرميدخت *āzarmīdukht*, or ازرميدخت *azarmīdukht*, Name of the daughter of Khusraw Parvez, who reigned four months. Name of her city.

P آزرميدن *āzarmīdan*, To honour, respect, favour.

A ازرنقاف *izrinkāf*, A going fast, making haste.

P آزرنگ *āzrang*, Adversity, misery. Destruction. *Āzrang*, (or *azrang*) A cucumber.

A ازريقاق *izrīkāk*, (v. n. 11 of زرق) Being of a blue or watery colour.

A ازرمّام *izrimmām*, (v. n. 11 of زرم) Sticking in the throat (word). Being cut off (flow of urine). Being contracted, drawn, puckered. Being born.

A ازز *azaz*, Fulness or overflow of an assembled council or convivial meeting Narrowness, tightness. Filled full. A large collection. A reckoning by the moon's course. Spare or intercalary days inserted between months and years.

A ازط *azatt*, Crooked-jawed, or cheek-boned. Smooth-chinned, beardless, thin of beard.

A ازعاج *izʿāj*, (v. n. 4 of زعج) Disturbing, moving from (its) place. Cholic, twisting of the guts.

A ازعاف *izʿāf*, (v. n. 4 of زعف) Killing one on the spot. Rushing on a wounded man to kill him.

A ازعاق *izʿāk*, (v. n. 4 of زعق) Terrifying. Oversalting meat. Causing to cry aloud (from fear or joy). Digging and finding muddy, brackish water. Travelling fast, quickening one's pace.

A ازعال *izʿāl*, (v. n. 4 of زعل) Exhilarating. Quickening. Uprooting.

A ازعام *izʿām*, (v. n. 4 of زعم) Exciting desire, alluring. Obeying. Being practicable. Becoming well-flavoured (milk). Beginning to put forth grass.

A ازعب *azʿab*, Short, squat, mean. Thick.

A ازعر *azʿar*, Thin of hairs. Bare, barren (spot).

A ازعرار *izʿirār*, (v. n. 9 of زعر) Being thin and few (hairs or feathers).

A ازعكيّ *azʿakīy*, Short, mean, and contemptible.

A ازعيرار *izʿīrār*, (v. n. 11 of زعر) Being thin and scattered (hairs).

A ازعيل *izʿīl*, Brisk, cheerful.

P آزغ *āzugh*, A slip, cutting, scion.

P ازغ *azgh*, A thing lopped (as vine-prunings).

A ازغاب *izghāb*, (v. n. 4 of زغب) Being covered with down (a young, callow, unfledged bird). Beginning to run and to leaf (a vine).

A ازغاد *izghād*, A suckling, a giving milk.

A ازغاف *azghāf*, (pl. of زغفة *zaghfat*) Coats of mail light but firmly woven.

A ازغال *izghāl*, (v. n. 4 of زغل) Flowing (blood from a wound). Pouring forth. Voiding (urine). Feeding (as a bird does her young).

A ازغان *izghān*, (pl. of وزغة *wazaghat*) Lizards.

A ازغب *azghab*, A large sort of fig. Pie-bald (horse). White and black (mountain). Downy (cucumber). Ash-coloured (camel).

A ازغباب *izghibāb*, (v. n. 9 of زغب) Having small yellow hairs (callow, unfledged birds).

P ازغج *azghich*, Ivy, convolvulus.

A ازغيباب *izghībāb*, (v. n. 11 of زغب) Having small yellow hairs (young unfledged birds).

A ازف *azaf*, (v. n. of ازف) Approaching, drawing near (time of departure). Hastening, coming suddenly upon. Being little, few, and small. Healing (a wound). Poverty, penury, straits.

A ازفّ *azaff*, Closely-feathered (ostrich).

A ازفاء *izfāʾ*, A transporting from place to place.

A ازفار *azfār*, (pl. of زفر *zifr*) Burdens, loads. Bottles, skins (for holding oil, &c.). Crowds, troops.

A ازفاف *izfāf*, (v. n. 4 of زفّ) Taking or sending a bride to her husband's house accompanied by music. Urging to a quick pace. Going fast (an ostrich or man).

A آزفة *āzifat*, (Approaching) judgment-day.

A ازفر *azfar*, (pl. زفر *zufr*) Large-sided (horse).

A ازفل *azfal*, Anger, passion, impetuosity.

A ازفلة *azfalat*, A crowd, troop, body.

A ازفلّة *izfallat*, Alacrity, lightness, sprightliness.

A ازفلي *azfalā'*, Promiscuously, indiscriminately.

P آزفنداك *āzfandāk*, (or آزفنداك) The rainbow.

A ازفي *azfā'*, Haste, expedition, celerity, alacrity, briskness, liveliness.

A ازق *azk* or *azak*, (v. n. of ازق) Being distressed; being overpowered (in battle). Difficulty, distress.

A ازقاق *azkāk*, (pl. of زقّ *zikk*) Leathern bottles.

A ازقام *izkām*, A causing to swallow.

A ازقان *izkān*, (v. n. 4 of زقن) Assisting (in carrying burdens).

A ازقّة *azikkat*, (pl. of زقاق *zukāk*) Streets, alleys. Narrow walks, spaces between rows of palm-trees.

A ازكاء *izkāʾ*, (v. n. 4 of زكا for زكو) Growing, increasing. Causing to grow.

A ازكات *izkāt*, (v. n. 4 of زكت) Filling (a leathern bottle). Bringing forth. Committing to memory, bottling up (a story).

P از كار دور *az kār dūr*, An idle vagabond.

P از كاره كردن *az kāra kardan*, To recall to mind. To write a history.

A ازكاك *izkāk*, (v. n. 4 of زكّ) Persevering, persisting. Predominating. Labouring under a suppression of urine.

A ازكام *izkām*, A giving of a cold in the head.

A ازكان *izkān*, (v. n. 4 of زكن) Teaching, giving to understand. Guessing, surmising, conjecturing the truth, hitting the nail on the head. Knowing, perceiving, understanding.

A ازكن *azkan*, One who judges very accurately. Sharper, sharpest, more or most clever.

A ازكي *azkā'*, More or most pious or pure. Very ingenious.

A ازكياء *azkiyāʾ*, (pl. of زكيّ *zakīy*) Good, just, virtuous, ingenuous. Possessing conveniences, abounding in comforts.

P ازگات *azgāt*, Wicked, villainous, depraved.

A ازل *azl*, (v. n. of ازل) Being inured to sorrow, conversant with distress and want. Keeping (one's flocks) from pasture on account of fear or scarcity. Falling into straits or scarcity. Keeping back from pasture, tethering. Imprisoning. Trouble, affliction, penury. *Izl*, A lie, falsehood. Calamity, misfortune. *Uzl*, (pl. of ازول *azūl*) Severe, barren (years). *Azal*, Eternity (having no beginning, ابد *abad*, implying eternity without end). ازل و آزال *azal u āzāl*, Eternity and eternities, *i. e.* from all eternity. ازل ازل *azlun azilun*, Extreme poverty, the deepest distress.

A ازلّ *azall*, (A wolf or man) lank and light about the legs and thighs. Swift. Broken-headed. السمع الازلّ *as simᶊu'l azall*, The mongrel whelp of a he-wolf and a she-hyena.

A ازلاج *izlāj*, (v. n. 4 of زلج) Bolting the door.

A ازلاع *izlāᶊ*, (v. n. 4 of زلع) Exciting a strong desire in any one to take a thing.

A ازلاف *izlāf*, (v. n. 4 of زلف) Bringing near.

A ازلاق *izlāk*, (v. n. 4 of زلق) Causing to slide or blunder in speaking. Looking grim. Casting her young (a camel). Shaving the head.

A ازلال *izlāl*, (v. n. 4 of زلّ) Causing to slide. Giving any one his due. Conferring a favour.

A ازلام *azlām*, (pl. of زلم *zalam* or *zulam*) Arrows without heads, which the Pagan Arabs made use of in drawing lots. Domestic animals resembling cats, but having short tails.

A ازلحفاف *izlihfāf*, (v. n. 4 of زلحف Q) Being removed; retiring, receding.

A ازلزل *izilzil*, A word used on the occasion of a violent tremor, as an earthquake.

A ازلعباب *izliᶊbāb*, (v. n. 4 of زلعب Q) Being dense (cloud). Increasing and dashing (a torrent).

A ازلغباب *izlighbāb*, (v. n. 4 of زلغب Q) Growing after shaving (hair). Producing down (a bird).

A ازلف *azlaf*, One who has a small straight nose.

A ازلق *azlak*, One who slips and slides much.

A ازلم *azlam*, (A goat) having two excrescences on the throat. (A camel) having one ear slit. الازلم الجذع *al azlamu'l jazaᶊ*, Misfortune. A mountain-goat. A lion.

A ازليّ *azalīy*, Eternal. God.

A ازليّة *azalīyat*, Life everlasting, eternity.

A ازليمام *izlīmām*, (v. n. 11 of زلم) Turning away the face instantaneously. Decamping, migrating. Standing bolt upright. Being high noon.

A آزم *āzim*, (pl. ازّم *uzzam*) A cheek-tooth, a grinder. One who keeps his lips closely shut.

P ازم *azm*, Progeny, offspring.

A ازم *azm*, (v. n. of ازم) Adhering (to a chief or friend). Abiding, sticking fast (in a place). Taking care of, overlooking (a farm or estate). Becoming contracted. Seizing and holding (with the teeth). Cutting with the teeth, a knife, or sword. Biting, champing (as a horse the bit). Keeping silence. Shutting (a door). Abstaining from, containing or commanding one's self. Neglecting food. Twisting (a rope or thread). Being unfavourable and severe (fortune, or a barren season). Extirpating, exhausting, destroying (men or cattle, during famine or other calamities). A fashion of twisting or plaiting the hair. Barren, disastrous (year). One who seizes with the teeth. *Azam*, (v. n. of ازم) Becoming contracted. Being pained. *Azim*, Barren, disastrous (year). *Izam*, (pl. of ازمة *azmat*) Meals. *Uzum*, (pl. of ازوم *azūm*) Cheek-teeth, grinders.

A ازّم *uzzam*, (pl. of آزم) Cheek-teeth, grinders.

P آزما *āzmā*, (from آزمودن *āzmūdan*) An experimenter. Skilled, experienced, tried.

P ازما *azmā*, Examining. An experimenter.

A ازماع *azmāᶊ*, (pl. of زمعة *zamaᶊat*) Small streams winding through valleys. Low grounds. *Izmāᶊ*, (v. n. 4 of زمع) Applying diligently to, and persevering in, any business. Developing themselves (the bearing spurs of a tree). Running (a hare). Shooting forth rapidly, unevenly, some parts being much finer than the rest (a plant).

A ازّمّال *izzimmāl*, (for ازدمال *izdimāl*, v. n. 8 of زمل) Wrapping or hiding one's self in a garment.

P آزمان *āzmān*, Repentance, regret, sorrow, grief, anguish. آزمان خوردن *āzmān khwurdan*, To devour grief, to repent.

A ازمان *azmān*, (pl. of زمان *zamān*) Times, seasons. *Izmān*, (v. n. 4 of زمن) Enduring a long time. Invading, pressing on one (time). Denying, disowning. Being ruined and desolate.

P آزماني *āzmānī*, An experiment, proof, trial.

P آزمانيدن *āzmānīdan*, To regret, grieve.

P آزمايش *āzmāyish*, Experiment, assay, proof.

P آزمائي *āzmāᶊī*, Experience, proof, test, trial.

A آزمة *āzimat*, (pl. اوازم) A cheek-tooth, grinder.

A ازمة *azmat*, (pl. ازم *azm* and *izam*) One meal, eating. Scarcity, dearth. *Azamat*, A bad season.

A ازمّة *azimmat*, (pl. of زمام *zimām*) Thongs, straps, fastenings. Reins, bridles, halters.

A ازمت *azmat*, More or most grave, or sedate. ازمت الناس *azmatu'n nās*, The gravest of men.

A ازمجرار *izmijrār*, A resounding, a crying aloud.

A ازمخرار *izmikhrār*, A being violent (noise).

P آزمرده *āzmurda*, Covetous. Lazy. Left.

A ازمع *azmaᶊ*, One who has a superfluous finger. (pl. ازامع *azāmiᶊ*) A calamity, misfortune. A disagreeable or iniquitous thing.

P ازمل *azmal*, Much, many: all. Voice, echo.

A ازمل *azmal*, (pl. ازامل *azāmil* or ازاميل *azāmīl*) Sound, murmur, confused noise. Family, domestics. الشيء بازمله *ash shayᶊu bi azmalihi*, The whole thing. *Azmal* or *azmul*, Household furniture, baggage. All, the whole.

A ازملة *azmalat*, Many, much. Universal. Household furniture, baggage. Family, domestics. The twanging of a bow.

A ازمن *azmun*, (or ازمنة *azminat*) (pl. of زمان *zamān*) Times, seasons. Ages.

P آزمند *āzmand*, Desirous, covetous, greedy.

P آزمندي *āzmandī*, Desire, lust, greediness.

P آزمودگي *āzmūdagī*, Experience. نا آزمودگي *nā āzmūdagī*, Inexperience.

P آزمودن *āzmūdan*, To try, prove, experiment.

P آزموده *āzmūda*, Tried, proved, experienced. آزمودها *āzmūdahā*, Experiments. كار آزموده *kār-āzmūda*, Experienced in business.

A ازمول *uzmūl*, (*izmawl*, ازمولة *izmawlat* or *uzmūlat*), Bleating (deer).

P آزمون *āzmūn*, A proof, trial, experiment.

A ازمهرار *izmihrār*, (v. n. 4 of زمهر Q) Being red with anger (the eye). Being austere, grim (the face). Being intensely cold (day). Twinkling (the stars).

A ازمهلال *izmihlāl*, (v. n. 4 of زمهل Q) Being dispelled (a cloud). Falling (rain). Flowing, running (melted snow).

A ازمئتات *izmiᶊtāt*, The being of various hues.

A ازمئرار *izmiᶊrār*, (v. n. 4 of زمار Q) Being incensed and having the eyes reddened with anger.

A ازميكاك *izmīkāk*, The being excessively angry.

A ازميل *izmīl*, A shoe-maker's paring knife. A kind of pike with which they hunt wild oxen. A mallet. Strong. Weak.

A ازميم *izmīm*, One of the last nights of a month.

A ازناء *iznāᶊ*, (v. n. 4 of زنأ) Causing to fly for refuge, or ascend a mountain. Giving a clyster.

A ازناد *aznād*, (or ازند *aznud*) (pl. of زند *zand*) Pieces of wood which, being rubbed against one another, produce sparks of fire. *Iznād*, (v. n. 4 of زند) Increasing. Having a return of pain.

A ازناق *iznāk*, (v. n. 4 of زنق) Keeping a family on short commons from avarice or poverty.

P آزناك *āznāk*, Desirous, greedy.

P آزناكي *āznākī*, Avidity, cupidity.

A ازنام *iznām*, (v. n. 4 of زنم not used) Beginning to put forth leaves (a tree).

A ازنان *iznān*, (v. n. 4 of زنّ) Entertaining an opinion (favourable or otherwise).

P ازناو *aznāv*, (or ازناوه *aznāva*) Name of a district in Hamadān.

P ازنب *aznab*, Displeasure, disgust.

A ازنب *aznab*, Fat.

P ازنك *azank*, A wrinkle. A frown. ازنك افكندن ميان دو ابرو *azank afgandan miyāni du abrū*, To knit the brows.

T ازنكميد *iznikmīd*, Nicomedia, in Bythinia.

P آزنكناك *āzanknāk*, Wrinkled, frowning.

A ازنم *aznam*, Slit-eared (camel). الازنم الجذع *al aznamu'l jazaᶊ*, Misfortune.

A ازني *azna'*, More or most salacious. ازني من قرد *azna' min kird*, More ruttish than an ape.

A ازنيّ *azanīy*, The spear of a king named ذو يزن *zū yazan*, who formerly reigned in حمير *himyar*.

P ازو *azu* or *azo*, From him.

A ازو *azw*, (v. n. of ازا for ازو) Diminishing, decreasing (a shadow).

A ازواء *azwāᶊ*, (pl. of زاي *zāy*) Letters ز *zayn*. *Izwāᶊ*, (v. n. 4 of زوي) Bringing another with one.

A ازواج *azwāj*, (pl. of زوج *zawj*) Pairs. Spouses.

A ازوار *azwār*, Men fond of female society.

A ازوال *azwāl*, (pl. of زول *zawl*) Elegant, ingenious, clever, witty youths. Powerful, strenuous. Wonderful. Wonders. Pudenda virorum.

A ازوج *uzūj*, (v. n. of ازج) Making haste. Hanging back, being loth to render assistance.

A ازوح *azūh*, Restive. One who fails in, or departs from, generous or noble deeds. ازوح انوح *azūh anūh*, Sordid, avaricious. *Uzūh*, (v. n. of ازح) Contracting one's self, shrinking up. Delaying, lingering, lagging. Stumbling, slipping, sliding. Beating (as the pulse). Approaching, drawing near.

P آزود *āzūd*, Intelligent, clear-sighted, acute.

P آزور *āzwar* or *āzūr*, Avaricious, greedy. Lewd.

A ازور *azwar*, (pl. زور *zūr*) An army. Inclined, leaning to one side. One who has an inequality in his breast-bones. (A dog) pigeon-breasted. One who looks out at one corner of his eye.

A ازورار *izwirār*, (v. n. 9 of زار for زور) Turning aside, shunning. Being crooked: falling crosswise.

A ازورة *azwirat*, (pl. of زوار *ziwār*) Ropes, straps, girths between the poitrel and the hind girth.

A ازورد *azward*, The lote-tree.

P ازوري *azwarī*, Name of a medicinal thorn.

A ازوش *azwash*, Proud, haughty, arrogant.

P آزوغ *āzūgh*, A lopping, a trimming. The prunings or loppings of trees.

A ازوف *uzūf*, (v. n. of ازف) Making haste. Approaching, drawing near (time of departure).

A ازول *azūl*, (pl. ازل *uzl*) Severe, barren (year).

A ازولال *izwilāl*, (v. n. 9 of زال for زول) Departing. Declining (as the sun from the meridian).

A ازوم *azūm*, One who sticks close (to a person or thing). Champing the bit (a horse). Barren, scarce (year). (pl. ازم *uzum*) A cheek-tooth, a grinder. *Uzūm*, (v. n. of ازم) Adhering, cohering. Seizing with the teeth.

A ازوي *azwī*, (pl. of زاي *zāy*) Letters ز *zayn*.

A ازويرار *izwīrār*, (v. n. 11 of زار for زور) Receding, turning aside. Being crooked, lying awry.

A ازهاء *izhāʼ*, (v. n. 4 of زها for زهو) Ripening (a date). Being proud. Being tall (a palm-tree). ما ازهاه *mā azhāhu*, How proud he is!

A ازهاد *izhād*, (v. n. 4 of زهد) Conjecturing, estimating by guess (a crop of corn while growing).

A ازهار *azhār*, (pl. of زهرة *zahrat*) Flowers.

P ازهار دسته *azhār-dasta*, A nosegay, a bunch of flowers. Several literary works bear the title of ازهار *azhār*, in the following manner: ازهار الروضتين في اخبار الدولتين *azhāru'r rawzatayn fī akhbāri 'd dawlatayn*, (The flowers of two gardens, in the history of two kingdoms) the history of the two royal families of Nūru'd dīn and Salāhu'd dīn (or Saladin), the famous sultāns of Egypt in the time of the crusades. *Izhār*, (v. n. 4 of زهر) Lighting a lamp: making (a fire) blaze. Flowering, blossoming.

A ازهاف *izhāf*, (v. n. 4 of زهف) Telling a lie, varnishing with falsehood. Exciting to mischief. Granting any one his request. Bringing near (a stab with speech or tongue). Rushing on a wounded man. Stirring up evil. Calumniating, whispering. Deceiving, betraying. Depressing, dishonouring. Hasting to do evil. Being delighted with. Giving pleasure. Referring, relating or tracing up to. Throwing (a rider). Carrying off. Destroying.

A ازهاق *izhāk*, (v. n. 4 of زهق) Shooting an arrow through the mark. Filling (a cup). Dissipating, destroying. Getting the saddle on his neck (a horse). Being full of marrow. Accelerating.

A ازهام *izhām*, (v. n. 4 of زهم) Being full of marrow (a bone).

A ازهر *azhar*, White, bright, brilliant, splendid, shining, clear, evident. The moon. A wild bull. Friday. Whitish-coloured (lion). Milk as soon as it is drawn. (A camel) straddling and cropping the extremities of a tree.

P ازهراك *azharāk*, Name of the tyrant Zahhāk.

A ازهران *azharāni*, (dual) The sun and moon.

A ازهيرار *izhīrār*, (v. n. 11 of زهر) Flowering.

A آزي *āzī*, Vehement, excessively warm, sultry.

A ازي *azy*, (v. n. of ازي) Being placed at, applied to, comprehended in. Being contracted, shrunk (a shadow). Studying to over-reach, circumvent, deceive or betray. Diminishing. Distressing, oppressing.

A ازيّ *uzīy*, (v. n. of ازي) Being placed at, applied to, comprehended in. Being contracted.

A ازياء *azyāʼ*, (pl. of زاي *zāy*) Letters ز *zayn*. (pl. of زيّ *ziy*) Costumes, habits, garbs, guises.

A ازيار *azyār*, (pl. of زير *zīr*) Those who delight in the company and conversation of women.

A ازياف *azyāf*, (pl. of زيف *zayf*) Clipt coins.

A ازيان *azyān*, (pl. of زين *zayn*) Ornaments. *Izyān*, (v. n. 4 of زان for زين) Adorning, decorating.

A ازّيّان *izzīyān*, A being decorated; ornateness.

A ازيب *azyab*, Cheerful, joyous. Vile, contemptible. One who takes short steps. Short. Satan. An iniquitous or disagreeable affair. Enmity, hostility. A hedgehog. Misfortune, calamity. Terror, tremor, Alacrity. Much water. A putative or adopted son, a bastard. The south-east wind. The south wind. *Azīb*, Long, tall.

A ازيبّ *izyabb*, Large (pudendum). ازيبّ البطش *izyabbu'l batsh*, Powerful in severity.

A ازيبّة *izyabbat*, Covetous (woman).

P آزيدن *āzīdan*, To injure, grieve, molest. To prick. To dye.

P آزير *āzīr*, Intelligent. Trouble.

P ازيرا *azīrā*, (for زيرا *zīrā*) Because.

P ازيرة *azīra*, A mattock, beetle, smith's hammer.

P آزيريدن *āzīrīdan*, To afflict. To draw.

A ازيز *azīz*, (v. n. of ازّ) Bubbling (a boiling cauldron). A thundering, crashing, rumbling, dreadful noise. Thunder. The sound proceeding from the clapper and other machinery of a mill. The noise of wind in the bowels. Frigid. Coldness. Vehemence, rapidity of motion.

P ازيش *azīsh*, From him.

A ازيع *uzayʻ*, A proper name.

P آزيغ *āzīgh*, Aversion, indignation.

P ازيغ *azīgh*, Perception, recollection.

A ازيل *azyal*, Wide between the thighs.

A ازيم *azyam*, (A camel) having no voice.

P ازين *azīn*, Such as this.

A ازينان *izyinān*, A being adorned: ornateness.

A ازيي *azyī*, (pl. of زاي *zāy*) Letters ز *zayn*.

A ازيينان *izyīnān*, The being greatly adorned.

P آژ *āj*, Rest, ease. Ingenious. Abstinent.

P آژخ *ājakh*, A wart. A mole on the skin.

P اژخ *ajakh*, A wart.

P آژخ ناك *ājakhnāk*, Full of warts, warty.

P اژدر *ajdar*, A dragon. The top of a standard.

P اژدرها *ajdarhā*, A dragon. A strong, brave man. A tyrant. Passionate, testy. A standard. Armorial bearings. The tyrant Zahhāk.

P آژدن *ājadan*, To sew, pierce, prick, puncture. To shave. To notch a mill-stone closely. To tinge, dye.

P اژدنك *ajdank*, Name of a demon.

P آژدة *ājada*, Pricked, punctured, sewed.

P اژدها *ajdahā*, A dragon. Brave, intrepid. A tyrant. Zahhāk. A standard. اژدهاي فلك *ajdahāyi falak*, The constellation of the Dragon.

P اژدها سران *ajdahā-sarān*, (pl.) Dragon-headed.

P اژدهاك *ajdahāk*, The tyrant Zahhāk.

P آژغ *ājugh*, The prunings of a vine.

P اژغ *ajgh*, Prunings, loppings.

P اژكان *ajkān*, Indolent, idle, lazy, slothful.

P اژكن *ajkan*, A latticed door.

P اژكهن *ajkahan*, (or اژكهان *ajkahān*) Indolent, idle, negligent, lazy, slothful. Vain, false.

P آژگن *ājgin*, Lattices, blinds.

P آژند *ājand*, Plaster, mortar, parget, cement.

P اژند *ajand*, Mortar. Clay, mud at the bottom of a cistern.

P آژندانيدن *ājandānīdan*, To make sew, or prick.

P آژندن *ājandan*, To prick, pierce. To sew.

P آژندة *ājanda*, Sewed. Bored, pierced.

P آژنديدن *ājandīdan*, To lay mortar between two bricks.

P آژنك *ājank*, A wrinkle: knitting of the brows.

P آژنك ناك *ājanknāk*, Frowning.

P آژنگ *ājang*, (or اژنگ) A wrinkle: a frown.

P آژنه كردن *ājana kardan*, To spread a table.

P اژنيان *ajnayān*, A chameleon.

P آژور *ājwar*, Covetous.

P آژوغ *ājūgh*, Slips, loppings. Palm-tree fibres.

P اژة *aja*, Quick lime, plaster, cement.

P اژهان *ajhān*, Idle, lazy, useless.

P اژهن *ajhan*, Lazy, indolent. A trifling thing.

P اژيانه *ajyāna*, A pavement of flags or brick.

P آژيخ *ājīkh*, Gummy exudations from the eyes.

P آژيدن *ājīdan*, To prick. To stitch, sew.

P آژير *ājīr*, Intelligent, learned, ingenious. Pious, devout. Chaste, modest. A lake, pool, ditch. A cistern wherein rain-water is collected. Victory, conquest. A cry, a shout. Abundance, surplus.

Preparation, arrangement.

P آژیر *ājir*, Intelligent, prudent. Pious, abstinent.

P آژیراك *ājirāk*, A shout, a cry.

P آژیریدن *ājirīdan*, To cry aloud. To appear wise and intelligent. To prepare, to arrange.

P آژینه *ājina*, A tool for notching mill-stones.

P آس *ās*, A mill-stone. Ground corn. A grinding of wheat, barley, &c. The ermine. A bald camel. A bow. Name of a village in Persia. آس کردن *ās kardan*, To grind, crush, bruise.

A آس *ās*, The myrtle. Cinders or ashes remaining in a fire-place. Honey; what remains in the hive. The ruins or remains of a dwelling. Secret remains of any thing in general. A tomb. A companion. آس برّي *āsi barrī*, The wild myrtle.

A اس *us*, A sound which tames serpents.

A اسّ *ass*, (v. n. of اسّ) Building, erecting an edifice. Enraging. Driving or checking sheep by crying *as as*. The excrement of a bee. *Ass*, *iss*, or *uss*, (pl. اساس *isās*) A foundation. The beginning or root of any thing. The earliest age, eternity. A spoiling, a marring. *Uss*, The vestige or trace of any thing. Ashes remaining in a place. The heart of man (as being the foundation of life). خذ اسّ الطريق *khuz ussa't tarīk*, Take for your guide on the road any footmarks or dung. علي اسّ الدهر *ʻala' ussi'd dahr*, In the beginning of time.

P آسا *āsā*, Manner, rule. Embellishment, decoration. Reverence, sternness, rigour. Authority, majesty, gravity. Quiet, tranquillity, repose. Gaping, yawning, stretching. آسا کشیدن *āsā kashīdan*, To yawn. (in compos. from آسودن *āsūdan*) Pacifying, soothing: as, روح آسا *rūh-āsā*, Soothing the mind. (an affix denoting) Like, resembling: as, مرد آسا *mard-āsā*, Manly, like a man. مشك آسا *mushk-āsā*, Like musk, odoriferous.

P اسا *asā*, Yawning. Like.

A اسا *asa'*, (v. n. of اسا for اسو) Curing, healing. Composing differences, making peace.

A اساء *isāʼ*, A making of horns to a bow.

A اساء *asāʼ* or *isāʼ*, A medicine, remedy. *Isāʼ* (v. n. 4 of ساء for سوأ) Corrupting, despoiling, destroying. Doing evil, injuring, maltreating. (pl. of آسي *āsī*) Physicians.

A اساءة *isāʼat*, An offence, crime, sin. Mischief, injurious treatment.

A آساب *āsāb*, (pl. of اسب *isb*) Fundaments. Hair about the fundament and genitals. Pubes.

A اسابذة *asābizat*, (pl. of اسبذيّ *asbazīy*) Name of a people in Persia, Magians.

A اسابل *asābil*, (pl. of اسطبل *istabl*) Stables.

A اسابيّ *asābīy*, (pl. of اسباءة *isbāʼat*) The passages or ducts for the blood.

A اسابيع *asābīʻ*, (pl. of اسبوع *usbūʻ*) Weeks.

A آساة *usāt*, (pl. of آسي *āsī*) Physicians, surgeons.

A اساتذة *asātizat*, (or اساتيذ *asātīz*) (pl. of P استاذ *ustāz*) Masters. اساتذهٔ عجم *asātizaʼi ʻajam*, Persian doctors or wise men.

A اساتير *asātīr*, (pl. of استار *istār*) Weights of 4½ miskāls, or 6½ drams.

A اساجيع *asājīʻ*, (pl. of اسجوعة *usjūʻat*) (Orations) written or delivered in rythm. اساجيع وليميّة *asājīʻi walīmīya*, Nuptial or festive verses.

A اساحة *isāhat*, (v. n. 4 of ساح for سيح) Causing to flow. Whisking his tail (a horse).

A اساحل *asāhil*, Channels for water.

A آساد *āsād*, (pl. of اسد *asad*) Lions.

A اساد *isʼād*, (v. n. 4 of سأد) Travelling quick: travelling all night without halting to refresh. Travelling night and day.

A اسادة *isādat*, (v. n. 4 of ساد for سود) Begetting a prince. Begetting black children. *Isādat* or *usādat*, (for وسادة *wisādat*) A cushion, pillow.

A اسآر *asʼār*, (pl. of سؤر *suʼr*) The remains after a meal, of whatever is gnawed or bitten. *Isʼār*, (v. n. 4 of سأر) Leaving remains of meat or drink.

A اسار *isār*, Captivity. (pl. اسر *usur*) A chain, fetter, ligament. (for يسار *yasār*) The left side.

A اسارة *isārat*, (v. n. 4 of سار for سير) Causing to go, driving.

G اسارون *asārūn*, Wild spikenard, asarum.

P آساره *āsāra*, Computation, calculation.

A اساري *asāra'* or *usāra'*, (pl. of اسير) Captives.

A اسارير *asārīr*, Beauty of face. (pl. of سرّ *sirr*) The lines, lineaments, wrinkles, or creases in the palms of the hand or on the forehead. The cheeks.

A اساريع *asārīʻ*, (pl. of اسروع *usrūʻ*) White worms with red heads found in sand. The fresh natural colour of the teeth. Shoots which grow from the roots of palm-trees, and which are occasionally eaten green. Lines or grooves on bows.

A آساس *āsās*, (pl. of اسس *asas*) Foundations.

A اساس *asās*, (pl. اسس *usus*) A foundation, basis, pedestal. اساس اللغات *asāsu'l lughāt*, (Foundation of speech) An Arabic grammar so called. اساس السياسة *asāsu's siyāsat*, (Foundation of rule) A treatise on political government. *Isās*, (pl. of اسّ *ass*) Foundations.

A اساسة *isāsat*, (v. n. 4 of ساس for سوس) Appointing a governor, throwing the government upon any one. Being affected by weevil (corn), by tike (sheep), by the moth (wool).

P اساسه *asāsa*, (or *isāsa*) A glance from a corner of the eye. Understanding, intellect. Revision, retrospect.

A اساطم *asātim*, (pl. of اسطمّة *ustummat*,) Domestics, relations.

A اساطير *asātīr*, (pl. of اسطار *astār*, pl. of سطر *satar*) Lines, rows, writings. (pl. of اسطار *istār*, اسطارة *istārat*, اسطير *istīr*, اسطيرة *istīrat*, اسطور *ustūr*, and اسطورة *ustūrat*) Stories, fables, tales, romances. اساطير الاوّلين *asātīru'l awwalīna*, Fables of the ancients.

A اساطين *asātīn*, (pl. of اسطوانة *ustuwānat*) Columns. Legs of quadrupeds. Veretra.

A اساعة *isāʻat*, (v. n. 4 of ساع for سوع) Losing. Destroying. Letting loose, sending camels grazing at random without a keeper. Entering (one hour into another). Remaining behind (one hour). Passing from hour to hour. Voiding seminal fluid. Allowing his pizzle to dangle (an ass).

A اساغة *isāghat*, (v. n. 4 of ساغ for سوغ) Giving time to swallow, to rest or pause. Being completed, made up (one thing by another).

A اساف *isāf*, or *asāf*, Name of an idol which عمرو بن لحيّ *ʻamr bin luhayy* set up on صفا *safā*, to which sacrifices were used to be offered in face of the Kaaba: according to others, a son of عمرو *ʻamr*, who for his wickedness was metamorphosed. *Isāf*, Name of a companion of Muhammad.

A اسافة *asāfat*, Grief, pain, sadness. Servitude, clientship. *Asāfat* or *usāfat*, Thin, light, unproductive soil. *Isāfat*, (v. n. 4 of ساف for سوف) Losing (cattle) by disease, (or children) by death. Unstitching (a leathern bottle). Stitching coarsely, so that the stitches afterwards burst. Patiently enduring. *Usāfat*, Leanness, barrenness of soil.

P آس افزون *ās-afzūn*, An iron instrument for notching a mill-stone.

A اسافل *asāfil*, Small camels. (pl. of اسفل *asfal*) Inferiors, lower classes, the canaille. Lower parts, the nether extremities. اعالي و اسافل *aʻālī u asāfil*, High and low, all ranks. اسافل ناس *asāfili nās*, The lowest of mankind.

A اساقة *asākat*, The strap of a stirrup. *Isākat*, (v. n. 4 of ساق for سوق) Causing to drive. Giving (camels) to be driven. Sending (a marriage-portion to a woman).

A اسّاقط *issākut*, (v. n. of اسّاقط, 6 of سقط, irregularly formed) Falling.

A اساقع *asākiʻ* (pl. of اسقع *askaʻ*) Small green birds with white heads.

A اساقف *asākif*, (or اساقفة *asākifat*) (pl. of اسقفّ *uskuff*) Bishops.

A اساقي *asākī*, (pl. of سقاء *sikāʼ*) Bottles (for wine or water): also those in which they churn milk.

A اساكفة *asākifat*, (or اساكيف *asākīf*) (pl. of اسكاف *iskāf*) Shoemakers. Handicraftsmen.

P آسال *āsāl*, A foundation, basis.

A اسآل *isʼāl*, (v. n. 4 of سأل) Granting, admitting or approving a request, allowing to ask.

A اسأل *asʼal*, More or most of an asker or beggar.

A اسال *asāl*, Likeness, resemblance. Signs.

A اسالة *asālat*, (v. n. of اسل) Becoming smooth, even, and long (a cheek or jaw-bone). *Isālat*, (v. n. 4 of سال for سيل) Shedding. Diffusing, causing to flow. Making long (the point of a spear.

A اسالق *asālik*, The parts about the uvula.

A اساليب *asālīb*, (pl. of اسلوب *uslūb*) Modes, manners, ways. Parts of doctrine or of knowledge. مكاتيب تهنيت اساليب *makātībi tanhiyat-asālīb*,

Letters in the way of congratulation.

G اساليطوس *asālītūs*, A kind of black clay which they rub on vines to destroy insects.

G اساليون *asāliyūn*, Parsley.

A آسام *āsām*, (pl. of اسم *ism*) Names.

A اسام *isām*, (v. n. 4 of سئم) Wearying.

A اسامة *isāmat*, (v. n. 4 of سام for سوم) Sending to graze. Darting a look at one. Raising a price, fixing a high price. Asking the price. Making a hole at the top of a well. *Usāmat*, A lion. اجرأ من اسامة *ajraʼ minusāmat*, Bolder than a lion.

A اسامع *asāmiɛ*, (pl. of سمع *samɛ*) Ears, hearing.

A اسامي *asāmī*, (pl. of اسم *ism*) Names. A An individual. A dependant, client. A tenant, renter. A debtor. The defendant of a suit. Office, place, appointment. The substitution of one for another.

A اساميّ *asāmīy*, (pl. of اسم *ism*) Names.

P اساميس *asāmīs*, Wild camomile.

P آسان *āsān*, Easy, convenient, commodious. Threads, strings. آسان داشتن *āsān dāshtan*, To make an abatement, to lower the price.

A آسان *āsān*, (pl. of اسن *usun*) Dispositions, tempers, manners, modes of living. Threads or twists of ropes. هو علىٰ آسان من ابيه *huwa ɛala' āsān min abīhi*, He takes after his father.

P آسان‌كار *āsān-kar*, Skilful, active, expeditious.

P آسان‌گير *āsān-gīr*, Easy of access, courteous.

P آساني *āsānī*, Facility, ease. Repose, sleep. Easy. Leave.

A اسانيد *asānīd*, (pl. of اسناد *isnād*) Allegations on other's authority. Imputations, attributes.

P آسانيدن *āsānīdan*, To facilitate, to expedite.

A اساوة *usāwat*, Medical art. Remedy, cure.

A اساود *asāwid*, (pl. of اسود) Black serpents.

A اساور *asāwir*, (or اساورة *asāwirat*) (pl. of سوار *siwār* or اسوار *uswār*) Bracelets. (pl. of اسوار *iswār* and *uswār*, q. v.)

A اساورة *asāwirat*, Name of a company of strangers who settled in Basra (as the احامرة *ahāmirat* did in Kufa).

A اساهيج *asāhīj*, Various modes of going.

A اساهيك *asāhīk*, A horse's pace. A gallop.

P آساي *āsāy*, (in comp.) Resting. Ceasing.

A اسايا *asāya'*, (pl. of آسية *āsiyat*) Sad, mournful (women).

P آسايانيدن *āsāyānīdan*, To give rest. To praise. To lift.

P آسايش *āsāyish*, Ease, quiet, rest, repose.

P آسايشكده *āsāyish-kada*, A place of rest.

A اسائن *asāʼin*, (pl. of اسينة *asīnat*) Bowstrings.

P آسائيدن *āsāʼīdan*, To rest, to cease.

P آسيب *āsīb*, Endeavour, effort. Nail, claw, hoof.

P اسب *asb*, A horse. The knight at chess. اسب آبي *asbi ābī*, The hippopotamus. اسب تيز رو *asbi tez-rav*, A swift horse. اسب جنگ *asbi jang*, A war-horse. اسب چوبين *asbi chūbīn*, (A wooden horse) A bier. اسب سرخ *asbi surkh*, A bay horse. اسب سركش *asbi sar-kash*, A restive horse. اسب لاشه *asbi lāsha*, A horse bred from an Arabian sire and an Anatolian dam. اسب نوبتي *asbi nawbatī*, A post-horse. اسب و اسباب *asb u asbāb*, A horse and his furniture or baggage. اسب و فرزين نهادن *asb u farzīn nihādan*, To win (at chess).

A اسب *isb*, (pl. آساب *āsāb*) The fundament, pubes, and the hair growing around those parts.

A اسباء *isbāʼ*, (v. n. 4 of سبأ) Humbling one's self, submitting to the authority of God. Being quiet. Being enamoured, insane, strongly inclined.

A اسباءة *isbāʼat*, (pl. اسابيّ *asābīy*) A duct or passage for the blood.

A اسباب *asbāb*, (pl. of سبب *sabab*) Causes, motives, arguments, reasons, incentives, stimulatives. Modes, ways, manners, means. Instruments, utensils, apparatus. Tracts, parts. Cloths, apparel, effects, moveables, goods, chattels, furniture. P اسباب جنگ *asbābi jang*, Military stores. اسباب رحله *asbābi rihla*, Baggage, necessaries for travelling. اسباب سفر *asbābi safar*, Necessaries, provisions, preparations for travelling. A اسباب السموات *asbābu's samawāt*, The tracts or quarters of the heavens. اسباب معيشه *asbābi maɛīsha*, The means of living. اسباب النوازل *asbābu'n nawāzil*, (Causes of the arrivals from heaven) Name of a work, shewing the causes for which each verse of the Kur'ān was sent from heaven.

A اسبات *isbāt*, (v. n. 4 of سبت) Resting. Keeping or entering on a Sabbath. Sabbatism.

A اسباح *isbāh*, (v. n. 4 of سبح) Causing to swim.

A اسباخ *isbākh*, (v. n. 4 of سبخ) Being saltish (ground). Reaching saltish ground when digging.

A اسباد *asbād*, (pl. of سبد *sibd*) Rogues, thieves. Wolves. Sable garments. Heads of the plant نصيّ *nasīy* ere they shoot forth. *Isbād*, (v. n. 4 of سبد) Shaving (the head). Growing (fresh shoots of the plant نصيّ *nasīy* upon the old ones).

A اسبار *asbār*, (pl. of سبر *sibr* or *sabr*) Forms. Origins, roots. Colours. Beauties.

A اسباط *asbāt*, (pl. of سبط *sibt*) Tribes, distinct bodies. The tribes of Israel. اولاد و اسباط *awlād u asbāt*, Sons and kindred. *Isbāt*, (v. n. 4 of سبط) Being silent from fright. Cleaving to the ground, lying outstretched from a sound drubbing. Sleeping with eyes half-closed. Slighting, disregarding. Being dilated, spread out. Falling and being unable to rise. Abounding in the plant سبط *sabat*.

A اسباع *asbāɛ*, (pl. of سبع *sibɛ*) (Camels) enduring thirst for seven days. (pl. of سبيع *sabīɛ*) Seventh parts. *Isbāɛ*, (v. n. 4 of سبع) Completing the number seven. Having camels which drink on the seventh day. Having one's flocks attacked by wild beasts. Feeding upon, or serving up, the flesh of wild beasts. Giving a child to nurse. Surrendering a flock to the wolf. Dismissing, setting at liberty, not making use of.

A اسباغ *isbāgh*, (v. n. 4 of سبغ) Completing. Conferring favours in perfection. Performing thoroughly a religious ablution, giving to each member its due share. Putting on an ample coat of mail.

P اسب افگن *asb-afgan*, One who charges (the enemy's) cavalry. One who urges his horse.

A اسباق *asbāk*, (pl. of سبق) Wagers stakes, bets.

A اسبال *asbāl*, Rims of water-buckets. *Isbāl*, (v. n. 4 of سبل) Letting down (drawers) through pride. Untying the knot of the drawers. Raining copiously. Weeping profusely. Having corn coming into ear. Coming into ear (corn). Talking immoderately. Being much frequented (a road).

P آسبان *āsbān*, A miller.

A اسبان *asbān*, Thin coifs or hoods. *Isbān*, (v. n. 4 of سبن) Putting on black trowsers, as are made at Saban, and worn by the women of Baghdād.

P اسبانبر *asbānbur*, Name of a city.

P اسب انگيز *asb-angez*, A spur.

P اسباه *isbāh*, A large army. A dog.

A اسبت *asbut*, (pl. of سبت *sabt*) Sabbaths. Drowsiness. Failings in the intellects. Bold, impudent (boys). Observations of the Sabbath. Braided tresses. Quick paces. Times, fortunes.

P اسب تاز *asb-tāz*, Level ground. The 18th of the month according to the æra of Jalālu'd din.

P اسبتان *asbatān*, Seed of the wild rue.

P اسب دزد *asb-duzd*, A horse-stealer.

P اسب دواني *asb-dawānī*, Horse-racing.

A اسبذيّ *asbazīy*, (pl. اسابذة) Persian Magi.

A اسبطرار *isbitrār*, (v. n. 4 of سبطر Q) Lying on one side. Stretching one's self at full length. Going with a quick pace (a camel). Being well regulated and in good order (a country).

A اسبع *asbuɛ*, (pl. of سبع *sabuɛ*) Beasts of prey.

A اسبغلال *isbighlāl*, (v. n. 4 of سبغل Q) Being sprinkled (a garment). Being anointed (the hair).

A اسبق *asbak*, Days of yore. Most excellent. Surpassing, super-eminent, transcendental.

A اسبكرار *isbikrār*, (v. n. 4 of سبكر Q) Being tall and well-proportioned (a damsel). Extending lengthwise. Lying on one side. Being in excellent order (a country).

A اسبل *asbal*, Long-mustachioed (man).

P اسب ماده *asb-māda*, A mare.

P اسب نمه *asb-nama*, The trappings of a war-horse. Any thing which dries up the sweat of a horse.

A اسبوبة *usbūbat*, A handle, an occasion. An occasion of endless reviling.

P اسبور *usbūr*, Stupid.

A اسبوع *usbūɛ*, (pl. اسابيع *asābīɛ*) A week.

A اسبوعًا *usbūɛan*, Seven times.

A اسبوعاني *usbūɛānī*, A fortnight, two se'nnights.

F اسبونتن *asbūnitan*, (in zand and Pāzand) To see. To cause to run.

P اسبه *isbah*, A troop of horse. A dog.

P اسبهان *isbahān*, Ispahān.

P اسبهبد *isbah-bad* or *isbah-bud*, A title assumed by the kings of Tabaristān. A general.

P اسبهبد خوره *isbah-bad khwura*, Speech.

A اسبيل *isbīl*, Name of a town in Yaman. Seville.

P اسپ *asp*, A horse. The knight at chess. اسپ تازي *aspi tāzī*, An Arabian horse. *Isp*, The hair about the privities.

G اسپاناج *ispānāj*, Spinage.

P اسپاه *ispāh*, A large army. A dog.

P اسپاهان *ispāhān*, (now Isfāhān) That part of Persia where the troops were generally quartered.

P اسپخول *ispikhūl*, Birds' dung.

P اسپدار *ispidār*, A general, a commander.

P اسپر *ispar*, A shield.

P اسپرايين *isparāyīn*, Isfarāyin, in Khurāsān.

P اسپرد *isparad*, Coagulated, curdled. Jelly.

P اسپ رز *asp-raz* (*isp-raz*, اسپ رس *asp-ras* or *isp-ras*), A race-course: an open space for exercise.

P اسپرز *uspurz*, Spleen, milt. Lingula pudendi.

P اسپرسب *asparsab*, (*isparsab*, اسپرسف *asparsaf* or *isparsaf*) A race-ground. An open space.

P اسپرش *isparish*, Completion. Perfection.

P اسپرغم *ispargham* or *asparghm*, Name of an odoriferous herb. Any green herb. Verdure. Any fragrant herb.

P اسپرگ *isparag*, A kind of yellow wood used in dyeing stuffs. Turmeric. The water-melon.

P اسپرلوس *isparlos*, A palace. A hall of justice.

P اسپرم *isparam*, Any flower or fragrant herb.

P اسپرم آب *isparam-āb*, Warm water medicinally prepared for washing the bodies of sick persons. An embrocation or medicated bath.

P اسپرنگ *isparang*, A city near Samarcand.

P اسپرود *isparūd*, A species of aquatic bird.

P اسپروز *ispuroz*, or *isparoz*, Name of a mountain.

P اسپرهم *isparham*, Any fragrant herb.

P اسپري *isparī*, Complete, perfect, entire, whole. Finished, exhausted, annihilated, destroyed. اسپري شدن *isparī shudan*, To be complete, to be finished, exhausted or annihilated.

P اسپريس *asp-res*, (*isp-res* or اسپريز *isp-rez*, اسپريش *asp-resh* or *isp-resh*) A course, a running-place for horses. Complete, entire.

P اسپس *uspus*, A louse. A small worm.

P اسپست *aspist*, Trefoil, clover.

P اسپست زار *aspistzār*, A clover-field.

P اسپغول *ispaghūl* (*aspaghūl*, or اسپغون *ispaghūn*) Seed of flea-wort.

P اسپك *aspak*, A little horse.

P اسپ کره *asp-kurra*, A colt, a foal.

P اسپلنج *aspalunj*, Goats' beard (a plant).

P اسپ ماده *asp-māda*, A mare.

G اسپناخ *ispanākh*, اسپناج *ispanānj*, Spinage.

P اسپند *ispand*, Wild rue, which they burn at marriages to drive away evil spirits.

P اسپندار *ispandār*, A wax-light. Name of the son of Gushtasp. The stay of the sun in Pisces.

P اسپندارمذ *ispandārmuz*, The earth. Name of the twelfth month of the Persian year; also the fifth day of each month. Name of the angel who presides over the month and day Ispandārmuz.

P اسپندان *ispandān*, Mustard-seed.

P اسپنديار *ispandyār*, Name of Gushtasp's son.

P اسپنوي *ispanūy*, Name of a woman.

P اسپه *aspa*, A colt, a horse rising two years old. *Ispah*, A troop of horse. A dog.

P اسپهان *ispahān*, The capital of Persian Irāk.

P اسپهبد *ispah-bad*, also *ispah-bud*, A prince (in Tabaristān). A general, commander-in-chief.

P اسپهبد خوره *ispahbad khwura*, Speech.

P اسپيچاب *ispechāb*, A town in Turkistān.

P اسپيد *isped*, White, colourless.

P اسپيدار *ispedār*, A sort of willow, the aspen.

P اسپيدبا *isped-bā*, A kind of broth made of the juice and small pieces of meat, together with spinage, flour, and vinegar.

P اسپيدرود *isped-rūd*, A river in Āzarbayjān.

P اسپيدكار *isped-kār*, A worker in tin, a tinman.

P اسپيل *aspīl*, A horse-stealer by profession.

P اسپيوش *ispayūsh*, Seed of flea-wort.

A آسة *āsat*, A single myrtle-tree.

P آست *āst*, (for آستا) Praise, commendation.

P است *ast*, Is (from بودن *būdan*, To be). He willeth, he seeketh. A mule. A bone. A seed, a kernel. *Ast* or *ust*, A commentary on the Zand and Pāzand. *Ist*, Stand thou. Praise. The anus. *Ust*, The buttocks. Throwing, flinging.

A است *ist*, The fundament. يا ابن استها *yā ibna istihā*, An expression when any one's father makes his mother desist from any work. تركته باست الارض *taraktuhu bi isti'l arz*, I left him poor and destitute. ما لك است مع استك *mā laka istun maʿ istika*, You have no assistance. على است الدهر *ʿala' isti'd dahr*, From the beginning of time, for ever, in every age. است الكلبة *istu'l kalbat*, Sorrow, trouble, a bad omen, an odious and disgusting thing. است المتن *istu'l matn*, A desert.

P استا *astā* or *ustā*, A commentary on the Zand or holy scriptures of the Magi or worshippers of fire. *Astā*, Name of a fort. *Istā*, Praising; an encomiast. A town in Samarkand. *Ustā*, Master, teacher.

A استاء *istāʾ*, (v. n. 4 of سني not in use) Fitting the warp to the loom. Weaving cloth.

A استاج *istāj*, A hollow stick or reel on which thread is wound by the fingers ready for weaving.

P استاخ *istākh*, A green branch. *Ustākh*, Impudent, audacious, unblushing, insolent, bold.

P استاد *ustād*, A master, teacher, tutor. An artificer, manufacturer, artisan. A barber. Ingenious, excellent, celebrated, famed for any art or work of ingenuity. استاد خياط *ustādi khiyāt*, A tailor. استاد هفت آسمان *ustādi haft āsmān*, Master of the seven heavens, the planet Jupiter.

P استادانيدن *istādānīdan*, (and استاداندن *istādāndan*) To make to stand, constitute, establish, fix.

P استادگي *istādagī*, Stability. A stop, a stay. استادگئ باران *istādagiʾi bārān*, A failure or want of rain. *Ustādgī*, A trade. Mastery of an art.

P استادن *istādan*, To stand, stop, dwell, halt.

P استاده *istāda*, Standing; set up, erected. A pole. An ensign-staff. The prop of a tent-door.

P استادي *ustādī*, (or استاذي *ustāzī*) An art, trade, workmanship. Excellence, skill in any art or profession. استادي كردن *ustādī kardan*, To work, to exercise any art or trade.

A استاذ *ustāz*, (pl. اساتذة *asātizat*) A teacher.

A استاذون *ustāzūn*, (pl. of استاذ *ustāz*) Masters.

P استار *astār*, Lining.

A استار *astār*, (pl. of ستر *sitr*) Veils.

G استار *istār*, (pl. اساتير *asātīr*) Four. A weight of 4½ miskāls, or 6½ drams.

P استاراباد *istārābād*, The city of Astārābād.

A استارة *istārat*, Any thing that covers or defends, as a veil, awning, shield, wall, &c.

P استاره *istāra*, A star. A canopy. A geometrical rule by which right lines are drawn. A kind of guitar with three strings. Name of a country, and of a fortress in the Dak'han.

G استافيل *istāfīl*, A grape.

G استاقوس *istākūs*, A kind of long sea-crab.

P استاك *istāk*, A cutting, a slip of a vine.

P استاگر *ustāgar*, (or استاكر) A skilful artist.

P استام *ustām*, Saddle-ornaments of gold and silver. Any thing to which one can trust; a confidant. A prop, a column. A patron.

P آستان *āstān*, A shoe-maker. Lying supine. A threshold. A king's court, royal palace. The Ottoman Porte. The tombs of prophets and other holy men. آستان برخاستن *āstān bar khāstan*, To exalt, to elevate. To be ruined. آستان سعادت *āstani saʿādat*, The palace of felicity. آستان عاليشان *āstāni ʿālī-shān*, The Sublime Porte, the court of high dignity. آستان عدم *āstāni ʿadam*, (or آستان فنا *āstāni fanā*) (The threshold of annihilation) The world. آستان گردون *āstāni gardūn*, The revolving heavens. *Āsitān*, Taking a person's horoscope.

P استان *astān*, A place of rest: a sleeping-place.

A استان *astān*, Roots of old trees. *Istān*, (v. n. 4 of ستن) Entering on a year of scarcity. *Ustān*, Name of four districts near Baghdad.

P آستانبوسي *āstān-bosī*, Threshold-kissing.

T استانبول *istāmbūl*, Constantinople.

P استاندن *istāndan*, To constitute, set up. To bring forth. To take, receive.

P آستانه *āsitāna*, A saint's tomb. A threshold. آستانۀ گردان *āsitānaʾi gardān*, The heavens.

P استانه *astāna*, A place of rest or sleeping.

P آستاني *āsitānī*, Belonging to a hall, or court.

P آستانيدن *āstānīdan*, To keep back, to prevent going.

A استاه *astāh*, (pl. of سته *satah*) Buttocks. و انتم اضيق استاهًا من ان تفعلوا *wa antum azyaha astāhan min an tafʻalū*, Ye are wholly unable to do (it).

P استاي *istāy*, Stand.

A استباء *istibāʼ*, (v. n. 8 of سبأ for سبي) Taking prisoner, making captive. Captivating the heart.

A استباءة *istibāʼat*, (v. n. 10 of باأ for بوأ) Preparing a habitation.

A استباب *istibāb*, (v. n. 8 of سبّ) Reviling one another.

A استباتة *istibātat*, (v. n. 10 of بات for بيت) Having or obtaining a night's food or lodging.

A استباثة *istibāsat*, (v. n. 10 of باث for بوث) Extracting, drawing forth.

A استباحة *istibāhat*, (v. n. 10 of باح for بوح) Deeming lawful. Making lawful. Permitting one to pursue his inclinations. Extirpating.

A استبار *istibār*, (v. n. 8 of سبر) Probing (a wound). Examining (an affair) to the bottom.

A استباع *istibāʻ*, (v. n. 8 of سبع) Stealing.

A استباعة *istibāʻat*, (v. n. 10 of باع for بيع) Wishing to sell. Asking to sell. Requesting one to purchase.

A استباق *istibāk*, (v. n. 8 of سبق) Contending for superiority in a race. Studying to excel. Getting off the road, losing the way.

A استبالة *istibālat*, (v. n. 10 of بال for بول) Holding, retaining urine.

P استبان *istabān*, Seed of the wild rue.

A استبانة *istibānat*, (v. n. 10 of بان for بين) Being evident, appearing. Knowing, understanding, having a distinct perception. Making clear. Making known.

A استبتال *istibtāl*, (v. n. 10 of بتل) Being separated, disunited.

A استبثاث *istibsās*, (v. n. 10 of بثّ) Begging a thing may be communicated or divulged to one.

A استبحاث *istibhās*, (v. n. 10 of بحث) Investigating, inquiring, examining.

A استبحار *istibhār*, (v. n. 10 of بحر) Being spread out. Having a copiousness of language at command (a poet).

A استبداد *istibdād*, (v. n. 10 of بدّ) Being alone in any business. Being obstinate and dogmatical, scorning to ask advice. Absolute dominion, despotism, usurpation of absolute authority, insisting upon a thing being done.

A استبداع *istibdāʻ*, (v. n. 10 of بدع) Esteeming as new or strange. Producing something new.

A استبدال *istibdāl*, (v. n. 10 of بدل) Changing. Desiring or requesting to change. Accepting a substitute. P استبدال كردن To change, exchange.

A استبذاذ *istibzāz*, (v. n. 10 of بذّ) Being alone (in any business), managing (it) one's self.

P استبر *istabr*, Great, thick, big, gross.

A استبراء *istibrāʼ*, (v. n. 10 of برأ) Cleaning the organ of generation from all remains of urine. Inquiring particularly into the news, so as to be free from doubt. Getting rid (of any business). Abstaining (from conjugal intercourse during the period of menstruation).

A استبراد *istibrād*, (v. n. 10 of برد) Finding or regarding (any thing) as cold.

A استبراز *istibrāz*, (v. n. 10 of برز) Causing to come forth. P استبراز كردن *istibrāz kardan*, To produce. To challenge. To provoke.

A استبراق *istabrāk*, A kind of thick satin.

A استبرق *istabrak*, A kind of thick satin. Satin embroidered with gold. A red thong.

A استبرقيّ *istabrakīy*, Satin, made of satin.

A استبرك *istabrak*, Thick brocade.

A استبزال *istibzāl*, (v. n. 10 of بزل) Drawing off clear wine from the cask, racking, broaching.

A استبسال *istibsāl*, (v. n. 10 of بسل) Exposing one's self to danger. Seeking death in the battlefield. Being killed. Habituating the mind to the thought of death.

A استبشار *istibshār*, (v. n. 10 of بشر) Rejoicing at, or announcing, good news. Certifying.

A استبشاع *istibshāʻ*, (v. n. 10 of بشع) Considering as nauseous, unwholesome, or unsuitable.

A استبصار *istibsār*, (v. n. 10 of بصر) Considering with attention, examining, scrutinizing.

A استبضاع *istibzāʻ*, (v. n. 10 of بضع) Sorting out goods for sale. A kind of marriage in which the woman was the suitor.

A استبطاء *istibtāʼ*, (v. n. 10 of بطؤ) Thinking (one) slow, regarding (one) as dilatory.

A استبطان *istibtān*, (v. n. 10 of بطن) Concealing. Becoming acquainted with the esoteric or internal part of a thing. Lying beneath, lining.

A استبعاء *istibʻāʼ*, (v. n. 10 of بعا for بعو) Requesting a loan. Borrowing (a dog) to hunt, or (a horse) to run.

A استبعاد *istibʻād*, (v. n. 10 of بعد) Thinking one to be at a distance. Retiring, withdrawing.

A استبعال *istibʻāl*, (v. n. 10 of بعل) Becoming a husband. Becoming a wife. Thriving (a palm-tree or a field) without artificial irrigation.

A استبغاء *istibghāʼ*, (v. n. 10 of بغي) Wishing, seeking, longing for. Begging one to make search.

A استبقاء *istibkāʼ*, (v. n. 10 of بقي) Preserving alive. Leaving a portion, allowing it to remain.

A استبكاء *istibkāʼ*, (v. n. 10 of بكي) Moving, bringing tears, forcing or inducing one to weep.

A استبلال *istiblāl*, A recovering of health.

A استبهاج *istibhāj*, (v. n. 10 of بهج) Rejoicing at, or announcing, good news.

A استبهال *istibhāl*, (v. n. 10 of بهل) Milking (a camel), having unloosed a bit of wood by which the teats were confined. Allowing people to live as they list (a governor). Affording refuge to those who wish to be without controul (a desert).

A استبهام *istibhām*, (v. n. 10 of بهم) Being obscure, ambiguous. Being dumb, or scarcely able to speak intelligibly. Appearing as a barbarian.

A استتابة *istitābat*, (v. n. 10 of تاب for توب) Intreating to relent, inducing to repent.

A استتار *istitār*, (v. n. 8 of ستر) Being hid. Concealing one's self. Abstaining, taking care, avoiding.

A استتاسة *istitāsat*, (v. n. 10 of تاس for تيس) Becoming a he-goat (a she-goat); applied to a low-born fellow on whom any mark of distinction has been conferred.

A استتال *istitāl*, (v. n. 8 of ستل) Following one another in succession.

A استتباب *istitbāb*, (v. n. 10 of تبّ) Being set in order, arranged, settled, completed.

A استتباع *istitbāʻ*, (v. n. 10 of تبع) Wishing, or asking to follow. Succession.

A استتراف *istitrāf*, (v. n. 10 of ترف) Being rebellious, insolent and impious.

A استتكاك *istitkāk*, (v. n. 10 of تكّ) Running the string into the drawers.

A استتلاء *istitlāʼ*, (v. n. 10 of تلا for تلو) Calling upon one to follow.

A استتمام *istitmām*, (v. n. 10 of تمّ) Fulfilling, completing, bringing to a close. Desiring, asking that a thing might be completed. Asking for a hoe or mattock.

A استتياس *istityās*, (v. n. 10 of تاس for تيس) Longing for the male (a she-goat).

A استثابة *istisābat*, (v. n. 10 of ثاب for ثوب) Asking for a remuneration. Taking back or asking for any thing back that had been given.

A استثآر *istisʼār*, (v. n. 10 of ثأر) Imploring help in order to avenge the death of another.

A استثارة *istisārat*, (v. n. 10 of ثار for ثور) Stirring up (war, tumult, dust). Turning up out of the ground.

A استثبات *istisbāt*, (v. n. 10 of ثبت) Seeking confirmation or stability. Hesitating. Proving.

A استثخان *istiskhān*, (v. n. 10 of ثخن) Overcoming any one (sleep).

A استثفار *istisfār*, (v. n. 10 of ثفر) Clapping his tail between his legs (a dog). Passing the end of a garment between the legs and tying it to the waist.

A استثقال *istiskāl*, (v. n. 10 of ثقل) Oppressing. Finding heavy. Pronouncing with difficulty.

A استثماد *istismād*, (v. n. 10 of ثمد) Seeking one's goodwill or kindness. Draining, emptying.

A استثناء *istisnāʼ*, (v. n. 10 of ثني) Excepting, excluding. Saying, "If God will." حرف الاستثناء *harfu'l istisnāʼ*, A particle of exception.

A استثنائيّ *istisnāʼīy*, Exclusive, exceptive. P قياس استثنائي *kiyāsi istisnāʼī*, A replicative syllogism, where, if the antecedent is denied, the consequence is denied also.

A استجابة *istijābat*, (v. n. 10 of جاب for جوب)

Hearing, receiving a petition. Giving an answer. Accepting, consenting.

A استجادة *istijādat*, (v. n. 10 of جاد for جود) Seeking, or finding (a thing) excellent. Looking out for a good horse. Appealing to one's liberality.

A استجارة *istijārat*, (v. n. 10 of جار for جور) Imploring aid or protection.

A استجازة *istijāzat*, (v. n. 10 of جاز for جوز) Asking leave, soliciting permission. Begging water for cattle, or irrigation.

A استجاشة *istijāshat*, (v. n. 10 of جاش for جيش) Asking for troops.

A استجاعة *istijāʻat*, (v. n. 10 of جاع for جوع) Appearing hungry. Being very hungry.

A استجافة *istijāfat*, (v. n. 10 of جاف for جوف) Discovering (a place) to be hollow. Being wide, ample, and spacious.

A استجبار *istijbār*, (v. n. 10 of جبر) Having one's broken fortune repaired.

A استجبال *istijbāl*, (v. n. 10 of جبل) Taking all that a man hath.

A استجداء *istijdāʼ*, (v. n. 10 of جدا for جدو) Asking for a donation.

A استجداد *istijdād*, (v. n. 10 of جدّ) Renewing. Making new.

A استجراء *istijrāʼ*, (v. n. 10 of جري) Appointing an envoy or attorney.

A استجراح *istijrāh*, (v. n. 10 of جرح) Being depraved, corrupted.

A استجرار *istijrār*, (v. n. 10 of جرّ) Drawing, dragging, pulling. Granting power to any one. Concealing, yielding, submitting to.

A استجزاز *istijzāz*, (v. n. 10 of جزّ) Being fit for reaping or gathering (corn or dates).

A استجعال *istijʻāl*, (v. n. 10 of جعل) Being in heat (a bitch).

A استجفاء *istijfāʼ*, (v. n. 10 of جفا for جفو) Esteeming one to be injurious and oppressive. Finding (a bed) hard and uncomfortable.

A استجفار *istijfār*, (v. n. 10 of جفر) Becoming four months old (a lamb).

A استجلاب *istijlāb*, (v. n. 10 of جلب) Begging that any thing might be brought or driven to him.

A استجمار *istijmār*, (v. n. 10 of جمر) Being kept a long time at the seat of war (an army). Being assembled, flocking together. Cleaning one's self with a flint or sherd after going to the necessary.

A استجماع *istijmāʻ*, (v. n. 10 of جمع) Being convened, assembled. Flowing together from all quarters (torrents). Drawing himself together in running (a horse). Enjoying a full tide of prosperity. Running with all his might (a horse).

A استجمال *istijmāl*, (v. n. 10 of جمل) Growing up, attaining maturity (a camel).

A استجمام *istijmām*, (v. n. 10 of جمّ) Reposing, resting. Recruiting one's strength. Putting forth herbage. Abounding, being plentiful (water).

A استجناب *istijnāb*, A being polluted.

A استجناح *istijnāh*, (v. n. 10 of جنح) Coming on (night), spreading (her) wings.

A استجنان *istijnān*, (v. n. 10 of جنّ) Covering one's self. Being concealed and protected. Exulting, rejoicing. Being possessed of a demon.

A استجواء *istijwāʼ*, (v. n. 10 of جوي) Loathing, nauseating (food).

A استجواب *istijwāb*, (v. n. 10 of جاب for جوب) Hearing, listening to. Accepting.

A استجواف *istijwāf*, (v. n. 10 of جاف for جوف) Being spacious and roomy.

A استجهال *istijhāl*, (v. n. 10 of جهل) Considering as ignorant and illiterate. Holding in contempt. Shaking a bough (the wind).

A استحاء *istihāʼ*, (v. n. 8 of سحي) Shaving (the head). Scraping (cinders). (v. n. 10 of حيي) Being ashamed of, blushing.

A استحاثة *istihāsat*, (v. n. 10 of حاث for حوث) Grubbing up the ground in search of something.

A استحار *istihār*, (v. n. 8 of سحر) Crowing betimes (the cock).

A استحارة *istihārat*, (v. n. 10 of حار for حور) Seeking or begging an answer. Trying to draw one out into conversation. (v. n. 10 of حار for حير) Staring with wonder. Being filled with water (a place). Coming to maturity (youth).

A استحاضة *istihāzat*, (v. n. 10 of حاض for حيض) Emitting blood (a woman), after the usual time of the monthly discharge has elapsed. The blood itself.

A استحاف *istihāf*, (v. n. 8 of سحف) (Wind) driving (a cloud). Stripping away fat from the back.

A استحالة *istihālat*, (v. n. 10 of حال for حول) Undergoing a change, passing from one state to another. Undulating (the surface of the ground). Being distorted (a bow). Being impossible, or absurd (an assertion, a story). Considering as such. Looking attentively (at any object) to see whether it will move or not.

A استحباب *istihbāb*, (v. n. 10 of حبّ) Taking a liking to, regarding, loving, choosing, preferring. Retaining water long (an animal's stomach).

A استحثاء *istihsāʼ*, (v. n. 10 of حثا for حثو) Throwing dust in the faces of each other.

A استحثاث *istihsās*, (v. n. 10 of حثّ) Instigating, urging.

A استحجاء *istihjāʼ*, (v. n. 10 of حجا for حجو) Smelling badly through disease (meat).

A استحجاب *istihjāb*, (v. n. 10 of حجب) Appointing a chamberlain. Requesting the office of chamberlain.

A استحجار *istihjār*, (v. n. 10 of حجر) Becoming hard like a stone, petrifying (clay). Making a closet, chamber, or cell. Being bold, brave, intrepid.

A استحداث *istihdās*, (v. n. 10 of حدث) Bringing out or doing something new.

A استحداد *istihdād*, (v. n. 10 of حدّ) Shaving about the pubes with a razor. Waxing angry.

A استحذاء *istihzāʼ*, (v. n. 10 of حذي) Asking for a shoe. Asking for a gift.

A استحرار *istihrār*, (v. n. 10 of حرّ) Waxing hot. Being strong and firm (a twist).

A استحرام *istihrām*, (v. n. 10 of حرم) Wishing for the male (spoken in general of those animals which part the hoof). Being associated with what is sacred and inviolate.

A استحسار *istihsār*, (v. n. 10 of حسر) Being exhausted with fatigue.

A استحسان *istihsān*, (v. n. 10 of حسن) Approving. Praising. Taking, or considering as a favour. Approbation, esteem.

A استحشاش *istihshāsh*, (v. n. 10 of حشّ) Withering (the hand). Rendering the shank thin (fat). Being thirsty. Being long (a branch). Being large (the fore-arm and the hand small withal).

A استحشاف *istihshāf*, (v. n. 10 of حشف) Drying up and shrivelling (a leathern bottle, udder, or ear). Putting on an old worn-out garment.

A استحصاد *istihsād*, (v. n. 10 of حصد) Being twisted tight (a rope). Ripening, being fit for the sickle (corn). Assembling, being mingled together and assisting each other. Being angry.

A استحصاف *istihsāf*, (v. n. 10 of حصف) Being confirmed, established. Being adverse and untoward (fortune). Being small and shrivelled.

A استحضار *istihzār*, (v. n. 10 of حضر) Coming to one's self. Urging to full speed. Occurring to the memory. Acquirement.

A استحطاب *istihtāb*, (v. n. 10 of حطب) Requiring to be pruned (a vine).

A استحطاط *istihtāt*, (v. n. 10 of حطّ) Begging that burdens may be removed, or sins remitted. Asking for an abatement, drawback, or discount.

A استحفاء *istihfāʼ*, (v. n. 10 of حفي) Interrogating, exploring, investigating, asking news.

A استحفاظ *istihfāz*, (v. n. 10 of حفظ) Desiring one to remember, or to take care of, any thing.

A استحقاف *istihfāf*, (v. n. 10 of حقّ) Taking the whole (of another's property).

A استحقاب *istihkāb*, (v. n. 10 of حقب) Taking behind one's back. Perpetrating a crime.

A استحقار *istihkār*, (v. n. 10 of حقر) Despising.

A استحقاق *istihkāk*, (v. n. 10 of حقّ) Claiming one's right. Deserving, being worthy. Merit, desert.

A استحكاك *istihkāk*, (v. n. 10 of حكّ) Itching, requiring to be scratched (the head).

A استحكام *istihkām*, (v. n. 10 of حكم) Being strengthened, confirmed, done firmly and effectually. Hardness, tightness, firmness.

A استحلاء *istihlāʼ*, (v. n. 10 of حلي) Esteeming, deeming to be sweet.

A استحلاب *istihlāb*, (v. n. 10 of حلب) Milking. Requesting leave to milk.

A استحلاس *istihlās*, (v. n. 10 of حلس) (Covering the face of the earth (grass). Sticking close to one, never leaving him (fear). Selling water, and not giving to drink. Having ducts of fat in the hinder part (a camel's bunch).

A استحلاف *istihlāf*, (v. n. 10 of حلف) Adjuring, causing to swear, commanding to be sworn.

A استحلاق *istihlāk*, (v. n. 10 of حلق) Longing insatiably for the male without conceiving.

A استحلال *istihlāl*, (v. n. 10 of حلّ) Considering lawful. Wishing a thing lawful, begging that it may be so. Asking absolution.

A استحماش *istihmāsh*, (v. n. 10 of حمش) Being in a fierce rage.

A استحماض *istihmāz*, (v. n. 10 of حمض) Finding (a thing or vegetable) salt and bitter.

A استحماق *istihmāk*, (v. n. 10 of حمق) Thinking one a fool. Being foolish, acting like a fool.

A استحمال *istihmāl*, (v. n. 10 of حمل) Desiring to bear, carry, or take upon one's self. Patience.

A استحمام *istihmām*, (v. n. 10 of حمّ) Washing in warm water. Taking a warm bath. Sweating.

A استحناذ *istihnāz*, (v. n. 10 of حنذ) Basking in the sun, in order to get a sweat.

A استحناط *istihnāt*, (v. n. 10 of حنط) Braving, despising death.

A استحناك *istihnāk*, (v. n. 10 of حنك) Eating heartily after eating sparingly. Being torn up by the roots (the plant عضاه *ɛizāh*).

A استحنان *istihnān*, (v. n. 10 of حنّ) Being under strong emotions, yearning greatly.

A استحواذ *istihwāz*, (v. n. 10 of حاذ for حوذ) Prevailing against, overcoming.

A استحواس *istihwās*, (v. n. 10 of حاس for حوس) Restraining one's self. Tarrying, lingering.

A استحواض *istihwāz*, (v. n. 10 of حاض for حوض) Flowing into a tank, making a pond or reservoir for itself (water).

A استحياء *istihyās*, (v. n. 10 of حيي) Blushing, being ashamed. Leaving alive, preserving alive.

A استخاذ *istikhāz*, (for اتّخاذ *ittikhāz*) A taking to one's self.

A استخارة *istikhārat*, (v. n. 10 of خار for خور) Making a fawn cry out that the dam may come within his reach (a hunter). Conciliating favour. Driving a stake in the mouth of a hyena's hole, that he may come out at another place. Making (a habitation) neat and clean. (v. n. 10 of خار for خير) Praying for the blessing of God, or for success, or for any thing that is good. Wishing or asking for the best.

A استخالة *istikhālat*, (v. n. 10 of خال for خول) Begging the loan of a horse. Regarding as a maternal uncle. (v. n. 10 of خيل) Being vain, proud.

A استخانة *istikhānat*, (v. n. 10 of خان for خون) Considering as perfidious, regarding as a traitor.

A استخباء *istikhbās*, (v. n. 10 of خبي) Pitching and entering into (a tent).

A استخبار *istikhbār*, (v. n. 10 of خبر) Interrogating, exploring, investigating, informing one's self, asking news, desiring advice.

A استخبال *istikhbāl*, A borrowing (of a camel).

A استخثان *istikhsān*, (v. n. 10 of خثن) Overpowering (sleep).

A استخدام *istikhdām*, (v. n. 10 of خدم) Seeking to obtain one as a servant. Taking any one into one's service. Stating a proposition in terms capable of a two-fold interpretation.

A استخذاء *istikhzās*, (v. n. 10 of خذأ) Humbling one's self, submitting. (v. n. 10 of خذي) Becoming weak and trampled upon.

P استخر *istakhr*, A lake, pool, ditch. The ancient Persepolis: the Persian fabulous tradition says, that it was built by the fairies in the time of Jān bin Jān, who ruled the world long before Adam.

A استخراب *istikhrāb*, (v. n. 10 of خرب) Being broken down by misfortune. Longing for, wishing.

A استخراج *istikhrāj*, (v. n. 10 of خرج) Wishing, purposing to bring out. Extracting, drawing out, making come forth. Deriving. Selecting, choosing.

A استخراط *istikhrāt*, (v. n. 10 of خرط) Persisting in crying, weeping sorely.

A استخساس *istikhsās*, (v. n. 10 of خسّ) Considering as base, discovering (one) to be despicable.

A استخشان *istikhshān*, (v. n. 10 of خشن) Finding (one) to be rough and unpolished.

A استخصاص *istikhsās*, (v. n. 10 of خصّ) Conferring a mark of distinction on any one, placing him amongst the nobility.

A استخفاء *istikhfās*, (v. n. 10 of خفي) Hiding one's self, lurking.

A استخفار *istikhfār*, A sueing for protection.

A استخفاف *istikhfāf*, (v. n. 10 of خفّ) Despising, holding in contempt, or in small esteem. Esteeming lightly. Finding (any thing) light, and carrying it away (the wind). Turning (any one) aside from what is reasonable and proper, and leading (him) to vanity.

A استخلاء *istikhlās*, (v. n. 10 of خلا for خلو) Being empty, void, deserted (a place). Requesting a private interview. Seeking privacy.

A استخلاب *istikhlāb*, (v. n. 10 of خلب) Scratching, tearing (with the nails). Cutting (grass).

A استخلاص *istikhlās*, (v. n. 10 of خلص) Desiring liberation, seeking liberty. Seeking to save. Appropriating to one's self. Making special and private. Claiming and taking the whole of any thing.

A استخلاط *istikhlāt*, (v. n. 10 of خلط) Covering without the assistance of man (a stallion-camel).

A استخلاف *istikhlāf*, (v. n. 10 of خلف) Appointing successors. Leaving posterity. Coming after, succeeding. Drawing water.

A استخمار *istikhmār*, A reducing to slavery.

A استخنان *istikhnān*, The stinking (of a well).

A استخوال *istikhwāl*, (v. n. 10 of خال for خول) Taking for servants or handmaids. Regarding (one) as a maternal uncle. Begging the loan of a horse.

P استخوان *ustukhwān*, A bone. A kernel, stone of fruit. A skeleton. The foundation of an edifice. The text of a book. An instrument of war. Noble.

استخوان در گلو گرفتن *ustukhwān dar gulū giriftan*, (To get a bone in the throat) To suffer distress.

P استخوان بزرگ *ustukhwān-buzurg*, Nobly-born.

P استخوان بند *ustukhwān-band*, A splint, fillet.

P استخوان خوار *ustukhwān-khwār*, (or استخوان ربا *ustukhwān-rubā*,), A kind of large eagle, which feeds upon, or carries off, bones.

P استخوان فروشي *ustukhwān-faroshī*, Roguery.

P استخوانك *ustukhwānak*, A small bone.

A استداء *istidās*, (v. n. 8 of سدي) Stretching forth the hand. Playing with nuts. Sweating.

A استداد *istidād*, (v. n. 8 of سدّ) Standing erect. Acting uprightly. Becoming closed (stitch-holes in a leathern bottle).

A استدارة *istidārat*, (v. n. 10 of دار for دور) Turning round, making a circle, revolving. Being or becoming round, assuming a circular form.

A استدامة *istidāmat*, (v. n. 10 of دام for دوم) Wishing to be quiet, permanent, perpetual. Seeking, wishing perpetuity. Being easy and lenient towards a debtor, by gentle means seeking to obtain, or obtaining, payment. Soaring in a circle. Procrastinating, putting off.

A استدانة *istidānat*, (v. n. 10 of دان for دين) Borrowing, contracting debts, getting in debt.

A استدبار *istidbār*, (v. n. 10 of دبر) Turning back, going backwards, retiring behind. Following, coming at the back or rear. Knowing at length something not known before. Choosing, selecting.

A استدراج *istidrāj*, (v. n. 10 of درج) Advancing or promoting by degrees, step by step, bringing near. Disturbing (one) and then leaving him to roam about the earth; or to roll on the ground. (God) consigning to punishment an obstinate ungrateful sinner, on whom he has conferred innumerable benefits. Causing any thing to roll about (as wind does the gravel). Deceiving. Loving to follow a new-born colt (a camel).

A استدرار *istidrār*, (v. n. 10 of درّ) Shaking (as the wind), forcing rain from the clouds. Flowing plentifully (milk). Longing for the male (a goat).

A استدراك *istidrāk*, (v. n. 10 of درك) Wishing, endeavouring to comprehend or obtain. Restoring, mending. Correcting, making accurate. Emendation. Restriction.

A استدعاء *istidɛās*, (v. n. 10 of دعا for دعو) Asking. Calling upon.

A استدفاء *istidfās*, (v. n. 10 of دفئ) Putting on warm clothing. Trying to get heat.

A استدفاع *istidfāɛ*, (v. n. 10 of دفع) Praying that (God) may avert, or ward off.

A استدفاف *istidfāf*, (v. n. 10 of دفّ) Fluttering, moving the wings and feet (a pigeon). Being right, straight, feasible, easy, possible, in one's power. Shaving the body.

A استدقاق *istidḳāḳ*, (v. n. 10 of دقّ) Being minute, fine, thin, and slender.

A استدلاق *istidlāḳ*, (v. n. 10 of دلق) Bringing out the coarse dervish's habit called دلق *dalaḳ*.

A استدلال *istidlāl*, (v. n. 10 of دلّ) Deducing arguments, getting a clue. Asking reason or proof.

A استدماء *istidmāʼ*, (v. n. 10 of دمي) By gentle means getting payment from a debtor.

P استدن *istadan*, To rise, stand, or work standing.

A استدناء *istidnāʼ*, (v. n. 10 of دنا for دنو) Asking leave to draw near. Begging one to approach.

A استذآب *istiẕʼāb*, (v. n. 10 of ذأب) Resembling a wolf, having a wolf-like appearance.

A استذابة *istiẕābat*, (v. n. 10 of ذاب for ذوب) Asking for honey or wax. Wishing to melt.

A استذراء *istiẕrāʼ*, (v. n. 10 of ذرا for ذرو) Rutting (a she-goat). Seeking shade or protection.

A استذراع *istiẕrāʻ*, (v. n. 10 of ذرع) Using (a thing) as a screen behind which to lurk (a hunter).

A استذفاف *istiẕfāf*, (v. n. 10 of ذفّ) Being right, straight, easy, feasible, in one's power.

A استذكاء *istiẕkāʼ*, (v. n. 10 of ذكي) Blazing much (a flame).

A استذكار *istiẕkār*, (v. n. 10 of ذكر) Recalling to recollection. Studying, committing to memory.

A استذلال *istiẕlāl*, (v. n. 10 of ذلّ) Soothing and coaxing (a camel) by picking the tikes off (him). Holding in contempt, despising.

A استذماء *istiẕmāʼ*, (v. n. 10 of ذمي) Recovering one's property from another. Investigating.

A استذمام *istiẕmām*, (v. n. 10 of ذمّ) Behaving in a manner deserving of censure.

A استذناب *istiẕnāb*, (v. n. 10 of ذنب) Following closely at the tail: treading in the steps of. Being finished, completed, and correct (business).

A استذهاب *istiẕhāb*, (v. n. 10 of ذهب) Wishing to go away, begging a departure.

A استذهان *istiẕhān*, (v. n. 10 of ذهن) Causing to forget, calling off or distracting the attention.

P آستر *āstar*, A kind of coarse thin stuff fit for lining garments. The inside of any thing, the lining of a garment. A star.

P استر *astar*, A mule (the first breeding of which is ascribed to Pharaoh). The lining of a garment.

A استرآء *istirʼāʼ*, (v. n. 10 of رأي) Wishing or asking to see. Taking for a hypocrite. Consulting, asking advice. Seeing, perceiving, knowing.

A استراء *istirāʼ*, (v. n. 8 of سرا for سرو) Choosing, selecting. Picking out the best for (his) prey (death). (v. n. 8 of سري) Travelling by night.

P استراباد *astarābād*, Name of a city in Māzendarān on the shore of the Caspian.

A استرابة *istirābat*, (v. n. 10 of راب for ريب) Doubting, suspecting, judging unfavourably, observing something which induces suspicion.

A استراثة *istirāsat*, (v. n. 10 of راث for ريث) Deeming lazy, slothful. Delaying, being dilatory. Asking a delay.

A استراحة *istirāhat*, (v. n. 10 of راح for روح) Smelling, scenting, nosing. Reposing, relying. Seeking or finding rest. Quiet, rest, tranquillity.

P استرار *istarār*, A lentil.

A استراضة *istirāzat*, (v. n. 10 of راض for روض) Being full of water (a reservoir or valley). Being very moist (a spot). Lying open and abounding in flowers. Being vigorous and cheerful (mind).

A استراط *istirāt*, (v. n. 8 of سرط) Swallowing.

A استراعة *istirāʻat*, (v. n. 10 of راع for ريع) Being astonished, bewildered.

A استراق *istirāḳ*, (v. n. 8 of سرق) Stealing, carrying off by stealth. Listening surreptitiously, overhearing, playing the eaves-dropper.

A استرآل *istirʼāl*, (v. n. 10 of رئل) Becoming large or very numerous (young ostriches). Shooting upwards (like the neck of an ostrich) a plant.

P استربا *astarbā*, (or استربان) A muleteer.

A استرباع *istirbāʻ*, (v. n. 10 of ربع) Being heaped together (sand). Being raised (dust). Travelling fast. Applying diligently (to work).

A استرتاج *istirtāj*, (v. n. 10 of رتج) Pronouncing with difficulty, stammering, stuttering.

A استرجاع *istirjāʻ*, (v. n. 10 of رجع) Applying to God in affliction, by repeating the ejaculation from the Kur'ān, انّا لله وانّا اليه راجعون *innā li'llāh wa innā ilayhi rājiʻūn*, Verily we belong to God, and verily we shall return to him. Asking or taking back the whole or part of any thing once given.

A استرحال *istirhāl*, (v. n. 10 of رحل) Asking leave to travel, craving permission to migrate.

G استرخا *istirkhā*, Red orpiment.

A استرخاء *istirkhāʼ*, (v. n. 10 of رخا for رخو) Hanging down. Being relaxed and flaccid. Having liquid stools. Looseness, flabbiness, flaccidness.

A استرخاص *istirkhāṣ*, (v. n. 10 of رخص) Valuing low. Buying cheap. Regarding as cheap.

A استرداد *istirdād*, (v. n. 10 of ردّ) Demanding restitution of any thing, whether given, deposited in trust, or taken without consent. Repelling.

A استرداف *istirdāf*, (v. n. 10 of ردف) Asking to be taken up behind another on horseback.

P استردن *usturdan*, To shave. To erase.

G استرديا *istiridiyā*, An oyster.

A استرذال *istirẕāl*, (v. n. 10 of رذل) Holding in contempt. Discovering (one) to be vile and base.

A استرزاغ *istirzāgh*, (v. n. 10 of رزغ) Esteeming, regarding, or finding weak and contemptible.

A استرسال *istirsāl*, (v. n. 10 رسل) Being allowed to hang loose (hair). Cultivating an intimacy. Being insolent and rude. Requesting one to send (camels) in separate herds. Acquiring a habit. Affability, freedom from reserve.

P استرش *usturash*, A ploughshare. A hoe.

A استرشاء *istirshāʼ*, (v. n. 10 of رشا for رشو) Desiring, asking a bribe. Letting suck. Obeying, submitting to, seeking to please and conciliate.

A استرشاح *istirshāh*, (v. n. 10 of رشح) Coming to its full size (the plant بهمي *buhma'*). Bringing up, rearing (young cattle). Waiting for a field to become fit for grazing or mowing.

A استرشاد *istirshād*, (v. n. 10 of رشد) Being well directed, going right. Seeking direction.

A استرشاش *istirshāsh*, (v. n. 10 of رشّ) Wishing to suck, putting its head between the dam's legs.

A استرضاء *istirzāʼ*, (v. n. 10 of رضي) Endeavouring, seeking or wishing to please and satisfy.

A استرضاع *istirzāʻ*, (v. n. 10 of رضع) Inquiring, and looking out for a wet-nurse.

A استرطاء *istirtāʼ*, (v. n. 10 of رطأ) Becoming silly, stupid, or foolish.

A استرطاط *istirtāt*, (v. n. 10 of رطّ) Esteeming to be a fool.

A استرعاء *istirʻāʼ*, (v. n. 10 of رعي) Asking one to feed, or take charge of any thing.

A استرعاف *istirʻāf*, (v. n. 10 of رعف) Laming a camel, making his feet bleed (a sharp stone). Running full speed (a horse). Trying to make (fat) drip.

A استرعال *istirʻāl*, (v. n. 10 of رعل) Following one another in a line (sheep). Leading the van.

A استرغاز *istirghaz*, (v. n. 10 of رغز) Esteeming or finding weak. Considering as soft, placid, gentle.

A استرغاس *istirghās*, (v. n. 10 of رغس) Considering as soft, or finding soft.

A استرفاد *istirfād*, (v. n. 10 of رفد) Seeking, needing, craving, or imploring help.

A استرفاض *istirfāz*, (v. n. 10 of رفض) Being widely extended (a valley).

A استرفاع *istirfāʻ*, (v. n. 10 of رفع) Wishing to raise or carry of. Requiring to be cleared (a table, the meal being ended).

A استرفاه *istirfāh*, (v. n. 10 of رفه) Reposing, remaining quiet, enjoying the pleasures of life.

A استرقاء *istirḳāʼ*, (v. n. 10 of رقي) Asking another to charm. Applying to one skilled in magic.

A استرقاع *istirḳāʻ*, (v. n. 10 of رقع) Needing repair, requiring a patch (a garment).

A استرقاق *istirḳāḳ*, (v. n. 10 of رقّ) Reducing to slavery. Being thin. Diffusing itself lightly (water). Sinking almost entirely into the ground.

G استرك *istarak*, Storax.

A استركاك *istirkāk*, (v. n. 10 of ركّ) Esteeming or discovering to be weak.

G استرلاب *usturlāb*, An astrolabe.

A استرماث *istirmās*, (v. n. 10 of رمث) Establishing, confirming in the possession of property.

A استرماك *istirmāk*, (v. n. 10 of رمك) Being little esteemed in their own account.

A استرمام *istirmām*, (v. n. 10 of رمّ) Requiring reparation, standing in need of repair (a house, &c.).

Asking for the means of making (a house) habitable.

P استرنگ *astarang*, or آسترنگ The mandrake.

A استرواح *istirwāh*, (v. n. 10 of راح for روح) Resting. Seeking or finding rest. Smelling. Relying, leaning on, trusting to.

P استرون *atarvan*, (Mule-like) Barren female.

P استرونتن *astarūnitan*, (in zand and Pāzand) To shut, to close.

P استرة *ustura*, A razor. استرة ليسيدن *ustura lisīdan*, (To lick a razor) To risk one's life, to evince daring and temerity.

A استرهاب *istirhāb*, (v. n. 10 of رهب) Terrifying, alarming.

A استزاتة *istizātat*, (v. n. 10 of زات for زيت) Asking for oil.

A استزادة *istizādat*, (v. n. 10 of زاد for زيد) Desiring an augmentation. Considering (a man) as having done less than (he) ought: wanting more from him. Egging a person on, encoring.

A استزارة *istizārat*, (v. n. 10 of زار for زور) Requesting a visit.

A استزراء *istizrāʼ*, (v. n. 10 of زري) Despising, holding in contempt.

A استزفاف *istizfāf*, (v. n. 10 of زفّ) Rendering light.

A استزلال *istizlāl*, (v. n. 10 of زلّ) Causing or wishing one to stumble, or blunder in speaking.

A استسخار *istiskhār*, (v. n. 10 of سخر) Mocking, deriding, making a laughing-stock.

A استسراج *istisrāj*, (v. n. 10 of سرج) Trimming a lamp.

A استسرار *istisrār*, (v. n. 10 of سرّ) Being concealed. Keeping a mistress privately.

A استسعاء *istisʻāʼ*, (v. n. 10 of سعي) Striving, endeavouring, being anxious to accomplish. Obliging a manumitted servant to work hard at a thing, in consequence of which he may obtain full liberty.

A استسعاد *istisʻād*, (v. n. 10 of سعد) Considering as happy, regarding as fortunate. Desiring happiness. Asking assistance.

A استسعاط *istisʻāt*, (v. n. 10 of سعط) Snuffing up the urine (of a she-camel).

A استسعال *istisʻāl*, (v. n. 10 of سعل) Resembling a hag. Brawling, being foul-mouthed.

A استسفاد *istisfād*, (v. n. 10 of سفد) Approaching (a camel) from behind, to vault upon (his) back.

A استسفار *istisfār*, (v. n. 10 of سفر) Requesting (a matter) to be made clear and plain.

A استسقاء *istiskāʼ*, (v. n. 10 of سقي) Asking for water, offering up public prayers for rain. Asking for drink. Labouring under a dropsy, being filled with yellow water (the belly). استسقاء زقي *istiskāʼi zikķī*, The anasarca. استسقاء طبلي *istiskāʼi tablī*, Tympany.

P استسقا گرفته *istiskā-girifta*, Dropsical.

A استسلاف *istislāf*, (v. n. 10 of سلف) Paying in advance. Asking for and receiving the money before the delivery of the goods.

A استسلام *istislām*, (v. n. 10 of سلم) Submitting to the authority of another, giving way to his judgment. Paying in advance.

A استسمان *istismān*, (v. n. 10 of سمن) Judging, or discovering to be fat. Asking for butter or something fat.

A استسناح *istisnāh*, (v. n. 10 of سنح) Enquiring, examining, exploring.

A استسنان *istisnān*, (v. n. 10 of سنّ) Having large teeth. Walking in a road or mode of life. Being stricken in years. Being travelled (a road).

A استسهال *istis-hāl*, (v. n. 10 of سهل) Esteeming easy. Rendering easy.

A استسهام *istis-hām*, (v. n. 10 of سهم) Wishing or requesting to draw lots.

A استشارة *istishārat*, (v. n. 10 of شار for شور) Consulting, asking advice. Smelling the female to discover if she be in foal. Putting on goodly raiment. Being plain and clear. Becoming fat and handsome (camels). Gathering honey.

A استشاطة *istishātat*, (v. n. 10 of شاط for شيط) Boiling with rage. Becoming fat (a camel). Laughing heartily. Flying fast (a dove). Being light, active, and expeditious.

A استشتات *istishtāt*, (v. n. 10 of شتّ) Being dispersed, scattered.

A استشحاج *istishhāj*, (v. n. 10 of شحج) Trying to make (a raven) croak.

A استشراء *istishrāʼ*, (v. n. 10 of شري) Being weighty and momentous. Being angry, quarrelsome.

A استشراب *istishrāb*, (v. n. 10 of شرب) Being deep, intense (colour, tincture, dye).

A استشرار *istishrār*, (v. n. 10 of شرّ) Becoming possessed of a large herd of camels.

A استشراط *istishrāt*, (v. n. 10 of شرط) Having murrain (a flock).

A استشراف *istishrāf*, (v. n. 10 of شرف) Looking upwards at some object, and screening the eyes (with the hand) from the glare of the sun. Demanding any thing noble and perfect. Attending closely to any thing lest it suffer damage. Defrauding another of his due.

A استشزار *istishzār*, (v. n. 10 of شزر) Twisting (a rope) from the left hand, or from the outside inwards. Being so twisted. Being high. Raising.

A استشعار *istishʻār*, (v. n. 10 of شعر) Putting on the garment شعار *shiʻār*. Being hairy (a fœtus). Being apprehensive and concealing one's fears.

A استشفاء *istishfāʼ*, (v. n. 10 of شفي) Seeking the recovery of health.

A استشفاع *istishfāʻ*, (v. n. 10 of شفع) Imploring (one) to intercede, begging (his) intercession.

A استشفاف *istishfāf*, (v. n. 10 of شفّ) Seeing through any transparent and diaphonous object (as a thin and flimsy garment or piece of stuff).

A استشلاء *istishlāʼ*, (v. n. 10 of شلا for شلو) Liberating. Being angry. Calling out to be rescued from danger and destruction.

A استشمام *istishmām*, (v. n. 10 of شمّ) Wishing to smell.

A استشناع *istishnāʻ*, (v. n. 10 شنع) Regarding as shameful, odious, deformed, and abominable.

A استشنان *istishnān*, (v. n. 10 of شنّ) Becoming lean. Becoming old and shrivelled (a leathern bottle). Thirsting for milk.

A استشهاد *istishhād*, (v. n. 10 of شهد) Taking evidence, summoning witnesses. (in the passive voice) Falling a martyr or witness for religion.

A استشهار *istishhār*, (v. n. 10 of شهر) Being published, proclaimed, or blazoned abroad.

A استصابة *istisābat*, (v. n. 10 of صاب for صوب) Deeming right, approving. Asking for or requiring what is right and proper.

A استصباح *istisbāh*, (v. n. 10 of صبح) Trimming a lamp. Asking for a lamp.

A استصبار *istisbār*, (v. n. 10 of صبر) Being thick and dense.

A استصباغ *istisbāgh*, (v. n. 10 of صبغ) Asking for colour or dye.

A استصحاب *istis-hāb*, (v. n. 10 of صحب) Associating with, becoming sociable. Wishing for or inviting the company of any person.

A استصحاح *istis-hāh*, (v. n. 10 of صحّ) Being restored to health and soundness (a sick person).

A استصراخ *istisrākh*, (v. n. 10 of صرخ) Asking aid, imploring help.

A استصراف *istisrāf*, (v. n. 10 of صرف) Praying (God) may avert.

A استصعاب *istisʻāb*, (v. n. 10 of صعب) Being difficult, perverse, untractable. Considering, finding, or discovering to be difficult.

A استصغار *istisghār*, (v. n. 10 of صغر) Despising, holding in small estimation, viewing with contempt.

A استصفاء *istisfāʼ*, (v. n. 10 of صفا for صفو) Choosing, selecting, taking the best or whole of any thing, exhausting. Considering as clear and pure.

A استصلاء *istislāʼ*, (v. n. 10 of صلي) Asking for roast meat.

A استصلاح *istislāh*, (v. n. 10 of صلح) Seeking peace. Wishing to amend, repair, or rectify.

A استصماغ *istismāgh*, (v. n. 10 of صمغ) Asking for gum. Extracting gum. Having a sore.

A استصواب *istisvāb*, (v. n. 10 of صاب for صوب) Approving, thinking well of, esteeming right. Asking or requiring what is right. P استصواب كردن *istisvāb kardan*, To approve. To consult.

A استضاءة *istizāʼat*, (v. n. 10 of ضاء for ضوء) Making bright. Asking for light, or counsel.

A استضارة *istizārat*, (v. n. 10 of ضار for ضور) Longing for the male.

A استضافة *istizāfat*, (v. n. 10 of ضاف for ضيف) Imploring help. Inviting one to be a guest.

A استضاقة *istizāķat*, (v. n. 10 of ضاق for ضيق)

Trying to contract by constrictive lotions (a woman).

A استضامة *istizāmat*, (v. n. 10 of ضام for ضيم) Diminishing. Defrauding.

A استضباع *istizbāɛ*, (v. n. 10 of ضبع) Wanting the male (a camel).

A استضحاك *istizhāk*, (v. n. 10 of ضحك) Desiring or wishing to laugh.

A استضراء *istizrāʼ*, (v. n. 10 of ضرا for ضرو) Deceiving, circumventing. Hunting stealthily.

A استضراب *istizrāb*, (v. n. 10 of ضرب) Becoming white and candied (honey). Deceiving, cheating.

A استضراع *istizrāɛ*, (v. n. 10 of ضرع) Being humble, supplicating.

A استضرام *istizrām*, (v. n. 10 of ضرم) Kindling (a fire).

A استضعاف *istizɛāf*, (v. n. 10 of ضعف) Esteeming, considering, or finding weak. Oppressing.

A استضلال *istizlāl*, (v. n. 10 of ضلّ) Wishing that (another) may err, miscarry or perish.

A استضمار *istizmār*, (v. n. 10 of ضمر) Conceiving in the mind.

A استضوار *istizwār*, (v. n. 10 of ضار for ضور) Wanting the bull (a cow).

A استضهال *istizhāl*, (v. n. 10 of ضهل) Enquiring, informing one's self.

A استطابة *istitābat*, (v. n. 10 of طاب for طيب) Relishing, liking, taking well, finding agreeable, approving. Finding or esteeming as pure and lawful. Asking for fresh water. Seeking purity. Cleaning, shaving, or washing the body (after the manner of the Muhammadans).

A استطار *istitār*, (v. n. 8 of سطر) Delineating, making lines, drawing, describing, writing.

A استطارة *istitārat*, (v. n. 10 of طار for طير) Diffusing itself abroad (the dawn). Being swift, fleet (horse). Drawing rapidly (a sword). Being in heat (a bitch). Giving flight (to a bird). Being dispersed. Being brisk and active (a market). Being riven (a wall). Terrifying, scaring.

A استطاعة *istitāɛat*, (v. n. 10 of طاع for طوع) Being able, capable. Submitting, yielding, obeying, complying with. Power, ability.

A استطافة *istitāfat*, (v. n. 10 of طاف for طوف) Going round, circumambulating.

A استطالة *istitālat*, (v. n. 10 of طال for طول) Being long, extended, raised, or elevated. Prevailing against, overcoming an enemy. Extolling one's self, yielding to nobody. Standing on tip-toe, stretching out the neck to see a distant object. Excelling, being eminent.

A استطباب *istitbāb*, (v. n. 10 of طبّ) Asking medical advice, demanding medicine.

A استطراب *istitrāb*, (v. n. 10 of طرب) Wishing to skip or dance for joy. Singing so as to make (camels) dance for joy. Driving (camels). Being under a strong emotion.

A استطراد *istitrād*, (v. n. 10 of طرد) Wishing to drive together from all quarters. Aiming at one thing and getting another. Feigning a retreat before the enemy.

A استطراف *istitrāf*, (v. n. 10 of طرف) Considering a thing as new. Procuring any thing which has been newly discovered, and being delighted with it. Producing something new, original, singular, or striking.

A استطراق *istitrāk*, (v. n. 10 of طرق) Begging the loan of a stallion. Asking another to divine by throwing pebble-stones or gravel.

A استطعام *istitɛām*, (v. n. 10 of طعم) Asking for food. Asking for instruction in reading.

A استطفاف *istitfāf*, (v. n. 10 of طفّ) Being possible, practicable, feasible.

A استطلاع *istitlāɛ*, (v. n. 10 of طلع) Seeking information, inquiring. Arriving. Going away with, carrying off.

A استطلاق *istitlāk*, (v. n. 10 of طلق) Taking (a camel) for one's own special use. Being loose and purging (the belly). Diarrhœa, looseness, flux.

A استطلال *istitlāl*, (v. n. 10 of طلّ) Hanging over, impending.

G استطلس *istatlus*, Jews' pitch.

A استطمام *istitmām*, (v. n. 10 of طمّ) Wanting cutting (hair), or clipping (wool).

A استطياب *istityāb*, (v. n. 10 of طاب for طيب) Finding (a thing) good or beautiful.

A استظآر *istizɛār*, (v. n. 10 of ظأر) Being in heat (a bitch).

A استظفاف *istizfāf*, (v. n. 10 of ظفّ) Following (the track of any one).

A استظلال *istizlāl*, (v. n. 10 of ظلّ) Sitting in or longing for the shade. Becoming interwoven (the branches of a vine which are loaded with clusters). Being sunk in the socket (the eye). Flowing from the body (blood).

A استظهار *istizhār*, (v. n. 10 of ظهر) Committing to memory. Reciting, repeating by heart. Imploring assistance or protection. Being strong in the back. Training, preparing (a camel) for use on every occasion.

A استعادة *istiɛādat*, (v. n. 10 of عاد for عود) Begging one to repeat, or do any thing over again, or to come back. Wishing to make a habit. Being accustomed to, having the habit of.

A استعاذة *istiɛāzat*, (v. n. 10 of عاذ for عوذ) Fleeing from evil to good, from the devil to God, and saying, نعوذ بالله من الشيطان الرجيم *naɛūzu bi'llāh mini sh'shaytāni'r rajīm*, We flee to God from the execrable devil.

A استعار *istiɛār*, (v. n. 8 of سعر) Beginning to appear in the groins and the arm-pits of a camel (scab). Being lighted, blazing (a fire). Bestirring themselves, being active (thieves). Spreading, being diffused (war or mischief).

A استعارة *istiɛārat*, (v. n. 10 of عار for عور) Borrowing. Passing (any thing) from hand to hand. Using a word metaphorically. A metaphor, a trope.

A استعاضة *istiɛāzat*, (v. n. 10 of عاض for عوض) Asking for, requiring, or needing a substitute or equivalent.

A استعاط *istiɛāt*, (v. n. 8 of سعط) Taking medicine or snuff up the nostrils, administering to one's self a sternutatory.

A استعانة *istiɛānat*, (v. n. 10 of عان for عون) Asking assistance, imploring help, seeking aid. Removing the hair from the pubes (عانة *ɛānat*) either by shaving, by plucking, or by a paste made of arsenic and quick-lime. Instrumentality.

A استعاية *istiɛāyat*, (v. n. 10 of عيي) Being unequal to, and unable to accomplish.

A استعباد *istiɛbād*, (v. n. 10 of عبد) Reducing to slavery. Treating as a servant or slave.

A استعبار *istiɛbār*, (v. n. 10 of عبر) Being sad, grieving. Asking the interpretation of a dream. Flowing (tears). Weeping.

A استعتاب *istiɛtāb*, (v. n. 10 of عتب) Requesting a favour. Desiring one to take a thing well, or to rest contented. Conferring a favour. Wishing, desiring. Refraining from evil.

A استعتام *istiɛtām*, (v. n. 10 of عتم) Delaying to milk (cattle), that the milk may accumulate in the udder. Being milked in the evening (camels).

A استعجاب *istiɛjāb*, (v. n. 10 of عجب) Being struck with astonishment. Astonishment, wonder.

A استعجال *istiɛjāl*, (v. n. 10 of عجل) Hastening, accelerating, ordering one to make haste, stimulating, despatching any business soon. Outstripping, getting before. Striving to outstrip. Wishing or endeavouring to make haste.

A استعجام *istiɛjām*, (v. n. 10 of عجم) Keeping silence, not responding, being unable to speak distinctly. Being barbarous, foreign, obscure, and unintelligible (a dialect or jargon). Being unable to read from somnolency.

A استعداء *istiɛdāʼ*, (v. n. 10 of عدا for عدو) Making (a horse) run. Asking assistance. Imploring help against an enemy.

A استعداد *istiɛdād*, (v. n. 10 of عدّ) Preparing, making preparation, getting ready for. Skill, aptness, aptitude, merit.

A استعدادات *istiɛdādāt*, Preparations.

A استعذاء *istiɛzāʼ*, (v. n. 10 of عذي) Liking (a place), finding (it) agreeable.

A استعذاب *istiɛzāb*, (v. n. 10 of عذب) Prohibiting. Giving to drink fresh and wholesome water. Discovering and drawing such (water). Considering and regarding as pure. Abandoning.

A استعراء *istiɛrāʼ*, (v. n. 10 of عري) Eating (dates) whilst on the tree.

A استعراب *istiɛrāb*, (v. n. 10 of عرب) Speaking coarsely or obscenely. Wanting the bull (a cow).

A استعرار *istiɛrār*, (v. n. 10 of عرّ) Spreading

amongst camels (the scab called عرّ *ʿurr*).

A استعراز *istiʿrāz*, (v. n. 10 of عرز) Being difficult, hard, and painful (business). Being strong and hard. Being contracted, drawn in, wrinkled.

A استعراض *istiʿrāz*, (v. n. 10 of عرض) Asking for a full disclosure of any affair. Giving promiscuously. Asking (anybody) indifferently. Killing indiscriminately. Becoming fat (a camel). Grazing in grassy land. Being suspected.

A استعراف *istiʿrāf*, (v. n. 10 of عرف) Shewing one's self with a desire of being recognised.

A استعراق *istiʿrāk*, (v. n. 10 of عرق) Exposing one's self to the heat in order to get a sweat. Sending forth roots into the ground (a tree).

A استعزاز *istiʿzāz*, (v. n. 10 of عزّ) Being close and compact (sand). Overpowering one (disease). Terminating any one's existence by disease (God).

A استعساب *istiʿsāb*, (v. n. 10 of عسب) Wanting the stallion (a mare). Disliking, disapproving.

A استعسار *istiʿsār*, (v. n. 10 of عسر) Being difficult, intricate, and embarrassing. Asking, seeking for difficulties. Sitting down without employ.

A استعسال *istiʿsāl*, (v. n. 10 عسل) Asking for honey. Seeking honey.

A استعسان *istiʿsān*, (v. n. 10 of عسن) Eating little (a camel).

A استعشاء *istiʿshāʾ*, (v. n. 10 of عشا for عشو) Finding (one) bewildered. Being guided and attracted at night by the light of a blazing fire.

A استعصاء *istiʿsāʾ*, (v. n. 10 of عصي) Charging with rebellion. Accusing falsely.

A استعصام *istiʿsām*, (v. n. 10 of عصم) Keeping back, withholding. Keeping one's seat on horseback by clinging to something fixed to the saddle for that purpose.

A استعضاد *istiʿzād*, (v. n. 10 of عضد) Cutting (a tree). Gathering (fruit).

A استعضاه *istiʿzāh*, (v. n. 10 عضه) Seeking to wizards, having recourse to magic or necromancy.

A استعطاء *istiʿtā*, (v. n. 10 of عطا for عطو) Begging, asking a present.

A استعطار *istiʿtār*, (v. n. 10 of عطر) Perfuming. Wishing, or desiring to perfume, requiring, calling for perfume.

A استعطاف *istiʿtāf*, (v. n. 10 of عطف) Begging one to become favourably inclined.

A استعظام *istiʿzām*, (v. n. 10 of عظم) Becoming proud. Conceiving highly of, admiring. Taking the larger part.

A استعفاء *istiʿfāʾ*, (v. n. 10 of عفا for عفو) Seeking to be disengaged, or begging to be released from an obligation. Cropping herbage close to the ground.

A استعفاف *istiʿfāf*, (v. n. 10 of عفّ) Abstaining from what is forbidden, restraining one's self. Desiring or requiring to abstain. Clearing away dry grass from the surface of the ground (camels).

A استعقاب *istiʿkāb*, (v. n. 10 of عقب) Inveighing against any one, enquiring into their characters or vices. Receiving an equivalent or substitute.

A استعقان *istiʿkād*, (v. n. 10 of عقد) Being a brimming, wanting the boar (a sow).

A استعقار *istiʿkār*, (v. n. 10 of عقر) Howling aloud and melodiously with joy (a wolf).

A استعكاد *istiʿkād*, (v. n. 10 of عكد) Lying close to any thing (a bird) from fear of birds of prey. Becoming fat (a camel or lizard).

A استعلاء *istiʿlāʾ*, (v. n. 10 of علا for علو) Being high. Being advanced (the day). Raising, elevating. Superiority, exaltation.

A استعلاب *istiʿlāb*, (v. n. 10 of علب) Beginning to stink (meat). Loathing, nauseating, discovering (a pasture) to be unwholesome.

A استعلاج *istiʿlāj*, (v. n. 10 of علج) Becoming hard (the skin).

A استعلاف *istiʿlāf*, (v. n. 10 of علف) Wanting provender, expressing a wish for corn (as a horse does by neighing).

A استعلام *istiʿlām*, (v. n. 10 of علم) Asking information, advice, or news, being desirous of knowing, eager to learn.

A استعمار *istiʿmār*, (v. n. 10 عمر) Causing people to inhabit and colonize.

A استعماش *istiʿmāsh*, (v. n. 10 of عمش) Thinking one a fool.

A استعمال *istiʿmāl*, (v. n. 10 of عمل) Causing to work. Employing, requiring one to labour. Making use of advice or implements. Seeking employment. Appointing (any one) as governor. Use, usage, application.

A استعمام *istiʿmām*, (v. n. 10 of عمّ) Choosing for one's paternal uncle. Putting on a turban.

A استعناد *istiʿnād*, (v. n. 10 of عند) Overcoming any one (sickness or vomiting). Making free use of the yard, fornicating. Bending outwards the rim of a leathern bottle so as to be able to drink. Seeking, tending towards, making for. Being unmanageable (a horse). Beating with a stick.

A استعناز *istiʿnāz*, (v. n. 10 of عنز) Retiring, receding, departing.

A استعواء *istiʿwāʾ*, (v. n. 10 of عوي) Calling (to a riot). Desiring to twist a rope.

A استعوار *istiʿwār*, (v. n. 10 of عور) Being alone.

A استعهاد *istiʿhād*, (v. n. 10 of عهد) Making an agreement with a salesman, to send back his goods if damaged. Making a covenant, treaty, deed, or contract in writing. Giving a guarantee, fine, or compensation.

A استعياء *istiʿyāʾ*, (v. n. 10 of عيي) Being embarrassed, unequal to.

A استغاثة *istighāsat*, (v. n. 10 of غاث for غوث) Calling for help, imploring assistance.

A استغارة *istighārat*, (v. n. 10 of غار for غور) Making a hostile incursion into an enemy's country. Begging zeal (of God). Swelling (a wound). Descending into any low country, or that part of Arabia called غور *ghawr*. Becoming fat. Preparing for, undertaking.

A استغثاث *istighsās*, (v. n. 10 of غثّ) Extracting the matter from a wound, dressing it.

A استغدار *istighdār*, (v. n. 10 of غدر) Becoming full of ponds, pools, and stagnant ditches.

A استغذاء *istighzāʾ*, (v. n. 10 of غذي) Throwing prostrate, dashing on the ground.

A استغراب *istighrāb*, (v. n. 10 of غرب) Wondering. Regarding as strange. Laughing until the tears flow, being in a roar of laughter.

A استغراد *istighrād*, (v. n. 10 of غرد) Inducing, requesting to sing. Causing (the flies) to buzz and hum (a meadow).

A استغرار *istighrār*, (v. n. 10 of غرّ) Being deceived. Being foolish, inconsiderate, thoughtless. Coming upon one suddenly.

A استغراق *istighrāk*, (v. n. 10 of غرق) Filling a girth so that the ends will not meet (a camel's belly). Laughing till the tears run. Taking the whole. Absoluteness, the absence of all restriction.

A استغزار *istighzār*, (v. n. 10 of غزر) Giving somewhat to receive more in return.

A استغشاء *istighshāʾ*, (v. n. 10 of غشي) Wrapping one's self up in a garment, so as neither to see or hear, or to be heard or seen.

A استغشاش *istighshāsh*, (v. n. 10 of غشّ) Considering as false and insincere. Deceiving, betraying. Seeking to deceive or betray.

A استغفار *istighfār*, (v. n. 10 of غفر) Asking forgiveness, begging pardon.

A استغلاء *istighlāʾ*, (v. n. 10 of غلا for غلو) Considering as dear.

A استغلاظ *istighlāz*, (v. n. 10 of غلظ) Finding (cloth) coarse, and for that reason declining to purchase it. Discovering (food) to be unwholesome. Being thick and coarse. Swelling with grains (an ear of corn).

A استغلاق *istighlāk*, (v. n. 10 of غلق) Not allowing the option of returning a purchase. Being of that description (a bargain). Foreclosing. Being obscure and unintelligible, and as it were locked up or sealed (a speech or book).

A استغلال *istighlāl*, (v. n. 10 of غلّ) Ordering (one's servants) to carry home grain (غلّه *ghalla*). Receiving grain from those who bring it. Gathering in grain or vegetables. Receiving wages.

A استغناء *istighnāʾ*, (v. n. 10 of غني) Acquiescing. Being contented, in want of nothing, wealthy, independent, and able to do without.

A استغوار *istighwār*, (v. n. 10 of غار for غور) Asking (God) for rain.

A استغيال *istighyāl*, (v. n. 10 of غيل) Being thick and entangled (trees). Giving suck whilst pregnant or cohabiting with a man (a woman).

A استفاء *istifāʾ*, (v. n. 8 of سفي) Using art

and cunning. Turning about.

A استفاءة *istifāʼat,* (v. n. 10 of فاء for فيأ) Receiving plunder, booty, or earnest-money. Returning.

A استفاجة *istifājat,* (v. n. 10 of فاج for فوج) Treating lightly, holding in little estimation.

A استفادة *istifādat,* (v. n. 10 of فاد for فيد) Acquiring. Receiving profit. Seeking profit or advantage. Imparting benefit.

P استفاضانه *istifāzāna,* Profusely, abundantly.

A استفاضة *istifāzat,* (v. n. 10 of فاض for فيض) Being divulged, spread abroad (news). Requesting that water may be poured out. Desiring abundance or profusion. Abounding in trees (a valley).

A استفاط *istifāt,* (v. n. 8 of سفط) Drinking up all the contents of a jug. Using one's utmost endeavour.

A استفاع *istifāʻ,* (v. n. 8 of سفع) Being excited, agitated, moved, stimulated. Changing from fear (colour) Becoming turbid (the sky).

A استفاف *istifāf,* (v. n. 8 of سفّ) Taking a medicinal powder. Scattering, throwing.

A استفاقة *istifākat,* (v. n. 10 of فاق for فوق) Recovering from indisposition, ebriety, passion, or madness. Milking after a proper interval. Abstaining (from drink).

A استفاهة *istifāhat,* (or استفاه *istifāh*) (v. n. 10 of فاه for فوه) Eating plentifully after fasting. Quenching the thirst.

A استفتاء *istiftāʼ,* (v. n. 10 of فتا for فتو) Consulting a lawyer or muftī, asking for his fatwa.

A استفتاح *istiftāh,* (v. n. 10 of فتح) Asking assistance. Beginning, commencing.

A استفتار *istiftar,* (v. n. 10 of فتر) Drawing, dragging, pulling the rider (a horse).

A استفتال *istiftāl,* (v. n. 10 of فتل) Quitting the ranks before coming into action.

A استفحال *istifhāl,* (v. n. 10 of فحل) Being weighty and momentous (an affair). Keeping for a stallion. Allowing a fine-made Arab free access to their women (as the natives of Kābul are said to do). Becoming فحّال *fuhhāl* (a palm-tree).

A استفخاذ *istifkhāz,* (v. n. 10 of فخذ) Humbling one's self, submitting.

A استفخار *istifkhār,* (v. n. 10 of فخر) Purchasing or seeking for something excellent.

A استفداح *istifdāh,* (v. n. 10 of فدح) Finding (a thing) difficult.

A استفذاذ *istifzāz,* (v. n. 10 of فذّ) Being alone, singular. Choosing any thing. Claiming as one's own exclusive right.

A استفراخ *istifrākh,* (v. n. 10 of فرخ) Keeping (pigeons) for the sake of their young. Looking out for a place where to rear their young (pigeons).

A استفراد *istifrād,* (v. n. 10 of فرد) Being fond of solitude. Accomplishing (a work) alone. Choosing one out of a number, and using that only. Leaving alone.

A استفراع *istifrāʻ,* (v. n. 10 of فرع) Beginning any thing, commencing a discourse. Sacrificing the firstlings of camels or sheep (a custom of the pagan Arabs).

A استفراغ *istifrāgh,* (v. n. 10 of فرغ) Vomiting, evacuating, rejecting, clearing out the stomach. Straining every nerve, exerting every endeavour.

A استفراك *istifrāk,* (v. n. 10 of فرك) Becoming plump and hard in the ear (grain).

A استفرام *istifrām,* (v. n. 10 of فرم) Washing (herself) with an astringent lotion (a woman).

A استفراه *istifrāh,* (v. n. 10 of فره) Acquiring a generous horse.

A استفزاز *istifzāz,* (v. n. 10 of فزّ) Making light of, despising. Exhilarating. Leading forth, turning out of doors. Rendering one light and active (fear). Removing, tearing from a place.

A استفساد *istifsād,* (v. n. 10 of فسد) Seeking to do mischief.

A استفسار *istifsār,* (v. n. 10 of فسر) Asking an explanation, informing one's self, enquiring.

P استفسار كردن *istifsār kardan,* To interrogate.

A استفصاص *istifsās,* (v. n. 10 of فصّ) Drawing forth.

A استفضال *istifzāl,* (v. n. 10 of فضل) Leaving a residue. Taking more than one's due. Bringing an increase. Seeking a benefit.

A استفظاع *istifzāʻ,* (v. n. 10 of فظع) Finding or discovering to be shameful.

A استفلاء *istiflāʼ,* (v. n. 10 of فلي) Requiring to be cleared of lice (the head). Asking any one to perform that office.

A استفلاح *istiflāh,* (v. n. 10 of فلح) Escaping, obtaining a victory, or deliverance. استفلحي بامرك *istaflahī bi amriki,* An expression employed when a divorce is pronounced.

A استفلال *istiflāl,* (v. n. 10 of فلّ) Taking a small part, decimating.

A استفنان *istifnān,* (v. n. 10 of فنّ) Raising (any one) above different sorts and classes.

A استفهام *istifhām,* (v. n. 10 of فهم) Desiring to know or to be taught, informing one's self by asking questions: interrogation. حرف استفهام *harfi istifhām,* A particle of interrogation.

A استفهاميّ *istifhāmīy,* Interrogative.

A استفهاميّة *istifhāmīyat,* Interrogation.

A استفيال *istifyāl,* (v. n. 10 of فال for فيل) Resembling an elephant (a camel).

A استقاء *istikāʼ,* (v. n. 8 of سقى) Drawing water. Asking for water. Growing fat.

A استقاءة *istikāʼat,* (v. n. 10 of قيأ) Vomiting. Retching violently.

A استقاتة *istikātat,* (v. n. 10 of قات for قوت) Asking for victuals.

A استقادة *istikādat,* (v. n. 10 of قاد for قود) Submitting, yielding, giving up the reins.

A استقاع *istikāʻ,* (v. n. 8 of سقع) Being changed (colour).

A استقاف *istikāf,* (v. n. 8 of سقف) Mounting.

A استقالة *istikālat,* (v. n. 10 of قال for قيل) Desiring one to rescind an agreement, cancel a contract, or give up a bargain.

A استقامة *istikāmat,* (v. n. 10 of قام for قوم) Standing erect, remaining, rising up, acting uprightly. Valuing goods. Being correct. Being middling and moderate. Being equable. Rectitude, integrity, fidelity, truth, purity of intention.

A استقباح *istikbāh,* (v. n. 10 of قبح) Regarding as ugly and odious. Detesting, hating, abhorring.

A استقبال *istikbāl,* (v. n. 10 of قبل) Going forth to meet, encountering, looking towards. Futurity.

A استقباليّ *istikbālīy,* Belonging to futurity.

A استقتال *istiktāl,* (v. n. 10 of قتل) Desiring to kill. Being regardless of danger, seeking, as it were, to be killed.

A استقداد *istikdād,* (v. n. 10 of قدّ) Continuing, persevering. Being level and smooth. Remaining in one state.

A استقدار *istikdār,* (v. n. 10 of قدر) Praying (that God) may over-rule or ordain (for good). Asking for strength and ability.

A استقدام *istikdām,* (v. n. 10 of قدم) Preceding. Wishing to get before. Surpassing in boldness or strength of mind.

A استقذار *istikzār,* (v. n. 10 of قذر) Abominating as filthy.

A استقراء *istikrāʼ,* (v. n. 10 of قرأ) Making the female lie down to ascertain if she be in foal (a stallion camel). (v. n. 10 of قرا for قرو) Intending, purposing. Making diligent search. Containing matter (a boil). (v. n. 10 of قري) Following. Passing from place to place, travelling over any country. Making diligent search. Wishing to be a guest.

A استقرار *istikrār,* (v. n. 10 of قرّ) Stopping, resting, dwelling, settling, fixing a residence. Remaining fixed in a female's womb (seed of a male).

A استقراض *istikrāz,* (v. n. 10 of قرض) Borrowing, asking to lend.

A استقراع *istikrāʻ,* (v. n. 10 of قرع) Asking the loan of a bull or he-camel. Wanting the bull (a cow), or the stallion (a she-camel). Being hard (a hoof). Losing its shagginess (the rough tripe).

A استقران *istikrān,* (v. n. 10 of قرن) Swelling in the veins (blood). Being able to bear a load. Becoming able and strong.

A استقسام *istiksām,* (v. n. 10 of قسم) Demanding one's portion, claiming one's share of spoil or property of any kind (which share is determined by throwing a kind of arrow, a practice common among the Arabians). Requiring one to swear.

A استقصاء *istiksāʼ,* (v. n. 10 of قصا for قصو) Curiously prying, or using every effort to get to the knowledge of any thing. Earnest endeavour, perseverance. Strict inquiry.

A استقصاد *istiksād*, (v. n. 10 of قصد) Seeking a middle course.

A استقصار *istiksār*, (v. n. 10 of قصر) Desiring to abbreviate, or to be abbreviated. Considering (a thing) as abridged or short.

A استقصاص *istiksās*, (v. n. 10 of قصّ) Desiring one to retaliate.

A استقضاء *istikzā*, (v. n. 10 of قضي) Demanding payment judicially; wishing to have a debt fixed and determined by the sentence of a judge. (in the passive form) Being constituted judge.

A استقضاض *istikzāz*, (v. n. 10 of قضّ) Finding (a bed) uneasy. Being incommodious and uneasy. Being gravelly (a place).

A استقضام *istikzām*, (v. n. 10 of قضم) Victualling one's household sparingly in a time of dearth.

A استقطار *istiktār*, (v. n. 10 of قطر) Wishing it to distil, or rain. Trying to catch droppings.

A استقفاء *istikfā*, (v. n. 10 of قفا for قفو) Striking (with a stick).

A استقفاف *istikfāf*, (v. n. 10 of قفّ) Being dry and wrinkled with age.

A استقفال *istikfāl*, (v. n. 10 of قفل) Being stingy, avaricious, and close-fisted.

A استقلال *istiklāl*, (v. n. 10 of قلّ) Lifting up (a water-pot). Taking up one's baggage. Soaring upwards (a bird). Seizing any one (a tremor). Being angry. Moving from place to place, departing. Esteeming little, considering as small. Being possessed of sovereign authority and absolute dominion. Growing (a plant).

P استقلالانه *istiklālāna*, Absolutely.

A استقلالي *istiklālī*, Invested with authority. Confirmation.

A استقناع *istiknā*, (v. n. 10 of قنع) Becoming high (the udder of a ewe).

A استقناف *istiknāf*, (v. n. 10 of قنف) Being firm in counsel, able in business.

A استقنان *istiknān*, (v. n. 10 of قنّ) Abiding with one's flocks, and drinking the milk. Regarding as little.

A استقواس *istikwās*, (v. n. 10 of قوس) Bending through age. Being bent as a bow (eyebrow).

A استقواه *istikwāh*, (v. n. 10 of قوه) Asking one to drive wild beasts into a net.

P استقيلا *ustukīlā*, Name of an ancient hero.

A استكارة *istikārat*, (v. n. 10 of كار for كور) Making haste. Carrying a bundle of clothes.

A استكاك *istikāk*, (v. n. 8 of سكّ) Becoming stopt up, and deaf (the ear). Growing wild, entangled, and luxuriant (a plant). Humbling one's self, supplicating, deprecating.

A استكان *istikān*, (v. n. 8 of سكن) Humbling one's self. Becoming low and contemptible.

A استكانة *istikānat*, (v. n. 10 of كان for كون) Humbling one's self, submitting.

A استكبار *istikbār*, (v. n. 10 of كبر) Being proud, haughty, arrogant, and presumptuous. Playing the great man. Viewing, regarding as great.

A استكتاب *istiktāb*, (v. n. 10 of كتب) Asking or ordering one to write. Dictating (a letter). Getting transcribed. Appointing an amanuensis.

A استكتام *istiktām*, (v. n. 10 of كتم) Desiring (one) to keep a secret.

A استكثار *istiksār*, (v. n. 10 of كثر) Wishing or asking for much. Flowering (a palm-tree). Using a large quantity. Asking much (water) to drink.

A استكثاف *istiksāf*, (v. n. 10 of كثف) Being thick and dense.

A استكداد *istikdād*, (v. n. 10 of كدّ) Plaguing, tormenting, wishing (any one) to take trouble.

A استكراء *istikrā*, (v. n. 10 of كرا for كرو) Hiring, renting. Taking on hire.

A استكراش *istikrāsh*, (v. n. 10 of كرش) Becoming fit for ruminating (the stomach of any beast that chews the cud), as when a kid begins to graze. Becoming big from over-eating (the belly of a boy).

A استكرام *istikrām*, (v. n. 10 of كرم) Wishing for, discovering or doing any thing noble and generous. Procuring generous horses. Acquiring greatness.

A استكراه *istikrāh*, (v. n. 10 of كره) Abhorring, abominating, disdaining, despising, contemning. Regarding as disgusting. Forcing to act reluctantly.

A استكشاف *istikshāf*, (v. n. 10 of كشف) Requesting any thing to be made manifest, or laid open.

A استكفاء *istikfā*, (v. n. 10 of كفأ) Begging the loan of a camel for the benefit of the hair, milk, and colt, for a year. (v. n. 10 of كفي) Asking to do what is sufficient. Considering as sufficient or competent.

A استكفاف *istikfāf*, (v. n. 10 of كفّ) Stretching forth the hand (to give or to receive alms). Screening the eye (with the hand) from the glare of the sun and looking at any object attentively. Flocking, gathering round any thing. Being matted (hair). Coiling up (as a serpent).

A استكلاء *istiklā*, (v. n. 10 of كلأ) Abounding in forage (ground). Asking for a delay.

A استكلاب *istiklāb*, (v. n. 10 of كلب) Imitating the barking of a dog to induce them to respond (one who has lost his way). Being greedy of human flesh (a dog).

A استكمال *istikmāl*, (v. n. 10 of كمل) Completing, perfecting. Wishing (any thing) finished, perfected, completed.

A استكنان *istiknān*, (v. n. 10 of كنّ) Concealing one's self.

A استكواء *istikwā*, (v. n. 10 of كوي) Requiring the cautery.

P استل *istal*, A fish-pond, a lake, a pool.

A استلاء *istilā*, (v. n. 8 of سلأ) Boiling, liquifying, melting, purifying (butter, &c.) by melting. (v. n. 8 of سلا for سلو) Becoming fat (a sheep). (v. n. 8 of سلي) Casting out the after-birth (a ewe).

A استلاب *istilāb*, (v. n. 8 of سلب) Seizing, plundering. Producing an abortion.

A استلات *istilāt*, (v. n. 8 of سلت) Wiping or scraping (a dish with the finger).

A استلاج *istilāj*, (v. n. 8 of سلج) Drinking much.

A استلاحة *istilāhat*, (v. n. 10 of لاح for لوح) Considering attentively, contemplating, knowing. Being thirsty.

A استلاطة *istilātat*, (v. n. 10 of لاط for لوط) Bringing on one's self, deserving. Adopting into one's family.

A استلال *istilāl*, (v. n. 8 of سلّ) Drawing (a sword, &c.).

A استلآم *istilām*, (v. n. 10 of لأم) Marrying amongst low and ignorant people. Having a bad sire. Putting on a coat of mail. Kissing the black stone at Mecca, or rubbing it with the hand.

A استلام *istilām*, (v. n. 8 of سلم) Submitting to another's opinion, surrendering. Rubbing the forehead against the black stone at Mecca. Coming out of the ear (corn).

A استلامة *istilāmat*, (v. n. 10 of لام for لوم) Behaving so as to merit or draw censure on one's self.

A استلانة *istilānat*, (v. n. 10 of لان for لين) Considering or finding smooth, soft, placid, or gentle.

A استلباء *istilbā*, (v. n. 10 of لبأ) Sucking the beestings from the ewe (a lamb).

A استلباث *istilbās*, (v. n. 10 of لبث) Regarding as dilatory.

A استلبان *istilbān*, (v. n. 10 of لبن) Asking milk.

A استلجاج *istiljāj*, (v. n. 10 of لجّ) Claiming for one's self. Persevering stoutly in an oath; swearing roundly without any allowance for the credibility and veracity of the opposite party.

A استلحاق *istilhāk*, (v. n. 10 of لحق) Adopting. Calling, or inviting to join or unite unto. Sowing the ground called لحق *lahak*.

A استلحام *istilhām*, (v. n. 10 of لحم) Following a wide road. Pursuing, surrounding, or hemming in (a foe). Killing. Being wide (a road).

A استلذاذ *istilzāz*, (v. n. 10 of لذّ) Considering as delicate, elegant, or agreeable. Tasting, relishing.

A استلزام *istilzām*, (v. n. 10 of لزم) Requiring, rendering necessary.

A استلسام *istilsām*, (v. n. 10 of لسم) Searching.

A استلطاف *istiltāf*, (v. n. 10 of لطف) Joining, uniting, causing to stick to one's arm or side.

A استلطام *istiltām*, (v. n. 10 of لطم) Wanting a slapping, buffeting, or cuffing.

A استلعاب *istilāb*, (v. n. 10 of لعب) Producing unripe dates after having been cut (a palm-tree). Wishing, asking, or requiring to play.

A استلغاء *istilghā*, (v. n. 10 of لغا for لغو) Listening to the language of any one, without putting any questions.

A استلفاث *istilfas*, (v. n. 10 of لفث) Prying curiously, using every effort to elicit or extract information. Concealing, suppressing (news) Accomplishing one's object. Leading to pasturage.

A استلقاء istilkāʼ, (v. n. 10 of لقي) Lying on one's back.

A استلقاح istilkāh, (v. n. 10 of لقح) Reaching the time when she ought to be covered (a camel), or when it should receive the fructifying pollen of the male (a female palm-tree).

A استلهام istilhām, (v. n. 10 of لهم) Wishing to be inspired. Beseeching (God) to reveal.

P استم istam, (for ستم) Oppression, injustice.

A استماء istimāʼ, (v. n. 8 of سما for سمو) Going a hunting. Putting on sandals to hunt the mountain-goat. Designing, proposing, intending a visit. Prognosticating good.

A استماتة istimātat, (v. n. 10 of مات for موت) Seeking on every side. Waxing fat after being lean.

A استماحة istimāhat, (v. n. 10 of ماح for ميح) Asking a gift. Intreating (one) to intercede.

A استمازة istimāzat, (v. n. 10 of ماز for ميز) Being separate, distinct. Being removed. Retiring.

A استماع istimāɛ, (v. n. 8 of سمع) Listening, hearing, giving ear.

A استماقة istimākat, (v. n. 10 of ماق for موق) Being foolish, playing the fool. Regarding as a fool.

A استمال istimāl, (v. n. 8 of سمل) Blinding, knocking out an eye, gouging.

A استمالة istimālat, (v. n. 10 of مال for مول) Being rich. (v. n. 10 of مال for ميل) Caressing, conciliating, giving good words, soothing, gaining the favour of any one. Seeking to incline, striving to bias. Measuring with the two expanded arms (a fathom).

A استمتاع istimtāɛ, (v. n. 10 of متع) Enjoying one's property, reaping the fruits, or receiving the usufruct. Celebrating the solemn festival called عمرة ɛumrat at Mecca.

A استمجاد istimjād, (v. n. 10 of مجد) Taking much. Desiring or asking for much. Emitting much fire (the trees مرخ markh and عفار ɛafār).

A استمحاض istimhāz, (v. n. 10 of محض) Asking for pure milk.

A استمخار istimkhār, (v. n. 10 of مخر) Turning one's back to the wind. Facing the wind and snuffing it up (a horse).

A استمداد istimdād, (v. n. 10 of مدّ) Asking supplies, subsidies, help. Taking a penful of ink.

A استمراء istimrāʼ, (v. n. 10 of مرأ) Digesting one's food, finding it very digestible.

A استمرار istimrār, (v. n. 10 of مرّ) Proceeding, going on. Persevering, persisting in one course. Remaining, continuing. Being able to bear. Perpetuity. استمرّت مريرته عليه istamarrat marīratuhu ɛalayhi, His malice against him remained.

A استمراري istimrārī, Perpetual, continuative.

A استمساك istimsāk, (v. n. 10 of مسك) Holding. Refraining.

A استمشاء istimshāʼ, (v. n. 10 of مشي) Purging. Suffering from a diarrhœa.

A استمصال istimsāl, (v. n. 10 of مصل) Taking a cathartic draught. Purging (a drastic medicine).

A استمطار istimtār, (v. n. 10 of مطر) Praying for rain.

A استمعاز istimɛāz, (v. n. 10 of معز) Striving, using exertion.

A استمكات istimkāt, (v. n. 10 of مكت) Being filled with matter (a pustule).

A استمكال istimkāl, (v. n. 10 of مكل) Marrying a wife.

A استمكان istimkān, (v. n. 10 of مكن) Having in one's power, getting possession or fast hold of.

A استملاء istimlāʼ, (v. n. 10 of ملأ) Lending to monied men. (v. n. 10 of ملا for ملو) Asking to indite. Asking for a delay.

A استملاح istimlāh, (v. n. 10 of ملح) Esteeming good, agreeable, or beautiful.

A استملال istimlāl, (v. n. 10 of ملّ) Being wearied, tired, feeling (a thing) to be irksome.

A استمناء istimnāʼ, (v. n. 10 of مني) Wishing to produce, or producing a seminal effusion; onanizing. Putting (a camel) in the condition of ممني mumnī.

A استمناح istimnāh, (v. n. 10 of منح) Asking for a gift.

A استمهاء istimhāʼ, (v. n. 10 of مهي) Breaking an enemy's rank irresistibly.

A استمهال istimhāl, (v. n. 10 of مهل) Petitioning for a delay, begging respite, asking for time.

P آستن āstin, The sleeve of a garment.

A استن astan, Old roots of trees. A tree, which at a distance resembles the human form.

P استن ustun, A column, a prop.

A استناء istināʼ or استناءة istināʼat, (v. n. 10 of ناء for نوأ) Setting in the west (a star) whilst another is rising in the east. Asking for a gift.

A استناحة istināhat, (v. n. 10 of ناح for نوح) Weeping, lamenting, mourning. Howling (a wolf). Moving to tears.

A استناخة istinākhat, (v. n. 10 of ناخ for نوخ) Kneeling down to receive the male (a she-camel). Endeavouring or wishing to make the female kneel.

A استناد istinād, (v. n. 8 of سند) Leaning against, supporting one's self by, or depending on.

A استنارة istinārat, (v. n. 10 of نار for نور) Shining, glistening. Seeking light. Putting to flight, making flee away in terror, overcoming, prevailing.

A استناصة istināsat, (v. n. 10 of ناص for نوص) Retreating, retiring. Moving himself when about to run (a horse). Putting in motion. Holding (any one) light and making use of (him) to suit one's own convenience.

A استناطة istinātat, (v. n. 10 of ناط for نوط) Asking the loan (of a camel) to carry provisions.

A استناعة istināɛat, (v. n. 10 of ناع for نوع) Preceding. Being shaken (branches by the wind).

A استنامة istināmat, (v. n. 10 of نام for نوم) Sleeping. Feigning to be asleep. Being quiet. Relying, trusting. Security, reliance.

A استنان istinān, (v. n. 8 of سنّ) Rubbing the teeth. Instituting or observing a certain mode of life. Galloping. Trembling, being unsteady (the vapour سراب sarāb). Capering, being restive.

A استنباء istimbāʼ, (v. n. 10 of نبأ) Enquiring, informing one's self. Asking news.

A استنباح istimbāh, (v. n. 10 of نبح) Making (a dog) bark. Endeavouring to make (a dog) bark.

A استنباط istimbāt, (v. n. 10 of نبط) Causing (a spring) to flow. Eliciting, extracting (generally confined to religious matters, or affairs of jurisprudence, as to make an extract from the Kur'ān). Causing something to appear which was previously concealed. Sojourning amongst, or becoming as one of, the Nabathean Arabs.

A استنبال istimbāl, (v. n. 10 of نبل) Asking for an arrow. Taking the best of a man's property.

T استنبول istambūl, Constantinople.

P استنبه istamba, Thick, coarse, hideous. Strong, powerful, brave. The night-mare. A demon.

A استنة astanat, The root of an old tree.

A استنتاء istintāʼ, (v. n. 10 of نتا for نتو) Being numerous (pimples of boils).

A استنتار istintār, (v. n. 10 of نتر) Squeezing out the last drop of urine.

A استنتال istintāl, (v. n. 10 of نتل) Leading, preceding, going in front of the rank. Preparing.

A استنتاج istintāj, (v. n. 10 of نتج) Becoming loose (one side of a load).

A استنثار istinsār, (v. n. 10 of نثر) Drawing up water through the nostrils and discharging it again.

A استنجاء istinjāʼ, (v. n. 10 of نجا for نجو) Obtaining, gaining. Being set at liberty. Making haste. Cutting boughs and sticks from a tree. Felling timber. Finding and eating fresh dates. Gathering fruit. Cleaning a gut and fitting it to a bow. Washing or cleaning one's self with a flint after easing nature. Drawing a bow. Ablution.

A استنجاث istinjās, (v. n. 10 of نجث) Going in the track of. Extracting, drawing forth. Throwing one's self in the way of, opposing.

A استنجاح istinjāh, (v. n. 10 of نجح) Despatching any business easily and successfully.

A استنجاد istinjād, (v. n. 10 of نجد) Asking assistance, or protection. Recovering from sickness. Taking courage after having been afraid.

A استنجاز istinjāz, (v. n. 10 of نجز) Doing any thing with success and despatch. Asking for the fulfilment of a promise.

A استنجاع istinjāɛ, (v. n. 10 of نجع) Growing fat, thriving on.

A استنجاف istinjāf, (v. n. 10 of نجف) Emptying, voiding (as the wind a cloud).

A استنجال istinjāl, (v. n. 10 of نجل) Being full of water (a valley).

A استحساس *istinhās*, (v. n. 10 of لحس) Inquiring, ascertaining.

A استنخاب *istinkhāb*, (v. n. 10 of نخب) Asking to be lain with. Choosing, picking out.

A استنخاج *istinkhāj*, (v. n. 10 of نخج) Becoming soft.

A استنداص *istindās*, (v. n. 10 of ندص) Drawing out one's due.

A استنداء *istindāh*, (v. n. 10 of ندء) Prospering, being well managed (business).

P استندن *istandan*, To take, to receive.

T استنديل *istindīl*, Tenedos, in the Archipelago.

A استنزال *istinzāl*, (v. n. 10 of نزل) Sending down. Bringing down. Receiving into one's house. Being removed from office, descending from one's station. Wishing to descend.

A استنساء *istinsāʼ*, (v. n. 10 of نسأ) Requesting a creditor to wait. Asking one to sell on credit.

A استنساب *istinsāb*, (v. n. 10 of نسب) Tracing one's genealogy. Mentioning, recording, or wishing to record a genealogy.

A استنساخ *istinsākh*, (v. n. 10 of نسخ) Transcribing, copying.

A استنسار *istinsār*, (v. n. 10 of نسر) Resembling or acting like a vulture.

A استنشاء *istinshāʼ*, (v. n. 10 of نشأ) Smelling. Inquiring into. (v. n. 10 of نشي) Smelling, perceiving a smell. Being overcome with drink.

A استنشاد *istinshād*, (v. n. 10 of نشد) Asking one to repeat a poem.

A استنشاط *istinshāt*, (v. n. 10 of نشط) Becoming wrinkled (skin). Shrivelling up (leather).

A استنشاق *istinshāk*, (v. n. 10 of نشق) Drawing up water through the nostrils; snuffing up the air, or odours.

A استنصات *istinsāt*, (v. n. 10 of نصت) Requesting one to keep silence.

A استنصاح *istinsāh*, (v. n. 10 of نصح) Esteeming one to be a faithful counsellor.

A استنصار *istinsār*, (v. n. 10 of نصر) Soliciting aid against an enemy. Asking supplies.

A استنصاف *istinsāf*, (v. n. 10 of نصف) Becoming quits, getting one's just due.

A استنصال *istinsāl*, (v. n. 10 of نصل) Drawing forth. Causing the prickles of the plant بهمي *buhma'* to fall (hot weather).

A استنضاح *istinzāh*, (v. n. 10 of نضح) Sprinkling water on the privities after making an ablution.

A استنضاض *istinzāz*, (v. n. 10 of نضّ) Collecting drop by drop. Requesting payment of a debt in coin. Trying to obtain a benefit.

A استنطاق *istintāk*, (v. n. 10 of نطق) Endowing with speech (God). Trying to make one speak. Searching, inquiring. Talking together.

A استنظار *istinzār*, (v. n. 10 of نظر) Begging a delay, asking to wait or give time. Asking credit.

A استنظاف *istinzāf*, (v.n. 10 of نظف) Taking all clean away. Exacting the whole (of tribute).

A استنعاء *istinʻāʼ*, (v. n. 10 of نعي) Approaching. Returning, fleeing. Galloping away with his rider (a camel). Calling (sheep) to follow him (a shepherd). Taking the lead. Preceding. Being scattered, dispersed. Being divulged, published. Overtaking a man (misfortune). Possessing, occupying (as the love of wine).

A استنعات *istinʻāt*, (v. n. 10 of نعت) Asking for an epithet, requesting one to describe or qualify.

A استنفاج *istinfāj*, (v. n. 10 of نفج) Drawing out (anger), enraging.

A استنفاد *istinfād*, (v. n. 10 of نفد) Emptying, exhausting. Putting forth all one's strength.

A استنفار *istinfār*, (v. n. 10 of نفر) Running away terrified (animal). Desiring one to run away. Making (an animal) to run away.

A استنفاض *istinfāz*, (v. n. 10 of نفض) Cleaning the penis from the remains of urine. Extracting. Sending forth scouts. Examining carefully.

A استنفاق *istinfāk*, (v. n. 10 of نفق) Laying out money, spending all.

A استنفاه *istinfāh*, (v. n. 10 of نفه) Reposing.

A استنقاذ *istinkāz*, (v. n. 10 of نقذ) Liberating, emancipating, rescuing. Putting to a distance.

A استنقاص *istinkās*, (v. n. 10 of نقص) Desiring or endeavouring to diminish or lessen the price of any thing. Regarding as deficient.

A استنقاع *istinkāʻ*, (v. n. 10 of نقع) Flowing into a place and stagnating (water); also becoming yellow in the body. Being high (the voice). Having a rattling in the throat (a dying person). Changing (colour). Steeping in water. Descending into a pond to wash and cool the body.

A استنقاه *istinkāh*, (v. n. 10 of نقه) Understanding. Interrogating.

A استنكاح *istinkāh*, (v. n. 10 of نكح) Marrying, taking a wife. Lying with a woman.

A استنكار *istinkār*, (v. n. 10 of نكر) Seeking to become acquainted with a subject of which one is ignorant. Being ignorant of, not knowing.

A استنكاف *istinkāf*, (v. n. 10 of نكف) Declining, refusing, rejecting, disdaining. Being proud, haughty, playing the great man. Tracking (a camel) over a sandy plain.

A استنكاه *istinkāh*, (v. n. 10 of نكه) Bidding another breathe in one's face to discover what he has been drinking. Smelling another's breath.

A استنواء *istinwāʼ*, (v. n. 10 of نوي) Throwing away date-stones.

A استنواق *istinwāk*, (v. n. 10 of ناق for نوق) Becoming a she-camel (a male camel), spoken of one who mingles his own stories with those of others.

A استنواك *istinwāk*, (v. n. 10 of ناك for نوك) Being foolish and silly.

A استنهاج *istinhāj*, (v. n. 10 of نهج) Adopting another's mode of life. Lying open (royal road).

A استنهار *istinhār*, (v. n. 10 of نهر) Flowing copiously. Lying open (a wound). Being wide and spacious. Turning the course of a river through a solid bed. Checking, shouting, calling out to.

A استنهاض *istinhāz*, (v. n. 10 of نهض) Rousing, ordering to rise.

A استواء *istiwāʼ*, (v. n. 8 of سوي) Being straight and even. Being equal, parallel. Being level with any thing, *i. e.* hiding or burying it (ground). Putting the whole of one thing into another. Being moderate, temperate. Sitting well or upright (on horseback). Arriving at full maturity of body and mind about the age of forty. Predominating. Coming to maturity (youth). Approaching, advancing. Tending towards, ascending (to heaven. Intending, proposing. Dropping a letter in reading. Leaving, quitting, neglecting. Being disgraced, rendered ignominious. Incurring impurity. Equality, uniformity. خط استوا *khatti istiwā*, A right line. The equator.

P استوار *ustuwār*, Firm, strong, solid. Faithful, true, worthy to be relied on. استوار شدن *ustuwār shudan*, To stick fast and firmly. استوار داشتن *ustuwār dāshtan*, To rely upon, to believe.

P استواري *ustuwārī*, Strength, firmness, constancy, resolution.

A استواط *istiwāt*, (v. n. 8 of ساط for سوط) Being confused, perplexed, disturbed.

P استوان *ustuwān*, Firm, solid. Trustworthy.

P استوانه *ustuwāna*, A cylinder.

P است و بست *ast u bast*, Particulars.

P استودان *ustūdān*, A cemetery of the Guebres.

P استور *ustūr*, A horse, mule, beast of burthen.

P استوربان *ustūrbān*, A horse-keeper. Barren.

P استوم *ustūm*, A bulrush.

P استون *ustūn*, A column, beam, mast. A kinsman (son-in-law, father-in-law). Odoriferous grass.

P استوه *istūh* or *ustūh*, Wearied, dispirited, sorrowful, afflicted, overwhelmed with ennui.

P استوي *ustuwī*, The back-bone.

P آسته *āsta*, A kernel. A bone. آستهٔ خرما *āstaʼi khurmā*, A date-stone.

P استه *asta*, The stone of a date, plum, or peach. A bone. *Istih*, Contention, altercation. *Istuh*, Dejected, dispirited, tired. *Usta*, The buttocks.

A استه *astah*, (pl. سته *sutuh*) Large-buttocked. One who finds a pleasure in large buttocks.

A استهاءة *istihāʼat*, (v. n. 10 of هوي) Bewitching, seducing, bewildering, stupefying.

A استهاب *istihāb*, (v. n. 8 of سهب) Giving much. Becoming very liberal.

A استهائة *istihāʼat*, (v. n. 10 of هيث not used) Doing, wishing, or asking much. Doing mischief.

A استهاف *istihāf*, (v. n. 8 of سهف) Esteeming lightly, holding in contempt.

A استهام *istihām*, (v. n. 8 of سهم) Casting lots.

A استهامة *istihāmat*, (v. n. 10 of هام for هيم)

Infatuating, bewitching.

A استهانة *istihānat*, (v. n. 10 of هان for هون) Making light of, despising.

A استهباع *istihbāʻ*, (v. n. 10 of هبع) Urging (a camel) so that he runs with outstretched neck.

A استهتار *istihtār*, (v. n. 10 of هتر) Being strongly inclined to drink. Being so greedy as to be lost to all sense of shame. Patronizing vanity and folly.

A استهجاج *istihjāj*, (v. n. 10 of هجّ) Taking one's own way without consulting any body. Hurrying forward travellers.

A استهجان *istihjān*, (v. n. 10 of هجن) Regarding as base and shameful.

A استهداء *istihdāʼ*, (v. n. 10 of هدي) Asking a gift, or guidance.

A استهداف *istihdāf*, (v. n. 10 of هدف) Being erect and tall. Setting one's self as a mark or butt (for criticism, &c.). Exhausting (a milker).

P استهدن *istihdan*, To squabble.

A استهزاء *istihzāʼ*, (v. n. 10 of هزأ) Deriding, joking, sneering.

P استهزانه *istihzāna*, Scornfully, deridingly.

A استهشاش *istihshāsh*, (v. n. 10 of هشّ) Considering as light.

A استهضاب *istihzāb*, (v. n. 10 of هضب) Becoming incessant (a shower). Becoming dry, giving little milk (a sheep).

A استهطاع *istihtāʻ*, (v. n. 10 of هطع) Stretching out the neck, hanging the head and going fast.

A استهكام *istihkām*, The being proud.

A استهلاك *istihlāk*, (v. n. 10 of هلك) Ruining, destroying, consuming, expending.

A استهلال *istihlāl*, (v. n. 10 of هلّ) Being glad, cheerful, shining with joy (the countenance). Flowing plentifully (tears, water, rain). Beginning to rain with noise. Giving the first cry (an infant). Raising the voice, invoking. Drawing (a sword). Appearing (the new moon). Beginning a month.

A استهمام *istihmām*, (v. n. 10 of همّ) Caring, being anxious about the concerns of one's people.

A استهناء *istihnāʼ*, (v. n. 10 of هنأ) Asking help, or a gift.

A استهناع *istihnāʻ*, The being unable to reply.

A استهواء *istihwāʼ*, (v. n. 10 of هوي) Bewitching, seducing, bewildering, stupefying.

P استهيدن *istihīdan*, To quarrel, litigate, strive.

P آستي *āsti*, The sleeve of a garment.

A استيّ *istiy*, Belonging to the anus, fundamental, anal. A follower. *Ustiy*, The warp of a garment. Fitted to the loom, stretched on the warp.

A استيآء *istiʼāʼ*, (v. n. 10 of وأي) Receiving or being gratified by a promise. Asking a promise.

A استياء *istiyāʼ*, (v. n. 8 of ساء for سوأ) Being displeased, disgusted, feeling hurt at any one.

A استياد *istiyād*, (v. n. 8 of ساد for سود) Killing, or taking prisoner, a chief. Asking (the chief woman of a tribe) in marriage.

A استيآر *istiʼār*, (v. n. 10 of وأر) Running away.

A استيار *istiyār*, (v. n. 8 of سار for سير) Taking provisions for the way. Living after the fashion, or adopting the habits of another.

A استيآس *istiʼās*, (v. n. 10 of يئس) Desponding, despairing.

A استئاسة *istiʼāsat*, (v. n. 10 of اوس not used) Asking for an equivalent.

A استياف *istiyāf*, (v. n. 8 of ساف for سوف) Smelling, snuffing up. (v. n. 8 of ساف for سيف) Fighting with swords. Being put to the sword.

A استياق *istiyāk*, (v. n. 8 of ساق for سوق) Driving, urging forward.

A استئاك *istiʼāk*, (v. n. 10 of ايك) Becoming a thick entangled forest (the tree اراك *arāk*).

A استياك *istiyāk*, (v. n. 8 of ساك for سوك) Cleaning the teeth with a stick. Making a dentifrice.

A استيام *istiyām*, (v. n. 8 of سام for سوم) Bidding against, raising the price. Fixing a price. Asking a price.

A استيباء *istībāʼ*, (v. n. 10 of وبأ) Discovering (a place) to be infected with plague or contagious disorder. Being heavy, unwholesome (food).

A استئباط *istiʼbāt*, (v. n. 10 of ابط) Excavating a pit narrow at the mouth and wide at the bottom (either for storing grain or catching wild beasts).

A استيباق *istībāk*, (v. n. 10 of وبق) Perishing. Wishing one may perish.

A استيبال *istībāl*, (v. n. 10 of وبل) Being unhealthy (air). Finding (air) so. Wanting the rain.

A استئتاء *istiʼtāʼ*, (v. n. 10 of اتي) Longing for the male. Thinking one slow, longing for his arrival.

A استئتان *istiʼtān*, (v. n. 10 of اتن) Purchasing a she-ass. Becoming a she-ass (a male: spoken of one who from being honourable becomes debased).

A استيتان *istītān*, (v. n. 10 of وتن) Becoming fat (sheep).

A استيثاج *istīsāj*, (v. n. 10 of وثج) Being entangled (as plants when growing too close together). Being complete. Being plentiful. Asking much.

A استئثار *istiʼsār*, (v. n. 10 of اثر) Choosing (any good thing) for one's self, and not for one's companions. Taking (any one) to himself at death (God). Accomplishing (a thing) alone.

A استيثار *istīsār*, (v. n. 10 of وثر) Importuning. Coming often.

A استيثاق *istīsāk*, (v. n. 10 of وثق) Taking a written compact or agreement.

A استيثان *istīsān*, (v. n. 10 of وثن) Growing fat. Increasing, abounding. Waxing strong. Remaining. Dividing itself into two parts (a palm-tree). Having colts full grown (camels).

A استيج *ustīj*, A weaver's shuttle, the woof about the quill.

A استيجاب *istījāb*, (v. n. 10 of وجب) Being worthy, deserving.

A استئجار *istiʼjār*, (v. n. 10 of اجر) Hiring.

A استئجاز *istiʼjāz*, (v. n. 10 of اجز not used) Bending over a pillow, without reclining upon it.

A استيجاف *istījāf*, (v. n. 10 of وجف) Smiting the heart (love).

A استئجال *istiʼjāl*, (v. n. 10 of اجل) Requesting a reprieve, or delay. Attaining to a fixed period.

A استيحاء *istīhāʼ*, (v. n. 10 of وحي) Putting in motion, exciting, stirring. Calling one in order to send him. Questioning, being inquisitive.

A استيحاد *istīhād*, (v. n. 10 of وحد) Being alone, single, unique. Knowing, perceiving, understanding.

A استيحاش *istīhāsh*, (v. n. 10 of وحش) Experiencing care, sadness, or terror. Taking fright.

A استيحال *istīhāl*, (v. n. 10 of وحل) Abounding in thin mud.

P استيخ *istīkh*, Tall and straight (column).

A استيخاء *istīkhāʼ*, (v. n. 10 of وخي) Asking news or information.

A استئخاذ *istiʼkhāz*, (v. n. 10 of اخذ) Taking possession of.

A استئخار *istiʼkhār*, (v. n. 10 of اخر) Remaining behind.

A استيخام *istīkhām*, (v. n. 10 of وخم) Being unable to digest heavy and unwholesome food. Being heavy and unwholesome.

A استئداء *istiʼdāʼ*, (v. n. 10 of ادي) Imploring help. Fining, amercing.

A استيداء *istīdāʼ*, (v. n. 10 of ودي) Acknowledging a debt.

A استئداب *istiʼdāb*, (v. n. 10 of ادب) Being instructed in morals. Acquiring learning.

A استيداع *istīdāʻ*, (v. n. 10 of ودع) Requesting any one to keep a deposit. Committing, commending.

A استيداف *istīdāf*, (v. n. 10 of ودف) Scrutinizing. Letting fall in drops, catching melted fat as it drops. Holding, containing, retaining (sperm in the uterus). Growing long (grass). Opening the head of a vessel to examine the milk.

A استيداق *istīdāk*, (v. n. 10 of ودق) Wanting the male (a mare or ass).

A استيداه *istīdāh*, (v. n. 10 of وده) Being driven together (camels). Being defeated and submitting to a conqueror. Being well managed (business). Despising, holding lightly.

P استيدن *istīdan*, To stand. To begin.

P استيده *istīda*, Standing.

A استئذان *istiʼzān*, (v. n. 10 of اذن) Asking leave, begging permission.

P استير *astīr*, A weight of 6½ dirhems.

A استيراء *istīrāʼ*, (v. n. 10. of وري) Striking fire by the friction of two pieces of wood.

A استئراب *istiʼrāb*, (v. n. 10 of ارب) Being overloaded with debt.

A استيراغ *istīrākh*, (v. n. 10 of ورغ) Being irrigated (the earth).

A استيراد *istīrād*, (v. n. 10 of ورد) Approaching water to drink. Bringing to water. Citing.

A استئراض *istiɛrāz*, (v. n. 10 of ارض) Becoming raw and angry (a sore).

A استيراط *istīrāt*, A plunging headlong.

A استيزاء *istīzāɛ*, (v. n. 10 of وزي) Ascending (a mountain).

A استيزار *istīzār*, (v. n. 10 of وزر) Preserving. Carrying off. Appointing a vazīr, choosing (one) to be prime minister. Soliciting the office of vazīr. Performing the duty of a vazīr. Collecting.

A استيزاع *istīzāɛ*, (v. n. 10 of وزع) Praying for divine inspiration, imploring a thankful spirit for divine favours.

A استئزاق *istiɛzāk*, (v. n. 10 of ازق) Being narrow, confined, close.

P استيزه *istīza*, Controversy, quarrel, anger.

A استئساء *istiɛsā*, (v. n. 10 of اسي) Seeking solace, desiring consolation.

A استيساء *istīsāɛ*, (v. n. 10 of وسي) Asking aid.

A استيساخ *istīsākh*, (v. n. 10 of وسخ) Being dirty, soiled (a garment).

A استئساد *istiɛsād*, (v. n. 10 of اسد) Being bold as a lion. Growing to maturity (a plant).

A استيساد *istīsād*, (v. n. 10 of وسد) Exciting, raising a commotion.

A استيسار *istīsār*, (v. n. 10 of يسر) Being easy, in a good train, well arranged, in good order, easily to be obtained.

A استيساع *istīsāɛ*, (v. n. 10 of وسع) Being wide, roomy, capacious, large enough.

A استيساق *istīsāk*, (v. n. 10 of وسق) Being collected.

A استيسان *istīsān*, (v. n. 10 of وسن) Being sleepy and drowsy.

A استيشاء *istīshāɛ*, (v. n. 10 of وشي) Making (a horse) run at full speed. Calling. Moving.

A استيشار *istīshār*, (v. n. 10 of وشر) Desiring (another) to make one's teeth thin and sharp.

A استيشاع *istīshāɛ*, A drawing of water.

A استيشاغ *istīshāgh*, (v. n. 10 of وشغ) Drawing water with a torn bucket.

A استيشام *istīshām*, (v. n. 10 of وشم) Desiring the marks وشم *washm* to be punctured on one's body.

A استيصاء *istīsāɛ*, (v. n. 10 of وصي) Receiving a charge, command, or testament. Enjoining.

A استيصاد *istīsād*, (v. n. 10 of وصد) Constructing a sheep-cote on a mountain.

A استيصاف *istīsāf*, (v. n. 10 of وصف) Asking (a physician) for a medical prescription.

A استئصال *istiɛsāl*, (v. n. 10 of اصل) Eradicating, erasing, exterminating, ruining.

A استيضاح *istīzāh*, (v. n. 10 of وضح) Requesting an explanation. Seeking to discern any object by raising the hand to the forehead.

A استيضاع *istīzāɛ*, (v. n. 10 of وضع) Asking for an abatement.

A استيضام *istīzām*, (v. n. 10 of وضم) Injuring, hurting, oppressing.

A استيطاء *istītāɛ*, (v. n. 10 of وطئ) Finding (a bed) soft.

A استيطان *istītān*, (v. n. 10 of وطن) Choosing for a residence.

A استيظاف *istīzāf*, (v. n. 10 of وظف) Taking the whole (property).

A استيعاء *istīɛāɛ*, (v. n. 10 of وعي) Cutting clean away, leaving nothing remain.

A استيعاب *istīɛāb*, (v. n. 10 of وعب) Taking (the whole).

A استيعار *istīɛār*, (v. n. 10 of وعر) Finding (a road) rugged.

A استيعال *istīɛāl*, (v. n. 10 of وعل) Taking refuge. Fleeing to a mountain.

A استيغال *istīghāl*, (v. n. 10 of وغل) Washing the groin or arm-pit.

A استيفاء *istīfāɛ*, (v. n. 10 of وفي) Demanding and receiving the whole of what is due.

A استئفاد *istiɛfād*, (v. n. 10 of افد) Approaching, coming suddenly.

A استئفار *istiɛfār*, (v. n. 10 of افر) Becoming fat and sprightly after being worn with fatigue.

A استيفار *istīfār*, (v. n. 10 of وفر) Receiving or paying what was due.

A استيفاز *istīfāz*, (v. n. 10 of وفز) Sitting bolt upright. Squatting on the tips of one's toes.

A استيفاض *istīfāz*, (v. n. 10 of وفض) Running fast. Making haste. Causing to make haste, driving. Being driven and scattered here and there. Expelling, banishing.

A استيفاق *istīfāk*, (v. n. 10 of وفق) Imploring or seeking divine guidance and grace.

A استيقاح *istīkāh*, (v. n. 10 وقح) Being hard (nails or hoofs).

A استيقاد *istīkād*, (v. n. 10 وقد) Kindling, lighting. Burning, blazing. Being in heat (a female).

A استيقار *istīkār*, (v. n. 10 of وقر) Taking a load from off any one's head. Becoming fat (camels).

A استيقاط *istīkāt*, (v. n. 10 of وقط) Abounding in hollows where water collects (a place).

A استيقاظ *istīkāz*, (v. n. 10 of يقظ) Watching, awakening. Awaking out of sleep. Making a tinkling noise (a necklace, or metal ring on the ankle).

A استيقاع *istīkāɛ*, (v. n. 10 of وقع) Being time for sharpening a sword. Anxiously expecting a thing to happen or fall out. Being terrified. Taking a sharp edge (a sword).

A استيقاف *istīkāf*, (v. n. 10 of وقف) Requesting one to wait, detain (another), or pause.

A استيقان *istīkān*, (v. n. 10 of يقن) Knowing for sure, ascertaining.

A استيقاه *istīkāh*, (v. n. 10 of وقه) Obeying.

A استيكاء *istīkāɛ*, (v. n. 10 of وكي) Being fat.

A استيكاث *istīkās*, (v. n. 10 of وكث) Partaking of a hasty meal. Breakfast.

A استيكاح *istīkāh*, (v. n. 10 of وكح) Being penurious, sordid, niggardly, refusing to give. Being fat and fleshy (young birds).

A استيكاع *istīkāɛ*, (v. n. 10 of وكع) Acquiring strength. Becoming consolidated and not leaking.

A استيكاف *istīkāf*, (v. n. 10 of وكف) Catching any thing dripping or distilling.

A استئكال *istiɛkāl*, (v. n. 10 of اكل) Begging a meal. Devouring the substance of the weak.

A استئكام *istiɛkām*, (v. n. 10 of اكم) Being full of hillocks. Finding (a bed soft).

A استيلاء *istīlāɛ*, (v. n. 10 of ولي) Having entire power or authority. Reaching the extremity. Hitting a mark. Authority, ascendancy, domination.

A استيلاخ *istīlākh*, (v. n. 10 of ولخ) Becoming moistened (ground).

A استيلاغ *istīlāgh*, (v. n. 10 of ولغ) Not caring for disgrace.

A استئلاك *istiɛlāk*, (v. n. 10 of الك) Bearing a message, going on an embassy.

P آستيم *āstīm*, A sleeve. Blood from a wound. A healed wound. A poultice. The orifice of a bottle.

P استيم *astīm*, A sleeve. The mouth of a vessel. *Istīm*, A wound affected by the cold and swollen. Cold which causes a wound to swell. A wound healed on the surface and full of matter within. Pus, matter.

A استئماء *istiɛmāɛ*, (v. n. 10 of امي) Purchasing a handmaiden, taking a maidservant.

A استئمار *istiɛmār*, (v. n. 10 of امر) Consulting, deliberating. Adjuring, causing to swear.

A استئماع *istiɛmāɛ*, (v. n. 10 of امع) Being weak-headed, and at every body's beck and call.

A استئمام *istiɛmām*, (v. n. 10 of امّ) Taking for a mother.

A استئمان *istiɛmān*, (v. n. 10 of امن) Confiding, considering trustworthy. Begging protection, taking refuge.

A استيمان *istīmān*, (v. n. 10 of يمن) Considering as fortunate. Being happy and blest. Administering an oath.

P آستين *āstīn*, A sleeve. آستين افشاندن *āstīn afshāndan*, To dance. To confer favours. To abandon, refuse, shake off. آستين برچيدن *āstīn bar chīdan*, (آستين بر زدن *āstīn bar zadan*, or آستين ماليدن *āstīn mālīdan*) To tuck up one's sleeve, *i.e.* to prepare for business. آستين بر گناه كشيدن *āstīn bar gunāh kashīdan*, To pass by a fault. آستين پوستين *āstīni postīn*, Fault, blemish. آستين تر داشتن *āstīn tar dashtan*, To shed tears. آستين تيريز كردن *āstīn tīrīz kardan*, To draw one's hand in. آستين كوتاه *āstīni kūtāh*, A garment without ornaments. آستين گرفتن *āstīn giriftan*, To compel one to work for nothing.

A استئناء *istiɛnāɛ*, (v. n. 10 of اني) Waiting.

A استئناس *istiɛnās*, (v. n. 10 of انس) Being intimate, familiar. Perceiving the presence of a man (a wild beast). Knowing. Asking leave.

A استئناف *istiɛnāf*, (v. n. 10 of انف) Commencing. An exordium, beginning, commencement.

P آستينه *āstina* (or استينه *istina*) A bird's egg.

A استئوار *istiswār*, (v. n. 10 of اور not used) Fearing, flying in terror. Running away (startled camels) over rough ground. Making haste, hurrying along in the dark. Waxing angry (people). Preparing to leap (a camel).

A استيهاب *istihāb*, (v. n. 10 of وهب) Asking for a present.

A استيهار *istihār*, (v. n. 10 of وهر) Knowing for a certainty. (v. n. 10 of يهر) Persevering in. Running away in fear (asses). Knowing for sure. Exchanging, swoping. Losing his wits (a man).

A استئهال *istiʼhāl*, (v. n. 10 of اهل) Being worthy, deserving. Buying and eating condiment called اهالة *ihālat*.

A اسج *usuj*, (for وسج *wusuj*) Swift she-camels.

A اسجاح *isjāh*, (v. n. 4 of سجح) Pardoning, sparing, acquitting, soothing, giving good words.

A اسجاد *asjād*, Tribute-money. *Asjād* or *isjād*, Jews and Christians, who are charged with paying homage to the figures on certain coins tendered for tribute. *Isjād*, (v. n. 4 of سجد) Bowing the head to the ground, paying adoration. Beholding any thing very attentively, and injuring the eyelids.

A اسجاع *asjāʻ*, (pl. of سجع *sajʻ*) Rhymes, compositions in rhythm. Cooings of turtles.

A اسجاف *asjāf*, (pl. of سجف *sajf*) Veils, curtains. *Isjāf*, (v. n. 4 of سجف) Letting fall (a curtain) before a tent-door. Closing in (night).

A اسجال *isjāl*, (v. n. 4 of سجل) Filling (a cistern). Giving a large bucket or two. Abounding in good things. Leaving. Sending, despatching.

A اسجام *isjām*, (v. n. 4 of سجم) Raining copiously. Causing to drop or flow.

A اسجح *asjah*, Fine, well-proportioned (face).

A اسجد *asjad*, Troubled with a swelled foot.

A اسجر *asjar*, One who has a blood-shot eye. Limpid (lake). A lion.

A اسجل *asjal*, Long and swaggy (camel's udder).

A اسجم *asjam*, Silent, not braying (camel).

A اسجوعة *usjūʻat*, (pl. اساجيع *asājīʻ*) Rhythm, cadence. An oration written or recited in rhythm. Cooing of turtles. The braying of a camel.

A اسجهرار *isjihrār*, (v. n. 4 of سجهر Q) Growing long and spreading out (a plant). Appearing and disappearing (mirage, or vapour سراب *sarāb*). Meeting, blowing towards one (winds).

A اسحاء *is-hāʼ*, (v. n. 4 of سحي) Covering or binding (a book) with a membrane of the papyrus. Possessing this membrane in abundance.

A اسحات *as-hāt*, (pl. of سحت *suht* or *suhut*) Unlawful gains. *Is-hāt*, (v. n. 4 of سحت) Extirpating. Making unlawful gain.

A اسحار *as-hār*, (pl. of سحر *sahr*) The lungs (of animals). (pl. of سحر *sahar*) Twilights, dawns. مقطعة الاسحار *mukattiʻatu'l as-hār*, A hare (the lungs of which often burst in running). *Is-hār*, (v. n. 4 of سحر) Rising, going, or coming early in the morning, at the dawn of day.

A اسحارة *is-hārrat*, *as-hārrat* (اسحار *is-hārr* or *as-hārr*) A certain pot-herb which fattens cattle.

G اسحارة *as-hāra*, Mallows.

A اسحاف *is-hāf*, (v. n. 4 of سحف) Selling the fat سحفة *sahfat*. Bearing the clouds along (wind).

A اسحاق *is-hāk*, (v. n. 4 of سحق) Removing. Putting to a distance. Becoming thread-bare (a garment). Being worn (the hoof of a camel). Shrinking after milking (the teats). Isaac.

A اسحاقية *is-hākiya*, Name of a sect.

A اسحال *as-hāl*, (pl. of سحل *sahl*) Stuffs made of white cotton. *Is-hāl*, (v. n. 4 of سحل) Discovering (one) to be an object of blame and abuse.

A اسحام *is-hām*, (v. n. 4 of سحم) Pouring forth rain (a cloud).

A اسحت *as-hat*, Barren (year).

A اسحر *as-har*, More or most of a magician.

A اسحفان *us-hufān*, Name of a plant used medicinally for sciatica.

A اسحل *is-hil*, Name of a tree from the wood of which they make dentifrices.

A اسحلان *us-halān*, Tall (youth) with long and lanky locks, shaved here and there.

A اسحلاني *is-hilānīy*, Long-bearded (man).

A اسحلانية *is-hilānīyat*, Tall, handsome, and attractive (woman).

A اسحم *as-ham*, Black. A horn. The nipple. A wine-bottle. A cloud. Blood, in which conspirators at the time of swearing dip their hands. A ringlet. Night. Name of an idol.

A اسحمان *is-himān*, Black. Name of a mountain. *Us-humān*, A kind of tree.

A اسحنطار *is-hintār*, (v. n. 3 of سحطر not used) Stretching one's self. Leaning, inclining. Being wide and long. Falling on the face.

A اسحنفار *is-hinfār*, (v. n. 3 of سحفر Q not used) Going quick. Being straight (a road). Being abundant (rain). Being diffuse and verbose (an orator). Preaching with fluency.

A اسحنكاك *is-hinkāk*, (v. n. 3 of سحكك Q) Being dark (the night). Being difficult and unintelligible (a speech).

A اسحوان *us-huwān*, Tall, handsome. A glutton.

A اسحوب *us-hūb*, A great eater and drinker.

A اسحوف *us-hūf* or *is-hawf*, (A camel) whose teats, having large orifices, give milk plentifully.

A اسحية *as-hiyat*, (pl. of سحاء *sihāʼ*) The bands of a book. (pl. of سحاية *sihāyat*) Parts peeled or scraped off, membranes.

A اسحية *us-hīyat*, The periosteum.

P اسخاره رومي *ishhāra rūmī*, A thorny grass.

A اسخاط *iskhāt*, (v. n. 4 of سخط) Enraging.

A اسخال *iskhāl*, (v. n. 4 of سخل) Keeping back, hindering. Leaving behind.

A اسخان *iskhān*, (v. n. 4 of سخن) Boiling (water). Heating. Causing to weep.

A اسخم *askham*, Black.

A اسخن *askhan*, Very hot, hotter, hottest.

A اسخنة *ishhinat*, Feverish heat, a disease, the opposite of ابردة *ibridat*.

A اسخي *askhaʼ*, More or most liberal.

A اسخياء *askhiyāʼ*, (pl. of سخي *sakhīy*) Liberal.

A اسخيتات *iskhītāt*, (v. n. 11 of سخت) Subsiding (a swelling).

A آسد *āsud*, (pl. of اسد *asad*) Lions.

A اسد *asd* (v. n. of اسد) Stirring up sedition. Making havock. (for ازد *azd*) Name of the founder of a tribe. *Usd*, (pl. of اسد *asad*) Lions. *Asad*, (v. n. of اسد) Being seized with horror at the sight of a lion. Resembling a lion. Being angry. Being silly and foolish. *Asad*, (pl. آساد *āsād*, اسود *usūd*, اسودة *usūdat*, اسد *usd*, آسد *āsud*, اسدان *usdān*, and ماسدة *maʼsadat*) A lion. The sign Leo. اسد الارض *asadu'l arz*, The lion of the earth, the humble lion, the chameleon. A species of plant. اسد العدس *asadu'l ʻadas*, (The lion of pulse) Broom-rape. اسد الله *asadu'llāh*, The lion of God, to which the Persians add generally الغالب *al ghālib* (the conqueror), by which epithets they distinguish the Khalif Alīy. اسد الدين *asadu'd dīn*, Lion of the faith; اسد الدولة *asadu'd dawlat*, Lion of the state: (Muhammadan surnames).

A اسّد *issad*, An aged goat.

A اسدّ *asadd*, Straight, even, firm (business).

A اسداء *isdāʼ*, (v. n. 4 of سدي) Fitting to the loom, fastening to the warp. Sending (a camel) to graze without a keeper. Hitting the nail upon the head. Having dates ripening at the stalk (a palm), becoming flaccid and pendulous (the envelope of the dates). Making peace, composing differences. Conferring a favour, doing a kindness.

P اسدآباد *asad-ābād*, A city near Hamadān.

A اسداد *asdād*, Obstacles, obstructions. *Isdād*, (v. n. 4 of سدّ) Going the right way to work, hitting the nail upon the head, or seeking to do so.

A اسدار *isdār*, (v. n. 4 of سدر) Dazzling the eyes (the sun).

A اسداس *asdās*, (pl. of سدس *suds* or *sudus*) Sixth parts. *Isdās*, (v. n. 4 of سدس) Being six in number. Having camels which drink on the sixth day. Shedding teeth in the eighth year.

A اسداف *isdāf*, (v. n. 4 of سدف) Throwing aside or lifting up a veil or curtain. Letting fall a veil. Showing light (as the dawn). Lighting (a candle or lamp). Growing dark (night). Sleeping. Waxing blind or dim-sighted (through age or hunger). Coming in or going away at day-break.

A اسدال *asdāl*, (pl. of سدل *sidl*) Veils. *Isdāl*, (v. n. 4 of سدل) Letting down her gown, hair, or veil, (a woman).

A اسدام *asdām*, (pl. of سدم *sadam* or *sadim*)

Widely diffused (waters). (pl. of سدم *sudum* or *sudm*) Concealed wells filled with earth.

A اسدان *asdān*, (pl. of سدن *sadan*) Veils, curtains. Awnings over camel-litters. *Usdān*, (pl. of اسد *asad*) Lions.

A اسدة *asadat*, A lioness. *Asidat*, A wooden enclosure, a sheep-fold. (A bitch) trained to hunt.

A اسدّة *asiddat*, (pl. of سدّ *sadd*) Infirmities of the body (as blindness, deafness, or dumbness).

A اسدران *asdarāni*, (du.) Two veins in the eye. جاء يضرب اسدريه *jāʼa yazribu asdarayhi*, He came striking his sides or shoulders, *i.e.* empty, without having attained his object.

A اسدف *asdaf*, Black.

A اسدل *asdal*, (pl. سدل *sudul*) Pendulous, dangling. *Asdul*, (pl. of سدل *sidl*) Veils. (pl. of سديل *sadīl*) Awnings, canopies over camel-litters.

A اسديّ *usdīy*, (Cloth) fitted to the loom. A kind of plant. *Usdīy* or *asdīy*, The warp of a web. *Asadīy*, Lion-like. Of the tribe of اسد *asad*.

A اسدية *asdiyat*, (pl. of سداة *sadāt*) Warps.

P آسر *āsur*, A thriving field of (corn).

A اسر *asr*, (v. n. of اسر) Binding, tying. Creating. A chain. باسره *bi asrihi*, The whole of it, *i.e.* it, chain and all. باسرهم *bi asrihim*, All of them. *Usr*, Retention or stoppage of urine, strangury. عود اسر *ʻūdu usrin*, A piece of wood placed under the belly of one troubled with suppression of urine. *Asar*, Glass. *Usur*, Feet or supporters of a bed or throne. (pl. of اسار *isār*) Bonds, fetters.

A اسرّ *asarr*, More or most joyous. Hollow. An intimate friend. One who meddles in another's business. (A camel) hurt or galled in the breast. One who comes uninvited. في اسرّ الازمان *fī asarri'l azmān*, In good time, in a convenient season, at the happiest of moments, to the purpose.

A اسراء *isrāʼ*, (v. n. 4 of سرأ) Being the time for locusts to deposit their eggs. (v. n. 4 of سرا for سرو) Banishing grief (from the mind). (v. n. 4 of سري) Carrying off by night. Travelling by night. Going to a part of Arabia called سراة *sarāt*. *Usarāʼ*, (pl. of اسير *asīr*) Captives.

A اسراج *isrāj*, (v. n. 4 of سرج) Saddling (a horse). Lighting a candle or lamp.

A اسراد *isrād*, (v. n. 4 of سرد) Bearing unripe sour dates (a palm-tree).

A اسرار *asrār*, (pl. of سرّ *sirr*) Secrets, mysteries, confidential concerns. (pl. of سرر *sarar* and *surar*) Lines, creases, lineaments on the face or palms of the hands. P اسرار زمين *asrāri zamīn*, Plants. A *Isrār*, (v. n. 4 of سرّ) Concealing. Divulging, discovering. Causing one's words to reach another. Entrusting with a secret.

A اسراع *isrāʻ*, (v. n. 4 of سرع) Making haste, being quick. Causing or ordering to make haste, hastening, quickening. Having swift-paced camels.

A اسراف *isrāf*, (v. n. 4 of سرف) Wasting, squandering, lavishing. Eating what is unlawful. Prodigality, waste, abuse of wealth, extravagance.

SY اسراف *isrāf*, A slave.

A اسرافيل *isrāfīl*, The angel of death, who is to blow the last trumpet. A seraph.

A اسرافين *isrāfīn*, The seraphim.

A اسراق *isrāk*, (v. n. 4 of سرق) Being weak and languid. Lagging behind in order to steal away.

A اسرال *isrāl*, Israel.

A اسرام *asrām*, Extremities of the intestines.

A اسراييل *isrāyīl*, (or اسرائيل *isrāʼīl*, اسرايين *isrāyīn*, or اسرائين *isrāʼīn*) Israel. بني اسرائيل *banī isrāʼīl*, The children of Israel.

A P اسرب *usrub*, (also اسربّ *usrubb*) Lead.

P اسرب گداخته *usrubi gudākhta*, Molten lead.

A اسربيّ *usrubīy*, Leaden.

P اسرپ *usrup*, Lead.

A اسرة *usrat*, (pl. اسر *usar*) An impenetrable coat of mail. Affinity, kindred. Kinsmen, paternal relations.

A اسرّة *asirrat*, (pl. of سرّ *sirr*) The best and richest parts of a valley. (pl. of سرّ *surr*) The parts of the navel-string which are cut off. (pl. of سرار *sirār*) Lines on the palm of the hand or on the forehead. (pl. of سرير *sarīr*) Thrones, couches.

A اسرع *asraʻ*, More or most swift, swifter, swiftest, fleeter, fleetest, quicker, quickest.

A P اسرف *usruf*, Lead.

A اسرق *asrak*, More or most addicted to stealing.

P اسرنج *isrinj*, Cinnabar, vermilion, red lead, sandyx, burnt ceruse (of which they make an ointment for wounds). Cymbals.

A اسرنداء *isrindāʼ*, (v. n. 15 of سرد) Being superior, overbearing: using opprobrious words.

P اسروش *usrosh*, An angel. An agreeable voice. Name of the 17th day of the month.

P اسروشنه *israwshana* or *usrūshana*, Name of a city in Turkistān.

A اسروع *usrūʻ*, (pl. اساريع *asārīʻ*) A kind of worm (found among pot-herbs). A nerve running along the inside of the fore and hind-leg of an antelope. A line traced on a bow.

A اسريٰ *asra'*, (pl. of اسير *asīr*) Captives.

A اسرياء *asriyāʼ*, (pl. of سريّ *sarīy*) Liberal.

A اسرية *asriyat*, (pl. of سريّ *sarīy*) Rivulets running to palm-trees.

P آسريس *āsrīs*, A race-ground.

P اسريشم *isrīsham*, Glue, gum, isinglass.

A اسس *asas*, (pl. آساس *āsās*) A foundation.

A اسس *usus*, (pl. of اساس *asās*) Foundations.

A اسطّ *asatt*, One who has long feet.

A اسطار *astār*, (pl. of سطر *satar*) Lines, rows, strings. Writings. *Istār*, (v. n. 4 of سطر) Skipping a line, passing over in reading. Blundering in reading. A fable, fiction, story, romance.

A اسطارة *istārat*, (pl. اساطير *asātīr*) A fable, fiction. Any thing trifling.

A اسطاعة *istāʻat*, (for استطاعة *istitāʻat*) Submission, obedience.

A اسطام *istām*, A poker. Chips, fuel. Iron.

A اسطان *astān*, Copper-vessels.

A اسطبّة *ustubbat*, The refuse of cotton or flax (which falls in the carding or dressing), stupe.

P اسطبر *istabr*, Thick.

G اسطبل *istabl*, A stable.

G اسطخدور *istakhdūr*, Rosemary.

P اسطخر *istakhr*, Persepolis.

A اسطر *astur*, (pl. of سطر *satr*) Lines, strings, rows. Writings.

G اسطر *ustur*, A balance. Name of a king.

G اسطراغيلس *istarāghilus*, A die, dice.

P اسطرخ *istarakh*, A lake. Persepolis.

P اسطرخا *astirkhā*, Red orpiment.

G اسطرلاب *usturlāb*, An astrolabe. P سطرلاب چهارم *usturlābi chahārum*, The sun.

G اسطرنونا *usturnūnā*, Astronomy.

A اسطع *astaʻ*, Long-necked (ostrich).

G سطفاين *istafīn*, A carrot.

G اسطفين *istafīn* or *ustafīn*, A carrot.

G اسطقس *ustukus*, An element. اسطقسات اقليدس *ustukusāti uklīdas*, Euclid's Elements.

A اسطمّ *ustumm*, The middle of the sea.

A اسطمّة *ustummat*, (pl. of اساطم *asātim*) The midst of the people. Nobles, chiefs. A place where people are assembled.

A اسطوان *usturwān*, High, lofty. Long-necked.

A اسطوانة *usturwānat*, (pl. اساطين *asātīn*) A column, cylinder. The leg of a quadruped. Veretrum. A portico supported by pillars. اهل الاسطوانة *ahlu'l ustuwānat*, Followers of the Stoics.

G اسطوخودوس *ustūkhūdūs*, French lavender.

G اسطور *ustūr*, (or اسطورة *ustūrat*) (pl. اساطير *asātīr*) A fable, story.

G اسطون *ustūn*, A carrot.

A اسطي *usta'*, A barber.

A اسطير *istīr*, (or اسطيرة *istīrat*) (pl. اساطير *asātīr*) A story, romance, or trifling thing.

A اسعاء *isʻāʼ*, (v. n. 4 of سعي) Stimulating to exertion, obliging or setting one to seek for a thing. Setting any one to accuse or calumniate. Giving any one a thing sought after.

A اسعاد *isʻād*, (v. n. 4 of سعد) Making happy or prosperous, blessing, favouring, assisting, seconding, supporting, aiding. Helping another woman to weep and lament (a woman).

A اسعار *asʻār*, (pl. of سعر *siʻr*) Prices fixed upon provisions. *Isʻār*, (v. n. 4 of سعر) Kindling (a fire). Stirring up (war). Fixing the price of provisions, assizing. Causing evil to overtake.

A اسعاط *isʻāt*, (v. n. 4 of سعط) Injecting medicine into the nostrils. Piercing (the nose) with a spear. Indoctrinating, instructing profoundly.

A اسعاف *isʻāf*, (v. n. 4 of سعف) Promoting or finishing any business. Going near. Coming within reach of the hunter (game). Coming down to and joining one's family.

A اسعال *isʿāl,* (v. n. 4 of سعل) Exhilarating. Causing any one to act and behave like a goblin.

A اسعان *isʿān,* (v. n. 4 of سعن) Making a canopy, awning, or shady booth (called سعنة *suʿnat*).

A اسعد *asʿad,* More or most happy. A kind of scab incident to camels.

A اسعر *asʿar,* Lean. Changed in colour.

A اسعف *asʿaf,* (A camel) scabby or mangy and therefore bald about the mouth. (A horse) having white hairs hanging over the forehead.

A اسغاب *isghāb,* (v. n. 4 of سغب) Enduring hunger and penury.

A اسغام *isghām,* (v. n. 4 of سغم) Feeding well, bringing up delicately. Vexing to the heart.

A اسغان *asghān,* Bad aliments.

P آسغده *āsaghda,* Prepared, ready. *Āsughda,* A fire-brand, half-burnt wood.

P اسغده *asaghda,* Prepared, ready.

P اسغديدن *asaghdīdan,* To fashion, finish.

P اسغر *usghur,* (or اسغرنه *usghurna*) A porcupine.

A آسف *āsif,* Grieved, indignant, angry.

A أسف *asifa,* (fut. يأسف *yaʾsafu*) He grieved.

A اسف *asaf,* (v. n. of اسف) Grieving exceedingly. Being angry with. Sadness, grief, anguish, pain. Name of a village. *Asif,* Lean, barren (soil). Grieved, indignant, angry.

A اسفاء *isfāʾ,* (v. n. 4 of سفو or سفي) Sweeping away the dust (wind). Carrying away earth. Hurrying on to levity and fickleness. Injuring, ruining, destroying. Running away (a camel) Purchasing a swift mule. Losing its down (a thistle). Losing flesh (a camel). Having a strong beard (corn). Choosing. Becoming light, silly, and senseless. *Usafāʾ,* (pl. of اسيف *asīf*) Grieved.

P اسفابور *asfābūr,* A city founded by Nūshirwān.

A اسفاح *isfāḥ,* (v. n. 4 of سفح) Being free from risk, secure from danger. Making (a horse) run without laying any stakes.

A اسفاد *isfād,* (v. n. 4 of سفد) Causing (goats, camels, kine, birds, or wild beasts) to generate.

A اسفار *asfār,* Travellers. (pl. of سفر *safr*) Files (for polishing). (pl. of سفر *sifr*) Books, volumes. (pl. of سفر *safar*) Journeys, travels. *Isfār,* (v. n. 4 of سفر) Breaking (like the morning), shining, becoming light, bright, or splendid. Putting a leathern or iron curb across (a camel's nose). Entering on the brightness of the morning. Losing its leaf, having it carried away (a tree). Raging (war). Feeding camels on dried leaves. Going about where they like (camels).

P اسفار *isfār,* Myrtle.

A اسفارينى *isfārayniy,* A native of Isfarain.

A اسفاط *asfāt,* (pl. of سفط) Chests, boxes, sacks.

A اسفاف *isfāf,* (v. n. 4 of سفّ) Weaving, platting (palm-leaves). Looking intently at any object. Flying low (a cloud, or a bird). Attending to the minutiæ of things. Having the face bespattered. Conquering, overcoming. Being changed, altered (the face). Lowering (his) head with intent to bite (a stallion). Pouring medicine into a wound. Engaging in mean pursuits. Running away, absconding. Giving (a camel) dry food. Putting the bit into (a horse's) mouth.

A اسفاق *isfāk,* (v. n. 4 of سفق) Shutting (a door). Opening (a door).

G اسفاناج *isfānāj,* (or اسفاناخ) Spinage.

P اسفانبر *asfāmbur,* Name of a city.

A اسفاه *isfāh,* (v. n. 4 of سفه) Causing one to drink much without quenching the thirst.

P آسفته *āsufta,* A fire-brand, quenched brand.

P آسفده *āsufda,* Prompt, ready.

G اسفراج *isfirāj,* Asparagus.

P اسفراين *isfarāyin,* Name of a city in Khurāsān.

A اسفرة *asfirat,* (pl. of سفار *sifār*) Curbs of leather or iron across the noses of camels.

P اسفرسب *asfrasb,* or اسفرسف A race-course.

P اسفرم *isfaram,* Myrtle: any odoriferous plant.

P اسفرنج *isfaranj,* (or اسفرنگ *isfarang*) Name of a district in Samarcand.

P اسفرود *isfarūd,* The bird called قطا *kaṭā* in Arabic, one of the tetraonidæ, or grouse family.

P اسفست *isfist* or *usfust,* A medicinal plant.

P اسفستى *isfistī,* Abounding in اسفست *isfist.*

A اسفع *asfaʿ,* A hawk. A wild bull. Black. Black inclining to red. Sheep ready to be milked.

A اسفل *asfal,* Lower, lowest. اسفل سافلين *asfalu sāfilīna,* The lowest of the low, the most infamous. Old age. Destruction, ruin. Vain, useless. Error, a devious road.

A اسفلنج *isfilanj,* Goat's beard (a shrub).

G اسفناج *isfināj,* Spinage. P اسفناج رومي *isfināji rūmī,* Orach.

G اسفنج *isfanj,* A sponge. A kind of dumpling.

P اسفنجه *isfanja,* A sponge.

P اسفند *isfand,* A species of rue. Name of a province of Nīshābūr. Name of the twelfth month. اسفند اسفيد *isfandi isfed,* White mustard-seed.

A اسفند *isfand* or *isfind,* Wine.

P اسفندارمذ *isfandārmuz,* Name of the twelfth month of the solar year. Name of the fifth day of every month. Name of the angel who presides over the twelfth month. The earth.

P اسفندمذ *isfandmuz,* Name of the third of the five intercalary days used in olden time.

P اسفنديار *isfandyār,* The son of Gushtāsp, of the first dynasty of Persian kings. Name of the genius who presides over the day and the month اسفندار *isfandār.* Divine power and goodness.

A اسفنط *isfint,* A kind of wine.

A اسفه *asfah,* More or most foolish.

P اسفهبد *isfah-bud,* A general, a commander-in-chief. A title of the kings of Persia.

P اسفهبد خوره *isfahbud khwara,* Speech.

P اسفهسالار *isfah-sālār,* Commander of an army.

A اسفى *asfaʾ,* Slow-paced (according to some), swift-paced (mule). (A horse) thin of hair about the fore-locks. *Asafaʾ,* Safi, a town in Morocco.

P اسفيجاب *isfījāb,* Name of a city in Turkistān.

P اسفيد *isfed,* White, bright, splendid.

P اسفيداج *isfedāj,* White water, ceruse, a paint used by women. اسفيداج الجصّاصين *isfedāju'l jassānīn,* Shell-lime.

P اسفيداد الرصاص *isfedādu'r rasās,* Whiting.

P اسفيدار *isfedār,* The white poplar; the aspen.

P اسفيدبا *isfed-bā,* (or اسفيدباج *isfed-bāj*) A kind of dish made of meat, onions, butter, cheese, &c., or of bread and milk.

P اسفيد دشت *isfed dasht,* Name of a village.

A اسفيذاج *isfīzāj,* (from P اسفيداج) Whiting.

G اسفيوش *isfayūsh,* Seed of flea-wort.

A اسقاء *iskāʾ,* (v. n. 4 of سقي) Watering, giving drink. Sending rain. Directing, guiding to water. Wishing well, saying سقاك الله *sakāka'llāh,* May God water thee! Bestowing a ready-made water-bottle, or a skin to be used as such. Defaming.

A اسقاب *iskāb,* (v. n. 4 of سقب) Being near. Bringing near.

A اسقاد *iskād,* (v. n. 4 of سقد) Extenuating, emaciating (a fat horse).

A اسقار *iskār,* (v. n. 4 of سقر) Distilling سقر *sakr* (a date-tree).

A اسقاط *askāt,* (pl. of سقط *sakat*) Goods, furniture of little value. The meanest sorts of utensils. *Iskāt,* (v. n. 4 of سقط) Causing to fall, dropping, letting fall. Shedding (a tooth). Endeavouring to make (any one) blunder, lie, or blab. Casting her young (a camel). Producing an abortion. Committing a blunder in writing or speaking. Repenting; being confounded. Taking away. اسقاط الاجنّة *iskātu'l ajinnat,* The producing of abortions.

A اسقاع *iskāʿ,* (v. n. 4 of سقع) Being changed (colour).

G اسقال *iskāl,* A squill. A wild onion, a scallion.

A اسقلان *askālān,* Askelon in Palestine.

A اسقام *askām,* (pl. of سقم *sakam*) Diseases, infirmities. *Iskām,* (v. n. 4 of سقم) Making sick.

A اسقان *askān,* Extenuated, lank sides. *Iskān,* (v. n. 4 of سقن) Polishing (a sword).

A اسقب *askub,* (pl. of سقب *sakb*) Male fœtuses (of camels).

A اسقح *askah,* Bald.

A اسقطرى *uskutraʾ,* The island of Socotra.

A اسقع *askaʿ,* (pl. اساقع *asākiʿ*) A small greenish bird with a white head. A horse or bird with a white head.

A اسقف *askaf,* Tall, large-boned (man). Bare, hairless (camel). Long and crooked-necked (ostrich). Crooked. Meal, flour. *Uskuf,* (or *uskuff*) (pl. اساقف *asākif* or اساقفة *asākifat*) A bishop.

A اسقفية *uskufiyat*, Episcopacy. A bishopric.
G اسقل *askal*, Squills.
G اسقليباس *askalbiyās*, The plant asclepias.
G اسقلطس *iskaltas*, Jew's-pitch.
P اسقنبه *iskimba*, Satan.
G اسقنقور *iskankūr*, The skink (a kind of lizard).
G اسقورديون *uskūrdiyūn*, Germander (a plant).
G اسقورون *uskūrūn*, Dross of metal, iron-scoria.
G اسقولو *uskūlū*, The sea-cow.
G اسقولوس *uskūlūs*, Glue, starch.
G اسقولوفندريون *iskūlūfandariyūn*, Sclopendrium, hart's tongue.

A اسقية *askiyat*, (pl. of سقاء *sikāʼ*) Leathern water-bottles. (pl. of سقي *siky*) Full of water. Particles of water. (pl. of سقيّ *sakīy*) Watery clouds.
G اسقيل *iskīl*, A wild onion, a scallion.
P آسك *āsak*, A place near ارّجان *arrajān*.
P اسك *isk* or *ask*, A courier. A post-horse.
A اسكّ *asakk*, Small-eared, or destitute of ears. Deaf. (pl. سكّ *sukk*) A male ostrich. A male ostrich with a looseness in the belly.
A اسكاب *iskāb*, A shoemaker. A blacksmith.
A اسكابة *iskābat*, The stopple of a leathern bottle.
A اسكات *askāt*, A wandering soldier. A strolling, dissolute fellow. The remains of a thing. The temperate season after the heat of summer. *Iskāt*, (v. n. 4 of سكت) Pacifying, soothing, silencing. Breaking off a discourse, ceasing to speak.
A اسكاتة *iskātat*, (v. n. of سكت) Being silent.
A اسكار *iskār*, (v. n. 4 of سكر) Intoxicating.
A اسكاف *iskāf*, (v. n. 4 of سكف) Being a shoemaker, or a mechanic in general. (pl. اساكيف *asākīf* or اساكفة *asākifat*) A shoemaker. A workman, mechanic, carpenter, or blacksmith. Clever at any thing. Wine-dregs or lees.
A اسكال *askāl*, Sorts of large black fish.
P اسكالش *iskālish*, Thought, reflection. Thoughtful, imaginative.
A اسكان *askān*, (pl. of سكن *sakn*) Victuals, aliments. *Iskān*, (v. n. 4 of سكن) Giving repose. Stilling, quieting. Making (a letter) quiescent, depriving it of a vowel. Causing one to stay, remain, continue to dwell, giving house-room. Making poor, miserable, or contemptible. Becoming so.
P اسكانه *iskāna*, The calf of the leg.
P اسكاوند *askāwand*, A mountain in Sīstān.
A اسكبّة *uskubbat*, The threshold of a door.
A اسكتان *askatāni* or *iskatāni*, (dual) (pl. اسك *ish*, *ask*, or *isak*) The two lips or sides of the matrix.
P اسكدار *askudār*, *uskudār*, or *iskudār*, A courier, a postman. A relay of post-horses or letter-carriers. A postman's bag. Name of a king.
P اسكردن *askardan*, To bruise, to grind.
P اسكرك *iskirk*, The hiccough.
P اسكره *uskara* or *uskarra*, A saucer, platter, dish.
A اسكف *askaf*, A shoemaker.
A اسكفّ *uskuff*, The extremity of the lower eyelid, from which the hairs grow.
A اسكفّة *uskuffat*, A threshold.
A اسكن *askan*, More or most quiet, placid, gentle. اسكن للعطش *askanu li'l ʻatash*, Better or best quencher of thirst.
P اسكنج *askanj*, Fetid breath.
P اسكند *askand*, A rope-dancer. Rope-dancing.
P اسكندان *askandān*, A lock. A tomb-stone.
G اسكندر *iskandar* or *askandar*, Alexander. Alexander is said to be the son of دارا *dārā*, who married ناهيد *nāhīd*, daughter of فيلقوس *fīlkūs*. On account of her fetid breath, her husband sent her back to her father, who cured her by the use of اسكندروس *iskandarūs*, Garlic. Hence she gave to her son, when born, the name of Alexander.
A اسكندرانيّ *iskandarānīy*, Alexandrian.
G اسكندروس *iskandarūs*, Garlic. Name of the mother or son of Alexander.
A اسكندرون *iskandarūn*, Alexandria or Alexandretta, near Aleppo in Syria (Scanderoon).
A اسكندريّ *iskandarīy*, Alexandrian.
A اسكندريّة *iskandarīyat*, Alexandria in Egypt. Sixteen cities of this name are ascribed to Alexander.
P اسكنك *iskinak*, A wimble, an auger.
P آس كننده *ās-kunanda*, Revolving mill-wheel.
P اسكنه *iskana*, An auger.
T اسكوار *askwār*, Scutari (in Turkey).
A اسكوب *uskūb*, Lightning flashing on the surface of the earth. A row of palm-trees. A shoemaker. A continued rain. A blacksmith. Flowing, current (water).
A اسكوبة *uskūbat*, A stopple, a plug.
A اسكوف *uskūf*, A shoemaker.
P اسكيز *iskīz*, (or اسكيزه) A kick, caper, bound.
P اسكر *usgur*, A porcupine.
P آسگون *āsgūn*, The Caspian. Name of a country.
A اسل *asal*, A bulrush. A tree having long prickles. A prickle, thorn, point of a spear, or ear of corn. Spears, arrows, prickles of palm-trees. Leafless branches of which mats are made.
A اسلاء *aslāʼ*, (pl. of سلا *salaʼ*) Membranes enveloping the fœtus in the womb, secundines. *Islāʼ*, (v. n. 4 of سلا for سلو) Consoling, comforting: causing to forget. Being secure from wild beasts.
A اسلاب *aslāb*, (pl. of سلب *salab*) Spoils. *Islāb*, (v. n. 4 of سلب) Losing leaves or fruit (tree).
A اسلاح *islāh*, (v. n. 4 of سلح) Causing to mute.
A اسلاس *islās*, (v. n. 4 of سلس) Producing an abortion (a camel). Having the roots of its branches torn up or laid bare (a palm-tree).
A اسلاع *aslāʻ*, (pl. of سلع *silʻ*) Fissures in mountains. Similes, similitudes. Alike, equals. اسلاع الفرس *aslāʻu'l faras*, The flesh adhering to the muscle running from the thigh to the heel in a horse that is fat. *Islāʻ*, (v. n. 4 of سلع) Receiving a blow, or cut, or fracture on the head.
A اسلاف *aslāf*, (pl. of سلف *silf*) The husbands of a man's wife's sisters. (pl. of سلف *salaf*) Ancestors, remote or ancient kindred. *Islāf*, (v. n. 4 of سلف) Attaining the age of forty-five (a woman). Paying before due, or in advance. Levelling (ground) for sowing.
A اسلاق *aslāk*, (pl. of سلقة *salkat*) Plain level grounds, of good soil. *Islāk*, (v. n. 4 of سلق) Passing a stick through the handles of two sacks for the conveniency of carriage. Hunting a she-wolf.
A اسلاك *aslāk*, (pl. of سلكة *silkat*) Sewing threads. *Islāk*, (v. n. 4 of سلك) Inserting one thing into another. Causing (one) to thread his way. Thrusting (one's hand into one's bosom).
A اسلال *aslāl*, (pl. of سلّة *sallat*) Canisters or wardrobes in which victuals or clothes are kept. *Islāl*, (v. n. 4 of سلّ) Extracting, drawing out gently. Visiting with consumption. Bribing. A present for the purpose of corruption and bribery. Theft.
• A اسلام *aslām*, (pl. of سلم *silm*) Those who cultivate peace and friendship. (pl. of سلم *salam*) Certain thorny trees. *Islām*, (v. n. 4 of سلم) Paying in advance. Producing the tree سلم *salam*. Yielding obedience to the will of God, submitting, humbling one's self, surrendering or resigning one's self to the divine disposal. Embracing the religion of Muhammad, turning Musulmān: conversion to the Muhammadan faith. The true or orthodox faith among the Muhammadans. A country in which Muhammadism reigns. Being in health, peace, and safety. Escaping, becoming free. Deceiving, betraying, abandoning. اهل اسلام *ahlu'l islām*, The faithful, true believers, Muhammadans.
T اسلامبول *islāmbūl* or *islāmbol*, Constantinople.
A اسلاميّ *islāmīy*, Faithful, orthodox. A Muhammadan, an Ottoman. احكام اسلاميّه *aḥkāmi islāmīya*, Precepts of religion. ممالك اسلاميّه *mamāliki islāmīya*, The Ottoman Empire.
A اسلة *asalat*, A bulrush. Any straight tree or stick. The tip (of the tongue or elbow). The point (of a spear or thorn). The sharp-pointed toe of a shoe. The pizzle (of a bull or camel).
A اسلت *aslat*, One whose nose has been cut off.
A اسلحباب *islihbāb*, (v. n. 4 of سلحب Q) Being straight, open, and extended (a road).
A اسلحة *aslihat*, (pl. of سلاح *silāh*) Military arms.
A اسلخ *aslakh*, Bald-headed. Very red.
A اسلخاخ *islikhkhākh*, A lying on one's side.
A اسلط *aslat*, More or most eloquent.
A اسلع *aslaʻ*, Cracked in the hoof. Leprous.
A اسلغ *aslagh*, Hard tough flesh of old cattle, unfit for cooking. Raw, exceedingly red. Leprous. Vile, abject, mean, sordid.
A اسلغباب *islighbāb*, (v. n. 4 of سلغب Q) Producing feathers (a bird).
A اسلف *asluf*, (pl. of سلف *salf*) Large wallets. Undressed leathers.
A اسلم *aslam*, More or most mild. *Aslum*, (pl.

of سلم *salm*) One-handled buckets.

P اسلنج *aslanj*, Horse-tail (a plant).

A اسلنطاء *islinṭāʼ*, (v. n. 3 of سلطا Q) Raising one's self up to look at any thing.

A اسلنطاح *islinṭāḥ*, (v. n. 3 of سلطح Q) Falling on the face. Being wide (a valley).

A اسلنطاع *islinṭāʻ*, A lying on one's back.

A اسلنقاء *islinḳāʼ*, A lying on one's back.

A اسلنقاع *islinḳāʻ*, (v. n. 3 of سلقع Q) Flashing, glaring (lightning). Becoming heated by the sun (gravel).

F اسلوب *uslūb*, A kind of food. Name of a sage and a king.

A اسلوب *uslūb*, (pl. اساليب *asālīb*) Order, way, mode, means, measure, manner, method, form. A lion's neck. A prominence of nose.

A اسلوبا *uslūban* Methodically.

A اسلوفة *uslūfat*, The relationship which a man bears to another who has married his wife's sister.

A اسلهباب *islihbāb*, (v. n. 4 of سلهب Q) Being long in the body and stretching out (a horse).

A اسلهمام *islihmām*, (v. n. 4 of سلهم Q) Changing (colour or smell).

A اسلي *aslīy*, Pronounced, or formed by the tip of the tongue.

A اسلئة *asliʼat*, (pl. of سلاء *silāʼ*) Melted butters (of cow's milk).

A اسليح *islīḥ*, A species of herb, the feeding on which increases the milk of camels.

A اسليخ *islīkh*, Name of a plant.

G اسليقون *islīḳūn*, Vermilion, red lead.

P اسليمي *islīmī*, A species of painting.

A اسم *ism* or *usm*, (pl. اسماء *asmāʼ*, اسماوات *asmāwāt*, اسامي *asāmīy*, اسامي *asāmī*, and آسام *āsām*) A name. A noun. اسم اعظم *ismi aʻzam*, or اسم عظيم *ismi ʻazīm*, The great name, the name of God. The great names or attributes of the Deity are 100, of which the following five are most generally made use of: الله *allāh*, (the He), رحمان *raḥmān*, (merciful), رحيم *raḥīm*, (compassionate), رب *rabb*, (Lord), مالك *mālik*, (King). اسم استفهام *ismi istifhām*, An interrogative particle. اسم اشارت *ismi ishārat*, A demonstrative pronoun. اسم آلت *ismi ālat*, Noun of instrument. اسم با مسمّى *ismi bā musamma'*, Worthy of the name (it bears), whose name is expressive of its qualities. اسم تامّ *ismi tāmm*, A perfect noun. اسم تصغير *ismi tasghīr*, A diminutive noun. اسم تفضيل *ismi tafẓīl*, A comparative or a superlative noun. اسم جامد *ismi jāmid*, A primitive noun. اسم جمع *ismi jamʻ*, The plural number. اسم جنس *ismi jins*, A generic or appellative noun. اسم زمان *ismi zamān*, Adverb of time. اسم سامي *ismi sāmī*, A noble or exalted name. اسم ضمير *ismi ẓamīr*, A pronoun. اسم ظرف *ismi ẓarf*, Adverb of time and place. اسم عدد *ismi ʻadad*, A noun of number. اسم فاعل *ismi fāʻil*, Noun of agency. اسم فعل *ismi fiʻl*, A verbal noun. اسم كثرت *ismi kasrat*, Noun of multitude. اسم مبالغة *ismi mubālagha*, Noun of excess, or intensity. اسم مرّة *ismi marra*, Noun of unity: as, قعدة *kuʻdat*, A single sitting. اسم مشتق *ismi mushtaḳḳ*, A derivative noun. اسم مصدر *ismi masdar*, Noun of action. اسم مصغر *ismi musaghghar*, A diminutive noun. اسم مضاف *ismi muẓāf*, A noun in construction. اسم معنى *ismi maʻna'*, An abstract noun. اسم مفعول *ismi mafʻūl*, The passive participle. اسم معارف *ismi maʻārif*, A determinate noun. اسم مكان *ismi makān*, Noun of place. اسم منسوب *ismi mansūb*, A relative noun. اسم موصول *ismi mawsūl*, A relative pronoun. اسم نكرة *ismi nakra*, An indeterminate noun. اسم نوع *ismi nawʻ*, A specific noun: as, كتبة *kitbat*, The art of writing. اسم وصف *ismi wasf*, An adjective. اسم وعا *ismi wiʻā*, Noun of the vessel: as, محلب *miḥlab*, A milk-pail, (from حلب *ḥalaba*, He milked).

A اسمّ *asamm*, Narrow-nostriled (nose).

A اسماء *asmāʼ*, (for وسماء) A woman's name.

A اسماء *asmāʼ*, (pl. of اسم *ism* for سمو *sumw*) Names. اسماء افعال *asmāʼi afʻāl*, Verbal nouns. اسماء صفت *asmāʼi sifat*, The names or attributes of God. علم اسما *ʻilmi asmā*, The knowledge of names, *i. e.* of the attributes of God. *Ismāʼ*, (v. n. 4 of سما for سمو) Naming, calling. Raising up. Going towards, taking the road to سماوة *samāwat*.

A اسماح *ismāḥ*, (v. n. 4 of سمح) Being easy, submissive, obedient, pliant, governable. Being generous, liberal, and humane.

P آسمار *āsmār*, (or اسمار *ismār*) The myrtle-tree.

A اسمار *asmār*, (pl. of سمر *samar*) Nocturnal conversations, evening entertainments, stories. *Ismār*, (v. n. 4 of سمر) Nailing.

A اسماط *asmāt*, Unbranded (camel). (pl. of سميط *samīt*) Single or thin breeches, not stuffed or lined with cotton, &c. Single shoes, slippers, or sandals. *Ismāt*, (v. n. 4 of سمط) Keeping silence.

A اسماع *asmāʻ*, (pl. of سمع *samʻ*) The ears. *Ismāʻ*, (v. n. 4 of سمع) Causing to hear, relating. Reproaching, reviling. Accepting, approving. Putting a handle (to a bucket or basket for drawing up earth). Singing.

A اسّماع *issimāʻ*, (v. n. 8 of سمع) Listening.

A اسماعيل *ismāʻīl*, Ishmael, whom the Muhammadans believe to have been the intended victim, and not Isaac.

A اسماعيليّة *ismāʻīlīyat*, Name of a sect.

A اسمال *asmāl*, Old, worn-out (garment). *Ismāl*, (v. n. 4 of سمل) Making peace, composing differences. Being old and worn out (a garment).

P آسمان *āsmān*, Heaven, the celestial orb. The ceiling of a house. Name of a genius who presides over the 27th day of every Persian solar month. Some consider this genius to be the same with Murdād or Asrael, the angel of death. آسمان برين *āsmāni barīn*, The ninth or uppermost heaven. آسمان و ريسمان *āsmān u rīsmān*, A proverbial expression employed to denote an evasive or impertinent reply. آسمان از ريسمان ندانستن *āsmān az rīsmān na dānistan*, (a proverbial expression, denoting) A total want of discrimination.

A اسمان *asmān*, Old, worn-out breeches. *Ismān*, (v. n. 4 of سمن) Buttering (any thing, as bread or meat). Possessing, buying, or giving away, fat (cattle). Abounding in butter. Being naturally fat.

P آسمان پيوند *āsmān-paywand*, Sky-reaching.

P آسمانجوني *āsmānjūnī*, A sapphire, hyacinth.

P آسماندرة *āsmān-dara*, The galaxy, milky way.

P آسمان صفت *āsmān-sifat*, Heaven-like.

P آسمان گير *āsmān-gīr*, (Catching or intercepting the sky) A projecting roof. An arbour, a bower.

P آسمانه *āsmāna*, A ceiling, roof.

P آسماني *āsmānī*, Heavenly. Azure, hyacinthine.

P آسماني تير *āsmānī-tīr*, A meteor, a falling star.

P آسماني زبان *āsmānī-zabān*, The language of angels. Angel-tongued, eloquent.

A اسماوات *asmāwāt*, (pl. of اسم *ism*) Names.

A اسمح *asmaḥ*, More liberal. Easier, easiest.

A اسمداد *ismidād*, A swelling with rage.

A اسمدرار *ismidrār*, (v. n. 4 of سمدر Q) Being weak (the sight).

A اسمر *asmar*, Brown, tawny, dusky. Does' milk.

A اسمرار *ismirār*, The being of a tawny colour.

A اسمران *asmarāni*, (dual, The two browns) Wheat and water. Water and a spear.

A اسمطة *asmitat*, (pl. of سماط *sumāt*) Tables covered with viands.

A اسمع *asmaʻ*, More or most quick of hearing. More or most proper, agreeable, or worthy of being heard. *Asmuʻ*, (pl. of سمع *samʻ*) Ears.

A اسمعداد *ismiʻdād*, (v. n. 4 of سمعد Q) Being filled (with rage). Swelling (the tips of the fingers).

A اسمعيل *ismaʻīl*, Ishmael, son of Abraham.

A اسمغداد *ismighdād*, (v. n. 4 of سمغد Q) Being in a rage. Swelling (the tips of the fingers).

A اسمقة *asmiḳat*, Pieces of wood on which bricks fresh from the mould are laid to dry.

A اسمن *asman*, More or most fat, jolly, plump, gross, lusty. *Asmun*, (pl. of سمن *samn*) Butters.

P آسمند *āsmand*, Lying. Bewildered, frightened, confounded.

P اسمند *asmand*, A village near Samarcand.

P اسمندر *asmandar*, A salamander.

G اسموسا *asmūsā*, Sort of marjoram: wild carrot.

P آسموغ *āsmūgh*, Name of a demon, one of the principal emissaries of Ahraman (the devil), according to the system of the Magi. His employment is to sow discords in families, law-suits among neighbours, and wars between princes.

A اسمهداد *ismihdād*, (v. n. 4 of سمهد Q) Being large (a camel's bunch).

A اسمهرار *ismihrār*, (v. n. 3 of سمهر Q) Becoming stiff and dry (a thorn). Being even and straight. Being thick (darkness).

A اسمي *ismīy*, Nominal.

A اسمية *asmiyat*, (pl. of سماء) Heavens. Rains.

A اسمية *ismīyat*, The state or condition of a noun.

A اسميداد *ismīdād*, A swelling with rage.

A اسمیرار *ismīrār*, The being of a tawny colour.

A اسمئلال *ismiʾlāl*, (v. n. 4 of سمال Q) Being thin, meagre. Being old, worn out (a garment).

A آسن *āsin*, Corrupted, stinking (water).

A اسن *asn*, (v. n. of اسن) Kicking the backside.

P اسن *asan*, A garment turned. An unripe melon.

A اسن *asan*, (v. n. of اسن) Fainting on going into a well or reservoir, being affected by foul air or any noxious effluvia. *Asin*, Affected by the foul air of a noisome pit, drain, or sewer. Corrupted, stinking water. *Usun*, (pl. آسان *āsān*) Disposition, temper, habit, mode of living. Name of a valley in Arabia. *Usun*, *isn*, or اسن *usunn*, (pl. آسان *āsān*) A single rope or thong, with several of which twisted together they make bridles or halters. Remains of fat (on an animal).

A اسنّ *asann*, Of a more advanced age, older. Large-toothed. *Asunn*, (pl. of سنّ *sinn*) Teeth.

A اسناء *isnāʾ*, (v. n. 4 of سني) Exalting, raising. Remaining a whole year at any place. Suffering from the barrenness or inclemency of a season. Entering a house, falling on the earth, or flying on a cloud (the lightning's flash).

A اسنات *isnāt*, A suffering from scarcity.

A اسناخ *asnākh*, Roots of the teeth.

A اسناد *asnād*, The steepness or declivity of a mountain. (pl. of سند *sanad*) Striped stuffs. A Credentials. Vouchers, warrants. A *Isnād*, (v. n. 4 of سند) Causing to lean. Imputing, attributing. Alleging; an allegation on the authority of another. Carrying up or tracing back a thing spoken to the person who first said it. Ascending a mountain. Causing to ascend a mountain. The steepness or declivity of a mountain.

A اسناط *asnāt*, (pl. of سناط) Beardless youths.

A اسناع *asnāʿ*, (pl. of سنع *sinʿ*) Ankle or pastern-joints. Wrist-joints. Joints connecting the fingers and wrists. *Isnāʿ*, (v. n. 4 of سنع) Being lame in the pastern. Being tall and handsome. Begetting handsome children.

A اسناف *isnāf*, (v. n. 4 of سنف) Putting on the girth called سناف *sināf*. Doing (business) well. Outstripping in a race (a mare). Taking the lead of others (a she-camel). Out-stretching his neck in travelling (a camel). Blowing hard, raising dust (wind). Appearing near (lightning or a cloud).

A اسناق *isnāk*, (v. n. 4 of سنق) Elating, puffing up, pampering, filling (riches).

A اسنام *asnām*, Camels' bunches. *Isnām*, (v. n. 4 of سنم) Raising up (smoke or blaze). Giving (a camel) a high bunch (fodder). The fruit of the plant حليا *hulayya'*.

A اسنان *asnān*, (pl. of سنّ *sinn*) Teeth. Ages, periods of life. P اسنان سي و دو *asnāni sī u du*, The two and thirty teeth. A *Isnān*, (v. n. 4 of سنّ) Being advanced in years. Shooting forth (the camel's tooth called سديس *sadīs*). Breeding teeth. Having large teeth. Making (the teeth) grow.

A اسنائي *isnāʾīy*, Of the town of Isna.

A اسنّة *asinnat*, (pl. of سنّ *sinn*) Teeth. (pl. of سنان *sinān*) Points of spears, halberds, lances, javelins, or arrows.

P آسنستان *āsinistān*, (اسنستان *asnistān* or اسنستّان *asinisittān*) Wāmik's wife's father.

A اسنع *asnaʿ*, Long, tall. Longer. Better.

A اسنمة *asnimat*, (pl. of سنام) Camels' bunches.

A اسنى *asnā'*, More or most high, or sublime. *Isna'* or *usna'*, Name of a town in Upper Egypt.

A اسو *asw*, (v. n. of اسا for اسو) Curing, healing, composing differences.

P اسو *asū*, A part, side. *Usū*, Robbery, seizure.

A اسوّ *asūw*, (pl. آسية) A medicine, remedy.

A اسوء *aswaʾ*, Ugly, ill-favoured. Offensive. More or most disagreeable, ugly, or offensive.

A اسواء *aswāʾ*, (pl. of سواء *sawāʾ*) Equals. *Iswāʾ*, (v. n. 4 of سوأ) Neglecting, abandoning. (v. n. 4 of سوي) Making equal, even, or level. Being on a par with a boy in temper or disposition. Fornicating. Being dishonoured, disgraced. Falling into trouble. Inserting completely one thing into another. Rejecting a letter from the Kur'ān. Neglecting, slighting, leaving, forsaking.

A اسواد *iswād*, (v. n. of ساد for سود) Begetting a prince. Begetting a black child.

P اسوار *aswār*, A horseman. A soldier who fights with a hatchet or mace. Name of a town in Upper Egypt.

A اسوار *aswār*, (pl. of سور *sūr*) Walls of a city. *Iswār* or *uswār*, (pl. اساور *asāwir*, and اساورة *asāwirat*) A groom skilled in horsemanship, sitting well on horse-back. A captain or leader amongst the Persians. A darter of javelins, one skilful in hurling the javelin. *Uswār*, (pl. اسورة *aswirat*, اساور *asāwir*, and اساورة *asāwirat*), A bracelet.

P اسواري *aswārī*, A mode of warfare with hatchets and maces.

A اسواط *aswāt*, (pl. of سوط) Scourges, whips.

A اسواع *iswāʿ*, (v. n. 4 of ساع for سوع) Moving, departing from hour to hour. Delaying an hour. Having a priapism and seminal effusion. Drawing, unsheathing (an ass).

A اسواغ *iswāgh*, (v. n. 4 of ساغ for سوغ) Being born with. Being born after.

A الاسواف *al aswāf*, Name of a place in Madīna.

A اسواق *aswāk*, (pl. of سوق *sūk*) Streets, market-places, squares, open places.

A اسوان *aswān*, Sad, afflicted, grieved. *Uswān*, Name of a town in Egypt (Syene).

P اسوبار *asūbār*, (in zand and Pāz.) A horseman.

A اسوة *iswat* or *uswat*, (pl. اسى *isa'* or *usa'*) A chief, leader, distinguished man, exemplar. Comfort, whatever alleviates pain. A comforter.

A اسود *aswad*, Black. Blacker, blackest. More or most illustrious or powerful (from سيّد *sayyid*, A lord). More or most liberal. Meeker, meekest. The heart's core. A sparrow. A lucky gaming arrow (as if black by frequent handling). (pl. اساود *asāwid*) A large kind of black serpent. The Arabians (other nations being by them called احمر *ahmar*, Red). اسود البرم *aswadu'l burm*, Name of a mountain from which they excavate large cauldrons of stone. *Usūd*, (pl. of اسد *asad*) Lions.

A اسوداد *iswidād*, (v. n. 9 of ساد for سود) Being black, or dark-coloured.

A الاسودان *al aswadāni*, The two blacks, as dates and water (being the chief food of the Arabians). A serpent and a scorpion.

A اسودة *aswadat*, The female large black serpent. *Aswidat*, (pl. of سواد *sawād*) Bodies. *Usūdat*, (pl. of اسد *asad*) Lions.

P آسودگي *āsūdagī*, Quiet, repose, tranquillity.

P آسودن *āsūdan*, To rest. To be satisfied, refreshed, regaled. To die. To quiet, pacify, silence. To lose moisture, to dry.

P آسوده *āsūda*, Peaceable, quiet, at rest, asleep. آسوده و آزاده *āsūda u āzāda*, Quiet and free.

P اسوده *usūda*, Feeling, handling, touching.

P آسوده حال *āsūda-hāl*, Tranquil. Full, replete.

P اسور *aswar*, (in zand and Pāzand) The day before yesterday.

A اسورة *aswirat*, (pl. of سوار *siwār* or اسوار *uswār*) Bracelets.

A اسوس *aswas*, Troubled with the disease سوس *sawas* in the buttocks (a horse).

A اسوغ *aswagh*, Easy in flowing down the throat.

A اسوف *asūf*, Sad, inclined to melancholy, easily affected, prone to grief, tender-hearted.

A اسوق *aswak*, Long and handsome-legged.

A اسوق *asuk*, (pl. of ساق *sāk*) Legs, shanks.

A اسوقة *aswikat*, (pl. of سويق *sawīk*) The meals of wheat, barley, and vetches, pounded and fried.

A اسول *asūl*, Swag-bellied. Low (cloud).

A اسولة *aswilat*, (pl. of سؤال *suʾāl*) Questions.

A اسون *usūn*, (v. n. of اسن) Becoming naught, stinking (water).

A اسوياء *aswiyāʾ*, (pl. of سوي *sawīy*) Right. Equal. Entire.

A اسويداد *iswīdād*, The being very black.

P آسه *āsa*, Tillage, sowing. A field ready for sowing. Liquorice-root.

A اسهاء *as-hāʾ*, Colours. Forms, sorts. *Is-hāʾ*, (v. n. 4 of سها for سهو) Constructing a bench.

A اسهاب *is-hāb*, (v. n. 4 of سهب) Talking much, babbling. Being insatiable in one's desires. Sucking the ewe (a lamb). Giving much. Allowing (cattle) to pasture without a keeper. Finding a stratum of sand when digging for water, digging to no purpose. Losing one's senses, changing colour (from love, fear, disease, or venomous bite).

A اسهاد *is-hād*, (v. n. 4 of سهد) Bringing forth a child at one throe (a woman).

A اسهار *is-hār*, (v. n. 4 of سهر) Rendering watchful. Keeping awake.

A اسهال *is-hāl*, (v. n. 4 of سهل) Loosening. Purging, producing a diarrhœa. Coming to soft ground. Dysentery. P اسهال خون *is-hāli khūn*, or اسهال دموي *is-hāli damawī*, A bloody flux.

A اسهام *is-hām*, (v. n. 4 of سهم) Talking much. Casting lots.

A اسهان *as-hān*, Soft sands.

A اسهد *as-had*, More or most wide awake. اسهد رأيا *as-hadu ra-yan*, More heedful or circumspect.

A اسهران *as-harāni*, (dual) The nose and penis. Two veins in the eye. Two spermatic vessels.

A اسهل *as-hal*, More easy, easier, easiest.

A اسهم *as-hum*, (pl. of سهم *sahm*) Arrows.

P آسي *āsī*, The wife of a man who has another wife, a rival wife.

A آسي *āsī*, Melancholy, solicitous, sorrowful. (pl. اساة *usāt* and اساء *isā*) A physician, surgeon.

A أسي *asiya*, (fut. يأسي *ya-sa'*) He was sad.

A اسي *asy*, (v. n. of اسي) Keeping, preserving (meat). *Asa'*, (v. n. of اسي) Being sorrowful, solicitous. Grief. *Isa'*, (v. n. of اسي) Applying a remedy. *Isa'* or *usa'*, (pl. of اسوة *iswat* or *uswat*) Chiefs, leaders, exemplars. Comforts, alleviations.

A اسيّ *asīy*, Healed, cured. *Usīy*, Traces or ruins of a habitation. Utensils of the meanest kind.

P آسيا *ās-yā*, A mill-stone. آسياي دستي *ās-yāyi dastī*, A hand-mill. خرآسيا, An ass-mill.

P اسيا *asyā*, Black. (in zand and Pāz.) A breast.

P آسيا آژن *āsyā-ājan*, An iron instrument for notching a mill-stone.

P آسياب *āsyāb*, (or آسياو *āsyāv*) A water-mill. آسياب بي آب *asyābi bī āb*, A mill without water.

P آسيابان *āsyābān*, A miller.

A اسياح *asyāh*, (pl. of سيح *sayh*) Running waters. Striped garments.

P آسيا زن *āsyā-zan*, A mill-wright.

P آسيا زنه *āsyā-zana*, An iron instrument for notching a mill-stone.

P آسيا سنگ *āsyā-sang*, A mill-stone.

A اسياف *asyāf*, (pl. of سيف *sayf*) Swords. Troops. Auxiliaries. (pl. of سيف *sīf*) Shores.

P آسياگر *āsyāgar*, A mill-wright. A miller.

P آسياگري *āsyāgarī*, The business of a miller, or of a mill-wright.

A اسيان *asyān*, Sad, mournful.

P آسيب *āsīb*, Trouble, molestation, perturbation, misery, calamity, wretchedness, affliction, hurt, injury, damage, loss. Dissension, discord, sedition. The shock or concussion of a body of men, pressing upon, struggling, or fighting with one another. آسيب نظر *āsīb-nazr*, A fatal accident in consequence of witchcraft.

A آسية *āsiyat*, (pl. اواسي *awāsī*) A female physician or surgeon, a woman who circumcises girls. A column, large pillar, prop, support, the main-beam of a house. Firm, strongly-built (edifice). (pl. اسايا *asāya'*) Sad, mournful (woman). Name of Pharaoh's wife. (pl. of اسوّ *asūw*) Medicines.

A اسيّد *usayyid*, (dim. of اسود) Blackish.

A اسيّديّ *usayyidīy*, Of a blackish colour.

A اسير *asīr*, (pl. اسراء *usarā*, اساري *usāra'*, *asāra'*, and اسري *asra'*) Bound with thongs, chained in fetters. A prisoner, captive, bondman. Imprisoned. Twisted, folded, entangled (plant). A man's name. اسير طبع *asīri tab'*, A sensualist.

P اسير كردن *asīr kardan*, To make prisoner.

P اسيرك *asīrak*, A slice of a melon.

P اسيرگير *asīr-gīr*, Taking prisoners. A slaver.

A اسيري *asīrī*, Captivity, slavery, bondage.

A اسيس *asīs*, A substitute, succedaneum, any thing used instead of another. Root, foundation.

A اسيف *asyuf*, (pl. of سيف *sayf*) Swords. *Asīf*, (pl. اسفاء *usafā*) Grieving, sorrowful. Easily affected, prone to grief, tender-hearted. A servant, a hired labourer, a mercenary. A slave. One that does not fatten. A frail decrepit old man.

A اسيفة *asīfat*, Barren (soil), producing nothing.

A اسيل *asīl*, Smooth, even, equal. Taper, long. اسيل الخدّ *asīlu'l khadd*, (A horse) having small and smooth cheek-bones.

A اسيلم *usaylim*, The vein running between the little and ring fingers, salvatella.

P آسيم *āsīm*, (in zand and Pāz.) A man of rank.

A اسيمر *usaymir*, Of a duskish colour.

P آسيمه *āsīma*, Astonished, amazed, stupefied, confused. Dark.

P آسيمه دماغ *āsīma-dimāgh*, Crack-brained.

A اسينة *asīnat*, (pl. اسائن *asā-in*) The thread of a bowstring. A leathern thong, with several of which, twisted or plaited, they make reins or halters.

A اسيوس *asyūs*, A stone which produces nitre. A powder growing on the top of a stone, like salt. Fixt alkaline salt.

A اسيوط *usyūt*, Suyūt in Upper Egypt.

P آسيون *āsyūn*, Stupefied, astonished. Dark.

P آسيه *āsiya*, Name of Pharoah's wife who educated Moses.

P آش *āsh*, Meat, victuals, viands, soup, broth, gruel, pottage. Drinking. A drinker. آش بچگان *āshi bachagān*, Castor (a medicine given to infants). آش پختن *āsh pukhtan*, To stir up one against another. آش تزوير *āshi tazwīr*, Gruel for the sick. آش جو *āshi jaw*, Barley-water, water-gruel. آش خليل الله *āshi khalīl allāh*, Pottage of lentils. آش دقيق *āshi dakīk*, Rice-gruel. آش كردن *āsh kardan*, To cook. آش مزور *āshi mazūr*, Rice-broth given to one convalescent.

P اش *ash*, when added to a noun ending in soft ه *he*, i. e. not sounded, signifies His, him, &c.: as, خانه اش *khāna ash*, His house.

A اش *ash*, (or ايش *aysh*) How? what? what thing? for what? Is it not? اش حالك *ash hāluka*, How's your state? how do you do?

A اشّ *ashsh*, (v. n. of اشّ) Rising up against, making a commotion, being stimulated to any thing bad. Calling out (to a sheep). Petulance, insolence. Dry bread.

A اشاء *ashā*, The dwarf palm-tree, or a palm-tree in general. Name of a place in Mauritania.

A اشاءة *ashā-at*, Name of a race in Hazramawt. *Ishā-at*, (v. n. 4 of شيأ) Forcing, compelling.

A اشابانيّ *ashābānīy*, Red, rosy, of a deep red.

A اشابة *ishābat*, (v. n. 4 of شاب for شيب) Making gray (sorrow). Having children who are becoming old. *Ushābat*, (pl. اشائب *ashā-ib*) A miscellaneous collection, a crowd of people. Wealth (whether fairly or villainously acquired).

A اشاجع *ashājiʻ*, (pl. of اشجع *ishja'*) The joints of the fingers which are next to the hand.

A اشاح *ishāh* or *ushāh*, (for وشاح *wishāh* or وشاح *wushāh*) A belt or girdle of leather, adorned with jewels, worn by ladies round their waists.

A اشاحة *ishāhat*, (v. n. 4 of شاح for شيح) Being diligent and persevering in doing any thing. Being cautious, guarded. Producing the plant شيح *shīh*.

A اشادة *ishādat*, (v. n. 4 of شاد for شيد) Raising the voice. Ruining, destroying. Giving information to the owner of a lost chattel. Referring or ascribing (a saying or sentiment).

A اشارات *ishārāt*, (pl. of اشارة) Signs, indices.

A اشارة *ishārat*, (v. n. 4 of شار for شور) Gathering honey, assisting to gather honey. Pointing, nodding, beckoning with the hand or eye. Commanding. Exercising (a horse), riding (him) to and fro to shew (him) off to a purchaser. Trying, proving, turning about (a horse or a female slave). Raising (fire). A sign, token, mark, signal, wink, nod, or wave with the hand. A note, an asterisk. P اشارت فرمود *ishārat farmūd*, He made a signal. اشارت كردن *ishārat kardan*, To point out, make a sign, hint, intimate.

A اشاري *ashāra'* or *ushāra'*, (pl. of اشران *ashrān*) Lively, sprightly, cheerful, joyous, wanton.

A اشارير *ashārīr* (pl. of اشرارة *ishrārat*, q. v.)

A اشآز *ish-āz*, (v. n. 4 of شأز) Agitating, making uneasy, disquieting.

A اشاش *ashāsh*, (or اشاشة *ashāshat*) (v. n. of اشّ) Being joyous, cheerful, glad. Agility, alacrity, mirth, exultation. Petulance, sauciness.

A اشاشة *ishāshat*, (v. n. 4 of شاش for شيش) Producing bad dates, not having been properly fructified by the male (a palm-tree).

A اشاصة *ishāsat*, (v. n. 4 of شاص for شوص)

Rubbing the teeth up and down, using the dentifrice سواك *siwāk*. (v. n. 4 of شاص for شيص) Producing the bad dates شيص *shīs* (a palm-tree).

A اشاطة *ishāṭat*, (v. n. 4 of شاط for شيط) Burning up. Destroying. Burning the bottom of a pot. Dividing (meat). Coming in for the last portion of a slaughtered camel. Bringing to be killed. Striving to compass the death of another.

A اشاعة *ishāʻat*, (v. n. 4 of شاع for شيع) Publishing, divulging, diffusing, spreading about or abroad. Appointing an attendant, a follower, a helper. Scattering, shooting, squirting urine. Calling (to camels) to make (them) stop.

A اشاعثة *ashāʻisat*, (or اشاعث *ashāʻis*) (Men) perplexed in their affairs.

A اشاعر *ashāʻir*, (pl. of اشعر *ashʻar*) Hairs about the hoofs of cattle. The lips of a camel's vulva.

A اشافة *ishāfat*, (v. n. 4 of شاف for شوف) Being at the point of. Fearing. Getting to know.

A اشافي *ashāfī*, (pl. of اشفى *ishfa'*) Cobblers' awls. (pl. of شفاء *shifāʼ*) Medicines, remedies.

P اشاق *ashāḳ*, A boy, a slave.

A اشاكة *ishākat*, (v. n. 4 of شاك for شوك) Wounding with a thorn. Bearing thorns (a tree).

A اشالة *ishālat*, (v. n. 4 of شال for شول) Lifting up (a stone). Cocking (her) tail (a camel).

P آشام *āshām*, Potation. Victuals. Water in which rice has been boiled. Spare diet. The country of Assam. (in comp.) A drinker: as شراب آشام *sharāb-āshām*, A drinker of wine. زهر آشام *zahr-āshām*, Poisoned. Envenomed. خون آشام *khūn-āshām*, Tinged with blood, bloody, sanguinary. شعلهٔ آشام *shuʻla-āshām*, Burning, inflamed.

A اشآم *ishʼām*, (v. n. 4 of شأم) Going to Syria.

A اشأم *ashʼam*, More or most unfortunate or disastrous. The left side. (pl. اشائم *ashāʼim*) Unlucky. طائر اشأم *tāʼir ashʼam*, An ominous bird. ما اشأمه *mā ashʼamahu*, How unfortunate he is!

P اشام *ashām*, Food sufficient to support life.

A اشامة *ishāmat*, (v. n. 4 of شيم) Entering.

P آشامنده *āshāminda*, A drinker, a sipper.

P آشاميدن *āshāmīdan*, To drink, to sip.

P آشاميدني *āshāmīdanī*, Any thing drinkable, fit to be drunk or sipped: a beverage.

A اشاوات *ashāwāt*, (pl. of شيء *shayʼ*) Things.

A اشاوز *ashāwiz*, (pl. of اشوز) Created beings.

A اشاوه *ashāwih*, (pl. of شاة *shāt*) Sheep. (pl. of شيء *shayʼ*) Things.

A اشاوي *ashāwa'*, (pl. of شيء *shayʼ*) Things.

A اشاهر *ashāhir*, (or آشاهر *āshāhir*) The whiteness of the narcissus.

A اشايا *ashāya'*, (pl. of شيء *shayʼ*) Things.

A اشائب *ashāʼib*, (pl. of اشابة *ushābat*) Crowds. Mixtures. Gains (just or unjust).

A اشائم *ashāʼim*, Unfortunate. Left hands.

P آشب *āshab* or *āshb*, Name of a place.

A اشب *ashb*, (v. n. of اشب) Mixing, mingling, involving, implying. Reprehending, abusing, reviling, despising. Intertwined (as palm-trees). Enmity, dissimulation. Intricate business. *Ashab*, (v. n. of اشب) Being intertwined (as trees). Intertwined (palm-trees). *Ashib*, Involved, mingled, confused. عدد اشب *ʻadad ashib*, A great number. بلدة اشبة *baldat ashibat*, A town having many palm-trees intertwined.

A اشباء *ishbāʼ*, (v. n. 4 of شبا for شبو) Begetting a clever ingenious lad. Taking after the father (a son). Honouring. Giving. Growing tall and luxuriant (a tree). Throwing into a well or into any thing disagreeable. Pushing, thrusting away.

A اشباب *ashbāb*, (pl. of شابّ *shābb*) Young men, youths. *Ishbāb*, (v. n. 4 of شبّ) Having children growing up. Growing old (an ox). Growing up (a girl). Exciting. Being determined, predestinated, appointed.

A اشباج *ishbāj*, (v. n. 4 of شبج not used) Driving back, repelling. Restoring. Shutting a door.

A اشباح *ashbāḥ*, (pl. of شبح *shabaḥ* or *shabḥ*) Bodies. Property known (as camels, sheep, &c.).

A اشبار *ashbār*, (pl. of شبر *shibr*) Spans. *Ishbār*, (v. n. 4 of شبر) Giving.

A اشباع *ishbāʻ*, (v. n. 4 of شبع) Satiating, satisfying, filling up. Making complete or perfect. Dyeing (cloth), impregnating (it) with a sufficient quantity of colour. Reading the vowels distinctly. Adding a letter to fill up when required by poetic license: as, كمالا *kamālā* for كمال *kamāla*, كمالو *kamālū* for كمال *kamālu*, or كمالي *kamālī* for كمال *kamāli*.

A اشباك *ishbāk*, (v. n. 4 of شبك) Digging wells near to each other (resembling net-work).

A اشبال *ashbāl*, (pl. of شبل *shibl*) Whelps of a lion or other wild beast. ابو اشبال *abū ashbāl*, (Father of the whelps) a lion. *Ishbāl*, (v. n. 4 of شبل) Shewing favour or fondness. Declining a second marriage that she may attend to the education of the children of her deceased husband. Aiding.

A اشبانيّ *ushbānīy*, Red-faced and red-whiskered. *Ashabānīy*, Extremely red.

A اشباه *ashbāh*, (pl. of شبه *shibh* or *shabah*) Pictures, images. Likes, equals. Brasses. *Ishbāh*, (v. n. 4 of شبه) Resembling, taking after. اشبه امّه *ashbaha ummahu*, He resembled his mother, *i.e.* He was weak. و ما اشبه ذالك *wa mā ashbaha zālika*, And the like to that, and so forth.

A اشبة *ushbat*, A wolf.

A اشبل *ashbul*, (pl. of شبل *shibl*) Lions' whelps.

P اشبو *ashbū*, A chafing-dish.

A اشبور *ushbūr*, A kind of fish.

A اشبونة *ushbūnat*, Lisbon.

A اشبه *ashbah*, More or most resembling.

A اشبيليّة *ishbīlīyat*, Seville in Spain.

P آشپز *āsh-paz*, A cook.

P اشپس *ushpus*, A louse.

P اشپشه *ishpisha*, A moth, a weevil.

P اشپغور *ashpaghūr*, Seed of the herb fleawort.

P اشپك *ashpak*, Roe of the sturgeon, caviar.

G اشپلاتوس *ashpalātūs*, A prickly shrub.

P اشپوختن *ishpūkhtan*, (or اشپختن *ishpikhtan*) To sprinkle, scatter. Sprinkled, scattered.

P اشپخته *ishpikhta*, Sprinkled, scattered. Aspergula (Ladies' bed-straw).

P اشتا *ushtā* or *ishtā*, Haste.

A اشتاء *ishtiʼāʼ*, (v. n. 8 of شاأ for شأو) Hearing. Preceding, taking precedency.

A اشتاء *ishtāʼ*, (v. n. 4 of شتا for شتو) Entering on the winter. Suffering from scarcity in winter.

P اشتاب *ushtāb* or *ishtāb*, Haste, despatch.

A اشتات *ashtāt*, (pl. of شتّ *shatt*) Distinct. Dispersed. *Ishtāt*, (v. n. 4 of شتّ) Dispersing.

P اشتاد *ashtād*, Name of the 26th day of the month, and of its presiding angel. A section of the book of Zardusht (Zoroaster).

A اشتار *ishtār*, (v. n. 4 of شتر) Rendering the eyelids inverted and relaxed.

P اشتار *ushtār* or *ishtār*, Haste.

A اشتاغ *ishtāgh*, (v. n. 4 of شتغ) Destroying.

P اشتافتن *ishtāftan*, To hasten.

P اشتالنگ *ishtālang*, The ankle. Dice.

A اشتباب *ishtibāb*, A making young.

A اشتباك *ishtibāk*, (v. n. 8 of شبك) Being intermingled and ravelled. Being pitchy dark (night). Being very brilliant (stars). Darkness. Doubt.

A اشتباه *ishtibāh*, (v. n. 8 of شبه) Being obscure, doubtful, and ambiguous. Resembling, bearing a striking resemblance to one another. Doubt, ambiguity. Obscurity. Similitude, resemblance. P بي اشتباه *bī ishtibāh*, Without doubt. قلعهٔ فلك اشتباه *ḳalʻaʼi falak-ishtibāh*, A citadel resembling heaven, high as the firmament

A اشتباهي *ishtibāhī*, Suspicious, doubtful.

A اشتة *ashtat*, A general name given to the collectors and reporters of traditions, natives of Isfahān.

A اشتجار *ishtijār*, (v. n. 8 of شجر) Putting the hand to the chin, and leaning on the elbow. Being intermingled (spears). Quarrelling, opposing each other. Departing from the eyes (sleep).

A اشتداد *ishtidād*, (v. n. 8 of شدّ) Becoming hard and strong. Being fortified, confirmed, strengthened. Being difficult and oppressive. Running. Becoming high (the day). Firmness, vehemence, force, violence, intensity, obstinacy.

A اشتداه *ishtidāh*, (v. n. 8 of شده) Being astonished, amazed, distracted. Being employed.

A اشتر *ashtar*, One who has inverted and relaxed eyelids.

P اشتر *ushtur*, A camel.

A اشترّ *ushturr*, Name of a Shīah sect in Kufa.

A اشتراء *ishtirāʼ* (v. n. 8 of شري) Buying. Selling. Trade, barter. Letting go one thing to lay hold of another.

P اشترابه *ushturāba*, A kind of woollen garment.

A اشتراط *ishtirāt*, (v. n. 8 of شرط) Imposing conditions, stipulating.

A اشتراف *ishtirāf*, (v. n. 8 of شرف) Standing erect, upright.

A اشتراق *ishtirāk*, (v. n. 8 of شرق) Cutting (raw meat) into long strips, and drying (it) in the sun.

A اشتراك *ishtirāk*, (v. n. 8 of شرك) Entering into partnership. Company, partnership, association, participation, society. P بر وجه اشتراك *bar wajhi ishtirāk*, In a partnership-way, by division.

A اشتران *ashtarāni*, Name of a king and son.

P اشتراوه *ushturāwa*, A kind of woollen garment.

P اشتربان *ushturbān*, A camel-driver or keeper.

P اشتربانه *ushturbāna*, (or اشترابه *ushturāba*) A garment made of wool and camel's hair, worn by the kings of Persia.

P اشتربين *ushtur-bīn*, Quick-sighted.

P اشترپاي *ushtur-pāy*, Penny-royal.

P اشترخار *ushtur-khār*, A thorn eaten by camels.

P اشترخوار *ushtur-khwār*, A serpent. A tike, camel-louse. A thorn of which camels are fond.

P اشتردار *ushtur-dār*, A camel-keeper or owner, one who has the charge or management of camels.

P اشترداري *ushtur-dārī*, The keeping of camels.

P اشتردل *ushtur-dil*, Camel-hearted: timid, pusillanimous. Malicious, revengeful, spiteful.

P اشترزهره *ushtur-zahra*, Timid, slow, languid.

P اشترغاز *ushtur-ghāz*, Root of the assafœtida.

P اشترغان *ushtur-ghān*, Sage, clary, or spurge.

P اشترك *ushturak*, A small camel. A wave.

P اشتركا *ashtar-kā*, A griffin.

P اشتر گاو پلنگ *ushtur-gāw-palang*, The cameleopard, or giraffe. (Camel, cow, leopard).

P اشترگيا *ushtur-giyā*, A thorn eaten by camels.

P اشترمرغ *ushtur-murgh*, The ostrich.

P اشتر مور *ushtur-mūr*, (Camel-ant) An animal in form like an ant, in size equal to a sheep.

P اشتروا *ushtur-wā*, A covering of camel's hair.

P اشتروار *ushturwār*, A camel's burden. Camel's hair.

P اشتروغ *ushturūgh*, A herb eaten by camels.

A اشتطاط *ishtitāt*, (v. n. 8 of شط) Giving an unjust verdict. Going a great distance to pasture.

A اشتعاب *ishtiʿāb*, (v. n. 8 of شعب) Overtaking any one (death).

A اشتعال *ishtiʿāl*, (v. n. 8 of شعل) Being kindled (a fire). Becoming dry and inflamed. Being hoary (the head). Hoariness.

A اشتغار *ishtighār*, (v. n. 8 of شغر) Being very many (numbers), and difficult to cast up. Exalting one's self from pride, affecting to lord it over. Being numerous and going to and fro. Being confused (business). Travelling far in the desert.

A اشتغال *ishtighāl*, (v. n. 8 of شغل) Occupying, employing one's self. Being kept employed and diverted. A grammatical form in which the object is placed before the verb, but represented by a pronoun subjoined to it: as, زيد ضربته *zayd zarabtuhu*, Zayd, I smote him, for ضربت زيدًا *zarabtu zaydan*, I smote Zayd. Employment.

A اشتفاء *ishtifāʾ*, (v. n. 8 of شفي) Recovering health, being healed.

A اشتفاف *ishtifāf*, (v. n. 8 of شفّ) Taking the whole of any thing. Filling his girth (a camel). Doing (a thing) attentively.

A اشتقاق *ishtikāk*, (v. n. 8 of شقّ) Deriving one noun from another. Being cloven asunder. Taking a half. Speaking discursively and little to the purpose (in a debate).

A اشتقاقي *ishtikākiy*, Derivative.

P اشتك *ishtak*, Swaddling clothes.

A اشتكاء *ishtikāʾ*, (v. n. 8 of شكا for شكو) Lamenting, complaining of aches and pains. Making a churn from the skin of a kid. Suspecting.

A اشتكار *ishtikār*, (v. n. 8 of شكر) Raining plentifully. Being collected in a large quantity in the udder (milk). Bringing forth small leaves called شكير *shakīr* (a tree). Bringing rain (the wind). Being intense (cold or heat). Exciting one's self greatly in running.

A اشتكال *ishtikāl*, (v. n. 8 of شكل) Being difficult, obscure, intricate.

A اشتلاء *ishtilāʾ*, (v. n. 8 of شلا for شلو) Liberating, rescuing. Crying out, intreating to be rescued from difficulty or danger.

P اشتلهونا *ishtalhūnā*, A sceptre.

P اشتلم *ushtulum*, Severity, violence, oppression. A forcible seizure. اشتلم كردن *ushtulum kardan*, To force, oblige, conquer, overcome. To rule, regulate, to reign despotically. To fight.

P آشتم *āshtim*, (or اشتم) The pus of a wound.

A اشتمات *ishtimāt*, The beginning of fatness.

A اشتماذ *ishtimāz*, (v. n. 8 of شمذ) Striking the ewe's tail that she may let him blissom (a ram).

A اشتمال *ishtimāl*, (v. n. 8 of شمل) Consisting of, comprising, comprehending, containing. Surrounding, enclosing. Wrapping one's self up in a garment. Making haste. Carrying (a sword) under one's garment.

A اشتمام *ishtimām*, A smelling, a snuffing up.

P آشتنگاه *āshtan-gāh*, A necessary, a privy.

P اشتو *ashtū*, A finger. Charcoal. *Ushtū*, Herbage. A finger.

P اشتوا *ashtuwā*, A live coal. A chafing-dish. *Ushtuwā*, Herbage.

A اشتواء *ishtiwāʾ*, (v. n. 8 of شوي) Roasting, or procuring roast. Being roasted.

P اشتوانه *ushtuwāna*, A finger-ring.

P اشتود *ashtawad*, Name of the second of the five intercalary days added to the Persian year.

P اشتوم *ashtūm*, Pease-haulm or straw. A besom of the same.

P آشتوه *āshtūh*, (اشتوه *ashtūh*, اشتوره *ashtūra*), A bitter thorny plant, of which camels are fond.

A اشته *ashtah*, Name of a company of traditionists of the people of Isfahān.

A اشتهاء *ishtihāʾ*, (v. n. 8 of شها for شهو) Wishing for, longing for. Appetite, desire, wish.

A اشتهاب *ishtihāb*, (v. n. 8 of شهب) Turning gray.

A اشتهار *ishtihār*, (v. n. 8 of شهر) Publishing, divulging, blazoning abroad. Being published, blazoned abroad. Being universally known. Fame, renown, celebrity, reputation, notice, publication. P اشتهار داشتن *ishtihār dāshtan*, To be famous. اشتهار شدن *ishtihār shudan*, To be famous, conspicuous, known, noted, notorious, clear, evident. اشتهار كردن *ishtihār kardan*, To publish, proclaim. خورشيد اشتهار *khwurshed-ishtihār*, Clear as the sun.

P اشتهار نامه *ishtihār-nāma*, A proclamation.

P آشتي *āshtī*, Peace, concord, reconciliation.

A اشتياب *ishtiyāb*, (v. n. 8 of شاب for شوب) Being mixed.

A اشتياذ *ishtiyāz*, (v. n. 8 of شوذ) Putting on a turban, girding one's head with a turban-sash.

A اشتيار *ishtiyār*, (v. n. 8 of شار for شور) Collecting honey from a hive.

A اشتئاز *ishtiʾāz*, (v. n. 8 of شأز) Being frightened and running away.

A اشتياف *ishtiyāf*, (v. n. 8 of شاف for شوف) Looking with out-stretched neck. Watching (the lightning) to discover whether it will rain. Becoming thick or rough (a sore place or wound).

A اشتياق *ishtiyāk*, (v. n. 8 of شاق for شوق) Wishing, longing, desiring (to see any absent person or thing). P اشتياق كردن *ishtiyāk kardan*, To desire. عرض اشتياق و محبت كردن *ʿarzi ishtiyāk u mahabbat kardan*, To express love and affection (at the beginning of letters).

P اشتياق نامه *ishtiyāk-nāma*, Letters expressive of desire or affection.

A اشتيال *ishtiyāl*, (v. n. 8 of شال for شول) Lifting up (a pitcher). Happening, occurring. Being exposed. Opposing, hindering. Reviling.

A اشتيام *ishtiyām*, (v. n. 8 of شام for شيم) Entering into.

A اشتئان *ishtiʾān*, A proposing, an intending.

A اشتية *ashtiyat*, (pl. of شتاء *shitāʾ*) Winters.

P آشتي خواره *āshtī-khwāra*, Sweetmeats sent from one to another on a reconciliation.

P اشتيم *ashtīm*, Pus, matter. Drawers.

P آشتينه *āshtīna*, An egg.

A اشج *ushshaj*, Gum ammoniac.

A اشجّ *ashajj*, Broken-headed.

A اشجاء *ishjāʾ*, (v. n. 4 of شجا for شجو) Overpowering, overcoming by force. Making sad. Causing to leap for joy.

A اشجاذ *ishjāz*, (v. n. 4 of شجذ) Raining gently. Injuring. Being severe upon. Ending, taking up after raining heavily.

A اشجار *ashjār*, (pl. of شجر *shajr*) Mouths.

Chins. (pl. of شجر *shajar*) Trees. *Ishjār*, (v. n. 4 of شجر) Abounding in or producing trees.

A اشجان *ashjān*, (pl. of شجن *shajan*) Necessary things. Anxieties, griefs, pains. *Ishjān*, (v. n. 4 of شجن) Grieving, afflicting. Having ripe stalks (a vine).

A اشجر *ashjar*, Abounding in trees, woody. More or most abundant in trees, more woody.

A اشجع *ashja'*, More or most brave, active, or nimble. Intrepid, brave, warlike. Long, tall. A lion. A serpent. Fortune. Time. *Ishja'* or *ashja'*, (pl. اشاجع *ashāji'*) The root or joint of the finger next to the hand; (the third joint of the finger and second of the thumb).

A اشجعة *ashji'at*, (pl. of شجيع) Bold, brave.

A اشجغ *ashjagh*, Advancing (camel).

A اشحاء *ish-hās*, (v.n.4 of شحا for شحو) Opening.

A اشحّاء *ashihhās*, (pl. of شحيح *shahīh*) Avaricious men, misers.

A اشحاذ *ish-hāz*, (v. n. 4 of شحذ) Sharpening, whetting (a knife).

A اشحاص *ash-hās*, (pl. of شحص *shahs*) Sheep giving no milk; also fat and barren. *Ish-hās*, (v. n. 4 of شحص) Tiring, fatiguing. Banishing.

A اشحاط *ish-hāt*, (v. n. 4 of شحط) Removing, putting to a distance.

A اشحام *ish-hām*, A giving of fat to eat.

A اشحان *ash-hān*, Passionate, angry, testy. Sad. *Ish-hān*, (v. n. 4 of شحن) Filling (a city with cavalry). Beginning to blubber (a boy). Putting a sword in a sheath. Drawing a sword. Preparing to shoot (an arrow).

A اشحّة *ashihhat*, (pl. of شحيح *shahīh*) Misers.

A اشحم *ash-ham*, More full of fat, lard, or pulp.

A اشحى *ash-ha'*, Passionate, angry (woman).

A اشخاذ *ishkhāz*, (v. n. 4 of شخذ not used) Instigating (a dog), setting (him) on.

P اشخار *ashkhār*, Potash. Sal ammoniac.

A اشخاس *ishkhās*, (v. n. 4 of شخس) Slandering, calumniating. Putting on a sour countenance in conversation.

A اشخاص *ashkhās*, (or اشخص *ashkhus*) (pl. of شخص *shakhs*) Persons, bodies. Individuals. Shapes, figures. *Ishkhās*, (v. n. 4 of شخص) Sending from place to place. Disturbing, making restless. Carrying away. Speaking evil of one absent. Tearing up from its place. Passing above the mark (an arrow). Being arrived (the hour for setting out on a journey).

A اشخام *ishkhām*, (v. n. 4 of شخم) Turning sour (milk).

P آش خانه *āsh-khāna*, A kitchen, a cook's shop.

A اشخر *ashkhar*, The gum-bearing tree *'ushar*.

A اشخم *ashkham*, Shining (hair). Unproductive (ground). (An ass) black in the head and muzzle.

A اشخوب *ushkhūb*, The sound made in milking.

P اشخون *ishkhūn*, A plant. A sort of dock.

A اشخيص *ishkhīs*, A sort of mezereon.

A اشخيمام *ishkhīmām*, (v. n. 11 of شخم) Being intermingled (fresh and withered plants).

A آشدّ *āshadd*, Name of a brother of Joseph.

A اشدّ *ashadd*, More or most vehement, strong, bold, severe. Stronger, strongest. Name of a brother of Joseph. *Ashudd* or *ushudd*, Strength and powers (particularly applied to a young man between eighteen and thirty).

A اشداء *ishdās*, (v. n. 4 of شدا for شدو) Becoming a skilful singer.

A اشدّاء *ashiddās*, (pl. of شديد *shadīd*) Strong, brave, bold, vehement, violent, severe, rigorous.

A اشداد *ishdād*, (v. n. 4 of شدّ) Possessing a strong beast. Imparting strength, invigorating.

A اشداف *ishdāf*, (v. n. 4 of شدف) Being dark (the night).

A اشداق *ashdāk*, (pl. of شدق *shidk* or *shadk*) Corners of the mouth, chops. Sides of a valley.

A اشدان *ishdān*, (v. n. 4 of شدن) Having her fawn strong and independent of herself (a doe).

A اشداه *ishdāh*, (v. n. 4 of شده) Stupefying.

A اشدح *ashdah*, Ample, large, capacious, wide.

A اشدخ *ashdakh*, (A horse) marked down the face with a streak of white. A lion.

A اشدف *ashdaf*, Left-handed. Wry-cheeked. Difficult, disastrous. (A horse) that leans to one side from fatigue. (A camel) that goes crosswise from friskiness. Bulky (horse).

A اشدق *ashdak*, Eloquent (orator).

A اشذاء *ishzās*, (v. n. 4 of شذا for شذو) Removing afar off, putting to a distance.

A اشذاب *ashzāb*, (pl. of شذب *shazab*) Household goods. Bits of wood, dry branches or barks of trees. Remains of fodder.

A اشذاذ *ishzāz*, (v. n. 4 of شذّ) Putting by itself. Employing any unusual form of speech. Removing far off, putting to a distance.

A آشر *āshir*, The jagged parts of the legs of a locust, the knob at the end of his tail, in which there are two crooked claws, and in general what he corrodes or saws with. A sawyer.

A أشر *ashara*, (fut. يأشر *ya'sharu*) He sawed.

A أشر *ashira*, (fut. يأشر *ya'sharu*) He exulted.

A اشر *ashr*, (v. n. of اشر) Sawing. Notching or sharpening (saw or teeth). *Ashar*, (v. n. of اشر) Exulting, rejoicing, triumphing. Being proud and insolent. Exultation, excessive joy, insolence, sauciness, frowardness, petulance. *Ashir*, *ashur*, *ashr*, or *ashar*, (pl. اشرون *ashirūna* or *ashurūna*) Exulting, rejoicing, sprightly. Proud, insolent. *Ashur*, The jagged grooves or notches of the teeth. The teeth of a sickle. *Ushur* and *ushar*, (pl. اشور *ushūr*) A notch or indentation in the teeth (either from nature or from wear). اشر المنجل *ushuru'l minjal*, The teeth of a reaping hook.

A اشرّ *asharr*, (little used) Worse, worst.

A اشراء *ashrās*, (pl of شري *shara'*) Sides, quarters, districts. *Ishrās*, (v. n. 4 of شري) Flashing repeatedly (lightning). Filling (a dish, vessel, or pond). Causing to incline, bending. Being open and staring (a camel's coat). Stirring up strife.

A اشرّاء *ashirrās*, (pl. of شرير) Wicked, bad.

A اشراب *ishrāb*, (v. n. 4 of شرب) Thirsting. Giving drink, watering (cattle). Causing to imbibe, imbuing. Arriving (the hour of drinking). Drinking water. Imputing, ascribing, telling a lie against, charging falsely. Making deep (a colour). (One colour) being mixed with or imbibing that of another. Being received into the heart (love). Putting a rope round the neck. Giving every male camel a female. Possessing camels, whether satiated with water, or thirsty. Admixture. اشربني ما لم اشرب *ashrabanī mā lam ashrib*, He imputed to me that which I did not.

A اشراج *ashrāj*, (pl. of شرج *sharaj*) Strings, thongs, or chains for fastening portmanteaus; also the loops or ouches through which those ligaments pass. *Ishrāj*, (v. n. 4 of شرج) Drawing together (a wallet). Coalescing, mixing.

A اشراد *ishrād*, (v. n. 4 of شرد) Driving away.

A اشرار *ashrār*, (pl. of شرير *sharīr*) Wicked, criminal, sinful. *Ishrār*, (v. n. 4 of شرّ) Calling another a rascal. Hanging or exposing to the air to dry. Disclosing (any thing).

A اشرارة *ishrārat*, (pl. اشارير *ashārīr*) A perforated wooden vessel, or one made of plaited rushes or reeds, into which they put cream or sour milk, after the whey is strained off; which, with the addition of salt, is then exposed to the sun, and preserved for winter use. Flesh dried in the sun. A large herd of camels.

A اشراز *ishrāz*, (v. n. 4 of شرز) Throwing into inextricable difficulty.

A اشراس *ashrās*, A kind of shoemaker's glue. *Ishrās*, (v. n. 4 of شرس) Having cattle feeding on the herb شرس *shirs*.

P اشراس *ishrās*, Shoemaker's or binder's paste.

A اشراط *ashrāt*, (pl. of شرط *shart*) Mean, low, base, vile. (pl. of شرط *sharat*) Signs or marks (by which men or cattle are distinguished, taken either in a good or bad sense). Nobles, grandees. Three stars in the head of Aries, two bright and one small. اشراط الساعة *ashrātu 's sā'at*, Signs of the last hour, or of the end of the world. اشراط القوم *ashrātu'l kawm*, Nobles of the people. اشراط المال *ashrātu'l māl*, The meanest parts of property or flock. *Ishrāt*, (v. n. 4 of شرط) Marking cattle and sending them to be sold. Binding, compelling by law. Expediting (an ambassador). Preparing, making ready. Marking, designating.

A اشراع *ashrā'*, (pl. of شرعة *shara'at*) Ships, sail. Verandas, porticoes, covered galleries. *Ishrā'*, (v. n. 4 of شرع) Opening (a door) upon a road.

Making (a way) clear. Pointing (a spear at one).

A اشراف *ashrāf,* (pl. of شريف *sharīf*) Nobles, grandees, gentlemen, men of high extraction. The ears and nose. اعيان و اشراف *aꜥyān u ashrāf,* Chiefs and nobles. *Ishrāf,* (v. n. 4 of شرف) Being high, exalted. Mounting, ascending. Looking down from an eminence. Being near, at the point of. Compassionating, pitying.

A اشراق *ishrāḳ,* (v. n. 4 of شرق) Rising (the sun). Shining, flashing, being brilliant, beautiful. Entering into the sunshine. Being tall (a palm-tree). Bearing unripe dates. Dyeing deeply (a garment). Causing (one) to choke with vexation. Splendour, lustre, refulgence, radiance.

A اشراقات *ishrāḳāt,* Rays, refulgences.

A اشراقين *ishrāḳīn,* The Platonists.

A اشراك *ashrāk,* (pl. of شرك *shirk*) Communions, companies. Religions in which a plurality of persons in the Godhead is maintained. (pl. of شريك *sharīk*) Companions, partners, associates in trade. *Ishrāk,* (v. n. 4 of شرك) Taking a partner (شريك *sharīk*). Giving companions to God, *i. e.* believing in the Trinity, which the Muhammadans consider as infidelity. Sharing, making common. Putting straps (شراك *shirāk*) to one's shoes.

A اشران *ashrān,* (pl. اشري *ashra'*, اشاري *ashāra'* and *ushāra'*) Exulting, joyous. Proud, insolent.

A اشربة *ashribat,* (pl. of شراب) Drinks, syrups.

A آشرة *āshirat,* Sawed, split (wood).

A اشرة *ashrat,* Exultation, sauciness, petulance. *Ushrat,* The jagged part of a locust's leg, or knob at the end of his tail, where are placed two crooked claws.

A اشرج *ashraj,* A horse which has one testicle larger than another.

A اشرحفاف *ishrihfāf,* (v. n. 4 of شرحف Q) Preparing for battle. Making haste. Being light.

P آشردن *āshurdan,* To bruise. To knead. To bake. To wash.

A اشرس *ashras,* Perverse, stubborn, wayward, intractable. Bold in battle. A lion. Adversity.

A اشرط *ashrat,* More or most vile or worthless.

A اشرع *ashraꜥ,* (A nose) whose tip is extended.

A اشرعة *ashriꜥat,* (pl. of شراع *shirāꜥ*) Sails of ships. The necks of camels. Strings of bows and musical instruments (in their tense state).

A اشرف *ashraf,* More or most noble. High (shoulder). A bat. اشرف المخلوقات *ashrafu'l makhlūḳāt,* The most noble of creatures, *i. e.* man.

P اشرفي *ashrafī,* An old Spanish coin, worth about 4 shillings, or 7 reals. The gold muhr of Hindūstān is valued at 16 sicca rupees; and the intrinsic value of that coined at Calcutta is estimated at 1*l.* 11*s.* 8*d.*, and the gold of it is better than English standard gold by 5*s.* in the ounce, or about $\frac{1}{16}$. By the Regulations of 1793, it should weigh 190,894 grains (troy).

A اشرك *ashruk,* (pl. of شراك) Shoe-latchets.

A اشرم *ashram,* Cut in the nose.

A اشري *ashra',* (pl. of اشران) Lively, joyous.

A اشرئباب *ishri-bāb,* (v. n. 11 of شرب) Looking with outstretched neck, or ascending an eminence in order to get a look or bird's eye view.

A اشرية *ashriyat,* (pl. of شري *shira'*) Bargains.

A اشريراء *ishrīrā-,* (v. n. 12 of شري) Being agitated, disturbed; shaking, tottering.

A اشريراق *ishrīrāḳ,* The being drowned in tears.

A اشزر *ashzar,* Milk of a reddish hue.

A اشساع *ashsāꜥ,* (pl. of شسع *shisꜥ*) Shoe-strings. *Ishsāꜥ,* (v. n. 4 of شسع) Putting strings to shoes.

A اشصاء *ishsā-,* (v. n. 4 of شصا for شصو) Looking up, fixing the eye.

A اشصاب *ashsāb,* (pl. of شصب *shisb*) Adversities. Barren (seasons). Lots, chances, portions. *Ishsāb,* (v. n. 4 of شصب) Making uncomfortable.

A اشصار *ashsār,* (pl. of شصر *shasar,* or شاصر *shāsir*) Young deer when their horns begin to appear.

A اشصاص *ishsās,* (v. n. 4 of شصّ) Putting to a distance. Denying, refusing, prohibiting, hindering. Giving little milk (a camel).

A اشطاء *ashtā-,* (pl. of شطء *shat-*) Suckers, shoots. Summits. *Ishtā-,* (v. n. 4 of شطأ) Shooting forth suckers, leaves, or blades. Growing up and taking after (his) father (a boy).

A اشطاط *ishtāt,* (v. n. 4 of شطّ) Giving an unjust sentence. Tyrannizing. Exceeding just bounds. Going deep, advancing far (in search of something). Travelling in a desert.

A اشطان *ashtān,* (pl. of شطن *shatan*) Long ropes. *Ishtān,* (v. n. 4 of شطن) Putting far off.

A اشطر *ashtur,* (pl. of شطر *shatr*) Parts, halves. Sides, tracts. حلب اشطر الدهر *halaba ashtura'd dahr,* He has milked both teats of fortune, *i.e.* he has experienced good and ill luck.

A اشظاء *ishzā-,* (v. n. 4 of شظي) Hurting the small bones or sinews of the elbows or knees.

A اشظاظ *ishzāz,* (v. n. 4 of شظّ) Fastening the mouth of a sack with a crooked billet. Driving away, scattering. Having a priapism. Cocking his tail or carrying it straight (a camel).

A اشظة *ashizzat,* (pl. of شظاظ *shizāz*) Crooked billets for fastening the mouths of sacks, or making tight the ropes with which loads are fastened.

A اشعاء *ishꜥā-,* (v. n. 4 of شعا for شعو) Taking thought for, minding, attending to, being concerned about. Sympathizing with. Sending forth predatory bands in all directions.

A اشعاب *ishꜥāb,* (v. n. 4 of شعب) Dying. Leaving one's friends, parting with them for ever.

A اشعار *ashꜥār,* (pl. of شعر *shaꜥr*) Hairs (of a man or of a beast). (pl. of شعر *shiꜥr*) Poesy, poems, verses. Sciences. *Ishꜥār,* (v. n. 4 of شعر) Making known, informing, acquainting. Using a symbol, sign, or watchword. Calling out the watchword to each other. Engrossing the mind (care), enveloping the soul. Joining, cementing, causing to stick. Fixing a round knob on the end of a knife-handle. Casting a hairy fœtus (a camel). Lining (a boot) with hair. Being hairy (an embryo, or a part of the body). Putting on another the inner garment called شعار *shiꜥār.* Marking a camel destined to be sacrificed at Mecca (which is done by cutting or piercing the skin till the blood appears). Killing (a king). Speaking poetry.

A اشعاع *ishꜥāꜥ,* (v. n. 4 of شعّ) Scattering urine from side to side (a camel). Darting forth rays (the sun). Coming into ear (grain). Having the grains compact (an ear of corn).

A اشعال *ishꜥāl,* (v. n. 4 of شعل) Setting on fire, kindling, inflaming. Bedaubing (camels) with pitch. Scattering (camels). Sending out predatory horse in every direction. Being spread about, or dispersed over a district of country, when making an excursion against the enemy, in order to render the attack general. Leaking on every side (water from a leathern bag). Gushing violently (blood from a wound). Flowing plentifully (tears). Watering abundantly.

A اشعان *ishꜥān,* (v. n. 4 of شعن) Catching, seizing (an opponent) by the forelock.

A اشعب *ashꜥab,* (pl. شعب *shuꜥb*) (A goat) having the horns distant from each other, also having the hips asunder. Name of a certain miser whose name has become a proverb.

A اشعث *ashꜥas,* (pl. شعث *shuꜥs*) One whose hair is dishevelled and soiled with dust. The prosodial foot وتد *watad.* The plant بهمي *buhma'* when dry. Uncurried (horse).

A اشعر *ashꜥar,* More happily poetical, a better poet. (pl. شعر *shuꜥr*) Flesh growing under the nails. A kind of wart growing between a sheep's claws. (pl. اشاعر *ashāꜥir*) Very hairy. Hair about the hoofs of cattle. The lip of a camel's vulva.

A اشعرة *ashꜥirat,* (pl. of شعار *shiꜥār*) Shirts, shifts, or under garments. Sheets. Horse-cloths. Signs, badges, symbols: watchwords, pass-paroles. Deaths. Trees (with thick intricate branches). Hairs.

A اشعري *ashꜥariy,* (pl. اشاعرة *ashāꜥirat*) Name of a celebrated Musulmān doctor, whose disciples are called Ashariyūn.

A اشعل *ashꜥal,* White-tailed (horse).

A اشعلال *ishꜥilāl,* (v. n. 9 of شعل) Being partially white about the tail (a horse). Staring, sticking up (hair on the body, coat of a beast).

A اشعّة *ashiꜥꜥat,* (pl. of شعّ *shuꜥꜥ* and شعاع *shuꜥāꜥ*) Rays, sunbeams. Lights, splendours.

A اشعيا *ishꜥiyā,* Isaiah the prophet.

A اشعيلال *ishꜥīlāl,* (v. n. 11 of شعل) Having white on the tail and forelocks (a horse). Having the hair (erect).

A اشعينان *ishꜥīnān,* (v. n. 11 of شعن) Being dishevelled (the hair).

A اشغاء *ishghā*, (v. n. 4 of شغا for شغو) Opposing, resisting. Letting one's urine fall drop by drop.

A اشغار *ishghār*, (v. n. 4 of شغر) Being distant from the highway (a house, a watering-place, or a company of travellers). Lifting up (a woman's) leg. Being intricate and perplexing (an account). Being widely extended and on a great scale (warfare).

A اشغال *ashghāl*, (pl. of شغل *shughl*) Affairs, employments, occupations, businesses. *Ishghāl*, (v. n. 4 of شغل) Employing, keeping occupied.

P اشغر *ushghur*, A porcupine.

A اشغل *ashghal*, More or most employed, busy. ما اشغله *mā ashghalahu*, How occupied he is!

A اشغولة *ushghūlat*, Occupation, employ. Any thing which hinders, or keeps a person employed.

A اشغي *ashgha'*, One who has redundant, distorted, or unequal teeth.

A اشفا *ishfā*, A saddler's needle, cobbler's awl.

A اشفاء *ashfā*, (pl. of شفا *shafa'*) Small remains (of life). Extremities, edges, sides, borders. *Ishfā*, (v. n. 4 of شفي) Being on the brink of any thing, at the point of (death). Administering a medicine by which health may be restored. Freeing from disease, imparting health, healing, curing.

A اشفار *ashfār*, (pl. of شفر *shafr* or *shufr*) Margins, sides. Edges of eye-lids. Labra vulvæ.

A اشفاف *ishfāf*, (v. n. 4 of شف) Preferring one to another. Augmenting. Diminishing.

A اشفاق *ashfāk*, (pl. of شفق *shafak*) Compassions, kindnesses, favours. Crepuscles, twilights. Coasts, shores. *Ishfāk*, (v. n. 4 of شفق) Compassionating, pitying. Fearing, being cautious of each other. Being affectionately solicitous about. Making small, diminishing. P اشفاق انگيز *ishfāk-angez*, Inspiring pity or sympathy.

P آشفتانيدن *āshuftānīdan*, To confound, disturb, make mad, or crazy.

A اشفترار *ishfitrār*, (v. n. 4 of شفتر Q) Being divided, scattered. Being broken (a stick). Being widely diffused (the light of a lamp). Dispersion.

P آشفتگي *āshuftagī*, Perturbation, consternation, confusion, contention, disquietude, disturbance, tumult, commotion, disorder.

P آشفتن *āshuftan*, To disturb, or be disturbed. To become foolish, distracted, confounded, enamoured, insane, amazed, astonished, thunderstruck, wretched, miserable. To change, alter.

P آشفته *āshufta*, Enamoured, mad, confounded. آشفته شدن *āshufta shudan*, To be distracted. آشفته كردن *āshufta kardan*, To distract, to disturb. كتابت آشفته *kitābati āshufta*, Illegible writing.

P آشفته حال *āshufta-hāl*, In a distressed state.

P آشفته خاطر *āshufta-khātir*, Disturbed in mind, distressed.

P آشفته روميان *āshufta-rūmiyān*, A live coal.

P آشفته مغز *āshufta-maghz*, Brain-sick.

P آشفته موي *āshufta-mūy*, (by some *moy*) Having dishevelled hair.

A اشفع *ashfa*, Tall of stature.

P اشفند *ashfand*, Name of a district of Nishābūr.

A اشفي *ashfa'*, More or most powerful, efficacious, medicinal, or salutary. Most skilful in medicine. (A man) whose lips do not close. *Ishfa'*, (pl. اشافي *ashāfī*) A cobbler's awl; a large needle.

A اشفية *ashfiyat*, (pl. of شفاء *shifā*) Medicines.

P ايشق *ushak*, Gum ammoniac, galbanum.

A اشق *ushshah*, Gum ammoniac.

A اشق *ashakk*, More or most difficult and troublesome. (A horse) taking the lead in a race, running right and left. (A horse) wide between the haunches. Long (horse).

A اشقاء *ishkā*, (v. n. 4 of شقا for شقو) Rendering miserable. Combing the hair.

A اشقاء *ashikkā*, (pl. of شقيق *shakīk*) Brothers.

A اشقاح *ashkāh*, Dogs' posteriors or chops. *Ishkāh*, (v. n. 4 of شقح) Removing (one) to a distance. Beginning to redden (dates). Going to a distance. Bearing dates beginning to redden (a palm-tree).

A اشقاذ *ishkāz*, (v. n. 4 of شقذ) Driving away.

A اشقاقل *ashkākul*, The root of an Indian tree. *Ishkākul*, A species of wild carrot.

A اشقان *ishkān*, (v. n. 4 of شقن) Having small property. Giving sparingly.

A اشقاه *ishkāh*, (v. n. 4 of شقه not used) Turning colour (unripe dates).

A اشقح *ushkah*, Of a bright red. A reddening, ripening date.

A اشقر *ashkar*, Of a fine bright red. Chesnut (horse) whose mane and tail are of the same colour. Ruddy-complexioned. Glutinous, viscous (blood).

A اشقرار *ishkirār*, (v. n. 9 of شقر) Being of a bright red or light chesnut colour.

G اشقرديون *ashkardiyūn*, Wild garlic.

P اشقره *ashkara*, An extinguished fire-brand.

A اشقياء *ashkiyā*, (pl. of شقي *shakīy*) Poor, miserable. Robbers, thieves, felons, criminals.

P اشك *ashk*, A tear. A drop. Devout, pious. Name of the first king of the Ashkāniyān dynasty of Persian monarchs, supposed by some to be a grandson of that Darius who was defeated by Alexander. He is by others called Arshak, from whence, according to them, the Arsacides took their family surname. اشك تلخ *ashki talkh*, Bitter tears. Wine. اشك خونين *ashki khūnīn*, Tears of blood. اشك شيرين *ashki shīrīn*, (or اشك طرب *ashki tarab*) Tears of joy.

A اشكاء *ishkā*, (v. n. 4 of شكا) Putting forth branches (a tree). (v. n. 4 of شكا for شكو) Finding one sick or complaining. Occasioning complaints, forcing one to complain, adding to his troubles. Putting a stop to, or checking complaints, either by soothing or chiding. Receiving from any one something to put a stop to the complaints of another.

A اشكاد *ishkād*, (v. n. 4 of شكد) Giving. Acquiring or possessing bad cattle.

P آشكار *āshkār*, (آشكارا *āshkārā* or آشكاره *āshkāra*) Clear, evident, manifest, open, public.

P اشكار *ishkār*, Prey, game. Hunting, the chase.

A اشكار *ishkār*, (v. n. 4 of شكر) Being full (the udder). Bearing شكير *shakīr* (a palm, other tree, or vine). Having camels yielding much milk.

P آشكارگي *āshkāragī*, Publicity.

P آشكاره *āsh-kāra*, A cook.

P اشكاري *ishkārī*, A hunter, sportsman, fowler.

A اشكاع *ishkā*, (v. n. 4 of شكع) Enraging. Vexing, annoying, wearying, disgusting.

A اشكال *ashkāl*, (pl. of شكل *shakl*) Forms, figures, shapes, semblances. Obscure, doubtful, intricate matters. Ear-rings made of pearls or pieces of silver resembling each other. *Ishkāl*, (v. n. 4 of شكل) Being difficult, obscure, intricate. Coming to maturity (dates, &c.). Having a redness in the eyes. Clearing (a book) of all obscurities and difficulties. Marking Arabic letters with vowels, or diacritical points.

A اشكام *ishkām*, (v. n. 4 of شكم) Remunerating, rewarding.

P اشكانيان *ashkāniyān*, The family name of the third dynasty of Persian kings, who reigned after Alexander the Great for about 160 years.

P اشكاوند *ashkāwand*, A mountain in Sīstān.

A اشكاه *ishkāh*, (v. n. 4 of شكه) Being difficult and obscure.

P اشكبار *ashk-bār*, Shedding tears, tears falling. ديدهء اشكبار *dīdaī ashk-bār*, Weeping eyes. اشكبار شدن *ashk-bār shudan*, To melt into tears.

P اشكباري *ashk-bārī*, Weeping.

P اشكبوس *ashkbūs*, A hero killed by Rustam.

P اشكره *ishkira*, A hunting-hawk.

A اشكز *ushkuzz*, A girth, belt, surcingle (of white leather), with which a saddle is fastened.

P اشكستن *ishkastan*, To break, bruise, squeeze.

P اشكش *ashkash*, Name of an ancient hero.

P اشكفت *ashkift*, Surprise. *Ishkaft*, A cave.

P اشكفه *ishkufa*, A blossom, bud. Vomiting.

A اشكل *ashkal*, The mountain lote-tree. White-thighed (sheep). Reddish-eyed (man). Any thing which has red and white mixed. Any thing white with an inclination to red and black. (A camel) whose dark colour has a mixture of red in it. More or most resembling. ماء اشكل *mā ashkal*, Water mingled with blood.

P اشكل *ishkil*, (A horse) whose right fore-foot and left hind-foot are white. Fraud, craft, imposture.

A اشكلة *ashkalat*, A single mountain lote-tree. Necessity, want. Mixture, confusion. Likeness.

P اشكم *ishkam*, (for شكم *shikam*) The belly.

P اشكنبه *ishkamba*, The stomach of beasts.

P اشكنج *ishkunj*, A nip, a pinch.

P اشكنجه *ishkanja*, Torment, torture, rack.

P اشكنه *ishkina*, A wrinkle. A musical note.

Bread crumbled into broth.

P اشكو *ishkū*, A roof. A layer or row in the covering of a house. A fowler, bird-catcher.

P آشكوب *āshkūb*, A ceiling, a stage, a story. A row of bricks in a wall. Heaven.

P اشكوب *ashkūb*, A row or layer in the roofing of a house. *Ushkūb*, The elbow: a cubit.

P اشكوخ *ishkokh*, A trip, stumble, slip, blunder.

P اشكوخيدن *ishkokhīdan*, To slip, slide, fall.

P اشكوفه *ushkūfa*, Vomiting. A flower, blossom.

P اشكوه *ushkoh*, Majesty, authority, greatness.

P اشكيل *ishkīl*, A horse whose right fore-foot and left hind-foot are white. Fraud, craft, imposture.

P اشكيل چشم *ishkīl chashum*, A kind of bramble.

P اشكيوان *ishkewān*, Name of a place.

P اشكيود *ashkyūd*, Compounded, mixed.

P اشگرف *ashgarf*, Agreeable, excellent. *Ishgarf*, Large, coarse, thick. Dignity, pomp.

P اشگفت *ishguft*, The expanding of a flower.

P اشگنش *ashganish* or *ishganish*, The building of a wall.

P آشگون *āshgūn*, Name of a country.

A اشل *ashl*, A Basra-measure of forty cubits.

A اشلّ *ashall*, One who has a withered hand.

A اشلاء *ashlās*, (pl. of شلو *shilw*) Members, joints, bodies. Remains (of water). Reins of a bridle. Thin-bitted (bridles). *Ishlās*, (v. n. 4 of شلا for شلو) Calling (a sheep, dog, or camel) by name. Calling (a horse) by holding out a corn-bag. Setting (a dog in pursuit of game).

A اشلال *ishlāl*, (v. n. 4 of شلّ) Being withered, dried up (the hand). Causing (the hand) to wither.

A اشلّة *ashillat*, (pl. of شليل *shalīl*) Clothes worn under armour. Cloths of hair or wool laid across the loins (of camels).

A اشم *asham*, (v. n. of اشم) Being pained.

A اشمّ *ashamm*, High (mountain). High (shoulder). High-nosed. Grave, dignified, respectable.

A اشمات *ishmāt*, (v. n. 4 of شمت) Causing (any one) to rejoice at another's misfortune.

A اشمار *ishmār*, (v. n. 4 of شمر) Making one to proceed quickly. Tying a camel's teats together. Impregnating the female. Folding, inserting.

A اشماس *ishmās*, (v. n. 4 of شمس) Being bright and sun-shiny.

A اشماط *ashmāt*, Pot-herbs and spiceries put into victuals whilst cooking. *Ishmāt*, (v. n. 4 of شمط) Mixing. Having hairs black and white.

A اشماع *ishmāع*, (v. n. 4 of شمع) Giving good light (a candle).

A اشمال *ashmāl*, (pl. of شمل *shamal*) Small quantities (of rain, men, or fruits). *Ishmāl*, (v. n. 4 of شمل) Being exposed to the north wind. Giving one a covering or clothing for the whole body. Wrapping up one's self in a garment, so that no part of the body appears. Surrounding on all sides, sending universally (evil). Tying the udders of cattle in bags, called شمال *shimāl*, that they may not be sucked. Gathering or pulling (dates and other fruit) leaving but a small part remaining. (A stallion camel) impregnating half a flock or two-thirds of camels; (when he is successful with the whole it is then expressed by اقمام *ikmām*).

A اشمام *ishmām*, (v. n. 4 of شمّ) Smelling. Giving or allowing to smell. Walking with the head erect. Extending the hand. Turning from any thing. Departing from. Turning to the right and left. Giving to a quiescent consonant a slight sound (or scent) of ضمّه *zamma* or كسره *kasra*, but not so as to lengthen the syllable, or make one syllable more. Circumcising partially. واو اشمام *vāvi ishmām*, Quiescent or silent و *vāv*, when preceded by خ and followed by either ا, د, ر, ز, س, ش, ن, ي, ه, or پ, quiescent, *i.e.* not having a vowel.

A اشمخرار *ishmikhrār*, (v. n. 4 of شمخر Q) Being tall and lofty.

A اشمذة *ashmazat*, Swift of flight (a bird).

A اشمط *ashmat*, (pl. شمط *shumt* and شمطان *shumtān*) Half gray, bi-coloured.

A اشمطاط *ishmitāt*, The being half gray-haired.

A اشمعطاط *ishmiعtāt*, (v. n. 4 of شمعط Q) Being filled with rage. Making haste, and distributing themselves all about in pursuit. Impatiently striking the ground (horses). Being dispersed (camels). Being erect (penis).

A اشمعلال *ishmiعlāl*, (v. n. 4 of شمعل Q) Being on the brink of. Going on a predatory excursion. Roving in a large pasture. Making haste, and dispersing themselves in search of any thing.

A اشمق *ashmak*, The foam of a camel's mouth mixed with blood.

A اشمل *ashmal*, More or most perfect, complete, universal, comprehensive, surpassing, transcendent. Larger, largest. *Ashmul*, (pl. of شمال *shimāl*) Left hands.

G اشموسا *ashmūsā*, A species of merow.

A اشموم *ushmūm*, Name of two districts in Egypt.

A اشمون *ashmūn*, Name of a city, and of a canal from the river Nile, near Damietta in Egypt.

A اشمونين *ashmūnīn*, A city of Egypt, where many pyramids, sphinxes, &c. still remain.

A اشمويل *ashmawīl*, The prophet Samuel.

P آشميد *āshamīd*, (for آشاميد) A draught.

A اشمئزاز *ishmiعzāz*, (v. n. 4 of شمأز Q) Drawing one's self together. Being affrighted. Creeping (as the skin does with terror). Disliking, detesting.

A اشمئطاط *ishmiعtāt*, The being half-gray.

A اشميطاط *ishmītāt*, (v. n. 11 of شمط) Being half-gray. Being mixed.

P اشن *ashan*, A turned vest. An unripe melon.

P آشنا *āshnā*, A friend, companion, comrade, acquaintance. Swimming, floating. A swimmer. آشنا و بيگانه *āshnā u bīgāna*, Known and unknown, friends and strangers. مذاق آشنا *mazāk-āshnā*, Having a delicate taste. معنى آشنا *maعna'-āshnā*, Intelligent, learned in mysteries, significations, or relations of things. سداد آشنا *sadād-āshnā*, Accustomed to what is right, knowing the right way.

P اشنا *ashnā*, A gem, precious stone. A swimmer.

P آشناب *āshnāb*, A swimmer.

P اشناب *ishnāb*, A swimmer.

P آشناباز *āshnā-bāz*, A swimmer.

P آشنابازي *āshnā-bāzī*, Swimming, natation.

P آشنا پرست *āshnā-parast*, Friendly.

P آشناد *āshnād*, The 25th day of the month.

A اشناع *ishnāع*, A going fast, a making haste.

A اشناف *ishnāf*, (v. n. 4 of شنف) Adorning (a girl) with ear-rings.

P اشنافتن *ishnāftan*, To understand, perceive.

A اشناق *ashnāk*, The intermediate numbers between any two, as between 10 and 40; and between 40 and 100 (especially with regard to the proportion of cattle taxed by the Muhammadan law from such herds or flocks for pious uses). Mulcts of expiation (for manslaughter), or rather, supplementary parts of larger fines formerly paid; also mulcts for maiming. *Ishnāk*, (v. n. 4 of شنق) Exacting those mulcts, or being obliged to pay them. Exalting one's self (from self-conceit). Checking (a camel) with the bridle till the back of his head touches the front of the saddle. Raising (his) head in that manner (a camel). Oppressing. Tying a string, called شناق *shināk* round the neck of a full bottle, and carrying or hanging it up thereby.

P آشناگر *āshnāgar*, A swimmer.

A اشنان *ishnān*, (v. n. 4 of شنّ) Sending a marauding party to plunder on all sides. Sprinkling (water). Becoming old and worn (a leathern bottle).

P اشنان *ushnān* or *ishnān*, The herb alkali, and the ashes which are made from it, with which they wash clothes. اشنان دارو *ushnān-dārū*, Hyssop.

A اشنانيّ *ushnāniy*, A seller of alkali. Name of several traditionists.

P آشناو *āshnāv*, A swimmer.

P آشناور *āshnāwar*, A swimmer.

P آشناه *āshnāh*, The art of swimming, natation. A swimmer.

P آشنايان *āshnāyān*, Acquaintances.

P آشنائي *āshnāī*, Friendship, acquaintance.

A اشنب *ashnab*, One who has a clean, fresh, and sweet mouth and teeth.

A اشنة *ushnat*, A sort of dodder that entwines itself around the oak and pine.

A اشنع *ashnaع*, Filthy, foul, odious, disagreeable. Unpleasant (day).

P اشنود *ashnawad*, Name of the second of the five days added to the last month of the Persian year, in order to make their twelve months, of 30 days each, equal to a solar year. *Ushnūd*, He heard.

P اشنوشه *ishnūsha*, Sneezing.

A اشنونة *ushnūnat*, Name of a fortress in Spain.

P اشنه *ashna*, Immature. *Ushna*, Alkali. Moss which grows on trees.

A اشنى *ushna'*, A village in Upper Egypt.

P اشنيدن *ishnīdan*, To hear, to listen.

P آشو *āshū*, Calamity, hurt, trouble.

P اشو *ashū*, (in zand and Pāzand) Heavenly.

A اشواء *ishwāʼ*, (v. n. 4 of شوي) Giving meat to roast. Preparing for roasting. Serving up roast meat. Being ripe and fit for parching (wheat). Turning yellow and withering (a palm-leaf). Wounding but not mortally. Leaving (meat) from dinner or supper. Acquiring the worst kinds of cattle.

A اشوار *ishwār*, (v. n. 4 of شور) Raising (fire).

A اشواط *ashwāt*, (pl. of شوط *shawt*) Lists, courses. Single heats. Turns, rounds. Rays of light which enter at crevices.

A اشواق *ashwāk*, (pl. of شوق *shawk*) Desires.

A اشواك *ashwāk*, (pl. of شوك *shawk*) Thorns. *Ishwāk*, (v. n. 4 of شوك) Abounding in thorns.

A اشوال *ashwāl*, (pl. of شول *shawl*) Small quantities of water left in the bottoms of vessels. (Camels) seven or eight months after foaling. (Camels) having the udders wrinkled from want of milk.

P آشوب *āshūb*, Terror, dread, fear. Grief, affliction, misfortune. Confusion, discord, disturbance, tumult, riot, sedition. (in comp.) Disturbing.

P اشوب *ashūb*, A poker, a coal-rake.

P آشوب انگيز *āshūb-angez*, An exciter of discord.

P آشوبتر *āshūbtar*, More grievous.

P آشوبناك *āshūbnāk*, Terrified, confused.

P آشوبيدن *āshūbīdan*, To be confused, disturbed.

A اشوذ *ashwaz*, Name of the son of Shem, son of Noah. (pl. اشاوذ *ashāwiz*) A created being.

A اشور *ushūr*, (pl. of اشر *ushur* and *ushar*) The notched indented surfaces of the teeth, or a saw.

P آشوردن *āshurdan*, To mix, mingle, intermix, join, associate, couple, conjoin. To ferment.

A اشوز *ashwaz*, Proud, haughty, arrogant.

A اشوس *ashwas*, One who contracts his eyes and knits his brow to look more steadily. Long.

A اشوص *ashwas*, One who winks with his eyes.

A اشوع *ashwaʻ*, One who has rough and disordered locks (of hair).

P اشوغ *ushūgh*, Of unknown family or country.

P آشوفتگي *āshūftagī*, Disquietude, uneasiness.

P آشوفتن *āshūftan*, To be disturbed.

P آشوفته *āshūfta*, Disturbed in mind.

A اشوق *ashwak*, Inflamed with love. Long, tall. More or most inclined or propense.

A اشول *ushūl*, Ropes for measuring.

A اشؤن *ashʼun*, (pl. of شأن) Lachrymal ducts.

A اشوه *ashwah*, Ugly. One with an evil or fascinating eye. Self-important, haughty, proud.

A اشه *ushah*, Gum ammoniac.

A اشهاء *ish-hāʼ*, (v. n. 4 of شها for شهو) Giving one what he longs for. Viewing with an evil eye.

A اشهاب *ish-hāb*, (v. n. 4 of شهب) Begetting white or ash-coloured foals. Emaciating or destroying cattle (a severe year).

A اشهاد *ash-hād*, (pl. of شاهد *shāhid*) Witnesses, such as have been present (eye-witnesses). *Ish-hād*, (v. n. 4 of شهد) Citing, summoning. Being a martyr. Being menstruous (a girl), arriving at the age of puberty. Having a seminal effusion.

A اشهار *ish-hār*, (v. n. 4 of شهر) Making known. Entering upon or spending a month. Drawing (a sword). Entering upon her ninth month (a pregnant woman).

A اشهب *ash-hab*, White or ash-coloured (camel or mule). Whitish (ambergris). Cold, frosty (day). Shining, polished (spear). Barren (year). A lion. A difficult business. A whitish she-goat. اشهب ادهم *ash-hab adham*, Dark red, chesnut-coloured. اشهب اخضر *ash-hab akhzar*, A light lively green. *Ash-hub*, (pl. of شهاب) Flaming fires.

A اشهباب *ish-hibāb*, (v. n. 9 of شهب) Being of an ash-colour (a horse).

A الاشهبان *al ash-habāni*, Two years without rain between two rainy and verdant years.

A اشهر *ash-har*, More or most celebrated, known, notorious. الاشهران *al ash-harāni*, The drum and standard. *Ash-hur*, (pl. of شهر *shahr*) Months. اشهر معلومات *ash-hur maʻlūmāt*, The four known or sacred months, viz. شوّال *shawwāl*, ذو القعده *zū'l kaʻda*, ذو الحجّه *zū'l hijja*, and محرّم *muharram*, during which it is reckoned unlawful to go to war (a prohibition which is more ancient among the Arabs than Muhammadism).

A اشهل *ash-hal*, Gray-eyed. Name of an idol.

A اشهلال *ish-hilāl*, (v. n. 9 of شهل) Having eyes of a darkish gray, with a shade of red or pink.

A اشهى *ash-ha'*, More desirous, or desirable.

A اشهيباب *ish-hībāb*, (v. n. 11 of شهب) Being of an ash-colour. Remaining green in some parts or patches (withered and dry corn).

A آشي *āsha'*, Jesse, the father of David.

A اشي *ashy*, (v. n. of اشي) Feigning, inventing. Finding necessary, having occasion, being forced.

A اشيّ *ashīy* or *ushīy*, The star on (a horse's) forehead. *Ushīy*, Whiteness of leg (in a horse). *Ushayy*, A small palm-tree. Name of a valley.

A اشياء *ashyāʼ*, (pl. of شيء *shayʼ*) Things. Clothes, effects. *Ishyāʼ*, (v. n. 4 of شاء for شيأ) Forcing (any one) to take refuge.

A اشياخ *ashyākh*, (pl. of شيخ *shaykh*) Old men, sages, senators, doctors, prelates, dervises, religious men. اشياخ النجوم *ashyākhu'n nujūm*, The originals of the stars, which are seven.

A اشياع *ashyāʻ*, (pl. of شيع *shayʻ*) Parts, quantities. Lions' whelps. (pl. of شيعة *shīʻat*) Companions, equals, peers. Followers, dependants.

P اشياف ماميثا *ashyāfi māmīsā*, Poppy-juice.

P آشيان *āshyān*, (or آشيانه *āshyāna*) A nest. A ceiling, roof. جنّت آشيان *jannat-āshyān*, (Having a nest in Paradise) the blessed, the deceased of happy memory, dwelling in Paradise. سعادت آشيان *saʻādat-āshyān*, The nest of felicity (one of the titles of the Ottoman Porte). آشيانه كردن *āshyāna kardan*, To build a nest.

A اشياوات *ashyāwāt*, (pl. of شيء *shayʼ*) Things.

A اشيايا *ashyāyā'*, (pl. of شيء *shayʼ*) Things.

P آشيب *āshīb*, Terror. Affliction. Confusion.

A اشيب *ashyab*, (pl. شيب *shīb* and *shuyub*) White, gray-haired. Cold and cloudy. Old man.

P آشيج *āshīj*, Opposite, adverse, contrary.

A اشير *ashyur*, (pl. of شيار *shiyār*) Saturdays.

P آشيگاه *āshīgāh*, A privy.

A اشيم *ashyam*, Distinguished by a mole or any other natural mark.

P آشين *āshīn*, A cook. A baker.

P آشينه *āshīna*, An egg.

A اشيه *ashyah*, More or most base, shameful. More or most reproachful. (A man) having various-coloured hair; (ابلق *ablak* is applied to a grizzled horse, and اذرأ *azraʼ* to a grizzled goat).

P آشيهه *āshīha*, (or اشيهه *ashīha*) The neighing of a horse. Echo.

A اصّ *ass*, (v. n. of اصّ) Breaking. Rendering smooth. Shining, glittering. Being firm in flesh, compact, and abounding in milk (a camel). Crowding, pressing, thronging. *Iss*, *ass*, or *uss*, (pl. اصاص *isās*) Root, origin.

A اصاء *isāʼ*, (v. n. 4 of صاي) Causing to chirp.

A اصاب *isāb*, (v. n. 4 of صئب) Having the head full of nits.

A اصابة *isābat*, (v. n. 4 of صاب for صوب) Overtaking, reaching, arriving at, finding, discovering, meeting with, obtaining. Injuring, hurting, afflicting. Speaking properly, conceiving well, hitting the mark. Striking, touching. Ascending. Accuracy. Want, necessity. Contagion.

A اصابع *asābiʻ*, (pl. of اصبع *asbaʻ*) Fingers. ذات الاصابع *zātu'l asābiʻ*, Name of a place in Syria. غايت اصابع *ghāyat asābiʻ*, The little finger. اصابع زينب *asābiʻi zaynab*, A kind of sweetmeats. اصابع العذاري *asābiʻu'l ʻazāra'*, A species of long black grape. اصابع الفتيات *asābiʻu'l fatayāt*, Sweet basil. اصابع صفر *asābiʻ sufr*, Turmeric. اصابع فرعون *asābiʻ firʻawn*, Name of a kind of pearl or stone like a finger found in the Red Sea. اصابع هرمس *asābiʻu hurmus*, Wild saffron.

A اصابل *asābil*, (pl. of اصطبل *istabl*) Stables.

A اصابيع *asābīʻ*, (pl. of اصبوع *usbūʻ*) Fingers.

A اصاتة *isātat*, (v. n. 4 of صات for صوت) Sounding, making a noise, exclaiming, shouting.

A اصاحيب *asāhīb*, (pl. of صاحب *sāhib*,) Lords, friends, companions, associates.

A اصاخة *isākhat*, A listening, an attending to.

A اصاد *isād*, A hollow place between mountains, where water stagnates, a marsh. A kind of dish or plate. ذات الاصاد *zātu'l isād*, Name of a place.

A اصادة *isādat*, (v. n. 4 of صاد for صيد) Injuring, hurting. Medicating, curing (a camel) of the disease called صاد *sād*.

A اصادق *asādik*, (pl. of صديق *sadīk*) Sincere, true. Friends.

A آصار *āsār*, (pl. of اصر *isr*) Oaths or formulæ used in divorcing, freeing slaves, or vowing to God.

A اصار *isār*, (or اصارة *isārat*) (pl. اصر *usur*) A short rope for fastening the lower parts of a tent to the pins. A tent-pin. A basket. Dry herbage, hay. A sheet or cloth in which fodder is gathered.

A اصارة *isārat*, (v. n. 4 of صار for صور) Causing to incline. Making crooked. Breaking. (v. n. 4 of صار for صير) Causing to become.

A اصارم *asārim*, (pl. of صرم *sirm*) Contiguous streets, adjoining houses. Blows. Crowds.

A اصاريم *asārīm*, (pl. of صرم) Blows. Crowds.

A اصاص *isās*, (pl. of آصّ *ass*, *iss*, or *uss*) Roots.

A اصاصة *isāsat*, (v. n. 4 of صاص for صيص) Producing the bad date صيص *sīs* (a palm-tree).

A اصاطل *asātil*, (pl. of اصطبل *istabl*) Stables.

A اصّاعد *issāɛud*, Ascent.

A اصاغر *asāghir*, (and اصاغرة *asāghirat*) (pl. of اصغر *asghar*) Smaller, less. Contemptible.

A اصافة *isāfat*, (v. n. 4 of صاف for صيف) Entering upon the summer-season. Begetting children in old age. Averting (evil from any one).

A آصال *āsāl*, (pl. of اصيل *asīl*) Evenings.

A اصالة *asālat*, (v. n. of اصل) Being firmly rooted, steady, immoveable. Being steady and solid (the judgment). Firmness, constancy, solidity of judgment. Radicalness.

A اصالةً *asālatan*, In one's own right.

A اصّالح *issāluh*, (v. n. 6 of صلح irregular) Making peace with one another, becoming reconciled.

A اصالف *asālif*, (pl. of اصلف) Hard lands.

A اصالق *asālik*, (pl. of صلق) Level grounds.

A اصائد *asāɛid*, (pl. of صاد *sād*) Veins between the eyes of a camel. Diseases in camels causing a discharge at the nose. Camels affected therewith.

A اصائل *asāɛil*, (pl. of اصيل *asīl*) Evenings.

A اصباء *asbāɛ*, (pl. of صبا *saba'*) East winds, zephyrs, gentle gales. *Isbāɛ*, (v. n. 4 of صبأ) Rising (a star). Growing (a tooth or nail). Directing, guiding an enemy against any one. Rushing upon, attacking unexpectedly. Putting one's fingers into the dish to help one's self to food. (v. n. 4 of صبا for صبو) Bearing a male child. Turning to the east wind. Inclining or inviting one to juvenile practices or frolics. Making frantic with love. Having an east wind (a day)

A اصباب *asbāb*, (pl. of صبب *sabab*) Sloping grounds. *Isbāb*, (v. n. 4 of صبّ) Entering upon a sloping ground, beginning to descend a declivity.

A اصباح *asbāh*, (pl. of صبح *subh*) Dawns, auroras, day-breaks, mornings. *Isbāh*, (v. n. 4 of صبح) Rising betimes. Coming, doing any thing, early in the morning. Bringing forth the morning. Entering on the morning. Becoming (learned). Diligence, application of mind. Knowing, being well-informed. Looking to the end or issue of any thing. The morning, the dawn.

A اصبار *asbār*, (pl. of صبر *sibr* and *subr*) White clouds. Sides, brinks, margins, brims. الي اصباره *ila' asbārihi*, (Filled) to the brim (vessel). باصباره *bi asbārihi*, In whole, the whole of it. *Isbār*, (v. n. 4 of صبر) Commanding one to exercise patience. Detaining one forcibly, and putting to death. Rendering (any one) patient. Eating a biscuit called صبيرة *sabīrat*. Falling into misfortune (called امّ صبّور *umm sabbūr*). Becoming acid even unto bitterness (milk). Putting the stopple into a cruet. Covering over (the mouth of a vessel). Sitting upon a cairn or heap of stones, called صبير *sabīr*.

A اصباغ *asbāgh*, (pl. of صبغ *sibgh*) Colours, tinctures, dyes. *Isbāgh*, (v. n. 4 of صبغ) Conferring benefits abundantly. Having dates partly ripe (a palm-tree). Bringing forth a hairy fœtus (a camel). Dipping the hands into the flesh and blood of swine, *i.e.* eating them.

A اصباهان *isbāhān*, Ispahān. One of the twelve modes of music.

A اصبح *asbah*, (fem. صبحاء *sabhāɛ*) Black, inclining to red. A lion. Hair naturally white and red mixed. One whose hair is of that colour.

A اصبحيّ *asbahīy*, A whipping. A scourge.

A اصبر *asbar*, More or most patient. ما اصبرهم علي النار *mā asbarahum ɛala'n nār*, How they will have to endure the fire!

A اصبرار *isbirār*, (v. n. 9 of صبر) Being patient.

A اصبرة *asbirat*, Camels, and other cattle, which go out in the morning and return in the evening without straying.

A اصبع *asbaɛ*, *asbiɛ*, *asbuɛ*, *isbaɛ*, *isbiɛ*, *isbuɛ*, *usbaɛ*, *usbiɛ*, and *usbuɛ*, (pl. اصابع *asābiɛ*) A finger. A favourable impression. A good sign. مغلّ الاصبع *mughillu'l isbaɛ*, Perfidious.

A اصبغ *asbagh*, (A horse) whose fore-lock and tip of the ear are white. White-tailed (bird). A torrent, a mighty stream. One who, when beaten, bedaubs his clothes. Thin black mud.

A اصبوحة *usbūhat*, The morning, dawn, aurora.

A اصبوع *usbūɛ*, (pl. اصابيع *asābīɛ*) A finger.

P اصبهان *isbahān*, Ispahān, capital of Persia.

A اصبهبذيّة *asbahbazīyat*, A certain coin current in Irāk. Name of a college in Baghdad.

A اصبي *asbi*, (or اصبية *asbiyat*) (pl. of صبيّ *sabīy*) Boys, youths. Edges of swords or knives. Princes, chiefs of the people. Sides of the cheek-bones or jaws. Those parts of the skull below the ears. Pupils, apples of eyes.

A اصبيحاح *isbīhāh*, (v. n. 11 of صبح) Being naturally of a red and white colour (hair).

A اصت *ast*, (v. n. of اصت) Being bare (a field).

A اصتقار *istikār*, (v. n. 8 of صقر) Being kindled, blazing (a fire).

A اصتلاح *istilāh*, (v. n. 8 of صلح) Being reconciled together. Coming together about one business.

A اصحّ *asahh*, More or most true or authentic. More or most accurate, correct, sound, or healthy.

A اصحاء *is-hāɛ*, (v. n. 4 of صحا for صحو) Becoming clear and serene (the sky). Recovering from ebriety. Going out, taking the air when fine.

A اصحّاء *asihhāɛ*, (and اصحّة *asihhat*) (pl. of صحاح *sahāh* and صحيح *salāh*) Free from blemish, sound, whole. Complete, perfect.

A اصحاب *as-hāb*, (pl. of صاحب *sāhib*) Lords. Possessors, masters. Friends, companions, intimates. Inhabitants. اصحاب اخبية و خيام *as-hābi akhbiya u khiyām*, Dwellers in pavilions and tents. اصحاب اعتبار *as-hābi iɛtibār*, Esteemed, confidential, honourable men. اصحاب النار *as-hābu'n nār*, Companions of fire, the damned. اصحاب بدع و ضلالت *as-hābi bidaɛ u zalālat*, Innovators, deviating from the right path. اصحاب تدبير *as-hābi tadbīr*, Sage ministers, prudent counsellors. اصحاب تواريخ *as-hābi tawārīkh*, Historians, writers of chronicles. P اصحاب جاه *as-hābi jāh*, Eminent, possessed of dignity. A اصحاب جحيم *as-hābi jahīm*, Inhabitants of hell. اصحاب دولت *as-hābi dawlat*, Grandees, nobles, great men, ministers. بعض اصحاب روايت *baɛzi as-hābi riwāyat*, Certain historians. اصحاب سيوف *as-hābi suyūf*, (Soldiers) possessed of swords, swordsmen. اصحاب علم *as-hābi ɛilm*, Learned men, the literati. اصحاب فهوم *as-hābi fuhūm*, Intelligent, sagacious, endowed with understanding. اصحاب قصص *as-hābi kisas*, Historians, masters of history. اصحاب كهف *as-hābi kahf*, Inhabitants of the cave, *i.e.* the seven sleepers. P اصحاب گزين *as-hābi guzīn*, Select friends, the companions of Muhammad. A اصحاب نفاق *as-habi nifāk*, Impious liars, hypocrites, infidels. T آل و اصحابي *āl u as-hābī*, The posterity and companions of Muhammad. A *Is-hāb*, (v. n. 4 of صحب) Associating, giving a companion, joining. Taking, receiving a companion. Leaving a leathern bottle hairy and undressed. Marching on without halting. Having a green film floating on its surface (water). Preventing. Having a son who has attained the age of puberty. Becoming gentle and tractable after having been stubborn and refractory. Tending, taking care (of a maniac).

A اصحاح *is-hāh*, (v. n. 4 of صحّ) Having one's family or stock safe and sound. Restoring to health.

A اصحار *is-hār*, (v. n. 4 of صحر) Going forth into the desert. Being wide and spacious (a place). Being one-eyed.

A اصحاف *is-hāf*, (v. n. 4 of صحف) Collecting or being collected (books).

A اصحب *as-hab*, (An ass) whitish dust-coloured, inclining to red.

A اصحر *as-har,* (An ass) whitish dust-coloured, inclining to red. A lion.

A اصحل *as-hal,* Hoarse.

A اصحم *as-ham,* Black, inclining to yellow.

A اصحن *as-hun,* (pl. of صحن *sahn*) Dishes.

A اصحيرار *is-hīrār,* (v. n. 11 of صحر) Turning reddish and white (withered grass).

A اصحيمام *is-hīmām,* (v. n. 11 of صحم) Becoming yellow (grass). Becoming of a bright green. From green, turning yellow with a mixture of black. Wanting rain (the earth). Being nipped by cold and beginning to wither (corn).

A اصخاد *iskhād,* (v. n. 4 of صخد) Basking in the sun.

A اصخار *iskhār,* (v. n. 4 of صخر) Coming to a rocky, stony place.

A اصخيتات *iskhītāt,* (v. n. 11 of صخت not used) Subsiding (the swelling of a wound). Being restored to health.

A اصد *usd,* A small shift. *Isad,* (pl. of اصدة *isdat*) Places where people assemble.

A اصدا *asdaₑ,* Rust-coloured. (A goat) of a reddish black colour.

A اصداء *isdāₑ,* (v. n. 4 of صدي) Returning an echo. Dying.

A اصداد *isdād,* (v. n. 4 of صدّ) Averting, preventing, hindering, prohibiting. Being purulent, full of corrupted matter.

A اصدار *isdār,* (v. n. 4 of صدر) Leading home from water.

A اصّداع *issidāₑ,* (v. n. 8 of صدع) Being split, cleft, divided, separated, scattered.

A اصداغ *asdāgh,* (pl. of صدغ *sudgh*) The temples, that part of the face from the eyes to the ears; the hair that flows around the temples.

A اصداف *asdāf,* (pl. of صدف *sadaf*) Shells, shell-fish, pearls. *Isdāf,* (v. n. 4 of صدف) Diverting from, alienating, estranging.

A اصداق *isdāk,* (v. n. 4 of صدق) Giving (a woman) her dowry.

A آصدة *āsidat,* A kind of dish.

A اصدة *isdat,* (pl. اصد *isad*) A place where people collect. *Usdat,* A small shirt, such as is called a Banyan shirt in India. A shift worn by girls.

A اصدح *asdah,* A lion (as roaring).

A اصدر *asdar,* Breasted, having a large breast.

A اصدران *asdarāni,* (dual) Two veins below the temples. جاء يضرب اصدريه *jāₑa yazribu asdarayhi,* He came empty.

A اصدغان *asdaghāni,* The two temporal veins.

A اصدف *asdaf,* (A horse) that straddles much, and whose feet point outwards.

A اصدق *asdak,* More or most true or veracious, truer, truest. اصدق القائلين *asdahu'l kāₑilīn,* The truest of speakers (an epithet of God).

A اصدقاء *asdikāₑ,* (pl. of صديق) True friends.

A اصدم *asdam,* Bald about the temples.

A اصر *asr,* (v. n. of اصر) Inclining, turning. Swearing to divorce or manumit. Vowing. Breaking. Detaining, imprisoning, coercing. Fixing the pin اصار *isār* to a tent. *Isr,* Whatever gives inclination or bias. (pl. آصار *āsār* or اصران *isrān*) An oath or formula used in pronouncing a divorce, manumitting a slave, or vowing to God. The orifice of the ear. *Isr, asr,* or *usr,* A compact, convention, treaty, agreement. A crime, sin, fault. A burthen, load, weight. *Usur,* (pl. of اصار *isār*) Short ropes with which they fasten the inner parts of tents to the poles. Sheets or cloths in which grass is gathered. Herbage, fresh grass, dry hay.

A اصراء *isrāₑ,* (v. n. 4 of صري) Selling a sheep that has been kept unmilked for several days.

A اصراب *isrāb,* (v. n. 4 of صرب) Giving, bestowing. Giving sour milk to drink.

A اصراح *isrāh,* (v. n. 4 of صرح) Speaking openly, shewing plainly.

A اصراخ *isrākh,* (v. n. 4 of صرخ) Assisting.

A اصراد *isrād,* A shooting beyond the mark.

A اصرار *isrār,* (v. n. 4 of صرّ) Pricking his ears (a horse). Being ready to come forth (an ear of corn). Going to a distance and making haste. Persevering, persisting in any thing bad, contracting a wrong habit. Obstinacy, stubbornness.

A اصراف *isrāf,* (v. n. 4 of صرف) Composing a poem whose verses end in different vowels. The last syllable of verses ending with different vowels.

A اصرام *asrām,* (pl. of صرم *sirm*) Adjoining streets or houses. Blows. Crowds. *Isrām,* (v. n. 4 of صرم) Being poor, destitute. Being the season for gathering ripe dates. Having dates fit for gathering (a palm-tree). Being needy, having a numerous family. Possessing a herd of camels.

A اصران *isrān,* (pl. of اصر *isr*) Orifices of ears. Oaths or formulæ used in pronouncing a divorce, freeing slaves, or vowing to God.

A آصرة *āsirat,* (pl. اواصر *awāsir*) Good-will, benevolence, grace, favour. Whatever renders one agreeable to another, as companionship, affinity, or merit of any kind. A short rope, with which the inner part of tents are fastened to the poles. (pl. of اصار *isār,* q.v.).

A اصرّة *asirrat,* (pl. of صرار *sirār*) Strings with which they tie the dugs of camels, to prevent the young from sucking.

A اصرع *asruₑ,* (pl. of صرع *sarₑ* or *sirₑ*) Modes, kinds, sorts, similitudes.

A اصرم *asram,* Poor, encumbered by a family.

A اصرمان *asramāni,* Night and day. The crow and the wolf. The crow and the bird صرد *surad.*

A اصرّي *asirra'* or *asirrī,* Labour, pains. Purpose, design, resolution.

A اصريباب *isrībāb,* The being smooth and sleek.

A اصص *usus,* (pl. of اصوص *asūs*) Fat (camels) not conceiving. Thieves, robbers.

A اصطباب *istibāb,* The being poured out.

A اصطباح *istibāh,* (v. n. 8 of صبح) Taking a morning draught. Lighting a lamp or candle.

A اصطبار *istibār,* (v. n. 8 of صبر) Striving to be patient. Being patient. Tracing, tracking.

A اصطباغ *istibāgh,* (v. n. 8 of صبغ) Being seasoned with sauce. Being dyed. Baptism.

A اصطبان *istibān,* A departing, a retiring.

G اصطبّة *ustubbat,* Hemp, tow, bards, oakum.

G اصطبل *istabl,* A stable, stall. اصطبل دوابّ *istabli dawābb,* A stable. A cow-house.

A اصطحاب *istihāb,* (v. n. 8 of صحب) Associating together. Keeping each other company. Keeping, taking care of. Fellowship, society.

A اصطحام *istihām,* The act of standing upright.

A اصطخاب *istikhāb,* (v. n. 8 of صخب) Being noisy and clamorous. Roaring (waves). Being noisy and confused (the chirping of birds).

A اصطخاد *istikhād,* (v. n. 8 of صخد) Standing upright in the sun.

A اصطخام *istikhām,* The act of standing erect.

P اصطخر *istakhr,* The ancient name of Persepolis, the capital of Persia during the three first dynasties; the royal residence being afterwards removed to Madāyin on the Tigris. A lake, pool.

A اصطداد *istidād,* The being covered, or veiled.

A اصطدام *istidām,* (v. n. 8 of صدم) Striking each other. Collision, clash.

A اصطر *astur,* (pl. of سطر *satr* or *satar*) Lines.

G اصطر *ustur,* A pound troy.

A اصطراب *istirāb,* (v. n. 8 of صرب) Collecting milk in small quantities in a leathern bottle, and leaving it to turn sour.

A اصطراخ *istirākh,* A crying out to one another.

A اصطراع *istirāₑ,* (v. n. 8 of صرع) Wrestling.

A اصطراف *istirāf,* (v. n. 8 of صرف) Turning about to gain any thing.

A اصطرام *istirām,* (v. n. 8 of صرم) Pruning, lopping. Reaping.

P اصطرخ *istarakh,* A lake, a pool. Istakhar.

G اصطرك *astarak,* A sweet gum called storax.

G اصطرلاب *usturlāb,* An astrolabe.

A اصطرلابي *usturlābiy,* A maker of astrolabes.

G اصطرة *ustura,* (or اصطور *ustūr*) A troy balance.

A اصطعاد *istiₑād,* (v. n. 8 of صعد) Ascending.

A اصطعاط *istiₑāt,* (v. n. 8 of سعط) Injecting a cephalic medicine into one's own nostrils.

A اصطفاء *istifāₑ,* (v. n. 8 of صفا for صفو) Choosing, electing, selecting.

A اصطفاف *istifāf,* (v. n. 8 of صفّ) Being drawn up in a row, set in array.

A اصطفاق *istifāk,* (v. n. 8 of صفق) Being struck (chords of a lyre). Being shaken by the wind (tree).

G اصطفلين *istaflīn,* A carrot.

G اصطفي *astafī,* Liquid storax.

G اصطفين *astafīn,* A carrot.

A اصطقار *istikār,* (v. n. 8 of صقر) Being kindled.

A اصطكاك *istikāk*, (v. n. 8 of صك) Knocking the knees together in walking (from weakness). Cutting (as one foot against another). Striking one another (with swords). P اصطكاك زند كردن *istikāki zand kardan*, To strike fire by friction.

A اصطكمة *istakmat* or *ustukmat*, Bread baked under the ashes.

A اصطلاء *istilā*, A being heated by the fire.

A اصطلاب *istilāb*, (v. n. 8 of صلب) Extracting marrow from bones.

A اصطلاح *istilāh*, (v. n. 8 of صلح) Being reconciled. A particular mode of speaking peculiar to certain classes, crafts, trades, arts, or professions. Phraseology, phrase, idiom: slang, cant.

A اصطلاحات *istilāhāt*, Forms of speech.

A اصطلاحيّ *istilāhīy*, Technical, conventional.

A اصطلاق *istilāk*, (v. n. 8 of صلق) Grinding with the teeth. Gnashing, grating.

A اصطلام *istilām*, (v. n. 8 of صلم) Eradicating.

A اصطمّة *ustummat*, The greater, or middle part of any thing, the centre of a mass, or collection, the aggregate, conflux.

A اصطناع *istināʿ*, (v. n. 8 of صنع) Receiving or bestowing a favour. Choosing, selecting for any special purpose. Ordering a seal or ring to be engraved. Educating, rearing, bringing up. Informing, teaching, exercising. Applying to any trade, study, or art. Preparing a feast, providing an entertainment. انواع مكارم و اصطناع *anwāʿi makārim u istināʿ*, Different kinds of obligations and favours.

A اصطهار *istihār*, (v. n. 8 of صهر) Eating dripping, fat, or marrow. Dissolving, causing to melt.

A اصطياد *istiyād*, (v. n. 8 of صاد for صيد) Hunting.

A اصطياف *istiyāf*, (v. n. 8 of صاف for صيف) Passing the summer (which is called صيف *sayf*).

A اصطيام *istiyām*, (v. n. 8 of صام for صوم) Fasting. Abstaining from meat, drink, talk, or venery.

A اصطيان *istiyān*, (v. n. 8 of صان for صون) Guarding, preserving, laying up, keeping.

A اصعاب *isʿāb*, (v. n. 4 of صعب) Being difficult. Being or becoming disobedient and troublesome. Possessing a stubborn, refractory camel. Finding (any body or thing) troublesome. Setting (a camel) at liberty, and not riding (him).

A اصعاد *isʿād*, (v. n. 4 of صعد) Ascending. Going or travelling by land (particularly to Mecca). Descending into a valley. Taking a liking to a colt of last year (a camel). Inducing a camel which has cast her foal to take a liking to her last year's colt. (A camel) being delivered of an untimely birth, and sucked by her colt of the former year, to preserve her milk. Causing a camel to bring forth an abortion.

A اصعار *isʿār*, (v. n. 4 of صعر) Averting the face, distorting the countenance, looking with indignation and contempt on any one.

A اصعاط *isʿāt*, (v. n. 4 of صعط) Injecting medicine or snuff into the nostrils (of another).

A اصعاق *isʿāk*, (v. n. 4 of صعق) Casting fire from heaven. Causing to swoon.

A اصعان *isʿān*, (v. n. 4 of صعن not in use) Having a small head and little sense.

A اصعب *asʿab*, More or most difficult. Strongly fortified, and difficult of capture.

A اصّعّد *issaʿʿud*, Ascent.

A اصعر *asʿar*, Wry-necked or mouthed. Wry-necked (camel). Perishing, going to ruin.

A اصعرّار *isʿirrār*, (v. n. 4 of صعرر Q) Turning round from pain. Drawing one's self together.

A اصعل *asʿal*, Small-headed and small-necked (man or ostrich). Small-headed (palm-tree).

A اصعنان *isʿinān*, (v. n. 9 of صعن not used) Being slender and small.

A اصعنرار *isʿinrār*, (v. n. 3 of صعرر Q) Turning round from pain. Drawing one's self together.

A اصعنفار *isʿinfār*, (v. n. 3 of صعفر Q) Being driven by fear in all directions. Being bent (neck).

A اصعيلال *isʿīlāl*, (v. n. 11 of صعل) Having a small head and slender neck.

A اصغاء *isghā*, (v. n. 4 of صغا for صغو) Hearing, listening, lending an ear. Turning the head, as if listening to any thing. Inclining (a vessel) to one side. Diminishing, rendering deficient and incomplete (any thing). Bending (a leathern bottle) when about to drink.

A اصغار *isghār*, (v. n. 4 of صغر) Lessening, diminishing. Rendering vile or contemptible, making abject and slavish. Sewing (a leathern bottle) with small and close stitches. Producing short, stunted grass, or small, weak, and tender plants (ground). Causing little ones to be brought forth.

A اصغر *asghar*, Less, least, smaller, smallest. (pl. اصاغر *asāghir* and اصاغرة *asāghirat*) Little, small, contemptible. الاصغران *al asgharāni*, (The two lesser or least) The heart and tongue.

A اصغى *asgha'*, Wry-headed.

A آصف بن برخيا *āsaf bin barkhiyā*, Name of a great man, supposed by the Arabians to have been Solomon's grand vazīr. By invoking the name of the Most High, in a twinkle he brought the throne of Balkīs to Solomon, a two month's journey.

A اصف *asaf*, The caper-tree or root.

A اصفاء *asfā*, (pl. of صفاة *safāt*) Large smooth stones. *Isfā*, (v. n. 4 of صفا for صفو) Straining, racking. Draining (a man) dry. Shewing a sincere regard. Choosing, electing, selecting, preferring. Taking the whole of any thing. Being destitute (of property), lacking (instruction). Laying no eggs (a hen). Being addle (a poet's brain).

A اصفاح *isfāh*, (v. n. 4 of صفح) Refusing a petitioner. Making broad. Turning the flat side of (a sword, or any other similar thing).

A اصفاد *asfād*, (pl. of صفد *safad*) Chains, fetters, bonds. Presents. *Isfād*, (v. n. 4 of صفد) Binding. Fastening, making fast.

A اصفار *asfār*, (pl. of صفر *sufr*, *sifr*, *safr*, *safir*, and *sufur*) Empty. (pl. of صفر *safar*) Name of the second month in the Arabian year, the next to Muharram. اناء اصفار *ināʾun asfārun*, An empty vessel. *Isfār*, (v. n. 4 of صفر) Being poor, empty-handed. Emptying, stripping (a house).

A اصفاغ *isfāgh*, (v. n. 4 of صفغ) Causing (a person) to take (a thing) up in the hand.

A اصفاف *isfāf*, (v. n. 4 of صف) Covering a saddle: making a seat (صفّة *suffat*) for a saddle.

A اصفاق *isfāk*, (v. n. 4 of صفق) Shutting the door. Milking cattle only once a day. Covering. Placing a dish (on a table). Consenting, suiting, agreeing. Turning (any one) back. Filling (a cup). Pouring (wine) from one vessel into another, racking it off. Encountering, lighting on. Meeting (with food or pasture) in abundance.

A اصفال *isfāl*, (v. n. 4 of صفل) Feeding (camels) on the herb صفصلّى *sifsilla'*.

P اصفاهانك *isfāhānak*, One of the twelve modes of music.

A اصفح *asfah*, One whose forehead is broad.

A اصفر *asfar*, Yellow, pale, livid. Black. More or most empty. More or most timid. A bird with a shrill note. بنو الاصفر *banū'l asfar*, The Greeks.

A اصفرار *isfirār*, (v. n. 9 of صفر) Being yellow. Turning pale.

A الاصفران *al asfarāni*, (The two yellows) Gold and saffron. The plant ورس *wars* and currants.

A اصفعند *isfaʿind*, Wine.

A اصفنط *isfint* or *isfant*, Grape-wine.

P اصفهان *isfahān*, The capital of Persia.

P اصفهسالار *isfah-sālār*, A general.

A اصفى *asfa'*, More or most pure.

A اصفياء *asfiyā*, (pl. of صفىّ *safīy*) Pure, just.

A اصفيرار *isfīrār*, (v. n. 11 of صفر) Being excessively yellow. Turning exceedingly pale.

A اصقاب *iskāb*, (v. n. 4 of صقب) Being near. Bringing near. Coming within shot (game).

A اصقار *iskār*, (v. n. 4 of صقر) Shining strong, darting forth heat (the sun).

A اصقاع *iskāʿ*, (v. n. 4 of صقع) Being covered with hoar frost. Going upon ground so covered. Covering the ground (hoar frost).

A اصقح *askah*, Bald about the forehead.

A اصقر *askar*, More or most honied (date) *Askur*, (pl. of صقر *sakr*) Kites, hawks, birds of prey.

A اصقرار *iskirār*, (v. n. 9 of صقر) Being exceedingly acid (milk).

A اصقع *askaʿ*, White-headed (horse or bird). Name of a bird, called also صفارية *sufāriyat*.

A اصقعرار *iskiʿrār*, (v. n. 4 of صقعر Q) Striking so hot upon a locust (the sun), that it goes away.

G اصقيل *iskīl*, A shrimp, a prawn. A squill.

A اصكّ *asakk*, Knock-kneed (particularly the ostrich). Strong, robust (man or beast). *Asukk*, pl. of صك sakk) Sentences signed by a judge.

A آصل āsul, (pl. of اصل asl) Roots. Foundations.

A اصل asl, (v. n. of اصل) Destroying. Springing at any one (the deadly serpent اصلة asalat). (pl. آصل āsul and اصول usūl) Root, stock, origin, principle, foundation, element, source, cause. Lineage, race, line, birth, family. Nobility, honour. Capital, principal, sum, stock in trade. An original, archetype, prototype, exemplar. اصل الارواح aslu'l arwāh, Quicksilver. اصل السوس aslu's sūs, Liquorice-root. اصل الغرب aslu'l gharb, Root of the mountain-pine. اصل المازريون aslu'l māzaryūn, Mezereon-root. اصل جمع asl jamaʻ, The original rents with which the lands (in India) were first charged in the books of the Emperor Akbar, exclusive of all additions and impositions made since from time to time by the Government. اصل قيمة asl kīmat, Prime cost. اصل كتاب asli kitāb, The original of a book, the first copy. اصل و فرع asl u farʻ, Root and branch. Cause and effect. اصل داران پاك asl-dārāni pāk, Holy men. Asal, (v. n. of اصل) Stinking (water), becoming tainted (meat). (pl. of اصلة asalat) Hideous and venomous serpents with large heads and small bodies. Asil, Uprooted. Usul, (pl. of اصيل asīl) Evening-times.

A اصلاً aslan, (اصلاً مطلقًا aslan mutlikan, or اصلاً و قطعًا aslan wa katʻan) Not at all, by no means, never, in no shape.

A اصلاء aslāʼ, (pl. of صلا salaʼ) Middles of backs. Lower parts of haunch-bones. Spaces between fundament and tails. Islāʼ, (v. n. 4 of صلا for صلو) Becoming relaxed about the haunches (a mare previous to foaling). (v. n. 4 of صلي) Putting (any thing) into the fire to heat, and keeping (it) there. Usalāʼ, (pl. of اصيل asīl) Noble, illustrious.

A اصلاب aslāb, (pl. of صلب sulb) The loins, sides, flanks, back-bones. Islāb, (v. n. 4 of صلب) Standing with outstretched neck (as if gibbeted), that her colt may suck abundantly (a camel).

A اصلات aslāt, (pl. of صلت salt) Naked swords. Large knives.

A اصلاح islāh, (v. n. 4 of صلح) Fitting, adapting. Amending, correcting, restoring, adjusting, improving. Dressing or manuring (land). Preparing, dressing (meat). Tuning (a musical instrument). Shewing kindness. P اصلاح كردن islāh kardan, To repair, to mend.

A اصّلاح issilāh, (v. n. 8 of صلح) Making peace with each other. Doing good to one another.

P اصلاح پذير islāh-pazīr, Corrigible.

A اصلاد islād, (v. n. 4 of صلد) Being hard (the ground).

A اصلاف islāf, (v. n. 4 of صلف) Making a person very disagreeable, making a wife hateful to her husband. Being of an unkind temper. Hating.

A اصلاق aslāk, (pl. of صلق saluk) Plain, level grounds. Islāk, (v. n. 4 of صلق) Sounding loud, croaking harshly.

A اصلال aslāl, (pl. of صلّ sill) Serpents which cannot be charmed. Islāl, (v. n. 4 of صلّ) Tingling when struck (iron). Beginning to putrefy (meat). Causing (water) to stink (time).

A اصلان uslān, (pl. of اصيل asīl) Evenings.

A اصلب aslab, Harder, hardest. Aslub, (pl. of صلب sulb) Loins, flanks, back-bones.

A اصلة asalat, Universality, the whole. (pl. اصل asal) A serpent of a dangerous species. جاؤا باصلتهم jāʼū bi asalatihim, They came together, they came all of them. اخذ الشيء باصلته akhaza 'sh shayʼ bi asalatihi, He took the thing by the root, wholly, totally, entirely, completely, radically.

A اصلّة asillat, (pl. of صلال silāl) The lining leathers of boots. Boot-legs.

A اصلتيّ aslatīy, An active, bustling man.

A اصلج aslaj, Very bare or bald. Deaf.

A اصلح asluh, Better, best. More or most correct, fine. اصلح الله aslaha'llāh, (pret. of 4 used optatively) May God amend!

A اصلخ aslakh, Deaf (as a post). Mangy (camel).

A اصلخاخ islikhākh, The act of lying on the side.

A اصلخداد islikhdād, The act of standing erect.

A اصلخمام islikhmām, (v. n. 4 of صلخم Q) Standing upright. Being angry.

A اصلد aslad, Very covetous, and hard.

P اصل زاده asl-zāda, Nobly-born, high-bred.

A اصلع aslaʻ, (pl. صلع sulʻ and صلعان sulʻān) Bald (man). Bright (spear-head).

A اصلف aslaf, (pl. اصالف) Hard ground.

A اصلم aslam, One whose ears appear as if cut close to his head. A flea. The last part of a verse consisting of a وتد مفروق watad mafrūk, q. v.

A اصلنطاح islintāh, (v. n. 3 of صلطح Q) Being wide (low-lying gravelly land).

A اصلهباب islihbāb, (v. n. 4 of صلهب Q) Being stretched out on the face. Being long, extended.

A اصلهمام islihmām, The state of being hard.

A اصليّ asliy, (fem. اصليّة asliyat) Radical, original, essential, principal. Noble, of noble origin. رطوبة اصليّة rutūbat asliyat, Radical humour.

A اصليان asliyān, (Pers. pl.) Nobles, gentlemen.

A اصليت islīt, Highly polished, keen (sword).

A اصمّ asamm, (pl. صمّ summ and صمّان summān) Deaf. Surd (in arithmetic). الاصمّ al asamm The *surd* conjugation of Arabic verbs. Deaf to all persuasion or intimidation. A deaf adder. A dreadful kind of serpent. A hard stone. شهر الله الاصمّ shahru'llāhi'l asamm, The month of Rajab, the seventh of the Arabian year (because then the noise of war is not heard).

A اصماء ismāʼ, (v. n. 4 of صمي) Knocking down and killing (game) on the spot. Champing the bit (a horse). Making haste. Turning. Rushing upon.

A اصمات ismāt, (v. n. 4 of صمت) Keeping silence. Silencing. Making a thing solid, without a cavity to give it sound. Reaching the end of the second year without being sown (land). Silence.

A اصمار asmār, (pl. of صمر sumr) The lips, edges or mouths of vessels. Ismār, (v. n. 4 of صمر) Refusing to complain. Preventing, hindering. Being avaricious. Being exceedingly salt or bitter. Entering on the hour of sunset.

A اصماغ ismāgh, (v. n. 4 of صمغ) Dropping gum (a tree). Having abundance of spittle (the corners of the mouth). Having thick milk (a sheep).

A اصماق ismāk, (v. n. 4 of صمق) Shutting or bolting a door. Spoiling, turning (milk or water).

A اصمام ismām, (v. n. 4 of صمّ) Becoming, making, or discovering to be, deaf. Corking a bottle. Making a stopple (صمام simām) for a bottle.

A اصمّة usummat, The greater or middle part of any thing, the aggregate or conflux.

A اصمت asmat, Silent. Ismita, (as بلد اصمت balad ismita or وحش اصمت wahsh ismita) A desert, a solitary, unsociable place.

A اصمح asmah, A fearless, daring fellow, who with sword or spear belabours the heads of the brave.

A اصمخة asmikhat, (pl. of صماخ simākh) Ears. Ear-holes. Tympana.

A اصمخداد ismikhdād, A swelling with rage.

A اصمع asmaʻ, High, elevated, eminent. (pl. صمعان sumʻān) Elegant plumage. Sharp (sword). Any tree whose fruit enlarges itself without bursting the pod or envelope in which it is enclosed. A handsome well-shaped ankle. Brisk, keen, acute, active (mind). Small-eared. Astonished, bewildered. اصمعان asmaʻāni, (dual) A bold heart and penetrating mind.

A اصمعداد ismiʻdād, A passing rapidly by.

A اصمعيّ asmaʻiy, Name of a grammarian.

A اصمقرار ismikrār, (v. n. 4 of صمقر Q) Being exceedingly acid (milk). Shining strong, darting heat (the sun).

A اصموخ usmūkh, The orifice of the ear.

A اصميكاك ismīkāk, (v. n. 11 of صمك) Being angry. Becoming thick (milk). Being wet with rain (ground).

A اصمئلال ismiʼlāl, (v. n. 4 of صمأل Q) Being strong. Being dry, hard. Being luxuriant (plant).

A اصنّ asann, One who feigns negligence.

A اصناء asnāʼ, (pl. of صنو sinw) Uterine brothers. Sons. Paternal uncles. Isnāʼ, (v. n. 4 of صنا for صنو) Sitting wistfully near a cauldron or pot.

A اصنات isnāt, A strengthening, a confirming.

A اصناخ asnākh, (pl. of صنخ) Roots of teeth.

A اصناع asnāʻ, (pl. of صنع sinʻ) Cisterns. Isnāʻ, (v. n. 4 of صنع) Assisting. Applying to the learned of any art, and acquiring it. Grooming and fattening (a horse).

A اصناعي asnāʻī, Clever, neat handed (men).

A اصناف asnāf, (pl. of صنف sinf) Forms, kinds, sorts, species, varieties. Subjects, peasants.

under-tenants. اصناف قبائل *asnāfi kabāʼil*, Various tribes. اصناف مختلفة *asnāfi mukhtalifa*, Different sorts, varieties. P مردم اصناف *mardumi asnāf*, A mechanic.

A اصناق *isnāk*, (v. n. 4 of صنق) Taking good care of the money, flocks, or effects of another. Persevering, persisting.

A اصنام *asnām*, (pl. of صنم *sanam*) Images, idols. Statues. P اصنام چين *asnāmi chīn*, The images of China (metaphorically implying the handsome of either sex). A عبادة الاصنام *ɛibādatu'l asnām*, The adoration of images, idolatry.

A اصنان *isnān*, (v. n. 4 of صنّ) Tossing the nose, looking proud, disdainful. Being averse from the male (a pregnant she-camel). Having the colt sticking in her womb and striking his head against her arse-gut (a mare). Persevering in assisting. Smelling, emitting a stench under the arm-pits. Turning, becoming bad (water), stinking (meat).

A اصنّة *asinnat*, (pl. of صنان) Arm-pit stenches.

A اصنع *asnaɛ*, More or most skilful or industrious, more or most of an artist. Very expert.

A اصنف *asnaf*, (pl. صنف *sunf*) (An ostrich) whose legs are excoriated.

A اصنوجة *usnūjat*, Troughs containing dough.

A اصو *asw*, (v. n. of اصا for اصو) Being thick and entangled (a plant).

A اصواء *aswāʼ*, (pl. of صوّة *suwat*) High and rugged grounds. Mile-stones. Herds of wild beasts. Echoes. *Iswāʼ*, (v. n. 4 of صوي) Withering (a palm-tree).

A اصوات *aswāt*, (pl. of صوت *sawt*) Voices, sounds. Fames, reputations. Imitative sounds.

A اصواع *aswāɛ*, (pl. of صاع) Certain measures.

A اصواف *aswāf*, (pl. of صوف *sūf*) Fleeces. Wools. Camelots.

A اصوب *aswab*, Better, best, straighter, truer.

A اصوبيّة *aswabiyatī*, Melioration, improvement.

A اصور *aswar*, (pl. صور *sūr*) Desirous, eager, keen, wishful, inclined to. Wry. Wry-necked.

A اصورة *aswirat*, (pl. of صوار *suwār* or *siwār*) Herds (of wild oxen). Bags of musk.

A اصوص *asūs*, (pl. اصص *usus*) Fat (camel) not conceiving. A robber.

A اصوع *aswuɛ*, (or اصؤع *asʼuɛ*) (pl. of صاع *sāɛ*) Certain dry measures.

A اصوف *aswaf*, Woolly, wool-bearing.

P اصول *usūl*, Tone, sound, musical note. Mode. اصول فاختة *usūli fākhta*, Name of a musical note.

A اصول *usūl*, (pl. of اصل *asl*) Roots, origins, causes. The roots or fundamentals of Muhammadism (opposed to فروع *furūɛ*). اصول و فروع *usūl u furūɛ*, Causes and effects. Ascent and descent in kindred, ancestors, and posterity. اصول عشرة *usūli ɛasharat*, The ten primary intelligences first created by God. اربعة الاصول *arbaɛatu'l usūl*, The four roots, masterwort, parsley, capers, and fennel. شراب اصول *sharābi usūl*, A syrup of roots.

A اصوليّ *usūlīy*, Solid, deep (reasoner, polemic).

A اصون *aswan*, Better or best preserver.

A اصونة *aswinat*, (pl. of صوان *sawān*, *siwān* or *suwān*) Drawers, chests of drawers, wardrobes.

A اصهاء *is-hāʼ*, (v. n. 4 of صها for صهو) Suffering from a gall or wound on the middle of the back (a horse). Exposing a child to the sun after being anointed with butter (by way of cure for a disease).

A اصهاب *is-hāb*, (v. n. 4 of صهب) Begetting red and white colts (a camel).

A اصهار *as-hār*, (pl. of صهر *sihr*) Near relations. Fathers-in-law. Brothers-in-law (sisters' husbands). Sons-in-law. Sepulchres (as being nearly related to man). *Is-hār*, (v. n. 4 of صهر) Approaching (as one army towards another). Being joined, allied, connected (by a matrimonial alliance).

A اصهب *as-hab*, (pl. اصهبيّات *us-habīyāt*) (A camel) red and white. A lion. Cold (day). Sandy (hair). اصهب صاهب *as-hab sāhib*, A word used in calling sheep to be milked.

A اصهرار *is-hirār*, (v. n. 9 of صهر) Approaching, drawing near each other (two armies).

A اصهيباب *ishībāb*, (v. n. 11 of صهب) Being of a reddish white colour.

A اصهيرار *is-hīrār*, (v. n. 11 of صهر) Being melted. Shining, glittering, glistening, from the heat of the sun (a cameleon's back).

A ابن آصى *ibn āsaʼ*, A sort of bird.

A اصياد *asyād*, (pl. of صاد *sād*) Veins between the eyes of camels. Diseases in camels causing a discharge at the nose. Camels affected therewith.

A اصياف *asyāf*, (pl. of صيف *sayf*) Summers (particularly the months May and June; the hotter months being called اقياظ *akyāz*).

A اصيّان *usayyān*, (for اصيلان) Short evenings.

A اصيبيّة *usaybīyat*, Little boys.

A آصية *āsiyat*, Inevitable evil. Relationship. Beneficence. A linctus. Drink made from the date.

A اصيد *asyad*, One who carries the head high (from pride). Wry-necked. (A camel) that holds his head elevated (from indisposition). A lion. A king. *Asīd*, The middle part between the outward gate and the house, a vestibule, a court.

A اصيداد *isyidād*, The being wry-necked.

A اصيدة *asīdat*, A sheep-fold: any inclosure for cattle, built of wood. A small shift worn by girls.

A اصير *asīr*, Near, neighbouring, approaching. Entangled (hair). Long and thick (eye-lashes).

A اصيص *asīs*, Tremor, terror. A broken vessel or half a water-pot in which odoriferous herbs are planted. A chamber-pot. A strong edifice. A vessel for transplanting clay.

A اصيصة *asīsat*, Neighbouring, adjacent (houses). هم اصيصة واحدة *hum asīsatun wāhidatun*, They are at one, they are agreed.

A اصيل *asīl*, Rooted, radical. Firm, constant, durable, permanent. Solid. An intelligent vicegerent. Death, destruction. Name of a city in Spain. اصيل الرأي *asīlu'r raʼy*, Sound in judgment. مجد اصيل *majdi asīl*, Solid glory. Noble. (pl. آصال *āsāl*, اصل *usul*, اصلان *uslān*, and اصائل *asāʼil*) Evening. *Usayl*, (dim. of اصيل *asīl*) Short evenings. Name of a companion of Muhammad.

A اصيلان *usaylān*, (sometimes اصيلال *usaylāl*) (dim. of اصلان *uslān*, Evenings) Short evenings.

A اصيلة *asīlat*, Hereditary possessions (as descending from the family-root). Death, destruction. Universality, the whole, universal.

A اصيلع *usayliɛ*, (dim. of اصلع *aslaɛ*) (Little bald-pate) Veretrum. Slender-necked (serpent).

A اضّ *azz*, (v. n. of اضّ) Causing difficulty and trouble (a thing). Rendering necessitous, forcing, compelling (poverty). Breaking. Longing for, seeking her nest (an ostrich). *Izz*, Root, origin.

A اضاء *izāʼ*, A melon-bed. A reed-bed, a marsh. A bed of the Indian willow. Stagnant pools.

A اضاءة *izāʼat*, (v. n. 4 of ضاء for ضوأ) Shining, lightening, flashing. Kindling, illuminating. Causing to shine. Rendering clear and visible. Scattering (urine) about.

A اضابير *azābīr*, (pl. of اضبارة *izbārat* or *azbārat*) Bundles of papers, piles of manuscript.

A اضاة *azāt*, (pl. اضوات *azwāt*, اضيات *azyāt*, اضاً *azan*, اضاء *izāʼ* and اضون *azūn*) Stagnant water; any place where it collects.

A اضاحيّ *azāhīy*, (pl. of اضحيّة *uzhīyat*) Sheep sacrificed in the forenoon. Goats or camels ordained for sacrifice.

A اضاحيك *azāhīk*, (pl. of اضحوكة) Jests, jokes.

A اضاد *izād*, (v. n. 4 of ضاد) Giving a cold.

A اضاض *izāz*, A sanctuary, asylum, place of refuge. The cries of a parturient camel.

A اضاعة *izāɛat*, (v. n. 4 of ضاع for ضيع) Ruining, destroying, wasting, squandering. Neglecting, losing. Having a number of farms or fields (ضيعة *zayɛat*). Being clear, evident, manifest, public.

A اضافة *izāfat*, (v. n. 4 of ضاف for ضيف) Receiving hospitably, making a guest. Causing to incline or decline. Bending. Being aware of. Oppressing. Fleeing away. Making one to fly for refuge. Being afraid of, or cautious. Running swift. Making haste. Looking from a height, looking down upon any thing. Being at the top, on the point of. Increase, surplus. The construction of one noun with another. The relation of the genitive case denoted by كسرة *kasra*, called in Persian كسرهٔ توصيفي *kasraʼi tawsīfī*, Descriptive kesra: as, پسر زيد *pisari zayd*, The son of Zayd.

A اضافيّ *izāfīy*, Constructive, relative.

A اضاقة *izākat*, (v. n. 4 of ضاق for ضيق) Making narrow. Being impoverished, losing property.

A اضآك *izʼāk*, (v. n. 4 of ضئك) Giving a cold in the head.

A اضالة *izālat*, (v. n. 4 of ضال for ضيل) Producing the white lote-tree.

A اضاميم *azāmīm*, (pl. of اضمامة *izmāmat*) Heaps, piles (of books). Herds, crowds. Stones.

A اضان *azān*, (pl. of ضأن *zaan*) Wethers. *Izsān*, (v. n. 4 of ضأن) Abounding in wethers.

A اضبّ *azabb*, (A camel) swollen in the feet or breast. *Azubb*, (pl. of ضبّ *zabb*) Lybian lizards.

A اضباء *izbā*, (v. n. 4 of ضبأ) Concealing, containing, suppressing, keeping in mind. Being silent about a misfortune, concealing it. Hiding enmity in the heart. (v. n. 4 of ضبا for ضبو) Impending, overhanging. Holding, detaining. Raising. Being near getting possession of. Disappointing in a search (a journey). Making small, breaking into little bits. Conquering, prevailing over. Becoming lean and emaciated.

A اضباب *izbāb*, (v. n. 4 of ضبّ) Being silent. Laying up in one's mind. Speaking, uttering, calling. Hating, bearing a secret grudge. Rising up in a mass to do any thing (people). Being numerous (hairs). Abounding in plants (ground), or in Lybian lizards (a country). Advancing, coming in scattered groups (cattle). Being allowed to trickle through a stitch-hole (water). Flowing with blood. Holding fast. Being on the point of obtaining one's wish. Sticking close to any one. Being misty (a day). Giving (a child) butter and new wine.

A اضباث *azbās*, Handsful, grasps.

A اضبارة *izbārat* or *azbārat*, (pl. اضابير *azābīr*) A collection or bundle of papers, a pile of books.

A اضباع *azbāʿ*, (pl. of ضبع *zabʿ*) The arms, armpits, the fleshy parts of the arms next the arm-pits.

A اضبان *azbān*, Places full of wild beasts of prey. *Izbān*, (v. n. 4 of ضبن) Enduring a long time. Making narrow; reducing to straits. Taking under the arm.

A اضبط *azbat*, An ambidexter. A lion. More or most tenacious.

A اضبع *azbuʿ*, (pl. of ضبع *zabuʿ*) Hyenas.

A اضبيكاك *izbīkāk*, (v. n. 11 of ضبك not used) Putting forth herbage (the ground).

A اضجاج *izjāj*, A crying aloud, a shouting.

A اضجار *izjār*, (v. n. 4 of ضجر) Grieving, afflicting, wearying.

A اضجاع *izjāʿ*, (v. n. 4 of ضجع) Making one recline upon one side on the ground, on a bed, &c. Thrusting down or depressing. Emptying a large sack. Composing verses terminating in different vowels or consonants. Putting the vowel كسر *kasr* under the last letter of the oblique case. Giving to فتحه *fatha* a sound inclining to كسره *kasra*.

A اضّجاع *izzijāʿ*, (v. n. 8 of ضجع) Lying on one side (on a bed or on the ground).

A اضجعرار *izjihrār*, (v. n. 4 of ضجعر Q) Being filled (a leathern bottle).

A اضجع *azjaʿ*, (A husband) who has an aversion to a wife. One whose fore-teeth are crooked.

A اضجم *azjam*, Wry-nosed. Distorted in any member (particularly about the head), as the lip, mouth, chin, neck, or shoulders.

A اضحاء *izhā*, (v. n. 4 of ضحا for ضحو) Making clear. Doing any thing in the forenoon. Basking in the sun. Continuing, persevering.

A اضحاة *azhāt*, (pl. اضحي *azha'*) The sacrifice of a sheep in the forenoon.

A اضحي *azha'*, White or gray (horse). The day whereon sacrifices are offered at Mecca.

A اضحاك *izhāk*, (v. n. 4 of ضحك) Making to laugh. Causing (any one) to wonder. Filling (a cistern) to overflowing. Producing herbage.

A اضحال *azhāl*, (pl. of ضحل) Shallow waters.

A اضحوكة *uzhūkat*, (pl. اضاحيك *azāhīk*) A ridiculous thing, jest, joke, laughable affair.

A اضحيان *izhiyān* or *uzhiyān*, Name of a plant. *Uzhuyān*, Bright (moon). Cloudless (day).

A اضحية *izhiyat*, (اضحيانة *izhiyānat* or *uzhiyānat*) (A night) serene and clear.

A اضحيّة *uzhiyat*, (pl. اضاحيّ *azāhīy*) A goat or camel ordered for sacrifice. A sheep sacrificed in the forenoon, half-way between sunrise and noon.

A اضخام *izkhām*, (v. n. 4 of ضخم) Doing (any thing) roughly. Making stout and lusty.

A اضخم *azkham*, Corpulent, fat, big. Thicker.

A اضخمّ *azkhamm*, Corpulent, fat, big.

A اضخومة *uzkhūmat*, A stuffing or bolstering of the petticoats, a pad which gives a prominent appearance to the hips (in modern phrase, a bustle).

A اضداء *izdā*, The act of filling (a vessel).

A اضداد *azdād*, Contraries, opposites, opponents. *Izdād*, (v. n. 4 of ضدّ) Being angry, enraged.

A اضرّ *azarr*, More or most hurtful, injurious.

A اضراء *izrā*, (v. n. 4 of ضري) Drinking date-wine. Training (a dog). Setting (a dog) in pursuit of game. Making greedy, causing to hanker.

A اضرّاء *azirrā*, (pl. of ضرير *zarīr*) Blind.

A اضراب *izrāb*, (v. n. 4 of ضرب) Leading (a camel) to cover. Causing (ground) to imbibe (its) moisture (a hot pestilential wind). Staying, stopping. Being well baked (bread). Hanging down the head. Turning away from any one. Remaining silent. Remaining at home. Striking any one (cold). Being overtaken by a misling rain or rime (called ضريب *zarīb*). Amplification.

A اضراح *izrāh*, (v. n. 4 of ضرح) Removing, repelling. Corrupting. Spoiling a market, preventing any thing from being sold.

A اضرار *azrār*, (pl. of ضرر *zarar*) Hurts, harms, injuries. *Izrār*, (v. n. 4 of ضرّ) Harming, hurting, injuring. Urging, compelling, forcing one against his will. Taking a second wife over the head of the first (thus injuring her). Approaching very near. Taking the bit between his teeth and biting it (a horse). Shewing speed, running.

A اضراس *azrās*, (pl. of ضرس *zirs*) Teeth, grinders. اضراس العقل *azrāsu'l ʿakl*, Teeth coming after the twentieth year, wisdom-teeth. اضراس الكلب *azrāsu'l kalb*, Polipody, a plant. *Izrās*, (v. n. 4 of ضرس) Striking, moving, astonishing, confounding. Setting the teeth on edge. Silencing.

A اضراط *izrāt*, (v. n. 4 of ضرط) Causing one to break wind. Making a noise with the mouth in contempt. Mocking, jeering, despising, treating with contempt.

A اضراع *izrāʿ*, (v. n. 4 of ضرع) Making one submissive, humbling, enfeebling. Giving milk a little while before the birth. Giving liberally.

A اضرام *izrām*, (v. n. 4 of ضرم) Inflaming, burning, setting on fire.

A اضرب *azrab*, More or most of a striker. *Azrub*, (pl. of ضرب *zarb*) Modes, forms.

A اضرس *azras*, Large-toothed (boy).

A اضرط *azrat*, Thin-bearded or thin-eyebrowed.

A اضرع *azruʿ*, (pl. of ضرع *zirʿ*) Similitudes, likes, equals. Threads of a rope.

A اضرغطاط *izrightāt*, (v. n. 4 of ضرغط Q not used) Bursting with rage. Overlapping the flesh (skin). Being abundant (flesh).

A اضرهزاز *izrihzāz*, (v. n. 4 of ضرهز Q) Creeping clandestinely towards.

A اضري *azrī*, (pl. of ضرو *zirw*) Hunting-dogs.

A اضريج *izrīj*, A kind of yellow garment. Crimson dye. A high-blooded swift horse. Red silk, raw or spun.

A اضريراء *izrīrā*, (v. n. 12 of ضرو or ضري) Having the stomach overloaded.

A اضزّ *azazz*, (pl. ضزّاز *zuzzāz*) Bad-tempered, ill-natured, passionate, capricious, testy. Inarticulate in pronunciation, from a bad formation of jaws, or adhesion of teeth. Hard and narrow (pubes).

A اضزاز *izzāz*, (v. n. 4 of ضزّ) Being avaricious. Champing the bit (a horse).

A اضطباء *iztibā*, (v. n. 8 of ضبأ) Lying hid, concealing one's self.

A اضطباث *iztibās*, (v. n. 8 of ضبث) Taking, seizing, grasping, griping.

A اضطباع *iztibāʿ*, (v. n. 8 of ضبع) Passing a cloak, robe, or scarf under the right arm and over the left shoulder, thus leaving bare the right, and covering the left shoulder.

A اضطبان *iztibān*, A taking under the arm.

A اضطجاع *iztijāʿ*, (v. n. 8 of ضجع) Lying on one's side: or on the breast in a posture of adoration.

A اضطراب *iztirāb*, (v. n. 8 of ضرب) Shaking, being ricketty. Tottering. Being irresolute. Fighting and quarrelling amongst themselves. Being poor, indigent. Being emaciated, extenuated. Being tall and flabby. Ordering a gold ring to be made. Acquiring. Requesting that lots may be drawn for one. Agitation, perturbation, commotion, fluctuation, perplexity. اضطراب الحبل *iztirābu'l habl*, Discordance and diversity of opinions.

A اضطراح *iztirāh*, (v. n. 8 of ضرح) Rejecting, throwing on one side.

A اضطرار *iztirār*, (v. n. 8 of ضرّ) Compelling, forcing. Being forced, and reduced to helplessness. Want, need, necessity. اضطرارا *iztirāran*, From necessity, by force, compulsion, or violence.

A اضطرام *iztirām*, (v. n. 8 of ضرم) Being kindled. Blazing. Hoariness.

A اضطغاث *iztighās*, (v. n. 8 of ضغث) Collecting handsful of grass dry and green for fuel.

A اضطغاغ *iztighāgh*, (v. n. 8 of ضغّ) Being moist and verdant (ground).

A اضطغان *iztighān*, (v. n. 8 of ضغن) Hating one another. Feeling a tendency to hate. Taking under the arm.

A اضطفاز *iztifāz*, A swallowing unwillingly.

A اضطفان *iztifān*, (v. n. 8 of ضفن) Kicking one's own hinder part with the heel.

A اضطلام *iztilām*, A submitting to injuries.

A اضطماخ *iztimākh*, A being profusely anointed.

A اضطمار *iztimār*, (v. n. 8 of ضمر) Being slender in the body, lank in the belly.

A اضطمام *iztimām*, (v. n. 8 of ضمّ) Contracting, drawing to one's self. Comprehending, containing, comprising.

A اضطناء *iztināʼ*, (v. n. 8 of ضنأ) Blushing. Being drawn in, contracted.

A اضطنان *iztinān*, The being avaricious.

A اضطواك *iztiwāk*, (v. n. 8 of ضاك for ضوك) Disputing, litigating.

A اضطهاد *iztihād*, An overcoming, a forcing.

A اضعاف *azʻāf*, (pl. of ضعف *ziʻf*) Resembling, alike, equal. Double, as much more, double the quantity, the same thing over again. The distances or intervals between the lines of a book; where the lines in a book are doubled (or in two columns), and where there is a double margin: also when explanatory interlineations or marginal notes are added. The members; also the bones of the body. *Izʻāf*, (v. n. 4 of ضعف) Doubling. Adding a double quantity, or increasing from one to three. Receiving double. Weakening, rendering infirm. Blinding. Having a weak beast.

A اضعف *azʻaf*, More or most weak, helpless, impotent. اضعف الخدّام *azʻafu'l khuddām*, The most weak (or humble) of servants.

A اضغاء *izghāʼ*, (v. n. 4 of ضغا for ضغو) Forcing (one) to cry out.

A اضغاث *azghās*, (pl. of ضغث *zighs*) Handsful (of herbs, part green and part dry). اضغاث الاحلام *azghāsu'l ahlām*, Confused dreams which cannot be interpreted.

A اضغاغ *izghāgh*, (v. n. 4 of ضغّ not in use) Having plenty of provision (chiefly of corn and other animal produce of lands. Being succulent and juicy (a plant). Being full of moisture (ground).

A اضغان *azghān*, (pl. of ضغن *zighn*) Hatreds.

A اضفيداد *izfīdād*, A swelling with rage.

A اضكل *azkal*, Naked.

A اضلّ *azall*, More or most astray. More or most seductive, or tending to lead astray.

A اضلاع *azlāʻ*, (and اضلع *azluʻ*) (pl. of ضلع *ziliʻ* and *zilaʻ*) Ribs. (pl. of ضليع *zalīʻ*) Strong-sided. Firm. Muscular, compact. *Izlāʻ*, (v. n. 4 of ضلع) Causing to incline, and preponderate. Bearing a heavy load. Overloading.

A اضلال *izlāl*, (v. n. 4 of ضلّ) Causing to err, leading astray. Leaving in error. Concealing, burying. اضلال حال *izlāli hāl*, A ruined situation.

P اضلال كردن *izlāl kardan*, To ruin, disgrace.

A اضلع *azlaʻ*, (pl. ضلع *zulʻ*) Strong, thick (man or horse). One whose teeth are bent inward, resembling the curvature of ribs.

A اضلولة *uzlūlat*, Error, wandering, aberration.

A اضم *azam*, (v. n. of اضم) Being angry and hating. Sticking to one and injuring him. Pursuing and biting the females (a he-camel). (pl. اضمات *azamāt*) Anger. Envy, hatred. *Izam*, Name of a mountain, and of a valley near Madina.

A اضماج *izmāj*, A cleaving to the ground.

A اضماد *izmād*, (v. n. 4 of ضمد) Collecting, bringing together. Sprouting (the plant عرفج *ʻarfaj*).

A اضمار *izmār*, (v. n. 4 of ضمر) Hiding, concealing. Concealing (a man) either by a journey or by death (a country). Suppressing. Thinking, musing, hatching in the mind. Prying curiously, using all diligence to attain the knowledge of a thing. Exercising (a horse). Feeding (a horse) sparingly to reduce his fat. The silence of the ت *te* of متفاعلن *mutafāʻilun* in the metre called كامل *kāmil*. اسرار واجب الاضمار *asrāri wājibu'l izmār*, Secrets necessary to be concealed.

A اضمامة *izmāmat*, (pl. اضاميم *azāmīm*) A heap or pile (of books). A crowd, herd, troop. A stone. سبّاق الاضاميم *sabbāqu'l azāmīm*, The leading horse (of a troop), the first horse (in a race).

A اضمحلال *izmihlāl*, (v. n. 4 of ضمحل Q) Vanishing, disappearing. Being scattered (a cloud).

A اضمحنان *izmihnān*, (v. n. 4 of ضمحن) Vanishing, disappearing,

A اضماك *izmihāk*, (v. n. 9 of ضمك not used) Being verdant (the ground).

A اضمى *azmaʼ*, Black-lipped.

A اضميكاك *izmīkāk*, (v. n. 11 of ضمك) Being green and succulent (a plant). Budding, blossoming. Swelling with rage. Being full of water and ready to rain (a cloud).

A اضناء *iznāʼ*, (v. n. 4 of ضنأ) Being fruitful, prolific, having many children. Having many cattle. (v. n. 4 of ضني) Emaciating, reducing (disease).

A اضوء *azwaʼ*, More luminous, brighter.

A اضواء *azwāʼ*, (pl. of ضوء *zawʼ*) Lights, splendours. *Izwāʼ*, (v. n. 4 of ضوي) Bringing forth a puny child. Braying. Pounding small. Being thin and slender. Becoming weak. Defrauding. Making incline. Weakening. Doing superficially.

A اضوات *azwāt*, (pl. of اضاة) Stagnant waters.

A اضواج *azwāj*, (pl. of ضوج) Windings of a river.

A اضواع *azwāʻ*, (pl. of ضوع *zuwaʻ* or *ziwaʻ*) Male-owls. Birds resembling crows, but eatable.

A اضوط *azwat*, Foolish, silly. One who has a small jaw and chin.

A اضؤن *azʼun*, (pl. of ضأن *zaʼn*) Wethers.

A اضهاء *azhāʼ*, (pl. of ضهوة *zahwat*) Ponds, cisterns. *Izhāʼ*, (v. n. 4 of ضهي) Feeding upon the shrub ضهياء *zahyāʼ*, (a camel). Marrying a woman who does not conceive.

A اضهاج *izhāj*, (v. n. 4 of ضهج) Casting her foal (a camel).

A اضهاد *izhād*, (v. n. 4 of ضهد) Oppressing, treating with cruelty.

A اضهال *izhāl*, (v. n. 4 of ضهل) Bearing ripe dates (a palm). Beginning to ripen (green dates).

A اضيات *azyāt*, (pl. of اضاة) Stagnant waters.

A اضياف *azyāf*, (pl. of ضيف *zayf*) Guests.

A اضيال *izyāl*, (v. n. 4 of ضيل not used) Producing the tree called ضال *zāl*.

A اضيع *azyaʻ*, More or most useless.

A اضيق *azyak*, Narrower, straiter.

P اطا *atā*, The white poplar.

A اطابة *itābat*, (v. n. 4 of طاب for طيب) Making beautiful, fragrant, soft, sweet, or delicate. Speaking soothingly, giving good words. Cleaning or shaving the body Musulmān fashion. Serving up delicate meats. Bearing well-disposed children. Taking a lawful wife.

A اطاحة *itāhat*, (v. n. 4 of طاح for طوح) Causing (the hair) to fall. Shedding the coat. Wasting, destroying (property). Throwing about. Ruining.

A اطار *itār*, A circle, any thing that surrounds another; the environs of the mouth; the hair about the hoofs of cattle; the wooden ring or hoop of a drum, sieve, &c. Cat-gut or bowstring wrapped round an arrow near the notch. The rim of the glans penis. The branches of a vine trained to form an arbour. A ring or circle of men.

A اطّار *attār*, One who makes and sells wooden rings or circles of the sort mentioned above.

A اطارة *itārat*, (v. n. 4 of طار for طير) Causing to fly. Putting to flight, urging one to fly, causing to move rapidly. Dividing (property) into proportions.

A اطاشة *itāshat*, (v. n. 4 of طاش for طيش) Shooting wide of the mark.

A اطّاط *attāt*, Loud-voiced, clamorous, noisy.

A اطاعة *itāʻat*, (v. n. 4 of طاع for طوع) Obeying. Obedience, submission, surrender, subjection. Bearing ripe fruit (a tree), and putting it within the gatherer's reach. Lying open (a field) for pasture. انقياد و اطاعت *inkiyād u itāʿat*, Submission and obedience. اطاعت اوامر سيّد الابرار *itāʿat awāmiri sayyidi'l abrār*, Obedience to the mandates of the prince of the just (*i.e.* Muhammad). P اظهار اطاعت كردن *izhāri itāʿat kardan*, To offer obedience, to surrender, to submit.

A اطافة *itāfat*, (v. n. 4 of طاف for طوف) Approaching, stealing upon any animal softly, in order to catch it. Alighting, going near any one.

A اطاقة *itāḳat*, (v. n. 4 of طاق for طوق) Being able, powerful. Being competent to grapple with (any thing). Giving power. Bearing, enduring. Ability for any thing.

A آطال *ātāl*, (pl. of اطل *itl*) The sides, especially under the short ribs.

A اطالة *itālat*, (v. n. 4 of طال for طول) Prolonging, extending, lengthening out. Bringing forth a child of a long shape, or tall. Prolixity. انّ القصيرة قد تطيل *inna'l ḳaṣīrata ḳad tutīlu*, Sometimes a dwarfish woman produces a tall son.

P اطاليق *atālīḳ*, A master, guardian, governor.

A آطام *ātām*, Name of a village in Yamāmah. (pl. of اطم *utum*) Fortresses of stone. Edifices square and flat-roofed.

A اطام *utām* or *itām*, Costiveness from indisposition. A strangury.

A اطاميم *atāmīm*, Legs of quadrupeds.

A اطاول *atāwil*, (pl. of اطول) Longer, longest.

A اطائب *atāʾib*, The best and choicest parts (of a slaughtered camel). Delicacies. (pl. of اطيب *atyab*) Better, best, more or most delightful.

A اطائم *atāʾim*, (pl. of اطيمة *atīmat*) Places where fires are lighted, hearths.

A اطباء *atbāʾ*, (pl. of طبي *tuby* and *tiby*) The dugs (of animals). اطباءُ الكلبة *atbāʾu'l kalbat*, (Bitch's dugs) Sebestens. *Itbāʾ*, (v. n. 4 of طبا for طبو) Shewing an affection for any one and then killing him. (v. n. 4 of طبي) Turning from, removing, averting. Calling to one.

A اطّباء *ittibāʾ*, (v. n. 8 of طبا for طبو) Calling. Choosing as a friend, accepting. (v. n. 8 of طبي) Choosing, selecting for one's self. Killing by stratagem. Calling.

A اطبّاء *atibbāʾ*, (pl. of طبيب *tabīb*) Physicians.

A اطّباخ *ittibākh*, (v. n. 8 of طبخ) Being cooked. Cooking for one's self. Cooking. Taking a decoction or apozem. Putting on the pot.

A اطباع *atbāʿ*, (pl. of طبع *tibʿ*) Rivulets, streams, channels made by torrents. Leathern bottles for churning. Rusts.

A اطباق *atbāḳ*, (pl. of طبق *tabaḳ*) Plates, dishes. Lids, covers. Strata of the earth. اطباق افلاك *atbāḳi aflāk*, The vaults of heaven. *Itbāḳ*, (v. n. 4 of طبق) Covering with a lid. Raining for a week. Consenting, agreeing. Being numerous and appearing (stars). Continuing (fever or madness). Placing a flag-stone over a hole.

A اطبال *atbāl*, (pl. of طبل *tabl*) Drums. اي اطبال هم *ayyu atbālin hum*, What people are these?

A اطبّة *atibbat*, (pl. of طبيب *tabīb*) Physicians. Leathern straps of a finger's length for covering the seams of a leathern bottle.

A اطبخ *atbakh*, Very foolish, extremely stupid.

A اطبع *atbaʿ*, More or most natural, skilful.

A اطبقة *atbiḳat*, (pl. of طبق *tabaḳ*) Lids, covers.

A اطبئنان *itbiʾnān*, (v. n. 4 of طبأن Q) Being still and quiet, reposing, resting. Tranquillity.

A اطثار *itsār*, (v. n. 4 of طثر) Increasing, multiplying, abounding, being many.

A اطّجاع *ittijāʿ*, (v. n. 8 of ضجع) Lying on one side (whether on a bed or on the ground)

A اطحاح *it-hāh*, (v. n. 4 of طحّ) Throwing. Letting fall.

A اطحار *it-hār*, (v. n. 4 of طحر) Extirpating the foreskin in circumcision.

A اطحل *at-hal*, Of the colour of dust. Neither dark-coloured nor bright-coloured (wolf, wine, or ashes). (Water) covered with moss. Name of a mountain. Spleen-coloured.

A اطخاف *itkhāf*, (v. n. 4 of طخف) Making the broth طخيفة *takhīfat*.

A اطخم *atkham*, (A ram) black-headed, the rest of the body of a sooty colour. (A horse) striped black from the withers to the tail. Chesnut, bright bay (horse). The tip of the nose (of man or horse). Dry flesh, of a blackish colour.

A اطخمام *itkhimām*, (v. n. 9 of طخم) Being dry and blackish (flesh).

A اطد *atad*, Wood of brambles.

A اطر *atr*, (v. n. of اطر) Bending (a bow). Surrounding, walling, hedging, or paling round. Wrapping a piece of cat-gut or bowstring round an arrow, near the notch, to strengthen it. The curve of a bow. A cloud. A rim, a circle. *Utur*, (pl. of اطار *itār*) Circles.

A اطراء *itrāʾ*, (v. n. 4 of طرأ) Praising immoderately. (v. n. 4 of طرا for طرو) Praising immoderately. Hyperbole, exaggeration. Pickling, seasoning with spiceries, preserving with sugar, honey, or vinegar.

A اطراب *atrāb*, The choicest odoriferous herbs. *Itrāb*, (v. n. 4 of طرب) Exhilarating, producing joy. Singing.

A اطرابلس *atrābulus*, Tripoli in Syria.

A اطّراح *ittirāh*, (v. n. 8 of طرح) Throwing away, putting to a distance.

A اطراد *itrād*, (v. n. 4 of طرد) Ejecting, banishing. Rejecting. Ordering to be banished, ejected, or exiled. Collecting, bringing together (camels) from different quarters. Betting, wagering. A remainder, sequel, consequence.

A اطّراد *ittirād*, (v. n. 8 of طرد) Being in good train (business). Flowing (rivers). Following in succession. Floating, hovering (the vapour *sarāb*).

A اطرار *itrār*, (v. n. 4 of طرّ) Cutting. Cutting off. Causing to fall. Holding in contempt. Irritating, instigating. Sprouting, coming forth (whiskers).

A اطراس *atrās*, (pl. of طرس *tirs*) Leaves of paper or of a book; especially where the writing has been erased and re-written.

A اطراف *atrāf*, (pl. of طرف *tarf*) Eyes (disallowed by some). (pl. of طرف *tirf*) Noble, eminent, high-born. Learned, distinguished (men). (pl. of طرف *taraf*) Sides, districts, tracts, coasts, shores, environs, confines, skirts, extreme parts. Ends, tips. The head, hands, feet, and other extremities of the body. The nearest kinsmen (as fathers, brothers, uncles, &c.). اطراف العذاري *atrāfu'l ʿazāraʾ*, (Maid's fingers) A sort of grape. اطراف و اكناف *atrāf u aknāf*, (or اطراف و آفاق *atrāf u āfāḳ*, Everywhere, throughout the globe, the whole world. امرائ اطراف *umarāʾi atrāf*, The neighbouring governors. *Itrāf*, (v. n. 4 of طرف) Giving any one something new, such as he never had before. Winking, shutting the eyes. Abounding in the plant نصيّ *nasiy*, compact and full-grown. Becoming acquainted, understanding, being up to.

A اطّراف *ittirāf*, (v. n. 8 of طرف) Buying something new. Tinging the tips of her fingers with privet (a woman).

A اطرافيّة *atrāfīyat*, Name of a sect.

A اطراق *atrāḳ*, (pl. of طرق *taraḳ*) Folds, or wrinkles (of the belly or a leathern bottle when almost empty). *Itrāḳ*, (v. n. 4 of طرق) Being dumb, keeping silence. Hanging the head. Fixing the eyes upon the ground. Being addicted to, or following (pastimes). Succeeding each other (portions of the night). Bringing ruin and destruction upon any one. Lending or hiring out (a camel-stallion). Covering any thing with leather, &c. Going one after another, following one another's foot-steps. Being clothed with skin and sinews.

A اطّراق *ittirāḳ*, (v. n. 8 of طرق) Going in different directions, leaving the high road. Being folded (the wings of a bird). Following each other's footsteps (camels).

A اطرام *itrām*, (v. n. 4 of طرم) Being dirty and covered with tartar (the teeth). Stinking (the breath, from shreds of meat sticking in the teeth).

A اطّرام *ittirām*, (v. n. 8 of طرم) Contracting a dirty colour (teeth).

A اطرة *utrat*, Flesh surrounding the nails. The cat-gut or bow-string which is twisted round an arrow, near the notch. The rim of the nut of the yard. The edge of the artery ابهر *abhar*. A species of glutinous substance mixed up with blood and ashes with which broken earthenware, &c., is cemented.

A اطرخمام *itrikhmām*, (v. n. 4 of طرخم Q) Carrying one's self haughtily, tossing the nose from pride. Being dim the (sight), dark (the night).

A اطرط الحاجبين *atratu'l hājibayn*, One who

has thin eye-brows.

A اطرغشاش *itrighshāsh*, (v. n. 4 of طرغش Q) Recovering health. Rising up, moving. Leaning from side to side in walking. Stirring in the nest (young birds). Being blessed with rain and fertility after a season of scarcity and discomfort.

A اطرغلات *utrughullāt*, Female turtle-doves. Wood-pigeons.

A اطرغمام *itrighmām*, The being proud.

A اطرق *atrak*, Weak in the knee. Bow-legged. *Atruk*, (pl. of طريق *tarīk*) Roads, ways.

A اطرقاء *atrikās*, (pl. of طريق *tarīk*) Roads, ways.

A اطرقة *atrikat*, (pl. of طريق *tarīk*) Roads, ways.

A اطرمساس *itrimsās*, (v. n. 4 of طرمس Q) Being dark (the night).

A اطروان *utruwān*, The earliest and most lively season of youth.

A اطروش *utrūsh*, Deaf.

A اطرهمام *itrihmām*, (v. n. 4 of طرهم Q) Being middle-sized and well-proportioned.

A اطرية *itriyat*, A vermicelli used in broths.

A اطريح *itrīh*, Oblong (bunch of a camel).

A اطريراء *itrīrās*, (v. n. 12 of طرو) Being oppressed with indigestion. Being puffed with pride or anger. Swelling (the belly).

A اطريفل *itrīfal*, A myrobalan-electuary.

G آطريلال *ātrīlāl*, (or اطريلال) Crow-foot.

A اطساء *itsās*, (v. n. 4 of طسأ) Causing indigestion (repletion or satiety).

A اطسمة *utsummat*, The greater or middle part of any thing, the aggregate, conflux.

A اطشاء *itshās*, (v. n. 4 of طشأ) Taking cold, suffering from rheum.

A اطشاش *itshāsh*, (v. n. 4 of طش) Misling.

A اطط *uttat*, Creaking (thongs).

A اطعام *itʿām*, (v. n. 4 of طعم) Feeding, giving victuals. Grafting. Being well-flavoured (ripening dates). Having ripe fruit (a palm-tree).

A اطّعام *ittiʿām*, (v. n. 8 of طعم) Being fine flavoured (fruit). Being instructed in literature and good breeding, or any thing useful. Eating food.

A اطّعان *ittiʿān*, (v. n. 8 of طعن) Seeking to spear (each other). Breaking a lance with another.

A اطعمة *atʿimat*, (pl. of طعام *taʿām*) Meats, victuals, viands. Wheats. اطعمهٔ نفيسه *atʿimasi nafīsa*, Exquisite meats.

A اطعن *atʿan*, More or most of a piercer.

A اطغاء *itghās*, (v. n. 4 of طغي) Seducing, leading into error. Rendering proud, petulant, insolent. Making exorbitant or excessive.

A اطفاء *itfās*, (v. n. 4 of طفئ) Extinguishing, putting out (a fire or life).

A اطفاح *itfāh*, (v. n. 4 of طفح) Filling till the liquor runs over, filling to the brim.

A اطّفاح *ittifāh*, (v. n. 8 of طفح) Throwing up scum (a boiling pot). Taking off the scum.

A اطفاذ *atfāz*, (pl. of طفذ) Sepulchres, graves.

A اطّفار *ittifār*, (v. n. 8 of طفر) Putting his feet under the armpit of a horse (a rider), which is regarded as bad horsemanship.

A اطفاف *itfāf*, (v. n. 4 of طفّ) Happening, occurring. Being possible, offering itself, coming in one's way. Impending. Filling to the brim. Bringing forth an imperfect colt (a camel). Understanding, knowing. Comprehending, containing. Being near, at the point of. Hitting (with a stone). Studying to deceive.

A اطفاق *itfāk*, (v. n. 4 of طفق) Fulfilling one's wishes (God).

P اطفال *atfāl*, A wife (considered more respectful than زن *zan*, and other similar words).

A اطفال *atfāl*, (pl. of طفل *tifl*) Infants, children, boys. P اطفال باغ *atfāli bāgh*, Fresh flowers, young plants. A *Itfāl*, (v. n. 4 of طفل) Being near sun-set, reddening, as at sun-set. Entering upon darkness.

A اطفئنان *itfisnān*, (v. n. 4 of طفأن Q) Being quiet, tranquil, good, and amiable.

A اطل *itl* or *itil*, (pl. آطال *ātāl*) The side, that part of the belly under the short ribs, the hypochondria. *Utl*, Any thing, a mouthful.

A اطلاء *atlās*, (pl. of طلا *tala'*) Fawns (when just brought forth). The young ones, especially of animals that divide the hoof. Sick, diseased. *Itlās*, (v. n. 4 of طلي) Inclining to one's own wishes. Bowing the head, submitting to death, or any other calamity. Anointing (with pitch).

A اطّلاء *ittilās*, (v. n. 8 of طلي) Being anointed, bedaubed. Anointing one's self with pitch, or the like. Removing hair from the body with a preparation of arsenic.

A اطلاب *atlāb*, (pl. of طلب *tilb*) Lovers, courtiers, suitors, fond of women. *Itlāb*, (v. n. 4 of طلب) Forcing (one) to seek or inquire. Granting a petition. Being far off, or a great way to seek (as water or forage).

A اطّلاب *ittilāb*, (v. n. 8 of طلب) Seeking, asking, exacting.

A اطلاح *atlāh*, (pl. of طلح *tilh*) Jaded (camels). Tikes, sheep-lice. Stewards, farming-bailiffs. Danglers after women. *Itlāh*, (v. n. 4 of طلح) Fatiguing or even killing (a camel). Being jaded.

A اطلاس *atlās*, (pl. of طلس *tils*) Worn smooth, bare, bald. Wolves whose hair is rubbed off quite bare; the thighs of camels in the same state. Things defaced or erased. Spots, stains.

A اطلاع *itlāʿ*, (v. n. 4 of طلع) Manifesting, imparting what one knows, informing, putting in possession of a secret. Knowing, understanding, considering. Bringing up or out, drawing forth. Putting forth buds or the spathes which enclose the dates (a palm-tree). Vomiting. Shooting or throwing beyond, above, or wide of the mark. Coming, approaching. Causing one to make haste. Doing a kindness, conferring a favour.

A اطّلاع *ittilāʿ*, (v. n. 8 of طلع) Ascending, rising (the sun or stars). Putting forth buds (a palm). Knowing. Inspecting, viewing, examining, penetrating deeply (into any business). Arriving, approaching. Being hidden. Information, report. P اطّلاع و شعور كردن *ittilāʿ u shuʿūr kardan*, To examine and animadvert upon.

A اطّلاعاً *ittilāʿan*, For the purpose of informing.

A اطلاف *itlāf*, (v. n. 4 of طلف) Giving, bestowing. Escaping with impunity. Suffering to go unpunished.

A اطلاق *atlāk*, (pl. of طلق *talk*) Fawns, young deer. (pl. of طلق *tulk* and *tuluk*) Free, unconfined (camels), pasturing at large. (pl. of طلق *talak*) Intestines. Sheaths (of horses). *Itlāk*, (v. n. 4 of طلق) Setting at liberty, liberating, releasing, dismissing, sending away. Loosening, relaxing. Using (a word) in a free, unrestricted, or universal sense. Opening (the hand), being liberal, giving bountifully. Divorcing, repudiating. Allowing (camels) to go freely to pasture and water when the day's journey is over; also, being possessed of such camels. Giving a poisoned draught to an enemy. Rendering the female palm fruitful by sprinkling the farina of the male tree. A diarrhœa. حروف الاطلاق *hurūfu'l itlāk*, The letters ا, و, and ي put after a homogeneous vowel to fill up: as, كمالو *kamālū* for كمال *kamālu*, كمالا *kamālā* for كمال *kamāla*, كمالي *kamālī* for كمال *kamāli*. علي الاطلاق *ʿala'l itlāk*, Absolutely, properly, universally. P اطلاق عنان كردن *itlāki ʿinān kardan*, To give the reins (to a horse).

A اطّلاق *ittilāk*, (v. n. 8 of طلق) Being carried away (the mind). Being joyous and glad.

A اطلال *atlāl*, A certain horse or camel said to have been endued with the gift of speech. (pl. of طلل *talal*) Bodies, substances. Ruins of a house. *Itlāl*, (v. n. 4 of طلّ) Being at the point of, impending. Knowing, understanding. Permitting blood to be shed unrevenged.

A اطّلام *ittilām*, (v. n. 8 of ظلم) Submitting to injuries.

A اطّلاه *ittilāh*, (v. n. 8 of طله) Ascending, rising. Inspecting, viewing; knowing, being cognizant.

A اطلب *atlab*, More or most of a seeker.

A اطلّة *atillat*, (pl. of طليل *talīl*) Mats.

A اطلخاخ *itlikhākh*, (v. n. 9 of طلخ) Being scattered. Flowing (tears).

A اطلخمام *itlikhmām*, (v. n. 4 of طلخم Q) Being high and haughty. Being very dark (the night). Being dim (the sight).

A اطلس *atlas*, Bare, smooth, bald. Satin. Dirty, soiled. Old (raiment). Tending to black; any thing of such a colour. Name of a dog. A thief. Black (Ethiopian). Blackened, stigmatized, suspected. P چرخ اطلس *charkhi atlas*, The crystalline sphere.

P اطلسي *atlasī*, An eunuch (black).

A اطلط *atlat*, More or most cunning, shrewder.

A اطلنساء *itlinsā*, (v.n.3 of طلسي Q) Flowing over the body (sweat). Going from place to place.

A اطلنفاء *itlinfā*, A cleaving to the ground.

A اطله *atlah*, Destitute of water (river). (pl. طله *tulh*) The same as اطلس *atlas* above.

A اطلية *atliyat*, (pl. of طلاء *tilā*) Liniments.

A اطم *atm*, (v. n. of اطم) Biting (the hand). Voiding dung. Narrowing (a well's mouth). Letting down a veil before a tent. Having a constipation and suppression of urine (a camel). Being enraged. Being bound, drawn together. *Utum*, (pl. آطام *ātām* and اطوم *utūm*) A fortress of stone. Any square edifice, with a flat roof. A stone fort. A fortress in Madina. اطم الاضبط *utumu'l azbat*, Name of a fortress in Yaman built by اضبط بن قريع *azbat bin kuray*.

A اطماح *itmāh*, (v.n.4 of طمح) Raising the face, lifting the eyes.

A اطمار *atmār*, (pl. of طمر *timr*) Old, worn-out clothes. *Itmār*, (v.n. 4 of طمر) Drawing his yard up into the sheath (a horse). Causing to leap.

A اطّمار *ittimār*, (v.n. 8 of طمر) Leaping, vaulting upon (a horse's) back from behind.

A اطماس *itmās*, (v.n. 4 of طمس) Putting out, quenching.

A اطماط *atmāt*, A species of Indian nut.

A اطماع *atmā*, (pl. of طمع *tama*) Soldiers' pay. The times at which they receive it, pay-days. (pl. of طامع *tāmi* and طمع *tami*) Greedy. *Itmā*, (v. n. 4 of طمع) Exciting a strong desire, causing to hanker.

A اطمال *itmāl*, (v.n.4 of طمل) Erasing (writing).

A اطّمال *ittimāl*, (v. n. 8 of طمل) Extracting even to the last drop from a cistern.

A اطمام *itmām*, (v. n. 4 of طمّ) Being fit for cutting, requiring to be cut and dressed (hair).

A اطمحرار *itmihrār*, (v.n. 4 of طمحر Q) Drinking to repletion.

A اطمخرار *itmikhrār*, (v.n.4 of طمخر Q) Drinking to repletion.

A اطمرّ *utmurr*, High-spirited, swift (horse).

A اطموط *atmūt*, A species of Indian nut.

G اطميسا *atmīsā*, Southernwood. Mugwort.

A اطمئنان *itmi-nān*, (v.n.4 of طمأن Q) Reposing, resting. Rest, tranquillity, repose, content, quiet, security, peace. اطمئنان خاطر *itmi-nāni khātir*, Peace of mind.

A اطناء *itnā*, (v.n. 4 of طنأ) Killing, stinging mortally (a scorpion). Wishing for an inn or place of repose (travellers). Reclining upon any thing in order to sleep. Lying down in order to drink. (v. n. 4 of طني) Poisoning, killing suddenly, stinging mortally (a serpent). Striking in a mortal part. Inclining to suspicion and scandal. Launching out into wickedness and debauchery. Having the spleen and lungs adhering to the left side. Buying. Selling. Liking to lounge on a sofa.

A اطنّاء *atinnā*, (pl. of طنين) Buzzings of flies.

A اطناب *atnāb*, (pl. of طنب *tunub*) Tent-ropes. *Itnāb*, (v. n. 4 of طنب) Raising a dust (wind). Speaking with sublimity, using glowing language. Sublimity of style. Bombast, hyperbole in praise or censure. Following one another (camels). Flowing to a distance (a river).

A اطنابة *itnabāt*, An umbrella, parasol, arbour, any place or thing that shades from the sun or rain. A thong which joins a bow-string to the horn of a bow. ابن الاطنابة *ibnu'l itnābat*, Name of a poet.

A اطناخ *itnākh*, The causing of an indigestion.

A اطناف *atnāf*, (pl. of طنف *tanf*) Promontories, extremities, protuberances, or mountain-peaks. *Itnāf*, (v. n. 4 of طنف) Standing on a pinnacle, mountain-top, or coping of a wall. Having a coping for one's wall, or a slab or pent over one's door.

A اطنان *atnān*, (pl. of طنّ *tunn*) Human bodies. *Itnān*, (v. n. 4 of طنّ) Making any thing to sound or ring (as a bason, drum, or a bell). Making a duck to quack, or a fly to buzz. Cutting the leg (from the sound which the blow makes).

A اطنب *atnab*, Long-legged, but lax withal. Long-backed.

A ما اطنفه *mā atnafahu*, What a little eater he is! How poor he is! How unwilling he is!

G اطنه *atana*, Athens. The Arabians call it مدينة الحكماء *madīnatu'l hukamā*, The city of philosophers; and زيتونة *zaytūnat*, The olive-garden.

A اطواء *atwā*, Wrinkles, folds, plies. Ducts of fat in the bunches of camels. *Itwā*, (v. n. 4 of طوي) Abstaining from food, fasting.

A اطّواء *ittiwā*, (v.n.8 of طوي) Being folded.

A اطواد *atwād*, (pl. of طود) Large mountains.

A اطوار *atwār*, (pl. of طور *tawr*) Times, turns, ways. مقامات و اطوار *makāmāt u atwār*, Places and countries. P اطوار سيه *atwāri siyah*, Black or wicked actions. اطوار ناهموار *atwāri nāhamwār*, Unworthy actions. اطوار حميده و آثار پسنديده *atwāri hamīda u āsāri pasandīda*, Praise-worthy actions and illustrious deeds. خوش اطوار *khwush-atwār*, Well-bred.

A اطوارًا *atwāran*, Occasionally.

A اطواس *atwās*, (pl. of طاؤس *tā-us*) Peacocks. Beaus, handsome men. (Grounds) luxuriant with herbage. Silvers.

A اطواط *atwāt*, (pl. of طوط) Libidinous stallions.

A اطواق *atwāk*, The milk of the cocoa-nut. (pl. of طوق *tawk*) Collars, chains for the neck.

A اطوال *atwāl*, (pl. of طول *tūl*) Longitudes. *Itwāl*, (v. n. 4 of طال for طول) Lengthening. Bringing forth a long-shaped infant (a woman).

A اطور *atwar*, End, extremity.

A اطورين *atwarīn*, A calamity, misfortune. بلغ في العلم اطوريه *balagha fi'l ilm atwarayhi* or *atwarīhi*, He attained the beginning and end of learning.

A اطوع *atwa*, More or most obedient.

A اطول *atwal*, (pl. اطاول *atāwil*) Longer, longest. (A camel) which has a long dangling upper lip.

A اطولاً *atwalan*, Prolixly, tediously.

A اطوم *atūm*, A sea-tortoise, turtle. A species of wild ox. A kind of thick-skinned fish. A bow whose string sticks close to the handle. A hedgehog. A sea-shell. *Utūm*, (pl. of اطم *utum*) Castles, fortresses, square buildings of stone with flat roofs.

A اطهاء *it-hā*, (v. n. 4 of طها for طهو) Being skilful, clever at any work or business.

A اطهار *at-hār*, (pl. of طهر *tuhr*) Purities. (pl. of طاهر *tāhir*) Clear, pure, chaste, unsullied, clean. الاطهار *al at-hār*, Days (of a woman's) cleanness.

A اطهاف *it-hāf*, (v. n. 4 of طهف not in use) Using a short for a long vowel. Discoursing plainly, simply, perspicuously. Being loose, flaccid (a leathern bottle). Giving away a part of one's wealth. Growing luxuriantly (the plant صليان *silliyān*). Sowing the kind of grass called طهف *tahf*.

A اطهر *at-har*, More or most pure.

A اطّهر *ittahhur*, (v. n. of اطّهر *ittahhara*) (for تطهّر *tatahhur*, v. n. 5 of طهر) Being purified. Being clean, free from vice.

A اطياب *atyāb*, (pl. of طيب *tīb*) Odours, unguents. *Ityāb*, (v. n. 4 of طاب for طيب) Relishing, liking well, approving.

A إطيار *atyār*, (pl. of طير *tayr*) Birds.

A اطّياف *ittiyāf*, (v. n. 8 of طاف for طوف) Going to the privy.

A اطيب *atyab*, Better, best, more or most sweet, fragrant, delicate, pleasant, delightful. الاطيبان *al atyabāni*, The two delights, Ceres and Venus, or youth and gay spirits. ما اطيبه *mā atyabuhu*, How delightful (is) it!

A اطير *atīr*, Sin, crime, fault. Straits. Speech, a word. Evil which comes from afar. اخذني باطير غيري *akhazanī bi atīri ghayrī*, He blamed me for the fault of another.

A اطيرق *utayrik*, A palm-tree.

A اطيش *atyash*, A kind of bird.

A اطيط *atīt*, (v. n. of اطّ) Making a creaking noise (the saddle of a camel). The sound itself. The rattling of the belly (from hunger). Hunger. The yearning of the bowels. The noise made by a camel's colt. The murmuring of a camel from fatigue, or desire for her young. اهل اطيط *ahli atīt*, Those who look after, or make use of, camels.

A اطيمة *atīmat*, (pl. اطائم *atā-im*) A grate, a hearth, or any place where fire is lighted.

A اطيوط *atyūt*, Name of an Indian nut.

A اظآر *azsār*, (pl. of ظئر *zi-r*) Nurses, foster-mothers, those who suckle the offspring of others. *Izsār*, (v. n. 4 of ظأر) Inducing (a camel) to suckle the colt of another. Hiring a nurse.

A اظافير *azāfīr,* (pl. of ظفر) Nails, claws, hoofs.

A اظاليف *azālīf,* (pl. of اظلوفة *uzlūfat,*) Grounds full of rugged and sharp stones (as mountains, &c.).

A اظانين *azānīn,* (pl. of ظنّ *zann*) Opinions. Doubts, waverings.

A اظبي *azbī,* (pl. of ظبة *zubat*) The points of arrows. The curved edges of swords. (pl. of ظبي *zaby*) Wild bucks, chevrils.

A اظراب *azrāb,* The roots of the teeth. Wisdom-teeth. Four teeth behind the نواجذ *nawājiz.*

A اظرار *izrār,* A walking upon sharp stones.

A اظراف *izrāf,* (v. n. 4 of ظرف) Bringing forth ingenious, witty children. Making a vessel.

A اظرّة *azirrat,* (pl. of ظرير *zarīr*) (Grounds) full of sharp stones.

A اظرف *azraf,* More or most elegant, beautiful, clean, neat. More or most facetious, witty.

A اظرور *uzrūr,* A round stone with a sharp edge.

A اظريراء *izrīrāʼ,* (v. n. 12 of ظري) Swelling (the belly). Suffering from over-eating. Being oppressed with fat.

A اظطلام *iztilām,* (v. n. 8 of ظلم) Being harrassed by, bearing patiently, or sinking under, tyranny, oppression, cruelty, or outrage.

A اظطئار *iztiʼār,* (v. n. 8 of ظأر) Hiring a nurse.

A اظعان *azʼān,* (pl. of ظعينة *zaʼīnat*) Litters in which women travel on the backs of camels. Women so carried. *Izʼān,* (v. n. 4 of ظعن) Causing (a man) to travel, or to migrate.

A اظّعان *izziʼān,* (v. n. 8 of ظعن) Travelling in the camel-litter ظعينة *zaʼīnat,* (a woman).

A اظفار *azfār,* A kind of perfume resembling uprooted nails. (pl. of ظفر *zufr*) Nails, claws, hoofs. Large tikes, which annoy camels, sheep, and other cattle. Certain small stars in front of the constellation of the eagle. اظفار الذئب *azfāru'z ziʼb,* Certain small stars near the constellation فرقدان *farkadān.* اظفار الطيب *azfāru't tīb,* Perfumed nails. *Izfār,* (v. n. 4 of ظفر) Wounding with the nails. Making conqueror, enabling one to triumph, or to attain his object.

A اظّفار *izzifār,* (v. n. 8 of ظفر) Being victorious. Sticking the nails in any thing. Seizing (a bird) by the head (a hawk).

A اظفر *azfar,* Possessed of long and broad nails.

A اظفور *uzfūr,* (pl. اظافير *azāfīr*) A nail, claw, talon. A tendril growing round the branch of a vine.

A اظلّ *azall,* (pl. ظلّ *zull*) The inside of a finger or of the sole of a camel's foot.

A اظلاف *azlāf,* (pl. of ظلف *zilf*) The hoofs of oxen, sheep, and other animals which divide the hoof. The animals themselves. *Izlāf,* (v. n. 4 of ظلف) Falling upon hard ground, with sharp and rugged stones. Concealing one's footsteps by walking upon hard, unyielding ground.

A اظلال *azlāl,* (pl. of ظل *zill*) Shadows. *Izlāl,* (v. n. 4 of ظلّ) Shading, casting a shadow. Turning the face to. Approaching. Being cloudy.

A اظلام *izlām,* (v. n. 4 of ظلم) Growing dark. Walking in darkness. Being bright (the front teeth. Meeting with oppression.

A اظّلام *izzilām,* The being tyrannized over.

A اظلم *azlam,* More or most unjust. لعن الله اظلمي و اظلمك *laʼana'llāh azlamī wa azlamaka,* May God curse the more unjust of me and thee!

A اظلوفة *uzlūfat,* (pl. اظاليف *azālīf*) Ground covered with sharp rugged stones.

A اظماء *azmāʼ,* (pl. of ظمء *zimʼ*) Thirsts. The spaces of time between drinking or watering of cattle. *Izmāʼ,* (v. n. 4 of ظمیٔ) Making thirsty. Making (a fat horse) lean.

A اظمیٰ *azmaʼ,* Brown and slender (spear). Black (cloud or shadow). One who has brown and bloodless gums.

A اظنان *iznān,* (v. n. 4 of ظنّ) Suspecting. Rendering liable to suspicion.

A اظّنان *izzinān,* (v. n. 8 of ظنّ) Suspecting.

A اظنّة *azinnat,* (pl. of ظنين *zanīn*) Suspected.

A اظواء *izwāʼ,* (v. n. 4 of ظوي) Being foolish.

A اظؤب *azʼub,* (pl. of ظأب *zaʼb*) Husbands of wives' sisters. Marriages. Noises, clamours.

A اظؤر *azʼur,* (pl. of ظئر) Nurses, foster-mothers.

A اظهار *izhār,* (v. n. 4 of ظهر) Revealing, discovering, publishing, evincing, displaying, exhibiting. Pretending, feigning, making an outward show. Exalting, rendering superior, assisting against an enemy. Entering upon or travelling in the noon-tide heat. Despising, rejecting, forgetting, treating slightingly, casting behind one's back. Reading off by heart. Being possessed of camels for the saddle. P اظهار خصومت كردن *izhāri khusūmat kardan,* To show enmity, become an open enemy. اظهار فرار كردن *izhāri firār kardan,* To make a feint retreat, to appear to fly.

A اظّهار *izzihār,* (v. n. 8 of ظهر) Throwing behind one's back. Forgetting. Neglecting. Despising.

A اظهر *azhar,* More or most clear, bright, evident. اظهر من الشمس *azhar mini' sh shams,* Clearer than the sun. *Azhur,* (pl. of ظهر) Backs. بين اظهرهم *bayna azhurihim,* In the midst of them.

A اظّئار *izziʼār,* (v. n. 8 of ظأر) Giving suck to another's child (a woman), another's colt (a camel).

A اع اع *uʼ uʼ,* The sound made in vomiting.

A اعاء *iʼāʼ,* A sheath, case, pure, or chest.

A اعابد *aʼābid,* (pl. of عبد *ʼabd*) Servants.

A اعاجم *aʼājim,* (pl. of اعجم *aʼjam*) Barbarians (those who cannot speak Arabic, or speak incorrectly; but more particularly the Persians).

A اعاجيب *aʼājīb,* (pl. of اعجوبة *uʼjūbat*) Miracles, wonders.

A اعادة *iʼādat,* (v. n. 4 of عاد for عود) Causing to return, bringing back. Making a habit or custom (عادة *ʼādat*). Repetition, reiteration, saying or doing any thing over again. P اعادت كردن *iʼādat kardan,* To repeat, to relate.

A اعادي *aʼādī,* (pl. of عدوّ *ʼadūw*) Enemies, foes.

A اعاذة *iʼāzat,* (v. n. 4 of عاذ for عوذ) Forcing to fly for refuge. Having recently brought forth young (camels, mares, deer, &c.). Wishing to hinder, prevent, or keep back. Saving, defending.

A اعارة *iʼārat,* (v. n. 4 of عار for عور) Lending. Borrowing. Being in fear. (v. n. 4 of عار for عير) Carrying. Turning (a horse) loose to pasture. Going to and fro. Turning away from one female to another (a male camel). Flying about, being spread far and wide (a poem). Making (an arrow-head) large in the middle.

A اعارض *aʼāriz,* (or اعاريض *aʼārīz*) (pl. of عروض *ʼarūz*) The concluding members in the first hemistichs of couplets.

A اعاريب *aʼārīb,* (pl. of اعراب *aʼrāb*) Wild wandering Arabs (the more civilized citizens being called عرب *ʼarab*).

A اعاسة *iʼāsat,* The withering (of corn).

A اعاشة *iʼāshat,* (v. n. 4 of عاش for عيش) Supporting, preserving life.

A اعاشير *aʼāshīr,* (pl. of اعشار *aʼshār*) Broken in ten pieces (pots).

A اعاصير *aʼāsīr,* (pl. of اعصار *iʼsār*) Whirlwinds, hurricanes, tornadoes.

A اعاضة *iʼāzat,* (v. n. 4 of عاض for عوض) Recompensing, rewarding, retaliating, giving one thing in return for another.

A اعاظم *aʼāzim,* (pl. of اعظم *aʼzam*) Great, chief, principal. اعاظم سلاطين مسلماني *aʼāzimi salātīni muslimānī,* The greatest of Muslim princes.

A اعافة *iʼāfat,* (v. n. 4 of عاف for عيف) Having (cattle) approaching water, and smelling to it, without drinking, although thirsty.

A اعالة *iʼālat,* (v. n. 4 of عال for عول) Becoming poor. Providing adequately for the maintenance of a family. Desiring eagerly. Exacting or levying more than what is due by law. (v. n. 4 of عال for عيل) Having a numerous family. Keeping a large establishment or household.

A اعالي *aʼālī,* (pl. of اعلیٰ *aʼla'*) The upper parts.

P اعالي مآب *aʼālī-maʼāb,* Of exalted deeds.

A اعامة *iʼāmat,* (v. n. 4 of عام for عيم) Leaving without milk. Being without milk.

A اعانة *iʼānat,* (v. n. 4 of عان for عون) Aiding, assisting. Assistance, help, aid, favour. (v. n. 4 of عان for عين) Keeping a look out from an eminence. Eying, following with a malignant eye. Causing water to come up at a spring.

A اعاور *aʼāwir,* (pl. of اعور) Nits in the head.

A اعاهة *iʼāhat,* (v. n. 4 of عاه for عوه or عيه) Suffering loss in cattle or corn.

A اعبّ *aʼabb,* Poor, needy. Thick-nosed.

A اعباء *aʼbāʼ,* (pl. of عبء *ʼibʼ*) Burthens, loads, bales (of merchandise). Like, resembling.

A اعباد *iʼbād,* (v. n. 4 of عبد) Receiving or

purchasing as a servant. Making (one) to serve another. Being fatigued, perishing through fatigue (cattle). Striking. Assembling, flocking together.

A اعبار *iʿbār*, (v. n. 4 of عبر) Remaining a whole year without being sheared (a sheep). Having much wool (sheep).

A اعباس *iʿbās*, (v. n. 4 of عبس) Being bedaubed with dry dung (tails of camels).

A اعباش *iʿbāsh*, (v. n. 4 of عبش) Circumcising (a boy). Adjusting, amending.

A اعباط *iʿbāt*, (v. n. 4 of عبط) Surprising (a man) whilst in the vigour of health (death).

A اعبال *aʿbāl*, (pl. of عبل *ʿabal*) Curled jagged leaves (as those of the tamarisk-tree). *Iʿbāl*, (v. n. 4 of عبل) (Trees) having leaves sprouting (as in spring). Having leaves falling (on the approach of winter). Having large, thick, red leaves (the plant ارطي *arta'*) proper for tanning hides. Being thick. Being white.

A اعبان *iʿbān*, The using a large, bulky camel.

A اعبد *aʿbad*, More or most devout or devoted servant. *Aʿbud*, (pl. of عبد *ʿabd*) Servants.

A اعبل *aʿbul*, White stones. A mountain where such stones are found. A stone rugged and thick, in which there is a mixture of white, red, and black.

A اعبنقاء *iʿbinkāʾ*, (v. n. 15 of عبق) Being a wicked wretch. Being extremely subtle.

A اعبئة *aʿbiʾat*, (pl. of عباء *ʿabāʾ*) Black striped cloaks worn by dervishes. Foolish fellows. Heavy, unwholesome (meats).

A اعتاء *aʿtāʾ*, (pl. of عتيّ *ʿatiy*) Low, vile. Destroyers. Proud, overbearing. Whoremongers.

A اعتاب *iʿtāb*, (v. n. 4 of عتب) Contenting, satisfying, making (one) to consent or acquiesce. Receiving into favour. Retiring.

A اعتاد *iʿtād*, (v. n. 4 of عتد) Disposing, placing in order, arranging, preparing one's self for any future occasion.

A اعتاق *iʿtāk*, (v. n. 4 of عتق) Setting at liberty, bestowing freedom. Urging on (a horse). Managing well (property). Digging (a well) and building up the sides of it. Settling on a spot and becoming owner of it.

A اعتام *iʿtām*, (v. n. 4 of عتم) Becoming dark (night). Being in the first division of the night, commencing after sunset. Doing any thing during that time. Having a portion of itself past (the night). Abstaining from that to which one had been addicted. Being slow and tardy. Being milked in the evening (camels). Collecting milk in the udder after the last milking.

A اعتان *iʿtān*, The being severe (to a debtor).

A اعتباء *iʿtibāʾ*, (v. n. 8 of عبأ) Stuffing, cramming. Repletion.

A اعتباد *iʿtibād*, (v. n. 8 of عبد) Reducing to slavery or servitude. Receiving as a servant.

A اعتبار *iʿtibār*, (v. n. 8 of عبر) Taking counsel. Taking an example or warning, and profiting by it. Reasoning, computing by comparison. Considering with attention. Being astonished, wondering. Esteem, honour, reverence, veneration, respect. Confidence, faith, belief. بعين اعتبار *ba ʿayni iʿtibār*, With the eye of esteem, respectfully.

A اعتباط *iʿtibāt*, (v. n. 8 of عبط) Slaughtering an unblemished (camel). Carrying off a man in his full vigour (death). Digging (a well). Lying hid (a man). Forging a lie. Peeling the surface of the ground (wind).

A اعتباطيّ *iʿtibātiy*, Violent (suppression).

A اعتتاب *iʿtitāb*, (v. n. 8 of عتب) Purposing to do any thing. Turning away from one thing, and turning to another. Leaving a smooth road, and turning into a rough one. Turning away from, retiring, departing. Ascending and not turning away.

A اعتثاث *iʿtisās*, (v. n. 8 of عثّ) Uprooting. Finding the way towards. Cleaving, sticking to.

A اعتثام *iʿtisām*, (v. n. 8 of عثم) Asking assistance. Being useful, beneficial. Doing to the best of one's ability. Stretching forth the hand to receive or to beckon. Sewing slightly (a wallet).

A اعتجار *iʿtijār*, (v. n. 8 of عجر) Putting on a coif or veil for the head (a woman). Putting on a turban without leaving any part of the sash to hang down. Bringing forth a boy or girl after having despaired of offspring.

A اعتجان *iʿtijān*, (v. n. 8 of عجن) Kneading. Taking dough.

A اعتد *aʿtud*, (pl. of عتاد *ʿatād*) Arms, instruments, utensils, equipments (for a journey).

A اعتداء *iʿtidāʾ*, (v. n. 8 of عدا for عدو) Transgressing, being iniquitous, unjust. Injustice.

A اعتداد *iʿtidād*, (v. n. 8 of عدّ) Counting, numbering. Taking pains, being anxious. Sufficing.

A اعتدار *iʿtidār*, (v. n. 8 of عدر) Raining heavily. Abounding in water. Being moist by rain.

A اعتدال *iʿtidāl*, (v. n. 8 of عدل) Being middling, moderate, just, or even. Being straight and upright. Equality, equilibrium. Moderation, temperature, mediocrity. اعتدال هوا *iʿtidāli hawā*, The temperature or salubrity of the air. اعتدال النهار و الليل *iʿtidālu'n nahār wa'l layl*, (Equality of day and night) The equinox; the Persians call the two equinoxes of spring and autumn نو روز *naw roz*, (new day, that being the beginning of their year) and مهرجان *mihrjān*, (the autumn) both of which they celebrate with festivals. حد اعتدال *hadi iʿtidāl*, Mediocrity, moderation. An equitable decision. P قامت بر اعتدال *kāmati bar iʿtidāl*, Middle stature. اعتدال كردن *iʿtidāl kardan*, To temperate, moderate.

A اعتدة *aʿtidat*, (pl. of عتود) Yearling kids.

A اعتذاب *iʿtizāb*, (v. n. 8 of عذب) Leaving both ends of the turban-sash to fall down behind.

A اعتذار *iʿtizār*, (v. n. 8 of عذر) Being effaced, obliterated. Excusing one's self, apologizing. Lamenting, complaining. Letting the ends of the turban-sash hang loose. Stopping, ceasing to flow. Deflowering. Expiation. Old, ancient. P اعتذار كردن *iʿtizār kardan*, To excuse, make an apology.

P اعتذار نامه *iʿtizār-nāma*, A letter of apology.

A اعتذاق *iʿtizāk*, (v. n. 8 of عذق) Letting both ends of the turban-sash fall down behind. Distinguishing, particularizing. Marking (a young she-camel) in order to catch (her).

A اعتذال *iʿtizāl*, (v. n. 8 of عذل) Blaming one's self. Receiving reproof. Pursuing with steadiness: resolution, perseverance. Going in the middle of the road. Shooting a second time.

A اعتراء *iʿtirāʾ*, (v. n. 8 of عرا for عرو) Coming upon, down upon, over one. Desiring, seeking.

A اعترار *iʿtirār*, (v. n. 8 of عرّ) Being in want, and shewing one's necessities without begging.

A اعتراس *iʿtirās*, (v. n. 8 of عرس) Being separated, divided, scattered.

A اعتراش *iʿtirāsh*, (v. n. 8 of عرش) Making a bower. Hanging from the top of a trellis (grapes). Being seated on horseback.

A اعتراص *iʿtirās*, (v. n. 8 of عرص) Playing. Being cheerful, sprightly, active. Beating, throbbing (the skin).

A اعتراض *iʿtirāz*, (v. n. 8 of عرض) Being mounted on horseback, and reviewing an army. Reviewing a book; criticism, animadversion. Meeting, encountering, lighting on. Intervening, intercepting. Being hindered by a jinn or disease from visiting one's wife. Opposing, hindering, resisting; refusal, denial. Speaking ill of, disparaging. Being untractable, disobedient to the rein (a horse). Going awry (a stubborn camel). Riding on such a beast. Lying (as a plank across a brook or a gutter). Feeding in a grassy spot (a camel). Spreading. Smiting with a dart an opponent. Commencing a month, but not at the beginning. Taking pains, striving. Occurrence.

A اعتراضات *iʿtirāzāt*, Oppositions.

A اعتراط *iʿtirāt*, A slandering of the absent.

A اعتراف *iʿtirāf*, (v. n. 8 of عرف) Knowing. Inquiring diligently. Being patient. Being humble, obedient, submissive. Telling one's name and business. Confessing, acknowledging, avowing.

A اعتراق *iʿtirāk*, (v. n. 8 of عرق) Stripping the flesh from a bone.

A اعتراك *iʿtirāk*, (v. n. 8 of عرك) Pressing one upon another in battle, or camels round a cistern. Stuffing herself with a menstrous cloth (a woman).

A اعترام *iʿtirām*, A being hard, violent, intense.

A اعتزاء *iʿtizāʾ*, (v. n. 8 of عزا for عزو) Claiming relationship. (v. n. 8 of عزي) Mentioning one's own name, relationship, or military watch-word in battle. Claiming relationship. A sign, mark, signal, pass-parole, or military watch-word.

A اعتزاز *iʿtizāz,* (v. n. 8 of عزّ) Priding one's self upon, esteeming one's self ennobled by.

A اعتزال *iʿtizāl,* (v. n. 8 of عزل) Separating one's self from the rest, renouncing, discarding, seceding. Being deposed from office. Abstaining from intercourse with women. Schism, secession, retirement, dissent. اهل اعتزال *ahli iʿtizāl,* A schismatic.

A اعتزام *iʿtizām,* (v. n. 8 of عزم) Pursuing any thing with steadiness, resolution, perseverance. Fixing one's heart upon. Endeavouring, striving. Travelling in the middle of the highway. Going in a canter, going at a moderate pace. Going in a headstrong and skittish manner (a horse). Bearing up patiently under troubles and afflictions. Application, attention, endeavour, fixed purpose, deliberation. Running full speed (a horse).

A اعتسار *iʿtisār,* (v. n. 8 of عسر) Bridling and riding on an unbroken camel. Compelling, forcing, using violence. Taking part of (a son's) property against his will.

A اعتساس *iʿtisās,* (v. n. 8 of عسّ) Acquiring, gaining. Going in amongst (camels) stroking their udders to induce them to give milk. Going the nightly round, patrolling. Keeping watch (a dog).

A اعتساف *iʿtisāf,* (v. n. 8 of عسف) Straying, deviating from the right way. Employing, using the labour of another. Oppression, injury.

A اعتسام *iʿtisām,* (v. n. 8 of عسم) Putting on old purchased boots. A shepherd placing the lambs (as soon as dropped) near their respective dams.

A اعتشاء *iʿtishāʾ,* (v. n. 8 of عشا for عشو) Travelling in the evening. Going near a fire or light in order to see better.

A اعتشاش *iʿtishāsh,* (v. n. 8 of عشّ) Building a nest. Laying in a small quantity of provisions.

A اعتشان *iʿtishān,* (v. n. 8 of عشن) Conjecturing, guessing. Seeking carefully for those dates which are gathered from the roots of the branches after the clusters are cut off. Assaulting or springing upon (any one) unjustly.

A اعتصاء *iʿtiṣāʾ,* (v. n. 8 of عصا for عصو) Leaning on a staff. Cutting a stick, felling a tree for the sake of a stick. Making a sword serve the purpose of a stick. (v. n. 8 of عصي) Being very hard (a date-stone).

A اعتصاب *iʿtiṣāb,* (v. n. 8 of عصب) Tying a rope round a camel's thigh to make her give milk more plentifully. Forming troops of from ten to forty. Being content.

A اعتصار *iʿtiṣār,* (v. n. 8 of عصر) Squeezing, expressing (juice from the grape) in one's own person, or for one's own self. Being pressed. Being avaricious and tenacious. Extorting money (as a debt or otherwise). Easing one's self. Visiting with a view of obtaining a present. Taking refuge. Refusing, preventing. Withholding property from a son (a father). Dissolving with a little water food sticking in the throat. Taking, seizing.

A اعتصاف *iʿtiṣāf,* (v. n. 8 of عصف) Labouring to gain a livelihood. Going with haste.

A اعتصام *iʿtiṣām,* (v. n. 8 of عصم) Preserving one's self from sin. Taking refuge. Keeping one's seat on horseback by laying hold of something fixed to the saddle for that purpose.

A اعتضاد *iʿtiẓād,* (v. n. 8 of عضد) Begging assistance. Taking or putting under the arm.

A اعتطاب *iʿtiṭāb,* (v. n. 8 of عطب) Taking fire in a bit of cloth (عطبة *ʿutbat*).

A اعتطاف *iʿtiṭāf,* (v. n. 8 of عطف) Putting on (the cloak or mantle عاطف *ʿāṭif*).

A اعتظال *iʿtiẓāl,* (v. n. 8 of عظل) Sticking fast when coupling (dogs or locusts).

A اعتفاء *iʿtifāʾ,* (v. n. 8 of عفا for عفو) Going to beg a favour. Cropping herbage close to the ground (camels).

A اعتفاد *iʿtifād,* (v. n. 8 of عفد) Shutting the door upon one's self and dying of hunger, without asking relief (a thing sometimes done in seasons of scarcity). Believing.

A اعتفار *iʿtifār,* (v. n. 8 of عفر) Soiling with dust. Assaulting, springing upon another. Rolling his prey in the dirt (a lion). Throwing on the ground.

A اعتفاس *iʿtifās,* (v. n. 8 of عفس) Grasping in wrestling. Being turbulent (people).

A اعتفاص *iʿtifāṣ,* (v. n. 8 of عفص) Exacting, extorting (a debt).

A اعتفاف *iʿtifāf,* (v. n. 8 of عفّ) Picking up dry herbage clean off the ground (a camel).

A اعتفاق *iʿtifāḳ,* (v. n. 8 of عفق) Springing upon his prey (a lion). Fighting with swords.

A اعتقاء *iʿtiḳāʾ,* (v. n. 8 of عقا for عقو) Being detained. Digging in the sides of a well to gain an increase of water. Bandying words to and fro. (v. n. 8 of عقي) Coming from any place.

A اعتقاب *iʿtiḳāb,* (v. n. 8 of عقب) Imprisoning. Withholding goods from a purchaser until the money be paid. Being brought at length to repentance. Settling, lodging.

A اعتقاد *iʿtiḳād,* (v. n. 8 of عقد) Being very hard, firm, and strong. Gaining, acquiring. Buying an estate. Laying up in store. Believing. Faith, belief, trust. A popular notion. P اعتقاد كردن *iʿtiḳād kardan,* To place confidence, to believe. بي اعتقاد *bī iʿtiḳād,* Faithless, an infidel.

A اعتقار *iʿtiḳār,* (v. n. 8 of عقر) Being wounded and galled in the back by the saddle (a beast of burden), and not driving off a bird that alights on it.

A اعتقاق *iʿtiḳāḳ,* (v. n. 8 of عقّ) Breeding excrescences at the root (a palm-tree or vine). Drawing (a sword). Being divided, split (a cloud).

A اعتقال *iʿtiḳāl,* (v. n. 8 of عقل) Being bound, imprisoned. Being tongue-tied. Tying up a camel's foot. Sitting cross-legged. (A horseman) carrying his spear between his leg and the side of his horse. Doubling the foot back upon the groin, or resting it on the fore part of the saddle, when riding. Twisting the legs between those of a sheep to make her steady whilst milking. Tripping up the heels in wrestling. Receiving a fine for murder.

A اعتقام *iʿtiḳām,* (v. n. 8 of عقم) Digging a well; and having penetrated to a short distance from the spring, boring a hole to try the quality of the water, in order to decide whether the work should be prosecuted or abandoned.

A اعتكاب *iʿtikāb,* (v. n. 8 of عكب) Being raised (dust). Raising (a dust).

A اعتكاد *iʿtikād,* A cleaving, a sticking to.

A اعتكار *iʿtikār,* (v. n. 8 of عكر) Being very thick (darkness). Raining heavily. Raising clouds of dust (wind). Rushing upon, assaulting. Renewing a charge. Being mixed, thrown into disorder and inextricable confusion (combatants). Being fat (camel's bunch). Lasting, being firm (youth).

A اعتكاس *iʿtikās,* (v. n. 8 of عكس) Being turned upside down. Being transposed or inverted.

A اعتكاف *iʿtikāf,* (v. n. 8 of عكف) Waiting, expecting. Restraining, curbing one's passions from religious motives. Seeking retirement and holy solitude. Remaining constantly in the mosque.

A اعتكال *iʿtikāl,* (v. n. 8 of عكل) Being obscure, intricate, perplexing. Butting (two bulls). Seeking retirement.

A اعتكام *iʿtikām,* (v. n. 8 of عكم) Poising on the back of a beast of burden (panniers, trusses, &c.). Being closely packed.

A اعتلاء *iʿtilāʾ,* (v. n. 8 of علا for علو) Raising, elevating. Being advanced (the day). Height.

A اعتلاث *iʿtilās,* (v. n. 8 of علث) Taking wood from the مرخ *markh* tree without knowing whether it will emit fire or not.

A اعتلاج *iʿtilāj,* (v. n. 8 of علج) Wrestling, boxing. Preparing for a fight or wrestling-match. Dashing together (billows). Producing the plant called علجان *ʿalajān.*

A اعتلاص *iʿtilāṣ,* (v. n. 8 of علص) Taking a small quantity.

A اعتلاط *iʿtilāṭ,* (v. n. 8 of علط) Litigating, contending, squabbling, stirring up strife.

A اعتلاف *iʿtilāf,* The eating of provender.

A اعتلاق *iʿtilāḳ,* (v. n. 8 of علق) Being attached, devoted to, loving.

A اعتلال *iʿtilāl,* (v. n. 8 of علّ) Being weak, sickly, ailing. Excusing one's self. Seeking for a pretext to injure any one. Turning (a man from a resolution), diverting (him) from (his) design. Being occupied by or satisfied with. Occurring.

A اعتلام *iʿtilām,* (v. n. 8 of علم) Knowing. Flowing (water).

A اعتلان *iʿtilān,* The being made public.

A اعتماء *iʿtimāʾ,* (v. n. 8 of عمي) Electing, choosing. Preparing for.

A اعتماد *iʻtimād*, (v. n. 8 of عمد) Leaning, depending, relying upon, trusting or committing one's self (to any thing). Resolving, purposing. Riding all night. Being baptized. Faith, confidence, dependence, reliance. A support, prop. اعتماد الدولة *iʻtimādu'd dawlat*, (Stay of the empire) A prime minister. P اعتماد كردن *iʻtimād kardan*, To rely.

A اعتمادًا *iʻtimādan*, Confidently. Expressly.

A اعتمادي *iʻtimādī*, Worthy of confidence.

A اعتمار *iʻtimār*, (v. n. 8 of عمر) Visiting, frequenting. Remaining at Mecca on a pilgrimage. Preparing for. Putting on a turban called عمارة.

A اعتماط *iʻtimāt*, (v. n. 8 of عمط) Disgracing, disparaging, reproaching.

A اعتماق *iʻtimāḳ*, (v. n. 8 of عمق) Making deep.

A اعتمال *iʻtimāl*, (v. n. 8 of عمل) Doing any thing one's self. Being constantly at work. Cultivating, peopling (the earth) Employing, using. Disturbance, perplexity, confusion.

A اعتمام *iʻtimām*, (v. n. 8 of عمّ) Being common. Coming to maturity, attaining the full growth (a youth, plant, &c.). Putting on a turban (عمامة *ʻimāmat*). Frothing (milk). Being high, foaming (waves). The mode of putting on a turban.

A P اعتميد *iʻtimīd*, (a corruption of اعتماد *iʻtimād*) Reliance.

A اعتناء *iʻtinās*, (v. n. 8 of عني) Taking pains, looking after, managing. Coming upon any one (business). Anxiety, care.

A اعتناز *iʻtināz*, (v. n. 8 of عنز) Declining, turning to one side. Travelling far, from place to place.

A اعتناس *iʻtinās*, (v. n. 8 of عنس) Being long and hairy (the tail of a she-camel).

A اعتناش *iʻtināsh*, (v. n. 8 of عنش) Seizing one another by the collar in a scuffle, grappling. Injuring. Seizing by force and under false pretences.

A اعتناف *iʻtināf*, (v. n. 8 of عنف) Grasping, seizing violently. Beginning any thing new. Being ignorant of. Coming unexpectedly. Loathing, disliking (food or a country). Disagreeing with, not suiting. Turning away, retiring. Grazing land hitherto ungrazed. A beginning, commencement.

A اعتناق *iʻtināḳ*, (v. n. 8 of عنق) Embracing or hugging one another (in friendship or in battle). Wearing (a chain) about the neck.

A اعتناك *iʻtināk*, (v. n. 8 of عنك) Walking with difficulty through mounds of sand (a camel).

A اعتنان *iʻtinān*, (v. n. 8 of عنّ) Presenting itself to view. Having one's affairs or history known.

A اعتواء *iʻtiwās*, (v. n. 8 of عوي) Making a wry mouth and shouting. Howling. Bending.

A اعتوار *iʻtiwār*, A borrowing from one another.

A اعتواك *iʻtiwāk*, (v. n. 8 of عاك for عوك) Thronging, crowding, pressing on one another.

A اعتوال *iʻtiwāl*, (v. n. 8 of عول) Weeping.

A اعتوان *iʻtiwān*, The aiding of one another.

A اعتوبة *uʻtūbat*, A mutual cause of quarrel, expostulation, or mutual recrimination.

A اعتهاد *iʻtihād*, (v. n. 8 of عهد) Seeking for something lost or missing. Renewing a treaty or covenant. Looking after, minding, attending to.

A اعتياد *iʻtiyād*, (v. n. 8 of عاد for عود) Coming step by step. Making a habit or custom. Being accustomed to any thing. Repetition. P مشرب داد اعتياد *mashrabi dād-iʻtiyād*, A disposition accustomed to justice. فؤاد مسرّت اعتياد *fuʼādi masarrat-iʻtiyād*, A heart habitually prone to joy.

A اعتياص *iʻtiyāṣ*, (v. n. 8 of عاص for عوص) Being difficult, intricate. Not holding to the male.

A اعتياض *iʻtiyāẓ*, (v. n. 8 of عاض for عوض) Accepting a substitute, receiving an equivalent. Coming and asking for a substitute.

A اعتياط *iʻtiyāt*, (v. n. 8 of عاط for عوط) Being difficult and intricate. (v. n. 8 of عاط for عيط) Not conceiving for several years though not barren.

A اعتياف *iʻtiyāf*, (v. n. 8 of عاف for عيف) Taking provisions for the way.

A اعتياق *iʻtiyāḳ*, (v. n. 8 of عاق for عوق) Hindering, preventing. Holding back.

A اعتيام *iʻtiyām*, (v. n. 8 of عام for عيم) Taking the best part of wealth or of sheep.

A اعتيان *iʻtiyān*, (v. n. 8 of عان for عين) Acting as a spy for any one. Keeping a look out from an eminence, watching. Viewing, surveying. Looking out for a place or for fodder. Taking the best part of any thing. Buying on credit.

A اعثار *iʻsār*, (v. n. 4 of عثر) Causing (one) to stumble or fall. Complaining of one to the king. Bringing down, abasing, destroying. Apprising.

A اعثاق *iʻsāḳ*, (v. n. 4 of عثق) Being fertile (the ground). Being abundant and plenteous (a year).

A اعثام *iʻsām*, (v. n. 4 of عثم) Sewing slightly.

A اعثان *aʻsān*, (pl. of عثن *ʻasan*) Little idols.

A اعثك *aʻsak*, Left-handed.

A اعثى *aʻsa'*, Blackish (colour). Blackish-coloured. Foolish. Very hairy. A male hyena.

A اعثيجاج *iʻsījāj*, (v. n. 12 of عثج) Making haste.

A اعجاء *iʻjās*, (v. n. 4 of عجا for عجو) Giving suck to a child after the proper time.

A اعجاب *iʻjāb*, (v. n. 4 of عجب) Causing surprise. Giving pleasure. (in passive) Being pleased.

A اعجاج *iʻjāj*, (v. n. 4 of عجّ) Blowing violently, making the dust fly. Being windy, stormy.

A اعجاز *aʻjāz*, The roots of palm-trees. (pl. of عجز *ʻajuz*, *ʻajaz*, or *ʻajiz*) The hinder parts, the buttocks. ركب في الطلب اعجاز الابل *rakiba fi't talabi aʻjāza'l ibli*, He endured hardship. He was patient under difficulties or the loss of his right. He strove hard in the attainment of any thing. *Iʻjāz*, (v. n. 4 of عجز) Discovering, detecting weakness and imbecility. Rendering weak. Escaping, slipping through one's fingers, disappointing. A miracle. اعجاز مسيحي *iʻjāzi masīḥī*, A miraculous cure, equalling those wrought by the Messiah.

A اعجازة *iʻjāzat*, Any kind of stuffing, quilting, or pad, which women use, to give a protuberance round the hips (in modern phrase, a bustle).

A اعجاس *aʻjās*, (pl. of عجس) Hinder parts.

A اعجاف *iʻjāf*, (v. n. 4 of عجف) Emaciating, making lean (cattle). Adapting one's self to the humours and wants of the sick by care and patience. Having lean (cattle).

A اعجال *aʻjāl*, (pl. of عجلة *ʻajalat*) Carriages. *Iʻjāl*, (v. n. 4 of عجل) Accelerating, stimulating, urging, instigating. Outstripping, getting before. Being delivered of an untimely fœtus (a camel). Hurrying a debtor, insisting on prompt payment. Keeping back, withholding.

A اعجالة *iʻjālat*, New milk, which the milkers send in presents to their friends.

A اعجام *aʻjām*, (pl. of عجم *ʻajam*) Persians. Foreigners (not Arabians). *Iʻjām*, (v. n. 4 of عجم) Speaking or writing Arabic improperly, incorrectly, barbarously, or like a foreigner. Marking a consonant with diacritical points.

A اعجان *iʻjān*, (v. n. 4 of عجن) Riding a fat she-camel. Being troubled with a swelling in the perinæum (عجان *ʻijān*).

A اعجب *aʻjab*, More or most astonishing, wondrous, strange. اعجب العجب *aʻjabu'l ʻajab*, Most marvellous of marvels. ما اعجبه برأيه *mā aʻjabahu bi raʼyihi*, How pleased with his own opinion!

A اعجر *aʻjar*, Large-bellied. Rough, fierce.

A اعجز *aʻjaz*, More or most impotent. Large about the buttocks. *Aʻjuz*, (pl. of عجز *ʻajuz*) Hips.

A اعجس *aʻjas*, Strong, hard in the centre.

A اعجف *aʻjaf*, (pl. عجاف *ʻijāf*) Thin, lean, meagre. Thin (spear-head).

A اعجل *aʻjal*, The shortest-lived, the one who is nearer or nearest his end.

A اعجم *aʻjam*, One who speaks barbarously (including all who cannot speak Arabic, or who speak it without elegance). A Persian. Dumb. Silent (wave making no noise). Ziyād the poet.

A اعجميّ *aʻjamīy*, A Persian. Persic. Barbaric, foreign. A barbarian.

A اعجنة *aʻjinat*, (pl. of عجان) Fools. Perinæa.

A اعجوبة *uʻjūbat*, (pl. اعاجيب *aʻājīb*) A miracle, a prodigy, a wonderful thing.

A اعدّ *aʻadd*, More or most ready.

A اعداء *aʻdās*, (pl. of عدي *ʻida'* or *ʻuda'*) Sides, quarters. (pl. of عدو *ʻadūw*) Strangers, persons afar off. Enemies. اعدائ دولت *aʻdāsi dawlat*, Enemies of the state. اعدائ دين *aʻdāsi dīn*, Enemies of the faith. *Iʻdās*, (v. n. 4 of عدا for عدو) Contaminating, infecting (either by disease or bad example). Carrying or communicating a contagious disease from one to another. (A judge) assisting or redressing any injury done by one to another. Helping, assisting, strengthening, reinforcing. Putting (a horse) to full speed. Causing to run.

Exceeding bounds (in speech), speaking improperly or wickedly. Being iniquitous, unjust. Passing over one thing to another.

A اعداد *aɛdād,* (pl. of عدّ *ɛidd*) Perennial fountains. Multitudes. (pl. of عدد *ɛadad*) Numbers. *Iɛdād,* (v. n. 4 of عدّ) Preparing, putting in order, making ready. Storing, laying up. P اعداد ثمن كردن *iɛdādi saman kardan,* To count out money.

A اعداق *iɛdāk,* (v. n. 4 of عدق) Thrusting the hand into any place full of water, and moving it from side to side in search of any thing.

A اعدال *aɛdāl,* (pl. of عدل *ɛadl*) Pairs, equals. (pl. of عدل *ɛidl*) Things equal to others in weight or quantity (as loads divided equally on each side of a horse or camel). It has a reference also to animate beings: as, just, equitable, honest (men).

A اعدام *iɛdām,* (v. n. 4 of عدم) Annihilating, destroying. Being wanting and not to be had. Escaping from. Depriving. Preventing. Wanting, lacking, or being deprived of; becoming poor.

A اعدل *aɛdal,* More or most just, equal, temperate. اعدل العادلين *aɛdalu'l ɛādilīn,* Most just of the just. اعدل اصحاب *aɛdali as-hāb,* Most just of the companions. اعدل سلاطين *aɛdali salātīn,* Most equitable of kings.

A اعدي *aɛda',* More or most dangerous, inimical. More or most swift of foot, a better runner.

A اعذاب *iɛzāb,* (v. n. 4 of عذب) Tormenting. Being sweet (water). Abandoning, leaving. Hindering, prohibiting, preventing. Clearing (water) from weeds, leaves, or other things which tend to spoil it. Having pure and sweet water.

A اعذار *aɛzār,* (pl. of عذر *ɛuzr*) Excuses. *Iɛzār,* (v. n. 4 of عذر) Excusing. Making apologies, inventing excuses. Deserving to be excused. Circumcising. Providing a feast on any novel occasion (as finishing a house, or circumcising a child). Being very sinful, criminal, vicious. Doing less than one ought, although appearing to exert one's self greatly. Exerting one's self to the utmost. Leaving a scar. Marking with stripes (the back). Bridling (a horse), putting on that part of the bridle called عذار *ɛizār.* Reaching maturity (a girl). Being full of rubbish and filth (a court-yard). Having one's life endangered. See انصاف *insāf.*

A اعذاق *aɛzāk,* (pl. of عذق *ɛizk*) Bunches of grapes or dates. *Iɛzāk,* (v. n. 4 of عذق) Distinguishing by a peculiar mark (a camel or a sheep). Flowering (the sweet rush).

A اعذب *aɛzab,* Sweeter, sweetest. الاعذبان *al aɛzabāni,* (The two sweets) Ceres and Venus, or saliva (of the mouth of a mistress) and wine.

A اعذبة *aɛzibat,* (pl. of عذاب *ɛazāb*) Torments.

A اعذق *aɛzuk,* (pl. of عذق *ɛazk*) Palm-trees with their fruit.

A اعرّ *aɛarr,* Scabby (camel). Itchy (man). Bunchless (camel). (An ass) fat about the neck.

A اعراء *aɛrāɛ,* (pl. of عرو *ɛirw* or عراء *ɛarāɛ*) Spacious open places, tracts of country. Idle, negligent. (pl. of عري *ɛury*) Horses without saddles. *Iɛrāɛ,* (v. n. 4 of عرا for عرو) Abandoning, retiring from, deserting (a friend). Giving away the produce of a grazing-field or of a palm-tree. Making a handle (عروة *ɛurwat*) to a jug or gugglet. (v. n. 4 of عري) Stripping, denuding, divesting. Walking or stopping in a clear open place. Giving away one year's produce of a palm-tree.

A اعراب *aɛrāb,* (pl. اعاريب *aɛārīb*) Wild, wandering Arabs (the more civilized Arabians who live in cities being called عرب *ɛarab*). *Iɛrāb,* (v. n. 4 of عرب) Reading or pronouncing accurately the Arabic language. Conforming a foreign word to the Arabic idiom. Speaking, reasoning in Arabic, plainly, without reserve. Speaking plainly, distinctly, clearly, accurately. Using shameful, indecent, and obscene language. Inflecting, declining an Arabic noun or verb. Marrying a woman called عروب *ɛarūb.* Restraining one from speaking indecently. Begetting a son of a dusky or Arabian complexion. Distinguishing, knowing accurately (a fine Arabian horse from any other by his neighing). Putting (a horse) to the gallop, putting him on his mettle. Giving earnest-money. Marrying, or hinting at it. Fetching water, sometimes every day, at other times every other day, and afterwards regularly at stated times. Explanation, exposition.

A اعرابيّ *aɛrābiy,* Relating to the wild Arabs. An Arab, an Arabian.

A اعراج *aɛrāj,* (pl. of عرج *ɛarj* or *ɛirj*) Troops of camels. *Iɛrāj,* (v. n. 4 of عرج) Making lame, crippling. Becoming possessed of lame camels. Giving a troop of camels called عرج *ɛarj.* Reaching the hour of sunset.

A اعرار *iɛrār,* (v. n. 4 of عرّ) Being dirtied with excrement (a house). Diminishing the size of a camel's bunch. Making (a camel) scabby.

A اعراز *iɛrāz,* (v. n. 4 of عرز) Corrupting, vitiating, spoiling.

A اعراس *aɛrās,* (pl. of عرس *ɛars* or *ɛurs*) Young camels weaned from the mother. (pl. of عرس *ɛirs*) Spouses (husband and wife). Lionesses. (pl. of عرس *ɛurs*) Nuptials. (pl. of عرس *ɛurs* and *ɛurus*) Marriage-feasts. *Iɛrās,* (v. n. 4 of عرس) Preparing for a marriage ceremony. Bringing a wife home to one's house and retiring with her. Conjugal intercourse. Alighting (as travellers at the end of the night) in order to take refreshment or rest, and then to pursue their journey. Sticking close to, persevering. Being necessary.

A اعراش *aɛrāsh,* (pl. of عرش *ɛarsh*) Thrones, chairs of state. Roofs, domes, arched ceilings. Upper or convex parts of the feet. Tents. Awnings, coverings from rain or sun. Props or buttresses. Glories. *Iɛrāsh,* (v. n. 4 of عرش) Erecting buildings of wood, as covers to wells, or props to vines.

A اعراص *aɛrās,* (pl. of عرصة *ɛarsat*) Courts, squares, areas, open places free from buildings. *Iɛrās,* (v. n. 4 of عرص) Going totteringly (a camel).

A اعراض *aɛrāz,* (pl. of عرض *ɛarz*) The villages of Hijāz. Large armies. The extremities of branches of trees. (pl. of عرض *ɛirz*) Honours, reputations. Valleys planted with trees. Souls. Bodies. Pores of the skin. Edges, borders. Upper parts. (pl. of عرض *ɛaraz*) Accidents. اعراض جسمانيّه *aɛrāzi jismānīya,* Corporeal faculties. اعراض ذاتيّه *aɛrāzi zātiya,* Essential properties. اعراض روحانيّه *aɛrāzi rūhānīya,* Spiritual endowments. اعراض المدينة *aɛrāzu'l madīnat,* Villages lying between Hijāz and Yaman. Tamarisk and اراك *arāk* trees. *Iɛrāz,* (v. n. 4 of عرض) Turning away the face, declining, shunning, avoiding, flying from, opposing. Appearing, being manifest. Making broad. Turning the broad side of any thing towards you. Happening, being possible, being in one's power. Standing erect and presenting a good mark (a deer). Travelling far and wide. Bearing a child of a broad squat form. Bringing forth a son illegitimately (a woman). Castrating.

A اعراف *aɛrāf,* The boundary which the Muhammadans have placed between their Paradise and Hell: by some it is supposed to resemble a veil; by others a thick and strong wall, guarded by angels and holy men. It is in general considered as their Purgatory, which, according to Sadī, appears a hell to the blessed, and a heaven to the damned. The uppermost currents of wind. A sort of palm-tree. (pl. of عرف *ɛurf*) Crests, manes, combs of birds. (pl. of عرفة *ɛurfat*) Sand-banks. *Iɛrāf,* (v. n. 4 of عرف) Having a long mane.

A اعراق *aɛrāk,* (pl. of عرق *ɛirk*) Roots. Veins, arteries. *Iɛrāk,* (v. n. 4 of عرق) Diluting wine with a little water. Putting water into a bucket, but not to the full. Shooting its roots in all directions (a tree). Going into Irāk. Being of a noble race. Being rooted in noble or in vicious qualities.

A اعراك *iɛrāk,* A being menstruous.

A اعران *iɛrān,* (v. n. 4 of عرن) Eating meat continually. Having the legs of young camels cracked from a disease having crept into the herd. Having the itch amongst one's camels.

A اعرب *aɛrub,* Fine Arabian horses.

A اعرج *aɛraj,* (pl. عرج *ɛurj* and عرجان *ɛurjān*) Lame by nature, cripple from the birth. A crow. تيمور اعرج *tīmūr aɛraj* Lame Tīmūr (Tamerlane).

A اعرف *aɛraf,* (pl. عرف *ɛurf*) Crested (serpent), thick-maned (horse). More or most knowing or intelligent. More or most known, better or best known.

A اعرقة *aɛrikat* (pl. of عراق *ɛirāk,* q. v.)

A اعرم *aɛram,* (pl. عرمان *ɛurmān*) Spotted black and white, piebald, dappled. Mixed (flock of sheep and goats). White-lipped (ram). Uncircumcised. A well, a ditch. An egg of the Kata bird.

A اعرنجاج *iɛrinjāj*, A striving, a taking pains.

A اعرنجام *iɛrinjām*, A becoming corrupt.

A اعرنزام *iɛrinzām*, (v. n. 3 of عرزم Q) Being collected, drawn together, contracted or wrinkled.

A اعرنفاز *iɛrinfāz*, (v. n. 3 of عرفز Q not used) Being almost dead with cold.

A اعرنفاط *iɛrinfāt*, (v. n. 3 of عرفط Q) Drawing one's self, being contracted.

A اعرنكاس *iɛrinkās*, (v. n. 3 of عركس Q) Being collected and sitting of a heap, closely packed. Being very black (the hair).

A اعروّاش *iɛriwwāsh*, (v. n. 13 of عرش Q) Riding on horseback.

A اعروّاف *iɛriwwāf*, (v. n. 13 of عرف) Preparing for mischief. Rolling high (billows). Being thick and branchy like a hyena's mane (a palm-tree). Being frothy (blood). Having a high mane (a horse). Being mounted on اعراف *aɛrāf* (a man).

A اعري *aɛra'*, More or most naked. اعري من المغزل *aɛra' mini'l mighzāl*, More bare than a distaff.

A اعرية *aɛriyat*, (pl. of عراء *ɛarā'*) Open spaces, extensive areas clear of every thing.

A اعريراء *iɛrīrā'*, (v. n. 12 of عري) Travelling alone. Perpetrating a vile and shameful thing. Riding (a horse) without a saddle.

A اعريراف *iɛrīrāf*, (v. n. 11 of عرف) Having a mane (a horse). Being bushy like a mane (a palm). Being frothy (blood). Climbing a palm. Being ready for mischief. Being tempestuous (sea).

A اعزّ *aɛazz*, More or most glorious, more or most esteemed. More or most precious. Dearer, dearest. More or most inaccessible. Glorious, excellent. Rare. Long, tall. Firm.

A اعزّاء *aɛizzā'*, (pl. of عزيز *ɛazīz*) Excellent, rare, incomparable, glorious. Powerful, magnificent. Dear, precious.

A اعزاب *aɛzāb*, (pl. of عزب *ɛazab*) Bachelors. Maids. *Iɛzāb*, (v. n. 4 of عزب) Being afar off. Arriving at a distant place. Finding distant pasture. Placing or driving to a distance.

A اعزاز *iɛzāz*, (v. n. 4 of عزّ) Strengthening, invigorating. Holding dear, loving. Honouring. Having the orifice of the teat very small (a cow or a sheep). Having a painful conception and gestation (a cow). Lighting upon hard ground. Appearing pregnant (a ewe). Being grieved and uneasy. Brooking ill. Magnificence, honour, respect. باعزاز و احترام *ba iɛzāz u ihtirām*, With honour and reverence, respectfully. P اعزاز كردن *iɛzāz kardan*, To honour, respect, revere.

A اعزاف *iɛzāf*, (v. n. 4 of عزف) Hearing the sound of the sands moving in the desert. Hearing the noise of palm-leaves when a rope is being twisted.

A اعزال *aɛzāl*, (pl. of اعزل *aɛzal* and عزل *ɛuzul*) Unarmed (men).

A اعزان *iɛzān*, (v. n. 4 of عزن) Dividing with another, and taking one's share.

A اعزب *aɛzab*, An unmarried man, a bachelor.

A اعزّة *aɛizzat*, (pl. of عزيز *ɛazīz*) Excellent, rare, incomparable, dear, precious, glorious, powerful.

A اعزل *aɛzal*, (pl. عزل *ɛuzl*, عزّل *ɛuzzal*, اعزال *aɛzāl*, عزلان *ɛuzlān*, and معازل *maɛāzil*) A man unarmed. A cloud without rain. Detached, separate (sand-hill). Deficient in the projecting hip-bone. (A horse) whose tail habitually inclines to one side. The portion of meat of an absent person. A separate portion or share of meat. السماك الاعزل *as simāku'l aɛzal*, Spica virginis, a star so called in the constellation Virgo.

A اعساب *iɛsāb*, (v. n. 4 of عسب) Running, fleeing away (a wolf).

A اعسار *iɛsār*, (v. n. 4 of عسر) Exacting a debt, pressing a debtor. Suffering pain in child-bearing. Not conceiving the first year. Being poor.

A اعساف *iɛsāf*, (v. n. 4 of عسف) Seizing a camel (the agonies of death). Being the owner of such a camel. Employing (a servant) in laborious work. Travelling in the night, being unable to see one's way. Drinking always from a large goblet.

A اعسال *aɛsāl*, Dispositions, manners, tempers. (pl. of عسل *ɛasal*) Honies. Bubbles.

A اعسام *aɛsām*, Shape, or points (of a horse). *Iɛsām*, (v. n. 4 of عسم) Rendering the limbs stiff and motionless. Giving that which was desired. Shedding tears. Winking (the eyes).

A اعسان *aɛsān*, Vestiges, impressions. Shoulder-blades of camels. (pl. of عسن *ɛasn*, *ɛisn*, or *ɛusn*) Fats, lards. Likes, equals. اعسان الارض *aɛsānu'l arz*, Old chumps, roots, or stocks of trees. Old pollards. *Iɛsān*, (v. n. 4 of عسن) Producing some little vegetation (ground).

A اعسيجاج *iɛsījāj*, (v. n. 9 of عسج) Bending with age (a man).

A اعسر *aɛsar*, Left-handed. More or most difficult. White on the left wing (a pigeon). Difficult. Disastrous, unfortunate, evil. ع اعسر يسر *aɛsaru yasarun*, Ambidexter.

A اعسم *aɛsam*, One whose hand or foot is withered or distorted.

A اعسي *aɛsa'*, More or most fit, worthy, proper. اعس به *aɛsi bihi*, How suitable and worthy he is!

A اعشاء *iɛshā'*, (v. n. 4 of عشا for عشو) Making purblind. Giving a supper. Giving.

A اعشاب *iɛshāb*, (v. n. 4 of عشب) Producing green herbage, being grassy. Discovering (when travelling through deserts) ground producing grass, and gathering much Feeding on fresh grass.

A اعشار *aɛshār*, (pl. of عشر *ɛushr*) Tenths. Decades of verses into which the Kur'ān is divided. Portions of slaughtered camels. The outside feathers in a bird's wing. (pl. اعاشير *aɛāshīr*, (A pot) broken in ten pieces. A cauldron which requires ten men to carry it. A broken (heart). اعشار شرعية *aɛshāri sharɛiya*, The ten commandments. *Iɛshār*, (v. n. 4 of عشر) Being in the tenth month of her pregnancy (a camel). Being ten in number (men). Driving camels, or being owner of camels which are driven, to water once only in ten days.

A اعشاش *aɛshāsh*, (pl. of عشّ *ɛushsh*) Birds' nests built in trees. تلمّس اعشاشك *talammas aɛsāshaka*, Look at home for faults. *Iɛshāsh*, (v. n. 4 of عشّ) Disturbing, moving (deer) from its place. Prohibiting, checking, turning any one aside. Extenuating, making lean. Molesting any one so as to oblige him to quit his habitation. Lighting upon dry ground (called عشّة *ɛashshat*).

A اعشاف *iɛshāf*, (v. n. 4 of عشف) Suffering, being ill from indigestion. Abominating, loathing.

A اعشاويّ *aɛshāwīy*, Relating to a purblind man.

A اعشر *aɛshar*, A fool.

A اعشراء *aɛshirā'*, (pl. of عشير *ɛashīr*) Tenths. Companions, friends, husband and wife. Tribes.

A اعشم *aɛsham*, Bicoloured. Purblind with age. Dust-dried (tree).

A اعشويّ *aɛshawīy*, Belonging to one purblind.

A اعشيٰ *aɛsha'*, Purblind. Blind at night.

A اعشية *aɛshiyat*, (pl. of عشاء *ɛashā'* or عشيٰ *ɛisha'*) Suppers.

A اعشيشاب *iɛshīshāb*, (v. n. 12 of عشب) Producing green herbage luxuriantly. Finding a place producing such herbage.

A اعصاء *aɛsā'*, (pl. of عصا *ɛasa'*) Canes, batons, rods, walking-sticks. *Iɛsā'*, (v. n. 4 of عصا for عصو) Putting forth branches, but having no fruit (a vine).

A اعصاب *aɛsāb*, (pl. of عصب *ɛasab*) Nerves, tendons, sinews. *Iɛsāb*, (v. n. 4 of عصب) Travelling fast (camels).

A اعصاد *iɛsād*, (v. n. 4 of عصد) Bending, twisting (the neck). Lending or hiring out a stallion.

A اعصار *aɛsār*, (pl. of عصر *ɛasr*) Ages, times. سلاطين اعصار *salātīni aɛsār*, The monarchs of the times. *Iɛsār*, (v. n. 4 of عصر) Becoming marriageable, being fit for pressure (a girl). Entering upon the afternoon. Staying at home on account of the menses. Bringing forth. (pl. اعاصير *aɛāsīr*) Hurricanes, gusts of wind which whirl up the dust in the form of columns, and drive to and fro, clouds fraught with thunder and lightning.

A اعصاف *iɛsāf*, (v. n. 4 of عصف) Blowing violently (wind). Being in blade (corn). Passing swiftly by (a horse). Carrying off, destroying (war). Perishing. Running round the wells, when thirsty, and driving the dust about (camels).

A اعصال *aɛsāl*, (pl. of عصل *ɛasal*) The small guts, intestines. *Iɛsāl*, (v. n. 4 of عصل) Taking up one's walking-staff.

A اعصام *aɛsām*, (pl. of عصم *ɛusm*) Whitenesses on the arms of deer. (pl. of عصمة *ɛusmat*) Dogs' collars. (pl. of عصمة *ɛasamat*) Defences, guards: collars. *Iʿṣām*, (v. n. 4 of عصم) Being attached, sticking close (to a friend). Holding fast. Taking hold of the skirt. Keeping one's self steady (on horseback) by laying hold of the mane. Sitting badly on horseback. Fastening a belt called عصام *ʿiṣām* round the mouth of a leather bottle, by which it is closed, and carried, or hung up. Fixing a loop or thing similar to a saddle for the rider to lay hold of, and thus save himself when in danger of falling.

A اعصان *iʿṣān*, (v. n. 4 of عصن not used) Being intricate and crooked (business).

A اعصبة *aʿṣibat*, (pl. of عصيب *ʿaṣīb*) Hearts, lights, and livers, dressed with other intestines.

A اعصج *aʿṣaj*, Bald on the forehead. Polished (spear-head).

A اعصر *aʿṣur*, (pl. of عصر *ʿaṣr*) Ages.

A اعصل *aʿṣal*, Much distorted (tooth). Bow or bandy-legged. One who sticks close to a thing. Inclined, bent. (pl. عصال *ʿiṣāl*) Crooked and hard.

A اعصم *aʿṣam*, (A crow) with white feathers in the wings; also (a crow) having a red beak and feet. (A stag) having white on either or both the fore-feet, the rest of the body black or red. *Aʿṣum*, (pl. of عصم *ʿiṣam*) Defences, guards. Collars.

A اعصمة *aʿṣimat*, pl. of عصام *ʿiṣām* The smaller extremities of the tails of animals. Chains or belts with which leathern bottles are fastened and carried.

A اعصي *aʿṣi*, (pl. of عصا *ʿaṣa'*) Staffs.

A اعصيصاب *iʿṣīṣāb*, (v. n. 12 of عصب) Being assembled in companies (men). Being heavy (misfortune), oppressively hot or disastrous (day). Travelling briskly (camels).

A اعصيلال *iʿṣīlāl*, (v. n. 11 of عصل) Taking a staff in hand.

A اعضاء *aʿẓāʾ*, (pl. of عضو *ʿizw* or *ʿuzw*) Members, limbs. اعضاء التناسل *aʿẓāʾu't tanāsul*, Organs of generation. اعضائ رئيسه *aʿẓāʾi raʾīsa*, The principal members, as heart, lungs, &c.

A اعضاب *iʿẓāb*, (v. n. 4 of عضب) Breaking a horn (a sheep). Slitting (a camel's) ear.

A اعضاد *aʿẓād*, (pl. of عضد *ʿazd*) Companions, assistants. The pent-houses over, or parapets round, or the side-posts, of wells, or by the road-side. *Iʿẓād*, (v. n. 4 of عضد) Flying right and left (an arrow).

A اعضاض *aʿẓāẓ*, (pl. of عض) Prickly shrubs. *Iʿẓāẓ*, (v. n. 4 of عض) Causing one to take (a morsel) in his teeth, or to bite. Giving one a blow (with a sword). Being narrow and deep (a well). Having camels feeding upon the prickly shrub عض *ʿuzz* or the food *ʿuzz*. Abounding with these shrubs.

A اعضال *iʿẓāl* (v. n. 4 of عضل) Being troublesome and difficult (business). Being dissatisfied and discontented. Wearying, harrassing. Puzzling, perplexing, baffling. Having a painful birth (a woman). Laying with difficulty (a hen).

A اعضاه *iʿẓāh*, (v. n. 4 of عضه) Accusing falsely, inventing lies against. Having camels feeding upon the thorns عضاه *ʿizāh*. Abounding in such trees.

A اعضب *aʿẓab*, (A ram) which has one horn broken. (A horse) which has more than a fourth part of his ear cut off. Bereaved of a brother. Defenceless, friendless. Short-handed. (In the metre وافر *wāfir*), مفاعلتن *mufāʿalatun* shortened into مفتعلن *muftaʿilun*.

A اعضد *aʿẓad*, Slender-armed: short in one arm.

A اعضمة *aʿẓimat*, (pl. of عضم *ʿazm*) Wooden harrows with which corn is winnowed.

A اعضيلال *iʿẓīlāl*, (v. n. 11 of عضل) Having many branches intertwined (a tree).

A اعط *aʿaṭṭ*, Long, tall (man).

A اعطاء *iʿṭāʾ*, (v. n. 4 of عطا for عطو) Giving, offering, bestowing, presenting. Receiving of one another. Being tractable and obedient (a camel). ما اعطاه للمال *ma aʿṭāhu li'l māl*, How liberal he is of his money! how disposed to give!

A اعطاب *iʿṭāb*, (v. n. 4 of عطب) Ruining, destroying. Being excessively enraged.

A اعطاش *iʿṭāsh*, (v. n. 4 of عطش) Keeping camels long from drinking. Having cattle dying of thirst. Finding (beasts) thirsty. Making thirsty.

A اعطاف *aʿṭāf*, (pl. of عطف *ʿaṭf*) Favours.

A اعطال *aʿṭāl*, (pl. of عطل *ʿaṭal*) Statues, figures, bodies. (pl. of عطل *ʿuṭul*) (Camels or horses) destitute of all distinguishing mark, halter, neck-harness. Unarmed (men). Unornamented, without necklaces or bracelets (women). Stringless (bows). *Iʿṭāl*, (v. n. 4 of عطل) Making empty and void, bare of ornament. Leaving, neglecting.

A اعطان *aʿṭān*, (pl. of عطن *ʿaṭan*) Places near wells where (camels) recline after drinking. *Iʿṭān*, (v. n. 4 of عطن) Having camels so reclining. Making (camels) lie down after drinking. Driving them from the well to such places before they have drank, in order to render them tractable, in expectation of being allowed to drink. Detaining (camels) at a cistern.

A اعطر *aʿṭar*, More or most scented, fragrant.

A اعطى *aʿṭa'*, More or most disposed to give.

A اعطية *aʿṭiyat*, (pl. of عطا *ʿaṭa'*) Gifts.

A اعظار *iʿẓār*, (v. n. 4 of عظر) Oppressing, indisposing the stomach. Being oppressed (stomach).

A اعظاظ *iʿẓāẓ*, (v. n. 4 of عظ) Making a man warlike (God).

A اعظام *iʿẓām*, (v. n. 4 of عظم) Magnifying, honouring, praising. Conceiving highly of. Giving (a dog) a bone (عظم *ʿazm*). Respect, reverence.

A اعظامة *iʿẓāmat*, Cushions, or any kind of stuffing which women use, to give them an apparent protuberance round the hips.

A اعظم *aʿẓam*, Greater, larger, bigger, greatest. Superior, supreme. Great. وزير اعظم *wazīri aʿẓam*, The grand vazīr. اعظم سلاطين عظام واكرم خواقين كرام *aʿẓami salāṭīni ʿiẓām u akrami khawākīni kirām*, The greatest of sovereign princes, and the most glorious of the mighty kings. *Aʿẓum*, (pl. of عظم *ʿazm*) Bones.

A P اعظمتر *aʿẓamtar*, Greater, bigger.

A اعفاء *iʿfāʾ*, (v. n. 4 of عفا for عفو) Permitting to grow long. Granting freedom, liberty, immunity. Preserving or restoring health. Preserving from trouble and affliction. Expending the best part of one's substance.

A اعفاء *aʿiffāʾ*, (pl. of عفيف *ʿafīf*) Chaste, temperate, abstaining from what is forbidden.

A اعفاج *aʿfāj*, (pl. of عفج *ʿifj*, *ʿafaj*, or *ʿafij*) The intestines into which the food descends from the stomach after digestion (in man and solid-hoofed animals; in the soft-footed beasts, and those which divide the hoof, they are called مصارين *maṣārīn*.

A اعفار *aʿfār*, (pl. of عفر *ʿufr*) Strong, robust, and valiant. (pl. of عفر *ʿafar* or *ʿafr*) Earth, dusts.

A اعفاص *iʿfāṣ*, (v. n. 4 of عفص) Stopping the mouth of a bottle.

A اعفاف *iʿfāf*, (v. n. 4 of عف) Making one to abstain (from things forbidden). Having milk remaining in the udder (a sheep).

A اعفاق *iʿfāk*, (v. n. 4 of عفق) Going to and fro unnecessarily. Returning frequently.

A اعفان *iʿfān*, (v. n. 4 of عفن) Having (leather) worm-eaten.

A اعفت *aʿfat*, Foolish, stupid, dull. Left-handed. One who cannot speak but with difficulty.

A اعفث *aʿfas*, One whose privities are exposed when he sits down. A silly talker.

A اعفج *aʿfaj*, One who has large intestines.

A اعفر *aʿfar*, (A deer) whose white is slightly tinged with red; or red-backed, and sides whitish.

A اعفش *aʿfash*, Weak or dim-sighted. One whose eyes continually water.

A اعفك *aʿfak*, Foolish, stupid. Left-handed. Unskilful at work. Incoherent, rambling from his subject. One who, leaving a work unfinished, sets about something else.

A اعفنجاج *iʿfinjāj*, A making haste.

A اعقاء *aʿkāʾ*, (pl. of عقى *ʿiky*) The first excrements of an infant. *Iʿkāʾ*, (v. n. 4 of عقي) Being very bitter. Spitting out any thing on account of its bitterness.

A اعقاب *aʿkāb*, (pl. of عقب *ʿakib*) Heels. Offsprings, children, grand-children, descendants. The last days of a month. على اعقابهم *ʿala' aʿkābihim*, On their heels, back to their former state. *Iʿkāb*, (v. n. 4 of عقب) Causing an immediate indisposition (any kind of meat of a pernicious quality). Succeeding (as a son to his father). Dying and leaving a son to succeed. Rising (as one star immediately after another). Substituting one for another. Riding alternately with another; ride and tie. Returning (as insanity, after intervals). Receiving one's due, or something in lieu of another. Returning a kettle which had been lent, with parts of the broth, by way of interest. Requiting. Recompensing services and obedience. Sending bad news. Making a channel whereby water may flow into a cistern.

A اعقاد aʻḳād, (pl. of عقد ʻakd) Arches. Iʻḳād, (v. n. 4 of عقد) Making thick, making any thing to coagulate or congeal by boiling.

A اعقار aʻḳār, (pl. of عقر ʻukr or ʻukur) Places behind lakes, wells, or watering ponds, where camels stand when they drink. Areas, plats of ground. Middles of houses. A kind of tree. Iʻḳār, (v. n. 4 of عقر) Astonishing, confounding, striking with amazement. Possessing many fields or estates. Making (the womb) diseased or barren (God). Causing (any one) to eat عقرة ʻukrat.

A اعقاق iʻḳāḳ, (v. n. 4 of عقّ) Making (water) bitter. Rotting (as a palm for want of pruning). Producing the shoots عقّان ʻikkān (a palm-tree). Practising disobedience. Being pregnant (a mare).

A اعقال iʻḳāl, (v. n. 4 of عقل) Discovering one to be wise. Having the shadow shortened or perpendicular at mid-day. Being obligatory (the tithe عقال ʻikāl). Going in the shade at mid-day.

A اعقام iʻḳām, (v.n.4 of عقم) Rendering barren.

A اعقب aʻḳub, (pl. of عقاب ʻuḳāb) Eagles.

A اعقّة aʻikkat, (pl. of عقيق) Channels of rivers.

A اعقد aʻḳad, One who has an impediment in the speech, tongue-tied. A dog of a particular species, with a knotty tail. Knotty-horned (ram). A wolf with a twisted tail. لئيم اعقد laʼīm aʻḳad, A confirmed miser.

A اعقر aʻḳar, More or most skilful at hamstringing. (A camel) whose teeth have dropped out.

A اعقص aʻḳas, (A goat) whose horns bend back towards the ear. (A man) whose fingers or front-teeth are distorted, and which cross each other. (In the measure وافر wāfir, or Exuberant) The مفاعلتن mufāʻalatun changed to مفعولن mafʻūlun.

A اعقف aʻḳaf, Poor, needy. Rude, cruel, savage (wild Arab). Crooked, curved.

A اعقل aʻḳal, More or most wise, prudent, or intelligent. Bow-legged, distorted-legged.

A اعقنفار iʻḳinfār, (v. n. 3 of عقفر Q) Overwhelming and destroying (misfortunes).

A اعقنفاس iʻḳinfās, The being bad-tempered.

A اعكاء iʻkāʼ, (v.n.4 of عكي) Dying. Tying fast.

A اعكاب iʻkāb, (v.n.4 of عكب) Smoking much.

A اعكاد iʻkād, (v. n. 4 of عكد) Taking refuge.

A اعكار iʻkār, (v. n. 4 of عكر) Making any thing dirty, muddy, turbid. Having a large troop of camels. Being thick, dark, cloudy (night). Being fat (camel's bunch).

A اعكاك iʻkāk, (v. n. 4 of عكّ) Changing the colour of the hair (as a camel does after conception).

A اعكال aʻkāl, (pl. of عكل ʻikl or ʻukl) Inglorious, mean, vile, abject, cowardly, avaricious, sordid. Iʻkāl, (v.n.4 of عكل) Being confused, doubtful, perplexed. Tying up (the leg of a camel).

A اعكام aʻkām, (pl. of عكم ʻikm) The halves of loads, single trusses or packages, such as beasts of burthen carry upon each side. Ropes, or things similar, for tying up bales. Iʻkām, (v. n. 4 of عكم) Assisting in tying up bales.

A اعكان aʻkān, (pl. of عكنة ʻuknat) Wrinkles on the belly (from fatness).

A اعكب aʻkab, Thick-lipped, and thick-toothed. Aʻkub, (pl. of عنكبوت ʻankabūt) Spiders.

A اعكي aʻkaʼ, Thick on both sides. Bunchy (part of a garment which in Arabia is wrapped round the middle). (A horse) that has the root of his tail strong and thick.

A اعلا aʻlā, (for اعلي aʻlaʼ) Higher, most high, sublime, excellent, superior, supreme. Excellently.

A اعلاء iʻlāʼ, (v. n. 4 of علا for علو) Exalting, elevating. Ascending. Being in the upper part or above (any thing). Arriving in that part of Arabia which is called عالية ʻāliyat. Retiring, receding. Dismounting, coming down from off (horseback). P اعلا كردن iʻlā kardan, To elevate.

A اعلاء aʻillāʼ, (pl. of عليل ʻalīl) Invalids.

A اعلاث aʻlās, Mixed, unsorted, jumbled together (applied in general to a kind of tree called مرخ markh in Arabia, some parts of which, when rubbed together, emit sparks of flame, and are made use of to kindle fires: these are carefully sorted from the others which have not that quality, and laid up for future service; when piled therefore in indiscriminate heaps, they are called اعلاث aʻlās). اعلاث الزاد aʻlāsu'z zād, Whatever is eaten without previous trial or habit. اعلاث الشجر aʻlāsu'sh shajar, Mixed bits of dry wood and grass.

A اعلاج aʻlāj, (pl. of علج ʻilj) Foreigners who become proselytes to the Arabians, especially in religious matters. Asses, wild or tame (especially when inclining to corpulency). Cakes of a particular kind, thick towards the edges. Stewards.

A اعلاز iʻlāz, (v. n. 4 of علز) Weakening.

A اعلاط aʻlāt, (pl. of علط ʻulut) (Camels) without bridles or marks burnt on the neck. Bright, sparkling stars not distinguished by any name.

A اعلاف aʻlāf, (pl. of علف ʻalaf) Grasses, and every species of fodder with which cattle are fed. Iʻlāf, (v. n. 4 of علف) Beginning to appear (the fruit of a thorn when the flowers drop off). Giving (cattle) provender, fattening (them).

A اعلاق aʻlāk, (pl. of علق ʻilk) More or most excellent (wines or clothes). Iʻlāk, (v. n. 4 of علق) Setting (a leech) to suck blood from any part. Fastening (one rope to another). Fixing the claws, nails, talons, into any thing. Catching and suspending (game or prey) in a noose. Fastening any thing to the horns of a bow by which it may be hung up or slung. Lifting a child up from the privy. Finding or lighting upon very valuable property. Bringing misfortune. Joining two camels to the rope of a large bucket.

A اعلال iʻlāl, (v. n. 4 of علّ) Making (camels) drink a second time, after the first draught. Driving (them) from the water before (they) have quenched their thirst. Debilitating, afflicting with any ailment or distemper (علّة ʻillat).

A اعلام aʻlām, (pl. of علم ʻalam) Flags, standards, ensigns, colours, banderols, streamers, pennants. Land-marks. Mile-stones or direction-posts upon a road. Mountains. Borders of cloth of different colours from the rest. Lords, princes. Proper names. اعلام المدارس aʻlāmu'l madāris, Professors of colleges, learned men. P علام نصرت ظفر فرجام aʻlāmi nusrati zafar-farjām, Victorious standards. A Iʻlām, (v. n. 4 of علم) Announcing, proclaiming, indicating, informing, teaching. Certifying. Marking cloth (as weavers, fullers, or bleachers). Distinguishing or making remarkable in battle (as a horseman does his charger, by ornamenting him with trappings of different colours). Distinguishing one's self (by bravery). Information, signification, advice. P اعلام دادن iʻlām dādan, To give information.

P اعلام نامه iʻlām-nāma, A proclamation.

A اعلان iʻlān, (v. n. 4 of علن) Publishing, divulging, manifesting. Acting openly.

A اعلاه aʻlāhu, The top or upper part of him or it.

A اعلط aʻlat, More or most offensive, displeasing.

A اعلطة aʻlitat, (pl. of علاط ʻilāt) Ropes about the necks (of camels). Traverse marks, made by burning, on the sides of (camels') necks.

A اعلم aʻlam, More or most learned. One who has a fissure in the upper lip. الله اعلم allāh aʻlam, God knows, or God knows best.

A اعلنباء iʻlimbāʼ, (v. n. 3 of علبي Q) Rising up, or putting one's self in a threatening attitude. Bristling up the hair or feathers (as dogs or cocks).

A اعلنداء iʻlindāʼ, (v. n. 3 of علدي Q) Being bulky, corpulent, and strong (a camel).

A اعلنكاس iʻlinkās, A being black (said of hair).

A اعلنكاك iʻlinkāk, (v.n. 3 of علكك Q) Being thick and plentiful (hair).

A اعلوّاد iʻliwwād, (v.n. 13 of علد) Being bulky and strong. Being grave and sedate.

A اعلوّاط iʻliwwāt, (v. n. 13 of علط) Hanging by (a camel's) neck and sitting on (his) back. Riding (a camel) without a bridle. Mounting the female (a camel). Entering upon any business rashly, without due thought or consideration. Laying hold of, detaining forcibly. Sticking close to.

A اعلومة uʻlūmat, An impression, a mark.

A اعلي aʻlaʼ, Higher, highest, upper. Of higher authority. Higher or highest part, topmost point.

A اعليط iʻlīt, Leaves of the tree called مرخ markh, or the pod, husk, and rind of its fruit. The fallen leaves of trees. (pl. علط ʻulut) A mark impressed crosswise on a camel's neck.

A اعلیلاء *iʻlīlāʼ*, (v. n. 12 of علو) Exalting, elevating. Being high. Ascending, being above.

A اعمّ *aʻamm*, More or most common, general, universal, concerning all. Coarse, thick. A great crowd. *Aʻumm*, (pl. of عمّ *ʻamm*) Paternal uncles.

A اعماء *aʻmāʼ*, (pl. of عمو *ʻamw*) Errors. Meannesses, submissions. (pl. of اعمی *aʻmaʼ*) Blind. Ignorant. Uncultivated (deserts). Tall. اعماء عامیه *aʻmāʼi ʻāmiya*, Blind deserts. ما اعماه *mā aʻmāhu*, How blind he is! *Iʻmāʼ*, (v. n. 4 of عمی) Making blind. Discovering one to be blind. Arriving at the hottest part of the day.

A اعماد *iʻmād*, (v. n. 4 of عمد) Supporting, sustaining, propping, strengthening (by pillars). Weakening, enfeebling, oppressing.

A اعمار *aʻmār*, (pl. of عمر *ʻumr*) Lives, life-times. *Iʻmār*, (v. n. 4 of عمر) Cultivating, rendering habitable. Causing to cultivate and render habitable. Visiting, frequenting the household of one's wife. Finding (a country) cultivated. Helping one to pay the sacred visit عمرة *ʻumrat*. Giving to one during life (a horse, or an estate). Rendering rich.

A اعماس *iʻmās*, (v. n. 4 of عمس) Hiding, concealing. Winking (the eye), being shut (eye-lids).

A اعماق *aʻmāk*, (pl. of عمق *ʻamk* or *ʻumk*) Widely extended (deserts). *Iʻmāk*, (v. n. 4 of عمق) Making deep (عمیق *ʻamīk*). Penetrating much.

A اعمال *aʻmāl*, (pl. of عمل *ʻamal*) Dependencies. Works, acts, labours. P اعمال پسندیده *aʻmāli pasandīda*, Approved works. A *Iʻmāl*, (v. n. 4 of عمل) Causing or bidding (one) to work. Making use (of advice or implements). Using one's own wits. Giving advice respecting a work (عمل *ʻamal*).

A اعمام *aʻmām*, (pl. of عمّ *ʻamm*) Paternal uncles. *Iʻmām*, (v. n. 4 of عمّ) Being paternal uncle.

A اعمان *iʻmān*, (v. n. 4 of عمن) Travelling towards عمّان *ʻammān*. Entering into or living constantly (in a place).

A اعمّة *aʻimmat*, (pl. of عمّ) Paternal uncles.

A اعمتة *aʻmitat*, (pl. of عمیتة) Clews of wool.

A اعمدة *aʻmidat*, (pl. of عمود *ʻamūd*) Pillars.

A اعمر *aʻmar*, More or most cultivated or inhabited. *Aʻmur*, (pl. of عمرو *ʻamr*) Amrs (names).

A اعمش *aʻmash*, Weak, or dim-sighted.

A ما ابعد اعمقها *mā abʻada aʻmakahā*, How deep (the well) is!

A اعمل *aʻmal*, More or most efficacious.

A اعمون *aʻmamūn*, Paternal uncles.

A اعمویّ *aʻmawiy*, Belonging to the blind. Ophthalmic.

A اعمی *aʻmaʼ*, (pl. عمی *ʻumy*, اعماء *aʻmāʼ* or عمیان *ʻumyān*) Blind. A desert. Tall. Ignorant. لقیته اعمی *lakītuhu aʻmaʼ*, I met him at the hottest part of the day.

A اعمیاء *iʻmiyāʼ*, (v. n. 9 of عمی) Being blind.

A اعمیاء *iʻmīyāʼ*, (v. n. 11 of عمی) Being blind.

A الاعمیان *al aʻmayāni*, (Two blinds) A torrent and conflagration; or night and a furious camel.

A اعناء *aʻnāʼ*, (pl. of عنو *ʻinw*) Tracks (in the heavens). Crowds or bodies of men of different ranks, families, or tribes. *Iʻnāʼ*, (v. n. 4 of عنا for عنو) Making or keeping prisoner. Depressing, humbling. Bringing forth, exhibiting, producing. (v. n. 4 of عنی) Fatiguing, afflicting. Detaining in captivity. Prefixing a title or frontispiece.

A اعناب *aʻnāb*, (pl. of عنب *ʻinab*) Grapes.

A اعنات *iʻnāt*, (v. n. 4 of عنت) Breaking again (a bone) which had formerly been broken and cured. Leading into difficulties.

A اعناج *iʻnāj*, (v. n. 4 of عنج) Leading a camel by the halter, exercising a camel. Pulling the check-rain. Settling, arranging firmly (business). Complaining of a pain in the loins (عناج *ʻināj*).

A اعناد *iʻnād*, (v. n. 4 of عند) Flowing but not drying (sweat). Bringing up one thing after another (in vomiting). Doing equal with another (either in harmony or in discord). Requiting kindness. Obstinacy, opposition.

A اعناز *iʻnāz*, (v. n. 4 of عنز) Making one to refuse, decline, or turn away from, any thing.

A اعناس *iʻnās*, (v. n. 4 of عنس) Remaining long in her parents' house unmarried (a marriageable virgin). Altering the features (age).

A اعناص *iʻnās*, (v. n. 4 of عنص) Having few and scattered hairs.

A اعناط *iʻnāt*, The begetting of a tall child.

A اعناف *iʻnāf*, (v. n. 4 of عنف) Incommoding, molesting.

A اعناق *aʻnāk*, (pl. of عنق *ʻunk* or *ʻunuk*) Necks. The lower orifices of stomachs; maws, guts. Princes, chiefs. Pieces of bread. اعناق الریح *aʻnāku'r rīh*, Particles of dust raised by the wind. *Iʻnāk*, (v. n. 4 of عنق) Ornamenting with a collar (a dog's neck). Making a collar. Being long and bearded (ears of corn). Setting (the stars called Pleiades). Looking with out-stretched neck. Travelling with an extended neck and a peculiar pace (camels). Driving (them) at that pace. Scattering dust (wind).

A اعناك *iʻnāk*, (v. n. 4 of عنك) Shutting, bolting (a door). Dealing in clothes. Meeting with impassable sands.

A اعنام *iʻnām*, (v. n. 4 of عنم) Eating of the عنام *ʻanām* tree (camels).

A اعنان *aʻnān*, Those parts of the heavens which are apparent to the sight. Extremities of trees. اعنان الشیاطین *aʻnānu'sh shayāṭīn*, The nature and manners of demons. *Iʻnān*, (v. n. 4 of عنّ) Putting on a rein to a bridle. Bridling, checking with the reins. Meeting, being exposed. Being impotent, fascinated, bewitched, or declared to be so judicially. Distinguishing a book by a title or inscription. Putting a direction on a letter. Making large or broad, laying open, rendering conspicuous. Exposing.

A اعنب *aʻnab*, Large-nosed.

A اعنّة *aʻinnat*, (pl. of عنان) Reins of bridles.

A اعنجة *aʻnijat*, (pl. of عناج *ʻināj*) Ropes or leathern straps which serve as handles to buckets. Pains in the loins, lumbagos.

A اعنز *aʻnuz*, (pl. of عنز *ʻanz*) She-goats.

A اعنش *aʻnash*, Six-fingered (man).

A اعنق *aʻnak*, Long-necked (dog). Marked with some white on the neck. Name of a famous stallion. بنات اعنق *banāt aʻnak*, The daughters of a wealthy farmer. *Aʻnuk*, (pl. of عنق *ʻunuh*) Necks. (pl. of عناق *ʻanāk*) Female kids.

A اعني *aʻnī*, I mean, that is to say, viz.

A اعنیناس *iʻnīnās*, (v. n. 12 of عنس) Being long and hairy (a camel's tail).

A اعواد *aʻwād*, (pl. of عود *ʻūd*) Lutes. Timbers, branches, trunks of trees, staves.

A اعواذ *iʻwāz*, (v. n. 4 of عوذ) Having lately brought forth (camels, mares, or does).

A اعوار *iʻwār*, (v. n. 4 of عور) Exposing one's self to the attack of a foe. Being possible. Appearing, being conspicuous. Coming within one's reach (game). Blinding, depriving of an eye.

A اعواز *iʻwāz*, (v. n. 4 of عوز) Being indigent. Standing in need of something without being able to procure it. Being near, at the point of. Impoverishing, reducing to poverty.

A اعواص *iʻwās*, (v. n. 4 of عاص for عوص) Rendering difficult. Adducing difficult arguments. Embarrassing, reducing (an opponent) to a nonplus.

A اعواض *aʻwāz*, (pl. of عوض *ʻiwaz*) Compensations, substitutes. *Iʻwāz*, (v. n. 4 of عاض for عوض) Compensating, countervailing.

A اعواق *aʻwāk*, (pl. of عوق *ʻawk* or *ʻūk*) Worthless, good for nothing. *Iʻwāk*, (v. n. 4 of عاق for عوق) Failing, being spent (a beast of burden, or travelling provisions).

A اعوال *iʻwāl*, (v. n. 4 of عال for عول) Weeping aloud, wailing. Having a numerous family to provide for. Using blandishments. Imposing a burden. Pouncing upon, attacking. Desiring earnestly, being greedy. Twanging (a bow-string).

A اعوام *aʻwām*, (pl. of عام *ʻām*) Years. Times.

A اعوان *aʻwān*, (pl. of عون) Helpers, allies.

A اعواه *iʻwāh*, (v. n. 4 of عوه) Suffering loss (in cattle or corn).

A اعوج *aʻwaj*, Crooked, curved. Of bad morals or manners. A horse in whose forelegs there is a curvature. Name of a celebrated horse and sire.

A اعوجاج *iʻwijāj*, (v. n. 9 of عوج) Being crooked. Crookedness, curvature, obliquity.

A اعوجيّ *aʻwajiy*, (A horse) bred from the celebrated sire اعوج *aʻwaj*.

A اعود *aʻwad*, More or most profitable. More or most useful, more or most conducive.

A اعور *aɛwar*, (pl. عور *ɛūr*, عيران *ɛīrān*, and عوران *ɛūrān*) One-eyed. A blind guide. A road with no direction-post. A crow. Weak, timorous, pusillanimous. Corrupt, bad (word or action). Illiterate, stupid. Obliterated, illegible (book). (A horseman) destitute of whip or switch. One who has no brother germain. Worthless, good for nothing. Disappointed and frustrated in the attainment of one's object. (pl. اعاور *aɛāwir*) A nit in the head. بدل اعور *badal aɛwar*, A bad substitute.

A اعورار *iɛwirār*, The being blind of an eye.

A اعوس *aɛwas*, Polish, lustre. A polisher, furbisher. A furbishing instrument. One who describes or praises ably. One who draws in the corners of his mouth when laughing.

A اعوص *aɛwas*, (pl. عوص *ɛūs*) Difficult (verse).

A اعولة *aɛwilat*, (pl. of عيال *ɛiyāl*) Families.

A اعويرار *iɛwīrār*, The being blind of an eye.

A اعهاء *iɛhāʼ*, (v. n. 4 of عهي not in use) Having a distemper (amongst one's cattle).

A اعهاد *iɛhād*, (v. n. 4 of عهد) Securing, guaranteeing, becoming surety for.

A اعياء *aɛyāʼ*, (pl. of عيّ *ɛayy*) Stammerers, stutterers. Awkward or embarrassed (in doing any thing). Name of an Arabian tribe. (pl. of عياء *ɛayāʼ*) Impotent, unable to generate. *Iɛyāʼ*, (v. n. 4 of عيّ) Being wearied with travelling. Fatiguing, tiring. Disabling, wearing out (disease). Becoming difficult, impeded, obstructed (business).

A اعياد *aɛyād*, (pl. of عيد *ɛīd*) Festivals.

A اعيار *aɛyār*, (pl. of عير *ɛayr*) Asses (wild or tame). Certain bright stars lying in the path of the feet of سهيل *suhayl*. *Iɛyār*, (v. n. 4 of عار for عير) Chasing (a horse) about. Putting the part called عير *ɛayr* to a spear-head.

A اعياس *iɛyās*, (v. n. 4 of عيس not used) Being without moisture (sown grain).

A اعياص *aɛyās*, (pl. of عيص *ɛīs*) Thick, shady, tall, trees. The Kuraysh Umayyades; namely, العاص *al ɛās*, ابو العاص *abū'l ɛās*, العيص *al ɛīs*, and ابو العيص *abū'l ɛīs*.

A اعيال *iɛyāl*, (v. n. 4 of عال for عيل) Having a numerous family. Supporting a family. Desiring eagerly.

A اعيان *aɛyān*, (pl. of عين *ɛayn*) Eyes. Fathers' or mothers' brothers. Great men, grandees. اعيان القوم *aɛyānu'l kawm*, The senators, the chiefs or elders of the people. اعيان دولت *aɛyāni dawlat*, (Eyes of the state) ministers. اعيان ممكنات *aɛyāni mumkināt*, The most excellent of creatures. اعيان ثابته *aɛyāni sābita*, Figures emblematic of the names of God. *Iɛyān*, (v. n. 4 of عان for عين) Boring to a spring of water.

A اعيرج *uɛayrij*, (pl. اعيرجات) An asp.

A اعيس *aɛyas*, Whitish-yellow (camel).

A اعيط *aɛyat*, Long-necked (camel or man). Backward, averse. Proud, stubborn. High, lofty, eminent (citadel or glory).

A اعيلة *aɛyilat*, (pl. of عيال *ɛiyāl*) Families.

A اعين *aɛyan*, (pl. عين *ɛīn*) One who has large or black eyes. A wild bull. (A man) possessed of many domestics. ما اعينه *mā aɛyanahu*, How malignant is his look! *Aɛyun*, (pl. under ten of عين *ɛayn*) Eyes. Fountains. اعين السراطين *aɛyunu's sarātīn*, Seeds of Agnus castus.

A اعينات *aɛyunāt*, (pl. of اعين *aɛyun*, pl. of عين *ɛayn*) Many eyes.

A اعينة *aɛyinat*, (pl. of عيان) Plough-shares.

A اعيى *aɛyaʼ*, More or most stammering (in speech). More or most dangerous and desperate (disease). Name of the father of a tribe.

A اعيياء *aɛyiyāʼ*, (pl. of عييّ *ɛayīy*) Stammering. Embarrassed, unequal to.

A اعيية *aɛyiyat*, (pl. of عييّ *ɛayīy*) Stammerers.

A اعييّة *uɛyiyat* or *iɛyiyat*, Any subject about which one stammers and speaks unintelligibly.

P آغا *āghā*, A great lord, nobleman, head, chief master, commander. An eunuch (as having the principal charge of the seraglio).

A اغابة *ighābat*, (v. n. 4 of غاب for غيب) Having her husband absent (a woman).

A اغاثة *ighāsat*, (v. n. 4 of غاث for غوث) Bringing help, succouring.

P آغار *āghār*, (or اغار *aghār*) A sinking of moisture into the ground. Mixed, kneaded. Moistened. Excited, instigated.

P آغارانيدن *āghārānīdan*, To throw down. To move.

A اغارة *ighārat*, (v. n. 4 of غار for غور) Coming into a low-lying hollow country (called غور *ghawr*) in Arabia. Travelling in a country. Having the eyes deep sunk in their sockets. Attacking, plundering, making a hostile excursion into an enemy's country. Coming or sending to any one for assistance. Mending the pace, making haste. Spurring (a horse). Twisting (a rope) firmly. Going full speed in making a predatory attack. Provoking to jealousy, making jealous. (v. n. 4 of غار for غير) Taking a second wife (so making the first jealous).

P آغارد *āghārad*, Bruising, crushing. Exciting.

P آغاردن *āghārdan*, (or اغاردن *aghārdan*) To moisten, macerate. To mix. To knead. To cause to move, to rouse, to excite. To sink, or to cause (water) to sink into the ground.

P آغاروز *āghāroz*, Beginning, commencement.

P آغاري *āghārī*, A vessel.

P آغاريدن *āghārīdan*, To moisten, wet, macerate, bring almost to a solution. To excite, instigate.

G اغاريقون *aghārīkūn*, Common agarick.

P آغاز *āghāz*, Beginning, commencement. Design, wish. Echo, call. آغاز كردن *āghāz kardan*, To commence, make a beginning. To design, will.

P اغاز *aghāz*, Will, intention, design. A voice, noise, echo. A beginning, commencement.

P آغازه *āghāza*, A cobbler's tool. Sole of a shoe

P اغازه *aghāza*, A cobbler's tool.

P آغازيدن *āghāzīdan*, To begin: to design, will.

P آغاش *āghāsh*, Recorded. Accumulated.

P آغاشتن *āghāshtan*, To accumulate, throw one above another, place one thing before another.

A اغاضة *ighāzat*, (v. n. 4 of غاض for غيض) Making (water) decrease, causing (it) to subside into the ground. Lowering, beating down (price).

A اغاظة *ighāzat*, (v. n. 4 of غاظ for غيظ) Enraging, raising indignation.

A اغافة *ighāfat*, (v. n. 4 of غاف for غيف) Causing to incline.

P آغال *āghāl*, Instigation, excitement. A setting in motion. The swallowing of food not masticated. A sheep-cote. A hive. A beginning, commencement. A moistening, macerating.

P آغال پشه *āghāl pasha*, The lote-tree. The gnat-tree, with large smooth stem and thick foliage.

A اغالة *ighālat*, (v. n. 4 of غال for غيل) (A woman) giving suck to a child while pregnant, or cohabiting with a man. Exposing a child to danger by cohabiting with the mother whilst suckling.

P آغالش *āghālish*, (or اغالش *aghālish*) Instigation, incitement to crime.

P آغالشتن *āghālishtan*, To accumulate, heap.

G اغالوخي *aghālūkhī*, Aloes.

P آغاليدن *āghālīdan*, (or اغاليدن *aghālīdan*) To excite, rouse, animate (to battle). To be hot, fiery, and contentious. To confine, reduce to straits.

A اغاليط *aghālīt*, (pl. of اغلوطة *ughlūtat*) Questions, doubts, or whatever matters are liable to error or reprehension; things which mislead.

A اغاليق *aghālīk*, (pl. of اغلوقة *ughlūkat*) Locks.

A اغامة *ighāmat*, (v. n. 4 of غام for غيم) Being cloudy, misty, foggy (the sky).

A اغانة *ighānat*, (v. n. 4 of غان for غين) Overspreading (as clouds the sky). Overwhelming (as grief the mind).

A اغانم *aghānim*, (pl. of غنم) Sheep. Flocks.

A اغاني *aghānī*, (pl. of اغنيّة *ughnīyat*) Songs.

P آغايان *āghāyān*, (pl. of آغا *āghā*) Great lords.

A اغباء *ighbāʼ*, (v. n. 4 of غبي) Raining slightly (with a small sprinkling rain called غبية *ghabyat*).

A اغباب *aghbāb*, (pl. of غبّ *ghubb*) Low grounds. Distant (waters). *Ighbāb*, (v. n. 4 of غبّ) Visiting every other day. Attacking every other day (a tertian fever). Watering (camels) every other day. Not failing or ceasing for a single day. Stinking (as meat). Passing the night with.

A اغبار *aghbār*, (pl. of غبر *ghubr*) The remains of any thing, the remains of milk in the breast, or of blood in menstruation. *Ighbār*, (v. n. 4 of غبر) Raising dust. Being of a dusty colour. Striving to the utmost. Raining fast.

A اغباس *ighbās*, (v. n. 4 of غبس) Growing dark. Being of a dusky colour.

A اغباش *aghbāsh*, (pl. of غبش *ghabash*) The latter parts of nights, especially when very dark. *Ighbāsh*, (v. n. 4 of غبش) Being dark (the latter part of the night).

A اغباط *ighbāt*, (v. n. 4 of غبط) Leaving unmoved (a pack-saddle on the back of a beast). Continuing without intermitting (a fever). Raining incessantly. Covering the ground (herbage).

A اغبث *aghbas*, Inclining to a dusty colour. Ash-coloured (lion).

A اغبثاث *ighbisās*, (v. n. 9 of غبث) Being of a dusty or ash-colour.

A اغبر *aghbar*, Soiled with dust. Scarce, barren (year). Departed (glory). A wolf.

A اغبرار *ighbirār*, (v. n. 9 of غبر) Being very dusty (the day). Being of a dusty colour.

A اغبس *aghbas*, Dun (wolf). Bay (horse). Dusky (rose).

A اغبساس *ighbisās*, (v. n. 9 of غبس) Growing dark. Being of a dusky colour.

A اغبش *aghbash*, Dark (night).

A اغبي *aghba'*, Thick, entangled (branch).

A اغبيساس *ighbīsās*, (v. n. 11 of غبس) Growing dark. Being of a dusty colour.

A اغتام *ightām*, (v. n. 4 of غتم not in use) Repeating visits or importunities till they become disgusting. Being oppressed with indigestion.

A اغتباط *ightibāt*, (v. n. 8 of غبط) Being in happy circumstances. Attaining the object of one's desire, being rendered happy thereby. Mirth.

A اغتباق *ightibāk*, (v. n. 8 of غبق) Drinking wine at even-tide.

A اغتبان *ightibān*, (v. n. 8 of غبن) Concealing (any thing) under the armpit.

A اغتتام *ightitām*, (v. n. 8 of غتم) Visiting frequently, so as to become wearisome. Being troubled with indigestion.

A اغتثاث *ightisās*, (v. n. 8 of غثّ) Feeding on spring-grass (horses).

A اغتداء *ightidā*, (v. n. 8 of غدا for غدو) Coming, going, or working in the morning.

A اغتدار *ightidār*, (v. n. 8 of غدر) Making the hasty pudding called غديرة *ghadīrat*.

A اغتداف *ightidāf*, (v. n. 8 of غدف) Taking much. Cutting a robe or garment.

A اغتذاء *ightizā*, (v. n. 8 of غذا for غذو) Being fed, nourished. Eating.

A اغتذار *ightizār*, (v. n. 8 of غذر) Preparing the food غذيرة *ghazīrat*, *i.e.* flour milked upon, and then heated with a hot stone.

A اغتذام *ightizām*, (v. n. 8 of غذم) Eating voraciously. Eating with difficulty. Draining the udder (a camel's colt). Drinking up the whole.

A اغتراب *ightirāb*, (v. n. 8 of غرب) Travelling from one's own country into foreign parts. Marrying a foreigner. Distance from home.

A اغترار *ightirār*, (v. n. 8 of غرّ) Being deceived. Being foolish, uncircumspect, inattentive, or thoughtless. Coming upon one suddenly.

A اغتراز *ightirāz*, (v. n. 8 of غرز) Putting the foot in the stirrup when going to mount. Drawing near (the time of departure).

A اغتراف *ightirāf*, (v. n. 8 of غرف) Drinking water (out of the hand). Exhausting (water) by lading (it) out with any thing.

A اغتراق *ightirāk*, (v. n. 8 of غرق) Intermingling with others (a horse), and then passing on and leaving them behind. Absorbing the gaze of the company (a beautiful woman). Filling the throat (a breath or braying). Filling a girth so that the ends cannot meet (a camel's belly).

A اغتزاء *ightizā*, (v. n. 8 of غزا for غزو) Being singled out from amongst one's companions. Intending, purposing, willing, wishing.

A اغتزاز *ightizāz*, (v. n. 8 of غزّ) Being sole proprietor. Particularizing, selecting from amongst.

A اغتزال *ightizāl*, (v. n. 8 of غزل) Spinning.

A اغتسال *ightisāl*, (v. n. 8 of غسل) Washing one's self. Ablution. Sprinkling one's self with perfume. Sweating all over. Copulating much.

A اغتشاش *ightishāsh*, (v. n. 8 of غشّ) Consenting to perfidy. Entertaining a suspicion of fraud, suspecting perfidy.

A اغتصاب *ightisāb*, The act of seizing violently.

A اغتصاص *ightisās*, (v. n. 8 of غصّ) Being choked, suffocated.

A اغتضاب *ightizāb*, A flying in a passion.

A اغتضار *ightizār*, (v. n. 8 of غضر) Dying in the flower of youth.

A اغتطاء *ightitā*, (v. n. 8 of غطا for غطو) Being covered and hidden. Covering.

A اغتطاط *ightitāt*, (v. n. 8 of غطّ) Making the female lie down (a male camel). Contending with and overcoming in a race.

A اغتفاف *ightifāf*, (v. n. 8 of غفّ) Having a sufficiency of spring-grass (cattle). Giving a little. Becoming fatter (camels).

A اغتفاق *ightifāk*, (v. n. 8 of غفق) Surrounding.

A اغتلاء *ightilā*, (v. n. 8 of غلا for غلو) Travelling fast, making haste. Celerity.

A اغتلات *ightilāt*, (v. n. 8 of غلت) Taking unawares. Receiving with indifference.

A اغتلاث *ightilās*, (v. n. 8 of غلث) Taking wood from the مرخ *markh* tree without knowing whether it will emit fire or not. Not striking fire.

A اغتلاف *ightilāf*, (v. n. 8 of غلف) Having a foreskin. Making a sheath or cover (غلاف *ghilāf*). Perfuming (hair or beard) with musk.

A اغتلال *ightilāl*, (v. n. 8 of غلّ) Perfuming the beard or mustachios with غالية *ghāliyat*, or civet. Suffering from thirst. Drinking. Putting on an inner garment. Being infected by a certain disease.

A اغتلام *ightilām*, (v. n. 8 of غلم) Being very lustful (from غلام *ghulām*, A boy). Buggering.

A اغتم *aghtam*, One who speaks indistinctly.

A اغتماد *ightimād*, (v. n. 8 of غمد) Entering (into the night), being enveloped (in darkness).

A اغتمار *ightimār*, (v. n. 8 of غمر) Tinging with saffron or any other liniment. Covering, overflowing (water). Plunging, descending into water.

A اغتماز *ightimāz*, (v. n. 8 of غمز) Censuring, condemning, reviling, reproaching, disgracing.

A اغتماس *ightimās*, (v. n. 8 of غمس) Tinging (her) hands all over without figures (a woman).

A اغتماص *ightimās*, (v. n. 8 of غمص) Despising, slighting, holding cheap.

A اغتماض *ightimāz*, (v. n. 8 of غمض) Winking. Dozing. علي اغتماض *ʿala' ightimāzin*, Without trouble or difficulty.

A اغتماط *ightimāt*, (v. n. 8 of غمط) Contending with and beating in a race, after having been first beaten. Talking loud and overpowering with words. Disappearing and leaving no sign or vestige.

A اغتمام *ightimām*, (v. n. 8 of غمّ) Being sad and gloomy. Sadness, gloom. Being long and luxuriant (a plant).

A اغتنام *ightinām*, (v. n. 8 of غنم) Getting spoil or plunder. Regarding as plunder. Seizing an opportunity.

A اغتهاب *ightihāb*, A travelling in the dark.

A اغتياب *ightiyāb*, (v. n. 8 of غاب for غيب) Traducing, inveighing against (the absent).

A اغتيار *ightiyār*, (v. n. 8 of غار for غور) Being profited, deriving benefit. (v. n. 8 of غار for غير) Victualling one's household, purveying. Carrying corn from country to country.

A اغتياظ *ightiyāz*, (v. n. 8 of غاظ for غيظ) Being angry, enraged.

A اغتيال *ightiyāl*, (v. n. 8 of غال for غول) Assaulting, rushing upon, or attacking suddenly, overcoming and destroying. Concealing, hiding (as a vast waste does footsteps), suppressing. (v. n. 8 of غال for غيل) Growing fat and plump (a boy).

A اغثاء *aghsā*, (pl. of غثاء *ghusā* or غثّاء *ghussā*) Leaves of trees, pieces of wood, and other rubbish floating upon water. *Ighsā*, (v. n. 4 of غثا for غثو) (A torrent) drawing fodder in a heap, and washing and extracting all the goodness out of it. Being covered with verdure (ground).

A اغثاث *ighsās*, (v. n. 4 of غثّ) Becoming lean. Being wicked, obscene, impure (speech): talking smut. Throwing out purulent matter (a wound).

A اغثار *ighsār*, (v. n. 4 of غثر) Emitting a substance called مغثور *mughsūr*, resembling honey, which exudes from a certain plant like tears.

A اغثر *aghsar*, Dust-coloured, mixed with green. A kind of marshy pulse. Water-moss. Low, plebeian. Ignorant. A certain bird with a long neck. A lion. Coarse woollen nappy cloth. Much.

A اغثم *aghsam*, (A head of hair) consisting more of white than black ones.

A اغثي *aghsa'*, A lion.

A اغثيرار *ighsīrār*, (v. n. 11 of غثر) Being long and thick (nap, pile, or shag on cloth).

A اغداد *ighdād*, (v. n. 4 of غدّ) Being seized with the plague (a camel). Having (camels) labouring under an infection. Being angry, exasperated, stimulated to rage.

A اغدار *ighdār*, (v. n. 4 of غدر) Abandoning, quitting, leaving, forsaking. Leaving a remainder. Leaving behind (a sheep or camel).

A اغداف *ighdāf*, (v. n. 4 of غدف) Loosing or dropping (a veil) over the face. Letting fall a net (upon birds). Diffusing darkness (the night). Cutting off (the foreskin). Lying with.

A اغداق *ighdāk*, (v. n. 4 of غدق) Being copious.

A اغدية *aghdiyat*, (pl. of غداء *ghadāʼ*) Breakfasts, victuals. كمّيّت اغديه *kammīyati aghdiya*, The quality of meats.

A اغديداق *ighdīdāk*, (v. n. 12 of غدق) Being very copious (rain).

A اغديدان *ighdīdān*, (v. n. 12 of غدن) Being long and bushy (hair). Being of a dark green through rankness (a plant).

A اغذاذ *ighzāz*, (v. n. 4 of غذّ) Suppurating (a wound). Flowing from a sore (matter). Making haste, going fast. Accelerating.

A اغذام *ighzām*, (v. n. 4 of غذم) Exhausting the dam's udder (a young camel).

A اغذية *aghziyat*, (pl. of غذاء) Aliments.

P آغر *āghar*, The bed of a river with a little water here and there.

A اغرّ *agharr*, (pl. غرر *ghurar* and غرّان *ghurrān*) White, bright. Illustrious, noble. (A horse) with a white spot on his forehead. Conspicuous for generous (acts). One whose beard covers almost the whole of his face. Most sultry (day).

A اغراء *aghrāʼ*, (pl. of غرا *ghara'*) Lean. *Ighrāʼ*, (v. n. 4 of غراء for غرو) Being wholly addicted to. Causing one to be intently eager. Instigating, stimulating. Setting (a dog) after game. Sowing enmity, setting one against another.

A اغرّاء *aghirrāʼ*, (pl. of غرير *gharīr*) Such as are deceived with vain hopes. Young people inexperienced in life, and liable to deception.

A اغراب *ighrāb*, (v. n. 4 of غرب) Becoming strange or foreign. Travelling to foreign parts, travelling far and wide. Bringing, performing or relating any thing new, foreign, strange, or wonderful. Drawing near sunset. Going westwards. Filling (a bottle). Being good and prosperous (a condition). Having white eye-brows or eye-lashes (man or beast). Having a white lip and white eyelashes (a horse). Running much (a horse). Riding (a horse) to death. Laughing immoderately. Being seized with violent pains. Having a shameful trick played upon one. Having the blaze upon the forehead extending to the eyes (a horse). Whiteness of the groin. An excellent condition.

A اغراد *ighrād*, (v. n. 4 of غرد) Singing (especially with a raised voice and motion of the body. Warbling in the throat, trilling, shaking.

A اغرار *aghrār*, Unskilled, inexperienced persons.

A اغراز *ighrāz*, (v. n. 4 of غرز) Abounding in the plant غرز *gharaz* (land).

A اغراس *aghrās*, (pl. of غرس *ghars*) Plants, saplings. (pl. of غرس *ghirs*) The membranes covering the heads (of young camels), and other substances which are brought forth along with the fœtus. *Ighrās*, (v. n. 4 of غرس) Planting, setting.

A اغراض *aghrāz*, (pl. of غرض *gharz*) Girths of camels' saddles: (those belonging to pack-saddles are called بطان *bitān*, and those of a horse-saddle حزام *hizām*). (pl. of غرض *gharaz*) Designs, intentions, ends, views, objects, purposes, wishes. Butts, marks, targets. *Ighrāz* (v. n. 4 of غرض) Filling (a bottle). Filling (it) not quite full. Tiring, fatiguing, vexing. Girthing (a camel). Procuring fresh food for one's household, and not giving it to them stale.

A اغراق *ighrāk*, (v. n. 4 of غرق) Drowning, plunging, immerging, throwing into (water). Filling (a cup). Bending or drawing (a bow) to the utmost of one's strength. Praising immoderately. Blaming immoderately (drawing the long bow).

A اغرام *ighrām*, (v. n. 4 of غرم) Mulcting, fining. Bringing into debt. Being addicted to, or fond of.

A اغران *aghrān*, (pl. of غرن *gharan*) Eagles.

A اغرب *aghrab*, More or most strange, wonderful. *Aghrub*, (pl. of غراب *ghurāb*) Crows, ravens.

A اغربة *aghribat*, (pl. of غراب *ghurāb*) Crows, ravens. The prominent parts of the hips of horses or camels. اغربة العرب *aghribatu'l ʻarab*, The swarthy of the Arabs.

A اغرّة *aghirrat*, (pl. of غرير *gharīr*) Young and inexperienced persons.

P آغرده *āgharda*, (A garment) thin and flimsy.

G اغرسطس *aghirustis*, Couch-grass, agrostis.

A اغرل *aghral*, Easy, agreeable (life). Plentiful (year). Uncircumcised (lad).

A اغرنداء *ighrindāʼ*, The being superior, overbearing by violence or opprobrious language.

A اغرنشام *ighrinshām*, (v. n. 3 of غرشم Q) Becoming flaccid (the body).

P اغره *aghra*, A mote of kings, nobles, or judges. An airy, windy place. *Ughra*, A wen, a kernel.

G اغريا *aghriyā*, A mountain.

A اغريراق *ighrīrāk*, (v. n. 12 of غرق) Overflowing with tears, being drowned in tears (the eye).

P اغريرث *ighrīras*, The brother of Afrāsyāb.

A اغريض *ighrīz*, The flowers of the palm-tree. Any thing fresh and shining.

A اغزاء *ighzāʼ*, (v. n. 4 of غزا for غزو) Sending upon a military expedition, compelling, inducing, or instigating (a man) to go to war. Preparing the materiel of war. Granting a delay in the payment of debt. Having (a husband) absent in the wars. Conceiving with difficulty (a camel).

A اغزار *ighzār*, (v. n. 4 of غزر) Conferring many benefits. Having (camels) abounding with milk.

A اغزاز *ighzāz*, (v. n. 4 of غزّ) Having many hard thorns (a tree). Having a hard pregnancy or gestation (a cow).

A اغزال *ighzāl*, (v. n. 4 of غزل) Twirling the spindle when spinning. Having a young one (a doe).

A اغزل *aghzal*, More or most of an erotic poet. A fever which returns at regular intervals.

A اغساء *ighsāʼ*, (v. n. 4 of غسا for غسو) Being dark. (v. n. 4 of غسي) Involving in darkness.

A اغساف *ighsāf*, The act of walking in darkness.

A اغساق *ighsāk*, (v. n. 4 of غسق) Growing very dark. Walking in, being in the dark. Calling the people, or announcing the hour of prayer at a late hour in the evening.

A اغسال *ighsāl*, (v. n. 4 of غسل) Covering much (a stallion).

A اغسام *aghsām*, Portions, bits of a cloud. *Ighsām*, (v. n. 4 of غسم) Being dark (the night).

A اغسان *aghsān*, Natures, tempers, dispositions of people. Tattered garments.

P آغستن *āghastan*, To fill, to cram.

P آغش *āghush*, An embrace.

A اغشاء *ighshāʼ*, (v. n. 4 of غشي) Covering, enveloping (with darkness). Spreading a veil. Blinding. Causing any thing to come, or bringing a thing upon one unexpectedly. Exciting, stirring up, leading into (rebellion).

A اغشاش *ighshāsh*, (v. n. 4 of غشّ) Deceiving, dissembling. Keeping back, withholding. Causing to make haste.

P آغشتانيدن *āghashtānīdan*, To cause to mix or macerate.

P آغشتگي *āghashtagī*, Alloy, mixture.

P آغشتن *āghashtan*, To moisten. To be moist. To cut, hash, or mince. To defile, or be defiled.

P آغشته *āghashta*, (or اغشته *aghashta*) Mixed. Moistened, smeared. Watered (ground).

P آغشك *āghashak*, Turpentine.

A اغشي *aghsha'*, White-headed or faced (horse).

A اغصاص *ighsās*, (v. n. 4 of غصّ) Choking, causing suffocation. Making one choke with grief. Rendering inconveniently narrow, straitening.

A اغصان *aghsān*, (pl. of غصن *ghusn*) Branches. *Ighsān*, (v. n. 4 of غصن) Having many berries (a bunch of grapes).

A اغصن *aghsan*, White on the tail (an ox).

A اغضّ *aghazz*, More or most fresh, green, tender.

A اغضاء *ighzāʼ*, (v. n. 4 of غضا for غضو) Being silent (about any thing). Being dark, and by the darkness concealing every thing (the night). Half closing the eyelids. Closing or averting the eye.

A اغضاب *ighzāb*, (v. n. 4 of غضب) Provoking, enraging, angering, putting in a passion.

A اغضاض ighzāz, (v. n. 4 of غض) Freshening.

A اغضاف ighzāf, (v. n. 4 of غضف) Being obscure, cloudy, dark (night). Being luxuriant in the branches (the palm), and therefore bearing worse fruit. Being weighed down with fruit (a palm-tree). Threatening rain. Being numerously stocked with beasts (a fold near water).

A اغضان ighzān, The act of raining continually.

A اغضب aghzab, The groin. Very angry.

A اغضّة aghizzat, (pl. of غضيض ghazīz) Languid (eyes). Deficient. Abject, submissive.

A اغضف aghzaf, (pl. غضف ghuzf) Bangle-eared (dog), whose ears fall backwards. Thickly feathered (arrow). Dark (night). Easy, comfortable, delicate (life). Flap-eared (lion). One whose upper eyelashes overhang the lower from rage or pride; supercilious.

A اغضن aghzan, One who wrinkles his eyes naturally (from anger, hatred, or pride).

A اغضيلال ighzīlāl, (v. n. 12 of غضل) Being very moist. Being very branchy and leafy (a tree).

A اغطّ aghatt, Rich, wealthy, opulent.

A اغطاء ightā, (v. n. 4 of غطا for غطو) Rising above and hiding. Diffusing branches, and extending them along the ground (a tree). Being full of sap, having its sap running (a vine).

A اغطاش ightāsh, (v. n. 4 of غطش) Being dark. Making dark.

A اغطال ightāl, (v. n. 4 of غطل) Being overcast (the sky). Being black by reason of density (clouds).

A اغطش aghtash, Weak-sighted.

A اغطف aghtaf, Comfortable, easy (life). Possessed of long eyelids.

A اغطية aghtiyat, (pl. of غطاء) Coverings.

A اغطيلال ightīlāl, (v. n. 11 of غطل) Riding one upon another. Coming in one after another in quick succession.

A اغفاء ighfā, (v. n. 4 of غفا for غفو) Sleeping, slumbering. (v. n. 4 of غفي) Sleeping, lying on straw in a mow. Abounding with bran (wheat). Cleaning (grain) from tares, darnel, or chaff.

A اغفار aghfār, (pl. of غفر ghafr) The young of wild goats. Ighfār, (v. n. 4 of غفر) Covering, hiding, laying up any thing in a case or repository. Being attended by her young one (a female mountain-goat). Bearing dates, which in their unripe state have on them a kind of husk (a palm-tree).

A اغفال aghfāl, (Deserts) without roads or signals to direct travellers. (Districts) without habitations or the traces of any. (Places) without owners. (Camels) without milk. Ighfāl, (v. n. 4 of غفل) Neglecting, overlooking. Forgetting. Causing one to forget or to be negligent. Finding (any one) negligent. Calling (any one) negligent. Leaving (any thing) to the recollection of another. Turning (a horse) loose without branding (him).

A اغفر aghfar, (A garment) more or most apt to take the dirt. More or most forgiving.

A اغفيرار ighfīrār, (v. n. 11 of غفر) Having much nap, being shaggy (cloth).

P آغل āghil, A sheep-cote.

P اغل aghil, A sheep-cote in a mountain.

A اغلاء ighlā, (v. n. 4 of غلا for غلو) Growing high, being thickly entangled (herbage). Buying dear. Making dear. Lightening (a tree) of its leaves. (v. n. 4 of غلي) Making (a pot) boil.

A اغلاءة ighlā,at, One single ebullition.

G اغلاجون aghlājūn, The aromatic aloe.

A اغلاس aghlās, (pl. of غلس ghalas) Darknesses. Ighlās, (v. n. 4 of غلس) Being, or doing, any thing about the end of the night.

A اغلاط aghlāt, (pl. of غلط ghalat) Errors. Ighlāt, (v. n. 4 of غلط) Leading into error.

A اغلاظ ighlāz, (v. n. 4 of غلظ) Making thick and stout. Using coarse or opprobrious language. Buying coarse (cloth), discovering (it) to be so. Going to rough, coarse, rugged grounds, and residing there. (The adjective is غليظ ghalīz).

A اغلاف ighlāf, (v. n. 4 of غلف) Sheathing, putting up in a scabbard or sheath (غلاف ghilāf). Preparing a sheath for any thing.

A اغلاق aghlāk, (pl. of غلق ghalk) Locks, bars, bolts. Ighlāk, (v. n. 4 of غلق) Shutting, locking, or fastening (a door). Forcing against one's will. Galling (a camel's back) by overloading (so that it cannot be cured).

A اغلال aghlāl, (pl. of غلّ ghull) Yokes or chains for the neck (of iron, or of leather with part of the hair adhering). (pl. of غلل ghalal) Waters flowing amongst trees. اغلال سلاسل aghlāli salāsil, Bolts, links, or rings of chains. P سزاور اغلال sazāwari aghlāl, Fit for the yoke. A Ighlāl, (v. n. 4 of غلّ) Defrauding, cheating of his share, acting perfidiously. Accusing of perfidy and malevolence. Producing corn or pulse called غلة ghallat (ground). Having rich produce of this kind (a farmer). Bringing home such produce. Producing the herbs called غلّان ghullān (a valley). Fixing (the countenance or the eye) directly (upon any object). Watering (camels) insufficiently so as to leave (them) thirsty. Having thirsty flocks. Pulling off, with too much violence, the skin of any slaughtered animal, so that part of the flesh and fat comes along with it. P اغلال کردن ighlāl kardan, To yoke. To pillory.

A اغلام ighlām, The act of provoking to venery.

A اغلب aghlab, Superior, stronger, strongest. More or most violent. The greater part, most part. Thick-necked. Brave, bold. الاغلب al aghlab, A lion. في الاغلب fi'l aghlab, For the most part.

A اغلظ aghlaz, Grosser, fatter, thicker, thickest. نجو اغلظ najwi aghlaz, Thick stools.

A اغلف aghlaf, Uncircumcised. Sheathed (sword). Hard, stubborn (heart), as being sheathed or plunged in vice. Affluent, comfortable (life). Abundant in produce, plentiful, smiling (year).

A اغلمة aghlimat, (pl. of غلام ghulām) Boys. Servants, slaves.

P اغلمش ughlumish, Name of a king of Persia.

A اغلنتاء ighlintā, (v. n. 3 of غلتي Q) Conquering, overpowering with words or abuse.

A اغلنساء ighlinsā, (v. n. 3 of غلسي Q) Conquering, overpowering with words or abuse.

A اغلوج ughlūj, A little branch, a twig.

A اغلوطة ughlūtat, (pl. اغاليط aghālīt) A doubtful question, any thing that may mislead a person. Any thing liable to error or misapprehension.

A اغلوقة ughlūkat, (pl. اغاليق aghālīk) A lock.

A اغلية aghliyat, (pl. of غلاء ghalā) Certain short-bodied fishes.

P اغليسون aghlīsūn, The rainbow.

A اغليلاء ighlīlā, (v. n. 12 of غلا for غلو) Growing long, being thick and entangled (herbage).

A اغليلاب ighlīlāb, (v. n. 11 of غلب) Being luxuriant and entangled (grass).

A اغمّ aghamm, One who has much hair on the forehead, or on the hinder part of the head. Dense (cloud) with no opening in it.

A اغماء aghmā, (pl. of غميٌ ghama') Fainted, swooned. Roofs of houses. The highest parts of a roof covered with reeds or any thing similar. Ighmā, (v. n. 4 of غمي) Speaking obscurely. Fainting, swooning. Causing to faint, throwing into a fit. Being misty, cloudy, or unintelligible. Being constantly clouded (the day). Veiling the moon (a cloud). Being obscure, uncertain, or unintelligible (news). Being uncertain, and at a loss how to act.

A اغماد aghmād, (pl. of غمد ghimd) Sheaths. Husks, pods. Ighmād, (v. n. 4 of غمد) Sheathing (a sword). Inserting one thing into another.

A اغمار aghmār, (pl. of غمر ghumr) Rude, inexperienced, unlearned (men). Ighmār, (v. n. 4 of غمر) Persevering in one's journey after the heat has somewhat subsided.

A اغماز ighmāz, (v. n. 4 of غمز) Disparaging, detracting from, railing against, blaming, reviling. Acquiring, gaining, possessing the worst kind of cattle. Growing cool, abating (the heat of the sun). Braving the heat, or travelling when the heat has begun to abate. Being fat on the bunch (a camel).

A اغماض aghmāz, (pl. of غمض ghamz) Low, flat (grounds). Ighmāz, (v. n. 4 of غمض) Looking with half-shut eyes. Winking at, indulging. Looking disdainfully. Allowing a discount. Beating down the price. Getting ahead of any one in running after he had previously taken the lead. Connivance, dissimulation. Superciliousness, neglect. Sharpening (the edge of a sword). ما اكتحلت اغماضا mā iktahaltu ighmāzan, I slept not a wink. P اغماض کردن ighmāz kardan, To connive at.

A اغماط *ighmāt*, (v. n. 4 of غمط) Continuing without intermission (a fever).

A اغمام *ighmām*, (v. n. 4 of غمّ) Saddening, making melancholy. Being overcast with clouds (the sky). Being very hot and suffocating (the day). Being uncertain and confused (intelligence).

A اغمراء *aghmirāʼ*, (pl. of غمير *ghamīr*) Grasses which are overtopped and sheltered from the sun by the taller and drier herbage; whatever green stuff vegetates at the roots of hay or grass.

A اغمص *aghmas*, Blear-eyed.

A اغمية *aghmiyat*, (pl. of غميٰ *ghama'*) Roofs of houses. House-tops covered with earth, reeds, &c.

A اغنّ *aghann*, One who speaks through the nose, or with a nasal twang. (Deer) braying through the nose. (A valley) abounding with trees or herbage, and resonant with the hum of insects. (A place) thronged with people (as a busy mart).

A اغناء *aghnāʼ*, The paraphernalia of a bride. *Ighnāʼ*, (v. n. 4 of غني) Enriching, rendering independent, enabling to do without. Contenting, satisfying. Sufficing. Supplying the place of another.

A اغناظ *ighnāz*, (v. n. 4 of غنظ) Overwhelming with grief, throwing into difficulty and trouble.

A اغنام *aghnām*, (pl. of غنم) Sheep, flocks.

A اغنان *ighnān*, (v. n. 4 of غنّ) Resounding with the humming of flies (a valley); also being verdant and grassy (in which the flies delight). Having fruits come to maturity (a palm-tree). Being filled (a bottle). Buzzing (flies).

P آغند *āghand*, Stuffed, crammed.

P آغندن *āghandan*, To fill, stuff, cram.

P آغنده *āghanda*, Filled, stuffed. Cramming. A stuffer. *Āghunda*, Ball of cotton. Sort of spider.

A اغنيٰ *aghna'*, Richer, richest. More or most independent. More or most useful.

A اغنّيّ *aghanniy*, The letters م *mīm* or ن *nūn*.

A اغنياء *aghniyāʼ*, (pl. of غنيّ *ghaniy*) Rich. اغنيا و فقرا *aghniyā u fuḳarā*, The rich and poor.

P اغنياءِ روزگار *aghniyāʼi rozgār*, The rich men of the world.

A اغنيّة *ughnīyat*, *ighnīyat*, اغنية *ughniyat* or *ighniyat*, (pl. اغاني *aghānī*) Music, melody, modulation, a certain musical mode. A song.

A اغواء *ighwāʼ*, (v. n. 4 of غوي) Seducing, leading astray, deceiving. Seduction, temptation.

P آغوات *āghawāt*, (Ar. pl. of آغا *āghā*) Lords.

A اغوار *aghwār*, (pl. of غار *ghār*) Caverns, dens.

A اغواط *aghwāt*, (pl. of غائط *ghāʼit*) Low, flat, hollow grounds, especially where one may lie hid.

A اغوال *aghwāl*, (pl. of غول *ghūl*) Kinds of demons or evil spirits (called in the Arabian tales غول *ghūls*) supposed to haunt woods and church-yards, and to devour human bodies, alive or dead. Those who by the art of magic are imagined to have power to change themselves into various shapes. Serpents, dragons. Whatever suddenly attacks and destroys men, or deprives them of their senses from terror. Calamities, deaths.

A اغوثا *aghūsā*, Help!

P آغوز *āghūz*, The beastings of a sheep.

A اغوز *aghwaz*, Just, kind towards kindred.

P آغوش *āghosh*, An embrace. The bosom. As much as the arms can embrace or contain, an armful. A servant, slave. آغوش كردن *āghosh kardan*, (or در آغوش كردن *dar āghosh kardan*) To embrace, hold, comprehend, contain.

P آغوشيدن *āghoshīdan*, To embrace.

P آغول *āghol*, (or اغول) Side-glance, angry look.

A اغول *aghwal*, Soft, easy, comfortable (life).

A اغويّة *ughwīyat*, A dangerous place. A pit dug for a lion. Danger, difficulty, evil, misfortune.

A اغياء *ighyāʼ*, (v. n. 4 of غيي) Raising (a standard). Remaining stationary (a cloud).

A اغيار *aghyār*, Rivals. (pl. of غير *ghīr*) Expiations for murder.

A اغياض *aghyāz*, (pl. of غيضة *ghīzat*) Forests, places abounding in trees, but having little water. Haunts, dens.

A اغيال *aghyāl*, (pl. of غيل *ghīl*) Woods, thickets. Reed-beds, marshes. Lions' haunts. Valleys full of trees and water. *Ighyāl*, (v. n. 4 of غال for غيل) Yeaning twice a year (a sheep). Being thick and shady (a tree). Giving suck to a child whilst pregnant or cohabiting with a man.

A اغيام *ighyām*, (v. n. 4 of غام for غيم) Being cloudy (sky). Being overtaken or enveloped in mist.

A اغيان *ighyān*, (v. n. 4 of غان for غين) Fainting, losing consciousness. Pressing one (debt). Overpowering the heart (desire).

A آغية *āghiyat*, (pl. اواغي *awāghī*) A channel by which water is brought upon tilled ground.

A اغيد *aghyad*, One who nods when asleep. Waving, flexible and soft (plant). A place abounding in plants.

A اغير *aghyar*, More or most zealous, or jealous.

P آغيرس *āghīras*, A walnut.

P اغيس *aghīs*, A kind of grain.

P آغيشتن *āghishtan*, To embrace. To be embraced. To cut, mince, hash, macerate. To hang, to be suspended.

P آغيشيدن *āghishīdan*, To fear, to dread. To embrace. To cut.

A اغيف *aghyaf*, One who nods his head though not asleep. Easy, comfortable (life).

P آغيل *āghīl*, A squint, oblique look, turning the corner of the eye, looking askance with anger.

P اغيل *aghīl*, A sheep-cote.

A اغيلمة *ughaylimat*, (dim. of اغلمة) Little boys.

A اغين *aghyan*, Long, tall. Of a dark green colour, inclining to black.

P آف *āf*, The sun. The musk-deer.

P اف *uf*, Fie! for shame! اف گفتن *uf guftan*, To detest, to say Fie!

A افّ *aff*, (v. n. of افّ) Saying افّ *uffa*, Fie! for shame! *Iff*, Time, season. *Uff*, Paucity, scarcity. Nail-parings. Ear-wax. Dirt that gathers about the ears or nails. A stick or reed picked off the ground. *Uffa*, (A particle expressive of loathing and disgust, and which may be written in forty ways) Fie! for shame!

A افا *afa'*, (pl. of افاة *afāt*) Flocks of sheep. Clouds emptied of their water.

A افاء *ifāʼ*, (v. n. 4 of فأو for فاٴ) Lighting upon a bare place. Wounding the head, making a wide open wound.

A افاءة *ifāʼat*, (v. n. 4 of فاء for فيأ) Returning. Bringing, causing to return, leading back. Putting in possession of the riches of the infidels (God).

A افاة *afāt*, (pl. افا *afa'*) A flock of sheep.

A آفات *āfāt*, (pl. of آفة) Misfortunes, losses.

A افاتة *ifātat*, (v. n. 4 of فات for فوت) Causing (one) to pass by, to fly, to run, or to slip an opportunity. Letting, allowing to slip or pass by.

A افاتيخ *afātīkh*, Small white funguses.

A افاجة *ifājat*, (v. n. 4 of فاج for فوج) Making haste, running. Sending to water in troops.

A افاحة *ifāhat*, (v. n. 4 of فاح for فوح) Pouring forth, spilling, shedding. Making (a pot) boil.

A افاحيص *afāhīs*, (pl. of افحوص) Katas' nests.

A افاخة *ifākhat*, (v. n. 4 of فاخ for فوخ) Diffusing fragrance (perfumes). Making a hissing noise (as in making water). Breaking wind. (v. n. 4 of فاخ for فيخ) Prohibiting, averting. Being feeble (the hand). Repenting, regretting. An evacuation accompanied by an explosion of wind.

A افاخم *afākhim*, (pl. of افخم *afkham*) Greatest.

A افادة *ifādat*, (v. n. 4 of فاد for فود) Killing, causing to perish. Deriving advantage. Imparting advantage. (v. n. 4 of فاد for فيد) Giving or allowing profit, emolument, or advantage. Reaping advantage. Teaching, instructing. Denoting. Removing with the hand (ashes from off bread).

P افاده كردن *ifāda kardan*, To convey a meaning or signification, to denote. افاده و تصريح كردن *ifāda u tasrīh kardan*, To teach and demonstrate. افادهٔ كلام *ifādaʼi kalām*, The explanation of words. افادهٔ مرام كردن *ifādaʼi marām kardan*, To explain one's intentions. باب افاده كشاده كرد *bābi ifāda kushāda kard*, He opened the door of instruction, he began to teach. A (v. n. of وفد) Coming, arriving on an embassy.

A افاديّة *afādīyat*, Heating medicines, as cloves, cinnamon, &c.

A افارة *ifārat*, The act of causing to boil.

A افاريق *afārīk*, (or افارقة *afārikat*) (pl. of افراق *afrāk*, pl. of فرق *firak*, pl. of فرقة *firkat*) Sects, tribes, clans. Assemblies. افاريق العرب *afārīku'l ʻarab*, Tribes or clans of Arabians.

A افاز *ifāz*, (for وفاز *wifāz*) Haste.

A افازة *ifāzat*, (v. n. 4 of فاز for فوز) Enabling

(one) to obtain (his) wish or purpose.

A افاصة *ifāṣat*, (v. n. 4 of فاص for فوص) Speaking softly and gently. Letting (a word) escape. (v. n. 4 of فيص not in use) Making clear or evident. An evident declaration or clear expression of any thing. Escaping out of the hand, slipping through the fingers. Scattering (urine). Standing apart (the fingers) when grasping any thing.

A افاضة *ifāẓat*, (v. n. 4 of فاض for فيض) Dilating. Becoming diffuse in narrative. Filling (a vessel) till (it) overflows. Sprinkling or pouring water upon one's person. Shedding (tears). Rushing with impetuosity (as the Muhammadan pilgrims do down Mount عرفات *ʿarafāt* to the valley of مني *mina*). Striking with an unfeathered arrow. Playing with gaming arrows. Throwing up the food from the stomach (as the camel and other animals do when chewing the cud). A single effort, thrust, shove, or push.

A افاضل *afāẓil*, (pl. of افضل *afẓal*) Learned, virtuous, excellent. Philosophers, doctors. P در نزد افاضل *dar nazdi afāẓil*, Amongst the learned.

A افاطير *afāṭīr*, (pl. of افطور *ufṭūr*) Fissures in the nose and other parts of the face of a youth.

A افاظة *ifāẓat*, (v. n. 4 of فاظ for فيظ) Killing, tearing the soul from the body. Occasioning the death of another.

A افاعي *afāʿī*, (pl. of افعي *afʿaʾ*) Serpents, vipers. Certain veins or ramifications from the two veins called حالبين *hālibayn*.

A افاعيل *afāʿīl*, (pl. of افعال *afʿāl*, pl. of فعل *fiʿl*) Acts, actions.

A افاغنة *afāghinat*, (pl. of افغان) The Afghans.

A افاف *ifāf*, Timidity. Time, opportunity.

A آفاق *āfāḳ*, (pl. of افق *ufḳ*) Horizons, quarters of the heavens, of the world, or universe. The surface of a road.

A افاق *affāḳ*, One who travels much in search of knowledge.

A افاقة *ifāḳat*, (v. n. 4 of فاق for فوق) Recovering (from a distemper, insanity, or ebriety). Returning from scarcity to plenty (seasons). Returning to one who has been sick (health). Fitting the notch of the arrow to the bow-string when going to shoot. (A camel) collecting milk in the udder between the times of milking. The resting time between the milkings of cattle.

P آفاق گرفته *āfāḳ-girifta*, Celebrated, famous.

A آفاقي *āfāḳīy*, One who has travelled much. آفاقي مكه *āfāḳīy makka*, One who appears not at the spot where the pilgrims meet at Mecca.

P افاقيا *afāḳiyā*, A kind of liquid flowing from minerals, or expressed from acid substances.

A افاك *affāk*, Addicted to lying (افك *ifk*).

A افاكل *afākil*, The descendants of افكل *afkal*.

A افاكيل *afākīl*, Crowds, troops.

A افال *ifāl*, (pl. of افيل) Yearling camels: weanels.

A افآم *ifʾām*, (v. n. 4 of فأم) Enlarging, widening a (camel's) saddle.

P افام *afām*, Colour. Debt.

A افان *iffān* or *affān*, A convenient season, suitable time, proper opportunity.

A افاني *afānī*, (pl. of افانية *afāniyat*) Fox-grapes. *Ufānaʾ*, A sort of plant.

A افانيّ *afānīy*, A crowd. Fox-grapes.

A افانية *afāniyat*, (pl. افاني *afānī*) A species of herb. Fox-grapes.

A افانين *afānīn*, (pl. of افنون *ufnūn*) Reasons, ways, modes, forms, kinds, arts (of speaking). (pl. of افنان *afnān* pl. of فنن *fanan*) Many branches.

A افاوج *afāwij*, (or افاويج *afāwīj*) (pl. of فوج *fawj*) Troops, bodies, squadrons.

A افاويق *afāwīḳ*, (pl. of فيقة *fīḳat*) Milk collected in the udder between two milkings. Rains fallen at intervals. Larger parts of the night.

A افاويه *afāwīh*, (pl. of افواه *afwāh*, which is pl. of فوه *fūh*) Aromatics, spices.

A افائك *afāʾik*, (pl. of افيكة) Lies, falsehoods.

A افائل *afāʾil*, Yearling camels or sheep.

P افپونتن *afpūnitan*, (in zand and Pāzand) To cook. To ripen.

A آفة *āfat*, (pl. آفات *āfāt*) A misfortune, calamity. A murrain amongst cattle, blight amongst corn. P آفت ديو *āfati dev*, Pustules breaking out on the lips, from terror, whilst asleep. A ringworm. آفت سماوي *āfati samāwī*, A year of scarcity arising from too much or too little rain, locusts, &c.

A افة *uffat*, A poltroon, coward. Poor: filthy.

A افت *aft*, (v. n. of افت) Averting, keeping back, withholding. A she-camel very patient and tractable. A swift she-camel, out-stripping the males. A generous camel. A branch of the tribe of هذيل *huzayl*. *Ift*, A fruitful she-camel. A prodigy, portent, extraordinary calamity. A lie.

P افتا *uftā*, (part. of افتادن *uftādan*) Falling.

A افتاء *aftāʾ*, (pl. of فتيّ *fatīy*) Young in years. *Iftāʾ*, (v. n. 4 of فتا) Desisting, ceasing, discontinuing, abstaining from. Passing by. (v. n. 4 of فتي) Resolving a question of law, or a case of conscience. Publishing, proclaiming, making manifest. Causing to separate and to become distinct.

P آفتاب *āftāb*, (Sunshine) The sun. A day. Wine. The soul. آفتاب عالمتاب *āftābi ʿālam-tāb*, The world-illuminating sun. آفتاب عالمسوز *āftābi ʿālam-soz*, The sun inflaming the world. آفتاب زرد رو *āftābi zard-rū*, (The yellow-faced sun) A melon. آفتاب ساده *āftābi sāda*, The pure sun (an epithet of Solomon). آفتاب بر ديوار رفتن *āftāb bar dīwār* (or بر كوه *bar koh*) *raftan*, The termination of life, grandeur, prosperity, happiness.

P آفتاب پرست *āftāb-parast*, A worshipper of the sun. Sun-flower. A chameleon. A water-lily.

P آفتابچي *āftābachī*, A ewer-holder.

P آفتاب خانه *āftāb-khāna*, The sun's house (in an astronomical sense). A summer-house.

P آفتاب دزدك *āftāb-duzdak*, (Intercepting the sun) A kind of parasol made of reeds.

P آفتاب رو *āftāb-rū*, Exposed to the sun (spot).

P آفتاب سوار *āftāb-suwār*, An early riser.

P آفتاب گاه *āftāb-gāh*, (The sun's place) A sunny place. A sun-shining day. The equinox.

P آفتاب گردش *āftāb-gardish*, The surface of the earth. The chameleon.

P آفتاب گردك *āftāb-gardak*, (Turning to the sun) The chameleon. The sun-flower.

P آفتابگير *āftāb-gīr*, (Sun-catching) A parasol.

P آفتابناك *āftābnāk*, Sunny.

P آفتابه *āftāba*, A water-pot. Traveller's bottle.

P آفتابي *āftābī*, A kind of parasol. An embossed shield (in shape like the sun).

A افتاح *iftāḥ*, (v. n. 4 of فتح) Having the orifices of the dugs large and open (a she-camel).

A افتاخ *iftākh*, (v. n. 4 of فتخ) Being wearied and falling down with fatigue.

P افتادگان *uftādagān*, (pl. of افتاده) The fallen.

P افتادگي *uftādagī*, Humility. Vileness. A fall.

P افتادن *uftādan*, To fall. To befal, to happen. To submit. To perish, be ruined. To be distant.

P افتاده *uftāda*, Fallen. Weakened. Oppressed.

A افتار *iftār*, (v. n. 4 of فتر) Making relaxed, languid, weak (disease or drink). Having weak eye-lids.

P افتافيا *aftāfiyā*, A kind of liquid flowing from minerals, or expressed from acid substances.

A افتاق *iftāḳ*, (v. n. 4 of فتق) Enjoying an open clear sky (the clouds being divided and dispersed). Going out into a clear open space. Having fat cattle. Being oppressed with want, disease, or debt. Being, or arriving in, a country destitute of rain, whilst the neighbouring districts are plentifully watered. Finding an opening in the sky and appearing through it (the upper limb of the sun's disk). Cleaning the teeth with dry date-stalks.

A افتاك *iftāk*, (v. n. 4 of فتك) Daring to perpetrate whatever one meditates.

P افتال *iftāl*, Dispersed, scattered. Rent, torn.

A افتال *iftāl*, (v. n. 4 of فتل) Producing pods (the سلم *salam* or سمر *samur* trees).

P افتاليدن *iftālīdan*, To scatter, spread, disperse. To tear. To destroy, spoil. To cleave, break.

A افتان *iftān*, (v. n. 4 of فتن) Trying, proving. Tempting, seducing, fascinating. Filling with astonishment. Being harrassed with misfortunes. Bringing into trouble.

P افتان *uftān*, Falling. He who falls. افتان و خيزان *uftān u khezān*, (or افتان خيزان *uftān khezān*) Sometimes falling and sometimes rising. Limping. Creeping along softly.

P افتانيدن *uftānīdan*, To let fall, throw down.

P آفتاوه *āftāwa*, (equiv. to آفتابه *āftāba*) A ewer.

P افتايانيدن *uftāyānīdan*, To cause or let fall. To throw down.

A افتتاح *iftitāh*, (v. n. 8 of فتح) Opening. Endeavouring to open. A beginning, commencement. Conquest, reduction.

A افتتان *iftitān*, (v. n. 8 of فتن) Being tried (gold in the fire). Losing property and reason. Being tempted, seduced, falling into temptation. Being involved in rebellion. Seducing, leading astray.

A افتثاث *iftis̤ās*, (v. n. 8 of فثّ) Conquering.

A افتجاء *iftijāʼ*, (v. n. 8 of فجأ) Falling upon unexpectedly, rushing upon unawares.

A افتجار *iftijār*, (v. n. 8 of فجر) Inventing, trumping up a story.

A افتجال *iftijāl*, (v. n. 8 of فجل) Originating.

A افتحاث *iftihās*, (v. n. 8 of فحث) Examining, inquiring, investigating. Investigation.

A افتحار *iftihār*, (v. n. 8 of فحر) Following one's own way, acting without, or contrary to advice given.

A افتحاص *iftihās*, (v. n. 8 of فحص) Investigating, enquiring. Investigation, enquiry.

A افتحال *iftihāl*, (v. n. 8 of فحل) Choosing an excellent camel-stallion.

A افتحام *iftihām*, (v. n. 8 of فحم) Drinking wine at evening-tide.

A افتخ *aftakh*, One whose palms of hand, soles of feet, or joints of fingers, are soft and limber. Broad-footed (lion). Weak or dim-sighted.

A افتخاخ *iftikhākh*, (v. n. 8 of فخّ) Snoring.

A افتخار *iftikhār*, (v. n. 8 of فخر) Glorying, boasting. Glory, honour, grace. Elegance, gracefulness. افتخار الاماجد و الاكارم *iftikhāru'l amājid wa'l akārim*, The most glorious of the most honoured and most noble (a mode of address in writing to great men). P افتخار كردن *iftikhār kardan*, To glory (in any thing), to boast of.

P افتد *aftid*, Strange! A wonderful thing. Admiration. Praising. An encomiast.

A افتداء *iftidāʼ*, (v. n. 8 of فدي) Being redeemed. Ransoming one's self.

P افتدستا *aftid-sitā*, Eulogy, praise, laud.

P افتدن *uftadan*, To fall. To happen.

A افتراء *iftirāʼ*, (v. n. 8 of فرا for فرو) Putting on a robe of fur. (v. n. 8 of فري) Inventing a lie. Calumny, falsehood, imposition, unjust imputation. P افترا كردن *iftirā kardan*, To defame, invent lies, traduce.

A افترار *iftirār*, (v. n. 8 of فرّ) Showing the teeth in laughing. Smiling sweetly. Flashing (as lightning). Smelling at, snuffing up.

A افتراز *iftirāz*, (v. n. 8 of فرز) Cutting off.

A افتراس *iftirās*, (v. n. 8 of فرس) Tearing (his) prey (a lion). Hunting.

A افتراش *iftirāsh*, (v. n. 8 of فرش) Being spread on the ground. Spreading (the arms) on the ground. Treading upon, trampling. Conquering, throwing prostrate. Making free with and disparaging the reputation of another. Saying whatever one pleases. Prevailing against, dashing to the ground. Following the steps of another, tracking. Seizing another's goods.

A افتراص *iftirās*, (v. n. 8 of فرص) Seizing an opportunity (which is called فرصة *fursat*).

A افتراض *iftirāz*, (v. n. 8 of فرض) Enjoining, prescribing. Becoming extinct (a people). Receiving their presents or stipend (troops).

A افتراط *iftirāt*, (v. n. 8 of فرط) Losing (a son) under age. Escaping, being lost. Dying.

A افتراع *iftirāʽ*, (v. n. 8 of فرع) Deflowering.

A افتراغ *iftirāgh*, (v. n. 8 of فرغ) Pouring water (for one's self).

A افتراق *iftirāk*, (v. n. 8 of فرق) Being divided, separated. Removal, absence, distance, separation. Disparity. بحالت افتراق *ba hālati iftirāk*, In a state of separation.

P افتراكار *iftirā-kār*, A slanderer.

P افتراكاري *iftirā-kārī*, The habit of lying, slander.

A افترام *iftirām*, (v. n. 8 of فرم) Wearing a menstruous cloth (a woman).

P آفت رسيده *āfat-rasīda*, Afflicted, unlucky.

A افتزاز *iftizāz*, (v. n. 8 of فزّ) Terrifying, frightening. Being victorious.

A افتشال *iftishāl*, (v. n. 8 of فشل) Sitting on the فشل *fishl* in a camel-litter (a woman).

A افتصاد *iftisād*, (v. n. 8 of فصد) Opening a vein, bleeding. Venesection, blood-letting.

A افتصاص *iftisās*, (v. n. 8 of فصّ) Separating, dividing. Drawing one thing out of another.

A افتصاع *iftisāʽ*, (v. n. 8 of فصع) Drawing back the foreskin. Exacting payment of a debt.

A افتصال *iftisāl*, (v. n. 8 of فصل) Weaning. Transplanting. Disjunction, separation. Dissection.

A افتضاح *iftizāh*, (v. n. 8 of فضح) Being detected in villainy and publicly exposed. Being apparent, evident. Disgrace, dishonour, ignominy.

A افتضاخ *iftizākh*, (v. n. 8 of فضخ) Cleaving (the skull), breaking any hollow substance.

A افتضاض *iftizāz*, (v. n. 8 of فضّ) Being poured out (water). Arriving at running water. Pouring out water little and little. Deflowering (a virgin). Putting off mourning (a widow), by touching perfumes or otherwise. Rubbing her person with a living creeping thing or bird (which was then thrown away and rarely survived).

A افتظاظ *iftizāz*, (v. n. 8 of فظّ) Drinking (water) from the stomach of a camel.

A افتعال *iftiʽāl*, (v. n. 8 of فعل) Inventing a lie.

A افتقاء *iftikāʼ*, (v. n. 8 of فقأ) Going over stitches a second time. Fixing a third piece of leather between two pieces already wrapped about the handle of any thing to strengthen it.

A افتقاد *iftikād*, (v. n. 8 of فقد) Losing. Searching for a thing lost. Investigation, search.

A افتقار *iftikār*, (v. n. 8 of فقر) Becoming poor. Humbling one's self. Poverty. Self-abasement. بلسان تضرّع و افتقار *ba lisāni tazarruʽ u iftikār*, With the tongue of supplication and humility.

A افتكار *iftikār*, (v. n. 8 of فكر) Thinking.

A افتكاك *iftikāk*, (v. n. 8 of فكّ) Redeeming, releasing (a pledge or pawn). Liberation.

A افتكال *iftikāl*, (v. n. 8 of فكل) Attending to, heeding, minding.

A افتل *aftal*, (A man) with wide-set knees or hands. (A camel) whose elbow is far from his side.

A افتلاء *iftilāʼ*, (v. n. 8 of فلا for فلو) Weaning. Grazing. Bringing up, rearing, taking care of.

A افتلات *iftilāt*, (v. n. 8 of فلت) Speaking without premeditation, extempore. Dying suddenly.

A افتلاذ *iftilāz*, (v. n. 8 of فلذ) Taking a bit.

A افتلاص *iftilās*, (v. n. 8 of فلص) Taking out of a person's hand.

A افتلاط *iftilāt*, The being taken by surprise.

A افتلاق *iftilāk*, (v. n. 8 of فلق) Bringing out something wonderful (a poet). Exerting one's self to admiration in running. Performing a wonderful feat.

A افتلال *iftilāl*, (v. n. 8 of فلّ) Being notched, broken (a sword). Being broken up, routed, and put to flight (an army).

A افتلام *iftilām*, A mutilating (of the nose).

G آفتمون *āftimūn*, Dodder of thyme.

P افتن *uftan*, (contraction of افتادن) To fall.

A افتنان *iftinān*, (v. n. 8 of فنّ) Using different modes of speech.

P آفته *āfta*, Understood, comprehended.

A افتئات *iftiʼāt*, (v. n. 8 of فأت) Saying or feigning any thing false. Being singular in one's opinion. Dying suddenly.

A افتيات *iftiyāt*, (v. n. 8 of فات for فوت) Flying from, eluding the pursuit of justice. Passing by. Acting of one's self, without receiving authority from another. Innovating, producing or saying something new. Exercising authority, ordering, commanding. فلان لا يفتات عليه *fulānun lā yuftātu ʽalayhi*, Such an one, nothing is done except by his command.

A افتئاد *iftiʼād*, (v. n. 8 of فأد) Lighting a fire. Roasting.

A افتياق *iftiyāk*, (v. n. 8 of فاق for فوق) Becoming poor. Sobbing to death.

A افتئال *iftiʼāl*, (v. n. 8 of فأل) Taking as a happy omen (فال *fāl*), prognosticating.

P افتيدن *uftīdan*, To fall. To happen.

A افثاء *ifsāʼ*, (v. n. 4 of فثأ) Being weary, tired, fatigued, languid; stopping from fatigue to take rest, breathing short (after running). Preparing (for one sick) stones, warmed, and sprinkled with water, that he may recline thereon, to get a sweat.

A افثاج *ifsāj*, (v. n. 4 of فثج) Leaving. Being wearied. Panting, breathing hard. Being exhausted (a well).

A افثاح *afsāh*, (pl. of فثح) Paunches, bellies.

A افج *afajj*, Wide between the feet, straddling.

A افجاء *ifjāʼ*, (v. n. 4 of فجا for فجو) Being at a great family-expense.

A افجاج *ifjāj*, (v. n. 4 of فج) Striding, straddling, spreading, laying asunder. Travelling along a broad road between two mountains. Hastening, making haste, walking fast. Muting (an ostrich). Ploughing (the ground) rudely, tearing it up.

A افجار *ifjār*, (v. n. 4 of فجر) Reaching, attaining the hour of day-break. Getting to a fountain or spring, causing it to burst forth. Causing to burst. Discovering (any one) to be a wicked, lewd fellow. Fornicating. Swerving from truth, lying. Denying the faith. Bringing great wealth.

A افجاس *ifjās*, A boasting falsely.

A افجان *ifjān*, (v. n. 4 of فجن) Eating frequently of rue (فيجن *fayjan*).

A افجر *afjar*, More or most wicked, flagitious.

A افجرة *afjirat*, (pl. of فجار *fijār*) Battles fought between the tribes قريش *kuraysh* and قيس *kays* (so called from فجار *fijār*, wickedness, because they were fought during the sacred months, when, by the old Arabian law, fighting was prohibited).

A افجل *afjal*, Wide between the legs, straddling.

A افجم *afjam*, Thick about the chops.

A افجن *afjan*, One who is in the constant habit of eating rue (فيجن *fayjan*).

A افجي *afjaʼ*, (A camel) wide and straddling between the thighs, knees, and legs, from fatness.

A افجيج *ifjīj*, A valley, a channel, or hollow. Wide and spacious. Narrow and confined.

P افچه *ufcha* or *afcha*, A scare-crow, a malkin.

A افحاء *afhāʼ*, (pl. of فحا *faha'*) Onions, or any other kinds of herbs or seasonings, put amongst victuals whilst cooking. *Ifhāʼ*, (v. n. 4 of فيح irreg.) Tempering the noon-day heat.

A افحاث *afhās*, (pl. of فحث) Paunches, bellies.

A افحاج *ifhāj*, (v. n. 4 of فحج) Departing from any design, retracting any proposal. Making (cattle) straddle for conveniency of milking them. Turning on one's heel and running away.

A افحاش *ifhāsh*, A speaking filthily, obscenely.

A افحال *ifhāl*, (v. n. 4 of فحل) Lending a stallion-camel or horse to a neighbour's she-camels or mares.

A افحام *ifhām*, (v. n. 4 of فحم) Silencing (in an argument). Finding one so silenced. (Grief) rendering (one) unable to repeat a verse. Sobbing and being unable to breathe or cry. Bleating hoarsely (a ram). Discovering one to be ignorant of, insensible to, poetry. Letting the first shades of the night pass away.

A افحج *afhaj*, Bow-legged, one who walks with his toes turned in, and his heels turned out.

A افحل *afhul*, (pl. of فحل) Males, stallions.

A افحوص *ufhūs*, (pl. افاحيص) The kata's nest.

A افخ *afkh*, (v. n. of افخ) Striking the part of the head called bregma (يافوخ *yāfūkh*).

A افخاذ *afkhāz*, (pl. of فخذ *fakhz*, *fikhz*, or *fakhiz*) Thighs.

A افخار *ifkhār*, (v. n. 4 of فخر) Preferring, promoting. Regarding one as finer and more glorious than another. Bringing forth fine children.

A افخام *ifkhām*, (v. n. 4 of فخم) Honouring.

A افخر *afkhar*, Finer, finest, braver, bravest, more or most sumptuous.

A افخم *afkham*, Greater, greatest.

P آفد *āfad*, A nephew by the brother or sister.

A افد *afida*, (fut. يافد *ya-fadu*) He made haste.

A افد *afd*, (v. n. of افد) Making haste. Delaying, proceeding slowly. Approaching, coming suddenly. *Afad*, Despatch. Term, limit, appointed time. *Afid*, Who makes haste, or approaches.

P افد *afid*, Strange! Any thing wonderful. Admiration. Praising; a praiser.

A افداء *ifdāʼ*, (v. n. 4 of فدي) Exacting a ransom from a captive Being big-bellied. Making a store-room for dates. Gathering (dates) and selling (them). Dandling (an infant).

A افداح *ifdāh*, (v. n. 4 of فدح) Finding (a thing) difficult and oppressive.

A افدار *ifdār*, (v. n. 4 of فدر) Becoming languid and turning away (a stallion).

A افداس *ifdās*, (v. n. 4 of فدس not in use) Having spiders in one's cup.

A افدام *ifdām*, (v. n. 4 of فدم) Dyeing red.

A افدان *afdān*, (pl. of فدن *fadan*) Citadels or palaces covered with plaster.

A افدة *afadat*, Delay, procrastination.

P افدر *afdar*, (or افدره *afdara*) A nephew. An uncle.

P افدستا *afdistā*, Admiration, praise.

A افدع *afdaʻ*, (A man) whose wrist or ankle is distorted. One, the sole of whose foot does not touch the ground. Crooked-legged (camel). One, the sole of whose foot turns inwords. (A camel) whose leg is crooked from the groin to the foot.

P افديدن *afdīdan*, To wonder, to admire.

A افذ *afazz*, Unfeathered (gaming arrow).

A افذاذ *afzāz*, (pl. of فذ) Only, sole, singular.

A افر *afara*, (fut. يافر *yaʼfiru*) He overstepped.

A افر *afira*, (fut. يافر *yaʼfaru*) He made clear.

P افر *afr*, Bravo! Name of a place in Persia.

A افر *afr*, (v. n. of افر) Passing, running, leaping. Assailing, attacking. Banishing, driving away. Boiling vehemently. Being sultry. Being brisk, active in waiting upon, attending, or serving. *Afr* or *afar*, (v. n. of افر) Becoming fat and sprightly after having been worn with fatigue (a camel).

A افر *afurr*, Name of a town in Irāk.

P افرا *afrā*, Bravo! Well done!

A افرء *afruʼ*, (pl. of فرأ *faraʼ*) Wild asses, onagers.

A افراء *afrāʼ*, (pl. of فرأ *faraʼ*) Wild asses, or their colts. *Ifrāʼ*, (v. n. 4 of فري) Cutting or slashing (a skin, and thereby destroying it). Preparing, dressing. Ordering to be prepared or dressed. Tearing (as a wolf the lamb). Opening (a vein). Blaming, reprehending.

A افراث *ifrās*, (v. n. 4 of فرث) Piercing the stomach, or liver, and letting out the contents. Accusing one's associates. Throwing into trouble. Explaining (any matter) to the chiefs of the people. Bringing forward (a person) that he may be a butt for censure or ridicule.

A افراج *ifrāj*, (v. n. 4 of فرج) Discovering (a murder): finding out (a way). Going aside. Leaving.

A افراح *afrāh*, (pl. of فرح *farah*) Delights, joys. *Ifrāh*, (v. n. 4 of فرح) Cheering, gladdening. Crushing, oppressing, weighing (one) down (debt).

A افراخ *afrākh*, (pl. of فرخ *farkh*) Young (birds or beasts). Buds, sprouts, young herbs or grasses. Vile, abject (men). The fore-parts of the brain. *Ifrākh*, (v. n. 4 of فرخ) Bringing forth or hatching (beasts, birds). Producing a chick (an egg). Showing openly, manifesting, publishing. Appearing clear and distinct, after having been ambiguous and doubtful. Departing, being surmounted (fear). Subduing fear, tranquillizing the mind.

P افراختگي *afrākhtagī*, Elevation, exaltation.

P افراختن *afrākhtan*, To exalt, raise, elevate.

P افراخته *afrākhta*, Raised, elevated.

A افراد *afrād*, (pl. of فرد *fard*) Individuals, singular numbers, single ones. (Stars) remarkably conspicuous and bright when rising in the horizon. Unique, incomparable. *Ifrād*, (v. n. 4 of فرد) Being single, solitary, alone. Putting in the singular number. Entering upon or achieving (any work) alone and by one's self. Making solitary or alone. Performing a pilgrimage alone. Bearing one child. Appropriating to one's sole use. Sending an ambassador, apostle, or special messenger. Removing, deposing.

A افرار *ifrār*, (v. n. 4 of فر) Putting to flight. Cleaving (with a sword the head of another). Changing the first or milk-teeth (a horse or camel). Doing to anybody that from which he runs away.

P افراز *afrāz*, Exalted, elevated, erect, high. Summit, height. A protuberance. Refractory, contumacious. A pulpit. Membrum virile. Before. Near, beneath, below. An assembly, multitude. Henceforth, afterwards. Bound, closed. Open, displayed. Extended, enlarged. Ample, wide. A shoe, slipper. (contracted participle of افراختن *afrākhtan* or افراشتن *afrāshtan*, used in compos.) Raising, exalting. سرافراز *sar-afrāz*, Exalting the head. گردن افراز *gardan-afrāz*, Stretching out the neck.

A افراز *ifrāz*, (v. n. 4 of فرز) Separating, distinguishing. Exposing itself to the hunter (game).

P افرازانيدن *afrāzānīdan*, To exalt.

P افرازرخ *afrāz-rukh*, The most prominent part of the cheek. Having large cheeks.

P آفرازه *āfrāza*, A flame.

P افرازي *afrāzī*, Elevation, extension, exaltation.

P افرازيدن *afrāzīdan*, To exalt. To adorn.

P افراس *afrās*, A tent. The walls of a tent.

A افراس *afrās*, (pl. of فرس *faras*) Horses.

P افراس آب *afrāsi āb*, (Water-horses) Bubbles.

A *Ifrās*, (v. n. 4 of فرس) Having (a sheep) carried off by the wolf (especially through the inattention of the shepherd). (A timid man) leaving his ass or other beast in the jaws of the lion, and saving himself by flight. Taking part of a remnant and leaving a remainder.

P افراسياب *afrās-yāb*, (Conqueror of Persia) Name of an ancient king, celebrated in Persian poetry, sovereign of Tūrān, and a Scythian or Turk by birth. One who moves leisurely on the road.

A افراش *ifrāsh*, (v. n. 4 of فرش) Spreading carpets and the like, making beds, laying any thing under a person. Paving or strewing with stones. Locking, bolting, barring. Traducing or reviling another whilst absent. Abounding in mud dried on the surface of the ground (a place). Giving one a small camel unfit for burdens. Whetting, sharpening (a sword). Remaining behind, desisting.

P افراشانيدن *afrāshānīdan*, To cause to exalt.

P افراشتگي *afrāshtagī*, Exaltation.

P افراشتن *afrāshtan*, To exalt, extol, raise.

P افراشته *afrāshta*, Exalted, elevated, erect.

P افراشته قد *afrāshta-kad*, Tall, of high stature.

A افراص *ifrāṣ*, (v. n. 4 of فرص) Assisting, favouring (opportunity, called فرصة *furṣat*).

A افراض *ifrāẓ*, (v. n. 4 of فرض) Ordaining, appointing, prescribing, ordering any thing to be observed in point of religion or law (فريضة *farīẓat*). Giving. Amounting to such a number as to be subject to decimation or tithes (cattle or corn).

A افراط *afrāt*, (pl. of فرط *fart*) Small hills. Sign-posts. (pl. of فرط *furut*) High hills. The crepuscles, or first dawnings of light. *Ifrāt*, v. n. 4 of فرط) Sending before. Despatching an ambassador on special business. Sprinkling late the female palm with the male flowers, when the pods are ready to burst. Accelerating, hastening. Making haste. Precipitating, falling quick, raining hard. Moving with rapidity, clapping suddenly (one's hand to one's sword in order to draw it). Forgetting. Filling, cramming (a bag). Making a vessel to overflow. Overloading. Exceeding bounds. Excess, superfluity. افراط اخلاط *afrāti akhlāt*, (or P افراط خون *afrātī khūn*) Plethora.

A افراع *ifrāʻ*, (v. n. 4 of فرع) Descending (a hill). Alighting and residing with any one. Going round (any place) in order to survey or reconnoitre (it). Going before (a caravan) to provide provender and water. Beginning (any thing), making the exordium (of a speech). Maintaining, providing for one's family. Sacrificing (the firstlings of camels or sheep). (Camels) being delivered of their first colts. Being possessed of such camels. Hurting (a horse) in the mouth by the bit of the bridle). Lying with a bride, deflowering her. Observing blood at child-bearing, or before menstruation (a woman). Laying waste (a flock), imbruing (it) in (its) gore (a hyena).

A افراغ *afrāgh*, Certain places around Mecca. *Ifrāgh*, (v. n. 4 of فرغ) Emptying, pouring out. Shedding. Clothing. Putting on a garment.

A افراق *afrāk*, (pl. of فرق *farak*) Divisions, separations. Differences. Dispersions, scatterings. Dawns, mornings. Distances, intervals (as between teeth; the divisions of the hoofs of camels, oxen, &c.; the manes of horses; the combs of cocks; beards or locks of hair, &c.). Inequalities in the height of a horse's hips, one being higher than the other. (Plants) growing in scattered clumps. (pl. of فرقة *firkat*) Troops, squadrons, crowds, bodies of men. *Ifrāk*, (v. n. 4 of فرق) Recovering from an indisposition (particularly the small-pox, or such diseases as people are in general only subject to once in their lives. Giving to a woman in child-birth the preparation called فريقة *farīkat*. Recovering part of her milk (a camel). Turning (camels) loose to pasture. Causing to void excrement.

A افراك *ifrāk*, (v. n. 4 of فرك) Being ripe or ready for rubbing (an ear of corn).

A افرام *ifrām*, (v. n. 4 of فرم) Filling (a vessel).

A افران *afrān*, Merry, cheerful.

P افراه *afrāh*, Victuals distributed amongst prisoners in jail.

A افراه *ifrāh*, (v. n. 4 of فره) Bringing forth a lively colt (a camel). Acquiring a clever servant.

P افراهام *ifrāhām*, Abraham.

P افراي *afrāy*, (in compos.) Creating.

G افربيون *afarbiyūn*, Gum of the euphorbium.

A افرة *afarat*, A crowd, troop, confused assemblage. Mixture, confusion. Violence, severity. Adversity, sorrow. The first part of the summer.

A افرّة *afurrat*, Violence, or beginning of heat.

A افرج *afraj*, One whose fore-teeth are distant. One whose buttocks sit wide apart. One whose privities (فرج *farj*) are exposed through negligence.

A افرخ *afrukh*, (or افرخة *afrikhat*) (pl. of فرخ *farkh*) The young of birds or other animals; also young grasses or herbage. The anterior parts of the brain. Vile, abject (men).

P افردستا *afardastā*, A spear's point. A summit.

A افرس *afras*, Better or best horseman.

P افرسب *ifrasb*, A beam, a roof-beam.

A افرض *afraz*, Well instructed in the precepts of the Kur'ān. Better or best acquainted with the law of inheritance (both called فريضة *farīzat*).

A افرط *afrut*, (pl. of فرط *fart*) Small hills, the summits or protuberances on mountains. Sign-posts.

A افرع *afraʻ*, (pl. of فرع *farʻ* and فرعان *farʻān*) (A man) having a fine head of (hair) (such was ابو بكر *abū bakr*). A suggester of evil things.

A افرغ *afragh*, Free, ceasing from labour, having just finished a work. More or most unemployed, more or most free, more or most at leisure.

A افرغة *afrighat*, (pl. of فراغ *firāgh*) Vacations, leisures. Large water-vessels made of leather. Large-uddered (camels). Broad heads of javelins. Bows which shoot far and inflict deep wounds.

A افرق *afrak*, (A man, horse, or cock) having a فرق *farak*, q. v. (pl. فرق *furuk*) A white cock. (A ram) having his testicles wide asunder. Slit-lipped (man). (A horse) with one testicle, a ridgel.

A افرقاء *afrikāʼ*, (and افرقة *afrikat*) (pl. of فريق *farīk*) Troops, crowds, bodies.

A افرم *afram*, Broken-toothed (man).

A افرنباج *ifrimbāj*, (v. n. 3 of فرنج Q) Being dried before the fire (the outside of a lamb's skin).

A افرنج *afranj*, The Franks, French. The crusaders of all nations. The Christians in Palestine and other places in the East, and in general, all Europeans. حديد افرنج *hadīdi afranj*, The iron of Europe, *i.e.* steel. P افرنج رنج كردار *afranji ranj-kardār*, The desolation-causing Franks.

A افرنجام *ifrinjām*, (v. n. 3 of فرجم Q) Being scorched on the surface, and not roasted (meat).

A افرنجة *ifranjat*, A race of men, the Franks.

P افرنجمشك *afranjamushk*, Tamarisk-berries; a kind of sweet basil; the musk of Europe (so called by Asiatics on account of their excellent flavour).

A افرنجه *afranja*, Name of a city founded by Nūshīrwān; of a country in Eastern Africa, and of a tract in Arabia. A bugbear to frighten children.

P افرنجي *afranjī*, (A افرنجيّ *afranjīy*) A Frank.

A افرنجيّة *afranjīyat*, Europe, so called by the Arabians from the Franks or French; a name which they gave indiscriminately to all the nations of Christendom engaged in the crusades.

P افرنجيون *afrinjiyūn*, (in astr.) The lower apsis.

P افرند *afrand*, Splendour. Beauty. Dignity. *Ifrind*, A sword. The lustre of a polished sword, &c.

P افرنديدن *afrandīdan*, To decorate, embellish.

A افرنساخ *ifrinsākh*, (v. n. 3 of فرسخ Q) Being dispelled (grief), kept out (cold), removed (disease).

A افرنقاع *ifrinkāʻ*, (v. n. 3 of فرقع Q) Pulling the fingers till the joints crack. Making a cracking noise when pulled (the fingers). Being uncovered. Being removed. Retiring. Turning away the face. Running. Scattering.

P افرنگ *afrang*, Elegance, dignity, grace. Magnificence, grandeur, power. Magnitude. A throne. A crown. Provisions, necessaries. *Afrang* or *ifring*, A European, a Frank.

P افرنگان *afiringān*, A chapter of Zand-avastā.

P افروختگي *afrokhtagī*, Combustion, blaze.

P افروختن *afrokhtan*, To inflame, set on fire. To kindle. To blaze, to flame. To polish.

P افروخته *afrokhta*, Inflamed, lighted; shining, radiant. Polished, furbished. چراغ افروخته *charāghi afrokhta*, A blazing lamp. A dependant.

P افروز *afroz*, (in composition) Burning. Illuminating. بوستان افروز *bostān-afroz*, Dazzling the garden (the anemone). عالم افروز *ʿālam-afroz*, (or جهان افروز *jahān-afroz*) Inflaming the world. گيتي افروز *gīti-afroz*, Firing the universe. مجلس افروز *majlis-afroz*, Illuminating the banquet. معركه افروز *maʿraka-afroz*, Animating the battle.

P افروزا *afrozā*, Burning. Polishing.

P افروزانيدن *afrozānīdan*, To make burn, kindle.

P افروزندن *afrozandan*, To be burnt, consumed.

P افروزنده *afrozanda*, A polisher. One who sets on fire. Bright, shining, radiant.

P افروزه *afroza*, The wick of a lamp.

P افروزيدن *afrozīdan*, To kindle. To polish, to make bright. To shine, to be very bright.

G افروساليين *afrūsāliyīn*, The moon-stone.

P آفروشه *āfrosha*, (or افروشه *afrosha*) A kind of dish made of butter, honey, and flour. Bruised wheat or barley, and victuals dressed with it. A confection made of almonds. A dish made of yolk of egg, milk, and syrup.

P افروغ *afrogh*, The rays of the sun. The beams of the moon. The light of a candle.

P افرهنج *afrahanj*, Flax-seed.

P افري *afrī* or *afarī*, Well done!

P آفريدگار *āfrīdgār*, (or آفريدهگار) The Creator.

P آفريدگان *āfrīdagān*, Creatures, created beings.

P آفريدن *āfrīdan*, To create. Creating. Creation.

P آفريدون *āfrīdūn*, (or افريدون *afrīdūn*) See فريدون *farīdūn*.

P آفريده *āfrīda*, Created.

G افريز *ifrīz*, The coping of a wall: a projection or slab over a door. A brick-house. A botcher.

G افريسموس *afrīsmūs*, A priapism.

P افريشم *afrīsham*, Silk. The string of a musical instrument.

A افريقي *afrīkiy*, An African.

A افريقية *afrīkiyat*, Africa.

P آفرين *āfirīn*, Praise, glory, applause, encomium, benediction, blessing. Blessed. Well done! bravo! Name of the first of the five intercalary days of the Persian year. (in composition) The Creator: as, جان آفرين *jān-āfirīn*, Creating the soul. جهان آفرين *jahān-āfirīn*, (or عالم آفرين *ʿālam-āfirīn*) The Creator of the world. آفرين خواندن *āfirīn khwāndan*, To applaud. آفرين كردن *āfirīn kardan*, To praise, applaud. To bless. To describe. To create.

P آفرينا *āfirīnā*, (or آفريننده) The Creator.

P آفرين خانه *āfirīn-khāna*, An oratory.

P آفرينش *āfirīnish*, Creation. خداوند آفرينش *khudāwandi āfirīnish*, The Lord of the creation.

P آفرينگان *āfirīnagān*, Feasts held in honour of the memory of departed friends.

A افز *afz*, (for وفز *wafz*) An assault, an attack.

P افزا *afzā*, More. Greater. Yawning. Increasing, multiplying. A mover, causer (used in compos.): as, بهجت افزا *bahjat-afzā*, Promoting cheerfulness. روح افزا *rūh-afzā*, Soul-refreshing.

P A افزار *afzār*, A shoe. A weaver's comb. An artificer's tool. Any herbs or hot seasonings with which victuals are dressed. The sail of a ship.

A افزار *ifzār*, (v. n. 4 of فزر) Pulling to pieces (a cloak or covering for the body).

P افزارپا *afzār-pā*, A shoe, a slipper.

P افزاردان *afzārdān*, A vessel wherein they keep seasonings for meat, a spicery-box.

A افزاز *afzāz*, (pl. of فز *fazz*) Light men. Wild calves. *Ifzāz*, (v. n. 4 of فز) Frightening, terrifying.

A افزاع *afzāʿ*, (pl. of فزع *fazaʿ*) Terrors. *Ifzāʿ*, (v. n. 4 of فزع) Frightening, terrifying, confounding, distracting. Assisting, aiding, succouring, redressing wrongs. Apprising, certifying. Dispelling fear. Awakening one from sleep.

P افزانيدن *afzānīdan*, To multiply. To grow.

P افزايا *afzāyā*, Adding.

P افزايانيدن *afzāyānīdan*, To cause to increase.

P افزايدن *afzāyidan*, (or افزائيدن *afzāīdan*) To add. To exalt. To be exalted, to be high. To fall. افزايدن در قيمت چيزي *afzāyidan dar kīmati chīze*, To offer higher for any thing, to raise the price.

P افزايش *afzāyish*, Abundance, increase, increment, augmentation. افزايش كردن *afzāyish kardan*, To increase. To grow. افزايش نمودن *afzāyish namūdan*, To augment. To be augmented.

A افزر *afzar*, (A man) who has a protuberance on the back or breast.

P افزود *afzūd*, Increase, addition. More.

P افزودن *afzūdan*, To add, to increase. To be increased, multiply, abound, overflow, remain over.

P افزوده *afzūda*, Increased.

P افزون *afzūn*, More, greater. More ample, spacious. Manifold. افزون آمدن *afzūn āmadan*, To superabound, be redundant. To prevail, excel. افزون ماندن *afzūn māndan*, To remain over and above. روز افزون *roz-afzūn*, Increasing daily.

P افزونتر *afzūntar*, More, greater, more excellent.

P افزوني *afzūnī*, Increase, enlargement, abundance, excess, superfluity. افزوني كردن *afzūnī kardan*, To ask more than enough, to exceed bounds, to be unreasonable. افزونيء نان *afzūnīi nān*, The fermentation or raising of bread.

P افژردن *afjardan*, To throw away, cast down. To grasp, tie, or hold fast. To press, squeeze.

P افژول *afjūl*, Incitement, impulse. Urgency, exaction. Scattered, dissipated.

P افژولانيدن *afjūlānīdan*, To cause to drink and quench thirst. To cause to excite.

P افژولنده *afjūlanda*, Exciting. Expelling.

P افژوليدن *afjūlīdan*, To instigate, rouse, stir up. To render bold. To bring to a head. To importune, dun. To scatter. To shake off dust settled on a garment. To quench thirst.

P افسا *afsā*, Fascinating. A wizard, an enchanter.

A افسأ *afsaʾ*, Hollow-backed, or protuberant-breasted. One whose backside, loins, or thighs, give (him) pain in walking; or one who, sitting down, finds a difficulty in rising.

A افساج *ifsāj*, (v. n. 4 of فسج) Departing from.

A افساح *ifsāh*, (v. n. 4 of فسح) Being spacious and roomy (a place).

A افساد *ifsād*, (v. n. 4 of فسد) Corrupting, vitiating, destroying, adulterating. Spoiling, laying waste, damaging, injuring.

P افسار *afsār*, Fascinating. A headstall. افسار دم *afsāri dum*, A crupper.

P افساردن *afsārdan*, To press, squeeze, strain, constrain. To speak idly, obscenely, profanely.

A افسال *ifsāl*, (v. n. 4 of فسل) Cutting slips off (a palm-tree) to plant. Adulterating (coin). Rendering (furniture or wares) useless or of no value.

P افسان *afsān*, Fascinating. A magician. A fable, story. An event, accident. A whetstone. سنگ افسان *sangi afsān*, A whetstone. A hone.

P افسانانيدن *afsānānīdan*, To cause to relate.

G افسانوس *ifsānūs*, The ocean.

P آفسانه *āfsāna*, (or افسانه *afsāna*) A charm, incantation. A fiction, tale, fable, romance, parable. A narrative, a story of past events. Public, notorious, noted. افسانه و افسون *afsāna u afsūn* Fictions and deceitful tales. افسانه گفتن *afsāna guftan*, To speak parables, tell stories.

P افسانه گو *afsāna-gū* or *go*, A romancer.

P افسانه گوئي *afsāna-gūī*, Story-telling.

P افسانيدن *afsānīdan*, To tell stories. To extend, grow. To make straight. To tame, make obedient.

P افساي *afsāy*, An enchanter.

P افسايانيدن *afsāyānīdan*, To make tell stories.

P افساييدن *afsāyidan*, To subdue by magic.

A افسح *afsah*, More and most spacious, roomy.

A افسد *afsad*, More or most corrupt, mischievous.

P افسر *afsar*, A crown, diadem. A bridle, halter. افسر ديراعظم *afsari dayri aʿzam*, The sun. افسر سر *afsari sar*, The crown of the head. افسر سگزي *afsari sigzī*, A kind of musical instrument. Melody. افسر شدن *afsar shudan*, To be crowned.

P افسرآرا *afsar-ārā*, (Gracing the diadem) Title of a princess.

P افسرانيدن *afsurānīdan*, To cause to freeze. To cause to become languid, dull, melancholy.

P افسردگي *afsurdagī*, Congelation. Dejection.

P افسردن *afsurdan*, To freeze, congeal. To grow faint, feeble, dejected: to flag, wither.

P افسرده *afsurda*, Congealed. Melancholy.

P افسرده خاطر *afsurda-khātir*, Dispirited.

P افسرده دل *afsurda-dil*, Faint-hearted, low-spirited, dull, lifeless.

P افسرگر *afsargar*, Crested. A bird of paradise.

A افسق *afsak*, More or most wicked, villainous.

A افسل *afsul*, (pl. of فسل *fasl*) Worthless men. Vine-tendrils.

G افسنتين *afsintīn*, Wormword.

P افسو *afsū*, A fork. (in zand and Pāz.) Come then.

P افسور *ufsūr*, Shame. A kind of wild beast.

P افسوس *afsos*, Irritation, vexation, sorrow, concern. Wit, humour, jest. Tyranny, oppression. Error. Ridicule, derision. Ah! alas! افسوس داشتن *afsos dāshtan*, To ridicule, to banter, to play upon, mock, deride, despise, affront. To complain, to groan. To lament. To play, divert one's self.

G افسوس *afsūs*, Ephesus.

P افسون *afsūn*, An incantation, a fascination, verses used in spells. Fraud deceit. افسون خواندن *afsūn khwāndan*, To utter spells or incantations.

P افسون پژوه *afsūn-pijūh*, An enchanter, wizard.

P افسون زده *afsūn-zada*, Enchanted, deceived by magical arts.

P افسونكن *afsūn-kun*, A conjurer, wizard.

P افسونگر *afsūngar*, A magician, an enchanter.

P افسونگري *afsūngarī*, Magic, incantation.

A افشاء *ifshāʼ*, (v. n. 4 of فشا) Being proud, arrogant, playing the great man. (v. n. 4 of فشا for فشو) Divulging, revealing, disclosing. Having one's fortune increasing (in cattle or money).

P افشادن *afshādan*, To strain, squeeze, press. To speak obscenely, profanely, boorishly.

P افشار *afshār*, (in compos.) Speaking idly or obscenely. Fixing, inserting. Pressing, squeezing out (water). A weaver's treadle, that which he moves with his feet. An assistant, associate, companion, partner, or abettor. A tribe of Turkomāns.

P افشاردن *afshārdan*, To speak idly or obscenely. To press.

P افشارده *afshārda*, Pressed, squeezed.

P افشاري *afshārī*, A firm step.

A افشاغ *ifshāgh*, (v. n. 4 of فشغ) Striking (with a whip). Being good for little.

A افشال *afshāl*, (pl. of فشل *fashl*) Cowards.

P افشان *afshān*, (in composition) Dispersing, scattering, diffusing. A disperser. تيغ افشان *tegh-afshān*, Brandishing a falchion. خون افشان *khūn-afshān*, Shedding blood. درّ افشان *durr-afshān*, (or جوهر افشان *jawhar-afshān*) Scattering gems. غبار افشان *ghubār-afshān*, Raising dust. Making water. گل افشان *gul-afshān*, Strewing flowers.

P افشانانيدن *afshānānīdan*, To cause to scatter.

P افشاندن *afshāndan*, To disperse, scatter, strew. To diffuse, sprinkle, shed.

P افشانده *afshānda*, Dispersed, scattered, shed.

P افشانيدن *afshānīdan*, To scatter, shed. دست افشانيدن *dast afshānīdan*, To applaud, clap hands.

P افشردگي *afshurdagī*, A squeeze, pressure.

P افشردن *afshurdan*, To press, squeeze, strain, compress, express (juice). To make firm, solid.

P افشرش *afshurish*, Compression, sqeezing.

P افشرگر *afshurgar*, A press. An oil-presser.

P افشره *afshura*, Juice expressed from pomegranates, quinces, and other fruits or plants.

P افشره گر *afshura-gar*, An oil-maker.

A افشغ *afshagh*, One whose fore-teeth are distant or projecting. Wide-horned (ram).

P افشك *afshak*, (or افشنگ *afshang*) Dew.

P افشنه *afshana*, Name of a village near Bukhārā.

P افشو *afshū*, (in zand and Pāzand) Come.

P افشون *afshūn*, A kind of winnowing-machine.

P افشه *afsha*, Barley or wheat coarsely ground.

P افشين *afshīn*, Name of a very liberal person.

A افصاء *ifṣāʼ*, (v. n. 4 of فصا for فصو) Being freed from, or escaping (evil). Ceasing (rain). Having no game in his toils (a hunter). Being set at liberty. Retiring (as winter or summer).

A افصاح *ifṣāḥ*, (v. n. 4 of فصح) Explaining clearly, relating distinctly. Being clear, evident, and perspicuous. Dawning (the morning). (A sheep, &c.) giving biestings, after the poor or thinner milk is exhausted. Giving clear milk (a sheep). Being free from froth (milk). Being clear (urine). Speaking (Arabic) elegantly and classically. Celebrating the passover, keeping Easter.

A افصاحاً *ifṣāḥan*, Clearly, distinctly.

A افصاد *ifṣād*, (v. n. 4 of فصد) (Trees) having leaves bursting (from the buds).

A افصاص *ifṣāṣ*, (v. n. 4 of فصّ) Producing, drawing out. Separating, laying on one side.

A افصام *ifṣām*, (v. n. 4 of فصم) Ceasing, going off, abating, subsiding (rain or fever).

A افصح *afṣaḥ*, More or most eloquent. More or most elegant (phrase, or mode of expression).

A افصع *afṣaʻ*, One whose foreskin being drawn back, leaves the gland uncovered.

A افصم *afṣam*, Broken (ornament for the ankle) without separation.

A افضاء *ifẓāʼ*, (v. n. 4 of فضأ not used) Feeding, giving to eat. (v. n. 4 of فضا for فضو) Going out, abroad, into the fields. Opening one's mind, communicating a secret. Bursting (a woman). Laying the palms of both hands upon the ground (in prayer). Going in unto (a wife).

A افضاح *ifẓāḥ*, (v. n. 4 of فضح) Dawning, breaking forth (the morning). Bearing red, purple, or yellow dates (a palm-tree). Treating with ignominy.

A افضاخ *ifẓākh*, (v. n. 4 of فضخ) Beginning to be ripe or ready for pressing (as grapes).

A افضال *ifẓāl*, (v. n. 4 of فضل) Causing excess, making a surplus, leaving a residue or remainder. Conferring a favour, benefit, or grace. Surpassing, excelling (in quality), exceeding (in quantity).

A افضح *afẓaḥ*, Of a whitish colour. A prattler, a great talker. الافضح *al afẓaḥ*, The lion. The camel (from his whitish colour).

A افضل *afẓal*, More or most excellent, virtuous, distinguished, eminent, learned, noble. The best. افضل المرسلين *afẓalu'l mursalīn*, The most distinguished of apostles (an epithet of Muhammad).

A P افضلتر *afẓaltar*, Better. Best.

A افضليّة *afẓalīyat*, Pre-excellence, pre-eminence, superiority, transcendency.

A افطّ *afaṭṭ*, Flat-nosed.

A افطأ *afṭaʼ*, Flat-nosed. Pigeon-breasted.

A افطاء *ifṭāʼ*, (v. n. 4 of فطأ) Feeding, giving victuals or refreshment. Cohabiting much. Becoming bad after having been amiable (temper). Being ample and diffused.

A افطار *ifṭār*, (v. n. 4 of فطر) Breaking a fast. Causing one to breakfast. Being time to breakfast, arriving at the hour to do so. Not saturating (a hide) with the tanning material, stinting (it).

A افطام *ifṭām*, (v. n. 4 of فطم) Being ready for weaning (a colt).

A افطح *afṭaḥ*, Broad-headed. Broad-nosed. Crooked-wristed. A bull. A chameleon.

A افطس *afṭas*, Flat-nosed. Flat (nose).

A افطور *ufṭūr*, A slit in the nose or face of a youth.

A افظاء *ifẓāʼ*, The being bad-tempered.

A افظاع *ifẓāʻ*, (v. n. 4 of فظع) Finding troublesome or shameful (business). Being entangled in any thing of that nature. Being shameful, troublesome, and disagreeable.

A افظع *afẓaʻ*, More or most shameful.

A افعا *afʻaʼ*, Pleasant odours.

A افعال *afʻāl*, (pl. of فعل *fiʻl*) Actions, offices, functions. Verbs.

A افعام *ifʻām*, (v. n. 4 of فعم) Filling (a vessel or a house) with perfumes. Diffusing themselves (perfumes), filling the olfactory nerves. Enraging.

A افعنجاج *ifʻinjāj*, (v. n. 4 of فعج Q) Going fast.

A افعوان *ufʻuwān*, A venomous serpent, a viper.

A افعي *afʻaʼ*, (pl. افاعي *afāʻī*) A large venomous serpent, a viper. Perfumes, sweet scents.

P افعي زرد فام *afʻaʼi zard-fām*, A pen. A flame. افعي قربان *afʻaʼi kirbān*, A bow. Sagittarius. افعي كاه ربا پيكر *afʻaʼi kāh-rubā paykar*, (or افعي مرجان عصب *afʻaʼi marjān-ʻaṣab*) A flame.

A افعيعام *ifʻiʻām*, (v. n. 12 of فعم) Being filled to the brim and to overflowing.

P افعي ناك *afʻaʼnāk*, Swarming with vipers.

A افغاء *ifghāʼ*, (v. n. 4 of فغا for فغو) Shooting forth flowers (the privet). Being rotten (a palm-tree). Eating dates called فغا *fagha'*. Becoming poor from being rich. Becoming ugly after having been beautiful. Becoming intractable from being obedient. Inflaming with rage.

A افغار *ifghār*, (v. n. 4 of فغر) Opening the mouth.

A افغام *ifghām*, (v. n. 4 of فغم) Filling (a place) with scent. Filling (a vessel) with water.

P افغان *afghān*, Lamentation, groaning, complaint, cries for help. Alas! Name of a race long inhabiting the mountains between Kandahār and the river Indus. افغان كردن *afghān kardan*, To lament, to complain.

A افغان *afghān*, (pl. افاغنة) An Afghān.

P افغانستان *afghānistān*, Afghānistān.

A افف *afaf*, A little, a trifle. Grief, vexation.

A آفق *āfak*, Uncircumcised. *Āfik*, Very generous. Extremely swift (horse). Name of a horse.

A افق *afk*, (v. n. of افق) Dressing (leather) by tanning or thickening (it). Lying. Overcoming. Circumcising. Giving some more than others. Following one's own whim, being opiniated. Travelling over the world. Excelling in liberality. *Ufk* or *ufuk*, (pl. آفاق *āfāk*) The horizon. A tract or region of the earth. The space between the two posts of the portico of a house. *Afak*, (v. n. of افق) Excelling (especially in liberality or science, as a man; or in good blood, as a horse). Travelling over the world. (pl. آفاق *āfāk*) The surface of a road. *Afak* or *ufuk*, (pl. of افيق *afīk*,) Leathers not quite tanned, or, when tanned, unsewed or unused. *Afīk*, Famous for liberality or learning. *Ufuk*, Fleet (horse or mare).

A افقاد *ifkād*, (v. n. 4 of فقد) Depriving, stripping, bereaving.

A افقار *ifkār*, (v. n. 4 of فقر) Making poor. Turning the side towards the hunter and presenting an easy mark (game). Lending (a camel for riding or carrying burdens).

A افقاع *ifkāʿ*, A bad plight, evil case.

A افقال *ifkāl*, (v. n. 4 of فقل) Abounding in produce (land).

A افقاه *ifkāh*, (v. n. 4 of فقه) Giving to understand, letting know. Instructing in law and divinity.

A آفقة *āfikat*, The waist. (pl. of افيق *afīk*) Leathers not quite tanned; or, when tanned, unsewed or unused. (pl. of فواق *fuwāk*) Intervals between two milkings.

A افقة *ufkat*, The foreskin. *Afakat*, The waist. A burying of a hide that the hair may fall off.

A افقر *afkar*, Poorer, poorest.

A افقع *afkaʿ*, (pl. فقع *fukʿ*) Intensely white.

A افقم *afkam*, One whose front teeth of the upper jaw project beyond those of the under: also the contrary. Intricate (business). A man's name.

A افقيّ *ufukīy* or *afakīy*, One who has travelled much. افقيّ مكّه *afakīy makka*, One who appears not at the spot where the Mecca pilgrims meet.

A افك *afk*, (v. n. of افك) Inverting, overturning. Diverting from any purpose. Frustrating, disappointing. Rendering weak, silly, irresolute. Making (any one) lie. Being weak and silly. Receiving no rain and yielding no produce (ground). *Ifk*, *afk*, or *afak*, (v. n. of افك) Lying. *Ufk*, (pl. of افوك *afūk*) Liars. *Afak*, The place of union of the jaws in man or animals, and of the upper and lower part of the beak of a bird.

A افكّ *afakk*, One who has weak, relaxed shoulder-blades, slip-shouldered. The jaw.

A افكار *afkār*, (pl. of فكر *fikr*) Thoughts, meditations, opinions, advices. Concerns, cares. *Ifkār*, (v. n. 4 of فكر) Thinking, considering attentively.

A افكاك *ifkāk*, (v. n. 4 of فكّ) Being near foaling (a camel), being relaxed behind and having a full udder. Wanting the male.

A افكاه *ifkāh*, (v. n. 4 of فكه) (A camel) giving thick milk before foaling, from plenty of fresh grass.

A افكة *afikat*, A barren year.

A افكل *afkal*, Trembling, consternation, tremor. A species of green magpye. A troop, crowd. Name of the father of a tribe. جاؤا بافكلهم *jāʾū bi afkalihim*, They came in a crowd, tumultuously.

A افكوهة *ufkūhat*, A miracle, prodigy, wonder.

P افگار *afgār*, A wound. Soreness of back of a beast of burden. Lame, crippled, wounded. Fatigued, jaded. افگار شدن *afgār shudan*, To be fatigued. افگاري مي *afgāri may*, Intoxicated, overloaded with wine. دل افگار پر افكار *dili afgār pur afkār*, A fatigued mind full of cares.

P آفگانه *āfgāna*, (or افگانه *afgāna*) An abortion.

P افگانيدن *afgānīdan*, To cause to throw.

P افگن *afgan*, Throwing, casting away (in composition). بيخ افگن *bekh-afgan*, Throwing down trees. تاب افگن *tāb-afgan*, Casting forth flames. سنگ افگن *sang-afgan*, Throwing stones. كوه افگن *koh-afgan*, Overturning mountains.

P افگندگي *afgandagī*, A falling off, decay, abjectness. Servitude. Excrement.

P افگندن *afgandan*, To throw, to cast away, up, off, or down. To contend for equality. To subtract. از شمار افگندن *az shumār afgandan*, To subtract.

P افگندني *afgandanī*, Fit only to be thrown away, refuse. The subtracter.

P افگنده *afganda*, Thrown away. Subtracted. Vile, abject. A slave.

P افگنده سم *afganda-sam*, Weakness, impotency. Lamentation.

A آفل *āfil*, (pl. اوافل *awāfil*) Setting, declining (sun). Pregnant (lioness).

A افل *afl* or *afal*, (v. n. of افل) Becoming dry (a mother). *Afal*, (v. n. of افل) Being brisk, lively.

A افلّ *afall*, (A sword) broke, jagged, nicked, or notched in the edge. Name of a sword.

A افلاء *aflāʾ*, (pl. of فلو *falūw*) Horse-colts when weaned from sucking. (pl. of فلاة *falāt*) Deserts. *Iflāʾ*, (v. n. 4 of فلا for فلو) Weaning (an infant or colt). Possessing a weaned colt. Having a colt fit to wean. Going to, or arriving at, a desert.

A افلات *iflāt*, (v. n. 4 of فلت) Escaping, flying away, giving the slip. Setting at liberty. Aiding (one) to make (his) escape, or to give the slip.

A افلاج *aflāj*, (pl. of فلج *falaj*) Rivulets, brooks. Waters streaming from the eyes. *Iflāj*, (v. n. 4 of فلج) Liberating, setting free, granting an escape. Rendering superior. Obtaining a triumph. Escaping, getting clear. Publishing, proclaiming, making evident, clear, and manifest. Justifying or espousing a cause. Establishing an argument or proof. Victory, triumph.

A افلاح *iflāh*, (v. n. 4 of فلح) Prospering, living. Escaping, obtaining a victory. Prosperity, success.

A افلاذ *aflāz*, (pl. of فلذ *filz*) The livers of camels. (pl. of فلذة *filzat*) Parts, pieces, segments. The treasures of the earth.

A افلاس *iflās*, (v. n. 4 of فلس) Becoming bankrupt. Penury, want. Insolvency, bankruptcy.

A افلاص *iflās*, (v. n. 4 of فلص) Being delivered, obtaining deliverance; escaping.

A افلاط *iflāt*, (v. n. 4 of فلط) Setting at liberty. Surprising, coming on, attacking. Escaping.

G افلاطون *aflātūn*, Plato, whom the Arabians call often افلاطون الٰهيّ *aflātūn ilāhīy*, The divine Plato. Gum bdellium.

A افلاق *aflāk*, Separate particles: small fragments (of an egg). *Iflāk*, (v. n. 4 of فلق) Bringing out something wonderful (a poet). Bringing misfortune.

A افلاك *aflāk*, (pl. of فلك *falak*) Heavens. Celestial orbits, heavenly bodies. *Iflāk*, (v. n. 4 of فلك) Being round (a damsel's breasts).

P افلاك شناسان *aflāk-shināsān*, Astronomers.

P افلاك ظلّ *aflāk-zill*, The shadow of heaven. Powerful protection.

P افلاكيان *aflākiyān*, Worshippers of the heavenly bodies. Stars and planets. Celestials.

A افلال *aflāl*, (pl. of فلّ *fall*) Routed (hosts). *Aflāl*, (pl. of فلّ *full* or *fill*) Grounds without rain or produce, deserts. *Iflāl*, (v. n. 4 of فلّ) Being spoiled of one's property. Travelling in a country destititute of rain and vegetation.

A افلة *afilat*, Pregnant (lioness).

A افلج *aflaj*, One who has wide-set teeth. One whose hands and breasts are wide apart.

A افلح *aflah*, Chapped, cut on the under lip.

A افلس *aflas*, Poorer, poorest. *Aflus*, (pl. of فلس *fals*) Small coins. Scales of fish. Bosses on the backs of books or on bridles.

A افلك *aflak*, One who moves round a circular hillock or sand-hill (called فلكة *falkat*).

P افلنجه *iflunja*, Name of a seed resembling mustard-seed, but of a fragrant smell.

A افلود *uflūd*, A grown youth, soft, easy, and fat.

A افليج *iflīj*, Name of a place. *A* Palsied.

A افليكان *iflīkāni*, Two bits of flesh encompassing the uvula.

A افن *afn*, (v. n. of افن) Weakening, impairing (the understanding). Exhausting the milk in (a camel's) udder, either by milking or sucking. Exhausting the udder (a camel's colt). Milking a camel at an unusual hour (which injures the animal). Having little milk (a camel). A sort of plant. *Afn* or *afan*, (v. n. of افن) Being bad and rotten (food or a nut). *Afan*, (v. n. of افن) Being weak of intellect. Weakness of intellect.

A افناء *afnāʾ*, افناء الناس *afnāʾu'n nās*, Men

unknown. *Ifnāʼ*, (v. n. 4 of فنى) Consuming, ruining, destroying, annihilating. P افنائ كفّار كردن *ifnāʼi kuffār kardan*, To destroy the infidels.

A افناد الليل *afnādu'l layl*, equivalent to اركان الليل *arkānu'l layl*. *Ifnād*, (v. n. 4 of فند not in use) Labouring under an imbecility of mind, doting. Telling a lie. Charging with mental imbecility.

A افنادًا *afnādan*, Singly, without a leader. In crowds of 30,000 men or 60,000 angels.

A افناق *afnāk*, (pl. of فنيق *funīk*) Large fine camels, kept as stallions. *Ifnāk*, (v. n. 4 of فنق) Living elegantly after having suffered difficulties.

A افناك *afnāk*, (pl. of فنك *funk*) Hay-weasels. Martens. Ferrets. Beavers. *Ifnāk*, (v. n. 4 of فنك) Insisting, urging, persevering. Lying. Sticking close to.

A افنان *afnān*, (pl. of فنّ *fann* and فنن *fanan*) Branches. (pl. of فنّ *fann*) Ways, manners, kinds.

A افنة *afinat*, (A camel) having little milk.

G افنجيون *afanjiyūn*, Apogeon.

P آفند *āfand*, War, strife.

P آفنداك *āfindāk*, The rainbow.

T افندي *afandī*, (pronounced *effendi*) A lord, master, gentleman.

P آفنديدن *āfandīdan*, (or افنديدن *afandīdan*) To stir up strife, enmity, or war.

A افنون *afnūn*, A mode, manner, form (of doctrine or prayer). *Ufnūn*, A various or involved kind of speech or prayer. A serpent. A languid old woman. A misfortune. Luxuriant, entangled branches. A mixed kind of running between that of a horse and camel. Beginning (of youth).

A افنيٰ *afnaʼ*, Different-coloured (hair). Fine and long (hair).

A افنية *afniyat*, (pl. of فناء *fināʼ*) Courts, areas.

A افنيك *ifnīk*, The joint of the chin-jaw. The side of the chin. The root of the tail.

A افوات *afwāt*, (pl. of فوت *fawt*) Spaces between the fingers.

A افواج *afwāj*, (pl. of فوج *fawj*) Crowds, troops, herds, flocks. Armies. افواج قاهرة *afwāji kāhira*, A victorious army. افواجًا *afwājan*, In crowds.

A افواح *afwāh*, (pl. of فوح *fawh*) Fragrant substances, odours.

A افواف *afwāf*, (pl. of فوف *fūf*) Membranes. White spots which grow at the ends of the nails. Whitish grains in the heart of the date-stones, from which originate the palm-trees. Things. برد افواف *burdu afwāfin*, A thin striped stuff.

A افواق *afwāk*, (pl. of فوق *fūk*) Notches of arrows. (pl. of فيقة *fīkat*) The milk in the udders (of camels) collected between the hours of milking.

A افواه *afwāh*, (pl. of فوه *fūh*) Mouths. The mouths or entrances of rivers or streets, embouchures. Modes, sorts, kinds. Aromatic herbs, whence odours and ointments are extracted.

A افواهي *afwāhī*, Famed, reported, noised abroad.

A افؤد *ufʼud*, Bread baked in the ashes.

P افور *ufūr*, An owl. A belch, eructation.

A افور *ufūr*, (v. n. of افر) Leaping, jumping, bounding, springing, running swiftly. Promptitude, activity (in serving). A driving away.

A افؤس *afʼus*, (pl. of فأس *faʼs*) Axes, hatchets.

A افوغ *afwagh*, Thick-mouthed.

A افوف *afūf*, Swift, active, keen, bustling. The young of a species of Asiatic woodcock.

A افوفة *ufūfat*, Frequent repetition of the word *uf*.

A افوق *afwak*, Broken-notched (arrow). افوق ناصل *afwak nāsil*, A broken arrow, without head or point. Broken fortune, bad luck.

A افوقة *afwikat*, (pl. of فواق *fuwāk*) Intervals between two milkings.

A افوك *afūk*, (pl. افك *ufk*) A liar. *Ufūk*, (v. n. of افك) Lying.

A افؤل *afʼul*, (pl. of فأل *faʼl*) Omens.

A افول *ufūl*, (v. n. of افل) Setting (the sun).

A افوه *afwah*, Large-mouthed. One whose teeth project, or are very long. Name of a poet.

A افهاء *ifhāʼ*, (v. n. 4 of فها for فهو) Auguring, taking an omen. Erring, mistaking (judgment).

A افهار *afhār*, (pl. of فهر *fihr*) Stones, held in the hand, for breaking nuts or pounding drugs: mullers. *Ifhār*, (v. n. 4 of فهر) Celebrating a Jewish festival (called *Purim*). Coming to the synagogue or college. Lying with a woman, and, before consummation, lying with another and consummating. Lying with a girl within the hearing of another. (Both these practices are forbidden by the Sunna or book of Muhammadan traditions). Circumcising a girl. Lying in collops or separate masses (flesh or fat). Lagging, or perishing on the road.

A افهاق *ifhāk*, (v. n. 4 of فهق) Filling (a bottle). Branding (a camel) on the first joint of the neck. Spreading, extending itself wide.

A افهام *afhām*, (pl. of فهم *fahm*) Intellects, understandings. *Ifhām*, (v. n. 4 of فهم) Giving to understand, making comprehend, teaching.

A افهاه *afhāh*, (pl. of فاه *fāh*) Mouths. *Ifhāh*, (v. n. 4 of فهه) (God) visiting any one with an impediment of speech, striking dumb. Causing to forget.

A افهد *afhud*, (pl. of فهد *fahd*) Hunting panthers, cheetas (in Persian called يوز *yūz*).

A افهم *afham*, More or most intelligent.

A افهود *ufhūd*, Fat, jolly (boy) near puberty.

A افياء *afyāʼ*, (pl. of فيء *fayʼ*) Shadows. Tributes. Preys. Returns. Bevies of birds.

A افياف *afyāf*, (pl. of فيف *fayf*) Level (grounds). Deserts without water.

A افياق *ifyāk* (v. n. 4 of فاق for فيق) Bringing out something wonderful (a poet).

A افيال *afyāl*, (pl. of فال *fāl*, فيل *fīl* or *fayl*) Weak in mind. (pl. of فيل *fīl*) Elephants.

A افيح *afyah*, Roomy (house). Wide (ocean).

A افئدة *afʼidat*, (pl. of فؤاد *fuʼād*) Hearts. Livers. Lungs.

A افيق *afīk*, (pl. افق *afak*, *ufuk*, and آفقة *āfikat*) Leather not quite dressed by the tanner; also leather fit for sewing, but not used. Famous for liberality or learning. Capacious (bucket).

A افيقة *afīkat*, Leather tanned fit for sewing, but not yet cut. A misfortune, strange, unheard of.

A افيك *afīk*, A liar. Weak in intellect, simple, irresolute. Self-deceived.

A افيكة *afīkat*, (pl. افائك *afāʼik*) A lie.

A افيل *afīl*, A yearling camel. A weanel.

P افيلون *afīlūn*, The wormwood of Pontus.

A افين *afīn*, Barren of genius, void of prudence. A vain boaster. A child or young camel weaned from the mother. Corrupted.

P افيوس *afyūs*, A wild radish.

A افيون *ifyawn*, Opium, poppy-juice. Black.

A افيوني *ifyūnī*, An opium-eater. P افيوني چيزي شدن *ifyūnī chīze shudan*, To adopt a custom, habit.

A اقاء *ikāʼ*, That by which a thing is preserved.

A اقاءة *ikāʼat*, (v. n. 4 of قاء for قيأ) Making vomit.

A اقاتة *ikātat*, (v. n. 4 of قات for قوت) Being able, powerful. Feeding (a fire).

A اقاحة *ikāhat*, (v. n. 4 of قاح for قوح) Deliberately refusing after being asked. Being purulent.

A اقاحي *akāhī*, Beginnings, preludes of things. (pl. of اقحوان *uk-huwān*) Camomiles, anthemis.

A اقادة *ikādat*, (v. n. 4 of قاد for قود) Giving (a horse) to be led. Giving a number (of horses). Punishing by the law of retaliation, eye for eye, &c. Ordering a slayer to be killed. Preceding, going before. Excelling. Spreading wide (rain).

A اقادح *akādih*, (pl. of قدح *kidh*) Arrows, ere they have received heads or wings.

A اقارب *akārib*, (pl. of قريب *karīb*) The nearest kindred, kinsmen, relations. P اقارب و خويشان *akārib u khweshān*, Kindred and allies, or relations.

A اقارع *akāriʻ*, Hard, strong (men).

G اقارون *akārūn*, Sweet flag. Wild myrtle.

A اقازل *akāzil*, (pl. of اقزل) Wolves. Snakes.

A اقاسم *akāsim*, (pl. of اقسومة) Parts, portions.

A اقاسيم *akāsīm*, (pl. of قسم *kism*) Parts, portions (of goods), allotments. Portions or shares divided amongst servants.

A اقاصر *akāsir*, (pl. of اقصر *aksar*) Very short.

A اقاصي *akāsī*, pl. of اقصيٰ *aksaʼ* Extreme parts.

A اقاضة *ikāzat*, The act of breaking, splitting.

A اقاط *ikāt*, (for وقاط *wikāt*) Hollows in mountains or hard grounds, where water collects.

A اقاطع *akātiʻ*, (pl. of قطيع *katīʻ*) Loppings, or small branches of trees, of which arrows are made.

A اقاطيع *akātīʻ*, (pl. of قطيع *katīʻ*) Herds, flocks.

G اقاقيا *akākiyā*, The acacia. All kinds of juices expressed from any thing of a styptic quality; but particularly juice of the pods of an Egyptian thorn.

P آقال *ākāl*, Any thing useless or worthless. Any kind of parings or husks, &c.

A اقالة *ikālat*, (v. n. 4 of قال for قول) Imputing to any one, or alleging that he said or did such a thing. (v. n. 4 of قال for قيل) Breaking a contract or engagement, declining to complete a bargain, rendering void, cancelling. Passing over a sin, forgiving slips and falls. Giving drink at mid-day.

A اقاليم *akālīm*, (pl. of اقليم *iklīm*) Climates, climes, countries, regions, kingdoms. اقاليم سبعه *akālīmi sabʻa*, The seven climates, the whole world.

A اقامة *ikāmat*, (v. n. 4 of قام for قوم) Stopping, resting, staying, standing still. Causing to stand. Constituting, appointing. Setting up, fixing. Perpetrating. Being intent (upon any thing). Causing to sit. Making straight. Persevering, persisting. Being earnest and persevering in prayer or supplication: urging, pressing. P اقامت حدود كردن *ikāmati hudūd kardan*, To put the laws in execution. اقامت خيام كردن *ikāmati khiyām kardan*, To pitch a tent. اقامت شهود آوردن *ikāmati shuhūd āwardan*, To bring or set up witnesses.

A اقانيم *akānīm*, (pl. of اقنوم) Persons; hypostases.

A اقاوز *akāwiz*, (pl. of قوز) Round hills of sand.

A اقاوم *akāwim*, (or اقاويم *akāwīm*) (pl. of قوم) Peoples, nations, tribes, families, men and women.

A اقاويز *akāwīz*, (pl. of قوز) Circular sand-hills.

A اقاويل *akāwīl*, (pl. of اقوال *akwāl*, which is pl. of قول *kawl*) Sayings, speeches, words. Opinions. Agreements, compacts, bargains.

A اقائم *akāʼim*, (pl. of قوم) Peoples, nations.

A اقبّ *akabb*, (pl. قبّ *kubb*) Slender-waisted.

A اقباح *ikbāh*, (v. n. 4 of قبح) Finding or discovering to be ugly or deformed (قبيح *kabīh*). Acting shamely, villainously, basely.

A اقبار *ikbār*, (v. n. 4 of قبر) Making a grave or tomb (قبر *kabr*) for one. Giving over to a tribe their dead for interment. Ordering or causing to be buried (and not to be thrown to the dogs).

A اقباس *ikbās*, (v. n. 4 of قبس) Giving (fire). Permitting another to light his fire from one's own. Asking for fire for another. Teaching, imparting knowledge, making clever and learned.

A اقباض *ikbāz*, (v. n. 4 of قبض) Making or fitting a handle (قبضة *kabzat* to a sword or knife).

A اقبال *ikbāl*, (v. n. 4 of قبل) Approaching, advancing, coming. Turning (the face) towards any person, thing, or place. Adhering steadily to. Recovering. Admitting, consenting, accepting (a bond, &c.). Placing over against. Applying successfully (to any thing). Supplying a shoe with the thongs called قبال *kibāl*. Looking towards the tip of the nose (the eye). Directing the eye towards the tip of the nose. Becoming intelligent after having been foolish. Approach, advance. Good fortune, prosperity, felicity. P اقبال نمودن *ikbāl namūdan*, To promise, agree, engage. اقبال يك هفته *ikbāli yak hafta*, Short-lived prosperity.

A اقبالاً *ikbālan*, Prosperously.

A اقبالة *ikbālat*, The slit part of the ears turned towards the fore part of the head. A bit of leather tied to (a sheep's ear) and left to dangle.

P اقبالمند *ikbālmand*, Prosperous, fortunate.

A اقبان *ikbān*, (v. n. 4 of قبن) Being routed. Running fast without fear.

A اقبح *akbah*, More or most base, mean, infamous. More or most ugly and objectionable.

A اقبس *akbas*, One whose glans protrudes prior to circumcision.

A اقبص *akbas*, One whose head is large and round. One who, in walking, throws up the dirt with his toes which falls where he sets his heel.

A اقبل *akbal*, One who squints inwardly.

A اقبية *akbiyat*, (pl. of قباء *kabāʼ*) Vestures.

A اقبيلال *ikbīlāl*, (v. n. 11 of قبل) Looking to the tip of the nose, being squint-eyed (اقبل *akbal*).

A اقبئنان *ikbiʼnān*, (v. n. 3 of قبأن Q) Drawing one's self. Being contracted.

A اقت *akt*, (v. n. of اقت) Fixing a time. (for وقت *wakt*) A definite time, a fixed hour.

A اقتاب *aktāb*, (pl. of قتب *kitb*) Intestines. (pl. of قتب *katab*) Saddles, pannels, dorsers for camels. *Iktāb*, (v. n. 4 of قتب) Saddling (a camel). Taking a solemn oath.

A اقتاد *aktād*, (pl. of قتد *katad*) The timbers of a packsaddle. (pl. of قتاد *katād*) Tragacanths.

A اقتار *aktār*, (pl. of قتر *kutr* and *kutur*) Coasts, shores, banks, margins, tracks (of the heavens), sides, parts, districts. *Iktār*, (v. n. 4 of قتر) Being parsimonious and screwing in one's expenditure. Keeping domestics on short commons. Sending forth a flavour (as meat, when dressing or otherwise). Perfuming with the wood of aloes (a woman). Lying hid in his lurking-place (a hunter). Adhering, sticking to. Being reduced to poverty.

A اقتال *aktāl*, (pl. of قتل *kitl*) Enemies, adversaries. Companions, associates, friends, seconds, cousins, relations. Brave, gallant, strong men. Horns. *Iktāl*, (v. n. 4 of قتل) Exposing (to danger or death), giving up to be killed.

A اقتان *iktān*, (v. n. 4 of قتن) Being scarce (as meat). Destroying the vermin called tike. Having little meat. Being lean or emaciated.

A اقتباء *iktibāʼ*, (v. n. 4 of قبا for قبو) Dressing, preparing. Making up cloth into the garment kabā.

A اقتباب *iktibāb*, The act of cutting off (the hand).

A اقتباس *iktibās*, (v. n. 8 of قبس) Borrowing, taking (fire from another). Acquiring knowledge. Imparting (knowledge). Asking. A quotation.

A اقتباع *iktibāʻ*, (v. n. 8 of قبع) Bending inward the mouth of a leathern bottle, when going to drink.

A اقتبال *iktibāl*, (v. n. 8 of قبل) Beginning, commencing. Extemporizing the خطبة *khutba*.

A اقتتاب *iktitāb*, The act of saddling (a camel).

A اقتتات *iktitāt*, (v. n. 8 of قتّ) Eradicating.

A اقتتال *iktitāl*, (v. n. 8 of قتل) Dying (from love or insanity). Fighting, slaying one another.

A اقتثاث *iktisās*, (v. n. 8 of قثّ) Tearing up.

A اقتثاد *iktisād*, (v. n. 8 of قثد) Cutting, or reaping the cucumber called قثد *kasad*.

A اقتثار *iktisār*, (v. n. 8 of قثر) Using, adopting any thing as household furniture (قثرة *kasarat*).

A اقتثام *iktisām*, (v. n. 8 of قثم) Eradicating. Sweeping off much wealth. Collecting.

A اقتحاء *iktihāʼ*, (v. n. 8 of قحو) Taking, seizing.

A اقتحاش *iktihāsh*, (v. n. 8 of قحش) Enquiring, examining, ascertaining.

A اقتحاف *iktihāf*, (v. n. 8 of قحف) Drinking the contents of a cup. Sweeping all away (rain).

A اقتحام *iktihām*, (v. n. 8 of قحم) Rushing headlong. Engaging in an enterprise rashly. Rushing among the females unsent (a he-camel). Despising, holding in contempt. Setting (a star).

A اقتد *aktud*, (pl. of قتاد *katād*) Tragacanths.

A اقتداء *iktidāʼ*, (v. n. 8 of قدا for قدو) Imitating. Following. P اقتدا كردن *iktidā kardan*, To take example, to make one an exemplar (قدوة *kudwat*).

A اقتداح *iktidāh*, (v. n. 8 of قدح) Striking fire with a flint and steel. Taking gravy out of a pot with a ladle. Managing, disposing, regulating.

A اقتداد *iktidād*, (v. n. 8 of قدّ) Arranging, regulating. Cutting, tearing lengthwise: cutting up by the root. Separating, distinguishing, analysing.

A اقتدار *iktidār*, (v. n. 8 of قدر) Being powerful or able. Power, authority. Boiling or dressing (in a pot). Dignity, excellence. صاحب اقتدار *sāhib iktidār*, A powerful, capable, or able man. P پادشاه بلند اقتدار *pādshāhi baland-iktidār*, A king of high authority, a most potent monarch. گردون اقتدار *gardūn-iktidār*, Powerful as heaven.

A اقتذاء *iktizāʼ*, A looking and then winking.

A اقتر *aktar*, Frugal, close in house-keeping.

A اقتراء *iktirāʼ*, (v. n. 8 of قرأ) Reading (especially the Kur'ān). (v. n. 8 of قرا for قرو) Intending, purposing. Searching, pursuing diligently. (v. n. 8 of قري) Wishing to be a guest. Pursuing, going from place to place. Entertaining hospitably.

A اقتراب *iktirāb*, (v. n. 8 of قرب) Approaching, drawing near. Being about to be fulfilled (a promise). Becoming near one another.

A اقتراح *iktirāh*, (v. n. 8 of قرح) Pronouncing an unpremeditated speech or extempore verses. An extempory composition or delivery (in prose or verse). Digging a well where there is no water. Having all his teeth come (a horse). Breaking or riding (a horse or camel) for the first time. Attempting a thing which had not been done before. Choice, election. Dominion, authority, usurpation.

A اقترار *iktirār*, (v. n. 8 of قرّ) Remaining fixed in the womb of the female (the seed of a stallion-camel). Seeking in the heart of a valley for any remaining forage. Becoming fat (a camel). Washing in cold water. Taking and seasoning one's bread with whatever remains or adheres to the bottom and sides of a kettle wherein victuals have been cooked. Repletion, satiety. Exceeding fatness.

A اقتراش *iktirāsh*, (v. n. 8 of قرش) Falling (one part upon another). Fighting with spears.

A اقتراض *iktirāz*, (v. n. 8 of قرض) Borrowing, taking on credit. Gnawing, corroding, destroying. Traducing, aspersing.

A اقتراع *iktirāʿ*, (v. n. 8 of قرع) Choosing, selecting. Kindling a fire. Casting lots (قرعة *kurʿat*).

A اقتراف *iktirāf*, (v. n. 8 of قرف) Being accused. Committing a crime. Acquiring.

A اقتران *iktirān*, (v. n. 8 of قرن) Being associated, joined, united. Company, association, union. Conjunction (of the planets). دولت اقتران *dawlat-iktirān*, Happy, associated with prosperity.

A اقتسار *iktisār*, (v. n. 8 of قسر) Forcing, compelling, obliging.

A اقتساط *iktisāt*, A dividing among themselves.

A اقتسام *iktisām*, (v. n. 8 of قسم) Dividing among themselves. Swearing amongst themselves. اقتسام ميراث *iktisāmi mīrās*, Division of inheritance.

A اقتشاب *iktishāb*, (v. n. 8 of قشب) Gaining praise or incurring censure.

A اقتصاب *iktisāb*, (v. n. 8 of قصب) Cutting up a sheep (a butcher called قصّاب *hassāb*). Cutting a hollow stalk or reed (قصب *kasab*).

A اقتصاد *iktisād*, (v. n. 8 of قصد) Being in a middle state, neither corpulent nor slender, neither prodigal nor sparing, neither swift nor slow. Keeping the middle path. Writing poetry, versifying.

A اقتصار *iktisār*, (v. n. 8 of قصر) Being satisfied and keeping within bounds. Abbreviation, abridgment. P اقتصار كردن *iktisār kardan*, To abridge.

A اقتصاص *iktisās*, (v. n. 8 of قصّ) Following, pursuing, tracking. Reciting, relating. Retaliating. Requesting (another) to retaliate.

A اقتصال *iktisāl*, A cutting. A being cut.

A اقتضاء *iktizās*, (v. n. 8 of قضي) Demanding, insisting upon, requiring, exacting (a debt). A decree. اقتضائ محلّ *iktizāsi mahall*, The exigency of the thing, time, or place. P اقتضا كردن *iktizā kardan*, To demand, exact, require.

A اقتضاب *iktizāb*, (v. n. 8 of قضب) Cutting off a part of any thing. Riding an unbroken camel. Speaking extempore.

A اقتضاض *iktizāz*, The deflowering of a virgin.

A اقتطاط *iktitāt*, (v. n. 8 of قطّ) Cutting. Cutting crosswise. Cutting any hard substance.

A اقتطاع *iktitāʿ*, (v. n. 8 of قطع) Cutting off a part. Taking a sheep from the flock.

A اقتطاف *iktitāf*, (v. n. 8 of قطف) Pulling, plucking, gathering (grapes).

A اقتع *aktaʿ*, More or most vile, mean or abject.

A اقتعاء *iktiʿās*, The act of a stallion's mounting.

A اقتعاث *iktiʿās*, (v. n. 8 of قعث) Excavating much earth from a pit or well.

A اقتعاد *iktiʿād*, (v. n. 8 of قعد) Mounting, sitting upon. Using (a camel) for the saddle.

A اقتعاط *iktiʿāt*, The act of wrapping the sash round the turban without passing it under the chin.

A اقتعاف *iktiʿāf*, (v. n. 8 of قعف) Being displaced. Falling with a crash (a wall). Seizing, grasping with avidity and zest.

A اقتعال *iktiʿāl*, (v. n. 8 of قعل) Removing, shaking off (vine-flowers called قعال *kuʿāl*).

A اقتفاء *iktifās*, (v. n. 8 of قفي) Going over stitches a second time. Putting a small thin piece of money between two other small thin bits. (v. n. 8 of قفا for قفو) Following, walking in the steps. Choosing, selecting, preferring. Receiving a guest. Distinguishing. Being peculiar, distinguished.

A اقتفار *iktifār*, (v. n. 8 of قفر) Following (another's steps). Picking (a bone).

A اقتفاط *iktifāt*, (v. n. 8 of قفط) Bringing up his hinder part close to the female (a he-goat).

A اقتفال *iktifāl*, (v. n. 8 of قفل) Being bolted and barred (a door).

A اقتفان *iktifān*, (v. n. 8 of قفن) Slaughtering (a sheep) in front and detaching the head.

A اقتلات *iktilāt*, (v. n. 8 of قلت) Having no surviving offspring (a woman).

A اقتلاد *iktilād*, (v. n. 8 of قلد) Being drowned.

A اقتلاز *iktilāz*, (v. n. 8 of قلز) Drinking, quaffing.

A اقتلاع *iktilāʿ*, (v. n. 8 of قلع) Pulling up, tearing out, extracting. Seizing, plundering. Being pulled up, torn out, extracted.

A اقتلاف *iktilāf*, (v. n. 8 of قلف) Uprooting. Being uprooted (a nail). Receiving without measure.

A اقتم *aktam*, Of the colour of dust with a mixture of red. Black.

A اقتماح *iktimāh*, (v. n. 8 of قمح) Putting any dry (as medicine) into the mouth. Becoming ripe (wheat). Raising the head. Drinking wine.

A اقتماع *iktimāʿ*, (v. n. 8 of قمع) Drinking the entire contents of a leathern bottle. Drinking with the mouth out of the orifice of a leathern bottle. Choosing, selecting the best part of any thing.

A اقتمام *iktimām*, (v. n. 8 of قمّ) Nibbling, picking up off the ground (a sheep). Devouring what is on the table. Managing any business well. Taking off (a load) without allowing (it) to touch the ground. Giving medicine to the sick. Remedying. Resolving, determining upon, and not failing. (v. n. 9 of قتم) Being black or of a dusty colour.

A اقتناء *iktinās*, (v. n. 8 of قنا for قنو) Acquiring, possessing, gaining, storing, receiving. Being habitually modest. Sticking close to. P اقتنا كردن *iktinā kardan*, To acquire.

A اقتناص *iktinās*, (v. n. 8 of قنص) Hunting.

G اقتنالوقي *aktinālūkī*, White thorn.

A اقتنان *iktinān*, (v. n. 8 of قنّ) Standing on a rock (a goat). Choosing a slave. Keeping silence.

A اقتواء *iktiwās*, (v. n. 8 of قوي) Being firm, strong, powerful, and vigorous. Outbidding, e[n]hancing. Claiming for one's self. A reproach[ful] speech. (v. n. 9 of قتا for قتو) Seeking to obta[in] one as a servant.

A اقتوار *iktiwār*, (v. n. 8 of قار for قور) Cutti[ng] (any thing) in the middle in a circular form.

A اقتياب *iktiwāb*, (v. n. 8 of قاب for [قو]ب) Choosing, selecting.

A اقتيات *iktiyāt*, (v. n. 8 of قات for [ق]وت) Feeding: supplying with fuel. Being fed.

A اقتياد *iktiyād*, (v. n. 8 of قاد for قود) Leading. Being led. Consenting to be led; submitting.

A اقتيار *iktiyār*, (v. n. 8 of قار for قور) Cuttin[g] any thing in the middle in a circular form. Need[-]ing, having occasion for. Investigating.

A اقتياز *iktiyāz*, (v. n. 8 of قاز for قوز) Devourin[g] any one (a leopard).

A اقتياس *iktiyās*, (v. n. 8 of قاس for قوس) Measuring, comparing. Bearing a resemblance to taking after (one's father). Agreeing with, answering to another in measuring or comparison.

A اقتياض *iktiyāz*, A tearing up by the roots.

A اقتياف *iktiyāf*, (v. n. 8 of قاف for قوف) Following, tracing, dogging, tracking.

A اقتيال *iktiyāl*, (v. n. 8 of قال for قول) Desiring to change. Accepting a substitute. Exercising authority (as dictator, قائل *hāsil*). Choosing.

A اقتيام *iktiyām*, A cutting off (of the nose).

A اقتيان *iktiyān*, (v. n. 8 of قان for قين) Appearing beautiful (plants). Flowering (a garden).

A اقتينان *iktīnān*, (v. n. 11 of قتن not used) Standing erect. Being beautiful (a plant), looking gaily (a meadow).

A اقثاء *iksās*, (v. n. 4 of قثأ obsol.) Abounding in cucumbers (a place). Being rich in cucumbers. (v. n. 4 of قثا for قثو) Collecting (wealth, &c.).

P اقجنوش *akajnosh*, Rust of iron.

T اقچه *akcha*, Money.

A اقحاح *ak-hāh*, (pl. of قحّ) True (Arabians).

A اقحاد *ik-hād*, (v. n. 4 of قحد) Having a large bunch (a camel). Making a camel's bunch.

A اقحاص *ik-hās*, (v. n. 4 of قحص) Removing, placing at a distance.

A اقحاط *ik-hāt*, (v. n. 4 of قحط) Suffering from drought and consequent scarcity. Sending drought and scarcity. Copulating without consummating.

A اقحاطيّ *ak-hātiy*, A descendant of Kahtān.

A اقحاف *ak-hāf*, (pl. of قحف *kihf*) Skulls. Broken heads. رماه باقحاف رأسه *ramāhu bi ak-hāfi rassihi*, A phrase denoting the silencing of any one by bringing upon him trouble, or the keeping of him back from any necessary business. *Ih-hāf*, (v. n. 4 of قحف) Collecting a number of stones, upon which to place household utensils.

A اقحال *ih-hāl*, The making dry or withered.

A اقحام *ik-hām*, (v. n. 4 of قحم) Throwing headlong. Forcing (a horse) into a river. Being compelled to migrate from famine.

A اقحد *ak-had,* Large-bunched (camel). *Ak-hud,* (pl. of قحدة *kahadat*) Bunches of camels, or the roots or middle parts of them.

A اقحر *ak-hur,* Decrepit (men). Aged (camels).

A اقحمة *ak-hamat,* Intense cold.

A اقحوان *uk-huwān,* (pl. اقاحي *akāhī* or اقاحيّ *akāhiy*) Camomile.

A اقدّ *akudd,* (pl. of قدّ *kadd*) Statures, bodies. Kid-skins. Quantities, portions, sections (of any thing). (pl. of قدّ *kidd*) Leathern vessels. Scourges. Strips cut from an undressed hide.

A اقداء *ikdā*, (v. n. 4 of قدا for قدو) Coming off a journey. (v. n. 4 of قدي) Making (meat) well-flavoured. ما اقداه *mā akdāhu,* How finely flavoured (the food is)!

A اقداح *akdāh,* (pl. of قدح *kadah*) Cups, bowls.

A اقداد *ikdād,* (v. n. 4 of قدّ) Cutting long-ways.

A اقدار *akdār,* (pl. of قدر *kadar*) Powers. Orders, degrees, appointments. Quantities, values, measures. *Ikdār,* (v. n. 4 of قدر) Giving power.

A اقداع *ikdāع,* (v. n. 4 of قدع) Preventing, prohibiting, curbing, restraining, hindering one another.

A اقدام *akdām,* (pl. of قدم *kadam*) Feet. Steps, paces. The toes. *Ikdām,* (v. n. 4 of قدم) Ordering (one) to advance or go before. Sending on before. Giving or inspiring spirit or courage, stimulating to any thing bold. Administering an oath. Approaching or proceeding readily and with spirit, going boldly against an enemy. Boldness, intrepidity. P اقدام نمودن *ikdām namūdan,* To be forward and eager. A اقدام و احجام *ikdām u ihjām,* Impulse and repulsion, boldness and timidity, being stimulated to any thing daring, yet shrinking. اقدام و اهتمام *ikdām u ihtimām,* Care and diligence.

A اقدّة *akiddat,* pl. of قدّ *kadd*) Kid-skins. Statures of bodies. Quantities, parts.

A اقدح *akdah,* A fly. *Akduh,* (pl. of قدح *kidh*) Arrows, before they have received heads or wings.

A اقدحرار *ikdihrār,* (v. n. 4 of قدحر Q) Preparing to do mischief, revile, or fight.

A اقدر *akdar* Short-necked (man). (A horse) that places his hind-feet in the track of his fore-feet, or that places them where he ought to place them. *Akdur,* (pl. of قدر *kidr*) Kettles.

A اقدس *akdas,* More or most pure, most holy.

A اقدم *akdam,* Former, first, more ancient. A lion. اقدم ملوك كفّار *akdami mulūki kuffār,* The foremost of the infidel kings. *Akdim,* (imp. of 4) Advance! proceed! get on! (a word made use of to a horse). *Akdum,* (pl. of قدم *kadam*) Steps.

A اقدى *akda',* More or most highly flavoured.

A اقذّ *akazz,* (pl. قذّ *kuzz*) An arrow without wings. A feathered arrow. An arrow straight and even. A small matter. Wealth, property. Folk. ما له اقذّ و لا مريش *mā lahu akazz wa lā marīsh,* He has neither a feathered nor unfeathered arrow.

A اقذاء *akzā*, (pl. of قذي *kiza'*) Pounded, pulverized earths. *Ikzā*, (v. n. 4 of قذي) Hurting (another's eyes) by throwing any small particle or mote into them. Extracting a mote from the eye.

A اقذاذ *ikzāz,* (v. n. 4 of قذّ) Feathering an arrow.

A اقذار *akzār,* Filth. *Ikzār,* (v. n. 4 of قذر) Being very talkative.

A اقذاع *ikzāع,* (v. n. 4 of قذع) Reviling, upbraiding contumeliously, attacking with sarcasms, reproaches, or rude language.

A اقذان *ikzān,* (v. n. 4 of قذن) Having many defects and blemishes.

A اقذر *akzar,* More or most filthy, nastier, nastiest.

A اقذعرار *ikziعrār,* (v. n. 4 of قذعر Q) Being ready for mischief, reviling, or fighting. Heaping abuse upon any one.

A اقذعلال *ikziعlāl,* The being difficult.

A اقذلة *akzilat,* (pl. of قذال *kazāl*) The back parts of the heads of horses behind the ears.

A اقر *ukur,* A valley or wide channel covered with water and salsuginous plants.

A اقراء *akrā*, (pl. of قرء *kar*) Times, seasons. The menses of women. Purifications, or periods when they are over. The intermediate space between two menses. Verses ending with the same letter, rhymes, kinds of poetry, modes of versification. دعي الصلوة ايّام اقرائك *daعi's salāta ayyāma akrāiki,* Let prayer alone the days of thy menstruation. (pl. of قرو *karw*) Cups, small vessels. Vessels from which dogs eat their food. Stumps of palm-trees. (pl. of قريّ *kariy*) Canals, aqueducts, streams drawn into sown fields. *Ikrā*, (v. n. 4 of قرأ) Giving, or ordering one to read. Communicating in writing tidings relative to health, &c. Approaching. Retiring, receding, delaying, departing, being gone or absent. Blowing (as periodical winds). Delaying to come (as rains in their proper season). Returning. Being pious, religious, devout, dedicated to the service of God. Being menstruous. Becoming purified. Remaining in the uterus of a camel (seed). Detaining (a damsel) until (she) become pure from menstruation. (v. n. 4 of قرا for قرو) Leaving a horse-cloth continually on a horse's back. Having a pain in the back. Seeking for hospitality. Remaining constantly in a village. (v. n. 4 of قري) Remaining constantly in a village (called قرية *karyat* or *kiryat*). Wishing to be a guest.

A اقراب *akrāb,* (pl. of قرب *kurb* and *kurub*) Those parts of the haunches or hips nearest to the belly, the hypochondria. *Ikrāb,* (v. n. 4 of قرب) Filling (a cup) almost full. Being about to shed their first teeth (a camel's colt or a mare's foal). Being near delivery (a woman, &c.). Urging forward a camel during a nocturnal journey in search of water. Having camels hastening to water, during nocturnal journeys (when they quicken their pace). Putting up a sword with its scabbard into a sheath.

A اقراح *ikrāh,* (v. n. 4 of قرح) Afflicting with ulcers. Having ulcerated cattle. Having the teeth completely grown (a horse).

A اقراد *akrād,* (pl. of قرد *kird*) Male baboons. *Ikrād,* (v. n. 4 of قرد) Being silent, speechless, unable to speak, from any ailment in the tongue. Being humble. Resting. Feigning to be dead.

A اقرار *ikrār,* (v. n. 4 of قرّ) Establishing, fixing (in a place). Confirming, settling, ratifying. Confessing, acknowledging a fault, telling the truth. Holding to the stallion (a she-camel). Lying safe in the womb (the fœtus of a camel). Smiting with cold. Refreshing, making (the eye) cool. Suffering by cold. Affirmation, attestation, confirmation. Assurance, promise, agreement. P اقرار آوردن *ikrār āwardan,* To confess, to make confession (of sins). اقرار كردن *ikrār kardan,* To promise. To acknowledge. اقرار عام *ikrāri ʿām,* A general acknowledgment, a public declaration.

P اقرار نامه *ikrār-nāma,* A written agreement, an indenture, a bond, a contract.

A اقراس *ikrās,* A chilling, a making cold.

A اقراش *ikrāsh,* (v. n. 4 of قرش) Speaking ill of any one. Rushing or falling upon. Cleaving (a bone) without making a fracture.

A اقراص *akrās,* (pl. of قرص *kurs*) Round loaves (of bread). Pastils, lozenges. Disks of the sun. اقراص الطين *akrāsu't tīn,* Bole-lozenges. اقراص راسن *akrāsi rāsan,* Elecampane-lozenges. اقراص كندر *akrāsi kundur,* Frankincense-lozenges. اقراص مورد *akrāsi mord,* Myrtle-lozenges. *Ikrās,* (v. n. 4 of قرص) Taking up with the tips of the fingers (as a pinch of snuff). Washing with the tips of the fingers.

A اقراض *ikrāz,* (v. n. 4 of قرض) Lending, giving credit. Sending on before (good or evil acts). Requiting any one by the gift of a piece of land.

A اقراط *akrāt,* (pl. of قرط *kurt*) Ear-rings.

A اقراع *ikrāع,* (v. n. 4 of قرع) Casting or drawing lots. Lending or hiring out (a stallion camel). Giving away the best parts of one's estate (whether in cattle or other effects). Taking good advice. Returning (to that which is right). Submitting and becoming obsequious. Refusing (counsel), being stubborn, high, and proud. Checking or curbing (a horse). Abstaining from, hanging back. Prohibiting, restraining, driving back. Approaching, drawing near to the inn or caravansera (a traveller). Being strong and powerful. Kicking one another (asses). Paving a house with bricks or tiles. Being perpetual, never ceasing (evil). Reaching the bottom (a diver or one who goes in search of water).

A اقراف *ikrāf,* (v. n. 4 of قرف) Accusing: exposing to suspicion. Making evil mention. Being near, approaching. Mixing with, holding intercourse. Visiting a sick household and catching the infection. Being bred from a blood mare, by a mean sire.

A اقرام *ikrām,* (v. n. 4 of قرم) Making master.

Honouring, reverencing, respecting. Preserving from labour (a stallion camel).

A اقران *akrān*, Peers, pairs, equals. *Ikrān*, (v. n. 4 of قرن) Elevating a spear, lest the point should hurt any one before. Being near bursting (a boil). Abounding in the veins (blood). Selling a quiver. Selling a rope. Giving power. Being weak and inadequate to. Deviating from the road. Discharging two arrows at once. Being able to manage an estate; also being unable. Grasping two teats. Bringing two captives in one cord. Sacrificing in the forenoon a horned ram. Being fully adequate to the performance of a thing. Riding an excellent-paced camel. Milking (a camel) whose fore and hinder teats are close together. Taking a companion. Anointing the eyes every night with one styleful. Continuing and not giving over (rain). Being high (the Pleiades). Performing at the same time the solemnities of حج *hajj* and عمرة *ʿumrat*.

G اقرانيا *ikrāniyā*, The cornel-tree.

A اقرب *akrab*, (pl. اقربون *akrabūna* and اقارب *akārib*) Nearer, nearest. في اقرب الوقت *fī akraba'l wakt*, In the shortest time, very shortly.

A اقرباء *akribāʼ*, Kindred, near relations, friends.

A اقربون *akrabūna*, Kindred, nearest relations.

A اقرح *akrah*, (pl. قرحان) A sort of mushroom.

A اقرحة *akrihat*, (pl. of قراح *karāh*) Sown fields. Places destitute of buildings and trees. Pure, limpid, unmixed (waters).

A اقردة *akridat*, (pl. of قرد *kird*) Male baboons.

A اقرط *akrat*, (A goat) with pendulous lobes.

A اقرطة *akritat*, (pl. of قرط *kurt*) Ear-rings.

A اقرع *akraʿ*, Most valiant, strenuous, vehement, bold, strong. (pl. قرع *kurʿ* and قرعان *kurʿān*) Bald (from disease). Bald-headed (serpent) by reason of the quantity of its venom. Stripped of its bark (a stick). Hard (place or shield). Sharp and excellent (sword). (A cup or an arrow) rubbed on the pebbles until the lines or grooves appear. Full, complete, strong (thousand).

A اقرعباب *ikriʿbāb*, (v. n. 4 of قرعب Q not used) Being drawn together from cold.

A اقرعفاف *ikriʿfāf*, (v. n. 4 of قرعف Q not used) Drawing one's self together.

A اقرف *akraf*, Intensely red. ما اقرفه *mā akrafahu*, (or اقرف به *akrif bihi*) How worthy he is!

A اقرم *akram*, A stallion-camel of great value, and exempted for that reason from labour.

A اقرن *akran*, One whose eye-brows meet.

A اقرنباع *ikrimbāʿ*, (v. n. 3 of قربع Q not in use) Contracting one's self, when sitting, from cold.

A اقرنداح *ikrindāh*, (v. n. 3 of قردح Q) Seeking to fix a crime upon any one.

A اقرنذاح *ikrinzāh*, (v. n. 3 of قرذح Q) Being attached, having a propensity or an inclination for Charging with a crime of which one is guiltless.

A اقرنشاع *ikrinshāʿ*, (v. n. 3 of قرشع Q not in use) Being brisk, lively, active, alert. Raising the head.

A اقرنصاع *ikrinsāʿ*, (v. n. 3 of قرصع Q) Wrapping one's self in a garment.

A اقرنفاط *ikrinfāt*, (v. n. 3 of قرفط Q) Drawing or collecting one's self together.

A اقرنفاع *ikrinfāʿ*, (v. n. 3 of قرفع Q) Fainting, and afterwards recovering.

A اقرنماط *ikrinmāt*, (v. n. 3 of قرمط Q) Shrivelling, being wrinkled (a skin).

A اقرؤ *akruʼ*, (pl. of قرء *karʼ*) The menses.

A اقروة *akriwat*, (or اقري *akrī*) (pl. of قرو *karw*) Cups, small vessels. Vessels from which dogs eat their food. Stumps of palm-trees.

A اقره *akrah*, Squalid, dirty (fellow).

A اقرية *akriyat*, (pl. of قري *kariy*) Canals, aqueducts; streams let into sown fields.

A اقريطش *akrītish*, The isle of Crete or Candia.

A اقزاء *ikzāʼ*, (v. n. 4 of قزو) Being tainted by vice after having been correct in one's conduct.

A اقزّاء *akizzāʼ*, (pl. of قزّ *kazz*) Free from stains.

A اقزاح *akzāh*, (pl. of قزح *kizh*) Pot-herbs, seasonings added to victuals whilst cooking.

A اقزاع *ikzāʿ*, (v. n. 4 of قزع) Contradicting.

A اقزام *akzām*, (pl. of قزم *kazam*) (Men) of a meaner race or rank; also weaker in body.

A اقزان *ikzān*, (v. n. 4 of قزن) Breaking (the leg).

A اقزع *akzaʿ*, A ram whose wool has partially fallen off in the spring.

A اقزل *akzal*, One who halts ungracefully, having emaciated legs. (pl. اقازل *akāzil*) A wolf. A species of snake. الاقزلان *al akzalāni*, Two feathers in the middle of the eagle's tail.

A اقساء *iksāʼ*, (v. n. 4 of قسا for قسو) Hardening (the heart). Inhabiting the mountain قساء *kusāʼ*.

A اقساح *iksāh*, (v. n. 4 of قسح) Having priapism.

A اقساط *iksāt* (v. n. 4 of قسط) Being just, equitable. Distributing justice (قسط *kist*).

A اقسام *aksām*, (pl. of قسم *kism*) Portions, divisions, classes. *Iksām*, (v. n. 4 of قسم) Swearing.

A اقسان *iksān*, (v. n. 4 of قسن) Having the hand callous by labour or drawing water.

A اقسرا *aksarā*, A city in Natolia (Asia Minor).

A اقسط *aksat*, More or most just. (A camel) the muscles of whose legs are dry and hard. (A horse) whose hind legs are nearly perpendicular (which is considered a blemish).

A اقسماء *aksimāʼ*, (pl. of قسيم *kasīm*) Coparceners. Portions.

T آقسنقر *āksunkur*, A certain bird of prey. An emperor of the Turks. A day. The sun.

A اقسومة *uksūmat*, (pl. اقاسيم *akāsīm*) A part, portion, division, allotment.

G اقسياقنتا *aksiyākantā*, The oxyacanth-tree.

A اقسيان *aksayān*, Name of a certain plant.

A اقسئنان *iksiʼnān*, A growing old.

A اقشاء *ikshāʼ*, (v. n. 4 of قشا for قشو) Becoming poor, from being rich.

A اقشاب *akshāb*, (pl. of قشب *kishb*) Poisons.

A اقشاش *ikshāsh*, (v. n. 4 of قش) Recovering from the small-pox, or other eruption. Roving without constraint. Being very dry (a country).

A اقشاع *ikshāʿ*, (v. n. 4 of قشع) Dissipating, dispelling. Being dispersed, dispelled (clouds or men). Retiring from water (men).

P آقشته *ākishta*, A pantry, cupboard, buttery.

A اقشر *akshar*, Stripped of the peel (قشر *kishr*), barked. One whose nose is peeled by the heat, and very red. Barren (year).

A اقشع *akshaʿ*, More or most exalted, noble.

A اقشعرار *ikshiʿrār*, (v. n. 4 of قشعر Q) Creeping (the skin with terror). Being barren (year).

A اقشف *akshaf*, Barren (year).

G اقشون *akshūn*, Name of a plant.

A اقصاء *iksāʼ*, (v. n. 4 of قصا for قصو) Removing far off. Preserving, protecting the distant part of an army. Reaching, extending to. Having she-camels distinguished by the epithet قصيّة *kasiyat*, or solitary (as kept apart from others, on account of their superior value; though sometimes so named, as being laid aside from their worthlessness).

A اقصاب *aksāb*, (pl. of قصب *kusb*) Intestines. Backs. *Iksāb*, (v. n. 4 of قصب) Having camels interrupting their drinking before their thirst is quenched. Producing hollow reeds (قصب *kasab*).

A اقصاد *aksād*, Broken (spear). *Iksād*, (v. n. 4 of قصد) Hitting fair, and killing (an arrow). Aiming at with a spear and striking without fail. Biting and killing (a serpent).

A اقصار *aksār*, (pl. of قصرة *kasarat*) Roots of necks. *Iksār*, (v. n. 4 of قصر) Beginning the evening, and doing any thing then. Coming in the evening. Containing one's self, refraining or abstaining from any thing, doing less than one is equal to. Shortening prayers. Bearing children short of stature (a woman). Becoming smooth and worn down from age (teeth of sheep or goats). Becoming deficient, unequal to. Being aged and having the teeth worn. انّ الطويلة قد تقصرو انّ القصيرة قد تطيل *inna't tawīlat kad tuksir, wa inna'l kasīrat kad tutīl*, A tall woman sometimes brings forth short children, and a short woman tall ones.

A اقصر *aksar*, (pl. اقاصر *akāsir*) Shorter, shortest. More or most deficient. Troubled with a stiff-neck.

A اقصاص *iksās*, (v. n. 4 of قصّ) Being at the point of (death). Bringing (one) to death's door. Drawing near to any one (death). (Ground) producing the herb called قصيص *kasīs*. Appearing to be pregnant (mares, sheep, &c., by refusing the male). Being able to retaliate and retaliating for one's self. Being weak, emaciated, and unable to labour (a camel). Inflicting the punishment of retaliation called قصاص *kisās* (a magistrate).

A اقصاف *iksāf*, (v. n. 4 of قصف) Being slender (the tree ارطي *artaʼ*).

A اقصام *aksām*, (pl. of قصم *kism* or *kasm*) Roots of pasture-lands.

A اقصعلال *iksiʻlāl*, (v. n. 4 of قصعل Q) Being in the meridian (the sun).

A اقصف *aksaf*, (or اقصم *aksam*) One whose teeth (especially before) are broken in the middle.

A اقصي *aksa'*, (pl. اقاصي *akāsī*) Far off, more or most remote, farther, farthest. Most of all, very much, for the most part. Crop-eared (camel). اقصي الغايات *aksa'l ghāyāt*, The extremes, terms, boundaries; the accomplishment, completion, perfection, end. اقصىٰ معمورالارض *aksa' maʻmūri'l arz*, The utmost bound of the habitable earth. مسجد اقصي *masjidi aksa'*, The most remote temple, *i. e.* the temple at Jerusalem (so called, because people from the most distant countries flock to visit it).

A اقصئلال *iksi·lāl*, (v. n. 4 of قصأل Q) Seizing hold of. Stopping in a place.

A اقضاء *ikzā*, (v. n. 4 of قضيٌ) Giving to eat.

A اقضاب *ikzāb*, (v. n. 4 of قضب) Producing abundance of clover called قضبة *kazbat* (a field).

A اقضاض *ikzāz*, (v. n. 4 of قضّ) Being covered with dry sand or gritty particles (meat). Putting sugar or candy into a ptisan. Being hard, rough, gravelly, incommodious (bed or resting-place). Making (a place of that kind) uneasy. Following bad habits. Prosecuting subtile enquiries.

A اقضام *ikzām*, (v. n. 4 of قضم) Giving corn to a horse, put into a nose-bag, and fastened round his head. Victualling one's household sparingly in a season of dearth. Chattering (the jaws of a camel).

A اقضم *akzam*, Notched and blackish-toothed.

A اقضيٰ *akza'*, More or most judicious, better or best judge (قاضي *kāzī*). اقضي القضاة *akza'l kuzāt*, The most intelligent, penetrating of judges.

A اقضية *akziyat*, (pl. of قضاء *kazā*) Judgments, decrees. Predestinations, fates.

A اقط *akt*, (v. n. of اقط) Dressing victuals with a preparation of milk called اقط *akit* or *ikt*, dried so as to be reducible to powder. Feeding any one with this food. Throwing prostrate. Mixing. *Akat*, (v. n. of اقط) Possessing much *akit*. *Akit*, *akat*, *akut*, or *ikt*, (pl. اقطان *uktān*) A preparation of sheep's milk, dried butter-milk: new-made cheese.

A اقطاب *aktāb*, (pl. of قطب *kutb*) Polar stars. Centres around which bodies revolve. Princes, chiefs. *Iktāb*, (v. n. 4 of قطب) Mixing (wine). Being assembled (men).

A اقطار *aktār*, (pl. of قطر *kutr*) Tracks (of the heavens). Districts. *Iktār*, (v. n. 4 of قطر) Causing to fall in drops. Laying prostrate on the back or side. Being time to distil, drop, or rain. Tying (camels) in a string (which is called قطار *kitār*).

A اقطاط *aktāt*, (pl. of قطّ) Curly-haired (men).

A اقطاع *aktāʻ*, Cut (as cloth for making garments). Lands assigned to any one on feudal tenure. (pl. of قطع *kitʻ*) Camels' saddle-cloths. (Arrows) having small but broad heads. (pl. of قطيع *katīʻ*) Herds (of oxen), flocks (of sheep), as being distinct and separate bodies. *Iktāʻ*, (v. n. 4 of قطع) Permitting one to lop (branches or trees). Suffering from a withholding of the rain from heaven. Crossing (a river) along with any one. Being sufficient for one's stature (cloth for a garment). Defeating by argument, silencing. Being silenced, defeated in argument. Checking, stopping (the mouth of an enemy by good offices). Being overpowered, so as to be unable to answer. Being sunk, gone, exhausted (the water in a well). Assigning lands on feudal or copyhold tenure (as a prince to a subject). Giving over laying eggs (a hen). Having dates fit for gathering (a palm-tree).

A اقطاف *iktāf*, (v. n. 4 of قطف) Being near the vintage season. Being almost ripe (grapes). Having vines in that state. Having a dull, heavy-paced horse, or one that takes short steps.

A اقطان *aktān*, (pl. of قطن *kutn*) Cottons. *Uktān*, (pl. of اقط *akit*) Preparations of milk so called.

A اقطة *akitat*, Something below the rough tripe of what belongs to the stomach.

A اقطّة *akittat*, (pl. of قطاط *kitāt*) Models or patterns whereon things are cut. Circumferences of hoofs of quadrupeds. Upper parts of sides of caverns. Edges of mountains, edges of cliffs.

A اقطرار *iktirār*, (v. n. 9 of قطر) Turning, beginning to wither (a plant). Conceiving (a she-camel), cocking her tail and tossing her head.

A اقطع *aktaʻ*, (pl. قطع *kutʻ* and قطعان *kutʻān*) One who has the hand amputated. Deaf. More or most acute, sharper, sharpest. More or most quenching. White-breasted (pigeon). A thief, a highway robber. مدّ ومتّ الينا بثدي غيراقطع *madda wa matta ilaynā bi sadyin ghayr aktaʻ*, He essayed to join himself to us on the score of near relationship. *Aktuʻ*, (pl. of قطع *kitʻ*) The points of arrows, small but broad. (pl. of قطيع *katīʻ*) Branches or loppings, of which they make arrows.

A الاقطعان *al aktaʻāni*, The sword and pen.

A اقطعة *aktiʻat*, (pl. of قطيع *katīʻ*) Small branches of trees of which arrows are made.

A اقطعرار *iktiʻrār*, (v. n. 4 of قطعر Q) Breathing short from over-exercise.

A اقطعنان *iktiʻnān*, (v. n. 4 of قطعن Q) Being spent, exhausted from puffing and blowing (breath).

A اقطف *aktaf*, Sharper, or sharpest. Nimbler.

A اقطن *aktan*, Crooked (back). *Aktin*, A sort of pulse. اقطن يمني *aktini yamanī*, A sort of vetch.

G اقطنالوقي *aktinālūkī*, White-thorn.

A اقطوعة *uktūʻat*, A token which, in Arabia, one woman sends to another, to intimate a renunciation of friendship, correspondence, and society.

A اقطيٰ *akta'*, The bel fruit. The elder-tree.

A اقطيرار *iktīrār*, (v. n. 11 of قطر) Turning, beginning to wither. Being angry. Running away.

A اقطيطاء *iktītā*, (v. n. 12 of قطا for قطو) Taking short steps. Stepping sprightly, but slowly.

A اقعاء *ikʻā*, (v. n. 4 of قعا for قعو) Being turned up (the nose). Sitting down, leaning the back against any thing. Kneeling with the buttocks resting on the heels (a lazy mode with some people in prayer). Sitting upon the hams (as a dog or other animal), having the fore-feet perpendicular. Pulling back, checking, or making to go backward.

A اقعاث *ikʻās*, (v. n. 4 of قعث) Being prodigal, extravagant. Making a valuable present.

A اقعاد *akʻād* or *ikʻād*, Lameness. Any infirmity which inclines one to sit much, or prevents man or beast from walking erect. *Ikʻād*, (v. n. 4 of قعد) Ordering or desiring one to sit. Compelling one to sit still (a disease). Serving, attending, waiting upon. Being contented (in point of gain or advantage). Digging superficially (for water) and leaving the ground so dug up, without finding any.

A اقعار *ikʻār*, (v. n. 4 of قعر) Digging deep.

A اقعاس *ikʻās*, Opulence, abundance, plenty.

A اقعاص *ikʻās*, (v. n. 4 of قعص) Killing suddenly, on the spot, the moment the blow is struck.

A اقعاط *ikʻāt*, (v. n. 4 of قعط) Being obscene (in conversation). Retiring from, leaving. Despising, regarding as light and despicable. Loud, vehement.

A اقعاظ *ikʻāz*, (v. n. 4 of قعظ) Being difficult, troublesome. Rendering painful and troublesome.

A اقعاع *ikʻāʻ*, A digging to thick, brackish water.

A اقعال *ikʻāl*, (v. n. 4 of قعل) Expanding (as the vine-flowers).

A اقعام *ikʻām*, (v. n. 4 of قعم) Biting and killing (as a serpent). Rising high (the sun).

A اقعب *akʻub*, (pl. of قعب *kaʻb*) Large wooden cups; small cups; such cups as hold as much as a man may drink off at a draught. The more profound or hidden parts (of a discourse).

A اقعد *akʻad*, Nearly related to the head of the family. ابنة اقعدي *ibnatu akʻidī*, A maid-servant.

A اقعدة *akʻidat*, (pl. of قعود *kaʻūd*) (Young camels) ready or beginning to be ready for the saddle (such as the camel-keeper rides upon occasionally).

A اقعس *akʻas*, (A horse) having a low place for the saddle, and high behind. Hollow-backed, with a protuberance in the breast. A sort of palm. Long (night). Grave (man). Solid (glory). (A camel) whose head, neck, and back are bent.

A اقعطرار *ikʻitrār*, (v. n. 4 of قعطر Q) Breathing hard from over exercise.

A اقعم *akʻam*, Flat-nosed.

A اقعنداد *ikʻindād*, A staying, an abiding.

A اقعنساس *ikʻinsās*, (v. n. 3 of قعسس Q) Returning, going backward.

A اقعنصار *ikʻinsār*, A squatting, cowering down.

A اقعنفاز *ikʻinfāz*, (v. n. 3 of قعفز Q) Sitting on tip-toes as if prepared to rise.

A اقعيٰ *akʻa'*, Pug-nosed, snub-nosed.

A اقعئلال *ikeilāl*, (v.n. 4 of قعأل Q) Expanding (as vine-flowers). Sitting erect on horseback.

A اقفاء *akfās*, (pl. of قفا *kafa'*) The hinder parts of the neck or head. *Ikfās*, (v.n. 4 of قفا for قفو) Preferring. Partaking of hospitality. Setting food before a guest. Making peculiar and special. Choosing, selecting for any particular work.

A اقفاخ *ikfākh*, (v. n. 4 of قفخ) Wishing for the male (a cow or she-wolf).

A اقفار *ikfār*, (v. n. 4 of قفر) Being ruined, desolate, desert (house or country). Discovering (a city) to be deserted. Going from home, travelling through a desert, wanting victuals. Hungering.

A اقفاص *akfās*, (pl. of قفص *kafs*) Cages, aviaries. *Ikfās*, (v. n. 4 of قفص) Having a bird-cage.

A اقفاف *akfāf*, (pl. of قفّ *kuff*) Clouds, resembling mountains (clustering one over another, and having at the same time the appearance of forests). Rugged hills. *Ikfāf*, (v. n. 4 of قفّ) Giving over laying eggs. Having eggs and keeping them in the belly. Departing from the eyes (tears), and going away (blackishness about the eyes).

A اقفال *akfāl*, (pl. of قفل *kufl*) Locks, bolts, bars. *Ikfāl*, (v. n. 4 of قفل) Locking or bolting (a door). Causing (a caravan) to return. Appointing a guardian. Following with one's eye. Collecting, drawing (people) together. Not allowing to proceed, laying an embargo.

A اقفان *ikfān*, (v. n. 4 of قفن) Slaughtering (a sheep) on the back of the head or neck.

A اقفد *akfad*, One who has a thick and flabby neck. One who walks on tip-toe. Short-toed and fingered. (A camel) whose feet point inwards.

A اقفر *akfar*, Barren, desert.

A اقفز *akfaz*, (A horse) whose fore-legs, as far as the knees, are white, resembling white stockings.

A اقفزة *akfizat*, (pl. of قفيز *kafīz*) Measures containing about eight مكاكيل *makākīl*. Spaces of ground, containing 144 cubits square.

A اقفس *akfas*, One whose father is not an Arab, but mother Arabian. Any thing long and curved.

A اقفع *akfaε*, One who habitually hangs his head. One whose toes are bent downwards.

A اقفعلال *ikfiεlāl*, (v. n. 4 of قفعل Q) Being contracted and withered (the hand).

A اقفل *akful*, (pl. of قفل *kufl*) Bolts, bars, locks.

A اقفي *akfī* or اقفية *akfiyat*, (pl. of قفا *kafa'*) Hind-heads, napes of the neck.

A اقلّ *akall*, Less, least. Poor. اقلّ عبدان *akalli εibdān*, Least or meanest of servants. اقلّ المالك *akallu'l mamālik*, Least of the kingdoms.

A اقلّاء *akillās*, Few persons. Thin.

A اقلاب *aklāb*, (pl. of قلب *kalb*) The piths of palm-trees. *Iklāb* (v. n. 4 of قلب) Turning, converting, inverting, revolving. Receiving to himself (God). Being fired or done upon one side, and ready for turning (bread). Having camels attacked with a distemper which affects the heart (called قلاب *kulāb*), to which they are subject. Being dried on the outside (grapes).

A اقلات *iklāt*, (v. n. 4 of قلت) Destroying or exposing to destruction.

A اقلاد *aklād*, (pl. of اقليد *iklīd*) Threads of copper wound round the nose-ring of a camel or round an ear-ring. Necks. *Iklād*, (v. n. 4 of قلد) Overwhelming, drowning (the sea).

A اقلاز *iklāz*, (v. n. 4 of قلز) Fixing its tail in the ground when depositing its eggs (a locust).

A اقلاص *iklās*, (v. n. 4 of قلص) Having a small bunch appearing (a camel). Becoming fat in summer (a she-camel), when she gives no milk.

A اقلاع *iklāε*, (v. n. 4 of قلع) Removing from a place, taking off. Abstaining, desisting (from any business). Intermitting or going off (a fever). Retiring (from water). Ceasing, giving over (rain). Navigating, hoisting sail, going with full sail. Being of a proper age for the saddle (she-camels). Shedding their first teeth, and getting those called رباعية *rabāεiyat*. Building a fortress.

A اقلاق *iklāk*, (v. n. 4 of قلق) Having the pack-saddle or baggage loose, and ready to fall off (a camel). Disturbing, disquieting.

A اقلال *iklāl*, (v. n. 4 of قلّ) Taking up a water-pot. Raising. Diminishing. Seizing any one (a tremor). Being rare, never occurring. Making few or small; discovering to be so. Bringing little. Becoming poor.

A اقلام *aklām*, (pl. of قلم *kalam*) Pens. Reeds of which they make pens. P اقلام بد ارقام *aklāmi bad-arkām*, Malignant writings, satires, libels.

A اقلب *aklab*, (A man) whose lips are inverted.

A اقلبة *aklibat*, (pl. of قليب) Wells, old wells.

A اقلح *aklah*, (A man) whose teeth are dirty and yellow. A beetle.

A اقلحمام *iklihmām*, A becoming old, decrepit.

A اقلط *aklat*, More or most despairing.

A اقلع *akluε*, (pl. of قلع) Shepherd's wallets.

A اقلعتات *ikliεtāt*, (v. n. 4 of قلعت Q not used) Being very crisp and curly (the hair). See اقلعداد.

A اقلعداد *ikliεdād*, (v. n. 4 of قلعد Q) Travelling, rambling, and roving over a country. Being very crisp and curly (hair).

A اقلعطاط *ikliεtāt*, (v. n. 4 of قلعط Q) Being crisp and curly (hair).

A اقلعفاف *ikliεfāf*, (v. n. 4 of قلعف Q) Becoming shrivelled and puckered from cold or age.

A اقلف *aklaf*, (pl. قلف *kulf*) Uncircumcised. Plenteous (year). Easy, comfortable (life). Single-edged (sword).

A اقلنساس *iklinsās*, (v. n. 3 of قلنس Q) Wearing a high cap called قلنسوة *kalansuwat*.

A اقلوّاد *ikliwwād*, (v. n. 13 of قلد) Overcoming one (sleep).

A اقليد *iklīd*, A key. A rope made of palm-leaves. (pl. اقلاد *aklād*) A copper thread put on the nose-ring of a camel or on an ear-ring. The neck.

G اقليدس *uklīdis*, Euclid.

A اقليلاء *iklīlās*, (v. n. 12 of قلا for قلو) Being moved, disturbed. Making haste. Expediting or pushing forward (any business). Being swift (ass). Rising up or soaring (birds). Climbing (a mountain), and standing or appearing on the summit. Departing, travelling. Not staying in one's place. Lighting and sitting upon a tree (a bird).

A اقليلي *iklīla'*, The whole.

G اقليم *iklīm*, (pl. اقاليم *akālīm*) A clime, climate, or country. P هفت اقليم *haft iklīm*, The seven climates, the whole world.

P اقليما *aklīmā*, Name of Adam's daughter.

P اقليميّا *iklīmiyā*, Name of Adam's daughter. The ore, scum, or dross of gold or silver. A kind of white earth. Litharge.

A اقليميّاء *iklimiyās*, Scoriæ or efflorescence on the surface of melted gold or silver. Name of the daughter of Adam.

A اقماء *ikmās*, (v. n. 4 of قمأ) Despising, undervaluing, treating with contempt. Having cattle becoming fat. Growing fat (sheep). Abiding in a place fruitful in herbage. Being proper (pasture or fodder) for fattening (cattle). Causing surprise, giving pleasure.

A اقماح *ikmāh*, (v. n. 4 of قمح) Raising the head. Tossing the nose, being high and haughty. Causing (any one) to take up in the hand. Casting down (the eye). Throwing into the ear (flour of wheat). Keeping a criminal's head raised (the pillory). Coming into grain (an ear of wheat).

A اقماخ *ikmākh*, (v. n. 4 of قمخ) Tossing the nose; being high and haughty.

A اقماد *ikmād*, (v. n. 4 of قمد) Exalting (the neck). Having an erection. A seminal effusion.

A اقمار *akmār*, (pl. of قمر *kamar*) Moons. (pl. of قمير *kamīr*) Those with whom you play at games of hazard. *Ikmār*, (v. n. 4 of قمر) Having bright moonlight (a night). Waiting for, watching the rising of the moon. Being bright. Being struck with frost before being ripe (dates). Lighting upon a plenteous pasture (camels).

A اقماز *ikmāz*, (v. n. 4 of قمز) Storing, treasuring. Acquiring, possessing the worst of any thing.

A اقماس *ikmās*, A dipping one in water.

A اقماع *ikmāε*, (v. n. 4 of قمع) Subduing, humbling, bringing into subjection. Running down the throat without any exertion of swallowing (water). Getting a bunch, and being long bunched (a camel's colt). Averting or repelling any thing threatened. Driving off.

A اقماعيّ *akmāεiy*, A kind of white grape, which at last turns yellow, having a round stone.

A اقمال *ikmāl*, (v. n. 4 of قمل) Putting forth the first and smaller leaves (an artichoke or a thistle). Breeding lice (قمل *kaml*).

A اقمام *ikmām*, (v. n. 4 of قمّ) Impregnating.

A اقمد *akmad*, Long-necked with thickness.

A اقمر *akmar*, Brilliant, clear (night). Moon-resembling (face). White. Of a whitish colour mixed with green.

A اقمشة *akmishat*, (pl. of قماش) Cloths, stuffs.

A اقمصة *akmisat*, (pl. of قميص *kamīs*) Shirts. Inner garments of linen or cotton. Surplices.

A اقمطرار *ikmitrār*, (v. n. 4 of قمطر Q) Bending its tail, drawing together its body (a scorpion). Being disastrous (day). Being very disagreeable.

A اقمع *akmaʻ*, (pl. قمع *kumʻ*) (A man) troubled with an incessant watering of the eye. Large-kneed or large-houghed (horse). One who has the bone of the wind-pipe large. Large-pointed (hough). Wry-nosed.

A اقمعطاط *ikmiʻtāt*, (v. n. 4 of قمعط Q) Being large above, shrunk below (belly): being collapsed.

A اقمهداد *ikmihdād*, (v. n. 4 of قمهد Q) Raising or holding up the head. Dwelling or remaining in any place. Trembling, fluttering whilst being fed (a young bird in the nest).

A اقن *ukan*, (pl. of اقنة) Structures of stone.

A اقناء *aknāʼ*, (pl. of قنو *kinw*) Bunches of dates.

A اقناء *iknāʼ*, (v. n. 4 of قنأ) Killing, or urging to kill. Spoiling (tanned leather). Investing with power. Being possible. (v. n. 4 of قنا for قنو) Being habitually modest. (v. n. 4 of قني) Being enriched (particularly by acquiring property). Laying up a store. Putting into one's power. Giving enough, contenting, satisfying. Giving over raining.

A اقناءة *aknāʼat*, The shady side of a wall.

A اقناب *iknāb*, (v. n. 4 of قنب) Increasing to a troop of thirty or forty. Owning such a troop. Withdrawing or absconding from king or creditor.

A اقنات *iknāt*, (v. n. 4 of قنت) Humbling one's self before God. Supplicating God, being long and earnest in prayer and praise, in performing pilgrimage, or in waging a religious war. Denouncing imprecations.

A اقناح *iknāh*, (v. n. 4 of قنح) Planing a door, and setting it up.

A اقناز *iknāz*, (v. n. 4 of قنز) Drinking (wine) from a small flagon.

A اقناس *iknās*, (v. n. 4 of قنس not used) Pretending, laying a groundless claim to nobility.

A اقناع *aknāʻ*, (pl. of قنع *kinʻ*) Arms, missile weapons. *Iknāʻ*, (v. n. 4 of قنع) Satisfying, rendering content. Going home, or to pasture (cattle). Sending (cattle) to water or pasture. Holding the head erect (as a player on a flute or other pipe). Stretching out the neck in order to drink (a camel). Having the eye intently fixed upon any thing, the head being raised and immoveable. Raising the hands in prayer. Residing in a valley between two rising hills. Being high, with no tendency to come down (a sheep's udder). Causing to want, rendering necessitous.

A اقناف *iknāf*, (v. n. 4 of قنف) Having a numerous army. Being firm in council, able in business. Being flagging and flapping (the ear). Having flagging ears.

A اقنان *aknān*, (and اقنّة *akinnat*) (pl. of قنّ *kinn*) Domestic servants (*i.e.* born in the family, and the property consequently of their master, if their fathers and mothers are slaves).

A اقنة *uknat*, (pl. اقن *ukan*) A structure of stone.

G اقنتالوقي *akantālawkī*, A kind of white thorn.

G افنتيون *akantiyūn*, A kind of thorn.

A اقنع *aknaʻ*, High-headed, low-necked (camel).

A اقنف *aknaf*, One who has small and thick ears sticking close to his head. (A horse) whitish on the back of the neck. Thick-nosed.

A اقنوم *aknūm* or *uknūm*, (pl. اقانيم *akānīm*) A substance or principle. A person of the sacred Trinity (which the Muhammadans acknowledge not).

A اقنى *akna'*, Hook-nosed, hawk-nosed.

A اقنيز *iknīz*, A small flagon or wine-vessel.

A اقنينان *iknīnān*, (v. n. 15 of قين) Being good (grass), being fresh and verdant (a mead).

A اقواء *ikwāʼ*, (v. n. 4 of قوي) Being empty, deserted, uninhabited. Going down into a desert unpeopled country. Having strong and robust (cattle). Being contented, in want of nothing, independent. Being poor, reduced to poverty, empty-bellied. Having all one's provisions run out. Making a rope of different-sized yarns; (metaphorically) composing verses ending with different vowels or an unequal number of consonants; verses so composed.

A اقواب *akwāb*, (pl. of قوب *kūb*) Chicks.

A اقوات *akwāt*, (pl. of قوت *kūt*) Victuals.

A اقواز *akwāz*, (pl. of قوز) Round heaps of sand.

A اقواس *akwās*, (pl. of قوس *kaws*) Bows.

A اقواط *akwāt*, (pl. of قوط *kawt*) Flocks. Hundreds of sheep.

A اقواع *akwāʻ*, (pl. of قاع *kāʻ*) Plains, level grounds. (pl. of قوع *kawʻ*) Places where they collect together dates or grain.

P اقواق *akwāk*, The white Indian poplar.

A اقوال *akwāl*, (pl. of قول *kawl*) Words, sayings, opinions. Agreements. (pl. of قيل *kayl*) Kings of the Himyarit Arabs (whose words all obey). ابن اقوال *ibn akwāl*, (Son of words) Eloquent. اقوال صداقت مآل *akwāli sadākat-maʼāl*, Words full of sincerity. *Ikwāl*, (v. n. 4 of قال for قول) Imputing to one, alleging that he said or did so and so.

A اقوام *akwām*, (pl. of قوم *kawm*) Peoples, nations, men (the human species, including women).

A اقود *akwad*, (A horse or camel) having a long neck or back. Strong-necked. Greedy, stingy of his victuals; one who, whilst eating, looks not around, that he may avoid seeing or inviting any one to partake. A long mountain. One who comes up to any thing and turns not away. More or most of a pimp قوّاد *kawwād*). Tractable (horse).

A اقورار *ikwirār*, (v. n. 9 of قار for قور) Being slender. Being fat. Being wrinkled. Being altered, varied. Disappearing (plants).

A اقورين *akwarīna*, (or اقوريّات *akwarīyāt*) Great misfortunes.

A اقوس *akwas*, Difficult, adverse (time). Crook-backed. High (sand-hill). Far (country). Long (day). احنى اقوس *ahna' akwas*, A sore calamity.

P آقوش *ākūsh*, A lion. A tiger. A leopard.

A اقوع *akwuʻ*, (pl. of قاع *kāʻ*) Plains, flats. Grounds where they collect dates or grain in heaps.

A اقوف *akwaf*, More, most skilful in tracking.

A اقوم *akwam*, More or most right or just. ما اقومه *mā akwamahu*, How straight or upright he is!

G اقومارثون *akūmārisūn*, Wild fennel.

G اقومالي *akūmālī*, Honey-water.

A اقوى *akwa'*, More or most strong, powerful, firm, robust, valiant. Stronger, strongest. اقوى الله *akwa' allāh*, May God strengthen, or confirm!

A اقوياء *akwiyāʼ*, (pl. of قويّ) Strong, powerful.

G اقويلاسمون *akūyilāsamūn*, Oil of balsam.

A اقة *ak-h*, (by metathesis for قاة) Obedience.

A اقهاء *ik-hāʼ*, (v. n. 4 of قهي) Being averse from, loathing. Rendering averse. Drinking coffee (قهوة *kahwa*) incessantly. Obeying (the king).

A اقهاب *ik-hāb*, (v. n. 4 of قهب) Abstaining from food, having no appetite.

A اقهار *ik-hār*, (v. n. 4 of قهر) Finding one conquered. Having one's allies defeated. Yielding, returning to a state of subjection.

A اقهال *ik-hāl*, (v. n. 4 of قهل) Interfering in what one has no concern. Bedaubing one's self.

A اقهام *ik-hām*, (v. n. 4 of قهم) Having no appetite. Loathing, abhorring. Wishing for meat. Being serene (the sky). Winking at. Regarding as small and trivial.

A اقهب *ak-hab*, Of a dark-brown, dusky hue. الاقهبان *al ak-habāni*, The elephant and the buffalo.

A اقهر *ak-har*, More or most oppressive, stronger.

A اقي *aky*, A loathing of food through disease.

A اقياء *ikyāʼ*, A making of one to vomit.

A اقياد *akyād*, (pl. of قيد *kayd*) Fetters, chains, shackles, straps, belts, ligaments. Restrictions.

A اقياص *akyās*, (pl. of قيص) Braying camels.

A اقياظ *akyāz*, (pl. of قيظ *kayz*) Midsummers, from the rising of the Pleiades to that of Canopus.

A اقيال *akyāl*, (pl. of قيل *kayl*) Kings of the Himyarit Arabs (whose words all obey).

A اقيان *akyān*, (pl. of قين *kayn*) Blacksmiths.

G اقيانوس *ikyānos*, The ocean.

A اقيحيّ *ukayhīy*, (dim. of اقحوان *uk-huwān*) A little camomile flower.

A اقير *akyar*, More or most bitter.

A اقيس *akyas*, More, most regular, analogous.

A اقيش *ukaysh*, Name of the father of a tribe,

the camels of which are apt to start and run away.

A اقيشر *ukayshir*, (dim. of اقشر *akshar*) Name of المغيرة *al mughīrat* the poet.

A اقيصر *ukaysir*, Name of an idol. ابن اقيصر *ibn ukaysir*, Name of a man proverbial for his knowledge of horses.

A اقيط *akīt*, Heavy, unwholesome.

P آك *āk*, (or اك *ak*) Calamity, misfortune. Vice, defect, blemish.

A اكّ *akk*, (v. n. of اكّ) Being hot (the day). Repelling. Hindering. Pressing upon. Labouring under anguish and low spirits. Warm, sultry.

A اكاء *ikāʼ*, (v.n. 4 of كاي) Loathing, abhorring.

A اكاء *ikāʼ*, A chain, or any thing fastening the mouth of a bottle, or the cover of a vessel. Any vessel whose head is covered over. *Ikāʼ*, (or اكاءة *ikāʼat*) (v. n. 4 of كاء for كيأ) Terrifying, frightening, causing to desist from any undertaking.

A اكآب *ikʼāb*, (v.n. 4 of كئب) Being sad, fretting. Falling into perdition. Making sorrowful.

A اكابر *akābir*, (pl. of اكبر *akbar*) The rich, powerful, grandees, nobles. اكابر و اصاغر *akābir u aṣāghir*, Great and small, grandees and plebeians.

A اكاحة *ikāhat*, (v. n. 4 of كاح for كوح) Conquering in battle, subduing. Giving, bestowing. Penetrating, piercing, and leaving a mark. Ruining. (v. n. 4 of كاح for كيح) Destroying. Making an impression, taking effect (a sword).

A اكاحل *akāhil*, (pl. of كحل) Certain pot-herbs.

A اكاد *ikād*, (pl. اكائد *akāʼid*) A rope, belt, girth. A thong connecting the bow with the saddle-flap.

A اكادر *akādir*, (pl. of اكدر *akdar*) Thick, muddy, turbid. Name of certain mountains.

A اكاديد *akādīd*, (Men) dispersed here and there.

A اكاذيب *akāẓīb*, (pl. of اكذوبة *ukẓūbat*) Lies.

P اكار *ukār*, A vine-dresser. A tiller of ground.

A اكّار *akkār*, (pl. اكرة *akarat*) A farmer, husbandman, tiller of the ground.

A اكارة *ikārat*, (v. n. 4 of كار for كور) Esteeming or finding weak, and treating with contempt.

P اكارس *akāris*, A mushroom, a fungus, a puff.

A اكارس *akāris*, (or اكاريس *akārīs*) (pl. of كرس *kirs*) Adjoining houses.

A اكارع *akāriʻ*, (pl. of كراع *kurāʻ*) The small parts of the legs of sheep or oxen, the shins. The extremities of any thing, the remoter extremities of the earth. The rocky projections of mountains.

A اكارم *akārim*, (pl. of اكرم *akram*) Most noble.

A اكاسة *ikāsat*, (v.n. 4 of كاس for كوس) Loading (a camel) till (he) limps on three feet. Throwing prostrate. (v. n. 4 of كاس for كيس) Having ingenious children. Begetting sharp, clever children.

A اكاسرة *akāsirat*, and اكاسر *akāsir*, (pl. of كسري *kisra'* or *kasra'*) The Khosroes, kings of Persia, a family title, like the Cæsars or the Ptolemies.

A اكاسم *akāsim*, Ready to ride over each other (numerous horsemen). (pl. of كيسوم *kaysūm*) (Gardens) full of herbs.

A اكاف *ikāf* or *ukāf*, (pl. اكف *ukuf*) A thick coarse cloth placed under pack-saddles of asses.

A اكّاف *akkāf*, One who makes or vends cloths for asses' pack-saddles.

A اكاكة *akkākat*, Adversity.

A آكال *ākāl*, (pl. of اكلة *iklat*) Itchings. آكال الملوك *ākālu'l mulūk*, Provisions for royal households. آكال الجند *ākālu'l jund*, Soldiers' rations. ذوا الآكال *zawū'l ākāl*, Chiefs of people or tribes who, in Pagan times, received a fourth of plunder.

A اكال *akāl*, (v. n. of اكل) Being diseased by having a hairy fœtus in the womb (a camel). Being broken (the teeth). Meat, food. *Ikāl*, (v. n. 3 of اكل) Eating together: eating with one another. *Ukāl*, The itch. A disease incident to a she-camel, from having a hairy fœtus in her womb. *Ukāl* or *akāl*, (v. n. of اكل) Itching, requiring to be scratched (the head). Corrosion, canker.

A اكّال *akkāl*, Eating. Corrosive. A glutton.

A اكالب *akālib*, (pl. of كلب *kalb*) Dogs.

A اكاليل *akālīl*, (pl. of اكليل) Crowns, diadems.

P آكام *ākām*, A mushroom, a fungus.

A آكام *ākām*, (or اكام *ikām*) (pl. of اكمة *akamat*) Hills, heights, or rising grounds. Heaps of stones, or earth: cairns.

A اكام *ikām*, A pack-saddle.

P اكامه *akāma* or *ukāma*, Stuffed chitterlings.

A اكاميم *akāmīm*, (pl. of كمّ *kimm*) Follicles of unblown flowers.

A اكانة *ikānat*, (v. n. 4 of كان for كين) Humiliating, depressing. Reducing to a miserable plight.

A اكائد *akāʼid*, (pl. of اكاد *ikād*) Belts, girths.

A اكباء *akbāʼ*, (pl. of كبا *kibāʼ*) The sweepings of a house. *Ikbāʼ*, (v. n. 4 of كبا for كبو) Failing (a flint to strike fire). Emitting smoke. Altering.

A اكباب *ikbāb*, (v. n. 4 of كبّ) Falling prostrate. Overturning. Throwing prostrate. Turning. Leaning to, inclining the face to, approaching. Being necessary. Being assiduous, persevering.

A اكباح *ikbāh*, (v. n. 4 of كبح) Pulling the bridle, checking a horse. Making high and lofty.

A اكباد *akbād*, (pl. of كبد *kabd*, *kibd* or *kabid*) Livers. سود الاكباد *sūdu'l akbād*, Black-livered (a term applied to enemies). يضرب اليه اكباد الابل *yuẓrab ilayhi akbādu'l ibil*, Camel's livers are spurred, *i.e.* People resort thereto from all quarters.

A اكبار *akbār*, (pl. of كبر *kabar*) Capers. *Ikbār*, (v. n. 4 of كبر) Considering any thing as great. Voiding excrement (a boy). Being menstruous (a woman). Experiencing a seminal effusion (a man).

A اكباش *akbāsh*, (pl. of كبش *kabsh*) Rams.

A اكبان *ikbān*, A restraining of the tongue.

A اكبح *akbah*, Strong (camel).

A اكبد *akbad*, Corpulent, especially about the middle. Diseased in the liver, troubled with an enlargement of the liver. Slow-paced. A sort of bird.

A اكبر *akbar*, (pl. اكابر *akābir*) Greater, greatest. الله اكبر *allāh akbar*, God is great. The Emperor Akbar, who reigned in India from 1555 to 1605. *Ikbir* or *akbar*, A kind of dry sweetish substance produced by the palm-tree.

P اكبرآباد *akbar-ābād*, (Akbarpolis) Agra.

A اكبران *akbarāni*, The two great ones, namely, ابو بكر *abū bakr* and عمر *ʻumar*.

A اكبرّة *ikbirrat* or *akbirrat*, Chief of a family.

P اكبري *akbarī*, Name of a gold coin (in India).

A اكبس *akbas*, One who has a preposterously-shaped forehead (the crown advancing, the forehead receding). One whose pudenda are prominent.

A اكبش *akbush*, (pl. of كبش *kabsh*) Rams. Princes (as being the chiefs of their flocks).

P اكبيا *akbiyā*, (in zand and Pāzand) A nerve.

A اكبئنان *ikbiʼnān*, The being drawn together.

P آكپ *ākup*, The inside of the mouth.

A اكّة *akkat*, Intense heat. Adversity, tribulation. An evil disposition. Hatred, rancour. Death. A fit of rage against any one. Pain, trouble, grief. Stillness, calmness of mind.

A اكتاء *iktāʼ*, (v. n. 4 of كتا for كتو) Being superior to, prevailing against a foe.

A اكتئاب *iktiʼāb*, (v.n. 8 of كئب) Being grieved, sad, and melancholy.

A اكتاب *iktāb*, (v. n. 4 of كتب) Tying tight, or closing the mouth of (a leathern bottle). Teaching to write. Dictating, inditing (a poem).

A اكتات *iktāt*, The act of whispering in the ear.

A اكتاد *aktād*, (pl. of كتد *katad*) The spaces or substances between the shoulders and the back, interscapulæ. Troops, crowds. Images, pictures. Swift, rapidly succeeding in the traces of each other.

A اكتاف *aktāf*, (pl. of كتف *katif* or *kitf*) Shoulders. علم الاكتاف *ʻilmu'l aktāf*, The science of the shoulders; thus named from the shoulder-bones of sheep (marked with certain characters in geomancy), which are employed in this mode of anticipating the knowledge of futurity. ذو الاكتاف *zū'l aktāf*, Name of Shāpūr, a king of Persia.

A اكتال *iktāl*, (v. n. 4 of كتل) Imprisoning.

A اكتان *iktān*, (v. n. 4 of كتن) Glueing, joining.

A اكتباء *iktibāʼ*, (v. n. 8 of كبا for كبو) Squatting over a chafing-dish. Being perfumed (cloth).

A اكتتاب *iktitāb*, (v. n. 8 of كتب) Writing, describing, delineating. Writing one's name in the muster-roll or army-list. Requesting (any one) to write; dictating (an epistle). Sewing (a leathern bottle) with two thongs. Being confined (the belly).

A اكتتات *iktitāt*, (v. n. 8 of كتّ) Whispering in the ear. Listening, hearing.

A اكتتام *iktitām*, (v. n. 8 of كتم) Concealing. Being concealed. Being yellow.

A اكتحال *iktihāl*, (v. n. 8 of كحل) Anointing or rubbing the eye with a collyrium or black powder. Being covered the first time with green herbage (the ground). Falling into troubles.

A اكتد *aktad,* Prominent in the shoulder-blades, high-shouldered. High in the withers (horse).

A اكتداح *iktidāh,* A gaining, acquiring, earning.

A اكتداد *iktidād,* (v. n. 8 of كدّ) Plaguing, tormenting, desiring one to take trouble. Hanging back, desisting. Parsimony, closeness.

A اكتداش *iktidāsh,* The receiving of a present.

A اكتراء *iktirāʼ,* (v. n. 8 of كري) Hiring, renting. Taking on hire.

A اكتراب *iktirāb,* (v. n. 8 of كرب) Being weighed down with grief.

A اكتراث *iktirās,* (v. n. 8 of كرث) Minding, regarding, caring for, attending to, fearing.

A اكتراص *iktirās,* (v. n. 8 of كرص) Collecting. A collection.

A اكتزاز *iktizāz,* A shrivelling from cold.

A اكتساء *iktisāʼ,* The act of dressing one's self.

A اكتساب *iktisāb,* (v. n. 8 of كسب) Gaining, acquiring. Striving, endeavouring to gain.

A اكتساح *iktisāh,* (v. n. 8 of كسح) Stripping any one of the whole of his property.

A اكتسار *iktisār,* The act of breaking in pieces.

A اكتساع *iktisāʻ,* (v. n. 8 of كسع) Putting his tail between his legs (a dog). Striking his hips with his tail (a stallion-camel).

A اكتشاف *iktishāf,* (v. n. 8 of كشف) Exposing herself in a state of complete nudity to her husband (a woman). Leaping on the ewe (a ram).

A اكتشام *iktishām,* (v. n. 8 of كشم) Cutting off entirely the nose.

A اكتصاص *iktisās,* (v. n. 8 of كصّ) Thronging, collecting (men).

A اكتظاظ *iktizāz,* (v. n. 8 of كظّ) Being unable to breathe from repletion. Being brim-full.

A اكتع *aktaʻ,* One whose fingers bend inwards to the palm, leaving the joints prominent.

A اكتعين *aktaʻīna,* All. رأيتهم اجمعين اكتعين *raʼaytuhum ajmaʻīn aktaʻīn,* I saw them all.

A اكتف *aktaf,* Wide-shouldered (man or horse). (A horse) lame in the shoulder.

A اكتفاء *iktifāʼ,* (v. n. 8 of كفأ) Inverting (a vessel). Being content and satisfied. (v. n. 8 of كفي) Being content and satisfied.

A اكتفات *iktifāt,* The act of taking the whole.

A اكتفار *iktifār,* (v. n. 8 of كفر) Cleaving to a village (كفر *kafr*), not quitting it.

A اكتفال *iktifāl,* (v. n. 8 of كفل) Putting something on the hinder parts of a horse. Taking on one's back. Throwing a cloth over a camel's bunch for the rider to sit on. Putting any business on the shoulders of another. Turning one's backside upon.

A اكتفان *iktifān,* (v. n. 8 of كفن) Lying with.

A اكتل *aktal,* Intense, violent. Temptation. Sorrow, misfortune. Name of a traditionist.

A اكتلاء *iktilāʼ,* (v. n. 8 of كلأ) Receiving a part of the price and granting a delay for the remainder. Being on one's guard. Keeping watch. Wakefulness. (v. n. 8 of كلي) Having a pain or being hurt in the kidneys (كلية *kulyat*).

A اكتلات *iktilāt,* (v. n. 8 of كلت) Drinking.

A اكتلال *iktilāl,* (v. n. 8 of كلّ) Being bright with lightning (a cloud).

A اكتم *aktam,* Gor-bellied, satiated.

A اكتماع *iktimāʻ,* (v. n. 8 of كمع) Drinking out of a bottle.

A اكتمان *iktimān,* The act of concealing one's self.

SY اكت مكت *akit makit,* A grain, to which many wonderful properties are ascribed.

A اكتناء *iktināʼ,* (v. n. 8 of كني) Being called or calling one's self by a name which has naturally another meaning, being dubbed, or styled.

A اكتنات *iktināt,* (v. n. 8 of كنت) Being humble, submissive. Acquiescing.

A اكتناز *iktināz,* (v. n. 8 of كنز) Being closely packed or set. Being filled. Being collected.

A اكتناع *iktināʻ,* (v. n. 8 of كنع) Assembling, flocking together. Being indulgent. Being contracted and drawn together with old age.

A اكتناف *iktināf,* (v. n. 8 of كنف) Encircling. Making for camels a fold of bushes called كنيف.

A اكتنان *iktinān,* (v. n. 8 of كنّ) Being hid, concealed. Concealing one's self. Hiding, veiling, concealing. Whiteness.

A اكتناه *iktināh,* (v. n. 8 of كنه) Scrutinizing, getting to the bottom of, endeavouring to become thoroughly acquainted with. Reaching or attaining to the full extent of. P اكتناه سبب كردن *iktināhi sabab kardan,* To penetrate into the true cause.

A اكتواء *iktiwāʼ,* (v. n. 8 of كوي) Searing, cauterizing, or branding one's self. Being seared. Commending one's self for what one does not possess.

A اكتهاء *iktihāʼ,* The act of speaking face to face.

A اكتهاف *iktihāf,* (v. n. 8 of كهف) Entering into a cavern or grotto (كهف *kahf*).

A اكتهال *iktihāl,* (v. n. 8 of كهل) Becoming of full age, *i. e.* between thirty and fifty. Being filled with flowers (a garden). Beginning to grow gray.

A اكتياء *iktiyāʼ,* (v. n. 8 of كوي) Cauterizing one's self. Commending one's self for what one does not possess.

A اكتئاب *iktiʼāb,* (v. n. 8 of كئب) Desponding, losing spirits; grief, melancholy.

A اكتياب *iktiyāb,* (v. n. 8 of كاب for كوب) Drinking out of a goblet.

A اكتياد *iktiyād,* (v. n. 8 of كيد) Being deceived, cheated, taken in.

A اكتيار *iktiyār,* (v. n. 8 of كار for كور) Falling down. Preparing to rail at or revile. Cocking the tail. Quickening one's pace. Putting on a turban.

A اكتياز *iktiyāz,* (v. n. 8 of كاز for كوز) Drinking out of a goblet. Taking water in a jug.

A اكتياس *iktiyās,* (v. n. 8 of كاس for كوس) Hindering one in his work.

A اكتيال *iktiyāl,* (v. n. 8 of كال for كيل) Measuring (corn). Measuring for another. Receiving by measure.

A اكتيام *iktiyām,* (v. n. 8 of كام for كوم) Sitting upon the tips of the fingers.

A اكتيان *iktiyān,* (v. n. 8 of كان for كون) Becoming surety for another. Being, existing. (v. n. 8 of كان for كين) Being sad and melancholy.

A اكتيتاء *iktītāʼ,* (v. n. 12 of كتي) Being lavish in self-commendation. Stammering, stuttering. Being filled with rage.

A اكثاب *aksāb,* (pl. of كاثبة *kāsibat*) The lower parts of the withers of a horse. *Iksāb,* (v. n. 4 of كثب) Allowing (the hunter) to advance near to them (wild beasts or other game). Approaching, drawing near. Giving one to drink a little milk or water remaining in a vessel.

A اكثاث *iksās,* The having a thick beard.

A اكثار *iksār,* (v. n. 4 of كثر) Increasing, multiplying. Using immoderately. Doing very much. Abounding in money or flocks. Being much increased (wealth). Flowering (the palm-tree). Being very talkative. Immoderate use.

A اكثاف *iksāf,* (v. n. 4 of كثف) Coming near, giving opportunity, putting one's self in the power.

A اكثام *iksām,* v. n. 4 of كثم) Filling (a bottle). Approaching near to the hunter (wild beasts or other game). Retiring and concealing one's self (at home).

A اكثبة *aksibat,* (pl. of كثيب) Hills, sand-heaps.

A اكثر *aksar,* More or most numerous, copious, plentiful. More, many, frequent, the most part. For the most part, in general. اكثر اوقات *aksar awkāt,* Often, generally, frequently.

A اكثري *aksarī,* (or اكثريًّا *aksariyan*) More copious, for the most part.

A اكثع *aksaʻ,* (A man) having turgid lips, or gums full of blood.

A اكثف *aksaf,* Thicker, denser.

A اكثم *aksam,* Wide, broad (way). Large-bellied. Full, replete, saturated. Fat, fleshy (pubes).

A اكثوث *aksūt,* Dodder.

P اكج *akaj,* A species of wild apple, a medlar. A long pole with an iron hook, used by ice-house people in breaking and pulling to the banks ice from rivers and other pieces of water; grappling-irons.

P اكچ *akaj,* A sort of wild apple, a medlar.

P آكح *ākah,* (آكحي or آكخ) A decoction.

A اكحال *ak-hāl,* (pl. of كحل *kuhl*) Collyriums. *Ik-hāl,* (v. n. 4 of كحل) Being covered for the first time with green herbage (ground). Dearth, scarcity.

A اكحت *ak-hat,* Short, squab, dwarfish (man).

A اكحل *ak-hal,* One who has black eye-lashes Black-eyed. الاكحل *al ak-hal,* The middle vein of the arm. A chrysoprasus.

A اكحوان *uk-huwān* or *ak-hawān,* Camomile.

A اكحيلال *ik-hīlāl,* (v. n. 11 of كحل) Being covered with green herbage for the first time (ground).

A اكد *akd*, (v. n. of اكد) Treading out (corn).

اكداء *ikdāʼ*, (v. n. 4 of كدأ) Stunting. (v. n. 4 of كدي) Being stingy, avaricious. Being good for nothing, giving little. Producing no gems (mines). Finding (the soil) hard when digging, coming to a more solid stratum. Finding one inexorable when asking a favour. Repelling, averting, restraining.

A اكداد *akdād*, (Men) dispersed here and there. *Ikdād*, (v. n. 4 of كدّ) Confining, imprisoning. Hanging back, desisting. Parsimony, closeness.

A اكدار *akdār*, (pl. of كدر *kadar*) Troubles, cares.

A اكداس *akdās*, (pl. of كدس) Corn-stacks.

A اكداش *ikdāsh*, The act of receiving a present.

A اكداف *ikdāf*, (v. n. 4 of كدف) Striking with his hoofs (a horse).

A اكدام *ikdām*, (v. n. 4 of كدم) Being firmly bound (a prisoner) by agreement or parole.

A اكدّة *akiddat*, Leavings of a meadow that has been depastured. Dispersed here and there (men).

A اكدر *akdar*, (pl. اكادر *akādir*) Thick, muddy, turbid. Dark-coloured. (A stream) which brushes away the surface of the ground. Name of a dog. بنات لاكدر *banātu'l akdar*, Wild asses.

A اكدرار *ikdirār*, The being turbid, muddy, opake.

A الاكدريّة *al akdariyat*, The spouse, mother, grandfather, paternal or maternal aunt, remaining alive (with what belongs to them in a legal sense).

P اكدش *ikdish* or *akdish*, Of a mixed breed. Mixture, union. Beloved, sought. Sentient soul.

A اكذاب *ikzāb*, (v. n. 4 كذب) Detecting a lie. Compelling or instigating (one) to lie. Proving, discovering one to be a liar. Returning no answer, but pretending to be asleep.

A اكذاذ *ikzāz*, (v. n. 4 of كذّ) Walking through lumps or clods of earth.

A اكذب *akzab*, More or most of a liar.

A اكذوبة *ukzūbat*, (pl. اكاذيب) A lie, falsehood.

A اكر *akr*, (v. n. of اكر) Digging, excavating a well or ditch. *Ukar*, (pl. of اكرة *ukrat*) Ditches.

P اكر *akar*, Wood of aloes.

A اكراء *ikrāʼ*, (v. n. 4 of كري) Hiring out (a horse). Letting a (house). Delaying (supper). Lengthening (a discourse). Being increased, augmented. Being diminished, decreased. Watching in obedience to the divine command.

A اكراب *ikrāb*, (v. n. 4 of كرب) Filling. Hastening. Tying a short rope to the cross bar of a bucket. خذ رجليك بالاكراب *khuz rijlayka bi'l ikrāb*, Bestir yourself.

A اكراث *ikrās*, (v. n. 4 of كرث) Oppressing, afflicting, giving pain.

A اكراج *ikrāj*, (v. n. 4 of كرج) Being stale and mouldy (bread).

A اكراح *akrāḥ*, (pl. of كرح *kirḥ*) Hermits' cells.

A اكراد *akrād*, (pl. of كرد *kurd*) Kurds, people inhabiting part of Chaldea, Assyria, and Mesopotamia.

A اكرار *akrār*, (pl. of كرّ *karr*) Cushions, napkins, on which they kneel at prayer. Ropes which fasten together the wooden bars in camels' saddles; also the trusses or loads which they carry on each side. (pl. of كرّ *kurr*) Certain measures.

A اكراس *akrās*, (pl. of كرس *kirs*) Adjoining houses. Buildings erected for young goats. Dovecotes. Strings of pearls or other beads in the form of a chain. Dungs of animals, consisting of different strata, and adhering together. قلادة ذات كرسين او ذات اكراس *kilādatun zāt kirsayn aw zāt akrās*, A necklace consisting of two chains or of (several) chains. *Ikrās*, (v. n. 4 of كرس) Putting (a pigeon) into a pigeon-house, or a young goat into its cote. Becoming possessed of a cote. Being full of the dung of cattle (a house).

A اكراع *ikrāʻ*, (v. n. 4 of كرع) Exposing (itself) to be taken, affording a fair mark (game to the hunter). Coming to standing water. Watering camels.

A اكراف *ikrāf*, (v. n. 4 of كرف) Being addle, rotten (egg). Smelling (as the male does the female).

A اكرام *ikrām*, (v. n. 4 of كرم) Honouring, respecting, venerating. Keeping clean from any thing impure. Begetting a noble, liberal-minded offspring. Giving in great abundance whatever is proper for the support and comfort of life. Speaking nobly and excellently.

A اكراه *ikrāh*, The act of forcing against one's will.

A اكربة *akribat*, (pl. of كرابة *kurābat* or *karābat*) Dates which are gathered from the roots of the branches after the clusters are cut off.

A اكرة *ukrat*, (pl. اكر *ukar*) A well or ditch in which water collects, whence it is drawn out pure. (for كرة *kurat*) A globe, sphere, ball. *Akarat*, (pl. of اكار *akkār*) Farmers, husbandmen.

A اكرع *akraʻ*, Spindle-shinned. *Akruʻ*, (pl. of كراع *kurāʻ*) The smaller parts of the legs of sheep or of the cow-kind, their shins. The rocky projections of mountains.

P اكرفس *akrifs*, Parsley.

A اكرم *akram*, More or most noble, great, or benign; greatest, supreme.

A اكرماء *akrimāʼ*, (pl. of كريم *karīm*) Generous.

G اكروفس *akrūfas*, A walnut-tree.

A اكرومة *ukrūmat*, Honour, glory, nobility, grandeur, generosity, liberality, benignity, beneficence, clemency, grace, goodness.

P اكروهك *akrūhak*, A kind of Persian gum or balsam, excellent for the closing of wounds.

A اكرياء *akriyāʼ*, (pl. of مكاري *mukārī*) Letters out of camels, horses, and the like.

T اكريت *ikrīt*, The island of Crete or Candy.

A اكزاز *ikzāz*, (v. n. 4 of كزّ) Affecting with intense cold, or with a shivering fit.

A اكزام *ikzām*, (v. n. 4 of كزم) Being contracted within one's self. Eating to satiety.

A اكزم *akzam*, Short-lipped (horse). اكزم البنان *akzamu'l banān*, Close-fisted, avaricious.

P آكس *ākus*, A mason's chisel. A hooked stick.

A اكسّ *akass*, (A man) short-teethed.

A اكساء *aksāʼ*, (pl. كسء *kusʼ*, كسوء *kusūʼ*, and كسي *kusy*) Hinder parts, rumps. ركب اكساءه *rakiba aksāʼahu*, He fell on the back of his head. *Iksāʼ*, (v. n. 4 of كسأ) Following, going after. Turning tail, retreating.

A اكساب *iksāb*, (v. n. 4 of كسب) Causing (one) to get or gain. Getting, gaining.

A اكساد *iksād*, (v. n. 4 of كسد) Being dull and languid (a market). Spoiling a market, preventing wares from being sold.

A اكسار *aksār*, (pl. of كسر *kasr* or *kisr*) The lower parts of tents, or the flaps next to the ground, in which are openings for the conveniency of going in and out. Sides of houses. Parts of the body, and of the members. Bones with little flesh upon them. جفنة اكسار *jafnatun aksār*, A large dish having many joinings in it.

A اكساس *aksās*, (pl. of كسّ *kuss*) Vulvæ.

A اكساف *aksāf*, (pl. of كسفة *kisfat*) Parts, portions, segments.

A اكسال *iksāl*, (v. n. 4 of كسل) Making lazy. Covering without consummating (beasts or men).

P آكسته *ākasta*, Bound, tied.

A اكسح *aksaḥ*, (pl. كسحان *kus-ḥān*) Weak, powerless in the hands and feet, lame, unable to move. ما اكسحه *mā aksaḥahu*, How heavy he is!

A اكسد *aksad*, Dull, flat (market).

A اكسع *aksaʻ*, (A bird) having white feathers under the tail.

A اكسوم *aksūm*, Full of herbs (a garden).

P اكسون *aksūn* or *iksūn*, Satin, particularly a black kind (worn by princes). A species of brocade.

P آكسه *ākasa*, Suspended, hanging, adhering.

A اكسى *aksa'*, Better dressed. More or most liberal in presenting a great number of dresses to a person, by way of honouring him. اكسى من بصلة *aksa' mim basalatin*, More clothed than an onion.

A اكسية *aksiyat*, (pl. of كساء) Clothes, dresses.

A اكسير *iksīr*, An elixir, the philosopher's stone. Alchemy. اكسير دولت *iksīri dawlat*, The elixir of life or prosperity (a book so called).

P اكسيري *iksīrī*, An alchemist.

P اكسيه *aksiya*, A general name for malt-liquor.

A اكشاء *ikshāʼ*, (v. n. 4 of كشأ) Roasting (meat) till it becomes dry.

A اكشاد *ikshād*, (v. n. 4 of كشد) Purifying, clarifying (butter).

A اكشاف *ikshāf*, (v. n. 4 of كشف) Laughing and shewing the sockets of the teeth. Having she-camels which take the male when pregnant, or two years successively. Bringing forth two years in succession (a camel). Covering (a camel) in foal.

P آكشته *ākashta*, Strong. Fastened. Full.

A اكشف *akshaf*, Destitute of a helmet or shield in battle. One who has the hair on the forehead twisted. A horse in the bone of whose tail is a twist. A run-away in battle.

A اكشم *aksham*, One who labours under a defect of the body, or blemish in his pedigree. The cheeta, or hunting panther.

A اكشوث *akshūs*, Flax-seed. *Ukshūs*, Dodder.

A اكصاص *ikṣās*, The being put to flight, fleeing.

A اكظام *akzām*, (pl. of كظم) Mouths: throats.

A اكعاء *akʻās*, Cowards.

A اكعاب *ikʻāb*, (v. n. 4 of كعب) Making haste. Ordering to make haste. Having a fast-going beast.

A اكعات *ikʻāt*, (v. n. 4 of كعت not used) Departing, going away quick. Sitting still. Riding off, swelling with rage.

A اكعاع *ikʻāʻ*, (v. n. 4 of كع) Making afraid. Restraining, checking, repressing.

A اكعان *ikʻān*, Remission of alacrity, languor.

A اكعب *akʻub*, (pl. of كعب *kaʻb*) Ankles, the projecting bones at the juncture of the leg and foot. The tops of the feet, insteps.

A اكعر *akʻar*, Fat, full-bellied (boy).

A اكف *ukuf*, (pl. of اكاف *ikāf*) Thick, coarse cloths placed under the pack-saddles.

A اكفّ *akuff*, (pl. of كفّ) Hands, or palms.

A اكفاء *akfās*, (pl. of كفء كف *kafs*) Equal, resembling; equals. *Ikfās*, (v. n. 4 of كفأ) Overturning, turning down in order to empty (a vessel). Inverting. Inclining. Causing to incline. Inclining the upper part of a bow, so as not to make it perpendicular, when shooting. Adding more skirts or folds to a tent. Giving away whatever a camel produces in a year (as her colt, hair, or milk). Dividing a stock of she-camels into two classes, that the first may be impregnated one year, and the other the next; so that every camel may rest a season. Composing verses which end with different vowels or consonants (a poet). Increasing, multiplying (young camels).

A اكفّاء *akiffās*, Rivals.

A اكفاح *ikfāh*, (v. n. 4 of كفح) Drawing in or checking with the bridle, bridling. Driving back.

A اكفار *ikfār*, (v. n. 4 of كفر) Calling (another) a كافر *kāfir*, or infidel. Cleaving to a village.

A اكفال *akfāl*, (pl. of كفل *kifl*) Those who sit badly on horseback. (pl. of كفل *kafal*) Hinder parts, buttocks. *Ikfāl*, (v. n. 4 of كفل) Entrusting (to another) the administration of one's affairs.

A اكفان *akfān*, (pl. of كفن) Winding-sheets.

A اكفح *akfah*, Black.

A اكفس *akfas*, Bow-legged. One who limps on the outer edges of his feet. Crooked-breasted.

P اكفوده *akfūda*, The Caspian Sea.

A اكفهرار *ikfihrār*, (v. n. 4 of كفهر Q) Being of a dark colour (the face). Looking grim. Appearing, being visible in thick darkness (a star).

P اكاكرا *akahrā*, (or الكلكرا *akalkarā*) Pellitory. Dracunculus.

A آكل *ākal*, More or most voracious. *Ākil*, (pl. اكلة *akalat*) An eater, a devourer. A tyrant (as devouring his subjects). آكل نفسه *ākil nafsahu*, (Self-devouring) A kind of gum, euphorbium.

A أكل *akala*, (fut. يأكل *yaʼkulu*) He ate.

A اكل *akl*, (v. n. of اكل) Eating. Devouring. A grazing, pasturing. اكل و شرب *akl u shurb*, Meat and drink. الحسد يأكل الايمان كما تأكل النار الحطب *al hasad yaʼkulu'l īmān kamā taʼkulu'n nāru'l hatab*, Envy eats out religion as fire consumes fuel. *Ukl* or *ukul*, (pl. آكال *ākāl*) Victuals, provisions. Fruit of trees (as dates). Abundance, prosperity. Density or firmness (of cloth or paper). Prudence, understanding. ذو اكل *zū ukl*, Fortunate, possessed of the comforts of life. Endued with intelligence. انقطع اكله *inkataʻa ukluhu*, His victuals failed him, (metaphorically) he died. *Akal*, (v. n. of اكل) Being corroded. *Akil*, A tyrant (as the devourer of his subjects). *Ukal*, (pl. of اكلة *uklat*) Victuals, eatables.

A اكلأ *aklaʼ*, More or most permanent. بلغ الله بك اكلأ العمر *ballagha 'llāh bika aklaʼa'l ʻumr*, May God prolong thy life to the end of time!

A اكلاء *iklāʼ*, (v. n. 4 of كلأ) Grazing (a camel). Abounding in pasture (land). Turning (the view) again and again. Lending without usury. Paying (a debt) before due. Bringing to its close (life).

A اكلاب *iklāb*, (v. n. 4 of كلب) Having rabid (camels).

A اكلاح *iklāh*, (v. n. 4 of كلح) Looking austere and shewing the teeth. Rendering austere.

A اكلاع *iklāʻ*, (v. n. 4 of كلع) Making dirty, soiling. Laying layer upon layer (dirt).

A اكلاف *iklāf*, (v. n. 4 of كلف) Causing (one) to be wholly devoted to a thing.

A اكلال *iklāl*, (v. n. 4 of كل) Fatiguing, jading. Bringing on a dimness of sight (much weeping). Having a needy family or needy relations.

A اكلب *aklub*, (pl. of كلب *kalb*) Dogs.

A آكلة *ākilat*, Flocks pasturing. Rust. Gangrene. آكلة اللحم *ākilatu'l lahm*, (Eater of flesh) A knife. A pointed stick. Fire. A scourge.

A اكلة *aklat*, One meal. *Iklat*, *aklat*, or *uklat*, A calumniating of the absent, secret detraction. *Iklat*, (v. n. of اكل) Itching, requiring to be scratched (the head). (pl. آكال *ākāl*) Pruriency, irritation, itch. Manner of eating: as, حسن الاكلة *hasanu'l iklat*, Graceful in his eating. *Uklat*, (pl. اكل *ukal*) One mouthful. A round loaf or cake; prog. ذو اكلة *zū uklat*, Name of a man. ما زالت اكلة خيبر تعاذني *mā zālat uklatu khaybara tuʻādduni*, The (poisoned) morsel (I ate) at Khaybar never failed to torment me every anniversary (a saying of Muhammad). *Akalat*, (pl. of آكل *ākil*) Eaters, consumers. هم اكلة رأس *hum akalat raʼs*, They are few; such as may be satisfied with one head or one sheep. *Akilat*, (A camel) having a hairy fœtus. A disease which corrodes the bones. Itch. *Ukalat*, A glutton (man or woman).

A اكلزاز *iklizāz*, A sitting unsteadily on the saddle.

A اكلس *aklas*, Brown-coloured (wolf).

A اكلظ *aklaz*, (or اكلط *aklat*) One who limps.

A اكلف *aklaf*, Of a dark-red colour. A lion.

A اكلنداء *iklindās*, The being hard and thick.

A اكلنداد *iklindād*, (v. n. 3 of كلدد Q) Being hard. Being contracted: refusing. Throwing one's self on.

A اكليزاز *iklīzāz*, (v. n. 11 of كلز) Being very much contracted. Preparing to pounce on prey (a hawk).

A اكليفاف *iklīfāf*, (v. n. 11 of كلف) Becoming of a blackish red (a wine-jar).

A اكليل *iklīl*, (pl. اكاليل *akālīl*) A crown, diadem, chaplet, wreath, or garland. The capsule of any flowering shrub. Flesh growing about the root of the nails. A cloud which appears to be covered with a membrane or gauze. اكليل الجبل *iklīlu'l jabal*, (The crown of the mountain) An herb smelling like frankincense, rosemary. اكليل الملك *iklīlu'l malik*, (The royal crown) The herb melilot. الاكليل *al iklīl*, Name of the 17th lunar mansion.

A اكليلي *iklīliy*, Belonging to a crown or garland.

P اكليون *akalyūn*, A kind of stuff made entirely of silk or of velvet, worked with flowers and other figures. The Gospel.

A اكم *akam*, *ukum*, also آكم *ākum*, (pl. of اكمة *akamat*) Hills. Heaps of stones. Cairns.

A اكماء *akmās*, (pl. of كميّ *kamiy*) Bold, brave. Armed. *Ikmās*, (v. n. 4 of كمأ) Eating mushrooms or giving them to be eaten. Abounding with mushrooms. Rendering aged. (v. n. 4 of كمي) Killing the valiant of a host. Concealing from the eyes of others. Suppressing evidence. Purposing, resolving.

A اكمات *ikmāt*, The being of a dark-bay colour.

A اكماح *ikmāh*, (v. n. 4 of كمح) Pulling the reins (to make a horse hold up his head or stop). Beginning to shoot forth leaves (a vine). Being conspicuous, rising up, appearing aloft.

A اكماخ *ikmākh*, A sitting in state. Pride.

A اكماد *ikmād*, (v. n. 4 of كمد) Rendering sad, grieving. Wearing out, being worn out and smooth.

P اكماك *akmāk*, (or اكمال) A vomiting: a vomit.

A اكمال *ikmāl*, (v. n. 4 of كمل) Perfecting, completing, accomplishing. Perfection, completion, fulfilment, consummation.

A اكمام *akmām*, (pl. of كمّ *kimm*) The cups, follicles, or outward leaves of young unblown flowers. (pl. of كمّ *kumm*) Sleeves. *Ikmām*, (v. n. 4 of كمّ) Producing follicles (a tree). Making sleeves.

A اكمان *ikmān*, (v. n. 4 of كمن) Concealing.

A اكمة *akamat*, (pl. اكم *akam*, *ukum*, آكم *ākum*, اكام *ikām*, and آكام *ākām*) A hill, hillock, knoll, bank. A heap of stones. Rising ground.

A اكمّة *akimmat*, (pl. of كمّ *kimm*) Sacks with provender, which they hang under the mouths of horses; nose-bags. The follicles, or cups, which contain the young leaves of flowers, rose-buds, or pods of the palm-flowers.

A اکمتات *ikmitāt*, The being bay-coloured.

A اکمس *akmas*, One who can scarcely see.

A اکمش *akmash*, Short-footed. One who sees with difficulty.

A اکمل *akmal*, More or most perfect, complete.

A اکملیّة *akmaliyat*, The greatest perfection.

A اکمؤ *akmu*, (pl. of کمء *kam*) Mushrooms.

P اکمون بزان *akmūn bazān*, The herb vervain.

A اکمه *akmah*, Blind from the birth. Plentiful (forage), embarrassing from its abundance.

A اکمهداد *ikmihdād*, (v.n. 4 of کمهد Q) Raising its head, fluttering when fed in the nest (a chick).

A اکمهلال *ikmihlāl*, A cowering down from cold.

A اکمیتات *ikmītāt*, The being of a bay colour.

A اکناء *iknā*, (v.n. 4 of کنا for کنو) Expressing or calling by a word which has naturally another meaning, dubbing, nicknaming.

A اکناب *iknāb*, (v.n. 4 of کنب) Growing hard from labour (the hand). Being thick, coarse, and rough. Constipation. Retention (of the tongue).

A اکناش *iknāsh*, (v.n. 4 of کنش) Ordering one to make haste, or to hurry away from any thing.

A اکناع *iknā'*, (v.n. 4 of کنع) Contracting the wings (as an eagle when descending). Being submissive and supplicant, bordering on meanness. Bringing near. Asking.

A اکناف *aknāf*, (pl. of کنف *kanaf*) Parts, sides, environs, quarters, tracts, coasts. Protections. guardianships. *Iknāf*, (v.n. 4 of کنف) Receiving under protection. Preserving. Assisting.

A اکنان *aknān*, (pl. of کنّ *kinn*) Veils, umbrellas, shades, or coverings, under which any thing is kept, sheltered, or preserved. *Iknān*, (v.n. 4 of کنّ) Concealing in one's mind. Protecting, preserving, screening.

A اکناه *iknāh*, (v.n. 4 of کنه) Arriving at a summit or last stage (called کنه *kunh*).

A اکنة *uknat*, (for وکنة *wuknat*) A bird's nest.

A اکنّة *akinnat*, (pl. کنان *kinān*) Veils.

P آکنج *ākanj*, A hook used by ice-house people in drawing ice from pools.

A اکنع *akna'*, (pl. کنع *kun'*) Defective and marred (business). Disabled in the hand.

P اکنون *aknūn*, Now, at this time. Already. Therefore. For, still. But, however.

P آکو *ākū*, An owl. A bird of ill omen.

A اکواب *akwāb*, (pl. of کوب *kūb*) Cups, goblets (such as have neither handles nor spouts).

A اکواث *akwās*, (pl. of کوث) Shoes, short boots.

A اکواخ *akwākh*, (pl. of کوخ *kūkh*) Cottages (those especially made of reeds with no windows).

A اکواد *akwād*, (pl. of کودة) Heaps (of earth).

A اکوار *akwār*, (pl. of کور *kawr*) Herds of camels, from 150 to 200 and upwards. Herds of oxen. (pl. of کور *kūr*) Camels' saddles.

A اکواز *akwāz*, (pl. of کوز) Cups, tankards, jugs.

A اکواع *akwā'*, (pl. of کوع *kū'*) Wrist-bones.

P اکوان *akwān*, Name of a demon destroyed by Rustam. *Akawān*, Flower of the ارغوان *arghawān*.

A اکوان *akwān*, (pl. of کون) Worlds: existences.

A اکور *akwur*, (pl. of کور *kūr*) Camels' saddles.

A اکؤس *ak-us*, (pl. of کأس *ka-s*) Drinking-cups. Cups filled with wine.

A اکوس *akwas*, Ingenious, clever, shrewd (man).

A اکوع *akwa'*, (A man) who has a distorted wrist. One who has a large wrist-bone.

A اکول *akwal*, Ground spreading in the form of hills. *Akūl*, A devourer, consumer, glutton.

A اکولة *akūlat*, (A sheep) separated from a flock in order to be fattened. Barren (ewe). *Ukūlat*, A sheep fixed as a bait for the wolf.

A اکوم *akwam*, High. The part below the breast.

A اکوهداد *ikwihdād*, (v. n. 4 of کوهد Q) Fluttering, trembling (as a young bird in the nest when about to be fed). Toiling, being fatigued.

A اکوئداد *ikwi-dād*, (v. n. 4 of کوأد Q) Tottering with age (an old man).

A اکویداد *ikwīdād*, The being old and tremulous.

A اکوئلال *ikwi-lāl*, The being short.

A اکهاء *ak-hā*, Knowing, intelligent (men). *Ik-hā*, (v. n. 4 of کهي) Abstaining (from meat). Warming the fingers' ends with the breath.

A اکهاد *ik-hād*, The being tired. A fatiguing.

A اکهام *ik-hām*, (v. n. 4 of کهم) Being weak, heavy, dull (the sight).

A اکهب *ak-hab*, Dark-red or brown (camel).

A اکهیٰ *ak-ha'*, Freckled, pimply on the face. (A stone) solid, free from fissure or flaw. Stinking-breathed. Weak, languid, pusillanimous.

A اکي *aky*, (v. n. of اکي) Taking a written agreement from a debtor in the presence of a witness.

A اکیات *akyāt*, Ingenious, (persons). Purses.

A اکیاح *akyāh*, (pl. of کاح *kāh* or کیح *kīh*) The broader parts, sides, or declivities of mountains.

A اکیار *akyār*, (pl. of کیر *kīr*) A smith's bellows.

A اکیاس *akyās*, (pl. of کیس *kīs*) Purses. (pl. of کیّس *kayyis*) Sagacious, ingenious, prudent. *Ikyās*, (v. n. 4 of کیس) Having ingenious children.

A اکیاش *akyāsh*, Wool or silk twice spun; also the refuse.

A اکیال *akyāl*, (pl. of کیل) Measures (of grain).

A اکیح *akyah*, Rough, hairy. Gross, thick.

A P اکیخ *akīkh*, A sausage. The intestines, guts. A tendon. Cat-gut. Lute, harp, or fiddle-strings.

A اکید *akīd*, Firm, steady. Strong. Valiant. Vehement, rigorous, severe. Constant, unalterable اکید و شدید *akīd u shadīd*, Strong and valiant.

A اکیراح *ukayrāh*, Certain stations visited by Christians on some of their festival-days.

A اکیس *akyas*, More or most prudent, sagacious, ingenious. Ingenious, sensible.

A اکیك *akīk*, Warm, hot, sultry (day).

A اکیل *akīl*, An eater: a glutton. A sheep fixed as a bait for a wolf. A quadruped devoured by wild beasts. A boarder, fellow-commoner, mess-mate.

A اکیلب *ukaylib*, Somewhat like a dog.

A اکیلة *akīlat*, Food (of wild beasts). A sheep fixed as a bait for the wolf. Eaten by wild beasts. (A sheep) separated from the flock to be fattened.

P آگ *āg*, Name of a poisonous milky tree which grows in India. (in zand and Pāz.) Wheat.

P آگاه *āgāh*, Aware, wary. Intelligent, knowing, acquainted with. Prudent. Vigilant, attentive. Notice, news, indication, information. آگاه شدن *āgāh shudan*, To be certified or informed, to be aware of. آگاه کردن *āgāh kardan*, To inform, advise, certify. ناگاه *nāgāh*, Unawares.

P آگاهانیدن *āgāhānīdan*, To indicate, inform, signify, announce, certify. To warn.

P آگاهي *āgāhī*, Notice, intelligence, news, information. Attention, vigilance. آگاهي داشتن *āgāhī dāshtan*, To be aware, or informed of. آگاهي نمودن *āgāhī namūdan*, To be careful, provident.

P آگاهیدن *āgāhīdan*, To inform, advise, certify.

P آگده *āgada*, Filled, stuffed, crammed.

P آگر *āgar*, (or اگر *agar*) The buttocks.

P اگر *agar*, If; although. Sweet-scented flag.

P اگرا *ugrā*, Gruel, pottage.

P اگرچند *agar-chand*, Although, nevertheless.

P اگرچه *agar-chi*, Although, notwithstanding.

P اگرنه *agar-na*, If not, otherwise.

P اگرفت *agirift*, A certain number of crimes.

P آگره *āgra*, Agra, once the capital of Hindustān.

P آگري *āgrī*, A native of Agra.

P اگریون *agaryūn*, The itch, the scab.

P اگست *agast*, The star Canopus.

P آگسته *āgasta*, Wetted. Smeared. Mixed. *Āgista*, Firmly bound.

P آگش *āgush*, An embrace. The bosom.

P آگشته *āgashta*, Wetted. Smeared. Mixed. *Āgishta*, Firmly bound.

P آگفت *āgaft* or *āgift*, Grief, sorrow, affliction. Murrain or blight.

G اگلیون *agaliyūn*, The Gospel.

P آگن *āgan*, The stuffing of a pillow. A stuffer.

P آگنبالین *āgam-bālin*, Flocks of wool, or other stuff with which they fill cushions, pillows, or saddles.

P آگنج *āganj*, A sausage. A sheep's pudding stuffed. Filled, full.

P آگند *āgand*, He filled. Filled. Stuffing.

P آگندگي *āgandagī*, Plumpness, fulness.

P آگندن *āgandan*, To fill, stuff, cram.

P آگنده *āganda*, Filled. Any thing stuffed or crammed. A sausage. Large, fat. Flourishing, cultivated. پشم آگنده *pashm-āganda*, Stuffed with wool. گوشت آگنده *gosht-āganda*, Full of flesh. آگنده کردن *āganda kardan*, To fill. *Āganda* or *āgunda*, A stable, stall, or manger.

P آگنده گوش *āganda-gosh*, One whose ears are

stopped. Deaf. Hardened in wickedness.

P آگنش *āganish*, Stuffing (of cotton or wool).

P اگنش *agnish*, The erection of an edifice.

P آگنه *āgana*, Stuffing, lining.

P آگنیدن *āganīdan*, To stuff, to fill, to cram.

P آگنیده *āganīda*, Stuffed, crammed.

P آگور *āgūr*, A burnt brick.

P آگوش *āgosh*, An embrace. The bosom. As much as the arms can contain. A servant, a slave.

P آگوشیدن *āgoshīdan*, To embrace.

P آگون *āgūn*, Inverted, reversed. Contrary.

P آگه *āgah*, Intelligent, conscious, wary.

P آگهي *āgahī*, Knowledge, wisdom. Wariness.

P آگیش *āgīsh*, Suspended. Drawn out.

P آگیلون *āgīlūn*, Flowered silk of Damascus.

P آگین *āgīn*, Fat. (in comp.) Full: عنبر آگین *ʻambar-āgīn*, Filled with amber. زیب جوهر آگین *zībi jawhar-āgīn*, An ornament set with gems.

P آل *āl*, A sort of fish. A whale. A fatal disorder to which women are liable till the seventh day after their confinement. Reddish yellow, shining, carnation. The appearance of something resembling water on sandy plains, exhaled by the heat of the sun at mid-day; it looks like the sea at a distance, and is called سراب *sarāb*. A royal mark or signature, prefixed to diplomas. Fraud, treachery, deceit, plot, snare. Forceps. آل معصفر *āli muʻasfar*, Fiery, ruddy. A kind of fish.

A آل *āl*, (pl. آوال *āwāl*) Offspring, posterity, progeny, descendants, family, house, race (used only when the family is noble; since one cannot say آل الاسکاف *ālu'liskāf*). Followers and friends. The highest part of a camel, that which is seen at a distance. The vapour سراب *sarāb*, especially at the beginning of the day. Wood, timber. A figure, body, person. A tent-pole. The sides of a mountain. آل عثمان *āli ʻusmān*, The posterity of Osmān or Othmān, the first king of the Turks, the royal family of Constantinople. آل عمران *āli ʻimrān*, The family of Amrām. آل غدر *āli ghadr*, Perfidious. علي آله *ʻala' ālihi*, On his children.

A ال *al*, The Arabic article answering to *the*.

P ال *il*, Name of a city and country. *Ul*, He.

SY ال *il*, God.

A الّ *all*, (v. n. of الّ) Going quick, hastening. Shining (colour). Being shaken, agitated, disturbed, disordered, frightened, put into confusion, abashed by the interjection ویل *wayl*, Woe! Pushing, impelling, wounding, piercing (with a javelin). Sewing or quilting (a garment). Accusing, laying to one's charge. Quivering when running (certain nerves and muscles in a horse's shoulder). Groaning (from sickness or grief). Raising the voice in prayer, or in affliction. (A horse) erecting his ears into a point. (A hawk) refusing to hunt or to approach the game. Impatience under affliction. (pl. of الّة *allat*) Broad-headed javelins. *Ill*, A treaty, an oath (by which it is confirmed). Revelation. Security, safety, peace, tranquillity. Impatience under affliction. Near, neighbouring. Propinquity, affinity, relationship. An excellent race, origin, family. A mine. Enmity, hatred. Dominion, supremacy. Deity, divinity. God the best, the greatest.

P آلا *ālā*, Reddish colour. (in compos.) Contaminating. Contaminated. A contaminator.

A آلاء *ālāʼ*, (pl. of الي *aly, ily*, الو *alw*, الي *ala'*, and *ila'*) Benefits, favours, kindnesses.

P الا *alā*, Ho! halloa! have a care!

A الا *a'lā*, Is it not? Up! Away! Come along! Halloa! Ho! Well done! Prythee! Know for sure. Verily, indeed, forsooth.

A الاء *alāʼ*, (or الا *ala'*) Name of a bitter tree used in thickening or tanning leather. Fleshy-hipped (women). *Alāʼ*, (A sheep) exceeding six years, having its teeth dropt out.

A الآء *alʼāʼ*, (pl. of لأي *laʼy*) Wild oxen. *Ilʼāʼ*, (v. n. 4 of لأي) Falling into misfortunes.

A الّا *allā*, Come on! (for ان لا *an lā*) That not. *Illā*, (for ان لا *in lā*) Unless, save, except, besides, unless that, but that, but what. والا *wa illā*, And if not, otherwise, yet, nevertheless.

A الّاء *allāʼ*, A vendor of sheep's tails.

A الابة *ilābat*, (v. n. 4 of لاب for لوب) Having thirsty camels.

A آلات *ālāt*, (pl. of آلة *ālat*) Instruments, utensils, apparatus, tools, arms, harness. Tent-poles. آلات بیت *ālāti bayt*, Household furniture. P آلات شکم *ālāti shikam*, The bowels.

A الاتة *ilātat*, (v. n. 4 of لات for لیت) Defrauding one of his right, cheating him of a debt. Detaining, retaining. Diverting from any pursuit.

A الاثة *ilāsat*, (v. n. 4 of لاث for لوث) Committing, commending, entrusting to the care of.

P الاچي *alāchī*, Small cardamoms.

A الاحة *ilāhat*, (v. n. 4 of لاح for لوح) Shining, flashing (as lightning, a rich habit, a sword). Appearing. Making (a sword) gleam. Destroying. Fearing, shunning, avoiding.

A الادة *ilādat*, (v. n. of ولد) Bearing children.

A الاذة *ilāzat*, (v. n. 4 of لاذ for لوذ) Surrounding, embracing, comprehending.

P آلار *ālār*, Name of the founder of a sect.

P آلاریان *ālāriyān*, Disciples, followers of Alār.

P آلاس *ālās*, A live coal.

A الاس *ulās*, Insanity, madness.

A الاصة *ilāsat*, (v. n. 4 of لاص for لوص) Turning or inclining (any one) to that which one wishes. Being terrified, trembling. (v. n. 4 of لاص for لیص) Bending or wagging (any thing) in order to draw (it) out. Begging, asking, demanding.

G الاطیني *alātīnī*, Ivy. Bind-weed.

A الاعة *ilāʻat*, (v. n. 4 of لاع for لوع) Being black or discoloured (a nipple).

P الاغ *ulāgh* or *ulāk*, A forcing of one to work gratis. A relay of post-horses. A courier. An ass.

A آلاف *ālāf*, (pl. of الف *alf*) Thousands. (pl. of الف *ilf*) Intimate, familiar; comrades.

A الاف *ilāf*, (v. n. of ولف) Flashing incessantly (lightning). (v. n. 3 of الف) Agreeing with one per thousand, giving a thousand.

A الّاف *ullāf*, (pl. of آلف *ālif*) Accustomed, familiar. Intimate friends.

A الاق *ilāk*, (v. n. of الق) Shining, flashing. False lightning (*i.e.* when no rain follows).

A الّاق *allāk*, A liar. Lightning without rain.

A الاقة *ilākat*, (v. n. 4 of لاق for لیق) Binding to one's self, causing to cleave unto. Putting raw silk into an ink-stand, and making the ink good.

A الاقي *alākī*, Misfortunes, adversities.

A الاکة *ilākat*, (v. n. 4 of لاك for لوك) Performing the duties of an ambassador, or envoy.

A الال *alāl*, Vain, false, trifling. الضلال ابن الالال *az'zalālu'bnu'l alāl*, Error, the son of error; one who persists in error. *Ilāl* or *ulāl*, (pl. of الّة *allat*) Broad-headed javelins.

A الالة *ilālat*, The act of beginning the night.

P آلاله *ālāla*, (or الاله *alāla*) A tulip.

A آلام *ālām*, (pl. of الم *alam*) Cares. Griefs. Pains, misfortunes. Sicknesses. P دل پر آلام *dili pur ālām*, A heart full of grief.

A الآم *alʼām*, (pl. of لئیم *laʼīm*) Likes, equals. *Ilʼām*, (v. n. 4 of لأم) Repairing, mending, stopping cracks. Reconciling. Doing any mean dirty work; shewing one's self in a contemptible light; begetting children of the same wretched principles.

A الأم *alʼam*, More or most vile, base, sordid.

A الام *ilāma*, (for الي ما *ila' mā*) How long?

P الام *ulām*, A message. A courier, messenger.

A الامان *al' āmān*, Calling for quarter or mercy in battle. *Alāmān*, (Allemanni) A German.

A الامة *ilāmat*, (v. n. 4 of لام for لوم) Reproving, blaming much. Deserving censure. Doing that for which one is blamed.

A الآن *al'ān*, Now, presently, at this time, now-a-days. الآن کما کان *al'ān kamā kān*, Just as heretofore, as usual, as formerly.

A الانة *ilānat*, A softening, a smoothing.

P آلانه *ālāna*, A falcon: a falcon's nest. A shadow. The ring of a door, by which it is shut. A crow.

A الآني *alānī*, Belonging to the present time.

G الانیون *alāniyūn*, Elecampane, helenium.

P آلاو *ālāw*, (or الاو *alāw*) A flaming fire.

P آلاوه *ālāwa*, A trevet, pot-hook, fire-place. Two sticks for playing at hockey.

A الاویّة *alāwiyat*, Fragrant woods.

A الاویح *alāwīh*, (pl. of الواح *alwāh*) Planks, boards. Tables. Surfaces.

A اله *ilāh*, (pl. آلهة *ālihat*) A god. A pagan deity (Omnipotence being expressed by الله *allāh*, contracted from ال اله *al ilāh*, the radical ا *a* coalescing with the article).

A الاهة *ilāhat*, (v. n. of اله) Worshipping, adoring. *Ilāhat* or *ulāhat*, Deity, divinity, godhead.

A الاهي *ilāhīy*, Divine. P علم الاهي *ʿilmi ilāhī*, Divine knowledge, theology, metaphysics.

A الاهيون *ilāhiyūn*, The divines (an epithet given to Socrates, Plato, Aristotle, and other philosophers of the academic or peripatetic schools).

P آلاي *ālāy*, (in comp.) Defiling; a defiler.

A الايا *ulāya'*, (pl. of الية *alyat*) Fat buttocks. Fleshy-hipped (women). (pl. of الية *alīyat*) Oaths.

P الايچي *ilāychī*, Cardamoms.

P آلايش *ālāyish*, Contamination, defilement, corruption, pollution, impurity. آلايش دنيوية *ālāyishi dunyawīya*, The corruptions of the world.

A الائف *alāʼif*, (pl. of اليف) Intimate associates.

P آلائيدن *ālāʼidan*, To contaminate. To confound, to mix. To be contaminated.

A الب *alb*, (v. n. of الب) Drawing together (an army); assembling from every quarter (in order to commit hostilities). Instigating, impelling, driving (camels); being active in driving them, making them travel fast. Being driven into a ruck and thronging each other (camels). Driving forwards its prey (the wild ass). Walking fast. Returning. Raining incessantly. A collection, congregation, crowd. The violence of heat, or a fever. Thirst. A propensity to love. A violent urging forwards. A lamb's skin. The skinning over of a sore when it begins to heal. The briskness of a cupbearer. A stratagem against a foe. Poison, venom. *Ilb*, Name of a tree, the juice of whose leaves is poisonous. A collection. The distance between the outstretched tips of the thumb and finger.

A البّ *alubb*, (pl. of لبّ *lubb*) Hearts. Marrows. Kernels. Understandings.

P البا *albā*, (in zand and Pāz.) Milk. Mallows.

P البا *ulbā*, Sheeps' heart and liver hashed and fried in oil.

A الباء *ilbāʼ*, (v. n. 4 of لبأ) Putting the kid to the goat in order to suck. Suckling a young one with biestings. Giving (any one) biestings to drink. Providing biestings for a journey. Sending out biestings (a sheep). Boiling biestings. (v. n. 4 of لبي) Staying in a place.

A البّاء *alibbāʼ*, (pl. of لبيب *labīb*) Wise, prudent, intelligent, ingenious, industrious, assiduous.

A الباب *albāb*, (pl. of لبّ *lubb*) Hearts, marrows, bowels. Substances. Nuts. The piths of a tree. Understandings, intellects. ارباب الباب *arbābu'lalbāb*, Learned doctors. (pl. of لبب *labab*) Throats, those parts in particular about which they hang ornaments, or where they slaughter animals. The poitrels, or breast-harness (of horses). Small heaps of sand. *Ilbāb*, (v. n. 4 of لبّ) Stopping, remaining in a place. Putting breast-harness (on a horse) to steady the saddle. Being manifest, occurring, exhibiting, or presenting itself (a thing). Forming a kernel (the milky grain of corn). Driving forwards its prey (the wild ass).

A الباث *ilbās*, The act of delaying, retarding.

A الباح *ilbāh*, (v. n. 4 of لبح) Growing old (a man).

A الباد *albād*, (pl. of لبد *libd*) Felt-cloths, such as are put under saddles. Affairs. *Ilbād*, (v. n. 4 of لبد) Mixing or entangling (any thing), joining one thing to another. Stopping, remaining. Mending, patching. Putting the felt-cloth on a horse, and making it firm, supporting the saddle by that or any thing similar. Covering (a bottle) with such cloth. Stooping (going into a house). Being fixed on the ground (the eye in prayer). Bedaubing his buttocks with dung and urine, which becomes caked (a camel). (A camel) beginning to fatten, renewing his coat and colour in the spring.

P الباد *illbād*, A carder or cleaner of cotton.

A الباس *albās*, Clothes. *Ilbās*, (v. n. 4 of لبس) Clothing, dressing. Covering, concealing.

A الباط *albāt*, Skins, hides.

P الباق *ulbāq*, A kind of winter-garment.

A الباك *ilbāk*, (v. n. 4 of لبك) Blundering in speech. Speaking obscenely. An error in speech.

A البان *albān*, (pl. of لبن *laban*) Milks. *Ilbān*, (v. n. 4 of لبن) Having milk in the udder (a camel). Having plenty of milk (a farmer). Making the mess called تلبينة *talbīnat*.

A البب *albub*, (pl. of لبّ *lubb*) Hearts, minds (the best parts of any thing). Veins or roots of the heart or pericardium, the heart-strings. Nuts. بنات البب *banāt albub*, (or *albab*) The heart-strings, the seat of tenderness and sympathy.

P البة *ulbat*, A congregation, assembly, crowd. Hunger. *Alubat*, A cuirass of leather.

A البتّة *albatta*, Certainly, necessarily, in every manner, altogether. P البتّه خواهم داد *al batta khwāham dād*, I will certainly give (it).

P البرز *alburz*, Name of a celebrated mountain near Hamadān in Persia, famous for a number of temples of the Magi. An athletic, courageous man.

A البسة *albisat*, (pl. of لباس *libās*) Clothes, garments. البسهٔ فاخره *albisaʼi fākhira*, Rich dresses.

A البوب *ulbūb*, Kernel of the stone of the lote.

P البه *ulba*, A kind of food.

A آلة *ālat*, (pl. آلات *ālāt*) State. An instrument, utensil, tool, apparatus. A bier. A tent-pole. Severity, intensity. آلة التعريف *ālatu't taʼrīf*, The definite article. آلت حرب *ālati harb*, Machines of war, military apparatus, arms. هو في آلة سوء *huwa fī ālati sawʼin*, He is in an evil case.

A الّة *allat*, (pl. الّ *all*, الال *ilāl* or *ulāl*) A broad-headed javelin. A ewe. A weapon. A forked stick. The noise of running water. A single stroke. *Illat*, (pl. الل *ilal*) Relationship. A kinsman, relation. A mode of groaning. *Ullat*, (pl. الل *ulal*) A flock pasturing at a distance.

P آلت *ālut*, Plump buttocks. The chine.

A الت *alata*, (fut. يألت *yaʼlitu*) He defrauded He retained or detained. He removed or averted He exacted an oath. He compelled to swear or to be bound by an oath.

A الت *alt*, A false accusation, or suspicion.

A الّت *allati* or *allat*, (fem. of الذي) Who, which.

A التاب *iltāb*, A causing, a rendering necessary.

A التباء *iltibāʼ*, (v. n. 8 of لبأ) Sucking biestings from its dam (a lamb). Giving one biestings to drink. Milking biestings (called لبأ *libaʼ*).

A التباد *iltibād*, (v. n. 8 of لبد) Sticking closely together, being impacted clotted, feltered (hair or leaves). Having very thick foliage (a tree).

A التباس *iltibās*, (v. n. 8 of لبس) Being obscure, intricate, confused, mixed, doubtful, perplexing. Confusion, intricacy, doubt, perplexity.

A التباط *iltibāt*, (v. n. 8 of لبط) Purposing, striving, attempting. Being astonished, confounded, disturbed. Drawing (his) legs together (a horse). Striking the fore-part of the foot against the ground in running (a camel). Hemming in. Adhering, sticking close to. Commotion, perturbation. Effort.

A التباك *iltibāk*, The being mixed, confused.

A التبان *iltibān*, A sucking of one's own milk.

A التة *ultat*, A small present. Perjury.

A التتاب *iltitāb*, The putting on of raiment.

A التثاء *iltisāʼ*, (v. n. 8 of لثي) Gathering gum.

A التثاق *iltisāk*, The being wet, moist, or dewy.

A التثام *iltisām*, (v. n. 8 of لثم) Covering (the mouth) with a veil. Kissing.

A التجاء *iltijāʼ*, (v. n. 8 of لجأ) Fleeing for refuge (to a man or place). (v. n. 8 of لجي) Assuming a false title, falsely claiming relationship.

A التجاج *iltijāj*, A being mixed, confused (voices).

A التجام *iltijām*, (v. n. 8 of لجم) Becoming speechless (the tongue).

A الته *altah*, More or most acute in discovering the meaning of a poem.

A التحاء *iltihāʼ*, (v. n. 8 of لحا for لحو) Stripping off the bark, peeling. Picking a bone. (v. n. 8 of لحي) Becoming bearded, getting a beard.

A التحاب *iltihāb*, (v. n. 8 of لحب) Beating, treading, walking (on a road).

A التحاج *iltihāj*, (v. n. 8 of لحج) Compelling, forcing. Being difficult, obscure, and intricate.

A التحاد *iltihād*, (v. n. 8 of لحد) Inclining to one side. Departing from the faith, becoming impious and unbelieving.

A التحاس *iltihās*, A receiving of any thing due.

A التحاص *iltihās*, (v. n. 8 of لحص) Compelling, coercing, forcing to. Hindering, keeping back. Imprisoning. Adhering. Sticking fast. Being stopped (a needle's eye). Being mixed, confused (voices). Sucking an egg. Tearing out a sheep's eye and swallowing it (a wolf). Being forced.

A التحاط *iltihāt*, (v. n. 8 of لحط) Being angry.

A التحاف *iltiḥāf*, (v. n. 8 of لحف) Being covered with a sheet or coverlet. Wrapping a garment about one's self. Clothing one's self with any kind of upper garment (called لحاف *liḥāf*).

A التحام *iltiḥām*, (v. n. 8 of لحم) Being filled up with flesh (لحم *laḥm*), healing (a wound). Uniting, sticking close together, becoming one. Waxing hot and bloody (a battle).

A التخاء *iltikhās*, (v. n. 8 of لخا for لخو) Feeding on pap (a babe). Cutting a piece of skin from the brisket of a camel). (v. n. 8 of لخي) Cutting out thongs from the breast of a camel.

A التخاخ *iltikhākh*, (v. n. 8 of لخ) Being entangled (herbage). Being perplexed (business). Confusion, perplexity, mixture.

A التخاط *iltikhāt*, The being intermixed.

A التداد *iltidād*, (v. n. 8 of لد) Swallowing medicine (called لدود *ladūd*) taken in at one corner of the mouth. Deviating, declining from.

A التدام *iltidām*, (v. n. 8 of لدم) Smiting the breast (in grief). Perturbation, violent emotion.

A التذاذ *iltizāz*, (v. n. 8 of لذ) Savouring, relishing.

A التذاع *iltizāʿ*, (v. n. 8 of لذع) Being burnt. Suffering excruciating pain. Ulceration.

A التزاق *iltizāḳ*, (v. n. 8 of لزق) Adhering, sticking.

A التزام *iltizām*, (v. n. 8 of لزم) Being necessary. Embracing. Being assiduous, sticking firm to. Taking upon one's self. *A* Hire, rent, lease.

A التزاماً *iltizāman*, (Pers. التزامانه *iltizāmāna*) Necessarily, consequently. By renting, hiring.

A التزامي *iltizāmīy*, Necessary, consequential.

A التساق *iltisāḳ*, The act of sticking, adhering.

P آلت شناس *ālat-shinās*, Skilled in arms.

A التصاص *iltiṣāṣ*, (v. n. 8 of لص) Firmly adhering, sticking close.

A التصاق *iltiṣāḳ*, The act of sticking, adhering.

A التطاط *iltiṭāṭ*, (v. n. 8 of لط) Being rubbed with musk. Veiling herself (a woman). Covering.

A التطاع *iltiṭāʿ*, (v. n. 8 of لطع) Drinking or lapping dry, a cup or a cistern.

A التطام *iltiṭām*, (v. n. 8 of لطم) Dashing furiously (waves).

A التظاء *iltizās*, (v. n. 8 of لظي) Burning, blazing, sending forth flame.

A التعاج *iltiʿāj*, The being wasted with grief.

A التعاق *iltiʿāḳ*, (v. n. 8 of لعق) Changing colour (the face).

A التعان *iltiʿān*, (v. n. 8 of لعن) Cursing, railing at one another. Keeping in the middle path in praying for one's self.

A التغاد *iltighād*, (v. n. 8 of لغد) Taking by the hand. Keeping one back from what he wishes to do.

A التفاء *iltifās*, (v. n. 8 of لفا) Peeling bark. Stripping, denuding.

A التفات *iltifāt*, (v. n. 8 of لفت) Turning towards another. Minding, attending to. Respect, courtesy, reverence. Attention, regard. (in rhetoric) An apostrophe. P التفات ملوكانه *iltifāti mulūkāna*, Royal favour.

A التفاع *iltifāʿ*, (v. n. 8 of لفع) Putting on an upper garment. Wrapping a cloak about one's self. Being covered with plants. Being changed (colour).

A التفاف *iltifāf*, (v. n. 8 of لف) Growing luxuriantly, being entangled. Wrapping one's self up in a garment. Wrapping a garment round one's body.

A التفام *iltifām*, (v. n. 8 of لفم) Putting a fillet (called لفام *lifām*) over the nose or mouth.

A التقاء *iltiḳās*, (v. n. 8 of لقي) Meeting, encountering. Interview, audience, conference.

A التقاص *iltiḳāṣ*, A taking, a receiving.

A التقاط *iltiḳāt*, (v. n. 8 of لقط) Collecting, gathering, picking up. Stumbling unexpectedly (upon one). Tale-bearing.

A التقاطاً *iltiḳātan*, Unexpectedly, suddenly.

A التقاع *iltiḳāʿ*, (v. n. 8 of لقع) Changing, fading.

A التقام *iltiḳām*, (v. n. 8 of لقم) Devouring, swallowing. Taking (لقمه *luḳma*) into the mouth.

A التكاك *iltikāk*, (v. n. 8 of لك) Thronging, crowding about a cistern. Being drawn up in close array (an army). Committing a blunder (in speaking). Pleading slowly and deliberately.

A التماء *iltimās*, (v. n. 8 of لما) Taking or laying by, any fragments (of meat) in a dish. Fading (colour). (v. n. 8 of لمي) Fading (colour).

A التماح *iltimāḥ*, The losing of one's sight.

A التماس *iltimās*, (v. n. 8 of لمس) Praying, supplicating, petitioning, beseeching. Seeking, searching. Prayer, request, entreaty.

A التماط *iltimāt*, A going off with, a taking away.

A التماظ *iltimāz*, (v. n. 8 of لمظ) Throwing (food) hastily into the mouth. Making a smacking noise with the lips. Taking away another's due. Twisting, wrapping. Being folded or wound about.

A التماع *iltimāʿ*, (v. n. 8 of لمع) Shining, flashing, being resplendent. Carrying away, clandestinely, snatching. Being changed (colour).

A التمام *iltimām*, (v. n. 8 of لم) Descending, alighting. Visiting. Being collected in a mass.

A التواء *iltiwās*, (v. n. 8 of لوي) Being bent, doubled, folded together. Being twisted (a rope). Coiling itself up (a serpent). Being distorted (an arrow or sand-hillock). Hanging back, turning aside from laziness. Laying by a part of the food called لويّة *lawīyat* (a woman).

A التهاء *iltihās*, The act of amusing one's self.

A التهاب *iltihāb*, (v. n. 8 of لهب) Burning, flaming. Heat, inflammation. P آتش گرم التهاب *ātishi garm-iltihāb*, A fire burning fiercely.

A التهاث *iltihās*, (v. n. 8 of لهث) Lolling out his tongue (a dog).

A التهاف *iltihāf*, (v. n. 8 of لهف) Flaming.

A التهام *iltihām*, (v. n. 8 of لهم) Swallowing quickly, bolting. Exhausting (the udder). Fading, changing (colour).

A الّتي *allatī*, Calamity, misfortune. (fem. of الّذي *allazī*, rel. pron.) Who, which.

A التئاء *iltiʾās*, (v. n. 8 of لأي) Becoming poor. Being sluggish, proceeding slowly. Slowness, delay.

A التياث *iltiyās*, (v. n. 8 of لاث for لوث) Mixing. Being mixed. Wrapping a garment round one's body. Minding, attending to. Mixture, confusion, intricacy. Luxuriancy, entanglement. Tardiness. Power, strength. Fatness. Imprisonment.

A التياح *iltiyāḥ*, (v. n. 8 of لاح for لوح) Being thirsty. Shining, flashing (lightning). Rising, appearing (a star).

A التياخ *iltiyākh*, (v. n. 8 of لاخ for لوخ) Being mixed. Fermenting (dough).

A التياذ *iltiyāz*, (v. n. 8 of لاذ for لوذ) Flying to, taking refuge with.

A التياط *iltiyāt*, (v. n. 8 of لاط for لوط) Plastering (a cistern) for one's own use. Adopting into one's family. Being near, dear, and close to the heart. Affiliation.

A التياظ *iltiyāz*, (v. n. 8 of لاظ for لوظ) Being difficult (an affair).

A التياع *iltiyāʿ*, (v. n. 8 of لاع for لوع) Being inflamed with love. Pining away. Sorrow, grief.

A التياق *iltiyāḳ*, (v. n. 8 of لاق for ليق) Acting with sincerity, so that the party becomes attached. Adhering, cleaving to. Being content, independent. Intimacy, adherence, devotedness.

A التئام *iltiʾām*, (v. n. 8 of لأم) Agreeing. Being healed, consolidated. Being restored to favour.

A التيام *iltiyām*, (v. n. 8 of لام for لوم) Being blamed, chidden, receiving censure.

A الثاء *ilsās*, (v. n. 4 of لثي) Being wet. Distilling juice or a thin gum (a tree). Giving to one the juice of a tree to drink.

A الثاث *ilsās*, (v. n. 4 of لث) Being importunate, urgent. Remaining in a place. Raining for several days successively.

A الثاق *ilsāḳ*, A wetting, moistening, bedewing.

A الثغ *alsaʿ*, One who stutters in pronouncing the letters ث *sa* or ع *ʿayn*.

A الثغ *alsagh*, A stammerer. One who pronounces the letter غ *gha*, ل *la*, or ي *ya*, instead of ر *ra*; or ث *sa* (literally *tha*), instead of س *sa*.

P الج *alj*, Proud. A pompous or mincing air.

A الجاء *iljās*, (v. n. 4 of لجا) Compelling, forcing. Referring a matter to God, and submitting to his will. Protecting, defending.

A الجاج *iljāj*, (v. n. 4 of لج) Braying aloud and foaming at the mouth (a camel).

A الجاف *aljāf*, (pl. of لجف *lajaf*) Cuts in the sides of a well, through which some part of the water runs off. The channels of torrents.

A الجام *iljām*, (v. n. 4 of لجم) Bridling. Coming up to the mouth (water). Burning the mark of a bridle (لجام *lijām*) upon a horse.

A الجبر *al jabr*, Algebra (as the reduction of parts

to a whole, or of fractions to integers).

A الجمة *aljimat*, (pl. of لجام *lijām*) Bridles, reins. Marks, resembling bridles branded upon cattle.

الجخت *al, il,* or *ulchakht*, Desire. Hope.

T الجي *ilchī*, An ambassador, plenipotentiary.

T الجيك *al chīchak*, Name of a Turkish prince.

A الحاء *ilhās*, (v. n. 4 of لحي) Doing a thing meriting censure. Requiring to be peeled (a branch).

A الحاج *alhāj*, (pl. of لحج *luhj* and *lahj*) Sockets of the eyes. Hollows, cavities. *Ilhāj*, (v. n. 4 of لحج) Compelling, forcing, constraining to repair.

A الحاح *ilhāh*, (v. n. 4 of لح) Importuning, soliciting, urging, dunning, harassing, teazing. Raining incessantly. Remaining fixed (a cloud). Being refractory, restive, lazy, lying down, when he should stand or proceed. Galling a camel's back.

A الحاد *alhād*, (pl. of لحد *lahd* or *luhd*) Niches dug in the side of a tomb or grave. *Ilhād*, (v. n. 4 of لحد) Preparing a niche in the side of a tomb for depositing the dead. Slighting. Inclining, deviating, departing from the true faith. Impiety, irreligion, infidelity, heresy, idolatry, polytheism. Dispute, contention, calumny. Burying. Storing up grain against times of scarcity. Oppression.

A الحاس *ilhās*, (v. n. 4 of لحس) Producing the first crop of grass (ground). Putting forth herbage (such as sheep may crop).

A الحاصل *al hāsil*, On the whole, in fine, to sum up.

A الحاف *ilhāf*, (v. n. 4 of لحف) Sweeping the ground with the train of a robe (from ostentation). Uprooting a nail. Importuning, urging, forcing, compelling. Walking near the foot of a mountain.

A الحاق *alhāk*, (pl. of لحق *lahak*) Parts of a valley sown after the overflowing waters have subsided. *Ilhāk*, (v. n. 4 of لحق) Arriving, reaching, overtaking, following. Joining. Affixing, suffixing.

A الحال *al hāl*, Now, at present. الحالة هذه *al hālat hāzihi*, This being the case, things being so.

A الحام *ilhām*, (v. n. 4 of لحم) Consolidating, joining together, soldering. Having a great deal of flesh-meat in the house. Giving flesh to eat. Filling up with flesh (a wound). Having grain in the ear (corn). Weaving. Versifying. Finishing (any thing begun). Surrounding any one (battle). Exposing (the honour of another) to the contumely of an enemy. Stopping, being restive, not proceeding far, till compelled by stripes. الحم ما اسديت *alhim mā asdayta*, Finish what you have begun.

A الحان *alhān*, (pl. of لحن *lahn*) Notes, sounds, modulations, or tones. P خوش الحان *khwush-alhān*, Singing melodiously, having sweet notes.

A *Ilhān*, (v. n. 4 of لحن) Making one to understand.

A الحذر *al hazar*, Take care! beware! shun (it)!

A الحق *al hahk*, Truly, certainly, the truth is.

A الحم *alhum*, (pl. of لحم *lahm*) Meats.

P الحمد خواندن *al hamd khwāndan*, To read the first chapter of the Kur'ān, which commences thus: الحمد لله *al hamdu li'llāh*, Praise be to God!

A الحن *alhan*, Melodious reader or chanter.

A الحى *alha'*, Large-bearded, or long-bearded (man). *Alhī*, (pl. of لحي *laha'*) Chins.

A الخ *alakh*, (for الي آخره *ila' ākhirihi*) And so forth, et cetera, to the end of it.

A الخاء *ilkhās*, (v. n. 4 of لخي) Giving of one's property. Injecting medicine into the nose or mouth.

A الخاص *ilkhās*, (v. n. 4 of لخص) Looking into the eye (of a camel) in order to disover whether he is fat enough for slaughter.

A الخص *alkhas*, One whose upper eye-lid is thick and hard.

A الخن *alkhan*, Uncircumcised. Offensive, rank.

A الخي *alkha'*, A babbler, a chattering, talkative fellow. Crooked. Unequal-kneed (camel).

A الدّ *aladd*, (pl. لدّ *ludd* and لداد *lidād*) An antagonist, insatiable and unfair. Quarrelsome, squabbling, litigious (man). Long-necked (camel).

A الداء *ildās*, (v. n. 4 of لدي) Having many cotemporaries (called لدة *lidat*).

A الداد *ildād*, (v. n. 4 of لدّ) Administering medicine to the sick through one corner of the mouth.

A الداس *aldās*, (pl. of لديس *ladīs*) Fat, fleshy. *Ildās*, (v. n. 4 of لدس) Putting forth herbage.

A الدام *ildām*, (v. n. 4 of لدم) Continuing to afflict (a fever).

A الدة *ildat*, (for ولدة *wildat*) A daughter. A girl. (pl. of ولد *walad*) Sons.

A الدّة *aliddat*, (pl. of لدود *ladūd* and لديد *ladīd*) Medicines poured into the corner of the mouth.

A الدعا *ad'duā*, Farewell, adieu (ال and دعا).

A الذّ *alazz*, Sweeter, more or most delicious.

A الذا *allazā*, Those two (men) who.

A الذام *ilzām*, (v. n. 4 of لذم) Rendering necessary, making inseparable, causing to adhere or remain constantly, fixing. Exciting, instigating, making greedy, inflaming. Being addicted to.

A الذّة *alizzat*, Those who take their pleasure.

A الذي *allazi*, (الذيّ *allazīy*, الذّ *allazi* or *alluz*) (relat. masc. pron.) Who, which.

A ال رأيت *al raayta*, (for هل رأيت *hal raayta*) Hast thou seen? perchance thou hast seen.

A الذين *allazīna*, (pl. of الذي *allazī*) Who.

P آلر *ālar*, Buttocks, hips.

P الرد *alard*, A net with wide meshes in which gardeners carry their vegetables to market.

A الز *alz*, (v. n. of الز) Adhering. Inhering. Being addicted or given up to any thing. *Alaz*, (v. n. of الز) Staggering, tottering.

A الزاء *ilzās*, (v. n. 4 of لزأ) Filling. Feeding to satiety (flocks).

A الزاز *ilzāz*, A glueing together, making adhere.

A الزاق *ilzāk*, A joining, cementing, glueing.

A الزام *ilzām*, (v. n. 4 of لزم) Rendering necessary, compelling. Fastening (a thing) upon (any one), tying (it) round his neck. Conviction. ممكن الالزام *mumkinu'l ilzam*, Capable of conviction.

P الزام كردن *ilzām kardan*, To use violence. To arraign. To convict. To sentence.

A الزم *alzam*, More or most necessary.

A الزن *alzan*, Most severe, disastrous (season).

A آلس *ālis*, Name of a river near Tarsus.

A الس *alasa*, (fut. يالس *yaalisu*) He deceived.

A الس *als*, (v. n. of الس) Being perfidious, deceitful. Being disturbed in intellect. Perfidy, treason, disloyalty, treachery, fraud. A lie. Theft, larceny. Doubt, suspicion, scandal. A change, deterioration of the disposition. Mental aberration, perturbation of mind, insanity, madness, frenzy. A bad stock, race, or family.

P السا *alsā*, Aniseed baked in bread.

A الساس *ilsās*, (v. n. 4 of لسّ) Bringing forth herbage (ground).

A الساع *ilsāع*, (v. n. 4 of لسع) Sowing divisions, promoting animosities, raising quarrels.

A الساق *ilsāk*, A joining, fixing, making adhere.

A السام *ilsām*, (v. n. 4 of لسم) Making one to taste. Seeking, searching. Ordering one to proceed (on the road), or forcing him to keep it. Instructing, teaching, informing.

A السان *ilsān*, (v. n. 4 of لسن) Lending a young camel that he may suck and induce a camel to give her milk Causing to arrive or happen.

P آلست *ālast*, (or الست) A fat, plump buttock.

A السن *alsan*, (pl. لسن *lusn*) Eloquent. *Alsun*, (or السنة *alsinat*) (pl. of لسان *lisān*) Tongues. Languages, dialects. السنة العصافير *alsinatu'l ع asāfīr*, Sparrow's tongue (a herb).

A الشام *ash'shām*, Syria. The city of Damascus.

A الصّ *alass*, One who has compact close-set eeth. One who has high, close shoulder-blades. More or most given to robbery, more or most of a thief (لصّ لصّ *liss, lass, luss*). الصّ الاليتين *alassu'l alyatayn*, One whose buttocks are closely set.

A الصاص *alsās*, (pl. of لصّ *liss*) Thieves, robbers.

A الصاق *ilsāk*, (v. n. 4 of لصق) Joining, glueing together: inseparableness, adhesion. Houghing.

A الط *alatt*, One whose teeth are dropped out, or eaten away, and the roots still remaining.

A الطاط *iltāt*, (v. n. 4 of لطّ) Covering, concealing. Denying a debt. Making one refuse to pay that which is justly due; abetting, aiding him in such refusal. Flattening, making (a grave) lie flat on the ground. Being violent in litigation.

A الطاع *altāع*, (pl. of لطع *latع*) Jaws.

A الطاف *altāf*, (pl. of لطف *lutf*) Benefits, favours. *Iltāf*, (v. n. 4 of لطف) Conferring favours. Joining, uniting, making stick to one's side.

A الطروهي *aluti rūmī*, A species of mint.

A الطجاع *iltijāع* for (اضطجاع), Lying on the side.

A الطست *altast*, Indian storax.

A الطع *altaع*, (A man) who has lost his teeth.

A الطف *altaf*, More or most kind or benevolent.

T آل طمغا *āl tamghā*, The royal seal or signature.

A الطوسيّ *at'tūsiy*, Native of Tūs in Khurāsān: many eminent men have taken this surname, especially a celebrated astronomer called Nāsiru'd dīn.

A الظاظ *ilzāz*, (v. n. 4 of لظّ) Being assiduous, industrious, attentive, unremitting. Importuning. Raining incessantly. Staying in a place.

A العاء *alʻās*, The bones of the fingers.

A العاب *ilʻāb*, (v. n. 4 of لعب) Slavering (an infant). Causing or exciting to play. Producing any thing ludicrous, with which sport may be made.

A العاج *ilʻāj*, A kindling, setting fire (to wood).

A العاط *alʻāt*, (pl. of لعط *laʻt*) Lines or marks, such as the Ethiopians and other barbarous nations make upon their faces: tattoo.

A العاع *ilʻāʻ*, (v. n. 4 of لعّ) Producing its first crop of grass (ground).

A العاف *ilʻāf*, (v. n. 4 of لعف not used) Licking blood with the tongue (a lion or camel). Being in a fierce rage and preparing to spring (a lion). Looking, knitting the brows and looking again. Going slowly, preparing to be restive (a camel).

A العبان *ulʻubān*, Addicted to play.

A العث *alʻas*, Slow, heavy.

A العس *alʻas*, Black-lipped. Luxuriant (plant).

A العوبة *ulʻūbat*, Play, fun. A playful woman.

A العياذ بالله *al ʻiyāz bi'llāh*, May God avert!

P الغ *aligh*, Effeminate, infamous.

T الغ *ulugh*, (or الوغ *ulūgh*) Powerful, great. الغ بيگ *ulugh beg*, A great prince. Name of a king of Parthia and India, grandson of Tīmūr Lang.

A الغاء *ilghās*, (v. n. 4 of لغا for لغو) Excluding, rejecting, disappointing, baulking, frustrating. Throwing out of account, not admitting into computation.

A الغاب *ilghāb*, (v. n. 4 of لغب) Fatiguing, tiring, jading, vexing. Fitting a bad feather to an arrow.

A الغاد *alghād*, (pl. of لغد *lughd*) The fleshy parts of the mouth from the jaws to the windpipe, round the throat. Exuberances of flesh in the inner part of the ears. The lobes of the ears.

A الغاز *alghāz*, (pl. of لغز *lughz, lughuz, laghaz*, and *lughaz*) Enigmas, riddles, mysteries, unintelligible discourses. Holes of moles, rabbits, field-mice, lizards, and other animals that live in subterraneous burrows. Labyrinths, mazes, intricate ways. *Ilghāz*, (v. n. 4 of لغز) Speaking obscurely and enigmatically, concealing one's meaning.

A الغاط *alghāt*, (pl. of لغط *laght*) Voices, noises, confused sounds, such as proceed from a crowd of people; unintelligible jargons. *Ilghāt*, (v. n. 4 of لغط) Making such obscure noise. Putting a hot iron into milk or water, and making it hiss. Hissing (milk into which a hot stone has been put).

A الغاف *ilghāf*, (v. n. 4 of لغف) Licking blood (a lion). Being prepared to spring. Making haste. Making one swallow morsels or mouthsful. Abetting, being a companion of thieves. Alacrity, despatch. Fraud, perfidy, deceit, injustice.

P آلغده *ālaghda*, Mixed. Angry, contentious.

P الغده *alaghda*, Mixed.

A الغرض *al gharaz*, To sum up all, in a word.

A الغز (ابن) *(ibn) alghaz*, Name of a man proverbially potent in venery.

P الغنجار *alghunjār*, Feigned anger of a mistress. A morel cherry. Calumny. Envy.

P الغنجيدن *alghanjīdan*, To gain, to acquire.

A الغوزة *ulghūzat*, An enigma.

P آلغونه *ālghūnah* (or آلغنونه *alghunūna*), Rose-coloured, scarlet, ruby-coloured paint for the face.

A الغينان *ilghīnān*, (v. n. 11 of لغن not in use) Being long, luxuriant, and involved (herbage).

A آلف *ālaf*, More or most tame or familiar. *Ālif*, One who associates or joins. One who becomes intimate. A giver of a thousand (الف *alf*). (pl. الّاف *ullāf*) Accustomed, familiar. A comrade, companion, intimate friend.

A الف *alf*, (v. n. of الف) Giving a thousand. (pl. الوف *ulūf* and آلاف *ālāf*) A thousand. *Ilf*, Intimacy, familiarity. A female friend. (pl. آلاف *ālāf*) An associate, companion, familiar friend. *Ilf* and *alf*, (v. n. of الف) Being familiar, intimate, or accustomed. *Alif*, (pl. الفات *alifāt*) Name of the first letter in the Arabian and Persian alphabets. One of any thing. A bachelor. A comrade, companion, intimate friend. A vein which lines the arm from the elbow to the shoulder. الف استوا *alifi istiwā*, The equinoctial line. الف اقليم *alifi iklīm*, The first of the seven climates of the earth. الف با تا *alif, bā, tā*, A slate, a pen, and stool. P الف بي *alif be*, The a, b, c, the alphabet. الف كردن *alif kardan*, To strip naked. الف كوفيان *alifi kūfiyān*, The Kūfic alif. Any thing bent. Penis. *Uluf*, (pl. of الوف *alūf*) Intimates.

A الفّ *alaff*, Populous, thronged, crowded (place). Slow of speech, having an impediment. (A man) who has thick fleshy thighs, and slow of motion. One whose eye-brows join together. Unequal to, and sinking under, business. A vein in the narrow part of the fore-leg of a quadruped.

A الفاء *ilfās*, (v. n. 4 of لفا) Preserving entire. (v. n. 4 of لفا for لفو) Finding, attaining, arriving at.

A الفاج *ilfāj*, (v. n. 4 of لفج) Forcing (one) to take refuge with strangers. Being poor and penniless.

P الفاختن *alfākhtan*, To gain, acquire, collect.

P الفاش *ulfāsh*, A hypocrite. A kind of thistle.

A الفاظ *alfāz*, (pl. of لفظة) Words, vocables.

A الفاف *alfāf*, (pl. of لفّ *liff*) Thick, intangled (trees). *Ilfāf*, (v. n. 4 of لفّ) Involving, folding, wrapping. Hiding one's head in one's vest. Hiding (its) head under (its) wing (a bird).

A الفام *ilfām*, A tying tight, a binding fast.

A الفان *alifāni*, (dual) Two veins inside the arms from the shoulder to the elbow.

A آلفة *ālifat*, (pl. آلفات *ālifāt* and اوالف *awālif*) An intimate, familiar female friend.

A الفة *ilfat*, A female friend. *Ulfat*, Friendship, attachment, familiarity, companionship, intimacy.

P آلفت *ālaft* or *āluft*, Affliction, grief, madness.

A الفت *alfat*, Crooked-horned (goat). Left-handed. A fool. A stammerer.

P آلفتگان *āluftagān*, (pl. of آلفته *ālufta*) Astonished, confounded, afflicted, mad. Enamoured.

P الفتگري *ulfatgarī*, Friendship, intimacy.

P آلفتن *āluftan*, To rage, grow mad (with love). To be confounded, afflicted, enamoured.

P آلفته *ālufta*, Astonished, furious, insane, mad. Broken, infirm, poor, disconsolate. A debauchee.

P الفت بنده *ulfati-banda*, Attached, intimate.

A الفث *alfas*, Foolish; a fool.

P الفخت *alfakht*, Acquisition, gain.

P الفختن *alfakhtan*, To gain, acquire.

P الفخته *alfakhta*, Gained.

P الفغدن *alfaghdan*, To gain.

A الفك *alfak*, Left-handed. Foolish.

P الف گرفته *ilf-girifta*, Habituated, accustomed.

P الفنج *alfanj*, Gained.

P الفنجيدن *alfanjīdan*, To gain, acquire, collect.

P الفندن *alfandan*, To gain.

P الفنديدن *alfandīdan*, To gain, to acquire.

A الفيّ *alifiy*, Tall, erect, straight as an ا *alif*.

P الفيدن *alfīdan*, To gain, to acquire.

P الفينه *alfīna*, (or الفيه *alfiya*) The penis.

A الق *alk*, (v. n. of الق), Flashing. Being mad. *Ilk*, A wolf. *Ilak*, (pl. of القة *ilkat*) She-wolves.

A الّق *illak*, Shining, flashing (lightning).

A القاء *alkās*, (pl. of لقوة *lakwat* or *likwat*) (Women or camels) of a quick conception. Female eagles. (pl. of لقيّ *laka'*) Things thrown away as despicable. *Ilkās*, (v. n. 4 of لقي) Throwing down, flinging. Casting, shedding (teeth). Imparting, communicating. Proposing, propounding. Injecting, infusing.

A القاب *alkāb*, (pl. of لقب *lakab*) Titles of honour, appellations, epithets, styles, surnames. Forms of address (in letters).

A القاح *ilkāh*, (v. n. 4 of لقح) Rendering the female palm-tree fruitful, by sprinkling over it the flowers of the male. Covering (as a he-camel the female). Impregnating. Shaking a tree (the wind).

A القاط *alkāt*, Dispersed and despicable (men).

A القاف *alkāf*, (pl. of لقف) Sides of cisterns.

A القام *ilkām*, (v. n. 4 of لقم) Making swallow. Trotting, or going in a peculiar kind of quick pace.

A القان *ilkān*, A learning quickly by heart.

A القة *ilkat*, (pl. الق *ilak*) A she-wolf. A she-ape. An intrepid woman.

A القرآن *al kur'ān*, The reading. That book, which is the repository of the Muhammadan religion and law, known to us by the title of the Kur'ān, or, with the article, Al Kur'ān. It was published at different times, verse by verse, as exigencies required (Muhammad giving out, that he received them directly from heaven, by the mouth of the angel Gabriel), and collected into its present form by the Khalif Abū bakr. It has several other names: as, مصحف *mus-haf* and كتاب *kitāb*, The book, by way of excellence; تنزيل *tanzīl*, implying, Descended from heaven; كلام شريف *kalām sharīf*, Sublime word; and كتاب عزيز *kitāb ɛazīz*, Precious book. When the Musulmān writers transcribe any passage from it into their works, they never mention the chapter or verse, but only write in large characters, or with red ink, قال تعالى *kāl taɛāla'*, The Supreme Being says, or some expression synonymous to these. A good Muslim will not touch the Kur'ān till he has washed; and, lest he might transgress this law through inadvertency, it is in general carefully kept in a case; upon one part of which, called لسان الكتاب *lisānu'l kitāb* (the tongue of the book), there are written these words, لا يمسّه الا المتطهّرين *la yamussahu illa'l mutatahhirīn*, Let none but the purified touch it.

A القصّة *al kissa*, On the whole, in a word.

A القى *alaku'*, Impatient, fretful (woman).

A القية *ulkiyat*, (pl. الاقي *alākī*) A proposition, question, problem, enigma. A misfortune, adversity.

P آلك *ālak*, Spikenard (also dim. of آل *āl*, q. v.).

A الك *alk*, (v. n. of الك) Champing the bit.

P الك *alik*, Hopeless, destitute, undone. A road.

P الكا *ulkā*, A country, kingdom, region.

A الكد *alkad*, Mean, base. Fixed, adhering to one's friends, party, or tribe.

A الكع *alkaɛ*, Sordid, mean, abject, servile.

A الكن *alkan*, A stutterer, a bad pronouncer.

P الكن *ulkan*, Avaricious. A miser. A drunkard.

A الكني *alkanī*, Stammering, barbarous.

P الكوس *alkūs*, Name of a champion of Turkistān killed by Rustam.

P الكه *ulka*, A province, dominion, possession.

P آلگونه *ālgūna*, A wash or paint for the face.

A الل *alal*, (v. n. of الّ) Groaning (a sick man), crying with pain. Wrestling in prayer. Stinking (a leathern bottle) Pricking his ears (a horse). Becoming decayed (the teeth). Refusing to hunt (a falcon). The surface of a knife-blade. (for يلل *yalal*) Shortness of teeth, especially bending inwardly. *Ilal*, (pl. of الّة *illat*) Kindreds, relations. *Ulal*, (pl. of الّة *ullat*) Flocks pasturing at a distance.

A اللاء *allaɛ*, (pl. of التي *allatī*) (The women) who.

A اللاء *allāɛ*, (pl. of ذا *zā* and ذه *zihi*) These. Those who.

A اللاء *allāɛ*, (pl. of التي) (The women) who.

A اللاءات *allaɛāt*, (pl. of التي) (The women) who.

A اللاءون *allāɛūna*, (oblique اللائين *allāɛīna*) (pl. of الذي *allazī*) (Those men) who.

A اللات *al lāt*, Name of an idol once worshipped at Mecca.

A اللات *allāti*, (pl. of التي) (The women) who.

A اللاتي *allāti*, (pl. of التي) (The women) who.

A اللان *alalāni*, (dual) The two sides of a knife-blade. The two sides of the shoulder. Two pieces of flesh on the shoulder-blades.

A اللاي *al lāy*, (pl. of التي) (The women) who.

A اللائي *allāɛī*, (pl. of التي) (The women) who.

A اللت *allati* or *allat*, (fem. of الذي) Who, which.

A اللتان *allatāni*, (اللتانّ *allatānni* or اللتا *allatā*) The two women who.

A اللتيا *allatiyā*, Calamity, misfortune.

A اللذان *allazāni*, (or اللذا *allazā*) (dual of الذي *allazī*) The two (men) who. Who, which.

A اللوا *allawā*, (pl. of التي) (The women) who.

A اللواء *allawāɛ*, (pl. of التي) (The women who.

A اللوات *allawāti*, (or اللواتي *allawāti*) (pl. of التي) (The women) which.

A الله *allāh*, (originally الاله *al ilāh*) God: The God, by way of eminence (being compounded of the article ال *al*, The, and اله *ilāh*, a God); to which the following and such like epithets are generally added; الله تعالي *allāh taɛāla'*, الله تبارك و تعالي *allāh tabāraka wa taɛāla'*, الله جلّ و علا *allāh jalla wa ɛala'*, الله سبحانه *allah subhānahu*, which imply, The most high, holy, blessed, and gorious God. الله اعلم *allāh aɛlam*, God knows. الله اكبر *allāh akbar*, God (is) greatest, omnipotent. Name of a mountain at Shīrāz. بارك الله *bāraka' llāh*, Blessed God! الله الله *allāh allāh*, O God! good God! (a mark of admiration). الله قادر *allāh kādir*, God (is) powerful! (used to express that he can avert any threatened calamity). الله كريم *allāh karīm*, God is good, beneficent (a consolatory ejaculation). والله *wa'llāh*, بالله *bi'llāh*, تالله *ta'llāh*, لله *li'llāh*, By God!—الله *allāh* is used by all the nations that profess Muhammadanism, whatever language they speak. It is likewise comprehended, by contraction, in several mysterious words: as, in صلعم *salɛam*, which is often subjoined to the name of Muhammad, being compounded of the initial, medial, and final letters of the following words: صلّي الله عليه و سلّم *salla' allāh ɛalayhi wa sallam*, The blessing and peace of God be upon him!

A آلم *ālim*, Grieving, afflicted, pained.

A الم *alam*, (v. n. of الم) Being in pain. المت بطنك *alimta batnaka*, You have a pain in the belly. (pl. آلام *ālām*) Grief, affliction, anguish, distress, pain, agony. *Alim*, Pained, grieved.

A الم *a'lam*, Is it not? Is it not yet? This is also one of the mysterious contracted words prefixed to some of the chapters of the Kur'ān, which is decyphered in various ways: as, انا الله اعلم *ana allāh aɛlam*, I am the most wise God (being formed by the initial of the first word, the medial of the second, and the final of the third). الله لطيف مجيد *allāh latīf majīd*, God the merciful and glorious (compounded of the initials); or الله جبرائيل محمّد *allāh jabrāīl muhammad*, God, Gabriel, (and) Muhammad (composed of the initial of the first, final of the second, and initial of the last).

P الم *alum*, A kind of vetch. *Ulum*, A company, a squadron. الم الم *ulum ulum*, In troops.

A آلمّ *ālamm*, is another mysterious abbreviation, placed at the beginning of the third chapter of the Kur'ān, implying آلاء لقاء محبّة الكريم *ālāɛ likāɛi mahabbati'l karīm*, The benefits of the perception of the Divine love.

A المّ *alumma*, Come on, approach, draw near.

A الماء *ilmāɛ*, (v. n. 4 of لما) Taking, seizing, comprehending, receiving, choosing. Stealing, carrying off. Taking or laying by (fragments of meat in a dish). Denying a debt. Leaving a place empty, deserting any ground (cattle). (v. n. 4 of لي) Stealing. Coming in the darkness of night (a thief).

A الماح *ilmāh*, (v. n. 4 of لمح) Glancing at, taking a slight view. Flashing, causing light (lightning). Affording an opportunity of stealing a glance at her charms (a lovely woman).

A P الماس *almās*, A diamond. Glass. A penknife. A tooth. Sharp, piercing or cutting iron. Strenuous, active.

P الماس تراش *almās-tarāsh*, A diamond-cutter. Diamond-dust. Cut into angles or facets (glass).

P الماسي *almāsī*, Cut into facets (like a diamond).

P الماسي رنگ *almāsī-rang*, Bright, transparent.

A الماص *ilmās*, (v. n. 4 of لمص) Being within reach of the hand (a tree).

A الماظ *ilmāz*, (v. n. 4 of لمظ) Pouring water upon or into the lips (of another). Filling (one) with rage.

A الماع *ilmāɛ*, (v. n. 4 of لمع) Seizing, snatching any thing towards one. Shining, making a brilliant appearance. Having the teats black and shining (a mare or ass in foal). Turning, changing (colour). Wagging the tail (a sheep). Having a child stirring in the womb (a woman). Having withered plants (the ground, and thus presenting a shining appearance).

A المالق *al mālak*, Name of a country in Turkistān.

A المام *ilmām*, (v. n. 4 of لم) Descending, arriving, reaching, approaching, betaking one's self to, or dwelling (in a place). Approaching puberty. Being nearly ripe (a date). Commiting a slight offence, or venial sins. Being near doing any thing, falling very little short of.

A المحي *almahīy*, One who glances much.

P المزده *alam-zada*, Afflicted, struck with grief.

A المظ *almaz*, (A horse) white on the under-lip.

A المظاظ *ilmizāz*, (v. n. 9 of لمظ) Being distinguished by a whiteness on his under-lip (a horse).

A المع *almaɛ*, Ingenious, keen, shrewd, judicious, sagacious, clever, witty.

A المعي *almaɛīy*, A liar. Ingenious, clever, witty.

A المعيّة *almaɛīyat*, Sagacity, penetration.

A المنّة لله *al minnat l'illāh*, Thanks be to God!

P الموت *alamūt*, (Eagle-nest) Name of a fortress betwixt Kazwin and Ghīlān.

P الموں ilimūn, A lemon.

A المي alma', Black, brown-lipped. Very brown and hard (spear). Dark (thicket, shade, or marrow). One whose spittle is cold. Thick, shady (tree).

P آلنج ālunj, A wild plum.

P النجان alinjān, Name of a province in Persia.

P النجج alunjaj (or النجوج alanjūj), Aloe-wood.

A الندد alandad, A formidable adversary, unfair and regardless of truth.

P النكه alanka, A flame.

P آلنگ ālang, (or النگ alang) An entrenchment. A wall of defence. A garrison. A besieging party.

P الني alni, A door-post.

G النيون alaniyūn, Helenium, elecampane.

P آلو ālū, Defiled, contaminated. A brick-kiln. A name of various fruits. A plum. A yam.

A الو alw, Sheep's dung. (pl. آلاء ālā,) A benefit, a favour. Alw, (or الوّ ulūw) (v. n. of الا for الو) Failing. Doing less than one ought. Being unequal to. Becoming able, capable. Omitting. Intermitting. Delaying, hesitating, being tardy. Becoming proud. Not leaving (aught). Ability.

A الو ulū, (pl. without a singular) Lords, masters; having, possessed of. الو الامر ulū'l amr, The companions of Muhammad: also their followers in learning and authority.

A الوّ ulūw, Fragrant wood.

P الوا alwā or ilwā, Aloes. Rustam's sword-bearer. Ulwā, A star, planet, constellation.

A الواء alwā,, The sinuosities of a river. Environs, coasts. (pl. of لوي liwa') Distorted sand-hills. Places where sand-hills terminate. Ilwā,, (v. n. 4 of لوي) Turning (the head). Moving or raising (the tail). Ruining, destroying. Breaking one's word. Denying (a debt). (An eagle) carrying off (any thing). Making a signal (with your garment). Becoming flaccid, withered (pot-herbs). Drying up (semen virile). Hastening to a place where the hills of sand terminate, and more solid ground is found. Sewing (a standard). Hoisting (a standard). Eating victuals which had been laid by. Seizing upon what is in any dish, to the exclusion of others. Wishing for a great deal.

A الواث ilwās, (v. n. 4 of لوث) Bringing forth fresh grass in a dry place, or amongst dry grass.

A الواح alwāh, (pl. of لوح lawh) Planks, boards, tables. Surfaces. A ship's timbers. الواح السلاح alwāhu's silāh, Glittering arms, as swords or spears.

A الواد alwād, (pl. of الود) Perverse, obstinate.

P الواذ alwāz, An asylum. A mountain.

A الواذ alwāz, (pl. of لوذ lawz) The windings of a river or valley. The skirts of a mountain.

A الواز alwāz, (pl. of لوز lawz) Almonds.

A الواع alwāh, (pl. of لاع lāɛ) Timid, fearful. Distempered. Insincere in friendship.

A الوان alwān, (pl. of لون lawn) Colours. Forms, species. P الوان خوردن ulwān khwurdan, To swallow voraciously.

A الوب alūb, Brisk, alert, ready (in drawing up a bucket out of a well). A high cold wind, sweeping the earth and whirling the dust.

P آلوبالو ālū bālū, An armarylla, or sour cherry.

A الوة alwat, The utmost stretch. Ease, affluence. Fragrant wood. At any time, ever. Alwat, ilwat, or ulwat, An oath.

A الوّة alūwat, Bow-shot distance. Fragrant wood. A lioness. Repose, quiet. Affluence, enjoyment. Alūwat, ilūwat, or ulūwat, An oath. Ulūwat, Aloe-wood.

A الوث alwas, Languid, flaccid, slow of speech or gait, drawling. Strong, robust. Mad.

P الوج alūj, Elecampane, an herb, which is a specific against the bite of serpents.

P آلوچه allūcha, A small plum. A currant. A cherry.

P آلود ālūd, (in composition) Contaminated, stained, polluted, dirtied, soiled, bespattered, besmeared, fouled. وجود خطأ آلود wujūdi khata-ālūd, A person stained with crimes. خواب آلود khwāb-ālūd, Drowned in sleep. چشم خون آلود chashmi khūn-ālūd, Having the eye bloody, blood-shot. غبار آلود ghubār-ālūd, Covered with dust. مجاز آلود majāz-ālūd, Polluted with crimes.

A الود alwad, Thick (neck). (pl. الواد alwād) Perverse, obstinate, refractory.

P آلودگي ālūdagi, Contamination, defilement.

P آلودن ālūdan, To stain, pollute, contaminate, defile. To anoint. To be polluted, defiled.

P آلوده ālūda, Stained, polluted, smeared, defiled. Anointed. Disturbed, confused. Overwhelmed. Mingled. آلودهٔ خون ālūda,i khūn, Smeared with blood. Weeping. آلودگان دهر ālūdagāni dahr, Worldlings, misers. Criminals, rebels.

P آلوده دامن ālūda-dāman, Having the tails of one's garments bespattered. A sinner, fornicator.

P آلوس ālūs, Glancing amorously or in anger.

A الوس alūs, A thing, any thing: as, ما ذقت الوسا mā zuktu alūsan, I did not taste any thing.

P آلوسن ālūsan, A sort of plum, an aperient.

G الوسن alūsan, Alysson, or madwort.

P آلو سيه ālū siyah, A certain Indian fruit.

P الوش alūsh, Provisions from the king's table.

A الوط alwat, Very close or dear to the heart.

A الوف alūf, (pl. الف uluf) Very familiar. Ulūf, (pl. of الف alf) Thousands.

A الوق alwah, Foolish.

A الوقة alūkat, A dish made with butter and dates. Fresh butter. اشهي من الوقة ashha' min alūkat, More desirable than fresh butter.

A الوك alūk, An ambassador, messenger, nuncio, legate, apostle. A letter. News. Ulūk, A mission, an embassy. The Evangelist Luke.

A الوكة alūkat, A mission, embassage. News.

P آلوگرده ālū garda, A kind of fruit.

A الومة alūmat, Meanness, avarice. Blame.

A الونان ilwinān, (v. n. 9 of لون) Being coloured, being of various colours.

P آلوند ālwand, (more commonly الوند alvand) Name of a high mountain in Hamadān.

P آلونه āluna, A wash, cosmetic, paint.

A الوهة ulūhat, (or الوهيّة ulūhiyat) (v. n. of اله) Worshipping. Worship. Deity, divinity, godhead.

A الويّ alwa', (pl. لي luyy) Crooked by nature, (as a horn or goat's tail). Dividing, separating, withdrawing from others, solitary, singular, retired. Long, unknown (way). Violent in litigation. A species of tree.

A الويّ ilawiy, Belonging to the particle الي ila'.

A الوية alwiyat, (pl. of لواء liwā,) Standards, ensigns, banners. (pl. of لوي liwa') Distorted sand-hills. Places where sand-hills terminate.

P آله ālu, Spikenard. Āluh, An eagle.

A آله ālih, Astonished, stupefied, distracted.

P اله ala, Blue bdellium. Ulah (or الّه) An eagle.

A اله alah, (v. n. of اله) Being astonied, stupefied, confounded, dazzled, distracted. Lamenting sorely over. Fleeing for refuge. Protecting, securing, making safe.

A الٰه ilāh, (for الاه ilāh) Worshipped, adored. A god; sometimes used to express Omnipotence: as, الٰه العالمين ilāhu'l ɛālamīn, The God of worlds.

A الهاء ilhā,, (v. n. 4 of لها for لهو) Amusing. (v. n. 4 of لهي) Neglecting things of importance through weakness, and attending to music. Hindering, preventing. اله عن الشي alhi ɛani 'sh shay, Let that alone, think no more of it.

A الهاب alhāb, (pl. of لهب lihb) Intermediate spaces between two mountains. Clefts, fissures, narrow passes in mountains. Steep precipices. Ilhāb, (v. n. 4 of لهب) Inflaming, kindling. Being heated in running (a horse) and raising the dust. Flashing repeatedly (lightning).

P الٰه آباد ilāh-ābād, The city of Allahabād.

A الهاج ilhāj, (v. n. 4 of لهج) Having young ones greedy of suck, so as to render it necessary to tie up the dugs of the mother.

A الهاد ilhād, (v. n. 4 of لهد) Oppressing, injuring. Despising, holding in contempt. Bending to the earth from heaviness. Holding one man, in order that he may be attacked by another, acting unfairly. Aiding one against another.

A الهاط ilhāt, (v. n. 4 of لهط) Dashing water against the privities.

A الهاف ilhāf, (v. n. 4 of لهف) Being greedy, gluttonous. Avidity, greediness, gluttony.

A الهام ilhām, (v. n. 4 of لهم) Inspiring, infusing into the mind. Inspiration, divine revelation. الهام الٰهي ilhāmi ilāhī, (and الهام ربّاني ilhāmi rabbānī) The inspiration of God.

P الهام پذير ilhām-pazir, Inspired.

A الهان *il-hān*, (v. n. 4 of لهن) Offering (a present) to any person coming off a journey.

A الهانيّة *ulhāniyat*, Worship. Divinity.

A آلهة *ālihat*, (pl. of الاه *ilāh*) Gods, deities.

A الهة *ilāhat*, (v. n. of اله) Worshipping, adoring. Worship, adoration. The sun. Name of a place. A serpent. An idol. The horned moon. *Alāhat* or *ulāhat*, The sun. *Ulāhat*, Worship. Divinity.

A الهوب *ulhūb*, Impetus of a galloping horse.

A الهوة *ulhūwat*, That whereby time is beguiled.

A الهيّ *ilāhiy*, Divine. علم الهي *ʿilmi ilāhī*, Divine knowledge.

A الهيّة *ilāhiyat*, Divinity, deity. الالهيّة *al ilāhiyat*, Metaphysics. Theology.

A الهيّة *ulhiyat*, Any question put for amusement.

A الهيجاج *ilhījāj*, (v. n. 11 of لهج) Beginning to coagulate (sour milk). Being heavy with sleep (the eye). Being mixed.

A آلي *āla'*, Large-buttocked (man). Fat-tailed (ram). *Ālī*, Fat-tailed (ram). Fleshy-hipped (man). (fem. آلية *āliyat*, pl. اوالي *awālī*) One who falls short.

P آلي *ālī*, Saffron-colour.

A الي *aly* or *ila'*, (v. n. of الي) Having large buttocks. *Aly*, *ily*, or *ala'*, (pl. الي *ila'* or آلاء *ālāʼ*) Beneficence. A favour, benefit. *Uly*, Fleshy-buttocked (men or women). (pl. of الياء *alyāʼ*) Large, fat-tailed (sheep). *Ila'*, To, towards, until. In. Even to, as far as. Along with. From. الي آخر الزمان *ila' ākhiri'z zamān*, Until the end of time. الي الآن *ila'l ān*, (or الي هذا الآن *ila' hāzā'l ān*) Till now, to this time, until this hour. الي ان *ila' an*, Until that. الي اين *ila' ayn*, Whither? الي غير ذالك *ila' ghayr zālika*, Et cetera. الي غير نهاية *ila' ghayr nihāyat*, Ad infinitum, for ever. الي ما *ila' mā*, So long as. الي متي *ila' matta'*, Until when? How long? الي يومنا هذا *ila' yawmnā hāzā*, Until this day. اليك عنّي *ilayka ʿannī*, Keep off from me. اليك كذا *ilayk kazā*, Take, hold this. ابيض الي السواد *abyaz ila's sawād*, White inclining to blackness. اذهب اليك *izhab ilayka*, Go about your business, what concern have you in it? *Ula'*, (for اول *uwal*) First. Those (females).

A الّي *alla'*, (v. n. of الا for الو) Failing, doing less than one ought. Delaying. Becoming proud.

A اليّ *aliy*, One who swears much. Fat-tailed (ram). *Ilayya'*, To me. *Uliy*, (v. n. of الا for الو) Failing, doing less than one ought. Delaying. Becoming proud.

G اليا *alyā*, Marsh-mallows.

A اليا *ilyā*, Jerusalem.

A اليّا *aliya'*, An oath.

A الياء *alyāʼ*, (A ewe) which has a large fat tail. *Ilyāʼ*, (v. n. 4 of ليا) Being slow. Jerusalem.

A الياس *ilyās* or *alyās*, Elias. الياسين *ilyāsīn*, The followers of Elias.

A الياط *alyāt*, (pl. of ليطة *līṭat*) Barks of canes or reeds. Bows.

A اليال *ilyāl*, The act of entering on the night.

A اليان *alyān* or *alayān*, Fat-tailed (ram). *Ilyān* (v. n. 4 of لان for لين) Making soft or smooth.

A اليانة *alyānat*, Large-hipped (woman). Fat-tailed (ewe).

P آلي بالي *ālī-bālī*, A cherry.

A اليبب *ulaybib*, (dim. of البب *albub*) The smaller heart-strings.

A الية *alyat*, The tail of an Asiatic ram, large and very fat, weighing about ten or twelve pounds. (pl. اليات *alyāt* and الايا *alāya'*) The buttocks. The calves of the legs, the balls of the thumbs, fingers, toes, the mons veneris, and other fat and fleshy protuberances. الية الحافر *alyatu'l hāfir*, The hinder part of the foot or hoof of a quadruped. *Ilyat*, The fore part. A side.

A اليّة *aliyat*, (pl. الايا *alāya'*) An oath. (fem. of اليّ *aliy*) Negligent: as, الا حظيّة فلا اليّة *illā haziyat fa lā aliyat*, If fortune is wanting, I will not be negligent of myself. *Iliyat*, Aloe-wood.

A اليث *alyas*, (pl. ليث *lis*) Brave, strong.

P آليختن *ālikhtan*, To take ill, to be enraged.

A اليّد *ulayyid*, (dim. of الندد) A little foe.

P آليدن *ālidan*, To commit a crime. To recede, to depart from an agreement. To blame, accuse. To quake with fear.

P آليز *āliz*, A kick. A bound, a leap.

P آليزنده *ālizanda*, Kicking, vicious (horse).

P آليزيدن *ālizidan*, To bound, rebound, kick. To mourn, become sad. To palpitate, shake, be in convulsions. To offend. To blame, accuse, criminate.

A اليس *a'laysa*, Is it not? *Alyas*, (pl. ليس *lis*) Intrepid, valiant, brave, courageous, strong. A lion. (A camel) bearing any burthen. One who never leaves home. A cuckold, without jealousy, or the least regard for his honour; consequently a butt for ridicule. Endowed with a noble disposition and accomplished manners.

A اليط *alyat*, Very close or dear to the heart.

A اليغ *alyagh*, Foolish, insane, mad. One who pronounces repeatedly the letter ي *ye*.

A اليف *alif*, (pl. الائف *alāʼif*) Familiar, intimate. A comrade, friend.

A اليق *alyak*, More or most proper or suitable.

A اليل *alīl*, (v. n. of الّ) Groaning (from pain or grief). Raising the voice in prayer or affliction. Refusing to hunt (a falcon). Pricking his ears (a horse). Bereavement. Restlessness (from fever). The clattering noise of stones or gravel. The murmuring of running water. A groan. *Alyal*, Very dark night (ليل *layl*).

A اليلة *alilat*, Bereavement. A flock pasturing at a distance.

A اليم *alīm*, Painful. عذاب اليم *ʿazābun alīmun*, An excruciating torment.

A الين *alyan*, Softer, more or most limber or subtile. *Alīn*, Name of a village in مرو *marv*.

A الينا *alyināʼ*, (pl. of ليّن *layyin*) Smooth. Placid, gentle.

A اليوم *al yawm*, To-day. اليوم في اليوم *al yawm fil yawm*, From day to day.

A اليون *alyūn*, Name of the ancient capital of Egypt, changed into فسطاط *fustāt*, when conquered by the Musulmāns.

A اليهة *alihat*, The sun.

A آم *ām*, Name of a city famous for the manufacture of clothing. ما له آم و عام *mā lahu ām wa ʿām*, He has neither wife nor flock.

A آمّ *āmm*, (pl. امام *imām*) A blow on the crown of the head which wounds the brain.

P ام *am*, (first person of بودن *būdan*, To be) I am: when added to nouns it signifies My, or rather Me; as, جامه ام *jāma am*, My robe, or robe of me. *Im*, when prefixed to some words, signifies, This: as, امشب *imshab*, To-night, امروز *imroz*, To-day (for اين شب *īn shab*, اين روز *īn roz*).

A ام *am*, Whether? Nay, rather. Yea.

A امّ *amm*, (v. n. of امّ) Intending, purposing, desiring, tending towards. Taking the lead in the exercise of prayer. Striking on the crown of the head, wounding in the head so as to touch the brain. Teaching, giving a good example. Becoming a mother.

A امّ *imm*, A mother. *Umm*, (pl. امّات *ummāt* for irrational beings, and امّهات *ummahāt* for rational ones) A mother. A nation. A people. A genus. A servant of the people. An aged wife. The root, origin, principle, the primary cause upon which any thing depends. That in which any thing is contained: as, A house, habitation, sepulchre. This word is often used in forming the rhetorical figure, called metonymy; امّ الاجساد *ummu'l ajsād*, Quicksilver. امّ ادراص *ummu adrās*, A mole. Adversity. امّ اربعة واربعين *umm arbaʿat wa arbaʿīn*, A scolopendra. امّ الارضين *ummu'l arzīn*, (Mother of countries) Mecca. امّ الاموال *ummu'l amwāl*, (Mother of wealth) A sheep. امّ البيض *ummu'l bayz*, (Mother of whiteness, or of the egg) The ostrich. امّ التنائف *ummu't tanāʼif*, (Mother of length) An extensive desert. امّ جابر *ummu jābir*, Frumenty. امّ الجراف *ummu'l jarrāf*, A shield. A bucket, an urn. امّ جرذان *umm jirzān*, A sort of date. امّ جندب *umm jundab*, A centinel, a watch. Perfidy. Oppression, tyranny. Wakefulness, watchfulness. Accident, calamity, oppression. امّ الجيش *ummu'l jaysh*, (Mother of armies) A standard. امّ حباب *umm hubāb*, (Mother Bubble) The world. امّ حباحب *umm hubāhib*, A kind of locust. امّ حبوكري *umm habawkara'*, Death. Sorrow. امّ حبين *umm hubayn*, The chameleon. امّ حثور *umm husūr*, The hyena. امّ حفصة *umm hafsat*, A hen. امّ حلس *ummu hils*, A she-ass. امّ حلقوم *umm hulkūm*, (Mother of the throat) A fairy so called, who is supposed either to bring on, or to cure a quinsy or sore throat. امّ الحوادث *ummu'l hawādis*, News of great importance. امّ حوار *umm hawār*, The eagle. امّ الخبائث *ummu'l khabāsis*, (Mother of evils) Wine. امّ خشاف *umm khashshāf*, Death. Adversity. امّ خفاش *umm khaffāsh*, Misfortune, calamity. امّ خنّور *ummu khannūr*, A hyena. امّ درزة *ummu darzat*, The world. امّ درين *umm darin*, Straits. Ground without grass. امّ دفر *umm dafr* or امّ دفار *ummu dafār* (Mother Stink) The world. امّ الدماغ *ummu'd dimāgh*, (The mother of the brain) The membrane called dura mater. امّ الدهيم *ummu'd duhaym*, Sorrow. امّ الرأس *ummu'r rass*, (Mother of the head) The crown of the head. The pia mater. The brain. امّ راشد *ummu rāshid*, A mouse. امّ الربيق *ummu'r rubayk*, Tribulation, calamity. امّ الرجل *ummu'r rajul*, (Mother of the man) A wife of a certain age. امّ رحم *umm ruhm*, Mecca. The world. امّ الرذائل *ummu'r razāsil*, (Mother of baseness) Ignorance. امّ الركوب *ummu'r rukūb*, Death. امّ الرمح *ummu'r rumh*, (Mother of spears) A standard (at the point of a spear). امّ الزبيق *ummu'z zubayk*, Great affliction. امّ زوبعة *umm zawbaȝat*, (Mother of the devil's gale) A whirlwind, a hurricane. امّ سالم *umm sālim*, Name of a place. امّ السخال *ummu's sikhāl*, A she-goat. امّ السماء *ummu's samās*, The milky way. امّ سويد *ummu suwayd*, The anus. امّ شملة *umm shamlat*, The sun. امّ الشوء *ummu'sh shaws*, The eagle. امّ صبّار *umm sabbār*, (or امّ صبّور *ummu sabbūr*) Adversity. A fierce battle. امّ الصبيان *ummu's sibyān*, (The mother of children) A ghost, a goblin, bugbear. The epilepsy. امّ طبق *ummu tabak*, A calamity. A serpent. امّ الطريق *ummu't tarīk*, A highway. A hyena. امّ الطعام *ummu't taȝām*, Wheat. The stomach. امّ الطفل *ummu't tifl*, A mother with her child. امّ طلحة *ummu talhat*, A louse. امّ طلبة *umm tilbat*, An eagle. امّ الظباء *ummu'z zibās*, A plain, a field. امّ عامر *ummu ȝāmir*, A hyena. امّ عبّور *umm ȝabbūr*, A hyena. Misfortune. امّ عتّاب *umm ȝattāb*, (or امّ عتبان *umm ȝitbān*) A hyena. امّ عريط *umm ȝiryat*, A scorpion. امّ عزم *umm ȝazm*, The anus. A horse. امّ عقبة *umm ȝakabat*, A louse. امّ العلوم *ummu'l ȝulūm*, (Grammar) The mother of sciences. امّ عوف *umm ȝawf*, A locust. امّ العيال *ummu'l ȝiyāl*, Name of a village in Arabia. امّ غيلان *umm ghilān*, The gum-arabic tree. امّ الفرج *ummu'l faraj*, A sop. امّ فروة *ummu farwat*, (Mother of riches) A sheep. A buffalo. امّ الفضائل *ummu'l fazāsil*, (Mother of excellence) Science. امّ القبور *ummu'l kubūr*, A hyena. امّ القرآن *ummu'l kursān*, (Mother of the book) The first chapter of the Kur'ān. Any unrepealed or unabrogated verse of the Kur'ān. امّ القردان *ummu'l kirdān*, The fetlock of a horse. امّ القري *ummu'l kira'*, Fire. A dish made of meat, wheaten flour, &c. *Ummu'l kura'*, (Mother of cities) Mecca. امّ قشعم *umm kashȝam*, Adverse fortune. Death. A hyena. A spider. امّ قوب *umm kūb*, Misfortune. امّ القوم *ummu'l kawm*, (Mother of the people) A king, a chief. امّ الكتاب *ummu'l kitāb*, (Mother of books) The Kur'ān (called also the book of divine decrees, in which, according to the Muhammadans, the destiny of every man is written in indelible characters). The first chapter of the Kur'ān. امّ كلب *umm kalb*, A tree whose leaf resembles that of the willow. امّ كلبة *ummu kalbat*, The fever. امّ لوح *umm lawh*, The eagle. امّ اللهين *ummu'l luhayn*, Death. امّ محبوب *umm mahbūb*, A serpent. امّ مرزم *umm mirzam*, The north wind. امّ المنزل *ummu'l manzil*, (or امّ المثوي *ummu'l maswa'*) A hostess, landlady, mother of a family. A wife. امّ مسلمين *umm muslimīn*, (Mother of the Muslims) Ayisha, the favourite wife, and widow of Muhammad, called also An'nabiya the Prophetess, on account of the great authority she obtained among the Muhammadans after her husband's death. امّ ملدم *ummu mildam*, A fever. امّ نافع *umm nāfiȝ*, (Mother profitable) A hen. امّ النجوم *ummu'n nujūm*, (Mother of the stars) The milky way, heaven, the starry vault. امّ الندامة *ummu'n nadāmat*, (Mother of repentance) Haste, precipitation. امّ النوفل *ummu'n nawfal*, A hyena. امّ الولد *ummu'l walad*, (Mother of children) A mother. (In a law sense) A female slave who has borne a child to her master. امّ الهام *ummu'l hām*, The pia mater. امّ الهنبر *ummu'l himbir*, The ass. امّ الهيثم *ummu'l haysam*, The eagle. امّ اليمن *ummu'l yaman*, Sanā the capital of Yaman. لا امّ لك *lā umma laka*, You have no mother (an expression of contempt, You are a foundling; though sometimes taken in a contrary sense).

A اما *a'mā*, Is it not? Verily, truly, indeed.

A امّا *ammā*, But. As for. Whether. Or. However. Notwithstanding. *Immā*, But if, unless, whether. Either. Or. امّا ان *immā an*, Would that!

A اماء *imās*, (pl. of امة *amat*) Handmaids, females, slaves. *Umās*, (v. n. of اما for امو) Mewing.

A امآء *imsās*, (v. n. 4 of مأي) Becoming a hundred in number (camels). Making up a hundred. (pl. of امة *amat*) Handmaids, female slaves

A امات *imāt*, High, unequal places.

A امّات *ummāt*, (pl. of امّ *umm*) Mothers, dams.

A اماتة *imātat*, (v. n. 4 of مات for موت) Putting to death. Losing flocks by a murrain. Losing her young. Being bereaved of her children. Rendering (meat) soft and flabby from overboiling. (in gram.) Rendering (a word or tense) obsolete.

A اماثل *amāsil*, (pl. of امثل *amsal*) Eminent, conspicuous. Peers, nobles, grandees, free-men.

P آماج *āmāj*, A plough. *Āmāj*, (or اماج *amāj*) Heaps (of earth) on which they place butts for shooting at with arrows. A target for archers. A throne. The 24th part of a firsang.

P اماج *amāj*, A plough. آهن اماج *āhani amāj*, A ploughshare. ساخت اماج *sākhti amāj*, Plough gear. *Umāj*, A kind of pottage.

A اماجد *amājid*, (pl. of امجد *amjad*) Most glorious, honourable.

P آماج ساختگی *āmāj-sākhtagī*, Plough-gear.

P آماجگاه *āmāj-gāh*, The world. A place on which a target is fixed.

A اماخيض *amākhīz*, (pl. of امخاض *imkhāz*) Milks as long as they are in the churn.

A اماد *imsād*, (v. n. 4 of مأد) Rendering (a plant) pliable, soft, and succulent (irrigation).

P آمادگي *āmādagī*, Preparation, readiness.

P آمادن *āmādan*, To prepare, make ready, equip, expedite, despatch. To be prepared. To fill.

P آماده *āmāda*, Prepared, ready. Arranged, disposed in order, equipped. Ripe. Made plain. Resolved, determined.

A اماديح *amādīh*, (pl. of امدوحة) Laudable acts.

P آمار *āmār*, Numeration, calculation. Inquisition, investigation. Minute search. Dropsy.

P امار *amār*, Starch. Weaver's glue.

A امار *amār*, Time. A promise. Time or place of promise. Sign, mark, signal. *Imār*, A command.

A امّار *ammār*, Imperious, despotic, tyrannical. Propense. نفس امّارة *nafs ammārat*, Concupiscence.

A امارة *amārat*, A sign, mark, signal, token, or symptom. Time. A promise. The time or place of a promise. *Imārat* or *amārat*, Dominion, power, authority, sovereignty, command. A government, a district under the authority of a governor. دار الامارة *dāru'l imārat*, The palace of the mayor, the house of prefecture. *Imārat*, (v. n. 4 of مار for مور) Making (the dust) fly (a wind). Causing (blood) to flow on the ground. (v. n. 4 of مار for مير) Laying in a stock (of provisions) Melting. Pouring water upon saffron. Cutting the jugular veins.

A امارد *amārid*, (pl. of امرد) Beardless youths.

P آماره *āmāra*, Enquiry, strict search. Dropsy.

P اماره *imāra*, Computation, reckoning.

P اماره گير *imāra-gīr*, An accomptant.

A امازة *imāzat*, (v. n. 4 of ماز for ميز) Separating, distinguishing, discriminating.

A امازر *amāzir*, (pl. of مزير *mazīr*) Brave, undaunted. Polished, elegant, accomplished.

P آماس *āmās*, A tumour, a swelling.

A آماس *āmās*, (pl. of امس *ams*) Yesterdays.

P آماسا *āmāsā*, Swelling.

P آماسانيدن *āmāsānīdan*, To cause to swell.

P آماسيدن *āmāsīdan*, To swell, become inflated.

P آماسيده *āmāsīda*, Swelled, swollen.

P آماسيده خايه *āmāsīda-khāya*, One who has swelled testicles.

A اماسيه *amāsiya*, A city in Cappadocia.

P آماش *āmāsh*, A roasting-spit.

A اماصيخ *amāsīkh*, (pl. of امصوخة *umsūkhat*) Leaves of the plant ثمام *sumām*.

A اماطة *imātat*, (v. n. 4 of ماط for ميط) Removing, taking away, putting to a distance. Departing from. Being far distant.

A اماعة *imāʿat*, The act of causing to flow.

A اماعز *amāʿiz*, (or اماعيز *amāʿīz*) (pl. of امعوز *umʿūz*) Herds of mountain-goats. Bevies of roes.

A اماعق *amāʿik*, (or اماعيق *amāʿīk*) Widely-extended deserts.

A آماق *āmāk*, (or اماق *amʾāk*) (pl. of موق *muʾk*) The inner corners of the eye. (pl. of موق *muʾk* and موق *mūk*) Low-lying grounds.

A اماق *imʾāk*, (v. n. 4 of مئق) Bursting into rage, or into tears with excessive sobbing. A fit of rage or sobbing. Fraud, deceit.

A اماكن *amākin*, (pl. of مكان *makān*) Places. Mansions, habitations. اماكن متبركه *amākini mutabarraka*, Holy places.

A اماكيد *amākīd*, Balances, remainders of fines for shedding blood.

A آمال *āmāl*, (pl. of امل *amal*) Desires, hopes. بني الآمال *banī'l āmāl*, Sons of hope. واهب الآمال *wāhibu'l āmāl*, (God) the granter of desires.

A امالة *imālat*, (v. n. 4 of مال for مول) Enriching. (v. n. 4 of مال for ميل) Causing to incline, bending. Feeding on a salt and bitter plant. Giving to fatha a sound like that of kasra (as when كتاب *kitāb* is pronounced as if written كتيب *kitīb*).

A امالس *amālis*, (pl. of امليس) Barren deserts.

A اماليت *amālīt*, Swift camels.

A اماليج *amālīj*, (pl. of املوج *umlūj*) Leaves of certain trees like the cypress. Wild date-stones.

A اماليس *amālīs*, (pl. of امليس) Barren deserts.

A امام *amām*, Before, prior to. امامك *amāmak*, Before thee, beware!

A امام *imām*, (pl. امام *imām* and ائمّة *aʾimmat*) A head, chief, leader in religious matters, prelate. Muhammad. A khalif. A king. A general officer. A guide, exemplar, pattern. Any book of instruction. The daily lesson of a child. The Kur'ān. A mason's line or rule. A bowstring. A driver. An open royal road. A tract of land leading to the temple of Mecca. *Imām*, is sometimes used to imply امام شافعيّ *imām shāfiʿīy*, The first of the four peers, equals or heads of the four chief Muhammadan sects, whom they call Imām, as our theologians say often the Apostle, meaning the Apostle Paul. (pl. of آمّ *āmm*) Blows which wound the brain.

P امام باره *imām-bāra*, A temple, conclave. A place illuminated at the festival of Muharram, where the shrines of the Imāms Hasan and Husayn are visited with great veneration.

A امامة *imāmat*, (v. n. of امّ) Setting an example. Taking the lead in religious matters, performing the functions of an Imām. The priestly office. *Umāmat*, A body of 300 camels. A woman's name. ابو امامة *abū umāmat*, Name of several men.

P امامزاده *imām-zāda*, The son of a priest.

P امام قلي *imām kuli*, The son of Nādir Shāh.

G امامون *amāmūn*, Stone-parsley. Ginger. Pepper.

A اماميّ *imāmīy*, Name of two traditionists.

A اماميّة *imāmīyat*, Name of a sect, that of Alīy.

A امان *amān*, (v. n. of امن) Being safe and secure. Security, safety, peace, tranquillity, protection. Any treaty or agreement tending to bestow security, liberty, or mercy. الامان *al amān*, Quarter! mercy! في امان الله *fī amān allāh*, Under the protection of God. P امان خواستن *amān khwāstan*, To sue for mercy, to beg quarter.

A امّان *ummān*, An ideot. Faithful, trusty. A sower, farmer. *Ummāni*, (du. of امّ) Two mothers; a mother and aunt; also parents, father and mother.

A امانة *amānat*, (v. n. of امن) Being faithful and trustworthy. Keeping (any thing) close and not repeating (it). A deposit, charge, any thing given in trust. Security, safety, protection. Fidelity. Rectitude, sincerity. An inward belief corresponding to the outward profession. Statutes of divine obligation. P امانت داشتن *amānat dāshtan*, To deposit, to place in trust.

P امانتدار *amānat-dār*, A depositary. Trusty.

P امانتداري *amānat-dārī*, Charge, trust, agency. Fidelity, faithfulness, honesty, trustiness.

P امانتكار *amānat-kār*, An agent, a factor.

A اماني *amānī*, Security. Trust, charge, deposit. (In India applied to land) that which is in charge of a collector on the part of government (in opposition to اجاره *ijāra*, that which is farmed).

A امانيّ *amānīy*, (pl. of امنيّة *umnīyat*) Desires.

P آماه *āmāh*, A tumour.

A يا اماه *yā umāh*, O mother!

A اماهة *imāhat*, (v. n. 4 of ماه for موه) Giving water to drink. Pouring water on the blade of a knife whilst grinding it, or into an ink-stand. Having water springing up and bursting forth (ground). Filling (a pond). Digging to a spring of water. Raining. Mixing. Impregnating (a stallion).

P آماهيدن *āmāhīdan*, To swell, to be stupefied.

P آماي *āmāy*, (in comp.) Filling: a filler. One who prepares or makes ready. An ornamenter.

A امائم *amāʾim*, (pl. of اميم *amīm*) Blows upon the head. Stones with which such blows are given.

P آمائي *āmāʾī*, Fullness, repletion.

P آمائيدن *āmāʾīdan*, To make ready, to prepare. To be ready. To fill.

G امبرباريس *ambar bārīs*, Barberries.

P امبرود *ambarūd*, A pear.

G امبروسير *ambarūsira*, Ambrosia.

A امّة *āmat*, Fruitfulness, plenty. Rain widely spread. The secundine which infolds the new-born child. Swaddling-clothes. A blemish, defect, loss.

A آمّة *āmmat*, (A wound) reaching the brain.

A امة *amat*, (pl. امَوات *amwāt*, اماء *imāʾ*, آمي *āmī*, اموان *amwān*, *imwān*, and *umwān*) A female servant, a handmaid. Name of four female companions of Muhammad.

A امّة *immat*, Grace, favour, benevolence. The priestly office. Submission to the guidance of an Imām. Religion, rule of life. State, condition, mode, form, manner. Affluence. *Ummat*, (pl. امم *umam*) A crowd, company. A nation, people. Religion, sect, cast. Rule of life. Persons of the same persuasion, followers, adherents: as, امّة عيسيٰ *ummat ʿīsa'*, The people of Jesus, *i.e.* Christians; امّة محمّد *ummat muhammad*, The people of Muhammad, *i.e.* Muhammadans. Any genus of animals. An open road, a highway. A head, chief, guide, pattern. A mother. Time, occasion, opportunity. Obedience, submission. One who abounds in good things. Figure, stature. Face, surface. A learned man. Creatures. امّة الله *ummatu'llāh*, Creatures of God. امّة الرجل *ummatu'r rajul*, The family of a man. Glee, sprightliness. A follower of the truth, opposed to all other forms of belief.

A امت *amt*, (v. n. of امت) Determining (by measure, manner, or time). Intending purposing. Guessing, conjecturing. Being depressed. Being steep and high. Weakness. A proper regulation for living. Curvature. A distortion about the mouth. A fold, a wrinkle in a garment. Inequality in ground. (pl. امات *imāt* and اموت *umūt*) High, prominent ground. A small hill. A protuberance: as, امتلأ السقا فما بها امت *imtalaʾa's sikā, fa mā bihā amt*, The skin is full, and there is no protuberance in it (being equally stretched in every part). Diversity of opinion, doubtfulness: الخمر حرّمت لا امت فيها *al khamr hurrimat lā amta fīhā*, Wine is forbidden, there is no doubt of it.

A يا امّت *yā ummati*, O my mother!

A امتاء *imtāʾ*, (v. n. 4 of متي) Walking badly, ungracefully. Abounding in the necessaries of life.

A امتاح *imtāh*, (v. n. 4 of متح) Fixing (her) tail in the ground when laying (her) eggs (a locust).

A امّتار *immitār*, The being extended, lengthened.

A امتاع *imtāʿ*, (v. n. 4 of متع) Enjoying. Being independent of, able to do without. Permitting to enjoy, bestowing, making plenty. Causing to grow, supplying growth.

A امتان *imtān*, A striking on the side of the back.

P امّتان *ummatān*, (Pers. pl. of A امّة *ummat*) Peoples, nations.

A امتتاح *imtitāh*, (v. n. 8 of متح) Tearing away. Carrying off. Enjoying. Reposing, resting on a journey. Making a wind with the hand.

A امتتاخ *imtitākh*, An extracting, a tearing up.

A امتثال *imtisāl*, (v. n. 8 of مثل) Obeying, submitting, conforming (to law). Making an example of, enforcing the lex talionis. Representing, exhibiting, rehearsing. Pourtraying. Imitating. امتثالاً للامر *imtisālan li'l amr*, In obedience to command.

A امتحاء *imtihāʾ*, (v. n. 8 of محا for محو) Becoming expunged, effaced, obliterated.

A امتحاش *imtihāsh*, The being burnt.

A امتحاض *imtihāz*, A drinking of pure milk.

A امتحاط *imtihāt*, (v. n. 8 of محط) Running (a camel). Drawing (a sword): extracting (a spear).

A امتحاق *imtihāk*, (v. n. 8 of محق) Being abolished or cancelled. Being burnt or scorched.

A امتحاك *imtihāk*, (v. n. 8 of محك) Being passionate, choleric. Wrangling, litigating.

A امتحان *imtihān*, (v. n. 8 of محن) Examining, weighing attentively, trying, proving, testing. Looking to the final result. Opening, enlarging the heart (God). An experiment, proof, examination. امتحانات الهيّة *imtihānāti ilāhiya*, Divine temptations.

A امتخاخ *imtikhākh*, The act of taking marrow.

A امتخار *imtikhār*, (v. n. 8 of مخر) Selecting the best of any thing. Extracting the marrow from a bone. Meeting and snuffing up the wind (a horse galloping at full speed).

A امتخاض *imtikhāz*, (v. n. 8 of مخض) Stirring itself (a fœtus). Being shaken in the churn (milk).

A امتخاط *imtikhāt*, (v. n. 8 of مخط) Blowing the nose. Unsheathing a sword. Drawing up (water) through the nostrils and discharging (it) again. Snatching (any thing) from the hand of another.

A امتداح *imtidāh*, (v. n. 8 of مدح) Praising. Being wide (the hypochondria). Being roomy enough (a habitation). Self-applause.

A امتداخ *imtidākh*, The being insolent, unjust.

A امتداد *imtidād*, (v. n. 8 of مدّ) Stretching one's self. Being extended. Protraction, prolongation, production, extension, prorogation. امتداد حيات *imtidādi hayāt*, Prolongation of life. امتداد زمان *imtidādi zamān*, Length, or process of time.

A امتدار *imtidār*, (v. n. 8 of مدر) Taking a clod or lump of clay (مدرة *madarat*).

A امتداش *imtidāsh*, The act of taking, snatching.

A امتذاق *imtizāk*, (v. n. 8 of مذق) Being diluted with water (milk).

A امتراء *imtirās*, (v. n. 8 of مري) Doubting. Doubt, scepticism. Dissolving the clouds in rain (wind). Pouring forth (tears). Drawing out (milk).

A امترار *imtirār*, (v. n. 8 of مرّ) Passing across, by, through, over. Persevering in, being perpetual.

A امتراز *imtirāz*, (v. n. 8 of مرز) Cozening, defrauding. Keeping a partner out of his property. Withdrawing one's own share out of a partnership concern. Injuring the reputation of another. Boxing.

A امتراس *imtirās*, (v. n. 8 of مرس) Rubbing one's self against any thing. Being at a loss for words when wrangling and quarrelling. Brawling, wrangling. Altercation. Rancour.

A امتراش *imtirāsh*, (v. n. 8 of مرش) Wrenching. Seizing. Snatching any thing from the hand of another. Gaining, acquiring.

A امتراط *imtirāt*, (v. n. 8 of مرط) Grasping, seizing. Collecting.

A امتراق *imtirāk*, (v. n. 8 of مرق) Flying swiftly and passing through (an arrow).

A امتزاج *imtizāj*, (v. n. 8 of مزج) Mingling. Being mixed, diluted, blended. Union, mixture. مزاج سعادت امتزاج *mizāji saʿādat-imtizāj*, A disposition tempered with excellence.

A امتساء *imtisās*, (v. n. 8 of مسا for مسو) Taking the whole of another's substance. (v. n. 8 of مسي) Being athirst.

A امتساح *imtisāh*, The unsheathing (of a sword).

A امتساخ *imtisākh*, (v. n. 8 of مسخ) Drawing, unsheathing (a sword).

A امتساغ *imtisāgh*, (v. n. 8 of مسغ) Retiring.

A امتساك *imtisāk*, The act of holding fast.

A امتسال *imtisāl*, The act of drawing (a sword).

A امتش *amtash*, Weak-sighted (man).

A امتشاء *imtishās*, (v. n. 8 of مشي) Having a numerous offspring, or prolific herds.

A امتشاش *imtishāsh*, (v. n. 8 of مشّ) Obtaining part of another's property. Milking the udder dry. Cutting the ornaments off her neck (a woman). Cleaning one's self with a flint or clod after stooling.

A امتشاط *imtishāt*, (v. n. 8 of مشط) Combing herself (a woman).

A امتشاع *imtishāʿ*, (v. n. 8 of مشع) Milking (the udder) dry. Twitching, snatching another's garment. Drawing a sword rapidly. امتشع منه ما مشع لك *imtashiʿ minhu mā mashaʿa laka*, Take thereof whatever thou canst find.

A امتشاق *imtishāk*, (v. n. 8 of مشق) Snatching a thing from another's hand. Milking (the udder) dry. Cutting off, separating. Drawing (a sword).

A امتشال *imtishāl*, The act of drawing a sword.

A امتشان *imtishān*, (v. n. 8 of مشن) Breaking, cutting off. Snatching, dragging away by force. Drawing (a sword). Receiving a wide but shallow wound. Milking (the udder) dry.

A امتصاح *imtisāh*, (v. n. 8 of مصح) Stripping the leaves from the plants ثمام *sumām* and نصيّ *nasīy*.

A امتصار *imtisār*, (v. n. 8 of مصر) Milking a camel with the ends of the fingers, or with the forefinger and thumb only. Being metamorphosed, and changed into another shape.

A امتصاص *imtisās*, (v. n. 8 of مصّ) Sucking.

A امتصاع *imtisāʿ*, A travelling, a journeying.

A امتطاء *imtitās*, (v. n. 8 of مطا for مطو) Using a horse or beast of burden (called مطيّة *matīyat*).

A امتطاح *imtitāh*, (v. n. 8 of مطح) Rising and swelling (a river).

A امتطال *imtitāl*, (v. n. 8 of مطل) Delaying the payment of a debt. Shooting forth (a plant).

A امتعاد *imtiʿād*, (v. n. 8 of معد) Drawing or seizing any thing rapidly. Travelling.

A امتعاس *imtiʿās*, (v. n. 8 of معس) Rubbing (the backside) on the ground.

A امتعاض *imtiʿāz*, (v. n. 8 of معض) Being difficult, troublesome. Being angry, grieved, vexed.

A امتعاط *imtiʿāt*, (v. n. 8 of معط) Falling off (hair). Advancing (the day). Drawing (a sword).

A امتعال *imtiʿāl*, (v. n. 8 of معل) Stabbing and seizing at one and the same time.

A امتعة *amtiʿat*, (pl. of متاع *matāʿ*) Goods, wares, merchandises. P امتعهٔ گران بها *amtiʿasi girān-bahā*, Merchandise of great value.

A امتغاط *imtighāt*, (v. n. 8 of مغط) Being stretched (a bow or any thing elastic). Advancing (the day). Drawing (a sword).

A امتقار *imtikār*, (v. n. 8 of مقر) Deepening a well when its water has been exhausted.

A امتقاط *imtikāt*, (v. n. 8 of مقط) Extracting.

A امتقاع *imtikāʿ*, (v. n. 8 of مقع) Sucking (the udder) dry. Changing colour from fear or terror.

A امتقاق *imtikāk*, A draining (of the udder).

A امتقال *imtikāl*, The act of diving repeatedly.

A امتكار *imtikār*, (v. n. 8 of مكر) Being coloured with red earth. Sowing seed.

A امتكاك *imtikāk*, (v. n. 8 of مكّ) Sucking. Exhausting the udder (a colt).

A امتلاء *imtilās*, (v. n. 8 of ملأ) Being filled.

A امتلاج *imtilāj*, The act of sucking (the teat).

A امتلاح *imtilāh*, (v. n. 8 of ملح) Mixing falsehood with truth.

A امتلاخ *imtilākh*, (v. n. 8 of ملخ) Unsheathing (a sword). Drawing (a tooth). Tearing out (an eye). Unbridling (a horse), unbitting (him).

A امتلاذ *imtilāz*, (v. n. 8 of ملذ) Receiving a gift.

A امتلاز *imtilāz*, (v. n. 8 of ملز) Tearing up, removing forcibly.

A امتلاس *imtilās*, (v. n. 8 of ملس) Being taken away (sight).

A امتلاط *imtilāt*, (v. n. 8 of ملط) Hauling, snatching, pulling to one's self.

A امتلاع *imtilāʿ*, (v. n. 8 of ملع) Travelling quick (a camel). Skinning a sheep (beginning at the neck). Snatching hastily. Passing quick.

A امتلاق *imtilāk*, (v. n. 8 of ملق) Extracting.

A امتلال *imtilāl*, (v. n. 8 of ملّ) Baking (bread) upon the embers. Walking fast. Embracing a certain religion, or sect (ملّة *millat*).

A امتن *amtan*, Stronger, strongest.

A امتناء *imtinās*, (v. n. 8 of مني) Arriving in the valley of Mina', close to Mecca.

A امتناح *imtināh*, (v. n. 8 of منح) Receiving a present. Being loaded with benefits (from God).

A امتناع *imtināʿ*, (v. n. 8 of منع) Being prevented. Abstaining, refraining. Being strong and powerful. Refusing, denying. P امتناع كردن *imtināʿ kardan*, To refuse, deny. To abstain.

A امتنان *imtinān*, (v. n. 8 of منّ) Upbraiding, twitting one with a benefit conferred (منّة *minnat*). Conferring a favour or obligation (منّة *minnat*).

A امتهاء *imtihās*, (v. n. 8 of مهي) Sharpening (a paring-knife).

A امتهاج *imtihāj*, (v. n. 8 of مهج) Swooning, fainting. Being drained of blood.

A امتهاد *imtihād*, (v. n. 8 of مهد) Attending to one's affairs and gaining. Being broad and level. Spreading out, making even and soft (a bed).

A امتهاش *imtihāsh*, (v. n. 8 of مهش) Being burned. Shaving (her) face with a razor (a woman).

A امتهان *imtihān*, (v. n. 8 of مهن) Taking one as a servant, making use of his service. Becoming a servant. Regarding as weak and contemptible.

A امتياث *imtiyas*, (v. n. 8 of ماث for ميث) Dyeing. Steeping, macerating in water. Obtaining an easy livelihood. Dissolving and drinking the coagulated milk اقط *akit*.

A امتياح *imtiyāḥ*, (v. n. 8 of ماح for ميح) Making a present. Making sweat behind the ears (sun).

A امتثاد *imtisād*, The act of gaining, acquiring.

A امتثار *imtisār*, (v. n. 8 of مأر) Hating.

A امتيار *imtiyār*, (v. n. 8 of مار for مور) Drawing (a sword). (v. n. 8 of مار for مير) Victualling one's household.

A امتياز *imtiyāz*, (v. n. 8 of ماز for ميز) Being separated. Separation, distinction, discrimination.

P امتياز كردن *imtiyāz kardan*, To make a distinction, to separate, to discriminate.

A امتيازي *imtiyāziy*, Possessing the quality of discriminating, discriminative.

A امتئاق *imtisāk*, (v. n. 8 of مأق) Sobbing, weeping, breathing hard. Being violent (anger).

A امتياه *imtiyāh*, (v. n. 8 of ماه for موه) Giving water to drink. Pouring water on the blade of a knife when grinding it.

A امثال *amsāl*, (pl. of مثل *masal*) Resemblances, likenesses. Proverbs, adages. *Imsāl*, (v. n. 4 of مثل) Punishing by way of example, retaliating (as eye for eye).

A امثل *amsal*, (pl. اماثل *amāsil*) Most excellent, most proper for imitation. Convalescent.

A امثلة *amsilat*, (pl. of مثال *misāl*) Exemplars. Pictures, images. Commands. Fables. Beds.

A امثن *amsan*, One unable to contain his urine.

A امثولة *umsūlat*, A verse, sentence, or saying, worthy of repetition or quotation.

A امج *amj*, (v. n. of امج) Travelling fast. *Amaj*, (v. n. of امج) Being very thirsty. Extreme heat or thirst. Very hot. صيف امج, A hot summer.

A امجاج *imjāj*, (v. n. 4 of مج) Travelling, making a tour. Beginning to run (a horse) before (he is) warm. Running (sap in a tree).

A امجاد *amjād*, (pl. of ماجد *mājid* or مجيد *majīd*) Glorious. *Imjād*, (v. n. 4 of مجد) Magnifying, praising, glorifying. Giving largely. Finding a pasture abundant in feed, and grazing almost to satiety (camels). Satiating or almost satiating. Bringing forth a noble, praiseworthy son (a woman).

A امجار *imjār*, (v. n. 4 of مجر not in use) Being large in the belly of the mother (a fœtus). Taking large profit. Pouring milk into an infant's mouth. Having a large fœtus, being unable to rise (a ewe).

A امجاع *imjāʿ*, (v. n. 4 of مجع) Giving (a weaned camel's colt) milk to drink from a bucket.

A امجال *imjāl*, (v. n. 4 of مجل) Contracting a hardness (the hand) from hard labour. Hardening the hand (hard labour).

A امجد *amjad*, More or most excellent or glorious.

A امح *amahh*, Fat.

A امّحاء *immihās*, The being obliterated.

A امحاح *imhāh*, (v. n. 4 of مح) Being thread-bare.

A امحاش *imhāsh*, A burning, scorching, searing.

A امحاص *imhās*, (v. n. 4 of محص) Shining (as the sun, after an eclipse). Recovering from disease.

A امحاض *imhāz*, (v. n. 4 of محض) Giving to drink pure milk, without any admixture of water. Possessing pure milk. Making a true relation. Demonstrating sincere friendship.

A امحاق *imhāk*, (v. n. 4 of محق) Depriving of a blessing. Perishing, dying away.

A امّحاق *immihāk*, (v. n. 8 of محق) Being cancelled or made void. Being burnt or scorched.

A امحاك *imhāk*, (v. n. 4 of محك) Being morose and surly. Being angry.

A امحال *imhāl*, (v. n. 4 of محل) Being barren. Suffering from barrenness. Giving no rain.

A امحان *amahān*, (v. n. of امح) Beating, throbbing (a wound).

A امحس *amhas*, An expert currier of leather.

A امحص *amhas*, One who receives the excuse of another, without examining into its truth or fallacy.

A امحوضة *umhūzat*, Sincere, disinterested, and faithful admonition.

A امخاء *imkhās*, (v. n. 4 of مخي) Being free, clear of. Excusing one's self.

A امخاخ *imkhākh*, (v. n. 4 of مخ) Being full of marrow (a bone). Becoming fat (a sheep). Being mealy (an ear of corn). Being full of sap (a branch).

A امخاض *imkhāz*, (v. n. 4 of مخض) Having camels enduring the pangs of labour. Being ready for the churn (milk). Being shaken in the churn (milk). Milk as long as it continues so in the churn.

A امخاط *amkhāt*, (pl. of مخط *mukhit*) Generous (princes). *Imkhāt*, (v. n. 4 of مخط) Shooting (an arrow) and making it pierce. Piercing and coming out at the other side (an arrow).

P آمختن *āmukhtan*, To teach.

P آمخته *āmukhta*, Taught.

P آمد *āmad*, He came. Arrival. Income.

A آمد *āmid*, A freighted ship. A man full of good or bad qualities. Name of a city.

P امد *amd*, Time, season, opportunity.

A امد *amad*, (v. n. of امد) Being angry with. End, extremity, boundary, age, term (of life), catastrophe. A goal. Anger. امد مديد و عهد بعيد *amadi madīd u ʿahdi baʿīd*, A long space of time. *Amida*, The capital of Mesopotamia (Diyār bakar).

A امدّ *amadd*, More or most extended.

A امداء *amdās*, (pl. of مدي *mudy*) Mudds, certain measures used in Egypt and Syria of different dimensions. *Imdās*, (v. n. 4 of مدي) Granting a delay, tolerating. Advancing in years, growing old. Drinking a great quantity of milk. Filling.

A امّداح *immidāh*, A being sufficiently spacious.

A امداد *amdād*, (pl. of مدّ *mudd*) Certain dry measures. *Imdād*, (v. n. 4 of مدّ) Assisting, aiding, helping, succouring. Giving, subsidizing. Furnishing with as much ink as the pen will hold. Putting ink into the ink-stand. Delaying, putting off (an appointed term), prolonging (life). Issuing from a sore (matter). Yielding fruit. Becoming juicy from the circulation of the sap (a vegetable). Giving camels the food مديد *madīd* to eat.

A امداش *imdāsh*, (v. n. 4 of مدش) Giving.

P آمد آمد *āmad āmad*, Approach.

A امّدان *immidān*, Water on the surface of the ground. Name of a place.

A امدّان *imiddān*, Very salt (water). *Imiddān*, (or امّدان *immidān*) A running fountain. A place where water springs either from the ground or from a rock.

P آمدانه *āmadāna*, (or آمداني *āmadānī*) Accidental, casual, fortuitous, adventitious. Imports.

A امدة *umdat*, The remains, the rest. A surplus.

A امدّة *amiddat*, The warp of a web in the loom. That whereby the edges of a piece of cloth are held fast in the loom.

A امدر *amdar*, Large-bellied (hyena) that shines from being besmeared with dung. One who stools in his clothes, whose excrement is copious, and cannot be retained. Uncircumcised. Dust-coloured. One whose sides swell out or are dirtied with clay.

P آمد رفت *āmad raft*, Coming and going, ingress and egress. Intercourse. Travellers. A road.

A امدش *amdash*, (A man) having a slender flexible hand. Weak in mind, possessed of little intelligence. Lean, emaciated.

P آمد شد *āmad shud*, Coming and going. آمد شد كردن *āmad shud kardan*, To come and go.

P آمدن *āmadan*, To come. Coming, arrival, entry.

P آمدنگاه *āmadan-gāh*, The time or place of coming, arriving, or meeting: a rendezvous.

P آمدني *āmadanī*, Income, impost, revenue. The season at which any merchandize generally arrives. Perquisites, any thing gained over and above.

A امدوحة *umdūhat*, Praise. A praiseworthy act.

A امدود *umdūd*, Custom, habit, usage.

P آمد و رفت *āmad u raft*, Intercourse.

P آمد و شد *āmad u shud*, Coming and going.

P آمده *āmada*, Come, arrived. A joke, pleasantry, impromptu.

P آمده گير *āmada-gīr*, Receiving, welcoming.

A امدي *amdaʾ*, More or most rare, greatest.

A امدية *amdiyat*, Ponds enclosed with stones.

A امذاء *imzās*, (v. n. 4 of مذي) Turning (a horse) to grass. Diluting very much (wine). Giving (a horse) the rein. Experiencing a seminal effusion. Playing the bawd to one's own wife.

A امذار *imzār*, (v. n. 4 of مذر) Causing to stink, spoiling (an egg).

A امذال *imzāl*, (v. n. 4 of مذل) Sleeping, being torpid (the foot).

A امذح *amzah*, Chafed between the thighs. Stinking, fetid. ما امذح ريحه *mā amzaha rīhahu*, How fetid his breath is!

A امذر *amzar*, One who often goes to stool.

A امذقرار *imzikrār*, (v. n. 4 of مذقر Q not used) Being separated (milk), the lacteal parts on one side, and the aqueous on the other. Being mixed with water (milk or blood).

A امذلال *imzilāl*, The being torpid, languid.

A آمر *āmir*, One who commands, orders, or issues mandates. Numerous, complete, perfect. The last of the five, or, according to some, seven days (called العجوز *al ʿajūz*) of the winter solstice. Name of the first month of the Muhammadan year, during which they are forbidden to fight. This is in the old dialect, the more modern name being Muharram (prohibited). آمر نون والقلم *āmiri nūn u'l kalam*, (Commander of the ink and pen) God. Muhammad.

A أمر *amara*, (fut. يأمر *yaʾmuru*) He commanded.

A امر *amr*, (v. n. of امر) Commanding. Becoming emir, prince, or governor. Multiplying, rendering numerous. (pl. اوامر *awāmir*) A mandate, edict, decree, precept, diploma, commission, ordinance, brief. (in gram.) The affirmative imperative of a verb. P امر كردن *amr kardan*, To command. A (pl. امور *umūr*) A thing, business, affair, action. امر معروف *amri maʿrūf*, A self-evident duty. امر مهم *amri muhimm*, An affair of importance. اولو الامر *ulū'lamr*, Chiefs, learned men. *Imr*, Grievous. A wonderful thing. امر امر *amrun imrun*, A disagreeable or strange affair. *Amar*, (v. n. of امر) Being numerous: being complete, perfect. Having numerous flocks. Being vehement, heavy, hard. Any one, some one. (pl. of امرة *amarat*) Small stones which they erect in the deserts to shew travellers the way. *Amir*, Happy, fortunate, blest.

A امّر *immar* also *ammar*, Weak, silly. Easy, pliable. *Immar*, A lambkin. ما له امّر و لا امّرة *mā lahu immar wa lā immarat*, He has nothing.

A امرّ *amarr*, More bitter. The intestines which contain the dung. امرّ عقداً *amarr ʿakdan*, More or most able in the management of business.

S آمرا *āmrā*, The mangoe.

A امرء *imraʾ* or *imruʾ*, A man. A he-wolf.

P امرا *amrā*, (in zand and Pāzand) An ass. *Amarā*, Wine.

A امراء *imrāʾ*, (v. n. 4 of مرأ) Agreeing with a man, being wholesome and digestible (food). (v. n. 4 of مري) Emitting milk in streams (a camel). *Umarāʾ*, (pl. of امير *amīr*) Commanders, governors, princes, grandees, amirs. امراءِ كرام *umarāʾi kirām*, Great princes, noble lords.

A امرءة *imraʾat*, A woman. A she-wolf.

A امرات *amrāt*, (pl. of مرت *mart*) Deserts, solitudes, wastes. Barren, desert.

A امراج *imrāj*, (v. n. 4 of مرج) (God) permitting (the seas) to flow freely. Feeding (flocks). Violating (a treaty). Bringing forth an abortion.

A امراح *imrāh*, (v. n. 4 of مرح) Putting (a horse) into great spirits (by giving him fodder).

A امراخ *imrākh*, (v. n. 4 of مرخ) Softening, macerating, or thinning (any mass of matter or dough), by diluting with water.

A امرار *amrār*, (pl. of مرّ *murr*) Bitternesses, bitter things. (pl. of مرّة *mirrat*) Galls, biles. Powers, strengths, durability of bodies. Intellects, faculties, powers of the understanding, strength of judgment, vigour of mind. (pl. of مرّة *murrat*) Certain bitter trees or herbs. *Imrār*, (v. n. 4 of مرّ) Being bitter. Embittering. Speaking bitter words. Causing to pass by or to cross over. Wrestling. Grasping the tail of a she-camel and turning her about in order to make her tame and gentle. Throwing prostrate. Having amongst it the black and bitter grain مريراء *murayrāʾ* (wheat).

A امراس *amrās*, (pl. of مرسة *marasat*) Ropes. *Imrās*, (v. n. 4 of مرس) Placing right on a pulley (a rope that had slipt off). Throwing (a rope) between the pulley and the cheek so as to make it stick.

A امراش *amrāsh*, (pl. of مرش *marsh*) Lands made smooth or level by the overflowing of water.

A امراض *amrāz*, (pl. of مرض *maraz*) Diseases, maladies, distempers. امراض بلغميّه *amrāzi balghamīya*, Phlegmatic diseases. امراض مائيّه *amrāzi maʾīya*, Pestilential disorders. امراض مختلفه *amrāzi mukhtalifa*, Various infirmities. *Imrāz*, (v. n. 4 of مرض) Making sick, throwing into a disorder. Finding (one) indisposed, and taking care of (him). Having distempered cattle. Being near the truth; following the dictates of reason.

A امراط *amrāt*, (pl. of مريط *marīt*) Unfeathered arrows. *Imrāt*, (v. n. 4 of مرط) (A palm-tree) being naked by the falling of the unripe dates. Being fit for pulling (hair). Being swift (a camel).

A امّراط *immirat*, (for امتراط *imtirāt*) (v. n. 8 of مرط) Falling off one after another (hairs).

A امراع *amrāʿ*, (pl. of مريع *marīʿ*) (Places) abounding with grass, herbage, or other produce. *Imrāʿ*, (v. n. 4 of مرع) Emitting (urine or excrement) through fear. Abounding with grass. Finding a fertile spot. Anointing the head abundantly.

A امراغ *imrāgh*, (v. n. 4 of مرغ) Spitting, slavering, foaming. Blabbing, chattering. Thinning (a mass of paste) with water.

A امراق *imrāk*, (v. n. 4 of مرق) Making broth in a sufficient quantity (a pot). Uncovering one's nakedness, shewing the privities. Being ready to be plucked (wool from a skin). Shooting deliberately, transfixing with an arrow.

A امران *amrān*, A tendon in the arm.

A امرّان *amarrāni*, (The two bitters) Poverty and old age. The aloe and the nasturtium.

A آمرة *āmirat*, (pl. اوامر *awāmir*) A command.

A امرة *amrat*, (v. n. of امر) Being numerous. Being complete, perfect. Having numerous flocks. A single command. *Imrat*, A government, principality, dominion. *Amarat*, (pl. امر *amar*) A small mile or way-stone, which is erected in the deserts.

A امّرة *immarat* or *ammarat*, Silly, indiscreet.

A امرجة *amrijat*, (pl. of مريج *marīj*) Small white bones in the middle of horns.

A امرخ *amrakh*, (A bull) spotted red and white.

A امرخة *amrikhat*, (pl. of مريخ *marīkh*) Soft bones inside the horns of animals.

A امرخداد *imrikhdād*, (v. n. 4 of مرخد Q) Being loose, lax, hanging down.

P آمرد *āmard*, The fruit of the tree اراك *arāk*.

A امرد *amrad*, (pl. مرد *murd*) Beardless and handsome (youth). Leafless (branch). (A horse) having little hair about his heels.

P امرداد *amurdād*, Name of a month.

P امرد پرست *amrad-parast*, A pederast.

P امرد پرستي *amrad-parastī*, Pederasty.

P آمرزا *āmurzā*, Remitting, absolving, forgiving.

P آمرزش *āmurzish*, Absolution, forgiveness.

P امرزش *amurzish*, Pardon, forgiveness. امرزش خواستن *amurzish khwāstan*, To crave forgiveness.

P آمرزگار *āmurzgār*, Forgiving, compassionate.

P آمرزگاري *āmurzgārī*, Compassion, forgiveness.

P آمرزندگان *āmurzandagān*, The merciful.

P آمرزنده *āmurzanda*, Pitying, forgiving.

P آمرزيدن *āmurzīdan*, To forgive, absolve.

A امرش *amrash*, A worthless scoundrel.

A امرط *amrat*, (pl. مرط *murt*) Smooth-cheeked (man). Thin-eyebrowed. Unfeathered (arrow). Weak-sighted, watery-eyed. Light-bodied (man). Bald (wolf). A robber.

A امرع *amruʿ*, (pl. of مريع *marīʿ*) (Places) abounding with grass, herbage, or other produce.

P آمرغ *āmurgh*, A little, few, somewhat. Quantity. Value, price. Gain, profit. Stock, capital. A store, hoard. Power, rank. *Āmurgh* or *āmargh*, Root, origin. The purest and choicest part.

A امرغ *amragh*, One that wallows in vice.

P امرود *amrūd*, (or امروت) A pear. A guava.

P امروز *imroz*, (for اين *īn* and روز *roz*) To-day.

P امروز فردا *imroz-fardā*, To-day or to-morrow.

P امروزي *imrozī*, (or امروزينه) Of to-day.

A امروعة *umrūʿat*, Fruitful, productive (land).

A امر و نهي *amr u nahy*, Command and prohibition, order and counter-order: absolute authority.

A امره *amrah*, Sore-eyed from neglecting to anoint them with eye-salve. Unmixed (wine).

A آمريّ *āmiriy*, Name of the father of a tribe.

A امرئة *amriʾat*, (pl. of مريء *marīʾ*) Gullets.

A امرئى *imra,īy*, Belonging to امرؤ القيس.

A امزّ *amazz*, Hard, difficult.

A امزاج *imzāj*, (v. n. 4 of مزج) Conducting (a vine) along the trellis or arbour, round which it twines and supports itself.

A امزجة *amzijat*, (pl. of مزاج *mizāj*) Mixtures. Humours of the body. Constitutions.

A امزهلال *imzihlāl*, (v. n. 4 of مزهل Q) Being dispelled (a cloud). Melting (snow).

A آمس *āmus*, (pl. of امس *ams*) Yesterdays.

A امس *amsi, amsa, amsu*, (الامس *al amsa* or بالامس *bi'l amsa*) (pl. آمس *āmus*, آموس *āmūs*, and آماس *āmās*) Yesterday.

A امساء *imsā,*, (v. n. 4 of مسأ) Exciting discord. (v. n. 4 of مسا for مسو) Becoming evening. Being, becoming (unfortunate).

A امساح *amsāh*, (pl. of مسح *mis-h*) Pack-saddles. Hair-cloths, sack-cloths. Bags, sacks. Highways.

A امساخ *imsākh*, (v. n. 4 of مسخ) Becoming relaxed, dispersed, or discussed (a swelling).

A امساد *amsād*, (pl. of مسد *masad*) Ropes made of the fibres of the palm-tree, or of any other substance firmly twisted.

A امساس *imsās*, (v. n. 4 of مسّ) Ordering or causing one to touch. Causing to rub.

A امساغ *imsāgh*, The act of retiring, receding.

A امساك *imsāk*, (v. n. 4 of مسك) Keeping, holding, detaining. Abstaining (from speaking). Parsimony, savingness. Tenacity.

P امسال *imsāl*, (for این سال *īn sāl*) This year.

A امسح *amsah*, Hurt in the hams by the friction of coarse raiment; also chafed between the thighs. One whose feet are even at the soles (not concave). A level, gravelly place.

A امسخ *amsakh*, More or most tasteless or insipid.

A امسكة *amsikat*, Holes in the ground which retain the water.

A امسلة *amsilat*, (pl. of مسل *masal*) Channels of torrents.

A امسوح *umsūh*, A ship-plank of an oblong form.

A امسوخ *umsūkh*, A plant of a knotty species, with leaves resembling the olive, and red fruit of an astringent bitter.

A امسىّ *imsīy*, Yesterday's, of yesterday.

A امسية *umsīyat*, Evening-tide.

A امشّ *amashsh*, Diseased in the eye (a camel).

A امشاء *imshā,*, (v. n. 4 of مشا for مشو) Causing a looseness in the belly, purging (medicine). Waiting, expecting medicine to produce that effect. (v. n. 4 of مشي) Ordering one to walk or go: driving. Being rich in cattle (ماشية *māshiyat*). Having very prolific cattle: having a numerous offspring.

A امشاج *amshāj*, (pl. of مشيج *mashīj*) Mixed. Miscellanies, mixtures. Sordes collected in the navel. نطفة امشاج *nutfat amshāj*, Semen mingled with blood.

A امشاح *imshāh*, (v. n. 4 of مشح) Being barren (the year). Being cloudless (the sky).

A امشار *imshār*, (v. n. 4 of مشر) Shooting forth sprigs and leaves. Producing herbage (grounds). Swelling. Stretching one's self in running.

P امشاسپند *amshāspand* or امشاسفند, An angel.

A امشاش *imshāsh*, (v. n. 4 of مشّ) Being full of marrow (a bone). Putting forth tender branches (the tree سلم *salam*).

P امشاش *imshāsh*, Measure, rule. Comparison.

A امشاط *amshāt*, (pl. of مشط *mushut*) Combs.

A امشاق *imshāk*, (v. n. 4 of مشق) Scourging.

P امشب *imshab*, (این *īn*, شب *shab*) To-night.

A امشق *amshak*, (A man) chafed between the thighs. (pl. مشق *mushk*) Split, cracked (skin).

A آمص *āmis*, (from P خاميز *khāmīz*) A kind of dish made with veal. Broth made of meat, flour, and vinegar, which is allowed to cool after the fat is skimmed off. Raw meat put into vinegar.

A امصاخ *imsākh*, (v. n. 4 of مصخ) Coming out (the leaves of the plant ثمام *sumām*.)

A امّصاخ *immisākh*, (v. n. 8 of مصخ) Being weaned from the mother.

A امصار *amsār*, (pl. of مصر) Cities, great cities.

A امصاص *imsās*, (v. n. 4 of مصّ) Making suck.

A امصاع *imsāع*, (v. n. 4 of مصع) Voiding dung (a bird). Bringing forth (a woman). Confessing, acknowledging (a debt). Possessing camels giving little milk. Shooting forth leaves (the box-thorn).

A امصال *imsāl*, (v. n. 4 of مصل) Exhausting sheep (by milking). Injuring, hurting, wasting (property). Bringing forth an immature fœtus.

A امصح *amsah*, Short, feeble (shadow).

A امصدة *amsidat*, (pl. of مصاد *masād*) High mountains.

A امصرة *amsirat*, (pl. of مصير) Intestines.

A امصوخة *umsūkhat*, (pl. اماصيخ *amāsīkh*) A leaf of a kind of thistle and of the herb ثمام *sumām*.

A امض *amaz*, (v. n. of امض) Being regardless of reproof. Resolving, planning in the mind, and declaring the contrary of one's intentions.

A امضاء *imzā,*, (v. n. 4 of مضي) Making pass or penetrate, transmitting, despatching. Holding valid. Accomplishing. Subscription, signature.

A امضاح *imzāh*, (v. n. 4 of مضح) Dishonouring.

A امضاض *imzāz*, (v. n. 4 of مضّ) Giving pain. Afflicting, grieving. (Acrid collyrium) burning (the eye). Pricking, itching, requiring to be scratched.

A امضاغ *imzāgh*, (v. n. 4 of مضغ) Bearing ripe dates (a palm-tree). Being fit to eat.

A امضحلال *imzihlāl*, A vanishing, disappearing.

A امضى *amza'*, More or most acute, penetrating.

A امطاء *amtā,*, (pl. of مطا *mata'*) Backs. (pl. of مطو *matw* or *mitw*) Things long, particularly long split branches of the palm-tree, with which they bind trees together. (pl. of مطيّة *matīyat*) Riding-camels, upon which people travel. Horses, beasts of burthen. *Imtā,*, (v. n. 4 of مطا for مطو) Employing as a beast of burden (مطيّة *matīyat*).

A امطار *amtār*, (pl. of مطر *matr*) Skins filled with oil or olives. (pl. of مطر *matar*) Rains. *Imtār*, (v. n. 4 of مطر) Causing to rain. Sending a superabundance of rain (God). Sweating (brow). Finding (a place) wet with rain. Keeping silence.

A امطىّ *umtīy*, Well-proportioned, tall in stature. A kind of gum which they eat.

A امظاظ *imzāz*, (v. n. 4 of مظّ) Seasoning green wood by stripping the bark, letting the moisture dry.

A امّع *immaع* or *ammaع*, (or امّعة *immaعat* or *ammaعat*) Weak in mind, fickle, changeable. One who is at the beck and call of any body: obedient, yielding, compliant. Who comes to table uninvited.

A امعاء *amعā,*, (pl. of معى *maعy* or *miعa'*) Intestines. امعاء الارض *amعā,u'l arz*, Earthworms.

A امعار *imعār*, (v. n. 4 of معر) Being destitute of travelling-provisions, poor. Feeding ground quite bare. Stripping of possessions. Being thin (hairs or plumage). Being nearly destitute of herbage.

A امعاز *imعāz*, (v. n. 4 of معز) Abounding in goats.

G امعاسيون *amعāsiyūn*, Juice of grapes.

A امعاص *amعās*, (pl. of معص *maعas*) Cramps.

A امعاض *imعāz*, (v. n. 4 of معض) Enraging, vexing, grieving. Setting on fire, burning.

A امّعاط *immiعāt*, (v. n. 7 of معط) Being bald. Being smooth and worn (a rope). Being stretched out and long (a rope). A scald.

A امعاق *amعāk*, (pl. of معق *maعk*) Wide-spread deserts. *Imعāk*, (v. n. 4 of معق) Making deep.

A امعال *imعāl*, (v. n. 4 of معل) Diverting from a purpose, turning one from any thing.

A امعان *imعān*, (v. n. 4 of معن) Advancing far (in any business). Going far (a horse). Confirming any one in his right, admitting it, acknowledging it. Denying. Flowing (water). Being saturated with moisture (land). Being possessed of wealth. Being poor. Hiding (as a lizard in the farthest part of its hole). Carrying off (what in justice belongs to another). Penetration, acumen.

A امعر *amعar*, One whose hair or nails are dropping off. (A place) bare of grass or other herbage. Thin-plumaged. Falling (hair). Hairless (boot). (A hoof) whose hair is long and overhanging.

A امعز *amعaz*, Hard, gravelly soil. ما امعزه من رجل *mā amعazahu mir rajulin*, How hard a man he is!

A امعط *amعat*, A wolf, one especially that is bare of pile, bald. Wolf-like, *i.e.* a robber, a thief. Destitute of hair. Sandy (place) without vegetation.

A امعوز *umعūz*, The goat kind. (pl. اماعز *amāعiz* or اماعيز *amāعīz*) A herd of wild goats: a bevy of roes.

A امغاد *imghād*, (v. n. 4 of مغد) Drinking much. Suckling a child.

A امغار *imghār*, (v. n. 4 of مغر) (A sheep) emitting (whilst milking) blood (along with the milk). Bringing out (blood, &c.). Causing to pass by. Becoming red (milk).

A امغاص amghās, (pl. of مغص maghas) Choice camels of the finest sort.

A امّغاط immighāt, (v. n. 7 of مغط) Being stretched (a bow or elastic substance).

A امغال imghāl, (v. n. 4 of مغل) Suckling, whilst pregnant. Conceiving twice in one year (a sheep or goat), bringing forth twice in every year. Bearing a child every year, and conceiving again before the year is gone. Having camels afflicted with a belly-ache in consequence of eating earth along with green herbage. The cholic in a sheep causing her to cast her young. Slandering.

A امغر amghar, Red-haired. Reddish-skinned. Of a ruddy face with pure white. Chesnut-coloured (horse). Of a red earth colour (a camel).

A امغيلان amughīlān or ammughīlān, An Egyptian thorn.

G امفاسيون umfāsiyūn, Juice of unripe grapes.

A امق amk or umk, The inner corner of the eye.

A امقّ amakk, Long-bodied (horse).

A امقار imkār, (v. n. 4 of مقر) Being bitter, acrid. Losing its flavour, being insipid (as milk). Steeping (salted fish in vinegar).

A امقاط amkāt, (pl. of مقط mukt) Ropes or gins for catching birds.

A ما امقتني له mā amkatanī lahu, How hateful I am to him! A ما امقته عندي mā amkatahu ʿindī, How odious he is to me!

A امقرار imkirār, (v. n. 9 of مقر) Standing out prominently (a vein).

A هو شرّاب بامقع huwa sharrābun bi amkuʿ, He perseveres until he has attained his object.

A امقه amkah, Grey-eyed. Distant, remote. Barren (place) without tree or plant. Thin of eyelashes; tender-eyed. Blue, water-coloured (wine).

A امكاء amkāʾ, (pl. of مكو makw) Hares' forms. Foxes' covers.

A امكان imkān, (v. n. 4 of مكن) Giving power, affording an opportunity. Being possible; possibility; contingency (in opposition to وجود wujūd, necessity, or necessary existence). Having eggs in the belly (a lizard). Taking eggs under her wing.

A امكاني imkānī, Possible.

A امكر amkar, More or most crafty.

A امكن amkana, (pret. of مكن 4) May be, it is allowed. ما امكنه عند الامير mā amkanahu ʿinda'l amīr, How great is his interest with the prince!

A امكنة amkinat, (pl. of مكان makān) Places.

P آمل āmul, Name of a town in Tabaristān, and of one situated on the river Oxus.

A أمل amala, (fut. يأمل yaʾmulu) He hoped.

A امل aml, (v. n. of امل) Hoping. Amal, aml, or iml, (pl. آمال āmāl) Hope. Umul, (pl. of اميل amīl) Large, wide-extended, sandy hills.

A املاء amlāʾ, (pl. of ملأ malaʾ) Opinions, dispositions, habits, manners. Fillings (of a vessel). Imlāʾ, (v. n. 4 of ملأ) Drawing (a bow-string) tight. Helping, assisting. Giving a cold in the head. (v. n. 4 of ملا for ملو) Lengthening (a rope or tether). Granting a delay. Allowing to continue in error and folly. Permitting to enjoy. Inditing. Writing correctly.

A املاءً imlāʾan, Orthographically. P بي املا bī imlā, Inaccurate, unorthographical (writing).

A املاج imlāj, (v. n. 4 of ملج) Suckling.

A املاح amlāh, (pl. of ملح milh) Brackish waters. (pl. of مليح malīh) Good, beautiful. Agreeable, gracious. Imlāh, (v. n. 4 of ملح) Salting too much (in cooking). Descending to drink salt water. Becoming salt or brackish (water which was once sweet). Giving such water (to camels).

A املاز imlāz, (v. n. 4 of ملز) Going away (with any one). Remaining behind.

A املاس imlās, (v. n. 4 of ملس) Being bare or naked (a sheep whose wool has dropped off). Escaping. The mixture of darkness and light.

A امّلاس immilās, (v. n. 7 of ملس) Escaping. Being smooth, bare.

A املاص imlās, (v. n. 4 of ملص) Bringing forth a dead child. Causing to slide. Slipping.

A امّلاص immilās, A being liberated, escaping.

A املاط amlāt, (pl. of ملط milt) Bad men. Thieves. Obscurely born. Imlāt, (v. n. 4 of ملط) (A camel) bringing forth an abortion (before the hair has begun to grow upon the fœtus).

A املاع imlāʿ, (v. n. 4 of ملع) Walking fast (a camel), or going with outstretched neck.

A املاغ amlāgh, Fools. Obscene talkers.

P املاق imlāk, Name of a country in Turkistān.

A املاق imlāk, (v. n. 4 of ملق) Being reduced to want, becoming impotent. Casting her foal (a mare). Washing (a garment). Poverty, destitution.

A امّلاق immilāk, (v. n. 7 of ملق) Being smooth. Escaping, withdrawing, passing by, being lost.

A املاك amlāk, (pl. of ملك malk) Kings. (pl. of ملك mulk) Goods, riches, possessions. Countries, estates. (pl. of ملك malak) Angels. Imlāk, (v. n. 4 of ملك) Putting in possession of a thing. Appointing a king. Being able to follow the dam. Causing to marry. Giving a wife. Kneading well (dough). Marriage, the marriage-contract. املكت مرها umlikat amrahā, She was divorced.

A املاكات amlākāt, (pl. of املاك amlāk) Goods and chattels; paraphernalia of a bride.

A املال imlāl, (v. n. 4 of ملّ) Being long and tedious (a journey). Annoying, vexing, wearying. Dictating, inditing a letter. Confession.

A املاه imlāh, (v. n. 4 of مله not in use) Arriving at the age of puberty (a girl). Making pretences or excuses. Stipulating, making conditions.

A املة imlat, Hope. ما اطول املته mā atwala imlatuhu, How long he hopes! how great his faith! Amalat, Assistants, defenders, guards, garrisons.

A املج amlaj, Brown, tawny, dusky. A barren waste. Poor. The myrabolan-tree.

A املح amlah, (A ram) variegated with black and white wool. Intensely blue-eyed.

A املحاح imlihāh, (v. n. 9 of ملح) Being black and white (a ram). Being blue and green.

A املد amlad, (amlud, imlid, املدان umludān or املدانيّ umludāniy Delicate (boy or branch).

A املس amlas, Even, smooth, sleek. Bare. Sound-backed (horse).

A املص amlas, Thin of hair about the head.

A املط amlat, Smooth-bodied. Thin-bearded. Featherless (arrow).

A املغ amlagh, Obscene (discourse).

A املوج umlūj, (pl. اماليج) The leaf of a certain tree like the cypress. The stone of the مقل mukl.

A املود umlūd, Tender, delicate (girl). Umlūd, (fem. املودة umlūdat) Tender (boy or branch).

A املودان umlūdān, (or املودانيّ umlūdāniy) Tender, delicate (boy or branch).

A املودانيّة umlūdāniyat, Tender, delicate (girl).

A املوك umlūk, A people of Arabia; the Himyaritic kings. (pl. of مالك mālik) Proprietors.

P آمله āmula (or امله amla), Name of an excellent eye-medicine. The myrabolan-tree.

A املئاء amliʾāʾ, (pl. of مليئ maliʾ) Opulent.

A امليجاج imlījāj, (v. n. 11 of ملج) Growing up (a boy). Breeding its milk-teeth (a child).

A امليد imlīd, Tender (boy or branch). A desert level and glittering.

A امليس imlīs, (or امليسة imlīsat) (pl. اماليس amālīs and امالس amālis) A barren desert.

A امليساس imlīsās, (v. n. 11 of ملس) Being smooth. Escaping, getting free.

A امليسيّ imlīsiy, (or امليسيّة imlīsiyat), A wild pomegranate hollow in the heart.

A امليص imlīs, A swift pace. A quick journey.

A امم amam, (v. n. of امّ) Being near. Intending, purposing. Approaching Manifest. Easy. Small, few, little. Nearness. A middle, centre. من امم min amam, Hard by, near at hand. امم داري amam dārī, Opposite my house. Umam, (pl. of امّة ummat) People, nations. Sects. امم خالية umam khāliyat, By-gone nations.

P آمن āman, Circumference, circuit (in general applied as a minor term, when compared to something of the same kind of a greater circumference).

A آمن āman, The best, soundest, or noblest. Āmin, Secure, safe, fearing nothing. Safety, security. The choicest and best of one's property.

A أمن amana, (fut. يأمن yaʾmunu) He confided. Amina, (fut. يأمن yaʾminu) He was secure. Amuna, (fut. يأمن yaʾmunu) He was trustworthy.

A امن amn, (v. n. of امن) Being safe, secure. Trusting, confiding in. Safety, security. Faith, religion. Imn, (v. n. of امن) Being safe, secure. Aman, (v. n. of امن) Being safe, secure. Faith, religion. Security, repose, peace, liberty, safety.

Amin, One who implores security and safety. Fearless, safe, secure. *Umun*, (pl. of امون *amūn*) Firm, safe (camels), not apt to stumble.

A امناء *amnāʼ*, (pl. of منا *mana'*) Minas, certain weights of about 2lbs. Scales, balances. Measures for dry goods. *Imnāʼ*, (v. n. 4 of مني) Arriving and living in the valley of Mecca, called Mina'. Being in the state when she is called ممني *mumnī* or ممنية *mumniyat* (a camel). Experiencing a seminal effusion. *Umanāʼ*, (pl. of امين *amīn*) Prefects. Tax-gatherers, revenue-collectors. Superintendants.

A امنان *amnān*, (pl. of منّ *mann*) Weights of about 2 lbs. *Imnān*, (v. n. 4 of منّ) Depriving of strength. Reaching the utmost of any one's power.

A آمنة *āminat*, Name of Muhammad's mother.

A امنة *amanat*, (v. n. of امن) Being safe and secure. Fidelity, sincerity. A trustee, depositary. Unsuspecting. *Umanat*, Unsuspecting, disposed to believe everybody. A trustee, a depositary.

A امنع *amnaʻ*, More or most inaccessible or impregnable, more or most strongly fortified.

P آمنه *āmana*, (or امنه *amana*) Split wood, put up in bundles for sale.

A امني *amnī*, (pl. of منا *mana'*) Certain weights or measures.

A امنيّة *umnīyat*, (pl. اماني) Desire, wish.

P آمو *āmū*, A tumour, swelling, inflation. *Āmū*, (or آب آمو *ābi āmū*) The name of the river Oxus.

A امواء *imwāʼ*, (v. n. 4 of ماء for موأ) Imitating the mewing of a cat.

A اموات *amwāt*, (pl. of ميّت *mayyit*) The dead. *Amawāt*, (pl. of امة *amat*) Maids, handmaids.

A امواج *amwāj*, (pl. of موج) Waves, billows.

A امواق *amwāk*, (pl. of موق *mūk*) Strong boots.

A اموال *amwāl*, (pl. of مال *māl*) Riches, goods, effects. Wished, desired (objects).

A اموان *amwān*, *imwān*, or *umwān*, (pl. of امة *amat*) Servant-maids, handmaidens.

A امواه *amwāh*, (pl. of ماء *māʼ*) Waters. *Imwāh*, (v. n. 4 of موه) Digging and finding water.

A اموة *amwat* or *amawat*, A maid-servant.

A امّوة *umūwat*, The becoming a maid-servant.

P آموت *āmūt*, The nest of a bird of prey.

A ما اموته *mā amwatahu*, How dead he is!

A اموت *umūt*, (pl. of امت *amt*) Unequal grounds. High grounds. Differences (in opinion). Doubts. Hills, hillocks or unequal rugged grounds. Altitudes, protuberances, projections. Proper regulations for living. Weaknesses. Distortions about the mouth. Wrinkles or folds in loose garments.

P آموتيا *āmūtiyā*, (in zand and Pāz.) A damsel.

P آموختن *āmokhtan*, To learn. To teach.

P آموخته *āmokhta*, Learnt. Taught. آموختگان ازل *āmokhtagāni azal*, (Taught of the Eternal) Prophets, seers, and saints.

P آمودن *āmūdan*, To prepare, to fashion. To cause to be made. To adorn. To be adorned. To mix. To be mixed. To fill.

P آموده *āmūda*, Full, filled. Adorned. Prepared, fashioned. Mixed. A pearl. A ruby.

P آمور *āmūr*, A tumour.

A امور *amūr*, Commanding, ordering. *Umūr*, (pl. of امر *amr*) Things, affairs, acts, deeds, businesses. امور دولت و دين *umūri dawlat u dīn*, Affairs of state and religion. امور جميله *umūri jamīla*, Good, beautiful, elegant things. امور عموم *umūri ʻumūm*, (or جمهور *jumhūr*) Public or state-affairs.

A امورات *umūrāt*, Things, matters, concerns.

P اموردیده *umūr-dīda*, Experienced in business.

P آموز *āmoz*, Teaching. Learned, skilful. دانش آموز *dānish-āmoz*, Skilled in science, a learned man. كار آموز *kār-āmoz*, Experienced, clever at business.

P آموزاننده *āmozānanda*, A teacher.

P آموزانيدن *āmozānīdan*, To make learn, to teach.

P آموزش *āmozish*, Instruction, teaching.

P آموزگار *āmozgār*, A teacher. A learner.

P آموزناك *āmoznāk*, A teacher. A student. A name of God.

P آموزنده *āmozanda*, Teaching: a teacher.

P آموزيدن *āmozīdan*, To learn. To teach.

P اموس *amūs*, (or آموس *āmūs*) Bishop's weed. A seed put into bread.

A اموس *umūs*, (pl. of امس *ams*) Yesterdays.

P آموسني *āmūsnī*, (or اموسني *amūsnī*) A woman who has a husband in common with another.

P آموغ *āmūgh*, Gravity, reverence, venerability. Terror. Quantity, measure. Stature.

G آمولن *āmūlan*, Starch.

A امومة *umūmat*, The being a mother; maternity.

P آمون *āmūn*, Brimful. Name of a river.

A امون *amūn*, Firm, steady, not apt to trip.

A اموه *amwah*, More or most full of water.

A آموي *āmūy*, Name of a town and of a tribe near the river Oxus or Jīhūn. Filling. A filler.

A امويّ *amawīy*, In the station of a maid-servant. *Umawīy* or *amawīy*, A descendant of اميّة *umayyat*.

P آمويه *āmūya*, The river Oxus.

P آمه *āma*, An ink-stand. A bundle of sticks.

A امه *amaha*, (fut. يامه *yaʼmuhu*) He enjoined.

A امه *amh*, (v. n. of امه) Being afflicted with pustules called اميهة *amīhat* (cattle). Commanding. Stipulating. *Amah*, (v. n. of امه) Forgetting. Confessing, acknowledging. Being disturbed in mind and bereft of reason. Oblivion, forgetfulness.

A امهاء *imhāʼ*, (v. n. 4 of مها for مهو) Grinding or sharpening (a sword, lancet, or knife). Making (milk) thin and watery. Finding water when digging a well. Giving (a sword) a fine water, making it very bright. Giving (a horse) the reins, driving him at full gallop, till he sweats and foams.

A امّهات *ummahāt*, (pl. of امّ *umm* spoken of human beings) Mothers. امّهات الابواب *ummahātu'l abwāb*, The mother conjugations, viz. the three first of the simple triliteral conjugations; viz. نصر *nasara*, ينصر *yansuru*, ضرب *zaraba*, يضرب *yazribu*, سمع *samiʻa*, يسمع *yasmaʻu*. P امّهات طبائع چهار اركان *ummahāti tabāʼiʻi chahār arkān*, The four maternal or elementary qualities (in man). چهار امّهات سفليّه و نه آبائ علويّه *chahār ummahāti suflīya u nuh ābāʼi ʻulwīya*, The four mothers below and the nine fathers above; *i.e.* The four elements and the nine heavens.

A امهاد *amhād*, (pl. of مهد *muhd*) High (grounds); also those low, plain, and level.

A امهار *amhār*, (pl. of مهر *muhr*) Foals, colts. *Imhār*, (v. n. 4 of مهر) Giving a marriage-portion to a woman, and marrying her to some one. Causing a camel to become of the kind مهريّة *mahrīyat*.

A امهال *imhāl*, (v. n. 4 of مهل) Prolonging, giving a delay, deferring, giving longer time. Behaving in a manner kind, easy, and gentle. See also مبالغة *mubālaghat* and اعذار *iʻzār*.

A امهان *imhān*, The act of making contemptible.

A امّهة *ummahat*, (for امّ *umm*) (pl. امّهات *ummahāt*) A mother, (applied to rational beings).

A امهج *umhuj*, (or امهجان) Thin milk or fat.

A امهدة *amhidat*, (pl. of مهاد *mihād*) Beds.

A امهق *amhak*, Of a dead white (like chalk).

A امهود *umhūd*, A pit dug for catching prey, or for cooking in.

P امهوسپند *amhūspand*, (or امهوسفند *amhūsfand*) An angel.

A امهيصاص *imhīsās*, (v. n. 11 of مهص) Becoming bare of vegetation.

A آمي *āmī*, (pl. of امة *amat*) Handmaidens.

A امّيّ *ummīy*, An idiot, who can neither read nor write (as he came from his mother's (*umm*) womb). امّيّ صادق *ummīy sādik*, Muhammad. نبيّ امّيّ *nabīy ummīy*, An illiterate prophet, an idiot (by which epithet they sometimes distinguish Muhammad).

P اميا *amyā*, (or اميان *amyān*) A purse, a scrip.

A اميال *amyāl*, (pl. of ميل *mīl*) Miles. Milestones put up in the deserts. Styles. Probes.

A اميّة *umayyat*, (dim. of امة *amat*) A little maid. Name of a woman. بنو اميّة *banū* (or بني *banī*) *umayyat*, A branch of the tribe of Kuraysh.

A امّيّة *ummīyat*, Maternity, being a mother.

A اميثال *umaysāl*, (pl. of مثيل *musayl*) Somewhat like.

P آميختگي *āmekhtagī*, Sociability. Mixture.

P آميختن *āmekhtan*, To mix, mingle. To be intermixed.

P آميخته *āmekhta*, Mixed. A mixture. Sociable.

P اميد *umīd* or *umed*, *ummīd* or *ummed*, Hope, expectation, dependence, trust. Desire, greediness. پيك اميد *payki umīd*, Attendant hope (as it always accompanies us). خلاف اميد Disappointment.

P اميد بخش *umed-bakhsh*, (Giver of hope). God.

P اميدگاه *umed-gāh*, A place of hope or refuge.

P اميدوار *umedwār*, Hopeful, confident, supported by hope. An expectant, dependant, candidate. امیدوارم که *umedwāram ki*, I hope that.

P امیدواري *umedwārī*, Hope, expectancy.

P آمیر *āmīr*, (or امیر *amīr*) A glutton. Lazy.

A امیر *amīr*, (pl. امراء *umarāʹ*) A commander, governor, emperor, chief, leader, lord, prince. A leader of the blind. A neighbour. A counsellor. امیر الامراء *amīru'l umarāʹ*, The amiru'l umarā, prince of princes, a viceroy or governor of a great province. P امیر زنبوران *amīri zambūrān*, A king-bee. A امیر البحر *amīru'l bahr*, Harbour-master. امیر الجیوش *amīru'l juyūsh*, The general of an army. امیر المومنین *amīru'l mūminīn*, Commander of the faithful, one of the titles of the khalifs. P امیر آبحیوان *amīri āb haywān*, The prophet Khizr. A امیر حج *amīri haj*, The prefect, or chief of the pilgrims, one of the most honourable employments in the appointment of the Khalifs. امیر صاحب دلق *amīri sāhibi dalak*, Muhammad. امیر علم *amīri ʻalam*, Governor of a city or small district. امیر المرأة *amīru'l marʹat*, The husband of a woman. P امیر آخور *amīri ākhwur*, Master of the horse. امیر داد *amīri dād*, Chief justice. امیر کردن *amīr kardan*, To play the prince, to act the emir. To reign properly.

P امیرانه *amīrāna*, Imperial, princely: imperially.

A امیرة *amīrat*, An empress, queen, princess.

P امیرزاده *amīr-zāda*, A king's son. A descendant of Muhammad, by his son-in-law Alīy and his daughter Fātima.

A امیري *amīrī*, Principality. P امیري کردن *amīrī kardan*, To erect a principality, to become sovereign.

P آمیز *āmez*, Mixing. Mixed. Mixture. Concubitus, coitus. حکمت آمیز *hikmat-āmez*, Mysterious, mixed with mystery or wisdom. رنگ آمیز *rang-āmez*, Mixed with colour, deceitful. ستم آمیز *sitam-āmez*, Mixed with threats; full of vexation. شهد آمیز *shahd-āmez*, Mixed with honey. جواب مژده آمیز *jawābi mujda-āmez*, An answer mixed with happy tidings, an agreeable or satisfactory answer. نیاز آمیز *niyāz-āmez*, Mingled with supplications.

A امیز *amyaz*, More or most distinguished.

P آمیزانیدن *āmezānīdan*, To cause to mix.

P آمیزش *āmezish*, Mixture: alloy. Sociableness.

P آمیزکاري *āmez-kārī*, Mixture. Sociableness.

P آمیزناك *āmeznāk*, Blended, mixed.

P آمیزنده *āmezanda*, Sociable.

P آمیزه *āmeza*, Mixed. Middle-aged, turning grey. Nature, temperament, bodily habit. Coitus.

P آمیزه مو *āmeza-mū*, One beginning to turn gray.

P آمیزیدن *āmezīdan*, To mix, mingle: to be mixed.

P آمیژ *āmej*, Mixing.

P آمیژه *āmeja*, Mixed. Gray, grizzled. Old. Weighed, adjusted. A versifier.

A آمیص *āmīs*, (from P خامیز *khāmīz*) A kind of dish made with veal. Broth made of meat, flour, and vinegar, left to cool after the fat is skimmed off.

P آمیغ *āmegh*, Copulation. Truth. Mixture.

P آمیغه *āmegha*, Mixed. Mixture, union: coitus.

P آمیغي *āmeghī*, True, sincere, unfeigned.

A امیل *amyal*, Inclining to one side (the shoulder, neck). Wry-necked. Sitting badly on a saddle, tottering. Having neither sword, shield, nor spear. Pusillanimous, terrified. Large (sand-hill). Branchy (tree). *Amīl*, (pl. امل *umul*) A sandy mountain, a mile in breadth, and in length a day's journey.

A ما امیلحه *mā umaylihahu*, How pretty he is!

P امیله *amīla*, The myrobalan.

A امیم *amīm*, Wounded in the head, so as to touch without injuring the dura mater. (pl. امائم *amāʹim*) The stone with which such wound is made. Elegantly formed.

A امیمة *umaymat*, (dim. of امّ *umm*) A little mother. A woman's name. (pl. امائم *amāʹim*) A stone fracturing the skull. A smith's hammer.

A آمین *āmīn*, So let it be! amen! God. آمین یا معین *āmīn yā muʻīn*, Amen, so be it! آمین یا ربّ العالمین *āmīn yā rabba'l ʻālamīn*, Amen, O Lord of the worlds! آمین بحرمة سیّد المرسلین *āmīn bi hurmati sayyidi'l mursalīn*, Amen, for the sake of the Prince of Apostles (different modes of concluding prayers).

A امین *amīn*, (pl. امناء *umanāʹ*) Secure, safe, free. Faithful, trusty. Strong, powerful. A name of God. A commissioner, superintendant. An arbitrator. An officer employed by government to collect the revenues of a district (in India). امین البیت *amīnu'l bayt*, One who wishes to visit the house (*i.e.* to perform a pilgrimage to the temple of Mecca). امین دیوان *amīni dīwān*, Receiver-general, the superintendant of the Dīwān. امین بن هارون *amīn bin hārūn*, Amīn the son of Hārūn Ar rashid, the sixth khalif of the house of Al Abbās. امین قلعهٔ بغداد *amīni kalʻaʹi baghdād*, Governor of the castle of Baghdād. الروح الامین *ar rūhu'l amīn*, The faithful spirit (a name by which the Muhammadans distinguish the angel Gabriel; it being by his ministry that they suppose Muhammad received the Kur'ān, verse by verse, as the faithful dictates of Omnipotence). بلد امین *baladi amīn*, The secure city, *i.e.* Mecca.

A آمّین *āmmīn*, A name of God.

P آمینه *āmīna*, Wood split, and bundled for sale.

A امیني *amīnī*, Security. Trust. Office of amīn.

A امّیّون *ummīyūn*, (pl. of امّي *ummīy*) Idiots.

A امیه *amyah*, More or most full of water.

A جامع بني امیّه (*jāmiʻi banī*) *umayya*, The temple of the sons of Umayyah (a church in Damascus, dedicated to St. John).

A امیهة *amīhat*, (v. n. of امه) (Being) afflicted with eruptions, not unlike the pustules of small-pox (cattle): the pustules themselves. Pustulous (cattle).

A امیّيّ *umayyīy*, Of the family of امیّة *umayya*.

P آن *ān*, That. Time. Salt. Taste, flavour. Beauty. Any thing elegant or excellent. Understanding. Wine. آن وقت *ān wakt*, Then, that time. آن طور *ān tawr*, Thus, in that manner. آن جهان *ān jahān*, That, or the next world, future life. آن *ān*, in composition denotes possession: as, از آن من *az āni man*, Of or belonging to me, mine. ان *ān* is added to animate nouns to form the plural: as, مرد *mard*, A man, مردان *mardān*, Men. It is added sometimes to form the pl. of inanimate objects: as, درخت *dirakht*, A tree, درختان *dirakhtān*, Trees. It also forms nouns of agency: افتان *uftān*, Falling, خیزان *khezān*, Rising.

A آن *ān*, Time, an hour. الآن *al ān*, Now, at this time. من الآن *mini'l ān*, From this time, henceforth. الي هذا الآن *ila' hāza'l ān*, To this moment, until this hour, hitherto.

P ان *an*, (in zand and Pāzand) A mother.

A ان *an*, That. الي ان *ila' an*, Until that. لمّا ان *lammā an*, After that. علي ان *ʻala' an*, So that, on condition that. *In*, If, if at any time, if so be. Certainly, doubtless. ان شاء الله *in shāʹ allāh*, If God pleases. ان صدقا و ان کذبا *in sidkan, wa in kizban*, If true and if false: true or false. Not: as, بالله ان فعلت *bi'llāh in faʻaltu*, By God I did not do it. ان لم *in lam*, If not, unless. حیث ان *haysa in*, Where, in which place.

A انّ *anna*, (fut. یئنّ *yaʹinnu*) He groaned.

A انّ *ann*, (v. n. of انّ) Groaning. Pouring out.

A انّ *anna*, (and انّه *annahu*) Since, because. But that. That. Perhaps. لا شكّ انّ *lā shakka anna*, There is no doubt but that. علي انّ *ʻala' anna*, So that. لانّ *li anna*, also لانّه *li annahu*, Since, because that. ما انّ *mā anna*, As far as, whilst, so long as: as, لا افعله ما انّ في السماء نجم *lā afʻaluhu mā anna fi's samāʹ najmun*, I will not do it so long as the stars are in heaven. ما انّ في الفرات قطرة *mā anna fi'l furāt katratun*, As long as one drop remains in the Euphrates. *Inna* and فانّ *fa inna*; انّه *innahu* and فانّه *fa innahu*, For, for certain, truly, verily, yes, indeed. و انّ *wa inna*, For. But. *Inna* is often expletive.

A انا *ana'*, (personal pronoun) I. *Ana'* or *ina'*, (v. n. of اني) Arriving (time). Coming to maturity.

A انّا *innā*, Indeed we, truly we: as, انا خلقناك خلیفة في الارض *innā khallafnāka khalīfat fi'l arz*, Indeed we appointed thee vicegerent upon earth.

A آناء *ānāʹ*, (pl. of انو *inw*) Times, portions of time. (pl. of اني *ina'* or *ana'*) Whole days. (pl. of نوي *nuʹy*) Trenches dug round tents. آناء اللیل *ānāʹu'l layl*, The hours of the night.

A اناء *anʹāʹ*, (pl. of نوي *nuʹy*) Trenches dug round tents. *Inʹāʹ*, (v. n. 4 of ناي) Putting to a distance. Making round a tent a trench (called نوي *nuʹy*) for keeping off the rain-water.

A اناء *anāʹ*, An impediment, delay. Arrival. Maturity. *Ināʹ*, (pl. آنیة *āniyat* and اواني *awānī*) A vase, urn, vessel.

A اناءة *ināʹat*, (v. n. 4 of ناء for نوأ) Oppressing, weighing down. Causing to incline.

A اناب *anāb*, Musk, perfume.

A انابة *ināmat*, (v. n. 4 of ناب for نوب) Repenting; penitence, repentance, conversion in religious matters. Making one supply another's place.

A انابيب *anābīb*, (pl. of انبوب *umbūb*) Joints (of reeds or canes). Spaces between the joints. Pipes, tubes, syphons. انابيب الرئة *anābību'r riat*, The tubes of respiration.

A انابيش *anābīsh*, (pl. of انبوش *umbūsh*) Roots of trees, pot-herbs, &c. Trees with their roots torn up.

A اناة *anāt*, Expectation, patience, delay. An indolent, languid woman, rising slowly upon her feet. اهل الاناة *ahlu'l anāt*, Dilatory people. طويل الاناة *tawīlu'l anāt*, Long-suffering, patient.

P اناتونتن *anātūnitan*, (in zand and Pāzand) To leave. To place.

A اناث *ināṡ*, Things inanimate (as trees or rocks). Small stars. *Ināṡ*, (or اناثى *anāsa'*) (pl. of انثى *unsa'*) Women, females. Goddesses. اناث و ذكور *ināṡ u zukūr*, Females and males.

A اناجير *anājīr*, (pl. of انجار) Flat house-roofs.

A اناجيل *anājīl*, (pl. of انجيل *injīl*) The gospels.

A اناخة *ināk͟hat*, (v. n. 4 of ناخ for نوخ) Obliging (a she-camel) to lie down (a male).

A انادر *anādir*, (pl. of اندر *andar*) Barns or other places where grain is threshed or trodden out, thrashing-floors. Heaps of corn laid up there.

A انادید *anādīd*, Dispersed, scattered (birds), and (adverbially) scatteredly, here and there.

P انار *anār*, A pomegranate. Fireworks.

A انار *anāra*, (pret. of 4) May God illuminate!

A انارة *ināmat*, (v. n. 4 of نار for نور) Illuminating. Shining bright. Being beautiful, clear, shining, conspicuous. Flourishing, flowering, blossoming. (v. n. 4 of نار for نير) Marking (cloth) with a border of different colours. Shouting.

P انارستان *anāristān*, A pomegranate garden.

P انار گیرا *anār-gīrā*, The poppy.

P انار گیوا *anār-gīwā*, The poppy.

P انار مشك *anār-mishk*, Name of a red fruit resembling the pomegranate.

P انارین *anārīn*, Rust.

A آناس *ānās*, (pl. of انسان) Men: certain men.

A اناس *unās*, Men. ابو اناس *abū unās*, Name of a historian. ام اناس *umm unās*, Name of a woman.

A اناسة *ināsat*, (v. n. 4 of ناس for نوس) Moving, agitating, setting in motion.

A اناسم *anāsim*, Men.

A اناسيّ *anāsiy*, اناسي *anāsī*, (and اناسية *anāsiyat*) (pl. of انسيّ *insiy*), Men. Pupils of eyes.

A اناشيد *anāshīd*, (pl. of انشودة *unshūdat*) Verses recited in public assemblies.

A اناصة *ināsat*, The act of wishing.

A اناصي *anāṣī*, (pl. of نصيّة *naṣīyat*) The best, choicest (men, animals, things). Remains.

A اناصيب *anāṣīb*, Mile-stones, direction-posts.

A اناصيل *anāṣīl*, (pl. of انصولة *unṣūlat*) Flowers or thistle-downs of the plant بهمى *buhma'*.

A اناض *ināẓ*, The half-ripe produce of a palm.

A اناضة *anāẓat*, The being half-dressed (meat). *Ināẓat*, (v. n. 4 of ناض for نوض) Betraying ignorance by looks. Bearing ripe fruit (a palm-tree).

A انأطار *inṭitār*, (v. n. 7 of اطر) Being bent.

A اناطة *ināṭat*, (v. n. 4 of ناط for نوط) (Camels) being afflicted with swellings (in the neck). Being covered with tamarisk-trees or Egyptian thorns.

T اناطولي *anāṭūlī*, Anatolia, Asia Minor.

G اناطيطس *anāṭīṭus*, A stone which is said to assist women in labour.

A اناظيم *anāẓīm*, (pl. of نظام *niẓām*) Bases, constitutions of things.

A اناعيم *anāʻīm*, (pl. of نعم) Sheep, cattle, camels.

G اناغاطس *anāg͟hāṭus*, A sort of stone.

G اناغالس *anāg͟hālis*, The herb pimpernel.

A آناف *ānāf*, (pl. of انف *anf*) Noses.

A انافة *ināfat*, (v. n. 4 of ناف for نوف) Increasing, augmenting, adding to. Exceeding, being over and above. Projecting, overhanging.

A انافح *anāfiḥ*, (pl. of انفحة *infaḥat*) Yellow substances taken from the stomachs of sucking lambs, used in curdling milk.

A انافيّ *unāfiy*, Large-nosed.

A انافيض *anāfīẓ*, Leaves of an Egyptian thorn, shaken from the tree and strewed upon coverlets.

T اناق *ināk*, Secure, safe, free from anxiety.

A اناقة *anākat* or *inākat*, Gracefulness, elegance (in manner or dress): as, له اناقة و لياقة *lahu inākat wa liyākat*, He possesses gracefulness and genius.

A انالة *inālat*, (v. n. 4 of نال for نول) Swearing by God. Being rich in ore (a mine). (v. n. 4 of نال for نيل) Causing to obtain: giving, bestowing.

G انالیقي *anālīkī*, A nettle.

A انام *anām*, (or آنام *ānām*) Mankind, mortals. The world. Angels, demons, giants, genii.

A انامة *ināmat*, (v. n. 4 of نام for نوم) Putting to sleep. Finding asleep. Enervating. Killing.

A انامل *anāmil*, (pl. of انملة *anmalat* or *anmilat*) Nails, claws. Tips of the fingers.

P آنان *ānān*, (pl. of آن *ān*) Those.

A انان *unān*, (v. n. of انّ) Groaning. A groan. One who groans much.

A انّان *annān*, A great groaner, one who groans.

A انّانة *annānat*, Groaning (woman).

A انانيّة *anānīyat*, (from انا *ana'*, I) Egotism.

G اناوافتيز *anāwāftīz*, An anabaptist.

A اناويض *anāwīẓ*, (pl. of نوض *nawẓ*) High places, from whence water flows.

P اناهيد *anāhīd*, The planet Venus.

A انايیب *anāyīb*, (pl. of ناب) Dog-teeth. Tusks.

P انب *anab*, The egg-plant.

A انباء *ambāʼ*, (pl. of نبأ *nabaʼ*) News, advices. (pl. of نبيء *nabīʼ*) Prophets. *Imbāʼ*, (v. n. 4 of نبأ) Announcing. Prophesying. Not making his arrow penetrate (an archer). (v. n. 4 of نبى) Removing, averting. Announcing. Prophesying. Wishing to remove from one's self.

A انبات *imbāt*, (v. n. 4 of نبت) Causing to grow or vegetate. Putting forth vegetation (the ground). Growing, sprouting (herbage). Shewing signs of virility, getting a pecten (a youth).

A انباج *imbāj*, (v. n. 4 of نبج) Uttering confused jargon. Sitting on a hill.

A انباح *imbāḥ*, The act of making (a dog) bark.

A انباخ *imbāk͟h*, (v. n. 4 of نبخ) Chewing or eating the root of the papyrus. Baking or kneading sour leaven. Sowing high grounds, of a light soil mixed with stones.

P انباخون *ambāk͟hūn*, A castle, a fortification.

P انباده *ambāda*, Vain-glorious. Purse-proud.

A انباذ *ambāẕ*, (pl. of نبذ *nabẕ*) Small quantities. The vulgar, rabble, canaille. *Imbāẕ*, (v. n. 4 of نبذ) Pressing grapes, making wine. Making malt liquor or beer. Throwing down.

P انبار *ambār*, Full to the brim, replete. A pond, a reservoir. Filth, dung, manure. Dilapidation, a falling to pieces of a house or a wall. Fodder. انبار دادن *ambār dādan*, To manure.

A انبار *ambār*, (pl. of نبر *nibr*) Short-bodied, deformed, hideous. Tikes. Flies. Wild beasts. Ricks, stacks of corn. Barns, granaries, magazines, repositories of grain and other provisions. (in India) The Government share of the produce. Keels, ships'-bottoms. Name of a city in Chaldea, and a village in Balkh. *Imbār*, (v. n. 4 of نبر) Building or establishing a granary. Storing up grain.

P انبار *imbār*, (for این بار *īn bār*) This time, now.

P انبارخانه *ambār-k͟hāna*, A magazine, a store.

P انباردار *ambār-dār*, The keeper of a magazine.

P انبارداري *ambār-dārī*, Whatever is laid up against a scarcity.

P انباردگي *ambārdagī*, Repletion. Competence.

P انبارده *ambārda*, Filled: full, replete. Affluent.

P انبارش *ambārish*, Stuffing, quilting.

P انباري *ambārī*, A howda for an elephant.

A ابن الانباريّ *ibnu'l ambāriy*, Name of an Arabian grammarian.

P انباریدن *ambārīdan*, (or انباردن *ambārdan*) To fill. To cause to fill. To pull down.

P انباز *ambāz*, A companion, associate, partner in trade. انباز شدن *ambāz shudan*, To participate in any thing.

A انباز *ambāz*, (pl. of نبز) Surnames: nick-names.

P انبازانیدن *ambāzānīdan*, To go partners.

P انبازده *ambāzada*, Proud of wealth or family.

P انبازناك *ambāznāk*, A partner in trade.

P انبازي *ambāzī*, Partnership, joint company.

P انبازي كردن *ambāzī kardan*, To go partners.

P انبازیدن *ambāzīdan*, To become a partner in any common fund of gain or labour. To increase.

P انباشتگي *ambāshtagī*, Moderate competency.

P انباشتن *ambāshtan*, To fill. To supply. To

sprinkle. To macerate, dilute. To lay in ruins.

P انباشته *ambāshta*, Filled. Choked (well).

A انباض *imbāẓ*, A making (a bow-string) twang.

A انباط *ambāt*, Nabatheans, natives of Nabathea. *Imbāt*, (v. n. 4 of نبط) Getting to a spring or fountain-head (by digging). Causing to appear (something concealed). Making an impression.

P انباغ *ambāgh*, A concubine; any woman whom a man lives with beyond one wife.

A انباغ *imbāgh*, (v. n. 4 of نباغ) Frequenting (a town or other place). Going and coming. Sifting.

P انباق *ambāḳ*, A (voluntary) cuckold.

A انباق *imbāḳ*, (v. n. 4 of نبق) Breaking wind.

A انبال *ambāl*, (pl. of نبل *nabl*) Arabian arrows. *Imbāl*, (v. n. 4 of نبل) Giving such arrows (to any one), bringing them in a confused heap. Shooting arrows. Teaching to shoot arrows. Bearing fresh dates (a palm-tree).

G انبالس *ambālus*, (or انبالش *ambālush*) A vine.

P انبان *ambān*, (or انبانه *ambāna*) Soft skins (of goats) of the finest kind, such as they call Spanish or Cordovan. A leathern bag, cloak-bag, portmanteau. A purse. انبان باد *ambāni bād*, The stomach.

P انبان بار *ambān-bār*, Fat, pursy: idle, useless.

P انبانك *ambānak*, A kind of purse or scrip.

A انباه *imbāh*, (v. n. 4 of نبه) Awaking, rousing from sleep. Forgetting.

A انبب *umbub* (pl. انابيب *anābīb*) The knot or joint of a reed; also the space between the joints. A pipe, tube, syphon, or sucker.

A انبت *ambat*, Most productive of vegetation.

A انبتات *imbitāt*, (v. n. 7 of بتّ) Being cut off. Breaking down, lagging. Failing (semen virile).

A انبتار *imbitār*, (v. n. 7 of بتر) Being cut off or mutilated. Being deprived of offspring. Running.

A انبتاع *imbitāʻ*, (v. n. 7 of بتع) Being broken, cut off, detached.

A انبتاك *imbitāk*, (v. n. 7 of بتك) Being cut off. Being drawn or dragged, pulled or plucked up.

A انبتال *imbitāl*, (v. n. 7 of بتل) Being cut off.

A انبثاث *imbisās*, (v. n. 7 of بثّ) Being separated, disunited (particles of bread steeped in water, teased wool, &c.).

A انبثاق *imbisāḳ*, (v. n. 7 of بثق) Being cleft asunder. Being burst (as a dam). Bursting out and flowing freely. Being let out and allowed to overflow (water). Coming down and overflowing without resistance (a torrent). Pouring forth a torrent of words. Proceeding (John xv. 26).

A انبج *ambaj* or *ambij*, An Indian fruit: a preserve.

A انبجات *ambijāt*, Confections, preserves.

A انبجاس *imbijās*, A bursting out, gushing forth.

A انبجان *ambajān*, Fermented paste, leaven.

A انبجاني *ambajāniy*, Belonging to, or made at, Mambij. Warm paste. ثريد انبجاني *sarīdi ambajānī*, Hot bread crumbled down.

A انبحاث *imbihās*, (v. n. 7 of بحث) Inquiring, examining, investigating.

A انبخ *ambakh*, Rough, hard, thick. Cloudy, opaque. Much (earth).

A انبخان *ambakhān*, Fermented (leaven).

A انبخاني *ambakhāniy*, Smoaking hot (paste). A kind of bread made with biscuit, oil, and water.

A انبخانية *ambakhāniyat*, Large and thick (loaf), or (a loaf) like a honey-comb.

A انبذة *ambizat*, (pl. of نبيذ) Grape or date-wines.

P انبر *ambur*, Tweezers, pincers, forceps.

A انبراء *imbirāʼ*, (v. n. 7 of بري) Being shaved, smoothed (an arrow). Occurring, happening.

A انبرباريس *ambarbārīs*, Barberries.

P انبرد *ambarud*, A pear.

P انبروت *ambarūt*, A pear.

P انبره *ambura* or *ambara*, A camel or other animal that has shed his coat. A camel or horse used for drawing water. A mountain-pass. A tube, pipe. *Ambura*, Tweezers, pincers, forceps.

A انبزاغ *imbizāgh*, (v. n. 7 of بزغ) Approaching (spring-season). Running a horse.

P انبزان *ambazān*, The last day of the month.

P انبس *ambas*, (or انبش *ambash*) A heap of grain trodden or thrashed out, and sifted.

A انبس *ambas*, Austere, crabbed, grim.

A انبساس *imbisās*, (v. n. 7 of بسّ) Dispersing everywhere. Flowing on the ground (water).

A انبساط *imbisāt*, (v. n. 7 of بسط) Being spread out. Being long (the day). Laying aside one's gravity, having a cheerful countenance. Gladness, cheerfulness, recreation, delight, mirth, gaiety.

P انبست *ambast*, Coarse, thick: bound, shut up.

P انبسته *ambasta*, Bound. Hard, stiff, difficult to be unloosed. Clotted (milk or blood).

A انبش *ambash*, More or most of a digger up of dead bodies (نبّاش *nabbāsh*).

A انبضاع *imbizāʻ*, (v. n. 7 of بضع) Being cut off.

A انبط *ambat*, (A horse) distinguished by the whiteness of the belly.

A انبطاح *imbitāh*, (v. n. 7 of بطح) Falling flat on the face. Being flattened, depressed. Being extended, diffused.

A انبطاش *imbitāsh*, (v. n. 7 of بطش) Striking against, being dashed or driven against.

G انبطرون *ambatarūn*, Samphire, empetron.

A انبعاث *imbiʻās*, (v. n. 7 of بعث) Being sent. Being roused up. Going about one's own business. Rising up, raising one's self. Going quickly.

A انبعاج *imbiʻāj*, (v. n. 7 of بعج) Being cleft. Being scattered (clouds after rain).

A انبعاق *imbiʻāḳ*, (v. n. 7 of بعق) Pouring forth rain (a cloud). Being diffuse, verbose, and hasty in speaking. Giving liberally. Committing an assault.

A انبغاء *imbighāʼ*, (v. n. 7 of بغي) Being sought after. Behoving. Being easy. Meetness.

A انبقاع *imbiḳāʻ*, The act of going off in haste.

A انبك *ambik*, An alembic, a still.

A انبل *ambal*, More or most excellent (in disposition or genius). Most skilful in archery.

A انبلات *imbilāt*, The being cut or divided.

A انبلاج *imbilāj*, A breaking forth (of the dawn).

A انبلاط *imbilāt*, The being very distant.

A انبلاق *imbilāḳ*, (v. n. 7 of بلق) Being opened wide (a door). Lying open.

P انبله *ambala*, A tamarind.

P انبمن *ambiman*, (in zand and Pāz.) A grape.

P انبوب *ambūb*, A bed, cushion, or mat.

A انبوب *umbūb*, (pl. انابيب *anābīb*) The joint (of a cane). The space between two joints of a reed or cane. A mountain-path. A row of trees. High ground. A road. A pipe, tube.

A انبوبة *umbūbat*, The joint of a cane.

P انبوبه *ambūba*, A reed used by weavers to wind thread upon. A tube, syphon, spout.

P انبوت *ambūt*, A root. انبوت الراعي *ambūtu'r rāʻī*, A sort of houseleek. انبوت ملكي *ambūti malikī*, The amaranth.

A انبوثة *umbūsat*, A game, in which something is hid in a hole, and whoever gets it out, gains.

P انبودن *ambūdan*, To gather. To throw down. To be seized with torpor. To miscarry.

P انبوذن *ambūzan*, Primary matter whence any substance is formed (according to the cosmogony of the Muhammadans).

P انبور *ambūr*, Stuffing, filling. Pincers, forceps. انبور آهنگر *ambūri āhangar*, Blacksmith's pincers.

P انبوس *ambūs*, Bread with seeds in it.

P انبوسيدن *ambūsīdan*, To appear, to be manifest. To become benumbed. To rot. To collect.

A انبوش *umbūsh*, (pl. انابيش *anābīsh*) Root of a tree or pot-herb. Uprooted, with roots and fibres.

P انبون *ambūn*, Broad, wide, ample, spacious.

P انبوه *ambūh*, (or انبه *ambuh*) Large, copious, ample. Full. Numerous. A multitude, concourse, mob. The falling of a house in ruins. Name of a district. انبوه كردن *ambūh kardan*, To smell, snuff up. To diffuse an odour. To press upon one another (as people in a crowd). To pull down, demolish.

P انبوه ريش *ambūh-rīsh*, Thick-bearded.

P انبوهناك *ambūhnāk*, Wide, broad. Copious.

P انبوهي *ambūhī*, Thickness, bushiness, luxuriancy. A multitude, a crowd. Tumult, bustle. انبوهي نمودن *ambūhī namūdan*, To crowd, throng.

P انبوي *ambūy*, Ample, copious. *Ambūy* or *amboy*, Odoriferous. Odour.

P انبوئيدن *ambūʼīdan* or *amboʼīdan*, To smell sweetly, to scatter perfume.

P انبه *amba*, The mangoe. *Ambuh*, A crowd.

A انبهار *imbihar*, (v. n. 7 of بهر) Falling down. Breathing hard from over-exercise.

A انبهاش *imbihāsh*, (v. n. 7 of بهش) Being black (meat).

A انبياء *ambiyāʼ*, (pl. of نبيّ *nabiʼ*) Prophets.

A انبياج *imbiyāj*, (v. n. 7 of باج for بوج) Overtaking one (misfortunes).

A انبياش *imbiyāsh*, (v. n. 7 of باش for بوش) Fleeing, scampering away. Contracting, shrinking.

A انبياص *imbiyāṣ*, (v. n. 7 of باص for بوص) Taking the lead. Passing off, making no stay.

A انبياع *imbiyāʿ*, (v. n. 7 of باع for بوع) Flowing (sweat). Unfolding itself to spring (a serpent). Lowering the price in selling any article. Stretching out the hand or inclining the body to testify one's assent. Measuring a fathom (a rope). (v. n. 7 of باع for بيع) Finding a ready sale (goods).

A انبياق *imbiyāḳ*, (v. n. 7 of باق for بوق) Overtaking, overwhelming. Entering into the presence of another uncalled for. Injuring, oppressing.

A انبياك *imbiyāk*, (v. n. 7 of باك for بوك) Being disturbed in mind, distracted in councils.

P انبير *ambīr*, A rose. Repletion. Religion, law, institute.

P انبيره *ambīra*, Chips, shavings, which, when laid on the roof of a house, are incrusted with mud.

P انبيس *ambīs*, A heap of winnowed grain.

P انبيسته *ambīsta*, (or انبيسه) A thing cold, chilly.

A انبيق *ambīḳ*, An alembic.

P انبيلا *ambīlā*, A rhinoceros.

P انپاشتن *ampāshtan*, To fill.

P انپاشته *ampāshta*, Filled.

P انپژ *impaj*, The herb southernwood.

A آنة *ānnat*, (ما له حانّة ولا آنّة *mā lahu hānnat wa lā ānnat*) He has neither camel nor sheep.

P آنت *ānt*, Bravo! *Ānt* or *ānat*, That for thee.

A انت *anta*, Thou (mas.). انت حسبي انت كافي يا ودود *anta hasbī anta kāfī yā wadūd*, Thou art my portion, thou art sufficient (for me), O indulgent (God). *Anti*, Thou (fem.).

A انتاء *intāʾ*, (v. n. 4 of نتا for نتو) Retiring or remaining behind. Bruising a man's nose, so as to make it swell. Agreeing with, or resembling another in shape or disposition.

A انتآء *intiʾāʾ*, (v. n. 8 of ناء for نوأ) Cutting a furrow (called نؤي *nuʾy*) round a tent to keep off the rain-water. Retiring to a distance.

A انتاج *intāj*, (v. n. 4 of نتج) Bringing forth, producing. Being near the birth. Going where she pleases, and colting in an unknown place (a she-camel). Having pregnant camels.

A انتاش *intāsh*, (v. n. 4 of نتش) Growing to a great height (a tree).

A انتاض *intāẓ*, (v. n. 4 of نتض) Protruding and displacing the others (a tooth or a mushroom).

A انتاع *intāʿ*, (v. n. 4 of نتع) Sweating profusely. Coming forth unchecked (vomit).

A انتاغ *intāgh*, (v. n. 4 of نتغ) Laughing, or partially suppressing a laugh. Smiling sarcastically.

A انتاق *intāḳ*, (v. n. 4 of نتق) Carrying a parasol. Lifting a hard stone. Marrying a prolific wife. Building (a house) opposite another. Shaking (a wallet) to keep (it) clear from moths. Fasting during the month of Ramazān.

A انتان *intān*, The act of stinking, a being fœtid.

A انتباث *intibās*, (v. n. 8 of نبث) Digging, scooping out the earth with the hand. Rubbing (meal) with the hand and moistening (it) with water. Taking, eating. Swelling in water (a ptisan). Tucking up one's skirts and sitting on the ground. Disclosing, shewing (what had been concealed).

A انتباج *intibāj*, The swelling (of a bone).

A انتباذ *intibāz*, (v. n. 8 of نبذ) Pressing. Retiring to one side. Retiring from an adversary in battle. Bestirring one's self. Throwing down. Being moved from its place. Making wine or a drink (called نبيذ *nabīz*) from dates or raisins.

A انتبار *intibār*, (v. n. 8 of نبر) Swelling (the body). Being sore and swollen from labour (the hands). Ascending a pulpit, mounting the rostrum.

A انتباق *intibāḳ*, (v. n. 8 of نبق) Extracting, drawing forth, deriving.

A انتباك *intibāk*, (v. n. 8 of نبك not in use) Being eminent, conspicuous, making an appearance, being published. Ascending a hill. Involving one's self in a scrape. Giving one's self up to any thing bad.

A انتبال *intibāl*, (v. n. 8 of نبل) Dying. Being killed. Killing. Carrying any thing off by a single attack. Adverting to, minding, heeding. Keeping watch. Giving away arrows (نبل *nabl*).

A انتباه *intibāh*, (v. n. 8 of نبه) Waking from sleep. Being on one's guard. Vigilance, circumspection, animadversion, consideration. اهل انتباه *ahli intibāh*, Vigilant, circumspect.

A انتتاء *intitāʾ*, (v. n. 8 of نتا) Coming forward. Being high and elevated.

A انتتار *intitār*, The being drawn or dragged.

A انتتاش *intitāsh*, (v. n. 8 of نتش) Beginning to swell (grain). Putting forth the first sprout before the root develops itself (grass).

A انتتاف *intitāf*, (v. n. 8 of نتف) Being plucked up (hair). Plucking (hair or wool).

A انتتام *intitām*, (v. n. 8 of نتم) Breaking out into abusive language.

A انتثار *intisār*, (v. n. 8 of نثر) Being scattered, dropping off. Discharging any thing through the nose, particularly water which had been drawn up. Drawing water into the nose.

A انتثال *intisāl*, The act of cleaning out (a well).

A انتثام *intisām*, A talking obscenely.

A انتجاء *intijāʾ*, (v. n. 8 of نجأ) Looking with a malignant eye. (v. n. 8 of نجا for نجو) Communicating privately together. Entrusting with a secret. Obtaining, gaining, recovering. Sitting on a hill.

A انتجاب *intijāb*, (v. n. 8 of نجب) Barking a tree. Choosing.

A انتجاث *intijās*, (v. n. 8 of نجث) Extracting, Swelling. Appearing, being perceptible (fat).

A انتجاخ *intijākh*, The act of breaking wind.

A انتجاع *intijāʿ*, (v. n. 8 of نجع) Seeking provender, foraging. Visiting with a view to gain.

A انتجاف *intijāf*, (v. n. 8 of نجف) Milking (a sheep) dry. Extracting, drawing out. (The wind) emptying (a cloud of its contents).

A انتجال *intijāl*, (v. n. 8 of نجل) Being evident, apparent. Passing, going by. Drawing off stagnant water from the foot of a wall. Laying bare the foundation of a wall (a land-spring).

A انتجام *intijām*, (v. n. 8 of نجم) Ending, being over (as rain or cold).

A انتجاه *intijāh*, A repelling, a driving away.

A انتحاء *intihāʾ*, (v. n. 8 of نحا for نحو) Going towards. Inclining to the left side (a camel in travelling). Seeking, aiming at. Inclining to one side. Relying. Exposing, laying open. (v. n. 8 of نحي) Striving, taking pains. Resolving, purposing. Leaning upon. Applying a knife to the throat.

A انتحاب *intihāb*, (v. n. 8 of نحب) Lamenting, complaining. Howling, shrieking. Breathing hard.

A انتحات *intihāt*, A being planed or chipped off.

A انتحار *intihār*, (v. n. 8 of نحر) Cutting one's own throat, committing suicide. Being extremely tenacious. Seizing each other by the throat.

A انتحاض *intihāẓ*, (v. n. 8 of نحض) Stripping the flesh (off a bone). Being lean, lank, stripped of its flesh (a bone).

A انتحال *intihāl*, (v. n. 8 of نحل) Falsely assuming, or attributing to one's self, that which belongs to another. Professing to belong to this or that religious society. Becoming thin, lean, and emaciated.

A انتحام *intihām*, (v. n. 8 of نحم) Applying the mind to any thing.

A انتخاء *intikhāʾ*, A boasting, a vaunting.

A انتخاب *intikhāb*, (v. n. 8 of نخب) Electing, choosing, selecting, picking out. Election, choice.

A انتخاص *intikhāṣ*, The wasting away (of flesh).

A انتخاط *intikhāt*, (v. n. 8 of نخط) Blowing the nose. Ejecting spittle. Resembling, taking after.

A انتخاع *intikhāʿ*, (v. n. 8 of نخع) Being very far from one's native soil. Pouring out rain (a cloud).

A انتخال *intikhāl*, (v. n. 8 of نخل) Separating, sifting, picking out the best.

A انتداء *intidāʾ*, The being convened in council.

A انتداب *intidāb*, (v. n. 8 of ندب) Listening, answering, being gracious (God). Hastening to recompense. Becoming surety for, or pledging the successful issue of any thing. Opposing, contradicting. Receiving ready money or prompt payment. Perspiring gently.

A انتداح *intidāh*, A being wide, spacious, roomy.

A انتداغ *intidāgh*, (v. n. 8 of ندغ) Laughing gently, smiling.

A انتدام *intidām*, The being easy, within reach.

A انتداه *intidāh*, (v. n. 8 of نده) Being well managed (business).

A انتذار *intizār*, (v. n. 8 of نذر) Making a vow.

P انترج *untruj*, An orange.

A انتزاع *intizāʻ*, (v. n. 8 of نزع) Tearing up, removing forcibly. Being torn up by the roots (trees). Refraining, abstaining, desisting, refusing. Keeping back, withholding.

A انتساء *intisāʼ*, (v. n. 8 of نسأ) Retiring, receding. Wandering, roaming to distant pastures.

A انتساب *intisāb*, (v. n. 8 of نسب) Being related to, or descended from. Tracing (one's self) back, claiming relationship to. Relation. عسکر ظفر انتساب *ʻaskari zafar-intisāb*, An army related to victory, a victorious army. جواب صواب انتساب *jawābi sawāb-intisāb*, An answer correlative with truth, a true answer.

A انتساخ *intisākh*, (v. n. 8 of نسخ) Obliterating, effacing, causing to vanish. Transcribing, copying.

A انتساع *intisāʻ*, (v. n. 8 of نسع) Dispersing themselves about the pasture (camels).

A انتساغ *intisāgh*, (v. n. 8 of نسغ) Striking his breast with the fore-foot (a camel tormented by the flies). Going to a great distance for pasture, and being widely scattered (camels).

A انتساف *intisāf*, (v. n. 8 of نسف) Eradicating, tearing up by the roots. Lifting up or off. Sweeping away the dust (wind). Pulling down to the foundation. Talking in a whisper. Not finishing a sentence. Changing colour through fear.

A انتساق *intisāk*, (v. n. 8 of نسق) Being regularly adjusted; adhering (one thing to another).

A انتشاء *intishāʼ*, (v. n. 8 of نشأ) Growing up. (v. n. 8 of نشي) Perceiving a smell. Being overcome with wine, being crop-sick.

A انتشاب *intishāb*, (v. n. 8 of نشب) Cleaving, clinging, sticking fast. Heaping together, accumulating. Collecting fuel or food or dressing.

A انتشار *intishār*, (v. n. 8 of نشر) Being scattered, diffused, propagated, spread. Spreading out its branches (a palm-tree). Being inflated (a nerve). Having a priapism. Lengthening itself out (a day). Being separated from their keeper (camels). Spread, propagation, circulation.

A انتشاص *intishās*, The act of uprooting a tree.

A انتشاط *intishāt*, (v. n. 8 of نشط) Stretching a rope till it breaks. Scraping the scales off a fish. Drawing a knot till it becomes unloosed. Nibbling, browsing (as a sheep).

A انتشاع *intishāʻ*, (v. n. 8 of نشع) Injecting medicine into one's nostrils. Throwing down. Pulling out, tearing up.

A انتشاغ *intishāgh*, (v. n. 8 of نشغ) Striking his breast with his fore-foot (a camel tormented by flies).

A انتشاف *intishāf*, (v. n. 8 of نشف) Drinking the froth of fresh milk. Being changed (colour).

A انتشال *intishāl*, (v. n. 8 of نشل) Taking (meat out of a cauldron) with the hands or with a flesh-hook.

A انتصاء *intisāʼ*, (v. n. 8 of نصي) Growing long (as hair). Being far-extended and elevated (table-land). Electing, choosing.

A انتصاب *intisāb*, (v. n. 8 of نصب) Being placed. Being erect, standing upright. Rising up and setting about a thing. (in gram.) Being inflected with the vowel fat'ha (َ *a*, called نصب *nasb*).

A انتصات *intisāt*, A keeping silence.

A انتصاح *intisāh*, (v. n. 8 of نصح) Listening to faithful admonition.

A انتصار *intisār*, (v. n. 8 of نصر) Conquering, overcoming. Taking revenge. Self-preservation.

A انتصاص *intisās*, (v. n. 8 of نصّ) Sitting on a throne (a bride). Drawing one's self in, becoming contracted. Being raised, erect.

A انتصاف *intisāf*, (v. n. 8 of نصف) Reaching to the middle. Being mid-day. Deciding equitably. Avenging one's self. Recovering the whole of a debt, getting one's due. Covering herself with a veil (a girl). Smiting the game (an arrow).

A انتصال *intisāl*, (v. n. 8 of نصل) Losing the point of a spear.

A انتضاء *intizāʼ*, (v. n. 8 of نضا for نضو) Wearing threadbare. Drawing (a sword). Emaciating.

A انتضاح *intizāh*, (v. n. 8 of نضح) Pouring forth tears. Sprinkling (water) on the privities after having made one's ablutions.

A انتضاخ *intizākh*, (v. n. 8 of نضخ) Being sprinkled (water). Sprinkling water.

A انتضاد *intizād*, A remaining, a standing still.

A انتضاف *intizāf*, (v. n. 8 of نضف) Sucking the whole of its mother's milk (a camel's colt).

A انتضال *intizāl*, (v. n. 8 of نضل) Contending with one another (in archery or in poetry). Boasting one against another. Choosing, picking out. Drawing forth. Throwing his fore-feet about in walking or running (a camel). Competition.

A انتطاح *intitāh*, The act of butting (as rams).

A انتطاق *intitāk*, (v. n. 8 of نطق) Putting on a garment called نطاق *nitāk* (a woman). Putting on a girdle. Talking.

A انتطال *intitāl*, (v. n. 8 of نطل) Pouring forth a small quantity (of water) from a leathern bottle.

A انتظار *intizār*, (v. n. 8 of نظر) Expecting, waiting (anxiously). P انتظار کردن, To anticipate.

A انتظام *intizām*, (v. n. 8 of نظم) Being arranged, strung in a line. Having eggs in her belly (a hen). Running any one through the body with a spear, enfilading. Order, disposition, regularity, arrangement, regulation.

A انتعات *intiʻāt*, (v. n. 8 of نعت) Qualifying with an epithet.

A انتعاش *intiʻāsh*, The act of taking, receiving.

A انتعاش *intiʻāsh*, (v. n. 8 of نعش) Recovering; regaining one's legs after stumbling; falling without hurting one's self. Recovering from disease.

A انتعاص *intiʻās*, (v. n. 8 of نعص) Regaining one's legs after falling. Being angry, enraged. Going as if heavily laden.

A انتعاظ *intiʻāz*, The being inflamed with lust.

A انتعاف *intiʻāf*, (v. n. 8 of نعف) Ascending a steep mountain. Leaving any thing in charge of one. Being conspicuous at a distance (a horseman).

A انتعال *intiʻāl*, (v. n. 8 of نعل) Putting on shoes. Travelling on foot. Sowing in a hard soil. Riding on hard ground.

A انتغاش *intighāsh*, A waving, nodding, bowing.

A انتفاء *intifāʼ*, (v. n. 8 of نفي) Being repulsed, removed, banished, exiled: retiring.

A انتفاج *intifāj*, (v. n. 8 of نفج) Bulging out (a camel's sides). Being roused and started (game).

A انتفاح *intifāh*, (v. n. 8 of نفح) Opposing, intervening, intercepting. Turning towards, veering.

A انتفاخ *intifākh*, (v. n. 8 of نفخ) Swelling, becoming inflated, blown up.

A انتفاد *intifād*, (v. n. 8 of نفد) Emptying, eating up, taking the whole. Annihilating. Milking.

A انتفاش *intifāsh*, (v. n. 8 of نفش) Setting its hairs erect (a cat), or a bird its feathers (from fear). Having the hairs on end.

A انتفاص *intifās*, (v. n. 8 of نفص) Sprinkling water on the privities through the fingers.

A انتفاض *intifāz*, (v. n. 8 of نفض) Being shaken, beaten (a garment). Diddering, shivering. Flourishing (a vine). Cleaning the yard from remains of urine.

A انتفاع *intifāʻ*, (v. n. 8 of نفع) Being useful, profitable, beneficial, availing. Deriving advantage, being benefited. Utility, profit, advantage.

A انتفاق *intifāk*, (v. n. 8 of نفق) Entering its burrow (a field-mouse); (contra) quitting (its) hole. Going along a narrow road.

A انتفال *intifāl*, (v. n. 8 of نفل) Praying oftener than what the law enjoins. Retiring, receding. Being freed, absolved, liberated. Seeking any thing to be done for one's self.

A انتقاء *intikāʼ*, (v. n. 8 of نقي) Extracting (marrow). Choosing.

A انتقاب *intikāb*, (v. n. 8 of نقب) Veiling her face (a woman).

A انتقاش *intikāsh*, (v. n. 8 of نقش) Extracting (marrow from a bone). Scrutinizing (any affair). Making haste, doing quickly. Digging, tearing up.

A انتقاح *intikāh*, (v. n. 8 of نقح) Extracting marrow from a bone.

A انتقاخ *intikākh*, The extracting of marrow.

A انتقاد *intikād*, (v. n. 8 of نقد) Separating good (coin) from bad. Receiving ready money. Grow-up, becoming an adult (a boy).

A انتقار *intikār*, (v. n. 8 of نقر) Being hollowed out. Hollowing out, carving. Writing. Scrutinizing. Electing, choosing. Inviting one person to the exclusion of the rest. Making holes in the ground with his feet (a horse). Pecking.

A انتقاز *intikāz*, (v. n. 8 of نقز) Suffering from a complaint called نقاز *nukāz* (a sheep). Giving another the worst part of the flock.

A انتقاش *intikāsh*, (v. n. 8 of نقش) Ordering (the stone of a ring) to be engraved. Striking the ground with the foot when trying to rid himself of a thorn that has pierced it. Extracting (a thorn) from the foot. Selecting, extracting.

A انتقاص *intikās*, (v. n. 8 of نقص) Diminishing. Being diminished. Letting water drop through the interstices of the fingers on the privities. Disgracing, dishonouring. Decrease, diminution.

A انتقاض *intikāz*, (v. n. 8 of نقض) Being demolished (a building), untwisted (a rope), violated (a treaty, a covenant). Untwisting. Demolishing. Dissolving. Becoming raw and running (a sore).

A انتقاع *intikāɛ*, (v. n. 8 of نقع) Slaughtering a camel (to provide an entertainment). Slaughtering a sheep ere the flock has been divided. Becoming changed (colour). Being saturated. Quenching thirst.

A انتقاف *intikāf*, (v. n. 8 of نقف) Splitting an apple, and cutting away rind or core. Extracting, drawing out, causing to come forth. Taking away.

A انتقال *intikāl*, (v. n. 8 of نقل) Being transported, transplanted, translated. Transferring one's self, going over to. Dying, passing to the other world. Removal, departure, migration.

A انتقام *intikām*, (v. n. 8 of نقم) Punishing, chastising. Taking vengeance. Loathing, abhorring. Reproving, rebuking. Vengeance. عزيز الانتقام *ɛazīzu'l intikām*, (God) the supreme avenger. P انتقام گرفتن *intikām giriftan*, To take vengeance.

A انتقاه *intikāh*, (v. n. 8 of نقه) Recovering health. Deriving spiritual health and solace from any promise or declaration. Understanding well.

A انتكاء *intikāɛ*, The receiving of any thing due.

A انتكاب *intikāb*, A shouldering (one's quiver).

A انتكات *intikāt*, (v. n. 8 of نكت) Falling headlong (any one wounded with a spear).

A انتكاث *intikās*, (v. n. 8 of نكث) Being untwisted (a rope). Being violated (a treaty). Turning from one business to another. Receding.

A انتكاس *intikās*, (v. n. 8 of نكس) Being turned upside down, capsized. Falling on the head.

A انتكاش *intikāsh*, A taking of mud out of a well.

A انتكاف *intikāf*, (v. n. 8 of نكف) Enduring a shower while it lasts. Turning away the face. Being broken and violated (a covenant or bargain). Emigrating. Discovering the mark of a camel's foot in soft level ground.

A انتلة *intulat*, A kind of medicinal shrub, with yellowish leaves, very bitter and aromatic. انتلة سوداء *intulat sawdāɛ*, Zedoary.

A انتم *antum*, You (mas. pl.).

A انتما *antumā*, You two (dual mas. and fem.)

A انتماء *intimāɛ*, (v. n. 8 of نمي) Soaring aloft (a hawk). Being related to another. Attributing any thing to another as the author. Relation, respect, or regard to, resemblance, tendency. جواب صواب انتما *jawābi sawāb-intimā*, A just answer, an answer related to truth. كلام حكمت انتما *kalāmi hikmat-intimā*, Words having a tendency to mystery or wisdom; an ambiguous or wise speech. P گردن رعونت انتما *gardani ruɛūnat-intimā*, A neck resembling pride, a stately or proud appearance.

A ما انتنه *mā antanahu*, How he stinks!

A انتواء *intiwāɛ*, (v. n. 8 of نوي) Intending, proposing. Aiming at. Abiding, halting. Despatching.

A انتوار *intiwār*, (v. n. 8 of نار for نور) Being bedaubed with a liniment of pitch for the scab.

L انتون *antūn*, Anthony.

P انتونتن *antūnitan*, (in zand and Pāz.) To have.

A انتهاء *intihāɛ*, (v. n. 8 of نهي) Being interdicted. Abstaining, desisting. Coming to an end, being finished. Arriving, reaching. End, extremity, termination. Summit, vertex. الي انتهاء الزمان *ila' intihāɛi'z zamān*, Until the end of time.

A انتهاب *intihāb*, (v. n. 8 of نهب) Seizing, making a prey of, spoiling. Winning a heat (a horse). Rapine, depredation, spoil, booty.

A انتهار *intihār*, (v. n. 8 of نهر) Shouting. Prohibiting, checking, chiding. Being loose, purging (the belly). Flowing profusely so as not to be stopped (blood from a vein). A diarrhœa.

A انتهاز *intihāz*, (v. n. 8 of نهز) Watching for, finding an opportunity. Laughing immoderately. Being near puberty (a lad).

A انتهاس *intihās*, A biting with the front-teeth.

A انتهاش *intihash*, (v. n. 8 of نهش) Tearing the meat off a bone with the teeth.

A انتهاض *intihāz*, The act of rising, getting up.

A انتهاك *intihāk*, (v. n. 8 of نهك) Enfeebling, emaciating. Milking an udder dry. Violation (of honour, virtue, or respect).

A انتئاء *intiɛāɛ*, (v. n. 8 of نأي) Making a trench (called نوي *nuɛy*) round a tent to keep off the rain-water. Being at a distance

A انتياب *intiyāb*, (v. n. 8 of ناب for نوب) Approaching, from time to time (نوبة *nawbat*), again and again. Repetition.

A انتيار *intiyār*, (v. n. 8 of نار for نور) Being bedaubed with a liniment of pitch for the scab.

A انتئاش *intiɛāsh*, (v. n. 8 of نأش) Loitering behind. Going from place to place with a flock.

A انتياش *intiyāsh*, (v. n. 8 of ناش for نوش) Leading forth, drawing out. Taking, receiving.

A انتياط *intiyāt*, (v. n. 8 of ناط for نوط) Being suspended, appended. Lying afar off. Cutting off (any thing) without taking the advice of any body. Lending any one (a camel) to carry provisions.

A انتياق *intiyāk*, The act of choosing, selecting.

G انتيلس *antīlis*, The sea-kidney vetch, anthyllis.

A انثاء *insāɛ*, (v. n. 4 of نثي) Disparaging, dispraising, slandering. Disdaining, loathing.

A انثار *insār*, (v. n. 4 of نثر) Breathing through the nose. Sneezing, and thereby discharging any thing disagreeable from the nostrils. Drawing water up the nose. Making any one's nose bleed by throwing him on his nose.

A انثاع *insāɛ*, (v. n. 4 of نثع) Vomiting. Bleeding immoderately at the nose. Flowing, coming up (vomit or blood). An irreducible hemorrhage.

A انثتام *insitām*, (v. n. 7 of ثتم) Breaking forth in obscene language.

A انثجاج *insijāj*, A flowing plentifully.

A انثجار *insijār*, A gushing forth: an overflowing.

A انثداغ *insidāgh*, A being broken (the head).

A انثداق *insidāk*, (v. n. 7 of ثدق) Being relaxed (the belly). Rushing, falling upon any one.

A انثرام *insirām*, (v. n. 7 of ثرم) Being broken off at the root, or disbanded by disease (teeth).

A انثطاء *insitāɛ*, (v. n. 7 of ثطو) Becoming flaccid and relaxed.

A انثعاب *insiɛāb*, (v. n. 7 of ثعب) Being set a flowing (water or blood).

A انثعاع *insiɛāɛ*, (v. n. 7 of ثع) Being cast up (vomit). Streaming from nose or wound (blood).

A انثقاب *insikāb*, The being drilled, perforated.

A انثلاغ *insilāgh*, (v. n. 7 of ثلغ) Being bruised (the head). Bearing soft and ripe dates (a palm).

A انثلال *insilāl*, (v. n. 7 of ثل) Being poured out.

A انثلام *insilām*, The being notched and broken.

A انثماء *insimāɛ*, A being fractured (as the skull).

A انثماغ *insimāgh*, (v. n. 7 of ثمغ) Being bruised by falling (ripe fruit). Becoming moist (a sore).

A انثمام *insimām*, (v. n. 7 of ثم) Being poured out. Being melted. Growing old. Languor.

A انثناء *insināɛ*, (v. n. 7 of ثني) Being bent. Receding, retreating.

A انثيٰ *unsa'*, (pl. اناث *ināṣ* or اناثي) A female. امرأة انثي *imraɛatun unsa'*, A perfect woman.

A انثيال *insiyāl*, (v. n. 7 of ثال for ثول) Being poured from above (dust). Being prolix (an invective against any one). Being assembled.

A انثيان *unsayāni*, (dual) The testicles. The ears.

P آنج *ānaj*, A medlar.

P انج *anj*, The cheek, the contour of the face. Going out. Drawing forth. About, round about.

P آنجا *ānjā*, There, in that place, thither.

A انجاء *injāɛ*, (v. n. 4 of نجا for نجو) Liberating. Disclosing, revealing. Farting. Being dissipated, dispelled (cloud). Voiding (by stool). Sweating. Removing, separating (skin from the body). Cutting (a branch from a tree). Ordering to cut (a tree). Having dates ripe and ready for cutting (a palm).

A انجاب *anjāb*, (pl. of نجيب *najīb*) Generous, honourable, noble, illustrious. *Injāb*, (v. n. 4 of نجب) Begetting such a son; (contra) one degenerate and worthless. Being excellent.

A انجاث *anjās*, (v. n. 4 of نجث *nujs* and *nujus*) Coats of mail. Pericardia.

A انجاح *injāh*, (v. n. 4 of نجح) Prospering, being successful. Overcoming. Giving success (God).

A انجاد *anjād*, (pl. of نجد *najd*) High lands. (pl. of نجد *najud*) Bold, brave, strenuous. هو طلاع انجاد *huwa tallāʿu anjādin*, He meditates high matters. *Injād*, (v. n. 4 of نجد) Helping, defending, assisting. Promoting, advancing, exalting one's self. Being high. Being clear and serene (the sky). Reading aloud. Listening to a petition. Going or coming to one's wife or relations. Arriving in, or travelling to نجد *najd*. Sweating.

A انجار *injār*, (pl. اناجير) The flat roof of a house.

A انجاز *injāz*, (v. n. 4 of نجز) Fulfilling a promise, consummating, accomplishing. Rushing on a wounded (man) with intent to kill (him).

A انجاس *anjās*, Impurities. انجاس اجناس شياطين *anjāsi ajnāsi shayātīn*, Devil's dung, *i. e.* infidels. *Injās*, (v. n. 4 of نجس) Soiling, staining, defiling, rendering impure.

A انجاص *injās*, (an incorrect mode of writing اجّاص *ijjās*) A plum.

A انجاع *injāʿ*, (v. n. 4 of نجع) Giving milk to, allowing to suck (a camel's colt). Escaping, being liberated. Being wholesome and efficacious (medicine, exhortation, &c.). Prospering, living by.

A انجاف *injāf*, (v. n. 4 of نجف) Tying a piece of leather called نجاف *nijāf* under the belly of a he-goat to prevent him from gendering.

P آنجا كه *ānjā ki*, In that place where. So that, by which.

A انجال *injāl*, (v. n. 4 of نجل) Sending (a horse) to pasture amongst a kind of grass called نجيل *najīl*. Being verdant (the earth).

P انجاليدن *anjālīdan*, To fill, saturate. To restrain impetuosity, to check audacity. To fatigue. To signify. To admonish. To twist.

P انجام *anjām*, End, extremity, termination, conclusion. An appendix, a supplement. Grief, anxiety, vexation, affliction, sorrow. (in composition) Finishing, accomplishing; who or what finishes or brings to an end. انجام يافت *anjām yāft*, Is it all finished? سلام سلامت انجام *salāmi salāmat-anjām*, An affectionate salutation. مضمون بلاغت انجام *mazmūni balāghat-anjām*, A letter completely elegant. تعظيم انجام *taʿzīm-anjām*, Most respectful. سعادت انجام *saʿādat-anjām*, Happy, fortunate. ظلام انجام *zalām-anjām*, Dark, obscure.

A انجام *anjām*, (pl. of نجم *najm*) Stars. *Injām*, (v. n. 4 of نجم) Appearing, arising. Ending, being over (as rain or cold). Becoming serene (the sky).

P انجامن *anjāman*, The end of any thing.

P انجاميدن *anjāmīdan*, To come to an end, be finished. To end, ensue. To finish, accomplish.

A انجانة *injānat*, A stone bottle, a phial, a cup, pitcher, water-pot, washing-vat, or tub.

A انجباذ *injibāz*, (v. n. 7 of جبذ) Being drawn.

P انجبار *anjabār* or *injabār*, A kind of plant growing on the banks of the Euphrates, which, with a preparation of sugar, &c., they apply to stop hemorrhages and bleedings of every kind.

A انجبار *injibār*, (v. n. 7 of جبر) Being set (a fractured limb). Being repaired (the broken fortune of a friend). Name of a useful plant from which a drink is prepared.

A انجه *anjah*, More or most beneficial.

A انجحار *injihār*, (v. n. 7 of جحر) Creeping into his hole (a lizard).

P انجخ *anjukh*, A wrinkle, crease, furrow.

P انجخت *anjukht*, Desire, concupiscence.

P انجختن *anjukhtan*, To desire. To be or become wrinkled (on the brow, belly &c.). To leap, bound.

P انجخيدن *anjukhīdan*, To become wrinkled.

A انجد *anjud*, (pl. of نجد *najd*) High grounds. طلاع انجد *tallāʿu anjud*, Meditating high matters.

A انجدال *injidāl*, (v. n. 7 of جدل) Being thrown down, falling down.

A انجدان *anjudān*, Pellitory, laserpitium, silphium; whence comes benzoin and assafœtida. An ape. A satyr.

A انجدة *anjidat*, (pl. of نجود *nujūd*) High grounds. هو طلاع انجدة *huwa tallāʿu anjidatin*, He meditates high matters.

A انجذاب *injizāb*, The being drawn or attracted. Attraction, enticement, inclination, affection.

A انجذاذ *injizāz*, The being broken or cut off.

A انجذار *injizār*, The being cut or clipped.

A انجذاف *injizāf*, (v. n. 7 of جذف) Flying fast.

A انجذام *injizām*, The being amputated.

A انجذان *anjuzān*, Assafœtida.

A انجر *anjar*, (from P. لنگر *langar*) An anchor.

A انجراح *injirāh*, (v. n. 7 of جرح) Being wounded.

A انجراد *injirād*, (v. n. 7 of جرد) Being extended, lengthened, protracted. Going on a journey. Being smoothed, mangled (as linen). Being sleek (a horse). Being stripped, denuded.

A انجرار *injirār*, (v. n. 7 of جرّ) Being drawn out. Grazing and walking about (camels). Allowing (a camel) to graze whilst mounted on her back. (in gram.) Being marked with the vowel كسر *kasr*. Protraction, extension, tediousness.

A انجرة *anjurat*, A nettle. انجرة سوداء *anjurat sawdāʾ*, Pellitory, bindweed, helxine, assafœtida.

P انجرك *anjirak*, Marjoram. Name of a desert.

P انجروت *anjarūt*, Flesh-glue.

P انجرة *anjara*, A nettle.

A انجزار *injizār*, (v. n. 7 of جزر) Retiring, ebbing (the sea). Appearing at ebb-time (an island).

A انجزاع *injizāʿ*, (v. n. 7 of جزع) Being cut (a rope), broken (a stick).

A انجزام *injizām*, (v. n. 7 of جزم) Being broken. Being marked with a جزم *jazm* (a letter).

A انجس *anjas*, Dirtier, nastier, most squalid.

G انجسا *anjisā*, A species of herb, bugloss.

A انجع *anjaʿ*, More or most wholesome.

A انجعاب *injiʿāb*, The being thrown prostrate.

A انجعار *injiʿār*, The dunging (of a beast).

A انجعاف *injiʿāf*, (v. n. 7 of جعف) Being thrown prostrate. Being plucked up.

P انجغ *anjugh*, A wrinkle, a furrow.

A انجفال *injifāl*, (v. n. 7 of جفل) Moving off from any place (people). Passing away and vanishing (a shadow). Being rooted up.

A انجكك *anjakak*, A kind of grain or kernel, which is black on the outside and white within.

A انجل *anjal*, (pl. نجل *nujl* and نجال *nijāl*) Long. Large. Broad. One who has large open eyes.

P انجل *anjil*, Marsh-mallows, or the root.

A انجلاء *injilāʾ*, (v. n. 7 of جلا for جلو) Being apparent or conspicuous. Being wiped away (grief from the mind). Going off. Brightness, shining. An apparition, appearance.

A انجلاب *injilāb*, (v. n. 7 of جلب) Being driven from place to place (slaves or cattle).

A انجلاع *injilāʿ*, (v. n. 7 of جلع) Being uncovered.

A انجم *anjum*, (pl. of نجم *najm*) Stars. P پادشاه انجم سپاه *pādshāhi anjum sipāh*, An emperor with an army (numerous) as the stars; a most potent monarch. انجم افشردن *anjum afshurdan*, To make firm. انجم روز *anjumi roz*, The sun.

A انجماد *injimād*, A congelation, a curdling.

A انجمال *injimāl*, (v. n. 7 of جمل) Accruing, becoming accumulated.

P انجمن *anjuman*, A company, assembly, banquet, congregation, synagogue, congress, any place where people meet and converse. A multitude. انجمن كهكشان *anjumani kahkashān*, The milky way. وحوش وطيور و انجمن مار و مور *wuhūsh u tuyūr u anjumani mār u mūr*, Wild beasts, and birds, and a multitude of serpents and ants.

P انجمنگاه *anjuman-gāh*, A place of assembling.

P انجن *anjan*, A pounding, pulverizing. A cutting. Trouble, chagrin. Collyrium, antimony.

P انجنيدن *anjanīdan*, To be broken. To divide. To afflict, vex. To be anxious. To be disgusted.

P انجو *anjū*, An island. Name of an island.

P انجوج *anjūj*, The wood of aloes.

P انجوخ *anjūkh*, Flaccid, withered, flat, wrinkled, changed in colour. A wrinkle. Spittle.

P انجوختن *anjūkhtan*, To be wrinkled. To acquire.

P انجوخيدگي *anjūkhīdagī*, Corrugation.

P انجوخيدن *anjūkhīdan*, To be full of wrinkles.

P انجوسا *anjūsā*, Bugloss.

P انجوغ *anjūgh*, A wrinkle, fold, plait. Spittle. انجوغ گرفتن *anjūgh giriftan*, To contract wrinkles.

P انجوغيدن *anjūghīdan*, To become wrinkled.

P انجوك *anjūk*, Name of an unknown desert.

A انجياب *injiyāb*, (v. n. 7 of جاب for جوب) Stretching her neck to be milked (a camel).

A انجئاث *injiʾās*, (v. n. 7 of جأث) Being split.

A انجئاف *injiʾāf*, The being uprooted.

A انجيال *injiyāl*, (v. n. 7 of جال for جول) Going round. Being raised and flying about (dust).

A انجية *anjiyat*, (pl. of نجيّ *najīy*) Partners in

secrets, confidants.

A انجيدة anjīdat, A species of herb, marrubium.

P انجيدن anjīdan, To crumble (bread). To cup. To extract. To irrigate. To irritate, vex.

P انجيدة anjīda, Pounded, crumbled. Wild leek.

P انجير anjīr, A fig. A hole. Foramen podicis. انجير آدم anjīri ādam, (or انجير دشتي anjīri dashtī) Adam's fig, a kind of Indian fruit, resembling a gourd, round and red, with a small white point in the middle. انجير وزيري anjīri wazīrī, A kind of fig, white and delicate.

P انجيردن anjīrdan, To bore a hole, drill, perforate.

P انجيرة anjīra, Foramen ani. A fig. Name of a fountain near يزد yazd. Travelling-apparatus.

A P انجيل injīl or anjīl, The gospel. اهل انجيل ahli injīl, Christians, gospellers.

A انجيليّ injīliy, An evangelist.

P انجين anjīn, Pulverized. A pulverizer. A plasterer.

P آنچنان ānchunān, Thus, so, in that or like manner. آنچنان كه ānchunān ki, So that, in the same way, like as, even as.

P آنچه ānchi, That which. Whatever.

A آنح ānih, (pl. انّح unnah) A miser, who sighs and groans when asked for any thing. One troubled with a difficulty in breathing.

A انح anh, (v. n. of انح) Breathing hard.

A انّح unnah, A miser who sighs and groans when asked for any thing. (pl. of آنح ānih) Misers.

A انحاء anhās, (pl. of نحو nahw) Ways, roads, paths, tracks, quarters, sides. (pl. of نحي nihy) Leathern bottles in which they keep butter. Earthen milk-vessels. Broad-headed arrows. Inhās, v. n. 4 of نحا for نحو) Turning aside (the face from another). Leaning to the left side (a camel in travelling). (v. n. 4 of نحي) Turning (arms against one).

A انحاز inhāz, (v. n. 4 of نحز) Having camels afflicted with a disease in the lungs called نحاز nuhāz.

A انحاف inhāf, (v. n. 4 of نحف) Making thin and lean (نحيف nahīf), emaciating.

A انحال inhāl, (v. n. 4 of نحل) Rendering (one) thin, lean, extenuated (grief or anxiety). Giving wealth, appropriating it to a particular use.

A انحباس inhibās, (v. n. 7 of حبس) Being withheld, being imprisoned. Mortmain.

A آنحة ānihat, A female miser, groaning when any thing is asked. Short of stature (woman).

A انحتات inhitāt, (v. n. 7 of حتّ) Being rubbed between the hands. Falling (leaves from a tree).

A انحجار inhijār, A retiring into a hole or den.

A انحجاز inhijāz, (v. n. 7 of حجز) Being restrained. Going into a part of Arabia called حجاز hijāz.

A انحجاف inhijāf, (v. n. 7 of حجف) Humbling one's self, submitting. Supplication.

A انحداد inhidād, (v. n. 7 of حدّ) Being sharp.

A انحدار inhidār, (v. n. 7 of حدر) Swelling. Descending a declivity. Being thrown (down a precipice). Foundering (a ship at sea).

A انحذاق inhizāk, (v. n. 7 of حذق) Being broken to pieces, or divided into portions.

A انحذام inhizām, (v. n. 7 of حذم) Being cut.

A انحراد inhirād, (v. n. 7 of حرد) Falling (a star).

A انحراف inhirāf, (v. n. 7 of حرف) Changing, becoming a turn-coat. Inclining, turning. Turning away. Swerving. Deflexion, inversion, change. Recantation. Declination (in astronomy). P انحراف ورزيدن inhirāf warzīdan, To swerve, to deviate. To sow rebellion.

A انحز anhaz, A disease in the lungs, to which camels are subject, creating a violent cough. Ulcers, with which they are also afflicted. انحزان anhazāni, (dual) Both these maladies.

A انحس anhas, More or most unlucky.

A انحسار inhisār The being naked and exposed.

A انحساس inhisās, (v. n. 7 of حسّ) Being scattered, fallen (leaves). Being plucked up. Being pulled out (a tooth).

A انحساف inhisāf, (v. n. 7 of حسف) Being crumbled small with the fingers. Being dispersed.

A انحسام inhisām, (v. n. 7 of حسم) Being amputated. Standing, stopping.

A انحشاء inhishās, (v. n. 7 of حشي) Being stuffed, filled, crammed.

A انحصار inhisār, (v. n. 7 of حصر) Being besieged, confined, detained, let, hindered. Being compressed. Being numbered, told, computed.

A انحصاص inhisās, (v. n. 7 of حصّ) Falling off (as hair). Being docked (a tail), losing one's tail.

A انحصام inhisām, The being broken (as a bough).

A انحضاج inhizāj, (v. n. 7 of حضج) Being hot with anger. Being dilated. Laying aside gravity.

A انحطاط inhitāt, (v. n. 7 of حطّ) Sinking, descending. Falling, being reduced (price of provisions), lowered (character). Descending, alighting. Walking fast. Pulling at the bridle and going towards a precipice (a camel). Decline, decay.

A انحطام inhitām, (v. n. 7 of حطم) Being broken.

A انحفطينا anhaftīnā, Flower of pomegranate.

A انحقاق inhikāk, (v. n. 7 of حقّ) Being close and firm (a knot).

A انحلاب inhilāb, (v. n. 7 of حلب) Flowing (sweat). Shedding tears (the eye), pouring forth saliva (the mouth).

A انحلال inhilāl, (v. n. 7 of حلّ) Being loosed, untied, relaxed, loosened.

A انحلام inhilām, (v. n. 7 of حلم) Dreaming.

A انحماص inhimās, (v. n. 7 of حمص) Subsiding (an inflammation). Being drawn in, contracted, wrinkled. Becoming thin and spare. Eating the plant قرظ karaz, and becoming red and slender (a locust). From being fat, becoming thin and small.

A انحماق inhimāk, (v. n. 7 of حمق) Becoming vile and abject. Being worn out. Being flat and dull (a market). Being foolish, playing the fool.

A انحمال inhimāl, The being instigated.

A انحناء inhinās, The being bent and curved.

A انحياز inhiyāz, (v. n. 7 of حاز for حوز) Abandoning one residence and going to another. Retreating. Turning aside, deviating.

A انحياش inhiyāsh, (v. n. 7 of حاش for حوش) Fleeing, scampering (from fear). Shrinking, drawing one's self together.

A انحياص inhiyās, A turning back or aside.

A انخاء inkhās, (v. n. 4 of نخا for نخو) Waxing greater in pomp, pride, and glory (نخوة nakhwat).

A انخاب inkhāb, (v. n. 4 of نخب) Begetting a brave, heroic son; also a mean, cowardly one.

A انخاص inkhās, (v. n. 4 of نخص) Extenuating, withering (age).

A انخاط inkhāt, A blowing the nose. A spitting.

A انخاف inkhāf, (v. n. 4 of نخف) Making a repeated noise resembling sneezing.

A انخباز inkhibāz, The being depressed.

A انختاع inkhitāع, A travelling, roaming about.

A انخداع inkhidāع, (v. n. 7 of خدع) Being deceived, cheated, duped. Submitting to be duped. Being flat (a market).

A انخرار inkhirār, (v. n. 7 of خرّ) Hanging loose.

A انخراط inkhirāt, (v. n. 7 of خرط) Being strung. Being refractory and unmanageable (a beast of burden). Doing any thing in an ignorant, headstrong manner. Assailing any one suddenly with abusive language, or in some other shameful manner. Running fast. Being slender-bodied.

A انخراع inkhirāع, (v. n. 7 of خرع) Being split open, or broken to pieces. Being dislocated (a joint). Being uprooted. Being weak.

A انخراق inkhirāk, (v. n. 7 of خرق) Being torn. Inventing a lie. Blowing violently across.

A انخرام inkhirām, A being notched, cleft, riven.

A انخزاع inkhizāع, (v. n. 7 of خزع) Being broken in two, cut off. Bending from age or weakness.

A انخزاق inkhizāk, (v. n. 7 of خزق) Being run through (with a dart).

A انخزال inkhizāl, (v. n. 7 of خزل) Being separated, broken off. Proceeding heavily. Not being anxious about.

A انخزام inkhizām, (v. n. 7 of خزم) Being bored. Being spoiled.

A انخساء inkhisās, (v. n. 7 of خسأ) Being driven to a distance from the society of men (dogs, swine).

A انخساف inkhisāf, (v. n. 7 of خسف) Being put out (the eyes). Being eclipsed (the moon).

A انخشاش inkhishāsh, (v. n. 7 of خشّ) Entering into any thing.

A انخشاف inkhishāf, (v. n. 7 of خشف) Engaging in any work.

A انخضاج inkhizāj, (v. n. 7 of خضج) Sinking on one side (a boat).

A انخضاد inkhizād, (v. n. 7 of خضد) Being broken (a green stick). Being burst (an apple).

A انخضاع *inkhizāɛ*, (v. n. 7 of خضع) Being humble, submitting to another.

A انخع *ankhaɛ*, More or most deadly or detrimental to one's self, or what entails great disgrace.

A انخفاس *inkhifās*, (v. n. 7 of خفس) Becoming fetid (water).

A انخفاض *inkhifāz*, (v. n. 7 of خفض) Being depressed. Falling into a low place. Being marked with the vowel كسر *kasr* (ِ). Humiliation.

A انخفاع *inkhifāɛ*, (v. n. 7 of خفع) Fainting, becoming attenuated from the want of food. Being torn up (a palm-tree). Being burst (the lungs).

A انخفة *ankhifat*, (pl. of نخاف *nikhāf*) Boots.

A انخلاء *inkhilāɛ*, (v. n. 7 of خلي) Being mowed.

A انخماس *inkhimās*, (v. n. 7 of خمس) Subsiding, going down (a swelling).

A انخناث *inkhināş*, The being flexible, limber.

A انخناس *inkhinās*, (v. n. 7 of خنس) Retiring, withdrawing, remaining behind.

A انخناق *inkhināk*, (v. n. 7 of خنق) Strangling one's self. Being throttled, suffocated.

A انخيات *inkhiyāt*, (v. n. 7 of خات for خوت) Pouncing on his prey (a falcon).

A انخياق *inkhiyāk*, The being broad, spacious.

P اند *and*, They are. Speaking doubtfully and uncertainly. Desire, hope. Surprise. Giving thanks. A period of 500 ages or 15,000 years. Some, any number between three and ten. So much, so many, as many as. Liquorice.

P اندا *andā*, Plastering the roof of a house. A plasterer. Calumny. A dream such as pious persons are occasionally favoured with.

A انداء *andāɛ*, (pl. of ندي *nada'*) Rains: day-dews. *Indāɛ*, (v. n. 4 of ندا for ندو) Moistening Feeding (camels) between two drinkings. Giving magnificently, liberally. Having a good voice.

A انداب *andāb*, (pl. of ندبة *nadbat*) Scars of wounds. *Indāb*, (v. n. 4 of ندب) Having scars. Leaving a scar. Exposing (one's self) to danger.

P اندابه *andāba*, A plasterer's trowel.

P انداچه *andācha*, (in zand and Pāzand) Consideration, thought.

A انداح *andāh*, (pl. of ندح *nadh*) Spacious tracts of land. Mountain-steeps.

A انداخ *indākh*, The causing (a ship) to drive.

P انداختن *andākhtan*, To throw, cast, dart, shoot, lance, hurl. To shake, drive about. To eject. To inject. To force away. To rush. To disperse, scatter, strew, diffuse. To do, make.

P انداد *andād*, The herb nose-smart. Plaster.

A انداد *andād*, (pl. of ند *nidd*) Like, similar. *Indād*, (v. n. 4 of ند) Dispersing.

P اندادن *andādan*, To incrust. To desire.

P اندار *andār*, A narrative, story, tale, fiction.

A اندار *indār*, (v. n. 4 of ندر) Causing to fall off, striking off. Subtracting. Drawing forth.

P اندارس *andāris*, Name of a person who despatched a messenger to عذرا *ɛazrā* and whose eyes عذرا *ɛazrā* tore out.

P انداز *andāz*, The incrustation of a wall, plaster, parget. An instrument, a trowel with which they plaster walls. A measure, a certain quantity. Valuation, guess. (in composition) Throwing, darting: diffusing, scattering. Seeking. A darter, thrower. آب انداز *āb-andāz*, One who plans or measures aqueducts. برق انداز *bark-andāz*, A matchlock-man. پرتو انداز *partav-andāz*, Diffusing rays. تير انداز *tīr-andāz*, Shooting arrows. دهشت انداز *dahshat-andāz*, Spreading terror.

P اندازا *andāzā*, Throwing.

P اندازه *andāza*, An ell, a yard. Measure, quantity, dimension. Proportion, symmetry. A specimen, copy. Strength. A belt, leathern strap, shoe-latchet. Worthy. اندازه كردن *andāza kardan*, To measure. To guess. To estimate, calculate.

P اندازي *andāzī*, A shot. حرف اندازي *harf-andāzī*, A threat.

P اندازيدن *andāzīdan*, To throw. To measure. To make.

P انداس *andās*, Measure. Guess, computation.

A انداس *andās*, Shrewd, bold, fearless (men).

P انداشگر *andāshgar*, A plasterer.

A انداص *indās*, (v. n. 4 of ندص) Drawing out, obtaining one's due, getting one's rights.

A انداع *indāɛ*, (v. n. 4 of ندع not in use) Following the example of bad men.

A انداغ *indāgh*, (v. n. 4 of ندغ) Doing evil, disgusting, offending.

A انداف *indāf*, (v. n. 4 of ندف) Driving violently, riding furiously. Listening to the sound of a lute. Giving drink (to a dog or other beast).

P اندام *andām*, The body. A member, a limb. Stature, figure, form (of the body). Exact proportion, justness, symmetry. Order, arrangement. Ornament. Beauty. Good-breeding. Rule, custom. A court, area. اندام پيش *andāmi pesh*, (or اندام شرم *andāmi sharm*) Pudendum. اندام دانا *andāmi dānā*, The fore-finger. اندام زدن *andām zadan*, To dismember. Commemorating, recalling past griefs. اندام نهاني *andāmi nihānī*, The privy member. جاريت سيم اندام *jāriyati sīm-andām*, A virgin splendid as the silver, of a silver form. اندام اندام كردن *andām andām kardan*, To dismember, to cut up. بي اندام *bī andām*, (or نا اندام *nā andām*) Ill-proportioned, disproportionate.

A اندام *indām*, (v. n. 4 of ندم) Making repent.

P اندامه *andāma*, A recollection, remembrance (of friends or past events). An historical narrative.

P اندان *andān*, Term, mode, manner. An ell.

P آنداو *āndāv*, Cement, plaster.

P انداو *andāv*, Garden-herbs, cresses. Cement.

P انداوش *andāwish*, The incrustation of a wall.

P انداوة *andāwa*, A trowel. Calumny: complaint.

P انداويدن *andāwīdan*, To plaster. Incrustation.

P انداويده *andāwīda*, Plastered, bedaubed.

P انداي *andāy*, Plastering. A plasterer. Cement, plaster. Complaint.

P اندايش *andāyish*, Plastering: cement, plaster.

P اندايشگر *andāyishgar*, A plasterer, a pargeter.

P اندايه *andāya*, A trowel. Slander, detraction.

P اندائيدن *andāīdan*, To incrust. To covet.

A اندباح *indibāh*, A stooping low (in prayer).

A اندباغ *indibāgh*, The being tanned (a hide).

A اندثار *indisār*, A being effaced, obliterated.

P اندجان *andajān*, Name of a city in Turkistān.

A اندحاح *indihāh*, A being dilated, distended.

A اندحاض *indihāz*, (v. n. 7 of دحض) Being demolished, effaced, obliterated.

A اندحاق *indihāk*, (v. n. 7 of دحق) Protruding, prolapsing (matrix of a camel) after the birth.

A اندخ *andakh*, A dull, doltish man, of few words.

A اندخاخ *indikhākh*, Fast-travelling (of an ass).

A اندخال *indikhāl*, An entering. Ingress.

P اندخس *andakhas*, (or اندخسو) A protector.

P اندخسواره *andakhas-wāra*, A citadel: asylum.

P اندخسيدن *andakhusīdan*, To protect. To take refuge.

P اندخش *andakhish*, An asylum: protection.

P اندخوارة *andakhwārah*, A sanctuary. A citadel, a fortress.

P اندخور *andakhwur*, Worthy, suitable, proper.

P اندر *andar*, In, into, within. *Andar*, when added to the words پدر *pidar*, مادر *mādar*, برادر *birādar*, and خواهر *khwāhar*, implies step-father, step-mother, half-brother, and half-sister.

A اندر *andar*, More or most rare. (pl. انادر *anādir*) A barn or other place where grain is thrashed or trodden out. A heap of grain placed there. Name of a village near Aleppo.

A اندراء *indirāɛ*, (v. n. 7 of درأ) Being propelled (a torrent). Spreading itself far and wide (a fire).

P اندراب *andar-āb*, (In the water) An islet. Name of a city on the confines of Khurāsān towards India, near Ghaznīn. Name of another city in Gilān, on the south-west side of the Caspian Sea.

A اندراج *indirāj*, (v. n. 7 of درج) Becoming extinct (a family). Being rolled together (as a scroll).

A اندراس *indirās*, A being obliterated, erased.

A اندراسيون *andarāsiyūn*, A kind of perfume.

A اندراع *indirāɛ*, (v. n. 7 of درع) Advancing. Being driven back. Being dislocated (a bone). Being full (the belly). Breaking forth from behind the clouds (the moon).

P اندران *andarān*, A species of gum.

A اندراني *andarānīy*, Large (bag, purse, wallet).

P اندرايين *indarāyīn*, The fruit of the colocynth.

P اندرباي *andar-bāy*, Necessity. Necessary. Suspended, inverted.

P اندربايست *andar-bāyist*, Requisite, necessary.

P T اندربيگ *andar-beg*, (Admitted) amongst the great; also amongst the higher order of demons.

P اندرجاه *andar-jāh*, An interior place. A supplemental day (of which five are added to the Persian year, to make their twelve months, of thirty days each, equal to a solar year).

P اندرجو *indirjav*, Sparrow's tongue (a plant).

P اندر خور *andar-khwar*, (اندر خورد *andar-khward*, Worthy, proper, deserving. Convenient.

P اندرخوردن *andar khwardan*, To deserve, to merit. To be proper, convenient, agreeable, suitable, well adapted.

P اندر خورند *andar-khwarand*, Worthy, proper.

P اندرز *andaraz*, A testament, last will, precept, admonition, counsel, advice. Relation, narrative. A book, a writing.

P اندر زا *andar-zā*, (Bred-within) A stone found in the gall-bladder of an ox.

P اندرز کرده شده *andaraz karda shuda*, Enjoined by a will. An administrator.

P اندرزکننده *andaraz-kunanda*, A testator.

P اندر گاهان *andar-gāhān*, Intermediate times. Five intercalary days added to the Persian year.

P اندرو *andarū*, Together, all at once. With himself, it is his.

P اندروا *andarwā*, (اندرواژ *andarwāj*, اندرواه *andarwāh*, or اندرواي) Inverted, head-downwards. Suspended. Astonished, bewildered. Desire, need.

P اندروائي *andarwāī*, Astonishment, stupor. A hanging down of the head. Desire, wish.

A P اندروب *andurūb*, Ring-worm: dry scab.

P اندروخورون *andarūkhūrūn*, Tares, darnel.

P اندروخون *andarūkhūn*, Name of a coarse prickly shrub.

P اندرود *andarūd*, Incrustation. Decoration.

A اندرورد *andarward*, (or اندروردية *andarwardīyat*) Short breeches (from the Persian).

A اندروس *andarūs*, Leander the lover of Hero.

P اندروز *andarūz*, An examiner, explorer, spy. Mortar, plaster. A court-house. A market-place.

G اندروصارون *andarūsārūn*, Honeysuckle.

G اندروصاقس *andarūsākas*, The herb navel-wort.

G اندروطاقس *andarūtākas*, The herb navel-wort.

P اندرون *andarūn*, Within. The inside. The heart, bowels. Intrinsic, interior, internal. اندرون مسجد *andarūni masjid*, Within the temple. در اندرون رفتن *dar andarūn raftan*, To go in, to enter.

A اندرون *andarūn*, A number of gay young fellows, men met for a drinking-bout.

P اندرون اندر *andarūn-andar*, A strap, a thong for measuring.

P اندرونه *andarūna*, A sheet. A shirt: a doublet.

P اندروني *andarūnī*, Internal. Fine linen.

P اندرهست *andarhast*, Wild saffron, dog's-bane.

A اندريّ *andariy*, A thick rope. Of Andar.

P اندريمان *andarīmān*, Name of a certain hero.

A الاندرين *al andarīn*, Name of a village in Syria; also of one in Mesopotamia.

P اندز *andaz*, Proposal, intention. Conjecture, opinion. Name of an herb, useful in curing diseases of horses. A celebrated man. *Andiz*, A bridle, strap, or leathern thong for measuring.

A اندساج *indisāj*, A falling flat on the face.

A اندساس *indisās*, (v. n. 7 of دسّ) Being hid, buried. Hiding, lurking, burying one's self.

P اندشمار *andishmār*, A lecture, a discourse.

P اندشمال *andishmāl*, A lecture. A clear voice.

A اندعاء *indiꜥāꜥ*, (v. n. 7 of دعا for دعو) Answering, accepting (when called upon).

A اندعاص *indiꜥāṣ*, (v. n. 7 of دعص) Becoming putrid (a corpse).

A اندفاع *indifāꜥ*, (v. n. 7 of دفع) Being repelled or carried off, going to a distance. Being propelled. Dilating, becoming diffuse in narrative. Arriving suddenly. Walking fast.

A اندفاق *indifāk*, A being poured forth (water).

A اندفان *indifān*, A being buried, hid, covered.

A اندقاق *indikāk*, A being pounded small.

A اندقام *indikām*, (v. n. 7 of دقم) Entering into any thing (wind).

P اندك *andak*, Little, few, small. اندك اندك *andak andak*, By little and little, by small degrees, a trifle at a time. بسپاه اندك شمار *ba sipāhi andak-shumār*, With an army, small in number.

A اندكاك *indikāk*, (v. n. 7 of دكّ) Being made smooth and level (uneven ground).

A اندكام *indikām*, (v. n. 7 of دكم) Rushing into.

P اندك مال *andak-māl*, Poor, indigent.

P اندكي *andakī*, A little. Littleness. Scarcity.

P اندگان *andagān*, Name of a country and city lying between Samarkand and China.

A اندلاث *indilās*, (v. n. 7 of دلث) Falling foul upon, rushing violently. Rushing into a business without thought and foresight. Defaming, reproaching, vilifying, inventing a lie against.

A اندلاص *indilāṣ*, (v. n. 7 of دلص) Slipping through the hand.

A اندلاظ *indilāz*, (v. n. 7 of دلظ) Being driven forward (a current).

A اندلاع *indilāꜥ*, (v. n. 7 of دلع) Being lolled out (the tongue). Being unsheathed (a sword). Being large and swagging (the belly).

A اندلاف *indilāf*, A being poured forth.

A اندلاق *indilāk*, (v. n. 7 of دلق) Going before, outstripping. Going out. Protruding (a gut). Falling (a sword from the sheath). Overflowing, inundating (a mighty stream or countless host).

A اندلال *indilāl*, (v. n. 7 of دلّ) Being directed, guided, led. Being poured out. Allowing one's self to be guided, submitting to guidance.

A اندلس *andalus*, Spain, so called by the Arabians, from Andalusia, the province which was first conquered in the year of the Hijra 92 (A.D. 710) by Tārik Bin Ziyād, under the khilāfat of Al Walīd the 13th successor to Muhammad.

P آن دم *ān dam*, Then, at that breath.

A اندم *andam*, More or most penitent.

A اندماج *indimāj*, (v. n. 7 of دمج) Adhering fast (one thing to another), being entangled.

A اندماس *indimās*, (v. n. 7 of دمس) Entering (a cave or bath called ديماس *dīmās*).

A اندماق *indimāk*, (v. n. 7 of دمق) Entering suddenly without permission. Falling, slipping from (its) place. Creeping into a lurking-place.

A اندمال *indimāl*, (v. n. 7 of دمل) Being healed and cicatrized (a wound).

P اندمه *andama*, Remembrance of past grief.

P اندو *andav*, Plaster. A pitcher. *Andū*, Within.

P اندوب *andūb*, (or اندوج) Ringworm, scab.

P اندوختن *andokhtan*, To acquire, collect. To pay a debt.

P اندوخته *andokhta*, Acquired, gained. Profit. A treasury. اندوختها *andokhtahā*, Gains.

P اندوخش *andokhish*, Gain, profit, emolument.

P اندود *andūd*, Plaster, mortar, incrustation. زر اندود *zar-andūd*, Washed, gilt, incrusted with gold. قار اندود *kār-andūd*, Besmeared with pitch.

P اندودن *andūdan*, To incrustate, plaster, cover over, anoint, smear. To gild, plate, wash over.

P اندوده *andūda*, Anointed. Incrusted.

P اندوز *andoz*, (in composition) Gaining, acquiring: seizing, occupying: collecting, gathering. Collected, gathered. شب ظلمت اندوز *shabi zulmat-andoz*, A night gathering darkness. بلدهٔ عبرت اندوز *baldaꜥi ꜥibrat-andoz*, A wonderful city.

P اندوزنده *andozanda*, Acquiring. A gainer.

P اندوزيدن *andozīdan*, To gain, acquire, collect. To repay a debt. To remove, to send away.

P اندوژه *andojah*, A violet. Endive.

P اندوشه *andosha*, Name of a flower.

P اندوك *andūk*, Anxiety, grief, trouble, care.

P اندول *andūl*, Throne of the kings of Zanguebar.

P آندون *āndūn*, There. Then. Thus.

P اندون *andūn*, Plaster, cement. Ointment.

P اندوند *andwand*, Upside down. Scattered.

P اندوه *andūh*, Anxiety, grief, care, anguish, aversion, disgust. اندوه خوردن *andūh khwurdan*, To be anxious and careful. To grieve.

P اندوهگين *andūhgīn*, (or اندوه ناك) Melancholy.

P اندوه ناكي *andūhnākī*, Grief, sadness.

P اندوهه *andūha*, A recollection of past sorrows.

P اندوهيدن *andūhīdan*, To mourn, grieve, fret.

P انده *anduh*, Grief, sadness. Care, anxiety.

A اندهاش *indihāsh*, The being astonied.

P اندهان *anduhān*, (pl. of انده *anduh*) Cares.

P انده قوقو *andahūkū*, The lote-tree.

A اندي *andaʼ*, More, most liberal. One whose voice (نداء *nidāꜥ*) can be heard at a great distance.

P اندي *andī*, Especially, particularly, chiefly. Perhaps, may be. Also. Surprise. Hope. Days of yore.

A انديّ *undiy*, A native of اندة *undat* in Spain.

A اندياح *indiyāh*, (v. n. 7 of داح for دوح) Hanging pendulous and swagging (the belly).

A اندياس *indiyās,* The being thrashed out.

A اندياص *indiyāṣ,* (v. n. 7 of داص for ديص) Escaping out of one's hand. Attacking unawares.

A اندياق *indiyāḳ,* (v. n. 7 of داق for دوق) Being swollen (the belly).

A انديال *indiyāl,* (v. n. 7 of دال for دول) Migrating. Being ample, swaggy, and hanging near the ground (belly). Being discharged (from the belly). Adhering.

A اندية *andiyat,* (pl. of نديّ) Rains: day-dews.

P انديدن *andīdan,* To be surprised or disturbed in mind. To speak obscurely, ambiguously, doubtfully, softly. To incrustate. To be lazy.

P انديسي *andīsī,* A mode of writing.

P انديش *andesh,* (in compos.) Thinking, meditating, devising, considering, reflecting. خير انديش *khayr-andesh,* Meditating on what is good, thinking well. خاطر صواب انديش *khāṭiri ṣawāb-andesh,* A mind reflecting justly. فجور انديش *fujūr-andesh,* Impious. فساد انديش *fasād-andesh,* Mischief-making. مرد صلاح انديش *mardi ṣalāḥ andesh,* A pacific man, or one prudent, judicious.

P انديشانيدن *andeshānīdan,* To cause to think.

P انديشمند *andeshmand,* (or انديشناك *andeshnāk*) Thoughtful. Also انديشه مند *andeshamand.*

P انديشه *andesha,* Consideration, thought, meditation. Jealousy. Suspicion. Fear. Reverie. Care, anxiety. انديشه كردن *andesha kardan,* To fear.

P انديشه گار *andeshagār,* Thoughtful.

P انديشه گاري *andeshagārī,* Thoughtfulness.

P انديشه ناك *andeshanāk,* Thoughtful.

P انديشيدگي *andeshīdagī,* Thoughtfulness, care.

P انديشيدن *andeshīdan,* To consider, meditate.

P انديك *andīk,* And therefore, therefore, because. Would to heaven! Perhaps, may be. A crowd.

P اندينا *andīnā,* A water-melon.

A انذار *inẕār,* (v. n. 4 of نذر) Warning, deterring, putting in fear. Preaching. Dehortation, solemn admonition, or caution, dissuasion.

A انذال *anẕāl,* (pl. of نذل *naẕl* or نذيل) Base.

A انذخاخ *inẕikhākh,* The act of labouring hard.

A انذراع *inẕirāʻ,* (v. n. 7 of ذرع) Being propelled. Walking fast. Coming unexpectedly.

A انذرانيّ *anẕarāniy,* Very white (salt).

P انذرو *anẕarū,* The bezoar-stone

A انذعاب *inẕiʻāb,* (v. n. 7 of ذعب) Flowing continually (water).

A انذعاف *inẕiʻāf,* (v. n. 7 of ذعف) Being slain, cut off. Suffering from a difficulty in breathing.

A انذلاء *inẕilāʼ,* (v. n. 7 of ذلي) Being gathered.

A انذلاغ *inẕilāgh,* (v. n. 7 of ذلغ) Ripening (dates). Becoming raw (a camel's back).

A انذياب *inẕiyāb,* The being melted.

A انذئاج *inẕiʼāj,* (v. n. 7 of ذأج) Being torn (a leathern bottle).

A انذياع *inẕiyāʻ,* A being published, divulged.

A انذئاف *inẕiʼāf,* (v. n. 7 of ذأف) Dying suddenly. Being broken (the heart).

P انر *anar,* Ugly, hideous. Bad.

P آنرا *ānrā,* Him. To him. That. To that.

A انروب *anrūb,* Itch, mange, scab, ringworm.

A انزاء *inzāʼ,* (v. n. 4 of نزا for نزو) Causing to leap. Sending forth in a gush.

A انزاح *inzāḥ,* (v. n. 4 of نزح) Exhausting, drying up (a well).

A انزار *inzār,* (v. n. 4 of نزر) Giving little (in a present). Rendering few and small.

A انزاز *inzāz,* (v. n. 4 of نزّ) Becoming hard, hardening. Being watery (ground).

A انزاع *inzāʻ,* (v. n. 4 of نزع) Having cattle returning eagerly to their accustomed habitation or pasture. Having part of the forehead bald.

A انزاف *inzāf,* (v. n. 4 of نزف) Exhausting (tears). Being destitute of water (a well). Possessing such a well. Passing by (wind). Going a foraging. Having one's wine exhausted. Becoming intoxicated.

A انزاق *inzāḳ,* (v. n. 4 of نزق) Raising the forefeet for a leap (a horse). Causing (a horse) to raise his feet. Laughing immoderately. From being wise, becoming a fool.

A انزال *anzāl,* (pl. of نزل *nuzl*) Provisions prepared for a guest. *Inzāl,* (v. n. 4 of نزل) Preparing to entertain a guest. Causing to reside. Causing to descend, sending down. Emitting. Seminal effusion.

A انزباق *inzibāḳ,* (v. n. 7 of زبق) Entering.

A انزبان *inzibān,* (v. n. 7 of زبن) Being removed, going on one side.

A انزجار *inzijār,* (v. n. 7 of زجر) Being repulsed, prohibited, reproved.

A انزراب *inzirāb,* A lurking (as a hunter).

A انزراف *inzirāf,* (v. n. 7 of زرف) Passing by. Driving along (wind). Going in search of water.

A انزراق *inzirāḳ,* (v. n. 7 of زرق) Entering (a hole) and lying hid. Remaining behind. Lying supine. Penetrating, passing through (an arrow).

P انزرو *anzarū,* The bezoar-stone.

A P انزروت *anzarūt,* Sarcocolla, flesh-glue.

A انزع *anzaʻ,* (A man) bald about the temples.

A انزعاج *inziʻāj,* (v. n. 7 of زعج) Being disturbed and moved from its place.

A انزعاق *inziʻāḳ,* (v. n. 7 of زعق) Being panic-struck. Being timid at night. Travelling fast (beast of burden). Taking the lead (a horse).

A انزقاب *inziḳāb,* (v. n. 7 of زقب) Entering (a field-mouse into its hole).

A انزكاب *inzikāb,* (v. n. 7 of زكب) Being thrown headlong into a ditch.

A انزل *anzil,* Descend thou (to fight in an arena).

A انزمام *inzimām,* The being tied or bound.

P آنزمان *ān zamān,* That time: then, at that time.

P انزن *anzan,* Breadth.

A انزواء *inziwāʼ,* (v. n. 7 of زوي) Retiring into a corner or cell (a recluse). Being removed to a distance. Shrivelling up before the fire (leather).

A انزه *anzah,* More or most pleasant and agreeable (country).

A انزهاق *inzihāḳ,* (v. n. 7 of زهق) Outstripping, taking the lead, from whipping or fright (a horse).

A انزهوة *inzahwat,* Proud, haughty.

A انزياح *inziyāḥ,* A being far off, a going away.

A انزيال *inziyāl,* (v. n. 7 of زال for زول) Quitting. (v. n. of زال for زيل) Being separated.

P انژه *anja,* A lentil.

A آنس *ānas,* More or most familiar. *Ānis,* Social, cheerful.

A انس *ins,* Mankind (the medium between جنّ *jinn,* a demon, genius, or spirit, and وحشيّ *wahshīy,* the brute creation). انسك *insuka,* Thine intimate friend. ابن انسك *ibnu insika,* The son of thine intimate friend. *Uns,* (v. n. انس) Being intimate. Being social and cheerful. Society, companionship, intimacy, familiarity. P انس گرفتن *uns giriftan,* To associate. A *Anas,* Intimacy. A company or society of people living together. Mankind. Name of a servant of Muhammad. انس ابن ابي اناس *anas ibn abī unās,* Name of a poet. *Unus,* (pl. of انوس *anūs*) Tame (dogs), not biting.

A انساء *ansāʼ,* (pl. of نسا *nasa'*) Nerves or tendons which extend from the hips to the heels. (pl. of نسي *nasy* or *nisy*) Things thrown away or left behind as useless. *Insāʼ,* (v. n. 4 of نسأ) Deferring, putting off, granting a delay. (v. n. 4 of نسي) Making (one) to forget.

A انساب *ansāb,* (pl. of نسب *nasab*) Genealogies. Generations. Families. Lines. Successors. Progenies, parentages. *Insāb,* (v. n. 4 of نسب) Blowing hard, scattering dust or gravel (wind).

A انساخ *insākh,* (v. n. 4 of نسخ) Making write. Finding, or discovering to be cancelled, abrogated.

A انساسا *unsāsā,* (Syriac) Raisins.

A انساع *ansāʻ,* (pl. of نسعة *nisʻat*) Bridles or reins made of twisted thongs of leather. *Insāʻ,* (v. n. 4 of نسع) Getting into the north wind. Annoying one's neighbours much.

A انساغ *insāgh,* (v. n. 4 of نسغ) Beating one severely (with whips or rods). Putting forth its pith (the young shoot of a palm-tree). (A tree) sprouting afresh (after being lopped).

A انساق *insāḳ,* A speaking in rhyme.

A انسال *ansāl,* (pl. of نسل *nasl*) Progenies, offsprings. *Insāl,* (v. n. 4 of نسل) Begetting or bringing forth. Moulting, shedding, or changing (feathers or hair). Being near moulting time (an animal). Putting forth or shedding their extreme parts (thistles). Excelling, preceding, outstripping.

A انسام *ansām,* (pl. of نسم *nasam*) Gentle breezes. Respirations.

A انسان *insān,* (pl. آناس *ānās* or اناسي *anāsī*) Man, mankind. A woman. The top, peak, or ridge of a mountain. The tip of the finger. The shadow of a man. Ground not sowed. انسان العين *insānu'l ʿayn*, The pupil of the eye. عين الانسان *ʿaynu'l insān*, The eye of a man, *i. e.* the glory or ornament of man.

A انسانة *insānat*, A woman.

A انسانيّ *insāniy*, Human.

A انسانيّة *insāniyat*, Human nature, humanity. Courtesy, civility, urbanity, politeness.

A انسب *ansab*, More or most convenient, agreeable, befitting, conformable, advisable, proper. More or most learned in genealogies. More or most tender in praise of a mistress (verse), more or most of an erotic character.

A انسباء *ansibāʾ*, (pl. of نسيب *nasīb*) Related. Nobly-allied. *Insibāʾ*, A being excoriated, flayed.

A انسبات *insibāt*, (v. n. 7 of سبت) Being long and extended. Being soft and smooth. Extension, prolongation. Length of visage.

A انسباك *insibāk*, The being melted (as silver).

A آنسة *ānisat*, (A girl) of good spirits.

A انسة *anasat*, (v. n. of انس) Being intimate, social, and cheerful. Intimacy.

P آنسته *ānasta*, *ānsta*, or انسته *anista*, Root of the herb سعد *suʿd* (galangale).

A انسجاح *insijāh*, (v. n. 7 of سجح) Forgiving, pardoning. Being liberal and generous.

A انسجار *insijār*, (v. n. 7 of سجر) Being let fall (hair). Following in regular succession.

A انسجال *insijāl*, The being poured out (as water).

A انسجام *insijām*, (v. n. 7 of سجم) Being poured out (water). Flowing (tears).

A انسحاء *insihāʾ*, (v. n. 7 of سحي) Being shaven.

A انسحاب *insihāb*, The being trailed along.

A انسحاج *insihāj*, The being peeled, excoriated.

A انسحاط *insihāt*, (v. n. 7 of سحط) Slipping through the hand. Losing one's hold and slipping down a palm-tree.

A انسحاق *insihāk*, (v. n. 7 of سحق) Being rubbed, pulverized. Becoming worn (a camel's hoof). Drying and becoming shrivelled up (an udder). Being wide, spacious, and roomy.

A انسحال *insihāl*, (v. n. 7 of سحل) Being smoothed and polished. Being peeled. Speaking diffusely.

A انسداح *insidāj*, A falling flat on the face.

A انسداح *insidāh*, A lying on the back or face.

A انسداخ *insidākh*, (v. n. 7 of سدخ) Being expanded, being broad and flat.

A انسداد *insidād*, (v. n. 7 of سدّ) Becoming closed up (stitches in a leathern bottle).

A انسدار *insidār*, (v. n. 7 of سدر) Being let loose, dishevelled (hair). Being distant. Descending, or being thrown down. Proceeding, persevering.

A انسدال *insidāl*, (v. n. 7 of سدل) Being let down (a woman's veil, garments, or hair).

A انسدام *insidām*, The being healed (sore back).

A انسر *ansur*, (pl. of نسر *nasr*) Vultures. Eagles.

A انسراء *insirāʾ*, (v. n. 7 of سرو) Being shaken off (fear, alarm, grief, or sadness).

A انسراب *insirāb*, (v. n. 7 of سرب) Entering his burrow (a fox). Being long.

A انسراح *insirāh*, (v. n. 7 of سرح) Undressing, stripping. Lying supine, stretching out the feet.

A انسراط *insirāt*, A gliding easily down the throat.

A انسراق *insirāk*, Weakness (of the joints).

A انسطاح *insitāh*, (v. n. 7 of سطح) Lying on the ground stretched out and motionless.

A انسعاب *insiʿāb*, The flowing (of water).

A انسفار *insifār*, (v. n. 7 of سفر) Being bare, naked, and exposed. Going off (camels).

A انسفاق *insifāk*, (v. n. 7 of سفق) Lying wide open (a door).

A انسفاك *insifāk*, A being shed (as blood, tears).

A انسكاب *insikāb*, (v. n. 7 of سكب) Being poured out: flowing (blood or water). Pouring out.

A انسكاك *insikāk*, The being closely compressed.

A انسلاء *insilāʾ*, (v. n. 7 of سلا for سلو) Being shaken off (sadness), being comforted.

A انسلات *insilāt*, (v. n. 7 of سلت) Stealing away privately, eloping.

A انسلاخ *insilākh*, (v. n. 7 of سلخ) Being drawn off (a skin). Being ended (a month). Quitting. Departing. Putting off a garment (a man), or a slough (a snake). Being drawn forth (the day from the night). Becoming raw (a camel's back).

A انسلاع *insilāʿ*, (v. n. 7 of سلع) Having fissures or cracks.

A انسلاق *insilāk*, (v. n. 7 of سلق) Being affected with a disease called سلاق *sulāk* (the eye).

A انسلاك *insilāk*, A being inserted, or threaded.

A انسلال *insilāl*, (v. n. 7 of سلّ) Stealing away privately, eloping. Falling or dropping out from the midst (as a sword from the sheath).

A انسماح *insimāh*, (v. n. 7 of سمح) Being liberal.

P آنسو *ān sū*, That side, thither, from the other side, through.

A انسي *ansaʾ*, Pained in the nerve نسا *nasaʾ*, afflicted with sciatica. A vein in the lower leg.

A انسيّ *insiy* or *anasiy*, (pl. اناسيّ *anāsiy*) A man. *Insiy*, The interior part, the inside (of a bow or of the foot). The left or near side (the off side being called وحشيّ *wahshiy*).

A انسياء *insiyāʾ*, (v. n. 7 of سيأ) Collecting at the extremity of the teats (milk).

A انسياب *insiyāb*, (v. n. 7 of ساب for سيب) Running or walking fast. Gliding along the ground swiftly (a serpent). Returning.

A انسياح *insiyāh*, (v. n. 7 of ساح for سيح) Being widely extended (urine). Being slit (a garment). Waxing large and fat (the belly).

A انسياع *insiyāʿ*, (v. n. 7 of ساع for سيع) Flowing (water or wine).

A انسئاف *insiʾāf*, (v. n. 7 of سأف) Being peeled and divided into fibres (a palm-tree).

A انسياق *insiyāk*, (v. n. 7 of ساق for سوق) Being stimulated, impelled, driven, urged forward.

A انسيّة *unsiyat*, Familiarity, intimacy.

A انشاء *inshāʾ*, (v. n. 4 of نشأ) Rising up, starting into existence. Creating, producing, causing to grow. Educating. Composing or reciting (verses). Beginning (to build a house), commencing (to relate a story). Going out. Conceiving (a camel). Raising (a cloud). Elegance of style. Form, style, composition. The belles lettres. The term *inshā* is particularly applied to the forms of letter writing. (v. n. 4 of نشي) Smelling, scenting.

A ان شاء *in shāʾ*, If (he) please. ان شاء الله تعالي *in shāʾ allāh taʿāla'*, Please God, God willing. When written in Persian it must be so, انشا الله.

A انشاب *inshāb*, (v. n. 4 of نشب) Fixing. Causing to stick or hitch. Laying snares, taking game. Blowing hard (wind), scattering dust and gravel.

P انشا پردازي *inshā-pardāzī*, Elegance of style.

A انشاج *anshāj*, (pl. of نشج) Aqueducts, canals.

A انشاد *inshād*, (v. n. 4 of نشد) Giving information concerning a thing lost. Inquiring or asking information about something that had been lost. Reading or reciting a poem. Improvising. Lampooning, satirizing.

A انشار *inshār*, (v. n. 4 of نشر) Recalling to life.

A انشاز *anshāz*, (pl. of نشز *nashz*) High places. *Inshāz*, (v. n. 4 of نشز) Raising (any thing) from its place. Collecting and carrying bones (which had been taken away) to their proper repository, and piling them one upon another.

A انشاشا *unshāsā*, (SYRIAC) Dried grapes.

A انشاص *inshās*, (v. n. 4 of نشص) Banishing or removing (people) from their native country, compelling (them) to emigrate.

A انشاط *anshāt* or *inshāt*, (A well) full of water, having water near to the mouth or pipe which can be drawn at a single pull of the bucket. *Inshāt*, (v. n. 4 of نشط) Making brisk, cheerful. Putting (a horse) in spirits by proper feeding. Biting (as a serpent). Loosing, untying (a knot). Making a long knot on a camel's tether. Ordering one to drive camels. Seizing, snatching. Having cheerful, well-fed domestics, horses, or cattle.

A انشاع *inshāʿ*, (v. n. 4 of نشع) Putting any thing into the mouth or nose of an infant. Giving (a fortune-teller) his fee. Assisting (to a draught).

A انشاغ *inshāgh*, A retiring to a great distance.

A انشاف *inshāf*, (v. n. 4 of نشف) Giving to drink the froth of new milk (نشفة *nushfat*). Bringing forth a male colt after a female (a camel).

A انشاق *inshāk*, (v. n. 4 of نشق) Snuffing up, or causing to snuff up (any thing cephalic). Catching (deer) by toils.

A انشائيّ *inshāʾiy*, Productive, creative, having the power of production.

A انشتات *inshitāt*, The being dispersed.

A انشتار *inshitār*, (v. n. 7 of شتر) Being inverted

and relaxed (the eye-lids).

A انشجار *inshijār*, (v. n. 7 of شجر) Departing from the eyelids (sleep). Escaping.

A انشخاب *inshikhāb*, (v. n. 7 of شخب) Flowing profusely, streaming (milk). Bursting forth.

A انشداح *inshidāh*, (v. n. 7 of شدح) Lying on the back and stretching out the feet.

A انشداخ *inshidākh*, (v. n. 7 of شدخ) Being broken (any thing hollow). Being cut open.

A انشراث *inshirās*, (v. n. 7 of شرث) Being cracked (the back of the hand); also being thick.

A انشراج *inshirāj*, (v. n. 7 of شرج) Being full of chinks or cracks. Lying open, gaping. Being cracked (the back of the hand).

A انشراح *inshirāh*, (v. n. 7 of شرح) Being opened, expanded. Being cheerful, breathing freely.

A انشراق *inshirāk*, (v. n. 7 of شرق) Being cleft.

A انشرام *inshirām*, (v. n. 7 of شرم) Being split.

A انشط *anshat*, More or most brisk or lively.

A انشطاء *inshitāʼ*, (v. n. 7 of شطا for شطو) Branching out in different ways; being scattered.

A انشطاب *inshitāb*, The flowing (of water).

A انشعاب *inshiʻāb*, (v. n. 7 of شعب) Branching out in many directions. Being absent; withdrawing to a distance. Making peace one with another. Parting from friends, *i. e.* dying.

A انشعاع *inshiʻāʻ*, (v. n. 7 of شعّ) Getting amongst the flock and wasting it (a wolf).

A انشقاق *inshikāk*, (v. n. 7 of شقّ) Branching out in many directions (a tree, a road, or a stream). Being divided, split, cleft, or broken up. Being threaded (a street). Breaking away from off the lightning (a cloud). انشقاق الفجر *inshikāku'l fajr*, The breaking forth of the dawn. انشقاق القمر *inshikāku'l kamar*, Splitting the moon (an operation which some credulous Muhammadans believe was performed by their prophet).

A انشلال *inshilāl*, (v. n. 7 of شلّ) Being driven forward. Descending (rain). Flowing, trickling (a torrent that has not yet attained its strength.)

A انشمار *inshimār*, (v. n. 7 of شمر) Preparing, getting ready for, or setting about (any business). Walking carefully or haughtily.

A انشماص *inshimās*, A being frightened, afraid.

A انشمال *inshimāl*, (v. n. 7 of شمل) Being ready, alert, despatching business. Drawing together one's skirts. Going fast.

A انشناج *inshināj*, (v. n. 7 of شنج) Being shrivelled (the skin).

A انشواء *inshiwāʼ*, (v. n. 7 of شوي) Being roasted.

A انشودة *unshūdat*, (pl. اناشيد *anāshīd*) Verse, when recited in public assemblies.

A انشوطة *unshūtat*, A running knot upon strings, which may easily be loosed (such as is used in the fastening of garments).

A انشياب *inshiyāb*, The being mixed.

A انشيال *inshiyāl*, (v. n. 7 of شال for شول) Being lifted up (a water-pot). Being taken away.

A انشيام *inshiyām*, (v. n. 7 of شام for شيم) Being regarded (with respect), revered. Penetrating.

G انشينية *anshīniya*, Commemoration-festivals.

A انصاء *ansāʼ*, (pl. of نصيّة *nasiyat*) The most excellent, selected. *Insāʼ*, (v. n. 4 of نصا for نصو) Apprehending (any one), taking (him) by his forelocks. (v. n. 4 of نصي) Abounding with a kind of white thistle called نصيّ *nasiy* (ground).

A انصاب *ansāb*, (pl. of نصب *nasb*) The stones erected round the temple of Mecca, to which they repeat لا اله الّا الله *lā ilaha illā allāh*, There is no god but God; and upon which sacrifices were offered up to idols. The seven sacred limits of Mecca. *Insāb*, (v. n. 4 of نصب) Wearing, paining (a disease). Tiring, vexing, wearying. Laying a snare. Fitting a handle, which is called نصاب *nisāb* (to a knife).

A انصات *insāt*, (v. n. 4 of نصت) Keeping silence. Commanding or making any one to keep silence. Listening, paying attention. Having a propensity to jesting and mimicry.

A انصار *ansār*, (pl. of ناصر *nāsir*) Assistants, defenders, auxiliaries, friends, confederates, warriors, protectors, applied particularly to the citizens of Madīna, who assisted Muhammad when obliged to fly from Mecca. This word signifies also Christians, though they are, by Muhammadans, more commonly called نصاري *nasāra'* (Nazarenes).

A انصاريّ *ansāriy*, Belonging to those friends of Muhammad who are called انصار *ansār*.

A انصاع *insāʻ*, (v. n. 4 of نصع) Acknowledging and discharging (a debt). Disclosing what is in one's mind. Preparing for mischief. Wishing for, or rushing to, battle. Holding to the stallion (a she-camel). Standing on end with horror (hair).

A انصاف *ansāf*, (pl. of نصف *nisf*) Halves. (pl. of نصف *nasaf*) Middle-aged (men or women). *Insāf*, (v. n. 4 of نصف) Dividing, taking half. Being mid-day, attaining its middle (the day). Adjusting (a difference) equitably. Serving. Doing (any thing) quickly. Equity, justice. Immediately. P انصاف ستاندن *insāf sitāndan*, To avenge. با انصاف *bā insāf*, With justice. Just. Justly. بي انصاف *bī insāf*, Unjust.

A انصافاً *insāfan*, Speedily, quickly.

A انصال *insāl*, (v. n. 4 of نصل) Taking off the head (نصل *nasl* of an arrow or spear). Fixing a head (upon a spear). Extracting (an arrow). Putting forth prickles (the plant بهمي *buhma'*).

A انصب *ansab*, Straight-horned (goat).

A انصباء *ansibāʼ*, (also انصبة *ansibat*) (pl. of نصيب *nasīb*) Parts, portions. Chances. Good fortunes. Prizes (in a lottery).

A انصباب *insibāb*, (v. n. 7 of صبّ) Being outpoured: being shed, spilled. Raining, flowing.

A انصبان *insibān*, A retiring, returning.

A انصداع *insidāʻ*, A being split asunder, disjoined.

A انصر *ansar*, Uncircumcised.

A انصراح *insirāh*, The being clear, plain, open.

A انصراع *insirāʻ*, A falling into epileptic fits.

A انصراف *insirāf*, (v. n. 7 of صرف) Retiring, going off, returning. Departing. Flowing. Being declined, or declinable (a noun). Departure.

A انصرام *insirām*, (v. n. 7 of صرم) Being broken off, cut off, or terminated.

A انصع *ansaʻ*, Purer, clearer, purest, cleanest.

A انصف *ansaf*, More or most just and equitable.

A انصفاق *insifāk*, (v. n. 7 of صفق) Retiring, returning, departing. Being shut. Being opened.

A انصل *ansul*, (pl. of نصل *nasl*) Sharp points, heads (of darts): pointed awns or beards (of corn).

A انصلات *insilāt*, A running full speed.

A انصلاح *insilāh*, A being restored or amended.

A انصلاع *insilāʻ*, (v. n. 7 of صلع) Breaking forth from behind a cloud, and coming to its zenith.

A انصماء *insimāʼ*, (v. n. 7 of صما) Being attacked. (v. n. 7 of صمي) Being poured out.

A انصماع *insimāʻ*, A walking off in a rage.

A انصولة *unsūlat*, (pl. اناصيل *anāsīl*) The flower or thistle-down of a kind of wall herb called نصل *nasl* or بهمي *buhma'*.

A انصهار *insihār*, The being melted, dissolved.

A انصياب *insiyāb*, (v. n. 7 of صاب for صوب) Being poured forth. Falling (rain).

A انصيات *insiyāt*, (v. n. 7 of صات for صوت) Hearing, answering, obeying when called, accepting, consenting. From being crooked, becoming straight. Going into concealment. Being erect and upright. Growing old. Becoming celebrated, ringing with the fame of any one (an age).

A انصياح *insiyāh*, (v. n. 7 of صاح for صوح) Being cleft (the earth). Being rent (a garment). Shining forth (the moon).

A انصياخ *insiyākh*, (v. n. 7 of صاخ for صيخ) Descending into the ground.

A انصيار *insiyār*, (v. n. 7 of صار for صور) Being inclined, propense. Being bent.

A انصياع *insiyāʻ*, (v. n. 7 of صاع for صوع) Becoming separated, dispersed. Turning back quickly. Being twisted. Passing quickly by.

A انصياغ *insiyāgh*, (v. n. 7 of صاغ for صوغ) Being fashioned, moulded. Being prepared, arranged.

A أنض *aniza*, (fut. يأنض *yaʼnizu*) (The meat) stunk. *Anuza*, (fut. يأنض *yaʼnuzu*) (The meat) was ill-dressed.

A انضاء *anzāʼ*, (pl. of نضو *nizw*) Emaciated (cattle). Iron bits, &c. (separate from the bridles). *Inzāʼ*, (v. n. 4 of نضا for نضو) Making lean, extenuating, dissolving, macerating. Giving away (an emaciated camel). Wearing (a garment) threadbare.

A انضاب *inzāb*, (v. n. 4 of نضب) Bringing or pulling towards you. Drawing a bow.

A انضاج *inzāj*, (v. n. 4 of نضج) Maturing, bringing to maturity, causing to ripen. Cooking properly or thoroughly.

A انضاح *anzāh*, (pl. of نضح *nazah*) Watering-ponds. *Inzāh*, (v. n. 4 of نضح) Beginning to fill (ears of corn). Scattering urine. Tarnishing (the honour of another).

A انضاد *anzād*, (pl. of نضد *nazad*) Bed-cloths laid one upon another. Counterpanes, carpets, cushions; the most valuable kinds of such furniture; the beds, couches, thrones, or places where those coverlets are spread. Noble, eminent (men). Nobilities. Fathers, uncles, or ancestors (eminent for birth, fortune, bravery, or merit). Fat camels. Clouds, which have the appearance of being heaped one upon another. Rocks (falling from mountains) piled one over another. Crowds or troops of men.

A انضار *inzār*, (v. n. 4 of نضر) Shining, being beautiful (face or colour). Endowing with beauty.

A انضاض *inzāz*, (v. n. 4 of نضّ) Giving little milk (to lambs or kids). Expediting, despatching.

A انضاف *inzāf*, (v. n. 4 of نضف) Causing to break wind. Trotting (a camel). Making (a camel) trot. Eating a great deal of organy or bastard-marjoram, which is called نضف *nazaf* (camels).

A انضال *inzāl*, A fatiguing, a making lean.

A انضباح *inzibāh*, (v. n. 7 of ضبح) Becoming changed by the action of fire (colour).

A انضّة *anizzat*, (pl. of نضيضة *nazīzat*) Moderate (rains).

A انضجاع *inzijāع*, (v. n. 7 of ضجع) Reclining on one side (on a bed or on the ground).

A انضر *anzar*, Florid, vivid, shining, bright. More or most flourishing. Gold or silver of the finest kind: a lump of pure gold or virgin silver. *Anzur*, (pl. of نضر *nazr*) Golds. Silvers.

A انضراء *inzirāع*, (v. n. 7 of ضرأ) Being killed, put to death (a camel). Withering (a tree).

A انضراج *inzirāj*, (v. n. 7 of ضرج) Being cleft, divided. Being very wide apart (saying and doing). Existing (a distance or separation). Pouncing on his prey (an eagle). Being ample, extended. Becoming burst (the pod which envelopes the blossoms of the date).

A انضراح *inzirāh*, The being wide asunder.

A انضفار *inzifār*, A being platted (two ropes).

A انضماخ *inzimākh*, A being profusely anointed.

A انضمار *inzimār*, A being flexible after emission.

A انضمام *inzimām*, (v. n. 7 of ضمّ) Being bound, drawn together. Being slender in the middle. Close contact, conjunction. Addition, increase.

A انضناط *inzināt*, A crowding round a well.

A انضواء *inziwāع*, An inclining towards.

A انضياج *inziyāj*, A lying widely extended.

A انضياع *inziyāع*, (v. n. 7 of ضاع for ضوع) Fluttering (as a young bird going to be fed). Writhing and throwing himself about (a boy when crying).

A انضية *anziyat*, (pl. of نضيّ *naziy*) Cattle emaciated with extreme labour. Arrows without heads or feathers. Gaming arrows newly polished but not used. Heads of arrows or javelins. Backs of necks or joints from the ears to the shoulders. Penes.

A انطّ *anatt*, Distant. A distant journey.

A انطاء *antāع*, (pl. of نطاة *natāt*) The pedicles of unripe dates. Branches whence the clusters hang. *Intāع*, (v. n. 4 of نطا for نطو in the dialect of Arabia Felix) Giving.

A انطابلس *antābulus*, Name of a city in Africa.

A انطاع *antāع*, (pl. of نطع نطع *nitع*) Sheets of dressed leather, which they spread out as a table or table-cloth, and used occasionally as a draught-board.

A انطاف *intāf*, (v. n. 4 of نطف) Rendering suspected, accusing of crimes, making notorious for any thing bad.

A انطاق *intāk*, (v. n. 4 of نطق) Bestowing the faculty of speech. Enabling to speak.

A انطاكيّ *antākiy*, Belonging to, or a native of, Antioch, in Syria. The herb scammony, or a medicine prepared with it (so called because carried into Persia from Antioch).

A انطاكية *antākiyat*, Antioch.

A انطباخ *intibākh*, (v. n. 7 of طبخ) Being cooked.

A انطباع *intibāع*, (v. n. 7 of طبع) Being stamped, sealed. Being printed. Being trained, disciplined.

A انطباق *intibāk*, The being covered with a lid.

A انطحاح *intihāh*, (v. n. 7 of طحّ) Being outstretched, expanded.

A انطراب *intirāb*, The being delighted.

A انطراح *intirāh*, The being thrown prostrate.

A انطسام *intisām*, A being obliterated.

A انطفاء *intifāع*, (v. n. 7 of طفئ) Being extinguished, quenched; going out (a fire).

A انطلاس *intilās*, (v. n. 7 of طلس) Being hidden or intricate (business).

A انطلاق *intilāk*, (v. n. 7 of طلق) Being dismissed, divorced. Departing, going away. Being cheerful (the countenance).

A انطلة *antalat*, Evils, misfortunes.

G انطليون *antalyūn*, The rainbow.

A انطماس *intimās*, A being obliterated, effaced.

A انطمال *intimāl*, An associating with thieves.

A انطواء *intiwāع*, (v. n. 7 of طوي) Being folded together, coiled up.

A انطياد *intiyād*, (v. n. 7 of طاد for طود) Ascending high in the air.

A انطيار *intiyār*, The being split, cleft.

A انطياع *intiyāع*, (v. n. 7 of طاع for طوع) Being or becoming obedient, submissive. Submission.

A انظار *anzār*, (pl. of نظر) Looks. Eyes. *Inzār*, (v. n. 4 of نظر) Listening, lending an ear. Deferring, delaying, putting off. Giving time.

A انظام *anzām*, Particles (of sand) adhering together. A string of pearls. A row of eggs; also the egg-bed (in fowls). *Inzām*, (v. n. 4 of نظم) Having a row of eggs in her belly (a hen). Having the lines called نظامان *nizāmāni* (a lizard or a fish).

A انظامان *inzāmāni*, Two white lines on the back of a Lybian lizard, from the head to the tail.

A انظلام *inzilām*, The submitting to injuries.

A انظمة *anzimat*, (pl. of نظام *nizām*) Bases, constitutions of things.

A انظور *anzūru*, (amongst some Arabians for انظر *anzuru*) I see, I behold.

A انظومتان *unzūmatāni*, Two white lines on the back of a fish or lizard, from the head to the tail.

A انعات *inعāt*, (v. n. 4 of نعت) Being endued with a handsome face, worthy of being described.

A انعاث *inعās*, (v. n. 4 of نعث) Preparing to proceed (on a journey). Squandering (money), being profuse, lavish. هم في انعاث *hum fī anعās*, They act or proceed diligently.

A انعاج *inعāj*, (v. n. 4 of نعج) Having fat camels.

A انعار *inعār*, (v. n. 4 of نعر) Producing fruit (the plant اراك *arāk*).

A انعاس *inعās*, (v. n. 4 of نعس) Begetting heavy, sleepy children. Putting (any one) to sleep.

A انعاش *inعāsh*, (v. n. 4 of نعش) Exalting.

A انعاظ *inعāz*, (v. n. 4 of نعظ) Being extremely libidinous (a man or woman). Causing an erection. Being mad a-horsing (a mare).

A انعاف *inعāf*, (v. n. 4 of نعف not in use) Sitting on the declivity of a mountain.

A انعال *inعāl*, (v. n. 4 of نعل) Shoeing (a horse). Putting on shoes. Having many slippers.

A انعام *anعām*, (pl. of نعم *naعam*) Camels, cattle, animals. *Inعām*, (v. n. 4 of نعم) Bestowing abundance, conferring a favour. Rendering soft and pleasant. Doing (any thing) well. Saying نعم *naعam*, Yes. Slipping, stealing upon one with naked feet or on tip-toe. Increasing. Striving, straining every nerve. Being comfortable, commodious (house). A donative, benefaction, gratuity, largess, favour. A gift from a superior to an inferior. A grant of land for charitable purposes.

P انعام فرمودن *inعām farmūdan*, To bestow a favour.

A انعامات *inعāmāt*, Presents. Favours.

P انعام دار *inعām-dār*, A holder of an انعام *inعām*, one enjoying rent-free land. A beneficiary.

A انعتال *inعitāl*, (v. n. 7 of عتل) Being dragged or treated roughly. Quitting a place, going with.

A انعجام *inعijām*, (v. n. 7 of عجم) Being difficult, closed, or impeded.

A انعدال *inعidāl*, (v. n. 7 of عدل) Deviating from the right way. Curvature, obliquity.

A انعراج *inعirāj*, (v. n. 7 of عرج) Being bent. Bending (one's) self. Inclining westward (the sun).

A انعزال *inعizāl*, (v. n. 7 of عزل) Retiring. Choosing retirement. Being dismissed.

A انعساف *inعisāf*, A being bent, folded, twisted.

A انعشاش *inعishāsh*, (v. n. 7 of عشّ) Being repaired, patched (shirt, shift, or other under garment).

A انعصاب *inعisāb*, The being firm and strong.

A انعصار *inعisār*, A being squeezed, expressed.

A انعصام ingisām, (v. n. 7 of عصم) Being preserved, defended. Keeping clear of sin and danger.

A انعطاط ingitāt, (v. n. 7 of عط) Being rent (a garment). Being bent without breaking, or rather being broken without any apparent fracture (wood).

A انعطاف ingitāf, A being bent, turned, folded.

A انعطان ingitān, (v. n. 7 of عطن) Being macerated with dung, salt, and the plant علقي galka' (hides). Stinking (a skin).

A انعفار ingifār, A being rolled in, soiled with dust.

A انعفاس ingifās, (v. n. 7 of عفس) Being covered with, or rolled in, the dust.

A انعفاق ingifāk, (v. n. 7 of عفق) Advancing rapidly in any work.

A انعقاد ingikād, (v. n. 7 of عقد) Being firmly bound, fixed, established, concluded, agreed upon, stipulated, bargained. Being set (fruit-blossoms). Being coagulated, curdled. Being tied (the tongue).

A انعقار ingikār, (v. n. 7 of عقر) Being hurt and galled (the back of a beast by the saddle).

A انعقاف ingikāf, The being bent, curved.

A انعقاق ingikāk, (v. n. 7 of عقّ) Being cleft, split, or divided. Being dissolved in rain (clouds). Flying about (dust). Being untied (a knot).

A انعكاس ingikās, (v. n. 7 of عكس) Being turned upside down. Being inverted or transposed. Reflection (from a mirror). Repercussion, reverberation.

A انعم angam, Softer. Softest. Angum, (pl. of نعم nugm) Successes, prosperities. Conveniences. (pl. of نعمة nigmat) Presents, gifts, benefits, favours.

A انعماد ingimād, (v. n. 7 of عمد) Being supported, propped up. Standing upon a column.

A انعمام ingimām, (v. n. 7 of عمّ) Wrapping a turban-sash (عمامة gimāmat) about the head.

A انعواء ingiwās, A being twisted, bent, distorted.

A انعياج ingiyāj, (v. n. 7 of عوج) Inclining, leaning; feeling an inclination towards.

A انغاء inghās, The act of speaking intelligibly.

A انغار inghār, (v. n. 4 of نغر) Yielding milk mixed with blood. Being rotten, addle (an egg).

A انغاص inghās, (v. n. 4 of نغص) Making (life) uncomfortable. Rendering muddy and dull.

A انغاض inghāz, (v. n. 4 of نغض) Moving the head (in wonder). Being moved.

A انغال inghāl, (v. n. 4 of نغل) Spoiling (a hide) in tanning. Sowing dissensions, breeding mischief.

A انغراز inghirāz, (v. n. 7 of غرز) Being thrust into.

A انغراف inghirāf, A being broken or cut off.

A انغساس inghisās, The being dipped in water.

A انغسال inghisāl, (v. n. 7 of غسل) Being washed.

A انغضاض inghizāz, (v. n. 7 of غضّ) Winking.

A انغضاف inghizāf, (v. n. 7 of غضف) Being enveloped in dust. Falling in, choking up (a well).

A انغفاء inghifās, A being broken. Rout, defeat.

A انغلال inghilāl, (v. n. 7 of غلّ) Being inserted (one thing into another). Entering, penetrating.

A انغمار inghimār, A sinking into the water.

A انغماس inghimās, A being plunged into water.

A انغماض inghimāz, (v. n. 7 of غمض) Winking. Being half-closed (the eye).

A انغمال inghimāl, (v. n. 7 of غمل) Being put under ground (a skin with the hair on). Becoming soft, stinking, and losing the hair (a skin).

A انغمام inghimām, (v. n. 7 of غمّ) Being closed, stopped up (the mouth or nostrils). Being covered over and concealed. Being sorrowful. Sadness.

A انغمان inghimān, A being buried under ground.

A انغواء inghiwās, Inclining. A falling down.

A انغياء inghiyās, (v. n. 7 of غوي) Being deceived, seduced. Bending. Falling down.

A انغياض inghiyāz, (v. n. 7 of غاض for غيض) Decreasing, falling, sinking into the ground (water).

A انغياط inghiyāt, The being bent (as wood).

A آنف ānaf, (A field) the quickest in producing vegetation. More or most ashamed. Ānif, High, disposed to resent an affront. (A camel) pained in the nose by the ring. Preceding. The first part of any given time. آنفا ānifan, A little before, a while ago. The first time. Now. آنفا و سالفا ānifan wa sālifan, Now and formerly. Ānuf, (pl. of انف anf) Noses.

A انف anf, (v. n. of انف) Striking the nose. Reaching as high as the nose (water). Treading upon fresh, untrodden pasture (camels). (pl. انوف unūf, آناف ānāf, and آنف ānuf) A nose, a ness. A lord, a prince. The beginning of any thing. The strongest or most vehement of any thing. The point of a tooth when it first appears. The tip of a camel's hoof. انف الارض anfu'l arz, That part of the ground which is exposed to the sun. انف البرد anfu'l bard, Intenseness of cold. انف الجبل anfu'l jabal, The nose or ness of a mountain, i.e. a promontory. انف رغيف anfi raghīf, A bit of of bread. انف الشدّ anfu'sh shadd, The greatest vehemence. انف القوم anfu'l kawm, The prince or chief of the people. انف اللحية anfu'l lihyat, The tip of the beard. انف المطر anfu'l matar, The first sprouts produced by the rain. حميّ الانف hamīyu'l anf, One who defends his nose, i.e. who preserves his dignity or gravity; lofty, fastidious. سميّ الانف samīyu'l anf, High-nosed, aquiline-nosed. جعل انفه في قفاه jagala anfahu fī kafāhi, He put his nose in his neck, i.e. he turned from the right way, he committed iniquity. يتتبّع انفه yatatab-bagu anfahu, He follows his nose, i.e. he goes right. انف في السماء واست في الماء anf fi's samās wa ist fi'l mās, Spoken of one who boasts much, but performs not. Anaf, (v. n. of انف) Disdaining. Colouring up, being ashamed. Loathing, desiring nothing (a pregnant woman). Being hurt by the nose-ring (a camel). Anif, (A camel) pained in the nose by the ring. Unuf, A handsome gait. امر انف amrun unuf, A new act hitherto performed by no one. روضة انف rawzat unuf A meadow not yet grazed. كاس انف kas unuf, A new cup (one out of which nobody has drank). من ذي انف min zi unufin, Anon, by and by.

A انفا anifan, A little while ago. The first time.

A انفاج infāj, (v. n. 4 of نفج) Removing the pail, for a moment, from under the dugs, whilst milking. Making (a hare) bounce; starting game.

A انفاد infād, (v. n. 4 of نفد) Consuming, exhausting. Failing (water in a well).

A انفاذ infāz, (v. n. 4 of نفذ) Transmitting, causing (any thing) to pass, penetrate, pervade, or be received. Performing, achieving. Entering into (a tribe) and becoming one of them. Walking through a crowd. Passing clean through and leaving behind. Sending (a letter or messenger).

A انفار anfār, (pl. of نفر nafar) Individuals, persons. Soldiers. Servants. Infār, (v. n. 4 of نفر) Aiding, assisting, relieving, redressing. Proclaiming conqueror, pronouncing victor. Terrifying, putting to flight. Extending, prolonging.

A انفاز infāz, (v. n. 4 of نفز) Turning (an arrow upon the nail, to try its goodness). Dandling.

A انفاس anfās, (pl. of نفس nafas) Breathings, spirits. Intervals, breathing times. Voices, words, utterings, songs, intonations. P انفاس مشكبار anfāsi mushk-bār, Sweet or musky words. A Infās, (v. n. 4 of نفس) Rendering wishful, desirous. Affording pleasure. Causing surprise. Being precious.

A انفاسا anfāsan, By intervals.

A انفاش infāsh, (v. n. 4 of نفش) Allowing (cattle) to pasture at night without a shepherd.

A انفاص infās, (v. n. 4 of نفص) Speaking fast. Laughing much. Making signs with the lips.

A انفاض infāz, (v. n. 4 of نفض) Having many young ones (camels). Losing many cattle. Being destitute, or having a scarcity of, or consuming all the provisions for a journey. Being rained upon. Shaking (dates) out of a basket. Being finished, exhausted, consumed.

A انفاط infāt, (v. n. 4 of نفط) Blistering the hand (labour). Scattering urine here and there.

A انفاع infāg, (v. n. 4 of نفع) Selling walking-sticks (called نفعة nafgat).

P انفاق infāk, Oil of olives.

A انفاق infāk, (v. n. 4 of نفق) Expending, disbursing. Spending (one's substance), waxing poor. Having goods easily vendible. Being spent (money). Having a brisk market, disposing rapidly of one's wares. Having their coat staring with fat (camels).

G انفاق unfāk, The juice of unripe grapes.

A انفال anfāl, (pl. of نفل nafal) Plunder, spoils (especially those taken from unbelievers in the Muhammadan religion). Presents, gifts. Infāl, (v. n. 4 of نفل) Giving presents, bestowing largely. Taking a hatchet to cut down the tragacanth-tree, wherewith to feed camels.

A انفان anfān, Large-nosed. Arrogant, haughty.

A انفاه *infāh*, (v. n. 4 of نفه) Debilitating, fatiguing. Giving away little.

A انفة *anfat*, The beginning or exordium (of a prayer). انفة الصبيّ *anfatu's sabīy*, The commencement or quickness of a child's growth.

A انفة *anafat*, (v. n. of انف) Disdaining, loathing. Colouring up, blushing. Loathing, desiring nothing (a pregnant woman). Being hurt by the nose-ring (a camel).

P انفت *anfat*, Loss, damage.

A انفتات *infitāt*, A being broken, or crumbled.

A انفتاح *infitāh*, (v. n. 7 of فتح) Being open (a door). Opening itself (a wound), bursting (a pod).

A انفتاق *infitāḳ*, (v. n. 7 of فتق) Being split, burst in sunder; cracking. Being very wide (a woman). Suffering under a fatal disorder (a camel), the seat of which is between the navel and the udder. Overtaking, overwhelming (as misfortune).

A انفتال *infitāl*, A being twisted. A receding.

A انفثاث *infisās*, A being broken. Defeat.

A انفجاء *infijāʿ*, The being opened (a door).

A انفجاج *infijāj*, (v. n. 7 of فجّ) Being wide between the handle and string (a bow).

A انفجار *infijār*, (v. n. 7 of فجر) Bursting out and flowing freely. Being dispelled by, and retiring before, the rising dawn (shades of night). Being diffusive in munificence. Bursting forth (dawn). Bursting in upon one from every quarter (misfortunes).

A انفجانيّ *anfajānīy*, A great and vain talker.

A انفحاق *infiḥāḳ*, A becoming open and wide.

A انفحة *infahat*, (انفحّة *infahhat* or *infihhat*) (pl. انافح *anāfih*) A kind of substance of a yellow colour which is taken from the stomachs of sucking lambs or kids, and preserved in cotton for curdling milk; rennet. The stomach of a sucking lamb or kid (when these animals begin to graze and ruminate, it is called كرش *kirsh* or *karish*). *Infahat*, A tree resembling the brinjal.

A انفحام *infiḥām*, The act of rushing into a thing.

A انفخ *anfakh*, One who has swelled testicles.

A انفخات *infikhāt*, (v. n. 7 of فخت) Being perforated, being full of holes (a roof).

A انفخان *infikhān*, (*unfukhān*, انفخانيّ *infikhānīy* or *unfukhānīy*) Swelling with fat (paunch).

P انفخت *anfakht*, Gain. Capital, stock.

P انفختن *anfakhtan*, To gain, to acquire.

A انفداء *infidāʿ*, (v. n. 7 of فدي) Being ransomed.

A انفداع *infidāʿ*, (v. n. 7 of فدع) Being crooked (the pastern joint of a quadruped).

A انفداغ *infidāgh*, The being weak from dryness.

A انفذ *anfaz*, More or most piercing, pervading.

A انفراء *infirāʿ*, A being cleft asunder, gaping wide.

A انفراث *infirās*, (v. n. 7 of فرث) Being pierced (the stomach or liver) and their contents let out. Falling into a swoon or fainting fit (such particularly as a pregnant woman is subject to).

A انفراج *infirāj*, (v. n. 7 of فرج) Gaping, cleaving asunder. Being separate, distant. Being dispelled (grief). Recreation, relaxation of mind. An interval, space, cleft, chink.

A انفراد *infirād*, (v. n. 7 of فرد) Choosing and using one thing only. Being alone. Retiring by one's self. Accomplishing (any work) alone. Singleness, singularity. علي الانفراد *ʿala' l infirād*, (or انفراداً *infirādan*) Singly, one by one.

A انفراش *infirāsh*, (v. n. 7 of فرش) Being spread out and flattened.

A انفراق *infirāḳ*, The being separated, divided.

A انفراك *infirāk*, (v. n. 7 of فرك) Being rubbed in the hands (an ear of corn, linen, &c.). Having the shoulder dislocated.

A انفزار *infizār*, (v. n. 7 of فزر) Being torn, rent.

A انفس *anfas*, More or most precious. *Anfus*, (pl. of نفس *nafs*) Minds, spirits, souls. Persons.

A انفساح *infisāh*, (v. n. 7 of فسح) Being spacious and roomy. Expanding (the bosom). Joy.

A انفساخ *infisākh*, (v. n. 7 of فسخ) Being broken, dissolved, violated, dislocated. Being nullified. Becoming loose and separated from the skin (wool). Being spoiled, and running (the colour of a garment). Being excommunicated, anathematized.

A انفساد *infisād*, (v. n. 7 of فسد) Being corrupted.

A انفساق *infisāḳ*, (v. n. 7 of فسق) Quitting its shell (a ripe date).

P انفست *anfust*, A spider's web.

A انفشاح *infishāh*, (v. n. 7 of فشح) Straddling in walking. Keeping the legs apart when in pain.

A انفشاش *infishāsh*, (v. n. 7 of فشّ) Escaping from a bladder or leathern bag (wind). Abating (a swelling or inflammation). Being slothful in the performance of any business.

A انفشاط *infishāt*, (v. n. 7 of فشط not used) Being broken (a green bough).

A انفشاغ *infishāgh*, (v. n. 7 of فشغ) Being many. Appearing, being conspicuous.

A انفصاء *infisāʿ*, The being set at liberty.

A انفصاد *infisād*, (v. n. 7 of فصد) Having leaves bursting from the pods (a tree).

A انفصاص *infisās*, (v. n. 7 of فصّ) Being separated; departing, going off.

A انفصاع *infisāʿ*, (v. n. 7 of فصع) Being brought forth, drawn out (the gland from a lad's foreskin).

A انفصال *infisāl*, (v. n. 7 of فصل) Being separated. Separation, division. Final adjustment, decision, settling, termination (of a cause).

A انفصام *infisām*, (v. n. 7 of فصم) Being broken without a separation of the parts. Being broken and cut off. A fracture, rupture. Interruption.

P انفصام پذير *infisām-pazīr*, Broken, interrupted.

A انفضاج *infizāj*, (v. n. 7 of فضج) Having the roots of the hair moist with perspiration. Being filled with fat (the body). Being wrinkled (a camel's body). Appearing clear (the horizon). Bursting (a boil). Leaking (as a leathern bottle). Being open (the navel). Being weak and languid (business). Becoming very fat.

A انفضاح *infizāh*, A being exposed to infamy.

A انفضاخ *infizākh*, (v. n. 7 of فضخ) Being opened and burst (an ulcer or boil), becoming wide (a sore). Weeping profusely. Pouring out its contents (a bucket). Being cut open (a camel's bunch). Being broken (a green branch).

A انفضاض *infizāz*, (v. n. 7 of فضّ) Being broken open (the seal of a letter). Becoming exhausted (an udder). Being separated, scattered, dispersed (flocks). Breaking up (an assembly).

A انفطار *infitār*, The being split, cleft, riven.

A انفطاش *infitāsh*, (v. n. 7 of فطش) Being broken (as wood), especially when green or wet.

A انفطام *infitām*, (v. n. 7 of فطم) Being prohibited. Abstaining. Arriving at the end or extremity.

A انفطينا *anfitīnā*, A wild rose.

A انفع *anfaʿ*, More or most useful, convenient, profitable, available, or serviceable.

A انفعاس *infiʿās*, A gaping, cleaving asunder.

A انفعال *infiʿāl*, (v. n. 7 of فعل) Being wrought. Shame, ignominy. P انفعال خوردن *infiʿāl khwurdan*, To blush, to be ashamed.

A انفغار *infighār*, (v. n. 7 of فغر) Opening, unclosing itself (the mouth).

A انفغام *infighām*, (v. n. 7 of فغم) Breaking up, being loosed and going off (a cold in the head).

P انفغده *anfaghda*, Liquid gold or silver.

A انفقاء *infiḳāʿ*, (v. n. 7 of فقأ) Being torn out (eye), burst by squeezing (imposthume). Being stripped off the head of a new-born child (the caul).

A انفقاس *infiḳās*, (v. n 7 of فقس) Being turned upon a bird, and holding him (a curved stick). Being burst (an egg-shell).

A انفقاع *infiḳāʿ*, (v. n. 7 of نقع) Being split, cleft.

A انفقاق *infiḳāḳ*, A being disjoined, separated.

P انفقده *anfaḳda*, Liquid gold or silver.

P انفقون رومي *anfaḳūni rūmī*, A species of inodorous rose.

A انفكاك *infikāk*, (v. n. 7 of فكّ) Being put out of joint. Being separated. Being set free. Being dispelled. Failing, ceasing to be.

A انفلات *infilāt*, (v. n. 7 of فلت) Being set at liberty, escaping, slipping by.

A انفلاص *infilās*, A being delivered, escaping.

A انفلاع *infilāʿ*, A being cut, or cleft asunder.

A انفلاق *infilāḳ*, (v. n. 7 of فلق) Being split, shivered. Being diffused. Separating, being parted.

A انفلال *infilāl*, (v. n. 7 of فلّ) Being notched (a sword). Being routed (an army).

P انفنج *anfanj*, Glue.

P انفوج *anfūj*, or *unfūj*, Contracted, wrinkled.

A انفهاق *infihāḳ*, (v. n. 7 of فهق) Spreading, diffusing itself widely (lightning).

A انفئاء *infiʾāʿ*, (v. n. 7 of فأو not used) Being split asunder, being wide open.

A انفياز *infiyāz*, A being single, alone, solitary.

A انفياق *infiyāḳ*, (v. n. 7 of فاق for فوق) Being broken (notch of an arrow). Being lean and dying.

A آنق *ānaḳ*, Extremely earnest in any pursuit.

A انق *anaḳ*, (v. n. of انق) Being joyful and glad. Liking, being pleased with. Joy, cheerfulness. Forage, fodder. *Aniḳ*, Pleasing, agreeable.

A انقاء *anḳāʼ*, (pl. of نقا *naḳaʼ*) Heaps of sand. The bones of the arms. (pl. of نقو *naḳw* or *niḳw*) Marrows. Marrow-bones. (pl. of نقي *niḳy*) Marrows. Fat parts of eyes. *Inḳāʼ*, (v. n. 4 of نقا for نقو) Choosing, selecting. Becoming fat. Having bones full of marrow. Being full of flour (wheat).

A انقاب *anḳāb*, The ears. (pl. of نقب *nuḳb*) Scabs. *Inḳāb*, (v. n. 4 of نقب) Having broken, worn, or tender feet (camels). Becoming chamberlain, or master of the ceremonies; also chief or leader. Having a camel whose feet are worn smooth or perforated. Running from country to country, seeking for a place of refuge.

A انقاح *inḳāḥ*, (v. n. 4 of نقح) Polishing verses. Selling the embossings of a sword and other ornaments, on account of the scarcity of provisions.

A انقاد *inḳād*, (v. n. 4 of نقد) Shooting forth leaves (a tree).

A انقاذ *inḳāẕ*, (v. n. 4 of نقذ) Setting at liberty. Turning or causing to go in one direction.

A انقار *inḳār*, (v. n. 4 of نقر) Sparing, abstaining from. Letting go.

A انقاز *inḳāz*, (v. n. 4 of نقز) Killing (an enemy), giving a signal to put him to death. Having cattle of the worst kind called نقز *naḳaz*. Continually drinking pure fresh water. Falling amongst cattle (the disease نقاز *nuḳāz*).

A انقاس *anḳās*, (pl. of نقس *niḳs*) Writing-inks.

A انقاش *inḳāsh*, (v. n. 4 of نقش) Pressing, prosecuting (a debtor). Eating great numbers of ripe dates. Being powerful in venery.

A انقاص *inḳāṣ*, A diminishing. An injuring.

A انقاض *anḳāẓ*, (pl. of نقض *niḳẓ*) (Camels) emaciated and fatigued with travelling. Ruins. Grounds raised up by mushrooms protruding. *Inḳāẓ*, (v. n. 4 of نقض) Applying the tongue to the roof of the mouth and making a noise to urge on a horse. Sounding (as an instrument, echo, or any thing inanimate). Making a noise in chewing the gum of pines. Calling (goats). Pulling the fingers till the joints crack. Striking the fingers until they make a noise. Causing mushrooms to spring out of the earth. Crying (an eagle). Pressing heavily (the back). (A sack) galling (the back of a beast of burthen). The cry of a young camel's colt (when full grown this sound is then called هدير *hadīr* and قرقرة *karkarat*).

A انقاع *inḳāʻ*, (v. n. 4. of نقع) Macerating or dissolving (a medicine in water) and applying it. Steeping, soaking, Killing (an enemy). Raising the voice and making a continued noise, ballooing. Satisfying thirst (water). Slaughtering (a camel on account of the arrival of strangers). Deflowering a virgin. Injuring or privately hatching mischief (against another). Filliping the nose (of another). Turning a house topsy-turvy. Burying (the dead). Adorning, beautifying a house. Stagnating in the body and becoming yellow (water).

A انقاف *inḳāf*, (v. n. 4 of نقف) Cutting or splitting a colocynth, and taking off the rind and core. Giving a bone (in order to have the marrow extracted). Filling (a valley) with eggs (locusts).

A انقال *anḳāl*, (pl. of نقل *naḳl*) Clouted, patched (shoes or clothes). *Inḳāl*, (v. n. 4 of نقل) Mending clothes by patching. Making a boot or leather shoe for a sore-footed camel.

A انقاه *inḳāh*, (v. n. 4 of نقه) Restoring to health.

A انقباء *inḳibāʼ*, A hiding one's self, a lurking.

A انقباس *inḳibās*, (v. n. 7 of قبس) Being drawn in, sheathed (a horse's yard).

A انقباض *inḳibāẓ*, (v. n. 7 of قبض) Being seized, grasped in the hand, drawn in, contracted. Drawing one's self in. Being contracted. Contracting the brow. Decreasing, becoming shorter (a shadow). Going, making haste. Detention, retention, impediment (in speech). Constipation.

A انقباع *inḳibāʻ*, (v. n. 7 of قبع) Being concealed. Settling in its nest snug and concealed (a bird).

A انقحال *inḳiḥāl*, The being full of years.

A انقحام *inḳiḥām*, (v. n. 7 of قحم) Being thrown headlong. Being forced into a river (a horse).

A انقحر *inḳahr*, Aged with remains of strength.

A انقحل *inḳahl*, Dry-skinned (old man).

A انقخ *anḳakh*, (An ostrich) having little brain.

A انقد *anḳad*, A hedge-hog. بات بليل انقد *bāta bi layli anḳada*, He led a sleepless night (he passed the night like a hedge-hog, as that animal, it is said, does not sleep during the night). الانقد *al anḳad*, A tortoise.

A انقداح *inḳidāḥ*, A striking fire.

A انقداد *inḳidād*, (v. n. 7 of قد) Being cut lengthwise into strips or thongs.

A انقدار *inḳidār*, (v. n. 7 of قدر) Being cut out exactly to the measure (a garment).

A انقداع *inḳidāʻ*, A ceasing, a refraining.

A انقدان *inḳadān*, A tortoise.

P آنقدر *ānḳadar*, (آن and قدر) So many, so much.

A انقذ *anḳaẕ*, A porcupine.

A انقذام *inḳiẕām*, A hastening, a making speed.

A انقراض *inḳirāẓ*, (v. n. 7 of قرض) Becoming extinct, disappearing without leaving a vestige. Being gnawed asunder. Extinction. Consummation, end, accomplishment. انقراض الزمان *inḳirāẓu'z zamān*, The end or consummation of time.

A انقراع *inḳirāʻ*, (v. n. 7 of قرع) Refusing, being stubborn. Turning and tossing one's self about all night. Abstaining from, hanging back.

A انقرة *anḳirat*, (pl. of نقير *naḳīr*) Ditches, trenches. Name of a town in Galatia (Ancyra). Name of a place near Kūfa.

G انقرديا *anḳardiyā*, A kind of Indian fruit.

A انقس *anḳas*, A bondman, born of a female slave. *Anḳus*, (pl. of نقس *niḳs*) Writing-inks.

A انقسام *inḳisām*, A being divided into parts.

A انقشار *inḳishār*, A being barked, peeled.

A انقشاش *inḳishāsh*, (v. n. 7 of قش) Departing, going away. (v. n. 9 of نقش) Pressing, prosecuting a debtor. Eating great quantities of dried dates sprinkled with water. Being potent in venery.

A انقشاط *inḳishāṭ*, (v. n. 7 of قشط) Being serene and free from clouds (the sky).

A انقشاع *inḳishāʻ*, (v. n. 7 of قشع) Being uncovered; being dispelled (a cloud). Being dispersed (an assemblage of people).

A انقص *anḳaṣ*, More or most deficient.

A انقصاد *inḳiṣād*, The being broken, or cleft.

A انقصاف *inḳiṣāf*, (v. n. 7 of قصف) Being broken to pieces. Being jostled, carried forward in a crowd. Retiring from, leaving and passing on.

A انقصال *inḳiṣāl* (v. n. 7 of قصل) Being cut.

A انقصام *inḳiṣām*, (v. n. 7 of قصم) Being broken, so that the parts become separated.

A انقضاء *inḳiẓāʼ*, (v. n. 7 of قضى) Being finished, accomplished, fulfilled, terminated, determined, elapsed. Becoming extinct, consumed, or annihilated. Expiration of a term.

A انقضاب *inḳiẓāb*, A being cut off, or separated.

A انقضاض *inḳiẓāẓ*, (v. n. 7 of قض) Pouncing on its prey (a hawk). Charging the enemy (a troop of horsemen). Being ready to tumble (a wall). Falling (a star).

A انقضاع *inḳiẓāʻ*, (v. n. 7 of قضع) Removing from one's kindred.

A انقضاف *inḳiẓāf*, A being separated.

A انقطاع *inḳiṭāʻ*, (v. n. 7 of قطع) Being broken, cut off, detached. Ceasing to flow. Being stanched, (blood). Being prevented from taking a journey. Being sunk, gone, exhausted (water in a well). Separation, disjunction. Cessation.

G انقطريون *inḳitriyūn*, Amber.

A انقع *anḳaʻ*, (A beverage) which effectually quenches the thirst. الرشف انقع *ar rashfu anḳaʻ*, Sipping is the best quencher of thirst (an expression employed to inculcate gentle measures). *Anḳuʻ*, (pl. of نقع *naḳʻ*) Hard places where water stagnates. Stagnant waters. Slaughters.

A انقعاث *inḳiʻās*, (v. n. 7 of قعث) Being pulled up by the roots. Falling down (any one struck).

A انقعار *inḳiʻār*, The being eradicated.

A انقعاش *inḳiʻāsh*, (v. n. 7 of قعش) Being torn up, and going away. Falling in ruin (a wall).

A انقعاص *inḳiʻāṣ*, A dying. A being bent.

A انقعاف *inḳiʻāf*, (v. n. 7 of قعف) Being dilapidated (wall), falling (precipice). Being displaced.

A انقعة *ankiʿat*, (pl. of نقيع) Wells full of water.

A انقفاش *inkifāsh*, (v. n. 7 of قفش) Retiring to his hole (a spider): also drawing in his legs.

A انقفاع *inkifāʿ*, (v. n. 7 of قفع) Lagging, remaining behind. Abstaining, refusing.

A انقفال *inkifāl*, (v. n. 7 of قفل) Being bolted, locked (a door).

A انقلاء *inkilāʾ*, A kind of Syrian date.

A انقلاب *inkilāb*, (v. n. 7 of قلب) Being turned. Revolution, vicissitude, change, turn. انقلاب زمان *inkilābi zamān*, The vicissitudes of time.

A انقلاع *inkilāʿ*, A being pulled up, torn out.

A انقلاف *inkilāf*, (v. n. 7 of قلف) Being large and spiral (a navel).

P انقله *ankula*, A kind of China-ginger; also an African plant, which is an antidote against poisons. Name of a city in Nubia.

G انقليا *inkiliyā*, Melilot, bugloss.

A انقليس *ankalīs* or *inkalīs*, An eel.

A انقماح *inkimāḥ*, (v. n. 7 of قمح) Raising the head when refusing to drink (a camel).

A انقماس *inkimās*, (v. n. 7 of قمس) Being plunged into water. Setting (a star).

A انقماع *inkimāʿ*, (v. n. 7 of قمع) Being humbled, brought into subjection. Being contemptible. Entering into a house in a clandestine manner.

A انقور *unkūr*, A small furrow in the stone of a date, from whence it germinates.

A انقوعة *unkūʿat*, Any place into which water flows from a canal. A furrow or hollow made in the top of a pudding, into which they pour fat, butter, or any other sauce.

A انقوفة *unkūfat*, That which a woman takes from off the spindle when her work is finished.

G انقون *ankūn*, A fetid rose, whose root has a caustic quality, bastard pellitory, pyrethrum.

A انقهال *inkihāl*, A falling down from weakness.

A انقي *ankaʾ*, Small-boned (man).

A انقياء *ankiyāʾ*, (pl. of نقيّ *nakīy*) Clean, pure.

A انقياب *inkiyāb*, (v. n. 7 of قاب for قوب) Being excavated. Being burst (an egg by a bird).

A انقياد *inkiyād*, (v. n. 7 of قاد for قود) Being led. Submitting. Shelving, sloping. Being clear, open (road). Submission, obedience, subjection.

A انقيار *inkiyār*, (v. n. 7 of قار for قور) Falling down in ruins (a well). Inclining.

A انقياس *inkiyās*, A being measured.

A انقياص *inkiyāṣ*, (v. n. 7 of قاص for قيص) Falling in (a well). Being poured out, falling down (sand or earth). Falling out (a tooth). Abundance of water in a well.

A انقياض *inkiyāz*, (v. n. 7 of قاض for قيض) Being overthrown. Being cracked, but without any separation. Being split lengthwise (a tooth).

A انقيض *inkīz*, Name of a certain aromatic.

A انقيضاض *inkīzāz*, (v. n. 11 of نقض) Being ready to fall (a wall).

P آنك *ānka*, (for آنكه) He who. That which.

P آنك *ānak*, Behold! lo! there! A pimple.

A آنك *ānuk*, Lead. Tin.

A انكاث *ankās*, Untwisted (rope).

A انكاح *inkāḥ*, (v. n. 4 of نكح) Marrying, taking a wife. Giving in marriage.

A انكاد *ankād*, (pl. of نكد *nakd*) Avaricious (men). Miseries.

A انكار *ankār*, (pl. of نكر *nakir*, *nakur*, and *nukur*) Ingenious, intelligent. *Inkār*, (v. n. 4 of نكر) Denying, disavowing. Being ignorant, not knowing, ignoring. Disapproving, disallowing, rejecting. Losing one's wits. Denial. Objection.

A انكاريّ *inkāriy*, Negative.

A انكاز *inkāz*, (v. n. 4 of نكز) Emptying (a well).

A انكاس *ankās*, (pl. of نكس *niks*) Weak, imbecile: unable to rise to any thing honourable. (Arrows) broken at the notches. (Spears) broken near the root so that the lower points are used as well as the heads. Bows and arrows, inversely and preposterously formed. Preposterous births.

A انكاظ *inkāz*, The act of ordering to make haste.

A انكاع *inkāʿ*, (v. n. 4 of نكع) Removing quickly. Repelling. Being wearied. Fatiguing.

A انكاف *inkāf*, (v. n. 4 of نكف) Removing (from a man) whatever is disagreeable (to him). Magnifying (God), declaring him to have no equal.

A انكال *ankāl*, (pl. of نكل *nikl*) Fetters, chains. *Inkāl*, (v. n. 4 of نكل) Driving, chasing away. Exciting (one) to retreat.

A انكب *ankab*, (A man) unarmed, wanting a bow. Oppressive, tyrannical.

A انكباب *inkibāb*, (v. n. 7 of كبّ) Falling on the face. Approaching. Sticking to, persevering.

A انكتار *inkitār*, An Englishman. This is the name which the Arabian historians of the Crusades have given to Richard Cœur de Lion king of England, famous among them for his heroic achievements, but particularly on account of the truce for which the great Salāhu'd dīn was obliged to sue.

A انكتال *inkitāl*, (v. n. 7 of كتل) Passing by.

A انكثاب *inkisāb*, (v. n. 7 of كثب) Being gathered into a heap (sand). Being poured or put into.

A انكثام *inkisām*, A grieving, a being sad.

A انكح *ankaḥ*, More or most addicted to venery.

A انكحة *ankihat*, (pl. of نكاح *nikāḥ*) Marriages.

A انكد *ankad*, Avaricious. Sinister. Vile.

A انكدار *inkidār*, (v. n. 7 of كدر) Hastening. Being poured out. Falling (a star). Rushing impetuously, pouncing upon.

A انكر *ankar*, More or most offensive, displeasing.

A انكراث *inkirās*, A being broken, cut off.

A انكراس *inkirās*, (v. n. 7 of كرس) Falling flat on the face. Entering in a stooping posture.

A انكرام *inkirām*, A being honoured.

S انكژ *ankuj*, An instrument for guiding elephants.

P آنكس *ān kas*, He, that person.

A انكساد *inkisād*, (v. n. 7 of كسد) Flocking together (sheep), returning (one flock to another).

A انكسار *inkisār*, (v. n. 7 of كسر) Being broken. Being routed, put to flight. Being inflected with كسر *kasr*, *i.e.* the vowel *i*. Despondency, loss of spirits or courage, despair. P انكسارپذيرشدن *inkisār-pazīr shudan*, To be broken, defeated.

A انكساف *inkisāf*, (v. n. 7 of كسف) Being eclipsed (the sun). A (solar) eclipse.

A انكشاح *inkishāḥ*, A being separated, dispersed.

A انكشاط *inkishāt*, (v. n. 7 of كشط) Being hushed (fears). Being exposed, uncovered, bared.

A انكشاف *inkishāf*, (v. n. 7 of كشف) Being uncovered: lying open. Being dispelled, dissipated. انكشاف عيوب *inkishāfi ʿuyūb*, Detection of vices.

A انكع *ankaʿ*, One who has an excoriated nose.

A انكفاء *inkifāʾ*, (v. n. 7 of كفأ) Being turned from a design. Returning. Being changed (colour).

A انكفات *inkifāt*, (v. n. 7 of كفت) Being diverted from. Being drawn together. Retiring, departing. Leanness, lankness. Compactness.

A انكفاس *inkifās*, (v. n. 7 of كفس) Being bent, distorted, curled, or drawn up together.

A انكفاف *inkifāf*, (v. n. 7 of كفّ) Retiring, departing, removing from a place.

A انكلات *inkilāt*, (v. n. 7 of كلت) Being poured (into a vessel). Being drawn together.

A انكلاث *inkilās*, A preceding, taking the lead.

A انكلال *inkilāl*, (v. n. 7 of كلّ) Smiling, shewing the teeth. Flashing (lightning). Gleaming (a thunder-cloud). Losing its edge (a sword).

A انكليس *ankalīs*, An eel.

A انكماء *inkimāʾ*, A being concealed, suppressed.

A انكماد *inkimād*, The being grieved, vexed.

A انكماش *inkimāsh*, (v. n. 7 of كمش) Making haste. Shrinking. Haste, speed, despatch.

P آنكه *ān ki*, He who. That which. آنكه را *ānki rā*, (for آنكه اورا *ānki urā*) He to whom.

A انكياف *inkiyāf*, A being cut off, separated.

A انكيال *inkiyāl*, (v. n. 7 of كال for كول) Attacking one another with blows and revilings.

A انكيس *inkīs*, A certain figure in geomancy.

P انگ *ang*, An aqueduct, earthern water-pipe.

S *Anga*, Name of a country in Hindūstān.

P انگار *angār*, A painter. An opinion, imagination, fancy, conception. An incomplete business. (in composition) Imagining, pourtraying, painting.

P انگارده *angārda*, A fable, story, narrative.

P انگارش *angārish*, A story, tale, narrative.

P انگاره *angāra*, A revenue-book, cash-account. A narrative of facts or accidents, story. A journal. Incomplete. A commencement of a narration of events from the beginning. A tedious narration. One who creeps behind from shame and bashfulness.

P انگاريدن *angārīdan*, (or انگاردن *angārdan*) To think, imagine, fancy, estimate, compute, suppose. To paint, figure, pourtray, draw, sculp.

P انگارین *angārin*, Computation. A cash-book.

P انگاز *angāz*, A tool, an implement.

P انگاشتن *angāshtan*, To think, consider, suppose, opine, imagine, fancy.

P انگام *angām*, Time, season.

P انگامه *angāma*, A crowd. A company of actors or story-tellers.

P آنگاه *ān gāh*, Then, at that time. Afterwards.

P آنگاهی *ān gāhī*, Of that time. Then.

P انگبار *angubār*, Name of a certain plant.

P انگبین *angubīn*, Honey. انگبین شیرین گوار *angubīni shīrīn-guwār*, Honey sweet and easily digested. *Angubīn*, is frequently given as a proper name, especially to black slaves.

P انگبین خانه *angubīn-khāna*, A bee-hive.

P انگبینه *angubīna*, Honey brought to a consistency, poured on a plate and left to harden.

P انگختن *angikhtan*, To excite, produce, create. To cover all over. To overwhelm.

P انگدان *angudān*, Assafœtida. Mace. A satyr.

P انگرده *angurda*, A single grape, a berry.

P انگرك *angurak*, A little grape.

P انگرو *angarū*, (or انگروا) A sheep-cote, fold.

T انگروس *angarūs*, Hungary.

P انگریز *angrez*, Tarragon, a kind of herb. *Angrez* or *ingrez*, The English (adopted in Hindūstān from the Portuguese). کنپني انگریز *kampanī angrez*, The English East-India Company.

P انگریزي *angrezī*, An Englishman.

P انگز *anguz*, A spade. An iron hook for guiding elephants.

P انگزك *anguzak*, A hook with which the elephant-guider guides the elephant.

P انگژد *angujad*, Assafœtida. Gum in general.

P انگژوا *angijwā*, A sheep-cote. A sheep. A fruit-stone.

P انگژه *anguja*, Assafœtida.

P انگشبه *angashba*, A rich farmer, a capitalist.

P انگشت *angisht*, Charcoal.

P انگشت *angusht*, A finger. A toe. A measure of nine inches. انگشت بدندان گزیدن *angusht ba dandān gazīdan*, To be amazed, astonished. To grieve. انگشت بر چشم نهادن *angusht bar chashm nihādan*, To accept, to approve. انگشت بر حرف نهادن *angusht bar harf nihādan*, To blame censure, criticise. انگشت بر دهان نهادن *angusht bar dahān nihādan*, (or انگشت بر گرفتن *angusht bar giriftan*,) To put the finger on the mouth (an Eastern manner of expressing surprise); which motion of the finger is called انگشت حیرت *angushti hayrat*, The finger of astonishment. انگشت برك *angushti burak*, A kind of mole whose flesh is poison. انگشت بزرگ *angushti buzurg*, The thumb. انگشت حلقه *angushti halka*, The ring-finger. انگشت خائیدن *angusht khāīdan*, To grieve, be sorry, or vexed, to repent. انگشت دراز *angushti darāz*, (انگشت مهین *angushti mihīn*, or انگشت میانه *angushti miyāna*) The long or middle finger. انگشت دشنام *angushti dushnām*, The fore-finger. انگشت شهادت *angushti shahādat*, (or انگشت شك *angushti shak*) The fore-finger, the index, the finger of testimony or profession (because the Muhammadans hold it up when they make a profession of their religion). انگشت شهین *angushti shahīn*, A fat finger. The thumb. انگشت زدن *angusht zadan*, To snap the fingers (in joy). انگشت سترك *angushti suturk*, The thumb. انگشت شکم *angushti shikam*, Membrum virile. انگشت عروس *angushti ʻarūs*, A kind of sweetmeat. A grape. انگشت کشیدن *angusht kashīdan*, To efface, obliterate. انگشت کنیزکان *angushti kanīzakān*, Sweet basil. A kind of grape. انگشت کوچك *angushti kūchak*, or انگشت کهین *angushti kihīn*, The little finger. انگشت گنده *angushti ganda*, Assafœtida. انگشت نر *angushti nar*, The thumb. The great toe. انگشت نهادن *angusht nihādan*, To censure. انگشت نیل کشیدن *angushti nīl kashīdan*, To abandon a work. Ignominy. Poverty. پاي انگشت *pāy-angusht*, A toe (foot-finger). بانگشت گرفتن *ba angusht giriftan*, To count with the fingers.

P انگشتال *angishtāl*, Weak, lean, sickly, ailing.

P انگشتان *angushtān*, A finger.

P انگشتانه *angushtāna*, A thumb-ring: a thimble.

P انگشت برك *angusht-burak*, A kind of mole whose flesh is poisonous.

P انگشت دان *angushtdān*, A thimble.

P انگشتري *angushtarī*, A ring worn on the finger. A seal, a signet.

P انگشترین *angushtarīn*, A ring. A thimble.

P انگشت زنه *angusht-zana*, A ferule for striking the fingers.

P انگشتك *angishtak*, Assafœtida. *Angushtak*, (dim. of انگشت *angusht*) A small finger. انگشتك عروس *angushtaki ʻarūs*, A kind of sweetmeat.

P انگشت نما *angusht-namā*, A pointing-stock. Famous. Pointed at with the finger.

P انگشتنه *angushtana*, A thimble.

P انگشتو *angushtū*, A pancake fried in oil. A kind of bread usually crumbled before it is eaten.

P انگشتوا *angishtwā*, Bread baked on the coals.

P انگشتوانه *angishtwāna*, A brazier. *Angushtwāna*, A ring or defence worn upon the thumb by those who dart the javelin. A thimble.

P انگشته *angashta* or *angishta*, A rich farmer, or merchant. *Angushta*, A fork for winnowing grain.

P انگشتیانه *angushtiyāna*, A thumbstall.

P انگل *angal*, A button-hole, loop, catch, eye. A clownish, boorish man, a disagreeable fellow.

E انگلش *ingilish*, English.

P انگلگون *angalgawn*, Amiable qualities.

E انگلند *ingiland*, England.

P انگلندو *angalandū*, A sort of child's rattle.

P انگله *angala*, A button. A button-hole.

P انگلیز *ingilīz*, England. An Englishman.

P انگلینه *angilīna*, Angelica, imperial (a herb).

P انگلیون *angalyūn*, Silk of a changing colour: also of various colours. A species of brocade, so named, because the Christians of the East generally kept the Evangelists carefully wrapped up in a rich stuff of this kind. The book of the painter and impostor Mānī. A cameleon. Flowers of different hues.

G انگلیون *angiliyūn*, The gospel.

P آنگندن *āngandan*, To fill, cram, stuff.

P انگوان *anguwān*, Assafœtida.

P انگوپا *angūpā*, (in zand and Pāz.) Endive.

P انگوتین *angūtin*, (in zand and Pāzand) The mountain-ox.

P انگور *angūr*, A grape, a raisin. Granulations in a healing sore. انگور دشتي *angūri dashtī*, Sebestens. انگور روباه *angūri rūbāh*, Fox-grapes, nightshade. انگور زیتوني *angūri zaytūnī*, A species of black grape, in shape like an olive.

P انگوردان *angūrdān*, A wine-press.

P انگورك *angūrak*, A little grape. انگورك چشم *angūraki chashm*, The pupil of the eye.

P انگوریه *angūriya*, Angora in Asia Minor.

P انگوریّه *angūrīya*, Ancyra in Asia Minor.

P انگوژه *angūja*, Assafœtida.

P انگوشیدن *angoshīdan*, To embrace.

P انگول *angūl*, A button-hole, a loop. A button.

P انگوله *angūla*, A button. A button-hole.

P آنگه *āngah*, Then. Afterwards. Continually. At the same time. Immediately, by and by. At length. تا آنگه که *tā āngah ki*, Until the time that, till which or when.

P انگیان *anguyān*, Assafœtida.

P انگیختن *angekhtan*, To excite, rouse; to instigate, provoke. To raise. To create, produce, make. To extract. To publish. To put to a distance.

P انگیخته *angekhta*, Excited. Produced, raised. Erected, set up. An image, a statue.

P انگیر *angīr*, A grape.

P انگیز *angez*, (in compos.) Exciting. خجلت انگیز *khajlat-angez*, Raising blushes. خفقان انگیز *khafakān-angez*, Causing a palpitation. خلوص انگیز *khulūs-angez*, Promoting sincerity. سعي ارشاد انگیز *saʻyi irshād-angez*, An endeavour producing salvation, a salutary effort. ظلمت انگیز *zulmat-angez*, Causing darkness. عبرت انگیز *ʻibrat-angez*, Exciting wonder. فتنت انگیز *fitnat-angez*, Raising a tumult. نظر التفات انگیز *nazari iltifāt-angez*, A look commanding respect.

P انگیزاندن *angezāndan*, (or انگیزانیدن *angezānīdan*) causal of انگیختن *angekhtan* or انگیزیدن *angezīdan*) To cause to excite. To erect (a statue). To revive (an agreement), renew (a confederacy).

P انگیزش *angezish*, Excitement.

P انگیزنده *angezanda*, An exciter.

P انگیزه *angeza*, A cause, motive, occasion.

P انگزیدن *angezīdan*, To excite, rouse, raise.

P انگیس *ingis*, A certain figure in geomancy.

P انگیل *angīl*, (or انگیله *angīla*) A loop. A button-hole. A button.

P انگیون *angiyūn*, A piece of variegated silk.

A انمّ *anamm*, More calumnious, greater tell-tale.

A انماء *inmāʼ*, (v. n. 4 of نمي) Increasing. Causing to increase. Divulging, blazoning abroad. Wounding (an animal, which instantly flees, hides itself, and dies). كل ما اصميت و دع ما انميت *kul mā asmayta wa daʻ mā anmayta*, Eat what thou knockest down and killest on the spot; but let alone what thou woundest, and which retires and dies.

A انّما *annamā*, That. *Innamā*, For. Surely. Only. Surely not: as, انّما الاحسان الّا بالتمام *innamā'l ihsān illā bi't tamām*, Surely (it is) not a favour, unless (it is) complete.

A انمّاء *animmāʼ*, (pl. of نمّ *namm*) Slanderers, whisperers, calumniators, tale-bearers.

P انمار *anmār*, Name of a city. Name of a tribe.

A انمار *anmār*, (pl. of نمر *namir*) Leopards. Lines on the legs of wild oxen. *Inmār*, (v. n. 4 of نمر) Finding sweet and wholesome water.

A انماس *inmās*, A sowing of dissensions.

A انّماس *innimās*, (v. n. 7 of نمس) Concealing one's self. Being concealed.

A انماش *inmāsh*, Calumny, slander.

A انماص *inmāṣ*, A budding, a sprouting.

A انماط *anmāt*, (pl. of نمط *namat*) Coverings, blankets, sheets, coverlets. Housings, saddle-cloths. Societies, companies, clubs of men. Sorts, kinds. Reasons, manners, modes of acting. Band-boxes.

A انماطيّ *anmātiy*, A maker of counterpanes, coverlets, housings, &c.

A انمال *anmāl*, (pl. of نمل *namil*) Slanderous. *Inmāl*, (v. n. 4 of نمل) Slandering privately.

A انمجاج *inmijāj*, (v. n. 7 of مجّ) Leaping. Flowing freely from the pen (ink).

A انمحاء *inmihāʼ*, A being erased, obliterated.

A انمحاص *inmihāṣ*, (v. n. 7 of محص) Coming to pass. Breaking forth, shining after an eclipse (the sun). Escaping, fleeing away. Being allayed, assuaged, going down (a swelling).

A انمذاق *inmizāk*, (v. n. 7 of مذق) Being diluted with water (milk).

A انمر *anmar*, Spotted, black and white, dappled. *Anmur*, (pl. of نمر *namir*) Leopards.

A انمراع *inmirāʻ*, A journeying, a travelling.

A انمس *anmas*, Brown, dark-coloured.

A انمساخ *inmisākh*, (v. n. 7 of مسخ) Being lank (the حماة of a horse, considered as a blemish).

A انمشاش *inmishāsh*, A coming, a falling to one.

A انمص *anmas*, Thin-haired (man).

A انمصار *inmisār*, (v. n. 7 of مصر) Being changed, metamorphosed.

A انمصاع *inmisāʻ*, (v. n. 7 of مصع) Travelling, journeying. Pricking his ears (an ass).

A انمصة *anmisat*, (pl. of نماص *numāṣ*) Months.

A انمعاط *inmiʻāt*, The falling off (of hair).

A انملاز *inmilāz*, An escaping from, getting clear.

A انملاس *inmilās*, (v. n. 7 of ملس) Escaping, obtaining deliverance.

A انملاص *inmilāṣ*, (or امّلاص *immilāṣ*) (v. n. 7 of ملص) Slipping out of the hand from lubricity.

A انملاع *inmilāʻ*, (v. n. 7 of ملع) Travelling quick.

A انملاق *inmilāk*, (or امّلاق *immilāk*) (v. n. 7 of ملق) Escaping, fleeing away. Being smooth, bare.

A انملال *inmilāl*, (v. n. 7 of ملّ) Snatching, stealing. Falling or dropping out from the midst (as a sword from the sheath),

A انملة *anmulat*, (*anmalat*, *anmilat*, *inm.* written nine ways, pl. انامل *anāmil* or انملات *anmulāt*) The tip of the finger covered by the nail. A nail, claw.

P انمودج *unmūdaj*, (also انموذج *unmūzaj*) A sample, specimen, model, copy, exemplar.

A انمهلال *inmihlāl*, (v. n. 4 of نمهل Q) Being erect, upright. Being moderate, temperate. Resting, reposing, ceasing. Quietness, remissness, languor.

A انميّ *unmiy*, A sack or pillow stuffed with straw.

A انمياث *inmiyās*, (v. n. 7 of ماث for موث) Being mixed. Being steeped in water, diluted.

A انميار *inmiyār*, (v. n. 7 of مار for مور) Being plucked (wool or camels' hair). Falling (hair from the body of a beast).

A انمياز *inmiyāz*, A being separated, distinguished.

A انمياع *inmiyāʻ*, The being melted (as fat).

A انمياق *inmiyāk*, The act of perishing.

A انن *unan*, Name of a bird resembling a pigeon, but black, and makes a cry of اوه اوه *ūh ūh*.

U انّناس *annanās*, A pine-apple.

A اننة *unanat*, One who groans much.

A انّني *annanī*, Perhaps I.

A انو *inw*, (pl. آناء *ānāʼ*) Time. A portion of time, as an hour, or a watch of the night.

A انوأ *anwaʼ*, Skilled in the science of the stars.

A انواء *anwāʼ*, (pl. of نوء *nawʼ*) Certain stars in the 28th mansion of the moon. (pl. of نويّ *nawaʼ*) Date-stones. *Inwāʼ*, (v. n. 4 of نوي) Throwing away (the stones of dates). Performing, completing (any business). Travelling to distant countries, retiring to a distance, making distant journeys. Covering a camel (fat). Forming a stone (a date).

A انواح *anwāh*, Weeping, wailing (women).

A انوار *anwār*, (pl. of نار *nār*) Fires. (pl. of نور *nawr*) Flowers (especially white). (pl. of نور *nūr*) Lights. Splendours. *Inwār*, (v. n. 4 of نار for نور) Being beautiful, shining, clear, conspicuous.

A انواري *anwārī*, Name of a famous Persian poet, who died about the year 1200.

A انواض *anwāz*, (pl. of نوض *nawz*) Higher grounds. Places from whence waters flow. Sutures, or joinings of the buttocks with the back).

A انواط *anwāt*, (pl. of نوط *nawt*) Things suspended or pendulous. Parcels hung or placed between the two larger trusses or loads carried on each side by a camel or other beast of burthen. Date-hampers. (pl. of نياط *niyāt*) Strings by which bows or bottles are hung up. Heart-strings. ذات انواط *zāt anwāt*, Name of a tree.

A انواع *anwāʻ*, (pl. of نوع *nawʻ*) Sorts, kinds, species, varieties. Ways, means.

A انواف *anwāf*, (pl. of نوف *nawf*) Camels' bunches (of the larger kind). Cries (of the hyena).

A انواق *anwāk*, (pl. of ناقة *nākat*) She-camels. *Inwāk*, (v. n. 4 of نوق) Hunting the pelican.

A انواك *inwāk*, A discovering one to be a fool.

A انوال *anwāl*, (pl. of نال *nāl*) Liberal men. (pl. of نول *nawl*) Weavers' beams. Modes, ways.

A انوام *anwām*, (pl. of نوم) Dreams, sleeps.

A انوان *anwān*, (pl. of نون *nūn*) Fishes. Swords, resembling fish. Ink-horns.

P انوپا *anūpā*, Bugloss. Endive.

A انوج *anwaj*, Fat, heavy, and breathing hard. *Unūj*, Hard breathing.

A انوح *anūh*, (A horse) making a snorting noise whilst he runs. A horse that takes the bit between his teeth and shakes his head when running. One who sighs when any thing is asked from him. A miser. *Unūh*, (v. n. of انح) Sighing, breathing hard.

A انور *anwar*, More or most bright, luminous, resplendent, or enlightened. Beautiful.

A انورة *anwirat*, (pl. of نار *nār*) Fires.

G انورسما *anūrasmā*, A hemorrhage.

A انوس *anūs*, (pl. انس *unus*) Tame (as a dog that does not bite).

P انوش *anosh*, Enos the son of Seth.

P انوشا *anoshā*, The religion of the Guebres. Joy, mirth. Equality, justice.

P انوشه *anūshah* or *unūshah*, Fortunate, happy, blessed. Prosperous. Desirable. A young king. Wine. Hail! welcome! God bless you!

A انوطة *anwitat*, (pl. of نياط) Heart-strings.

A انوف *anūf*, (A woman) breathing through her nose an agreeable perfume. Modest, bashful, attentive to reputation, avoiding every thing bad. *Unūf*, (pl. of انف *anf*) Noses.

A انوق *anūk*, An eagle. A pelican. A black-coloured, crested, or bald-headed bird with a yellow beak. اعزّ من بيض الانوق *aʻazz mim bayzi'l anūk*, More rare than the egg of the *anūk*. *Anwuk* or انؤق *anʼuk* (pl. of ناقة *nākat*) She-camels.

A انوك *anwak*, (pl. نوكى *nawkā* and نوك *nūk*) Foolish, stupid. ما انوكه *mā anwakahu*, What a fool he is! *Unūk*, (v. n. of انك) Being large. Being coarse and thick. Being long-bodied (a camel). Being pained. Shewing symptoms of grief. Coveting.

A ما انوله *mā anwalahu*, How bountiful he is!

A انوم *anwam*, Sleepy, somnolent, drowsy.

G انوميا *anūmiyā*, The anemone.

A انوه *unūh*, A breathing hard. Envying.

P انوييد *anūyīd*, A wailing, lamentation.

P انوييدن *anūyīdan*, To weep, lament, sigh.

A انّ anh, (v. n. of انّ) Breathing hard. Envying. *Anih,* Envious.

P انَ āna, A particle, which, when added to substantives, gives them an adverbial signification: as, A اتّفاق ittifāk, Union; P اتّفاقانه ittifākāna, Unanimously, شاهانه shāhāna, Royally.

A انّه unnah, Those who sigh when any thing is asked of them. Misers. Enviers.

A انّهُ annahu, Because that. Since, for as much as. *Innahu,* Certainly, indeed, surely, yes.

P آنها ānhā, (pl. of آن ān) They.

A انهاء anhāء, (pl. of نهي nahy or nihy) Ditches, pools, trenches, puddles. *Inhāء,* (v. n. 4 of نهأ) Not dressing meat sufficiently, leaving it half raw. Doing (any thing) incompletely. (v. n. 4 of نهي) Causing to arrive. Bringing, conveying, transmitting. Coming to a pool. Giving over, leaving off. Arriving, reaching. Announcement, publication.

A انهاج inhāj, (v. n. 4 of نهج) Following the road. Shewing the way. Being clear, open, main (a road). Making a road open, plain, and clear. Proceeding on the way. Wearing out (a garment). Being worn out. Breathing quick whilst travelling.

A انهاد inhād, (v. n. 4 of نهد) Extolling, magnifying, esteeming as great (a present). Filling (a cup or lake) three parts full.

A انهار anhār, (pl. of نهر nahr) Rivers. *Inhār,* (v. n. 4 of نهر) Digging till you find water. Making (blood) to flow. Flowing profusely (blood from the vein), so as not to be stopped. Widening, enlarging (a river). Being, happening, or doing any thing in the day-time (نهار nahār). Becoming fat (a woman). Slacking speed (a horse). Acquiring nothing good.

A انهاض inhāz, (v. n. 4 of نهض) Exciting, rousing, causing to stand. Beginning to fill, or swell (a leathern bottle).

A انهاك inhāk, (v. n. 4 of نهك) Severely punishing, or tormenting, harassing, overworking. Weakening, emaciating, grinding the faces. Being extremely scrupulous in washing and cleaning.

A انهال inhāl, (v. n. 4 of نهل) Satisfying the thirst of a camel, causing him to drink the first draught. Having camels plentifully watered. Exciting anger. Giving. Making thirsty. Satisfying with drink. A tomb, tumulus, grave.

A انهباس inhibās, A laughing immoderately.

A انهباط inhibāt, (v. n. 7 of هبط) Falling, descending, lowering. Being diminished. Depression.

A انهباك inhibāk, (v. n. 7 of هبك) Yielding, giving way beneath the feet (ground).

A انهتاك inhitāk, (v. n. 7 of هتك) Being torn, rent (a curtain). Being ravished.

A انهجاس inhijās, (v. n. 7 of هجس) Being repulsed, driven away from any thing. Abstaining.

A انهجام inhijām, (v. n. 7 of هجم) Shedding (tears). Falling down (a house).

A انهداد inhidād, (v. n. 7 of هدّ) Falling down with a crash (a cliff).

A انهداش inhidāsh, (v. n. 7 of هدش) Being irritated (a dog).

A انهداغ inhidāgh, (v. n. 7 of هدغ) Becoming soft (a dry thing). Being squashed (a fresh date).

A انهدام inhidām, (v. n. 7 of هدم) Being thrown down. Falling down (a house). Destruction, demolition, ruin, overthrow.

A انهدان inhidān, (v. n. 7 of هدن) Growing remise, slackening one's ardour in any pursuit.

A انهر anhar, Clear, serene (day). *Anhur,* (pl. of نهر nahr) Rivers. (pl. of نهار nahār) Days.

A انهراج inhirāj, A being overcome with ale.

A انهراس inhirās, A being thumped and bruised.

A الانهران al anharāni, A name given to two stars because they portend much rain. See عوّاء ɛawwāء and سماك simāk.

A انهرة anhirat, (pl. of نهار nahār) Young قطا katas (grouse or bustards). Male owls or bustards.

A انهزاع inhizāɛ, A being bruised, brayed, broken.

A انهزام inhizām, (v. n. 7 of هزم) Being broken with a loud crack (a stick). Being pressed inwards (an apple, wax, &c.). Being routed, put to flight. Fleeing away. Defeat, discomfiture, overthrow.

A انهشام inhishām, (v. n. 7 of هشم) Being broken (any thing not solid, as the skull, the nose, a bone, or an egg). Being weak and languid (camels).

A انهصار inhisār, The being bent or broken.

A انهض anhuz, (pl. of نهض) The parts in camels between the upper and lower part of the shoulder.

A انهضاض inhizāz, A being broken to pieces.

A انهضام inhizām, (v. n. 7 of هضم) Being well digested. Sinking inwards, being depressed. بطئ الانهضام batiɛu'l inhizām, Slow of digestion. سريع الانهضام sariɛu'l inhizām, Quick of digestion.

A انهفات inhifāt, The being diminished.

A انهقاع inhikāɛ, (v. n. 7 of هقع) Hungering. Falling in (the belly).

A انهكاك inhikāk, (v. n. 7 of هكّ) Being overcome with wine. Being relaxed about the hips (a lying-in woman). Being out of joint. Lying close to the ground. (v. n. 9 of نهك) Being separated.

A انهلاب inhilāb, (v. n. 7 of هلب) Being stripped of bristles. Being plucked out (bristles).

A انهلات inhilāt, (v. n. 7 of هلت) Stealing away privately: removing to a distance. Forgetting.

A انهلاك inhilāk, (v. n. 7 of هلك) Precipitating one's self into danger, exposing one's life.

A انهلال inhilāl, (v. n. 7 of هلّ) Pouring violently (rain). Shedding plentifully (tears). Being so shed. Rolling, falling down (a heap of sand).

A انهماء inhimāء, The being worn out (garment).

A انهمار inhimār, (v. n. 7 of همر) Being poured out (water). Flowing. Being stripped of its leaves (a tree). Being ruined, demolished, falling down.

A انهماز inhimāz, (v. n. 7 of همز) Being marked with همزة hamza (ء). Being squeezed.

A انهماغ inhimāgh, (v. n. 7 of همغ) Being burst open (a ripe date). Being moist (pudendum).

A انهماك inhimāk, An applying diligently.

A انهماكا inhimākan, (P انهماكانه) Diligently.

A انهمال inhimāl, (v. n. 7 of همل) Rising, becoming erect and stiff. Raining gently but incessantly. Overflowing with tears (eyes). Delaying.

A انهمام inhimām, (v. n. 7 of همّ) Being liquefied (fat), melted (hailstones). Drooping from age. Being harassed with care and anxiety.

A انهواء inhiwāء, (v. n. 7 of هوي) Falling, descending from a height. Passing by.

P انهوبا anhūbā, (in zand and Pāzand) Jupiter.

A انهي anhī, (pl. of نهي nahy or nihy) Ditches, pools, puddles.

A انهياء anhiyāء, (pl. of نهيّ) Prudent, wise.

A انهيار inhiyār, (v. n. 7 of هار for هور) Flowing down (a heap of sand). Falling into ruins.

A انهياض inhiyāz, (v. n. 7 of هاض for هيض) Being broken again (a bone). Muting (a bird).

A انهياع inhiyāɛ, (v. n. 7 of هاع for هيع) Spreading, diffusing itself (a mist, a vapour).

A انهياك inhiyāk, (v. n. 7 of هاك for هوك) Falling into difficulties from inattention.

A انهيال inhiyāl, (v. n. 7 of هال for هيل) Being poured out, shed (flour). Pursuing (him) one after another with invectives and blows.

A آني ānī, Reaching, or attaining to the highest degree. Patient, long-suffering (man).

A اني any, (v. n. of اني) Arriving (time). Coming to maturity. Waiting, expecting. Attaining its maximum. Patience, delay, long-suffering. *Any* or *iny,* Time, part of time, as a watch of the night. *Iny,* (v. n. of اني) Causing to lag or delay. *Ana'* or *ina',* The highest degree (of any thing). Maturity. *Ina',* (v. n. of اني) Lagging, delaying, proceeding slowly. Arriving (time). *Ina'* or *ana',* (pl. آناء ānāء or انيّ uniy) A whole day.

A انّى anna', Where, wherever. Whence, from what place? When. How? Howsoever. *Annī,* Perhaps I. *Innī,* Indeed, surely, or since I.

A انيّ aniy, Arrived. Come to maturity. *Uniy,* (v. n. of اني) Lagging, delaying, proceeding slowly. (pl. of انى ina' or ana') Whole days.

A انياء inyāء, A leaving (of meat) half-dressed.

A انياب anyāb, (pl. of ناب nāb) Canine teeth. Aged she-camels.

A انيار anyār, (pl. of نير nīr) Reeds. Threads collected together. Borders of garments. Yokes. Hems, fringes. Woofs of a web. ذات انيار zāt anyār, Aged (camel) with some remains of strength.

A انياق anyāk, (pl. of نيق nīk) Mountain-tops.

A انيب anyab, Large-tusked or canine-toothed. *Anyub,* (pl. of ناب nāb) Tusks. Canine teeth.

P انيبا anībā, (in zand and Pāzand) Myrtle.

A آنية āniyat, (pl. of اناء ināء) Vessels, vases.

A انيت *anīt*, (v. n. of انت) Sighing. Envying. Measuring, defining. The object of envy.

P انيتا *anītā*, (in zand and Pāzand) Myrtle.

A انيث *anīs*, Soft (literally female) iron.

A انيثة *anīsat*, Soft ground fruitful in produce.

A انيح *anīh*, (v. n. of انح) Breathing hard.

A انير *anyar*, More or most clear, or evident.

P انير *anīr*, A bad temper or disposition.

P انيران *anīrān*, Name of the 30th day of every solar month of the ancient Persian calendar; and also of an angel or genius, who was supposed to have the superintendency of whatever happened upon that day, and also of all marriages.

P انيژ *anīj*, The plant southernwood.

A انيس *anīs*, A companion, friend, comrade, familiar acquaintance, of the same temper, disposition, or genius. Thursday. A cock. انيس اعضا *anīsi aʻzā*, The eye. Any object of desire. ما بالدار انيس *mā bi'd dār anīs*, No one at home.

P انيسان *anīsān*, A jest, joke, drollery. A frivolous story, a lie. Raillery. Opposition.

A انيسة *anīsat*, A fire (as being a companion).

P آنيسته *ānīsta*, Congealed, frozen, coagulated.

P آنيسون *ānīsūn*, Resistance, opposition.

G انيسون *anīsūn*, (or انيسو) Anise, aniseed.

P انيسه *anīsa*, Congealed, frozen. Coagulated.

A انيسيّة *anīsīyat*, Association, intimacy.

P انيش *anīsh*, A little garden. A vineyard.

P انيشه *anīsha*, A spy. A flatterer. Congealed.

A انيض *anīz*, (v. n. of انض) Being tainted, corrupted in smell (meat). Raw or half-dressed. The throbbing of the intestines through terror.

A انيف *anīf*, Pained in the nose, complaining of a broken nose. A mountain earlier in producing than any other part of the country. (A field) of quick vegetation. Soft iron. *Unayf*, Name of several men. انيف فرع *unayf farʻ*, Name of a place.

P انيق *anīk*, Name of a depilatory drug.

A انيق *anīk*, Beautiful, excellent, charming.

A انيم *anīm*, Men, creatures.

P آنين *ānīn*, A churn. A churning-stick.

A انين *anīn*, (v. n. of انّ) Groaning. A groan. A churn. P آه و انين و نالۀ حزين *āh u anīn u nālaʻi hazīn*, Sighs, groans, and lamentations.

A انيه *anīh*, A breathing hard. *Inīh*, No, not.

A انئياد *inʻiyād*, A being, or a becoming bent.

P آو *āv*, (equivalent to آب *āb*) Water.

A او *aw*, Whether. Or. Unless. Except. Ere. To, unto. Either. Nay. That. When او *aw* is used as a noun it is doubled: as, دع الاوّ جانباً *dāʻi 'l awwa jāniban*, Lay aside the or (or the unless).

P او *u*, He, she, it (relating to man). كتاب او *kitābi u*, His book. او مرغ اين انجير نيست *u murghi īn anjīr nīst*, He is no bird for this fig; *i. e.* it is not bread for his teeth; it is not for him.

A اوّ *aww*, Alas!

P آوا *āwā*, A voice, sound, echo, rumour, clamour. Fame. A nightingale. Food. Frumenty. گوشت آوا *gosht-āwā*, A kind of dish made of minced or hashed meat. برنج آوا *birinj-āwā*, Rice-meat, a dish made with rice. هزار آوا *hazār-āwā*, (Thousand-note) The nightingale.

P اوا *awā*, Voice, sound, echo. Broth, soup.

A اواء *iwāʻ*, (v. n. of اوي) Repairing to any place, in order to dwell there.

A آواب *āwāb*, (pl. of اوب) Tracts, districts.

A اوّاب *awwāb*, A sincere penitent. One who praises God. Name of a tribe. صلوة الاوّابين *salātu'l awwābīn*, The prayer of the forenoon. *Ūwāb*, (pl. of آئب *āʻib*) Returners.

A اوابد *awābid*, (pl. of آبدة *ābidat*) Timorous, untamed animals. Wild beasts (not dying a natural death). Notable calamities. النعم اوابد فقيّدوها بالشكر *an niʻam awābid; fa kayyidūhā bi'shshukr*, Favours are fleeting: secure a continuance of them by gratitude. اوابد الاشعار *awābidu'l ashʻār*, Celebrated poems flying from mouth to mouth. اوابد القصائد *awābidu'l kasāʻid*, Rare verses. اوابد الكلام *awābidu'l kalām*, Outlandish forms of speech.

A اوابل *awābil*, Numerous camels.

A اوّابيّ *awwābīy*, Of the tribe of اوّاب *awwāb*.

P آواخ *āwākh*, Ah! alas! A share, portion.

A اواخر *awākhir*, (pl. of آخرة *ākhirat* and اخير *akhīr*) Ends, hinder parts. The last ten days of the month (See اوائل *awāʻil* and اواسط *awāsit*). Moderns. فريد الاوائل و الاواخر *farīdu'l awāʻil wa'l awākhir*, Phœnix of the ancients and moderns.

A اواخيّ *awākhīy*, (pl. of اخيّة *akhīyat*) Tethers, pegs. Things necessary to be attended to.

P آوادان *āwādān*, Cultivated, cheerful.

A اوادم *awādim*, (pl. of آدم) Browns. Men.

A اواذيّ *awāzīy*, (pl. of آذيّ) Waves of the sea.

P آوار *āwār*, Injustice, iniquity. Oppression. Calculation, reckoning. Ruined, depopulated. A vagrant, outcast, exile. Quantity, measure.

P اوار *awār*, A cash-book.

A اوار *uwār*, (pl. اور *ūr*) Warmth, heat (of the sun, fire, or thirst). Smoke. Flame. The south wind.

A اوارجة *awārijat*, (pl. اوارجات *awārijāt*) (from P اواره *awāra*) A register, an account-book.

P اوارجه *awārja*, A cash-book, a book of receipts and disbursements. A diary, journal, or register.

A اوارك *awārik*, (pl. of آركة *ārikat*) Camels feeding on the plant اراك *arāk*.

P آوارگي *āwāragī*, Vagrancy. Wretchedness.

P آواره *āwāra*, Computation. Certainty, assuredness. Lost, annihilated. Ruined. Scattered. Destitute of name or character. An exile, outcast, vagabond, vagrant. Iron filings. Oppression, injustice. Ruin, desolation. آواره شدن *āwāra shudan*, To be oppressed, injured. آواره كردن *āwāra kardan*, To harass. To tear. آواره گرديدن *āwāra gardīdan*, To roam, to wander. آواره و سرگردان شدن *āwāra u sar-gardān shudan*, To be stupid, bewildered, and to wander about like a fool.

P اواره *awāra*, An account-book. The hall of prefecture, a court. Iron filings. *Uwāra*, Heat.

P آواره گير *āwāra-gīr*, A book-keeper, accountant.

P آواري *āwārī*, Idleness, vagrancy.

A اواريّ *awārīy*, (pl. of آريّ *ārīy*) Stables, mangers. Stakes or tethering ropes, for cattle.

P آواريدن *āwārīdan*, (or اواريدن) To swallow.

P اوارين *awārīn*, Wicked, bad, ugly.

P آواز *āwāz*, Voice, sound, noise, clamour: tone. Fame, rumour, report. Echo. آواز دادن *āwāz dādan*, (زدن *zadan* or كردن *kardan*) To make a noise, to call out, halloo, invite. آواز گشتن *āwāz gashtan*, To become divulged, celebrated, illustrious.

P اواز *awāz*, The time during which the sun continues in the constellation Pisces. With, in the possession of. Against. اواز و *awāzi u*, With him.

P آوازك *āwāzak*, A little noise. A smack.

A اوازم *awāzim*, (pl. of آزمة *āzimat*) Cheek-teeth grinders. Hardships, distresses.

P آوازناك *āwāznāk*, Noisy.

P آوازه *āwāza*, Voice, sound, loud talk. Fame, rumour, echo. A note in music in a high key, of which six are enumerated; viz. سلمك *salmak*, شهناز *shahnāz*, گردانيه *gardāniya*, گوشت *gosht*, مايه *māya*, and نوروز *nawroz*.

P اوازي *awāzī*, With.

P آوازيدن *āwāzīdan*, To cry out, make a noise, vociferate, make loud acclamations, halloo, huzza.

A اواسط *awāsit*, Middles, centres. The ten middle days of a month. See اوائل and اواخر.

A اواسي *awāsī*, (pl. of آسية *āsiyat*) Female circumcisers. Firmly built houses. Columns.

A اواصر *awāsir*, (pl. of آصرة *āsirat*) Benevolent affections. Qualities which render one agreeable.

A اواصل *awāsil*, (originally وواصل *wawāsil*) (pl. of واصلة) Women wearing borrowed hair.

A اواضح *awāzih*, The days of bright moon-shiny nights, *i. e.* the 13th, 14th, and 15th of the month.

A اواطب *awātib*, (pl. of وطب) Milk bottles.

A اواعس *awāʻis*, (pl. of اوعس *awʻas*) Soft, sandy (grounds, plains, or hills, such as produce abundance of those pot-herbs which are eaten raw).

A اواغي *awāghī*, (pl. of آغية *āghiyat*) Channels whereby tilled grounds are irrigated. Blight, mildew.

A اوافل *awāfil*, (pl. of آفل *āfil*) Setting (suns).

A اواقي *awākī*, (pl. of واقية) Female protectors.

A اواقيّ *awākīy*, A weaver's shuttle. *Awākīy*, (or اواقي *awākī*) (pl. of اوقيّة *ūkīyat*) Ounces.

A اوال *awāl*, Name of a fruitful island belonging to the district of Bahrayn in Arabia Felix where there is a pearl-fishery. Name of an idol formerly worshipped by the tribes Bakr and Taghlib.

A اوالف *awālif*, (pl. of آلفة *ālifat*) Intimate female friends.

A اوالي *awālī*, (pl. of اوّل *awwal*) The firsts. (pl. of اولي *awla'*) Nearer. Better, worthier. (pl. of

آلية *āliyat*) Coming short. Negligent.

P اوام *awām*, Debt. Colour.

A اوام *uwām*, Violent thirst, or the heat attending it. Smoke. Giddiness, the vertigo. A bow-string.

A اوامر *awāmir*, (pl. of امر *amr*) Commands, mandates, edicts.

A اوان *awān*, (or *iwān*, pl. آونة *āwinat*) Time. Season. (pl. اون *ūn*) An arched gallery, portico.

A اواني *awānī*, (pl. of اناء *ināʼ*) Vessels, vases. اوانيء صينيّة *awānīʼi sīniya*, China vases.

P اوانيدن *awānīdan*, To sleep, to be drowsy.

A اواوين *awāwīn*, (pl. of ايوان *īwān*) Porticoes, arched galleries, corridors, piazzas.

P آواه *āwāh*, (or اواه *awāh*) Echo.

A اوّاه *awwāh*, Merciful, compassionate (one of the names of God). A lawyer. A theologian. A believer. Certain of any thing. Invocation, prayer.

P آواها *āwāhā*, Labours, works. Victuals.

A اواهد *awāhid*, (pl. of اوهد *awhad*) Mondays.

P آواي *āway*, A loud voice.

A اوائل *awāʼil*, (pl. of اوّل *awwal*) The first (men), principals, chiefs. The ancients. Beginnings. The first ten days of every month. في اوائل شهر رجب *fī awāʼili shahri rajab*, On one the first ten days of the month of Rajab.

A اوائن *awāʼin*, (pl. of آئنة *āʼinat*) Easy, convenient, tranquil. Name of a city. ثلاث ليال اوائن *salāsa liyāli awāʼin*, Three easy nights (journey, without trouble or inconvenience).

A اوب *awb*, (v. n. of آب for اوب) Returning. Repentance, conversion. Coming in the night (especially to seek for water). Flocking to from all quarters. Celerity, agility, quickness of step (in camels), an ambling pace. Rectitude. A way, a road. The wind. A cloud. A bee. An intention, design. A custom. A mode, manner. (pl. of آئب *āʼib*) Returners. من كل اوب *min kulli awbin*, From every quarter. In every manner. *Awab*, (v. n. of اوب) Being angry.

A اوباء *awbāʼ*, (pl. of وبأ *wabaʼ*) Pestilences.

A اوبات *awbāt*, (pl. of اوبة) Legs of quadrupeds.

A اوباد *awbād*, (pl. of وبد *wabad*) Large indigent families. Men in wretched circumstances.

P اوبار *awbār*, Any thing swallowed. A house. Strong poison. Devouring fire. (in compos. from اوباريدن *awbārīdan* or اوباشتن *awbāshtan*) Devouring, swallowing. A devourer, glutton. Any animal that devours other animals. اژدهاىء مردم اوبار *ajdahāʼi mardum-awbār*, A dragon devouring men. ماهيء كشتي اوبار *māhīʼi kishtī-awbār*, A fish swallowing a boat. *Obār*, Lamentation.

A اوبار *awbār*, (pl. of وبر *wabar*) The hairs of camels, hares, and other animals that have soft piles.

P اوباريدن *awbārīdan*, To ingulph, swallow, devour. To throw in, cast. *Obārīdan*, To groan.

P اوباش *awbāsh*, (or اوباشه *awbāsha*) A dunder-headed, ignorant, vulgar, self-opiniated, obstinate, unmanageable fellow. Dissolute, rakish.

A اوباش *awbāsh*, (pl. of وبش *wabash*) The common people, the canaille. Ruffians. Mixed multitudes of every class.

P اوباشتن *awbāshtan*, To fill. To throw away. To devour, swallow.

P اوباشي *awbāshī*, Rakishness; dissoluteness. Attendance at games and public shows.

P اوبانيدن *awbānīdan*, To doze. To be laid flat.

A اوبة *awbat*, (v. n. of آب for اوب) Returning. (pl. اوبات *awbāt*) The leg of a quadruped.

A اوبر *awbar*, Hairy (camel). بنات اوبر *banātu awbara*, A kind of mushroom or fungus covered with an earth-coloured down. Misfortune.

P اوبردن *awburdan*, To swallow unmasticated.

P اوبس *ūbis*, Kindred, connexions.

P اوبه *obih*, Name of a village in هراة *harāt*.

P اوبئة *awbiʼat*, (pl. of وباء *wabāʼ*) Plagues.

P اوپچه *awpcha*, An officer of the court.

P اوپچه خانه *awpcha-khāna*, Guard-house: picket.

A آوة *āwat*, Name of a town near Ray.

A اوّة *ūwat*, (pl. اوو *uwaw*) Accident, misfortne.

P اوت *ut*, (for او و تو *u ʼu tu*) He and thou.

A اوتاد *awtād*, (pl. of وتد *watad*) Stakes, poles, pegs, pins, props. Grandees, chiefs (as being pillars of the state). Mountains. Teeth.

A اوتار *awtār*, (pl. of وتر) Chords, bow-strings.

P اوتاق *otāk*, (or اوداغ) A large tent, pavilion.

P اوتانيدن *awtānīdan*, To sleep. To faint.

A اوّتاه *awwatāh*, (or اوتاه *awatāh*) Alas!

A او ترما *aw tara mā*, Especially.

A اوتك *awtak*, (or اوتكيّ *awtakaʼ*) A sort of date.

A اوتل *awtal*, (pl. اتل *utul* or وتل *wutul*) (A man) full to satiety of wine or other liquor, drunk.

A اوتنة *awtinat*, (pl. of وتين) Heart-strings.

P اوتي *oti*, A kind of hot iron, with which they take stains out of cloth, by pressing it upon blotting-paper laid upon the spot.

A اوثان *awsān*, (pl. of وثن *wasan*) Idols.

A اوثر *awsar*, as الاوثر *al awsar*, Enmity.

A اوثم *awsam*, Bare. Barren. ما اوثم *mā awsam*, How bare! How barren!

P اوج *awj*, Name of a note in music.

A اوج *awj*, (from P اوك *awk*) Top, summit, vertex. Altitude, ascendant. اوج شرف *awji sharaf*, The fortunate aspect or ascendant of a planet.

A اوجاح *awjāh*, (pl. of وجحة) Low grounds.

A اوجار *awjār*, (pl. of وجرة *wajrat* and *wajarat*) Holes dug to entrap wild beasts.

A اوجاع *awjāʻ*, (pl. of وجع *wajaʻ*) Pains, aches, diseases, complaints.

A اوجال *awjāl*, (pl. of وجل *wajal*) Fears, alarms.

A اوجام *awjām*, (pl. of وجم *wajam*) Large heaps of stones, thought to be the work of عاد *ʻād*. Stones erected in the desert as a direction for travellers.

A اوجان *awjān*, Name of a city in Azarbayjān.

A اوجب *awjab*, More or most necessary.

A اوجر *awjar*, Timid, timorous.

A اوجرة *awjirat*, (pl. of وجار) Hyenas' dens.

A اوجس *awjas*, Somewhat, a little. الاوجس *al awjas*, *al awjasu* or *awjusu*, An age. سجيس الاوجس *sajīsa'l awjasi*, Never, at any time.

A اوجل *awjal*, Timid, afraid.

A اوجم *awjam*, The larger part of a tract of sand.

A اوجن *awjan*, Thick (rope).

A اوجه *awjah*, More or most fair, beautiful, or plausible. More or most respectable or dignified. *Awjuh*, (pl. of وجه *wajh*) Faces, surfaces. *A* A paper specifying the amount of several particulars.

A اوجية *awjiyat*, (pl. of وجاء) Little sacks, trusses,

s اوجين *awjīn*, Name of a town in India, 126 measured coss from Agra (each 4000 English yards).

P اوچ *ūch*, A wager. اوچ كردن, To lay a wager.

P اوچت پمن *awchat pamun*, (in zand and Pāzand) A finger. A toe.

P اوچه *ochcha*, Name of a city.

P اوچيزي *ūchīzī*, Quality, or manner of a thing.

A اوحاج *awhāj*, (pl. of وحجة) Low places.

A اوحاش *awhāsh*, (pl. of وحش) Famished.

A اوحال *awhāl*, (pl. of وحل *wahal*) Soft clays.

A اوحد *awhad*, Singular, only, unique. الاوحد *al awhad*, A title of God. هو اوحد اهل زمانه *huwa awhadu ahli zamānihi*, He is an incomparable man, the phœnix of his age. اوحد الدين *awhadu'd dīn*, Singular in the faith.

A اوحش *awhash*, More or most unsavoury.

P آوخ *āwakh*, A share, portion. Good, elegant. Auspicious, happy. Ah! alas!

A اوخاش *awkhāsh*, (pl. of وخش *wakhsh*) Vile, worthless, base.

A اوخام *awkhām*, (pl. of وخم *wakhm*) Heavy, disagreeable men. (pl. of وخم *wakhim*) Indisposed from indigestion or a pain in the stomach.

A آود *āwad*, (fem. اوداء *awdāʼ*) Curved, crooked.

A اود *awd*, (v. n. of آد for اود) Bending: inclining. Weighing down, oppressing. Keeping employed. Returning. Proper name of a man. Name of the father of a tribe. ذو اود *zū awd*, Name of a king (dynasty?) that reigned in Yaman 600 years. *Awad*, (v. n. of اود) Becoming crooked. Crookedness.

A اوّد *awidd* or *awudd*, Lovers, dear friends.

A اوداء *awdāʼ*, (اوداة *awdāt*, اودية *awdiyat*, or اوداية *awdāyat*) (pl. of وادي *wādī*) Valleys, low grounds between hills. Rivers. Banks, beds, or channels of rivers.

A اوداء *awiddāʼ*, (pl. of وديد) Lovers, friends.

A اوداج *awdāj*, (pl. of ودج) The jugular veins.

A اوداد *awdād*, Lovers, cordial friends.

G اوداساليون *awdāsāliyūn*, Rock-parsley.

P اوداغ *odāgh*, A splendid tent of a circular form, used by princes, generals, or other grandees.

P اودر *awdir*, A father's brother.

G اوذر *ūzar*, Water.

P اودردن *ūdurdan*, (in zand and Pāz.) To die.

P اودس *awdas*, (or اودست *awdast*) A span.

A اودع *awdaᶓ*, The jerboa. (A pigeon) having a white crop.

A اودك *awdak*, as بنات اودك *banāti awdak*, Misfortunes. ما ادري اي اودك هو *mā adrī ayyu awdaka huwa*, I do not know what man he is.

A اودن *awdan*, Soft, smooth.

P اوده *awda*, Name of a city.

A اودية *awdiyat*, (pl. of وادي) Valleys: rivers.

A اوذح *awzah*, Base, abject (slave).

P آور *āwar*, Certainty. True, certain. The seventh heaven. Ugly, deformed, ill-favoured. Bad language. Bringing; a bringer. Master, possessor: as, بيخ آور *bekh-āwar*, Having a root, *i.e.* strongly rooted. جنگ آور *jang-āwar*, A warrior. دل آور *dil-āwar*, One who hath a heart, *i.e.* bold. زورآور *zor-āwar*, Having strength, *i.e.* strong.

A اور *awr*, (v. n. of آر for اور) Lying with a woman. The north. The sailing motion of clouds to and fro. *Ūr*, The east wind. (pl. of اوار *uwār*) Heats of sun, fire, or thirst. Smokes, flames. South winds. *Awir*, (A country) heated by the sun or south wind. *Urar*, (pl. of ارة *irat*) Fires. Hearths.

P اور *ūr*, The fist. A blow with the fist. An almond, pistachio, or walnut, whose kernel is rotten. *Awar*, Obscene discourse.

P اورا *awrā*, A fortress, citadel. *Urā*, (oblique of او *u*) Him, her, it. To him, of him.

A اوراب *awrāb*, (pl. of ورب *warb*) The tops or mouths of the holes of mice or scorpions.

A اوراد *awrād*, (pl. of ورد *ward*) Roses. Rosy. (pl. of ورد *wird*) Continual praises or commemorations; also certain portions of the Kur'ān, which the Muhammadans recite at different hours, espetially at their morning and evening service. Leaves of a tree or book.

P اوراز *awrāz*, Exalting. Erect, high. Height.

G اوراساليون *awrāsāliyūn*, Mountain-parsley.

P اوراشتن *awrāshtan*, To exalt, raise, elevate.

A اوراع *awrāᶓ*, (pl. of ورع) Weak, small, puny.

A اوراق *awrāk*, (pl. of ورق *wark*) Monies. (pl. of ورق *warak*) Leaves (of a tree or of a book).

P اوراق پريشان *awrāki parishān*, Scattered leaves. *Awrāk* is a title given to many books, especially, by way of modesty, to small works.

A اوراك *awrāk*, (pl. of ورك) Hips, haunches.

A اورال *awrāl*, (pl. of ورل *waral*) Reptiles resembling the Lybian lizard.

A اورام *awrām*, (pl. of ورم) Tumours, swellings.

P اورامن *orāman*, (or اورمه *orāma*) A peculiar manner of reading or chanting Pahlavī poetry, which derives its name from a village in the dependencies of جوشقان where the inventor of it lived.

P اورتاق *ortāk*, (in Khwārazm) A merchant.

P آورجه *āwarja*, A cash-book, a book of receipts and disbursements. A distribution of items of account under appropriate heads.

P آورد *āward*, Battle, conflict, engagement, war. آورد كردن *āward kardan*, To make war, to fight.

A اوردة *awridat*, (pl. of وريد) Jugular veins.

P آوردگاه *āward-gāh*, A field of battle.

P آوردن *āwardan*, To bring, fetch, or adduce. To relate. To cause or produce. بجا آوردن *ba jā āwardan*, To perform, to exhibit. بصلاح آوردن كار *ba salāh āwardani kār*, To bring a work to perfection, to finish any thing properly, to adjust. بيرون آوردن *birūn āwardan*, To bring forth, to produce (as the earth). در آوردن *dar āwardan*, To carry in. To conceal a cause, to cloak. هجوم آوردن *hujūm āwardan*, To assault. ياد آوردن *yād āwardan*, To remember, to bring to memory.

P آوردني *āwardanī*, Worthy of being presented.

P اوردو *ordū*, A court, palace, camp. A horde (of Tartars). زبان اوردو *zabāni ordū*, Hindūstānī.

P آورده *āwarda*, Brought, introduced. آب آورده *āb-āwarda*, A distemper in the hoof, nail, or claw; a whitlow. آورده آمدن *āwarda āmadan*, To admit, to infer. To come brought, or be introduced. آورده شدن *āwarda shudan*, To be introduced, adduced, or brought. آورده اند *āwarda and*, They say: as, آورده اند كه امير صاحب بعد شاديء خود خواهد آمد *āwarda and ki amīr sāhib baᶓd shādīi khud khwāhad āmad*, They say that the governor will come after his marriage.

P آورديدن *āwardīdan*, To fight. To carry off.

A اورس *awiras*, The cypress. The juniper-tree.

P آورسر *āwarsar*, The planet Jupiter.

P اورسيا *ūrsiyā*, Roots of the iris or white lily.

A اورشليم *ūrshalīm*, Jerusalem.

A اورق *awrak*, (pl. ورق *wurk*) Brown, tawny, dusky-coloured. A year without rain. Milk with two-thirds water. Ashes.

P آورك *āwrak*, (or اورك) A swing, see-saw.

A اورك *awrak*, Large-hipped (man).

P اوركوه *awarkūh*, A city in Persian Irāk.

P اورگنج *ūrganj*, Name of a city in Khwārazm.

A اورم *awram*, Men, people, a crowd. A military host bristling with arms. Name of four villages near Aleppo.

G اورمالي *ormālī*, The gummy exudation of a certain tree.

P اورمان *ūrmān*, Difficulty, trouble. A forest.

P اورمز *ormuz*, The planet Jupiter. Name of the first of the month; also of its angel. Name of the son of Bahman and grandson of Isfandyār.

P اورمزد *ormuzd*, The name of the angel or genius supposed to preside over the first day of the ancient Persian solar year. Name of the grandson of Isfandyār. The planet Jupiter.

P اورمك *ūrmak*, A cap, a hat, a woollen cowl.

P اورنج *awranj*, Nightshade. *Oranj*, The stalk of a bunch of eaten grapes.

P اورنجن *awranjan*, (or اورنجين *awranjīn*) A bracelet. An anklet.

P آورند *āwrand*, Tigris. Nile. Fraud, deceit.

P اورند *awrand*, A throne. Glory, honour, dignity, pomp, grandeur, power. Beauty. Ornament. Fortune, destiny. Life. Any large river. The sea. Blackness. Name of a grandson of Kaykubād. Fraud, deceit, imposture. A crown.

P اورندن *awrandan*, To throw away.

P آورنده *āwaranda*, Bringing. A bringer.

P اورنديدن *awrandīdan*, To deceive.

P اورنگ *awrang*, A throne. Wisdom, understanding. Beauty, gracefulness. Life. A manufacturing village. Fraud, deceit. Mirth. A worm which eats into wood. A line whereon things are hung to dry. Glory, honour. A man's name. (for آب رنگ *āb-rang*) Water-colour, paint.

P اورنگاباد *awrang-ābād*, A city in India.

P اورنگزيب *awrang-zīb* or *zeb*, (Ornament of the throne) Name of an emperor of Hindūstān (who died in 1707, after a glorious reign of fifty years).

P اورنگ زيبي *awrang-zībī*, A kind of cloth.

P اورنگ شاهي *awrang-shāhī*, A kind of silk.

P اورنگ نشين *awrang-nishīn*, (Sitting on a throne) A reigning prince.

P اورنگي *awrangī*, An air of music. Name of the third of the thirty notes in music.

G اوروبنخي *ūrūbankhī*, Broomrape.

P اوروختن *avrokhtan*, To inflame, blaze.

P آوره *ār-rah*, A canal, a conduit.

A اوره *awrah*, Foolish, unskilful.

P اوره *awra*, The outside of a garment. The best side of cloth. The surface of any thing. اورۀ افلاك *awrai aflāk*, The heaven of heavens.

P آوري *āwarī*, A man of truth or certainty.

A اورياء *ūriyāᵃ*, Uriah (the Hittite).

P اوريب *urīb*, (or اوريو) Inverted, transposed.

P آوريدن *āwarīdan*, To bring. To attack, charge. *Āwrīdan*, To swallow. To hold a conference.

P اوريدن *awrīdan*, To be slothful. To deceive. To finish. To bring.

P آوريز *āv-rez*, (for آبريز *āb-rez*) A water-closet.

P اوريسي *awrīsī*, Set with jewels.

A اوريم *ūrīm*, The Urim.

P آورين *āwarīn*, (or آورن *āwarin*) Juniper.

P اوريه *ūriya*, The province of Orissa in India.

A اوز *awz* or *awaz*, A mode of reckoning drawn from the lunar motions.

P اوز *ūz*, (in Khwārazm) Ingenious, dexterous.

A اوزّ *iwazz*, A gander. A thick dwarf.

P اوزار *awzār*, The sail of a ship. A shoe. Tools. Spiceries, hot seasonings.

A اوزار *awzār*, (pl. of وزر *wizr*) Burthens, loads, whatever oppresses. Sins, crimes. Arms, weapons. (pl. of وزر *wazar*) Mountains, or other places of refuge, sanctuaries, asylums. Fortifications. (pl. of وزير *wazīr*) Vazīrs, counsellors, ministers of state.

P اوزاردان *awzārdān*, A spicery or pepper-box.

A اوزاع *awzāᶓ*, Bodies, crowds. Name of a tribe.

A اوزاعيّ *awzāʻīy*, Of the tribe of اوزاع *awzāʻ*.
A اوزاغ *awzāgh*, (pl. of وزغة) Lizards. Weak.
A اوزان *awzān*, (pl. of وزن *wazn*) Weights. Measures. Metres. اوزان فارسيّه *awzāni fārisīya*, Persian weights and measures.
P اوزايش *avzāyish*, Abundance, increase.
P اوزبك *ūzbak*, Name of a Tartar dynasty.
P اوزّة *iwazzat*, A goose. A nimble woman.
P اوزجند *ozjand*, Name of a place.
P اوزك *awzak*, A particular seal.
P اوزن *awzan*, Strong, vigorous. A lion.
A اوزن *awzan*, Stronger, more or most weighty, respectable, influential.
P اوزند *awzand*, Military accoutrements.
P اوزون *avzūn*, (equivalent to افزون *afzūn*) Ample, spacious. Increase, augmentation.
A اوزّونا *iwazzūna*, (pl. of اوزّ *iwazz*) Ganders. Dwarfs. Active men.
A اوزّي *iwazza'*, A waddling, goose-like pace.
A اوزّيّ *iwazzīy*, Goose-like.
P آوزيدن *āwizīdan*, (or آويزيدن) To suspend.
P آوزين *āwzīn*, Juniper.
P اوزين *awzīn*, A ring. A buckle.
P اوژن *awjan*, Murder, slaughter. (in compos.) Throwing, casting. مرد اوژن *mard-awjan*, A hero.
P اوژنديدن *awjandīdan*, To throw, cast, hurl.
P اوژول *awjūl*, Instigation. Haste, speed.
P اوژولنده *awjūlanda*, Exciting, instigating.
P اوژوليدن *awjūlīdan*, To raise, excite, stir up. To exact, demand. To pluck up. To hasten. To dissipate, scatter. To render bold. To perplex.
A اوس *aws*, (v. n. of آس for اوس) Giving in exchange or return, requiting, repaying. A gift. A wolf. Name of a tribe. Occasion, opportunity.
P اوس *aws*, Hope.
A اوساخ *awsākh*, (pl. of وسخ) Filths, dirts.
A اوساط *awsāt*, (pl. of وسط *wasat*) Middle parts, centres, waists.
P اوسان *awsān*, A whetstone.
A اوسان *awsān*, Things needful to be done. Whatever materially concerns one's self.
P اوسبيد *usabīd* or *avsabīd*, Sort of water-lily.
P اوست *ust*, (for او است *u ast*) He is.
P اوستاخ *ūstākh*, Boldness, impudence, incivility.
P اوستاد *ūstād*, A master in any art or profession.
P اوستادگي *ūstādgī*, A trade. Mastership.
P اوستادي *ūstādī*, A trade. Skill, mastership. اوستادي كردن *ūstādī kardan*, To fabricate, manufacture. To act the master.
P اوستام *ostām*, A pillar, prop. A prince, patron. A threshold. Faithful, trustworthy. Ornaments for a saddle and bridle. Confidence.
P اوستان *ostān*, A threshold. Trustworthy. Ornaments of a saddle or bridle, trappings.
P اوستره *ostura*, (for استره *ustura*) A razor.
P اوستيم *awstīm*, A sleeve. Blood. Pus, matter.
A اوسخ *awsakh*, Nastier, nastiest.

A اوسط *awsat*, A middle, mean. Middlemost. Middle proposition in a syllogism (The extremes being اعلى *aʻla'*, Highest, and ادنى *adna'*, Lowest). Most excellent. اوسط القامة *awsatu'l kāmat*, Of a middling stature. خير الامور اوسطها *khayru'l umūr awsatuhā*, Virtue consists in moderation.
A اوسطي *awsatī*, Middle, middling, moderate.
A اوسع *awsaʻ*, More or most ample. Larger, largest, wider, widest. Ampler, amplest.
A اوسق *awsuk*, (pl. of وسق) Camels' loads.
P اوسن *awsan*, Short, brief.
P اوسو *ūsū*, Robbery, spoliation. *Ūsū* or *awsū*, Grief, lamentation.
P اوسون *avsūn*, Enchantment, fascination, spell.
P اوسه *awsa*, (or *ūsa*) Taken, seized. Robbery.
G اوسيرس *osīris*, The Egyptian God.
G اوسيمون *awsīmūn*, Mallows.
P اوش *awsh* or *ūsh*, A city in Transoxania.
A اوشاب *awshāb*, (pl. of وشب) Crowds, mobs.
A اوشاز *awshāz*, Assistants, allies. Men of low condition, mean. Joints. Troubles, adversities. علي اوشاز *ʻala' awshāz*, On the road, in haste.
P اوشال *awshāl*, A pond, tank, reservoir.
A اوشال *awshāl*, (pl. of وشل *washal*) Small quantities of water. Few, and also, many tears.
A اوشالاً *awshālan*, (Men) following in ranks or files.
P اوشان *avshān*, Scattering. *Oshān*, Those.
P اوشاندن *avshāndan*, To scatter.
P اوشانده *avshānda*, Scattered. A button.
P اوشانيدن *avshānīdan*, To cause to scatter.
A اوشحة *awshihat*, (pl. of وشاح *wishāh* or *wushāh*) Belts of leather, ornamented with gems or gold-studs, worn by the Arabian ladies.
P آوشن *āwshin*, Origany.
A اوشن *awshan*, One who goes to another, sits down, and eats his food.
P اوشندنه *awshandana*, A button: a button-hole.
P اوشنگ *awshang*, A line for clothes or grapes.
P اوش و بوش *awsh u bawsh*, Ostentation, pride.
P اوشه *awsha*, Dew. *Osha*, Origany.
P اوشهنگ *oshhang*, See هوشنگ *hoshang*.
P اوشين *awshīn*, (or آوشن) Wild marjoram.
A اوصاب *awsāb*, (pl. of وصب *wasab*) Diseases.
A اوصاف *awsāf*, (pl. of وصف *wasf*) Specifications, descriptions, titles, epithets. Attributes, qualities, endowments. Praises, encomiums. Famous actions. اوصاف جميله *awsāfi jamīla*, Excellent qualities. اوصاف و القاب *awsāf u alkāb*, Titles and epithets. P شاه زادهٔ حميده اوصاف *shāh-zādaʼi hamīda-awsāf*, A prince of noble endowments.
A اوصال *awsāl*, (pl. of وصل *wasl*) Joints, joinings. (pl. of وصل *wisl* or *wusl*) Bones that break not, or which are not joined to other bones. Places of joining of two bones, articulations.
A اوصر *awsar*, High ground.
P اوصو *ūsū*, Grief, lamentation for the dead.

A اوصياء *awsiyāʼ*, (pl. of وصيّ *wasīy*) Giving or receiving orders. Testators. Executors.
A اوضاح *awzāh*, (pl. of وضح *wazah*) Bracelets, necklaces, ornaments for the ankles and other parts of the body. Good coins. Lights, lustres, splendours. White spaces (especially on the foreheads or feet of horses). Hoary or white hairs. Milks. Leprosies. The best parts of a road. Certain kinds of young green herbage. (All these being so named on account of their light or bright colours).
A اوضار *awzār*, (pl. of وضر *wazar*) Putrid, rancid, corrupted qualities (of meat, fat, water, or milk).
A اوضاع *awzāʻ*, (pl. of وضع *wazʻ*) Postures, positions, actions, gestures. اوضاع و اطوار *awzāʻ u atwār*, Actions and motions. P اوضاع نا هموارة *awzāʻi nā hamwāra*, Unsuitable acts or behaviour.
A اوضام *awzām*, (or اوضمة *awzimat*) (pl. of وضم *wazam*) Mats, boards, or such things, upon which meats are placed to keep them clean.
A اوضح *awzah*, More or most clear, evident.
A اوضع *awzaʻ*, Lower, lowest, meaner, meanest.
A اوضياء *awziyāʼ*, (pl. of وضيء) Clean, neat, pure.
A اوطاب *awtāb*, (pl. of وطب *watb*) Bottles, made of the leather of full-grown cattle.
A اوطار *awtār*, (pl. of وطر *watar*) Things needful to be done; what materially concern one's self.
P اوطاق *otāk*, A tent. A room, chamber.
A اوطان *awtān*, (pl. of وطن *watan*) Countries, mother-countries. Homes. Stalls for cattle. ترك اوطان *tarki awtān*, Abandonment of one's country.
A اوطب *awtub*, (pl. of وطب *watb*) Leathern milk-bottles (the same as اوطاب *awtāb*).
A اوطف *awtaf*, Hairy about the eyebrows. Hovering (darkness). Easy (life).
A اوظفة *awzifat*, (pl. of وظيف *wazīf*) The slenderest parts of the limbs of animals, the parts between the knees or houghs and the ankles and pasterns; shanks, cannon-bones.
A اوعاء *awʻāʼ*, (pl. of وعاء) Sheaths, cases.
A اوعار *awʻār*, (pl. of وعر) Rugged grounds.
A اوعال *awʻāl*, (pl. of وعل *waʻl*) Nobles, princes. Asylums. (pl. of وعل *waʻil*) Mountain-goats. Months of Shaabān.
A اوعب *awʻab*, More or most capable of holding or receiving the whole of a thing.
A اوعر *awʻar*, Rugged, rough (road). Intricate (question). *Awʻur*, (pl. of وعر *waʻr*) Rough, rugged, and uneven (places).
A اوعس *awʻas*, (pl. وعس *wuʻs* and اواعس *awāʻis*) Soft sandy soil, of a high exposure, fruitful in such kinds of herbs as are eaten raw.
A اوعية *awʻiyat*, (pl. of وعاء *wiʻāʼ* or *wuʻāʼ*) Repositories, sheaths, vessels, cases.
A اوغا *awghā*, Air, wind.
A اوغاب *awghāb*, (pl. of وغب *waghb*) Large sacks. The inferior sorts of household furniture (as pots or pans). Weak. Fools. Strong (camels).

A اوغاد *awghād*, (pl. of وغد *waghd*) Servants (particularly those who serve for their victuals). Weak in body, enervated (men). People, men, boys.

A اوغام *awghām*, (pl. of وغم *waghm*) Hatreds.

P اوغان *avghān*, Lamentation.

P اوغر *awghar*, An assembly. An airy place.

P اوغل *awghal*, Name of a certain people.

P اوغن *oghun*, An aqueduct, a canal.

A اوفاد *awfād*, (pl. of وفد *wafd*) Comers. هم على اوفاد *hum ʿala' awfād*, They are on a journey.

A اوفاز *awfāz*, (pl. of وفز *wafz*) High places. Hastes. هو على اوفاز *huwa ʿala' awfāz*, He is on the road, he is making haste.

A اوفاض *awfāz*, (pl. of وفض *wafz*) Hastes. (pl. of وفض *wafaz*) Chopping-blocks. Different sects, bodies. Multitudes, crowds, especially meeting and conversing together at market, each carrying a scrip. على اوفاض *ʿala' awfāz*, In haste.

A على اوفاط *ʿala' awfāt*, In, or making haste.

P اوفتادن *uftādan*, To fall.

P اوفتانيدن *uftānīdan*, To cause to fall.

A اوفر *awfar*, Complete, perfect (leathern bottle).

P اوفسانه *ofsāna*, A tale, a story.

A اوفق *awfak*, Most convenient or apposite.

A اؤفوفة *uʾfūfat*, One who oft says اف *uff*.

A اوفي *awfa'*, More, most sufficient, abundant.

A اوق *awk*, (v. n. of اوق for آق) Overhanging. Being at the point of. Inclining. Bringing any thing disastrous, disagreeable. A burden, weight, trouble: any thing oppressive or disagreeable.

A اوقاب *awkāb*, (pl. of وقب *wakb*) Fools. Low, mean men. Household furniture, utensils.

A اوقات *awkāt*, (pl. of وقت *wakt*) Times, seasons. اوقات عزيز *awkāti ʿazīz*, Precious hours.

P اوقات گذري *awkāt-guzarī*, Stipend, pension.

A اوقار *awkār*, (pl. of وقر *wikr*) Burthens, loads.

A اوقاس *awkās*, A few scattered people. Profligate (people), of bad reputation. Slaves.

A اوقاش *awkāsh*, An adventurer. A vagabond, vagrant. A mixed assembly, mob, crowd.

A اوقاص *awkās*, (pl. of وقص *wakas*) Those numbers under ten, and above five, in relation to the taxing of cattle for sacrifice (supposing the owner of cattle to be assessed to the value of a sheep for every five oxen; whatever number he has above five, and under ten, pays nothing). Scattered, dispersed (people). اوقاص من بني فلان *awkās min banī fulān*, The rabble of such a tribe. صاروا اوقاصا *sārū awkāsan*, They became dispersed.

A اوقاف *awkāf*, (pl. of وقف) Legacies, bequests.

A اوقال *awkāl*, (pl. of وقل *wakl*) Dwarf palm-trees; also their fruits when dry.

A اوقب *awkab*, Salacious, often ready (penis).

A اوقة *awkat*, An assembly, a crowd. *Ūkat*, (pl. اوقات *ūkāt* and اوق *ūk*) A subterraneous canal, a common sewer. The nest of a bird on the top of a mountain.

T اوقدر *awkadar*, So much, so many, the more.

A اوقر *awkar*, More or most grave or modest.

A اوقص *awkas*, Short-necked. Nearest road.

G اوقطاريون *awkatāriyūn*, Hemp agrimony.

A اوقل *awkal*, More or most addicted to climbing and standing on a hill (a mountain-goat).

G اوقليدس *ūkulīdis*, Euclid.

G اوقيانوس *awkiyānūs*, The ocean.

A اوقية *ūkiyat*, (pl. اواقي *awākīy* or اواقي *awākī*) An ounce. Forty dirhems. An استار *istār* and two-thirds. Seven مثاقيل *masākīl*.

G اوقيمن *awkay*, or *awkīman*, Wild sweet basil.

P اوك *awk*, (for اوج *awj*) A summit.

A اوكار *awkār*, (pl. of وكر *wakr*) Nests, eyries.

A اوكاف *awkāf*, (pl. of وكف *wakaf*) Deviations, excesses. Faults, crimes. Projections like wings over a doorway.

A اوكة *awkat*, Anger, rage, vehemence. Malice, wickedness. Affliction.

A اوكح *awkah*, Earth, sand, and stones.

A اوكد *awkad*, More or most firm or solid.

P اوكر *awkar*, A weaver's trench.

A اوكر *awkur*, (pl. of وكر *wakr*) Birds' nests.

A اوكس *awkas*, A man of the very worst class.

A اوكع *awkaʿ*, (A man) having the great toe pressing upon the next, and protuberant at the joint. Tall, but stupid. Worthless (servant).

A اوكن *awkun*, (pl. of وكنة *wuknat*) Birds' nests.

P اوكو *ūkū*, A bird of ill omen. An owl.

A اوكية *awkiyat*, (pl. of وكاء *wikāʾ*) Chains, strings, or things which connect the stopple to the neck of the bottle, or fastens it more firmly in the mouth. Close-handed men.

P اوگار *awgār*, Soreness of back of a beast of burden. Crippled. Loaded. Drunk.

P اوگنج *awganj*, Repentance, contrition.

P اوگندن *avgāndan*, (for افگندن) To throw.

A اول *awl*, (v. n. of اول for آل) Returning, retiring. Losing flesh, becoming lean (a camel). Escaping. Administering well, managing with propriety. Governing, presiding. Becoming thick (liquor). Thickening, making thick. *Awal*, (v. n. of اول) Preceding, taking the lead. *Ūwal*, (or اوّل *ūwal*) (pl. of اولي *ūla'*, fem. of اوّل *awwal*) First.

A اوّل *awwal*, (pl. اوائل *awāʾil*, اوالي *awālī*, and اوّلون *awwalūna*) First, prior. Best, principal. اوّل ما *awwal mā*, As soon as, or ever. اوّل باوّل *awwal bi awwal*, Successively. اوّل بهار *awwali bahār*, The beginning of spring. اوّل البيت *awwalu'l bayt*, The fane at Mecca. اوّل قنوت *awwali kunūt*, Break of day. اوّل ولد *awwali walad*, A first-born. اوّل وهلة *awwal wahlat*, At first, at the first onset. مذ اوّل من امس *muz awwal min ams*, Since the day before yesterday, three days ago. A P اوّل طعام پس كلام *awwal taʿām pas kalām*, First dinner, then conversation.

A اولا *awla'*, (for اولي *awla'*) Nearer. More or most apt. Better, preferable. It is enough. ما اولاه للمعروف *mā awlahu li'l maʿrūf*, How conspicuous he is for beneficence!

A اولاء *ūlāʾ*, (pl. of ذا *zā* and ذه *zihi*) These.

A اوّلاً *awwalan*, In the first place, before all things. اوّلاً و آخراً *awwalan wa ākhiran*, (or اوّل و آخر *awwal u ākhir*) From beginning to end, from first to last, at length, finally.

A اولات *ūlāt*, (pl. of ذات *zāt*) Female possessors.

A اولاج *awlāj*, (pl. of ولجة *walajat*) Caverns, or places, into which passengers retire to shelter from rain, &c. Windings of rivers or valleys.

A اولاد *awlād*, (pl. of ولد *walad*) Sons, children, descendants. Offspring.

P اولاد *ūlād*, Name of a certain demon.

A اولائك *ūlāʾika*, (fem. اولاك *ūlāka* and اولالك *ūlālika*) (pl. of ذاك *zāka* and تاك *tāka*) These.

A اولائلك *ūlāʾilika*, (pl. of ذالك *zālika*) Those.

A اوّلة *awwalat*, The first. The beginning.

P اولج *awlij*, A small grape-stalk. Nightshade.

G اولسطيون *olustiyūn*, The herb flitchwort.

A اولع *awlaʿ*, Madness. به الاولع *bihi'l awlaʿ*, Madness is in him.

A اولق *awlak*, Madness, insanity, or something like it. Insane, foolish. The sword of خالد بن وليد.

T اولقدر *awlkadar*, Only, so much, many, far.

A اولم *awlam*, Is it not? اولمّا, Is it not?

P اولنج *awlanj*, Knowledge, understanding, intellect. A throne. Mirth. Mode of living. Nightshade. Fraud, deceit. Pomp, splendour. *Ūlanj*, A bunch from which the grapes have been eaten.

A اولو *ūlū*, (pl. of ذو *zū*) Lords, masters, possessors. اولو الابصار *ūlū'l absār*, Having eyes, *i.e.* prudent, sagacious, penetrating. اولو الارحام *ūlū'l arhām*, Related by birth. اولو الالباب *ūlū'l albāb*, Prudent, intelligent. اولو الامر *ūlū'l amr*, Emperors, generals, commanders-in-chief, especially endued with wisdom and piety. The friends and companions of Muhammad, and they who follow them in wisdom. اولو الطريق *ūlū't tarīk*, Priors, abbots, or other chiefs of religious orders. اولو العزم *ūlū'l ʿazm*, (Endued with constancy) Noah, Abraham, Moses, and Jesus.

A اولون *awlawna*, (pl. of اولي *awla'*) Nearer. Better. More eligible.

A اوّلون *awwalūna*, (pl. of اوّل) First: forefathers.

A اولوية *ūluwiyat*, Majority, superiority, pre-excellence, priority, precedence. بطريق اولويت *bi tarīki ūluwiyat*, By right of majority.

P آوله *āwla* or *āvila*, A blister, pimple, felon, freckle, small-pox, or other eruption on the skin.

P اوله *awla* or *ūla*, An eagle, a falcon. A brute.

A اولي *awla'*, in Persian *awlī*, (pl. اوالي *awālī* and اولون *awlūna*) Nearer. Best, more or most excellent, worthy, fit, sufficient, proper. Worthier, fitter. اولى لك *awla' laka*, Woe be to thee! ما اولاه للمعروف *mā awlahu li'l maʿrūf*, How greatly disposed he is to acts of kindness! *Ūla'*, (fem. of اوّل *awwal*) (pl. اول *uwal* and اوّل *ūwal*) First: as, درجة اولى *darajatun ūla'*, A first step. (pl. of ذا *zā* and ذه *zihi*) These. *Ūlī*, (oblique of اولو *ūlū*) Possessed of, endowed with: as, اولي الاجنحة *ūli'l ajnihat*, Winged animals. اولي العزم *ūli'l ʻazm*, Resolute (men). اولي العلم *ūli'l ʻilm*, Scientific (men). اولي النهي *ūli'n nahy*, Wise, prudent (men).

A اوّلي *awwalī*, First, best, chief. A first principle. A self-evident proposition: an axiom, general maxim.

A اوّليّ *awwalīy*, First, earliest.

A اولياء *awliyā*, (pl. of وليّ *walīy*) Near, contiguous. Of the same profession. Equals, companions. Assistants, patrons, defenders, allies. Fathers. Lords, masters. Friends (of God), saints, prophets. اوليائ دولت *awliyā-i dawlat*, Fathers of the state, *i.e.* Princes, ministers, nobles.

A اولية *awliyat*, Showers upon showers.

A اوّلية *awwalīyat*, Priority, primacy. Earliness.

P اوليتر *awlītar*, (or اولى تر *awla' tar*) Better.

G اوليرا *ūlīrā*, Starch-wheat.

G اوليقوس *ūlīkūs*, Six oboli.

A اولئك *awlaʼika*, (pl. of ذلك *zālika*) Those.

A اوليل *awlīl*, Salt-pits in Western India.

A اوّلين *awwalīn*, (in Persian pronounced *avvalīn*) (obliq. pl. of اوّل *awwal*) First. اوّلين حرف *awwalīn harf*, The letter alif. Knowledge infused. اوّلين نقش *awwalīn nakhsh*, Destiny, fate. اوّلين و آخرين *awwalīn u ākhirīn*, Ancients and moderns.

A اوم *awm*, (v. n. of آم for اوم) Breathing with difficulty (a thirsty person). Smoking. Destroying (bees) by fumigation. Governing, ruling. *Uwam*, as ليال اوم *layālī uwam*, Nights of misfortune.

A اوَمّ *awamm*, Better or best fitted for an Imām.

P اوماج *ūmāj*, A mark, butt. A kind of pottage.

G اومادا *awmādā*, Juice of the wild cucumber.

G اومالي *ūmālī*, (or اوومالي *uwūmālī*) Elæomeli, a honied oil which exudes from certain trees.

P اومان *awmān*, Name of a village in Hamadān.

P اوميد *ūmīd*, (*omed* or اوميز *ūmīz*) Hope.

P آون *āwan*, Any thing suspended.

A آون *āwin*, Easy, tranquil.

A اون *awn*, (v. n. of آن for اون) Going softly. Convenience. Quiet. Peace, tranquillity. Gentleness, mildness. A gentle pace. A counterpoise to a load. One side of a wallet. Name of a place.

A اون *ūn*, (pl. of اوان *iwān*) Galleries, porticoes.

A اوناديا *ūnādiyā*, A wild cucumber.

P اونار *awnār*, A fire. Fragrance. Drowsiness.

P اونانيدن *awnānīdan*, To slumber. To hope.

P اونانيس *awnānīs*, Pomegranate-buds.

A آونة *āwinat*, Tortoises. (pl. of اوان) Times.

A آونةً *āwinatan*, Repeatedly, frequently, often.

P اونج *uwanj*, Friendship, intimacy, familiarity.

P آونـد *āwand*, Furniture, particularly belonging to the kitchen, as pots, pans, or other vessels. A line on which they hang clothes or grapes to dry. A tennis-racket. A chess-board. Argument, proof. A throne. *Āwand* or *āwind*, First.

P اوند *awand*, A vessel. *Awind*, Fraud, deceit.

A آوندي *āwandī*, A vat in which wine is made.

A اونق *awnuk*, (pl. of ناقة *nākat*) She-camels.

P اونكه *awinka*, A prickly kind of shrub.

P آونگ *āwang*, A mortar in which things are pounded. Any thing suspended. A line on which clothes or bunches of grapes are hung up to dry.

P آونگان *āwangān*, Pendulous, hanging.

P اوننگ *awnang*, A clothes-line.

G اونو *awnū*, Wine.

P آونوس *āvnūs*, (for آبنوس *ābnūs*) Ebony.

G اونومالي *awnūmālī*, Honey and wine mixed.

P اوني *ūnī*, A kind of grain like barley.

P اونيا *awniyā*, A medlar. *Ūniyā*, Pressed juice.

P اونيدن *awanīdan*, To rest, slumber. To hope.

P آوو *āwaw*, Name of a city.

A اوو *uwaw*, (pl. of اوّة *ūwat*) Misfortunes.

A اوور *awūr*, The east wind.

A اووك *uwawūk*, A kind of gum.

A آوّه *āwūh*, Alas!

A اووي *awawīy*, Corporeal. Miraculous.

P آوه *āwa*, A forge. A brick-kiln. A fringe. Name of a city. Whatever makes an echo. Ah! alas!

A اوه *awh*, (v. n. of آه for اوه) Crying oh! in pain. *Awh*, (اوّه *awwah* or *awwih*) Alas!

A آوّه *āwwah*, Alas! Well a day!

P آوها *āwhā*, (equivalent to آبها *ābhā*) Waters.

A اوهاط *awhāt*, Quarrels, squabbles, lawsuits.

A اوهاق *awhāk*, (pl. of وهق *wahak*) Nooses, which are thrown to catch man or beast, lassoes.

A اوهام *awhām*, (pl. of وهم *wahm*) Opinions, conjectures, suppositions, imaginations, doubts, suspicions. Large and tractable camels.

A اوهد *awhad*, (pl. اواهد *awāhid*) Monday. *Awhud*, (pl. of وهد) Low, sloping, hollow lands.

A اوهز *awhaz*, Graceful in walking.

A اوهية *awhiyat*, Breaches, fissures, cracks.

A اوهيّة *ūhiyat*, A space between mountains, a valley, the declivity of a hill, from top to bottom.

A آوي *āwī*, (pl. اويّ *uwīy*) One who repairs to a place to pass the night. One who pities, condoles, or is tenderly affected towards.

A اوي *awy*, (اويّ *uwīy* or *iwīy*) (v. n. of اوي) Repairing to any place in order to dwell there; taking a house, carrying to, or receiving into, a house. Receiving hospitably.

P اوي *uwī*, He, she, it. Lo! behold!

A اويّ *uwīy*, (pl. of آوي *āwī*) Flocking together. طير اويّ *tayri uwīy*, Birds flocking together.

P اويا *ūyā*, A lazy, slothful, idle fellow.

P اويان *ūyān*, A mountain. The middle month of autumn.

A اوياه *awīyāh*, Alas!

A اوية *awyat*, (v. n. of اوي) Pitying, being tenderly affected towards.

P آويج *āwej*, (for آويز *āwez*) Any thing suspended.

A اويجه *uwayjih*, (dim. of وجه *wajh*) The face. نظروا الي باويجه سوء *nazarū ilayya bi uwayjihi sūʼin*, They looked upon me with a face of evil.

P آويختن *āwekhtan*, To hang, to suspend.

P آويخته *āwekhta*, Suspended, hanging loose, pendulous.

A اويد *awīd*, The murmur or hum of people.

P آويدن *āwīdan*, To twist. To fatigue.

P اويرا *uwīrā*, (for اورا *ūrā*) Him, her, it: to him.

P اويرش *awīrash*, (in zand and Pāzand) A certain number of crimes.

P آويز *āwez*, Any thing suspended. A place where things are hung up. A hook upon which meats are hung. A flesh-hook. The shambles. A border, margin, circuit.

P آويزان *āwezān*, (pl. of آويز *āwez*) Suspended.

P آويزانيدن *āwezānīdan*, To cause to hang up.

P آويزش *āwezish*, A hanging on. Suspension, pendulosity. War, trouble.

P آويزگن *āwezgin*, A petitioner who addresses everybody: a hanger-on. An importunate beggar. An infamous boy. Left, dismissed. Contagious.

P آويزگي *āwezagī*, Pendulousness.

P آويزه *āweza*, An ear-ring, a drop, pendant.

P آويزه بند *āweza-band*, An ear-ring, pendant.

P آويزيدن *āwezīdan*, To hang up. To adhere.

P آويژگان *āwejgān*, Adherents, lovers, friends.

P آويژه *āweja*, (or اويژه *aweja*) Wine. Chaste. Pure, unmixed.

A اويس *uways*, A wolf. A man's name.

P آويشن *āwīshan*, Hanging, suspended. Drawing a sword. Marjoram, organy.

P اويشن *awīshin*, Sight.

P آويشه *āwīsha*, Marjoram, organy.

A اويل *uwayl*, (dim. of آل *āl*) A small number of people. A little family.

A اويمّة *uwaymmat*, (dimin. of ائمّة *aʼimmat*) Little Imāms.

P آوينا *āwīnā*, Expressed juice (of fruit, &c.).

P آويندن *āwīndan*, To hope. To sleep, to slumber.

P A آه *āh*, Ah! alas! A sigh. آه آتشبار *āhi ātish-bār*, An ardent sigh. آه آتشين *āhi ātishīn*, The sigh of one in pain. آه جان كاه *āhi jān-kāh*, A sigh from the bottom of the heart. آه در جگر نداشتن *āh dar jigar na dāshtan*, To be penniless. آه جگر سوز *āhi jigar-soz*, A heart-burning sigh. آه عنبرين *āhi ʻambarīn*, The sigh of one in pain. آه كشيدن *āh kashīdan*, To fetch a sigh.

A آه *āh*, (an abbreviation of الي آخره *ila' ākhirihi*) To the end of it, et cetera.

P اه *ah*, Ah! alas!

A آهّ *ahh*, (v. n. of آهّ) Sighing from grief, mourning, pronouncing *ah*!

A اهاب *ahāb*, Name of a place near Madina. *Ihāb*, (pl. آهبة *āhibat*, اهب *uhub* and *ahab*) A skin, a raw hide, not tanned or otherwise prepared.

A اهابة *ihābat*, (v. n. 4 of هاب for هيب) Calling to camels or cattle to make them stop or return.

A اهاجة *ihājat*, (v. n. 4 of هاج for هيج) Withering or drying plants (wind). Finding land having dry and withered plants.

P آهار *āhār*, Starch. Food. Polished steel.

P اهار *ahār*, Starch for glazing.

P آهازيدن *āhāzidan*, To draw (a sword).

P آهازيده *āhāzida*, Drawn out, extended. Lofty.

A اهاضيب *ahāzib*, Showers of large drops.

A اهال *ahāl* (or آهال *āhāl*) (pl. of اهل *ahl*) Families, relations. Domestics. Peoples.

A اهالة *ihālat*, (v. n. 4 of هال for هيل) Pouring out (sand or flour). (pl. اهالات *ihālāt*) Fat, grease, tallow, marrow. Oil. Condiment to bread.

A اهالي *ahālī*, (pl. of اهل *ahl*) Inhabitants, citizens, commons. Consorts, spouses. Domestics, family-folk. Possessors. Worthy. اهالي مملكت *ahālīi mamlakat*, Inhabitants of a kingdom.

A اهاليب *ahālīb*, (pl. of اهلوب *uhlūb*) Kinds, modes, manners. Frauds. Delays.

P اهالي كس *ahālī-kas*, The common people.

A اهاليل *ahālīl*, Rains. New moons.

P اهان *ahān*, Glue, starch. Border, fringe, list. Contamination, defilement. Pap, panado, gruel.

A اهان *ihān*, A trunk whose top and branches have been cut off: pollard. A bunch of dates (dry).

A اهانة *ihānat*, (v. n. 4 of هان for هون) Despising. Disdain, contempt, insult, affront. Hostility, enmity, treachery. P اهانت كردن *ihānat hardan*, To despise, treat with contempt.

A اهانذ *ahānid*, Hindoos.

P آهانه *āhāna*, (or اهانه *ahāna*) The crown of the head. The summit of a mountain. A hillock. An upper chamber, open gallery, or principal apartment in eastern houses. The top of a house. Villainy. A disgraceful action. Deformity.

A اهب *ahab* or *uhub*, (pl. of اهاب *ihāb*) Skins not tanned. *Uhab*, (pl. of اهبة *uhbat*) Warlike instruments, accoutrements, provisions, equipments.

A اهباء *ahbāʼ*, (pl. of هباء *habāʼ*) (Men) of weak understandings. *Ihbāʼ*, A raising of the dust.

A اهباب *ahbāb*, A garment, ragged or worn.

A اهباذ *ihbāz*, A running, flying, making haste.

A اهبار *ihbār*, (v. n. 4 of هبر) Growing very fat.

A اهباط *ihbāt*, A throwing down, precipitating.

A اهبال *ihbāl*, (v. n. 4 of هبل) Depriving of offspring, bereaving. Being quick, speedy, hasty.

A آهبة *āhibat*, (pl. of اهاب) Skins, raw hides.

A اهبة *uhbat*, (pl. اهب *uhab*) Provision made for any undertaking. (Warlike) apparatus. اخذ اهبة الشي *akhaza uhbata'sh shay*, He took the apparatus of the thing, he made himself master of it.

A اهبر *ahbar*, (A camel) full of flesh.

A اهبرة *ahbirat*, (pl. of هبير *habīr*) The lowest parts of mountains, low-lying grounds, valleys.

A اهبنقاع *ihbinkāʻ*, (v. n. 3 of هبقع Q) Sitting in the fashion called هبنقعة *habankaʻat*.

P آهبنيابه *āhbanyāba*, Yawning, gaping.

A اهبياخ *ihbīyākh*, A going with a strut.

A آهة *āhat*, Measles. Ah! آهة لك, Woe to thee!

A اهة *ahhat* or *ihhat*, A crying *ah*! from grief.

A اهتأ *ahtaʼ*, Hump-backed.

A اهتار *ahtār*, (pl. of هتر *hitr*) Lies. Idle, foolish speeches. Blunders, slips of the tongue. Wonders. Misfortunes. *Ihtār*, (v. n. 4 of هتر) Being delirious, talking incoherently (from folly, sickness, or age).

A اهتام *ihtām*, A knocking out of the front teeth.

A اهتباب *ihtibāb*, (v. n. 8 of هبّ) Cutting a stick. Rattling at rutting time (a he-goat).

A اهتباد *ihtibād*, (v. n. 8 of هبد) Gathering colocynths, bruising them, extracting the seeds, and macerating them, so that the bitterness may depart.

A اهتباذ *ihtibāz*, A hastening, running, flying.

A اهتبار *ihtibār*, (v. n. 8 of هبر) Amputating with a sword. Becoming quite extenuated (a camel).

A اهتباش *ihtibāsh*, (v. n. 8 of هبش) Being assembled, convened. Meeting with, obtaining.

A اهتباص *ihtibās*, (v. n. 8 of هبص) Laughing immoderately. Hastening. Alacrity, cheerfulness.

A اهتبال *ihtibāl*, (v. n. 8 of هبل) Providing for the wants of a family. Prizing much the words of wisdom. Watching for an opportunity or for prey. Lying much. Being bereft of a son. Deceit, machination. اهتبل هبلك Mind your business.

A اهتتاش *ihtitāsh*, A being irritated (a dog).

A اهتجاج *ihtijāj*, A persevering, protracting.

A اهتجار *ihtijār*, A separating from each other.

A اهتجاس *ihtijās*, (v. n. 8 of هجس) Turning.

A اهتجال *ihtijāl*, (v. n. 8 of هجل) Inventing, producing something new.

A اهتجام *ihtijām*, A milking (of the udder dry).

A اهتجان *ihtijān*, A lying with a young girl.

A اهتداء *ihtidāʼ*, (v. n. 8 of هدي) Being directed right. Taking the lead. Finding the right way. Conducting (a bride to her husband).

A اهتذاذ *ihtizāz*, (v. n. 8 of هذّ) Cutting off quickly. Reading fast.

A اهتراش *ihtirāsh*, (v. n. 8 of هرش) Growling, fighting (dogs).

A اهتراع *ihtirāʻ*, (v. n. 8 of هرع) Breaking a stick.

A اهتزاز *ihtizāz*, (v. n. 8 of هز) Being shaken, agitated (tree by the wind). Fluttering. Tottering. Exultation, joy. Falling with glittering light (star). Growing long (grass). The noise of a cavalcade.

A اهتزاع *ihtizāʻ*, (v. n. 8 of هزع) Being shaken (a tree), brandished (a sword), vibrated (a lance). Making haste.

A اهتزام *ihtizām*, (v. n. 8 of هزم) Falling with noise (rain). Making a noise when running (a horse). Slaughtering a sheep. Hastening to sacrifice a victim, or to do any thing.

A اهتشال *ihtishāl*, (v. n. 8 of هشل) Taking (a camel) without the owner's consent, and returning him when the journey is over.

A اهتشام *ihtishām*, (v. n. 8 of هشم) Milking with the whole hand. Applying (the mind) unwillingly to any pursuit.

A اهتصار *ihtisār*, (v. n. 8 of هصر) Twisting, breaking. Binding and training the branches (of a palm-tree), so that the clusters (of dates) may hang conveniently. Being bent, twisted, or broken.

A اهتضاب *ihtizāb*, A talking loud and much.

A اهتضاض *ihtizāz*, (v. n. 8 of هضّ) Breaking in pieces. Regarding one's self as inadequate.

A اهتضام *ihtizām*, (v. n. 8 of هضم) Forcing, compelling. Injuring, defrauding, diminishing. Withholding part of another's due.

A اهتفاف *ihtifāf*, A humming or buzzing in the ear. The refulgence of vapours caused by the reflection of the sun, which, at a distance, makes the Arabian deserts to resemble the ocean.

A اهتقاع *ihtikāʻ*, (v. n. 8 of هقع) Keeping (another) back from any enterprise, and marring his success. Leaving any one for a day and then returning (a fever). Making (a she-camel) lie down and mounting (her). Changing colour.

A اهتكاع *ihtikāʻ*, (v. n. 8 of هكع) Being modest, submissive. Keeping (one) back from any enterprise and thwarting him. Manifesting impatience.

A اهتلاس *ihtilās*, A being stupid and senseless.

A اهتلاك *ihtilāk*, (v. n. 8 of هلك) Exposing one's self to danger.

A اهتلال *ihtilāl*, (v. n. 8 of هلّ) Shining with lightning (a cloud). Exposing to view white teeth.

A اهتلام *ihtilām*, A carrying off, going away with.

A اهتم *ahtam*, One whose fore-teeth are broken or dropt out.

A اهتماج *ihtimāj*, (v. n. 8 of همج) Being debilitated, enervated by heat. Becoming flabby (face).

A اهتمار *ihtimār*, (v. n. 8 of همر) Running (a horse).

A اهتماش *ihtimāsh*, (v. n. 8 of همش) Mixing one with another, tumultuously and with clamour. Advancing and receding. Being topsy turvy (locusts). Creeping along (an animal).

A اهتماص *ihtimās*, (v. n. 8 of همص) Throwing prostrate. Overcoming. Killing.

A اهتماط *ihtimāt*, (v. n. 8 of همط) Taking unduly of a thing, seizing, plundering. Injuring the reputation of another.

A اهتماع *ihtimāʻ*, A being changed (colour).

A اهتمام *ihtimām*, (v. n. 8 of همّ) Taking thought for, minding, attending to. Being concerned about. Being oppressed with cares. Solicitude, anxiety, care, attention. Endeavour, effort. Favour.

P اهتمام بندي *ihtimām-bandī*, An account specifying the number of Pergunnahs and the names of the Zamindārs in a province.

P اهتمام دار *ihtimām-dār*, An under-collector of revenue who acts on commission from a Zamindār. A responsible person.

A اهتناء *ihtināʼ*, (v. n. 8 of هنأ) Managing well (property), looking well after one's camels.

A اهتوار *ihtiwār*, (v. n. 8 of هار for هور) Perishing.

P آهته *āhta*, Drawn out (sword). Lofty.

A اهتياب *ihtiyāb*, A fearing, a being in awe of.

A اهتياج *ihtiyāj*, The being raised (dust).

A اهتياض *ihtiyāz*, (v. n. 8 of هاض for هيض) Breaking a bone again before it has been well set.

A اهتياف *ihtiyāf*, A suffering from thirst.

A اهتيال *ihtiyāl*, (v. n. 8 of هال for هول) Being terrified, fearing. Trembling.

A اهتيام *ihtiyām*, The act of deceiving, cheating.

A اهجاء *ihjāʼ*, (v. n. 4 of هجأ) Feeding, giving to eat, satisfying hunger. Paying (debts). Stopping (camels) in order to graze. (v. n. 4 of هجا for هجو) Discovering (a verse) to be satirical.

A اهجاد *ihjād*, (v. n. 4 of هجد) Sleeping. Causing to sleep. Finding asleep. Touching the ground with his neck (a camel).

A اهجار *ahjār*, (pl. of هجر *hajr*) Fruitful (countries). *Ihjār*, (v. n. 4 of هجر) Talking deliriously. Speaking obscenely. Cursing, reviling, reproaching, laughing to scorn. Leaving, abandoning. Growing up into beauty, improving in her paces (a she-camel). Going abroad in the heat of the day.

A اهجاع *ihjāʻ*, (v. n. 4 of هجع) Satisfying hunger.

A اهجال *ahjāl*, (pl. of هجل *hajl*) Extensive and level plains, especially between mountains *Ihjāl*, (v. n. 4 of هجل) Allowing to travel slow (camels). Enlarging (a thing). Losing, destroying (wealth).

A اهجام *ahjām*, (pl. of هجم *hajm* or *hajam*) Cups, goblets, bowls. *Ihjām*, (v. n. 4 of هجم) Coming in suddenly, entering unexpectedly. Introducing. Putting in a stable (camels). Removing a distemper (God).

A اهجان *ihjān*, (v. n. 4 of هجن) Having many camels of a white and excellent kind. Giving a girl in marriage ere she has attained the age of puberty. Covering a young camel.

A اهجر *ahjar*, More or most excellent, nobler, noblest. Longer, longest. Broader, broadest.

A اهجوة *uhjūwat*, (or اهجية *uhjiyat*) A satire.

A اهجيج *ihjīj*, A deep valley.

A اهجيراء *ihjīrāʼ*, (اهجيري *ihjīra'* or اهجورة *uhjūrat*) Custom, habit. Manner, state.

A اهجيري *ihjīra'*, (v. n. of هجر) Raving, doting (in sleep or sickness).

P آهختن *āhikhtan*, To unsheath, draw (a sword).

P آهخته *āhikhta*, Unsheathed, drawn (sword).

A اهدّ *ahadd*, A coward.

A اهدأ *ahdaʼ*, Curved, crook-backed. A shoulder swollen on the top and relaxed.

A اهداء *ihdāʼ*, (v. n. 4 of هدأ) Pacifying (a child, by patting it gently, and making it sleep). Giving ease from toil. Relaxing (the shoulder). Making decrepit (old age). (v. n. 4 of هدي) Offering, presenting. Sending. Leading (a bride home to her husband).

A اهداب *ahdāb*, (pl. of هدب *hadab*) Slender leaves of plants somewhat resembling hair. Hairy or tufted branches (of palms). *Ihdāb*, (v. n. 4 of هدب) Having long hanging branches (a tree).

A اهداد *ihdād*, The being strong and powerful.

A اهدار *ihdār*, (v. n. 4 of هدر) Permitting (blood) to be shed with impunity.

A اهداف *ahdāf*, (pl. of هدف *hadaf*) Targets, butts for archers. *Ihdāf*, (v. n. 4 of هدف) Approaching near (to fifty years of age). Looking down from an eminence. Being erected, exposed on an eminence (as a mark to shoot at). Being so large as to present a mark like a target (buttocks). Fleeing to, taking refuge. Happening, befalling. Going to meet, encountering.

A اهدام *ahdām*, (pl. of هدم *hidm*) Worn or tattered (garments). Mended, patched. Old (shoes).

A اهدان *ihdān*, (v. n. 4 of هدن) Making lean.

A اهدب *ahdab*, One who has long eye-lashes.

A اهدر *ahdar*, Swollen, inflated (belly).

A اهدل *ahdal*, Long-lipped (camel).

A اهدي *ahdā'*, Better or best guide or director.

A اهديدار *ihdīdār*, The falling (of rain).

A اهذاء *ihzāʼ*, (v. n. 4 of هذي) Over-boiling, or otherwise dressing meat, till the parts are dissolved.

A اهذاب *ihzāb*, (v. n. 4 of هذب) Proceeding expeditiously (in walking, flying, or talking). Pouring forth rain rapidly (a cloud).

A اهذار *ihzār*, (v. n. 4 of هذر) Babbling, doting.

P اهر *ahr*, A town between Ardabīl and Tabrīz. *Ahar*, The seed of the ash-tree. The ash-tree.

A اهر *ahar*, (pl. of اهرة *aharat*) Household goods.

A اهراء *ahrāʼ*, (pl. of هري *hury*) Barns, granaries, magazines. *Ihrāʼ*, (v. n. 4 of هرأ) Dressing (meat) till the flesh separates from the bone. Killing, injuring, blasting. Refreshing (the evening). Making a long oration in vain, talking balderdash.

A اهراب *ihrāb*, (v. n. 4 of هرب) Compelling, urging, putting to flight. Driving the dust (wind). Travelling expeditiously, quickening one's pace (from fear). Being deeply engaged or immersed.

A اهراج *ihrāj*, (v. n. 4 of هرج) Urging on (a camel) till he becomes uneasy.

A اهرار *ihrār*, (v. n. 4 of هرّ) Making (a dog) whine. Calling sheep (to water).

A اهراط *ahrāt*, (pl. of هرط) Aged (she-camels).

A اهراع *ihrāʻ*, (v. n. 4 of هرع) Pointing a spear at an enemy. Going, walking, or travelling fast. Trembling (from rage, fear, fever, or debility).

A اهراف *ihrāf*, (v. n. 4 of هرف) Increasing in wealth. Producing an early crop (palm-trees).

A اهراق *ihrāk*, (v. n. 4 of هرق) Pouring out (water). Shedding (blood).

A اهرام *ahrām*, (or الاهرام *al ahrām*) (pl. of هرم *haram*) The pyramids of Egypt (from their age). *Ihrām*, (v. n. of 4 هرم) Making decrepit, enfeebling.

P اهرامن *ahrāman*, A seducer. The devil.

P اهران *ahrān*, A hatchet, an adze, an axe.

A اهرة *aharat*, (pl. اهر *ahar* and اهرات *aharāt*) Household furniture, utensils. A good condition. Form, figure, shape.

A اهرت *ahrat*, (or اهرد) Wide-mouthed (lion).

A اهرشفاف *ihrishfāf*, (v. n. 4 of هرشف Q) Drying up (cotton in an inkstand).

P اهرم *ahram*, A pestle.

A اهرمّاع *ihrimmāʻ*, (v. n. 4 of هرمع Q) Walking quickly. Being swift, agile. Being contentious. Talking much. Feigning to weep. Flowing (water or tears).

P آهرمن *āhraman*, (*āharman*, اهرامن *ahraman*, or *ahriman*) Leading into wickedness: a seducer. A demon: the devil. The principle of Evil, in opposition to Ormuzd, the principle of Good.

P آهرمن‌خوي *āhraman-khū*, Devilish-tempered.

P آهرن *āhran*, (or آهزن *āhzan*) Naphtha, a kind of very inflammable bituminous substance, gathered from the surface of water, of a clear pale yellow colour. *Āhran*, A seducer. The devil.

P اهرن *ahran*, A seducer. The devil.

P اهرون *ahrūn*, Name of a Jewish physician.

A اهرياق *ihriyāk*, The effusion of water.

P آهريمن *āhrīman*, (or اهريمن *ahrīman*, آهريمه *āhrīma*, or اهريمه *ahrīma*) A seducer. The devil.

A اهزاء *ihzāʼ*, (v. n. 4 of هزأ) Bearing, and exposing one's self to, intense cold. Killing (a camel) by cold. Making haste, travelling swiftly.

A اهزاج *ihzāj*, (v. n. 4 of هزج) Writing in الهزج *al hazaj* verse.

A اهزاق *ihzāk*, (v. n. 4 of هزق) Laughing much.

A اهزال *ihzāl*, (v. n. 4 of هزل) Having lean cattle. Confining cattle through straits and penury. Finding one playful, jocose, jesting, and trifling.

A اهزع *ahzaʻ*, The last arrow in the quiver (whether unused from its badness, or reserved for its excellence till some critical occasion). ما في الدار اهزع *mā fi'd dār ahzaʻ*, Nobody in the house.

P آه زنان *āh-zanān*, Sighing.

P اهزون *ahzūn*, Now. *Uhzūn*, A barren woman.

P آهستگي *āhistagī*, Lenity, gentleness, softness, mildness. Calmness, deliberation. بآهستگي گفتن *ba āhistagī guftan*, To speak in a whisper.

P آهسته *āhista*, Soft, tender, delicate. Gentle. Grave, sedate, modest, quiet. Calmly. Slowly, gently, by degrees, step by step, softly. Whisperingly, in a low voice, piano. سخن آهسته *sukhani āhista*, A whisper. سخن آهسته گفتن *sukhani āhista guftan*, To whisper, to speak a word in the ear.

P آهسته راي *āhista-rāy*, Wise, skilful, learned.

P آهسته رو *āhista-rav*, Walking gently. Slow.

A اهشاء *ahshāʼ*, Astonished, bewildered persons.

A اهشال *ihshāl*, (v. n. 4 of هشل) Lending (a horse) without, or against, the consent of the owner.

P آهشتگي *āhishtagī*, Lowness, softness of voice.

A اهصاء *ahsā*, Strong, intrepid, brave, gallant.

A اهضاء *ahzā*, Crowds, bodies of men.

A اهضاب *ihzāb*, A being verbose, speaking loud.

A اهضال *ihzāl*, (v. n. 4 of هضل) Raining abundantly. Striking (a bucket) against the side of a well, and drawing out all the water.

A اهضام *ahzām*, (pl. of هضم *hazm* and هضم *hizm*) Low, extensive grounds. Bottoms of valleys. (pl. of هضم *hazam*) Certain aromatic substances. الليل و اهضام الوادي *al layla wa ahzāma'l wādī*, The night and the deep valley (*i. e.* Take care of the night and places of danger)! *Ihzām*, (v. n. 4 of هضم) Shedding the milk-teeth (cattle).

A اهضم *ahzam*, One who has thick fore-teeth. Shrunk, lank. Gaunt-bellied. Slender-waisted.

A اهضوبة *uhzūbat*, A shower with large drops.

A اهطاع *ihtāʿ*, (v. n. 4 of هطع) Stretching out the neck, hanging the head, and travelling fast.

A اهفاء *ahfāʾ*, Fools, coxcombs, simpletons.

A اهقاء *ihkāʾ*, A corrupting (in morals).

P آهك *āhak*, (or اهك *ahak*) Quick-lime, plaster, cement. Ointment compounded of quick-lime and arsenic (used in the baths as a depilatory). آهك سياه *āhaki siyāh*, A kind of strong cement. آهك صدف *āhaki sadaf*, Shell-lime.

A اهكاء *ahkāʾ*, Astonished, stupefied (people).

A اهكاك *ahkāk*, Persons labouring in mind.

P آهك پز *āhak-paz*, A lime-burner.

A اهكومة *uhkūmat*, Derision, mockery.

A آهل *āhil*, Peopled (place).

A أهل *ahala*, (fut. يأهل *yaʾhilu* or *yaʾhulu*) He married. *Ahila*, (fut. يأهل *yaʾhilu*) He associated with.

A اهل *ahl*, (pl. اهلون *ahlūna*, اهالي *ahālī*, آهال *āhāl*, اهلات *ahlāt*, and *ahalāt*) People (belonging to any particular person, place, order, or profession). An inhabitant. A family. Kindred, relations. A lord, master. A husband. A spouse, a wife. A domestic. Worthy, fit, apt. Capable, skilful. Endowed with, possessed of. اهل اتّقا *ahli ittikā*, The faithful, pious. اهل ادراك *ahli idrāk*, Intelligent, sagacious. اهل الارض *ahlu'l arz*, Demons. T اهل ازنيك *ahli iznīk*, A citizen of Nice. A اهل اسلام *ahli islām*, A true believer, orthodox. اهل الردّة *ahlu'r riddat*, An apostate. اهل السنّة *ahlu's sunnat*, An observer of the law, a Musulmān. One who is circumcised. اهل الله *ahlu'llāh*, People of God. The people of Mecca. اهل اهلة *ahlu ahilatin*, Wealthy persons. اهل اهواء *ahli ahwāʾ*, Heretics, visionaries. اهل ايمان *ahli īmān*, A believer. اهل باطن *ahli bātin*, Contemplative, pious, spiritual. P اهل بچه *ahli bacha*, A sodomite. A اهل بصيرت *ahli basīrat*, Provident, prudent, sagacious. اهل بغي *ahli baghy*, Wicked, tyrannical. P اهل بهشت *ahli bihisht*, The blessed, the inhabitants of Paradise. A اهل بيت *ahli bayt*, (P اهل خانه *ahli khāna*) People of the house, domestics. P اهل پرهيز *ahli parhez*, Continent, abstinent. A اهل تصوّف *ahli tasawwuf*, Contemplative. An anchorite. اهل تعدّي *ahli taʿaddī*, Unjust, cruel. A tyrant. اهل تفسير *ahli tafsīr*, A doctor in theology, a commentator on holy writ. اهل تقويٰ *ahli takwa'*, (or اهل متورّع *ahli mutawarriʿ*) Pious, devout. اهل تواضع *ahli tawāzuʿ*, Submissive. اهل جماعت *ahli jamāʿat*, A member of the community. اهل جنّت *ahli jannat*, The inhabitants of Paradise. اهل جهنم *ahli jahannam*, The damned. اهل حال *ahli hāl*, Skilled or conversant in the state of things. اهل حجاب *ahli hijāb*, Veiled. Modest. اهل حرفت *ahli hirfat*, (or اهل صنعت *ahli sanʿat*) An artificer. اهل حق و يقين *ahli hak u yakīn*, Wise, contemplative, pious. اهل حكمت *ahli hikmat*, Wise, philosophical. A worker of miracles. اهل خبرت *ahli khubrat*, A censor, critic, connoisseur. اهل الدار *ahlu'd dār*, (People of the house) Domestics. P اهل دانش انتباه *ahli dānish-intibāh*, Cautious and vigilant. اهل درون *ahli darūn*, Confidants. اهل دكّان *ahli dukkān*, A shop-keeper. اهل دل *ahli dil*, Brave, spirited, generous. A اهل دنيا *ahli dunya'*, Inhabiting the world, worldly. اهل دول *ahli dawl*, A monied man. اهل ديوان *ahli dīwān*, A counsellor of state, senator, minister. اهل ذكر *ahli zikr*, Conversant with the Scriptures. اهل ذوق *ahli zawk*, Addicted to pleasure, a voluptuary. اهل رجا *ahli rajā*, A supplicant, expectant. اهل الرجل *ahlu'r rajul*, Neighbours. Domestics. P اهل روزگار *ahli rozgār*, A man of the world. A اهل زمان *ahli zamān*, Observant of, conforming to, the times. P اهل زمين *ahli zamīn*, Inhabiting the earth. A اهل زهد و ورع *ahli zuhd u waraʿ*, Pious, devout, self-denying. اهل سخاوت *ahli sakhāwat*, Liberal, munificent. اهل سياحت *ahli siyāhat*, A traveller. اهل شرع *ahli sharʿ*, A legislator, lawyer, public teacher of the law. اهل شرف *ahli sharaf*, Noble, eminent. اهل شقاق *ahli shikāk*, Seditious, inimical. اهل شوكت *ahli shawkat*, Great, powerful. اهل شهود *ahli shuhūd*, A professor of religion. Holy, inspired. اهل صفا *ahli safā*, Pure in heart. A voluptuary. اهل صورت *ahli sūrat*, Superficial, one who skims the surface of things. اهل ضلال *ahli zalāl*, An infidel, heretic. اهل طاعت *ahli tāʿat*, Obedient to God, faithful. اهل طبقة *ahli tabka*, Unobservant of the precepts of Muhammad. اهل طرف *ahli tirf*, Noble. اهل طريق *ahli tarīk*, An observer of the laws of Muhammad. اهل ظاهر *ahli zāhir*, Hypocrites, having only the external appearance of goodness. اهل عذاب *ahli ʿazāb*, The damned. اهل عرفان *ahli ʿirfān*, Learned, scientific. اهل عرفت *ahli ʿurfat*, Artificers, artisans. اهل عقول *ahli ʿukūl*, Prudent, judicious. اهل علم *ahli ʿilm*, Learned. اهل علم رقم *ahli ʿilmi raham*, An arithmetician. اهل علم كلام *ahli ʿilmi kalām*, An orator, rhetorician. اهل علم منطق *ahli ʿilmi mantik*, A logician. اهل علم نجوم *ahli ʿilmi nujūm*, An astronomer, astrologer. اهل عهد و ذمّت *ahli ʿahd u zimmat*, Tributary. اهل عيافة *ahli ʿiyāfa*, Soothsayers. اهل عيال *ahli ʿiyāl*, The father or master of a family. اهل غدر *ahli ghadr*, Fraudulent, perfidious. اهل غوايت *ahli ghawāyat*, Vagrants. اهل فراش *ahli firāsh*, Bed-ridden. اهل فساد *ahli fasād*, A scoundrel, villain. اهل قبلة *ahli kibla*, Knowing which way to turn in prayer. اهل القبور *ahlu'l kubūr*, (Inhabitants of the tomb) The dead. اهل قريت *ahli karyat*, A villager. اهل قلم *ahli kalam*, A scribe. P اهل كار *ahli kār*, A workman, clerk. A اهل كتاب *ahli kitāb*, A learned man, a doctor in theology. Jews and Christians. اهل كرم *ahli karam*, Liberal, generous. اهل كلام *ahli kalām*, Eloquent; an orator. P اهل كين *ahli kīn*, An enemy. A اهل مجلس *ahli majlis*, Assistants, assessors. Members of good society, courtiers. اهل محاسبه *ahli muhāsaba*, An accountant. اهل محشر *ahli mahshar*, Those who rise at the day of judgment. اهل مدر *ahli madar*, The Arabs who inhabit cities. اهل مذهب *ahli mazhab*, A religionist. اهل مشورت *ahli mashwarat*, A counsellor, an adviser. اهل معرفت *ahli maʿrifat*, Learned. Possessed of the knowledge of God. اهل معنيٰ *ahli maʿna'*, Spiritual, intellectual, one who penetrates into divine mysteries. اهل مكه *ahli makka*, An inhabitant of Mecca. اهل مناجات *ahli munājāt*, Attending to prayer, supplicating God. اهل منزل *ahli manzil*, A household. اهل منصب *ahli mansab*, A minister, an official. اهل النبيّ *ahlu'n nabīy*, The family of the prophet, *i.e.* his wives, daughters, ʿAlīy his son-in-law and his wives, &c. اهل نظر *ahli nazr*, Perspicacious, clear-sighted. P اهل نشست *ahli nishast*, Hermits, recluses. A اهل نعيم *ahli naʿīm*, The inhabitants of Paradise, the blessed. اهل نفاق *ahli nifāk*, Perfidious, impious. اهل نفس *ahli nafs*, Sensualists. اهل نقيصت *ahli nakīsat*, Vicious. اهل وبر *ahli wabar*, The Scenite Arabs, who dwell in tents. اهل وقار *ahli wakār*, Grave, majestic, dignified. اهل وقوف *ahli wukūf*, Skilful. اهل هدا *ahli hada'*, (or هديٰ *hada'*) Following the right way, orthodox. P اهل هنر *ahli hunar*, Skilful. A اهل هوا *ahli hawā*, Licentious, libertine. *Ahal*, (v. n. of اهل) Associating with, being intimate and familiar. *Ahil*, Domestic, tame.

A اهلاً *ahlan*, (in supplication) God be with you! Heaven bless you! welcome. اهلاً و مرحباً *ahlan wa marhaban*, Welcome and welcome.

A اهلاب *ihlāb*, (v. n. 4 of هلب) Continuing his speed (a horse).

A اهلات *ahlāt* or *ahalāt*, (pl. of اهل *ahl*) Families, relations, kindreds.

A اهلاج *ihlāj*, (v. n. 4 of هلج) Hiding, concealing.

A اهلاس *ihlās*, (v. n. 4 of هلس) Concealing

any thing said or done. Ridiculing slily. Laughing gently. Talking in a whisper.

A اهلاك *ihlāk*, (v. n. 4 of هلك) Causing to perish. Ruining, destroying, proving fatal. Selling. P اهلاك نفس كردن *ihlāki nafs kardan*, To restrain the passions, mortify the desires.

A اهلال *ihlāl*, (v. n. 4 of هلّ) Looking at the new moon (هلال *hilāl*). Beginning to appear (the new moon). Observing the beginning of the month. Beginning (a month). Raising the voice, crying (as a child). Pronouncing the word لبّيك *labbayka* (I am obedient to thee). Invoking God by saying بسم الله *bi' smi'llāh* In the name of God (when sacrificing or consecrating any animal). Rolling the tongue about the mouth, when thirsty, in order to collect moisture. Cutting one (a sword).

A اهلام *ihlām*, (v. n. 4 of هلم) Saying to one هلم.

A اهلب *ahlab*, Hairy, bristly. Rainy (year). الاهلب *al ahlab*, A tail docked, without hair; also one abounding with hair.

P اهلبوب *ahlabūb*, (in zand and Pāz.) Heaven.

A اهلة *ahlat*, (a noun of unity) One people. A wife. *Ahilat*, Wealth, property.

A اهلّة *ahillat*, (pl. of هلال *hilāl*) New moons (especially on the first nights of their appearance).

A اهلك الله للخير *ahhalaka'llāh li'l khayr*, God bless you.

A اهلوب *uhlūb*, (pl. اهاليب *ahālīb*) A species, kind, sort. A mode, manner (of speaking).

A اهلول *uhlūl*, Vain, trifling, insignificant.

A اهلون *ahlūn*, (pl. of اهل) Families, kindreds.

A اهلي *ahlīy*, Domestic, tame, gentle. Belonging to a house or garden.

A اهلية *ahlīyat*, Worthiness. Aptitude. Ability. Possession.

A اهليلج *ihlīlij*, The myrobalan-tree, a kind of citron. اهليلج كابلي *ihlīliji kābilī*, Chebulic myrobalans. اهليلجات *ihlīlijāt*, Myrobalan-trees.

A اهلية *ahlīya*, A wife.

A اهمّ *ahamm*, More or most important, needful. اهمّ امور *ahammi umūr*, The most important things. P اهمّ كار *ahammi kār*, An affair of consequence.

A اهماء *ahmāʼ*, (pl. of هِمء *himʼ*) Worn-out clothes. *Ihmāʼ*, (v. n. 4 of هما) Tearing, wearing.

A اهمات *ihmāt*, A laughing or a speaking low.

A اهماج *ihmāj*, (v. n. 4 of همج) Straining every nerve, running at full gallop. Concealing, hiding.

A اهماد *ihmād*, (v. n. 4 of همد) Remaining quiet in a place. Being quiet, sedate. Proceeding expeditiously. Running hastily (to victuals). Pacifying. Causing to rest or remain. Keeping silence (with regard to any thing disagreeable).

A اهمار *ihmār*, (v. n. 4 of همر) Striking (the ground) violently with his feet (a horse).

A اهمال *ihmāl*, (v. n. 4 of همل) Letting alone, not making use of. Slighting, neglecting. Overlooking. Negligence, carelessness, indifference, indolence. Delay.

A اهمالاً *ihmālan*, (P اهمالانه) Carelessly.

A اهمام *ahmām*, (pl. of هِمّ *himm*) Frail old men. *Ihmām*, (v. n. 4 of همّ) Rendering solicitous, keeping in suspense. Waxing old and frail.

P اهمر *uhmar*, A jackall.

A اهمكاك *ihmikāk*, (or اهميكاك *ihmīkāk*) The being filled with rage.

P آهمند *āhmand*, A liar.

P اهمه *ahama*, A piece, portion. Deficient.

P آهن *āhan*, Iron. A sword. آهن افسرده *āhani afsurda*, A sword rusty and blunt. آهن نر *āhani nar*, Male iron or steel. آهن جفت *āhani juft*, (or آهن گاو *āhani gāv*) A ploughshare. آهن سرد *āhani sard*, (Cold iron) The human heart. آهن سرد كوفتن *āhani sard koftan*, (To beat cold iron) To waste time. آهن نرم *āhani narm*, Soft iron.

A آهن *āhin*, Hereditary wealth. Ready money.

A اهناء *ihnāʼ*, (v. n. 4 of هنا) Giving, bestowing. Giving food easy of digestion.

A اهناد *ahnād*, (pl. of هند *hind*) Hindas (a name).

P آهن آشيان *āhan-āshyān*, A thimble.

A اهناف *ihnāf*, (v. n. 4 of هنف) Making haste. Smiling ironically (a female). Beginning to cry.

A اهناق *ihnāk*, (v. n. 4 of هنق) Rendering restless, heating, chafing.

P اهنامه *ahnāma*, Disgrace, ignominy. Pomp, ostentation. Self-commendation. Fortune. Love. Transitory, evanescent.

A اهنان *ihnān*, (v. n. 4 of هنّ) Making fat and strong. Causing to weep.

P آهن بايه *āhambāya*, A yawning, a gaping.

P آهن بر *āhan-bar*, A robber, housebreaker.

P آهن پاره *āhan-pāra*, A splinter of iron.

P آهن پايه *āhan-pāya*, The foot of a spit.

P آهنج *āhanj*, A design, intention, resolution. A commencement. (in compos.) Casting, throwing, flinging, hurling. Extracting, drawing (a sword). Drinking, taking.

P آهن جان *āhan-jān*, Iron-hearted. Having a soul of iron. Tried in adversity.

P آهنجانيدن *āhanjānīdan*, To cause to drink.

P آهنجد *āhanjad*, A windlass, capstan.

P آهنجه *āhanja*, (or آهنچه *āhancha*) An iron ring. The knocker of a door. A weaver's instrument for stretching and keeping tight cloth in the loom. A rope, by means of which weavers fix to the wall or roof of the work-shop the extreme threads of the web, when near finished, and too short to be fastened to the beam.

P آهنجيدن *āhanjīdan*, To drink. To drag. To fling. To swim. To weigh. To peel.

P آهنخاي *āhan-khāy*, A bravo. A strong horse.

A اهند *ahnud*, (pl. of هند *hind*) Hindas.

P آهن دل *āhan-dil*, Brave, fearless, intrepid.

P آهنديگ *āhan-deg*, An iron cauldron.

P آهن ربا *āhan-rubā*, (Iron-attracting) A magnet.

P آهن رگ *āhan-rag*, A strong horse.

P آهن ساي *āhan-sāy*, A file. An iron coal-rake.

A اهنع *ahnaʻ*, Hump-backed. (A horseman) unable to sit erect. The son of a noble lady.

P آهن قبا *āhan-kabā*, A coat of mail.

P آهنكش *āhan-kash*, (Attracting iron) A magnet.

P آهنگ *āhang*, Concord, symphony, harmony, modulation, melody, pitch, tune. Design, institution, purpose, intention. Canon, regulation. Rule, custom, manner of proceeding. A row, a series. The side (of a cistern). The curve or arch of a cupola or dome. A tether, stable, stall. Haste, expedition. Behold! آهنگ حجاز *āhangi hijāz*, A kind of music introduced into Persia from Arabia. آهنگ ستيز كردن *āhangi sitez kardan*, To draw up in order of battle, to clear or make ready for an engagement. آهنگ كردن *āhang kardan*, To sound, resound, to make a noise, to cry aloud. To sing. To tune an instrument. To prepare for, to undertake (a journey). آهنگ گريز ساختن *āhangi gurez sākhtan*, To prepare for flight. دراز آهنگ *dirāz-āhang*, Stretching out (as a lion when going to spring). شمشير آتش آهنگ *shamshīri ātish-āhang*, A flaming sword, a sword striking fire.

P اهنگاه *ahangāh*, Then, after.

P آهنگر *āhangar*, A blacksmith. A dealer in iron.

P آهنگري *āhangarī*, Smithcraft.

P آهنگي *āhangī*, Consonance, harmony.

P آهنگيدن *āhangīdan*, To intend, design, propose. To draw out, tear, pull off, peel, or skin. To swim, float. To break.

P آهنو *āhnū*, Seeds, grains. A scare-crow. *Āhnū*, (or آهنوا) Provisions carried to working people.

P اهنوخوشي *ahnūkhwashī*, The fourth or lowest class, that of the artisans, instituted by Jamshed.

P اهنود *ahnavad*, Name of the first of the five days added to the Persian year, to make their twelve months, of thirty days each, equal to a solar year.

P آهنه *āhana*, An iron ring.

P آهني *āhanī*, Made of iron.

P آهنيابه *āhunyāba*, A yawning, a gaping.

P آهنين *āhanīn*, Iron, made of iron.

P آهنين پنجه *āhanīn-panja*, Iron-handed: strong, powerful, oppressive.

P آهنين جان *āhanīn-jān*, Inured to distress. Cruel, unfeeling, iron-hearted.

P آهنين جگر *āhanīn-jigar*, Cruel. Intrepid.

P آهنين خفتان *āhanīn-khaftān*, An iron cuirass.

P آهنين دوش *āhanīn-dosh*, Strong, stout, sturdy.

P آهنين رگ *āhanīn-rag*, A muscular horse.

P آهنين كرسي *āhanīn-kursī*, An anvil.

P آهنين كمر *āhanīn-kamar*, A brave veteran.

P آهو *āhū*, A vice, fault, defect, stain, spot, villainy. Flight, escape. An exclamation, cry for help. An asthma. A deer, roe, gazelle. Any object of pursuit or chace. A beautiful eye. A mistress. آهوي چين *āhūʼi chīn*, The China or musk-deer. آهوي

آهوئِ خانۂ خاوري *āhū-i khāna-i khāwarī*, (آهوئِ خاور *āhū-i khāwar* or خاوري *khāwarī*, The sun) The sun. The sovereign of China and Tartary. The emperor of China. آهوئِ زرين *āhū-i zarīn*, The sun. A golden goblet. آهوئِ سياه *āhū-i siyāh*, The black antelope. آهوئِ سيمين *āhū-i sīmīn*, A fair-skinned cup-bearer. آهوئِ شيرافگن *āhū-i sher-afgan*, (The lion-subduing fawn) The eye of a mistress. A cup-bearer, a page. آهوئِ فلك *āhū-i falak*, The sun. آهوئِ كسي بودن *āhū-i kase badan*, To be taken prisoner. آهوئِ مانده گرفتن *āhū-i mānda giriftān*, (To seize a wearied doe) To oppress. آهوئِ نر *āhū-i nar*, A black and white cloud.

A اهواء *ahwā*, (pl. of هوي *hawa'*) Loves, desires, affections. Musical airs. Erroneous notions in religion, heresies. *Ihwā*, (v. n. 4 of هوي) Falling, descending from a height. Holding a sword in a menacing posture. Stretching forth the hand to receive any thing, or to beckon any one.

P اهوار *ahwār*, Astonished, amazed, stupefied.

A اهوار *ahwār*, (pl. of هور *hawr*) Pools, ditches, marshes, or quagmires, into which one easily sinks. Flocks of sheep, especially when numerous and tumbling one over the other.

A اهواز *ahwāz*, A name of nine towns lying between Basra and Persia; each town has a distinct name, but they are all comprised under the collective name Ahwāz. They are, رامهرمز *rāma hurmuz*, عسكر مكرم *ʿaskaru mukram*, تستر *tustar*, جنديسابور *junday sābūr*, سوس *sūs*, سرق *surrak*, نهرتيري *nahru tīra'*, ايذج *ayzah*, and مناذر *manāzir*.

A اهوال *ahwāl*, (pl. of هول *hawl*) Terrors, dangers, frightful things. P سفرِ پر اهوال *safari pur ahwāl*, A dangerous journey.

P آهوان *āhwān*, A fawn. The nape.

P اهواند *ahwānd*, (or اهوانه *ahwāna*) The first of the five supplemental days added to the Persian year.

P آهواي *āhwāy*, Name of a town on the Oxus.

P آهوبره *āhū-bara*, A fawn. آهوبرۂ فلك *āhū-bara-i falak*, The sign Aries. The sun.

P آهو پاي *āhū-pāy*, Swift-footed. A house of an hexagonal form. A parlour to which you ascend by a winding or spiral staircase.

A اهوج *ahwaj*, Tall. Foolish, precipitate.

A اهود *ahwad*, The old Arabic name of Monday.

P اهور *ahwar*, A beloved object.

P آهوري *āhorī*, Mustard.

P اهوز *ahwaz*, Name of a celebrated archer.

A اهوس *ahwas*, A consumer, eater, devourer. النّاس هوسي و الزمان اهوس *an nās hawsa' wa'z zamān ahwas*, Men consume (the fruits of the earth) and time devours (them).

A اهوعة *ahwiʿat*, (pl. of هواع *huwāʿ*) Months of ذو القعدة *zū'l kaʿda*.

P آهو كردن *āhū kardan*, To blame, find fault.

P آهوگان *āhūgān*, (pl. of آهو *āhū*) Fawns.

P آهول *āhūl*, A vice. A subterraneous passage.

A اهول *ahwal*, More or most terrible. ما اهول *mā ahwala*, O how dreadful! *Uhūl*, (v. n. of اهل) Marrying a wife. Founding a family. Becoming familiar with, or accustomed to, any thing.

A اهوم *ahwam*, Large-headed (man).

P آهو ماده *āhū-māda*, A doe, hind, gazelle, roe.

P آهون *āhūn*, (or اهون *ahūn*) A cavern, grotto, pit, mine, or any subterraneous place. A hole in a wall, especially one made by a house-breaker.

A اهون *ahwan*, Easy, smooth. More or most contemptible. More or most easy. Lighter. An old Arabic name for Monday.

A اهوناء *ahwinā*, (pl. of هيّن *hayyin*) Quiet, easy. Despicable.

P آهونبر *āhūn-bar* or *āhūn-bur*, A house-breaker. A miner. A well-digger.

P آهو وره *āhū-vara*, (for آهو بره) A fawn.

P آهوي *āhuwī*, Belonging to a fawn. Fawn-like.

A اهوي *ahwa'*, Dearer, more agreeable (to me than aught else). Name of a mountain and place.

A اهوية *ahwiyat*, (pl. of هواء) Airs, atmospheres.

A اهويّة *uhwīyat*, Air, atmosphere. A very low-lying place, a deep valley or pit.

A اهوينان *ihwīnān*, (v. n. 11 of هان for هون) Lying low and spacious (a country).

P آهويي *āhūyī*, Terror, fright. Vice, fault, blemish. Escape.

P آهي *āhī*, (in zand and Pāzand) A fawn.

A اهي *ahy*, (v. n. of اهي) Laughing aloud.

4 اهياج *ihyāj*, (v. n. 4 of هاج for هيج) Finding land with dry and withered plants.

P آهيانه *āhiyāna*, (or اهيانه *ahiyāna*) The skull. The throat. The palate. One side of the head.

A اهيب *ahyab*, More or most revered.

A اهيجنة *uhayjinat*, Boys married too young.

P آهيختن *āhekhtan*, To draw (a sword). To educate. To intend. To hang, suspend.

P آهيخته *āhekhta*, Extracted. Educated. Intended. Hung, suspended,

P آهيز *āhez*, Modestly. Softly! stop! halt!

A اهيس *ahyas*, Bold, strenuous, unshrinking.

A اهيغ *ahyagh*, Fertile, plentiful (year). The conveniences of life, abundance of good things. Plenty (of water). الاهيغان *al ahyaghāni*, (du.) Meat and drink. Food and venery.

A اهيف *ahyaf*, Slender-waisted.

A اهيق *ahyak*, Long-necked.

A اهيل *ahyal*, Spread, scattered, poured out (sand). *Uhayl*, A little family. Name of a place.

A اهيم *ahyam*, Dark, starless (night).

A اهيمان *ahyamāni*, A torrent, and resty camel.

A آهين *āhīn*, (for آهن *āhan*) Iron.

P آي *āy*, (imper. of آمدن *āmadan*) Come. (in compos.) Coming. A comer.

A آي *āy*, (pl. of آية *āyat*) Signs. Miracles. Verses of the Kur'ān. Individuals.

P اي *ay*, O! ho! hallo! Namely, that is to say. اي بار خدا *ay bārī khudā*, O great God!

A اي *ay*, That is, to wit, viz. Who? which? what? O (vocative particle). *Ī*, Yes, ay, indeed.

A ايّ *ayy*, (fem. ايّة *ayyat*) Whoever, whosoever. Who? which? what? ايّ رجل *ayyu rajulin*, Whatever man; or what man? What a man! ايّكم *ayyukum*, Any of you; or, which of you? ايّ حين *ayya hīnin*, In whatever time; or, in what time? لايّ سبب *li ayyi sababin*, On whatever account; or, on what account? ايّهم في الدار *ayyuhum fī' d dār*, Who is in the house?—When the same noun that is governed by ايّ *ayy* also precedes, it implies something indefinite: as, مررت برجل وايّ رجل *marartu bi rajulin wa ayyu rajulin*, I passed a man; but what man (I do not know); or, by way of admiration: as, وقع بلاء وايّ بلاء *wakaʿa balāʾun, wa ayyu balāʾin*, Trouble befel (him), but such trouble! *Ayy*, The vocative O! A particle of calling, Ho! do you hear? hark-ye! hola! have a care!

P آيا *āyā*, Whether or not? is it not? May be, perhaps, perchance, possibly. A particle of interrogation: as, آيا زيد استاده است يا عمر *āyā zayd istāda ast yā ʿamr*, Is Zayd or Amr standing (there)? آيا زيد اين جا نيست *āyā zayd injā nīst*, Is not Zayd here?

P ايا *ayā*, Ho! hark ye! Ah! alas!

A ايا *ayā*, O! ho! hola! *Iya'* Light, brightness.

A ايّا *iyā*, Have a care! ايّاك و الاسد *iyāka wa'l asad*, Beware of the lion! ايّاك ان تفعل كذا *iyāka an tafʿala kazā*, Beware of doing so. ايّاك و المخالفة *iyāka wa'l mukhālafat*, Beware lest thou contend. *Īyā* is a pleonastic particle prefixed to personal pronouns: as, ايّاي *iyāya'*, Me. ايّاك *iyāka*, Thee. ايّاه *iyāhu*, Him. ايّاكما *iyākumā*, You two. ايّاهما *iyāhumā*, Them two. ايّانا *iyānā*, Us. ايّاكم *iyākum*, You. ايّاهم *iyāhum*, Them; and are governed by the verb, either following: as, ايّاك نعبد *iyāka naʿbudu*, Thee we adore; or preceding: as, ضرب ايّاك *zaraba iyāka*, He beat thee. When the action operates upon the agent it becomes equivalent to نفس *nafs*, Soul, self: as, ضربت ايّاي *zarabtu iyāya'*, I beat myself.

A اياء *ayāʾ*, (or آياء *āyāʾ*) (pl. of آية *āyat*) Signs. Verses of the Kur'ān. Persons. *Ayāʾ*, (or اياء *iyyāʾ*) Light, brightness. Splendour of the sun.

A ايآب *īʾāb*, (v. n. 4 of وأب) Provoking, enraging. Outraging decency, putting to the blush. Averting shamefully from (his) business.

A اياب *ayāb*, (v. n. of آب for اوب) Setting (the sun). *Iyāb*, (v. n. of آب for اوب) Returning. The setting of the sun. A return.

A ايّاب *ayyāb*, A water-seller. A cup-bearer. *Īyāb*, A return. *Uyyāb*, (pl. of آئب *āʾib*) Returners.

A ايابس *ayābis*, (pl. of ايبس *aybas*) Legs (especially the fore parts of them), dry, hard, fleshless. Hard substances, upon which they prove swords.

A اياة *ay,at*, Form, figure, aspect.

A اياة *ayāt* or *iyāt*, Splendour (of the planets).

A آيات *āyāt*, (pl. of آية *āyat*) Signs, miracles. Verses of the Kur'ān. Persons, individuals. آيات متشابهات *āyāti mutashābihāt*, Verses which may be variously interpreted. آيات محكمات *āyāti mukkamāt*, Incontrovertible, unambiguous verses.

A ايات *ay,āt*, Begone! away!

A اياد *iyād*, Whatever preserves, defends, or protects. A fortification, castle, asylum. A fortified hill. A veil, curtain. Air, ether, atmosphere. A side, edge, margin, shore. Mounds of clay or earth raised round tents, houses, or cisterns, to keep out, or hold in, water. The right or left wing of an army (both wings are called ايادان *iyādāni*). A hill or large heap (of sand). A great number of camels. هو في اياد الله *huwa fī iyādi'llāh*, He is under the protection of God.

A ايادي *ayādī*, (pl. of يد *yad*) Hands.

A ايادم *ayādim*, Rugged hills. (pl. of اندامة *i,dāmat*) Hard grounds without stones.

A آيار *āyār*, (pl. of اير *ayr*) Veretra.

A ايآر *ī,ār*, (v. n. 4 of وار) Terrifying, causing to fly. Announcing, proclaiming, making known.

P ايار *ayār*, Computation.

A ايار *ayār*, Copper.

G ايار *iyār*, Air, atmosphere.

A ايّار *ayyār*, A Syro-Macedonian month, May.

G ايارج *iyārij*, An aperient medicine.

P ايارده *iyārida* or *ayārda*, A commentary on the Zand, and called Pāzand.

P ايارگير *ayār-gīr*, An accountant.

P اياره *ayāra*, A bracelet. A laxative medicine. A register, an account-book. Quantity. Space. Number. Measure.

P اياره گير *ayāra-gīr*, A scribe, an accountant.

A اياري *uyāriy*, Magno veretro præditus.

P اياز *āyāz*, (or اياز *ayāz*) Name of a favourite of Sultān Mahmūd of Ghaznah. Name of one of the Emirs of Sultān Ibrahim bin Massūd bin Mahmūd Ghaznawīy.

P ايازي *ayāzī*, A woman's black veil.

P اياس *ayās*, Name of a favourite of Mahmūd.

A اياس *iyās*, (v. n. of ايس) Despairing. Name of seventeen companions of Muhammad, and of several compilers of traditions. Name of a judge in Baghdad, who was so excellent a physiognomist, that he discovered the guilt or innocence of prisoners by their looks; hence the proverb افرس من اياس *afras min iyās*, Better physiognomist than Iyās; and فراسة اياسيّة *firāsat iyāsiyat* implies physiognomy, or the conjecture of Iyās.

A اياسة *iyāsat*, A causing one to depair.

P اياسرم *iyāsaram*, The fourth period consisting of thirty days, in which the trees were created (according to ancient Persian cosmogony).

P اياسه *ayāsa*, Desire, wish. A ring. A hook.

P اياسي *ayāsī*, A sort of woman's veil.

A اياسين *ayāsin*, (pl. of ايسان *īsān*) Men.

A اياصر *ayāṣir*, or اياصي, Short ropes with which the lower parts of tents are fastened to the pegs.

A اياطل *ayāṭil*, (pl. of ايطل *ayṭal*) Those parts of the belly and sides under the short-ribs.

P اياغ *ayāgh*, A cup, drinking vessel.

A ايّاك *iyyāka*, Begone! Take heed Beware!

A ايآل *ī,āl*, (v. n. 4 of وال) Being full of the dung of sheep and camels (a place). Filling a place with dung (sheep and camels).

A ايال *iyāl* (v. n. of آل for اول) Thickening. Ruling, governing (as a king). Administering, managing well. Becoming thick. A vessel.

A ايالات *iyālāt*, Valleys. Rivers.

A ايالة *iyālat*, (v. n. of آل for اول) Governing. Administering, managing property. Dominion, prefecture, administration, rule. حسن ايالت *husni iyālat*, Good government. P ايالت كردن *iyālat kardan*, To govern.

A ايام *iyām*, (v. n. of آم for ايم) Making a smoke. Destroying bees by fumigation. Taking honey from a hive. Troubling. *Uyām* or *iyām*, A disease peculiar to a camel. (pl. اوم *uyum*) Smoke.

A ايّام *ayyām*, (pl. of يوم *yawm*) Days. Favours, benefits. Times, seasons. Wind, weather. Battles. ايّام باحور *ayyāmi bāhūr*, The dog-days. ايّام عشر *ayyāmi ʻashar*, The ten days' festival at the Muharram. ايّام معدودات *ayyāmi maʻdūdāt*, Three days after slaying the sacrifices at Mecca. ايّام معلومات *ayyāmi maʻlūmāt*, The ten first days of Z'ul hajjah. P ايّام بوقلمون *ayyāmi būkalamūn*, Changeable times, untoward circumstances. ايّام شادي *ayyāmi shādī*, Holidays allowed at a marriage. A ذو ايّام *zū ayyām*, Disastrous (day).

A ايّا ما *ayyan mā*, (for ايّ اسم ما *ayyu ismi mā*) Of whatever name.

A ايامن *ayāmin*, (pl. of ايمن *ayman*) Prosperous, successful. (pl. of يمين *yamīn*) Right sides.

A ايامي *ayāmā'*, (pl. of ايّم *ayyim*) Widows. Single or unmarried women.

A ايامين *ayāmīn*, (pl. of يمين) Right hands.

P آيان *āyān*, (pl. of آي *āy*) Comers.

A ايّان *ayyāna* or *īyāna*, When? ايّان ما *ayyāna mā*, Whensoever. *Ayyāni*, (du. of ايّ *ayy*) Which two?

A ايّانا *iyyānā*, Us.

A اينق *ayānik*, (pl. of ناقة *nākat*) She-camels.

A ذو اياوم *zū ayāwim*, Disastrous (day).

A ايا وين *ayāwīn*, (pl. of ايوان) Galleries.

A ايّاه *iyyāhu*, Him, it. ايّاها *iyyāhā*, Her. ايّاهم *iyyāhum*, Them. ايّاهما *iyyāhumā*, Them two. ايّاهنّ *iyyāhunna*, Them (fem.).

A ايّاي *iyyāya'*, I, me.

A ايايا *ayāyā*, Courage! Get on! gee!

A ايابر *uyāyir*, Name of a place in the Hawrān.

A ايائل *ayā,il*, (pl. of ايّل *iyyal*, *uyyal*, or *ayyul*) Harts.

A ايائم *ayā,im*, (pl. of ايّم *ayyim*) Widows.

A آئب *ā,ib*, (pl. اوب *awb*, اوّاب *uwwāb*, and ايّاب *uyyāb*) One who returns. Who turns towards.

A ايباء *ībā,*, (v. n. 4 of وبأ) Suffering from the plague. Making a sign, pointing with the finger; beckoning for one to approach (ايما *īmā* being the word used when one is beckoned to retire). The sign so made with the finger. Having the stomach overloaded with milk (a camel's colt).

A ايباد *ībād*, A separating (from the flock).

A ايبار *ībār*, (v. n. 4 of وبر) Being hairy (a camel).

A ايباس *ībās*, (v. n. 4 of يبس) Drying. Producing withered plants (ground). Inhabiting, or travelling through such a country. Keeping a profound silence.

A ايباش *ībāsh*, (v. n. 4 of وبش) Hastening. (Ground) producing, shooting forth (luxuriant and entangled plants or herbage).

A ايباص *ībāṣ*, (v. n. 4 of وبص) Abounding with herbage (grounds). Producing flame, beginning to burn (fire).

A ايباط *ībāt*, (v. n. 4 of وبط) Enfeebling. Inflicting wounds. Slaying. Conquering.

A ايباق *ībāk*, (v. n. 4 of وبق) Destroying, ruining. Imprisoning.

A ائبال *i,bāl*, The possessing of many camels.

A ايبال *ībāl*, Herds, flocks, or flights (of camels, oxen, sheep, or birds), following one another in rows.

A ايبالة *ībālat*, A bundle of grass or hay.

A ايباه *ībāh*, (v. n. 4 of وبه) Considering, understanding, perceiving, turning the mind to.

A آئبة *ā,ibat*, Water drunk at noon.

A ايبة *aybat* or *ībat*, (v. n. of آب for اوب) Returning. A return. The foot of a quadruped. *Ībat*, A noon-day potation.

P ايبد *aybad*, A spark of fire.

A ايبد *aybad*, A plant, having a grain like barley, with which they fatten cattle.

A ايبس *aybas*, (pl. ايابس *ayābis*) Dry. The fore-part of the leg, hard and fleshless. Harder, hardest. A hard substance used for proving swords.

P ايبك *ebak*, An idol. *Aybak*, Name of a village in Badakshān.

A ايبل *aybal* or *aybul*, A Christian monk.

A ايبليّ *aybulīy* or *aybalīy*, A Christian monk.

A آية *āyat*, (pl. آيات *āyāt*, آي *āy*, اياء *ayā,*, and آياء *āyā,*) A sign, miracle. An individual, a single person, body. A verse of the Kur'ān, of which there are 6236. A crowd, congregation, convocation, congress, assembly. الآية *al āyat*, See the text in the Kur'ān. آية الرجل *āyatu 'r rajul*, The person of a man. آية كريمة *āyat karīmat*, A verse of the Kur'ān. الآيتان *al āyatāni*, (or آيتان *āyatāni*) The two verses, confessions, or attestations, called الشهادتان *ash' shahādatāni*, لا اله الاّ الله و محمّد رسول الله *lā ilaha illā 'llāh, wa muhammad rasūlu'llāh,* There is no god but God, and Muhammad (is) the apostle of God.

A آيّة *ayyat,* (or ايّتما *ayyatumā* with the pleonastic ما *mā,* fem. ايّ *ayy,* Above) Whoever, whatsoever. What!

A ائتاء *iʼtāʼ,* (v. n. 4 of اتي) Bringing or giving a present. Compensating, requiting. A gift.

A ايتاح *ītāh,* (v. n. 4 of وتح) Bringing a little present (a poor man). Being indigent. Being importunate, in order to obtain any thing. Bringing into trouble and difficulty.

A ايتاخ *ītākh,* A conquering. An excelling.

A ايتاد *ītād,* (v. n. 4 of وتد) Driving or fixing firmly (a stake or peg called وتد *watad*).

A ايتار *ītār,* (v. n. 4 of وتر) Repeating the separate prayer called الوتر *al witr.* Stretching the bowstring, and bending the bow. Stringing a bow, or fixing to it a string for hanging it by. Making an even number an odd one (وتر *witr* or *watr*).

A ايتاغ *ītāgh,* (v. n. 4 of وتغ) Ruining. Afflicting. Corrupting (one's religion by sin). Detaining, imprisoning.

A ايتام *aytām,* (pl. of يتيم *yatīm*) Orphans. Incomparable. *Ītām,* (v. n. 4 of يتم) Having her children fatherless (a woman). Bereaving, orphaning, rendering orphans (يتيم *yatīm*).

A ائتام *iʼtām,* (v. n. 4 of اتم) Forcing (a woman), bursting and making both passages one.

A ايتان *ītān,* (v. n. 4 of يتن) Bringing forth preposterously, with the feet foremost (any female).

A ائتباب *iʼtibāb,* (v. n. 8 of ابّ) Preparing for a journey or other undertaking. (v. n. 9 of اتب) Putting on the garment called اتب *itb.*

A ائتبار *iʼtibār,* (v. n. 8 of ابر) Digging a well. Desiring one to look after or dress sown fields or palm-trees. Being impregnated (a female palm).

A ائتباض *iʼtibāz,* (v. n. 8 of ابض) Being hurt in the thigh-tendon, and disabled by the contraction.

A ائتباط *iʼtibāt,* (v. n. 8 of ابط) Being plain and even. Being heavy, disturbed (the spirits).

A ائتبال *iʼtibāl,* (v. n. 8 of ابل) Sitting steadily (on a camel). Tending diligently (camels) grazing.

A ائتثار *iʼtisār,* A following of the footsteps.

A ائتجاج *iʼtijāj,* (v. n. 8 of اجّ) Being hot (the day). Being kindled, made to blaze.

A ائتجار *iʼtijār,* (v. n. 8 of اجر) Giving alms in expectation of a reward (اجر *ajr*). Demanding or receiving wages or reward (اجرة *ujrat*).

A ائتخاذ *iʼtikhāz,* A laying hold of one another.

A ائتدام *iʼtidām,* (v. n. 8 of ادم) Joining (bread or other concomitant to meat). Reviving, being moist and fresh (a tree).

A ائتراء *iʼtirāʼ,* (v. n. 8 of اري) Making honey (a bee). Remaining in one place.

A ائترار *iʼtirār,* (v. n. 8 of ارّ) Making haste. Hastening, pressing.

A ائتراش *iʼtirāsh,* (v. n. 8 of ارش) Demanding or taking any thing as a compensation for an injury.

A ائتراق *iʼtirāk,* A being watchful, or sleepless.

A ائتراك *iʼtirāk,* (v. n. 8 of ارك) Being full-grown, firm, and strong (the tree ارك *arāk*).

A ائتزار *iʼtizār,* (v. n. 8 of ازر) Putting on trowsers, breeches, or drawers (called ازار *izār*).

A ائتزاز *iʼtizāz,* (v. n. 8 of ازّ) Boiling (a pot). Causing one to make haste.

A ائتساء *iʼtisāʼ,* (v. n. 8 of اسا for اسو) Imitating, making one a pattern or exemplar (اسوة *iswat* or *uswat*). Deriving comfort, getting relief.

A ايتسار *ītisār,* (v. n. 8 of يسر) Distributing by lot (the limbs of a slaughtered camel). Playing at dice, drawing lots.

A ائتشاء *iʼtishāʼ,* (v. n. 8 of اشي) Being set and healed (a broken bone).

A ايتشاء *ītishāʼ,* (v. n. 8 of وشي) Being set (a broken bone).

A ائتشاب *iʼtishāb,* The being mixed together.

A ائتشار *iʼtishār,* (v. n. 8 of اشر) Asking one to notch and sharpen (her) teeth (a woman).

A ائتصار *iʼtisār,* (v. n. 8 of اصر) Being long and rank (vegetation), touching each other (plants). Being very numerous (people).

A ائتصاص *iʼtisās,* (v. n. 8 of اصّ) Assembling, flocking together.

A ائتضاض *iʼtizāz,* (v. n. 8 of اضّ) Being forced, constrained. Seeking, asking. Striking.

A ائتطام *iʼtitām,* (v. n. 8 of اطم) Being constipated. Labouring under a strangury.

A ائتعاد *iʼtiʻād,* (v. n. 8 of وعد) Receiving or being gratified by a promise.

A ائتفاظ *iʼtifāz,* (v. n. 8 of افظ not used) Taking.

A ائتفاك *iʼtifāk,* (v. n. 8 of افك) Lying. Being overthrown (by an earthquake).

A ائتقاط *iʼtikāt,* (v. n. 8 of اقط) Using acid milk as condiment. Making the cheese اقط *akit.*

A ائتكاك *iʼtikāk,* (v. n. 8 of اكّ) Knocking one against another (legs). Being very hot (a day). Thronging, pressing round a watering-place. Being oppressed by any arduous and irksome business.

A ائتكال *iʼtikāl,* (v. n. 8 of اكل) Being eaten into, corroded. Being inflamed with anger.

P ايتگين *etgīn,* A householder, proprietor.

P ايتگيني *etgīnī,* Ownership, rightful possession.

A ائتلاء *iʼtilāʼ,* (v. n. 8 of الا for الو) Swearing. Being able and capable. Being proud. Failing, doing less than one's duty.

A ائتلاف *iʼtilāf,* (v. n. 8 of الف) Cultivating friendship. Agreeing. Assembling, flocking together. Friendship, familiarity, company, society.

A ائتلاق *iʼtilāk,* A shining, flashing of lightning.

A ائتماء *iʼtimāʼ,* An intending, proposing.

A ائتمار *iʼtimār,* (v. n. 8 of امر) Submitting. Consulting. Thinking anxiously about. Acting upon one's own opinion. Commanding one another.

A ائتمام *iʼtimām,* (v. n. 8 of امّ) Taking for guide, leader, model, or exemplar: accepting as one's Imām. Following, imitating. Intending, purposing.

A ائتمان *iʼtimān,* A trusting, confiding, relying.

A ائتناف *iʼtināf,* (v. n. 8 of انف) Beginning any thing anew. Beginning, commencement.

P ايتند *ītand,* An uncertain sum or number.

A ائتواء *iʼtiwāʼ,* (v. n. 8 of اوي) Repairing to a place for a temporary or a permanent residence. Being tenderly affected towards.

P ايتوك *ītūk,* Happy news, good tidings.

A ائتياب *iʼtiyāb,* (v. n. 8 of آب for اوب) Coming to water at night-time.

A ائتياد *iʼtiyād,* The being bent.

A ائتيال *iʼtiyāl,* (v. n. 8 of آل for اول) Administering well, managing properly.

A ائتيام *iʼtiyām,* (v. n. 8 of آم for ايم) Marrying a widow (ايّم *ayyim*).

A ايثاء *īsāʼ,* (v. n. 4 of وثأ) Making soft, bruising (flesh by beating without touching the bone). Spraining (the hand). (v. n. 4 of وثي) Having any kind of vehicle broken or injured (as a carriage, a ship; also a beast of burden).

A ايثاب *īsāb,* A causing to leap or spring.

A ايثار *īsār,* (v. n. 4 of اثر) Presenting, offering (a gift). Preferring, choosing. Honouring. Causing to follow.

P ايثار بخش *īsār-bakhsh,* A title of Hūshang.

A ايثاف *īsāf,* An underpropping (of a kettle).

A ايثاق *īsāk,* A binding, a tying fast.

A ائثام *iʼsām,* A seducing, the making to sin.

A ايثان *īsān,* (v. n. 4 of وثن) Giving liberally. Being numerous (flocks), abundant (wealth).

P ايجا *ījā,* (for اينجا *injā*) Here, this place.

A ايجاء *ījāʼ,* (v. n. 4 of وجأ) Repelling, removing, prohibiting, hindering, averting. Seeking for something in rain. Failing (water in a well). (v. n. 4 of وجي) Discovering one to be avaricious and worthless. Hurting or wearing thin (the hoof of a horse). Being tenacious, avaricious, granting nothing to a petitioner. Giving. Selling small trusses or bundles of clothes, or portmanteaus. Returning without game (a hunter). Reaching the hard stratum or rock (when digging for water) without finding a spring. Refraining, abstaining, turning away from.

A ايجاب *ījāb,* (v. n. 4 of وجب) Rendering necessary. Doing any thing extremely good or bad (deserving of reward or punishment in the life to come). Making (the heart) palpitate. Eating once only in twenty-four hours. (in logic) Affirmation. (in Muhammadan law) The first proposal made by one of the parties in negociating or concluding a bargain. P ايجاب است *ījāb ast,* It is requisite or necessary, it behoves. ايجاب كردن *ījāb kardan,* To render necessary, to cause to be done. To exact or demand performance.

A ايجابيّ *ījābiy,* Affirmative.

A ايجاح *ījāh*, (v. n. 4 of وجح) Digging down to smooth stones. Forcing to flee for refuge. Appearing, becoming manifest. Covering (a tent), roofing (a house). Causing pain in being discharged (urine). Hanging down before a house or tent (a curtain).

A ائجاد *iʼjād*, (v. n. 4 of اجد) Corroborating, strengthening. Restoring to wealth or affluence. Creating she-camels strong in the vertebræ (God).

A ايجاد *ījād*, (v. n. 4 of وجد) Causing (one) to find. Giving an existence. Making rich and happy. Invigorating, strengthening. Compelling one to do any thing. Vexing, molesting. Invention, discovery, production.

A ايجاز *ījāz*, A forcing against the will.

A ائجار *iʼjār*, (v. n. 4 of اجر) Letting out on hire. Prostituting (herself) for hire. Stabbing in the mouth with a spear. Replacing a disjointed bone crookedly. Repaying. Hiring, taking on hire.

A ايجار *ījār*, (v. n. 4 of وجر) Stabbing in the mouth or the breast with a spear. Putting medicine into the mouth of a child.

A ايجاز *ījāz*, (v. n. 4 of وجز) Abridging, curtailing, epitomizing. Giving quickly. Being short, abridged, laconical, and compendious. Compendium, abridgement, summary, epitome.

A ايجازا *ījāzan*, (P ايجازانه) Compendiously.

A ايجاس *ījās*, A thinking, feeling, conceiving.

A ايجاع *ījāʻ*, An incommoding, a giving pain.

A ايجاف *ījāf*, (v. n. 4 of وجف) Making to travel quickly. Using, employing. Fatiguing.

A ائجال *iʼjāl*, (v. n. 4 of اجل) Applying a remedy for a pain in the neck. Imprisoning.

A ائجام *iʼjām*, (v. n. 4 of اجم) Exciting disgust, causing a loathing. Entering into a thicket (a lion).

A ايجانة *ījānat*, A stone-bottle, phial, pitcher.

A ايجاه *ījāh*, (v. n. 4 of وجه) Rendering respectable, illustrious, celebrated (وجيه *wajīh*). Discovering (one) to be respectable.

A ايجل *ījil*, (imper. of وجل *wajala*) Fear thou.

P ايچ *ech*, (for هيچ *hech*) Any.

A ايحاء *īhāʼ*, (v. n. 4 of وحي) Suggesting, revealing, inspiring. Fearing. Raising, sending.

A ايحاج *īhāj*, A forcing, compelling to seek refuge.

A ايحاد *īhād*, (v. n. 4 of وحد) Making the unique or phœnix of the age. Leaving alone, abandoning to enemies. Bringing forth one lamb (a ewe).

A ايحار *īhār*, (v. n. 4 of وحر) Poisoning (meat or drink) with its venom (the reptile وحرة *waharat*).

A ايحاش *īhāsh*, (v. n. 4 of وحش) Finding (a land) desolate. Being deserted (a city). Being destitute of provisions. Dying of hunger.

A ايحاف *īhāf*, (v. n. 4 of وحف) Making haste. Being inconvenient, disagreeable (fold for camels).

A ايحال *īhāl*, (v. n. 4 of وحل) Plunging into, throwing amongst, mud. Afflicting, distressing.

A ايخ *īkhi*, A word used to make a camel lie down.

A ايخاش *īkhāsh*, (v. n. 4 of وخش) Injuring another's credit. Giving little. Mixing, jumbling together. Replacing repeatedly the arrows used in drawing lots into the quiver.

A ايخاص *īkhās*, (v. n. 4 of وخص) Giving away the smallest part. (A horseman) riding through the vapour called سراب *sarāb*, and raising and lowering it alternately.

A ايخاف *īkhāf*, (v. n. 4 of وخف) Striking mallows until they become viscous. Making haste.

P ايخان *īkhān*, Name of a country in Turkistān.

P ايخشت *ayukhshut*, Bits of divers sorts of metals, as gold or silver.

A ايد *ayd*, (v. n. of آد for ايد) Being strong and firm. Strength, power, vigour, hardness.

A ايّد *ayyid*, Powerful, strong.

A ائداء *iʼdāʼ*, (v. n. 4 of ادي) Assisting. Preparing for a journey. Being numerous and opulent. Being strong. Giving strength. Becoming numerous, and difficult for the owner to manage and overlook (flocks). Assistance, relief.

A ايداء *īdāʼ*, (v. n. 4 of ودي) Preparing either to stale or to cover (as a horse). Voiding something after having made water. Perishing. Removing any one (death). Casing one's self in armour. (v. n. 4 of يدي) Conferring a favour.

A ائداب *iʼdāb*, (v. n. 4 of ادب) Inviting to a feast. Administering justice, governing well.

A ايداح *īdāh*, (v. n. 4 of ودح not used) Submitting, humbling one's self, being obsequious. Restoring, repairing (a cistern). Standing still (a ram not caring to touch the ewe). Being clean and plump (camels). Owning, acknowledging (even to a falsehood, or the merest trifle).

A ايداع *īdāʻ*, (v. n. 4 of ودع) Intrusting and confiding (a secret). Depositing, giving in deposit. Making peace with. Receiving a deposit. (v. n. 4 of يدع) Rendering obligatory.

A ايداق *īdāk*, (v. n. 4 of ودق) Raining. Wanting the male (a mare or an ass).

A ائدام *iʼdām*, (v. n. 4 of ادم) Adding one thing to another (as bread to meat). Making peace, reconciling. Concord, harmony. Friendship, intimacy.

A ائدامة *iʼdāmat*, Hard ground without stones.

A ايدان *īdān*, (v. n. 4 of ودن) Bringing forth a puny extenuated child. Making short, shortening.

A ايداه *īdāh*, (v. n. 4 of وده) Calling to in a threatening manner. Prohibiting, checking.

P ايدر *īdar*, Now. Here, in this place. Behold!

P ايدرا *īdrā*, Now. Here.

P ايدري *īdarī*, Belonging to this place.

A ايدع *aydaʻ*, Saffron. Dragon's-blood, and another kind of red gum brought from an island called Socotra. Brasil-wood; also a species of privet for dyeing. Name of a bird.

P ايدماميد *īdamāmīd*, Name of a medicine.

P ايدند *īdand*, Any number from three to ten.

P ايدون *aydūn*, God. *Aydūn* or *īdūn*, Thus, in this manner. Now.

A ايدي *aydaʼ*, More or most dexterous. ما ايدي فلانة *mā aydaʼ fulānat*, How dexterous such a female is! *Aydī*, (pl. of يد *yad*) Hands. Favours, benefits.

P ايدي *aydī*, Also.

A أئذا *aʼizā*, (for أ اذا *a izā*) Whether, when?

A ائذاء *iʼzāʼ*, (v. n. 4 of اذي) Oppressing, injuring, afflicting. Pain, inconvenience, injury.

A ايذام *īzām*, (v. n. 4 of وذم) Fastening a chain or rope (وذم *wazam*) to the ears (of a bucket). Engaging to perform the pilgrimage (to Mecca).

A ائذان *iʼzān*, (v. n. 4 of اذن) Proclaiming. Summoning to prayer. Striking upon the ear. Prohibiting, hindering, denying access, secluding, precluding. Causing surprise. Giving pleasure.

A ايذج *ayzaj*, Name of a town in Kurdistān.

P ايذون *īzūn*, Thus, in this manner.

A ائر *aʼir*, A man greatly addicted to venery.

A آير *āyur*, (pl. of اير *ayr*) Veretra.

A اير *ayr*, (pl. ايور *uyūr*, آيار *āyār*, and آير *āyur*) Veretrum. Male offspring. *Ayr* or *īr*, The east-wind. *Īr*, Cotton. Silver-filings.

P اير *īr*, A kind of itchy eruption on the body, whose pustules are larger than measles or small-pox.

A ايّر *ayyir*, East-wind. Large-yarded (man).

A ايرّ *ayarr*, Hard (stone).

P ايرا *īrā*, (for زيرا) Since, therefore, because.

A ائراء *iʼrāʼ*, (v. n. 4 of اري) Coupling (cattle) to the same manger, or in the same stall.

A ايراء *īrāʼ*, (v. n. 4 of وري) Striking fire from a steel, or from the friction of two pieces of wood.

A ائراب *iʼrāb*, A prospering. An overcoming.

A ايراث *īrās*, (v. n. 4 of ورث) Making one an an heir (وارث *wāris*), entailing. Producing.

A ائراخ *iʼrākh*, (v. n. 4 of ارخ) Dating (a letter).

A ايراخ *īrākh*, An attenuating (dough or paste).

A ايراد *īrād*, (v. n. 4 of ورد) Producing, exhibiting. Citing, bringing to the مورد *mawrid*. Bringing proof, adducing, alleging. Purpose, design.

A ائرار *iʼrār*, An emaciating, an extenuating.

A ايراس *īrās*, (v. n. 4 of ورس) (Ground) producing great quantities of the plant called ورس *wars*, growing only in Arabia Felix, with which they paint the face of a yellow colour. Growing yellow like saffron. Producing leaves (a tree).

A ايراص *īrās*, (v. n. 4 of ورص) Laying an egg at once, without difficulty (a hen). Voiding excrement by a single effort.

A ائراض *iʼrāz*, An afflicting with the rheum ارض.

A ايراض *īrāz*, (v. n. 4 of ورض) Voiding excrement at one effort (a man, or a hen sitting on eggs).

A ائراط *iʼrāt*, (v. n. 4 of ارط) (Ground) producing the tree called ارطى *artaʼ*.

A ايراط *īrāt* (v. n. 4 of ورط) (A man) mixing (his camels) among others, so that they cannot be discovered. Driving to destruction (ورطة *wartat*). Tying a rope tight round a camel's throat.

A ايراع *īrāʿ*, An interposing, intercepting.

P ايراف *īrāf*, Name of the father of اردا *ardā*, whom the fire-worshippers revere as a prophet.

A ايراف *īrāf*, (v. n. 4 of ورف) Being long and broad (a shadow).

A ائراق *iʾrāk*, (v. n. 4 of ارق) Rendering sleepless, keeping awake.

A ايراق *īrāk*, (v. n. 4 of ورق) Producing leaves (a tree). Growing rich. Getting no game nor plunder (a sportsman, or a soldier).

P ايراك *īrāk*, (for زيرا كه *zīrā ki*) Because that.

A ايرام *īrām*, (v. n. 4 of ورم) Having a swelling.

P ايران *īrān*, The kingdom of Persia, so named from ايرج *īraj*, son of Farīdūn, to whom this part of Persia was given. Hoshang son of Siyāmak.

P ايرانشهر *īrān shahr*, The old name of Nīshābūr.

P ايراني *īrānī*, A native of Irān; a Persian.

P ايرج *īraj* or *eraj*, The sun. Name of the eldest son of Farīdūn. Name of a king of Babylon.

G ايرسا *īrsā*, The rainbow. The root of the iris.

G ايرسون *īrsūn*, Talc.

G ايرقان *īrhān*, A species of privet.

P ايرگ *īrg*, (in zand and Pāzand) A man.

P ايرمان *īrmān*, Repentance, contrition. Wish. A sigh. An uninvited guest. A parasite. A loan.

P ايرمانخور *īrmān-khwur*, Desirous, hankering.

P ايرمانسراي *īrmān-sarāy*, (or ايرمان خانه *īrmān-khāna*) A hired house. The head of a street where the object of intense desire is found. The house of sighs or regret. The present world.

A ايرميّ *ayramīy*, A stone erected in the desert to guide travellers. *Ayramīy* or *īramīy*, Any one.

P ايرون *īrūn*, Sulphur. Here. Now.

P ايري *īrī*, (in zand and Pāzand) A man. Manliness, bravery.

A ايريداد *īrīdād*, (v. n. 11 of ورد) Being rose-coloured, between كميت *kumayt* and اشقر *ashkar*.

A ايريقاق *īrīkāk*, (v. n. 11 of ورق) Beginning to colour (grapes).

A ائزاء *iʾzāʾ*, (v. n. 4 of ازي) Making the conduits or aqueducts called ازاء *izāʾ*. Answering to, agreeing with, facing. Surpassing, excelling. Fearing, dreading. Harassing, oppressing.

A ايزاء *īzāʾ*, (v. n. 4 of وزي) Supporting, propping up. Bedaubing, plastering (a wall with clay).

A ايزاب *īzāb*, The act of wandering, travelling.

A ايزار *īzār*, (v. n. 4 of وزر) Preserving, guarding. Making a place of refuge, providing an asylum. Binding, fastening. Making up a heavy burden for any one. Concealing. Carrying off.

P ايزاره *īzāra*, A screen, low wall before a house. Any support for one's back when sitting down.

P ايزاري *īzārī*, A handkerchief. A towel, napkin.

A ايزاع *īzāʿ*, (v. n. 4 of وزع) Dividing, distributing. Exciting, instigating, impelling. Inspiring.

A ائزاف *iʾzāf*, A causing to make haste.

A ايزاف *īzāf*, (v. n. 4 of وزف) Making haste.

A ايزان *īzān*, (v. n. 4 of وزن) Applying the mind.

P ايزد *īzid*, (by some *ezid*) God.

P ايزد گشسب *īzid-gashasb*, Worshipper of God.

P ايزدي *īzidī*, Any thing bestowed for God's sake. Whatever is given as one's due.

P ايزغنج *ezghunj*, A sack, a bag.

P ايژك *ejak*, A spark of fire.

A آيس *āyas*, More or most despairing.

A أيس *ayisa*, (fut. يأيس *yaʾyasu*) He despaired.

A ايس *ays*, (v. n. of ايس) Despairing. Being soft, mild, gentle, placid. Making despair. Force.

P ايسا *īsā*, Now, already. A proper name. Name of a book revealed from heaven to Abraham.

A ائساء *iʾsāʾ*, (v. n. 4 of اسي) Consoling.

A ايساء *īsāʾ*, A shaving (of the head). A cutting.

A ايساب *īsāb*, A producing of herbage.

A ايساج *īsāj*, The making (a camel) go faster.

P ايساخ *īsākh*, A dirtying, soiling (of a dress).

A ائساد *iʾsād*, (v. n. 4 of اسد) Setting (one dog) against another, or after game. Setting one man at variance with another.

A ايساد *īsād*, (v. n. 4 of وسد) Setting (a dog) in pursuit of game. Walking fast (a camel).

A ايسار *aysār*, (pl. of يسر *yasar*) Easy. Ready, prepared. Numbers of people assembled for play, gamesters. Those who preside, shake, or draw the gaming arrows. (pl. of يسرة *yasarat*) Lines on the palms of the hand when distant one from another. Marks burnt upon the thighs. (pl. of ياسر *yāsir*) Gamesters. Those who preside and distribute the joints of a slaughtered camel according to lots. Camel-butchers. Easy. Left. *Īsār*, (v. n. 4 of يسر) Being opulent: wealth. Bringing forth with ease.

A ايساع *īsāʿ*, (v. n. 4 of وسع) Enlarging, widening, making large and wide. Being or becoming powerful, able, or affluent. Giving power or wealth.

A ائساف *iʾsāf*, A making sad. An enraging.

A ايساق *īsāk*, (v. n. 4 of وسق) Loading (a camel). Being loaded with fruit (a palm-tree).

A ائسان *iʾsān*, A leaving, an allowing to remain.

A ايسان *īsān*, (pl. اياسين *ayāsīn*) A man. (v. n. 4 of وسن) Causing to faint (the vapour of a well).

P ايستا *īstā*, (from ايستادن *īstādan*) Standing.

P ايستادگي *īstādagī*, Stability, steadiness, stillness. ايستادگيء باد *īstādagī-i bād*, A calm.

P ايستادن *īstādan*, To stand, stop, stay, remain, tarry, wait for. باز ايستادن, To stand back, desist.

P ايستاده *īstāda*, Standing.

P ايستاندن *īstāndan*, To make rise or stand up. To rouse, stir. To erect, fix, place, constitute, appoint.

P ايستانيدن *īstānīdan*, To make stand, establish.

P ايستيدن *īstīdan*, To stand. To begin, set about.

P ايستيده *īstīda*, Standing.

A ايسر *aysar*, Left. The left hand. Easier, easiest; the most moderate. More fortunate. ايسر ايّام *aysari ayyām*, Prosperous times. A fair wind.

A ايش *aysh*, (and اش *ash*) (for ايّ شيءٍ *ayyu shayʾin*) What? what thing? how? why? wherefore? لايش *liʾaysha*, For what reason? ايش حالكم *aysh hālukum*, How do you do?

P ايش *esh*, A spy, a scout.

P ايشا *īshā*, (for ايشان *īshān* or *eshān*) They.

A ائشاء *iʾshāʾ*, The setting a broken bone, healing.

A ايشاء *īshāʾ*, (v. n. 4 of وشي) Exercising, breathing, trying, making (a horse) run at full speed. Being found to contain little gold (a mine). Drawing out gently. Considering (an oration or poem) in order to discover the sense. Despatching, finishing, doing. Rousing, stirring up. Restoring health (medicine). (Ground) producing herbage, or (a palm-tree) bearing fruit (for the first time). Abounding in wealth. Taking a part (of money).

A ايشاع *īshāʿ*, (v. n. 4 of وشع) Blossoming, flowering (a tree, a herb). Injecting medicines into the mouth of a horse.

A ايشاغ *īshāgh*, (v. n. 4 of وشغ) Scattering by little and little (urine). Injecting medicines into the mouth or nostrils. Giving a very little.

A ايشاق *īshāk*, An adhering tenaciously.

A ايشاك *īshāk*, (v. n. 4 of وشك) Making haste, proceeding with expedition. Approaching, being on the point of.

A ايشال *īshāl*, (v. n. 4 of وشل) Procuring a little (water), drop by drop. Diminishing (the fortune of another). Teaching (a camel's colt) to suck.

A ايشام *īshām*, (v. n. 4 of وشم) Putting forth conspicuous plants (the earth). Flashing faintly (lightning). Beginning (to do any thing). Beginning to have breasts very apparent (a woman). Having ripe grapes (a vine). Finding a grassy pasture (camels). Gaining upon any one (hoariness). Defaming the character of another. Examining.

P ايشان *īshan* or *eshān*, They (rational beings).

P ايشانه *īshāna*, A brood of young chickens.

P آيشم *āyishm*, (in zand and Pāz.) Moonlight.

P آيشنه *āyishna*, A flatterer. A spy, scout.

P آيشه *āyisha*, A spy. A flatterer.

P ايشه *esha*, A thicket, brake. A spy. A flatterer.

P ايشهريار *īshahryār*, Name of the thirtieth day of the month according to the æra of Jalālu'd din.

P ايشي *eshī*, A lady, a matron.

A ايصاء *īsāʾ*, (v. n. 4 of وصي) Admonishing, counselling, ordering, charging, commanding. Making a will or testament. Making (one) executor.

A ايصاب *īsāb*, (v. n. 4 of وصب) Being continual, perennial. Being firm, fixed, constant, assiduous. Adhering, persevering. Being sick. Making sick. Begetting weakly children.

A ايصاد *īsād*, (v. n. 4 of وصد) Shutting (a door). Erecting a sheep-cote or fold of stone. Setting (a dog) after any thing.

A ايصاف *īsāf*, (v. n. 4 of وصف) Being of age

for service, becoming a servant, performing service. Being mature.

A اتّصال *isāl*, (v. n. 4 of اصل) Coming in the evening. Beginning the time of the evening اصيل.

A ايصال *īsāl*, (v. n. 4 of وصل) Causing to arrive. Introducing, causing to unite. Conveying, paying.

A ايصر *aysar*, (pl. اياصر *ayāsir*) A short rope with which they fasten the lower parts of tents to the pins. Any kind of cloth in which they gather grass. Herbage, fresh grass, dry hay.

A ايض *ayz*, (v. n. of آض for ايض) Returning. Becoming, undergoing a change.

A ايضا *ayzan*, As above, as before, in the same manner. Ditto. Again, anew, afresh. Hitherto. Also, likewise.

A ايضاح *īzāh*, (v. n. 4 of وضح) Making evident, rendering clear. Coming in view, appearing plain. Explanation, exposition, elucidation.

A ايضاحا *īzāhan*, Clearly, evidently.

A ايضاخ *īzākh*, (v. n. 4 of وضخ) Filling (a bucket) about half-way. Containing little water (a well). Drawing or giving a small quantity of water.

A اتّضاض *iʼzāz*, (v. n. 4 of اضّ) Longing, seeking for her nest (an ostrich).

A ايضاع *īzāʻ*, (v. n. 4 of وضع) Spurring or urging (a horse or camel) to a quicker pace. Suffering loss (in merchandize). Going fast (a camel). Feeding upon the plant حمض *hamz* (camels).

A ايضاف *īzāf*, A going fast. Urging forward.

A ايضام *īzām*, (v. n. 4 of وضم) Placing (meat) on a block or tray. Making a mat for that purpose.

A ايطاء *ītāʼ*, (v. n. 4 of وطئ) Consenting, agreeing. Putting (one upon horseback), making one to sit or mount easily. Giving (any thing) to be trampled upon. Depressing, subjecting to oppression. Repeating the last syllable of a verse. Setting (one) to work in ignorance.

A اتّطام *iʼtām*, (v. n. 4 of اطم) Locking (a door).

A ايطان *ītān*, (v. n. 4 of وطن) Considering or making (any place) one's home. Residing.

A ايطب *aytab*, (for اطيب *atyab*) ما ايطبه *mā aytabahu*, How excellent it is!

A ايطبّة *aytabbat*, (or ايطبة) Heat in sheep.

A ايطل *aytal*, (pl. اياطل *ayātil*) The belly and sides under the short ribs, the hypochondria.

A ايعاء *īʻāʼ*, (v. n. 4 of وعي) Collecting, preserving. Laying up in a repository. Being covetous, parsimonious, and sparing in one's expenditure. Cutting clean away, allowing nothing to remain.

A ايعاب *īʻāb*, (v. n. 4 of وعب) Taking the whole. Putting the whole of one thing into another. Sheathing. Tearing up by the roots. Collecting, assembling, heaping up.

A ايعاث *īʻās*, (v. n. 4 of وعث) Plunging into a quagmire, as soft or new-dug ground. Being prodigal, profuse, lavish.

A ايعاد *īʻād*, (v. n. 4 of وعد) Promising. Threatening, terrifying.

A ايعار *īʻār*, (v. n. 4 of وعر) Being difficult, rough (road). Finding (a way) difficult; getting into a bad road or a dangerous place. Bringing (any person) into a rugged place. Diminishing, abating, lessening. Being poor.

A ايعاز *īʻāz*, (v. n. 4 of وعز) Making a signal, beckoning. Commanding.

A ايعاس *īʻās*, (v. n. 4 of وعس not in use) Travelling with difficulty through a soft sandy plain.

A ايعاط *īʻāt*, (v. n. 4 of وعط obsol.) Crying, the wolf; giving the alarm on the approach of an enemy, by calling out يعاط *yiʻāti*.

A ايعاق *īʻāk*, A causing to make haste.

A ايعاك *īʻāk*, (v. n. 4 of وعك) Crowding upon one another (camels when running to the watering-place). (Dogs) rolling (their prey) in the dust. Falling with violence when running. A fierce battle in which the combatants are intermixed.

A ايغار *īghār*, (v. n. 4 of وغر) Putting in a rage, inflaming with anger. Making (water) boil. Heating (milk) by putting a hot stone into it. Being in the heat of the day. Exacting, receiving (tribute or tax). Permitting to be free (from tribute). Paying the tribute to the chief magistrate to escape the vexatious exactions of the tax-gatherers. Taking refuge. Forcing one to take refuge. Appointing (time or place). Farming imposts.

A ايغاف *īghāf*, (v. n. 4 of وغف) Walking fast, running. Travelling with a fatigued or drawling pace. Having a weak sight. Striking marsh-mallows until they become viscous. Lolling (the tongue). Eating enough. A wriggling motion, agitation.

A ايغال *īghāl*, (v. n. 4 of وغل) Penetrating suddenly (into any place) and hiding there. Forcing (one) to enter suddenly. Compelling (one) to go from place to place. Travelling with expedition, and going far into any country. Making great progress (in science). Causing (one) to make haste.

P ايغده *ī* or *ayghuda*, A silly prating coxcomb.

P ايغور *īghūr*, Igūra, a country inhabited by oriental Turks or Scythians; the eastern extremity of which extends to China.

A ايفاء *īfāʼ*, (v. n. 4 of وفي) Paying, satisfying. Performing a promise, fulfilling an engagement, keeping faith. Filling a measure, making good measure. Approaching, arriving. Being near, at the point of, impending. ايفاءِ مراسم صداقت *īfāʼi marāsimi sadākat*, Observing the laws of truth.

A ايفاد *īfād*, (v. n. 4 of وفد) Sending (an ambassador). Overtopping, hanging over. Walking fast, proceeding with expedition. Holding the head high, and pricking the ears (a deer). Elevation.

A ايفاز *īfāz*, A hastening, an accelerating.

A ايفاض *īfāz*, (v. n. 4 of وفض) Dispersing, separating. Spreading any thing under another to keep it from the ground. Running, making haste.

A ايفاع *ayfāʻ*, (pl. of يفع *yafaʻ*) Tall youths. *Īfāʻ*, (v. n. 4 of يفع) Being tall (a youth). Entering on his twentieth year.

A ايفاق *īfāk*, (v. n. 4 of وفق) Being near. Assenting, agreeing. Being disposed in order (camels). Happening suddenly and unexpectedly. Fitting the notch of the arrow properly to the bow-string when shooting. Meeting, encountering. Looking for, finding.

P آيفت *āyift*, A petition. Necessity, need.

P ايفده *īfada*, A silly, prating coxcomb: a boaster.

A ايق *ayk*, A small bone at the pastern-joint (of camels or horses); the joint itself.

A ايقاب *īkāb*, (v. n. 4 of وقب) Putting (butter or sauce) into a hole made in a pudding. Starving.

A ايقاح *īkāh*, (v. n. 4 of وقح) Being hard (the hoof). Being shameless, brazen-faced.

A ايقاد *īkād*, (v. n. 4 of وقد) Lighting, kindling, inflaming. Abandoning, leaving (an infant). ايقاد النار *īkādu'n nār*, (or P ايقاد نار *īkādi nār*) Lighting a fire. P ايقاد نائرهٔ جنگ *īkādi nāʼira-i jang*, A kindling of the flames of war.

A ايقاذ *īkāz*, A leaving one indisposed.

A ايقار *īkār*, (v. n. 4 of وقر) Loading a beast of burthen. Being loaded with fruit (a palm-tree). Being pregnant. Being heavily laden. Hurting a horse in the hoof, laming him, and causing him to stumble. Cracking or splitting a bone.

A ايقاص *īkās*, A making one short-necked.

A ايقاظ *aykāz*, (pl. of يقظ *yakiz*) Watchful, provident. *Īkāz*, (v. n. 4 of يقظ) Awaking, raising, stirring up, exciting.

A ايقاع *īkāʻ*, (v. n. 4 of وقع) Causing to fall. Striking a blow. Casting, throwing into distress, or into battle; fighting furiously. Making harmonic cadences (a singer). Containing water (a garden).

A ايقاف *īkāf*, (v. n. 4 of وقف) Causing to stand, stopping, restraining: detaining at home. Abstaining. Keeping silence. Bequeathing. Checks, arrests.

A ايقام *īkām*, (v. n. 4 of وقم) Humbling, subduing.

A اتّقان *iʼkān*, A making sure.

A ايقان *īkān*, (v. n. 4 of يقن) Being sure, knowing for certain.

A ايقاه *īkāh*, (v. n. 4 of وقه) Lending an ear. Understanding. Obeying.

G ايقون *īkūn*, A stinking rose.

G ايقونة *aykūnat*, An image, a picture.

A ايك *ayk*, (v. n. of ايك) Becoming a thick entangled forest (the tree اراك *arāk*). Thick entangled trees. A forest full of the سدر *sidr*, اراك *arāk*, اثل *asl*, and other trees, which intertwine their branches; any number of trees growing close together. ايك آئك *ayki āʼik*, A forest of fruit-trees.

A ايكاء *īkāʼ*, (v. n. 4 of وكأ) Causing to recline against, or lie down upon, placing a sofa for any one. Throwing one down on the left side. Leaning upon a staff. (v. n. 4 of وكي) Binding or stopping the mouth (of a bottle). Stopping one's mouth. Causing or keeping silence. Filling. Being tenacious, covetous, parsimonious, refusing to give.

A ايكاب *īkāb*, (v. n. 4 of وكب) Keeping close to a troop of horse (a camel). Preparing to fly (a bird): also clapping the wings (in falling, or supporting itself). Irritating.

A ايكاح *īkāh*, (v. n. 4 of وكح) Coming to a stratum of stone (in digging a well). Breaking or cutting off. Refusing to give (a present). Desisting from. Being fatigued. Making special (a gift).

A ايكار *īkār*, A filling (of a vessel or the belly).

A ايكاس *īkās*, (v. n. 4 of وكس) Being spent, or wasted (money). Suffering a loss (in trade).

A ايكاع *īkāʻ*, (v. n. 4 of وكع) Making hard (a leathern bottle). Being hard and difficult (business). Being firm, established, adjusted. Engaging (in an arduous affair). Having robust, plump (camels). Being poor and good for nothing (man).

A ائكاف *iʼkāf*, (v. n. 4 of اكف) Placing the saddle-cloth اكاف *ikāf* upon an ass.

A ايكاف *īkāf*, (v. n. 4 of وكف) Distilling, dropping, running. Rendering culpable or criminal, causing to fall into sin. Saddling (an ass).

A ائكال *iʼkāl*, (v. n. 4 of اكل) Giving or offering any thing to eat. Furnishing food (a tree). Inviting (any one) to eat. Giving up any thing to be consumed. Whispering, creating animosities by detraction. Empowering one against another.

A ايكال *īkāl*, (v. n. 4 of وكل) Trusting in God. Leaving one's affairs in the hands of another.

A ايكة *aykat*, A number of trees close together.

A ايّكم *ayyukum*, Who or which of you?

P ايگ *ig*, Name of a country in Persia.

P ايگ باون *ig-bāwan*, Name of a religious book of the fire-worshippers.

P ايگر *aygar*, Sweet cane.

A آئل *āʼil*, (pl. ايّل *uyyal*) Thick, thickening (milk or the vessel which contains it).

A ايل *īl*, God. Name of a mountain.

A ايّل *iyyal*, *uyyal*, and *ayyil*, (pl. ايائل *ayāʼil*) A deer, hart, wild-goat. *Uyyal*, Thick milk. Water in the womb.

A ايلّ *ayall*, One who has short teeth (particularly the upper ones). Short (nail). High (hill).

A ائلاء *iʼlāʼ*, (v. n. 4 of الو for الا) Swearing. Being full of sheep's dung. (v. n. 4 of الي) Swearing.

A ايلاء *īlāʼ*, (v. n. 4 of ولي) Appointing to a government, setting over. Charging, giving command. Causing to follow, subjoining. Conferring a favour, giving. Bringing or placing near.

A ايلات *īlāt*, (v. n. 4 of ولت) Diminishing, impairing, defrauding.

A ايلاج *īlāj*, (v. n. 4 of ولج) Inserting, introducing, causing to enter.

A ايلاد *īlād*, (v. n. 4 of ولد) Being near the birth (a woman), bearing (a child).

A ايلاس *īlās*, (v. n. 4 of ولس) Relating any thing obscurely and ambiguously.

A ايلاع *īlāʻ*, (v. n. 4 of ولع) Exciting, impelling, inspiring with desire. Being enslaved by passion, greatly addicted to any thing.

A ايلاغ *īlāgh*, The allowing (of a dog) to lap.

A ائلاف *iʼlāf*, (v. n. 4 of الف) Rendering familiar, accustoming, habituating, using to. Being accustomed to, often frequenting (a place). Making, completing, or becoming a thousand (الف *alf*). Browsing upon trees and drinking alternately (camels). Protection, safe-guard.

P ايلاق *īlāk*, Name of the capital of خطا *khatā* and ايغور *ighūr*. Name of a tree.

A ائلام *iʼlām*, An afflicting, tormenting, paining.

A ايلام *īlām*, (v. n. 4 of ولم not in use) Preparing a nuptial entertainment or banquet. Being strong in body and firm in mind.

P ايلاول *aylāwil*, Name of a mountain.

A ايلاه *īlāh*, (v. n. 4 of وله) Making a mother distracted (from excess of affection for her children).

A ايلة *aylat*, Name of a town on the coast of the Red Sea (the Elana of Ptolemy). Name of a mountain between Mecca and Madīna.

T P ايلچي *īlchī*, An ambassador, an envoy.

P ايلخان *īl-khān*, A commander. A title of the Mogul emperors.

P ايلخي *īlkhī*, A herd of horses.

P ايلدانه *eldāna*, The lesser cardamom.

P ايلقي *īlkī*, A herd of horses.

P ايلك *ay* or *īlik*, Name of a city in Turkistān.

A ايلمة *aylamat*, Pain, anguish. Motion, noise from motion: as, ما سمعت له ايلمة *mā samiʻtu lahu aylamatan*, I did not hear sound or motion from him.

P ايلول *aylūl*, The twelfth month of the Syrian or Chaldean calendar, answering to October.

P ايله *ila*, Elah on the Red Sea.

A ايلياء *īliyāʼ*, (or ايليا) Elia, Jerusalem. Elias.

A ايم *aym*, (v. n. of آم for ايم) Being bereaved, left a widow or widower. ايم هو *ayma huwa*, Whoever he be. *Īm*, (pl. ايوم *uyūm*) A serpent particularly slender and white. *Uyum*, (pl. of ايام *iyām*) Smokes.

P ايم *īm*, A widower. *Īm* or *em*, We are.

A ايّم *ayyim*, (pl. ايائم *ayāʼim*, ايامي *ayāmaʼ*, and ايوم *uyūm*) Unmarried, single (man or woman), a widower, a widow. Free, excellent, unblemished. Relationship. Female relations (as daughter, sister, or aunt). A slender white serpent.

A ايمّ *ayamm*, Better or best fitted to be an Imām.

A ايما *aymā* or *īmā*, (for امّا *ammā*) But, or whether. ايما الي جنّة ايما الي نار *īmā ilaʼ jannatin, īmā ilaʼ nārin*, Either to a heaven or to a hell.

P ايما *īmā*, We, us, our. ايمارا *īmārā*, To us.

A ايّما *ayyumā*, (fem. ايّتما *ayyatumā*) Whoever, whatever. What!

A ائماء *iʼmāʼ*, (v. n. 4 of امو or امي) Becoming a handmaid (امة *amat*).

A ايماء *īmāʼ*, (v. n. 4 of وما) Nodding, beckoning. A nod, sign, signal. A sign made by the finger for any one to retire. Intimation, hint, or emblem. P ايما كردن *īmā kardan*, (or ايما وُ اشارت كردن *īmā u ishārat kardan*) To make a sign with the head or hand; to nod, beckon.

A ائمار *iʼmār*, (v. n. 4 of امر) Multiplying, rendering numerous. Ordering, commanding.

A ايمار *īmār*, A command.

A ايماس *īmās*, (v. n. 4 of ومس) Being impudent, shameless, addicted to prostitution (a woman). Rubbing the body against a post.

A ايماض *īmāz*, (v. n. 4 of ومض) Shining, glancing slightly (lightning). (When more diffusive it is called خفو *khafw*; and when it flashes furiously it is named عقيقة *ʻakīkat*). Stealing a look at a man, making him a private signal (a woman).

A ايم الله *aymu'llāh*, By God!

A ايمان *aymān*, A widower.

A ايمان *aymān*, (also ايمن *aymun*) (pl. of يمين *yamīn*) Right hands or sides. Oaths (because, in swearing, one man touched the other upon the right hand). P ايمان شداد كردن *aymāni shidād kardan*, To swear much, vehemently, roundly. A رجل ايمان عيمان *rajulun aymān ʻaymān*, A man whose wife and cattle are dead. *Īmān*, (v. n. 4 of يمن) Coming to Yaman. Holding on the right side.

A ائمان *iʼmān*, (generally written ايمان *īmān*) (v. n. 4 of امن) Protecting, securing, making safe. Crediting, acknowledging as true, believing. Faith, belief, religion. ائمان بالله العزيز العلّام *iʼmān bi'llāhi'l ʻazīzi'l ʻallām*, Faith in God, the glorious, the omniscient. ائمان بالله و رسوله *iʼmān bi'llāh wa rasūlihi*, Faith in God and his prophet. ائمان باطل *iʼmāni bātil*, Superstition. ارباب ائمان *arbābi iʼmān*, The faithful, orthodox, believers. P ايمان داشتن *īmān dāshtan*, To believe, to give credit.

P ايمان دار *īmān-dār*, Faithful. A believer.

P ايمبار *īmbār*, (for اينبار *īn bār*) This time.

A ايمة *aymat*, (v. n. of آم for ايم) Becoming a widow. Widowhood.

A ائمّة *aʼimmat*, (written ايمّة *ayimmat*) (pl. of امام *imām*) Prelates, priests, imāms. نذر ائمّه *nazri aʼimma*, A grant to attendants at a saint's tomb.

P ايمد *aymad*, A plough-share. A plough.

P ايمر *aymar* or *īmar*, A coulter, a ploughshare.

A ايمن *ayman*, More or most happy, fortunate, illustrious, august. (pl. ايامن *ayāmin*) Happy, fortunate, prosperous. Secure, off one's guard. Right-handed. امّ ايمن *ummi ayman*, Name of the nurse of Muhammad's children. *Ayyuman*, Whosoever.

P ايمن *emin*, (from A آمن *āmin*) Free, secure.

P ايمن آباد *ayman-ābād*, A place of security.

A ايمن الله *aymanu 'llāh* also *īmanu'llāh*, By God. The following words or particles (as well as ايمن *ayman*) are sometimes joined with الله *allāh* in the same sense: ليمن *laymunu*, ايم *aymu* or *īmu*,

هیم *haymu*, ام *imu, imi*, or *ima*, من *manu, minu, munu, muni*, and م *mu, ma, mi*. They say likewise, لیمنك *laym..nuka* or لیمنك یا رب *laymunuka yā rabb*, By thee, O God!

P ایمنی *aymanī* or *eminī*, Security, protection.

P ایمه *ayma*, Now, this moment. Vain, futile. *Īma*, Thus, so. (for ایمسه *imasa*) A yoke of oxen.

A ایمه *ayma*, (or ایمّه *ayimma*) Land given as a reward or favour by the king, at a very low rent, a fief (when no rent is paid the land is called لا خراج *lā kharāj*, Allodial). Charity-lands.

P ایمه دار *ayma-dār*, One who holds lands in *ayma*, a feoffee, an occupier of charity-lands.

A ایمه مدد *ayma-madad*, (ملك *milk*, or P پیران *pirān*) The names of particular tenures of free lands.

A ایمي *ayma'*, A woman who thirsts for milk. امراة ایمي عیمي *imra-at ayma' ʻayma'*, A woman whose husband and cattle are dead.

P ایمید *aymīd*, Twins. Ploughing-oxen.

P ایمین *imin*, A plough: a team. Free from care.

P آین *āyan*, (for آهن) Iron. *Āyin*, Rite, custom.

A آئن *ā-in*, Quiet, tranquil. (A man) who conducts himself peaceably, easily, quietly.

A این *ayn*, (v. n. of آن for این) Arriving (time). Fatigue. Convenient, fit, or proper time. A man. A camel. A serpent. آن اینك *āna aynuka*, (or *inuka*) Your time is come. *Ayna*, Where? این مقرّك *ayna makarruka*, Where is your residence? الی این *ila' ayna*, Whither? من این *min ayna*, Whence? *A'in*, Whether if?

P این *in*, This. Doubt, irresolution. این جهان *in jahān*, This world (in contra-distinction to آن جهان *ān jahān*, That world, or the life to come). این طرف *in taraf*, This side. این قدر *in kadar*, This much. این معنی *in maʻna'*, This cause. این همه آوردهٔ تست *in hama āwarda-i tu'st*, All this comes of you, all this is owing to you. این و آن *in u ān*, This and that. This world and the next.

A ایناء *i-nā*, (v. n. 4 of انی) Detaining, delaying. Deferring, retarding, playing a slow, irresolute part.

A اینا *inā*, (v. n. 4 of ونی) Fatiguing, weakening.

A ایناث *inās*, (v. n. 4 of انث) Being brought to-bed of a girl (انثی *unsa'*).

A ایناس *inās*, (v. n. 4 of انس) Rendering familiar or sociable. Exhilarating, rejoicing, comforting, making merry. Knowing. Seeing, perceiving, looking. Hearing. Familiarity.

A ایناض *i-nāz*, The act of dressing (meat) badly.

A ایناع *inā*, A coming to maturity, a ripening.

A ایناف *i-nāf*, (v. n. 4 of انف) Making the nose (انف *anf*) sore. Reaching as high as the nose. Exciting (any one) to loathing. Expediting business. Leading (camels) to fresh untouched pasture.

A ایناق *i-nāk*, (v. n. 4 of انق) Delighting. Exciting admiration.

P اینان *inān*, Bravo! Well done!

P اینك *inak*, (for اینك *inak*) Behold!

P اینان *inān*, (pl. of این *in*) These.

P اینبار *imbār*, (این *in* and بار *bār*) This time.

A آئنة *ā-inat*, (pl. آئنات *ā-ināt* or اوائن *awā-in*) Easy (nocturnal journey). (pl. of اوان *awān*) Times, seasons. P هر آئنه *har ā-ina*, Always, at all times.

A آینة *āyinatan*, Oftentimes, frequently.

P اینت *inat*, Take this. Bravo! Well done!

P اینجا *injā*, This place. Here. از اینجا *az injā*, Hence. از اینجاست *az injāst*, Here or hence it is.

P اینجانب *in jānib*, This side, this part.

P اینجائی *injā-ī*, Of or belonging to this place.

P اینجیدن *injīdan*, To crumble bread. To eat or destroy (as a moth). To irritate, vex. To be cleft.

P اینچنین *inchunin*, Thus, so, in this manner.

P ایند *inad*, Numeration. An uncertain number, any part of an unknown number. Fascination, enchantment, charm.

P آیندگان *āyandagān*, Living beings.

P آینده *āyanda*, Coming. Ensuing, next. A comer or guest. وقت آینده *wakti āyanda*, The future, the time to come. آینده و رونده *āyanda u ravanda*, Going and coming, travellers, passengers.

P اینست *inast*, This is.

P اینسو *insū*, Hither.

P اینسه *inasa*, Bound, hard to unloose. Frozen.

P اینفت *inaft*, A petition. Need, want.

A اینق *aynuk*, (pl. of ناقة *nākat*) She-camels.

P اینك *inak*, Behold! Lo! Now. اینك ترازو *inak tarāzū*, Behold the balance; come to the proof. اینکیم *inakīm*, Behold us! *Īnuk*, A pimple, pustule.

P اینگر *ingar*, Vermilion.

A اینما *aynamā*, Wherever, everywhere.

P ایند *inand*, So much, so many. A strange word. A thing spoken in doubt, opinion, or conjecture. They are. Any number from three to nine.

P آینه *āyina*, A mirror, a looking-glass, sometimes made of polished steel. آینهٔ اسکندری *āyina-i iskandarī*, A mirror made by Aristotle and placed on the summit of a tower erected by Alexander at Alexandria. The sun. آینهٔ چینی *āyina-i chīnī*, A mirror made of polished metal. The sun. آینهٔ خاکیان *āyina-i khākiyān*, The Creator. Adam. The human heart. آینهٔ زانو *āyina-i zānū*, The knee-pan. آینهٔ زرین *āyina-i zarīn*, The sun. آینهٔ شش جهت *āyina-i shash jihat*, (Six-faced mirror) The heart of Muhammad. The seven sleepers. Persons acquainted with mysteries and revelations. آینهٔ فیل *āyina-i fīl*, Steel mirrors on the armour of an elephant. The colour of an elephant. آینهٔ گردان *āyina-i gardān*, (The revolving mirror) The sun. آینهٔ گیتی *āyina-i gītī*, The sun. آینهٔ مقصود *āyina-i maksūd*, Name of the verse in the Kur'ān, اطیعوا الله و اطیعوا الرسول و اولي الامر منکم *atīʻū 'llāh wa atīʻū'r rasūl wa ūli'l amr minkum*, Obey God and obey the apostle, and those who are in authority among you.

P اینها *inhā*, (pl. of این *in*) These (things).

P آینه افروز *āyina-afroz*, A polisher.

P آینه دار *āyina-dār*, The mirror-holder, a male or female attendant on the great in the east.

P آینه دان *āyinadān*, A case for a looking-glass.

P آینه زدای *āyina-zidāy*, A polisher of mirrors.

P اینهسه *inhasa*, Fast, hard to unloose. Frozen.

P آینه محل *āyina-mahal*, A glazed house. A room hung round about with mirrors.

A ایواء *i-wā*, (v. n. 4 of اوي) Receiving hospitably.

P ایوار *ewār*, The evening. ایوار کردن *ewār kardan*, To travel late in the evening.

P ایواز *ewāz*, (or ایوازه *ewāza*) Adorned, decorated.

P A ایوان *aywān*, A portico, open gallery, veranda, balcony on the top of the house, for the benefit of the prospect and fresh air. ایوان زرکاري *aywāni zarkārī*, (or سیمابي *simābī*) The heavens.

A ایوان *iwān*, (pl. ایوانات *iwānāt* and اواوین *awāwīn*) A portico, an arched gallery. ایوان اللجام *iwānu'l lijām*, The fore part of a bridle-bit.

A ایوانات *aywānāt*, Porticoes, galleries.

P ایوانس *ayvānis*, Name of a city of the Franks wherein is a church. Every year at the time the sun enters Capricorn many starlings arrive, each bearing an olive in its beak, which they drop in the church, and which suffice the inhabitants of the place for a whole year. There is not an olive-tree within a hundred leagues of the spot.

P ایواه *aywāh*, Fie! pho! alas!

A ایوب *uyūb*, (v. n. of آب) Setting (the sun).

A ایّوب *ayyūb*, Job. ابو ایّوب A camel.

A ایور *uyūr*, (pl. of ایر *ayr*) Veretra.

P ایوره *iwara*, Adorned.

P ایوز *iwaz*, (or ایوزه *iwaza*) Adorned, decorated.

A ایوم *aywam*, A very clear day. An evil day. *Uyūm*, (v. n. of آم for ایم) Being left a widow. (pl. of ایم *īm*) Serpents. (pl. of ایّم *ayyim*) Bachelors.

P ایومن *ayūmin*, (in zand and Pāzand) The eye.

A ایّون *ayyūna*, (pl. of ايّ *ayy*) Who? which?

A ایه *iha* or *ihi*, Well done! bravo! come on!

A ایها *ayhā*, Begone! get away! *Īhā*, Silence!

A ایّها *ayyuhā*, O!

A ایهاء *īhā*, (v. n. 4 of وهی) Dissolving, breaking, disjointing. Hurting (the hand) by striking.

A ایهاب *ihāb*, (v. n. 4 of وهب) Preparing, making ready. Being possible, being within one's reach. Being perpetual, perennial.

A آیهات *ayahāta*, Begone! away!

A ایهات *ayhāta*, Begone! away! *Īhāt*, (v. n. 4 of وهت) Stinking (meat).

A ایهاج *ihāj*, (v. n. 4 of وهج) Lighting, kindling.

A ایهاط *ihāt*, (v. n. 4 of وهط) Debilitating. Throwing one into any unpleasant business. Cast ing to the ground. Killing, slaying.

A ایهاف *ihāf*, (v. n. 4 of وهف) Happening.

A ایهال *ihāl*, (v. n. 4 of اهل) Marrying. Admitting into a family. Regarding as fit, worthy.

A ايهام *īhām*, (v. n. 4 of وهم) Causing a blunder, deceiving, misleading, puzzling. Exciting suspicion. Omission, neglect. Persuading. Ambiguity, amphibology. Insinuation.

A آيهان *āyahān*, Begone! away!

A ايهان *ayhān*, Begone! away! *Īhān*, (v. n. 4 of وهن) Enervating, debilitating. Entering upon the middle of the night.

A ايّتها *ayyatuhā* (or ايّهذا *ayyuhāzā*) O!

P ايهقان *ayhukān*, The herb rocket.

A ايهقان *ayhukān*, Name of a broad-leaved, red-flowered, esculent plant. Wild rocket.

A ايهك *ayhaka*, Well done! Come along!

A ايهم *ayham*, Foolish, stupid. Deaf. Bold, brave (man). A smooth flint-stone. A steep or inaccessible mountain. Land. Continent. A desert through which there is no way.

A ايّهم *ayyahum*, Whomsoever.

A ايّهما *ayyuhumā*, Which of the two. من ايّهما *min ayyihimā*, From whichever of the two.

A الايهمان *al ayhamāni*, The two great evils; (to the Nomade Arabs) A torrent and a camel in rut; (to those dwelling in towns) A flood and a fire.

A ائياس *iyās*, A causing to despair.

A ائيافة *iyāfat*, (v. n. 4 of آف for اوف) Suffering from a murrain amongst cattle, or a blight amongst corn (the same being called آفة *āfat*).

A ائيام *iyām*, A widowing, a bereaving.

P آييان *āyyān*, Perhaps no? Any thing eatable.

A ايئة *ayat*, Form, figure, aspect of the heavens.

A ايّيّة *uyayyat*, (dim. of ا *a*) A little alif.

P آييدن *āyīdan*, To come.

P آييژ *āyīj*, (or آييژك *āyījāk*) A spark of fire.

P آييشه *āyīsha*, A spy, informer. Intelligence.

A ايّيمة *uyayyamat*, (dim. of ائمّة) Little Imāms.

P آيين *āyīn*, An institution, rite, custom, ordinance, canon, usage, prescription. Common law (in contradistinction to the laws delivered by Muhammad, and which are called شرع *sharع*). Mode, form, manner. Ornament, decoration. Name of a mountain where mummies are found. خلفائ كرام عدل آيين *khulafāi kirāmi ءadl-āyīn*, Illustrious khalifs, (making) just laws. آيين بستن *āyīn bastan*, To prepare, adorn. آيين جمشيد *āyīni jamshed*, A sort of flute. A note in music. صفا آيين *safā-āyīn*, Pure, unsullied.

P آيين برگ *āyīn-barg*, Armed, bearing arms.

P آيين بندي *āyīn-bandī*, An alcove, a bower.

P آيين پرستي *āyīn-parastī*, Servitude.

A ايينقات *uyaynikāt*, Small she-camels.

P آيينه *āyīna*, (also آئينه *āina*) A mirror, a looking-glass. آيينهٔ اسكندري *āyīnai iskandarī*, The mirror of Alexandria, representing the whole world, formerly supposed to have been in the library of Alexandria. The sun. آيينهٔ آسمان *āyīnai āsmān* (آيينهٔ چرخ *āyīnai charkh* or آيينهٔ خاوري *āyīnai khāwarī*) The sun. آيينهٔ پيل *āyīnai pīl*, The accoutrements or armour of an elephant. آيينهٔ چيني *āyīnai chīnī*, A mirror made of polished metal. آيينهٔ خاكيان *āyīnai khākiyān*, The Creator. Adam. The human heart. آيينهٔ شش جهت *āyīnai shash jihat*, (The six-faced mirror) The heart of Muhammad. The sleepers in the cave. Those acquainted with mysteries and revelations. آيينهٔ گردان *āyīnai gardān*, The sun.

P آيينه دار *āyīna-dār*, The mirror-keeper, an office at some Eastern courts. The female attendant upon a great lady, who has the care of the looking-glass. A beggar, mendicant. A barber, cupper.

P آئينه داري *āina-dārī*, Office of mirror-holder.

P آيينه دان *āyīna-dān*, A looking-glass case.

P آيينه زداي *āyīna-zidāy*, A polisher of mirrors.

P آيينه فروز *āyīna-faroz*, A furbisher.

A ايّيّيب *uyayyib*, (dim. of ايّوب) Little Job.

ب

ب *bā* or *be*, (called بائ ابجد *bāi abjad*, بائ موحّده *bāi muwahhada*, بائ عربي *bāi ءarabī*, or بائ تازي *bāi tāzī*) The second letter of the Arabic and Persian alphabet. It expresses Two in arithmetic, Monday as the second day of the week, and the constellation Gemini. By way of abbreviation it is put likewise for the month Rajab (the seventh month of the lunar year), especially in the dates of letters: as, تحريرا في ١٥ ب سنه ٨٣ *tahrīran fī khamsata ءashara rajab sana salās u samānīn*, Written (or given) on the 15th of the month Rajab, in the year 83 (contracted for the year 1083). In naming this letter the Arabs call it با *bā* and the Persians بي *be*. In Persian it is sometimes changed for و *vāv*: as, آو *āv* for آب *āb*, Water; خواو *khwāv* for خواب *khwāb*, Sleep: also for ف *fe*: as, زفان *zafān* for زبان *zabān*, Speech; and for م *mīm*: as, غژم *ghujm*, A grape-stone, for غژب *ghujb*.

P ب *ba*, pronounced like the short e in "bet," (the inseparable Persian preposition, instead of which the separate particle به *ba* is often used) To. With. In. For. By. On. According to. Examples of words, to which these prepositions are prefixed, will frequently occur hereafter in alphabetical order. ب *ba* is often prefixed to the future, imperative, and other tenses of Persian verbs; either to determine the signification, to heighten the energy, or merely to prevent a cacophony or harshness of sound, by the concurrence of too many vowels. Before a vowel بد *bad* is substituted for ب *ba* or به *ba*, to prevent the hiatus: as, بدو *badu* for به او *ba u*, To him. It is sometimes a pleonasm: as, بجز *ba juz*, بغير *ba ghayr*, Beside, except; بدر *ba dar*, In. داخل شد بشهر در *dākhil shud ba shahr dar*, He entered into the city; در آمد بخانه در *dar āmad ba khāna dar*, He came into the house. Before a verb this ب *ba* may always be read *bi*: as, برو *bi rav*, Go thou; بكرد *bi kard*, He did; but prefixed to an imperative, of which the first letter is moveable by پيش *pesh*, it may itself receive that vowel: as, بكن *bi kun* or *bu kun*, Do thou.

A ب *bi*, (the inseparable Arabic preposition) With. In. Because, for, on account of. By. At the distance of. To. It is frequently an expletive.

P با *bā*, With. Possessed of, endowed with. Worthy of. Though, notwithstanding. To. At the expense of. با احترام *bā ihtirām*, With honour; venerable, honourable, honoured, worthy of esteem. جوان با استعداد *jawānī bā istiءdād*, A youth endowed with capacity. شاه با افسر *shāhi bā afsar*, A king possessed of a crown, a crowned head. با نان *bā nān*, Possessing bread. با آنكه *bā ānki*, (or با اين همه *bā in hama*) Notwithstanding that, although. با اينهمه كه *bā in hama ki*, Notwithstanding all this, that. با اين جمله *bā in jumla*, With all these, besides all these, notwithstanding. باكه *bā ki*, With whom? to whom? Other examples will be found alphabetically, the particle forming one word with the noun.

P با *bā*, A kind of gruel or other species of spoonmeat. (for باد *bād*) May it be!

A بأا *basa'*, (for بأو *basawa* or بأي *basaya*) (fut. يبأي *yabsa'*) He was proud.

A باء *bāsa*, (for بوأ *bawasa*) (fut. يبوء *yabūu*) He returned. He was separated. He departed. He confessed. He tarried. He agreed with. He alighted. He levelled (a spear).

A باء *bās*, (pl. باءات *bāsāt*) The letter ب *bā*. Conjugal intercourse.

P با آب *bā āb*, With or having water. Watery.

P با ابرو *bā abrū*, Honourably, respectably.

A باءة *bāsat*, A place to which people turn aside, in travelling, for repose; an inn, a caravansera. A house, habitation. Conjugal intercourse, coition.

P با او *bā u*, With him. با او پا گرفت *bā u pā girift*, He opposed him.

P با اوش *bā osh*, A species of large cucumber reserved for seed. A small cluster of grapes.

A باب *bāba*, (fut. يبوب *yabūbu*) He discharged the office of porter (بوّاب *bawwāb*). He dug a pit.

P باب *bāb*, A father. Worthy, suitable. Regard, respect. در باب فلاني *dar bābi fulāne*, In regard to So and so. باب القوم *bābu'l kawm*, A leader of the people. (for باد *bād*) Wind.

A باب *bāb*, (pl. ابواب *abwāb*, بيبان *bībān*, and ابوبة *abwibat*), A gate. A door. The chapter of a book. An affair, business, point, matter. Reason, manner, mode, kind, species, method, sort. The extreme terms in numbers, or the extreme boundaries in limits, confines, or marches. (in grammar) Conjugation. باب التوبة *bābu't tawbat*, The door of repentance. باب الخلاف *bābu'l khilāf*, Irresistible. باب السماء *bābu's samās*, The milky way. باب سعادت *bābi saءādat*, The port of felicity, the king's court. باب مفاعله *bābi mufā'ala*, The third conjugation. باب استفعال *bābi istif'āl*, The tenth conjugation. P باب لا ينصرف خواندن *bābi lā yansarif khwāndan*, To be parsimonious. A هو من هذا الباب *huwa min hāzā'l bāb*, So far (is) to the point. P در باب فلان *dar bābi fulān*, Respecting such and such a person, or thing. در اين باب *dar īn bāb*, In this affair.

P بابا *bābā*, A father. A grandfather. The head of an order of monks called Calendars.

A بأباء *ba'bā*, Intelligent, sagacious. Learned.

A بأباة *ba'ba'at*, (v. n. of بأبأ Q) Saying "Papa," papaing. Saying "May my father be a ransom for you." Running.

A بابات *bābāt*, (pl. of بابة *bābat*) The extreme terms in numbers, the extreme boundaries in limits or confines. Faces. بابات الكتاب *bābātu'l kitāb*, The lines of a book.

P بابا خان *bābā-khān*, Father-king, a royal title.

P با باران *bā bārān*, With rain, rainy.

G باباري *bābāri*, Black pepper.

P بابا شيخي *bābā-shaykhī*, A kind of melon.

A باب الابواب *bābu'l abwāb*, The gate of gates, called by the Persians "Dar-band," or The Barrier, is a strong fortress on the Caspian Sea, formerly the boundary of the Persian and the Turkish empires on that quarter.

A باب الزقاق *bābu'z zukāk*, (or باب الاسواق *bābu'l aswāk*) Gate of the way, Straits of Gibraltar.

A باب المندب *bābu'l mandib*, The gate of tears, the straits into the Red Sea, called "Babelmandel."

P بابايان *bābāyān*, (pl. of بابا) Fathers, ancestors.

P بابايانه *bābāyāna*, Like a father, according to ancient custom, in the manner of ancestors.

A بابة *bābat*, The extreme term in numbers, or in boundaries. The face. هذا بابته *hāzā bābatuhu*, This is best for him, it suits him, it is his business. هذا من بابتك *hāzā min bābatika*, This agrees with you; this is your affair. البابه *al bāba*, The Pope.

P بابت *bābat*, An item. For, on account of. بابت او *bābati u*, On account of him or of it.

P بابر *bābar*, Name of an emperor of Hindūstān, the second of the Mogul race.

P بابره *bābira*, A bracelet.

P بابري *bābari*, Belonging to Sultān Bābar.

P بابزن *bābzan*, A spit.

P بابسر *bābasir*, Senna.

P بابك *bābak*, (dimin. of باب *bāb*) A little father. One who educates. Faithful, constant, firm, strong. A turquoise stone. Name of a king.

A بابل *bābil* or *bābul*, Babylon, renowned for wine and magic.

P بابل خانه *bābul-khāna*, A bawdy-house, stew.

G بابلس *bābilas*, Devil's-milk. Poppy-seed.

A بابله *bābala*, Liquid storax.

A بابليّ *bābiliy*, Poison. Wine.

A بابليّة *bābiliyat*, Wine.

A بابليون *bābilyūn*, The Babylon of Egypt, afterwards called الفسطاط *al fustāt*, The tent, and then القاهرة *al kāhira*, The victorious.

P بابندن *bābandan*, To give, to bestow.

P بابو *bābū*, A kind of wandering monk.

P بابوار *bābwār*, Item by item. A chapter.

P بابوته *bābūta*, An earthen pitcher full of water.

A بابوس *bābūs*, A young child. A camel's colt. The young of any animal. Adulterated camphor.

A بابوسر *bābūsir*, Adulterated camphor.

P بابوك *bābūk*, Camomile-flowers. Ground ivy. The earth-apple (on account of the roundness of its flowers). Foolish, insane.

A بابول *bābūl*, Babylon.

A بابونج *bābūnaj*, or بابونك Camomile-flowers.

P بابونه *bābūna*, Camomile. Wild ivy. بابونۀ گاو *bābūna-i gāv* or *gāo*, Camomile-flowers.

P بابه *bāba*, Stuffed with wool. Worthy, suitable.

A بابيّة *bābīyat*, A wonderful thing.

P بابيزان *bābīzān*, A surety, sponsor, middleman. (for باد بيزن *bād-bīzan*) A fan, ventilator.

P با بي زباني ساختن *bā bī zabānī sākhtan*, To keep silence.

P بابيزن *bābīzan*, A spit. A sponsor, a surety.

P با پايان *bā pāyān*, Camels. Short, finite: shoal.

A باة *bāt*, A place of repose, an inn. Coitus.

A بات *bāta*, (for بيت *bayata*) (fut. يبيت *yabītu* or يبات *yabātu*) He passed the night.

A باتّ *batt*, Who or whatever cuts, breaks, or weakens. A fool. Lean, emaciated. Drunk, drunken. Complete, finished, settled.

P باتاب *batāb*, Similitude, equality. Opposition.

P باتّاب *battāb*, Equal, alike, consistent. Contradiction, opposition, aversion. A kind of dervish.

P باتب *batab*, Worthy, suitable.

P باتر *bātar* or *bātir*, A crane. A man's name.

A باتر *bātir*, Who or what cuts. (pl. بواتر *bawātir*) A sharp sword.

P باتره *bātara*, A drum, a tambourin.

P باتس *bātus*, (or باتش *bātush*) (in the dialect of the people of شبانكاره *shabānkāra*) An orange.

A باتّفاق *bi ittifāk*, With (one) consent.

A باتك *bātik*, Sharp (sword). Name of a sword.

P با تمكين *bā tamkīn*, Majestic.

P باتنگان *bātingān*, The egg-plant.

P باتنگل *bātangal*, Name of a book of the Hindūs.

A باتنيّ *bātiniy*, Name of a man.

P باتو *bātū*, An orange. The grain called حب السلاطين *habbu's salātīn*. Name of a king.

P باتوته *bātūta*, An earthen pitcher full of water.

P باتون *bātūn*, A falcon distinguished by some natural mark.

P باتونه *bātūna*, A jug or pitcher full of water.

A باث *bāsa*, for بوث *bawasa*, (fut. يبوث *yabūsu*) He searched diligently.

A باث *bāsi*, Dispersed, here and there.

A باثر *bāsir*, Water which issues forth without digging. Environs.

A باثعة *bāsi'at*, A lip full of blood, ready to burst.

A باثق *bāsik*, Abundant (in liberality).

A باثقة *bāsikat*, Full, overflowing (well).

P باج *bāj*, Tribute. Toll levied by the road-patrol. A silence observed by the Magi at meals and whilst performing their ablutions. باج و خراج *bāj u kharāj*, Tribute and contribution, duties, taxes.

A بأج *ba'j*, (v. n. of بأج) Changing, turning. Shouting, crying aloud. *Ba'j*, (or باج *bāj*) A species, sort, mode, or manner. هم في امر بأج *hum fī amrin ba'jin*, They are in a bad business.

A باج *bāja*, (for بوج *bawaja*) (fut. يبوج *yabūju*) (Misfortune) overtook (him).

P باجبان *bājbān*, A revenue-collector.

A بأجة *ba'jat*, A kind of food.

P باجدار *bāj-dār*, A collector of the revenues.

A باجر *bājir*, (pl. بجرة *bajarat*) One who has a swelled belly. *Bājir* or *bājar*, Name of an idol formerly worshipped by the tribe of ازد *azd*.

H باجرا *bājrā*, A species of Indian corn.

P باجگذار *bāj-guzār*, Tributary, taxed, taxable.

P باجگير *bāj-gīr*, A collector of revenue.

A باجل *bājil*, Very fat (man or camel). Rich, fruitful. Joyous. In good condition.

A باجمعين *bi ajma'īna*, All, the whole.

P باج نامه *bāj-nāma*, Household stuff. Service, drudgery. Favour. Pomp, pride.

P باجنگ *bājang*, A small window.

P باجه *bāja*, A wicket. A large window.

H باجي *bājī*, Nitre.

P باجيان *bājyān*, A revenue-collector.

P باچنگل گرفتن *bā changal* (or باچنگ *bā chang*) *giriftan* To tickle, twitch, scratch with the fingers.

P باچو *bāchū*, A title given to Tartar princes.

A باح *bāha*, (for بوح *bawaha*) (fut. يبوح *yabūhu*) It was manifest. He was tired. He communicated (a secret).

A باحة *bāhat*, (pl. بوح *būh*) A gulf, great body of water. A whirlpool. Many palm-trees, a palm-plantation. A court, area, or quadrangle. باحة الطريق *bāhatu't tarīk*, The middle of the road.

A باحث *bāhis*, An examiner, scrutineer.

A باحثاء *bāhisā*, Earth resembling the nest of the field-mouse.

A باحر *bāhar*, Name of an idol. *Bāhir*, Foolish, stupid: stupefied, confounded, struck with amaze. A liar, idle talker. Blood of a pure red. Blood of the womb. دم باحر *dami bāhir*, Black blood.

A باحرة *bāhirat*, Name of a thorny tree. A camel yielding plenty of milk.

A باحريّ *bāhiriy*, Blood of a bright red.

P با حفصان *bā hafsān*, A schoolmaster.

P باحفصانه *bā hafsāna*, Lispingly, like a child.

A باحور *bāhūr*, Intense heat, heat of midsummer or the dog-days. Exhalation from the earth in hotweather. The moon. ايّام باحور *ayyāmi bāhūr*, Dog-days.

A باحوراء *bāhūrā*, The heat of the dog-days.

A باحوريّ *bāhūriy*, Critical. يوم باحوري *yawmi bāhūrī*, The critical day (in a fever).

P باخ *bākh*, A road, a way.

P باخبر *bā khabar*, Informed. Intelligent, wary.

P باختر *bākhtar*, The west. The east. Bactria.

P باختن *bākhtan*, To play. To lose at play. To give. قمار باختن *kimār bākhtan*, To play at dice.

P باخته *bākhta*, Played. The plaster, incrustation, smoothing, or polishing of a wall.

A باخر *bākhir*, One who waters sown fields. (for بآخر *bi ākhir*) At length. At last.

P باخرز *bākharz*, A note in music. In Khurāsān.

A باخريق *bākharīk*, Name of a village, the birth-place of an eminent Muhammadan lawyer, who gave sentence for the shedding the blood of his own son, when convicted of a capital offence.

A باخس *bākhis*, One who deprives another of his due; a sharper, a swindler. Deficient.

A باخسة *bākhisat*, A female sharper.

P باخسه *bākhsa*, A lancet. A private entrance.

P باخصوص *bā khusūs*, Particularly, especially.

A باخع *bākhiʻ*, Who kills himself (with sorrow).

A باخق *bākhik*, One-eyed.

A باخقة *bākhikat*, Sightless (eye).

A باخل *bākhil*, (pl. بخّل *bukhkhal*) Covetous.

P باخنامه *bākh-nāma*, A surname, nickname, title.

P باخود *bā khwud*, By himself, by herself.

P باخور *bākhūr*, Name of Abraham's grandfather. (They say that money was first coined in his time).

G باخوس *bākhūs*, Bacchus.

P باخويش *bā khwesh*, Alone. Solitude, loneliness. A dip, plunge.

P باخه *bākha*, A tortoise. باخهٔ دريائي *bākhasi daryāsī*, A sea-tortoise or turtle. باخهٔ برّي *bākhasi barrī*, A land-tortoise.

P باخه زن *bākha-zan*, (or باخيزان) A plasterer.

P باد *bād*, Let it be, so be it! هرچه بادا باد *har chi bādā bād*, Let it be as it may, or, as God will.

P باد *bād*, Wind, air. Breath. A word. A sigh, a groan. Pride, haughtiness. Praise, encomium. Sharp, fierce. A horse. Annihilated. (for باده *bāda*) Wine. باد آهنگ *bādi āhang*, An echo. باد بروت *bādi burūt*, Pride, airs, conceit. باد برين *bādi barīn*, The north-east wind. The south-west wind. باد بهار *bādi bahār*, The gale of the spring. باد پس پشت *bādi pas pusht*, The west wind. باد پسين *bādi pasīn*, Future happiness. باد پيش *bādi pesh*, The east wind. باد پيمودن *bād paymūdan*, (To measure the wind) To engage in any foolish undertaking. To drink wine. باد تند *bādi tund*, A hurricane, tempest. باد تنگ بسته *bādi tang-basta*, A horse. باد در دست داشتن *bād dar dast dāshtan*, To be empty-handed. To hold the reins of a horse. باد دبور *bādi dabūr*, A south-west wind. باد سرد *bādi sard*, A deep cold sigh. Despair. باد سخت *bādi sakht*, (or باد شديد *bādi shadīd*) A violent wind. باد سليمان *bādi sulaymān*, The wind that wafted Solomon and his hosts everywhere. Magnificence, grandeur. باد سموم *bādi samūm*, A sultry, unwholesome, and pestilential air. باد سموم جان گداز *bādi samūmi jān-gudāz*, A scorching wind, melting the soul, fatal to life. باد سنجيدن *bād sanjīdan*, (To weigh the wind) To talk nonsense. باد شدن *bād shudan*, To go to the winds. To disappear. To fly. باد شرطه *bādi shurta*, A favourable wind, prosperous gale. باد صبا *bādi sabā*, The zephyr, the north-east or morning wind. باد عيسيٰ *bādi ʻīsa'*, (or باد مسيح *bādi masīh*) The breath of Jesus (or of the Messiah); an expression used by the Persians to imply a skilful physician; as if endowed, like the Messiah, with the power of recovering the sick, or recalling the dead, by a breath. باد فرنگ *bādi farang*, St. Anthony's fire. باد فروردين *bādi farvardīn*, The south-west wind. باد كردن *bād kardan*, To fan. باد كنجي *bādi kunjī*, The cholic. باد كژ *bādi kaj*, A north-west wind. A side wind. باد گند *bādi gund*, A rupture. باد گيسو *bādi gīsū*, Pride, airs, affectation. باد مخالف *bādi mukhālif*, A contrary wind. باد مراد *bādi murād*, A fair wind. باد نوا *bādi nawā*, An echo. باد نو روز *bādi nawroz*, Vernal breezes. Name of a modulation in music. باد هوا *bādi hawā*, Gratis, for nothing, gratuitously. The law of the country (*i.e.* when a criminal is apprehended and punished in any place of which he is not a native). *Bād* is also the name of an angel or genius, who, like the Æolus of the Greeks, presides over the winds. He also presides over marriage, and has the superintendency of every thing that happens on the 22d day of the month, which is consecrated to this spirit, and called by his name. The second of Khusraw's treasures.

A باد *bāda* (for بيد *bayada*) (fut. يبود *yabūdu* or يبيد *yabīdu*) He perished.

A بادّ *bādd*, The inner part of the thigh.

P بادا *bādā*, Let it be, so be it! يا ربّ اينچنين بادا *yā rabb īnchunīn bādā*, O Lord! so let it be.

P باداباد *bād-ā-bād*, Be it so.

P باد آبله *bād-ābila*, A boil, blain. Small-pox.

A باداة *bādāt*, A desert.

P باداد *bā dād*, With equity, justly.

P بادارنگ *bādārang*, An orange.

P باداش *bādāsh*, A requital of kindness.

P بادافراش *bād afrāsh*, Punishment. Revenge.

P باد آفراه *bād-āfrāh*, Punishment. A toy.

P بادافراه *bād afrāh*, (or افره *afrah*) Punishment, penance, chastisement. Revenge. A child's toy.

P باد افزا *bād-afzā*, Revenge. Retribution.

P بادام *bādām*, An almond. Spiceries. A slit in a horse's ear. The eye of a mistress. بادام دو مغزي *bādāmi du maghzī*, A slit, a fissure. Cracked. بادام شگوفه فشان *bādāmi shigūfa-fishān*, A weeping eye. بادام شگوفه كردن *bādāmi shigūfa kardan*, To shed tears. بادام كوهي Mountain-almond.

P بادامتره *bādāmtara*, The herb basil.

P باد آمدن *bād āmadan*, To congratulate.

P بادامستان *bādāmistān*, An almond-grove.

P بادام فروش *bādām-farosh*, A seller of almonds.

P بادامه *bādāma*, The cocoon of the silk-worm. A seal shaped like an almond. A kind of silk. habit, made of rags sewed together, worn by Dervishes or Fakīrs. Any kind of stuff printed or stamped. The bezel of a ring. A stone in the form of an eye which they sew on a child's cap. A link. A mole on the cheek.

P بادامي *bādāmī*, Buff-coloured. Sort of eunuch.

P بادان *bādān*, Populous. A recompense.

A بادّان *bāddāni*, (dual of بادّ *bādd*) The inside of the thighs. The parts of the horse which are pressed by the rider's thighs.

P باد انجير *bād-anjīr*, A kind of early hollow fig.

P بادان فيروز *bādān-fīroz*, The city of Ardabil.

P باد انگيز *bād-angez*, (Wind-exciting) A kind of plant which the Persian peasants hold in their hands when they winnow their corn, and suppose to have the power of raising the wind, especially when they rub it and throw it in the air. Saffron.

P باد آور *bād-āwar*, A sort of thorny shrub. One of the seven treasures of Khusraw. Riches acquired without labour; a windfall. Name of a note in music.

P باد آورد *bād-āward*, (or باد آورده *bād-āwarda*) A kind of white thorn or thistle, of which camels are fond. A place exposed to the wind. Ventilated. A fan. Name of a musical note. A windfall.

P باد آوله *bād-āvila*, A fatal kind of boil.

P باد آهنج *bād-āhanj*, A ventilating window.

P بادبار *bād-bār*, A fan. Ventilation.

P بادباز *bād-bāz*, A fan. Easy. Fortunate.

P بادبان *bādbān*, A sail. A fan. The collar or sleeve of a garment. A ship's mast. Sociable.

بادبان اخضر *bādbāni akhzar*, The blue firmament. بادبان چرخ *bādbāni charkh*, Moon-light. بادبان كشيدن *bādbān kashīdan*, To set sail.

P بادبانه *bādbāna*, Name of an herb.

P باد بدست *bād-ba-dast*, (Wind in the hand) Empty-handed, poor. Luckless.

P بادبر *bād-bar*, A paper kite. A boaster, bragger. *Bād-bur*, A whipping-top.

P بادبرك *bād-barak*, A paper kite.

P بادبروت *bād-burūt*, Proud, haughty, boasting, assuming; one who arrogates to himself what he never performed, cannot do, or is not entitled to.

P بادبره *bād-bara*, The 22d of the month Bahman. *Bād-bura*, A little round piece of wood put upon a spindle to give it a circular motion, a whirl.

P باد بمشت *bād-ba-musht*, (Wind in the fist) Fruitless, unproductive.

P باد بيزن *bād-bīzan*, A sort of fan. Idle, useless.

P بادپا *bād-pā*, (or باد پاي *bād-pāy*) (A horse)

fleet as the wind. باد پاي وهم bād-pāyi wahm, Quick of conception, of a lively imagination.

P بادپالا bād-pālā, Racking wine: a wine-strainer

P بادپر bād-par, A boaster. A beam. A whirligig.

P باد پرّان bād-parrān, An empty boaster.

P باد پروا bād-parwā, A ventilator. Any aperture made for the admission of air. One to whom all things come alike. An airy house.

P باد پره bād-para, A shaving of wood which the wind carries away. The down of a plant.

P باد پزان bād-pazān, Flattering. A welcome.

P باد پسین bād-pasīn, A fart.

P باد پیچ bād-pech, A swing.

P بادپیما bād-paymā, (Measuring the air) Swift. A traveller. Talkative. A liar. Sensual. A glutton. A drunkard. A curling lock. Penniless.

P باد تخم bād-tukhm, Fennel. Aniseed.

P باد خان bād-khān, Airy room. A ventilator.

P باد خانه bād-khāna, A ridge, top. A ventilator.

P باد خاني bād-khānī, Name of a fountain in the province of Dāmghān; so called because at a certain season of the year there rushes from it a wind so violent and impetuous, that it sweeps away men and animals, and even uproots the strongest trees.

P بادخایه bād-khāya, Rupture: swelled testicle.

P باد خن bād-khan, A storm, tempest, hurricane. A ventilator. An airy house.

P باد خوار bād-khwār, (Devouring the wind) Name of a bird. The rupture.

P باد خوان bād-khwān, An idle talker, jester. Facetious. A flatterer.

P بادخور bād-khwur, (Breeze-devouring) A window, especially in the roof, for the benefit of fresh air, and the advantage of a fine prospect.

P باد خورا bād-khwurā, A scald-head.

P باد خورك bād-khwurak, A small black bird said to live in the air, and to feed on the wind. (If he happen to alight he is unable to rise again.)

P باد خون bād-khūn, A ventilator. A country retirement, garden-house, or villa. The flowing of water. Household furniture. The plan, delineation, or figure of a house.

P باد دار bād-dār, Windy. Swollen. Puffed up with pride. Independent. Worldly-minded. Possessed of an evil spirit. Destructive.

P باد درتام bād-dar-tām, Rheum.

P باد درسر bād-dar-sar, (Wind in the head) Arrogance, haughtiness, foppishness.

P باد در كف bād-dar-kaf, (also باد در مشت bād dar musht, (Wind in the fist) Poor, penniless.

P باد دژم bād-dajam, A species of disease occasioned by the wind; (breaking forth into bloody wheals all over the body).

P باد دژنام bād-dijnām, A superfluity of blood in the body, breaking out in sores and boils.

P باد دست bād-dast, Lavish. A spendthrift.

P باد دم bād-dam, Puffed up with pride, vain.

P بادر bādar, The 29th day of the month or moon. Moist, fresh, green. Lettuce. The erysipelas.

A بادر bādir, Full (moon). Full-grown (youth). Ripe (fruit).

P بادرام bādrām, Vain, foolish, idle, silly, futile, unprofitable. Wicked, depraved. A subject.

P باد ران bād-rān, A fan. Haughty, aspiring. Name of an angel presiding over (driving) the wind.

A بادرة bādirat, (pl. بوادر bawādir) Cutting. An event happening suddenly and unexpectedly. Impetuosity, vehemence. Ardour, warmth. The leaf of the حوّاءة huwāsat. The first opening of a plant. The choicest and youngest of the saffron. The edge or keenness of a sword. The fleshy part between the neck and shoulder: the fleshy part between the bottom of the breast and the nipple.

P بادرس bād-ras, Airy. A flue, funnel, vent.

P باد رفتار bād-raftār, Going like the wind.

P بادرم bād-rum or bād-ram, Vain, foolish, idle, silly, futile, unprofitable. A subject.

P بادرنگ bād-rang, A species of cucumber. An orange. A kind of disease caused by grief. A fleet horse. A kind of swinging cradle.

P بادرنگبویه bādrang-būya, (or boya) (in Arab. بادرنجبویه bādranjbūya) Mountain-balm.

P بادرنگین bād-rangīn, A species of large cucumber. A poem.

P بادرو bād-rū, Balm. A kind of cucumber. A herb that smells like an orange.

P بادروج bādrūj, A fragrant kind of herb.

P بادروچه bādrūcha, Name of an herb.

P بادروز bādroz, A gift, a present. Sweet basil.

P بادروز بویه bādroz-būya, (or boya) A kind of plant which smells like an orange.

P بادروزه bādroza, Continual, perpetual; daily bread, common fare; a garment for daily wear.

P بادروم bādrūm, (or بادرونه) Mountain-balm.

P بادره bādra, Speaking without reflection; haste. *Bādra* or *bādara*, Breeches, drawers.

P بادریس bādrīs, (or بادریسه bādrīsa) A little round piece of wood or leather fixed on a spindle or distaff to wind the thread upon. A flat piece of wood circular and perforated to receive the top of a tent-pole. A whirl. A fan.

P بادریسه چشم bādrīsa-chashm, One-eyed. The devil.

P بادریشه bādresha, (or بادریش bādresh) A cucumber. Rice. Sickness.

P بادریه bādriya, A kind of large wooden fan or ventilator suspended from the roof, to promote a circulation of air, and drive away the flies, a punka.

P بادزد bād-zad, A whirlwind, hurricane.

P بادزم bādzam, Treacle. Trifles, frivolities.

P بادزنه bād-zana, A fan, ventilator.

P بادزهر bād-zahr, The bezoar-stone.

P باد زهره bād-zahra, A swelled throat, quinsey.

A بادزهریّة bādzahrīyat, The property or virtue of the bezoar-stone, counterpoison.

P بادزین bād-zīn, The zephyr.

P بادژ bādij, A pestilential carbuncle or inflammatory appearance of the skin. Red wine.

P بادژفام bādijfām, (or بادژكام bādijkām) An inflammatory red, purple, or livid hue on the face.

P بادژنام bādijnām, An inflammatory red, purple, or livid hue on the face. Red wine. Bile.

P بادژوام bādijwām, An inflammatory disease.

P بادسار bād-sār, Vain, light, trifling. Swift.

P بادسخا bād-sakhā, Generous. The world.

P بادسر bād-sar, Proud, vain, affected, airy.

P بادسره bād-sara, A girth. Sickly, ailing.

P بادسري bād-sarī, Pride, folly, affectation.

P بادسنج bād-sanj, (Weighing wind) Idly speculative, vain. Vain hopes, delusive dreams. Proud.

P بادسوار bād-suwār, A horseman. A fleet horse.

P بادسیر bād-sayr, Travelling like the wind.

P بادش bādash, An inflammatory, livid appearance of the face regarded as precursor of leprosy.

P بادشاه bādshāh, A king.

P بادشاهت bādshāhat, Kingdom, government.

P بادشاهي bādshāhī, A kingdom.

P باد شرطه bād-shurta, A favourable wind.

P بادشفام bādishfām, (بادشنام bādishnām or بادشوام bādishwām) Red wine. The prickly heat, an inflammatory appearance of the face.

P بادشه bādshah, A king.

P باد عنان bād-ʻinān, Swift, fleet (horse).

P بادغر bādghar, (بادغرد bādghard, بادغد bād-ghad, or بادغند bād-ghand) A house having a number of windows, an airy summer-house.

P بادغس bād-ghas, A vent, chimney, funnel.

P بادغن bād-ghan, An airy house. A vain boaster.

P بادغیس bādghīs, A district in Khurāsān.

P بادفت bādaft, Name of a fragrant tree.

P بادفر bād-far, A small top or gig, a plaything that hums. A large fan or ventilator suspended from the roof for promoting a circulation of air, a punkah. Punishment, retribution. A boaster.

P باد فراه bād-farāh, A child's plaything. *Bādafrāh*, Punishment, retribution.

P بادفره bādafra, Vain, foolish, boasting, brag. Punishment, retribution. *Bādfara*, A child's game.

P باد كردار bād-kirdār, Swift, hasty, expeditious.

P بادكش bād-kash, A large fan. A punkah. Bellows. Cupping, scarification. باد كش فراشي bād-kashi firāshī, A large sort of fan.

P باد كن bād-kin, A rupture.

P بادگان bādgān, A keeper, guardian: treasurer. The fore and hinder part of the collar of a garment.

P بادگانه bād-gāna, A latticed window.

P بادگاه bād-gāh, A draught-house, a privy.

P بادگذار bād-guzār, An air-hole. A fabler.

P بادگر bādgar, (or بادگرد bād-gird) A whirlwind.

P بادگنجي bād-gunjī, (or بادگنج) The cholic.

P بادگي bād-gī, (or بادگیر gīr) An airy house. A funnel perforated in every part for the admission of air.

A بادل ba‑ādil, (pl. of بادلة bādilat) Quick paces. Fleshy parts between arm-pits and breasts.

P بادل bā dil, Generous, brave, noble-hearted.

A بادلة bādilat, (pl. بادل ba‑ādil) The flesh between the arm-pit and breasts. The flesh of the breast. A quick pace.

P بادلجان bādiljān, The egg-plant or brinjal.

P با دل و جان bā dil u jān, With heart and soul.

P بادليجه bādalīja, A sort of cannon.

P بادم bādam, (for بادام) An almond. Spiceries.

P بادمهره bād-muhra, Antidote for a snake's bite.

A بادن bādin, (pl. بدن budun and بدّن buddan) Old (man or woman). Fat, corpulent.

A بادنة bādinat, Corpulent (woman).

P بادنج bādinj, A cocoa-nut.

P بادنجان bādinjān, The egg-plant or brinjal.

P بادنگ bādang, Swaddling-clothes.

P بادنگان bādingān, The egg-plant or brinjal.

P باد نما bād-namā, A vane, pennant, weathercock, showing the quarter whence the wind blows.

P بادوان badwān, The sail of a ship. The collar of a garment. A shirt, shift. A cup, goblet.

P بادوبان bādūbān, The front and back of the collar of a garment.

P باد و بيد bād u bīd, Useless, unprofitable.

P باد و دم bād u dam, Pride, self-complacency.

P بادويز bād-wīz, (or بادويزن) A ventilator, fan.

P باده bāda, Wine. A cup, vessel full of wine. بادهٔ مست bāda‑i mast, Strong, intoxicating wine. بادهٔ نو bāda‑i naw, New wine. باده پيمودن bāda paymūdan, To measure out wine; to give to drink.

P باده پالا bāda-pālā, Racking wine: a strainer.

P باده پرست bāda-parast, Given to wine, a sot.

P باده پيمان bāda-paymān, Measuring wine.

P باده پيماني bāda-paymānī, Crop-sickness.

P باد هرزه bād-harza, An incantation employed by house-breakers to lull the watchmen to sleep.

P باده گسار bāda-gusār, A wine-drinker.

P بادهنج bād-hanj, (or بادهلج bād-hilj) A building on the top of houses in the East, in the form of a chimney, having an opening face to the west, which, catching the breeze, gives a refreshing coolness to the apartments with which it communicates.

P باده نوش bāda-nosh, A wine-biber, a drunkard.

P باد هوائي bād-hawā‑ī, Fruitlessness, waste.

P بادي bādī, Be thou. Mayest thou live for ever! The signs Gemini, Libra, and Aquarius. Flatulent, full of wind, windy. Aerial, airy.

A بادئ bādi‑, Who or what appears, comes out.

A بادي bādī, (pl. بادون bādūn, بدّا buddan, and بدّاء buddā‑) A peasant, countryman, inhabitant of the desert. A beginning. Conspicuous. Author, cause. البادي اظلم al bādī azlam, The author is most to blame. بادي الانقاض bādi'l infāz, Evidently destitute. بادي الراي bādi'r ra‑y, First thought. بادي النظر bādi'n nazar, The first glance.

A باديات الجن bādiyātu'ljinn, Fairies' desert.

P باديار bādyār, A falcon trained for hunting.

P باديان bādyān, (or باديانه) Fennel, anise.

P باديا وند bādyāwand, Strong, robust. Strength.

P باديا وندي bādyāwandī, Bodily strength, force.

A بادئة bādi‑at, A new and original saying.

A بادية bādiyat, A desert. The deserts of Arabia, inhabited by the Badawīns. اهل البادية ahlu'l bādiyat, Inhabitant of the desert, a Bedouin. باديهٔ تيه bādiya‑i tih, The desert of the Israelites.

P باديهٔ غولدار bādiya‑i ghūl-dār, Present world.

P باديج bādīj, Large boots or stockings.

P باديد bā dīd, Openly. Manifest, conspicuous.

P باديدار bā dīdār, Sightly, pleasing to the eye.

P بادير bādīr, A pillar, prop, support, buttress.

P باديه bādya, A capacious earthen vessel, in which wine is kept; also a large deep jug in which wine is brought to table; and, thence, filled into the smaller cups, to prevent the spirit from evaporating.

P باديه پيماي bādiya-paymāy, (Measuring the desert) A swift horse. A traveller.

P باديه نشين bādiya-nishīn, An inhabitant of the desert.

A باذّ bāzz, Bad, old, worn, torn, squalid.

P باذارنگ bāzārang, A citron, a quince.

P باذام bāzām, (for بادام) An almond. Mcn.

A باذامك bāzāmak, A kind of willow.

P باذاورد bāzāward, A white thorn.

A باذخ bāzikh, (pl. بواذخ) High, exalted.

P باذذم bāzzam, A trifle, a thing of no importance.

A باذرنجبوية bāzaranjbūyat, The herb melissa.

P باذرو bāzaro, Parsley.

A باذروج bāzarūj, Mountain-balm.

A باذغيش bāzghīsh, (from P بادخيز bād-khez) Name of a village dependent on Harāt.

P باذفت bāzaft, Name of a tree which emits a sweet perfume when shaken by the wind.

A باذق bāzik also bāzak, (from P باده bāda) The juice of the grape slightly boiled. حاذق باذق hāzik bāzik, Endowed with quickness of parts.

A باذل bāzil, One who expends, uses, puts out. Liberal, munificent. P باذل مقدور كردن bāzili makdūr kardan, To employ (every) endeavour.

A باذنة bāzanat, Knowledge. Confession. Submission, self-abasement.

A باذنجان bāzinjān, The egg-plant or brinjal.

P بار bār, A burden, load, weight, charge. Baggage. A pack, a bale. A fœtus. Fruit, flowers, blossoms. Sorrow, grief. The imposition of a burden not to be endured. A court, congress, assembly. A tribunal. A curtain at the door of a pavilion. Entrance. Free access, admittance. Opportunity. A petition, written memorial, request. Leave, license. Root, cause, origin, foundation. A branch. A fortification, a wall. A ditch, a moat. A granary, storehouse. God. Greatness, eminence, dignity. Fault, crime. Dung, manure. Adulteration, alloy. A trivet. A musical instrument. Rice or any other grain from which beer is made. Name of a village near Tūs. Food in general. Filling a plate with food. A time, turn. يك بار دو بار yak bār du bār, Once or twice. بار سوم bāri siwum, The third time. هر بار har bār, Every time, as often as, always. Precisely, exactly. بار بار bār-bār, Oft, repeatedly, time after time. Great, elevated, high: اي بار خداي ay bār khudāy, Great God! (participle of باريدن bāridan, To rain, used in composition) Raining, pouring, shedding, scattering: اشك بار ashk-bār, Tear-shedding. دربار dur-bār, Scattering pearls. عنبر بار ʻambar-bār, Fragrant as ambergris. مشك بار musk-bār, Breathing musk. (An affixing implying) Conflux or multitude: as, جوي بار jūy-bār, A river, a place abounding in streams. A region: as, زنگبار zangabār, Zanguebār. مالبار mālbār, Malabār. هندوبار hindūbār, India. بار بر دل نهادن bār bar dil nihādan, To lay a burden on the heart, to afflict. بار دادن bār dādan, To hold a levee. To give the road to a superior. To manure land. بار دل bāri dil, Heart-ache, grief of heart, worldly cares. بار ساختن bār sākhtan, To make up a bundle, to pack up. بار شدن bār shudan, To be loaded, burdened. بار عام bāri ʻām, A public audience, a levee. بار پذيرفتن bār paziruftan, To conceive. بار كردن bār kardan, To load. To draw up in battle-array. بار كشتي bāri kishtī, The freight of a ship. بار گرفتن bār giriftan, To conceive, become pregnant. بار نهادن bār nihādan, To bring forth. بار و ديوار bār u dīwār, Walls and bulwarks. بار يافتن bār yāftan, To gain or find admittance.

A بأر ba‑r (v. n. of بأر) Digging (a well, ditch, or corn-vault). Hiding, concealing. Laying up in a magazine, or a store of merit. Doing good secretly.

A بار bāra, (fut. يبور yabūru) He perished.

A بارّ bārr, (pl. ابرار abrār and بررة bararat) Beneficent, pious. Just, true. Dutiful. One who abstains from any thing unjust or unlawful.

P باراب bār-āb, Agricultural produce raised by water drawn from the beds of rivers or by artificial canals. Name of a district in Turkistān.

P بارات bārāt, An assignment for money, draft.

P باراج bārāj, A midwife.

P بار آغوش bār-āghosh, An armful.

P باران bārān, Rain. باران شتاب bārāni shitāb, Heavy rain. باران رسيده bārān-rasīda, (also باران زده bārān-zada) Rained upon.

P باران ريز bārān-rez, A spout.

P باران گريز bārān-girez, The eaves of a house. Shelter from rain.

P باران گير bārān-gīr, A shelter from rain.

P باران ناك bārānnāk, Rainy (day).

P بارانه bārāna, The main-beam of a house. The herb melissa. بارانه كردن bārāna kardan, To fall into danger. To throw away. To boast, brag.

P بارانی *bārānī*, A riding-coat or cloak which keeps out the rain. Name of a Turkomān tribe.

P بارانیدن *bārānīdan*, To cause to rain.

P باراهی کند *bārāhī-kand*, An Indian plant.

P باربار *bār-bār*, Frequently, repeatedly. Murmuring, crying. Name of a prophet.

P باربد *bārbud*, Name of a famous Persian musician, native of Jahram, a town near Shīrāz.

P باربر *bār-bar*, (or باربردار *bār-bardār*) A carrier, porter. A day-labourer. A beast of burden. A devious course.

P باربرداری *bār-bar-dārī*, Travelling expenses, carriage-hire.

P باربغه *bār-bugha*, A load, baggage. Gently. Small wares.

P باربنگاه *bār-binigāh*, A load ready adjusted.

T باربیگی *bār-begī*, Master of the ceremonies.

P بارتنگ *bāritang*, The plantane-tree.

P بارج *bāraj*, Nightshade. Name of a fruit.

A بارج *bārij*, A skilful sailor.

P بارجا *bār-jā*, A royal court.

P بارجات *bārjāt*, An oppressive custom of forcing to purchase goods above the market-price.

P بارجامه *bār-jāma*, A large pair of saddle-bags with a mouth on the side.

P بارجای *bārjāy*, A free grant of a spot of ground made by a Zamīndār to any one of his relations.

A بارجة *bārijat*, A great ship of war. Wicked man.

P بارچا *bār-chā*, Judgment-hall, court of justice.

A بارح *bārih*, (pl. بوارح *bawārih*) A sultry wind. A strong wind raising the dust. (Game) passing from the right side of the hunter to the left. Unfortunate, unhappy. بنت بارح *bintu bārihin*, (pl. بنات بارح *banātu bārihin*) A calamity. هو كبارح الاروى *huwa ka bārihi'l arwa'*, It appears like the mountain-goat (*i.e.* it is seldom seen, applied to any thing uncommonly strange).

A بارحة *bārihat*, The last part of the preceding day or night. البارحة *al bārihat*, Yesterday. البارحة الاولى *al bārihatu'l ūla'*, The day before yesterday.

P بارخانه *bār-khāna*, A tent, or cloth stretched upon poles, under which goods and baggage are kept from rain, when halting upon a journey. A sack. Dorsers or pack-saddles for beasts of burden, upon which loads are placed. Baggage, particularly such as kings and great men travel with. Merchandize transported from place to place.

P بارخدا *bār-khudā*, Lord God. A king, a prince. An excellent poem.

P بارخدایا *bār khudāyā*, O mighty Lord God!

P بارخیمه *bār-khayma*, A collector of revenue. A custom-house. An exchequer.

A بارد *bārid*, Cold, frigid. Firm, solid, established. Competent. (pl. بوارد *bawārid*) Sharp sword. اوضاع بارد *awzāʿi bārid*, Cold, unfriendly actions. سموم بارد *samūmi bārid*, A hot wind blowing incessantly. عیش بارد *ʿayshi bārid*, An agreeable life. الغنم البارد *al ghanamu'l bārid*, A prize taken without fighting. بارد المزاج *bāridu'l mizāj*, Cold by nature.

P بارداد *bār-dād*, Leave. A porter, chamberlain.

P باردار *bār-dār*, Pregnant. Fruitful.

P باردان *bārdān*, A fruit-basket. A repository for travellers, goods and baggage. Household furniture. Poles, upon which travellers mount awnings or tilts for the preservation of their goods from rain. A large wallet. A cloak-bag, a portmanteau. A flagon of wine.

A باردة *bāridāt*, A woman's name.

P باردست *bārdast*, Ebony.

P باردو *bār-du*, A forked stick used in propping up the branches of a tree overloaded with fruit.

P باردیج *bārdīj*, Any kind of damp cloth fastened to a long pole, with which bakers clean their oven and temper the heat.

P باررنگ *bārrang*, Infants' swaddling bands. Ropes, girths, bandages, or fastenings for loads. Bandages for the breasts, to prevent their swagging

P بارروج *bārrūj*, Baroach, a city in India.

A بارز *bāriz*, Who or what issues forth. Stretching out, extended. Prominent, projecting. Apparent, evident. The third or last page of a letter.

P بارزد *bārzad*, A gum, benzoin or benjamin.

P بارزمان *bār-zamān*, The vicissitudes of fortune.

P بارسا *bārsā*, Done hastily. A commencement.

H برسات *bārsāt*, The rainy season (in India).

G بارسطلارون *bārastalārūn*, (or بارسطاریون *bāristārayūn*) Valerian.

P بارسنج *bār-sanj*, (or بارسنجن *bār-sanjin*) Weighing a load. Any thing placed in an opposite scale as an equilibrium.

P بارش *bārish*, Rain.

P بارشك *bā rashk*, With jealousy, jealous.

P بارشكنی *bār-shikanī*, Provision, especially brought from abroad.

A بارض *bāriz*, The first appearance of grass above ground, when the species is not discernible.

A بارع *bāriʿ*, One who excels in virtue or knowledge. Beautiful, elegant, good, fair.

A بارعة *bāriʿat*, Witty and beautiful (woman).

A بارق *bārik*, Shining, flashing (cloud). Bright (sword). Name of the father of a tribe; also of a place near Kūfa.

A بارقة *bārikat*, Refulgent, bright, dazzling, sharp (sword). Refulgence. Lightning.

P بارك *bārik*, Thin, slender, minute. The membrane which envelopes the fœtus.

A بارك *bārik*, Recumbent (camel), kneeling.

A بارك الله *bārak allāh*, Good God! strange!

P باركش *bār-kash*, A porter, a day-labourer. A bandage tying over all. Carriage, means of conveyance. Oppressed. Sympathizing, condoling.

P باركشی *bār-kashī*, Porterage, a carrying of loads, a bearing of burdens.

P باركی *bāraki* or *bāriki*, A strong horse (particularly a baggage-horse). All together, all at once.

P بارگان *bārgān*, A ditch, a puddle.

P بارگاو *bārgāw*, An agreement, a treaty.

P بارگاه *bār-gāh*, Place of leave or dismission (applied to ambassadors and supplicants of every denomination); *i.e.* the king's court, palace, tent, tribunal, hall of audience. A court, where they load or unload beasts of burden. The womb.

P بار گرفتن *bār giriftan*, To become pregnant.

P بارگه *bār-gah*, (for بارگاه) A hall of justice.

P بارگی *bāragī*, A pack-horse. An excellent strong horse. Strength, power. A courtezan.

P بارگیر *bār-gīr*, A bearer of loads: a beast of burden; a baggage-horse. A camel. One who puts a load on man or beast. One upon whom any burden is laid, or to whom any crime or fault is imputed: charged, convicted. A horse-soldier who has his horse found him. Conceiving, pregnant, gravid. A female. A camel-litter. A lender.

P بارگیری *bār-gīrī*, Conviction, criminal charge.

P بارگین *bārgīn*, A cistern. A sink. Stagnant, fetid, or putrid water.

P بارمان *bārmān*, Name of a champion of Tūrān.

P بارمبوی *bāramboy*, (or بارنبوی) Sweet basil.

A بارنامج *bār-nāmaj*, (P بارنامه) An account-book.

P بارنامه *bār-nāma*, Example, rule, regulation, form, formula, canon. An edict, order, command. Obligation. A numerous household, retinue. Pride, haughtiness, vain-glory. Boasting. Praise, encomium. Glory, exaltation. Leave, dismissal. Throwing, hurling, darting. Interceding, mediating, reconciling. Custom. Military apparatus.

P بارنج *bāranj*, A cocoa-nut.

P بارندگی *bārandagī*, Raining. The rainy season.

P بارنده *bāranda*, (part. of باریدن) Raining.

P بارنگ *bārang*, Swaddling-bands. An orange.

P بارنگبوی *bārangboy*, Southernwood.

P بارنگبویه *bārangboya*, Balm-gentle, parsley.

P بارنگو *bārangū*, Mountain-balm, calamint.

H بارو *bārū*, Sand.

P بارو *bārū*, A wall, rampart, bulwark, fortification. A fort. A tower. Battlements, embrasures.

P باروت *bārūt*, Gunpowder.

P باروت خانه *bārūt-khāna*, A powder-magazine.

P باروچه *bārūcha*, A vessel for carrying clay.

P بارود *bārūd*, Saltpetre. Gunpowder.

P بارور *bārwar*, Fruitful. Plentiful.

P باروزنه *bārawzana*, Name of a note in music.

P باروزه *bā roza*, An every-day garment. Daily bread.

G باروق *bārūk*, Ceruse of white lead or tin.

A باروك *bārūk*, A coward. The night-mare.

P باره *bāra*, God. The presence of God. A curl, a ringlet. An intimate friend. Form, manner. Rule, custom. A time, a turn. Walls, fortifications. Any thing which divides or separates two objects. Ugly, deformed. Covetous, avaricious. Addicted, given to. A bribe to a judge. The curved extremities of the beam of a balance to which the scales or weights are suspended. A horse. A herd, flock. An intoxicating liquor made from barley, beer, ale. Regard, respect. Good, excellent. Beautiful. True, just. Countenance, aspect. The eye-brow. Leave, dismissal. State, condition. Arms. دربارهٔ من *dar bāraʼi man*, With regard to me. بارهٔ نهم *bāraʼi nuhum*, The ninth heaven. زنباره *zan-bāra*, Fond of women; a whoremonger. غلام باره *ghulām-bāra*, Addicted to boys; a sodomite.

P بارها *bārhā*, (pl. of بار *bār*) Burdens. Often, many times, frequently.

P بارهي *bārhī*, Zedeoary.

A بارئ *bāriʼ*, God the divine Creator. (pl. براء *birāʼ*) Healed, cured, restored to health. حضرت بارئ تعالى عزّ شانه *hazrat bāriʼ taʻāla' ʻazza shānuhu*, The Lord God most high and glorious.

P باري *bāre*, Once. A time, a turn. Any time. Sometimes. I wish, would to God! At length. At least, in short, at all events. يك باري *yak bāre*, Once. دو سه باري *du sih bāre*, Twice or thrice. *Bārī*, Loaded, heavy. God. A king. Rank. Excuse, pretext. Walls, fortifications. Name of a town in India. See كعبتين قلب *kaʻbatayni kalb*.

A باري *bārī*, A mat-maker. A maker of arrows. اعطيت القوس باريها *aʻtayta'lkawsa bārihā*, You have given the bow to him who knows how to use it.

A باريّ *bārīy*, (بارياء *bāriyāʼ*, or باريّة *bārīyat*) A mat made of woven reeds.

P باريا *bāryā*, O great God! A hypocrite.

P بارياب *bār-yāb*, Admitted at court.

P بارياني *bār-yābī*, Admittance at court.

P بارياز *bār-yār*, A flower. Fruit. A castle. A burden. A beast of burden. A street having no thoroughfare. *Bār-yār*, when added to numerals, signifies Times: as, دوباريار *du bār-yār*, Twice.

P باريافته *bār-yāfta*, (or باريدار *bārīdār*) Admitted. A servant, a guard, a sentinel at a Haram.

P باريدگي *bārīdagī*, Rain. A cut, rent, fissure.

P باريدن *bārīdan*, To rain.

P باريز *bārīz*, The autumn.

G باريقون *bārīkūn*, Fennel. Hellebore.

P باريك *bārīk*, Subtile, slender. Penetrating. Small, fine, delicate, thin, minute, little, indistinct. وزراي باريك رأي *wuzarāʼi bārīk-raʼy*, Vazirs of a subtile or penetrating genius. رشتهٔ باريك *rishtaʼi bārīk*, A small cord.

P باريك آواز *bārīk-āwāz*, A babbler.

P باريك بين *bārīk-bīn*, Discerning, intelligent.

P باريك بيني *bārīk-bīnī*, Quickness, acuteness.

P باريك ميان *bārīk-miyān*, Slender-waisted.

P باريكي *bārīkī*, Subtilty; slenderness, slimness.

A بارين *bārīn*, Name of a town near Hamāt.

P باز *bāz*, Back, again. Anew, afresh. Also. Towards. Return, repetition. Descent, declivity. Inversion, contrariety. The shoulder. The arm, or the upper part of it. A span, cubit. The distance between each hand when the arms are horizontally extended in an opposite direction. A fathom. A finger-joint. A bundle, armful. Choice, distinction, separation. A ford, ferry. Open. Wine. Tax, tribute. A falcon. باز آزردن *bāz āzurdan*, Gratifying (the reverse of annoying). باز استادن *bāz istādan*, To remain behind, desist, or cease. To be detained, checked, prohibited. To supersede. باز افتادن *bāz uftādan*, To fall back, relapse, recede. باز آمدن *bāz āmadan*, To return. To desist. To repent. باز آوردن *bāz āwardan*, To bring back, restore. باز آورده كردن *bāz āwarda kardan*, To bring back an apology, to excuse, exculpate (one's self). باز بردن *bāz burdan*, To flatten (a cake). باز بستن *bāz bastan*, To rebind, to set (a broken bone). To trace (one's self or one's pedigree) back, to claim relationship. باز بگو *bāz bu gu*, Repeat. باز خميدن *bāz khamīdan*, To taunt, reproach. باز خواندن *bāz khwāndan*, To charge, to accuse openly and publicly. باز پس رفتن *bāz pas raftan*, To retrace one's steps. باز خورد *bāz khwurd*, He swallowed it, he met it, he hit upon it. باز دادن *bāz dādan*, To give back, to return. پشت بچيزي باز دادن *pusht ba chīze bāz dādan*, To turn the back upon any thing. باز داشتن *bāz dāshtan*, To hold back, restrain, prohibit. To hide, conceal, seclude. To delay. باز راندن *bāz rāndan*, To repel. To recollect, reconsider. To explain, relate. باز زدن *bāz zadan*, To retreat, to withdraw. To rebel. باز طلبيدن *bāz talbīdan*, To demand restitution. باز كردن *bāz kardan*, To open or unfold. To take to pieces, undo, demolish. To strip off (skin). To gather (fruit). To wean. To roll out (a lump of dough). باز كشادن *bāz kushādan*, To open. باز گردان شدن *bāz gardān shudan*, To fall back. To suffer a relapse. باز گردانيدن *bāz gardānīdan*, To cause to return, to recall. To correct. To restore, repay. باز گفتن *bāz guftan*, To say again, repeat. To rehearse, relate. باز ماندن *bāz māndan*, To stay behind. To remain or survive. To desist, cease, stop, leave off. To be separated. باز نمودن *bāz namūdan*, To shew again; to explain, to clear up. To expose. باز يافتن *bāz yāftan*, To resume. *Bāz*, (in comp. from بازيدن *bāzīdan*) Playing; a player: as, شطرنج باز *shatranj-bāz*, A chess-player; حقه باز *hukka-bāz*, A player with cups and balls.

A بأز *baʼz*, (pl. ابؤز *abʼuz*, بؤوز *buʼūz*, and بئزان *biʼzān*) A hawk, a falcon.

A باز *bāz*, (pl. ابواز *abwāz* and بيزان *bīzān*) A falcon. باز خشين *bāzi khashīn*, A kind of falcon with a dark-coloured back and a red eye. P باز سپهر *bāzi sipihr*, The sun. باز سفيد پر *bāzi safed-par*, The white-winged falcon (epithet of the sun). A day.

P بازا *bāz ā*, Come back. A weight equal to 90 استير *astīr*, each astīr weighing four مثقال *mis̤kāl*.

P بازار *bāzār*, A market. A market-day. A bargain. Usage, currency. Beauty, splendour. *Bāz ār*, Bring back (imperat. of باز آوردن *bāz āwardan*). بازار جدال و قتال *bāzāri jidāl u kitāl*, War, battle. بازار خاك *bāzāri khāk*, The human body. Pomp, pride. The attractions of the present or of the future world. بازار زد و خورد *bāzāri zad u khwurd*, Strife, battle. بازار عجل *bāzāri ʻajal*, War, fight. بازار ماكيان *bāzāri mākiyān*, A poultry-market. بازار كردن *bāzār kardan*, To fix a price. To trade. بازار كشيدن *bāzār kashīdan*, To babble.

T بازار خلقي *bāzār-khalkī*, Market-folk.

P بازارگان *bāzārgān*, A merchant.

P بازاري *bāzārī*, Belonging to a market, mercantile. A market-man. بازاري كردن *bāzārī kardan*, To market.

P بازاريا *bāzāriyā*, A small trader, huckster.

P بازافگن *bāz-afgan*, A piece, section, morsel, bit, shred, rag. A pad, wadding, or stuffing.

P بازام *bāzām*, A swing, a see-saw.

P بازان *bāzān*, A large brazen vessel in which they wash clothes. The basin of a fountain.

P بازآورد *bāz-āward*, Gift offered to a superior.

P باز ايستادگي *bāz istādagī*, A standing back.

P بازآيندگي *bāz-āyandagī*, Return, coming back.

P بازبام *bāz-bām*, (بازبان or بازبار) A falconer.

P بازبر *bāzbar*, The bezoar-stone, an antidote.

P بازبزه *bāzbaza*, Loving women. A lover.

P بازپرس *bāz-purs*, Repeated inquiry, minute search. A revision, an examination.

P بازپره *bāz-para*, A butterfly. A bat.

P بازپس *bāz-pas*, Back, behind. The remains of any thing. Restitution. بازپس نگارستن *bāz-pas nigāristan*, To look back.

P باز پسان *bāz pasān*, The canaille.

P بازپسين *bāz-pasīn*, Last, hindmost.

P بازپيچ *bāz-pech*, A swing, see-saw. A cradle. A string of beads suspended from the top of a cradle for the amusement of infants.

P بازجاي *bāz-jāy*, Back, behind. Remains.

P بازخ *bāzakh*, A sound, a voice.

P بازخاست *bāz-khāst* (or بازخيز) Resurrection.

P باز خريدن *bāz kharīdan*, To redeem.

P باز خميد *bāz-khamīd*, Resurrection. Taunt.

P باز خواست *bāz-khwāst*, Answer. Question. Demand of restitution. Retrospect. Investigation.

P بازد *bāzud*, The fleshiness of the arms.

P بازدار *bāz-dār*, A falconer. A sower. An agriculturist. Keeping back. A revenue-collector.

P بازداري *bāz-dārī*, Charge of falcons or hawks.

P بازداشت *bāz-dāsht*, A hindering, a preventing, keeping back. An interval; a partition. Confinement, imprisonment, durance. A prison. باز داشت كردن *bāz dāsht kardan*, To hinder, restrain.

P بازرگان *bāzargān*, A merchant, a trader.

P بازرگاني *bāzargānī*, Trade, merchandize. بازرگاني كردن *bāzargānī kardan*, To trade, to buy and sell.

P بازرنجویه *bāzranjoya,* The herb melissa.

P بازرنگ *bāzrang,* Infants' swaddling-clothes. Girths, surcingles, ropes, fastenings of loads or saddles.

P بازرو *bāzrū,* or بازرون An every-day garment.

P باز شدگی *bāz shudagī,* A receding or retreat.

P باز شده *bāz shuda,* Receded, retreated.

A بازغ *bāzigh,* Rising (sun or moon).

P بازك *bāzak,* (or بازي) A sparrow-hawk, merlin.

P بازكشا *bāz-kushā,* Discriminating.

P بازگان *bāzgān,* (for بازرگان) A merchant.

P بازگذار *bāz-guzār,* Returning. Agreeing, apt, fit.

P باز گردان شدن *bāz gardān shudan,* To return.

باز گردان کردن *bāz gardān kardan,* To bring back.

P باز گردیدگی *bāz gardīdagī,* Return. Relapse.

P بازگشا *bāz-gushā,* The discriminative faculty.

P بازگشتن *bāz gashtan,* To turn back. To repent. To retire. To depart from.

P بازگشته *bāz-gashta,* Turned back, returned.

P بازگون *bāz-gūn,* Inverted, turned upside down, preposterous. Inversion. Inversely.

P بازگونه *bāz-gūna,* Inverted. Unfortunate.

P بازگیر *bāz-gīr,* A falconer. A chronologist. A revenue-collector.

A بازل *bāzil,* (pl. بزّل *buzzal* and بوازل *bawāzil*) (A camel) breeding a front or side-tooth called ناب *nāb,* in his ninth year; one that has cut his four lancet-teeth. (pl. بوازل *bawāzil*) The front or side-tooth ناب *nāb.* (A man) perfected in experience.

A بازلة *bazalat,* A quick pace. Contention, strife.

A بازلة *bāzilat,* Any thing, some, somewhat, a part. Any fracture of the skin from whence blood issues. شجّة بازلة *shajjat bāzilat,* A wound on the head from whence blood flows.

P بازمان *bāz mān,* Halt! stop! A delay.

P بازماندگی *bāz-māndagī,* A staying behind. A being detained, detention.

P بازمانده *bāz-mānda,* Left behind. A survivor, relict. Incapacitated, knocked up.

P بازمانیدن *bāz mānīdan,* To remain: be present.

P بازن *bāzan,* A cuckold.

P بازنامه *bāz-nāma,* Release, deed of acquittance.

P بازنانه کردن *bāznāna kardan,* To dart, to throw. To put one's self in danger. To boast. To intercede. To reconcile.

P بازنج *bāzinj,* A swing, a see-saw. Rocking. A cloth or curtain thrown over a cradle, in order to set a child to sleep.

P بازنجان *bāzinjān,* (for بادنجان) The brinjāl.

P بازنده *bāzinda,* A player. A kind of pigeon.

P بازنیچ *bāznīch,* (for بازپیچ *bāz-pech*) A swing.

P بازو *bāzū,* The arm, or the upper part of it. Strength, power. The cloth wrapped round the middle whilst bathing. The post of a door. The side of a bedstead. A friend, companion. One who accompanies in a song. A buck, doe, deer. A cubit, an ell. A perch. بازوی عضل *bāzūᵢ ʻazil,* A strong muscular arm. آهنین بازو *āhanīn-bāzū,* Having an arm of iron, strong-armed.

P بازو بند *bāzū-band,* A bracelet, an armlet.

P بازو دادن *bāzū dādan,* To help, lend an arm.

P بازو دراز *bāzū-dirāz,* Long-armed. Powerful.

P بازور *bāzūr,* Name of an eastern enchanter.

P بازوشتن *bāzūshtan,* To twist: to plait: to hem.

P بازو کشاده *bāzū-kushāda,* A petitioner.

P بازه *bāza,* A fathom. A sheep-hook. A walking-stick. A street, valley, or opening which separates houses, &c. A kind of hawk. A scale-beam.

P بازي *bāze,* One falcon. *Bāzī,* Play, sport. A little sphere or ball. بازي خوردن *bāzī khwurdan,* To be cheated or gulled. قمار بازي *kimār-bāzī,* Any forbidden game, as dice or cards.

A بازي *bāzī,* (pl. بزاة *buzāt,* بوازي *bawāzī,* ابؤز *abʼuz,* بؤوز *buʼuz,* and بيزان *bīzān*) A falcon.

P بازيار *bāz-yār,* A farmer, sower. A falconer.

P باز يافت *bāz-yāft,* The resumption of any thing; a deduction, a stoppage. باز يافت چاكر *bāz-yāfti chākar,* Lands appropriated for the payment of (public) servants.

P بازيج *bāzīj,* The watch of the night. Little globes, or things suspended above infants' cradles for their amusement. A collar, chain, wreath, chaplet.

P بازي جا *bāzī-jā,* A playhouse.

P بازيچه *bāzīcha,* Any little trifling amusement, child's play, fun, sport. بازيچه گذار كردن *bāzīcha-guzār kardan,* To play at children's pastimes. بازيچهٔ روم و زنگی *bāzīchaᵢ rūm u zangī,* Day and night. The freaks or vicissitudes of fortune.

P بازيدن *bāzīdan,* To play. To cause one to play. To lose at play, and to be agitated or affected by it. To spoil. To fly. To do repeatedly. To strive. To consecrate, devote.

P بازيره *bāzera,* An hour, a watch of the night. A lover of women. Wanton.

P بازيزه *bāzīza,* A lover of women.

P بازي كنان *bāzī-kunān,* Making sport, sportive.

P بازيگاه *bāzī-gāh,* A playhouse.

P بازيگر *bāzīgar,* A rope-dancer. Frolicsome.

P بازيگرن *bāzī-garn,* (or بازيگرني) An actress.

P بازيگوش *bāzī-gosh,* Cheerful, playful, wanton.

P بازيور *bā zīwar,* Adorned. Repetition: again.

P باژ *bāj,* Tribute, toll, duty, revenue, tax, impost; any grievous imposition which distresses the poor or the conquered. Silence observed by the Pārsīs whilst eating or performing their ablutions. A fathom. The shoulder. The distance between each hand when the arms are horizontally extended in an opposite direction. The arm, or the upper part of it. A finger-joint. Name of a town in the dependencies of Tūs, and birth-place of Firdawsī.

P باژبان *bājbān,* A revenue-collector. A tribe of Turkomāns.

P باژدار *bāj-dār,* A collector of the revenues.

P باژدان *bājdān,* The court of exchequer, the fisc.

P باژرند *bāj-rand* (or باژرنگ *bājrang*) A girdle for women or children.

P باژستان *bāj-satān,* A tax-gatherer, collector.

P باژ گونه *bāj gūna,* Inverted. Unfortunate.

P باژگیر *bāj-gīr,* A revenue-collector.

P باژن *bājan,* A ram or he-goat leading the flock.

P باژنامه *bāj-nāma,* A surname. A companion.

P باژه *bāja,* Revenue, tax, duty, impost, tribute.

A بأس *baʼs,* (v. n. of بؤس) Being bold and dauntless. Adversity. Pain, severity, torment, evil. Fortitude, intrepidity, boldness. Power, strength, ability. لا بأس *lā baʼs,* No harm, well and good.

P باس *bās,* Ancient. Fear. A husbandman.

A بأساء *baʼsāʼ,* (Bodily) hardship. Misfortune.

P باسامان *bā sāmān,* An honest man. Patient. Abstinent, continent. Wise, intelligent.

P باسان *bāsan,* The balm-tree; balsam.

P باسبوس *bāsbūs,* Sweet marjoram.

P باسّة *bāssat,* Mecca.

P باستار *bāstār,* Of the same kind, equal, alike. One, any one, such a one. An accessory word in a speech or sentence. An absurd answer to any argument. باستارو بيستار *bāstār u bīstār,* So and so.

P باستان *bāstān,* Past, preceding, old. The world, fortune. Solitary. (in zand and Pāz.) Date.

P باستان نامه *bāstān-nāma,* Name of a history.

P باستراك *bāstarāk,* (also باسترك *bāstarak*) A kind of starling or thrush.

P باستي *bāstī,* Humility, lowliness.

P باستين *bāsitīn,* Fruit on the middle of a branch.

A باسر *bāsir,* Grim, truculent (visage).

A باسرة *bāsirat,* Of an ugly appearance, detestable look. Crabbed, austere (countenance).

P باسرشدن *bāsir shudan,* To retreat, run away.

P باسرم *bāsram,* A field prepared for sowing.

P باسره *bāsara,* Tillage, agriculture.

A باسره *bi asrihi,* (Rope and all) Et cætera, and so forth, and thus with regard to the rest. باسرهم *bi asrihim,* (or باسرها) All, the whole, every one.

A باسط *bāsit,* One who spreads abroad or stretches out. A name of God, who dispenses riches to whom he will. One who spreads carpets. A bed-maker. Distant, remote, far off (from water). باسط اليد *bāsituʼl yad,* Invested with power, exercising controul. خمس باسط *khimsun bāsitun,* Camels, unwatered for five days, hasting to the cistern. قامة باسطة *kāmat bāsitat,* (A well) which does not flow.

G باسطيوس *bāstiyūs,* An emperor.

P باسغاق *bāsghāk,* (باسقاق *bāsikāk,* and باسقان *bāsikān*) (in Khwārazm) A viceroy, governor.

A باسق *bāsik,* (pl. بواسق *bawāsik*) Tall (palm-tree). A delicious yellow fruit.

A باسقة *bāsikat,* A white cloud. Calamity.

P باسلك *bāsuk,* A gaping, yawning. Drowsiness.

A باسل *bāsil,* (pl. بسلاء *busalāʼ* and بسل *busl*) A strong intrepid man, a hero. A lion. Austere, angry. Harsh, abominable (language). Sour (milk). Strong (urine).

G باسلوس *bāsilūs,* A king.

G باسليق *bāsilīk,* The basilik, or great artery.

A باسم *bāsim,* Smiling. A smiler,

A باسفان *bāsinān,* Name of a town in Khūzistān.

A باسنة *bāsinat,* (pl. باسن *bāsin*) A ploughshare, coulter. A tool. A large sack of coarse stuff.

P باسنگ *bā sang,* Heavy. Great, powerful.

A باسور *bāsūr,* (pl. بواسير *bawāsīr*) Emerods, piles. An hemorrhage or flux of blood, at the nose and other parts of the body.

P باسوس *bāsūs,* Caper-root.

A باسوط *bāsūt,* A (camel's) saddle made in a certain form (the reverse of مفروق *mafrūk*).

P باسه *bāsa,* Black-faced. Criminal, disgraced.

P باسيج *bāsīj,* A swallow.

P باسيدن *bāsīdan,* To guard, preserve.

P باسيره *bāsīra,* A poet, repeater of verses. A reciter of history, teller of tales. A sown field.

P باش *bāsh,* Stay, remain, wait, be still. Ancient. Living in, inhabiting. An inhabitant.

A بأش *baɪsh,* (v. n. of بأش) Throwing (one) down unexpectedly. Repelling or keeping back.

P باشا *bāshā,* Being, existing. A basha (a corruption of بادشاه *bādshāh*), governor of a province, counsellor of state, great lord; also sometimes the grand vazīr. A kind of falcon, a hawk.

P باشام *bāshām,* Fat. A veil. A note in music.

P باشامه *bāshāma,* A veil.

P باشانه *bāshāna,* Fat. The oil of nuts. Things scattered, dispersed. Selected, chosen.

P باشت *bāsht,* The main beam of a house.

P باشترك *bāshtarak,* A starling or stare.

P باشتين *bāshtīn,* Fruit growing from the midst of a tree without any previous blossom. Name of a village in the district of سبزهوار *sabzahwār.*

P باشد *bāshad,* Be it so! Entreaty. باشد كه *bāshad ki,* It may be that. Would that it were!

A باشر *bāshir,* One who rejoices at good news. Prudent, skilful. One who mixes gentleness with severity. Name of a fortress near Aleppo.

P باشش *bāshish,* Residence, stay.

A باشق *bāshak,* (pl. بواشق) A sparrow-hawk.

P باشقه *bāshika,* Dirt adhering to the hands.

P باشكو *bāshkū,* Hold fast! take care!

P باشكوك *bāshgūk,* Skilful, knowing. Dexterous, expert in the management of affairs.

P باشگونه *bāsh-gūna,* Inverted, reversed. A cross-birth (the side or feet of the infant lying nearest to the orifice of the womb).

P باشگونگي *bāsh-gūnagī,* Contrariety.

P باشنامه *bāshnāma,* Favour, obligation. Pride, boast. A title or nickname (good or bad).

P باشنده *bāshinda,* Being. Staying. An inhabitant. باشندگان *bāshindagān,* Inhabitants.

P باشنك *bāshank,* (or باشنگ) A bunch of grapes hanging from the tree. A small cluster of grapes dried on the stalk. A cucumber kept for seed.

P باشنگان *bāshingān,* A melon-bed.

P باشنين *bāshnīn,* Loppings, branches, or bark, cut or torn from the extremities of trees.

P باشو *bāshū,* A lizard.

P باشومه *bāshūma,* A woman's veil.

P باشه *bāsha,* A sparrow-hawk. باشهٔ فلك *bāsha-i-falak,* The sun. The Eagle (a constellation).

P باشيدن *bāshīdan,* To be. To stand, stay, stop, tarry, remain, dwell. To trample, tread. To spurn.

P باشين *bāshīn,* Chips. Loppings of trees.

A باص *bāsa,* (fut. يبوص *yabūsu*) He preceded.

A باصر *bāsar,* A small saddle for a camel's bunch. *Bāsir,* Penetrating, quick-sighted, perspicacious. لمح باصر *lamhun bāsirun,* A penetrating glance.

A باصرة *bāsirat,* The eye. Vision, sight.

P باصفا *bā safā,* Pure, clean, free.

A باصور *bāsūr,* Flesh, meat. A small saddle-cloth. A medicament which assists the sight.

A باضة *bāzzat,* Fat (girl) with a thin, soft skin.

A باضع *bāziɛ,* (pl. بضعة *bazaɛat*) Cutting, keen (sword). Wholesome (water). A broker or dealer in camels. One who transports the stock of a tribe from place to place. Name of an island.

A باضعة *bāziɛat,* (pl. بواضع *bawāziɛ*) A troop, herd, (or flock of camels or of sheep), or a portion separated from the herd. A blow on the head which cuts the skin and causes the blood to drop (when it flows it is then named دامية *dāmiyat*).

A باضك *bāzik,* Cutting, sharp (sword).

A باضوض *bāzūz,* Moisture.

A باطخ *bātikh,* Who licks: a licker. باطخ الماء *bātikhu'l māɪ,* A blockhead (licker of water).

G باطس *bātis,* The bramble.

P باطسه *bātisa,* (or باطيسه) A field, a plain.

A باطش *bātish,* One who seizes fast hold.

A باطل *bātil,* (pl. اباطيل *abātīl*) False. Vain, idle, trifling, absurd, ineffectual, frivolous, futile. The devil, the lying one. كلام باطل *kalāmi bātil,* Vain conversation, idle talk.

A باطلاً *bātilan,* Vainly, foolishly, falsely.

A باطن *bātin,* Interior, internal. Esoteric. (pl. ابطنة *abtinat* and بطنان *butnān*) The inward part. Low ground. (pl. بواطن *bawātin*) Hidden, concealed. Knowing the hidden and concealed; hence God is named الباطن *al bātin.* A water-course in rugged ground. ظاهر و باطن *zāhir u bātin,* Exterior and interior. في الباطن *fi'l bātin,* Inwardly.

P باطن بين *bātin-bīn,* A close observer.

A باطنة *bātinat,* Houses and shops of Basra and Kūfa contiguous to one another. Borders of a town.

A باطنيّه *bātinīya,* Name of a sect of Shiahs.

A باطية *bātiyat* or باطئة *bātiɪat,* (pl. بواطي *bawātī*) An earthen or other vessel in which wine is kept. A flagon or tankard from which the wine at table is poured into smaller cups.

A باع *bāɛ,* (pl. ابواع *abwāɛ*) A fathom. Nobility, rank, honour. طويل باعًا *tawīl bāɛan,* Liberal.

A باع *bāɛa,* (fut. يبيع *yabīɛu*) He sold.

A باعة *bāɛat,* Area, court-yard. A gutter on the house-top. (pl. of بائع *bāɪiɛ*) Sellers. Informers.

A باعث *bāɛis,* One who sends, or excites. An author, cause, occasion, subject. A name of God. باعث ليل و نهار *bāɛisi layl u nahār,* God. The sun.

A باعثيّة *bāɛisīyat,* Quality of causing, causality.

A باعجة *bāɛijat,* The wide open part of a valley.

A باعد *bāɛid,* (pl. بعد *baɛad*) Remote, distant.

A باعر باي *bāɛir bāy,* Those who have no locks on their doors.

A باعق *bāɛik,* Excessive rain, a deluge.

A باعك *bāɛik,* Foolish, stupid.

A باعوث *bāɛūs,* The feast of Easter; particularly the second day of it (from بعث *baɛasa* He arose).

A باعورا *bāɛūrā,* Beor, the father of Balaam.

P باغ *bāgh,* A garden. A vineyard. The world. باغ باغ *bāgh bāgh,* Joy! Pleasure! باغ بديع *bāghi badīɛ,* (باغ رفيع *bāghi rafīɛ,* باغ قدس *bāghi kuds,* or باغ وسيع *bāghi wasīɛ*) The firmament. Paradise. باغ پرستاره *bāghi pur sitāra,* A garden full of flowers. باغ رنگين *bāghi rangīn,* The world. باغ زاغان *bāghi zāghān,* Name of a garden in Harāt. باغ سخا *bāghi sukhā,* (Garden of liberality) The world. A liberal man. باغ سياوشان *bāghi siyāwishān,* Name of a note in music. باغ شيرين *bāghi shīrīn,* Name of a note in music. The 4th of the 30 musical modulations invented by Bārbud. باغ ليل و نهار *bāghi layl u nahār,* (Garden of night and day) God. The sun.

A باغ *bāgha,* (fut. يبيغ *yabīghu*) He perished.

A باغات *bāghāt,* (pl. of P باغ *bāgh*) Gardens.

P باغبان *bāghbān,* A gardener, a vine-dresser.

P باغباني *bāghbānī,* The care of a garden, horticulture. باغباني نمودن *bāghbānī namūdan,* To keep or dress a garden, to practise horticulture.

P باغچ *bāghach,* Unripe grapes.

P باغچوان *bāghchiwān,* A gardener.

P باغچه *bāghcha,* A garden, a little garden.

P باغره *bāghira,* A swelling in the body, a wen.

A باغز *bāghiz,* Obscene, villainous, dishonourable. Agility, briskness. Eagerness, vehemence.

A باغزيّة *bāghizīyat,* A garment made of raw silk called خز *khazz.*

P باغستان *bāghistān,* A vineyard.

A باغش *bāghish,* Small (rain).

P باغل *bāghil,* A cow-house. A sheep-fold.

P باغم *bā gham,* Sad, sorrowful.

A باغمة *bāghimat,* Said in a modest low voice.

P باغمي *bā ghamī,* Sadness, sorrowfulness.

P باغنج *bāghanj,* Unripe grapes.

P باغند *bāghand* (or باغنده *bāghanda*) Picked, teased, or carded cotton.

P باغوان *bāghwān,* A gardener.

A باغوث *bāghūs,* (probably a corruption of باعوث *bāɛūs*) Name of a Christian festival.

P باغوش *bāghosh*, Immersion.

P باغي *bāghī*, Grown in a garden. Hortulan.

A باغي *bāghī*, (pl. بغاة *bughāt* and بغيان *bughyān*) A seeker, an inquirer. Rebellious. A rebel, mutineer, traitor. A tyrant, oppressor, extortioner. A sinner. (A stallion) not impregnating.

P باف *bāf*, (in composition, from بافتن *bāftan*) Weaving. كناري باف *kanārī-bāf*, A lace-maker.

P بافت *bāft*, Texture, textile.

P بافتگي *bāftagī*, Texture.

P بافتن *bāftan*, To weave, intertwine, plait, twist.

P بافته *bāfta*, Woven, twisted. Mohair-buttons. A rope. A kind of cotton-cloth. A colour in pigeons.

A بافد *bāfd*, Name of a town in Caramania.

P بافدم *bāfdam* or *dum*, Last. End. Henceforth.

P بافكار *bāf-kār*, A weaver.

P بافل *bāfal*, An idiot, ignoramus. Reviling.

P بافندگي *bāfandagī*, Weaving, texture.

P بافنده *bāfanda*, A weaver.

P بافنگ *bāfanag*, A kind of marten or sable.

P بافيدن *bāfīdan*, To weave, plait, or twist.

A باق *bāka*, (fut. يبوق *yabūku*) He injured.

A باقة *bākat*, A bundle of herbs.

A باقر *bākir*, A herd of oxen (with their keepers). Great, large. Abounding (in knowledge). A dissension producing breach of friendship. A lion. A vein in the corner of the eye. Cows.

A باقرة *bākirat*, Sharp (sword).

P باقرخاني *bākir-khānī*, Bread, butter, and milk.

A باقع *bākiʿ*, A female hyena. Mottled black and white (crow or dog).

A باقعة *bākiʿat*, An evil, calamity, misfortune. Sagacious, intelligent, subtile, whom nothing escapes. A bird that dares not approach the water to drink, in dread of being taken.

A باقل *bākil*, (Ground) producing herbs, shrubs, or verdure. Name of a stupid, ignorant man, who, having bought a doe for eleven pieces of money, and not being able to tell what he had given in words, held up his ten fingers and lolled out his tongue, the doe in the mean time running off; whence the proverb, اعيي من باقل *aʿyaʾ min bākil*, More stupid than Bākil. A green-grocer.

A باقلاء *bākilāʾ*, (باقله *bākila*, باقلي *bākiliy*, or باقلّي *bākillaʾ*, A bean. A pea. A pot-herb. الباقلّي القبطي *al bākillaʾl kibtiy*, The Egyptian bean.

A باقلاني *bākillāniy*, A vender of beans.

P باقو *bākū*, The planet Mars. Name of a man.

A باقور *bākūr*, (also باقورة *bākūrat*) A herd of oxen. Black cattle, bulls, or cows: beeves.

A باقورة *bākūrat*, (in Yaman) An ox. A cow.

A باقي *bākī*, Remaining, left. Alive. Permanent, durable, fixed, firm. Immortal, everlasting, eternal. Remainder, rest. Balance, arrears. As to the rest. A name of God. امر باقي *amri bākī*, A permanent, solid, fixed thing. P باقي شدن *bākī shudan*, To remain, continue, endure. A باقي والسلام *bākī wa's salām*, (or باقي و الدعا *bākī wa'd duʿā*) And with this, farewell. باقي و السلام علىٰ من اتّبع الهدىٰ *bākī wa's salām ʿala'man ittabaʿa'l huda'*, As to the rest, peace be upon him who follows the right way. P باقي هموارة بر مسند صحّت و سلامت پايدار باد *bākī hamwāra bar masnadi sihhat u salāmat pāy-dār bād*, For the rest, may his foot be continually upon the throne of health and peace. باقي هميشه عمر و دولت دائم و عز و رفعت قائم باد *bākī hamīsha ʿumr u dawlat dāʾim, wa ʿizz u rifʿat kāʾim bād*, Upon the whole, may your life and prosperity be perpetual, and your glory and dignity everlasting. With these and similar prayers they conclude letters.

A باقيات *bākiyāt*, (pl. of باقية *bākiyat*) Remainders. Balances. Permanent (things). الباقيات *al bākiyāt*, Good works (as being permanent and always remaining with us). Such expressions as, سبحان الله *subhāna'llāh*, الحمد لله *al hamdu li'llāh*, لا اله الا الله *lā ilaha illa'llāh*, الله اكبر *allāh akbar*, and a few others. The five daily prayers.

A باقية *bākiyat*, (v. n. of بقي) Remaining. (pl. بواقي) Alive. Remaining. Permanent. Remainders.

P باقي دار *bākī-dār*, Owing a balance, in arrear.

P باقي ماندگي *bākī-māndagī*, Continuance, permanency. A remaining or a being left behind.

P باقي مانده *bākī-mānda*, A remainder. A survivor. Leavings. The balance of an account.

P باك *bāk*, Fear, dread, timidity. Care, solicitude. Attention. Species, sort. باك داشتن *bāk dāshtan*, To dread. To be anxious, careful, timid, apprehensive. بي باك *bī bāk*, Fearless, bold.

A باكّ تاكّ *bākk tākk*, An arrant fool.

A باكر *bākir*, Early in the morning.

A باكرة *bākirat*, (pl. بواكر *bawākir*) Early-bearing (date-tree). An unblemished virgin.

P باكمال *bā kamāl*, Exquisite, excellent, perfect. جمال باكمال *jamāli bā kamāl*, (Her) perfect beauty.

P باكند *bākand*, A ruby. Red. Wine.

P باكو *bākū*, Name of a city and fortress.

A باكور *bākūr*, The first rain in the spring. Any thing which soon reaches maturity.

A باكورة *bākūrat*, (pl. بكر *bukr*) First-fruits, early fruits, first of any thing.

P باكويه *bākawayh*, Name of a city in Persia.

P با كه *bā ki*, With whom?

A باكي *bākī*, (pl. بكاة or بكيّ *bukiy*) A weeper.

P باكيدن *bākīdan*, To fear.

P باكيده *bākīda*, A kind of silken stuff. A ruby.

P باگره *bāgra*, A swelling on the body, a wen.

P باگل *bāgal*, Milk-warm water.

P بال *bāl*, An arm. A wing. Stature. The upper part, top. A kind of large scaly fish. Growing.

A بال *bāl*, (pl. بالات *bālāt*) The heart, mind, soul. State, condition. A spade. Solicitude, care, heed, regard. Affluence, easy circumstances, conveniences. رخيّ البال *rakhīyu'l bāl*, In easy circumstances, and comfortable in mind. امرٌ ذو بال *amrun zū bālin*, A serious and important business.

P بالا *bālā*, Stature. Tallness. The upper hand. A horse led for parade. High, exalted, elevated, supreme. Above, upwards. بالا گرفتن *bālā giriftan*. To get the upper hand. بالاي آسمان *bālāyi āsmān*, Above the heavens. بالا و پستي *bālā u pastī*, Altitude and humility. زير و بالا *zīr u bālā*, Up and down (lit. down and up). زير و بالا كردن *zīr u bālā kardan*, To reverse, turn upside down. عالم بالا *ʿālami bālā*, Heaven, the world above.

S بالا *bālā*, An odoriferous grass.

P بالا بال *bālā-bāl*, Firm. Strongly, vehemently.

P بالا بالا *bālā-bālā*, Deceitfully, fraudulently.

P بالابر *bālā-bar*, Part of the dress which laps over the thigh.

P بالا بر امدگي *bālā bar āmadagī*, Height.

P بالا بر آمده *bālā bar āmada*, Risen high.

P بالابند *bālā-band*, A turban. Upper garment.

P بالاپوش *bālā-posh*, An outer garment. A counterpane, coverlet.

P بالاتر *bālātar*, Higher, superior, more eminent.

A بالاتفاق *bi'l ittifāk*, With (one) consent.

P بالاخانه *bālā-khāna*, An upper chamber, gallery, or balcony on the top of the house, a parlour. بالاخانهٔ وزارت *bālā-khānaʾi wizārat*, Rank of vazīr.

A بالآخر *bi'l ākhir*, At length, finally.

P بالاخواني *bālā-khwānī*, Hyperbole. Eulogy.

P بالاد *bālād*, (or بالاذ *bālāz*) A baggage-horse.

P بالادست *bālā-dast*, Superior, uppermost. The chief seat. Precedency. Exquisite, precious.

P بالادستي *bālā-dastī*, Clandestine exactions.

P بالادوي *bālā-davī*, Velocity, speed.

P بالاده *bālāda*, A led-horse, a horse of state.

P بالار *bālār*, The main beam of a house. A son dutiful to his mother.

P بالا رستگي *bālā-rustagī*, Germination, growth.

P بالاز *bālāz*, A led-horse. A pack-horse.

P بالاس *bālās*, (or پالاس *pālās*) A kind of fine, soft, thin armosin silk. An old piece of cloth. A kind of coarse woollen stuff, such as they put under burdens on the backs of horses or camels. (The richer people spread it in the vestibules, in order to leave their slippers upon it; the poorer sort lay it at the door of their bed-chambers; and some dervishes wear habits made of it).

A بالاضطرار *bi'l iztirār*, By force, unwillingly.

P بال افگندن *bāl afgandan*, To drop the wing.

A بالاقتضا *bi'l iktizā*, From necessity.

P بالاگر *bālāgar*, The main beam of a house.

P بالال *bālāl*, The main beam of a house.

P بالان *bālān*, Growing, increasing, extending. Moving, oscillating. A springe. A space between two doors; or between a gate and the house.

P بالاندن *bālāndan*, To grow. To cause to grow.

P بالانده *bālānda*, Growing. Moving: shaken.

P بالا نشين *bālā-nishīn*, Sitting high, occupying the chief seat. كم قادر و بالا نشين *ham-kādir u bālā-nishīn*, Inferior in dignity, yet sitting in the chief seat. بالا نشين مسند سلطاني *bālā-nishīni masnadi sultānī*, Sitting upon a royal throne.

P بالانه *bālāna*, Growing, increasing. Moving, oscillating. A space between two doors, a vestibule.

P بالاني *bālānī*, Moveable, oscillatory. A pack-horse. A covering for the head.

P بالانيدن *bālānidan*, To extol, to commend. To let the hair grow. To cause to move.

P بالا و پست *bālā u past*, Above and below. Heaven and earth. The world.

P بالاور *bālāwar*, A pitcher full of water.

P بالا همّت *bālā-himmat*, Magnanimous, noble-minded. Generous. Beneficent. Most favourable.

P بالاي *bālāy*, A horse led for parade.

P بالايانيدن *bālāyānidan*, (and بالائيدن *bālā-idan*) To extend, enlarge, spread, reach, arrive at, overtake. To become long. To equal, match. To ripen. To roll, wallow, toss. To become turbid, muddy. To fear, dread. To commend highly.

P بالايك *bālāyik*, A gnat, a small fly.

P بالائين *bālāīn*, (from بالا) Above, superior.

P بالائي يافت *bālāī-yāft*, Perquisites.

A بالبداهه *bi'l badāha*, Suddenly, unexpectedly.

P بالبوس *bālbūs*, The kingdom of Kandahār.

P بالپر *bāl-par*, The adoption of better habits.

A بالة *baʻālat*, (v. n. of بوّل) Being small, weak.

A بالة *bālat*, Heed, regard, consideration. A perfume-box, perfumer's tray. A flask, decanter. A wallet. An iron instrument for catching fish.

A بالّة *ballat*, Moisture. Any thing good.

A بالتفصيل والاجمال *bi't tafsīl wa'l ijmāl*, Prolixly and compendiously, diffusively and succinctly.

A بالتقدير *bi't takdīr*, By chance, providentially.

A بالتمام *bi't tamām*, Totally, entirely.

A بالجملة *bi'l jumla*, Totally, generally, or universally. On the whole, in a word, to sum up all.

A بالح *bālih*, Barren (ground).

A بالحق *bi'l hakk*, In truth. Justly, deservedly.

A بالحلال *bi'l halāl*, Lawfully.

A بالخطر *bi'l khatar*, With danger: dangerously.

A بالخير *bi'l khayr*, Happily, fortunately.

A بالد *bālid*, An inhabitant, a resident.

A بالدفعات *bi'd dafʻāt*, At times. Often.

A بالذات *bi'z zāt*, In person, by himself.

P بالزن *bāl-zan*, (بال *bāl*, Wing, زن *zan*, Striking) Moving, striking the wings, flying. Business.

P بالزين *bāl-zīn*, The flap of a saddle.

P بالست *bālast*, A virgin, a maid.

P بالستن *bālustan*, To bless, invoke blessings.

P بالش *bālish*, A cushion, pillow. A staple. A weight of gold (eight miskāls and two dānaks). Growth, increase: development. Vegetation. بالش تكيه *bālishi takya*, A cushion to put under one's elbow. بالش عالي *bālishi ʻālī*, A high throne.

P بالشت *bālisht*, A cushion, a pillow. A span.

P بالشتك *bālishtak*, A little cushion, a pad. A bandage for a broken bone.

P بالشتن *bālushtan*, To invoke a blessing.

P بالشچه *bālishcha*, A little cushion put upon a saddle. بالشچهٔ سرين *bālishchaʼi surīn*, A pad worn by women to give a prominence to the hips.

P بالشك *bālishak*, The flap of a saddle. A pad.

A بالصدق و الاخلاص والصاف *bi's sidk wa'l ikhlās wa's sāf*, In truth, sincerity, and purity.

A بالصواب *bi's sawāb*, Justly, reasonably.

A بالضرورة *bi'z zarūra*, Of necessity, by force.

A بالطوع والرضا *bi't tawʻ wa'r rizā*, (or بالطوع و الاختيار *bi't tawʻ wa'l ikhtiyār*) Spontaneously, freely, with good will.

A بالطول و العرض *bi't tūl wa'l ʻarz*, In length and breadth.

A بالع *bāliʻ*, A swallower. Name of one of the two stars called سعد بلع *saʻd bulaʻ*.

A بالعز و الاكرام *bi'l ʻizz wa'l ikrām*, With reverence and honour.

A بالعشي و الابكار *bi'l ʻashīy wa'l ibkār*, Morning and evening.

P بالغ *bālagh*, Name of a country north of Persia.

A بالغ *bāligh*, Penetrating, passing. Received or obeyed every where. Insinuating, lodged (venom in the body). Arrived at maturity or at puberty (boy or girl). Good, excellent. Arrant, downright. بالغ اقصي الغايات كمالات *bālighi aksa'l ghāyāti kamālāt*, Reaching the highest perfection of virtue or art. P بالغ شدن *bāligh shudan*, To come of age.

P بالغ *bālugh* or *bāligh*, A cup made of horn, in use among the Georgians. A goblet of wine.

A بالغاء *bālighāʼ*, Shanks of sheep, or the like.

A بالغة *bālighat*, Arrived at maturity (a girl).

A بالغدوّ و الآصال *bi'l ghudūw wa'l āsāl*, Morning and evening.

A بالغضب *bi'l ghazab*, In anger, indignantly.

A بالفعل *bi'l fiʻl*, In fact, actually, really, effectually. At this hour, now, presently. بالفعل و القوّة *bi'l fiʻl wa'l kuwwat*, In act and in power.

G بالقس *bālkis*, Bugloss, borage.

A بالقصد *bi'l kasd*, On purpose, designedly.

P بالكانه *bālkāna*, A lattice-window.

A بالكل *bi'l kull*, (or بالكلّيّة *bi'l kulliyat*) Totally, entirely, wholly, universally, all together.

A بالكمال *bi'l kamāl*, Perfectly, completely.

A باللغو *bi'l laghw*, Inconsiderately.

A بالله *bi'llāh*, By God! بالله العظيم *bi'llāhi'l ʻazīm*, By the great God! P بالله رفتن *bi'llāh raftan*, To go to school.

A بالمرّة *bi'l marra*, At once.

A بالمشافهه *bi'l mushāfaha*, Face to face.

A بالمعني *bi'l maʻnaʼ*, Really, truly, in reality. Mysteriously. حديث بالمعني *hadīsi bi'l maʻnaʼ*, A mysterious but true oracle. نقل بالمعني *nahli bi'l maʻnaʼ*, Wonderful but certain accounts.

A بالمواجهه *bi'l muwājaha*, In presence of.

P بالنده *bālanda*, Growing.

P بالنگ *bālang*, An orange. A cucumber.

P بالنگو *bālingū*, A species of sweet basil. A citron. The mountain-balm or calamint. بالنگوي خورد *bālangūyi khwurd*, A species of sweet basil.

P بالو *bālū*, A wart. A whole brother. The cry of one in sadness. Ring-worm. A cherry.

P بالوا *bālawā*, A disorder making the nails drop.

A بالواجب *bi'l wājib*, Necessarily, properly.

P بالواد *bālwād*, A bustard.

P بالوار *bālwār*, Winged.

P بالوازه *bālwāza*, A swing, a see-saw.

P بالواسه *bālwāsa*, Cloth in the loom, the warp.

P بالوانه *bālwāna*, A small black bird, by the people of Shīrāz called واشه *wāsha*.

P بالواه *bālwāh*, A swallow.

P بالوايه *bālwāya*, A swallow.

P بالود *bālūd*, Increase.

P بالودن *bālūdan*, To grow, to increase.

P بالور *bālwar*, Winged.

A بالورا *bi'l warā*, Openly, in sight of all men.

P بالورته *bālwarta*, A sparrow. A swallow. A butterfly. A bat.

P بالورگي *bālūrgī*, A cullender or strainer.

P بالوس *bālūs*, Adulterated camphor.

P بالوش *bālūsh*, An idol. A louse. Impure, nasty. Adulterated camphor.

A بالوعة *bālūʻat*, (pl. بواليع *bawāliʻ*) A hole or sink in the middle of houses in the East, into which they sweep the filth, and in which rain-water falls. A sewer. A place for washing the face and hands.

A بالول *bālūl*, A drop of water.

P بالويه *bālūya*, A swallow. A bird of Paradise.

P باله *bāla*, A kind of sack.

A بالي *bālī*, Old, worn (garment).

P باليد *bālīd*, He increased. A rustic shoe.

P باليدگي *bālīdagī*, Growth, vegetation. Pride.

P باليدن *bālīdan*, To grow, to wax great.

P باليده *bālīda*, Extended. Grown (hair).

P باليسر *bālesar*, The town of Balasore in India.

P باليك *bālīk*, A shoe, a slipper.

P بالين *bālīn*, A pillow, a cushion.

P بالين پرست *bālīn-parast*, Lazy, unemployed.

P باليوس *bālyūs*, The country of Candahār.

P بام *bām*, Morning, dawn, break of day. A roof. A ceiling of a room (external or internal). A terrace. The thickest string or base of a viol. (for فام *fām*) Colour: as, سرخ بام *surkh-bām*, Inclining to red. (for وام *wām*) Debt. بام بديع *bāmi badīʻ*, بام رواق بديع *bāmi rafīʻ*, بام رفيع *bāmi riwāki badīʻ*, بام فراخ *bāmi farākh*, بام گشاده رواق *bāmi gushāda riwāk*, بام نهم *bāmi nuhum*, or بام وسيع *bāmi wasīʻ*) The ninth or empyrean heaven. بام بلند *bāmi baland*, Any lofty building. The sky. بام چشم *bāmi chashm*, The eye-lid. بام خضرا *bāmi khazrā*, Heaven. بام زمانه *bāmi zamāna*, The lower heaven, the firmament. بام مسيح

bāmi masīh, The fourth heaven. بام نشستن *bām nishastan*, To be ruined and desolate.

P با ما *bā mā*, (from با *bā* and ما *mā*) With us.

P بامال *bā māl*, Wealthy.

P بامبره *bāmbara*, Dignity, order, degree.

P بام پوش *bām-posh*, A roof-covering. A roof.

P بامداد *bāmdād*, (or بامدادان *bamdādān*) In the morning. At break of day.

P بامدادي *bāmdādī*, Matutinal, matutine.

P بامدن *b'āmadan*, To enter, come in.

A بامر الله تعالي *bi amri'llāh taʻāla'*, By the command of God most high.

P بامره *bām-rah*, (Way to roof) A ladder, stair.

P بامزد *bām-zad*, A kettle-drum.

P بامزه *bā maza*, Sweet, savoury, relishing.

P بامس *bāmas* or *bāmus*, Sated with the world. Weary of foreign travel, but unable to return home.

P بامستون *bām-sitūn*, A terrace, or balcony.

P با مسكنت *bā maskanat*, Modest. Poor.

P بامشاد *bāmshād*, Name of a famous musician.

P بامگاه *bām-gāh*, Morning. Morrow-morning.

P بام گلان *bām-gulān*, (or بام گردان *bām-gardān*) A large stone-roller used for smoothing and hardening the flat mud-plastered roofs of houses.

P با من *bā man*, With me.

P بامنشين *bām-nishīn*, Ruined, destroyed.

P بامون *bāmūn*, A scoundrel, coward: catamite.

P بامه *bāma*, A long beard. Long-bearded (man).

P با مهر *bā muhr*, Sealed, closed. Suspended.

P بامي *bāmī*, Name of the city of بلخ *balkh*.

P باميان *bāmiyān*, An indifferent writer, an inaccurate scribe. Name of a district in Kohistān.

P باميره *bāmī-rah*, A step. A window in a gate.

P بامين *bāmīn*, (or باميين) A town in Harāt.

P بان *bān*, A prince, lord, chief, or governor. The gum-herb lāda. The tamarisk-tree. An iron rocket used in war. (for بام *bām*) A roof. (for بانگ *bāng*) A cry. *Bān*, when affixed to a noun, signifies a keeper or a guardian: as, باغبان *bāghbān*, A gardener; دربان *darbān*, A door-keeper.

A P بان *bān*, Name of a tree, the myrobalan, whence the fine balsam called Benzoin or Benjamin is extracted. It resembles the tamarisk, and grows in great abundance in Arabia Felix.

A بان *bāna*, (fut. يبين *yabīnu*) He excelled.

A باناة *bānāt*, A bow sticking close to the string. A man who leans over the bowstring in shooting.

H بانات *bānāt*, Broad-cloth.

P بانات فروش *bānāt-farosh*, A woollen-draper.

S بانارس *bānāras*, Benares, in India, situated on the bank of the Ganges, held sacred by the Brahmans.

A بانب *bānab*, Name of a town in Bukhārā.

P بان بربيتا *bān-barbītā*, (in zand) An elephant.

S بان پرست *bānparast*, An anchoret.

A بانة *bānat*, An interstice, interval. Distinction.

P بانجا *b'ān jā*, There, to that place.

S بانس *bāns*, A bamboo.

P بانقش *bānkish*, A berry called بن *ban* or ون *van*, from which, when pounded, they make a decoction.

P بانكش *bānkash*, A (male) pigeon.

P بانگ *bāng*, Voice, sound, noise, cry, clamour. Name of a fragrant shrub, and of a medicinal seed. (بانگ الله *bāngi allāh* or بانگ نماز *bāngi namāz*) The call to prayer, by the crier, from the minarets or towers of the mosques, which is made five times a day. بانگ بر ابلق زدن *bāng bar ablak zadan*, To exclaim against fortune. بانگ رواړو *bāngi rū-ā-rū*, The blast of a trumpet announcing the approach of a great man. بانگ زدن *bāng zadan*, To withhold, keep. To drive, repel. بانگ كردن *bāng kardan*, To crow. بانگ عنقا *bāngi ʻanḳā*, Name of a note in music. بانگ هاون *bāngi hāwin*, A public profession of the Muhammadan religion. A knowledge of the Muhammadan law.

P بانگ زن *bāng-zan*, The muezzin.

P بانگشت گرفتن *b'angusht giriftan*, To reckon.

P بانگه *bānga*, An extending of the voice.

H بانگه *bāngah*, Raw cotton.

P بانگيدن *bāngīdan*, To cry with a loud voice.

P بانو *bānū*, A princess. A lady. A bride. A flagon of wine. A goblet of rose-water. بانوي مشرق *bānūyi mashrik*, The sun. بانوي مصر *bānūyi misr*, Zulaykhā (Potiphar's wife). بهار بانو *bahār-bānū*, The blooming princess. همايون بانو *humāyūn-bānū*, The august princess. نرگس بانوي شهلا چشم *nargis bānūyi shahlā chashm*, The lady Narcissa with black eyes (*i.e.* the narcissus), or figuratively (a beautiful woman).

P با نوا *bā nawā*, Having a sweet voice. Rich. Fortunate. A man's name.

P بانوج *bānūj*, (or بانوچ *bānūch*) A swing, see-saw.

A بانوقة *bānūkat*, Name of a certain woman.

P بانو گشسب *bānū gashasb*, Rustam's daughter.

P بانه *bāna*, Pubes: the hair about those parts.

A باني *bānī*, A builder, architect. A composer. An author. One who goes in unto a wife.

A بانيّ *bāniy*, Erect as the tamarisk (stature).

P با نيازان *bā niyāzān*, The indigent. Creatures.

A بانياس *bāniyās*, A town and river in Syria.

A بانية *bāniyat*, A bow sticking close to the string.

P باني كار *bānī-kār*, An architect. A composer.

P باني كاري *bānī-kārī*, Architecture.

A باو *baw*, (or باواء *bawāʼ*) (v. n. of باّ for باو) Becoming proud, vain-glorious; boasting, bragging. Raising, exalting one's self.

P باو *ba' u*, (from با *bā*, With, and او *u*, Him) روزگار باو بسر برد *rozgār ba' u ba sar burd*, He passed his time with him.

P باوتا *bāwtā*, An idol. باوتا شكن *bāwtā-shikan*, (Abraham) The iconoclast.

A P با وجود *bā wujūd*, (from با *bā*, With, and وجود *wujūd*, Existence) Existing, being present. In consequence. Excepting, with the exception. Nevertheless, notwithstanding. Particularly, chiefly, especially. Namely.

P باور *bāwar*, True, creditable. Belief, credit, acceptance. باور كردن *bāwar kardan*, (also باور داشتن *bāwar dāshtan*) To believe, to credit.

P باورچي *bāwarchī*, (in Khwārazm) An officer who takes care of a great man's table. A cook.

P باورچيخانه *bāwarchī-khāna*, A kitchen.

P باورچي گري *bāwarchīgarī*, The culinary art.

P باورد *bāward*, Name of a hero; also of a city.

P باوردي *bāwardī*, A kind of pottage.

P باورس *bāwars*, Games with dice or cards. A woman whose husband has another prolific wife.

P باوريدن *bāwarīdan*, To believe, to give credit.

P باوسني *bāwusnī*, The wife of a husband who has another wife and a child, a rival wife. One of several wives of the same husband. A wife whom her husband does not love and seldom visits.

P باوصف *bā wasf*, Notwithstanding.

P باوقار *bā wakār*, Majestically, with dignity.

P باول *bāwal*, Name of a place famed for its silks.

P باولي *bāwlī*, A bird whose wings being partially deprived of their feathers is turned loose, that a young falcon may easily catch him, and thus be taught to hunt. A large well.

P باوي *bā way*, (from با *bā* and وي *way* for او *u*) With him. *Bāwī*, Come along. Go to.

P باوين *bāwīn*, A basket, a woman's work-basket.

P باه *bāh*, Lust. Sperm.

A باء *bāʼ*, (v. n. of باٌ) Considering, attending to.

A باه *bāh*, Coitus.

P باها *bāhā*, A kind of food.

P باهار *bāhār*, A cup. A mode of reading.

A باهة *bāhat*, An open space free from buildings.

P باهت *bāhat*, A stone which is said to make any person laugh whose eyes should chance to light upon it. Astonished, thunderstruck.

A باهت *bāhit*, A liar, a calumniator.

P باهده *bā huda*, True, just.

P باهر *bā har*, With every, with all.

A باهر *bāhir*, Superior, excellent. Open, public, manifest. A vein in the skin of the head reaching to the bregma. كلام باهر الانتظام *kalāmi bāhiru'l intizām*, A discourse excellently arranged. باهر الشرف *bāhiru'sh sharaf*, Most noble. P شاه باهر الاقبال *shāhi bāhiru'l ikbāl*, The most prosperous king. باهر و ظاهر كردن *bāhir u zāhir kardan*, To make manifest and clear.

A باهراً *bāhiran*, Excellently. Publicly.

A باهرات *bāhirāt*, Ships.

A باهرة *bāhirat*, (fem. of باهر *bāhir*) Excellent. Excellence, superiority. كمالات باهره *kamālāti bāhira*, Eminent perfections. P باهرة الاشراق شدن *bāhiratu'l ishrāk shudan*, To be bright, to shine.

A باهظ *bāhiz*, Troublesome, difficult. A calamity, misfortune. P باهظ كردن *bāhiz kardan*, To vex.

A باهغ *bāhigh*, Asleep, sleeping.

P باهك *bāhak*, Pain, torture, rack.

P باهكيدن *bāhakīdan*, To put to the rack.

A باهل *bāhil*, (pl. بهل *buhl* and بهّل *buhhal*) (A she-camel) having no marks of a ring through the nose, or of the wooden machines which they usually fasten to their udders to prevent colts from sucking. (A woman) at her own disposal, sauntering about, doing nothing. A shepherd without his crook. Free from controul.

A باهلة *bāhilat*, Free from marriage.

P باهم *bā ham*, Together, along with. باهم آمدن *bā ham āmadan*, To come together. To fly in a passion. باهم سودن *bā ham sūdan*, To chafe, to rub against one another. باهم راست كردن *bā ham rāst kardan*, To confront, compare, collate. باهم باهن كشيدن *bā ham ba āhan kashīdan*, To chain, to fetter. با همديگر *bā hamdīgar*, Together, along with. By mutual endeavours. باهم شير و شكر بودن *bā ham shīr u shakar būdan*, To be milk and sugar together, to be on very friendly terms.

P باهم *bāhum*, A fair wind, the wind in poop.

P باهمان *bāhmān*, He, such an one.

P باهمه كه *bāhama ki*, Though, notwithstanding.

P باهو *bāhū*, A walking-stick, club. A shepherd's staff. The arm from the elbow to the shoulder.

A باهي *bāhī*, Empty, deserted (house).

A باهيّ *bāhīy*, Aphrodisiacal, provocative.

A باهية *bāhiyat*, Wide-mouthed (well).

A باهين *bāhīn*, A palm which has always some buds and clusters of green, fresh, and ripe dates.

P باي *bāy*, A city.

A بأي *baʼy*, (v. n. of بأي) Becoming proud, vainglorious, boasting, bragging. Running hard.

P بايا *bāyā*, It is proper, it behoveth.

P باأيّام برآمدن *b' ayyām bar āmadan*, To grapple with adversity, to contend against misfortune.

A بائت *bāʼit*, Who or what is in the night-time, passing the night, watching. Yesterday's victuals, the remains of what has been eaten and drunk the day before. Stale bread.

A البائج *al bāʼij*, Name of a vein in the thigh.

A بائجة *bāʼijat*, (pl. بوائج *bawāʼij*) Misfortune.

A بائح *bāʼih*, (or بائخ *bāʼikh*) Fatigued.

A باييّحال *biayyi hāl*, How? In whatever state.

P بايد *bāyad*, It is necessary, behoves. بايد شايد *bāyad shāyad*, As it should be, fit, proper.

A بائدة *bāʼida*, Besides, unless, except. Because.

A بائر *bāʼir*, (pl. بور *bawr* and *būr*) Confused, confounded, astonished, struck with amazement. حائر بائر *hāʼir bāʼir*, Irresolute, perplexed in mind, incapable of acting by his own power or following the advice of others. *Bāʼir*, (and بائرة *bāʼirat*) Uncultivated ground.

A بائز *bāʼiz*, One who is living at his ease.

P بايزيد *bāyizīd*, A proper name (Bajazet).

A بائس *bāʼis*, Miserable, pressed with want.

P بايست *bāyist*, It is necessary, it behoveth. بايست وقت *bāyisti wakt*, As the case requires.

P بايستگاه *bāyistagāh*, The heart's desire, wish.

P بايستن *bāyistan*, To be necessary or requisite.

P بايستني *bāyistanī*, Necessary to be done.

P بايسته *bāyista*, Required. Necessary.

P بايستهٔ هستي *bāyistaʼi hastī*, Whose existence is necessary, self-existent.

P بايسك *bāyisk*, Physiognomy. A man's name.

A بائض *bāʼiz*, (pl. بيض) Oviparous. A hen.

A بائع *bāʼiʻ*, (pl. بوائع *bawāʼiʻ*) A buyer. A seller, vender. (A woman) much courted on account of beauty, whom many men wish to marry. (pl. بوع *būʻ*) A young deer bounding at full speed. (pl. باعة *bāʻat*) An informer, a calumniator.

A بائق *bāʼik*, (Merchandize) of little value.

A بائقة *bāʼikat*, (pl. بوائق) Misfortune. Calamity.

A بائك *bāʼik*, A young plump camel.

P بايكديگر *bā yak dīgar*, (or دگر *digar*) With one another, together, mutually, reciprocally.

P بايگان *bāygān*, A guardian, a treasurer.

A بائل *bāʼil*, One who makes water, mingent.

P باين *baʼ in*, (contrac. of با اين *bā īn*) With this.

A بائن *bāʼin*, Distinct, separate, divided. Repudiated, divorced (woman). Manifest, clear, evident, notorious. Complete, final (divorce). Declared. Those who milk cattle on the left side (such as milk on the right side being named معلّي *muʻallī*). That part of a bow most distant from the string. Deep and full (well).

A بائنة *bāʼinat*, (pl. بوائن *bawāʼin*) The evidence of four witnesses. Complete, final (divorce). (A bow) distant from the string. Deep (well).

P بايونيستي *bāyūnīstī*, Annihilable, destructible.

A بائهة *bāʼihat*, Lean, extenuated (sheep).

A البايية *al bāyiyat*, The feast of palms.

P بائيدن *bāʼīdan*, To be necessary. To behove.

A ببّ *babb*, Species, kind, sort. A fat youth.

P ببا *ba bā*, A door. A decoction from بن *ban*.

P ببارة *balāra*, A stalk, stem. An esculent root.

P ببالا *ba lālā*, Above, upwards.

P ببال ديگر پريدن *ba bāli dīgar parīdan*, To fly with another's wings: to succeed by another's aid.

A ببّان *babbān*, (or ببان *babān*) Habit, custom, mode, way of living. هم ببّان واحد *hum babbān wāhid*, (or على ببّان واحد *ʻala' babbānin* (or *balānin*) *wāhidin*) They are equals, peers, of the same sort, following the same mode of life.

P بباي *ba bāy*, Remain thou.

A ببّة *babbat*, The voice of an infant, crying Papa. A handsome young man inclining to corpulency. A fool, blockhead, lazy, indolent fellow.

P ببتك *bibtak*, Part of a bunch of grapes or dates.

P ببدي *ba badī*, Wickedly, naughtily.

P ببر *babr*, A tiger. *Babar*, Bread soaked in butter. A wild animal like a cat, but not having a tail. *Bi bar*, (imp. of بردن *burdan*) Bear, carry, or take thou. A mouse. *Bi bur* or *bu bur*, (imp. of بريدن *burīdan*) Cut thou, strike off.

A ببر *babr*, (from P.) (pl. ببور *bubūr*) A tiger.

P ببربيان *babri bayān*, A kind of military cloak made of a leopard's skin (such as was worn by the famous Rustam Zāl, the Persian Hercules). Brisk, alert, nimble. A kind of changing-coloured silk.

A ببرالة *bubrāllat*, Birthwort, aristolochy.

P ببراله *bubrāla*, Long birthwort.

P ببروج *babrūj*, The mandrake.

P ببسوده *bibsūda*, Rubbed, stroked. Bored.

A ببغاء *babghāʼ*, (or ببّغاء *babbaghāʼ*) A parrot. A nightingale. Name of a poet, so called from an impediment in his speech. P ببغائ شيرين ادا *babghāʼi shīrīn-adā*, The nightingale with sweet notes.

P ببك *babak*, The pupil of the eye. Children.

P ببلس *bablus*, Bread with butter or syrup.

A ببنيّ *babnīy*, Name of a collector of traditions.

A ببور *bubūr*, (pl. of ببر *babr*) Tigers. Soldiers.

P ببول *babūl*, A species of mimosa yielding gum.

P ببا باش *ba pā bāsh*, Stand up.

P بپاي *ba pāy*, Stand up. بپاي اندر آمدن *ba pāy andar āmadan*, (or ماندن *māndan*) To slip, fall.

P بپاي دادن *ba pāy dādan*, To throw away.

P بپاي شدن *ba pāy shudan*, To stand upright.

P بپساويدن *bipsāwīdan*, To wipe, to rub.

P بپسودان *bipsūdān*, Rubbing, touching.

P بپسودن *bipsūdan*, To anoint. To rub gently.

P بپسوده *bipsūda*, Anointed. Rubbed. Bored.

P بپغا *bapghā*, A parrot.

P بپكن *bapgan*, Throw thou. Nauseating.

P بپيش *ba pesh*, Before, in presence of.

P بت *bat*, A line drawn to distinguish separate names in a catalogue, or articles in an account; a mark, a score. A weaver's brush. Weaver's size. A duck. *But*, An idol, an image, any figure that is an object of adoration. God. Truth.

A بتّ *batt*, (v. n. of بتّ) Cutting. Incapacitating from arriving with a caravan. Breaking down, halting on the road. Performing, doing. A cutting or breaking off. (pl. بتوت *butūt*) A kind of hood, coif, mantle, or scarf. A rope twisted from left to right. طحن بتّا *tahana battan*, He ground (the corn), beginning to turn to the left.

P بتا *batā*, Till when? how long? Rice dressed with milk and butter. *Bitā* or *butā*, Let alone, leave.

P بتّا *battā*, Rice dressed with milk and butter.

A بتاء *butāʼ*, Plain, smooth, soft ground.

A بتات *batāt*, (v. n. of بتّ) Divorcing for ever. A cutting-off, separation. (pl. ابتّة *abittat*) Viaticum, provision for a journey. Tapestry, carpeting. Marriage-preparations. Household furniture or utensils. على بتات امر *ʻala' batāti amrin*, On the point of (doing) a thing.

A بتاتا *batātan*, Irrevocably.

A بتّات *battāt*, A maker or vender of the hood, coif, mantle, or lappet, called طيلسان *taylasān*.

A بتّار *battār*, (or بتار *butār*) Sharp, cutting (sword).

P بتارة *batāra*, A machine for glazing linens.

P بتازگي *ba tāzagi*, Recently, lately.

P بتاشه *batāsha*, A sweetmeat, confection.

A بتّاك *battāk*, Keen, sharp (sword).

A بتّان *battān*, Name of a tract in حرّان *harrān*.

P بتانج *butānj*, A wife, a spouse; particularly one of many who have one husband in common.

P بتاوار *batāwār*, End, consummaton. Health.

P بتاور *batāwar*, Health, safety.

A بتائل *batā,il*, (pl. of بتيلة *batīlat*) The fleshy parts of the body. Shoots, cions of a palm-tree.

P بتاييدن *bitāyīdan*, To quit, leave, pass by.

P بتپرست *but-parast*, An idolater. A fane.

P بتپرستي *but-parastī*, Idolatry.

A بتة *bitat*, (v. n. of وبت) Abiding (in a place).

A بتّة *battat*, (v. n. of بتّ) Cutting. Incapacitating from arriving with a caravan. Breaking down, halting. Performing. Divorcing for ever. A cutting off. A section. *Battat*, (or البتّة *al battat*) Altogether, totally. Certainly, irrevocably.

P بت تراش *but-tarāsh*, An idol-maker, sculptor.

P بتخ *batkh*, Squeezing, straining, pressing.

P بتخاك *butkhāk*, Name of a place near Kābul.

P بتخال *bat* or *but-khāl*, Name of an idol-temple.

P بتخانه *but-khāna*, An idol-temple. A tavern.

A بتر *batara*, (fut. يبتر *yabturu*) He cut off.

A بتر *batr*, (v. n. of بتر) Cutting off. Docking. Tearing up. Keeping incomplete. Rejecting, eliding, cutting off (a syllable by apocope). *Batar*, (v. n. of بتر) Being docked. Being childless. Being good for nothing.

P بتر *batar*, (or بتّر *battar* by elision or insertion) (for بدتر *badtar*) Worse.

A بتراء *batrā,*, (fem. of ابتر *abtar*) Docked. Sharp, piercing, penetrating. Muhammad's coat of mail. Name of a place on the road to Tabūk, near which is Muhammad's mosque. خطبة بتراء *khutbat batrā,*, A Muhammadan prayer, or rather the mutilated preamble to it, two solemn articles being omitted, in one of which they praise God, and in the other they bless the prophet.

A بترة *batrat*, A she-ass.

P بترجا *batarjā*, Pudenda. Flesh under the nail.

A بترية *butrīyat*, Name of a Muhammadan sect.

P بت شكن *but-shikan*, An image-breaker.

P بت شكني *but-shikānī*, Iconoclasm.

A بتع *bataع*, (v. n. of بتع) Going far away. Making the wine بتع *bitع*. *Bitع*, Wine. Tall (man). *Bitع* or *bitaع*, Wine made from honey or the juice of the grape. *Butع*, (pl. of ابتع *abtaع* and بتعاء *batعā,*) Firmly knit in the joints and ligaments. *Bataع*, (v. n. of بتع) Having the joints and ligaments firmly knit. Doing a thing without consulting any one. Length of neck, with firm well-knit joints. *Batiع*, (A horse) having a long and strong neck. One whose joints and ligaments are firmly knit. *Butaع*, All (the women).

A بتعاء *batعā,*, (fem. of ابتع *abtaع*) All, universal. Firmly knit in the joints and ligaments (woman).

P بت فريب *but-firīb*, Twenty-fourth day of the month according to the æra of Jalālu'd dīn.

P بتفوز *batfūz*, The parts around the mouth, chops or snout. The circumference of a cap.

A بتك *batk*, (v. n. of بتك) Cutting, dividing, amputating. Catching hold of any thing, plucking, pulling, laying violent hands upon. *Bitak*, (pl. of بتكة *bitkat*) Parts, portions.

P بتك *bitik*, Writing. A letter. A book.

P بتك *butak*, (dim. of بت *but*) A little idol.

A بتكة *bitkat* also *butkat*, (pl. بتك *bitak*) A part or portion of any thing (particularly of a thing contained in another). The darkness (of the night). Any thing plucked up (as feathers or hair).

P T بتكچي *bitikchī*, A writer, a scribe.

P بتكده *but-kada*, An idol-temple. A tavern.

P بتكن *bitkan*, A head-ache produced by indigestion. A rake. A harrow.

P بتكنديدن *bithandīdan*, (or بتكندن *bitkandan*) To suffer from indigestion. To nauseate one's food.

P بتكوب *batkob*, (or بتكوت *batkot*) A kind of food made of cream or milk, walnuts, and anise.

P بتكيش *batkesh*, A quiver.

A بتل *batl*, (v. n. of بتل) Cutting. Dividing. Separating, distinguishing. Any thing cut off and separate. عطاء بتل *ataع batl*, A final gift. *Butul*, (pl. of بتيل) Channels at the bottom of valleys.

A بتلاء *batlā,*, The sacred visitation called عمرة *عumrat* without the pilgrimage. مرّ علي بتلاء من رأيه *marra عala' batlā, mir ra,yihi*, He followed his determination without flinching.

P بتلاب *bitlāb*, The envelope of the flower of dates, the spathe. The plant southernwood.

A بتلة *batlat*, A cutting off, a separation. Any thing cut off and separate. صدقة بتلة *sadakat batlat*, Alms irrevocably given away.

P بتلخ و ترش رضا دادن *ba talkh u tursh rizā dādan*, To bear trials and hardships contentedly

A بتم *butm*, *batam*, or بتّم *buttam*, Name of a tract, fortress, or mountain in Farghāna.

A بتماميها *bi tamāmihā*, Entirely, altogether.

P بتنها *ba tanhā*, Sole, alone, one, separate.

P بتنج *batanj*, Compression. *Bitanj*, Squeeze.

P بت نگار *but-nigār*, A painter, a limner.

A بتو *batw*, (v. n. of بتو for بتا) Dwelling.

P بتو *bataw*, The East. A place much exposed to the sun. *Batū*, A funnel. A knot in the stalk of a plant. A pestle. A stone-mortar. *Bitū*, A cask. A handle. A pestle. *Ba tu*, To thee.

P بتواز *batwāz*, A perch, a roost for falcons.

A بتوت *butūt*, (v. n. of بتّ) Being lean, emaciated. Emaciating. (pl. of بتّ *batt*) Hoods, coifs, lappets. Mantles, scarfs, cloaks.

P بتوراك *batūrāk*, A subterraneous granary. A tambourin.

A بتوع *butūع*, (v. n. of بتع) Being broken, cut off, severed. Travelling to a great distance.

P بتوك *batūk*, A kind of wooden basket or tray, in which garden-stuff, fish, or bread, is carried about and sold.

A بتوك *batūk*, Sharp (sword).

A بتول *batūl*, A virgin averse from marriage and worldly concerns from religious motives, a vestal, a nun. With the addition of the article (البتول *al batūl*), the Eastern Christians use it as one of the names of the Virgin Mary; whilst the Muhammadans apply it to Fātima, the daughter of Muhammad, and wife of the Khalif Alīy. *Batūl* signifies also the shoot of a palm, when ready to be planted by itself; or a young shoot already planted.

P بته *bata*, A muller. A pestle. Dried rice.

P بتّه *batta*, A pestle. A muller.

H بتّه *battah*, Extra allowance to troops in the field. Ebb-tide.

P بتهوا *bat-huwā*, Orach.

A بتيّ *batīy*, A table-cloth, a napkin.

A بتّيّ *battīy*, A maker or vender of hoofs, coifs, lappets, mantles, or scarfs.

P بتيا *batyā* or *bityā*, The breast.

P بتيار *batyār*, Ugly, detestable. *Bityār*, Trouble, affliction. A glass urinal.

P بتياره *batyāra*, Any thing ugly, odious, and detestable. A demon inhabiting the woods. *Bityāra*, Grief, trouble, affliction, injury.

A بتيراء *butayrā,*, (dim. of بتراء *batrā,*) Partially docked, incomplete. The sun.

A بتيرة *butayrat*, (dim. of بترة) A little she-ass.

P بتيغ خاستن *ba tegh khāstan*, To stand on end (the hair).

A بتيل *batīl*, The Virgin Mary. The shoot of a palm-tree separate from the parent stock and growing by itself. Name of a mountain in Yamāmah. (pl. بتل *butul*) A channel in the bottom of a valley. A tree whose clusters hang down.

A بتيلة *batīlat*, (pl. بتائل *batā,il*) A shoot from a palm-tree planted and flourishing at a distance from the parent tree. Any joint or member of the body, with the flesh belonging to it, a fleshy part. Buttocks. An unflinching determination. A nun.

P بتيله *batīla*, The wick of a candle or lamp.

P بتينه *butīna*, (or بتينا) Penitence, repentance.

P بتيّه *bitiya*, The town of Battiah in Bahār.

A بثّ *bass*, (v. n. of بثّ) Publishing, disseminating news. Scattering (dust). Strewing, spreading. State, condition. Any thing dispersed, scattered, published. Sickness. Need. Grief, sorrow. تمر بثّ *tamr bass*, Dates scattered here and there.

A بثاء *basā,*, (or بثاءة) Plain, even, soft ground.

A بثاث *bisās*, The communicating (of a secret).

A بثبثة *basbasat*, A scattering. A divulging.

A بثة *bisat*, Ashes.

A بثر *basr*, A country covered with white stones. Much, many. Little, few. Sand adhering to the ground, and when dug emitting water. *Basr* or *basar*, (v. n. of بثر) Being covered with pimples (the face). A pustule, pimple, or eruption on the body. *Basir*, Covered with pimples.

A بثرة *basrat*, A single pimple.

A بثط *basat*, (v. n. of بثط) Swelling (the lip).

A بثع *basaع*, (v. n. of بثع) Protuberating from a surcharge of blood (a lip). Becoming inverted when laughing (the lips).

A بثعاء *basعās*, (A woman) whose lips are swollen with blood and ready to burst.

A بثعة *basعat*, (pl. بثع *basع*) A bit of flesh growing from the lip adjoining the gum.

A بثغ *basagh*, Blood ready to burst from the skin (especially in the lips).

A بثق *basaka*, (fut. يبثق *yabsuku*) He rent, he tore.

A بثق *bash*, (v. n. of بثق) Tearing, lacerating. Breaking down banks, dikes, or mounds (a river). Starting in the eye (tears). *Bash* or *bisk*, (pl. بثوق) A place or breach through which water bursts.

A بثلة *buslat*, Fame, celebrity, renown, notoriety.

A بثن *bisan*, Soft sands. *Busun*, Gardens, meads.

A بثنة *basnat*, A beautiful woman with a soft skin. Soft sand. Butter. Riches upon riches. Finest kind of wheat (so called either from the soft rich soil which produces it, or from the following country where it grows). البثنة *al basnatu*, Bethania, a rich level country near Damascus, where the patriarch Job is said to have been born. *Basnat* or *bisnat*, Plain, equal, level, and soft ground.

A بثنون *basnūn*, Name of a town in Egypt.

A البثنيّة *al basnīyat*, Bethanian wheat, and in general all wheat grown on plains (as distinct from جبليّة *jabalīyat*, which grows on hilly grounds).

A بثو *basw*, (v. n. of بثا for بثو) Sweating.

A بثور *busūr*, (v. n. of بثر) Being covered or afflicted with pimples (a body). (pl. of بثر *basr*) Pustules, pimples, tubercles.

A بثوق *busūk*, (v. n. of بثق) Being filled to overflowing (a well). (pl. of بثق *bash* or *bisk*) Breaches made by floods in banks of rivers.

A بثي *bisa'*, (pl. of بثة *bisat*) Ashes.

A بثيّ *basīy*, Possessed of a numerous retinue. Lavish in the praises of others.

A بثير *basīr*, Covered with pimples. *Basīr*, (or بثير كثير *basīr kasīr*) Many, much.

A بثينة *busaynat*, (dim. of بثنة *basnat*) A little softish ground. Name of a woman; and of a place between Basra and Bahrayn. ابو بثينة *abū busaynat*, Name of a certain poet.

P بج *baj*, A strainer for water, or wine. Inside of the mouth. The cheek, ball of the cheek, external part of the cheek and mouth. *Bij*, Rice. *Buj*, A goat. The hair on the forehead.

A بجّ *bajj*, (v. n. of بجّ) Cutting open (a boil). Piercing (with a spear). Conquering, overcoming. Swelling almost to bursting (cattle from eating much). *Bujj*, The young of any bird.

P بجا *ba jā*, In place: true, accurate, right, proper.

A بجاء *bujās*, Name of a tribe in Arabia.

A بجّاء *bajjās*, An eye having the lashes far asunder. Open, wide (eye).

P بجا آمدن *ba jā āmadan*, To be accomplished.

P بجا آوردن *ba jā āwardan*, To accomplish, to execute. To bring to bear. To know.

A بجابج *bujābij*, Fat, corpulent.

A بجاجة *bajājat*, Low, vile (persons).

A بجاد *bijād*, (pl. بجد *bujud*) A kind of Arabian cloak or upper garment of striped cloth.

A طفيل بجادي *tufayl bijādīy*, Name of a poet.

A ذو البجادين *zū'l bijādayn*, Name of a man who served as a guide to Muhammad.

A بجارم *bajārim*, Adversities, evils.

A بجاريّ *bajārīy*, (pl. of بجريّ) Calamities.

A بجال *bajāl*, (or بجّال *bajjāl*) A prince, an aged chief, a great lord, a powerful man. An old, corpulent, and, on that account, respectable man (the Eastern nations in general considering corpulent men as the peculiar favourites of God).

P بجال *bujāl*, A live coal. An extinguished coal.

A بجالة *bajālat*, (v. n. of بجل) Being great, portly. A woman distinguished for beauty and greatness.

P بجام عدل دادن *ba jāmi عadl dādan*, To give with the cup of justice, *i. e.* what is just.

P بجان *ba jān*, With all one's soul, heartily. بجان آمدن *ba jān āmadan*, To be wearied out, displeased, disgusted: to be ready to die. بجان آوردن *ba jān āwardan*, To perform. To distress, to kill.

P بجانب *ba jānib*, Towards (the city). بجانب او *ba jānibi u*, Towards him, on his side.

P بجان من *ba jāni man*, On my account.

P بجان واحد *ba jāni wāhid*, By one's self, alone.

A بجاوة *bujāwat*, The country of Nubia.

A بجاويّات *bujāwīyāt*, Camels from Bujāwat.

P بجاي *ba jāy*, In lieu. بجاي او, In lieu of him.

A بجاية *bijāyat*, Name of a city of Africa.

P بجاي جا *ba jāy jā*, Everywhere, in all places.

P بجاي رسيدن *ba jāy rasīdan*, To arrive at, to attain, to accomplish.

A ببجاج *bajbāj*, (or ببجاجة *bajbājat*) A man whose flesh shakes on account of his corpulency. A fool. A great talker. *Bajbāj*, Sand heaped together in a bulky mass.

A بجبج *bujbuj*, Leathern bottles split and torn. Name of a traditionist, a native of Morocco.

A بجبجة *bajbajat*, Any kind of song, dangling, playfulness, or amusement, with which infants are coaxed into good humour, or put to sleep.

A بجّة *bajjat*, A pimple or sty on the eye-lid. Blood drawn from a vein (particularly of a camel, which being fried is eaten in a season of scarcity). *Bajjat*, (or البجّة *al bajjat*) Name of an idol.

A بجح *bajiha*, (fut. يبجح *yabjahu*) He rejoiced.

A بجح *bajah*, Joy, gladness. Greatness of rank.

A بجد *bajd*, A company of people. A hundred or more of horses.

P بجدّ *ba jidd*, Diligent, serious, attentive. Urgent, pressing. Quick. Diligence. Diligently.

P بجدا *ba judā*, Separately, asunder.

A بجدة *bajdat*, *bujdat*, or *bujudat*, Root, origin. The pith or substance (of any business). A desert. *Bajdat*, Knowledge, science. ابن بجدة *ibn bajdat*, (Son of knowledge) A skilful, intelligent, able man. One who swerves not from his word.

A بجر *bujr*, (pl. اباجر *abājir* and اباجير *abājīr*) Evil, misfortune. An important and dangerous affair. A marvellous thing. (pl. of ابجر *abjar*) Affected with a swelling at the navel. *Bajar*, (v. n. of بجر) Having a tumour, rupture, or other distemper affecting the navel. Having a projection of the belly. Having the belly filled with milk or water without being satisfied. Hanging down, being relaxed. *Bajir*, Filled with milk or water without the thirst being satisfied. *Bujar*, Defects. ذكر عجره و بجره *zakara عujarahu wa bujarahu*, He mentioned his defects and every thing relating to him.

A بجراء *bajrās*, (fem. of ابجر *abjar*) (A woman) afflicted with a swelled belly, rupture, or disease of the navel. High ground.

A بجران *bujrān*, (pl. of ابجر *abjar*) Persons afflicted with a swelled body, or a tumour at the navel.

H بجر بهانگ *bajjir b'hāng*, Tobacco.

A بجرة *bujrat*, (pl. بجر *bujar*) The navel. An excrescence on the body, face, or neck. ابن بجرة *ibn bujrat*, Name of a vintner at Tāif, celebrated by the poets. *Bajarat*, (pl. of باجر *bājir*) Those with swelled bellies. شبيب بن بجرة *shabīb bin bajarat*, Name of one of those engaged in the murder of Alīy. *Bujarat*, Name of a kinsman of Ishmael.

H بجرة *bajara*, A barge used in India, a budgerow.

A بجريّ *bujrīy*, (or بجريّة *bujrīyat*) (pl. بجاريّ *bajārīy*) An accident, calamity, misfortune.

P بجز *ba juz*, Besides, except. See جز *juz*.

A بجس *bajs*, (v. n. of بجس) Flowing (water). Making (water) flow. Splitting open (a boil). (Water) which bursts or gushes out. *Bujs*, (or بجّس *bujjas*) (Clouds) pouring down rain.

P بجس *bajas*, The cartilage of the nose. Softness.

P بجست *bajast*, A voice, sound, or echo.

P بجشاك *bijashāk*, A farrier. A corn-dealer.

P بجشك *bijishk*, A physician. A sparrow.

A بجع *bajع*, (v. n. of بجع) Cutting with a sword.

P بجكله *bajkala*, (or بچكله *bachkala*) A flagon, stone bottle, or stout vessel in which wine is kept.

P بجكم *bajkam*, A kind of stone seat in the porches of houses in the East, raised pretty high above the ground, upon which they sit or recline in warm weather. The lower part of the house where they live in winter-time. Name of a Turkomān tribe.

A بجل *bajl*, (v. n. of بجل) Being in good condition, rich in produce and joyous. *Bajal*, A low, growelling disposition. Yes, even so, very well. ذو البجل *zu'l bajal*, A low, grovelling fellow. *Bajal* or *bajl*, Sufficient. *Bajal* or *bujl*, A false imputation, a calumny. A marvellous thing.

P بجل *bujul*, The ankle-bone.

A بجلة *bajlat*, A small tree. A pleasing, handsome appearance. Name of a family.

A بجم *bajm*, (v. n. of بجم) Being quiet. Lying still through fear or fatigue. Delaying. Being contracted. Contracting one's self.

P بجم *bujm* or *bijm*, The fruit of the tamarisk.

A بجميع *bi jamīʿ*, With all, on all sides.

P بجنس *ba jins*, In kind, sort, species. Pure.

P بجوار حق پيوستن *ba jiwāri hak paywastan*, To die (to join the neighbourhood of truth).

P بجوجيا *bajūjiyā*, (in zand) A female. Vulva.

A بجود *bujūd*, (v. n. of بجد) Abiding in a place.

P بجور *bijwar*, A country bordering upon India.

A بجوس *bujūs*, (v. n. of بجس) Reviling, treating with contumely.

P بجول *bujūl*, The ankle-bone.

A بجول *bujūl*, (v. n. of بجل) Being great, portly. Being in good condition, rich in produce, and joyous.

A بجوم *bajwam*, Full of water (pool).

P بجهت *ba jihat*, Because, on which account.

A بجيد *bujayd*, Name of a man. امّ بجيد *ummu bujayd*, (Mother of Bujayd) Name of a woman.

A بجير (كثير *kasīr*) *bajīr*, Very plentiful, extremely numerous. *Bujayr*, (dim. of ابجر *abjar*) Hence عيّر بجير بجرة *ʿayyara bujayr bujrata*, A proverb, implying, one who censures another for a vice which he himself has in a higher degree; similar to which is the next: نسي بجير بجرة *nasiya bujayr bajarahu*, The swag-bellied forgets his swag belly.

A بجيس *bajīs*, Copious, overflowing (fountain).

A بجيل *bajīl*, Corpulent, portly (old man). A prince, chief, or elder. Large. Coarse, thick.

A بجيلة *bajīlat*, Name of the branch of a tribe.

A بچ *buch*, The inside of the mouth. The hair on the forehead.

P بچبچ *buch buch*, A low tone, whisper. A word used by goatherds in calling together their flocks.

P بچراغ رسيدن *ba charāgh rasīdan*, To enter the service of a great man. To make one's fortune.

P بچرك *bichrak* or *bichirk*, Derided. A dupe.

P بچش *bachash*, The cartilage of the nose. Languor. Grief.

P بچشك *bichishk*, Nature. A physician. A vender of simples.

P بچشم *ba chashm*, With the eye, *i. e.* most readily, willingly. بچشم آمدن *ba chashm āmadan*, To befal (as a misfortune). To be hurt by an evil eye. بچشم كردن *ba chashm kardan*, To inspect narrowly. To look with a malignant eye. To impress. To choose.

P بچك *bachak*, A kind of weapon.

P بچكاندن *ba chakāndan*, To drop, to distil.

P بچكم *bachkam* or *bichkam*, A summer-house. A court. A hall of audience. A wolf.

P بچگان *bachagān*, (pl. of بچه *bacha*) Infants, children. The young of any animal. بچگان ديده *bachagāni dīda*, Tears. زن و بچگان *zan u bachagān*, Wife and children.

P بچگانه *bachagāna*, Childish, fit for children.

P بچل *bachal*, One used to bedaub his clothes.

P بچم *bicham*, Order, method, disposition, arrangement, manner, train. كارم بچم گرفت *kāram bicham girift*, My affairs are in an excellent train.

P بچند *ba chand*, For how much?

P بچه *bacha* or *bachcha*, An infant, boy, child, son. A whelp, cub. Ivy. بچۀ خور *bachaʾi khwur*, (or بچۀ خورشيد *bachaʾi khwurshed*) A ruby. Gold. Silver. بچۀ خونين *bachaʾi khūnīn*, Tears of sorrow. بچۀ طاوس علوي *bachaʾi tāwusi ʿulwī*, The sun. A sun-shiny day. Fire. A ruby. بچۀ ناتمام افگني *bachaʾi nā tamām-afganī*, Abortion, miscarriage. بچۀ نو *bachaʾi naw*, Any new discovery or incident? Young shoots. *Ba chi*, Why? wherefore? for what?

P بچه دار *bacha-dār*, Having young. Pregnant.

P بچه دان *bachadān*, The womb.

P بچه كشي *bacha-kashī*, Child-bearing.

P بچه كو *bacha-kū*, (Child of the street) A foundling. A bastard.

P بچه گاو *bacha-gāw*, (*gāv* or *gāo*) A calf.

P بچه ناك *bachanāk*, A parent of male children.

P بچيچ *bachīch*, (or بچيج *bachīj*) A whisper, any thing spoken secretly, whisperingly. A word used by goatherds in managing goats.

P بچيچه *bachīcha*, Quieting of an infant, lullaby. A word used by shepherds in calling their flocks.

P بچيز *ba chīz*, Small, diminutive. Mean. بچيزي نگرفتن *ba chīze na giriftan*, To make no account of.

A بحّ *bahh*, (بحح *bahah*, بحاح *bahāh*, بحاحة *bahāhat*, or بحوح *buhūh*) (v. n. of بحّ) Having a hoarse, rough voice. *Buhh*, (pl. of ابحّ *abahh*) Hoarse. Fat. Thick timbers. Games of chance, or the arrows with which they play. Denarii, ducats.

A بحّاء *bahhāʾ*, (fem. of ابحّ *abahh*) Hoarse, or gruff-voiced. A hillock in the desert.

A بحابح *bahābih*, (pl. of بحبوحة *buhbūhat*) Middles of houses, courts, quadrangles.

A بحاث *bihās*, An investigating. A disputing.

A بحّاث *bahhās*, A disputant, controversialist.

A بحاثة *buhāsat*, Earth scratched up for playing the game of بحثة *bahsat*.

A بحاح *buhāh*, Hoarseness, gruffness of voice.

A بحار *bihār*, A level country begirt by seas and mountains. (pl. of بحر *bahr*) Seas. Great rivers. Gulphs. (pl. of بحرة *bahrat*) Countries, inhabited places. Towns having water. Low-lying grounds. Large gardens. بحار اوامر *bihāri awāmir*, Commands flowing on all sides. بحار بحريّة *bihāri bahrīya*, Tempestuous seas.

A بحّار *bahhār*, A seaman.

A بحّارة *bahhārat*, Seamen, sailors.

P بخارزندان *buhārzandān*, A city in Bukhārā.

A بحارم *bahārim*, Misfortunes, evils.

A بحارين *bahārīn*, Turns of a distemper.

P بحال *ba hāl*, In its proper state or condition. Right, true. Reinstated (in service or condition), happy, flourishing, prosperous. بحال آمدن *ba hāl āmadan*, To come to a state or condition: to recover.

A بحباح *bahbāh*, Of equal length and breadth. *Bahbāhi*, An exclamation of regret uttered at the loss or destruction of a thing.

A بحباحة *bahbāhat*, Offensive, perverse (woman).

A بحبحة *bahbahat*, (v. n. of بحبح Q) Settling, taking up one's abode. A multitude, a crowd.

A بحبحيّ *bahbahīy*, Gay, profuse. Affluent.

A بحبشة *bahbashat*, A being collected together.

A بحبوح *buhbūh*, A root. Middle, pith, heart.

A بحبوحة *buhbūhat*, (pl. بحابح *bahābih*) The middle of a house, a court, an area.

A بحبور *bahbūr*, A young bustard.

A بحّة *bahhat*, Hoarse, gruff-voiced (woman). *Buhhat*, Hoarseness. A gruffness in the voice.

A بحت *baht*, Pure, genuine, unmixed (as wine with water, bread with victuals). عربيّ بحت *ʿarabīy baht*, (and عربيّة بحتة *ʿarabīyat bahtat*) True, genuine Arabians.

A بحتر *buhtur*, Short and compact-bodied. Name of the progenitor of a tribe. Name of a stallion.

A بحث *bahs*, (v. n. of بحث) Investigating, examining. Controversy, debate, dispute, contest, argument, question. (pl. بحوث *buhūs*) A mine. A large serpent. A wager. بحث و جدل *bahs u jadal*, Contention and altercation. P بحث كردن *bahs kardan*, To debate, dispute, argue. To wager.

A بحثا بحثي *bahsā-bahsī*, Argumentation.

A بحثة *bahsat*, A sort of game played with earth.

A بحثجات *bahsajāt*, Shepherd's staff (a herb).

A بحثرة *bahsarat*, (v. n. of بحثر Q) Separating, scattering, dispersing. Investigating, examining. Extracting, drawing out. Discovering, unveiling. Being divided into granulated particles (milk).

A بحثنة *bahsanat*, A proceeding languidly.

P بحجّت برنيامدن *ba hujjat bar nayāmadan*, To fail in logic.

A بحح *bahah*, Hoarseness, gruffness of voice.

A بحدريّ *buhdurīy*, Badly fed, stunted (child).

A بحدلة *bahdalat*, (v. n. of بحدل Q) Being wry-shouldered. Running. Agility, lightness of step.

P بحدّي *ba hadde*, To a degree (that).

A بحذق *buhzuk*, Seed of flea-wort.

A بحر *bahr*, (v. n. of بحر) Splitting, making wide. Slitting (the ear). (pl. ابحر *abhur*, بحور *buhūr*, and بحار *bihār*) A sea, estuary, or great river. A large collection of water. A generous man. A fleet horse. Luxuriant produce. Fundus uteri. A slit made in a camel's ear. The seat of a saddle. A fleet. (A horse) having a long step. All kinds of Arabic verse, of which there are fifteen. بحرابيض و بحراسود *bahri abyaz u bahri aswad*, The White and Black Sea (*i.e.* the Egean with the Mediterranean and Euxine). بحر اخضر *bahri akhzar*, Heaven. بحر الاخضر *bahru'l akhzar*, (and بحر الهند *bahru'l hind*) The Green Sea. The Indian Ocean. The Indus. بحر الحسب *bahru'l hasab*, Name of a certain treatise on arithmetic. بحر الخزر *bahru'l khazar*, The Caspian Sea. بحر الخوارزم *bahru'l khwārazm*, Name of a lake into which the river Jihūn flows. بحر الرحم *bahru'r rihm*, Fundus uteri. بحر الروم *bahru'r rūm*, The Grecian or Mediterranean Sea. بحر الزخّار *bahru'z zakhkhār*, A swelling sea. A numerous army. بحر الصين *bahru's sīn*, The China Sea. بحر الغمام *bahru'l ghamām*, Name of a lake in Kāshgar. بحر الفارس *bahru'l fāris*, The Persian Gulf. بحر القلزم *bahru'l kulzum*, (or بحر الاحمر *bahru'l ahmar*) The Red Sea. P بحر بيگران خندق *bahri bīgirān khandak*, The highest heaven. بحر دمان زيبق عمل *bahri damāni zībak-ʿamal*, Clouds distilling rain. بحر زنگي *bahri zangi*, The Ethiopic Sea. بحر الماس *bahru'l mās*, A sea wherein are islands containing diamond-mines. A بحر عمان *bahri ʿumān*, The Sea of Omān (extending from the Straits of Bābu'l mandib to the Persian Gulf). Name of a town. The eye. بحر مسحور *bahri mashūr*, The enchanted or heavenly waters (those which the Muhammadans suppose to be under the throne of God). بحر محيط *bahri muhīt*, The ocean. P بحر نهنگ آثار *bahri nahang-āsār*, A bright sword. A بحر و برّ *bahrun wa barrun*, Sea and land. بحر وسيع *bahri wasīʿ*, The firmament. A liberal hand. بنات بحر *banāti bahr*, (Daughters of the sea) Vapours, thin clouds, which rise from the sea, especially before summer. ماء بحر *māʾun bahrun*, Salt water. *Buhr*, (pl. of بحرة *bahrat*) Countries, inhabited places, towns. Low-lying grounds. Large gardens. Places where waters stagnate. *Bahar*, (v.n. of بحر) Being astonished from terror (as بطر *batar* expresses surprise from joy). Wasting away (flesh). Exerting himself in running till he is weak and black in the face (a camel). Having an unquenchable thirst. Slitting a (camel's) ear. Consumption, phthisy. *Bahir*, Astonished from terror. Tormented with an unquenchable thirst. Emaciated, consumptive. Weak and black in the face from exertion in running (a camel).

A بحران *bahrān*, The country usually called بحرين *bahrayn*. Name of a town between بصرة *basra* and عمان *ʿumān*. *Buhrān*, Crisis of a disease. يوم بحران *yawmi buhrān*, A critical day of disease.

A بحرانيّ *bahrāniy*, The blood of the womb. A native of Bahrayn. *Buhrāniy*, Pure, red (blood). Foolish (man).

A بحرة *bahrat*, (pl. بحر *buhr* and بحار *bihār*) A country, region, territory. Low-lying ground. A large garden. A place where water lodges. Madīna. Any town possessed of water, running or stagnant. هذه بحرتنا *hāzihi bahratunā*, This is our territory. صحرة بحرة *sahrata bahrata* or *sahratan bahratan*, Plainly, clearly, openly, without a veil.

P بحردست *bahr-dast*, Bountiful (as the sea).

P بحرگان *bahrgān*, Sea-faring. A mariner.

A بحرم *bahram*, Abounding in water (pool).

P بحروزۂ تر *bahrozaʾi tar*, Chios or Cyprus turpentine. بحروزۂ خوشك *bahrozaʾi khwushk*, Frankincense.

A بحريّ *bahriy*, Marine, maritime. Of the colour of the sea. A native of Bahrayn. A pearl, the produce of the fishery of Bahrayn.

A بحريّة *bahriyat*, A ship's crew, sailors, seamen.

A بحريت *bihrīt*, Pure, unsullied, unveiled.

P بحري قطاس *bahri-kutās*, A sea-ox, the tail of which in some countries they are accustomed to fix to the top of a spear.

A بحرين *bahrayn*, (dual of بحر *bahr*) The two seas, the White and the Black, the Mediterranean and the Euxine. Name of an island in the Persian Gulf, near the Arabian shore (called also Bahrayn), celebrated for a great pearl-fishery. . Name of a town between Basrah and عمان *ʿumān*. *Bahrayni* signifies also, in the Kur'ān, two waters, *i. e.* the salt water of the sea and sweet water of rivers.

A بحز *bahz*, A striking on the breast with the fist.

A بحزج *bahzaj*, A camel's colt. A calf. A dwarf. Short, and large-bellied.

A بحسب *bi hasbi*, According to, in the manner. بحسب الشرع *bi hasbi'sh sharʿ*, According to law. بحسب الظاهر *bi hasbi'z zāhir*, From outward appearance. بحسب المقدمات المذكورة *bi hasbi'l muhaddamāti'l mazkūrat*, According to the premises.

A بحشلة *bahshalat*, A dancing the Negroes' dance.

A بحصل *buhsal*, Thick, gross, big. Corpulent.

A بحظلة *bahzalat*, (v. n. of بحظل Q) Leaping and frisking like mice or jerboas.

A بحقّ *bi hakk*, By the truth (in swearing): as, بحقّ النبيّ و آله *bi hakki'n nabiy wa ālihi*, By the prophet and his posterity. P بحق پيوستن *ba hak paywastan*, To unite with truth, *i. e.* to die. بحق شريك شدن *ba hak sharīk shudan*, To be a partner in truth, *i. e.* to be answerable for life or safety.

P بحقد *bihuhad*, Hiccup.

A بحكم *bi hukmi*, According to, from, agreeable to, in conformity with. بحكم البشريّة *bi hukmi'l bashariyat*, From the frailty of human nature. بحكم الديانة *bi hukmi'd diyānat*, In conformity with religion. P بحكم ضرورت *ba hukmi zarūrat*, Agreeable to the exigency; forced by necessity.

A بحل *bahl*, A strong impulse.

P بحل *bihil*, Pardon, remission, absolution.

A بحمد الله تعالى *bi hamdi'llāhi taʿāla'*, God be praised! By God's grace! P بحمد الله كه *ba hamdi'llāh ki*, Thank God that.

A بحناء *bahnāʾ*, A large date-basket made of palm-leaves. A cantonment or township, of the larger size, peculiar to the Campestrian or wild Arabs. A great body of men living together.

A بحنانة *bahnānat*, A large spark. A large date-basket made of palm-leaves.

A بحنة (بنات *banātu*) *bahnat*, Scourges, lashes.

A بحوتة *buhūtat*, The being pure, and unmixed.

A بحوث *bahūs*, A camel which paws the ground with her fore-feet. A great disputant or controversialist. The chapter of توبة *tawbat* in the Kur'ān. *Buhūs*, (pl. of بحث *bahs*) Mines. Large serpents.

A بحوحة *buhūhat*, (v. n. of بحّ) Having a hoarse, gruff voice.

A بحور *bahūr*, A fleet, wide-stepping horse. A horse improved in swiftness by running. *Buhūr*, (pl. of بحر *bahr*) Seas. Gulfs, bays. Great rivers or lakes. Kinds of Arabic verse.

A بحون *bahwan*, A pile of sand. One who takes short, quick steps. A kind of date. Big-bellied.

A بحونة *bahwanat*, Small-sized (woman). Big-bellied (bottle).

A بحيثي *buhhaysaʾ*, A game played with earth.

A بحيح *bahīh*, (as شحيح بحيح) Covetous.

A بحير *bahīr*, Consumptive.

A بحيرا *buhayrā*, Name of a Nestorian monk.

A بحيرة *bahīrat*, (pl. بحائر *bahāʾir* or بحر *buhur*) A camel or sheep, which, in Pagan times, after giving birth to a tenth young one had its ear slit, and was then let loose to wander where it pleased. At its death, the men partook of its flesh, but not the women. A camel turned loose without a keeper. A camel whose fifth young one, if a male, was slaughtered and eaten both by men and women: if a female, its ear was slit, and it was forbidden to taste its flesh or to ride upon it. A sheep which, having brought forth five times, had its ear slit and was turned loose. A female with much milk. Name of a woman. *Buhayrat*, A small sea, a lake. Madīna. A name common to fifteen places. بحيرة طبريه *buhayrat tabarīya*, The Sea of Tiberias.

A بخ *bahh*, (or بخ بخ *bakh bakh*, *bakhi bakhi*, or *bakhkhin bakhkhin*) Bravo! well done!

A بخّ *bakhkha*, (fut. يبخّ *yabukhkhu*) (The business) was important. (The heat) raged. (The sleeper) snored.

A بخّ *bakhkh*, (v. n. of بخّ) Snoring. Growing cool after being angry. Liberal, generous.

A بخات *bakhkhāt*, A possessor of the Bactrian camel بختيّ *bukhtiy*.

A بخاتج *bakhātij*, (pl. of بختج) Decoctions.

A بخاتي *bakhāti*, (or بخاتيّ *bakhātiy*) (pl. of بختيّة *bukhtiyat*) Strong Bactrian camels.

P بخار *bukhār*, (in zand) Wisdom, learning.

A بخار *bukhār*, Vapour, steam, exhalation, fog, mist. Miasma. Fever. بخار العود *bukhāru'l ʿūd*, Incense of aloe-wood. بخار الماء *bukhāru'l māʾ*, (or P بخار آب *bukhāri āb*) Exhalations of water, fog.

P بخارا *bukhārā*, (A بخاراء *bukhārā'*), Bukhārā.

A بخاري *bukhāriy*, A native of Bukhārā. One who perfumes with incense of aloe-wood.

A بخارية *bukhāriyat*, Name of a wide street in Basrah where Ziyād located a thousand slaves brought from Bukhārā.

P بخاطر *ba khātir*, To one's mind. بخاطر آوردن *ba khātir āwardan*, To bring to mind, regard, pay attention to, recollect.

A بخاع *bikhā'*, A vein or nerve in the loins.

A بخاعة *bakhā'at*, (v. n. of بخع) Acknowledging a debt. Humbling one's self, submitting. Over-sticking (a sheep).

A بخاق *bukhāq*, A he-wolf.

P بخاك بردن *ba khāk burdan*, To bear through life, carry to one's grave. بخاك نشاند *ba khāk nishānd*, (or بخاك راه نشاند *ba khāki rāh nishānd*) He has depressed or rendered (him) contemptible, (he has laid him on the earth).

A بخّال *bakhkhāl*, (or بخال) Very avaricious.

A بخاند *bakhānid*, (pl. of بخنداة *bakhandāt* or بخندي *bakhanda'*) Women full-grown, firmly knit in their finger-joints.

T بخاو *bakhāv*, Fetters, tethers.

A بخبخة *bakhbakhat*, (v. n. of بخبخ Q) Making an audible noise (flabby flesh). Snoring. Braying (a camel). Growing cool in the afternoon.

P بخت *bakht*, Fortune, prosperity, felicity, happiness. Luck (good or bad). A horoscope, nativity, planet, constellation. The nightmare. A kind of locust. بد بخت *bad-bakht*, (or شور بخت *shor-bakht*) Unfortunate, inauspicious, unhappy. Ignoble, sordid, inglorious. قوي بخت *kawī-bakht*, Ever glorious, fortunate, happy, prosperous. نيك بخت *nek-bakht*, Fortunate, happy. بخت دندان خاي *bakhti dandān-khāy*, An ill star or fortune.

A بخت *bakht*, (v. n. of بخت) Striking. Pusillanimous, Fortune, happiness. *Bukht*, A species of large, strong, and hairy Bactrian camel, with two bunches, used in general for winter labour. The king who sacked Jerusalem (Nebuchadnezzar).

P بختاور *bakht-āwar*, Happy, prosperous: rich.

P بخت برگشته *bakht-bar-gashta*, Unfortunate.

P بخت بيدار *bakht-bīdār*, Whose fortune is awake; fortunate.

A بختج *bukhtaj*, (P پخته *pukhta* Arabicised) (pl. بخاتج *bakhātij*) Boiled, decocted, cooked.

P بخت خفته *bakht-khufta*, Whose fortune is asleep; unlucky.

P بختر *bakhtar*, The east. Hence the Persians call the sun شاه بختر و خاور *shāhi bakhtar u khāwar*, King of the east and west. Hence too is named that noble and extensive region (Khurāsān), called by the ancients Bactriana; and also the great river Bactrus (Amū or Jihūn), on account of their eastern situations with regard to Persia.

A بخترة *bakhtarat*, A stately gait.

A بختريّ *bakhtarīy*, One who has a handsome person and a stately gait. Haughty, airy, proud.

A بخترية *bakhtarīyat*, An airy, jaunty, flaunting gait. A handsome woman with a stately gait.

P بختك *bakhtak*, Little fortune.

P بختگار *bukhtagār*, Lightness.

P بختگاره *bukhtigāra*, Levity. Suspended.

P بختگاري *bakhtigārī*, Skill, cleverness, stratagem.

P بختگاو *bukhtgāw*, Warm water medicinally prepared, and poured from a vessel slowly over the head; an embrocation.

P بختمند *bakhtmand*, Fortunate.

P بختمندي *bakhtmandī*, Good fortune.

P بخت نصر *bakhti nassar*, (A بخت نصّر *bukhta nassara*) Nebuchadnezzar.

P بختو *bukhtū* or *bakhtū*, Thunder. Rapacious.

P بختور *bakhtwar* or *bakhtūr*, Fortunate. *Bukhtūr* or *bakhtūr*, Thunder. A roaring lion.

P بختوه *bukhtūh* or *bakhtūh*, Thunder. A roaring animal.

P بخته *bakhta*, A ram three or four years old. Any animal having a thick hide and a fat tail. A collector (of revenue).

A بختي *bukhtīy*, (fem. بختيّة *bukhtīyat*) (pl. بخاتيّ *bakhātīy* or بخاتي *bakhātī*) A large, strong, hairy camel with two bunches.

P بختيار *bakht-yār*, Fortunate. Rich.

P بختياري *bakht-yārī*, Prosperity, riches.

P بختياور *bakhtyāwar*, Fortunate.

A بختير *bikhtīr*, Handsome in person and stately in gait. Airy, proud, haughty.

A بخثرة *bakhsarat*, (v. n. of بخثر Q) Scattering, dispersing. Any kind of impurity or filth (particularly such as is seen in water); dirt on a garment.

A بخثنة *bakhsanat*, A proceeding languidly.

P بخجد *bakhjad*, Dross, especially of iron.

P بخدا *bakhudā*, By God, to God, for God's sake.

A بخدج *bakhdaj*, Fat, swelled (camel's colt).

A بخدجة *bakhdajat*, A straddling mode of walking with the toes in and heels out.

A بخدن *bakhdan*, A delicate girl.

A بخر *bakhr*, (v. n. of بخر) Steaming, sending forth steam. بنات بخر *banātu bakhrin*, Vapours, thin clouds which rise from the sea before summer. *Bakhar*, (v. n. of بخر) Having a stinking breath. Stinking. Fetid breath. Any odour diffusing itself. *Bakhir*, A strong smell.

A بخراء *bakhrā'*, Stinking, offensive. Name of a district, and fetid well in Arabia. A kind of plant.

A بخرة *bakhrat*, Name of a plant.

P بخرد *bikhrad*, Intelligent. بخرد بخردان *bikhradi bikhradān*, The wisest of the wise (a title of the prime-minister in some Eastern countries).

P بخردي *bikhradī*, Wisdom, sagacity.

P بخرك *bukhrak*, A species of wild mountain, or forest-almond, of a hot and humid nature.

P بخريدن *bukhrīdan*, To be epileptical, to groan, writhe in agony.

P بخريده *bukhrīda*, Epileptical.

A بخز *bakhz*, (v. n. of بخز) Tearing out (an eye).

P بخس *bakhs*, (or پخس *pakhs*) Heat. Anguish of mind, sickness at heart, faintness, decay, consumption. A pining or wasting away with grief or malady. Blandishment, coquetry. A stately gait or graceful air. Withered, shrivelled. Base coin. *Bikhs*, The soft parts of the nose. Softness. Debility. *Bakhis*, Vile, mean. Cheap.

A بخس *bakhs*, (v. n. of بخس) Tearing out (the eye), blinding. Withholding what is due, defrauding. Lessening, diminishing. Defect, deficiency, decrease, damage. Injustice, oppression, cruelty. Taxes received from shopkeepers. Money extorted by the collectors over and above what is due. Deficient, defective, short, scanty. Sown land which produces grain without being watered. بخس الكيل *bakhsu'l kayl*, Defective in measure. ثمن بخس *samani bakhs*, A low price. لا بخس فيه و لا شطط *lā bakhs fīhi wa lā shatat*, Neither too little (is given) for it, nor too much; it is a just price.

P بخسان *bakhsān*, Fusible, melting, dissolving. Contracted, withered, shrivelled. One who has gone through much trouble. Walking gracefully.

P بخسانيدن *bakhsānīdan*, To melt, to cause to become liquid. To afflict. To walk gracefully.

P بخست *bakhast*, Noise, sound, voice, echo.

P بخّست *bukhkhast*, A snore.

P بخستانيدن *bakhustānīdan*, To cause to snore.

P بخستن *bukhastan*, To snore, to snort.

P بخسلوس *bakhsilūs*, Name of an ancient king.

P بخسم *bakhsum*, A drink from wheat or millet.

P بخسودن *bakhsūdan*, To beat, bruise, hammer (so as to make a convexity) concave. To reap, mow, clip, shear. To saw. To pluck up. To fear. To palpitate. To be in anguish. To melt. To change.

P بخسي *bakhsī*, Weak and limber plants which grow without irrigation. Melted. A twitching.

A بخسيّ *bakhsīy*, (pl. بخوس *bukhūs*) Land not watered, and which brings grain without watering.

P بخسيدن *bakhsīdan*, To cause to melt. To inflict anguish, pain, affliction, sickness, distraction of mind. To cause to wither.

P بخسيده *bakhsīda*, Heated. Melted. Withered. Drawn together. Walking pompously.

P بخش *bakhsh*, Fortune, lot, part, portion. A dove-cote. A tower. A celestial sign. A fish. (in composition from بخشيدن *bakhshīdan*) A giver, donor. A distributer, or divider: as, حيات بخش *hayāt-bakhsh*, Life-giving. God. خطا بخش *khatā-bakhsh*, Sin-pardoning. صفا بخش *safā-bakhsh*, Producing pleasure; exhilarating, delightful. مراد بخش *murād-bakhsh*, The granter of desires. نور بخش *nūr-baksh*, Light-giving. The sun. بخش كردن *baksh kardan*, To give, distribute, divide. بخش ناكرده *bakhsh-nākarda*, Undistributed.

P بخشا *bakhshā*, A giver. (in composition) Bestowing, presenting. مالك ممالك مملكت بخشا *māliki mamāliki mamlakat-bakhshā*, (God) the King of kingdoms, the Bestower of empires.

P بخشاد *bakhshād*, May (God) forgive.

P بخشانيدن *bakhshānīdan*, To bestow. To pity, To forgive.

P بخشانيده *bakhshānīda*, Bestowing. Forgiving.

P بخشاي *bakhshāy*, Give thou. Granting, giving.

P بخشايا *bakhshāyā*, Remitting, forgiving.

P بخشايدن *bakhshāyidan*, To pity, to forgive.

P بخشايش *bakhshāyish*, Forgiveness. A gift. باران رحمت بخشايش *bārāni rahmat-bakhshāyish*, A shower of mercy.

P بخشايشگر *bakhshāyishgar*, Merciful.

P بخشايندگي *bakhshāyandagī*, Liberality: pity.

P بخشاينده *bakhshāyanda*, Bountiful: merciful.

P بخشبندر *bakhsh-bandar*, A royal custom-house.

P بخشش *bakhshish*, A gift, a present. Pisces.

P بخشش نامه *bakhshish-nāma*, A deed of gift.

P بخشندگي *bakhshandagī*, Liberality. Pardon.

P بخشنده *bakhshanda*, Liberal. Forgiving.

P بخشودن *bakhshūdan*, To give, bestow: forgive.

P بخشوده *bakhshūda*, Pardoned (by God).

P بخشه *bakhsha*, A portion.

P بخشي *bakhshī*, Fortune. A portion, a lot. Pay. A giver. A paymaster.

P بخشي جز *bakhshī-juz*, Paymaster of the house.

P بخشي خانه *bakhshī-khāna*, The pay-office.

P بخشيدن *bakhshīdan*, To give, grant, bestow. To remit. To pardon, forgive, spare.

P بخشيش *bakhshīsh*, A present. An honorary or pecuniary gratuity. Drink-money. A (Christmas) box. بخشيش كردن *bakhshīsh kardan*, To make a present. بخشيش وعطا دادن *bakhshīsh u ʿatā dādan*, To make an offering, to give a largess.

P بخشي كل *bakhshī-kul*, A paymaster-general.

P بخشي گري *bakhshīgarī*, Rank of commander-in-chief. بخشي الممالك *bakhshī'l mamālik*, Commander-in-chief.

A بخص *bakhs*, (v. n. of بخص) Tearing out an eye. *Bakhas*, (v. n. of بخص) Having protuberant flesh around the eyes. The fleshy parts of the fingers and of the feet: also of a camel's hoof. Protuberant flesh about the eyes. Unsound flesh of a whitish hue. *Bakhis*, Fleshy and veiny (udder), which with difficulty allows the milk to flow.

A بخصل *bakhsal*, Thick, fleshy, corpulent.

A بخع *bakhʿ*, (v. n. of بخع) Killing one's self, dying (with grief). Digging, excavating, till the water appears. Admonishing faithfully, pressing sincere counsel. Working, exhausting (land) by incessant tillage. Believing, crediting (a rumour). Slaughtering so hard as to reach the spinal cord.

A بخق *bakhk*, (v. n. of بخق) Making blind. Giving one a blow on the eye, so that it is either struck out, or he is deprived of the use of it. Becoming blind of, or losing an eye. *Bakhak*, (v. n. of بخق) Being very blind (the eye, the lid not meeting to cover the pupil).

A بخقاء *bakhkhāʾ*, Sightless (eye).

A بخل *bukhl* or *bakhal*, (v. n. of بخل) Being avaricious. *Bukhl, bakhal, bukhul*, or *bakhl*, Avarice, parsimony. *Bakhal*, Very covetous (man).

A بخّل *bukhkhal*, (pl. of باخل *bākhil*) Misers.

A بخلاء *bukhalāʾ*, (pl. of بخيل *bakhīl*) Misers.

P بخلاف *ba khilāf*, Contrary to.

P بخلوت *ba khalwat*, Apart, alone.

P بخله *bukhla*, A bean. Purslain.

P بخم *bakhm* or *bakham*, Name of a country famous for its musk.

P بخمه *bakhma*, An artichoke.

A بخن *bakhn*, Tall, long.

A بخنداة *bakhandāt* (or بخنديٌ *bakhanda'*) (pl. بخاند *bakhānid*) A woman full grown, having the finger-joints firmly knit, and the legs stout.

A بخنق *bukhnak* or *bukhnuk*, A kind of cloth which the Arabian women put under the معجر *miʿjar* to keep it from being greased. A small veil or hood for the face. The shell on a locust's neck.

A بخنك *bukhnak*, equiv. to بخنق *bukhnuk*.

P بخنو *bakhnaw*, Thunder. A father-in-law.

P بخنود *bakhnūd*, Thunder.

P بخنونه *bakhnūna*, Thunder. Lightning.

P بخنوه *bukhnūh* or *bakhnava*, Lightning.

P بخنويدن *bakhnawīdan*, To thunder and lighten.

A بخو *bakhw*, Dates of a bad sort. Soft, relaxed.

P بخود *ba khwud*, To, with, or by one's self. بخود آمدن *ba khwud āmadan*, To come to one's self. بخود فرو رفت *ba khwud faro raft*, (or شد *shud*) He hung his head (from shame or grief). بخودي خود *ba khwude khwud*, Solitary, by one's self.

A بخور *bakhūr*, (pl. بخورات *bakhūrāt*) Perfume, odour, or any thing which diffuses fragrance, as aloes, musk, thyme, storax, frankincense, &c. بخور مريم *bakhūri maryam* or بخور الاكراد *bakhūru'l akrād*, Maiden-weed. Hog's fennel. بخور البربر *bakhūru'l barbar*, A kind of plant which shoots a number of twigs along the surface of the ground, with small round leaves and white flowers.

P بخور *bukhūr*, Liquid storax.

P بخورانيدن *ba khwurānīdan*, To cause one to eat.

P بخوردان *bakhūrdān*, A censer for incense.

P بخور شيشه *bakhūr-shīsha*, A censer. Perfumes moistened and laid upon the fire to scent a room.

P بخوره *bakhūra*, A musk-bag.

P بخوريده *bukhūrīda*, Epileptical: horror-struck.

A بخوس *bukhūs*, (pl. of بخسيّ *bakhsīy*) Sown lands which produce grain without requiring water.

A بخوع *bukhūʿ*, (v. n. of بخع) Confessing, owning (a debt). Humbling one's self, submitting.

A بخول *bukhūl*, Avarice, parsimony.

P بخون *ba khūn*, Difficult. The planet Mars.

A بخي *bakhīy*, (or بخّي *bakhkhīy*) (Money) inscribed with the word بخ *bakh*.

A بخيت *bakhīt*, Fortunate, happy.

P بخيدن *bakhīdan*, To card wool or cotton.

P بخيده *bakhīda*, Carded, teased. Pickled.

P بخير *bakhīr*, (or بخيل *bakhīl*) A kind of artichoke.

P بخيز *bi khez*, Rise. An ambush.

A بخيق *bakhīk*, One-eyed. Sightless (eye).

A بخيقة *bakhīkat*, One-eyed (woman).

A بخيل *bakhīl*, (pl. بخلاء *bukhalāʾ*) Avaricious, covetous. A miser.

P بخيله *bakhīla*, Purslain.

A بخيلي *bakhīlī*, Avarice. P بخيلي نمودن *bakhīlī namūdan*, To be stingy, niggardly, avaricious.

P بخيه *bakhya*, Quilting, sewing very thick and strong. Sewing with long stitches, basting. A piece of sewed cloth. بخيه اش بر روي كار افتاد *bakhya ash bar rūyi kard uftād*, (The cloth has fallen from his face) *i.e.* the secret is discovered. بخيه زدن *bakhya zadan*, To sew with long stitches, to baste. *Bukhya*, A line, plumb-line. A wedge or iron instrument for cleaving wood. Touching, squeezing, twitching with the fingers.

P بخيه دار *bakhya-dār*, Quilted.

P بخيه زن *bakhya-zan*, A stitcher, quilter, botcher.

P بد *bad*, Bad, wicked, naughty. Evil, calamity. Wickedness. Linen rags half-burned, tinder. Touchwood. جامهٔ بد *jāmaʾi bad*, A torn or worn-out garment. *Bud*, A lord, master. A servant. (for بود *būd*), It was.

A بدّ *badda*, (fut. يبدّ *yabuddu*) He separated.

A بدّ *badd*, (v. n. of بدّ) Separating, disjoining. Driving, putting to a distance. Lassitude, fatigue. *Bidd*, Like, resembling. *Budd*, (P بت *but*) (pl. بددة *bidadat* and ابداد *abdād*) An idol, image. A gnat. An idol-temple. A part, portion. Separation. Flight, escape. لا بد *lā budd*, There is now no flight, no retreat, or remedy; it becomes necessary.

A بدء *badʾ*, (v. n. of بدأ) Beginning. Creating or giving a beginning. Going out, departing from one's own country. Being seized with an indisposition (as the measles). Commencement, a beginning, a turn to begin. A new, unheard-of thing, first invented. A lord, a chief. The first-created. A new well (such being so called as have been dug since the æra of Muhammadism). (pl. ابداء *abdāʾ* and بدوء *budūʾ*) The prime joint of a slaughtered camel. A sensible intelligent youth. P بدء كلام كردن *badʾi kalām kardan*, To begin a discourse, sermon, speech, or conversation.

A افعله بدأً *ifʿalhu badʾan*, Do it at the first, at the outset, before all other things. Synonymous with which are اوّل بدء *awwala badʾin*, بادي بدء *bādiya badʾin*, بادي بديّ *bādiya badiyin*, بادي بدأة *bādiya badʾatin*, بدءة ذي بدء *badʾata zī badʾin*, بدءة ذي بداءة *badʾata zī badāʾatin*, بدءة ذي بدأة *badʾata zī badʾatin*, بدءة ذي بديء *badʾata zī badiʾin*, بداءة ذي بديء *badāʾata zī badi-*

-ʾin, بدءة بدء badʾata badʾin, بدئ بدء badiʾa badʾin, بادء بدء badʾa badʾin, بادئ بدئ bādiʾa badiʾin, بادئ بدء bādiʾa badiʾin, بدي ذي بدء badiʾa zi badʾin, بادئ بدا bādiʾa badʾin, بادئ بدء bādiʾa badā, بدا بدء badā badʾin, بدءة بدءة badʾata badʾata, بادي بدء bādī badʾin, and بادي بدا bādī badā. رجع عوده علي بدئه rajaʿa ʿawdahu ʿala' badʾihi, He returned by the way he came. Also, في عوده وبدئه fī ʿawdihi wa badʾihi, في عودته وبدأته fī ʿawdatihi wa badʾatihi, or عودا وبدأ ʿawdan wa badʾan.

A بدا badaʾ, (pl. ابداء abdāʾ) Thin excrement. A joint. Name of a place in Syria.

P بدا badā, Wickedness, obscenity, profane talk.

A بدأ badaʾa, (fut. يبدأ yabdaʾu) He began.

A بدّا buddaʾ, People living in the desert.

A بداء badāʾ, (v. n. of بدأ) Coming in the mind (a scheme). (v. n. of بدا for بدو) Appearing. Going forth into the desert.

A بدّاء baddāʾ, (fem. of ابدّ abadd) Corpulent (female), or one who straddles from corpulency. Buddāʾ, (pl. of بادي bādī) Inhabitants of the desert.

A بداءة badāʾat, (v. n. of بدا for بدو) Appearing. Entering the mind (an idea). Badāʾat or budāʾat, A beginning, a turn to begin, the first turn.

A بدأة badʾat, A mushroom. A kind of earth. The principal part or joint of a slaughtered camel. Badʾat or budʾat, A beginning, a turn to begin. Budʾat, Beginning, first turn. Name of a plant.

A بداح badāh, (pl. بدح buduh) A widely-extended tract of soft land. Bidāh, (pl. of بدح bidh) Fields or wide tracts of uncultivated ground.

P بد اختر bad-akhtar, Ill-starred, unfortunate.

P بداخشان badākhshān, A country in Persia.

P بد اخلاق bad-akhlāk, Of depraved morals.

A بداد badād, A sallying-forth to battle, a going down to fight (particularly applied to those who engage man to man in an amphitheatre, &c.). A contribution to a general fund. يا قوم بداد بداد yā kawm badādi badādi, O soldiers, one by one, single out each his antagonist. بداد بداد badādi badādi or badāda badāda, Scattered. Bidād, (v. n. 3 of بدّ) Bartering, exchanging. Contributing to a general fund. (pl. بدائد badāʾid and ابدّة abiddat) A saddle-cloth, a felt-cloth to save the horse's back. Bidād or badād, A portion, lot, share.

A بدادان bidādāni, Two wadded sides.

A بدار badāri, Make haste. Bidār, (v. n. 3 of بدر) Outstripping. Hastening, making haste.

P بدآرام bad-ārām, A knave. A pleasant place.

P بداز badāz, A shoemaker's wedge.

P بداسلوب bad-uslūb, Ill-shaped: of bad conduct.

P بداصل bad-asl, Of a bad stock, or mean race.

A بداعة badāʿat, (v. n. of بدع) Being wonderful, surprising. Outstripping in courage, learning, &c.

P بدآغاز bad-āghāz, Innately bad.

A بداغة badāghat, A stooling in one's clothes.

P بداق bidāk, The lower part of breeches, drawers, or trousers.

P بداك badāk, Angry, malevolent.

A بدال bidāl, (v. n. 3 of بدل) Exchanging, bartering, trucking.

A بدّال baddāl, A seller of eatables.

P بدامتزاج bad-imtizāj, (Bad mixture) Wicked.

P بدآموز bad-āmoz, Ill-bred. Teacher of evil.

P بدان badān, (from به ba and آن ān) To, or with, that. For that purpose, with that design.

A بدان badān, A becoming corpulent: corpulency.

A بدانة badānat, A becoming fat and corpulent.

P بد انديش bad-andesh, Malicious, malevolent.

P بد انديشان bad-andeshān, (pl. of بدانديش bad-andesh) The malevolent.

P بد انديشي bad-andeshī, Malevolence.

P بدانگونه badān-gūna, Of that kind.

P بداو badu, (from به ba and او u) To, with him.

A بداوة badāwat, First appearance. A mushroom. A kind of earth. Badāwat or bidāwat, A country life (in opposition to حضارة hazārat, A town life).

A بداوي badāwiy also bidāwiy, Rural, rustic, belonging to the desert.

A بداه bidāh, A coming upon one suddenly.

A بداهة badahat or budāhat, An unexpected accident. The beginning of any thing. An impromptu.

P بد آهوش bad-āhosh, Malevolent.

A بدائد badāʾid, (pl. of بداد) Saddle-stuffings.

A بدائع badāʾiʿ, (pl. of بديعة) New, strange. بدائع معنوي badāʾiʿi maʿnawī, Style, sentiment.

A بدائه badāʾih, Strange, things, novelties.

P بد آيين bad-āyīn, Irreligious: perverse; ill-bred. لعين بدآيين laʿīni bad-āyīn, A wicked wretch.

P بدباز bad-bāz, A mimic, a jester.

P بدباطن bad-bātin, Intrinsically bad.

P بد بافتگي bad-bāftagī, Flimsiness of texture,

P بد بافته bad-bāfta, Badly woven; flimsy.

P بد بخت bad-bakht, Ill-fated, unfortunate.

P بدبختيوار bad-bakhtīwār, Unlucky, inglorious.

A بد بد bad bad, Bravo! well done!

P بدبدك budbudak, The hoopoo or puet (called also مرغ سليمان murghi sulaymān, Solomon's bird).

P بدبردن bad burdan, To molest, to afflict.

P بدبو bad-bo, Fœtid. Bad smell, funk, stench.

P بدبوك bad-būk, Malignant, malevolent.

P بد بوگ bad-būg, Timid.

P بدپدر bad-pidar, (Bad father) A step-father.

P بد پرتو bad-partav, Unfortunate. Sinister, of a bad aspect. Of a wretched character.

P بدپرهيز bad-parhez, Intemperate. Heedless, imprudent. Inattentive to medical advice.

P بدپرهيزي bad-parhezī, Inattention to medical advice. Carelessness about one's health.

P بدپسند bad-pasand, A lover of difficulties.

P بدپشت bad-pusht, (Bad back), A young unbroke beast of burden, that will bear no load.

P بدپوز badpūz, The environs of the mouth.

A بدّة baddat or biddat, Power. ما له به بدّة mā lahu bihi biddat or baddat, He has not power to do it. Buddat, (pl. بدد bidad) A portion, lot, share. End, extremity.

P بد تبار bad-tabār, Of mean birth, ignoble.

P بدتر badtar, Worse, more villainous.

P بدترين badtarīn, Worst, most infamous.

P بدجلوي bad-jalwī, Deviation. Disaffection.

P بدجنس bad-jins, Ignoble, base-born, mean.

P بد چشم bad-chashm, Having a bad or unlucky eye, of a malignant aspect. Coveting the property of another. Weak-sighted (horse), one that shies. بد چشمي كردن bad-chashmī kardan, To shy.

A بدح badh, (v. n. of بدح) Cutting, splitting, tearing. Hitting, striking. Coming upon one with an affair suddenly and unexpectedly. Revealing, disclosing. Walking elegantly (a woman). Pressing heavily. Breaking down under a load (a camel). A kind of fish. Bidh, (pl. بداح bidāh) An extensive plain, a spacious area. Buduh, (pl. of بداح badāh) Widely-extended tracts of soft land.

A بدحا badhan, Clearly, openly, evidently.

A بدحاء badhāʾ, Wide, roomy (woman).

P بد حال bad-hāl, In bad circumstances.

P بد حالي bad-hālī, Grief, despondency. Badness of condition, evil plight.

A بدحة budhat, Middle court, area of a house.

A بدخاء budakhāʾ, (pl. of بديخ) High in rank.

P بدخش badakhsh, (more usually بدخشان badakhshān) Name of a country between India and Khurāsān, from whence they bring rubies, and famous for its large sheep. كوه بدخشان kohi badakhshān, The mountain where they dig them. لعل بدخشان laʿli badakhshān, The finest kind of rubies brought from thence. بدخشان تابدار badakhshāni tāb-dār, A ruby of the finest colour.

P بدخش مذاب badakhsh-muzāb, A ruby. Red, ruby-coloured wine.

P بدخشي badakhshī, (Of Badakhsh) A ruby.

P بد خصال bad-khisāl, Of a bad disposition. بد خصالان انام bād-khisālāni anām, The most vicious or perverse of mankind.

P بدخط bad-khat, Writing ill: a bad penman.

P بدخلق bad-khulk, Ill-tempered, perverse.

P بدخو bad-kho, (or khu, خوي khoy or khuy) Bad-tempered, ill-bred, rude. Vicious, wicked.

P بدخوار bad-khwār, Ill-fed.

P بدخوارگي bad-khwāragī, Poorness of living.

P بد خواه bad-khwāh, Malevolent, invidious.

P بد خواهي bad-khwāhī, Malevolence, hatred.

P بد خورش bad-khwurish, Ill-fed.

P بدخوئي bad khoʾī, Badness of temper. Vice.

P بدخيم bad-khīm, Sour, crabbed, ill-tempered.

A بدد badad, (v. n. of بدد) Straddling from corpulency (man or animal). Exchange, barter. Necessity, need, lack. Space between two things. Power, ability. ما لك به بدد mā laka bihi bada-

dun, Thou art not a match for him. *Badada badada* or *badadan badadan,* (The horses came in) scattered. *Bidad,* (pl. of بدّة *buddat*) Portions.

A بددا *bidadan,* In shares, by lots.

A بددة *bidadat,* (pl. of بدّ *budd*) Idols, images.

P بددعا *bad-duɛā,* An imprecation, malediction.

P بد دل *bad-dil,* Dastardly, cowardly, timid, pusillanimous. Weak, silly. Suspicious.

P بددلي *bad-dilī,* Cowardice. Suspicion.

P بد دماغ *bad-dimāgh,* Difficult to please.

P بد دول *bad-dawl,* Ill-shaped, ungraceful.

P بد دين *bad-dīn,* Impious, irreligious, heretical.

P بد ذات *bad-zāt,* Base-born. Vicious.

P بدذهن *bad-zihn,* Slow of apprehension, stupid.

A بدر *badara,* (fut. يبدر *yabduru*) He made haste.

A بدر *badr,* (v.n. of بدر) Becoming perfect and full-grown (a young man). Becoming ripe (fruit). Integrity, plentitude, fulness. (pl. بدور *budūr*) The full moon. A tray. A youth arrived at maturity. A lord, a prince. Name of a well between Mecca and Madīna. ليلة البدر *laylatu'l badr,* The night of full moon. The fourteenth of every lunar month. بدرالدين *badru'd dīn,* The full moon of religion (a proper name). يوم بدر *yawm badr,* The day or battle of Badr, or the victory gained there by Muhammad. *Bidar,* (pl. of بدرة *badrat*) Skins of lambs or kids used for carrying milk.

P بدر *ba dar,* Without, out of doors. بدر آمد *ba dar āmad,* He came out. بدررفت *ba dar raft,* He went out. بدرافتادن *ba dar uftādan,* To fall out. بدر آوردن *ba dar āwardan,* To bring out, to extract. بدر بردن *ba dar burdan,* To lead or carry out, to eject, expel. بدرزدن *ba dar zadan,* To go, proceed, or flee. بدرن كردن *ba dar kardan,* To drive out, eject, expel, emit.

A بدرام *badrām,* A pleasant, elegant, delightful place, garden, or house. An assembly, banquet, or entertainment. *Bad-rām,* Wild, vicious, unbroke (horse). Continually.

P بدران *badrān,* A kind of stinking herb. A kind of dish. Wicked.

P بدراه *bad-rāh,* Deviating from the right path, in a wrong road. Wicked. دشمن بدراه *dushmani bad-rāh,* A malignant enemy.

P بدر آي *ba dar āy,* Come forth.

P بد راي *bad-raꜥy,* Erroneous. Heretical.

P بد رائحه *bad-rāꜥiha,* Fetid. A stink, stench.

A بدرة *badrat,* A quick, brisk eye. An eye in its badar or full moon. A weight of 10,000 dirhems, or 7000 dinars. (pl. بدور *budūr* and بدر *bidar*) A bag made of the skin of a lamb or kid, in which they carry milk (the skin in which they put butter is called مسأدة *misꜥadat*; and both have these names only when they have been just taken from the mother; for if they were sucking lambs or kids, the milk-bag is then called شكوة *shakwat,* and that for butter عكة *ɛukkat*: and when the lambs or kids have been one or two years old, the first is named وطب *watb,* and the other نحي *nihy*).

P بدرج *badruj,* The purple amaranth.

P بد رخته *bad-rakhta,* Melancholy, gloomy.

P بدررو *badar-rav,* (Going out) A drain, sewer.

P بدرزق *bad-rizk,* Disliked, unacceptable.

P بدرزه *badarza,* A portion, part, share. *Bidruza* or *bidraza,* Victuals carried home from an entertainment by the guests.

P بدرستي *ba durustī* or *ba drustī,* Indeed, truly.

P بدر شب *badr-shab,* A full-moonlight night.

P بد رفتار *bad-raftār,* Going badly. Patient. *Bidruftār,* A surety, a sponsor.

P بدرفتاري *bidruftārī,* Surety, sponsorship.

P بدرقه *badraka,* A guide, guard, escort, convoy. Protection. A vehicle. Any thing ordered to be taken with medicine (as water-gruel with salts). An observer of the moon. A confidant. Patient. لشكر بدرقه *lashkar-badraka,* An army-guide. ورقهٔ محبت بدرقه *warakaꜥi mahabbat-badraka,* Letters of friendship.

P بدركاب *bad-rikāb,* Ill-paced, hard to mount.

P بدرگ *bad-rag,* Of a bad stock. Malevolent.

P بدرگي *bad-ragī,* Baseness. Malevolence.

P بد رنگ *bad-rang,* Of a bad colour or kind.

P بدر نويسي *ba dar navīsī,* Error. The auditing of charges.

P بدر نيامدن *ba dar nayāmadan,* To be distressed and helpless. To lag, be tired, remain behind.

P بدرو *bad-rav,* A bad goer. A pack-horse.

P بدرود *bidrūd,* Farewell! Health. Fronting. Parting, leaving, quitting.

P بدروزگار *bad-rozgār,* Wicked. Unfortunate.

P بدروش *badrūsh,* (or بدروشت) A pass, a narrow pass on an enemy's confines. Expectation.

P بدروغ *ba durogh,* Falsely.

P بدرة *badra,* A weight of 10,000 dirhems. A small pocket, purse, or bag, nearly square, full of money. A barren tree. *Bidra,* A ship-worm.

P بدري *badrī,* A purse full of money. A wrapper.

A بدري *badara',* Precedency, advance.

A بدري *badrīy,* One present at the battle of Badr. Rain falling before winter. A fat camel's colt.

P بدريا دادن *ba daryā dādan,* (To give to the sea) To wash. To remove out of sight.

A بدرية *badrīyat,* Name of a quarter in Bagdad.

P بد زبان *bad-zabān,* Foul-mouthed, ill-tongued, back-biting, scurrilous. Indecent language, abuse.

P بد زباني *bad-zabānī,* Scurrility, abuse.

P بد زندگاني *bad-zindagānī,* Wicked, vicious. A bad-liver. One who fares meanly or coarsely.

P بدزهره *bad-zahra,* Malignant. Timid, fearful.

P بدزيب *bad-zīb,* Ungraceful, inelegant.

P بدس *badas,* Make haste!

P بدساعت *bad-sāɛat,* An unlucky moment. Ill-timed.

P بدست *bidast, bidist,* or *badast,* A span.

P بدست آوردن *ba dast āwardan,* To procure.

P بدست باش *ba dast bāsh,* Be at hand! make ready! be quick! attend!

P بدست بودن *ba dast būdan,* To be in hand. To be aware, to be informed of. To be on the alert. To number, to count. To obtain.

P بدست چپ شمردن *ba dasti chap shumurdan,* To count with the left hand. (As the fingers of the left hand stand for thousands the expression implies, To be very numerous).

P بدست ديگر مار گرفتن *ba dasti dīgar mār giriftan,* To take hold of the serpent *i. e.* to engage in a perilous undertaking) with the hand of another.

P بدست شدن *ba dast shudan,* To come to hand. بدست گرفتن *ba dast giriftan,* To take in hand, to handle.

P بدستور *ba dastūr,* According to custom. As heretofore.

P بدسج *bad-saj,* Ungraceful, ill-favoured.

P بدسغان *badisghān,* (or بدسگان *badisgān*) Ivy, convolvulus.

P بدسگال *bad-sikāl,* Malevolent, malignant.

P بد سگاليدن *bad sigālīdan,* To plot mischief.

P بد سلوك كردن *bad-sulūk kardan,* To maltreat.

P بد سوار *bad-suwār,* A bad horseman. A stallion, fierce and untractable. A horse that will not carry well or double.

P بد سيرت *bad-sīrat,* Ill-tempered or behaved.

P بدشغان *badishghān,* Ivy, convolvulus.

P بد شكل *bad-shakl,* Deformed, ill-shaped.

P بد شگون *bad-shugūn,* Unlucky, ill-omened.

P بد شگوني *bad-shugūnī,* Ill-luck.

P بد صورت *bad-sūrat,* Ugly. Badly formed.

P بد طريق *bad-tarīk,* A bad habit (religiously).

P بد طينت *bad-tīnat,* Ill-tempered, malignant.

P بد طينتي *bad-tīnatī,* Malignity, malevolence.

P بد ظن *bad-zan,* Suspicious, distrustful.

A بدع *badaɛa,* (fut. يبدع *yabdaɛu*) He invented.

A بدع *badɛ,* (v. n. of بدع) Producing something new, originating, beginning. Causing a spring to flow. *Bidɛ,* New, original. A novelty. A man of a noble disposition, and far ahead of his cotemporaries in learning and valour. A body full of flesh. (pl. ابداع *abdāɛ* and بدع *buduɛ*) Wonderful, surprising, incomparable. هو بدع في هذا الامر *huwa bidɛun fī hāzā'l amr,* He is quite original in this affair. *Budɛ,* (pl. of بديع *badīɛ*) Fat men. *Badaɛ,* (v. n. of بدع) Being fat. *Bidaɛ,* (pl. of بدعة *bidɛat*) Wonderful, incomparable (women). Novelties, innovations; heresies, schisms. *Buduɛ,* (pl. of بدع *bidɛ*) Wonderful, incomparable men.

A بدعة *bidɛat,* (pl. بدع *bidaɛ*) Novelty, innovation in matters of religion: heresy, schism. Oppression. A hog. (pl. بدع *bidaɛ*) Wonderful (woman). اهل بدعت *ahli bidɛat,* A heretic, sectary.

P دو سه بدعت *du sih bidɛat,* Two or three hogs.

A بدعتي *bidɛatī,* A tyrant, oppressor. An innovator in religious matters: schismatical, heretical.

P بد علف *bad-ʻalaf*, Unobservant of the distinction between clean and unclean meats; unscrupulous.

P بد عمل *bad-ʻamal*, Evil-doer, wrong-doer.

P بد عهد *bad-ʻahd*, A liar. A promise-breaker. كافر بد عهد *kāfiri bad-ʻahd*, A perfidious infidel.

P بد عهدي *bad-ʻahdī*, Breach of faith, perfidy.

A بدعيّ *bidʻiy*, Heretical.

A بدغ *badgh*, (v. n. of بدغ) Breaking (a nut or almond). The fragments of a broken nut or almond. *Bidgh*, One who bedaubs himself by stooling in his clothes. *Badagh*, (v. n. of بدغ) Being bedaubed with excrement. Being tainted with evil. Sliding with one's bottom on the ground. *Badigh*, Bedaubed. Contaminated. (pl. بدغون *badighūna*) Plump, fat, in a good habit of body.

P بد فرجام *bad-farjām*, Ending badly: malignant, ill-meant.

P بد فعال *bad-fiʻāl*, Operating badly, having an unlucky tendency, doing mischief. Of bad habits (in a religious sense).

P بد فوز *badfūz*, The inside of the mouth. The environs of the mouth, the corners, or dimples. Fortunate, succeeding in one's wishes.

P بدق *badak*, A pawn at chess.

P بد قمار *bad-kimār*, A rascally cheat, who gets money any how. Ill-tempered. Habitually wicked.

P بد قيافه *bad-kiyāfa*, Sinister, ill-looking.

P بدك *budak*, A hoopoo, a puet.

P بدكار *bad-kār*, (or بدكاره *bad-kāra*) Iniquitous, villainous, sinful. Adulterous.

P بد كاري *bad-kārī*, Wickedness, villainy.

P بد كردار *bad-kirdār*, An evil-doer, a malefactor. كفّار بد كردار *kuffāri bad-kirdār*, Vile infidels.

P بد كرداري *bad-kirdārī*, Wickedness, mischief.

P بد كرزام *bad-kajrām*, Doing any thing badly,

P بد كند *bad-kand*, A bribe offered to a judge.

P بد كنش *bad-kunish*, (or بد كنشت *bad-kunisht*) An evil-doer. Bad, evil.

P بدكيش *bad-kesh*, Impious. Inhuman.

P بدگمان *bad-gumān*, Suspicious. Suspected. Scandalous. Malevolent. Suspicion. بدگمان شدن *bad-gumān shudan*, To be jealous, suspicious.

P بدگماني *bad-gumānī*, Suspicion, scandal.

P بد گند *bad-gand*, Stinking. A bribe proffered to a judge.

P بدگو *bad-go* (or *gū* بد گوي *bad-goy* or *gūy*) A slanderer, detractor.

P بد گوهر *bad-gohar*, (or گهر *guhar*) Essentially bad. Bad by nature: of a wicked, base, mean origin.

P بد گويان *bad-goyān* (or *gūyān*) Evil-speakers. Calumniators, backbiters.

P بد گوئي *bad-goī* (or *gūī*), Evil-speaking.

A بدل *badal* or *bidl*, (pl. ابدال *abdāl*) A succedaneum, substitute, equivalent. Exchange, substitution. Retaliation. Noble, generous. For. Because. From. Out of. عين بدل عين *ʻayn badal ʻayn*, Eye for eye. P بدل فراغت *badali farāghat*, A bribe for a benefice, simony. بدل مال *badali māl*, Exchange, barter, price. بدل آن *badali ān*, In lieu of that. بدل دادن *badal dādan*, To make an exchange, give an equivalent. A حروف البدل *hurūfu'l badal*, The letters of change are contained in the following technical words: انجدته يوم صال زط *anjattuhu yawma sāla zuttun*. The letters of change without insertion are لجدّ صرف شكس آمن طيّ ثوب عزّته *li jiddin sarafa shakisun āmana tayyun sawba ʻizzatihi*. بدلاً عن *badalan ʻan*, As a substitute for, in lieu of. *Badal*, (v. n. of بدل) Being pained in the joints or hands, or flesh of the breast. The pain itself. *Badil*, Pained in the joints or hands.

P بدل *ba dil*, With the heart, heartily.

A بدلاء *budalāʼ*, (pl. of بديل *badīl*) Substitutes.

A بدلة *bidlat*, A suit or change of raiment.

P بد لگام *bad-ligām*, Hard-mouthed, headstrong.

P بدله *bidla*, A kind of tree which bears no fruit. A tree fit only for the fire. An every-day garment.

P بد لهجه *bad-lahja*, Ill-tongued, malignant.

A بدليس *bidlīs*, Name of a town near Khilāt.

SY بدليون *badliyūn*, A kind of gum, bdellium.

P بد محبّت *bad-mahabbat*, Unamiable.

P بد مذهب *bad-mazhab*, A sectary: an idolater.

P بد مزاج *bad-mizāj*, Peevish.

P بد مزاجي *bad-mizājī*, Peevishness

P بد مزگي *bad-mazagī*, Insipidity. Coolness betwixt friends.

P بد مست *bad-mast*, Intoxicated. Refractory.

P بد مستي *bad-mastī*, Intoxication. Dissoluteness, profligacy.

P بد مصاحبتي *bad-musāhabatī*, Evil company.

P بد مظنّه *bad-mazinna*, Suspicious, mistrustful.

P بد معاش *bad-maʻāsh*, Of a bad life, profession, or trade.

P بد معاملگي *bad muʻāmalagī*, Unfair dealing.

P بد معامله *bad-muʻāmala*, Unfairness.

P بد موم *bad-mimūm*, (in zand and Pāzand) Fearing, running away.

P بد مهري *bad-mihrī*, Unkindness, ill-will.

A بدن *badn* or *budn*, (v. n. of بدن) Becoming corpulent. *Badan*, (pl. ابدان *abdān*) The body (especially when lifeless). A headless trunk. P بدن در جامه نگنجيد *badan dar jāma na gunjīd*, (His) garment could not contain (him for joy). A A rampart, a battlement. The walls of a tent. Aged (man). (pl. ابدن *abdun*) An old mountain-goat. The limbs of a slaughtered camel. A short coat of mail. Paternal kindred. Lineage, race, stock, family. Dignity. Reputation, respect. *Badin*, Aged (man or woman). Fat, thick. *Budun*, Fatness. (pl. of بدين *badīn*) Fat (men or women). (pl. of بدنة *badanat*) Oxen or camels sacrificed at Mecca in discharge of a vow.

P بدن *budan*, (for بودن *būdan*) To be, to become.

A بدّن *buddan*, (pl. of بدين *badīn*) Corpulent.

P بد نام *bad-nām*, A bad name. Having a bad name, infamous. An evil-speaker. A disease to which horses and mules are subject. بدنام دادن *bad-nām dādan*, To calumniate.

P بد نامي *bad-nāmī*, Infamy, bad repute, disgrace.

A بدنة *badanat*, (pl. بدن *budun*) An ox or camel sacrificed at Mecca in discharge of a vow.

P بد نژاد *bad-nijād*, Base-born, descended from mean ancestors. A horse, got by an Arabian sire, out of a Turkish mare (and not highly esteemed on account of his dam).

P بد نسل *bad-nasl*, Of a bad stock. A bastard.

P بد نعل *bad-naʻl*, (A horse) unsure-footed, apt to stumble. Troublesome (horse), bad to shoe.

P بد نفس *bad-nafs*, Having a depraved mind, sensual. *Bad-nafas*, Stinking-breathed. Having an unpleasing voice.

P بد نفسي *bad-nafsī*, Sensuality.

P بدنك *budank*, Water-cresses.

P بد نگر *bad-nigar*, Seeing badly, weak-eyed.

P بدنما *bad-namā*, A bad sign or appearance. Deformed, ungraceful, inelegant. عجوز بد نما *ʻajūzi bad-namā*, A deformed, ugly old woman.

P بدنهاد *bad-nihād*, Depraved, perfidious.

P بد نهادي *bad-nihādī*, Malignity, depravity.

A بدنيّ *badaniy*, Corporeal, bodily. Corpulent.

P بدنيّت *bad-nīyat*, Mal-intentioned.

A بدو *badw*, (v. n. of بدا for بدو) Appearing. Entering the mind (an idea). Departing for the desert. Voiding excrement. A desert.

P بدو *badu*, (for باو *ba u* or for به او *ba u*, to avoid the cacophony) To, for, by him, or it. *Ba du*, To two. *Badav*, Fleet (horse).

A بدوّ *budūw*, (v. n. of بدا for بدو) Appearing.

A بدوء *budūʼ*, (v. n. of بدو) Appearing. (pl. of بدء *badʼ*) The prime joints of a slaughtered camel.

A بدوات *badawāt*, Opinions, notions, schemes. ذو بدوات *zū badawāt*, Full of (new) schemes.

P بدوار *badwār*, Of evil thoughts: mischievous.

P بدواز *badwāz*, Flying. A roost, a perch.

A بدوان *badawān*, A new opinion. ذو بدوان *zū badawān*, Unjust, tyrannical, despotic.

A بدوة *badwat*, A river-side. Name of a place. دارة بدوتين *dārat badwatayn*, Name of a place.

A بدوح *budūh*, (v. n. of بدح) Walking gracefully (a woman).

A بدور *budūr*, (v. n. of بدر) Making haste. Taking precedency. (pl. of بدر *badr*) Full-moons. (pl. of بدرة *badrat*) Lambskins.

P بدوره *badwara*, A share, portion. Sweetmeats, delicacies carried away by guests from a feast.

P بدّوره *baddūra*, Sweetmeats from a feast.

P بدوس *badūs*, Good-will, affection. Hope. A sharp sword.

A بدوع *budūʻ*, (v. n. of بدع) Being wonderful, surprising. Outstripping (one's cotemporaries) in learning, bravery, and nobility.

P بدون *ba dūn*, Without, besides.

A بدوي *badawiy*, Wild, rude (as the Arabs of the desert). A Bedouin.

A بدة *badh*, (v. n. of بده) Coming suddenly, surprising. Happening unexpectedly. Meeting one accidentally with any thing, or bringing it to him when he does not expect it. An impromptu. *Badh* or *budh*, The beginning of any thing. Sudden, unexpected.

P بده *bada*, Boiled rice. Name of a very hard tree. Any tree which bears not fruit. A debt, a loan. The willow. *Buda*, Linen-tinder.

P بدهاد *ba dihād*, May (God) grant.

P بده كار *bada-kār*, A debtor.

P بدهشه *bad-hisa*, Deformed, mishapen, ugly.

A بدي *bady*, (v. n. of بدي) Beginning.

P بدي *badī*, Badness. (for بادي) Live for ever!

A بديّ *badiy*, Newly invented, created, discovered, found out. First. A well newly dug (or any that has been made since the Muhammadan era).

A بديء *badīʼ*, Any thing new.

P بديج *badīj*, The myrobalan or citron-tree.

A بديح *budayh*, Name of a celebrated singer.

A بديخ *badīkh*, (pl. بدخاء *budakhāʼ*) Eminent in rank or dignity.

A بديد *badīd*, An open plain. A cloak-bag or wallet. (pl. بدائد *badāʼid* and ابدّة *abiddat*) A saddle-cloth, a felt-cloth. Like, resembling.

A بديدة *badīdat*, Calamity, misfortune. Like, فلاة بديدة *falāt badīdat*, A desolate plain.

A بدير *budayr*, (diminutive of بدر *badr*) A little full moon (a term expressive of endearment).

P بديسه *badīsa*, A circular bit of wood or leather fixed on the top of a spindle. A circular bit of wood bored for receiving the top of a tent-pole.

P بديشان *badeshān*, (for بايشان *ba eshān*, to avoid the hiatus) To, for, with, by them.

A بديع *badīʻ*, Wonderful, surprising, marvellous, astonishing, strange, rare. Alien from, inconsistent with. An originator, inventor, a producer of something new. A thing invented, an invention. A rope, which ere it has been well twisted, is untwisted, respun, and twisted again. A new leathern wine-bottle. (pl. بدع *budʻ*) A fat man. يا قادر بديع المظاهر *yā kādir badīʻu'l mazāhir*, O omnipotent creator of visible things! كلام بديع الانتظام *kalāmi badīʻu'l intizām*, A discourse wonderfully arranged. علم بديع *ʻilmi badīʻ*, Elegance of composition, metrical arrangement. بديع الجمال *badīʻu'l jamāl*, Of astonishing beauty. بديع السموات و الارض *badīʻu's samawāt wa'l arz*, Creator of the heavens and of the earth. بديع صنيع *badīʻ sanīʻ*, The holy spirit. The human frame.

A بديعة *badīʻat*, (fem. of بديع *badīʻ*) (pl. بدائع *badāʼiʻ*) A strange thing (often used in a neuter sense, like other feminines of Arabic adjectives).

P بديل *badīl*, Name of a celebrated king.

A بديل *badīl*, (pl. ابدال *abdāl*) A substitute. A good, just, religious man.

P بديمن *bad-yumn*, Ominous, inauspicious.

P بدين *badīn*, To, in, or with this. بدين گونه *ba dīn gūna*, In this manner.

A بدين *badīn*, (pl. بدن *budun* and بدّن *buddan*) Corpulent, fat, lusty (man or woman).

P بديه *badya*, A wine-butt. *Bidya*, Desire.

A بديها *badīhan*, Extempore, suddenly.

A بديهة *badīhat*, Any thing said or done inconsiderately, without regard to time or place. The first of any thing. A turn to begin. An unexpected event. A sally or fancy. An impromptu. Extempore. اجاب علي البديهة *ajāba ʻala'l badīhat*, He replied extempore. P ببديهه گفتن *ba badīha guftan*, To speak extempore.

A بديهيّ *badīhīy*, (fem. بديهيّة *badīhīyat*) Extempore, unpremeditated. بديهيّ الظهور *badīhīyu'z zuhūr*, Happening unexpectedly or suddenly.

P بديهي گفتن *badīhī guftan*, To speak extempore.

A بديهيّات *badīhīyāt*, Unlooked-for accidents.

A بديئة *badīʼat*, A beginning, a turn to begin, the first turn. See بديهة *badīhat*.

A بذّ *bazza*, (fut. يبذّ *yabuzzu*) He conquered.

A بذّ *bazz*, (v. n. of بذّ) Conquering. Victory, conquest. Old, worn, torn. Squalid. Scattered (dates). Alike, equal. فذّ بذّ *fazz bazz*, Odd, single, uneven. البذّ *al bazz*, Name of a country between Irān (Persia) and Azarbayjān (Media).

A بذء *bazʼ*, (v. n. of بذأ) Despising, treating with contempt. Observing something in the conduct of another which is deserving of detestation. Finding fault with the pasture in any place.

A بذاء *bazāʼ*, (or بذاءة *bazāʼat*) (v. n. of بذؤ) Being impudent, immodest, obscene in conversation. *Bizāʼ*, (v. n. 3 of بذأ) Talking obscenely. Obscenity, indecency.

A بذّاخ *bazzākh*, Braying (camel) that protrudes the substance شقشقة *shikshikat* from his mouth.

A بذاخيّ *buzākhīy*, Great, large.

A بذاذ *bazāz*, (or بذاذة *bazāzat*) (v. n. of بذّ) Being in a bad state or habit. *Bizāz*, (v. n. 3 of بذّ) Pressing on, preventing, pre-occupying.

A بذاذة *bazāzat*, A bad habit or condition. Deformity, filth, nastiness.

A بذاذيك *bazāzayka*, Hold off! Keep back!

A بذار *bizār*, (pl. of بذر *bazr*) Seedlings.

A بذارة *bazārat*, A becoming a babbler of secrets.

A بذّارة *bazārrat*, (or بذارة *bazārat*) A squandering of money. *Buzārat*, Offspring, progeny. Increase, abundance.

A بذامة *bazāmat*, (v. n. of بذم) Being strong.

P بذبار *bazbār*, A mimic, buffoon, jester.

A بذة *bizzat*, A portion.

A بذج *bazaj*, (pl. بذجان *bizjān*) A lamb weaned and able to eat grass.

A بذح *bazh*, (v. n. of بذح) Slitting the tongue (of a young animal) to wean it. Stripping the skin from the flesh. Giving. (pl. بذوح *buzūh*) The place of a fissure. *Bizh*, A gash in the hand. *Bazah*, An excoriation of the thighs.

A بذخ *bizkh* or *bazikh*, Braying (camel) that protrudes the substance شقشقة *shikshikat* from his mouth. *Bazakh*, (v. n. of بذخ) Being proud. Pride. *Bizikh bizikh*, Bravo! well done!

A بذذ *bazaz*, (v. n. of بذّ) Being in a bad state.

A بذر *bazara*, (fut. يبذر *yabzuru*) He sowed.

A بذر *bazr*, (v. n. of بذر) Coming forth, appearing (a seedling). Sowing seed, disseminating, scattering. Disclosing a secret. Squandering money. Seed-corn. Offspring, progeny. (pl. بذور *buzūr* and بذار *bizār*) A seedling. Flax or pot-herb seed. بذر الكتّان *bazru'l kattān*, Lint-seed. *Bazir*, A sower. A winnower. A chatterer, a babbler. Plenteous, abundant (food for entertainment) *Buzur*, (pl. of بذور *bazūr*) Blabbers, tell-tales. شذر بذر *shazara bazara* or *shizara bizara*, Here and there, everywhere, on all sides.

P بذرام *bazrām*, A delightsome place.

A بذرة *bazrat*, A seed. A child, a son.

P بذرفتن *bizruftan*, To accept, be pleased with.

A بذرق *bazrah*, Contemptible, abject (man).

A بذرقة *bazrakat*, (v. n. of بذرق Q) Being a guide, escort. Extreme bashfulness. A guide, escort.

P بذرگر *bazirgar*, A farmer, ploughman, sower.

P بذرگري *bazirgarī*, Husbandry, agriculture.

A بذروج *bazrūj*, Basil-royal, ocymum.

P بذره *bazra*, A talent.

A بذرّي *buzurra'*, Vain, idle. Prodigal, lavish.

P بذست *bizist*, (or بذشت *bizisht*) A span.

A بذع *bazʻ*, (v. n. of بذع) Frightening, terrifying. Dropping water (a jar). Emanation, a dropping. *Bazaʻ*, Terror.

A بذق *bazk*, (pl. بذوق *buzūk*) A guide through unknown roads. Small, slight.

A بذقطة *bazkatat*, A wasting of time or of talk.

A بذل *bazl*, (v. n. of بذل) Giving liberally. A gift, a present. Expense. A pace which a horse reserves against a time of need. P بذل سيمين *bazli sīmīn*, Excessive liberality. بذل كردن *bazl kardan*, To present. To expend. To put forth.— In construction it implies, sometimes, Study, endeavour, care, attention: as, P بذل همّت كردن *bazli himmat kardan*, (also بذل مقدور و سعي موفور دادن *bazli makdūr u saʻyi mawfūr dādan*) To employ every endeavour, use all diligence, make it the whole study, bestow every care or attention.

A بذلاخ *bazlākh*, A promiser, but not performer. *Bizlākh*, (v. n. of بذلخ Q) Promising, but not doing.

A بذلة *bizlat*, A garment for daily use, of which no care is taken.

A بذلخة *bazlakhat*, (v. n. of بذلخ Q) Promising, but not performing.

P بذله *bazla*, The recital of a poem in a cadence. A joke, jest, pleasantry, raillery, witticism, bon-mot, any thing pleasant and entertaining.

P بذله باز *bazla-bāz*, A buffoon, jester; witty.

P بذله پوش *bizla-posh*, Clad in an every-day garment.

P بذله گوي *bazla-goy*, A jester, a droll: jocular.

A بذم *bazuma*, (fut. يبذم *yabzumu*) He had his wits about him, and was in full possession of himself (though in a passion).

A بذم *buzm*, Intellect, understanding: soul, spirit. Toleration, patience. Power, strength. Skin, hide. Fatness, fleshiness. Thickness, substance (of cloth).

A بذو *bazw*, (v. n. of بذو) Being obscene.

A بذوح *buzūh*, (pl. of بذح *bazh*) Fissures, cracks.

A بذوذة *buzūzat*, (v. n. of بذ) Being in a bad state. A miserable condition. Filthiness, squalor.

A بذور *bazūr*, Much, many. A calumniator, an accuser. One who cannot keep a secret. *Buzūr*, (pl. of بذر *bazr*) Sprouts, germs, buds. Seeds.

A بذوق *buzūk*, (pl. of بذق *bazk*) Road-guides. Small, slight.

A بذول *bazūl*, Liberal, munificent. A giver.

P بذه *bazh*, A lie, fiction, falsehood. *Biza* or *buza*, A barren tree, used only as fire-wood.

A بذي *baziy*, Obscene, immodest (in conversation). Destitute or scarce of fodder or provision.

A بذئة *bazi*ء*at*, Immodest (woman).

A بذية *baziyat*, Shameless, obscene (woman).

A بذيذ *bazīz*, Alike, equal.

A بذيذة *bazīzat*, A portion. Scanty fare and coarse clothing. Conquest, victory.

A بذير *bazīr*, A calumniator, accuser. Unable to keep a secret. كثير بذير *kasīr bazīr*, Much.

A بذيم *bazīm*, Strong. Stinking (mouth). In full possession of one's faculties, although in a passion.

A بذيمة *bazīmat*, In full possession of one's wits, though in a passion. Name of a man.

P بذيون *bazyūn*, A costly garment of silk.

A بذيئة *bazī*ء*at*, Destitute of pasture (land).

P بر *bar*, On. Up. Upon. In. Into. At. Forth. With. Back. Away. Against. Near. Before. According to. On account of. When placed before a number of words, it either changes or strengthens the sense, as will appear from the following examples, and from many others which will be found in their proper alphabetical places. Prefixed to a verb it is often redundant. برحسب *bar hasb*, According to. برسيد *bar rasīd*, It has happened. He has taken it, he understands it. برسبيل تواضع *bar sabīli tawāẓuع*, In humility, by way of submission. برصحت شدن *bar sihhat shudan*, To be in health. برطرف *bar taraf*, Apart. برطرف كردن *bar taraf kardan*, To put away, remove, lay aside. برقرار *bar karār*, Firm, solid, immoveable. برقرار سابق *bar karāri sābik*, In pristine vigour, (restored) to former strength. بركشيد *bar kashīd*, He proceeded, advanced, surpassed, excelled. برگرفت *bar girift*, He took, received, accepted. برمنوال مشروح *bar minwāli mashrūh*, In the manner above-mentioned. بر موجب فرمان شاهي *bar mūjibi farmāni shāhī*, According to the commands of the king. بروجه *bar wajhi*, In the manner of. برحق *bari hak*, Near to God, in the sight of God. (When بر *bar* signifies Near, it then takes كسره *kasra*).

P بر *bar*, Height, top, summit. A continent, earth, globe. An arid desert. A burden, a load. Fruit. Profit, advantage. Pulse. Seed. The bosom, breast, embrace, armpit or lap. The cheek-bone. Memory, recollection. Preservation, custody. A palace. A door. Lot, portion. Breadth. A side, part. A kind of tree, the Indian fig. A young woman. A bird. برعربستان *bari ع arabistān*, The desert of Arabia. برگ و بر *barg u bar*, Leaves and fruit. سمن بر *saman-bar*, Jasmine-bosomed. (for برگ *barg*) A leaf.

P بر *bar*, (contracted participle of بردن *burdan*, To bear) Seizing, carrying off. A porter, carrier. دل بر *dil-bar*, A ravisher of hearts. نامه بر *nāma-bar*, A letter-carrier. *Bur*, (contracted participle of بريدن *burīdan*) Cutting. ناخن بر *nākhun-bur*, Scissors for paring the nails.

A برّ *barr*, (v. n. of برّ) Overcoming, prevailing against in word and deed. (pl. بررة *bararat* and ابرار *abrār*) Good, beneficent. Just, equitable, true, righteous. Pious towards God; dutiful to parents; affectionate to children. Truth in an oath. God. The continent, earth, globe. A desert, a large uncultivated barren plain. Sylvan, wild, desert. بحر و برّ *bahr u barr*, Sea and land. بحرًا و برًّا *bahran wa barran*, By sea and land. عسل البرّ ع*asalu'l barr*, Wild honey. P برّ بيابان *barri biyābān*, An extensive desert. A *Birr*, Piety, reciprocal affection between parents and children, demonstrations of love and obedience. Extensive kindness, expansive benevolence. A gift. Goodness, innocence. Truth, sincerity. Truth in an oath. A fox's cub. A female mouse. A kind of field-mouse. Pilgrimage to Mecca. A driving of camels. The heart. Paradise. The driving of sheep, or the calling of them to pasture. The bleating of sheep. لا يعرف هرًّا من برّ *lā ya*ع*rafu hirran mim birrin*, He knows not a foe from a friend, or a kitten from a mouse; or calling sheep from driving them, &c. برّ احسان *barri ihsān*, (or برّ و احسان *barr u ihsān*) Beneficence, the bestowment of favours, the making of contributions. *Birr* or *burr*, (v. n. of برّ) Being accepted by God (a pilgrimage). Accepting a pilgrimage (God). Observing truth and fidelity in an oath. *Burr*, (pl. ابرار *abrār*) Wheat.

A برء *bar*ء, (v. n. of برأ) Creating. (v. n. of بروّ or برئ) Being free, safe, out of danger. *Bur*ء, (v. n. of بروّ and برئ) Being free, safe, out of danger. Recovering from illness, being cured of a wound. A cure. برء الساعة *bur*ء*u's sā*ع*at*, An immediate cure, the cure of an hour.

A برأ *bara*ء*a*, (fut. يبرأ *yabra*ء*u*) He created.

A برا *bara'*, (fut. يبرو *yabrū*) He created.

P برا *barā*, A sort of savoury dish made of minced meat and spices. (for براي *barāy*) For, on account of.

A برأ *bura*ء, (pl. of برأة *bura*ء*at*) Lurking-places in which the hunter waits for his prey.

A برًّا *barran*, Without, out of doors.

P برّا *burrā* or *burā*, Acute, sharp, cutting.

A براء *bura*ء*ā*ء, (pl. of برئ *barī*ء) Free, clear. Discharged, absolved.

A براء *barā*ء, (v. n. of برأ) Being free, clear, exempt. (wanting fem. dual and plural) Free, clear, exempt. The first or last day or night of a lunar month. A proper name. *Birā*ء or *burā*ء, (pl. of برئ *barī*ء) Free, clear, quit, absolved. Healed, cured. *Burū*ء, (sing.) Free, clear. (pl. of براية *burāyat*) Chips, laths, shavings, scrapings. Nail-parings.

A برّاء *barrā*ء, An arrow-maker, one who chips and fashions arrows.

A براءة *barā*ء*at*, (v. n. of برأ) Being free (from faults or crimes). Recovering health. Innocence. براءت تام *barā*ء*ati tām*, Perfect health. براءة ذمّة *barā*ء*atu zimmatin*, Acquittance of obligation, discharge of debt or dues. يمين البراءة *yamīnu'l barā*ء*at*, An oath of excommunication, or renunciation of the divine protection and favour (Rom. ix. 3).

P برآب *bar āb*, On the water. A field sown and watered. برآب آمدن *bar āb āmadan*, To become divulged. برآب فلان *bar ābi fulān*, After the manner of so and so. برآب گفتن *bar āb guftan*, To speak fast. To repartee.

A برابخ *barābikh*, (pl. of بربخ *barbakh*) Earthen pipes for conveying water; sewers of earthen pipes.

P برابر *bar-ā-bar*, (Breast-to-breast) Equal, alike, on a par. Plain, even, level, smooth. Uniform. Accurate, exact. Equally, in the same manner. Abreast, opposite, over against. برابر كردن *bar-ā-bar kardan*, To level. To oppose. زمين برابر كردن *zamīn bar-ā-bar kardan*, To level with the ground.

A برابر *barābir*, (or برابرة *barābirat*) Natives of Barbary or Western Africa. Barbarians, Africans.

P برابران *barābarān*, Name of a medicinal herb.

P برابري *bar-ā-barī*, An equality. برابري كردن *bar-ā-barī kardan*, To contend, to oppose one's self to another, to dispute for equality.

A برابط *barābit*, (pl. of بربط) Harps, lutes.

A برابير *barābīr*, A kind of dish made of old wheat (newly taken from the ears) and milk.

A براة *barāt*, A knife for fashioning bows.

A برأة *bur*ء*at*, (pl. برأ *bura*ء) The lurking-place of a hunter waiting for game.

P برات *barāt*, (or A ليلة البرات *laylatu'l barāt*) A night in the eighth month, *Sha*ع*bān*, consecrated to the memory of forefathers. Weariness, disgust.

A برات *barāt*, A letter, epistle. A royal diploma,

brevet, commission, patent, or privilege. An assignment, a draft. برات سلطان *barāti sultān*, برات عاليشان *barāti ʿālī-shān*, or P برات همايون *barāti hamāyūn*, Royal, imperial, or august diplomas, letters, or privileges. برات بر شاخ آهو *barāt bar shākhi āhū*, Vain promises, lies (a draft on Whitechapel-pump). *Burāt*, (pl. of برة *burat*) Rings worn on the ankles.

A برّات *barrāt* or *birrāt*, (pl. of برّ) Good works.

P برات دار *barāt-dār*, One who holds an assignment, privileged. A patentee.

A براتك *barātik*, Little hills.

P براتي *barātī*, A worn-out garment. Relations who conduct the bridegroom to the bride's house.

A براث *birās*, (pl. of برث) Soft, level grounds.

A براثن *barāsin*, (pl. of برثن *bursun*) The soft parts under the claws of birds or beasts. Claws.

A براثي *barāsī*, The sabine plant.

A برّاج *barrāj*, Belonging to tower or dove-cot. برّاج الحمام *barrāju'l hamām*, A carrier-pigeon.

A براجد *barājid*, (pl. of برجد *burjud*) Garments of thick, hairy, shaggy stuff.

A براجم *barājim*, (pl. of برجمة *burjumat*) Joints of the fingers. The middle talons of a bird. Knuckles of clenched fists.

P براجيل *barājīl*, Parsley.

A براح *barāh*, (v. n. of برح) Ending, desisting, ceasing, terminating. Receding, deserting, flying. Going into an uncultivated country. A wide-extended desert. A woman's name. حبيل براح *habīl barāh*, A bold man. A lion. لا براح *la barāha* or *hu*, Firmly. Unceasingly, continually, without end. جاءنا بالامر براحا *jāʾanā bi'l amri barāhan*, He explained to us the matter clearly. رأي براح *raʾyun barāhun*, Wicked counsel. *Birāh*, The sun.

A براد *burād*, (v. n. of برد) Being blunt, dull (a sword). Being weak and languid. Sending a messenger (بريد *barīd*). Cold (water).

P براداندر *birād andar*, A half-brother.

A برادة *burādat*, Filings, scrapings, saw-dust. Chips. Rust.

A برّادة *barrādat*, A vessel for cooling water, a refrigerator: a narrow-necked goblet used for that purpose. A place for drinking water.

P برادر *birādar*, A brother. برادر اندر *birādar andar*, A half-brother. برادر پدر *birādari pidar*, A father's brother, an uncle. برادر حقيقي *birādari hakīkī*, Own brother, full brother. برادر خورد *birādari khwurd*, A younger brother, a cadet. برادر رضاعي *birādari rizāʿī*, A foster-brother. برادر زن *birādari zan*, A wife's brother, a brother-in-law. برادر شوهر *birādari shawhar*, A husband's brother. برادران دين *birādarāni dīn*, Brothers in the faith, religious fraternities.

P برادرانه *birādarāna*, Brotherly, like a brother.

P برادرپرور *birādar-parwar*, Kind to brethren.

P برادر خواندگي *birādar-khwāndagī*, A calling of one's self a brother, fraternization.

P برادر خوانده *birādar-khwānda*, An adopted brother.

P برادرزاده *birādar-zāda*, Brother's son, nephew.

P برادر كهتر *birādar-kihtar*, A younger brother.

P برادر مادر *birādar-mādar*, Maternal uncle.

P برادر مهتر *birādar-mihtar*, An elder brother.

P برادرنده *birādaranda*, A half-brother.

P برادر نسبت *birādar-nisbat*, A brother-in-law.

P برادري *birādarī*, Brotherhood, the fraternal relation. Relationship. برادري كردن *birādarī kardan*, To enter into a fraternity. To exercise or show brotherly love, to fraternize.

P برادر *birāzar*, A brother.

A برادع *barāziʿ*, (pl. of برذعة *barzaʿat*,) Woollen saddle-cloths.

A براذين *barāzīn*, (pl. of برذون *birzawn*) Beasts for burden or for the saddle (implying especially the slow and sluggish).

P برآر *bar ār*, Peace, concord. (part. of برآوردن *bar āwardan*) One who carries off, draws out, ravishes, bears away, raises up. An extractor, bearer, elevator. One who receives favourably. An approver, accepter, supporter.

P برار *barār*, A province in the Dak'han (India).

A برارث *barāris*, (pl. of برث *bars*) Soft, smooth, level grounds.

P برآرنده *bar āranda*, An extractor, bearer. A receiver. An approver, accepter.

A براري *barārī*, (and برارِيت *barārīt*) (pl. of بَرِّيَّة *barrīyat* and بَرِّيت *barrīt*) Deserts.

P برآريدن *bar ārīdan*, To spread branches.

P براربر *barārir*, (or برار يز *barārīz*) The year before last.

P براز *barāz*, Joining, fastening, glueing. A patch. Beauty, grace, elegance, ornament, decoration. A shoemaker or carpenter's wedge. Well then! despatch! finish! An axis. A goad. Plough-gear.

A براز *barāz*, An extensive open plain. براز الروز *barāzu'r rawz*, Name of a طسوج *tassūj*, (a sort of weight) current in Baghdad. *Birāz*, (v. n. 3 of برز) Fighting (especially single combat, in an amphitheatre or other place). Human excrement (a more decent word than غائط *ghāʾit*).

P برازبان *birāzbān*, That part of a knife or dirk which enters into the handle; the shank.

A برازة *barāzat*, (v. n. of برز) Becoming clever, skilful, adroit.

A برازخ *barāzikh*, (pl. of برزخ *barzakh*) Impediments, bars. برازخ الايمان *barāzikhu'l īmān*, That which lies between the beginning and end of faith, debatable ground between doubt and belief.

P برازد *barāzad*, Convenient, fit, proper, suitable, elegant, graceful, beautiful. Good manners. Ornament, decoration. It agrees, suits, accords. *Birāzad*, A brother, friend, or companion.

P برازده *barāzda*, A mass of leaven.

P برازر *birāzar*, A brother. Goodness. Elegance.

P برازش *barāzish*, Decoration. A patching.

A برازق *barāzik*, (also برازيق *barāzīk*) (pl. of برزيق *birzīk*) Crowds, bodies, fraternities. Troops of horses. Horsemen. By-paths.

P برازندگي *barāzandagī*, Decoration.

P برازوان *birāzwān*, That part of a knife or dirk which enters into the handle, the shank.

P برازيدن *barāzīdan*, To act with propriety, behave with decency, proceed in conformity to. To appear beautiful and elegant. To join, unite. To coincide, quadrate. To deserve. To decorate.

A براساء *barāsāʾ*, A body of men.

P (راه) براستا (*rāh*) *barāstā*, A skilful guide.

P برآسودن *bar āsūdan*, To rest. To give rest.

P براش *barāsh*, A quenching. A stilling. A scratch, a wound. A sprinkling, a scattering.

P برآشفتگي *bar āshuftagī*, Excitement.

A براشم *burāshim*, Clear-sighted.

A براشن *burāshin*, One who gazes intently.

P براشيدن *barāshīdan*, To quell. To ask.

A براص *birās*, (pl. of برصة *bursat*) The habitations of demons. Sandy deserts without herbage.

A براض *birāz*, (pl. of برض *barz*) Few, little. *Burāz*, A little. Scarcity of water.

A برّاض *barrāz*, Name of a noted robber. One who has squandered away all his substance.

A براطم *burātim*, Thick-lipped.

A براطيل *barātīl*, Bribes. Long stones.

A براعة *barāʿat*, (v. n. of برع) Excelling. Being perfect in virtue and beauty. Excellence, pre-eminence. براعت استهلال *barāʿati istihlāl*, The meeting of several synonymous words in a sentence.

A براعث *barāʿis*, (pl. of برعث *burʿus*) Podices.

A براعيم *barāʿīm*, Summits of mountains. Name of a place. (pl. of برعوم *burʿūm*) Buds. Pods.

A برّاغ *barrāgh*, A phlebotomist, a bleeder.

P براغاليدن *barāghālīdan*, (or براغليدن *barāghalīdan*) To instigate, stimulate, stir up. To put to flight, chase, cause to run. To extract, pluck up.

A براغيث *barāghīs*, (pl. of برغوث) Fleas.

A براغيس *barāghīs*, Noble, high-bred animals.

A براغيل *barāghīl*, (pl. of برغيل *birghīl*) Districts situate near to water, or lying between an inhabited country and a desert.

P برافتادن *bar uftādan*, To dwindle, die away.

P برافراشتن *bar afrāshtan*, To exalt, erect, raise.

P برافروختن *bar afrokhtan*, To kindle, light up.

P برافروخته *bar afrokhta*, Inflamed, fired, lit up.

P برافرود *bar afrod*, Topsy-turvy, pell-mell.

P برافروسيدن *bar afrosīdan*, To excite desire. To walk with a fastidious, pompous air. To abuse one by menacing actions or opprobrious words.

P برافژوليدن *bar afzhūlīdan*, To incite, to stir up. To extract. To pluck out. To throw away.

P برافشاندن دست *bar afshāndani dast*, Dancing (literally, waving the hands).

P برافگندن *bar afgandan,* To throw up. To remove. To send.

A براق *burāk,* (or البراق *al burāk*) The celebrated animal smaller than a mule and bigger than an ass in the Kur'ān, upon which Muhammad is said to have gone from Jerusalem to heaven. He is likewise called براق سعادت مساق *burāki saʿādat-masāk,* The ass of the fortunate impulse.

P براق برق تاز *burāki bark-tāz,* A steed fleet as lightning. براق جم *burāki jam,* The wind which wafted Solomon's throne from place to place. براق چهارم فلك *burāki chahārum falak,* The sun. The seventh heaven. سمند براق رفتار *sumandi burāk-raftār,* A steed swift as البراق *al burāk.*

A برّاق *barrāk,* Flashing, glittering, bright.

A برّاقة *barrākat,* Handsome, brilliant (woman).

A براقش *barākish,* Name of a bitch. ابو براقش *abū burākish,* Name of a changing-coloured bird.

A برّاقية *barrākiyat,* Splendour, brilliancy.

A براك *birāk,* (v. n. 3 of برك) Pronouncing a blessing. (pl. of برك *burk*) A species of the sword-fish.

A براكاء *barākāʼ,* (pl. براكئ *barāʼik*) Firmness, stedfastness in battle. A kneeling down.

A براك براك *barāki barāki,* Courage! courage! (an animating ejaculation to one another in battle).

P براكوه *barākūh,* A mountain in Farghūna.

A براكية *burākiyat,* A kind of ship.

P براكنده *barāganda,* (or براكند) A bribe to corrupt a judge, a present, gift, offering, donation.

A برألة *barʼalat,* (v. n. of برأل Q) Swelling the feathers of his neck (a game-cock going to fight).

A برام *birām,* (pl. of برمة *burmat*) Stone kettles. *Burām,* (pl. ابرمة *abrimat*) A tike.

P براماهيدن *bar āmāhīdan,* (also برامهيدن *barāmahīdan* or براماسيدن *bar āmāsīdan*) To swell, to blow up (as dough).

P برآمد *bar āmad,* A rising or coming up. Issue. Expenditure, outgoings. Informing (more particularly of bribery), accusation, impeachment. برآمد كار *bar āmadi kār,* The execution of any business.

P برآمدگي *bar āmadagī,* A projection, rising, or swelling. A setting in, an overspreading of darkess.

P برآمدن *bar āmadan,* To ascend, arise, come forth, appear, emerge, grow out. To surprise, to come suddenly and unexpectedly. To succeed in one's wishes, to triumph, overcome. To result. To honour, exalt, magnify. To pass through. To be disgusted or tired out. To be replete.

P برآمده *bar āmada,* Prominent. A balcony.

A برامكة *barāmikat,* (pl. of برمكي *barmakiy*) Barmecides, persons of the family of Barmak.

P برآن *bar ān,* Upon that. برآن شدن *bar ān shudan,* To agree upon. To will, desire, intend.

P بران *birān,* Passing, past.

P برّان *burrān,* Sharp, cutting. تيغ برّان *teghi burrān,* A sharp sword.

P برانداختن *bar andākhtan,* To throw out or down. To scatter, throw about, discomfit, defeat. To break an engagement, to rescind a purchase or sale.

P برانداف *burandāf,* Intestines.

P براندن *burāndan,* To lose at play.

P برّاندن *burrāndan,* To be sharp and cutting.

A برانس *barānis,* (pl. of برنس *burnus*) Caps, hats.

P برانغار و جوانغار *baranghār u juwanghār,* The right and left wings of an army.

A برانك *barānik,* (pl. of برنكان *barnakān*) Black gowns, barracanes.

P برانگار *barangār,* The right hand.

P برانگيختگي *bar angekhtagī,* Instigation.

P برانگيختن *bar angekhtan,* To raise or pull up, tear out, draw forth, eradicate. To excite, stir up, rouse, awake. To cause to happen. To learn, know.

P برآنند *bar ān and,* On that they are agreed.

P برانه *barāna,* Name of a city.

P براني *barānī,* A glass or earthen vessel in which flowers, sugar, confections, or medicines are kept.

A براني *barāniy,* (pl. of برنية *barnīyat*) Vessels of earthenware. Young cocks.

A برّاني *barrāniy,* Outer. Native of Barrānīyat.

P برانيدن *burānīdan,* To kiss or be kissed. To go away. To agree. To put to flight.

P براو *barāv,* A sweeper of the streets, a dustman.

P برآور *bar-āwar,* Fruit-bearing (tree). Fruitful.

P برآورد *bar āward,* An estimate, calculation. A specimen. A citadel. برآورد كردن *bar āward kardan,* To strike out (a muster-roll). To calculate, estimate, carry to account.

P برآوردگي *bar āwardagī,* A bringing forth.

P برآوردن *bar āwardan,* To bring up. To draw out, bring forth, pluck, pull, or tear up. To draw (a breath). To elevate, raise up, erect, build. To repair, restore, correct, accomplish, bring to perfection. To relieve (indigence or necessity). To close, to fill up. To breed (teeth or horses). To produce, to bear. To accept, receive favourably. To insert. To break the peace. To represent. To counterfeit, feign, imitate, mimick.

P برآورده *bar āwarda,* Brought up or forth. Built, constructed, erected. Mimicked, imitated, counterfeited. Taken up (in the arms). Raised to honours. Invested with authority. A raised building. A rampart. A fortress. Deducted or stopped. Produced, alleged. Separated. Given. Heard, accepted. Completed, finished. Accustomed to any thing. برآوردهٔ زبان كردن *bar āwardaʼi zabān kardan,* To speak, utter, pronounce

P برآويختن *bar āwekhtan,* To suspend, hang up.

P براه *ba rāh,* To the way, by the way. Ornament, beauty, elegance. Adorned. Beautiful. Good. Goodness. براه كردن *ba rāh kardan,* To dismiss, send away, despatch. To depart, set out, begin, or proceed on a journey.

P براهام *barāhām,* Name of a notorious miser.

P برآهيختن *bar āhikhtan,* (also برآهيختن *bar āhekhtan,* To unsheath, to draw (a sword).

A براهم *barāhim,* براه *barāh,* or براهيم *barāhīm* (pl. of ابراهيم *ibrāhīm*) Abrahams.

A براهمة *barāhimat,* (pl. of براهمن *barāhman*) Brāhmans. (pl. of ابرهيم *ibrāhīm*) Abrahams.

P برآهنجيدن *bar āhanjīdan,* To draw, lead out.

P براهيدن *barāhīdan,* To send. To travel.

A براهين *barāhīn,* (pl. of برهان *burhān*) Proofs.

P براي *barāy,* For, because, on account of. In respect of, for the sake of. براي ادب *barāyi adab,* By way of civility. براي آن *barāyi ān,* For that. براي آنكه *barāyi ānki,* Because that. براي او *barāyi u,* On his account, for him. براي اين *barāyi īn,* For this. براي چه كار *barāyi chi kār,* On what account? براي ضبط اطراف *barāyi zabti atrāf,* In order to overawe the neighbourhood. براي قرابت *barāyi karābat,* For the sake of the relationship. براي كار دربار *barāyi kāri darbār,* On the business of the Durbār.

A برايا *barāyaʼ,* (pl. of بريئة *bariʼat*) Free, clear, absolved (women). (pl. of بريّة *barīyat*) Creatures. People, men. Patricians, nobles. Vassals. خالق البرايا *khāliku'l barāyaʼ,* The Creator of men.

A براية *burāyat,* (pl. براء *burāʼ*) A chip, a shaving. Nail-pairings. Fat, flesh. Capability of enduring a long journey.

A برائق *barāʼik,* (pl. of بريقة *barīkat*) Milks into which a little butter or fat has been poured.

A برائك *barāʼik,* (pl. of بركان *barkān*) Black robes or garments of a particular fashion.

A برائل *burāʼil,* (or برائلى *burāʼilaʼ*) The smaller feathers (called hackles) in the neck of a bird, particularly in that of a cock or the crest of a bustard. ابو برائل *abū burāʼil,* A cock. برائل الارض *burāʼilu'l arz,* (Feathers of the earth) Plants.

A برائلي *burāʼiliy,* (or برائلى *burāʼila'*) A cock.

P برايه *barāya,* (or براي) A pretext, cause, reason.

A بربّ العباد *bi rabbi'l ʼibād,* By the lord of servants! by God! (as in the conclusion of letters). باقي هميشه عزت باد بربّ العباد *bāki hamīsha ʼizzat bād bi rabbi'l ʼibād,* With regard to the rest, may your highness remain for ever, by God (or which God grant)!

P برباد *bar bād,* To the wind. Destroyed, overthrown, laid waste. برباد بودن *bar bād būdan,* To be undone. برباد داده *bar bād dāda,* Given to the wind, ruined. برباد رفتن *bar bād raftan,* To be dispersed. برباد ساختن *bar bād sākhtan,* To destroy.

P بربار *barbār,* (or بربارہ) An upper chamber.

A بربار *barbār,* Murmuring, angry. Noisy, clamorous. Noisy, creaking (bucket). A lion.

P برباران *bar bārān,* Fields sown in time of rain.

P بربارہ *barbāra,* A private entrance to a house.

A برباريس *barbārīs,* The barberry-tree.

A برباس *birbās,* A deep well.

L برباشك *barbāshk,* (Verbascum) Mullein.

B بربال *birbāl,* Coral.

P بر بالاي پاردم گوزيدن bar bālāyi pārdum gūzīdan, To boast. To attempt above one's strength.

A بربخ barbakh, (pl. برابخ) A large sewer made of earthen pipes. An earthen pipe for carrying water.

P بربد barbad, Name of a country called Sīstān.

P بربر bar bar, Upon. Above. Besides. Upon the breast. Barbar, A barber. A surgeon. Foolish, prating, quarrelsome. بربر سر barbari sar, A shaver of the head.

A بربر barbar, (or البربر al barbar) (pl. برابرة barābirat) The people of Barbary. Birbir, A word for calling sheep. Burbur, Noisy, clamorous.

A بربرة barbarat, (v. n. of بربر Q) Talking much, shouting. The bleating of a goat. Sounds, clamours, mixed noises. Birbirat, A call to sheep. Burburat, One who makes many noises.

P بربر خانه barbar-khāna, A barber's shop.

P بربردن bar burdan, To appear, rise (the sun).

A بربسة barbasat, A seeking, inquiring, searching.

P بربرستان barbaristān, Barbary.

P بربري barbarī, A barberry.

T بربريس barbarīs, A gooseberry, or the tree.

A بربريّة barbariya, Barbary in Africa.

P بربست bar bast, (pl. بربستگان bar bastagān) Usage, established custom.

P بربستن bar bastan, To shut or fasten up. To be shut up by frost. To freeze. To prepare.

P بربسته bar basta, Shut up. Frozen, congealed. Incapable of growth, inorganic.

A بربصة barbasat, An irrigating copiously.

P بربط barbat, A harp or lute. بربط زن barbat-zan, A player upon the lute. بربط نواز barbat-nawāz, A harper, a lutanist.

A بربط barbat, (pl. برابط barābit) A lute.

P بربلند bar baland, Very high. An upper chamber in Eastern houses, open in the front.

P بربلندين bar balandīn, Ringlets dangling upon the forehead. Ornamental work over a doorway.

P بربند bar band, Collected. A collar. A girdle.

A بربور burbūr, Corn coarsely ground.

A بربوز barbūz, The blite (a kind of grass).

G بربوسيوس barbūsiyūs, A kind of ivy.

P بربهين barbahīn, Purslain.

A بربيطاء birbītāʼ, A plant. Name of a place celebrated for embroidery.

P برپا bar pā, Raised, fixed, established, erect. برپا بودن bar pā būdan, To stand, to be on foot. برپا خاستن bar pā khāstan, To rise upon the feet; to stand. برپا كردن bar pā kardan, To erect, set up, fix, plant, or pitch. برپاي خاك زدن bar pāyi khāk zadan, To hold in contempt, to degrade or render contemptible. برپاي داشتن bar pāy dāshtan, To support. To be raised, pitched, or established.

P برپروشان bar paroshān, Co-religionists.

P برپژ barpaj, Heaven, firmament. Barpuj, A plum. The root of the ear. Declivity of a mountain.

P برپوز barpoz, The parts round the mouth.

P برپوس barpos, The same. Purslain.

P برپون barpūn, The itch, the scab.

P برپهن barpahan, Purslain. A throne. Flying.

P برپيچيده bar pechīda, Twisted. Shrivelled.

P برپيخته bar pekhta, Twisted together, coiled.

A برة birat, (v. n. of وبر) Abiding. Burat, (pl. برات burāt, برين burīn, birīn, and بري bura') A garter. An ankle-ring worn by the Arabian ladies. A bracelet. An ear-ring. A bridle or ring of iron, brass, or hair, running through a camel's nose.

A برّة barrat, Dutifulness, obedience. Beneficent (woman). Name of the well Zamzam. Name of the place where Cain killed Abel.

A برت bart, (v. n. of برت) Cutting. Being astonished, confounded. An axe. A guide. A section, a segment. Birt, A guide. Burt, A guide. A hatchet. Sugar-candy.

P برتاس bartās, Name of a wrestler. Name of a city on the confines of Russia: also a country in Turkistān from whence costly furs are brought.

P برتاسي bartāsī, A fur brought from Bartās.

P برتاشك bartāshk, (or برتراشك) Mugwort.

P برتافتگي bar tāftagī, Distortion.

P برتافتن bar tāftan, To twist. To turn away. To bore, pierce, perforate.

A برتة burtat, Acuteness, shrewdness, cleverness.

P برتر bartar, Higher. Cause, reason, sake.

P برترين bartarīn, Highest, most exalted.

P بر تقدير bar takdīr, On supposition.

A برتكة bartakat, (v. n. of برتك Q) Tearing. Cutting piecemeal. A mixture of falsehood with truth. Defamation.

P برتل bartal, Great, vehement, tremendous.

P برتله bartula, A gift, present. A kind of Tartar cap worn under a wreath or turban of fine linen. A wreath, bandage.

P برتميدن bartamīdan, To break out in pustules upon the lips, to have the lips chapped (after a fever). To have a pain in the abdomen from excessive heat. To have the shingles, or St. Anthony's fire. To stuff, to cram (as cotton into a sack). To rush headlong. To tumble, to fall prostrate. To throw down. To grow fat. To boil (meat).

P برتن bartan, An Arabian. A tribe. A leader.

P برتنگ bartang, The bittern. A narrow kind of cloth. Swaddling-clothes. A girth.

P برتني bartanī, A strut: haughtiness, vain-glory.

P برته barta, Name of a hero of Tūrān.

P برتهيدن bartahīdan, To throw upon the ground. To destroy, subvert, overturn, overwhelm, deface. To heap together.

P برتيبا bartībā, (in zand and Pāz.) A swallow.

A برث bars, (pl. براث birās, ابراث abrās, بروث burūs, and برارث barāris) Soft, smooth, fertile ground. A sand-hill. A skilful, intelligent guide. Baras, (v. n. of برث) Being blessed abundantly with the conveniences and comforts of life.

A برثطة barsatat, (v. n. of برثط Q) Sitting in one's house. Keeping close at home. Falling into a dangerous place. Ascending a mountain. Sitting on the hams with the knees apart.

A برثمة bursumat, Power, strength.

A برثن bursun, (pl. براثن barāsin) The soft part under the claws of birds and beasts. The hand with the fingers. A brand on a camel.

A برثنة bursunat, Power, strength.

A برثوطة bursūtat, A dangerous place.

P برج barj, A cylinder. A rolling-pin. Burj, A dove-cote. Baraj, A sweet-scented flag.

A برج burj, (pl. بروج burūj and ابراج abrāj) A tower. A star, constellation. The house or station of the moon or any other planet. A sign of the zodiac. P برج آبي burji ābī, (or A دلو dalw) Aquarius. برج آذري burji āzarī, The signs Aries, Leo, and Sagittarius. برج آسمان burji āsmān, The zodiac, the celestial signs. A برج ثريّا burji surayya', The Pleiades. (met.) The face of a mistress. برج ثور burji sawr, Taurus. P برج چهل ساله burji chihal sāla, An angel. The human understanding. A برج حمل burji hamal, The sign Aries. P برج خوشه burji khosha, The sign Virgo. برج دريدن burj darīdan, To be unveiled. برج سيم burji siyum, The sign Gemini. A برج شرف burji sharaf, A noble house. The highest degree of dignity and prosperity. برج هلال burji hilāl, The sign Cancer. Baraj, (v. n. of برج) Having the white of the eye exactly surrounding the black. Such a formation of the eye. Eating and drinking plentifully, or possessing meat and drink in abundance. (pl. ابراج abrāj) Beautiful, lovely-faced, clear.

P برجا bar jā, On the ground; prostrate, quiet. In place. Properly placed. True, accurate, right. برجا شدن bar jā shudan, To be finished, arranged. برجا كردن bar jā kardan, To observe, pay attention, arrange. عقل برجا بودن ʻakl bar jā būdan, To be in sound understanding.

A برجاء barjāʼ, (fem. of ابرج abraj) Beautiful-eyed (woman). Intensely black and white (eye).

P برجاس burjās, A butt to shoot at (especially elevated high in the air). A stone thrown into the water, in order to put it in motion and make it flow fresh from the spring. A way-side milestone.

P برجاسب burjāsb, An ancient warrior of Tūrān.

P برجاف burjāf, A species of bean.

P بر جامه bar-jāma, A rich and valuable dress.

A برجان burjān, Name of a famous robber, or gang of robbers. اسرق من برجان asraka mim burjān, More fierce or thievish than Burjān. حساب البرجان hisābu'l burjān, The sum of any number multiplied by itself, the original number being added thereto. Thus 12 is the برجان burjān of 3.

A برّجان barrajān, Name of a Sūfī commentator.

P برجان قدم نهادن bar jān kadam nihādan, (To set the foot on life) To despair of life.

P برجاي *bar jāy,* On the spot.

P برجاي ماندگي *bar jāy māndagī,* Paralysis. Ailment, lassitude. A remaining on the spot.

P برجاي مانده *bar jāy mānda,* Tired, worn down with fatigue. Paralytic.

A برجد *barjad,* Name of a man. *Burjud,* (pl. براجد) A garment of a thick, hairy, shaggy stuff.

P برجزوي *bar juzwī,* Somewhat, a little, in part.

P برجستگي *bar jastagī,* A springing or leaping upon. An eruption, a pustule.

P برجستن *bar jastan,* To leap up, to start up, to bound. To have any pustulous complaint (as the small-pox or measles). To palpitate, to beat.

P برجسته *bar jasta,* Befitting, proper, right, opportune. Salient.

A برجمة *barjamat,* Grossness of speech. *Burjumat,* (pl. براجم *barājim*) The middle joint of the finger, nearest to the first joint (which is called راجبة *rājibat,* that which is next to the hand being named اشجع *ashjaʿ,* as the strongest). A finger-joint in general. The middle talon of a bird. A knuckle of the clenched fist.

P برجوشيدگي *bar joshīdagī,* Small-pox, measles.

P برجوشيدن *bar joshīdan,* To boil up, ferment.

P برجهانيدن *bar jahānīdan,* To cause to leap.

P برجهنده *bar jahanda,* Springy, elastic.

A برجيس *birjīs,* Jupiter. A milch camel.

P برچاف *burchāf,* Pease. Beans.

P برچخ *barchakh,* A small spear of the Hindūs.

P برچدن *bar chidan,* (for برچيدن) To collect.

P بر چفسيدن *bar chafsīdan,* To clot, to felter.

P برچند *birchand,* Name of a village in Khurāsān.

P برچه *barcha,* A kind of large spear.

H برچي *barchī,* A small spear.

P برچيدن *bar chīdan,* To collect, gather, assemble. To gird up the loins, prepare, make haste. To pick, choose. To clench (a nail). دامن برچيدن *dāman bar chīdan,* To gird up one's loins.

P برچينا *bar chīnā,* Gathering. A collector.

P برچيندن *barchīndan,* (or برچينيدن *barchīnīdan*) To gather, collect.

P برچين گاه *barchīn-gāh,* A seat, a chair.

A برح *barh,* (v. n. of برح) Being angry. Affliction, calamity, distress, evil. برح بارح *barhun bārihun,* A sore calamity. ابن برح *ibn barh,* (pl. بنو برح *banū barh*) or بنت برح *bint barh,* (pl. بنات برح *banāt barh*) Trouble, calamity. *Barah,* (v. n. of برح) Becoming clear, evident, manifest. *Birah,* A distressing affair. *Burah,* (pl. of برحة *burhat*) Excellent she-camels.

A برحة *burhat,* (pl. برح) An excellent she-camel.

A برحاء *burahāʾ,* Paroxysm of a fever. Grief.

P برحسب *bar hasbi,* According to.

P برحق *bar hak,* In truth, indeed, forsooth.

A برحي *barhaʾ,* An interjection or exclamation, used when one misses the mark (as مرحي *marhaʾ* is employed when the shot takes place, or when any favourite point is gained).

A برحين *barhayn, birhayn,* or *burhayn,* Difficulties. Afflictions.

P برخ *barkh,* A little, somewhat, some, a few. A lot, portion. A house, edifice, parlour, dining-room, or open apartment at the top of Eastern houses. A cavern, a subterraneous habitation, den. A cistern. Conveniency. Household furniture. Lightning. A fish. A spark. *Barkh* or *burkh,* Dew.

A برخ *barkh,* Increase, growth, abundance. A low price put upon provisions or other goods (by edict of a magistrate). Power, authority, dominion. Slenderness, or weakness, or a breaking of the neck or back. A blow with a sword which cuts away part of the flesh.

P برخاج *barkhāj,* A spindle, a whirl.

P برخار *bar khār,* Ascent, elevation.

P برخاست *bar khāst,* Adjournment. Recal.

P برخاستگي *bar khāstagī,* A rising up, uprising.

P برخاستن *bar khāstan,* To rise, to arise. To rise against, make an insurrection. To stand, to become erect. To stir up, rouse, instigate, excite. To enkindle. To stand still, stop, desist. To break up (as an assembly). To grow, increase.

P برخاست نامه *barkhāst-nāma,* Order of recal.

P برخاسته *barkhāsta,* Raised. برخاسته شدن *bar khāsta shudan,* To be raised. To become loud (as the clamour of a mob).

A برخاش *birkhāsh,* Confusion.

P برخان *barkhān,* Clamour. Name of a country.

P برخچ *barkhach* or *barakhch,* Deformed, ugly.

A برخداة *burakhdāt,* A delicate, succulent woman.

P برخش *barakhsh,* Back of a beast of burden.

P برخفچ *barkhafch,* (or برخفنج) The night-mare.

P برخفچي *barkhafchī,* Litigation, emulation.

P برخ كردن *barkh kardan,* To create.

P برخلاف *bar khilāf,* Contrary, opposite.

P برخلد سر كردن *bar khuld sar kardan,* To obtain immortality.

P برخنجو *barkhanjū,* A granary, storehouse. A pruning. Joy, shouts of triumph, exultation.

P برخوابه *bar khwāba,* A mattrass. A bed-fellow.

P برخواج *bar khwāj,* (or برخواش) A spindle.

P برخوار *bar-khwār,* Glory. Fortune. A partner.

P برخواندن *bar khwāndan,* To attribute.

P برخودار *barkhū-dār,* Prosperous. Glorying.

P برخود پيچيدن *bar khwud pechīdan,* To writhe in pain. To be greatly distressed.

P برخود گرفتن *bar khwud giriftan,* To take upon one's self. To make one's self responsible.

P برخور *barkhwar* or *bar-khwur,* Glory, prosperity, good fortune. A daily allowance. A barn, granary. A companion, partner in trade. Pounding small. *Barkhwar,* Having a share.

P برخوردار *bar-khwur-dār,* Happy, enjoying long life and prosperity. Receiving a daily allowance. Glorying, boasting. Household furniture, utensils.

P برخورداري *bar-khwur-dārī,* Maintenance. Happiness, felicity, glory, reputation, good fortune. برخورداري دادن *bar khwurdārī dādan,* To bestow, confer, permit freely to enjoy. برخورداري گرفتن *bar-khwurdārī giriftan* or يافتن *yāftan,* To enjoy.

P برخوردن *bār khwurdan,* To eat fruit, enjoy.

P برخوز *barkhūz,* A large earthen vessel.

P برخوش *bar khwush,* Good, right, very well.

P برخوهل *bar khwahl,* Crooked, awry.

P برخه *barkha,* A piece, a morsel.

P برخي *barkhī,* Some, a little, somewhat, a particle. An offering, a ransom. A substitute.

P برخيدن *barkhīdan,* To extract, draw out. To pluck, pull. To reap, mow. To unravel, loose, resolve, tease (cotton or wool). To shave. To fortify, fence (with thorns). To be inverted, changed, converted. To clench or rivet nails. To surround or set (jewels with gold). To find, invent. To magnify. To remain quiet, to wait.

P برخيز *barkhez,* Arise. Rising.

P برخيزا *barkhezā,* Rising up. An insurgent.

P برخيزانيدن *barkhezānīdan,* To erect: to rouse.

P برخيزش *barkhezish,* A rising, insurrection.

P برخين *barkhīn,* A little ransom, a small portion.

P برد *bard,* An enigma. Stand off! give way! hold off! take care! begone! retire! Reverence, dread, terror. A captive, a prisoner of war. A stone. (in the Karmānian dialect) A city.

A برد *baruda,* (fut. يبرد *yabrudu*) It was cold.

A برد *bard,* (v. n. of برد) Making cold. Hailing. Applying cool antimony to the eye. Being cool, striking cold (the night). Dying. Becoming thin (marrow). Being blunt (a sword). Pouring water upon bread. Filing. Being easy. Being necessary or due. Cold, chill. Cold, chilliness. Spittle. Sleep. برد النهار *bardu'n nahār,* The beginning of day. برد الخيار *bardu'l khiyār,* A kind of title. برد و شتا *bard u shitā,* Cold and winter. حرّ و برد *harr u bard,* Heat and cold. *Burd,* (pl. ابراد *abrād,* ابرد *abrud,* and برود *burūd*) Striped cloth. An upper garment or surtout. A locust's wing. برد الشباب *burd'ush shabāb,* The vesture of youth. بردمزاج *burdi mizāj,* The habit of the constitution. برد يماني *burdi yamānī,* Striped stuff of Yaman. *Barad,* Hail. *Barid,* Cold. Hailing (cloud). سحاب برد *sahābi barid,* Hailing clouds. *Burud,* (pl. of بريد *barīd*) Arranged, disposed, prepared. Messengers, couriers. Guides. Animals (called likewise بروانق *barwānak* or فرانق *furānik*), which serve as guides to the lion; jackals, lions' providers. Post-horses, relays. Journeys made by post-horses. Measures of three parasangs or twelve miles: also, measures of two parasangs (the fourth part of a day's journey). Nocturnal stages on horseback.

P برد *burd,* (pret. of بردن *burdan*) He carried, bore, supported, carried off. A carrying, a bearing. (at chess) When only the king is left to the party. An enigma. *Barad,* He may carry.

P بردا *bardā,* Noise of combatants. An enigma.

A برداء *buradāʼ,* An ague.

P بردابرد *bard-ā-bard,* (A word used by guards, ushers, tipstaves, or beadles in clearing the way) Have a care! stand by! Confusion.

P بر دادن *bar dādan,* To quit, release, free.

P بردار *bar dār,* Exalted, lifted up. Suspended, hanged, crucified. A summer-house. بردار كردن *bar dār kardan,* To crucify, to hang. بردار بودن *bar dār būdan,* To be hanged. *Bardār,* (in composition from برداشتن *bardāshtan*) Bearing, supporting, raising or holding up. Observing, obeying, executing. فرمان بردار *farmān-bardār,* (or حكم بردار *hukm-bardār*) Obeying commands. حقه بردار *hukka-bardār,* The servant who prepares the hukka in India. *Bar-dār,* Bearing fruit. *Burdār,* (a contraction of بردبار *burdbār*) A bearer of burdens. Patient, long-suffering.

P بردار كشيده *bar dār kashīda,* Gibbeted.

P برداريدن *bar dāridan,* To raise. To hang.

P برداشت *bardāsht,* Endurance. A musical instrument pertaining to royalty. برداشت كردن *bardāsht kardan,* To suffer, endure, bear patiently.

P برداشتن *bar dāshtan,* To exalt, raise, elevate. To bear up, support, prop, sustain. To pick up. To take, assume. To take upon one's self. To remove, carry off. To offer. To fly for refuge. To overlook, disregard. آب برداشتن *āb bar dāshtan,* To draw water.

P برداشتني *bar dāshtanī,* Bearable, supportable. Possibility, certainty.

P برداشته *bar dāshta,* Borne, carried. Exalted. A man who flies to avoid punishment; one who takes refuge in a sanctuary. Exposed to hazard, left to the wide world.

P برداشته خاطر *bardāshta-khātir,* Uneasy.

P برداغ *bardāgh,* Name of a herb used in dyeing.

P بردال *bardāl,* A pair of compasses.

L بردال *burdāl,* (Burdigala) Bordeaux.

P بردان *bardān,* The juice of a certain plant.

A بردان *bardān,* Cold, shivering with cold, patient of cold. *Baradān,* Name of a place. البردان *al bardāni,* (The two colds) Morning and evening.

P بردانه *bardāna,* Bread, steeped in milk, and fried with butter.

P بردبار *burd-bār,* A bearer of burdens. Forbearing. Patient, long-suffering. The tedious winding-up of any business.

P بردباري *burd-bārī,* Patience. Long-suffering.

P برد برد *bard bard,* Give place! make way!

A بردة *bardat,* A name for a sheep. هو لي بردة يميني *huwa li bardati yamīnī,* He is perfectly known to me. هي لك بردة نفسها *hiya laka bardata nafsihā,* She is yours with her whole heart. *Bardat* or *baradat,* Indigestion, heaviness at the stomach, dyspepsy, bradypepsy. *Burdat,* A kind of habit sometimes of black checkered stuff, sometimes striped, worn by the Arabians: a cassock or habit, worn by the dervishes, or by the mendicants. بردة الضأن *burdatu'z zaʼn,* A kind of milk. هما في بردة اخماس *humā fī burdati akhmāsin,* They are both engaged about the same thing. *Baradat,* The middle of the eye. Name of a woman.

A بردج *bardaj,* (P برده) A captive, prisoner.

P بردر *bar dar,* The lintel over a door. A brother.

A بردس *birdis,* An overbearing, proud, supercilious man. Deformed, of an ugly aspect.

P بردع *bardaʻ,* Name of a country and city.

A بردعة *bardaʻat,* A cloth stuffed with wool, placed under the saddle. A pannel, pack-saddle, dorser. Name of a city in Azarbayjān.

A بردعيّ *bardaʻiy,* A maker of saddle-cloths.

P بر دفتر افگندن *bar daftar afgandan,* To register, to enrol.

P بردك *bardak,* A fable, fiction, parable. A charm. *Bardak* or *burdak,* An enigma, riddle.

P بردگان *bardagān,* (pl. of برده *barda*) Slaves.

P بردگي *bardagī,* Captivity, slavery, bondage.

P بردم *bar dam,* A moment, instant. The old name of the city بردع *bardaʻ.* *Burdam,* I carried.

P بردميدن *bardamīdan,* To shoot forth, to grow. To breathe. To be angry.

P بردن *birdan,* Velocity. A swift horse.

P بردن *burdan,* To carry, bear, bring, lead, conduct, transfer, transport. To take, assume, carry off, draw, remove, abstract, take away. To gain at play. To throw away, lose, lower (dignity). To go, run, fly. To obey, execute. اعتقاد بردن *iʻtikād burdan,* To believe. حسد بردن *hasad burdan,* To bear malice, to envy. حمله بردن *hamla burdan,* To make an attack, assault, insult. در پناه كسي بردن *dar panāhi kase burdan,* To flee for refuge to any one. روزگار بردن *rozgār burdan,* To live or associate. To waste time. شك بردن *shakk burdan,* To doubt. فرمان بردن *farmān burdan,* To obey commands, execute orders. خدا برد *khudā burd,* Whither does God conduct you?

P بردنگ *bardang,* A hillock in a desert.

P بردو *bardū,* Expectation, hope.

P بر دوام *bar dawām,* Always, continually. بر دوام باد *bar dawām bād,* May it endure for ever!

P بردوامي *bar dawāmī,* Perpetuity, duration.

S بردوان *bardwān,* A district and city in Bengal.

A برد و سلام *bard wa salām,* Ribwort.

P بر دوش *bar dosh,* On the shoulders. خرقه بر دوش *khirka bar dosh,* Clad in shreds and patches: a religious mendicant.

P بردون *birdūn,* A gelding.

P برده *barda,* A captive, prisoner of war. A slave, servant. برده بردن *barda burdan,* To make prisoner, to take captive. *Burda,* Borne, carried away. برده شدن *burda shudan,* To be carried off.

P برده فروش *barda-farosh,* A slave-dealer.

P بردي *bardī,* A masquerade. Mirth, jollity, festivity. A vase of polished marble. Papyrus. An excellent kind of date. *Burdī,* Thou barest.

A بردىٰ *barada',* Name of a stream in Damascus.

A برديّ *bardiy,* The papyrus. A branch. A locust's wing. *Burdiy,* An excellent sort of date.

P برد يافتن *burd yāftan,* To win at play, to gain.

P برديدن *bardīdan,* To retire, withdraw, retreat.

A برديس *birdīs,* Overbearing, supercilious.

P برديق *bardīk,* Ignorant, uninformed.

P بردين *bardīn,* Dregs, filth, refuse. Rust.

A برذج *burzaj,* The roaring of a lion. (a corruption of P برزه *purzu*) Nap of cloth.

A برذعة *barzaʻat,* (pl. براذع *barāziʻ*) A woollen saddle-cloth. A pack-saddle for an ass. Ground neither hard nor soft. A town in Azarbayjān.

A برذنة *barzanat,* (v. n. of برذن Q) Oppressing, overpowering. Being unable to reply. Travelling sluggishly like a pack-horse.

A برذون *birzawn,* (pl. براذين *barāzīn*) A horse or beast of burden, dull and sluggish: a pack-horse.

P براه *bar rāh,* An ornament. Decorated.

A بررة *bararat,* (pl. of بارّ) Just, pious (men).

P بر رستن *bar rastan,* To arise.

P بررسته *bar rusta,* A stalkless plant. Clownish.

P بر رسيدن *bar rasīdan,* To arrive. To investigate, to obtain information.

P بر رفتن *bar raftan,* To precede.

P بر روي آب آمدن *bar rūyi āb āmadan,* To be evident. بر روي افتادگي *bar rūy uftādagī,* A falling flat on the face, proneness. بر روي دويدن *bar rūy dawīdan,* To speak fluently.

P بره *bar rih,* Adorned. Ornament.

P برريق *bar rīk,* (On spittle) Fasting. Ignorant.

A برز *baraza,* (fut. يبرز *yabruzu*) He went forth.

P برز *barz,* A sown field. Seed. Agriculture. *Barz* or *burz,* Stature, height, tallness, elegance of shape. Tall. A trowel. Perfect, complete. The trunk of a tree. *Burz,* Youthfulness. Greatness.

A برز *barz,* Respectable, intelligent. Abstinent, temperate, honourable. An open country.

A برزاغ *birzāgh,* Full-grown (youth).

A برزة *barzat,* A woman of mature age who converses modestly with men. The summit of a mountain. A steep declivity. Name of a place.

P برزج *burzaj,* The roaring of a lion.

A برزخ *barzakh,* (pl. برازخ *barāzikh*) An interval, partition, bar. The grave. The interval of time, according to the Kur'ān, between the death of a man and the resurrection; before which period the Muhammadans do not imagine that departed spirits receive either their rewards or punishments. An ape is said to be the *barzakh* (connecting link) between man and the brute; the palm-tree between animals and vegetables; and coral between plants and fossils. The Holy Spirit.

P برزدن *bar zadan,* To strike up. To raise,

elevate. To level or equal. To count or play with the fingers. To collect. To separate. To cast anchor. بانگ برزدن *bāng bar zadan*, To make a noise, raise the voice. دامن برزدن *dāman bar zadan*, To tuck up the skirt, to prepare for business.

P برزده *bar zada*, Raised, shot forth.

A برزعة *barzaʿat*, A couch, bed. A carpet, mat.

A برزغ *burzugh*, Cheerfulness, alacrity (of youth). A young man filled out and full grown.

P برزغه *barazgha*, A saddle or pannel-cloth.

A برزق *barzak*, Name of a plant.

P برزقي *barzakī*, Examination, penetration.

P برزك *barzak*, The seed of lint of hemp.

P برزكار *barz-kār*, A farmer.

P برزگر *barzgar*, A farmer, a ploughman.

P برزگري *barzgarī*, Agriculture.

A برزل *burzul*, A heavy, corpulent man.

P برزم *barzam*, A sack. A wink, nod, amorous glance. Name of a fortress near the Jīhūn or Oxus.

P برزمان *bar zamān*, Formerly, sometimes.

P برزن *barzan*, A mansion, dwelling. A street, especially a long one. The top or extreme part of a street, the corner of a square or court. A plain, desert. *Birzan*, An earthen pan for baking bread.

P برزندن *barzandan*, To sow. To agree, tally.

A برزوغ *burzūgh*, Full-grown (youth). Buoyancy of spirits.

P برزويلا *burzūyalā*, Name of an ancient wrestler.

P برزه *barza*, Seed. A branch. Sowing, agriculture. A stuff made of silk and thread. *Burza*, A sort of the gum-arabic tree.

P برزه برز *barza-barz*, A sown-field, a seed-plot. Cloth, or a garment, made of silk and wool.

P برزه كار *barza-kār*, A farmer.

P برزه گاو *barza-gāw*, An ox used in agriculture.

P برزه گر *barzagar*, A sower, a farmer.

A برزهي *barzahīy*, Native of برزة *barzat*.

P برزي *barzī*, A husbandman.

A برزي *barzīy*, Respectable, moral. Intelligent.

P برزيدن *barzīdan*, To sow. To quadrate, agree, to correspond with. To persevere. To be habitually engaged in. *Barazīdan*, To dress becomingly.

P برزيق *barzīk*, A rude, unpolished clown.

A برزيق *birzīk*, (pl. برازيق *barāzīk*) A body, society, assembly. A by-path.

P برزيگر *barzīgar*, An agriculturist, farmer.

P برزيگري *barzīgarī*, Husbandry, agriculture,

P برزين *barzīn*, Fire. Name of one of the chief priests of the religion of Zardusht, who built a fire-temple which he called آذر برزين *āzuri barzīn*. A plain, a desert. A street or quarter of a city. Name of an ancient champion.

A برزين *birzīn*, A drinking-cup made out of a branch of the palm-tree.

P برزين كروس *barzīn kurūs*, Name of a wise man or priest of the fire-worshippers.

A برزيه *barziya*, Name of a fortress in Syria.

P برژ *barj*, Perfect, complete, entire. High, sublime. Power. Full splendour. A whirlpool.

P برس *bars*, A bridle, a halter. A kind of wooden forceps put upon the nose of an unruly horse when shoeing; a similar bit of wood, through which the camel's bridle runs. A spur. *Burs*, Fruit of the mountain-cypress. Juniper-berries.

A برس *bars*, (v. n. of برس) Being severe upon a debtor. An electuary compounded of opium, spices, and honey. *Birs* or *bars*, Skill of a guide in shewing the way. *Birs* or *burs*, A sort of coarse cotton, gathered from the tops of the reed papyrus.

A برساء *barsāʾ*, A crowd, body, assembly of men

H برسات *barsāt*, The rainy season (in India).

P برساختن *bar sākhtan*, To instruct, to render accomplished.

P برسام *bar-sām*, (from بر *bar*, The breast, and سام *sām*, Swelling) A pain in the breast, an oppression, wind, or swelling in the stomach. Pleurisy.

A برسام *birsām*, Pleurisy.

P برسان *barsān*, Syrup dark-coloured and of a fragrant smell. *Barsān* or *birsān*, People of the same religion, co-religionists. *Bursān*, A dragon.

P برسبيل *bar sabīl*, In the way of, by way of.

P برسد *ba rasad*, May it come to pass!

P برسر *bar sar*, On or at the head, end, or point. These two words are much used in composition, as in the following examples: برسر آمدن *bar sar āmadan*, To conquer, to be at the head. To augment, to amplify. برسر آوردن *bar sar āwardan*, To bring to the point, to discover. برسرپا ايستادن *bar sari pā īstādan*, To stand on the point of the foot; to stand. برسرچشم *bar sari chashm*, On the point of the eye; most willingly. برسرحساب آمدن *bar sari hisāb āmadan*, To come to the end of the account; to be reconciled, satisfied, contented. برسررسيدن *bar sar rasīdan*, Upon the point of arriving. برسرسخن رفتن *bar sari sukhun raftan*, To go to the head of the discourse; to explain. برسرزدن *bar sar zadan*, To lose one's senses. To be deep in thought. برسركار *bar sari kār*, On the point of business; when there is occasion.

P برسرافگندني *bar sar afgandanī*, A coif or veil for throwing over the head.

P برس غنچه *burs-ghuncha*, Juniper-berries.

P برسكيزيدن *bar sikīzīdan*, To leap.

P برسم *barsam*, Rods of a span long used by the fire-worshippers in their ceremonies. برسم چين *barsam-chīn*, The knife for cutting the rods. برسمدان *barsamdān*, The case for holding the rods.

P برسن *birsun*, Cotton. *Bursun*, A ring of wood, or of hair, passed through a camel's nose, to which the bridle is fastened. A nose-jewel, worn by ladies in the East. A bride. A yoke.

P برسنگ *barsang*, A counterpoise, equilibrium, any thing hung at one side to counterbalance the load upon the other.

P برسو *bar sū*, The top, the head. برسوي گوش *bar sūyi gosh*, The top of the ear. برسوي ران *bar sūyi rān*, The hip-bone.

P برسوله *barsūla*, A lozenge composed of nuts, mace, and other hot spices.

P برسي *barsī*, Weariness, irksomeness.

P برسيان *barsiyān*, (or برسياوشان *barsiyāwishān*), Shepherd's crook; maiden-hair (herbs).

P برسيانا *barsiyānā*, Name of a plant whose seed resembles parsley.

P برسياه *bar siyāh*, Brown, tawny. Black bile.

P برسيدن *ba rasīdan*, To be ended, completed. To be annihilated, erased, abolished, consumed.

A برسيم *birsīm*, Name of a certain grain or seed.

P برسين *barsīn*, Clover.

P برسينا *barsīnā*, Name of a plant, the seed of which is good for the itch.

P برش *barsh*, Desire. *Birsh*, A halter. *Barash*, Upon him. His breast. *Barish*, A pair of compasses. The shingles. *Burish*, A chip, shaving. A cutting off, scission.

A برش *barash*, Small spots or hairs upon a horse, of a different colour from the rest. A white speck on the nail.

A برّش *burrish*, The sharpness of a sword.

A برشاء *barshāʾ*, (fem. of ابرش *abrash*) (Ground) variegated with herbage of different kinds. Fruitful in grass (year). A body, crowd, society. ما ادري اي البرشاء هو *mā adrī ayyu'l barshāʾ huwa*, I know not who he is.

P برشاخ آهوان *bar shākhi āhuwān*, (On the horns of antelopes) Impossible, unattainable.

A برشاع *birshāʿ*, Foolish, headstrong. Thick, corpulent. Rough. Malignant. Deformed.

A برشام *birshām*, (v. n. of برشم Q) Colouring with different colours. A sharp piercing eye.

A برشان *barshān*, People of the same religion. *Burshān*, Bread, or the consecrated wafer, used by the Eastern Christians in the Eucharist.

A برشة *burshat*, Spots upon a horse.

P برشترنشستن *bar shutur nishastan*, (To sit upon a camel) To get abroad (a secret).

P برشتن *burushtan*, To fry, roast, broil. To bake.

A برشتوك *barashtūk*, A kind of sea-fish.

P برشته *burushta*, Fried, roasted, broiled, toasted, baked. گل برشته *gili burushta*, Baked clay.

P برشدن *bar shudan*, To ascend, to be superior. To be collected.

A برشطة *barshatat*, A cutting (of meat) in pieces.

A برشع *birshiʿ*, A tall corpulent man. A fool. Malignant.

A برشقة *barshakat*, (v. n. of برشق Q) Cutting (meat). Scourging.

P برشك *barshak*, A wine or oil-press. A belt.

H برشكال *barshakāl*, The rainy season.

A برشكة *barshakat*, (v. n. of برشك Q) Cutting up, dividing (a slaughtered animal).

P برشكستن *bar shikastan,* To shun, quit, retire.

A برشم *burshum,* A veil for the face.

A برشمة *barshamat,* (v. n. of برشم Q) Being silent from grief. Drawing (the face) in wrinkles. Looking stedfastly. Colouring with different colours.

P برشمردن *bar shumurdan,* To sum up, count.

P برشن *barshan,* Ivy.

P برشنان *barshunān,* People of the same religion.

P برشوم *barshūm,* A kind of dried date.

A برشوم *burshūm* or *barshūm,* A very early date grown at Basrah.

P برشهي *barshahī,* Down growing on a bird's wing. A wing.

P برشيان دارو *barshiyān-dārū,* The herb shepherb's staff.

P بر شير نر زين نهادن *bar sheri nar zīn nihādan,* (To saddle the male lion) To be very valiant and daring. (To bell the cat).

P بر شير نشستن *bar shīr nishastan,* To hide.

A برص *bars,* An insect generated in wells. *Burs,* (pl. of ابرص *abras*) Leprous. *Baras,* (v. n. of برص) Being leprous. Leprosy. White spots upon cattle from the bites of insects or any other cause.

A برصاء *barsās,* (fem of ابرص *abras*) Leprous. (Pasture-ground) cropped short by cattle. Shining-skinned (serpent).

A برصة *bursat,* (pl. براص *birās*) The mansion of a demon. A barren sandy desert without herbage. *Birasat,* (pl. of سامّ ابرص *sāmm abras*) Certain large poisonous lizards.

P بر صحرا نهادن *bar sahrā nihādan,* To disclose.

P برص زده *baras-zada,* Afflicted with leprosy.

A برصوم *bursūm,* A leathern case (for a flask).

A برصيصا *barsīsā,* Name of a certain devotee who afterwards became an apostate.

A برض *barz,* (v. n. of برض) Giving little. Flowing slowly (water from the fountain). (pl. براض *birāz,* بروض *burūz,* and ابراض *abrāz*) A few.

A برضة *burzat,* A place where trees grow not. A little water.

A برطاس *bartās,* Name a city in Turkistān famous for its fox furs.

P بر طاق نهادن *bar tāk nihādan,* To exalt, promote. To quit. To forget.

A برطام *birtām,* Swollen-lipped. Thick-lipped. A thick lip.

G برطانيقي *bartānīkī,* The herb betony.

P برطايل *bartāyil,* Name of a fabulous island in India, pictured as a most enchanting place. Loud noises are said to issue from a certain tree there; and from a mountain therein the melodious sounds of musical instruments are heard in the night-time.

P برطبق *bar tabak,* According to.

P برطرف *bar taraf,* Aside, apart. Discharge, dismissal. برطرف ساز بودن *bar taraf sāz būdan,* To be set aside, or delayed till another time. To be finished, concluded. برطرف كردن *bar taraf kardan,* To set aside, dismiss, discharge, cashier. برطرف نهادن *bar taraf nihādan,* To set apart, remove, displace, throw away, reject. To preserve, lay by. To terminate, conclude. لطيفه برطرف *latīfa bar taraf,* Let joking cease! raillery apart!

P برطرفي *bar tarafī,* Dismissal, discharge.

A برطل *burtul* or *burtull,* A high-crowned cap.

A برطلة *bartalat,* (v. n. of برطل Q) Placing a large stone in front of a cistern. Bribing (a judge).

A برطلة *burtullat,* A narrow canopy or parasol.

P A برطله *bartala* or *bartula,* A cap worn under the turban.

A برطم *bartam,* A stammerer.

A برطمة *bartamat,* (v. n. of برطم Q) Enraging. Being enraged. Growing dark (night). A swelling with rage. A kind of game.

A برطنة *bartanat,* Sport, amusement, play.

G برطيسقون *bartīskūn,* Red clay.

A برطيل *birtīl,* (pl. براطيل *barātīl*) A hard, long stone, or a long piece of iron, with which they notch a millstone. A kind of long crow of iron used by miners and others in splitting of stones. A bribe to corrupt a judge.

A برعث *burʿus,* (pl. براعث *barāʿis*) Podex.

A برعس *birʿis,* Abounding in milk and finely-shaped (camel).

P برعكس *bar ʿaks,* Inversely. On the contrary.

A برعل *burʿul,* A young hyena. The young of the animal called وبر *wabr.*

A برعم *burʿum,* (or برعوم *burʿūm*) (pl. براعيم *barāʿīm*) An unblown bud.

A برعمة *barʿamat,* (v. n. of برعم Q) Budding (a tree). *Burʿumat,* A bud.

A البرعوم *al burʿūm,* Name of a place in Arabia.

A برعومة *burʿūmat,* A pod, bud, or envelope.

A برعيس *birʿīs,* Patient under adversity. (A camel) abounding in milk and finely shaped.

P برغ *bargh, barigh,* or *baragh,* A dam, dike, mound, bank, weir, or any kind of water-inclosure.

A برغ *bargh,* Spittle, slaver. *Baragh,* (v. n. of برغ) Enjoying abundantly the conveniences of life.

P برغاب *bargh-āb,* A dam. A place where water stagnates.

A برغاز *birghāz,* (برغز *barghaz, burghuz,* or برغوز *burghūz*) A calf when able to follow the cow.

P برغاليدن *barghālīdan,* To excite. To throw. To pluck up.

A برغثة *barghasat,* Ash-colour, spleen-colour.

A برغز *burghuz,* Malicious.

P برغست *barghast,* A certain wild pot-herb resembling spinage, and growing on the banks of rivers. A yellow flowering shrub with which they feed cattle and asses. Water-moss. A canal cut for the purpose of irrigation.

P برغستوا *barghast-wā,* Soup made from برغست.

A برغش *barghash,* A gnat.

A برغل *burghul,* Wheat prepared by first softening the grain in hot water, and then breaking it and unhusking it by means of a hand-mill: it is afterwards dried in the sun, and thus preserved for use.

P برغلانيدن *barghalānīdan,* To excite, animate.

A برغلة *barghalat,* (v. n. of برغل Q) Inhabiting a برغيل *birghīl.*

P برغمان *barghamān,* A large serpent.

P برغندان *barghandān,* A carnival.

P برغو *burghū,* A musical pipe.

A برغوث *burghūs,* (pl. براغيث *barāghīs*) A flea.

A البرغوثي *al burghūsiy,* Flea-wort.

P برغول *barghol,* A kind of sweetmeat. *Burghol* or *barghol,* Wheat, barley, corn (epecially bruised); also a dish made of grain.

A برغيس *birghīs,* Patient, indifferent, careless.

A برغيل *birghīl,* (pl. براغيل *barāghīl*) A district situated near water, or between an inhabited country and a desert.

P برف *barf,* Snow. برف باريدن To snow.

P برف آب *barf-āb,* Snow-water, water as cold as snow. Spittle. برف آب دادن *barf-āb dādan,* To damp the spirits.

P برفان *barfān,* Lamb's fleece. A leathern vest.

P برفخج *barfukhj,* The night-mare, the incubus.

P برفدان *barfdān,* An ice-house. The gullet.

P برفر *barfar,* (or برفره *barfara*) Dignity, rank.

P برفراخيدن *bar farākhīdan,* To stand on end.

P برفرازنده *bar farāzinda,* An illuminator.

P بر فراغ كردن *bar farāgh kardan,* To finish.

P برفرود *bar farod,* Above and below. An arched building.

P برفروشان *bar faroshān,* People of one nation.

P برف زدي *barf-zadī,* Injury caused by snow.

P برفشاندن دست *bar fishāndani dast,* To dance. Dancing.

P بر فلان چكيدن *bar fulān chakīdan,* To fall upon one. To suspect. To be fixed or firm on one.

P برفناك *barfnāk,* Snowy. Covered with snow.

P برفنج *barfanj,* Rough, difficult, arduous (road or business). Any thing new, uncommon, recently happened. First-fruits.

P برفنجك *barfanjak,* Nightmare. Intoxicating.

P برفند *barfand,* Fraud, deceit, treachery. A foolish speech. An agreeable speech. Any deep place or thing. A valley, a ditch. A zone, a belt. An arched building. An army.

P برفندار *barfandār,* A commentator, a lecturer. A wise man, who solves difficulties in religion, law, or the abstract sciences. A master of any art or profession. A musician, singer.

P برفنده *barfanda,* A clothes-chest or press. A fruit-pannier.

P برفوز *barfoz,* Purslain. Parts round the mouth.

P برفوس *barfos,* The parts about the mouth.

P برفي *barfī,* A kind of sweetmeat.

G برفير *barfīr,* Purple. The purple-shell-fish.

A برق *bark*, (v. n. of برق) Glittering. Sparkling (the eye). Having the eyes so dazzled with glare as scarcely to be able to shut them. Being astonished, confounded. Seasoning (meat) with a little oil or butter. Rising (a star). Adorning herself (a woman). Giving false signs of pregnancy (a camel). (pl. بروق *burūk*) Lightning. A flashing cloud. A thunderbolt. برق خاطف *barki khātif*, A thunderbolt. برق خلب *barki khullab*, Flashing clouds without rain (a proverb applied to those who brag much). P برق شدن *bark shudan*, To go swiftly. برق کردن *bark kardan*, To lighten, to flash. برق يماني *barki yamānī*, A sword with a Yaman-blade. A *Burk*, Lybian lizards. *Barah*, (pl. ابراق *abrāk* برقان *birkān* or *burkān*) A lamb. A ram. (v. n. of برق) Having the eyes so dazzled with glare as scarcely to be able to shut them. Being astonished, confounded. Being heated (a churn) so that the milk will not concrete. Having the gripes (a sheep) from eating of the herb بروق *barwak*. Amazement, bewilderment. *Barik*, Heated so (a churn) that the milk will not concrete. *Burak*, (pl. of برقة *burkat*) Stony, sandy grounds.

A برقاء *barkā*, (fem. of ابرق *abrak*) An eye (as shining, glossy, and being of different colours). Black and white, pie-bald (she-goat). (pl. برقاوات *barkāwāt*) Stony, sandy ground mixed with clay.

P برقاعده *bar kāida*, According to rule.

P برقان *barkān*, A lamb-skin.

A برقان *barkān*, (v. n. of برق) Lightning, flashing, thundering. Menacing, threatening. *Birkān* or *burkān*, (pl. of برق *barak*) Lambs. *Burkān*, Glittering (substance). Variously coloured (locust).

P برق انداز *bark-andāz*, A matchlock-man.

A برقاوات *barkāwāt*, (pl. of برقاء *barkā*) Stony places mixed with clay.

A برقة *barkat*, Barca in Africa. Amazement. *Burkat*, (pl. برق *burak*) A name common to more than a hundred places in Arabia. Coarse ground, consisting of clay, sand, and stones. Necessary business.

A برقحة *barkahat*, Ugliness of face.

P برقرار *bar karār*, Firm, solid, immoveable, fixed, constant, uniform. Firmly. برقرار شدن *bar karār shudan*, To be established. برقرار کردن *bar karār kardan*, To establish, confirm, ratify.

A برقش *birkish*, A small bird called شرشور.

A برقشة *barkashat*, (v. n. of برقش Q) Painting or forming any thing of various colours. Mixing, jumbling a discourse. Being scattered. Being of diverse colours. Advancing, preparing to eat.

A برقطة *barkatat*, (v. n. of برقط Q) Looking behind the back. Taking very short steps in walking. Scattering, dispersing. Talking at random.

A برقع *birkiɛ* or *burkuɛ*, The seventh heaven (with some the fourth, and others the first). *Burkuɛ* or *burkaɛ*, A lady's veil, through which only the eyes are seen. P برقع كشاي هر مشكل *burkaɛ kushāyi har mushkil*, Unveiling and resolving every difficulty. *Burkuɛ*, A mark branded on a camel's thigh. A word used in calling the goats to be milked.

A برقعة *barkaɛat*, (v. n. of برقع Q) Putting a veil on one. Striking with a stick between the ears. برقع لحيته *barkaɛa lihyatuhu*, He was infamous.

A برقعيد *barkaɛīd*, Name of a town near Mawsil.

P برقك *barkah*, Talc. Gilt paper.

A برقلة *barkalat*, (v. n. of برقل Q) Lying.

A برق نحره *barika nahruhu*, (His throat shone) A nickname given to a certain individual.

P برقندان *barkandān*, (or برقدان *barkadān*) A carnival or time of festivity, before the commencement of the month of fasting called *Ramazān*, the ninth of the Muhammadan year.

A برقوع *burkūɛ*, A veil through which the eyes only are seen. *Burkūɛ* or *barkūɛ*, Intense hunger.

A برقوق *burkūk*, An apricot. A kind of bad yellow plum.

P ذو البرقه *zū'l barka*, Alīy, son-in-law of Muhammad.

A برقيل *birkīl*, A cross-bow for shooting balls, &c.

A برك *bark*, (pl. بروك *burūk*) A troop of camels (especially reclining). The breast of a man. The inside of the breast. The part or parts of a camel's breast which touch the ground when he is recumbent. *Birk*, A reservoir. *Burk*, (pl. of بريك *barīk*) Dishes of fresh dates and butter. (pl. of براك *birāk*) Sword-fishes. *Birak*, (pl. of بركة *birkat*) Basins of fountains. *Burak*, A kind of tree, saltish, bitter, and short-stemmed. The month ذو الحجة *zū'l hijjat*. A coward. The nightmare. Firm, fixed, steadily seated at any thing. (pl. of بركة *burkat*) Small white ducks.

A برك *baraka*, (fut. يبرك *yabruku*) He kneeled.

P برك *barak*, A garment made of camel's hair. A short vest. The star Canopus. Name of a river and of a country.

P بركاپوز *barkāpoz*, (بركاپوس *barkāpos*, بركافوز *barkāfoz*, or بركافوس) The parts round the mouth.

A بركات *barakāt*, (pl. of بركة *barakat*) Blessings. Abundance, prosperity. محصول عميم البركات *mahsūli ɛamīmi'l barakāt*, A plentiful harvest.

P بركاردارنده *bar kār dāranda*, A practitioner.

P بركاريدن *barkārīdan*, To cut a slice (of a melon). To cut out the collar of a coat or a shift.

P بركاشتن *barkāshtan*, To sow.

A بركان *birkān*, A salt and bitter sort of shrub. Any plant not putting forth a long stem. Any slender plant. *Burkān* or *birkān*, (pl. of بركة *burkat*) Certain aquatic birds small and white.

A بّركان *barrakān*, (or بّركانيّ *barrakānīy*) A kind of black gown or habit, a barracane.

P بركاويدن *barkāwīdan*, To cut out a piece (of cloth or melon). To slit a garment. To dig.

A بركة *birkat*, The outside of the breast. The part of a recumbent camel's breast which is next the ground. The manner of a camel's reclining on it. A striped stuff of Yaman. (pl. برك *birak*) A large reservoir of water, lake, pond. A milch ewe. The flowing of milk from the udder of a recumbent camel, and the making her stand up to be milked. *Birkat* or *barkat*, One morning's milking. *Burkat*, (pl. برك *burak*, ابراك *abrāk*, بركان *burkān* and *birkān*) An aquatic bird, a species of white duck. Frogs. Tribute; also those who collect it. An assembly of nobles. Toll taken by the miller for grinding. *Burkat*, *barkat*, or *birkat*, Those who demand expiatory fines for manslaughter. *Barakat*, A blessing. Abundance, increase. Fertility. Prosperity, happiness. Recompense.

P بركر *barkar*, Fortune, good luck.

P بركرائيدن *barkarāīdan*, To be modest. To feel.

P بركردن *bar kardan*, To commit to memory, to learn by heart. To kindle (a fire). To uproot.

P بر كرسي نشاندن *bar kursī nishāndan*, To bring an affair to a happy termination. To set a person's mind at rest (to place him on velvet).

P بركست *barkast*, Flying to God. God forbid!

P بركشيدن *bar kashīdan*, To draw up. To extract, draw, lead, or bring out. To wrinkle, shrivel.

A بركع *burkuɛ*, A man of short stature. A camel's colt whose neck does not reach to the ground.

A بركعة *barkaɛat*, (v. n. of بركع Q) Cutting, amputating. Throwing prostrate. Standing on all fours. Falling on the knees.

P بركم *barkam*, A prohibition, refusal. An impediment, delay. A restrainer, hinderer.

P بركمال *bar kamāl*, In perfection. Complete.

P بركنار *bar kanār*, On one side, free, clear of.

P بركنج *barkanj*, A kind of sweetmeat.

P بركند *barkand*, A bribe to a judge. A plucking up. An owl. A robust, strong, beardless youth.

P بركندن *bar kandan*, To dig up, extirpate.

P بركنده *barkanda*, Dug up. بركنده آمدن *bar kanda āmadan*, To be extirpated.

P بركنه *barkana* or *birkana*, An electuary made from gold and silver-dust. Any thing beaten and mixed together (especially perfumes).

A بركوع *burkūɛ*, Intense hunger. A veil.

P بركوه *burkūh*, Name of a city in Persian Irāk.

P بركوهان *barkūhān*, Melody of voice. Harmony of instruments. The voice of a parrot.

P بركه *birka*, A reservoir of water, a pond, pool, ditch. بركهٔ اردشير *birkaʼi ardshīr*, Name of a city so called from a large reservoir built by one of the ancient kings of Persia. بركهٔ لاجورد *birkaʼi lājaward*, The sky. *Burka*, A kind of white duck.

P بركي *barakī*, A species of high-crowned cap made of felt. A kind of rollers which the poorer people wrap round their head.

P بركينه *barkīna*, An exhilarating electuary.

P برگ *barg*, The leaf of a tree, a blade of grass. An instrument. Arms. Intention, aim, design.

End. Power, strength. Intellect. A musical instrument. Provision for soldiers, travellers, or guests. Wealth. A workshop. The dress of Kallenders (a kind of monk). Collectedness. برگ تنبول *bargi tambūl*, Betel-leaf. برگ چشم *bargi chashm*, (The leaf of the eye) The eye-lid. برگ سبز *bargi sabz*, (برگ سبزك *bargi sabzak* or برگ تر *bargi tar*) A green leaf (the gift of a poor man). برگ كازروني *bargi kāzarūnī*, Wild aniseed. مفلس بي برگ *muflisi bī barg*, Poor, indigent.

P برگاشتن *bargāshtan*, To turn. To avert the face.

P برگان *bargān*, Name of a village near Shīrāz.

P برگ بيد *barg-bīd*, (by some *bed*) A kind of spear, the head of which resembles the leaf of a willow.

P برگدار *barg-dār*, Leafy, bearing leaves. برگدار ساختن *barg-dār sākhtan*, To cover with leaves. برگدار شدن *barg-dār shudan*, To be in full leaf (trees).

P برگذار *bar guzār*, A present, a gift.

P برگرد *bar gird*, About. برگرد ماه *bar girdi māh*, About the moon.

P برگردانيدگي *bar gardānīdagī*, Transportation, transposition, change, inversion.

P برگرديدگي *bar gardīdagī*, Inversion, change. Removal, departure.

P برگرديدن *bar gardīdan*, To be turned, inverted: to recede.

P برگرديده *bar gardīda*, Turned. Tumbled over.

P برگرديده بوي *bar gardīda-boy*, Stinking.

P برگرفتن *bar giriftan*, To take, accept, seize, carry off. To lift or pick up. To bring. To bear. To cause to put on. To drive away. To erase.

P برگريزان *barg-rezān*, (Scattering leaves) The fall of the leaf, autumn, November. The autumn of mortality the decline of the life.

P برگ ريزي *barg-rezī*, Fall of the leaf, autumn.

P برگزيدگان *bar guzīdagān*, The elect.

P برگزيدگي *bar guzīdagī*, Choiceness. Choice.

P برگزيدن *bar guzīdan*, To prefer, choose, select.

P برگزيده *bar guzīda*, Chosen. برگزيدهٔ عالم *bar guzīdasi ʿālam*, The most select of men.

P برگس *bargas*, (or برگست *bar gast*) Mercy upon us! Heaven forbid!

P برگستان *bar gustān*, (or برگستوان *bar gustuwān*) Horse-armour worn in battle.

P برگسه *bargasa*, Hidden, concealed.

P برگشت *bargusht*, A plant growing like dishevelled hair.

P برگشتگي *bar-gashtagī*, Change. Inversion. Apostacy, recession.

P برگشتن *bar gashtan*, To turn. To recede, retire, return. To apostatize.

P برگشته *bar gashta*, Turned. Topsy turvy. Broken. Afflicted. Murdered. Dead. برگشته اختر *bar-gashta-akhtar*, Unfortunate. برگشته حال *bar gashta-hāl*, (pl. برگشته حالان *bar gashta-hālān*) Most afflicted. برگشته روزگار *bar gashta-rozgār*, Unfortunate in the world, desperate, abandoned.

P برگشه *bar-gasha*, Covered, concealed.

P برگ گاه *barg-gāh*, (Place of leaf) A shoot, stalk.

P برگماشتگي *bar gumāshtagī*, Power, delegated authority. Delegation, appointment to any post.

P برگماشتن *bar gumāshtan*, To put in authority, to appoint, to instal, to delegate.

P بر گماشته *bar gumāshta*, Delegated.

P برگ نيل *barg-nīl*, Indigo, woad.

P برگ و بار *barg u bār*, Leaves and fruit.

P برگ و ساز *barg u sāz*, (or برگ و نوا *barg u nawā*) Means of subsistence.

P برگوك *bargūk*, A structure, an edifice.

P برگي *baragī*, A kind of high-crowned cap.

P بر لنگ زدن *bar lang zadan*, To run away.

P برم *barm*, A committing to memory. Expectation. A reservoir for rain-water. Name of a water-bird. *Baram*, A trellis. A two-pronged fork.

A برم *barm*, (v. n. of برم) Doing (business) well. *Burm* or *buram*, (pl. of برمة *burmat*) Stone-kettles. *Baram*, (v. n. of برم) Being wearied and disgusted. Being anxious of adducing proof or argument, but being unable to recal it to memory. (pl. ابرام *abrām*) Vexation, fatigue, languor, disgust. One who refuses to go partner with gamesters (from avarice). Fruit of a dwarf-thorn called عضاه *ʿizāh*. Sour, unripe grapes. Liquid collyrium. The summit of a mountain. *Barim*, A man disgusted with himself, odious and shunned for his deceitfulness.

P برماس *barmās*, The touch. A rubbing with the hand. The sense of feeling.

P برماسيدن *barmāsīdan*, To feel, touch: to rub one limb against another. To inquire, examine.

P برمال *bar māl*, Running away. The peak of a mountain. The breast. برمال زدن *bar māl zadan*, (or بر مال كردن *bar māl kardan*) To run away.

P برماليدن *bar mālīdan*, To fold, to twist. To tuck up the sleeves. To run away.

P بر ماه مشك انداختن *bar māh mushk andākhtan*, (To throw musk on the moon's face) To have a mole on the cheek.

P برماهه *barmāha*, (or برماه *barmāh*) An auger gimlet, wimble. A surgeon's trepan.

P برمايون *birmāyūn*, The famous cow belonging to king Farīdūn of Persia. A kind of silk.

P برمايه *bir* or *barmāya*, Farīdūn's cow.

A برمة *burmat*, (pl. برم *burm*, *buram*, and برام *birām*) A large cauldron or kettle used in Khurāsān hollowed out of stone. *Baramat*, (pl. برم *baram* and برام *birām*) The fruit of a thorny shrub.

A برمّتها *bi rummatihā*, All, the whole.

P برمچ *barmach*, Touch: a stroking with the hand.

P برمچيدن *barmachīdan*, To handle, touch, try, feel, examine by the hand: to rub. To creep. To drag.

P برمخيدن *bar makhīdan*, To be disobedient.

P برمخيده *barmakhīda*, Refractory, disobedient, self-willed. Undutiful.

P برمر *barmar*, Desire. Hope. Expectation. A bee.

P برمراد *bar murād*, According to (one's) wishes.

P برمسيدن *barmasīdan*, To handle, try, feel.

P برمشيدن *bar mashīdan*, To creep. To snatch.

P برمغاز *bar maghāz*, (or برمغازه) A present over and above his hire given by a master to his boy.

P برمقتضا *bar muktazā*, According to. برمقتضائ صلح *bar muktazāsi sulh*, Agreeable to the (treaty of) peace.

P برمك *barmak*, Name of a noble family, originally from Balkh in Khurāsān, and highly celebrated all over the East for their generosity, magnificence, and distinguished patronage of men of genius. Name of a place and of a country.

P برمكي *barmakī*, Of the family of Barmacides. A hero, a noble liberal man.

A برمكيّ *barmakīy*, (pl. برامكة *barāmikat*) One of the family of Barmak, a Barmecide.

P برمكيه *barmakya*, The aloe dressed with sugar and sauce.

P برمگان *baramgān*, The hair of the pubes.

P برملا *bar malā*, Openly, in the sight of all. برملا افتادن *bar malā uftādan*, To become public.

P برمو *barmū*, Expectation, hope, desire.

P برموجب *bar mūjib*, According to. برموجب عادت *bar mūjibi ʿādat*, According to custom.

P برموده *barmūda*, Any thing, a thing in general.

P برموز *barmūz*, Desire, wish. Provender. A bee.

P برموزه *barmoza*, The son of سادة شاه.

P برمون *bar mūn*, (poet. for برما *bar mā*) On us.

P برمه *barma*, A gimblet, a wimble, an auger.

A برميل *barmīl*, A tun, a butt, a hogshead.

P برميو *barmiyū*, The strangury, heat of urine.

P برن *barn*, Name of a star. Any place above which something is extended. A broad vessel. A drinking-cup of earth or metal. A bundle of rods wattled together. A harrow for breaking clods. A grate of brass or wood. The new moon. *Baran*, Name of a city in India.

P برنا *barnā* or *burnā*, A youth. Young. Good. Elegant, handsome. The dyeing shrub hinna.

P برناخن ايستادن *bar nākhun istādan*, To stand on tip-toe. To obey promptly.

P برناس *barnās*, Ignorant, unskilful. Ignorance.

A برناساء *barnāsās*, Men.

P برناق *barnāk*, A young man, a youth.

P برناك *barnāk*, *burnāk*, (برناه *barnāh* or *burnāh*) A young man. Young. Privet.

P برنامه *bar nāma*, A model, an exemplar. An account-book. Title. Exordium of a book or letter.

P برنان *birnān*, Name of a tree growing in Ajmīr (in Hindūstān) used for making rosaries.

P برنانه *birnāna*, A mud cottage.

P برنايشتي *barnāyishtī*, Alliance, protection, support. Partiality, strong attachment.

P برنائي *barnāsī*, Youth, the season of youth.

P برنبور *barambūr*, A child's game.

A برنتي *baranta'*, Bad, evil-disposed.

P برنج baranj, A man nearly blind and thus groping his way. A most delicious species of the date. Biranj, A kind of medicine which promotes a discharge of phlegm. Birinj, Rice. برنج زرد birinji zard, Rice dressed with turmeric. برنج شماله birinji shamāla, A kind of curry. Burinj, Copper.

P برنجار birinjār, (for برنج زار) Rice-grounds.

P برنج آري birinj-ārī, One who follows a camp with grain, a brinjarrie.

P برنجاسف birinjāsf, (برنجاسب birinjāsb or برنجاسه) Dungwort, motherwort. Mugwort.

P برنجمشك baranj-mushk, The musk of Europe, the tamarisk. Mountain-balm.

P برنجن baranjan, (or برنجين baranjīn) A metal ring worn by females on their wrists or ankles. Any female ornament. A little pendulous fringed decoration of silk or wool, worn by the Turkomān women, hanging to their hair, by camels at their sides, and by horses from their manes.

P برنجه كردن ba ranja kardan, To torment, afflict.

P برنجين burinjīn, Brazen, made of copper.

P برند barand, Plain silk. Burand or barand, A sharp sword. Tonsure.

A برند birind, A sword bearing marks of age. Birind or birand, The glittering surface of a sword.

P برنداف barandāf, The intestines. A stirrup-leather, a strap.

P برندك barandak, A little hill. A lock, bolt, bar. Dross of iron. A species of the myrobalan.

P برندكام birandakām, A medicine made of camomile-flowers.

P برندن burundan, To compress, to squeeze.

P برنده baranda, Operating, acting. A moth. A carrier. Burinda, Cutting. A sharp sword. Acid milk. برندۀ گوشت burindasi gosht, A butcher.

P برنس barnas, Shears. Barnas, (barnis or برنش barnish) A pain in the bowels, cholic, gripes.

A برنس burnus, (pl. برانس barānis) A kind of high-crowned cap, worn formerly in Barbary and Spain. Any upper garment or cloak which covers the head together with the body.

A برنساء barnasā‛, Men. اي برنساء هو ayyu barnasā‛ or baranasā‛ huwa, (or اي البرنساء هو ayyu'l barnasā‛ or baranasā‛ huwa) Of what people or family is he? what man is he?

A برنشاء barnashā‛, Men.

P برنشاندن bar nishāndan, To make sit: to seat. To set (a stone in a ring), fix (a head on a spear).

P برنشست bar nishast, Riding. ستور برنشست sutūri bar nishast, A beast for riding; a saddle-horse or camel, a hack, a nag.

P برنشستن bar nishastan, To sit up or upon. To mount, to ride. To propose, intend.

P برنشستني bar nishastanī, Fit for riding (nag).

P برنشسته bar nishashta, Mounted, sitting on.

P برنغار baranghār, The right wing of an army.

P برنك baranh, A bell. A key. A lock. A bolt. Root, origin. Assault, inroad. Silken stuff.

A برنكان barnakān, (or برنكانيّ barnakāniy) (pl. برانك barānik) A kind of black gown, a barracane.

P برنگ barang, An allowance of provisions. A bell. A key. A bar, bolt. Biring, A kind of the myrobalan. Burung, Gain, acquisition; hoard.

P برنو barnū, Brocade.

P برنوس barnos, An army. Barnos or barnosh, A general. A soldier. Name of a general.

A برنوف burnūf, Name of an Egyptian tree.

P برنون barnūn, Brocade. Sewing-silk.

P برنهادن bar nihādan, To place above. Coire.

P برني barnī, An earthen or glass vessel, in which they keep flowers, confections, medicines, or sugar.

A برنيّ barnīy, A delicious kind of date. Baranīy, Foreign, external.

P برنيان barniyān, A silken garment.

P برنيان خوي barniyān-khoy, Of a mild temper.

A برنيّة barnīyat, (pl. برانيّ barānīy) A vessel of earth in which any thing is preserved. A cockerel.

P برنيس birnīs, An acorn. Large shears.

P برنيش burnesh, The cholic.

A برنيق birnīk, The mud of a river. A kind of mushroom oblong and red; or small and blackish.

P برنيك barnīk, Delicious fruit. A kind of date.

P برو barv, The planet Jupiter. Bar u, Upon, on, above, him, her, or it. Barū, The eyebrow. Birav, Go. Burū, (for بروت burūt) Whiskers.

A برو barw, (v. n. of برا for برو) Creating. Shaving (a stick, arrow, or pen). Putting the ring برة burat (of copper or hair) through a camel's nose.

A بروء burū‛, (v. n. of برأ) Creating. (v. n. of برؤ for برئ) Recovering from sickness, being healed. Being, free, safe, out of danger. (v. n. of برئ) Being free, clear, exempt.

A بروات barawāt, (pl. of برات barāt) Diplomas, patents, privileges. بروات شريفه barawāti sharīfa, Royal diplomas.

P بروار barwār, A summer-house.

P برواره barwāra, A parlour. An upper chamber. A private way to a house.

P برواز barwāz, Rest, repose. A roost, a perch.

P بروازه barwāza, A nuptial fire. Victuals which people carry to eat in the fields or gardens.

A برواق barwāk, Asphodel. Shoemaker's paste.

P بروان barwān, A stomacher, handkerchief. Any thing thrown over the shoulders. A long flowing robe. A high cap.

G بروانيا barwāniyā, A tree resembling ivy, the fruit of which is used in tanning.

P بروت burūt, Whiskers, mustaches.

A بروث burūs, (pl. of برث bars) Soft grounds.

P بروج barwaj, Broach, a city in Guzerat.

A بروج burūj, (pl. of برج burj) Towers. Zodiacal signs. Fortresses, citadels. Barbacans.

P بروجه bar wajh, By way of, in the manner of. بروجه تعجيل bar wajhi ta‛jīl, In haste, quickly.

A بروح barūh, (Game) which passes from the right side of the hunter to the left. Burūh, (v. n. of برح) Turning the left side to you when passing from right to left (a deer, or any other species of game, esteemed unlucky by the Arabians).

P برود barūd, Bayrūt, a city in Syria.

A برود barūd, Cold, frigid. (Bread) moistened by cold water poured upon it. برود العين barūdu'l ‛ayn, A cold refreshing collyrium, or wash for the eyes. Burūd, (v. n. of برد) Being blunt (a sword). Being weak and languid. Sending a messenger. (pl. of برد burd) Striped stuffs.

A برودة burūdat, (v. n. of برد) Being cold. Coldness, lukewarmness. برودة وكدورة burūdat wa kudūrat, A coldness in friendship. P برودت انگيز burūdat-angez, Exciting coldness, disgusting.

P برودر افتاده barū dar uftāda, Fallen prostrate.

P برور barwar, Fruitful, pregnant. Lace, fringe, edge. (in zand and Pāzand) A brother.

A برور burūr, (v. n. of برّ) Being sworn with truth (an oath): keeping truth and fidelity in an oath.

P بروز barūz, A roost. A fray. Burūz, A bed, a couch. Fringe.

P بروز ba roz, By day, in the day. روز بروز roz ba roz, Daily, from day to day, de die in diem.

A بروز burūz, (v. n. of برز) Going forth into the open country. Being clear, made manifest, published.

P بروسان barūsān or بروشان barūshān, A people, nation, community.

P بروشك burūshak, Dust, earth.

A بروض barūz, A well which gives little water. Burūz, (v. n. of برض) Appearing above ground, whilst the species as yet remains indiscernable (grass). Coming out in a small quantity (water from a well). (pl. of برض barz) Few, some.

A بروع barwa‛, Name of a woman. Name of a camel. Burū‛, (v. n. of برع) Excelling. Being perfect in virtue or beauty.

P برو فرود bar u firod, Up and down. Ascent and descent.

P بروفه burūfa, A turban, a sash.

A بروق barwak, A shrub green in cloudy weather; asphodel. Barūk, A camel which appears pregnant when she is not. Burūk, (v. n. of برق) Shining, glittering, dazzling (a sword). Flashing (the heavens). Being struck with the heat (a leathern churning bottle), so that the butter melts and will not unite. Having the eyes so dazzled with glare as scarcely to be able to shut them. Being astonished, confounded. Rising (a star). Seasoning (meat) with a little oil or butter. Casting forth lightnings. Menacing, threatening. (pl. of برق bark) Lightnings, thunderbolts.

P بروك barūk, A species of dwarf tree.

A بروك barūk, A woman who marries after having a son grown up. Burūk, (v. n. of برك) Kneeling. Lying down on his breast (a camel).

Being firm and solid. Striving, exerting one's self. Raining incessantly. Stopping, staying. Exertion in running. (pl. of برك *bark*) Troops of camels (especially when reclining). A sweetmeat made of dates and butter.

A بروكاء *barūkā‚*, Firmness, steadfastness in battle. A kneeling down.

A بروكة *barwakat*, A female porcupine.

P برومند *barūmand*, Rich, fertile. Wealthy, prosperous, fortunate, happy. Satisfied. Powerful.

P برومندي *barūmandī*, Increase. Happiness.

P برون *birūn*, Without, out, abroad. Not having. For the sake of, on account of. برون آمدن *birūn āmadan*, To come out. To rebel. *Burūn*, A ring. A ring put through a camel's nose.

P بـرّون *barrūn*, (in zand and Pāzand) A ram leading the flock. A mountain goat.

P برونده *barwanda*, A basket. A clothes-bundle.

P برون سرا *birūn-sarā*, Base money (not coined at the mint).

P برونوس *barūnūs*, (or برونوش *barūnūsh*) An army. A soldier. Name of a general.

P بروي *bar vay* or *way*, (for براو *bar u*) Above, upon, to him, or it.

P بره *bara*, A lamb. The sign Aries. A fawn. A pruning-hook (for vines). The exterior surface of a garment. Infirm, weak, برهٔ دو مادري *bara‚i du mādarī*, (A lamb sucking two ewes) Well off, fortunate; having two strings to one's bow. برهٔ فلك *bara‚i falak*, The sign Aries. بره گرفتن *bara giriftan*, To help the weak. *Ba rah*, On the road. Provisions for a journey. An aqueduct. Handsome, beautiful, decorated.

A بره *barah*, (v. n. of بره) Recovering its former state after sickness (the body). Being ruddy and white. Moistness, juiciness, freshness.

A برهاء *barhā‚*, White, fair, and ruddy (woman).

P برهان *barhān*, Joy, gladness.

A برهان *burhān*, (v. n. of بره) Recovering health after sickness. Being fair (the complexion). (pl. براهين *barāhīn*) Demonstration, proof. Conviction. A clear judgment or decision. An indisputable argument. A sign. A prince, chief. برهان قاطع *burhāni kātiʻ*, A convincing proof. برهان مسيح *burhāni masīh*, A demonstration equal to those adduced by the Messiah, viz. Healing the sick or raising the dead.

H برهان پور *barhān-pūr*, A city in Kandesh (India).

P برهانج *barhānaj*, A gusset.

P برهانراج *burhān-rāj*, Convincing discourse.

A برهانيّ *burhāniy*, Demonstrative. Decisive.

P دليل برهاني *dalīli burhānī*, A Convincing proof.

A برهة *barhat* or *burhat* A long space of time. برهة من الزمان *barhat mini'z zamān*, During a long space of time.

P برهختن *barhakhtan* or *barhikhtan*, To extract, draw forth. To educate, instruct, teach good manners. To wound.

P برهخته *barhikhta*, Instructed, educated.

A برهرهة *barahrahat*, A woman (when young, beautiful, delicate, and full of animal spirits).

G برهليا *barhiliyā*, Hay-seed. The herb fennel.

P برهم *bar ham*, Together. Collected, assembled. Confused, perplexed, embroiled, intricate, entangled. Confusion. برهم زدن *bar ham zadan*, To shut close. To slam (a door or window). To mix, confuse. To embroil. To interfere. To prevent. To upset, overthrow, destroy. برهم شدن *bar ham shudan*, To be entangled, embroiled. To be multiplied. To be diversified.

S برهمپتر *barahmaputar*, (Brahma's son) Name of a large river which joins the Ganges near Dakka.

A برهمة *barhamat*, (v. n. of برهم Q) Looking stedfastly, fixing the eyes. *Barhamat* or *burhumat*, The buds of trees or flowers.

P برهم خوردگي *bar ham khwurdagī*, Commotion.

P برهم درهم *barham darham*, Entangled, confused, topsy-turvy.

P برهم ديگر خوردن *bar ham dīgar khwurdan*, To knock (as the knees) against each other, to cut.

P برهم دوزي كردن *bar ham dozī kardan*, To close up a seam (in a ship's plank).

P برهم زدگي *bar ham zadagī*, Confusion, broil. Commotion, agitation

A P برهمن *barhaman*, *barahman*, برهمند *barahmand*, or برهمه (pl. براهمه *barāhima*) A Brahman.

P برهم نشسته *bar ham nishasta*, Thick (darkness).

A برهنة *barhanat*, Establishment of proof.

P برهنگي *barahnagī*, Nakedness, nudity.

P برهنه *barahna*, Naked, bare. A clear, serene sky. برهنه كردن *barahna kardan*, To unveil, make naked, despoil, denude.

P برهنه استخوان *barahna-ustukhwān*, Raw-boned.

P برهنه پا *barahna-pā*, (or پاي *pāy*) Barefoot.

P برهنه جو *barahna-jaw* or *jav*, Huskless barley.

P برهنه سر *barahna-sar*, Bare-headed: a pilgrim.

P برهنه سري *barahna-sarī*, The being uncovered, as a pilgrim on his way to Mecca. Prohibition, repulse, disappointment.

A برهوت *barahūt* or *burhūt*, A well, in which the Muhammadans imagine the souls of all infidels to be confined. They suppose it to be in Hazramawt, to the eastward of the Straits of Bābu'l mandib in Arabia. Name of a medicinal plant. (The Muhammadans say that the best well in the world is Zamzam, and the worst is Barahūt).

P برهود *barhod*, Vain, foolish, absurd. Slightly burned, singed.

P برهودن *barhodan*, To burn, scorch, singe. To be discoloured by the heat of fire. To wander, stray.

P برهون *barhūn*, A halo round the moon. A collar. A girdle. A circle described by compasses. A wooden fence. A thorny hedge. A cottage. Ornament, decoration. The girth or belt-place. The swell of a mountain.

P برهوه *barhūh*, Soap. Marriageable (woman).

P برهيختن *barhekhtan*, To draw forth. To educate, teach.

A بري *bary*, (v. n. of بري) Cutting, chipping, hewing. Making (a pen or arrow), shaping (the nails). Tiring, fatiguing, emaciating (travelling). *Bara'*, Earth. Dust. *Bura'*, (pl. of برة *burat*) Rings through a camel's nose.

A بريء *bari‚*, (pl. بريئون *bari‚un*, براء *bura‚ā‚*, براء *birā‚*, ابراء *abrā‚*, ابرئاء *abri‚ā‚*, or براء *burā‚*) Clear, quit, absolved, innocent, guiltless. (pl. براء *birā‚*) Healed, cured, restored to health.

A بريّ *burra'*, A good, kind, agreeable word.

A بريّ *bariy*, Cut out and smoothed (arrow).

A برّيّ *barriy*, Sylvan, rustic, wild. External. Level (road). Growing on land (in contradistinction to بحريّ *bahriy*, Sea-born, or نهريّ *nahriy*, Fluviatic). A landsman.

A بريئات *bari‚āt*, (or بريّات *bariyāt*) (pl. of بريئة *bari‚at*) Free, clear, absolved (women).

A بريّات *bariyāt*, (pl. of بريّة *bariyat*) Creatures.

P برياش *baryāsh*, Dispersion. Dispersed.

P بريان *biryān*, Roasted, broiled, grilled, baked. Toasted. بريان كردن *biryān kardan*, To bake, roast.

P بريان محلا *biryān-muhallā*, Roast meat, bread, and onions.

A بريئة *bari‚at*, (fem. of بريء *bari‚*) (pl. بريئات *bari‚āt*, بريّات *bariyāt*, and برايا *barāya'*) Free, clear, absolved (woman). (pl. برايا *barāya'*) A creature, created being.

A بريّة *bariyat*, (pl. بريّات *bariyāt* or برايا *barāya'*) A creature. People.

A برّيّة *barriyat*, (pl. براري *barārī*) A desert.

A برّيت *barrīt*, (pl. براريت *barārīt*) A desert, a plain without vegetation. *Birrīt*, An intelligent guide. Level ground.

P بريج *barīj*, An account comprising the amount and then the particulars. Name of a tribe of Afghāns.

P بريجن *barījan*, A portable oven, furnace, stove.

A بريح *barīh*, Game which passes from the right side of the hunter to the left. ابن بريح *ibn barīh*, A crow. امّ بريح *umm barīh*, A crow. A misfortune.

A بريخ *barīkh*, Broken-backed.

A بريد *barīd*, (pl. برد *burud*) Disposed, ready prepared (especially for carrying royal dispatches). A barid, veredus, courier, messenger, running footman. The siyāh-gosh, or black-ear, which constantly attends upon the lion, and is therefore called his running footman. A measure of two parasangs or twelve miles. خيل البريد *khaylu'l barīd*, Posthorses, relays of horses. سير في البريد *sayr fi'l barīd*, A travelling by post. صاحب البريد *sāhibu'l barīd*, A postmaster. P بريد خوش نويد *barīdi khwush-nawīd*, A messenger of good news.

A بريد فلك *barīdi falak*, The moon. Saturn.

P بريدگان *buridagān*, (pl. of بريده *burida*) Cut. Circumcised.

P بريدگي *buridagī*, A cut, fissure, incision. Separation, division.

P بريدن *barīdan*, To send a messenger. *Burīdan*, (or بّريدن *burridan*) To cut, sever. To circumcise. To cut or desert (one's kindred).

P بريده *barīda*, A narrow pass. A ferry, ford. *Burīda*, Cut. Clotted. دم بريده Docked.

P بريده دم *burīda-dum*, Docked.

P بريده زبان *burīda-zabān*, Tongue-tied, mute.

P بريده گوش *burīda-gosh*, Crop-eared.

A برير *barīr*, The early fruit of the tree اراك *arāk*.

P بريزن *barezan*, An oven. *Birezan*, A sieve, a strainer. A frying-pan. An oven made of clay. Galbanum.

P بريزه *bireza*, A kind of gum, benzoin. Metallic cement, solder. A liniment rubbed on a wound.

P بريسال *barīsāl*, Name of the governor or prefect of Yaman.

P بريسمان *ba rīsmān*, With a rope. بريسمان كس در چاه مرو *ba rīsmāni kas dar chāh ma rav*, Descend not into the well by another's rope (Risk not your life at the instance of another).

A بريش *barīsh*, (A horse) having spots of a different colour from the rest of his hair, dappled.

P بريش *birīsh*, Dispersion.

P بريشم *barīshim*, (for ابريشيم *abrīshīm*) Silk.

G بريشوي *barīshawī*, The eve of the sabbath, Easter, or any other festival, the preparation.

A بريص *barīṣ*, Bright, shining. Leprous. A plant resembling galangale. ابو بريص *abū barīṣ*, A certain speckled bird.

A بريعة *barīʿat*, A woman witty or beautiful.

P بريغ *biregh*, A bunch of grapes.

A بريق *barīk*, (v. n. of برق) Flashing, dazzling. Seasoning (meat) with a little oil or butter. Rising (a star). Lightning. Splendour, brilliancy. Flash, gleam, glitter. *Burayh*, Name of a poet.

A بريقة *barīkat*, (pl. برائق *barāïk*) Milk into which a little butter or other fat substance is poured.

A بريك *barīk*, (pl. برك *burk*) Blessed with abundance. Plenteous. Fresh dates eaten with butter.

A بريكة *barīkat*, A kind of dish made with fresh dates and butter.

A بريم *barīm*, Formed of two or more things twisted together (especially of black and white or brown hair). A wreath, made in general of white and red threads twisted together, and often adorned with jewels, which the women fasten about their waists or their arms. A kind of amulet or charm hung round a child, as a preservative against fascinating or malignant eyes. An army (from the different coloured ensigns). The dawn (from the various tints of the clouds). Part of the liver and of the bunch of a camel, which are cut into oblong slices, strung upon a thread, and dressed together (being so called from the difference of their colours, the first being black and the other white). Flocks of two kinds of cattle (sheep and goats, camels and oxen). A miscellaneous assembly, a crowd, mob. A tear mixed with antimony. Suspected, accused. البريمان *al albarīmāni*, Heart and bunch of a camel.

A بريمة *barīmat*, An auger, gimlet. A trepan.

P برين *barīn*, (for براين *bar in*) On, or upon, this. High, sublime, eminent (in situation, quality, or dignity). Upper, higher, highest. Superior, supreme. Perpetual, eternal. Pleasant, agreeable. Excellence of any thing, the principal part. The north-east wind. A notch, fissure. Name of a fire-temple. پايهٔ برين *pāyaï barīn*, The highest step. چرخ برين *charkhi barīn*, The heavens, the celestial sphere. فردوس برين *firdawsi barīn*, (or خلد برين *khuldi barīn*) Paradise above, eternal, delightful. *Birīn*, An opening. Door of an oven. Fetid water. A sink. *Burīn*, A slice of a melon.

A برين *burīn* or *birīn*, (pl. of برة *burat*) Rings in camels' noses.

A بّرين *barrayni*, (dual of بّر *barr*) The provinces adjacent to the White and Black Seas (the Mediterranean and Euxine).

P برينش *burīnish*, A scissure. A flux, diarrhœa.

P برينقدر *bar īn kadar*, Moreover, nevertheless.

P برينكه *bar īn ki*, To wit; videlicet.

P برينه *birīna*, A hole. Mouth of a furnace.

P بريون *baryūn*, The parts round the mouth. *Barewan*, *biryawn*, or *biryūn*, A ring-worm.

A بريئون *barīūn*, (pl. of بريء *barīʾ*) Clear, quit.

A بريه *burayh*, (or بريهيم *burayhīm*) (dim. of ابراهيم *ibrāhīm*) A little Abraham.

P بز *baz*, A habit, a rich dress. Fine linen. A bull's dewlap. High ground. A hill. Manner, custom, rule. (for بزم *bazm*) A feast. *Biz*, A bee. *Buz*, A she-goat, the goat species.

A بزّ *bazza*, (fut. يبزّ *yabuzzu*) He seized forcibly.

A بزّ *bazz*, (v. n. of بزّ) Seizing, carrying away forcibly. Fine linen. A garment, clothing. Arms, armour. Furniture, drapery. Victory, conquest, superiority. The extremity of a river. من عزّ بزّ *man ʿazza bazza*, The strong carries off the spoil.

A بزا *baza'* (v. n. of بزا) Being hump-backed. A protuberance of the breast, with a hollow back. A hump-back.

A بزابز *buzābiz*, A smart, active lad. A quick walker. Strong and not courageous.

A بزاة *buzāt*, (pl. of بازي *bāzī*) Kites. Falcons.

A بزاج *bizāj*, A boasting. A contending with.

A بزاخة *buzākhat*, Name of a place where a battle was fought in the caliphat of Abū bakr.

P بزاختن *buzākhtan*, To melt, liquify. To clean.

P بزاد بر آمده *ba zād bar āmada*, An old woman.

A بزادرة *bazādirat*, (pl. of P بازدار) Falconers.

P بزادي *bazādī*, A beryl, a sea-green stone.

A بزار *bazzār*, A dealer in linseed or linseed-oil.

P بزاريدن *buzārīdan*, To melt, to liquefy.

P بزاز *bazāz*, A shoe-latchet, a leathern thong. *Buzāz*, A carpenter or shoemaker's wedge.

A بزّاز *bazzāz*, A dealer in cloths, a linen-draper. A general merchant, trader, shopkeeper. An inn-keeper. Name of several reporters of traditions.

A بزازة *bizāzat*, The drapery or furniture business.

P بزّازستان *bazzāzistān*, A market-place.

A بزاع *buzāʿ*, A light, nimble, clever servant.

A بزاعة *bazāʿat*, (v. n. of بزع) Being polished, well-bred (a young man). Possessing good abilities. *Buzāʿat* or *bizāʿat*, Name of a town near Aleppo.

A بزاغه *bazāgha*, Name of a place near Aleppo.

A بزاق *buzāk*, Spittle.

A بزال *bizāl*, A spigot. *Buzāl*, A hole at which the liquor of a vessel is let out.

P بزان *bazān*, Leaping. Blowing. Wind.

A بزان *bizān*, (v. n. 3 of بزن not in use) Bringing.

P بزانه *bazāna*, Blowing (wind).

A بزواء *bazāwāʾ*, Hump-backed (woman).

P بزايانيدن *ba zāyānīdan*, To assist a woman in labour, to help to bring forth.

P بزباز *bazbāz*, The cover of nutmeg, mace.

A بزباز *bazbāz*, An active lad. A fast walker. The nozzle of a pair of bellows. The privities.

A بزبز *buzbuz*, A smart, nimble lad. An active walker. Strong but not courageous.

A بزبزة *bazbazat*, (v. n. of بزبز Q) Walking fast. Urging forward, stimulating. Moving very much and fast. Curing, remedying, adjusting. Forcing to do any thing against the will. Spoiling, seizing. Shooting one without design. Flight, escape.

P بزپونتن *bazpūnitan*, (in zand) To give.

A بزّة *bizzat*, A rich dress, presented by a prince, or great man as a mark of honour. Arms, armour. Form, figure.

A بزج *bazj*, (v. n. of بزج) Boasting, contending for pre-eminence. Irritating (one against another).

P بزجامه *baz-jāma*, (or برجامه) A rich dress.

A بزخ *bazkh*, (v. n. of بزخ) Sweeping all away. Striking on the back with a stick. *Bazakh*, A protuberance of breast and a hollowness of back.

A بزخاء *bazkhāʾ*, Protuberant-breasted, hollow-backed (woman).

P بزداغ *bazdāgh*, *bizdāgh*, or *buzdāgh*, A polishing or furbishing instrument.

P بزداييدن *bizdāyīdan*, To furbish, remove rust.

P بزدل *buz-dil*, (Goat-hearted) A coward.

A بزر *bazr*, (v. n. of بزر) Beating. Sowing seed, disseminating. Blowing the nose. Filling. Throwing herbs into the pot to season victuals. Offspring. Suivel. *Bazr* or *bizr*, (pl. بزور *buzūr*) A pot-herb seed. Seed. The egg of the silk-worm. (pl. ابزار *abzār* and ابازير *abāzīr*) A pot-herb seasoning for meat. بزر البنج *bazru'l banj*, Henbane-seed. بزر الكتّان *bazru'l kattān*, Linseed.

P بزرا *bazrā*, (in zand and Pāz.) Seed, grain.

A بزراء *bazrūʼ*, (A woman) with a numerous seed.

A بزرج *buzurj*, (P. بزرگ *buzurg*) Great, grand.

P بزرجمهر *buzurj-mihr*, Name of the prime minister of Naushirwān King of Persia.

P بزرخانه *bazr-khāna*, An oil-mill.

P بزرقطونا *bazr-katūnā*, Fleawort; its seed.

P بزرك *bazrak*, A small seed.

P بزركار *bazr-kār*, A farmer.

P بزرگ *bazurg*, Linseed. *Buzurg*, Great, large, immense. Powerful, grand, magnificent. Adult, elder. A saint. Name of a note in music. بزرگ شدن *buzurg shudan*, To grow up. بزرگ داشتن *buzurg dāshtan*, To honour, to revere, magnify.

P بزرگ آميد *buzurg-umed*, (Great hope) Name of a sage, tutor to Parvez the son of Naushīrwān.

P بزرگان *buzurgān*, (pl. of بزرگ *buzurg*) Grandees, nobles. Doctors, wise men, philosophers.

P بزرگانه *buzurgāna*, Magnificent, grand. Befitting the great. Magnificently. بزرگانه آواز *buzurgāna-āwāz*, A loud voice. In a high key.

P بزرگتر *buzurgtar*, Greater, larger, bigger.

P بزرگ تن *buzurg-tan*, Corpulent, big-bodied.

P بزرگر *bazrgar*, A farmer, ploughman, sower.

P بزرگ زادگي *buzurg-zādagī*, High birth.

P بزرگزاده *buzurg-zāda*, Of noble race, high-born.

P بزرگ زانو *buzurg-zānū*, Large-kneed.

P بزرگسال *buzurg-sāl*, Aged, stricken in years.

P بزرگ سالي *buzurg-sālī*, Greatness of age.

P بزرگ منش *buzurg-manish*, Proud, haughty.

P بزرگ منشي *buzurg-manishī*, Pride, disdain.

P بزرگوار *buzurgwār*, Great, excellent. Powerful, magnificent. Noble, illustrious. A learned man, doctor, philosopher. (This word is applied only to man; بزرگ *buzurg* above, being used indiscriminately to express, as well inanimate substances as animate beings: as, سنگ بزرگ *sangi buzurg*, A large stone).

P بزرگواري *buzurgwārī*, Grandeur, greatness, magnificence. Honour, glory. Highness, nobility.

P بزرگ همّت *buzurg-himmat*, High-minded.

P بزرگي *buzurgī*, Grandeur, greatness.

P بزرور *bazrwar*, Employed. Full of seed.

A بزري *bazaraʼ*, Hollow-backed, protuberant-breasted (young woman).

A بزز *bazaz*, Arms, armour.

P بزستان *bazistān*, A cloth-hall: market-place.

P بزسك *buzisk*, A lentil.

P بزشك *bizishk*, A physician. A horse-doctor.

P بزشكي *bizishkī*, Physic, medical practice. بزشكي نمودن *bizishkī namūdan*, To profess physic.

P بزشم *buzashm*, (from بز *buz* and پشم *pashm*) Fine goat's hair growing at the root of the long hair, and employed in the manufacture of shawls.

P بزغ *bazgh*, A ditch wherein water stagnates. *Bazagh*, A frog. A dam, a weir. Water-lentils, or any herbage that vegetates in water, amongst which the frogs live.

A بزغ *bazgh*, (v. n. of بزغ) Bleeding, breathing a vein. Rising (the sun). Coming forth, appearing (a camel's tooth).

P بزغاله *buz-ghāla*, (pl. بزغالگان *buzghālagān*) A kid. A calf. بزغالهٔ فلك *buzghālaʼi falak*, Aries.

A بزغة *bazghat*, (v. n. of بزغ) Opening a vein.

A بزغر *buzghur*, Malicious.

P بزغسمه *bazagh-sama*, (or بزغمه) Water-moss.

P بزغش *buzghush*, Name of a saint.

P بزغم *bazgham*, A thorny tree, the acacia.

P بزغنج *buzghunj*, (or بزغند *buzghund*) The pistachio-tree or nut.

P بزغه *bazgha*, A support for a vine. *Buzgha*, A kind of hatchet. *Bazagha*, A kind of lizard.

P بزفل *bazful*, (or بزقل *bazkal*) A rose-worm.

P بزفند *bazfand*, Idle, lazy, sluggish. Weak.

A بزق *bazk*, (v. n. of بزق) Spitting, spawling. Sowing (ground). Rising (the sun).

P بزق *bazak*, A frog. Name of a herb.

P بزقدم *buz-kadam*, Timid: a coward: abject.

P بزك *buzh*, Name of a black-coloured, long-beaked bird.

P بزكوهي *buzi kohī*, The mountain-goat. A doe.

A بزكي *bazakaʼ*, Quickness of pace.

P بزگله *buz-gala*, A flock of goats.

A بزل *bazl*, (v. n. of بزل) Cleaving. Breaking off (an affair, or an opinion). Tapping, broaching (a barrel), drawing off (wine). Straining, purifying, racking (wine). امر ذو بزل *amrun zū bazlin*, An important and unfortunate event. *Buzl*, (v. n. of بزل) Appearing (the camel's tooth called ناب *nāb*). A she-goat. *Buzul*, (or بزّل *buzzal*), (pl. of بازل *bāzil* and بزول *bazūl*) (Camels) whose fore and side teeth called ناب *nāb* are appearing.

A بزلاء *bazlāʼ*, Good thoughts. Wholesome advice, excellent counsel. A dreadful calamity. Adversity, troubles. خطّة بزلاء *khuttat bazlāʼ*, A line separating truth from falsehood. نهّاض ببزلاء *nahhāzun bi bazlāʼi*, One who understands and executes affairs of importance.

P بزله *bazla*, A jest, a bon-mot.

P بزم *bazm*, A banquet, entertainment, assembly, convivial meeting. Society. A pavilion.

A بزم *bazm*, (v. n. of بزم) Biting with the front teeth. Milking (a camel) with the fore-finger and thumb. Stealing (a garment). Carrying a load. Twanging (a bow-string). Coarse language. A fraction. A resolution to accomplish any thing.

P بزماده *buz-māda*, A she-goat.

P بزم افزون *bazm-afzūn*, Name of a lady.

P بزمان *bazmān* or *buzmān*, Drunk. Sorrowful. Desire, wish, will.

P بزماورد *bazm-āward*, Viands or sweetmeats carried home from a feast. A kind of sandwich.

P بزمايون *bazmāyūn*, Name of Farīdūn's cow.

A بزمة *bazmat*, A single meal. A weight of thirty dirhems.

A بزمخة *bazmakhat*, A being proud or arrogant.

P بزمگاه *bazm-gāh*, (or بزمگه *bazm-gah*) A banqueting-house: a jovial company. Name of a book. بزمگاه بلاغت *bazm-gāhi balāghat*, Field of eloquence, place for disputation, oratory, or conversation.

P بزمونه *bazmūna*, The second day of the month according to the æra of Jalālu'd dīn.

P بزموي *buz-moy* or *mūy*, Goat's hair.

P بزمه *bazma*, A nook of a banqueting-house.

P بزن *bazan*, A harrow. A ploughshare.

P بزندار *bazindār*, (in zand) A window, balcony.

L بزنطيه *bizantīh*, Byzantium, Constantinople.

P بزنگ *bazang*, A bolt, a bar. A key.

A بزو *bazw*, (v. n. of بزا for بزو) Overpowering, seizing. An equilibrium, equipose, equivalent.

A بزواء *bazwāʼ*, Protuberant-breasted, hollow-backed (woman). Name of a tract between Mecca and Madīna.

A بزوان *bazawān*, (v. n. of بزا for بزو) Attacking, overpowering. Assault, attack: impetuosity.

P بزودي *ba zūdī*, With speed. Quickly.

P بزور *ba zūr* or *ba zor*, By force, forcibly.

A بزور *buzūr*, (pl. of بزر *bazr*) Herb-seeds. Seeds.

A بزوري *buzūrīy*, A green-grocer: seedsman.

P بزوش *buzvash*, Goatish, goat-like, like a goat.

P بزوشم *buz-washm*, (for بزيشم) Goat's hair.

P بزوشه *buzawsha*, Lamb's tongue (an herb).

P بزوغ *buzūgh*, The rising of the sun, moon, or stars.

A بزوغ *buzūgh*, (v. n. of بزغ) Breaking (day). Rising (the sun). Cutting (a tooth). Opening (a vein).

A بزول *bazūl*, (pl. بزل *buzul*) (A camel) breeding a front or side-tooth called ناب *nāb*, which occurs in his ninth year. *Buzūl*, (v. n. of بزل) Having a fore or side-tooth (called ناب *nāb*) projecting from the gums (a camel). Cleaving.

P بزونه *bazūna*, (in zand and Pāz.) The knee.

P بزه *baza*, A sin, crime. Disappointed, frustrated. Poor. Injustice, oppression. *Buza*, Unequal ground. A kind of odoriferous fruit.

P بزهش *buzhish*, Opposition. Comparison, collation.

P بزه كار *baza-kār*, A sinner.

P بزه گار *bazagār*, Sinful, criminal.

P بزه مند *bazamand*, Culpable, criminal.

A بزيٓ *bazaʼ*, A protuberance of the breast with a hollowness of the back.

A بزيّ *bazīy*, A foster-brother.

A بزيج *bazīj*, One who returns benefits, who requites a favour; grateful.

P بزيچه *buzīcha*, A kid. A butcher's block.

P بزيدن *bazīdan*, To blow as the wind. *Buzīdan*, To tickle. To pluck off hair or wool.

P بزيده *bazīda*, Blown (as the wind). *Buzīda*, Tickled. Plucked, pulled off.

P بزير *ba zīr*, Downwards. بزير آمدن *ba zīr āmadan*, To descend. بزير زنخ دست ستون كردن *ba zīri zanakh dast sutūn kardan*, To be pensive and dejected. بزير گرفتن *ba zīr giriftan*, To detract, take down. بزير نگين آوردن *ba zīri nigīn āwardan*, To bring under subjection.

A بزيزا *bizzīza'*, Victory, conquest, superiority.

P بزيشه *bazesha*, Sesame-flour. The dregs of sesame-oil.

A بزيع *bazīꜥ*, Ingenious, intelligent (youth). Light, nimble. Eloquent. Shameless, impudent.

A بزيم *bazīm*, A young sucker with which they tie pot-herbs. A bundle or handful of pot-herbs. The remains of broth at the bottom of a pot.

P بزين *bazīn*, Blowing. Name of a fire-temple in Nishābūr.

P بزيون *bizyawn* or *buzyūn*, Brocade.

P بژ *baj*, Snow, sleet. A hill. A heap.

P بژج *bajuj*, Invention, a new discovery.

P بژرني *bajarnī*, Magnificence, majesty.

P بژغرده *bajghurda*, A rolling-pin. A kind of thorny plant.

P بژکم *bajkam*, A keeping back, a preventing.

P بژکول *bajkūl* or *bijkūl*, Strong, robust. Patient. Laborious. Eager, earnest.

P بژم *bajm*, Dew.

P بژمان *bajmān* or *bijmān*, Sad, melancholy, mournful, dejected. Faint, flagging.

P بژمژه *bujmaja*, A chameleon.

P بژن *bajan*, Mud at the bottom of a well.

P بژند *bajand*, Name of a herb used in cookery.

P بژندي *bajandī*, Disappointment. Poverty.

P بژنگ *bajang*, A key.

P بژوال *bajwāl*, An echo.

P بژوج *bajūj*, An invention, a new discovery.

P بژول *bujūl*, The ankle.

P بژهان *bujhān*, Strong desire, without envy.

P بژير *bajīr*, A wing, a feather. Wool.

P بس *bas*, Often. Only. Enough, it is sufficient! no more! A great number, many, more. Very much, greatly. Yes, indeed, certainly, it is so, very true, surely, undoubtedly, unquestionably. بس کردن *bas kardan*, To stop, leave off, give over. *Bus*, A spit. A kiss, a buss.

A بسّ *bass*, (v. n. of بسّ) Driving (a camel) gently. Turning (cattle) loose. Being crumbled to dust (a mountain). Losing part of his property (a man). Preparing a kind of dish made with barley-meal or flour, and mixed with oil or butter, called بسيسة *basīsat*. Sending into different parts (money, merchandize, or spies). Calling (a camel) to be milked by the words *bas bas*. A petition, request; demand. Power, strength, vigour. Labour, study. Enough, sufficiency. *Bass* or *biss*, A domestic cat. *Bass, biss, buss*, The noise by which they call sheep.

A P بسوء *basū*, (*basaw* or بساء *basāū*) (v. n. of بسا) Becoming habituated, intimate, or familiar.

P بسا *basā*, Many, some, something, somewhat, how many soever. Oh! enough! Name of a city in Persia. چند چند بسا *chand chand basā*, (or بسا بسا *basā basā*) Many, in great numbers.

P بسا بزرگ *basā-buzurg*, Very great, very noble.

A بسابس *basābis*, (pl. of بسبس *basbas*) Desert lands. Trifling amusements, foolish words.

A بساتين *basātīn*, (pl. of بستان *bustān*) Gardens. P بساتين خوش نما و دلکشا *basātīni khwush-namā u dil-kushā*, Gardens beautiful and delighting the heart.

A بساتيني *basātīniy*, A gardener.

A بساتينية *basātīniyat*, Gardeners.

P بساج *basāj*, (or بساخ) Depravity, wickedness.

P بسا دست *basā-dast*, Earnest-money.

A بسار *bisār*, (pl. of بسر *busr*) Rains newly fallen.

A بسارة *bisārat*, Summer-rains, rains in India.

P بساردادن *bi* or *basārdādan*, (or بساردن *bi* or *basārdan*) To plough, to break up fallow ground.

P بسارده *basārda*, Watered. *Bisārda*, Ploughed.

P بساروب *basā-rob*, Gleanings after harvest.

P بساره *ba* or *bisāra*, A bench: a portico, verandah.

P بساز *bisāz*, A day. (imp. of ساختن) Do thou.

P بساس *basās*, Length.

A بساسة *bassāsat*, Mecca.

A بساط *basāt*, Extensive (tract of country). A large cauldron. A wide plain, an open, level country. *Bisāt*, (pl. بسط *busut*) A bed, covering, carpet, cushion, or any thing spread upon the ground for sitting, reclining, or sleeping, or for receiving leaves or fruit shaken from a tree. An extensive tract of country. (v. n. 3 of بسط) Laying aside modesty. (pl. of بسط *bist, bust*, and *busut*) Camels left with their sucking colts. P بساط خاك *bisāti khāk*, The earth. بساط ساختن از رخسار *bisāt sākhtan az rukhsār*, To fall prostrate. To lie on the bare ground. A بساط شطرنج *bisāti shatranj*, A chequered carpet for the game of chess. بساط فلك *bisāti falak*, The terrestrial globe. بساط كون و مكان *bisāti kawn u makān*, The surface of the globe, whole world, universe. بساط مقراضي *bisāti mikrāzī*, A carpet curiously cut out and wrought.

A بساطة *basātat*, (v. n. of بسط) Speaking freely.

A بساطي *bisātī*, A pedlar, a toyman.

A بساق *bisāk*, (pl. of بسقة *baskat*) Stony countries. *Busāk*, Spittle, saliva when spit out (whilst in the mouth it is called ريق *rīk*).

P بساك *basāk*, A garland of flowers.

A بسال *basāl*, (v. n. of بسل) Being strong, strenuous, powerful. *Bisāl*, (v. n. 3 of بسل) Surrounding (an enemy).

A بسالة *basālat*, (v. n. of بسل) Being brave, valiant. Valour.

P بساله كردن *basāla kardan*, To rub, to bray.

A بسّام *bassām*, One who smiles much. A name.

P بسامان *ba sāmān*, Good, upright. A pledge.

P بسان *ba sān*, Like, resembling.

P بسانج *basānij*, A kind of herb.

P بسانيدن *basānīdan*, To water, to irrigate.

P بساوند *basāwand*, The last consonant in a verse with which all the other distichs rhyme.

P بسباس *basbās*, Vain, unmeaning conversation.

A بسباس *basbās*, The herb fennel.

A بسباسا *basbāsā*, Wild rue.

A بسباسة *basbāsat*, Mace, the nutmeg's envelope.

P بسبب *ba sabab*, For that reason, therefore.

A بسبس *basbas*, (pl. بسابس *basābis*) A desert, uncultivated ground. Trifling amusement. Foolish words. A tree whence they make saddle-timbers.

A بسبسة *basbasat*, (v. n. of بسبس Q) Calling (camels). Making haste. Being unremitting, constant, persevering.

P بسپايه *bas pāya*, (Many footed) Polypody.

A بسّة *bissat*, (pl. بسس *bisas*) A domestic cat.

P بست *bast*, He bound or connected. A lover, a sweetheart, one in whom the heart is bound up. A turban, wreath for the head. A knot. A hundred. A sanctuary, asylum. A bank, a rampart. A mountain. Distribution of water into canals, ditches, or drains. *Bist*, Twenty. *Bust*, Name of a country and of a fortress. A rose-garden.

A بست *bast*, A kind of running, straddling pace.

P بستا *bastā*, A cloth in which a bundle is tied up.

P بستاخ *bustākh*, Impudent, forward, rash.

P بستار *bistār*, Inconstant. Weak. Fresh water.

P بستام *bistām*, Coral.

P بستان *bi satān*, (imper. of ستاندن *satāndan*) Take. Buy. *Bustān*, A garden for flowers or herbs (a fruit-garden being expressed by باغ *bāgh*). A place where odoriferous fruits grow.

A P بستان *bustān*, (Ar. pl. بساتين *basātīn* or بساتون *basātūn*) A garden.

P بستان افروز *bustān-afroz*, Inflaming the garden (an epithet applied to the anemone, the purple amaranth, and other flowers).

P بستان پيرا *bustān-perā*, Gardener, vine-dresser.

P بستان سراي *bustān-sarāy*, A palace-garden.

P بستان شيرين *bustān-shīrīn*, A note in music.

P بستاني *bustānī*, Hortulan. A gardener.

P بستاوند *bustāwand*, Hillocks: uneven ground.

P بستج *bustaj*, (*bustij*, or بسج) Frankincense.

P بستر *bistar*, A bed, mattress, bolster, pillow, cushion. بر بستر عيش و حضور *bar bistari ꜥish u huzūr*, Upon the bed of ease and pleasure. بستر سمندر *bistari samandar*, The salamander's bed, *i. e.* Fire. بستر شدن *bistar shudan*, To be abed, lie down.

P بستر آهنگ *bistar-āhang*, A coverlet: a sheet.

P بستردن *bistardan*, To obliterate. To clean.

P بسترم *busturm*, An eruption on the body.

P بستر نشين *bistar-nishīn*, Lying on a bed.

P بستري *bistarī*, Bed-ridden.

A بستق *bastak*, A servant, minister, attendant.

A بستقان *bustakān*, A gardener. A keeper of a vineyard, one who watches sown fields to keep them from accidental injury.

P بستك *bustak*, Frankincense.

P بستگي *bastagī*, The being bound or fastened.

The setting of a broken limb. Tightness, stricture, fastness. A band, swathe. A stammering, stuttering, impediment in speech. بستگيِ بول *bastagī-i bawl*, Strangury. بستگيِ سخن *bastagī-i sukhan*, Impediment in the speech. بستگيِ فرج *bastagī-i farj*, A female hernia.

P بستم *bistum*, The twentieth.

P بستن *bastan*, To bind, shut, close up. To contract, get, acquire, incur. To congeal, coagulate, clot. بستنگاه كشتيها *bastan-gāhi kashtīhā*, An anchorage or mooring for ships.

P بستني *bastanī*, A cloth for binding together bundles of paper, books, inkstands, and the like.

P بستو *bastū*, A small glazed earthenware vessel. A churn-stick.

P بست و بند *bast u band*, Arrangement, adjustment. Controul.

A بستوقة *bustūkat*, Earthenware, pottery.

P بستوه *bistūh*, Sad, melancholy, afflicted.

P بسته *basta*, Bound, obliged, tied, fastened, chained. Closed, shut, locked, barred, bolted. Set (broken limb or fruit-blossoms). Coagulated, clotted, congealed. Concreted. Stopped up, obstructed, blocked up. Fixed, established, determined, concluded. Benumbed. Bewitched, and so rendered impotent. Planted, driven in. Coloured silk stretched on a frame to be embroidered. A bale of goods. A poem consisting of four verses. Name of a note in music. بسته شدن *basta shudan*, To be bound. بسته كردن *basta kardan*, To bind. بستهٔ زنجير بودن *basta-i zinjīr būdan*, To be made prisoner, taken captive and bound in chains. دست و گردن بسته *dast u gardan-basta*, Bound hand and neck. يخ بسته *yakh-basta*, Ice-bound, frozen. *Bistuh*, Sad, melancholy. *Busta*, A filbert nut.

P بسته رحم *basta-rahim*, Barren.

P بسته زبان *basta-zabān*, Tongue-tied.

P بسته فرج *basta-farj*, Impervious (woman).

P بسته نگار *basta-nigār*, Name of a note in music.

P بستي *bustī*, A gardener. Gardening. Relating to a garden. A native of Bust.

P بستيباج رومي *bastibāji rūmī*, Name of a creeping plant.

P بستيغ *bastīgh*, A village near Nishābur.

P بسخندن *baskhandan*, To cause fermentation (with yeast).

P بسخن رسيد *ba sukhan rasīd*, A reasonable man.

P بس خواسته *bas-khwāsta*, Much sought after.

P A بسد *busd*, A flower-garden. A fruit-garden.

P بسّد *bussad* or *bissad*, Coral, and its root.

P بسدك *basadk*, A handful of wheat or barley in the straw. *Basdak*, The herb melilot.

P بسدين *busdīn*, Red.

P بسّدين *bussadīn*, Red, coral-colour.

A بسّذ *bussaz*, (from P بسّد *bussad*) Coral.

A بسر *basr*, (v. n. of بسر) Doing or asking (any thing) prematurely or unseasonably. Sprinkling before the proper time the female palm-tree with the flowers of the male, or causing a she-camel to be covered. Covering a she-camel before she is in season. Pressing the payment of a debt before the time. Laying bare the scar of an unhealed wound. Expressing the juice from ripe dates, amongst which unripe ones are mixed. Eating grass before it is fit to be grazed. Emptying the churn before the butter has been made. Beginning, commencing. Looking austere. Having a stern, awful countenance. Oppressing, overcoming by force. Cold water. The beginning of any thing. *Busr*, Unripe dates full grown, and beginning to ripen. Herbs nearly of full growth. (pl. بسار *bisār*) Fresh rain just fallen. Any thing fresh, new, and tender. Tender herbage. A young man, a youth. A young woman. Name of a place. *Busur*, (pl. of بسرة *busrat*, q. v.).

P بسر *ba sar*, At or to the head, end, point, or extremity: as, بسر آمدن *ba sar āmadan*, To come to an end; to be finished. To die. بسر بردن *ba sar burdan*, To bear or carry to an end. To finish, accomplish. To fulfil a promise. To pass the time, to live. To agree, harmonize. To condole, sympathize. To kill.

A بسراط *bisrāt*, Name of a place abounding in crocodiles near Damietta.

P بسر بردگي *ba sar burdagī*, The fulfiment (of a promise). Accomplishment.

A بسرة *busrat* or *busurat*, One single unripe date. The sun just rising. Small glass beads and other similar ornaments with which the poorer people decorate themselves. The point of a dog's penis. Name of the foster-mother of Muhammad.

P بسر در آمدگي *ba sar dar āmadagī*, A slip, fall.

P بسر در آينده *ba sar dar āyanda*, One who falls on his head.

P بسر و چشم *ba sar u chashm*, (With head and eye) Willingly, cheerfully.

P بسريا *bisriyā*, (in zand and Pāz.) Meat, flesh.

A بسس *bisas*, (pl. of بسّة *bissat*) Domestic cats. *Busus*, (She-camels) gentle and easily milked. Barley flour (after being soaked one night in water, and then fried) rubbed, shaken, and mixed together. Shepherds, keepers.

A بسط *basata*, (fut. يبسط *yabsutu*) He stretched.

A بسط *bast*, (v. n. of بسط) Stretching out (the hand). Spreading abroad. Enlarging, widening. Whipping, scourging. Receiving (an apology). Containing, holding, being wide enough for. Exhilarating. Preferring, exalting. Removing shame from any one. A name given to an inebriating paste made from hemp-flowers mixed with tobacco. A she-camel left with her sucking colt. P بسط كردن *bast kardan*, To expand. بسط جناح كردن *basti janāh kardan*, To expand the wings. A *Bist*, *bust*, or *busut*, (pl. ابساط *absāt*, بسط *busut*, and بساط *bisāt*) A she-camel left with her sucking colt. *Bust*, *bist*, or *busut*, Open, expanded (hand). *Busut*, (pl. of بسط *bist*, *bust*, and *busut*) She-camels left to pasture with their colts. (pl. of بساط *bisāt*) Carpets or any thing spread upon the ground (for sitting or sleeping). (pl. of بسيط *basīt*) Wide, ample, spacious. Simple. Open, liberal.

A بسطاء *bastā*, Large and broad (ear).

A بسطام *bastām*, Name of a city. *Bistām*, Name of a man. Name of a city.

A بسطامّي *bastāmīy*, Native of Bastām.

A بسطة *bastat* or *bustat*, Excellence. Extensive and profound literary acquirements. Tallness, fulness of stature.

A بسطيّ *bastīy*, A vender of the intoxicating electuary بسط *bast*.

P بسغ *basagh*, A cupola, a high apartment surrounded with windows, for prospect and air.

P بسغده *basaghda* or *basughda*, Ready, prepared. An accomplisher.

P بسغديدن *basaghdīdan*, *bisaghdīdan*, or *bisughdīdan*, To be finished, arranged, prepared.

A بسفايج *basfāyaj*, (from P بس پايه) Polypody.

A بسق *bask*, (v. n. of بسق) Spitting, spawling.

G بسقپوس *biskupos*, A bishop.

A بسقة *baskat*, A stony, burnt-up country.

P بسك *bask*, A handful of wheat in the ear. Yawning. *Basak*, Melilot. *Busuk*, Cotton-twist.

A بسكل *buskul*, The last horse in a race.

P بسكله *bashala*, The bar of a door.

P بسكليدن *bishilīdan*, To tickle. To embrace.

P بسگوي *bas-goy*, Talkative, prating, verbose.

A بسل *basula*, (fut. يبسل *yabsulu*) He was valiant.

A بسل *basl*, (v. n. of بسل) Accelerating. Sifting with a sieve. Taking by little at a time. Detaining, imprisoning. Unlawful, illicit, illegal. Lawful. Intenseness, violence, severity. The beard. Reproof, blame, censure. Torment. Eight months held sacred by a portion of the tribes of Ghatafān and Kays. The expressed juice of saffron and privet. Disagreeable and repulsive in one's aspect. *Busl*, (pl. of باسل *bāsil*) Heroes. Lions. *Basal*, Yes, even so. *Basil*, Bold, brave. Austere, angry. *Busul*, (pl. of باسل *bāsil*) Brave men.

P بسل *basal*, Millet. The heel.

A بسلاء *busalā*, (pl. of باسل *bāsil*) Heroes. Lions.

A بسلاً بسلاً *baslan baslan*, Amen! amen!

A بسلاً له *baslan lahu*, Woe be to him!

P بسلانيدن *bisilānīdan*, To drag. To break.

A بسلة *buslat*, The hire of an enchanter.

P بسله *basla*, A pea, pease.

A بسم *basm*, (v. n. of بسم) Smiling. Tasting. بسم *bi'smi*, (for باسم *bi ismi*) In the name of. بسم الله *bismi'llāh*, In the name of God (an ejaculation frequently used by Muhammadans, especially when going to commence any thing). At the beginning of the sūras or chapters of the Kur'ān, and indeed prefixed to almost every Arabic, Persian, or Turkish book, is the following line بســــــم الله الرحمٰن الرحيم *bismi'llāhi'r rahmāni'r rahīm*, In the name of God, the compassionate, the merciful (often extending the connecting stroke between س *sin* and م *mim* to an uncommon length; and sometimes adding و به نستعين *wa bihi nastaʿīn*, And of Him we implore aid). This verse is often followed by another of the same rhyme. نعوذ بالله من الشيطان الرجيم *naʿūzu bi'llāh mini'sh shaytāni'r rajīm*, Let us fly to God from the execrable devil!

P بسمل *bismil*, Sacrificed, slaughtered. Meek, forbearing. بسمل کردن *bismil kardan*, To sacrifice, to slaughter. (*Bismil* is contracted from *bismillāh*, and is used in this sense, because, when they kill an animal, they always say, or ought to say, *bismillāh*, in the name of God).

A بسملة *basmalat*, (v. n. of بسمل Q) Pronouncing the sentence بسم الله *bismi'llāh*, In the name of God.

P بسملگاه *bismil-gāh*, Slaughter-house, butchery.

P بسمه *basma*, A collyrium, tincture, or medicine for the eyes. A gold or gilded thread.

A بسن *basan*, Handsome, beautiful.

P بسناس *bisnās*, Name of a certain learned man or prince.

P بسنج *bisanj*, A freckle.

P بسنجیدن *basanjīdan*, To draw a curtain, to hide or conceal from view. To prepare, make ready.

P بسنخدن *basanakhdan*, To ferment, to leaven.

P بسند *basand*, Complete, entire. Sufficient, worthy. Sufficiency, competency. Contentment. بسند آمدن *basand āmadan*, To satisfy, to suffice. بسند کردن *basand kardan*, To be satisfied.

P بسندکار *basand-kār*, Content, satisfied.

P بسنده *basanda*, Sufficient, complete. Worthy. بسنده کردن *basanda kardan*, To be satisfied.

P بسنده کار *basanda-kār*, Contented, satisfied.

P بسنده کاری *basanda-kārī*, Contentment.

P بسنگ *bisang*, The herb melilot. A palm-tree.

P بسنگ آمدن *ba sang āmadan*, To be weak.

P بسنه *basna*, An unbroke horse. A bullock, steer.

A بسوء *basūʾ*, Quiet, gentle (she-camel when milking). *Busūʾ*, (v. n. of بسأ) Becoming accustomed, habituated, familiar.

P بسوته *basota* or *bisota*, A curl, a lock of hair.

P بسودن *bisūdan*, To handle, feel, touch, seize, rub. To bore. To repel, thrust back. To throw from the hand. To abolish, erase, remove. To swallow, ingulph. To mix, mingle.

P بسوده *bisūda*, Felt, touched, or handled.

A بسور *basūr*, Sharp, sour, crabbed. Grim, stern. A lion. *Busūr*, (v. n. of بسر) Having a stern, crabbed look. Making haste. Doing prematurely, unseasonably. Oppressing, overpowering.

P بسور *busūr*, Malediction, imprecation.

P بسوریدن *busūrīdan*, To curse, to execrate.

A بسوس *basūs*, A she-camel, whose milk comes with difficulty from her, making in the pail the sound *bissi bissi*. The name of an Arabian woman, from whom originated a war, called from her name حرب بسوس *harbi basūs* (which has since become a proverb to express, Great events from little causes); two Arabian tribes having fought above forty years because a camel belonging to this woman broke a hen's egg: the owner of the egg wounded the camel's udder with an arrow; an arrow pierced him in return; and the tribes were instantly in arms. اشأم من بسوس, More dire than Basūs.

A بسوق *basūk*, A sheep with a long udder. *Busūk*, (v. n. of بسق) Being tall (a palm-tree). Being superior to one's fellows. Growth.

P بسول *busūl*, A curse, imprecation.

A بسول *busūl*, (v. n. of بسل) Frowning, looking stern (from anger or valour).

P بسولیدن *busulīdan*, To curse.

P بسوي *ba suwī*, Towards. Against.

P بسه *basa*, The herb melilot.

P بسی *basī*, Many. Abundance, plenty. Enough.

P بسیا *basyā*, (in zand and Pāzand) Wine.

P بسیار *bisyār*, Many, much. Numerous. Frequent. Copious. Very. Exceedingly. بسیار بودن *bisyār būdan*, To be numerous. بسیار شدن *bisyār shudan*, To be multiplied. بسیار کردن *bisyār kardan*, To multiply, to increase.

P بسیاربر *bisyār-bar*, Very fruitful.

P بسیار خسپ *bisyār-khasp*, Drowsy, lethargic.

P بسیار خوار *bisyār-khwār*, A great eater, glutton.

P بسیاردان *bisyār-dān*, Very learned. (Many-grained) A kind of pomegranate.

P بسیاردانه *bisyār-dāna*, (Many-grained) A species of pulse.

P بسیار گو *bisyār-go* or *gū*, Talkative, verbose.

P بسیار وام *bisyār-wām*, Burdened with debt.

P بسیاري *bisyārī*, Abundance, plenty, multitude.

P بسیج *basej* or *bisej*, Arms, armour. Apparatus for a journey. Furniture, gear. Purpose, design, enterprise. Finished, prepared.

P بسیجنده *basejanda*, Preparing, arming for war.

P بسیجیدن *bisejīdan*, To arm. To prepare for. To finish, to complete. To manage.

P بسیجیده *bisejīda*, Prepared, arranged, disposed.

A بسيّد الانام *bi sayyidi'l anām*, By the prince of men (Muhammad).

A بسيس *basīs*, Little (food).

A بسيسة *basīsat*, (v. n. of بسّ) Sending (spies) amongst people. Flour of wheat or barley, toasted or fried with butter or oil, and honey. A whispering, a creating of animosities by detraction.

A بسيط *basīt*, (pl. بسط *busut*) Expanded, spread. Extended, level. Ample, spacious. Superficial. Simple (in opposition to compound). Single. Free in the use of one's tongue. (in prosody) The metre مستفعلن فاعلن *mustafʿilun fāʿilun* repeated eight times. بسيط الوجه *basītu'l wajh*, Of an open, joyful countenance. بسيط اليدين *basītu'l yadayn*, Open-handed, liberal.

A بسيطة *basītat*, A simple thing. The earth. An extensive plain, an open, level country. Surface, superficies. A sun-dial. An astronomical quadrant. Name of a village in Syria. A camel left with her colt. ذهب بسيطة *zahaba busaytata*, He travelled through the earth.

A بسيل *basīl*, Ugly, hideous, repulsive. Austere, stern (from courage or wrath). Remains of wine left in a cup after drinking over-night.

A بسيلة *basīlat*, Remains, leavings of wine left in a cup by another person, or after drinking over-night. Bitterness in the taste of any thing.

P بسیله *basīla*, A kind of bean.

P بسیم *basīm*, (in zand and Pāz.) Well-flavoured.

A بسيم *basim*, Smiling. Cheerful, jovial, merry, buxom, blithe. P خندان و بسیم *khandān u basim*, Of a joyous, open, smiling countenance. بسیم بودن *basim būdan*, To be cheerful.

P بش *bash*, A bandage. A hoop. A padlock. A watered field. *Bush*, A horse's mane. Incomplete. A fringe, flounce. A lock, ringlet.

A بشّ *bashsh*, A cheerful, open countenance. Courtesy, affability in asking a question. A turning towards any one with a smile. The joy of an interview between two friends.

A بشاعة *bashāʿat*, Name of a place.

P بشار *bishār* or *bashār*, Scattered (money). Inlaid with gold or silver. Stamped silver (to specify its fineness). Beaten (gold). Tired, wearied. A prisoner. A gentle rubbing. Touch.

A بشار *bushār*, The lowest of the people.

A بشّار *bashshār*, A proper name.

A بشارة *bashārat*, (v. n. of بشر) Rejoicing. *Bashārat*, *bishārat*, or *bushārat*, Joyful tidings, happy news. P بشارت کردن *bishārat kardan*, To announce good news. To preach the Gospel. A *Bushārat*, Scrapings of the skin.

P بشاسب *bushāsb*, (for بوشاسب *būshāsb*) Sleep.

A بشاشة *bashāshat*, (v. n. of بشّ) Turning towards one with a smile. Being cheerful, smiling. Joviality, cheerfulness, openness, freshness of countenance. Courtesy, sweetness in asking a question, &c.

A بشاع *bashāʿ*, The operation of meat, or any thing which disagrees with the stomach or the mind.

A بشاعة *bashāʿat*, (v. n. of بشع) Having a bad flavour, being bitter, unwholesome, or disagreeable (meat). Having a fetid breath. Being austere, sour, morose. Abhorring, being indisposed by any thing. Being narrow (channel too small for a body of water). Being unequal to any business, sinking under it.

A بشّاك *bashshāk*, A great liar.

A بشام *bashām*, Name of a fragrant shrub, growing near Mecca, with the branches and tufts of which they clean the teeth, and from whose leaf a black dye for the hair is made.

A بشامة *bashāmat*, Name of two poets.

P بشاورد *bushāvard*, Uneven ground.

A بشائر *bashāïr*, (pl. of بشيرة) Bringers of good news. Drums beaten on any joyful occasion.

P بشبش *bashbash* or *bushbush*, Colocynth-leaves.

P بشبق *bashbak*, (or بشبه *bashba*) Name of a village in the dependency of مرو *marv*.

P بشبيون *bashbayūn* or *bashbiyūn*, Fat.

P بشپول *bishpol*, Scattering. Scattered, dispersed.

A بشت *busht*, Name of a country in Khurāsān.

P بشتاب *bi'shtāb*, (imp. of شتافتن) Hasten.

P بشتالم *bishtālam*, (or بشتام *bishtām*) A parasite.

P بشتر *bashtar*, The archangel Michael (who they say has the distribution of riches to mankind). An angel who presides over rain and vegetation. A cloud. *Bushtar*, Pimples, pustules; thrush.

P بشترغ *bashturagh*, A herb with which they dye stuffs. Part of a cluster of grapes or dates.

P بشترم *bushturam*, A pimple, eruption, rash.

P بشتري *bushtarī*, Suffering from an eruption.

P بشتك *bashtuk*, *bashtak*, or *bushtak*, A small jar.

P بشجير *bushjīr*, A mountain-tree of which they make bows, arrows, or javelins.

A بشخانة *bashkhanat*, (from P پيشخانه *pesh-khāna*) A vestibule, an antechamber.

P بشخاييدن *bishkhāyidan*, To tear with the nails.

P بشخشم *bishakhsham*, A sliding, a stumbling.

P بشخوار *bishkhwār*, (or بشخور *bushkhwur*) The remainder of water in a vessel after drinking.

P بشخودن *bishkhūdan*, To tear with the nails.

P بشخوده *bishkhūda*, Scratched. Enlarged, widened. Ruined. Trodden down.

P بشخيدن *bashkhīdan*, To shine. To sprinkle. To steal.

A بشر *bashara*, (fut. يبشر *yabshuru*) He brought joyful news.

A بشر *bashr*, (or بشور *bushūr*) (v. n. of بشر) Relating news in general, good or bad. Meeting, receiving, looking at one with a smiling countenance. Taking, handling, touching, on the surface (the skin). Shaving, scraping, peeling. Shaving or trimming the whiskers close so that the skin is seen through. Feeding upon the fields (locusts). Beauty, comeliness, plumpness. *Bishr*, An openness of countenance, demonstrative of happiness and joy. Name of a well in Arabia, and of a mountain in Diyārbakr (Mesopotamia). *Bashar*, (pl. of بشرة *basharat*) Skins, cuticles. (pl. ابشار *abshār*) Man, mankind; mortals, the human race. ابو البشر *abū'l bashar*, The father of mankind, Adam. ابو بشر *abū bashar*, Sweetmeats, the dessert at a feast.

P بشرّ *ba sharr*, Maliciously, malevolently.

A بشرة *basharat*, (pl. بشر *bashar*) The skin, cuticle, or outward skin (the interior being called ادمة *adamat*). Outside, exterior. Surface of the ground covered with herbage. Humanity, constitution.

P بشرط آن كه *ba sharti ān ki*, On condition that.

A البشرود *al bashrūd*, Name of a town in Egypt.

P بشرونتن *bashrūnitan*, (in zand) To worship.

A بشرى *bushra'*, (v. n. of بشر) Communicating good news. (pl. بشراوات *bushrāwāt*) Joyful news. The Gospel. Name of a man. بشرى الانجيل *bushra'l injīl*, The publication of the Gospel.

A بشريّ *bashariy*, Human. P ضعف بشري *zuʻfi basharī*, Human weakness. عقول بشري *ʻukūli basharī*, Human intellect.

A بشريّة *bashariyat*, (or طبع بشريت *tabʻi bashariyat*) Human nature.

P بشستن *bishistan*, To sit. *Bishustan*, To wash.

A بشع *bashaʻ*, (v. n. of بشع) Having a bad flavour, being bitter, unwholesome, or disagreeable (meat). Having a fetid breath. Being narrow, too small for the volume of water (a river's bed). Being unequal to any business, sinking under it. *Bashiʻ*, Disgusting, ill-flavoured, bitter (food). One who has eaten such food. Stinking-breathed from unpicked teeth. Disagreeable, offensive (in morals, manners, or person). Knotty, gnarly (wood).

A بشغ *bashgh*, Small rain which does not run.

P بشغره *bashghara*, Made, formed, finished.

A بشق *bashk*, (v. n. of بشق) Striking (with a stick). Looking intently. Tarrying (a traveller, either on account of heavy rains, weariness, or inability to proceed). Taking no prey (a hawk).

P بشك *bashk*, Amorous blandishment. Lightning. Dew. Hail. A curtain hung before a door. Name of a tree. (for باشد كه *bāshad ki*) It may be that. *Bushk*, Curly hair. The forelocks.

A بشك *bashk*, (v. n. of بشك) Lying. Sewing slightly. Making haste. Unloosing fetters. Urging forward rapidly. Cutting. Mixing. Speed, haste, precipitancy. Bad workmanship. *Bashk* or *bashak*, (A horse's) picking up (his) feet quickly or lifting up his legs without advancing his fore-feet.

P بشكاري *bashkhārī*, A walk. Agriculture, tillage.

A بشكانيّ *bushkhāniy*, Foolish, ignorant of Arabic.

P بشكستن *bishkhastan*, To break. To extinguish.

P بشكل *bishkhal*, (or بشكله *bishkhala*) A crooked stick for opening a lock, a sort of key.

P بشكليد *bishkalīd*, A scratch.

P بشكليدن *bishkalīdan*, To scratch, to tear. To enlarge, to widen.

P بشكم *bashkam* or *bishkam*, A summer-house, an airy house. A balcony, a verandah.

P بشكنج *bashkanj*, The arm. The left hand.

P بشكنه *bishkina*, The stocks. A key.

P بشكوفه *bishkūfah*, A flower. A vomit.

P بشكول *bishkol* or *bashkol*, Swift, expeditious, active, eager, strong. Intelligent. Woad.

P بشكوليدن *bashkolīdan* or *bishkolīdan*, To set eagerly about a thing.

P بشكون *bashkūn*, Nimble, active, notable.

P بشكونه *bishkūna*, A flower. Frequent vomiting.

P بشكوه *bishkoh*, Magnificent, majestic, stately.

A بشكى *bashaka'*, Fast-going, sprightly (she-camel). Nimble, active-fingered (woman).

P بشگر *bishgar*, The chace; game.

P بشگرد *bishgard*, A hunter, a fowler. A place for hunting. The chace; game.

P بشگير *bashgīr*, A towel.

P بشل *bashal*, Suspended, pendulous.

G بشلشكه *bishilshaka*, Gentian, bitter-wort.

P بشلنگ *bishlang*, Name of a fort in Hindūstān.

P بشليدن *bashlīdan*, To hang. To adhere, stick.

P بشم *bashm*, Hoar-frost. Dew. A heretic, a man of no religion. Name of a place. *Basham*, Weary, disgusted. Sad. Of a weak digestion.

A بشم *basham*, (v. n. of بشم) Suffering from indigestion. An indisposition arising from indigestion. *Bashim*, Troubled with indigestion.

P بشما *ba shumā*, To you.

P بشماط *bishmāt*, Biscuit, bread baked twice.

P بشماق *bashmāk*, A shoe, sandal, slipper.

P بشمخ *bashmakh*, A form of invocation.

P بشمه *bashma*, Undressed leather. A certain black grain used in anointing the eyes.

P بشن *bashn*, Stature, height. The body. The head. A root. A side.

A بشنة *bishnat*, A species of millet.

P بشنج *bashanj*, Splendour. Freshness of the cheek. Elegance, beauty. *Bishanj*, A freckle or spot on the face or hands.

P بشنجه *bishanja*, Weavers' glue; also glue-brush.

P بشنزه *bushnaja*, Paste of meal and date-syrup.

P بشنگ *bishing*, A plasterer's or mason's chisel with which they peck holes. An auger. A mattock.

P بشنيز *bashnīz*, (or بشنيزه) Southernwood.

A بشنين *bushnīn*, The Egyptian lot-tree, the root of which they call بيارون *bayārūn*.

P بشوتن *bashūtan*, Of bad principles. *Bishūtan* or *bashūtan*, An ape. Name of the son of Gushtāsb, and brother to Isfandiyār.

P بشودن *bushūdan*, To wash. To be bad-tempered.

A بشور *bushūr*, Announcement of good news.

P بشورنتن *bashūrintan*, (in zand and Pāzand) To worship, to adore.

P بشوريدن *bishūrīdan*, To curse. To be disturbed, to be angry.

P بشول *bishūl* or *bushūl*, Active, skilful, intelligent. Confusion, broil.

P بشولانيدن *bushūlānīdan*, To cause to move to and fro. To agitate, to shake. To excite.

P بشولش *bishūlish*, Perturbation. Performance, execution. Knowledge. Sight.

P بشوليدن *bishūlīdan* or *bashūlīdan*, To move to and fro, shake, waver. To sit down fatigued and bewildered. To see. To mix, confuse, embroil. To scatter. To execute.

P بشوليده *bishūlīda*, Seen. Known. Expert, skilled. Disturbed, confused. Accomplished.

P بشيج *bashīj*, Equal. Death, destruction.

A بشير *bashīr*, A messenger of good news. Beautiful. A proper name. Name of a province in Spain. Name of 26 companions of Muhammad; also of several traditionists. *Bushayr*, A proper name.

P بشيز *bashīz*, A leathern water-bottle.

A بشيش *bashīsh*, Fresh, cheerful, happy (faced).

A بشيشة *bashīshat*, Money in one's possession.

A بشيع *bashīع*, Stinking-breathed. Offensive. اطوار بشيعة *atwār bashīعat*, Wicked, shameful acts.

P بشيك *bashīk*, Peculiarity. Special.

A بشيل *bashyal*, Name of a Greek interpreter attached to the court of Ar Rashīd.

P بشيمه *bashīma*, An undressed hide.

P بشين *bishīn*, Essence, existence.

P بشيون *bashyūn*, Fat.

A بصاء *bisāء*, Castration.

A بصابص *busābis*, A bright bay colour.

A بصار *bisār*, (v. n. 3 of بصر) Trying who shall see first. (pl. of بصرة *basrat*) Whitish and soft stones.

A بصارة *basārat* or *bisārat*, (v. n. of بصر) Seeing, perceiving. Intimate knowledge.

A بصّاص *bassās*, Flashing eyed, bright-eyed.

A بصّاصة *bassāsat*, The eye.

A بصاق *bisāk*, (pl. of بصقة *baskat*) Elevated stony countries. *Busāk*, Spittle, saliva when spit out (whilst in the mouth it is called ريق *rīk*). A species of the palm-tree. A superior kind of camel.

A بصاقة *busākat*, Name of a place near Mecca. بصاقة القمر *busākatu'l kamar*, The selenites or moonstone in Arabia (having a number of shining white spots, which increase and decrease with the moon).

A بصّال *bassāl*, A seller of onions.

A بصان *busān*, (or بصّان *bussān*) (pl. ابصنة *absinat*) The month Rabīع the second.

A بصائر *basāءir*, (pl. of بصيرة) Attentions, pains.

A بصباص *basbās*, Rapid (nocturnal journey in quest of water). Slender (camel). Milk. Little (water). Fodder remaining on a stick, and presenting the appearance of jerboas' tails. Bread.

A بصبصة *basbasat*, (v. n. of بصبص Q) Opening the eyes (a whelp). Travelling quickly a nocturnal journey in search of water. Fawning, flattering, caressing. Wagging the tail (a dog). Shewing the first signs of vegetation (the earth).

A بصر *basr*, (v. n. of بصر) Cutting. Sewing together two pieces of leather. A skin. *Basr*, *bisr*, or *busr*, A thick stone. *Busr*, Cotton. Bark, skin, crust. A skin. A side, border, margin. *Basar*, (v. n. of بصر) Seeing, discerning. (pl. ابصار *absār*) The sight, vision. The eye. Understanding, mind, capacity. Knowledge, science. صلوة البصر *salātu'l basar*, Prayer of evening and morning twilight. P بصري بي بصيرت *basari bī basīrat*, An eye without vision, mind without foresight. A العامل بلا بصر كالرامي بلا وتر *al عāmil bilā basar ka'r rāmī bilā watar* (a proverb).

A بصراء *busarāء*, (pl. of بصير *basīr*) Clear-sighted. Intelligent.

A بصرة *basrat*, (pl. بصار *bisār*) Whitish and soft stone. A kind of gross earth, out of which they dig stones. *Basrat*, *bisrat*, *basarat*, or *basirat*, The city of Basra or Bassora (as situated on such ground). *Busrat*, Red and rich soil. A little remains of milk.

A البصرتان *al basratāni*, Basra and Kūfa.

A بصروي *busrawīy*, Native of Busra (Bozra).

A بصره بالي *basra bālī*, Manna.

A بصري *busra'*, Name of a city in Syria. (Is. lxiii. 1.) Name of a village near Baghdād.

A بصري *basrīy*, (pl. بصريون) Native of Basra.

A بصط *bast*. (See بسط *bast*).

A بصع *basaعa*, (fut. يبصع *yabsaعu*) He collected.

A بصع *basع*, (v. n. of بصع) Collecting. Flowing, running (water). A narrow chink, through which water will hardly penetrate. The space between the fore and middle finger. *Bisع*, A part of the night, the beginning of the night. *Busع*, (pl. of ابصع *absaع*) All, universal. Foolish (men). (pl. of بصيع *basīع*) Sweatings, emanations of sweat.

A بصعاء *basعāء*, (fem. of ابصع *absaع*) All, universal.

A بصق *bask*, (v. n. of بصق) Spitting. Milking a teeming ewe.

A بصقة *baskat*, An elevated stony country.

A بصل *basal*, An onion. The bulbous root of the lily, tulip, onion, or garlic. An iron helmet. بصل الذئب *basalu'z ziءb*, Bulbus esculentus. بصل العنصل *basalu'l عunsul*, (or بصل الفار *basalu'l fār*) A squill. بصل القي *basalu'l kay*, Bulbus vomitorius. أكسي من البصل *aksa' mini'l basal*, More clothed than an onion. اقليم البصل *iklīmu'l basal*, The onion country (a province of Spain).

A بصلة *basalat*, A single onion.

A بصليّة *basalīyat*, Name of a quarter in Baghdad.

A بصم *busm*, An interval, distance between the extremities of the ring and the little fingers (as, عتب *عatab* is the space between the middle and ring-fingers; رتب *ratab* between the middle and fore; فتر *fitr* between the index and thumb; شبر *shibr* (a span) from the thumb to the little finger; and فوت *fawt* the interval between any two). ذو بصم *zū busmin*, Gross, thick (man or cloth).

A بصنّي *basanna'*, A village from which veils are brought.

A بصوة (ما في الرماد *mā fi'r ramādi*) *baswatun*, There is not a spark or live coal among the ashes.

A بصوق *basūk*, The cattle in the flock which give least milk.

A بصي *basa'*, (fut. يبصي *yabsa'*) He pressed hard (upon a debtor).

A بصيّ (خصيّ *khasīy*) *basīy*, An eunuch.

A بصير *basīr*, (pl. بصراء *busarāء*) Seeing, perceiving, discerning, penetrating. Intelligent. A connoisseur. The all-seeing God. A dog. P بصير شدن *basīr shudan*, To look at.

A بصيرة *basīrat*, (pl. بصائر *basāءir*) Sight. Foresight, prudence: penetration, judgment: watchfulness, attention: caution, circumspection, carefulness. A sentence, opinion. An evident or convincing proof, demonstration. A witness. Blood, indicative of a wound inflicted. Signs of virginity. An admonition, monitory, or subject of serious reflection. Any thing firmly believed. A coat of mail. A shield, buckler. Whatever is comprehended within the sides of a house. اهل بصيرت *ahli basīrat*, (or ارباب بصيرت *arbābi basīrat*) Prudent, circumspect. P چشم بصيرت *chashmi basīrat*, Eyes of prudence. بصيرت كردن *basīrat kardan*, To foresee. بي بصيرت *bī basīrat*, Improvident.

A بصيص *basīs*, (v. n. of بصّ) Giving little. Flowing, distilling, trickling. Flashing, shining. Tremor. حصيصهم و بصيصهم *hasīsuhum wa basīsuhum*, A number of them.

A بصيع *basīع*, (pl. بصع *busع*) Flowing sweat.

A بضّ *bazz*, (v. n. of بضّ) Flowing little and little. Giving sparingly. Tuning (a lute). Thin, fat, and soft-skinned. Sour milk. ما يبضّ حجره *mā yabizzu hajaruhu*, His stone sweats not, *i. e.* he gives nothing.

A بضابض *buzābiz*, Strong, powerful.

A بضاض *bizāz*, Wells nearly dry.

A بضاضة *bazāzat*, (v. n. of بضض) Having a thin and soft skin and tender body. *Buzāzat*, A little water.

A بضاع *bazāع*, (v. n. of بضع) Quenching thirst. An island. *Bizāع*, (v. n. 3 of بضع) Lying with. Coition. (pl. of بضعة *bazعat*) Parts, slices. كمعلّمة امّها البضاع *ka muعallimatin ummahā'l bizāع*, Like one teaching her mother. . . . . .

A بضاعة *bizāعat*, (pl. بضائع *bazāءiع*) A capital or stock in trade. A share in a mercantile adventure; property entrusted to another to be employed in trade. قليل البضاعة *kalīlu'l bizāعat*, Having a small capital, a poor man. بئر بضاعة *biءr buzāعat* or *bizāعat*, Name of a well at Madīna.

A بضان *buzān*, The fourth Arabian month, otherwise called ربيع الاخر *rabīعu'l ākhir*.

A بضائع *bazāءiع*, (pl. of بضاعة) Goods, wares.

A بضباض *bazbāz*, Mushrooms.

A بضباضة *bazbāzat*, Thin, fat, soft-skinned (girl).

A بضّة *bazzat*, Sour milk. Fat and soft-skinned (woman).

A بضر *bazr*, An excrescence, a caruncle, which is usually cut off by those who practise female circumcision. بضرا مضرا *bizran mizran*, Blood was shed) with impunity, without retaliation or revenge.

A بضرة *bazrat*, Abortiveness, futility.

A بضض *bazaz*, Little water.

A بضع *bazع*, (v. n. of بضع) Cutting in pieces, cutting off a part. Cleaving, splitting. Quenching thirst. Marrying, contracting a marriage. Having commerce with a woman. Divorcing. Declaring, making clear. Starting in the eye, but not running over (a tear). Being melancholy and uneasy. (pl. of بضيع *baziɛ*) Partners. *Bazɛ* or *bizaɛ*, (pl. of بضعة *bazɛat* or *bizɛat*) Parts, segments. *Bizɛ* or *bazɛ*, A part (of the night). A small number of people (from three to nine or to five, or from one to four, or from four to nine, or as far as twenty). The number seven. *Buzɛ*, Genitale arvum. The contracting of a marriage. Divorce. Coition.

A بضعات *bazaɛāt*, (pl. of بضعة) Parts, slices.

A بضعة *bazɛat* or *bizɛat*, (pl. بضع *bazɛ*, *bizaɛ*, and بضاع *bizāɛ*) A part, section, piece (of meat). *Bazaɛat*, (pl. of باضع *bāziɛ*) Cutting (swords).

A بضك *bazk*, (v. n. of بضك) Cutting, amputating.

A بضم *bazm*, (v. n. of بضم) Being large in the grain (wheat). Being softish (grain). *Buzm*, Soul, self. A full-grown ear of corn.

A بضوض *bazūz*, (pl. بضاض *bizāz*) (A well) containing little water. *Buzūz*, (v. n. of بضّ) Flowing by little and little. Giving sparingly.

A بضوضة *buzūzat*, The being thin-skinned.

A بضوع *buzūɛ*, (v. n. of بضع) Understanding, apprehending. Becoming tired of, disgusted with. Quenching thirst.

A بضوك *bazūk*, Sharp (sword).

A بضيض *baziz*, (v. n. of بضّ Flowing slowly, and in a small quantity (water). Hence the proverb ما يبضّ حجره *ma yabizzu hajaruhu*, His stone does not sweat: there is no water on his stone (applied to a miser, from whom nothing is to be got).

A بضيضة *bazizat*, Little water. Small misling rain. Thin, fat, soft-skinned (girl). Whatever is in one's possession.

A بضيع *baziɛ*, (pl. بضع *bazɛ*) A partner. Sweat. Flesh. An island in the sea. The sea. Wholesome (water) easy of digestion. Name of an anchorage below Judda towards Yaman. كثير البضيع *kasīru'l baziɛ*, Very fleshy.

A بضيعة *baziɛat*, A led camel.

P بط *bat*, A goose, a duck. A sort of large cup. بط سرخاب زاي *bati surkh-āb zāy*, A goblet of pure wine.

A بط *bat*, (for باطل *bātil*) False.

A بطّ *batt*, (v. n. of بطّ) Cutting open (a boil). A duck. A goose.

A بطء *butɂ*, (v. n. of بطؤ) Being slow, proceeding slowly. Slowness, delay. بطأ *butɂan*, (or بطأي *butɂa'*) At no time, never

A بطاء *bitāɂ*, (v. n. of بطؤ) Being slow, proceeding slowly. (pl. of بطيء *batiɂ*) Slow.

A بطاح *bitāh*, (pl. of بطح *batih*) Low, gravelly lands. *Butāh*, A disease resembling the pleurisy, which sometimes follows a fever.

A بطاحيّ *butāhiy*, Indisposed with the disease بطاح *butāh*.

A بطاخيّ *butākhiy*, Thick, bulky, corpulent.

P بطارش *batārish*, Fern.

A بطارق *butārik*, Long, tall.

A بطارقة *batārikat*, (pl. of بطريق *bitrīk*) Patriarchs. Commanders of 10,000. Vain, haughty, proud. Fat (birds).

A بطاريك *batārīk*, (pl. of بطريك) Patriarchs.

A بطاقة *bitākat*, The pupil of the eye. A label affixed to a piece of cloth marking the price. A letter sent by a pigeon. حمام البطاقة *hamāmu'l bitākat*, A carrier-pigeon.

A بطال *battāl*, Idle, unemployed. Fruitless, empty, vain. Old, obsolete, unfashionable, antiquated. Abolished, repealed, abrogated, suppressed. A brave man, a champion. P بطّال كردن *battāl kardan*, To abolish.

A بطالة *batālat*, (v. n. of بطل) Being idle, unemployed (a hireling). Talking idly, jesting. Being courageous. Valour, bravery.

A بطآن *butɂāna* or *batɂāna*, (equivalent to بطؤ *batuɂa*) He was slow.

A بطان *bitān*, (pl. ابطنة *abtinat* and بطن *butun*) A girth. (pl. of بطن *batin*) Rich, purse-proud. Gluttonous. عريض البطان *ɛarīzu'l bitān*, Rich.

A بطانة *bitānat*, The lining of a garment. The heart of a city. A sincere, confidential friend. A secret. Sincere friendship.

A بطائح *batāɂih*, (pl. of بطيحة *batīhat*) Low, gravelly lands.

A بطائط *butāɂit*, Large (vulva). حطائط بطائط *hutāɂit butāɂit*, Thick and fat.

A بطائق *batāɂik*, (pl. of بطاقة *bitākat*) Letters sent by pigeons.

A بطائن *batāɂin*, (pl. of بطينة) Sofa-linings.

A بطباط *batbāt*, Shepherd's staff (a plant).

A بطبطة *batbatat*, (v. n. of بطبط Q) Stooling from fright. Cackling or diving in the water (ducks or geese). Weakness of judgment.

A بطّة *battat*, A single duck or goose. A she-bear. A flask, flagon, decanter.

A بطح *bataha*, (fut. يبطح *yabtahu*) He prostrated.

A بطح *buth*, Sticking close, lying flat. *Batih*, (pl. بطاح *bitāh*) Low-lying, gravelly ground, upon which, at certain seasons, the waters descend from the higher countries, though dry best part of the year.

A بطحاء *bathāɂ*, A spacious channel bedded with pebbles. Any large open place for exercises, horse-course, race ground. A place near Mecca.

A بطحان *batihān*, A swampy valley near Madina.

A بطحة *bathat*, The stature of a man. *Buthat*, Nature, quality, property.

A بطخ *bathh*, (v. n. of بطخ) Licking.

A بطخة *batikhat*, Thick, bulky (men or camels).

A بطر *batr*, (v. n. of بطر) Dividing, splitting, cleaving, bursting (an imposthume). *Batar*, (v. n. of بطر) Exulting, being insolent with joy, petulant, inconsiderate, ungrateful to the Supreme Being, returning no thanks for prosperity. Loathing, disliking without a cause. Being thunder-struck, lost in amazement. Briskness, liveliness. Insolence, petulance, pertness, sauciness. Inability to bear prosperity suitably. ذهب دمه بطرًا *zahaba damuhu bitran*, His blood was shed unrevenged. *Batir*, Full of spirits. Petulant, insolent.

G بطرا *batrā*, A stone, a rock.

G بطراخو *batrākhū*, (or بطراخوس) A frog.

G بطراساليون *batrāsāliyūn*, Rock-parsley.

G بطرالاون *batrālāvan*, Petrolium, rock-oil.

A بطرك *bitrak*, *bitark*, or *batrak*, A patriarch. A chief of the Magi.

A بطرير *bitrīr*, Clamorous, brawling, shameless. Far gone in error.

A بطريق *bi tarīk*, By way of, in the manner of, on account of. بطريق حقّ *bi tarīki hakk*, For the love of God, for the sake of justice.

G بطريق *bitrīk*, (pl. بطارقة *batārikat*) A commander of 10,000 men. Vain, haughty, proud. Fat (bird). A patriarch.

A بطريقان *bitrīkāni*, (dual) Shoe-latchets.

A بطريكية *batrīkiyat*, (or بطراكة) A patriarchate.

A بطش *batasha*, (fut. يبطش *yabtushu*) He seized.

A بطش *batsh*, (v. n. of بطش) Seizing, carrying away by force. Rushing upon with violence. Recovering (from a fever, although still weak). Power, vigour, strength, sternness, severity. قهّار شديد البطش *kahhāri shadīdu'l batsh*, The Lord powerful in severity.

A بطشة *batshat*, Power, superiority over others, force, violence. البطشة الكبري *al batshatu'l kubra'*, The grand drubbing, *i.e.* the battle of Badr.

A بطغ *batagh*, (v. n. of بطغ) Being bedaubed (with excrement), polluted (with crimes). Sliding along on the buttocks.

P بطك *batak*, A duckling. A small goblet. A drinking-cup made in the form of a duck.

A بطل *batala*, (fut. يبطل *yabtulu*) It was vain.

A بطل *butl*, (v. n. of بطل) Being vain, abortive, of no effect. Being idle. *Batal*, (pl. ابطال *abtāl*) A brave man, a champion.

A بطّلات *buttalāt*, Vain words, foolish things, idle tales, trifles.

A بطلان *butlān*, (v. n. of بطل) Being vain, abortive, fruitless. Idleness. شبهت بطلاني *shubhati butlānī*, A foolish doubt, a vain scruple.

A بطلة *batalat*, A heroic, masculine woman. Magicians, wizards (dealing in vain things).

G بطلميوس *batlamiyūs*, (or بطلميوس) Ptolemy.

A بطليوس *batalyūs*, Name of a town in Spain.

A بطم *butm* or *butum*, The turpentine-tree and fruit. A kind of greenish grain, of a turpentine quality. A greenish sore.

A بطماج *bitmāj*, The fruit of the معاث *muɛās*.

A بطن *batn*, (v. n. of بطن) Striking upon the belly. Being an intimate and confidential friend. Going into the middle. Penetrating into a business. Having a clear view of a thing. (pl. ابطن

abtun, بطون *butūn*, and بطنان *butnān*) The belly, paunch. The interior part or middle of any thing. The interior of the city of Mecca. Whatever is contained in the belly, as a fœtus. The esoteric meaning of the Kur'ān (in contradistinction to the ظهر *zahr*). A small tribe, an offset of a larger one. The second degree of consanguinity. The longest side of a feather. بطنا عن بطن *batnan ɛan batnin*, From tribe to tribe, all, universally. ذو بطن *zū batnin*, Dung, excrement. The contents of the belly; a fœtus, an egg. القت المرأة ذا بطنها *alkati'l marɛatu zā batnihā*, The woman brought forth. القت الدجاجة ذا بطنها *alkati'd dajājatu zā batnihā*, The hen laid an egg. *Batan*, (v. n. of بطن) Having the belly ready to burst from over-eating. Being big-bellied. A pain in the belly. *Batin*, (pl. بطان *bitān*) A glutton. Purse-proud. *Butun*, (pl. of بطان *bitān*) Girths.

A بطنان *butnān*, (pl. of بطن *batn*) Bellies. Middles, centres. Longest sides of feathers. (pl. of باطن *bātin*) Inward parts. Low grounds. Water-courses through rugged places. بطنان الجنة *butnānu'l jannat*, The middle of Paradise.

P بطن پرست *batn-parast*, A worshipper of the belly, a glutton.

A بطنة *bitnat*, Exultation, joy, insolence, sauciness, petulance. Fulness of belly from eating, indigestion from repletion.

A بطوط *butūt*, (pl. of بطّ *batt*) Ducks. Pots, cups. Bottles.

A بطول *butūl*, (v. n. of بطل) Being vain, fruitless, abortive. Vanity, folly.

A بطولة *butūlat*, Valour, bravery.

A بطون *butūn*, (v. n. of بطن) Lying hid. Being intimate with. (pl. of بطن *batn*) Bellies. Interior parts, cells. Smaller sections of a tribe.

A بطئ *batiɛ*, Slow, tardy. بطئ المشرب *batiɛu'l mashrab*, Lazy by nature. بطئ الحركة *batiɛu'l harakat*, Slow in motion.

A بطية *bityat*, Delay.

A بطيحة *batīhat*, (pl. بطائح *batāɛih*) A gravelly, a low-lying ground overflown with waters at certain seasons of the year. البطيحة *al batīhat*, Name of a low marshy ground between Wāsit and Basrah, and of another between Basrah and Ahwāz.

A بطّيخ *bittīkh*, (and بطّيخة *bittīkhat*) A melon, musk-melon. A pumpkin: a cucurbitaceous plant. بطّيخ زقّي *bittīkhi zikkī*, A water-melon. بطّيخ مستطيل *bittīkhi mustatīl*, (or بطّيخ هندي *bittīkhi hindī*) The citrul.

A بطّيخي *bittīkhīy*, Seller of melons or pumpkins.

A بطير *batīr*, Split, cloven. A veterinary surgeon.

A بطيش *batīsh*, Powerful, severe, stern.

A بطيط *batīt*, A wonderful thing. A lie. The top of a boot without a leg. Misfortune.

A بطيطة *batītat*, A ship-worm. The white ant.

A بطيّطة *butayyitat*, A ship-worm. The white ant.

A بطين *batīn*, Large, gorbellied. Rich. Far distant, remote. *Butayn*, (dim. of بطن *batn*) A little belly. The second mansion of the moon, distinguished by three small stars in the belly of Aries.

A بطيئ *batīɛ*, (pl. بطاء *bitāɛ*) Slow.

A بظّ *bazz*, (v. n. of بظّ) Tuning (a musical instrument). فظ بظ *fazz bazz*, Thick, gross.

A بظا *buza'*, Compact portions of flesh.

A بظارة *bazārat* or *buzārat*, An excrescence which they who practise female circumcision are accustomed to cut off. *Bizārat*, The smack of the lips in kissing. *Buzārat*, An excrescence on the middle of the upper lip, resembling a kernel. The point of the privities of a ewe.

A بظر *bazr*, (pl. بظور *buzūr*) The clitoris. A finger-ring. *Bazar*, (v. n. of بظر) Having an excrescence in the middle of the upper lip (a man). Having a clitoris (a woman). A seal-ring.

A بظراء *bazrāɛ*, (A girl) with a large clitoris.

A بظراً *bizran*, With impunity, unrevenged.

A بظرة *bazrat*, A scarcity of hair under the arms. *Buzrat*, An excrescence in the centre of the upper lip.

A بظرم *bazram*, A seal-ring: hence, تبظرم *tabazrum*, The making an idle display of a ring, by waving the hand when speaking.

A بظريرة *bizrīrat*, Clamorous, noisy (woman).

A بظماج *bizmāj*, A kind of velvet garment, or a stuff plain in the centre and figured on the sides.

A بظو *bazw*, (v. n. of بظو) Being full and compact (flesh).

A بظور *buzūr*, (pl. of بظر *bazr*) Clitorises.

P بظهور آمدن *ba zuhūr āmadan*, To come to pass, be put in execution, to be accomplished.

A بظی *baza'*, (v. n. of بظي) Being fat and full of flesh (a woman).

A بظيظ *bazīz*, Fat. Soft.

A بعّ *baɛɛ*, (v. n. of بعّ) Remaining fixed in one place (a cloud). Raining copiously. Shedding (wine). A copious effusion.

A بعابعة *baɛābiɛat*, Indigent (men), dervishes.

A بعاث *buɛās*, Name of a place near Madīna, where a battle was fought.

A بعائط *baɛāɛit*, (pl. of بعثط *buɛsut*) Middles.

A بعاد *biɛād*, (v. n. 3 of بعد) Removing far. Retiring. Separation, distance. Removal. *Buɛād*, Remote, distant.

A بعار *biɛār*, (v. n. 3 of بعر) Dunging (a camel or sheep). *Buɛār*, The lote-tree; also the fruit, of which the Egyptians make bread.

A بعاس *biɛās*, Emaciated, milkless camels.

A بعاع *baɛāɛ*, (v. n. of بعّ) Raining incessantly. Remaining fixed in one place (a cloud). Household furniture. Carpets or garments which a traveller carries with him. Those things which a bride brings to her husband's house. What is dropped on the way when any place is plundered. The heaviness of a cloud from rain. A certain delicate plant. القي عليه بعاعه *alka' ɛalayhi baɛāɛahu*, He threw himself on it. القي السحاب بعاعه *alka's sahābu baɛāɛahu* The cloud poured down what was in it.

A بعاق *buɛāk*, (v. n. of بعق) Raining, soaking, drenching (the earth). *Buɛāk*, *baɛāk*, or *biɛāk*, A cloud pouring down rain. Excessive rain, a deluge. A hideous noise, the sound of a torrent.

A بعال *biɛāl*, (v. n. 3 of بعل) Sporting; toying with a spouse. Conjugal intercourse. (pl. of بعل *baɛl*) Husbands. Wives. Spouses.

A بعائس *baɛāɛis*, Lean, milkless camels.

A بعبع *baɛbaɛ*, The noise made by decanting the contents of a bottle. The dawn of youth.

A بعبعة *baɛbaɛat*, Precipitancy of speech. Flight from battle, or from an enemy. The confused noise of a mixture of voices.

A بعّة *buɛɛat*, The colt of a camel between هبع *hubaɛ* and ربع *rubaɛ*.

A بعث *baɛasa*, (fut. يبعث *yabɛasu*) He sent.

A بعث *baɛs*, (v. n. of بعث) Sending. Rousing, stirring up. Awakening. Raising the dead. Resurrection. (pl. بعوث *buɛūs*) An army, a detachment. بعث اموات *baɛsi amwāt*, The resurrection of the dead. بعث و نشر *baɛs u nashr*, Raising and dispersing; the resurrection. يوم البعث *yawmu'l baɛs*, The day of resurrection. *Baɛas*, (v. n. of بعث) Remaining awake. An army. *Baɛis*, Wakeful.

A بعثة *biɛsat*, Mission, embassy, detachment.

A بعثرة *baɛsarat*, (v. n. of بعثر Q) Looking, beholding. Investigating, examining. Separating, discriminating. Scattering, wasting. Inverting, turning upside down. Extracting, drawing forth. Uncovering, displaying. Raising, stirring up. Ruining, demolishing (a cistern). A disturbed, disordered state of mind. Dirty colour: dirt, nastiness.

A بعثط *buɛsut*, (or بعثوط *buɛsūt*) (pl. بعائط *baɛāsit*) The middle of any place. The navel. Podex. هو ابن بعثطها *huwa ibn buɛsutihā*, He knows it well.

A بعثقة *baɛsakat*, (v. n. of بعثق Q) Flowing or leaking (water) from a pond, cistern, or jar, through any fissure or broken part.

A بعج *baɛj*, (v. n. of بعج) Cutting open (the belly with a knife). Tormenting (love). بعج بطنه لك *baɛaja batnahu laka*, He diligently exhorted thee. *Baɛij*, One who walks languidly.

A بعد *baɛd*, After, afterwards. Hitherto. Not yet. This word generally begins Eastern letters, immediately after the preamble (or short prayer for the health and prosperity of the person to whom it is addressed): as, بعد اظهار مراتب اشتياق و آرزوي مواصلت *baɛd izhāri marātibi ishtiyāk u ārzūyi muwāsalat*, After evincing a high desire and wish for an interview, &c. (a form of compliment like some in our European letters, which means nothing, as wishes for an interview are often expressed in despatches to those whom they neither hope nor desire to see). بعد الاجلاس *baɛda'l ijlās*, After having desired (him) to sit down. بعد الخراب البصرة *baǥda'l kharābi'lbasarat*, Shutting the stable-door when the steed is stolen. بعد السلام *baǥda's salām*, (or بعد السلام و الكلام *baǥda's salām wa'l kalām*) After the usual salutations and compliments. بعد الظهر *baǥda'z zuhr*, Afternoon. بعد ما *baǥda mā*, After that, on which. بعد المشورة *baǥda'l mashwarat*, After consulting. بعد الموت *baǥda'l mawt*, After death. بعد الوقوع *baǥda'l wukūǥ*, After it happens, when it it is done. بعد اليوم *baǥda'l yawm*, Henceforth, or the time to come. امّا بعد *ammā baǥd*, After these premises. Now to begin. في ما بعد *fī mā baǥd*, But then, now however (a transition from one part of the subject to another, very common in letters). من بعد *mim baǥd*, Afterwards. For the future. و بعد *wa baǥd*, And then. P بعد از اين *baǥd az īn*, After this. بعد از آن *baǥd az ān*, After that. بعد از آنكه *baǥd az ān ki*, After which, after that which. A *Buǥd*, (v. n. of بعد) Being distant. Dying. Distance. Death. بعد باعد *buǥdun bāǥidun*, A very remote distance. بعد المشرقين *buǥdu'l mashrikayn*, The distance between the two easts (*i. e.* between the east and west, or between the solstices). ذو بعد *zū buǥdin*, (or بعدة *buǥdatin*) Prudent, intelligent. علي بعد *ǥala' buǥdin*, At a distance. *Baǥad*, (v. n. of بعد) Being distant. Dying. Remote, distant. (pl. of باعد *bāǥid*) Very distant. *Buǥad*, Profit, benefit, good. غير بعد *ghayr buǥadin*, Worthless. *Buǥud*, (pl. of بعيد *baǥīd*) Distant.

A بعداء *buǥadāǥ*, (or بعدان *buǥdān*) (pl. of بعيد *baǥīd*) Distant.

A بعدا لك *buǥdan laka*, Evil be to thee! قربا و بعدا *kurban wa buǥdan*, Near and far.

A بعدة *buǥdat*, Distance (of place or kin).

A بعده *baǥdahu*, After, afterwards, then, after that. بعديكما *baǥdaykumā*, After you both.

A بعذارة *biǥzārat*, (v. n. of بعذر Q) Moving, setting in motion, shaking.

A بعر *baǥr*, (v. n. of بعر) Voiding dung (a camel or sheep). Extreme poverty. *Baǥr* or *baǥar*, (pl. ابعار *abǥār*) The globular dung of animals. *Baǥar*, (v. n. of بعر) Becoming full-grown and fit for labour (a camel, then called بعير *baǥīr*).

A بعران *buǥrān* or *biǥrān*, (pl. of بعير *baǥīr*) Camels nine years old, or four years old.

A بعرة *baǥrat*, The wrath of (God). *Baǥarat*, Camels' dung. Glans penis.

A بعزقة *baǥzakat*, (v. n. of بعزق Q) Scattering.

A بعساكرهم *bi ǥasākirihim*, With their troops.

A بعص *baǥs*, Leanness of body. Agitation.

A بعصوص *buǥsūs* or *baǥasūs*, Slender, thin. The hip-bone.

A بعصوصة *buǥsūsat*, Kind of white shining insect.

A بعض *baǥz*, (pl. ابعاض *abǥāz*) Some, certain, sundry. A part. بعض كرة *baǥz kurat*, Sometimes. بعض الليالي *baǥzu'l layālī*, On a certain night. بعض لبعض *baǥzun li baǥzin*, One with another, each other, reciprocally, mutually.

A بعضة (ارض *arzun*) *baǥizatun*, A place abounding with musquitoes. ليلة بعضة *laylatun baǥizatun*, A night infested by gnats.

A بعضوضة *buǥzūzat*, An insect like the beetle.

A بعضي *baǥze*, Some, a little. بعضي بابت *baǥze bābat*, Particular taxes, so called from their being entered under this vague head, specifying no particular account on which they are levied. بعضي جمع *baǥze jamǥ*, Sundry impositions (as fines for theft or fornication; fees on marriage, &c.) or taxes forming a total of revenue exclusive of the ground-rent. P بعضي خرچ *baǥze kharch*, Petty charges. بعضي زمين *baǥze zamīn*, Lands exempted from the payment of revenue.

A بعط *baǥt*, (v. n. of بعط) Killing, sacrificing, slaughtering. Turpitude (either in word or deed).

A بعق *baǥk*, (v. n. of بعق) Killing (a camel). Digging (a well). Making a loud noise. Detecting, unveiling, making clear.

A بعقط *buǥkut*, Small in size, a dwarf.

A بعقطة *buǥkutat*, Ball of dung rolled by a beetle.

A بعقوباء *baǥkūbāǥ*, Name of a village near Bagdad: hence, بعقوبيون *baǥkūbiyūn*, Certain reporters of Muhammadan traditions.

A بعقوط *buǥkūt*, Short, dwarfish.

A بعقوطة *buǥkūtat*, Ball of dung rolled by a beetle.

A بعك *baǥk*, (v. n. of بعك) Striking (with a sword). *Baǥak*, Thickness, grossness; also a contraction of the body.

A بعكرة *baǥkarat*, A cutting with a sword.

A بعكن *baǥkan*, (Sand) difficult to be crossed.

A بعكوك *buǥkūk*, Intensity of heat. بعكوك القوم *buǥkūku'l kawm*, Marks left by a party that has been sitting.

A بعكوكاء *baǥkūkāǥ*, Evil. Clamours, noises.

A بعكوكة *buǥkūkat*, An assembly (of men). Heat. *Buǥkūkat*, *baǥkūkat*, (or بعكوك *buǥkūk*) The marks left where people have been sitting. A body of men (or of camels). Nobles. The middle of any thing. A numerous herd. The throng and dust raised by a large herd. بعكوكة الصيف و الشتاء *buǥkūkatu's sayf wa'sh shitāǥ*, The meeting of heat and cold.

A بعل *baǥl*, (pl. بعال *biǥāl*, بعولة *buǥūlat*, and بعول *buǥūl*) A husband. A wife. A lord, master, possessor. The idol Baal. High ground, a hill (especially such as receives rain only once a year). A burden, load, weight. A male palm-tree. A palm or any other tree, shrub, or plant, watered only by rain, not by art. A price paid for the watering of palm-trees. *Baǥal*, (v. n. of بعل) Being astonished, frightened out of one's wits. *Baǥil*, (fem. بعلة *baǥilat*) Astonished, frightened out of one's wits.

A بعلبك *baǥalbakk*, (or *baǥlabakk*) Baalbak in Syria (Heliopolis).

A بعلة *baǥlat*, A wife. *Baǥilat*, Astonied, amazed (woman). A woman who dresses ungracefully.

A بعلزبوب *baǥalzabūb*, Beelzebub.

A بعليّ *baǥlīy*, Grown in a field or garden watered by rain only. Belonging to Baalbak.

P بعمل *ba ǥamal*, To use: as, بعمل آمدن *ba ǥamal āmadan*, To come to use; to be put in practice. بعمل آوردن *ba ǥamal āwardan*, To bring to use, to put in practice, carry into execution, perform. بعمل در نيامدن *ba ǥamal dar nayāmadan*, Not to come to use, to fail, or become ineffectual.

A بعناية الله تعالي *bi ǥināyati'llāh taǥāla'*, By the help of the Most High God.

A بعنس *baǥnas*, A foolish girl.

A بعنسة *baǥnasat*, (v. n. of بعنس Q) Being abject, vile; degrading one's self (by servitude).

A بعنقاة *baǥankāt*, Sharp-taloned (eagle).

A بعو *baǥw*, (v. n. of بعا for بعو) Committing a crime. Oppressing, overcoming by force. Borrowing. Borrowing (a dog) for hunting, (a horse) for a race. Darting a malignant look. Striking, occasioning trouble to another. A crime. A mistake. A thing borrowed or lent.

A بعوث *buǥūs*, (pl. of بعث *baǥs*) Armies, bodies of men.

A بعوس *baǥūs*, (pl. بعائس *baǥāǥis* and بعاس *biǥās*) An extenuated milkless camel.

A بعوض *baǥūz*, (or بعوضة *baǥūzat*, noun of unity) A gnat. مخّ بعوضة *mukhkhu baǥūzat*, The marrow of a gnat (a proverb expressing any thing which either does not exist or is difficult to be found). جناح بعوضة *janāhu baǥūzatin*, The wing of a gnat (any thing of small value).

A بعول *buǥūl*, (pl. of بعل *baǥl*) Husbands. Wives.

A بعولة *buǥūlat*, (v. n. of بعل) Becoming a husband. Becoming a wife. Marrying. Refusing, rebelling against. (pl. of بعل *baǥl*) Husbands. Wives.

A بعون الله تعالي *bi ǥawni'llāhi taǥāla'*, By the assistance of the Most High God.

A بعيث *baǥīs*, Sent, despatched. Name of a poet.

A بعيج *baǥīj*, Burst in the belly, cut open. A woman with a numerous offspring.

A بعيد *baǥīd*, (pl. بعد *buǥad*) Distant, absent. Remote (in point of relationship). شقاق بعيد *shikāki baǥīd*, A wide schism. عهد بعيد *ǥahdi baǥīd*, A long time ago. غير بعيد *ghayr baǥīd*, Not far off, near at hand. من البعيد *mini'l baǥīd*, From afar. بعيد عن الصواب *baǥīd ǥani's sawāb*, Far from right, unreasonable. بعيد الغور *baǥīdu'l ghawr*, (A man) of a deep impenetrable mind. P بعيد شدن *baǥīd shudan*, To be separated. بعيد كردن *baǥīd kardan*, To remove, absent one's self, be hid.

A بعيد *buǥayd*, A little after. A little way off, at a short distance. بعيد زمان *buǥayd zamān*, or بعيدات بين *buǥaydāti baynin*, After a little while, at intervals, in a short time, by and by, presently.

A بعيدا *baǥīdan*, Afterwards.

A بعير *baǥīr* or *biǥīr*, (pl. ابعرة *abǥirat*, اباعر

abāṣir, اباعير abāṣīr, بعران buṣrān and biṣrān) A camel nine years old, or four years old, when certain teeth project from his jaws. An ass. Any beast of burden.

A بعيم baṣīm, A wooden statue. Name of an idol. One who can neither read nor compose verses. A picture without colouring.

A بعينه bi ṣaynihi, Really, truly, justly, properly, in a genuine style, to the point, to the life, plainly, clearly, exactly, literally, word for word, faithfully. بعينه حضرت سليمان biṣaynihi hazrat sulaymān, Just as the prophet Solomon, *i.e.* exactly, neither more or less.

P بغ bagh, A ditch. Name of an idol.

A بغ baghgh, (v. n. of بغ) Boiling (blood).

P بغا baghā, A whore, adultress. An infamous boy.

A بغاء bighā, (v. n. 3 of بغي) Playing the whore, committing adultery. *Bughāṣ*, (v. n. of بغي) Desiring. Seeking.

A بغاة bughāt, (pl. of باغي bāghī) Wishers. Seekers, inquirers. Prevaricators, transgressors. Oppressors, tyrants. Ruffians, rebels. بغاة واشقياء bughāt wa ashkiyāṣ, Rebels and plunderers.

A بغاث baghās, bighās or bughās (pl. بغثان bighsān) A sort of kite. بغاث الطير baghāsu't tayr, Any bird of the inferior kind of the hawk species.

A بغاددة baghādidat, (pl. of بغداديّ baghdādiy) Natives of Baghdad.

P بغار baghār, A nail, spike, wedge. *Baghār*, (or بغاره baghāra) A breach in a wall. A wound. *Bighār*, A river.

A بغاري baghāra' or bughāra', (pl. of بغير baghir) (Camels) affected by a disease produced by an unquenchable thirst.

P بغاز baghāz, A wedge used by carpenters to split timber, and by shoemakers to stretch the leather on their lasts.

A بغاضة baghāzat, The being hated. A hating.

A بغال bighāl, (pl. of بغل baghl) Mules.

A بغّال baghghāl, A muleteer or owner of mules.

A بغام bughām, (v. n. of بغم) Calling their young (does or mountain-goats). Speaking indistinctly.

P بغامه baghāma, A demon inhabiting the woods.

P بغان baghān, A wedge, a wooden peg.

P بغانوش baghānūsh, A quick-going horse.

A بغاوة baghāwat, Rebellion. P بغاوت كردن baghāwat kardan, To assault, injure.

A بغايا baghāya', (pl. of بغيّ baghīy) Whores. The advanced guard, picket, or forlorn hope of an army.

A بغاية bi ghāyat, Extremely, exceedingly, immoderately, vehemently. Until, down to. *Bughāyat*, A thing greatly in request.

A بغبغ bughbugh, A well whose water is near the mouth. A fat hart.

A بغبغة baghbaghat, The braying of a camel. The noise of one snoring or trampling. *Bughbughat*, A piece of ground at Madīna; also a very copious fountain; also a palm-grove belonging to the family of Muhammad.

A بغبور bughbūr, A stone or altar upon which they sacrifice to idols. The title of the Emperor of China.

A بغت baght, (v. n. of بغت) Coming upon unawares. Any sudden or unexpected event.

P بغتاف baghtāf, A fissure.

P بغتاق baghtāk, A high cap. A cleft.

A بغتة baghtat or baghatat, (v. n. of بغت) Happening unexpectedly. بغتةً baghtatan, Suddenly, unexpectedly.

A بغث baghas, (v. n. of بغث) Being variegated, piebald (sheep).

A بغثاء baghsāṣ, (fem. of ابغث abghas) (A ewe) marked with white and black spots. A mob, mixed company of men.

A بغثان bighsān, (pl. of بغاث baghās) Kites. Mischievous birds.

A بغثة baghsat, Small gentle rain. *Bughsat*, A black colour mixed with white in cattle.

A بغثر baghsar, Foolish. Weak. Heavy, unwholesome. Dirty, nasty. Large, bulky (camel).

P بغثرانيدن bughsarānīdan, To cause to scatter.

A بغثرة baghsarat, (v. n. of بغثر Q) Separating, scattering. (See بعثرة baṣsarat). Commotion, tumult, mixture, confusion. A palpitation or disorder of the heart, arising from any thing which disturbs the mind. القوم في البغثرة al kawm fi'l baghsarat, The people (are) in a tumult.

P بغثري bughsarī, Afterwards, a little after.

P بغثريدن bughsarīdan, To scatter, strew, sow.

P بغچه bughcha, A bundle.

A بغداد baghdād, (sometimes written بغذاذ baghzāz, بغذاد baghdāz, بغدان baghdān, بغدين baghdīn, and مغدان maghdān) The city of Baghdad, situated on the eastern side of the Tigris, the capital of Babylonian or Arabian Irāk (the ancient Chaldea or Assyria). It was built (A.C. 762) by the Khalif Almansūr; and named also مدينة السلام madīnatu's salām, The city of peace. The belly. The second line upon the cup of Jam. P بغداد خرابست baghdād kharābast, Baghdad is ruined (metaphorically, the stomach (or the wine-cup) is empty). بغداد معموره baghdād maṣmūra, Fulness, repletion.

A بغداديّ baghdādiy, (pl. بغاددة baghādidat) A native of Baghdad.

A بغر baghr, (v. n. of بغر) Pouring down a heavy and sudden shower (the sky). Moistening the earth (rain). Watering, irrigating. *Baghr* or *baghar*, A sudden and heavy fall of rain. *Baghar*, (v. n. of بغر) Drinking without quenching the thirst, and being diseased thereby (a camel). A disease incident to camels from excessive thirst. Bad water, injurious to the cattle that drink it. *Baghir*, (A camel) troubled with a disease caused by an inextinguishable thirst.

P بغرا baghrā, A boar. *Bughrā*, Quadrangular sections of paste (or macaroni) dressed with soup or milk. Name of a king of Khwārazm. A heron that takes the lead in flight.

P بغراخاني bughrā khānī, A certain kind of soup called *bughrā*, of which Bughrā Khān, king of Khwārazm, was the inventor.

A بغراس baghrās, Name of a city near Antioch.

P بغراو bughrāw, Clamour, noise.

A بغرة baghrat, Seed sown after rain, and remaining moist until it puts forth the blade. A perennial gift.

A بغز baghz, (v. n. of بغز) Beating with a stick. Kicking. Causing to move with alacrity. Agility, briskness. Eagerness, violence of temper.

A بغس baghs, (in Yaman) Blackness.

A بغش baghsh, (v. n. of بغش) Raining small. Screaming and running frightened (a child to its mother). Entering (as a mote in the sun-beams through a lattice). *Baghsh*, (or بغشة baghshat) Small misling rain, dew.

P بغشور baghshūr, Name of a village near Harāt.

A بغض baghz, (v. n. of بغض) Hating. بغض جدّك baghiza jadduka, Perish thy grandfather! *Bughz*, Hatred. بغض خفي bughzi khafī, Concealed hatred.

A بغضاء baghzāṣ, Excessive hatred.

A بغضة bighzat, Intense hatred.

P بغطاق baghtāk, A turban. A fissure.

A بغل baghl, (v. n. of بغل) Rendering (offspring) base and mongrel. (pl. بغال bighāl and مبغولاء mabghūlāṣ) A mule.

P بغل baghl, Name of a Jewish coiner of money. *Baghal*, The arm-pit. The embrace. A fathom. بغل دست baghali dast, The arm-pit. بغل ران baghali rān, The groin. بغل باز نمودن baghal bāz namūdan, To receive with open arms. بغل رفتن baghal raftan, To go on one side. بغل زدن baghal zadan, To rejoice at another's distress. بغل گشادن baghal gushādan, To exercise. To prove. To display strength.

A بغّل baghghal, Slow, tardy, fatigued. A certain pace of a camel, neither good nor bad.

P بغل بند baghal-band, A rope tied under the arm-pits.

A بغلة baghlat, A she-mule. A herd of mules.

P بغلتاق baghltāk, The accoutrements of a horse. A cap, a head-dress. A cleft.

P بغل تري baghal-tarī, Shame, bashfulness, funk.

P بغلطاق baghltāk, The accoutrements of a horse. A cap, a head-dress. A cleft.

P بغلك baghalak, A swelling under the arm-pits, a bubo. بغلك زدن baghalak zadan, To rejoice at another's misfortunes.

P بغل گير baghal-gīr, Embracing: an embracer.

P بغل گيري baghal-gīrī, Embracement, clasp, hug.

P بغلنقار baghlankār, (or بغلنقاز baghlankāz) Name of a bird.

P بغلي *baghlī*, A disorder in camels, rubbing the thigh against the belly. A kind of dumb bell used in exercise. Money of the coinage of Baghl the Jew.

P بغماز *bughmāz*, Circumference. *Bughmāz*, (or بغمار *bughmār*) A mould for making bricks.

P بغنج *bughunj*, Coriander-seed.

P بغند *baghand*, An inquiry. A river. A kind of leather.

A بغو *baghw*, (v. n. of بغا for بغو) Observing, considering. The blossoms of the trees عرفط *ʻurfut* and سلم *salam*). The fruit of a wild tree, small, green, and never ripening.

A بغوّ *baghūw*, A whore.

A بغوة *baghwat*, An unripe date. A pod of a palm-tree, bursting and shooting forth flowers.

A بغور *bughūr*, (v. n. of بغر) Setting (stars, particularly the pleiades) and causing rain.

A بغوم *baghūm*, (A doe or mountain-goat) bleating. *Bughūm*, (v. n. of بغم) Leaving off braying (a she-camel). Bellowing, bleating (does, camels, and mountain-goats) when calling their young. Speaking obscurely, ambiguously, or indistinctly.

A بغويّ *baghawīy*, Native of بغشور *baghsūr*.

A بغي *baghy*, (v. n. of بغي) Watching, expecting, waiting for. Considering attentively, examining. Transgressing (the) bounds (of propriety). Being overbearing, immoderate, unjust, insolent, oppressive. Strutting, walking pompously. Raining hard. Filling a valley (a torrent). Lying. Playing the whore. Swelling (a wound). Being brisk, active, swift (a horse). Injustice, tyranny, oppression, violence. Insolence. Defection, revolt, rebellion. Excoriation. *Bughy*, (v. n. of بغي) Begging, asking, searching. Assisting one in seeking for any thing lost.

A بغيّ *baghīy*, (pl. بغايا *baghāya'*) A whore, an adulteress. A maid-servant. One who makes great search or strict observation.

P بغياز *baghyāz*, Drink-money. A present of sweetmeats. Good news.

P بغيازي *baghyāzī*, Good news. Drink-money.

A بغيان *bughyān*, (pl. of باغي *bāghī*) Seekers, inquirers, wishers.

A بغيبغ *bughaybigh*, A little well whence water is easily drawn. عدا طلقا بغيبغا *ʻada' talkan bughaybighan*, He ran a little way.

A البغيبغة *al bughaybighat*, Name of an estate and of a well belonging to Alīy.

A بغية *bighyat* or *bughyat*, (v. n. of بغي) Desiring, seeking. Any thing wanted, lost, sought after. لي في فلان بغية *lī fī fulān bighyat*, I have something to do with such a one.

A بغيّة *baghīyat*, (pl. بغايا *baghāya'*) Any thing lost or sought after. An advanced guard, a reconnoitering party.

A بغيث *baghīs*, Wheat: wheat mixed with barley.

A بغيثاء *bughaysāʼ*, The part of a camel wheron a portmanteau or pad is placed.

A بغير *baghīr*, (pl. بغاري *baghāra'* or *bughāra'*) (A camel) affected by a disease brought on by an unextinguishable thirst. *Bi ghayr*, Without, besides, except, unless. بغيري *bi ghayrī*, (or P بغير ازمن *ba ghayr az man*) Except me. A بغير روية *bi ghayr rūyat*, Rashly.

A بغيض *baghīz*, Hated. Name of a person whose name was changed by Muhammad to حبيب *habīb*.

P بف *baf*, A weaving instrument.

P بفار *bafār*, A wedge.

P بفتري *baftarī*, The yarn-beam. The sley of a weaver's loom. Any instrument used in weaving.

P بفج *bafj*, Spittle. A slaverer. A blubber-lip.

P بفجم *bafjam*, Much, many. Copious. Cloths stretched upon spars of wood in which people catch the money so scattered.

P بفردا *ba fardā*, To-morrow. See فردا *fardā*.

P بفرما *bifarmā*, (imp. of فرمودن *farmūdan*) Command, say.

P بفرود *ba firod*, Down, downward.

P بفش *bafsh*, Magnificence, elegance, pomp.

A بفضله سبحانه و تعالى *bi fazlihi subhānahu wa taʻāla'*, By the grace of God, by divine favour.

P بفكين *baflīn*, (in zand and Pāz.) An upper chamber, gallery, or balcony on the top of a house.

P بفم *bafm* or *bafam*, Sorrow. Weak, tired. Sad.

P بفنج *bafnaj*, A kind of venomless serpent.

A بقّ *bakk*, (v. n. of بقّ) Bringing forth many children. Dispersing abroad (one's family). Shooting forth (a plant). Scattering (wealth). Raining abundantly. Talking much. Splitting (a leathern wallet). Becoming powerful and grand. A gnat. لق بق *lakk bakk*, Talkative. شجرة البق *shajaratu'l bakk*, The gnat-tree, so called from the immense number of gnats found in its pods. It is described as very large, having a smooth trunk requiring three or four men to clasp it, and capable of sheltering two hundred horsemen. In Persian it has a variety of names: as, آغال پشه *āghāl-pasha*, پشه غال *pasha-ghāl*, پشه دار *pashsha-dār*, دردار *dardār*, سارخكدار *sārakh-dār*, سارشكدار *sārashk-dār*, لامشگر *lāmishgar*, گژم *gujm*, كنجك *kanjak*, and نازين *nājīn*. بق الحيطان *bakku'l hītān*, A wall, wood, or paper-louse. A bug.

A بقاء *bakāʼ*, (v. n. of بقي) Remaining. Continuing. Life, living. Permanency, perpetuity, duration. دار بقا *dāri bakā*, (or P كشور بقا *kishwari bakā*) The other world, the everlasting kingdom, eternity.

A بقّار *bakkār*, A dealer in cattle, a drover. A blacksmith. البقّار *al bakkār*, The name of a valley and of a desert, said to be inhabited by demons. A sort of game. *Bukkār*, (pl. of بقرة *baharat*) Cows, oxen.

A بقّاري *bukkāra'*, A lie. Misfortune, calamity.

A بقّاريّ *bakkārīy*, A stout stick, a cudgel.

A بقاط *bukāt*, A handful of اقط *akit* (or sour milk, allowed to concrete, and reduced to powder, which is kept for future use, and dressed in a variety of ways).

A بقّاط *bukkāt*, Sediment of the grains of the colocynth, sweetened by pouring water upon them.

A بقاع *bikāʻ*, (pl. of بقعة *bukʻat* or *bakʻat*) Low places where water stagnates. (pl. of بقعة *bukʻat*) Tracts, districts. Irregular tracts of land. Countries. Buildings. Temples. Monasteries. Name of several places in Syria. بقاع كلب *bikāʻ kalb*, Name of a place near Damascus where the tomb of Elias is to be seen. بقاع خير *bikāʻi khayr*, Sacred places, monasteries. P بقاع سپهر ارتفاع *bikāʻi sipihr-irtifāʻ*, Fabrics high as the heavens. A خرؤ بقاع *khurʻu bakāʻ*, Dust or sweat, whereof traces yet remain on the body.

A بقاق *bakāk*, (v. n. of بقّ) Being very talkative. Goods, furniture of little value. A certain noisy bird. Rubbish, sticks, and straws in a valley or river.

A بقاقة *bakākat*, Talkative.

A بقال *bakāl*, (Ground) fruitful in pot-herbs.

A بقّال *bakkāl*, (incorrectly for بدّال *baddāl*) A vender of provisions in general. A green-grocer.

A بقّالة *bakkālat*, A garden of pot-herbs.

A بقامة *bukāmat*, Weak in mind. Coarse or uncombed wool. The coarse part of flax or hemp. Chips, shavings.

A بقاوة *bakāwat*, (v. n. of بقي) Looking upon. Considering. Expecting. Guarding, keeping.

P بقاول *bakāwal*, (for بكاول) Overseer of the kitchen.

A بقايا *bakāya'*, (pl. of بقيّة *bakīyat*) Remains, fragments. Balances. بقاياي باقي *bakāyāyi bākī*, Outstanding balances.

A بقباق *bakbāk*, Prating, talkative. The mouth.

A بقبقة *bakbakat*, (v. n. of بقبق Q) Sounding (as a bottle when decanting, or a jug in water). Scattering (words).

A بقّة *bakkat*, A gnat. A bug. Prolific (woman).

A بقت *bakt*, (v. n. of بقت) Mixing up the preparation of milk called اقط *akit*.

A بقش *baks*, (v. n. of بقش) Mixing, confounding.

P بقچه *bukcha*, A knapsack, wallet, small bundle.

A بقدر *bi kadri*, (P *ba kadri*) According to, with regard to, as to, in consideration of. بقدر الاحتياج *bi kadri'l ihtiyāj*, According to the exigency, in consideration of the necessity. بقدر الامكان *bi kadri'l imkān*, (or بقدر الطاقة *bi kadri't tākat*) As far as possible. P بقدر مراتبش *ba kadri marātibash*, According to his rank.

A بقر *bakara* (fut. يبقر *yabkaru*) He clave asunder.

A بقر *bakr*, (v. n. of بقر) Cleaving, splitting. Knowing people's affairs, prying into them. Sighing. Being scarcely able to see. Being fatigued. Widening, opening. Looking for and discovering water (the lapwing). *Bakar,* (v. n. of بقر) Being astonished and wild with joy on seeing an ox (a dog). Sighing. Being scarcely able to see. Being fatigued. (pl. of بقرة *bakarat*) Black cattle, beeves. اقاطع البقر *akāṭiʿu'l bakar,* Herds of oxen. جوع البقر *jūʿu'l bakar,* An insatiable appetite, the stomach of an ox. عيون البقر *ʿuyūnu'l bakar,* An ox-eye, a kind of fine large black grape, but not of a genuine sweetness. The damasc plum. بقر عيد *bakar-ʿīd,* A feast held in commemoration of Abraham's offering to sacrifice his son (Ismāīl, and not Is-hāk, according to the Muhammadans). *Buhar,* A lie. An evil, misfortune, calamity. *Bukur,* (pl. of بقرة *bakarat*) Oxen. Cows, beeves.

A بقرات *bakarāt,* (pl. of بقرة *bakarat*) Oxen. Cows, beeves. Flocks (of sheep).

G بقراط *bukrāt,* Hippocrates. A بقراط مالك الصحة *bukrāt māliku's sahhat,* Hippocrates, the king of health.

A بقرة *bakarat,* (pl. بقر *bakar,* بقرات *bakarāt,* بقر *bukur,* بقار *bukkār,* ابقور *ubkūr,* بواقر *bawākir,* باقر *bākir,* or بقير *bakīr*) A cow, ox. (pl. بقر *bakar*) A kind of bird, white, pie-bald, or ash-coloured.

A بقس *baks,* (or بقسيس *baksīs*) The box-tree.

A بقط *bakt,* Household furniture. A collecting together of household goods. Separation, dispersion. A letting out of a garden (for a third or a fourth part of its produce). *Bakat,* Dates which fall to the ground when the clusters are carelessly cut. A part or fragment of any thing. A scattered body of men.

A بقطة *buktat,* A scattered body of men.

A بقطرية *bukturīyat,* Garments white and ample.

A بقع *bakʿ,* (v. n. of بقع) Going into any country. Provoking by opprobrious words and false imputations. *Bukʿ,* Persons clad in patched garments. Drawers of water whose clothes, being wet in places, present a spotted appearance. Name of a well at Madina. *Bakaʿ,* (v. n. of بقع) Being marked with black and white spots. Becoming desert and uninhabited. Sprinkling water on the body. Being satisfied with. An intermixture of colours in birds and dogs (particularly of black and white). *Bakiʿ,* Ground whereon are speckled locusts. *Bukaʿ,* (pl. of بقعة *bukʿat*) Spots.

A بقعاء *bakʿāʾ,* (fem. of ابقع *abkaʿ*) Black and white (crow). (A year) barren or scarce of provisions; (or rather) partly fruitful and partly barren, as expressive of variety. Name of a city.

A بقعان *bukʿān,* (pl. of بقيع *bakīʿ*) Servants, Ethiopian slaves. بقعان الشام *bukʿānu'sh shām,* The servants or slaves of the people of Syria, some white and others black, Europeans and Ethiopians.

A بقعة *bukʿat* or *bakʿat,* (pl. بقع *bukaʿ* and بقاع *bikāʿ*) A low place in which water stagnates. A place, country, region, district. An edifice. A temple. A monastery. A caravansera. كل بقعة *kullu bukʿatin,* Everywhere.

A بقل *bakl,* (v. n. of بقل) Growing, appearing (the herbage; the beards of young men; the teeth of camels). Producing herbage (ground). Flourishing, putting forth leaves. Gathering pot-herbs for one's camels. Fruitful in pot-herbs (ground). (pl. بقول *bukūl*) Herbage produced from seed. *Bukl,* Spring-herbs. Spring.

A بقلة *baklat,* A pot-herb. Purslain. A bean. A kitchen-garden. A verdant spot of ground. البقلة الاترجية *al baklatu'l utrujīyat,* Balm. بقلة الانصار *baklatu'l ansār,* Cauliflower, cabbage. البقلة البادرة *al baklatu'l bāridat,* Pellitory. Ivy. بقلة الحمقاء *baklatu'l hamkāʾ,* The insipid herb, purslain. بقلة بقلة الخراسانية *baklatu'l khurāsānīyat,* Sorrel. بقلة الخطاطيف *baklatu'l khatātīf,* Turmeric. Saffron. Celadine. البقلة الذهبية *al baklatu'z zahabīyat,* Orage. بقلة الرماة *baklatu'r rumāt,* A kind of herb. بقلة الضب *baklatu'z zabb,* A species of sweet basil. بقلة الغزال *baklatu'l ghazāl,* Dittany. البقلة اللينة *al baklatu'l layyinat,* Purslain. البقلة المباركة *al baklatu'l mubārakat,* Endive. Purslain. بقلة الملك *baklatu'l malik,* Fumitory. البقلة اليمانية *al baklatu'l yamānīyat,* Beet, spinage. بقلة يهودية *baklat yahūdīyat,* Sow-thistle, a kind of lettuce.

T بقلنقاز *baklankāz,* Name of a certain animal with a black and white neck, long legs, and a broad blueish snout.

P بقم *bakam,* Wood, like Brazil wood; the red dye extracted from it. *Buhum,* The thorn-apple.

A بقم *bakkam,* The wood of a large tree, whose leaf is like the almond and trunk red, used in dyeing. *Bukham,* The thorn-apple.

A بقوة *bakwat,* (v. n. of بقي) Looking upon. Observing, considering. Expecting, waiting for. Respecting, regarding. Guarding, keeping.

A بقول *bukūl,* Herbs, pot-herbs. بقول الاوجاع *bukūlu'l awjāʿ,* A certain herb good for the gripes.

A بقوي *bakwa'* or *bukwa',* A remainder, any thing reserved. Life, living. Pity.

A بقي *baky,* (v. n. of بقي) Considering, observing. Expecting, waiting for. *Baky* or *baka',* (v. n. of بقي) Remaining.

A بقيا *bukya',* A remainder, any thing reserved. Pity. Life, living.

A بقية *bakīyat,* A remainder, residue, remnant, what is preserved or reserved. Remains of strength or beauty. A balance, surplusage. What God has left indifferent. Life, living. Prudence, intelligence. Pity. Probity, rectitude amongst people. بقية الله *bakīyatu'llāh,* Obedience rendered to God, in the expectation of a future reward. بقية السيوف *bakīyatu's suyūf,* The remains of the sword (*i.e.* of a scattered army after a defeat). P بقية سپاه *bakīyaʾi sipāh,* The rest of the soldiers.

A بقير *bakīr,* Split. A camel whose belly is cut open to let the foal come out. A herd of oxen. *Bakīr,* (or بقيرة *bakīrat*) A shift or inner garment, slit, and without sleeves, worn by women. (pl. of بقرة *bakarat*) Cows. *Bukayr,* A foal born in a caul.

A بقيري *bukhayra',* A sort of boy's game.

A بقيع *bakīʿ,* A place in which there are roots of a number of trees. بقيع الغرقد *bakīʿu'l gharkad,* The cemetery of Madīna. ابن بقيع *ibn bukayʿ,* A dog.

A بقيل *bakīl,* Fruitful in pot-herbs (ground).

A بقيلة *bakīlat,* Meat dressed with broth, peas, and other herbs. *Bukaylat,* (dim. of بقلة *baklat*) A small pot-herb.

P بك *bak,* Wild cucumber. A retreat, an asylum. A frog. A forest. A wild uncultivated country. Name of a city in Transoxania. *Bik,* A live coal. *Buk,* The cheek, face, A pitcher with a short neck. Ignorance, unskilfulness.

A بكا *bakʾ* or *bukʾ,* (v. n. of بكأ) Having little milk (a camel or a sheep). *Bahaʾ,* Name of a plant.

A بكا *baka',* (fut. يبكي *yabkī*) He wept.

A بكا *baka',* A sort of plant. *Buka',* (v. n. of بكي) Shedding tears, weeping.

A بكاء *bikāʾ,* (pl. of بكيء *bakīʾ*) (Camels) giving little milk. *Bukāʾ,* (v. n. of بكي) Weeping, crying, bewailing, lamenting. A complaint, lamentation, exclamation. P زار و بكا كردن *zār u bukā kardan,* To lament and complain.

A بكاء *bakkāʾ,* One who weeps much.

A بكابك *bukābik,* Joyous, sprightly.

P بكار *ba kār,* At work. To use, useful. بكار آب بودن *ba kāri āb būdan,* To be constantly drinking. بكار آمدن *ba kār āmadan,* To come to use, to serve, to be of use, to be fit or useful. بكار آوردن *ba kār āwardan,* To bring to use, to use, effect, perfect. To kill, to slay. بكار بردن *ba kār burdan,* To use, to employ. بكار نيامدني *ba kār nayāmadanī,* (or بكار نا آينده *ba kār nā āyanda*) Unserviceable, useless.

A بكار *bikār,* (v. n. 3 of بكر) Coming early in the morning. (pl. of بكرة *bakrat*) Young (she-camels).

A بكارة *bakārat,* (v. n. of بكر) Being a virgin. Virginity. *Bakarat* or *bikarat,* (pl. of بكر *bakr*) Young (camels). P بكارت گرفتن *bakārat giriftan,* (or ازالهٔ بكارت كردن *izālaʾi bakārat kardan*) To deflower a virgin.

A بكاس *bakās,* A strong place near Antioch.

P بكاغذ بردن *ba kāghiz burdan,* To promote to the highest degree of honour.

A بكالة *bakālat,* A kind of dish made of flour. See بكيلة *bakīlat.*

A بكامة *bakāmat,* (v. n. of بكم) Being dumb. Restraining one's self from speaking. Abstaining (from a wife).

A بكان *bukkān,* (pl. of ابك *abakk*) Severe years (destroying cattle). Very wise. Herdsmen. Farming-bailiffs. Hirelings.

P بكاول *bakāwul,* A head cook, a superintendant of the kitchen (a term much used in India).

A بكايا *bakāya'*, (pl. of بكيئة *bakī,at*) (Camels) which yield little milk.

P بكاين *bakāyin*, The Persian lilac.

A بكباك *bakbāk*, A toddling dwarf.

P بكبر *bakbar*, The purging cassia.

A بكبكة *bakbakat*, (v. n. of بكبك Q) Throwing one on another, crowding, squeezing, thronging. Going and coming. Shaking or turning upside down. The treatment of a she-goat to her young.

P بكبكه *bakbaka*, Frumenty, pottage. A villain, corrupter, spoiler.

A بكّة *bakkat*, (v. n. of بكّ) Crowding together, thronging, assembling tumultuously. Pitying. Hindering. Tearing, separating, dividing, scattering, disjoining, dissolving. Urging, pressing. Humbling, depressing. Breaking (the neck). Overworking with venery. Being reduced to poverty. Having a hairy body, the mark (according to the Arabians) of a bold and active mind. Mecca, or the interior part of it, lying between two mountains.

A بكت *bakt*, (v. n. of بكت) Striking with (a sword or stick). Offering or placing before any one what he detests. Receiving with a bad grace.

P بكتاش *baktāsh*, Name of a prudent man mentioned in the Gulistān; also of a king of Khwārazm.

P بكتانوش *baktānosh*, A king of the genii.

P بكتر *baktar*, A coat of mail, a cuirass.

P بكترپوش *baktar-posh*, Clad in armour.

P بكتري *baktarī*, An armourer, who makes coats of mail.

P بكتوسان *baktūsān*, Name of a certain intelligent man; also of a poet.

P بكتوش *baktūsh*, A man's name.

P بكجا *ba kujā*, Whither?

P بكخا *bikhkhā*, Plain silk.

P بكدامين *ba kudāmīn*, How? in what manner?

A بكر *bakara*, (fut. يبكر *yabkuru*) He rose betimes.

A بكر *bakr* or *bukr*, (pl. ابكر *abkur*, بكران *bukrān*, بكارة *bakārat* or *bikārat*) A young camel. Name of the father of a tribe. ابو بكر *abū bakr*, Name of Muhammad's father-in-law and successor. ديار بكر *diyār-bakr*, Mesopotamia, and also the capital city, formerly Amida. *Bikr*, (pl. ابكار *abkār*) A maid, virgin, girl. A camel which has brought forth her first colt. A woman delivered of her first and only child. A heifer which has not yet borne a calf. The first, the first-born (male or female, man or beast). A vine bearing for the first time. A cloud fraught with rain. An unprecedented affair. الضربة البكر *az zarbatu'l bikr*, A blow which penetrates, a mortal wound. P بكر پوشيده روي *bikri poshīda-rūy*, (The veiled-faced virgin), (or بكر مشاطه خزان *bikri mashāta-khizān*) (The autumn-attired maiden) An unbroached cask of wine. A *Bakar*, (v. n. of بكر) Making haste. The morning, dawn. (pl. of بكرة *bakrat* or *bakarat*) Pullies. *Bakir* or *bakur*, One who rises betimes and does any thing in the morning. *Bukr*, (pl. of بكور *bakūr* and بكير *bakīr*) Ripe dates. All fruits which ripen soon.

A بكرا *bakaran*, In the morning, early.

A بكرات *bakarāt*, The ornamental rings of the sheaths of Eastern cimeters, by which they are suspended by chains to the girdle. (pl. of بكرة *bakrat* or *bakarat*) Pullies.

P بكران *bukrān* The inside of a pot, the bottom of a pot; also what is contained in it, or, being burnt, adheres to the bottom. Scalded in a pot.

A بكران *bukrān*, (pl. of بكر *bakr*) Young camels.

P بكران چرخ *bikrāni charkh*, (or بهشت *bihisht*) Virgins of Paradise. The stars.

A بكراويّ *bakrāwiy*, Belonging to the tribe of بني ابي بكر *banī abī bakr*.

P بكرائي *bakrā,ī*, Name of a fruit like the citron.

A بكرة *bakrat*, (pl. بكار *bikār*) A young she-camel. A troop, a crowd. *Bakrat* or *bakarat*, (pl. بكر *bakar* and بكرات *bakarāt*) A pulley. ابو بكرة *abū bakrat*, Name of one of Muhammad's companions, (so called because he let himself down by a pulley from a fortress at the battle of Taif).

A بكرة *bukrat*, (pl. بكر *bukar*) The morning, the dawn. جاء بكرةً *jā,a bukratan*, He came betimes. بكرةً وعشيّةً *bukratan wa ʻashīyatan*, Morning and evening.

P بكردار *ba kirdār*, After the manner of, like.

P بكروي *bakrawī*, A kind of fruit between an orange and a lemon. A great drinker.

A بكريّ *bakriy*, Of the family of Abū bakr, or of بني بكر بن عبد مناة *banī bakr bin ʻabd manāt*, or of بكر بن وائل *bukr bin wā,il*. *Bikriy*, Virgin, belonging to a virgin.

A بكس *baks*, (v. n. of بكس) Subduing, overcoming (an adversary).

A بكسة *buksat*, A ball made of cloth, with which boys play at كجّة *kujjat*. A piece of potsherd.

P بكسر *baksir*, Buxar, a town in Bahār (India).

P بكستن *buksistan*, To break. To be broken.

P بكسمات *baksamāt*, Biscuit taken on a journey.

P بكسه *buksa*, A fragment of meat.

A بكش *baksh*, (v. n. of بكش) Loosing the camel's rope عقال *ʻikāl*.

P بكشه *baksha*, A swelling or tubercle on the neck or body.

A بكع *bakʻ*, (v. n. of بكع) Offering or placing before another whatever he detests. Checking or silencing by upbraiding. Striking one with repeated blows upon different parts of the body. Giving any thing entirely. Cutting in pieces. Going away, departing for any place.

P بكف آوردن *ba kaf āwardan*, To acquire. To exhibit, to display.

A بكك *bukuk*, Robust youths. Sprightly asses.

A بكل *bakl*, (v. n. of بكل) Speaking foolishly. Preparing the dish بكيلة *bakīlat*. Mixture, confusion. Booty, spoil, prey, plunder.

A بكلة *biklat*, Nature, form, figure, habit, state, condition, shape.

A بكم *bukm*, (pl. of ابكم *abkam*) Dumb (persons). *Bakam*, (v. n. of بكم) Being dumb (either from nature or disease). Refraining from speech. Abstaining (from the marriage-bed). Dumbness.

P بكم *bakam*, Brazilian wood.

P بكمار *bukmār*, A conqueror, a superior.

A بكمان *bukmān*, (pl. of بكيم *bakīm*) Dumb.

P بكن *bi kan*, Tear thou up, dig. *Ba kun* or *bu kun*, Do thou.

P بكنك *bakang* or *bikang*, An animal that has lost its tail.

A بكوء *bukū,*, (v. n. of بكأ) Having little milk.

A بكور *bakūr*, (pl. بكر *bukr*) Ripe dates, and in general all fruits which ripen soon. Early spring rain. *Bukūr*, (v. n. of بكر) Rising, going, coming, visiting, or doing any thing early in the morning. Making haste.

A بكوريّة *bukūriyat*, Primogeniture.

P بكوك *bakūk*, A butt, mark, or target to shoot at. *Bakūk*, (or بكول *bakūl*) A drinking-cup.

P بك و لك *buk u luk*, Unequal. Ignorance.

P بكونك *bakūnak*, (or بكونه) A wooden cimeter.

P بكهان *bak-hān*, (or بكهاين) A sort of grain.

P بكهوجتان *bak-hūjtān*, Any thing high in the middle and sloping at each end.

A بكيّ *baka'*, Name of a plant. *Buka'*, (v. n. of بكي) Weeping, crying.

A بكيّ *bakiy*, Ready to weep. One who weeps much. Little. *Bukiy*, (pl. of باكي *bākī*) Weepers.

A بكّيّ *bakkiy*, Belonging to Baalbak.

A بكيء *bakī,* or بكيئة *bakī,at*, (pl. بكاء *bikā,* and بكايا *bakāya'* (A camel) having little milk.

P بكياسا *bikyāsā*, A small load placed on a larger.

A بكير *bakīr*, Ripe dates, and all early fruits.

A بكيك *bakīk*, (A sword) which fells any one to the ground.

A بكيل (جميل *jamīli*) *bakīl*, Extremely nice and circumspect with regard to dress and deportment.

A بكيلة *bakīlat*, A kind of miscellaneous dish, made in different manners, of meat, flour, or slices of thin paste, dates, new wine, milk, pulse, oil, and water. A mixed flock of sheep and goats. Spoil, booty, prey, plunder. Nature, disposition.

A بكيم *bakīm*, (pl. بكمان *bukmān*) Dumb, silent.

P بگاه *ba gāh*, In time. Morning; the dawn. بگاهست *ba gāhast*, It is time.

P بگتر *bagtar*, A coat of mail, a cuirass.

P بگذار *bu guzār*, Send away, dismiss, let pass.

P بگذاشتن *bu guzāshtan*, To send away, dismiss, discharge, disband, permit to pass.

P بگردانيدن *ba gardānīdan*, To turn, convert, avert, divert. To turn the back. To take a turn.

P بگرد رفت *ba gard raft*, He is gone to dust, he is annihilated. It is evaporated in smoke.

P بگرديدن *ba gardīdan*, To walk, to wander. To

turn, change, alter. بگردیدن از چیزي *ba gardīdan az chīze*, To decline or turn away from any thing.

T P بگزاده *beg-zāda*, A prince's son, a cavalier.

P بگشان *bagshān*, An assembly of nobles.

P بگم *bagam*, Brazilian wood used in dyeing. *Bigum*, A queen. The queen-mother. A lady of rank. A respectable matron.

P بگماز *bagmāz*, Sorrow, grief. A drinking-glass. An entertainment, a banquet. بگماز کردن *bagmāz kardan*, To give a wine-party. *Bigmāz*, Wine. A drinking-glass. Wine-drinking.

P بگند *bagand*, A bird's nest.

P بگنگ *bagang*, An animal which has lost its tail.

P بگني *bagnī*, Malt-liquor, beer. بگنيء ارزن *bagnīʼi arzan*, Beer from millet.

P بگو *ba go* or *bu gū*, (from گفتن *guftan*) Say thou.

P بگه *ba gah*, In time, in a certain time, timely.

P بل *bal*, The heel. *Bil*, (for بهل *bihil*) Let alone, touch not, dismiss, send away. Name of a fruit. *Bul*, Much. Very. Many.

A بل *bal*, But. Nay, no, on the contrary. Assuredly. What do I say?

A بل *balla*, (fut. يبل *yabullu*) He moistened.

A بلّ *ball*, (v. n. of بلّ) Moistening, softening, sprinkling. Soaping the beard or head when going to shave. Travelling. Bestowing upon. Recovering from indisposition. Sowing (ground). Conquering. A union of friends. Greedy. One who withholds just dues. Quarrelsome, contentious. Cruel, unjust, oppressive. *Bill*, (v. n. of بلّ) Uniting; enjoying the society of friends. Recovery from indisposition. Any thing allowed or permitted, in which every one enjoys a common right. هو بذي بلّ *huwa bizī billin*, He is gone no one knows where. *Bull*, (pl. of ابلّ *aball* and بلّاء *ballāʼ*) Wicked, perjured, adulterous (men or women).

A بلا *bala'*, (fut. يبلو *yablū*) He tempted.

A بلا *bilā*, Without, beyond. بلا امهال *bilā imhāl*, Without delay. بلا اهمال *bilā ihmāl*, Without neglect. بلا تأخير *bilā taʼkhīr*, Immediately, without delay. بلا ترتيب *bilā tartīb*, Disorderly, irregular, inordinate. بلا تردّد *bilā taraddud*, Without hesitation, without opposition. بلا تسيّل *bilā tasayyul*, Without running or flowing. بلا تشبيه *bilā tashbīh*, Beyond comparison, incomparably. بلا تعب *bilā taʻb*, Without trouble or fatigue. بلا تعبير *bilā taʻbīr*, Inexplicable. بلا توقّف *bilā tawakkuf*, Without waiting, immediately, at once. بلا حجّة *bilā hujjat*, Without proof. بلا حركة *bilā harakat*, Motionless, immoveable. بلا سبب *bilā sabab*, (or بلا موجب *bilā mūjib*) Without cause. بلا شرط *bilā shart*, Unconditional. بلا طلب *bilā talab*, Without seeking. بلا عوض *bilā ʻiwaz*, Without recompense. بلا فائده *bilā fāʼida*, Unprofitable. بلا فرق *bilā fark*, Indifferently. بلا قصور *bilā kusūr*, Without fail. بلا مهارشه *bilā muhārasha*, Without dispute.

A بلاء *balāʼ*, (v. n. of بلا for بلو) Tempting, trying, making an experiment. Doing good, conferring a favour. بلاه الله بلاءً حسناً *balahu llāh balāʼan hasanan*, God tried him with a beneficent temptation (or simply, Bestowed a benefit upon him). (v. n. of بلي) Becoming old, worn, and threadbare (a garment). (v. n. 3 of بلي) Caring for, heeding, minding, regarding. Evil, misfortune, sorrow, trial, trouble. P بلائی سياه *balāʼi siyāh*, Confusion, opposition, trouble.

A بلّاء *ballāʼ*, (fem. of ابلّ *aball*) Perjured. An adultress. Smooth.

A بلابل *bulābil*, (pl. *balābil*) Light, active, nimble in whatever one sets about.

P بلابه *bilāba*, An adultress, a courtezan. An obscene or idle-talker. Cajolery. Bad, naught, worthless. ابن بلابه *ibn bilāba*, A son of a whore.

P بلابه كار *bilāba-kār*, Unchaste, adulterous. A whoremonger. A whore.

A بلاتة *balātat*, The being wise, intelligent.

A بلاثيق *balāsīk*, (pl. of بلثوق *bulsūk*) Stagnating waters, extending a great way over the surface of the ground.

P بلاج *balāj*, Reeds from which mats are made. A mat.

A بلاخ *bilākh*, Large-hipped (woman). *Bulākh*, The holm-oak.

A بلا خلاف *bilā khilāf*, Without contradiction.

A بلاخيّة *bulākhīyat*, A noble lady, a matron.

A بلاد *bilād*, (v. n. 3 of بلد) Fighting with swords. Cudgel-playing. (pl. of بلدة *baldat*) Cities, countries, regions, habitations. تخطيط بلاد *takhtīti bilād*, Geography, chorography. خطّاط البلاد *khattātu'l bilād*, A drawer of countries, a geographer.

P بلاد خوشنما *bilādi khwush-namā*, Splendid cities.

A بلادة *balādat*, (v. n. of بلد) Being stupid: stupidity, stolidity.

P بلادر *balādar*, The ornaments of a woman, particularly ornaments of gold worn on the head.

A بلادر *balādar*, A kind of Indian fruit, in shape and colour resembling the heart; the anacardium or Malacca bean.

P بلادري *balādarī*, An anacardium electuary.

P بلادور *balādūr*, Anacardia. See بلادر *balādar*.

P بلاده *balā-dih* (or *bilā-dih*) Giving trouble. Seditious: an evil-doer.

P بلار *balār*, Root of a thorny shrub called آذربويه.

P بلار *ballār*, Crystal.

A بلارج *balāraj*, A stork.

P بلارك *balārak*, Indian steel: an Indian sword.

P بلاري *ballārī*, Crystalline.

A بلأز *bulʼaz*, Short. Satan. Hard, robust (youth).

A بلأزة *balʼazat*, (v. n. of بلأز Q) Fleeing, running away. Eating to repletion.

P بلا زده *balā-zada*, Stricken with adversity.

P بلاژ *bilāj*, Without cause or reason.

A بلاس *balās*, (pl. بلس *bulus*) A hair-cloth, sackcloth. A mattrass.

A بلّاس *ballās*, A seller of hair-cloths.

P بلاساغون *balāsāghūn*, A city in Turkistān.

P بلاسيدن *balāsīdan*, To have a wrinkled, rugged, or unequal surface (especially any thing of a globular form, as a melon). To wither, dry, and shrivel (as fruit) before it be ripe.

P بلاش *balāsh*, Scientific, skilful. Name of a king; also of a city. *Bilāsh*, Without cause or reason, without a why or wherefore.

P بلاشجرد *balāshjird*, Name of a city four leagues from Marw.

A بلا شك *bilā shakk*, Assuredly.

A بلأصة *balʼasat*, The act of running away.

A بلاصيّ *balāsīy*, (pl. of بلنصاة *balansāt*) Birds of a particular species whose eggs are green.

A بلاط *balāt*, Level ground, a smooth pavement of stones, bricks, tiles, or earth. A flag-stone or brick used in pavements. The surface of ground. The termination of hard rocky ground. Name of a place near Madīna. *Bilāt*, (v. n. 3 of بلط) Fighting with a sword. Coming down upon an enemy in battle. Exerting one's self in swimming. Disparaging, disgracing.

A بلاطح *bulātih*, Broad.

A بلاطنس *balātunus*, A small town in Syria.

A بلّاعة *ballāʻat*, A sewer or drain in the middle of the house.

A بلاعق *balāʻik*, Spacious, open (places).

A بلاغ *balāgh*, Arrival. Whatever is brought. Conveyance. A sufficiency, enough. ما علينا الّا البلاغ *mā ʻalaynā illa'l balāgh*, We have only to deliver our message. *Bilāgh*, (v. n. 3 of بلغ) Striving, using diligence. Doing to excess.

A بلاغات *balāghāt*, (pl. of بلاغة) Whisperings.

A بلاغة *balāghat*, (v. n. of بلغ) Being eloquent. Eloquence, flow of words. مضمون بلاغت مشحون *mazmūni balāghat-mashhūn*, The eloquent contents.

A بلاغن *balāghin*, (pl. of بلغن *bilaghn*) Eloquent.

P بلاغور *balāghūr*, A stranger, a refugee.

A بلاغيٰ *ba* or *bulāgha'*, Clear, distinct, eloquent.

P بلاق *balāk*, The feet of long trousers or drawers.

A بلاقع *balākiʻ*, (pl. of بلقع *balkaʻ*) Uncultivated, uninhabited grounds. (Women) destitute of every good quality.

P بلاكش *balā-kash*, Unhappy, miserable, afflicted.

P بلال *balāl*, Root of the plant آذربويه.

A بلال *balāl*, Moisture, humidity, freshness (of youth or young plants). Water. A visit to, or intercourse with, kindred. Any thing good. Beneficence, benefit. *Bilāl*, (v. n. of بلّ) Uniting, enjoying the society of friends. Milk, water, or any thing moistening the mouth. Moisture. Name of the crier who announced to the people when Muhammad said prayers. (pl. of بلّة *bullat*) Moistures. Remains of love. Benefits. *Bulāl*, Water.

A بلال *ballāl,* Flax or pot-herb seed. A noisy peacock.

A بلالة *balālat,* (v. n. of بلّ) Sticking close to. Being tempted, tried, proved. *Ba* or *bulālat,* Remains of love. *Bulālat,* Evil, wickedness. Moisture.

P بلالك *balālak,* Excellent steel. An Indian sword.

A بلالير *balālīr,* (pl. of بلّور *ballūr* or *billawr*) Crystals. Beryls.

A بلاليط *balālīt,* Level grounds, pavements.

A بلاليع *balāliʻ,* (pl. of بالوعة) Drains, sewers.

A بلاليق *balālīk,* (pl. of بلوق *ballūk*) Deserts. Soft and level grounds. (Tracts of land) producing nothing but the tree رخامي *rukhāma'.*

A بلام *bulām,* A green salsuginous plant.

A بلامدار *balā-madār,* Afflicted, wretched.

A بلّان *ballān,* A bath. An attendant at a bath.

A بلّانة *ballānat,* A bathing-woman.

A بلاهة *balāhat,* (v. n. of بله) Doating, being simple, weak in judgment, foolish, ignorant. (in a better sense) Being extremely bashful. Being careless and regardless of one's actions, yet always meaning well. Carelessness, thoughtlessness.

A بلاهي *balāhī,* (or بلاهن *balāhin*) (pl. of بلهنية *bulahniyat*) Luxurious modes of living.

A بلايا *balāya',* (pl. of بليّة *baliyat*) Misfortunes.

P بلايه *ba* or *bilāya,* A whore. An impudent man or woman. Corrupted, degenerate, bad, sorry.

P بلايه قز *balāya-kaz,* A kind of coarse silk of little value.

P بلايه كار *bālaya-kār,* Whorish (woman).

A بلبال *balbāl,* (v. n. of بلبل Q) Exciting, stirring up. (pl. بلابل *balābil*) Anxiety, anguish, grief, vexation, affliction. Excitement. A discontented turn of mind. A wolf. *Bilbāl,* (v. n. of بلبل Q) Being subject to evil suggestions or temptations. Exciting, stirring up.

A بلبالة *balbālat,* Anguish, grief.

P بلبكه *balbaka,* Fresh butter.

A P بلبل *bulbul,* (pl. بلابل *balābil*) The bulbul, a bird with a melodious voice, a great favourite with the Eastern poets; the European bird which most nearly resembles it is the nightingale. A little king, viceroy. P بلبل بستان ما زاغ *bulbuli bustāni mā zāgh,* The nightingale of the garden of us crows, *i.e.* poor miserable creatures (an epithet of Muhammad). بلبل گنج *bulbuli ganj,* An owl.

A بلبل *bulbul,* Nimble, active in travelling. A fish of the size of the hand. A spout, a syphon. One who helps much.

P بلبلاني *balbalānī,* A kind of sweetmeat.

A بلبلة *balbalat,* (v. n. of بلبل Q) Exciting, stirring up. Grief, anguish of spirit. Mixture, confusion of languages. Evil suggestions. A black pearl or any thing similar in a shell. Division, schism in opinions. A scattering of furniture. *Bulbulat,* A jug with a spout at the side of the head. A travelling litter for ladies.

P بلبل چشم *bulbul-chashm,* A sort of silk.

P A بلبله *balbala,* The guggling of water when poured from a bottle. Anguish of spirit. A drinking-vessel with a spout. Butter. Liquor. Leather. A root. A camel-litter.

P بلبلي *bulbulī,* A firkin. Wine. Leather, thin and delicate. A kind of apricot.

A بلبليّ *bulbuliy,* Light, expeditious in travelling. An able assistant.

P بلبن *balban,* Purslain.

P بلبوس *balbūs,* A wild onion. Garlick. A kind of poppy.

A بلبول *bulbūl,* Name of a place in Bahrayn.

A بلبيس *balbays* or *bulbays,* A town in Egypt.

A بلّة *bulat,* A bundle of grass, wood, and the like.

A بلّة *ballat,* One single drop. Moisture. Remains of love. *Billat,* (v. n. of بلّ) Sprinkling, moistening. Riches, fortune. Moisture. Fluency of tongue, clearness of enunciation, distinctness. Eloquence. *Bullat,* Juice of young plants. (pl. بلال *bilāl*) Remains of love. Vice, wickedness.

A بلت *balata,* (fut. يبلت *yablitu*) He cut.

A بلت *balt,* (v. n. of بلت) Cutting, splitting, slitting, dividing, separating. *Balat,* (v. n. of بلت) Being cut, divided. *Bulat,* The name of a bird, whose feathers, it is said, consume those of every other bird with which they are mixed.

A بلتاة *baltāt,* A cutting, dividing, splitting.

A بلتع *baltaʻ,* Cunning, crafty, sly, sagacious.

A بلتعانيّ *baltaʻāniy,* A person pluming himself on qualifications to which he has no pretensions.

A بلتعة *baltaʻat,* Clamorous, talkative (woman).

A بلتعيّ *baltaʻiy,* Eloquent. Bold.

A بلتم *baltam,* Men, people. A stammerer.

P بلتيس *biltīs,* Name of a medicine.

A بلثوق *bulsūk,* (pl. بلاثيق *balāsīk*) A wide extent of stagnant water.

A بلج *balj,* (v. n. of بلج) Shining forth, appearing (dawn). Opening. Of an open countenance. Name of an idol. حمّام بلج *hammām balj,* A certain bath in Egypt. *Balaj,* (v. n. of بلج) Rejoicing. Separation of the eye-brows; space between them. *Buluj,* Partings of the hair.

A بلجة *baljat* or *buljat,* Light. The latter part of the night, just before the dawn. بلجة الصبح *baljatu's subh,* The morning twilight, the first appearance of dawn. *Buljat,* Space between the eye-brows.

P بلجم *baljam,* (equiv. to بلغم *balgham*) Phlegm.

A بلجمة *baljamat,* (v. n. of بلجم Q) Swathing the distempered legs of a horse.

A بلح *balh,* (v. n. of بلح) Drying up (the ground). Passing, being lost (shame). *Balah,* Unripe dates (being in the middle state between بسر *busr* and خلال *khalāl,* which signify also unripe dates in different stages). *Bulah,* (pl. بلحان *bulhān*) (An eagle or vulture) infirm through age. A large kind of bird, whose feathers, it is said, consume those of every other bird with which they are mixed.

A بلحارث *balhāris,* The tribe of بني الحارث *banī'l hāris.*

A بلحتة *bilihtat,* A kind of plant which spreads upon the ground, from whose leaf a gargle is made for bringing up a leech sticking in the throat.

A بلحلح *balahlah,* A dish without a bottom.

A بلخ *balkh* or *bilkh,* Proud, haughty, exalting one's self, elated. *Balkh,* A kind of oak. Length, tallness. One of the capitals of Khurāsān (Transoxania), about ten parasangs or leagues from the Oxus or Jīhūn. It is called likewise شهر ابراهيم *shahri ibrāhīm,* The city of Abraham, and was as highly venerated by the ancient Persians as Mecca is now by the Muhammadans. A goblet of wine. *Balakh,* (v. n. of بلخ) Being proud, haughty.

A بلخاء *balkhā',* (fem. of ابلخ *ablakh*) Foolish.

A بلخحتة *bilikhtat,* A species of dwarf-tree, which extends its branches a great way over the surface of the ground; a gargarism of which is used to make leeches upon the gums drops off.

P بلخچ *bal* or *balakhach,* Vitriol, black tincture.

A بلخص *balkhas,* Thick, coarse, rude, gross.

P بلخم *balkham,* A sling.

A بلخيّة *balakhiyat,* A tree, resembling the pomegranate, with beautiful flowers.

P بلد *balad,* A guide, escort, convoy.

A بلد *balad,* (pl. ابلاد *ablād* and بلدان *buldān*) A city, town, district, province, country. Habitation, abode. Mecca. Earth, ground (especially where it has not been dug, nor any fire lighted). A mark, sign, trace. An ostrich's nest, or the place where her eggs are hatched (whence the proverb اذلّ من بيضة البلد *azall mim bayzati'l balad,* More contemptible than the egg left by the ostrich). A sepulchre, tomb, grave. A part of the heavens which has few stars (being, in astrology, the twenty-first mansion of the moon, distinguished by six stars in Sagittarius). The isthmus of the jaws, the throat and parts adjacent. The space between the eye-brows and the root of the nose. The breast. The palm of the hand. Land yet undug, whereon no fire has been lighted. The element or principle of any thing. A plummet, lead, particularly such as is used at sea. Name of a town in Diyār-bakar (Mesopotamia) and of another in Persia. بلد الامين *baladu'l amīn,* The secure city, *i.e.* Mecca. *Buld,* A globe of gold, silver, or lead for measuring out water.

A بلدام *bildām,* (or بلدامة *bildāmat*) Loosely and shamblingly built.

A بلدان *buldān,* (pl. of بلد *balad*) Cities.

A بلدة *baldat,* (pl. بلاد *bilād*) A city; or the quarter where any one resides. One's country. The twenty-first mansion of the moon. A part of the heavens having few stars. Mecca. The breast, the chest. The space between the eye-brows and the root of the nose. بلدة طيّبة *baldat tayyibat*, A glorious city, Constantinople. بلدة فاخرة *baldat fākhirat*, A superb city. *Buldat*, The space between the eye-brows. بلدة الوجه *buldatu'l wajh*, The form of the face.

A بلدح *baldah*, Name of a valley near Mecca, and of a mountain near Juddah. Fat (woman).

A بلدحة *baldahat*, (v. n. of بلدح Q) Throwing one's self on the ground. Promising, not performing.

A بلدم *baldam*, The most prominent part of the breast and throat, and that part of the windpipe which is connected with the breast. The projecting part of the throat of a horse. The top of the windpipe. Dull, heavy looking. Loosely and shamblingly built. A blunt sword.

A بلدمة *baldamat*, A being silent from fear.

P بلده *balda*, Eve, the first woman.

A بلديّ *baladiy*, Of a city. A fellow-townsman.

A بلز *biliz*, Plump, fat, light (woman). Short.

A بلزّ *bilizz*, Thick, stout (woman).

A بلس *balas*, Wicked, profligate (man). A kind of white fig, or a fruit resembling it in Arabia Felix. *Balis*, Despairing. Silent, one who keeps his thoughts to himself. *Bulus*, (pl. of بلاس *balās*) Hair-cloths, sackcloths. *Bulus, balis*, or *buls*, Lentils.

A بلسام *bilsām*, The pleurisy.

A بلسان *balasān*, The balsam-tree. Balsam.

P بلست *bilist*, A span.

P بلسك *balask*, A swallow. *Bilish*, An iron spit. A piece of iron, flat at one end, for detaching bread from the sides of the oven.

A بلسك *balsak* or *bilsik*, A plant which adheres fast to the clothes.

A بلسكى *balsaka'*, A kind of plant.

A بلسمة *balsamat*, (v. n. of بلسم Q) Being silent from fear. Making an ugly face.

A بلسن *bulsun*, A lentil, or any pulse similar to it.

P بلشك *bulushk*, An iron or stick with which meat is hung up to roast.

A بلشون *balashūn*, see بو تيمار *bū tīmār*.

A بلصّ *biliss*, A kind of bird like the *surad*.

A بلصام *bilsām*, (or بلصمة *balsamat*) (v. n. of بلصم Q) Running away.

A بلصوّ *balasūw*, (or بلصوّة *balasūwat*) A kind of bird resembling the صرد *surad*.

A بلصوص *balasūs*, or *bullasūs*, Name of a bird.

A ابن بلصى *ibn balasa'*, A kind of bird.

A بلصّى *bilissa'*, A sort of bird, called صرد *surad*.

A بلط *balt*, (v. n. of بلط) Paving with stones. *Balt* or *bult*, A turner's lathe. *Bulut*, Deserters, runaways. Impudent, daring, shameless (fellows).

P بلطاون *baltāwan*, Beet, spinage.

A بلطة *bultat*, A house. A long space of time. An unexpected thing. A hill. Fate, fortune. Insolvent, poor, penniless.

A بلطحة *baltahat*, (v. n. of بلطح Q) Throwing one's self on the ground. Promising, not performing.

A بلطف الله تعالى *bi lutf allāh taʿāla'*, By the favour of God Most High.

A بلع *baliʿa*, (fut. يبلع *yablaʿu*) He swallowed.

A بلع *balaʿ*, (v. n. of بلع) Swallowing. *Bulaʿ*, A hole in the centre of mill-stones or pullies. A glutton. سعد بلع *saʿdi bulaʿ*, The twenty-third lunar mansion (distinguished by two stars, the one bright, the other faint, as if devoured by the other).

A بلعاء *balʿāʾ*, A man's name. Name of a horse.

A بلعام *balʿām*, Balaam the soothsayer.

P بلعبيدن *balaʿbīdan*, To swallow, devour.

A بلعبيس *bulaʿbīs*, Miracles, wonders.

A بلعة *bulʿat*, The hole in the centre of a pulley-wheel. *Bulaʿat*, A glutton.

A بلعث *balʿas*, Fat, relaxed from corpulency.

A بلعثة *balʿasat*, Fat (woman). Bad-tempered.

A بلعس *balʿas*, A camel relaxed from fatness.

A بلعص *bulʿus* or *balʿas*, The inside of the female privity.

A بلعق *balʿak*, The best date grown in Omān.

A بلعك *balʿak*, A she-camel having loose flesh, old, gross, and stooping. A stupid, contemptible man. A kind of date.

A بلعكة *balʿakat*, A cutting with a sword.

A بلعلع *buluʿluʿ*, A long-necked water-bird.

A بلعم *balʿam*, A glutton, one who greedily devours. *Bulʿum*, The gullet.

A بلعمة *balʿamat*, (v. n. of بلعم Q) Devouring greedily, swallowing.

A بلعوس *bilʿaws*, A foolish woman.

A بلعوم *bulʿūm*, A gutter entering into the ground on a hill. The gullet. A white spot on an ass's lip.

A بلغ *balagha*, (fut. يبلغ *yablughu*) He attained.

A بلغ *balgh*, *bilgh*, or *bilagh*, Clear, distinct. Eloquent. جيش بلغ *jayshun balghun*, An overpowering army. امر الله بلغ *amru'llāh balgh*, The command of God is paramount and irresistible. اللّهمّ سمع لا بلغ *allāhumma samʿ lā balgh*, O God, let not that be confirmed which is heard! God forbid! (A common mode of expression when any disagreeable news is related). احمق بلغ *ahmaku balgh*, (*bilgh* or بلغة *balghat*) Completely stupid. One who, with all his stupidity, attains his object. بلغ ملغ *bilghu milghu*, Impure, wicked, base.

A بلغاء *bulaghāʾ*, (pl. of بليغ *baligh*) Eloquent.

A بلغار *bulghār*, Bulgaria. Perfumed leather.

P بلغاك *bulghāk*, Clamour, altercation.

A بلغة *bulghat*, (pl. بلغ *bulagh*) A little. Sufficient to sustain life.

A بلغث *balghas*, Coarse and flabby.

A بلغثة *balghasat*, Softness, or flabbiness, with coarseness and fatness. Coarse and flabby (woman).

P بلغد *bulghud*, A heap, a pile.

P بلغده *balghada*, Fetid, addled. *Bulghuda*, Heaped up. A quilting or padding.

A بلغر *bulghar*, Bulgaria.

P بلغر *bulghur*, Coarsely ground wheat.

P بلغراد *balghirād*, Belgrade.

P بلغشنه *bulghushna*, A running knot, a noose.

T P بلغم *balgham*, Phlegm (one of the four humours of the body).

A بلغميّ *balghamīy*, Phlegmatic.

A بلغن *bilaghn*, (pl. بلاغن *balāghin*) Eloquent.

P بلغند *bulghund*, A heap. Heaped.

P بلغندر *balghandar*, An expression of praise; also of reviling. *Bulghandar*, A man of no religion.

P بلغنده *balghunda*, A knapsack, a wallet, a load for a man's back. Stopped (circulation of blood). *Bulghunda*, Heaped up.

P بلغور *bulghūr*, Bruised barley or wheat. A dish made of the same. Any thing pounded.

P بلغونه *bulghūna*, Paint for the face (especially of yellow colour).

A بلغين *bilaghīn* or *bulaghīn*, Misfortune. Danger. Perfection, end.

P بلفخشن *balfakhtan*, To gain, to acquire.

A بلق *balaka*, (fut. يبلق *yabluku*) He made haste.

A بلق *balk*, (v. n. of بلق) Having the legs white as high as the thighs (a horse). Opening wide (a door). Shutting (a door). Deflowering (a virgin). *Balak*, (v. n. of بلق) Having the legs white as high as the thighs (a horse). Being astonished, confounded. Variety of colour (especially black and white). A tent of goat-hair cloth. Slight madness. A door, a gate. Marble. A kind of transparent stone, found in Arabia Felix. A dense crowd.

A بلقاء *balkāʾ*, (fem. of ابلق *ablak*) Variegated, black and white. Name of a city.

A بلقار *bulkār*, Red Russia leather.

A بلقة *bulkat*, Variety, mixture of colour.

P بلقدر *bulkadar*, A fellow of no religion.

A بلقط *bulkut*, Short, dwarfish.

A بلقع *balkaʿ*, (or بلقعة *balkaʿat*) (pl. بلاقع *balākiʿ*) An uncultivated, uninhabited country. A woman destitute of every good quality.

A بلقعة *balkaʿat*, (v. n. of بلقع Q) Being desert, desolate (a country).

A بلقعيّ *balkaʿīy*, Bright-pointed (spear).

P بلقندر *balkandar*, Reproach. *Bulkandar*, Faithless.

A بلقوط *bulkūt*, Short. A kind of bird.

A بلقيس *bilkīs*, Name of the queen of Sheba.

A بلك *balk*, (v. n. of بلك) Mixing. *Buluk*, The sound made when the finger is put into the mouth, and brought out with a jerk against the cheek.

P بلك *bilk*, A spark. Fire. *Balki*, But, however. *Bilak*, First-fruits. Any thing new or elegant. A pretty little bird. A gift. *Bilik*, Adhesiveness. *Buluk*, A large prominent eye.

P بلكامه *bulkāma*, Eager, desirous, sanguine.

A بلكثة *balkasat*, A large kind of mouse.

P بلكس *bilkis* or *bulkus*, The coping of a wall.

A بلكعة *balkaʿat*, (v. n. of بلكع Q) Cutting.

P بلكفد *bulkafd* or *bilkifd*, A bribe given to a judge.

P بلكفده *bulkafda*, A bribe to a judge.

P بلكك *bilkak*, (or بلكل *bilkal*) Tepid water.

P بلكن *balkan*, A machine for raising or throwing stones; a balista. The coping of a wall.

P بلكه *balki*, But, however, perhaps. Nay, no. Still more. Moreover; besides.

P بلكنجك *bulgunjak* or *bulganjak*, Any thing new, strange, or laughable.

A بلل *balal*, (v. n. of بلّ) Obtaining a victory. Getting or having possession of. Sticking close to. Being tempted, tried, or proved. Recovering from sickness. Knowing. Being wicked, unjust, tyrannical, and oppressive. Committing adultery. Moisture, humidity. A trifling matter. Health, safety. A banquet. Freshness of youth. Riches after poverty. Remains of forage. Patience, long-suffering. The fruit of the قرظ *karaz*. The blossom of the عضاه *ʻizāh*, or the down which succeeds the blossom. The flower of the عرفط *ʻurfut* or سمر *samur*, or the gum of the عرفط *ʻurfut*. *Bilal*, The gum of the plant عرفط *ʻurfut*. *Bulal*, Seed. Seed-sowing.

A بللات *balalāt*, Remains of love.

A بللة *balalat*, Dampness, moisture (of a leathern bottle). *Balalat* or *bululat*, A remainder, a remnant. Remains of love. Evil, mischief. *Bulalat*, Form, habit, state. *Bululat* or *bulalat*, Moisture, humidity.

A بلم *balam*, (v. n. of بلم) Wanting the male (a camel). Small fry. A jack, a pike.

P بلما *balmā*, Thick. A vast pile. Smooth (beard).

A بلماء *balmāʼ*, The fourteenth night of the moon.

P بلماج *bulmāj* or *bulamāj*, Soup, broth.

A بلمة *balamat*, A tumour on the lips. Lust in a she-camel.

P بلمليدن *balmalīdan*, To mutter to one's self, to be vexed, indignant, to bear with impatience.

P بلمون *balmūn*, A thorny plant, called in Arabic عرفج *ʻarfaj*.

P بلمه *balma*, Long-haired (man). A step, a stair. *Balma* or *bulma*, Hair thick and long.

P بلمه ريش *balma-rīsh*, A large beard.

A بلنتع *balantaʻ*, Cunning, clever, shrewd.

A بلنتعة *balantaʻat*, Noisy, talkative (woman).

P بلنج *balanj* or *bilinj*, Measure. Quantity.

P بلنجا *bulanjā*, (for جاي بلند) A high place.

P بلنجاسپ *bilinjāsp*, (or بلنجاسف *bilinjāsf*) Southernwood.

P بلند *baland*, (by some *buland*) High, sublime, elevated, exalted, tall. Dignified. The lintel of a door or window. ببلند آواز خواندن *ba baland āwāz khwāndan*, To read with a loud voice. بلند پروازي كردن *baland-parwāzī kardan*, To aspire, soar. بلند ديدن *baland dīdan*, To look or behave respectfully, to admire, revere, honour. بلند كردن *baland kardan*, To elevate, raise, exalt, aggrandize. جايِ بلند *jāʼi baland*, A high place. سلطان بلند سايه *sultāni baland-sāya*, A most gracious or merciful prince. مرغ بلند پرواز *murghi baland-parwāz*, A bird flying high. *Baland* or *bilind*, The four posts (*i. e.* jambs, lintel, and threshold) of a door.

A بلند *baland*, The root of the shrub حنّا *hinnā*.

P بلند آختر *baland-ākhtar*, High-starred, lucky.

P بلند اراده *baland-irāda*, Ambition: ambitious.

P بلندارکان *baland-arkān*, Raised on lofty pillars.

P بلند اقتدار *baland-iktidār*, High in power.

P بلند آواز *baland-āwāz*, Having a loud voice. In high repute.

P بلند بانگ *baland-bāng*, Sonorous-voiced.

P بلند بين *baland-bīn*, Aspiring. Spiritual.

P بلندپايه *baland-pāya*, Placed in a high situation.

P بلند پرواز *baland-parwāz*, Of lofty flight.

P بلند ترين *balandtarīn*, The highest.

P بلند جاه *baland-jāh*, Exalted in dignity.

A بلندح *balandah*, Short of stature. Fat.

P بلند حوصله *baland-hawsala*, Ambitious.

P بلند دوش *baland-dosh*, High-shouldered.

P بلندر *balandar*, (for بلندتر *balandtar*) Higher.

P بلندرين *balandarīn*, (for بلندترين) Highest.

P بلند كوكب *baland-kawkab*, Of lucky star.

P بلند گراي *baland-girāy*, Aspiring.

A بلندم *balandam*, Loosely and shamblingly built.

P بلند مرتبه *baland-martaba*, High in rank.

P بلند نظر *baland-nazar*, Aspiring.

P بلند و پست *baland u past*, High and low. Heaven and earth.

P بلند همّت *baland-himmat*, High-minded.

A بلنديٰ *balanda'*, Broad, large, wide, expanded.

P بلندي *balandī*, Sublimity, height, exaltation. Summit, eminence.

P بلنديدن *balandīdan*, To exalt. To be exalted.

P بلندين *balandīn*, The jambs, beams, or posts of a doorway. The lintel.

A بلنزيٰ *balanza'*, Thick and strong (camel).

A بلنسم *balansam*, Liquid pitch, tar.

A بلنسية *balansiyat*, Valentia, in Spain.

A بلنصاة *balansāt*, (pl. بلنصيٰ *balansa'*) A kind of herb. (pl. بلاصي *balāsī*) A bird whose eggs are green.

A بلنصيٰ *balansa'*, A kind of bird. (pl. of بلنصاة *balansāt*) Certain pot-herbs.

A بلنط *balnat*, A kind of coarse marble.

A بلنقع *balankaʻ*, Clear, plain, open (road).

P بلنگمشت *balangmusht*, The wild tamarisk.

P بلنگيدن *bulangīdan*, To halt, to limp.

L بلنياس *bilniyās*, Pliny.

A بلو *balw*, (v. n. of بلا for بلو) Examining, trying, making an experiment. Tying a camel to the grave of her deceased master. (pl. ابلاء *ablāʼ*) A manager of property, a steward. *Bilw*, (pl. ابلاء *ablāʼ*) (A she-camel) spent, emaciated with fatigue. A steward or person who ably manages revenue. بلو اسفار *bilwu asfārin*, Worn down by care, travel, or trials. بلو شرّ *bilwu sharrin*, Inured to adversity.

P بلوا *balwā*, Disturbance. Disobedience. A concourse.

P بلواز *bilwāz*, (*balwāz* or بلوازه *balwāza*) The extremity of a beam or joist, projecting beyond the wall.

P بلوايه *balwāya*, A swallow.

A بلوة *bilwat*, Sorrow, trouble: trial, temptation.

P بلوتك *bulūtak*, A drinking-vessel.

P بلوچ *bulūch*, A wart. A cock's comb. A bit of flesh, which they who practise female circumcision cut off. A vane, a weather-cock. A coping-stone on a wall or a roof. *Bulūch* or *buloch*, Name of a wild tribe living on the bank of the Indus.

A بلوح *baluh*, (A well) empty, by the draining of the water. Alienated from relations, having no correspondence or society with them. *Bulūh*, (v. n. of بلح) Being fatigued. Flowing, wasting (water).

P بلود *bulūd*, Oldness, antiquity.

A بلود *bulūd*, (v. n. of بلد) Dwelling, residing. Establishing a solid, permanent settlement; fighting either to gain or maintain it.

P بلوده *bulūda*, Old.

A بلور *bilawr*, Crystal. Beryl.

A بلّور *ballūr* or *billawr*, (pl. بلالير *balālīr*) Crystal. Beryl. *Billawr*, Brave. Thick, large, bulky. Name of a king.

P بلّورين *billawrīn* or *ballūrīn*, Made of crystal.

P بلوز *balūz*, A large table-cloth.

P بلوس *balūs*, A deceiver, a flatterer. Supplication, entreaty. Deceit, flattery. *Bulūs*, A deceiver.

A بلوس *balūs*, Any thing (especially eatable).

L بلوس *bulūs*, Paul (the apostle).

G بلوسطيون *balūstiyūn*, Pomegranate-flowers.

A بلّوط *ballūt*, An acorn. An oak. The ward of a key. بلّوط الارض *ballūtu'l arz*, (The ground oak) The herb germander, chamædrys. شاه بلوط *shāh-ballūt*, (The royal oak) A chesnut-tree. انقطع بلّوطي *inkataʻa ballūtī*, I am destitute of all assistance.

A بلوع *balūʻ*, Wide, open (mouth of a pot).

A بلّوعة *ballūʻat*, (pl. بلاليع *balālīʻ*) A hole in the middle of a house or court, into which all kind of filth is thrown; the mouth of a sewer, a gulley-hole.

A بلوغ *bulūgh*, (v. n. of بلغ) Arriving at a place; obtaining an object. Consummating, terminating any thing. Arriving at the age of puberty, the years of discretion or reason. Adolescence. Consummation. P دندان بلوغ *dandāni bulūgh*, A wisdom-tooth.

A بلوغيّة *bulūghīyat*, Puberty, the age of reason.

A بلوق *bulūk*, (v. n. of بلق) Making haste, going quick, making dispatch. (A torrent) sweeping away (stones). Opening the whole (gate), or opening it violently. Deflowering (a virgin). Shutting.

A بلّوق *ballūk*, (pl. بلاليق *balālīk*) A desert. Ground producing nothing but the رخاميٰ *rakhāma'*.

A بلوقة *balūkat* or *bulūkat*, A desert, solitude. Plain, level, bare ground, producing nothing excepting the tree رخاميٰ *rakhāma'*. Name of a place in Bahrayn in Arabia, supposed by the natives to be inhabited by demons.

P بلوك *bulūk*, A cup of wine. A tract of country which a subject obtains either by gift, purchase, or succession, holding of the sovereign upon feudal tenure. Camel's dung.

P بلوكات *bulūkāt*, Peoples, nations.

A بلول *bulūl*, (v. n. of بلّ) Being cold and moist (a wind). Recovering from sickness. Escaping. Sticking close to. Being tempted, tried, proved. An evil deed. Remains of love.

A بلولة *bulūlat*, A remainder, a remnant. Remains of love. State, condition. Evil, mischief.

P بلون *balūn*, A chaplet, garland. A gorget. A handkerchief. A road, way. *Bulūn*, A servant.

P بلوندك *balwandak*, A wooden sword.

P بلونك *balūnak*, (or بلونه) A wooden sword.

A بلويٰ *balwa'*, Trial. Temptation. Affliction.

A بلويّ *balawiy*, One of the tribe of Kuzāat.

A بله *baliha*, (fut. يبله *yablahu*) He was silly.

A بله *bulh*, (pl. of ابله *ablah*) Weak, ignorant, simple-minded. *Balah*, (v. n. of بله) Being weak, silly, simple, ignorant, unskilful. Being foiled in argument. Being careless of actions or behaviour, yet knowing what is right and meaning well. Carelessness, thoughtlessness. *Balha*, Let alone, meddle not. Yes, indeed, certainly. Besides, except. How? بله ما *balha mā*, Besides that. ما بلهك *mā balhaka*, What is it to thee?

A بلهاء *balhās*, (fem. of ابله *ablah*) Simple, silly, weak (woman). Noble (lady). (A camel) that shrinks from nothing.

H بله بند *bila-band*, Settlement, regulation.

A بلهسة *balhasat*, The act of walking fast.

A بلهصة *balhasat*, (v. n. of بلهص Q) Running from terror. Making haste.

A بلهق *bilhik*, Talkative and ruddy (woman).

A بلهنية *bulahniyat*, (pl. بلاهي *balāhī* or بلاهن *balāhin*) An easy life, free from care.

A بلهور *balahwar*, A spacious, roomy place.

A بلي *bily*, (pl. ابلاء *ablās*) (A she-camel) emaciated and worn out (with fatigue). بلي اسفار *bilyu asfārin*, Worn down by care, travel, or trials. بلي شرّ *bilyu sharrin*, Inured to adversity. بلي مال *bilyu mālin*, A skilful manager of property, an able steward. *Bala'*, (v. n. of بلي) Becoming old, worn, and threadbare (a garment). Yes, indeed, certainly, surely. *Bila'*, (v. n. of بلي) Becoming old, worn, or rotten (a garment).

P بلي *bale*, Yes.

A بلّيٰ *bulla'*, Riches after poverty. هو بذي بلّيٰ *huwa bi zī balla'*, (بليٰ *bila'* or بلّيٰ *baliy*) He went no one knows where. *Bi zī baliyin*, Men dispersed in disorder, without chief, guide, or leader.

A بليّ *baliy*, The Arabian tribe of Kuzāat.

A بليّات *baliyāt*, (pl. of بليّة *baliyat*) Misfortunes, griefs, trials.

P بلياد *balyād*, A plain garment.

P بليار *balyār*, An elegant garment.

P بليان *balyān*, Name of a prophet, and village.

A بلّيان *billayān*, (*ballayān*, *billiyān*, or بليان *balyān*) One who departs nobody knows where. بذي بليان *bi zī balayān* or *biliyān*, One who goes to an unknown place.

A بليّة *baliyat*, (pl. بلايا *balāya'*) Temptation, a sore trial. Sorrow, misfortune. A camel which the Arabs in times of Paganism were wont to fasten beside the grave of her deceased master, and there leave to perish; that in the resurrection he might be enabled to ride to the place of judgment, and not be compelled to go on foot, considered disgraceful.

A بليت *billīt*, A taciturn man. A wise man.

A بليث *balīs*, Fodder two years old, and black.

P بليج *bilij*, Quantity, measure. A span.

A بلّيج *billij*, An oar, a paddle.

A بليحا *bulayhā*, The plant اسليخ *islīkh*.

A بليخ *balīkh*, Name of a river in Mesopotamia.

A بليد *balīd*, Stupid, doltish, one who cannot by any means be stimulated to exertion.

A بليدة *bulaydat*, (dim. of بلدة *baldat*) A hamlet.

A بلّز *bilsiz*, Hard, robust (youth).

A بليغ *balīgh*, (pl. بلغاء *bulaghās*) Eloquent. Effectual, efficacious. Extreme, cogent. Mature, perfect. Numerous, copious. سعي بليغ *sa'yi balīgh*, A great effort. فصيح و بليغ *fasīh u balīgh*, Rhetorical and eloquent.

P بليغانه *balīghāna*, Eloquently.

A بليق *bulayk*, Name of a swift but despised horse (hence a proverb expressive of any one who behaves well and yet is blamed, يجري بليق و يذمّ *yajrī bulayk, wa yuzamm bulayk*, Bulayk runs, yet Bulayk is despised.

P بليل *balīl*, Belleric myrobalan.

A بليل *balīl*, Voice, sound, noise. A humid wind, cold and rainy. *Bulayl*, An open road. A drinking-place at Siffīn. Name of a man.

P بليلا *balīlā*, Name of Muhammad, said to be mentioned in the Gospel.

A بليلة *balīlat*, A humid wind, cold and rainy.

P بليله *balīla*, (or A بليلج) Belleric myrobalan.

P بم *bam*, The bass or lowest string, having the deepest tone. Beating and thumping the head.

A بم *bima*, So that. By what? How! in what manner? By that which.

A بمّ *bamm*, (pl. بموم *bumūm*) The base string of a lute or harp. *Bumm*, (for بوم *būm*) An owl.

P بما *ba mā*, To us.

A بما *bi mā*, So that. How? With that which, notwithstanding.

A بماذا *bi māzā*, In which? To which? Why?

P بمان *bi mān*, (from ماندن) Remain, stay.

P بمانده *ba mānda*, Fixed. Tired, fatigued, spent.

A P بمجرّد *bi* or *ba mujarrad*, Immediately, instantly. P بمجرّد ديدن او *ba mujarradi dīdani u*, At the bare sight of him.

A بمدّ نظر *bi maddi nazr*, As far as eye can see.

A بمشتا *bi mashtā*, In winter-quarters.

P بمعنيٰ آنكه *bamaʿna' ānki*, To the intent that.

A بمقتضا *bi muktazā*, In conformity with, according to the requirement of.

P بمنگ *bamang*, Affliction, distress.

P بمنگيدن *bamangīdan*, To murmur. To be afflicted. To perish. To be buried. To set (as the sun).

P بمواجهه *ba murājaha*, In presence, face to face.

A بموجب *bi mūjib*, According to, conformably to.

A بموم *bumūm*, (pl. of بمّ *bamm*) Bass strings.

A بمه *bi mah*, By what?

P بمهر *ba muhr*, Sealed. كيسهٔ سر بمهر *kīsa-i sar ba muhr*, A sealed bag (or purse).

P بن *ban*, A garden, a sown field. Harvest. A certain fruit (called also ون *wan*). بن كوهي *bani kohī*, A kind of herb used in cooking. *Bun*, Root, basis, foundation. Podex. The bottom. The stern of a ship. Extremity, point, end, tip (of any thing). A kind of sourish drink or gruel prepared for assisting and promoting digestion. A cluster of dates. The trunk of a tree. Issue, result. بن بغل *buni baghal*, The arm-pit (or root of the arm). بركندن بن *bar kandani bun*, Tearing up by the roots, eradicating. از بن بر كندگي *az bun bar kandagī*, Extirpation. بن بيني *buni bīnī*, The tip of the nose. The root or higher part of the nose next to the eyebrows. بن دامان *buni dāmān*, The ground. بن دامان شبستان كردن *buni dāmān shabistān kardan*, To sleep upon the ground. To keep watch. بن دامن *buni dāman*, The extremity or hem of a garment. بن دندان *buni dandān*, The gums. Submission, obedience. Purpose, intention. A treasure, a store. Savings laid by. بن ران *buni rān*, The groin. بن كشتي *buni kishtī*, The poop or stern of a vessel. بن كوه *buni koh*, The base of a mountain. بن گوش *buni gosh*, The soft part of the ear. Respectful, attention, submission. بيخ و بن *bekh u bun*, The root and foundation. خرما بن *khurmā-bun*, A palm-tree. The pith of a palm-tree. A cluster of dates.

A بن *ban*, (equivalent to بل *bal*) But. *Bin*, (for ابن *ibn*, occurring between two proper names) A son. ابن عبد الله *ibn ʿabda' llāh*, A son of a servant of God (a name given by Muhammadans to apostate Christians who embrace Muhammadism).

A بنّ *binn*, Fat. A stinking place. بنّ عليٰ بنّ *binn ʿala' binn*, Fat upon fat (one good thing upon another). *Bunn*, A coffee-bean. A sour and bitter gruel for creating an appetite or assisting digestion.

A بنا *binā*, With, by, for, to us.

A بناء *binās*, (v. n. of بني) Building, erecting an edifice. Conferring favours. Giving orders for a bride to be conducted home. Going into unto (a wife). Fattening the body (food). Sticking close to the string (a bow). (in gram.) Being indeclinable (built). (pl. ابنية *abniyat*) An edifice, fabric, structure, building. Form, construction. Conjugation. P بنا كردن *binā kardan*, To build, erect, rear.

A بنّاء *bannās*, A builder. P بنّا و كاركر *bannā u kārgar*, Builder and workman. بنّا و معمار *bannā u miamār*, Architect and builder.

P بنابر *banābar*, Because. بنابر آن *banābar ān*, Because of that, therefore. بنابرين *banābar in*, Because of this, wherefore.

P بنابه *banāba*, A time, a turn.

A بناة اللحم *banātu'l lahm*, Firm-fleshed (girl).

A بنات *banāt*, (pl. of بنت *bint*) Daughters. Children's dolls. بنات آوي *banātu āwa'*, (pl. of ابن آوي *ibn āwa'*) Jackals. بنات البحر *banātu'l bahr*, (Daughters of the sea) Mermaids. بنات الارض *banātu'l arz*, (Daughters of the earth) Rivulets. بنات الاربعة *banātu'l arbaєat*, Quadriliteral words. بنات الخمسة *banātu'l khamsat*, Quinqueliteral words. بنات الدهر *banātu'd dahr*, Events, circumstances. بنات الرعد *banātu'r raєd*, (Daughters of thunder) Mushrooms. بنات الفلا *banātu'l fala'*, Camels straying in the desert. بنات گردون *banāti gardūn*, The stars. Three stars in the Great Bear. بنات اللهو *banātu'l lahw*, Lute-strings. بنات الليل *banātu'l layl*, Events of the night: pollution. بنات الماء *banātu'l mās*, Name of a water-fowl. بنات المنايا *banātu'l manāya'*, An arrow. بنات نبات *banāti nabāt*, (The daughters of grass) The tender herbage. بنات النعش *banātu'n naєsh*, The constellation of the Bear (as having the stars scattered, in opposition to the Pleiades where they cluster). بنات وردان *banātu wardān*, Name of a certain animal. جارية بنات اللحم *jāriyat banātu'l lahm*, A girl fat and plump.

A بنادر *banādir*, (pl. of بندر *bandar*) Sea-ports.

A بنادرة *banādirat*, (pl. of بندار *bundār*) Dealers in precious stones, who keep close to the mines. Forestallers, regraters.

A بنادق *banādik*, (pl. of بندق *bunduk*) Balls for cannon, musquetry, or cross-bows.

A بنادك *banādik*, Square bits of cloth, gores.

A بناديق *banādīk*, (pl. of بندوق *bundūk*) Muskets.

S بنارس *banāris*, Benares.

P بنارنج *banārinj*, A shepherd, a pastor.

P بناست *bināst*, Turpentine.

A بناصر *banāsir*, (pl. of بنصر) The ring-fingers.

A بناغ *banāgh*, Thread twisted round a spindle. A secretary, a notary. See also بنانج *banānj*.

A بناقيس *banākīs*, (pl. of بنقوس *bunkūs*) The blossoms of melons. بناقيس الطرثوث *banākīsu't tursūs*, A small substance growing up along with the plant طرثوث *tursūs*.

P بناگر *bināgar*, (or بناكر *binākar*) A builder.

P بناگوش *binā-gosh*, The cavity behind the ear, or the lower part of the ear. بناگوش كردن *binā-gosh kardan*, To raise the uvula of a new-born babe. To submit, to obey.

A بنام *banām*, (for بنان *banān*) The fingers. The tip of the finger.

P بنام *bi nām*, Of the same name. Synonymous.

P بناميزد *ba nāmi ezid*, In the name of God! O heaven! How beautiful! Charming! Excellent!

A بنان *banān*, The finger. The tips of the fingers. *Binān*, (pl. of بنة *bannat*) Odours, smells.

A بنانة *banānat*, The tip of the finger. *Bunānat*, A delightsome garden, a pleasant mead.

P بنانج *banānj*, (or بنانجه *banānja*) A second wife among the Muhammadans, in respect of another whom the husband had before married. A man who has two wives, a bigamist.

P بناور *bun* or *ban-āwar*, A sore called a felon.

P بناوند *bināwand*, Restraining, confining.

A بناية *bināyat*, (v. n. of بني) Building, rearing. Height, eminence.

A بنائق *banāsik*, (pl. of بنيقة *banīkat*) Gores of shifts, or any triangular pieces of stuff, inserted into garments, in order to enlarge their circumference.

P ببنبا *bam-bā*, A dish composed of the fruit بن *ban*.

P بنبر *bambar*, An Indian medicine, Sebestens.

A بنبك *bumbuk* or *bambak*, A fish which bites men through the middle (perhaps a shark).

P بنبل *bambal*, A sour apple, a crab. Acidity.

A بنّة *bannat*, The odour of the dung of deer when they feed on flowers. (pl. بنان *binān*) Odour, flavour (whether good or bad).

A بنت *bint*, (pl. بنات *banāt*) A daughter, a girl. This word like ابو *abū*, Father, and امّ *umm*, Mother, is frequently employed with other substantives in forming the rhetorical figure metonymy: as, بنت الارض *bintu'l arz*, (Daughter of the earth) Mud, clay. A kind of vegetable. A rivulet. بنت البحر *bintu'l bahr*, (or بنت الماء *bintu'l mās*) The syren or mermaid (daughter of the sea or of the water). بنت الجبل *bintu'l jabal*, (Daughter of the mountain) Echo. بنت الشفة *bintu'sh shafat*, (Daughter of the lip) Speech. بنت العنب *bintu'l єinab* or بنت العنقود *bintu'l єunkūd*, (Daughter of the grape) Wine. بنت العين *bintu'l єayn*, (Daughter of the eye) Tears. بنت الفكر *bintu'l fikr*, (Daughter of reflection) Prudence. Advice. Poetry. بنت الكرم *bintu'l karm*, (Daughter of the vine) Wine. بنت المنيّة *bintu'l maniyat*, بنت اجل *binti ajal*, (Daughter of death) Fever. بنت نارين *binti nārin*, (Daughter of brightness) Flame, fire. Boiling water.

P بنتومه *bantūma*, Missletoe, missledine.

A بنتيّ *bintiy*, Daughter-like, daughterly.

A بنج *banj*, (v.n. of بنج) Returning to its root or origin. Henbane, a soporific herb. *Binj*, Root, origin, stock, family.

P بنجشك *binjishk*, A sparrow.

P بنجشك زوان *binjishk-zuwān*, Sparrow's tongue, a herb.

P بنجك *bunjak*, Carded cotton.

A بنجنجست *banjanjust*, (P پنج انگشت *panj angusht*) Cinquefoil.

P بنجيدن *banjīdan*, To be friendly, to assist. To cut into pieces, divide, bruise. To do, make. To rise.

P بنچه *bunicha*, A corporate body of artificers.

A بنح *banh*, (v.n. of بنح) Cutting in bits (meat). *Bunuh*, Gifts.

P بن خوشه *buni khosha*, Stalk of grapes or corn.

P بند *band*, A band, tie, fastening, ligament, ligature, bandage, chain, shackle, fetter, manacle. A knot, joint, belt, girdle, or any thing by which bodies are joined, bound, or fastened together. A joint of the finger, knee, or any other part. A mound, dam, dike, or any inclosure of water. A lock. An iron plate, band, or hoop. A tent-rope. A yoke (of oxen). The handle of a knife, the hilt of a sword. A quantity of paper (equal to ten دسته *dasta*), half a ream. A roll (of parchment). A bundle. A kind of verse, wherein the same line recurs at stated intervals as a burden. Durance, captivity. Affliction, sorrow. A pledge, a deposit. Oath, treaty, agreement. Hope, expectation, desire. Idea. Imposture, deceit, hypocrisy, trick. A twist, trick, sleight, or manœuvre in wrestling. A share of spoil. A kite. Name of a country. (imp. of بستن *bastan*) Bind thou. بند و بست *band u bast*, A settlement or agreement for the payment of revenue, &c. Military discipline. بند انگشت *bandi angusht*, The knuckle. بند آهنين *bandi āhanīn*, An iron chain. بند جان كشيدن *bandi jān kashīdan*, To be violently in love. بند دست *bandi dast*, The wrist. بند شدن *band shudan*, To be bound, restrained, prohibited, prevented. در بند شدن *dar band shudan*, To be labouring. بند شمشير *bandi shimshīr*, A sword-belt. بند شهريار *bandi shahr-yār*, Name of a note in music. بند فرمودن *band farmūdan*, To put in prison. بند كردن *band kardan*, To bind, to tie. To imprison, confine, detain. To compose. پاي بند *pāy-band*, Fetters. When added to some nouns it implies a maker, causer, contriver, artificer, &c. حيله بند *hīla-band*, A contriver of fraud, a deceiver, a cheat. ديباجه بند *dībāja-band*, One who makes an exordium or preface, a beginner. عدوّ بند *єadūw-band*, A binder of enemies, a conqueror. ميان بند *miyān-band*, A girder of the loins, a belt. نعل بند *naєl-band*, A blacksmith, a farrier. نقل بند *nakl-band*, A composer of narrations, a writer of history.

A بند *band*, (pl. بنود *bunūd*) A large standard, a banner. A legion or body of 10,000 men. A stratagem. A pawn at chess. A water which intoxicates.

P بنداب *band-āb*, A dyke, embankment.

P بنداد *bundād*, A foundation. A prop. Origin, root.

P بندار *bun-dār*, Firm, solid, fundamental, certain, established. Knowing, intelligent. Rich, possessing warehouses, granaries, or other repositories. A forestaller, regrater, engrosser; whoever lays up any thing in magazines, in order to enhance the price; also a dealer in slaves or horses, who sets them off to advantage, in order to sell them dearer.

Name of an ancient poet.

A بندار *bundār,* (pl. بنادرة *banādirat*) A dealer in precious stones, who keeps close to the mine. A forestaller, a regrater.

P بنداري *bandārī,* A particle of similitude.

G بندافلون *bandāfilūn,* Cinquefoil.

P بنداق *bandāk,* A kind of high mitre-like cap worn by the dervishes or kalandars.

P بندامير *band-amīr,* Name of an embankment near Shīrāz, so called from امير *amīr* the maker.

P بند بازي *band-bāzī,* Rope-dancing.

P بند باگوري *band bāgorī,* A species of herb.

P بندخانه *band-khāna,* Prison, house of captivity.

P بندخت *bundukht,* The face, the countenance.

P بندد *bun-dad,* (for بنداد) Root: foundation.

P بندر *bandar,* A city. An emporium: a port, harbour, trading town, to which numbers of foreign merchants resort. *Bundur,* Name of a city.

A بندر *bandar,* A port, harbour, anchorage.

P بندرز *bandarz* or *bundarz,* A packing-needle.

P بندرگاه *bandar-gāh,* A port. Emporium: pass.

P بندروغ *bandrūgh,* A dam or barrier, either to form a reservoir of water, or to divert its course.

P بندش *bandash,* Carded cotton. *Bandish,* Termination, resolve. Fastening. Engraving, enchasing (of gold or silver). Invention, contrivance. The preparing a false story, trumping up a false account. Elegance of style. Name of a country.

A P بندق *bunduk,* (pl. بنادق *banādik*) A filbert nut. A cannon or musket-ball; also any ball of clay which is shot from cross-bows, balistas, &c. بندق هندي *bunduki hindī,* An Indian nut. بندق شکستن *bunduk shikastan,* To smack the lips.

A بندقة *bandakat,* (v. n. of بندق Q) Making into round balls. Looking keenly. *Bundukat,* Name of the father of a tribe.

P بندقه *bunduka,* A little ball. A round stone.

A بندقي *bundukiy,* A costly kind of linen garment.

P بندك *bandak,* Cotton cleansed of the seed, and ready for spinning.

P بند کشاد *band-kushād,* A joint, a ligament.

P بند کشه *band-kasha,* A bolt, bar. Servitude.

P بندگان *bandagān,* (pl. of بنده *banda*) Bondmen, servants, slaves. بندگان بي ريا *bandagāni bī riyā,* Sincere servants. بندگان حضرت *bandagāni hazrat,* Servants of God.

P بندگاه *band-gāh,* A joint. Place (of a joint).

P بندگي *bandagī,* Servitude, ministry, devotion. Bondage. Compliment. بندگيم *bandagiyam,* My devotion. بندگيش *bandagiyash,* His service.

P بندگير *band-gīr,* A fine cement made of chalk, with oil and cotton, or ox-hair, employed in the construction of baths. A large beam, the main support of a house. Name of a tree.

P بندمه *bandima,* A button.

P بندن *bandan,* To bind, fasten. To propose, design, desire.

P بندنايژه *band-nāyija,* Litter from stalks.

P بندنه *bandina,* (or بندمه) A coat-button.

P بندني *bandanī,* Any thing used for tying or binding. A bundle, a truss.

P بندو *bandū,* The tike. The canker-worm.

P بندوا *bandawā,* Acid. A certain bitter plant.

P بندوانه *bandawāna,* A kind of water-melon.

P بند و بست *band u bast,* Settlement for rent or taxes. Arrangement. Securing, management.

P بند و بستي *band u bastī,* Belonging to a settlement. A fine.

P بندور *bandūr,* The imaginative faculty. *Bundūr,* Packthread.

P بندوروغ *bandūrugh* or *bandiwargh,* A dam, weir.

A بندوق *bundūk,* (pl. بناديق *banādīk*) A musket.

P بنده *banda,* Bound, fastened, fixed, chained. Included, contained, shut up. A servant, slave, bondman, domestic. Quicksilver. (in compos.) A keeper. بندهٔ بي مقدار *bandaʼi bī mikdār,* A servant without power, a most humble servant. بندهٔ درگاه *bandaʼi dargāh,* The slave of (your) threshold. بندهٔ شکم *bandaʼi shikam,* The slave of his belly. بندهٔ صادق الاخصاص *bandaʼi sādiku'l ikhsās* (for بندهٔ مخلص *bandaʼi mukhlis*) A most devoted and affectionate servant. بندهٔ فرمان *bandaʼi farmān,* Obeying commands, subject to the orders, obedient, obsequious. بنده و بسته کردن *banda u basta kardan,* To bind and oblige.

P بنده پرور *banda-parwar,* Cherisher of slaves (a respectful expression used in addressing a superior).

P بنده خانه *banda-khāna,* House of (your) servant, *i. e.* my house (when speaking to a superior).

P بنده زاده *banda-zāda,* Son of your slave, *i. e.* my son.

P بنده گرفتگي *banda-giriftagī,* Captivity, slavery.

P بنده گرفته *banda-girifta,* Taken prisoner.

P بنده نواز *banda-nawāz,* Kind to servants.

P بندي *bandī,* Bound, chained, imprisoned; a prisoner. A Muhammadan captive.

P بنديان *bandiyān,* Prisoners, captives.

P بنديخانه *bandī-khāna,* House of bondage, prison.

P بنديدن *bandīdan,* To bind, to shut up, confine.

P بنديشه *bandīsha,* Imagination, fancy.

P بندينه *bandīna,* (or بنديمه) A coat-button.

P بنران *bun-rān,* (Root of the thigh) The groin.

A بنس *banas,* (v. n. of بنس) Shunning (evil).

P بنساله *bunsāla,* Old, worn-out.

A بنش *bansh,* (v. n. of بنش) Being remiss.

P بنشاختن *binshākhtan,* To place, to erect.

P بنشاندن *binshāndan,* To make sit, set, erect.

P بنشين *bi nishīn,* (imp. of نشستن) Sit down.

A بنصر *binsir,* (pl. بناصر *banāsir*) The ring-finger.

A G (بحر *bahri*) بنطش *buntush,* Sea of Pontus.

A بنظر *bunzur,* The clitoris.

A بنظيان *binziyān,* A shrew, scold, brawler.

A بنفحة *binfahat,* A yellow curdling substance taken from the stomach of a sucking kid.

P بنفسج *banafsaj,* A violet. Violet-colour.

A بنفسه *bi nafsihi,* In person, himself. Identically.

P بنفش *bunafsh,* Blue, violet-colour.

P بنفشه *bunafsha* or *binafsha,* Violet. Violet-colour. A certain aquatic plant.

P بنفشه گون طارم *binafsha-gūni tāram,* The purple sky. بنفشه گون مهد *binafsha-gūn-mahd,* Heaven and earth.

A بنق *banaka,* (fut. يبنق *yabnuku*) He arrived.

A بنق *bank,* (v. n. of بنق) Arriving. Planting a single palm-shoot.

A بنقة *binakat,* The upper opening of the shirt at the breast. A gore in a woman's shift. A gusset.

A بنقوس *bunkūs,* (pl. بناقيس) Melon-blossom.

P بنقه *bunka,* A grain resembling a lentil.

P بنك *bunk,* The bark of the Egyptian thorn. *Banak,* (dim. of بن *ban*) A sort of fruit. A kind of satin. A pimple. Drops of sweat on the face. *Bunak,* A shrub. A sign, mark, vestige.

A بنك *bunk,* The root, origin, best, or soundest part of any thing. An hour of the night. Nascaptha, an odoriferous root.

P بنكران *bunkarān,* Any thing burnt in a pot, and adhering to the bottom.

P بنكشيدن *bunkushīdan,* To swallow without masticating, to bolt (one's food).

P بنكلك *bunkulak,* A rose-bush. A sort of fruit.

P بنكن *ban-kan,* An instrument for levelling the ground, a rake. *Bun-kan,* A hoe, weeding-hook.

P بنكو *bankū,* Cotton-seed.

P بنكول *bankūl,* Bencoolen.

P بنگ *bang,* An inebriating, maddening draught, made of hemp-leaves, hemlock, henbane, opium, or masloc. An allurement, bait, enticement. بنگ ساختن *bang sākhtan,* To allure, to entice.

P بنگاله *bangāla,* Bengal.

P بنگالي *bangālī,* A native of Bengal.

P بنگان *bingān,* A goblet. A cup. A bason. A copper bowl or bason with a hole bored in the bottom, which being placed in water is suffered to fill, and thus serves to measure the time that each cultivator is allowed to have water turned upon his land from a canal for the purposes of irrigation.

P بنگاه *bun-gāh,* A place or dwelling. The rear of an army. A magazine, storehouse. An iron chest. بار و بنگاه *bār u bangāh,* Moveables, tents, household furniture, and utensils.

P بنگر *bangar,* An agreement for clearing lands.

P بنگ رنگ *banag-rang,* Asthma: asthmatic.

P بنگره *bangara,* A song to quiet babes, a lullaby. *Bingara,* Spinning thread.

P بنگش *bangish,* Name of a country in Turkistān. *Bungush,* Deglutition.

P بنگشتن *bungushtan,* To swallow without masticating.

P بنگل *bungul,* Name of a certain tree and fruit.

P بنگلك *bungulak* or *bungalak,* A certain fruit.

P بنگلور *bangalor*, Bangalore in Mysore.

P بنگله *bangala*, Of or belonging to Bengal, as the language. A thatched house, a bungalow.

P بنگو *bangū*, Seed of fleawort.

P بنگه *bunga*, An extending of the voice. *Bungah*, A place or dwelling. A place where money or goods are deposited.

P بنگی *bangī*, One who inebriates himself with بنگ *bang*, q. v.

P بنلاد *bunlād*, Foundation, basis: a prop. A wall.

P بنمين *banmīn*, (in zand and Pāzand) A son.

P بنند *banand*, An unknown number.

P بنو *banū*, Harvest. Corn reaped and stacked.

A بنو *banū*, (pl. of ابن *ibn*) (in composition from بنون *banūn*) Sons, posterity. بنو اصفر *banū asfar*, The posterity of Esau; (a name by which the Arabian historians distinguish the Greeks and Romans, whom they suppose to be of Idumean descent). بنو الصليب *banū's salīb*, Sons of the cross, Christians. *Banaw*, (always written ابن *ibn*) A son.

A بنو الجانّ *banū'l jānn*, The children of angels. (These are considered as the same with those whom Moses calls The children of God, or the angels.)

P بنوان *banwān* or *bunwān*, The superintendant or bailiff of a farm.

A بنوّة *bunūwat*, Filiation, sonship.

A بنود *bunūd*, (pl. of بند *band*) Royal standards, banners. Legions of 10,000 men. (pl. of Pers. بند *band*) Tricks. كثير البنود *kasīru'l bunūd*, Full of deceit, teeming with evil.

A بنّودة *bannūdat*, The posteriors.

P بنوردن *banwardan*, Wild berries.

P بنوره *banawra*, A foundation, a basis.

P بنو سرخ *bunū-surkh*, A lentil.

P بنو سياه *bunu-siyāh*, Peas, pulse.

P بنوعي *ba nawʻe*, In such a manner as.

P بنوك *banūk*, Warmth with festivity, gladness, joy; walking or moving briskly. بنوك كرم *banūk kirm*, A lizard.

P بنو ماش *bunū-māsh*, A black bean or vetch.

A بنون *banūn*, (pl. of ابن *ibn*) Sons. مال و بنون *māl u banūn*, Wealth and children, any thing dear.

P بنونخله *bunū-nakhla*, A kind of wild vetch.

P بنوند *binawand*, Kept (as water in a jar).

P بنوه *banwa* or *banūh*, A harvest. A stack of grain in the straw.

A بنويّ *banawīy*, Filial. Barbarous, relating to aliens residing in Arabia Felix.

P بنه *bana*, A dunghill. A slender rope. *Buna*, Household furniture, goods, and chattels. Baggage. Foundation, bottom, basis. A place. A shop. A house. A tree. بنه بستن *buna bastan*, To pack up, to set off on a journey.

A بني *bany*, (v. n. of بني) Building, rearing. *Banay*, (written ابن *ibn*) A son. *Banī*, (in composition oblique pl. of ابن *ibn*) Sons. بني آدم *banī ādam*, The sons of Adam, men, mortals. بني نوح *banī nūh*, The sons of Noah, mankind. *Bina'* or *buna'*, A fabric. The structure of the human frame. (pl. of بنية *binyat* or *bunyat*) Buildings, structures.

A بنّي *bunnī*, A dish, a plate.

A بنيّ *bunayy*, (dim. of ابن *ibn*) A young son. يا بنيّ *yā bunayya'* or *bunayyī*, O my little son.

A بنّيّ *bunnīy*, A species of fish, the bonito.

P بنيا *banyā*, Victuals which people carry into the country. A pic nic.

A بنيّات *bunayyāt*, Small cups or goblets. بنيّات الطريق *bunayyātu't tarīk*, (Little daughters of the road) Lanes branching from a main road.

P بنياد *bunyād*, A foundation, basis. A fabric. A wall. بنياد كردن *bunyād kardan*, To lay a foundation, to build.

P بنيادگر *bunyādgar*, A builder.

A بنيامين *binyāmīn*, Benjamin, Joseph's brother.

A بنيان *banyān*, Work, labour. Bad, corrupt (speech). *Bunyān*, (v. n. of بني) Building, rearing. A wall, rampart. A fabric, building. Root, basis. Name of a certain cistern of brackish water which on the mission of Muhammad is said to have become sweet. عقيدت بنيان *ʻakīdat-bunyān*, Loyal. Faithful. P بنيان نهادن *bunyān nihādan*, To lay a foundation, to build.

A بنية *binyat*, (v. n. of بني) Building, rearing. Form, mode, manner, nature of the construction or formation of any creature, its build. *Binyat* or *bunyat*, (pl. بني *bina'* or *buna'*) A structure. The constitution or construction of the human body. صحيح البنية *sahīhu'l binyat*, Sound in body.

A بنيّة *baniyat*, A building, structure. The temple of Mecca.

P بنيچ *banīch*, A garment.

P بنيچه *banīcha*, A company of artisans, a corporate or associated body. بنيچه بستن *banīcha bastan*, To wind up an account.

P بنيز *binīz*, Never. Also. Haste. God forbid!

A بني طيّ *banī tayy*, Name of an Arabian tribe.

A بني فاطمة *banī fātima*, The children of Fatima, *i.e.* the descendants of Muhammad.

A بنيقة *banīkat*, The bearing spur of a vine. Hair that turns different ways on a horse's flank. The gore of a woman's shift, or any kind of oblong triangular piece of cloth inserted into a garment to give to it a greater circumference, or adapt it to any particular shape. The upper orifice of a shirt, or opening at the breast. بنيقتان *banīkatāni*, Two small circles or hairy stars upon horses' throats.

P بنيك *banīk*, Coarse raw silk.

A بنين *banīn*, Firm, established. Prudent, wise.

P بنيوش *biniyūsh*, Hear or listen thou.

P بنيوشيدن *biniyūshīdan*, To hear, to listen.

P بو *bū* or *bo*, Odour, smell, flavour, fragrance, scent, perfume. Hope. Flesh of the mountain-goat. بو بردن *bo* (or *bū*) *burdan*, To suspect, to get wind of any thing. عنبر بو *ʻambar-bo*, Fragrant as ambergris. *Bū*, Be thou. (also contraction of بود *buvad*, باشد *bāshad*, بوم *buvam*, and باشم *bāsham*).

A بو *bū*, (for ابو *abū*) A father. بو العجب *bū'l ʻajab*, (Father of admiration) A wonderful thing. A leap, spring, dance. بو الهوس *bū'l hawas*, (Father of desire) Curious. Libidinous. A man who lives well. A fool.

A بوّ *baww*, The young of a camel. The skin of a sucking camel's colt, stuffed with straw, and placed before the mother, which she supposes to be alive, and either gives milk plentifully, or suckles another colt; in Scotland, a tulchan. Ashes, embers, cinders. (fem. بوّة *bawwat*) Foolish, silly.

A بوء *baws*, (v. n. of باء for بوأ) Returning. Taking upon one's self, bearing, sustaining. Being killed in the stead of another. Being equal (as blood for blood). Lying with a woman. Confessing, acknowledging (a fault or a debt). باءُ بغضب من الله *bāʼu bi ghazabin min allāh*, They incurred the wrath of God.

P بوا *buvā*, Be it so!

A بواء *bawās*, (v. n. of باء for بوأ) Confessing. Opposing. Taking upon one's self, bearing, sustaining. Being killed in the stead of another. Equality, equivalent, parity, retaliation. دم بواء دم *dam bawās dam*, Blood for blood. اجابوا عن بواء واحد *ajābū ʻan bawāsin wāhidin*, They replied in the same manner.

A بوّا (جوز *jawzu*) *bawwā*, A nutmeg.

A بوّاب *bawwāb*, A porter, warder, door-keeper.

P بوّابان زرّين سر *bawwābāni zarrīn-sar*, Porters with heads (*i.e.* caps) of gold.

A بوابة *biwābat*, The office of a porter.

A بوّابيّ *bawwābīy*, Belonging to a porter.

A بواتر *bawātir*, (pl. of باتر *bātir*) Sharp swords.

A بواحا *bawāhan*, Openly, publicly.

A بواد *bawād*, (v. n. of باد for بود) Perishing, dying. Going away, departing from friends.

A بوادر *bawādir*, The fleshy parts between the neck and shoulders (in men and animals). (pl. of بادرة *bādirat*) Violent emotions of the soul (particularly in anger).

A بوادي *bawādī*, (pl. of بادية *bādiyat*) Uninhabited deserts.

A بواذخ *bawāzikh*, (pl. of باذخ *bāzikh*) High (mountains).

A بوار *bawār*, (v. n. of بار for بور) Perishing. Laying waste, destroying. Ruin, destruction, perdition. Badness of markets, when a merchant cannot dispose of his goods. (A woman) remaining at home, unasked and unmarried. (pl. بور *būr*) Uncultivated fields. دار البوار *dāru'l bawār*, The house of perdition, *i.e.* Hell.

A بوارح *bawārih*, (pl. of بارح *bārih*) Hot winds.

A بوارد *bawārid*, (pl. of بارد *bārid*) Sharp swords. (pl. of باردة *bāridat*) Cold (things). مرهفات بوارد *murhafāti bawārid*, Death-giving swords.

P بوارد *biwārad*, Acidity, tartness.

P بوارغ *bawārigh*, A chair for a lying-in (woman).

A بوارق *bawārik*, (pl. of بارق *bārik* or بارقة *bārikat*) Flashing (clouds). Glittering (swords).

A بواريّ *bawāriy*, A maker of reed mats.

A بوازل *bawāzil*, (pl. of بازل *bāzil*) (Camels) having the anterior or lateral teeth projecting. The teeth themselves.

A بوازي *bawāzī*, (pl. of بازي *bāzī*) Falcons.

A البوازيج *al bawāzīj*, A place near Takrīt.

P بواس *bawās*, Affliction, calamity, misfortune.

P بواسحاق *bū is-hāk*, Name of a tribe; of a turquoise-mine at Nishābūr; of a king; and of a person eulogized by Hāfiz.

P بواسطه *ba wāsita*, Because, on account of, by means of. بواسطه انكه *ba wāsita ānki*, Because that, for the reason that.

A بواسق *bawāsik*, (pl. of باسق *bāsik*) Tall palms.

A بواسير *bawāsīr*, (pl. of باسور) Emerods, piles.

A بواشق *bawāshik*, (pl. of باشق *bāshik*) Sparrow-hawks.

P بواشه *bawāsha*, A grain-winnowing machine.

A بواضع *bawāziʻ*, (pl. of باضعة *bāziʻat*) Flocks of sheep, herds of cattle. Wounds from whence the blood drops, but does not flow.

A بواطن *bawātin*, (pl. of باطن *bātin*) Concealed. (pl. of باطنة *bātinat*) Interior parts.

A بواطي *bawātī*, (pl. of باطية *bātiyat*) Flagons.

A بواعث *bawāʻis*, (pl. of باعث *bāʻis*) Causes.

A بواقر *bawākir*, (pl. of بقرة) Cows. Oxen.

A بواقي *bawākī*, (pl. of باقية *bākiyat*, fem. of باقي *bākī*) Remaining. Permanent. Remainders.

A بواكر *bawākir*, (pl. of باكرة *bākirat*) Early-bearing (date-trees).

A بواكي *bawākī*, (pl. of باكية *bākiyat*) Weepers.

A بوال *buwāl*, A continual discharge of urine.

A بوّال *bawwāl*, One who makes water much; one who pisses in his bed. Diabetic.

A بوالحسن *bū'l hasan*, The father of Hasan, *i.e.* Aliy.

P بوالخجدر *bū'l khajdar*, A profane, impious wretch.

A بوالعجب *bū'l ʻajab*, Strange. Wonders. A fool.

A P بوالعجيبها *bū'l ʻajībhā*, Wonders.

P بوالفضول *bū'l fuzūl*, (or بوالقاسم) Idle-talker.

P بوالكفد *bū'l kafd*, A bribe to a judge.

P بوالكنجك *bū'l ginjak*, Curious. Any thing playful, ludicrous, curious, or entertaining.

P بوالهوسي *bū'l hawasī*, Folly. Sensuality. Curiosity.

A بواليع *bawālīʻ*, (pl. of بالوعة) Sinks, sewers.

P بوان *bawān*, A narrow pass between mountains. Name of a country abounding in currants and pomegranates.

A بوان *biwān* or *buwān*, (pl. ابونة *abwinat*, بون *būn* and *buwan*) A tent-pole.

A شعب بوّان *shiʻb bawwān*, One of the four paradises of the world, situated in Persia.

A بوانة *buwānat*, Name of a hill behind Yambuʻ.

A بواني *bawānī*, The curved bones of the breast. The legs of a camel. القي بوانيه *alka' bawāniyahu*, He stood firm.

A بواهد *bawāhid* Evils, misfortunes.

A بواهمه *bi wāhima*, In fear of, for fear.

A بوائج *bawāʼij*, (pl. of بائجة *bāʼijat*) Misfortunes.

A بوائع *bawāʼiʻ*, (pl. of بائع *bāʼiʻ*) Purchasers.

A بوائق *bawāʼik*, (pl. of بائقة *bāʼikat*) Evils, calamities, misfortunes. Injuries, oppressions.

A بوائك *bawāʼik*, (pl. of بائكة *bāʼikat*) Young fat she-camels.

P بوب *būb*, (equiv. to يوب *yūb*) A rich carpet.

A بؤب *buʼab*, A species of horses, short and full of flesh, with a long step.

P بوبا *bo-bā*, A dish made of goat's flesh.

A بوباة *bawbāt*, A desert, solitude.

P بوباش *bū būsh*, Ancient, perpetual, everlasting.

P بوب اندين *būb-andīn*, A palace. A tent.

P بوبراقش *bū-barākish*, The chameleon.

P بوبرد *būbard*, (or بوبردك) The nightingale.

P بو بردن *bo bardan*, To get scent, be apprised.

P بوبش *būbash*, A lapwing. Desire. A comb.

P بوبك *bobak*, A virgin. A hoopoo, puet.

A بوبكر *bū bakr*, (for ابوبكر *abū bakr*) The father-in-law of Muhammad.

A بؤبؤ *buʼbuʼ*, The pupil of the eye. Root, origin. The middle or principal part of any thing. The body of a locust. A nobleman, grandee. Ingenious, intelligent. A learned man. The ornamented lid of a little box, in which they keep a kind of black collyrium, called كحل *kuhl*, with which they tinge the eyelids. هو في بؤبؤ المجد *huwa fī buʼbuʼi'l majd*, He is in the eye-ball, or pinnacle of glory. هو بؤبؤ دهره *huwa buʼbuʼ dahrihi*, He is the glory of his age.

P بوبو *būbū*, A hoopoo; also its cry. A term by which a woman addresses her sister. Desirous.

P بوبويه *būbūya*, A hoopoo.

P بوبه *būba*, Wish, desire. A hoopoo or puet.

A بوت *būt*, Name of a tree resembling a medlar.

A بوتاتي *būtātī*, Relating to household expense.

A بوتراب *bū turāb*, Name of the khalīf Aliy.

A بوتقة *būtakat*, (from P بوته *bota*) A crucible.

P بوته *bota*, A crucible, melting-pot. A bush. A butt for shooting at. Brushwood. The young of man or beast. A young camel. A spot. A flower.

بوتهٔ خاك *bota-i khāk*, The human body.

P بو تيمار *bū tīmār*, A heron.

A بوث *baws*, (v. n. of باث for بوث) Inquiring. Dispersing.

P بوج *bawj*, Pride, ostentation.

A بوج *bawj*, (or بوجان *bawajān*) (v. n. of باج for بوج) Being tired. Flashing vividly (lightning). Making a noise. Falling upon, overtaking (misfortune). Lassitude. Exclamation, clamour.

P بوجاسب *būjāsb*, Name of a hero of Tūrān.

P بوجيپا *būjīpā*, (in zand) A sort of cucumber.

P بوجهي *ba wajhe*, On any account. In a way.

P بوچ *bawch*, Pomp, conceit. *Būch*, The inside of the mouth.

A بوح *bawh*, (v. n. of باح for بوح) Appearing, being evident. Disclosing secrets. *Būh*, Root, origin. The sun. The sensitive soul. Confusion in business. Pudenda. Coition. ابن بوحك *ibn būhika*, Thine own son.

G بوحا *būhā*, Zedoary.

A بو حفصان *bū hafsān*, A schoolmaster.

A بوحك *bawhaka*, An exclamation of pity.

A تركهم بوحي *(tarakahum) bawha'*, (He left them) prostrate.

A بوخ *bawkh*, (v. n. of باخ for بوخ) Becoming quieted, pacified (rage), extinguished (fire). Being fatigued. *Būkh*, Confusion in business, perturbation of mind.

P بوخت *bokht*, A son.

P بوخل *būkhal*, or بوخله *būkhala*, Purslain.

P بوخلاف *bū khilāf*, (Father of opposition) The devil.

A بود *bawd*, (v. n. of باد for بود) Departing. Being cut off. A well.

P بود *būd*, It was. Existence, being. A dwelling-place. بود و باش *būd u bāsh*, Residence. *Buvad*, Let him be. It may, might, or will be.

P بو دار *bo-dār*, Scented. Perfumed leather.

P بودانه *bo-dāna*, A medicinal seed.

P بودباش *būd-bāsh*, Place of abode. Service; maintenance.

P بودش *būdish*, Existence.

A بودقة *būdakat*, (from P بوته *bota*) A crucible.

P بودن *būdan*, To be. To become. To exist.

P بودنگ *būdang*, Pennyroyal, pulecium.

P بودنه *būdana*, A small partridge. A quail.

P بودني *būdanī*, Possible, contingent. Future. Essence, existence. بودني بود *būdanī būd*, What is to be, will be.

P بود ونا بود *būd u nā būd*, Riches and poverty. Existence and non-existence.

P بوده *būda*, Been, existent. بوده آمدن *būda āmadan*, To exist. بوده نان *būda-nān*, Unleavened bread, dried forty days in the sun.

P بودي *būdī*, Thou wast. Existence, reality.

A بوذ *bawz*, Injury, outrage, oppression. Poverty. Humiliation, self-abasement. *Būz*, Name of a mountain in Ceylon, where Adam descended.

A بور *bawr*, (v. n. of بار for بور) Perishing, dying. Being fruitless (undertaking). Being languid, dull (market, where nothing can be sold). Proving, trying. Examining, discovering, (particularly applied to a he-camel discovering by the smell whether a she-camel is pregnant or not). Bringing a she-camel to the male for that purpose. Ruin, destruction. Land not sown, nor ready for it. Land that has lain fallow for one season. *Būr*, (mas. fem. du. or pl.) A wicked man, ruffian, villain, scoundrel; one in danger of perdition. Uncultivated ground. *Būr* or *bawr*, (pl. of بائر *bāʼir*) Helpless, unable to help themselves, and destitute of the assistance of others. Uncultivated lands.

P بور *bor*, A bay horse. A pheasant. Bring thou.

P بورا *būrā*, A sack, bag. A nail's head or point.

P بوراق *būrāk*, Borax.

P بوراني *būrānī*, Food made from the egg-plant.

A بورانيّة *būrānīyat*, A kind of food invented by a woman called بوران *būrān*.

A بؤرة *buʼrat*, A ditch, pit (especially any place dug in the ground, where they light a fire and dress victuals). A treasure, stores, provisions.

A بورق *būrak*, (from P بوره *būra*) Borax, nitre.

P بورك *būrak*, A kind of food. A sort of triangular paste or macaroni. Money given to a bystander at dice. Mouldiness of bread.

A بورك *būrah*, Borax, nitre, saltpetre.

P بورنگ *bo-rang*, A fragrant mountain-plant.

P بورنيه *būrniya*, A large jar filled with drugs.

P بورو *būrū*, A trumpet, hunting-horn. A tube, canal. The gripes. بورو زن *būrū-zan*, A trumpeter.

P بوروره *būrūra*, Name of a king, and island.

P بوره *būra*, Nitre, borax. Pastry. Lump-sugar. بورهٔ ارمني *būraʼi armanī*, Nitre, borax, used in soldering gold.

P بوري *būrī*, A trumpet. A hunting-horn. The point of any thing (especially of a nail). A split reed, or a mat made of such. بوري زدن *būrī zadan*, To sound a trumpet. البوري *al būrī*, A kind of fish.

A بوريّ *būrīy*, (بوريّة *būrīyat* or بورياء *būriyāʼ*) A mat made of split reeds. *Būrīy*, A kind of fish found in Egypt.

P بوريا *būriyā*, (بوريه *būriya* or بوري *būrī*) A mat made of split reeds. A carpet. A case for any instrument. بوريا باف *būriyā-bāf*, (or بوريا بان *būriyābān*) A maker of mats; or instrument-cases.

P بورياكوبي *būriyā-kobī*, A mat-treading (house-warming).

A ارسله ببوريّة *arsalahu bi būrīyatin*, He left him alone without correction or controul.

G بوريطش *būrītash*, The fire-stone pyrites.

P بوز *bawz*, Mouldiness of bread. A large black bee. The trunk of a tree. *Boz*, A roan horse. Swift. Intelligent. Shrewd.

A بؤز *buʼuz*, (pl. of بازي *bāzī*) Falcons, hawks.

P بوزا *bozā*, (equivalent to بوزه *boza*) Beer.

P بوزار *bozār*, Hot spices mixed up with food.

P بوزاگر *bozāgar*, A brewer of beer.

P بوزاگري *bozāgarī*, Brewing, making of beer.

A بوزع *bawzaʻ*, Name of a tribe. Name of a woman. Name of a sandy tract.

P بوزك *bawzak*, Mouldiness of bread.

P بوزكند *būzkand*, A kind of settee placed before the doors in the East. A veranda, a portico.

P بوزمند *būzmand*, (بورمند *būrmand* or بوزمه *būzama*) Name of a certain fragrant herb.

P بوزنه *būzina*, (بوزينه or بوزنيه) An ape.

P بوزه *boza*, A beverage made from rice, millet, or barley: beer. The trunk of a tree.

P بوزه خانه *boza-khāna*, A beer-shop, ale-house.

P بوزه كباب *būza-kabāb*, Roast lamb.

P بوزيدان *būzīdān*, Name of a fattening drug.

P بوژ *bawj*, A whirlpool. *Būj*, Weight. A raging fever.

P بوژنه *būjuna*, A rose-bud not yet expanded, a follicle, a pod.

A بوس *baws*, (v. n. of باس for بوس) Kissing. Being rough. Mixture. *Būs*, Adversity, indigence. Humility, lowness.

P بوس *bos*, A kiss, buss. Kissing. دامن بوس دادن *dāman bos dādan*, To kiss the hem of a garment. بوس رخسار كردن *bosi rukhsār kardan*, To kiss the cheek. پا بوس *pā-bos*, Kissing the feet. زمين بوس *zamīn-bos*, Kissing the ground. بوس و كنار *bos u kanār*, Kissing and embracing.

A بؤس *buʼs*, (v. n. of بؤس) Becoming poor, indigent, and miserable. (pl. ابؤس *abʼus*) Misfortune, evil, misery, adversity.

P بوسانه *bosāna*, Humility.

P بوسانيدن *bosānīdan*, To cause to kiss, or rot.

P بوستان *bostān*, (Place of perfume) A garden, a kitchen-garden, a green spot. Name of a city. Name of many Arabian and Persian books, the most celebrated of which is the Bostān of سعدي *saʻdī*, a native of Shīrāz; which, together with his Gulistān, is in the highest esteem in every country where the Persian language is known. بوستان سندس *bostāni sundus*, Flowers of various hues. بوستان گل نماي *bostāni gul-namāy*, The firmament.

P بوستان افروز *bostān-afroz*, Cock's comb.

P بوسحاق *būs-hāk*, Name of a tribe. Name of a turquoise-mine at Nīshāpūr.

P بوسك *bosak*, A little kiss. The wing of a bird. Any thing hollow or excavated.

P بوسگاه *bos-gāh*, (بوسا گه *bosā-gah*, بوسه گاه *bosa-gāh*, or بوسه گه *bosa-gah*) The place of kissing, *i. e.* The royal apartment (because every one going there kisses, or ought to kiss, the gate).

P بوسليك *būsalīk*, Name of a note in music.

P بوسليمان *būsulaymān*, A roost-cock: a hoopoo.

P بوسنج *būsanj*, Name of a city.

P بوسنه *būsna*, The province of Bosnia.

P بوسه *bosa*, A kiss. بوسه دادن, To kiss.

P بوسه بازي *bosa-bāzī*, Kissing and toying.

P بوسه جاي *bosa-jāy*, (Place of kissing) Lips.

P بوسه شكستن *bosa shikastan*, To smack the lips, in kissing.

A بؤسي *buʼsaʼ*, (v. n. of بئس) Becoming needy and miserable. Adversity, injury, loss, misfortune.

P بوسي *bose*, One kiss.

P بوسيدگي *bosīdagī*, Rottenness. Submission.

P بوسيدن *bosīdan*, To kiss. To rot.

P بوسيده *bosīda*, Rotten, stale.

A بوسير *bawsīr*, (for بوصير *bawsīr*) Hemorrhoids.

P بوسير *būsīr*, Possibility.

P بوسين *būsīn*, Accusation, upbraiding, reproof.

P بوش *bawsh*, Celebrity. Ostentation, boast. Magnificence. *Būsh*, A kind of eye-salve brought from Dar-band. *Bavish*, Predestination, fate. *Buvish*, Existence.

A بوش *bawsh*, (v. n. of باش for بوش) Making a confused noise (a mob). Stretching forth the hand to receive something. *Bawsh* or *būsh*, (pl. اوباش *awbāsh*) A multitude, crowd, troop, or band. A mixed company of various tribes. A kind of dish made from baked wheat and lentils. The sound or noise made by a mob or other great body of men. تركتهم هوشا بوشا *taraktuhum hawshan bawshan*, I left them confused and tumultuous. بوش بائش *būsh bāʼish*, A crowd of all ranks. *Būsh*, A place in Egypt where stuffs are manufactured.

P بوشا *būshā*, Meditation, thoughtfulness, solicitude, anxiety.

G بوشاد *boshād*, The rape-root. A turnip.

P بوشاسب *boshāsb*, Sleep. Pollution.

P بوشپاس *būshpās*, Sleep. A dream, a vision.

P بوشنج *boshanj*, Name of a town.

P بوشنك *būshanh*, Name of a village near Harāt.

A بوشيّ *bawshīy*, A poor man, with a large family. *Bawshīy* or *būshīy*, Of the meanest rank of men. *Būshīy*, (Stuff) manufactured at Būsh.

P بوشيدن *būshīdan*, To begin any work. To consider.

A بوص *baws*, (v. n. of باص for بوص) Preceding, going before, being superior, excelling. Making haste. Flying, absconding. Being hid, concealed. Importuning, teasing. Colour. A woman's hips. A precipitate pace. Fatigue, lassitude. (pl. ابواص *abwās*) Kind, sort (of cattle). *Būs* or *baws*, Softness of the fat of the buttocks. *Būs*, Colour. Name of a fruit. A woman's hips. حال بوصه *hāla būsuhu*, His colour changed.

A بوصاء *bawsāʼ*, Large-hipped (woman). A game, in which a torch being lighted at one end is whirled round with velocity.

A بوصيّ *būsīy*, A little boat, a skiff.

A بوصير *būsīr*, The plant bear's ear. A kind of hemlock. (corruption of باسور *bāsūr*) Piles.

A بوض *bawz*, (v. n. of باض for بوض) Standing, remaining, staying, abiding. Being beautiful, clean in the face, after being foul (with freckles).

A بوط *bawt*, (v. n. of باط for بوط) Becoming poor after having been rich, and despicable after having been honourable.

A بوطانيّة *būtānīyat*, A creeper called black vine.

A بوطة *būtat*, (from P بوته *bota*) A crucible.

A بوظ *bawz*, (v. n. of باظ for بوظ) Becoming fat. Discharging in the womb.

A بوع *bawʻ*, (v. n. of باع for بوع) Expanding the hand, stretching it out when giving money. Taking long steps in running (a horse or camel).

Measuring with a fathom or with the arms extended. *Bawʻ* or *būʻ*, (pl. ابواع *abwāʻ*) Declivity of a mountain, or any part which has fallen into a slope. A fathom. *Būʻ*, (pl. of بائع *bāʼiʻ*) Young deer bounding at full speed.

A بوغ *bawgh*, (v.n. of باغ for بوغ) Boiling (blood).

P بوغ *būgh* or *bogh*, Any outward covering or wrapper (especially of leather). A pouch.

A بوغاء *bawghāʼ*, Soft, friable earth. Unsettled, crazy, insane (men). Confusion. Aromatic fragrance.

P بوغبند *bogh-band*, A cloth in which any thing is wrapped up.

P بوغرا *būghrā*, (or بوغراق *būghrāk*) A kind of food (made of boiled meat, flour, &c.)

G بوغلصن *būghulsun*) Borage.

P بوغما *boghmā*, Trumpery, trifles, scraps, rags. Fragments, broken victuals, stores of a wallet. A fat and ugly woman.

P بوغنج *būghanj*, Coriander. Name of a city.

P بوغند *būghand*, Convolvulus, ivy, bindweed.

P بوف *būf*, An owl.

P بوفروش *bo-firosh*, A perfumer, a druggist.

A بوق *bawk*, (v. n. of باق for بوق) Oppressing, distressing, injuring. Befalling (as a misfortune). Surrounding, hedging in. Attacking with united force, and killing unjustly. Rushing (into the inner or forbidden apartments). Being affected by any malady and perishing (cattle). Rising and coming upon any one from an ambush. Robbing, stealing, kidnapping. A blab. *Būk*, (pl. ابواق *abwāk* and بيقان *bīkān*) A trumpet, clarion, hunting-horn, and often used to signify a flute, pipe, or any musical instrument (in allusion to which one who cannot keep a secret is called *būk*, as being full of holes). A kind of pipe into which a miller blows. Vain, foolish. False, unjust. *Buwak*, (pl. of بوقة *būkat*) Thunder-showers, violent rains. Disagreeable things.

P بوق *bok*, A large sheet.

A بؤق *baʼuk*, Evil, calamity, severity.

A بوقات *būkāt*, (pl. of بوق *būk*) Trumpets, cornets.

A بوقال *būkāl*, A tankard without a handle.

A بوقة *būkat*, (pl. بوق *buwak*) A violent rain, a thunder-shower, coming down with uncommon impetuosity. A disagreeable thing.

P بوقلمون *bū kalamūn*, A chameleon. A tortoise. A turkey. A bird which as often as it plunges into the water appears of a different colour. Various-coloured stuffs or habits. (In general) any thing of various colours, or whose surface reflects different rays from a change of position. A variable, capricious man. The inconstancy of fortune. Changeable world.

P بوقلمونی *būkalamūnī*, Variegated, motley.

G بوقيصا *būkīsā*, The elm-tree.

A بوك *bawk*, (v. n. of باك for بوك) Leaping (as the male ass upon the female). Conversing with a woman. Forming little balls of clay between the palms of the hands. Buying or selling merchandize. Removing with a stick rubbish from a fountain or aqueduct to make the water flow more freely. Being in confusion (business). Being disturbed in mind (men). Becoming fat. اوّل بوك *awwal bawk*, The first time or thing.

P بوك *būk*, By chance, perhaps, haply, may be. Except. A divine precept. A pit in which they lay up (wheat). A fire-shovel. Tinder.

بوك و مگر *būk u magar*, Perhaps, may be.

A بوّك *būwak*, (pl. of بائك *bāʼik*) Fat camels.

A بوكاء *bawkāʼ*, Mixture, confusion.

P بوكلك *būkalak*, Juniper-berries. A kind of fruit in Persia called بن *ban*.

P بوكند *būkand*, Ivy.

P بوكه *bū ki*, Perhaps it may; would that it were!

P بوگان *būgān*, The womb. A flower-bed.

A بول *bawl*, (v. n. of بال for بول) Making water. Bursting out, flowing freely. Becoming liquid, melting. A great number, a multitude. A son. (pl. ابوال *abwāl*) Urine. بول الابل *bawlu'l ibl*, A kind of medicine for wounds (produced in Arabia Felix). بول العجوز *bawlu'l ʻajūz*, Milk. P بول كردن *bawl kardan*, To urine.

A بولة *bawlat*, A daughter. *Buwalat*, One who voids urine copiously.

A بؤولة *buʼulat*, (v.n. of بؤل) Being small and weak.

P بوالحكيم *bū'l hakīm*, Wise, learned.

P بوالخجدر *bū'l khajdar*, An unbeliever, heretic.

P بولدان *bawldān*, A chamber-pot, a urinal.

A بولس *būlas*, Name of a dungeon in hell.

P بولس *bolus*, Paul.

A بولع *bawlaʻ*, A glutton.

P بوالكنجك *bū'l kunjak*, Any thing new or wonderful. The first-fruits. A masquerade, pastime, frolic.

P بولنجك *bū lanjak*, Any thing strange, curious, and entertaining.

G بولوبودبون *būlūbūdabūn*, Polypody.

G بولوطريخون *būlūtarīkhūn*, Maiden's hair.

P بوله *būla*, A tube, tunnel.

A بولهب *bū lahab*, (for ابولهب *abū lahab*) Name of one of Muhammad's uncles (Kur'ān, chap. cxi.). P بولهبان وقت *būlahabāni wakt*, (The Bū lahabs of the age) Obstinate unbelievers.

L بوليناس *būlīnas*, (Plinius) Pliny.

P بوم *būm*, A country, region. Desert land not yet cultivated. The boundaries or frontiers of inimical states, whose hostile inroads are always to be dreaded. A garrison. A mansion or place where one dwells in safety. Embroidered cloth. Nature, disposition, temperament. بوم آباد *būmi ābād*, An inhabited country. بوم ويران *būmi werān*, A desolate country. *Buvam*, I may be.

A بوم *būm*, (or بومة *būmat*) An owl. البوم المشؤم *al būmu'l mashʼum*, The owl of bad omen.

P بومادران *būmādarān*, (or بوماران *būmārān*) The plant southernwood.

P بومارة *būmāra*, A kind of bird.

P بومبر *būm-bar*, Dominion, lordship, seigniory.

P بومكند *būm-kand*, A subterraneous dwelling.

P بومه *būma*, Fire struck by a horse's shoe.

P بومهن *būmhan*, An earthquake. *Būmahan*, An earthquake. The intestines of sheep not cleaned.

P بومهين *būmahīn*, An earthquake.

P بون *bawn*, A portion, share. *Būn*, Foundation, root, origin. End, limit. Intestines of sheep or cattle not cleaned. The womb. The heavens. بون ستون *būni sitūn*, The base of a column, the pedestal of a statue.

A بون *bawn*, (v. n. of بان for بون) Excelling. *Bawn* or *būn*, Difference. Interval, space. بون مديد *bawni madīd*, A long interval (of time). *Būn* or *buwan*, (pl. of بوان *biwān*) Pillars, tent poles, or the wooden work which supports the top of the doorway, and the curtains of tents.

A بونافع *bū nāfiʻ*, Wine.

A بونة *bawnat*, A little daughter. *Būnat*, A town in Africa.

P بوند *buvand*, They may be. *Buvand* or *buvind*, Proud, arrogant. *Buwund*, Lenity, meekness.

P بونده *buvanda* or *buvinda*, Proud. Majestic. *Buwunda*, Modest, gentle, grave.

P بونيز *būnīz*, (equiv. to نيزه *nīza*) A short spear.

A بؤوح *baʼūh*, One who cannot keep a secret. *Buʼūh*, (or بؤوحة *buʼūhat*) (v. n. of باح for بوح) Disclosing a secret.

A بؤوخ *buʼūkh*, (v. n. of باخ for بوخ) Turning, stinking, becoming tainted (as meat).

A بؤوز *buʼūz*, (pl. of باز *baʼz*) Falcons.

A بؤوس *buʼūs*, (v. n. of بئس) Becoming indigent and miserable.

A بؤوق *baʼūk*, (v. n. of بأق) Overtaking (misfortune).

A بؤولة *buʼūlat*, (v. n. of بؤل) Being small, weak.

A بوه *bawh*, (v. n. of باه for بوه) Lying with a woman. Cursing. An imprecation, curse. *Būh*, (v. n. of باه for بوه) Directing one's attention, minding, adverting to. A moulted hawk. A male owl. A large owl or a bird resembling it.

P بوه *buwa*, A tree which does not bear fruit. Grave, modest.

A بوهة *būhat*, A she-owl. A kind of hawk that has moulted. Feathers driven about by the wind. Wool or cotton put into an ink-holder and not yet wet. Thin-bodied. Small-boned. Extenuated, emaciated. Foolish, absurd, silly, flighty.

P بوهمان *būhmān*, The womb. Some one, somebody, so and so.

P بوهه *būha*, Desire. Perturbation of mind. The hoopoo.

P بوي *boy* or *būy*, Odour, fragrance, perfume, scent, spice. Hope, wish, desire: search, quest. Love. Nature, disposition. Portion, part. عنبربوي *ʻam-*

bar-boy, Fragrant as amber. بوي بردن *boy burdan*, To give a hint. To hear. To suspect. بوي دادن *boy dādan*, To diffuse fragrance. بوي سوختني *boy sokhtanī*, Incense. بوي شنيدن *boy shanīdan*, To smell. بوي كردن *boy kardan*, To smell, to scent of. To snuff up, to smell to. بوي گرفتن *boy giriftan*, To contract a smell, to stink. بوي يكرنگي *boy yakrangī*, Sincere affection. *Buv*, Thou mayest be.

A بوّيّ *bawwīy*, A fool.

P بويا *boyā*, Odoriferous, fragrant. Fetid. Coriander-seed.

P بوي افزا *boy-afzā*, Spice, seasoning.

P بوي افزار *boy-afzār*, A censer. Spice, seasoning.

P بويان *boyān*, Smelling. Name of a country.

P بويانك *boyānak*, Parsley. Southernwood.

P بوي پرست *boy-parast*, A hound. A pard. A parasite. A demon. An angel.

A بويت *buwayt*, (dim. of بيت *bayt*, not approved) A small house, a cottage.

P بويچه *būycha*, Ivy, convolvulus.

A بو يحيا *bū yahyā*, Name of the angel of death.

P بوي دار *boy-dār*, Scented. Hunting by the scent (a dog).

P بويدان *boydān*, A perfume-box.

P بوي رنگ *boy-rang*, A rose.

P بوي سا *boy-sā*, A stone for rubbing powders.

P بوي سوز *boy-soz*, A censer, a chafing-dish.

P بويش *boyish*, Smelling. The sense of smelling.

P بوي فروش *boy-farosh*, A perfumer.

P بوي كلك *boy-kalik*, A kind of berry with a green bark, noxious to the teeth and stomach.

P بوي گرفتگي *boy-giriftagī*, Stink, taint.

P بوي گرفته *boy-girifta*, Fetid, stinking.

P بوي مادران *boy-mādarān*, Southernwood, melissa, parthenion, apiastrum, balm-gentle.

P بوي ناك *boynāk*, Rank-smelling.

P بويناكان *boy-nākān*, Destitute of the sense of smelling.

P بوينگ *boyang*, A kind of sweet basil.

P بويه *boya*, Hope, desire. Fumitory.

A بويه *buwayh*, The founder of a certain dynasty.

P بوئيدن *boīdan*, To smell, scent, diffuse perfume. To have a smell. To smell to, snuff up. To live in the country.

P بوي يكرنگي *boy-yak-rangī*, Fidelity, love.

P به *ba*, To. For. In. On. With. By. According to. It is sometimes pleonastic: as, به آب اندر *ba āb andar*, In the water. *Bih*, Good, excellent. Better. Safe, sound. Elegant. A quince. به شدن *bih shudan*, To be healed, to recover.

A به *bah*, Well done! bravo! excellent! *Bihi*, With, for, from, in, or by him, or it. مامور به *mamūr bihi*, Ordered, commanded.

A بهّ *bahh*, (v. n. of بهّ) Rising in dignity, being promoted by the monarch.

A بهأ *bahaʼa*, (fut. يبهأ *yabhaʼu*) He emptied (the house) of furniture. He tore (the garment). He understood. ما بهأت له *mā bahaʼtu lahu*, I did not attend to it.

A بهأ *bahʼ*, (v. n. of بهأ) Being accustomed.

A بها *bahaʼ*, (fut. يبهو *yabhū* or يبهى *yabhī*) (It) was beautiful, elegant, or graceful.

P بها *bahā*, Price, value. بهاى خلعت *bahāʼi khilʼat*, A tax to defray the expense of honorary dresses. بهاى خون *bahāʼi khūn*, The price of blood (which is paid to the relations of a person killed, as an atonement). بها قطع كردن *bahā katʼ kardan*, To fix a price. بها كردن *bahā kardan*, To value, appraise. پر بها و شرف *pur bahā u sharaf*, Most precious and noble. گران بها *girān-bahā*, Dear, precious. *Bihā*, Goodness. Beauty, ornament.

A بهاء *bahāʼ*, (v. n. of بهأ) Being accustomed, familiar. (v. n. of بهو) Being fair and handsome. (v. n. of بهى) Being torn and demolished (a tent). Beauty, elegance. Lustre, splendour. The shining of the froth of milk. A camel easy to be milked. حسن و بهاء *husn wa bahāʼ*, Beauty and elegance.

P بها پيشي *bahā-peshī*, Money advanced, prepayment.

A بهّات *bahhāt*, A calumniator, a slanderer.

A بهاتر *bahātir*, (pl. of بهتر *buhtur*) Short in stature.

A بهاجة *bahājat*, (v. n. of بهج) Being beautiful.

P بهادر *bahādur*, Brave, bold, valiant, courageous, magnanimous, warlike, strong, athletic. A soldier, champion, hero, chevalier, knight, horseman. *Bahādur* forms part of the title of honour conferred by the Great Mogul and other Eastern potentates, upon the nabobs (nuwwāb) and other great men, bearing some resemblance to the European title of military knighthood: as, عمدة الممالك افتخار الملك قمر الدولة محمد خان بهادر *ʼumdatu'l mamālik, iftikhāru'l mulk, kamaru'd dawlat, muhammad khān bahādur*, The pillar of empires, the glory of the kingdom, the full moon of the state, Muhammad Khān, the brave.

P بهادران *bahādurān*, (pl. of بهادر *bahādur*) Valiant soldiers.

P بهادرانه *bahādurāna*, Bravely, like a champion.

P بهادري *bahādurī*, Valour, military gallantry.

P بهار *bahār*, Spring, beginning of summer. A blossom. Orange-flower. A Budhist temple. An idol. The haram of a prince. Camomile, anthemis. Name of an island. فصل بهار *fasli bahār*, The spring-season. The harvest of that season. بهار دانش *bahāri dānish*, The title of a well-known work on ethics. *Bihār*, The province of Behar in India. Half a horse-load.

A بهار *bahār*, Any thing beautiful and splendid. A species of odoriferous herb; buphthalmus, ox-eye. The inferior hollow part in the throat of a horse, next to the thorax, and also a whitish appearance there. *Bihār*, (v. n. 3 of بهر) Boasting, glorying. *Buhār*, An idol. A swallow. A white fish. Cotton taken from the pods. Sea-baggage, every thing necessary for accommodation on ship-board. An equipoise weighing 400 *ratl*. A weight of about 300, 400, 600, or 1000 *ratl*. A vessel with a spout resembling an ewer.

P بهار آرا *bahār-ārā*, Vernal showers, or blossoms.

P بهاران *bahārān*, The spring. Orange-flower.

P بهار بانو *bahār-bānū*, The blooming princess.

P بهار بشكنه *bahār-bushkana*, A note in music.

P بهار پيرا *bahār-perā*; (Spring-adorning) Vernal showers, buds or blossoms.

P بهار خانه *bahār-khāna*, An idol-temple.

P بهار خوش *bahār-khwush*, Flesh smoke-dried.

P بهارستان *bahāristān*, Spring. Vernal blossoms.

P بهاري *bahārī*, Belonging to the spring, vernal.

P بهاز *bihāz*, A high-bred horse kept for stock.

A بهازر *bahāzir*, (pl. of بهزرة *buhzurat* or *bahzarat*) Large she-camels. Tall palm-trees.

A بهازرة *bahāzirat*, Fat camels.

P بهاشتن *bahāshtan*, To weep, to cry.

P به افتاده *bih-uftāda*, Healthy, vigorous.

P به آفرين *bih-āfirīn*, The sister of Isfandiyār.

A بهاكن *bahākin*, (pl. of بهكن *bahkan*) Fresh and full of vigour (youths).

P بها گير *bahā-gīr*, Precious, valuable, costly.

A بهاليق *bahālīk*, Trifles, vanities.

A بهام *bihām*, (pl. of بهم *bahm*) Lambs, kids, and camel's colts comprehended in one flock. سعد البهام *saʼdu'l bihām*, One of the lunar mansions.

P به آمدن *bih āmadan*, To come well; to succeed, to prosper.

P بهامين *bahāmīn*, Spring.

A بهانس *buhānis*, Tame, tractable camel. Lion.

P بهانستن *bahānistan*, To weep.

P بهانه *bahāna*, Pretence, excuse, evasion. Motive, cause. بهانه جستن *bahāna justan*, To seek a pretext. بهانه كردن *bahāna kardan*, To make an excuse. بهانه يافتن *bahāna yāftan*, To find a pretence. بهانه فروش *bahāna-farosh*, A vender of apologies, a maker of false excuses.

P بهاور *bahāwar*, Precious, valuable.

A بهائم *bahāʼim*, (pl. of بهيمة *bahīmat*) Beasts, brutes, wild beasts. بهائم مخصوص *bahāʼim makhsūs*, Wild, ferocious.

A بهباه *bahbāh*, Hoarsely-braying (camel).

P بهبود *bih-būd*, Welfare, safety. Healthy.

P بهبودي *bih-būdī*, Well-being. Health, vigour.

A بهبهة *bahbahat*, (v. n. of بهبه Q) Crying out Bravo! well done! A loud braying noise.

A بهبهيّ *bahbahīy*, Large, great, corpulent.

A بهت *baht*, (v. n. of بهت) Attacking suddenly and defeating or overwhelming (an individual or body of men). Rupture, separation, disjunction. Stupor. Amazement. A kind of stone. *Baht* or *bahat*, (v. n. of بهت) Slandering, accusing falsely. *Buht*, A lie, calumny, slander, false accusation.

P بهت *buht*, A planet's motion in a given time.

H بهت *bahat*, Rice dressed in milk.

A بهتان *buhtān*, (v. n. of بهت) Slandering, accusing falsely. A calumny, lie, slander, false accusation, malignant imputation, malevolent suspicion. P بهتان شدن *buhtān shudan*, To be defamed. بهتان گفتن *buhtān guftan*, To slander.

P بهتانگوي *buhtān-goy*, A slanderer, defamer.

A بهتر *bahtar*, A lie. *Buhtur*, (fem. بهترة *buhturat*) (pl. بهاتر *bahātir*) Short in stature.

P بهتر *bihtar*, Better.

P بهترك *bahtarak*, Somewhat better. *Bihtarak*, A Persian intercalary month, introduced once in 120 years, and celebrated with one continued festival. The old Persian year consisted of twelve months of thirty days; to the last of which they added five, making thereby their year 365 days; but with regard to the excess of six hours, instead of our more regular mode of leap-year, they thought of no further intercalation till the surplus hours amounted to thirty days, when the 120th year was made to consist of thirteen months.

P بهترين *bihtarin*, Best. بهترين خلق *bihtarīni khalk*, Best of created beings, *i. e.* Muhammad.

A بهث *bahs*, (v. n. of بهث) Receiving with an open countenance, expressive of joy and kindness.

A بهثة *buhsat*, The wild cow.

A بهج *bahj*, (v. n. of بهج) Making glad, exhilarating. *Bahaj*, (v. n. of بهج) Rejoicing being glad. *Bahij*, Glad, cheerful.

P بهج *bahaj*, A certain fattening drug.

A بهجة *bahjat*, (v. n. of بهج) Being joyful and glad. Being beautiful. Beauty, elegance, grace, excellence. Gladness, cheerfulness, alacrity. Exultation. P پر بهجت *pur-bahjat*, Full of joy.

P بهدانه *bih-dāna*, The seed of a quince.

A بهدريّ *buhduriy*, A child that does not thrive.

A بهدل *bahdal*, A hyena's whelp. A species of green bird.

A بهدلة *bahdalat*, (v. n. of بهدل Q) Being large (the flesh on a man's chest). Lightness, quickness.

P بهدله *bahdala*, A woman's name; also a man's.

P بهدين *bih-dīn*, The religion of Zardusht or Zoroaster. Religious, faithful, pious, devout.

A بهذا الداخلية *bihāza'd dākhiliya*, Mean time.

A بهر *bahr*, (v. n. of بهر) Shining, excelling (in beauty, grace, virtue). Excellence, pre-eminence. Conquest. Superiority. A filling up, completing. Distance. Love, friendship. Grief. Calumny. The imposition of a burden beyond the strength. Astonishment, wonder. *Buhr*, Shortness of breath, asthma, breathing hard from overload. A city, town, or province. An extensive district. The middle of a valley, a channel.

P بهر *ba har*, At, by, to, or in every or each. بهرحال *ba har hāl*, In every shape, however it be, in whatever condition. بهرسال *ba har sāl*, In every year. بهر سه نوع *ba har sih nawʻ*, Animal, vegetable, and mineral. بهرماه *ba har māh*, In every month. بهروقتي *ba har wakte*, At all times. *Bahr*, For, because, on account of. بهر آزمودن *bahri āzmūdan*, By way of trial, in order to discover. بهر تو *bahri tu*, For thy sake. بهراين *bahri īn*, On this account. بهرچه *bahri chi*, For why? wherefore? بهر شما *bahri shumā*, For you. بهر كسي *bahri kase*, For some one. از بهر سود *az bahri sūd*, On account of gain. از بهر خود *az bahri khwud*, For his own sake. از بهر نماز *az bahri namāz*, In order to pray. *Bahr*, A part, portion, lot, chance, fortune. Name of a country. *Buhr*, Continually. A herb with a stalk like that of barley.

P بهرا *bahrā*, On account of, for the sake of.

A بهرًا *bahran*, A curse upon it! may he perish!

P بهرام *bahrām*, The planet Mars. Name of several kings of Persia, and of other kingdoms in the East (corrupted by the Greeks into that of Varanes). The twentieth day of every month. Name of an angel.

A بهرام *bahrām*, Bastard saffron.

P بهرام تل *bahrām-tal*, An obelisk or pyramid, which Bahrām-chūbīn caused to be constructed with the skulls of the Turks slain in a bloody engagement.

A بهرامج *bahrāmaj*, A species of willow.

P بهرام چوبين *bahrām-chūbīn*, Name of a celebrated general, so called from his lankiness.

P بهرامگور *bahrām-gor*, Name of one of the kings of Persia, so called from his passion for the chase of the wild ass.

P بهرامن *bahrāman*, A ruby. A kind of variegated silk. Safflower. Rouge, paint for the face.

P بهرامه *bahrāma*, A species of willow. A robe of green silk.

P بهران *buhrān*, A hot pestilential wind.

P بهراي *bih-rāy*, Prudent, fit for business, proper for the administration of public affairs. Ingenious, thinking judiciously.

A بهرة *buhrat*, The middle (of the day or night; of a valley; of a horse; of a ring). An extensive tract of country.

A بهرج *bahraj*, Vain, fruitless, futile. A lie. Wicked, base, wretched, bad. Open to the opinion or use of every man. (from P نبهره *nabahra*, said to be originally Indian نبهلا *nabahlā*) Base (coin).

A بهرجة *bahrajat*, (v. n. of بهرج Q) Allowing (blood) to be shed with impunity. Bringing one's cattle by a way not travelled, through fear of the tithe-collector. Deviation from the highway.

P بهرك *bahrak*, One whose hands and feet are hardened by labour. Filth, ordure, dregs, dross.

P بهركيف *ba har kayf*, By any means, in every way soever.

P بهرگي *bahragī*, Riches, wealth. Opulent, affluent.

P بهرم *bahram*, Bastard saffron. (for بهرام *bahrām*).

A بهرم *bahram*, Saffron in the flower. Privet.

P بهرمان *bahramān*, The finest ruby. Fine silk interwoven or painted with flowers. Safflower. Paint.

A بهرمة *bahramat*, (v. n. of بهرم Q) Staining the beard with privet. The religious worship of the Brahmins and other Hindū casts. A kind of Indian flower.

P بهرمن *baharman*, An idol-temple. A ruby.

P بهرمند *bahramand*, (for بهره مند) Fortunate.

P بهرمه *bahrama*, An auger, a gimblet.

P بهروج *bihroj*, (or بهروجه *bihroja*) Crystal of a transparent blue colour, and of little value. Cheap. Indian frankincense.

P بهروز *bihroz*, (or بهروزه *bihroza*) A species of blue crystal. Indian frankincense.

P بهرون *bihrūn*, Name of Alexander the Great.

P بهره *bahra*, A part, portion, quota, share, lot. Profit, gain, advantage. Happiness, prosperity, fortune, favour. A burden, as much as an ass, camel, or horse carries upon one side. بهرهٔ وصيّت *bahraʼi waṣiyat*, A legacy. بهره بهره كردن *bahra bahra kardan*, To divide into portions. بهره يافتن *bahra yāftan*, To find favour. *Buhra*, A people living in Guzerat. *Bihra*, A town near Lahore.

P بهره بر *bahra-bar*, (or بهره ور) A partner.

P بهره دار *bahra-dār*, A sharer, participator, partner. Enjoying one's wishes, fortunate. بهره دار عطيّه و انعام كردن *bahra-dāri ʻaṭīya u inʻām kardan*, To make a partner of gifts and presents.

P بهره مند *bahramand*, Sharing, participating. Fortunate, prosperous, happy, contented. بهره مند شدن *bahramand shudan*, To accomplish an object, to obtain what we desire, to be fortunate, prosperous, successful. To participate, share.

P بهره ور *bahrawar*, Favoured, happy.

P بهره ور بانو *bahrawar-bānū*, Name of a princess.

P بهره ياب *bahra-yāb*, One who finds favour. A partaker, a sharer.

P بهري *bahre*, A little, somewhat, a part. Any thing. Any one.

P بهريك *bahri yak*, For some one, for the sake of one. *Ba har yak*, For every one.

A بهز *bahz*, (v. n. of بهز) Removing, repelling, thrusting away. Striking one (upon the breast) with feet and hands, or with the elbow. Name of a tribe.

P بهزاد *bih-zād*, Isfandiyār. Name of a horse.

A بهزر *bahzar*, Nimble, active. Intelligent, wise, sound in judgment. Noble, illustrious.

A بهزرة *buhzurat* or *bahzarat*, (pl. بهازر *bahāzir*) A large she-camel. A tall palm-tree.

A بهس *bahs*, Boldness, bravery, courage.

P بهش *bahsh*, The fruit of the dwarf palm-tree.

A بهش *bahsh*, (v. n. of بهش) Searching, investigating. Having an affection for any one, being benevolently disposed. Catching without retaining, endeavouring to catch without succeeding. Extending (the hand in order to seize any thing). Being ready to cry. Being light, glad, and cheerful. Being ready to laugh. Assembling (men). Fresh or moist mastich or bdellium, an Arabian gum. Cheerful, humane, benign. اهل البهش *ah-*

lu'l bahsh, The Arabians of Hijāz. بلاد البهش *bilādu'l bahsh,* The country of Hijāz. وجوه البهش *wujūhu'l bahsh,* Faces of a deformed black appearance.

P بهشت *bihisht,* Paradise. Heaven. بهشت دنيا *bihishti dunya',* A title of the Sughd of Samarkand; also of the city of Damascus. شهزادۀ بهشت خرام *shah-zādaʼi bihisht-khirām,* The glorious prince who has departed for Paradise.

P بهشت گنگ *bihisht-gang,* Name of a city.

P بهشت نشين *bihisht-nishīn,* (Settled in Paradise) Blessed.

P بهشته *bahishta,* Placed, deposited. Left.

P بهشتي *bihishtī,* Paradisiacal. Handsome. A water-carrier. (The last is Hindustāni).

P به شدگي *bih-shudagī,* Cure, convalescence.

P به شده *bih-shuda,* Cured, healed.

A بهشمية *bahshamīyat,* A Muhammadan sect.

A بهص *bahas,* Thirst.

A بهصل *buhsul,* Thick in body. White.

A بهصلة *bahsalat,* (v.n. of بهصل Q) Stripping off one's clothes and staking them at dice. Eating flesh upon the bone stripped off every part. Ejecting (people) from (their) possessions. Very white (female). Short (woman). *Buhsulat,* (fem.) Short. Clamorous. Intensely white.

A بهصم *buhsum,* Hard, firm.

A بهصوص *buhsūs,* Something, any thing.

A بهض *bahz,* An afflicting, vexing, fatiguing.

H بهطّ *bahatt,* Rice dressed with milk and butter.

A بهظ *bahz,* (v. n. of بهظ) Afflicting, vexing, fatiguing, tiring. Being above one's strength or ability (any thing heavy or oppressive). Catching by the beard. Weighing down (debt).

P بهفت آب شستن *ba haft āb shustan,* (To wash with seven waters) To perform one's ablutions with great nicety and circumspection.

A بهق *bahak,* (P بهك *bahak*) Leprosy, white morphew (distinct from برص *baras*). Ringworm. بهق الحجر *bahaku'l hajar,* Lichen. Sandix-gum. *Bahih,* Afflicted with tetter or ringworm.

A بهكثة *bahkasat,* Quickness, expedition.

A بهكل *bahkal,* (fem. بهكلة *bahkalat*) (or بهكن *bahkan*) (fem. بهكنة *bahkanat*) Full of health and juices, smooth, sleek, shining (young person, animal).

P به گزين *bih-guzīn,* Choosing, picking; discriminating easily between good and bad money. Select, chosen. Camphor.

A بهل *bahl,* (v. n. of بهل) Leaving any one at liberty to do what he pleases, free from every impediment. Cursing, execrating any one (God). A curse. Freedom from marks of a nose-ring, or of the machine for preventing sucking (in a she-camel). A little, small quantity, somewhat. *Buhl,* (or بهّل *buhhal*) (pl. of باهل *bāhil*) She-camels having no marks of a ring through the nose, or of the wooden machines which they usually fasten to their udders to prevent colts from sucking. *Bahal,* (v. n. of بهل) Being left at full liberty to be sucked by her colt (a she-camel).

A بهلا *bahlan,* Fair and softly! give a little time!

P بهل *bihil,* Let alone, give over. Absolution.

A بهلة *bahlat* or *buhlat,* A malediction, anathema.

A بهلق *bahlak,* A great misfortune or calamity. *Bihlik, bahlak,* or *buhluk,* A ruddy woman. Chattering, talkative (woman), without mind or intellect. *Bihlik,* A bawler. A discontented morose man.

A بهلقا *bihlikan* or *bihlakan,* (Saying any thing) openly, to one's face.

A بهلقة *bahlakat,* Pride, vanity. Traducing, railing, scolding, abusing. Vain boasting. A misfortune, evil, calamity. Lying, a lie.

A ضلال بن بهلل و بهلل *zalālu'bnu bahlala, wa buhlula,* A lying, trifling, idle fellow.

A بهلول *buhlūl,* One who laughs or smiles. A prince with every accomplishment. Name of a man.

P بهله *bahla,* A falconer's glove. Privy purse.

A بهم *bahm* or *baham,* Lambs, kids, and calves, comprehended in one flock. *Buhm* or *buhum,* (pl. of ابهم *abham*) Dumb. Naked, empty. Free from blemish, sound, whole, entire. حفاة عراة بهما *hufātan ʻurātan buhman,* (On the resurrection-morn mankind will be raised) barefooted, naked, (and) free from blemishes (such as lameness, leprosy, &c.). (pl. of بهيم *bahīm*) Animals of one colour. *Buham,* (pl. of بهمة *buhmat*) Rocks, stones. Brave, invincible soldiers, gallant heroes. Troops of horse. Arduous affairs.

P بهم *ba ham,* Together, one with another, one against another. At once. Rage, anger, indignation. بهم آمدن *ba ham āmadan,* (or بهم برآمدن *ba ham bar āmadan,* To be contracted, drawn together. To assemble. To be constipated, bound. To be offended, enraged, disgusted, vexed, confounded. To be wrung with anguish. بهم بر كردن *ba ham bar kardan,* To distress. بهم در شدن *ba ham dar shudan,* To be mixed, confounded, jumbled together. دل بهم در آمدن *dil ba ham bar āmadan,* To have a pain at the heart. To be disturbed or perplexed. بهم رسيدن *ba ham rasīdan,* To be met with, to come to hand, to be acquired. To appear, to come into being. *Bi ham,* Yes.

A بهماة *buhmāt,* A single plant بهمي *buhma'.*

P بهمار *bahmār,* Many, numerous. A multitude.

P بهم آميختگي *ba ham āmekhtagī,* Commixture.

P بهمان *bihmān,* Some one, a certain person. Any thing unknown.

P بهم بر بسته *baham bar basta,* Suspicious. Suspected. Suspicion.

P بهم برزدن *ba ham bar zadan,* To be hasty.

A بهمة *bahmat,* A lamb. *Buhmat,* (pl. بهم *buham*) A rock, a stone. A brave invincible soldier. A difficult, arduous affair. A troop of horse. An army. *Bahimat,* (Ground) abounding in the wild herb بهمي *buhma'.*

P بهمتان *bahmatān,* A white lily. A red lily.

P بهم رسانيدن *ba ham rasānīdan,* To procure.

P بهم زده *ba ham zada,* Overturned, overwhelmed. Dejected.

P بهمزگ *bahmazag,* A hedgehog. A porcupine.

P بهم سائي *baham sāʼī,* Confrication.

P بهمن *bahman,* Intelligent, acute, adroit. The supreme intelligence. A cloud pouring rain. An avalanche of snow from a mountain produced by the heat of the sun. A certain vegetable that flowers in winter, having a root red and white. Name of a note in music. The middle month of winter, answering to our January. One who speaks and acts right. The second day of every month. Long-armed, powerful, oppressive. Name of a demon or genius, supposed by the old Persians, and by their descendants the Parsī, Magi, or Guebres, to preside over all beasts of burden. Name of Ardshīr, son of Isfandiyār. Name of a citadel and of a lofty mountain. Name of a fountain in Jurjān. بهمن زمان و تهمتن دوران *bahmani zamān u tahamtani dawrān,* The monarch of his time, the hero of his age.

A بهمن *bahman,* The root of a plant resembling a large radish. It is crooked, red and white, and is used medicinally.

P بهمنچه *bahmancha,* (or بهمنجنه *bahmanjana*) Name of a festival celebrated by the kings of Persia upon the second day of the month of Bahman.

P بهمنيار *bahmanyār,* A disciple of Avicenna.

P بهمنين *bahmanīn,* Name of a plant which flowers in winter, and whose root is red and white.

P بهمه *buhma,* Of inestimable value. Invincible.

A بهمي *buhma',* Name of a plant.

A بهن *bahan,* The being cheerful and joyous.

A بهنانة *bahnānat,* A woman smelling sweetly, particularly in the breath; also one gentle and placid, who laughs and smiles.

P بهنانه *bahnāna,* An ape. *Bihnāna,* White bread.

A بهنس *bahnas,* A camel, gentle and tractable. Fat and heavy. A lion.

P به نسبت *ba nisbat,* In proportion, comparison.

A بهنسة *bahnasat,* (v. n. of بهنس Q) Walking haughtily and stately like a lion.

P بهنه *bahna,* A boy's whipping-top.

P بهو *bahw,* A balcony. A portico, a veranda.

A بهو *bahw,* (pl. ابهاء *abhāʼ,* بهوّ *buhūw,* or بهيّ *buhīy*) A house or tent projecting in front of the rest, and detached. A wild bull's den or retreat, of the largest size; also a large stable for tame cattle. (pl. ابهاء *abhāʼ,* ابهى *abhī,* بهيّ *bihīy,* and *buhīy*) A wide extended country. Any thing large. Broad-headed (cow). The cavity of the breast. The space between the breasts and the throat. The place between the haunches, the womb.

A بهوء *buhūʼ,* (v. n. of بهأ) Being accustomed.

A بهوت *bahūt*, (pl. بهت *buht* and بهوت *buhūt*) A great inventor of lies.

P بهود *buhod*, Cloth singed, and having a yellow appearance.

A بهور *bahwar*, A lion. *Buhūr*, (v. n. of بهر) Being distinguished for any perfection. Shining, excelling in brightness (as the moon among the stars).

P بهور *buhūr*, The eye, the sight.

A بهوص *buhūs*, Somewhat, any thing.

A بهوغ *buhūgh*, A going to sleep. Sleep.

A بهونيّ *bahwaniy*, A camel betwixt a كرمانيّ *karmāniy* and and عربيّ *ɛarabiy*.

A بهي *bihy*, (v. n. of بهي) Being empty and deserted (a house).

P بهي *bihī*, Recovery, cure. Thou art good. Goodness. A quince. O! (an interjection, when the person addressed is near at hand).

A بهيّ *bahīy*, Beautiful, elegant, graceful. Dear, precious. *Buhīy*, (pl. of بهو *bahw*) Houses or tents projecting beyond the rest. Wild bulls' dens of the largest size. *Buhīy* or *bihīy*, (pl. of بهو *bahw*) Extensive countries. Cavities of breasts. Wombs.

A بهيّة *bahīyat*, (fem.) Beautiful. Precious. هديّهٔ بهيّه *hadiyaɛi bahīya*, A valuable present. هداياي لائقهٔ بهيّه *hadāyāɛi lāɛikaɛi bahīya*, Rich and suitable presents.

A بهيتة *bahītat*, A false imputation, a gross lie.

A بهيج *bahīj*, Glad, cheerful. Beautiful, lovely.

P بهيد *bahīd*, Name of a grain.

P بهيدن *bahīdan*, To squeeze, grasp with the hands, to press with the feet, to kick, to trample.

P بهير *bahīr*, Baggage, camp-followers.

A بهير *bahīr*, Breathing hard, fatigued. A corpulent woman, who can hardly breathe when walking.

P بهيرا *baherā*, Belleric myrobalan.

A بهيرة *bahīrat*, A woman of a slender shape, beautiful and delicate. A woman of distinction.

A بهيصل *buhaysil*, Weak, bad, naught.

A بهيلة *bahīlat*, Free (woman), one of distinction, who has a high dowry.

P بهيم *bahīm*, A balcony, portico.

A بهيم *bahīm*, (pl. بهم *buhum*) (A horse) of one colour, without any distinguishing mark. Black. Dark. A black sheep. Wholly unknown. Giving little or no sound, an almost imperceptible echo, a heavy dull tone. Sincere, unmixed, without mark or blemish. Excellent, incomparable.

A بهيمة *bahīmat*, (pl. بهائم *bahāɛim*) A quadruped, an animal wild or tame. A lamb, calf, kid. The infernal pit.

A بهيميّ *bahīmiy*, Brutal, bestial, brutish.

P بهين *bihīn*, Better, best. Selected, picked out. Opulence. A cotton-carder. A week. مهين سلاطين روي زمين و بهين خواقين دنيا و دين *mihīni salātīni rūyi zamīn, u bihīni khawākīni dunya' u dīn*, The greatest of the kings of the earth, and most excellent of the monarchs of the world and the faith.

A بهينس *buhaynis*, A lion.

P بهينه *bihīna*, A week. A carder of cotton. Best, choicest.

P بي *bī* or *be*, (A privative particle or preposition) Without. When prefixed to nouns, it is equivalent to *in*, *un*, *im*, *ir*, *less*, &c., in English, implying wanting, or being destitute: as, بيبصر *bī basar*, Imprudent. بيبقا *bī bakā*, Inconstant. بيبهره *bī bahra*, Unfortunate. بي پروا *bī parwā*, Heedless, fearless. بي ترتيب *bī tartīb*, Irregular; with many others, which will be found in alphabetical order. A moth.

A بيّ *bayy*, (v. n. of بوي) Imitating, mimicking. A mean, wretched, abject man. ابن بيّ *ibnu bayyin* or هيّ بن بيّ *hayyu bnu bayyin*, One of the sons of Adam who, at the dispersion of the family, went no one knows where and was never heard of.

P بيا *bayā*, Full. A door. *Biyā*, (imp. of آمدن *āmadan*) Come, come hither, approach.

P بي آب *bī āb*, Without water. Flat, insipid, dull. Sottish, silly. Disgraced, ashamed. بي آب شدن *bī āb shudan*, To be ashamed, disgraced.

A بيّاب *bayyāb*, A cup-bearer, one who presents water publicly (giving drink gratis, which is done from motives of piety). One who sells water about the streets.

P بيابان *biyābān*, Uncultivated, desert: a desert.

P بيابان باش *biyābān-bāsh*, An inhabitant of the desert. تازيان بيابان باش *tāziyāni biyābān-bāsh*, Bedouin Arabs.

P بيابان نشين *biyābān-nishīn*, A hermit: a gipsy.

P بيابان نورد *biyābān-naward*, Travelling in the desert.

P بياباني *biyābānī*, Wild, savage, desert, scenite.

A بيابانيّات *bayābānīyāt*, Stars which lie out of the track of the sun and moon.

P بي ابر *bī abr*, Cloudless.

P بي آبرو *bī ābrū*, Dishonoured, disgraced, degraded. Shameless.

P بي آبروي *bī ābrūī*, A disagreeable thing.

P بي آبي *bī ābī*, Want of water. Want of lustre. Insipidity. Folly.

P بيات *bayāt*, Grief, anxiety, care.

A بيات *bayāt*, (v. n. of بات for بيت) Passing the night. Doing any thing in the night. A nocturnal invasion, a hostile surprise by night.

A بياتا *bayātan*, By night. Nightly.

P بي اتفاق *bī ittifāk*, Without union, discordant.

P بي اثر *bī asar*, Unimpressive, inefficacious.

A بياح *biyāh*, (or بيّاح *bayyāh*) A species of fish.

A بيّاحة *bayyāhat*, A fishing-net.

P بياحتياط *bī ihtiyāt*, Heedless, uncircumspect.

P بياختيار *bī ikhtiyār*, Involuntary, forced, constrained. Without self-possession or controul.

P بياختيارانه *bī ikhtiyārāna*, Unwillingly; forced, compelled.

P بي اختياري *bī ikhtiyārī*, Helplessness.

P بي اخلاصي *bī ikhlāsī*, Unfriendliness.

A بياد *bayād*, A being separated, cut off.

P بياد *biyād*, Watchfulness, vigilance.

P بيادب *bī adab*, Uncivil, rude, ill-mannered.

P بيادبانه *bī adabāna*, Rudely, disrespectfully, indecently. Uncivil. بيادبانه وضع *bī adabāna waze*, An indecent, unbecoming action.

P بي ادبي *bī adabī*, Ill-breeding, rudeness, incivility. Presumption.

P بيادراك *bī idrāk*, Without understanding. Unintelligent.

A بيادقة *bayādikat*, (pl. of بيدق) Pawns at chess.

A بياذق *bayāzik*, (pl. of بيذق *bayzak*) Road-guides. Foot-soldiers. Pawns at chess.

A بياذقة *bayāzikat*, Men on foot. Pawns at chess.

A بئار *biɛār*, (pl. of بئر *biɛr*) Wells.

P بيار *biyār*, (imp. of آوردن *āwardan*) Bring thou.

P بياراستن *biyārāstan*, To adorn. To invent a fiction, to lie.

P بيارام *bī ārām*, Restless, unquiet, having no repose, in perpetual disquietude. بي آرام وبي قرار *bī ārām u bī karār*, Restless and inconstant.

P بي آرامي *bī ārāmī*, Restlessness.

P بيارش *bayārish*, Regimen, cure.

A بيارق *bayārik*, (Arab. pl. of بيرق.) Flags.

P بيارکان *bī arkān*, Immodest, uncivil, ill-bred.

A بيارون *bayārūn*, The root of the lot-tree.

P بياره *bayāra*, Any plant whose stalk does not grow erect, as cucumbers, melons, or pumpkins.

P بي آزار *bī āzār*, Innoxious, harmless, inoffensive.

A بيازر *bayāzir*, (pl. of بيزر *bayzar*) Fullers' beetles. Thick clubs.

A بيازرة *bayāzirat*, (pl. of بيزار *bayzār*) Falconers. Labourers, ploughmen.

P بي آزرم *bī āzarm*, Shameless, brazen-faced.

A بيأس *bayɛas*, Strong, bold. A lion. عذاب بيأس *ɛazābun bayɛasun*, A severe torment.

A بيّاس *bayyās*, Bais, a maritime town near Antioch in Syria.

P بي استحضار *bī istihzār*, Unpremeditated.

P بياستحقاق *bī istihkāk*, Unjustly, undeservedly.

P بياستو *biyāstū*, Yawning. Fetid breath.

A بياسرة *bayāsirat*, (pl. of بيسريّ *baysariy*) Baysarians, a people in Scinde, hired to fight by commanders of ships.

P بي اشتباه *bī ishtibāh*, Undoubtedly. True.

P بياشفاق *bī ishfāk*, Merciless, ruthless. Impious.

P بياصل *bī asl*, Unfounded. Causeless. Ignoble, mean. The offspring of a free father and a slave mother. Unprincipled.

A بياض *bayāz*, Whiteness. Milk. Paper. Leprosy. A common-place book. بياض البيض *bayāzu'l bayz*, The white of an egg. بياض العين *bayāzu'l ɛayn*, A white speck on the eye. بياض اليوم *bayāzu'l yawm*, The whole day (as long as the light continues). P بياض خور *bayāzi khwur*, A sun-beam. Day.

A بياضة *bayāzat*, Whiteness. Brightness, splendour.

A بياضي *bayāzī*, An elegant poem.

A بياطرة *bayātirat*, (pl. of بيطار *baytār*) Veterinary surgeons.

P بي اطلاع *bī ittilāع*, Uninformed, ignorant.

A بيّاع *bayyāع*, A seller. A broker. An appraiser. An auctioneer.

A بياعة *biyāعat*, Merchandize, goods. Commerce.

P بياعتبار *bī iعtibār*, Contemptible, disesteemed.

P بي اعتباري *bī iعtibārī*, Disesteem.

P بي اعتدالي *bī iعtidālī*, Injustice. Inequality.

P بياغاريد *biyāghārīd*, Steeped in water or blood.

P بياغاريدن *biyāghārīdan*, To steep, soak: to mix.

P بياغاشتن *biyāghāshtan*, (or بياغشتن *biyā ghashtan*) To steep, soak. To mix.

P بياغاليدن *biyāghālīdan*, To stir up strife.

P بياقران *bī akrān*, Peerless, matchless.

P بياگاه *bī āgāh*, Ignorant, uninformed. Unlooked-for. Careless, thoughtless, forgetful.

P بي آگاهي *bī āgāhī*, Carelessness, thoughtlessness, forgetfulness. Want of information.

P بي آگهي *bī āgahī*, Unexpectedly.

P بيالبان *biyālbān*, The language and characters which, according to Eastern tradition, were peculiar to those beings, whom they suppose to have inhabited the world before the creation of man.

P بي التفاتي *bī iltifātī*, Incivility.

P بي امان *bī amān*, Merciless, pitiless, unrelenting, unsparing. همچو زمان بيامان بلا امهال *hamchu zamāni bī amāni bilā imhāl*, Like unrelenting time (giving) no delay.

P بيامتياز *bī imtiyāz*, Undiscerning. Ill-bred, rude.

P بيامدن *biyāmadan*, To enter. To come.

P بي املا *bī imlā*, Incorrect, unorthographical.

P بي آميختگي *bī āmekhtagī*, Freedom from admixture.

P بيآميختن *biyāmekhtan*, To mix, to mingle.

P بي آميغ *bī āmegh*, Unmixed.

P بيان *bayān*, A species of tiger.

A بيان *bayān*, (v. n. of بان for بين) Being clear, distinct, manifest. Speaking clearly and distinctly. Being eloquent. A relation, explanation, declaration, exposition, evidence, proof, or illustration. Eloquence. A section, division of a chapter. سحر البيان *sihru'l bayān*, The magic of eloquence. P بيان كردن *bayān kardan*, To explain, demonstrate, elucidate, comment upon, illustrate, declare, to render clear, evident, manifest. To relate.

A بيّان *bayyān*, Vile, abject. Name of a place. ابن بيّان or هيّان بن بيّان *ibnu bayyāna* or *hayyānu'bnu bayyān*, An unknown son of an unknown father. ابو علي بن بيّان *abū عaliy bin bayyān*, Name of a certain holy man.

P بيانان *bayānān*, Name of a contemptible race.

A بيانانيّات *bayānānīyāt*, Certain stars lying out of the track of the sun or moon.

P بيانتها *bī intihā*, Immense, infinite, boundless.

P بيانجام *bī anjām*, Infinite, boundless, endless.

P بياندازه *bī andāza*, Immense, immeasurable.

P بي اندام *bī andām*, Out of proportion.

P بياندامي *bī andāmī*, Disproportionateness.

P بي انصافي *bī insāfī*, Injustice.

P بي انفعال *bī infiعāl*, Shameless.

P بيانك *biyānah*, A reed whence mats are made.

P بيانوار *bayānwār*, Explanation, detail of items.

P بيانه *bayāna*, A town in India, whence indigo is brought. *Biyāna*, An earnest, advance, pledge.

A بيانيّ *bayāniy*, Explanatory.

P بياوار *bayāwār*, Work, business, employ.

P بياوان *biyāwān*, A desert, solitude.

P بياور *bayāwar*, Gain, profit.

P بياوردن *biyāwardan*, To contract (as the joints or muscles). To become irritated, to grow worse (a wound). To bring.

P بياه *biyāh*, Name of a river in Lahore.

P بياهنگ *bī āhang*, Dissonant, discrepant, discordant. Unprepared, without proper apparatus.

P بياهنگي *bī āhangī*, Discord.

P بي ايمان *bī īmān*, Without religion, or faith.

A بيب *bīb*, A canal: pipe or conduit of a cistern.

P بيباعث *bī bāعis*, Without cause or reason, why or wherefore.

P بيباق *bī bāk*, (for بيباقي *bī bākī*) Complete, entire.

P بيباقي *bī bākī*, Without a balance, quits. Completion.

P بيباك *bī bāk*, Fearless, intrepid, bold. Impudent. بي باك خرام *bī bāk khirām*, Walking fearlessly, treading firmly.

P بي باكانه *bī bākāna*, Fearlessly, impudently.

P بيباكي *bī bākī*, Fearlessness. Frowardness, sauciness, impudence.

A بيبان *bībān*, (pl. of باب) Doors. Chapters.

P بيبد *bī bad*, Without blemish, faultless.

P بيبدل *bī badal*, Without equivalent: matchless.

P بيبر *bī bar*, Without fruit. Barren, fruitless.

P بي برگ و بر *bī barg u bar*, Barren. Poor.

P بي برگي *bī bargī*, Destitution, poverty.

P بيبس *bī bas*, Helpless. Uncontrolled.

P بيبصر *bī basar*, Sightless, blind. Without foresight. Improvident, imprudent.

P بي بصيرت *bī basīrat*, Blind, ignorant.

P بيبقا *bī bakā*, Unstable, frail, transient.

P بيبل *bī bal*, Weak, wretched, poor.

P بي بند *bī band*, Insecure, not secured. Unfettered. بي بند و بست *bī band u bast*, Unsettled (as a country).

P بي بها *bī bahā*, Invaluable, inestimable.

P بيبهار *bī bahār*, Out of season, inopportune.

P بيبهره *bī bahra*, Destitute, indigent, deprived. Unfortunate, out of favour. چهرهٔ بيبهره *chihraʼi bī bahra*, An unlucky, disagreeable countenance.

P بيبي *bībī*, A lady, a matron. (It is particularly applied by the Persians to those whom they mean to honour: they therefore call the Virgin Mary Bībī Maryam, which implies The Lady Mary).

P بيپايان *bī pāyān*, Immense, infinite, endless.

P بيپدر *bī pidar*, Fatherless. An orphan.

P بي پر و بال *bī par u bāl*, Mutilated, destitute, without feather or wing. Without resource.

P بي پردگي *bī pardagī*, Disgrace, dishonour.

P بيپرده *bī parda*, Without veil; open, exposed.

P بيپروا *bī parwā*, Without fear, scruple, or reflection. Intrepid. بيپروا شدن *bī parwā shudan*, To be bold, to have no fear or hesitation.

P بي پروائي *bī parwāʼī*, Carelessness, thoughtlessness, inattention, independence, indifference.

P بيپرهيز *bī parhez*, Incontinent, dissolute. Incautious. Inattentive to medical advice.

P بيپرهيزي *bī parhezī*, Incontinence. Indifference to, carelessness about, one's health.

P بي پژمان *bī pajmān*, Intimate, familiar.

P بي پژماني *bī pajmānī*, Intimacy, familiarity. Freedom from melancholy, sadness, or fear.

P بي پژماي *bī pajmāy*, High-spirited. Cheerful.

P بي پير *bī pīr*, Without spiritual guide; vicious.

P بي پيرايگي *bī perāyagī*, Absence of ornament.

P بي پيرايه *bī perāya*, Unadorned (woman).

A بثّة *biʼat*, The plague.

A بيت *bayt*, (pl. بيوت *buyūt*) A house, temple, edifice, fabric. A citadel. The Kaaba. A family, domestics. Marriage, wedlock. The floor or pavement of a house. A grave, a tomb. (pl. ابيات *abyāt*) A distich, verse, couplet. Noble. Nobility. بيت الله *baytu'llāh*, بيت الحرام *baytu'l harām*, or بيت العتيق *baytu'l عatīk*, (or رحم *ruhm*) The house of God, the sacred temple, the ancient fabric, the temple of Mecca. بيت الحمد *baytu'l hamd*, A temple. بيت الخلا *baytu'l khalā*, A privy. بيت السرّ *baytu's sirr*, The cabinet of secrets. بيت السقر *baytu's sakar*, Hell. بيت الشرف *baytu'sh sharaf*, A sign of the zodiac. The highest mansion of a planet. بيت الشعر *baytu'sh shaعr*, A tent composed of felt or hair, used by the Arabs. بيت الشمس *baytu'sh shams*, Heliopolis. بيت عنكبوت *bayti عankabūt*, A spider's web. بيت لحم *bayt laham*, Bethlehem. بيت ما *bayti mā* or بيت الفراغ *baytu'l farāgh*, A water-closet. بيت المال *baytu'l māl*, The treasury. The effects of one who dies intestate or without heirs (perhaps a corruption of بي تن مال *bī tan māl*). خزانهٔ بيت المال *khizānaʼi bayti'l māl*, The royal treasury, the public revenues. بيت المعمور *baytu'l maعmūr*, The heavenly temple (*i.e.* Mecca, being built in imitation of the vault of heaven). The seventh heaven. بيت معمور شريعت *bayti maعmūri sharīعat*, The tabernacle of justice. بيت المقدّس *baytu'l mukaddas*, Jerusalem. بيت الملك *baytu'l malik*, The king's palace. P بيت شهريار *bayti shahr-yār*, The royal palace. A *Bayt*, (v. n. of بات for بيت) Passing the night. Doing any thing in the night. *Bit*, (or بيتة *bītat*) Provisions, victuals of every kind. بيت ليلة *bīt laylat*, Provisions for one night or day.

P بي تا *bī tā*, Without a wrinkle; beautiful.

P بيتا *bītā*, (in zand and Pāzand) A house.

P بيتاب *bī tāb*, Impotent, feeble, faint. Impatient, restless. بي تاب و توان كردن *bī tāb u tawān kardan*, To debilitate or render impotent.

P بيتابانه *bī tābāna*, Instantly. Voluntarily.

P بي تابي *bī tābī*, Impatience. Inability.

P بيتال *bītāl*, Out of time. Ill-timed.

P بي تأمّل *bī taʼammul*, Inconsiderate. Thoughtlessly, without consideration or reflexion.

P بيتان *bītān*, Out of tune.

P بيتانه *bītāna*, (in zand and Pāz.) A stranger.

P بيت بيت *bayta bayta*, From house to house. فلان جاري بيت بيت *fulānun jārī bayta bayta*, Such an one is my next-door neighbour.

A بيتة *bītat*, A night's lodging. Food, victuals.

P بي تحاشا *bī tahāshā*, Rash, precipitate.

P بي تحاشي *bī tahāshī*, Fearlessness, rashness.

P بي تدبير *bī tadbīr*, Incautious, unwitting, inconsiderate, improvident.

P بيترتيب *bī tartīb*, Irregular. Disorderly.

P بي تردّد *bī taraddud*, Unhesitating.

P بي تشويش *bī tashwīsh*, Without mixture, pure.

P بي تعلق *bī taʻalluk*, Independent.

P بي تعلقي *bī taʻalluḳī*, Independence, freedom.

P بي تقريب *bī taḳrīb*, Without cause, without apparent motive or reason. بي تقريب و بي وقت *bī taḳrīb u bī waḳt*, Absurd and ill-timed.

P بي تقصير *bī taḳsīr*, Without defect, or fail.

P بي تكلف *bī takalluf*, Without ceremony, or compliment. Abruptly. Inconsiderately. All at once.

P بي تميز *bī tamīz*, Undiscerning, injudicious.

P بي تميزي *bī tamīzī*, Want of judgment and discrimination.

P بي تمييز *bī tamyīz*, Undiscerning. Indiscreet. Unpolite.

A بيتوتة *baytūtat*, (v.n. of بات for بيت) Passing the night. Doing any thing during the night.

P بي توزكانه *bī tūzakāna*, Contrary to custom; irregular.

P بي توشگي *bī toshagī*, Scarcity of provisions.

P بي توشة *bī tosha*, Unprovided, poor, helpless.

P بي توفيق *bī tawfīḳ*, Graceless, destitute of the directing grace of God.

P بي توقف *bī tawaḳḳuf*, Without delay.

P بي ته *bī tah*, Impatiently. Without a vestige. Bottomless.

A بيتيّ *baytiy*, Pertaining to a house, domestic.

P بي تيمار *bī tīmār*, Unwatched, untended, unguarded, neglected, uncared for.

A بيث (تركهم حيث *tarakahum haysa*) *baysa*, He left them dispersed here and there.

P بيجا *bī jā*, Out of place, unseasonable, wrong.

P بيجاپور *bījāpūr*, Name of a city in India.

P بيجاد *bejād*, (or بيجادة *bejāda*) Amber. A stone resembling a ruby.

A بيجادق *bayjādaḳ*, (Ar. of P. بيجادة *bejāda*) A stone resembling a ruby.

P بيجادة آب *bejāda-āb*, Red, or yellow-coloured. Wine. بيجادة شدن *bejāda shudan*, To become yellow. To err.

P بيجادة گون تيغ *bejāda-gūn-tegh*, Bloody sword.

P بيجادة لب *bejāda-lab*, Red or coral-lipped.

P بيجادة مذاب *bejāda-muzāb*, Blood. Red wine. Saffron-coloured wine.

P بيجان *bī jān*, Lifeless. Faint. Valiant.

P بيجرم *bī jurm*, Faultless, innocent.

P بيجك *bījak*, An invoice, a list.

P بيجگر *bī jigar*, Timid, chicken-hearted.

P بي جمالي *bī jamālī*, Want of beauty, homeliness.

P بيجواب *bī jawāb*, Unable to reply, speechless.

P بيجوهر *bī jawhar*, Unskilful, ignorant.

P بيچارگان *bī chāragān*, The helpless, unfortunate.

P بيچارگي *bī chāragī*, Helplessness, necessity.

P بيچارة *bī chāra*, Without remedy. Remediless, hopeless. Helpless, destitute, desperate, miserable, reduced to the last extremity.

P بيچال *bī chāl*, Unprincipled.

P بيچالي *bī chālī*, Misdemeanour, ill-behaviour.

P بي چراغ *bī charāgh*, Without lamp or light; depopulated. A desolated, unpeopled village.

P بيچند *bīchand*, A tree.

P بيچوبة *bī chūba*, A small tent without poles.

P بيچون *bī chūn*, Incomparable, unparalled. Unscrutable, inexplicable. Pure, eternal, divine (one of the attributes of God). حضرت خالق پروردگار بيچون *hazrati khālik parwardagāri bī chūn*, The omnipotent Creator, ineffable, inscrutable.

P بي چوني *bī chūnī*, Matchlessness, incomparableness (an attribute of God).

P بيچه *baycha*, A peculiar kind of roof which contributes much to the comfort of a winter habitation.

P بيچيز *bī chīz*, Poor, possessed of nothing.

P بيچيزي *bī chīzī*, Poverty, destitution.

P بيحارژون *bīhārjūn*, Delicate food.

P بي حاصل *bī hāsil*, Fruitless, unprofitable, barren.

P بيحاصلي *bī hāsilī*, Unprofitableness.

P بيحال *bī hāl*, Ill-circumstanced.

A بيحان *bayhān*, (or بيّحان *bayyahān*) One who reveals his secrets. Name of a man who was founder of an Arabian tribe; whence certain camels are denominated بيحانية *bayhāniya*.

P بيحجاب *bī hijāb*, Unveiled. Immodest.

P بيحدّ *bī hadd*, Boundless, immense, unbounded, infinite. Immensely. بي حدّ وشمار *bī hadd u shumār*, Infinite and innumerable.

P بيحرمت *bī hurmat*, Disgraced, debased.

P بيحرمتي *bī hurmatī*, Disgrace.

P بيحس *bī hiss*, Destitute of feeling, insensible.

P بيحساب *bī hisāb*, Countless. Inconsistent.

P بي حضور *bī huzūr*, Absent, inattentive. Disturbed. Offended, irritated, enraged. بيحضور شدن *bī huzūr shudan*, To be confused, irritated. بيحضور كردن *bī huzūr kardan*, To molest, to trouble.

P بيحضوري *bī huzūrī*, Disquietude. Anger. Inattention, a want of presence of mind.

P بي حفاظ *bī hifāz*, Impudent, indelicate.

P بيحقيقت *bī haḳīḳat*, Insincere. Ungrateful. Insincerely.

P بيحكمت *bī hikmat*, Unskilful.

P بي حلم *bī hilm*, Merciless, severe, inclement.

P بي حلمي *bī hilmī*, Severity, inclemency.

P بيحميّت *bī hamīyat*, Spiritless, dastardly, having no sense of honour.

P بيحميّتي *bī hamīyatī*, Want of zeal or spirit.

P بيحواس *bī hawāss*, Bereft of sense.

P بيحيا *bī hayā*, Impudent, shameless.

P بيحيائي *bī hayāʼī*, Impudence, effrontery.

P بيخ *bekh*, A root, origin. Base, foundation. Origin. بيخ كوهي *bekhi kohī*, Fennel. بيخ انجبار *bekhi anjabār*, Bistort of snake-weed (an herb). بيخ پشم *bekhi pashm*, Flesh. بيخ كندن *bekh kandan*, To uproot. بيخ گل عبّاس *bekhi guli ʻabbās*, Jalap.

P بيخار *bī khār*, Without thorn, fear, or anxiety.

P بيخانمان *bī khānmān*, Without a domicile; a traveller.

P بيخاور *bekh-āwar*, Having many roots. Ivy.

P بيخايب *bī khāyib*, Wakefulness, sleeplessness.

P بيخايه *bī khāya*, Without a testicle; a eunuch.

P بيخبر *bī khabar*, Ignorant, uninformed. Incautious. بي خبر شدن *bī khabar shudan*, To be unacquainted with, to have no information of.

P بيخبري *bī khabarī*, Ignorance. Imprudence.

P بيختن *bekhtan*, To sift. To enslave. To render impotent, deprive of motion. To become weak.

P بي ختنه *bī khutna*, Uncircumcised. بي ختنه مانده *bī khutna-mānda*, Left uncircumcised. بي ختنه ماندگي *bī khutna māndagī*, A being left, or a remaining uncircumcised: uncircumcision.

P بيخرد *bī khirad*, Destitute of judgment, dull.

P بيخرو خاوند *bī khar u khāwind*, Without master or owner.

P بيخزان *bī khizān*, Perennial.

P بيخستن *bīkhastan*, To be unfortunate and destitute. To be enfeebled. To take prisoner.

P بيخسته *bīkhasta*, Unfortunate, destitute. Captive. A prisoner.

P بيخشت *baykhusht*, A tree torn up by the roots.

P بيخطر *bī khatar*, Free from danger; safe.

P بيخ كن *bekh-kan*, Tearing up by the roots. A judge (as extirpating thieves), a marauder (as destroying the subjects).

P بيخ كني *bekh-kanī*, Eradication, uprooting.

P بي خميرمايه *bī khamīr māya*, Unleavened.

P بيخوابي *bī khwābī*, Wakefulness, sleeplessness.

P بيخواني *bī khwānī*, Flavourless. Insipidity.

P بيخواهش *bī-khwāhish*, Without inclination or spirit; without pursuit, object, or hobby-horse.

P بيخود bī khwud, Out of his senses, beyond himself, in ecstasy, enraptured, mad, insane.

P بيخودي bī khwudī, Ecstasy, rapture: madness.

P بيخور و خواب bī khwur u khwāb, Disinclined to eat or sleep.

P بيخوف bī khawf, Fearless of danger.

P بيخوفي bī khawfī, Fearlessness. Security, unconsciousness of danger.

P بيخويش bī khwesh, (or بيخويشتن bī khweshtan) Friendlessness. Mad, insane.

P بيخه bīkha, Weak, impotent, feeble, frail.

P بي خيله bī khīla, Purslain.

A بيد bayd, (v. n. of باد for بيد) Perishing. Being separated from one's kindred. Noxious, unwholesome (meat). *Bayda*, Besides, except, unless. Because. بيد ان bayda an, Except that. بيد انه bayda annahu, Except that he. *Bīd*, (pl. of بيداء baydā,) Deserts.

P بيد bīd or bed, A willow: rattan. A mouse. A moth which eats books or woollen cloths. Useless, unprofitable. Name of an evil spirit. (for بويد buvīd and باشيد bāshīd) May ye be! بيدوش لرزان bīdwash larzān, Trembling like the aspen. بيد خام bīdi khām, A green branch. بيد سرخ bīdi surkh, (or بيد طبري bīdi tabarī) A species of willow. بيد مجنون bīdi majnūn, The weeping willow. بيد مشك bīdi mushk, A tree from which perfume is drawn. *Bed*, The Vedas, or scriptures of the Hindūs. Knowledge.

A بيداء baydā, (pl. بيد bīd) A desert, an uninhabited dengerous region. Name of a flat and extensive tract between Mecca and Madīna.

P بيداد bī dād, Injustice. Unjust, iniquitous. Name of a city in Turkistān.

P بيدادگر bīdādgar, A tyrant, an oppressor.

P بيدادي bīdādī, Injustice, lawlessness, tyranny.

P بيدار bīdār, Awake, waking: wakeful, attentive. Play, sport. بيدار داشتن bīdār dāshtan, To keep awake. بيدار شدن bīdār shudan, To awake from sleep. To be vigilant, alert, attentive. بيدار كردن bīdār kardan, To awake, to rouse.

P بيداربخت bīdār-bakht, Of wakeful fortune.

P بيداردل bīdār-dil, Vigilant, alert, quick, sharp.

P بيداردلي bīdār-dilī, Alertness, quickness.

P بيدارمغز bīdār-maghz, Prudent, intelligent.

P بيداره bīdāra, Timid. Inflamed with love.

P بيداري bīdārī, Wakefulness. Vigilance, attention. Conscious. چشم بيداري chashmi bīdārī, (His) wakeful eye.

P بيداشت bī dāsht, Careless, negligent.

P بيداشتي bī dāshtī, Carelessness, inattention (particularly not taking care of cattle).

P بيداغ bīdāgh, Without scar or freckle. Spotless.

P بيدام bīdām, Unjust. Injustice.

A بيدانة baydānat, (pl. بيدانات) A wild she-ass.

P بيدانجير bīd-anjīr, The shrub Palma Christi.

P بيدانش bī dānish, Ignorance. Ignorant.

P بيدانشي bī dānishī, Ignorance. An unwise act, any thing inconsistent with one's profession.

P بيدانه bī dāna, Seedless.

P بيد باف bīd-bāf, One who works on rattans; a basket-maker.

P بيد بافي bīd-bāfī, The art of weaving with rattans (as bottoms of chairs and pannels of doors).

P بيد برگ bīd-barg, A spear, especially of a limber texture. An arrow whose head resembles the leaf of a willow.

P بيدپاي bīdpāy, Name of a famous Indian philosopher, known to us by the name of Pīlpāy. He was vazīr to Dābshalīm, an ancient king of the Indies, and author of the Testament of Hoshang (second king of Persia of the first dynasty), which has received a variety of names according to the different translations it has undergone: as, Jāvidān-Khirad, Humāyūn Nāmah, Kalīla u Dimna, Anvāri Suhailī, and Pīlpāy's fables. A part of it was translated into French, at Paris, in the year 1644, by one David Said of Ispahān, from which our English version is taken. As the word Bīdpāy is not known to the Hindūs, some suppose it to be a corruption of Vidyā-priya, or Veda-priya, Sanskrit words, signifying Dear to science, or A lover of the Veda. The original of the book abovementioned, in Sanscrit, is called Hitopadesa, and its author Vishnu Sarmā. It has been translated into English under the same title.

A بيدح baydah, Old (woman). Fat.

P بيدخ baydahh or bīdukh, An excellent horse. Fierce, untractable.

A بيدخة baydakhat, Fat, moist, juicy (woman).

P بيدخت bedukht, The planet Venus.

P بيدخل bī dakhl, Dispossessed, excluded. Withholding, keeping back part of the revenue.

A بيدر baydar, A threshing-floor. A corn-bin. A stack of unthrashed corn.

A بيدرة baydarat, (v. n. of بيدر Q) Stacking corn.

P بيدرمان bī darmān, Hopeless, remediless.

P بيدرنگ bī dirang, Without delay, suddenly, instantaneously. Quick, alert, nimble, brisk.

P بيدره bīdara, A blacksmith's ditch (these artificers, as well as the weavers in Persia, do not sit upon benches, but dig circular or square holes about two feet in depth, where they place their anvils, round which they sit upon the ground, with their feet in the ditch).

A بيدري baydara', Even, smooth (tongue).

P بي دريغ bī diregh, Undeniable, evident, incontestible, readily acknowledged. Unsparing, ungrudging, unstinted, liberal. Remorseless, ruthless, unpitying. عون بي دريغ ʻawni bī diregh, The (divine) aid freely given. تيغ بي دريغش teghi bī direghash, His irresistible or remorseless cimeter. بيدريغ شدن bī diregh shudan, To receive no denial. بيدريغ كردن bī diregh kardan, To agree, to grant without regret, not to refuse.

P بيدستان bīdistān, Grove of willows, osier-bed.

P بيدستر bedastar, The beaver.

P بيدست و پا bī dast u pā, Without power or authority. Astonished, stupefied.

P بيدستور bī dastūr, Ill-bred. Without precedent, unusual.

P بيدعوي bī daʻwa', Free from claims.

A بيدق baydak, A pawn at chess. Single, unmarried. P بيدق سيم baydaki sīm, A star.

P بيد گيا bīd-giyā, A sort of artichoke.

P بيدل bī dil, Heartless, dispirited, out of heart. Pusillanimous. Love-sick. Ignorant. Melancholy, dejected, sad, stupid.

P بيدلا bedalā, Vain words, idle talk.

P بيدلي bī dilī, Heartlessness. Cowardice.

P بيدماغ bī damāgh, Brainless. Ill-tempered, easily provoked, irritable, testy, impatient.

P بيدماغي bī damāghī, Impatience, irritability.

P بيدمال bīdmāl, A dagger. A bright sword. *Bīd-māl*, Rubbing the rust from a sword or mirror with a willow-stick.

P بيدموش bīd-mosh, Name of a fragrant shrub.

P بيدمي bī dumī, Absence of tail.

P بي دندان bī dandān, Toothless. بي دندان شدن bī dandān shudan, To lose the teeth.

P بيدواز bedwāz, A mountain in Transoxania.

A بيدودة baydūdat, (v. n. of باد for بيد) Departing. Being cut off, separated.

P بيدوس bī dos, Innocent, faultless (little used).

P بيدول bī dawl, Shapeless. Uneducated, ill-bred.

P بيدولت bī dawlat, Unfortunate, unhappy.

P بيدون bīdūn, Without.

P بيدوند bīdwand, A stone used medicinally.

P بيدهشت bī dahshat, Undismayed, unappalled.

P بيدي bīde, A willow, a single willow.

P بي ديانت bī diyānat, Irreligious, unjust.

P بي ديده bī dīda, Blind. Saucy. Ungrateful.

P بي دين bī dīn, Irreligious, heretical. An infidel.

A بيذار bayzār, (and بيذارة bayzārat) A scatterer of words, a prater, a blabber.

P بيذاره bīzāra, (or بيداره bīdāra) Fraud, deceit.

A بيذخ bayzahh, A fat woman. A palm-plantation.

A بيذراني bayzarānīy, A prater, a babbler.

P بيذق bayzak, A commander. A falcon.

A بيذق bayzak, (pl. بياذق bayāzik) A road-guide. A foot-soldier. A pawn at chess.

A بيذمان bayzumān, A kind of plant.

A بئر bi,r, (pl. آبار ābār, ابار ab,ār, ابؤر ab,ur, آبر ābur, and بئار bi,ār) A well, a pit.

P بير bīr, Lightning. Thunder. A thunder-bolt. A deluge. A bed, bed-clothes. A handsome vest. Learning by heart.

P بيراز berāz, The horn of any animal.

P بيراسته bīrāsta, A village abounding in palms.

P بيراق bayrāk, A standard, ensign. A troop.

P بيراقدار bayrāk-dār, A standard-bearer, cornet.

H بيراگي bayrāgī, A Hindū mendicant and penitent, who, having forsaken the world, leads a wandering life.

P بيرام *bayrām*, A Muhammadan solemn festival.

P بيران *berān*, (for ويران *werān*) Desolate.

P بيرانه *berāna*, (for ويرانه) A place full of ruins.

P بيراه *bī rāh*, A wanderer, who deviates, errs, or loses the way. Astray. Unprincipled, dissolute. A courtezan. Anger. Misdeeds, unbecoming acts. The two sides of a road, but without a highway. بيراه شدن *bī rāh shudan*, To wander, stray, deviate. بيراه شوا *bī rāh shawā*, Wandering, straying.

P بيراهي *bī rāhī*, Deviation from the right way. بيراهي كردن *bī rāhī kardan*, To be guilty of excess.

P بيراي *bī rāy*, A fool, ideot, imprudent man.

P بيربط *bī rabt*, Irregular, undisciplined.

P بيربوشا *bīrbūshā*, (zand and Pāz.) A cucumber.

H بيربهم *bīrbhum*, Name of a district in Bengal.

A بئرة *bi‚rat*, A treasure, store, provisions.

P بي رحم *bī rahm*, Merciless, cruel, savage. آن بي رحم قاطع الرحم *ān bī rahmi kātiʿu'r rahim*, That pitiless wretch who abandons parents and relatives.

P بيرز *biraz*, A fuller's beetle.

P بيرزد *bīrzad*, Iron filings. Solder. Galbanum.

A بئر زمزم *bi‚ri zamzam*, The well Zamzam.

P بيرزة *bīrza*, (or بيرزي *bīrzay*) Galbanum.

P بي رستاي عيد *bī rustāyi ʿīd*, Innocent mirth.

P بيرشك *bī rashk*, Unambitious. Spiritless.

P بيرضا *bī rizā*, Without leave.

P بيرق *bayrak*, A standard, flag, pennant, colours. A troop. بيرق نور *bayraki nūr*, Peep of dawn.

P بيرگ *bī rag*, Heartless, without emulation.

P بيرگند *birgand*, Name of a city.

P بيرم *bayram*, A kind of silken stuff.

A بيرم *bayram*, A gimlet. Liquid collyrium. A long stone. A hoe, a pickaxe.

P بيرن *bīrun*, (for بيرون *bīrūn*) Out, without.

P بيرنجاسب *bīrinjāsb*, The plant southernwood.

P بيرنگ *bī rang*, Colourless. *Berang*, The sketch or outline (of a picture), the plan (of an edifice). The Divine essence divested of attributes.

P بي رو *bī rū*, Shameless, scurrilous. Bold, rash, inhuman. A purse.

A بيروت *bayrūt*, A maritime city in Syria.

P بيروج *bīrūj*, The herb mallows.

A بيروح *bayrūh*, The root of the wild mandrake.

P بي روز *bī roz*, Unfortunate. A green stone of little value.

A بيروزج *bīrozaj*, (for P پيروزة) A turquoise.

P بيروزن *bīrozan*, A precious stone. A load.

P بيروزة *bīroza*, A garment for daily wear.

P بي روزي *bī rozī*, Destitute of daily bread.

P بيرون *bīrūn* or *berūn*, Without, out of doors. Exterior, extrinsic, foreign. The outside. From, a great way from. بيرون آمدن *bīrūn āmadan*, To come out, sally forth. To revolt. بيرون فرستادن *bīrūn faristādan*, To send abroad, to emit, send out, despatch away. بيرون كردن *bīrūn kardan*, To extract, draw forth, lead out, export, throw out, eject. To except, exclude. بيرون شهر *bīrūni shahr*, Without the city. از بيرون *az bīrūn*, From without.

P بيرون آمدگي *bīrūn-āmadagī*, A turning out. A projection, prominence, protuberance.

P بيرونتر *bīrūntar*, More foreign or external.

P بيرون جستگي *bīrūn-jastagī*, Saliency.

P بيرون سرا *bīrūn-sarā*, Not stamped at a mint.

P بيرون شو *bīrūn-shav*, Termination, exit.

P بيرونه *bīrūna*, An outside garment, a cloak.

P بيروني *bīrūnī*, External. The outside. A shirt, a shift. Excluded. Excepted.

P بيرونين *bīrūnīn*, External.

P بيرة *bīra*, A wimble, an auger. A mouthful, chew. Name of a fortified place on the Euphrates.

P بيرة زن *bera zan*, An earthen pan for baking.

P بيري *bīrī*, A bed. A cushion, a carpet.

P بيريا *bī riyā*, Sincere. Sincerity. Sincerely.

P بيريب *bī rayb*, Without doubt, indubitably.

P بيريش *bī rīsh*, Beardless.

P بيريشة *bī rīsha*, Without fibres, fibreless.

P بيرين *bīrīn*, Fetid water.

A بيز *bayz*, (v. n. of باز for بيز) Perishing. Escaping, fleeing away.

P بيز *bez* or *bīz*, (in composition) Sifting. Stricken. فتنه بيز *fitna-bez*, Sowing sedition.

A بيزار *bayzār*, (pl. بيازرة *bayāzirat*) Penis. A falconer. (from P بازدار) A labourer, plowman.

P بيزار *bīzār*, Free, clear. Absolved. Healed. Wearied, disgusted. بيزار شدن *bīzār shudan*, To have an aversion, loath, abhor, detest. To be free from fault or debt. To become languid or low-spirited, to despair. بيزار كردن *bīzār kardan*, To fatigue, vex, disgust.

A بيزارة *bayzārat*, A large club.

P بيزارة *bīzāra*, Magnanimous. A lover.

P بيزاري *bīzārī*, A royal diploma. A charter of liberty, a letter of manumission. Vexation. Anger, ill-humour, displeasure.

A بئزان *bi‚zān*, (pl. of باز *ba‚z*) Falcons.

A بيزان *bīzān*, (pl. of بازي *bāzī*) Falcons.

P بيزبان *bīzabān*, Without a tongue: mute, dumb.

P بي زباني *bī zabānī*, Dumbness, silence.

A بيزر *bayzar*, (pl. بيازر) A bleacher's beetle.

P بيزر *bīzar*, Moneyless. A miser. Avaricious.

A بيزرة *bayzarat*, (pl. بيازر *bayāzir*) A large club.

P بيزر خريد *bī zar kharīd*, (Obtaining) without purchase.

P بي زنگ *bī zang*, Free from rust, untarnished.

P بي زن و فرزند *bī zan u farzand*, Without wife or child.

P بي زني *bī zanī*, Bachelorship.

P بي زوال *bīzawāl*, Unchangeable, imperishable.

P بيزور *bī zor*, Weak, impotent.

P بيزهرة *bī zahra*, Without bile; good-tempered, patient, forbearing; indefatigable. Shameless.

P بي زيب و زينت *bī zīb u zīnat*, Ugly, awkward, inelegant.

P بيزيدن *bīzīdan* or *bezīdan*, To sift.

P بيزين *bī zīn*, Unsaddled.

P بيژن *bejan*, Name of a hero or giant.

P بيژنوار *bejanwār*, Hercules-like, Sampson-like.

P بيژة *bīja*, Pure, genuine. Special, private.

A بئس *bi‚s*, (v. n. of بئس) Being unfortunate, unhappy, miserable. Pinched with poverty, miserable. عذاب بئس *ʿazābun bi‚sun*, A sore punishment. بنات بئس *banātu bi‚sin*, Calamities, misfortunes. *Bi‚sa*, Fie! out upon! بئس رجلاً زيد *bi‚sa rajulan zaydun*, A bad fellow is Zayd. بئس القرين *bi‚sa'l karīn*, Bad is the companion. بئس المصير *bi‚sa 'l masīr*, Miserable is the abode (whither they return). *Ba‚is*, Bold, brave. Sore, severe. قراءة البعض عذاب بئس *kirā‚atu'l baʿz ʿazābun ba‚isun*, The mode of reading of some people is a sore infliction.

A بيس *bays*, (v. n. of باس for بيس) Being proud; overbearing, domineering. A word used in soothing a child.

P بي ساختگي *bī sākhtagī*, Sincerity, artlessness.

P بيساخته *bī sākhta*, Undisguised, plain, artless.

P بي ساز *bī sāz*, Unprepared, unaccoutred. Useless.

P بي سامان *bī sāmān*, Poor. Wicked. Disproportioned. Stupid. سر بيسامان *sari bī sāmān*, A brainless head, a dunce, a dunderhead.

P بي ساماني *bī sāmānī*, Poverty.

A بيسان *baysān*, Name of two places.

P بيسبب *bī sabab*, Causeless, without motive.

P بيست *bīst*, Twenty. *Best*, Stand! stop! wait!

P بيستاخ *bīstākh*, Impudent, shameless, rash.

P بيستار *bestār*, Superfluous. Such a person.

P بي ستارگان *bī sitāragān*, Without stars, starless (night).

P بيستارة *bī sitāra*, Unfortunate, ill-starred.

P بيستگاني *bīstagānī*, A monthly pension, which used to be paid upon the twentieth day. Wages.

P بيستگي *bīstagī*, Impunity. The leprosy.

P بيستم *bīstum*, The twentieth.

P بيستون *bīstūn*, Name of a mountain in Persia. The heavens.

P بيستي *bīstī*, A Persian coin of 20 deniers. A water-carrier. (The last is Hindustānī).

P بيستين *bīstīn*, The twentieth.

P بيسج *bī saj*, Shapeless, ill-made.

P بيسخن *bī sukhun*, Dumb, silent. Doubtless.

P بيسر *bī sar*, Peerless. *Besar*, A hawk.

P بيسراك *besurāk* or *besarāk*, A young and strong camel. A camel's colt two years old. A young camel whose dam is Arabian and sire double-hunched. An ass. *Besurāk*, A mule.

P بيسران *bī sarān*, (Without masters) Persons who attain eminence without parental instruction.

P بي سرمگي *bī surmagī*, A want of collyrium. A neglect of the application of collyrium to the eyes.

P بي سر و پا *bī sar u pā*, Without head or feet.

Weak, powerless, totally destitute. Immethodical. A circular shell or bead.

P بيسر و دلي *bī sar u dilī*, Absence of mind.

P بيسر و سامان *bī sar u sāmān*, Unfurnished, destitute, helpless. Confused, intricate. Deplorable. Depraved, villainous. Mean, grovelling. Dirty, unclean. Wicked, impudent, lascivious.

P بيسرة *besra*, A sparrow-hawk, merlin. A mule.

A بيسري *baysariy*, (pl. بياسرة *bayāsirat*) A certain people living in Scinde, employed by ship-commanders to man their vessels of war.

P بيسعادت *bīsaʿādat*, Unfortunate. Unhappy.

A بيسك *baysaka*, (for ويسك *waysaka*) (A particle of condolence; also of contempt) Alas! wo! fy! pho! out out upon thee!

P بي سكه *bī sikka*, Unstampt (coin). Without respect or esteem, without freshness or beauty.

P بيسليقة *bī salīka*, Immethodical: inexpert.

P بيسن *bīsan*, Deadly poison.

P بيسنك *bī sang*, Without weight or gravity. Without respect or influence.

P بيسور *besūr*, Name of a city.

P بي سوز *bī soz*, The extinguisher of a candle.

H بيسوة *bīswa*, The sixtieth part of an acre.

A بئسي *biʾsaʾ*, (v. n. of بئس) Becoming indigent and miserable.

P بيش *besh*, Much. More. Great. Good, proper. Best. Well. Excellent, elegant. Delightful. بيش قيمت *besh-kīmat*, A high value or price. *Bīsh*, Name of an Indian poisonous herb. بيش موش *bīsh-mosh* (or فارة البيش *fāratu'l bīsh*) A mouse, which lives amongst the roots of this herb.

A بيش *bīsh*, A certain plant resembling ginger, in which frequently a deadly poison is found.

P بيشائبه *bī shāʾiba*, Without doubt.

P بيش بها *besh-bahā*, Of great price or value.

P بيش بهار *besh bahār*, Sempervivum, houseleek.

P بيشبهه *bī shubha*, Without doubt. Undoubted.

A بئشة *biʾshat*, (or بيشة *bīshat*) Name of a valley in Yaman abounding in lions.

P بيشتر *beshtar*, Oftener, for the most part. More. Broader. Longer. Exceeding. دو چيز يا بيشتر *du chīz ya beshtar*, Two or more things.

P بيشترين *beshtarīn*, The most, the greatest.

P بي شرم *bī sharm*, Shameless, indecent.

P بي شرمي *bī sharmī*, Immodesty, shamelessness.

P بيشعور *bī shuʿūr*, Ignorant, unconscious. A blockhead.

P بيشفقت *bī shafkat*, Pitiless, harsh, unkind.

P بيشك *bī shakk*, (or بي شك و شبهه *bī shakk u shubha*) Without doubt, doubtless; without question, unquestionably.

P بيشكار *beshkār*, Unremunerated labour.

P بيشكيب *bī shakīb*, Impatient.

P بشمار *bī shumār*, Innumerable.

P بيش و كم *besh u kam*, More or less. A moderate quantity.

P بي شوي *bī shūy*, Husbandless.

P بي شوئي *bī shūʾī*, A maiden state, celibacy.

P بيشه *bīsha* or *besha*, A forest, wood, wild, uncultivated country. A country overgrown with reeds and the like. A shepherd's pipe. بيشهٔ بي توشه *bīshaʾi bī tosha*, The nook of poverty.

P بيشي *beshī*, Excess, increase.

A بيص *bays* or *bīs*, Adversity, calamity. Confusion. Difficulty, straits. وقع في حيص بيص *wakaʿa fī hays bays* or *hīs bīs*, He fell into confusion and difficulty.

P بي صبر *bī sabr*, Impatient, not brooking delay.

P بي صبري *bī sabrī*, Impatience, restlessness.

P بي صدا *bī sadā*, Dumb, returning no echo.

P بي صرفه *bī sarfa*, Useless, inconsiderate. Nonsense.

P بي صرفه گو *bī sarfa-go* or *gū*, An idle talker.

P بي صلاح *bī salāh*, Ill-advised, headstrong.

P بي صيقل *bī saykal*, Unpolished, unfurbished.

A بيض *bayz*, (v. n. of باض for بيض) Excelling in whiteness. Having a white swelling on the fore-foot (a horse). Having the whites (fluor albus). Laying an egg. Becoming intense (heat). Being stripped of its prickles (the plant بهمى *buhma'*). Remaining in a place. Raining. Becoming dry (wood). Whiteness, brightness. A swelling on the fore-foot of a horse. Intense heat. A mark fixed to public writings by the magistrate or any principal officer. (pl. of بيضة *bayzat*) Eggs. *Bīz*, (pl. of بيوض *bayūz*) Hens which lay many eggs. (pl. of بيضة *bīzat*) White kinds of light soil. White dates. (pl. of ابيض *abyaz* and بيضاء *bayzāʾ*) White. The fair sex. ايّام البيض *ayyāmu'l bīz*, The 12th and 13th (or, according to some, the 13th, 14th, and 15th) days from the new moon, as being the brightest. الدراهم البيض *ad darāhimu'l bīz*, Silver coins. *Buyuz*, (pl. of بائض *bāʾiz* or بيوض *bayūz*) Hens which lay many eggs.

A بيضاء *bayzāʾ*, (fem. of ابيض *abyaz*) White. Bright. The sun. Blank paper. Untrodden (ground). A misfortune, calamity. Wheat or barley without husk, and moist. A leathern bag, scrip, purse. A pot. A hunter's rope, gin, or noose. Aleppo. Name of a horse; of a place in Basra; of four towns in Egypt; of one in Persia; and of a province in Morocco, and of many more places. امّ بيضا *ummi bayzā*, A boiler, kettle. دينار البيضاء *dīnāru'l bayzāʾ*, The sun. منارهٔ بيضا *manāraʾi bayzā*, The White Tower, or Tower of Damascus (where the Muhammadans believe that Jesus Christ descended from heaven). يد بيضا *yadi bayzā*, A white hand, the white hand of Moses; or simply, the hand.

P بيضابي *bayzābī*, (for بيضوي *bayzawī*) A species of Persian writing where the curvatures (or دامن *dāman*) of the letters are oval.

A بيضان *bīzān*, White men (in opposition to سودان *sūdān*, Negroes).

P بيضانه *bayzāna*, The official mark of a superior officer. The perquisites of a magistrate for marking public papers.

P بي ضبط *bī zabt*, Irregular, unrestrained, wanton.

P بي ضبط و ربط *bī zabt u rabt*, Without order or connexion.

A بيضة *bayzat*, (pl. بيوض *buyūz*) An egg. A testicle. A helmet. The headache (a lasting pain seizing the whole head). The middle (of a country, of a city, of the head). Fluor albus. A ring or circus formed by a number of people; also the area comprehended by a circular disposition of tents. بيضهٔ آفتاب *bayzaʾi āftāb*, The sun. بيضة البلد *bayzatu'l balad*, The chief of a city. A white fungus. An ostrich's egg. اذلّ من بيضة البلد *azall mim bayzati'l balad*, More lowly than a fungus. بيضة الخدر *bayzatu'l khidr*, (The egg of the female apartments) A virgin. بيضة العقر *bayzatu'l ʿukr*, A cock's egg (because he is supposed to lay one only in his life; and thence it is used as a proverb for any thing that either exists not, or is very rare). بيضة القصب *bayzatu'l kasab*, Gum exuding from a sugar-cane. بيضة النهار *bayzatu'n nahār*, The light of the day (as long as the light continues). بيضة مكنونة *bayzat maknūnat*, A beautiful girl kept closely confined. P بيضهٔ آتشين *bayzaʾi ātishīn*, The world-illuminating sun. بيضه بر آوردن *bayza bar āwardan*, To castrate. بيضه پروردن *bayza parwardan*, To hatch, or to brood. بيضهٔ خاكي *bayzaʾi khākī*, The terrestrial globe. بيضه در آب *bayza dar āb*, An egg in which the bird has not begun to be formed. Boiled. بيضه در كلاه *bayza dar kulāh*, An egg which jugglers conceal in their cap. The human heart. بيضه در كلاه شكست *bayza dar kulāh shikast*, The egg in his hat is broken. (met.) His deceit has become known. بيضهٔ زر *bayzaʾi zar*, An ancient Persian coin (so called from its elliptical form). The sun. بيضهٔ صبح *bayzaʾi subh*, The sun. بيضهٔ كافور *bayzaʾi kāfūr*, Snow. The sun. The moon. Lightning. بيضهٔ ماهي *bayzaʾi māhī*, Fish-spawn. بيضه نهادن *bayza nihādan*, To lay an egg. بيضهاى زرين *bayzahāʾi zarīn*, The stars. A *Bīzat*, (pl. بيض *bīz*) A white kind of light soil. A kind of whitish date.

A بيضوي *bayzawiy*, Oval. Elliptical. Name of Abū Saʿīd, a native of the city of Bayzah, and author of a celebrated commentary on the Kur'ān. P خط بيضوي *khati bayzawī*, A form of Persian writing, in which the curved tails of the letters are segments of an oval; opposed to خط آفتابي *khati āftābī*, in which they are portions of a circle.

P بيضهگر *bayzagar*, Oviparous.

A بيضي *bayzī*, Whiteness, purity.

A بيط *bayt*, The egg of an ant or ostrich.

A بيطار *baytār*, A horse-doctor.

P بي طاقت *bī tākat*, Without power, impotent.

P بيطاقت و تاب شدن *bī tākat u tāb shudan*, To

be deprived of all power.

P بي طاقتي *bī tākatī*, Impotency, imbecility.

A بيطر *baytar* or *biyatr*, A horse-doctor. *Biyatr*, A tailor.

P بي طراوتي *bī tarāwatī*, Want of moisture or sap: siccity.

A بيطرة *baytarat*, (v. n. of بيطر Q) Practising the veterinary art.

A بيطري *baytarī*, The veterinary art. P بيطري كردن *baytarī kardan*, To practise farriery.

P بي طعم *bī taɛm*, Without flavour, insipid. Without food.

P بي طلب ورجا *bī talab u rajā*, Without request or petition.

P بي طمعي *bī tamaɛī*, Disinterestedness.

P بي طور *bī tawr*, Ill-mannered.

A بيظ *bayz*, (v. n. of باظ for بيظ) Discharging into the womb. Seed (of animals). The womb.

A بيظر *bayzar*, The clitoris. يا بيظر *yā bayzar*, A term of reproach addressed to a young woman.

P بي ظرف *bī zarf*, Without the power of containing.

A بيع *bayɛ*, (v. n. of باع for بيع) Selling. Buying. Accusing or reporting (any one) unfavourably to the government. Purchase. (pl. بيوع *buyūɛ*) Commerce, dealing. بيع و شرا *bayɛ u sharā*, Purchase and sale. P بيع كردن *bayɛ kardan*, To buy. To sell. To trade, to traffic. A باع على بيعه *bāɛa ɛala' bayɛihi*, He shewed his rank and superiority and triumphed over him. *Biyaɛ*, (pl. of بيعة *biɛat*) Christian churches.

A بيّع *bayyiɛ*, (pl. بيعاء *biyaɛā*, and ابيعاء *abyiɛā*) A buyer. A seller. A merchant, dealer, chapman. A bidder, one who raises the price upon another. A horse that takes long steps.

A بيعاء *biyaɛā*, (pl. of بيّع) Sellers. Buyers.

A بيّعان *bayyiɛānī*, (dual) Buyer and seller.

P بيعانه *bayɛāna*, Earnest-money.

A بيعة *bayɛat*, Inauguration, salutation, or acknowledging the authority of a great man. An agreement, compact, treaty, covenant. P بيعت دادن *bayɛat dādan*, To stipulate, to give the hand upon making an agreement. To administer the oath of loyalty or fealty. بيعت كردن *bayɛat kardan*, To agree with, to receive a promise or pledge for the settling of a bargain. To promise or plight loyalty or fealty. A *Biɛat*, (pl. بيع *biyaɛ*) A temple, a Christian church. The mode or manner of selling. Buying and selling.

P بي عدل *bī ɛadl*, Unjust, lawless.

P بي عديل *bī ɛadīl*, Incomparable, unequalled.

P بي عزت *bī ɛizzat*, Inglorious, dishonourable.

P بي عزتي *bī ɛizzatī*, Dishonour.

P بي عقل *bī ɛakl*, Without judgment or intellect. Infatuated. Foolishly.

P بي عقلي *bī ɛaklī*, Want of sense and understanding. Infatuation. Levity.

P بي علاقگي *bī ɛilākagī*, Want of connexion.

P بي علاقه *bī ɛilāka*, Unconnected.

P بي علت *bī ɛillat*, Without cause or reason. Safe, secure, free from accident. Independent.

P بيع نامه *bayɛ-nāma*, A bill of sale.

P بي عنايت *bī ɛināyat*, Unkind, rude. Reckless, unconcerned.

P بي عيب *bī ɛayb*, Without blemish, faultless.

A بيغ *baygh*, (v. n. of باغ for بيغ) Boiling (blood). Perishing.

P بيغار *bayghār*, (or بيغاره *bayghāra*) Reproach, reproof, chiding.

P بيغال *bīghāl*, A short spear, demi lance, pike.

P بي غايت *bī ghāyat*, Endless.

P بي غرض *bī gharaz*, Disinterested; independent; indifferent.

P بيغرضانه *bī gharazāna*, Sincere, pure. Disinterested. Sincerely. محبّت بي غرضانه *mahabbati bī gharazāna*, Sincere, disinterested friendship.

P بي غرضي *bī gharazī*, Disinterestedness.

P بي غشّ و غلّ *bī ghashsh u ghill*, Without hatred or dissimulation. A sincere friend.

P بي غمّ *bī ghamm*, Without grief or anxiety. Free from sorrow. At ease.

P بي غمّي *bī ghammī*, Freedom from sorrow.

P بي غور *bī ghawr*, Shallow. Inconsiderate.

P بيغه *bīgha*, Fuel, fire-wood.

P بيغي *bayghī*, Removal, repulse.

P بي غيرت *bī ghayrat*, Spiritless. A cuckold.

P بيفائده *bī fāɛida*, Without advantage: useless, unprofitable. Ineffectual.

P بي فرزند *bī farzand*, Bereaved (parent).

P بي فروغ *bī furūgh*, Without success. Inconclusive.

P فرنگ بي فرهنگ *farangi bī farhang*, The imprudent Franks (or Christians in general).

P بيفكر *bī fikr*, Thoughtless: rash. Content.

P بي فهمي *bī fahmī*, Slowness of apprehension.

P بيفهميد *bī fahmīd*, Slow in comprehending.

P بيفيض *bī fayz*, Unprofitable, possessing but not bestowing (as a learned man who does not communicate his knowledge, or a rich man from whose wealth no one receives advantage).

P بيقابو *bī kābū*, Without restraint. Secure.

P بيقاعده *bī kāɛida*, Without order; irregular.

P بيقال *bī kāl*, Dumb, speechless.

A بيقان *bīkān*, (pl. of بوق *būk*) Trumpets, clarions.

A بيقة *bīkat*, A kind of pulse or pease, when stripped of its husk it is fattening for cattle.

P بيقدر *bī kadr*, Without dignity.

P بي قدم *bī kadam*, Without a footing, unfortunate.

A بيقر *baykar*, A weaver. Name of a place.

P بيقرار *bī karār*, Inconstant, unsettled, variable. Impatient, passionate. Afflicted, impotent.

P بيقراري *bī karārī*, Instability, restlessness.

A بيقران *baykurān*, Name of a plant.

A بيقرة *baykarat*, (v. n. of بيقر Q) Starting and running away (as a dog at the sight of an ox). Sighing. Being fatigued. Perishing. Corrupting, vitiating. Walking in a stately manner. Doubting. Dying. Alighting at a house. Taking up a town-residence. Abiding. Leaving one's family in the country and going none knows where. Running fast with the head thrust forward. Being wholly given up to the accumulation of wealth, and tenaciously keeping it. Pawing with his fore-feet (a horse). Departing from Syria to Chaldea. Wandering from one country to another. Abundance of property.

P بي قرينه *bī karīna*, Irregular.

P بي قصد و اختيار *bī kasd u ikhtiyār*, Unintentional, involuntary. Unwillingly. Suddenly. Casually, accidentally.

P بيقصور *bī kusūr*, Without defect, without fail. Completely, entirely. Faultless, innocent.

P بيقلعي *bī kalɛī*, Untinned (as a pot).

A بيقور *bayhūr*, Black cattle, oxen.

P بيقول *bī kawl*, Regardless of one's word, faithless, perfidious.

P بيقياس *bī kiyās*, Incomprehensible. Immense, infinite, inexplicable, contrary to the common order of things, abnormal.

A بيقية *bīkiyat*, A kind of pulse.

P بيقيد *bī kayd*, Unrestrained, irregular.

P بي قيمت *bī kīmat*, Inestimable.

A بيقين *bi yakīn*, Certain, for certain.

P بيك *ba yak*, To one, with one. بيك نيم نهاد *ba yak nīm nihād*, He left it half-finished. بيك راه *ba yak rāh*, At once, at one stroke.

A بيّك *buyyak*, (pl. of بائك *bāɛik*) Fat camels.

P بيكار *bī kār*, Without employment or profession, an idle, lazy fellow, vagabond, vagrant. Incapable of work, useless.

P بيكاري *bī kārī*, Want of employ, idleness.

P بيكام *bī kām*, Disappointed.

P بيك بار *ba yak bār*, At once. Suddenly.

P بيكس *bī kas*, Friendless, destitute. An orphan.

P بي كسي *bī kasī*, A friendless condition, solitude.

P بي كفش *bī kafsh*, Shoeless, barefoot.

P بي كفشي *bī kafshī*, Bareness of feet. Want of shoes, discalceation.

P بيكم *baykam*, A portico, vestibule, veranda.

P بي كم و كاست *bī kam u kāst*, Without increase or diminution, without defect. Complete, perfect, entire. Accurate.

P بيكند *baykand*, A city built by Jamshed.

T بيگ *beg*, A lord, a prince.

P بيگاده *bīgāda*, Averse from women, impotent.

P بيگار *begār*, Employing any one without a remuneration.

P بيگاره *bīgāra*, Impotent.

P بيگانگي *bīgānagī*, The situation of a stranger or person unknown; the being a stranger or alien. Foreignness.

P بيگانه *bīgāna*, Unknown, a foreigner, stranger, alien. بیگانه و خویش *bīgāna u khwesh*, Strangers and relations, foreigners and natives.

P بیگاه *begāh*, Unseasonable. Delay. Evening.

P بیگران *bī girān*, Inestimable, infinite.

P بي گزند *bī gazand*, Unharmed, unblemished.

P بي گزندگي *bī gazandagi*, Freedom from hurt.

T بیگلربیگي *beglar begi*, Prince of princes.

P بیگم *begam*, A lady of rank.

P بیگمان *bī gumān*, Without doubt.

P بي گماني *bī gumānī*, Certainty.

P بیگناه *bī gunāh*, Innocent, guiltless, harmless.

P بیگه *bīgah*, Ill-timed. Delay. Evening.

H بیگهه *bīgha*, A measure of a third of an acre.

P بیل *bel*, A shovel, spade. An oar, a paddle. The loins. A basket for carrying away rubbish. A gunner. A gardener, a vine-dresser. (in zand and Pāz.) A well. بیل کشتي *beli kishtī*, An oar.

H بیل *bel*, An Indian fruit containing in a hard shell a pulp resembling the apricot in flavour.

P بیلا *bīlā*, Money to be distributed in charity.

P بیلا بردار *bīlā-bardār*, One of the retinue of a great man who scatters money amongst the populace, an almoner.

P بیلاق *belāk*, A flower. A garden. A cool grot.

P بیلاك *bīlāk*, A gift, a present.

P بیلاي *bīlāy*, (in zand and Pāzand) A well.

A بیلة *bīlat*, A making water, or a doing any thing similar.

P بیلچه *belcha*, A hoe, a small mattock.

P بیلحاظ *bī lihāz*, Inattentive, indiscreet, ill-bred.

P بیلدار *bel-dār*, A digger, delver. A pioneer.

P بیلسته *belasta*, A finger. A kind of rose.

P بیلطافت *bī latāfat*, Unpleasant, harsh.

P بیلفت *bīluft*, Name of the planet Venus.

P بیلفختن *biyalfakhtan*, To gain, to collect.

P بیلفخند *bīlfakhand*, A collection, assembly.

P بیلقان *baylkān*, Name of a city in Armenia Major, near the ports of the Caspian Sea. Name of a district in Persia.

P بیلك *baylak*, A royal mandate. Title-deeds. A two-headed arrow. *Belak*, A hoe or small spade. A kind of arrow resembling a small spade.

A بیلم *baylam*, (pl. بیالم *bayālim*) The pod in which the cotton grows; also the stuff, resembling a coarser cotton, on the top of the Egyptian papyrus. A wimble, auger, gimlet.

A بیلمان *baylamān*, Name of a place in Yaman: also one in India or Scinde celebrated for its swords.

P بیلوا *belwā*, A druggist, an apothecary.

P بیله *bela*, A mattock. An arrow with a broad head resembling a hoe. An oar, a paddle. An island. A sort of medicine. A tray on which drugs are exposed for sale. A royal mandate. The title-deeds to an estate. Pus. The silk-worm's cone. A cheek. A side.

P بیم *bīm*, Fear, terror, dread, danger. بیم جان *bīmi jān*, The danger of life. دربیم هلاك *dar bīmi halāk*, In dread of destruction. ازبیم سطوتش *az bīmi satwatash*, From fear of his power.

P بیحاصل *bī mā hasal*, Useless, unprofitable. Unfortunate, unlucky.

P بي مادر *bī mādar*, Motherless.

P بیمار *bīmār*, Sick, infirm, afflicted. The eye of a mistress. بیمار سیاه *bīmāri siyāh*, A black or burning fever attended with perspiration.

P بیمارباریك *bīmār-bārīk*, Phthisic, consumption.

P بیمارپرست *bīmār-parast*, A nurse of the sick.

P بیمارپرسي *bīmār-pursī*, Visitation of, or inquiry about, the sick. بیمارپرسي نمودن *bīmār-pursī namūdan*, To visit the sick.

P بیمارجگر *bīmār-jigar*, Diseased in the liver.

P بیمارچشم *bīmār-chashm*, Languid-eyed.

P بیمارخانه *bīmār-khāna*, An hospital, infirmary.

P بیمارخیز *bīmār-khez*, Convalescent.

P بیماردار *bīmār-dār*, An attendant on the sick.

P بیمارداري *bīmār-dārī*, Attendance on the sick. بیمارداري کردن *bīmār-dārī kardan*, To tend the sick.

P بیمارژون *bīmār-jūn*, Regimen of invalids. Sickly, ailing.

P بیمارسان *bīmārsān*, Like a sick person. (for بیمارستان *bīmāristān*) An hospital.

P بیمارغنج *bīmār-ghanj*, Infirm, ailing. Love-sick.

P بیمارگران *bīmār-girān*, Having a chronic disease.

P بیمارگون *bīmār-gūn*, Sickly-coloured.

P بیمارگین *bīmār-gīn*, Diet of the sick. Valetudinary.

P بیماره *bīmāra*, Sick, infirm, indisposed. آن دلداربیماره *ān dildāri bīmāra*, That charming patient, that beautiful sick woman.

P بیماري *bīmārī*, Disease, sickness, infirmity. بیماریت *bīmāriyat*, Thy sickness. بیماريء باریك *bīmārī-i bārīk*, A consumption. بیماريء کودك *bīmārī-i kūdak*, Diseases incident to children.

P بیماريناك *bīmārīnāk*, Sickly (country).

P بي مآل *bī maāl*, Absurd, vain, fruitless. سؤال بیمآل *suāli bī maāl*, An absurd demand.

P بي مالك *bī mālik*, Without owner or master. ممالك بي مالك *mamāliki bī mālik*, A kingdom without a king.

P بیمان *bīmān*, Dishonoured. Dishonourable.

P بي مانند *bī mānand*, Incomparable, unparalleled. Effaced, obliterated.

P بي ماوي *bī mawā'*, Uninhabited, inhospitable.

P بیمایگي *bī māyagī*, Indigence, poverty.

P بي مایه *bī māya*, Poor, indigent.

P بیم بر *bīm bar*, Price, value. Frightened.

P بي مثال *bī misāl*, Incomparable, unequalled. درکمال حسن و جمال بیمثال *dar kamāli husn u jamāli bī misāl*, In the perfection of beauty and elegance unequalled.

P بیمجال *bī majāl*, Powerless, impotent.

P بیمحابا *bī muhābā*, Unceremonious, disrespectful. Unsparing. بي محابا پلنگ *bī muhābā palang*, The world; fortune; death.

P بي محاسبه *bī muhāsaba*, Without calculation, at a venture.

P بیمحل *bī mahall*, Impertinently, ill-timed.

P بي محلي *bī mahallī*, Incivility.

P بیمدد *bī madad*, Unaided, destitute, unassisted.

P بي مر *bī mar*, Immeasurable, innumerable.

P بي مرحمت *bī marhamat*, Ruthless, pitiless.

P بي مروت *bī murūwat*, Clownish, rude. Ungenerous, uncivil, brutal, inhuman.

P دزد بي مزد *duzdi bī mazd*, An infamous robber.

P بیمزگي *bī mazagī*, Distaste, disgust. Insipidity, a nauseous taste.

P بیمزه *bī maza*, Insipid, tasteless. Nauseous. بیمزه کردن *bīmaza kardan*, To disgust.

P بي مساس *bī masās*, Without foundation.

P بي مشقت *bī mashakkat*, Without trouble.

P بي معني *bī maʿnā'*, Unmeaning: vain, frivolous, absurd, unreasonable, ill-founded. Vainly, foolishly.

P بي مغ *bī magh*, Without depth, shallow.

P بیمغز *bī maghz*, Brainsick, brainless, giddy, superficial. بي مغزان تردامن *bī maghzāni tar-dāman*, Fornicators, adulterers.

P بي مقال *bī makāl*, Dumb, speechless, silent.

P بي مقدار *bī mikdār*, (or بي مقدور *bī makdūr*) Without authority. Without resource. Poor.

P بي ملاحظه *bī mulāhaza*, Inconsiderately.

P بي من *bī man*, Spiritless.

P بیمناك *bīmnāk*, Fearful, afraid, timorous.

P بي منت *bī minnat*, Without the necessity of asking, without entreaty. Without favour or obligation. Independent. Disinterested.

P بیمند *bīmand*, The mill-clapper. Rattles used by watchmen and boys. Any noisy instrument by which birds are frightened from gardens. Gravel scattered on a mill-stone.

A بیمن همتکم العلیة *bi yumni himmatikimi'l ʿaliyat*, Under your favourable auspices.

P بي موجب *bī mūjib*, Without cause or reason.

P بیموري *bīmūrī*, Majesty, reverence, awe, severity.

P بیموس *bīmūs*, Unleavened bread.

P بي موشدگي *bī mū shudagī*, Baldness.

P بي موشده *bī mū shuda*, Become bald. Bald.

P بي موقع *bī mawkiʿ*, Out of place, unseasonable.

P بي موي *bī mūy*, Bald, without hair.

P بیمه *bīma*, Insurance against risk. بیمه کردن *bīma kardan*, To insure.

P بیمهر *bī mihr*, Unkind.

P بي مهري *bī mihrī*, Unkindness.

A بین *bayn*, (v. n. of بان for بین) Excelling. Excellence. Being placed at a distance, separated (one thing from another). Separation. Distance. Interval, interstice. Absence. A desert. Conjunction, connection, union. ذات البین *zātu'l bayn*, Friendship, concord. غراب البین *ghurābu'l bayn*, A crow of different colours, a crow with a black body and red feet and beak. A crow that never approaches any spot till it has become deserted by its inhabitants. *Bayna,* (used constantly as a preposition) Between, among. بين الاقران *bayna'l akrān,* Between equals. بين ذلك *bayna zālika,* In the meanwhile. بين الصلوتين *bayna's salātayn,* Between the two prayers (which are said in the mosques every Friday about mid-day). بين الناس *bayna'n nās,* Among men, among the people. بينهما بين بعيد *baynahumā bayn baʿīd,* Between both the difference is great, the one is much unlike the other. بين يديه *bayn yadayhi,* Between his hands (*i.e.* before him, made use of particularly when an inferior appears before a superior). شيء بين بين *shay-un bayna bayna,* Indifferent, neither good nor bad. A hamza made light. في ما بين *fī mā bayn,* Between: mutual. لقيه بعيدات بين *lakiyahu buʿaydāti bayn,* He met him after an interval; then held back from him, and afterwards came to him.

P بين *bīn,* (in composition) Seeing. See thou (imperat. of ديدن *dīdan*). چشم حق بين *chashmī hak-bīn,* (or ديدهٔ حقيقت بين *dīdasi hakīkat-bīn,* The eye discerning truth. جهان بين *jahān-bīn,* Seeing the world, comprehending the idea of the whole universe. خردهٔ بين *khwurda-bīn,* Seeing minute objects, subtile in judgment, acute, penetrating. دوربين *dūr-bīn,* Far-seeing. A telescope. مصلحت بين *maslahat-bīn,* Despatching business, skilful in managing affairs.

A بين *bīn,* (pl. بيون *buyūn*) A tract of country. A rugged eminence. Confines, marches between two countries or places. As far as eye can reach.

A بيّن *bayyin,* (pl. ابيناء *abyināʾ* and بينة *bīnat*) Clear, evident, manifest, apparent, distinct, perspicuous, evidencing. (pl. ابيناء *abyināʾ,* ابيان *abyān,* and بيناء *buyanāʾ*) Eloquent. كلام بيّن الانتاج *kalāmi bayyinu'l intāj,* Words clearly expressing, evidently concluding. بيّن الخلاف *bayyinu'l khilāf,* Showing the contrary, demonstrating to be false or repugnant.

A بينا *baynā,* In the mean time, whilst.

P بينا *bīnā,* (pl. بينايان *bīnāyān*) Seeing, clearly-sighted. A sort of long grass. A month.

A بيناً *baynan,* (or بيّناً *bayyinan*) Distinctly.

A بيناء *buyanāʾ,* (pl. of بيّن *bayyin*) Eloquent.

P بيناب *bīnāb,* A vision.

A بيّنات *bayyināt,* (pl. of بيّنة *bayyinat*) Evident proofs, evidences.

P بينارة *bīnāra,* A gigantic demon. A frightful, detestable face.

P بيناس *benās,* (or بيناسگ *benāsg*) A window.

P بينام *bī nām,* Without a name: nameless, anonymous. Without character or reputation. The finger-ring.

P بي ناموس *bī nāmūs,* Without law or religion. Uncivilized, rude, rustic. بي ناموس و ننگ *bī nāmūs u nang,* Clownish, without politeness or shame.

P بينائي *bīnāī,* The eye. Perspicacity, strength of sight or of mind, penetration, vision. A lunar month (in the Zand avestā). بينائي رفته *bīnāī-rafta,* Sightless, whose sight is gone.

A بينب *bīnab,* Periwinkle, spurge-laurel.

A بينة *bīnat,* (pl. of بيّن *bayyin*) Clear, evident.

A بيّنة *bayyinat,* (pl. بيّنات *bayyināt*) An evident demonstration, a positive proof. P بيّنت آوردن *bayyinat āwardan,* To bring proof, to demonstrate clearly (by witnesses).

P بيجيدن *biyanjīdan,* To sift. To be taken prisoner. To be made captive, helpless, and impatient.

P بيند *bīnad,* Hope. A number. *Biyand,* They are.

P بينش *bīnish,* Vision, sight. Providence.

P بي نشان *bī nishān,* Without sign, mark, or trace.

P بينصيب *bī nasīb,* Destitute, poor, portionless.

A بينط *biyant,* A weaver.

P بينظير *bī nazīr,* Matchless, unrivalled.

P بينظيري *bī nazīrī,* Pre-excellence, incomparableness, matchlessness.

P بي نعل *bī naʿl,* Destitute, poor.

P بينك چشم *bīnaki chashm,* The pupil of the eye.

A بينما *baynamā,* In the mean time, whilst.

P بي نمازي *bī namāzī,* Ceremonial impurity in women (disqualifying them for engaging in prayer).

P بينمك *bī namak,* Insipid, saltless, tasteless. Ill-favoured.

P بينمكي *bī namakī,* Insipidity. Ill behaviour. Ingratitude.

P بي نمود *bī namūd,* Invisible.

P بينند *bīnand,* (from ديدن *dīdan*) They see, will see, or may see. Hope, expectation. More. How many?

P بينندگي *bīnandagī,* Seeing, sight.

P بينندة *bīnanda,* A spectator, beholder. The eye. Provident.

P بيننگ *bī nang,* Shameless. Disreputable, without honour or reputation, Faultless.

P بيننگي *bī nangī,* Shamelessness.

P بي نوا *bī nawā,* Helpless, unfortunate, unprovided. A beggar.

P بي نوائي *bī nawāī,* Indigence, poverty, beggary. Destitution, fasting.

P بينور *bī nūr,* Without light. Blind. بي نور كردن *bī nūr kardan,* To extinguish.

A بينونة *baynūnat,* (v. n. of بان for بين) Being placed at a distance, separated, or distinguished (one from another). Being joined. Separation of parts.

P بينهايه *bī nihāya,* Without end, endless, infinite.

P بيني *bīnī,* The nose. The snout. The brain. The toe of a boot. (from ديدن *dīdan*) Thou seest, wilt see, mayest see. بينيء چراغ *bīnīsi charāgh,* The wick or flame of a candle. بينيء خوك *bīnīsi khūk,* The snout of a hog. بينيء كوه *bīnīsi koh,* The nose of a mountain; a promontory, peak, ness. بيني فشاندن *bīnī fishandan,* To sneeze. To blow the nose. To grunt.

P بينياز *bī niyāz,* Without prayers or entreaty, in want of nothing, independent, able to do without. Free. بينياز كردن *bī niyāz kardan,* To relieve from indigence, to guard one against want, to give charity.

P بي نيازي *bī niyāzī,* Independence, fortune.

P بيني بند *bīnī-band,* (or بيني ور *bīnīwar*) The nose-coverer, *i.e.* a veil worn by the Arabian ladies.

A بينيث *baynīs,* The fish called bonito.

P بيني دار *bīnī-dār,* Pointed at the toe (boot, shoe).

P بيني در *bīnī-dar,* The curtain of the door of a chamber or tent. A cramp-iron which fastens planks.

P بيني دراز *bīnī-darāz,* Long-nosed. A sturgeon.

P بيني درة *bīnī-dara,* The nostril.

P بيو *bayo,* A bride. *Bev,* A moth.

P بي وارث *bī wāris,* Heirless, without an owner.

P بيوارة *bewāra,* A foreigner, stranger. Destitute. A rolling-pin. Without rank, or consideration.

P بيواز *bewāz,* Quiet. A bat. Acceptance, reply.

P بيواسطة *bī wāsita,* Without means. Causeless.

P بيوالي *bī wālī,* Without a patron or protector.

P بيوان *biwān,* Leave.

P بي وايگي *bī wāyagī,* Independence, no want.

P بي واية *bī wāya,* Independent, without want.

P بيو باريدن *biyo* or *biyav bārīdan,* To bolt in eating, to swallow without masticating.

A بيوت *buyūt,* (pl. of بيت *bayt*) Houses.

A بيّوت *bayyūt,* Stale bread. Cold water. Nocturnal labour. امر بيّوت *amri bayyūt,* The work of the night, any thing done with great care, that smells of the lamp.

A بيوتات *buyūtāt,* (pl. of بيوت *buyūt,* pl. of بيت *bayt*) Many houses. *A* Out-houses. House-expenses; household; house-tax. An office for registering the effects of deceased persons.

A بيوتاتي *buyūtātī,* Holder of the above charge.

A بيّوتة *bayyūtat,* A tooth not shedding or falling out (when the time of changing arrives).

P بي وجود *bī wujūd,* Non-existing. Humble, low. Mean, vile.

A بيود *buyūd,* (v. n. of باد for بيد) Departing from one's friends. Dying. Setting (the sun). Perishing. Perdition.

P بيور *bīwar,* Ten thousand. The kernel of a walnut when dry and bitter. Name of Zahhāk.

P بيورد *beward,* Name of an ancient champion. Name of a city in Khurāsān.

P بيورسب *bīwarasb,* Zahhāk, a king of Persia.

P بيورنبارة *biyawrambāra,* A town in Egypt.

A بيوز *buyūz,* (v. n. of باز for بيز) Perishing. Escaping, fleeing away.

P بيوس *bayūs,* Avarice, cupidity. Hope, expectation. Humility. Flattery.

P بيوسندة *bayūsanda,* Abasing one's self. Hoping.

P بيوسيدن *bayūsīdan,* To hope. To excite hope. To flatter.

P بيوش *buyūsh,* Humility. Listening. Hope. Sham poverty.

P بيوشانيدن *buyūshānīdan*, To cause to submit.

A بيوض *bayūz*, (pl. بيض *bīz* and *buyuz*) (A hen) laying many eggs. *Buyūz*, (pl. of بيضة *bayzat*) Eggs.

P بيوضعي *bī wazaʿī*, Breach of good manners.

A بيوع *buyūʿ*, (pl. of بيع *bayʿ*) Sales. Purchases. Commercial dealings.

P بيوفا *bī wafā*, Faithless, insincere, deceitful. Fickle. Ungrateful.

P بي وفائي *bī wafāʾī*, Want of faith. Perfidy. Ingratitude. Fickleness.

P بي وقت *bī wakt*, Ill-timed, unseasonable.

P بيوقر *bī wakr*, Without character; dishonorable.

P بي وقوف *bī wukūf*, Inexpert. Uninformed.

P بيوگ *bayūg* or *buyūg*, A bride.

P بيوگاني *bayūgānī*, Nuptials. A marriage-feast.

P بيوگندن *biyavgandan*, To throw.

P بيوگي *bīwagī*, Widowhood.

P بيوليدن *buyūlīdan*, To hope: trust: consider.

P بيون *bayūn*, Opium.

A بيون *bayūn*, (A well) deep and full of water. *Buyūn*, (v. n. of بان for بين) Being separated, detached. (pl. of بين *bīn*) Tracts of ground. Districts within view.

P بيوند *bīwand*, Treachery, fraud, perfidy.

P بيوه *bīwa*, A widow. A widower. A stranger. Wild cucumber.

A بيه *bayh*, (v.n. of باه for بيه) Directing one's attention to, minding, attending to.

P بيهده *bayhuda*, Singed. *Bī huda*, (for بيهوده *bī hoda*) Vain, absurd. Useless. Villainous.

P بي هراس *bī hirās*, Fearless, intrepid.

A بيهس *bayhas*, A lion. A strong courageous man. A woman who walks well. Name of a man proverbial for taking retaliation, or Lynch-law.

A بيهسيّة *bayhasīyat*, A Muhammadan sect.

P بيهق *bayhak*, Name of a city.

P بيهمال *bī himāl*, Incomparable, excellent. Peerless, without equal or fellow.

P بيهمّت *bī himmat*, Without exertion or resolution. Humble, unambitious. Lazy, slothful. Mean, vile. Pusillanimous.

P بيهمتا *bī hamtā*, Incomparable, inimitable.

A بيهن *bayhan*, A narcissus.

P بيهن *bīhan*, A porcupine.

P بيهنر *bī hunar*, Ignorant, unskilful.

P بي هنري *bī hunarī*, Unskilfulness.

P بيهنگام *bī hangām*, Ill-timed, unseasonable.

P بيهود *bayhūd* or *bīhūd*, Cloth singed and yellow, from being too nigh the fire.

P بيهودگي *bī hodagī*, Absurdity, folly, levity.

P بيهودن *bayhūdan*, To singe. *Bihodan*, To talk nonsense.

P بيهوده *bayhūda*, Singed. *Bihoda*, Immodest, obscene. Vain, futile, impertinent, absurd, ridiculous, foolish, ill-applied, without foundation, ill-timed. Unprofitable. Useless. False, villainous. كوشش بيهوده *koshishi bīhoda*, Labour in vain, a foolish attempt. گذاف بيهوده *guzāfi bīhoda*, Idle words, trifles.

P بيهوده شدن *bayhūda shudan*, To be singed and yellow by fire.

P بيهوده كار *bīhoda-kār*, Frivolous, trifling. Jocose, jocular.

P بيهوده گو *bīhoda-gū*, Raving, doting; a dotard.

P بيهوده گوئي *bīhoda-gūʾī*, Vain talk, balderdash.

P بيهوش *bī hosh*, Insane, mad, distracted. Unconscious, insensible, fainted, swooned. بي هوش بيهوش شدن *bī hosh shudan*, To lose one's senses. گرديدن *bī hosh gardīdan*, To lose one's senses, to swoon. To become infatuated.

P بي هوشي *bī hoshī*, Insanity. Fainting, a fainting fit, a swoon. Stupefaction.

P بيهين *bīhīn*, Better. Swift-paced.

P بي يارمند *bī yārmand*, Friendless, defenceless.

A بيئة *bīʾat*, State, condition. A lodging, mansion, habitation. A hospitable reception.

A بييت *buyayt* or *biyayt*, (diminutive of بيت *bayt*) A small house.

A بئيرة *baʾīrat*, Whatever is laid up in a treasury or granary.

A بئيس *baʾīs*, Strong, bold. Stern, severe. عذاب بئيس *ʿazābi baʾīs*, A severe punishment.

A بييضة *buyayzat*, A hexagonal building. A house ornamented with pictures. The world.

A بئيل *baʾīl*, Small and weak.

پ

پ *pā* or *pe*, (called بائ فارسي *bāʾi fārsī* or بائ عجمي *bāʾi ʿajamī*) The third letter of the Persian alphabet, which, having the exact power of *p*, is herein represented by that letter. It is interchangeable with ف *fe*: as, فارسي *fārsī* or پارسي *pārsī*, سپيد *saped* or سفيد *safed*; and often with ب *be*: as, پادشاه *pādshāh* and بادشاه *bādshāh*. پ *pe* does not occur in the Arabic alphabet; thus for پيل *pīl* they write فيل *fīl*.

P پا *pā*, The foot. A footstep, vestige. Cause, pretence, pretext. Power, strength. Opposition, resistance. پائ دامن *pāʾi dāman*, That part of a skirt which sweeps the ground. پا پس آوردن *pā pas āwardan*, To abandon, recede, give up a pursuit. To be routed. پا بستن *pā bastan*, To be imprisoned. پا پس داشتن *pā pas dāshtan*, To have an aversion to a wife, to approach her seldom. پا بدامن كردن *pā ba dāman kardan*, To court retirement. To be contented. پا كوفتن *pā koftan*, To stamp the foot. To be offended, or ashamed of.

P پا افزار *pā-afzār*, A shoe, a slipper.

P پا افشار *pā-afshār*, (Foot-pressed) A treadle.

P پا انداز *pā-andāz*, A carpet spread at the entrance of a room, on which the feet are cleaned.

P پا آورنجن *pā-awranjan*, An ankle-ornament.

P پا آهو *pā-āhū*, A building of a hexagonal form. An apartment hung round with pictures. The world.

P پاب *pāb*, A father. The pope.

P پا بر جا *pā bar jā*, Firm, immoveable.

P پا برنجن *pā-baranjan*, An ankle-ornament.

P پا بست *pā-bast*, Foot-bound.

P پا بلند كردن *pā baland kardan*, To lift up the feet, to run.

P پا بند *pā-band*, Fetters. Swathes. Fettered.

P پا بوس *pā-bos*, Kissing the feet. Reverencing. The heel.

P پا بوسي *pā-bosī*, Reverence, worship, adoration.

P پاپا *pāpā*, Father. The Pope.

P پاپژ *pāpaj*, Uneven ground. Soft clay.

P پاپوش *pā-posh*, (Foot-cover) A shoe, slipper.

P پاپياده *pā-piyāda*, On foot.

P پات *pāt*, A throne.

P پاتابه *pā-tāba*, The ribands or straps of sandals. Wreaths. Bandages, rollers. A sock.

P پاتان *pātān*, Together with.

P پاتاوه *pātāwa*, A sock. Plenitude. A kind of cushion.

P پاتپراس *pātiprās*, (in zand and Pāzand) Recompense, retribution.

P پاتت *pātat*, Worthy, suitable.

P پاتخته *pā-takhta*, A shoe of undressed leather. The treadle of a weaver's loom.

P پاترگاه *pātrigāh*, A patriarch.

P پاتله *pātila*, A copper saucepan.

P پاتو *pātū*, The signs Gemini and Virgo; or, (according to others) Aries and Scorpio. A large earthen pot.

P پاتوا *pātawā*, A kind of shoe. A sock.

P پاتيله *pātīla*, A cauldron, kettle, pot (of copper or brass).

P پاتيمار *pātīmār*, Haste.

P پاتيني *pātīnī*, A sieve.

P پاجامه *pā-jāma*, Trowsers, long drawers.

P پاجه *pāja*, A piece, portion, fragment.

P پاجي *pājī*, Mean, low, grovelling.

P پاجيانه *pājiyāna*, Meanly.

P پاجي پرست *pājī-parast*, A patronizer of mean upstarts.

P پاجي مزاج *pājī-mizāj*, Mean-spirited.

P پاچال *pāchāl*, The treadle of a weaver's loom. A cook's shop, a place where they sell heads, feet, and intestines (of oxen or sheep). A fruiterer, green-grocer, or baker's shop.

P پاچان *pāchān*, (for پاشان *pāshān*) Scattering.

P پاچاه *pā-chāh*, (or پاچاهه *pā-chāha*) A weaver's treadle, or hole in which he places his feet.

P پاچايه *pāchāya*, Ordure, urine, filth.

P پاچك *pāchak*, Dried cow-dung used for fuel.

P پاچله *pā-chila*, A snow-shoe.

P پاچنامه *pāch-nāma*, A surname. An ally.

P پاچنگ *pāchang*, Small loop-holes in forts,

through which they can look with one eye only; garret-windows, fan-lights over doors. A shoe, a sandal.

P پاچوك *pāchūk*, Cow-dung dried for fuel.

P پاچه *pācha*, Feet (of sheep, calves, or other animals, especially when boiled), trotters.

P پاچه فروش *pācha-farosh*, Cooks who sell the heads of animals ready dressed.

P پاچیدن *pāchīdan*, To scatter. To go softly.

P پاچیله *pāchīla*, A shoe, sandal. A snow-shoe.

P پاخ *pākh*, Gold or silver full of dross or bad alloy, unrefined. Adorned, ornamented, decorated. Beautiful. Ingratitude. Vile, base. Lime, plaster, mortar, cement. An ambassador, envoy, legate. A beautiful form. Yesterday.

P پاخاك كردن *pā-khāk kardan*, To trudge.

P پاخته *pākhta*, A bricklayer's plummet.

P پاخره *pākhara*, *pākhira*, or *pākhra*, *pā-khara*, *pā-khira*, or *pā-khra*, A seat, a stool, a bench.

P پا خوردن *pā-khwurdan*, To be cheated.

P پاخوست *pā-khwust*, Trodden under foot.

P پاخیره *pākhīra*, Lowest row of stones in a wall.

P پاخیره زن *pākhīra-zan*, A builder. A mixer of mortar.

P پاد *pād*, Protecting, guarding. A guardian. Great. Firm, durable. A throne. Power, possession.

P پادادن *pā dādan*, To send. To give rank.

P پادار *pā-dār*, Permanent, fixed, immoveable. Always, continually. A spirited, mettlesome horse. The 20th day of the month of the æra of Jalālu'd dīn.

P پاداش *pādāsh*, پاداشت *pādāsht*, or پاداشن *pādāshan*, Revenge, vengeance, retaliation, reprisals. Reward, compensation. Retribution (good or bad).

P پادام *pā-dām*, A gin, a springe, made of horse-hair for catching birds. A bird tied by the foot to decoy others. An oratory. One who prays with great devotion.

P پادامان *pā-dāmān*, That part of a skirt which touches the ground.

P پادانیا *pādāniyā*, A root like a carrot.

P پادبان *pādbān*, A foot-band, a tether.

P پادر *pādar*, A trembling in the limbs.

P پادراز *pā-darāz*, Content, at ease. Boastful.

P پادرازي *pā-darāzī*, Boasting, arrogance.

P پا در ركاب *pā dar rikāb*, (Foot in the stirrup) Mounted on horseback. Prepared for a journey. In dying circumstances. Beginning to turn sour. Any thing beginning to go, become bad and spoilt.

P پا در گل *pā dar gil*, Stuck in the mire. Embarassed, entangled, bewildered.

P پادزهر *pād-zahr*, The bezoar-stone.

P پادست *pā-dast*, Buying or selling on credit.

P پادش *pādash*, Recompense, retribution.

P پادشاه *pād-shāh*, (from پاد و شاه *pād u shāh*, Protector and Lord, or from پاد *pād*, A throne, and شاه *shāh*, Lord) An emperor, sovereign, monarch, king. پادشاه عالم پناه *pādshāhi ʿālam-panāh*, A king the asylum of the world. پادشاه عالي جاه *pādshāhi ʿālī-jāh*, The emperor of exalted dignity. پادشاه چین *pādshāhi chīn* or پادشاه ختن *pādshāhi khutan*, The sun. پادشاه نیمروز *pādshāhi nīm roz*, The king of Sīstān. The sun. An upright man. Adam. Muhammad.

P پادشاهانه *pādshāhāna*, Royally, imperially, befitting a king.

P پادشاهت *pādshāhat*, Royalty.

P پادشاه زاده *pādshāh-zāda*, King's son, prince.

P پادشاهي *pādshāhī*, Kingdom, empire, monarchy, royal dignity. A reign. Royal, imperial. پادشاهي كردن *pādshāhī kardan* or پادشاهي راندن *pādshāhī rāndan*, To reign, to govern. To oppress. *Pādshāhe*, A king, a certain king.

P پادشه *pādshah*, (for پادشاه *pādshāh*) A king.

P پادكانه *pādkāna* or *pādikāna*, A high roof. A window.

P پادل *pādal*, A flower.

P پادنگ *pāding*, (or پادنگه *pādingah*) A flail. A pestle for separating rice from the husk.

P پاده *pāda*, A herd of oxen. A drove of asses. A walking-stick. A meadow, a pasture.

P پاده بان *pādabān*, A shepherd, a pastor.

P پادیاب *pād-yāb*, (or پادیاو *pād-yāv*) Washing, purifying (a thing) by prayer.

P پادیر *pā-dīr*, (or پاذیر *pā-zīr*, or پازیر *pā-zīr*) A prop, support, buttress.

P پار *pār*, Past, elapsed. Heretofore. A bit, a piece. A skin, a tanned hide. Last year. Flight.

P پاراج *pārāj*, A present to a superior, or guest.

P پاراو *pārāv*, An old woman. Name of a district of Kazvīn.

P پارچه *pārcha*, A piece, segment, section, morsel. Cotton or linen-cloth. A garment, a robe.

P پارد *pārad*, A tike, or cattle-louse.

P پاردان *pārdān*, A sack. A goblet. Wine.

P پاردم *pār-dum*, A crupper.

P پاردو *pārdū*, Balm.

P پارس *pārs*, A pard. An animal smaller than a leopard and trained to hunt. Persia. Pahlū, son of Shem.

P پارسا *pārsā*, Pure, chaste, devout, pious, holy, religious, abstinent, continent, above reproach. Legitimate, lawfully born. Clever, skilful, adroit in business. Persian, Persic. پارسا زن *pārsā-zan*, Pure, chaste, devout woman. The wife of a holy man.

P پارسال *pār-sāl*, The last year.

P پارسائي *pārsāʼī*, Chastity, purity, abstinence.

P پارسنگ *pār-sang*, A makeweight.

P پارسه *pārsa*, Indigence. Poor: mendicant.

P پارسي *pārsī*, A Persian. Persic.

P پارسیان *pārsiyān*, Pārsīs, fire-worshippers.

P پارسي نامه *pārsī-nāma*, Persian history.

P پارش *pārsh*, A pard. A leopard.

P پارگي *pārgī*, Prostitution. A sink.

P پارگین *pārgīn*, A sink, sewer. Dirty water.

P پارنج *pā-ranj*, (Foot-labour) Money given to singers and dancers at weddings and other entertainments. A remuneration to messengers or errand-boys. *Pāranj*, An orange.

P پارنجن *pā-ranjan*, An anklet. A garter.

P پارو *pāro*, (or پاروب *pārob*) A shovel. A paddle. An oar. An old woman. پارو كشیدن *pāro kashīdan*, To row.

P پاره *pāra*, A piece, portion, fragment, morsel. An iron mace. Flight. A gift. A bribe. Born. A kind of sweetmeat. A blemished damsel. The isle of Paros. يك پاره *yak pāra*, Solid, in one piece. پارهٔ آرد *pāraʼi ārd*, Gruel for the poor. پارهٔ آتش *pāraʼi ātish*, A spark of fire. پاره دادن *pāra dādan*, To bribe. پارهٔ زرد *pāraʼi zard*, A strip of yellow cloth which the Jews in some countries are obliged to wear. پاره زدن جامه *pāra zadani jāma*, The mending or patching of a garment. پاره كردن *pāra kardan*, To tear in pieces.

P پاره پاره *pāra-pāra*, In pieces, piece-meal. By instalments. پاره پاره شدن *pāra pāra shudan*, To evaporate in steam (boiling water). پاره پاره كردن *pāra pāra kardan*, To divide into portions. To tear to pieces.

P پاره پاره شده *pāra pāra shuda*, In pieces.

P پاره دوز *pāra-doz*, A botcher. A tent-maker.

P پاره دوزي *pāra-dozī*, Patching, botching.

P پاره زده *pāra-zada*, Patched.

P پاره كار *pāra-kār*, Airy, saucy; a coquette.

P پاري *pārī*, Succeeding well, any thing which happens fortunately. Fruit. Of last year.

P پاریاب *pāryāb*, (or پاریاو *pāryāv*) Tillage by means of irrigation.

P پاریدن *pārīdan*, To fly.

P پارین *pārīn*, Last year. Of the last year.

P پارینه *pārīna*, Old, ancient.

P پاز *pāz*, Sincere. Elegant, graceful.

P پازاج *pāzāj*, A midwife. A wet-nurse.

P پازار *pāzār*, A peasant's shoe made of raw leather, or the bark of a tree. Any kind of bandages wrapt round the feet. An infant's swaddling-clothes.

P پازبا *pāzbā*, The bezoar-stone.

P پازتاري *pāztārī*, A portion, a part.

P پازخ *pāzakh*, A voice. A sigh, lamentation.

P پازده *pā-zada*, Trampled, trodden under foot.

P پازش *pāzish*, A weeding up, rooting of weeds.

P پازگیر *pāzgīr*, Tail of a serpent or dragon.

P پازن *pāzan*, The mountain-goat.

P پازند *pā-zand*, A commentary on the Zand.

P پازوم *pāzūm*, Meat, food, victuals.

P پازه *pāza*, A shepherd's crook.

P پازهر *pāzahr*, Treacle, an antidote against poison or venom. The bezoar-stone.

P پازیب *pā-zīb* or *zeb*, A chain-anklet, or female ornament, consisting of heavy rings of silver resembling a curb-chain, occasionally set with a fringe of small spherical bells charged with shot, all of which tinkle at every motion of the legs.

P پازيده *pāzīda*, A butterfly. A bat.

P پازير *pā-zīr*, A buttress, a shore for a wall.

P پازيژه *pāzīja*, (or پازين) A little of the night.

P پاژ *pāj*, A place in the dependencies of Tūs.

P پاژخ *pājakh*, A voice, a noise. Friction. *Pājukh*, An answer.

P پاژنامه *pāj-nāma*, A surname, style, title. A peer. A friend.

P پاژند *pā-jand*, A commentary on the Zand.

P پاژنگ *pājang*, A shoe. A little window.

P پاژو *pājū*, Beet. Spinage. A door-post.

P پاژه *pāja*, Feet (of sheep, &c.) dressed.

P پاژير *pājīr*, The bezoar-stone.

P پاس *pās*, A watch of the day or night, three hours. Guard, watch. A guard, sentinel; defence, protection. Regard for, in consideration of. Sadness, heartache. A part, portion. پاس داشتن *pās dāshtan*, To guard, to protect. پاس نمك *pāsi namak*, Faithful service. پاس خاطر *pās khātir*, For sake of, in deference to.

P پاساخت *pā-sākht*, Ready prepared.

P پاساد *pāsād*, Defence, preservation. Abstinence from every thing bad.

P پاسار *pāsār*, (or پاسپار) A kick, wince. A cuff.

P پاسبان *pāsbān*, A sentinel, guard, watchman. A shepherd. پاسبان خطهٔ اوّل *pāsbāni khittaʼi avval*, Angels. پاسبان طارم نهم *pāsbāni tārami nuhum*, (or فلك *falak*) The planet Saturn.

P پاسباني *pāsbānī*, Watching; watch and ward.

P پا سبك *pā-sabuk*, Swift of foot. A long arrow with four wings for shooting at a mark.

P پاسپردگي *pā sipurdagī*, A treading, trampling.

P پاسپرده *pā sipurda* (or پا سپر كرده *pā-sipur karda*) Trodden, beaten (road).

P پا ستاده *pā's tāda*, Standing on foot, ready, in order. آماده و پاستاده *āmāda u pā's tāda*, Ready, prepared, and on foot.

P پاستان *pāstān*, Former.

P پاستاني *pāstānī*, Of former times.

P پاستانيان *pāstāniyān*, The ancients.

P پاسخ *pāsukh*, An answer. پاسخ دادن *pāsukh dādan*, To give an answer. شكر پاسخ *shakar-pāsukh*, Giving a mild, sweet, gentle answer.

P پاسدار *pās-dār*, A sentinel, guard, watchman.

P پاسداري *pās-dārī*, Guardianship. Partiality.

P پاسره *pāsara*, Ground rent-free for wages.

P پاسك *pāsak* or *pāsuk*, Yawning.

P پاسنگ *pā-sang*, A makeweight.

P پاسوار *pā-suwār*, A nimble pedestrian.

P پاسوان *pāswān*, A watchman, guard.

P پاسه *pāsa*, Propensity. Grief, sadness.

P پاسي *pāse*, A watch of the night.

P پاسيدن *pāsīdan*, To guard, keep watch, wake.

P پاش *pāsh*, (in comp. from پاشيدن *pāshīdan*) Diffusing, scattering. شعله پاش *shuʻla-pāsh*, Scattering flames. ضيا پاش *ziyā-pāsh*, Light-diffusing.

T پاشا *pāshā*, (for باشا *bāshā*) A lord, a bashā.

P پاشام *pāshām*, The membrane enveloping the pia mater. The caul containing the bowels. Oil extracted from nuts.

P پاشامه *pā-shāma*, Long drawers.

P پاشته *pāshta*, The heel, the fleshy part of the foot. پاشتهٔ در *pāshtaʼi dar*, The foot of a door.

P پاشك *pāshak*, Yawning.

P پاشنا *pāshnā*, The heel. A cucumber, melon, or pumpkin kept for seed.

P پاشنامه *pāshnāma*, A surname. Peer, equal.

P پاشنگ *pāshang*, (or پاشنگه) A small cluster of grapes. A cucumber or melon kept for seed.

P پاشنه *pāshina*, The heel. The sole of a shoe, particularly that part answering to the heel. A pumice-stone with which they rub the heels when in the bath. The foot of a door, or that part which revolves in a socket, in the threshold or lintel, and serves the purpose of a hinge.

P پاشنه كوب *pāshina-kob*, Close on the heels.

P پاشو *pāshū*, A crook. A pilgrim's staff.

P پاشي *pāshī*, A diffusion, scattering. A sprinkling. Irrigation.

P پاشيب *pā-shīb*, The round of a ladder. The declivity of a mountain. A foot-stool.

P پاشيدن *pāshīdan*, To sprinkle, scatter. To be sprinkled or scattered. To be filled.

P پاشيده *pāshīda*, Sprinkled, dispersed. Scattered, diffused. A cucumber, melon, pumpkin. A bunch of grapes.

P پاشينه *pāshīna*, The heel.

P پاغر *pāghar*, The main beam of a house.

P پاغره *pā-ghura*, The elephantiasis.

P پاغند *pāghund*, (or پاغنده *pāghunda* or *pāghanda*) Carded cotton.

P پاغوش *pā-ghosh*, Dip, plunge, immersion.

P پافزار *pā-fazār*, A shoe, a slipper.

P پاك *pāk*, Pure, chaste, innocent, clean, neat. Perfect, full, complete. All, entire. پاك آب *pāk-āb*, Pure water. پاك و پاكيزه *pāk u pākīza*, Quite pure, polished, neat, clean. Totally, entirely. پاك شدن *pāk shudan*, To become obliterated. پاك كردن *pāk kardan*, To purify, wash, polish, furbish. To obliterate.

P پاكار *pā-kār*, A sub-collector of revenue. A nightman. Second in command. A servant.

P پاكان خطّ اوّل *pākāni khatti awwal*, The angels who bear the throne of God.

P پاك باز *pāk-bāz*, Having a fortunate aspect, or a fine countenance. Sporting harmlessly. An honourable lover. A fair dealer. A saint. پاكباز چرخ *pāk-bāzi charkh*, The moon. Moonlight.

P پاك بازي *pāk-bāzī*, Purity of mind.

P پاك بوم *pāk-būm*, Pure earth.

P پاكبوي *pāk-boy* or *būy*, Chaste.

P پاك دامن *pāk-dāman*, Chaste, pure.

P پاكردن *pā kardan*, To stand in presence of.

P پاكرو *pāk-rū*, Beautiful-faced. *Pāk-rao*, Pure in one's walk.

P پاك سوختن *pāk sokhtan*, To burn clean up.

P پا كشاده رواق *pā-kushāda-rawāk*, The sky.

P پاكشان *pāk-shān*, Noble, illustrious, exalted.

P پاك شده *pāk-shuda*, Obliterated.

P پاك صاف *pāk-sāf*, Pure, clean, undefiled.

P پاكند *pākand*, A ruby.

P پاك نهاد *pāk-nihād*, Pure, holy.

P پا كوب *pā-kob*, A dancer, a jumper.

P پا كوفتن *pā koftan*, To dance.

P پاكي *pākī*, Purity, chastity, cleanliness. Completion. A razor.

P پاكيدن *pākīdan*, To purify, to clean.

P پاكيزگي *pākīzagī*, Purity, cleanness, neatness.

P پاكيزه *pākīza*, Pure, chaste. Innocent. Purity, chastity. پاكيزه كردن *pākīza kardan*, To winnow.

P پا گاه *pā-gāh*, A privy. The step of a ladder or staircase. The foot-way or pavement at the side of a street. Stones placed like steps for mounting to any place. A stable. Extremity.

P پالا *pālā*, (in composition) Straining. A colander or strainer, made of brass or earth, for washing rice and draining the juice of grapes from the stones, stalks, &c. Hung, suspended. A horse led for parade. (in zand and Pāzand) Lamentation.

P پالاپال *pāl-ā-pāl*, Strained hard. The sail of a ship. Swift, rapid. Hard, firm.

P پالاد *pālād*, A led horse, a horse of state.

P پالادن *pālādan*, To strain.

P پالاده *pālāda*, A led horse. Villainous.

P پالار *pālār*, (or پالارخانه *pālār-khāna*) The highest beam, that which supports the roof. A roof.

P پالارنگ *pālārang*, Indian iron or steel.

P پالاري *pālārī*, A main-beam. A rafter, joist.

P پالاش *pā-lāsh*, One with dirty feet.

P پالاگر *pālāgar*, The main-beam of a house.

P پالان *pālān*, A pack-saddle. A vestibule.

P پالاندوز *pālān-doz*, A maker of pack-saddles.

P پالانگر *pālāngar*, A pack-saddle maker.

P پالانده *pālānanda*, Increasing, augmenting.

P پالانه *pālāna*, A balcony, a belvidere.

P پالاني *pālānī*, A sluggish beast of burden. A maker of pack-saddles. An artificer's tool. اسب پالاني *asbi pālānī*, A packhorse.

P پالانيدن *pālānīdan*, To strain. To press, to squeeze. To cause to strain.

P پالاوان *pālāwān*, (or پالاون *pālāwan*) A colander, strainer. Any vessel full of holes through which liquor is drained. A skimmer.

P پالاهنگ *pālāhang*, (contract. of پالا *pālā*, A led horse, and آهنگ *āhang*, Drawing) A rein, bridle, halter, rope, cord. The pillory, or four cross pieces of wood, in which they enclose the necks of men or cattle. A noose, a buck-stall. A medium. The galaxy.

P پالاي *pālāy*, Straining. Augmenting. Led horse.

P پالاي اسپ *pālāy-asp*, A horse led for parade.

P پالايش *pālāyish*, Filtration, percolation.

P پالاييدن *pālāyidan*, To strain. To increase.

P پالدم *pāl-dum*, The crupper-leather.

P پالش *pālish*, Increase, augmentation.

P پالغ *pālugh*, A cup made of horn or ivory.

P پالغز *pā-laghz*, A false step, slip, trip: ruin.

P پالغزيده *pā-laghzīda*, Slipping, tripping.

P پالك *pālak*, A shoe, slipper. Spinage.

P پالكانه *pālkāna*, A high roof. A window. The beginning of harvest. Any thing put into a scale to maintain the equilibrium.

P پالكي *pālkī*, A travelling litter, a palanqueen.

P پالنده *pālanda*, Growing, increasing.

P پالنگ *pālang*, A kind of rustic shoe made of cow's leather. A small window. A bed. Name of a fruit. A certain river.

P پالنگ پوش *pālang-posh*, A quilt, coverlet.

P پالو *pālū*, A wart.

P پالواسه *pālwāsa*, Grief, anguish of mind.

P پالوانه *pālwāna*, A bird of paradise, said to live chiefly in the air. A colander.

P پالوايه *pālwāya*, A swallow.

P پالود *pālūd*, Strained. A lamb-skin garment.

P پالودگي *pālūdagī*, A straining, a racking off.

P پالودن *pālūdan*, To strain, squeeze, press, drain, filter, purify. To become pure. To increase, to be large. To make large. To deliver. To escape.

P پالوده *pālūda*, Strained, filtered. Gilded. A kind of sweet beverage made of water, flour, and honey. The bason of a pair of scales. پالودۀ رواق ربعي *pālūda-i rawāki ribʿī*, Vernal showers.

P پالودي *pālūdī*, A garment of lamb-skin.

P پالوزه *pālūza*, A wart.

P پالوسه *pālūsa*, Sickness, grief, anguish, agony.

P پالوش *pālosh*, Adulterated camphor.

P پالونه *pālūna*, A colander or strainer.

P پالهنگ *pālhang*, A bridle, halter, rope. Four cross pieces of wood in which they enclose the necks of men or cattle. A pillory. A noose with which any thing is caught. A medium.

P پاليال *pālyāl*, Always, perpetual. Joined.

P پاليدن *pālīdan*, To purify. To see. To inquire, search.

P پاليده *pālīda*, Strained, purified. Increased. Searched, investigated.

P پاليز *pālez*, Kitchen-garden. Melon-ground.

P پاليزبان *pālezbān*, (or پاليزوان *pālezwān*) A gardener. Name of a note in music.

P پاليك *pālik*, A leathern shoe. Bandages.

P پام *pām*, Like. Colour. Debt.

P پامال *pā-māl*, Trampled upon, trodden under foot, beaten (as a path). Dashed. Plunder, spoil, destruction. پامال خيول شدن *pā-māli khuyūl shudan*, To be trodden under foot by the cavalry. پامال كردن *pā-māl kardan*, To trample, lay waste.

P پامرد *pā-mard*, Powerful. An assistant. An intercessor.

P پامردي *pā-mardī*, Strength. Intercession.

P پامزد *pā-muzd*, Gain earned by foot-labour.

P پامس *pāmas*, Tied by the leg, wearied with but unable to quit the place one is in.

P H پان *pān*, A plant bearing an aromatic leaf chewed with the areca or beetle-nut. The name in India is *tāmbūl*. The word *pān* is used for the whole composition as made up for chewing.

P پانجاه *pānjāh*, (for پنجاه *panjāh*) Fifty.

P پانزده *pānzdah* or *pānzadah*, Fifteen.

P پانزده سالگي *pānzdah-sālagī*, Age of fifteen.

P پانزدهم *pānzdahum*, The fifteenth.

P پانزهر *pānzahar*, Bezoar-stone, an antidote.

P پانسند *pānasand*, Sought for, inquired after.

P پانمشك *pānmushk*, The turpentine-tree.

P پانصد *pānsad*, (for پنج صد) Five hundred. پانصد هزار *pānsad hazār*, Five hundred thousand.

P پانه *pāna*, A shoemaker's or carpenter's wedge. A wedge put under a door to keep it from flying open.

P پانهاده *pā-nihāda*, Brought into existence, appearing. Set on foot.

P پاني پت *pānī-pat*, A town 50 miles from Delhi.

P پانيذ *pānīz*, Sugar-candy, a sweetmeat.

P پاو *pāw*, Washing, cleansing. A foot.

P پاوپر *pāvpar*, Power, authority.

P پاوچك *pāwchak*, Dry cow-dung for fuel.

P پاورنجن *pā-waranjan*, A metal ring worn on the ankle by females.

P پاوند *pā-wand*, A fetter.

P پاه *pāh*, Meat, victuals.

P پاها *pāhā*, (pl. of پا *pā*) Feet.

P پاهك *pāhak*, The torture, torment.

P پاهكيدن *pāhakīdan*, To torture.

P پاهنگ *pāhang*, A small window. A make-weight. An ornament for the female ankle.

P پاهنگه *pā-hanga*, A slipper. An ankle-ring.

P پاي *pāy*, The foot. A footing. Vestige, track, footstep. Base, bottom. Basis, foundation. Firmness, durability, permanency. Resistance. Power, force. The hinder or latter part. End, limit. Excuse, pretext, pretence. پاي فكر *pāyi fikr*, The foot of thought. پاي بز افگندن *pāyi buz afgandan*, To be uneasy and restless. To charm (in allusion to a practice with butchers, of writing an incantation and tying it to the leg of a goat; which being turned loose among a herd, attracts the whole herd about him, so that the butcher can catch whichever he chooses). پاي كوفتن *pāy koftan*, To dance. با فلان پاي ندارم *bā fulān pāy na dāram*, I am not upon a footing with such a one. I cannot resist such a one. بپاي داشتن *ba pāy dāshtan*, To stand upright. To put forth, to publish. بپاي داشتن نمازرا *ba pāy dāshtan namāzrā*, To assist at prayers. برپاي داشتن *bar pāy dāshtan*, To support, preserve, maintain. برپاي كردن *bar pāy kardan*, To rise, stand up.

P پايا *pāyā*, Existing, standing, continuing.

P پاياب *pā-yāb*, Power, strength, force. Resistance. A well, any shallow stone reservoir of water easy of access. The bottom of the sea, pond, or piece of water. Eternity, perpetuity, duration. Shallow, fordable, shoaly. A ford.

P پاي ابرنجن *pāy-abranjan*, An ankle ring.

P پايابي *pā-yābī*, Shallowness, shoaliness.

P پايازي *pāyāzī*, Pain, anguish, grief.

P پاي افراز *pāy-afrāz*, A shoe. Swift messenger.

P پاي افزار *pāy-afzār*, Shoes which tie with strings. A treadle.

P پاي افزاه *pāy-afzāh*, Promoting in rank.

P پاي افشار *pāy-afshār*, A weaver's treadle.

P پايان *pāyān*, End, extremity. Limit, boundary, margin. The point of contact of two circles. A place to leave the shoes. Low, inferior. پايان روزي بخوردن *pāyāni roze ba khurdan*, To terminate one's life. بپايان بردن كار *ba pāyān burdani kār*, To accomplish, execute, or finish any business. بي پايان *bī pāyān*, Endless. Immense.

P پاي انداز *pāy-andāz*, Shoes which tie with strings. Carpets spread on the pavement on the public entry of a king.

P پاي آور *pāy-āwar*, Powerful, great.

P پاي اوژاره *pāy-awjāra*, A weaver's treadle.

P پاي باف *pāy-bāf*, A weaver.

P پاي باقي *pāy-bākī*, Balance of account.

P پاي بدامن كردن *pāy ba dāman kardan*, To desist, refrain.

P پاي برافگندن *pāy bar afgandan*, To be restless, impatient. To be weak. To fascinate, bewitch.

P پاي بر پي نهادن *pāy bar pay nihādan*, To follow, obey.

P پاي برجاي *pāy bar jāy*, Firmly fixed.

P پاي برچشم نهادن *pāy bar chashm nihādan*, (To place the foot on the eye) To salute.

P پاي برداشتن *pāy bar dāshtan*, To have power.

P پاي برسنگ آمدن *pāy bar sang āmadan*, To risk one's life, to encounter danger.

P پاي بركابست *pāy ba rikāb ast*, He is on a journey, his foot is in the stirrup.

P پاي برميان آوردن *pāy bar miyān āwardan*, To be overwhelmed with business.

P پاي برهنه *pāy-barahna*, Barefoot.

P پاي بس آوردن *pāy bas āwardan*, To retreat.

P پاي بست *pāy-bast*, (or پاي بسته *pāy-basta*) A prisoner, captive. Standing, waiting. Foundation.

P پاي بند *pāy-band*, Tied by the leg. Encumbered with a family. A fetter. Deceit, treachery.

P پاي بندي *pāy-bandī*, Fettered, in fetters.

P پاي بوس *pāy-bos*, Kissing the feet; a ceremony said to have been originally instituted by Kayumars, king of Persia, who reigned near 900 years before the Christian æra, as a mark of fidelity, respect, and homage, from the subordinate kings who acknowledged him as their lord paramount.

P پاي پوزان *pāy-pūzān*, A fear-inspiring voice.

P پاي پوش *pāy-posh*, A shoe. پاي پوش زدن *pāy-posh zadan*, To beat with a shoe (degrading).

P پاي پوشي *pāy-poshī*, Covering for the feet.

P پاي پيچيدن *pāy pechīdan*, To turn away the feet. To run. To fly. To give up the ghost.

P پاي پيل *pāy-pīl*, A cup made in the form of an elephant's foot. A spear used by the Ethiopians.

P پاي تابه *pāy-tāba*, A shoe-sock. پاي تابه گشادن *pāy-tāba gushādan*, (To draw off one's socks) To come off a journey.

P پاي تخت *pāy-takht*, The foot of the throne. The metropolis.

P پاي تراب *pāy-turāb*, Change of ground or place, following quick. First stage of a journey.

P پاي ثبات *pāy-sabāt*, Firmness, steadfastness.

P پاي جامه *pāy-jāma*, Drawers, trowsers (either loose or scant).

P پايچال *pāy-chāl*, A weaver's treadle.

P پاي چوبين *pāy-chūbīn*, (or *chobīn*) Stilts.

P پايچه *pāycha*, Breeches, drawers, or trowsers. The feet of sheep or calves ready dressed. Cow-heel. The frontstall of a bridle. A frontlet, or any ornament for the forehead.

P پاي حوض *pay-hāwz*, A place of ill fame.

P پاي خاكي كردن *pāy-khākī kardan*, To travel. To seek.

P پاي خانه *pāy-khāna*, A necessary, privy.

P پاي خرچ *pāy-kharch*, Balance, residue.

P پاي خوان *pāy-khwān*, Interpretation.

P پاي خوست *pāy-khwust*, (پاي خست *pāy-khast*, or پاي خسته *pāy-khasta*) Trodden down, trampled upon, kicked. Any thing laid under foot.

P پاي خوشه *pāy-khosha*, (Ground) become hard from the trampling of men or animals.

P پاي دادن *pāy dādan*, To erect, set on foot. To have lost, to be disheartened.

P پايدار *pāy-dār*, Having feet. Firm, fixed, permanent, constant, uninterrupted, durable, steady. Standing (corn). Long-lived. An epithet of God. Confirming. Strong, mettlesome (horse). (equiv. to كعبتين قلب *kaʻbatayni kalb*, Auricles? of the heart).

P پاي داره *pāy-dāra*, An assistant. Succour.

P پايداري *pāy-dārī*, Stability. پايداري كردن *pāy-dārī kardan*, To tread firmly. To do any thing often, over and over again, substantially. To injure, abuse. To suffer patiently. To wait, expect. To be firm.

P پاي داشتن *pāy dāshtan*, To keep in custody.

P پاي دام *pāy-dām*, A hair-noose to catch birds, a springe, gin. A rope-ladder for climbing trees. A decoy-bird.

P پاي دامن خود كشيدن *pāyi dāmani khwud kashīdan*, To draw in one's skirts. (met.) To return from ill ways to good.

P پايدامه *pāy-dāma*, A fetter: a noose. A gin.

P پايدان *pāydān*, A shoe. A treadle. Perpetual.

P پايدان آب *pāydān-āb*, Running water.

P پاي در راه نهادن *pāy dar rāh nihādan*, To proceed, set out.

P پاي در سنگ *pāy dar sang*, Immoveable. پاي در سنگ آمدن *pāy dar sang āmadan*, To stumble, to fall on a stone.

P پاي درگشتن *pāy dar yashtan*, To be weak.

P پاير *pāyir*, The time of the sun's stay in Cancer.

P پاي رنج *pāy-ranj*, (Foot-labour) Money given to messengers or dancers. پاي رنج كشيدن *pāy ranj kashīdan*, To be prepared.

P پايز *pāyiz*, The autumn.

P پايزار *pāyzār*, A shoe, a slipper.

P پاي زاغ كردن *pāy zāgh kardan*, To be drawn into a snare.

P پايزن *pāy-zan*, A cut-throat, foot-pad. A slave.

P پاي زنجير *pāy-zanjīr*, Chained, tied by the leg. Encumbered with a family.

P پايزه *pāyiza*, Delegated regal authority.

P پاي زهر *pāy-zahr*, The bezoar-stone.

P پاي زيب *pāy-zīb*, A woman's foot-ornament.

P پايژه *pāyija*, A tent-rope.

P پايستن *pāyistan*, To wait. To be firm. To trample on.

P پاي ستور *pāy-sutūr*, A sort of musical instrument, made from the hoof of an animal, in use amongst shepherds.

P پايسته *pāyista*, Firm, permanent.

P پاي سخن *pāyi sukhun*, Eloquence.

P پاي شكم *pāyi shikam*, The lower belly.

P پاي شيب *pāy-shīb*, A solemnity performed in the valley of Mina near Mecca, in which they defy and throw stones at a figure representing the devil. The place of future punishment.

P پاي فرو كشيدن *pāy faro kashīdan*, To wait.

P پاي فشردن *pāy fashurdan*, To remain, be firm, constant. To continue in a morbid and melancholy state of mind.

P پاي كار *pāy-kār*, Expert. A sub-revenue-collector. An attendant on a revenue-collector. A sweep.

P پايكاشت *pāy-kāsht*, (Land) let out to non-resident tenants.

P پاي كشانيده *pāy-kashānīda*, Emancipated. A fugitive.

P پاي كشيدن *pāy kashīdan*, To quit, refrain.

P پاي كم آوردن *pāy kam āwardan*, To run off.

P پاي كوب *pāy-kob*, A dancer.

P پاي كوبان *pāy-kobān*, Prancing.

P پاي كوفتن *pāy koftan*, To dance. To be going, or dying.

P پايگاه *pāy-gāh*, A vestibule, portico, or court before a house. A place for depositing shoes. A stable. An inn or any place where travellers put up. A step of a stair or ladder. Dignity, rank, office, employment. Root, stock. A necessary. The projecting part of a roof. The bottom of a piece of water. A ford.

P پاي گذار *pāy-guzār*, An assistant.

P پاي گرد كردن *pāy gird kardan*, To supplant.

P پاي گرفتن *pāy giriftan*, To walk, to travel.

P پاي گشادن *pāy gushādan*, To return. To run away. To divorce.

P پايگه *pāy-gah*, A place for leaving one's shoes. A stable. Dignity, rank, office. Root, stock. A ford.

P پايگي *pāygī*, Degree, rank. A troop.

P پاي لغز *pāy-laghz*, A false step; error, fault.

P پايم *pāyam*, My foot.

P پاي ماچان *pāy-māchān*, The lowest order of priest. A place for leaving the slippers. A sort of penance practised by the Sūfis, in which the offender is made to stand on one foot, his left hand touching his right ear, and his right hand his left ear. پاي ماچان رفتن *pāy-māchān raftan*, To excuse one's self.

P پاي مال *pāy-māl*, Trampled upon, trodden under foot, bruised, kicked. Ruined, destroyed. Defeated, dissipated, dispersed, despised. Vile, contemptible. Remission made to a renter on account of the depredation of an enemy, &c. پايمال كردن *pāy-māl kardan*, To ruin.

P پايمالي *pāy-mālī*, Devastation, ruin, occasioned by an army or cattle overrunning and trampling fields or gardens.

P پايمرد *pāy-mard*, An assistant. An intercessor. Courageous.

P پايمردي *pāy-mardī*, Assistance. Intercession. Courage.

P پاي مزد *pāy-muzd*, Hire for running about.

P پايموز *pāymoz*, A kind of pigeon.

P پاين *pāyin*, Low, below, inferior. At the foot of. Of less value.

P پايانداز *pāy-andāz*, Cloths of silk and other rich stuff, which in some places are spread upon the streets when the king makes a public entry. Gold, silver, jewels, or other presents made to great men (as being laid at their feet).

P پايندان *pāyandān*, A security, surety, cautioner, sponsor. A hostage. A pledge. Imprisonment, durance. A place where shoes are pulled off.

P پايندان كار *pāyandān-kār*, A factor, agent.

P پايندانى *pāyandānī*, Security, pledge, caution. پايندانى كردن *pāyandānī kardan*, To give surety, to become bound for.

P پايندگان *pāyandagān*, The blessed. The damned. The throne of God.

P پايندگي *pāyandagī*, Firmness, permanency.

P پايندن *pāyandan*, To delay. To wait.

P پاينده *pāyanda*, Firm, solid, substantial, durable, lasting, permanent, perennial, perpetual, continual, subsisting, remaining. Always, constantly. A royal diploma, granting an immunity from taxes. The prop (of a wall) somewhat curved. One who keeps his eye stedfastly fixed on any object.

P پايني *pāyinī*, Inferiority, meanness.

P پاي و پر *pāy u par*, Power, strength.

P پاي وجود درگل اجل رفتن *pāyi wujūd dar giliajalraftan*, To sink into the fatal slough. To die.

P پايون *pāyūn*, An ornament of jewels, gold, or silver.

P پايوند *pāywand*, A fetter.

P پايه *pāya*, The step of a stair, the round of a ladder. A staircase. A ladder. Basis, foundation. Dignity, rank, promotion, office, degree. A three-legged piece of wood on which they hang clothes. Low, vile. Lost. Trampling under foot, kicking. Thrashing, beating. Quantity. Rain. پايۀ اعلىٰ *pāyaʼi aʻlaʼ*, The highest step or rank. پايۀ حوض *pāyaʼi hawz*, A place of ill fame. پايۀ سرير *pāyaʼi sarīr*, The foot of the throne.

P پايه پايه *pāya pāya*, By degrees, according to rank, in due order or gradation, step by step.

P پايه دار *pāya-dār*, Possessed of authority.

P پائي *pāʼī*, Humility. Permanent, stable.

P پاييدن *pāyīdan*, (or پائيدن *pāʼīdan*) To stand firm, to be constant, steady, fixed, established; to subsist independently of any thing. To fix the look steadily on any object. To trample upon, wear, beat, or make smooth with the feet. To kick. To wait, expect. To become satiated, fatigued, tired.

P پائير *pāʼīr*, Time of the sun's stay in Cancer.

P پاييز *pāyīz*, Autumn. Old age, decline of life.

P پائي كار *pāʼī kār*, A person who purchases goods from the manufacturer to sell to the merchant.

P پائين *pāʼīn*, Lower part, bottom, foundation.

P پايين پرستي *pāyīn-parastī*, Obedience.

P پپتك *piptak*, A small cluster of dates or grapes. A part of a cluster.

P پپره *papara*, (in zand and Pāz.) Old, aged.

P پپريشيدن *paprīshīdan*, To disperse, scatter.

P پپلس *paplus*, Bread soaked in oil and syrup.

P پپليپا *paplīpā*, (in zand and Pāzand) A garment, a short vest.

P پپنو *papanū*, Sour milk from which the butter is taken; when coagulated, and the thinner part strained off, it is dried in the sun, and preserved with salt, &c., for winter use.

P پت *pat*, Starch, size. Goats' hair which is soft, fine, and inner. Any thing soft. *Put*, A worm which pierces ships' bottoms.

P پتادق *patādak*, (A word used to express celerity or the noise of any thing falling) Impetuously, thunderingly.

P پتاره *patāra*, A brush for sprinkling cloth in the loom.

P پتت *pitat*, Repentance. Asking forgiveness.

P پتخ *pathh*, Astonished, stupefied. Foolish.

P پتسر *patar*, Amulets of gold or silver.

P پتسو *patsū*, Acidulated milk dried. (See پپنو).

P پتفت *pataft*, Repentance, resipiscence.

P پتفوز *patfoz*, The parts round the mouth. The snout (of an animal), the beak (of a bird). The circumference of a cap. پتفوز زبر *patfozi zabar*, The upper lip of a quadruped.

P پتفوز بسته *patfoz-basta*, Muzzled.

P پتفوز بند *patfoz-band*, A muzzle.

P پتك *puth*, A smith's hammer.

P پتگير *patgīr*, A hair-sieve, a searce.

P پتل *patal*, A mat.

P پتلاد *putlād*, (or پتلادە) A bar for a door.

P پتل بند *patal-band*, A mat-maker.

P پتلوب *patlūb*, A kind of food made of sour milk, milk, and walnuts.

P پتنگ *patang*, A paper kite. *Pitang*, Window.

P پتنگ بازي *patang-bāzī*, Flying kites.

H پتنه *patna*, The capital of Bahār (India).

P پتني *patanī*, A hopper for seed-corn.

P پتو *patav*, A place constantly exposed to the sun. (for پرتو *partav*) A ray of light. *Patū*, A kind of woollen cloth. Camlet.

P پتواز *patwāz*, A perch, a roost.

P پتوله *patūla*, A kind of Indian silken stuff.

H پتّه *pattah*, A lease. A grant or lease specifying the quantity of land possessed by each tenant, and the amount of rent with which it is assessed. A broadsword. Bosses on a bridle.

H P پتّه دار *patta-dār*, A leaseholder.

P پتيا *putyā*, Penitence, repentance.

P پتياره *patyāra*, Affliction, misery, misfortune. Any thing ugly, terrific, and shocking. Modesty. Severity, vehemence. Fraud, stratagem. Shame. Contention, strife. Hidden, concealed.

H پتياله *patyāla*, A town N. W. of Delhi.

P پتيره *patīra*, Disgusting, shocking.

P پتيل *patīl*, A wick for a lamp, lint-stock.

P پتيل سوز *patīl-soz*, A lamp-stand.

P پتيله *patīla*, Wick of a candle, or lamp.

P پج *paj*, A mountain. *Puj*, A kind of fruit, a large strawberry. Plain, broad, open, wide. Confused. Disproportioned. Immense. Unbecoming, unhandsome, uncivilized.

P پجار *pajār*, A mountain.

P پجاوه *pajāwa*, A brick-kiln.

P پجول *pujūl*, The leg-bone, the ankle.

P پجيو *pajīv*, Hypocrisy, deceit.

P پچ پچ *pach pach*, Hush! A call to goats.

P پچپچه *puchpucha*, Any thing whispered about.

P پچشك *puchushk*, Dung of sheep, goats, or camels. A druggist. A physician. پچشك ستور *puchushki sutūr*, A leech, a veterinary surgeon.

P پچشكي *puchushkī*, The practice of medicine.

P پچكم *pichkam*, A court, hall of audience. A wolf. *Pichkam* or *pachham*, A house whose sides are latticed.

P پچل *pachal*, One who often bedaubs himself.

P پچواك *pachwāk*, An interpreter. (according to some) A translation.

P پچوه *pachūh* or *pachwah*, A translation.

P پچه *pacha*, Ivy.

P پچيدن *pichīdan*, To twist, entwine.

P پخ *pakh*, Well, good. A side. O! bravo! well done! excellent! When doubled, *pakh pakh*, it gives a greater energy to the interjection. *Pikh* or *pakh*, Get away! begone! (said to a cat or dog).

P پخپخو *pikhpikhū*, A tickling under the arms.

P پخت *pakht*, Trodden, pressed flat. *Pukht*, He cooked. A kick.

P پختري *pukhtarī*, Cakes (or bread) which are laid over dishes when bringing to table, and under which the meat is kept warm. Cakes imbued with clarified butter.

P پختگان حقيقت *pukhtagānihakīkat*, Matured, skilled in the knowledge of sacred truths: wise men, saints.

P پختگي *pukhtagī*, Ripeness.

P پختن *pukhtan*, To boil, cook, make ready. To concoct. To ripen. To be cooked.

P پختني *pukhtanī*, Fit for cooking. Boiled.

P پخته *pakhta*, Cotton.

P پخته *pukhta*, Boiled, dressed, cooked. Ripe, mature. Expert, skilful, versed in business. Sly. A large lamb. Contemptible. Strong, well built. پخته تدبيرها *pukhta tadbīrhā*, Prudent counsels.

P پخته جوش *pukhta-josh*, Lambs' flesh boiled in spiced wine.

P پخته خوار *pukhta-khwār*, A son-in-law. Beggar.

P پخته كاو *pukhta-kāv*, Warm water medicinally prepared and poured from a vessel slowly over the head. An embrocation.

P پختي *pukhtī*, Jelly (of fish); congealed broth.

P پخچ *pakhch*, Trodden. Ample, wide.

P پخچودن *pakhchūdan*, To trample. To pound. To widen.

P پخچوده *pakhchūda*, Trampled on. Extended, widened, flattened.

P پخچيدن *pakhchīdan*, To trample on. To widen.

P پخچيده *pakhchīda*, Trampled. Expanded, widened.

P پخس *pakhs*, Liquefaction. A melting or wasting away. Diminution. Heart-burning, distress. Shrivelled, dried up. Withering. Blandishment.

P پخسان *pakhsān*, Drying, withered. Amorously playful, blandishing. Melting. Sorrowful.

P پخسيدن *pakhsīdan*, To walk pompously.

P پخسينه *pakhsīna*, Withered, shrivelled.

P پخش *pakhsh*, Trodden. Expanded. Withered, shrivelled. Soft, tender.

P پخشا *pakhshā*, Refusal, denial. Oppression. Straitness, distress.

P پخشان *pakhshān*, Afflicted, sad.

P پخشانيدن *pakhshānīdan*, To strut. To dissolve with grief.

P پخشاييدن *pakhshāyīdan*, To afflict, grieve.

P پخشودن *pakhshūdan*, To beat, trample on.

P پخشوده *pakhshūda*, Trampled upon. Expanded, wide, broad.

P پخشيدن *pakhshīdan*, To trample, tread upon.

To burn. To strut. To waste away with grief. To shine, glitter. To be wide and ample.

P پخشیده *pakhshīda*, Trodden. Enlarged, widened.

P پخل *pukhl*, (or پخله *pukhla*) Purslain.

P پخلوچه *pakhlūcha*, A tickling under the arms.

P پخلیچه *pakhlīcha*, A tickling under the arms.

P پد *pad*, A guard, guardian. The white poplar. *Pid*, (for پدر *pidar*) A father. *Pud*, Touchwood, tinder.

P پد آسیا *pad-āsyā*, The sail of a wind-mill, or the tooth of a water-mill wheel. A mill-stone.

P پدپود *pudpūd*, Touchwood: tinder. Fuel.

P پدر *pidar*, A father. پدر پدر *pidari pidar*, A paternal grandfather. پدر سببي *pidari sababī*, A father-in-law. پدر کلان *pidari kalān*, A grandfather. پدر مادر *pidari mādar*, A maternal grandfather.

P پدرام *pidrām*, Adorned. Good, charming. A bed-chamber. Always, continual.

P پدر اندر *pidar-andar*, A stepfather.

P پدرانه *pidarāna*, Paternal. Paternally.

P پدرخته *padrakhta*, Sorrowful. Anxious.

P پدر زن *pidar-zan*, A wife's father.

P پدرزه *padarza*, A wrapper in which clothes are folded up. Victuals tied up in a handkerchief. A portion, a share.

P پدرفتار *pidruftār*, (or پدیرفتار) Patient.

P پدر مرده *pidar-murda*, An orphan.

P پدرندر *pidar-andar*, A stepfather.

P پدر نویسی *pidar-navīsī*, Abatement of extraordinary charges.

P پدروار *pidarwār*, Like a father.

P پدرود *padrūd*, Leave, dismissal. Farewell. پدرود کردن *padrūd kardan*, To bid adieu.

P پدري *pidarī*, Paternal. Fatherhood.

P پدريّه *pidarīya*, Paternity.

P پدمه *padma*, A part, portion. A bundle.

P پدندر *pidandar*, *padandar*, or *padnadar*, A father-in-law.

P پدواز *padwāz*, The parts round the mouth. A perch, roost.

P پده *pada*, The white poplar-tree. *Pada* or *puda*, A barren tree, proper for firewood. Touchwood.

P پدید *padīd*, Open, public, clear, evident, manifest, conspicuous, in sight. Openly, evidently. پدید آمدن *padīd āmadan*, To appear, to become manifest.

P پدیدار *padīdār*, Manifest, appearing. پدیدار شدن *padīdār shudan*, To appear, show one's self. پدیدار کردن *padīdār kardan*, To rouse. To evince.

P پدیسار *padīsār*, Taking up any business which has already been begun upon.

P پذر *pizar*, (equiv. to پدر *pidar*) A father.

P پذرفتار *pizruftār*, Surety, bail. Acceptance.

P پذرفتاریدن *pizruftārīdan*, To make one's self responsible.

P پذرفتاري کردن *pizruftārī kardan*, To bear patiently. To accept. To pledge one's self. To entrust, to give in charge.

P پذرفتکار *pizruft-kār*, Accepting; who accepts or approves. Acknowledging; who acknowledges or confesses. Obeying; obedient.

P پذرفتن *pizruftan*, To accept. To own, confess.

P پذرفته *pizrufta*, Confessed, owned. Accepted.

P پذور *pazūr*, Mint, spearmint.

P پذیر *pazīr*, (in composition) Receiving, accepting, admitting. Having, being possessed of, endowed with. پوزش پذیر *pozish-pazīr*, Accepting an apology. خلل پذیر *khalal-pazīr*, Disturbed. Altered. زینت پذیر *zīnat-pazīr*, Adorned, possessed of ornaments. صفا پذیر *safā-pazīr*, Endowed with integrity, pure, sincere. صورت پذیر *sūrat-pazīr*, Having the appearance of, resembling. صورت پذیر گرفتن *sūrat-pazīr giriftan*, To assume the appearance. فنا پذیر *fanā-pazīr*, Corruptible, corrupted.

P پذیرا *pazīrā*, Accepting. Hearing. Obeying. Going along, flowing, passing. Accepted. A leader. Meeting, encountering. Matter. The first principle of every thing material.

P پذیرا سخن *pazīrā-sukhun*, Acceptable word.

P پذیرانیدن *pazīrānīdan*, To make be accepted.

P پذیرائي *pazīrāī*, Acceptance. Obedience.

P پذیرش *pazīrish*, Acceptance. Obedience.

P پذیرفتار *pazīruftār*, An accepter. A surety. A chief. Acceptance.

P پذیرفتاري *pazīruftārī*, Suretyship. پذیرفتاري کردن *pazīruftārī kardan*, To bear patiently.

P پذیرفتاریدن *pazīruftārīdan*, To take upon one's self, to be security for another. To bear patiently. To render accceptable.

P پذیرفتکار *pazīruftkār*, Accepting, taking in good part. Obedient. Confessing, acknowledging. A leader, a chief.

P پذیرفتگاري *pazīruftagārī*, Acceptance.

P پذیرفتن *pazīruftan*, To accept, receive, take in good part, approve of, assent to, admit. To answer for, become surety. To consult what is just and right.

P پذیرفته *pazīrufta*, Accepted, approved.

P پذیرفتي *pazīruftī*, Affliction, grief, shame.

P پذیرنده *pazīranda*, Who approves, accepts.

P پذیره *pazīra*, Acceptable. A meeting, encounter. A going before. Acceptance. Obedience. An accepter. A leader. پذیره شدن *pazīra shudan*, To go or appear before, to meet, to encounter. To return. To follow. To be angry.

P پر *par*, A wing. A feather. A leaf. The arm from the collar-bone to the tip of the finger. The sails or paddles of a mill. A side, skirt, or margin. Light, ray. (in compos., Flying. One who flies). پر آسیا *pari āsyā*, The sweep of a wind-mill. P پرافشاردن *par afshārdan*, To flap the wings. پر و بال *par u bāl*, Feather and wing. پر و بال اقبال *par u bāli ikbāl*, The feather and wing of prosperity. پروانۂ پرسوخته آسا *parwānaʼi par-sokhta āsā*, Like a moth with burnt wings. *Pur*, Full. Laden, charged. Complete. پربار *pur-bār*, Loaded, laden, charged. Pregnant. سلطان پر زور *sultāni pur-zor*, A powerful prince. پر شعور *pur-shuʿūr*, Wise. پر کردن *pur kardan*, To fill. پر هنر *pur-hunar*, Skilful.

P پرا *purā*, Fulness. Fatness.

P پراپر *pur-ā-pur*, Filled to the brim, quite full.

P پرادران *parāzrān*, A species of royal falcon.

P پراریر *parārīr*, (or پراریز) The year before last.

P پرارین *pirārīn* or *parārīn*, (in zand and Pāzand) Good, excellent.

P پراز *purāz*, Scattering. Plough-harness.

P پرازده *pa* or *pirāzda*, A lump of dough.

P پراژ *purāj*, Dispersed, scattered.

P پراس *parās*, Expansion. Perfection. Delivery, surrender.

P پراسال *parāsāl* (or پراسالینه *parāsālīna*) The year before the last, the third from the present year.

P پراستن *parāstan*, To clean.

P پراش *parāsh*, Dispersion, scattering.

P پراشیدن *parāshīdan*, To disperse, scatter. To put down, quell, appease. To be disordered in mind.

P پراشیده *parāshīda*, Scattered. Insane.

P پراکوه *parā-koh*, The further side of a mountain. A channel made by a mountain-torrent.

P پراگندگي *parāgandagī*, Dispersion, scatteredness. Distraction.

P پراگندن *parāgandan*, To disperse, dissipate, scatter. To send everywhere. To disband (an army).

P پراگندني *parāgandanī*, Any thing to be strewed or scattered (as sweet herbs over dead bodies).

P پراگنده *parāganda*, Dispersed, scattered, disbanded. Dissipated; inattentive. Prose (opposed to پیوسته *paywasta*, Poetry). پراگنده کردن *parāganda kardan*, To disperse, scatter. پراگنده و پریشان شدن *parāganda u pareshān shudan*, To be dissipated and ruined.

P پراگنده دل *parāganda-dil*, Disquieted.

P پراگندیدن *parāgandīdan*, To scatter. To cause to scatter.

P پراگي *parāgī*, A helmet. A skull-cap.

P پرالك *parāluk*, Excellent steel. A sword.

P پر آمد قفیز *pur āmad kafīz*, The measure (of his days) is full.

P پران *parān*, Flying.

P پرانداخ *parāndākh*, Goat's-skin leather.

P پر انداختن *par andākhtan*, To moult (as birds). To grow weak, to become dispirited and contemptible. To chew the cud. To court retirement. To be cheerful.

P پرانه *parāna*, Name of a city and a river.

P پرانیدن *parānīdan*, To cause to fly. To define.

P پر آور *par-āwar*, Flying. Swift.

P پراوند *parāwand*, The bar of a door.

P پراهام *parāhām*, (in zand and Pāzand) Abraham. Name of a certain wealthy Jew.

P پرباد *pur-bād*, Full of wind, inflated.

P پربار *parbār*, (or پرباره) A summer-house.

P پربار *pur-bār*, Freighted. Lading, cargo.

P پربال *parbāl*, (or پرباله) A summer-house.

P پر بر آمدن *par bar āmadan*, To be fledged.

P پر بر ناوش *par bar nāwash*, The sky.

P پربون *parbūn*, A kind of painted China silk.

P پرپایه *pur-pāya*, (Full of feet) A centipede.

P پرپر *purpar*, An herb like water-mint.

P پرپرم *parparam*, (or پرپر) A young partridge.

P پرپره *parpara*, Small, thin, light coin.

P پرپوز *parpoz*, The parts round the mouth.

P پرپهلو *pur pahlū*, A displeasing word.

P پرپهن *parpahan* or *parpahn*, Purslain.

P پرپي *purpay*, An assessment to defray the expense of lighting Musulmān temples.

P پرپين *parpīn*, Zedoary.

P پرتاب *partāb*, An arrow that flies far. A leap, spring, throw. Shining, brilliancy, resplendency, brightness, flashing. Tumbling. Shooting, casting, hurling, lancing.

P پرتابيان *partābiyān*, Archers, bowmen.

P پرتاد *partād*, Slander, whisperings.

P پرتاش *partāsh*, A district in Turkistān.

P پرتاو *partāv*, (for پرتاب *partāb*) A bow-shot.

P پرتر *partar*, Starch, size.

P پرتگال *purtugāl*, Portugal.

P پرتله *partala*, (or پرتاله *partāla*) A belt.

P پرتو *partav*, A ray, light. Shock, collision.

P پرتو انداز *partav-andāz*, Darting rays.

P پرتوه *partava*, A far-flying arrow.

P پرتير *par-tīr*, A pointless four-winged arrow.

P پرچم *parcham*, A lock of hair (especially waving over the forehead). The tail of the sea-cow which they hang round the necks of horses. The sea-cow. The Yak or Tartary ox. A black fringe or tassel tied round the neck of a spear.

P پرچه *parcha*, A bit, piece. Cotton-cloth.

P پرچيدن *parchīdan*, To strike, drive, clench.

P پرچين *parchīn*, Curved, crooked, bent. Nails driven through any thing, and then clenched in the points. A hedge of briars. Thorns placed on a wall as a fence. A shed. A hovel constructed of sticks, leaves, &c. *Pur-chīn*, Full of wrinkles.

P پرخاش *purkhāsh*, War, battle. A quarrel.

P پرخاشجو *purkhāsh-jū*, پرخاشخور *purkhāsh-khwur*, (or پرخاشخر *purkhāsh-khar*) Disposed for war, pugnacious.

P پرخچ *parakhch*, A horse's buttocks.

P پرخش *parakhsh*, A horse's buttocks.

P پر خطر *pur khatar*, Full of hazard.

P پرخو *parkhav* or *purkhū*, A magazine, granary. A buttery, larder. Meat, victuals. Cheerfulness. A pruning of trees.

P پرخور *pur-khwur*, (Eating to the full) A glutton.

P پرخوري *pur-khwurī*, Fulness of food, gluttony.

P پرخون *pur-khūn*, Full of blood.

P پرخوني *pur-khūnī*, A blood or black pudding.

P پرخيدن *purkhīdan*, To pull up by the roots. To shave. To reap, mow. To fence with thorns.

P پرخيده *parkhīda*, A wink, nod, sign.

P پرد *pard*, An enigma. The plush of velvet, &c. A time. A fold, plait, ply. يك پرد *yak pard*, Once. دو پرد *du pard*, Twice. Two-fold. *Purd*, Difficult, obscure. An enigma. A bridge.

P پردا *pardā*, To-morrow.

P پرداخ *pardākh*, Splendour.

P پرداخت *pardākht*, Finished, complete, polished. Finish, polish, correction. Completion, perfection. Engagement, employment. Patronage.

P پرداختن *pardākhtan*, To finish, complete, accomplish. To polish, furbish, adorn, bring to perfection. To clean, clear, free. To be busily and attentively engaged: to attempt, care about. To excite. To set out. To raise, take up, remove. To prepare, arrange. To evacuate, abandon, leave. To come to an end, to be completed. To be disengaged and free from all attachments. To take, rob, seize. To be bound or closely connected with any one. To sing. To play on an instrument.

P پرداخته *pardākhta*, Finished. Left. Adorned. Polished. Disengaged, freed from all attachments or hindrances. Excited. Employed, busily engaged. Put to a distance. از همه پرداخته *az hama pardākhta*, Wholly and entirely disengaged, freed from business of every kind.

P پردار *par-dār*, Winged.

P پرداز *pardāz*, (in compos. from پرداختن *pardākhtan*) Performing. Completing. Adorning. براعت پرداز *barāʻat-pardāz*, Perfect in excellence. ترانه پرداز *tarāna-pardāz*, Composing tunes, a musician, singer. سخن پرداز *suhkan-pardāz*, Composing sentences, an orator. طبع نكته پرداز *tabʻi nukta-pardāz*, Of an acute genius, subtile, penetrating. مهمه پرداز كردن *muhimma pardāz kardan*, To prepare necessaries, provide, lay in, lay up.

P پردازنده *pardāzanda*, Becoming disengaged.

P پردازي *pardāzī*, Completion, elegance, ornament, perfection. انشا پردازي *inshā-pardāzī*, Elegance of composition.

P پرداس *pardās*, Consummation. Stability.

P پردال *pardāl*, A pair of compasses. A gusset.

P پردان *pur-dān*, (or پرداني) Wise, prudent.

P پردختن *pardakhtan*, To finish.

P پردخته *pardakhta*, Completed, finished, accomplished. Disengaged. Employed. Polished.

P پر درد *pur-dard*, Full of pain, painful.

P پردك *pardak*, An enigma. Sincere, pure.

P پردگي *pardagī*, A modest, chaste woman, one who is confined at home. Concealed. Concealment. A chamberlain. پردگي رز *pardagī-raz*, Wine. پردگي هفت رنگ *pardagīʼi haft-rang*, The world.

P پردگين *pardagīn*, Veiled, hid by a curtain.

P پردگين كرده شده *pardagīn karda shuda*, Confined at home, secluded from the view of men.

P پردل *purdal*, A plate, trencher, dish. *Pur-dil*, Full of courage, intrepid, magnanimous. Intelligent. Liberal.

P پردلي *pur-dilī*, Valour, courage.

P پردن *pardan*, A boundary, a limit.

P پردو *pardo*, A roof. A balcony. A small beam.

P پرده *parda*, A veil, curtain, tapestry, caul, film, membrane. A partition between two rooms. A fence or wall for dividing fields. A coating, a layer, a lamina. The sky. A plait, fold. A musical tone or sound, a note. A melody. The key of an organ, harpsichord, or similar instrument. Frets, or divisions upon the neck or finger-board of a guitar or lute. The walls of a tent. Modesty. پردهٔ آهن *pardaʼi āhan*, The firmament. پرده بردن *parda burdan*, To seize. To ravish. پرده بر گرفتن *parda bar giriftan*, To lift the veil; to reveal, to shew. To behave in a shameless manner. پردهٔ تنگ *pardaʼi tang*, Bed-curtains. پرده كردن *parda kardan*, To veil, hide, conceal. To divide (fields). پرده گرفتن *parda giriftan*, To make evident. در پرده داشتن *dar parda dāshtan*, To shut up (in a haram), to keep women from the view of men. در پرده شدن *dar parda shudan*, To be veiled, concealed, or shut up (as women in the haram or seraglio). پردهٔ آهريماني *pardaʼi āharīmānī*, Wicked spirits. پردهٔ بيني *pardaʼi bīnī*, The cartilage that separates the nostrils. پردهٔ چشم *pardaʼi chashm*, The eyelid. پردهٔ چغانه *pardaʼi chaghāna*, Name of a note in music. پردهٔ حجاز *pardaʼi hijāz*, پردهٔ صفاهان *pardaʼi sifāhān*, and پردهٔ عشاق *pardaʼi ʻushshāk*, Names of three sorts of musical airs or melodies. پرده خاكي كردن *parda khākī kardan*, To disclose, reveal. پردهٔ خرم *pardaʼi khurram*, Name of a note in music. پردهٔ خماهن *pardaʼi khumāhan*, Heaven. پردهٔ دخاني *pardaʼi duhhānī*, A dark night. پردهٔ دل *pardaʼi dil*, The veil of the heart, the pericardium. The lungs. پردهٔ ديرسال *pardaʼi dīr-sāl*, Name of a note in music. Heaven. پردهٔ زجاجي *pardaʼi zujājī*, A dark night. A black cloud. Heaven. پردهٔ زنبور *pardaʼi zambūr*, Name of a musical note. Curiously wrought tapestry. پردهٔ زنبوري *pardaʼi zambūrī*, Heaven. پردهٔ سرا *pardaʼi sarā* The veil before women's apartments. پردهٔ عنكبوت *pardaʼi ʻankabūt*, A cobweb. A disease or web in the eye. The arachnoid tunic of the eye. پردهٔ عيسي گراي *pardaʼi ʻīsaʼ girāy*, The fourth heaven. پردهٔ غوك *pardaʼi ghūk*, Scum on stagnant water. پردهٔ قمري *pardaʼi kamarī*, Name of a note in music. پردهٔ مكدر *pardaʼi mukaddir*, Wicked spirits. پردهٔ ناموسي *pardaʼi nāmūsī*, Honour, reputation. پردهٔ نيلگون *pardaʼi nīl-gūn*, The firmament. پردهٔ هفت رنگ *pardaʼi haft rang*, The world. The vicissitudes of life. The seven heavens. پردهٔ ياقوت *pardaʼi yākūt*, Name of a note in music. آتش پرده *ātish-parda*, A fire-screen. A parasol. باران پرده *bārān-parda*, An umbrella, parapluie. ديوار پرده *dīwār-parda*, The veil or membrane of the wall, tapestry. مغز پرده *maghz-parda*, The pia mater. *Purda*, An enigma.

P پردها *pardahā*, (pl. of پرده *parda*) Veils.

P پرده آراي *parda-ārāy*, Entertainment.

P پرده باز *parda-bāz*, A musician, a singer.

P پرده بر انداز *parda bar andāz*, Letting the cat out of the bag.

P پرده برگرفتن *parda bar giriftan*, To reveal, disclose. To act in a shameful manner.

P پرده پوش *parda-posh*, Putting on a veil, keeping a secret.

P پرده دار *parda-dār*, Holding the veil. A chamberlain, porter of the inner chamber, the eunuch who has the care of the women's apartments. A spider. A woman, who holds a veil over another's acts. A confidant. پرده دار فلك *parda-dāri falak*, The moon.

P پرده در *parda-dar*, A veil-tearer, an impudent, immodest man, ravisher of women, slanderer or defamer of the sex. A betrayer of secrets. A strumpet.

P پرده دريدگي *parda-darīdagī*, Defamation.

P پرده سرا *parda-sarā*, A curtain, a pavilion. *Pardā-sirā* (or سراي *sirāy*) A musician.

P پرده شناس *parda-shinās*, A musician. Religious. پرده شناسان, Musicians. Intelligent.

P پرده فاش *parda-fāsh*, A betrayer of secrets.

P پرده كش *parda-kash*, Drawing a veil.

P پرده گاه *parda-gāh*, A theatre, a stage.

P پردهن *pur-dahan*, Full-mouthed.

P پرده نشين *parda-nishīn*, Sitting behind the veil. A modest woman, who remains constantly at home veiled from the eyes of men. An army stationed on the frontiers of a country.

P پرده نشينان *parda-nishīnān*, Women. Angels. Confidants.

P پرده نشيني *parda-nishīnī*, A retired, home-life.

P پرريختن *par rekhtan*, To moult. To grow weak. To retire from society and creature-dependance.

P پرز *purz*, Nap upon cloth. Raw silk put into an ink-horn.

P پرزد *parzad*, A drug resembling gum.

P پرزدن *par zadan*, To fly.

P پرزمبوري *purzambūrī*, The firmament.

P پرزه *parza*, A powder or fine collyrium for the eyes. A ploughing-ox. A noble or princely dwelling. Pile or nap upon cloth.

P پرزه *purza*, (or پرژه *purja*) Shavings, shearings, clippings, pollings (of cloth, &c.). A scrap, a bit, a piece. Frippery, rags. A tinder-box. Fuel. An account.

P پرزه دار *purza-dār*, Nappy, shaggy.

P پرزيدن *parzīdan*, To fill a well with stones. To fortify or repair a well on the inside.

P پرزيوند *parzīwand*, Evident, undisguised.

P پرژك *parjak*, Weeping, wailing.

P پرس *pars*, A curtain, a veil. A panther. Livid, pale. *Purs*, (imperative of پرسيدن *pursīdan*) Ask thou. A question. (in compos.) Asking.

P پرسا *pursā*, An inquirer.

P پرسال *par-sāl*, Last year. Inquiry after health.

P پرساله *pur-sāla* Old and full of years.

P پرسان *pursān*, Interrogating, asking, inquiring, demanding. An interrogator.

P پرسانيدن *pursānīdan*, To cause to ask.

P پرست *parast*, A worshipper. آتش پرست *ātish-parast*, A fire-worshipper. بت پرست *but-parast*, An idolater. خدا پرست *khudā-parast*, A worshipper of God. خود پرست *khwud-parast*, A worshipper of himself, self-conceited; an egotist.

P پرستار *parastār*, (or پرستا) A worshipper. A servant, slave, male or female, Obedient, submissive.

P پرستاري *parastārī*, Worship. Servitude.

P پرستان *parastān*, A bird resembling a peacock. An iron stove. (pl. of پرست *parast*,) Worshippers. واهمه پرستان *wāhima-parastān*, Speculative, visionary people. Suspicious. Jealous. پرستان خيال *parastāni khayāl*, Poets. پرستان زمانه *parastāni zamāna*, Worshippers of the world, worldly-minded.

P پرستش *parastish*, Adoration, worship. Attendance on the sick. پرستش كردن *parastish kardan*, To adore, worship.

P پرستش خانه *parastish-khāna*, A house of worship, a temple.

P پرستشگاه *parastish-gāh*, An oratory.

P پرستش گري *parastishgārī*, Adoration, worship.

P پرستك *piristuk*, A swallow.

P پرستگاري *parastagārī*, Servitude, slavery.

P پرستنده *parastanda*, A worshipper, adorer. A servant. پرستندۀ خيال *parastandaï khayāl*, A visionary. A poet.

P پرستو *piristū*, A swallow.

P پرستوك *piristūk*, A swallow.

P پرسته *parasta*, Any object of worship. *Pirista*, A handmaid.

P پرستيدن *parastīdan*, To worship, adore, pray to. To serve.

P پرسش *pursish*, A question, interrogation. مراسم پرسش خاطر *marāsimi pursishi khātir*, Inquiries after one's health.

P پرسق *pursuk*, A weasel.

P پرسم *parsum*, Flour scattered on the table to prevent the dough from sticking to it, *Pursam*, An entertainment, feast.

P پرسنده *pursinda*, An interrogator. پرسندۀ خيال *pursandaï khayāl*, A poet.

P پرسوز *pur-soz*, Blazing. شمع پرسوز *shamʿi pur-soz*, A lighted candle.

P پرسه *parsa*, Poverty. *Pursa*, Attendance upon the sick. Condolence. Inquiry. A condoler.

P پرسي *pursī*, A cess, a fine.

P پرسيان *parsayān*, Ivy, convolvulus. پرسيان دارو *parsiyān-dārū*, Maiden's hair (an herb).

P پرسياوش *parsiyāwush*, Maiden's hair (an herb). A part of the heavens containing twenty-nine stars called رأس الغول *rasu'l ghūl*, The dragon's head.

P پرسياوشان *parsiyāwushān*, Maiden's hair.

P پرسيدن *pursīdan*, To ask, inquire.

P پرش *parsh*, Cholic, gripes. Agitation. Ivy. A fountain. *Parish*, Flight.

P پرشاش *parshāsh* or *purshāsh*, Name of a country in Turkistān.

P پرشگال *purshigāl*, A cloudy, rainy sky.

P پرشنبه *parshambih*, (for پنجشنبه) Thursday.

P پرشوم *pirshūm*, A reed.

P پرشهي *parishahī*, A wing. Down on a wing.

P پرشيدن *parshīdan*, To scatter. To swallow. To salt.

P پرشير *pur-shīr*, Full of milk, milch.

P پرشيرگي *pur-shīragī*, Fullness of milk.

P پرطاس *partās*, A species of ermine.

P پرغازه *par ghāza*, (or پرغزه *parghaza*) A root. A bird's wing.

P پرغور *purghūr*, A dish of bruised corn.

P پرغول *parghūl*, Wheat or barley coarsely ground. Gruel. A kind of sweetmeat, barley-sugar.

P پرغونه *parghūna*, Filthy, ugly, displeasing.

P پرفان *parfān*, Melancholy, full of sorrow.

P پرفائده *pur-fāida*, Full of instruction, edifying. Advantageous. پرفائده ترين *pur-fāida-tarīn*, Most advantageous.

P پرفغان *pur fighān*, Full of bustle.

P پرك *park*, Lint-seed. The noise made by a crackling fire, or by wood when splitting. *Pirk*, The eye-lash. *Parak*, The star Canopus. An echo. Name of a river.

P پركار *pur-kār*, Skilful. Thick, close, and well executed; full of work, or workmanship.

P پركاري *pur-kārī*, Thickness,

P پركاش *par-kāsh*, Saw-dust. Attention.

P پركاله *parkāla*, A spark. A pane of glass.

P پركام *parkām*, The womb.

P پركان *parkān*, Ignorance, inability to reply.

P پركاوش *parkāwish*, The pruning of trees.

P پركاه *pur-kāh*, Stuffed with straw.

P پركر *parkar*, Expectation, hope.

P پركردن *pur kardan*, To fill: multiply. To repeat.

P پركردني *pur kardanī*, Stuffing, quilting.

P پركسون *puraksūn*, (or پرگسون) A rich housing put over the saddle by way of ornament.

P پركم *parkam*, Idle. Reduced to nothing.

P پركن *parkan*, A curry-comb.

P پركنده *parkanda*, Impotent. Scattered.

P پركين *parkīn*, A hearth. Temple of the Magi.

P پركينه *pur-kīna*, Malicious, spiteful.

P پرگار *pargār*, A pair of compasses. A circle made by them. Furniture. Worldly things. A tool. A collar. A collection. پرگار فلك *pargāri falak*, (or چرخ *charkh*) The circle of the heavens.

P پرگاره *pargāra*, A small pair of compasses. A little circle made by them. A bit, a piece of linen. A wardrobe. Worldly things.

P پرگاري *pargārī*, Work done with a compass.

P پرگاس *pargās*, Suspending. Inquiring. Sunrise.

P پرگال *pargāl*, A pair of compasses. Worldly things. Furniture. A collection.

P پرگاله *pargāla*, A little bit of cloth, rag, strip. The pen of the compass. A piece, portion. A patch.

P پرگر *pargar*, A collar of precious stones worn by the ancient kings of Persia, and sometimes put round a horse's neck. A pair of compasses.

P پرگشت *pargasht*, An herb which creeps along the ground, twisting itself like a rope.

P پرگندگي *pargandagī*, Dispersion, diffusion.

P پرگنده *parganda*, Dispersed, scattered.

P پرگنه *pargana*, A district, a division of a province so called. *Pargana* or *pirgana*, An electuary or compound of various fragrant substances.

P پرگنه دار *pargana-dār*, Chief of a parganah.

P پرگو *pur-go* or *gū*, Full of talk, talkative.

P پرگوك *pargūk*, A lofty building. A hospital, house of refuge, bede-house.

P پرگوئي *pur-goī*, (or *gūī*) Talkativeness.

P پرگيري *purgīrī*, An ortolan.

P پرگين *pargīn*, Public.

P پرماس *parmās*, Touch. A rubbing of the hand gently on any thing. Knowledge. Liberation, freedom. Salvation. Growth, extension. Consummation, finish.

P پرماسه *parmāsa*, A smoothing, planing. Touch. Extension. Liberation. Knowledge.

P پرماورد *parmāward*, A kind of sweetmeat.

P پرماه *parmāh*, A wimble, gimlet: a trepan.

P پرمايه *pur māya*, Stocked.

P پرمخيده *parmakhīda*, Contradicting. Self-opiniated. Disobedient, undutiful to parents.

P پرمر *parmar*, Expectation, hope. A bee.

P پرمگس *pari magas*, A fly's wing. Any thing of a very delicate texture. A kind of silken garment. An excellent sword. The wavy lustre of a sword or steel. A manner of playing music or singing. A kind of weapon.

P پرمو *parmū*, Hope, expectation. A bee.

P پرموته *parmūta*, A thing: matter, substance.

P پرموده *parmūda*, The son of سادة شاه.

P پرمور *parmūr*, Hope, expectation. A bee.

P پرموز *parmūz*, Hope. A bee. *Purmūz*, Hay.

P پرموزه *parmūza*, Expectation, hope. A bee. Name of the son of Sāda shāh.

P پرمون *parmūn*, Ornament, decoration with gold, silver, and jewels.

P پرمه *parma*, Something. A part. A wimble, drill. *Pirma*, Sloth. *Purma*, Song, air. A piece.

P پرمهره *par-muhra*, A cud of feathers, &c., which birds of prey bring up from their crop.

P پرمهه *pirmaha*, Procrastination. Sloth.

P پرمي *pur-may*, A sort of grape.

P پرميو *parmiyo*, Gonorrhœa, clap.

P پرن *paran*, The pleiades. Yesterday.

P پرنا *parnā*, Painted or embroidered silk.

P پرناك *parnāk*, Feathery, full of, or clothed with feathers. *Purnāk*, A youth. A Turkomān tribe.

P پرنان *parnān*, Mouldiness of bread.

P پرنج *paranj*, A grain smaller than wheat.

P پرند *parand*, The glittering surface of a polished sword. A sword. A kind of fine figured, painted silk. Plain silk. A bird. A saddle-cloth. The Pleiades. A sort of grass. Wild cucumber. Goat's-skin leather.

P پرنداخ *parandākh*, Goat's-skin leather.

P پرندامت *pur-nadāmat*, Deeply penitent.

P پرنداور *parand-āwar*, A glittering sword.

P پرندخ *parandakh*, An arrow.

P پرندك *parandak*, A hillock in a plain.

P پرندوار *parandwār*, The night before last.

P پرندوش *parandosh*, The night before last.

P پرنده *paranda*, Flying, volatile: a flyer. A bird. A winged animal. A bark, small ship. Quicksilver. پرندۀ چراغ *paranda-i charāgh*, (Flying round the lamp) A moth.

P پرندين *parandīn*, Silken stuff.

P پرنگ *pirang*, The lustre or undulatory surface (of a glittering sword). *Piring*, Copper.

P پرنم *pur-nam*, Full of tears.

P پرنو *parnū*, (or پرنون) Embroidered silk.

P پرنهادن *par nihādan*, To dislodge, eject, repel. To divert another from his purpose.

P پرنيان *parniyān*, A kind of fine painted China silk; also garments made of it. لحاف پرنيان *lihāfi parniyān*, A mantle of such silk.

P پرنيان خوي *parniyān-khoy* or *khuy*, Cheerful, gay. Mild-tempered. Contented. Tender-hearted.

P پرنيخ *parnīkh*, A stone or marble-slab.

P پرنيش *pur-nīsh*, (Full of sting) Cholic, gripes. Pained in the bowels, griped.

P پرو *parv*, The Pleiades.

P پروا *parwā*, Cessation from labour, leisure, quiet, rest. Patience. Power, force, strength. Possession, hold. Occasion, opportunity. Desire, inclination, affection, appetite, concupiscence. A turning towards. Study, endeavour, effort. Vigilance. Flight. Knowledge. Rhetoric. Care, concern, solicitude, anxiety. Honour, respect. Education. Protection, Fear, terror, stupor. Bringing up, rearing. Known. Easy. Skilful. پروائ كار *parwā-i kār*, Leisure, freedom from toil. پروائ وي كرد *parwā-i way kard*, He cared about him (or it). پروا داشتن *parwā dāshtan*, To care, or be concerned. بي پروا *bī parwā*, Without fear; careless, intrepid. Boldly, undauntedly.

P پروار *parwār*, Education. Fatted, crammed, stall-fed. A washerwoman's beetle. A summer-house latticed on all sides for the admission of air. A turret open all sides. A treasury. Planks for the roofing of a house. A thing known. An easy thing. A strong propensity. Liberality. Enough, sufficient. Fumigation with aloes. The urine of a sick person which is shewn to the physician.

P پرواره *parwāra*, A summer-house. An upper chamber. A treasury. Fatted. Planks for the roofing of a house. Aloe-wood for fumigation. A glass urinal.

P پرواري *parwārī*, Fatted, stall-fed. گاو پرواري *gāvi parwārī*, A fatted ox.

P پرواز *parwāz*, Flight. Leaping, springing. Light, glory, radiance. A residence, resting-place. A roost, perch. A small beam or batten for roofing a house. A porch or portico. Money scattered about on certain festive occasions. A veil, a shirt, shift, any thing that covers or conceals. A certain progress or stage in the divine life. Whatever is veiled or hid from public view. شهبازهما پرواز *shah-bāzi humā-parwāz*, A falcon soaring like an eagle. پرواز كردن *parwāz kardan*, To fly, to fly or run to, to take wing. To set on, to cause to fight.

P پروازه *parwāza*, The fire of festivity, which used to be lighted before the bride. The nuptial fire. Wormwood strewed at the feet of a bride. Money or scraps of gilt paper scattered about at marriages. Gladness, cheerfulness, enjoyment of life. Victuals which people carry along with them to make a repast in fields or gardens, pic nic.

P پروازه گر *parwāzagar*, A gilt-paper maker.

P پروازي *parwāzī*, The hem of a garment.

P پرواس *parwās*, Feel, touch. Knowledge. Growth, extension. Smoothing. Cessation. Deliverance. Fear. پرواس كردن *parwās kardan*, To know. To feel: to rub. To play. To lengthen.

P پرواسيدن *parwāsīdan*, To examine, feel with the hand whether any thing is hard or soft, fat or lean. To imagine, fancy. To apprehend, fear.

P پرواش *parwāsh*, Negligent, careless: secure. Astonished, stupefied. A buttock. A corner. End.

P پرواك *parwāk*, A watch, guard. Echo.

P پروال *parwāl*, A gusset. Compasses.

P پروان *parwān*, Flue of silk. A parrot. A crime. A spectacle, show, any thing wonderful. Liberality, beneficence. Walking, recreating. Name of a city near غزنين *ghaznīn*.

P پروانجات *parwānajāt*, Orders, passes.

P پروانچه *parwāncha*, Order, licence, permit.

P پروانچي *parwānchī*, A government-officer.

P پروانك *parwānak*, The lion's provider, otherwise called the سياه گوش *siyāh-gosh*, A small lynx with ears tipped with black hairs, which are used for painting. (He is said to eat the lion's leavings). A guide, escort. A messenger, courier, running footman. A general.

P پروانگي *parwānagī*, An order, permission.

P پروانه *parwāna*, A moth, particularly such as fly about a candle at night. A candle, lantern. A messenger. The animal called the lion's provider. Any military monument set up as a road-direction, or to commemorate any spot. A general, commander. A supervisor, inspector. A midwife. A royal patent or diploma. A grant or letter under the great seal from any man in power. A pass, licence, leave, permit, command, precept, warrant, written order or commission. Sentence of a judge. The middle. A locust. An ingenious, elegant youth.

P پرواوه *parwāwa*, A guard, sentinel.

P پرواي *parwāy*, Easy: soft. Nimble. Plump.

P پروائي *parwāī*, Indigent, necessitous.

P پر و بال داشتن *par u bāl dāshtan*, (To possess feathers and wings) To be powerful.

P پر و پاي *par u pāy*, Power, strength.

P پرور *parwar*, (in composition) Nourishing, fostering, educating. A patron, protector. Lace, fringe, edging. A joint, connexion. تن پرور *tan-parwar*, Nourishing or comforting the body, self-indulgent. جان پرور *jān-parwar*, (or نفس پرور *nafs-parwar*) Improving the mind. سايه پرور *sāya-parwar*, Educated in the shade: soft, delicate, knowing little of the world. علما پرور *ʿulamā-parwar*, A cherisher of learned men. غريب پرور *gharīb-parwar*, Cherisher of the poor. *Parūr*, A link, connexion, joint.

P پروراندن *parwarāndan*, (or پرورانيدن *parwarānīdan*) To cause to cherish.

P پرورد شانه *parward-shāna*, Shining. Lightning.

P پروردگار *parwardagār*, Omnipotence (as nourishing all). پروردگار گونه *parwardagāri gūna*, (Protector of the species) A king.

P پروردگي *parwardagī*, A fostering, rearing.

P پروردن *parwardan*, To nourish, foster, educate. To worship. To make up, to dispense (medicine). To pickle, to preserve.

P پرورده *parwarda*, Educated, bred, reared. Nourished, fed, fattened. A pupil, scholar, ward. A slave. Pickled. Made up, dispensed (medicine). پرورده شدن *parwarda shudan*, To be nourished, fostered, educated. پرورده كردن *parwarda kardan*, To educate, to nourish.

P پرورش *parwarish*, Education. A fostering, rearing. Protection. Worship. Knowledge, learning. پرورش كردن *parwarish kardan*, To educate. To cherish.

P پرورش آموختگان *parwarish-āmokhtagān*, Prophets. Poets.

P پرورش آموز *parwarish-āmoz*, A teacher. A spiritual father. God.

P پرورنده *parwarinda*, Cherishing: a cherisher. A protector, patron.

P پرورنديدن *parwarandīdan*, (or پرونديدن) To pack or put up in bundles or trusses.

P پروره *parwara*, Fed, nourished, stall-fed, fatted.

P پروري *parwarī*, Education. One who educates. Educated.

P پروريدن *parwarīdan*, To bring up. To nourish. To begin.

P پروريش *parwarish*, Sugar of roses, conserve of roses.

P پروز *parwaz*, A kind of border or selvedge round a garment. A shirt, any thing that is put on the body or spread upon a bed. Origin, root, stock. A patch. A garment of two colours, called شب اندر روز *shab andar roz*, Night in day (pepper and salt). A sort of grass called مرغ *margh*. Array. A circular disposition of an army.

P پروزن *parwizan*, A sieve, searce. Any thing perforated all over with holes. A fishing-net.

P پروژ *parwaj*, Interred, buried.

P پروسنّا *parvasannā*, People of the same religion or society, co-religionists.

P پروش *parosh*, Pimples, pustles.

P پرون *parwan*, Flue of silk. Name of a city.

P پروند *parwand*, A pimp, pander. A beardless youth. A pear. Name of a plain near Kazwīn.

P پرونده *parwanda* or *parūnda*, A bundle, roll, or truss (of clothes). Any coarse cloth in which they put up linens, a packing sheet. A clothes press or chest. A bleacher's beetle. A rope with which they fasten linens together when washing. A large wallet that opens on the side.

P پرونديدن *parwandīdan*, To pack, truss.

P پروه *parwa*, Plunder. Bedding. Pleiades.

P پروهان *parwahān*, Manifest, clear, evident.

P پرويز *parwez*, Victorious. Fortunate, happy. Dear, excellent, precious. Propriety of behaviour. A sieve. Liberality. The Pleiades. Splendour. A sugar-refinery. A fish. A proper name among the ancient Persians; but particularly of one of their kings, called Khusrau Parvez, son of Noshīravān (cotemporary with Muhammad). پرويز فلك *parwezi falak*, The sun.

P پرويزن *parwīzan*, A hair-sieve, a searce.

P پرويش *parwesh*, Carelessness. Careless.

P پروين *parwīn*, Pleiades. *Purwīn*, Filth. Sordid.

P پرّه *parra*, A side, border, edge, margin, extremity. A spindle. A circular disposition of troops for hunting or other purposes. A rank or file of soldiers. The broad leaf of wheaten straw. The white poplar-tree, also another kind of barren tree. The bolt of a door, the bolt of a lock, also what they call the iron wings of the locks. پرّهٔ آسيا *parrasi āsyā*, The sail of a windmill. The board of a water-wheel upon which the stream falls. پرّهٔ بيني *parrasi bīnī*, The nostrils. پرّهٔ سر *parrasi sar*, The sharp point of a bone. A part of the head. پرّه بستن *parra bastan*, To arrange in order of battle.

P پرهازه *parhāza*, Touchwood, tinder.

P پرهام *parhām*, (in zand and Pāz.) Abraham.

P پرهختن *parhakhtan* or *parhikhtan*, To correct, instruct, teach good manners.

P پرهوده *parhūda*, Singed. Frothy talk.

P پرهون *parhūn*, A halo round the moon. A periphery, a circle made by compasses. A hoop. A collar.

P پرهيختن *parhekhtan*, To teach, educate.

P پرهيز *parhez*, Abstinence. Continence, chastity, controul over the passions. Care, forbearance, caution. Distance. Fear. پرهيز داشتن *parhez dāshtan*, To abstain, fast, take care, be heedful. پرهيز فرمودن *parhez farmūdan*, To enjoin abstinence. پرهيز كردن *parhez kardan*, To abstain. بدي پرهيز *badī-parhez*, Abstaining from evil.

P پرهيزانه *parhezāna*, Food given to the sick.

P پرهيزگار *parhezgār*, Sober, abstinent. Chaste. Cautious, careful.

P پرهيزگاري *parhezgārī*, Carefulness, caution. Chastity. Sobriety.

P پرهيزناك *parheznāk*, Abstaining from sin.

P پرهيزي *parhezī*, Fit for one under regimen.

P پرهيزيدن *parhezīdan*, To restrain one's self. To take heed.

P پري *parī*, Winged. A good genius, a fairy. (for پرير *parīr*) The day before yesterday. *Purī*, Thou art full. Plenitude, fulness.

P پري افساي *parī-afsāy*, An exorcist. An amulet. Epileptic. One who subdues or gains ascendancy.

P پريان *paryān*, Silk. Muslin. Camel-leather.

P پري پيكر *parī-paykar*, Fairy-faced.

P پريچه *parīcha*, Fibrous bark of the palm.

P پريخوان *parī-khwān*, Exorcist, magician.

P پريدار *parī-dār*, A necromancer, magician, one having familiar spirits at command. Possessed of a spirit of divination. Mad. Pandemonium.

P پريداري *parī-dārī*, Magic, necromancy.

P پريدخت *parī-dukht*, Name of the daughter of an Emperor of China.

P پريدگان *parīdagān*, Fliers. Birds.

P پريدگي *parīdagī*, Flight.

P پريدن *parīdan*, To fly in the air, to flutter. To throb. *Purīdan*, To fill.

P پرير *parīr*, The day before yesterday. پرير پرير *parīr parīr*, Four days ago. پريرسال *parīr-sāl*, The year before last.

P پري رخسار *parī-rukhsār*, (or پري رخ *parī-rukh*) Angel-cheeked, fairy-faced.

P پريرفت شدن *parīraft shudan*, To be affected with convulsions, or eruptions on the lips, from disturbed dreams.

P پريرم *parīram*, Four days ago.

P پري روز *parī-roz*, Day before yesterday.

P پري روي *parī-rūy*, Fairy or angel-faced.

P پريره *parīra*, Golden, red gold, or golden red.

Of the day before yesterday. Bread baked upon the coals. Interrupting.

P پریرینه *parirīna*, Of the day before yesterday.

P پریز *parez*, Complaint, lamentation. A herb growing on the banks of rivers. A hair-sieve.

P پري زاده *parī-zāda*, Fairy-born. Parisatis.

P پریزبان *parezbān*, A sifter of meal or flour.

P پري زده *parī-zada*, Fairy-struck, bewitched.

P پریزن *parezan*, A hair-sieve.

P پري سال *parī-sāl*, The year before last.

P پري ساي *parī-sāy*, A magician.

P پریستار *paristār*, An ambassador.

P پري سوز *parī-soz*, Name of a temple built by Khusraw Parvez.

P پریش *paresh*, Disperse thou. Dispersing, or who disperses. Dispersion. Perturbation, confusion, perplexity.

P پریشان *pareshān*, Dispersed, scattered. Dishevelled. Disturbed, perplexed, confounded, distracted, agitated, afflicted, vexed, sad, melancholy. Unfortunate. Disgusted. اوراق پریشان *awrāki pareshān*, Disordered papers lying here and there. زلف پریشان *zulfi pareshān*, Dishevelled hair. سخنهای پریشان *sukhanhā-i pareshān*, A rambling incoherent discourse. پریشان کردن *pareshān kardan*, To disjoin, disperse, dissipate. To offend, provoke, disgust. پریشان گفتن *pareshān guftan*, To talk nonsense.

P پریشان اوراق *pareshān-awrāk*, Scattered leaves, (a book) written upon scraps or separate leaves, unarranged, unrevised.

P پریشان حال *pareshān-hāl*, In a ruined state.

P پریشان حالي *pareshān hālī*, A distressed, melancholy, sad, or ruined state.

P پریشان خاطر *pareshān-khātir*, Afflicted in mind. Disturbed. Offended.

P پریشان روزگار *pareshān-rozgār*, Distressed in one's circumstances.

P پریشان ساز *pareshān-sāz*, Scattering.

P پریشان مشرب *pareshān-mashrab*, Of depraved morals.

P پریشاني *pareshānī*, Dissipation, dispersion. Distraction, confusion. Disgust. Distress, perplexity. پریشاني کردن *pareshānī kardan*, To vex.

P پریشانیدن *pareshānīdan*, To distract and distress. To be distracted and distressed.

P پري شب *parī-shab*, Night before last.

P پریشم *parisham*, Silk.

P پریشن *pareshan*, Dispersion. A mark.

P پریشیدن *pareshīdan*, To disperse. To lose one's senses.

P پري گرفته *parī-girifta*, A soothsayer.

P پریون *paryūn*, A distemper about the nails, making them drop off. Tetter, ring-worm, mange.

P پز *paz*, A sweet cane, the root of which is eaten for a pain in the stomach. (in composition, from پختن *pukhtān*) Cooking. Boiling.

P پزاختن *pazākhtan* or *pizākhtan*, To melt.

P پزانیدن *pazānīdan*, To cook. To cause, request, or order to cook.

P پزاوه *pazāwa*, (or پژاوه *pajāwa*) A brick-kiln; a lime-kiln.

P پزپونتن *pazpūnitan*, (in zand and Pāzand) To give. پزپونمي *pazpūnamī*, I give. پزپونید *pazpūnid*, Give ye.

P پزد *pazd*, Blood. Soul, spirit.

P پزدك *pazdak*, A weevil.

P پزسك *pazask*, An owl. *Pizish*, A physician.

P پزشك *pizishk*, A physician, surgeon.

P پزشکي *pizishkī*, The art of healing.

P پزغ *pazagh* or *pazgh*, A young vine-shoot.

P پزغند *puzghand*, A certain tanning fruit.

P پزگر *pazgar*, A cook.

P پزوند *pazwand*, A bundle of clothes.

P پزوي *pazwī* or *pazavī*, Ignoble, vile, base.

P پزه *piza*, Sweet cane. Arms, armour.

P پزي *pazī*, Side, part, toward.

P پزیدن *pazīdan*, To cook. To be cooked.

P پزیره *pazīra*, (or پژیره) Meal, flour.

P پژ *paj*, Uneven ground. Old and soft mud. Old, obliterated. Filth, dregs, dross. The summit of a mountain. *Pūj*, Sleet. Sweet cane.

P پژاد *pajād*, Aged. A venerable old man.

P پژاد برآمده *pajād bar āmada*, Aged.

P پژار *pajār*, A pace, a step.

P پژآسمان *paj-āsmān*, Empyrean heaven.

P پژاگن *pajāgin*, Impure, filthy, sordid.

P پژاوند *pajāwand*, The bar of a door or gate (particularly such as they thrust into a groove in the wall when the gate is to be opened, and draw out when shut, to make it fast). The beetle of a fulling-mill.

P پژاوه *pajāwa*, A brick-kiln.

P پژپژ *pujpuj*, A word used by shepherds in calling their goats.

P پژسر *paj-sar*, Bald.

P پژغم *pajgham*, The acacia, a thorn from which they extract a styptic medicine: (they imitate this in Europe by sloe-juice).

P پژغند *pujghand*, Curriers' sumach, a kind of bushy shrub with which leather is dressed. The braying of the mule.

P پژغه *pajgha*, A vine-prop or arbour.

P پژقله *pajkala*, The scolopendra.

P پژقند *pajkanad*, Vain, idle discourse.

P پژکاله *pajkāla*, Part, portion, bit: patch.

P پژم *pajm* or *pijm*, A mountain.

P پژماپون *pajmāpūn*, Name of a hero.

P پژمان *pijmān*, *pajmān*, or *pujmān*, Sad, melancholy, mournful, dejected. Drunk. Bedimmed. *Pujmān*, Desire, wish.

P پژماني *pijmānī*, Grief, care, sadness.

P پژمایه *paj* or *pijmāya*, Farīdūn's cow.

P پژمردگي *pijmurdagī*, A withered state.

P پژمردن *pijmurdan*, (or پژمریدن *pijmurīdan*) To wither, fade, flag, faint, become lean, emaciated, pale. To be sad and melancholy. To die.

P پژمرده *pijmurda*, Withered. Bedimmed. Sad, mournful, melancholy. پژمرده روي و پریشان موي *pijmurda-rūy u pareshān-mūy*, Pale-faced and dishevelled-haired.

P پژن *pajan*, A kite. End of a street.

P پژنامه *pajnāma*, A surname, nickname.

P پژند *pajand*, A wild gourd, or purging phlegm, a species of cucumber, the colocynth. A kind of self-growing, sweet-smelling, edible plant, which resembles spinage.

P پژنگار *pajangār*, A carpenter: smith; tanner.

P پژنگر *pajangar*, A tanner, a currier.

P پژنگره *pajangara*, (or پژنگژه) A coney, rabbit.

P پژو *pajū*, Blood. Life.

P پژواك *pajwāk*, An echo.

P پژوده (خبر *khabar*) *pujūda*, A spy.

P پژوك *pujūk*, An alarming noise.

P پژول *pajūl*, The ankle. A filbert. The female breast. A ball with which boys play.

P پژول باز *pajūl-bāz*, A player at such a game.

P پژول پستان *pajūl-pistān*, Plump-breasted.

P پژولش *pijūlish*, Intricate. Scattered.

P پژولید *pijūlīd*, Withered, faded.

P پژولیدن *pajūlīdan*, To intermix. *Pijūlīdan*, To search, inquire, investigate. To wither. To mix. To be scattered, perplexed, disturbed. To advise. To cut off the tail.

P پژولیده *pijūlīda*, Withered. Soft. Docked. Advised. Questioned. Impotent, feeble, faint. Flat, insipid.

P پژوم *pajūm*, Poor. Despised.

P پژومان *pajūmān*, Beggars.

P پژوند *pajwand*, A bar, bolt. A fuller's beetle. *Pajwand* or *pajawand*, A pimp.

P پژوه *pijūh*, (in compos.) Examining. An examiner, searcher, explorer, investigator, inquirer. Examination, search, inquiry. A mountain. The lining of a garment. حکم پژوه *hikam-pijūh*, Contemplating abstract subjects. خرد پژوه *khirad-pijūh*, An examiner into the opinions of others. دانش پژوهان *dānish-pijūhān*, Investigators of science.

P پژوهش *pijūhish*, Inquiry, examination.

P پژوهندگي *pijūhandagī*, Strict search, minute examination.

P پژوهنده *pijūhanda*, Examining, searching. Intelligent, wise. An inquisitor.

P پژوهیدن *pijūhīdan*, To examine, inquire.

P پژوهیده *pijūhīda*, Investigated. Wise.

P پژوي *pajawī* or *pujuwī*, Base, ignoble.

P پژوین *pajwīn*, Filthy, nasty. Squalor.

P پژه *paja*, A mountainous country. The lining of a garment. *Pijuh*, Search.

P پژهان *pujhān*, Honest ambition, laudable emulation. Desire. پژهان بردن *pujhān burdan*, To be solicitous. To desire. To envy.

P پس *pas*, After, afterwards, behind: finally, at last, at length, after all. The last, latter part. But, moreover, however. Then, therefore, consequently, accordingly. For this reason. پس از آن *pas az ān*, After that, thenceforth. پس ازاین *pas az īn*, After this, henceforth. پس از بسیار ایّام *pas az bisyār ayyām*, After many days. پس از جنگ *pas az jang*, After the battle. پس افکندن *pas afkandan*, To lay up in store. To bequeath. پس آمدن *pas āmadan*, (or درپس آمدن *dar pas āmadan*) To follow, to come behind. پس انداز کرد *pas andāz kard*, (or پس سرکرد *pas sar kard*) He despised, discarded, or reviled. پس آنگاه *pas ān gah*, Afterwards, then. پس پا شدن *pas pā shudan*, To return, to retreat, to turn back. پس پرده *pasi parda*, Behind the curtain. پس پشت کردن *pas pusht kardan*, To put behind one's back, to stand before, to hide, conceal. پس جا نشین *pasi jā nishīn*, An assistant in a shop. پس چون *pas chūn*, When therefore. پس خانه *pasi khāna*, Behind the house. پس خم زدن *pas kham zadan*, To run away. پس دست کردن *pas dast kardan*, To conceal, to store. پس دیوار *pasi dīwār*, Behind the wall. پس رفتن *pas raftan*, To follow. پس سر نمودن *pas sar namūdan*, To turn away the face through shame. To divert, call off the attention. پس غیبت *pasi ghaybat*, Behind one's back, in one's absence. پس فردا *pasi fardā*, The day after to-morrow. پس گوش انداختن *pasi gosh andākhtan*, To pretend not to hear, to dismiss from one's mind. پس ماندن *pas māndan*, To remain behind, to survive. پس و پیش *pas u pesh*, Behind and before, here and there. Demur, hesitation, evasion. از این پس باز *az īn pas bāz*, In future, henceforth. پاپس *pā pas*, (or پس ازپس *pas az pas*) Successively, one after another. Behind. درپس *dar pas*, Behind, after, in the rear. *Pus*, A son.

P پسا *pasā*, Name of a city in Persia.

P پساچین *pasā-chīn*, Gleanings.

P پسادست *pasā-dast*, Credit. Borrowed. Buying on credit.

P پس افتاده *pas-uftāda*, Lagging behind.

P پس افگند *pas-afgand*, Any thing laid up for future use, either in reference to this world or the next. Inheritance.

P پسانتن *pasānitan*, (zand and Pāz.) To scatter.

P پس انداز *pas-andāz*, Clear profit. Savings, a reserve against old age or want of employment.

P پسانیدن *pasānīdan*, To irrigate.

P پس اوگند *pas-avgand*, A hoard, a reserve.

P پساوند *pas-āwand*, The last consonant in a verse with which all the other distichs rhyme. Rhyme, metre, verse.

P پساویدن *pasāwīdan*, To rub gently, touch. To intoxicate.

P پساهنگ *pas-āhang*, A nail. A horse-shoe. A piece of iron nailed to the heel of a shoe.

P پس آینده *pas āyanda*, A follower.

P پسپاي *pas-pāy*, Sitting cross-legged, as the Asiatics; or like tailors. A manœuvre for tripping up another's heels.

P پست *past*, Low. Humble. Plain, level ground. Abject, mean, base, vile. Avaricious, sordid, grovelling. Destroyed, ruined, depopulated. پست کردن *past kardan*, To render miserable, to crush, to depress. To lower. پست و خوار *past u khwār*, Base and mean. *Pist*, Bruised corn. Meal of wheat, barley, or vetches, especially when toasted (in Arabic called سویق *sawīk*). A kind of food made of deer's liver, almonds, &c., and of which a bit of the size of a pistachio-nut will support the life of a dervīsh several days. پست جو *pisti jaw*, Barley-meal.

P پستا *pastā*, Carrying forward any business already begun. *Pistā*, The pistachio-nut.

P پستادست *pastā-dast*, Buying on credit.

P پستان *pastān*, (pl. of پست *past*) The most humble. The basest, lowest, meanest, most avaricious of mankind. *Pistān*, The breast, nipple. A place abounding with pistachio-nuts. The pine-tree. پستان سگ *pistāni sag*, Sebestens. پستان کردن *pistān kardan*, To give milk. پستان مادر بریدن *pistāni mādar burīdan*, To cut off a mother's breast. (met.) To be insatiable and guilty of the basest ingratitude.

P پست آواز *past-āwāz*, Low-voiced.

P پست ترین *past tarīn*, Nethermost.

P پست داشتگي *past-dāshtagī*, A holding down. پست داشتگیء سر *past-dāshtagī-i sar*, A hanging down of the head.

P پست داشته *past-dāshta*, Held down.

P پستر *pastar*, Posterior, later.

P پسترك *pasturak*, Somewhat lower, inferior. Later. Humbler. More base, more avaricious. Any thing laid under paper to keep it clean whilst being polished.

P پسترم *pasturum*, Ice. Frost, hoar-frost.

P پسترین *pastarīn*, The last.

P پست فطرت *past-fitrat*, Small-minded.

P پست قد *past-kad*, Dwarfish, low of stature.

P پستك *pistak*, The jujube-tree.

P پستکردن *past kardan*, To squeeze, press.

P پستگي *pastagī*, Lowness, depression.

P پستنك *pistank*, The jujube-tree.

P پسته *pista*, The pistachio-nut. پستهٔ شکرفشان *pista-i shakar-fishān*, The lip of a mistress.

P پست همّت *past-himmat*, Mean-spirited. Unambitious.

P پستي *pastī*, Lowness. Inferiority. Humility. Baseness. A swamp, marsh. *Pistī*, A pistachio.

P پستي رنگ *pistī-rang*, Pea-green.

P پستیوار *pastīwār*, A clumsy mechanic.

P پسچین *pischīn*, A hard wood for making bows

P پسخوار *pas-khwār* or *pasi-khwār*, Fragment of meat or drink.

P پس خورده *pas-khwurda*, The fragments of a meal, orts. A sip, a draught.

P پس دیوار *pas-dīwār*, The back-wall.

P پسر *pisar* or *pusar*, A son, boy, youth. پسر عمّ *pisari ɛamm*, An uncle's son, a cousin.

P پسراندر *pisar-andar*, A step-son.

P پسرپستك *pisar-pistak*, A fruit like the jujube.

P پسرخواندگي *pisar-khwāndagī*, Adoption.

P پسرخوانده *pisar-khwānda*, Adopted son.

P پسرزاده *pisar-zāda*, A son's son, a grandson.

P پسرك *pisarak*, A little boy: a child, infant.

P پسرگیر *pisar-gīr*, An adopted son.

P پسرمردگي *pisar-murdagī*, Bereavement.

P پسرمرده *pisar-murda*, Bereaved of a son.

P پسرو *pasrav*, A follower, an attendant. An imitator. Dependants. Train, equipage. *Pisarū*, A little boy.

P پسري *pisarī*, Boyhood. Filiation, sonship.

P پسریچه *pisarecha*, A froward son.

P پس شام *pas-shām*, A meal which the Muhammadans make a little before day-break during the month of Ramazān to enable them to fast till sunset.

P پسغده *pasaghda*, Prepared, arranged.

P پسك *pisk*, A lot which is cast. Curly hair. Globular dung.

P پس کش *pas-kash*, Recoil, repercussion.

P پسکل تارگي *pishkali tāragī*, Pistachio.

P پسکله *paskulla*, A wooden bar or bolt.

P پسکوهه *pas-koha*, Back part of the saddle.

P پس گردن *pas-gardan*, Neck, hind-head.

P پسگك *pasagak*, Dew, hoar-frost, rime.

P پس لشکر *pas lashkar*, The rear-guard.

P پسمان *pasmān*, A wager.

P پس مانده *pas-mānda*, A survivor. Old, antiquated, out of fashion.

P پسند *pasand*, Approbation. Choice. Praised, approved. Selected. Grateful, agreeable, excellent. (in comp.) Approving, admiring, loving: as, اهالي پسند *ahālī-pasand*, Approved by the learned. خود پسند *khwud-pasand*, Admiring or praising one's self. دل پسند *dil-pasand*, Grateful to the heart, cordial. سماحت پسند *samāhat-pasand*, Delighting in liberality. هدایایٔ سلاطین پسند *hadāyā-i salātīn-pasand*, Presents worthy of a prince. یاران پسند *yārān-pasand*, Agreeable to friends. پسند کردن *pasand kardan*, To approve. To choose.

P پسندر *pusandar* or *pisandar*, A brother by the father, not by the mother, or vice versa.

P پسندن *pasandan*, To approve, choose.

P پسنده *pasanda*, Chosen, approved,

P پسندیدگي *pasandīdagī*, Approbation.

P پسندیدن *pasandīdan*, To approve, be content.

P پسندیده *pasandīda*, Approved, admired,

esteemed. Selected, chosen. Agreeable, acceptable. Praiseworthy, laudable. Warranted. Purified, holy. پسنديده شدن *pasandīda shudan*, To be agreeable, to please. پسنديدهٔ كبار *pasandīda-i kibār*, Agreeable to the great. پسنديده كردن *pasandīda kardan*, To render agreeable. To approve. اعمال پسنديده *aʿmāli pasandīda*, Worthy actions. نا پسنديده *nā pasandīda*, Hateful, disapproved.

P پسنديده خصال *pasandīda-khiṣāl*, Of excellent morals.

P پسنديده رو *pasandīda-rav*, Of good conduct.

P پسنگك *pasangak*, Hail.

P پس نهاد *pas-nihād*, A treasure, store, reserve. A heritage.

P پس و پيش نمودن *pas u pesh namūdan*, To hesitate, demur, waver.

P پسوده *pasūda*, Struck. Rubbed. Reached. Bored.

P پسور *paswar*, Carrying back. *Pusūr*, Imprecation, curse.

P پسوريدن *pusūrīdan*, To curse, execrate.

P پسهانتن *pas-hānitan*, (in zand) To scatter.

P پسيج *pasīj*, Prepared. Provision for a journey.

P پسين *pasīn*, Posterior, last, newest, hindmost. The afternoon, between mid-day and sunset. جنگ پسين *jangi pasīn*, The last battle.

P پسينيان *pasīniyān*, The moderns.

P پش *pash*, The mane of a horse. A forelock. A tuft hanging loose at the end of a turban, sash, or belt. Ignoble. Defective. Like, resembling. *Pish*, Before. *Push*, An owl.

P پشام *pashām*, Dark-coloured, opake.

P پشان *pashān*, A passage. A mace.

P پشاور *pashāwar*, A province of Persia.

P پش بنهاد *pish ba nihād*, Favour, regard.

P پشت *pusht*, The back. The outside. A support, prop. A protector, patron. A pannel, pack-saddle, knot, upon which porters in the East carry their burdens. Generation, descent. A catamite. Name of a town in Khurāsān, and of a district in the vicinity of Nishābūr. پشت به پشت *pusht ba pusht*, Generation to generation. پشت بام *pushti bām*, The flat surface of a roof or a terrace. A partisan. پشت پا خاريدن *pushti pā khārīdan*, To rejoice, to be in high spirits. پشت پا زدن *pushti pā zadan*, To take to one's heels. To abandon. پشت پاي *pushti pāy*, The convex or upper part of the foot. پشت پلنگ *pushti palang*, Mottled, dappled. پشت چمن *pushti chaman*, A grass-plot. پشت داد *pusht dād*, (or پشت نمود *pusht namūd*) He gave (or shewed) his back, he fled. He backed or supported. پشت كردن *pusht kardan*, To turn the back. پشت دست گزيدن *pushti dast gazīdan*, To bite the back of the hand. (met.) To repent. پشت ماهي *pushti māhī*, A fish's back. Night. پشت و پناه *pusht u panāh*, A protector and an asylum.

P پشتاره *pushtāra*, A truss, pack, load.

P پشت انداز *pusht-andāz*, An infamous boy, who submits to be abused.

P پشت بست *pusht-bast*, A large wrapper. A truss, load. A horse-cloth.

P پشت پاي *pusht-pāy*, Infamous. A term of reproach.

P پشت پناه *pusht-panāh*, An ally.

P پشت پوزي *pusht-pozī*, A crupper.

P پشت خار *pusht-khār*, (Scratch-back) A curry-comb. بپشت خار خاريدن *ba pusht-khār khārīdan*, To curry (a horse).

P پشت خاريده *pusht-khārīda*, Curried (horse).

P پشت خم *pusht-kham*, Hump-backed.

P پشت خم شده *pusht kham shuda*, Humble, stooping, having the back bent.

P پشت دار *pusht-dār*, A prop. A bar. Thick clothing. Propped, backed, supported.

P پشت ريش *pusht-resh*, Sore-backed, galled.

P پشتك *pashtak*, Dew, hoar-frost. Curled hair. The pill-like dung of sheep or goats. Canine teeth. *Pushtak*, A kick, a wince. The game of leap-frog. A disease incidental to the hoofs of horses, asses, or mules. A waistcoat, doublet.

P پشتكر *pashathar*, The canine teeth.

P پشتك زن *pushtak-zan*, Kicking, wincing.

P پشتگاني *pushtagānī*, A pension, stipend.

P پشت گرمي *pusht-garmī*, Warm support.

P پشتلنك *pushtlang*, Lagging behind. Vicious, faulty. Unintelligible, unmeaning.

P پشت مازه *pusht-māza*, (or پشتمزه *pusht-maza*) Loins, joints in the back. Flesh inside the back-bone.

P پشتمال *pusht-māl*, An apron.

P پشتنك *pushtank*, A surcingle, girth.

P پشتو *pashtū*, A glass bottle. *Pushto*, The language spoken by the Afghāns.

P پشتوار *pushtwār*, (or پشتواره *pushtwāra*, A burden, load; as much as a man can carry on his back.

P پشتوان *pushtwān*, A prop, support for a tottering wall. The bar of a door. A helper, protector.

P پشته *pushta*, A little hill, an embankment. Declivity. A heap. The shoulder-blades. A load. A faggot. A buttress, prop. A vault. A quay. پشتهٔ باغ *pushta-i bāgh*, A meadow.

P پشته بندي *pushta-bandī*, A rate levied for embankments.

P پشتي *pushtī*, Return. A protector, support, safeguard, or prop. Alliance, aid. A kind of large cushion, pillow, or carpet, upon which they sit. A waistcoat, a doublet. پشتي كردن *pushtī kardan*, To back, to help.

P پشتيبان *pushtībān*, The bar of a door. A prop. Whatever is leant upon, trusted to, or adds to strength or security.

P پشتيمان *pushtīmān*, (پشتيوان *pushtīwān* or پشتيون *pushtīwan*) A bar. A prop.

P پشخانه *pash-khāna*, A mosquito-curtain.

P پشخوان *pash-khwān*, A beating, flattening. A gift. A table carried with one on a journey.

P پشخودن *pashkhūdan*, To express, compress, squeeze, strain.

P پشخور *push-khwur*, Vain conversation.

P پشخوره *pash-khwura*, Sweets, dessert.

P پشخون *pishkhūn*, A table, a bench.

P پشخه *pashkha*, A clothes-brush. A bleacher's beetle.

P پشخيدن *pashkhīdan*, To shine, flash, glitter. To scatter.

P پش ديد *pish-dīd*, Favour, regard, wish.

P پشرو *pish-rav*, Going before. An overture in music.

P پشك *pashk*, Evenness, equality. Love. Suspending. A beetle. An owl. A disease in horses. *Pishk*, Lot. The dung of sheep or deer. *Pushk*, Sheep's or camel's dung. A small wine-jar. Name of a tree. *Pashak*, Dew. *Pushak*, A cat.

H پشكال *pushkāl*, The rainy season.

P پشكر *pishkir*, (پشكره *pishkira*) Sheep's, goat's, or deer's dung.

P پشكردن *pash* or *push kardan*, To fight. To contract, shrivel, wrinkle. To be trusted, believed.

P پشكش *pish-kash*, A present.

P پشكل *pishkil*, The orbicular dung of sheep.

P پشكل ناك *pishkilnāk*, Full of dung.

P پشكله *pishkila*, A hooked stick with which they open a lock, a key. Dung of sheep or deer.

P پشكليدن *pishkalīdan*, To mark with the nails, to scratch.

P پشكم *pish* or *pashkam*, A court, vestibule.

P پشگن *pishgan*, Easy to cook.

P پشل *pishil* or *pashal*, Two things twisted or stuck together.

P پشلنگ *pash-lang*, Lagging behind. A pick-axe. Name of the father of Afrāsyāb. *Pashlung*, A mountain-fortress. Defective. Vain, unmeaning. Vicious.

P پشم *pashm*, Wool. Down. Camels' or asses' hair. پشم انداختن *pashm andākhtan*, To cast his coat (a camel). پشم بريدن *pashm burīdan*, To shear sheep. Sheep-shearing. پشم دوات *pashmi dawāt*, Cotton, wool, or any spongy substance which is put into an ink-holder. پشم در كلاه ندارد *pashm dar kulāh na dārad*, He has no wool in his cap, (met.) He has neither rank, knowledge, or spirit. پشم شدن *pashm shudan*, To be frittered away, to fall to pieces. To scatter. پشم كشيدن *pashm kashīdan*, To become contemptible. To despise. To parry, to ward off.

P پشماگند *pashm-āgand*, Stuffed with wool (as saddle-cloths). The stuffing of a saddle.

P پشمالو *pashm-ālū*, A kind of peach.

P پشمان *pishmān*, Penitent.

P پشم بريده *pashm-burīda*, Shorn (sheep).

P پشم فريز *pashm-firez*, Shearings of wool.

P پشمك *pashmak*, Name of a sweetmeat.

P پشم ناك *pashmnāk*, Hairy, woolly.

P پشميدن *pashmīdan*, To scatter, separate.

P پشمين *pashmīn*, Woolly, woollen. لباس پشمين *libāsi pashmīn*, Woollen garments (particularly of the coarser kind).

P پشمينه *pashmīna*, Woollen. خرقۂ پشمينه بر دوش *khirkaꜙi pashmīna bar dosh*, Having a coarse woollen cloak upon the shoulders.

P پشن *pashan*, Name of the father of Afrāsyāb. A field of action celebrated for a battle.

P پشنج *pashanj*, A furrow. A sown field.

P پشنجش *pashanjash*, A sprinkling.

P پشنجه *pishanja*, A handful of grass with which weavers and glazers starch cloth in the loom.

P پشنجيدن *pishanjīzan*, To sprinkle. To be sprinkled.

P پشندده *pushnuda*, A Persian dish made of flour dressed with dates. Frost.

P پشنگ *pashang*, A kind of vessel with which they carry earth away. A mason's chisel. Oppression. Anguish, affliction. Exudation. Name of the father of Afrāsyāb. *Pishing*, Exudation.

P پشور *pushūr*, Imprecation, curse.

P پشول *pushūl*, Imprecation, curse.

P پشوليدن *pushūlīdan*, To curse.

P پشوليده *pisholīda*, Scattered. Entangled.

P پشه *pashsha*, A gnat. پشۂ زرين *pashshaꜙi zarīn*, A spark of fire. پشۂ زعفران *pashshaꜙi zaꜙfarān*, A live coal, a firebrand.

P پشه خانه *pashsha-khāna*, A hair tent to keep off flies. A mosquito-curtain. The gnat-tree, a tree with a very large smooth stem and thick foliage.

P پشه خورد *pashsha-khwurd*, A sore to which people in Balkh are liable, thought to be caused by the sting of a gnat.

P پشه دار *pashsha-dār*, (or پشه غال *pashshaghāl*) The gnat-tree (so called from the swarms of gnats which are bred in its pods).

P پشه دان *pashshadān*, A mosquito-curtain.

P پشه ناك *pashshanāk*, Swarming with gnats.

P پشي *pishī*, A small, thin, copper coin.

P پشيج *pashīj*, Circular (as a piece of money, fish-scale, &c.). Abundant, ample. Many. Apparatus for a journey.

P پشيجيدن *pashījīdan*, To be armed: to prepare.

P پشيچ *pashīch*, Large, abundant.

P پشيخ *pashīkh*, Even, equal. Provisions for the way.

P پشير خرما *pashīr-khurmā*, Caliculus of a date.

P پشيز *pishīz*, Any thing small, round, and flat. A small piece of money. A fish-scale.

P پشيز نشان *pishīz-nishān*, A coiner of money.

P پشيزه *pishīza*, The scale of a fish. A small, thin piece of money. The skirt of a tent. A thin layer of metal between the handle and blade of a knife. پشيزۂ خرما *pishīzaꜙi khurmā*, The caliculus of a date, resembling a navel where it adheres to the stalk.

P پشيم *pashīm*, Penitent. Dispersion, separation. پشيم شدن *pashīm shudan*, To be penitent, sorry. To be separated, scattered. To be ignorant.

P پشيمان *pashīmān*, Penitent. Sorry. Ashamed, abashed, disgraced.

P پشيمان شدگان *pashīmān-shudagān*, Penitents.

P پشيماني *pashīmānī*, Repentance. Regret. پشيماني خوردن *pashīmānī khwurdan*, To repent.

P پشين *pashen*, Name of the third (according to some the first) son of Kaykubād.

P پغار *pughār*, Pride, arrogance, conceit.

P پغاز *paghāz*, A wedge.

P پغنه *paghna*, A step, a stair.

P پف *puf*, A puff, a blast. Breathing, respiration. چراغرا پف كردن *charāghrā puf kardan*, To puff out the candle.

P پفيدن *pufīdan*, To puff, to blow out.

P پفيوز *pafyūz*, Sour, crabbed, austere, proud.

P پك *pak*, The round of a ladder. Ignorant, silly, conceited, vain. *Pik*, A joint of the finger or toe. *Puk*, Uneven, prominent. Thick, coarse. Ignorant, silly, conceited. Hollow. One side of the ankle-bone. A sledge-hammer. A leap, bound.

P پكمال *pakmāl*, An iron instrument with which they draw lines or figures on leather.

P پكند *pakand*, (in Khwārazm) Bread.

P پكنه *pakna*, Fat and short.

P پكوك *pakūk*, A smith's hammer. A balcony. A projecting gallery of wood.

P پكول *pakūl*, Balcony. Main beam of a roof.

P پكولك *pak u lak*, Ignorance, unskilfulness. Inquiry, search. Household furniture. Useless, unprofitable. *Pukūluk*, Rough, uneven. Thick.

P پگ *pag*, A female who has round breasts. A child's plaything. Millet.

P پگاه *pagāh*, Dawn. پگاه تر, Early dawn.

P پگوي *pagawī*, (in zand) A philosopher.

P پگه *pagah*, The dawn.

P پگين *pagīn*, (in zand and Pāzand) Millet.

P پل *pal*, A field with a raised border. *Pil*, The foot (also the head) of a door, revolving in a socket, in the way of a turnstile. A bit of wood, answering to a brace or button, for uniting the different parts of a tent. The piece of wood which is struck in the game of tipcat or hockey. A humming-top. *Pul*, A bridge, an arch. An embankment. A small coin. پل آبگون آتش بار *puli ābgūni ātish-bār*, The celestial vault. پل بالان *pulbālān*, Name of an embankment near Harāt. پل چكنم *pul-chikunam*, Name of a bridge near Shīrāz. پل شكستن *pul shikastan*, To fail, to break down. To drown. پل صراط *puli sirāt*, The bridge over the eternal fire, across which the Muhammadans imagine they shall pass into Paradise. پل هفت طاق *puli haft tāk*, The seven heavens.

P پلاد *palād*, A led horse. *Pulād*, Steel.

P پلارك *palārak*, A cimeter (of Damascus), a sword of the finest Indian steel.

P پلاژور *palājūr*, (or پلازور *palāzūr*) Mastic.

P پلاس *palās*, Coarse woollen cloth worn by Dervīshes. A woollen carpet. Sackcloth. Fraud, deceit. A cheat, an impostor. پلاس انداختن *palās andākhtan*, To apostatize, to become reprobate. To disperse, to scatter.

P پلاس پوش *palās-posh*, Clad in Dervīsh-attire.

P پلاسك *palāsak*, Evil, misfortune.

P پلاطير *palātīr*, A window.

P پلالك *palālak*, A sword of excellent steel.

P پلان *pilān*, A pack-saddle.

P پلانه *palāna*, A bad or indecent action.

P پلاني *palānī*, A sluggish beast.

P پلاو *palāw*, A dish composed of flesh or fish highly seasoned, first roasted and afterwards fricasseed or stewed, covered and heaped over with rice newly boiled, seasoned, and sometimes coloured, and garnished with eggs, onions. Affluence, ease, good things.

P پلاهنك *palāhank*, A rein, bridle, halter.

P پل بندي *pul-bandī*, Construction of bridges and embankments: the tax imposed for such works.

P پلپل *pulpul* or *pilpil*, Pepper. پلپل خام *pulpuli khām*, White Pepper. پلپل مشك *pulpuli mushk*, A kind of black berry of a musky odour. پلپل مويه *pulpul mūya*, Root of the long pepper-tree.

P پلچي *pulchī*, Glass beads, small shells.

P پلچي فروش *pulchī farosh*, A vender of small shells or glass beads.

P پلخ *palakh*, The throat.

P پلخم *palakhm*, (or پلخمان) A sling.

P پلستك *pilistuk*, A swallow.

P پلسگي *pilasgī*, A crimson dye.

P پلشت *palasht*, Impure. Carrion. Contemptible, worthless.

P پلغده *palaghda*, Rotten, putrid, addle.

P پلفته *palafta*, Burnt provender.

P پلك *palk* or *pilk*, An eyelid. *Palak*, An eyelid. Pendulous, hanging loose. پلك چشم *palaki chashm*, The eyelid. پلك چشم جنبانيدن *palaki chashm jumbanīdan*, To twinkle the eye. پلك دريا *palaki daryā*, Clouds.

H پلكر *palkar*, Revenue from orchards.

P پلكن *pulukan*, Ambiguous, obscure.

P پلكه *puluka*, Reproach. Ambiguous.

P پلم *palm*, Earth, soil, dust.

P پلمس *palmas*, (or پلمسه *palmasa*) Perturbation. A losing of the use of hands and feet. A lie. Calumny, unjust imputation.

P پلمه *palma*, Lie, calumny. Suspicion. A board on which children learn to read. A loss of the use of hands and feet.

P پلنك *palank*, (or پلنگ *palang*) A leopard,

a panther. A giraffe. Any thing of a motley colour. A bedstead. The entire breadth of a doorway. *Piling*, A door-post.

P پلنگ پوش *palang-posh*, A coverlet.

P پلنگر *pilangar* or *palangar*, Name of a king slain by Alexander.

P پلنگ رنگ *palang-rang*, (or پلنگ گون *palang-gūn*, (A horse) spotted like a leopard, leopard coloured.

P پلنگ مشك *palang-mishk*, A herb growing at Baghdād, musky, and spotted like a leopard.

P پلنگ موش *palang-mūsh*, A fragrant plant.

P پلنگي كردن *palangī kardan*, To growl like a leopard or panther.

P پلنگين *palangīn*, Of, or like a leopard.

P پلنگينه *palangīna*, Like or belonging to a leopard. A kind of royal vest.

P پلوازه *palwāja*, Glass. A glass vessel.

P پلواس *palwās*, Deception, flattery.

P پلوان *pulwān*, A hero. (Bridge-like) A raised path round a field. A truss of straw.

P پلوس *pulos*, (equiv. to چاپلوس) Flattery.

P پلوك *paloh*, A smith's hammer. An upper chamber. A balcony. *Pulūk*, Camel's dung.

P پلوگ *palūg*, A beam. A projecting roof.

P پلول *palwal*, Name of an Indian pulse.

P پلون *pulvan*, (Bridge-like) A raised path or balk round a field.

P پلونده *palwanda*, A truss, bale, bundle.

P پله *pala*, A scale. A small capital. The hair on the temples. A humming-top. Biestings. A certain tree. The round or step of a ladder. *Pila*, Silk. The silkworm's cocoon. A willow. A tipcat.

P پلّه *palla*, The round or step of a ladder. *Pilla*, The bason of a balance, a scale. The round of a ladder.

P پله چوب *pila-chob*, The game of tipcat.

P پلّه دار *pilla-dār*, Carrying far (a gun).

P پلّه كش *pilla-kash*, Partial. An adherent.

P پلّه كشي *pilla-kashī*, Partiality.

P پلهنگ *palhang*, A bridle, halter, rope.

P پليته *palīta*, The wick of a candle or lamp. A tent, a roll of lint to be put into a wound, a suppository.

P پليد *palīd*, Impure, defiled, polluted, contaminated, unwashed. Foul. پليد شدن *palīd shudan*, To be impure. پليد كردن *palīd kardan*, (or ساختن *sākhtan*) To defile.

P پليد چشم *palīd-chashm*, Malignant eye.

P پليدزبان *palīd-zabān*, Foul-tongued, scurrilous.

P پليدكار *palīd-kār*, Flagitious. Defiled.

P پليدن *palīdan*, To search, investigate.

P پليدناك *palīdnāk*, Dirty, nasty, filthy.

P پليدي *palīdī*, Uncleanness, foulness. Excrement, dung, ordure. پليدي انداختن, To mute.

P پليشدن *palīshudan*, To be nasty. To abhor.

P پليندي *palyandī*, A fine kind of melon.

P پن *pan*, But.

P پناد *panād*, The air, the atmosphere.

P پناغ *pinägh*, A ball of raw thread or yarn. A thread of silk. A writer, a secretary.

P پنافتن *panāftan*, To be obstructed (as a water-course, or the lacteal veins).

P پناگاه *panā-gāh*, An asylum, a refuge.

P پناگير *panā-gīr*, A market, a fair.

P پنام *panām*, Certain acts performed to avert the influence of the evil eye. An amulet or charm. Hidden, covered, concealed. A kerchief with which the followers of Zardusht cover their faces in prayer. چشم پنام *chashm-panām*, Averting the influence of malignant eyes (an amulet, inscribed with sacred characters, as a supposed charm against fascination).

P پناميدن *panāmīdan*, To prohibit, avert.

P پنانك *panānak*, A kind of gum.

P پناوه *panāwa*, Trust (in God), resignation.

P پناه *panāh*, An asylum, refuge, protection. Shade, shelter. پناه بردن *panāh burdan*, (or گرفتن *giriftan*) To take refuge. پناه خدا *panāhi khudā*, The protection of God. God save you! افضال پناه *afzāl-panāh*, A retreat for learned men. سعادت پناه *saɛādat-panāh*, or دولت پناه *dawlat-panāh*, The asylum of felicity, happy, august, glorious. مسند دولت پناه *masnadi dawlat panāh*, The throne of felicity, a royal throne. شفقت پناه *shafakat-panāh*, Most merciful, clement, compassionate. عالم پناه *ɛālam-panāh*, The asylum of the world, where all the world resorts. عصمت پناه *ɛismat-panāh*, Most chaste. فتوا پناه *fatwa-panāh*, Most excellent in the decision of law-controversies. كرامت پناه *karāmat-panāh*, Miraculous.

P پناه جاي *panāh-jāy*, A place of refuge.

P پناهگاه *panāh-gāh*, An asylum, sanctuary.

P پناهنده *panāhanda*, Seeking refuge.

P پناهيدن *panāhīdan*, To fly, take refuge. To consult safety, take care of one's self. To be defeated.

P پناهيده *panāhīda*, A refugee. Protecting.

P پنبون *pambūn*, Going, walking.

P پنبه *pamba*, (by some *pumba*) Cotton. پنبه از گوش بر آوردن *pamba az gosh bar āwardan*, To take the cotton from the ear; to be attentive. پنبه در گوش نهادن *pamba dar gosh nihādan*, To put cotton in the ear; to be inattentive to what is said. پنبه شدن *pamba shudan*, To be soft as cotton. To be pure and white. To disperse. To run away. پنبه كردن *pamba kardan*, To run away. To be scattered. To deny. To keep silence. To be impotent. To repel, rout. To obliterate. پنبه نهادن *pamba nihādan*, To deceive. To satisfy, put to rest.

P پنبه پاي *pumba-pāy*, A sort of shoe.

P پنبه پز *pamba-paz* or وز *waz*, Cotton-carder.

P پنبه دار *pamba-dār*, Having cotton.

P پنبه دانه *pumba-dāna*, Cotton-seed.

P پنبه دوز *pumba-doz*, A carder of cotton.

P پنبه زار *pumbazār*, A cotton-field.

P پنبه زن *pamba-zan*, A dresser of cotton.

P پنبه كن *pumba-kan*, Flue of cotton or silk. *Pamba-kun*, Obliterate. Deny. Keep silence. Flee.

G پنتافيليون *pantāfīlyūn*, Cinquefoil.

P پنج *panj*, Five. Fifth. In fives. The five senses. *Pinj*, A pinch. A button.

P پنجاب *panjāb*, (The five waters or rivers, viz. Sutlej, Rāvi, Chināb, Jilam, and Attock or Indus) Name of a country N. W. of Hindūstān.

P پنج اركان *panj arkān*, The five pillars (of Muhammadanism: Unitarianism, Prayer, Fasting, Pilgrimage, and Alms-giving).

P پنجال مرغ *panjāli murgh*, A bird's beak. Bird's dung.

P پنج انگشت *panj angusht*, Cinquefoil.

P پنجاه *panjāh*, Fifty.

P پنجاه ساله *panjāh sāla*, Fifty years old.

P پنجاهم *panjāhum*, The fiftieth.

P پنجاهه *panjāha*, The Christian Lent.

P پنجايانه *panjāyāna*, Henbane.

P پنج آيت *panj āyat*, The five chapters of the Kur'ān which are read during the mourning of a Musulmān.

P پنجايه *panjāya*, Prayers said in Lent.

P پنج بيچاره *panj bīchāra*, The five wanderers, viz. Saturn, Jupiter, Mars, Venus, and Mercury.

P پنج پايك *panj-pāyak*, (or پنجپايه *panj pāya*) A crab. The sign Cancer.

P پنجپهلو *panj-pahlū*, Quinquelateral.

P پنج تاه *panj-tāh*, (A rope) of five threads.

P پنج ترياق *panj-tiryāk*, A syrup of treacle.

P پنج تن پاك *panj tani pāk*, Five holy ones, *i.e.* Muhammad, Fātimah, Alīy, Hasan, and Husayn.

P پنج توسن سلامت *panj tawsani salāmat*, The five senses.

P پنج چوبه *panj-choba*, A kind of tent.

P پنج دعا *panj duɛā*, The five daily prayers.

P پنجر *panjar*, A window, balcony, wooden lattice before a window. A cage, coop. Watch (on board ship).

P پنج روز *panj roz*, Five days. Human life.

P پنجره *panjara*, A cage. One who keeps a look out from a ship's mast. پنجرهٔ لاجورد *panjarasi lājaward*, The firmament. *Pinjara*, Name of a country.

P پنجره دار *panjara-dār*, Latticed.

P پنج سال *panj sāl*, Five years. Five years old.

P پنج سالگي *panj sālagī*, A lustre, five years.

P پنج ساله *panj sāla*, Of five years: quinquennial.

P پنجش *pinjash*, A ball of carded cotton.

P پنج شاخ دست *panj shākhi dast*, Five fingers. Cinque-foil.

P پنج شاخه *panj-shākha*, Five-pronged.

P پنج شعبه *panj shuɛba*, The five senses.

P پنجشنبه *panj shambih*, Thursday.

P پنجشيدن *panjshīdan*, To press, squeeze, or tickle with the fingers. To disperse.

P پنج عيب شرعي *panj ɛayb sharɛī*, Very vicious (guilty of five vices; namely, robbery, adultery, gaming, drunkenness, and falsehood).

P پنجك *panjak*, A sort of ivy. *Punjak*, A ball of carded cotton.

P پنجگان *panjagān*, Fives.

P پنجگانه *panj gāna*, Five.

P پنج گنج *panj ganj*, The five senses. The five daily prayers of the Muhammadans.

P پنج گوشه *panj gosha*, Pentangular.

P پنجم *pānjum*, (or پنجمين *panjumin*) A fifth. پنجم رواق *panjum rawāk*, The fifth heaven. The orbit of the planet Mars.

P پنجمير *panjmīr*, A province in توران *tūrān*.

P پنجنگشت *panj angusht*, Five fingers. Cinquefoil, and several other similar plants, with their seeds. A fork with five prongs. A place near Tabrīz.

P پنج نوبت *panj nawbat*, The five daily prayers of a Muhammadan. The five times a day that music is played before the house of a great man. The five instruments of war, دهل *duhul*, دمامه *damāma*, طبل *tabl*, دف *daf*, and صنج *sanj*. پنج نوبت زدن *panj nawbat zadan*, To rejoice. To play the great man.

P پنجنوش *panj nosh*, An electuary made up of five ingredients.

P پنج ورق *panj warah*, Cinquefoil.

P پنج وشش و هفت و چهار *panj u shash wa haft u chahār*, The five (senses), the six (sides) of the world, seven (planets), and four (elements).

P پنجه *panja*, The palm of the hand with the five fingers, or the sole of the foot with the five toes. The fist. The hand with the fingers expanded. The extended talons of a bird, the claws. A prong. A sort of link or torch resembling five fingers. A hand made of ivory to scratch the back. A handle, a hilt. Gripe. Loose stones placed on the parapet of a fort. A stone hurled out of a balista, or for sinking an enemy's ship. Ivy. A kind of dance, in which they take hold of each other's hands. پنجهٔ بیچاره *panjaᵢi bīchāra*, The five wanderers, *i.e.* Saturn, Jupiter, Mars, Venus, and Mercury. پنجه تیز کردن *panja tez hardan*, To prepare for war. پنجهٔ دزدیده *panjaᵢi duzdīda*, Five intercalary days added to the Persian year. پنجهٔ دلیرانه *panjaᵢi dilīrāna*, War. پنجهٔ کبك دري *panjaᵢi habk darī*, Name of a note in music. پنجه کردن *panja hardan*, To grasp. To box, slap. پنجهٔ گربه *panjaᵢi gurba*, Cat's claw (a plant). پنجهٔ مریم *panjaᵢi maryam*, Sow-bread. *Pinja*, Ivy. *Panjah*, (for پنجاه *panjāh*) Fifty. A fish. A net. A fish-hook. A grappling-iron.

P پنجه دار *panja-dār*, Pronged.

P پنجه زن *panja-zan*, Striking the nails into.

P پنجه کش *panja-hash*, An iron instrument resembling a hand with which wrestlers exercise themselves, by locking their fingers within those of the instrument. A kind of bread bearing the marks of five fingers.

P پنجه گیر *panja-gīr*, A wrestler, pugilist.

P پنجيانه *panjiyāna*, Hog's bean.

P پنجيدن *panjīdan*, The fifth.

P پنجيره *panjīra*, (or پنجهير) A cage: window.

P پنج يك *panj yak*, One of five, a fifth.

P پنجين *panjīn*, Division into parts.

P پنجيوده *panj yoda*, Five, five units.

H پنچايت *panchāyat*, Arbitration by five.

P پنچه *puncha*, The front, forehead. The forelocks, ringlets hanging down the forehead. پنچه بر روي كسي زدن *puncha bar rue kase zadan*, To disgrace, distress, ruin.

P پنچه بند *puncha-band*, A front band, wreath, fillet, worn by women. A curled or braided lock.

P پند *pand*, Counsel, advice. Admonition, exhortation. Doctrine, moral. Rite, ceremony. A kite. پند پدر *pandi pidar*, Paternal admonition. پند دادن *pand dādan*, (or پند گفتن *pand guftan*) To give advice. پند دلپسند *pandi dil-pasand*, Cordial exhortation, good counsel. *Pind*, A seat. Posteriors. *Pund*, Cotton prepared for spinning.

P پندار *pandār*, One who takes advice. *Pindār*, Thought, imagination, fancy, opinion. Pride, conceit, a high opinion of one's self. (in composition) Pondering, thinking, weighing. Revolving. دور پندار *dūr-pindār*, Thinking deeply, penetrating into futurity.

P پندارانيدن *pindārānīdan*, To cause to understand, suppose, imagine, or consider.

P پندارگان *pindāragān*, Ideas, fancies.

P پنداره *pindāra*, Thought, fancy. Conceit.

P پنداري *pindārī*, You understand or consider. Conceit. تا نپنداري *tā na pindārī*, That you may not think.

P پنداشتن *pindāshtan*, (or پنداريدن) To think, imagine, consider, understand, presume. To be proud.

P پندر *pandar*, Name of a fort near Shīrāz.

P پندره *pindara*, A blockhead. A supposititious child.

P پندش *pundash*, (or پندك *pundak*) A ball of carded cotton.

P پندند *pandand*, (in zand and Pāz.) A son.

P پندوره *pandūra*, Cresses. A half-brother.

P پنده *pinda*, A drop, spot, point.

P پنديدن *pandīdan*, To give or take counsel.

P پنزه *panza*, A kind of dance with joined hands.

G پنطافلون *pantāfīlūn*, Cinquefoil.

P پنك *pink*, A pinch. *Panak*, A span. *Panik*, (in zand and Pāz.) A kind of wild black plum.

P پنگ *pang*, A bunch of dates. A rod, stick, baton, piece of wood. A window. Dawn, daybreak, morning. A copper bason with a small hole in the bottom, for water in which it is placed to flow through, used for measuring time. *Ping*, A ten-thousandth part of a night and a day.

P پنگاره *pangāra*, A platter, dish, bowl, cup.

P پنگال *pingāl*, A cup, glass. An hour-glass.

P پنگان *pingān*, A bowl, a cup. A copper bason with a small hole in the bottom for water in which it is placed to flow through, used in measuring time; a clepsydra.

P پنگانچه *pingāncha*, A small cup.

P پنگاه *pungāh*, A hill.

P پنگره *pang* or *pingara*, A large kettle. A small dish, pan, plate, or cup. A winnowing-fan made of straw.

P پننگ *panang* or *pinang*, A window.

P پنه *panah*, A dunghill.

P پنهاله *panhāla*, Confection of almonds.

P پنهان *panhān* or *pinhān*, Concealed, hid. Clandestine, secret. پنهان بودن *pinhān būdan*, To be concealed, to abscond. پنهان داشتن *pinhān dāshtan* (or كردن *kardan*) To conceal, suppress.

P پنهان ديدگي *pinhān dīdagī*, Asly, stolen glance.

P پنهانگر *pinhāngar*, A place expected to contain something.

P پنهاني *pinhānī*, Concealment. به پنهاني *ba pinhānī*, (or در پنهاني *dar pinhānī*) In secret.

P پنهانيدن *pinhānīdan*, To abscond, lie hid.

P پنير *panīr*, Cheese.

P پنير آب *panīr-āb*, Whey from new cheese.

P پنيرخرما *panīr-khurmā*, Pith of a palm-tree.

P پنيرك *panīrak*, Sun-flower. Chameleon.

P پنير كيسه *panīr-kīsa*, A cheese suspended in a cloth that the serum may run out.

P پنير مايه *panīr-māya*, Rennet.

P پنيره *panīra*, A sun-flower. The chameleon.

P پنيري *panīrī*, Made of cheese. Cheesy.

P پنيز *panīz*, Ever. Never. Quick, speedy.

P پنيزه *panīza*, (or پنيسه) Fumitory (a herb).

P پنيلو *panīlū*, A market-place.

P پنين *panīn*, Ever. Never. Quick, speedy.

P پنيوش *panyūsh*, Pulsation. Labour.

P پنيون *panyūn*, Going away, walking.

P پو *pū*, Inquiry, search. A moderate pace, a trot. A running about. تك و پو كردن *tah u pū hardan*, To inquire diligently, to run about in search of.

P پواچ *puwāch*, Wicked, base, low, vile.

P پوازي *pawāzī*, Heat, pain.

P پوانه *pawāna*, A pass leading into Persia.

P پوب *pūb*, Tapestry, carpeting, or any thing spread in a house by way of ornament. The comb of a cock. A father. *Pob*, A bird's crest.

P پوپ *pūp*, (or پوپش) The hoopoo or puet.

P پوپشمن *pūpishman*, (zand and Pāz.) A helmet.

P پوپك *pūpah*, A hoopoo. A virgin.

P پوپل *pūpal*, Betel-nut.

P پوپو *pūpū*, A hoopoo; also its cry.

P پوپه *pūpa*, A hoopoo.

P پوت *pūt*, Sheep's liver. Victuals. A kind of melon.

P پوتاب *pūtāb*, A butt for shooting at.

P پوتنك *pūtank*, Pulecium, pennyroyal.

P پوته *pūta*, A treasury. A crucible.

P پوتي *pūti*, (A fry) of sheep's liver.

P پوج *pūj*, (or پوچ *pūch*) Injudicious, ignorant, absurd. Irregular, inconsistent, immoderate, inordinate. Round, convex, bunching out, hilly. Low, vile, base. Plain, smooth. Empty, vacant. A prater, babbler, blabber.

P پوج بيني *pūj bīnī*, Large or hook-nosed.

P پوچ گو *pūch-go* or *gū*, Talking nonsense.

P پوچيات *pūchiyāt*, Foolish prattle.

P پوخ *pūkh*, Gumminess about the eyes.

P پوختن *pokhtan*, To cook.

P پود *pūd*, Meat or food (for man and beast). Bait (for fish). Tinder, touchwood. The woof or weft, *i.e.* the cross-threads (in contradistinction to the warp or threads stretched lengthwise, and which are called تار *tār*). Cloths (particularly linens) woven in streaks or stripes of different colours. Old. دو پود *du pūd*, Wrought in two colours.

P پودات *pūdāt*, Perceived, felt.

P پود بند *pūd-band*, A fillet for the mouth. A thing forgotten.

P پودنه *pūdina*, Mint.

P پوده *pūda*, Rubbed, worn. Fallen to pieces. Empty. Old. Weak. Rotten, addle. Meat (for men), food (for cattle), bait (for fish). Tinder, touchwood. The woof or weft.

P پودينه *pūdīna*, Mint, spearmint.

P پوذش *pozish*, Excuse, apology.

P پور *pūr*, A son. A horse. One who shams ignorance. Steel. A woodcock. Porus king of Kanoge. شاه پور *shāh-pūr*, The son of a king, name of a king of Persia, whom the Greek and Roman writers called Sapores.

P پور آتبين *pūri-ātabīn*, Farīdūn king of Persia.

P پور آذر *pūr-āzar*, The patriarch Abraham.

P پوران *pūrān*, Kanoge. A successor. Sons.

P پوران دخت *pūrān-dukht*, Name of the daughter of Khusraw Parvez.

P پورتكال *pūrtakāl*, Portugal.

P پوردستان *pūr-dastān*, Name of Rustam.

P پوردگان *pordagān*, (or پورديان) Five intercalary days added to the end of the Persian year.

P پور سبكتكين *pūr sabuktigīn*, Sultan Mahmūd.

P پور سينا *pūr sinā*, Avicenna.

P پورشسب *pūr-shasb*, The father of Zardusht.

P پور صدف *pūri sadaf*, (Oyster's son) A pearl.

P پورعمران *pūr-ɛamrān*, Aaron and Moses.

P پورعنقا *pūr-ɛankā*, The father of Rustam.

P پورفان *pūrfān*, Saucy beggars.

P پور قباد *pūri kubād*, Nūshīravān king of Persia.

P پوركند *porkand*, A balcony. A mansion.

P پورمند *pormand*, A kind of fragrant herb. *Pūrmand*, Having a numerous offspring.

P پوره *pūra*, A son. Trunk of a tree.

P پور هاجر *pūri hājar*, Ishmael, Hagar's son.

P پوريان *pūriyān*, The citizens of Kanoge.

P پوز *poz*, The lip, mouth, and environs. The beak of a bird, the snout of a quadruped. The space between the nose and lip. The trunk of a tree.

P پوز بند *poz-band*, A muzzle.

P پوزش *pozish*, An excuse, apology. پوزش كردن *pozish kardan*, To excuse, make an apology.

P پوزش پذير *pozish-pazīr*, Accepting excuses.

P پوزمال *poz-māl*, A farrier's twitch.

P پوزن *pozan*, Land prepared for sowing.

P پوزه *poza*, The parts round the mouth. The trunk of a tree.

P پوزيدن *pozīdan*, To make excuse, apologize.

P پوژنگ *pūjang*, A piece, portion, morsel.

P پوس *pūs*, Cajolery, servile civility.

P پوسانه *pūsāna*, Fraudulently. Cajolery.

P پوست *post*, Skin. A raw hide, undressed skin. Rind, outward coat. Crust. Bark of a tree. A shell. Poppy-head. Slander, detraction. پوست بازكردن *post bāz kardan*, (or دادن *dādan*) To draw back the skin. To reveal the secrets of the heart. پوست بركردن *post bar kardan*, To peel (fruit). پوست بيضه *posti bayza*, An egg-shell. پوست جوز *posti jawz*, A nut-shell. پوست خايه *posti khāya*, The scrotum. پوست سگ برروي كشيدن *posti sag bar rū kashīdan*, To draw a dog's skin over the face. To be indecent. پوست كردن *post kardan*, To be intimate. To slander. To deceive. بپوست كسي افتادن *ba posti kase uftādan*, To traduce. پوست كندن *post kandan*, To flay. پوست مار *posti mār*, A snake's slough. پوست مس *posti mis*, Blue vitriol.

P پوست بازرفتگي *post-bāz raftagī*, Excoriation.

P پوست بازرفتة *post bāz rafta*, Excoriated.

P پوست بازكرده *post bāz karda*, Skinned.

P پوستپاره *post-pāra*, The standard of كاو *kāv*.

P پوست پيرا *post-perā*, A currier, leather-dresser.

P پوست پيراي *post-perāy*, A tanner. A currier.

P پوست رفتگي *post-raftagī*, Excoriation.

P پوست رفتة *post-rafta*, Excoriated.

P پوستگال *postgāl* (or پوست گاله *post-gāla*) The smooth skin under the tail of a sheep.

P پوستي *postī*, One who intoxicates himself with an infusion of poppy-heads. Lazy, indolent.

P پوستين *postīn*, Leathern. Leather. A fur garment. Slander, detraction. پوستين دريدن *postīn darīdan*, To blab a secret. پوستين كردن *postīn kardan*, (or درپوستين افتادن *dar postīn uftādan*) To speak ill of; to tell the faults.

P پوستين دوز *postīn-doz*, A furrier.

P پوسه *posa*, The thread, which in spinning is coiled round the spindle

P پوسيدن *posīdan*, To rot, corrupt, spoil, wither; become putrid.

P پوسيده *posīda*, Rotten, rancid, putrefied.

P پوسيده چوب *posīda-chūb* or *chob*, Rotten wood. Wood which ignites and burns as a candle.

P پوش *posh*, A covering, mantle, garment. A coat of mail. A cover, veil, lid. A certain plant, which, when pounded, forms a medicament for the eye. (in compos.) Clothing, dressing, covering. پاپوش *pā-posh*, (Covering the feet) Shoes, slippers. جرم پوش *jurm-posh* or خطا پوش *khatā-posh*, Concealing or pardoning sins. سبز پوش *sabz-posh*, Clothed in green. كله پوش *kalla-posh*, (Covering the head) A turban or other head-dress.

P پوشا *poshā*, Covering, concealing: a garment.

P پوشاك *poshāk*, Clothes, raiment, attire.

P پوشاكي *poshākī*, Fit for making garments.

P پوشانيدن *poshānīdan*, To clothe another.

P پوشش *poshish*, A covering, garment, dress. A coverlet, sheet, blanket. پوشش تن *poshishi tan*, A covering for the body, a habit, coat. پوشش رهگذر *poshishi rah-guzar*, A covered way between two houses. A corridor. زمين بي پوشش *zamīni bī poshish*, (Ground without covering) A desert; uncultivated lands.

P پوشك *poshak*, (in Tūrān) A cat, puss.

P پوشگان *poshgān*, A point in the divine life attainable only by the very spiritually-minded. Name of a place near Nīshāpūr. *Poshagān*, Invisible things. Name of a note in music.

P پوشله *poshala*, Covered. Clothing.

P پوشند *poshand*, A veil touching the ground.

P پوشندگي *poshandagī*, A garment, a covering.

P پوشنده *poshinda*, Who clothes. پوشندۀ كسوت محبت *poshindaɪ kiswati mahabbat*, Wearing the habit of friendship.

P پوشنگ *poshnag*, A cat.

P پوشنه *poshna*, A lid, cover. Concealed.

P پوشه *posha*, A veil, a curtain.

P پوشيدگي *poshīdagī*, Ambiguity, dubiousness.

P پوشيدن *poshīdan*, To cover, conceal, clothe. To dress, to wear clothes. To shut.

P پوشيدني *poshīdanī*, Fit to be put on, proper to be worn. Clothing, dress.

P پوشيده *poshīda*, Clothed, dressed, concealed, covered, hid. A chaste, retired woman. پوشيده بودن *poshīda būdan*, To be concealed, abscond, lie hid. To be clothed, dressed.

P پوشيده چشم *poshīda-chashm*, Hood-winked. Blind. Blind to the failings of others.

P پوك *pūk*, Tinder, touchwood. Wind from the throat in blowing a fire. Corn laid up in a pit, which is then strewed over with thorns and rubbish that it may not be discovered by thieves or enemies. Hollow.

P پول *pūl*, A bridge. A small piece of copper coin. A fish-scale. پول گرفتن *pūl giriftan*, To scrape the scales off a fish, to scale. An inn.

P پولاب *pūlāb*, Sense, feeling.

P پولابي *pūlābī*, Palpable, tangible, evident.

P پولاد *pūlād*, The finest Damascus steel, which, with that of قوم *kūm*, is esteemed the best in the East. Steel generally, a sword. Name of a demon and of a famous warrior. A club.

P پولاد بازو *pūlād-bāzū*, With arm of steel.

P پولاد خاي *pūlād-khāy*, (or رگ *rag*) Headstrong.

P پولاد سنجان *pūlād-sanjān*, Hardy warriors.

P پولاد مخلب *pūlād-mikhlab*, Steel-taloned.

P پولاد نهاد *pūlād-nihād*, As hard as steel.

P پولادوند *pūlādwand*, Hard as steel.

P پولاني *polānī*, Pottage, gruel.

P پولك *pūlak*, The scales of a fish.

P پوله *pola*, A withered melon. Any fruit soft and rotten inside.

P پون *pūn*, Felt-cloth, any kind of saddle-cloths for horses, camels, or other beasts of burden.

P پونيكا *pūnīkā*, Phœnicia.

P پوي *pūy*, A moderate pace, a trot.

P پويا *pūyā*, (or پويان *pūyān*) Running, trotting. A runner. پويان بودن *pūyān būdan*, To meander up and down.

P پويان هزبر *pūyān-hizbar*, A horse.

P پوي پوي *pūy-pūy*, Running, trotting. Fie!

P پويچه *pawīcha*, Ivy.

P پويدن *pūyidan*, To wander. To trot.

P پويش *pūyish*, A trotting up and down.

P پويگان *pūygān*, The womb. Water sprinkled.

P پويندگي *pūyandagī*, A running, trotting.

P پويه *pūya* or *poya*, A canter, hand-gallop, run. پويه دويدن *poya dawīdan*, To canter.

P پوييدن *pūyīdan*, To run to and fro, to trot. To examine, search.

P په په *pah*, Bravo! well done! په كردن *pah kardan*, To puff or breathe in one's face.

H P پهانسي كردن *phānsī kardan*, To strangle.

P پهانه *pahāna*, A wedge: one under a door.

P پهتان *phatān*, An Afghān tribe. A Patan.

P پهر *pahr*, Fourth. دو پهر شب *du pahri shab*, Two watches of the night. *Puhr*, A Jewish school.

P پهره *pahra*, A guard. Protection. A watch or fourth part of the night.

P پهره دار *pahra-dār*, A watchman, guard.

P پهلو *pahlav*, A hero. A wrestler. A saint. A city. Name of a country where Pehlevi is spoken. Shem, son of Noah. The parts about Ispahān. *Pahlū*, The side. Utility. Profit, advantage. پهلو تهي كردن *pahlū tihī kardan*, To withdraw, retire. To shun, avoid, abstain. پهلو دادن *pahlū dādan*, To assist. To retire. To avoid. پهلو زدن *pahlū zadan*, (or پهلو سابيدن *pahlū sāyīdan*) To associate, be on a footing with. پهلو كردن *pahlū kardan*, To run away. To turn away the face, avoid, beware of. پهلوي لشكر *pahlūyi lashkar*, The wing of an army. پهلو نهادن *pahlū nihādan*, To sleep. بپهلو افتادن *ba pahlū uftādan*, To fall on the side. To die, be killed.

P پهلوان *pahlawān*, A hero, champion, brave warrior, strong athletic man. Rough, rugged in figure or in speech. پهلوان سپهر *pahlawāni sipihr*, The celestial warrior, Mars. پهلوان پر زور *pahlawāni pur-zor*, A brave champion.

P پهلوانانه *pahlawānāna*, Heroic: heroically.

P پهلواني *pahlawānī*, Heroism. A citizen. Ancient Persian. Heroic. Belonging to a city.

P پهلو دار *pahlū-dār*, A helper. Scurrility.

P پهلو ساي *pahlū-sāy*, An equal. Intimate.

P پهلوي *pahlavī*, Belonging to a city. A citizen. An ancient Persian, and what relates to him. Saintly. زبان پهلوي *zabāni pahlavī*, The language of the ancient Persians, the Pahlavi language.

P پهله *pahla*, Ispahān, Ray, and Dīnawar.

P پهمزك *pahmuzak*, A porcupine.

P پهن *pahn*, Wide, large, broad, ample, extensive. پهن كردن *pahn kardan*, To extend. *Pahan*, Milk which boils in the breast of the mother through maternal affection.

P پهنا *pahnā*, Broad. Latitude, breadth, width.

P پهنانه *pahnāna*, Buttered toast. An ape.

P پهناور *pahnāwar*, Broad, wide, ample. دشت پهناور *dashti pahnāwar*, A widely-extended desert.

P پهنائي *pahnāʼī*, Breadth, width.

P پهن بيني *pahn-bīnī*, Flat or broad-nosed.

P پهند *pahand*, A toil for catching deer.

P پهنور *pahnūr*, The colocynth.

P پهنه *pahna*, A kind of racket, such as they play with at tennis, a battledore. Breadth. The inside of the thigh toward the root of the tail. A boy's spinning-top. A race-ground. *Pahana*, A flowing of milk through maternal affection.

P پهني *pahnī*, Flatness, breadth.

P پهنيدن *pahnīdan*, To expand, stretch.

P پهي *pahī*, The bitter purging apple.

P پي *pay*, A foot. A nerve, tendon, sinew. A footstep, track, trace, mark, vestige. Pursuit. The heel. Rank. Power, strength. Pretence, pretext, false appearance. Inclination. A time, turn. Because, for, on account of. After; behind. پي بردن *pay burdan*, To trace, discover, find out. پي كردن *pay kardan*, To abandon, give up, lose. از پيء تو *az paysi tu*, On thy account. از پي رفتن *az pay raftan*, (or در پي آمدن *dar pay āmadan*) To go behind, follow, trace. از پيء تفريح *az paysi tafrīh*, By way of recreation. پي رسيدن *pay rasīdan*, To arrive quickly. پي باز نهادن *pay bāz nihādan*, To retreat. پي كردن *pay kardan*, To follow. To hamstring. *Pī*, Fat, grease, tallow.

P پياب *pay-āb*, Power, strength. Bottom of the sea, river, lake, cistern, or piece of water. Foot or extremity of any thing, end.

P پياپي *pay-ā-pay*, Step by step, successively, repeatedly, incessantly, continuously, consequently. Continuous. پياپي شدن *pay-ā-pay shudan*, To follow in succession.

P پياده *piyāda*, A footman. A foot-soldier. Infantry. A peon. A pawn at chess. A bailiff, catchpoll. Ignorant, uninformed, illiterate. The tendril of a vine. A kind of willow. A sort of rose. پياده شدن *piyāda shudan*, To be on foot. To alight from a horse. پياده نهادن *piyāda nihādan*, To regard or set down as base and weak. پيادهء ملتزم *piyādasi multazim*, A servant in constant pay.

P پياده پا *piyāda-pā*, On foot.

P پياده نفرات *piyāda-nafarāt*, Infantry.

P پيارك *piyārak*, A bird resembling the nightingale in shape and song, but smaller and very green.

P پياز *piyāz*, An onion. پياز دشتي *piyāzi dashtī*, A wild onion, sea-onion, bulbous root, scallion, squill. Ratsbane, wolfsbane. پياز موش *piyāzi mūsh*, Sea-onion or squill.

P پياز فروش *piyāz-farosh*, A seller of onions.

P پيازك *piyāzak*, A rattan. A mace. Name of a village.

P پيازكي *piyāzakī*, A ruby from Piyāzak.

P پيازليز *piyāz-līz*, A wild onion.

P پيازو *piyāzū*, A sea-onion, a squill.

P پيازوا *piyāz-wā*, Light, unsatisfying food.

P پيازي *piyāzī*, A wild onion. A kind of ruby. An iron mace, a war-mace.

P پيازي رنگ *piyāzī-rang*, Pinky, rosy.

P پياله *piyāla*, A cup, goblet, or drinking-glass. The pan of a musket-lock. پيالهء جور *piyālasi jawr*, A cup filled to the brim. پياله كشيدن *piyāla kashīdan*, To drink. پياله گردانيدن *piyāla gardānīdan*, To circulate the bowl.

P پياله نواله *piyāla-nawāla*, Meat and drink (a cant word amongst debauchees).

P پيام *payām*, News, advice. A message. Salutation (in letters). پيام مودّت اختتام *payāmi mawaddat-ikhtitām*, Salutations sealed with affection, friendly compliments.

P پيام آور *payām-āwar*, An envoy. A prophet.

P پيامبر *payām-bar*, An apostle: a messenger.

P پياميغ *pay-āmegh*, Muscular, sinewy flesh. The fleshy part or brawn of meat. A piece of flesh or fish without bone. Name of an herb.

P پياهو *pay-āhū*, A house of a hexagonal form. An upper room having an ascent by a spiral staircase.

P پيبس *pības*, Dry mouldy bread, spoiled by the mice. A tumour. A louse. A kind of butter, or fat of mutton, the eating of which is said to be good for disorders in the eyes.

P پيبند *pay-band*, A fetter, a tether.

H پيپل *pīpal*, The holy fig-tree.

H پيپلا مول *pīpalā-mūl*, Long-pepper root.

P پيتام *paytām*, (in zand and Pāzand) News.

P پيترسب *pītarasb*, Zardusht's grandfather.

P پيتك *pītak*, A moth fretting a garment.

P پيتكاني *pītkānī*, An engine (for throwing stones). A lever.

H پيتل *pītal*, Brass.

P پيته *pīta*, A wick; a lint-stock.

P پيتيشهيم *pītīshahīm*, The third period, lasting 75 days, during which the earth was created.

P پيچ *pech*, Twisted, folded, rolled up, curled, intertwined, coiled, crooked, complicated, intricate.

Curvature, bending. A curl, ringlet, fold, plait wreath, twist, roll. A worm which infests the bottom of ships. A screw. A vortex. A coat-button. Difficulty, perplexity. Deceit. Envy. بهزار پيچ و تاب *ba hazār pech u tāb*, With a thousand folds and writhings. رشتهٔ پر پيچ و تاب *rishta-i pur pech u tāb*, Thread, full of twists and turns. پيچ در پيچ *pech dar pech*, Roll within roll. پيچ زدن *pech zadan*, To screw.

P پيچاپيچ *pech-ā-pech*, Involved, intricate, distorted, crooked, rolled in a circle. Crisped, curled.

P پيچاك شكم *pechāki shikam*, A twisting of the guts, gripes.

P پيچان *pechān*, Complicated, twisted.

P پيچانيدن *pechānīdan*, To twist, involve.

P پيچاى ناف *pechā-i nāf*, Contortion of the navel, a violent, excruciating pain, incident to women in labour.

P پيچپا *pech-pā*, (Crooked foot) A crab.

P پيچپيچ *pech-pech*, The rack.

P پيچ پيچان *pech pechān*, Inclining, leaning from side to side.

P پيچتاب *pech-tāb*, A knot. High words, angry discourse. Silence through anger. Restlessness, suspense, perplexity.

P پيچدار *pech-dār*, Twisted, coiled.

P پيچش *pechish*, Contortion, inflexion, curve. Gripes. Circumvention. Disobedience, rebellion. پيچش روده *pechishi rūda*, A twisting of the guts.

P پيچش زده *pechish-zada*, Griped.

P پيچك *pechak*, A ball of thread or silk. The bottom on which thread is wound. A fillet for confining a lady's head-dress. A ship-worm. Ivy. A bone ring without a bezel.

P پيچ كش *pech-kash*, A turn-screw.

P پيچند *pechand*, A fillet for the hair. Ivy.

P پيچوان *pechwān*, Twisted, coiled.

P پيچه *pecha*, An auger, wimble, piercer. A pent or projection over a door. A creeping plant, ivy. A lock of curling hair. An ornament set with jewels worn on the head of a bride. A fillet for the hair. A wall (between two other walls it does not touch) upon which the roof rests in a peculiar manner, conducing to warmth. A wink, nod, sign.

P پيچيدگي *pechīdagī*, A twisting, twist, distortion.

P پيچيدن *pechīdan*, To twist, distort, bend, involve, wreath or coil as a serpent, wind in a serpentine form, surround, envelope, involve. To twist a bit of camel's nerve or bowstring round the end of an arrow. To screw, wreath, make intricate. To assemble, meet. To disobey, rebel. To wound. To divulge. To be confused in speech. To assist, aid. *Paychīdan*, To associate or keep company with.

P پيچيده *pechīda*, Twisted. A bracelet, particularly one quadrangularly platted. Ivy. Perverse.

P پيخ *pīkh*, Gum adhering to the eye-lashes.

P پيخال *pīkhāl*, The dung of birds. Excrement of any kind. پيخال انداختن *pīkhāl andākhtan*, To mute, (said of birds, beasts, or flies). پيخال آلودگي *pīkhāl-ālūdagī*, Defilement with dung. پيخال آلوده *pīkhāl-ālūda*, Defiled with dung.

P پيختن *pekhtan*, To twist.

P پيخس *paykhas*, Suspicion, guess: discovery.

P پيخست *pay-khast*, Undermined. Trampled and softened under the foot. Imprisoned. Sick, infirm, weak. Fetid, stinking. A discovery.

P پيخسته *pay-khasta*, Trampled under foot. Impotent, helpless. Suspicion, fancy, doubt. Fetid. Stuffed. A man or beast confined in a narrow place whence they cannot escape. An undermined wall.

P پيد *pīd*, Scattered. Singed, spoiled: useless.

P پيدا *paydā*, Discovered, invented. Clear, evident, manifest, apparent. Exhibited. Public. Born, produced. Invention; discovery. Publication, exhibition, production. Openly, publicly, clearly, evidently, manifestly. پيدا شدن *paydā shudan*, To be evident. To become public. To come forward (as a boil or other sore). To labour under any disorder. To originate (as a malady). To rise or appear (as the sun). پيدا كردن *paydā kardan*, To invent, discover, declare, make public. To engender. To afford.

P پيداد *paydād*, Open, public, manifest.

P پيداش *paydāsh*, Creation, production.

P پيداوار *paydāwār*, Produce. Profits.

P پيداوسي *paydāwasī* or *pīdāwasī*, A coin of the value of five dīnārs, that passed current in Persia during the reigns of the Kayānians.

P پيدايش *paydāyish*, Production, birth. Creation. Genesis. Earnings, profit.

P پيدائي *paydā-ī*, Manifestation, appearance.

P پي در پي *pay dar pay*, Step by step, one after another. Repetition.

P پير *pīr*, An old man. A founder or chief of any religious body or sect. Monday. An old woman. پير بر تاتن *pīri bar tātan*, The world. پير برناوش *pīri barnāwash*, The world. The sky. پير تعليم *pīri ta'līm*, A spiritual guide. پير چهل ساله *pīri chihl sāla*, Maturity of intellect. An angel. Adam. A turquoise stone. پير خدا *pīri khudā*, Name of Othmān. پير خرد *pīri khirad*, Wisdom. پير خسيس *pīri khasīs*, The planet Saturn. The devil. پير دو تا *pīri du tā*, The vault of heaven. پير دو موي *pīri du moy*, The world (as subject to the interchange of day and night). پير دهقان *pīri dihkān*, Old wine. پير زال *pīri zāl*, An old decrepit man. The father of Rustam. A title of honour (similar to Senior, Seigneur, Senor, or Senhor, among the French, Italians, and Spaniards). پير سال خورده *pīri sāl-khwurda*, Old wine. پير سرانديب *pīri sarāndīb*, The old man of Ceylon, *i.e.* Adam. پير ششم چرخ *pīri shashum charkh*, The planet Jupiter. پير طريقت *pīri tarīkat*, A spiritual guide. پير فرتوت *pīri fartūt*, A delirious old man. پير فلك *pīri falak*, The planet Saturn. پير كشتهٔ غوغا *pīri kushta-i ghawghā*, The old man killed in the fray, *i.e.* Othmān. پير كنعان *pīri kan'ān*, The patriarch Jacob. پير مغان *pīri mughān*, A chief priest of the Magi or worshippers of fire. A prior of a Christian monastery. A keeper of a tavern or house of promiscuous entertainment. پير هشت خلد *pīri hasht khuld*, Rizwān, porter of Paradise. پير هفت فلك *pīri haft falak*, Saturn. Jupiter. پير و جوان *pīr u jawān*, Old and young. پير درويشان *pīri darwīshān*, The superior of the Dervīshes (an order of Muhammadan monks).

P پير *piyar*, A father.

P پيرا *perā* or *payrā*, One who decorates, polishes, writes, or executes with elegance and accuracy. A pruner. One who shaves, clips, trims, or plucks up superfluous hairs. نادره پيرا *nādira-perā*, A writer of memorable events.

P پيرار *pīrār*, The year before last. The day before yesterday.

P پيرار سال *pīrār-sāl*, The year before last.

P پيراستن *perāstan*, (by some *payrāstan*) To adorn, decorate, ornament, embellish (by cutting, clipping, or taking away). To prune, clip, trim. To diminish. To tan.

P پيراسته *perāsta*, Adorned. Trimmed, clipped, polled. Tanned. Arranged, adjusted. A village abounding in palm-trees.

P پيراسيدن *pīrāsīdan*, To rub, to grind.

P پيراگند *pīrāgand*, Scattered, dispersed.

P پيراگندن *pīrāgandan*, To disperse, scatter.

P پيرامن *perāman*, (or پيرامون *perāmūn*) Environs, adjacent places. A circuit. A border, margin, skirt, lappet, flap. About, around. پيرامن سراي *perāmani sarāy*, The environs of the house, whatever surrounds it.

P پيران *pīrān*, (pl. of پير *pīr*) Old men. Land granted for the erection or preservation of a tomb over a Muhammadan saint. Name of one of Afrāsyāb's generals.

P پيرانه *pīrāna*, Elderly, like an old man, or saint: saintly. Growing old. A hunter.

P پيرانه سر *pīrāna-sar*, Old age.

P پيرانيدن *pe* or *payrānīdan*, (trans. of پيراستن *pe* or *payrāstan*) To cause to adorn.

P پيراه *perāh*, A leather-dresser, currier.

P پيراهش *perāhish*, Decoration. Tanning.

P پيراهن *pīrāhan*, (or پيراهان *pīrāhān*) A loose vest, shirt, shift. پيراهن كاغذي *pīrāhan kāghizī*, A petition for justice. Dawn. The rays of the sun. پيراهن قبا كردن *pīrāhan kabā kardan*, To tear a shirt.

P پيراهيدن *perāhīdan*, To tan, dress leather.

P پيراي *perāy*, Adorning. Pruning. Shaving the head. Tanning.

P پيرايش *perāyish*, Ornament, decoration. Tanning. Preparation.

P پيرايگي *perāyagī*, Female ornament.

P پیرایندة *perāyinda*, Clipping, pruning. Adorning. One who clips, prunes, trims, or adorns.

P پیرایه *perāya* or *payrāya*, Ornament, decoration (but always with the idea of shaving, trimming, lopping, or diminishing, and not of adding). A cradle. A vessel, a plate (of gold or silver).

P پیراییدن *perāyidan*, To adorn.

P پیربنیه *pīr-bunya*, A young man gray.

P پیرپنبه *pīr-pamba*, A hairy old man.

P پیر زاد *pīr-zād*, (Old) born decrepit. An old man of authority, an aged prince. The father of Rustam (the Persian Hercules). (The father of this hero is called likewise پیر زال *pīr-zāl*, (Old hair), and زال زر *zāl-zar*, (Golden hair).

P پیرزر *pīr-zar*, An old man.

P پیرزن *pīr-zan*, An old woman. پیزرن چرخ *pīr zani charkh*, Heaven.

P پیرزة *payrza*, A thing tied up in a bundle.

P پیرزي *pīruzī*, Victory, triumph.

P پیرمرد *pīr-mard*, An old man.

P پیرمن *pīraman*, A circuit. About.

P پیرنداخ *pīrandākh*, Goat's leather, morocco.

P پي رو *pay-rav*, A follower.

P پي روان *pay-ravān*, Followers.

P پیروج *perūj*, A turkey.

P پیروز *pīroz*, Victorious. Prosperous, favoured by fortune and opportunity. A champion of Irān.

P پیروز رام *pīroz-rām*, Name of a city in India.

P پیروزة *pīroza*, A turquoise, a kind of blue gem.

P پیروزة چادر *pīroza-chādir*, طشت *tasht*, مغز *maghz*, or مغفر *mighfar*, The sky.

P پیروزي *pīrozī*, Victory, triumph.

P پیروي *pay-ravī*, A following, pursuit. Search. Dependence. Consequence. پیروي کردن *pay-ravī kardan*, To follow.

P پیرة *pīra*, Bald. Virgin honey. Sugar. A successor. A recluse.

P پیرة زن *pīra-zan*, An old woman.

P پیرهن *pīrahan*, A shirt, shift, tunic.

P پیرهنچه *pīrahancha*, A short shirt.

P پیرهند *pīrhand*, A shirt, shift, tunic.

P پیري *pīrī*, Old age, decrepitude.

P پي زدة *pay-zada*, Wounded, hamstrung.

P پیزر *pīzar*, A pedlar. Name of a disease.

P پي زن *pay-zan*, One who hamstrings.

P پي زني *pay-zanī*, Hamstringing.

P پیس *pes*, Leprosy. A dwarf palm-tree, of the twigs or fibres of which they make ropes. White. Vile, ignoble.

P پیس اندام *pes-andām*, Leprous.

P پي سپار *pay-sipār*, (or پي سپر *pay-sipur*) Trampled. A traveller.

P پي سپردن *pay sipurdan*, To trample.

P پیست *pest*, Leprous.

P پیستان *pīstān*, The past, those gone.

P پیسکي *pīskī*, Youth.

P پیسگی *pesagī*, An intermixture of colours, piebaldness.

P پیسودن *pesūdan*, To incline. To desire.

P پیسة *paysa*, A small weight, twenty-four to a pound, used only for weighing copper money. A copper coin. Money. *Pesa*, Piebald, dappled, variegated.

P پیسي *pesī*, The leprosy.

P پیش *pesh*, Before. In front. Forward. Past. Future. Further, beyond. Preamble, premises. An example, model, exemplar, coryphæus, chief, superior, commander, leader. (in gram.) The vowel point ـُ *u*. A palm-branch. A dwarf palm-tree. Intelligent, wise. پیش از آن *pesh az ān*, Before that. پیش از آنکه *pesh az ānki*, Before that which, previous to which, sooner than. پیش ازاین *pesh az in*, Henceforth, hereafter. Before this, heretofore, sometime. پیش آمدن *pesh āmadan*, To come before, meet, oppose, obstruct. To occur, happen. پیش آوردن *pesh āwardan*, To bring, produce before. پیش پاي *peshi pāy*, The toe. پیش پا شدن *pesh-pā shudan*, To be in advance; to go forward, proceed. پیش رفتن *pesh raftan*, To go before, advance, precede. اسپ پیش رو *aspi pesh-rav*, A horse outstripping all others. پیش شدن *pesh shudan*, To be superior, to excel. پیش شمردن *pesh shumurdan*, To count beforehand; to anticipate. پیش فرستادن *pesh faristādan*, To send to, towards, before. پیش قاضي *peshi kāzī*, Before the judge. پیش کردن *pesh kardan*, To prefix, to preface. To shut (a door). پیش کشیدن *pesh kashīdan*, To attract. پیش گرفتن *pesh giriftan*, To learn, to teach. To precede, to excel in doing or learning any thing. To exhibit, stretch out. To propose any thing to one's self. از پیش رفتن *az pesh raftan*, To go ahead, to advance. پیش و پس *pesh u pas*, Before and after. (They generally say پس و پیش *pas u pesh*).

P پیشاب *pesh-āb*, Urine.

P پیشاپیش *pesh-ā-pesh*, Equal, parallel. Equally, before. پیشاپیش گرفتن *pesh-ā-pesh giriftan*, To take the lead.

P پیشادست *peshā-dast*, Ready money, cash paid down. Wages paid in advance.

P پیشار *pesh-ār*, (Brought before) Urine (of a sick person, shown to a physician).

P پیشاران *pesh-ārān*, Doctors' prescriptions.

P پیش افتاد *pesh-uftād*, The forlorn hope.

P پیش امام *pesh-imām*, A high-priest.

P پیش آمد *pesh-āmad*, Advance, coming into the presence. Elevation, advancement. Access, admittance.

P پیشان *peshān*, The utmost extremity in front, the furthest of all. The best side of cloth, the best end which is shown to a buyer. (pl. of پیش *pesh*) Those before.

P پیش انداز *pesh-andāz*, A necklace. A napkin.

P پیش اندیشي *pesh-andeshī*, Forethought.

P پیشاني *peshānī*, Front, forehead, brow. Ringlets hanging over the forehead. Sauciness. Strength. Hardness. Opposite, over against, even. Fortune. پیشاني کردن *peshānī kardan*, To be forward or saucy.

P پیشاني بند *peshānī-band*, Fillet for the hair.

P پیشاني دار *peshānī-dār*, Expert. Successful, prosperous.

P پیشاني گشادة *peshānī-gushāda*, Candid.

P پیشاهنگ *pesh-āhang*, A general, a colonel (as being the chief of an army or a regiment). The leader of the flock or a caravan. The vanguard: forlorn hope.

P پیشایگي *peshāyagī*, Forwards.

P پیش آیندة *pesh-āyanda*, Opposer, obstructer.

P پیش باز *pesh-bāz*, Meeting, a going out to meet a person of distinction. A kind of garment. پیشباز آمدن *pesh-bāz āmadan*, To run to and fro.

P پیش بند *pesh-band*, The belt that passes over a horse's breast, to prevent the saddle from slipping back, breast-harness.

P پیش بندي *pesh-bandī*, Premises. Foresight.

P پیش بین *pesh-bīn*, Foreseeing; wise, prudent.

P پیش بیني *pesh-bīnī*, Foresight. Anticipation.

P پیشپا *pesh-pā*, A wardrobe.

P پیشپار *pesh-pār*, Sweetmeats presented to a guest. A woman bringing forth an abortion.

P پیشپارة *peshpāra*, (پیشپارچه *peshpārcha* or پیشارة *peshāra*) A cake made of flour, honey, and oil or butter.

P پیش پائی *pesh-pāī*, Precedency.

P پیش پیش رفتگي *pesh pesh raftagī*, Precedence.

P پیشتختة *pesh-takhta*, A portfolio: a desk.

P پیشتر *peshtar*, Prior, more forward. Forward.

P پیشترین *peshtarīn*, Foremost.

P پیشخانة *pesh-khāna*, A portico; a gallery or projecting balcony. Tents of state sent in advance when travelling. Camp-equipage.

P پیشخورد *pesh-khwurd*, An early breakfast. Parched corn or grain of different kinds, toasted, and rubbed between the hands. (It is eaten before meals, and often carried by people when travelling.) Corn or fruit sold before it is ripe. Money paid down in advance.

P پیش خیمة *pesh-khayma*, A public audience-tent. A sort of dagger.

P پیشداد *pesh-dād*, A law-giver. The first to redress the wrongs of the oppressed. Earnest-money. Hoshang, the first of the line of Peshdādian kings.

P پیشدادیان *peshdādiyān*, The Peshdādians, or first dynasty of the kings of Persia. They were six: هوشنگ *hoshang*, طهمورث *tahmūras*, جمشید *jamshed*, ضحاك *zahhāk*, فریدون *farīdūn*, and منوچهر *minūchihr*. According to other authorities they were 11, who reigned 2450 years. Their names were کیومرث *kayūmars*, هوشنگ *hoshang*, طهمورث *tahmūras*, جمشید *jamshed*, ضحاك *zahhāk*, فریدون *farīdūn*, منوچهر *minūchihr*, نودر *nawdar*, افراسیاب *afrāsyāb* (of Turkistān), زو پسر طهماسب بن

منوچهر *zaw pisari tahmāsb bin minūchihr*, and گوشاسپ *gūshasp*.

P پیش دار *pesh-dār*, A javelin for killing hogs.

P پیشدر *pesh-dar*, A frontispiece.

P پیشدست *pesh-dast*, Surpassing, excelling. Outstripping. An assistant. Right of precedency, chief seat. Earnest-money, money paid in advance.

P پیش دستي *pesh-dastī*, An outstripping, surpassing. Pre-eminence, precedency, pre-excellence. پیش دستي نمودن *pesh-dastī namūdan*, To excel, surpass. پیش دستي کرد *pesh-dastī kard*, He performed it soon, he quickly accomplished it, he made great haste. He made an aggression.

P پیشدل *pesh-dil*, Deliberation.

P پیش دید *pesh-dīd*, In view.

P پیش دین *pesh-dīn*, A spiritual guide.

P پیش رس *pesh-ras*, First-fruits. Provident.

P پیش رفت *pesh-raft*, Impressive, forcible.

P پیش رفتگي *pesh-raftagī*, A going before, a leading of the van.

P پیش رفته *pesh-rafta*, Gone before, bygone.

P پیشرو *pesh-rav*, (*raw* or *rao*) A general, chief, leader. A guide, forerunner, escort. The advanced guard, van, forlorn hope. Preface, preamble, exordium. Prelude or symphony in music. پیشرو لشکر صحرا *peshravi lashkari sahrā*, The wild ass.

P پیش شاخ *pesh-shākh*, A female garment.

P پیشطاق *pesh-tāk*, Portico, hall, anteroom.

P پیش قبضه *pesh-kabza*, A dagger worn in front.

P پیش قدمي *pesh-kadamī*, Alacrity, activity.

P پیشك *peshak*, A little before.

P پیشکار *pesh-kār*, An assistant, helper. A domestic, a serving-man, a hired labourer. A steward. A disciple. A subordinate officer whose business it is to write the accounts.

P پیشکاره *pesh-kāra*, A midwife. A matron. A lady superior. Tapestry or carpets, with which they decorate the best apartments or principal seats. A serving-man, a hired labourer.

P پیشکاري *pesh-kārī*, Deputyship.

P پیشکش *pesh-kash*, What is first drawn. First-fruits. A magnificent present, such as is only presented to princes, great men, superiors, or sometimes to equals (particularly on receiving a great appointment). Tribute, quit-rent. پیشکش نویش *peshkash-navīs*, A registrar of presents.

P پیشکوهه *pesh-koha*, The front of the eyebrow. The bow or pommel of the saddle.

P پیشگاه *pesh-gāh*, The front. Vestibule, portico. Area, court. The principal seat for the most noble of the company. A kind of high altar in a mosque. The breast, the chest. Tapestry. A carpet. A king, a lord of a throne. پیشگاه نشور *pesh-gāhi nushūr*, The resurrection. درپیشگاه سپاه *dar pesh-gāhi sipāh*, In the front of the army.

P پیشگر *peshgar*, An artificer: a help, servant.

P پیشگو *pesh-go*, (*gū*, گوي *goy*, or *gūy*) One who presents petitions. One who introduces at court, a chamberlain, master of the ceremonies.

P پیشگه *pesh-gah*, The frontispiece.

P پیشگهي *peshgahī*, Breakfast.

P پیشگي *peshgī*, Advance of money.

P پیشگیر *pesh-gīr*, Choosing. A towel, napkin.

P پیشمان *peshmān*, (for پشیمان) Penitent.

P پیشمزد *pesh-muzd*, Handsel, the first money which a merchant receives in a morning. Workmen's wages. Good luck.

P پیشن *pīshan*, (or پیشند *pīshand*) The fibrous substance of palm-tree, from which ropes are made.

P پي شناس *pay-shinās*, Clever at tracking.

P پیش نشین *pesh-nishīn*, A midwife. A friend.

P پیش نماز *pesh-namāz*, A leader at prayer.

P پیش نمازي *pesh-namāzī*, The high-priesthood.

P پیشنهاد *pesh-nihād*, What is placed before. Custom, mode, manner, use. Rule, regulation. Intention, design. پیش نهاد کردن *pesh nihād kardan*, To habituate one's self, to follow any regulation, or propose to one's self a model for imitation.

P پیشوا *peshwā*, Exemplar, model, guide, leader: the head of a party. The chief of a religious sect, general of an army. The first executive officer among the Marhattas. A sort of woman's garment. پیشوا رفتن *peshwā raftan*, To go to meet (out of respect). پیشوا کردن *peshwā kardan*, To be a model, or a chief. پیشوائ محافظان حصار *peshwāi muhāfizāni hisār*, The commandant of a fort.

P پیشوار *peshwār*, A garment open before.

P پیشواز *peshwāz*, Going out to meet a person of distinction. A full-dress gown, reaching a little below the knee.

P پیشوائي *peshwāī*, High-priestship: leadership.

P پیش و پس رفتگي *pesh u pas raftagī*, A going to and fro, fore and aft.

P پیشه *pesha*, Art, skill. Work, business, craft, trade, calling, profession. Custom, habit. A shepherd's pipe. سپاه جهاد پیشه *sipāhi jihād-pesha*, Soldiers inured to war, hardy veterans. صداقت پیشه *sadākat-pesha*, Sincere, professing veracity. معرفت پیشه *maʿrifat-pesha*, Studying virtue or science. نخوت پیشه *nakhwat-pesha*, Behaving proudly. هم پیشه *ham-pesha*, Of the same trade, profession, or rank. پیشهٔ آتش *peshai ātish*, Diabolical deeds. پیشه کردن *pesha kardan*, To choose, elect, prefer. *Pīsha*, A rope made from the fibres of the palm-tree.

P پیشه شاگرد *pesha-shāgird*, Servants.

P پیشه گار *peshagār* (or پیشه‌گر) An artisan.

P پیشه گاه *pesha-gāh*, Work-shop, laboratory.

P پیشه مرغ *pesha-murgh*, A carrion bird.

P پیشه وار *peshawār*, (or پیشه ور) An artisan.

P پیشي *peshī*, The chief seat, precedency, superior rank. Money paid in advance. پیشي گرفتن *peshī giriftan*, To take the lead, precede, surpass.

P پیشیاب *pesh-yāb*, Foresightful, provident.

P پیشیار *pesh-yār*, A glass urinal, in which the physicians examine the water of their patients. Urine. A servant, serving man, hired labourer. A disciple. Earnest-money.

P پیشیاره *pesh-yāra*, A tray whereon sweetmeats and flowers are brought into a room.

P پیشین *peshīn*, Anterior, ancient, antique, prior, former. Anticipated, per advance. Morning, forenoon. Mid-day prayer. پیشین کردن *peshīn kardan*, To anticipate, pre-occupy, give per advance. پیشین گفتن *peshīn guftan*, To predict, prognosticate. بر آیین پیشین *bar āyīni peshīn*, According to ancient custom. بر وجه پیشین *bar wajhipeshīn*, By anticipation, in advance, paid down.

P پیشین گه *peshīn-gah*, Mid-day prayer.

P پیشینه *peshīna*, Prior, antecedent. A predecessor. Money paid in advance.

P پیشینهگان *peshīnagān*, (or پیشینیان *peshīniyān*) Forefathers, predecessors. The ancients.

P پیغاره *payghāra*, Slander. Railing, abuse.

P پیغاله *payghāla*, A goblet of wine.

P پیغام *payghām*, A message. Fame, rumour, report: news, advice. An embassy, mission. عرض پیغام کردن *ʿarzi payghām kardan*, To deliver credentials, to explain the cause of an embassy.

P پیغاماپیغامي *payghām-ā-payghāmī*, Mutual messages, mediation, correspondence.

P پیغامبر *payghām-bar*, A messenger. A prophet, apostle. An ambassador, envoy, legate.

P پیغامبري *payghām-barī*, Prophetical office.

P پیغام گذار *payghām-guzār*, A messenger.

P پیغام گذاري *payghām-guzārī*, The delivery of a message. The office of messenger.

P پیغان *peghān*, Promise, agreement. Vain.

P پیغله *payghula*. See پیغوله *payghūla*.

P پیغلوش *pīghlūsh*, The root of a flower. A sort of lily. An ant's nest. The mouth. The ear.

P پیغم *paygham*, A message. Report.

P پیغمبر *paygham-bar*, A prophet.

P پیغمبري *paygham-barī*, The prophetical office, prophecy.

P پیغن *payghan*, Rue.

P پیغو *payghū*, The country of Pegu. *Pīghū*, A species of falcon. A bird's beak.

P پیغور *payghūr* or *pīghūr*, A vessel small and glazed with a narrow neck. A small mouth.

P پیغوله *payghūla*, A corner, angle. A narrow street, bye-path. پیغولهٔ دهن *payghūlai dahan*, The corner of the mouth.

P پیغون *payghūn*, A condition, covenant.

P پیغه *pīgha*, Rotten wood, touchwood.

P پي فشردن *pay fashurdan*, To be firm.

P پیفه *pīfa*, Rotten wood, touchwood.

P پیك *payk*, A footman, lacquey. A running footman. A carrier, messenger. A guard. A watchman. پیك اجل *payki ajal*, The angel of death, fate. پیك رایگان *payki rāygān*, The moon. A merchant. A traveller. The zephyr. پيك فلك *payki falak*, The moon. *Payak*, A parasite.

P پيكان *paykān*, Point of a spear or arrow. An arrow, javelin, spear, dart. پيكان خاره گذار *paykāni khāra-guzār*, A marble-piercing spear. پيكان كمان *paykāni kamān*, The sun. The stars. پيكان مقراضه *paykāni mikrāza*, A double-headed halbert.

P پيكان كش *paykān-kash*, An instrument for extracting arrows.

P پيكانه سم *paykāna-sum*, Pointed like a spear. The claw or talon of a bird.

P پيكاني *paykānī*, A kind of ruby. A turquoise (so called from its resemblance to a spear-head). Sal-ammoniac.

P پيكر *paykar*, Face, countenance. Form, figure, mould, model. Portrait, likeness. An idol-temple. پيكر ملكوت *paykari malakūt*, The face, heavenly effigy or intelligence. پري پيكر *parī-paykar*, Fairy-faced, lovely. زبرجدي پيكر *zabarjadī-paykar*, Azure, of a cerulean appearance. پيكران درخش *paykarāni dirakhsh*, The stars. Disembodied spirits. پيكران مانا *paykarān mānā*, An intermediate world, the world of spirits. ماه پيكر *māh-paykar*, Moon-faced, beautiful as the moon.

P پيكر پرست *paykar-parast*, An idolater.

P پيكرستان *paykaristān*, The land of fairies.

P پيكرگار *paykargār*, A painter, limner.

P پيكر گاو *paykar-gāw*, *gāo*, or *gāv*, A drinking-vessel in the form of an ox.

P پيكر گده *paykar-gada*, An idol-temple.

P پي كن *pay-kan*, A hamstringer.

P پيكند *pīkand*, The city of Samarkand.

P پيكندن *paykandan*, To join. To collect. To draw out. *Pay kandan*, To hamstring.

P پيكور *pay-kūr*, Trackless. Blind.

P پيگ *payg*, A newsman, messenger.

P پيگار *paygār*, Battle, combat, war. Wish, design, aim. پيگار كردن *paygār kardan*, To fight.

P پيگار پرستان *paygār-parastān*, Warriors.

P پيگو *pegū*, The king of Pegu.

P پيگور *pay-gūr*, The foot or tail of an ass.

P پيل *pīl*, An elephant. The heel. A purse, a small bag. A knot. A glandular swelling. پيل آبكش *pīli āb-kash*, (A water-carrying elephant) A cloud. پيل امرود *pīl amrūd*, A species of pear. پيل معلق درهوا *pīli muᶜallak dar hawā*, (An elephant suspended in the air) A cloud. پيل هوائي *pīli hawāī*, (Airy elephant) A cloud.

P پيلارام *pīl-ārām*, Name of a certain fortress.

P پيل افگن *pīl-afgan*, Elephant-oversetting.

P پيلاو *pīlāw*, Boiled rice and meat.

P پيل بالا *pīl-bālā*, Of an elephantine stature. Lofty. Bulky. A heap of unthrashed corn.

P پيلبان *pīlbān*, Elephant-driver or keeper.

P پيلباني *pīlbānī*, Charge, care of elephants.

P پيلپا *pīl-pā*, (Elephant-foot) Elephantiasis. A large cup handed round after dinner. A weapon used by the Moors. A beam.

P پيلپايه *pīl-pāya*, A pillar, a prop.

P پيلتن *pīl-tan*, (Elephant-bodied) Large, bulky. A horse. Rustam (the Persian Hercules).

P پيل زور *pīl-zor*, Strong as an elephant.

P پيلسته *pīlasta*, Ivory. Cheek. Face. Arm. The finger. Goat's leather perfumed, morocco.

P پيلسم *pīlsam*, Name of a hero killed by Rustam. *Pīl-sum*, Massive silver. A dark night.

P پيلغوش *pīlghosh*, Flowers, of different colours, with jagged leaves; particularly the iris, or elephant's ears. A large shovel for removing ashes or rubbish.

P پيلكش *pīl-kash*, A kind of weapon.

P پيلگوش *pīl-gosh*, Variegated iris: dragonwort.

P پيلگوشك *pīl-goshak*, Sorrel.

P پيل مال *pīl-māl*, Trampling under foot.

P پيل مرغ *pīl-murgh*, (Elephant-bird) A turkey.

P پيلو *pīlū*, A wood with which the teeth are rubbed; also the fruit called in Arabic اراك *arāk*.

P پيلوا *pīlawā*, An apothecary, a druggist.

P پيلوار *pīl-wār*, An elephant-load, much.

P پيلوايه *pīlwāya*, A swallow.

P پيلور *pīlwar*, A druggist. A pedlar.

P پيله *pela*, Merchandise of an inferior kind, or small wares, hawked by pedlars. A silkworm, the silkworm's cocoon. A purse. A certain medicinal plant. A button, knot. A blotch rising in the midst of a bubo or boil. Pus of a sore. An open champaign lying between two rivers. The eyelid. The hairs of the eyelid. The eye. The head of an arrow. پيلهٔ فلك *pelaī falak*, The expanse of the firmament.

P پيله بيني *pīla* or *pīlaī bīnī*, The nostrils.

P پيله ور *pelawar*, A huckster, a petty dealer.

P پيم *payam*, A message. Rumour, fame.

P پيما *paymā*, (in compos.) Measuring. A measurer, weigher. سخن پيما *sukhun-paymā*, A measurer of words, an orator. ملامت پيما *malāmat-paymā*, Opprobrious. رهرو باديه پيما *rah-ravi bādiya-paymā*, A traveller measuring the desert.

P پيمان *paymān*, Measuring. Promise, agreement, compact, convention, treaty, stipulation, pledge, security, confirmation. Asseveration, oath. Kindred. ابد پيمان *abad-paymān*, Eternal. عهد و پيمان *ᶜahd u paymān*, Capitulations, alliances, treaties, peace. پيمان بستن *paymān bastan*, To form an alliance, to make peace.

P پيمان شكن *paymān-shikan*, A breaker of faith.

P پيمان شكني *paymān-shikanī*, Breach of faith.

P پيمان فرهنگ *paymān-farhang*, Name of a certain work replete with prudential and political maxims, ascribed to مه آباد *mah-ābād*, an early apostle sent to Persia.

P پيمانه *paymāna*, A cup, goblet, bowl. A measure either for dry or wet goods. A bushel. پيمانه اش پر شد *paymāna ash pur shud*, His measure is full, his days are numbered.

P پيمانه گاه *paymāna-gāh*, A cupboard.

P پيمانه نوش *paymāna-nosh*, A drinker.

P پيماي *paymāy*, Measuring. A measurer.

P پيمايش *paymāyish*, Measure, measurement. Survey, measuring of lands.

P پيمبر *payam-bar*, An apostle.

P پيمودن *paymūdan*, To measure. To pass over, traverse. Measuring.

P پيموده *paymūda*, Measured. Dimensions. A draught of wine. A trifle. An iniquitous thing. Any thing estimated beyond its size or worth. پيموده شدن *paymūda shudan*, To be measured.

P پيناك *paynāk*, Sinewy.

P پينگي *pīnagī*, Slumber.

P پينگي رسيده *pīnagī-rasīda*, Sleepy.

P پينگي زننده *pīnagī-zananda*, Slumbering.

P پينو *pīnū*, (or پينوك) New cheese, cream-cheese. Butter-milk. Any thing eaten with bread.

P پينوا *pīnuwā*, (or پينووا) Sour-milk pottage.

P پينه *pīna*, A piece, clout, patch (of cloth). The skin of the hand or foot grown hard from labour. The arm. The match of a lamp, wick of a candle, a gunner's lint-stock, or any thing in that form. پينه زدن *pīna zadan*, To mend clothes.

P پينه دوز *pīna-doz*, A patcher, botcher.

P پيو *payū*, A brick-bat. A moth. *Payo*, A kind of disease which breaks out in the limbs in the form of a thread, a disease to which the natives of لار *lār* are subject.

P پيواز *pīwāz*, A bat.

P پيواسته *pīwāsta*, A fortress. A bastion. Breast-work on the outside of fortified towns.

P پيوس *piyos*, Hope, expectation.

P پيوسانيدن *piyosānīdan*, To give hope.

P پيوست *paywast*, Conjunction, coherence. Arrival, meeting, union. Union with the Supreme Spirit. Friendship. Continual. Continually.

P پيوستگان *paywastagān*, Animals. Vegetables. Minerals.

P پيوستگي *paywastagī*, Continuity, conjunction. Union, junction.

P پيوستن *paywastan*, To join, fasten, tie, bind, connect, attach. To graft a tree. To be joined, attached, linked. برحمت ايزدي پيوستن *ba rahmati ezidī paywastan*, To be joined to divine mercy (*i.e.* to die).

P پيوسته *paywasta*, Joined. Contiguous, adjacent, touching, sticking close. Continually, without interruption, one following another perpetually. Unable to speak for weeping. Poetry. پيوسته شدن *paywasta shudan*, To be joined, connected. To arrive, to meet. پيوستهٔ اختتام بودن *paywastaī ikhtitām būdan*, To be brought to a conclusion.

P پيوسته ابرو *paywasta-abrū*, One whose eye-brows meet.

P پيوسته گري *paywastagarī*, Union, concord.

P پیوسیدن *piyosīdan*, To hope, to expect.

P پیوکان *payūkān*, A bridegroom. A bride.

P پیوگ *payavg* or *payūg*, A bride.

P پیوگانی *payūgānī*, Nuptials.

P پیوند *paywand*, Bound, fastened; touching, reaching, tending towards, belonging to. A member. A joint. Connexion, conjunction (and in general whatever joins things together). Kindred, relations, allies. پیوند استخوان *paywandi ustukhwān*, Articulation, joint of bones. پیوند انگشت *paywandi angusht*, A knuckle. پیوند بیخ انگشتان *paywandi behhi angushtān*, The knuckle at the root of the fingers. پیوند پای *paywandi pāy*, The ankle (in a man), the pastern (in a horse). پیوند دست *paywandi dast*, The wrist. پیوند سردست *paywandi sar-dast*, The wrist (in a man), the pastern (in a horse). پیوند کردن *paywand kardan*, To join. To engraft. ابد پیوند *abad-paywand*, Joined to eternity, eternal, everlasting. آسمان پیوند *āsmān-paywand*, Heavenly, tending heavenward. آسمان پیوند شدن *āsmān-paywand shudan*, To be exalted to heaven.

P پیوندانیدن *paywandānīdan*, To make unite.

P پیوند پذیرفته *paywand-pazīrufta*, Set (broken bone). Joined, mended, repaired.

P پیوند خورده *paywand-khwurda*, Joined.

P پیوند کاری *paywand-kārī*, Patching: graft.

P پیوندن *paywandan*, To join, tie, connect.

P پیوندی *paywandī*, Engrafted.

P پیه *pīh*, Fat, grease, tallow. Pith. Pride, arrogance. *Paya*, A follower.

P پیه سوز *pīh-soz*, A kind of lamp in the shape of a platter, three feet in height from the base, and about six inches diameter at the top; having in the middle a small tube with two holes, through which the wick is fed by the oil or grease, kept in a state of constant liquefaction by the flame. A travelling case for a candle which, by the inversion of the top, serves also the purpose of a candlestick.

P پیه قاوندی *pīh-kāwandī*, An oily extract from a certain nut, good for a cough.

P پیه ناك *pīhnāk*, Fat, obese.

P پیه ناکی *pīhnākī*, Fatness, obesity.

P پی هم *payham*, Quickly, successively. Thick.

P پیهو *payhū*, A leech, bloodsucker.

P پیهودن *payhūdan*, To singe.

ت

ت *tā* or *te*, (called تاءِ قرشت *tāʼi karashat* or تاءِ مثنّاة فوقانی *tāʼi musannāti fawkānī*, *tā* doubly dotted above) is the third letter of the Arabic and Persian alphabets, and denotes 400 in Arithmetic. In Arabic, when prefixed, it expresses swearing: as, تربّ الکعبة *ta rabbi'l kaʻbat*, By the Lord of the Kaaba! In Persian ت (pronounced with a short vowel before it) when found at the end of a noun, stands for تو *tu*, Thou (or the genitive case "Of thee"): as, دلت *dilat*, for دل تو *dili tu*, Thy heart; and affixed to a verb it represents the oblique case of that pronoun, namely, ترا *turā*: as, میگویدت *mī goyadat*, for میگوید ترا *mī goyad turā*, He tells thee. Occasionally it is redundant at the end of a word: as, بالشت *bālisht*, for بالش *bālish*, A cushion. Words which in Arabic terminated in ة, when occurring in Persian are written sometimes with ت, and sometimes with ه: as, for همّة *himmat*, they write همّت: and for مکاشفة *mukāshafat*, مکاشفه *mukāshafa*. ت *tā* is commutable with د *dāl*: as, دنبوره *dambūra*, for تنبوره *tambūra*.

P تا *tā*, To, unto, until, as far as, as long as, whilst, even to. To the end that, in such a manner that, in order that, so that. Before, ere, as soon as. Since. Beware! Behold! For shame! Never. آمدم تا ترا بینم *āmadam tā turā bīnam*, I am come in order to see thee. رفتم تا بمکّه *raftam tā ba makka*, I went as far as Mecca. تا آن جا *tā ān jā*, Thitherto, so far. تا این جا *tā īn jā*, Hitherto, thus far. تا بزیست *tā ba zīst*, While life remains. تا بکجا *tā ba kujā*, How far? تا بکی *tā ba kay*, How long? how much? till what time? to what length then? تا چند بار *tā chand bār*, How often? how many times? تا چنین *tā chunīn*, Hitherto, thus far. تا حال *tā hāl*, Yet, hitherto. تا که *tā ki*, Until, so that, so long. تا کی *tā kay*, How long? تا هم *tā ham*, Yet, nevertheless. تا هنوز *tā hanūz*, Yet, still, hitherto. حکیم فرمود تا غلام را بدریا انداختند *hakīm farmūd tā ghulāmrā ba daryā andākhtand*, The physician commanded, so that they threw the lad into the sea. *Tā*, A fold, plait or ply. Single. A single sheet of paper. A unit. Like, resembling. A half-load. The form or cut of a garment. (for تار *tār*) A warp. The string of a lute. یك تا *yak tā*, Simple or single. دو تا *du tā*, Double. Two-fold. سه تا *sih tā*, Triple. Three-fold.

A تا *tā*, (The feminine demonstrative article of ذا *zā*) That (woman).

P تاء *tāʼ*, A milch-cow.

A تاء *tāʼ*, The third letter of the alphabet.

A تآوی *taʼāwī*, (v. n. 6 of اوی) Flocking together into one place.

A تاب *tāba*, (fut. یتوب *yatūbu*) He repented.

P تاب *tāb*, Strength, power, ability. Heat, warmth, burning, inflaming, illuminating. Light, splendour, lustre, radiance. A ray. A waving, bending, twisting, intertwining. A curling lock, waving ringlet. Pain, torment. Affliction, grief. Anger, indignation, wrath. Heated iron. (for تا *ba*) As far as. (in composition) Shining, irradiating, kindling, burning. Twisting, folding. آفتاب عالم تاب *āftābi ʻālam-tāb*, The world-irradiating sun. شمشیر جهان تاب *shimshīri jihān-tāb*, A cimeter dazzling the world. تاب دادن *tāb dādan*, To inflame. To polish. To sharpen, give an edge. To twist. To spin. تاب باز دادن *tāb bāz dādan*, To untwist.

A تابّ *tābb*, (pl. اتباب *atbāb*) Tall and weak (man). Sore-backed (camel or ass).

P تابا *tābā*, (in zand and Pāzand) Gold.

A تاباق *tābāk*, A walking-stick, a thick staff.

P تابان *tābān*, Light, luminous, resplendent, radiant, dazzling, brilliant, shining, glittering. A gleam, flash. Pith of a tree. ماه تابان *māhi tābān*, The bright moon. تابان بودن *tābān būdan*, To be luminous.

P تابانی *tābānī*, Splendour, light.

P تابانیدن *tābānīdan*, To cause to twist.

A تأبّب *taʼabbub*, (v. n. 5 of ابّ) Labouring under a hoarseness. Being astonished, struck with admiration. Being delighted.

A تابة *tābat*, (v. n. of تاب for توب) Repenting, turning from sin to God. Returning, relenting, becoming gracious (God). Repentance.

A تأبّت *taʼabbut*, The glowing (of embers).

P تابخانه *tāb-khāna*, A hot-house. A winter habitation. A warm bath. Summer-quarters. A house entirely glazed.

A تأبّد *taʼabbud*, (v. n. 5 of ابد) Being wild, untameable. Fleeing, scudding away from fear. Shunning society. Being deserted by its inhabitants (a place) and haunted by wild beasts. Being a long while absent and debarred from female society (a man). Being marked with freckles, tanned, sun-burnt (the face).

P تابداده *tāb-dāda*, Inflaming. Inflamed. Twisted. Spun.

P تابدار *tāb-dār*, Warm, hot, ardent, fervent, burning. Shining, luminous, bright, brilliant. Waving, curling. Twisted. آب تابدار *ābi tāb-dār*, Warm water. الفاظ تابدار *alfāzi tāb-dār*, Warm words. گوهر تابدار و نافهٔ مشك تاتار *gawhari tāb-dār u nāfaʼi mushki tātār*, Brilliant jewels, and bags of the musk of Tartary.

P تابدان *tābdān*, A stove in a bath. A forge. A chimney. A window. A skylight. A globe.

P تابده *tāb-dih*, Giving splendour. A rope-maker: a spinner.

A تأبّر *taʼabbur*, (v.n.5 of ابر) Being impregnated (the female palm-tree with the flowers of the male).

A تأبّس *taʼabbus*, (v. n. 5 of ابس) Being changed, troubled, disquieted. Being despised. Sinking into contempt.

P تابستان *tābistān*, Summer. Hot weather. تابستانه دادن *tābistāna dādan*, To give wages for the summer.

P تابستانی *tābistānī*, Summer-like. Estival. A summer or country-house. The delightfulness of the summer. تابستانی کردن *tābistānī kardan*, To summer, to pass the summer.

P تابسه *tābasa*, A meadow abounding in pasture and water.

P تابش *tābish*, Splendour, brilliancy. Heat. Power, strength. Grief, sorrow. Contortion. A twisting. Declivity. A span.

A تأبض *ta-abbuz*, (v. n. 5 of ابض) Binding the fore-foot of a camel with a rope (the knee being bent) to the shoulder or thigh. Being so bound. Being contracted (the tendons) by such ligature.

A تأبّط *ta-abbut*, (v. n. 5 of ابط) Putting or carrying (any thing) under the arm. Letting (a mantle or upper vest) fall from under the right arm, and throwing it over the left shoulder. Becoming full to tightness.

P تاب طاقت *tāb-tākat*, Power, ability.

A تأبّط شرّا *ta-abbata sharran*, (He carried destruction under his arm) Surname of Thābit bin Jābir, one of the رآبيل *ra-ābīl* of the Arabians, and a poet, who continually carried under his arm a bow, quiver, and sword, instruments of destruction: hence, a brave, fearless man.

A تأبّطيّ *ta-abbatiy*, Of, resembling, or descended from, Ta-abbatasharran: hence intrepid, formidable.

A تابع *tābiẓ*, (pl. تبع *tabaẓ* and تابعون *tābiẓūna*) A follower, dependant. Charge, custody. A familiar spirit that attends a man wherever he goes. One who has seen any of the associates of Muhammad, who are called اصحاب *as-hāb*. تابع النجم *tābiẓu'n najm*, The bull's eye, a star called also الدبران *ad'dabarān*.

A تابعة *tābiẓat*, (fem.) A follower: a familiar spirit.

A تابعيّ *tābiẓiy*, (fem. تابعيّة *tābiẓiyat*) (pl. تابعيّون *tābiẓiyūna*) A follower, particularly one who has seen or conversed with any of the associates of Muhammad.

A تأبّق *ta-abbuk*, (v. n. 5 of ابق) Being hidden, concealed. Absconding, lurking in secret. Denying, disavowing. Restraining one's self, abstaining from.

P تاب كرده *tāb-karda*, Heated, warmed.

A تابل *tābal* or *tābil*, (pl. توابل *tawābil*) Herbs or spiceries with which they season meat.

A تأبّل *ta-abbul*, (v. n. 5 of ابل) Feeding on fresh grass (a camel or other beast of the field), and thereby needing no water. Purchasing, acquiring camels. Bewailing (as Adam the death of his son Abel). Abstaining from conjugal intercourse (during the days of mourning).

A تأبّن *ta-abbun*, A tracking, a tracing.

P تابناك *tābnāk*, Bright, shining, resplendent, radiant, glittering, brilliant, luminous, illuminating, fiery. Passionate, choleric. Mixed, intricate.

P تابندگي *tābandagī*, Lustre, luminousness.

A تابوت *tābūt* (or تابوه *tābūh*) A coffin, bier. A wooden box. The ark of the covenant.

P تابوغ *tābūgh*, Public apology, confession.

P تابوك *tābūk*, A balcony or projection from a building.

A تابول *tābūl*, (properly تامبول) Betel-leaf.

P تابه *tāba*, A frying-pan. A brick. A tile. تابهٔ زر *tāba-i zar*, The sun. تابهٔ ماهي *tāba-i māhī*, A fish, first boiled, and afterwards fried in oil.

A تأبّه *ta-abbuh*, (v. n. 5 of ابه) Thinking highly of one's self. Being pure, free from.

P تابه بريان *tāba-buryān*, Meat fried in a pan.

P تابي *tābī*, Splendour, brightness. Light.

A تأبّي *ta-abbī*, (v. n. 5 of ابا for ابو) Calling one "father." Considering in the light of a father, regarding as a father. (v. n. 5 of ابي) Refusing, denying, resisting, being refractory.

A تأبيب *ta-bīb*, (v. n. 2 of ابّ) Shouting (when charging a foe). Noise, shout, cry.

A تأبية *ta-biyat*, (v. n. 2 of ابا for ابو) Calling one "father." Saying, "May my father be a ransom for you!"

A تأبيخ *ta-bīkh*, A chiding, a rebuking.

A تأبيد *ta-bīd*, (v. n. 2 of ابد) Making eternal, giving an endless duration. Frightening away, rendering averse from society. Duration, continuance.

P تابيدن *tābīdan*, To twist, spin. To shine. To be powerful, strong, or equal to any burden.

A تأبير *ta-bīr*, (v. n. 2 of ابر) Impregnating, fecundating a palm-tree. Dressing, fertilizing arable land.

A تأبيس *ta-bīs*, (v. n. 2 of ابس) Despising, debasing, degrading. Imprisoning.

A تأبيش *ta-bīsh*, (v. n. 2 of ابش) Listening to an unconnected discourse. Collecting, assembling.

A تأبيل *ta-bīl*, (v. n. 2 of ابل) Buying, procuring camels. Picking out camels for breeding and for milking. Being rich in camels. Making fat. Overcoming, conquering. Abstaining, refraining. Speaking in praise of the dead.

A تأبين *ta-bīn*, (v. n. 2 of ابن) Reproaching, reviling to one's face, disparaging. Watching narrowly. Following the steps of another. Speaking in praise of the dead. Drawing blood from an animal and preparing it for food.

A تأبيه *ta-bīh*, (v. n. 2 of ابه) Reminding (of a thing forgotten). Exciting one's attention. Causing to know, informing. Suspecting.

P تاپاك *tāpāk*, Disquietude, restlessness.

P تاپال *tāpāl*, Trunk of a tree. Cow-dung.

P تاپو *tāpū*, An earthen vessel for baking bread.

P تاپه *tāpa*, Cow-dung.

P تات *tāt*, (for تاترا *tā turā* or تا كه ترا *tā ki turā*) Until (I see) thee, till (I give) to thee.

P تاتا *tātā*, Impediment in the speech.

A تأتاء *ta-tā-*, (v. n. of تأتأ Q) Stammering. One who stammers, faulters, or pronounces with difficulty the letter ت *tā*. A word used in calling a he-goat to the female.

A تأتأة *ta-ta-at*, (v. n. of تأتأ Q) Stammering. A vicious pronunciation of the letter ت. The tottering gait of an infant. A stately warlike appearance. A word used in calling a he-goat.

P تاتار *tātār*, A Tartar. Tartary. تاتار باد رفتار *tātāri bād-raftār*, Tartars swift as the wind.

T تاتار بازار *tātār-bāzār*, A town in Thrace.

P تاتاري *tātārī*, Scythian, Tartaric. A kind of slashed doublet open at the sides, usually worn by the Tartars. Fine musk. An agreeable friend (male or female).

A تأتّب *ta-attub*, (v. n. 5 of اتب) Putting on a kind of short shift or inner garment without sleeves, worn by the women of Arabia. Carrying a bow across the shoulders. Making ready for battle. Growing hard.

P تاتلي *tātilī*, A napkin, tablecloth, towel.

P تاتو *tātū*, A certain insect bred in baths.

P تاتوره *tātūra*, Fetters for horses.

P تاتول *tātūl*, Wry-mouthed.

P تاتوله *tātūla*, The thorn-apple.

P تاتونك *tātawnak*, Decrepit old man. Union.

A تاته *tātah*, (an African word) A chameleon.

A تأتّه *ta-attuh*, (or تعتّه *taẓattuh*) A feigning of ignorance or insanity. Delirium, insanity, madness.

A تأتّي *ta-attī*, (v. n. 5 of اتي) Preparing for any thing. Being easily despatched (business). Coming to ask a favour. Occurring, happening, befalling. Being kind, friendly, accommodating.

A تأتيّ *ta-tiy*, (v. n. 2 of اتي) Facilitating the course of water, opening a free passage for it.

A تأتيب *ta-tīb*, (v. n. 2 of اتب) Putting on (another), or ordering (another) to put on, a short shift or drawers. (pass.) Being made up into a shift.

A تأتية *ta-tiyat*, (v. n. 2 of اتا for اتو) Bringing (especially water to one's own land from another's ground). (v. n. 2 of اتي) Making an opening or outlet (for water), causing to run or spring up.

A تأتير *ta-tīr*, (v. n. 2 of اتر) Bending a bow. Stringing (a bow).

A تأتيم *ta-tīm*, A bursting two holes into one.

A تأتين *ta-tīn*, (v. n. 2 of اتن) Bringing forth (a child) with the feet foremost (a woman).

P تاتينا *tātīnā*, A species of kite.

A تأثّر *ta-assur*, (v. n. 5 of اثر) Treading in the steps of. Following, tracking. Being marked, receiving an impression (a skin).

A تأثّف *ta-assuf*, (v. n. 5 of اثف) Remaining still, keeping one's place. Sticking to, following close, associating familiarly with. Importuning, teasing, dunning. Exciting, ceaselessly stirring up. Making of any place a store-room for grain. Surrounding, encompassing, hemming in.

A تأثّل *ta-assul*, (v. n. 5 of اثل) Being firm, fixed, radical, noble. Taking the best part of any thing. Amassing wealth. Digging a well. Becoming great, eminent, glorious. Being collected, assembled. Collecting, bringing together.

A تأثّم *ta-assum*, (v. n. 5 of اثم) Abstaining from, repenting of, sin. Regarding one's self as a sinner.

A تأثيث *taʼsīs*, (v. n. 2 of اثّ) Trampling upon. Subduing. Softening by beating or treading.

A تآثير *taʼāsīr*, (pl. of تؤثور *tuʼsūr*) Serjeants, beadles, life-guardsmen.

A تأثير *taʼsīr*, (v. n. 2 of اثر) Making an impression, leaving a mark. Affecting, influencing. Effect. P تدبير زود تأثير *tadbīri zūd-taʼsīr*, Persuasive counsel.

A تأثيرات *taʼsīrāt*, (pl. of تأثير) Impressions. The penetrating influences of the stars.

A تأثيف *taʼsīf*, (v. n. 2 of اثف) Placing (a pot) on (its) trivet.

A تأثيل *taʼsīl*, (v. n. 2 of اثل) Causing to take root. Considering, receiving as from an excellent origin or stock, of a noble family. Ennobling. Strengthening. Purifying wealth (*i.e.* paying a tenth part towards religious uses, and thereby rendering the rest more valuable). Amassing riches. Dressing one's dependants richly. Behaving generously.

A تأثيم *taʼsīm*, (v. n. 2 of اثم) Charging, accusing, convicting of crime. Sinning, committing evil. Sin, iniquity, transgression, guilt, moral evil.

P A تاج *tāj*, (pl. تيجان *tījān*) A crown, diadem. A crest. The comb of a bird. P تاج خروس *tāji khurōs*, A cock's comb. The amaranth. The herb staves-acre. Drop-wort. Pipe-weed. تاج سعدان *tāji saʻdān*, The planet Saturn. تاج فيروزه *tāji fīroza*, The sky. The crown of Kay Khusrav. تاج گردون *tāji gardūn*, The sun. تاج كياني *tāji kayānī*, A royal crown. تاج گل *tāji gul*, A wreath of flowers. تاج مفخرت *tāji mafkhirat*, A crown of glory.

A تأجّ *taʼajj*, (v. n. 5 of اجّ) Being hot (day).

P تاجبخش *tāj-bakhsh*, Distributing crowns; a maker of kings.

P تاجپوش *tāj-posh*, A cock's comb. The hoopoo or puet.

A تاجة *tājat*, Name of the daughter of ذو الشفر *zū'sh shufr*, and queen of Yaman. She was cotemporary with Joseph when governor of Egypt.

A تأجّج *taʼajjuj*, (v. n. 5 of اجّ) Burning, blazing, flaming. Being inflamed, set on a blaze. Being hot (the day).

P تاجدار *tāj-dār*, Wearing a crown. A king, sovereign, crowned head. A keeper of the crown. A jewel-house.

P تاجداري *tāj-dārī*, Royal. Royal dignity.

A تاجر *tājir*, (pl. تجار *tijār*, تجّار *tujjār*, تجر *tajr* and *tujr*) A merchant. A vintner. Clever, acute, expeditious, and adroit in business. تاجر او تاجرة *tājir aw tājirat*, (A she-camel) sought after and finding a ready sale in the market.

P تاجران *tājurān*, An interpreter.

A تاجرة *tājirat*, (fem. of تاجر *tājir*) Dexterous. هو علي اكرم تاجرة *huwa ʻala' akrama tājiratin*, He rides a noble horse, or one for which he would find a ready purchaser.

P تاجك *tājak*, A little crown. A crest, a bird's comb. *Tājik*, One not an Arab or Turk; a Persian. One of Arabian origin brought up in Persia.

P تاجكى *tājakī*, A garment worn at Tabrīz.

A تأجّل *taʼajjul*, (v. n. 5 of اجل) Arriving at an appointed term. Being assembled, flocking from all quarters. Being confined, dammed up (as water). Lagging, being slow. Being divided, or collecting in herds, flocks, and bevies (oxen, sheep, and deer). Begging for a delay.

A تأجّم *taʼajjum*, (v. n. 5 of اجم) Being scorching hot (the day). Burning, blazing (fire). Being angry against. Entering into a thicket (a lion).

P تاجور *tājwar*, Wearing a crown, crowned.

A تاجيّة *tājiyat*, Name of a cemetery in Baghdād, and of a river at Kūfa.

A تأجيج *taʼjīj*, (v. n. 2 of اجّ) Kindling, setting on fire, causing to blaze.

A تأجير *taʼjīr*, (v. n. 2 of اجر) Making bricks.

A تأجيل *taʼjīl*, (v. n. 2 of اجل) Delaying, protracting, deferring, putting off. Prescribing a fixed period or term. Reprieving. Hindering, restraining, preventing. Curing, applying a remedy to, a crick in the neck called اجل *ijl*. Gathering, bringing (water) into one place.

P تا چند *tā chand*, How many? by how much? تا چند بار *tā chand bār*, How oft? how many times?

P تا حال *tā hāl*, Hitherto, until this moment.

P تا حد *tā had*, (or تا حدي *tā hade*) So far as.

A تأحّد *taʼahhud*, A uniting, a becoming one.

A تاحم *tāhim*, A weaver.

A تاحي *tāhī*, Overseer of a garden, gardener.

A تأحية *taʼhiyat*, (v. n. 2 of احي) Repeating a sound as *ah ah*, hemming, hawing.

A تأحيد *taʼhīd*, (v. n. 2 of احد) Making two into one, or ten into eleven. Swearing by holding up one finger to denote that God is one.

P تاخ *tākh*, A certain tree, fit only for fuel.

A تاخّ *tākhkh*, One who rises having no appetite.

A تأخاذ *taʼkhāz*, Receipt, acceptance.

P تاخت *tākht*, Spoil, plunder, prey. Assault. Invasion. تاخت آوردن *tākht āwardan*, To assail, charge (an enemy).

P تاخت تاراج *tākht tārāj*, Assault, plunder.

P تاختن *tākhtan*, To hasten, walk fast, run. To rush upon, to assault. To pursue, hunt, chase. To urge, force, put to the gallop. To twist, spin. To bend, render curved or convex. To break out in an orbicular tumour upon the body. To contend, dispute, or wager. To bore. To spread, diffuse, pour out, pour in.

P تاختني *tākhtanī*, A canter: race. A post-horse.

P تاخت و تاز *tākht u tāz*, Assault. Plunder.

P تاخته *tākhta*, Twisted. Running, run. Put to full speed. Poured out.

A تأخّر *taʼakhkhur*, (v. n. 5 of اخر) Remaining behind. Being retarded, coming late. Going back.

A تآخي *taʼākhī*, A behaving like brothers.

A تأخّي *taʼakhkhī*, (v. n. 5 of of اخا for اخو) Choosing, receiving as a brother. Choosing the best. Behaving as a brother or a friend. Applying diligently.

A تأخية *taʼkhiyat*, (v. n. 2 of اخي not in use) Making a rope, stake, peg, or ring for tethering (a horse). Sitting on the left foot, and holding the right foot straight.

A تأخيذ *taʼkhīz*, (v. n. 2 of اخذ) Keeping (her husband) back from going after other women by means of a charm (a wife). Turning (milk) sour.

A تأخير *taʼkhīr*, (v. n. 2 of اخر) Delaying, procrastinating, postponing. Remaining behind. Keeping back, hindering. Leaving behind. Making last, putting behind. تقديم و تأخير *takdīm u taʼkhīr*, Transposition, reversing. P تأخيركردن *taʼkhīr kardan*, To delay. A بلا تأخير *bilā taʼkhīr*, Without delay. P در تاخير انداختن *dar tākhīr andākhtan*, To throw back, delay, postpone.

P تاخيره *tākhīra*, Fate, destiny. Portion, fortune. Origin, first condition. تاخيرهٔ فلان همچنين بود *tākhīrasi fulān hamchunīn būd*, The destiny of so and so was in such a manner.

A تأدّب *taʼaddub*, (v. n. 5 of ادب) Being instructed (in literature, politeness, and good manners): submitting to be taught. Being trained, broke in. Instruction, institution, discipline.

A تأدّد *taʼaddud*, (v. n. 5 of ادّ) Waxing strong, increasing, prevailing.

A تآدي *taʼādī*, (v. n. 6 of ادا for ادو) Preparing, making suitable arrangements for accomplishing any thing. Weighing down, oppressing.

A تأدّي *taʼaddī*, (v. n. 5 of ادا for ادو) Preparing to do any thing. Providing one's self with arms and other necessaries for averting evil. (v. n. 5 of ادي) Paying. Arriving (intelligence).

A تأديب *taʼdīb*, (v. n. 2 of ادب) Teaching good manners. Correcting, chastising. Training, breaking in. Correction, chastisement. P تأديب كردن *taʼdīb kardan*, To instruct, render learned or polite. To chastise. To teach good manners.

A تأديبات *taʼdībāt*, (pl. of تأديب) Instructions.

A تأدية *taʼdiyat*, (v. n. 2 of ادي) Causing to arrive. Leading to. Sending, despatching, bringing. Bringing tribute. Performing a promise. Paying a debt. Receiving, taking.

A تأديم *taʼdīm*, (v. n. 2 of ادم) Mixing much bread with condiment.

A تأذّن *taʼazzun*, (v. n. 5 of اذن) Giving certain information. Making known. Proclaiming, promulgating. Swearing. Making a threatening proclamation, making people's ears tingle.

A تأذّي *taʼazzī*, (v. n. 5 of اذي) Being injured.

A تأذين *taʼzīn*, (v. n. 2 of اذن) Lending an ear. Granting leave, giving permission. Striking (one) upon the ear, rubbing, twisting the ear. Making a handle to a vessel, or latchet for a shoe. Calling to prayers from the balcony of the minaret. Signifying, intimating, advertising frequently. Driving from water, not giving to drink.

P تار *tār*, Top, summit, vertex, pinnacle, head or higher part of any thing. The warp of a web in the loom, *i.e.* the threads stretched lengthwise. The string of a musical instrument. A thread. A wire. A curl. Dark, obscure. A bit, a piece. A species of palm-tree from which an intoxicating liquor (toddy) is extracted. چشم تار *chashmi tār*, A cloudy eye, blind. تار عنكبوت *tāri ʿankabūt*, A spider's web. تار و پود *tār u pūd*, Warp and woof.

A تأر *taʾr*, (v. n. of تأر) Flowing (blood that cannot be stopped).

A تارّ *tārr*, Moist, juicy, succulent. Fat, fleshy, and smooth-skinned. Weak and languid (from hunger). A stranger far from home.

P تارا *tārā*, A star. The pupil of the eye.

P تاراب *tārāb*, A village near Bokhārā.

P تارات *tārāt*, Spoil, plunder. Separation.

A تارات *tārāt*, Malevolence. Times, turns.

P تاراج *tārāj*, Spoil, plunder, sack. تاراج ويغما كردن *tārāj u yaghmā kardan*, To plunder and sack.

P تاراجگر *tārājgar*, A spoiler, pillager, robber.

P تاراس *tārās*, A bringing under subjection.

P تاران *tārān*, Dark.

A تأرّب *taʾarrub*, (v. n. 5 of ارب) Being drawn extremely tight (a knot). Applying unremittingly (to business). Resisting, obstinately refusing.

A تارة *tārat*, (pl. تئر *tiʾar* or تارات *tārāt*) A time, turn. Once, one time. Sometimes. تارة اخري *tāratuhkhra'*, Another time. تارة بعد تارة *tārat baʿd tārat*, Time after time, oftentimes, frequently.

A تارّة *tārrat*, Succulent, bonny (lass).

P تارتار *tār-tār*, Piecemeal. To atoms.

P تارتن *tār-tan*, A weaver: silkworm: spider.

P تارتنك *tār-tanak*, A spider.

P تارتور *tārtūr*, Piecemeal. Hard. Dark.

A تأرّث *taʾarrus*, (v. n. 5 of ارث) Being kindled (a fire), stirred up (strife).

P تارچوبه *tār-choba*, Asparagus.

A تارح *tārah*, Terah, Abraham's father.

P تارخ *tārukh* or *tārakh*, Name of Āzar, an idol-sculptor. Name of Abraham's father.

A تارز *tāriz*, Hard. Dry. Withered. Spiritless, evaporated. Dead.

A تارس *tāris*, Armed with a shield.

A تارش *tārish*, Light, volatile, unsteady.

A تارص *tāris*, Firmly built, compact (horse).

A تأرّض *taʾarruz*, (v. n. 5 of ارض) Putting forth the blade (grass), being fit for grazing or mowing. Meeting. Happening, befalling. Bending to the earth with weight.

P تارك *tārak*, The top, the crown of the head. A helmet. A little hill, a heap.

A تارك *tārik*, A leaver, a forsaker, a deserter. تارك الدنيا *tāriku'd dunya'*, One who abandons the world. P تارك كردن *tārik kardan*, To abandon.

P تاركاري *tār-kārī*, Filigree-work.

P تاركش *tār-kash*, A wire-drawer.

P تارم *tāram*, Name of a city whose inhabitants are renowned for their comeliness.

P تارميغ *tār-megh*, A dense fog, a wintry mist.

P تارو *tārū*, A tike or louse infesting cattle.

P تار و تور *tār u tūr*, Very dark. In pieces, piecemeal, to atoms.

P تار و مار *tār u mār*, Scattered. Destroyed. Topsy-turvy, in confusion.

P تارون *tārūn*, Dark.

P تاره *tāra*, The crown of the head. A cupola. A lute-string. Obscure, dark. The warp of cloth. The scale or bason of a balance. A bucket. A wooden building of a circular form.

P تاري *tārī*, Darkness, obscurity. Dark. A liquor exuding from a certain tree; toddy. *Tāre*, A single thread or wire.

A تأرّي *taʾarrī*, (v. n. 5 of اري) Standing quiet (as one horse behind another in the same stall). Abiding in one place. Bending the mind, devoting the whole attention to. Making honey (a bee). Withdrawing, lurking behind.

A تأريب *taʾrīb*, (v. n. 2 of ارب) Tying fast (a knot). Defining, setting bounds to. Completing, performing. Doing much.

A تأرية *taʾriyat*, (v. n. 2 of اري) Strengthening, establishing. Making a tethering post. Lighting (a fire). Stirring up (a fire). Concealing, suppressing.

A تأريث *taʾrīs*, (v. n. 2 of ارث) Kindling a fire. Stirring up strife.

A تأريج *taʾrīj*, (v. n. 2 of ارج) Raising, fomenting dissensions. Keeping a good account-book.

A تأريخ *taʾrīkh*, (v. n. 2 of ارخ) Dating (a letter). Registering. Chronicling. A chronicle, calendar, æra, epoch, year, date. End, boundary, extremity. تأريخ الهجرة *taʾrīkhu'l hijrat*, The æra of the Hijrat or flight. تأريخ اسكندري *taʾrīkhi iskandarī*, The æra of Alexander, commencing 312 years before Christ. تأريخ جلالي *taʾrīkhi jalālī*, The æra of Jalālu'd dīn, beginning in the year 1079 of the Christian æra. تأريخ رومي *taʾrīkhi rūmī*, The æra of Alexander. تأريخ الشهداء *taʾrīkhu'sh shuhadāʾ*, The æra of the martyrs under Diocletian in the year 284. تأريخ الصفر *taʾrīkhu's safar*, The æra of Safar (used by the Arabs in Spain, not extending beyond 38 of our years). تأريخ قبطي *taʾrīkhi kibtī*, The Coptic æra, *i.e.* The æra of the martyrs. تأريخ يزدجرد *taʾrīkhi yazdajird*, The æra of Yazdajird, the last monarch of the Sassanian dynasty, instituted in the year 632 of the Christian era. في التأريخ *fi't taʾrīkh*, On this date.

P تأريخ دار *taʾrīkh-dār*, A chronologer. Daily.

A تاريخي *tārīkhī*, A chronologist, a chronicler.

A تأريز *taʾrīz*, The making (a peg) fast.

A تأريس *taʾrīs*, (v. n. 2 of ارس) Cultivating land, becoming an agriculturist. Employing, making use of, another's service.

A تأريش *taʾrīsh*, (v. n. 2 of ارش) Kindling a fire. Stirring up strife.

A تأريض *taʾrīz*, (v. n. 2 of ارض) Causing grass to be depastured. Seeking for pasture. Purposing and making preparatives for keeping a fast. Using chaste, polished language. Adapting, correcting, adjusting. Making a leathern bottle fit for use by lining it with milk, water, butter, or inspissated juice. Making heavy. Delaying, putting off.

A تأريف *taʾrīf*, (v. n. 2 of ارف) Making a boundary, setting up a mete. Tying a knot (on a rope).

A تأريق *taʾrīk*, A rendering sleepless.

A تأريك *taʾrīk*, (v. n. 2 of ارك) Decorating with a throne. Ornamenting a bridal chamber with a sopha or couch.

P تاريك *tārīk*, Dark. Obscure, cloudy.

P تاريك چشم *tārīk-chashm*, Short-sighted.

P تاريك دل *tārīk-dil*, Benighted. Depraved.

P تاريكي *tārīkī*, Darkness, obscurity.

P تارين *tārīn*, Dark, obscure. The juice of a certain tree called toddy.

A تأز *taʾz*, (v. n. of تأز) Healing (a wound). Encountering one another in battle.

P تاز *tāz*, A greyhound. Ignoble, base. A beloved object. A beardless youth; especially one who behaves himself unseemly and talks indecently. (in comp.) Running, hastening, making an assault.

P تازانه *tāzāna*, A lash, whip. Correction.

P تازانيدن *tāzānīdan*, To cause to run at.

A تأزّب *taʾazzub*, (v. n. 5 of ازب) Dividing amongst themselves.

P تازباز *tāz-bāz*, Playing with boys; a pederast.

A تأزّح *taʾazzuh*, (v. n. 5 of ازح) Being drawn together. Being slow, tedious, longwinded. Failing, flinching, giving way.

A تأزّر *taʾazzur*, (v. n. 5 of ازر) Putting on breeches or trowsers (called ازار *izār*).

A تأزّز *taʾazzuz*, The boiling, bubbling (of a pot).

P تازش *tāzish*, A running here and there.

A تآزف *taʾāzuf*, (v. n. 6 of ازف) Approaching, being side by side.

A تأزّف *taʾazzuf*, A walking with short steps.

A تآزق *taʾāzuk*, The being reduced to straits.

A تأزّق *taʾazzuk*, (v. n. 5 of ازق) Being straitened, distressed. Being overpowered in battle.

P تازك *tāzik*, An Arab's son reared in Persia.

P تازگي *tāzagī*, Freshness, youthfulness. Novelty. Plumpness, fatness.

A تأزّل *taʾazzul*, (v. n. 5 of ازل) Being oppressed with anguish.

A تأزّم *taʾazzum*, The making a long stay.

P تازنده *tāzanda*, Running, making haste.

P تازنگ *tāzang*, A column or pilaster of stone

and mortar.

P تازه *tāza*, Fresh. Young. New, recent. Raw. تازه جوانست *tāza-jawānast*, He is a fresh, tender youth. سپاهِ تازه *sipāhi tāza*, A raw recruit. تازه شدن *tāza shudan*, To be tender and fresh. تازه کردن *tāza kardan*, To make fresh or clean.

P تازه بتازه *tāza ba tāza*, Fresh and fresh.

P تازه بيضه *tāza-bayza*, A fresh egg.

P تازه دم *tāza-dam*, Good spirits, elasticity.

P تازه رس *tāza-ras*, New, fresh, lately come.

P تازه روي *tāza-rūy*, Fresh-faced, florid. Cheerful, smiling, joyous.

P تازه روئي *tāza-rūī*, Freshness, beauty of face.

P تازه ظهور *tāza-zuhūr*, Newly produced.

P تازه قلم *tāza-kalam*, A postscript.

P تازه کن *tāza-kun*, Refreshing: a reviver.

P تازه وارد *tāza-wārid*, A fresh comer.

P تازه و تر *tāza u tar*, Fresh and green.

P تازي *tāzī*, Arabic. An Arabian horse. A greyhound. An assault. تازيان *tāziyān*, Arabians. بتازي *ba tāzī*, In Arabic.

A تأزي *taʼazzī*, (v. n. 5 of ازي) Retiring, desisting from timidity. Making a conduit called ازاء *izāʼ*. Hitting the mark and vibrating in it (an arrow). Sitting near one another.

P تازيان *tāziyān*, Running. Pursuing. (pl. of تازي *tāzī*) Arabians. Arabian horses.

P تازيانه *tāziyāna*, A scourge, lash, whip. تازيانه خوردن *tāziyāna khwurdan*, To receive a scourging. تازيانه کردن *tāziyāna kardan*, (or زدن *zadan*) To scourge, to flog.

P تازيانه خور *tāziyāna-khwur*, Scourged. Whipt.

P تازيانه زن *tāziyāna-zan*, A whipper, scourger.

A تأزية *taʼziyat*, (v. n. 2 of ازي) Making a conduit to a reservoir.

A تأزيج *taʼzīj*, (v. n. 2 of ازج) Building an oblong arched edifice or corridor with vaulted roof.

P تازيخانه *tāzī-khāna*, A dog-kennel.

P تازيدن *tāzīdan*, To run. To wander. To make an assault. To be born. To set on fire, to inflame. To twist. To bend. To bore. To wager. To strive. To suit.

A تأزير *taʼzīr*, (v. n. 2 of ازر) Covering one's breeches. Backing, strengthening, supporting.

P تازي زبان *tāzī-zabān*, The Arabic language.

P تازي سوار *tāzī-suwār*, Mounted on an Arab.

P تازيك *tāzīk*, One neither an Arab or a Turk. One of Arab blood born and brought up in Persia.

P تازي کارد *tāzī-kārd*, A big butchering knife.

P تازي نژاد *tāzī-nijād*, An Arab by birth.

P تاژ *tāj*, A tent, pavilion of cotton or muslin. Delicate. Elegant.

P A تاس *tās*, Playing cards. A fainting, restlessness, or longing desire to which pregnant women are subject. A cup, dish, plate.

P تاسا *tāsā*, Sorrow, grief, heaviness of heart.

P تاسانيدن *tāsānīdan*, To strangle.

P تاس باز *tās-bāz*, A conjuror: a card-player.

A تأسّر *taʼassur*, (v. n. 5 of اسر) Delaying, proceeding slowly. Seeking or finding an excuse against.

A تاسع *tāsiʻ*, The ninth. One who makes nine. يوم التاسع من شهر *yawmu't tāsiʻ mish shahri*, The ninth day of the month . . . . . .

A تأسّف *taʼassuf*, (v. n. 5 of اسف) Sighing, grieving, lamenting, bemoaning, regretting, pining, brooding over affliction. Grief. P تأسّف خوردن *taʼassuf khwurdan*, To sigh.

A تأسّل *taʼassul*, A taking after the father.

P تاسمصت *tāsimsat*, (Moorish) An orange.

P تاسمه *tāsma*, A strap. Hair combed over the forehead.

A تأسّن *taʼassun*, (v. n. 5 of اسن) Being changed, corrupted (water). Calling up an old agreement; seeking for a pretence, putting off, procrastinating. Taking after (his) sire.

A تاسوعاء *tāsūʻāʼ*, The ninth of Muharram.

A تاسومة *tāsūmat*, A sandal.

P تاسه *tāsa*, Disquietude, anxiety, grief, restlessness. A difficulty in breathing. A panting from heat or running. A sob. Blackness of the face from grief. The longing of pregnant women.

P تاسه زده *tāsa-zada*, Broken-winded.

A تاسهمت *tāsihamt*, (Moorish) Wild sorrel.

P تاسه واسه *tāsa wāsa*, Disquiet, restlessness.

A تآسي *taʼāsī*, (v. n. 6 of اسا for اسو) Consoling, solacing, or reciprocally assisting.

A تأسّي *taʼassī*, A receiving of comfort.

A تأسية *taʼsiyat*, (v. n. 2 of اسي) Administering consolation. Grieving, feeling grief or sympathy.

A تأسيد *taʼsīd*, The setting (a dog) at any thing.

P تاسيدن *tāsīdan*, To be sad or afflicted.

A تآسير *taʼāsīr*, Girths (of a saddle).

A تأسير *taʼsīr*, (v. n. 2 of اسر) Binding tight.

A تأسيس *taʼsīs*, (v. n. 2 of اسّ) Marking out a foundation. Laying a foundation. Making firm and solid. (in poetry) The last letter of a hemistich, with which all the following rhyme. The quiescent ا *alif*, which belongs to the penultimate syllable of a poem, and is separated from the رويّ *rawīy* or final by another letter: as in مکارم *makārim*, where ا *alif* is the تأسيس *taʼsīs*, ر *re* the ردف *ridf*, and م *mīm* the رويّ *rawīy*. The employment of a new word, imparting a different sense to the word previously used (in contradistinction to تأکيد *taʼkīd*, which means strengthening or corroborating). P تاسيس نهادن *tāsīs nihādan*, To lay a foundation, establish, fix, consolidate.

A تأسيل *taʼsīl*, (v. n. 2 of اسل) Sharpening, bringing to a point. Reaching the summit, tip, or extremity of a thing.

P تاش *tāsh*, A freckle. A companion, consort, partner in trade. A lord, master, householder. خواجه تاش *khwāja-tāsh*, A school-fellow.

A تأشّب *taʼashshub*, (v. n. 5 of اشب) Being mixed (a concourse of people). Being assembled, gathered, blended. Being intertwined (trees). Sticking close (as a client to his patron).

P تاشك *tāshak*, Whey. Fresh butter. Quick.

P تاشکل *tāshkil*, A wart.

A تأشّن *taʼashshun*, A washing with potash.

A تأشيب *taʼshīb*, (v. n. 2 of اشب) Setting (men) at variance. Mixing, intertwining.

A تأشير *taʼshīr*, (v. n. 2 of اشر) Sharpening, notching (the teeth). (pl. تآشير *taʼāshīr*) That by which a locust bites; his mandible.

A تأصّص *taʼassus*, An assembling, flocking.

A تأصّل *taʼassul*, A taking firm root.

A تأصية *taʼsiyat*, The being difficult.

A تأصيد *taʼsīd*, (v. n. 2 of اصد) Causing one to put on a small shift (called اصدة *usdat*).

A تأصيص *taʼsīs*, (v. n. 2 of اصّ) Binding, tying fast. Confirming, strengthening. Joining, cementing.

A تأصيل *taʼsīl*, (v. n. 2 of اصل) Causing to take root. Confirming, strengthening. Ennobling. Declaring to be of noble origin.

A تآطر *taʼātur*, (v. n. 6 of اطر) Being bent.

A تأطّر *taʼattur*, (v. n. 5 of اطر) Being bent. Vibrating (as a lance carried across the shoulder). Remaining in her father's house unmarried (a woman). Being imprisoned, confined, restrained.

A تأطّم *taʼattum*, (v. n. 5 of اطم) Being filled with rage. Dashing furiously (waves). Snoring. Purring (a cat in her sleep). Growing dark (night). Curbing one's self, refraining (from talk or acting).

A تأطيد *taʼtīd*, An establishing, confirming.

A تأطير *taʼtīr*, (v. n. 2 of اطر) Bending, making crooked. Wrapping a bit of catgut round an arrow near the notch to strengthen it.

A تأطيم *taʼtīm*, (v. n. 2 of اطم) Throwing a veil or covering over the camel-litter هودج *hawdaj*.

A تاعة *tāʻat*, A little mass, lump, ball.

A تاعس *tāʻis*, Perishing, dying. Trembling. Fallen prostrate. Thrown or laid down. Remote.

P تاغ *tāgh*, A tree, a fire of which will burn for a long time. An egg. Name of a fort in Sistān.

P تا غايت *tā ghāyat*, Until.

P تاغستان *tāghistān*, A grove of تاغ *tāgh* trees.

A تاغندست *tāghandast*, (Moorish) Pellitory.

A تافة *tāfat*, Vice, blemish, defect. Necessity, need, lack. Excess. Delay.

P تافتگي *tāftagī*, Vexation, fatigue. Distortion.

P تافتن *tāftan*, To set on fire, burn, inflame, scorch, heat. To be warm, hot. To shine, sparkle, glitter, dazzle, send forth rays. To twist. To bend, crook, render convex. To curl hair. To turn away. To turn away the face, to decline. To be disturbed and vexed. To sigh.

P تافته *tāfta*, Turned, bent, averted. Twisted. Woven. Shining, sparkling, glittering. A garment woven of linen. A kind of silken cloth. Taffeta. Hair, thread, or any thing similar capable of being platted, twisted, or curled. Heated, inflamed. Sad, afflicted, disturbed. Discomfort, uneasiness.

P تافته جگر *tāfta-jigar*, Hectic. In love.

A تافر *tāfir*, A sordid, dirty, squalid fellow.

P تافشك *tāfashak*, A ship-worm, wood-louse.

A تأفف *ta*ʼ*affuf*, (v. n. 5 of اف) Crying out with vexation and loathing اف *uffa*, Fie! for shame! out upon it!

A تأفق *ta*ʼ*affuk*, A coming from افق *ufuk*.

A تأفل *ta*ʼ*afful*, A being proud and haughty.

A تأفن *ta*ʼ*affun*, (v. n. 5 of افن) Being lessened, impaired. Accusing, reproaching. Making pretensions to what one does not possess. Boasting falsely. Exploring diligently the minutiæ of things.

A تافه *tāfih*, Small, few. Mean. Insipid.

A تأفيف *ta*ʼ*fīf*, (v. n. 2 of اف) Crying out اف *uffa*, Fy! shame! out upon it. Suffering from blight amongst corn, or murrain amongst cattle.

A تأفيك *ta*ʼ*fīk*, (v. n. 2 of افك) Lying.

A تأفيل *ta*ʼ*fīl*, (v. n. 2 of افل) Making complete or perfect. Multiplying, increasing.

A تاق *tāka*, (fut. يتوق *yatūku*) He desired.

A تأق *ta*ʼ*ak*, (v. n. of تئق) Being filled (a leathern bottle). Being full (of grief). Burning (with rage).

P تاق *tāk*, A tree, the fire of which will burn for seven days.

A تأقة *ta*ʼ*akat*, Excess of anger. Rashness, hastiness, passion. Haste, despatch. A disposition to rush into mischief.

A تأقط *ta*ʼ*akkut*, (v. n. 5 of اقط) Becoming new cheese, which is called اقط *akit* (milk)

A تأقيت *ta*ʼ*kīt*, The fixing of a time.

P تاك *tāk*, The tendril of a vine.

A تاك *tāka*, (fem. of ذاك *zāka*) This.

A تاكّ *tākk*, (pl. تاكون *tākkūn*, تككة *takakat*, تكاك *tukkāk*, and تكك *tukak*) Foolish, dull, stupid. Thin, emaciated. Perishing, on the brink of ruin.

P تا كجا *tā kujā*, How far? whither? How long?

A تأكد *ta*ʼ*akkud*, (v. n. 5 of اكد) Being confirmed, strengthened.

A تأكر *ta*ʼ*akkur*, (v. n. 5 of اكر) Trenching (land), preparing (it) for the reception of trees.

A تاكرّني *tākurruna*ʼ, A town in Spain, Tarragona.

A تآكل *ta*ʼ*ākul*, (v. n. 6 of اكل) Eating together. Slaying one another in battle (warriors).

A تأكّل *ta*ʼ*akkul*, (v. n. 5 of اكل) Being corroded (a tooth). Being devoured with rage. Gleaming (a sword, lightning, silver, &c.).

A تاكوت *tākūt*, (Moorish) Gum euphorbium.

P تاكي *tā kay*, Whither? To what length? How long?

A تآكيد *ta*ʼ*ākīd*, Belts, girths, thongs, holding together the fore parts of a camel's saddle.

A تأكيد *ta*ʼ*kīd*, (v. n. 2 of اكد) Tying tight, binding fast. Joining, uniting. Strengthening, satisfying, confirming, corroborating. Insisting. Corroboration. Stress. An order, injunction.

A تأكيدا *ta*ʼ*kīdan*, Strongly. Diligently.

A تأكيف *ta*ʼ*kīf*, (v. n. 2 of اكف) Laying the saddle-cloth upon (an ass). Making the coarse saddle-cloth اكاف *ikāf* or *ukaf*.

A تأكيل *ta*ʼ*kīl*, (v. n. 2 of اكل) Giving to eat. Inviting one to eat.

A تأكيم *ta*ʼ*kīm*, (v. n. 2 of اكم) Being thick about the buttocks. Thickness of buttock.

A تال *tāl*, Palm-shoots, or young palm-leaves.

H تال *tāl*, The fan palmyra-tree, the leaves of which are used to write on with an iron style. Copper. A dish of silver or brass. A sort of cymbal of bell-metal played with a stick. P A pond.

A تالّ (and ضالّ *zāll*) *tāll*, (and الضلال بن التلال *az zalālu'bnu't talāl*) Wandering, erring.

P تالاب *tālāb*, (تال *tāl* and آب *āb*) A pond.

P تالار *tālār*, A bedchamber or saloon, built of wood and supported by four columns. (for تالاب *tālāb*) A pond, a reservoir.

P تالاش *tālāsh*, A voice, clamour, tumult. Flame. Search.

P تالان *tālān*, Depredation, plunder, pillage.

A تألان *ta*ʼ*alān*, One who tosses his head in walking, or walks as if he had a load on his back.

P تالانك *tālānak*, An apricot.

P تالانه *tālāna*, A fruit resembling a peach.

A تألب *ta*ʼ*lab*, A tree from which bows are made. Robust (man, wild-ass, or mountain-goat).

A تالد *tālid*, Wealth inherited from one's ancestors. Cattle bred at the owner's home.

A تألّد *ta*ʼ*allud*, (v. n. 5 of الد) Being struck with astonishment.

A تألس *ta*ʼ*allus*, (v. n. 5 of الس) Feeling pain. Being moved.

P تالسان *tālisān*, (or تالشان *tālishān*) A kind of coif wreathed round the head, with a lappet or sash hanging down.

P تالش *tālish*, Name of a people in Gīlān.

A تألف *ta*ʼ*alluf*, (v. n. 5 of الف) Being united, associated. Contracting an acquaintance, cultivating friendship, holding social intercourse, agreeing. Finding to be suitable and agreeing with. Speaking kindly and soothingly. Conciliating the affections of another. Assembling, flocking together.

A تألق *ta*ʼ*alluk*, (v. n. 5 of الق) Flashing, glittering, gleaming (lightning). Tiring, adorning herself (a woman). Preparing, raising the head for a quarrel or for some mischievous purpose.

A تالك *tālika*, (fem. of ذالك *zālika*) That.

P تالكي *tālkī*, Wild coriander.

A تألّم *ta*ʼ*allum*, (v. n. 5 of الم) Suffering pain. Grief, torment.

P تألّم خانه *ta*ʼ*allum-khāna*, An hospital.

P تالمن *tālmin*, (in zand and Pāzand) A fox.

P تالواسه *tālwāsa*, Perturbation, disquietude, restlessness. Inclination, desire.

P تال و مال *tāl u māl*, Dispersed. Piecemeal.

A تألّه *ta*ʼ*alluh*, (v. n. 5 of اله) Worshipping, paying adoration. Being devout and pious.

A تاله العقل *tālihu'l ʻakl*, Mad, insane.

A تالي *tālī*, Following. Consequent. A reader. The fourth horse in a race. تالي النجم *tālī'n najm*, The bull's eye (a star).

A تألّي *ta*ʼ*allī*, (v. n. 5 of الى) Swearing.

A تأليب *ta*ʼ*līb*, (v. n. 2 of الب) Instigating, exciting, provoking. Sowing dissensions. Corrupting, laying waste. Urging forward.

A تألية *ta*ʼ*liyat*, (v. n. 2 of الو) Doing less than one's duty, coming short. Stopping, delaying.

A تالية *tāliyat*, Extremity: tail, foot.

A تآليد *ta*ʼ*ālīd*, Generations.

P تاليدن *tālīdan*, To cry (like a fowl that is caught, or a boy that is whipped). To weep. To sack, spoil, pillage.

A تأليف *ta*ʼ*līf*, (v. n. 2 of الف) Making, completing, or becoming one thousand. Writing the letter ا *alif*. Joining, uniting. Connecting in friendship, reconciling. Conciliating, winning (hearts). Collecting, bringing together, compiling. A compilation, literary composition, publication. تاليف قلوب *tālīfi kulūb*, The conciliating of hearts.

A تأليل *ta*ʼ*līl*, (v. n. 2 of ال) Sharpening. Pricking the ears.

A تأليم *ta*ʼ*līm*, (v. n. 2 of الم) Paining.

A تأليه *ta*ʼ*līh*, (v. n. 2 of اله) Causing or commanding to worship.

P تام *tām*, Few. Small. Little. Weak.

A تامّ *tāmm*, Entire, complete, perfect, full. تامّ الشعر *tāmmu'sh shaʻar*, One who has a full head of hair. تامّ الوزن *tāmmu'l wazn*, Of full weight. غير تامّ *ghayr tāmm*, Incomplete.

P H تامبول *tāmbūl*, Betel-leaf.

A تآمر *ta*ʼ*āmur*, (v. n. 6 of امر) Consulting, deliberating. Commanding one another.

A تامر *tāmir*, Rich or abounding in dates.

A تأمّر *ta*ʼ*ammur*, (v. n. 5 of امر) Being set over as commander. Commanding, bearing sway. Consulting.

A تأمريّ *ta*ʼ*muriy*, A man, some one.

A تامشطة *tāmashtat*, (Moorish) Fennel.

A تأمّع *ta*ʼ*ammuʻ*, (v. n. 5 of امع) Being weak in mind. Being at every body's beck and call.

A تامك *tāmik*, A camel's bunch, especially large and oblong. A camel's bunch in general. A camel having a large bunch.

A تأمّل *ta*ʼ*ammul*, (v. n. 5 of امل) Looking steadfastly (at any thing), regarding attentively. Reflecting, musing. Pausing. Contemplation, thought, meditation.

A تأمّم *ta*ʼ*ammum*, (v. n. 5 of امّ) Tending towards. Design, purpose, intention. Taking for, considering as, a mother. (for تيمّم *tayammum*) Purifying or rubbing the hands, face, and other parts of the body with sand or dust (agreeable to the Muhammadan law), where water cannot be got, before engaging in religious duties.

A تامور *tāmūr*, (or تأمور *taʼmūr*) Any one, some one. Any thing. Soul, spirit, breath. Blood. The life's blood. The heart; the heart's core. Saffron. Water. Wine. The monastic institution or mode of living. A monk's cloister. A lion's haunt or lair. The membrane which encloses the fœtus in the womb. A fœtus. A prime minister, a vazīr. A puppet. A purse or case for holding any thing. A round box for holding jewels or drugs. An ewer with a spout.

A تامورة *tāmūrat*, A cloister, a cell. The pericardium. Wine. Water. A round box for holding jewels or drugs. A lion's den. An ewer.

A تأموريّ *taʼmūriy*, A man; some one.

P تامول *tāmūl*, (تانبول *tāmbūl*) Betel-leaf.

A تأمّه *taʼammuh*, The taking a mother.

A تأمّي *taʼammī*, (v. n. 5 of امي) Purchasing a female slave (امة *amat*).

A تأمية *taʼmiyat*, (v. n. 2 of امي) Making (one) a handmaid (امة *amat*).

A تأميت *taʼmīt*, (v. n. 2 of امت) Determining, defining. Guessing, conjecturing.

A تأميد *taʼmīd*, (v. n. 2 of امد) Shewing a term or boundary, terminating, finishing.

A تآمير *taʼāmīr*, (pl. of تؤمور *tuʼmūr*) Direction-stones set up in the desert.

A تأمير *taʼmīr*, (v. n. 2 of امر) Appointing a governor (amir). Sharpening. Producing a mark, impression, or scar. Fixing a point to a lance. Rendering numerous.

A تأميل *taʼmīl*, (v. n. 2 of امل) Hoping.

A تأميم *taʼmīm*, (v. n. 2 of امّ) Proposing.

A تأمين *taʼmīn*, (v. n. 2 of امن) Saying Amen. Trusting, confiding in.

A تان *tān*, Sewing thread.

P تان *tān*, Your, yours. The mouth. The inside of the mouth. كاشانهٔ تان *kāshānaʼi tān*, Your parlour. رخت تان *rakhti tān*, Your furniture. (for تا آن *tā ān*) Until that, or he. (for تار *tār*) The warp of a web. Sundry cross threads which are left unwoven.

A تان *tāni*, (fem. dual of ذا *zā*) These two.

P تانك *tānak*, One who, in speaking, frequently pronounces the letter ت *tā*.

A تأنان *taʼnān*, (v. n. of انّ) Groaning.

P تانبول *tāmbūl*, Betel-leaf.

A تأنّث *taʼannus*, (v. n. 5 of انث) Becoming soft. Speaking tenderly, using soft words.

P تاند *tānad*, He is able. It is possible.

A تأنّس *taʼannus*, (v. n. 5 of انس) Becoming tame and gentle (an animal).

P تانست *tānist*, He is, or was, able.

A تأنّف *taʼannuf*, (v. n. 5 of انف) Desiring, longing intensely for one thing after another.

A تأنّق *taʼannuk*, (v. n. 5 of انق) Doing any thing properly and wisely. Displaying great neatness. Being neat and spruce. Fine, elegant workmanship. Viewing any object (as a garden) with wonder and delight, liking (a place).

P تانك *tānk*, A weight of about two ounces.

A تانك *tānika*, (or تانّك *tānnika*) (fem. dual of ذاك *zāka*) Those two.

P تانگو *tāngū* or *tānagū*, A barber.

P تانم *tānam*, I am able. (for دانم) I know.

A تأنّن *taʼannun*, (v. n. 5 of انّ) Being pleased with. Pleasing, rendering satisfied.

P تانول *tānūl*, The environs of the mouth. Wry-mouthed.

P تانه *tāna*, The warp of a web in the loom.

A تانئ *tāniʼ*, A villager, a peasant.

A تأنّي *taʼannī*, (v. n. 5 of اني) Waiting, expecting. P تأنّي كردن *taʼannī kardan*, To go slowly, deliberately, or patiently to work. To conduct business with care, skill, and industry. To delay, defer, hesitate.

A تأنيب *taʼnīb*, (v. n. 2 of انب) Treating harshly, with unkindness. Chiding any one and speaking through the nose.

A تأنية *taʼniyat*, (v. n. 2 of اني) Lagging, delaying, proceeding slowly.

A تأنيث *taʼnīs*, (v. n. 2 of انث) Putting in the feminine gender. Making soft. Flattering, using blandishments.

P تانيدن *tānīdan*, To prevail against.

A تأنيس *taʼnīs*, (v. n. 2 of انس) Making familiar, habituating. Exhilarating, rejoicing. Seeing, perceiving.

P تانيسر *tānīsar*, A city in Hindūstān.

A تأنيف *taʼnīf*, (v. n. 2 of انف) Sharpening, giving a sharp point. Exciting (any one) to disgust. Leading (camels) to fresh untouched pasture. Seeking pasture. Putting a handle to.

A تأنيق *taʼnīk*, A filling with astonishment.

A تأنين *taʼnīn*, (v. n. 2 of انّ) Being pleased with. Pleasing, rendering satisfied.

P تاو *tāv*, (for تاب *tāb*) Strength. Heat. Splendour. Fever, anguish. Trouble. Power. A curl, a twist. (in comp.) Twisting. Polishing.

P تاوا *tāwā*, A frying-pan, skillet.

P تاواتاو *tāv-ā-tāv*, Power, strength.

P تاوان *tāwān*, A mulct, fine. A substitute. Damage, loss. A crime, sin, fault, sinfulness. تاوان انداختن *tāwān andākhtan*, To impose a mulct. تاوان دادن *tāwān dādan*, To pay a fine, to expiate.

P تاوانا *tāwānā*, Power, strength.

P تاوان زده *tāwān-zada*, Amerced, fined.

P تاوانه *tāwāna*, A hot-house.

P تاوانيدن *tāwānīdan*, To cause to roll.

A تأوّب *taʼawwub*, (v. n. 5 of آب for اوب) Arriving at night, especially about nightfall. Returning.

P تاوتك *tāwtak*, Double, two-fold.

A تأوّخ *taʼawwukh*, Purpose, design, intent.

P تاوخانه *tāv-khāna*, A hot-house, conservatory. A bath. A stove. A summer-residence, summer-quarters for soldiers.

A تأوّد *taʼawwud*, (v. n. 5 of اود) Being bent. Oppressing, weighing down. Crookedness.

P تاور *tāwar*, Accident, contingency.

P تاورمان *tāwarmān*, Up and down, above, below.

P تاوريده *tāwarīda*, Accidental, contingent.

P تاوسه *tāvasa*, Pasture, a watered mead.

A تأوّق *taʼawwuk*, (v. n. 5 of آق for اوق) Hanging back, being discouraged.

P تاوقتي *tā wakte*, Till the time, or hour.

P تاوك *tāwak*, A young ass. A bullock.

P تاوكردن *tāv kardan*, To heat. To drink health.

P تاول *tāwal*, An ass-colt. An unbroke steer. A heifer. A calf. *Tāwil*, A blister on the hand or foot.

A تأوّل *taʼawwul*, (v. n. 5 of آل for اول) Explaining, rendering.

A تأوّن *taʼawwun*, (v. n. 5 of آن for اون) Eating and drinking till his belly is blown out like a pair of panniers (an ass).

P تاوه *tāwa*, A frying-pan, skillet. A burnt brick, a large tile. پاي تاوه *pāy-tāwa*, Bandages swathed round the feet.

A تأوّه *taʼawwuh*, (v. n. 5 of اوه) Crying ah!

A تاوي *tāwī*, One who falls or perishes.

A تأوّي *taʼawwī*, (v. n. 5 of اوي) Assembling, coming together in one place. Repairing to a place to make a temporary or permanent stay.

A تاويّ *tāwiy*, Terminating in تا *tā* (verses).

A تأويب *taʼwīb*, (v. n. 5 of آب for اوب) Travelling the whole of the day and halting at night. Striving against another in travelling. Returning.

A تأوية *taʼwiyat*, (v. n. 2 of اوي) Repairing to any place either to make a temporary or permanent stay. Receiving hospitably.

A تأويد *taʼwīd*, (v. n. 2 of آد for اود) Bending.

P تاويدن *tāwīdan*, To twist. To shine. To heat. To revolve. To be strong. To shave.

A تأويق *taʼwīk*, (v. n. 2 of آق for اوق) Imposing a burden. Overloading. Oppressing. Vexing. Hindering, preventing. Putting on short commons. Despising. Slighting.

A تأويل *taʼwīl*, (v. n. 2 of آل for اول) Bringing (any thing) back to (its) original state. Analyzing. Expounding, commenting upon. Arranging (especially words or sentences in metrical order). Making a passage which will bear a double interpretation to conform to the outward and apparent meaning. Elucidation, paraphrase. Explanation, interpretation (of dreams or obscure points in science). A certain fragrant pot-herb. P تأويل كردن *taʼwīl kardan*, To explain, comment upon, interpret, expound.

A تاويلة *tāwīlat*, Name of a plant.

A تأويليّ *taʼwīliy*, Explanatory, expository.

A تأويم *ta*ʼ*wīm*, (v. n. 2 of آم for اوم) Fattening. Augmenting the bulk of the body (as food or pasture). Making thirsty.

A تأوين *ta*ʼ*wīn*, (v. n. 2 of آن for اون) Eating and drinking (an ass) till his belly becomes blown out like a pair of panniers. Proceeding gently.

A تأويه *ta*ʼ*wīh*, A groaning from pain.

P تاه *tāh*, A plait, fold, ply. An odd number. Rust. يكتاه *yak tāh*, Single. دوتاه *du tāh*, Double.

A تأهّب *ta*ʼ*ahhub*, A being prepared, arranged.

A تأهّل *ta*ʼ*ahhul*, (v. n. 5 of اهل) Marrying a wife. Founding a family. Being worthy.

P تاهم *tā ham*, Still, yet, nevertheless.

A تأهّم *ta*ʼ*ahhum*, (v. n. 5 of تهم irregular) Visiting Tihāma.

P تاهمچنين *tā hamchunīn*, Thus far, thus much.

P تاهو *tāhū*, Spirituous liquor.

A تاهور *tāhūr*, A cloud.

A تأوّه *ta*ʼ*ahhuh*, (v. n. 5 of آه) Sighing.

A تأهيب *ta*ʼ*hīb*, A preparing, getting ready for.

A تأهيل *ta*ʼ*hīl*, (v. n. 2 of اهل) Regarding as proper, fit, worthy. Saying to any one اهلاً و مرحباً *ahlan wa marhaban*, You are welcome.

A تأي *ta*ʼ*a*ʼ, (fut. يتأي *yat*ʼ*a*ʼ) He preceded.

P تاي *tāy*, Like, resembling. A garment. Odd, single, unit. Number. A single (piece or sheet). Half a load. Fold. يكتاي *yak tāy*, Single. دوتاي *du tāy*, Two-fold.

P تاياق *tāyāk*, A bundle of sticks, a faggot.

A تائب *tā*ʼ*ib*, Repentant, returning (to God).

A تأيّب *ta*ʼ*ayyub*, (v. n. 5 of آب for ايب) Arriving at night. Returning.

A تاية *tāyat*, (for طاية *tāyat*) The flat roof of a house. A place where they dry dates. A large stone in sandy ground.

A تئيّة *ti*ʼ*ayyat*, Sojourn, stay, residence.

A تائج *tā*ʼ*ij*, One being crowned. One who wears a crown, crowned.

A تأيّد *ta*ʼ*ayyud*, (v. n. 5 of آد for ايد) Being corroborated, confirmed, strengthened.

A تائر *tā*ʼ*ir*, One who sets seriously about any thing (beginning after some intermission).

A تأيّس *ta*ʼ*ayyus*, (v. n. 5 of ايس) Being soft, gentle, lenient. Being changed, troubled, disquieted.

A تائق *tā*ʼ*ik*, Eager after.

A تائك *tā*ʼ*ik*, Arrant (fool).

A تأيّم *ta*ʼ*ayyum*, (v. n. 5 of آم for ايم) Continuing unmarried. Becoming a widow.

A تائه *tā*ʼ*ih*, Proud, haughty, boastful. One who wanders about as lost.

A تآيي *ta*ʼ*āyī*, (v. n. 6 of اي) Searching for.

A تأيّي *ta*ʼ*ayyī*, (v. n. 5 of اي) Abiding, dwelling, tarrying. Going in quest of the very thing or person (آية *āyat*).

A تائيّ *tā*ʼ*iy*, Terminating in تا *tā* (verses).

A تأييب *ta*ʼ*yīb*, (v. n. 2 of ايب) Returning.

A تأييد *ta*ʼ*yīd*, (v. n. 2 of آد for ايد) Strengthening, infusing fresh vigour. Assisting. Corroboration, confirmation. P با تاييد كردگار *bā tāyīdi kirdigār*, (or الهي *ilāhī*) By the divine assistance.

A تأييدات *ta*ʼ*yīdāt*, (pl. of تأييد) Aids, helps.

P تاييدن *tāyīdan*, To resemble, be like unto.

A تأييس *ta*ʼ*yīs*, (v. n. 2 of ايس) Making desperate. Softening, unbracing, relaxing. Making an impression, leaving a mark. Regarding as small and contemptible.

A تأييم *ta*ʼ*yīm*, (v. n. 2 of آم for ايم) Making (a man) a widower.

A تأييه *ta*ʼ*yīh*, (v. n. 2 of ايه) Calling (to camels). Crying aloud يا ايّه الرجل *yā ayyuha'r rajulu*, O man!

P تب *tab*, A fever. تب داشتن *tab dāshtan*, To rave, talk incoherently. تب دق *tabi dikk*, Hectic fever. تب ربع *tabi rubʻ*, Quartan fever. تب غبّ *tabi ghibb*, Tertian fever. تب لرزه *tabi larza*, Ague. تب محرق *tabi muhrik*, Ardent fever. تب مواظبه *tabi muwāzaba*, Quotidian fever. تب نوبت *tabi nawbat*, Intermittent fever. تب گرفته *tab-girifta*, Seized with a fever. پرتاب و تب *pur tāb u tab*, Full of fire and ardour.

A تبّ *tabb*, (v. n. of تبّ) Cutting, amputating. Loss, injury, damage, detriment, ruin, perdition, destruction. تبّاً له *tabban lahu*, May he perish!

A تباب *tabāb*, A perishing. Loss, destruction.

A تبابعة *tabābiʻat*, (pl. of تبّع *tubbaʻ*) Kings of Arabia Felix. دار التبابعة *dāru't tabābiʻat*, A house in Mecca where Muhammad was born.

A تبأبؤ *taba*ʼ*bu*ʼ, A running with haste.

A تبابيع *tabābīʻ*, (pl. of تبّع *tubbaʻ*) Shadows. Queen-bees.

A تبابيل *tabābīl*, (pl. of تبل) Hates. Sicknesses.

A تبابين *tabābīn*, (pl. of تبّان *tubbān*) Short sailors'-breeches.

A تباخس *tabākhus*, A defrauding of each other.

A تبادّ *tabādd*, (v. n. 6 of بدّ) Attacking each other severally, one by one. Choosing one's equal for any work.

A تبادح *tabāduh*, (v. n. 6 of بدح) Pelting each other with any soft substance (as melons, &c.).

A تبادر *tabādur*, A making haste simultaneously.

A تبادل *tabādul*, (v. n. 6 of بدل) Changing, transposing. Interchange, transfer; permutation (as of the letter ب *bā* with و *wāw*).

A تبادلات *tabādulāt*, Permutations.

A تباده *tabāduh*, (v. n. 6 of بده) Vying with, or exercising one another in the reciting of extemporary verses.

A تبادي *tabādī*, (v. n. 6 of بدا for بدو) Resembling, imitating the manners of those who live in the desert (بادية *bādiyat*). Manifesting enmity.

A تباديد *tabādīd*, Scattered: as, طير تباديد *tayr tabādīd*, Scattered birds.

P تبار *tabār*, A tribe, family, kindred. Root, origin. شهريار عالي تبار *shahryāri ʻāli-tabār*, A monarch of an illustrious house.

A تبار *tabār*, Ruin, destruction. دار التبار *dāru't tabār*, (The house of ruin) Hell.

A تبارز *tabāruz*, (v. n. 6 of برز) Marching forth against each other. Separating from one's party in order to grapple alone with an adversary.

A تبارك *tabāruk*, (v. n. 6 of برك) Being blessed. Being exalted, pure, holy, undefiled (applied exclusively to God). Taking a good omen, auguring well from. حق تبارك و تعالي *hakk tabāraka wa taʻāla'*, (literally, Blessed and exalted be God!) (though, in common acceptation) (God) The just, the blessed, and most high.

A تباري *tabārī*, (v. n. 6 of بري) Striving together. Opposing one another.

A تباريح *tabārīh*, Vehemence of desire.

A تباريق *tabārīk*, Meat moderately seasoned.

A تبازج *tabāzuj*, (v. n. 6 of بزج) Contending for pre-eminence, boasting against each other.

A تبازخ *tabāzukh*, (v. n. 6 of بزخ) Hanging back, receding (from business). Having protuberant hips (a woman).

A تبازي *tabāzī*, (v. n. 6 of بزي) Going with a wide step. Raising the hips in walking. Glorying in what (he) does not possess.

P تباسيدن *tabāsīdan*, To faint from heat.

A تباشر *tabāshur*, (v. n. 6 of بشر) Communicating reciprocally good news.

P تباشير *tabāshīr*, Sugar of bamboo. Chalk, clay, plaster.

A تباشير *tabāshīr*, (pl. of تبشير *tabshīr*) Happy tidings, agreeable intelligence, good news. The beginnings or preludes of good news. Lines, furrows upon sand produced by the wind. Warbles, raws upon the sides of a beast of burden. Early-bearing palm-trees. The colour and beauty of dates at the season of ripening. تباشير صباح *tabāshīri sabāh*, The prelude to the dawn, the break of day.

A تباصر *tabāsur*, (v. n. 6 of بصر) Seeing or looking at one another.

A تبأطّ *taba*ʼ*ut*, (v. n. 5 of بأط not used) Lying on one's breast. Being in easy and affluent circumstances. Disliking, loathing.

A تباطؤ *tabātu*ʼ, (v. n. 6 of بطؤ) Delaying, lingering, loitering.

A تباع *tibāʻ*, (v. n. 3 of تبع) Following, imitating. Doing any thing perfectly, certainly, and solidly. (A field) thoroughly fattening (a camel). Giving every member its due. Continuation. (pl. of تبيع *tabīʻ*) Followers, sectaries, clients. Assistants. Debtors. Calves. تبّاع العسكر *tubbāʻu'l ʻaskar*, Camp-followers.

A تباعة *tabāʻat*, (v. n. of تبع) Following. Pursuing, overtaking. Punishment, penal suffering. Attendance. *Tibāʻat*, A bad end.

A تباعد *tabāʻud*, A withdrawing to a distance.

A تباعل *tabāʻul*, A toying with a spouse.

A تابعيّة *tabāʻiyat* Obedience.

A تباغض *tabāghuz*, A hating of one another.

A تباغي *tabāghī*, (v. n. 6 of بغي) Being insolent and overbearing towards each other.

P تباك *tabāk*, Fever.

A تباكّ *tabākk*, (v. n. 6 of بكّ) Crowding, thronging. Being heaped, pressed together.

A تباكي *tabākī*, (v. n. 6 of بكي) Forcing one's self, or being forced to shed tears. Pretending to cry, feigning to weep.

A تبّال *tabbāl*, One who seasons victuals.

A تبالة *tabālat*, Name of a town in Yaman.

A تبالي *tabāluh*, A denying to each other.

A تبالط *tabālut*, (v. n. 6 of بلط) Fencing, fighting with swords.

A تبالغ *tabāligh*, (pl. of تبلغة *tablighat*) Ropes which communicate with the water-drawer, and the rope of the water-bucket.

A تباله *tabāluh*, (v. n. 6 of بله) Feigning ignorance or simplicity, pretending to be ابله *ablah*.

A تبًّا له *tabban lahu*, May he perish!

A تبالي *tabālī*, A proving, trying, assaying.

A تبّان *tabbān*, A dealer in straw. *Tubbān*, (pl. تبابين *tabābīn*) Short sailors'-breeches.

A تبانة *tabānat*, (v. n. of تبن) Looking steadily. Being intelligent and penetrating.

P تبانچه *tabāncha*, A box, blow, slap. Sort of food.

A تباوء *tabāwuʼ*, An equalling one of another.

A تبائس *tabāʼus*, (v. n. 6 of بؤس) Being mutually poor. Pleading poverty, abasing one's self.

A تباوس *tabāwus*, A kissing one another.

A تباوش *tabāwush*, (v. n. 6 of باش for بوش) Taking, receiving (food).

P تباه *tabāh*, Bad, wicked. Spoiled, ruined, destroyed, laid waste. Useless, incapable of being turned to account. Rotten (nut). Stinking, bad (egg). A divider, distributor. تباه كردن *tabāh kardan*, To kill, destroy, corrupt, spoil, taint, infect. تباه شدن *tabāh shudan*, To be spoiled or rotten. وضع تباه *wazʻi tabāh*, A wicked act.

A تباهث *tabāhus*, (v. n. 6 of بهث) Receiving with an open countenance, expressive of pleasure and satisfaction.

A تباهج *tabāhuj*, (v. n. 6 of بهج) Blooming, blossoming (a garden).

P تباهچه *tabāhcha*, Meat stewed down.

P تباه دست *tabāh-dast*, One who has a withered, shrivelled, or palsied hand.

A تباهش *tabāhush*, A contending greedily for.

P تباه كار *tabāh-kār*, Destroyer, corrupter; corrupt.

A تباهل *tabāhul*, (v. n. 6 of بهل) Cursing, execrating one another.

P تباهه *tabāha*, Stewed meat. A light kind of food made of the egg-plant, with a preparation of sour milk and herbs. Eggs, dressed with meat, vinegar, pepper, and pulse.

P تباهي *tabāhī*, Destroyed, lost, never come to perfection. Discord. تباهي كردن *tabāhī kardan*, To corrupt.

A تباهي *tabāhī*, (v. n. 6 of بهي) Contending for pre-eminence. Glorying against one another.

P تباهيدن *tabāhīdan*, To rot, corrupt, spoil.

P تباهي زده *tabāhī-zada*, Ruined. Afflicted.

P تبايانيدن *tabāyānīdan*, To cause to tremble. To bore. To warm with a fire.

A تبائع *tabāʼiʻ*, (pl. of تبيع) Yearling calves.

A تبايع *tabāyuʻ*, (v. n. 6 of باع for بيع) Selling from one to another. Dealing, trafficking, bartering, contracting, bargaining.

A تباين *tabāyun*, (v. n. 6 of بان for بين) Being separate, distinct from each other. Parting. Going away. Difference. Opposition, contradiction. (in arithmetic) The not having any common divisor except unity; incommensurability.

A تبب *tabab*, Loss. Death. Destruction.

P تب باده *tab-bāda*, The trembling, shivering paroxysm or periodical fit of a fever.

A تبّة *tibbat*, An afflicted condition.

P تبت *tibit*, Soft goat's hair, from which the finest shawls are made.

P تبّت *tibbat* or *tubbat*, Tibet in Tartary, whence comes the finest musk.

A تبتبة *tabtabat*, A growing old.

A تبتّت *tabattut*, (v. n. 5 of بتّ) Being provided with necessaries for a journey. Using, enjoying, deriving advantage.

A تبتّك *tabattuk*, The being cut off.

A تبتّل *tabattul*, (v. n. 5 of بتل) Withdrawing from the world and devoting one's self to God. Being cut, divided, separated. Being separate from, and independent of, the parent tree (a sucker).

P تبّتي *tibbatī* or *tibtī*, Musk, or any thing belonging to Tibet.

A تبتيت *tabtīt*, (v. n. 2 of بتّ) Providing with travelling necessaries.

A تبتيك *tabtīk*, (v. n. 2 of بتك) Cutting off (sheep's ears). Cutting off with violence.

A تبتيل *tabtīl*, (v. n. 2 of بتل) Retiring from the world, to dedicate one's self to religious duties. Cutting, dividing.

A تبثاق *tabsāk*, (v. n. of بثق) Breaking down a river's bank that the waters may overflow.

A تبثيث *tabsīs*, A dispersing, scattering.

A تبثير *tabsīr*, (v. n. 2 of بثر) Causing pustules to break out on the skin.

A تبثيع *tabsīʻ*, (v. n. 2 of بثع) Swelling with blood (a wound).

A تبثيق *tabsīk*, (v. n. 2 of بثق) Breaking down (a river's bank) to allow the water to overflow.

A تبجبج *tabajbuj*, (v. n. 2 of بجبج Q) Being abundant and flabby (flesh on a man).

A تبجّح *tabajjuh*, (v. n. 5 of بجح) Rejoicing, being overjoyed. Glorying. Displaying greatness.

A تبجّر *tabajjur*, (v. n. 5 of بجر) Sticking to the bottle, not giving over drinking.

A تبجّس *tabajjus*, (v. n. 5 of بجس) Being set a flowing (water).

A تبجيح *tabjīh*, (v. n. 2 of بجح) Exhilarating, giving joy. Honouring, esteeming great.

A تبجيد *tabjīd*, (v. n. 2 of بجد) Abiding.

A تبجيس *tabjīs*, (v. n. 2 of بجس) Causing (water) to burst forth, setting (it) a flowing. Opening (a sore).

A تبجيل *tabjīl*, (v. n. 2 of بجل) Extolling, magnifying. Saying to any one, "You have sufficient." على وجه التبجيل *ʻala' wajhi't tabjīl*, In a respectful manner. P تبجيل كردن *tabjīl kardan*, To honour, revere, esteem.

A تبجيلات *tabjīlāt*, Ceremonies.

A تبجيم *tabjīm*, (v. n. 2 of بجم) Delaying, proceeding slowly. Contracting one's self. Looking intently.

A تبحبح *tabahbuh*, (v. n. 2 of بحبح Q) Alighting at a place, settling, taking up one's abode. Occupying the middle of a house. Raining extensively.

A تبحتر *tabahtur*, (v. n. 2 of بحتر Q) Being allied or claiming affinity to the tribe of بحتر *buhtur*.

A تبحّث *tabahhus*, (v. n. 5 of بحث) Investigating, inquiring, examining.

A تبحثر *tabahsur*, A being separated, scattered.

A تبحّر *tabahhur*, (v. n. 5 of بحر) Penetrating in the depths (of science). Being profoundly learned. Abounding, rolling in riches. (by those living in Egypt) Going towards the sea, *i.e.* towards the north.

A تبحلس *tabahlus*, A coming empty.

A تبحيح *tabhīh*, (v. n. 2 of بحّ) Dwelling (in a place).

P تبخال *tab-khāl*, Pustules breaking out upon the lips after a fever. Fever-heat.

P تبخاله *tab-khāla*, Pustules breaking out upon the lips after a fever. The thrush. Air-bubbles in a glass full of wine.

A تبخبخ *tabahhbuhh*, (v. n. 2 of بخبخ Q) Subsiding (heat, anger). Resting, reposing (sheep).

A تبختر *tabakhtur*, (v. n. 2 of بختر Q) Walking very stately. A pompous, stately, jaunty, or graceful carriage.

A تبخترية *tabakhtarīyat*, A pompous gait.

A تبخثر *tabakhsur*, A being scattered, dispersed.

A تبخدجة *tabakhdajat*, A manner of walking with the toes turning in and the heels turning out. A pigeon-toed gait.

A تبخّر *tabakhkhur*, (v. n. 5 of بخر) Perfuming one's self. Fumigation.

A تبخّس *tabakhkhus*, (v. n. 5 of بخس) Drying (marrow in a bone).

A تبخّص *tabakhkhus*, (v. n. 5 of بخص) Seeing clearly, looking steadfastly. Being turned up (the eyelashes).

A تبخضل *tabakhzul*, (or تبخلص *tabakhlus*) Thickness and plenteousness (of flesh).

A تبخيت *tabkhīt*, (v. n. 2 of بخت) Silencing.

A تبخير *tabkhīr*, (v. n. 2 of بخر) Perfuming. Raising a smoke. Fumigation. Causing the breath to smell offensively.

A تبخيس *tabkhīs,* (v. n. 2 of بخس) Drying (marrow in a bone).

A تبخيل *tabkhīl,* (v. n. 2 of بخل) Esteeming, or calling one a miser (بخيل *bakhīl*).

P تبد *tibid,* Soft goat's hair.

A تبدّح *tabadduh,* (v. n. 5 of بدح) Walking gracefully (a woman).

A تبدّخ *tabadduhh,* (v. n. 5 of بدخ) Being proud, arrogant, haughty.

A تبدّد *tabaddud,* (v. n. 5 of بدّ) Being dispersed, scattered. Dividing amongst themselves by lots. Covering the entire bosom of a girl (ornaments).

A تبدّع *tabadduʿ,* (v. n. 5 of بدع) Turning, changing, becoming a propagator of something new.

A تبدّل *tabaddul,* (v.n. 5 of بدل) Being changed. Receiving one (thing) in the stead of another.

A تبدّلات *tabaddulāt,* Permutations.

A تبدّي *tabaddī,* (v. n. 5 of بدا for بدو) Abiding in the desert (بادية *bādiyat*).

A تبديد *tabdīd,* (v. n. 2 of بدّ) Scattering, wasting. Being tired and dozing in a sitting posture.

A تبديع *tabdīʿ,* (v. n. 2 of بدع) Calling one مبتدع *mubtadiʿ,* innovator or propagator of new opinions. Regarding as a novelty.

A تبديل *tabdīl,* (v. n. 2 of بدل) Changing, altering, substituting, transposing. Inversion. قابل تبديل *kābili tabdīl,* Reversible.

A تبديلاً *tabdīlan,* (P تبديلانه) In disguise.

A تبديلات *tabdīlāt,* Ministerial changes.

A تبدين *tabdīn,* (v. n. 2 of بدن) Growing old. Becoming feeble. Casing, clothing (another) in a coat of mail.

A تبذار *tibzār,* A scatterer of words, babbler.

A تبذارة *tibzārat,* A prodigal, spendthrift.

A تبذّح *tabazzuh,* (v. n. 5 of بذح) Raining.

A تبذّخ *tabazzukh,* (v. n. 5 of بذخ) Becoming proud, playing the great man. Being high, elated.

A تبذّر *tabazzur,* (v. n. 5 of بذر) Becoming yellow, and bad-tasted (water).

A تبذّل *tabazzul,* (v. n. 5 of بذل) Taking no care of one's clothes, wearing them every day. Being lavish of one's strength.

A تبذير *tabzīr,* (v. n. 2 of بذر) Sowing, scattering seed. Disseminating, scattering. Dissipating, spending prodigally. Revealing, blabbing (a secret). Trying, proving.

A تبذيع *tabzīʿ,* (v. n. 2 of بذع) Terrifying.

A تبر *tabara,* (fut. يتبر *yatbiru*) He brake.

A تبر *tabr,* A breaking. Ruin, destruction, perdition. *Tibr,* (pl. تبور *tubūr*) Gold or silver just from the mine, before it has felt the fire or the hammer. Fragments or particles of gold or glass. Any particle of brass or copper which can be made available. بلاد التبر *bilādu't tibr,* The country of gold or gold-dust, that part of Africa called the Gold Coast. *Tabar,* (v. n. of تبر) Perishing.

P تبر *tabar,* A hatchet, axe, or mattock. *Tibir,* Name of a bird.

A تبراك *tabrāk,* (v. n. of برك) Kneeling.

A تبرأل *tabarʾul,* (v. n. 2 of برأل Q) Ruffling its feathers (a bird preparing to fight). Putting (himself) in an attitude of defence.

A تبربس *tabarbus,* (v. n. 2 of بربس Q) Running like a dog, tripping lightly.

A تبرة *tibrat,* A bit of native gold or silver.

A تبرّج *tabarruj,* (v. n. 5 of برج) (A woman) dressing in order to shew herself (to men). Ostentatious decoration.

P تبرخون *tabar-khūn,* The jujube-tree, and fruit. A kind of willow. Brazilian wood. Tarragon. A club.

A تبرّد *tabarrud,* (v. n. 5 of برد) Washing or steeping in cold water. Being collected.

P تبردار *tabar-dār,* A hatchet-man, pioneer.

A تبرّر *tabarrur,* (v. n. 5 of برر) Being godly, devout. Being dutiful to parents.

A تبرّز *tabarruz,* (v. n. 5 of برز) Appearing, coming forth. Being published. Walking into the fields (to ease nature).

P تبرزد *tabar-zad,* Rock-salt. White sugar. The aloe. A kind of grape.

P تبرزن *tabar-zan,* Striking with a hatchet; a wood-cutter.

P تبرزه *tabarza,* Rock-salt. A sort of grape. White sugar. The aloe.

P تبرزين *tabar-zīn,* A battle-axe (usually fixed to the saddle). Rock-salt.

P تبرستان *tabaristān,* The ancient Hyrcania.

A تبرّص *tabarrus,* (v. n. 5 of برص) Grazing (a field) so closely as to leave no herbage.

A تبرّض *tabarruz,* (v. n. 5 of برض) Receiving (any thing) by little and little. Earning a scanty livelihood. Living poorly.

A تبرطل *tabartul,* (v. n. 2 of برطل Q) Taking a bribe (a judge).

A تبرطم *tabartum,* A swelling with rage.

A تبرّع *tabarruʿ,* (v. n. 5 of برع) Doing voluntarily what one is not obliged to do: giving gratis.

A تبرّعا *tabarruʿan,* (P تبرّعانه) Gratuitously.

A تبرعص *tabarʿus,* (v. n. 2 of برعص Q not used) Being disturbed, troubled. Writhing. The motion of a serpent.

A تبرعم *tabarʿum,* The budding (of a tree).

A تبرغص *tabarghus,* (v. n. 2 of برغص Q) Being disturbed, troubled. Trembling. (The) convulsive motion (of an amputated limb).

A تبرّق *tabarruk,* (v. n. 5 of برق) Decorating (herself), setting (herself) off (a woman).

A تبرقش *tabarkush,* (v. n. 2 of برقش Q) Being dressed, painted, or formed of motley colours.

A تبرقط *tabarkut,* (v. n. 2 of برقط Q) Falling on the back of one's head. Pasturing to and fro.

A تبرقع *tabarkuʿ,* The being veiled.

P تبرك *tabrak,* A flat dish. A table (especially with a high rim or border). The top of a drum. Sieves. Fruit-baskets. A fort. The castle of Isfahān.

A تبرّك *tabarruk,* (v. n. 5 of برك) Imploring the divine blessing. Blessing. Praising. Succeeding, prospering by the blessing of God. Taking a good omen, auguring well from. Abundance, plenty. A portion of presents (or of what is left of food presented to great men) given to their dependants. Sacred relics. تبرّكا و تيمّنا *tabarrukan wa tayammunan,* With the blessing and favourable auspices of God. In a happy hour. God be praised!

A تبرّكات *tabarrukāt,* (pl. of تبرّك) Benedictions. Plenty. Offices, honours, dignities.

A تبركة *tabrakat,* (v. n. of تبرك Q) Staying.

A تبركع *tabarkuʿ,* (v. n. 2 of بركع Q) Being thrown prostrate. Falling on the buttocks, or back.

A تبرّكي *tabarrukī,* A compliment.

P تبركيدن *tabarkīdan,* To slit the hoof or nail.

P تبرگون *tabar-gūn,* Hollow-backed (horse).

P تبرلگام *tabar-ligām,* A rein, bridle, bit.

P تبرم *tabram,* A great lady, a matron.

A تبرّم *tabarrum,* (v. n. 5 of برم) Being sated, wearied, disgusted.

A تبرنس *tabarnus,* (v. n. 2 of برنس Q) Wearing the high-crowned cap called برنس *burnus.*

A تبرّؤ *tabarruʾ,* (v. n. 5 of برأ) Being acquitted, cleared, absolved. Being free (from crimes).

A تبرّي *tabarrī,* (v. n. 5 of بري) Opposing, hindering, obstructing. Acquittal, justification.

A تبرئة *tabriʾat,* (v. n. 2 of برأ) Absolving (from a fault). Acquitting, setting at liberty. Healing.

A تبرية *tibriyat,* Scales or scurf on the head.

A تبريج *tabrīj,* (v. n. 2 of برج) Making a display of (his) merit (a man); also of (her) attire (a woman). Building a tower (برج *burj*).

A تبريح *tabrīh,* (v. n. 2 of برح) Injuring, vexing. Using cruelty in putting an animal to death (as throwing a fish on the fire alive).

A تبريخ *tabrīkh,* (v. n. 2 of برخ not used) Humbling one's self, submitting.

A تبريد *tabrīd,* (v. n. 2 of برد) Cooling, allowing, leaving to cool. Refreshing. Mixing with snow. Giving cold water to drink. Weakening.

A تبرير *tabrīr,* (v. n. 2 of برر) Overcoming, oppressing, subduing by word or deed. Justifying, declaring innocent. Any thing, somewhat.

P تبريز *tabrīz* or *tibrīz,* The capital of Azarbayjān (Media). *Tibrīz,* A table, a round piece of leather on which they lay victuals. A sofa, bench.

A تبريز *tabrīz,* (v. n. 2 of برز) Causing to come forth. Calling forth, challenging. Bringing to view, shewing openly. Being superior to, excelling. Excelling in swiftness (a horse), winning a race, saving his rider.

A تبريس *tabrīs,* A softening (ground) for culture.

A تبريص *tabrīs,* (v. n. 2 of برص) Shaving the

head. Raining on the ground before it is ploughed.

A تبريض *tabrīz*, (v. n. 2 of برض) Producing young grass just sprouting above ground.

A تبريق *tabrīk*, (v. n. 2 of برق) Opening the eyes, and keeping them fixed upon an object. Adorning herself (a woman). Travelling afar off. Decorating (one's house), giving (it) a brilliant appearance. Plunging into crimes. Being difficult, troublesome, impeded (business).

A تبريك *tabrīk*, (v. n. 2 of برك) Giving a blessing, pronouncing a blessing, congratulating, wishing joy. Imploring a blessing. Kneeling (a camel).

P تب زده *tab-zada*, Attacked by fever.

A تبزر *tabazzur*, (v. n. 5 of بزر) Belonging to the tribe of بزري *bazara'*.

A تبزع *tabazzuع*, (v. n. 5 of بزع) Being elegant, polished in (his) manners (a young man). Inspiring terror. Increasing, abounding. Being important (an affair).

A تبزعر *tabazعur*, (v. n. 2 of بزعر Q) Being of a harsh, disagreeable temper.

A تبزق *tabazzuk*, (v. n. 5 of بزق) Spitting.

A تبزل *tabazzul*, (v. n. 5 of بزل) Being cloven, split. Tapping (a barrel), drawing off wine.

A تبزلة *tibzilat*, (or تبزّلة *tibzillat*) Dwarfish (man).

A تبزيج *tabzīj*, (v. n. 2 of بزج) Adorning, beautifying. Doing well or handsomely.

A تبزيخ *tabzīkh*, (v. n. 2 of بزخ) Humbling one's self. Submitting.

A تبزيغ *tabzīgh*, A bleeding, breathing a vein.

A تبزيل *tabzīl*, A cleaving, a splitting.

A تبسبس *tabasbus*, The flowing of water.

P تبست *tabast*, Ruined, spoiled. Annihilated. Ugly. *Tabist*, Religion, sect, rite. Weak.

P تبستغ *tabastugh*, Eloquent, rhetorical.

A تبسّر *tabassur*, (v. n. 5 of بسر) Being cold (a day). Devouring the dry roots of plants from a ditch (a bull). Inquiring diligently into. Being torpid and asleep (the foot). Asking for any thing unseasonably.

A تبسّط *tabassut*, (v. n. 5 of بسط) Being extended far and wide. Ranging at large over length and breadth.

A تبسّق *tabassuk*, A being long and tall.

A تبسّل *tabassul*, (v. n. 5 of بسل) Contracting the visage, scowling from anger or any other cause. Being hideous and repulsive (the countenance). Being shunned and avoided.

A تبسّم *tabassum*, (v. n. 5 of بسم) Smiling. Shining, flashing (lightning). A smile, simper.

P تبسيدن *tabsīdan*, To have the lips cracked with heat, to be fainting or uneasy in sultry weather.

A تبسيط *tabsīt*, (v. n. 2 of بسط) Spreading out.

A تبسيق *tabsīk*, (v. n. 2 of بسق) Favouring, benefiting, conferring an obligation.

A تبسيل *tabsīl*, An abhorring, loathing, detesting.

P تبش *tabish*, Heat, warmth. Fire. Light.

A تبشبش *tabashbush*, (v. n. 2 of بشبش Q) Manifesting gladness. A manifestation of the divine favour and good will.

A تبشّر *tubushshir*, A kind of bird.

A تبشّش *tabashshush*, (v. n. 5 of بشّ) Being of an open, cheerful, smiling countenance.

P تبشي *tabshī*, A dish with a rim made of gold, silver, or brass.

P تبشير *tabshīr*, Clay, fuller's earth, plaster.

A تبشير *tabshīr*, (v. n. 2 of بشر) Communicating news, (good or bad), preaching.

A تبشيط *tabshīt*, A making haste. A hastening.

A تبصبص *tabasbus*, (v. n. 2 of بصبص Q) Wagging the tail. Caressing, flattering, blandishing.

A تبصّر *tabassur*, (v. n. 5 of بصر) Descrying, considering with attention, contemplating, understanding, perceiving. P تبصّر دادن, To give attention.

A تبصّص *tabassus*, A shining, a flashing.

A تبصّع *tabassuع*, (v. n. 5 of بصع) Flowing from the roots of the hair (sweat).

A تبصّل *tabassul*, (v. n. 5 of بصل) Being constituted like an onion, coat upon coat (bark). Stripping. Exhausting, draining by frequent asking.

A تبصية *tabsiyat*, (v. n. 2 of بصو) Castrating.

A تبصير *tabsīr*, (v. n. 2 of بصر) Rendering quick-sighted, intelligent. Shewing, demonstrating, declaring, making evident. Opening its eyes (a whelp). Going to Basrah. Cutting. Dissecting every joint. Beheading.

A تبصيص *tabsīs*, (v. n. 2 of بصّ) Opening its eyes (a whelp). Flattering, wheedling. Bringing forth its earliest produce (ground).

A تبصيل *tabsīl*, The peeling, barking (of a tree).

A تبضبض *tabazbuz*, (v. n. 2 of بضبض Q) Living delicately and luxuriously.

A تبضّض *tabazzuz*, (v. n. 5 of بضض) Recovering (a debt) by degrees. Taking away the whole of any one's property.

A تبضّع *tabazzuع*, (v. n. 5 of بضع) Flowing from the roots of the hair (sweat). Sweating (the forehead).

A تبضيض *tabzīz*, (v. n. 2 of بضّ) Enjoying in abundance the conveniences of life.

A تبضيع *tabzīع*, (v. n. 2 of بضع) Cutting. Declaring, making clear.

A تبطّح *tabattuh*, (v. n. 5 of بطح) Diffusing itself over a low-lying gravelly plain (a torrent).

A تبطرق *tabatruk*, The walk of a fine stallion or of a chaste woman.

A تبطّش *tabattush*, (v. n. 5 of بطش) Being tired and unable to wag.

A تبطّل *tabattul*, (v. n. 5 of بطل) Bandying to and fro vanity, folly, and lies. Being bold and courageous. Being removed, stopped. Folly, jest.

A تبطّن *tabattun*, (v. n. 5 of بطن) Placing under the belly. Lining (a female). Penetrating into the heart or inner part of any thing. Walking through the middle of a garden or field.

A تبطئة *tabtiat*, A retarding, a delaying.

A تبطيح *tabtīh*, A strewing with gravel.

A تبطيط *tabtīt*, (v. n. 2 of بطّ) Trading in ducks and geese (بطّ *batt*). Tiring, fatiguing.

A تبطين *tabtīn*, (v. n. 2 of بطن) Lining (a garment). Striking on the belly. Girthing (a beast). Entertaining inwardly. Shaving under the chin.

A تبظير *tabzīr*, (v. n. 2 of بظر) Circumcising a girl. Bidding (one) suck a clitoris (بظر *bazr*).

A تبع *tibع*, A suitor, wooer, lover. *Tabaع*, (v. n. of تبع) Following. Pursuing. Attending, accompanying. (pl. اتباع *atbāع*) A follower. The foot of a quadruped. Followers. Studious (people), carefully searching for any thing. Familiar spirits, supposed to accompany men wherever they go. *Tubaع*, One who pursues an oration, and connects one part with another, or rather who employs double words: as, حسن بسن *hasan basan*, قبيح شقيح *kabīh shakīh*.

A تبّع *tubbaع*, (pl. تبابعة *tabābiعat*) The surname of the kings of Yaman. The star Aldebarān. (pl. تبابيع *tabābīع*) The queen-bee (as having a number of subjects). *Tubbaع* or *tubbuع*, A shadow (as attending the sun). A kind of bird. ما ادري ايّ تبّع هو *mā adrī ayyu tubbaع huwa*, I know not who he is.

A تبعة *tabiعat*, Punishment, torture. Bad end.

A تبعّث *tabaععus*, (v. n. 5 of بعث) Flowing (from one, a poem).

A تبعثر *tabaعsur*, (v. n. 2 of بعثر Q) Being disturbed (the mind).

A تبعثق *tabaعsuk*, (v. n. 2 of بعثق Q) Leaking through a crack (water in a cistern).

A تبعّج *tabaععuj*, (v. n. 5 of بعج) Being scattered (clouds after rain).

A تبعّد *tabaععud*, A going to a distance.

A تبعصص *tabaعsus*, (v. n. 2 of بعصص Q) Being agitated, disturbed. Writhing (as a snake when crushed beneath the feet).

A تبعّض *tabaععuz*, A being divided into parts.

A تبعضض *tabaعzuz*, (v. n. 2 of بعضض Q) Receiving, taking, carrying off one another.

A تبعّق *tabaععuk*, (v. n. 5 of بعق) Coming down suddenly on one. Being diffuse in speaking. Raining.

A تبعّل *tabaععul*, (v. n. 5 of بعل) Obeying (a husband بعل *baعl*), or adorning herself for him.

A تبعي *tabعa'*, (A cow) following the bull.

A تبعيّ *tabaعiy*, Dependent, secondary.

A تبعيّة *tabعiyat*, A following, imitating, obeying.

A تبعيج *tabعīj*, A cutting open.

A تبعيد *tabعīd*, (v. n. 2 of بعد) Removing, sending to a distance, causing to go far off.

A تبعير *tabعīr*, (v. n. 2 of بعر) Purging the intestines, voiding the dung (بعر *baعr*).

A تبعيض *tabعīz*, (v. n. 2 of بعض) Parting, dividing into portions. Partage, participation.

A تبلّل *taballul*, (v. n. 5 of بلّ) Being moistened. Recovering health. Tearing the ground (a lion).

P تبلونستن *tablūnistan*, (zand and Pāz.) To break.

A تبلّه *taballuh*, (v. n. 5 of بله) Behaving simply, meaning well. Feigning ignorance or simplicity. Seeking for a strayed thing. Straying without a guide, or inquiring the way.

A تبلهص *tabalhus*, (v. n. 2 of بلهص Q) Pulling off clothes, undressing.

A تبلية *tabliyat*, (v. n. 2 of بلي) Consuming. Tying a camel to the grave of her deceased master.

A تبليح *tablīh*, A failing. A being enfeebled.

A تبليد *tablīd*, (v. n. 2 of بلد) Throwing one's self upon the ground. Being careless, inattentive, or forgetful. Being covetous. Being without rain (clouds). Refusing to proceed (a horse).

A تبليص *tablīs*, (v. n. 2 of بلص) Receiving all, leaving nothing. Having little milk (sheep).

A تبليط *tablīt*, (v. n. 2 of بلط) Paving with stones. Being fatigued. Striking (the ear with the fore-finger, so as to cause pain).

A تبليع *tablīʻ*, (v. n. 2 of بلع) Beginning to appear (gray hair). Causing to swallow, pouring down the throat.

A تبليغ *tablīgh*, (v. n. 2 of بلغ) Causing to arrive. Conveying. Sending (letters or compliments). Relaxing the reins to induce a horse to quicken his pace.

A تبليق *tablīk*, (v. n. 2 of بلق) Strengthening with teak-planks the sides of a well in soft soil.

A تبليل *tablīl*, (v. n. 2 of بلّ) Making very wet, moistening well.

A تبليم *tablīm*, (v. n. 2 of بلم) Exposing a foul deed. Longing intensely for the male.

A تبن *tabn*, (v. n. of تبن) Feeding (cattle) with straw. Selling straw. *Tibn*, A noble, generous lord or master. A capacious bowl (for twenty men). A wolf. *Tibn* or *tabn*, (pl. اتبان *atbān* and تبون *tubūn*) Straw. تبن مكّي *tibni makkiy* An odoriferous bullrush. *Taban*, (v. n. of تبن) Looking attentively. Being intelligent, penetrating. *Tabin*, Sharp-sighted, intelligent. One whose fingers are toying with every thing.

P تبنا *tubnā*, (in zand and Pāzand) Straw.

P تبنان *tubnān*, Trowsers, long drawers.

A تبنة *tibnat*, A bit of straw, a single straw.

A تبنّج *tabannuj*, A pretending to a noble origin.

P تبند *taband*, Deceit, fraud. A cheat.

P تبندر *tabandar*, The bar of a door.

P تبنده *tabinda*, Shining, resplendent.

P تبنك *tabanh* or *tubnak*, A crucible. A mould.

A تبنّك *tabannuk*, (v. n. 5 of بنك) Remaining in one place. Being grand and pompous.

P تبنكه *tabanka*, A baker's tray. An oven.

P تبنگ *tabang*, A large green-grocer's tray. A loud, shrill sound. A drum.

P تبنگو *tabangū*, A wicker-basket: chest: canister. A barber's case of instruments. A money-till.

A تبكية *tabkiyat*, (v. n. 2 of بكي) Weeping, wailing, lamenting. Deploring, bewailing. Moving to tears. Causing to bewail.

A تبكيت *tabkīt*, (v. n. 2 of بكت) Terrifying (by threats). Rebuking, upbraiding. Silencing. Convincing by clear proofs. Offering or placing before any one that which he detests.

A تبكير *tabkīr*, (v. n. 2 of بكر) Arriving before prayer begins. Preceding, going before. Doing any thing before the ordinary time. Setting out before daybreak. Causing one to rise early and get the start of his companions.

A تبكيع *tabkīʻ*, (v. n. 2 of بكع) Cutting in pieces. Silencing.

P تب گرفته *tab-girifta*, Shaking with ague.

A تبل *tabl*, (v. n. of تبل) Weakening, making sick. Destroying the intellect. Afflicting, wasting, destroying. Seasoning with herbs and spices. (pl. تبول *tubūl* and تبابيل *tabābīl*) Hatred. (pl. اتبال *atbāl*) Sickness. *Tabil*, Destructive.

P تبل *tabal*, A wrinkle, fold, plait.

P تبلاب *tablāb*, The hull enclosing the date.

P تبلاد *tablād*, A wooden shore for a wall.

A تبلبل *tabalbul*, (v. n. 2 of بلبل Q) Being confounded (tongues). Eating up clean all before him.

A تبلتع *tabaltuʻ*, (v. n. 2 of بلتع Q) Discoursing with fluency and readiness. Making pretensions to be witty.

A تبلّج *taballuj*, (v. n. 5 of بلج) Dawning, breaking forth (the dawn)

A تبلّخ *taballukh*, A being proud, supercilious.

A تبلخص *tabalkhus*, A being thick and numerous.

A تبلّد *taballud*, (v. n. 5 of بلد) Shewing stupidity, dulness. Wringing the hands from grief. Turning the palms of the hands outwards. Clapping the hands together. Astonishment. Falling on the ground. Coming into an uninhabited region. Taking possession of another's country.

A تبلدح *tabalduh*, A breaking one's promise.

P تب لرزه *tab-larza*, The paroxysm of a fever. An ague-fit.

A تبلسم *tabalsum*, (v. n. 2 of بلسم Q) Keeping silence (from fear). Making an ugly face.

A تبلّص *taballus*, (v. n. 5 of بلص) Cropping a field quite bare (cattle). Causing (a field) to be eaten quite bare. Asking (any thing) privately. Coveting, desiring.

A تبلصق *tabalsuk*, (v. n. 2 of بلصق Q) Asking (any thing) privately, or by flattery or fraud. Studying to contract an alliance.

A تبلّغ *taballugh*, (v. n. 5 of بلغ) Striving to attain. Having enough. Being content. Growing worse (a disease).

A تبلغة *tablighat*, (pl. تبالغ *tabāligh*) A rope communicating with the hand of the drawer of water, and with the rope of the water-bucket.

A تبلّق *taballuk*, (v. n. 5 of بلق) Flashing.

A تبعيق *tabʻīk*, (v. n. 2 of بعق) Cleaving, dividing (any thing) and pouring out (its) contents. Cutting (a camel's) throat.

A تبغثر *tabaghsur*, (v. n. 2 of بغثر Q) Being in a disordered state (the mind).

A تبغدد *tabaghdud*, (v. n. 2 of بغدد Q) Being connected or related to Baghdād. Imitating the manners of the Baghdādians. Storming Baghdād.

A تبغدن *tabaghdun*, A going to Baghdād.

A تبغّض *tabaghghuz*, A showing of hatred.

A تبغّم *tabaghghum*, A crying aloud.

A تبغنج *tabaghnuj*, (v. n. 2 of بغنج Q) Using all the endearing words and attitudes of lovers.

A تبغّي *tabaghghī*, A searching, inquiring.

A تبغيض *tabghīz*, A rendering odious.

A تبغيل *tabghīl*, (v. n. 2 of بغل) Being dull, heavy, lazy, sluggish. Going at an easy pace (a camel). Marrying amongst strangers, and begetting a mongrel race (from بغل *baghl*, A mule).

P تبفوز *tabfoz*, The beak of a bird. The parts round the mouth or snout (of man or animal).

A تبقّر *tabakkur*, (v. n. 5 of بقر) Being profoundly learned. Abounding in wealth. Remaining in the city or village (whilst one's family continues in the field). Being open, wide, and spacious.

A تبقّط *tabakkut*, (v. n. 5 of بقط) Taking or picking up (news) by little and little.

A تبقّع *tabakkuʻ*, A being covered with spots.

A تبقّل *tabakkul*, (v. n. 5 of بقل) Eating vegetables or pot-herbs. Going out to cull pot-herbs. Having cattle feeding on pot-herbs (بقل *bakl*).

A تبقّم *tabakkum*, (v. n. 5 of بقم) Being heavy with young (a ewe).

A تبقّي *tabakkī*, (v. n. 5 of بقي) Reserving a residue. Preserving, keeping alive.

A تبقية *tabkiyat*, (v. n. 2 of بقي) Reserving a remainder. Preserving alive. Sparing.

A تبقير *tabkīr*, (v. n. 2 of بقر) Playing at a boy's game called بقيري *bukkayra'*.

A تبقيط *tabkīt*, (v. n. 2 of بقط obsol.) Ascending (a mountain). Being quick (in speech or step). Overcoming in argument. Scattering.

A تبقيع *tabkīʻ*, (v. n. 2 of بقع) Departing, going away. Dyeing (a garment) in patches.

A تبقيق *tabkīk*, (v. n. 2 of بقّ) Scattering, squandering (money).

A تبقيل *tabkīl*, (v. n. 2 of بقل) Ruling, governing. Sprouting (the beard of a youth).

A تبكاء *tabkāʼ* or *tibkāʼ*, Excessive weeping.

A تبكبك *tabakbuk*, A thronging, a crowding.

A تبكّر *tabakkur*, A preceding, going before.

A تبكّل *tabakkul*, (v. n. 5 of بكل) Speaking perplexedly, confusing one's self in relating any thing. Opposing, obstructing. Overwhelming one with blows or reproaches. Conquering. Carrying off plunder. Walking haughtily. Plunder, booty.

A تبكّم *tabakkum*, A pronouncing with difficulty.

P تبنگوي *tabangūy,* A baker's tray. A chest.

A تبنّن *tabannun,* (v. n. 5 of بنّ) Staying or being confined in a place.

A تبنّي *tabannī,* (v. n. 5 of بني) Adopting or calling one son. Resembling a house. Sitting squat, straddling through fatness, so as to resemble a tent.

A تبنية *tabniyat,* A building much and well.

A تبنيت *tabnīt,* (v. n. 2 of بنت not in use) Asking, inquiring diligently. Rebuking, upbraiding, silencing. Telling (another) all one knows.

A تبنيج *tabnīj,* (v. n. 2 of بنج) Giving (any one) henbane (بنج *banj*) to eat, drugging (any one) with it. Piping in its nest (a partridge).

A تبنيس *tabnīs,* A lagging, staying behind.

A تبنيش *tabnīsh,* A being slack, remiss.

A تبنيق *tabnīk,* (v. n. 2 بنق) Standing in one place. Drawing together and finishing off (a discourse). Inventing (a lie). Making raw (the back with a whip). Putting (any thing) round the neck. Enlarging (a shirt), making the opening of the breast. Making (a quiver) wideat top and narrow at bottom. Planting a single palm-shoot.

A تبنيك *tabnīk,* (v. n. 2 of بنك not in use) Meeting and telling one another what is said and done at home (as gossiping girls). Performing, concluding, finishing.

A تبنين *tabnīn,* (v. n. 2 of بنّ) Tying up a sheep to fatten. Name of a citadel near Ptolemais.

A تبو *tabw,* (v. n. of تبو) Fighting : plundering.

A تبوّء *tabawwuʼ,* (v. n. 5 of باء for بوأ) Taking possession of, settling, abiding, inhabiting. Obtaining (a wife).

A تبّوب *tabbūb,* A desert, or dangerous place. That which is encircled by the ribs.

A تبوّب *tabawwub,* (v. n. 5 of باب for بوب) Making, taking for a porter. Constructing a door.

A تبوت *tabūt,* An ark, chest. A bier.

A تبوّج *tabawwuj,* (v. n. 5 of باج for بوج) Flashing (lightning). Coruscation.

A تبوذك *tabūzak,* One who sells the livers or gizzards of fowls. Name of a place.

P تبوراك *tabūrāk,* A drum, tabor, tambourin. A drum beaten to drive away the birds. A baker's or green-grocer's tray. A sieve, searce. A robust, handsome youth.

A تبوّش *tabawwush,* (v. n. 5 of باش for بوش) Being mixed together (men).

A تبوّط *tabawwut,* (v. n. 5 of باط not used) Lying on the side. Being in ease and affluence. Being averse, disliking.

A تبوّع *tabawwuʻ,* (v. n. 5 of باع for بوع) Being measured with a pole or perch. Measuring with a fathom. Making wide steps. Being long (a rope). The end or bottom of any thing.

A تبوّع الشمس *tabbūʻu'sh shams,* The wind of the sun (which blows in some countries from the east at sunrise, and follows the sun in his course through every point of the compass).

A تبوّغ *tabawwugh,* (v. n. 5 of باغ for بوغ) Boiling (blood). Conquering.

A تبوّق *tabawwuk,* (v. n. 5 of باق for بوق) Attacking the flock (a destructive murrain).

P تبوك *tabūk,* A large platter, tray, dish.

A تبوك *tabūk,* A place situated on the road from Syria to Madīna.

A تبوكيّ *tabūkiy,* A kind of grape.

A تبول *tubūl,* (pl. of تبل *tabl*) Hatreds. Enmities. Sicknesses.

A تبوّل *tabawwul,* (v. n. 5 of بال for بول) Making water. Receiving one with blows and abuse.

A تبوّن *tabaʼʼun,* A tracking, a tracing.

A تبويب *tabwīb,* (v. n. 2 of باب for بوب) Making a door. Dividing (a book) into chapters.

A تبوئة *tabwiʼat,* (v. n. 2 of باء for بوأ) Bringing back. Preparing a habitation. Receiving hospitably. Coming to a place (intending there to dwell). Levelling (a spear at any one).

A تبويج *tabwīj,* The flashing (of lightning).

A تبويش *tabwīsh,* (v. n. 2 of باش for بوش) Being mixed, jumbled together. Collecting people.

A تبويص *tabwīs,* (v. n. 2 of باص for بوص) Bearing the fruit called بوص *būs.* Being large, protuberant (the hips). Taking the lead in a race, outstripping. Being clear, transparent (colour).

A تبويل *tabwīl,* (v. n. 2 of بال for بول) Staling, pissing. Watering with urine.

A تبويئ *tabwīʼ,* (v. n. 2 of باء for بوأ) Lying with. Receiving hospitably.

P تبه *tabah,* Savoury meat, delicately dressed. Spoiled, destroyed. A divider, distributor.

A تبهبه *tabahbuh,* (v. n. 2 of بهبه Q) Being honoured, renowned, made much of. Being haughty.

A تبهّر *tabahhur,* (v. n. 5 of بهر) Being filled. Being bright (a cloud).

P تبه رأي *tabah-raʼy,* Of a depraved mind.

A تبهرس *tabahrus,* A strutting, looking big.

A تبهرم *tabahrum,* Redness, sandiness of hair.

P تبهره *tabahra,* Savoury meat stewed.

A تبهّش *tabahhush,* An assembling, meeting.

P تبه كار *tabah-kār,* A criminal, offender.

A تبهكن *tabahkun,* (v. n. 2 of بهكن Q) Being fresh and full of vigour (a woman).

A تبهّل *tabahhul,* (v. n. 5 of بهل) Cursing, wishing evil to one another. Independence, ability to do without.

A تبهلس *tabahlus,* (v. n. 2 of بهلس Q) Coming from any quarter naked and destitute of every thing.

A تبهلص *tabahlus,* (v. n. 2 of بهلص Q) Pulling off clothes, undressing.

A تبهلق *tabahluk,* The telling a lie : a lie.

A تبهلل *tabahlul,* (v. n. 2 of بهلل Q) Laughing.

A تبهّم *tabahhum,* (v. n. 5 of بهم) Being doubtful, obscure, and unintelligible. Being concealed.

A تبهنس *tabahnus,* A walking with a strut.

A تبهية *tabhiyat,* (v. n. 2 of بهي) Enlarging, widening (a tent).

A تبهيج *tabhīj,* (v. n. 2 of بهج) Beautifying.

A تبهيم *tabhīm,* (v. n. 2 of بهم) Weaning. Staying in a place.

A تبّيّ *tabbiy,* A sort of date.

P تبيازه *tabyāza,* A fever, caused by an enlargement of the spleen.

A تبيان *tibyān* or *tabyān,* (v. n. of بان for بين) Appearing distinct. Making clear. A declaration, a manifesto.

A تبيب *tabīb,* Harm. Death : destruction.

A تبيّت *tabayyut,* (v. n. 5 of بات for بيت) Diverting (one) from (his) purpose.

P تبير *tabīr,* (or تبيره *tabīra*) A drum, a kettle-drum. A mixen, dunghill.

A تبيزلة *tubayzilat,* Short, dwarfish (man).

A تبيع *tabīʻ,* (fem. تبيعة *tabīʻat*) A follower. (pl. تباع *tibāʻ* and تبائع *tabāʼiʻ*) A calf one year old still following the mother. A debtor. The bull's eye, the star Ad'dabarān. A defender, an assistant. Diligently searching, urgently asking.

A تبيّغ *tabayyugh,* (v. n. 5 of باغ for بيغ) Being intricate, perplexed, confused (business). Overcoming. Being in a boiling and inflammable state (blood). Bubbling up (water). Abounding (milk).

A تبيقر *tabaykur,* (v. n. 2 of بيقر Q) Being wide, ample, and spacious.

A تبيّن *tabayyun,* (v. n. 5 of بان for بين) Being distinct, becoming manifest, plain, and clear. Making clear. Making known. Desiring explanation. Slowness, caution.

A تبيّؤ *tabayyuʼ,* A purposing, resolving upon.

A تبيهس *tabayhus,* (v. n. 2 of بيهس Q) Walking pompously. جاء يتبيهس *jāʼa yatabayhasu,* He came with nothing.

A تبيّي *tabayyī,* (v. n. 5 of بيّ) Purposing, designing. Putting (a sword) into the scabbard.

A تبيئة *tabyiʼat,* An explaining, expounding.

A تبيية *tabyiyat,* (v. n. 2 of بيّ) Making laugh. Bringing near, giving access. Making manifest.

A تبييت *tabyīt,* (v. n. 2 of بات for بيت) Invading or surprising (an enemy) in the night-time. Keeping (one) back from (his) purpose. Doing any thing at night, conversing, meditating, lucubrating. Barking (a palm-tree).

A تبيّئ *tabʼīj,* A changing. A shouting.

A تبييح *tabyīh,* (v. n. 2 of باح for بيح) Cutting, dividing (meat) into small portions. Entrusting with a secret.

A تبييش *tabyīsh,* (v. n. 2 of بيش not in use) (God) making any one of a fair countenance.

A تبييض *tabyīz,* (v. n. 2 of باض for بيض) Making white, bleaching. Writing out fair : a fair copy. Filling (a vessel) with milk and water. Evacuating, emptying. Losing its prickles (the plant بهمي *buhma'*).

A تبييغ *tabyīgh*, (v. n. 2 of باغ for بيغ) Remaining behind, or being alone.

A تبيين *tabyīn*, (v. n. 2 of بان for بين) Separating. Giving (a daughter) in marriage. Illustrating, declaring, making clear. Making known. Appearing evident. Budding, shooting forth (a horn, a plant). Explication, elucidation.

P تپ *tap*, Fever, heat, ardour. Perturbation, disquietude, restlessness. تپ دق *tapi dikh*, A hectic fever, consumption.

P تپاك *tapāk*, Uneasiness, restlessness.

P تپانچه *tapāncha*, A blow, box. A billow, wave.

P تپايانيدن *tapāyānīdan*, To cause to tremble.

P تپره *tapra*, A kettle-drum.

H تپره *tapra*, The country Tiparah in India.

P تپره زن *tapra-zan*, Who beats the kettle-drum.

P تپش *tapish*, A swoon, fainting-fit from heat.

P تپ گرفته *tap-girifta*, Feverish.

P تپناك *tapnāk*, Feverish (place).

P تپنچه *tapancha*, A box, a slap.

P تپنگ *tapang*, A large green-grocer's tray. *Tupang*, A crucible, a mould.

P تپنگو *tapangū*, A chest. A casket. A case for a barber's instruments. A granary, magazine. A till. A crucible.

P تپه *tappa*, A high hill. Frontlet of pearls.

P تپيدن *tapīdan*, To be in great agitation. To grow hot. To totter, leap or spring. To stumble. To palpitate, be restless, uneasy (from indisposition). To lay a snare.

A تتاءن *tatā,un*, (v. n. 6 of تأن not used) Coming now from this side, and now from that. Fraud, deceit, trick.

A تتابع *tatābuʿ*, A following in succession.

P تتار *tatār*, A Tartar. Tartary.

P تتارچه *tatārcha*, A kind of arrow, or dart.

A تتارك *tatāruk*, (v. n. 6 of ترك) Quitting, leaving off (business).

P تتاري *tatārī*, Tartarian. Scythian.

A تتافل *tatāfil*, (pl. of تتفل) Foxes. Foxes' cubs.

A تتالع *tatāluʿ*, A walking erect (from pride).

A تتالي *tatālī*, (v. n. 6 of تلا for تلو) Following in continued succession.

A تتامّ *tatāmm*, (v. n. 6 of تمّ) Being finished, completed. Coming and drinking (the whole of them). Being in full tale.

A تتاون *tatāwun*, (v. n. 6 of تان for تون) Approaching (game) sometimes on the left and sometimes on the right. Fraud, deceit, trick.

A تتايع *tatāyuʿ*, (v. n. 6 of تاع for تيع) Rushing headlong (into mischief). Attempting, engaging in any thing against the wish of others. Shaking in walking (a camel's shoulder). Rising up. Carrying away (dust or leaves, as the wind). Quarrelling, wrangling.

A تتبّع *tatabbuʿ*, (v. n. 5 of تبع) Searching diligently, examining, exploring. Following. Loving, liking.

A تتبيب *tatbīb*, (v. n. 2 of تبّ) Injuring, destroying. Saying, "May you perish!" Injury.

A تتبير *tatbīr*, A breaking in pieces. Ruining.

A تتبيع *tatbīʿ*, A seeking, inquiring diligently.

A تتبيل *tatbīl*, (v. n. 2 of تبل) Seasoning (a pot) with herbs and spices.

A تتبين *tatbīn*, (v. n. 2 of تبن) Fixing the eye and the mind on any thing, perceiving clearly. Being intelligent, skilful, shrewd.

A تتحتح *tatahtuh*, (v. n. 2 of تحتح Q) Being moved, moving one's self.

A تتر *tatar*, A Tartar, Scythian. Tartary.

P تترا *tatrā*, (in zand and Pāzand) Summer.

P تتربو *tatrabū*, (*tatarbū* or تتربوه *tatrabūh*) Elegance, gracefulness. Jesting, jocularity, pleasantry, buffoonery.

A تترتر *tatartur*, (v. n. 2 of ترتر Q) Being agitated. Staggering.

A تترّح *tatarruh*, A being grieved, made sad.

A تترّس *tatarrus*, (v. n. 5 of ترس) Being armed, or arming one's self with a shield (ترس *turs*).

A تترّع *tatarruʿ*, A rushing headlong (to evil).

A تترّف *tatarruf*, (v. n. 5 of ترف) Being affluent, enjoying plenty.

P تترونتن *tatrūnatan*, (zand and Pāz.) To rain.

P تتره *tatra*, Drollery, buffoonery, jocularity.

A تتري *tatra'*, Singly, one after another.

P تتري *tatrī* or *tutrī*, Sumach, used as a condiment. The poppy. *Tatarī*, Tartarian. Tartaric. كلاه تتري *kulāhi tatarī*, A Tartarian cap (worn by great men or by soldiers).

A تتريب *tatrīb*, (v. n. 2 of ترب) Strewing, soiling, with dust or earth. Having enough. Having little wealth.

A تتريح *tatrīh*, A making sad, melancholy.

A تتريس *tatrīs*, The arming one's self, or the causing another to arm with a shield.

A تتريص *tatrīs*, (v. n. 2 of ترص) Making even, straight, just, and equal.

A تتريع *tatrīʿ*, (v. n. 2 of ترع) Shutting.

A تتريف *tatrīf*, (v. n. 2 of ترف) Enervating, corrupting, rendering effeminate and dissolute, ruining.

P تتريك *titrīk*, Sumach.

A تتعتع *tataʿtuʿ*, A hesitating, a reflecting.

A تتفل *tatfal*, *titfal*, *tutfal*, *titfil*, *tatful*, and *tutful*, (pl. تتافل *tatāfil*) A fox. A fox's whelp. *Tatful*, Withering shrubs.

A تتفيف *tatfīf*, (v. n. 2 of تفّ not in use) Pronouncing pho! fie! with a tone of detestation.

P تتق *tutuk*, A veil, curtain. A kind of network in tents for keeping off gnats. Coats of an onion. تتق سپهرگون *tutuki sipihr-gūn*, A blue veil. A saucer made of lapis lazuli. تتق نيلي *tutuki nīlī*, The sky. A black cloud.

A تتقتق *tataktuk*, (v. n. 2 of تقتق Q) Falling from a mountain. Being deep in the sockets (eyes).

A تتقين *tatkīn*, (v. n. 2 of تقن not in use) Irrigating (ground) with a slimy kind of water.

A تتلّع *tatalluʿ*, (v. n. 5 of تلع) Extending the neck, or raising the head to see or hear any thing.

A تتلّي *tatallī*, (v. n. 5 of تلي) Following. Dunning for payment.

A تتليب *tatlīb*, (v. n. 2 تلب) Filling.

A تتلية *tatliyat*, (v. n. 2 of تلي) Following. Repeating supererogatory prayers in discharge of a vow. Fetching the last breath.

A تتليد *tatlīd*, (v. n. 2 of تلد) Collecting. Obstructing, hindering.

A تتليص *tatlīs*, (v. n. 2 تلص not in use) Making smooth, soft, and even.

P تتم *tutum*, *tutm*, or *tatum*, Sumach.

P تتما *tatmā*, (in zand and Pāzand) A bear.

A تتمّات *tatimmāt*, Supplements.

P تتماج *tutmāj*, Thin slices of paste, vermicelli.

A تتمّة *tatimmat*, Completion. An appendix, supplement.

P تتمتن *tatmitan*, (in zand and Pāz.) A jackall.

A تتمّم *tatammum*, (v. n. 5 of تمّ) Unclosing itself, appearing (a fracture). Walking with pain from a broken bone.

A تتمير *tatmīr*, (v. n. 2 of تمر) Ripening, becoming تمر *tamr* (a moist date رطب *rutab*). Feeding with ripe dates. Drying (meat) cut into small pieces and fresh dates.

A تتميم *tatmīm*, (v. n. 2 of تمّ) Completing, accomplishing. Satisfying. Giving (to another) his share at dice. Consuming. Destroying. Hastening to despatch (a wounded man). Tying an amulet round the neck (of a child). Opening, becoming apparent (a fracture). Persisting, persevering. Becoming like the tribe of تميم *tamīm*, as regards climate, judgment, locality, &c.

A تتنّن *tatannun*, (v. n. 5 of تنّ) Deserting one's friends, and associating with others.

A تتنيت *tatnīt*, The act of weaving well.

A تتنيخ *tatnīkh*, An abiding in one place.

A تتو *tatw*, The lappet of a high-crowned cap.

A تتوبة *tatwibat*, (v. n. of تاب for توب) Repenting, turning from sin (to God). Turning, becoming gracious (as God to man).

A تتوّج *tatawwuj*, A being crowned.

A تتوّق *tatawwuk*, (v. n. 5 of تاق for توق) Evincing a strong desire.

A تتويب *tatwīb*, (v. n. 2 of تاب for توب) Causing to turn away or desist; inducing to repent.

A تتويج *tatwīj*, The act of crowning.

A تتويه *tatwīh*, (v. n. 2 of تاه for توه) Ruining. Astonishing, astounding.

A تتهّم *tatahhum*, A travelling to Tihāma.

P تتي *titī*, Gingerbread-figures for the amusement of children. A word used to entice birds.

A تتيّز *tatayyuz*, (v. n. 5 of تاز for تيز) Being turned (out of one's path). Desiring, feeling a propensity.

A تتيّع *tatayyuʻ*, A rushing headlong into evil.

A تتيية *tatyiyat*, (v. n. 2 of تيي) Writing well the letter ت *te*.

A تتييس *tatyīs*, A training, a breaking in.

A تتييع *tatyīʻ*, (v. n. 2 of تيع) Dipping (bread) into butter, taking (butter) up with bread.

A تتييم *tatyīm*, The act of enslaving.

A تتييه *tatyīh*, (v. n. 2 of تيه for تاه) Bewildering, confounding, losing.

A تثاءب *tasāʼub*, (v. n. 6 of ثأب) Yawning, gaping. Being dronish, sluggish.

A تثابر *tasābur*, A rushing one upon another.

A تأثأ *tasaʼsuʼ*, (v. n. 2 of ثأثأ Q) Fearing, standing in dread of. Flocking to the watering trough (camels). Purposing to travel, and then judging it most expedient to stay at home.

A تثاقل *tasākul*, (v. n. 6 of ثقل) Being heavy and slow. Being loth (to perform), abstaining from.

A تثألل *tasaʼlul*, A being troubled with warts.

A تثاون *tasāʼun*, (v. n. 6 of ثأن not used) Approaching (game) sometimes from the right, sometimes from the left.

A تثاون *tasāwun*, (v. n. 6 of ثون not used) Lying in wait, looking left and right for prey. Craft, cunning.

A تثباق *tasbāk*, (v. n. of ثبق) Running fast (a plenteous river).

A تثبّت *tasabbut*, (v. n. 5 of ثبت) Being fixed, established. Delaying.

A تثبّج *tasabbuj*, (v. n. 5 of ثبج) Holding a stick behind the back, thus keeping the arms pinioned (as shepherds do when sauntering).

A تثبّط *tasabbut*, (v. n. 5 of ثبط) Knowing, understanding, being aware of. Being let, hindered, keeping back.

A تثبّن *tasabbun*, (v. n. 5 of ثبن) Putting any thing in a purse or pocket. Carrying with both hands.

A تثبية *tasbiyat*, (v. n. 2 of ثبي) Collecting. Persevering in any thing. Praising the living. Complaining of one's circumstances and of want. Gathering what is good; also what is bad. Correcting, amending. Augmenting. Finishing. Extolling, magnifying. Imploring help against an enemy. Walking in the ways of one's father.

A تثبيت *tasbīt*, (v. n. 2 of ثبت) Establishing, fixing, making firm, steady. Detaining in a place. التثبيت *at tasbīt*, The Christian rite of confirmation.

A تثبيج *tasbīj*, (v. n. 2 of ثبج) Confounding (speech or writing); not easily understanding them. Holding a stick behind the back, thus keeping the arms pinioned (as shepherds do when walking).

A تثبير *tasbīr*, (v. n. 2 of ثبر) Restraining, hindering, detaining.

A تثبيط *tasbīt*, (v. n. 2 of ثبط) Hindering, turning one (from business). Occupying, making busy.

A تثتّم *tasattum*, (v. n. 5 of ثتم) Breaking forth into obscene language. Being rent (a vest). Falling in pieces (meat over-boiled).

A تثجثج *tasajsuj*, A flowing of water.

A تثجير *tasjīr*, (v. n. 2 of ثجر) Enlarging, making broad, amplifying. Making (water) flow. Flabbiness.

A تثدية *tasdiyat*, A maintaining, a feeding.

A تثدين *tasdīn*, (v. n. 2 of ثدن) Making fleshy, filling up the flesh.

A تثريب *tasrīb*, (v. n. 2 of ثرب) Chiding.

A تثرية *tasriyat*, (v. n. 2 of ثري) Moistening (earth). Sprinkling (a place). Pouring water on the cheese اقط *akit*. Having moist earth sticking to one's hands in consequence of leaning upon them on the ground. Putting on a fur garment.

A تثريد *tasrīd*, (v. n. 2 of ثرد) Slaying a sheep without cutting the jugular veins. A little, a small quantity, a sprinkle (of rain).

A تثرير *tasrīr*, (v. n. 2 of ثرّ) Wetting.

A تثطعم *tasatʻum*, (v. n. 2 of ثطعم Q) Prevailing against in words.

A تثطيع *tastīʻ*, (v. n. 2 of ثطع) Breaking.

A تثعّم *tasaʻʻum*, (v. n. 5 of ثعم) Delighting.

A تثعيط *tasʻīt*, A pounding small.

A تثغّب *tasaghghub*, (v. n. 5 of ثغب) Bleeding profusely (gums).

A تثفرق *tasafruk*, (v. n. 2 of ثفرق Q) Not becoming thick (milk).

A تثفّل *tasafful*, (v. n. 5 of ثفل) or تثفّي *tasaffī*, (v. n. 5 of ثفي) Interposing obstacles to (a man's) achieving deeds of renown (meanness of his birth).

A تثفية *tasfiyat*, (v. n. 2 of ثفي) Underpropping (a kettle), placing (it) on a trivet.

A تثفيد *tasfīd*, The act of lining (a coat of mail).

A تثفير *tasfīr*, (v. n. 2 of ثفر) Stimulating, impelling, driving.

A تثفيل *tasfīl*, (v. n. 2 of ثفل) Eating frumenty. Spreading a cloth under the mill to catch the flour.

A تثقّب *tasakkub*, (v. n. 5 of ثقب) Being perforated. Being worm-eaten (leather). Perforating. Kindling.

A تثقّر *tasakkur*, A wavering, fluctuation. Impatience, lamentation, complaint.

A تثقيب *taskīb*, (v. n. 2 of ثقب) Piercing, perforating repeatedly. Lighting (a fire). Becoming conspicuous (gray hairs).

A تثقيف *taskīf*, The making (a spear) straight.

A تثقيل *taskīl*, (v. n. 2 of ثقل) Making heavy. Inflecting with a vowel a silent consonant.

A تثل *tasl*, A kind of aromatic unguent.

A تثلّل *tasallul*, (v. n. 5 of ثلّ) Being overthrown (a house).

A تثلّم *tasallum*, (v. n. 5 of ثلم) Being notched (a sword-blade). Being full of flaws or chinks.

A تثليث *taslīs*, (v. n. 2 of ثلث) Dividing into three parts. Trebling. Making triangular. Asserting to be three. Professing (one's self) a trinitarian. Inflecting a consonant with the three vowels *a i u*: as, نصر *nasr*, *nisr*, *nusr*. Ripening the third part (of a date). Tying up three teats of a camel. Coming in third (a horse). Compounding an electuary called مثلث *musallas*. Making three efforts to rise. The Trinity. A trine (an aspect of the planets). القائلون بالتثليث *al kāʼilūn bi't taslīs*, Trinitarians.

A تثليخ *taslīkh*, A staining, soiling, bedaubing.

A تثليم *taslīm*, A nipping, notching much.

A تثمثم *tasamsum*, (v. n. 2 of ثمثم Q) Retiring, receding. Waiting.

A تثمّل *tasammul*, (v. n. 5 of ثمل) Drinking off.

A تثميد *tasmīd*, A draining, an exhausting.

A تثمير *tasmīr*, (v. n. 2 of ثمر) Shedding its blossoms and producing the first appearance of fruit (a tree). Increasing, causing to augment (wealth). Multiplying. Having particles of butter adhering to its sides (a leathern milk-bottle).

A تثميغ *tasmīgh*, (v. n. 2 of ثمغ) Perfuming (the head) with civet. Covering (the head).

A تثميل *tasmīl*, (v. n. 2 of ثمل) Leaving (something) at the bottom of a vessel or cistern.

A تثميم *tasmīm*, (v. n. 2 of ثمّ) Trampling upon. Breaking a bone clean asunder.

A تثمين *tasmīn*, (v. n. 2 of ثمن) Valuing, appraising. Making octangular.

A تثنّي *tasannī*, (v. n. 5 of ثني) Being bent, folded. Being doubled. Stooping much in walking. Walking pompously.

A تثنية *tasniyat*, (v. n. 2 of ثني) Making two, doubling. Putting in the dual number. Marking a letter with two points, as ت *tā* or ي *yā*. Bending. Making two efforts to rise. Praising. Disparaging, defaming. The dual number. Duality.

A تثوّب *tasaʼʼub*, (v. n. 5 of ثأب) Yawning, gaping. Being sluggish, torpid. Searching carefully, inquiring into news.

A تثوّب *tasawwub*, (v. n. 5 of ثاب for ثوب) Going over the prayers a second time, and so deserving a reward (ثواب *sawāb*).

A تثوّر *tasawwur*, (v. n. 5 of ثار for ثور) Making an assault or an effort. Being raised (dust). Rising from the ground (locusts or the bird قطا *katā*). Being visible (blood).

A تثوّل *tasawwul*, (v. n. 2 of ثال for ثول) Getting the better of. Insulting, reproaching, striking. Swarming (bees).

A تثوّي *tasawwī*, (v. n. 5 of ثوي) Receiving hospitably, being a host.

A تثويب *taswīb*, (v. n. 2 of ثاب for ثوب) Recompensing, rewarding. Calling to prayers at dawn of day. Reiterating the call, repeating the phrase, الصلوٰة خير من النوم *as salāt khayr mini'n nawm*, Prayer is better than sleep. Returning. Exchanging. Earnestness, perseverance in prayer. Prayers of supererogation.

A تثوية *taswiyat*, (v. n. 2 of ثوي) Detaining. Receiving hospitably. Dying.

A تثوير *taswīr*, (v. n. 2 of ثار for ثور) Exciting

(rebellion), raising (dust), obliging to rise (camels). Examining, scrutinizing (the Kur'ān to discover its true meaning).

A تثي *tasy*, Peeled fruit of a dwarf palm-tree. A date-husk.

A تثيّب *tasayyub*, (v. n. 5 of ثيب) Leaving her husband after having once lain with him (a woman).

A تثيتل *tasaytul*, (v. n. 2 of ثيتل Q) Appearing to be a fool after having appeared wise.

A تثييب *tasyīb*, (v. n. 2 of ثيب) Being depucelated (a woman). Separating (husband and wife). Becoming old (a camel).

P تجا *tajā*, Rough, sharp, cutting.

A تجاب *tijāb*, What is extracted the first time by smelting, from the silver stone, some silver still remaining.

A تجابّ *tajābb*, (v. n. 6 of جبّ) Marrying each other's sister (two men).

A تجاثي *tajāsī*, (v. n. 6 of جثا for جثو) Sitting together knee to knee.

A تجأجؤ *taja,ju,*, (v. n. 2 of جأجأ Q) Repelling. Retreating from timidity. Finishing. Dreading.

A تجاحد *tajāhud*, A denying one another.

A تجاحف *tajāhuf*, (v. n. 6 of جحف) Fencing with foils or sticks. Bandying a ball to and fro at the game of shinty.

A تجادع *tajāduع*, (v. n. 6 of جدع) Fighting, opposing one another, litigating, squabbling. Devouring one another.

A تجادل *tajādul*, (v. n. 6 of جدل) Litigating, quarrelling among themselves.

A تجاذب *tajāzub*, (v. n. 6 of جذب) Pulling one another about. Contending together. Being pulled, hauled, dragged.

A تجاذل *tajāzul*, A hating of one another.

A تجاذي *tajāzī*, (v. n. 6 of جذي) Lifting with both hands. Stealing away privately. Trying each other's strength in lifting a stone.

P تجار *tajār*, A thorough-bred, unbroken colt. A well-paced horse. (in zand and Pāzand) Travelling. A traveller.

A تجار *tijār*, (or تجّار *tujjār*) (pl. of تاجر *tājir*) Merchants. Vintners.

A تجارب *tajārib*, (pl. of تجربة) Experiments.

A تجارة *tijārat*, (v. n. of تجر) Trading. Merchandize, commerce. اصحاب تجارت *as-hābi tijārat*, Merchants. P تجارت كردن To trade.

A تجارز *tajāruz*, (v. n. 6 of جرز) Reviling, abusing each other. Hurting in word and deed.

P تجاره *tajāra*, A colt not yet broke in. (in zand and Pāzand) A traveller.

A تجاري *tajārī*, (v. n. 6 of جري) Conversing. Meeting. Agreeing.

A تجّاريّ *tujjārīy*, Suited to a trader, mercantile.

A تجاريد *tajārīd*, Detachments sent out.

A تجازر *tajāzur*, A reviling one another.

A تجازي *tajāzī*, (v. n. 6 of جزي) Entreating earnestly (a person to do any thing). Demanding payment of a debt.

A تجاسر *tajāsur*, (v. n. 6 of جسر) Raising the head. Carrying it high and insolently. Domineering. Boldness, firmness, intrepidity, temerity. Shaking a stick at any one.

A تجاشع *tajāshuع*, (v. n. 6 of جشع) Pressing on one another round a cistern (thirsty persons).

A تجاعل *tajāعul*, (v. n. 6 of جعل) Taking (any thing) between them.

A تجافي *tajāfī*, (v. n. 6 of جفا for جفو) Being separated, distant, not touching. Not staying in its place.

A تجافيف *tajāfīf*, Horse-armours.

A تجال *tajāll*, A making one'self great.

A تجالد *tajālud*, A fighting, fencing.

A تجالس *tajālus*, A sitting together: a session.

A تجالل *tajālul*, (v. n. 6 of جلّ) Taking the best (of any thing). Being old and stricken in years.

A تجالي *tajālī*, A disclosing to one another.

A تجاليد *tajālīd*, A body, person, shape.

A تجانّ *tajānn*, (v. n. 6 of جنّ) Appearing mad, furious. Being mad.

A تجانب *tajānub*, (v. n. 6 of جنب) Receding, avoiding. Shunning.

A تجانف *tajānuf*, (v. n. 6 of جنف) Declining, deviating, leaning.

A تجانن *tajānun*, (v. n. 6 of جنّ) Appearing mad, furious. Being mad.

A تجانؤ *tajānu,*, A falling flat upon.

A تجاوب *tajāwub*, (v. n. 6 of جاب for جوب) Answering one another.

A تجاود *tajāwud*, (v. n. 6 of جاد for جود) Examining, trying which was best in argumentation.

A تجاور *tajāwur*, (v. n. 6 of جار for جور) Being neighbours; neighbourhood. Protecting one another.

A تجاوز *tajāwuz*, (v. n. 6 of جاز for جوز) Exceeding, transgressing (just bounds). Straying. Passing by. Forgiving a fault. Winking, conniving. Outrage, insolence.

A تجاول *tajāwul*, (v. n. 6 of جال for جول) Going round one another (combatants).

A تجاويد *tajāwīd*, Rains.

A تجاويز *tajāwīz*, (pl. of تجواز) Striped garments.

A تجاويف *tajāwīf*, (pl. of تجويف) Cavities.

A تجاه *tajāh*, *tijāh*, or *tujāh*, Opposite, over against. تجاهك *tajāhaka*, In opposition to you, opposite to, or before your face.

A تجاهد *tajāhud*, (v. n. 6 of جهد) Labouring hard, putting forth strength, studying how to accomplish a thing. Care, effort, study.

A تجاهر *tajāhur*, An appearing openly in public.

A تجاهل *tajāhul*, (v. n. 6 of جهل) Pretending ignorance. Connivance, apathy, indifference. P تجاهل كردن *tajāhul kardan*, To feign ignorance, play the simpleton.

A تجباب *tijbāb*, A vein of silver conspicuous in a mineral stone.

A تجبار *tajbār*, Pride, arrogance.

A تجبّر *tajabbur*, (v. n. 5 of جبر) Being haughty, contumacious. Putting forth leaves (a tree). Beginning to look fresh (a field which had been grazed close). Having one's broken fortunes repaired. Being restored to health (a sick person). Obtaining (wealth). Recovering something of which one had been deprived.

A تجبّس *tajabbus*, A walking pompously.

A تجبّل *tajabbul*, (v. n. 5 of جبل) Entering into a mountain. Taking all, exacting the whole.

A تجبّن *tajabbun*, (v. n. 5 of جبن) Coagulating, curdling, becoming cheese (milk).

A تجبيب *tajbīb*, (v. n. 2 of جبّ) Being terrified. Flying (from battle). Watering cattle. Having the legs white as far as the knee (a horse).

A تجبية *tajbiyat*, (v. n. 2 of جبي) Bending forward the body. Putting the hands and knees on the ground, and falling flat on the face.

A تجبير *tajbīr*, (v. n. 2 of جبر) Restoring, setting (a broken bone). Repairing the broken fortune (of a friend).

A تجبيع *tajbīع*, (v. n. 2 of جبع) Becoming altered in appearance from leanness (the buttocks).

A تجبيل *tajbīl*, (v. n. 2 of جبل) Cutting in several pieces, hacking, mincing.

A تجبين *tajbīn*, (v. n. 2 of جبن) Imputing, attributing to pusillanimity. Making, calling, or knowing one to be, a coward (جبان *jabān*). Curdling (milk) turning (it) into cheese (جبن *jubn*).

A تجبيه *tajbīh*, (v. n. 2 of جبه) Receiving ungraciously. Treating with contempt. Turning away the head. Marking an adulterer and adultress on the face with ruddle, and parading them about on a camel or ass looking different ways.

A تجثجث *tajasjus*, (v. n. 2 of جثجث Q) Becoming thick (the hair). Shaking herself (a bird).

A تجثّم *tajassum*, (v. n. 5 of جثم) Laying (any thing) beneath one's breast.

A تجثيم *tajsīm*, A causing to lie on the breast.

A تجحدر *tajahdur*, (v. n. 2 of جحدر Q) Shaking her wings, moving and flying (a bird).

A تجحدل *tajahdul*, (v. n. 2 of جحدل Q) Rolling.

A تجحّر *tajahhur*, (v. n. 5 of جحر) Creeping into its hole (a lizard). Being sunk in the socket (an eye).

A تجحفل *tajahful*, (v. n. 2 of جحفل Q) Being assembled (men).

A تجحّم *tajahhum*, (v. n. 5 of جحم) Burning with greediness and covetousness.

A تجحيظ *tajhīz*, A regarding stedfastly.

A تجحيل *tajhīl*, A dashing to the ground.

A تجحيم *tajhīm*, A looking with fixed attention.

A تجحين *tajhīn*, A keeping on short allowance.

A تجخجخ *tajakhjukh*, (v. n. 2 of جخجخ Q) Being loose and languid; stretching one's self out. Being very dark (the night). Lying with.

A تجخّر *tajakhkhur*, (v. n. 5 of تخخر) Becoming cracked (clay of a cistern) so that the water leaks.

A تجخّي *tajakhkhī*, (v. n. 5 of تخخي) Perfuming one's self. Being overturned (a flagon, rundlet).

A تجخية *tajkhiyat*, (v. n. 2 of تخخي) Pushing forward the belly and opening both arms in prayer. Declining (the night). Bending (an old man).

A تجخير *tajkhīr*, (v. n. 2 of تخخر) Widening (the mouth of a well).

A تجدّب *tajaddub*, (v. n. 5 of جدب) Finding (a place) unhealthy.

A تجدّد *tajaddud*, (v. n. 5 of جدّ) Being new. Innovation, novelty. Having no milk (udder).

A تجدّل *tajaddul*, (v. n. 5 of جدل) Being thrown down, falling on the ground. Throwing down.

A تجديح *tajdīh*, (v. n. 2 of جدح) Dirtying, defiling. Mixing, stirring up a ptisan.

A تجديد *tajdīd*, A renewing, a making new.

A تجدير *tajdīr*, (v. n. 2 of جدر) Carrying (a wall) up high. Being attacked by the small-pox. Putting forth the first rudiments of fruit, as it were tubercles or small-pox (a tree). Rendering worthy.

A تجديع *tajdīʿ*, (v. n. 2 of جدع) Cropping the ears of an ass. Stunting the growth of vegetation (drought). Giving unwholesome food to a child. Wishing evil to any one by saying جدعا *jadʿan*, *i.e.* May thy hands, nose, ear, or lip be cut off!

A تجديف *tajdīf*, (v. n. 2 of جدف) Being ungrateful for the blessings of Providence; murmuring and blaspheming whilst enjoying them.

A تجديل *tajdīl*, A levelling with the ground.

A تجذّب *tajazzub*, A drinking, an imbibing.

A تجذّم *tajazzum*, A being amputated.

A تجذّي *tajazzī*, (v. n. 5 of جذي) Sweeping the ground with his tail in circles around the female (a pigeon).

A تجذيذ *tajzīz*, (v. n. 2 of جذّ) Wishing or asking (one) to follow (you), but in vain.

A تجذير *tajzīr*, (v. n. 2 of جذر) Eradicating, extirpating. The produce of any number multiplied by itself, a square number.

A تجذيم *tajzīm*, An amputating, a mutilating.

A تجر *tajara*, (fut. يتجر *yatjuru*) He traded.

A تجر *tajr*, (v. n. of تجر) Trading. *Tajr* or *tujur*, (pl. of تاجر *tājir*) Merchants. Wine-merchants.

P تجر *tajar*, Winter-quarters. A storehouse.

A تجربة *tajribat*, (v. n. 2 of جرب) Trying, proving. (pl. تجارب *tajārib*) Experiment, proof, assay.

P تجربه كردن *tajriba kardan*, To try, prove, hazard, make an experiment.

P تجربه كار *tajriba-kār*, Versed in business. An experienced agent. تجربه كاران روزگار *tajriba-kārāni rozgār*, Experienced in worldly affairs.

P تجربه كاري *tajriba-kārī*, Experience, practice.

A تجرثم *tajarsum*, (v. n. 2 of جرثم Q) Being collected, assembled. Falling from a height. Abiding in a place. Taking the greater part of a thing.

A تجرثي *tajarsī*, (v. n. 2 of جرثي Q) Being prominent (the wind-pipe).

A تجرجر *tajarjur*, (v. n. 2 of جرجر Q) Running down the throat with a gurgling noise (liquor). Taking a long draught.

A تجرجم *tajarjum*, (v. n. 2 of جرجم Q) Crouching and lying still in his lair (a wild beast). Coming to a close (night). Falling, being prostrated. Falling into a well. Falling to pieces, being demolished. Eating and drinking to excess.

A تجرّد *tajarrud*, (v. n. 5 of جرد) Being stripped, denuded. Resembling a pilgrim on pilgrimage. Going alone on pilgrimage. Cutting the envelope (an ear of corn). Subsiding (fermentation of liquor). Giving intense application. Nudity.

P تجرد گزين *tajarrud-guzīn*, Choosing solitude.

A تجرّس *tajarrus*, A speaking, talking.

A تجرّع *tajarruʿ*, (v. n. 5 of جرع) Drinking draughts of liquor. Forgetting (one's griefs, care, or anger). P تجرع كردن *tajarruʿ kardan*, To sip.

A تجرّف *tajarruf*, (v. n. 5 of جرف) Carrying away much. Sweeping, shovelling clean.

A تجرّم *tajarrum*, (v. n. 5 of جرم) Being completed (a year). Passing, elapsing (a night). Picking up dates which have dropped. Charging with a crime falsely. Committing a crime.

A تجرمز *tajarmuz*, (v. n. 2 of جرمز Q) Passing by (night). Rushing upon. Coming together.

A تجرّه *tajarruh*, (v. n. 5 of جره) Being made public, displayed to view.

A تجرّي *tajarrī*, (v. n. 5 جرو) Taking a whelp or young one. (v. n. 5 of جري) Appointing an attorney or sending a deputy (جري *jarīy*).

A تجريب *tajrīb*, A proving, trying; assay.

A تجرئة *tajrisat*, An inspiring with courage.

A تجرية *tajriyat*, (v. n. 2 of جري) Appointing an attorney, or sending a deputy (جريّ *jarīy*).

A تجريج *tajrīj*, (v. n. 2 of جرج not used) Shaving the head. Making wide, loose, and shaking.

A تجريح *tajrīh*, A wounding dangerously.

A تجريد *tajrīd*, (v. n. 2 of جرد) Stripping, pulling off the skin. Divesting, denuding. Drawing, unsheathing (a sword). Depriving (a skin) of the hair. Putting on a threadbare garment. Taking (cotton) out of the pod. Leaving (a manuscript) without the vowel or diacritical points. Going alone on a pilgrimage to Mecca. Sending a detachment. Asking people who refuse, or who give unwillingly.

A تجرير *tajrīr*, A drawing much and well.

A تجريس *tajrīs*, (v. n. 2 جرس) Proving, trying. Making one to have a sound opinion. Appointing (one) a governor or comptroller. Causing to hear. Rendering known or celebrated.

A تجريع *tajrīʿ*, (v. n. 2 of جرع) Causing to drink. Making one forget (grief, care, or anger).

تجريف *tajrīf*, (v. n. 2 of جرف) Carrying away every thing. Sweeping, shovelling away. Carrying away a part of the land with it, cutting a channel (a torrent).

A تجريم *tajrīm*, (v. n. 2 of جرم) Abandoning, withdrawing from. Completing (a year).

A تجريه *tajrīh*, A publishing, manifesting.

A تجريئ *tajrīs*, An inspiring with courage.

A تجزّر *tajazzur*, (v. n. 5 of جزر) Leaving (corpses) a prey for wild beasts.

A تجزّع *tajazzuʿ*, (v. n. 5 of جزع) Being broken (a stick). Taking an allotted portion.

A تجزّف *tajazzuf*, (v. n. 5 of جزف) Entering.

A تجزّم *tajazzum*, A being split and cracked.

A تجزّؤ *tajazzus*, (v. n. 5 of جزأ) Having enough, being contented.

A تجزئة *tajzisat*, (v. n. 2 of جزأ) Dividing, distributing. Having enough. Satisfying (a camel) with fresh grass, and enabling him to do without water. Fixing a handle (جزأة *juzsat*) on an awl or knife.

A تجزيع *tajzīʿ*, (v. n. 2 of جزع) Being almost ripe (green dates called بسر *busr*). Having but little water remaining (a cistern). Removing (any person's) impatience.

A تجزيم *tajzīm*, (v. n. 2 of جزم) Filling (a bottle). Being pusillanimous, weak. Being silent.

A تجسّد *tajassud*, (v. n. 5 of جسد) Assuming a body. Incarnation.

A تجسّس *tajassus*, (v. n. 5 of جسّ) Searching carefully, examining. Curiously prying into that which God has thought fit to conceal. Exploring, playing the spy.

A تجسّم *tajassum*, (v. n. 5 of جسم) Becoming incarnate, assuming a body. Being large-bodied. Choosing from amongst (other men). Going directly to the person or thing itself. Proposing to one's self, and undertaking a great achievement. Mastering the most difficult part (of any business). Ascending the steepest part of a mountain.

A تجسير *tajsīr*, A making or calling bold.

A تجسيم *tajsīm*, A making large-bodied.

A تجشّع *tajashshuʿ*, A being covetous, greedy.

A تجشّم *tajashshum*, A labouring hard.

A تجشّؤ *tajashshus*, Eructation, belching.

A تجشئة *tajshisat*, (v. n. 2 of جشأ) Belching.

A تجشير *tajshīr*, (v. n. 2 of جشر) Emptying (a vessel). Turning (horses) out to pasture, so that (they) do not return home at night. Leaving.

A تجشيم *tajshīm*, (v. n. 2 of جشم) Making (one) to labour hard at.

A تجصيص *tajsīs*, (v. n. 2 of جصّ) Plastering, whitewashing. Opening its eyes (a whelp). Filling (a vessel). Beginning to bud (a tree). Charging, attacking (an enemy).

A تجضّم *tajazzum*, A snatching with the mouth.

A تجضيض *tajzīz*, (v. n. 2 of جضّ) Going at a quick pace. Rushing on one with a sword.

A تجعّب *tajaʿʿub*, (v. n. 5 of جعب) Being thrown on the ground, falling down. Making a quiver. Using a quiver (جعبة *jaʿbat*).

A تجعبي *tajaʿbī*, (v. n. 2 of جعبي Q) Being thrown prostrate. Riding over one another (troops).

A تجعثم *tajaʿsum*, A being drawn together.

A تجعثن *tajaʿsun*, (v. n. 2 of جعثن Q) Being contracted, collected, drawn together.

A تجعجع *tajaʿjuʿ*, (v. n. 2 of جعجع Q) Throwing one's self upon the ground from excess of pain or grief.

A تجعّد *tajaʿʿud*, (v. n. 5 of جعد) Being curly, crisp (locks or beard). Being drawn together.

A تجعّر *tajaʿʿur*, (v. n. 5 of جعر) Fastening a rope round the waist when going down into a well.

A تجعّس *tajaʿʿus*, (v. n. 5 of جعس) Being squalid and talking obscenely. Voiding excrement.

A تجعّم *tajaʿʿum*, (v. n. 5 of جعم) Greedily desiring meat (a man), provender (a camel), a bone (a dog). Emitting a twanging sound (a lute).

A تجعيب *tajʿīb*, (v. n. 2 of جعب) Throwing prostrate. Making a quiver (جعبة *jaʿbat*).

A تجعيد *tajʿīd*, The act of curling (hair).

A تجفاف *tajfāf*, (v. n. 2 of جف) Drying (a garment) properly. *Tijfāf*, The armour of a horse; also of a soldier. Any cloth or covering that dries up the sweat of a horse.

A تجفجف *tajafjuf*, (v. n. 2 of جفجف Q) Becoming dry (a garment) so that still some moisture remains. Setting up, ruffling its feathers (a bird). Covering its eggs with its wings (a bird).

A تجفّر *tajaffur*, (v. n. 5 of جفر) Becoming four months old (a lamb, then called جفر *jafr*).

A تجفّف *tajaffuf*, (v. n. 5 of جف) Being dried (a garment).

A تجفّل *tajafful*, (v. n. 5 of جفل) Ruffling his feathers (a cock).

A تجفّؤ *tajaffuʾ*, Departure (of a country's weal).

A تجفير *tajfīr*, A becoming languid, spent.

A تجفيف *tajfīf*, (v. n. 2 of جف) Drying properly (a garment). Putting on a horse-cloth that dries up the sweat. Casing in armour (a horse).

A تجفيل *tajfīl*, (v. n. 2 of جفل) Peeling, stripping. Shovelling away (dirt).

A تجفين *tajfīn*, (v. n. 2 of جفن) Indulging much in venery. Serving up food in a large dish.

A تجلّب *tajallub*, A bringing, a fetching.

A تجلبب *tajalbub*, (v. n. 2 of جلبب Q) Being put on (a veil or pelisse). Putting on a veil.

A تجلّة *tajillat*, Reverence, respect. من تجلّتك *min tajillatika*, From respect to thee.

A تجلجل *tajaljul*, (v. n. 2 of جلجل Q) Being moved, agitated. Sinking into soft ground.

A تجلّد *tajallud*, (v. n. 5 of جلد) Contending, grappling. Bearing up under difficulties: sturdiness.

A تجلّس *tajallus*, (v. n. 5 of جلس) Sitting down, sitting (as judges to determine causes).

A تجلّق *tajalluḳ*, (v. n. 5 of جلق) Opening (the mouth), laughing.

A تجلّل *tajallul*, (v. n. 5 of جلّ) Becoming superior (in dignity). Taking what is greatest and most illustrious. Mounting the female (a camel).

A تجلّي *tajallī*, (v. n. 5 of جلا for جلو) Being revealed, discovered (as God to man). Raising its head and looking keenly (a falcon). An apparition with splendour. The Epiphany. Lustre, brightness, brilliancy. عيد التجلّي *ʿīdu't tajallī*, The feast of the Epiphany. تجلّي قدّامهم *tajalla' kuddāmahum*, He was transfigured before them. P تجلّي كردن *tajallī kardan*, To illuminate. To polish, adorn. To illustrate, make plain. A (v. n. 5 of جلي) Being above, superior to. Looking at any thing.

A تجلّيات *tajalliyāt*, Beatific visions.

A تجليب *tajlīb*, (v. n. 2 of جلب) Crying out, raising a clamour. Carrying together, collecting. Shouting to a horse. Hindering. Anointing a lock of wool and tying it round a camel's teat that the colt may not suck.

A تجلية *tajliyat*, (v. n. 2 of جلا for جلو) Polishing, scouring, making bright. Explaining (one's thoughts), revealing, declaring. Darting a glance. Raising his head, and looking keenly (a falcon). Coming in first (a horse). Presenting a handmaid to his bride (a bridegroom). (v. n. 2 of جلي) Revealing, discovering, making clear.

A تجليح *tajlīḥ*, (v. n. 2 of جلح) Making a great effort. Giving undivided attention to any thing. Springing, bounding (a wild beast).

A تجليد *tajlīd*, (v. n. 2 of جلد) Pulling off the skin (from the body of a slaughtered camel). Binding (a book) in leather.

A تجليز *tajlīz*, (v. n. 2 of جلز) Binding, folding, or wrapping round in order to strengthen. Extending. Removing. Pulling off, carrying away. Drawing a bow up to the head of the arrow. Travelling expeditiously.

A تجليف *tajlīf*, (v. n. 2 of جلف) Being fatal, destructive (year).

A تجليق *tajlīḳ*, A shooting with a balista.

A تجليل *tajlīl*, (v. n. 2 of جلّ) Covering (a horse) with cloth. Enveloping. Calling, taking to one's self.

A تجمجم *tajamjum*, A speaking low, a muttering.

A تجمّر *tajammur*, (v. n. 5 of جمر) Being kept long at the seat of war without being withdrawn (an army).

A تجمّع *tajammuʿ*, (v. n. 5 of جمع) Being collected carefully. Being assembled, flocking from all quarters.

A تجمّل *tajammul*, (v. n. 5 of جمل) Dressing, adorning one's person. Eating melted fat. Plenty of provisions, abundance of wealth. Dignity, retinue.

A تجمّلات *tajammulāt*, Moveables, household furniture. Conveniences, articles of luxury.

A تجمّم *tajammum*, (v. n. 5 of جمّ) Being thick and widely spreading (a plant). A present to a woman divorced from her husband.

A تجمّؤ *tajammuʾ*, (v. n. 5 of جمأ) Gathering one's clothes about one. Assembling, flocking together. Seizing and hiding.

A تجمهر *tajamhur*, A being oppressive, iniquitous.

A تجمّي *tajammī*, (v. n. 5 جمي not used) Assembling, flocking together.

A تجميد *tajmīd*, (v. n. 2 of جمد) Congealing, curdling. Beginning to freeze.

A تجمير *tajmīr*, (v. n. 2 of جمر) Cutting away the pithy, pulpy substance (called جمّار *jummār*) growing on the top of the date-tree. Keeping (an army) long at the seat of war without withdrawing them. Being assembled and crowding close together. Collecting. Gathering up (as women do their hair, and fastening it on the crown of the head).

A تجميش *tajmīsh*, (v. n. 2 of جمش) Flattering, soothing. Toying, playing.

A تجميع *tajmīʿ*, (v. n. 2 of جمع) Collecting with care and diligence. Collecting (her) eggs in her belly (a hen). Assembling with others to prayers on Friday (called يوم الجمعة *yawmu'l jumʿat*).

A تجميل *tajmīl*, (v. n. 2 of جمل) Adorning, embellishing, beautifying. Keeping (troops) in long confinement. Giving (one) camel's flesh to eat.

A تجميم *tajmīm*, (v. n. 2 of جمّ) Heaping up (a measure of corn). Growing thick, bushy (a plant).

A تجنّب *tajannub*, (v. n. 5 of جنب) Retiring, declining, avoiding, shunning. Being polluted.

A تجنّث *tajannus*, (v. n. 5 of جنث) Pretending to be of another family. Loving, yearning upon. Covering, enveloping. Expanding the wings; also, sitting (as a bird). Calling home the thoughts (in prayer) from idolatry. Abstaining from sin.

A تجنّح *tajannuḥ*, (v. n. 5 of جنح) Extending both arms. Resting on the palms of the hand in an act of adoration.

A تجنّس *tajannus*, A being homogeneous.

A تجنّن *tajannun*, (v. n. 5 of جنّ) Appearing mad, making one's self look furious. Being mad. Budding, bringing forth (ground).

A تجنّي *tajannī*, (v. n. 5 of جني) Accusing falsely. Seeking a pretext to injure another. Gathering fruit.

A تجنيب *tajnīb*, (v. n. 2 of جنب) Rendering one averse, causing to shun, or abstain. Shunning. Having a foot turned inwards (reckoned a good property in a horse). Giving little milk (a camel). Keeping (a stallion) apart from the females.

A تجنيح *tajnīḥ*, (v. n. 2 of جنح) Furnishing with wings. Causing to incline. Resting on the palms of the hands in adoration. Standing and extending both arms.

A تجنيد *tajnīd*, The collecting of an army.

A تجنيز *tajnīz*, The laying (a corpse) on a bier.

A تجنيس *tajnīs*, (v. n. 2 of جنس) Making homogeneous. Classing according to genus. Becoming ripe all over (a date). Resembling. Alliteration (Behemoth biggest born). A pun.

A تجنيص *tajnīs*, (v. n. 2 of جنص not used) Dying. Voiding dung. Running away in terror, and staring with fright. Looking stedfastly.

A تجنيق *tajnīk*, (v. n. 2 of جنق) Throwing stones with a balista (منجنيق *manjanīk*).

A تجنين *tajnīn*, A making mad.

A تجواب *tajwāb*, The traversing (of a country).

A تجواز *tijwāz*, (pl. تجاويز *tajāwīz*) A kind of striped garment.

A تجوال *tajwāl*, A circumambulating.

A تجوب *tajūb*, A section of the tribe of حمير *himyar*, of which was ابن ملجم *ibn muljam*, the assassin of Alīy.

A تجوّخ *tajawwukh*, (v. n. 5 of جاخ for جوخ) Falling in, filling up (a well). Bursting (a boil).

A تجوّد *tajawwud*, A choosing of what is good.

A تجوّر *tajawwur*, (v. n. 5 of جار for جور) Being laid prostrate. Falling. Being overthrown, pulled down.

A تجورب *tajawrub*, A putting on of socks.

A تجوّز *tajawwuz*, (v. n. 5 of جاز for جوز) Passing by. Forgiving. Doing business slightly, easily, or by the by. Allowing, tolerating, conniving at, indulging. Reducing (a work) into a compendious form. Receiving money although spurious. Abridging, cutting short. Speaking metaphorically.

A تجوّش *tajawwush*, (v. n. 5 of جوش not used) Having a portion of it passed (the night). Entering, descending into.

A تجوّظ *tajawwuz*, (v. n. 5 of جاظ for جوظ) Purposing, striving, attempting.

A تجوّع *tajawwuʿ*, (v. n. 5 of جاع for جوع) Starving one's self, bearing hunger voluntarily, abstaining purposely from food.

A تجوّف *tajawwuf*, (v. n. 5 of جاف for جوف) Penetrating into the middle or cavity, and lying hid.

A تجوّق *tajawwuk*, A being collected, assembled.

A تجوّن *tajawwun*, (v. n. 5 of جان for جون) Painting white the door of a bridegroom. Making black the gate of a deceased person.

A تجويب *tajwīb*, (v. n. 2 of جاب for جوب) Making the collar or breast of a shirt or garment.

A تجوبة *tajwiyat*, A patching a leathern bottle.

A تجويح *tajwīh*, (v. n. 2 of جاح for جوح) Making barefoot. Covering the foot.

A تجويخ *tajwīkh*, (v. n. 2 of جاخ for جوخ) Carrying along, sweeping (a current). Throwing down.

A تجويد *tajwīd*, (v. n. 2 of جاد for جود) Saying, doing, or making good. Doing well. Running swiftly (a horse).

A تجوير *tajwīr*, (v. n. 2 of جار for جور) Accusing of injustice. Beating. Levelling with the ground. Throwing down, prostrating.

A تجويز *tajwīz*, (v. n. 2 of جاز for جوز) Causing to go or pass by. Causing (an opinion) to pass, penetrate, or be received. Permitting, allowing, approving. Watering (camels). Contrivance, endeavour, plan. P تجويز كردن *tajwīz kardan*, To devise. To examine, try, prove, seek.

A تجويظ *tajwīz*, A purposing, striving; attempt.

A تجويع *tajwīʿ*, (v. n. 2 of جاع for جوع) Starving, famishing (one).

A تجويف *tajwīf*, (v. n. 2 of جاف for جوف) Hollowing, making concave.

A تجويفات *tajwīfāt*, Hollows, caverns.

A تجويق *tajwīk*, (v. n. 2 of جاق for جوق) Collecting, assembling. Crying out, raising a clamour.

A تجويل *tajwīl*, A going round about much.

A تجه *tajh*, (v. n. of تجه) Proceeding, turning towards. Paying attention to.

A تجهجه *tajahjuh*, A retiring, abstaining.

A تجهّز *tajahhuz*, (v. n. 5 of جهز) Being adorned, fitted out, furnished. Preparing for any thing.

A تجهضم *tajahzum*, (v. n. 2 of جهضم Q) Carrying one's self high, being proud, domineering over.

A تجهّم *tajahhum*, (v. n. 5 of جهم) Looking at, or receiving ungraciously, with stern countenance.

A تجهية *tajhiyat*, (v. n. 2 of جهي) Enlarging, extending, widening.

A تجهيز *tajhīz*, (v. n. 2 of جهز) Betrimming (a bride), fitting out (a traveller, or a troop of soldiers), furnishing (a funeral). Carrying to the grave. Making up (a bed). Causing (a horse) to run.

A تجهيل *tajhīl*, (v. n. 2 of جهل) Calling a fool, charging with ignorance. Imputing, ascribing to want of information.

A تجيب *tujīb* or *tajīb*, A section of the tribe of كندة *kindat*, of which was ابن بشر *ibn bishr*, the assassin of Othmān.

A تجير *tajīr*, Seed after the oil has been expressed; caput mortuum.

A تجيّش *tajayyush*, (v. n. 5 of جاش for جيش) Being greatly agitated (the mind).

A تجيّف *tajayyuf*, (v. n. 5 of جاف for جيف) Being putrid (a dead body).

A تجيئة *tajyiʾat*, (v. n. 2 of جاء for جيأ) Sewing (a leathern bottle).

A تجييش *tajyīsh*, The levying of an army.

A تجييض *tajyīz*, A declining, a turning from.

A تجئيف *tajʾīf*, (v. n. 2 of جأف) Terrifying.

A تجييف *tajyīf*, (v. n. 2 of جاف for جيف) Stinking, turning to a putrid corpse. Rendering vile and despicable. Terrifying. Striking.

A تجييم *tajyīm*, A writing the letter جيم *jīm*.

A تحابّ *tahābb*, (v. n. 6 of حبّ) Loving each other. Mutual love.

A تحابب *tahābub*, A loving of each other.

A تحاتّ *tahātt*, (v. n. 6 of حتّ) Falling (leaves) being scattered. Being rubbed in the hand. Being peeled.

A تحاتن *tahātun*, A being equal, resembling.

A تحاثّ *tahāss*, A stimulating one another.

A تحاجّ *tahājj*, A disputing, wrangling.

A تحاجز *tahājuz*, (v. n. 6 of حجز) Receding from each other (two squadrons in battle).

A تحاجي *tahājī*, (v. n. 6 of حجا for حجو) Proposing questions or enigmas alternately as an exercise of genius.

A تحادّ *tahādd*, A resisting mutually.

A تحادب *tahādub*, The being hump-backed.

A تحادث *tahādus*, (v. n. 6 of حدث) Conversing, telling stories.

A تحادر *tahādur*, The act of dropping, falling.

A تحادل *tahādul*, (v. n. 6 of حدل) Bending over a bow. Acting unjustly towards each other.

A تحادي *tahādī*, (v. n. 6 of حدا for حدو) Driving one another forwards (camels).

A تحاذي *tahāzī*, (v. n. 6 of حذي) Dividing among themselves.

A تحارب *tahārub*, (v. n. 6 of حرب) Fighting together, duelling, waging mutual war.

A تحارير *tahārīr*, (pl. of تحرير *tahrīr*) Writings. Manumissions.

A تحازن *tahāzun*, (v. n. 6 of حزن) Being grieved and sad. Pretending to be sad.

A تحاسد *tahāsud*, An envying of one another.

A تحاسين *tahāsīn*, (pl. of تحسين *tahsīn*) Beauties.

A تحاشد *tahāshud*, (v. n. 6 of حشد) Congregating, flocking together for mutual aid. Assembling for one object.

A تحاشي *tahāshī*, (v. n. 6 of حشي) Standing apart. Excepting against, by pronouncing حاشا *hāshā*. Exception, separation.

A تحاصّ *tahāss*, (or تحاصص *tahāsus*) (v. n. 6 of حصّ) Distributing amongst themselves, taking their shares (creditors).

A تحاصب *tahāsub*, (v. n. 6 of حصب) Pelting one another with pebbles or gravel.

A تحاضّ *tahāzz*, A stimulating each other.

A تحافي *tahāfī*, (v. n. 6 of حفي) Referring a matter to the judge by mutual consent.

A تحاقّ *tahākk*, A contending, disputing, injuring.

A تحاقر *tahākur*, (v. n. 6 of حقر) Appearing contemptible, shewing one's self contemptible.

A تحاكّ *tahākk*, (v. n. 6 of حكّ) Cutting (as one foot against the other, or as the knees trembling).

A تحاكم *tahākum*, A going together to a judge.

A تحالز *tahāluz*, A holding of a dialogue.

A تحالف *tahāluf*, (v. n. 6 of حلف) Conspiring together, entering into an alliance, leaguing. Swearing (plaintiff and defendant).

A تحالق *tahāluk*, (v. n. 6 of حلق) Shaving the head for one another.

A تحالل *tahālul*, A descending, alighting together.

A تحالم *tahālim*, (pl. of تحلمة *tahlimat*) Female kids infested by tikes. *Tahālum*, (v. n. 6 of حلم) Appearing mild or affable, though really not so.

A تحالي *tahālī*, (v. n. 6 of حلا for حلو) Displaying sweetness (a woman).

A تحامق *tahāmuk*, (v. n. 6 of حمق) Feigning or appearing to be a fool.

A تحامل *tahāmul*, (v. n. 6 of حمل) Laying upon any one more than he can bear. Undertaking a work with labour and difficulty. Labouring under a difficulty or misfortune. Inclining. Rising.

A تحامي *tahāmī*, (v. n. 6 of حمي) Being cautious. Avoiding. Shunning, keeping clear of.

A تحانّ *tahānn*, (v. n. 6 of حنّ) Being under a strong emotion.

A تحاني *tahānī*, A leaning towards.

A تحاور *tahāwur*, (v. n. 6 of حار for حور) Carrying on a dialogue, answering one another.

A تحاوز *tahāwuz*, (v. n. 6 of حاز for حوز) Being mutually repulsed, retreating severally (two hosts).

A تحاوش *tahāwush*, Interception, surrounding.

A تحاويل *tahāwīl*, Alternate seasons of plenty and scarcity.

A تحايي *tohāyī*, (pl. of تحياة *tahyāt*) Three stars in the sixth mansion of the moon, in Gemini.

A تحبّب *tahabbub*, (v. n. 5 of حبّ) Showing love. Trying, proving love or affection. Drinking water sufficient (an ass). Granulating.

A تحبجر *tahabjur*, (v. n. 2 of حبجر Q) Having a twisting of the guts.

A تحبّس *tahabbus*, (v. n. 5 of حبس) Being imprisoned, confined, restrained. Restraining one's self.

A تحبّك *tahabbuk*, (v. n. 5 of حبك) Drawing tight the waistband of the breeches. Tucking up the garment. Girding the waist.

A تحبكر *tahabkur*, (v. n. 2 of حبكر Q) Being astonished, amazed, confounded.

A تحبّل *tahabbul*, A netting, a catching in a net.

A تحبيب *tahbīb*, The making one a friend.

A تحبية *tahbiyat*, A protecting, a defending.

A تحبيذ *tahbīz*, (v. n. 2 of حبذ not used) Saying حبّذا *habbazā*, Excellent! bravo!

A تحبير *tahbīr*, (v. n. 2 of حبر) Beautifying, doing a thing elegantly. Writing elegantly. Adorning (a speech or poem).

A تحبيس *tahbīs*, (v. n. 2 of حبس) Retaining, imprisoning. Bequeathing to pious uses (prohibiting alienation). Retaining a thing in one's own possession, but dedicating the fruits of it to pious purposes. Spreading bed-clothes upon a bed.

A تحبيش *tahbīsh*, A collecting, gaining, getting.

A تحبيض *tahbīz*, A making light, alleviating.

A تحبيق *tahbīk*, (v. n. 2 of حبق) Collecting together (goods or furniture). Doing well, firmly, and effectually.

A تحبيك *tahbīk*, (v. n. 2 of حبك) Strengthening, making fast. Drawing lines well.

A تحبيل *tahbīl*, (v. n. 2 of حبل) Rendering pregnant. Throwing seed upon seed.

A تحت *taht*, The interior part. *Tahtu*, Under, below. *Tuhut*, The lower orders, the rabble.

A تحتانيّ *tahtānīy*, Lower. (Applied to letters or diacritical points) Small, short, or inferior: placed beneath, pointed below.

A تحتحة *tahtahat*, Motion, sound (made by motion or walking).

A تحتحت *tahathut*, A fall (of leaves from a tree).

A تحترش *tahatrush*, (v. n. 2 of حترش Q) Being assembled (people). Striving to apprehend, but without success.

A تحترف *tahatruf*, A being scattered.

A تحتّك *tahattuk*, (v. n. 5 of حتك) Going with a quick, short step.

A تحتّم *tahattum*, (v. n. 5 of حتم) Eating the remains of victuals left upon a table. Eating soft (bread or meat). Making pure and genuine. Wishing well to any one. ذو تحتّم *zū tahattumin*, Cheerful, easy, polite.

A تحتيّ *tahtīy*, Low, inferior: placed beneath.

A تحتيت *tahtīt*, Brokenness, weakness.

A تحتيد *tahtīd*, (v. n. 2 of حتد) Choosing on account of purity and excellence.

A تحتير *tahtīr*, (v. n. 2 of حتر) Giving victuals to builders, providing an entertainment on the completion of a new house. Putting a حتر *hitr* to a tent.

A تحتيش *tahtīsh*, An exciting, stirring up.

A تحثيث *tahsīs*, A stimulating, instigating.

A تحثير *tahsīr*, (v. n. 2 of حثر) Making up (medicine) into pills.

A تحجّب *tahajjub*, A being veiled, secluded.

A تحجّر *tahajjur*, (v. n. 5 of حجر) Petrifying, becoming hard as stone. Becoming purulent and hard (a wound). Making a closet, chamber, or cell. Pressing close up, straitening.

A تحجّز *tahajjuz*, A girding of one's waist.

A تحجّم *tahajjum*, (v. n. 5 of حجم) Burning with greediness and avarice.

A تحجّن *tahajjun*, The being crooked.

A تحجّو *tahajjuw*, (v. n. 5 of حجا) Being greedy, tenacious of. Being much addicted to.

A تحجّي *tahajjī*, (v. n. 5 of حجا for حجو) Remaining in one place. Pre-occupying, keeping possession. Designing, doing deliberately. Being greedily addicted to. A whispering, buzzing sound.

A تحجيب *tahjīb*, A veiling, secluding.

A تحجير *tahjīr*, (v. n. 2 of حجر) Being surrounded with a small thin circle (the moon). Being burnt round the eye (a camel).

A تحجيل *tahjīl*, (v. n. 2 of حجل) Having white feet (a horse). Dyeing the tips of (her) fingers (a woman). Preparing a bridal chamber, or bringing the bride into it. Diluting copiously with water (the hospitable milk-bowl) in a season of scarcity. Being sunk (the eye). White on the fore and hind feet of a horse, or on the two hind feet and one fore foot; or on the hind feet alone, never on the two fore feet exclusive of the hinder, nor of one fore foot without the other, except with the hind feet. White on the teat of a camel produced by the صرار *sirār*. A mark set on a camel.

A تحجيم *tahjīm*, A looking intently.

A تحجين *tahjīn*, (v. n. 2 of حجن) Bending (a stick). A crooked or curved brand or scar.

A تحدّب *tahaddub*, (v. n. 5 of حدب) Being friendly, benevolently inclined. Cleaving to. Declining a second marriage that she may attend to the education of her deceased husband's children.

A تحدّث *tahaddus*, (v. n. 5 of حدث) Relating. Discoursing, conversing.

A تحدّر *tahaddur*, (v. n. 5 of حدر) Descending.

A تحدّس *tahaddus*, (v. n. 5 of حدس) Inquiring, examining. Endeavouring to acquire the knowledge of any thing privately.

A تحدّم *tahaddum*, A burning with rage.

A تحدّي *tahaddī*, (v. n. 5 of حدي) Giving serious attention to. Doing any thing equal to another. Challenging (a rival). Striving to overcome.

A تحديث *tahdīs*, (v. n. 2 of حدث) Relating, telling. Suggesting, commanding. Conversing, talking. Reporting traditions of Muhammad.

A تحديج *tahdīj*, A looking with fixed attention.

A تحديد *tahdīd*, (v. n. 2 of حدّ) Sharpening (a sword, knife, or the sight). Describing or prescribing limits. Coming forth slowly for want of rain (corn). Tending towards. Defining logically.

A تحدير *tahdīr*, (v. n. 2 of حدر) Causing to descend. Making haste. Swelling from a blow (the skin).

A تحديق *tahdīk*, A looking intently.

A تحذّق *tahazzuk*, (v. n. 5 of حذق) Affecting cleverness, studying to appear clever when not so.

A تحذّل *tahazzul*, (v. n. 5 of حذل) Compassionating. Fearing for any one.

A تحذلق *tahazluk*, A laying claim to what is not one's due, a making undue pretensions to cleverness.

A تحذلم *tahazlum*, (v. n. 2 of حذلم Q) Receiving instruction and putting away one's folly. Walking fast and waddling.

A تحذير *tahzīr*, (v. n. 2 of حذر) Threatening. Admonishing, cautioning, warning, bidding beware.

A تحذيف *tahzīf*, A preparing and finishing.

A تحراش *tahrāsh*, A hunting the Lybian lizard.

A تحرّج *taharruj*, (v. n. 5 of حرج) Abstaining from wickedness, repenting of it, and turning from it. Being freed from straits.

A تحرّد *taharrud*, (v. n. 5 of حرد) Being stripped of the hair (a skin). Keeping aloof, retiring to a distance.

A تحرّر *taharrur*, A burning. A being free.

A تحرّز *taharruz*, (v. n. 5 of حرز) Abstaining from, being timid, cautious. Taking heed.

A تحرّس *taharrus*, A preserving one's self.

A تحرّص *taharrus*, (v. n. 5 of حرص) Waiting, longing for an expected time.

A تحرّف *taharruf*, (v. n. 5 of حرف) Being changed, inverted. Declining, turning from.

A تحرفص *taharfus*, A being collected, contracted.

A تحرّق *taharruk*, (v. n. 5 of حرق) Being burnt.

A تحرّك *taharruk*, (v. n. 5 of حرك) Moving one's self. Being moved.

A تحرّم *taharrum*, (v. n. 5 of حرم) Being prohibited. Seeking the protection of any one.

A تحرمز taharmuz, (v. n. 2 of حرمز Q) Being acute, intelligent. Bastardy (a word coined from P حرام زاده haram-zāda, Unlawfully born).

A تحرّي taharri, (v. n. 5 of حري) Choosing the most worthy and fitting. Intending, designing, giving deliberate attention to. Delaying. Staying.

A تحريب tahrīb, (v. n. 2 of حرب) Irritating, inflaming, enraging. Making sharp. Giving dates.

A تحريث tahrīs, A causing to plough.

A تحريج tahrīj, (v. n. 2 of حرج) Reducing to straits or difficulties. Forbidding. Making narrow. Taking a solemn oath.

A تحريد tahrīd, (v. n. 2 of حرد) Bending, curving. Twisting (ropes). Tying a band of rushes round an enclosure or fold for camels. Repairing into (a structure) of reeds without windows. Intending, proposing. Hindering, keeping back.

A تحرير tahrīr, (v. n. 2 of حرّ) Setting at liberty, giving freedom. Dedicating to the service of God. Writing elegantly and accurately. تحرير اقليدس tahrīri uklīdis, Euclid's elements. الي وقت التحرير ila' wakti't tahrīr, Up to the time of writing.

A تحريرا tahrīran, (P تحريرانه tahrīrāna) In (or by) writing. Written, dated, given: as, تحريرا في غرّة شهر tahrīran fī ghurrati shahri, Given, (written, or dated) in the beginning of the month of . . .

P تحريركش tahrīr-kash, A writer, a scribe.

A تحريز tahrīz, (v. n. 2 of حرز) Strengthening, fortifying. Preserving most carefully, sheltering, protecting.

A تحريش tahrīsh, (v. n. 2 of حرش) Irritating, setting (men or dogs) by the ears.

A تحريص tahrīs, A making greedy, an inflaming.

A تحريض tahrīz, (v. n. 2 of حرض) Instigating, exciting, provoking to, inflaming. Having a worn out fringe (a garment). Dyeing (garments) with saffron. Dealing in alkali, investing one's all in it.

A تحريضات tahrīzāt, Provocations.

A تحريف tahrīf, (v. n. 2 of حرف) Changing, inverting, transposing (letters), forming an anagram. Turning, diverting. Cutting the nib of a pen slantwise or diagonally.

A تحريفات tahrīfāt, Changes; anagrams.

A تحريق tahrīk, (v. n. 2 of حرق) Consuming by fire. Making thirsty.

A تحريك tahrīk, (v. n. 2 of حرك) Putting in motion. Marking a consonant with a vowel point. Inflecting every consonant (being at least two) with fatha (as مطر matar, ظلمة zalamat).

A تحريم tahrīm, (v. n. 2 of حرم) Prohibiting, interdicting. Rendering venerable or sacred. Being held sacred and inviolate. Girding on the pilgrim's garb for prayer. Entering on the sacred month. Being connected with what is sacred and inviolable. Being incompletely broken in (a quadruped). Not completely dressing leather. Beating at dice.

A تحريمة tahrīma, Assumption of a pilgrim's garb.

A تحريميّ tahrīmiy, Prohibited by law.

A تحزّب tahazzub, (v. n. 5 of حزب) Being assembled in crowds, confederating.

A تحزّز tahazzuz, A being cut or notched.

A تحزفر tahazfur, A being proud and haughty.

A تحزّق tahazzuk, A being covetous, close-fisted.

A تحزّم tahazzum, (v. n. 5 of حزم) Girding the waist with (a rope). Being girthed (a horse).

A تحزّن tahazzun, A being afflicted, grieving.

A تحزّو tahazzū, A divining, auguring, presaging.

A تحزّي tahazzī, A divining, auguring.

A تحزيب tahzīb, (v. n. 2 of حزب) Collecting, bringing a crowd together. Distributing into parts (especially the Kur'ān, into sixty sections, called احزاب ahzāb).

A تحزية tahziyat, (v. n. 2 of حزي) Guessing by the eye at the produce of a palm-tree. Crying out (to birds) and driving (them) away. (Vapour) raising up the human figure.

A تحزيز tahzīz, (v. n. 2 of حزّ) Notching, indenting (teeth). Hacking, mincing. Grating the teeth. Measuring. Guessing.

A تحزين tahzīn, (v. n. 2 of حزن) Making sorrowful. Reading (the Kur'ān) in a plaintive tone.

P تحس tahs, A heart overwhelmed with grief.

A تحسّب tahassub, (v. n. 5 of حسب) Reclining on a pillow. Making into a pillow. Inquiring with a view to learn, seeking instruction, purposing.

A تحسحس tahas-hus, (v. n. 2 of حسحس Q) Being moved. Falling off (a camel's hair).

A تحسّر tahassur, (v. n. 5 of حسر) Sighing. Grieving for, sorrowing after. Being full and plump in various parts of the body. Losing flesh from several days' travelling and loss of spring pasture (a camel). Having her face exposed (a woman). Moulting and getting new feathers (a bird). Falling off a (camel's) coat. Grief, regret.

A تحسّس tahassus, (v. n. 5 of حسّ) Exploring, examining, inquiring into. Listening, hearing of.

A تحسّف tahassuf, (v. n. 5 of حسف) Falling off (hair or fur). Eating up all, leaving nothing.

A تحسّن tahassun, (v. n. 5 of حسن) Beautifying, adorning, decorating. Doing (a thing) well.

A تحسّي tahassī, A sipping by little and little.

A تحسيب tahsīb, (v. n. 2 of حسب) Giving enough, contenting. Causing one to lean upon a cushion. Causing one to eat and drink to the full. Sleeping in the place where pilgrims throw stones in the valley of Mina. Burying (a corpse) among stones or in a winding-sheet.

A تحسية tahsiyat, A giving to sip.

A تحسيد tahsīd, (v. n. 2 of حسد) Envying much.

A تحسير tahsīr, (v. n. 2 of حسر) Wearying. Casting its feathers, moulting (a bird). Causing to sigh, throwing into a fit of grief. Despising, scorning. Hurting, afflicting.

A تحسيس tahsīs, (v. n. 2 of حسّ) Feeling, perceiving, seeing, finding, knowing. Broiling (meat) on the ashes. Raking the fire over bread baking in the embers.

A تحسيف tahsīf, A shaving (of the mustachios).

A تحسين tahsīn, (v. n. 2 of حسن) Doing well and handsomely. Beautifying. Commending, attributing to goodness. Approbation, applause, acclamation. P تحسين كردن tahsīn kardan, To approve, applaud. To bless.

A تحشحش tahashhush, (v. n. 2 of حشحش Q) Being separated, divided, scattered. Being moved; moving one's self.

A تحشّم tahashshum, A blushing, being ashamed.

A تحشّن tahashshun, (v. n. 5 of حشن) Gaining, acquiring. Striving, endeavouring.

A تحشّي tahashshī, (v. n. 5 of حشي) Excepting. Saying God forbid! Being ashamed of.

A تحشية tahshiyat, (v. n. 2 of حشي) Causing to puff, blow, or pant. Trimming the edge of a garment with fringe or lace. Making marginal notes (حاشية hāshiyat) to a book.

A تحشيد tahshīd, A convening, bringing together.

A تحشيف tahshīf, A looking with half-shut eyes.

A تحشيم tahshīm, A vexing, an enraging.

A تحصّب tahassub, (v. n. 5 of حصب) Going forth in quest of food (a dove).

A تحصحص tahas-hus, (v. n. 2 of حصحص Q) Cleaving to the ground. Being even.

A تحصّل tahassul, (v. n. 5 of حصل) Being collected. Remaining, being constant.

A تحصّن tahassun, (v. n. 5 of حصن) Defending one's self. Being chaste (a woman). Retiring to a fortress. Becoming a stallion (حصان hisān).

A تحصّي tahassī, (v. n. 5 of حصي) Being kept, preserved, guarded.

A تحصيب tahsīb, (v. n. 2 of حصب) Strewing with gravel. Flinging gravel at. Turning away the face. Lying down at night a little while at the place called محصّب muhassab.

A تحصية tahsiyat, (v. n. 2 of حصي) Defending, guarding. Giving protection.

A تحصيص tahsīs, An appearing, a being manifest.

A تحصيل tahsīl, (v. n. 2 of حصل) Causing to come to pass, or to be realized. Collecting, gathering, gaining. Summing up, getting at the sum and substance of (a discourse). Raising gold from the mine and sifting it. Bearing green and unripe dates or yellow flowers (a palm-tree). Collection, gain, acquisition. تحصيل دنيا و دين tahsīli dunya' u dīn, The acquisition of wealth and advancement of religion, *i.e.* The present world and the next. تحصيل علوم tahsīli ʿulūm, The acquisition of the sciences. تحصيل الكلام tahsīlu'l kalām, The sum and substance of the discourse. P تحصيل كردن tahsīl kardan, To amass, gather, gain, acquire. To collect (the public revenue). To produce, make manifest.

P تحصيل دار *tahsīl-dār*, A collector of revenue.

P تحصيل داري *tahsīl-dārī*, The office of revenue-collector.

P تحصيل ضابطه *tahsīl-zābita*, (in India) An account shewing the daily payments of the ryots to the circar.

A تحصين *tahsīn*, (v. n. 2 of حصن) Fortifying, defending, surrounding with a wall. Strengthening. Preserving, keeping (a young girl) at home. High breed in a stallion.

A تحضب *tahazzub*, (v. n. 5 of حضب) Entering on a rough and stony road.

A تحضر *tahazzur*, (v. n. 5 of حضر) Being present. Coming into the presence of.

A تحضيج *tahzīj*, (v. n. 2 of حضج) Speaking little.

A تحضيض *tahzīz*, (v. n. 2 of حضّ) Making greedy. Instigating, exciting.

A تحطم *tahattum*, (v. n. 5 of حطم) Being broken (through age). Burning with rage.

A تحطيط *tahtīt*, The act of eating food.

A تحطيم *tahtīm*, A breaking violently.

A تحظرب *tahazrub*, (v. n. 2 of حظرب Q) Being filled to distension (a leathern bottle). Being strung tight (a bow). Being filled (with enmity, food, &c.).

A زمن التحظير *zamanu't tahzīr*, The time when the Khalif Omar divided the territory called وادي القري *wādī'l hura'* between the Mussulmāns and بني عذرة *banī ʿuzrat* after the expulsion of the Jews. (This event forms an epoch with Muhammadans).

A تحف *tuhaf*, (pl. of تحفة *tuhfat*) Presents, valuable gifts.

A تحفاية *tahfāyat*, (v. n. of حفي) Treating with the greatest respect. Inquiring minutely into a person's state. Rejoicing.

A تحفة *tuhfat* or *tuhafat*, (pl. تحف *tuhaf*) A gift, present. A benefit, favour, kindness. An excellent, rare thing, worthy of being presented. Tribute from an inferior to a superior ruler. P تحفه دادن *tuhfa dādan*, To give a present. (This word is used as a title to many books: as, تحفة السلاطين *tuhfatu's salātīn*, (Present for kings) Treatise on politics.

P تحفجات *tuhfajāt*, Rarities. Presents.

A تحفز *tahaffuz*, (v. n. 5 of حفز) Preparing, hastening to rise. Sitting on the point of the toe.

A تحفش *tahaffush*, (v. n. 5 of حفش) Dwelling in a small house, box, or cell. Shewing love to a man (a woman).

A تحفظ *tahaffuz*, (v. n. 5 of حفظ) Being vigilant, cautious; taking heed to one's self. Committing to memory. Recollecting one by one.

P تحفگي *tuhfagī*, A rarity, treat, present.

A تحفل *tahafful*, (v. n. 5 of حفل) Meeting. Being numerously attended (a meeting). Flowing together (milk or water). Dressing, adorning one's person. Being polished. Weeping bitterly.

A تحفّي *tahaffī*, (v. n. 5 of حفي) Being beneficent; behaving humanely and generously. Striving to accomplish, or gain. Inquiring kindly after. Caressing much. Doing good. Exulting, rejoicing.

A تحفيش *tahfīsh*, (v. n. 2 of حفش) Dwelling in a small house, box, or cell (حفش *hifsh*).

A تحفيض *tahfīz*, (v. n. 2 of حفض) Throwing away. Drying, making dry. Leaving behind. Alleviating. Sowing.

A تحفيظ *tahfīz*, (v. n. 2 of حفظ) Giving in trust to another. Causing to commit to memory.

A تحفيف *tahfīf*, (v. n. 2 of حف) Going, turning, or carrying round, surrounding. Being pinched with want, poverty-stricken.

A تحفيل *tahfīl*, (v. n. 2 of حفل) Collecting, bringing together. Omitting to milk (a sheep) for some days, that she may appear to greater advantage when exposed to sale (she is then called محفل *muhaffal*). Ornamenting.

A تحقّد *tahakhud*, A hating, a wishing ill.

A تحقق *tahakhuk*, (v. n. 5 of حق) Discovering, knowing for certain, verifying. Being true (news).

A تحقير *tahkīr*, (v. n. 2 of حقر) Despising, contemning, treating with contempt. Scorn, disdain.

A تحقيرا *tahkīran*, (P تحقيرانه) Contemptuously.

A تحقيق *tahkīk*, (v. n. 2 of حق) Making, doing what is right, just, and true. Rendering necessary. Ascertaining the truth, verifying. Verification. Acknowledging as true, believing. اهل تحقيق *ahlī tahkīk*, Philosophers, doctors.

A تحقيقا *tahkīkan*, Certainly, verily.

A تحقيقات *tahkīkāt*, Certainties, verities.

A تحقيقي *tahkīkiy*, Sure, certain, confirming.

A تحكّر *tahakkur*, (v. n. 5 of حكر) Hoarding grain against a scarcity. Sighing, grieving, sorrowing after.

A تحكك *tahakkuk*, (v. n. 5 of حك) Struggling, opposing, resisting.

A تحكل *tahakkul*, (v. n. 5 of حكل) Squabbling, litigating ignorantly.

A تحكم *tahakkum*, (v. n. 5 of حكم) Commanding, lording over, obtaining the ascendancy. Bearing orders. Dominion, authority, usurpation.

A تحكيم *tahkīm*, (v. n. 2 of حكم) Putting in authority. Constituting (prince, lord, or judge). Giving power over (one's estate). Restraining one from doing as he wishes.

A تحل *tahill*, (v. n. 2 of حل) Loosing or making void an oath.

A تحلاق *tahlāk*, A shaving (of the head).

A تحلب *tahallub*, (v. n. 5 of حلب) Flowing (sweat from the body, spittle from the mouth, tears from the eyes). Watering (as the mouth does from desire or from taking any thing acid).

A تحلبة *tahlabat, tihlibat, tuhlabat, tuhlibat, tuhlubat*, or تحلابة *tihlābat*, A ewe having milk flowing from her dugs (before taking the ram).

A تحلّة *tahillat*, (v. n. 2 of حل) Making lawful. Loosing, getting clear off, or making void an oath.

A تحلج *tahalluj*, (v. n. 5 of حلج) Being in commotion and flashing (clouds). Entering.

A تحلحل *tahalhul*, (v. n. 2 of حلحل Q) Being removed (from its place).

A تحلز *tahalluz*, (v. n. 5 of حلز) Remaining, enduring (any thing). Being pained (the heart). Preparing for (business).

A تحلس *tahallus*, (v. n. 5 of حلس) Going round, circumambulating. Abiding in one place.

A تحلق *tahalluk*, (v. n. 5 of حلق) Being encircled by a halo (the moon). Sitting in circles (people).

A تحلل *tahallul*, (v. n. 5 of حل) Making an exception (when swearing). Making sick. Knocking one up (a journey).

A تحلم *tahallum*, (v. n. 5 of حلم) Being patient, mild, gentle. Persevering in acquiring the habit of mildness, striving so to be. Dreaming. Employing a dream. Pretending to have dreamed. Becoming fat and corpulent (a child or Lybian lizard, locust or cattle).

A تحلمة *tahlimat*, (pl. تحالم *tahālim*) (A female kid) infested by tikes.

A تحلئ *tihliʾ*, Hair or dirt scraped off a skin. Any part of a hide injured by the currier's knife.

A تحلي *tahallī*, (v. n. 5 of حلا for حلو) Eating sweetmeats. Finding (a thing) to be sweet. (v. n. 5 of حلي) Being adorned with bracelets and other female ornaments.

A تحلئة *tahliʾat*, (v. n. 2 of حلأ) Driving from water (camels). Giving money. Sweetening a ptisan. *Tihliʾat*, Hair or dirt scraped off a skin. Any one who sticks close to another and makes him sad.

A تحلية *tahliyat*, (v. n. 2 of حلا for حلو) Sweetening (a ptisan). (v. n. 2 of حلي) Dressing (a woman) with jewels and other ornaments. Decorating the hilt and sheath of a sword. Rendering (a thing) pleasant to the eye. Describing, pourtraying (a man) by (his) form and external appearance. Procuring ornaments for a woman.

A تحليف *tahlīf*, (v. n. 2 of حلف) Making swear. Exacting an oath.

A تحليق *tahlīk*, (v. n. 2 of حلق) Shaving close (the head). Marking (a camel) with circles. Soaring high in the air and skimming in circles (a bird). Lifting up the eyes towards heaven. Being encircled by a halo (the moon). Becoming two-thirds ripe (a date). Making the belly swell (milk and water). Being high in the udder (camel's milk). Being deeply sunk in the socket (the eye). Being high (a star). Flinging, throwing at.

A تحليل *tahlīl*, (v. n. 2 of حل) Making lawful. Untying (a knot). Loosing, getting clear of, or making void an oath. Causing to alight and sojourn in a place. Dissolving or discussing (in a medical sense). Inflicting stripes below the number authorized by law. Digestion, concoction, solubility. *Tihlil*, The orifice of the nipple or penis.

A تحليم *tahlīm*, (v. n. 2 of حلم) Rendering patient, tractable. Enjoining long-suffering and clemency. Esteeming one to be long-suffering. Picking grubs out of a hide.

A تحليئ *tahlīʼ*, (v. n. 2 of حلأ) Driving away from water. Giving (money). Sweetening a ptisan.

A تحم *tahm*, A staining, printing of stuffs.

A تحمّال *tihimmāl*, (v. n. 5 of حمل) Bearing, carrying a load. Enduring patiently.

A تحمة *tuhmat*, A deep black colour. *Tahamat*, Stuffs striped with yellow. ثياب التحمّة *siyābu't tahimmat*, Raiment which a man gives to a repudiated wife.

A تحمّت *tahammut*, (v. n. 5 of حمت) Being bright (colour).

A تحمحم *tahamhum*, (v. n. 2 of حمحم Q) Neighing (as a horse) on the sight of provender at a distance. A noise more subdued than neighing. The peculiar sound made by a bull at rutting-time.

A تحمّد *tahammud*, (v. n. 5 of حمد) Being praised; deserving it. Upbraiding with a benefit conferred.

A تحمّر *tahammur*, (v. n. 5 of حمر) Calling (a man) an ass. Speaking in the dialect of the Himyarit Arabs, the ancient inhabitants of Arabia Felix.

A تحمّس *tahammus*, (v. n. 5 of حمس) Maintaining one's ground. Waxing valiant in fight. Being zealous, firm, unshaken (in religion).

A تحمّش *tahammush*, A being angry.

A تحمّص *tahammus*, (v. n. 5 of حمص) Being contracted. Drying and shrivelling (flesh).

A تحمقس *tahamkus*, A being filthy and impure.

A تحمّل *tahammul*, (v. n. 5 of حمل) Bearing, carrying a load. Enduring patiently, putting up with. Taking up one's baggage and carrying one's self off. Patience, endurance, long-suffering, resignation. Truce, peace. Meekness, humility. P تحمّل كردن *tahammul kardan*, To load. To bear, to suffer. تحمّل گداز *tahammul-gudāz*, (Melting patience) Impatient. Intolerant. نا تحمّل *nā tahammul*, Intolerable.

A تحمّم *tahammum*, (v. n. 5 of حمّ) Being black. Going into a warm bath (حمّام *hammām*).

A تحموت *tahmūt*, A leathern bottle lined with a coating of inspissated juice. Very sweet (date).

A تحمّي *tahammī*, (v. n. 5 of حمي) Abstaining from, avoiding. Protecting one's self.

A تحميج *tahmīj*, (v. n. 2 of حمج) Half closing the eyes to see better. Looking long and intently at. Having the eyes sunk deeply in the sockets. Rolling the eye-balls from fear, or when threatening. Changing colour from anger. Being lean, emaciated.

A تحميد *tahmīd*, (v. n. 2 of حمد) Praising much. Thanking God, saying الحمد لله *al hamdu li'llāh*, God be praised!

A تحمير *tahmīr*, (v. n. 2 of حمر) Painting red. Reddening. Calling one an ass. Using the dialect of the Himyarit Arabs. Dividing with a blow so that a part falls off. Dressing or tanning leather badly. *Tahamyur*, (v. n. 2 of حمير Q) Speaking the Himyaritic dialect. Being bad-tempered.

A تحميس *tahmīs*, (v. n. 2 of حمس) Putting in a rage. Making (a thing) hard and rough. Warming or heating slightly (any medical preparation), holding it over the fire to simmer.

A تحميش *tahmīsh*, (v. n. 2 of حمش) Inflaming with rage. Collecting, bringing together.

A تحميص *tahmīs*, (v. n. 2 of حمص) Hunting (deer) at mid-day. Parching vetches.

A تحميض *tahmīz*, (v. n. 2 of حمض) Doing little, and that with indifference. Diminishing, lessening. Holding between the thighs (modus cœundi).

A تحميط *tahmīt*, (v. n. 2 of حمط) Shading a vine by means of a tree. Diminishing. Beating in moderation.

A تحميق *tahmīk*, (v. n. 2 of حمق) Calling or esteeming one a fool (احمق *ahmak*). Drinking wine.

A تحميل *tahmīl*, (v. n. 2 of حمل) Imposing a burden. Causing, requesting, or commanding to carry (a load) or convey (a letter).

A تحميم *tahmīm*, (v. n. 2 of حمّ) Making a provision for a repudiated wife. Boiling water. Blackening (the face) with charcoal. Becoming black (the head) after shaving. Sprouting (a young man's beard). Becoming black with hair (a head that has been shaved). Becoming fledged (a young bird). Growing (grass of a dark green colour).

A تحناذ *tahnāz*, (v. n. of حنذ) Roasting (a sheep) by laying hot stones upon (it).

A تحنّب *tahannub*, (v. n. 5 of حنب) Being bent (a man's back). Pitying, feeling an affection for.

A تحنبل *tahambul*, (v. n. 2 of حنبل Q) Stooping, crouching, lowering the head.

A تحنّث *tahannus*, (v. n. 5 of حنث) Avoiding, shunning, refraining from (sin). Worshiping for several nights. Putting away idols.

A تحندس *tahandus*, (v. n. 2 of حندس Q not used) Growing dark (the night). Falling, blundering. Being weak.

A تحنّط *tahannut*, (v. n. 5 of حنط) Being buried with sweet herbs (the dead).

A تحنظر *tahantur*, (v. n. 2 of حنظر Q not used) Going to and fro. Surrounding, turning round. Making a circle.

A تحنّف *tahannuf*, (v. n. 5 of حنف) Following the true religion. Circumcising one's self, and renouncing idolatry. Inclining towards.

A تحنّك *tahannuk*, (v. n. 5 of حنك) Passing the turban-sash under the chin.

A تحنّن *tahannun*, (v. n. 5 of حنّ) Being moved with pity towards. Inclination, desire, love, pity.

A تحنّؤ *tahannuʼ*, (v. n. 5 of حنأ) Being tinged or coloured with حناء *hinnāʼ* (cyprus or privet).

A تحنّي *tahannī*, (v. n. 5 of حني) Being curved, bent. Feeling an affection for, yearning over.

A تحنيب *tahnīb*, (v. n. 2 of حنب) Being curved or bent in the loins and pastern (a horse). Having the hind-legs wide apart, without a turning in of the toe. Bending any thing that is firmly put together. Turning upside down. Building an oblong arched edifice or corridor called ازج *azaj*.

A تحنئة *tahniʼat*, (v. n. 2 of حنأ) Tinging (the beard) with the cyprus or privet-herb and dust.

A تحنية *tahniyat*, A bending, a twisting.

A تحنيط *tahnīt*, (v. n. 2 of حنط) Burying (the dead) with odours. Becoming ripe and white (the plant رمث *rims*).

A تحنيف *tahnīf*, A making bow-legged.

A تحنيق *tahnīk*, (v. n. 2 of حنق) Coming out into ear (corn).

A تحنيك *tahnīk*, (v. n. 2 of حنك) Rubbing the palate (of a new-born child) with chewed date or honey to induce (it) to suck. Putting on barnacles or a kind of farrier's twitch. Tying a cloth under the chin of a dead person. Rendering expert (age or trials). Proving, trying.

A تحنين *tahnīn*, (v. n. 2 of حنّ) Blossoming (a tree). Causing to be tenderly affected. Retreating, being cowardly. Calling out الله الله *allāh! allāh!* when going to battle. Charging with falsehood, treating as a liar.

A تحنيئ *tahnīʼ*, (v. n. 2 of حنأ) Colouring with the herb حناء *hinnāʼ* (privet).

A تحوّب *tahawwub*, (v. n. 5 of حاب for حوب) Refraining from (crimes), repenting. Being distressed by grief or bodily torment.

A تحوت *tuhūt*, People of the lowest rank.

A تحوّج *tahawwuj*, (v. n. 2 of حاج for حوج) Seeking things needful.

A تحوّز *tahawwuz*, (v. n. 5 of حاز for حوز) Being coiled up (like a serpent). Absconding, retiring, receding.

A تحوّس *tahawwus*, (v. n. 5 of حاس for حوس) Displaying intrepidity. Being hindered, or halting in one place to make preparations for a journey. Being pained, grieving for.

A تحوّش *tahawwush*, (v. n. 5 of حاش for حوش) Retiring, receding, being far distant. Blushing. Living apart from her husband (a woman).

A تحوط *tahūt*, A barren year.

A تحوّط *tahawwut*, (v. n. 5 of حاط for حوط) Guarding, watching, minding, attending to.

A تحوّف *tahawwuf*, (v. n. 5 of حاف for حوف) Lessening, chipping away sides or edges.

A تحوّل *tahawwul*, (v. n. 5 of حال for حول) Being changed, turned, converted. Moving from place to place. Turning away from, retiring from. Leaping from horse to horse. Seeking a favourable opportunity to impart seasonable admonition. Sitting upright on horseback. Carrying a bundle of clothes on one's head, packing clothes in a bundle and carrying them on one's back. Hatching mischief. Craft, wile, shrewdness. Power.

A تحوّن *tahawwun*, Submission, subjection. Ruin.

A تحوّي *tahawwī*, (v. n. 5 of حوي) Being collected, contained, comprehended. Being drawn together. Being round. Coiling itself (a serpent). Circumference.

A تحوية *tahwiyat*, (v. n. 2 of حوي) Taking, receiving, grasping. Being drawn together. Contracting, drawing together in a circular form. Putting a coarse cloth on a camel's bunch to sit upon. Forming a circle.

A تحويج *tahwīj*, (v. n. 2 of حاج for حوج) Causing to turn aside. Quitting one's road through affection for one's friend.

A تحوير *tahwīr*, (v. n. 2 of حار for حور) Making white and bright. Making (bread) round. Cauterizing (a camel) round the eyes. Bringing back. Disappointing, frustrating. Lining (a boot) with red leather.

A تحويز *tahwīz*, (v. n. 2 of حاز for حوز) Driving (camels) to water. Bringing within the margin, border, or edge.

A تحويش *tahwīsh*, A collecting with care.

A تحويص *tahwīs*, (v. n. 2 of حاص for حوص) Sewing (a garment) in various parts.

A تحويض *tahwīz*, (v. n. 2 of حاض for حوض) Making a pond. Enclosing any place after the manner of a fish-pond. Making a small ditch for watering palm-trees. Longing, seeking after. Moving round.

A تحويط *tahwīt*, (v. n. 2 of حاط for حوط) Building a wall. Fencing about. Guarding, preserving, minding. Going round.

A تحويف *tahwīf*, (v. n. 2 of حاف for حوف) Placing on a brink. Encircling a place (the plant وسمي *wasmīy*). Changing, turning, setting in another direction.

A تحويق *tahwīk*, A twisting, a perverting.

A تحويل *tahwīl*, (v. n. 2 of حال for حول) Turning about. Changing. Causing to pass to another. Removing, transplanting. Causing to squint. Supposing or rendering absurd and impossible. Becoming changed. Becoming in the middle of the sky (the galaxy). Not conceiving though covered (a camel). Migration.

A تحويلات *tahwīlāt*, Revolutions.

P تحويلدار *tahwīl-dār*, Cash-keeper, treasurer.

P تحويلداري *tahwīl-dārī*, Office of cash-keeper.

A تحويم *tahwīm*, (v. n. 2 of حام for حوم) Being assiduous, sticking close to.

A تحيّات *tahīyāt*, Salutations, greetings.

A تحيّة *tahiyat*, (v. n. 2 of حيّ) Creating king. Saluting, greeting. Keeping, preserving. Constituting possessor. Approaching, being hard upon. (pl. تحيّات *tahīyāt* and تحايا *tahāya*) A salutation, compliment, congratulation, prayer, benediction. Possession. Permanency, duration. A kingdom. بعد التحيّة *baʻda't tahīyat*, After compliments.

A تحيت *tuhayt*, (dimin.) Somewhat below.

A تحيّر *tahayyur*, (v. n. 5 of حار for حير) Being astonished, confounded, disturbed. Being dazzled, overpowered (the eye-sight). Whirling in an eddy and being collected together (water). Wandering, flying in no fixed direction (a cloud). Being filled with water (a place). Being filled with meat or fat (a dish). Being completed (the season of youth).

A تحيّز *tahayyuz*, (v. n. 5 of حاز for حيز) Being coiled up, coiling itself up (a serpent).

A تحيّش *tahayyush*, (v. n. 5 of حاش for حيش) Being scared and greatly afraid.

A تحيّض *tahayyuz*, (v. n. 5 of حاض for حيض) Abstaining from public prayer (a woman) on account of ceremonial uncleanness.

A تحيط *tuhīt*, *tahīt*, or *tihīt*, A barren year.

A تحيّف *tahayyuf*, (v. n. 5 of حاف for حيف) Lessening by paring down the edge.

A تحيفس *tahayfus*, A moving of one's self in bed. A being removed from one's place. A being unloosed or untied.

A تحيّل *tahayyul*, (v. n. 5 of حال for حيل) Using stratagems. Craft, wile, sagacity. Power.

A تحين *tahīn*, Time, space of time.

A تحيّن *tahayyun*, (v. n. 5 of حان for حين) Waiting, longing for, an expected time. Fixing a time of night or day for milking. Being destroyed, cut off. The arrival of time, its being at hand.

A تحييد *tahyīd*, (v. n. 2 of حاد for حيد) Making projections or knots.

A تحييس *tahyīs*, (v. n. 2 of حاس for حيس) Preparing the dish called حيس *hays*.

A تحييض *tahyīz*, (v. n. 2 of حاض for حيض) Causing to flow. Lying with a menstruous woman.

A تحيين *tahyīn*, (v. n. 2 of حان for حين) Fixing a time. Destroying, cutting off.

P تخ *takh*, Dregs of sesame.

A تخّ *takhkhh*, (v. n. of تخّ) Fermenting, turning sour (leaven). Oil expressed from sesame. A sour mass of paste.

A تخاتل *takhātul*, (v. n. 6 of ختل) Deceiving each other. Being deceived.

A تخاتن *takhātun*, (v. n. 6 of ختن) Intermarrying.

A تخاجؤ *takhājuʼ*, (v. n. 6 of خجأ) Walking slowly. Delaying.

A تخادع *takhāduʻ*, (v. n. 6 of خدع) Pretending to be deceived. Deceiving one another.

A تخادن *takhādun*, (v. n. 6 of خدن) Acting sincerely towards one another in friendship.

A تخاذل *takhāzul*, (v. n. 6 of خذل) Withholding assistance from each other, deserting one another. Being infirm (the feet). Staying with her young (a doe).

A تخارج *takhāruj*, (v. n. 6 of خرج) Dividing amongst themselves (one party taking the house, and the other the land).

A تخارش *takhārush*, (v. n. 6 of خرش) Growling and fighting (dogs).

A تخاريب *takhārīb*, (pl. of تخريب *takhrīb*) Holes resembling a honeycomb or wasp's nest.

A تخازر *takhāzur*, (v. n. 6 of خزر) Contracting the eyelids, in order to look more accurately.

A تخاصّ *takhāss*, (v. n. 6 of خصّ) Doing any thing alternately. Making haste simultaneously.

A تخاسؤ *takhāsuʼ*, (v. n. 6 of خسأ) Throwing stones at one another.

A تخاسي *takhāsī*, (v. n. 6 of خسي) Pelting each other with pebbles.

A تخاشع *takhāshuʻ*, (v. n. 6 of خشع) Being humble, obsequious, submissive.

A تخاصر *takhāsur*, A walking hand in hand.

A تخاصل *takhāsul*, (v. n. 6 of خصل) Contending with one another in throwing the javelin (when the stakes are deposited).

A تخاصم *takhāsum*, (v. n. 6 of خصم) Altercating, being at variance. Litigation, squabble.

A تخاطب *takhātub*, A conversing face to face.

A تخاطر *takhātur*, (v. n. 6 of خطر) Depositing the bets, and then disputing or contending. Laying down the stakes.

A تخاطف *takhātuf*, (v. n. 6 of خطف) Carrying off (a ball with a shinty).

A تخاطؤ *takhātuʼ*, (v. n. 6 of خطئ) Erring, blundering (a man). Imputing to any one an error.

A تخافت *takhāfut*, (v. n. 6 of خفت) Reading any thing in a muttering low voice. Communicating secrets to one another.

A تخافف *takhāfuf*, (v. n. 6 of خفّ) Being light.

A تخالج *takhāluj*, (v. n. 6 of خلج) Exciting doubts in the mind.

A تخالس *takhālus*, (v. n. 6 of خلس) Snatching from one another. Drawing, tugging to one's self.

A تخالص *takhālus*, (v. n. 6 of خلص) Acting sincerely towards one another.

A تخالط *takhālut*, A mixing in society.

A تخالع *takhāluʻ*, (v. n. 6 of خلع) Divorcing, separating (as husband and wife). Dissolving partnership (a company). Violating an agreement.

A تخالف *takhāluf*, An opposing one another.

A تخامص *takhāmus*, (v. n. 6 of خمص) Being somewhat dark (the night) soon after the setting, and before the rising of the sun. Paying a debt and receiving a discharge. Being lifted off and laid on one side.

A تخاوز *takhāwuz*, A stipulating.

A تخاوض *takhāwuz*, (v. n. 6 of خاض for خوض) Considering together. Keeping up a conversation together. Agreeing.

A تخاويف *takhāwīf*, Hobgoblins. Scarecrows.

A تخايل *takhāyul*, (v. n. 6 of خال for خيل) Appearing probable. Being vain and proud.

A تخبّث *takhabbus*, A being filthy and impure.

A تخبخب *takhabkhub*, (v. n. 2 of خبخب Q) Being soft, flabby, and pendulous. Becoming lean after being fat. Subsiding (heat).

A تخبّر *takhabbur*, (v. n. 5 of خبر) Inquiring, asking news or information. Being acquainted, conversant with. تخبّروا خبرة *takhabbarū khubrat*, They bought a sheep, and divided her (when slaughtered) amongst themselves.

A تخبّس *takhabbus*, A seizing as plunder.

A تخبّش *takhabbush*, A carrying off, a taking.

A تخبّص *takhabbus*, (v. n. 5 of خبص) Cooking the preparation called خبيص *khabīs*.

A تخبّط *takhabbut*, (v. n. 5 of خبط) Losing one's way. Becoming silly. Pawing the ground (a camel). Hurting, harming one (Satan).

A تخبّق *takhabbuk*, (v. n. 5 of خبق) Being high, sublime, elevated.

A تخبّي *takhabbī*, (v. n. 5 of خبي) Erecting a tent called خباء *khibāʼ*. Putting out (the fire).

A تخبيب *takhbīb*, A seducing, deceiving.

A تخبئة *takhbiʼat*, (v. n. 2 of خبأ) Concealing.

A تخبية *takhbiyat*, The pitching of a tent.

A تخبيث *takhbīs*, (v. n. 2 of خبث) Corrupting.

A تخبير *takhbīr*, (v. n. 2 of خبر) Giving information, advising, imparting, communicating, certifying.

A تخبيص *takhbīs*, (v. n. 2 of خبص) Cooking the dish خبيص *khabīs*.

A تخبيط *takhbīt*, A mistake, blunder.

A تخبيل *takhbīl*, (v. n. 2 of خبل) Making silly, insane. Mutilating, depriving of the use of limbs.

A P تخت *takht*, (pl. تخوت *tukhūt*) A royal throne, chair of state. A seat, sopha. A bed. Any place raised above the ground for sleeping, sitting, or reclining. A saddle. A capital, the royal residence. P تخت آبنوسي *takhti ābnūsī*, Night. تخت آراسته *takhti ārāsta*, An ornamented throne. تخت اردشير *takhti ardshīr*, Name of a musical note. تخت جمشيد *takhti jamshed*, Persepolis. تخت چوبي *takhti chūbī*, A gun-carriage. تخت خورشيد برسر ضرغام *takhti khwurshed bar sari zirghām*, The sun in the sign Leo. تخت راهي *takhti rāhī*, The royal road, the highway. تخت روان *takhti ravān*, (or تخت رونده *takhti ravanda*) A travelling-bed, a litter with poles, like our sedan-chairs, but borne by mules. The throne of Solomon. An easy-paced horse. The sky. Name of four stars in the constellation of the Bear. تخت سراج *takhti sarāj*, Name of the college of Abū Is-hāk. تخت سليمان *takhti sulaymān*, The famous fortress of Kāshghar. تخت طاقديسي *takht-tāḳdīsī*, Name of a throne belonging to Farīdūn. Name of a note in music. تخت فيروزه *takhti fīroza*, The firmament. Name of the throne of Khusraw. تخت كلاه *takhti kulāh*, A wooden cap worn by criminals as a punishment. تخت همايون *takhti humāyūn*, The august, royal, or imperial residence.

A تخت *takht*, (pl. تخوت *tukhūt*) A wardrobe, clothes-press, chest.

A تختاخ *takhtākh*, (or تختخانيّ *takhtakhānīy*) A stammerer, a stutterer. One who speaks Arabic unintelligibly, being a barbarian or foreigner.

P تخت بخت *takht-bakht*, Throne and fortune.

A تختج *takhtaj*, (from P تخته *takhta*) (pl. تخاتج *takhātij*) Boards, planks, tables.

A تخ تخ *tikh tikh*, Said when driving poultry.

A تختخة *takhtakhat*, An impediment in speech; bad pronunciation.

P تخت دار *takht-dār*, A species of cloth, either white or black, which the kings of Persia, especially the Dārās (Darius), used to spread over their throne. Bed-clothes.

P تختر *tukhtar*, (for دختر) A daughter.

A تختّر *takhattur*, (v. n. 5 of ختر) Being delirious, intoxicated (with drink). Flagging, hanging down. Going at a lazy, sluggish pace. Labouring under a fever. Being lazy, slow, weak, relaxed.

P تختگاه *takht-gāh*, Royal residence, capital.

P تختله *takhtala*, A walking-staff. Shoes.

A تختّم *takhattum*, (v. n. 5 of ختم) Putting on a seal-ring. Dissembling, feigning negligence. Being silent. Covering, enveloping, wrapping up. Wrapping a turban round the head.

A تختمة *takhtimat*, Dissimulation, secresy. The wrapping a turban round the head.

P تخت نشان *takht-nishān*, Throne-bestowing.

P تخت نشين *takht-nishīn*, Sitting on the throne. A reigning prince. تخت نشينان خاك *takht-nishīnāni khāk*, Dwellers upon earth. Kings. Spirits. Devout men.

P تخت نشيني *takht-nishīnī*, Accession, reign.

P تخته *takhta*, A board, plank. A table. A table upon which dead bodies are stretched and washed before interment. Tablets, memorandum-book. A single sheet of paper. A little bed, couch. The pedestal of a statue. تختهٔ آسيا *takhtaʼi āsyā*, A plough-beam. تختهٔ اوّل *takhtaʼi avval*, The table of the divine decrees. A school-boy's writing-board. تختهٔ جامه *takhtaʼi jāma*, A large press; a calender, beetle, or any thing similar, by which linens are beat, pressed, or smoothed. An instrument of torture, made like a horse. تختهٔ جوهري *takhtaʼi jawharī*, The colours red and blue. تختهٔ خاك *takhtaʼi khāk*, The surface of the earth. تختهٔ در *takhtaʼi dar*, The panel of a door. تختهٔ زرنيخ *takhtaʼi zarnīkh*, A live coal. تختهٔ سالخورد *takhtaʼi sāl-khwurd*, Stories of old times. تختهٔ شطرنج *takhtaʼi shatranj*, A chess-board. تختهٔ عاج *takhtaʼi ʻāj*, A throne of ivory. Milk-white hips. Day. تخته كردن *takhta kardan*, (or تخته زدن *takhta zadan*) To clean cotton. تختهٔ كشتي *takhtaʼi kishtī*, The plank of a ship. تختهٔ كفشگر *takhtaʼi kafshgar*, A shoemaker's board, upon which he cuts out his leather. تخته گردن *takhta-gardan*, Broad, thick, straight-necked (horse). تختهٔ گوي *takhtaʼi gūī*, The mace or club with which the ball is struck. تختهٔ محاسبان *takhtaʼi muhāsibān*, The earth. تختهٔ ميانه *takhtaʼi miyāna*, The sky. تختهٔ مينا *takhtaʼi mīnā*, The firmament. تختهٔ نان *takhtaʼi nān*, A baker's kneading-board. A plain flat table. A large flat dish, with a brass rim round it. تختهٔ نرد *takhtaʼi nard*, A dice-table, backgammon-board. تختهٔ نرد آبنوسي *takhtaʼi nardi ābnūsī*, The zodiac. آهن تخته *āhan-takhta*, A plate of iron. تخت يا تخته *takht yā takhta*, A throne or a bier (spoken on engaging in a desperate enterprise) (A coronet or Westminster Abbey).

P تخته *tukhta*, Paid, discharged.

P تخته بند *takhta-band*, A splinter bound upon a broken bone. A floor. Confined, guarded.

P تخته بندي *takhta-bandī*, Boarding, wainscot.

P تخته پوش *takhta-posh*, Stage, wooden floor.

P تخته كشيده *takhta-kashīda*, Floored; floor.

P تختي *takhtī*, Becoming a throne. A board on which children learn to write. A signet of stone. The breast.

A تختير *takhtīr*, (v. n. 2 of ختر) Inebriating, making drunk. Disordering the intellects.

A تختيم *takhtīm*, (v. n. 2 of ختم) Sealing well.

A تخثّر *takhassur*, A being thick and turbid.

A تخثيث *takhsīs*, (v. n. 2 of خثّ not used) Collecting. Repairing, mending.

A تخثير *takhsīr*, (v. n. 2 of خثر) Allowing or causing (milk) to thicken.

A تخثيم *takhsīm*, A making broad.

P تخجم *takhjum*, Covetous, greedy, selfish.

A تخجيل *takhjīl*, A putting to the blush.

A تخدّب *takhaddub*, A moderate pace.

A تخدّد *takhaddud*, (v. n. 5 of خدّ) Wrinkling, shrivelling. Becoming lean and emaciated.

A تخدّع *takhadduʻ*, A striving to deceive.

A تخديد *takhdīd*, (v. n. 2 of خدّ) Being emaciated, shrivelled (flesh, skin). Being meagre, lank. Making lean. Splitting, cleaving.

A تخدير *takhdīr*, (v. n. 2 of خدر) Keeping (a woman) concealed. Occasioning a torpor in the limbs. Being concealed behind a veil from the gaze of men (a girl). Concealing one's self.

A تخديع *takhdīʻ*, (v. n. 2 of خدع) Deceiving remarkably. A blow or cut that does not penetrate.

A تخديم *takhdīm*, (v. n. 2 of خدم) Having a white ring on the lower part of the hind legs (a horse).

A تخذرف *takhazruf*, (v. n. 2 of خذرف Q) Striking any one (a date-stone).

A تخذّم *takhazzum*, (v. n. 5 of خذم) Cutting. Being broken or cut off.

A تخذيع *takhzīʻ*, (v. n. 2 of خذع) Mincing, hacking. Inflicting a blow which penetrates not.

A تخذيل *takhzīl*, (v. n. 2 of خذل) Alienating, causing a breach between friends.

A تخذيم *takhzīm*, (v. n. 2 of خذم) Cutting well.

A تخرب *takharrub*, A corroding, a cankering.

A تخرج *takharruj*, (v. n. 5 of خرج) Acquiring polite learning.

A تخرخر *takharkhur*, (v. n. 2 of خرخر Q) Being big and rattling (the belly).

A تخرد *takharrud*, (v. n. 5 of خرد) Being bashful. Being silent from timidity, or speaking low.

A تخرس *takharrus*, (v. n. 5 of خرس) Taking the food خرسة *khursat* (a woman in child-bed).

A تخرص *takharrus*, (v. n. 5 of خرص) Lying, speaking falsehood.

A تخرط *takharrut*, (v. n. 5 of خرط) Extracting the oily matter from his rump (a bird).

A تخرق *takharruk*, (v. n. 5 of خرق) Being torn, pierced full of holes. Sweeping across (as the wind). Inventing a lie. Being profusely liberal. Being oppressively, ridiculously troublesome. Rent, cleft.

A تخرم *takharrum*, (v. n. 5 of خرم) Being broken, burst (as sewing). Being pierced (as pearls, beads, or the septum of the nose). Destroying (him) entirely (fortune). Embracing the Khurramiyan sect (See خرمية *khurramīyat*). Being appeased (anger).

A تخرمل *takharmul*, A being torn (a garment).

A تخرور *tukhrūr*, (A man) not brisk and active, not yet thick and dense.

A تخريب *takhrīb*, (v. n. 2 of خرب) Destroying, demolishing, razing, devastating far and wide.

A تخريج *takhrīj*, (v. n. 2 of خرج) Bringing out, educing. Instructing in learning and politeness. Writing on one part (of a tablet) and not on another. Doing work in a party-coloured manner. Grazing one part of a field and leaving the other untouched. Being in some respects barren, in others fruitful (a season).

A تخريس *takhrīs*, (v. n. 2 of خرس) Preparing and giving food (to a woman in child-bed). Making dumb (اخرس *akhras*).

A تخريش *takhrīsh*, (v. n. 2 of خرش) Putting forth the ears (corn).

A تخريص *tikhrīs*, (or تخريصة *tikhrīsat*) The gore of a shift or other garment.

A تخريط *takhrīt*, (v. n. 2 of خرط) Loosening the belly (a cathartic).

A تخريف *takhrīf*, (v. n. 2 of خرف) Charging (any one) with dotage.

A تخريق *takhrīk*, (v. n. 2 of خرق) Tearing, lacerating very much. Telling many lies.

A تخريم *takhrīm*, The bursting (of sewing).

A تخزب *takhazzub*, (v. n. 5 of خزب) Swelling, being fat. Being swelled (the udder), and thence a contraction of the teats.

A تخزبز *takhazbuz*, (v. n. 2 of خزبز Q not used) Carrying one's self haughtily. Scowling, looking sour and grim. Striking with his foot whatever he meets (a camel).

A تخزبوب *takhzabūb*, Excellent, active (camel).

A تخزع *takhazzuع*, (v. n. 5 of خزع) Remaining behind, deserting one's associates. Cutting the flesh off a slaughtered camel. Cutting and dividing (among themselves).

A تخزل *takhazzul*, (v. n. 5 of خزل) Proceeding slowly, heavily (as a cloud charged with rain).

A تخزلج *takhazluj*, (v. n. 2 of خزلج Q) Walking fast, proceeding rapidly.

A تخزم *takhazzum*, (v. n. 5 of خزم) Piercing the foot (a thorn).

A تخزير *takhzīr*, A straitening, compressing.

A تخزيع *takhzīع*, (v. n. 2 of خزع) Hindering, detaining, letting. Cutting. Remaining behind, deserting.

A تخزيم *takhzīm*, (v. n. 2 of خزم) Passing a hair ring through the perforated nose of a camel.

P تخس *takhs* or *takhas*, Anguish, anxiety, change of temper or constitution, from grief or indisposition.

A تخس *tukhas*, A dolphin or certain marine animal said to save a man from drowning by taking him on his back.

A تخسية *takhsiyat*, (v. n. 2 of خسي) Playing at nuts, odd or even.

A تخسير *takhsīr*, (v. n. 2 of خسر) Causing loss, ruining, destroying.

P تخش *taksh*, A cross-bow. An arrow. A rocket. The chief seat.

P تخشا *takhshā*, One who tries to do any thing with energy.

A تخشب *takhashshub*, (v. n. 5 of خشب) Eating sticks and dry fodder.

A تخشخش *takhashkhush*, (v. n. 2 of خشخش Q) Rattling, clashing, rustling (as arms, papers, silks, dry leaves, &c.) Entering amongst trees and concealing one's self.

A تخشع *takhashshuع*, (v. n. 5 of خشع) Humbling one's self, becoming or being humble.

A تخشل *takhashshul*, (v. n. 5 of خشل) Being rejected. Being vile, abject, depressed.

A تخشم *takhashshum*, (v. n. 5 of خشم) Spoiling, stinking (meat).

A تخشن *takhashshun*, (v. n. 5 of خشن) Becoming rough (in habit, face, converse, or mode of life).

A تخشي *takhashshī*, (v. n. 5 of خشي) Dreading, standing in awe.

A تخشية *takhshiyat*, A striking with terror.

P تخشيدن *takhshīdan*, To sit on the high seat.

A تخشيف *takhshīf*, (v. n. 2 of خشف) Conducting others boldly (a guide in the night).

A تخشيم *takhshīm*, (v. n. 2 of خشم) Intoxicating (the fumes of wine).

A تخشين *takhshīn*, (v. n. 2 of خشن) Making rough. Irritating, exasperating.

A تخصة *takhissat*, (v. n. of خص) Marking especially, distinguishing peculiarly.

A تخصر *takhassur*, (v. n. 5 of خصر) Putting the hand on the hypochondria when tired. Taking a staff in the hand to lean upon.

A تخصص *takhassus*, (v. n. 5 of خص) Being distinguished. Peculiarity.

A تخصيب *takhsīb*, (v. n. 2 of خصب) Fattening.

A تخصير *takhsīr*, Slenderness.

A تخصيص *takhsīs*, (v. n. 2 of خص) Making peculiar and special. Particularizing. Playing with a lighted reed.

A تخصيف *takhsīf*, (v. n. 2 of خصف) Making (the hairs) equally white and black (hoariness). Being bad-tempered. Making great pretensions to what one is not entitled.

A تخصيل *takhsīl*, (v. n. 2 of خصل) Cutting in pieces. Separating into pieces (a tree). Cutting for a camel the tips of limber twigs.

A تخضج *takhazzuj*, The act of limping.

A تخضخض *takhazkhuz*, (v. n. 2 of خضخض Q) Being stirred about (water or a ptisan). Shaking.

A تخضد *takhazzud*, (v. n. 5 of خضد) Being broken (a green stick). Being bent double.

A تخضع *takhazzuع*, A humbling one's self.

A تخضعب *takhazعub*, Confusion (of business).

A تخضلب *takhazlub*, (v. n. 2 of خضلب Q) Being weak and confused (a business).

A تخضور *takhzūr*, Green.

A تخضيب *takhzīb*, A tinging beautifully.

A تخضيد *takhzīd*, A splitting, cutting asunder.

A تخضير *takhzīr*, (v. n. 2 of خضر) Making green. Blessing. Green.

A تخضيض *takhzīz*, (v. n. 2 of خض) Adorning (a maid) with beads called خضض *khazaz*.

A تخضيع *takhzīع*, (v. n. 2 of خضع) Cutting in pieces, mincing (meat). Causing to stoop (old age).

A تخطر *takhattur*, (v. n. 5 of خطر) Missing the mark (an arrow).

A تخطرب *takhatrub*, A telling lies of any body.

A تخطرف *takhatruf*, (v. n. 2 of خطرف Q) Walking fast, making long strides.

A تخطف *takhattuf*, A seizing, carrying off.

A تخطل *takhattul*, (v. n. 5 of خطل) Walking with a swinging air.

A تخطؤ *takhattuء*, (v. n. 5 of خطؤ) Erring, blundering, offending lightly. Imputing a fault to another, and reproaching him for it.

A تخطي *takhattī*, (v. n. 5 of خطا for خطو) Transgressing, passing beyond, overstepping.

A تخطئة *takhtiءat*, (v. n. 2 of خطئ) Leading into error. Blaming for a fault, charging with error or crime.

A تخطية *takhtiyat*, (v. n. 2 of خطا for خطو) Repelling, averting (evil).

A تخطيط *takhtīt*, (v. n. 2 of خط) Eating little. Weaving or marking (cloth) with stripes. Drawing lines well.

A تخطيم *takhtīm*, (v. n. 2 of خطم) Putting a halter over the nose of a (camel).

A تخطيئ *takhtīء*, A charging with a fault.

A تخظية *takhziyat*, (v. n. 2 of خظا for خظو)

Rendering stout, bulky, and fleshy.

A تخفّج takhaffuj, An inclining. A deviating.

A تخفّر takhaffur, (v. n. 5 of خفر) Being extremely bashful. Imploring protection from a patron. Recommending one's self to the protection of. Protecting. Excessive bashfulness.

A تخفّس takhaffus, (v. n. 5 of خفس) Being thrown down, falling or lying upon the ground, being spurned, being trampled upon.

A تخفّف takhaffuf, A being booted.

A تخفّي takhaffī, A concealing of one's self.

A تخفية takhfiyat, A hiding, a concealing.

A تخفير takhfīr, (v. n. 2 of خفر) Protecting, patronizing. Acting as guide. Causing to blush much.

A تخفيس takhfīs, A diluting wine with water.

A تخفيش takhfīsh, (v. n. 2 of خفش) Throwing down, levelling with the ground. Demolishing, making desolate. Trampling upon. Being feeble (the body). Cleaving to the ground.

A تخفيض takhfīz, (v. n. 2 of خفض) Speaking or doing any thing gently, submissively, or with ease. Pressing down (a camel's head) to make him kneel down.

A تخفيف takhfīf, (v. n. 2 of خفّ) Making light, alleviating. Abbreviating, by scratching out, or erasing a word or letter (as ضلع zalaʿ into zalʿ, بتر batar for بدتر badtar), or taking off the tanwīn. Abatement, alleviation, relief, remission.

A تخقين takhḳīn, (v. n. 2 of خقن not used) Appointing خاقان khāḳān or emperor (in Turkistān).

A تخلّج takhalluj, (v. n. 5 of خلج) Waving, nodding, shaking, or tottering from side to side, as if the joints were paralyzed.

A تخلخل takhalkhul, (v. n. 2 of خلخل Q) Wearing the ankle-ring خلخال khalkhāl (a woman).

A تخلّس takhallus, A seizing, a snatching.

A تخلّص takhallus, (v. n. 5 of خلص) Being saved, delivered from evil. Saving one's self. Obtaining, gaining. The transition from the description of one's owns feelings to the eulogium of a person in a poem. A titular name assumed by poets.

A تخلّع takhalluʿ, (v. n. 5 of خلع) Going wide between the feet. Sticking close to the bottle, drinking immoderately.

A تخلّف takhalluf, (v. n. 5 of خلف) Remaining behind. Being left behind.

A تخلّق takhalluḳ, (v. n. 5 of خلق) Inventing a lie. Imitating the manner of another. Perfuming with a spice called خلوق khalūḳ.

A تخلّل takhallul, (v. n. 5 of خلّ) Passing through. Separating with the fingers (the beard). Picking (the teeth). Perforating, boring. Piercing through with thrust after thrust. Entering into the alleys about a house. Entering amongst. Being partial (rain). Seeking for (ripe dates) amongst unripe ones. Being finished, exhausted, annihilated.

P تخله takhla, A staff. A shoe. Bits, scraps.

A تخليّ ti or takhlī, The world. Meat and drink.

A تخلّي takhallī, (v. n. 5 of خلي) Retiring. Abandoning, leaving empty or alone. Being alone. Being vacant, at leisure.

A تخلية takhliyat, (v. n. 2 of خلي) Vacating, abandoning, leaving empty or alone.

A تخليد takhlīd, (v. n. 2 of خلد) Adorning (with bracelets or ear-rings). Abiding. Growing old by slow degrees.

A تخليص takhlīs, (v. n. 2 of خلص) Showing sincere love. Saving, delivering, rescuing, preserving from evil. Clearing, freeing from. Taking the purest and best of any thing.

A تخليط takhlīt, (v. n. 2 of خلط) Mixing, confounding, disturbing, perplexing any business. Spoiling, marring. A clumsy job, a mess.

A تخليع takhlīʿ, (v. n. 2 of خلع) Straddling much in walking. In the metre called بسيط basīt changing the cæsura مستفعلن mustafʿilun into مفعولن mafʿūlun.

A تخليف takhlīf, (v. n. 2 of خلف) Leaving behind. Appointing a substitute. Tying up a (camel's) teat, that the milk may not run out.

A تخليق takhlīḳ, (v. n. 2 of خلق) Forming well, completing. Anointing with an aromatic called خلوق khalūḳ, or with saffron.

A تخليل takhlīl, (v. n. 2 of خلّ) Turning (any thing) sour. Exposing unripe dates to the sun, sprinkling them with vinegar, and laying them up in a jar. Becoming sour, turning to vinegar. Picking and cleaning the teeth. Pinning (clothes) with a skewer. Letting (water) run amongst the beard and between the fingers. Being peculiar, private, and special.

A تخليم takhlīm, (v. n. 2 of خلم) Choosing.

A تخم takhm (v. n. of تخم) Suffering from indigestion. Takhm or tukhm, The boundary or limits (of a province, palace, or town). A march-stone. Tukham, (pl. of تخمة) Indigestions, dyspepsies.

P تخم tukhm, Seed. Sperm. An egg. Origin, principle. Cholera morbus, flux and vomit. تخم خليل tukhmi khalīl, (or خلال khilāl) Seed of crow's foot. تخم ريحان tukhmi rayhān, Purslain. تخم كتّان tukhmi kuttān, Lintseed. تخم بنگ tukhmi bang, Henbane-seed. تخم جاروب tukhmi jārob, Crow's foot (a herb). تخم جهود tukhmi juhūd, Dispersed, scattered, ruined. تخم سپيد tukhmi saped, White seed. Mustard-seed. Mustard. تخم ماهي tukhmi māhī, Fish-spawn. تخم مرغ tukhmi murgh, A bird's egg. تخم نهادن tukhm nihādan, To lay an egg. Tukham, A cloth stretched upon two sticks, in which they catch such things as are thrown to the people upon rejoicing days.

P تخمار tukhmār, A dart having no point.

P تخم بد tukhm-bad, Of bad stock, low-bred.

A تخمة tukhamat or tukhmat, (pl. تخم tukham and تخمات tukhamāt) Disagreement of food with the stomach, indigestion, dyspepsy.

P تخمدان tukhmdān, A nursery-ground.

A تخمّر takhammur, (v. n. 5 of خمر) Putting on the veil or coif خمار khimār.

P تخم ريز tukhm-rez, Sowing. A sower. A sown field. An omelet. Hashed meat, upon which eggs are poured and fried.

P تخم ريزي tukhm-rezī, Seed-sowing: seedness.

A تخمّط takhammut, (v. n. 5 of خمط) Swelling with pride or anger; being furious, enraged. Being tempestuous (the sea). Braying (as a stallion camel).

P تخمگان tukhmugān, Purslain. The testicles. Any thing growing from seed.

A تخمّم takhammum, (v. n. 5 of خمّ) Eating up the orts left on the table.

P تخمه tukhma, Flux and vomit, cholera. Origin, principle. Root, stock.

P تخمه زده tukhma-zada, Dyspeptic.

A تخمير takhmīr, (v. n. 2 of خمر) Causing to ferment. Covering (the face, or a vessel). Suppressing (evidence). Fermenting, forming into leaven. ضمير محبّت تخمير zamīri mahabbat-takhmīr, A mind mixed or leavened with friendship.

A تخميس takhmīs, (v. n. 2 of خمس) Dividing into five parts. Making a pentagon, or any thing of five angles.

A تخمين takhmīn, (v. n. 2 of خمن) Conjecturing, guessing. Estimating, judging. Guess. Appraisement, valuation.

A تخميناً takhmīnan, (P تخمينانه) By conjecture or guess, by appraisement, nearly, about, more or less.

A تخميني takhmīnī, Conjectural.

A تخنّب takhannub, (v. n. 5 of خنب) Being proud, haughty, tossing the nose.

A تخنّث takhannus, (v. n. 5 of خنث) Being flexible, limber. Being bent. Becoming a catamite.

A تخندف takhanduf, (v. n. 2 of خندف) Claiming relationship with the tribe of خندف khindif.

A تخنذذ takhanzuz, (v. n. 2 of خنذذ Q) Becoming reprobate, outcast, and turning robber.

A تخنّس takhannus, (v. n. 5 of خنس) Slandering the absent. Concealing, rendering invisible.

A تخنيث takhnīs, A bending, a twisting.

A تخنيع takhnīʿ, A cutting with a hatchet.

A تخنيق takhnīḳ, (v. n. 2 of خنق) Strangling. Overspreading or covering almost entirely over. Being hard upon (forty). Filling (a vessel).

P تخوار tukhwār, The king of دهستان dahistān.

A تخوت tukhūt, (pl. of تخت takht) Wardrobes, chests. Chairs of state, thrones.

A تخوّت takhawwut, (v. n. 5 of خات for خوت) Diminishing, lessening (wealth). Stealing, robbing, carrying away by force. Breaking away from, abandoning, relinquishing.

A تخوخة tukhūkhat, (v. n. of تخ) Turning sour.

A تخوّد takhawwud, (v. n. 5 of خاد for خود) Being bent (a branch).

A تخوّش *takhawwush*, (v. n. 5 of خاش for خوش) Diminishing. Becoming lean.

A تخوّص *takhawwus*, (v. n. 5 of خاص for خوص) Receiving presents one after another.

A تخوّض *takhawwuz*, (v. n. 5 of خاض for خوض) Being forced, or feigning to be forced, to ford a river. Undertaking to cross a river.

A تخوّط *takhawwut*, (v. n. 5 of خاط for خوط) Approaching again and again.

A تخوّع *takhawwuع*, (v. n. 5 of خاع for خوع) Being diminished. Diminishing, weakening, by taking away a part. Hawking, vomiting.

A تخوّف *takhawwuf*, (v. n. 5 of خاف for خوف) Being terrified. Dreading, lest any evil should befal another. Diminishing. Being light.

A تخوّق *takhawwuk*, (v. n. 5 of خاق for خوق) Being enlarged, amplified. Withdrawing to a distance.

A تخوّل *takhawwul*, (v. n. 5 of خال for خول) Observing, discovering. Visiting, frequenting. Visiting, attending the sick. Appointing, choosing a manager of property (خال *khāl*).

A تخوم *takhūm*, (pl. تخوم *tukhūm* or تخم *tukhum*) A limit, a boundary. *Tukhūm*, A state which one desires. (pl. *tukhūm* or تخم *tukhum*) Limit, boundary.

A تخومة *takhūmat*, A limit, boundary.

A تخوّن *takhawwun*, (v. n. 5 of خان for خون) Withholding a due. Diminishing. Minding, attending to, managing.

A تخوية *takhwiyat*, (v. n. 2 of خوي) Failing (as stars, when, by their appearance at setting, they prognosticate rain, which does not happen). Becoming very fat (cattle). Digging a hole and lighting a fire in it, and compelling (diseased cattle) to lie therein. Having the belly distant from the ground when reclining (a camel). Stretching the limbs wide from one another (in worship). Expanding the wings (a bird). Giving food to a child-bed woman.

A تخويد *takhwīd*, (v. n. 2 of خاد for خود) Going fast. Turning a stallion camel amongst the herd. Taking a little food.

A تخوير *takhwīr*, Weakness, feebleness.

A تخويش *takhwīsh*, The act of diminishing.

A تخويص *takhwīs*, (v. n. 2 of خاص for خوص) Accepting (a present) though small. Conferring honour, first upon the chief guests, and then upon the rest. Beginning to appear (gray hairs). Adorning (a diadem) with plates of gold.

A تخويض *takhwīz*, (v. n. 2 of خاض for خوض) Plunging into and crossing (a river).

A تخويع *takhwīع*, (v. n. 2 of خاع for خوع) Lessening, taking from. Eating its banks away (a stream). Weakening by caning, cudgeling. Paying off (a debt).

A تخويف *takhwīf*, (v. n. 2 of خاف for خوف) Terrifying, putting in fear. Rendering formidable. A bugbear, hobgoblin, scarecrow.

A تخويق *takhwīk*, (v. n. 2 of خاق for خوق) Enlarging, widening, making roomy.

A تخويل *takhwīl*, (v. n. 2 of خال for خول) Giving possession, granting a request, giving one a preference to others. Appointing king.

A تخوين *takhwīn*, (v. n. 2 of خان for خون) Accusing of treachery, declaring any thing perfidious. Diminishing. Minding, attending to.

A تخيّب *tukhuyyib*, وادي تخيّب *wādī tukhuyyib*, Vanity, disappointment.

A تخيّر *takhayyur*, (v. n. 5 of خار for خير) Choosing, selecting, preferring. Doing aught for one's self.

A تخيّط *takhayyut*, (v. n. 5 of خاط for خيط) Beginning to grow gray (hairs).

A تخيعل *takhayعul*, (v. n. 2 of خيعل Q) Being dressed in a sleeveless shirt.

A تخيّف *takhayyuf*, (v. n. 5 of خاف for خيف) Being changed (in colour). Changing (colour).

A تخيّل *takhayyul*, (v. n. 5 of خال for خيل) Passing before the mind, appearing probable. Imagining, fancying. Judging, suspecting. Being overcast with clouds (the sky), portending rain. Being imagined, fancied, or suspected. Thinking vainly of one's self. Imagination, fancy.

A تخيّلات *takhayyulāt*, Imaginations.

A تخيّم *takhayyum*, (v. n. 5 of خام for خيم) Pitching a tent. Adhering (as perfume to a garment).

A تخييب *takhyīb*, (v. n. 2 of خاب for خيب) Prohibiting, barring from hope, disappointing, baulking, frustrating.

A تخييث *takhyīs*, Bigness and flaccidity of belly.

A تخيير *takhyīr*, (v. n. 2 of خار for خير) Giving the option. Preferring, giving the preference over others. Choosing, selecting. Choice.

A تخييس *takhyīs*, (v. n. 2 of خاس for خيس) Subduing, mastering. Forcing.

A تخييط *takhyīt*, (v. n. 2 of خاط for خيط) Appearing like threads (the beginning of grey hairs).

A تخييف *takhyīf*, (v. n. 2 of خاف for خيف) Retiring to, or alighting at (any place). Retreating (from battle). Being divided, distributed.

A تخييل *takhyīl*, (v. n. 2 of خال for خيل) Fancying, imagining. Suspecting. Making one suppose or fancy; deceiving. Pretending to, practising deception. Threatening thunder or rain (clouds). Putting (for a she-camel) any thing frightful, resembling an apparition, near her colt, to frighten the wolf. Hanging back, being timid, cowardly.

A تخييليّ *takhyīlīy*, Imaginary, imaginative.

A تخييم *takhyīm*, (v. n. 2 of خام for خيم) Pitching a tent and going into it. Covering with any thing (for shade). Stopping, or sitting in a place.

A تد *tid*, (imp. of وتد) Drive (the stake).

A تداءم *tadāءum*, (v. n. 6 of دأم) Being piled (as one thing upon another), weighing down.

A تدابر *tadābur*, (v. n. 6 of دبر) Deserting, neglecting one another, turning the back on each other.

A تدابير *tadābīr*, (pl. of تدبير *tadbīr*) Regulations. Counsels.

A تداثر *tadāsur*, (v. n. 6 of دثر) Being demolished, destroyed, old, or worn out.

A تداخل *tadākhul*, (v. n. 6 of دخل) Entering partially. Interfering with one another.

A تدأدؤ *tadaءduء*, (v. n. 2 of دأدأ Q) Being stirred. Being stilled. Being covered. Being turned over, rolled, revolved. Uttering a cry of affection from her inmost bowels (a she-camel). Travelling slowly, tarrying (news). Leaning to one side (a load). Inclining from side to side in walking. Thronging, pressing (crowd). Turning away from.

A تدارس *tadārus*, A studying under another.

A تدارك *tadāruk*, (v. n. 6 of درك) Repairing, mending. Following one another, the last following close, or overtaking the first.. Remedy. The instrument or means to procure justice, as writing, lawyers or witnesses. Provision, ammunition.

P تدارك پذير *tadāruk-pazīr*, Reparable.

A تدارؤ *tadāruء*, (v. n. 6 of درأ) Repelling, thrusting each other back in strife, litigation, or hostility.

A تداري *tadārī*, A sheltering of one's self.

A تداعب *tadāعub*, A jesting, playing together.

A تداعة *tadāعat*, Quiet, tranquillity, comfort.

A تداعك *tadāعuk*, (v. n. 6 of دعك) Rubbing against each other, being scratched in battle. Hating bitterly.

A تداعي *tadāعī*, (v. n. 6 of دعي) Striving together about questions, puzzling one another, propounding enigmas. Challenging each other. Approaching (an adversary). Assembling to hold a council. Threatening ruin (a wall). Falling down.

A تداغش *tadāghush*, (v. n. 6 of دغش) Mixing noisily and tumultuously.

A تدافّ *tadāff*, A riding one another's back.

A تدافع *tadāfuع*, (v. n. 6 of دفع) Thrusting one another back in battle. Passing, conveying (a guest) from tribe to tribe.

A تدافف *tadāfuf*, A riding upon one another.

A تدافن *tadāfun*, (v. n. 6 of دفن) Doing any thing privately together. Concealing among themselves. Being concealed.

A تدافي *tadāfī*, (v. n. 6 of دفا for دفو) Following one another, the last being close upon or overtaking the foremost. Doing any thing alternately. Rolling from side to side (an overloaded camel).

A تداقّ *tadākk*, (v. n. 6 of دقّ) Computing minutely together.

A تداكم *tadākum*, (v. n. 6 of دكم) Thrusting one another back in battle.

A تداكؤ *tadākuء*, (v. n. 6 of دكأ) Thrusting, pressing one another.

A تدالج *tadāluh*, (v. n. 6 of دلج) Carrying any thing between them, as upon a pole.

A تدامج *tadāmuj*, An assisting reciprocally.

A تدامل *tadāmul*, A being reconciled together.

A تدامير *tadāmīr*, (pl. of تدمير) Devastations.

A تداني *tadānī*, The being neighbours.

A تداوك *tadāwuk*, (v. n. 6 of داك for دوك) Fighting, crowding, pressing one another in battle.

A تداول *tadāwul*, (v. n. 6 of دال for دول) Handing from one to another. Doing any thing alternately. Taking turn and turn about. Bandying talk.

A تداوم *tadāwum*, (v. n. 6 of دام for دوم) Flying or skimming round in circles (like a swallow) without moving the wings.

A تداوي *tadāwī*, (v. n. 6 of دوي) Medicating one's self, preparing and taking medicine one's self. Preparing a medicine, applying a remedy, healing, curing. Dressing a wound.

A تداوير *tadāwīr*, (pl. of تدوير) Revolutions.

A تداهي *tadāhī*, (v. n. 6 of دهي) Being clever, shrewd, crafty, or malicious.

A تداين *tadāyun*, (v. n. 6 of دان for دين) Giving mutual credit, buying and selling on credit.

A تدبّر *tadabbur*, (v. n. 5 of دبر) Meditating upon, understanding, perceiving. Deliberating. Looking to the end or result of an affair.

A تدبّق *tadabbuk*, A being taken with bird-lime.

A تدبيب *tadbīb*, (v. n. 2 of دبّ) Walking very gently, creeping.

A تدبئة *tadbi,at*, (v. n. 2 of دبأ) Concealing.

A تدبية *tadbiyat*, (v. n. 2 of دبي) Exercising a trade. Trade, craft, profession.

A تدبيج *tadbīj*, Ornament.

A تدبيح *tadbīh*, (v. n. 2 of دبح) Bowing the head and putting it forward in humility and submission. Cleaving the ground (mushrooms) without protruding. Keeping within doors. Being mean and contemptible.

A تدبيخ *tadbīkh*, A bending forward.

A تدبير *tadbīr*, (v. n. 2 of دبر) Setting in order, arranging, disposing, administering, regulating, managing. Planning, plotting. Looking to the end or result of any affair. Relating, naming; quoting one thing after another. Giving liberty to a slave after one's death. (pl. تدابير *tadābīr*) Government, order, disposition, regulation, able management. Deliberation, council, opinion. تدبير امور البيت *tadbīru umūri'l bayt*, Management of the affairs of the house, domestic economy. تدبير سلطنت *tadbīri sultanat*, Politics. تدبير غذا *tadbīri ghizā*, Regimen. تدبير منازل *tadbīri manāzil*, Household economy. P تدبير دلپذير *tadbīri dil-pazīr*, An opinion agreeable to the heart. تدبير كار كردن *tadbīri kār kardan*, To manage an affair.

A تدبيرات *tadbīrāt*, Regulations, opinions.

P تدبير شناس *tadbīr-shinās*, Wise, prudent.

A تدبيس *tadbīs*, (v. n. 2 of دبس) Concealing. Lying hid, being concealed. Striking a boot against any thing so as to make a noise.

A تدبيق *tadbīk*, (v. n. 2 of دبق) Rubbing with bird-lime and catching a bird.

A تدبيل *tadbīl*, (v. n. 2 of دبل) Rolling into a lump, making up into mouthsful.

A تدبيه *tadbīh*, (v. n. 2 of دبه) Lighting on a sandy place. Persevering in a good way.

A تدبيئ *tadbī,*, A hiding, covering, concealing.

A تدة *tidat*, The fixing firmly (of a stake).

A تدثّر *tadassur*, (v. n. 5 of دثر) Wrapping one's self in a cloak. Mounting on the bunch of the female (a he-camel). Rushing at and springing upon (an antagonist).

A تدثير *tadsīr*, (v. n. 2 of دثر) Building a nest (a bird). Piling a heap of stones over a slain body.

A تدثين *tadsīn*, (v. n. 2 of دثن not used) Flying and hastening to alight in adjacent spots (a bird). Making a nest in a tree.

A تدجّج *tadajjuj*, (v. n. 5 of دجّ) Casing one's self in armour. Being cloudy (the sky).

A تدجدج *tadajduj*, Darkness (of night).

A تدجّي *tadajjī*, Darkness (of the night).

A تدجيج *tadjīj*, Cloudiness (of the sky).

A تدجيل *tadjīl*, (v. n. 2 of دجل) Gleaning. Covering with a false appearance. Gilding with gold or silver so as to have the appearance of those metals. Anointing with pitch. Lying, falsehood.

A تدجيه *tadjīh*, (v. n. 2 of دجه) Lying in wait.

A تدحدر *tadahdur*, A being rolled over.

A تدحرج *tadahruj*, (v. n. 2 of دحرج Q) Being turned or revolved.

A تدحّي *tadahhī*, (v. n. 5 of دحا for دحو) Ambling, prancing about (a horse). (v. n. 5 of دحي) Being extended far and wide.

A تدخدخ *tadakhdukh*, (v. n. 2 of دخدخ Q) Being contracted, shrunk.

A تدخّل *tadakhkhul*, (v. n. 5 of دخل) Entering. Getting in by degrees. Busying one's self gratuitously, interfering in matters.

A تدخّن *tadakhkhun*, (v. n. 5 of دخن) Being troubled with smoke.

A تدخين *tadkhīn*, The emitting of smoke.

A تدرأ *tudra,*, (and تدرأة *tudra,at*, The means by which a man repels an enemy without assistance. Power, glory, dignity.

A تدرّب *tadarrub*, (v. n. 5 of درب) Becoming habituated; being accustomed.

A تدربس *tadarbus*, A going before.

A تدربؤ *tadarbu,*, A being rolled, turned.

A تدرّة *tadirrat*, A copious flow of milk.

A تدرّج *tadarruj*, (v. n. 5 of درج) Being promoted, advanced. Ascending step by step. Approaching gradually.

A تدردر *tadardur*, Quivering of flesh or muscle.

A تدرّع *tadarruꜥ*, The putting on a coat of mail.

A تدرّؤ *tadarru,*, (v. n. 5 of درأ) Deceiving, circumventing, surprising (game). Getting the superiority and insulting over.

A تدره *tudrih*, The charge of driving off or protecting. هو ذو تدرهم *huwa zū tudrihim*, He is their defender or protector.

A تدرّي *tadarrī*, (v. n. 5 of دري) Hiding one's self (in order to seize or kill game). Combing the hair (a woman), setting it a flowing.

A تدريب *tadrīb*, (v. n. 2 of درب) Exercising, habituating. Training, teaching to hunt. Displaying patience in war. Firmness in retreat.

A تدريج *tadrīj*, (v. n. 2 of درج) Advancing, promoting by degrees. Folding (or rather) rolling together (a book or cloth). Oppressing intolerably (as business or meat).

A تدريجاً *tadrījan*, Step by step, gradually.

A تدريس *tadrīs*, A reading attentively.

A تدريع *tadrīꜥ*, (v. n. 2 of درع) Putting armour (on a man), a shift (on a woman). Advancing. Strangling. Making manifest.

A تدريق *tadrīk*, (v. n. 2 of درق) Softening.

A تدريك *tadrīk*, (v. n. 2 of درك) Following in close succession (drops of rain in a shower).

A تدريم *tadrīm*, (v. n. 2 of درم) Polishing and smoothing the nails after paring them.

A تدريه *tadrīh*, (v. n. 2 of دره) Augmenting, adding to. Being disagreeable to, disliking.

A تدسّس *tadassus*, (v. n. 5 of دسّ) Being concealed, hiding one's self.

A تدسية *tadsiyat*, (v. n. 2 of دسي) Concealing. Seducing, corrupting. Repeating, delivering (a saying) repeated by another.

A تدسيم *tadsīm*, (v. n. 2 of دسم) Making (meat) fat and greasy. Wetting (rain). Blackening the dimple in a child's chin (as a charm against fascinating eyes).

A تدشّن *tadashshun*, A taking, a receiving.

A تدعّب *tadaꜥꜥub*, (v. n. 5 of دعب) Bantering, in pretended love.

A تدعة *tudꜥat* or *tudaꜥat*, Quiet, tranquillity. Easy circumstances.

A تدعّث *tadaꜥꜥus*, (v. n. 5 of دعث) Being filled with anger and hatred.

A تدعدع *tadaꜥduꜥ*, The pace of an old man.

A تدعّر *tadaꜥꜥur*, (v. n. 5 of دعر) Being of a foul complexion and covered with spots.

A تدعّص *tadaꜥꜥus*, (v. n. 5 of دعص) Decaying (meat, a carcase).

A تدعكس *tadaꜥkus*, (v. n. 2 of دعكس Q) Dancing with joined hands after the manner of the Magi.

A تدعيس *tadꜥīs*, A piercing with a spear.

A تدفّق *tadaffuk*, (v. n. 5 of دفق) Going swiftly, taking wide steps. Being poured forth (water).

A تدفّن *tadaffun*, (v. n. 5 of دفن) Being concealed. Being buried.

A تدفّؤ *tadaffu,*, (v. n. 5 of دفئ) Being warmed. Putting on warm clothing.

A تدفيف *tadfīf*, A making haste to kill.

A تدفيق *tadfīk*, A pouring out properly.

A تدقيق *tadkīk*, (v. n. 2 of دقّ) Making thin, slender, fine. Pounding small. Considering minutely. Speaking abstrusely.

A تدكدك *tadakduh,* (v. n. 2 of دكدك Q) Becoming hillocks (mountains).

A تدكل *tadakkul,* (v. n. 5 of دكل) Delaying, lingering. Carrying one's self haughtily, disdaining, or feigning disdain. Being spread out.

A تدكيك *tadkīk,* A mixing, a mingling.

A تدكيل *tadkīl,* (v. n. 2 of دكل) Allowing (a horse) to wallow.

A تدكيم *tadkīm,* (v. n. 2 of دكم) Putting (one thing in another). Striking, giving one a push upon the throat with the head.

A تدكين *tadkīn,* (v. n. 2 of دكن) Piling (goods or furniture) one upon the other.

A تدلث *tadallus,* (v. n. 5 of دلث) Falling suddenly in or upon any thing. Rushing violently.

A تدلدل *tadaldul,* (v. n. 2 of دلدل Q) Fluctuating, hesitating. Hanging pendulous.

A تدلس *tadallus,* (v. n. 5 of دلس) Being concealed (a thing). Taking food by little and little. Licking any thing for pastime (a sheep).

A تدلف *tadalluf,* (v. n. 5 of دلف) Approaching. Advancing by degrees, step by step.

A تدلق *tadalluk,* (v. n. 5 of دلق) Overflowing, inundating (a mighty stream).

A تدلك *tadalluk,* (v. n. 5 of دلك) Rubbing one's body when bathing, or perfuming it with دلوك *dalūk.*

A تدلل *tadallul,* (v. n. 5 of دل) Toying, fondling, caressing. Being forward and impudent. Pretending anger or disdain (like lovers). Hanging down and swinging to and fro.

A تدلمز *tadalmuz,* (v. n. 2 of دلمز Q) Assembling, collecting, agreeing on any matter.

A تدلمص *tadalmus,* A being bald in front.

A تدله *tadalluh,* (v. n. 5 of دله) Being rendered frantic (by love).

A تدلي *tadallī,* (v. n. 5 of دلي) Hanging down (any thing from a tree). Approaching. Letting one's self down by a pulley. Abasing one's self.

A تدلية *tadliyat,* (v. n. 2 of دلي) Pulling, drawing up a bucket. Bringing a man into any disagreeable predicament, and keeping him there.

A تدليس *tadlīs,* (v. n. 2 of دلس) Concealing the faults of goods on sale. Not bringing sufficient proofs of what one alleges.

A تدليص *tadlīs,* (v. n. 2 of دلص) Polishing, rendering smooth (a coat of mail). Copulating outside the female organ.

A تدليه *tadlīh,* (v. n. 2 of دله) Rendering careless or frantic (love), fascinating, bewitching.

A تدمر *tadmur,* Tadmor.

A تدمري *tadmurīy,* A small short field-mouse. Unworthy of respect, base. ما رأيت تدمريًّا احسن منها *mā ra,aytu tadmurīyan ahsana minhā,* I have seen no one fairer than her. *Tadmurīy* or *tudmurīy,* Some man, some one.

A تدمرية *tadmurīyat,* Little (ear).

A تدمس *tadammus,* (v. n. 5 of دمس) Being contaminated, defiled.

A تدمشق *tadamshuk,* A besieging of Damascus.

A تدمل *tadammul,* (v. n. 5 of دمل) Being dunged (land).

A تدملك *tadamluk,* (v. n. 2 of دملك Q) Being round (breasts). Being smooth and round.

A تدمن *tadammun,* (v. n. 5 of دمن) Being defiled with dung (any place). Being manured.

A تدمية *tadmiyat,* (v. n. 2 of دمي) Wounding so that the blood flows, causing to bleed. Making access easy, opening a way. Appearing.

A تدميث *tadmīs,* (v. n. 2 of دمث) Making (a bed) smooth and soft. Relating a saying or action.

A تدميح *tadmīh,* (v. n. 2 of دمح not in use) Bending the back. Standing with the head inclined upon the breast.

A تدمير *tadmīr,* (v. n. 2 of دمر) Ruining, utterly destroying. Perfuming his hiding-place (a hunter) with the burnt hair of wild beasts, that they may not be able to get scent of him. Perdition, ruin.

A تدميس *tadmīs,* (v. n. 2 of دمس) Burying, hiding under ground.

A تدميغ *tadmīgh,* A making (a sop) in the pan.

A تدميق *tadmīk,* (v. n. 2 of دمق) Inserting one thing in another. Sprinkling (a mass of leaven) with flour that it may not stick to the fingers.

A تدميم *tadmīm,* (v. n. 2 of دم) Anointing with a medicinal unguent the outside of a child's eyes.

A تدمين *tadmīn,* (v. n. 2 of دمن) Remaining close to. Dirtying any place with dung. Relaxing in any point. Permitting, allowing.

A تدنس *tadannus,* (v. n. 5 of دنس) Becoming contaminated, nasty, filthy, blemished, tarnished.

A تدنؤ *tadannu,* (v. n. 5 of دنأ) Urging on to mean, low, or vicious practices.

A تدني *tadannī,* An approaching nearer.

A تدنية *tadniyat,* (v. n. 2 of دنا for دنو) Causing one to approach. Pursuing, examining into trifles as well as matters of importance.

A تدنيح *tadnīh,* A being humble and submissive.

A تدنيخ *tadnīkh,* (v. n. 2 of دنخ) Humbling or letting one's self down, hanging the head, becoming abject. Keeping close (at home). Becoming shrivelled and uneven, bumping out and sinking in (a melon). Being mis-shapen (hind-head).

A تدنير *tadnīr,* (v. n. 2 of دنر not in use) Shining (as the countenance). Being rich, abounding in gold coin (دينار *dīnār*).

A تدنيس *tadnīs,* (v. n. 2 of دنس) Staining, defiling, sullying, profaning.

A تدنيق *tadnīk,* (v. n. 2 of دنق) Fixing the eye steadily. Being attentive to any thing. Curiously prying. Being sunk in the socket (an eye). Descending to the west (the sun). Looking negligently or feebly.

A تدنيم *tadnīm,* Vileness, meanness, baseness. The twang of a bowstring, the ringing of a bason.

A تدنين *tadnīn,* (v. n. 2 of دن) Buzzing (as a fly), humming (as a hornet). Speaking indistinctly, unintelligibly.

P تدو *tadav,* A pheasant.

A تدورة *tadwirat,* A circular heap of sand.

A تدؤم *tada,,um,* (v. n. 5 of دأم) Covering any thing (water). Leaping on the female (a camel). Raining continuously. Rolling over any one (waves or troubles).

A تدوم *tadawwum,* An expecting, waiting for.

A تدون *tadawwun,* (v. n. 5 of دان for دون) Having quite a competency. Complete independence.

A تدوه *tadawwuh,* (v. n. 5 of داه for دوه) Changing, becoming spoiled. Becoming thick.

A تدوية *tadwiyat,* (v. n. 2 of دوي) Braying in a low tone (a he-camel). Being covered with a thin scum (milk or broth). Giving away or causing to eat such milk or broth. Being covered with whatever is brought by the wind (water). Coursing a field, traversing a desert.

A تدويح *tadwīh,* (v. n. 2 of داح for دوح) Making free with (one's wealth).

A تدويخ *tadwīkh,* (v. n. 2 of داخ for دوخ) Making base and abject. Subduing, subjugating. Roaming through cities.

A تدويد *tadwīd,* (v. n. 2 of داد for دود) Being full of worms (meat). Playing with a swing.

A تدوير *tadwīr,* (v. n. 2 of دار for دور) Causing to turn in a circle. Making round. Revolution. Circumference. Epicycle. Rotundity.

A تدويص *tadwīs,* (v. n. 2 of دوص not in use) Descending or letting one's self down from a height.

A تدويم *tadwīm,* (v. n. 2 of دام for دوم) Remaining fixed in one place. Stilling (a boiling pot) with cold water. Whirling (a wheel) with such velocity as to give (it) the appearance of being at rest. Making (a top) spin. Seizing (the drinker) with a reeling giddiness (wine). Going or flying round, whirling in circles, orbits, or eddies. Skimming the air in circles, without moving the wings (as swallows). Raining incessantly. Having circles of fat floating on its surface (broth). Rolling (as the eyeballs). Revolving (as the sun). Moving the tongue within the mouth to gather moisture. Running to a great distance (a dog). Moistening (safflower) with water.

A تدوين *tadwīn,* (v. n. 2 of دان for دون) Collecting (poems) into one book. Inscribing (names) in public books or muster-rolls (ديوان *dīwān*).

A تدويه *tadwīh,* (v. n. 2 of دوه not in use) Calling a camel to her colt by saying داه داه *dāhi dāhi.*

P تده *tada,* Spun. A web.

A تدهدم *tadahdum,* A falling, dropping out.

A تدهده *tadahduh,* The being rolled (a stone).

A تدهدي *tadahdī,* A being turned, rolled.

A تدهقن *tadahkun*, (v. n. 2 of دهقن Q) Being constituted head man of a village, or president of the board of agriculture. Practising farming business.

A تدهكر *tadahkur*, (v. n. 2 of دهكر Q) Being rolled. Shaking (a woman). Rushing upon, overcoming.

A تدهكم *tadahkum*, (v. n. 2 of دهكم Q) Precipitating one's self into any business, engaging in an arduous affair. Opposing, thwarting, resisting.

A تدهّن *tadahhun*, (v. n. 5 of دهن) Oiling one's body. Being anointed, greased.

A تدهور *tadahwur*, (v. n. 2 of دهور Q) Coming to a close and departing (night).

A تدهّي *tadahhī*, (v. n. 5 of دهي) Acting like a shrewd, cunning fellow (داهية *dāhiyat*).

A تدهية *tadhiyat*, (v. n. 2 of دهي) Declaring one to be ingenious and intelligent, regarding him as a shrewd, clever fellow (داهية *dāhiyat*). Dishonouring. Visiting with misfortune (داهية *dāhiyat*).

A تدهيش *tadhīsh*, A confounding, astonishing.

A تدهيم *tadhīm*, (v. n. 2 of دهم) Blackening (as a fire the pot).

A تدهين *tadhīn*, An anointing, an oiling.

A تديّث *tadayyus*, (v. n. 5 of داث for ديث) Playing the bawd, pimping. Panderism.

A تديّن *tadayyun*, (v. n. 5 of دان for دين) Borrowing, getting into debt, begging a loan. Being tenacious of, or upright and stedfast in, one's religion.

A تدييث *tadyīs*, (v. n. 2 of داث for ديث) Rendering abject, enslaving, subduing, rendering tame. Calling one a cuckold (ديّوث *dayyūs*).

A تدييخ *tadyīkh*, (v. n. 2 of ديخ not in use) Subduing (a country). Taming, rendering submissive.

A تدييد *tadyīd*, (v. n. 2 of ديد obsol.) Being troubled with worms, breeding worms (meat).

A تدييم *tadyīm*, A raining incessantly.

A تديين *tadyīn*, (v. n. 2 of دان for دين) Tolerating one in his religion. Possessing, controlling.

A تذابح *tazābuh*, A cutting one another's throats.

A تذاذؤ *tazāzuʼ*, A vacillating motion in walking.

A تذاكر *tazākur*, A remembering each other.

A تذامر *tazāmur*, An exciting each other (to fight).

A تذامم *tazāmum*, A blaming reciprocally.

A تذاؤب *tazāʼub*, (v. n. 6 of ذأب) Placing the figure of a wolf near a camel in order to excite in her a liking for another's colt. Blowing from various quarters (wind). Eating (food) at stated times.

A تذاوق *tazāwuk*, A crossing (of spears).

A تذاول *tazāwul*, A debasing of one's self.

A تذاؤن *tazāʼun*, (v. n. 6 of ذأن) Gathering the plant ذؤنون *zuʼnūn*.

A تذايل *tazāyul*, (v. n. 6 of ذال for ذيل) Being slighted, humbled (state).

A تذبذب *tazabzub*, (v. n. 2 of ذبذب Q) Shaking, waving, flapping. Uncertainty, doubt.

A تذبّل *tazabbul*, (v. n. 5 of ذبل) Walking like a man (a woman), stepping majestically.

A تذبيب *tazbīb*, (v. n. 2 of ذبّ) Drawing near to a close (day). Shrivelling from thirst (the lip). Passing the night in a wearisome search for water, without finding any, except in the vicinity of a town.

A تذبيح *tazbīh*, (v. n. 2 of ذبح) Bowing the head lower than the haunches.

A تذبير *tazbīr*, A writing or inditing.

A تذحلم *tazahlum*, (v. n. 2 of ذحلم Q) Being thrown down into a hollow. Being rolled or collected together.

A تذراف *tazrāf*, (v. n. of ذرف) Flowing (tears). Shedding tears.

P تذرج *tazarj*, A pheasant.

A تذرّع *tazarruʻ*, (v. n. 5 of ذرع) Being talkative. Measuring by the cubit. Cutting any thing into cubit-lengths. Approaching with a gift, studying to recommend one's self. Plunging into a pit of rain-water with the fore-legs (a camel). Splitting palm-leaves to form a mat (a woman). Making any thing a cause, motive, or occasion (ذريعة *zarīʻat*). Excessive talkativeness.

A تذرفة *tazrifat*, The shedding of tears.

A تذرّق *tazarruk*, (v. n. 5 of ذرق) Bathing the eyes with milk and water. Anointing the eyes with a collyrium made from trefoil.

P تذرو *tazarv*, A cock pheasant. The jungle cock. تذرو زرنيخ *tazarvi zarnīkh*, A live coal. تذرو زرين پر *tazarvi zarīn-par*, Fire. The sun.

A تذروة *tazriwat*, (v. n. 2 of ذرا for ذرو) Raising the dust, making it fly about (the wind).

A تذرّي *tazarrī*, (v. n. 5 of ذري) Getting on the top of a mountain or camel's bunch. Forming an alliance with a family of the highest rank. Being driven before the wind (dust), sifted (chaff).

A تذريب *tazrīb*, (v. n. 2 of ذرب) Making sharp. Carrying a child until it eases itself (a woman). Poisoning (a sword).

A تذرية *tazriyat*, (v. n. 2 of ذري) Ventilating. Sweeping any thing away (wind). Sifting, winnowing. Marking a shorn camel or sheep by leaving a tuft (of wool) uncut. Praising, extolling one's own condition.

A تذريح *tazrīh*, (v. n. 2 of ذرح) Poisoning (food) with cantharides. Besmearing a new (water-pot) with mud.

A تذريع *tazrīʻ*, (v. n. 2 of ذرع) Tossing the hands in walking. Stretching out the arms and hands (when bringing joyful news). Tying (a camel's) fore-leg by the end of his halter. Using both hands and shaking them in drawing water. Stretching out both arms in swimming. Strangling. Confessing. Communicating a portion of intelligence.

A تذريف *tazrīf*, (v. n. 2 of ذرف) Exceeding (a hundred in number). Shedding tears. Bringing one to the verge (of death).

A تذعّب *tazaʻʻub*, A terrifying (by demons).

A تذعذع *tazaʻzuʻ*, (v. n. 2 of ذعذع Q) Being scattered, squandered (money), published (a secret), shaken (a tree by the wind).

A تذعّر *tazaʻʻur*, A being terrified.

A تذعلب *tazaʻlub*, (v. n. 2 of ذعلب Q) Lying on the side. Putting on a light garment.

A تذفيف *tazfīf*, (v. n. 2 of ذفّ) Running to despatch a wounded man. Making light, lightening.

A تذقّح *tazakkuh*, A charging with a crime falsely.

A تذقّط *tazakkut*, A taking by little and little.

A تذقين *tazkīn*, (v. n. 2 of ذقن) Resting the chin on the hand or the head of a staff.

A تذكار *tazkār*, (v. n. of ذكر) Remembering. Recalling to one's recollection. An attestation of genealogy. *Tizkār*, Remembrance. Help to memory.

A تذكّر *tazakkur*, (v. n. 5 of ذكر) Remembering, keeping in one's memory. Recalling to one's recollection. Being of the masculine gender.

A تذكرة *tazkarat*, A billet, schedule, obligation, hand-writing. Biographical memoirs (especially of poets). *Tazkirat*, Memory, remembrance. Any thing that aids the memory (as a knot tied on the pocket-handkerchief).

A تذكية *tazkiyat*, (v. n. 2 of ذكا for ذكو) Slaughtering. Stirring a fire. Growing old (man). Becoming fat and corpulent. Rising six or seven (a horse).

A تذكير *tazkīr*, (v. n. 2 of ذكر) Reminding, admonishing. Putting in the masculine gender. Fixing steel on the head of an axe.

A تذلذل *tazalzul*, (v. n. 2 of ذلذل Q) Being lax and flabby. Shewing submission. Lamenting, groaning, crying for help.

A تذلّل *tazallul*, (v. n. 5 of ذلّ) Submitting. Supplicating. Submission, humility, tameness.

A تذلّي *tazallī*, A being humble, submissive.

A تذليق *tazlīk*, (v. n. 2 of ذلق) Making any thing sharp or pointed. Making lean. Giving a volubility to the tongue. Pouring water into a lizard's hole to make him run out.

A تذليل *tazlīl*, (v. n. 2 of ذلّ) Debasing, degrading. Mastering, subjugating. Holding in contempt. Conciliating and coaxing a stubborn camel by picking the tikes off him. Beating, treading (a path). Having its clusters hang perpendicularly or made even (a vine). Having its bunches laid upon the branch for a support (a palm-tree). Abasement, depression. P تذليل كردن *tazlīl kardan*, To subdue. To despise.

A تذمّر *tazammur*, (v. n. 5 of ذمر) Blaming one's self for neglect, or anger, or for allowing a thing to escape. Being alienated from, slighting. Being provoked to anger. Threatening.

A تذمّم *tazammum*, (v. n. 5 of ذمّ) Being led or induced by the shame of any thing, fearing censure.

A تذمير *tazmīr*, (v. n. 2 of ذمر) Searching the uterus of a camel to ascertain whether her foal be male or female. Measuring, fixing, disposing in order, arranging.

A تذميل *tazmīl*, (v. n. 2 of ذمل) Causing to

go faster, or to go an easy pace.

A تذنّب *tazannub*, (v. n. 5 of ذنب) Letting the extremities (of a turban sash) stream down the side or back of the head. Taking a road.

A تذنوب *taznūb* or *tuznūb*, (Dates) ripening at the stalk.

A تذنيب *taznīb*, (v. n. 2 of ذنب) Fixing, or adorning with, a train or tail. Ripening at the stalk.

A تذنين *taznīn*, (v. n. 2 of ذنّ) Being snotty.

P تذو *tazav*, A kind of winged insect propagated chiefly in baths.

A تذؤّب *tazaʼʼub*, (v. n. 5 of ذأب) Becoming like a wolf in wickedness. Placing any thing resembling a wolf near a camel that she may take a liking for another camel's colt. Blowing gently and veering about (wind). Taking (any thing) in turns.

A تذوّق *tazawwuk*, A tasting repeatedly.

A تذؤّن *tazaʼʼun*, (v. n. 5 of ذأن) Gathering the plant ذؤنون *zuʼnūn*.

A تذوّن *tazawwun*, A being rich. Affluence.

A تذويب *tazwīb*, (v. n. 2 of ذاب for ذوب) Melting, causing to dissolve. Making the hair to flow in ringlets (ذؤابة *zuʼābat*).

A تذويح *tazwīh*, (v. n. 2 of ذاح for ذوح) Sending (camels) into different directions. Scattering. Squandering, dissipating (money)

A تذويل *tazwīl*, A writing the letter ذ *zāl*.

A تذهيب *tazhīb*, (v. n. 2 of ذهب) Gilding.

A تذيّل *tazayyul*, (v. n. 5 of ذال for ذيل) Walking haughtily or majestically, with the train sweeping the ground. Casting a shadow. Laying aside one's gravity. Being impudent, saucy. Inclining.

A تذيّؤ *tazayyuʼ*, (v. n. 5 of ذيأ not in use) Being overdressed (meat). Being so putrid (a sore) that the flesh falls off. Swelling (the face).

A تذييء *tazyīʼ*, (v. n. 2 of ذيأ not in use) Boiling, stewing (meat) so as to cause it to separate from the bone.

A تذئيب *tazʼīb*, (v. n. 2 of ذأب) Adorning the forehead (of a boy) with forelocks. Making a vacant space under the pommel called ذئبة *ziʼbat*.

A تذييخ *tazyīkh*, (v. n. 2 of ذاخ for ذيخ) Bringing under subjection, humbling, subduing. Not receiving the fecundating blossom (the palm-tree).

A تذيير *tazyīr*, (v. n. 2 of ذار for ذير) Rubbing with dung (a camel's teats) to prevent the colt from sucking. Tying up (a camel's) teats to prevent her from giving suck. Becoming black (teeth).

A تذييل *tazyīl*, (v. n. 2 of ذال for ذيل) Making the train of a robe long. Amplifying. Causing to shine. Appendix.

P تر *tar*, A particle, which, added to the Persian adjectives, forms the comparative degree: as, به *bih*, Good, بهتر *bihtar*, Better; بد *bad*, Bad, بدتر *badtar*, Worse.

P تر *tar*, Moist, wet, juicy. Fresh, green. Tender, soft. A small bird with a melodious voice, called in Arabic صعوة *saʻwa*. A restless fellow. A quarrelsome gamester, who takes up what he has staked. A fornicator. Polluted, impudent, obscene. A stake. تر نهادن *tar nihādan*, To steep, to soak. تازه و تر *tāza u tar*, Fresh and moist. تر و تازه كردن *tar u tāza kardan*, To refresh. تر و خشك *taru khushk*, Moist and dry. Much or little.

A ترّ *tarr*, (v. n. of ترّ) Appearing, being distinctly seen (a bone). Being cut. Cutting. Being remote, distant, absent, retiring. Being full (of flesh), stretched, distended. Being moist and juicy (a bone). The casting forth of what is in the belly of the ostrich. A well-paced (post-horse) that picks up his feet sharply. Well-proportioned (horse). Oppressed with labour and oppression. *Turr*, Root, origin. A plumb-line, or other mason's rule for making buildings perpendicular and level. لاقيمنّك علي الترّ *la ukīmannaka ʻala't turr*, I will surely fix thee on the *turr* (a threatening expression).

P ترا *tarā*, High (wall such as surrounds a palace or citadel). *Turā*, Thee, to thee, on account of thee (oblique case of the personal pronoun تو *tu*).

P تراب *tarāb*, (imp. of ترابيدن *tarābīdan*) Flow. (Water) flowing or oozing. Oozy, plashy. Elegance. Address, skill.

A تراب *tirāb*, The root of the fore shank-bones of a sheep. *Turāb*, (pl. اتربة *atribat* and تربان *tirbān*) Ground, earth, dust. تراب صيدا *turābi saydā*, Sidonian earth. تراب القيء *turābu'l hayʼ*, The emetic earth, arsenic. تراب الهالك *turābu'l hālik*, Arsenic. ابو تراب *abū turāb*, Name of Alīy.

P ترابش *tarābish*, A flowing: a wave, flow, flux.

A ترأبل *taraʼbul*, (v. n. 2 of رأبل Q) Robbing, plundering, marauding without a leader.

A ترابل *tarābul*, (v. n. 6 of ربل) Bearing a resemblance to a lion.

A ترابيّ *turābīy*, Earthly, earthen, earthy.

P ترابيدن *tarābīdan*, To flow, ooze, exude.

A تراتر *tarātir*, Great, important (affairs). Adversities, distresses.

A تراتير *tarātīr*, (pl. of ترّة *turrat*) Handsome, foolish (girls).

P تراتيزك *tarā-tezak*, Rocket (an herb).

A تراث *turās*, (v. n. of ورث) Inheriting: heritage.

P تراج *turāj*, A woodcock.

A تراجز *tarājuz*, (v. n. 6 of رجز) Contending in the verse رجز *rajaz*.

A تراجع *tarājuʻ*, (v. n. 6 of رجع) Turning back.

A تراجم *tarājim*, (pl. of ترجمان *turjumān*) Interpreters, translators. (pl. of ترجمة *tarjamat*) Translations. *Tarājum*, (v. n. 6 of رجم) Throwing stones at each other.

A تراجيل *tarājīl*, Parsley.

A تراح *tarāh*, The beaver.

A تراحم *tarāhum*, A pitying of each other.

P تراختن *ta* or *tirākhtan*, To make great haste.

A تراخي *tarākhī*, (v. n. 6 of رخو) Proceeding slowly, becoming remiss, negligent, indolent. Deferring (to remedy an evil). Raining slowly. Delay, protraction, procrastination.

A ترادّ *taradd*, (v. n. 6 of ردّ) Bandying about from one to another. Squabbling. Dissolving a contract.

A ترادف *tarāduf*, (v. n. 6 of ردف) Following each other. Helping one another. Being bi-nominous. Intermarrying. Uninterrupted succession.

A ترارة *tarārat*, (v. n. of ترّ) Being moist, juicy, fresh (a bone), and tender.

P ترارة *tarāra*, Timid. Fear. A dunghill.

A ترارية *tarārīh*, (pl. of ترّهة *turrahat*) Vain words, foolish things, trifles. Calamities. Animalcules in sand.

P تراز *tarāz*, Raw silk. A fir-tree. Name of a city in Turkistān.

A تراز *turāz*, Sudden death. A fatal distemper which carries off sheep immediately.

A ترازن *tarāzun*, A being opposite or facing.

P ترازو *tarāzū*, A balance, scale, weight. Comprehension, understanding. The sign Libra. Equilibrium, counterpoise. Equity, justice. ترازو چشمه داشتن *tarāzū chashma dāshtan*, To outweigh (as one scale the other). ترازو شدن *tarāzū shudan*, To be a match for each other (two antagonists) in strength and valour. ترازوي انجم *tarāzūyi anjum*, An astrolabe. ترازوي پولاد سنجان *tarāzūyi pūlād-sanjān*, A short spear, dart, pike. ترازوي چرخ *tarāzūyi charkh*, (or ترازوي فلك *tarāzūyi falak*) The sign Libra. ترازوي زر *tarāzūyi zar*, The sun. ترازوي كلام *tarāzūyi kalām*, Measure of a verse, the quantity of a poetical foot.

P ترازودان *tarāzūdān*, The scale of a balance.

A تراس *tirās*, (pl. of ترس *turs*) Shields.

A ترأّس *taraʼʼus*, (v. n. 5 of رأس) Being appointed head or chief.

A ترّاس *tarrās*, A shield-bearer. A target-maker or vender.

A تراسّ *tarāss*, A telling one another secrets.

A تراسة *tirāsat*, The manufacture of shields.

A تراسل *tarāsul*, A sending reciprocal advices.

P تراش *tarāsh*, Desire, expectation. Erasure. Pared. A razor. A penknife. (in composition) Shaving, scraping, erasing, paring. مضمون تراش *mazmūn-tarāsh*, Scraping out the meaning, eliciting the sense. قلم تراش *kalam-tarāsh*, A penknife.

P تراش خراش *tarāsh-kharāsh*, A neat form.

P تراشش *tarāshish*, A graven image: a piece of sculpture. A shaving, a paring.

P تراشه *tarāsha*, Pared. A shaving, chip, splinter. Nail-pairings. A slice of a melon.

P تراشيدن *tarāshīdan*, To shave, pare, scrape, erase, cancel; to smoothe (as in a lathe), cut, hew; to make a pen.

P تراشيده *tarāshīda*, Shaved, scraped, pared.

A تراصّ *tarāss*, (v. n. 6 of رصّ) Standing close together. Being set in close array.

A تراصة *tarāṣat*, A being firm, compact.

A تراصص *tarāṣuṣ*, (v. n. 6 of رصّ) Being set in close array (soldiers).

A تراصع *tarāṣuꜥ*, The coupling (of sparrows).

A تراصف *tarāṣuf*, (v. n. 6 of رصف) Being drawn up in close array. Fitting, joining, adjusting one thing upon another.

A تراضخ *tarāẓukh*, (v. n. 6 of رضخ) Throwing stones at each other.

A تراضي *tarāẓī*, (v. n. 6 of رضي) Acquiescing, being content and satisfied with each other; mutual satisfaction.

A تراطن *tarāṭun*, (v. n. 6 of رطن) Speaking Persian or any language (not Arabic), talking barbarously; muttering, murmuring.

A تراع *tarrāꜥ*, (Waters from higher grounds) filling the channel. A doorkeeper.

A تراعية *turāꜥiyat* or *tirāꜥiyat*, One who looks well after camels.

A تراغي *tarāghī*, (v. n. 6 of رغي) Braying, roaring, one here and another there (camels).

A تراغيف *tarāghīf*, Flat, round cakes.

A ترافد *tarāfud*, (v. n. 6 of رفد) Helping one another. Storing up food.

A ترافص *tarāfuṣ*, A drawing water (in turns).

A ترافع *tarāfuꜥ*, (v. n. 6 of رفع) Referring (any thing) to a judge by mutual agreement. Raising any thing by the joint effort of two individuals.

A ترافق *tarāfuḳ*, (v. n. 6 of رفق) Travelling in company. Verses composed in such a manner that any two hemistichs thereof may be taken indifferently, and yet form a complete distich, without the poem suffering injury either in signification, in rhyme, or in measure.

A ترافؤ *tarāfuꜣ*, (v. n. 6 of رفأ) Agreeing together, consenting mutually. Strengthening each other.

A تراقص *tarāḳuṣ*, A dancing together.

A تراقي *tarāḳī*, (pl. of ترقوة *tarḳuwat* or *turḳuwat*) Collar-bones, shoulder-blades.

P تراك *tarāk*, A crack, split, cleft. The noise of any thing when splitting or cleaving. Thunder.

A تراك *tarāk*, Let alone; meddle not.

P تراكاستن *tarākāstan*, To distil, drop, exude.

A تراكب *tarākub*, (v. n. 6 of ركب) Being joined, rivetted, or firmly set.

A تراكض *tarākuẓ*, (v. n. 6 of ركض) Running together, towards. Making (horses) run together towards any object.

A تراكل *tarākul*, A kicking one another.

A تراكم *tarākum*, (v. n. 6 of ركم) Being collected. Being heaped, pressed together, condensed. A crowd, throng, press. Condensation.

A تراكمة *tarākimat*, (pl. of تركمان *turkmān*) The Turkomāns who rove about and live in tents.

P تراكه *tarāka*, Inheritance, heritage.

A تراكيب *tarākīb*, (pl. of تركيب) Compounds.

P تراكيدن *tarākīdan*, To split, cleave. To be split. To make a noise in splitting.

A ترامز *turāmiz*, A strong, well-made camel. Full-grown, come to maturity.

A ترامس *tarāmis*, Globes, balls of silver.

A ترامي *tarāmī*, (v. n. 6 of رمي) Darting, throwing at one another. Ejecting. Railing, scolding. Being remiss, relaxed (any business). Being gathered, heaped one on another (clouds). Tending (as a wound to corruption). Tending (either to triumph or disappointment).

P ترانگبين *tar angubīn*, Manna.

P ترانه *tarāna*, A handsome youth. Modulation, voice, song, melody, symphony, harmony; a trill, quaver, shake. A tetrastic. Jest, sarcasm, bad temper. Slyness, subtlety.

P ترانه پرداز *tarāna-pardāz*, Composing songs.

P ترانيدن *tarānīdan*, To exude, to sweat.

P تراو *tarāv*, An oozing forth.

P تراوانيدن *tarāwānīdan*, To cause to flow.

A تراوح *tarāwuḥ*, (v. n. 6 of راح for روح) Doing any thing alternately or by turns (first with the right hand, then with the left).

P تراوش *tarāwish*, Exudation, trickling, oozing.

A تراوض *tarāwuẓ*, The exercise of discipline.

A تراوغ *tarāwugh*, (v. n. 6 of راغ for روغ) Going round (as wrestlers).

P تراول *tarāwil*, The blade of a certain grass.

A تراوي *tarāwī*, Twenty-two genuflexions which the Muhammadans are wont to make after the last prayer of Ramazān.

A تراويح *tarāwīḥ*, (pl. of ترويح) Perfumes.

P تراويد *tarāwīd*, Expressed juice flowing.

P تراويدن *tarāwīdan*, To drop, distil, flow, exude, trickle, ooze.

P تراه *tarāh*, Timidity, terror.

A تراهص *tarāhuṣ*, (v. n. 6 of رهص) Being piled upon each other firmly (stones).

A تراهن *tarāhun*, (v. n. 6 of رهن) Laying a wager, laying down the stakes.

P تراهي *tarāhī*, First-fruits: young unripe fruit.

A تراهي *tarāhī*, (v. n. 6 of رها for رهو) Making peace together. Reposing, resting.

A ترأي *taraꜣꜣī*, (v. n. 5 of رأي) Beholding one's self in a mirror. Appearing, shewing one's self.

A ترائب *tarāꜣib*, (pl. of تريبة) Breast-bones.

A ترائق *tarāꜣiḳ*, (pl. ترقوة *tarḳuwat*) Shoulder-blades, collar-bones.

A ترائك *tarāꜣik*, (pl. of تريكة *tarīkat*) Things which have been forsaken. Women who have not been asked in marriage.

P ترايمان *tarāymān*, A sash worn round the loins. Dysentery.

A ترائي *tarāꜣī*, (v. n. 6 of رأي) Seeing each other. Looking from over-against, facing each other so that the fires may be distinctly seen (two houses). Looking into, examining. Appearing (a spectre). Beholding one's self (in a mirror or in a sword-blade). Exposing one's self to be seen. Bearing dates of various kinds (a palm-tree).

P ترابيدن *tarāyīdan*, To drop, distil, trickle.

P ترب *tarb*, Deceit, fraud. Eloquence, fluency. *Turb* or *turub*, A radish.

A ترب *tarb*, (v. n. of ترب) Throwing earth, covering with earth, dusting, sprinkling. Acquiring or possessing (a slave) thrice. Earth. *Tirb*, (pl. اتراب *atrāb*) A friend, companion, equal, coeval, contemporary. *Turb*, Earth, dust, ground. *Tarab*, (v. n. of ترب) Having much earth. Holding earth in the hand. Lying on, cleaving to, the ground. Becoming poor, suffering loss. *Tarib*, Earthy. Poor.

A ترباء *tarbāꜣ*, Wild senna. *Ta* or *turbāꜣ*, Earth.

A ترباض *tirbāẓ*, Saffron in the flower.

P تربالي *tarbālī*, Name of a large inn built in one of the cities of Persia by Ardeshīr Bābgān.

A تربامان *tarbāmān*, Agrimony, water-hemp.

A تربان *tirbān*, (pl. of تراب) Earths, soils.

A تربّب *tarabbub*, (v. n. 5 of ربّ) Accumulating, collecting. Educating. Claiming a right to, pretending to lord over.

A تربة *tarbat*, Weakness. *Turbat*, Earth, ground. A grave. A tomb. A monument; or rather, a mausoleum open at the top (with the exception of a brass grate to exclude the birds), so as to admit the rain to the shrubs planted about the grave. تربت طيّبه *turbati tayyiba*, The city of Madīna. *Turibat*, The tip of the finger. *Taribat* or *tarabat*, Wild senna. ريح تربة *rīh taribat*, Wind whirling up dust.

A تربّة *taribbat*, An educating, a bringing up.

P تر بتر *tar ba tar*, Completely wet.

A تربتيّ *turbatiy*, Earthy. Sepulchral.

A تربّث *tarabbus*, (v. n. 5 of ربث) Tarrying, delaying, lingering. Walking at a snail's pace. Being divided, separated.

A تربّج *tarabbuj*, (v. n. 5 of ربج) Feeling an affection toward her offspring (a woman), taking care of her children.

A تربّح *tarabbuh*, A being bewildered, confounded.

A تربّخ *tarabbukh*, A being loose and relaxed.

P تربد *tirbid*, A hollow pipe. Name of a cathartic medicine. Name of a city. *Turbud*, A purgative Indian root.

A تربّد *tarabbud*, (v. n. 5 of ربد) Being clouded (sky). Having an austere countenance, and changing colour from anger.

P تربره *tarbara*, A species of grape.

P تربز *tarbuz*, A water-melon. *Turbuz*, A radish.

P تربزه *tarbuza*, Water-melon. *Turbuza*, Radish.

P تربسه *tarbusa*, The rainbow.

A تربّص *tarabbus*, (v. n. 5 of ربص) Expecting, waiting for. Seizing. Hoarding up grain in expectation of a high price, regrating. (A woman) exacting the stipulated time (when a husband does not return in a certain period the wife may marry another). Being upon one's guard with respect to.

A تربض *tarabbuz*, A making of a pudding.

A تربّع *tarabbuʻ*, (v. n. 5 of ربع) Being quadrangular. Sitting in a quadrangular form. Fattening with spring grass. Having a long bunch (a camel). Passing the spring anywhere.

A تربّق *tarabbuk*, A suspending from the neck.

P تربك *turbak*, A sort of grape.

A تربل *tarbal* or *tirbil*, Name of a place.

A تربّل *tarabbul*, (v. n. 5 of ربل) Being very fleshy about the thighs and breasts. Being covered with verdure in the autumn (the earth). Producing leaves in autumn (a tree) from the coolness of the atmosphere without rain. Browsing upon such leaves. Going in search of such trees.

P تربن *tarbun*, Very hard ground.

A تربّن *tarabbun*, The navigating (of a vessel).

P تربند *tar-band*, A wet bandage on a wound.

P تربو *tarbū*, A term applied to cloth which is white, thick, and fine.

A تربوت *tarabūt*, Obedient, tractable (camel).

P تربه دار *turba-dār*, A keeper of a mausoleum.

A تربي *tirbī*, A female of the same age as another.

A تربّي *tarabbī*, (v. n. 5 of ربا for ربو) Feeding, rearing. Fostering, tending upon. Preserving (fruits) in inspissated juice. Being reared, brought up, educated.

A تربيب *tarbīb*, (v. n. 2 of ربّ) Educating, bringing up. Preparing (oil) with new wine for use.

A تربئة *tarbiʼat*, A carrying off, causing to depart.

A تربية *tarbiyat*, (v. n. 2 of ربي) Educating. Nursing, rearing, feeding. Relieving (any one) from an asthma, giving (him) ease. Seasoning, preserving. Dressing, compounding. Education, instruction, correction. Improvement. Composition. Augmentation. P تربيت كردن *tarbiyat kardan*, To educate, instruct. To inculcate. To compose. To season. To mix.

A تربيّة *turbīyat*, A reddish kind of wheat.

A تربيت *tarbīt*, (v. n. 2 of ربت not in use) Feeding (a child). Educating, bringing up. Putting to sleep by giving gentle taps on the side.

P تربيت پذير *tarbiyat-pazīr*, Docile, teachable.

A تربيث *tarbīs*, A hindering, letting, preventing.

A تربيح *tarbīh*, (v. n. 2 of ربح) Gaining by merchandize. Giving profit or advantage. Taking an ape (ربّاح *rubbāh*) into one's house.

A تربيز *tarbīz*, A filling (of a leathern bottle).

A تربيس *tarbīs*, The filling (of a bottle).

A تربيض *tarbīz*, (v. n. 2 of ربض) Putting as much into a vessel as will cover the bottom of it. Giving room.

A تربيع *tarbīʻ*, (v. n. 2 of ربع) Making a quadrangular or square figure, squaring. Multiplying any number by itself. Looking at one another from the fourth house (stars). An angle of 90 degrees.

A تربيق *tarbīk*, (v. n. 2 of ربق) Making a noose or loop for tying a lamb. Interlarding (a story) with lies. *Tirbīk*, A string for tying up a sheep.

P ترپ *tarp*, Black broth.

P ترپك *tarpak*, Black broth.

A ترة *tirat*, (v. n. of وتر) Avenging murder. Prosecuting, promoting any thing bad. Inflicting any thing disagreeable and disgusting. Defrauding. Terrifying. Prompting to revenge. Making an even number odd. Stringing (a bow). Ill-will.

A ترّة *turrat*, Handsome, soft, but foolish woman. False, vain, trifling.

P ترت *turt*, Confused, jumbled, mixed.

A ترتب *turtab*, Perpetuity. A bad servant. *Turtab* or *turtub*, Solid, well-arranged (business). Earth, dust. جاؤا ترتبا *jāʼū turtuban*, They all came.

A ترتّب *tarattub*, (v. n. 5 of رتب) Being firm, solid, well arranged. Being motionless.

A ترتبّة *turtubbat*, Similitude of way or manner. The likeness of a beaten path.

P ترتبيدن *tartabīdan*, To tremble.

A ترتة *turtat*, A stuttering, stammering.

A ترترة *tartarat*, (v. n. of ترتر Q) Moving, agitating, shaking backwards and forwards. Shaking a drunken man, and bidding him breathe, to discover what he has been drinking. Talkativeness. Languor in body or speech.

P ترترك *tartarak*, A sparrow with a red head. *Tirtirak*, Light, weak, undignified. *Turturak*, Name of a pleasant spot near Shirāz.

P ترتك *turtuk*, A pheasant. The jungle cock. A partridge.

A ترتّل *tarattul*, (v. n. 5 of رتل) Singing or speaking with a sweet distinct musical voice.

A ترتم *turtam* or *turtum*, Continual, uninterrupted (evil).

A ترتّم *tarattum*, (v. n. 5 of رتم) Having a string tied round the finger as a memorandum.

P ترتند *tartand*, Vain, useless.

A ترتني *tartanaʼ*, A girl. A whore.

A ترتور *turtūr*, The turtle-dove. A revenue-collector, king's officer, collector's servant.

P ترت و مرت *tart u mart*, Scattered, dispersed. Topsy turvy, higgledy piggledy.

A ترتيب *tartīb*, (v. n. 2 of رتب) Making firm, solid. Arranging. Observing the order prescribed in performing one's ablutions. Composition. Order, disposition, arrangement, method. P ترتيب كردن *tartīb kardan*, To arrange, to put in order. بر ترتيب حروف هجا *bar tartībi hurūfi hijā*, In alphabetical order.

P ترتيب دادة *tartīb-dāda*, Arranged.

A ترتيل *tartīl*, (v. n. 2 of رتل) Reciting in a clear melodious voice, chanting, singing.

A ترثّن *tarassun*, (v. n. 5 of رثن) Painting her face (a woman).

A ترثّي *tarassī*, (v. n. 5 of رثي) Lamenting, panegyrizing the dead.

A ترثية *tarsiyat*, A lamenting, praising (the dead).

A ترج *tarj*, (v. n. of ترج) Being hid. Name of a place abounding in lions; hence the proverb اجرأ من الماشي بترج *ajraʼ mini'l māshi bi tarj*, Bolder than he who walks in Tarj; *i.e.* among the lions. *Taraj*, (v. n. of ترج) Being obscure, intricate.

A ترجّح *tarajjuh*, (v. n. 5 of رجح) Palpitating, shaking. Travelling with a swinging motion (a camel). Being moved to and fro (as a swing or any thing suspended).

A ترجرج *tarajruj*, A shaking, a quivering.

A ترجّز *tarajjuz*, (v. n. 5 of رجز) Rumbling (as thunder). Being moved very gently by the wind (a cloud fraught with rain). Singing to his camels in the verse called rajaz (a camel-driver).

A ترجّع *tarajjuʻ*, (v. n. 5 of رجع) Selling (a camel) and buying another with the proceeds.

A ترجّل *tarajjul*, (v. n. 5 of رجل) Walking on foot: being foot-sore from walking. Placing (زند *zand*) under the feet. Going down into a well. Alighting from on horseback. Being high noon. Combing hair. Shining (sun). Acquiring masculine habits (a woman).

A ترجمان *turjumān*, *tarjamān*, or *tarjumān*, (pl. تراجم *tarājim*) An interpreter, translator. A present, bribe, or fine. A petition.

A ترجماني *turjumānī*, Interpretation.

A ترجمة *tarjamat*, (v. n. of ترجم Q) Interpreting, translating. *Tarjamat* or *tarjumat*, (pl. تراجم *tarājim*) Interpretation, translation.

P ترجمه نويس *tarjuma-navīs*, A translator.

A ترجّي *tarajjī*, (v. n. 5 of رجا for رجو) Hoping. Supplicating. Interceding.

A ترجيب *tarjīb*, (v. n. 2 of رجب) Revering, honouring, respecting. Supporting the branches of trees, to prevent their being broken down by the weight of fruit. Tying clusters of dates to the branches of palm-trees to prevent their being broken off by the wind. Straightening and making level (the shoots of a vine). Fencing a palm-tree with thorns to prevent any one from eating the dates. Sacrificing in the month Rajab.

A ترجية *tarjiyat*, A hoping, desiring.

A ترجيح *tarjīh*, (v. n. 2 of رجح) Swinging (any one) causing him to move to and fro in a swing. Preferring, considering as more valuable or important. Preponderance. ترجيح بلا مرجّح *tarjīh bilā murajjah*, Unreasonable preference.

A ترجيد *tarjīd*, A trembling, a being terrified.

A ترجيز *tarjīz*, (v. n. 2 of رجز) Composing or reciting a poem in the verse called رجز *rajaz*.

A ترجيع *tarjīʻ*, (v. n. 2 of رجع) Making a noise to and fro in the throat, warbling. Playing a tune. Raising and falling the voice alternate (in prayer, or in making the solemn attestation, لا اله الا الله و محمد رسول الله *lā ilah illā allāh, wa muhammad rasūlu'llāh*, There is no god but God, and Muhammad is the apostle of God). Repeating the ejaculation from the Kur'ān, انا لله و انا اليه راجعون *innā li'llāh wa innā ilayhi rājiʿūna*, "Verily we belong to God, and verily to Him we shall return," which the Muhammadans are used to do in seasons of perplexity and distress. Ambling (a horse). The bending of a horse's fore-feet (in ambling). Drawing lines upon the face with the point of a needle, which they rub over with indigo or woad. Retouching a faded painting or lines which have become faint. In rhythmical prose, a parallelism, of which the second member terminates in the same letter as the first.

P ترجيع بند *tarjīʿ-band*, A kind of verse in which the same line recurs at stated intervals.

A ترجيعي *tarjīʿiy*, Abounding in parallelisms (a literary composition).

A ترجيل *tarjīl*, (v. n. 2 of رجل) Making (hair) partly crisp partly smooth. Strengthening. White on one foot of a horse. A shade.

A ترجيم *tarjīm*, (v. n. 2 of رجم) Laying a stone over a grave, convex and shelving at both ends. Speaking with consideration.

A ترجين *tarjīn*, (v. n. 2 of رجن) Keeping a horse in the stable and bringing him down by poor food.

A ترح *tariha*, (fut. يترح *yatrahu*) He was sad.

A ترح *tarh*, Poverty, indigence. *Tarah*, (v. n. of ترح) Becoming sad and melancholy. Descending, alighting. (pl. اتراح *atrāh*) Melancholy, grief, anguish, care. Descent, fall, declivity. *Tarih*, Good for little.

A ترحاب *tarhāb*, (v. n. 2 of رحب) Saying مرحبا *marhaban*, Welcome.

A ترحال *tirhāl*, A journey, a departure.

A ترحب *tarahhub*, (v. n. 5 of رحب) Welcoming.

A ترحرح *tarahruh*, (v. n. 2 of رحرح Q) Spreading his legs out (a horse) when about to stale.

A ترحل *tarahhul*, (v. n. 5 of رحل) Departing, emigrating, travelling. Compelling one against his inclination.

A ترحم *tarahhum*, (v. n. 5 of رحم) Pitying, commiserating, feeling a tender sympathy towards. Saying to any one, "God have mercy on you." Pity, compassion.

A ترحي *tarahhī*, A coiling up (as a serpent).

A ترحيب *tarhīb*, (v. n. 2 of رحب) Welcoming a guest by saying مرحبا *marhaban*, God bless you! you are welcome. Inviting to whatever is agreeable. Enlarging, making spacious.

A ترحيل *tarhīl*, (v. n. 2 of رحل) Sending, ordering to depart. Patiently enduring any annoyance. Standing over one with a sword. A grayness or redness upon the shoulders.

A ترحيم *tarhīm*, (v. n. 2 of رحم) Having compassion upon. Saying to any one رحمك الله *rahimaka'llāhu*, "God have mercy on thee!"

P ترخ *tarkh*, Dragon-wort. An orange.

P ترخ *tarkh*, (v. n. of ترخ) Scarifying slightly (a cupper). A slight incision. Scarification.

P ترخان *tarkhān*, Free, exempted from tribute or taxes, not amenable to punishment. At large, uncontrolled. Dragon-wort. A certain tribe of Turks.

G ترخان *tarkhān*, A commander of 5000.

P ترخته *tarakhta*, A sort of flat fish.

P ترخچه *tarakhcha*, A vine-prop; a vine-shoot newly planted.

P ترخر *tarakhar*, Wild cresses.

A ترخش *tarakhkhush*, A being moved.

A ترخص *tarakhkhus*, (v. n. 5 of رخص) Being remiss, easy, slack. Being low-priced (provisions. Obtaining leave.

P ترخفنج *tarakh* or *tarkhafanj*, The nightmare.

A ترخم *turkham*, (*turkhum*, ترخمة *tarkhamat* or *tarkhumat*) Man, mankind. ما ادري اي ترخم هو *mā adrī ayyu turkhamin huwa*, I know not what man he is.

P ترخنده *tarkhanda*, Fraud, falsehood. Contumely, taunt. Vain, foolish.

P ترخوانه *tarkhwāna*, Thick pottage, frumenty, portable soup.

A ترخوم *tarkhūm*, A male pelican.

P ترخون *tar-khūn*, Blood-thirsty. Dragon-wort. A strolling soldier. A daring ruffian, robber, footpad, murderer. Brazilian wood.

A ترخيص *tarkhīs*, (v. n. 2 of رخص) Rendering cheap, lowering the market. Permitting, allowing, giving leave, conniving. Freeing from trouble; rendering easy, remiss.

A ترخيم *tarkhīm*, (v. n. 2 of رخم) Causing (a hen) to sit. Sitting on eggs (a hen). Making thin, fine, delicate, or soft. Cutting off (a syllable). Abbreviation, contraction, apocope.

P ترخينه *tarkhīna*, A sort of food.

P ترد *turd*, Any thing thin, delicate, fragile.

A ترداد *tardād*, (v. n. 2 of ردّ) Causing to turn very much. Wavering.

P تر دامن *tar-dāman*, Scandalous, criminal, soiled, polluted by every kind of shameful practice. A whoremonger.

P تردامني *tar-dāmanī*, Debauchery, immorality.

A تردّب *taraddub*, Grace, elegance. Affection.

A تردّد *taraddud*, (v. n. 5 of ردّ) Going to and fro. Wavering, hesitating. Refusal, resistance, opposition. Irresolution, fluctuation of opinion, suspension of judgment. Conversation, correspondence. Application, labour, exertion, endeavour. Contrivance. Cultivation, improvement. P بي تردّد و تكلّف *bī taraddud u takalluf*, Without hesitation or dissimulation, without ceremony.

A تردّدات *taraddudāt*, Labours, exertions. تردّدات دنيويّه *taraddudāti dunyawīya*, Worldly engagements.

P تردّد ضابطه *taraddud-zābita*, An account shewing the species and quantity of seed sown, the extent of land under cultivation, and the quantity remaining fallow (a term used in India).

A تردّس *taraddus*, (v. n. 5 of ردس) Falling (into a well). Falling from a mount. Putting on a cloak. See also تردّي *taraddī*.

P تردست *tar-dast*, Adroit, dexterous.

P تردستي *tar-dastī*, Dexterity, adroitness.

P تردك *tardak*, (or تزدك *tazdak*) A weevil.

A تردّم *taraddum*, (v. n. 5 of ردم) Having an affection (as a mother for her offspring). Being worn or torn (as a garment), and requiring to be mended. Being mended. Mending, patching. Feeling cattle if fat. Protracting (a law-suit). Following. Animadverting, noticing. Observing what is done from an eminence. Punishing for a fault.

P ترده *tarda*, Title-deeds. The price paid for grinding.

A تردّي *taraddī*, (v. n. 5 of ردي) Falling (into a well). Tumbling (from a mountain). Putting on a cloak or long robe. Wearing a girdle or belt adorned with jewels (a lady).

A ترديّة *tardiyat*, (v. n. 2 of ردي) Clothing another with a long robe, cloak, or upper garment. Throwing (into a well). Destroying. Pelting with stones.

A ترديد *tardīd*, (v. n. 2 of ردّ) Reiterating, repeating. Driving to and fro. Turning over in one's mind. Repelling. Resisting. Repulsion. Opposition, discord. P حرف ترديد *harfi tardīd*, The disjunctive particle يا *yā*, Or.

A ترديم *tardīm*, (v. n. 2 of ردم) Shutting (a door). Closing (a hole). Mending (a garment). Completing (a discourse). Being affectionate (as a mother to her offspring).

A تردين *tardīn*, A putting sleeves (to a garment).

A ترز *tarz*, (v. n. of ترز) Becoming hard. Throwing on the ground. Eating wet grass. Losing the hair (a camel's tail). Hunger. The cholic, to which cattle are subject by eating grass wet with dew. Epilepsy. *Taraz*, (v. n. of ترز) Freezing, congealing (water). Hunger.

P ترزبان *tar-zabān*, Moist, glib-tongued. An interpreter.

P ترزده *tarzada* or *tarazda*, Title-deeds.

P ترزفان *tar-zafān*, An interpreter. Eloquent. A fine, amercement. A bribe.

A ترزّن *tarazzun*, (v. n. 5 of رزن) Being respected, honoured. Being modest, mild, gentle, grave, sedate.

A ترزيح *tarzīh*, (v. n. 2 of رزح) Fatiguing, weakening, emaciating.

A ترزيز *tarzīz*, (v. n. 2 of رزّ) Strewing, spreading. Making easy, arranging. Smoothing, levelling. Polishing, glazing (paper).

A ترزيف *tarzīf*, (v. n. 2 of رزف) Approaching, advancing.

A ترزيم *tarzīm*, (v. n. 2 of رزم) Collecting in a bundle. Knocking one's self on the ground. Lying on the ground without stirring from the place.

A ترزين *tarzīn*, (v. n. 2 of رزن) Rendering grave, modest, and respectable.

P ترس *tars*, Fear, terror. (imp. of ترسيدن *tarsīdan*) Fear thou. *Turs*, Hard, strong. *Turus* or *tarus*, Hard soil.

A ترس *turs*, (pl. اتراس *atrās*, ترسة *tirasat*, تراس *tirās*, and تروس *turūs*) A shield, target, buckler. Hard soil.

P ترسا *tarsā*, (from ترسيدن *tarsīdan*) Fearing. Timid. A Christian. A worshipper of fire.

P ترسابچه *tarsā-bacha*, Son of a Christian.

P ترس استودن *tars-astūdān*, (Fear of the grave) Certain prayers, or portions of the Zand, which the Parsis read during three days and nights at the cemetery of a deceased person.

P ترسان *tarsān*, Timid, fearful.

P ترسانيدن *tarsānīdan*, To frighten, terrify.

A ترسة *tirasat*, (pl. of ترس *turs*) Shields.

P ترست *tirist*, A kind of measure. Three hundred. A weaver's beam.

A ترسّل *tarassul*, (v. n. 5 of رسل) Doing (any thing) softly, easily, gently, smoothly, deliberately. Being deliberate in writing.

A ترسّم *tarassum*, (v. n. 5 of رسم) Reading and committing to memory. Observing the marks of any thing. Tracing the outlines of an intended building. Looking for the vestiges of a habitation.

P ترسناك *tarsnāk*, Terrified, afraid. Timid. Terrible, dangerous.

P ترسناكي *tarsnākī*, Fear, timidity.

P ترسندگي *tarsindagī*, Fear, timidity.

P ترسندة *tarsinda*, Who fears. Timid: fearful.

P ترسة *tarsa*, Fancy. *Tursa*, A rainbow.

A ترسيّ *tursiy*, Of a shield, shield-like.

P ترسيدن *tarsīdan*, To fear, dread, apprehend.

P ترسيدة كار *tarsīda-kār*, (or گار *gar*) A fearer.

A ترسيع *tarsīʻ*, (v. n. 2 of رسع) Having sore eyelids. Being glued together. Platting (thongs).

A ترسيغ *tarsīgh*, (v. n. 2 of رسغ) Reaching the fetlock (water). Enlarging, making wide. Sprinkling, moistening ground. Embellishing (a story).

A ترسيل *tarsīl*, (v. n. 2 of رسل) Giving milk to weanlings. Abounding in milk. Reading in a clear, melodious voice.

A ترسيم *tarsīm*, (v. n. 2 of رسم) Appointing (any one) to mark or stamp. Writing well. Marking, painting (a garment with stripes). Those employed in sealing corn in the public granaries, or in the department of stamps generally.

A ترش *tarsh* or *tarash*, (v. n. of ترش) Being light, volatile, unsteady. Lightness, levity. Badness of disposition. *Tarish*, Light.

P ترش *tursh*, Acid, tart, sour. Morose, stern, cynical. Hard-favoured, ugly. ترش گشتن *tursh gashtan*, To become sour.

A ترشاه *tirshāʼ*, A rope, the rope of a bucket.

A ترشاش *tarshāsh*, A sprinkling. A pain-giving blow.

P ترشانيدن *turshānīdan*, To make acidulate.

P ترشائي *turshāʼī*, Sourness, acidity, harshness.

P ترشبا *tursh-bā*, Sour gruel, acid broth.

P ترشت *turusht*, *tirshit*, or *turshut*, A gardener's sack.

A ترشّح *tarashshuh*, (v. n. 5 of رشح) Sweating, exuding. Being fit to go (a colt) with (his) dam.

P ترشدن *tar shudan*, To be played upon, bantered, molested.

P ترش رو *tursh-rū*, Of a sour countenance.

P ترش روئي *tursh-rūʼī*, Crabbedness, austerity, sourness of countenance.

A ترشّش *tarashshush*, (v. n. 5 of رشّ) Being sprinkled: trickling, dropping.

P ترش شرين *tursh-shirīn*, Sour-sweet: sub-acid.

P ترش طبع *tursh-tabʻ*, (or مزاج *mizāj*) Sour-tempered, harsh.

P ترش طعم *tursh-taʻm*, Acid, sour-flavoured.

A ترشّف *tarashshuf*, A sipping, a sucking.

P ترشك *turshak*, Name of a bird; and herb.

P ترش گيا *tursh-giyā*, A sour herb; wild sorrel.

P ترش مزگي *tursh-mazagī*, Acidity of flavour.

P ترش مزة *tursh-maza*, Of an acid flavour.

P ترشناك *turshnāk*, Very acid.

P ترشة *turusha*, A sort of fruit.

P ترشة شيرين *tursha-shīrīn*, Sub-acid.

P ترشي *turshī*, Sourness. Pickles. Sad, sorrowful. Crabbed.

A ترشّي *tarashshī*, An acting or dealing gently.

P ترشي بادي *turshī-bādī*, Acid. Flatulent.

P ترشي پالان *turshī-pālān*, Strainer, colander.

A ترشية *tarshiyat*, (v. n. 2 of رشي) Bribing.

A ترشيح *tarshīh*, (v. n. 2 of رشح) Administering well (an estate). Educating from tender years, rendering qualified for any office. Licking the moisture off a fawn just dropt (a doe).

P ترشيدن *turshīdan*, To turn sour. To ferment.

P ترشيش *tarshīsh*, A kind of stone.

A ترشيف *tarshīf*, A sipping, a sucking.

P ترشي گرفتة *turshī-girifta*, Turned sour (milk).

A ترشيم *tarshīm*, A writing. A painting.

P ترشينك *turshīnak*, Garden-sorrel.

A ترصّد *tarassud*, (v. n. 5 of رصد) Observing steadily; expecting, waiting for. Hoping.

A ترصّع *tarassuʻ*, (v. n. 5 of رصع) Being cheerful. Joy, gladness.

A ترصيص *tarsīs*, (v. n. 2 of رصّ) Joining closely, pitching, soldering, glueing. Laying over with tin. Covering the face with a veil, the eyes only seen.

A ترصيع *tarsīʻ*, (v. n. 2 of رصع) Framing, fashioning, constructing, measuring. Adorning with jewels or gold. Briskness, cheerfulness. When the author in prose or verse divides his sentence into distinct parts, and assigns to each word another corresponding with it in measure and in rhyme.

A ترصيف *tarsīf*, (v. n. 2 of رصف) Joining well together (stones in pavements, or feet in prayer). Binding a macerated nerve round an arrow's head.

A ترصين *tarsīn*, (v. n. 2 of رصن) Mastering (a subject), becoming thoroughly acquainted with it.

A ترضّب *tarazzub*, A sucking saliva lasciviously.

A ترضّح *tarazzuh*, (v. n. 5 of رضح) Being bruised, pounded, crushed.

A ترضّخ *tarazzukh*, (v. n. 5 of رضخ) Receiving uncertain news. Being bruised (a serpent's head).

A ترضرض *tarazruz*, (v. n. 2 of رضرض Q) Being broken by pounding.

A ترضّي *tarazzī*, (v. n. 5 of رضي) Satisfying. Striving to please.

A ترضية *tarziyat*, A satisfying, a contenting.

A ترضيض *tarzīz*, A breaking in large pieces.

A ترطّب *tarattub*, A being very moist.

A ترطّم *tarattum*, A keeping in (of excrement).

A ترطيب *tartīb*, (v. n. 2 of رطب) Moistening, macerating. Wetting (a garment). Being moist (dates). Passing from the state بسر *busr* to that of رطب *rutab* (a date). Eating fresh dates. Feeding with fresh dates.

A ترطيل *tartīl*, (v. n. 2 of رطل) Rendering any thing limber and soft by anointing with oil, oiling the hair. Weighing with a pound weight.

A ترع *tarʻ*, (v. n. of ترع) Turning one away from his purpose. *Taraʻ*, (v. n. of ترع) Being full. Hastening precipitately into any thing bad. Plunging into business (with eagerness and cheerfulness). Turning away. A bottle, a vessel, or cistern full. *Tariʻ*, Full. Prone to anger. *Turaʻ*, (pl. of ترعة *turʻat*) Gates, doors.

A ترعاب *tarʻāb*, (v. n. 2 of رعب) Terrifying.

A ترعابة *tirʻābat*, Timid, terrified.

A ترعاية *turʻayat* or *tirʻāyat*, One who looks well after camels.

A ترعبل *taraʻbul*, (v. n. 2 of رعبل Q) Being torn or worn out (a garment).

A ترعة *turʻat*, (pl. ترع *turaʻ*) A gate, door. A pleasant garden having an elevated situation. A step, especially to a pulpit. A face, appearance. An open place. The mouth of a well where cattle drink. A fountain-head or spring.

A ترعّث *taraʻʻus*, A putting in ear-rings.

A ترعّد *taraʻʻud*, A shaking (of buttocks).

A ترعرع *taraʻruʻ*, (v. n. 2 of رعرع Q) Moving, growing (a lad). Being loose and shaking (a tooth).

A ترعّظ *taraʻʻuz*, (v. n. 5 of رعظ) Endeavouring to make the camel's load equal, when it leans.

A ترعّي *tirʻiy*, (ترعيّة *tarʻiyat*, *tirʻiyat*, *turʻiyat*, or ترعية *tarʻiyat*, *tirʻiyat*, or *turʻiyat*) One who feeds well and takes good care of camels (especially about the house). One whose own and whose father's business has been to look after camels.

A ترعّي *taraʻʻī*, A feeding: a going to pasture.

A ترعيب *tarʻīb*, (v. n. 2 of رعب) Striking with

terror. Cooing, mourning aloud (a dove). Cutting a (camel's) bunch. Repairing the hole in a spear-staff called رعب *ruʻb*.

A ترعيبة *tirʻībat*, A slice of a camel's bunch.

A ترعيّة *tirʻiyat* or *turʻiyat*, One who looks well after cattle.

A ترعيظ *tarʻīẕ*, (v. n. 2 of رعظ) Rendering languid and slothful. Making brisk. Moving (the fingers, or to pull up a stake).

A ترعيم *tarʻīm*, (v. n. 2 of رعم) Wiping away snot (رعام *ruʻām*) running from a sheep's nose.

P ترغ *turugh*, A chesnut or bay horse.

P ترغازه *targhāza*, Powerful. Overbearing. Headstrong.

P ترغاق *turghāk* or *targhāk*, A (night) watch against an enemy or a robber.

P ترغده *taraghda* or *targhada*, A joint stiff, motionless, and unserviceable. Bruised. Squeezed.

P ترغيش *targhish*, A sort of apricot.

A ترغم *taraghghum*, A being angry.

P ترغو *targho*, A kind of vest of scarlet silk.

P ترغون *targhūn*, A royal mandate.

A ترغيب *targhīb*, (v. n. 2 of رغب) Exciting desire. Making wishful. Stimulating, encouraging. Tempting. (opposed to ترهيد *tazhīd*) Temptation.

A ترغية *targhiyat*, (v. n. 2 of رغا for رغو) Foaming, being frothy (milk). Putting in a passion.

A ترغيف *targhīf*, A making of cakes.

A ترغيم *targhīm*, (v. n. 2 of رغم) Saying to another رغماً رغماً *raghman raghman*, *i.e.* Whether you like it or not, nolens, volens. Exasperating, mortifying.

P ترف *tarf*, Sour clotted milk, strained and dried in the sun for winter use.

A ترف *taraf*, (v. n. of ترف) Enjoying in abundance the conveniences of life. Persisting in insolence or disobedience.

A ترفاس *turfās*, (in Moorish) Toadstools.

P ترفان *tarfān*, Eloquent. An interpreter. A fine.

P ترفبا *turf-bā*, Food made from clotted cream.

A ترفة *turfat*, Any thing rare presented to a friend. Any thing elegant or gallant presented to a sweetheart. The conveniences or luxuries of life. Delicate meats. A little protuberance in the middle of the upper lip.

A ترفّت *taraffut*, (v. n. 5 of رفت) Being broken.

P تر فروش *tar-farosh*, A hypocrite, dissembler.

A ترفّض *taraffuẕ*, (v. n. 5 of رفض) Being dispersed. Being broken.

A ترفّغ *taraffugh*, (v. n. 5 of رفغ) Living delightfully. Sitting between the thighs (of a woman). Being in danger of a tumble from a camel's back.

A ترفّق *taraffuk*, (v. n. 5 of رفق) Being benevolent, friendly. Becoming a friend or fellow-traveller.

A ترفّل *taraffal*, A walking pompously.

A ترفلة *tarfalat*, A walking pompously.

P ترفنج *tarfanj*, A narrow pass, difficult way.

P ترفند *tarfand*, A falsity, a thing totally impossible. A vain, idle promise. Fraud, deceit.

P ترفنده *tarfanda*, A lie, falsehood. Fraud. Fear.

P ترفوا *tarf-wā*, Meat prepared with the milk described under ترف *tarf*.

A ترفّه *taraffuh*, (v. n. 5 of رفه) Being secure, quiet, and comfortable.

A ترفّي *taraffī*, (v. n. 5 of رفا for رفو) Saying to a newly-married couple, بالرفا و البنين *bi'r rafā wa'l banīn*, With concord and children (may you live!).

A ترفئة *tarfiʼat*, (or ترفيع *tarfīh*) (v. n. 2 of رفأ) Congratulating new-married people by saying, بالرفاء و البنين *bi'r rafāʼ wa'l banīn*, With concord and children.

A ترفية *tarfiyat*, (v. n. 2 of رفا for رفو) Saying to one, بالرفاء و البنين *bi'r rifāʼ wa'l banīn*, With concord and with children.

A ترفيد *tarfīd*, (v. n. 2 of رفد) Choosing a chief or lord. Reverencing, exalting, magnifying. Trotting.

A ترفيش *tarfīsh*, (v. n. 2 of رفش) Allowing the beard to grow until it becomes like a spade or shovel.

A ترفيض *tarfīẕ*, (v. n. 2 of رفض) Leaving a little water (in a leathern bottle). Hanging loose, dangling (a horse's yard).

A ترفيع *tarfīʻ*, (v. n. 2 of رفع) Exalting, raising. Going one while fast, and at another time slow (an ass). Retreating from battle.

A ترفيل *tarfīl*, (v. n. 2 of رفل) Magnifying, making great, choosing a chief, lord, or prince. Putting in possession of. Filling (a well with water). Debasing, degrading. In the measure كامل *kāmil* adding a foot, so that متفاعلن *mutafāʻilun* becomes متفاعلاتن *mutafāʻilātun*. (A man) who allows his garments to drag, and who swings his arms in walking.

P ترفينه *tarfīna*, A kind of black broth.

A ترفيه *tarfīh*, (v. n. 2 of رفه) Making easy and convenient. Enabling one to live peacefully and comfortably. Allowing (camels) to drink (their) fill daily. Using lenity, allowing breathing time to (a debtor). Peace, tranquillity.

A ترفيئ *tarfīʼ*, (v. n. 2 of رفأ) Congratulating a newly-married couple by saying بالرفاء و البنين *bi'r rifāʼ wa'l banīn*, May you be blessed with concord and children!

A ترقاة *tarkāt*, A hurting of the collar-bone.

A ترقّب *tarakkub*, A watching, waiting, hoping.

A ترقّح *tarakkuh*, A providing (for a family).

A ترقرق *tarakruk*, (v. n. 2 of رقرق Q) Moving, trembling (vapour over a plain). Going and coming. Starting, rolling in the eye (a tear). Shining. Appearing to revolve (the sun).

A ترقّش *tarakkush*, (v. n. 5 of رقش) Being polished, adorned. Adorning, decorating.

A ترقّص *tarakkus*, A being moved up and down.

A ترقّط *tarakkut*, (v. n. 5 of رقط) Being spotted (as a garment with ink and the like).

A ترقّع *tarakkuʻ*, A gaining, studying to gain.

A ترقّق *tarakkuk*, (v. n. 5 of رقّ) Being tenderly affected towards.

A ترقّن *tarakkun*, (v. n. 5 of رقن) Tinging the palms, nails, or hair with privet, or with saffron.

P ترقنده *tarkanda*, Futile, vain. Fraud, deceit: lie.

A ترقوة *tarkuwat* or *turkuwat*, (pl. تراقي *tarākī* and ترائق *tarāʼik*) The collar-bone.

A ترقّي *tarakkī*, (v. n. 5 of رقي) Ascending. Making a progress (in learning) step by step. Ascendant, climax. Promotion, advancement. Increase (of salary). Augmentation. Proficiency.

A ترقّيات *tarakkiyāt*, Augmentations.

A ترقية *tarkiyat*, (v. n. 2 of رقي) Causing to ascend. Reporting, telling that which has been heard elsewhere. Informing against, denouncing.

A ترقيح *tarkīh*, (v. n. 2 of رقح) Taking proper care of an estate, making a right use of riches.

A ترقيد *tarkīd*, A certain manner of walking.

P ترقيدن *tarkīdan*, To break, split, crack, cleave.

A ترقيش *tarkīsh*, (v. n. 2 of رقش) Adorning, embellishing (a discourse). Tale-bearing.

A ترقيص *tarkīs*, The act of dandling (an infant).

A ترقيع *tarkīʻ*, (v. n. 2 of رقع) Mending a garment by inserting a patch. Taking proper care of (an estate or flocks).

A ترقيق *tarkīk*, (v. n. 2 of رقّ) Reducing to servitude. Thinning. Whetting. Speaking properly. Proceeding with a slow step. Turning (any word or thing) into a nickname or metonymy.

A ترقيم *tarkīm*, (v. n. 2 of رقم) Writing. Pointing orthographically, placing the vowel-points so that the meaning may be plain. Marking with the price (cloth or goods). Weaving (a garment) in stripes. A mark or sign employed by tax-gatherers, revenue-collectors, or accountants, to fill up any blank spaces which may occur in their arithmetical columns.

P ترقين *tarkīn*, An interlineation.

A ترقين *tarkīn*, (v. n. 2 of رقن) Tinging (the beard) with privet. Dyeing with saffron. Marking. Drawing lines near one another. Writing well, decorating (a book). Dotting (letters). A mark (answering to our dot or nought) employed by revenue-collectors or accountants to fill up any blank spaces occurring in their columns of figures.

A ترك *taraka*, (fut. يترك *yatruku*) He left.

P ترك *tark*, A helmet. The sash of a turban. The strings of a tent. Name of a town in Azarbayjān. *Tarak*, A ditch, trench, moat. A kind of sweetmeat. A virgin, a maid. Thunder. The noise made in splitting. A split, a notch. Name of a river. (dim. of تر *tar*) Somewhat moist.

A ترك *tark*, (v. n. of ترك) Abandoning, forsaking, leaving. Putting, placing, making. Keeping, preserving. Marrying a neglected woman.

P ترك كردن *tark kardan*, To abandon, desert, leave, quit, forsake, throw off. ترك گرفتن *tark giriftan,* To take leave, abandon. ترك ادب *tarki adab,* Rudeness, unpoliteness, incivility. ترك ديار كردن *tarki diyār kardan,* To abandon one's country. ترك سر كردن *tarki sar kardan,* To risk one's life.

A P ترك *turk,* (pl. اتراك *atrāk*) A Turk, comprehending likewise those numerous nations of Tartars between Khwārazm and China, who all claim descent from Turk, the son of Japhet. (As those people have in general fine countenances, with large black eyes, the Persian poets make frequent use of this word to express beautiful youth of both sexes). A Scythian, barbarian, robber, plunderer, villain, vagabond. غزال الترك *ghazālu't turk,* The gazel roving at large. ترك اشقر *turki ashkar,* The sanguinary Turk. (met.) The planet Mars. ترك چين *turki chīn,* The Chinese Tartar. (met.) The sun. ترك حصاري *turki hisārī,* The sun. The moon. ترك روستايان *turki rūstāyān,* Garlic. ترك سلطان شكوه *turki sultān-shukoh,* The majestic Turk. (met.) The world-illuminating sun. ترك فلك *turki falak,* The planet Mars. The sun. ترك معربد *turki muąarbid,* The planet Mars. ترك نيمروز *turki nīm-roz,* The sun.

A تركات *tarikāt,* (pl. of تركة *tarikat*) Things left after death, inheritances, bequests, legacies.

H تركاري *tarkārī,* Garden-stuff.

A تركان *tirkān,* An abandoning, a leaving.

P تركان *turkān,* (pl. of ترك *turk*) Turks. (figur.) Beautiful women. تركان چرخ *turkāni charkh,* (Roving Tartars of the sphere) The seven planets.

P تركانه *turkāna,* Like a Turk, Turk-like.

P تركاني *turkānī,* A kind of spacious upper garment worn by the women of Turkistān.

A تركب *tarakkub,* (v. n. 5 of ركب) Being inserted (one thing into another, as a stone in a ring). Being fixed (as the head upon a spear).

A تركة *tarkat,* A square-bodied woman. A helmet. *Tarikat,* A legacy, bequest. An inheritance.

P تركتازي *turk-tāzī,* A plundering excursion conducted with rapidity, A roving about.

P ترك جوش *turk-josh,* Coddled, parboiled.

P تركچه *turkcha,* Turkish, like a Turk.

A تركح *tarakkuh,* (v. n. 5 of ركح) Delaying. Being easily contained. Sitting at ease in an assembly. Using freely; following one's discretion.

P تركردن *tar kardan,* To moisten, bedew. To steep, dye. تركردن زبان *tar kardani zabān,* Speaking harshly. Keeping any thing in the mouth.

A تركرك *tarakruk,* A shaking (of a churn).

P تركز *tarkaz,* A field sown with seeds and reaped. The second ploughing, or second crop. A furrow. A fallow field.

P تركژ *tarkaj,* Seed. A field ready for sowing.

P تركستان *turkistān,* Turkomānia, Transoxania.

P ترك سوار *turk-suwār,* A horseman, cavalier.

P تركش *tarkash,* A quiver. تركش جوزا *tarkash-jauzā,* Name of a constellation in the sign Gemini resembling a quiver. The wires of a stringed instrument. تركش ريخت *tarkash rekht,* He exhausted his quiver, *i.e.* he was conquered or surrendered.

P تركش بند *tarkash-band,* Wearing a quiver.

P ترك غري *turk-gharī,* Name of a cruel people in Turkistān.

A تركل *tarakkul,* (v. n. 5 of ركل) Striking (a spade) with the foot to make it enter the ground.

P تركمان *turkmān,* Turk-like. A Turkomān.

P تركمانستان *turkmānistān,* Turkomānia.

P تركماني *turkmānī,* Turkish, Turkomān.

P ترك مزاج *turk-mizāj,* Wicked, deceitful, sly.

A تركن *tarakkun,* (v. n. 5 of ركن) Being firmly established. Being grave and sedate.

P تركند *tarkand,* Vain, useless. Fraud, deceit.

P تركنده *tarkanda,* Foolish, trivial conversation. Deceit.

P تركي *turkī,* Turkish, Turk-like. A porcupine. تركى كردن *turkī kardan,* To oppress, injure.

A تركيات *turkiyāt,* Turkish writings, Turkish affairs (which are considered as barbarous by the Arabians and Persians).

A تركيب *tarkīb,* (v. n. 2 of ركب) Composing. Setting (a stone in a ring). Fixing (a head upon a spear). Causing to mount. Lending one (a horse) on condition that the owner receive half the spoil. Composition, compound, compost, mixture. Make, form, mechanism. The body. A note in music. An adjunct epithet in composition, an adjective compounded and composing, a compounding particle; the contracted Persian particle, used in compounding words; the second part of a compounding word: as, باز *bāz* in عشقباز *ąishk-bāz,* Sporting with love.

P تركيب بند *tarkīb-band,* A kind of poetry.

A تركيبي *tarkībī,* Compounded, mixed. Artful, artificial.

P تركيدگي *tarkīdagī,* A splitting, a cracking.

P تركيدن *tar* or *tirkīdan,* To cleave. To crack.

A تركيز *tarkīz,* (v. n. 2 of ركز) Fixing (a halberd) in the ground. (God) fixing in the earth mines (of gold and silver).

A تركيك *tarkīk,* (v. n. 2 of رك) Raining gently. Attenuating much. Folly.

P ترگون *targūn,* A strap attached to the fore or hinder part of a saddle, by which a portmanteau is made fast. A thong for tying a captive's hands.

P ترلك *tirlik,* (or ترليك *tirlīk*) A short-sleeved garment open in front.

A ترم *taram,* Pain in the fundament of animals.

A ترما (لا *lā*) *taramā,* Especially, first of all.

A ترماء *tarmāą,* (v. n. 3 of رمي) Contending in shooting or throwing the javelin.

P ترمانيدن *tarmānīdan,* To cause to throw.

P ترمتاي *turmtāy,* A species of falcon.

P ترمد *tirmid,* Name of a city.

A ترمرم *taramrum,* (v. n. 2 of رمرم Q) Moving the lips to speak and not speaking. Muttering.

A ترمز *tarammuz,* (v. n. 5 of رمز) Being confounded by a blow. Being in commotion, tumultuous. Preparing one's self, girding up the loins. Breaking wind violently.

P ترمزدن *tarmazdan,* To be silent.

P ترمس *tarmus,* A certain acid vegetable.

A ترمس *tar* or *turmus,* The Egyptian bean.

A ترمسة *tarmasat,* (v. n. of ترمس Q) Being absent, withdrawing from war or strife. *Turmusat,* A place constructed under ground for cool air in summer, or for preserving provisions.

P ترمسه *tarmasah,* A weight of eight grains, or two beans.

P ترمش *tarmush,* A certain sour vegetable.

P ترمشير *tarmashīr,* A species of elixir.

A ترمض *tarammuz,* (v. n. 5 of رمض) Hunting (a doe) under the noon-day sun, when the animal becomes an easy prey. Being disturbed (the mind).

A ترمع *tarammuą,* (v. n. 5 of رمع) Trembling with rage. Wandering in error. Defiling one's self with one's own ordure.

A ترمق *tarammuk,* (v. n. 5 of رمق) Drinking (milk or water), by sipping it at several times.

P ترمك *tirmak,* Hardness of heart.

A ترمل *tarammul,* A being stained with blood.

A ترمم *tarammum,* (v. n. 5 of رم) Being separated, dispersed, scattered.

P ترمنشت *tar-manisht,* Wickedness.

P ترمه *tarma* or *turma,* A saddle-cloth. A radish.

A ترمي *tarammī,* A shooting, throwing, hurling.

A ترميث *tarmīs,* (v. n. 2 of رمث) Leaving milk in the udder. Exceeding (fifty).

A ترميج *tarmīj,* (v. n. 2 of رمج not used) Erasing, scratching out (writing).

A ترميد *tarmīd,* (v. n. 2 of رمد) Roasting in the ashes (رماد, *ramād*). Giving milk (a ewe).

P ترميدن *tarmīdan,* To shoot, throw, hurl.

A ترميض *tarmīz,* (v. n. 2 of رمض) Tarrying (for another) some time, and then proceeding. Pasturing (flocks) beneath a scorching sun. Purposing to fast, or observe a رمضان, *ramazān.*

A ترميع *tarmīą,* (v. n. 2 of رمع) Being pale-faced from a pain in the vulva (a woman). Producing an abortion (a beast).

A ترميغ *tarmīgh,* (v. n. 2 of رمغ) Embellishing (a story). Anointing (the head). Seasoning (a flour-pudding) with fat or dripping.

A ترميق *tarmīk,* (v. n. 2 of رمق) Turning the face, looking all round, persevering in looking. Larding (a speech) with rhetorical flowers, embellishing with fictions. Sipping milk. Any work indifferently performed, but with which one is satisfied.

A ترميل *tarmīl,* (v. n. 2 of رمل) Tinging, besmearing with blood. Putting meat amongst sand (by way of preservation). Weaving (a mat) of a flimsy texture. Becoming a widow (ارملة *armalat*).

P ترن *taran*, Dog-rose. A field. A desert.

A ترن *taran*, (for درن *daran*) Filth, dirt.

P ترناس *tarnās*, The twang of a bow-string.

P ترنانه *tar-nāna*, Condiment eaten with bread.

P ترنج *taranj*, A placing together. *Turanj* or *turunj*, Wrinkled, squeezed, drawn together. Hard, rough, dry. A wrinkle, fold, plait. *Turunj*, An orange. ترنج زر *turunji zar* (or ترنج مهرگان *turunji mihrgān*) The sun.

P ترنجان *turunjān*, Balm-gentle, parsley.

A ترنجبين *taranjubīn*, (from Persian) Manna.

A ترنجة *turunjat*, A single orange.

A ترنجح *taranjuh*, A passing round of converse.

P ترنجي *taranjī*, A squeezing with the tips of the fingers, and the impression left by them. *Turunjī*, Orange-coloured.

P ترنجيدگي *taranjīdagī* or *turunjīdagī*, Corrugation, wrinkle, pucker.

P ترنجيدن *turunjīdan* or *taranjīdan*, To be squeezed, compressed, drawn together. To shrivel, pucker, wrinkle. To become rough and hard.

P ترنجيده *taranjīda* or *turunjīda*, Squeezed, puckered, wrinkled.

A ترنح *tarannuh*, (v. n. 5 of رنح) Staggering (with drink). Sipping. A sip.

A ترنخ *tarannukh*, (v. n. 5 of رنخ) Being weak and contemptible. Adhering, sticking the claws into. Cleaving to.

P ترند *tarand*, A very small yellow bird.

P ترندر *tarandar*, A red-headed sparrow.

P ترندك *taran* or *tirindak*, A sort of wild beast.

A ترنق *tarannuk*, (v. n. 5 of رنق) Being muddy.

P ترنگ *tarang*, The twang of a bowstring. The snapping of a sword. The noise of an arrow, mace, or sword striking an object. The sound of a musical cord when played upon. The crown of the head. A whirlpool. A wound. (in comp.) Stirring up. *Tirang*, Handsome. Good. *Tiring*, The twang of a bowstring. *Turang*, A prison. A pheasant.

P ترنگاترنگ *tarang-ā-tarang*, The twanging of a (bow) string.

P ترنگان *turangān*, Balm.

P ترنگانيدن *tarangānīdan*, To cause to twang.

P ترنگبين *tar-angubīn*, Manna.

P ترنگيدن *tarangīdan*, To twang. To be parted.

A ترنم *tarannum*, (v. n. 5 of رنم) Singing, modulating. Reading the Kur'ān with a pleasing tone. Cooing (as a dove). Creaking (as a locust's wing). Twanging (as a bow-string). Song, rhythm.

A ترنموت *tarnamūt*, A singing, a modulating. قوس ترنموت *kaws tarnamūt*, A twanging bow.

P ترنند *tarnand*, The dashing of the waves.

A ترنوء *tarannuʻ*, A tinging with privet.

A ترنوق *tarnūk*, (*turnūk*, or ترنوقاء *turnūkāʼ*) Mud at the bottom of a river or cistern.

A ترنوك *turnūk*, Vile, base. Lean.

A ترنومة *tarnūmat* or *turnūmat*, A musical voice; melody, rhythm.

P ترنهادگي *tarnihādagī*, A moistening, soaking.

P ترنهادن *tar nihādan*, To moisten, steep, soak.

P ترنهاده *tar nihāda*, Moistened, soaked, steeped.

A ترنى *turna'*, A maid-servant. A whore. ابن ترني *ibn turna'*, The son of a whore.

A ترني *tarannī*, A looking intently upon.

P ترنيان *tarniyān*, A wicker basket.

A ترنية *tarniyat*, (v. n. 2 of رنا for رنو) Causing to gaze incessantly. Singing with taste and execution. A shrill voice.

A ترنيح *tarnīh*, (v. n. 2 of رنح) Throwing into a fainting-fit. Being seized with a fit of shivering.

A ترنيخ *tarnīkh*, A bringing into subjection.

A ترنيع *tarnīʻ*, A moving or shaking the head.

A ترنيف *tarnīf*, A besmearing with blood.

A ترنيق *tarnīk*, (v. n. 2 of رنق) Rendering turbid. Making clear, clearing away a mote from the eye. Consulting together. Weighing down the eyelids (sleep). Continuing in one place. Retaining, confining. Fluttering with (his) wings, yet remaining stationary in the air (a bird). Looking attentively, gazing a long while. Weakness (in sight, body, or business). A fracture in a bird's wing disabling it from flying.

A ترنيم *tarnīm*, (v. n. 2 of رنم) Singing. Cooing (a dove). Creaking (locust's wing). Twanging (a bow-string).

A ترنين *tarnīn*, The making (of a bow) to sound.

P تروال *tarwāl*, A blade of grass.

A تروج *tarawwuj*, (v. n. 5 of راج for روج) Obtaining currency. Going round about any thing.

A تروح *tarawwuh*, (v. n. 5 of راح for روح) Ventilating, fanning. Growing luxuriant (plants). Contracting a smell from any neighbouring substance (water). Doing any thing, setting out or returning about sunset. Visiting in the evening.

A تروخ *tarawwukh*, A falling into the mud.

A ترؤد *taraʼʼud*, (v. n. 5 of رأد) Shaking, exulting in riches. Blustering, blowing (the wind). Standing and being seized by a tremour. Waving (a branch). Being bent (the neck).

A ترور *turūr*, (v. n. of تر) Being cut, severed. Cutting. Being moist and juicy (a bone). Being remote, absent. Appearing, being distinctly seen (a bone). Falling out (seed or kernels).

A تروز *turūz*, Thickness, coarseness. Firmness.

A تروس *turūs*, (pl. of ترس) Shields, bucklers.

A ترؤس *taraʼʼus*, A being appointed head.

P تروشه *turūsha*, A sort of fruit.

A تروع *tarawwuʻ*, A being terrified. Terror.

A تروعة *tarwiʻa*, The blast of a trumpet. P تروعه زدن *tarwiʻa zadan*, To sound taratantara.

A تروغ *tarawwugh*, (v. n. 5 of راغ for روغ) Rolling, wallowing (as a horse).

A ترؤم *taraʼʼum*, (v. n. 5 of رأم) Pitying, commiserating, feeling a tender sympathy towards. Love, tenderness, compassion.

A تروم *tarawwum*, A mocking, a ridiculing.

P ترومیده *taro* or *tiromīda*, Mixed. Gained.

P تروند *tarwand*, A false promise, broken faith. A vain, idle, impossible tale. First-fruits, early fruits.

P تروندہ *tarwanda*, Early fruits. First-fruits. Novelties. Fraud, deceit. A lie.

P ترووه *tarwoh* or *tirūva*, A pair, a match.

P تروه *tarūh* or *turwa*, A pair.

P تروهیده *taro* or *tirohīda*, Mixed. Gotten.

A تروي *tarawwī*, (v. n. 5 of روي) Slaking, quenching one's thirst. Being well moistened. Being green and succulent (a tree). Being middling and moderate. Being thick. Reporting a story, relating the words of another. Reflecting, meditating.

A ترويأ *tarwiʼ*, (or تروئة *tarwiʼat*) (v. n. 2 of روأ not in use) Considering with attention. Answering with deliberation.

A ترويب *tarwīb*, (v. n. 2 of راب for روب) Thickening (milk). Wearying, fatiguing. Intoxicating, making drunk.

A ترويه *tarwiyat*, (v. n. 2 of روي) Carrying water to one's family, satisfying their thirst. Wetting, moistening. Compelling one to repeat the words of another. Giving attention to, taking notice of. يوم التروية *yawmu't tarwiyat*, The eighth day of ذو الحجة *zu'l hijjat*, whereon certain rites are performed at Mecca.

A ترويج *tarwīj*, (v. n. 2 of راج for روج) Placing a value upon (goods, &c.), making them to be sold. Blowing about from nobody knows where (wind). Making to pass or go current, giving currency.

A ترويح *tarwīh*, (v. n. 2 of راح for روح) Stilling, quieting, causing to repose, giving rest. Fanning. Visiting in the afternoon. Driving (camels) home (in the evening). Perfuming.

A ترويز *tarwīz*, (v. n. 2 of راز for روز) Thinking, exercising the judgment on one thing after another.

A ترويض *tarwīz*, (v. n. 2 of راض for روض) Laying out a garden; making any place pleasant by planting herbs and flowers. Abiding in a garden. Training, instructing, exercising, making tractable, breaking in (a boy or a colt).

A ترويع *tarwīʻ*, (v. n. 2 of راع for روع) Terrifying. Soaking (bread) in melted butter.

A ترويغ *tarwīgh*, (v. n. 2 of راغ for روغ) Seasoning (a flour-pudding) with fat or dripping.

A ترويق *tarwīk*, (v. n. 2 of راق for روق) Straining off, making clear. Stretching abroad, spreading forth her sablest veil (night). Covering the cieling with a kind of matting. Selling off common ware and purchasing better. Raising the price of wares, so that the purchaser will not buy them. Bepissing himself (a drunkard).

A ترويل *tarwīl*, (v. n. 2 of رال for رول) Letting (his) saliva run into his nose-bag (a horse). Preparing to stale (a horse). Buttering (bread) or soaking (it) in fat. Experiencing a seminal effusion before coition.

A ترويم *tarwīm*, (v. n. 2 of رام for روم) Setting one to seek for. Delaying, tarrying. Turning the attention to one thing after another.

P تره *tarh*, Wards of a key. Beards of corn. *Tara* or تره *tarra*, Garden-herbs in general, especially beets, spinnage, cresses, or parsley. ترهٔ خراساني *tara-i khurāsānī*, A very acid kind of herb. ترهٔ شير *tara-i sher*, A very bitter kind of herb. ترهٔ گربه *tara-i gurba*, Balm.

A تره *tarh*, (v. n. of تره) Mixing one's self up with vanities and trifles.

A تره *turrah*, (pl. تراريه *tarārīh*) Vain, foolish, futile. A lie.

A ترهات *turrahāt*, (pl. of ترهة *turrahat*) Vain words, foolish things, idle tales, trifles, bagatelles. Calamities, troubles.

A ترهّب *tarahhub*, (v. n. 5 of رهب) Devoting one's self to religion, embracing a monastic life. Threatening greatly. Dreading.

A ترهبل *tarahbul*, A walking in a certain mode.

A ترهة *turrahat*, (pl. ترهات *turrahāt* and تراريه *tarārīh*) A foolish word, idle story, trifle. A narrow by-road, branching from a main road. Misfortune, calamity. An animalcule living in the sand. Wind. A cloud. An extensive piece of level ground.

P تره تيزك *tara-tezak* or تندك *tundak*, Rocket.

P تره دوغ *tara-dogh*, Herbs and sour milk.

A ترهره *tarahruh*, (v. n. 2 of رهره Q) Being soft, white, and shining (the body). Glittering (the vapour سراب *sarāb*).

P تره زار *tarazār*, A kitchen-garden.

A ترهّس *tarahhus*, A being moved, agitated.

P تره فروش *tara-farosh*, A green-grocer.

A ترهّل *tarahhul*, A being soft, loose, flabby.

P تره ميره *tara-mīra*, Wild mustard.

P ترهنده *tarhanda*, Fresh, elegant, delicate.

A ترهوط *turhūt*, A swallower of large gobbets.

A ترهوك *tarahwuk*, (v. n. 2 of رهوك Q) Walking with a swinging motion.

A ترهيب *tarhīb*, (v. n. 2 of رهب) Sitting and refreshing with fodder (a camel almost worn out upon a journey). Making one a monk (راهب *rāhib*). Striking with terror: deterring.

A ترهيد *tarhīd*, A displaying of egregious folly.

A ترهيط *tarhīt*, (v. n. 2 of رهط) Devouring voraciously, gobbling down large mouthsful.

A ترهيق *tarhīk*, (v. n. 2 of رهق) Suspecting. Calling (any one) unjust or oppressive.

A ترهيل *tarhīl*, (v. n. 2 of رهل) Making (flesh) soft and flabby, causing (it) to swell.

A ترهيؤ *tarahyu-*, (v. n. 2 of رهيأ Q) Meditating upon, setting about (business). Walking with a tottering gait. Being disposed to rain.

P تري *tarī*, Freshness, moisture. *Tare*, A high wall. A mound, a dam.

A ترّي *turra'*, An amputated hand.

A ترياض *tiryāz*, A woman's name.

A ترياق *tiryāk*, Treacle, theriaca, a composition made up of many ingredients. Antidotes of every kind against poisons. Wine. A sovereign remedy. (That of Baghdād has been long esteemed as an immediate remedy for the bites of the most venomous serpents). ترياق تركي *tiryāki turkī*, Mummy. P ترياق روستائيان *tiryāki rūstā-iyān*, Garlic. A ترياق فارسي *tiryāki fārsī*, The bezoar-stone. A stone in the corner of the eye of the mountain-ox. ترياق فاروق *tiryāki fārūk*, Treacle against poisons.

A ترياقة *tiryākat*, Wine.

A ترياقي *tiryākī*, Inebriated. A debauchee.

P ترياك *tiryāk* or *taryāk*, The bezoar-stone. Opium. ترياك اكبر *tiryāki akbar*, The bezoar-stone.

P تريان *tar* or *tiryān*, A wicker basket or sieve.

A تريب *tiryab* or *tarīb*, Earth.

A تريبة *tarībat*, (pl. ترائب *tarā-ib*) The four upper ribs on each side, or on the left only. The place above the collar-bone, where necklaces and other ornaments are suspended. The breast, the bosom, the neck. Hands. Eyes. Feet.

P تريت *tarīt*, (or تريد *tarīd*) Bread crumbled into milk or broth. A sop.

A تريّث *tarayyus*, A delaying, a hesitating.

A تريج *tarīj*, Violent (wind). Brawny (man).

P تريدن *tarīdan*, To extract, draw out. *Turīdan*, To be greatly afraid.

P ترير *tarīr*, Terrifying. A threatener.

P تريز *tīrez*, A gusset. A bird's wing.

A تريص *tarīs*, Strong. A well-poised scale. Any thing twisted.

A تريع *tarīꜥ*, One who plunges into, or enters upon, business cheerfully and with alacrity.

A تريّع *tarayyuꜥ*, (v. n. 5 of راع for ريع) Moving here and there (a floating mist). Being convened (people). Delaying. Stopping. Being astonished. Shining and shaking (floating fat).

A تريّغ *tarayyugh*, (v. n. 5 of راغ for ريغ) Being seasoned with fat, or dripping (a flour pudding).

A تريّف *tarayyuf*, (v. n. 5 of راف for ريف) Coming into that kind of country called ريف *rīf*.

A تريّق *tarayyuk*, (v. n. 5 of راق for ريق) Shining on the ground like water and appearing to flow (a vapour floating over a sandy plain).

A تريك *tarīk*, A stalk stripped of its grapes. (pl. of تريكة *tarīkat*, q. v.)

A تريكة *tarīkat*, (pl. ترائك *tarā-ik* and تريك *tarīk*) A helmet. Any thing left, neglected (as a woman by lovers, or a field by cattle). Water remaining after a flood. An egg left by an ostrich. An eggshell quitted by the chick.

A تريم *tarīm*, Submissive to the divine will. Stained, defiled with dust or with sins. *Tiryam*, Name of a place.

P ترين *tarīn*, Moist, fresh, recent, good. Added to an adjective it forms the superlative: as, خوب *khūb*, Good, خوبترين *khūbtarīn*, Very good, best.

P ترينان *tarīnān*, A wicker basket.

P ترين وا *tarīn-wā*, A kind of Turkomān food.

P ترينه *tarīna*, A kind of food or sowings eaten by the poor. Pot-herbs.

P تريو *taryo*, A flimsy kind of garment.

P تريوه *tarewa*, An up-and-down-hill road.

A تريّه *tarayyuh*, (v. n. 5 of راه for ريه) Moving to and fro, appearing and disappearing (the vapour سراب *sarāb*).

A ترئية *tar-iyat*, (v. n. 2 of رأي) Exposing to view. Holding a mirror. Playing the hypocrite. Beauty, elegance of looks.

A تريئة *taryi-at*, (v. n. 2 of راأ for ريأ) Easing of a quinsey or strangulation. Considering attentively.

A تريّيث *taryīs*, (v. n. 2 of راث for ريث) Softening. Fatiguing. Speaking slowly. Calling (any one) slow.

A تريّخ *taryīkh*, An enervating, a relaxing.

A تريير *taryīr*, (v. n. 2 of رار for رير) Having a plentiful year. Being oppressed by fat and unable to walk. Abounding in produce (a country).

A ترئيس *tar-īs*, (v. n. 2 of رأس) Giving authority, constituting head or chief, giving precedence.

A تربيش *taryīsh*, The feathering (of an arrow).

A تربيع *taryīꜥ*, An assembling, being convened.

A تريّغ *taryīgh*, (v. n. 2 of راغ for ريغ) Seasoning (a flour pudding) with fat or dripping.

A تريّيم *taryīm*, (v. n. 2 of رام for ريم) Remaining in one place. Augmenting, increasing. Being turbid or obscure.

P تز *taz*, A small bird of an ash colour. The wards of a lock. Leaves just sprouted. A head marked with scars.

A تزابي *tazābī*, A slow and self-important air.

A تزاجر *tazājur*, (v. n. 6 of زجر) Exciting each other (soldiers).

A تزاحف *tazāhuf*, (v. n. 6 of زحف) Drawing near each other to battle.

A تزاحك *tazāhuk*, (v. n. 6 of زحك) Approaching one another. Retiring from one another.

A تزاحم *tazāhum*, (v. n. 6 of زحم) Thronging. A crowd, mob, press, throng.

A تزأر *taza-ur*, A growling inwardly (of a lion).

A تزأزؤ *taza-zu-*, (v. n. 2 of زأزأ Q) Being moved, terrified. Being shaken. Being concealed, lying hid. Yielding, knocking under from fear.

A تزاعم *tazāꜥum*, (v. n. 6 of زعم) Holding with one another communications on which no reliance can be placed. Opposing, contradicting each other.

A تزانط *tazānut*, A thronging, pressing, crowding.

P تزاو *tazāv*, Name of a hero of Turkistān.

A تزاوج *tazāwuj*, (v. n. 6 of زاج for زوج) Marrying. Intermarrying.

A تزاور *tazāwur*, (v. n. 6 of زار for زور) Visiting

one another. Turning away, declining from.

A تزاوف *tazānuf*, (v. n. 6 of زاف for زوف) Playing at a certain game (boys).

A تزأوك *tazāuk*, A blushing, a being ashamed.

A تزاول *tazānul*, (v. n. 6 of زال for زول) Joining mutual endeavours, taking joint care. Occupying, employing one's self. Being kept employed.

A تزاهد *tazāhud*, (v. n. 6 of زهد) Despising, regarding as contemptible.

A تزايد *tazāyud*, (v. n. 6 of زاد for زيد) Increasing. Amplifying, making additions to a story. تزايد عزّ و منزلت *tazāyudi ʿizz u manzilat*, Increase of glory and dignity.

A تزايغ *tazāyugh*, An inclining, leaning, tottering.

A تزايل *tazāyul*, (v. n. 6 of زال for زيل) Being opposed, contrary to each other. Being separate, distant from each other. Being ashamed.

A تزبّب *tazabbub*, (v. n. 5 of زبّ) Foaming at the mouth when speaking.

A تزبتر *tazabtur*, A walking pompously.

A تزبّد *tazabbud*, (v. n. 5 of زبد) Foaming, frothing. Swallowing. Taking the choicest part. Making haste, being eager to swear.

A تزبرة *tazbirat*, An autograph. انا اعرف تزبرتي *ana aʿrifu tazbiratī*, I know my own handwriting. *Tazburat*, (v. n. of زبر) Writing.

A تزبّع *tazabbuʿ*, (v. n. 5 of زبع not in use) Being malignant, of a bad disposition, irascible, furious, and abusive. Going in an evil way. Becoming changed.

A تزبّي *tazabbī*, The digging of a pit for a lion.

A تزبيب *tazbīb*, (v. n. 2 of زبّ) Drying (grapes or figs) in the sun. Foaming (the mouth). Being near setting (the sun).

A تزبية *tazbiyat*, (v. n. 2 of زبي) Driving away. Digging a pit for a lion and strewing meat in it.

A تزبيد *tazbīd*, (v. n. 2 of زبد) Separating (cotton) with strokes of the bow-string. Foaming, frothing (at the mouth).

A تزبير *tazbīr*, (v. n. 2 of زبر) Writing.

A تزبيل *tazbīl*, (v. n. 2 of زبل) Dunging land.

A تزتّت *tazattut*, The being adorned (a bride).

P تزتك *tuztak*, A tube for shooting clay balls by the breath.

A تزتيت *taztīt*, The adorning (of a bride).

A تزجّي *tazajjī*, A being content (with a little).

A تزجية *tazjiyat*, (v. n. 2 of زجي) Driving gently, thrusting away. Passing time.

A تزجيج *tazjīj*, (v. n. 2 of زجّ) Extending in length and thinning the eye-brows (a woman). Making (a thing) straight and even.

A تزحّر *tazahhur*, (v. n. 5 of زحر) Being griped (the belly), and purging. Breathing hard. Groaning in travail (a woman).

A تزحزح *tazahzuh*, (v. n. 2 of زحزح Q) Retiring, going to a distance. Being distant.

A تزحّف *tazahhuf*, (v. n. 5 of زحف) Advancing, going towards.

A تزحّل *tazahhul*, A departing, going away from.

A تزحلف *tazahluf*, (v. n. 2 of زحلف Q) Being rolled, impelled. Being removed; retiring, receding.

A تزحلق *tazahluk*, A being turned over, revolved.

A تزحلك *tazahluk*, A being turned, revolved.

A تزحّن *tazahhun*, (v. n. 5 of زحن) Advancing slowly. Doing any thing against one's will: drinking, because being forced to it against one's will.

A تزحول *tazahwul*, A departing, going off.

A تزحير *tazhīr*, (v. n. 2 of زحر) Groaning (a travailing woman). Stopping the nostrils of a camel which has lost her newly-born colt, and stuffing a clout into her matrix; which after remaining there a night is drawn forth; when she, imagining herself to have been in foal, readily takes a liking to another's colt, and lets her milk flow freely.

A تزحيل *tazhīl*, A driving to a distance.

A تزخّر *tazakhkhur*, (v. n. 5 of زخر) Growing full, overflowing (a channel). Swelling (the sea).

A تزخّف *tazakhkhuf*, An adorning one's self.

A تزخور *tazakhwur*, A glorying in possessions.

A تزخيف *tazkhīf*, (v. n. 2 of زخف) Talking much and mouthing. Taking with the fingers.

A تزدّغ *tazaddugh*, A reclining on a bolster.

P تزده *tazda*, The miller's hire. Title-deeds.

P تزر *tazar*, A summer-house, country seat.

A تزرّر *tazarrur*, A being furnished with buttons.

A تزرزر *tazarzur*, A being moved; moving.

A تزرّع *tazarruʿ*, A hasting to do mischief.

A تزرنق *tazarnuk*, (v. n. 2 of زرنق Q) Being changed, altered, turning sour, becoming rotten. Drawing water with the machine زرنوق *zurnūk* for hire. Putting on clothes, concealing one's person therein.

P تزره *tazra*, The iron axle of a mill-stone.

A تزرّي *tazarrī*, A defaming, reproaching.

A تزريف *tazrīf*, (v. n. 2 of زرف) Talking much. Cleaning, winnowing. Removing, putting to a distance. Increasing, augmenting. Becoming putrid (a sore).

A تزريم *tazrīm*, (v. n. 2 of زرم) Interrupting, cutting short (the flow of urine, or of tears, or of conversation). Confining, blocking up, reducing to straits. Appearing as a miser.

A تزعّب *tazaʿʿub*, (v. n. 5 of زعب) Being brisk, lively, sprightly. Raging furiously. Eating and drinking immoderately. Dividing property amongst themselves.

A تزعزع *tazaʿzuʿ*, (v. n. 2 of زعزع Q) Being shaken (a tree by the wind). Commotion, agitation.

A تزعّل *tazaʿʿul*, A being brisk and cheerful.

A تزعّم *tazaʿʿum*, A lying, telling a lie.

P تزغ *tazgh* or *tuzgh*, A tree, the fire of which will continue for a week.

A تزغّم *tazaghghum*, (v. n. 5 of زغم) Sputtering the foam round the mouth. Speaking in a passion. Crying with a shrill voice (a camel's colt).

A تزغيب *tazghīb*, (v. n. 2 of زغب) Having down or small yellow hair (young unfledged birds).

P تزف *tazf* or *tazuf*, Barley-sugar. Freshness, moisture. Ease, affluence. Rest.

P تزفان *tazfān*, (for ترزفان) An interpreter.

A تزفزف *tazafzuf*, A diddering (from cold).

A تزفّي *tazaffī*, (v. n. 5 of زفي) Frightening.

A تزفيت *tazfīt*, An anointing with pitch.

A تزقّف *tazakkuf*, (v. n. 5 of زقف) Snatching greedily (as a starving man does meat).

A تزقّم *tazakkum*, (v. n. 5 of زقم) Swallowing meat. Seizing and devouring greedily.

A تزقيب *tazkīb*, The whistle or chirp of a bird.

A تزقيق *tazkīk*, (v. n. 2 of زقّ) Flaying, skinning an animal, beginning at the head.

A تزكّر *tazakkur*, (v. n. 5 of زكر) Being full (a leathern bottle). Growing, thriving (as a child). Being collected (wine).

A تزكزك *tazakzuk*, (v. n. 2 of زكزك Q) Laying up provisions for any needful occasion.

A تزكّي *tazakkī*, (v. n. 5 of زكا for زكو) Growing. Being augmented. Studying purity: almsgiving.

A تزكية *tazkiyat*, (v. n. 2 of زكا for زكو) Sanctifying, purifying (that part of a man's wealth which is dedicated to pious uses). Receiving alms. Praising (one's self). Causing to grow.

A تزكيت *tazkīt*, (v. n. 2 of زكت) Filling (a leathern bottle). Relating a story to another and causing him to lay it up in his mind.

A تزكير *tazkīr*, (v. n. 2 of زكر) Filling. Thriving.

A تزكيم *tazkīm*, The giving a cold (زكام *zukām*).

A تزكين *tazkīn*, (v. n. 2 of زكن) Comparing, likening. Soliloquizing. Concealing the truth, cheating, deceiving. Opinion, suspicion.

P تزلب *tazlab*, The fat of a sheep's tail.

A تزلّج *tazalluj*, (v. n. 5 of زلج) Sliding. Gulping, drinking largely (wine).

A تزلجب *tazaljub*, A slipping, sliding.

A تزلّح *tazalluh*, (v. n. 5 of زلح) Tasting.

A تزلحف *tazalhuf*, (v. n. 2 of زلحف Q) Being removed; retiring, receding.

A تزلزل *tazalzul*, (v. n. 2 of زلزل Q) Being shaken (the earth). Commotion, agitation, trembling, trepidation. An earthquake. (in prosody) Changing the vowel-point of one letter so as completely to alter the sense of the word. (Gladwin's Dissert.)

A تزلّع *tazalluʿ*, (v. n. 5 of زلع) Being cracked, chapped (hands or feet). Being broken.

A تزلّغ *tazallugh*, (v. n. 5 of زلغ) Being chapped and cracked (the foot).

A تزلّف *tazalluf*, (v. n. 5 of زلف) Proceeding, advancing, preceding. Being dispersed.

A تزلّق *tazalluk*, (v. n. 5 of زلق) Being so highly adorned and in such good case that the surface of the skin shines. Sliding, slipping.

A تزليج *tazlīj*, (v. n. 2 of زلج) Leading a frugal

life. Uttering, sending forth words.

A تزليخ *tazlīkh*, (v. n. 2 of زلخ) Smoothing, making smooth and shining.

A تزليف *tazlīf*, (v. n. 2 of زلف) Telling a long story, being talkative.

A تزليق *tazlīk*, (v. n. 2 of زلق) Shaving (the head). Making slippery. Anointing (the body) till (it) become quite slippery. Being a long while sharpening (a tool).

A تزليم *tazlīm*, (v. n. 2 of زلم) Filling (a lake or cistern). Smoothing and making straight (an arrow). Preparing or dressing badly (victuals), making them disagreeable or unwholesome. Turning (a mill). Taking the edge off a millstone.

P تزم *tazm*, A mist, a fog.

A تزمّت *tazammut*, Modesty. ما اشدّ تزمّته *mā ashadda tazammutahu*, How intense is his gravity!

A تزمجر *tazamjur*, The roaring (of a lion).

A تزمخر *tazamkhur*, Growl of an angry leopard.

A تزمّر *tazammur*, The crying (of a male ostrich).

A تزمزم *tazamzum*, The braying (of a camel).

A تزمّل *tazammul*, (v. n. 5 of زمل) Wrapping up, or hiding one's self in a garment.

A تزميح *tazmīh*, (v. n. 2 of زمح not used) Killing the bird زمّح *zummah*.

A تزمير *tazmīr*, (v. n. 2 of زمر) Piping, playing the flute. Filling (a bottle). Psalmody.

A تزميك *tazmīk*, (v. n. 2 of زمك not in use) Irritating (one against another). Filling (a bottle).

A تزميل *tazmīl*, (v. n. 2 of زمل) Wrapping another in a garment. Following.

A تزميم *tazmīm*, (v. n. 2 of زمّ) Fastening a rein through the nose of a camel. Being tied together on account of their number (camels).

A تزنبر *tazambur*, The being proud and haughty.

A تزنتر *tazantur*, A walking proudly.

A تزنّح *tazannuh*, (v. n. 5 of زنح) Drinking again and again. Carrying one's self above one's situation. Speaking openly.

A تزنّخ *tazannukh*, (v. n. 5 of زنخ) Speaking freely, in a dictatorial and dogmatical manner. Being proud.

A تزنّد *tazannud*, (v. n. 5 of زند) Being puzzled, nonplused, unable to reply. Being angry.

P تزندر *tazandar*, Name of a small bird.

A تزندق *tazanduk*, (v. n. 2 of زندق Q) Embracing the religion of Zoroaster, maintaining the doctrine of the two principles. Entertaining heretical or atheistical notions, as those of a زنديق *zindīk*.

A تزنّر *tazannur*, (v. n. 2 of زنر) Putting on a girdle. Being thin, slender. Being beaten, pounded.

A تزنّف *tazannuf*, A being angry.

A تزنئة *taznīat*, A reducing to straits.

A تزنية *tazniyat*, A making narrow. (v. n. 2 of زني) Playing the whore. Accusing of whoredom or adultery. Calling one a whoremonger.

A تزنيج *taznīj*, (v. n. 2 of زنج) Giving little.

A تزنيح *taznīh*, A drinking again and again.

A تزنيخ *taznīkh*, (v. n. 2 of زنخ) Speaking openly in an imperious manner. Raising his head when sucking (a lamb) from suffocation or dryness.

A تزنيد *taznīd*, (v. n. 2 of زند) Lying, telling falsehoods. Punishing above desert. Striking fire with two pieces of wood. Tying and skewering up the matrix of a camel which has suffered a prolapsus uteri after foaling. Filling.

A تزنيق *taznīk*, (v. n. 2 of زنق) Keeping (servants) on short commons (from avarice or poverty).

A تزنيم *taznīm*, (v. n. 2 of زنم not in use) Rousing, stirring up, sending any one to annoy and pick up a quarrel.

A تزنين *taznīn*, (v. n. 2 of زنّ) Eating habitually of the pulse زنّ *zinn*.

A تزواج *tazwāj*, A conjunction.

P تزوال *tazwāl*, (or تژوال *tajwāl*) The leaf or blade of a plant.

A تزوّج *tazawwuj*, (v. n. 5 of زاج for زوج) Marrying, taking a wife. Stealing upon, overpowering (as sleep).

A تزوّد *tazawwud*, (v. n. 5 of زود not in use) Being provided or providing one's self with necessaries for a journey.

A تزورق *tazawruk*, (v. n. 2 of زورق Q) Voiding the contents of the belly.

A تزوّع *tazawwuʿ*, (v. n. 5 of زاع for زوع) Becoming separate from the muscles (flesh).

A تزوّل *tazawwul*, (v. n. 5 of زال for زول) Saying or doing any thing good. Being very witty, clever, and sagacious.

A تزوّي *tazawwī*, (v. n. 5 of زوي) Retiring into a corner (زاوية *zāwiyat*). Becoming contracted.

A تزوية *tazwiyat*, A retiring into a corner.

A تزويج *tazwīj*, (v. n. 2 of زاج for زوج) Joining, associating, giving in marriage, causing to marry.

A تزويد *tazwīd*, (v. n. 2 of زود not in use) Providing with travelling necessaries or other things.

A تزوير *tazwīr*, (v. n. 2 of زار for زور) Giving a false colouring to, adorning a lie, adulterating. Marking, stamping with falsehood. Doing well and uprightly. Adorning. Establishing, setting on foot. Invalidating evidence. Causing to incline. Adulteration, deception. Imposture, fraud. A lie. Honour, respect shown to a visitor.

A تزويط *tazwīt*, A making up large mouthsful.

A تزويع *tazwīʿ*, (v. n. 2 of زاع for زوع) Turning (camels) different ways. Scattering (as the wind the withered parts of a plant).

A تزويق *tazwīk*, (v. n. 2 of زوق not in use) Overlaying with quicksilver. Executing well. Doing elegantly. A painting of gold impressed on iron by means of quicksilver.

A تزويل *tazwīl*, (v. n. 2 of زال for زول) Moving a thing from its place. Saying or doing any thing good.

A تزهّد *tazahhud*, A being abstinent and devout.

A تزهّف *tazahhuf*, (v. n. 5 of زهف) Prohibiting, checking. Turning away the face.

A تزهلج *tazahluj*, (v. n. 2 of زهلج Q not used) Being projected, going straight (a spear).

A تزهلق *tazahluk*, A being white, fat, and sleek.

A تزهنع *tazahnuʿ*, A being dressed, tired (a maid).

A تزهية *tazhiyat*, (v. n. 2 of زها for زهو) Changing colour (a ripening date).

A تزهيد *tazhīd*, (v. n. 2 of زهد) Making or striving to render abstinent and devout. Diminishing, making small. Considering as small. Holding in honour. Making thin and spare. Regarding as avaricious.

A تزيّب *tazayyub*, (v. n. 5 of زاب for زيب) Being compact, firm (flesh).

A تزيّخ *tazayyukh*, A being separated, dispersed.

A تزيد *tazīd*, Name of the father of a tribe.

A تزيّد *tazayyud*, (v. n. 5 of زاد for زيد) Increasing (the price of provisions). Adding observations (to a narrative). Yawning and stretching himself when roaring (a lion). The straddling pace of a jaded beast. Dearness. A lie.

P تزيدن *tazīdan*, To draw up. To extract.

A تزيديّ *tazīdīy*, A kind of red-striped garment.

A تزيّغ *tazayyugh*, (v. n. 5 of زاغ for زيغ) Adorning herself (a woman).

A تزيّق *tazayyuk*, (v. n. 5 of زاق for زيق) Ornamenting, dressing herself (a woman). Tinging the eyes with a black collyrium.

P تزيك *tazīk*, One neither an Arab nor Turk.

A تزيّل *tazayyul*, A being separated, dispersed.

A تزيّم *tazayyum*, (v. n. 5 of زام for زيم) Being dispersed, scattered. Being cut piecemeal. Being stowed very compactly (meat).

A تزيّن *tazayyun*, (v. n. 5 of زان for زين) Dressing, adorning one's person. Being adorned.

A تزيّي *tazayyī*, (v. n. 5 of زيي) Wearing a costume. Assuming a dress. تزيّا بزيّ الصلحاء *tazayya bi zīyi ṣ' ṣulahāʾ*, He clothed himself in the garb of the virtuous. Being invested with a form.

A تزيية *tazyiyat*, (v. n. 2 of زيي) Investing with shape, figure, habit, garb, or costume.

A تزييت *tazyīt*, A providing with, giving oil.

A تزييد *tazyīd*, An augmenting, amplifying.

A تزيير *tazyīr*, (v. n. 2 of زير not in use) Making (a horse) to stand still or become tractable by twisting his upper lip with a twitch.

A تزييغ *tazyīgh*, The straightening (of a curve).

A تزييف *tazyīf*, (v. n. 2 of زاف for زيف) Adulterating or clipping (coin).

A تزييل *tazyīl*, (v. n. 2 of زال for زيل) Separating, distinguishing. Dispersion.

A تزئيم *tazʾīm*, (v. n. 2 of زأم) Frightening.

A تزيين *tazyīn*, (v. n. 2 of زان for زين) Adorning, dressing, garnishing, decking, bedizening.

P تژ *tij*, A certain small bird with a plaintive note. A new leaf. Young grass.

P تژاو *tajāv*, Name of Afrāsyāb's son-in-law.

P تژاول *tajāwil*, The leaf or blade of a plant.

P تزدك *tajdak*, A weevil destructive to wheat.

P تزده *tajda*, The miller's hire for grinding. The notching of a mill-stone. The wards of a key. A rose-bud.

P تزم *tajm* or *tijm*, A mist, a fog.

P تزوال *tajwāl*, The leaf or blade of a plant.

P تزه *taja*, The bud of a flower. The beard of rye or barley. The main beam of a house. The wards of a key.

P تس *tas*, A slap. *Tus*, Wind which escapes gently. Spitting.

A تسائل *tasāul*, (v. n. 6 of سأل) Asking, inquiring of one another.

A تسابّ *tasābb*, (v. n. 6 of سبّ) Railing at, reviling one another. Being cut asunder, severed.

A تسابغ *tasābugh*, Neck-armour, a texture of iron rings hanging from the helmet.

A تسابق *tasābuk*, (v. n. 6 of سبق) Running, throwing, contending in any manner for a wager.

A تسابي *tasābī*, (v. n. 6 of سبي) Taking one another prisoners. Captivating hearts.

A تساتل *tasātul*, (v. n. 6 of ستل) Being joined, connected, following one another (as men, tears, or pearls on a string).

A تساجل *tasājul*, A boasting to one another.

P تساچه *tasācha*, A crocodile, an alligator.

A تساخين *tasākhīn*, Boots. A kind of hood such as learned men formerly wore on their heads.

A تسارّ *tasārr*, A telling one another secrets.

A تسارع *tasāruɛ*, A hastening together.

A تسأسؤ *tasa-sus*, (v. n. 2 of سأسأ Q) Being diverse, discordant, opposed, contrary (affairs).

A تساعيّ *tusāɛiy*, Consisting of, completing nine.

A تسافح *tasāfuh*, A whoring. Debauchery.

A تسافد *tasāfud*, The copulating (of beasts).

A تسافه *tasāfuh*, (v. n. 6 of سفه) Being light, foolish, and unsteady.

A تساقب *tasākub*, (v. n. 6 of سقب) Being near.

A تساقط *tasākut*, (v. n. 6 of سقط) Falling. Falling step by step. Throwing one's self into.

A تساقي *tasākī*, A giving drink reciprocally.

A تساكر *tasākur*, A feigning drunkenness.

A تسال *tasāl*, (v. n. of سأل) Asking, praying.

A تسالف *tasāluf*, (v. n. 6 of سلف) Being connected by affinity (as the husbands of two sisters).

A تسالم *tasālum*, (v. n. 6 of سلم) Making peace, being reconciled.

A تسامح *tasāmuh*, (v. n. 6 of سمح) Conniving. Reciprocal indulgence, the exercise of mutual kindness and forgiveness.

P تسامح پيشه *tasāmuh-pesha*, Easy, pliable.

A تسامع *tasāmuɛ*, (v. n. 6 of سمع) Listening (as the populace). Hearing from one another. Being spread abroad (news).

A تسامي *tasāmī*, A contending for pre-eminence.

A تسانّ *tasānn*, A biting one another.

A تساند *tasānud*, (v. n. 6 of سند) Leaning, staying upon. Assisting one another.

A تساور *tasāwur*, (v. n. 6 of سار for سور) Appearing, shewing one's self from a height.

A تساوق *tasāwuk*, (v. n. 6 of ساق for سوق) Following one another (camels), being tame, quiet. Thronging, tumbling over one another (sheep).

A تساوك *tasāwuk*, (v. n. 6 of ساك for سوك) Walking weakly (emaciated cattle).

A تسأول *tasāul*, An asking of one another.

A تساوم *tasāwum*, (v. n. 6 of سام for سوم) Bidding one against another. Setting a price.

A تساوي *tasāwī*, (v. n. 6 of سوي) Being equal, co-equal. Resembling one another. Being even. Equality, similarity, sameness. Neutrality.

A تساهل *tasāhul*, (v. n. 6 of سهل) Remitting, pardoning, conniving at. Reciprocal indulgence, the exercise of mutual kindness.

A تساهم *tasāhum*, (v. n. 6 of سهم) Casting lots (amongst themselves).

A تساير *tasāyur*, (v. n. 6 of سار for سير) Walking for a bet; going together.

A تسايف *tasāyuf*, (v. n. 6 of ساف for سيف) Fighting, fencing, skirmishing, using a broadsword.

A تسايل *tasāyul*, (v. n. 6 of سال for سيل) Flocking from all parts (troops).

P تسبانيدن *tasbānīdan*, (trans. of تسبيدن *tasbīdan*) To cause fissures in the lips. To heat. To suffocate, strangle.

A تسبّب *tasabbub*, (v. n. 5 of سبّ) Causing, employing means, labouring. Being caused, arising.

A تسبّج *tasabbuj*, (v. n. 5 of سبج not in use) Arraying one's person in a black dress called سبجة *subjat*.

A تسبّخ *tasabbukh*, (v. n. 5 of سبخ) Being assuaged, allayed; subsiding (heat).

A تسبسب *tasabsub*, The flowing (of water).

A تسبغ *tasbigh* or *tasbagh*, Neck-armour.

A تسبغة *tasbighat* or *tasbaghat*, (pl. تسابغ *tasābigh*) Neck-armour, a texture of rings hanging from the helmet.

A تسبيب *tasbīb*, (v. n. 2 of سبّ) Causing, giving cause. Reproaching, reviling, cursing.

A تسبيح *tasbīh*, (v. n. 2 of سبح) Celebrating the praises of God. Using a rosary or chaplet for that purpose. Ejaculating the phrase سبحان الله *subhāna'llāh*. Purity. A hymn, the praise of God, when saying بسم الله *b'ismi'llah*, In the name of God! سبحان الله *subhāna'llāh*, O holy (Creator! mercy on us! deliver us from! or such similar ejaculations). A rosary, a chaplet of beads. P تسبيح كردن *tasbīh kardan*, To praise God, to say prayers by the telling of beads.

A تسبيحات *tasbīhāt*, Hymns, anthems.

P تسبيح خانه *tasbīh-khāna*, A chapel, oratory.

P تسبيح خوان *tasbīh-khwān*, A singer of praises to God. One hired to pray, a private chaplain.

P تسبيح خواني *tasbīh-khwānī*, Chaplainship.

A تسبيخ *tasbīkh*, (v. n. 2 of سبخ) Making light. Erasing a syllable or a letter, making a short syllable instead of a long one. Quieting, stilling. Throwing away the refuse (of cotton, wool, or camel's hair), whilst carding. Being assuaged (heat), allayed (the throbbing of a wound). Rest. Stillness. Deep sleep.

A تسبيد *tasbīd*, (v. n. 2 of سبد) Smoothing the head by extirpating the hair, either by shaving or by pulling them up with an unguent. Letting the hair flow loose and moistening it. Leaving off unguent. Growing again (hairs, or fresh shoots of the plant نصيّ *nasiy* on the old one). Becoming fledged (a bird).

P تسبيدن *tasbīdan*, To have fissures or chaps in the lips. To strangle. To be strangled, suffocated. To grow hot, be fierce.

A تسبيط *tasbīt*, (v. n. 2 of سبط) Falsely shewing herself to be in foal (a camel) by refusing the male. Bringing forth a castling (a camel or sheep).

A تسبيع *tasbīɛ*, (v. n. 2 of سبع) Dividing into seven parts. Making septangular. Washing (a vessel) seven times. Recompensing sevenfold. Stipulating with one that he read the Kur'ān through once in seven days. Remaining with a wife seven nights. Making up the number seventy. Completing the number seven hundred.

A تسبيغ *tasbīgh*, (v. n. 2 of سبغ) Casting her foal (a camel) already covered with hair. A pouring forth. A certain kind of prosodial usage.

A تسبيق *tasbīk*, (v. n. 2 of سبق) Receiving the stakes (a winner). Paying the stakes. Casting her young before the time (a ewe).

A تسبيك *tasbīk*, (v. n. 2 of سبك) Melting (gold or silver), casting, pouring into a mould.

A تسبيل *tasbīl*, A consecrating to God.

P تست *tast*, A cup, goblet. *Tast* or *tust*, (for توست *tu'st*, or more properly تو است *tu ast*).

P تستر *tustar*, Name of a city in Khurāsān, the walls of which were the first built after the flood.

A تستّر *tasattur*, (v. n. 5 of ستر) Being hidden, veiled, or covered. Concealing one's self, absconding. Putting to a distance, avoiding.

A تستوق *tustūk*, Base coin washed with silver.

P تستي *tustī*, Thou art.

A تستير *tastīr*, The veiling, concealing (a damsel).

A تسجام *tasjām*, A causing to drop or flow.

A تسجية *tasjiyat*, (v. n. 2 of سجا for سجو) Covering (a dead body) with a winding sheet, or the like.

A تسجيح *tasjīh*, (v. n. 2 of سجح) Forgiving, pardoning. Speaking ambiguously.

A تسجير *tasjīr*, (v. n. 2 of سجر) Causing (water) to burst forth. Letting (the hair) fall.

A تسجيس *tasjīs*, A troubling, muddying (water).

A تسجيع *tasjīɛ*, A speaking or writing in rhythm.

A تسجيف *tasjīf*, A letting fall (a curtain).

A تسجيل *tasjīl*, (v. n. 2 of سجل) Confirming, ratifying. Throwing down from a height. Filling (a cistern). Signing (any thing) judicially. Being libidinous.

A تسجيم *tasjīm*, A causing to drop or flow.

A تسجين *tasjīn*, (v. n. 2 of سجن) Splitting. Digging a pit round the root of a palm-tree.

A تسحّب *tasahhub*, (v. n. 5 of سحب) Feigning aversion (lovers).

A تسحّج *tasahhuj*, (v. n. 5 of سحج) Being scratched, clawed (the face).

A تسحّح *tasahhuh*, (v. n. 5 of سحّ) Flowing (water), falling from a height.

A تسحّر *tasahhur*, (v. n. 5 of سحر) Rising, or setting out before daybreak, and breakfasting at that early hour.

A تسحسح *tasahsuh*, (v. n. 2 of سحسح Q) Flowing (as water), falling from a height.

A تسحّن *tasahhun*, (v. n. 5 of سحن) Examining the exterior, or the softness and beauty of the skin.

A تسحية *tas-hiyat*, (v. n. 2 of سحي) Covering or binding (a book) with the membrane of the papyrus.

A تسحيج *tas-hīj*, (v. n. 2 of سحج) Excoriating.

A تسحير *tas-hīr*, (v. n. 2 of سحر) Enchanting, fascinating, deceiving.

A تسخان *tashhān*, (for تسخن *taskhan*) (pl. تساخين *tasākhīn*) A boot. A sort of hood or coif formerly worn on the head by learned men.

A تسخر *taskhar*, Irony, raillery, buffoonery.

P تسخر كردن *taskhar kardan*, To jest, jeer, ridicule.

A تسخّر *tasakhkhur*, (v. n. 5 of سخر) Oppressing, compelling one to work for nothing. Making obedient or tractable. Being made submissive, obeying, yielding to.

A تسخّط *tasakhkhut*, (v. n. 5 of سخط) Considering as small (a present). Being discontented, disliking, loathing, detesting. Being enraged. Giving at an improper time or place.

A تسخّم *tasakhkhum*, (v. n. 5 of سخم) Being filled with hatred and malevolence.

A تسخّي *tasakhkhī*, (v. n. 5 of سخي) Diligently devising liberal things. Striving to outdo (one's companions) in acts of liberality.

A تسخئة *taskhiʼat*, (v. n. 2 of سخأ) Making room for fire to burn beneath a cauldron.

A تسخيد *taskhīd*, (v. n. 2 of سخد) Being pale and swollen. Being moist, and lying one upon another (leaves of trees).

A تسخير *taskhīr*, (v. n. 2 of سخر) Subduing, conquering, taking (a strong place or prisoners). Oppressing, compelling to work for nothing. Making obedient or tractable. Subjugation.

A تسخيل *taskhīl*, (v. n. 2 of سخل) Being sickly (a palm), bearing dates with soft stones. Possessing such dates. Casting its fruit. Reproaching, reviling, stigmatizing. Regarding as weak and contemptible. Shaking (a palm-tree).

A تسخيم *taskhīm*, (v. n. 2 of سخم) Blackening (the face). Warming (water). Enraging. Stinking (meat).

A تسخين *taskhīn*, A warming (of water).

A تسدّج *tasadduj*, A lying; a weaving falsehood.

A تسدّد *tasaddud*, (v. n. 5 of سدّ) Being pointed, levelled (a spear). Being stopped, closed (a gap).

A تسدّل *tasaddul*, A hanging down (of the hair).

A تسدّي *tasaddī*, (v. n. 5 of سدي) Ascending, sitting on the top. Following. Stretching the warp. Weaving. Riding on a wide-stepping she-camel.

A تسدية *tasdiyat*, (v. n. 2 of سدي) Stretching the warp. Washing (cloth in the loom) with size or gum-water. Doing a kindness.

A تسديح *tasdīh*, A killing, a slaying.

A تسديد *tasdīd*, (v. n. 2 of سدّ) Directing properly, leading in a right way. Pointing (a spear) well. Directing (an arrow) straight at game. Seeking right guidance. Taking the middle path.

A تسديس *tasdīs*, (v. n. 2 of سدس) Making of an hexagonal form. Dividing into six parts. An hexangular aspect of the stars.

A تسديك *tasdīk*, (v. n. 2 of سدك) Piling (hampers of dates) one upon another.

A تسرّب *tasarrub*, (v. n. 5 of سرب) Entering, creeping into a hole.

A تسربل *tasarbul*, (v. n. 2 of سربل Q) Being clad with a coat or shirt called سربال *sirbāl*.

A تسرّة *tasirrat*, A making glad.

A تسرّح *tasarruh*, A being carded (flax).

A تسرّر *tasarrur*, (v. n. 5 of سرّ) Keeping privately (a female slave as a concubine).

A تسرسر *tasarsur*, (v. n. 2 of سرسر Q) Weaving a garment closely. Weaving with small threads.

A تسرّط *tasarrut*, (v. n. 5 of سرط) Swallowing.

A تسرّع *tasarruʿ*, A hastening, making speed.

A تسرعف *tasarʿuf*, (An infant's) being well fed.

A تسرّق *tasarruk*, (v. n. 5 of سرق) Stealing one thing after another. A system of pilfering.

A تسرّم *tasarrum*, A falling to pieces.

A تسرمط *tasarmut*, (v. n. 2 of سرمط Q) Being few, scanty (hairs).

A تسروك *tasarwuk*, A sluggish gait from disease or fatigue.

A تسرول *tasarwul*, A being put into breeches.

A تسرّي *tasarrī*, (v. n. 5 of سرا for سرو) Pluming one's self on liberality. Keeping (a female slave) privately as a mistress (سرّيّة *surrīyat*).

A تسريب *tasrīb*, (v. n. 2 of سرب) Sending in crowds (camels). Filling a leathern bottle with water that it may swell at the seams. Digging (a well) from side to side.

A تسرئة *tasriʼat*, (v. n. 2 of سرأ) Laying eggs (a locust). Bearing many children (a woman).

A تسرية *tasriyat*, (v. n. 2 of سرا for سرو) Banishing grief from the mind. (v. n. 2 of سري) Raising or sending forth a detachment (سريّة *sarīyat*).

A تسريج *tasrīj*, (v. n. 2 of سرج) Adorning, dressing. Plaiting the hair, beautifying.

A تسريح *tasrīh*, (v. n. 2 of سرح) Sending (cattle) to graze. Repudiating (a wife). Combing (hair). Letting hair flow loose before combing. Making easy.

A تسريد *tasrīd*, (v. n. 2 of سرد) Sewing (a leathern bottle). Perforating.

A تسرير *tasrīr*, (v. n. 2 of سرّ) Reaching to the navel which is called سرّة *surrat* (water).

A تسريق *tasrīk*, A calling one a thief.

A تسريم *tasrīm*, A cutting to pieces.

A تسس *tusus*, Mean origins or families.

P تس سك *tus-sak*, A kind of medicinal herb.

A تسطيح *tastīh*, A making flat and level.

A تسطير *tastīr*, (v. n. 2 of سطر) Writing or relating fables or romances. Collecting, bringing together. Being put in authority or installed.

A تسطيع *tastīʿ*, (v. n. 2 of سطع) Marking (a camel) in the neck lengthwise by burning.

A تسطين *tastīn*, (v. n. 2 of سطن obsol.) Strengthening (a pillar).

A تسع *tasʿ*, (v. n. of تسع) Taking a ninth of one's property. Making up the number nine. *Tisʿ*, Nine (females). The interval between two waterings of a camel, the duration of his thirst. تسع آيات *tisʿ āyāt*, Nine signs, *i.e.* the rod, famine, sea, locusts, lice, blood, white hand, frogs, and flood. *Tusʿ*, A ninth part. *Tusaʿ*, The 7th, 8th, and 9th nights of the month.

A تسعّب *tasaʿʿub*, (v. n. 5 of سعب) Flowing in long threads (as honey, syrup, or spittle).

A تسعة *tisʿat*, Nine (males).

A تسعة عشر *tisʿat ʿashara*, (mas.) Nineteen.

A تسعّد *tasaʿʿud*, (v. n. 5 of سعد) Seeking the plant سعدان *saʿdān*. Taking a favourable omen.

A تسعّر *tasaʿʿur*, A being kindled (fire).

A تسعسع *tasaʿsuʿ*, (v. n. 2 of سعسع Q) Becoming old and decrepit. Shrinking and leaving the teeth bare (the lips). Decreasing (a man's means). Waning (a month).

A تسع مأية *tisʿa miʼat*, Nine hundred.

A تسعّن *tasaʿʿun*, A being full of fat.

A تسعون *tisʿūn*, (obliq. تسعين *tisʿīn*) Ninety.

A تسعير *tasʿīr*, (v. n. 2 of سعر) Kindling (fire). Exciting (war). Fixing a price (سعر *siʿr*) upon provisions or commodities of any kind, assizing.

A تسعيف *tasʿīf*, A mixing of perfumes.

A تسغبل *tasaghbul*, A putting on a coat of mail.

A تسغسغ *tasaghsugh*, (v. n. 2 of سغسغ Q) Being loose (a front tooth). Entering into the ground.

A تسغيم *tasghīm*, A causing to drink (water).

A تسفّد *tasaffud*, A going in a narrow road.

A تسفّر *tasaffur*, (v. n. 5 of سفر) Undertaking, beginning a journey. Eating fallen leaves (a camel). Feeding, grazing between sunset and the first watch of the night (camels). Being marked, impressed (a skin). Obtaining a part of a needed object. Endeavouring or requesting to have a woman's face unveiled. Asking of any one the half of a thing as his share of a fine for damage or loss.

A تسفّط *tasaffut*, A drinking, imbibing.

A تسفّع *tasaffuع*, A being heated by the fire.

A تسفّل *tasafful*, (v. n. 5 of سفل) Descending. Being in the meanest or lowest place.

A تسفّه *tasaffuh*, (v. n. 5 of سفه) Playing the fool. Bending the trees (wind). Deceiving, cheating, leading astray, befooling.

A تسفيح *tasfīh*, (v. n. 2 of سفح) Doing a work productive of no advantage.

A تسفيد *tasfīd*, (v. n. 2 of سفد) Putting (meat) on a spit (سفّود *saffūd*), spitting (meat).

A تسفير *tasfīr*, (v. n. 2 of سفر) Putting a curb of iron or leather across a camel's nose. Turning (camels) to pasture between sunset and the first watch of the night. Kindling (a fire), making it burn. Sending (any one) upon a journey.

A تسفيط *tasfīt*, A plastering with clay (a cistern).

A تسفيع *tasfīع*, (v. n. 2 of سفع) Blackening, swarthing a man's face (the sun).

A تسفيل *tasfīl*, (v. n. 2 of سفل) Depressing.

A تسفيه *tasfīh*, A charging with folly.

A تسقّط *tasakhut*, (v. n. 5 of سقط) Searching for the worst part of any thing. Hunting for an error, causing one to blunder, endeavouring to make one blab or fall. Receiving information by little and little.

A تسقّف *tasakhuf*, A being ordained bishop.

A تسقّي *tasakkī*, (v. n. 5 of سقي) Imbibing, being imbued with. Eating the plant حوذان *hawzān* fresh, and growing fat upon it (camels).

A تسقية *taskiyat*, (v. n. 2 of سقي) Giving to drink. Watering much. Saying سقاك الله *sakāka'llāh*, May God water thee!

A تسقيد *taskīd*, (v. n. 2 of سقد) Extenuating, emaciating (a horse that had been fat).

A تسقيع *taskīع*, A departing no one knows were.

A تسقيف *taskīf*, (v. n. 2 of سقف) Covering (a house) with a roof, roofing. Creating, ordaining, consecrating a bishop (اسقفّ *uskuff*), elevating to the episcopal dignity.

A تسقيم *taskīm*, (v. n. 2 of سقم) Making sick.

A تسكاب *taskāb*, A pouring out of water.

A تسكّع *tasakkuع*, (v. n. 5 of سكع) Contending for trifles; and being solely employed about them. Going into a corner. Wandering about distracted.

A تسكّف *tasakkuf*, (v. n. 5 of سكف) Making the heel of a door, or that part which revolves in a socket in the lintel or threshold, and serves the purpose of a hinge.

A تسكّك *tasakkuk*, (v. n. 5 of سكّ) Humbling one's self, supplicating, deprecating.

A تسكّن *tasakkun*, (v. n. 5 of سكن) Being poor, weak, wretched: resembling a pauper.

A تسكيت *taskīt*, A striking dumb, a silencing.

A تسكير *taskīr*, (v. n. 2 of سكر) Shutting or vailing the eyes. Dazzling, overpowering with light. Strangling. Making drunk.

A تسكين *taskīn*, (v. n. 2 of سكن) Quieting, stilling, allaying, assuaging. Suppressing a vowel. Extinguishing. Habitually riding a swift ass. Straightening (a spear) by fire.

P تسكين بخش *taskīn-bakhsh*, Assuasive, mitigating, solacing.

A تسلّب *tasallub*, (v. n. 5 of سلب) Laying aside her ornaments (a woman) and putting on widow's weeds (called سلاب *silāb*).

A تسلّج *tasalluj*, A drinking a great deal.

A تسلّح *tasalluh*, (v. n. 5 of سلح) Arming, accoutring one's self, wearing arms (سلاح *silāh*).

A تسلّخ *tasallukh*, (v. n. 5 of سلخ) Being excoriated, from disease or any other cause (the skin).

A تسلسل *tasalsul*, (v. n. 2 of سلسل Q) Being poured out (water). Running down the throat. Being joined, adhering as the links of a chain. Flowing like a chain (water whose surface is ruffled by a gentle breeze). Being worn quite thin (a garment). Concatenation (of ideas), sequence, series.

A تسلّط *tasallut*, (v. n. 5 of سلط) Ruling, bearing sway. Exercising absolute dominion. Being invested with authority. Commanding despotically.

A تسلطن *tasaltun*, (v. n. 2 of سلطن Q) Becoming a سلطان *sultān* or emperor.

A تسلّع *tasalluع*, A being split, cleft, chapped.

A تسلّف *tasalluf*, (v. n. 5 of سلف) Borrowing, receiving money per advance for goods to be afterwards delivered.

A تسلّق *tasalluk*, (v. n. 5 of سلق) Ascending or standing upon the top (of a wall). Tossing about in bed from care or pain. Disquietude, uneasiness.

A تسلّل *tasallul*, (v. n. 5 of سلّ) Advancing stealthily. Withdrawing, stealing away privately.

A تسلم *taslam*, (in swearing) Truly, by all means. بذي تسلم *bi zī taslam*, By God! اذهب بذي تسلم *izhab bi zī taslam*, Go in peace!

A تسلّم *tasallum*, (v. n. 5 of سلم) Having (any thing) consigned to one; receiving a consignment. Turning Musulmān. Keeping the road without missing one's way.

A تسلّي *tasallī*, (v. n. 5 of سلي) Being consoled. Solace, comfort. P تسلّي كردن *tasallī kardan*, To calm, soothe, solace, or comfort.

A تسليب *taslīb*, (v. n. 2 of سلب) Dressing in, causing to put on, mourning habits (سلاب *silāb*).

A تسلية *tasliyat*, (v. n. 2 of سلا for سلو) Quieting, contenting, assuring. Relieving from anguish, consoling, solacing. (v. n. 2 of سلي) Ridding (a camel or ewe) of the after-birth, pulling it out.

A تسليح *taslīh*, (v. n. 2 of سلح) Causing one to arm himself. Causing to purge. Anointing a leathern butter-bottle with inspissated juice.

P تسليخ *taslīkh*, A carpet for kneeling on to pray.

A تسليس *taslīs*, An arranging, stringing (pearls).

A تسليط *taslīt*, (v. n. 2 of سلط) Giving absolute dominion, investing with paramount authority.

A تسليع *taslīع*, (v. n. 2 of سلع) Tying a lighted branch of the trees سلع *salaع* and عشر *ع̤ushar* to the tails of wild oxen and making them descend the mountain with it (a rite observed by the Pagan Arabs with a view to obtain rain).

A تسليف *taslīf*, (v. n. 2 of سلف) Sending before. Paying before due or in advance. Breakfasting. Giving a breakfast. Taking any kind of victuals before dinner.

A تسليك *taslīk*, (v. n. 2 of سلك) Causing to thread, walk, or pass.

A تسليم *taslīm*, (v. n. 2 of سلم) Saluting, pronouncing a benediction, by saying السلام عليه *as salām ع̤alayhi*, Peace be with him! Preserving safe and sound, rescuing, delivering. Delivering, committing, consigning, handing over (to any person). Submitting to, and acquiescing in, the judgment of another. Health, safety, security, peace. Delivery, consignment. Resignation.

P تسلية بخش *tasliya-bakhsh*, Consolatory.

A تسمّت *tasammut*, (v. n. 5 of سمت) Keeping in the middle of the road. Walking uprightly.

A تسمّط *tasammut*, A being suspended.

A تسمّع *tasammuع*, (v. n. 5 of سمع) Listening, hearing, giving ear. Hearing by little and little.

A تسمعة *tasmiع̤at*, (v. n. 2 of سمع) Causing to hear. تسمعة لك *tasmiع̤atan laka* or تسمعتك *tasmiع̤ataka*, For thee to hear (I did it).

A تسمّل *tasammul*, (v. n. 5 of سمل) Swallowing (wine). Drinking remains of water (سملة *samalat*) in a vessel, cistern, or well.

A تسمّن *tasammun*, (v. n. 5 of سمن) Being fattened, becoming fat.

P تسمه *tasma*, A raw hide. A thong of undressed leather. Hair combed over the forehead.

A تسمّي *tasammī*, (v. n. 5 of سما for سمو) Giving one's self a name. Being related to, called after.

A تسمية *tasmiyat*, (v. n. 2 of سما for سمو) Giving a name, naming. Calling by name. Pronouncing the name of God. Making a proper name of.

A تسميت *tasmīt*, (v. n. 2 of سمت) Blessing any person or thing, as when one sneezes, saying يرحمك الله *yarhamuka'llāh*, God bless you! Adherence to the right way.

A تسميج *tasmīj*, A making deformed, hideous.

A تسميح *tasmīh*, (v. n. 2 of سمح) Making straight (a spear). Tripping softly and easily. Making haste, flying.

A تسميد *tasmīd*, (v. n. 2 of سمد) Manuring (land) with dung and ashes. Making bald, eradicating hair.

A تسمير *tasmīr*, (v. n. 2 of سمر) Diluting (milk) with water. Blinding. Nailing, fastening with nails. Sending, despatching. Discharging (an arrow) rapidly.

A تسميط *tasmīt*, (v. n. 2 of سمط) Being silent. Discharging (a debtor). Fastening (any thing) to thongs attached to the saddle for that purpose.

A تسميع *tasmīʿ*, (v. n. 2 of سمع) Ordering or causing one to listen. Divulging, making known or celebrated (either for good or bad). Defaming, disparaging, slandering. A sermon.

A تسميل *tasmīl*, (v. n. 2 of سمل) Being very scanty (water in a cistern). Bringing up a small quantity of water, or bringing up mud and dirt (a bucket). Cleaning out (a cistern). Using kind, soft, bland, and conciliatory language.

A تسمين *tasmīn*, (v. n. 2 of سمن) Dressing or preserving with butter. Making provision of butter. Fattening. (in the dialect of Yaman) Allowing (meat) to cool before eating it.

A تسميه *tasmīh*, (v. n. 2 of سمه) Sending (camels) pasturing at large without a herdsman.

A تسنت *tasannut*, (v. n. 5 of سنت) (A rich man but of mean birth) marrying a noble lady without fortune.

A تسنح *tasannuh*, (v. n. 5 of سنح) Searching, inquiring, investigating. Going round.

A تسنم *tasannum*, (v. n. 5 of سنم) Being on the top of. Taking suddenly, seizing unawares.

A تسنن *tasannun*, (v. n. 5 of سن) Walking. Regulating one's self, following a سنة *sunnat*.

A تسنه *tasannuh*, (v. n. 5 of سنه) Becoming mouldy and musty (as bread or wine, from age). Turning and becoming bad. Being old, and feeling the effects of age. Sojourning or working for a year with any one. Suffering from a year of scarcity. Becoming old and worn out (a palm-tree), and bringing no fruit for many years.

A تسني *tasannī*, (v. n. 5 of سنا for سنو) Living a year or many years with any one. Suffering from a year of scarcity. Satisfying. Being spoiled. Fascinating. Ascending, mounting. Becoming easy.

A تسنية *tasniyat*, (v. n. 2 of سنا for سنو) Exalting, elevating. Making easy. Opening.

A تسنيت *tasnīt*, (v. n. 2 of سنت not in use) Dressing (meat) with cummin-seed (سنوت *sannūt* or *sinnawt*). Putting cummin (into the pot).

A تسنيخ *tasnīkh*, A requesting, begging, seeking.

A تسنيد *tasnīd*, (v. n. 2 of سند) Propping, shoring (a wall). Wearing the striped stuff سند *sanad*.

A تسنيم *tasnīm*, (v. n. 2 of سنم) Making (a grave or tomb) convex, shelving at both ends. Causing a camel to have a high bunch (fodder). Being on the top of a thing. Filling (a vase). Name of a fountain in Paradise.

A تسنين *tasnīn*, (v. n. 2 of سن) Sharpening, whetting. Discoursing eloquently. Directing, levelling (a spear).

P تسو *tasū*, A weight of four barley-corns. The twenty-fourth part of a weight, measure, or day.

A تسوخ *tasawwukh*, A falling into the mud.

A تسود *tasawwud*, (v. n. 5 of ساد for سود) Marrying. Being dubbed a lord (سيد *sayyid*).

A تسور *tasaʾʾur*, A drinking the remains of wine.

A تسور *tasawwur*, (v. n. 5 of سار for سور) Putting on bracelets. Mounting and sitting on (a wall). Flying to the head (wine).

A تسوف *tasawwuf*, (v. n. 5 of ساف for سوف) Remaining firm, enduring.

A تسوق *tasawwuk*, (v. n. 5 of ساق for سوق) Buying and selling, frequenting market, marketing.

A تسوك *tasawwuk*, (v. n. 5 of ساك for سوك) Rubbing the mouth and teeth with a kind of wood as a dentifrice called مسواك *miswāk*.

A تسوم *tasawwum*, (v. n. 5 of سام for سوم) Setting a distinguishing mark upon one's self in battle.

A تسومة *tasūmat*, A sandal.

A تسون *tasawwun*, Looseness in the belly.

A تسوي *tasawwī*, (v. n. 5 of سوي) Being straight. Being level with any thing (the ground), *i.e.* burying it.

A تسوئة *taswiʾat*, (and تسويء *taswīʾ*) (v. n. 2 of ساء) Chiding any one by saying "You did wrong" (سوء *sūʾ*). Fixing a stigma upon.

A تسوية *taswiyat*, (v. n. 2 of سوي) Making equal, level, parallel. Straightening. Making erect. Composing differences. Equality, parity. A parallel.

A تسويد *taswīd*, (v. n. 2 of ساد for سود) Blackening. Begetting black children. Making a plaster for a (camel's) back with old bruised hair-cloth. Choosing a chief, lord, or prince. Begetting a prince. A sketch, plan, delineation, rough draft, foul copy. Boldness (especially in killing a prince).

A تسوير *taswīr*, (v. n. 2 of سار for سور) Putting bracelets (on another). Building a wall round a town (سور *sūr*). Climbing, scaling a wall.

A تسويس *taswīs*, (v. n. 2 of ساس for سوس) Appointing as governor, ruler, or chief. Taking that office upon one's self. Being affected by the moth (garments), by the weevil (corn). Adorning, rendering attractive and inviting.

A تسويط *taswīt*, (v. n. 5 of ساط for سوط) Mixing (especially liquids, by stirring). Confounding. Taking زماليق *zamālīk* out of the stalk of garlic.

A تسويغ *taswīgh*, A permitting. A giving.

A تسويغات *taswīghāt*, A magnificent present especially made to kings.

A تسويف *taswīf*, (v. n. 2 of سوف) Promising again and again سوف *sawf*, *i.e.* I will do it hereafter; procrastinating, delaying. Abandoning one's affairs to another, allowing him to do as he likes.

A تسويق *taswīk*, (v. n. 2 of ساق for سوق) Driving well. Committing (business to the management of another). Having a stem or trunk (a tree).

A تسويك *taswīk*, (v. n. 2 of ساك for سوك) Rubbing the mouth or teeth with a certain wood.

A تسويل *taswīl*, (v. n. 2 of سال for سول) Adorning, garnishing. Deluding, beguiling, suggesting evil. A fiction.

A تسويلات *taswīlāt*, (pl. of تسويل *taswīl*) Ornaments. Fictions. تسويلات شيطانيه *taswīlāti shaytāniya*, Diabolical fictions, Satanical delusions.

A تسويم *taswīm*, (v. n. 2 of سام for سوم) Sending (cattle) to pasture. Despatching horse. Setting at liberty. Making an excursion (against an enemy). Making depredations, injuring, damaging. Marking (a horse) by an impression. Compelling. Making one an overseer or manager of affairs. Allowing one to act as he pleases.

A تسهر *tasahhur*, A being awake.

A تسهل *tasahhul*, A becoming easy.

A تسهوك *tasahwuk*, (v. n. 2 of سهوك Q) Dying. Walking softly. Turning the back.

A تسهيد *tas-hīd*, (v. n. 2 of سهد) Stimulating to watchfulness, allowing (one) to take no sleep.

A تسهيل *tas-hīl*, (v. n. 2 of سهل) Loosening. Rendering easy, facilitating, making smooth. (in grammar) The assumption, by hamza, of a sound approaching in softness to that of *alif*, *wāw*, or *ye*.

A تسهيم *tas-hīm*, A weaving a striped garment.

A تسيار *tasyār*, A walking, a travelling.

A تسيج *tasayyuj*, (v. n. 5 of ساج for سيج) Being fenced about with a hedge (سياج *siyāj*).

A تسير *tasayyur*, (v. n. 5 of سار for سير) Being peeled (the skin). Instituting, adopting a certain mode of living (سيرة *sirāt*).

A تسيطر *tasaytur*, (v. n. 2 of سيطر Q) Presiding as inspector. Being appointed.

A تسيطل *tasaytul*, A coming empty-handed.

A تسيع *tasīʿ*, A ninth part.

A تسيؤ *tasayyuʾ*, (v. n. 5 of سيأ) Emitting milk from the udder before milking-time (a camel). Acknowledging (a debt) after having denied it. Being discordant and contradictory.

A تسييب *tasyīb*, (v. n. 2 of ساب for سيب) Giving. Allowing to go free.

A تسيئة *tasyiʾat*, (v. n. 2 of سيأ) Milking what is in the teats and flows spontaneously.

A تسييج *tasyīj*, A fencing a wall with thorns.

A تسييح *tasyīh*, A weaving a striped garment.

A تسيير *tasyīr*, (v. n. 2 of سار for سير) Causing to march or go, sending. Driving, banishing a great way off. Spreading abroad, giving circulation. Removing (the housing or covering from the back of a horse). Weaving (cloth) with stripes. Putting on henna in streaks (a woman).

A تسييع *tasyīʿ*, (v. n. 2 of ساع for سيع) Bedaubing (walls) with mud and short straw, or (a leathern-bottle) with grease.

A تسييل *tasyīl*, A causing (water) to flow.

P تش *tash*, A hatchet, an axe. Fire. *Tish*, A louse. Thirst. *Tush*, Grief.

A تشاءم *tashāʾum*, (v. n. 6 of شأم) Going to the left. Considering as ominous, and sinister.

A تشابر *tashābur*, (v. n. 6 of شبر) Advancing

close to one another, as though within a شبر *shibr*, or hand's breadth (in battle array).

A تشابك *tashābuk*, (v. n. 6 of شبك) Being perplexed, intricate. Leaping, springing (wild beasts).

A تشابه *tashābuh*, (v. n. 6 of شبه) Being similar, bearing a striking resemblance to each other. Resemblance, likeness.

A تشاتم *tashātum*, (v. n. 6 of شتم) Scolding. Reviling one another. Mutual reproach.

A تشاجب *tashājub*, (v. n. 6 of شجب) Being mixed, jumbled (one within the other).

A تشاجر *tashājur*, (v. n. 6 of شجر) Contending, opposing each other. Eating up all the grass. Entering (one thing into another).

A تشاجي *tashāji*, (v. n. 6 of شجا for شجو) Being firm and strong. Being inaccessible. Becoming sad. Pretending to be sad.

A تشاح *tashāhh*, (v. n. 6 of شح) Keeping (any thing) close amongst themselves. Displaying avarice or selfishness (شحة *shihhat*).

A تشاخز *tashākhuz*, (v. n. 6 of شخز) Falling out together, quarrelling.

A تشاخس *tashākhus*, (v. n. 6 of شخس) Grinning, uncovering the teeth (an ass when running to bite). Being uneven (teeth, some leaning and others falling out). Being bent or inclined. Being split, cleft in twain (the head). Being discordant.

A تشارش *tashārush*, A carrying on hostilities.

A تشارك *tashāruk*, Being partners: partnership.

A تشازب *tashāzub*, (v. n. 6 of شزب) Waiting, expecting amongst themselves, each man his fortune or share.

A تشازر *tashāzur*, (v. n. 6 of شزر) Looking at one another askance through half-shut eyes.

A تشاشؤ *tashasshuـ*, (v. n. 2 of شأشأ Q) Being separated, divided, scattered. Coming to naught.

A تشاطر *tashātur*, (v. n. 6 of شطر) Being drawn up in two lines in battle array.

A تشاعر *tashāـur*, (v. n. 6 of شعر) Professing or pretending to be a poet.

A تشاف *tashāff*, (v. n. 6 of شف) Doing any thing diligently and accurately. Drinking all that is in a vessel. Carrying off any gain or overplus.

A تشاكس *tashākus*, (v. n. 6 of شكس) Being hard, cruel. Opposing each other.

A تشاكل *tashākul*, (v. n. 6 of شكل) Agreeing with, suiting. Resembling one another.

A تشاكه *tashākuh*, A being like one another.

A تشاكي *tashākī*, A complaining one to another.

A تشام *tashāmm*, (v. n. 6 of شم) Smelling each other. Coming in sight of the foe.

A تشامم *tashāmum*, (v. n. 6 of شم) Smelling each other. Coming near or within scent of.

A تشان *tashānn*, (v. n. 6 of شن) Becoming dried up and good for nothing (a leathern bottle). Becoming wrinkled (skin). Being mixed, diluted.

A تشانؤ *tashānuـ*, A hating of one another.

A تشاور *tashāwur*, A consulting together.

A تشاوس *tashāwus*, (v. n. 6 of شاس for شوس) Looking through half-shut eyes from (pride or anger), and screwing up one cheek in so doing.

A تشاوش *tashāwush*, A being mixed together.

A تشاوظ *tashāwuz*, A cursing of one another.

A تشاول *tashāwul*, A fighting (with spears).

A تشاوم *tashāـum*, (v. n. 6 of شأم) Going towards the left. Taking a sinister omen.

A تشاهير *tashāhīr*, (pl. of تشهير) Shining marks.

A تشايخ *tashāyukh*, (v. n. 6 of شاخ for شيخ) Assuming the garb or appearance of a شيخ *shaykh*.

A تشايظ *tashāyuz*, A cursing of one another.

A تشايع *tashāyuـ*, (v. n. 6 of شاع for شيع) Professing one's self a Shiite. Associating together, being partners.

A تشائي *tashāـī*, (v. n. 6 of شأو) Separating, going in different directions. Being far asunder.

A تشبب *tashabbub*, (v. n. 5 of شب) Praising the beauty (of a woman) when making love. The description of one's feelings in love.

A تشبث *tashabbus*, (v. n. 5 of شبث not in use) Seizing and holding firmly. Fixing the nails or claws in any thing. P تشبث دامن کردن *tashabbusi dāman kardan*, To lay hold of the skirts (of another's garments).

A تشبح *tashabbuh*, (v. n. 5 of شبح) Stretching itself at full length on a bough (a chameleon).

A تشبر *tashabbur*, A carrying one's self high.

A تشبص *tashabbus*, (v. n. 5 of شبص) Being thickly entangled (a tree).

A تشبع *tashabbuـ*, (v. n. 5 of شبع) Pretending to be satiated, appearing to be satisfied, though not really so. Being ample, abundant. Eating repeatedly.

A تشبك *tashabbuk*, (v. n. 5 of شبك) Being mixed together, ravelled. Being perplexed, intricate.

A تشبه *tashabbuh*, (v. n. 5 of شبه) Imitating. Resembling, being similar, appearing.

A تشبيب *tashbīb*, (v. n. 2 of شب) Praising the beauty (of a woman) when making love (especially in verse). Commencing, making a beginning about any object aimed at. The description of one's feeling in love.

A تشبيح *tashbīh*, (v. n. 2 of شبح) Expanding, making wide. Growing old and seeing double.

A تشبير *tashbīr*, (v. n. 2 of شبر) Measuring, defining. Magnifying, honouring.

A تشبيع *tashbīـ*, A being almost satiated.

A تشبيك *tashbīk*, (v. n. 2 of شبك) Twisting. Intermingling. Clasping, locking (the fingers). Making lattice or network (شبكة *shabakat*).

A تشبيم *tashbīm*, (v. n. 2 of شبم) Putting the stick شبم *shibamm* into (a kid's) mouth, gagging, muzzling (him) to prevent (him) from sucking.

A تشبيه *tashbīh*, (v. n. 2 of شبه) Comparing, likening. Causing to resemble, making like. Rendering doubtful, intricate, and obscure. Comparison. Simile; allegory, metaphor. Similitude. Likeness. حرف تشبيه *harfi tashbīh*, A particle of similitude. P تشبيه کردن *tashbīh kardan*, (or تشبيه دادن *tashbīh dādan*) To compare, to liken.

A تشبيهات *tashbīhāt*, (pl. of تشبيه) Comparisons.

P تشت *tasht*, A bason. A salver. A ewer-stand. تشت آتش *tashti ātish*, The sun. تشت بلند *tashti baland*, The sky. The sun. تشت خوان *tashti khwān*, A table-bason, a platter. تشت زر *tashti zar*, (or تشت زرين *tashti zarīn*) The sun. تشت سيمين *tashti sīmīn*, The moon. تشت او از بام افتاد *tashti u az bām uftād*, His bason fell from the cover, *i. e.* His secrets were discovered. He was disgraced.

A تشتت *tashattut*, (v. n. 5 of شت) Being separated, dispersed, scattered.

P تشتخانه *tasht-khāna*, A place where bowls and basons are kept, a scullery. Bed-clothes, sheets. A wardrobe. A privy.

P تشتخوان *tasht-khwān*, A dining-table.

P تشتدار *tasht-dār*, An ewer-holder. A scullion.

P تشتر *tashtar*, Michael the archangel.

P تشت گر *tashtgar*, A maker of basons.

P تشتن *tashtan*, A large axe.

P تشت و خايه *tasht u khāya*, Filling an egg-shell with a fluid (in Persian شبنم *shabnam*, Dew) more rare than the atmosphere, and setting it (when heated) afloat in the air like a balloon. Heaven and earth. Astronomy. Magic.

A تشتي *tashattī*, A wintering, passing the winter.

A تشتية *tashtiyat*, (v. n. 2 of شتي) Passing the winter. Sufficing for, being acceptable in winter.

A تشتيت *tashtīt*, A dispersing, separating.

A تشتير *tashtīr*, (v. n. 2 of شتر) Derogating, reproaching. Rendering (the eyelids) inverted and relaxed.

P تشتيوان *tashtīwān*, Polypody. Dog's tooth.

A تشجب *tashajjub*, A being sad, grieving.

A تشجع *tashajjuـ*, (v. n. 5 of شجع) Boasting of courage, persevering, taking pains to acquire or display bravery.

A تشجن *tashajjun*, (v. n. 5 of شجن) Recollecting, recalling to mind. Being entangled (foliage).

A تشجيج *tashjīj*, (v. n. 2 of شج) Wounding much (the head). Resolving deliberately.

A تشجير *tashjīr*, (v. n. 2 of شجر) Painting in the form of a tree. Supporting a bunch of dates by a palm-branch.

A تشجيع *tashjīـ*, (v. n. 2 of شجع) Making or calling bold. Inspiring with courage.

A تشح *tashah*, Firmness, strength of mind. Avidity. Wickedness. Anger. Fear.

A تشحة *tushhat*, Boldness, firmness, energy, strength of mind. Avidity. Wickedness. Anger. Cowardice, fear. A disease in the leg of a camel.

A تشحذ *tashahhuz*, A driving away, banishing.

A تشحط *tashahhut*, (v. n. 5 of شحط) Weltering

in blood (a wounded man). Being besmeared with blood. Stirring, shaking in the secundine (a child).

A تشحّي tashahhī, (v. n. 5 of شحا for شحو) Opening the mouth wide against any one.

A تشحيذ tashḥīz, A sharpening, whetting.

A تشحيط tashḥīt, (v. n. 2 of شحط) Besmearing (with blood). Rolling (a wounded man in his blood).

A تشخّص tashakhkhus, (v. n. 5 of شخص) Being separated, distinct, distinguished.

A تشخيت tashkhīt, A causing to arrive.

A تشخير tashkhīr, (v. n. 2 of شخر) Supporting a bunch of dates by a palm-branch. Taking the coarse cloth from off a horse's back in order to saddle him.

A تشخيص tashkhīs, (v. n. 2 of شخص) Discerning, distinguishing. Identifying, particularizing. Knowing perfectly (a word much used by physicians to denote their having ascertained the disorder of a patient). Valuation, assessment. تشخيص امراض tashkhīsi amrāz, Diagnosis of diseases.

A تشخيم tashkhīm, A marring, spoiling (of meat).

A تشدّخ tashaddukh, A being broken (the head).

A تشدّد tashaddud, (v. n. 5 of شدّ) Becoming hard. Being hard and difficult. Seizing and holding firmly. Being stingy, covetous.

A تشدّق tashadduk, (v. n. 5 of شدق not in use) Twisting the corners of the mouth whilst speaking, mouthing. Babbling, prating (pompously).

A تشديخ tashdīkh, (v. n. 2 of شدخ) Breaking any thing not solid (as the head, or an apple). Bruising soft dates. Bruising the head (of any thing).

A تشديد tashdīd, (v. n. 2 of شدّ) Corroborating, confirming, strengthening. Pressing heavily on. Being hard and severe. Using the utmost caution, abstaining with the greatest care. Putting the orthographical mark tashdīd (ّ) over letters, which denotes that they should be doubled; also the name of the character itself.

A تشذّب tashazzub, A being separated, scattered, divided.

A تشذّر tashazzur, (v. n. 5 of شذر not in use) Being angry, threatening, putting in fear. Discovering forage, shaking her head and whisking her tail for joy (a camel). Leaning on one side and moving (a whip). Being brisk, lively. Making haste. Preparing for battle. Protracting a war, carrying it beyond bounds. Riding behind another on horseback. Passing the train of a garment through the legs, and tucking it up to the breast. Clapping the tail between the thighs close to the belly (a dog). Being dispersed (a crowd).

A تشذيب tashzīb, (v. n. 2 of شذب) Pruning, lopping, unbarking, peeling (a tree). Trimming (the trunk of a palm-tree). Hewing out roughly (an arrow). Dividing. Impelling, repelling. Separating. Dispersing, scattering. Tearing, dissipating.

A تشذيذ tashzīz, (v. n. 2 of شذّ) Separating, dividing. Putting alone and by itself.

A تشراب tashrāb, A drinking. A draught.

A تشرّب tasharrub, (v. n. 5 of شرب) Imbibing, drinking up. Passing from one thing to another.

A تشرّج tasharruj, A being mixed (two things).

A تشرّد tasharrud, (v. n. 5 of شرد) Suddenly taking flight through fear. Being singular, opiniated, wedded to one's own ideas.

A تشرّز tasharruz, A stirring up of mischief.

A تشرّط tasharrut, A considering attentively.

A تشرّع tasharruع, (v. n. 5 of شرع) Being open and clear (a way). Acting in conformity to the laws of Muhammad, which are called شرع sharع.

A تشرّف tasharruf, (v. n. 5 of شرف) Being honoured, renowned, rendered glorious. Being ornamented with pinnacles (a house). Looking out for or towards, expecting. Having their nobles killed (a people). Being at the top. Esteeming, counting, considering as great and noble. Being proud and haughty.

A تشرّق tasharruk, (v. n. 5 of شرق Sitting, walking in, or being exposed to, the heat of the sun.

A تشرّم tasharrum, A being torn, lacerated.

A تشرّي tasharrī, (v. n. 5 of شري) Becoming a heretic, schismatic. Being separated, scattered.

A تشريب tashrīb, (v. n. 2 of شرب) Giving to drink. Making free use of another's property. Rubbing a new leathern bottle with a kind of odoriferous clay, in order to give a fine flavour to the water. Imbuing, tinging, staining.

A تشرية tashriyat, (v. n. 2 of شري) Exposing to the sun and wind in order to dry.

A تشريث tashrīs, (v. n. 2 of شرث) Not being made straight (an arrow).

A تشريج tashrīj, (v. n. 2 of شرج) Shutting a purse, drawing the strings close. Sewing with wide stitches, basting. Embroidering. Fastening a leathern strap to a portmanteau.

A تشريح tashrīh, (v. n. 2 of شرح) Declaring, explaining clearly and minutely. Cutting (meat). Dissecting (a body). Anatomy.

A تشريد tashrīd, (v. n. 2 of شرد) Putting to flight. Dispersing. Spreading a bad report, defaming.

A تشرير tashrīr, (v. n. 2 of شرّ) Exposing to the sun or wind (in order to dry). Promulgating, celebrating, magnifying, rendering glorious, publishing the praise of another.

A تشريز tashrīz, (v. n. 2 of شرز) Punishing, tormenting. Cursing.

A تشريط tashrīt, A scarifying. Scarification.

A تشريع tashrīع, (v. n. 2 of شرع) Leading (cattle) to water, no pulley or bucket being needed. Making (the way) clear.

A تشريف tashrīf, (v. n. 2 of شرف) Ennobling, exalting. Raising, elevating. Decorating (a house) with pinnacles or turrets. Ascending a watch-tower. P تشريف آوردن tashrīf āwardan, To honour with a visit. This word is much used in speaking of, or to, superiors, as more respectful than *he* and *you*.

A تشريفات tashrīfāt, (pl. of تشريف tashrīf) Honours, dignities. *A* The book in which is described the manner of receiving ambassadors, with the usual expenses allowed to them.

A تشريفاتي tashrīfātī, The keeper of this book.

A تشريق tashrīk, (v. n. 2 of شرق) Drying (flesh in the sun). Tending towards, reaching unto the east. Turning the face eastwards. Praying on the day of a solemn festival. Being fair and beautiful. ايّام التشريق ayyāmu't tashrīk, Three days after the feast of sacrifice at Mecca (either because the flesh of the victims is then dried, or because they are not slain till after sunrise).

A تشريك tashrīk, (v. n. 2 of شرك) Selling part of of a thing purchased for as much as was given for the whole. Putting latchets (to shoes).

A تشريم tashrīm, (v. n. 2 of شرم) Tearing, lacerating, splitting. Returning, looking back (as wounded beasts).

A تشرين اوّل tashrīni awwal, A Syro-Macedonian month, answering to October. تشرين ثاني tashrīni sānī, November.

A تشزّر tashazzur, (v. n. 5 of شزر) Being angry; preparing to fight.

A تشزّن tashazzun, (v. n. 5 of شزن) Being hardy, strong, or intense. Standing up to oppose (in law, &c.). Throwing prostrate. Laying (a sheep) down to be slaughtered.

A تشزيب tashzīb, (v. n. 2 of شزب) Making lean. Rendering dry and withered. Weakening.

A تشزين tashzīn, A prostrating in wrestling.

A تشسيع tashsīع, A putting thongs to a shoe.

A تشصير tashsīr, (v. n. 2 of شصر) Inserting in the nose of a she-camel the wood شصار shisār.

A تشطيب tashtīb, (v. n. 2 of شطب) Cutting (leather or a camel's bunch).

A تشطية tashtiyat (v. n. 2 of شطي) Flaying (a slaughtered camel), and cutting up (his) flesh. Diminishing, impairing.

A تشطير tashtīr, (v. n. 2 of شطر) Tying up two teats (of a camel). Milking (a camel) of two teats. Halving (a thing).

A تشطيط tashtīt, (v. n. 2 of شطّ) Exceeding all bounds in injustice and oppression.

A تشطيئ tashtīء, (v. n. 2 of شطأ) Running, flowing (the two sides of a river).

A تشظّي tashazzī, (v. n. 5 of شظي) Being split into shivers. Branching out in many directions (nerves and sinews).

A تشظية tashziyat, A separating, scattering.

A تشظيظ tashzīz, A scattering (of men).

A تشعّب tashaععub, (v. n. 5 of شعب) Being divided, propagated. Being scattered. Branching in many directions (a road or a tree). Removing to a distance. Dying. Making peace together.

A تشعّث tashaععus, (v. n. 5 of شعث) Being

scattered, dispersed. Branching. Spreading into separate and distinct parts and subdivisions. Taking, seizing. Eating little food. Being dishevelled and entangled (locks of hair).

A تشعّر *tashaʿʿur*, A being hairy.

A تشعشع *tashaʿshuʿ*, (v. n. 2 of شعشع Q) Being nearly expired, having little remaining (a month).

A تشعّل *tashaʿʿul*, A being kindled.

A تشعيب *tashʿīb*, (v. n. 2 of شعب) Dividing into branches. Repairing a broken vessel. Parting from friends and never returning.

A تشعيث *tashʿīs*, (v. n. 2 of شعث) Separating with the fingers. Blaming, reproaching, slandering. Repelling, averting. Keeping off.

A تشعير *tashʿīr*, (v. n. 2 of شعر) Lining (a boot) with hair (شعر *shaʿr*). Being hairy (a fœtus).

A تشعيل *tashʿīl*, The kindling (of a fire).

A تشغبر *tashaghbur*, A veering (of the wind).

A تشغّر *tashaghghur*, (v. n. 5 of شغر) Going well, travelling vigorously (a camel). Going to great lengths in any thing shameful or disgraceful.

A تشغزب *tashaghzub*, A veering (of the wind).

A تشغيب *tashghīb*, (v. n. 2 of شغب) Raising a tumult, exciting any thing ruinous to another, stirring up mischief.

A تشغية *tashghiyat*, (v. n. 2 of شغا for شغو) Suffering from a continual discharge of urine.

A تشفّع *tashaffuʿ*, (v. n. 5 of شفع) Interceding, deprecating. Being even (a number).

A تشفّي *tashaffī*, (v. n. 5 of شفي) Returning to calmness of mind (after anger), being placid, pacified.

A تشفية *tashfiyat*, (v. n. 2 of شفي) Being profitable. Increasing.

A تشفير *tashfīr*, (v. n. 2 of شفر) Being consumed and wasted (property). Being near setting (the sun). Being at the brink or point of. Having connexion with a woman in labris vulvæ (شفر *shufr*).

A تشفيع *tashfīʿ*, (v. n. 2 of شفع) Admitting the intercession of one person (for another).

A تشفيف *tashfīf*, (v. n. 2 of شفّ) Being profitable. Increasing, augmenting.

A تشفيق *tashfīk*, (v. n. 2 of شفق) Making small. Weaving in the worst manner.

A تشقّق *tashakkuk*, (v. n. 5 of شقّ) Being cracked, split. Being clearly, distinctly delivered (a speech). Flashing most conspicuously (lightning).

A تشقية *tashkiyat*, (v. n. 2 of شقا for شقو) Rendering miserable. Overcoming.

A تشقيح *tashkīh*, (v. n. 2 of شقح) From being yellow, beginning to redden (dates). Bearing such sorts of dates (a palm-tree).

A تشقيص *tashkīs*, (v. n. 2 of شقص) Dividing among partners (joints of a slaughtered animal).

A تشقيق *tashkīk*, (v. n. 2 of شقّ) Splitting. Bringing out well one's words.

A تشقيه *tashkīh*, (v. n. 2 of شقه not used) Turning colour (unripe dates).

A تشكّر *tashakkur*, (v. n. 5 of شكر) Returning thanks for favours, being grateful.

A تشكّك *tashakkuk*, (v. n. 5 of شكّ) Doubting.

A تشكّل *tashakkul*, (v. n. 5 of شكل) Being beautiful. Being half-ripe (grapes). Being pourtrayed, fashioned, figured, fancied. Appearance, semblance.

A تشكّي *tashakkī*, (v. n. 5 of شكا for شكو) Complaining (of aches and pains). Making a milk-bottle from the skin of a sucking kid.

A تشكية *tashkiyat*, (v. n. 2 of شكا for شكو) Making a milk-bottle or churn (called شكوة *shakwat*) from the skin of a sucking kid. Restraining. Perfuming one's self. Contenting, satisfying. Desisting, remaining behind.

A تشكيد *tashkīd*, (v. n. 2 of شكد) Giving.

A تشكير *tashkīr*, (v. n. 2 of شكر) Giving thanks.

A تشكيك *tashkīk*, (v. n. 2 of شكّ) Creating doubt, causing to doubt.

A تشكيل *tashkīl*, (v. n. 2 of شكل) Forming, framing, figuring. Fettering (a horse). Tying a string to (a bird's) foot. Platting (her) hair in two braids upon (her) forehead (a woman). Being half ripe (grapes). Being obscure, intricate.

A تشلشل *tashalshul*, (v. n. 2 of شلشل Q) Scattering (urine) here and there. Letting (water) flow drop by drop. Coming drop by drop. Trickling with blood (a sword).

A تشليح *tashlīh*, (v. n. 2 of شلح) Stripping naked, denuding, making bare.

P تشليخ *tashlīkh*, A cushion for kneeling on.

A تشليخ *tashlīkh*, (v. n. 2 of شلخ) Killing. Blood and slaughter.

A تشمّت *tashammut*, (v. n. 5 of شمت) Returning disappointed of booty.

A تشمّر *tashammur*, (v. n. 5 of شمر) Preparing for, being ready for work. Going fast. Walking with nicety or a haughty air.

A تشمّز *tashammuz*, (v. n. 5 of شمز) Being contracted, knit (brow). Becoming changed (the colour of the face).

A تشمّس *tashammus*, (v. n. 5 of شمس) Being exposed to the sun. Being strong and powerful. Being very avaricious.

A تشمّص *tashammus*, (v. n. 5 of شمص) Being contracted, puckered, wrinkled, shrivelled.

A تشمعل *tashamʿul*, A being divided, scattered.

A تشمّق *tashammuk*, (v. n. 5 of شمق) Being brisk and lively. Being jealous.

A تشمّل *tashammul*, (v. n. 5 of شمل) Being covered, concealed. Putting on, or being possessed of a wrapper which encloses the entire body.

A تشمّم *tashammum*, (v. n. 5 of شمّ) Smelling at gently. Getting scent of.

A تشمية *tashmiyat*, The act of smelling.

A تشميت *tashmīt*, (v. n. 2 of شمت) Blessing any one (particularly when coughing or sneezing). Collecting. Blasting (one's) hopes, disappointing.

P تشمير *tashmīr*, (or تشتمير *tashtmīr*) Polipody.

A تشمير *tashmīr*, (v. n. 2 of شمر) Tucking up the garment. Collecting, drawing together. Being ready, alert; dispatching business. Expediting, sending away (a ship). Purposing, striving, aiming at. Walking haughtily.

P تشميزج *tashmīzaj*, A black shining grain resembling the pippin of a quince, with which, when pulverized, they anoint the eyes, by the natives of Shīrāz called چشم *chashm*.

A تشميس *tashmīs*, (v. n. 2 of شمس) Exposing to the sun. The worship of the sun.

A تشميص *tashmīs*, (v. n. 2 of شمص) Urging (a steed) forward: poking (him) with a stick.

A تشميع *tashmīʿ*, (v. n. 2 of شمع) Causing one to play. Exposing to ridicule, making contemptible. Covering (cloth) with wax, making a cerement.

A تشميل *tashmīl*, (v. n. 2 of شمل) Making haste, being expeditious. Being covered, concealed. Gathering in, drawing together one's skirt. Possessing a wrapper which covers the whole body.

A تشميم *tashmīm*, (v. n. 2 of شمّ) Smelling.

P تشن *tashan* or *tishan*, A small round blackish grain (larger than a lentil) with which camphor is made up into an eye-salve.

A تشنّج *tashannuj*, (v. n. 5 of شنج) Being shrivelled, puckered, wrinkled (leather). Cramp.

A تشنّع *tashannuʿ*, (v. n. 5 of شنع) Making haste, exerting one's self much in running. Mounting on horseback. Arming, preparing for battle. Sending out detachments of soldiers in every direction. Plundering, pillaging (a marauding party). Being split, falling to pieces from age (a garment).

A تشنّف *tashannuf*, (v. n. 5 of شنف) Adorning one's self, or being adorned with ear-rings.

P تشنك *tashnak*, The part of the head which in infants is soft.

P تشنگي *tishnagī*, Thirst. A hankering after.

A تشنّن *tashannun*, (v. n. 5 of شنّ) Being wrinkled, shrivelled (skin). Becoming old and dried up (a leathern bottle).

P تشنه *tishna*, Thirsty, parched with thirst. Eager, greedy, insatiable. تشنه شدن *tishna shudan*, To be thirsty.

P تشنه جگر *tishna-jigar*, (or تشنه دل *tishna-dil*) Thirsty, desirous. Desire, wish.

P تشنه خون *tishna-khūn*, Blood-thirsty.

P تشنه لب *tishna-lab*, Thirsty, parched-lipped.

A تشنيج *tashnīj*, (v. n. 2 of شنج) Wrinkling.

A تشنيع *tashnīʿ*, A reproaching, a defaming.

A تشنيخ *tashnīkh*, (v. n. 2 of شنخ) Cutting the prickles off a palm-tree.

A تشنير *tashnīr*, (v. n. 2 of شنر) Detecting villainies and exposing them to infamy. Reproaching, disparaging.

A تشنيط *tashnīt*, A roasting (of meat).

A تشنيع *tashnīʿ*, (v. n. 2 of شنع) Reproaching,

blaming, disparaging, taunting. Running to excess in what is shameful, foul, and odious. Being dull and melancholy. Regarding as filthy and hideous. Divulging, proclaiming. Making haste, going well.

A تشنيف *tashnīf*, (v. n. 2 of شنف) Causing one to put jewels in the ears. Adorning with ear-rings.

A تشنيق *tashnīk*, (v. n. 2 of شنق) Cutting (meat) in pieces. Adorning, dressing, garnishing. Putting the cross-bar شنيق *shanīk* into a bee-hive.

A تشوّد *tashawwud*, (v. n. 5 of شود not used) Being high, culminating (the sun).

A تشوّذ *tashawwuz*, (v. n. 5 of شاذ for شوذ) Wearing a turban, wreathing the sash round it. Sunrise.

A تشوّر *tashawwur*, (v. n. 5 of شار for شور) Being made to blush (as if by having the person exposed).

A تشوّش *tashawwush*, (v. n. 5 of شوش not in use) Being disturbed, discordant. Disquietude, distraction. (Some lexicographers deny this word).

A تشوّط *tashawwut*, (v. n. 5 of شاط for شوط) Fatiguing, over-driving (a horse).

A تشوّف *tashawwuf*, (v. n. 5 of شاف for شوف) Being dressed, adorned. Looking, viewing from a height. Fixing the eyes. Listening attentively. Being wishful, desiring anxiously.

A تشوّق *tashawwuk*, (v. n. 5 of شاق for شوق) Discovering or manifesting a vehement desire.

A تشؤّم *tashaʼʼum*, (v. n. 5 of شأم) Going to the left. Taking an unfavourable omen. Calling himself a Syrian, native of Syria (شأم *shaʼm*).

A تشوّن *tashawwun*, Levity of mind.

A تشوّه *tashawwuh*, (v. n. 5 of شاه for شوه) Making one's self so altered as not to be recognised. Hunting wild oxen. Viewing with an evil eye.

A تشويب *tashwīb*, (v. n. 2 of شاب for شوب) Repelling, defending one's self moderately.

A تشوية *tashwiyat*, (v. n. 2 of شوي) Roasting. Giving to roast. Serving up roast meat. Wounding, but not mortally.

A تشويج *tashwīj*, A denying, disavowing.

A تشويد *tashwīd*, (v. n. 2 of شود not used) Being high, culminating (the sun).

A تشويذ *tashwīz*, (v. n. 2 of شوذ not in use) Causing one to put on a turban. Rising above the horizon (the sun). Inclining to its setting (the sun). Covering the sun (a thin cloud without rain).

A تشوير *tashwīr*, (v. n. 2 of شار for شور) Beckoning, making a sign with the hand or eye. Causing (another) to blush (as if by uncovering his nakedness). Fattening (a horse). Exercising (a horse), riding (him) backwards and forwards to shew (him) off to a buyer. Trying, proving, turning about (a horse or a female slave). Raising (fire). Dyeing (a garment) with saffron.

A تشويش *tashwīsh*, (v. n. 2 of شوش not in use, and disapproved of by some lexicographers) Mixing, confounding. Disturbing, troubling, rendering uneasy and uncomfortable. Confusion, distraction, disquietude, alarm, apprehension, annoyance, bother.

A تشويص *tashwīs*, A rubbing (of the teeth).

A تشويط *tashwīt*, (v. n. 2 of شاط for شوط) Being long (a journey). Making a pot to boil. Stewing (meat) till it dissolves. Nipping, pinching herbage (the frost). Urging (a horse) forward till he knocks up.

A تشويق *tashwīk*, (v. n. 2 of شاق for شوق) Inflaming, exciting (desire). Filling with desire.

A تشويك *tashwīk*, (v. n. 2 of شاك for شوك) Turning white (as grain before it fills). Having thick mustachios (a young man). Fencing with thorns (a garden-wall). Producing side-teeth (a camel's jaw). Breeding the rudiments of quills (an unfledged bird). Putting forth hair after having been shaved (the head). Pointing, swelling (the breasts of a girl).

A تشويل *tashwīl*, (v. n. 2 of شول) Having a shrivelled udder without milk (a camel). Having little water in it (a large bucket). Leaving a little water in a bottle. Having their bellies drawn up to their backs (camels). Being diminished (milk or water). Failing (as water) in a leathern bottle. Dangling, being flaccid (penis).

A تشوين *tashwīn*, A cleaving (of skulls).

A تشويه *tashwīh*, (v. n. 2 of شاه for شوه) Making deformed, ugly. Looking with a malignant eye.

P تشّه *tashsha*, Name of an oil-measure; a hin.

A تشهاق *tashhāk*, (v. n. of شهق) Sighing, sobbing. The braying of an ass. Noisy (laughter).

A تشهجب *tashahjub*, (v. n. 2 of شهجب Q) Being mixed, jumbled together (business).

A تشهّد *tashahhud*, (v. n. 5 of شهد) Making a profession of religion, saying اشهد ان لا اله الا الله و اشهد ان محمدًا رسول الله *ashhadu an lā ilāha il-la'llāh, wa ashhadu an muhammadan rasūlu'-llāh*, I do testify that (there is) no god but God, and I acknowledge that Muhammad (is) the apostle of God; to which they sometimes add, by way of amplification, و اشهد ان محمدًا عبده و رسوله *wa ashhadu an muhammadan ʻabduhu wa rasūluhu*, And I testify that Muhammad (is) his servant and his apostle.

A تشهّق *tashahhuk*, (v. n. 5 of شهق) Wounding deeply with a malignant eye.

A تشهّل *tashahhul*, A fading (of the complexion).

A تشهّي *tashahhī*, (v. n. 5 of شها for شهو) Wishing, desiring eagerly, having a continued longing.

A تشهيب *tashhīb*, (v. n. 2 of شهب) Changing a person's colour (sun or wind). Distressing cattle (a severe season).

A تشهية *tashhiyat*, (v. n. 2 of شهي) Rendering desirable and appetible.

A تشهيد *tash-hīd*, A seminal effusion.

A تشهير *tashhīr*, (v. n. 2 of شهر) Divulging, proclaiming, blazoning abroad, praising the merit of another. Drawing a sword, and flourishing it round the heads of others.

P تشي *tashī*, A porcupine. *Tishī*, Lousy.

A تشيّخ *tashayyukh*, (v. n. 5 of شاخ for شيخ) Showing old age. Assuming the character of a شيخ *shaykh*, *i.e.* an elder or a learned man.

A تشيّد *tashayyud*, (v. n. 5 of شاد for شيد) Rubbing the body with perfumes.

P تشيرة *tashīra*, A ball of coloured stones.

A تشيّط *tashayyut*, (v. n. 5 of شاط for شيط) Being burnt, scorched. Becoming emaciated from indulging too freely in venery.

A تشيطن *tashaytun*, (v. n. 2 of شيطن Q) Deporting one's self like Satan, by being stubborn, proud, and headstrong.

A تشيظم *tashayzum*, A going fast, getting before.

A تشيّع *tashayyuʻ*, (v. n. 5 of شاع for شيع) Professing to be of the sect of Aliy (شيعة *shiʻat*).

P تشيّع مذهب *tashayyuʻ-mazhab*, Heretical.

A تشيّم *tashayyum*, (v. n. 5 of شام for شيم) Taking after, resembling (one's father). Walking, going, entering into. Appearing (gray hairs).

A تشيّؤ *tashayyuʼ*, A being appeased (anger).

A تشييب *tashyīb*, (v. n. 2 of شاب for شيب) Making gray (sorrow). Turning loose.

A تشيئة *tashyiʼat*, (v. n. 2 of شيئ) Making willing, egging on. Making deformed, covering with confusion.

A تشييح *tashyīh*, (v. n. 2 of شاح for شيح) Admonishing, cautioning. Frightening. Watching (an adversary) narrowly, hemming (him) in.

A تشييخ *tashyīkh*, (v. n. 2 of شاخ for شيخ) Growing aged. Calling any one شيخ *shaykh*, *i.e.* doctor (a title of respect). Rendering aged. Reproaching, reviling on account of age.

A تشييد *tashyīd*, (v. n. 2 of شاد for شيد) Raising high, erecting. Extolling (a name). Plastering.

A تشييز *tashyīz*, (v. n. 2 of شيز not used) Marking (a garment) with stripes.

A تشييص *tashyīs*, (v. n. 2 of شاص for شيص) Punishing, tormenting annoying.

A تشييط *tashyīt*, (v. n. 2 of شاط for شيط) Burning up the wool of a sheep's head and trotters that they may be more easily cleaned. Throwing meat on the fire till it frizzles and smells. Victuals dressed (for the people). Any thing fetid. A bad smell.

A تشييع *tashyīʻ*, (v. n. 2 of شاع for شيع) Accompanying, following. Coming after others are gone, and then following them. Going out with one to bid him farewell and bring him on his way. Burning, scorching. Blowing his pipe (a shepherd). Fasting six days after Ramazān. Inspiring with courage. Feeding a fire with fuel.

A تشييف *tashyīf*, (v. n. 2 of شاف for شيف) Forming (any thing) into a remedy for sore eyes.

A تشئيم *tashʼīm*, (v. n. 2 of شأم) Causing to go to the left. Sending to Syria (شأم *shaʼm*).

A تشييم *tashyīm*, (v. n. 2 of شام for شيم) Entering into. Dividing, apportioning. Seizing by the head or garment to fight.

A تشيين tashyīn, A writting well the letter ش.

A تصابب tasābub, (v. n. 6 of صبّ) Drinking the remains (of water) in a pot.

A تصابي tasābī, (v. n. 6 of صبي) Inflaming (a woman) with love, and deceiving (her). Playing with boys, being boyish.

A تصاتّ tasātt, A fighting among themselves.

A تصاخب tasākhub, (v. n. 6 of صخب) Calling out, bawling to each other. Fighting, squabbling.

A تصادق tasāduk, (v. n. 6 of صدق) Cultivating sincere friendship. Acting with fidelity and affection towards each other.

A تصادم tasādum, (v. n. 6 of صدم) Dashing one against another. Thronging, pressing, crowding.

A تصاديع tasādīɛ, Headaches. Troubles.

A تصارخ tasārukh, A crying out to one another.

A تصارف tasārif, (and تصارفات tasārifāt) Absolute commands, sovereign mandates.

A تصارم tasārum, A cutting asunder, disjoining.

A تصاريف tasārīf, (pl. of تصريف tasrīf) Absolute commands. Conversions. Revolutions. Changes, vicissitudes. (in gram.) Inflexions.

A تصاصؤ tasaṣu, (v. n. 2 of صاصأ Q) Fearing, apprehending, cowering down to.

A تصاعد tasāɛud, A being difficult. Ascension.

A تصاغر tasāghur, (v. n. 6 of صغر) Debasing one's self. Becoming contemptible.

A تصافّ tasāff, (v. n. 6 of صفّ) Being drawn up in two lines in battle array.

A تصافح tasāfuh, A shaking hands.

A تصافق tasāfuk, A striking hands on a bargain.

A تصافن tasāfun, A dividing (water) in portions.

A تصافي tasāfī, An acting sincerely to each other.

A تصالج tasāluj, A feigning deafness.

A تصالح tasāluh, A being reconciled together.

A تصالخ tasālukh, A pretending to be deaf.

A تصاليب tasālīb, Pictures of the cross.

A تصامم tasāmum, A feigning to be deaf.

A تصانيف tasānīf, Literary works.

A تصاول tasāwul, An attacking each other.

A تصاوير tasāwīr, (pl. of تصوير) Images, pictures.

A تصايح tasāyuh, (v. n. 6 of صاح for صيح) Calling to one another. Being split (the sheath of a sword).

A تصائي tasāʼī, (v. n. 6 of صأي) Twittering (the young of any animal).

A تصبّب tasabbub, (v. n. 5 of صبّ) Being poured out, disembogued. Flowing from a height, falling in a cascade. Being elapsed, escaped.

A تصبّح tasabbuh, (v. n. 5 of صبح) Slumbering in the morning. Taking breakfast. Amusing one's self in the morning.

A تصبّر tasabbur, (v. n. 5 of صبر) Being patient. Enduring patiently, making an effort so to do.

A تصبصب tasabsub, (v. n. 2 of صبصب Q) Elapsing, being spent (the best part of the night). Being very bold. Being intense (heat). Contradicting, disputing. Being scattered, put to flight. Being erased, cancelled.

A تصبّغ tasabbugh, The embracing a religion.

A تصبّي tasabbī, (v. n. 5 of صبي) Inflaming with love and deceiving (a woman). Desiring, inclining to, entertaining an affection for.

A تصبيح tasbīh, (v. n. 2 of صبح) Saluting in the morning. Coming in the morning. Giving a morning draught. Causing to arrive in the morning. Breakfast.

A تصبير tasbīr, (v. n. 2 of صبر) Desiring one to have patience. Restraining one's self or another from doing any thing. Taking by the gross.

A تصبيغ tasbīgh, (v. n. 2 of صبغ) Having dates ripening at the stalk (a palm-tree). Being delivered of a hairy abortion (a camel). Colouring, dyeing deeply.

A تصبين tasbīn, A rubbing with soap, soaping.

A تصتّع tasattuɛ, (v. n. 5 of صتع) Going backwards and forwards, to and fro, here and there, irresolute and uncertain. Coming naked and alone.

A تصتّم tasattum, A running hard.

A تصتيم tastīm, (v. n. 2 of صتم obsol.) Completing (a number). Making firm and strong.

A تصتيه tastīh, A rendering vile, an abasing.

A تصحّب tasahhub, A being ashamed of.

A تصحّت tasahhut, A blushing, being ashamed.

A تصحّف tasahhuf, (v. n. 5 of صحف not in use) Committing an error in reading or writing.

A تصحّن tasahhun, A questioning.

A تصحيح tas-hīh, (v. n. 2 of صحّ) Amending, correcting, making sound. Verifying, illustrating. Putting in order, arranging. Correction.

P تصحيحه tas-hīha, Muster. داغ تصحيحه dāghi tas-hīha, The office in which the horses entertained in service are marked.

A تصحيف tas-hīf, (v. n. 2 of صحف not in use) Making an error in reading or writing. An orthographical mistake, an error in spelling.

P تصحيف خواني tas-hīf-khwānī, Bad reading.

A تصخير tashkhīr, (v. n. 2 of صخر not used) Subduing, conquering. Oppressing, forcing to labour without remuneration.

A تصدّد tasaddud, (v. n. 5 of صدّ) Opposing, presenting one's self to. Happening.

A تصدّر tasaddur, (v. n. 5 of صدر) Being placed or sitting in the chief seat. Taking the lead with outstretched chest (a race-horse). Precedency.

A تصدّع tasadduɛ, (v. n. 5 of صدع) Becoming cleft, split, divided, separated, dispersed, scattered, dissipated. Being lost, disappearing.

A تصدّف tasadduf, (v. n. 5 of صدف) Declining, receding, turning away from.

A تصدّق tasadduk, (v. n. 5 of صدق) Giving alms. Bestowing, giving up to public use from religious motives. Alms given in grain at the time of thrashing.

A تصدّؤ tasadduʼ, (v. n. 5 of صدأ) Coming up in front of. Opposing, disturbing.

A تصدّي tasaddī, (v. n. 5 of صدي) Happening, coming to pass. Coming before, opposing.

A تصدئة tasdiʼat, The polishing (of a mirror).

A تصدية tasdiyat, A clapping with the hands.

A تصديد tasdīd, (v. n. 2 of صدّ) Striking with vehemence, clapping the hands together (so that the sound is heard). Flapping the wings (a bird). Striking (the lyre). Shaking (as the wind). Pouring (wine) from one vessel into another. Leading (cattle) from pasture to pasture.

A تصدير tasdīr, (v. n. 2 of صدر) Causing to spring forth. Leading back from water. Taking the lead with a stretched-out breast (a race-horse). Yielding precedence, giving the highest place or chief seat at table. Beginning a letter with a proœmium or exordium. Passing a rope from the ring in a camel's nose behind the callous part of his breast. Putting the breast-harness on a horse. Breast-harness.

A تصديع tasdīɛ, (v. n. 2 of صدع) Splitting, cleaving asunder. Separating, scattering. Suffering from a violent headache. (pl. تصاديع tasādīɛ) The headache. Perplexity, trouble. P تصديع دادن tasdīɛ dādan, To inflict.

A تصديغ tasdīgh, A branding on the temple.

A تصديق tasdīk, (v. n. 2 of صدق) Assuring of the truth of, proving, attesting, verifying. Believing, crediting, acknowledging as true. Receiving contributions for pious uses. Naming the amount of a woman's marriage-portion. Running away (a wild beast) without looking behind him.

A تصديقي tasdīkīy, Confirmatory. مطالب تصديقيّه matālibi tasdīkiya, Confirmative questions (tending to prove the truth).

A تصرّخ tasarrukh, (v. n. 5 of صرخ) Crying out, exclaiming vehemently. Endeavouring to cry out.

A تصرّف tasarruf, (v. n. 5 of صرف) Holding at one's own disposal. Using one's own discretion. Using, consuming. Taking, seizing, claiming. Being skilled, well practised in. Employing dexterity and cunning. Possession, use, occupancy, controul. Expenditure, embezzlement, extravagance. Power, influence, art. P تصرّف داشتن tasarruf dāshtan, To possess, enjoy, usurp, have in one's power. تصرّف كردن tasarruf kardan, To use, to dispose of. To spend.

A تصرّفات tasarrufāt, Possessions. Usages. Sum total of expenses. تصرّفات عروض tasarrufāti ɛarūz, Poetic licenses.

A تصرّفي tasarrufī, Common provisions given to dependents.

A تصرّم tasarrum, (v. n. 5 of صرم) Being cut off. Being finished, consumed. Being hard, robust, stubborn, obstinate.

A تصريب *tasrib*, (v. n. 2 of صرب) Drinking sour milk. Eating red gum.

A تصرية *tasriyat*, (v. n. 2 of صري) Taking little or no milk (from a sheep), in order to increase it.

A تصريج *tasrij*, (v. n. 2 of صرج not used) Plastering (a cistern) with a cement called صاروج *sāruj*.

A تصريح *tasrīh*, (v. n. 2 of صرح) Speaking openly. Showing plainly. Being open, plain, sincere, pure, clear. Losing its froth (wine). Evidence, manifestation. تصريح كحل *tasrīhi kahl*, Suffering distress from dearth. Becoming pure and free from admixture. Shooting but missing aim. P تصريح كردن *tasrīh kardan*, To make manifest.

A تصريد *tasrīd*, (v. n. 2 of صرد) Giving a very little to drink, not sufficient to quench the thirst. Giving a small present.

A تصرير *tasrīr*, A taking the lead.

A تصريع *tasrīɛ*, (v. n. 2 of صرع) Overthrowing, throwing completely prostrate. Putting folding doors to a gate. Beginning a poem with a hemistich, to the last syllable of which all the verses in the piece must rhyme.

A تصريف *tasrīf*, (v. n. 2 of صرف) Changing, turning. Drinking pure and neat (wine). Appointing a man to manage affairs, with full powers. Explaining, making clear (verses). Deriving (one word) from another. Spending, disbursing. Easily selling one's goods. Shifting, veering from one quarter to another (wind). (pl. تصاريف *tasārīf*) Inflection, conjugation, etymology.

A تصريم *tasrīm*, (v. n. 2 of صرم) Breaking, cutting in pieces. Cutting a tree.

A تصعاق *tasɛāk*, A fainting, falling into a swoon.

A تصعّب *tasaɛɛub*, A rendering difficult.

A تصعّد *tasaɛɛud*, (v. n. 5 of صعد) Being important, difficult, above one's power. Ascending.

A تصعّر *tasaɛɛur*, (v. n. 5 of صعر) Having a wry face. Being wry-necked.

A تصعرر *tasaɛrur*, A being spherical, globular.

A تصعصع *tasaɛsuɛ*, (v. n. 2 of صعصع Q) Moving one's self. Being moved. Being divided, scattered. Being cowardly. Being easy, submissive, humble, or depressed. Giving way, quitting the ranks (troops). Scattering, destroying.

A تصعفر *tasaɛfur*, A being bent (the neck).

A تصعلك *tasaɛluk*, (v. n. 2 of صعلك Q) Becoming indigent. Casting their coat (camels). Poverty, indigence.

A تصعيب *tasɛīb*, A making difficult, troublesome.

A تصعيد *tasɛīd*, (v. n. 2 of صعد Q) Ascending a mountain. Descending into a valley. Going on a declivity. Melting; distilling, sublimating.

A تصعير *tasɛīr*, (v. n. 2 of صعر) Making faces in contempt. A wryness of face from natural causes.

A تصغير *tasghīr*, (n. n. 2 of صغر) Diminishing. Rendering contemptible, despising. Putting (a noun) into the diminutive form. Diminution. A diminutive noun.

A تصفّت *tasaffut*, (v. n. 5 of صفت) Being strong, powerful, obstinate.

A تصفتت *tasaftut*, (v. n. 2 of صفتت Q) Being strong, powerful, hard, stern.

A تصفّح *tasaffuh*, (v. n. 5 of صفح) Examining minutely, considering accurately. Comparing, revising page after page.

A تصفّق *tasaffuk*, (v. n. 5 of صفق) Moving from side to side on the back. Going to and fro, being irresolute. Opposing, hindering. Inversion.

A تصفية *tasfiyat*, (v. n. 2 of صفي) Straining, drawing off water. Rendering clear, bright.

A تصفيح *tasfīh*, (v. n. 2 of صفح) Making broad, expanding, beating out (a ploughshare or sword-blade). Clapping (the hands).

A تصفيد *tasfīd*, A fastening, binding, tying.

A تصفير *tasfīr*, (v. n. 2 of صفر) Dyeing yellow. Emptying, stripping (a house of furniture). Whistling, singing. Calling (an ass) to water.

A تصفيف *tasfīf*, (v. n. 2 of صفّ) Arranging, drawing up in order of battle. Standing in a row.

A تصفيق *tasfīk*, (v. n. 2 of صفق) Shaking a tree (wind). Clapping (the hands) together. Going, passing on. Circumambulating. Pouring (wine) from one vessel into another. Leading (cattle) from pasture to pasture. Filling.

A تصفين *tasfīn*, (v. n. 2 of صفن) Laying in order side by side (the cells of a wasp's nest).

A تصقّر *tasakkur*, (v. n. 5 of صقر) Hunting with the bird صقر *sakr*. Being lighted, blazing (a fire). Delaying, tarrying.

A تصقير *taskīr*, The kindling (of a fire).

A تصقيع *taskīɛ*, (v. n. 2 of صقع) Swearing.

A تصلّب *tasallub*, A being hard, firm, inflexible.

A تصلصل *tasalsul*, (v. n. 2 of صلصل Q) Resounding (as thunder, artillery, a smith's forge, &c.), tingling (as bells or other bodies of a smaller and shriller sound). Becoming dry and rattling (as clay).

A تصلّع *tasalluɛ*, (v. n. 5 of صلع) Bursting from behind a cloud (the sun), reaching the meridian.

A تصلّف *tasalluf*, (v. n. 5 of صلف) Caressing, flattering. Boasting, gasconading. Becoming satiated with the plant خلّة *khullat* (a camel), and longing for the حمض *hamz*. Coming to hard, rugged ground.

A تصلّق *tasalluk*, (v. n. 5 of صلق) Crying out (a woman in labour). Rolling in pain (from the bellyache). Going in and out of the water.

A تصلّي *tasallī*, (v. n. 5 of صلي) Being burnt, scorched, singed. Growing hot, being heated before the fire. Straightening (a stick) by heat.

A تصليب *taslīb*, (v. n. 2 of صلب) Crucifying, gibbeting. Impaling. Making the sign of the cross; painting, or forming in the shape of a crucifix. Making very hard. Becoming hard and firm. Growing hard (a soft date). Taking the fat from meat. A mode of covering the head with a veil.

A تصلية *tasliyat*, (v. n. 2 of صلي) Putting any thing into the fire to heat. Roasting. Making straight by heat (a stick). Praying to, supplicating God. Being propitious, merciful (God). Blessing. Coming in second at a race (a horse). Driving the female before him (an ass).

A تصليح *taslīh*, The doing (a thing) well.

A تصليد *taslīd*, A being very covetous.

A تصليط *taslīt*, (v. n. 2 of صلط) Giving absolute dominion, investing with paramount authority.

A تصليع *taslīɛ*, (v. n. 2 of صلع) Making an apology. Being visible and uncovered by the earth (a grain). Spreading out, stretching (a skin). Stretching both hands on the ground, and easing nature.

A تصليك *taslīk*, (v. n. 2 of صلك not in use) Tying the string صرار *sirār* around a camel's dugs.

A تصليل *taslīl*, (v. n. 2 of صلّ) Beginning to stink (meat). Making a tinkling noise (a bridle-bit).

A تصليم *taslīm*, A cutting up by the root. A maiming (especially in the ears or nose).

A تصمّع *tasammuɛ*, A being stained (with blood).

A تصميت *tasmīt*, (v. n. 2 of صمت) Keeping silence. Ordering or putting to silence.

A تصمير *tasmīr*, (v. n. 2 of صمر) Being avaricious. Preventing, hindering. Entering on the hour of sunset.

A تصميع *tasmīɛ*, (v. n. 2 of صمع) Heaping, piling up to a point. Intending, designing, resolving.

A تصميغ *tasmīgh*, (v. n. 2 of صمغ) Gumming (any thing). Turning to gum.

A تصميم *tasmīm*, (v. n. 2 of صمّ) Intending, designing, resolving deliberately, determining firmly. Proceeding upon a journey, going on briskly. Penetrating to the bone, or hitting a joint exactly (a sword). Biting, fixing, or holding with the teeth. Putting (a horse) into forage, so that he becomes fat. Resolution, determination. Making one the repository of any communication.

A تصندل *tasandul*, (v. n. 2 of صندل Q) Talking politely to the ladies.

A تصنّع *tasannuɛ*, (v. n. 5 of صنع) Adorning herself (a woman). Making a display of art. Studying to make a fair appearance. Showing a specious outside.

A تصنّف *tasannuf*, (v. n. 5 of صنف) Being ready to burst into leaf (a tree). Becoming excoriated (the lip).

A تصنّي *tasannī*, (v. n. 5 of صنو) Sitting wistfully nigh a cauldron.

A تصنيج *tasnīj*, A throwing prostrate.

A تصنيع *tasnīɛ*, (v. n. 2 of صنع) Dressing elegantly (a girl). Feeding, fattening, making plump and comely (a girl).

A تصنيف *tasnīf*, (v. n. 2 of صنف not in use) Sorting, ranging, distributing (in classes). Compiling, composing (a book). Leafing (a tree). (pl.

تصانيف tasānīf) Invention, literary composition.

A تصنيم tasnīm, (v. n. 2 of صنم not in use) Forming an idol. Painting. Leaving (a camel) unmilked every other time that the milk may be increased.

A تصوّب tasawwub, (v. n. 5 of صاب for صوب) Falling, descending (rain). Reaching.

A تصوّح tasawwuh, (v. n. 5 of صاح for صوح) Becoming divided (hair in ringlets). Being split, cleft, riven. Being dried, withered, particularly on the top (herbage).

A تصوّر tasawwur, (v. n. 5 of صار for صور) Being painted, pourtrayed, framed, fashioned, formed, imagined, conceived. Imagining, fancying. Falling under a blow. Imagination, fancy, supposition, reflection, image, idea. P تصوّر كردن tasawwur kardan, To imagine, to picture to one's self.

A تصوّريّ tasawwuriy, Imaginative.

A تصوّع tasawwuʻ, (v. n. 5 of صاع for صوع) Being dispersed and going to a distance (people). Being withered (a plant). Being dirty, dishevelled, flying about and falling off (hair).

A تصوّف tasawwuf, (v. n. 5 of صاف for صوف) Being dark and mystical (a saying). An obscure and enigmatical mode of speaking (peculiar to the Eastern sophs or religious devotees). Jargon. Contemplation. Mysticism, Sufiism. A society of men (particularly a religious order). اهل تصوّف ahli tasawwuf, An anchoret. علم تصوّف ʻilmi tasawwuf, The science of mystery, theology. (This word is not found in the Kāmus).

A تصوّق tasawwuk, A being dirtied with ordure.

A تصوّك tasawwuk, (v. n. 5 of صاك for صوك) Being bedaubed with one's own excrement.

A تصويب taswīb, (v. n. 2 of صاب for صوب) Regarding (one) as a correct speaker, or as saying what is right and true. Approving, praising. Putting a horse to the gallop, urging to full speed. Lowering the head.

A تصوية taswiyat, (v. n. 2 of صوي) Leaving a ewe not milked dry, in order that the milk may thicken. Exempting a stallion-camel from all kinds of labour. Withering (a palm-tree). Reserving a son for a widow, or a daughter for a widower.

A تصويت taswīt, (v. n. 2 of صات for صوت) Resounding. Exclaiming. Causing to cry out.

A تصويح taswīh, (v. n. 2 of صاح for صوح) Drying up (as the sun or wind). Withering, becoming withered (herbs, particularly on the tops).

A تصويد taswīd, A writing the letter ص sād.

A تصوير taswīr, (v. n. 2 of صار for صور) Forming, fashioning. Painting, limning. A picture, image, effigy, likeness. P تصوير كردن taswīr kardan, To paint. To represent.

A تصويع taswīʻ, (v. n. 2 of صاع for صوع) (Wind) drying (plants). Preparing (a place) for carding cotton. Sharpening (a thing) at the head and rounding (it) at the sides. Jumping to the right and left of the female (an ass).

A تصويل taswīl, (v. n. 2 of صال for صول) Carrying or upraising any thing by water. Sweeping (a barn or granary). Burning and mixing one thing with another.

A تصهمم tasahmum, (v. n. 2 of صهمم Q) Doing the work of a صهميم sihmīm.

A تصيّح tasayyuh, (v. n. 5 of صاح for صيح) Drying up (herbs). Being divided (hair).

A تصيّد tasayyud, A hunting, looking for game.

A تصيّر tasayyur, (v. n. 5 of صار for صير) Resembling, taking after (his) father.

A تصيطر tasaytur, (v. n. 2 of صيطر Q) Being appointed to any office or post of authority. Presiding as inspector.

A تصيّع tasayyuʻ, (v. n. 5 of صاع for صيع) Moving to and fro on the surface of the ground (water) Withering (a plant).

A تصيّف tasayyuf, (v. n. 5 of صاف for صيف) Living any where in the summer season, summering.

A تصيّؤ tasayyuʼ, A washing (the head) slightly.

A تصيئة tasyiʼat, (v. n. 2 of صيأ not in use) Washing (the head) slightly. Bearing dates turning to a purple colour (a palm-tree).

A تصييح tasyīh, (v. n. 2 of صاح for صيح) Drying (as the sun or wind).

A تصيير tasyīr, (v. n. 2 of صار for صير) Effecting, causing to become, placing, constituting. Sending back. Causing to incline.

A تصييص tasyīs, (v. n. 2 of صيص) Producing the bad dates صيص sīs (a palm-tree).

A تصييغ tasyīgh, A saucing (of meat).

A تصييف tasyīf, A sufficing for the summer.

A تضاءل tazāʼul, (v. n. 6 of ضأل) Being thin, lean, spare, and contemptible. Concealing (one's self) by sitting down. Making one's self appear contemptible.

A تضاجر tazājur, (v. n. 6 of ضجر) Appearing (in truth or semblance only) wearied and disgusted.

A تضاجع tazājuʻ, (v. n. 6 of ضجع) Lying down together, each on one side.

A تضاجم tazājum, (v. n. 6 of ضجم) Being controverted. Being wry-mouthed. Disagreement, diversity. An obliquity in the mouth.

A تضاحك tazāhuk, (v. n. 6 of ضحك) Laughing at one another. Laughing amongst themselves.

A تضادّ tazādd, (v. n. 6 of ضدّ) Being enemies, opponents. Contradiction, contrariety, opposition. Absurdity, inconsistency.

A تضارب tazārub, (v. n. 6 of ضرب) Being in commotion, distracted among themselves. Fighting with swords. Squabbling.

A تضارس tazārus, (v. n. 6 of ضرس) Being unequal, consisting of uneven projecting parts. Making war, fighting with one another.

A تضازن tazāzun, (v. n. 6 of ضزن) Giving to one another. Fighting or overcoming one another.

A تضاعف tazāʻuf, (v. n. 6 of ضعف) Increasing, doubling. Becoming doubled. Pretending to be weak.

A تضاعيف tazāʻīf, (pl. of تضعيف tazʻīf) Augmentations.

A تضاغط tazāghut, A crowding, pressing.

A تضاغن tazāghun, (v. n. 6 of ضغن) Hating one another. Feeling a tendency to hate.

A تضافّ tazāff, (v. n. 6 of ضفّ) Pressing, crowding one upon another (camels, when running to water in a light state).

A تضافر tazāfur, A helping each other.

A تضافط tazāfut, A being compact, firm (flesh).

A تضافن tazāfun, A helping one another.

A تضالّ tazāll, (v. n. 6 of ضلّ) Pretending to have lost one's way.

A تضامّ tazāmum, (v. n. 6 of ضمّ) Being joined, accumulated, drawn towards.

A تضاؤل tazāʼul, (v. n. 6 of ضؤل) Being thin, lean, spare, and contemptible. Concealing one's self by sitting down. Making one's self appear contemptible.

A تضايف tazāyuf, (v. n. 6 of ضيف) Being narrow, confined (a channel). Coming down on both sides to a river. Attacking the game from both sides (dogs).

A تضايق tazāyuk, (v. n. 6 of ضيق) Being narrow (mind or place). Being crowded, jammed.

A تضبّب tazabbub, (v. n. 5 of ضبّ) Becoming fat and short-necked (a boy).

A تضبّط tazabbut, (v. n. 5 of ضبط) Taking by force and imprisonment. Snatching a mouthful of grass, grazing quickly and becoming strong (sheep).

A تضبيب tazbīb, (v. n. 2 of ضبّ) Fastening the door. Feeding (a boy) with butter from a leathern vase. Hooping (a vessel). Comprehending, observing, laying a thing up in mind. Making fat.

A تضبيد tazbīd, (v. n. 2 of ضبد obsol.) Calling to the recollection of another something which puts him in a passion.

A تضبير tazbīr, (v. n. 2 of ضبر) Collecting. Being firmly knit (the joints). Compactness or squareness of the animal frame.

A تضبيع tazbīʻ, (v. n. 2 of ضبع) Being pusillanimous. Preventing a sportsman from killing game, by coming between. Going with a long trot, throwing out the fore-legs (a horse).

A تضجّر tazajjur, (v. n. 5 of ضجر) Being oppressed and wearied in mind, complaining.

A تضجّع tazajjuʻ, (v. n. 5 of ضجع) Doing less than one ought, being negligent, indolent. Abiding in one place. Remaining fixed (a cloud).

A تضجيج tazjīj, (v. n. 2 of ضجّ) Going, departing. Inclining. Poisoning (birds and beasts). Exciting (any one) to scream aloud.

A تضجيع tazjīʻ, (v. n. 2 of ضجع) Doing less than one ought, being negligent. Being near setting (the sun), inclining to set (a star).

A تضحضح *tazahzuh*, Undulation (of a vapour).

A تضحك *tazahhuk*, (v. n. 5 of ضحك) Laughing.

A تضحّي *tazahhī*, (v. n. 5 of ضحا for ضحو) Dining, lunching. Basking in the sun. Sacrificing. Praying in the forenoon. Beginning to graze in the forenoon (camels).

A تضحية *tazhiyat*, (v. n. 2 of ضحا for ضحو) Proceeding slowly. Sacrificing a sheep (when the forenoon is far advanced). Leading sheep to pasture between sunrise and midday. Causing (any one) to eat at luncheon. Entertaining at dinner.

A تضحيك *tazhīk*, A causing to laugh.

A تضخيم *tazkhīm*, A making big.

A تضرّب *tazarrub*, (v. n. 5 of ضرب) Being moved, stirred, agitated. Shaking.

A تضرّة *tazirrat* or *tazurrat*, Necessity, want, indigence, bad plight, evil case.

A تضرّج *tazarruj*, (v. n. 5 of ضرج) Being smeared, stained (with blood). Being florid (the cheek). Expanding, bursting from the envelope, bud, or pod (a flower or fruit). (A woman) dressing herself to show herself to men. Shooting (lightning).

A تضرّر *tazarrur*, A being injured, suffering loss.

A تضرّع *tazarruʻ*, (v. n. 5 of ضرع) Humbling one's self. Surrendering one's self up to the divine disposal. Supplicating, deprecating. Petitioning, making known one's wants. Diminishing, contracting (a shadow). Running with short steps. Submission, supplication.

A تضرغم *tazarghum*, (v. n. 2 of ضرغم Q) Resembling a lion (ضرغام *zirghām*) in fierceness.

A تضرفط *tazarfut*, (v. n. 2 of ضرفط Q) Riding upon any one, and withdrawing the feet from under his arm-pit, and placing them on his neck.

A تضرّم *tazarrum*, (v. n. 5 of ضرم) Kindling, blazing (fire or rage). Being fired with rage.

A تضريب *tazrīb*, (v. n. 2 of ضرب) Striking. Stirring up debate. Mixing. Stitching a garment lined with cotton. Drinking the milk of several camels mixed in one bowl. Being deeply sunk in the socket (an eye). Going in, or being exposed to, the snow. Tale-bearing.

A تضرية *tazriyat*, (v. n. 2 of ضري) Making greedy, causing to hanker after. Setting a dog in pursuit of game. Training, exercising, habituating. Hemming the edge of a wallet.

A تضريج *tazrīj*, (v. n. 2 of ضرج) Dyeing (a garment) of a red colour. Imbruing, smearing (with blood). Speaking with elegance. Spurring (a steed) when making a hostile incursion. Slackening, unloosing the breast of a garment.

A تضريس *tazrīs*, (v. n. 2 of ضرس) Making expert (frequent wars or travels).

A تضريط *tazrīt*, (v. n. 2 of ضرط) Causing to break wind. Making a noise with the mouth in contempt. Holding up to ridicule.

A تضريع *tazrīʻ*, (v. n. 2 of ضرع) Being about to set (the sun). Being nearly cooked (meat in a pot). Cooking incompletely the inspissated juice called ربّ *rubb*. Taking short steps in running.

A تضريم *tazrīm*, (v. n. 2 of ضرم) Making burn.

A تضع *tuzʻ*, (v. n. of وضع) Bringing forth a child. *Tuzʻ* or *tuzuʻ*, (v. n. of وضع) Conceiving a little before menstruation. Travelling quickly.

A تضعضع *tazaʻzuʻ*, (v. n. 2 of ضعضع Q) Being desolated, falling in ruins. Becoming depressed. Waxing poor. Humbling one's self. Destruction.

A تضعّف *tazaʻʻuf*, (v. n. 5 of ضعف) Considering as weak. Being unknown, obscure, vile.

A تضعيف *tazʻīf*, (v. n. 2 of ضعف) Increasing, doubling, multiplying. Making weak, enfeebling. Esteeming, regarding as, or calling weak. Reduplication. A chemical wash or adulteration.

A تضغيث *tazghīs*, Rain moistening the earth.

A تضفير *tazfīr*, (v. n. 2 of ضفر) Twisting, plaiting, braiding (hair).

A تضكضك *tazakzuk*, (v. n. 2 of ضكضك Q) Rejoicing, exulting, having an open countenance.

A تضلال *tazlāl*, (v. n. 2 of ضلّ) Leading astray. Seduction. ضلّ بتضلال *zulla bi tazlālin*, Vain, false.

A تضلّع *tazalluʻ*, (v. n. 5 of ضلع) Being satiated (with victuals) till the ribs (ضلع *zilaʻ*) swell out.

A تضلّل *tuza* or *tuzullil*, Vain, empty, false, silly.

A تضلّي *tazallī*, (v. n. 5 of ضلي) Choosing the society of the lost and abandoned.

A تضليع *tazlīʻ*, (v. n. 2 of ضلع) Embroidering (a garment) with a pattern of ribs (ضلع *zilaʻ*).

A تضليل *tazlīl*, (v. n. 2 of ضلّ) Seducing, causing to wander. Accusing of error. Losing (one's horse or camel). Ruining, destroying.

A تضمّخ *tazammukh*, (v. n. 5 of ضمخ) Being profusely anointed (the body).

A تضمّد *tazammud*, (v. n. 5 of ضمد) Being bound up, dressed with a plaster (a wound). Being bound with a fillet (ضماد *zimād*).

A تضمّر *tazammur*, (v. n. 5 of ضمر) Falling away, becoming lean and withered (the face).

A تضمّن *tazammun*, (v. n. 5 of ضمن) Comprehending, containing, including. Accepting. Undertaking for, becoming security (for the performance of any thing). A bond with sureties.

A تضمّني *tazammuniy*, Elliptical.

A تضميخ *tazmīkh*, (v. n. 2 of ضمخ) Anointing copiously (the body).

A تضميد *tazmīd*, (v. n. 2 of ضمد) Binding (the head) with a fillet of any kind (excepting the عمامة *ʻimāmat* or sash of fine linen). Applying a plaster or poultice.

A تضمير *tazmīr*, (v. n. 2 of ضمر) Making lean. Giving (a horse) little fodder.

A تضميز *tazmīz*, A putting to silence.

A تضمين *tazmīn*, (v. n. 2 of ضمن) Intrusting another, causing to be accepted. Fining. Putting in a purse or strong box. Taking under protection. Comprehending or including one thing in another. Inserting the verses of another in one's own poem. An ellipsis.

A تضوّج *tazawwuj*, (v. n. 5 of ضاج for ضوج) Meandering greatly (a river).

A تضوّر *tazawwur*, (v. n. 5 of ضار for ضور) Fluttering the wings round the mother (young birds when wanting food). Howling from hunger (a wolf, dog, lion, or fox). Writhing and throwing himself about (as a boy when crying from a blow or hunger).

A تضوّع *tazawwuʻ*, (v. n. 5 of ضاع for ضوع) Diffusing odours (any thing when moved). Fluttering (as a young bird when about to be fed). The contortions of a boy when weeping.

A تضوّك *tazawwuk*, (v. n. 5 of ضاك for ضوك) Being defiled (with one's own excrement).

A تضوكع *tazawkuʻ*, (v. n. 2 of ضوكع Q) Walking heavily, because barefoot.

A تضوّن *tazawwun*, Numerousness of offspring.

A تضوّي *tazawwī*, (v. n. 5 of ضوأ) Sitting in a dark place (in order to get a sight of its inhabitants by the light of a fire).

A تضوئة *tazwiʼat*, (v. n. 2 of ضوأ) Making bright, pellucid, illuminating, causing to shine, shining. Declining, turning away from.

A تضوية *tazwiyat*, A causing to incline.

A تضويح *tazwīh*, (v. n. 2 of ضاح for ضوح) Diluting (milk) with water. Giving such milk and water to drink.

A تضويط *tazwīt*, An assembling, a collecting.

A تضهيب *tazhīb*, (v. n. 2 of ضهب) Broiling upon a hot stone; roasting, but not quite enough. Holding (a spear, arrow, or stick) to the fire in order to make them straight.

A تضهية *tazhīh*, (v. n. 2 of ضهّ) Resembling.

A تضيّح *tazayyuh*, (v. n. 5 of ضاح for ضيح) Being diluted with water (milk). Drinking such milk.

A تضيّر *tazayyur*, (v. n. 5 of ضار for ضير) Roaring, crying out (a wolf, dog, or lion). Howling with hunger (a fox). Crying aloud for help. Writhing from hunger, blows, or pain.

A تضيّع *tazayyuʻ*, (v. n. 5 of ضاع for ضيع) Diffusing a perfume (musk).

A تضيّف *tazayyuf*, (v. n. 5 of ضاف for ضيف) Declining, inclining (as the sun to the west). Bending, inclining. Being received hospitably (a guest).

A تضيّق *tazayyuk*, A being narrow and strait.

A تضيئة *tazyiʼat*, (v. n. 2 of ضيأ not used) Having many children (a woman).

A تضييح *tazyīh*, (v. n. 2 of ضاح for ضيح) Diluting (milk) with water. Giving such milk and water to drink.

A تضييع *tazyīʻ*, (v. n. 2 of ضاع for ضيع) Losing, wasting, consuming. Destroying, wasting. Allowing to be lost, suffering to sink into oblivion.

A تضييف *tazyīf,* (v. n. 2 of ضاف for ضيف) Receiving and entertaining hospitably. Causing to incline or decline. Fearing for one's self. Reducing to shifts. Inclining westward (the sun).

A تضييق *tazyīk,* (v. n. 2 of ضاق for ضيق) Making narrow. Astricting. Contracting (expenditure). Restraining, compressing, reducing to straits; hemming in (an enemy). Arguing closely, putting an antagonist to a nonplus.

A تطابق *tatābuk,* (v. n. 6 of طبق) Agreeing.

A تطارد *tatārud,* A repelling of each other.

A تطارش *tatārush,* A feigning deafness.

A تطارق *tatāruk,* (v. n. 6 of طرق) Following one another, treading in each other's steps.

A تطاريف *tatārīf,* Tips of the fingers. Edging.

A تطأطؤ *tataṣtuṣ,* (v. n. 2 of طأطأ Q) Being inclined downwards (the head). Lowering (the head). Stooping, crouching, submitting to another.

A تطاعم *tatāṣum,* (v. n. 6 of طعم) Billing (turtles).

A تطاعن *tatāṣun,* (v. n. 6 of طعن) Piercing mutually with spears.

A تطالل *tatālul,* (v. n. 6 of طلّ) Standing on tiptoe, and stretching out the neck to see any distant object.

A تطامن *tatāmun,* A depression.

A تطاؤ *tatāṣu,* A becoming dear (of provisions).

A تطاوح *tatāwuh,* A throwing at one another.

A تطاوع *tatāwuṣ,* (v. n. 6 of طاع for طوع) Giving application. Showing obedience.

A تطاول *tatāwul,* (v. n. 6 of طال for طول) Exalting one's self (especially from pride). Stretching out the neck to look at any thing. Boasting about the length and height of a building. Unjustly usurping another's right. Usurpation, tyranny, conquest, extension of dominion. Rudeness.

P تطاول پيشه *tatāwul-pesha,* Used to domineer.

A تطاير *tatāyur,* (v. n. 6 of طار for طير) Being dispersed, scattered. Being long (hair). Covering the face of the sky (clouds).

A تطبّب *tatabbub,* The practising of physic.

A تطبّج *tatabbuj,* (v. n. 5 of طبج) Introducing variety in conversation.

A تطبطب *tatabtub,* (v. n. 2 of طبطب Q) Dashing with a loud noise (a torrent).

A تطبّع *tatabbuṣ,* (v. n. 5 of طبع) Being agreeable to nature. Adopting any habit until it becomes a second nature, imitating nature. Being completely replenished, filled to the brim or top. الطبع يغلب التطبّع *at tabṣ yaghlibu't tatabbuṣ,* Nature overcomes art.

A تطبّق *tatabbuk,* (v. n. 5 of طبق) Being congruous, consonant, conformable. Being covered with a lid. Being folded. Covering any thing fold upon fold, layer upon layer.

A تطبيب *tatbīb,* (v. n. 2 of طبّ) Shaking (a bottle, suspended from a tent-pole, in order to churn butter). Letting in a gore or gusset called بنيقة *banīkat,* in order to enlarge a vest. Covering the seams of a water-bottle with strips of leather.

A تطبيخ *tatbīkh,* (v. n. 2 of طبخ) Growing (a boy or a lizard). Growing old.

A تطبيس *tatbīs,* A bedaubing with clay.

A تطبيع *tatbīṣ,* (v. n. 2 of طبع) Filling (a bottle) till (it) runs over. Staining, besmearing, tinging, daubing, defiling.

A تطبيق *tatbīk,* (v. n. 2 of طبق) Covering with a lid. Adapting, laying one thing exactly over another, doubling, folding. Putting the hind-foot into the print of the fore-foot when walking (a horse). Overspreading (as clouds the sky, or water the earth). Taking in, comprehending, comprising. Placing the hands upon or between the thighs, in the sacred inclination of the body at prayer, called ركوع *rukūṣ.* Striking exactly at the joint (when dividing any animal with an axe or sword; صمم *samam* being the word used when hitting the bone). Raining universally. Drawing the fore-feet near to the hind-feet when going to leap (a horse).

A تطبيل *tatbīl,* A beating a drum, drumming.

A تطحين *tathīn,* (v. n. 2 of طحن) Grinding.

A تطرّب *tatarrub,* (v. n. 5 of طرب) Singing. Causing one to dance for joy.

A تطرتم *tatartum,* A wallowing in the mire.

A تطرثث *tatarsus,* (v. n. 2 of طرثث Q) Culling, picking the plant or root called طرثوث *tursūs.*

A تطرّز *tatarruz,* (v. n. 5 of طرز) Being embroidered or ornamented (the border of a garment).

A تطرّس *tatarrus,* (v. n. 5 of طرس) Disdaining, abstaining from. Being curious; being nice, dainty, squeamish, with respect to food.

A تطرّش *tatarrush,* (v. n. 5 of طرش) Recovering from indisposition. Disagreeing. Bringing (quadrupeds), and taking (them) away. Opposition, contradiction.

A تطرّف *tatarruf,* (v. n. 5 of طرف) Pasturing (a she-camel) at the extremity of a field, and not mixing with the others. Acquiring a habit.

A تطرّق *tatarruk,* (v. n. 5 of طرق) Crossing (another) in the road. Thwarting, injuring. Travelling. Branching out, being separated. Opposition: division, distraction: opposition of synonyms.

A تطرّم *tatarrum,* (v. n. 5 of طرم) Stammering in speech. Speaking in a whisper.

A تطريب *tatrīb,* (v. n. 2 of طرب) Causing to leap for joy or writhe in pain. Drawing. Singing with great taste and execution. Lengthening out the voice.

A تطرية *tatriyat,* (v. n. 2 of طرا for طرو) Freshening. Damping (a garment). Mixing. Rendering (musk) more fragrant by an admixture of other perfumes.

A تطريح *tatrīh,* (v. n. 2 of طرح) Projecting greatly, throwing far. Lengthening out (a building or a wall).

A تطريد *tatrīd,* (v. n. 2 of طرد) Ordering to be driven away or banished. Holding out or brandishing (a scourge).

A تطريز *tatrīz,* (v. n. 2 of طرز) Embroidering, ornamenting the edge (طراز *tirāz*) of a garment.

A تطريس *tatrīs,* (v. n. 2 of طرس) Blackening. Tracing the pen over any writing a second time.

A تطريش *tatrīsh,* A dispersing, scattering.

A تطريف *tatrīf,* (v. n. 2 of طرف) Fighting at the wing of an army when attacking the enemy. Forcing (an enemy) to retreat. Shedding his teeth (a camel). Driving back (the foremost horses of a troop). Staining the tips of her fingers (a woman).

A تطريق *tatrīk,* (v. n. 2 of طرق) Opening a way. Being in labour (a woman, also an animal); being near chipping her eggs (the bird *kata*). Acknowledging a debt formerly denied. Restraining a camel from pasture; permitting him to pass to it.

A تطسيس *tatsīs,* A wandering about.

A تطعّم *tataṣṣum,* A tasting, trying, sipping.

A تطعيم *tatṣīm,* (v. n. 2 of طعم) Being full of marrow (a bone). Engrafting a branch of one tree upon another to give a flavour to its fruit.

A تطغّم *tataghghum,* (v. n. 5 of طغم) Feigning ignorance and folly.

A تطفّش *tataffush,* Filth.

A تطفّل *tataffal,* A going uninvited to a feast.

A تطفئة *tatfiṣat,* (v. n. 2 of طفأ) Extinguishing.

A تطفيح *tatfīh,* A filling to overflowing.

A تطفير *tatfīr,* (v. n. 2 of طفر) Turning to cream on the surface (milk).

A تطفيف *tatfīf,* (v. n. 2 of طفّ) Not quite filling a place or vessel. Expanding the wings (a bird). Approaching. Leaping with one (a horse).

A تطفيل *tatfīl,* (v. n. 2 of طفل) Being near setting (the sun), reddening towards the west. Beginning to darken (the night). Labouring, arranging a discourse. Driving slowly (camels, to enable their colts to keep pace). Pondering and understanding (a discourse). Rearing her young one well (a camel). Going uninvited to a feast. Becoming soiled with dust (a plant).

A تطلاب *tatlāb,* Search, quest.

A تطلّب *tatallub,* (v. n. 5 of طلب) Inquiring, interrogating, searching, seeking diligently, requesting again and again.

A تطلّس *tatallus,* (v. n. 5 of طلس) Being erased, defaced (writing).

A تطلّع *tatalluṣ,* (v. n. 5 of طلع) Being filled (a measure). Looking out for, expecting. Looking at attentively. Knowing, being aware of. Staggering, tottering, going with a swinging air.

A تطلّق *tatalluk,* (v. n. 5 of طلق) Flying rapidly without looking behind (a doe). Staling after a heat (a horse). Causing joy to be lighted up in the countenance.

A تطلّه *tatalluh*, (v. n. 5 of طله) Being various, diversified, discordant.

A تطلّي *tatallī*, (v. n. 5 of طلي) Being anointed, besmeared, bedaubed (with oil or pitch). Being addicted to play and pastime.

A تطليب *tatlīb*, A seeking leisurely.

A تطلية *tatliyat*, (v. n. 2 of طلي) Anointing. Rendering diseased. Singing. Reproaching.

A تطليث *tatlīs*, An increasing, an exceeding.

A تطليح *tatlīh*, (v. n. 2 of طلح) Fatiguing or even killing (a camel). Importuning, urging. Being jaded (a camel).

A تطليس *tatlīs*, Erasure (of writing).

A تطليع *tatlīʿ*, (v. n. 2 of طلع) Lifting up, causing to ascend. Filling a measure. Beginning to put forth buds (a palm-tree).

A تطليف *tatlīf*, (v. n. 2 of طلف) Superadding.

A تطليق *tatlīk*, (v. n. 2 of طلق) Dismissing, divorcing, repudiating a wife. Impregnating the female palm-tree (by sprinkling over it the male flowers). Being relieved from pain, being restored to one's self (from the bite of a serpent).

A تطليم *tatlīm*, (v. n. 2 of طلم) Forming bread into shape with the hands; baking it under the ashes.

A تطمّس *tatammus*, (v. n. 5 of طمس) Being obliterated, effaced, or erased.

A تطمّع *tatammuʿ*, (v. n. 5 of طمع) Desiring vehemently, being greedy.

A تطمّل *tatammul*, (v. n. 5 of طمل) Being smeared, anointed, or defiled.

A تطميح *tatmīh*, (v. n. 2 of طمح) Rearing, standing on his hind-legs (a horse), Scattering (urine) in the air.

A تطمير *tatmīr*, (v. n. 2 of طمر) Folding together. Loosing a veil.

A تطميع *tatmīʿ*, An exciting avarice, tempting.

A تطميل *tatmīl*, A scenting with perfume.

A تطميم *tatmīm*, (v. n. 2 of طمّ) Alighting or hopping upon a branch (a bird).

A تطنثر *tatansur*, (v. n. 2 of طنثر Q) Being oppressed by eating fat and indigestible things.

A تطنّف *tatannuf*, (v. n. 5 of طنف) Being affected with a strong desire (the mind). Being aware of, looking for, expecting. Covering, concealing. Coming unawares, surprising.

A تطنّي *tatannī*, (v. n. 5 of طني) Branding (a camel) on the side.

A تطنيب *tatnīb*, (v. n. 2 of طنب not in use) Abiding, continuing (in one place). Being long in the back (a horse). Stretching out (a tent or curtain) with ropes. Tying tight. Covering the seams of a water-bottle with strips of leather. Barking, howling (a wolf).

A تطنية *tatniyat*, (v. n. 2 of طني) Curing one of a distemper of the spleen, or giving medicine as a preventive. Branding (a camel) on the side.

A تطنيخ *tatnīkh*, The causing an indigestion.

A تطنيف *tatnīf*, (v. n. 2 of طنف) Suspecting. Applying the mind to, coveting. Fencing (a wall) with thorns.

A تطنين *tatnīn*, A sounding, tinkling, buzzing.

A تطواف *tatwāf*, (v. n. of طاف for طوف) Going round much and often. *Tatwāf* or *titwāf*, The garment in which the sacred perambulation of the Kaaba is made.

A تطوّح *tatawwuh*, A wandering at random.

A تطوّد *tatawwud*, (v. n. 5 of طاد for طود) Going (about mountains). Wandering o'er the world.

A تطوّس *tatawwus*, (v. n. 5 of طاس for طوس) Dressing gaudily, like a peacock (a woman).

A تطوّع *tatawwuʿ*, (v. n. 5 of طاع for طوع) Doing a good action to which one is not obliged. Making pretensions to a power one does not possess. An act of supererogation.

A تطوّعات *tatawwuʿāt*, (pl. of تطوّع) Spontaneous actions, works of supererogation.

A تطوّف *tatawwuf*, Going round (in procession).

A تطوّق *tatawwuk*, (v. n. 5 of طاق for طوق) Adorning one's self, being adorned with a chain, collar, or necklace; wearing it round the neck.

A تطول *titwal*, A long tethering rope, a fetter.

A تطوّل *tatawwul*, (v. n. 5 of طال for طول) Conferring benefits and obligations.

A تطوّي *tatawwī*, (v. n. 5 of طوي) Coiling up, twisting or writhing spirally (as a serpent).

A تطويح *tatwīh*, (v. n. 2 of طاح for طوح) Throwing stones. Striking with a stick. Chasing, driving about from pillar to post. Causing to wander about in astonishment. Exciting (one) to rush into an arena of danger. Banishing to the desert or other unknown place. Sending one to a place from whence there is little chance of a return. Forcing to love, drawing into sensuality.

A تطويد *tatwīd*, (v. n. 2 of طاد for طود) Wandering about. Going among the mountains.

A تطويس *tatwīs*, (v. n. 2 of طوس not in use) Leading away, going off with.

A تطويش *tatwīsh*, (v. n. 2 of طاش for طوش) Castrating, making one a eunuch. Giving time (to a debtor).

A تطويع *tatwīʿ*, (v. n. 2 of طاع for طوع) Consenting, agreeing, complying with. Submitting to, obeying. Inspiring with courage. Aiding, assisting, rendering capable of doing. Making feasible and practicable.

A تطويف *tatwīf*, (v. n. 2 of طاف for طوف) Going round again and again, circumambulating.

A تطويق *tatwīk*, (v. n. 2 of طاق for طوق) Granting one his desire, consenting, acquiescing. Enabling, imparting ability. Ornamenting with a collar. Appointing to a government. Making (any one) a revenue-collector. Compelling. Imposing a heavy burden.

A تطويل *tatwīl*, (v. n. 2 of طال for طول) Lengthening a (horse's) tether. Extending, prolonging, stretching out. Proroguing, giving a delay. تطويل بلا طائل *tatwīl bilā tāʾil*, Prolixity without utility.

A تطويلاً *tatwīlan*, (P تطويلانه) Prolixly.

A تطهّر *tatahhur*, (v. n. 5 of طهر) Becoming purified, cleansed. Being pure, abstaining from vice or sin. Purification, cleansing, sanctifying, washing (with water).

A تطهّل *tatahhul*, A becoming corrupted (water).

A تطهّم *tatahhum*, (v. n. 5 of طهم not in use) Loathing, abhorring. Being afraid of or scared at.

A تطهمل *tatahmul*, (v. n. 2 of طهمل Q) Going about utterly destitute and endeavouring to circumvent.

A تطهير *tathīr*, A purifying, cleansing.

A تطهيم *tathīm*, (v. n. 2 of طهم) Being terrified, scared, running away. Thickness, bulkiness.

A تطياب *tatyāb*, (v. n. of طاب for طيب) Being pleasing, agreeable, good, elegant, handsome. Abounding in pasturage (land).

A تطيّب *tatayyub*, (v. n. 5 of طاب for طيب) Being embalmed, anointed, perfumed with aromatics or sweet herbs. Perfuming one's self.

A تطيّخ *tatayyukh*, A being befouled, bedaubed.

A تطيّر *tatayyur*, A considering as a bad omen.

A تطيله *tutīla*, Tudelah, in Spain.

A تطيليق *tutaylīk*, A gentle flux.

A تطيّن *tatayyun*, A being bedaubed with clay.

A تطييب *tatyīb*, (v. n. 2 of طاب for طيب) Making pure and lawful. Perfuming, scenting. Finding good or beautiful, approving.

A تطييح *tatyīh*, (v. n. 2 of طاح for طيح) Throwing to perdition, exposing to destruction, losing, consuming. Causing to wander about in astonishment.

A تطييخ *tatyīkh*, (v. n. 2 of طاخ for طيخ) Contaminating, defiling. Filling any one (fat). Prevailing over and destroying (pain or torture).

A تطيير *tatyīr*, (v. n. 2 of طار for طير) Causing to fly or move with rapidity. Dividing, apportioning. Impregnating (camels).

A تطييش *tatyīsh*, (v. n. 2 of طاش for طيش) Rendering light, vain, and trifling.

A تطييف *tatyīf*, (v. n. 2 of طاف for طيف) Going round again and again.

A تطيين *tatyīn*, (v. n. 2 of طان for طين) Bedaubing with clay, plastering (a roof) with clay.

A تظالم *tazālum*, (v. n. 6 of ظلم) Injuring one another. Complaining of mutual injuries.

A تظاهر *tazāhur*, (v. n. 6 of ظهر) Deserting, neglecting one another, turning the back (ظهر *zahr*) on each other. Assisting, backing one another.

A تظبظب *tazabzub*, (v. n. 2 of ظبظب Q) Falling easily. Making a slight impression.

A تظرّف *tazarruf*, (v. n. 5 of ظرف) Affecting elegance, gracefulness, or wit, taking pains to appear witty and graceful (ظريف *zarīf*).

A تظرمط *tazarmut*, (v. n. 2 of ظرمط Q) Falling (in the mire) and being bedaubed.

A تظريب *tazrīb*, (v. n. 2 of ظرب) Being hard (hoof, nail, or claw).

A تظفير *tazfīr*, (v. n. 2 of ظفر) Praying that victory may attend one. Wounding with the nails or claws. Shooting forth excrescences resembling nails (a plant). Perfuming (a garment) with the perfume اظفار *azfār*. Bringing forth grass which may be uprooted by the nails. Rubbing a skin till the nails shine.

A تظلّل *tazallul*, A being shaded, seeking shade.

A تظلّم *tazallum*, (v. n. 5 of ظلم) Injuring, oppressing, defrauding of one's due. Causing oppression to recoil upon one's self. Exclaiming against oppression. P اظهار تظلّم كردن *izhāri tazallum kardan*, To complain of an injury.

A تظلّي *tazallī*, (v. n. 5 of ظلي not used) Remaining quiet in the shade.

A تظليف *tazlīf*, (v. n. 2 of ظلف) Superadding.

A تظليل *tazlīl*, (v. n. 2 of ظلّ) Holding up a rod or whip in terrorem.

A تظليم *tazlīm*, (v. n. 2 of ظلم) Charging with injury and oppression (ظلم *zulm*).

A تظمئة *tazmiʼat*, (v. n. 2 of ظمي) Rendering extremely thirsty. Making (a horse) lank and lean.

A تظنّي *tazannī*, (for تظنّن *tazannun*) A thinking, deeming, supposing.

A تظؤّر *tazaʼʼur*, (v. n. 5 of ظأر) Nursing the young of another, shewing affection to it.

A تظهّر *tazahhur*, (v. n. 5 of ظهر) Being protected, backed, supported. Pronouncing to a wife a kind of formula when repudiating her عليّ انت كظهر امّي *ɛalayya anti ka zahri ummī*, Upon me thou art like the back of my mother. Going any where at mid-day (ظهر *zuhr*).

A تظهير *tazhīr*, (v. n. 2 of ظهر) Pronouncing words importing a divorce. Throwing behind the back. Despising, slighting, neglecting. Forgetting. Entering upon or travelling in the noontide heat.

A تظيياً *tazyīɛ*, A vexing, distressing.

A تع *taɛ*, (for تعالي *taɛāla'*) The Most High.

A تعّ *taɛɛ*, (v. n. of تعّ) Stammering, breaking down. Stumbling in a sandy road. *Taɛɛ*, (and تعّة *taɛɛat*) Languor, laxness. A vomiting.

A تعابي *taɛābī*, A siding with a party.

A تعاتب *taɛātub*, (v. n. 6 of عتب) Expostulating with, recriminating, accusing one another.

A تعاتع *taɛātiɛ*, Idle words; fruitless deeds.

A تعاثث *taɛāsus*, A driving hard.

A تعاجل *taɛājul*, A making haste together.

A تعاجيب *taɛājīb*, Wonders.

A تعادّ *taɛādd*, The exceeding in number 1000.

A تعادي *taɛādī*, (v. n. 6 of عدا for عدو) Carrying on mutual hostilities. Contending in running. Going afar off. Disagreeing, differing. Being uneven (a place). Dying one after another. Uneven places. Discord, depravity. Distance.

A جرح تعار *jurhun taɛɛār*, A wound that cannot be stopped from bleeding.

A تعارّ *taɛārr*, (v. n. 6 of عرّ) Being waked from a dream, and tumbling in bed with exclamations or mutterings.

A تعارج *taɛāruj*, A going limpingly.

A تعارز *taɛāruz*, (v. n. 6 of عرز) Corrupting, vitiating. Being wrinkled, contracted, drawn together.

A تعارض *taɛāruz*, (v. n. 6 of عرض) Opposing, contradicting one another. Opposition, resistance.

A تعارف *taɛāruf*, (v. n. 6 of عرف) Knowing one another. Mutual acquaintance. Rule, fashion.

A تعازل *taɛāzul*, A retiring from each other.

A تعازي *taɛāzī*, (v. n. 6 of عزي) Condoling with one another, recommending patience to one another.

A تعاسر *taɛāsur*, (v. n. 6 of عسر) Being difficult, perplexed. Being hard and firm. Being mutually difficult and troublesome.

A تعاشر *taɛāshur*, (v. n. 6 of عشر) Associating together, living on terms of intimacy.

A تعاشق *taɛāshuk*, (v. n. 6 of عشق) Being in love with each other.

A تعاشي *taɛāshī*, (v. n. 6 of عشا for عشو) Feigning purblindness or ignorance.

A تعاشيب *taɛāshīb*, Different kinds of grasses and plants.

A تعاضّ *taɛāzz*, A biting one another.

A تعاضد *taɛāzud*, A helping each other.

A تعاطس *taɛātus*, (v. n. 6 of عطس) Making an effort to sneeze, sneezing voluntarily.

A تعاطف *taɛātuf*, (v. n. 6 of عطف) Having a mutual affection. Walking with a reeling, mincing, or swaggering gait.

A تعاطي *taɛātī*, (v. n. 6 of عطا for عطو) Taking any thing to eat or drink. Giving reciprocal presents. Taking with the hand. Giving the attention to, courageously attempting any thing. Taking what is not one's due. Perpetrating. Doing a good and noble deed. Raising one's self on tiptoe, and holding out the hand toward any thing. Contending, wrangling in taking.

A تعاظل *taɛāzul*, (v. n. 6 of عظل) Adhering, sticking fast when coupling (dogs or locusts).

A تعاظم *taɛāzum*, (v. n. 6 of عظم) Appearing great, weighty, important (business). Increasing in size, and being a match for.

A تعافّ *taɛāff*, (v. n. 6 of عفّ) Milking (a camel) twice. Taking medicine.

A تعافر *taɛāfur*, (v. n. 6 of عفر) Making white (the dish ثريد *sarīd*).

A تعافس *taɛāfus*, (v. n. 6 of عفس) Grasping one another in wrestling.

A تعافي *taɛāfī*, A recovering of health.

A تعاقب *taɛākub*, (v. n. 6 of عقب) Following, pursuing. Overtaking.

A تعاقد *taɛākud*, (v. n. 6 of عقد) Forming confederacies. Adhering (a dog and bitch).

A تعاقر *taɛākur*, (v. n. 6 of عقر) Wounding, hamstringing, or killing each other. Contending together who is the most expert at hamstringing.

A تعاقل *taɛākul*, (v. n. 6 of عقل) Pretending to knowledge. Contending for superiority of understanding. Contributing amongst themselves to expiate the shedding of blood, taking the fine upon themselves.

A تعاقم *taɛākum*, Succession (of day and night).

A تعاكر *taɛākur*, (v. n. 6 of عكر) Being mixed together (men) when quarrelling or fighting, intermingling their spears.

A تعاكظ *taɛākuz*, (v. n. 6 of عكظ) Contending for glory, boasting. Playing together. Disputing, jarring, fighting, wrangling. Lampooning, satirizing one another in verses at the fair of عكاظ *ɛukāz*.

A تعال *taɛāl*, Be exalted. Ascend! Come!

A تعالّ *taɛāll*, (v. n. 6 of علّ) Exhausting (a camel) towards the end of a journey by excessive driving. Recovering from childbirth.

A تعالج *taɛāluj*, (v. n. 6 of علج) Practising. Being employed about any thing. Striving together.

A تعالم *taɛālum*, (v. n. 6 of علم) Knowing an affair universally (all people).

A تعالى *taɛālī*, (v. n. 6 of علي) Being high, ascending. Coming, approaching, drawing near. Elevation. The third person preterite *taɛāla'* (which serves also for the optative, Be he exalted) is often joined to the name of God, and explained in an adjective sense: as, خداىٔ تعالى *khudāʼi taɛāla'*, The most high God. تعالى الله عن ذلك علوًّا كبيرًا *taɛāla' llāhu ɛan zālika ɛulūwan kabīran*, God be raised far above (such an imputation as) that!

A تعالين *taɛālayna*, Come along (ye women)!

A تعامس *taɛāmus*, (v. n. 6 of عمس) Feigning ignorance or negligence. Leaving any one in doubt and uncertainty.

A تعامش *taɛāmush*, (v. n. 6 of عمش) Neglecting, slighting, being inattentive.

A تعامه *taɛāmuh*, (v. n. 6 of عمه) Wandering in error: being bewildered in argument, losing one's way.

A تعامي *taɛāmī*, A feigning blindness.

A تعانق *taɛānuk*, An embracing each other.

A تعانيق *taɛānīk*, (pl. of تعنوق) Level grounds.

A تعاود *taɛāwud*, (v. n. 6 of عاد for عود) Running in a tumultuous manner to the general (an army); resorting to their own people. Turning against one another (parties). Inclining, leaning.

A تعاوذ *taɛāwuz*, (v. n. 6 of عاذ for عوذ) Fleeing for refuge to one another.

A تعاور *taɛāwur*, (v. n. 6 of عار for عور) Borrowing from one another. Speaking by turns.

A تعاوك *taɛāwuk*, A fighting among themselves.

A تعاون *taɛāwun*, An assisting each other.

A تعاوي *taɛāwī*, An assembling, flocking to.

A تعاويذ *taɛāwīz*, (pl. of تعويذ) Amulets, charms.

A تعاهد *taʻāhud*, (v. n. 6 of عهد) Confederating, covenanting, conspiring. Renewing a treaty. Managing the affairs of a kingdom. Writing out a treaty or covenant. Seeking for something lost. Visiting. Doing often.

A تعاهدات *taʻāhudāt*, (pl. of تعاهد) Conspiracies, mutual compacts, leagues, or agreements.

A تعاير *taʻāyur*, A reproaching each other.

A تعايش *taʻāyush*, A living together.

A تعايي *taʻāyi*, (v. n. 6 of عيّ) Being difficult, hindered, obstructed. Hesitating, being unequal to.

A تعب *taʻab*, Trouble. Labour. *Taʻib*, Tired.

A تعبان *taʻbān*, Fatigued, tired.

A تعبّب *taʻabbub*, A being given (to wine).

A تعبّد *taʻabbud*, (v. n. 5 of عبد) Receiving as a servant. Being pious, devout, cultivating devotional feelings. Over-fatiguing, overworking (a camel). Being refractory and stubborn (a camel). Excess of devotion, superstition.

A تعبّس *taʻabbus*, A scowling, looking grim.

A تعبشم *taʻabshum*, (v. n. 2 of عبشم Q) Belonging to the tribe of عبد شمس *ʻabd shams*.

A تعبعب *taʻabʻub*, (v. n. 2 of عبعب Q) Invading the whole. Destroying.

A تعبقس *taʻabkus*, (v. n. 2 of عبقس Q) Joining, claiming relationship, or tracing one's self to the tribe of عبد القيس *ʻabdu'l kays*.

A تعبئة *taʻbiʼat*, The drawing up of an army.

A تعبية *taʻbiyat*, (v. n. 2 of عبا for عبو) Arranging (household furniture). Fixing, laying up. Drawing up (soldiers) in array. P تعبيه كردن *taʻbiya kardan*, To fix.

A تعبيد *taʻbīd*, (v. n. 2 of عبد) Reducing to slavery. Going, flying all over the country. Delaying, hesitating. Taming, making quiet and gentle. Despising. Holding in honour.

A تعبير *taʻbīr*, (v. n. 2 of عبر) Crossing (a river). Causing to cross (a river). Explaining, interpreting (a dream). Telling what is in one's mind. Relating any thing for, or in the stead of, another. Reading (a book) in silence. Ruining, destroying. Shewing to another the heat of one's eyes. Pressing heavily upon one (business). Weighing (gold coins) one by one. Measuring (grain). Explanation, interpretation. P تعبير خواب *taʻbīri khwāb*, The interpretation of a dream. تعبير نامه *taʻbīr-nāma*, A book for teaching the interpretation of dreams.

P تعبيرگو *taʻbīr-go*, An interpreter of dreams.

A تعبيس *taʻbīs*, A frowning, knitting the brows.

A تعبيق *taʻbīk*, (v. n. 2 of عبق) Slaughtering. Kindling (a fire).

A تعبيل *taʻbīl*, (v. n. 2 of عبل) Putting a long broad point on an arrow.

A تعبيئ *taʻbīʼ*, (v. n. 2 of عبأ) Drawing up an army in military array.

A تعتاب *taʻtāb*, (v. n. of عتب) Reproaching, chiding. Hopping on one leg (a man), halting on three legs (a camel).

A تعتّب *taʻattub*, (v. n. 5 of عتب) Reviling, reproaching. Making a threshold (عتبة *ʻatabat*) for a door. Being angry.

A تعتّت *taʻattut*, (v. n. 5 of عتّ) Being inconstant, not persevering, or acting up to what one has spoken.

A تعتّد *taʻattud*, (v. n. 5 of عتد) Excelling (in any art), displaying great skill and neatness.

A تعترف *taʻatruf*, (v. n. 2 of عترف Q) Showing pride and haughtiness. The opposite of تعفرت.

A تعتع *taʻtaʻ*, A stuttering in the pronunciation of the letter ت or ف. Perturbation. (pl. تعاتع *taʻātiʻ*) False or foolish words; trifling actions. تع تع *tuʻ tuʻ*, (imper.) Abase yourself.

A تعتعة *taʻtaʻat*, (v. n. of تعتع Q) Stammering, stuttering. Sinking in the sand (a horse). Moving, shaking from side to side. Forcing one to do any thing against his will.

A تعتور *taʻatwur*, (v. n. 2 of عتور Q not used) Resembling, taking after, or being related to, the tribe of عتوارة *ʻitwārat*.

A تعتّه *taʻattuh*, (v. n. 5 of عته) Being furious, insane, or stupid. Feigning ignorance, stupidity, or insanity. Going to excess in dress, finery, and eating. Affecting neatness and cleanness. Madness, distraction.

A تعتّي *taʻattī*, A being exorbitant, proud.

A تعتيب *taʻtīb*, (v. n. 2 of عتب) Making a threshold (عتبة *ʻatabat*). Drawing together the waistband and folding it in front.

A تعتيد *taʻtīd*, (v. n. 2 of عتد) Preparing for.

A تعتيق *taʻtīk*, (v. n. 2 of عتق) Making old. Keeping long. Seizing with the teeth.

A تعتيم *taʻtīm*, (v. n. 2 of عتم) Delaying, hesitating. Doing any thing slowly and late. Abstaining from any thing to which one had been addicted. Collecting milk in the udder after the evening milking (cattle). Travelling late in the evening. Hovering over a man's head (a bird).

A تعثّر *taʻassur*, A stumbling, falling.

A تعثكل *taʻaskul*, (v. n. 2 of عثكل Q) Having many and entangled branches (a palm-tree).

A تعثلب *taʻaslub*, (v. n. 2 of عثلب Q) Being lean, in a bad condition.

A تعثيث *taʻsīs*, A shaking, modulating the voice.

A تعثير *taʻsīr*, (v. n. 2 of عثر) Causing to stumble or fall, tripping up.

A تعثين *taʻsīn*, (v. n. 2 of عثن) Perfuming. Emitting smoke. Mixing. Stirring up mischief.

A تعجابة *tiʻjābat*, A wonder-working man.

A تعجّب *taʻajjub*, (v. n. 5 of عجب) Being struck with astonishment. Inflaming and deceiving with love. Amazement, surprise, admiration.

A تعجّج *taʻajjuj*, (v. n. 5 of عجّ) Being full of smoke (a house).

A تعجّر *taʻajjur*, (v. n. 5 of عجر) Being wrinkled (the belly from fatness).

A تعجرف *taʻajruf*, (v. n. 2 of عجرف Q) Being troublesome, annoying, disgusting, having no sense of shame or reverence. Making haste. Being proud. Precipitancy, heedlessness.

A تعجّز *taʻajjuz*, (v. n. 5 of عجز) Mounting upon, or riding on the crupper (of a camel or a horse). Being folded and twisted.

A تعجّس *taʻajjus*, (v. n. 5 of عجس) Searching diligently, considering attentively the end or tendency of an affair. Following, dodging any one in his business. (Rain) continually moistening (the earth). Going out after midnight. Detaining, hindering, delaying. Remaining behind. Putting to the blush, reproaching. Being proud. Causing one to fail or come short.

A تعجّل *taʻajjul*, (v. n. 5 of عجل) Making haste. Exciting, ordering to make haste. Paying in advance. Making up اقط *akit* into pieces called عجاجيل *ʻajājīl*. Sending the new milk اعجالة *iʻjālat*. Taking quickly.

A تعجّلاً *taʻajjulan*, (P تعجّلانه) In haste, hastily.

A تعجلد *taʻajlud*, (v. n. 2 of عجلد Q) Being important and difficult (an affair).

A تعجّن *taʻajjun*, (v. n. 5 of عجن) Being fat.

A تعجّه *taʻajjuh*, (v. n. 5 of عجه not in use) Feigning ignorance. Being intricate (business).

A تعجهن *taʻajhun*, (v. n. 2 of عجهن Q) Being a servant, cook, sewer, or table-decker. Wooing a woman until her consent is obtained.

A تعجيب *taʻjīb*, A filling with astonishment.

A تعجية *taʻjiyat*, A turning away (of the face).

A تعجيج *taʻjīj*, (v. n. 2 of عجّ) Filling with smoke (a house). Raising the dust (wind).

A تعجيز *taʻjīz*, (v. n. 2 of عجز) Growing old (a woman). Having large buttocks. Regarding as weak, charging with weakness, imputing imbecility. Hindering, letting, keeping back.

A تعجيف *taʻjīf*, (v. n. 2 of عجف) Eating not to excess, stopping short of fulness. Abstaining, though hungry, that another may have enough.

A تعجيل *taʻjīl*, (v. n. 2 of عجل) Making haste. Hastening, urging, accelerating. Outstripping, getting before. Giving in advance, anticipating. Dressing meat quickly. Making up the new cheese اقط into pieces called عجاجيل *ʻajājīl*. Haste, despatch.

A تعجيلاً *taʻjīlan*, (P تعجيلانه) Hastily.

A تعجيم *taʻjīm*, (v. n. 2 of عجم) Dotting, pointing a letter or consonant.

A تعجيه *taʻjīh*, (v. n. 2 of عجه not in use) Endeavouring by sarcasms to promote a quarrel.

A تعداء *taʻdāʼ*, The act of running.

A تعداد *taʻdād*, Numbering, enumeration. Computation. P تعداد نمودن *taʻdād namūdan*, To count.

A تعدّد *taʻaddud*, (v. n. 5 of عدّ) Exceeding in number (1000).

A تعدّف *taʻadduf*, An eating, a tasting.

A تعدّي *taʻaddī*, (v. n. 5 of عدا for عدو) Passing from one to another, leaving. Transgressing, being unjust. Finding milk which renders one independent of wine, or pasture that saves one from purchasing provender. Receiving a dowry with a wife. Being active, transitive (a verb). Being infected with a contagion, and communicating it to another. Tyranny, oppression, excess, violence.

A تعدية *taʻdiyat*, (v. n. 2 of عدا for عدو) Causing to pass, transmitting. Averting, diverting from. Converting a neuter into an active verb. The transitive or active signification of a verb.

A تعديد *taʻdīd*, (v. n. 2 of عدّ) Counting with the utmost accuracy and strictness. Disposing in order, arranging, preparing (for a future occasion).

A تعديق *taʻdīk*, (v. n. 2 of عدق) Being uncertain, irresolute as to what to think, do, or ask. Letting down into a well a crooked instrument for drawing any thing out.

A تعديل *taʻdīl*, (v. n. 2 of عدل) Rectifying, straightening, adjusting. Justifying. Making one (scale) equal to another. Having one's belly as big as one side of a load from drinking. Considering as lawful (witnesses, proofs, &c.). Equation.

A تعدين *taʻdīn*, (v. n. 2 of عدن) Dunging (ground). Being filled (a drinker). Striking the ground with a pointed hammer or pickaxe.

A تعذّر *taʻazzur*, (v. n. 5 of عذر) Being difficult. Being impossible. Not going on straight-forwardly (a business). Being stained, besmeared with dung. Being defaced, obliterated. Making an apology for one's self and running away. Remaining behind.

A تعذفر *taʻazfur*, A being provoked to anger.

A تعذّل *taʻazzul*, (v. n. 5 of عذل) Bearing reprehension, taking reproof.

A تعذلق *taʻazluk*, (v. n. 2 of عذلق Q) Shaking one's self in walking.

A تعذيب *taʻzīb*, (v. n. 2 of عذب) Punishing, scourging, tormenting. Hindering. Punishment.

A تعذير *taʻzīr*, (v. n. 2 of عذر) Making an apology, advancing a false and inadmissible excuse. Besmearing with dung. Preparing a circumcision-feast, and inviting guests thereto. Effacing (the vestiges of a house). Beginning to appear (down upon a boy's cheek).

A تعذيق *taʻzīk*, A lopping branches (of a palm).

A تعذيل *taʻzīl*, A blaming, chiding. Reproof.

A تعر *taʻr*, (v. n. of تعر) Shouting, crying aloud. *Taʻar*, Heat of war or battle.

A تعرّب *taʻarrub*, (v. n. 5 of عرب) Being Arabic, or Arabian. Becoming like an Arabian. Sojourning in the desert. Talking obscenely.

A تعرّج *taʻarruj*, (v. n. 5 of عرج) Having an oblique, scalene, or irregular form (a building). Tying or confining (a beast) in the stable.

A تعرّز *taʻarruz*, (v. n. 5 of عرز) Being obdurate, hardened. Being difficult, hard, painful (business). Detaining hospitably.

A تعرّس *taʻarrus*, (v. n. 5 of عرس) Showing love (for a wife). Uxoriousness.

A تعرّش *taʻarrush*, (v. n. 5 of عرش) Fixing a residence. Being addicted to, fond of.

A تعرّص *taʻarrus*, A staying, an abiding.

A تعرّض *taʻarruz*, (v. n. 5 of عرض) Happening, occuring. Coming before, presenting one's self. Being exposed. Opposing, hindering, withstanding. Being curved, oblique, crooked, or angular. Walking from side to side in climbing a mountain (a camel). Going in the footsteps. Opposition, obstacle, impediment. Oppression, injury, loss. P تعرّض كردن *taʻarruz kardan*, To oppose, hinder, prevent. To injure, oppress.

A تعرعر *taʻarʻur*, (v. n. 2 of عرعر Q) Being afflicted with the disease عرّ *ʻurr* (a camel).

A تعرّف *taʻarruf*, (v. n. 5 of عرف) Inquiring with the view to learn, or till one learns any thing. Seeking knowledge.

A تعرّق *taʻarruk*, (v. n. 5 of عرق) Picking the flesh from the bone. Getting the antagonist's head under one's arm and throwing him down (in wrestling). Being benefited, profited.

A تعرقب *taʻarkub*, (v. n. 2 of عرقب Q) Walking through narrow, winding mountain-passes. Deviating, turning aside.

A تعرّم *taʻarrum*, (v. n. 5 of عرم) Picking a bone; barking a tree.

A تعروش *taʻarwush*, (v. n. 2 of عروش Q) Being fond of, addicted to, cleaving unto. Mounting upon, riding (a horse).

A تعرّي *taʻarrī*, (v. n. 5 of عري) Being naked, denuded, or free. Stripping one's self.

A تعريب *taʻrīb*, (v. n. 2 of عرب) Pronouncing Arabic agreeably to the rules. Conforming a foreign word to the Arabic idiom. Polishing, arranging a discourse accurately. Speaking plainly. Making an Arabian bow. Relating words as spoken by another. Adducing an argument in favour of any one. Speaking indecently. Reproving. Using one opprobriously. Giving earnest. Making (a squeamish stomach) sick. Cutting off the broken branch of a palm-tree. Cutting open or lancing and cauterizing (a sore). Inflaming a cow (as a bull). Drinking a quantity of clear water.

A تعرية *taʻriyat*, (v. n. 2 of عرا for عرو) Putting ears or handles to (a wallet). (v. n. 2 of عري) Laying bare, exposing, stripping, denuding.

A تعريج *taʻrīj*, (v. n. 2 of عرج) Being intent upon, attending to. Rearing an irregular or oblique structure. Causing to lean. Staying (with a host, hospitably entertained). Detaining, confining at an inn. Reaching the hour of sunset.

A تعريد *taʻrīd*, (v. n. 2 of عرد) Fleeing, running away. Piercing, passing through any thing struck (an arrow). Quitting (the road). Rising (a star), being at its highest altitude, and declining to set.

A تعريز *taʻrīz*, (v. n. 2 of عرز) Hiding, concealing. Corrupting, vitiating. Being wrinkled, contracted. Being ambiguous, speaking enigmatically.

A تعريس *taʻrīs*, (v. n. 2 of عرس) Alighting (travellers) in the end of the night for refreshment, and then pursuing a journey. ليلة التعريس *laylatu't taʻrīs*, The night the prophet went to sleep.

A تعريش *taʻrīsh*, (v. n. 2 of عرش) Making a vine-arbour; propping (a vine). Training a vine over a trellis. Roofing (a house). Proceeding slowly in an affair. Remaining constantly lighted (fire-wood). Raising the head when braying (an ass about to cover).

A تعريص *taʻrīs*, (v. n. 2 of عرص) Putting rafters on a house in order to roof it.

A تعريض *taʻrīz*, (v. n. 2 of عرض) Enlarging, extending, making broad. Setting a broad mark upon. Giving a broad hint. Making conspicuous. Rendering obnoxious, exposing. Opposing. Being constant and unremitting in eating yearling kids (عرضان *ʻirzān*). Giving provisions by way of reward. Selling goods for any thing except money. Being ambiguous in speech, speaking enigmatically. Being possessed of eloquence. Laying one thing upon another crosswise. Making writing illegible. Not dressing meat enough.

A تعريف *taʻrīf*, (v. n. 2 of عرف) Making known, signifying. Giving information to the owner of any thing lost. Making definite or determinate, determining. Imparting an agreeable odour, perfuming. Seeking for any thing lost. Staying on Mount Arafāt from religious motives. Affirmation, assertion. Explanation, notification, definition. A tariff. تعريف لفظي *taʻrīfi lafzī*, Verbal definition or explanation: as when the unusual word غضنفر *ghazanfar*, meaning A lion, is explained by the more familiar term اسد *asad*.

A تعريفات *taʻrīfāt*, (pl. of تعريف) Definitions.

A تعريفيّ *taʻrīfīy*, Commendable, notable.

A تعريق *taʻrīk*, (v. n. 2 of عرق) Diluting (wine) with a little water. Filling (a vessel) not to the brim.

A تعريك *taʻrīk*, (v. n. 2 of عرك) Pinching, wringing hard, pressing, squeezing.

A تعريم *taʻrīm*, A mixing, intermingling.

A تعزّ *taʻizz*, Name of the capital of Yaman.

A تعزّب *taʻazzub*, (v. n. 5 of عزب) Being in a state of celibacy, abstaining from matrimony.

A تعزّز *taʻazzuz*, (v. n. 5 of عزّ) Being rendered powerful. Becoming rare or exquisite. Making one's self inaccessible. Being firm (as flesh). Having a small orifice to the teat (a camel).

A تعزعز *taʻazʻuz*, (v. n. 2 of عزعز Q) Going off when spoken to (a goat).

A تعزّل *taʻazzul*, (v. n. 5 of عزل) Being removed from office. Receding, retiring. Seceding, discarding.

A تعزّم *taɛazzum*, (v. n. 5 of عزم) Pursuing with steadiness, applying the mind. Striving.

A تعزوة *taɛzuwat*, Patience.

A تعزيْ *taɛza'*, A word expressive of a desire to conciliate affection.

A تعزّي *taɛazzī*, (v. n. 5 of عزا for عزو) Belonging, claiming relationship, professing to belong (whether truly or falsely). A being consoled.

A تعزيب *taɛzīb*, A going to a distant pasture.

A تعزية *taɛziyat*, (v. n. 2 of عزي) Consoling. Enjoining or recommending patience. Mourning for the dead. A representation of the shrines of Hasan and Husayn, sons of Alīy. P تعزيت كردن *taɛziyat kardan*, To console, condole.

P تعزيت پرسي *taɛziyat-pursī*, Condolence.

P تعزيت نامه *taɛziyat-nāma*, Note of condolence.

A تعزير *taɛzīr*, (v. n. 2 of عزر) Reproving, censuring. Assisting, strengthening, reinforcing. Honouring, magnifying. Beating, inflicting stripes below the full number appointed by law.

A تعزيز *taɛzīz*, (v. n. 2 of عزّ) Rendering powerful, glorious, victorious, excellent, rare, precious, magnificent. Strengthening, backing. Making difficult and painful. Moistening the earth sufficiently (rain).

A تعزيل *taɛzīl*, A deposing (from office).

A تعزيم *taɛzīm*, (v. n. 2 of عزم) Reading verses of the Kur'ān as preventives against enchantments.

A تعس *taɛs*, (v. n. of تعس) Perishing. Stumbling, falling, sinking, descending. Destroying any one (God). Perdition, ruin, destruction. A fall, trip, stumble. Evil. Distance. تعساً لك *taɛsan lah*, Perdition catch thee! تعست العجلة *taɛisati'l ɛajalat*, Out upon haste! *Taɛis*, Perishing.

A تعسّر *taɛassur*, (v. n. 5 of عسر) Being difficult. Being obscure, inexplicable (a passage).

A تعسعس *taɛasɛus*, (v. n. 2 of عسعس Q) Hunting for, or catching (game). Smelling out.

A تعسّف *taɛassuf*, (v. n. 5 of عسف) Straying, losing one's way. Oppressing. Oppression, extortion.

A تعسّق *taɛassuk*, (v. n. 5 of عسق) Adhering. Being assiduous, keeping close.

A تعسّن *taɛassun*, (v. n. 5 of عسن) Resembling one's father. Searching diligently the vestige or place of any thing. Producing some vegetation.

A تعسير *taɛsīr*, (v. n. 2 of عسر) Rendering difficult. Opposing. Cocking (her) tail in running (a she-camel). Coming from the left.

A تعسيف *taɛsīf*, A forcing to toil and drudge.

A تعسيل *taɛsīl*, (v. n. 2 of عسل) Giving honey. Dressing victuals, or making sweetmeats with honey. Making and storing honey in the hive (bees).

A تعسين *taɛsīn*, (v. n. 2 of عسن) Lightening (a camel) of a part of (his) fat (a season of scarcity).

A تعشّب *taɛashshub*, (v. n. 5 of عشب) Pasturing on green herbage. Becoming fat (camels).

A تعشّق *taɛashshuk*, (v. n. 5 of عشق) Making demonstrations of love.

A تعشّم *taɛashshum*, A drying up, a withering.

A تعشّن *taɛashshun*, (v. n. 5 of عشن) Seeking carefully for those dates which are gathered from the roots of the branches, after the clusters are cut off.

A تعشنط *taɛashnut*, (v. n. 2 of عشنط Q) Continually scolding and rating her husband (a shrew).

A تعشّي *taɛashshī*, (v. n. 5 of عشي) Supping, eating supper. Pasturing by night. Being blind at night. P تغدّي و تعشّي كردن *taghaddī u taɛashshī kardan*, To dine and sup.

A تعشيب *taɛshīb*, (v. n. 2 of عشب) Being luxuriant in herbage, producing fresh grass.

A تعشية *taɛshiyat*, (v. n. 2 of عشي) Giving a supper. Giving (camels) their supper. Dazzling the eyes of birds in the night-time by a blaze of light, and thereby catching them. Proceeding slowly, dealing gently with.

A تعشير *taɛshīr*, (v. n. 2 of عشر) Decimating. Dividing into ten. Receiving tithes. Marking or distinguishing any thing by tens (as the verses of the Kur'ān). Emitting ten snores when braying (an ass), or cawing thus (a raven). Being already ten months gone with young (a camel).

A تعشيش *taɛshīsh*, (v. n. 2 of عشّ) Having a slender trunk and few branches (a palm-tree). Building a nest (a bird). Becoming dry and mouldy (bread). Becoming dry (fodder or ground).

A تعشين *taɛshīn*, A conjecturing, guessing.

A تعص *taɛas*, (v. n. of تعص) Having a cramp in the tendon of the leg from over-walking. A spasm, cramp, contraction.

A تعصّب *taɛassub*, (v. n. 5 of عصب) Binding the head with a fillet. Girding one's waist tight through hunger. Being content (with any thing). Being attached to one's kindred. Partiality, attachment: bigotry, obstinacy: severity, inflexibility.

A تعصّر *taɛassur*, (v. n. 5 of عصر) Being squeezed. Taking refuge.

A تعصفر *taɛasfur*, (v. n. 2 of عصفر Q) Being dyed saffron-colour (a garment). Being bent (the neck).

A تعصود *taɛaswud*, A shouting and fighting.

A تعصوصة *tuɛsūsat*, A white, shining insect.

A تعصّي *taɛassī*, A being hard and difficult.

A تعصيب *taɛsīb*, (v. n. 2 of عصب) Binding the head with a fillet. Appointing one as chief or head of a family. Keeping one hungry, famishing. Reducing people to misery (a scarce year). Destroying. Causing an individual to inherit what should be divided amongst those relations who are included in the term عصبة *ɛasabat*.

A تعصية *taɛsiyat*, The giving of a stick.

A تعصير *taɛsīr*, (v. n. 2 of عصر) Coming in the afternoon. Bringing forth. Arriving at the age of puberty (a girl). Staying at home on account of menses. Putting forth the ear (corn).

A تعصيص *taɛsīs*, (v. n. 2 of عصّ) Being hard and severe (towards a debtor).

A تعصيل *taɛsīl*, A delaying. A being crooked.

A تعضّل *taɛazzul*, (v. n. 5 of عضل) Being difficult, perplexing, and baffling (a medical case).

A تعضوض *taɛzūz*, A kind of black sweet date.

A تعضوضة *taɛzūzat*, Narrow (woman).

A تعضية *taɛziyat*, A dividing, dismembering.

A تعضيد *taɛzīd*, (v. n. 2 of عضد) Going right and left (an arrow).

A تعضيض *taɛzīz*, (v. n. 2 of عضّ) Biting the lips in anger. Biting hard. Feeding one's camel's on the preparation عضّ *ɛuzz*. Drawing water from a narrow well. Playing, sporting with one's maid.

A تعضيل *taɛzīl*, (v. n. 2 of عضل) Having a difficult, painful birth. Laying with difficulty (a hen). Being too narrow for its inhabitants (a country). Hindering, straitening, perplexing. Tyrannically hindering (a woman) from marrying.

A تعطّر *taɛattur*, (v. n. 5 of عطر) Perfuming one's self. Being perfumed. Dwelling in her father's house (an unmarried girl).

A تعطّش *taɛattush*, (v. n. 5 of عطش) Enduring voluntary thirst.

A تعطّط *taɛattut*, (v. n. 5 of عطّ) Being torn lengthwise (a garment).

A تعطّف *taɛattuf*, (v. n. 5 of عطف) Being indulgent, propitious, favourably inclined. Commiserating. Putting on (a cloak).

A تعطّل *taɛattul*, (v. n. 5 of عطل) Being idle, unemployed, and disengaged. Having no bracelets or other ornaments (a woman).

A تعطّن *taɛattun*, (v. n. 5 of عطن) Lying down near the well (camels that have drunk their fill).

A تعطّي *taɛattī*, (v. n. 5 of عطا for عطو) Begging a present. Making haste. Giving attention to, attempting.

A تعطيب *taɛtīb*, (v. n. 2 of عطب) Medicating wine to give it an agreeable scent. The appearance of spurs on a vine.

A تعطية *taɛtiyat*, (v. n. 2 of عطا for عطو) Working for, serving. Bidding to hasten, accelerating.

A تعطير *taɛtīr*, A perfuming, diffusing odours.

A تعطيس *taɛtīs*, A causing to sneeze.

A تعطيش *taɛtīsh*, (v. n. 2 of عطش) Keeping long from drink. Making thirsty.

A تعطيط *taɛtīt*, (v. n. 2 of عطّ) Tearing (a garment) lengthwise without separation.

A تعطيف *taɛtīf*, (v. n. 2 of عطف) Bending (wood). Converting one garment into a covering for another person. Regarding, favouring. Inducing (a camel) to take a liking to another's colt. Doubling, folding (a pillow).

A تعطيل *taɛtīl*, (v. n. 2 of عطل) Causing to be unemployed. Rendering useless. Taking off her ornaments (a woman). Leaving free, vacant, and empty, emptying. Leaving out every letter that is marked with a diacritical point. Laying waste. Vacation, holiday.

A تعطين *taʻtīn*, (v. n. 2 of عطن) Macerating (a hide) with dung and salt to bring off the hair. Constructing a fold for camels or sheep hard by a watering-place. Drinking their fill and lying down.

A تعطعط *taʻaṭʻuṭ*, (v. n. 2 of عطعط Q) Wavering, or turning in the flight (an arrow). Wagging the tail and travelling uneasily. Retiring, retreating from battle, swerving through cowardice. Going up (a hill).

A تعطّل *taʻaṭṭul*, (v. n. 5 of عطل) Assembling together (people). Riding upon one another.

A تعطلم *taʻaṭlum*, A being very dark (the night).

A تعظّم *taʻazzum*, (v. n. 5 of عظم) Carrying one's self haughtily. Accounting one to be great, dignified, exalted. Magnificence, grandeur, pride.

A تعظيب *taʻzīb*, (v. n. 2 of عظب) Putting off, delaying, promising again and again to do a thing.

A تعظيل *taʻzīl*, A flowing from all quarters.

A تعظيم *taʻzīm*, (v. n. 2 of عظم) Making great, enlarging. Magnifying, honouring. Cutting up (a sheep) bone by bone. Reverence, respect, honour. Ceremonious and respectful treatment.

P تعظيم كردن *taʻzīm kardan*, To honour, magnify.

A تعظيما *taʻzīman*, In honour of. تعظيما لشانه *taʻzīman li shānihi*, From respect to his dignity.

A تعفّج *taʻaffuj*, A going obliquely.

A تعفّر *taʻaffur*, (v. n. 5 of عفر) Being rolled in, or soiled with, dust. Becoming fat (a wild animal).

A تعفرت *taʻafrut*, (v. n. 2 of عفرت Q) Acting in a powerful, independent manner. Doing any thing attentively, artfully, or masterly. Being a demon. Manifesting demonical propensities, playing the devil, behaving like an عفريت *ʻifrīt*.

A تعفّف *taʻaffuf*, (v. n. 5 of عفّ) Being chaste, abstaining from what is forbidden, and from asking questions. Taking pains, striving to shew purity. Drinking milk remaining in the udder.

A تعفّق *taʻaffuk*, (v. n. 5 of عفق) Fleeing unto, taking refuge. Lying hid behind any thing.

A تعفّن *taʻaffun*, (v. n. 5 of عفن) Becoming putrid, rotten, and falling to pieces (a rope).

A تعفّي *taʻaffī*, A being obliterated, effaced.

A تعفية *taʻfiyat*, (v. n. 2 of عفا for عفو) Obliterating, defacing. Amending, restoring, adjusting. Falling upon one (any thing deadly).

A تعفير *taʻfīr*, (v. n. 2 of عفر) Rolling (one) in the dust: sprinkling or soiling with dust. Burying in the ground. Rubbing the nipple with a kind of earth to wean a child. Putting (meat) amongst dust and drying it in the sun. Mixing the black cattle of a flock with those of a reddish white. Making white, marking of a white colour. Keeping the teat from its young in order to wean it (a beast).

A تعفيص *taʻfīs*, A dyeing with gall-apples.

A تعفيف *taʻfīf*, (v. n. 2 of عفّ) Giving one to drink milk remaining in the udder.

A تعفيق *taʻfīk*, (v. n. 2 of عفق) Driving back one over the other (a flock of sheep).

A تعفيل *taʻfīl*, (v. n. 2 of عفل) Remedying or treating surgically a female rupture (عفل *ʻafal*). Ascribing to any one such a complaint.

A تعفين *taʻfīn*, (v. n. 2 of عفن) Corrupting (meat), tainting, causing (it) to stink.

A تعقّب *taʻakkub*, (v. n. 5 of عقب) Considering the end or tendency of any thing. Doubting the truth of a statement, and inquiring a second time. Railing against, or inquiring into, a man's vices. Punishing one for a fault. Doubting and tracing intelligence. Learning the happy event of one's good advice.

A تعقبل *taʻakbul*, A following, coming behind.

A تعقّد *taʻakkud*, (v. n. 5 of عقد) Being arched (the rainbow). Being narrow at bottom and wide at top (a well). Being knotted and entangled. Being heaped up (as sand). Being thick and concrete (must or honey).

A تعقّر *taʻakkur*, (v. n. 5 of عقر) Continuing (a widely-spread rain). Filling up every part compactly (fat on a camel's body). Being long (a plant).

A تعقّف *taʻakkuf*, A being curved, bent, crooked.

A تعقفر *taʻakfur*, Being overwhelmed, ruined.

A تعقّل *taʻakkul*, (v. n. 5 of عقل) Foreseeing, comprehending, understanding. Coming to one's senses. Joining the hands and intermixing the fingers. Sitting cross-legged.

A تعقّم *taʻakkum*, (v. n. 5 of عقم) Going to and fro, prowling about.

A تعقيب *taʻkīb*, (v. n. 2 of عقب) Following, coming closely behind. Looking back, waiting, expecting, lingering. Leaving behind. Doing any thing twice. Delaying, procrastinating. Being diligent, going to and fro, in searching after any thing. Having finished one excursion against the infidel, to undertake another the same year. Remaining in the mosque after the hour of public prayer is over. Receiving a substitute or equivalent. Turning yellow, and beginning to dry (the fruit of the plant عرفج *ʻarfaj*).

A تعقية *taʻkiyat*, (v. n. 2 of عقي) Giving a new-born infant something to make it void its excrement. Shooting an arrow in the air. Soaring high (a bird).

A تعقيد *taʻkīd*, (v. n. 2 of عقد) Setting (as fruit). Building an arch and any thing which connects the different parts of an edifice. Swearing with due consideration, without any reserve. Boiling (a thing) till it becomes thick.

A تعقير *taʻkīr*, A wounding desperately.

A تعقيف *taʻkīf*, A making crooked or curved.

A تعقيل *taʻkīl*, (v. n. 2 of عقل) Being intellectual. Rendering intelligent. Ascribing intellect to any one. Tying a camel's leg near to the knee. Bringing forth sour grapes (a vine).

A تعقيم *taʻkīm*, (v. n. 2 of عقم) Commanding silence. Rendering (the womb) unfit for conception.

A تعكّب *taʻakkub*, (v. n. 5 of عكب) not in use) Crowding upon one and rendering anxious (cares).

A تعكبس *taʻakbus*, (v. n. 2 of عكبس Q) Being mounted or piled (one thing upon another).

A تعكبش *taʻakbush*, (v. n. 2 of عكبش Q) Sticking, holding fast (a thorn).

A تعكّر *taʻakkur*, A being turbid, disturbed.

A تعكّز *taʻakkuz*, (v. n. 5 of عكز) Leaning upon a ferruled stick or crutch (عكّازة *ʻukkāzat*).

A تعكّيس *taʻakkus*, A crawling like a viper.

A تعكّش *taʻakkush*, (v. n. 5 of عكش) Being difficult. Being contracted and entering into itself. Being entangled, curled, and heaped together (hair). Contracting the legs to weave his web (a spider).

A تعكّص *taʻakkus*, (v. n. 5 of عكص) Being avaricious and parsimonious; refusing to give.

A تعكّظ *taʻakkuz*, (v. n. 5 of عكظ) Being perplexed, intricate, and difficult. Being confined, or confining one's self, in order to look after one's affairs. Being long, toilsome, and painful (a journey).

A تعكّف *taʻakkuf*, (v. n. 5 of عكف) Being curled (hair). Restraining one's self.

A تعكّن *taʻakkun*, (v. n. 5 of عكن obsol.) Being wrinkled (from fat) lying fold upon fold.

A تعكيب *taʻkīb*, (v. n. 2 of عكب) Smoking.

A تعكية *taʻkiyat*, (v. n. 2 of عكا for عكو) Wrapping round with a fresh sinew (the handle of a spear). (v. n. 2 of عكي) Dying.

A تعكير *taʻkīr*, (v. n. 2 of عكر) Making dirty, rendering impure, feculent, and muddy.

A تعكيز *taʻkīz*, (v. n. 2 of عكز) Strengthening the end (of a spear with a ferrule of iron).

A تعكيش *taʻkīsh*, A becoming mouldy.

A تعكيظ *taʻkīz*, (v. n. 2 of عكظ) Interrupting, diverting from. Preventing the execution of any business. Enjoining diligently, enforcing (an admonition, will, or testament).

A تعكيف *taʻkīf*, (v. n. 2 of عكف) Being threaded (pearls). Being plaited (hair).

A تعكيم *taʻkīm*, (v. n. 2 of عكم) Becoming fat.

A تعل *taʻal*, Violent heat in the throat, heart-burn.

A تعلامة *tiʻlāmat*, A very learned man. A skilful genealogist.

A تعلّة *taʻillat*, Whatever amuses or diverts the attention from any pursuit. Any thing employed as an excuse or pretext.

A تعلّث *taʻallus*, (v. n. 5 of علث) Being suspended, hanging. Deceiving, laying snares. Doing (any work) loosely and badly. Delaying, deferring to enforce the statutes.

A تعلثم *taʻalsum*, Delay, hesitation in speaking.

A تعلّج *taʻalluj*, (v. n. 5 of علج) Being thick and rough (flesh). Bearing a message. Being heaped together (sands).

A تعلعل *taʻalʻul*, (v. n. 2 of علعل Q) Tottering,

shaking, staggering: being irresolute. Being relaxed.

A تعلق taʻalluk, (v. n. 5 of علق) Being suspended to, dependent upon. Being devoted, wholly given up to. Suspending, putting off. Being content with little. Dependance, connexion. Parentage, relationship. Property, possession. A manor, lordship. A lease in perpetuity. A small zamīndārī, a talook or division of a district.

A تعلّقات taʻallukāt, (pl. of تعلّق taʻalluk) Dependencies, connexions, appurtenances, estates, substance, attachments, claims. تعلّقات دنيويّ taʻallukāti dunyawīy, Worldly concerns.

P تعلّقدار taʻalluk-dār, One who holds a talook.

A تعلّقه taʻalluka, Connexion, relationship. Lordship, possession of land. A see, manor.

P تعلّقه دار taʻalluka-dār, Possessor of an estate, lord of a manor, landlord, feoffee.

A تعلّل taʻallul, (v. n. 5 of علّ) Recovering from childbed (a woman). Being contented, satisfied. Being occupied with. Amusing one's self innocently, beguiling the time.

A تعلّم taʻallum, (v. n. 5 of علم) Submitting to be taught. Learning. Knowing. Doing any thing well. تعليم و تعلّم taʻlīm u taʻallum, Teaching and learning.

A تعلمة tiʻlimat, A very learned man. A skilful genealogist.

A تعلوط taʻalwut, A hugging, clinging to.

A تعلّي taʻallī, (v. n. 5 of علا for علو) Being high, above, over, or superior to. Ascending by degrees, slowly and softly. Recovering (from childbed labour, or from sickness).

A تعليب taʻlīb, (v. n. 2 of علب) Signing, marking, making an impression. Cutting. Scraping, erasing. Aiming at the nerve of a camel's neck with the sharp part of a sword. Wrapping the sinew of a camel's neck round the haft of a sword.

A تعلية taʻliyat, (v. n. 2 of علا for علو) Elevating, raising, pulling, or hoisting up. Unloading goods from a beast's back. Ascending, surmounting, being superior. Putting the title to a book.

A تعليس taʻlīs, (v. n. 2 of علس) Giving to taste. Increasing, making greater inroads (a disease). Being clamorous and noisy.

A تعليص taʻlīs, (v. n. 2 of علص) Griping the belly (indigestion).

A تعليط taʻlīt, (v. n. 2 of علط) Making a deep transverse mark upon a (camel's) neck. Taking a chain from off the neck. Speaking evil of.

A تعليف taʻlīf, (v. n. 2 of علف) Tying a knot. Being scattered (the blossom of the tree طلح talh). Beginning to put forth its berries (the acacia).

A تعليق taʻlīk, (v. n. 2 of علق) Suspending, hanging. Delaying. Shutting, fastening (a door). Captivating, or being captivated by love. Sending with any one a camel for carrying provisions. Giving corn to a horse. The Persian character called talīk (properly taʻlīk).

A تعليك taʻlīk, (v. n. 2 of علك) Making a proper use of money, managing property well. Tanning well (a leathern bottle). Holding fast (money).

A تعليل taʻlīl, (v. n. 2 of علّ) Soothing, quieting, amusing, diverting. Quenching, saturating after being saturated. Gathering fruit time after time. Causality, causation. حرف التعليل harfu't taʻlīl, A causal particle.

A تعليم taʻlīm, (v. n. 2 of علم) Teaching, instructing, informing. Erudition, instruction, tuition. Marking, distinguishing.

P تعليم خانه taʻlīm-khāna, A school.

P تعليم گر taʻlīmgar, A teacher, instructor.

A تعمّج taʻammuj, (v. n. 5 of عمج) Writhing, going tortuously (a serpent). An obliquity in walking.

A تعمّد taʻammud, (v. n. 5 of عمد) Doing deliberately. Designing, intending, purposing.

A تعمّدا taʻammudan, Deliberately, purposely.

A تعمّق taʻammuk, (v. n. 5 of عمق) Speaking profoundly and mysteriously. Being elegant and nice in one's apparel. Deepness. Penetration.

A تعمّل taʻammul, (v. n. 5 of عمل) Studying, applying to, labouring, toiling, taking pains. (in grammar) The application of the radical sense of a noun to a verbal use; as, from ترس turs, A shield, تترّس tatarrasa, He armed himself with a shield.

A تعمّم taʻammum, (v. n. 5 of عمّ) Putting on a turban. Calling (one) uncle.

A تعمّي taʻammī, (v. n. 5 of عمي) Being blind.

A تعمية taʻmiyat, (v. n. 2 of عمي) Blinding. Making obscure and enigmatical (a verse or sentence). Blindness. Obscurity. P درزبان تعميه dar zabāni taʻmiya, In enigmatical language.

A تعميت taʻmīt, (v. n. 2 of عمت) Clewing (wool) round the hand (preparatory to spinning).

A تعميد taʻmīd, (v. n. 2 of عمد) Arresting, blocking up, damming (a current). Baptizing.

A تعمير taʻmīr, (v. n. 2 of عمر) Repairing, mending. Rebuilding. Making habitable, cultivated, and populous. Granting long life. Praying to God to bless with a long life. Swearing, adjuring. Ascribing long duration to, characterizing by perpetuity. Praising God. Studying, reading. Restraining one's self from worldly conversation. Keeping clean and pure. Enlightening with a lamp. Measuring for one's self a fixed measure. Granting one (any thing) for his life. Excellent spinning and weaving.

A تعميش taʻmīsh, (v. n. 2 of عمش) Being purposely negligent and remiss. Healing. Making fat. Removing weakness and disease of the eye.

A تعميق taʻmīk, (v. n. 2 of عمق) Making deep, deepening. Penetrating deeper, pushing farther. Being far-sighted.

A تعميل taʻmīl, (v. n. 2 of عمل) Appointing one governor of a province or collector of revenue. Giving an employment. Paying hire for work.

A تعميم taʻmīm, (v. n. 2 of عمّ) Rendering universal. Comprehending, reaching all. Crowning with a turban. Setting (any one) over a nation (particularly the Arabs). Frothing (milk).

A تعمين taʻmīn, (v. n. 2 of عمن) Travelling towards عمان ʻumān or عمّان ʻammān. Entering into or abiding (in one place).

A تعميه taʻmīh, (v. n. 2 of عمه) Oppressing, treating harshly with injustice.

A تعنّت taʻannut, (v. n. 5 of عنت) Seeking the depression or destruction (of an adversary).

A تعنفص taʻanfus, Lightness. Boast. Pride, arrogance, vain-glory, vanity.

A تعنّق taʻannuk, (v. n. 5 of عنق) Entering his hole (a field-mouse). Hiding her head and neck in her form (a hare). Laying the hand on the neck (عنق ʻunk, ʻunuk, or ʻunuk) of each other.

A تعنقش taʻankush, (v. n. 2 of عنقش Q) Being bent, twisted. Becoming strong, robust, strengthened.

A تعنّك taʻannuk, (v. n. 5 of عنك) Being difficult to pass (sands).

A تعنكث taʻankus, An assembling together.

A تعنكش taʻankush, (v. n. 2 of عنكش Q) Being contracted. Being matted together (hair).

A تعنوق tuʻnūk, (pl. تعانيق) Level ground.

A تعنّي taʻannī, (v. n. 5 of عني) Fatiguing. Toiling, enduring toil and trouble. Enduring evil with all its consequences. Being tired. Resisting roughly. Contending, opposing, litigating. Bestowing pains. Being anointed with a liniment composed of urine and dung (a scabby camel).

A تعنيب taʻnīb, (v. n. 2 of عنب) Bearing clusters of grapes (a vine).

A تعنية taʻniyat, (v. n. 2 of عنا for عنو) Afflicting. Taking or detaining a captive. Smearing a mangy (camel) with a mixture of dung and urine. The mixture itself. (v. n. 2 of عني) Fatiguing. Prefixing a title or frontispiece to a book.

A تعنيت taʻnīt, (v. n. 2 of عنت) Leading (one) into trouble, forcing (him) into difficulties whence he cannot extricate himself.

A تعنيس taʻnīs, (v. n. 2 of عنس) Remaining, or being detained long in her parent's house unmarried (a marriageble girl). Keeping (her) so (her family).

A تعنيف taʻnīf, (v. n. 2 of عنف) Incommoding, molesting. Reproaching harshly, blaming severely. Inconvenience. Reproach.

A تعنيق taʻnīk, (v. n. 2 of عنق) Grasping the neck of another. Walking or ascending on high and rugged ground. Disappointing. Swelling and being almost ripe (dates). Growing long (flowers of the palm-tree).

A تعنين taʻnīn, (v. n. 2 of عنّ) Putting a title or inscription to a book. Fixing a rein to a bridle. Being impotent (especially declared so judicially). Impotency, aversion to women.

A تعنينة taʿnīnat, Impotency, aversion to women.

A تعوّث taʿawwus, Being astonied, bewildered.

A تعوّج taʿawwuj, A being bent, crooked, curved.

A تعوّد taʿawwud, (v. n. 5 of عاد for عود) Being accustomed. Making a habit or custom. Being angry. Usage.

A تعوّذ taʿawwuz, (v. n. 5 of عاذ for عوذ) Fleeing (to God), taking refuge.

A تعوّر taʿawwur, A borrowing from one another.

A تعوّض taʿawwuz, (v. n. 5 of عاض for عوض) Receiving a substitute or equivalent.

A تعوّط taʿawwut, (v. n. 5 of عاط for عوط) Not conceiving for several years (a camel), although not barren. Having a long neck.

A تعوّف taʿawwuf, (v. n. 5 of عاف for عوف) Prowling in the night (a lion).

A تعوّق taʿawwuk, (v. n. 5 of عاق for عوق) Being hindered, turned away from: hanging back.

A تعوية taʿwiyat, (v. n. 2 of عوي) Twisting (a rope). Bending (a bow). Calling a liar.

A تعويث taʿwīs, (v. n. 2 of عاث for عوث) Restraining, keeping back even to bewilderment.

A تعويج taʿwīj, (v. n. 2 of عوج) Bending, making crooked. Twisting. Perverting. Setting in ivory, inlaying with ivory or tortoise-shell.

A تعويد taʿwīd, (v. n. 2 of عاد for عود) Habituating, training (a dog for hunting). Introducing or prescribing a custom, manner, or fashion. Becoming old (a camel). Eating victuals the second time they are served up, or after others have finished.

A تعويذ taʿwīz, (v. n. 2 of عاذ for عوذ) Forcing (one) to flee for refuge. Wishing to imprison, detain, or keep back. An amulet or charm against sorceries or enchantments. A gold or silver case inclosing quotations from the Kurʼān, some mystical writing or vegetable substance, or the teeth or nails of a tiger, &c., worn by the Muhammadans on the neck, arm, or waist. P تعويذ آسمان taʿwīzi āsmān, Gemini.

A تعوير taʿwīr, (v. n. 2 of عار for عور) Depriving of an eye, rendering blind. Refusing, receding. Disappointing, rejecting (a petitioner). Stamping weights or measures with standard marks. Exposing to the hyenas. Bringing a ewe to the ram.

A تعويص taʿwīs, (v. n. 2 of عاص for عوص) Repeating a poetic verse or employing language difficult to be understood.

A تعويض taʿwīz, (v. n. 2 of عاض for عوض) Recompensing, rewarding, compensating. Giving or doing in exchange or return. Substituting.

A تعويق taʿwīk, (v. n. 2 of عاق for عوق) Delaying. Hindering, preventing, restraining.

A تعويل taʿwīl, (v. n. 2 of عال for عول) Placing confidence. Pouncing upon, attacking. Laying a burden upon. Crying, wailing, howling. Dissembling, resisting gently, feigning disdain. Making an umbrella, constructing a shelter from the rain called عالة ʿālat. Asking assistance, imploring help.

A تعويم taʿwīm, (v. n. 2 of عام for عوم) Laying down corn (when reaping) by handsful. Bearing fruit every second year (a palm-tree). Making swim.

A تعوين taʿwīn, (v. n. 2 of عان for عون) Reaching the meridian of life. Becoming a matron, or mistress of a family. Entering on the lot of another. Helping, assisting.

A تعويه taʿwīh, (v. n. 2 of عاه for عوه) Stopping on a journey, especially at the end of the night (for rest). Being imprisoned. Suffering from a murrain amongst cattle, or blight in corn. Calling an ass's colt by saying ʿawhi ʿawhi.

A تعهّد taʿahhud, (v. n. 5 of عهد) Minding, attending to, looking after, tending, taking care of. Seeking for something lost or missing. Making new. Renewing a treaty. Attacking any one frequently (an epileptic fit). Promise, agreement. Lease, contract, engagement. P تعهّد تسليم كرد taʿahhudi taslīm kard, He agreed to surrender.

A تعيّب taʿayyub, (v. n. 5 of عاب for عيب) Reproaching, accusing, defaming, stigmatizing.

A تعيّد taʿayyud, (v. n. 5 of عاد for عود) Looking intently with a malignant eye. Keeping holiday (عيد ʿīd). Being angry, scolding.

A تعيّس taʿayyus, (v. n. 5 of عاس for عيس) Becoming white with a mixture of black (camels).

A تعيّش taʿayyush, (v. n. 5 of عاش for عيش) Procuring a livelihood by labour and industry, labouring for a living.

A تعيّط taʿayyut, (v. n. 5 of عاط for عيط) Emitting watery exudations (as wood or stone). Flowing (water). Having a long neck. Noise, clamour, shouts of exultation or insolence. See also تعوّط.

A تعيّل taʿayyul, A walking gracefully.

A تعيّن taʿayyun, (v. n. 5 of عان for عين) Keeping a sharp look-out upon from an eminence. Influencing (particularly with a malignant eye). Seeing for certain. Feigning ignorance. Being full of small circles or eyes (a skin). Contemplating or looking continually at one thing. Waiting deliberately to strike with the eye. Being peculiar, special, specific. Being necessary and obligatory.

A تعيّنات taʿayyunāt, (pl. of تعيّن taʿayyun) Existences, qualities of matter. Appointment, attendance, service.

A تعيهر taʿayhur, A playing the whore.

A تعيّي taʿayyī, (v. n. 5 of عي) Being difficult. Being embarrassed, unequal to any business.

A تعييب taʿyīb, (v. n. 2 of عاب for عيب) Damaging, making faulty and vicious. Fixing a stigma, reproaching, accusing, rendering infamous.

A تعيية taʿyiyat, (v. n. 2 of عي) Stammering, speaking unintelligibly.

A تعييث taʿyīs, (v. n. 2 of عاث for عيث) Searching or groping with the hand. Beginning, setting about any thing. Being mingled.

A تعييد taʿyīd, Celebration of a festival.

A تعيير taʿyīr, (v. n. 2 of عار for عير) Putting to the blush, reproaching, reviling, disgracing. Weighing (gold coins) one by one. Being covered with weeds (water). عيّره الامر ʿayyarahuʼl amra, He reproached him with the affair.

A تعييش taʿyīsh, A supporting, preserving life.

A تعييط taʿyīt, (v. n. 2 of عاط for عيط) Crying out (either when drunk or in a tumult, but only once).

A تعييع taʿyīʿ, (v. n. 2 of عيع not in use) Desisting from any purpose (men thwarted or fatigued).

A تعييق taʿyīk, Vociferation, crying out.

A تعييل taʿyīl, (v. n. 2 of عال for عيل) Taking into a family. Setting (a horse) loose in a field. Feeding poorly. Missing, losing a thing without being able to find it. Supporting a family, providing adequately for its maintenacne.

A تعيين taʿyīn, (v. n. 2 of عان for عين) Specifying, particularizing. Rendering conspicuous and plain. Reproaching a man with a fault, setting his misdeeds before his face. Keeping up hostilities. Appropriating, determining (the property). Making checkered or mosaic work. Boring (pearls). Forming the letter ع ʿayn. Selling goods to be paid for at a given time, and afterwards repurchasing them at a lower rate than they were sold for. Receiving or paying money in advance. Borrowing or lending without interest. Filling with water (a new leathern bottle) in order to close up the eyes or holes made by the stitches, and make it leak-proof. Being green, blossoming (a tree). Deputation, designation. Daily allowance to ambassadors, &c., out of the treasury.

A تعيينات taʿyīnāt, (pl. of تعيين) Appointments.

A تغ تغ tigh tigh, The sound or giggle made by continued laughter. Tittering.

A تغابن taghābun, (v. n. 6 of غبن) Defrauding, cheating one another. Peevishness, fretfulness. يوم التغابن yawmuʼt taghābun, The day of judgment.

A تغابي taghābī, (v. n. 6 of غبي) Neglecting, taking no heed. Shamming negligence.

P تغار taghār, A provision-bag hung by a horseman at each side of his horse. An earthen dish or bowl. Any certain allowance of provisions, or stipend, on which a person depends. A measure.

A تغّار taghghār, Copiously bleeding (wound).

A تغّارة taghghārat, (A she-camel) running with rapidity straight forward and foaming.

P تغاره taghāra, A measure. A wash-tub.

A تغاريد taghārīd, (pl. of تغريد) Warblings.

A تغاريز taghārīz, Shoots, slips, offsets.

A تغازّ taghāzz, A disputing, contending with.

A تغازل taghāzul, (v. n. 6 of غزل) Soothing each other with blandishments, entertaining one another with amatory verses, sending valentines.

A تغازي taghāzī, A waging mutual war.

A تغاضي *taghāzī*, (v. n. 6 of غضي) Neglecting, being careless; being uninformed.

A تغاط *taghātt* A ducking each other in water.

A تغاطس *taghātus*, (v. n. 6 of غطس) Feigning negligence. Ducking one another into water.

A تغاطش *taghātush*, (v. n. 6 of غطش) Neglecting, not caring for. Shamming blindness.

A تغافل *taghāful*, (v. n. 6 of غفل) Feigning negligence. Being intentionally negligent, conniving. Negligence, inadvertency, carelessness.

A تغالب *taghālub*, An overcoming one another.

A تغالي *taghālī*, (v. n. 6 of غلا for غلو) Growing tall (herbage), or becoming entangled. Losing flesh, falling away (a camel). Exceeding bounds, being lavish in praise. Being dear (a price). Contending with each other in shooting an arrow.

A تغامج *taghāmuj*, A drinking. A sucking.

A تغامز *taghāmuz*, A winking to each other.

A تغامس *taghāmus*, A ducking one another.

A تغاني *taghānī*, (v. n. 6 of غني) Being able to do without one another, giving up intercourse. Exciting each other to fight (soldiers) by singing martial songs.

A تغاور *taghāwur*, (v. n. 6 of غار for غور) Making inroads upon one another for the sake of plunder.

A تغاوط *taghāwut*, A ducking one another.

A تغاوي *taghāwī*, (v. n. 6 of غوي) Assembling from every quarter for some mischievous design. Helping and joining to destroy others.

A تغايب *taghāyub*, (v. n. 6 of غاب for غيب) Being absent. Withdrawing. Slandering the absent.

A تغايد *taghāyud*, (v. n. 6 of غاد for غيد) Being tender, delicate, extremely flexible (girl).

A تغب *taghb*, Doubt. *Taghab*, (v. n. of تغب) Perishing. Corruption, loss, destruction. Penury. Barrenness, scarcity. Hunger. Vice, defect, blemish. Filth.

A تغبّة *taghibbat*, False testimony.

A تغبّر *taghabbur*, (v. n. 5 of غبر) Milking out the remains of milk in a camel's udder. Taking any thing that is left and remaining. Having offspring of any woman (particularly if she be of an advanced age).

A تغبّش *taghabbush*, (v. n. 5 of غبش) Injuring, oppressing. Laying a false claim.

A تغبّق *taghabbuk*, A milking in the evening.

A تغبيب *taghbīb*, (v. n. 2 of غبّ) Being negligent in business, taking (a matter) easily. Averting, prohibiting, beating back. Seizing (a sheep) by the throat (a wolf).

A تغبية *taghbiyat*, (v. n. 2 of غبي) Hiding, concealing. Clipping very close or uprooting the hair.

A تغبير *taghbīr*, A raising, or soiling with, dust. Exciting, stirring up, stimulating. Reiterating the phrase لا اله الا الله *lā ilāh illa'llāh*, There is no god but God.

A تغبيض *taghbīz*, (v. n. 2 of غبض not used) Refusing to weep (the eye).

A تغبيط *taghbīt*, (v. n. 2 of غبط) Making (one) to long for, causing to wish.

A تغبين *taghbīn*, (v. n. 2 of غبن) Leading into error, causing to blunder, misleading.

A تغترف *taghatruf*, Pride, petulance.

P تغتز *taghtaz*, A pancake, a fritter.

P تغتغ *taghtagh* or *tughtugh*, A corn-measure, equal to four ass-loads. A pancake, fritter.

A تغتغة *taghtaghat*, (v. n. of تغتغ Q) Stammering. Sound, proceeding from the collision or fall of bodies; also the sound of laughter.

A تغثيث *taghsīs*, A fattening little by little.

T تغدري *taghdarī*, A bustard.

A تغدّن *taghaddun*, (v. n. 5 of غدن) Leaning from side to side. Being indulgent or favourable.

A تغدّي *taghaddī*, (v. n. 5 of غدا for غدو) Eating early, breakfasting. Dinner.

A تغدية *taghdiyat*, A causing to breakfast.

A تغديد *taghdīd*, (v. n. 2 of غدّ) Receiving one's portion. Being troubled with the plague (a camel).

A تغذرم *taghazrum*, (v. n. 2 of غذرم Q) Swearing flatly without qualification or hesitation.

A تغذغذ *taghazghuz*, A jumping, a leaping on.

A تغذّم *taghazzum*, (v. n. 5 of غذم) Tasting. Devouring voraciously. Cutting.

A تغذمر *taghazmur*, (v. n. 2 of غذمر Q) Vociferating. Talking confusedly.

A تغذّي *taghazzī*, (v. n. 5 of غذا for غذو) Being nourished, fed. Eating.

A تغذية *taghziyat*, (v. n. 2 of غذا for غذو) Maintaining, feeding. Rearing, bringing up. Restraining urine; stopping whilst making water. Spurting out blood (a vein). Cutting.

A تغر *taghr*, (v. n. of تغر) Bleeding copiously (a vein). Issuing from a crevice in a waterbottle (water).

A تغران *tagharān*, (v. n. of تغر) Boiling (a pot).

A تغرّب *tagharrub*, (v. n. 5 of غرب) Being, becoming, or pretending to be foreign. Going to a great distance and being separated. Travelling to foreign parts. Coming from the west.

A تغرّة *taghirrat*, A risking of one's life.

A تغرّد *tagharrud*, A singing, a warbling.

A تغرّض *tagharruz*, (v. n. 5 of غرض) Being broken but not separated (a branch).

A تغرغر *tagharghur*, A gargling the throat. Overflowing with tears (the eye).

A تغرّف *tagharruf*, (v. n. 5 of غرف) Stripping (one) of all his property, carrying off every thing.

P تغري *tughra'*, An emperor's sign manual.

A تغريب *taghrīb*, (v. n. 2 of غرب) Banishing, expelling, exiling. Going towards the west. Being absent, concealed, invisible. Travelling to foreign parts. Bringing forth white children; also black ones. Collecting snow and hoar-frost and eating it.

A تغرية *taghriyat*, (v. n. 2 of غرا for غرو) Anointing, smearing. Gluing. Being wholly addicted to.

A تغريث *taghrīs*, (v. n. 2 of غرث) Starving, allowing to starve, suffering to become hungry.

A تغريد *taghrīd*, A singing, a warbling.

A تغرير *taghrīr*, (v. n. 2 of غرّ) Exposing one's self to danger. Beginning to appear (the fore-teeth). Filling (a bottle). Pasturing, tending (camels). Flowing, running, sinking (as water into the earth). Eating the herb غرغر *ghirghir*. Preparing to fly, meditating flight (a bird).

A تغريز *taghrīz*, (v. n. 2 of غرز) Thrusting the tail into the ground (as a locust when laying eggs). Being left without milking (a camel), especially every other milking-time; having her teats bathed with cold water to prevent the milk from flowing. (pl. تغاريز *taghārīz*) A shoot or slip.

A تغريض *taghrīz*, (v. n. 2 of غرض) Exhausting, emptying (a vessel or ocean). Leaving space, not filling (a vessel). Eating tender, fresh, or young meat. Eating fruit, enjoying. Cutting or gathering any thing new and fresh. Weaning prematurely.

A تغريق *taghrīk*, (v. n. 2 of غرق) Immerging, ducking, drowning. Suffocating, strangling. Killing. Drawing (a bow) with all one's might.

A تغريم *taghrīm*, (v. n. 2 of غرم) Compelling (one) to pay (especially what he does not owe). Bringing into debt. Fining, mulcting.

A تغزّل *taghazzul*, (v. n. 5 of غزل) Devoting one's self to, bestowing pains in, writing erotic poetry.

A تغزية *taghziyat*, (v. n. 2 of غزا for غزو) Sending or compelling (people) to go upon an expedition against an enemy.

A تغزير *taghzīr*, (v. n. 2 of غزر) Omitting to milk (a camel) every other time, that the milk may be increased. Thickening (the hair).

A تغس *taghs*, A small cloud.

A تغسّر *taghassur*, (v. n. 5 of غسر) Being intricate, obscure (business). Being twisted, entangled (thread). Having sticks fallen into it (a pond).

A تغسّل *taghassul*, A washing (of the body).

A تغسيل *taghsīl*, (v. n. 2 of غسل) Washing the members very much, performing ablutions most scrupulously. Cohabiting much to no purpose.

A تغشّم *taghashshum*, (v. n. 5 of غشم) Acting oppressively and iniquitously.

A تغشمر *taghashmur*, (v. n. 2 of غشمر Q) Taking forcibly. Being angry.

A تغشّن *taghashshun*, The floating (of dung).

A تغشّي *taghashshī*, (v. n. 5 of غشي) Covering one's self. Covering. Coming on one unexpectedly.

A تغشية *taghshiyat*, (v. n. 2 of غشي) Covering, veiling, hiding. Spreading a veil. Causing to come on one unexpectedly. Lashing, scourging.

A تغشيش *taghshīsh*, (v. n. 2 of غشّ) Deceiving, being insincere, persuading treacherously.

A تغصّب *taghassub*, A being constrained.

A تغضّب *taghazzub*, A being provoked to anger.

A تغضّر *taghazzur*, A declining, receding.

A تغضغض *taghazghuz*, A being lessened.

A تغضّف *taghazzuf*, (v.n. 5 of غضف) Falling in ruins, tumbling in (a well). Being complicated, wrinkled. Being bent, folded. Inclining. Being favourable, propitious (fortune). Twisting, coiling up (a serpent). Breaking. Covering (night).

A تغضّن *taghazzun*, (v. n. 5 of غضن) Being wrinkled. Having a wrinkled face.

A تغضوض *taghzūz*, A sweet sort of date.

A تغضيض *taghzīz*, (v. n. 2 of غضّ) Eating any thing fresh or green. Being fresh, tender, soft, delicate. Sustaining loss, injury, or diminution.

A تغضيف *taghzīf*, (v. n. 2 of غضف) Letting down, allowing to drop. Stealing away the understanding (love).

A تغضين *taghzīn*, (v. n. 2 of غضن) Wrinkling. Bringing forth an abortion (a camel).

A تغضيه *taghzīh*, (v. n. 2 of غضه) Cutting the thorny plant عضاه *ʻizāh*.

A تغطرس *taghatrus*, (v. n. 2 of غطرس Q) Being inflamed with anger. Walking flauntingly or pompously. Being avaricious. Losing one's way.

A تغطرش *taghatrush*, A pretending to be blind.

A تغطرف *taghatruf*, (v. n. 2 of غطرف Q) Being proud, self-important. Walking in a pompous manner. Arrogance, pride, vanity, folly.

A تغطّش *taghattush*, A being dim (the eye).

A تغطغط *taghatghut*, (v. n. 2 of غطغط Q) Raging (as the waves). Being dispersed, scattered.

A تغطّف *taghattuf*, (v. n. 5 of غطف) Shying, going right and left (a horse).

A تغطمط *taghatmut*, A hoarse gruff voice. The bubbling of a boiling pot. Dashing of waves. Noise of mirth.

A تغطّي *taghatti*, (v. n. 5 of غطي) Being covered. Covering, concealing.

A تغطية *taghtiyat*, (v. n. 2 of غطا for غطو) Covering. Enveloping in its darkness (night). Rising above and hiding.

A تغطيش *taghtīsh*, (v. n. 2 of غطش) Making open and plain (a road). Contriving or suggesting a manner of doing any thing.

A تغفّر *taghaffur*, (v. n. 5 of غفر) Collecting certain gummy drops called مغافير *maghāfīr*.

A تغفّق *taghaffuk*, A drinking (wine) all day.

A تغفّل *taghafful*, (v. n. 5 of غفل) Being intentionally careless and negligent. Rendering negligent and inattentive.

A تغفيق *taghfīk*, (v. n. 2 of غفق) Sleeping. Dozing, yet so as to overhear conversation. Applying a remedy to one bitten by a snake. A nap in the midst of wakefulness.

A تغفيل *taghfīl*, (v. n. 2 of غفل) Reproving for negligence, calling (one) negligent and forgetful, regarding (one) as such. Trusting to another and neglecting one's own affairs. Supplying the place of another, sufficing for his negligence and carelessness. Covering, veiling.

A تغلب *taghlib*, Name of an Arabian tribe.

A تغلّب *taghallub*, (v. n. 5 of غلب) Subjugating, taking possession (of a city). Power, superiority, predominance. Tyranny, oppression. Pretence, cheating.

A تغلبيّ *taghlabiy*, (rarely *taghlibiy*) Of, or belonging to, the tribe of Taghlib.

A تغلّت *taghallut*, A receiving with indifference.

A تغلّج *taghalluj*, (v. n. 5 of غلج) Being unjust, iniquitous, disobedient, and rebellious. Rolling the tongue from side to side in drinking (an ass).

A تغلّس *tughullis*, Evil, misfortune.

A تغلّط *taghallut*, (v. n. 5 of غلط) Falling into error. Leading into error, causing to blunder.

A تغلغل *taghalghul*, (v. n. 2 of غلغل Q) Flowing amid trees (water). Making haste. Entering. Perfuming one's self with غالية *ghāliyat* or civet.

A تغلّف *taghalluf*, (v. n. 5 of غلف) Perfuming one's person with civet. Having a foreskin.

A تغلّل *taghallul*, (v. n. 5 of غلّ) Perfuming the beard and mustachios with civet. Entering.

A تغلّي *taghalli*, A perfuming with غالية *ghāliyat*.

A تغليب *taghlīb*, (v. n. 2 of غلب) Rendering superior or victorious. Prevalence.

A تغلية *taghliyat*, (v. n. 2 of غلي) Causing to boil. Saluting from a distance, pointing, nodding.

A تغليس *taghlīs*, (v. n. 2 of غلس not in use) Travelling by night. Coming to a watering-place towards the end of the night.

A تغليط *taghlīt*, (v. n. 2 of غلط) Accusing of an error, charging with a blunder.

A تغليظ *taghlīz*, (v. n. 2 of غلظ) Thickening. Making a thing rough and oppressive to any one.

A تغليف *taghlīf*, (v. n. 2 of غلف) Perfuming (the beard and mustachios) with civet. Covering with a sheath (غلاف *ghilāf*), encasing.

A تغليق *taghlīk*, (v. n. 2 of غلق) Shutting, slamming, or fastening (a door).

A تغليل *taghlīl*, (v. n. 2 of غلّ) Perfuming with civet. Accusing of fraud or treachery.

A تغماض *taghmāz*, A wink of sleep.

A تغمّد *taghammud*, (v. n. 5 of غمد) (God) covering with mercy; saving (a sinner). Covering, overspreading. Filling a vessel.

A تغمّر *taghammur*, (v. n. 5 of غمر) Tinging the face with saffron or other liniment. Drinking out of a small cup called غمر *ghumar*. Drinking little (a camel), barely sufficient to quench his thirst. Cropping a sort of grass called غمير *ghamīr* (a sheep). Pushing, shoving, thrusting away. Throwing, darting, shooting. Giving (a horse) to drink from a small cup on account of scarcity of water.

A تغمّط *taghammut*, (v. n. 5 of غمط) Throwing earth upon, covering, hiding.

A تغمغم *taghamghum*, Shouting of conquerors. Roaring of an affrighted bull. An obscure, unintelligible speech.

A تغمّل *taghammul*, (v. n. 5 of غمل) Sitting wide in an assembly, having plenty of room: roominess.

P تغمه *taghma*, A badge of honour. A mark which artists put on their productions. The device on a shield or medal.

A تغمية *taghmiyat*, (v. n. 2 of غمي) Covering the roof of a house with earth, reeds, &c.

A تغميد *taghmīd*, (v. n. 2 of غمد) Hiding, keeping (one's secret). Concealing, suppressing (any thing shameful).

A تغمير *taghmīr*, (v. n. 2 of غمر) Tinging (her face) with the yellow liniment غمرة *ghumra* (a woman). Throwing to a distance, removing afar off. Giving (a horse) to drink from a cup on account of the scarcity of water.

A تغميس *taghmīs*, A drinking little and seldom.

A تغميض *taghmīz*, (v. n. 2 of غمض) Half shutting the eyes. Conniving at, indulging. Passing over an affair known. Abating the price of an article, allowing a discount. Rushing back from the cistern with closed eyes upon the driver (a camel). Speaking unintelligibly, mysteriously, profoundly. A wink of sleep. ما اكتحلت تغميضاً *mā iktahaltu taghmīzan*, I have not slept a wink.

A تغميم *taghmīm*, A causing to cover.

A تغنّث *taghannus*, (v. n. 5 of غنث) Cleaving, adhering. Heaviness, torpor, sluggishness.

A تغنثر *taghansur*, (v. n. 2 of غنثر Q) Drinking without being thirsty.

A تغنّج *taghannuj*, (v. n. 5 of غنج) Darting amorous glances; walking with a graceful step; employing alluring airs (a woman). Coquetry.

A تغنّم *taghannum*, A considering as plunder.

A تغنّي *taghanni*, (v. n. 5 of غني) Singing. Praising. Satirizing, ridiculing. Being contented, able to do without.

A تغنية *taghniyat*, (v. n. 2 of غني) Singing. Cooing (a turtle-dove). Celebrating (a lady) in verse. Speaking in praise of. Satirizing, ridiculing.

A تغنيم *taghnīm*, A giving away spoil or plunder.

A تغنين *taghnīn*, (v. n. 2 of غنّ) Making one speak through the nose.

A تغوّج *taghawwuj*, A being bent, doubled, folded.

A تغور *tughūr*, (v. n. of تغر) Boiling (a pot). Bursting with rain (a cloud). Squirting (urine).

A تغوّر *taghawwur*, (v. n. 5 of غار for غور) Going into any low-lying country called غور *ghawr*.

A تغوّط *taghawwut*, (v. n. 5 of غاط for غوط) Going down into a low place to ease nature.

A تغوّل *taghawwul*, (v. n. 5 of غال for غول) Being variously coloured. Assuming different shapes. Destroying.

A تغوّن *taghawwun*, (v. n. 5 of غون not in use) Displaying valour in war. Pursuing an enemy. Persevering in crime.

A تغوية *taghwiyat*, (v. n. 2 of غوي) Seducing,

A تفاصيل *tafāṣīl*, (pl. of تفصيل *tafṣīl*) Divisions into sections, distinct disourses. Assortments. Clothes. P بر تفاصيل *bar tafāṣīl*, In detail.

A تفاضل *tafāẓul*, (v. n. 6 of فضل) Contending for, or pretending to, pre-excellence.

A تفاطم *tafāṭum*, (v. n. 6 of فطم) Having weanlings that long for their dams.

A تفاطؤ *tafāṭus*, (v. n. 6 of فطأ) Hanging back, retreating. Being routed, put to flight. Having a depression of the back with a prominence of the breast. Refusing to work, being refractory.

P تفاغ *tifāgh*, A cup.

A تفاقح *tafāḳuh*, A joining backs.

A تفاقد *tafāḳud*, (v. n. 6 of فقد) Missing each other. Seeking for one another in vain.

A تفاقر *tafāḳur*, (v. n. 6 of فقر) Pleading poverty, abasing one's self. Glorying amongst themselves in their poverty.

A تفاقس *tafāḳus*, (v. n. 6 of فقس) Pulling each other by the hair.

A تفاقع *tafāḳuʻ*, Whiteness (of the eye).

A تفاقم *tafāḳum*, A being important.

A تفاكه *tafākuh*, (v. n. 6 of فكه) Jesting together, bandying jokes with one another.

A تفال *tufāl*, Spittle, saliva. Froth, foam.

A تفأل *tafaʼʼul*, (v. n. 5 of فال obsol.) Taking a good omen from a name or other circumstance.

A تفألاً *tafaʼʼulan*, A prognosticating well.

A تفالج *tafāluj*, A pretending to be paralytic.

A تفالي *tafālī*, (v. n. 6 of فلي) Lousing each other. Wanting, requiring, needing to be loused.

A تفان *tiffān*, A seasonable time. بتفانه *bi tiffānihi*, or علي تفانه *ʻala' tiffānihi*, Opportunely.

A تفاني *tafānī*, A destroying each other (in war).

A تفاوت *tafāwut*, (v. n. 6 of فات for فوت) Being absent, far asunder. *Tafāwat*, *tafāwut*, or *tafāwit*, Difference, distinction, separation, disparity, discrepancy, contradiction. Distance, space. Absence. Defect, gap, flaw, blemish.

A تفاود *tafāwud*, (v. n. 6 of فاد for فود) Benefitting one another in learning or skill.

A شركة تفاوز *shirkatu tafāwuz*, Copartnership.

A تفاوص *tafāwus*, Separation, distinction, distance from each other.

A تفاوض *tafāwuz*, (v. n. 6 of فاض for فوض) Being reciprocally the equal, peer, associate, help of each other. Consulting together. Partnership.

A تفاؤل *tafāʼul*, An auguring, foreboding.

A تفاوه *tafāwuh*, A speaking, a talking.

A تفايد *tafāyud*, (v. n. 6 of فاد for فيد) Availing, helping one another.

A تفة *tufat*, A contemptible, despicable woman.

A تفة *tuffat*, A slighted, despised woman. The siyāh-gosh, an animal of the lynx-kind, having the ears tipped with long black hair. تفة له *tuffat lahu*, Fie on him!

P تفت *taft*, Warm, hot. Heat, warmth. Rage.

A تف *tuff*, (pl. تففة *tifafat*) Nail-parings. Dirt under the nails. (pl. اتفاف *atfāf* and تفوف *tufūf*) A shred of meat sticking between the teeth.

A تفا *tuffan*, Fie! for shame!

A تفاتح *tafātuh*, A holding private conversation.

A تفاتف *tafātif*, (pl. of تفتاف *taftāf*) Idle, sauntering fellows, who pick up and retail the sayings of women. Short poems, scraps of verse.

A تفاتي *tafātī*, (v. n. 6 of فتي) Being noble, generous, liberal. Appealing to a man learned in the law (a مفتي *muftī*) to determine any point.

A تفاج *tafājj*, A straddling in walking.

A تفاجي *tafājī*, (v. n. 6 of فجا for فجو) Being distant (time) or space). Being cleft.

A تفاح *tuffāh*, An apple. تفاح الارض *tuffāhu'l arz*, (Earth-apple) The camomile or anthemis. تفاح ارمني *tuffāhi armanī*, (Armenian apple) The apricot. تفاح بري *tuffāhi barrī*, The medlar. تفاح الجن *tuffāhu'l jinn*, (Genii or demon's apple) The mandrake. تفاح فارسي *tuffāhi fārsī*, (Persian apple) The peach. P تفاح ماهي *tuffāhi māhī*, (Moon-apple) The orange or lemon.

A تفاحة *tuffāhat*, A single apple. The head of the thigh-bone.

A تفاحش *tafāhush*, (v. n. 6 of فحش) Abusing one another with filthy words. Speaking obscenely. Being shameful. Exceeding bounds in wickedness.

A تفاحية *tuffāhīyat*, A costermonger.

A تفاخر *tafākhur*, A mutual boasting.

A تفادي *tafādī*, (v. n. 6 of فدي) Rescuing or ransoming one another. Avoiding, shunning, being ware of. Keeping clear of. Retiring from, seeking escape.

A تفار *tafārr*, A fleeing from each other.

A تفارر *tafārur*, A fleeing from each other.

A تفارص *tafārus*, A doing any thing by turns.

A تفارط *tafārut*, (v. n. 6 of فرط) Preceding, getting the start, contending, striving to get before. Existing, happening, or taking place late. Overtaking, befalling one (sudden and heavy afflictions.

A تفاريج *tafārīj*, Openings, interstices.

A تفاريق *tafārīḳ*, (pl. of تفريق *tafrīḳ*) Intervals, distinct parts. بالتفاريق *bi't tafārīḳ*, In parts, in divisions. By instalments.

A تفازز *tafāzuz*, (v. n. 6 of فز) Marching forth against each other.

A تفاسح *tafāsuh*, (v. n. 6 of فسح) Extending, enlarging, making room (as people at a public assembly). Sitting at their ease without being crowded.

A تفاسد *tafāsud*, (v. n. 6 of فسد) Violating friendship. Being alienated, refractory, rebellious. Breaking off all connexions (relations).

A تفاسي *tafāsī*, (v. n. 6 of فسا for فسو) Raising the hinder parts in order to break wind.

A تفاسير *tafāsīr*, (pl. of تفسير) Commentaries.

A تفاصح *tafāsuh*, (v. n. 6 of فصح) Being rhetorically affected, striving to be eloquent.

leading astray. Cheating, deceiving. Making (milk) thick.

A تغويث *taghwīs*, (v. n. 2 of غوث) Calling for assistance by the word واغوثاه, Help! help!

A تغوير *taghwīr*, (v. n. 2 of غار for غور) Being defeated and put to flight. Attaining the hour of noon. Travelling at noonday, or alighting and reposing at that time. Passing by. Coming into a low-lying country. Flowing from higher grounds (water). Sinking below the horizon (the sun).

A تغويط *taghwīt*, (v. n. 2 of غاط for غوط) Digging deep (a well). Swallowing well (mouthsful of meat), taking large mouthsful.

A تغاء *tighaʼ*, (v. n. of تغي) Bursting into a loud laugh, tittering (a girl). Perishing (a man). A loud burst of laughter.

A تغيب *taghayyub*, A being absent or concealed.

A تغيث *taghayyus*, A becoming fat. Fatness.

A تغير *taghayyur*, (v. n. 5 of غار for غير) Being changed, altered, disturbed. Turning, becoming tainted or rotten (meat or fruit). A change.

A تغيرات *taghayyurāt*, Alterations, changes.

A تغيظ *taghayyuz*, (v. n. 5 of غاظ for غيظ) Furiously raging. Being intense (afternoon heat).

A تغيف *taghayyuf*, (v. n. 5 of غاف for غيف) Nodding, waving from side to side (branches). Inclining, going from side to side (a horse).

A تغيق *taghayyuḳ*, A being dark, dim (an eye).

A تغيل *taghayyul*, (v. n. 5 of غال for غيل) Being thick, entangled, and shady (trees). Being numerous. Having numerous flocks.

A تغيم *taghayyum*, (v. n. 5 of غام for غيم) Being overcast and misty (the sky).

A تغيهق *taghayhuḳ*, (v. n. 2 of غيهق Q) Being weakened by darkness (the sight).

A تغييب *taghyīb*, (v. n. 2 of غاب for غيب) Causing to be absent, removing. Concealing (in a tomb, burying).

A تغيية *taghyiyat*, A raising of a standard.

A تغيير *taghyīr*, (v. n. 2 of غار for غير) Altering, making a change (either for the better or the worse). Dismissing from office. Provoking to jealousy.

A تغييض *taghyīz*, (v. n. 2 of غاض for غيض) Diminishing. Restraining (tears). Haunting a forest (a lion).

A تغييظ *taghyīz*, An enraging, putting in a fury.

A تغييف *taghyīf*, (v. n. 2 of غاف for غيف) Being pusillanimous, cowardly: fleeing, running off.

A تغييق *taghyīḳ*, (v. n. 2 of غاق for غيق) Being confused, distracted; inconstant, irresolute. Making dark (the eye). Squandering, dissipating (one's property).

A تغييم *taghyīm*, (v. n. 2 of غام for غيم) Being clouded (the sky). Coming on like a mist (night).

P تف *taf*, Flame, heat, warmth. Brightness, effulgence. Vapour, exhalation. Corruption, rottenness, stink. *Tuf*, Spittle.

Haste, expedition. Waving, walking in a stately manner. Name of an intoxicating root. Name of a place in Persia.

A تفتاف *taftāf*, (pl. تفتافون *taftāfūn* and تفاتيف *tafātīf*) An idle sauntering fellow (who picks up and retails the sayings of women).

A تفتّت *tafattut*, A being broken or crumbled.

A تفتّح *tafattuh*, A being opened, unlocked.

A تفتر *taftar*, (for دفتر *daftar*) A book, journal.

A تفتّر *tafattur*, (v. n. 5 of فتر) Being delirious, intoxicated with drink. Going at a lazy, sluggish pace. Being lazy, slow, weak, relaxed. Labouring under a fever.

A تفتّغ *tafattugh*, (v. n. 5 of فتغ) Being broken between the teeth.

A تفتّق *tafattuk*, (v. n. 5 of فتق) Being split, broken, cleft, unsewed.

A تفتّك *tafattuk*, (v. n. 5 of فتك) Setting about business without consulting anybody.

P تفتگی *taftagī*, Heat, warmth. Anguish, teen.

A تفتّل *tafattul*, The being twisted (a rope).

P تفتن *taftan*, To burn, to be hot. To warm, to heat. To put in a rage.

P تفته *tafta*, Hot. Melted. Twisted. Displeased. Weighed down. Disturbed. A maddening root.

P تفته جگر *tafta-jigar*, Hectic. Inflamed with love.

P تفته دل *tafta-dil*, Heart-sick, desponding.

A تفتّي *tafattī*, (v. n. 5 of فتي) Being noble, liberal, generous. Becoming a grown girl.

A تفتية *taftiyat*, (v. n. 2 of فتي) Being considered as a grown girl, and kept confined at home, not being allowed to romp with boys.

A تفتيت *taftīt*, A breaking, a crumbling.

A تفتيح *taftīh*, An opening wide, an unbarring.

A تفتيخ *taftīkh*, Contraction and expansion of the fingers.

P تفتيدن *taftīdan*, To wax hot.

A تفتير *taftīr*, (v. n. 2 of فتر) Rendering weak or relaxed. Causing to slacken and flag. Being scattered and remaining immoveable (a cloud) and threatening rain.

A تفتيش *taftīsh*, (v. n. 2 of فتش) Investigating, examining, searching diligently. Inquiry, examination. Inquisitiveness.

A تفتيشى *taftīshī*, Investigation, research. An inquisitor, commissary, investigator, examiner.

A تفتيق *taftīk*, (v. n. 2 of فتق) Splitting, breaking, bursting (any thing sewed). Opening, loosing.

P تفتيك *taftīk*, Goats' hair resembling silk, growing at the roots of the long hair, and often more valuable (of which shawls are made).

A تفتيك *taftīk*, A carding of cotton.

A تفتيل *taftīl*, The twisting (of a rope).

A تفتين *taftīn*, (v. n. 2 of فتن) Exciting sedition, raising tumults. Bringing into trouble. Seducing or infatuating. Trying, proving (gold by fire, or man by temptations).

A تفث *tafas*, (v. n. of تفث) Purifying, before performing the sacred ceremony at Mecca, of throwing stones at the devil or Mina (when the devotee cuts off his hair, shaves his beard and the rest of his body, pares his nails, and cleanses himself from all filth). Filth, dirt in the head. *Tafis*, One who has neglected hair, or a squalid beard.

A تفشيج *tafsīj*, A bearing heavily.

A تفئيد *tafsīd*, (v. n. 2 of فئد) Lining (a cuirass).

A تفجّج *tafajjuj*, (v. n. 5 of فجّ) Straddling.

A تفجّر *tafajjur*, (v. n. 5 of فجر) Being set a flowing, bursting out and running rapidly (water). Sending forth its first glimmering (the dawn). Being diffusive (in munificence). Suppuration.

A تفجّس *tafajjus*, A being lofty, haughty, proud.

A تفجّع *tafajjuʻ*, (v. n. 5 of فجع) Being afflicted, shewing marks of grief. Condoling, lamenting the fate of another.

A تفجية *tafjiyat*, An uncovering: a displacing.

A تفجيج *tafjīj*, A making raw. Straddling.

A تفجير *tafjīr*, (v. n. 2 of فجر) Causing to burst forth, setting a flowing, permitting (water) to run or diffuse itself.

A تفجيع *tafjīʻ*, A giving of pain.

A تفجيل *tafjīl*, (v. n. 2 of فجل) Making broad. Exposing, rendering conspicuous.

A تفحاح *tafhāh*, The hissing of a serpent.

A تفحّج *tafahhuj*, (v. n. 5 of فحج) Sitting with the toes turned inwards.

A تفحّش *tafahhush*, (v. n. 5 of فحش) Speaking obscenely or foolishly.

A تفحّص *tafahhus*, (v. n. 5 of فحص) Inquiring diligently. Investigation, disquisition, search.

A تفحّل *tafahhul*, (v. n. 5 of فحل) Living well (in meat, drink, and clothing). Living or clothing roughly. Resembling a stallion (فحل *fahl*).

A تفحية *tafhiyat*, (v. n. 2 of فحا for فحو not in use) Meaning, having a tendency towards, pointing to any thing (a speech). Seasoning properly (a pot) with herbs and spiceries.

A تفحيج *tafhīj*, (v. n. 2 of فحج) Sitting with the toes turned inwards.

A تفحيم *tafhīm*, (v. n. 2 of فحم) Making (the face) black. Letting the first shades of night pass.

A تفخّت *tafakhkhut*, (v. n. 5 of فخت) Being struck with astonishment. Walking like the فاختة *fākhita* or ring-dove.

A تفخّذ *tafakhkhuz*, (v. n. 5 of فخذ) Delaying, tarrying, remaining behind.

A تفخّر *tafakhkhur*, (v. n. 5 of فخر) Being proud, boasting, and vain. Pride, arrogance.

A تفخّز *tafakhkhuz*, A being proud; haughtiness.

A تفخّل *tafakhkhul*, (v. n. 5 of فخل) Being grave and modest. Putting on one's best clothes.

A تفخيذ *tafkhīz*, (v. n. 2 of فخذ) Separating (men) and distributing (them) into families. Calling them by their families. Comprehending. Scattering. Disappointing. Sitting knee to knee. Putting, or holding between the thighs (فخذ *fakhiz*).

A تفخير *tafkhīr*, (v. n. 2 of فخر) Considering as excelling in glory, preferring.

A تفخيم *tafkhīm*, (v. n. 2 of فخم) Magnifying, honouring. Pronouncing (a letter) full or open (opposed to امالة *imālat*). Awe, solemnity. الف التفخيم *alifu't tafkhīm*, The broad swelling alif in such words as صلوة *salāt*, Prayer, حيوة *hayāt*, Life.

A تفدية *tafdiyat*, (v. n. 2 of فدي) Saying to another جعلت فداك *juʻiltu fidāka*, For thee I devote my head.

A تفديد *tafdīd*, (v. n. 2 of فدّ) Walking proudly, swaggering, strutting. Calling out, speaking loud (people buying and selling).

A تفدير *tafdīr*, (v. n. 2 of فدر) Breaking stones. Becoming languid and turning away (a stallion).

A تفديع *tafdīʻ*, (v. n. 2 of فدع) Distorting the wrist or ankle-joint.

A تفديك *tafdīk*, A carding, separating cotton.

A تفديم *tafdīm*, (v. n. 2 of فدم) Covering (the mouth). Making a stopple or plug for any vessel. Placing a lid or stopple on or in a water-pot.

A تفدين *tafdīn*, (v. n. 2 of فدن) Fattening (camels). Extending far, lengthening (a building).

A تفذّح *tafazzuh*, A preparing to stale.

A تفذّذ *tafazzuz*, (v. n. 5 of فذّ) Being alone, singular. Choosing any thing. Contending, quarrelling. Finishing and completing business by one's self. Claiming as one's own exclusive right.

A تفر *tafir*, (or تفران) Dirty, squalid (man).

A تفراجة *tifrājat*, Weak, pusillanimous.

A تفراق *tafrāk*, A being divided, scattered.

A تفرة *tifrat*, *tufrat*, *tafirat*, or *tufarat*, The small furrow from the nose to the upper lip. *Tafirat*, Whatever begins to sprout or bud. Grass which cattle cannot crop from its shortness. A species of plant. Any thing growing under a tree.

A تفرّث *tafarrus*, (v. n. 5 of فرث) Fainting (to which pregnant women are subject).

A تفرّج *tafarruj*, (v. n. 5 of فرج) Enjoying social intercourse. Relaxation, recreation. Amusement, fun. P تفرّج كردن *tafarruj kardan*, To be amused, delighted, entertained.

A تفرجاء *tifrijāʻ*, Weak, languid. A coward.

A تفرجة *tifrijat*, (pl. تفاريج *tafārīj*) An opening in a garment. An interstice (between the fingers or lattice-work). Weak, cowardly.

P تفرّج گاه *tafarruj-gāh*, A delightful place for recreation (as a garden, meadow, or theatre).

P تفرچاغ *tafarchāgh*, Finished, prepared.

A تفرّد *tafarrud*, (v. n. 5 of فرد) Accomplishing (a work) alone. Singularity, separation (from the rest of the world). Pertinacity, obstinacy.

A تفرّر *tafarrur*, (v. n. 5 of فرّ) Laughing.

A تفرزة *tafrizat*, (v. n. 2 of فرز) Prescribing to any one. Cutting out work for any one.

A تفرزع *tafarzuʿ*, (v. n. 2 of فرزع Q) Being divided into handsful (fodder).

A تفرّس *tafarrus*, (v. n. 5 of فرس) Judging from physiognomy. Looking steadily at. Shewing firmness and stability. Wishing to be thought a good horseman. Shewing one's self off on horseback.

A تفرسخ *tafarsukh*, (v. n. 2 of فرسخ Q) Being checked (cold); allayed (fever); dispelled (grief).

A تفرّش *tafarrush*, (v. n. 5 of فرش) Hovering with expanded wings and remaining in the same place (a bird in the air).

A تفرشح *tafarshuh*, A straddling to be milked.

A تفرّع *tafarruʿ*, (v. n. 5 of فرع) Being propagated, multiplied (branches), branching out, becoming evolved (as propositions from a root). Marrying the chief woman of a tribe. Excelling, being superior to, or at the summit.

A تفرعن *tafarʿun*, (v. n. 2 of فرعن Q) Resembling Pharaoh in pride and tyranny.

A تفرّغ *tafarrugh*, (v. n. 5 of فرغ) Being vacant, at leisure, having finished work. Reserving one's self in order to give one's whole attention to any thing.

P تفرغه *tafragha* or *tafrigha*, A city in China.

A تفرّق *tafarruk*, (v. n. 5 of فرق) Being separated, divided, scattered, terrified, routed. Becoming dispersed. Discrimination, separation.

A تفرقة *tafrikat*, (v. n. 2 of فرق) Scattering, dispersing, dissipating. Distinction, discrimination. Discord, disunion, misunderstanding. Dispersion.

A تفرقع *tafarkuʿ*, (v. n. 2 of فرقع Q) Making a cracking noise when pulled (the fingers).

A تفرّك *tafarruk*, (v. n. 5 of فرك) Trembling, stumbling (in walking). Blundering (in speech).

A تفرنق *tafarnuk*, (v. n. 2 of فرنق Q not in use) Being spoiled. Being high and tall (the ear).

A تفروق *tufrūk*, The stalk of a date.

A تفرّي *tafarrī*, (v. n. 5 of فري) Being split, divided, cut. Being parted (night from its morning). Flowing (as water through fissures of rock or earth).

A تفريب *tafrīb*, (v. n. 2 of فرب not in use) Laving, bathing, washing (herself) with constringent lotions (a woman).

A تفرية *tafriyat*, (v. n. 2 of فري) Splitting.

A تفريث *tafrīs*, (v. n. 2 of فرث) Loosening, letting out the bowels. Striking (the liver) of an animal whilst yet alive.

A تفريج *tafrīj*, (v. n. 2 of فرج) Banishing grief, dispelling care. Carrying, bearing. Making wide, widening. Dividing asunder. Becoming decrepit.

A تفريح *tafrīh*, (v. n. 2 of فرح) Exhilarating, rejoicing. Diversion, recreation, amusement.

A تفريخ *tafrīkh*, (v. n. 2 of فرخ) Hatching (birds). Producing a chick (an egg). Shooting forth branches (a plant). Being about coming into ear (corn). Being pusillanimous, cowardly, chicken-hearted. Departing, being surmounted (fear).

A تفريد *tafrīd*, (v. n. 2 of فرد) Retiring, leading a solitary life (on account of devotion). Being learned in law and divinity.

A تفريز *tafrīz*, (v. n. 2 of فرز) Prescribing a mode to any one. Cutting out work for any one. Subtraction in arithmetic.

A تفريش *tafrīsh*, (v. n. 2 of فرش) Spreading (a carpet or the like). Paving (a house with stones). Extending branches along the surface of the ground (a plant). Getting into the broad leaf (growing corn). Fluttering (a bird when desirous of pouncing on its prey or of alighting).

A تفريص *tafrīs*, (v. n. 2 of فرص) Making dots (on the sole of a shoe) with a pointed iron.

A تفريض *tafrīz*, (v. n. 2 of فرض) Cutting (in notches). Ordering any thing to be observed (as an article of religion). Rendering necessary by little and little. Separating. Cutting off. Displaying, making public. Being due, obligatory (tithe).

A تفريط *tafrīt*, (v. n. 2 of فرط) Acting carelessly, failing in the performance of any duty, forgetting, relinquishing, losing an opportunity. Leaving behind. Preceding. Sending an ambassador. Averting, warding off evil. Putting to a distance. Praising beyond bounds. Displaying weakness.

A تفريع *tafrīʿ*, (v. n. 2 of فرع) Drawing forth, bringing out, evolving propositions from an original principle. Climbing a mountain. Descending. Sacrificing the firstlings of sheep or camels, called فرع *faraʿ* (as practised by the pagan Arabians).

A تفريغ *tafrīgh*, (v. n. 2 of فرغ) Emptying a vessel. Giving a vacation, causing a cessation from work or study. Pouring forth, causing to gush out.

A تفريق *tafrīk*, (v. n. 2 of فرق) Separating, discriminating. Scattering. Receiving (a debt or due) by instalments. Intimidating. Division. Distribution, partition. Jealousy, suspicion, misunderstanding. Schism. Subtraction. Department.

A تفريقا *tafrīkan*, (P تفريقانه) Separately.

A تفريه *tafrīh*, (v. n. 2 of فره) Bearing a lively colt (a camel).

A تفزّر *tafazzur*, (v. n. 5 of فزر) Being split, burst, rent; falling to pieces from age (a garment).

A تفزّز *tafazzuz*, A prevailing against.

A تفزّع *tafazzuʿ*, A being terrified.

A تفزيع *tafzīʿ*, (v. n. 2 of فزع) Striking with terror. Delivering from fear or apprehension.

P تفس *tafs*, Heat, warmth.

P تفسان *tafsān*, Hot.

A تفسّح *tafassuh*, (v. n. 5 of فسح) Being ample, capacious (place). Making plenty of room for any one in a public assembly. Sitting at ease, not being crowded.

A تفسّخ *tafassukh*, (v. n. 5 of فسخ) Falling in pieces (a dead mouse in water). Dropping off (hair from a dead body). Falling under a load (a four-year old camel).

A تفسّر *tafassur*, (v. n. 5 of فسر) Being expounded, rendered plain and intelligible.

A تفسرة *tafsirat*, The urine of a sick person; or rather, the inspection of it. A symptom. A medical prescription.

A تفسّؤ *tafassuʾ*, (v. n. 5 of فسأ) Being rent (a garment). Spreading, being propagated (an epidemical disease). Striking on the back with a stick.

P تفسه *tafsa* or *tufsa*, A mole on the face. Grief, uneasiness, restlessness. An inclination. A longing (as in pregnant women or opium-eaters).

G تفسيا *tafsiyā*, The deadly carrot, thapsia.

A تفسئة *tafsiʾat*, A tearing by over-stretching.

A تفسيج *tafsīj*, (v. n. 2 of فسج) Standing with the legs apart when making water.

A تفسيح *tafsīh*, (v. n. 2 of فسح) Making room for any one in an assembly.

A تفسيد *tafsīd*, A destroying, overthrowing.

P تفسيدن *tafsīdan*, To grow warm.

P تفسيده *tafsīda*, Burned, warmed.

P تفسيده لبان *tafsīda-labān*, Chapped-lipped.

A تفسير *tafsīr*, (v. n. 2 of فسر) Explaining, expounding. Discovering the meaning of a difficult passage. Inspecting the urine of a sick person (a physician). (pl. تفاسير *tafāsīr*) Explanation, commentary, paraphrase; an interpretation of the Kur'ān.

A تفسيق *tafsīk*, (v. n. 2 of فسق) Making crooked or unjust, perverting.

P تفسيله *tafsīla*, A kind of rich silken stuff.

P تفش *tafsh*, Reproach. *Tafish*, Heat, warmth. Foam. Spittle.

A تفشّج *tafashshuj*, (v. n. 5 of فشج) (Sitting) with the legs wide asunder. Opening the legs (when making water).

A تفشّح *tafashshuh*, (v. n. 5 of فشح) Straddling in walking, or when about to stale. Lying with a woman.

A تفشّغ *tafashshugh*, (v. n. 5 of فشغ) Being scattered (grey hairs on the head). Being diffused over the body (blood). Entering amongst the houses and hiding one's self. Concealing one's self under any thing. Putting on one's smartest clothes notwithstanding old age and grey hairs. Clinging to a tree (bind-weed). Overcoming. Forcing (a woman). Laxness. Slowness.

A تفشّق *tafashshuk*, (v. n. 5 of فشق) Putting on a vest after the fashion of a sword-belt.

A تفشّل *tafashshul*, (v. n. 5 of فشل) Flowing (waters). Marrying. Sitting on the فشل *fishl* in a camel-litter (a woman).

P تفشله *tafshila*, A dish of meat, eggs, carrots, and honey.

A تفشّؤ *tafashshuʾ*, (v. n. 5 of فشأ) Spreading, being propagated (a contagion). Laughing at, turning into ridicule.

P تفشه *tafsha*, (or تفشل *tafshal*) A reproach, curse, chiding, railing.

A تفشّي *tafashshī*, (v. n. 5 of فشا for فشو) Being propagated (as a contagion). Being large, open (an ulcer or sore).

A تفشية *tafshiyat*, A causing to spread.

A تفشيج *tafshīj*, A standing with the legs apart.

A تفشيح *tafshīh*, (v. n. 2 of فشح) Stretching wide the legs. Turning away from.

A تفشيخ *tafshīkh*, A relaxation in the joints.

A تفشيغ *tafshīgh*, (v. n. 2 of فشغ) Overtopping and covering. Overcoming, conquering. Overpowering one (sleep).

A تفشيل *tafshīl*, (v. n. 2 of فشل) Putting under (her) that part of the camel-litter called فشل *fishl* (a woman). Milk remaining in the udder.

P تفشيله *tafshīla*, A dish of meat, eggs, carrots, and honey.

A تفصّح *tafassuh*, (v. n. 5 of فصح) Taking pains to be eloquent. Talking Arabic (a foreigner). Being an eloquent speaker (an Arabian).

A تفصّد *tafassud*, (v. n. 5 of فصد) Flowing.

A تفصفص *tafasfus*, (v. n. 2 of فصفص Q) Being dispersed, flying in disorder. Assembling, being met.

A تفصّم *tafassum*, (v. n. 5 of فصم) Being broken, bruised, without separation of the parts.

A تفصّي *tafassī*, (v. n. 5 of فصا for فصو) Being separated. Being liberated, freed. (v. n. 5 of فصي) Liberating. Separating.

A تفصيح *tafsīh*, Freedom (of milk) from froth.

A تفصيد *tafsīd*, (v. n. 2 of فصد) Dividing, trenching. Macerating, dissolving with a small quantity of water. Being saturated with a very little water. A trench, a gutter.

A تفصيص *tafsīs*, An opening wide the eyes.

A تفصيع *tafsīʿ*, (v. n. 2 of فصع) Drawing or leading out. Farting aloud, or breaking wind gently. Drawing the nut out from within the prepuce (a boy). Giving a part of one's property.

A تفصيل *tafsīl*, (v. n. 2 of فصل) Separating or distinguishing one thing from another. Dissecting (a sheep), dividing any thing into joints. Cutting out (a garment). Dividing (a book) into chapters, or (a speech) into sentences. Making distinct, clear, evident. (pl. تفاصيل *tafāsīl*) Separation. Distinction, division (into chapters). Analysis, detail, particulars. Dissection. An assortment. Statistics. Prolixity. Wearing apparel.

A تفصيلاً *tafsīlan* or علي التفصيل *ʿala't tafsīl*, (P تفصيلانه *tafsīlāna*) Distinctly, at full length, clearly explained in detail.

A تفضّج *tafazzuj*, (v. n. 5 of فضج) Having the roots of the hair wet (with sweat). Being filled with fat (a body). Being extended.

A تفضّض *tafazzuz*, A being scattered.

A تفضّل *tafazzul*, (v. n. 5 of فضل) Excelling, being eminent, assuming a superiority. Conferring a favour, favouring, obliging. Wearing the same garments every day (especially when at work or at home). Extracting much. Wearing a garment and throwing the ends over the shoulders. Extracting much. A favour, obligation.

A تفضّلات *tafazzulāt*, Favours, kindnesses.

A تفضيج *tafzīj*, (v. n. 2 of فضج) Having sweat at the roots of the hairs of the head, but not running. Having fat well distributed (the body). Being wrinkled. Being lean. Being open and wide.

A تفضيح *tafzīh*, A disgracing, a shaming.

A تفضيض *tafzīz*, (v. n. 2 of فضّ) Beating silver. Covering or ornamenting by inlaying with silver (فضّة *fizzat*).

A تفضيل *tafzīl*, (v. n. 2 of فضل) Preferring, exalting. Passing a judgment on the excellence of any one. Becoming proud, elevating one's self. Preference. اسم تفضيل *ismi tafzīl*, A comparative or superlative noun, noun of comparison.

A تفطّح *tafattuh*, (v. n. 5 of فطح) Being broad. Being wide open.

A تفطّر *tafattur*, A being split, cleft, divided.

A تفطيح *taftīh*, A making broad.

A تفطير *taftīr*, A causing to breakfast.

A تفطيس *taftīs*, A speaking to one's face.

A تفطين *taftīn*, (v. n. 2 of فطن) Making one to understand, to look at, or to consider (any thing).

A تفظّع *tafazzuʿ*, (v. n. 5 of فظع) Finding (a thing) to be disagreeable and shameful.

A تفعفع *tafaʿfuʿ*, A making haste.

A تفعّي *tafaʿʿī*, A being viperous, malicious.

A تفغّم *tafaghghum*, The expanding (of a flower).

A تففة *tifafat*, (pl. of تفّ *tuff*) Dirt of the nails. *Tufafat*, A worm that eats leather.

A تفقّح *tafakkuh*, An expanding, being blown.

A تفقّد *tafakkud*, (v. n. 5 of فقد) Searching for any thing lost, seeking for in vain. Inquiring diligently, wishing to know. Inspecting a wound.

A تفقّع *tafakkuʿ*, A being split, cleft in pieces.

A تفقّم *tafakkum*, (v. n. 5 of فقم) Taking by the jaw. Laying hold of by the end of the nose.

A تفقّؤ *tafakkuʾ*, (v. n. 5 of فقأ) Being torn out (an eye), burst (an imposthume or pod). Opening and pouring forth water (a cloud).

A تفقّه *tafakkuh*, (v. n. 5 of فقه) Studying divine subjects. Being skilled in jurisprudence.

A تفقئة *tafkiʾat*, (v. n. 2 of فقأ) Tearing out the eye, blinding, gouging. Bursting by squeezing (an imposthume).

A تفقيح *tafkīh*, (v. n. 2 of فقح) Opening the eyes for the first time (a whelp).

A تفقير *tafkīr*, (v. n. 2 of فقر) Digging, excavating. Digging a furrow for planting palm-trees. Piercing beads.

A تفقيع *tafkīʿ*, (v. n. 2 of فقع) Moving the corners of the mouth in speaking. Pulling the fingers till the joints crack. Striking (a rose-leaf) on the palm of the hand and making a smacking noise. Making (goat's leather) red.

A تفقيه *tafkīh*, (v. n. 2 of فقه) Teaching, instructing in law and jurisprudence (فقه *fik-h*).

P تفك *tufak*, A tube for shooting clay-balls through by the force of the breath. A musket.

A تفكّر *tafakkur*, (v. n. 5 of فكر) Thinking, reflecting, meditating, considering. Anxiety. P تفكر كردن *tafakkur kardan*, To consider.

A تفكّك *tafakkuk*, (v. n. 5 of فكّ) Being disjoined, dissolved, separated, broke open. Being relaxed behind and large uddered (as when about to foal). Being debilitated by insanity.

A تفكّن *tafakkun*, (v. n. 5 of فكن) Being penitent. Wondering. Penitence. Meditation. Vexation from losing hope of possession.

A تفكّه *tafakkuh*, (v. n. 5 of فكه) Admiring, being filled with astonishment. Being penitent. Enjoying. Eating fruit. Abstaining from fruit. The use and enjoyment of (any thing).

A تفكير *tafkīr*, A considering, reflecting.

A تفكيك *tafkīk*, (v. n. 2 of فكّ) Disjoining. Liberating, releasing. Futility.

A تفكيه *tafkīh*, (v. n. 2 of فكه) Delighting with amusing stories. Bringing fruit to any one.

A تفل *tafl*, (v. n. of تفل) Spitting, ejecting small saliva from the mouth. A bad smell from leaving off perfumes. *Tufl*, Spittle, saliva. Froth, foam. *Tafal*, (v. n. of تفل) Being disagreeable (a smell), stinking. *Tafil*, Smelling disagreeably, stinking-breathed.

A تفّل *tuffal*, A fox. A fox's cub.

A تفلة *tafilat*, Stinking-breathed (woman).

A تفلّت *tafallut*, (v. n. 5 of فلت) Escaping. Desiring, having a propensity. Leaping or rushing upon. Fighting.

A تفلّج *tafalluj*, A being cracked, chapped.

A تفلحس *tafalhus*, (v. n. 2 of فلحس Q not used) Going uninvited to a feast, playing the part of the beggar فلحس *falhas*.

A تفلّص *tafallus*, A being saved, escaping.

A تفلطس *tafaltus*, Broadness (of a man's nose).

A تفلّع *tafalluʿ*, (v. n. 5 of فلع) Being cut, split, cleft, cracked, or chapped.

A تفلفل *tafalful*, (v. n. 2 of فلفل Q) Being black (a teat). Walking with a starched air, taking short steps. Cleaning the teeth with a kind of wood.

A تفلّق *tafalluk*, (v. n. 5 of فلق) Being split, cut, cloven. Being separated into particles. Exciting one's self to admiration in running.

A تفلقح *tafalkuh*, A bringing good news.

A تفلّك *tafalluk*, A being round, orbicular.

A تفلّل *tafallul*, (v. n. 5 of فلّ) Being broken, blunted, or notched, in the edge or point (a sword or spear). Being routed (an army).

A تفلية *tafliyat*, A lousing the head.

A تفليج *taflīj*, (v. n. 2 of فلج) Dividing.

A تفليح *taflīh*, (v. n. 2 of فلح) Deriding, joking, sneering. Plotting. Cheating, cozening.

A تفليخ *taflīkh*, (v. n. 2 of فلخ) Striking.

A تفليز *taflīz*, A cutting in pieces.

P تفليس *taflīs* or *tiflīs*, A city in Georgia.

A تفليس *taflīs*, A declaring one a bankrupt.

A تفليص *taflīs*, The act of liberating.

A تفليع *taflīʿ*, A dividing, cutting, breaking.

A تفليق *taflīk*, A cleaving, splitting, dividing.

A تفليك *taflīk*, (v. n. 2 of فلك) Swelling (the breasts of a maiden). Having swelling breasts (a virgin). Being in heat (a bitch). Wrangling, quarrelling about any business. Making a muzzle of hair or wool to prevent a camel's colt from sucking.

A تفليل *taflīl*, (v. n. 2 of فلّ) Breaking, notching (a sword). Breaking the line, and putting (soldiers) to flight.

A تفن *tafan*, Dirt.

P تفناك *tafnāk*, Stinking, ill-smelling.

A تفنّد *tafannud*, (v. n. 5 of فند Urging, pressing, wishing one to do something. Repenting of, regretting. Repentance.

A تفنشخ *tafanshukh*, A spreading open the legs.

A تفنّق *tafannuk*, (v. n. 5 of فنق) Being delicately brought up. Living delicately and luxuriously.

P تفنگ *tufang*, A musket: an iron war-rocket.

T تفنگچي *tufăngchi*, A musqueteer.

A تفنّن *tafannun*, (v. n. 5 of فنّ) Being of different sorts. Diversion, amusement, fun.

P تفنود *tafnūd*, Courage, fortitude.

P تفنه *tafna*, (or تفني *tafnī*) A spider's web.

A تفنيخ *tafnīkh*, An overcoming, conquering.

A تفنيد *tafnīd*, (v. n. 2 of فند) Accusing of falsehood. Urging to the performance of an act. Charging with error. Making (a horse) lean. Tarrying long at wine. Sitting on the summit of a mountain. Pronouncing one to be insane or weak. Despising, treating with contempt.

A تفنيش *tafnīsh*, A being remiss, languid.

A تفنيق *tafnīk*, (v. n. 2 of فنق) Treating indulgently, pampering.

A تفنين *tafnīn*, (v. n. 2 of فنّ) Dividing into different sorts, distributing into classes. Mixing. Finding (cloth) to be stout in one part and thin in another. Being worn out without any rent (a garment). Inequality in the substance of cloth. Lines in cloth different from the rest.

P تفو *tafū*, Pho! fie! *Tufū*, Spittle.

A تفوّت *tafawwut*, A passing beyond, escaping.

A تفوّد *tafaʾud*, A being kindled, burning.

A تفوّد *tafawwud*, (v. n. 5 of فود not used) Standing perched on an eminence (a mountain-goat).

P تفور *tafūr*, (or تفوز *tafūz*) Clay.

A تفوف *tufūf*, (pl. of تفّ *tuff*) Shreds of meat sticking between the teeth.

A تفوّق *tafawwuk*, (v. n. 5 of فاق for فوق) Living at ease. Doing a thing by degrees. Milking (a camel) at intervals. Drinking milk at intervals. Reading small portions at a time.

A تفوّل *tafaʾul*, (v. n. 5 of فأل) Taking as a good omen, augering.

A تفوّل *tafawwul*, (for تفأّل *tafaʾul*, (v. n. 5 of فأل) Presaging happily, taking a good omen from a name. Presaging from a passage in a book opened by chance; bibliomancy.

A تفوّن *tafawwun*, Abundance, increase, growth.

A تفوه *tufūh*, (v. n. of تفه) Being little, mean, vile. Being silly, sottish. Being tasteless (food).

A تفوّه *tafawwuh*, (v. n. 5 of فاه for فوه) Speaking, pronouncing, delivering (a speech). Being talkative. Entering into a mouth or entrance.

A تفويت *tafwīt*, A letting escape or pass by.

A تفويج *tafwīj*, A cooling, allowing to cool.

A تفوير *tafwīr*, (v. n. 2 of فار for فور) Making a preparation of fenugreek and dates (called فيرة *fīrat*) for a woman in childbed.

A تفويز *tafwīz*, (v. n. 2 of فاز for فوز) Departing, travelling through the desert (with camels, &c.). Dying. Appearing clear, open, patent (a way).

A تفويض *tafwīz*, (v. n. 2 of فاض for فوض) Recommending, enjoining, committing, consigning, resigning, confiding, referring to another. Giving (a woman) in marriage without a dower.

A تفويف *tafwīf*, The printing (of a stuff).

A تفويق *tafwīk*, (v. n. 2 of فاق for فوق) Making a notch (to an arrow). Allowing (a camel's colt) to suck at intervals.

A تفويم *tafwīm*, A baking of wheaten bread.

A تفويه *tafwīh*, (v. n. 2 of فاه for فوه) Making large-mouthed. Making (one) to have long and projecting teeth (God).

A تفه *tafh*, (v. n. of تفه) Being little, mean, vile, filthy, contemptible. Being insipid (meat). *Tafih*, Foolish. Contemptible. Insipid (food). *Tufah* or تفّه *tuffah*, An animal of the lynx-kind.

A تفهّر *tafahhur*, (v. n 5 of فهر) Being wealthy.

A تفهّق *tafahhuk*, (v. n. 5 of فهق) Spreading or extending wide, being abundant. Flowing (blood).

A تفهّم *tafahhum*, (v. n. 5 of فهم) Understanding by little, perceiving one thing after another.

A تفهير *tafhīr*, A being fatigued, breathing hard.

A تفهيم *tafhīm*, (v. n. 2 of فهم) Giving to understand. Teaching, instructing.

A تفهيه *tafhīh*, (v. n. 2 of فهه) (God) making speechless, visiting with an impediment of speech. Causing to forget. Weakening.

A تفيأة *tafyaʾat*, The casting a shade.

A تفيحس *tafayhus*, A walking pompously.

A تفيّد *tafayyud*, (v. n. 5 of فاد for فيد) Receiving profit. Walking pompously.

P تفيدن *tafīdan*, To crack or chap (as the lips). To scrape (money) together. To sit in the sun, to expose to the fire or sun.

A تفيّش *tafayyush*, (v. n. 5 of فاش for فيش) Pretending to, making a false claim. Turning from one thing to another.

A تفيّظ *tafayyuz*, A breathing forth the soul.

A تفيّل *tafayyul*, (v. n. 5 of فال for فيل) Being weak or wandering (the mind), erring in opinion or conjecture. Being full grown and flowering (a shrub). Increasing (youth). Growing (fat).

A تفيلق *tafayluk*, (v. n. 2 of فيلق Q) Being bulky and fat. Exerting one's self to admiration in running.

A تفيلم *tafaylum*, A being fat and bulky.

A تفيّؤ *tafayyuʾ*, (v. n. 5 of فيأ) Doing any thing, sitting, in the shade. Turning itself (a shadow).

A تفيهر *tafayhur*, (v. n. 2 of فيهر Q) Being fatigued, breathing hard (a horse). Abounding in riches.

A تفيهق *tafayhuk*, (v. n. 2 of فيهق Q) Being talkative, diffusive in speech or prayer.

A تفيئة *tafyiʾat*, (v. n. 2 of فاء) Casting a shadow. Causing to wave (wind). At the heels of. تفيئة الشيء *tafiʾatu'sh shayʾ*, The proper season for a thing.

A تفييد *tafyīd*, (v. n. 2 of فيد) Drawing an ill omen from the note of the owl.

A تفئيل *tafʾīl*, (v. n. 2 of فأل) Presaging happily, taking a good omen. Causing to take an omen.

A تفييل *tafyīl*, (v. n. 2 of فال for فيل) Accusing one of silliness or weakness of mind. Rendering imprudent. Perverting the judgment.

A تفئيم *tafʾīm*, (v. n. 2 of فأم) Enlarging (a camel's saddle). Having his mouth full of grass (a camel).

A تقاء *tikāʾ*, (v. n. of تقى) Fearing.

A تقابل *takābul*, (v. n. 6 of قبل) Encountering, standing face to face, looking at one another.

A تقاة *tukāt*, Abstinence, piety, religion. The fear of God.

A تقاتر *takātur*, (v. n. 6 of قتر) Deceiving, circumventing each other.

A تقاتق *takātik*, Swift, rapid (nocturnal journey in quest of water).

A تقاتل *takātul*, A fighting, slaying one another.

A تقادع *takāduʿ*, (v. n. 6 of قدع) Piercing one another with spears in battle. Treading close one upon another in pursuit of any thing, trying who shall get first. Flying to the flame (a moth). Dying one after another.

A تقادم *takādim*, (pl. of تقدمة *takdimat*) Presents. *Takādum*, (v. n. 6 of قدم) Being ancient, antique, old. Preceding, going before. Fronting each other. (in law) Such a distance of time as suffices to prevent punishment.

A تقادير *takādīr*, (pl. of تقدير) Fates, decrees.

A تقاذع *takāzuʿ*, (v. n. 6 of قذع) Reviling, abusing. Bandying ribaldry.

A تقاذف *takāzuf*, (v. n. 6 of قذف) Throwing stones at one another. Abusing each other. Galloping (a horse).

A تقارّ *takārr*, (v. n. 6 of قرّ) Standing firm. Stopping, staying, being established in any place.

A تقارب *takārub*, (v. n. 6 of قرب) Approaching one another. Being near. Being few in number and galled-backed (camels). Approaching maturity (fruit or corn).

A تقارش *takārush*, (v. n. 6 of قرش) Mixing in battle. Being intermingled in battle (spears).

A تقارض *takāruz*, (v. n. 6 of قرض) Retaliating (either good or bad). Praising or censuring each other in verse. Looking at one another askance. Sending to one another any thing good or bad.

A تقارظ *takāruz*, A praising one another.

A تقارع *takāruع*, A casting lots.

A تقارير *takārīr*, (pl. of تقرير *takrīr*) Recitals.

A تقازيح *takāzīh*, Seasoning for victuals, herbs for the pot.

A تقاسم *takāsum*, (v. n. 6 of قسم) Dividing, sharing among one another. Swearing to each other.

A تقاصّ *takāss*, (v.n.6 of قصّ) Retaliating upon one another. Equalling numbers (in calculation).

A تقاصر *takāsur*, (v. n. 6 of قصر) Pretending to be short. Drawing one's self together. Being unequal to the performance of any thing, and desisting.

A تقاصف *takāsuf*, (v.n.6 of قصف) Assembling, flocking together. Being dashed to pieces (a ship).

A تقاصير *takāsīr*, (pl. of تقصار *tiksār* or تقصارة *tiksārat*) Collars, short and close. (pl. of تقصير *taksīr*) Deficiences, failures, short-comings.

A تقاضا *takāzā*, (for تقاضي *takāzī*) (v. n. 6 of قضي) Dunning, exacting. A demand. Exaction by means of a suit at law. Urgency, importunity. تقاضائ سنّ *takāzāi sinn*, The customs or habits of different ages, as of childhood, youth, manhood, &c. تقاضائ شديد *takāzāi shadīd*, Inexorable dunning. P تقاضا كردن *takāzā kardan*, To exact.

A تقاضي *takāzī*, (v.n.6 of قضي) Receiving (a debt).

A تقاطر *takātur*, (v. n. 6 of قطر) Being continuous. Arriving in bands, following one another. Facing each other (sides, tracts, or quarters).

A تقاطع *takātuع*, (v. n. 6 of قطع) Being disunited, alienated, giving each other the cut.

A تقاعد *takāعud*, (v. n. 6 of قعد) Not foregoing one's claims (upon another).

A تقاعس *takāعus*, (v. n. 6 of قعس) Receding, hanging back, lagging behind. Being refractory.

A تقافز *takāfuz*, A leaping together.

A تقافس *takāfus*, (v. n. 6 of قفس) Jumping together. Lugging each other's hair.

A تقافص *takāfus*, (v. n. 6 of قفص) Being intermingled. Being interlaced like network.

A تقافط *takāfut*, (v. n. 6 of قفط) Assisting each other to generate (applied especially to animals which part the hoof).

A تقافي *takāfī*, (v. n. 6 of قفا for قفو) Slandering, accusing falsely. Inventing a lie.

A تقالّ *takāll*, (v. n. 6 of قلّ) Considering as small, trifling. Ascending, rising high (the sun).

A تقالد *takālud*, (v. n. 6 of قلد) Observing rotations, taking one's turn in drawing water.

A تقاليب *takālīb*, Changes, revolutions.

A تقامر *takāmur*, (v. n. 6 of قمر) Playing together at dice or games of chance: wagering, betting.

A تقاود *takāwud*, (v. n. 6 of قاد for قود) Guiding, directing, pointing the way. Being tractable.

A تقاول *takāwul*, A conversing together.

A تقاوم *takāwum*, (v. n. 6 of قام for قوم) Rising one against another, getting up to fight. Opposing an enemy.

A تقاوه *takāwuh*, (v. n. 6 of قاه for قوه) Shouting together. A watchword.

A تقاوي *takāwī*, (v. n. 6 of قوي) Increasing (partners). Passing the night fasting. Money advanced to tenants to pay for seed.

A تقاويم *takāwīm*, (pl. of تقويم) Almanacks.

A تقايل *takāyul*, (v. n. 6 of قال for قيل) Dissolving mutually a contract, releasing each other.

A تقايي *takāyī*, A vomiting, a throwing up.

A تقبّب *takabbub*, (v.n.5 of قبّ) Entering a vaulted building (قبّة *kubbat*).

A تقبّص *takabbus*, A flocking around.

A تقبّض *takabbuz*, (v. n.5 of قبض) Being collected, contracted, wrinkled (the skin). Drawing one's self together. Being frightened. Leaping upon.

A تقبّل *takabbul*, (v. n. 2 of قبل irregular) Causing a workman to work. Accepting from a workman or a revenue-collector a surety or sponsor. (v. n. 5 of قبل) Receiving favourably, admitting, accepting. Going or turning to the south.

A تقبّي *takabbī*, (v. n. 5 of قبي) Putting on a short tunic open before, called قبا *kabā*. Stealing on one from behind. Resembling a cupola or dome.

A تقبيب *takbīb*, (v. n. 2 of قبّ) Making an arch or cupola. Drying up (a date).

A تقبية *takbiyat*, (v. n. 2 of قبي) Adjusting, adapting, arranging, preparing. Making the garment or tunic called قبا *kabā*.

A تقبيح *takbīh*, (v. n. 2 of قبح) Exposing a foul deed. Doing (any thing) in a coarse and ugly manner. Making ugly. Opening a boil and letting out the matter. Breaking (an egg). Reprobating and abandoning (God).

A تقبيص *takbīs*, (v. n. 2 of قبص) Taking up with the tips of the fingers.

A تقبيض *takbīz*, (v. n. 2 of قبض) Collecting in a heap. Causing one to take, putting within his grasp. Seizing, grasping.

A تقبيط *takbīt*, A frowning, a looking austere.

A تقبيل *takbīl*, (v. n. 2 of قبل) Kissing. A kiss. (v. n. 5 of قبل irregular) Doing work, managing an affair. Giving surety (a workman or collector).

A تقتاق *taktāk*, Swift, rapid (nocturnal journey in search of water).

A تقتال *taktāl*, A killing. Slaughter, murder.

A تقتّر *takattur*, (v. n. 5 of قتر) Preparing for any business. Retiring, remaining behind. Being angry. Breathing hard. Circumventing by fraud.

A تقتقة *taktakat*, A hard trot, uneasy motion.

A تقتّل *takattul*, (v. n. 5 of قتل) Going slowly, deliberately, and patiently about a thing. Walking with a graceful air (a woman).

A تقتيت *taktīt*, (v. n. 2 of قتّ) Publishing and censuring the opinions of others. Collecting and cooking herbs for the pot. Imbuing (oil) with the scent of fragrant flowers. Whispering, talebearing. Perfuming by boiling (unguents).

A تقتيد *taktīd*, (v. n. 2 of قتد) Cutting the shrub goat's thorn, burning it, and giving it to camels to eat.

A تقتير *taktīr*, (v. n. 2 of قتر) Sparing expense, keeping domestics at short allowance. Sending forth a flavour (meat when roasting). Putting a piece of meat in a hole, to allure wild beasts, or fumigating a place with burnt camel's hair, that they may not scent the hunter. Throwing any one into the dust. Drawing near, bringing together. Short commons, a bare sustenance.

A تقتيل *taktīl*, (v. n. 2 of قتل) Killing numbers. Wholesale slaughter.

A تقثّر *takassur*, (v. n. 5 of قثر not in use) Being timid, fearing. Being irresolute and undecided.

A تقحّز *takahhuz*, (v. n. 5 of قحز) Speaking rudely, harshly, and roughly.

A تقحزم *takahzum*, A sticking (to business).

A تقحزن *takahzun*, (v. n. 2 of قحزن Q) Falling down when struck, being levelled with the ground.

A تقحّل *takahhul*, (v. n. 5 of قحل) Having withered flesh upon the bones (an old man). Being old and full of years.

A تقحلز *takahluz*, (v. n. 2 of قحلز Q) Being thrown down, falling down from the effect of a blow.

A تقحّم *takahhum*, (v. n. 5 of قحم) Throwing his rider (a horse). Rushing violently.

A تقحيب *tak-hīb*, (v. n. 2 of قحب) Coughing, being seized with a fit of coughing.

A تقحيز *tak-hīz*, (v. n. 2 of قحز) Striking with a stick; making the (person) so struck to jump or spring. Using harsh (language).

A تقحيص *tak-hīs*, A removing, placing far off.

A تقحيط *tak-hīt*, (v. n. 2 of قحط) Making the female palm-tree fruitful by sprinkling the flowers of the male.

A تقحيم *tak-hīm*, (v. n. 2 of قحم) Precipitating, thrusting one into another. Throwing his rider on his face (a horse).

A تقخية *takhkhiyat*, (v. n. 2 of قخي not in use) Spitting out rheum. Throwing away mucus in a dirty manner.

A تقدة *tik*, *tak*, or *takidat*, Coriander-seed.

A تقدّد *takaddud*, (v. n. 5 of قدّ) Being split or cut into several parts. Being cut lengthwise. Being divided and dispersed (people). Being dry or dried. Being partially lean (a camel).

A تقدّر *takaddur*, (v. n. 5 of قدر) Preparing for any thing, being prepared.

A تقدّس *takaddasa*, (3d pers. sing. pret. of

قدس in the fifth conjug. used optatively) May he be sanctified! تقدّس و تعالىٰ *takaddasa wa taʻāla'*, May (He) be sanctified and exalted!

A تقدّس *takaddus*, A being pure and holy.

A تقدّع *takadduʻ*, (v. n. 5 of قدع) Preparing (mischief), becoming prepared (for mischief).

A تقدّم *takaddum*, (v. n. 5 of قدم) Preceding. Stepping forward, advancing. Being afore-mentioned. Being bold and intrepid. Laying a statement or narrative before any one. Commanding, giving a charge. Projecting beyond, jutting out. Standing before. Precedence, pre-excellence, preference, priority. One high in authority.

A تقدّمات *takaddumāt*, (pl. of تقدّم) Premises.

A تقدمة *takdimat*, The proposition of a syllogism. A government, lieutenancy. Final adjustment of an account. *Tukdamat*, A going before, a leading of the van.

A تقدمية *tukdumīyat*, A going before, a leading of the van.

A تقدّي *takaddī*, (v. n. 5 of قدا for قدو) Keeping the middle of the road.

A تقديح *takdīh*, (v. n. 2 of قدح) Making (a horse) slim or gaunt. Sinking in its socket (the eye).

A تقديد *takdīd*, (v. n. 2 of قدّ) Cutting or tearing (a garment) the long way. Cutting up by the root.

A تقدير *takdīr*, (v. n. 2 of قدر) Measuring. Dividing, apportioning subsistence or daily bread. Ordering. Thinking, considering, supposing. Confining, reducing to difficulties. Making one a professor of the doctrine of free-will. Thinking about doing a thing evenly. Predestination, inevitable decree, fixed fate. P بر تقدير *bar takdīr*, On the supposition. A على اي تقدير *ʻala' ayyi takdīrin*, In every possible case, on every supposition. على التقديرين *ʻala't takdīrayn*, In both cases.

A تقديرات *takdīrāt*, (pl. of تقدير) Decrees. تقديرات الهيّة *takdīrāt ilāhiyat*, Divine decrees.

A تقديريّ *takdīrīy*, Having the efficacy without the sensible or material part; real, virtual.

A تقديس *takdīs*, (v. n. 2 of قدس) Purifying, sanctifying, consecrating, calling holy.

A تقديم *takdīm*, (v. n. 2 of قدم) Giving precedence; preferring, promoting. Serving up, setting (food) before any one. Presenting. Preparing. Causing to proceed boldly. Sending forward, sending on before (virtuous or vicious deeds). Standing before. Swearing. Prefixing. Transposing, putting one before another.

A تقذّح *takazzuh*, A stirring up mischief.

A تقذّر *takazzur*, (v. n. 5 of قذر) Abhorring, detesting, considering as sordid or filthy. Regarding (food) as impure.

A تقذّع *takazzuʻ*, A preparing (of mischief).

A تقذقذ *takazkuz*, (v. n. 2 of قذقذ Q) Ascending a mountain. Falling into a well and perishing. Following one's own inclination.

A تقذية *takziyat*, (v. n. 2 of قذي) Taking a mote out of, or throwing one into, the eye.

A تقذير *takzīr*, (v. n. 2 of قذر) Soiling, dirtying (a garment). Charging with filthy practices.

A تقذيع *takzīʻ*, A dirtying, a soiling.

A تقذيف *takzīf*, (v. n. 2 of قذف) Cursing.

A تقر *takir*, Herbs, roots, spiceries, seasonings.

A تقرّاب *tikirrāb*, A striving to draw near.

A تقرار *takrār*, Stability, firmness, constitution.

A تقرّب *takarrub*, (v. n. 5 of قرب) Seeking admittance, striving to draw near. Hoping to render (the Deity) propitious by sacrifices. Placing the hands upon the hypochondria or space between the haunches and short ribs. Being quick, making haste. Propinquity, nearness. P كسب تقرّب كردن *kasbi takarrub kardan*, To gain admission, to get the ear (of a great man), to procure favour. A *Takarrab*, (imper. of the 5th conj.) Make haste.

A تقرة *takirat*, Caraway.

A تقرّة *takirrat*, (v. n. of قرّ) Remaining still. Being established in a place.

A تقرثع *takarsuʻ*, (v. n. 2 of قرثع Q not in use) Assembling, flocking together. Having his hair standing on end (a goat).

A تقرّح *takarruh*, (v. n. 5 of قرح) Being corroded with ulcers, becoming raw and sore. Being ready and prepared for.

A تقرد *tikrid*, Spiceries, seasonings. Caraways.

A تقرّد *takarrud*, (v. n. 5 of قرد) Being crisp and curly (hair). Being matted, impacted (wool).

A تقرّر *takarrur*, (v. n. 5 of قرّ) Being made fast, established. Being imposed (taxes). Staling on his legs (a camel). Eating dry meat and voiding turbid urine (a camel). Confirmation. Approbation.

A تقرزم *takarzum*, A writing bad poetry.

A تقرّش *takarrush*, (v. n. 5 of قرش) Collecting, wrapping one's self in a garment. Being collected, assembled from all quarters. Being pure, free from vice or stain. Taking any thing, first one part and then another.

A تقرّط *takarrut*, A being adorned with ear-rings.

A تقرطس *takartus*, (v. n. 2 of قرطس Q) Perishing.

A تقرطق *takartuk*, (v. n. 2 of قرطق Q) Being clad in the vesture called قرطق *kurtak*.

A تقرّع *takarruʻ*, (v. n. 5 of قرع) Turning and tossing one's self about in bed all night.

A تقرعث *takarʻus*, A being collected together.

A تقرعف *takarʻuf*, A drawing one's self together.

A تقرّف *takarruf*, (v. n. 5 of قرف) Being laid bare (a wound or sore).

A تقرفص *takarfus*, (v. n. 2 of قرفص Q) Wrapping (herself) up in her garments (an old woman).

A تقرفع *takarfuʻ*, A drawing one's self together.

A تقرقف *takarkuf*, (v. n. 2 of قرقف Q) Trembling. Gnashing the teeth.

A تقرّم *takarrum*, (v. n. 5 of قرم) Eating gently (as an infant), nibbling the herbage (as a young camel).

A تقرّؤ *takarruʼ*, (v. n. 5 of قرأ) Reading the scriptures. Being pious, religious, devoted to the service of God. Understanding.

P تقره *takira*, Caraway-seeds.

A تقرّي *takarrī*, A following of the stream.

A تقريب *takrīb*, (v. n. 2 of قرب) Giving access, causing to approach. Complaining of a pain in the hypochondria. Saying to any one حيّاك الله و قرّب دارك *hayyāka'llāhu wa karraba dāraka*. Cantering (a horse). A gallop, a mode of running in which the forefeet are raised together. Appearance, probability. Pretence, motive. Recommendation, mention. Occasion, conjuncture.

A تقريبًا *takrīban*, Near to, about.

A تقريبيّ *takrībīy*, Conjectural, probable.

A تقريح *takrīh*, (v. n. 2 of قرح) Causing a sore, making raw and sore. Encountering, meeting any one (with the truth).

A تقريد *takrīd*, (v. n. 2 of قرد) Being silent (especially from any impediment). Picking tikes off cattle. Soothing, cajoling, amusing, deceiving. Humbling, abasing, bringing into subjection. Humbling one's self, being submissive and depressed.

A تقرير *takrīr*, (v. n. 2 of قرّ) Fixing in a place, confirming. Constituting, appointing. Imposing (a tribute). Forcing to confess. Extorting the truth by torture. Staling at one gush. Relating, explaining. A narrative, relation, recital, account, detail. An official report. Pleasure, delight.

A تقريس *takrīs*, A chilling, a congealing.

A تقريش *takrīsh*, (v. n. 2 of قرش) Acquiring. Irritating, setting by the ears.

A تقريص *takrīs*, (v. n. 2 of قرص) Washing, squeezing, or pressing any thing out with the tips of the fingers. Cutting (dough) into several pieces. Making up (paste) into balls.

A تقريض *takrīz*, (v. n. 2 of قرض) Praising (a companion), exalting with praise. Censuring.

A تقريط *takrīt*, (v. n. 2 of قرط) Putting in ear-rings on any one. Bridling (a horse). Cutting (scallions) to season a pot. Snuffing a candle. Giving little. Putting (a horse) to his utmost speed.

A تقريظ *takrīz*, (v. n. 2 of قرظ) Praising the living (justly or unjustly).

A تقريع *takrīʻ*, (v. n. 2 of قرع) Reproaching, reviling, reproving, chiding. Striking the head. Incommoding, molesting, disturbing, disquieting. Curing a camel's colt of pustules called قرع *karaʻ*. Exciting a stallion to mount. Wetting the head of her colt with the milk of the other teat (a camel).

A تقريم *takrīm*, (v. n. 2 of قرم) Teaching to eat.

A تقرين *takrīn*, (v. n. 2 of قرن) Joining together many captives with one chain.

A تقريئ *takrīʼ*, (v. n. 2 of قرأ) Being confined at home by menstruation (قرء *karʼ* or *kurʼ*).

A تقزّع *takazzuʻ*, A spreading into many branches.

A تقزّز *takazzuz*, (v. n. 5 of قزّ) Hating impurity, regarding as unclean.

A تقزع *takazzuʻ*, A being ready to run.

A تقزية *takziyat*, A throwing down and killing.

A تقزيح *takzīh*, (v. n. 2 of قزح) Seasoning (a pot) with herbs. Decorating (a story). A substance on the head of a plant or tree, branching out like the soft parts under the claws of a dog.

A تقزيع *takzīʻ*, (v. n. 2 of قزع) Making (a horse) gallop or leap. Shaving (the head, but leaving some places hairy). Preparing (a horse) to run. Keeping (any one) purposely disengaged that he may be employed on a certain work. Sending (an ambassador or messenger). Running violently.

A تقسس *takassus*, A seeking, pursuing, desiring.

A تقسّط *takassut*, (v. n. 5 of قسط) Dividing equally amongst themselves. Receiving one's share.

A تقسقس *takaskus*, A listening, a hearing.

A تقسّم *takassum*, (v. n. 5 of قسم) Dividing, separating. Scattering. Being divided, scattered.

A تقسيس *taksīs*, A feeding (camels) well.

A تقسيط *taksīt*, (v. n. 2 of قسط) Dividing equally among themselves. Sparing expense, keeping domestics on short allowance.

A تقسيم *taksīm*, (v. n. 2 of قسم) Distributing, dividing, scattering, dispersing. Giving to be divided. Division in arithmetic. تقسيم جمع *taksīmi jamʻ*, An assessment of land. A rent-roll.

P تقسيم نمودن *taksīm namūdan*, To distribute, allot.

A تقسيمى *taksīmī*, An assessment of taxes in lots.

A تقشّر *takashshur*, (v. n. 5 of قشر) Being peeled, unbarked, excoriated.

A تقشّط *takashshut*, Serenity (of the sky).

A تقشّع *takashshuʻ*, (v. n. 5 of قشع) Being dispelled, separated, scattered, dispersed. Disappearing, vanishing.

A تقشّف *takashshuf*, (v. n. 5 of قشف) Living poorly. Being scantily fed and coarsely clothed. Becoming dry.

A تقشقش *takashkush*, (v. n. 2 of قشقش Q) Recovering from measles. Being healed (skin).

A تقشيب *takshīb*, (v. n. 2 of قشب) Contaminating, defiling. Affecting one (the poisonous smell of any thing).

A تقشية *takshiyat*, (v. n. 2 of قشا for قشو) Unbarking or chipping (wood). Skinning, stripping off a snake's slough. Preventing, hindering.

A تقشير *takshīr*, (v. n. 2 of قشر) Peeling, unbarking, excoriating.

A تقشيش *takshīsh*, (v. n. 2 of قش) Eating (upon every occasion).

A تقصار *tiksār*, (or تقصارة *tiksārat*) (pl. تقاصير *takāsīr*) A collar or necklace (short and close).

A تقصبة *taksibat*, A lock twisted, not plaited.

A تقصّد *takassud*, (v. n. 5 of قصد) Being broken in pieces (a spear). Dying (a dog).

A تقصّر *takassur*, (v. n. 5 of قصر) Amusing one's self, beguiling the time. Keeping (any one) amused, quieting, contenting.

A تقصّص *takassus*, (v. n. 5 of قص) Following (the steps of another). Preserving in memory (the speech of another).

A تقصّع *takassuʻ*, (v. n. 5 of قصع) Being full of matter (a boil).

A تقصّف *takassuf*, (v. n. 5 of قصف) Being broken, dashed, bruised. Assembling, flocking together. Joking, playing at meal-time.

A تقصّم *takassum*, A being broken, torn asunder.

A تقصّي *takassī*, (v. n. 5 of قصي) Curiously prying, using every effort to get at the knowledge of.

A تقصيب *taksīb*, (v. n. 2 of قصب) Coming into stalk (corn). Curling (hair), twisting, but not plaiting it. Accusing, blaming, reproaching. Tying the hands to the neck.

A تقصيبة *taksībat*, A lock twisted, not plaited.

A تقصية *taksiyat*, (v. n. 2 of قصا for قصو) Cutting the nails; cropping the tips of the ears.

A تقصيد *taksīd*, A breaking, splitting (wood).

A تقصير *taksīr*, (v. n. 2 of قصر) Subsiding (as anger or pain). Being deficient, unequal to. Desisting from what one cannot perform. Doing less than one ought. Falling short. Proceeding slowly. Abridging. Making a scanty gift. Shortening prayers (by performing two, instead of four, inclinations). Bleaching, fulling (a garment). Marking (a camel) on the neck. (pl. تقاصير *takāsīr*) Defect, failure, deficiency, short-coming. Abbreviation. Error, guilt, fault. A mark or cautery branded on a beast.

A تقصيرات *taksīrāt*, Errors, failings.

P تقصيروار *taksīrwār*, Faulty, culpable.

A تقصيص *taksīs*, A plastering with mortar.

A تقصيع *taksīʻ*, (v. n. 2 of قصع) Quenching thirst (water). Emerging from a mountain-pass. Wrapping one's self up in a garment. Throwing the soil out of his hole (the jerboa). Keeping close at home. Appearing above ground (wheat).

A تقضّب *takazzub*, (v. n. 5 of قضب) Being lopped, pruned (a vine). Emitting rays (the sun).

A تقضّض *takazzuz*, (v. n. 5 of قضّ) Sousing on prey (a hawk).

A تقضّع *takazzuʻ*, A being cut, separated, divided.

A تقضقض *takazkuz*, (v. n. 2 of قضقض Q) Being separated, divided, scattered.

A تقضّو *takazzuw*, (v. n. 5 of قضو) Seeking to sully a person's character, regarding as mean.

A تقضّي *takazzī*, (v. n. 5 of قضي) Vanishing. Being ended. Pouncing upon prey (a hawk).

A تقضيب *takzīb*, (v. n. 2 of قضب) Lopping off branches, pruning. Darting forth rays (the sun).

A تقضية *takziyat*, (v. n. 5 of قضى) Performing, finishing, consummating, executing. Constituting a judge. (God) sending calamity among men.

A تقضيع *takzīʻ*, Great aching (of the teeth).

A تقطّاع *tikittāʻ*, A cutting, amputating, dividing.

A تقطّب *takattub*, (v. n. 5 of قطب) Being grim, truculent, and austere.

A تقطّر *takattur*, (v. n. 5 of قطر) Dropping, being ready to drop, trickle, or distil. Being thrown down (the trunk of a palm-tree). Preparing for battle. Throwing one's self from a height. Falling on one's side. Throwing one on his side. Perfuming herself with wood of aloes (a woman). Retiring, remaining behind.

A تقطرب *takatrub*, (v. n. 2 of قطرب Q) Moving the head and resembling the قطرب *kutrub*.

A تقطّع *takattuʻ*, (v. n. 5 of قطع) Being cut into several parts. Being dissolved. Falling in pieces. Being diluted (as wine). Dividing (departments of business among one another).

A تقطقط *takatkut*, (v. n. 2 of قطقط Q) Being let down (a bucket). Taking short steps, and going fast. Travelling through a country. Following one's own way.

A تقطّل *takattul*, (v. n. 5 of قطل) Being cut up by the root (a palm-tree). Throwing on the side or prostrating.

A تقطّي *takattī*, (v. n. 5 of قطا for قطو) Being drawn up very gently from a well (a bucket). Being slow. Turning away the face. Deceiving, circumventing. Riding behind on a horse's rump.

A تقطيب *taktīb*, (v. n. 2 of قطب) Knitting the brows, scowling, looking austere. Mixing (wine).

A تقطير *taktīr*, (v. n. 2 of قطر) Causing to drop, or to come away drop by drop. Piercing with a spear, and levelling with the ground. Throwing (one) on (his) side. Perfuming (a garment) with the wood of aloes. Tying (camels) in a string. Distillation. A diabetes. A gonorrhœa.

A تقطيط *taktīt*, (v. n. 2 of قطّ) Cutting, turning, shaping a little box.

A تقطيع *taktīʻ*, (v. n. 2 of قطع) Cutting in several pieces, hacking, hashing, mincing. Dissecting. (In prosody) Scanning. Stopping, breaking off (as one does in making water). Inflicting punishment of diverse kinds (God). Diluting (wine with water). Leaving another behind (a horse in a race). Being sufficient for one's stature (cloth for a garment). The cesura or pause in verse. The stature of man. Gripes.

A تقطيف *taktīf*, (v. n. 2 of قطف) Gathering grapes. Scratching.

A تقطيل *taktīl*, (v. n. 2 of قطل) Cutting. Throwing (one) down on (his) side, or prostrating.

A تقطين *taktīn*, (v. n. 2 of قطن) Putting forth shoots or buds (a vine).

A تقع *takaʻ*, (v. n. of تقع) Being hungry. Hunger. تقع تقع *takaʻun takiʻun*, Hunger of the keenest kind, starvation.

A تقعثل *takaʻsul*, (v. n. 2 of قعثل Q) Moving heavily (one overloaded).

A تقعّد *takaʻʻud*, (v. n. 5 of قعد) Attending to,

minding business. Delaying (business). Preventing, hindering. Being unable, or unwilling, to do any thing. Hanging back.

A تقعّر *takaʿʿur*, (v. n. 5 of قعر) Being deep (well or ditch). Making efforts to be eloquent. Mouthing the words much when speaking.

A تقعّف *takaʿʿuf*, A being moved (from its place).

A تقعفز *takaʿfuz*, (v. n. 2 of قعفز Q) Kneeling.

A تقعقع *takaʿkuʿ*, (v. n. 2 of قعقع Q) Being removed with noise (as the poles of a tent when preparing to migrate). Being shaken. A noise made by the joints of the feet in walking.

A تقعوس *takaʿwus*, (v. n. 2 of قعوس Q) Becoming decrepit (an old man). Being destroyed, tumbling in ruins (a house).

A تقعوش *takaʿwush*, The same.

A تقعيب *takʿīb*, (v. n. 2 of قعب) Making deep. Being shaped like a cup (the hoof of a horse). Being carried far (in an argument).

A تقعيث *takʿīs*, A pulling up by the roots.

A تقعيد *takʿīd*, (v. n. 2 of قعد) Attending, serving, waiting upon. Praying that God may preserve. Satisfying, being sufficient in point of gain or advantage.

A تقعير *takʿīr*, (v. n. 2 of قعر) Going to the bottom. Being carried on (in a speech). Moving the mouth much when speaking. Shouting.

A تقعيط *takʿīt*, (v. n. 2 of قعط) Being obscene in talk. Straitening, narrowing. Driving forcibly.

A تقفّر *takaffur*, A following (the steps).

A تقفّز *takaffuz*, (v. n. 5 of قفز) Drawing on a glove. Tinging the (hands or feet) with privet.

A تقفّس *takaffus*, A leaping, hopping, skipping.

A تقفّص *takaffus*, A being collected, assembled.

A تقفّع *takaffuʿ*, (v. n. 5 of قفع) Being contracted, or becoming wrinkled, shrivelled.

A تقفقف *takafkuf*, (v. n. 5 of قفقف Q) Trembling (especially with cold), chattering (the teeth). Withering (as a plant).

A تقفّي *takaffī*, (v. n. 5 of قفا for قفو) Following the steps. Striking with a stick. Exulting, rejoicing. Shewing extraordinary kindness and benevolence. Making many inquiries about one.

A تقفية *takfiyat*, (v. n. 2 of قفا for قفو) Ordering or causing to follow, sending in the track of. Tracking, tracing, following the steps.

A تقفير *takfīr*, (v. n. 2 of قفر) Collecting, heaping together (earth).

A تقفيع *takfīʿ*, (v. n. 2 of قفع) Preserving, laying by, taking care of.

A تقفيل *takfīl*, (v. n. 2 of قفل) Locking (doors). Becoming dry (the skin). Keeping, guarding, preserving. Collecting, hoarding (grain).

A تقفين *takfīn*, A decapitating.

A تقلّب *takallub*, (v. n. 5 of قلب) Rolling, tossing one's self (as a snake writhing on hot sand). Carrying on one's business. Being expert in business, handling dexterously. Change.

A تقلّبات *takallubāt*, Changes, turns.

A تقلّح *takalluh*, (v. n. 5 of قلح) Making immoderate profits during a season of scarcity.

A تقلّد *takallud*, (v. n. 5 of قلد) Being adorned with a necklace (a woman), with a collar (an animal). Being preferred to, or confirmed in, an office. Receiving an investiture. Putting a sword-belt round the neck, or over the shoulder. Putting on a necklace (قلادة *kilādat*).

A تقلّز *takalluz*, (v. n. 5 of قلز) Being sprightly, brisk, and cheerful. Running (the mountain goat).

A تقلزم *takalzum*, (v. n. 2 of قلزم Q) Swallowing. Dying from avarice.

A تقلّس *takallus*, (v. n. 5 of قلس) Putting on the high-crowned cap قلنسوة *kalansuwat*.

A تقلسي *takalsī*, (v. n. 2 of قلسي Q) Being coifed with a hat or cap (قلنسوة *kalansuwat*).

A تقلّص *takallus*, (v. n. 5 of قلص) Contracting, shrinking (a shadow or clothes in washing). Being shrivelled (the lips).

A تقلّع *takalluʿ*, (v. n. 5 of قلع) Being torn up. Moving about.

A تقلعث *takalʿus*, (v. n. 2 of قلعث Q) Walking as if impeded by adhesive mire.

A تقلق *tiklik*, Name of an aquatic bird.

A تقلقل *takalkul*, A being moved, shaken.

A تقلنس *takalnus*, (v. n. 2 of قلنس Q) Being coifed with a hat or cap (قلنسوة *kalansuwat*).

P تقلي *tuklī*, A lamb six months old.

A تقلّي *takallī*, A shewing hatred.

A تقليب *taklīb*, (v. n. 2 of قلب) Revolving, inverting, turning upside down. Turning inside out.

A تقليح *taklīh*, A cleaning the teeth.

A تقليخ *taklīkh*, (v. n. 2 of قلخ) Striking a severe blow. Thriving (a plant).

A تقليد *taklīd*, (v. n. 2 of قلد) Adorning (a woman's neck) with a chain. Putting a wreath round the neck of a victim destined to be slain at Mecca. Putting a belt to a sword. Investing with authority. Imitation, representation. A counterfeiting. اهل تقليد *ahli taklīd*, A mimic, comedian, buffoon. P تقليد كردن *taklīd kardan*, To represent, counterfeit, feign. To imitate the voice, manner, or hand of another.

A تقليدي *taklīdī*, Imitated, forged, counterfeit.

A تقليز *taklīz*, (v. n. 2 of قلز) Causing one to empty a cup. Fixing its tail in the ground to lay its eggs (a locust).

A تقليس *taklīs*, (v. n. 2 of قلس) Beating a kind of Arabian drum, called دفّ *daff*, and meeting or going before kings and other great men, with that and other musical instruments, on triumphant and other public occasions. Placing the hand on the breast and making a reverential salutation.

A تقليص *taklīs*, (v. n. 2 of قلص) Drawing one's self together. Tucking up (a garment). Continuing, persevering. Being tucked up (a garment).

A تقليع *taklīʿ*, (v. n. 2 of قلع) Removing, tearing up. Extracting.

A تقليف *taklīf*, (v. n. 2 of قلف) Caulking (a ship). Dates stoned and laid up in hampers.

A تقليل *taklīl*, (v. n. 2 of قل) Diminishing, causing to look less. Giving little. Paucity.

A تقليم *taklīm*, A paring (of the nails).

A تقمّح *takammuh*, (v. n. 5 of قمح) Raising the head when refusing to drink (a camel).

A تقمّر *takammur*, (v. n. 5 of قمر) Gaining at dice. Visiting one by moonlight. Going out a hunting by moonlight. Prowling forth at that time (a lion in quest of prey). Bringing home (a wife) by moonlight. Marrying a woman. Stealing upon a woman unawares.

A تقمّش *takammush*, (v. n. 5 of قمش) Eating whatever one can get hold of, although refuse.

A تقمّص *takammus*, (v. n. 5 of قمص) Putting on a shirt or shift (قميص *kamīs*).

A تقمّع *takammuʿ*, (v. n. 5 of قمع) Taking the best part (of any thing). Sitting alone in astonishment. Shaking the head to drive away the flies.

A تقمقم *takamkum*, (v. n. 2 of قمقم Q) Being on the top of any thing. Being plunged under water. Mounting the female when recumbent (a camel).

A تقمّل *takammul*, The smallest perceptible degree of fatness.

A تقمّم *takammum*, (v. n. 5 of قمّ) Ascending to the highest part. Copulating (beasts). Searching, examining things swept together.

A تقمّن *takammun*, (v. n. 5 of قمن not in use) Endeavouring (to accommodate one's self to the humour of another).

A تقمّؤ *takammuʾ*, (v. n. 5 of قمأ) Collecting, scraping together. Taking the best part of any thing. Agreeing with any one (a place).

A تقمّه *takammuh*, (v. n. 5 of قمه) Wandering no one knows where, in uncertainty and irresolution.

A تقميح *takmīh*, (v. n. 2 of قمح) Putting one off with a little instead of much which was due.

A تقميش *takmīsh*, (v. n. 2 of قمش) Raking together (small things) from any place.

A تقميص *takmīs*, (v. n. 2 of قمص) Putting a shirt (قميص *kamīs*) upon any one.

A تقميط *takmīt*, (v. n. 2 of قمط) Binding the hands and feet (of a captive), or the four feet (of a sheep). Swaddling an infant.

A تقميع *takmīʿ*, (v. n. 2 of قمع) Taking the stalk (from a date).

A تقن *tikn*, Nature. Skilful (man). Clay or soil at the bottom of rivers, wells, or ditches. ابن تقن *ibn tikn*, Name of a famous shooter.

A تقنّب *takannub*, (v. n. 5 of قنب) Setting (the sun). Being 30 or 40 in number (a troop of horse).

A تقنّح *takannuh*, (v. n. 5 of قنح) Refusing to drink. Retiring from water after being filled.

Drinking short of repletion.

A تقنز *takannuz*, A hunting, seeking for game.

A تقنسر *takansur*, (v. n. 2 of قنسر Q) Growing old and contracted (a man).

A تقنّص *takannus*, (v. n. 5 of قنص) Hunting. Looking for game.

A تقنّع *takannuꜥ*, (v. n. 5 of قنع) Putting on a coif or cap called قناع *kināꜥ*. Wrapping one's self up in a garment. Striking on the head with a whip. Erecting his neck-feathers, about to fight (a cock).

A تقنفذ *takanfuz*, A striking with a staff.

A تقنّؤ *takannus*, (v. n. 5 of قنأ) Dyeing (the beard) with privet. Being intensely red.

A تقنّي *takanni*, (v. n. 5 of قنا for قنو) Living within one's income, and laying by.

A تقنيب *taknīb*, (v. n. 2 of قنب) Putting forth the broad leaf (corn). Being 30 or 40 in number (a troop of horse). Being owner of such a troop.

A تقنئة *takniꜣat*, (v. n. 2 of قنأ) Tinging with a very red colour. Dyeing (the beard) black.

A تقنية *takniyat*, (v. n. 2 of قنا for قنو) Sticking close to. Keeping up a sense of modesty.

A تقنيح *taknīh*, (v. n. 2 of قنح) Fitting a long crooked key to the lock of a door.

A تقنيش *taknīsh*, (v. n. 2 of قنش not used) Being frugal in housekeeping.

A تقنيط *taknīt*, A driving to desperation.

A تقنيع *taknīꜥ*, (v. n. 2 of قنع) Making contented. Putting on a head-dress, veiling, hooding. Wrapping a whip round the head. Ruffling up the feathers of his head even with his neck (a cock). Making or assisting (a woman) to put on her coif.

A تقنيف *taknīf*, (v. n. 2 of قنف) Cutting in pieces with a sword.

A تقنيء *taknīꜣ*, (v. n. 2 of قنأ) Tinging with a very red colour. Dyeing black (the beard).

A تقوا *takwa'*, (for تقوي *takwa'*) Piety. The fear of God.

A تقواء *tukawāꜣ*, (pl. of تقيّ *takiy*) Religious, God-fearing men.

A تقواد *takwād*, The act of leading.

A تقوالة *tikwālat*, Loquacious, talkative.

A تقوّب *takawwub*, (v. n. 5 of قاب for قوب) Being excoriated, unbarked. Being broken, torn, or pulled up. Being hollow (ground). Being broken (an egg).

A تقوّت *takawwut*, (v. n. 5 of قات for قوت) Supporting one's self, subsisting upon.

A تقوّح *takawwuh*, Suppuration (of a wound).

A تقوّر *takawwur*, (v. n. 5 of قار for قور) Twisting, coiling (as a serpent). Being elapsed (the best part of the night).

A تقوّز *takawwuz*, (v. n. 5 of قاز for قوز) Being sprightly, brisk, and cheerful. Falling from the top to the bottom. Being pulled down, demolished, destroyed, disjointed, and falling to pieces. Running (the mountain-goat).

A تقوّس *takawwus*, (v. n. 5 of قاس for قوس) Being crooked, curved, bent like a bow (قوس *kaws*). Arming one's self with a bow.

A تقوصر *takawsur*, (v. n. 2 of قوصر Q) Pretending to be short. Entering (one part into another).

A تقوصرة *takawsarat*, The making an appearance of being short.

A تقوّض *takawwuz*, (v. n. 5 of قاض for قوض) Being disjointed, demolished, falling to pieces. Going and coming. Breaking up and dispersing.

A تقوع *takūꜥ*, Tekoa (noted for its honey).

A تقوّع *takawwuꜥ*, (v. n. 5 of قاع for قوع) Inclining to one side. Walking as if treading upon thorns. Climbing (a tree as the chameleon).

A تقوّف *takawwuf*, (v. n. 5 of قاف for قوف) Checking one when speaking, desiring him to say this or that.

A تقوّل *takawwul*, A telling a lie of another.

A تقولة *tikwilat*, Loquacious, talkative.

A تقوّن *takawwun*, Transgression with the tongue. Full praise.

A تقوي *takwa'*, Fear of God, piety. Abstinence. اهل تقوي *ahli takwa'*, One who fears God; pious, devout. God (as worthy of being feared).

A تقوّي *takawwi*, (v. n. 5 of قوي) Becoming powerful, strong. Being withheld (rain).

A تقويب *takwīb*, (v. n. 2 of قاب for قوب) Digging. Tearing up, eradicating. Making an impression, penetrating.

A تقوية *takwiyat*, (v. n. 2 of قوي) Strengthening. Reinforcing. Suspecting. Reviling. Aid.

A تقويح *takwīh*, The sweeping (of a house).

A تقويد *takwīd*, The act of leading.

A تقوير *takwīr*, (v. n. 2 of قار for قور) Paring (an apple). Cutting (any thing) in the middle in a circular form.

A تقويز *takwīz*, (v. n. 2 of قاز for قوز) Being great in quantity (vegetation).

A تقويس *takwīs*, (v. n. 2 of قاس for قوس) Becoming crooked, decrepit (old men). Becoming crooked, curved, bent like a bow (قوس *kaws*).

A تقويض *takwīz*, (v. n. 2 of قاض for قوض) Demolishing a structure (such as pulling up the pegs and ropes), but not utterly destroying it.

A تقويف *takwīf*, Tracking footsteps, following.

A تقويل *takwīl*, (v. n. 2 of قال for قول) Reporting that another said so and so (generally falsely).

A تقويم *takwīm*, (v. n. 2 of قام for قوم) Making straight, straightening. Setting in order, fixing, adjusting. Putting a price upon. Estimating, rating. A calendar, almanack. علي احسن تقويم *ꜥala' ahsana takwīmin*, In the most perfect symmetry.

A تقويه *takwīh*, (v. n. 2 of قوه not in use) Making a clamour. Driving (wild beasts) into (a net).

P تقه *tuka*, A button, buckle, clasp.

A تقهقر *takahkur*, A retiring back.

A تقهّل *takahhul*, (v. n. 5 of قهل) Drying, withering (the skin). Having dry and withered flesh upon the bones (an old man). Unaccustoming the body to the use of water, keeping one's person squalid. Being of a horrible figure. Being poor and miserable. Speaking in a shrill, feeble tone of voice. Walking or proceeding slowly. Complaining of want.

A تقهوس *takahwus*, (v. n. 2 of قهوس Q) Making haste, going fast. Bending and tottering as one goes. Celerity. A trembling, tottering gait.

A تقي *takī*, (fem. imperative) Fear thou (woman). *Tuka'*, (v. n. of تقي) Fearing. Piety, the fear of God. اصحاب تقي *as-hābi tuka'*, The pious.

A تقيّ *takiy*, (pl. اتقياء *atkiyāꜣ* and تقواء *tukawāꜣ*) Pious, God-fearing.

A تقيّة *takiyat*, (v. n. of تقي) Fearing. Fear, caution. Piety.

A تقيّث *takayyus*, A collection. Prohibition.

A تقيّح *takayyuh*, Suppuration (of a wound).

A تقيّد *takayyud*, A binding one's self. Superintendence, oversight. Attention, diligence, application, assiduity.

A تقيّس *takayyus*, (v. n. 5 of قاس for قيس) Resembling, or adhering to, the tribe of Kays.

A تقيّص *takayyus*, (v. n. 5 of قاص for قيص) Braying (a camel). Falling in (a well).

A تقيّض *takayyuz*, (v. n. 5 of قاض for قيض) Being broken (an egg), demolished (a wall), falling, crumbling in ruins. Resembling (one's father). Being caused, arising.

A تقيّظ *takayyuz*, (v. n. 5 of قاظ for قيظ) Summering, passing the summer (قيظ *kayz*).

A تقيّل *takayyul*, (v. n. 5 of قال for قيل) Resembling, taking after, one's father. Sleeping at mid-day; also drinking then. Being assembled, met, flowing (water).

A تقيّن *takayyun*, (v. n. 5 of قان for قين) Being adorned (a bride).

A تقيّؤ *takayyuꜣ*, (v. n. 5 of قيأ) Vomiting. Pretending or striving to vomit. Throwing herself in her husband's way (a woman).

A تقيئة *takyiꜣat*, A causing to vomit.

A تقييح *takyīh*, (v. n. 2 of قاح for قيح) Making purulent (a wound). Making or yielding matter.

A تقييد *takyīd*, (v. n. 2 of قاد for قيد) Binding, restraining, repressing. Securing (her husband) by charms and amulets (a woman). Fettering, shackling. Pointing a book. Measuring. Making the رويّ *rawiy* of a poem quiescent. A tax.

A تقيير *takyīr*, The pitching (a ship or wine-jar).

A تقييض *takyīz*, (v. n. 2 of قاض for قيض) Determining, defining. Predestinating. Giving birth to a cause. Exposing for sale or barter. Exchanging, bartering. Marking (camels) with a hot stone or iron. Bringing and preparing.

A تقييظ *takyīz*, (v. n. 2 of قاظ for قيظ) Passing the summer (any where). Sufficing for the summer.

A تقييل *takyīl*, (v. n. 2 of قال for قيل) Giving drink, drinking, or milking a camel at mid-day.

A تقيين *takyīn*, (v. n. 2 of قان for قين) Adorning, dressing (a bride). Putting a house in order.

P تك *tak*, A species of grass growing among wheat. Name of a plant growing in the water, of which, in Egypt, they make paper, and which, in Arabic, they call برديّ *bardiy*. The bottom of a well. A stroke. The pace of a horse. Little, small, moderate in quantity. The full speed of a horse, a gallop. A heat, race. A smart blow, a rap. Striking the dice-box to make the dice lie even. (imperative and participle of تكيدن *takīdan*) Run thou. Running. اسب تك *asb-tak*, (Fleet) as a horse. تك و پو *tak u pū*, Run and search. Diligent inquiry. تك و پو كردن *tak u pū kardan*, To search or examine carefully. *Tik*, A mouthful, morsel. Before. Near. *Tuk*, The beak of a bird. The point of a dagger or spear. A small lamp which gives but little light.

A تكّ *takk*, (v. n. of تكّ) Cutting. Treading, trampling. Breaking. Overcoming, intoxicating.

A تكاءد *takāʼud*, A being difficult, troublesome.

P تكاب *tak-āb*, A channel hollowed out by a torrent. A pass between two mountains. Uneven grounds, partly under water, partly dry, partly verdant, partly sterile. A funnel. Name of a country.

A تكابر *takābur*, (v. n. 6 of كبر) Playing the great man upon one another, behaving superciliously.

P تكاپوي *tak-ā-pūy*, Diligent search. A running to and fro. A bustling about here and there.

A تكأة *tukaʼat*, A prop, support. A walking-stick. A cushion, pillow. One who reclines much upon his side.

A تكاتب *takātub*, (v. n. 6 of كتب) Writing to one another. Writing off his slavery, engaging to give his master a certain sum for his ransom (a slave).

A تكاتع *takātuʻ*, A following in succession.

A تكاتم *takātum*, (v. n. 6 of كتم) Concealing among themselves.

A تكاثح *takāsuh*, A fighting (with swords).

A تكاثر *takāsur*, (v. n. 6 of كثر) Disputing for superiority (in number, affluence, or offspring).

A تكاثف *takāsuf*, (v. n. 6 of كثف) Being thick, compressed, condensed. Thickness, density.

A تكادر *takādur*, A fixing the eye stedfastly.

A تكادم *takādum*, A biting each other.

A تكاذب *takāzub*, (v. n. 6 of كذب) Lying, deceiving each other. Lying for one another in friendship.

P تكار *tak-ār*, Running. A swift horse.

A تكارم *takārum*, A being honourable, pure.

A تكاره *takāruh*, (v. n. 6 of كره) Disliking, detesting, disapproving. علی التكاره, Reluctantly.

A تكاري *takārī*, A hiring, renting, taking on hire.

A تكاشف *takāshuf*, (v. n. 6 of كشف) Disclosing each other's faults.

A تكاسّ *takāss*, A thronging (of men).

A تكاظّ *takāzz*, A persecuting one another.

A تكافّ *takāff*, (v. n. 6 of كفّ) Repelling, keeping back one another.

A تكافؤ *takāfuʼ*, (v. n. 6 of كفأ) Answering exactly. Equality.

A تكّاك *tukkāk*, (pl. of تاكّ *tākk*) Foolish, dull, stupid. Thin, emaciated. Perishing.

A تكاكرة *takākirat*, (pl. of تكّري *takkurī*) Generals, leaders.

A تكأكؤ *takaʼkuʼ*, (v. n. 2 of كأكأ Q) Being weak, cowardly. Retiring from fear. Congregating, being collected together. Stammering.

A تكالب *takālub*, A rushing on one another.

A تكالم *takālum*, (v. n. 6 of كلم) Revisiting, conversing after a separation.

A تكاليف *takālīf*, (pl. of تكليف *taklīf*) Troubles. Impositions, exactions, levies, burdens, taxes.

A تكامر *takāmur*, (v. n. 6 of كمر) Inspecting each other's كمرة *kamarat*, to see which is the biggest.

A تكامل *takāmul*, A being perfect, complete.

P تكانيدن *takānīdan*, To brush or shake off.

P تكاو *tak-āv*, A channel hollowed by a torrent. Uneven grounds, partly under water and partly dry.

A تكاوح *takāwuh*, A treating one another ill.

P تكاور *tak-āwar*, Swift, running. An ambling horse. A camel. تكاور ابلق *tak-āwari ablak*, The world. Day and night.

A تكاوس *takāwus*, (v. n. 6 of كاس for كوس) Being compressed. Being firm in flesh (youth). Being thick (herbage).

A تكاول *takāwul*, (v. n. 6 of كال for كول) Pretending to be short. Hanging back.

A تكايد *takāyud*, (v. n. 6 of كاد for كيد) Laying snares for one another. Being arduous and difficult. Stinginess, covetousness.

A تكايس *takāyus*, A being sharp, clever.

A تكايل *takāyul*, (v. n. 6 of كال for كيل) Measuring to one another. Reviling each other.

A تكبّب *takabbub*, (v. n. 5 of كبّ) Breaking down from disease (a camel). Being shrivelled or contracted (from disease or cold).

A تكبّد *takabbud*, (v. n. 5 of كبد) Being in the meridian (the sun). Being in the highest altitude (a star). Becoming thick (milk). Pursuing, aiming at any object.

A تكبّر *takabbur*, (v. n. 5 of كبر) Being proud. Being stubborn and rebellious. Pride, haughtiness, arrogance, loftiness, presumption, grandeur.

A تكبرانيّة *takbirānīyat*, The height of glory.

A تكبّس *takabbus*, A being trodden.

A تكبكب *takabkub*, (v. n. 2 of كبكب Q) Breaking down from disease or leanness (a camel).

A تكبّن *takabbun*, A becoming fat.

P تكبند *tak-band*, A silken or woollen girdle with a hook and eye at the ends.

A تكبّي *takabbī*, (v. n. 5 of كبا for كبو) Being perfumed (clothes). Holding (a garment) over a censer that it may become scented. Squatting over a censer or chafing-dish.

A تكبيب *takbīb*, (v. n. 2 of كبّ) Cutting meat into bits for roasting, making a كباب *kabāb*.

A تكبية *takbiyat*, (v. n. 2 of كبا for كبو) Perfuming (garments). Covering up (live coals) with ashes.

A تكبيث *takbīs*, (v. n. 2 of كبث) Heeling, as a ship when unloading her cargo or transferring it on board another vessel.

A تكبيد *takbīd*, (v. n. 2 of كبد) Attaining its highest altitude above the horizon (the sun or star).

A تكبير *takbīr*, (v. n. 2 of كبر) Making, calling, or esteeming great. Magnifying God by saying الله اكبر *allāh akbar*, God is greatest.

A تكبيع *takbīʻ*, A cutting, hacking, hashing.

A تكبيل *takbīl*, (v. n. 2 of كبل) Fettering (a captive). Mixing. Deferring payment of a debt.

A تكّة *takkat*, (v. n. of تكّ) Intoxicating (wine). Cutting. Trampling, bruising under foot. *Tikkat*, (pl. تكك *tikak*) Strings for long drawers or trowsers.

P تكتاز *tak-tāz*, Haste, speed. Be quick!

A تكتّب *takattub*, A being drawn up in troops.

A تكتّف *takattuf*, (v. n. 5 of كتف) Walking with high shoulders.

A تكتكة *taktakat*, A treading. A breaking.

A تكتكت *takatkut*, A taking short, quick steps.

A تكتّل *takattul*, A going like a dwarf.

A تكتم *tuktam*, The well Zamzam at Mecca.

A تكتيب *taktīb*, (v. n. 2 of كتب) Writing. Teaching or causing to write. Assembling or drawing up (an army) in divisions or squadrons.

A تكتيع *taktīʻ*, (v. n. 2 of كتع) Cutting small, chopping, mincing.

A تكتيف *taktīf*, (v. n. 2 of كتف) Hooping (a barrel). Pinioning. Being high in the withers (a horse). Moving his shoulders in walking (a horse). Mincing, hashing (meat).

A تكتيل *taktīl*, (v. n. 2 of كتل) Working (dough or clay) with the hand.

A تكتيم *taktīm*, (v. n. 2 of كتم) Concealing, covering, hiding. Causing to conceal.

A تكثّح *takassuh*, (v. n. 5 of كثح) Being struck (with gravel). Putting (gravel) in motion.

A تكثّر *takassur*, (v. n. 5 of كثر) Boasting of, pretending to abound.

A تكثّم *takassum*, (v. n. 5 of كثم) Stopping short, delaying, halting. Being astonished. Retiring, withdrawing, lurking, crouching.

A تكثيب *taksīb*, Paucity, fewness, smallness.

A تكثئة *taksiʼat*, (v. n. 2 of كثأ) Gathering cream (milk). Throwing up fat or scum (a pot). Floating on the surface of whey (milk). Growing long, spreading (as plants, the beard, or camels' hair). Eating cream.

A تكثيح *taksīh*, An uncovering (one's posteriors).

A تكثير *taksīr*, (v. n. 2 of كثر) Multiplying,

augmenting, enlarging. Doing too much, overdoing.

A تكثيع *taksīʿ*, (v. n. 2 of كثع) Having a flux, voiding liquid stools. Gathering cream (milk). Throwing up scum (a pot). Skinning, healing over (a wound). Growing long (plants, the beard). Eating cream.

A تكثيف *taksīf*, A rendering thick, condensing.

A تكحّل *takahhul*, (v. n. 5 of كحل) Tinging the eyes with crude antimony, or lead-ore reduced to an impalpable powder. Beginning to look green with young herbage (ground).

A تكحيب *tak-hīb*, (v. n. 2 of كحب) Producing unripe grapes (a vine). Being numerous (unripe grapes).

A تكحيص *tak-hīs*, (v. n. 2 of كحص) Erasing, defacing, obliterating (a book).

A تكحيل *tak-hīl*, An anointing with collyrium.

A تكدّح *takadduh*, (v. n. 5 of كدح) Being scratched with the nails.

A تكدّر *takaddur*, (v. n. 5 of كدر) Being turbid, impure, dark (colour or liquour). Being disturbed, troubled (life). Dregs. Dulness.

A تكدّس *takaddus*, (v. n. 5 of كدس) Travelling as if over-loaded and fatigued (a horse or camel). Making haste, running well, shaking the shoulders. Going with the chest much raised up.

A تكدكد *takadkud*, (v. n. 2 of كدكد Q) Driving away, thrusting, pushing with violence.

A تكدّه *takadduh*, A being broken in pieces.

A تكدئة *takdiʾat*, (v. n. 2 of كدأ) (Cold) nipping (a plant), making it lie flat on the ground. Producing herbage slowly by reason of the cold.

A تكديح *takdīh*, A scratching violently (the face).

A تكديد *takdīd*, (v. n. 2 of كدّ) Driving away, thrusting, pushing, persecuting with virulence.

A تكدير *takdīr*, (v. n. 2 of كدر) Rendering turbid, tarnishing. تكدير خاطر *takdīri khātir*, Perturbation of mind.

A تكديم *takdīm*, (v. n. 2 of كدم) (A sheep) biting gently without cropping (herbage).

A تكديه *takdīh*, (v. n. 2 of كده) Scratching, disfiguring (the face). Striking, wounding. Breaking. Combing and parting the hair.

A تكذّاب *tikizzāb*, A liar.

A تكذّب *takazzub*, (v. n. 5 of كذب) Feigning a lie, inventing a poetic fiction, taking pains to tell a lie. Considering as false.

A تكذيب *takzīb*, (v. n. 2 of كذب) Accusing of falsehood, giving one the lie, treating as a liar. Denying stoutly, disapproving. Taking the male and not conceiving (a camel). Diverting any one from his purpose. Skipping and looking back (a wild animal). Delaying, hesitating, desisting. Failing, going off (a camel's milk).

A تكرار *takrār*, (v. n. of كرّ) Returning. Attacking, rushing upon. Causing to return time after time. Inclining to, shewing kindness. Repetition. Tautology. Altercation, dispute, strife: objection.

P تكرار كردن *takrār kardan*, To repeat, reiterate.

A تكرار باقي *takrār bākī*, A doubtful balance, a balance objected to.

A تكرّب *takarrub*, A gathering dates called كرابة.

A تكربش *takarbush*, A being wrinkled.

A تكرّة *takirrat*, (v. n. 2 of كرّ) Causing to return time after time.

A تكرتب *takartub*, A being turned upon.

A تكرتح *takartuh*, A going swiftly.

A تكرثؤ *takarsuʾ*, Closeness, thickness (of hair).

A تكرّج *takarruj*, (v. n. 5 of كرج) Being musty and mouldy (bread).

A تكردح *takarduh*, (v. n. 2 of كردح Q) Rolling. Reeling. Going swiftly.

A تكردس *takardus*, (v. n. 2 of كردس Q) Being contracted, compressed.

A تكردم *takardum*, A running in terror.

A تكرّر *takarrur*, (v. n. 5 of كرّ) Being repeated, reiterated. Being uncertain and irresolute. Repetition.

A تكرسف *takarsuf*, (v. n. 2 of كرسف Q) Being inserted, entering (one part into another).

A تكرّش *takarrush*, (v. n. 5 of كرش) Being drawn up (the face). Assembling, meeting (men).

A تكرّع *takarruʿ*, (v. n. 5 of كرع) Washing and purifying before prayer.

A تكرفس *takarfus*, (v. n. 2 of كرفس Q) Being contracted, compressed.

A تكرفؤ *takarfuʾ*, Bushiness (of the hair).

A تكركر *takarkur*, (v. n. 2 of كركر Q) Being driven to and fro in the air. Hesitating, being irresolute in business. Flowing back (water).

A تكرّم *takarrum*, (v. n. 5 of كرم) Being liberal, disdaining every thing base. Making pretensions to generosity, striving to be liberal. Being far removed from every thing censurable. Honour, glory, nobility, dignity. Liberality.

A تكرمة *takrimat*, A cushion placed for a man to do him honour.

P تكرونتن *takrūnitan*, (zand and Pāz.) To twist.

A تكرّه *takarruh*, (v. n. 5 of كره) Loathing, detesting, disliking, disapproving. Esteeming lightly. Giving inopportunely. Putting on a sour face. على تكرّه *ʿala' takarruhin*, Reluctantly.

A تكّري *takkurī*, (pl. تكاكرة) A general, leader.

A تكرّي *takarrī*, (v. n. 5 of كرو) Sleeping.

A تكريب *takrīb*, (v. n. 2 of كرب) Eating the dates called كرابة *kurābat*. Tying a short rope to the cross-bar (of a bucket). Making a noise (a baker's rolling-pin).

A تكريت *takrīt*, A city and fortress in Mesopotamia, the birth-place of Salāhu'd din (Saladin).

A تكريج *takrīj*, Mouldiness (of bread).

A تكرير *takrīr*, (v. n. 2 of كرّ) Repeating, reiterating. Causing to return time after time. Repetition, reply, revisal, renewal.

A تكريز *takrīz*, The moulting (of a falcon).

A تكريس *takrīs*, (v. n. 2 of كرس not in use) Laying the foundation of a house (with a row of stones). Dedication.

A تكريش *takrīsh*, (v. n. 2 of كرش) Frowning, knitting the brows. Dressing the tripe or paunch of an animal chewing the cud. Making a haggess.

A تكريشة *takrīshat*, Meat, &c., stuffed into the maw of a beast, and dressed; a haggess.

A تكريص *takrīs*, (v. n. 2 of كرص) Eating the preparation of milk, &c., called كريص *karīs*.

A تكريم *takrīm*, (v. n. 2 of كرم) Honouring, revering. Calling (one) generous and noble. Keeping clear from vices and blemishes. Pouring rain (a cloud). Honour, respect, reverence, salutation. A cushion placed for a man to do him honour.

A تكريمات *takrīmāt*, (pl. of تكريم) Reverences.

A تكريه *takrīh*, (v. n. 2 of كره) Rendering hateful and abominable.

A تكزّم *takazzum*, The eating of unpeeled fruit.

A تكزيم *takzīm*, (v. n. 2 of كزم) Preserving, laying by, taking care of. Contracting, causing to shrivel.

P تكژ *tahaj*, *takuj*, or *takij*, A grape-stone.

P تكژدان *takaj-dān*, (or تكژدانه *takaj-dāna*) The membrane which envelops the grape-stone. The husk of the grape.

P تكس *takas*, Grape-stones.

A تكسّب *takassub*, (v. n. 5 of كسب) Gaining, collecting: seeking a livelihood: studying hard to gain.

A تكسّر *takassur*, (v. n. 5 of كسر) Being broken, spent, debilitated. Being dashed to pieces. Carrying (figures in arithmetic).

A تكسّس *takassus*, (v. n. 5 of كسّ) Taking trouble upon one's self gratuitously. Undertaking any thing spontaneously.

A تكسّف *takassuf*, A cutting into many portions.

P تكسك *takask*, (*tikask* or تكسل *takasl*) A grape-stone or husk.

A تكسّي *takassī*, (v. n. 5 of كسا for كسو) Putting on apparel. Being clothed, clad, invested.

A تكسيح *taksīh*, A barking, skinning, peeling.

A تكسير *taksīr*, (v. n. 2 of كسر) Breaking in pieces. Making and declining (a noun) as a broken or irregular plural. Carrying (in arithmetic). Dividing so as to produce a fraction. Superficial measure. جمع التكسير *jamʿu't taksīr*, The irregular plural (in which the singular is often changed into a word of a very different form).

A تكسيف *taksīf*, A cutting in pieces.

P تكسين *taksīn*, Name of a Turkish chieftain.

P تكش *takash*, Grape-stones. Name of a king.

A تكشّح *takashshuh*, A lying with.

A تكشّر *takashshur*, (v. n. 5 of كشر) Putting on a crabbed, austere countenance.

A تكشّف *takashshuf*, (v. n. 5 of كشف) Being uncovered, unveiled, revealed, exposed. Illuminating the whole heaven (lightning).

A تكشّؤ *takashshuʾ*, (v. n. 5 of كشأ) Being filled

with food. Being peeled, skinned, unbarked.

A تکشيب *takshīb*, A greedy devouring (of meat).

A تکشيح *takshīḥ*, (v. n. 2 of کشح) Applying the cautery under the short ribs. Peeling off (bark).

A تکشيخ *takshīkh*, A calling one a cuckold.

A تکشير *takshīr*, A shewing the teeth, grinning.

A تکشيف *takshīf*, (v. n. 2 of کشف) Revealing, uncovering, disclosing. Apocalypse. Forcing (any one) against his will to make a disclosure.

A تکظکظ *takaẓkuẓ*, A sitting bolt upright at meals from having the stomach overcharged.

A تکظّي *takaẓẓī*, A swelling (with fat).

A تکعبش *takaʻbush*, A being wrinkled.

A تکعثب *takaʻsub*, Roundness (of a sack).

A تکعکع *takaʻkuʻ*, (v. n. 2 of کعکع Q) Being timid, cowardly, weak. Being checked, prohibited.

A تکعّل *takaʻʻul*, An adhering closely.

A تکعنش *takaʻnush*, (v. n. 2 of کعنش Q) Plunging into. Sticking fast in a net (a bird).

A تکعيب *takʻīb*, (v. n. 2 of کعب) Having swelling breasts (a girl). Making of a cubic form.

A تکفّت *takaffut*, (v. n. 5 of کفت) Being contracted or drawn together.

A تکفّر *takaffur*, A being covered or cased.

A تکفّف *takaffuf*, (v. n. 5 of کفّ) Asking with a stretched-out hand.

A تکفکف *takafkuf*, (v. n. 2 of کفکف Q) Going (from a place). Hanging back, desisting.

A تکفّل *takafful*, (v. n. 5 of کفل) Becoming security, giving caution for another, undertaking.

A تکفّؤ *takaffuʼ*, (v. n. 5 of کفأ) Walking in a stately manner, without looking at the right or left.

A تکفّي *takaffī*, The growing tall (of a tree).

A تکفيت *takfīt*, (v. n. 2 of کفت) Heaping up, receiving. Grasping, clutching.

A تکفير *takfīr*, (v. n. 2 of کفر) Covering. Expiating a crime or the breach of an oath (doing penance or paying a mulct as atonement). Humbling one's self before another (putting the hand upon the breast, and inclining the head), shewing distant respect. Crowning (a king) with a diadem, at the sight of which prostration is required. Making one an unbeliever. A name for a royal diadem.

A تکفيل *takfīl*, (v. n. 2 of کفل) Maintaining, supporting, educating. Giving surety. Causing to be accepted. Attending to, managing. Putting trust in, giving management to.

A تکفين *takfīn*, (v. n. 2 of کفن) Shrouding (the dead). Making a winding sheet (کفن *kafan*).

A تکك *tikak*, (pl. of تكّة *tikkat*) Drawer-strings. *Tukah*, (pl. of تاكّ *tākk*) Foolish, dull, stupid. Thin, emaciated. Perishing.

A تككة *takakat*, (pl. of تاكّ *tākk*) Foolish, dull, stupid. Thin, emaciated. Perishing.

A تکل *takal*, (v. n. of تکل) Relying on.

P تکل *takil* or *tikil*, A handsome, unbearded youth. A horned and pugnacious sheep. A dolt. Disproportionate.

A تکلاب *taklāb*, A rushing upon one another.

A تکلّام *tikillām*, A speaking, conversing.

A تکلامة *taklāmat*, (تکلّامة *takhlāmmat*, تکلام *taklām*, or تکلّام *taklāmm*) Eloquent. Talkative.

A تکلان *tuklān*, Trust, confidence (in God).

A تکلة *tuklat*, Trust, confidence in God. *Tukalat*, One who trusts his affairs to others, and depends upon them.

P تکلتو *takaltū*, Felt cloth placed under a saddle to prevent the galling of the horse's back. Whiskers.

A تکلّح *takalluḥ*, (v. n. 5 of کلح) Looking austere and grim, shewing the teeth. Flashing incessantly (lightning).

A تکلّد *takallud*, A being thick and hard.

A تکلّس *takallus*, A being moist, juicy, succulent.

A تکلّع *takalluʻ*, (v. n. 5 of کلع) Being assembled. Conspiring, entering into alliance, leaguing.

A تکلّف *takalluf*, (v. n. 5 of کلف) Taking any thing upon one's self without being commanded to do it. Taking trouble on one's self. Attempting, undertaking. Enduring, undergoing. Striving, taking pains. Pains, attention, industry, perseverance. Inconvenience, trouble. Ceremony, dissimulation, insincerity. P تکلّف برطرف *takalluf bar taraf*, Waving ceremony.

A تکلّفات *takallufāt*, (pl. of تکلّف *takalluf*) Troubles, inconveniences. Ceremonies, compliments. Elaborations. تکلّفات رسمي *takallufāti rasmī*, Ceremonious attentions, empty compliments. تکلّفات مجلس *takallufāti majlis*, The ceremonies of society, etiquette.

A تکلفة *taklifat*, A laborious enterprise, a painful exertion, difficulty.

P تکلّف مزاج *takalluf-mizāj*, Ceremonious.

A تکلّل *takallul*, (v. n. 5 of کلّ) Being crowned. Being destitute of relations. Gleaming (a cloud). Surrounding, enclosing, holding, comprehending.

A تکلّم *takallum*, (v. n. 5 of کلم) Speaking, talking. Conversation. P تکلّم کردن *takallum kardan*, To converse, speak, relate, tell.

A تکلّؤ *takalluʼ*, (v. n. 5 of کلأ) Receiving earnest. Asking for a delay. Receiving part of a price, and granting a delay for the remainder.

P تکله *tukla*, Mad, insane. Name of one of the Atābaks who reigned in Shīrāz.

A تکلّي *takallī*, (v. n. 5 of کلي) Staying in the rear, or standing in the rear rank (of the army).

A تکليب *taklīb*, A training dogs for the chace.

A تکلئة *takliʼat*, (v. n. 2 of کلأ) Moving to the bank of a river; getting to shore, keeping a vessel in port (especially in stormy weather). Getting to a place sheltered from the wind. Detaining (a man). Proceeding towards or against. Looking steadily at any person. Receiving part of a price, and granting a delay for the remainder. Taking, or causing to take food before dinner.

A تکلية *takliyat*, A coming to a hiding-place.

A تکليد *taklīd*, A heaping, accumulating, piling.

A تکليز *taklīz*, A collecting, assembling.

A تکليس *taklīs*, (v. n. 2 of کلس) Making an attack, impression, or assault. Losing courage, flying. Being moist and succulent.

A تکليف *taklīf*, (v. n. 2 of کلف) Proposing to, or obliging another to, undertake any thing difficult or above his strength. Imposing, laying on a burden. The imposition of a burden. (pl. تکاليف *takālīf*) Trouble, difficulty, molestation, distress, inconvenience, annoyance.

A تکليل *taklīl*, (v. n. 2 of کلّ) Crowning. Being blunt (a sword), dim (the sight). Being dispirited, unable to do any thing. Proceeding or striking boldly, springing, assaulting (a wild beast). Striving. Going away, deserting friends, leaving them to ruin and perdition.

A تکليم *taklīm*, A wounding much. Speaking.

A تکليء *taklīʼ*, (v. n. 2 of کلأ) Receiving earnest. Bringing (a ship) near shore, or mooring it.

P تکمار *tukmār*, (or تکمر *tukmur*) An arrow without a point, but with a button in its place.

A تکمّش *takammush*, (v. n. 5 of کمش) Hastening. Being wrinkled, shrivelling (the skin).

A تکمکم *takamkum*, (v. n. 2 of کمکم Q) Wrapping one's self (in a garment). Wearing a round cap.

A تکمّل *takammul*, (v. n. 5 of کمل) Being entire, perfect, finished. Completing, perfecting.

A تکمّم *takammum*, (v. n. 5 of کمّ) Being covered.

A تکمّؤ *takammuʼ*, (v. n. 5 of کمأ) Being averse, loathing, disliking. Hiding from view (the earth).

P تکمه *tukma*, A button. تکمهٔ جيب کشادن *tukmaʼi jayb kushādan*, To unbutton the pocket.

A تکمّه *takammuh*, (v. n. 5 of کمه) Being self-willed, departing (he) knows not where. Wandering, roaming, rambling.

A تکمهل *takamhul*, A being collected.

A تکمّي *takammī*, (v. n. 5 of کمي) Aiming at. Minding, attending to. Hiding, concealing. Overwhelming (as a sudden misfortune). Being killed (armed warriors).

A تکمئة *takmiʼat*, A giving one mushrooms to eat.

A تکميت *takmīt*, (v. n. 2 of کمت) Tinging (a horse) of a dark red or bay. Restraining anger.

A تکميد *takmīd*, (v. n. 2 of کمد) Fomenting a distempered limb, and applying warm bandages to the affected part.

A تکميش *takmīsh*, (v. n. 2 of کمش) Spurring, driving, impelling, urging onwards vigorously.

A تکميل *takmīl*, (v. n. 2 of کمل) Finishing, completing, perfecting. Performing, satisfying.

A تکميم *takmīm*, (v. n. 2 of کمّ) Putting forth buds (کمّ *kimm*) before flowering (a tree).

A تکنبث *takambus*, A being drawn together.

A تکنبش *takambush*, Mixture of people.

A تکنثر *takansur*, (v. n. 2 of کنثر Q) Being thick,

large, corpulent. Having the hairs or feathers erect (a cat or a bird from fright).

P تکند *ta* or *tikand,* A poultry-yard. A nest.

A تکنس *takannus,* (v. n. 5 of کنس) Hiding among foliage (a doe). Entering a tent (a man). Mounting and riding in a camel's litter (a woman).

A تکنظ *takannuz,* (v. n. 5 of کنظ) Annoying, teazing, vexing. Filling.

A تکنع *takannuʿ,* (v. n. 5 of کنع) Being contracted, shrunk. Being kept closely chained (a prisoner). Being suspended to, dependent on.

A تکنف *takannuf,* A surrounding, hedging in.

A تکني *takannī,* (v. n. 5 of کني) Being described by a کنية *kunyat* or کناية *kināyat, i.e.* a word which has properly another meaning.

A تکنية *takniyat,* (v. n. 2 of کني) Calling (a person or thing) by another name, dubbing: as, ابو جابر *abū jābir,* Father Restorative (*i.e.* bread); ام الخبائث *ummu'l khabāʾis,* Mother of evils, *i.e.* wine; ابن السبيل *ibnu's sabīl,* Son of the way, *i.e.* a traveller.

A تکنيس *taknīs,* A moving the nose sneeringly.

A تکنيع *taknīʿ,* (v. n. 2 of کنع) Contracting. Maiming, by disjointing or mutilating (the hand). Wounding with a sword. Deviating, turning away from. Tying the feet with a strap.

A تکنيف *taknīf,* A surrounding, enclosing.

A تکنين *taknīn,* (v. n. 2 of کنّ) Covering. Preserving. Screening from (the sun).

P تکو *takū,* Curly, entangled hair. Cakes baked with butter.

P تك وپوي *tak u pūy,* Run! search! Inquiry.

P تك و تاز نمودن *tak u tāz namūdan,* To run. To search diligently.

A تکوثر *takawsur,* (v. n. 2 of کوثر Q) Being plentiful, and piled up, stifling (dust).

A تکوّد *takawwud,* (v. n. 5 of کأد) Applying diligently to some arduous business. Becoming callous to evil, and bearing it with all its inconveniences. Being difficult and troublesome.

A تکوّذ *takawwuz,* A putting on a girdle.

A تکوّر *takawwur,* (v. n. 5 of کار for کور) Being gathered in. Distilling, dropping. Falling. Being thrown down, dejected, confounded. Setting about, preparing to do any thing.

A تکوّس *takawwus,* A being inverted.

A تکوّع *takawwuʿ,* (v. n. 5 of کاع for کوع) Being distorted in the wrist (a hand).

A تکوّف *takawwuf,* (v. n. 5 of کاف for کوف) Being round and circular (a heap of sand or a crowd of people). Removing (a sand-hill). Being one of Kūfa in Chaldea, studying to resemble, or persevering in imitating the manners, or calling one's self a native of Kūfa.

P تکوك *takok,* A cup made in the form of an animal. Glass. *Tukūk,* A large parlour or upper room. A butt for shooting at with arrows.

A تکوك *tukūk,* (v. n. of تكّ) Being out of one's senses. Being lean. Perishing.

A تکوّل *takawwul,* (v. n. 5 of کال for کول) Being assembled (against any one). Overwhelming with blows or reproaches.

A تکوّن *takawwun,* (v. n. 5 of کان for کون) Being, becoming. Deriving existence. Being moved.

A تکوّه *takawwuh,* (v. n. 5 of کاه for کوه) Being divided, diffused, scattered, or extended.

P تکوي *takawī,* Thin cakes. Curly hair.

A تکوّي *takawwī,* (v. n. 5 of کوي) Entering or squeezing one's self into a narrow place. Being contracted, drawn together. Drawing close (husband and wife for reciprocal warmth).

A تکويب *takwīb,* A braying with the stone *fihr.*

A تکويث *takwīs,* (v. n. 2 of کاث for کوث) Putting out four or five leaves (corn). Voiding excrement resembling hares' heads.

A تکويح *takwīh,* (v. n. 2 of کاح for کوح) Conquering in fight. Repelling. Depressing, dishonouring.

A تکويد *takwīd,* An accumulating, heaping up.

A تکويذ *takwīz,* (v. n. 2 of کاذ for کوذ) Reaching the middle of the body (an apron). Stabbing in the groin. Whipping the posteriors.

A تکوير *takwīr,* (v. n. 2 of کار for کور) (God) ordering (darkness) to succeed (the day). Causing to cover or hide. Throwing one down. Piercing one with a spear, and throwing (him) down gathered in a heap. Wrapping the turban round the head in a spiral form. Increasing, augmenting. Heaping goods together and tying them in bales.

A تکويس *takwīs,* (v. n. 2 of کاس for کوس) Turning, inverting. Throwing down, causing to fall upon the head, precipitating head foremost into the fire.

A تکويع *takwīʿ,* (v. n. 2 of کاع for کوع) Wounding with a sword, so as to distort the wrist-bones.

A تکويف *takwīf,* (v. n. 2 of کاف for کوف) Cutting (leather). Writing the letter ك *kāf.* Going to Kūfa (a city of Chaldea).

A تکويم *takwīm,* An accumulating, heaping up.

A تکوين *takwīn,* (v. n. 2 of کان for کون) Giving a being (کون *kawn*) or beginning to, causing to exist, originating, creating. Genesis.

P تکه *taka,* A he-goat that leads the flock. A single volume. Dry cow-dung flattened into cakes used for fuel. *Tika,* A mouthful, piece. تکه تکه *tika tika,* Piecemeal. *Tuka,* The string of the drawers. An arrow without a point, but with a knob at the end. A little hill, an eminence.

A تکهّف *takahhuf,* (v. n. 5 of کهف not in use) Having caverns and grottoes (a mountain). Entering a cavern. Eating into the sides of a well, so that a commotion and noise occur (water).

A تکهّل *takahhul,* (v. n. 5 of کهل) Resembling a middle-aged man (کهل *kahl*). Claiming relationship to the tribe of کهلان *kahlān.*

A تکهّن *takahhun,* (v. n. 5 of کهن) Predicting, presaging. Turning augur or soothsayer. Divination.

A تکهيف *tak-hīf,* (v. n. 2 of کهف) Making in the form of a cave or grot (کهف *kahf*).

A تکّي *tikkīy,* A vender or maker of strings for long drawers.

P تکيدن *takīdan,* To shake (a carpet). To run to and fro.

P تکيز *takīz,* A grape-stone.

A تکيّس *takayyus,* (v. n. 5 of کاس for کيس) Shewing sagacity or cunning. Being anxious to display cleverness (کيس *kays* or کياسة *kiyāsat*).

A تکيّف *takayyuf,* (v. n. 5 of کاف for کيف) Being described, defined, as to form and quality. Disgracing, affronting, blaming. Diminishing.

A تکيّل *takayyul,* A standing in the rear.

P تکين *takīn,* A grape-stone. Lower, inferior. Name of a king.

P تکيه *takya,* A place of repose. An alcove. An elbow-chair. A pillow. Any thing upon which one leans: a prop. The reserve of an army. تکيه زدن *takya zadan,* (or تکيه نمودن *takya namūdan*) To recline, lean. To rest. تکيهٔ مسيحي *takya-i masīhī,* A Christian monastery.

P تکيه دار *takya-dār,* A monk. A dervish.

P تکيه کلام *takya-kalām,* (or سخن تکيه *sukhun-takya*) A cant word introduced into conversation without any meaning (merely to rest upon).

P تکيه گاه *takya-gāh,* A resting-place. A sofa.

P تکيه نشين *takya-nishīn,* Sitting in a monastery (*i.e.* a monk or dervish who never goes out).

A تکييت *takyīt,* (v. n. 2 of کات for کيت) Filling (a purse), stuffing (a sack). Facilitating. Preparing, expediting (furniture).

A تکييس *takyīs,* A making sharp, clever, shrewd.

A تکييف *takyīf,* (v. n. 2 of کاف for کيف) Describing by a certain quality or form. Cutting into several parts. Cutting (leather).

A تکييل *takyīl,* A being timid, pusillanimous.

P تگ *tag,* Bottom. Earth, ground. A cry for help. A race or heat. Running. (in zand and Pāzand) A ripe date. تگ دريا *tagi daryā,* The bottom of the sea. بتگ نشستن *ba tag nishastan,* To sink to the bottom.

P تگاب *tag-āb,* (or تگاو *tag-āv*) Verdant patches of sloping ground from which the water has retired. A flagon with a spout. A funnel. Enmity, strife. Name of a note in music. Name of a village dependant on گنجه *ganja.*

P تگانيدن *tagānīdan,* To shake off (dust).

P تگاور *tag-āwar,* A running horse, one having good paces.

P تگ بن *tag-bun,* A shallow well.

P تگتاز *tag-tāz,* Running. Searching, seeking.

P تگ دو *tag-dav,* Running about on business, or in search of employ. Inquiry, search. Fatigue.

P تگرگ *tagarg,* Hail, sleet, storm, tempest. تگرگ باريدن *tagarg bāridan,* To hail. *Tagrag,*

The foundation of a wall.

P تگل *tagl*, A troop of soldiers. *Tigl*, A patch to put on a garment. A handsome youth.

P تگلتو *tagaltū*, Dorsers. Felt cloth used to prevent the saddle from galling the beast's back. Whiskers, mustachios.

P تگمر *tugmar*, An arrow with a wooden head.

P تگین *tigīn*, Name of a wrestler. Fire.

P تل *tal*, Any thing poured out into a heap. A hill. A beardless youth. *Tul*, A tailor's bag for needles, thread, and thimble.

A تلّ *tall*, (v. n. of تلّ) Throwing one prostrate, the cheek touching the ground. Giving, delivering, or throwing into the hand of another. Humbling one's self, supplicating, deprecating. Falling. Pouring forth sweat from the forehead. Letting down (a rope into a well). Making (a camel) lie down. Causing to be suspected of something bad. (pl. تلال *tilāl*) A little hill, hillock: a heap of sand. (pl. اتلال *atlāl*) A cushion. A sort of garment. تلّ باشر *tall bāshir*, تلّ السلطان *tallu's sultān*, تلّ الصافية *tallu's sāfiya*, تلّ خالد *tall khālid*, Names of fortresses.

A تلا *tala'*, (fut. يتلو *yatlū*) He followed.

A تلاء *talā'*, A treaty. Protection, guard. A portion, lot.

A تلّاء *tallā'*, A great reader (of the Kur'ān).

A تلاءم *talā'um*, A being restored to favour.

P تلاب *ti* or *talāb*, Poured out as water. A pond.

A تلأبيبة *tula'bībat*, Well-ordered business.

P تلاتف *talātuf*, (or تلاتوف) Dirty, nasty, sordid, filthy, shunned by society. Clamour, riot, noise.

A تلاتل *talātil*, (pl. of تليل *talīl*) Necks. Misfortunes. *Tulātil*, Fat, sleek, coarse, and thick.

P تلاتين *talātīn*, Perfumed or Russia leather.

P تلاج *talāj* or *tilāj*, Noise, tumult, shout.

A تلاجّ *talājj*, A quarrelling, wrangling mutually.

A تلاحز *talāhuz*, (v. n. 6 of لحز) Vying in reciting verses. Contending clamorously.

A تلاحق *talāhuk*, (v. n. 6 of لحق) Following successively, the one touching the other.

A تلاحك *talāhuk*, A sticking close together.

A تلاحم *talāhum*, (v. n. 6 of لحم) Being joined. The juncture or joint (of bones).

A تلاحي *talāhī*, A disputing, mutually blaming.

P تلاد *talād*, A large city bordering on China.

A تلاد *tilād*, Hereditary wealth.

A تلاديّ *tilādiy*, Vernacular, domestic.

A تلازم *talāzum*, (v. n. 6 of لزم) Being inserted within one another.

A تلازن *talāzun*, A thronging, a crowding.

P تلاس *talās*, Name of a city in Turkistān.

P تلاش *talāsh*, Dispersion. Search. Study.

P تلاشان *talāshān*, A grove in Ispāhān.

P تلاشيدن *talāshīdan*, To be scattered. To perish. To search.

A تلاطش *talātush*, (v. n. 6 of لطش) Dashing (waves). Striking one another with the hands.

A تلاطف *talātuf*, (v. n. 6 of لطف) Shewing favour mutually. Benevolence. Reciprocal kindness.

A تلاطم *talātum*, (v. n. 6 of لطم) Fighting, buffetting, slapping, or cuffing one another. تلاطم امواج *talātumi amwāj*, Dashing of waves.

A تلاظّ *talāzz*, (v. n. 6 of لظّ) Repelling each other, rushing on one another.

A تلاع *tilāع*, (pl. of تلعة *talعat*) High grounds. Streams flowing from high lands into a valley.

A تلاعب *talāعub*, A playing often, trifling.

A تلاعة *talāعat*, Length of neck.

A تلاعن *talāعun*, (v. n. 6 of لعن) Cursing one another. Being mutually impudent, indecent.

A تلافق *talāfuk*, (v. n. 6 of لفق) Having their affairs well arranged and consolidated. Composing differences. Being reconciled.

A تلافي *talāfī*, (v. n. 6 of لفا for لفو) Obtaining, trying to obtain; discovering a remedy. Amending one's ways. Arriving at, or comprehending. Compensation, amends.

A تلافيف *talāfīf*, Luxuriant entangled grass.

A تلاق *talāk*, Meeting, intercourse.

P تلاق *tilāk*, Long drawers. The clitoris.

A تلاقس *talākus*, A calling bad names.

A تلاقي *talākī*, (v. n. 6 of لقي) Meeting each other. Encountering in battle. A meeting, reunion, interview. يوم التلاقي *yawmu't talākī*, The day of meeting *i. e.* the day of judgment.

A تلاكن *talākun*, (v. n. 6 of لكن) Stammering on purpose for the entertainment of a company.

A تلال *tilāl*, (pl. of تلّ *tall*) Hills.

P تلالا *talālā*, Sound of singing or reading.

A تلالة *talālat*, An error.

A تلألؤ *tala'lu'*, (v. n. 2 of لألأ Q) Flashing, gleaming, glittering (lightning or a sword).

A تلام *talām*, (contraction of تلاميذ *talāmīz*) Scholars. *Tilām*, (pl. of تلم *tilm*) Boys. Servants. Husbandmen. Goldsmiths. Tubes through which the air passes. امّ تلام *umm tilām*, Fever.

A تلأّم *tala''um*, A being restored to favour.

A تلامذة *talāmizat*, (pl. of تلميذ *tilmīz*) Scholars, pupils, disciples.

A تلاميّ *talāmiy*, (for تلاميذ) Disciples, scholars.

A تلاميع *talāmīع*, Bright streaks.

A تلان *talān*, (for الآن *al ān*) Now.

P تلانج *talānaj* or *talānj*, Vociferation, noise.

A تلاوة *tilāwat*, (v. n. of تلا for تلو) Reading, meditating. Saying prayers omitted before. Buying a colt. *Tulāwat*, A balance of debt, a remainder of any thing.

A تلاؤم *talā'um*, (v. n. 6 of لأم) Healing, growing well (a sore).

A تلاوم *talāwum*, (v. n. 6 of لام for لوم) Accusing, blaming one another. Mutual accusation.

A تلاوي *talāwī*, An agreeing, being of accord.

A تلاهي *talāhī*, (v. n. 6 of لها for لهو) Playing, beguiling the time. Lying with.

A تلايس *talāyus*, (v. n. 6 of لاس for ليس) Being of an excellent disposition. Being indulgent, merciful, overlooking faults.

A تلب *talb*, Loss, destruction. تبًّا له و تلبًا *tabban lahu wa talban*, May perdition overtake him!

P تلبا *talbā*, (in zand and Pāz.) Fat, grease.

A تلبّب *talabbub*, (v. n. 5 of لبّ) Tucking up the garments. Girding one's self round the middle. Preparing for work.

A تلبّث *talabbus*, A delaying. Pause, delay.

A تلبّخ *talabbukh*, (v. n. 5 of لبخ) Being perfumed, or perfuming one's self with musk.

A تلبّد *talabbud*, (v. n. 5 of لبد) Adhering to the ground. Sitting (as a bird upon eggs). Sticking closely together. Being clotted, impacted, or feltered (hair, leaves, or wool).

A تلبّس *talabbus*, (v. n. 5 of لبس) Being covered; clothing one's self. Being engaged in, and mixed up with (business). Sticking to the hands (fat or grease).

A تلبّط *talabbut*, (v. n. 5 of لبط) Running. Being agitated, afflicted. Lying down, rolling on the ground. Tending, going on, turning towards.

A تلبّك *talabbuk*, A being confused, intricate.

A تلبّن *talabbun*, A delaying, deferring, tarrying.

A تلبيب *talbīb*, (v. n. 2 of لبّ) Seizing by the throat and dragging, collaring. Containing a kernel (a berry). Being irresolute and uncertain. Garments worn about the throat.

A تلبئة *talbi'at*, (v. n. 2 of لبأ) Having biestings in her udder (a ewe). Suckling a young one with biestings. Acquitting one's self of the obligation of going on pilgrimage (to Mecca).

A تلبية *talbiyat*, (v. n. 2 of لبي) Saying, What is your command? Here I am. Going a pilgrim (to Mecca). Staying in a place.

A تلبيث *talbīs*, (v. n. 2 of لبث) Delaying, retarding. Bidding one delay.

A تلبيخ *talbīh*, A growing old.

A تلبيد *talbīd*, (v. n. 2 of لبد) Covering the ground thick (dew). Putting any glutinous substance upon the head to prevent the hair from flowing about. Carding wool, and putting it when moistened about the head of a sword-sheath to protect the belt. Mending, patching. Trampling on.

A تلبيس *talbīs*, (v. n. 2 of لبس) Concealing (the truth, the faults of goods on sale, &c.), cheating, deceiving. Mixing. Misrepresentation. Fraud, fallacy, imposture. Mixture, confusion. P تلبيس كردن *talbīs kardan*, To adulterate, falsify, corrupt.

A تلبيق *talbīk*, (v. n. 2 of لبق) Softening (crumbled bread with soup).

A تلبيك *talbīk*, A mixing (wheat with honey).

A تلبين *talbīn*, (v. n. 2 of لبن) Making bricks. Transacting any business undertaken from generous motives. Transacting grave and important business. A kind of pottage.

A تلبينة *talbīnat*, Soup of bran, milk, and honey.

A تلّة *tallat*, A drinking-cup made out of a palm-tree. One pouring out. One lying down. *Tillat*, Sluggishness, indolence. A mode of lying down. State, condition. Moisture. تلّة سوء *tillat sūʼin*, A disagreeable affair.

A تلتّخ *talattukh*, (v. n. 5 of لتخ) Being stained, defiled, or contaminated.

A تلتلة *taltalat*, (v. n. of تلتل Q) Moving, shaking, agitating. Driving violently. A hard, disagreeable trot or other pace. (pl. تلاتل *talātil*) Hardship, adversity, intenseness, severity. A cup made of a palm. تلتلة بهراء *taltalatu bahrāʼ*, The inflecting of the ت *tā* of تفعلون *tafʻalūna* with كسر *kasr*, pronouncing it *tifʻalūna*.

A تلتيب *taltīb*, (v. n. 2 of لتب) Tying a horse-cloth upon a horse.

A تلثلث *talaslus*, (v. n. 2 of لثلث Q) Wavering, being inconstant. Being thrown down or rolled in the dust or the sand.

A تلثّم *talassum*, A veiling the mouth.

A تلثّي *talassī*, A gathering of gum.

A تلثيق *talsīk*, (v. n. 2 of لثق) Spoiling.

A تلج *tulaj*, An eaglet.

A تلجّج *talajjuj*, A wish to claim for one's self.

A تلجّف *talajjuf*, (v. n. 5 of لجف) Digging round the sides of a well. Being dug in the sides (a well).

A تلجلج *talajluj*, (v. n. 2 of لجلج Q) Being agitated, moving, shaking. Hesitating, vacillating. Taking from another. Being irresolute. Stammering.

A تلجّم *talajjum*, A tying on a menstruous cloth.

A تلجّن *talajjun*, (v. n. 5 of لجن) Washing, yet not cleaning (the head). Feeding (camels) with leaves of trees mixed with meal, barley, and date-stones. Being viscous (plants).

A تلجيب *taljīb*, (v. n. 2 of لجب) Being quite dry (a ewe). Having much milk (a sheep or goat).

A تلجئة *taljiʼat*, (v. n. 2 of لجأ) Forcing against the will. Lying at a sale.

A تلجيج *taljīj*, (v. n. 2 of لجّ) Launching into, sailing through the mighty deep (a ship).

A تلجيف *taljīf*, (v. n. 2 of لجف) Digging in the sides of a well. Working at the sides in coitu.

A تلجيم *taljīm*, (v. n. 2 of لجم) Coming up to the mouth (water).

A تلجين *taljīn*, (v. n. 2 of لجن) Feeding (camels) with leaves mixed with meal or barley. Striking (mallows) to thicken (them).

A تلحّز *talahhuz*, (v. n. 5 of لحز) Being avaricious, narrow-minded. Retiring, staying behind. Preparing one's self for. Tucking up the garments preparatory to fighting or travelling. The watering of the mouth (from desire or any thing acid).

A تلحّظ *talahhuz*, Narrowness. A sticking together. Anguish, affliction, toil.

A تلحّف *talahhuf*, (v. n. 5 of لحف) Taking, or making up, a sheet or outer garment (لحاف *lihāf*).

A تلحلح *talahluh*, A remaining in one place.

A تلحّي *talahhī*, (v. n. 5 of لحي) Passing the end of the turban-sash under the chin.

A تلحيب *talhīb*, (v. n. 2 of لحب) Striking with a sword. Making an impression.

A تلحيج *talhīj*, (v. n. 2 of لحج) Involving, confusing, not making one's meaning sufficiently clear.

A تلحيس *talhīs*, (v. n. 2 of لحس) Asking straitly, seeking news. Detailing one thing after another. Corroborating, strengthening. Making (a place) narrow.

A تلحيظ *talhīz*, A brand under a sheep's eye.

A تلحيف *talhīf*, (v. n. 2 of لحف) Sweeping the ground pompously with the train.

A تلحين *talhīn*, (v. n. 2 of لحن) Speaking badly, pronouncing the vowels with impropriety. Speaking melodiously, reading with a sweet or tender intonation of voice (لحن *lahn*). Accusing one of error in pronunciation (لحن *lahn*).

P تلخ *talkh*, Bitter. Acrimonious, malicious. Sad. Bitterly.

P تلخا *talkhā*, Grain, parched and pulverized, and afterwards mixed up with water into paste.

P تلخاب *talkh-āb*, Bitter water. Salt water.

P تلخ ارتيج *talkh-artīj*, A live coal. A portable stove, a brasier.

P تلخبار *talkh-bār*, Wild, unwholesome fruit.

P تلخجكوك *talkh-jukūk*, (or تلخ جوك *talkh-jūk*) Wild succory.

P تلخ جوان *talkh-jwān*, Poison. Death.

P تلخ خو *talkh-kho* or *khū*, Of a bitter temper.

P تلخ خوان *talkh-khwān*, The gall-bladder.

P تلخ دانه *talkh-dāna*, Darnel, tares.

P تلخ رو *talkh-rū*, Morose, crabbed, sullen.

P تلخ روده *talkh-rūda*, The dung-holding guts.

P تلخ عيش *talkh-ʻaysh*, One whose life is bitter.

P تلخك *talkhak*, Somewhat bitter. The colocynth or bitter purging apple. Endive. Name of a favourite of Sultān Mahmūd.

P تلخ كام *talkh-kām*, Having a bitter taste in the mouth. Disappointed, baulked.

P تلخ كامي *talkh-kāmī*, Bitterness of taste. Disappointment.

P تلخ كردار *talkh-kirdār*, Stern.

P تلخ گفتار *talkh-guftār*, Bitter-spoken (man).

P تلخ گو *talkh-gū*, Speaking bitterly. Harsh, keen, sharp, sarcastic.

P تلخ مزاج *talkh-mizāj*, Splenetic, peevish.

P تلخناك *talkhnāk*, Very bitter. Bitterly.

P تلخ و ترش *talkh u tursh*, Bitter and sour.

P تلخه *talkha*, Tares, darnel. Bile. Bitter, styptic food.

P تلخي *talkhī*, Bitterness. Endive.

P تلخي چشيده *talkhī-chashīda*, Tasted sorrow.

A تلخيص *talkhīs*, (v. n. 2 of لخص) Declaring, making public. Explanation, declaration, report or abstract of state affairs presented to the king by referendaries.

P تلخينه *talkhīna*, Milk soured and dried.

A تلد *talada*, (fut. يتلد *yatlu* or *ladu*) He abode.

A تلد *tald*, *tuld*, or *talad*, Hereditary wealth. Cattle bred under the master's eye. *Tuld*, An eaglet. *Talad*, Born in foreign parts, but brought up at home (as slaves among the Arabians).

A تلداغ *taldāgh*, The act of stinging, biting.

A تلدّد *taladdud*, (v. n. 5 of لدّ) Looking right and left. Delaying, pausing, standing in amazement.

A تلدّم *taladdum*, (v. n. 5 of لدم) Mending (a garment), patching (a shoe). Being worn and requiring mending (a garment).

A تلدّن *taladdun*, A delaying, tarrying at.

A تلديد *taldīd*, A publishing, revealing.

A تلديس *taldīs*, (v. n. 2 of لدس) Shoeing (a camel) for hard ground. Mending, patching (shoes or slippers).

A تلديم *taldīm*, (v. n. 2 of لدم) Mending (a garment). Uniting, cementing.

A تلدين *taldīn*, (v. n. 2 of لدن) Moistening (cloth). Making (a spear) limber.

A تلذّذ *talazzuz*, (v. n. 5 of لذّ) Taking pleasure, enjoying one's self.

A تلذّع *talazzuʻ*, (v. n. 5 of لذع) Walking elegantly and expeditiously. Looking right and left.

A تلزّج *talazzuj*, (v. n. 5 of لزج) Going in search of grass (cattle). Being viscous (plants). Remaining dirty after being washed (the head).

A تلزّح *talazzuh*, Secretion of spittle from eating sour fruit.

A تلزّق *talazzuk*, A sticking, an adhering.

A تلزلز *talazluz*, A being moved, a moving.

A تلزّؤ *talazzuʼ*, (v. n. 5 of لزأ) Being filled.

A تلزيب *talzīb*, An adhering firmly.

A تلزئة *talziʼat*, (v. n. 2 of لزأ) Giving. Feeding (camels) well.

A تلزيز *talzīz*, (v. n. 2 of لزّ) Giving a strong constitution (God).

P تلسك *tilisk*, A small bunch of grapes, part of a larger.

A تلسّن *talassun*, (v. n. 5 of لسن) Being lent (a camel's colt) that the camel may give milk plentifully. Giving out flame, flaming (live coals).

A تلسي *tulsī*, Sweet basil.

A تلسين *talsīn*, A making a tongue or latchet.

A تلصّص *talassus*, A robbing, plundering.

A تلصيص *talsīs*, A joining closely, making firm.

A تلطّخ *talattukh*, (v. n. 5 of لطخ) Being contaminated, defiled. Being anointed. A liniment.

A تلطّط *talattut*, A denying a debt legally due.

A تلطع *tiltiʻ*, (A camel) toothless from age.

A تلطّع *talattuʻ*, A being toothless from age.

A تلطّف *talattuf*, (v. n. 5 of لطف) Favouring, shewing kindness. Attaining gradually (to the knowledge of any thing).

A تلطّفاً *talattufan*, (P تلطّفانه) By favour.

A تلطّفات *talattufāt*, Caresses, favours.

A تلطّم *talattum*, (v. n. 5 of لطم) Being of a dark, ashy colour (the face).

A تلطّي *talattī*, (v. n. 5 of لطي) Waiting for (an enemy). Taking advantage of the negligence of others. Denying a debt.

A تلطيخ *taltīkh*, A bedaubing, dirtying, anointing.

A تلطيف *taltīf*, A making elegant or delicate.

A تلطيم *taltīm*, The sealing (of a letter).

A تلظلظ *talazluz*, (v. n. 2 of لظلظ Q) Turning or shaking the head in a rage. Twisting, writhing (as a serpent).

A تلظّي *talazzī*, A burning, flaming.

A تلظية *talziyat*, A causing to burn or flame.

A تلع *talaʿ*, (fut. يتلع *yatlaʿ*) (The day) advanced. He stretched out his neck to see and hear.

A تلع *talaʿ*, (v. n. of تلع) Being long-necked. Being full. Length of neck. *Taliʿ*, One who looks about or turns his head often. Full (vessel).

A تلعاب *talʿāb*, A playing: sport, play. *Tilʿāb*, *talʿāb*, (or تلّعاب *tiliʿʿāb*) Given to play, sportive.

A تلعابة *tilʿābat*, (*talʿābat*, or تلّعابة *tiliʿʿābat*) Given to play, sportive.

A تلعّب *talaʿʿub*, A playing, trifling, toying.

A تلعة *talʿat*, (pl. تلاع *tilāʿ*) High ground. Low ground. A river flowing from a rising ground into a valley. The channel of such a stream. لا اخاف الّا من سيل تلعتي *lā akhāfu illā min sayli talʿati*, I have no fear except from my own kin.

A تلعثم *talaʿsum*, (v. n. 2 of لعثم Q) Delaying, hesitating. Not daring. Considering attentively. Being deficient.

A تلعّج *talaʿʿuj*, Lust (in a woman).

A تلعذم *talaʿzum*, An eating, devouring.

A تلعّس *talaʿʿus*, A being voracious, eating much.

A تلعّص *talaʿʿus*, (v. n. 5 of لعص not in use) Becoming difficult, pressing hard upon.

A تلعّف *talaʿʿuf*, (v. n. 5 of لعف) Preparing to leap in, on, over. Preparing to be restive (a camel).

A تلعلع *talaʿluʿ*, (v. n. 2 of لعلع Q) Moving. Shining (as a vapour over the plain). Being broken (a bone). Writhing, being in commotion from hunger or thirst. Lolling the tongue from thirst (a dog). Being weak (from sickness or fatigue). Saying لعا لك *laʿan laka*, May you rise from your fall (a formula of sympathetic benediction, used when any one stumbles).

A تلعلم *talaʿlum*, A delaying, hesitating.

A تلعّي *talaʿʿī*, (v. n. 5 of لعي) Concreting, becoming candied (honey). Licking. Gathering or grazing the young herbage called لعاع *luʿāʿ*.

A تلعيب *talʿīb*, (v. n. 2 of لعب) Playing, sporting, jesting, joking, trifling.

A تلعيبة *tilʿībat*, Given to play, sportive.

A تلعين *talʿīn*, (v. n. 2 of لعن) Imprisoning. Tormenting, torturing.

A تلغّب *talaghghub*, (v. n. 5 of لغب) Removing, driving away. Fatiguing, tiring, wearying.

A تلغّف *talaghghuf*, (v. n. 5 of لغف) Preparing to leap, spring, or become refractory.

A تلغّم *talaghghum*, (v. n. 5 of لغم) Anointing the parts round the mouth (with perfumed unguents). Moving those parts (in speaking).

A تلغيب *talghīb*, A fatiguing, wearying out.

A تلغيط *talghīt*, (v. n. 2 of لغط) Making a murmuring noise, or a confused unintelligible jargon.

P تلف *tulf*, Repletion from eating grapes.

A تلف *talaf*, (v. n. of تلف) Perishing. Profusion, waste, prodigality, consumption. Ruin, destruction, loss.

A تلفا *talafan*, With impunity.

A تلفاق *tilfāk*, Two garments sewed together.

A تلفّت *talaffut*, (v. n. 5 of لفت) Bending, turning away (the face).

A تلفّظ *talaffuz*, A pronouncing, articulating.

A تلفّع *talaffuʿ*, (v. n. 5 of لفع) Being covered with a cloak (man or woman); with leaves (a tree); with grey hairs (the head). Wrapping a garment about one's body or head. Burning, flaming.

A تلفّف *talaffuf*, (v. n. 5 of لفّ) Wrapping one's self up (in a garment).

A تلفّق *talaffuk*, A being joined, reaching.

P تلفكار *talaf-kār*, Prodigal, lavish; spendthrift.

P تلف كرده *talaf-karda*, Wasted, squandered.

A تلفّم *talaffum*, (v. n. 5 of لفم) Binding or covering the tip of the nose or the mouth with a fillet or veil called لفام *lifām*. Veiling the head.

A تلفية *talfiyat*, A withholding, a defrauding.

A تلفيظ *talfīz*, Pronunciation, articulation.

A تلفيع *talfīʿ*, (v. n. 2 of لفع) Covering the head (grey hairs). Eating plentifully. Drawing, pressing to one's self. Turning a wallet inside out.

A تلفيف *talfīf*, (v. n. 2 of لفّ) Involving, covering up, folding, wrapping. Procuring false witnesses). Bringing together from various places.

A تلفيق *talfīk*, (v. n. 2 of لفق) Sewing together. Dressing, adorning. Adulterating, falsifying.

A تلقاء *tilkāʾ*, (v. n. of لقي) Arriving at, meeting with, falling upon, encountering. A meeting, encounter. تلقاء النار *tilkāʾaʾn nār*, Towards the fire. من تلقاء نفسه *min tilkāʾ nafsihi*, Of himself.

A تلقاع *tilikhāʿ*, A babbler, a prater.

A تلقاعة *tilikhāʿat*, A babbler, prater. A fool. One who calls nicknames.

A تلقام *tilhām*, (or تلقامة *tilhāmat*) One who swallows large mouthsful.

A تلقّب *talakkub*, (v. n. 5 of لقب) Assuming a surname or title. Being styled, titled, dubbed.

A تلقّح *talakkuh*, (v. n. 5 of لقح) Accusing falsely. Making motions with the hands whilst speaking. Spurning the male (a she-camel) and thus intimating that she is pregnant when she is not so.

A تلقّط *talakkut*, (v. n. 5 of لقط) Collecting everywhere, picking up here and there. Carrying from place to place.

A تلقّع *talakkuʿ*, The using abusive language.

A تلقّف *talakkuf*, (v. n. 5 of لقف) Swallowing, devouring, snatching greedily (like a starving wretch). Falling ruinous (a wall), bursting at the lower part.

A تلقلق *talakluk*, A being moved, agitated.

A تلقّم *talakkum*, (v. n. 5 of لقم) Eating or swallowing (any thing) leisurely. The murmuring noise of a rapid stream.

A تلقّن *talakkun*, (v. n. 5 of لقن) Being taught. Learning by heart.

A تلقّي *talakkī*, (v. n. 5 of لقي) Meeting, encountering. Learning (from one). Conceiving.

A تلقيب *talkīb*, (v. n. 2 of لقب) Giving a surname, style, title, or nickname.

A تلقية *talkiyat*, (v. n. 2 of لقي) Throwing (one thing into another), adding. Throwing to any one, injecting (a divine inspiration). Administering (an oath).

A تلقيث *talkīs*, A mixing. Mixture.

A تلقيح *talkīh*, (v. n. 2 of لقح) Making the female palm fruitful by sprinkling the male flowers.

A تلقيف *talkīf*, (v. n. 2 of لقف) Swallowing. Causing to swallow, giving a mouthful of meat. Raising and throwing the feet forward (a horse), not lifting them towards his belly. Striking his brisket when he travels (a camel).

A تلقيم *talkīm*, A causing to swallow.

A تلقين *talkīn*, (v. n. 2 of لقن) Instructing, informing, making to understand.

P تلك *talk*, Gold leaf. A kind of stuff. (for تلخ *talkh*) Bitter. *Tilk*, Green ginger. *Tulk*, A bean. *Tulak*, One whose beard has fallen off. A man with large mustachios. *Tilak*, The medlar-tree. A sleeveless garment. , A gown. A shoe.

A تلك *tilka*, (fem. of ذلك) She. That.

A تلكّد *talakkud*, (v. n. 5 of لكد) Embracing or hugging one another in friendship or in battle. Being joined, firm, compact. Being fleshy, thick, plump, fat, gross.

A تلكّؤ *talakkuʾ*, (v. n. 5 of لكأ) Stopping, delaying. Desisting, deserting. Being sickly, ailing.

A تلكيم *talkīm*, A patching, mending.

A تلل *talal*, Moisture. *Tulul*, (pl. of تليل) Necks.

A تلم *talm*, (v. n. of تلم) Ploughing. *Talam*, (pl. اتلام *atlām*) A trench, furrow (in corn-fields). *Tilam*, (pl. تلام *tilām*) A boy, servant; a ploughman. A goldsmith. A long tube, an air-pipe.

A تلمّاء *tilimmāʾ*, (v. n. 5 of لمي) Turning, changing (colour), becoming of a dark and tawny colour.

A تلماح *talmāh*, (v. n. of لمح) Shining, twinkling (a star), flashing (lightning).

A تلمّاظ *tilimmāz*, Inconstant in friendship.

A تلمّاظة *tilimmāzat*, Talkative (woman).

A تلمّج *talammuj*, (v. n. 5 of لمج) Taking a

whet before dinner, tasting.

A تلمّخ *talammukh*, (v. n. 5 of لمخ) Speaking obscenely, using foul language.

A تلمّز *talammuz*, (v. n. 5 of لمز) Asking repeatedly. Haste in walking.

A تلمّس *talammus*, An asking repeatedly.

A تلمسان *tilimsān*, The capital of Morocco.

A تلمّظ *talammuz*, (v. n. 5 of لمظ) Rolling the tongue about the mouth to clean the teeth after eating. Licking the lips. Rolling food about in the mouth to taste the flavour of it. Darting out the tongue, and moving it swiftly (a serpent).

A تلمّع *talammuʿ*, A snatching, catching at.

A تلمّق *talammuk*, (v. n. 5 of لمق) Tasting.

A تلمّك *talammuk*, (v. n. 5 of لمك) Tasting. Twisting his jaws or rolling his tongue about (a camel).

A تلمّل *talammul*, (v. n. 5 of لمل) Rolling the tongue about the mouth (after eating).

P تلمن *talmin*, (in zand and Pāzand) The nose, snout, beak.

A تلمّو *talammuʾ*, (v. n. 5 of لمأ) Covering, concealing (as the earth). Taking or laying by any fragments (of meat) in a dish.

A تلمّي *talammī*, A fading, vanishing (of colour).

A تلميج *talmīj*, (v. n. 2 of لمج) Breakfasting.

A تلميح *talmīh*, (v. n. 2 of لمح) Indicating, shewing. A glance. An illusion.

A تلميذ *tilmīz*, (pl. تلام *talām*, تلاميّ *talāmīy*, تلاميذ *talāmīz*, and تلامذة *talāmizat*) A scholar, student. A disciple.

A تلميظ *talmīz*, The paying of a debt.

A تلميع *talmīʿ*, (v. n. 2 of لمع) Having spots on his body differing in colour from the rest (a horse).

A تلنّة *tu* or *talunnat*, Delay. A thing necessary.

P تلندة *talanda*, A stutterer, a stammerer.

P تلنگ *talnag*, A fruit resembling a peach. *Tilang*, Name of a country in the Dak'han. *Tiling*, The beating of a tambourin. A small bunch of grapes. *Tulang*, Need, occasion. Inclination, wish. Supplication.

P تلنگبين *talangubīn*, (for ترنگبين) Manna.

P تلنگي *tulangī*, Indigent. A supplicant, a sturdy beggar. *Tulnigī*, A beardless youth. Large, corpulent. Fearless. A murderer.

P تلنه *tulna*, Poverty. Want, wish, desire.

A تلو *talw*, (v. n. of تلا for تلو) Purchasing a young mule. *Tilw*, (pl. اتلاء *atlāʾ*) Consecutive. High, exalted. Any thing following another (as the colt the dam). An ass-colt.

P تلو *talū*, A briar. *Tulū*, Shaft of an arrow.

A تلوّ *talūw*, One who follows without intermission. *Tulūw*, (v. n. of تلا for تلو) Following. Abandoning; withholding assistance.

A تلواذ *talwāz*, A mutual seeking of refuge.

P تلوازة *talwāza*, A wooden house.

P تلواسه *talwāsa*, Commotion, restlessness. Grief. Inclination.

A تلوة *tilwat*, A kid more than four months old. A she-ass colt. Lambs or kids dropt before the rising of the star Canopus.

A تلوّث *talawwus*, A being stained.

P تلوّث پذير *talawwus-pazīr*, Dirty, soiled.

A تلود *tulūd*, (v. n. of تلد) Being old (a possession), descending by heritage.

P تلوسه *talwsa*, The sheath in which the date is enveloped. A hatchet. *Talwasa*, Commotion, restlessness. Grief. *Talūsa* or *tulūsa*, A scabbard.

A تلوّص *talawwus*, A being twisted, inverted.

A تلوّط *talawwut*, (v. n. 5 of لاط for لوط) Committing an unnatural crime, doing as Lot's people.

A تلوع *tulūʿ*, Advance (of the day).

P تلوك *talok*, A butt for shooting at. A drinking vessel made in the shape of an animal.

A تلول *talūl*, Sluggish, led with difficulty (beast).

A تلوّم *talaʾʾum*, (v. n. 5 of لأم) Healing, becoming well (a wound).

A تلوّم *talawwum*, (v. n. 5 of لام for لوم) Being slow, dilatory. Waiting, expecting. Being blamed.

A تلون *tulūn*, (and تلونة *tulūnat*) Necessary business. Delay.

A تلوّن *talawwun*, (v. n. 5 of لان for لون) Being coloured. Changing colour: versatility, variableness.

A تلوّنات *talawwunāt*, Changes.

P تلوّن طبع *talawwun-tabʿ*, Capricious, whimsical, fitful, fretful.

P تلوّن مزاجي *talawwun-mizājī*, Caprice.

P تلونه *talūna*, A blossom.

A تلوّه *talawwuh*, (v. n. 5 of لاه for لوه) Shining (the vapour سراب *sarāb*). Trembling, wavering.

A تلوّي *talawwaʾ*, A small kind of ship. *Talawwī*, (v. n. 5 of لوي) Being bent, distorted, twisted. Turning away. Playing zigzag (lightning).

A تلويب *talwīb*, (v. n. 2 of لاب for لوب) Mixing a perfume. Smearing with saffron.

A تلوية *talwiyat*, (v. n. 2 of لوي) Twisting, bending, shaking the head.

A تلويث *talwīs*, (v. n. 2 of لاث for لوث) Befouling. Imprisoning, detaining. Mixing. Macerating, dissolving. Sucking his finger (a child).

A تلويج *talwīj*, Crookedness (of a road).

A تلويح *talwīh*, (v. n. 2 of لاح for لوح) Causing to change colour. Making tawny, yellow, or fiery-coloured (as the sun, fire, or thirst). Making the head white (hoariness). Heating. Shining in glistening garments or with a sword. Making (a garment) glossy. Making (a sword) glitter and gleam. Giving (a child) any thing to eat (which it can hold in its hand).

A تلويز *talwīz*, (v. n. 2 of لاز for لوز) Stuffing (dates or figs) with almonds (لوز *lawz*).

A تلويص *talwīs*, (v. n. 2 of لاص for لوص) Eating pure honey, called لواص *lawās*.

A تلويق *talwīk*, (v. n. 2 of لاق for لوق) Preparing, preserving, or dressing (meat) with butter. Dressing soft as butter (meat).

A تلويم *talwīm*, (v. n. 2 of لام for لوم) Reprehending, blaming, reproving. Writing the letter ل *lām*.

A تلوين *talwīn*, (v. n. 2 of لون not in use) Colouring. Varying, diversifying. Beginning to colour (dates).

P تله *tala*, A gin for catching birds. A place where cattle are tied up. A hot iron with which stains are taken out of cloth. *Tila*, Drawn gold. The step of a stair, the round of a ladder.

A تله *talah*, (v. n. of تله) Perishing. Being sad, distracted. Being made to forget, being rendered unmindful. Ruin, destruction. Mental perturbation.

P تلّه *talla*, Step of a stair; round of a ladder.

A تلهّب *talahhub*, A burning, flaming.

A تلهجم *talahjum*, (v. n. 2 of لهجم Q) Being greedy of, addicted to. Lying open (a beaten road). Thrusting the muzzle into.

A تلهذم *talahzum*, A cutting off. An eating.

A تلهّع *talahhuʿ*, Diffuseness, verbosity.

A تلهّف *talahhuf*, (v. n. 5 of لهف) Lamenting, regretting (any thing neglected, missed, or lost).

A تلهّق *talahhuk*, (v. n. 5 of لهق) Being of a dead white (linen).

A تلهلو *talahluʾ*, (v. n. 2 of لهلأ Q not in use) Retiring, desisting through timidity.

A تلهله *talahluh*, (v. n. 2 of لهله Q) Searching diligently, exploring the smaller particles of forage.

A تلهّم *talahhum*, A devouring, gulping up.

A تلهّن *talahhun*, A breakfasting, taking a whet.

A تلهوق *talahwuk*, (v. n. 2 of لهوق Q) Speaking or acting carelessly.

A تلهّي *talahhī*, (v. n. 5 of لها for لهو) Playing, sporting, unbending. Forgetting, dismissing. Being negligent and careless.

A تلهيب *talhīb*, A setting on fire, making blaze.

A تلهية *talhiyat*, (v. n. 2 of لها for لهو) Causing to love or delight in. Inducing one to unbend the mind or take amusement (in order to forget grief). Any thing by which time is beguiled.

A تلهيج *talhīj*, A giving breakfast or a whet.

A تلهيد *talhīd*, (v. n. 2 of لهد) Pushing away (in contempt). Accusing, reproaching.

A تلهيز *talhīz*, (v. n. 2 of لهز) Striking on the breast with the fist.

A تلهيع *talhīʿ*, (v. n. 2 of لهع) Prating, babbling: discoursing fluently. Making pretension to wit.

A تلهيف *talhīf*, (v. n. 2 of لهف) Crying out in anguish وا نفساه *wā nafsāhu*, Alas! my soul.

A تلهين *talhīn*, (v. n. 2 of لهن) Giving breakfast or a whet. Bringing a present from off a journey.

A تلي *tily*, One who swears much. Wealthy. *Tala'*, Remaining (part of a month).

P تلي *tilī*, Gold. *Tule*, An artificer's tool. A barber's case of instruments. A bag wherein a tailor keeps his needle, thread, and thimble.

A تلّي *talla'*, (pl. of تليل *talīl*) Prostrate. *Tulla'*,

A slaughtered sheep.

P تليبار *talebār*, A house for keeping silkworms.

A تلية *tilyat*, (or *taliyat*) Remainder (of a debt).

A تليث *talis*, A date-tree growing in salt ground.

A تلّيث *talayyus*, (v. n. 5 of ليث obsol.) Being bold, strenuous, resembling a lion in gracefulness.

A تليد *talid*, Born in foreign parts and educated at home (as slaves among the Arabians). Hereditary wealth.

A تلّيسة *tillisat*, A sack. A testicle. A basket.

A تليع *taliʿ*, Long-necked. Long, erect (neck).

A تلّيغ *talayyugh*, A feigning to be foolish.

A تليل *talil*, (pl. تلّي *talla'*) Prostrate. (pl. اتلّة *atillat*, تلل *tulul*, and تلاتل *talātil*) The neck.

P تليمان *talimān*, Name of a hero of Irān.

A تليّن *talayyun*, (v. n. 5 of لان for لين) Being softened, smoothed. Making professions of regard, caressing, blandishing.

P تليوار *talewār*, A house for keeping silkworms.

A تلييث *talyis*, (v. n. 2 of لاث for ليث) Resembling a lion in greediness and voracity.

A تلييط *talyit*, A joining, glueing.

A تلييف *talyif*, (v. n. 2 of لاف for ليف) Using (the bark of the palm). Being thick and having much bark (the shoot of a palm-tree).

A تلئيم *talʾim*, A bringing again into favour.

A تليين *talyin*, The act of smoothing.

P تم *tam*, A disease in the eye, the web or cataract on the pupil, which causes blindness.

A تمّ *tamma*, (fut. يتمّ *yatimmu*) It was finished.

A تمّ *tamm*, (v. n. of تمّ) Being entire, complete, full, finished. Completing, making up the number. Amulets of camel's hair. This word (or تمّ الكتاب *tamma'l kitāb*, The book is finished) is generally written at the end of a book, similar to our Finis, or The End. تمّ الكتاب بعون الملك الوهّاب *tamma'l kitāb bi ʿawni'l maliki'l wahhāb*, The book is finished, with the assistance of (God) the munificent king. *Timm*, A hoe, spade, axe, or mattock. *Timm*, *tamm*, or *tumm*, (v. n. of تمّ) Becoming perfect and complete. Completing. Persisting, persevering. Perfection, accomplishment, end, complement. ولدته لتمّ *waladathu li timmin*, She brought him forth perfectly formed.

A تماءر *tamāʾur*, A boasting against each other.

A تماتر *tamātur*, (v. n. 6 of متر) Flying here and there (sparks of fire). Being dispersed or scattered. Dragging, pulling one against another.

A تماته *tamātuh*, A being very far asunder.

A تماتين *tamātin*, (pl. of تمتان) Tent-strings.

A تماثل *tamāsul*, (v. n. 6 of مثل) Being convalescent (an invalid). Being equal, like each other.

A تماثيل *tamāsil*, (pl. of تمثال) Pictures.

P تماج *tumāj*, Goat's leather. A purse.

A تماجد *tamājud*, (v. n. 6 of مجد) Rehearsing the glory of one. Contending for, parading glory.

A تماجع *tamājuʿ*, (v. n. 6 of مجع) Sneering, ridiculing; being petulant, impudent, saucy; talking obscenely among themselves.

A تماجن *tamājun*, (v. n. 6 of مجن) Talking obscenely together among themselves.

A تماحك *tamāhuk*, A litigating, wrangling.

P تماخره *tamākhra*, A word. *Tamākhara*, A joke, jest. Wit, humour. Buffoonery.

A تمادح *tamāduh*, A praising one another.

A تمادخ *tamādukh*, (v. n. 6 of مدخ) Weighing down, oppressing. Shrinking from, hanging back. Insolence, rebellion.

A تمادي *tamādi*, (v. n. 6 of مدي not in use) Continuing a long time. Perseverance.

A تمّار *tammār*, A date-seller.

A تمارّ *tamārr*, (v. n. 6 of مرّ) Being broken off (friendship). Wrestling.

P تمارخ *tamārakh*, An excellent kind of grass.

A تمارس *tamārus*, A being in commotion, distracted among themselves, fighting, squabbling.

A تمارض *tamāruz*, The feigning a disease.

A تمارن *tamārun*, Failure of a camel's milk.

A تماري *tamāri*, (v. n. 6 of مري) Doubting (of any thing). Contending, quarrelling.

A تماريّ *tumāriy*, A sort of tree.

A تماريد *tamārid*, (pl. of تمراد *timrād*) Small houses within dove-cotes for pigeons to lay in.

A تمازّ *tamāzz*, The being wide apart.

A تمازح *tamāzuh*, A jesting together.

A تماسّ *tamāss*, (v. n. 6 of مسّ) Touching one another. Copulating.

A تماسح *tamāsuh*, (v. n. 6 of مسح) Acting fairly towards each other. Joining hands on a bargain.

A تماسك *tamāsuk*, (v. n. 6 of مسك) Holding together. Repressing, containing one's self.

A تماسي *tamāsi*, (v. n. 6 of مسي) Being dissolved, falling in pieces. Accidents, misfortunes.

A تماسيح *tamāsih*, (pl. of تمساح) Crocodiles.

A تماشا *tamāsha'*, (for تماشي *tamāshi*) (v. n. 6 of مشي) Walking abroad for recreation. Beholding. Looking at any thing comic or tragic. An entertainment, show, theatrical representation. Sport, amusement, pleasure. P تماشا كردن *tamāshā kardan*, To behold, to enjoy a sight.

P تماشا بين *tamāshā-bin*, A rake, epicure.

P تماشا بيني *tamāshā-bini*, Libertinism.

P تماشا گاه *tamāshā-gāh*, A place of amusement. A theatre, amphitheatre.

P تماشاگري *tamāshāgari*, A debauch.

A تماشق *tamāshuk*, A snatching from one another.

A تماشي *tamāshi*, A walking abroad together.

A تماصع *tamāsuʿ*, A fighting together.

A تماضّ *tamāzz*, A quarrelling, a wrangling.

A تماضر *tumāzir*, Name of a woman.

A تماظظ *tamāzuz*, An opposing, contending. A biting one another with the tongue.

A تماقل *tamākul*, A ducking one another.

A تماكس *tamākus*, A bidding against each other.

A تمالغ *tamālugh*, A laughing at, ridiculing.

A تمالك *tamāluk*, A maintaining self-possession.

A تمالؤ *tamāluʾ*, (v. n. 6 of ملأ) Mutually agreeing and aiding. Collecting together, forming a crowd.

A تمام *tamām*, Entire, perfect, complete, consummate. All. Whole. Conclusion, end, termination. Finished, accomplished, performed. Completely, totally, absolutely, entirely. The supplement of a hemistich in poetry. تمام العيار *tamāmu'l ʿiyār*, Of full weight. P تمام شدن *tamām shudan*, To be completed. To die. A *Tamām*, *timām*, or *tumām*, (v. n. of تمّ) Being full, complete, finished. Terminating. Completing. Persevering, persisting. P تمام كردن *tamām kardan*, To complete. A شيء بتمامه *shayʾ bi timāmihi*, The entire thing. ولدته لتمام *waladathu li timāmin*, She brought him forth fully formed. قمر تمام *kamari timām*, Full moon. ليل تمام *layli timām*, The longest night in the year.

A تماما *tamāman*, (also بتمامه *bi tamāmihi*, P تمامانه *tamāmāna*) Wholly, entirely, in toto.

P تمام اندام *tamām-andām*, Fat, full of flesh.

A تمامة *tamāmat*, End, completion, perfection. *Tamāmat* or *timāmat*, (v. n. of تمّ) Being complete; finishing. Persevering, persisting. *Tumāmat*, Remains, reversion, remainder.

P تمام عيار *tamām-ʿiyār*, Of full standard.

A تمامي *tamāmi*, Perfection. Conclusion, end.

A ليل تماميّ *laylun timāmiy*, The longest night in the year.

A تمامير *tamāmir*, (pl. of تمّرة *tummarat*) Certain birds smaller than sparrows.

A تمانع *tamānuʿ*, (v. n. 6 of منع) Receding from each other (two squadrons in battle).

A تماني *tamāni*, (v. n. 6 of منو) Gambling with the fingers, playing at the game called la morre.

A تماوت *tamāwut*, A feigning to be dead.

A تماؤر *tamāʾur*, A boasting, a glorying.

A تماؤن *tamāʾun*, (v. n. 6 of مأن) Arriving.

A تماهة *tamāhat*, (v. n. of تمه) Being corrupted, smelling (meat).

P تماهچه *tamāhcha*, Meat well dressed.

A تماهك *tamāhuk*, A litigating, wrangling.

A تمأّي *tamaʾʾi*, (v. n. 5 of مأّ) Being spread (evil), being propagated (sedition). Being wide by stretching (a skin). (v. n. 5 of مأي) Being stretched (a skin).

A تمايح *tamāyuh*, (v. n. 6 of ماح for ميح) Staggering, reeling (a drunken man).

A تماير *tamāyur*, Interruption (of friendship).

A تمايط *tamāyut*, (v. n. 6 of ماط for ميط) Being far distant, absent, retiring. Being estranged from each other, sundering the ties of friendship.

A تمايل *tamāyul*, (v. n. 6 of مال for ميل) Inclining, leaning from side to side in walking. Inflection, declination.

A تمائم *tamāʾim*, (pl. of تميمة) Amulets, charms.

A تمّة *tammat*, A charm against enchantments, made of camels' hair. *Tummat*, A present. (pl. تمم *tumam* or *timam*) A little hair or the like given to one to finish withal his blanket.

A تمت *tamt*, Name of an uneatable herb.

A تمتام *tamtām*, One who stutters, and pronounces with difficulty the letters م *mīm* and ت *tā*. One who speaks indistinctly.

A تمتامة *tamtāmat*, A difficulty in pronouncing ت *tā* and م *mīm*.

A تمتان *timtān*, (pl. تماتين) A tent-string.

A تمتّح *tamattuh*, (v. n. 5 of متح) Reposing.

A تمتّع *tamattuع*, (v. n. 5 of متع) Using, enjoying, reaping advantage. Assisting at the solemnities of Mecca. Performing the عمرة *ʿumrat* and the حجّ *hajj* together. Delight, enjoyment.

A تمتّك *tamattuk*, A sipping (wine or water).

A تمتم *timtim* or *tumtum*, The plant sumach.

P تمتم *tumtum*, The tail of the wild ox.

A تمتمة *tamtamat*, (v. n. of تمتم Q) Hesitating, pronouncing indifferently the letters ت *tā* or م *mīm*.

A تمتّن *tamattun*, A being firm and solid.

A تمتّه *tamattuh*, (v. n. 5 of مته) Commending one's self, fishing for applause. Walking very stately. Suffering toil, trouble, and misery. Intensity, exaggeration, hyperbole. A secret. Error, mistake.

A تمتّي *tamattī*, (v. n. 5 of متي) Drawing a bowstring. Being lengthy. Leaning on a rope in order to cut it in two.

A تمتيح *tamtīh*, (v. n. 2 of متح) Fixing her tail in the sand when laying her eggs (a locust).

A تمتيع *tamtīع*, (v. n. 2 of متع) Permitting freely to enjoy. Bestowing, conferring, granting. Prolonging, extending. Giving a divorced woman a present. Granting a long life. Causing to grow, supplying growth. A favour.

A تمتين *tamtīn*, (v. n. 2 of متن) Pitching a tent with its cords. Saying to any one, "Go on before to such a place and I will overtake you." Strengthening the skirting of a tent that the ends of the tent-poles may not tear it. Whipping a bow round with a sinew. Seasoning a leathern bottle with inspissated juice. (pl. تماتين *tamātīn*) A tent-string.

A تمثال *tamsāl*, Comparison, similitude. *Timsāl*, (pl. تماثيل) Image, effigy, portrait, semblance.

P تمثالگر *timsālgar*, A portrait-painter, limner.

A تمثّع *tamassuع*, The trotting (of a hyena).

A تمثّل *tamassul*, (v. n. 5 of مثل) Resembling, imitating. Appearing before, standing in the presence. Punishing by way of example, as eye for eye. Applying or employing a fable or proverb.

A تمثيل *tamsīl*, (v. n. 2 of مثل) Making an example of (a homicide) by mutilating (him) in the nose, ears, lips, or extremities. Taking a portrait. Describing accurately, giving a lively representation of. Likening, comparing, applying an allegory. Comparison, similitude, resemblance. Exemplification. An allegory, parable, fable, apologue. Impression.

A تمثيلات *tamsīlāt*, Examples, allegories.

A تمجّح *tamajjuh*, A boasting, a being proud.

A تمجّس *tamajjus*, (v. n. 5 of مجس not in use) Embracing the Persian religion of the Magi, or the worship of fire.

A تمجّع *tamajjuع*, (v. n. 5 of مجع) Eating dates and milk together, or drinking the milk afterwards. Taking a sip of milk and eating dates.

A تمجمج *tamajmuj*, (v. n. 2 of مجمج Q) Shaking (the buttocks of a horse). Endeavouring to disparage, wishing to disgrace.

A تمجّن *tamajjun*, Impudent, random talk.

A تمجيج *tamjīj*, A reproaching, disgracing.

A تمجيد *tamjīd*, (v. n. 2 of مجد) Satiating, or nearly satiating (camels) with green pasture. Giving abundantly. Giving glory to, glorifying. The glorification of God.

A تمجيس *tamjīs*, (v. n. 2 of مجس not used) Making one of the Magi, proselyting to the religion of the fire-worshippers.

A تمحّق *tamahhuk*, (v. n. 5 of محق) Being effaced, abolished. Being burned.

A تمحّك *tamahhuk*, A being morose, quarrelsome.

A تمحّل *tamahhul*, (v. n. 5 of محل) Deceiving, betraying, laying snares. Trying to recover (debt).

A تمحمح *tamahmuh*, (v. n. 2 of محمح Q) Alighting at a place, settling, taking up one's abode. Occupying the middle of a house. Being near delivery (a woman).

A تمحّن *tamahhun*, (v. n. 5 of محن) Toiling, undergoing trouble and vexation (محنة *mihnat*).

A تمحية *tamhiyat*, An erasing, defacing.

A تمحيص *tamhīs*, (v. n. 2 of محص) Proving, trying, making an experiment. Lessening, pulling the nerves out of meat.

A تمحيط *tamhīt*, (v. n. 2 of محط) Making (a bowstring) smooth and even with the fingers.

A تمحيق *tamhīk*, (v. n. 2 of محق) Erasing, effacing, annulling, destroying.

A تمحيل *tamhīl*, (v. n. 2 of محل) Strengthening.

A تمحين *tamhīn*, (v. n. 2 of محن) Taking off the bark or any thing similar. Smoothing (leather).

A تمخّج *tamahkhuj*, (v. n. 5 of مخج) Shaking, agitating (water) in a well with a bucket.

A تمخّخ *tamahkhuhkh*, The extracting of marrow.

A تمخّر *tamahkhur*, (v. n. 5 of مخر) Facing the wind and snuffing it up (a horse). Turning one's back to the wind. اذا اراد احدكم البول فليتمخّر الريح *izā arāda ahadukumu'l bawl, fa'l yatamakhkhari'r rīh*, When any one of you wants to make water, let him turn his back to the wind.

A تمخّس *tamahkhus*, (or تمخّش *tamahkhush*) Violent motion.

A تمخّض *tamahkhuz*, (v. n. 5 of مخض) Being agitated (milk) in churning. Being taken with the pains of labour. Bringing trials and difficulties (fortune). Shaking a churning-bottle. Stirring (as a fœtus). Conceiving (a ewe).

A تمخّط *tamahkhut*, (v. n. 5 of مخط) Blowing the nose. Drawing up water into the nostrils, and discharging it again. Vacillating in one's walk.

A تمخّي *tamahkhī*, (v. n. 5 of مخي) Being free, quit, clear. Abstaining, refraining from. Excusing one's self, apologizing.

A تمخية *tamkhiyat*, A removing, carrying away.

P تمخيثا *tamkhīsā*, An ejaculation on an emergency. Name of one of the seven sleepers in the cave near Ephesus.

A تمخيخ *tamkhīkh*, The extracting of marrow.

A تمخيض *tamkhīz*, (v. n. 2 of مخض) Being taken with the pains of labour. Seizing a female (the pangs of labour).

A تمخيط *tamkhīt*, (v. n. 2 of مخط) Taking off the caul from the nose of a newly-born lamb or kid.

A تمدّح *tamadduh*, (v. n. 5 of مدح) Commending one's self, fishing for applause, glorying in what one does not possess. Being ample, sufficiently extensive (a town or country). Praising.

A تمدّخ *tamadduhh*, (v. n. 5 of مدخ) Crawling onwards (a camel). Being proud (a man). Being filled with fat (camels).

A تمدّد *tamaddud*, (v. n. 5 of مدّ) Being extended. Yawning, stretching one's self. Extending, lengthening out. Walking with self-importance.

A تمدرع *tamadruع*, (v. n. 2 of مدرع Q) Putting on a woollen jerkin.

A تمدّل *tamaddul*, (v. n. 5 of مدل) Wiping one's self. Folding a fillet or sash (called منديل *mindīl*) round the body, and the fillet (called دستار *dustār*) round the head.

A تمدّن *tamaddun*, A residing in a city.

P تمده *tamda*, A stammerer, a stutterer.

A تمدّه *tamadduh*, (v. n. 5 of مده) Boasting, courting applause. Praise, eulogium.

A تمدهن *tamadhun*, (v. n. 2 of مدهن Q) Using or making an oil-bottle (مدهن *mudhun*).

A تمديح *tamdīh*, A praising greatly.

A تمديد *tamdīd*, An extending, lengthening.

A تمدير *tamdīr*, (v. n. 2 of مدر) Covering with clay; cementing the chinks of a bath, pond, or reservoir. Voiding excrement.

A تمديش *tamdīsh*, (v. n. 2 of مدش) Giving little.

A تمدين *tamdīn*, (v. n. 2 of مدن) Building (cities). Establishing and settling in a place. *Tamadyun*, A being brought up delicately.

A تمذّج *tamazzuj*, (v. n. 5 of مذج) Ripening (a melon). Becoming filled (a vessel). Swelling. Being ample, extended.

A تمذّح *tamazzuh*, (v. n. 5 of مذح) Rising, swelling (the sides with drink). Sucking.

A تمذّخ *tamazzukh*, (v. n. 5 of مذخ) Sucking the honey of pomegranate-flowers. Walking against each other (a camel and a man).

A تمذر *tamazzur*, (v. n. 5 of مذر) Being indisposed. Being scattered, dispersed. Falling into cheesy particles (milk), the serous particles being separated. Being rotten (a nut).

A تمذقر *tamazkur*, A turning, stinking (of water).

A تمذهب *tamazhub*, (v. n. 2 of مذهب Q) Embracing a sect.

A تمذية *tamziyat*, A sending (a horse) to pasture.

A تمذيح *tamzīj*, An enlarging, amplifying.

A تمذير *tamzīr*, A scattering, dispersing.

P تمر *tamr* or *timr*, A pearl in the eye. *Tumr*, Iron. *Timir*, Darkness, obscurity.

A تمر *tamr*, (v. n. of تمر) Giving away dates to eat. (pl. تمور *tumūr* and تمران *tumrān*) A ripe date. The various names for the date whilst growing are, طلع *talʿ*, The spathe, bud or flower: سيّاب *sayyāb*, when set: جدال *jadāl*, سراد *sarād*, or خلال *khalāl*, when round and green: بغو *baghw*, middle-sized: بسر *busr*, come to its full size. Afterwards, through the different stages of ripening, it is called مخطّم *mukhattam*, موكّت *muwakkit*, تذنوب *tuznūb*, جميسة *jamīsat*, ثعدة *saʿdat*, خالع *khāliʿ*, and خالعة *khāliʿat*. When fully ripe, رطب *rutb* and معو *maʿw*: last of all, تمر *tamr*. تمر الهند *tamru'l hind*, A tamarind.

A تمرات *tamarāt*, (pl. of تمرة *tamrat*) Dates.

A تمراد *tamrād*, (v. n. 2 of مرد) Making a تمراد *timrād*. *Timrād*, (pl. تماريد *tamārīd*) A small house within a dove-cote for pigeons to lay in.

A تمراغ *tamrāgh*, A dipping, a soaking.

A تمران *tumrān*, (pl. of تمر *tamr*) Dates.

A تمرة *tamrat*, One date. Lively spirits. *Tumrat*, A slender string for the notch of an arrow. A sinew thin at the notch of an arrow. *Tummarat*, (or ابن تمّرة *ibn tummarat*) (pl. تمامير *tamāmīr*) Name of a bird smaller than a sparrow.

A تمرّد *tamarrud*, (v. n. 5 of مرد) Being refractory, stubborn, obstinate, disobedient, insolent. Continuing beardless beyond the usual time (a youth), and afterwards getting a beard. Laying siege to Mārdīn (Timūr).

A تمرّدي *tamarrudī*, Obstinacy, stubbornness.

A تمرز *tumariz*, (or *tummariz*) Short, dwarfish.

A تمرّس *tamarrus*, (v. n. 5 of مرس) Rubbing one's self, or being rubbed against.

A تمرّص *tamarrus*, (v. n. 5 of مرص) Flying off (the husk of a barley called سلت *sult*). Unbarking any thing.

A تمرّض *tamarruz*, (v. n. 5 of مرض) Being weak, deficient in business.

A تمرّط *tamarrut*, The dropping off (of hair).

A تمرّع *tamarruʿ*, (v. n. 5 of مرع) Hastening, walking fast. Being moved, quivering with rage (the nose). Seeking for a cultivated place full of green herbage.

A تمرّغ *tamarrugh*, (v. n. 5 of مرغ) Being tumbled or turned over. Tumbling or rolling (as a horse upon the ground). Writhing with agony. Delaying, pausing, wavering, hesitating. Sliding (the foot). Remaining long at pasture. Being pure, free from vice or stain. Anointing one's self with oil. Spitting, sputtering, shedding slaver.

A تمرفق *tamarfuk*, The using a cushion.

A تمرّق *tamarruk*, (v. n. 5 of مرق) Coming forth. Being plucked, falling off (hair).

T تمرقزك *tamir* or *tamur kazak*, The word of God, the glorious Kur'ān.

A تمرمر *tamarmur*, (v. n. 2 of مرمر Q) Shaking, quivering. Trembling, tottering, moving (sand).

A تمرّن *tamarrun*, (v. n. 5 of مرن) Behaving elegantly. Excelling, being eminent. Being accustomed, acquiring a habit.

A تمرّؤ *tamarruʾ*, (v. n. 5 of مرأ) Shewing, pretending to, humanity or fortitude. Building reputation on the disparagement of others.

A تمرّي *tamarrī*, An adorning, dressing one's self.

A تمريّ *tamrīy*, Fond of dates.

A تمريء *tamrīʾ*, (v. n. 2 of مرؤ) Saying to any one "May your food digest, and do you good!"

A تمريث *tamrīs*, (v. n. 2 of مرث) Causing (a lamb or kid) to smell offensively, so as to excite the dam's aversion. Breaking, crumbling minutely.

A تمريج *tamrīh*, (v. n. 2 of مرج) Filling (a leathern bottle) with water, to close up the holes or stitches. Cleaning (wheat) from rubbish with a besom. Oiling (the skin). Going to battle.

A تمريخ *tamrīkh*, An anointing the body with oil.

A تمريد *tamrīd*, (v. n. 2 of مرد) Smoothing (a wall), making a building smooth and shining. Pruning. Constructing within a dove-cote the small house تمراد *timrād*, for pigeons to lay in.

A تمرير *tamrīr*, (v. n. 2 of مرّ) Making bitter.

A تمريش *tamrīsh*, A little rain.

A تمريض *tamrīz*, (v. n. 2 of مرض) Weakening, enervating. Taking care of, tending the sick. Being deficient (in business), doing less than one ought. Winnowing corn.

A تمريط *tamrīt*, (v. n. 2 of مرط) Pulling (hair) off the body. Making (a dress) with short sleeves.

A تمريغ *tamrīgh*, (v. n. 2 of مرغ) Allowing to wallow (a horse). Buttering much (a dish of food).

A تمريق *tamrīk*, (v. n. 2 of مرق) Singing (implying that of a female slave, or man of mean rank).

A تمرين *tamrīn*, (v. n. 2 of مرن) Smoothing, softening (leather). Looking sternly. Accustoming. Being familiar. Striking on the ground. (in grammar) Testing the proficiency of a student by proposing all sorts of difficult questions relating to the form assumed by a given root when carried into a given measure of inflection.

A تمزّر *tamazzur*, (v. n. 5 of مزر) Sipping, sucking. Drinking once. Milking the remains of milk.

A تمزّز *tamazzuz*, (v. n. 5 of مزّ) Sipping, sucking. Milking out the remains of milk in the udder. Drinking once. A moderate draught.

A تمزّع *tamazzuʿ*, (v. n. 5 of مزع) Growling, grumbling, being enraged: trembling, quivering with rage. Being torn up, off, away. Dividing between.

A تمزّق *tamazzuk*, (v. n. 5 of مزق) Being torn (cloth or garment). Being burst (skin). Being disbanded (an army).

A تمزمز *tamazmuz*, (v. n. 2 of مزمز Q) Moving up and down. Being driven here and there. Fleeing, scampering, being scattered. Preparing (to rise).

A تمزّن *tamazzun*, (v. n. 5 of مزن) Pretending to too much. Conferring favours. Affecting elegance. Diligently devising liberal things. Acquiring a habit. Going where one likes.

A تمزّي *tamazzī*, (v. n. 5 of مزي) Conferring favours or obligations.

A تمزية *tamziyat*, A bestowing praise.

A تمزيج *tamzīj*, (v. n. 2 of مزج) Turning yellow (corn). Giving, presenting.

A تمزيح *tamzīh*, (v. n. 2 of مزح) Putting forth its fruit (the vine). Beginning to colour (grapes).

A تمزير *tamzīr*, (v. n. 2 of مزر) Filling (a leathern bottle) so as to leave no bump on the surface.

A تمزيع *tamzīʿ*, (v. n. 2 of مزع) Dispersing, separating. Teazing (cotton).

A تمزيق *tamzīk*, A tearing. A dissipating.

A تمزين *tamzīn*, (v. n. 2 of مزن) Conferring favours. Filling (a bottle). Praising, eulogising.

P تمژه *tamja*, A flat roof or platform.

A تمساح *tamsāh*, A lie. *Timsāh*, (pl. تماسيح *tamāsīh*) A crocodile. A liar. Bad-tempered.

A تمسح *timsah*, A liar. Contumacious, stubborn, base, wicked. A crocodile.

A تمسّح *tamassuh*, (v. n. 5 of مسح) Passing the hand over any thing liquid. Rubbing one thing against another. Wiping one's self. Blessing another for any excellence. Being poor, naked, and bare.

A تمسّخ *tamassukh*, A being metamorphosed.

A تمسخر *tamaskhur*, Ridicule, buffoonery.

A تمسّك *tamassuk*, (v. n. 5 of مسك) Holding, keeping fast hold. Striking the claws into. Hanging back. Perfuming with musk. An obligation, bond, note of hand, writing, instrument, receipt. تمسّك حاضر ضامني *tamassuki hāzir-zāmini*, A recognisance for personal appearance.

A تمسّكات *tamassukāt*, Obligations, bonds.

A تمسكن *tamaskun*, (v. n. 2 of مسكن Q) Growing poor. Resembling a pauper. Being base and contemptible.

A تمسلم *tamaslum*, The being called a Muslim.

A تمسّؤ *tamassuʾ*, (v. n. 5 of مسأ) Being old, and falling to pieces (a garment).

A تمسّي *tamassī*, A falling into different pieces.

A تمسية *tamsiyat*, (v. n. 2 of مسا for مسو) Making it evening. Saying "How do you do this evening?" or, "I wish you a good evening."

A تمسيح *tamsīh*, (v. n. 2 of مسح) Passing the hand over any dirty object, that the dirt may be removed, or over a liquid surface. Fatiguing and extenuating by overwork. Flattery, cajolery.

A تمسيخ *tamsīkh*, An altering, a spoiling.

A تمسيخا *tamsīkhā*, Name of a prayer.

A تمسيك *tamsīk*, (v. n. 2 of مسك) Holding, keeping, preserving. Perfuming with musk. Giving earnest.

A تمش *tamsh*, A collecting, bringing together.

A تمشاء *timshās*, A mode of walking; step, gait.

A تمشّر *tamashshur*, (v. n. 5 of مشر) Putting forth leaves and young green branches. Appearing to be rich. Clothing itself with green (a leaf). Covering, clothing one's self. Striving to earn wherewithal to clothe one's family.

A تمشش *tamashshush*, (v. n. 5 of مش) Gnawing the end of a bone, and sucking out the marrow.

A تمشّع *tamashshuع*, (v. n. 5 of مشع) Removing filth from one (particularly excrement with a flint). Eating the entire contents of a dish.

A تمشّق *tamashshuk*, (v. n. 5 of مشق) Being torn. Retiring (night). Being stripped of its bark.

A تمشّي *tamashshī*, (v. n. 5 of مشي) Exhilarating (wine). Walking.

A تمشية *tamshiyat*, (v. n. 2 of مشي) Walking. Causing to walk. Passing, voiding. Furthering (business). Promotion, preferment, advancement.

A تمشير *tamshīr*, (v. n. 2 of مشر) Shooting forth branches or suckers. Dividing, scattering (any thing). Clothing. Disclosing, making manifest. Briskness, ardour for copulation.

A تمشيش *tamshīsh*, A taking out marrow.

A تمشيط *tamshīt*, (v. n. 2 of مشط) Combing. Having collops of fat on her sides resembling a comb (a camel).

A تمشيغ *tamshīgh*, (v. n. 2 of مشغ) Tarnishing (the reputation of another). Staining, dyeing with reddle, ruddling.

A تمشيق *tamshīk*, A tinging with vermilion.

A تمشيل *tamshīl*, (v. n. 2 of مشل) Giving little milk (a camel). Drawing (a sword).

A تمشين *tamshīn*, (v. n. 2 of مشن) Giving milk unwillingly. Milking (the udder) dry.

A تمصّخ *tamassukh*, (v. n. 5 of مصخ) Stripping the leaves off the plant called ثمام *sumām*.

A تمصّر *tamassur*, (v. n. 5 of مصر) Milking with the tips of the three fingers or the tip of the fore-finger and thumb. Being little or few. Searching diligently, exploring. Following, imitating. Being divided, scattered. Milking out the remains in the udder. Becoming a city (a place).

A تمصّص *tamassus*, A sucking, sipping.

A تمصيح *tamsīh*, (v. n. 2 of مصح) (God) removing (a disease).

A تمصير *tamsīr*, (v. n. 2 of مصر) Giving little milk. Diminishing. Giving by very small instalments. Founding cities, and bringing people to people them.

A تمصيع *tamsīع*, (v. n. 2 of مصع) Cutting green wood, and letting it lie with the bark, which seasons and prevents it from cracking.

A تمضّح *tamazzuh*, An oozing, or being extracted.

A تمضّر *tamazzur*, (v. n. 5 of مضر) Being inflamed, enraged. Being related, or claiming relationship, to the tribe of مضر *muzar*.

A تمضمض *tamazmuz*, (v. n. 2 of مضمض Q) Being oppressed with sleep (the eye). Performing the sacred ablution of the mouth. Flowing into the mouth (water for the performance of an ablution). Barking after any one (a dog).

A تمضّي *tamazzī*, (v. n. 5 of مضي) Being transmitted, passing through or beyond.

A تمضير *tamzīr*, (v. n. 2 of مضر) Afflicting, destroying. Referring, relating, or allying (any one) to the tribe of مضر *muzar*. مضّرها الله في النار *mazzarahā'llāh fi'n nār*, God tormented her (or may God torment her) in the fire.

A تمضيض *tamzīz*, A drinking brackish water.

A تمطّر *tamattur*, (v. n. 5 of مطر) Exposing one's self to the rain, going out in a cold rain. Travelling, perambulating a country. Flying downwards, pouncing rapidly (a bird). Coming along at full gallop (horses).

A تمطّط *tamattut*, (v. n. 5 of مطّ) Being diffusive in discourse, using circumlocution. Being extended. Being raised (the eyebrows). Becoming thick (water). Yawning.

A تمطّق *tamattuk*, (v. n. 5 of مطق not in use) Tasting, licking. Making a noise with the tongue against the palate.

A تمطمط *tamatmut*, Thickness, muddiness.

A تمطّي *tamattī*, (v. n. 5 of مطا for مطو) Yawning. Stretching. Being extended. Being long (the day). Walking with a haughty air.

A تمطيط *tamtīt*, (v. n. 2 of مطّ) Affronting, outraging, treating with disrespect. Extending.

A تمظّع *tamazzuع*, (v. n. 5 of مظع) Licking up all. Following a shadow from place to place. Remaining behind (in grazing).

A تمظيع *tamzīع*, (v. n. 2 of مظع) Softening a bowstring. Cutting down green wood, and letting it lie with the bark, which seasons and prevents it from cracking. Anointing with butter or fat.

A تمعّج *tamaععuj*, (v. n. 5 of معج) Being bent, doubled, folded. Going fast. Running rapidly (a stream). Going with a writhing motion (a serpent).

A تمعّد *tamaععud*, Freshness (of a date).

A تمعدد *tamaعdud*, (v. n. 2 of معدد Q) Being related to the tribe of معدّ *maعadd*. Aping their manners, adopting their costume. Being scantily fed and poorly clad. Recovering health (a sick person). Growing fat (a lean person). Waxing strong (a boy).

A تمعّر *tamaععur*, (v. n. 5 of معر) Being changed (colour of the face) from anger. Falling off (hair).

A تمعّز *tamaععuz*, (v. n. 5 of معز) Being contracted (brow). Being furious or swift in career (a camel).

A تمعّص *tamaععus*, A making (the bowels) ache.

A تمعّط *tamaععut*, (v. n. 5 of معط) Losing the hair (from sickness). Falling off (hair).

A تمعّق *tamaععuk*, (v. n. 5 of معق) Going deep or far into any place. Speaking profoundly and mysteriously. Being bad (the disposition).

A تمعّك *tamaععuk*, The wallowing (of a horse).

A تمعّي *tamaععī*, (v. n. 5 of معي) Stretching one's self, yawning. Being divulged (a secret).

A تمعير *tamعīr*, (v. n. 2 of معر) Having no travelling necessaries. Causing (the countenance) to undergo a change when enraged.

A تمعيض *tamعīz*, (v. n. 2 of معض) Enraging, vexing, grieving. Rendering (a business) difficult and troublesome to any one.

A تمعيك *tamعīk*, (v. n. 2 of معك) Allowing to tumble or wallow.

P تمغا *tamghā*, A wooden seal for sealing the doors of public granaries. A stamp. A stamp-tax generally for imports. An impression burnt upon the thigh (of a horse). Tribute.

P تمغاچي *tamghāchī*, A revenue-collector, a tax-gatherer.

A تمغثر *tamaghsur*, (v. n. 2 of مغثر Q not used) Gathering the juice مغثور *mughsūr*.

A تمغّص *tamaghghus*, (v. n. 5 of مغص) Causing (the bowels) to ache. Aching, being griped (the bowels).

A تمغّط *tamaghghut*, (v. n. 5 of مغط) Stretching out greatly the fore-feet in running (a horse or camel). Stifling any one under a ruin (dust).

A تمغفر *tamaghfur*, (v. n. 2 of مغفر Q) Collecting certain gummy drops called مغافير *maghāfīr*.

A تمغّل *tamaghghul*, (v. n. 5 of مغل) Imitating the manners of a Mogul.

A تمغمغ *tamaghmugh*, (v. n. 2 of مغمغ Q) Taking a little fodder. Being in prime condition (a flock).

A تمغّي *tamaghghī*, (v. n. 5 of مغي) Being soft (leather). Inventing a tale of another (good or bad).

A تمغير *tamghīr*, (v. n. 2 of مغر) Reciting the poetry of ابن مغراء *ibn maghrās*.

P تمفوز *tamfoz*, The parts round the mouth.

A تمقّت *tamakkut*, A hating one another.

A تمقّحس *tamak-hus*, Disturbance of the mind.

A تمقّس *tamakkus*, (v. n. 5 of مقس) Being indisposed from eating (the mind).

A تمقّق *tamakkuk*, (v. n. 5 of مقّ) Sipping at several times. Receiving a wound, but not sustaining any injury from it.

A تمقيت *tamkīt*, (v. n. 2 of مقت) Hating.

A تمقيس *tamkīs*, A pouring out much (water).

A تمقيط *tamkīt*, A throwing down.

A تمقيق *tamkīk*, (v. n. 2 of مقّ) Stinting (domestics). Feeding her young (a bird). Preparing her young for flight (a bird).

A تمك tamk, (v. n. of تمك) Being long and high (a camel's bunch); also being close-grained and succulent.

A تمكث tamakhus, (v. n. 5 of مكث) Delaying. Being tedious, slow, dilatory.

A تمكك tamakkuk, (v. n. 5 of مك) Sucking the whole (marrow from a bone). Being severe to a debtor, taking his all.

A تمكن tamakkun, (v. n. 5 of مكن) Having in one's power. Possessing authority. Being firmly fixed and well established.

A تمكحل tamak-hul, (v. n. 2 of مكحل Q) Making or procuring a collyrium-box.

A تمكى tamakkī, (v. n. 5 of مكا for مكو) Being wet with sweat. Rubbing his eye upon his knee (a horse).

A تمكير tamkīr, (v. n. 2 of مكر) Laying up corn against a scarcity, regrating.

A تمكين tamkīn, (v. n. 2 of مكن) Establishing, confirming. Investing with authority, giving power, enabling, affording opportunity. Rubbing. Majesty, dignity, authority, power. P گردون تمكين gardūn-tamkīn, (equal to) Heaven in dignity.

A تملاق tamlāḳ, Demonstration of love.

A تملاق timillāḳ, (v. n. 5 of ملق) Making professions of love; flattering, fawning.

A تملان timlān, (pl. of تميلة) Cats. Badgers.

A تملح tamalluh, A being fat. Fatness.

A تملخ tamallukh, A tearing out, extracting.

A تملز tamalluz, (v. n. 5 of ملز) Going along with another. Being saved, rescued, delivered. Remaining behind.

A تملس tamallus, (v. n. 5 of ملس) Escaping, getting free. Becoming smooth and shining. Desisting, receding.

A تملص tamallus, An escaping, getting free.

A تملط tamallut, (v. n. 5 of ملط) Being unfeathered and shining (an arrow).

A تملغ tamallugh, (v. n. 5 of ملغ obsolete) Feigning foolishness.

A تملق tamalluḳ, (v. n. 5 of ملق) Flattering, fawning. Making professions of love. Blandishment.

A تملك tamalluk, (v. n. 5 of ملك) Taking forcible possession of. Reigning.

A تملل tamallul, (v. n. 5 of مل) Tossing and tumbling in bed (from heat or indisposition). Making one perspire (a fever). Being hot within one's bones. Making the wooden part of a sword hilt, or the handle of a bow. Embracing a particular religion or sect (ملة millat).

A تململ tamalmul, A rolling about in bed.

A تملؤ tamallu', (v. n. 5 of ملأ) Being filled, satiated (with meat). Being glutted (with wealth). Swelling (with rage).

A تملوك tumlūk, A species of wild olive.

P تملول tamlūl, Name of a wild pot-herb.

A تملول tumlūl, Name of an early spring pot-herb.

A تملي tamallī, (v. n. 5 of ملا for ملو) Living long. Enjoying long (the society of a friend).

A تملئة tamli'at, (v. n. 2 of ملأ) Filling full. Drawing tight (a bowstring).

A تملية tamliyat, A permitting to enjoy.

P تمليت tamlīt, A light load laid on the back of a beast of burden, on which the rider sits. Half a load.

A تمليح tamlīh, (v. n. 2 of ملح) Over-salting (the pot). Producing any thing elegant (a poet). Being fit for killing (a camel). Fatness.

A تمليد tamlīd, A softening of leather.

A تمليز tamlīz, (v. n. 2 of ملز) Setting at liberty, saving, delivering.

A تمليس tamlīs, (v. n. 2 of ملس) Smoothing, making sleek and smooth.

A تمليط tamlīt, (v. n. 2 of ملط) Plastering a wall. Shaving. Repeating half a verse, which another finishes.

A تمليق tamlīḳ, (v. n. 2 of ملق) Plastering and smoothing (a wall). Levelling (ploughed ground).

A تمليك tamlīk, (v. n. 2 of ملك) Constituting possessor. Appointing master or chief. Giving in perpetuity. Making a king. Taking a wife. Kneading well (dough). Following the dam (a full-grown colt). Drying in the sun the wood of the tree نبعة nabʻat, from which they make bows and arrows. Possession.

A تمليكي tamlīkīy, Possessory. Hereditary, special, private.

A تمليكية tamlīkīyat, Hereditary right.

A تمليل tamlīl, (v. n. 2 of مل) Causing one to make haste. Making one restless in bed (any thing).

A تمم tamam, Perfectly formed. Tumam and timam, An amulet of camels' hair. (pl. of تممة tummat or تمي tumma') Bits of hair, &c., given to any one to finish therewith his blanket.

P تمن taman, A mist, a fog. Tuman, Ten thousand. The sum of five thousand aspers.

A تمنا tamannā, (for تمني tamannī) Wishing, asking for. P تمناى دل tamannā-i dil, Hearts' wish.

P تمنچه tamancha, A pistol.

A تمنح tamannuh, (v. n. 5 of منح) Feeding, giving victuals or refreshment to any one.

P تمندار tuman-dār, Commander of a tuman.

P تمنداري tuman-dārī, Command of a tuman.

A تمندل tamandul, (v. n. 2 of مندل Q) Using a towel. Wrapping a sash round the body.

P تمنده tamanda, One who hesitates in pronouncing ف fe.

A تمنطق tamantuḳ, A putting on a girdle.

A تمنع tamannuʻ, (v. n. 5 of منع) Being hindered, prohibited, excluded. Being inaccessible. Abstaining from. Being strong, firm. Prevailing against. Fortifying one's self.

P تمنگ taming or timing, The oxyacanth-tree.

A تمنن tamannun, A debilitating, fatiguing.

A تمني tamannī, (v. n. 5 of مني) Wishing for. Making known one's wishes. Reading (a book). Interweaving with lies. Inventing, dealing in fictions. Petition, request, supplication.

A تمنيات tamanniyāt, Prayers.

A تمنية tamniyat, (v. n. 2 of مني) Causing to wish or request. Giving the option. Filling with hopes. Requiting. Spilling sperm (مني maniy).

A تمنيع tamnīʻ, (v. n. 2 of منع) Hindering, driving away. Refusing, denying.

P تمودان tamūdān, Turks.

A تمور tumūr, (pl. of تمر tamr) Dates.

A تمور tamawwur, (v. n. 5 of مار for مور) Going to and fro. Falling right and left (the hair). Falling (wool or hair from the body).

P تمورخان timūr khān, Son of the Persian historian Mīrkhond, whose works he abridged.

A تموز tamūz, The Syrian month July: summer.

P تموك tamūk, A butt for archers. Broad-headed arrows used in shooting at marks. An arrow difficult to be extracted.

A تموك tumūk, (v. n. of تمك) Being high and broad (a camel's bunch); also being full and juicy.

A تمول tamawwul, A being, or becoming, rich.

A تمولي tamawlī, (v. n. 2 of مولي Q not in use) Making himself a great man, pretending to be so, or looking like one.

A تمون tamawwun, (v. n. 5 of مان for مون) Bestowing much on one's dependants (as provisions and other necessaries.

A تمويت tamwīt, A killing, putting to death.

A تمويص tamwīs, (v. n. 2 of ماص for موص) Washing or cleaning clothes. Dealing in straw.

A تمويل tamwīl, An enriching, making wealthy.

A تمويه tamwīh, (v. n. 2 of ماه for موه) Becoming full of water). Pouring much into a pot (when cooking). Gilding or silvering (brass or iron). Adulterating, falsifying (intelligence). P دليل بي تمويه dalīli bītamwīh, Arguments without fallacy.

A تمه tamah, (v. n. of تمه) Being corrupted, smelling (as meat).

A تمهد tamahhud, (v. n. 5 of مهد) Being broad and level (the bunch of a camel). Applying, accustoming (the mind) to any thing. Having, or acquiring, power and ability.

A تمهر tamahhur, A being penetrating, ingenious.

A تمهص tamahhus, A being plunged in water.

A تمهق tamahhuḳ, A drinking every hour.

A تمهك tamahhuk, (v. n. 5 of مهك) Doing (work) neatly and well. Painting, pourtraying. Embroidering.

A تمهل tamahhul, (v. n. 5 of مهل) Proceeding slowly, being tedious in business. Asking a delay.

A تمهمه tamahmuh, An abstaining, desisting.

A تمهية tamhiyat, A whetting (a cobbler's knife).

A تمهيد tamhīd, (v. n. 2 of مهد) Spreading

equally (a bed). Making smooth or level. Arranging, disposing, adjusting. Pleading an excuse. Receiving an apology. Arrangement, settlement.

A تمهير *tamhīr*, (v. n. 2 of مهر) Asking for, or receiving, a dower (مهر *mahr*).

A تمهيص *tamhīs*, A cleaning, a whitening.

A تمهيق *tamhīk*, (v. n. 2 of مهق) Drinking much milk. Giving much milk to an infant.

A تمهيك *tamhīk*, A pulverizing (of aromatics).

A تمهيل *tamhīl*, A giving time, granting delay.

A تمّي *tumma'*, (pl. تمم *tumam* or *timam*) A little hair given to any one to complete therewith his blanket. A present.

A تميال *tamyāl*, An inclining, a leaning to.

A تميّث *tamayyus*, (v. n. 5 of ماث for ميث) Being softened and cooled by rain (ground).

A تميّح *tamayyuh*, (v. n. 5 of ماح for ميح) Walking pompously (a woman).

A تميّخ *tamayyukh*, A strutting.

A تميز *tamīz*, Discernment, discretion.

A تميّز *tamayyuz*, (v. n. 5 of ماز for ميز) Being separated. Being distinguished. Being discerned. Bursting with rage.

A تميّس *tamayyus*, A walking flauntingly.

P تمّيشه *tammesha*, Name of a city in Īrān, formerly the residence of Farīdūn. Name of a forest near the city of Amul.

A تميّع *tamayyuʼ*, (v. n. 5 of ماع for ميع) Flowing. Being rendered fluent.

P تميك *tamīk* or *timīk*, A kind of bramble.

A تميلة *tumaylat*, (pl. تملان *timlān* or تميلات) An animal like a cat found in Hijāz. A badger.

A تميم *tamīm*, Well-formed, solid, firm. Name of a tribe. (pl. of تميمة *tamīmat*) Amulets.

A تميمة *tamīmat*, (pl. تميم *tamīm* and تمائم *tamāʼim*) An amulet or charm against witchcraft (hung round children's necks, bridles of camels, &c.).

A تميميّ *tamīmiy*, Of the tribe of Tamīm.

A تمئنة *tamʼinat*, (v. n. 2 of مأن) Directing properly, amending. Informing, certifying. Thinking. Seeing, viewing.

A تمييت *tamyīt*, A putting to death.

A تمييث *tamyīs*, A dissolving (in water). Dying.

A تمييز *tamyīz*, (v. n. 2 of ماز for ميز) Separating, distinguishing. Judgment, discernment, discrimination, distinction, discretion.

A تمييس *tamyīs*, (v. n. 2 of ماس for ميس) Making (the train of a garment) long.

A تمييل *tamyīl*, (v. n. 2 of مال for ميل) Causing to incline, giving a bias. Doubting, hesitating between two things. Complaining.

P تن *tan*, Body, stature, person; the whole man. Matter. The thing itself. Silent. This, that. دو تن *du tan*, Two persons. تن در دادن *tan dar dādan*, To consent, acquiesce. تن زدن *tan zadan*, To be silent. To be patient. To rest. To escape. To caress. تن محرم آسا *tani muhrim-āsā*, A naked body. تني چند *tane chand*, Several persons.

P تن *tun*, (A تنّ *tunn*) The thunny fish (which when dried is used as an antidote to the poison of serpents). A hot furnace (as in baths or glass-houses). A yellow flower used in dyeing.

A تنّ *tinn*, (pl. اتنان *atnān*) Alike, resembling. A companion, fellow, peer. Equal (in dignity, age, ability, or wealth).

A تنّاء *tunnāʼ*, (pl. of تانئ *tāniʼ*) Villagers.

A تناءة *tināʼat*, Residence, stay.

A تناءش *tanāʼush*, (v. n. 6 of نأش) Remaining or loitering behind. Retiring, being absent.

A تنابز *tanābuz*, (v. n. 6 of نبز) Calling one another names. Reproaching each other.

A تنابيل *tanābīl*, (pl. of تنبال *timbāl* and تنبول *tumbūl*) Dwarfs.

A تناتف *tanātuf*, (v. n. 6 of نتف) Being plucked up (hair). Flowing.

A تناتل *tanātul*, (v. n. 6 of نتل) Being thick, entangled (herbage).

A تناثّ *tanāss*, A communicating of secrets.

A تناثر *tanāsur*, (v. n. 6 of نثر) Being dispersed. Falling here and there by disease and death (men).

A تناثل *tanāsul*, (v. n. 6 of نثل) Rushing upon or into any thing. Running out in crowds (men).

A تناثي *tanāsī*, A remembering each other.

A تناجث *tanājus*, (v. n. 6 of نجث) Scattering, dispersing. Solitude. Sadness, care.

A تناجح *tanājuh*, (v. n. 6 of نجح) Being verified, falling out true (a dream).

A تناجخ *tanājukh*, A boasting against each other.

A تناجز *tanājuz*, A fighting among themselves.

A تناجش *tanājush*, (v. n. 6 of نجش) Praising, or bidding for goods, in order to enhance the price to others, without any intention of purchasing.

A تناجل *tanājul*, A disputing, fighting together.

A تناجي *tanājī*, (v. n. 6 of نجا for نجو) Communicating secrets to one another, speaking privately together.

A تناحب *tanāhub*, A fixing a time (for battle).

A تناحر *tanāhur*, (v. n. 6 of نحر) Flying at one another's throats (in battle). Flying greedily together at any business, as if they would cut each other's throats. Going out of the way. Being opposite (two houses).

A تنادّ *tanādd*, (v. n. 6 of ندّ) Being struck with horror, alarmed. Being dispersed, flying in disorder from one another.

A تنادس *tanādus*, A reviling one another.

A تنادم *tanādum*, (v. n. 6 of ندم) Conversing familiarly, sitting together at a convivial party.

A تنادي *tanādī*, (v. n. 6 of ندي) Calling to one another. Sitting together in council or conversation. يوم التناد *yawmu't tanādi*, The day of calling upon one another, *i. e.* The day of judgment.

A تناديد *tanādīd*, Scattered (birds). Flying in disorder (men).

A تناذر *tanāzur*, (v. n. 6 of نذر) Mutually admonishing or deterring.

A تنّار *tannār*, A builder, constructor, or fixer of ovens or furnaces.

A تنازب *tanāzub*, A calling one another names.

A تنازع *tanāzuʼ*, (v. n. 6 of نزع) Disputing, litigating. Receiving (victuals and drink). Eating and drinking.

A تنازق *tanāzuk*, A reproaching one another.

A تنازل *tanāzul*, (v. n. 6 of نزل) Rushing down into a plain against each other (two bodies of men). Decline (of price), loss (of rank).

P تناسان *tan-āsān*, Quiet. Healthy in body.

P تن آساني *tan-āsānī*, Bodily ease, indulgence.

A تناسب *tanāsub*, (v. n. 6 of نسب) Resembling. Being proportionate to each other. Being related. Conformity.

A تناسخ *tanāsukh*, The death of one heir after another before the partition of the inheritance. The death and uninterrupted succession of heirs to an inheritance, unimpaired, undivided. The revolution or succession of ages. التناسخ *at tanāsukh*, The metempsychosis, or Pythagorean system of the transmigration of souls.

A تناسخيّ *tanāsukhīy*, A believer in metempsychosis, or transmigration of souls.

A التناسخيّة *at tanāsukhīyat*, Metempsychosis.

A تناسف *tanāsuf*, (v. n. 6 of نسف) Communicating privately, whispering together.

A تناسق *tanāsuk*, An adhering, being arranged.

A تناسل *tanāsul*, A begetting. Generation. آلة التناسل *ālatu't tanāsul*, The organ of generation.

A تناسي *tanāsī*, (v. n. 6 of نسي) Pretending to forget. Forgetting.

A تناشب *tanāshub*, (v. n. 6 of نشب) Adhering, being connected, hanging together.

A تناشد *tanāshud*, (v. n. 6 of نشد) Repeating verses together. Satirizing one another. Asking, or being asked, to recite verses.

A تناشير *tanāshīr*, Writing-copies for boys.

A تناصر *tanāsur*, (v. n. 6 of نصر) Assisting one another. Mutually confirming, corroborating each other (news).

A تناصف *tanāsuf*, (v. n. 6 of نصف) Acting equitably towards each other.

A تناصيب *tanāsīb*, Mile-stones, direction-posts.

A تناضل *tanāzul*, (v. n. 6 of نضل) Throwing or darting at one another. Contending for superiority in darting.

A تناطح *tanātuh*, The butting (of rams).

A تناطي *tanātī*, (v. n. 6 of نطا for نطو) Remedying, curing. Contending, trying to outstrip. Pulling one another about. Exchanging (words).

A تناظر *tanāzur*, (v. n. 6 of نظر) Facing and looking at one another. Being opposite (as palm-trees). Exercising discipline. Undergoing trouble and labour.

P تناع *tunāʻ*, (and تناغ *tunāgh*) The stirrup-cup, last bottle when a company is just going.

A تناعس *tanāʻus*, A feigning sleep; somnolency.

A تناعم *tanāʻum*, (v. n. 6 of نعم) Being blessed with the conveniences of life.

A تناعي *tanāʻī*, (v. n. 6 of نعي) Animating one another to vigorous exertion in battle, by announcing the death of their comrades.

A تناغر *tanāghur*, A shewing, feigning ignorance.

A تناغص *tanāghus*, The thronging (of camels).

A تنافد *tanāfud*, A going before a judge.

A تنافذ *tanāfuz*, (v. n. 6 of نفذ) Going to law. Carrying a cause before the judge, adducing arguments on either side.

A تنافر *tanāfur*, (v. n. 6 of نفر) Flying from one another in a panic. Going together upon business before a judge.

A تنافز *tanāfuz*, A leaping together.

A تنافس *tanāfus*, (v. n. 6 of نفس) Wishing for, aspiring or panting after. Envying one another.

A تنافط *tanāfut*, (v. n. 6 of نفط) Plucking hair and eating it in a time of famine. Casting up scum (a boiling pot).

P تنافور *tanāfūr*, A certain measure of crimes.

A تنافي *tanāfī*, (v. n. 6 of نفي) Expelling, pursuing, persecuting, seeking to ruin one another.

A تنافيج *tanāfīj*, Gores of shifts.

A تناقض *tanāḳuz*, (v. n. 6 of نقض) Being dissolved, loosened, slackened. Being discordant. Breaking an agreement. Demolishing a building. Untwisting a rope. Contradiction.

A تناقل *tanāḳul*, A communicating together.

A تناقيص *tanāḳīs*, Defects, deficiencies.

A تناكث *tanākus*, (v. n. 6 of نكث) Violating promises or treaties.

A تناكح *tanākuh*, An intermarrying.

A تناكد *tanākud*, A being severe to one another.

A تناكر *tanākur*, (v. n. 6 of نكر) Pretending ignorance. Not knowing. Hating each other. Hostility, discord.

A تناكف *tanākuf*, A speaking in turns.

P تناليدن *tanālīdan*, To pour, or to be poured. To clean by washing, rubbing, or polishing.

A تنامّ *tanāmm*, (v. n. 6 of نمّ) Increasing, being numerous. Sleeping.

A تنانؤ *tanānuʼ*, (v. n. 2 of نانأ Q) Being weak in mind and confused. Being impotent, unequal to.

P تناني *tanānī*, Corporeal.

P تنانيدن *tanānīdan*, To cause to weave.

A تنانير *tanānīr*, (pl. of تنّور *tannūr*) Stoves, furnaces. Ovens. بنات التنانير *banātu't tanānīr*, Cakes baked in the oven.

A تنانين *tanānīn*, (pl. of تنّين *tinnīn*) Dragons.

A تناوب *tanāwub*, (v. n. 6 of ناب for نوب) Observing rotations, keeping time, or turn and turn about. Watering in turn.

A تناوة *tināwat*, Neglect of conference or study.

A تناوح *tanāwuh*, (v. n. 6 of ناح for نوح) Blowing from adverse quarters (wind). Being opposite, facing one another (mountains).

P تناور *tan-āwar*, Corpulent. Incarnate.

A تناؤش *tanāʼush*, (v. n. 6 of نأش) Receiving. Remaining or loitering behind: retiring, being absent.

A تناوش *tanāwush*, (v. n. 6 of ناش for نوش) Stretching forth the hand in order to take something. Returning.

A تناول *tanāwul*, (v. n. 6 of نال for نول) Carrying off: taking (meat and drink): receiving presents.

A تناوم *tanāwum*, A feigning to be asleep.

A تناهب *tanāhub*, The raising of a dust.

A تناهد *tanāhud*, (v. n. 6 of نهد) (Travellers) making a joint purse (for road expenses).

A تناهز *tanāhuz*, (v. n. 6 of نهز) Hastening in emulation (towards the attainment of any object), trying to get the start of each other. Pre-occupying, preventing.

A تناهض *tanāhuz*, (v. n. 6 of نهض) Rushing against, assaulting each other (hostile parties).

A تناهي *tanāhī*, (v. n. 6 of نهي) Extending, reaching to the end. Arriving (intelligence). Being brought to a termination. Abstaining. Prohibiting, forbidding one another. Being prohibited. Stagnating (water). (pl. of تنهية *tanhiyat*) Water-marks of torrents.

A تناية *tināyat*, Neglect of conference or study.

A تنائف *tanāʼif*, (pl. of تنوفة *tanūfat*) Extensive deserts. تنائف تنف *tanāʼif tunnaf*, Deserts far and wide.

A تنايك *tanāyuk*, (v. n. 6 of ناك for نيك) Being overcome by sleep. Overcoming one (sleep). Being closed (the eye-lids).

A تنائي *tanāʼī*, (v. n. 6 of نأي) Retiring far, or being distant from each other. Absence.

A تنباح *tambāh*, (v. n. of نبح) Barking (a dog), bleating (a sheep or deer), hissing (a serpent).

P تنباكو *tambākū*, Tobacco.

A تنبال *timbāl*, A dwarf.

A تنبالة *timbālat*, Dwarfishness. A dwarf.

P تنبان *tumbān*, Short breeches. Drawers. Wrestlers' leathern breeches.

A تنبّب *tanabbub*, (v. n. 5 of نبّ) Being set a-flowing, running (water).

P تن بتن *tan ba tan*, Man by man: man for man.

A تنبّج *tanabbuj*, The swelling (of a bone).

P تنبد *tambad*, Silence. A fit of shivering. *Tam-bud*, Universal matter.

P تنبسه *tambasa*, A small carpet, rug.

P تنبسيدن *tambasīdan*, To twist a rope.

A تنبّط *tanabbut*, (v. n. 5 of نبط) Making water to flow or spring up. Drawing, eliciting speech. Resembling, or being related to a Nabathean.

A تنبّع *tanabbuʻ*, A flowing, coming by degrees.

P تنبك *tambak* or *tumbak*, The flap of a saddle. *Tumbak*, Taking food with the fingers. Bagpipes.

P تنبل *tambal*, Lazy, sluggish. Unemployed. A buffoon. *Tambul*, Betel-leaf, paan. *Tumbul*, Fraud. Necromancy.

A تنبل *timbal*, A dwarf.

A تنبّل *tanabbul*, (v. n. 5 of نبل) Excelling, being ingenious, of a noble, generous disposition. Displaying dexterity. Taking whatever one has, choosing the best. Pretending to excellence. Being possessed of, or carrying (arrows). Taking thick, rough arrows one by one. Dying. Cleaning one's self with a flint (after voiding fæces).

P تنبليت *tambalīt*, Any thing placed on a pack-saddle on which the rider sits. Half a horse-load.

A تنبّؤ *tanabbuʼ*, (v. n. 5 of نبأ) Commencing prophet. Pretending to be prophet, laying claims to the prophetical office.

P تنبور *tambūr*, A lute, lyre, guitar. A drum.

P تنبوك *tambūk*, A weak bow. The flap of a saddle. A saddle-tree. A stirrup-leather.

P تنبول *tambūl*, Betel-leaf. A weak bow.

A تنبول *tumbūl*, (pl. تنابيل) A dwarf.

P تنبه *tamba*, The bar of a door.

A تنبّه *tanabbuh*, (v. n. 5 of نبه) Awaking from sleep. Being awake, keeping a sharp look out. Having one's wits about one. Allowing one's attention to be directed to.

A تنبّي *tanabbī*, A pretending to prophecy.

A تنبيب *tambīb*, The jointing (of a cane).

A تنبئة *tambiʼat*, A prophesying, announcing.

A تنبيت *tambīt*, (v. n. 2 of نبت) Causing to grow. Educating, nourishing, bringing up. Planting (trees). *Tambīt* or *timbīt*, Any thing that germinates, large or small.

P تنبيدن *tambīdan*, To lay snares. To tremble. To palpitate, to be restless. To plait, spin.

A تنبيذ *tambīz*, (v. n. 2 of نبذ) Throwing away. Pressing. Making malt-liquor or beer.

A تنبيز *tambīz*, (v. n. 2 of نبز) Reviling. Calling names. Giving a surname or title.

A تنبيس *tambīs*, A speaking, uttering.

P تنبيسه *tambīsa*, A small carpet, a rug.

A تنبيط *tambīt*, A making (a spring) to flow.

A تنبيق *tambīḳ*, (v. n. 2 of نبق) Planting (palm-trees) in a line. Breaking wind gently. Writing.

P تنبيك *tumbīk*, Bagpipes. A saddle-flap.

A تنبيل *tambīl*, (v. n. 2 of نبل) Giving one (victuals) by little and little at a time (and thereby coaxing him). Providing any one with flints (نبل *nabal*) (for cleaning his person). Giving an arrow.

A تنبيه *tambīh*, (v. n. 2 of نبه) Awaking, rousing from sleep. Rendering attentive. Teaching, insinuating, putting in mind, calling attention to. Raising from obscurity. Calling by name. Admonition. An edict, advertisement. P تنبيه و تاكيد كردن *tambīh u tākīd kardan*, To admonish repeatedly and severely.

A تنبيهات *tambīhāt*, Admonitions.

P تن پرست *tan-parast,* A pamperer of his belly. Sensual. Lazy.

P تن پرور *tan-parwar,* Self-indulgent. Nice.

P تن پروري *tan-parwarī,* A pampering of the body. تن پروري كردن *tan-parwarī kardan,* To pamper the flesh.

P تنپك *tumpak,* A mould. A crucible.

A تنة *tinat,* (v. n. of وتن) Running continually (water). Striking on the vein وتين *watīn.*

A تنّة *tunnat,* The thunny.

A تنتاش *tantāsh,* A traducing; secret slander.

P تنتاك *tantāk,* Name of a man; and a king.

A تنتالة *tintālat,* A dwarf.

A تنتّت *tanattut,* (v. n. 5 of نتّ) Becoming dirty after being clean.

A تنتّج *tanattuj,* A groaning in travail.

A تنتل *tintal,* A dwarf.

P تنتنه *tantana,* A cry, shout, uproar, fray.

P تنته *tanta,* A cobweb. *Tunta,* A red bee.

A تنتّي *tanattī,* (v. n. 5 of نتا for نتو) Leaping, being spurred on. Leaping on the female.

A تنتيت *tantīt,* An explaining, a detailing.

A تنتيف *tantīf,* A plucking up much hair.

A تنتيل *tuntīl,* Short, dwarfish.

A تنتين *tantīn,* (v. n. 2 of نتن) Rendering fetid, causing to stink.

A تنثّر *tanassur,* A being dispersed, scattered.

A تنثير *tansīr,* A scattering abroad very much.

A تنثيط *tansīt,* An appeasing, quieting.

P تنج *tanj,* A fixing, a planting. A twisting or rolling together. A squeezing or pressing. A coming in the rear.

P تنجامه *tan-jāma,* A garment, vest, doublet.

A تنجّث *tanajjus,* A scrutinizing, examining.

A تنجّح *tanajjuh,* (v. n. 5 of نجح) Despatching easily, successfully. Wishing for success.

A تنجّد *tanajjud,* A being high, elevated.

A تنجّز *tanajjuz,* (v. n. 5 of نجز) Expediting any thing properly and successfully. Demanding the fulfilment of a promise. Pressing to drink.

A تنجّس *tanajjus,* (v. n. 5 of نجس) Being polluted, defiled. Doing (any thing) to remove defilement from one's self.

A تنجّع *tanajjuʻ,* (v. n. 5 of نجع) Going in quest of provender. Coming to any one to obtain a benefit.

A تنجّم *tanajjum,* (v. n. 5 of نجم) Observing the stars. Lying awake, star-gazing.

A تنجنج *tanajnuj,* (v. n. 2 of نجنج Q) Being moved. Being astonished, stupefied. Being sound, hale, and healthy. Being haughty, contumacious.

A تنجّؤ *tanajjuʼ,* A looking (with an evil eye).

A تنجّه *tanajjuh,* (v. n. 5 of نجه) Repulsing, affronting, treating cavalierly.

A تنجّي *tanajjī,* (v. n. 5 of نجا for نجو) Seeking the highest ground. Eyeing malignantly.

A تنجّي *tunjiy,* Name of a bird.

A تنجيب *tanjīb,* The unbarking (of a tree).

A تنجية *tanjiyat,* (v. n. 2 of نجي) Setting free, rescuing, saving. Escaping, being liberated. Casting or causing to fall on high ground. Raising (a mound of earth) against inundations.

A تنجيد *tanjīd,* (v. n. 2 of نجد) Ornamenting a house with tapestry or painted cloths. Exercising, teaching, proving, trying (as misfortune). Running.

P تنجيدن *tanjīdan,* To squeeze. To twist, to roll together. To draw tight.

P تنجيده *tanjīda,* Drawn tight. Squeezed, pressed. Twisted.

A تنجيس *tanjīs,* (v. n. 2 of نجس) Polluting, defiling. Amulets against the fascination of malignant eyes (composed of dead men's bones, fetid rags, or other species of filth, and hung round the neck), fetiche. P تنجيس كردن *tanjīs kardan,* To pollute. To profane, to desecrate.

A تنجيع *tanjīʻ,* (v. n. 2 of نجع) Being salutary, doing good (as medicine or exhortation).

A تنجيف *tanjīf,* (v. n. 2 of نجف) Sloping off, or carrying away parts of high ground (the wind). Putting by a little milk for anybody. Milking partially (a sheep).

A تنجيم *tanjīm,* (v. n. 2 of نجم) Prognosticating or calculating any event by the aspect of the stars. Paying at stated periods.

A تنجيه *tanjiya,* Tangiers.

P تنچه *tancha,* (or تمچه *tamcha*) A wallet).

A تنحار *tanhār,* A hurting the throat.

A تنحّس *tanahhus,* (v. n. 5 of نحس) Examining (especially a messenger with news). Bearing hunger, fasting; also making (any one) fast (medically). Abstaining from flesh (in Lent).

A تنحّل *tanahhul,* (v. n. 5 of نحل) Falsely arrogating to one's self (sayings or verses of another). Professing to belong to this or that religious society.

A تنحنح *tanahnuh,* (v. n. 2 of نحنح Q) Hemming and hawing. Rumbling (the belly).

A تنحّي *tanahhī,* (v. n. 5 of نحا for نحو) Being removed. Retiring to a distance, receding. Tending to, inclining, purposing. (v. n. 5 of نحي) Being moved from one's place.

A تنحيب *tanhīb,* (v. n. 2 of نحب) Being diligent (in business). Travelling expeditiously to reach water. Being near water. Harassing, tiring.

A تنحية *tanhiyat,* (v. n. 2 of نحا for نحو) Setting at liberty, freeing. Removing. Putting to a distance.

A تنحيت *tanhīt,* The act of paring (a hoof).

A تنخ *tanukh,* A suffering from indigestion.

A تنخّذ *tanakhkhuz,* (v. n. 5 of نخذ not used) Being a ناخوذاة *nākhūzāt, i.e.* Commander or supercargo of a ship.

A تنخّش *tanakhkhush,* (v. n. 5 of نخش) Moving one's self, being moved; inclining towards.

A تنخّع *tanakhkhuʻ,* (v. n. 5 of نخع) Spitting out phlegm. Raining, emptying itself (a cloud).

A تنخّل *tanakhkhul,* (v. n. 5 of نخل) Choosing the best. Sifting.

A تنخّم *tanakhkhum,* A spitting, blowing the nose.

A تنخنخ *tanakhnukh,* A reclining, a kneeling.

P تنخواه *tan-khwāh,* An assignment on lands, or order on the treasury for the payment of a stipend, salary, and the like.

P تنخواه دار *tan-khwāh-dār,* One who receives a salary. A holder of an order for wages.

P تنخواه داري *tan-khwāh-dārī,* A receiving pay.

A تنخير *tankhīr,* Speech, discourse.

P تند *tund,* Rough, fierce, severe, stern, austere, hot-spirited, choleric, quarrelsome. Acrid, astringent. High, tall, lofty. Fat. Anger. Bold, impetuous, strong. Swift, rapid, brisk, active. Height. The summit of a mountain. Any thing prominent or projecting. The devil. A demon of the woods. شهباز تند پرواز *shahbāzi tund-parwāz,* A falcon of rapid flight.

P تن دادن *tan dādan,* To consent, acquiesce.

P تند باد *tund-bād,* A hurricane, whirlwind.

P تند بار *tund-bār,* Noxious, destructive.

P تند باز *tund-bāz,* Name of a rapacious bird.

P تند بور *tund-bor,* A leaping, a dancing.

P تند پرواز *tund-parwāz,* Flying swiftly.

P تند تيز *tund-tez,* Choleric, contentious. Mettlesome. Swift.

A تندّح *tanadduh,* (v. n. 5 of ندح) Becoming fat or distended with feeding and straying (sheep).

A تندّخ *tanaddukh,* (v. n. 5 of ندخ) Being vain, arrogant, pretending to what one does not possess.

P تند خوي *tund-khoy,* Hasty, obstinate.

P تندر *tan* or *tundar,* Thunder. A nightingale.

P تندرست *tan-durust,* Healthy, vigorous.

P تندرستي *tan-durustī,* Health, bodily vigour.

P تند رفتار *tund-raftār,* Swift, fleet.

P تند رو *tund-rav,* Swift, a quick goer. *Tund-rū,* Austere, crabbed, passionate. Avaricious.

P تند زبان *tund-zabān,* Eloquent, fluent.

P تندس *tan-das,* An image, a portrait. *Tandas* or *tandis,* Like a body.

A تندّس *tanaddus,* (v. n. 5 of ندس) Falling. Inquiring strictly (news of a messenger). Putting the hand upon the mouth. Exuding (water through the side of a well).

P تندسه *tan-dasa,* Resemblance, portrait. *Tandisa,* Resembling, like.

P تند عنان *tund-ʻinān,* Fast-going (horse).

A تندّل *tanaddul,* (v. n. 5 of ندل) Wiping one's self (with a cloth). Rolling a turban, fillet, or sash round the body.

P تند لجام *tund-lijām,* Hard-mouthed (horse).

A تندّم *tanaddum,* A being penitent, repenting.

P تند مزة *tund-maza,* Astringent, styptic.

P تندو *tandū,* A spider.

P تند و خند *tund u khund* or *tand u khand,* Scattered. Topsy turvy.

P تندور *tandūr,* Thunder. The nightingale. *Tun-*

dūr, Thunder.

P تن ده *tan-dih*, (Giving the body) Diligent.

P تنده *tunda*, Bud, follicle, pod. A red bee.

P تن دهي *tan-dihī*, Application, exertion.

P تندي *tundī*, A prominence, protuberance, bump. Violence. Sharpness, smartness. Ruggedness. Quickness, swiftness. Astringency, stypticity.

A تندّي *tanaddī*, (v. n. 5 of ندا for ندو) Shewing one's self liberal (beyond others). Feeding (camels) between their two drinkings.

A تندية *tandiyat*, (v. n. 2 of ندا for ندو) Feeding (camels) between their two drinkings. Leading (camels) from a bitter or salt to a sweet pasture. Wetting, moistening, soaking.

A تنديد *tandīd*, (v. n. 2 of ندّ) Declaring, divulging, publishing. Tearing (a veil). Defaming. Dispersing (camels).

P تنديدن *tundīdan* or *tandīdan*, To thunder. To murmur, mutter. To be in a rage. To chide. To put forth flowers, buds, or leaves (trees).

P تنديس *tandes*, (تن *tan*, Body, and ديس *des*, Like) Body, figure (of man or beast). A picture, effigy.

P تنديسه *tan-desa*, A picture, portrait, effigy.

A تنديغ *tandīgh*, A sprinkling dough with flour.

P تنديور *tundīwar*, Jumping, leaping.

P تنديه *tan-dīh*, The human shape or figure.

P تنزدن *tan zadan*, To be silent, modest.

P تنزده *tan-zada*, Taciturn, modest.

A تنزّر *tanazzur*, (v. n. 5 of نزر) Becoming small or few. Resembling, associating with, or being allied to the tribe of نزار *nizār*.

A تنزّع *tanazzuʿ*, A hasting, a making speed.

A تنزّل *tanazzul*, (v. n. 5 of نزل) Descending slowly, softly and gently. Sinking, submitting.

P تنزه *tunza*, (equiv. to تنده) A bud, a pod.

A تنزّه *tanazzuh*, (v. n. 5 of نزه) Being far (from water and pasture). Being pure, keeping one's self free from vice or stain. Being modest, chaste. (incorrectly used in the sense of) Walking in pleasant gardens. Going abroad to ease nature. Pastime, diversion.

A تنزّي *tanazzī*, (v. n. 5 of نزي) Making haste. Leaping, being excited. Causing to leap.

P تن زيب *tan-zīb*, (Ornament of the body) A sort of fine cotton-cloth rather thicker than muslin, in Bengal commonly called tanjibs (the *z* not existing in any Hindū language). An under-waistcoat.

A تنزية *tanziyat*, (v. n. 2 of نزا for نزو) Leaping upon, mounting. Causing to leap.

A تنزير *tanzīr*, (v. n. 2 of نزر) Slighting, giving a trifling present. Importuning, dunning.

A تنزيز *tanzīz*, (v. n. 2 of نزّ) Removing. Keeping one away from. Nourishing, rearing.

A تنزيف *tanzīf*, (v. n. 2 of نزف) Emitting blood, flooding (a woman).

A تنزيق *tanzīk*, (v. n. 2 of نزق) Making (a horse) leap or win a race.

A تنزيل *tanzīl*, (v. n. 2 of نزل) Sending any thing down (especially as God does from heaven). Causing (a traveller) to alight, or come into your house; lodging and treating him hospitably. Arranging, setting in order. Revelation from heaven. The Kur'ān.

A تنزيه *tanzīh*, (v. n. 2 of نزه) Purifying, cleansing, keeping one's self at a distance from every thing unclean. Declaring (God) to be without an equal, and free from every kind of mixture.

A تنساس *tansās*, (v. n. of نسّ) Approaching, coming to water. Flowing rapidly. A quick pace.

P تنسان *tan-sān*, Quiet, tranquil.

A تنسّب *tanassub*, (v. n. 5 of نسب) Pretending to or claiming relationship.

P تنسته *tanasta*, A spider's web.

P تنسخ *tansukh*, Curious, precious, rare.

A تنسّر *tanassur*, (v. n. 5 of نسر) Being untwisted (a rope). Being torn from one and scattered (fortune). Falling in pieces, going away bit by bit (a garment or paper).

A تنسّس *tanassus*, A perceiving, getting wind of.

A تنسّف *tanassuf*, (v. n. 5 of نسف) Seizing the (adversary's hands), and with the foot throwing down (in wrestling).

A تنسّق *tanassuk*, (v. n. 5 of نسق) Being arranged (an oration). Being disposed in order, connected together.

A تنسّك *tanassuk*, The being devout, pious.

A تنسّم *tanassum*, (v. n. 5 of نسم) Breathing. Exhaling an odour. Smelling any thing fragrant, snuffing up a breeze. Perceiving, getting wind of.

A تنسئة *tansiʾat*, (v. n. 2 of نسأ) Driving, urging onward. Shouting (at camels).

A تنسية *tansiyat*, A causing to forget.

A تنسيس *tansīs*, (v. n. 2 of نسّ) Inducing (an infant) to ease nature by crying *is is*. Causing to walk.

A تنسيع *tansīʿ*, Looseness (of the teeth).

A تنسيغ *tansīgh*, (v. n. 2 of نسغ) Being loose (teeth). Sprouting afresh (a tree that has been cut down). Producing branches closely set (a young palm-tree).

A تنسيق *tansīk*, (v. n. 2 of نسق) Arranging, disposing in order (a speech), stringing (pearls).

A تنسيم *tansīm*, (v. n. 2 of نسم) Beginning any business. Quickening, reviving. Letting out a refreshing breeze or pent breath.

A تنشّد *tanashshud*, An inquiring after news.

A تنشّر *tanashshur*, A being unfolded, spread open.

A تنشّز *tanashshuz*, (v. n. 5 of نشز) Being prepared. Opposing.

A تنشّط *tanashshut*, (v. n. 5 of نشط) Being brisk, lively, active, alert. Cheerfully doing any thing. Travelling well. Traversing the desert.

A تنشّغ *tanashshugh*, (v. n. 5 of نشغ) Groaning inwardly, sighing.

A تنشّف *tanashshuf*, (v. n. 5 of نشف) Imbibing, sucking up. Wiping one's self.

A تنشّق *tanashshuk*, A snuffing, a smelling.

A تنشّم *tanashshum*, (v. n. 5 of نشم) Making a beginning. Attaining gradually to the knowledge of a thing.

A تنشّؤ *tanashshuʾ*, A rising up to begin.

P تنشوي *tan-shūy*, A table on which dead bodies are washed. A cistern, fountain, or brook.

A تنشّي *tanashshī*, (v. n. 5 of نشي) Perceiving a smell. Being overcome with wine, getting drunk.

A تنشيب *tanshīb*, (v. n. 2 of نشب) Attacking, beginning (any thing). Causing a colour to change. Fixing.

A تنشئة *tanshiʾat*, (v. n. 2 of نشأ) Causing to grow. Educating.

A تنشير *tanshīr*, (v. n. 2 of نشر) Displaying, diffusing, extending. Writing an incantation, preparing an amulet or charm (نشرة *nushrat*).

A تنشيط *tanshīt*, (v. n. 2 of نشط) Making cheerful, lively, brisk. Fattening (a horse). Tying knots (upon a rope).

A تنشيف *tanshīf*, (v. n. 2 of نشف) Imbibing (water, as cloth, the earth, &c.). Wiping, sucking up (water with a cloth). Drying up. Giving frothy milk (a camel).

A تنشيل *tanshīl*, The giving a breakfast.

A تنشيم *tanshīm*, (v. n. 2 of نشم) Beginning, and adhering tenaciously (especially to any thing bad). Having water springing up (ground). Raising (the fame of any one). Making a beginning. Beginning to corrupt (meat).

A تنصّب *tanassub*, (v. n. 5 of نصب) Rising on the feet. Being erect. Being raised (dust). Standing about the male (she-asses).

A تنصّح *tanassuh*, (v. n. 5 of نصح) Resembling a faithful monitor. Being well watered (camels). Sewing a garment.

A تنصّر *tanassur*, (v. n. 5 of نصر) Becoming a Christian (Nazarene). Endeavouring, striving, attempting to assist another.

A تنصّف *tanassuf*, (v. n. 5 of نصف) Being a servant. Wanting or receiving as a servant. Veiling (a woman). Recovering the whole of one's due. Asking, begging. Submitting, being obsequious. Demanding justice at the hand of the magistrate. Covering the head (hoariness). Receiving any one amongst themselves.

A تنصّل *tanassul*, (v. n. 5 of نصل) Being absolved (from a crime). Taking away every thing. Taking or drawing out, extracting. Choosing. Losing its dye (a beard).

A تنصّي *tanassī*, (v. n. 5 of نصي) Curling (her) long flowing locks (a woman). Combing her hair (a woman). Being closely united. Marrying into a noble tribe.

A تنصيب *tansīb*, (v. n. 2 of نصب) Pricking his ears (a horse). Laying by a portion for any one. Setting up a column. Laying snares, hatching mischief. Putting down. Taking up.

A تنصير *tanṣīr*, (v. n. 2 of نصر) Converting to Christianity, christianizing.

A تنصيص *tanṣīṣ*, The harassing (a debtor).

A تنصيف *tanṣīf*, (v. n. 2 of نصف) Dividing in the middle, or into two equal parts. Being half white, half black (the beard or hair). Bearing dates half red, half green (a palm-tree). Covering (the face of a girl) with a veil.

A تنصيل *tanṣīl*, (v. n. 2 of نصل) Taking the head (off a spear). Putting the head on a spear. Piercing with, or fixing an arrow into.

A تنضاح *tanẓāḥ*, Exudation (of a leathern bottle).

A تنضال *tanẓāl*, (v. n. 3 of نضل) Contending in throwing the javelin.

A تنضب *tanẓub*, A thorny tree, of which arrows are made.

A تنضّح *tanaẓẓuḥ*, (v. n. 5 of نضح) Being repulsed, removed; retiring. Pouring forth tears (the eye).

A تنضّض *tanaẓẓuẓ*, (v. n. 5 of نضّ) Despatching (business). Getting by little and little what another owes him. Instigating, urging.

A تنضّل *tanaẓẓul*, A drawing forth.

A تنضّي *tanaẓẓī*, An emaciating, consuming.

A تنضيب *tanẓīb*, (v. n. 2 of نضب) Giving little milk (a camel). Flowing, sinking (water into the ground).

A تنضيج *tanẓīj*, (v. n. 2 of نضج) Going over the year without foaling (a camel).

A تنضيد *tanẓīd*, (v. n. 2 of نضد) Laying in order one on another, or one by the side of another.

A تنضير *tanẓīr*, (v. n. 2 of نضر) (God) blessing with beauty and every ornamental excellence.

A تنضيض *tanẓīẓ*, (v. n. 2 of نضّ) Having abundance of gold and silver coin. Disturbing, disquieting.

A تنطّس *tanaṭṭus*, (v. n. 5 of نطس) Being curious, inquisitive, accurate; nicely attentive to dress, speech, or victuals.

A تنطّع *tanaṭṭuʻ*, (v. n. 5 of نطع) Being attentive, considering attentively. Shewing subtilty, cleverness, and tact. Speaking profoundly, mysteriously. Serving up broken victuals. Pronouncing from the palate.

A تنطّف *tanaṭṭuf*, (v. n. 5 of نطف) Putting rings in the ears (a girl). Abstaining. Looking for, expecting news. Considering, understanding. Being contaminated, defiled.

A تنطّق *tanaṭṭuḳ*, The putting on a girdle.

A تنطنط *tanaṭnuṭ*, A being distant, retiring.

A تنطيف *tanṭīf*, (v. n. 2 of نطف) Adorning (another) with ear-rings. Accusing, impeaching.

A تنطيق *tanṭīḳ*, (v. n. 2 of نطق) Putting on a sash, belt, or girdle. Rising to the middle or waist of the bank (water).

A تنظار *tanẓār*, A looking, a viewing.

A تنظّر *tanaẓẓur*, (v. n. 5 of نظر) Granting a delay, waiting. Looking at, beholding, viewing. Waiting for, expecting.

A تنظّف *tanaẓẓuf*, (v. n. 5 of نظف) Cleaning, purifying one's self. Being, affecting, studying, or striving to be neat, spruce, nice, and clean.

A تنظّم *tanaẓẓum*, (v. n. 5 of نظم) Being arranged, strung (pearls).

A تنظير *tanẓīr*, A selling on credit.

A تنظيف *tanẓīf*, A purifying, cleaning.

A تنظيم *tanẓīm*, (v. n. 2 of نظم) Composing (verses). Threading (pearls). Ordering, arranging. Having the lines نظامان (a fish or a lizard).

A تنعاب *tanʻāb*, A croaking. A crowing.

A تنعّل *tanaʻʻul*, A putting on of shoes.

A تنعّم *tanaʻʻum*, (v. n. 5 of نعم) Being blessed with, enjoying in abundance the conveniences and comforts of life. Becoming soft and enervated. Suiting, agreeing with, being salubrious (a country). Walking barefoot, taking no care of the feet. Searching, seeking. Urging forward (a beast). Happiness, enjoyment. Prosperity.

A تنعنع *tanaʻnuʻ*, (v. n. 2 of نعنع Q) Being distant. Nodding, tottering, leaning from side to side.

A تنعير *tanʻīr*, (v. n. 2 of نعر) Turning (an arrow on the nail to try its smoothness or straightness).

A تنعيس *tanʻīs*, (v. n. 2 of نعس) Putting to sleep, causing to sleep.

A تنعيش *tanʻīsh*, (v. n. 2 of نعش) Exalting. Saying to any one نعّشك الله *naʻʻashaka'llāh*, May God exalt you!

A تنعيل *tanʻīl*, (v. n. 2 of نعل) Shoeing a horse (with iron), or a camel (with leather).

A تنعيم *tanʻīm*, (v. n. 2 of نعم) Bestowing plenty. Pampering. Rendering soft, delicate, and effeminate; enervating. Saying نعم *naʻam*, "Yes," in confirmation of any assertion.

A تنعمة *tanʻimat*, A kind of tree having a delicate leaf.

A تنغّر *tanaghghur*, (v. n. 5 of نغر) Boiling with rage, taking offence. Being changed, transformed. Putting the finger down any one's throat.

A تنغّش *tanaghghush*, (v. n. 5 of نغش) Trembling, nodding (as the head), being tremulous (a bird).

A تنغّص *tanaghghuṣ*, (v. n. 5 of نغص) Being unhappy, wretched, and uncomfortable (life).

A تنغّض *tanaghghuẓ*, A being moved (the head).

A تنغّم *tanaghghum*, A reading or singing low.

A تنغير *tanghīr*, (v. n. 2 of نغر) Calling to. Tickling (a child).

A تنغيص *tanghīṣ*, (v. n. 2 of نغص) Making life wretched, annoying, vexing.

A تنف (تنائف *tanāʼifi*) *tunnaf*, Vast deserts.

A تنفّج *tanaffuj*, A boasting vainly and falsely.

A تنفّذ *tanaffuz*, (v. n. 5 of نفذ) Entering. Passing through and leaving behind.

A تنفّر *tanaffur*, (v. n. 5 of نفر) Avoiding, shunning. Aversion, disgust.

A تنفّس *tanaffus*, (v. n. 5 of نفس) Breathing. Fetching a deep, cold sigh. Breaking (the dawn). Drinking at three draughts; also at one draught. Diffusing, throwing spray about (a wave). Being split (a bow). Respiration.

A تنفّش *tanaffush*, (v. n. 5 of نفش) Bristling up from fear (as a cat her pile, or a bird her feathers). Being teazed (wool or cotton).

A تنفّض *tanaffuẓ*, (v. n. 5 of نفض) Exploring, examining well (a place) to see if (it) be safe.

A تنفّط *tanaffuṭ*, (v. n. 5 of نفط) Boiling with rage. Having hands blistered from hard labour.

A تنفّغ *tanaffugh*, (v. n. 5 of نفغ) Swelling or having pustules (the hand from hard labour).

A تنفّق *tanaffuḳ*, (v. n. 5 of نفق) Dragging the jerboa out from its hole. Being entirely consumed.

A تنفّل *tanafful*, (v. n. 5 of نفل) Doing more than the law requires: saying prayers of supererogation. Receiving a larger share of booty (than one's associates).

A تنفيخ *tanfīkh*, A blowing, a puffing.

A تنفيذ *tanfīz*, (v. n. 2 of نفذ) Transmitting. Causing to pass or penetrate. Sending (an ambassador).

A تنفير *tanfīr*, (v. n. 2 of نفر) Terrifying, causing to fly. Pronouncing one victor. Giving (a man) an opprobrious epithet, and marking (him) as an object of aversion.

A تنفيز *tanfīz*, (v. n. 2 of نفز) Dandling (a child). Trying (the straightness of an arrow) on the nail.

A تنفيس *tanfīs*, (v. n. 2 of نفس) Consoling, comforting, easing, refreshing. Treating gently, granting respite, or breathing time. حرف التنفيس *harfu't tanfīs*, An optative particle.

A تنفيش *tanfīsh*, (v. n. 2 of نفش) Teazing (cotton or wool). Bristling up (angry dog or cock).

A تنفيض *tanfīẓ*, (v. n. 2 of نفض) Shaking violently (trees or garments).

A تنفيق *tanfīḳ*, (v. n. 2 of نفق) Selling fast (goods). Quitting its hole (a field-mouse). Making a hole (a field-mouse).

A تنفيل *tanfīl*, (v. n. 2 of نفل) Presenting with a gift or with plunder. Defending a companion. Adjuring. Driving away.

A تنقاد *tankād*, (v. n. of نقد) Separating (good money from bad).

A تنقاص *tankāṣ*, Detriment, deficiency, loss.

A تنقام *tinikkām*, (v. n. 2 of نقم) Punishing. Avenging one's self. Punishment.

A تنقّب *tanakkub*, A veiling of the face.

A تنقّش *tanakkus*, (v. n. 5 of نقش) Caressing, conciliating, gaining the good graces of any one. Making haste.

A تنقّد *tanakkud*, (v. n. 5 of نقد) Separating good from bad coin.

A تنقّذ *tanakkuz*, (v. n. 5 of نقذ) Receiving. Pulling (out of a ditch), rescuing.

A تنقّر *tanakkur*, An examining, scrutinizing.

A تنقّص *tanakkus*, (v. n. 5 of نقص) Disgracing, dishonouring, reproaching. Diminishing. Deficiency, diminution.

A تنقّض *tanakkuz*, (v. n. 5 of نقض) Being burst, split (the earth) by mushrooms springing up. Being split, divided in parts. Falling in drops (blood). Making a cracking noise (the bones).

A تنقّط *tanakkut*, (v. n. 5 of نقط) Containing patches of grass (a place). Getting hold of (any intelligence) bit by bit).

P تنقطار *tunkutar*, *tunkatār*, or *tunktār*, A watchman. A taper, rushlight.

A تنقّل *tanakkul*, (v. n. 5 of نقل) Travelling, being transported from place to place. Turning. Eating sweet cakes after having drunk a glass of wine. Migration.

A تنقّي *tanakkī*, A choosing, selecting.

A تنقيب *tankīb*, (v. n. 2 of نقب) Examining (a messenger). Sapping, undermining. Going from place to place (as merchants). Flying for refuge.

A تنقية *tankiyat*, (v. n. 2 of نقي) Cleaning, winnowing (grain). Cleaning (a well). Gutting (an animal) preparatory to cooking (it).

A تنقيث *tankīs*, (v. n. 2 of نقث Making haste, doing any thing quickly.

A تنقيح *tankīh*, (v. n. 2 of نقح) Extracting (marrow). Lopping (a branch). Cleaning, cutting off superfluities. Polishing (verses). Investigation, examination, search, inquiry.

A تنقيذ *tankīz*, (v. n. 2 of نقذ) Setting at liberty, freeing, rescuing. Pulling one (out of a ditch).

A تنقير *tankīr*, (v. n. 2 of نقر) Examining, inquiring into, scrutinizing. Whistling, singing (a bird). Making a place suited to lay her eggs (a bird). Naming, calling by name.

A تنقيز *tankīz*, (v. n. 2 of نقز) Causing to dance. Dandling (an infant). Making (a deer) bound.

A تنقيس *tankīs*, (v. n. 2 of نقس) Putting ink (into a standish). Giving a surname or title.

A تنقيش *tankīsh*, (v. n. 2 of نقش) Painting in colours, printing, staining.

A تنقيص *tankīs*, (v. n. 2 of نقص) Diminishing.

A تنقيض *tankīz*, An allowing, letting dangle.

A تنقيط *tankīt*, (v. n. 2 of نقط) Marking with points, dotting: putting a diacritical point to a letter.

A تنقيل *tankīl*, (v. n. 2 of نقل) Transporting from place to place. Mending (a garment or shoe). Shoeing (a camel) with leather. Breaking or shivering a bone (a blow).

P تنك *tunuk* or *tunak*, Thin, slender, slight, weak, delicate. Effeminate. A thin cake or fritter.

A تنكاع *tankāʻ*, A milking (cattle) hastily.

A تنكّب *tanakkub*, (v. n. 5 of نكب) Turning (out of the way). Shunning, avoiding. Slinging (a bow) across the shoulder.

P تنك حواس *tunuk-hawāss*, Sensible: sensitive.

P تنك حواسّي *tunuk-hawāssī*, Sensibility.

A تنكّر *tanakkur*, (v. n. 5 of نكر) Being disguised, travestied, transformed. Disguising one's self, making one's self unknown, becoming incognito. Disliking. Being indefinite, indeterminate. Being intense (darkness). A transition from a state which is agreeable to one which is disagreeable.

P تنكره *tankara*, A copper boiler, cauldron.

P تنك ريش *tunuk-rīsh*, Thin-bearded.

A تنكّس *tanakkus*, A being inverted.

P تنك صبر *tunuk-sabr*, Impatient.

A تنكّظ *tanakkuz*, (v. n. 5 of نكظ) Twisting one's self. Enduring hardships on a journey. Avarice.

P تنك ظرف *tunuk-zarf*, (A weak vessel) A tale-bearer, tattler, simpleton. Smooth, simple, unblemished. A tabula rasa.

P تنك مزاج *tunuk-mizāj*, Whimsical, peevish.

P تنك موي *tunuk-mūy* or *moy*, Thin-haired.

P تنكوب *tankūb*, A dish of sour milk, garlic, and walnuts.

P تنكه *tanka*, Gold. Money. A certain coin.

A تنكيب *tankīb*, (v. n. 2 of نكب) Misguiding, misleading. Diverting, averting. Retiring, deserting, letting alone. Distressing.

A تنكير *tankīr*, (v. n. 2 of نكر) Altering, transforming, disguising, rendering incapable of being recognised. Making indefinite or undetermined.

A تنكيس *tankīs*, (v. n. 2 of نكس) Turning upside down, capsizing, inverting.

A تنكيظ *tankīz*, (v. n. 2 of نكظ) Accelerating, causing to make haste.

A تنكيع *tankīʻ*, (v. n. 2 of نكع) Annoying, vexing, over-hurrying.

A تنكيف *tankīf*, (v. n. 2 of نكف) Having a protuberance behind the ears called *nakafāt* (a camel).

A تنكيل *tankīl*, (v. n. 2 of نكل) Treating opprobriously, tormenting. Giving an example. Prohibiting, restraining, diverting, turning (any one) aside. Punishing, chastising.

P تنگ *tang*, Narrow, strait. A strait, defile, narrow pass. (met.) The mouth of a mistress. Scarce, rare; incomparable, unattainable. A swallowing. Numerous, many. Near, neighbouring. A concealing, a putting out of sight. Strong, hard. Barren. Languid, melancholy, sad. Anger, indignation. The press of an oil-mill. An ass-load of sugar. A horse-girth. A strap for fastening a load. A package, bundle, sack. Half a horse or camel-load, as much as is carried upon one side. A body of troops. A plain surface, either of canvas or wood, on which painters or sculptors trace their first sketch. A pavilion. Name of a book written by the heresiarch Mānī. Name of the tenth book of the works of Zardusht. Name of a place in Turkistān. Name of a district in Badakshān. تنگ كردن *tang kardan*, To confine, block up, reduce to difficulties. تنگ نمودن *tang namūdan*, To contract. بتنگ آوردن *ba tang āwardan*, To annoy greatly, to reduce to distress. ديدهٔ تنگ *dīdaʼi tang*, An avaricious eye. سال تنگ *sāli tang*, A barren year. *Ting*, A bird's beak. *Tung*, A narrow-necked vessel.

P تنگ آب *tang-āb*, Shallow.

P تنگاتنگ *tangātang*, Straits. A throng.

P تنگار *tangār*, Borax.

P تنگبار *tang-bār*, A narrow way. Half a horse-load, a package. One who will not give place to another; inaccessible. Rare, scarce, invaluable. An epithet of God.

P تنگبيز *tang* or *tanug-bez*, A fine sieve, strainer.

P تنگ پيغوله *tang-payghūla*, The world.

P تنگت *tingit*, Name of a place.

P تنگ تركان *tangi turkān*, Name of a place, the inhabitants of which are remarkable for the comeliness of their persons.

P تنگ چشم *tang-chashm*, One with narrow, close eyelids. Insatiable, covetous, devouring all with the eyes. A Turk. The eye of a mistress. A woman who has had but one husband.

P تنگحال *tang-hāl*, Straitened, poor.

P تنگحالي *tang-hālī*, Poverty, distress, straits, narrow circumstances, adversity.

P تنگ خو *tang-kho* or *khu*, Bad-tempered.

P تنگ خوئی *tang-khoʼī* or *khuʼī*, Ill-temper.

P تنگدست *tang-dast*, Tight-handed. Poor. A cushion.

P تنگدستي *tang-dastī*, Parsimony. Poverty. Weakness.

P تنگدل *tang-dil*, Heartsick, desponding. Compassionate. A miser.

P تنگدلي *tang-dilī*, Heartache, grief. Compassion. Niggardliness.

P تنگ دهن *tang-dahan*, Small-mouthed. A sweetheart.

P تنگ روزي *tang-rozī*, Poor.

P تنگ روي *tang-rūy*, Tender-cheeked. *Tang-rūy*, One who accepts a petition without importunity.

P تنگز *tangiz*, Name of a thorny tree.

P تنگ زيست *tang-zīst*, Pinched, distressed.

P تنگس *tangis*, Name of a thorny tree.

P تنگسار *tang-sār*, Weakness of intellect. Transmigration, metempsychosis.

P تنگسال *tang-sāl*, Scarcity. A barren season.

P تنگ سالي *tang-sālī*, Dearth, scarceness.

P تنگست *tangast*, Name of a place famous for its beautiful crystal.

P تنگ شراب *tang-sharāb*, (or تنگ ظرف *tang zarf*) Soon drunk (as holding little).

P تنگ شكر *tang-shakar*, A mistress's mouth.

P تنگ عيش *tang-ʻaysh*, Poor. Melancholy.

P تنگ گير *tang-gīr*, One who presses hard or squeezes. Parsimonious, frugal.

P تنگ گيري *tang-gīrī*, Parsimony, frugality.

P تنگلوش *tanglosh*, (or تنگه لوشه *tanga losha*)

Name of the works of a famous Grecian artist, as celebrated in the East as those of the painter Mānī. The study or workshop of a Grecian painter.

P تنگناي *tang-nāy*, A difficulty. A defile. تنگناي خاك *tang-nāyi khāk*, The world. The body. The grave.

P تنگ نشين نهنگ *tang-nishīmani nahang*, The world. The sky. Time.

P تنگو *tango*, The king of Khata or Khutan.

P تنگه *tanga*, Cash, gold or copper coin. Thin paste, macaroni.

P تنگي *tangī*, Narrowness, closeness, straitness, tightness. Difficulty. Anguish. Constraint. Poverty, want. A sack.

P تنگياب *tang-yāb*, Difficult to be found, rare. Care-crazed.

P تنگيره *tangīra*, A brazen kettle, cauldron.

A تنم *tanm*, (v. n. of تنم) Eating of the tree تنّوم *tannūm* (a camel).

A تنماص *tanmās*, (v. n. 2 of نمص) Pulling the hairs from the face with tweezers or unguents.

A تنمّر *tanammur*, (v. n. 5 of نمر) Being angry, ill-humoured. Threatening with a long growl. Resembling a male panther when enraged. Becoming changed.

A تنمّص *tanammus*, (v. n. 5 of نمص) Giving one's self up to have the hairs plucked out. Being plucked up (hairs).

A تنمّل *tanammul*, A moving to and fro like ants.

A تنمّي *tanammī*, The soaring about (of a hawk).

A تنمية *tanmiyat*, (v. n. 2 of نمي) Adulterating (intelligence), spreading false reports, calumniating. Throwing wood upon a fire, and making it burn fiercer. Growing. Swelling, increasing. Causing to swell, increase, or grow up. Referring (to an author, (quoting his authority).

A تنمير *tanmīr*, (v. n. 2 of نمر) Being of an angry, ill-humoured disposition.

A تنميس *tanmīs*, (v. n. 2 of نمس) Covering. Imposing upon. Concealing, cheating.

A تنميش *tanmīsh*, (v. n. 2 of نمش) Keeping a secret. Whispering, telling tales.

A تنميص *tanmīs*, A plucking (hair off the face).

A تنميط *tanmīt*, A pointing out, shewing.

A تنميغ *tanmīgh*, A mixture of black, red, and white.

A تنميق *tanmīk*, (v. n. 2 of نمق) Writing. Writing a fine ornamented hand. Inditing.

P تنند *tanand*, A spider. Slow, sluggish.

P تنندو *tanandū*, A spider. A cobweb. A weaver's instrument (round which the warp is rolled, and then carried over the comb).

P تننده *tananda*, A spider. A cobweb.

P تنو *tanū*, Power, strength.

A تنوء *tunūء*, An abiding, dwelling (in a town).

A تنواء *tanwāء*, (v. n. of ناء for نوء) Rising with difficulty, and endeavouring to get up with a heavy load. Oppressing (any one) and making (him) stoop (a heavy load). Falling down (especially when heavily laden).

A تنواط *tanwāt*, Whatever is hung round a camel's litter (for ladies) by way of ornament.

A تنّوب *tannūb*, The pitch-tree, the pine.

P تنوتاس *tanūtās*, Learned. A man of business.

A تنوّح *tanawwuh*, (v. n. 5 of ناح for نوح) Vibrating (any thing pendulous).

A تنوخ *tanūkh*, Name of an Arabian tribe. *Tunūkh*, (v. n. of تنخ) Abiding, staying. Indigestion.

A تنوّخ *tanawwukh*, (v. n. 5 of ناخ for نوخ) Obliging (a she-camel) to lie down to receive him (a male). Lying down for this purpose (a she-camel).

A تنوخيّ *tanūkhīy*, Of the tribe of Tanūkh.

A تنوّد *tanawwud*, (v. n. 5 of ناد for نود) Being shaken (a branch).

P تنودن *tanūdan*, To draw. To twist, plait, spin.

A تنّور *tannūr*, (pl. تنانير *tanānīr*) An oven. The surface of the earth. Any place where water gushes out, or collects together in a valley.

A تنوّر *tanawwur*, (v. n. 5 of نار for نور) Seeing a fire at a distance. Shining. Turning the back, being put to flight. Anointing one's body with an unguent which pulls up hair by the roots. Being bedaubed with a liniment of pitch for the scab.

P تنّور آشوب *tannūr-āshūb*, A coal-rake.

P تنّورخانه *tannūr-khāna*, A bakehouse.

P تنّوره *tannūra*, A part of dress (like a furnace, of leather) worn by dervishes, from their middle. A sort of armour. A tunnel through which water rushes on a mill-wheel. Forming a ring or circle.

A تنّوري *tannūrīy*, A maker or fixer of iron furnaces or ovens.

A تنوّش *tanawwush*, (v. n. 5 of ناش for نوش) Wiping (the hands) with a napkin.

A تنوّط *tunawwit* or *tanawwut*, A certain bird which constructs a hang-nest suspended like a flask from the branch of a tree. اصنع من تنوّط *asnaع min tunawwit*, More of an artist than a Tunawwit.

A تنوّع *tanawwuع*, (v. n. 5 of ناع for نوع) Being shaken (branches by the wind). Being divided into distinct parts or species. Getting before, preceding.

A تنوفة *tanūfat*, or تنوفيّة *tanūfīyat* (pl. تنائف *tanāیif*) A dangerous desert, without water or inhabitant, though grassy. A widely-extended region.

A تنوّق *tanawwuk*, (v. n. 5 of ناق for نوق) Being elegant (in apparel), nice (in eating), neat (in doing a thing). Doing a thing properly, wisely.

A تنّوم *tannūm*, A tree growing in Arabia, producing specifics for worms and warts. Hemp-seed.

A تنوّم *tanawwum*, (v. n. 5 of نام for نوم) Sleeping. Dreaming. Browsing on the tree تنّوم *tannūm*.

A تنومة *tanwamat*, (v. n. of تنوم Q) Eating of the tree تنّوم *tannūm* (a camel).

P تنومند *tanūmand*, Robust, corpulent. Strong, powerful. Tall. Broad, fat. Contented, cheerful, in good case.

P تنومندي *tanūmandī*, Robustness, corpulence.

P تنوي *tannī*, One whose eye is fixed upward.

A تنوّي *tanawwī*, An intending, purposing: aim.

A تنوية *tanwiyat*, (v. n. 2 of نوي) Executing (business). Causing one to propose or endeavour. Throwing away (date-stones). Beginning to have stones called نواة *nawāt* (ripening dates).

A تنويخ *tanwīkh*, A forcing to lie down.

A تنوير *tanwīr*, (v. n. 2 of نار for نور) Shining. Illuminating, giving light. Flowering (a shrub), blossoming (a tree). Ripening (corn). Producing a kernel (a date). Pricking figures upon the arm with a needle, and then rubbing over the punctures with indigo, leaving an indelible impression. Appearing (the light of day). Covering, falsifying, misrepresenting, rendering obscure and difficult. Frightening (a female), causing (her) to run away with terror. Fascinating. Illumination.

A تنويز *tanwīz*, The act of making little.

A تنويس *tanwīs*, A remaining (in one place).

A تنويش *tanwīsh*, The giving of a present.

A تنويض *tanwīz*, A dyeing cloth.

A تنويط *tanwīt*, (v. n. 2 of ناط for نوط) Turning out (a leathern bottle) in order to anoint (it).

A تنويع *tanwīع*, (v. n. 2 of نوع not in use) Distinguishing, making different kinds. Shaking the branches of a tree (wind).

A تنويل *tanwīl*, A giving, bestowing.

A تنويم *tanwīm*, A lulling to sleep.

A تنوين *tanwīn*, (v. n. 2 of نون not in use) Marking the final letters of nouns with the nasal vowels ٌ *un*, ً *an*, or ٍ *in*. Nunnation.

P تنويه *tanwīh*, Greatness, grandeur.

A تنويه *tanwīh*, (v. n. 2 of ناه for نوه) Praising. Exalting. Calling.

P تنه *tana*, A web. The body. The trunk of a tree. Acceptance. Content, satisfaction. تنه شدن *tana shudan*, To accept. To be pleased or satisfied. تنهٔ عنكبوت *tanaی ع ankabūt*, A spider's web.

P تنّه *tunna*, The thunny fish.

P تنها *tanhā*, (pl. of تن *tan*) Bodies. Alone, solitary. An odd number.

A تنهاء *tanhāء*, The greatest height to which waters, rivers, or torrents rise in channels or vallies.

P تنهاگانه *tanhāgāna*, Solitary.

P تنهائي *tanhāی ī*, Solitude, loneliness, solitariness.

A تنهّد *tanahhud*, (v. n. 5 of نهد) Sighing.

P تنه دار *tana-dār*, Trunked (tree).

A تنهكة *tanhikat*, Punishment, torture.

A تنهنه *tanahnuh*, An abstaining, desisting.

A تنهية *tanhiyat*, (v. n. 2 of نهى) Prohibiting, forbidding. Bringing to an end. Reaching the bottom, summit, end, or extremity. Coming to. (pl. تناهي *tanāhī*) The greatest height to which waters, rivers, or torrents, rise in channels or vallies.

A تنهيد *tanhīd*, (v. n. 2 of نهد) Having round

plump breasts. Rising, being plump (the breasts).

P تني *tanī*, Corporeal, bodily.

P تنيان *taniyān*, Material (substances).

A تنيّب *tanayyub*, The sprouting (of a plant).

P تنيد *tanīd*, A web.

P تنيدن *tanīdan*, To twist, weave, spin, involve. To deceive. To effect. To be silent. To be twisted.

P تنيده *tanīda*, Woven. Silent. A cobweb.

A تنيرب *tanayrub*, (v. n. 2 of نيرب Q) Sweeping, marking (as the wind does sand or water, with long furrows or waves).

P تنيزه *tanīza*, A side, border, skirt, edge.

A تنّيس *tinnīs*, A city in Lower Egypt.

A تنيّق *tanayyuk*, (v. n. 5 of ناق for نيق) Being elegant (in apparel), nice (in diet). Doing any thing properly and wisely.

A تنين *tinīn*, Alike, resembling, equal.

A تنّين *tinnīn*, (pl. تنانين *tanānīn*) A large serpent, a dragon. التنّين *at tinnīn*, The constellation of the dragon. A shark. ذنب تنين *zanabi tinnīn*, The dragon's tail, a star. تنين فلك *tinnīni falak*, (in astronomy) The head and tail of the dragon.

A تنييب *tanyīb*, (v. n. 2 of ناب for نيب) Biting (an arrow) to try the quality of the wood. Being aged (a she-camel). Sprouting (a plant).

A تنيئة *tanyiʼat*, (v. n. 2 of نيأ) Leaving (meat) half-dressed, or (business) half-finished.

A تنييح *tanyīh*, (v. n. 2 of نيح not in use) Making solid (bones which were before soft). Debilitating, bruising (bones). Giving, bestowing.

A تنيير *tanyīr*, (v. n. 2 of نار for نير) Marking (cloth) with a different-coloured border.

A تنييف *tanyīf*, (v. n. 2 of ناف for نيف) Exceeding, going beyond, being upwards of. Augmenting, adding to.

P تو *taw*, Heat, warmth. Twist, turn. A fold. A ditch, pool, or hole where water stagnates. *To*, A curtain. A fold. A skin formed on the surface of milk. In, into, within. (in India) Thou. يك تو *yak to*, One fold, single. دو تو *du to*, Two-fold, double. تو بر تو *to bar to*, Fold upon fold. *Tu*, Thou. A feast, an entertainment. Self. When followed by است *ast*, Is, ا and و are sometimes omitted: as, از آن تست *az āni tust*, It is thine.

A تَوّ *taww*, (pl. اتواء *atwāʼ*) Alone, single. A rope of a single twist. A careless man (of here and hereafter). A troop of 1000 horse. A tent set up. An edifice. جاء توًّا *jāʼa tawwan*, He came post-haste without delay.

P توا *tawā*, Ruin. Ruined, destroyed, lost.

A تواء *tawāʼ*, (v. n. of توي) Perishing. *Tiwāʼ*, A cross made on the neck and thigh of an animal.

A تواءص *tawāʼus*, (v. n. 6 of وأص) Assembling, thronging about a pit.

A توّاب *tawwāb*, Penitent, contrite. Relenting.

A تؤابة *tuʼābat*, Disgrace, shame, ignominy.

A توابع *tawābiʻ*, Dependences, appurtenances. Adjuncts, appositives. Words following each other: as, حسن بسن *hasan basan*.

A توابل *tawābil*, (pl. of تابل *tābil*) Seasonings for meat, herbs.

P توابه *tawāba*, A champion of Tūrān.

A توابيت *tawābīt*, (pl. of تابوت *tābūt*) Planks, boards. Arks, chests. Coffins.

A تواتر *tawātur*, (v. n. 6 of وتر) Following in succession, with or without intervals.

A تواثب *tawāsub*, A rushing on one another.

A تواثير *tawāsīr*, (pl. of تؤثور *tuʼsūr*) Officers or beadles under the collectors of revenue.

A تواجه *tawājuh*, (v. n. 6 of وجه) Looking back on each other. Turning the face towards one another, encountering, standing face to face.

A تواجها *tawājuhan*, Opposite, over against.

A تأد *tawʼad*, A slow, gentle pace.

A توادّ *tawādd*, The loving of one another.

A توادع *tawāduʻ*, (v. n. 6 of ودع) Making peace. Being reconciled. Releasing, or forgiving mutually.

A توادي *tawādī*, (pl. of تودية *tawdiyat*) Pieces of wood (put beneath the udder to prevent a camel's being sucked). Dwarfs.

P توار *tawār*, A rope for tying on a load.

A توارع *tawāruʻ*, (v. n. 6 of ورع) Making peace together. Reposing, resting.

A توارك *tawāruk*, A reclining on the hip.

P توارة *tawāra*, A straw hut, in which the keepers of the vineyard take shelter. *Tuwāra*, A structure of reeds, under which is the dunghill, the privy, and such like. Thorns fixed on a wall.

A تواري *tawārī*, (v. n. 6 of وري) Lying hid, concealing one's self.

A تواريخ *tawārīkh*, (pl. of تأريخ *taʼrīkh*) Epochs, dates. Histories, chronicles. اهل تواريخ *ahli tawārīkh*, A historian. Chroniclers.

A توازف *tawāzuf*, An expending equally with.

A توازن *tawāzun*, A being equal in weight.

P تواسي *tiwāsī*, A carpet, embroidered rug.

A تواشظ *tawāshuz*, (v. n. 6 of وشظ) Rubbing against, pressing each other's belly (two lewd men).

A تواشق *tawāshuk*, (v. n. 6 of وشق) Drying oblong strips of meat. Cutting.

A تواصف *tawāsuf*, (v. n. 6 of وصف) Mutually praising, describing, recounting, or relating.

A تواصل *tawāsul*, (v. n. 6 of وصل) Being joined together. Acting in concert. Conjunction.

A تواصلات *tawāsulāt*, Conjunctions.

A تواصي *tawāsī*, (v. n. 6 of وصي) Commanding, enjoining, charging one another. Being united, allied, joined. Growing thick and tangled (herbage).

A تواضخ *tawāzukh*, (v. n. 6 of وضخ) Striving about drawing water. Contending in walking.

A تواضع *tawāzuʻ*, (v. n. 6 of وضع) Humbling, abasing one's self. Being remote, distant. Humility, submission. Pretended kindness, empty compliment. تواضع سمرقندي *tawāzuʻi samarkandī*, False politeness. P برسبيل تواضع *bar sabīli tawāzuʻ*, By way of submission.

A تواطح *tawātuh*, (v. n. 6 of وطح) Fighting. Bandying mischief to and fro. Flocking in crowds (as camels to a watering-trough).

A تواطخ *tawātukh*, A handing from one to another.

A تواطس *tawātus*, (v. n. 6 of وطس) Rushing. Being high (billows), dashing (waves). Slapping, boxing. Agreeing.

A تواطؤ *tawātuʼ*, A consenting, agreeing.

A تواعد *tawāʻud*, (v. n. 6 of وعد) Promising to one another. Appointing a time and place.

P تواغج *tuwāghaj*, The bark of a certain tree.

A توافق *tawāfuk*, (v. n. 6 of وفق) Agreeing together. Helping one another. Concord, good understanding. League, conspiracy. (in arithmetic) Being divisible by the same quantity without leaving a remainder; commensurability.

A توافي *tawāfī*, A coming in great numbers.

A توّاق *tawwāk*, Wistful, most propense.

A تواقص *tawākus*, A being short in the neck.

A تواقف *tawākuf*, A facing one another.

A تواقيع *tawākiʻ*, (pl. of توقيع) Royal letters.

A تواكظ *tawākuz*, Intricacy (of business).

A تواكف *tawākuf*, A declining, turning away.

A تواكل *tawākul*, (v. n. 6 of وكل) Trusting to each other's support. Deserting, forsaking. Mutual confidence. تواكلة القوائم *tawākilatu'l kawāʼim*, Wanting feet.

A تواكيد *tawākīd*, Girths, belts, surcingles. Straps with which the fore-parts of a camel's saddle are held together. (pl. of توكيد *tawkīd*) Emphases.

A توالد *tawālud*, (v. n. 6 of ولد) Begetting, propagating. Becoming numerous (offspring). Generation, birth. Succession.

A توالس *tawālus*, (v. n. 6 of ولس) Helping one another to deceive. Abetting each other in fraud and mischief.

A توالي *tawālī*, (v. n. 6 of ولي) Following in succession. Beginning to dry (fresh dates). Continuation. على التوالي *ʻala't tawālī*, In succession. (pl. of تالية *tāliyat*) The extremities, the hinder parts (as the feet or tail). The last beasts of a herd, those in the rear.

A توأم *tawʼam*, (pl. توائم *tawāʼim* and توأم *tuʼām*) A twin. The sign Gemini. The second lot or throw at dice. The second gaming arrow. علم ظفر توأم *ʻalami zafar-tawʼam*, The twin-brother of victory, *i.e.* A victorious standard.

A تؤام *tuʼām*, (pl. of توأم *tawʼam*) Twins.

A توءمان *tawʼamān*, A certain small plant.

A توأمان *tawʼamāni*, (dual of توأم) Twins.

A توأمة *tawʼamat*, (fem. of توأم *tawʼam*) A twin. A kind of litter for women open at the top.

A تؤاميّة *tuʼāmiyat*, A pearl.

P توان *tuwān* or *tawān*, Power, strength. It is possible, one may. A cloud. (in comp.) Able, powerful. فرمان قضا توان *farmāni kazā-tuwān,* Commands powerful as fate, *i.e.* irresistible.

P توانا *tawānā,* Powerful, strong, able.

P توانائي *tuwānā,ī,* Power, strength. A hand.

P توانچه *tawāncha,* A slap.

P توان دخت *tuwān-dukht,* Name of the daughter of Khusraw Parvez.

P توانستن *tuwānistan,* To be powerful, able, equal to. To get the mastery.

P توانگر *tuwāngar,* Great, powerful. Rich.

P توانگران *tuwāngarān,* The rich and powerful.

P توانگري *tuwāngarī,* Powerfulness. Wealth.

P توانگی *tuwāngī,* Riches, goods, wealth.

A تواني *tawānī,* (v. n. 6 of وني) Coming short. Being torpid and languid. Delay. Slowness, languor, lassitude. بلا تواني *bilā tawānī,* Without delay.

P توانيدن *tuwānīdan,* To be able.

A تواوص *tawā,us,* (v. n. 6 of وأص) Assembling about a drinking-place.

A تواهب *tawāhub,* A making presents mutually.

P تواهچه *tawāhcha,* Meat well dressed.

A تواهس *tawāhus,* A quickening of the pace.

A تواهق *tawāhuk,* (v. n. 6 of وهق) Doing any thing alike. Travelling together at the same pace.

P تواهه *tawāha,* Fried. An omelet. Roast meat.

P تواهي *tawāhī,* Destroyed. Incomplete.

A توايل *tawāyul,* A crying to one another, woe!

A توائم *tawā,im,* (pl. of توأم *taw,am*) Twins. توائم النجوم *tawā,imu'n nujūm,* Stars intermingled.

A توائي *tawā,ī,* An assembling, flocking together.

A توب *tawb,* (v. n. of تاب for توب) Repenting, returning (from sin to God). Turning, relenting, becoming gracious (God to man).

P توب *tob,* A fold, twist. Multiplicity. Power. The eye.

P توباره *tūbāra,* A he-goat.

P توبال *tūbāl,* (or توپال *tūpāl*) Filings. Brass. Copper. A توبال الحديد *tūbālu'l hadīd,* Particles of heated iron that fly off under the stroke of the sledge hammer. P توبال مس *tūbāli miss,* Blue vitriol.

G توباملن *tūbāmulun,* Name of a plant yielding a milky juice. A sort of broom.

P توبان *tūbān,* Wrestler's breeches, very short, and besmeared all over with oil or grease.

A توبة *tawbat,* (pronounced توبه *toba*) (v. n. of تاب for توب) Vowing to sin no more (*i.e.* to drink no more wine). Repenting. Repentance. Conversion. P توبه كردن *toba kardan,* To repent. توبه شكستن *toba shikastan,* To break a vow.

A تؤبة *tu,abat,* Shame, disgrace.

P تو بر تو *to bar to,* Fold on fold. Step by step. At the tail of one another. Sheep's tripe. A sweetmeat. Self-willed. A scoundrel. A term of abuse.

P توبره *tūbra,* A huntsman's bag. The nose-bag of a horse.

P توبزه *tobaza,* The root of a water-melon.

P توبك *tūbak* or *tawbah,* A treasury, magazine, strong box. A larder.

P توبكي *tūbkī,* A coin formerly current.

A توبل *tawbal,* (pl. توابل *tawābil*) Herbs or spiceries for seasoning the pot.

A توبلة *tawbalat,* The seasoning (of a pot).

P توبه *tūba,* The rainbow.

P توبه كار *toba-kār,* (or توبه دار *toba-dār*) Penitent. Restrained by a vow.

P توبه كاري *toba-kārī,* Penitence. A vow of abstinence.

A توبئة *tawbi,at,* An arranging, drawing up.

A توبيخ *tawbīkh,* (v. n. 2 of وبخ not in use) Threatening, chiding, rebuking. A reproach. P توبيخ كردن *tawbīkh kardan,* To blame. To threaten.

A توبيخا *tawbīkhan,* (P توبيخانه) Invectively.

A توبيخيّ *tawbīkhīy,* Objurgatory.

A توبير *tawbīr,* (v. n. 2 of وبر) Running to hard ground (a hare, badger, or fox, that their footsteps may not be seen). Fleeing through fear. Being alienated, entertaining aversion. Staying at home, not stirring abroad. Sprinkling the male flowers on the female palm-tree. Producing down, becoming callow (a young ostrich).

A توبيش *tawbīsh,* (v. n. 2 of وبش) Blowing (a coal alive) till (it) flames. Flocking to a place (people from all quarters).

A توبيص *tawbīs,* (v. n. 2 of وبص) Giving little. Opening the eyes (a whelp).

A توبيع *tawbīʻ,* A breaking wind.

T توپ *top,* A cannon. A division of troops, a band. P توپ زدن *top zadan,* To cannonade. توپ اسب رو *topi asb-rav,* Horse-artillery.

P توپا *tūpā,* (in zand and Pāzand) An apple.

P توپال *tūpāl,* Bits of gold, silver, iron, copper.

T P توپانداز *top-andāz,* An artillery-man.

T توپچي *topchī,* Commissary of ordnance.

T P توپ خانه *top-khāna,* An arsenal. A park of artillery.

P توپك *tūpak* or *tawpak,* A magazine or storehouse. A money-chest.

P توپ هوائی *top-hawā,ī,* Blank shot.

A توّة *tawwat,* An hour (of the day or night).

A توت *tūt,* A mulberry. The mulberry-tree. توت وحشي *tūti wahshī,* (P توت سه گل *tūti sih gul*) The blackberry.

A توتّر *tawattur,* A being hard, stiff (nerve or neck).

P توتك *tawtak,* A money-chest. A pantry, storehouse. *Totak,* A parrot. A sort of bread. A shepherd's pipe. A street in Shīrāz.

P توتماج *tūtmāj,* Vermicelli-soup.

T توتن *tūtan,* Tobacco.

P توتو *to to,* Covering each other (as the coats of an onion).

P توته *tūta,* A sty on the eyelid. *Tota,* A parrot.

P توتي *tūtī,* A parrot. A ship.

A توتياء *tūtiyā,* Tutty. توتياء *tūtiyā,* توتياى اكبر *tūtiyā,i akbar,* A shell whence they make tutty. توتياى دولت *tūtiyā,i dawlat,* State-tutty, a remedy for national affairs. توتياى ديده *tūtiyā,i dīda,* A collyrium or medicine for the eyes. توتياى زرد *tūtiyā,i zard,* The Basrah stone. توتياى سبز *tūtiyā,i sabz,* Green vitriol.

P توتيا مثال *tūtiyā-misāl,* Like tutty.

A توتيح *tawtīh,* The making a small present.

A توتيخ *tawtīkh,* (v. n. 2 of وتخ) Striking a palm-branch or a date-stalk.

A توتيد *tawtīd,* (v. n. 2 of وتد) Fixing firmly (a stake). Planting (one's feet) firmly. A priapism.

A توتير *tawtīr,* (v. n. 2 of وتر) Putting on a bow-string. Drawing (a bow) vigorously. Placing singly, one by one. Repeating prayers separately.

A توث *tūs,* (for توت *tūt*) A mulberry. توث حلو *tūsi halw,* The sweet or white mulberry. توث حامض *tūsi hāmiz,* The acid or black mulberry.

A توثّب *tawassub,* A seizing unjustly an estate.

A تؤثور *tu,sūr,* (pl. توائير *tawāsīr* or تآثير *ta,āsīr*) A beadle, officer, or attendant upon the collector of revenue. The iron with which they mark the soles of the camel's feet (to know their footsteps).

A توثيب *tawsīb,* (v. n. 2 of وثب) Placing a cushion for another, desiring or causing him to sit.

A توثير *tawsīr,* A softening by beating or treading.

A توثيف *tawsīf,* The underpropping (a pot).

A توثيق *tawsīk,* (v. n. 2 of وثق) Establishing, strengthening, making fast. Declaring or esteeming any one to be trusty and worthy of confidence.

A توثيل *tawsīl,* (v. n. 2 of وثل not in use) Joining. Strengthening, rendering powerful. Acquiring (wealth or cattle).

A توج *tawj,* (v. n. of تاج for توج) Sinking into a soft substance (the finger).

P توج *tūj,* A quince.

A توّج *tawwaj,* Name of a place abounding in lions; also of a city in Persia.

P توجبه *tūjaba,* An inundation. An angel.

A توجّد *tawajjud,* (v. n. 5 of وجد) Being indisposed from, and complaining of, want of sleep. Lamenting (the fate of another). Being ravished, entranced, rapt in extacy (وجد *wajd*).

A توجّر *tawajjur,* (v. n. 5 of وجر) Swallowing (medicine). Drinking (water) unwillingly.

A توجّز *tawajjuz,* (v. n. 5 of وجز) Performing expeditiously. Asking, petitioning, or wishing one's business might be expedited.

A توجّس *tawajjus,* (v. n. 5 of وجس obsol.) Hearing a low sound, and turning the ear to it. Tasting a little at a time. Becoming afraid.

A توجّع *tawajjuʻ,* (v. n. 5 of وجع) Being pained, shewing marks of grief. Grieving for, condoling.

A توجّن *tawajjun,* A submitting, supplicating.

A توجّؤ *tawajju,,* A striking (with hand or knife).

A توجّه *tawajjuh,* (v. n. 5 of وجه) Turning to go any where. Proceeding towards. Fleeing away. Being routed. Approaching. Bending through old age. Conversion. Kindness, favour, obligingness. توجّه خاصّ *tawajjuhi khāss*, A turning (of the face) God-ward. P توجّه نمودن *tawajjuh namūdan*, To set out. توجّه نياز آميز *tawajjuhi niyāz-āmez*, Prayers mixed with humility, a humble prayer.

A توجّي *tawajjī*, (v. n. 5 of وجي) Having a pain, or being hurt, or worn in the hoof.

A توجيب *tawjīb*, (v. n. 2 of وجب) Rendering necessary. Imposing a necessity. Declaring to be obligatory. Accustoming one's self to. Eating once in a day. Milking (camels) every twenty-four hours. Curdling in the udder (biestings). Being fatigued (camels).

A توجئة *tawjiʼat*, A finding (a well) without water.

A توجين *tawjīn*, (v. n. 2 of وجن) as, ما ادري ايّ من وجّن الجلد هو *mā adrī ayyu man wajjana'l jilda huwa*, I know not who he is.

A توجيه *tawjīh*, (v. n. 2 of وجه) Turning towards. Planting (a palm-tree) and inclining it towards the north. Sending one to another (on business). Setting in order, arranging. Promoting to honour. Appointing to a government. Sending, wafting. Countenancing (in wickedness). Giving an uniform appearance to the earth (rain). Ambiguity of speech, double-facedness. Manumission promised to a slave after his master's death. A closeness of the thighs in a horse with a straddling of the feet. The penultimate consonant at the end of a verse, usually inflected with the vowels ـُـ *u* or ـَـ *a*. The vowel itself. Adjustment. Assessment. A description-roll.

P توجيه نويس *tawjīh-navīs*, A keeper of description-rolls, clerk of the pipe.

A توح *tawh*, A being prepared.

A توحّد *tawahhud*, (v. n. 5 of وحد) Being single, sole, unique, unparalleled. Taking (any one) under his special and sole protection (God).

A توحّش *tawahhush*, (v. n. 5 of وحش) Being desolate, deserted (a city). Clinging with hunger. Fasting before taking medicine. Aversion, horror.

A توحّل *tawahhul*, An abounding in thin mud.

A توحّن *tawahhun*, Largeness of belly. Baseness, meanness of spirit. Ruin, destruction.

A توحوح *tawahwuh*, (v. n. 2 of وحوح Q) Shewing affection for, sitting upon (her eggs, an ostrich).

A توحّي *tawahhī*, A making haste.

A توحية *tawhiyat*, A causing to make haste.

A توحيد *tawhīd*, (v. n. 2 of وحد) Making one. Declaring to be one. التوحيد *at tawhīd*, A belief in the unity of God; unitarianism, anti-trinitarianism. P توحيد كردن *tawhīd kardan*, To make one. To acknowledge one God.

A توحيش *tawhīsh*, (v. n. 2 of وحش) Throwing away (cloak and arms) in flight. Desolating.

A توحيف *tawhīf*, (v. n. 2 of وحف) Striking with a stick. Throwing one's self on the ground, lying down (a man or a camel). Making haste. Cutting up (a slaughtered camel) into large joints.

A توحيم *tawhīm*, (v. n. 2 of وحم) Giving a pregnant woman what she longs for. Sacrificing, slaughtering. Exuding (sap from a green stick).

A توخ *tawkh*, (v. n. of توخ for تاخ) Being thrust, sinking (the finger into a soft mass).

P توختن *tokhtan*, To pay a debt. To return any thing borrowed. To acquire, gain, collect by degrees. To wish, want: to search, seek. To draw. To shew, spread, display, let off. To sew, stitch.

P توخته *tokhta*, Paid. Collected, gained, acquired. Drawn. Spread. Sewed.

P توخش *tawakhsh*, Drawing.

A توخّم *tawakhkhum*, (v. n. 5 of وخم) Being unhealthy, unwholesome (as a country, meat, &c.). Being unable to digest (heavy, unwholesome food).

A توخّن *tawakhkhun*, Tending to good or bad.

A توخّي *tawakhkhī*, (v. n. 5 of وخي) Purposing. Seeking the right way. Having rather.

A توخية *tawkhiyat*, (v. n. 2 of وخي) Sending towards. Designing, seeking, striving after.

A توخيش *tawkhīsh*, (v. n. 2 of وخش) Giving little. Throwing, casting. Obeying.

P تود *tūd*, (for توت *tūt*) The mulberry. *Tod*, A hill. Top, summit. A heap. A camel's bunch.

A تود *tūd*, Name of a tree.

A تؤدة *tuʼadat* or *tuʼdat*, Slowness, sedateness.

A تودّد *tawaddud*, (v. n. 5 of ودّ) Shewing love. Gaining the love of another. تودّد و محبّت *tawaddud u mahabbat*, Love and friendship.

A تودّر *tawaddur*, (v. n. 5 of ودر) Plunging headlong into (business). Being squandered, dissipated (property). Bringing one's friend to ruin.

P تودره *todara*, A bustard.

P تودري *tūdarī*, Mallows. Sumach.

G تودريون *todaryūn*, Hellebore.

A تودّس *tawaddus*, (v. n. 5 of ودس) Pasturing upon early herbage called وداس *widās*.

P تودستي *tūdastī*, Aid, assistance.

A تودّع *tawadduʻ*, (v. n. 5 of ودع) Being deposited, put away safe, given in charge. Depositing, laying by. Being careless in preserving, neglecting.

A تودّف *tawadduf*, (v. n. 5 of ودف) Inquiring (news). Appearing on the top of a hill (a goat).

A تودّن *tawaddun*, (v. n. 5 of ودن) Being soft and smooth (a skin).

A تودّؤ *tawadduʼ*, (v. n. 5 of ودأ) Carrying destruction among those who suspect no danger. Being prevented from arriving (news). Being equalled, levelled, thrown down (earth). Taking one's money and keeping it.

P تودوه *todūh*, A pair, a brace.

P توده *toda*, A heap. A rick, stack. A hillock, tumulus. The butt or mark at which arrows are shot. تودهٔ خاك *todaʼi khāk*, A mound of earth. تودهٔ كافور *todaʼi kāfūr*, A heap of snow. A fair skin. تودهاي خاك *todahāʼi khāk*, Tropics, climes, degrees of latitude. The human frame.

A تودئة *tawdiʼat*, (v. n. 2 of ودأ) Levelling the ground (over any thing).

A تودية *tawdiyat*, (v. n. 2 of ودي) Voiding something after having made water. A dwarf, short of stature. (pl. توادي *tawādī*) A piece of wood put on the udder to prevent a camel from being sucked.

A توديج *tawdīj*, (v. n. 2 of ودج) Bleeding (a horse) in the vein ودج *wadaj*.

A تودير *tawdīr*, (v. n. 2 of ودر) Driving (one) into danger or destruction, or exciting him to what will prove his ruin. Seducing. Being prodigal, extravagant, squandering one's property. Sending an envoy. Removing, warding off (evil). Turning away (the face from any one).

A توديس *tawdīs*, (v. n. 2 of ودس) Being hidden, concealed. Beginning to look verdant with young herbage (ground).

A توديع *tawdīʻ*, (v. n. 2 of ودع) Laying up (a garment) in its place. Leaving. Bidding adieu, taking leave. Rearing a stallion. Suspending a small white shell to any thing.

A توديك *tawdīk*, (v. n. 2 of ودك) Placing in fat or dripping, making greasy.

A تودين *tawdīn*, (v. n. 2 of ودن) Moistening, dissolving in water. Shortening. Striking with a stick.

A توذّف *tawazzuf*, A walking fast, but proudly.

A توذّل *tawazzul*, (v. n. 5 of وذل) Cutting flesh, but not dividing it.

A توذّن *tawazzun*, Conversion, change. Admiration of one's self.

A توذير *tawzīr*, (v. n. 2 of وذر) Cutting (meat) in pieces. Putting a lancet into a wound.

A توذيف *tawzīf*, A walking fast, but proudly.

A توذيم *tawzīm*, (v. n. 2 of وذم) Exceeding fifty in number. Cutting in pieces. Curing (a camel) of warts in the uterus called وذم *wazam*. Putting a collar round a dog's neck.

A تور *tawr*, (v. n. of تور) Running, flowing. (pl. اتوار *atwār*) An internuncio, mediator, ambassador (sent to conciliate differences). A vessel (out of which water is drank, or the hands and face are washed). A cake of wax.

P تور *tūr*, Name of the eldest son of Farīdūn. The country of Tūrān. A Turk. A sturdy wrestler, a champion. Bold, warlike, brave. A sweetheart. Beloved. Search, inquiry. Hospitality. Alarm, terror. Departure. A certain acid culinary herb. A little. Name of the daughter of Iraj, and wife of Minuchihr. *Tawar*, An axe, hatchet. A jewel.

P تورا *torā*, (in zand and Pāz.) An ox. A cow.

A توراب *tawrāb*, (better تراب *turāb*) Earth.

A توراة *tawrāt*, The Pentateuch.

P توران *tūrān*, Turkomania, Turkistān, Transoxania, so named from Tūr, eldest son of Farīdūn, to whom his father gave it for an inheritance.

P توران دخت *tūrān-dukht*, Name of the daughter of Khusraw Parvez, who reigned in Persia sixteen months.

P تورانشاه *tūrān-shāh*, The king of Tūrān. The proper name of many distinguished men.

P توراني *tūrānī*, A Scythian, Turkomān.

A تورب *tawrab*, Earth, dust.

A تورة *tawrat*, A girl sent between two lovers.

P تورتيز *turtiz*, Ease, comfort, competency.

P تورج *tūraj*, Name of the eldest son of Farīdūn, who obtained from his father the empire of Tūrān. He is also called Tūr.

A تورّخ *tawarrukh*, (v. n. 5 of ورخ) Being soft and thin (a mass of paste). Being irrigated, moistened (the earth).

A تورّد *tawarrud*, (v. n. 5 of ورد) Blushing like the rose. Entering by troops (horsemen). Going into water in order to drink. Seeking a halting or watering-place.

P تورزي *tawarzī*, (or تورزين) A battle-axe.

A تورّس *tawarrus*, (v. n. 2 of ورس) Staining one's self with the plant ورس *wars*.

P تورش *tūrsh*, (for ترش *tursh*) Acid, sour.

A تورّط *tawarrut*, (v. n. 5 of ورط) Falling into difficulty or destruction (ورطة *wartat*).

A تورّع *tawarruʻ*, (v. n. 5 of ورع) Abstaining; being restrained.

A تورّق *tawarruk*, (v. n. 5 of ورق) Plucking and devouring leaves (ورق *warak*).

P تورك *tūrak* or *tuvurk*, Purslain. A hero.

A تورّك *tawarruk*, (v. n. 5 of ورك) Reclining on the hip. Sitting (at prayer) with one buttock upon the right foot and the other on the ground (prohibited by the Muhammadan law). Turning up one leg, and sitting upon one hip on horseback, either when sore with riding, or when going to alight. Carrying a child on one hip (a woman). Delaying, hesitating, suspending business. Staying in a place. Bedaubing one's self. Being equal to any business, succeeding.

A تورّم *tawarrum*, A being seized with a swelling.

A تورّن *tawarrun*, The frequent use of unguents. A pampering, a rendering soft and effeminate.

P تورنج *tūrunj*, An orange.

P تورنگ *torang*, A pheasant. A jungle cock.

P تورنگان *tūrangān*, God, the creator and bestower of life.

A تورّؤ *tawarruʼ*, A being levelled (the earth).

A توررو *tusrūr*, An assistant to a police magistrate, an unpaid militia-man.

P توروه *to rūh*, A pair, a brace.

P توره *tawra*, Beloved (son or daughter).

P توره *tora*, Law, regulation. Custom, rite. A jackall. A fetter. A law instituted by Changiz Khān.

A تورّه *tawarruh*, A being ignorant, unskilful.

A توري *tawarrī*, A withdrawing, a lurking.

P توريان *tūriyān*, (pl. of توري) Turkomāns.

A توريب *tawrib*, A withdrawing, avoiding.

A تورئة *tawriʼat*, A knowing, being aware.

A تورية *tawriyat*, (v. n. 2 of وري) Concealing, dissembling. Receiving private intelligence, and publishing something different. Wishing one thing and pretending another. Turning away (the face from one). Striking fire with a steel or from two pieces of wood. Bringing on a disease of the lungs (called وري *wara'*). Ending with similar consonants (the periods of an oration, قافية *kāfiyat* expressing poetic rhymes). Baffling medical skill (an ugly wound). An enigma.

A توريت *tawrīt*, The books of Moses. اهل توريت *ahli tawrīt*, Those who adhere to the law of Moses, the Jews.

A توريث *tawris*, (v. n. 2 of ورث) Appointing an heir (وارث *wāris*). (equiv. to تأريث *taʼris*) Stirring (the fire) to make (it) burn brisker.

A توريخ *tawrīkh*, The dating (a letter).

A توريد *tawrīd*, (v. n. 2 of ورد) Blossoming (a tree). Painting the cheeks of a rose-colour (women).

P توريدن *toridan*, To be very much ashamed. To run away, retire, depart.

P توريز *tawrīz*, The capital of Azarbayjān.

A توريس *tawrīs*, (v. n. 2 of ورس) Dyeing (cloth) yellow with the plant ورس *wars*.

A توريش *tawrīsh*, (v. n. 2 of ورش) Instigating one against another. Exciting dissensions, tumults.

A توريص *tawrīs*, (v. n. 2 of ورص) Laying an egg at once (a hen). Easing nature without difficulty (an old man), the ring of the anus being relaxed.

A توريض *tawrīz*, (v. n. 2 of ورض) Going round a country in quest of forage. Resolving to fast. Laying an egg with ease (a hen). Easing nature without difficulty.

A توريط *tawrīt*, (v. n. 2 of ورط) Precipitating to destruction. Concealing (his camels) among others, so that they cannot be distinguished (when the tithing-man comes to number them).

A توريع *tawrīʻ*, (v. n. 2 of ورع) Checking, repressing, driving away; abstaining, keeping off.

A توريف *tawrīf*, (v. n. 2 of ورف) Being long, broad, and ample. Extending a great way (a shadow). Pressing with the lips in order to suck. Dividing (land).

A توريق *tawrīk*, (v. n. 2 of ورق) Being full of leaves (ورق *warak*), very leafy (a tree).

A توريك *tawrīk*, (v. n. 2 of ورك) Placing (any thing) near the haunch. Being equal to any business, succeeding. Turning up one leg and sitting on one haunch on horseback. Going by the side of a mountain. Leaning to a side. Rendering necessary. Accusing of a crime. Swearing with a different intention from what the oath purposes.

A توريم *tawrīm*, (v. n. 2 of ورم) Making swell. Making angry. Being high-nosed, proud, haughty.

P توز *toz*, (imp. and participle of توختن *tokhtan*) Gain. Draw. Seek. Pay, restore. Collecting, gaining. A collector, gainer. Paying, refunding. Sewing. Drawing. A drawer. Searching, seeking. The thin bark of a tree, like the papyrus, which is wrapped round bows by way of ornament, or to make them more smooth. Spoil, plunder. Heat, study. Assault. Name of a city.

A توز *tawz*, (v. n. of تاز for توز) Being thick, rugged, coarse. *Tūz*, Nature, quality. Origin, root. Name of a tree. A stick used in a game called كجه *kujja*, a bandy, a shinty.

A توّز *tawwaz*, Name of a place in Persia.

A توزان *tiwzān*, (or توزانة) Opposite.

A توزّر *tawazzur*, (v. n. 5 of وزر) Being chosen to, or exercising, the office of vazir or prime-minister.

A توزّع *tawazzuʻ*, (v. n. 5 of وزع) Dividing among themselves. Distraction, perplexity, grief.

P توزك *tūzak*, Institute, regulation.

A توزلي *tawzala'*, (or توزلاء) Calamity, evil.

A توزّؤ *tawazzuʼ*, (v. n. 5 of وزأ) Being filled (a leathern bottle).

P توزه *toza*, A thin bark put on a saddle or over the handle of a bow.

P توزي *tozī*, A light summer-garment, manufactured at Toz. A ship.

A توزّي *tawziy*, (v. n. 2 of ازي) Making a conduit called ازاء *izāʼ* to a cistern.

A توزّي *tawwaziy*, Made at Tawwaz (cloth).

A توزئة *tawziʼat*, (or توزيء *tawzīʼ*) (v. n. 2 of وزأ) Throwing his rider (a camel). Filling (a leathern bottle). Shutting (a purse) and tying firmly what is in (it). Binding (one) by oath.

P توزيدن *tozīdan*, To pay. To gain, collect. To draw, spread. To sack, plunder. To shew.

A توزيع *tawzīʻ*, (v. n. 2 of وزع) Dividing, distributing amongst several. Guarding, rendering inaccessible. Scattering. A schoolboy's picnic.

A توزيغ *tawzīgh*, (v. n. 2 of وزغ) Forming, or being formed, in the womb.

A توزيف *tawzīf*, A going fast.

A توزيم *tawzīm*, (v. n. 2 of وزم) Restraining one's self to one meal a day.

P توژ *toj*, Thin bark resembling the papyrus.

P توژي *tojī*, A schoolboy's picnic.

A توس *tūs*, Nature, disposition. Origin. توساً عليه وجوساً *tūsan ʻalayhi wa jūsan*, An imprecation.

P توست *tu'st*, (as از آن توست) It is thine.

A توسّخ *tawassuhh*, The being dirtied, soiled.

A توسّد *tawassud*, (v. n. 5 of وسد) Leaning, reclining upon a cushion. Putting (any thing) under the head for a pillow. Laying the Kur'ān under the pillow (implying both neglect and study).

A توسّط *tawassut*, (v. n. 5 of وسط) Being the middle. Becoming a mediator or umpire. Sitting in the midst. Penetrating into the marrow of any thing. Taking the medium between good and bad.

A توسّع *tawassuʻ*, (v. n. 5 of وسع) Sitting with

ease, not crowded. Width, roominess. Extensive and profound (literary attainments).

A توسعة *tawsiʿat*, Amplitude.

A توسّف *tawassuf*, (v. n. 5 of وسف) Being excoriated or peeled. Becoming fat. Casting the old and getting a new coat (a camel).

A توسّل *tawassul*, (v. n. 5 of وسل not in use) Endeavouring to recommend one's self to the notice and favour of God. Attaining (to any thing by the help of another). Thieving, taking away by stealth. Reliance. Introduction, conjunction.

A توسّم *tawassum*, (v. n. 5 of وسم) Discovering by physiognomy, and prognosticating good. Seeing. Imagining, fancying. Painting or dyeing one's self. Pasturing upon early spring forage.

P توسن *tawsan*, Wild, unmanageable. A young unbroke horse. A high-blooded steed. توسن تند عنان *tawsani tund-ʿinān*, A hard-mouthed, unmanageable steed.

A توسّن *tawassun*, (v. n. 5 of وسن) Stealing upon (a woman) asleep.

P توسنگ *tosang*, Contentment.

P توسني *tawsanī*, Refractoriness, restiffness.

A توسيخ *tawsīkh*, A dirtying, soiling (clothes).

A توسيد *tawsīd*, (v. n. 2 of وسد) Placing a cushion, or causing one to recline on a cushion.

A توسيط *tawsīt*, (v. n. 2 of وسط) Placing in the middle. Dividing in the middle, into two halves.

A توسيع *tawsīʿ*, (v. n. 2 of وسع) Enlarging. Making room. Making wide. Giving facility, affording opportunity. Investing with power. Enriching. Amplification, development. توسيع بلاد *tawsīʿi bilād*, The extending of the territories.

A توسيق *tawsīk*, (v. n. 2 of وسق) Dividing into distinct loads called وسق *wask* (corn).

A توسيل *tawsīl*, (v. n. 2 of وسل obsol.) Striving to obtain nearness and access. Seeking the favour of God by good works.

A توسيم *tawsīm*, (v. n. 2 of وسم) Assembling from all quarters to celebrate the festival of Mecca.

P توش *tosh*, Power, strength, vigour. Body. Food sufficient for a meal. (for تو اورا *tu urā*) Thou to him. *Tavish*, (for تبش) Heat, warmth.

P توشت *tawshat*, A spade, hoe. *Tawisht*, Heat.

A توشّح *tawashshuh*, (v. n. 5 of وشح obsol.) Putting on the sash or belt وشاح *wishah*. Girding on a sword. Putting on a vest. Embracing, hugging.

P توشدان *toshdān*, (or توشه دان *toshadān*) A beggar's wallet. A traveller's provision-bag. A pouch, cartouche-box.

A توشّز *tawashshuz*, Preparation for mischief.

A توشّع *tawashshuʿ*, (v. n. 5 of وشع) Climbing a mountain. Commencing to ascend right and left. Appearing in a great quantity (gray hairs).

A توشّغ *tawashshugh*, (v. n. 5 of وشغ) Disgracing one's self (by any thing base, as a lie).

P توشك *tūshak*, A kid. A cat. A small carpet with a short pile. Bedding. A mattress for sleeping on.

P توشك خانه *tūshak-khāna*, A wardrobe.

P توشكان *toshkān*, The stove of a bath.

A توشّن *tawashshun*, A paucity of water.

A توشوش *tawashwush*, (v. n. 2 of وشوش Q) Being mingled, confounded. Being agitated, in commotion. Much talking.

P توشه *tosha*, Provisions, necessaries. توشه بر داشتن *tosha bar dāshtan*, To set out upon a journey. توشهٔ چشم *toshaʾi chashm*, A wistful look. توشهٔ راه *toshaʾi rāh*, Provisions for the road. توشه و گوشه *tosha u gosha*, Food and lodging. گوشهٔ بي توشه *goshaʾi bī tosha*, A nook barren of provisions: a barren district.

P توشه خانه *tosha-khāna*, Wardrobe: storeroom.

P توشه‌دان *toshadān*, A wallet, provision-bag.

P توشي *toshī*, Children's picnic.

A توشّي *tawashshī*, (v. n. 5 of وشي) Being conspicuous. Shining (as gray hairs among black).

A توشية *tawshiyat*, (v. n. 2 of وشي) Dyeing, printing, painting, or embroidering (cloth) well.

A توشيج *tawshīj*, (v. n. 2 of وشج) Connecting firmly (propinquity). Binding a thing with ropes or straps, so that it cannot fall off.

A توشيح *tawshīh*, (v. n. 2 of وشح) Putting a girdle upon a lady. Adorning. (In poetry) Arranging the verses, so that the initial of each line being put together may form some word or verse. An acrostic. Putting a belt on another.

A توشيع *tawshīʿ*, (v. n. 2 of وشع) Winding (cotton-wool) into clews fit for weaving or spinning: rolling in spiral hanks round the thumb and little finger. Marking, printing (cloth). Appearing (as gray hairs).

A توشيغ *tawshīgh*, (v. n. 2 of وشغ) Staining garments with blood.

A توشيق *tawshīk*, (v. n. 2 of وشق) Drying parboiled flesh cut into long slices. Dividing, separating, scattering.

A توشيك *tawshīk*, A being swift, expeditious.

A توشيم *tawshīm*, (v. n. 2 of وشم) Pricking (the skin) with needles in various figures, and rubbing the punctures with woad or indigo (thereby making an indelible impression). Producing herbage.

A توصّب *tawassub*, A being sick, ailing.

A توصّل *tawassul*, (v. n. 5 of وصل) Being joined. Arriving. Obtaining any thing by stratagem or cajolery.

A توصّم *tawassum*, (v. n. 5 of وصم) Being broken down (by fever).

A توصيب *tawsīb*, A being sick, ailing.

A توصية *tawsiyat*, (v. n. 2 of وصي) Recommending. Admonishing, charging. Making a will or testament. بلا توصية *bilā tawsiyat*, Intestate.

A توصيد *tawsīd*, (v. n. 2 of وصد) Threatening, putting in fear, admonishing, warning, prohibiting.

A توصيص *tawsīs*, (v. n. 2 of وصّ not in use) Veiling (her) face (a woman), so as to leave no part visible except (her) eyes. Doing (a thing) firmly and well.

A توصيف *tawsīf*, A describing: a qualifying.

A توصيفيّ *tawsīfiy*, Significant of an attribute.

A توصيل *tawsīl*, A joining, connecting closely.

A توصيم *tawsīm*, (v. n. 2 of وصم) Weakening, breaking down the body (as a fever). Torpor, languor, debility.

A توضّح *tawazzuh*, A being manifest, clear, plain.

A توضّر *tawazzur*, A being nasty and dirty.

A توضّم *tawazzum*, (v. n. 5 of وضم) Lying with.

A توضّن *tawazzun*, (v. n. 5 of وضن) Being low, base, and vile. Submission, supplication, humility.

A توضّؤ *tawazzuʾ*, (v. n. 5 of وضأ) Performing ablutions before prayer. Bathing, washing the body. Arriving at the age of puberty (boys or girls), when ablutions must be observed.

A توضيح *tawzīh*, A making clear, manifest.

A توضير *tawzīr*, A being dirty, nasty, greasy.

A توضيع *tawzīʿ*, (v. n. 2 of وضع) Depressing, humbling, putting down. Laying her eggs side by side (an ostrich). Quilting a garment with cotton.

A توضيء *tawzīʾ*, A washing, cleaning.

A توطّد *tawattud*, (v. n. 5 of وطد) Being firm, established. Being heavy.

A توطّن *tawattun*, (v. n. 5 of وطن) Fixing one's residence anywhere. Applying, accustoming (the mind) to any thing.

A توطّؤ *tawattuʾ*, (v. n. 5 of وطئ) Treading upon, trampling on, compressing. Agreeing, consenting. Repeating the last syllable of a verse.

A توطوط *tawatwut*, The cries of an infant.

A توطئة *tawtiʾat*, (v. n. 2 of وطئ) Treading upon, trampling on. Allowing or causing to be trodden or trampled on. Expanding, rendering soft and level, making a bed. (God) making (the ground) low. Arranging, disposing in order. Lying in wait for an ambuscade. Repeating the last syllable or rhyme of a poem.

A توطيد *tawtīd*, (v. n. 2 of وطد) Putting one's foot on a place. Making firm. Making heavy.

A توطيش *tawtīsh*, (v. n. 2 of وطش) Repulsing, warding off, striking. Opening or referring (any thing) to another. Speaking obscurely and indistinctly. Relating any thing in part. Giving something. Making an impression, leaving a mark.

A توطين *tawtīn*, (v. n. 2 of وطن) Choosing as a place of residence. Habituating the mind to, fixing the heart on (any thing). Giving rest.

A توظيف *tawzīf*, (v. n. 2 of وظف) Assigning, writing an order, paying (any one) a daily stipend.

A توع *tawʿ*, A dipping bread in cream or butter.

A توعّد *tawaʿʿud*, A menacing, a terrifying.

A توعّر *tawaʿʿur*, (v. n. 5 of وعر) Being rough, uneven (a path). Being bewildered, embarrassed (in speaking). Being difficult, at a stand-still (business). Being hard, morose (man).

A توعّل *tawaʿʿul*, (v. n. 5 of وعل) Climbing, or standing on a hill.

A توعّن *tawaʿʿun*, (v. n. 5 of وعن not in use) Taking the whole. Becoming very fat (camels).

A توعيث *tawʿīs*, (v. n. 2 of وعث) Detaining, imprisoning. Changing, turning, converting.

A توعير *tawʿīr*, (v. n. 2 of وعر) Making rough or difficult. Preventing, prohibiting. Bewildering, embarrassing, perplexing.

A توعيز *tawʿīz*, (v. n. 2 of وعز) Commanding. Making a sign to another to do any thing.

A توعيق *tawʿīk*, (v. n. 2 of وعق) Playing, trifling. Calling one morose, refractory, stubborn, or ill-tempered. Delaying, protracting. Opposing, thwarting, hindering, preventing.

P توغ *togh*, A wood which burns several days.

G توغاج *tūghāj*, A bark, white and very bitter.

A توغّر *tawaghghur*, A burning, firing with rage.

A توغّل *tawaghghul*, (v. n. 5 of وغل) Travelling to a distance. Going deep into learning.

A توغّم *tawaghghum*, A being enraged against.

A توغّن *tawaghghun*, Intrepidity in battle.

A توغير *tawghīr*, (v. n. 2 of وغر) Stimulating to hatred. Heating milk, by putting into it a hot stone.

A توغيض *tawghīz*, The filling (of a vessel).

A توف *tawf*, Bewilderment (of the sight).

P توف *tūf*, Echo, clamour, noise.

A توفاق *tawfāk*, The time when any thing happens, or takes its rise. Season, opportunity.

P توفان *tūfān*, Noise, sound, din; the confused hum of men or animals. The roaring of the sea. A storm. Name of Wāmik's friend.

A توفة *tawfat*, (pl. توفات *tawfāt*) A trip, stumble, blunder, fault, crime. *Tūfat*, Vice, defect, blemish. Necessity, need, lack. Excess. Delay, hesitation.

A توفّد *tawaffud*, (v. n. 5 of وفد) Overtopping, overhanging, excelling.

A توفّر *tawaffur*, (v. n. 5 of وفر) Respecting, reverencing. Paying every thing which one owes.

A توفّز *tawaffuz*, A preparing to commit evil.

A توفق *tawfak*, The time when any thing happens. A convenient season.

A توفّق *tawaffuk*, A being happy, prosperous.

A توفّن *tawaffun*, Defect, deficiency, diminution.

A توفّي *tawaffī*, (v. n. 5 of وفي) Receiving the whole of what is due. Receiving to himself (as God the souls of the just).

A توفية *tawfiyat*, A paying in full.

A توفيد *tawfīd*, A sending, despatching.

P توفيدن *tūfīdan*, To cry aloud. To call for help. To roar, to bray. To raise a tumult.

A توفير *tawfīr*, (v. n. 2 of وفر) Making complete or perfect. Multiplying, increasing. Cutting (a garment) sufficiently large. Exacting and receiving the whole of what was due. Paying a debt completely. Sparing (a person's reputation), not reviling. Permitting to grow long. Increase, abundance, surplus revenue.

A توفيق *tawfīk*, (v. n. 2 of وفق) Causing to happen prosperously (Divine Providence); making events to conspire happily; seconding, prospering. The guidance, grace, or favour of God. Agreement. The completion of one's wishes. The time when any thing happens. و بالله التوفيق و اتوب اليه *wa bi'llāhi't tawfīk wa atūbu ilayhi*, Success is from God: to him I return by repentance.

A توفيل *tawfīl*, (v. n. 2 of وفل) Multiplying. A kind of fragrant herb.

A توق *tawk*, (v. n. of تاق for توق) Desiring ardently, being anxious to accomplish. Inclining to, favouring. Compassionating, commiserating. Being light. Flowing (tears). Turning up favourably (a gaming arrow). Spending one's strength willingly in the service of another. Drawing (a bow) with one's whole might. Desire. *Tūk*, The crookedness of a stick.

A توق *tuwuk*, A desiring ardently.

A توقان *tawakān*, (v. n. of تاق for توق) Desiring, longing. Favouring. Being anxious to accomplish. Being lavish of life for another. Shedding (tears). Drawing a bow. Being light. Compassionating, commiserating. Desire.

A توقّة *tawakat*, Convalescents.

A توقّد *tawakkud*, (v. n. 5 of وقد) Burning, blazing. Kindling a flame, lighting a fire.

A توقّر *tawakkur*, (v. n. 5 of وقر) Being modest, mild, gentle, sedate, grave. Respect, honour.

A توقّش *tawakkush*, A being moved, agitated.

A توقّص *tawakkus*, (v. n. 5 of وقص) Going at a pace so as to break whatever he treads upon (a horse). Going at a middling pace.

A توقّع *tawakkuʿ*, (v. n. 5 of وقع) Expecting any thing to be done, to fall out, or happen. Request, hope. Reliance, expectation.

A توقّف *tawakkuf*, (v. n. 5 of وقف) Stopping, delaying. Being firm, patient, persevering. Expecting. Delay, stoppage, pause. P توقّف نمودن *tawakkuf namūdan*, To pause.

A توقّل *tawakkul*, (v. n. 5 of وقل) Ascending, standing on a hill.

A توقلة *tawkalat*, A horse that goes well over rocks and stones.

A توقّم *tawakkum*, (v. n. 5 of وقم) Killing (game). Remembering another's saying. Threatening. Purposing. Going far and wide. Walking pompously.

A توقّن *tawakkun*, (v. n. 5 of وقن) Taking pigeons from their nest. Ascending, standing on a hill.

A توقّي *tawakkī*, (v. n. 5 of وقي) Fearing, being afraid of, shunning. Protecting, defending one's self.

A توقية *tawkiyat*, (v. n. 2 of وقي) Preserving, guarding from. Custody, guardianship.

A توقيت *tawkīt*, (v. n. 2 of وقت) Appointing a time (for any thing), limiting to a time.

A توقيح *tawkīh*, (v. n. 2 of وقح) Repairing (a pond or a well) with clods, turfs, boards, or stones. Hardening the hoof by anointing it with grease.

A توقيذ *tawkīz*, A leaving one indisposed.

A توقير *tawkīr*, (v. n. 2 of وقر) Honouring, revering, respecting. Regarding as grave or sedate. Trying, proving. Making grave, modest, respectable. Quieting, making steady (a horse). Leaving scars and marks. Wounding. Reverence.

A توقيص *tawkīs*, A throwing billets on the fire.

A توقيط *tawkīt*, (v. n. 2 of وقط) Abounding in hollows where water collects. Making a hollow in the ground (running water or water dropping from a height).

A توقيع *tawkīʿ*, (v. n. 2 of وقع) Making sharp, or giving a high polish to (a sword, spear, knife). Beating the hoof of a horse (a rugged road). Hurting the back (of a horse or camel). Signing (a letter) with the royal signet. Imagining, turning the thoughts to. Erecting a vine-arbour or prop. Raising and throwing the feet forward (a horse). Raining gently, hardly wetting the ground. The glittering polish of a sword. The royal signet put to diplomas, letters patent, and other public deeds (of an intricate formation, containing the king's name and titles). Opinion, conception, idea, thought. The shooting of an arrow, or any thing similar, so as to fall near the mark.

A توقيف *tawkīf*, (v. n. 2 of وقف) Causing to stand. Retaining, detaining, preventing, prohibiting, restraining, causing one to remain in a place. Standing one behind another (a regiment). Bequeathing a horse. Making a saddle so that it will not hurt the horse's back. Causing one to understand, making him acquainted. Adorning with bracelets (a woman); putting something similar round the feet of a horse. Strengthening the extremities of a bow, by twisting round the nerve of a camel's neck steeped in the blood of a stag. Making punctures on the hands, and rubbing them with *mendhī* (lawsonia inermis). Going to Mount عرفات *ʿarafāt* to celebrate the festival of Mecca. The make of the part where a bracelet is fixed. The adjusting of the saddle, so as not to hurt the horse's back. The expounding of sacred writ. A mark set upon arrows.

P توك *tūk*, The eye. A clew of wool. A lock of hair. Forelocks.

A توكاف *tawkāf*, A dropping of rain from a house.

A توكّد *tawakkud*, (v. n. 5 of وكد) Being confirmed. Being closely connected or drawn together.

A توكّر *tawakkur*, (v. n. 5 of وكر) Being filled with meat and drink (the belly of a lad). Being crammed (a bird's crop).

A توكّز *tawakkuz*, (v. n. 5 of وكز) Being filled.

Preparing (for evil). Leaning (on a staff). Being marked with black spots.

A توكف *tawakkuf*, (v. n. 5 of وكف) Expecting, looking out for (a person, or some advantage). Visiting (people) often relative to (their) affairs.

A توكل *tawakkul*, (v. n. 5 of وكل) Depending upon, trusting to, any one when unable to act for one's self. Confidence in God.

A توكن *tawakkun*, (v. n. 5 of وكن) Being firmly fixed and well established.

A توكؤ *tawakkuʼ*, (v. n. 5 of وكأ) Leaning (on a staff). Crying (as a camel in labour).

A توكوك *tawakwuk*, An ambling pace.

A توكيب *tawkīb*, (v. n. 2 of وكب) Turning blackish (ripe dates). Gathering dates.

A توكية *tawkiyat*, (v. n. 2 of وكي) Filling (a vessel). Shutting one's mouth, keeping silence.

A توكيت *tawkīt*, (v. n. 2 of وكت) Becoming covered with black specks (ripening dates). Filling.

A توكيد *tawkīd*, (v. n. 2 of وكد) Confirming, strengthening, connecting strongly. Energy. Making a league. (pl. تواكيد *tawākīd*) Emphasis.

A توكير *tawkīr*, (v. n. 2 of وكر) Giving a feast on the finishing of a building. Filling (a bottle).

A توكيس *tawkīs*, (v. n. 2 of وكس) Terrifying. Reproaching, reproving. Deficiency, decrease.

A توكيف *tawkīf*, The putting on a pack-saddle.

A توكيل *tawkīl*, (v. n. 2 of وكل) Appointing a lieutenant, deputy, substitute, factor, or agent (وكيل *wakīl*). Entrusting a business to any one.

A تول *tawl*, A practising magic.

P تول *tūl*, War, contention. The circumference of the mouth. Wry-mouthed. *Tol*, Flight, elopement.

A تولا *tūlā*, (or تولات *tūlāt*) Misfortunes.

A تولب *tawlab*, A wild (or tame) ass's colt. A calf. ام تولب *umm tawlab*, (Colt's mother) An ass.

A تولة *tuwalat*, *tawlat*, or *tūlat*, A misfortune, a dreadful calamity. *Tuwalat* and *tiwalat*, A philtre or charm used by a wife to conciliate the affection of her husband. A fascinating blandishment, or any thing which deceives and ravishes the heart. Magic, enchantment.

A تولج *tawlaj*, The lair of a wild beast.

P تولچه *tūlcha*, Name of a weight.

A تولد *tawallud*, A being generated, born: birth.

A تولع *tawalluʻ*, A being eager, intent upon.

A تولغ *tawallugh*, (v. n. 5 of ولغ) Forcing one's way, getting a footing.

P تولك *tūlak*, Ingenious, quick, intelligent. Moulting. تولك كردن *tūlak kardan*, To moult.

A تولن *tawallun*, A wailing, a lamenting.

P توله *tūla*, A hound that hunts by the scent. Name of a plant. A whelp. Name of an Indian weight of 2½ *mishḳāls*.

A توله *tawalluh*, (v. n. 5 of وله) Being amazed, stupid (with love, sorrow, or fear). Being distracted at the loss of her child (a mother). وادي توله *wādi tuwallihin*, Destruction.

A تولي *tūlaʼ*, A misfortune.

A تولي *tawallī*, (v. n. 5 of ولي) Being appointed to, or assuming, or being confirmed in, an office. Turning the back, taking flight. Cultivating friendship. Choosing a friend, taking for one's lord, master, or protector. Attending to any one's concerns. Conferring an appointment. A right still retained over a freedman by his emancipator, or by one who has furnished him with the means of obtaining his manumission. Government, jurisdiction. Recession.

A تولية *tawliyat*, (v. n. 2 of ولي) Appointing to a government, setting over. Turning the back, flying, retiring, going off. Shunning, deserting. Declining (the day). Turning towards. Assisting. Causing (one) to turn (himself). Selling at a price originally fixed, without any increase. Withering (a date). The superintendency of the affairs of mosques, churches, or other religious foundations.

A توليج *tawlīj*, (v. n. 2 of ولج) Causing to enter. توليج المال *tawlīju'l māl*, A father assigning his estate to his son during his own life, that people may no longer importune him for legacies.

A توليد *tawlīd*, (v. n. 2 of ولد) Procreating, begetting, engendering. Playing the midwife, assisting at a birth. Producing. Educating, bringing up. Generation, birth. Any action which produces another action (as opening a lock with a key).

P توليدن *tolīdan*, To flee, depart, retire.

A توليع *tawlīʻ*, (v. n. 2 of ولع) Causing one to be intently eager. Being marked with long black and white spots (a bull or pack-horse).

A توليه *tawlīh*, (v. n. 2 of وله) Rendering (a mother) distracted by taking (her) child from (her).

A توم *tūm*, and توم *tuʼam*, (pl. of تومة *tūmat*) Pearls. Ear-rings distinguished by large pearls. Ostrich's eggs.

P توما *tūmā*, (in zand and Pāzand) Garlic.

P تومار *tūmār*, A book, volume, roll. A doomsday-book. An amulet-case (of gold or silver) which they suspend round the necks of children.

A التومان (كتف *kitfu't*) *tawmān*, Name of the sixth lunar mansion in the Zodiac.

P تومان *tomān*, A myriad, 10,000. A sum of money equal to 10,000 Arabic silver drachmas (which are about one-third less than those of the Greeks; also a sum equal to fifteen dollars and a half). Districts into which a kingdom is divided, each being supposed to furnish 10,000 fighting men: when the city of Samarkand, for example, therefore, is put down for seven tomāns, it implies that she must hold 70,000 men ready on the requisition of her sovereign. A large division of a tribe.

P توماندار *tomān-dār*, Commander of a tomān.

P توماندارى *tomān-dārī*, Command of a tomān.

A تومة *tūmat*, (pl. توم *tūm* and توم *tuʼam*) A pearl. An ear-ring distinguished by a large pearl. A substance resembling pearls found in silver-mines. An ostrich-egg. ام تومة *ummi tūmat*, Mother of pearl. An ostrich.

A تومري *tuʼmuriy*, Some, any one.

A تومز *tawammuz*, (v. n. 5 of ومز) Springing forward in order the sooner to reach or catch an object. The motion of the glans beginning to rise.

A تومق *tawammuḳ*, (v. n. 5 of ومق) Shewing love.

P تومن *toman*, A district of a hundred villages.

A تومن *tawammun*, A multitude of children.

A تومور *tuʼmūr*, Any one. (pl. تامير *taʼāmīr*) A direction-stone set up in the desert.

A تومى *tūmaʼ*, Thomas.

A تومئة *tawmiʼat*, (v. n. 2 of وما) Making a sign. A nod, a sign.

P تون *tūn*, The stove of a bath. The womb. An intestine not cleaned. Name of a country in Khurāsān. *Tawan*, The body.

A تون *tūn*, A leathern chess-board.

P توند *tuʼnd*, (for تو *tu*, اند *and*) They are thine.

A تونس *tūnus*, Tunis in Africa, built on the ruins of Carthage.

A تونسي *tūnusiy*, Native of Tunis.

P تونك *tūnak* or *tawnak*, (or تونكه *tūnaka* or *tawnaka*) A store-house.

P تونگر *tawangar*, Rich, powerful. A barber.

P تونگر دل *tawangar-dil*, (or همّت *himmat*) Liberal-minded.

P تونگري *tawangarī*, Wealth. Power.

P تونگو *tawangū*, A barber. A wardrobe. A till. A halter.

P تونه *tūna*, Fringe, edge, border, selvage.

P توني *tūnī*, One who takes care of the furnaces in a bath. One who comes from afar, and has no home: a beggar, a gipsy. A thief, rogue, footpad. A native of Tūn in Khurāsān.

A تونيب *tawnīb*, A reproaching, accusing.

A تونية *tawniyat*, (v. n. 2 of وني) Discovering (one) to be slothful in business.

A تونير *tawnīr*, An exalting, raising.

A توءد *tawaʼʼud*, (v. n. 5 of وأد) Proceeding gently, easily. Concealing, hiding from view.

P تووه *tūwa*, A pair, a brace.

A توه *tawh*, (v. n. of تاه for توه) Perishing. Being proud. Being confused in the intellect. Departing. (pl. توه *tūh*, اتواه *atwāh*, and اتاويه *atāwīh*) Astonished, bewildered. *Tawh* or *tūh*, Ruin, destruction.

P توه *toh*, A pair, a brace. A fold, plait. *Tawa*, (for تبه *taba*) Destroyed, ruined.

A توهش *tawahhush*, An advancing far.

A توهج *tawahhuj*, (v. n. 5 of وهج) Being kindled; burning. Sparkling (gem). Being strong and diffused (perfume).

A توهد *tawahhud*, (v. n. 5 of وهد) Lying with.

A توهر *tawahhur*, (v. n. 5 of وهر) Interrupting,

confounding (any one) in speaking. Beginning to abate in darkness (night). Becoming milder (winter). Beginning to diminish (hills of sand).

A توهرِيّ *tawhariy*, A long camel's bunch.

A توهّز *tawahhuz*, (v. n. 5 of وهز) Treading heavy on the ground (a loaded camel). Rushing upon.

A توهّس *tawahhus*, (v. n. 5 of وهس) Treading heavy, striking the ground. Travelling fast and well (camels). The pace of any one overloaded.

A توهّش *tawahhush*, Bare-footedness. The step (of any one) overloaded.

A توهّط *tawahhut*, (v. n. 5 of وهط) Being sunk (in clay). Making equal, smooth, and easy (a bed).

A توهّق *tawahhuk*, (v. n. 5 of وهق) Disturbing, interrupting (any one) in speaking, urging him until he becomes bewildered. Being extremely hot (gravel or pebbles).

A توهّل *tawahhul*, A causing (one) to err.

A توهّم *tawahhum*, (v. n. 5 of وهم) Thinking, suspecting, imagining, supposing. Suspicion, imagination, doubt.

A توهّن *tawahhun*, A being weak and languid.

A توهوه *tawahwuh*, The growling (of a lion).

A توهيد *tawhīd*, A spreading, making soft (a bed).

A توهير *tawhīr*, (v. n. 2 of وهر) Bringing (one) into a disagreeable affair from which he cannot extricate himself.

A توهيل *tawhīl*, A terrifying, frightening.

A توهيم *tawhīm*, (v. n. 2 of وهم) Causing to err. Throwing into doubt. Persuading.

A توهين *tawhīn*, An enervating, relaxing.

P توي *tūy* or *toy*, Fold, ply. Inside. توئ شير *toï* or *tūï shīr*, Cream. *Toy*, Feast, entertainment.

A تويٰ *tawa'*, (v. n. of توي) Perishing. Destruction. *Tawī*, One who perishes or falls.

A تويّ *tawiy*, Standing fast, steady. One who abides in a place.

A تويبع *tuwaybiꜥ*, The star Aldeberān.

P تويج *toyaj*, Ivy.

P تويك *tūyak*, The inside. A store-room.

P تويل *tawīl*, Bald on the forehead. *Tuwīl*, The crown of the head. The top of the forehead. A sign which hunters set up in the fields with a view to drive the affrighted game into their net.

A تويّل *tawayyul*, An imprecating woe.

P توين *tuwīn*, Friendly, affectionate.

P تويه *tūya*, The rainbow.

P تويي *tuī*, Thou art. Thouism. Name of a bird.

A توئير *tawīr*, A drawing (one) into mischief.

A تويل *tawyīl*, A denouncing of woe.

A توئيم *tawīm*, (v. n. 2 of وأم) Making (one) large-headed and deformed in person.

P ته *tah*, A fold, ply. Single, odd. Rust. Under. The bottom, deep, or inner part. ته آب *tahi āb*, Bottom of water. ته دل *tahi dil*, The deep of the heart. *Tuh*, Spit.

A ته *tih* and *tihi*, (for ذه *zih* and *zihi*) (fem. of ذا *zā*) She. This.

A تهاتر *tahātir*, (pl. of تهتر *tahtar*) Contradictory testimonies. Testimony which convicts both parties of falsehood. *Tahātur*, (v. n. 6 of هتر) Contending, disputing about trifles. Convicting each other of uttering falsehood. Laying false charges against each other.

A تهاتم *tahātum*, (v. n. 6 of هتم) Stickling, contending about trifles.

A تهاتن *tahātun*, (v. n. 6 of هتن) Pouring down continued rain. See هتن *hatn*.

A تهاته *tahātih*, Vain things, trifles.

A تهاجر *tahājur*, A separating from each other.

A تهاجي *tahājī*, A satirizing one another.

A تهادّ *tahādd*, A coming behind one another.

A تهادر *tahādur*, (v. n. 6 of هدر) Permitting slaughter with impunity, or passing it over without punishment.

A تهادم *tahādum*, A leaving blood unrevenged.

A تهادن *tahādun*, (v. n. 6 of هدن) Being right, well arranged (any thing). Cultivating peace and amity amongst themselves.

A تهادي *tahādī*, (v. n. 6 of هدي) Offering reciprocal presents. Leaning from side to side in walking (a woman).

A تهارش *tahārush*, A growling and fighting.

A تهارط *tahārut*, A reviling, chiding one another.

A تهارم *tahārum*, A feigning extreme old age.

A تهافت *tahāfut*, (v. n. 6 of هفت) Falling one part after another (as leaves). Throwing one's self into. Rushing consecutively (a crowd). Waxing old (a garment). Flying to the flame (a moth).

A تهاكل *tahākul*, A disputing, a striving.

P تهال *tahāl*, A cave, cavern, grot.

A تهالك *tahāluk*, (v. n. 6 of هلك) Running headlong (to ruin). Tumbling (into bed). Walking trippingly (a woman).

A تهام *tahām*, (pl. تهامون) Belonging to Tihāmat.

A تهامة *tihāmat*, Mecca. An adjacent province.

A تهامس *tahāmus*, Whisper, private conference.

A تهامش *tahāmush*, (v. n. 6 of همش) Mixing, entering one within another, being in commotion.

A تهامي *tahāmī*, A native of Tihāma.

A تهاميّ *tihāmiy*, A native of تهامة *tihāmat*.

P تهانانيدن *tahānānīdan*, To make empty.

A تهانف *tahānuf*, A smiling ironically.

A تهانؤ *tahānuꜥ*, (v. n. 6 of هنأ) Congratulating one another. Provoking, challenging each other.

H تهانه *t'hāna*, A small fort. The head station of a district.

H P تهانه دار *t'hāna-dār*, Commander of a small fort. A man who has the management of a district.

A تهاني *tahānī*, (pl. of تهنئة) Congratulations.

A تهاوش *tahāwish*, (pl. of تهواش *tahwāsh*) Multitudes, crowds. Tumults, mobs. *Tahāwush*, (v. n. 6 of هاش for هوش) Mixing (a crowd, mob).

A تهاون *tahāwun*, (v. n. 6 of هان for هون) Despising, neglecting, slighting. Negligence, carelessness, sloth; neglect, contempt. P تهاون كردن *tahāwun kardan*, To despise, slight, neglect.

A تهاوي *tahāwī*, A falling one after another.

A تهاويش *tahāwīsh*, (pl. of تهواش) Crowds, mobs.

A تهاويل *tahāwīl*, (pl. of تهويل *tahwīl*) Apparitions, ghosts. Objects which strike with terror. Things of various colours. Painted robes. Bracelets, jewels, or necklaces (as striking with surprise, or dazzling the eyes of beholders).

A تهايج *tahāyuj*, (v. n. 6 of هاج for هيج) Rushing on each other, fighting hand to hand.

A تهايط *tahāyut*, (v. n. 6 of هاط for هيط) Assembling together to adjust any business (تمايط *tamāyut* implying Meeting to disturb). Arranging.

A تهايؤ *tahāyuꜥ*, A consenting, agreeing.

P ته بازاري *tah-bāzārī*, Ground-rent of a stall in the market.

A تهبّب *tahabbub*, A being worn, rent.

P ته بته *tah ba tah*, Plait by plait, every fold.

A تهبّج *tahabbuj*, A being troubled with a swelling.

A تهبّد *tahabbud*, (v. n. 5 of هبد) Extracting, bruising and boiling the seeds of the colocynth or bitter purging apple (هبد *habd* or هبيد *habīd*).

A تهبرس *tahabrus*, A walking pompously.

A تهبّش *tahabbush*, (v. n. 5 of هبش) Assembling. Being collected. Collecting, scraping together for one's family.

A تهبّط *tihibbit*, Name of an ash-coloured bird said to suspend itself, and cry انا اموت انا اموت *ana' amūt, ana' amūt*, I shall die, I shall die!

A تهبّل *tahabbul*, A providing (for a family).

P ته بند *tah-band*, A strip worn round the loins.

A تهبهب *tahabhub*, A being shaken: tottering.

A تهبّي *tahabbī*, (v. n. 5 of هبا for هبو) Shaking the hand. Being empty or out of work.

A تهبيب *tahbīb*, (v. n. 2 of هبّ) Calling (a he-goat). Tearing much.

A تهبيج *tahbīj*, A causing to swell.

A تهبير *tahbīr*, (v. n. 2 of هبر) Cutting (meat) so that a part falls.

A تهبيش *tahbīsh*, A gaining industriously.

A تهبيل *tahbīl*, (v. n. 2 of هبل) Oppressing any one (corpulence). Gaining with industry provision (for a family).

P ته پيچ *tah-pech*, A cap worn under a turban.

A تهتار *tahtār*, Foolishness, impertinence.

A تهتال *tahtāl*, A raining with little intermission.

A تهتان *tahtān*, (v. n. of هتن) Raining for several days, at least for a third part of the day or night. Continual gentle rain, unaccompanied by thunder or lightning.

A تهتر *tahtar*, (pl. تهاتر) Contradictory evidence.

A تهتّر *tahattur*, Folly.

A تهتّك *tahattuk*, (v. n. 5 of هتك) Being torn, rent (as a veil or a covering). Being disgraced. Haste, precipitancy. Disgrace, dishonour.

A تهتّم *tahattum*, A being broken (front teeth).

A تهتّؤ *tahattuʼ*, A being torn, cut, worn.

P ته ته *tah tah*, Multiplied, crowded.

A تهتهة *tahtahat*, (v. n. 2 of تهته Q) Giving one's self up to trifling pursuits. Stammering, pronouncing Arabic improperly.

A تهتير *tahtīr*, (v. n. 2 of هتر) Tearing any one's reputation, slandering, defaming.

A تهتيك *tahtīk*, (v. n. 2 of هتك) Tearing (a veil or a curtain so as to expose those who are concealed by them).

A تهتيم *tahtīm*, A disabling, enfeebling by blows.

P تهجا *tahjā*, Expressing the juice of grapes.

A تهجاء *tahjāʼ*, A satirizing, lampooning.

A تهجاع *tahjāʻ*, A light slumber, a nap.

A تهجّد *tahajjud*, (v. n. 5 of هجد) Being sleepless, walking at night. Sleeping sound in bed. Sleep. A prayer repeated during the night.

A تهجّر *tahajjur*, (v. n. 5 of هجر) Looking like one who has left his country (on account of persecution). Going abroad in the hottest part of the day.

A تهجع *tahjaʻ*, Wide (road).

A تهجّع *tahajjuʻ*, A going to sleep.

A تهجّؤ *tahajjuʼ*, (v. n. 5 of هجا) Repeating the letters of the alphabet. Syllabing, spelling.

A تهجّي *tahajjī*, (v. n. 5 of هجا for هجو) Spelling. حروف التهجّي *hurūfu't tahajjī*, The letters of the alphabet.

A تهجية *tahjiyat*, The act of spelling.

A تهجيد *tahjīd*, A causing to sleep or awake.

A تهجير *tahjīr*, (v. n. 2 of هجر) Travelling in the heat of the day. Making haste, coming early, arriving before prayer begins. Magnifying.

A تهجيع *tahjīʻ*, (v. n. 2 of هجع) Allowing or desiring to sleep.

A تهجيل *tahjīl*, (v. n. 2 of هجل) Reviling, slandering. Talking obscenely. Striking with a stick or scourge.

A تهجين *tahjīn*, (v. n. 2 of هجن) Disgracing, exposing a foul deed, reprobating. Rendering (offspring) base and mongrel (هجين *hajīn*).

P تهخانه *tah-khāna*, A cave, cavern, cellar, vault.

A تهدار *tahdār*, (v. n. of هدر) Being hot (wine). Cooing (a dove).

A تهدّج *tahadduj*, (v. n. 5 of هدج) Crying to her colt in a shrill and affectionate tone (a camel). Failing (the voice from fear).

A تهدد *tahaddud*, A terrifying, threatening.

P تهدرز *tah-darz*, New.

A تهدّك *tahadduk*, (v. n. 5 of هدك) Reproaching, reviling, using hard words, frightening.

A تهدكر *tahadkur*, (v. n. 2 of هدكر Q) Being satiated with milk, so as to occasion drowsiness. Being contented and cheerful. Trembling, shaking in going (flesh and bones). Rushing upon (men).

A تهدّل *tahaddul*, (v. n. 5 of هدل) Hanging down, dangling (the scrotum, a camel's lip, or the branches of a tree). Laxity, pendulousness.

A تهدّم *tahaddum*, (v. n. 5 of هدم) Being pulled down, destroyed. Rushing upon (any one) in a threatening manner.

A تهدّي *tahaddī*, (v. n. 5 of هدي) Being conducted (by God) into the way of righteousness. Being guided, finding the way (to a house, in a road).

A تهدية *tahdiyat*, (v. n. 2 of هدي) Separating, dispersing. Offering, presenting.

A تهديد *tahdīd*, (v. n. 2 of هدّ) Terrifying. Threatening. Letting (sheep) follow one another. P جوابِ تهديد آميز *jawābi tahdīd-āmez*, An answer mixed with menaces. تهديد كردن *tahdīd kardan*, To threaten, menace, alarm.

A تهديدات *tahdīdāt*, (pl. of تهديد) Threats.

A تهدير *tahdīr*, (v. n. 2 of هدر) Roaring (as a lion). Cooing (a dove). Making a muttering noise in the throat (like a he-camel when tied up in a pen).

P ته ديگي *tah-degī*, Scrapings of a pot; the burnt part of victuals sticking to the bottom of a pot.

A تهديم *tahdīm*, An overthrowing: a destroying.

A تهدين *tahdīn*, (v. n. 2 of هدن) Soothing (an infant). Hindering.

A تهذار *tahzār*, Adoting, raving, talking nonsense.

A تهذخر *tahazhkhur*, (v. n. 2 of هذخر Q) Walking with a graceful air or flauntingly (a woman).

A تهذكر *tahazkur*, (v. n. 2 of هذكر Q) Rejoicing. Being satiated with milk, so as to be overcome with sleep. Trembling, shaking in going (flesh and bones). Being contented and cheerful. Rushing upon.

A تهذّؤ *tahazzuʼ*, The bursting (of an ulcer).

A تهذيب *tahzīb*, (v. n. 2 of هذب) Purifying. Adjusting, adorning. Correcting, amending. Walking or flying fast (a man or bird).

A تهرّش *taharrush*, A being dispelled (mist).

A تهرشف *taharshuf*, (v. n. 2 of هرشف Q) Sipping by little and little.

A تهرّع *taharruʻ*, (v. n. 5 of هرع) Being levelled (a spear at a foe).

A تهرّؤ *taharruʼ*, (v. n. 5 of هرأ) Being boiled to dissolution (meat).

A تهرموز *taharmuz*, A perishing, a dying.

A تهرّي *taharrī*, A beating (with a great stick).

A تهريب *tahrīb*, A putting to flight.

A تهرئة *tahriʼat*, A boiling to dissolution (meat).

A تهرية *tahriyat*, (v. n. 2 of هري) Beating (with a great stick). Making or dressing cloth like that of هراة *harāt* (a city in Khurāsān). Dyeing yellow (the sash of a turban or tiara).

A تهريت *tahrīt*, A boiling to dissolution (meat).

A تهريج *tahrīj*, (v. n. 2 of هرج) Urging forward a camel until he becomes stupefied. Overcoming a man (wine). Frightening by cries (a wild beast).

A تهريد *tahrīd*, (v. n. 2 of هرد) Putting on a garment dyed yellow. Boiling till soft (meat).

A تهريس *tahrīs*, (v. n. 2 of هرس) Cooking (meat) till it falls to rags.

A تهريش *tahrīsh*, (v. n. 2 of هرش) Setting by the ears (men or dogs).

A تهريص *tahrīs*, (v. n. 2 of هرص) Being corroded by the dry scab.

A تهريع *tahrīʻ*, A levelling a spear (at a foe).

A تهريف *tahrīf*, (v. n. 2 of هرف) Making haste (to prayer). Producing early (a palm-tree).

A تهريق *tahrīk*, (v. n. 2 of هرق) Keeping close, tarrying long (at wine).

A تهريم *tahrīm*, (v. n. 2 of هرم) Making decrepid (age). Cutting into small portions. Magnifying, exalting.

A تهزّج *tahazzuj*, (v. n. 5 of هزج) Singing, warbling, shaking, trilling. Twanging (a bowstring).

A تهزّز *tahazzuz*, (v. n. 5 of هزّ) Being shaken (a tree by the wind).

A تهزّع *tahazzuʻ*, (v. n. 5 of هزع) Making haste, being swift. Walking with a tottering gait. Scowling, looking austere and grim. Making one's self unknown. Being broken (a stick). Shaking, vibrating (a spear or sword).

A تهزّل *tahazzul*, A being jocose, facetious.

A تهزّم *tahazzum*, (v. n. 5 of هزم) Twanging (a bowstring). Thundering. Being broken with a crash (a stick). Drying and bursting (a leathern bottle). Falling with noise (rain).

A تهزّؤ *tahazzuʼ*, A mocking, exposing to ridicule.

A تهزهز *tahazhuz*, (v. n. 2 of هزهز Q) Being moved. Exulting, being joyful.

A تهزيج *tahzīj*, A warbling, a quavering.

A تهزيز *tahzīz*, (v. n. 2 of هزّ) Shaking a tree.

A تهزيع *tahzīʻ*, A breaking, bruising.

A تهزيل *tahzīl*, An extenuating, emaciating.

A تهسهس *tahas-hus*, (v. n. 2 of هسهس Q) Whispering, muttering, grumbling. Clashing, jingling, rustling (as coats of mail, or necklaces).

A تهشّم *tahashshum*, (v. n. 5 of هشم) Being broken, bruised (any thing dry, hard, or hollow, as the head, the nose, a bone, or an egg). Breaking. Breaking any dry or withered vegetable (wind). Honouring, praising, magnifying. Milking with the whole hand. Making weak and languid. Being weak and languid (camels). Having an affection for. Conciliating the love of another.

A تهشيش *tahshīsh*, (v. n. 2 of هشّ) Making cheerful. Esteeming or finding weak.

A تهشيم *tahshīm*, An honouring, praising.

A تهصيص *tahsīs*, (v. n. 2 of هصّ) Having bright eyes. Opening the eyes and looking sharp.

A تهضّم *tahazzum*, (v. n. 5 of هضم) Injuring, defrauding, oppressing. Keeping back (another's due). Submitting. Coming off with loss.

A تهضيج *tahzīj*, A pasturing (flocks) poorly.

A تهطال *tahtāl*, (v. n. of هطل) Raining incessantly. Incessant, small rain.

A تهطّر *tahattur*, The falling to ruins (of a well).

A تهطرس *tahatrus*, A pompous manner of

walking, or a waving from side to side.

A تهطّل tahattul, (v. n. 5 of هطل) Employing stratagem (as a thief). Recovering from sickness.

A تهطلس tahatlus, (v. n. 2 of هطلس Q) The same.

A تهطلؤ tahatlu', A recovering from sickness.

P تهغربالي tah-ghirbālī, Siftings: small grain.

A تهقّع tahakkuʻ, (v. n. 5 of هقع) Lying down when wanting the male (a camel). Going off (a disease). Behaving proudly, playing the fool. Flocking to a watering-place. Acting basely.

A تهقّل tahakkul, A going as if heavily laden.

A تهقّم tahakkum, (v. n. 5 of هقم) Taming, subduing, overcoming. Swallowing by large mouthsful.

P تهك tahak, Empty, naked. Earth, loam.

A تهكّر tahakkur, A being stupefied with wonder.

A تهكّك tahakkuk, (v. n. 5 of هك) Being large-breasted and relaxed about the haunches (a woman near labour).

A تهكّم tahakkum, (v. n. 5 of هكم obsol.) Being inflamed with rage. Strutting pompously. Falling in (a well). Singing (to one) by way of ridicule. Being content. Contempt, mockery, derision. Pride. Repentance. Incessant rain which cannot soak in. Continued stabbing or reproach.

A تهكّن tahakkun, Penitence, repentance.

A تهكيد tahkīd, Heavy pressure (on a debtor).

A تهكيل tahkīl, The pace of a war-horse; and a haughty woman.

A تهكيم tahkīm, A singing to one in derision.

A تهلّب tahallub, (v. n. 5 of هلب) Being stripped of (his) bristles.

A تهلّز tahalluz, (v. n. 5 of هلز not in use) Preparing for. Tucking up the garment. Strutting.

A تهلّق tahalluk, A making haste, going fast. وادي تهلّك wādī tuhullika, False, vain, idle, trifling.

A تهلكة tahlukat, tahlakat, or tahlikat, (v. n. of هلك) Perishing, dying. Tahlukat, Any thing ending in destruction. Ruin, perdition.

A تهلّل tahallal, Vain, foolish (thing). Tahallul, (v. n. 5 of هلّ) Brightening up (the face). Shining, flashing (lightning). Being transparent (cloud). Flowing from the eyes (tears).

A تهلوك tuhlūk, A dying, a perishing.

A تهلهل tahalhul, A weaving of a garment closely. Weaving with small threads.

A تهلّي tahallī, The going fast (of a horse).

A تهليب tahlīb, (v. n. 2 of هلب) Pulling out hairs or bristles (هلب hulb); plucking an animal. Treating contumeliously, satirizing.

A تهليس tahlīs, Leanness, meagreness.

A تهليك tahlīk, A ruining, a destroying.

A تهليل tahlīl, (v. n. 2 of هلّ) Being timid, pusillanimous. Flying, retiring, remaining behind, hanging back, departing, receding. Praising God, by saying لا اله الا الله lā ilāha illa' llāh, There is no god but God. Calling out الله الله allāh allāh, when going to battle. Making in the form of the new moon (هلال hilāl), gibbous or curved. Writing (a letter). Joy, exultation, cheerfulness.

A تهم tahm, A district on the sea-coast. Taham, (v. n. of تهم) Being fetid (as flesh or oil). Being impotent, confounded. Disliking his pasture (a camel). Excessive heat. Want of wind, a calm. Tahim, Fetid. Tuham, A girl's name.

P تهم taham or tahm, Brave, warlike. Incomparable, unrivalled in stature or courage.

A تهماع tahmāʻ, A pouring forth, a shedding.

A تهمة tahmat, Mecca and the neighbouring province. A city. Tuhmat, Evil opinion, suspicion. P تهمت نهادن tuhmat nihādan, To suspect. To charge with a crime, to lay an accusation. A Tahamat, Fetidness. The sea-coast.

P تهمتره tahamtara, Name of Rustam.

P تهمت زده tuhmat-zada, Suspected.

P تهمت كرده شده tuhmat-karda shuda, Rendered suspected.

P تهمتن taham-tan, Powerful, mighty, formidable. Incomparable. A general, commander. A title of Rustam. Name of Bahman. Obedience.

A تهمتي tuhmatī, Suspicious. Ignominious.

A تهمرش tahamrush, A being set in motion.

A تهمّش tahammush, A flowing softly.

A تهمّط tahammut, (v. n. 5 of همط) Seizing by violence (any thing to which one has no right).

A تهمّع tahammuʻ, A feigning to weep.

P تهمك tahmak, Naked, empty, bare.

A تهمّك tahammuk, (v. n. 5 of همك Q) Giving one's whole attention to (any particular object). Precipitating one's self into folly or mischief.

A تهمّم tahammum, (v. n. 5 of همّ) Seeking for Endeavouring to find by groping. Striking with a sword (the head). Hunting lice in any one's head.

A تهمّؤ tahammu', A being torn or worn.

P تهمورس tahmūras, The third king of Persia of the Peshdādian dynasty. The rational soul.

P تهمير tahmīr, A hero of Rustam's family.

P تهميشه tahmīsha, Name of a forest.

A تهميم tahmīm, Gentle rain.

A تهن tahan, A sleeping. Tahin, Asleep.

A تهنبس tahambus, An inquiry after news.

A تهنّج tahannuj, (v. n. 5 of هنج) Beginning to quicken (a fœtus).

P ته نشان tah-nishān, Inlaid (iron with gold).

P ته نشين tah-nishīn, Sitting below. Sediment.

A تهنّؤ tahannu', (v. n. 5 of هنأ) Being refreshed with food, digesting easily.

A تهنئة tahni-at, (v. n. 2 of هنأ) Congratulating. Saying, "May it do you good!" Congratulation.

A تهنيد tahnīd, (v. n. 2 of هند not in use) Alluring, ravishing the senses, distracting the soul (a woman). Being deficient, unequal to any thing. Lagging, loitering, remaining behind. Hooting like an owl. Reviling opprobriously. Accusing of falsehood, treating as a liar. Bearing reproaches and making no return. Whetting (a sword).

A تهنيف tahnīf, A making haste.

A تهنيء tahnī', A congratulating.

P تهو tihū, A bird resembling a small partridge, a quail. Tuhū, Spittle.

A تهواء tahwā' or tihwā', Part of the night.

A تهواد tahwād, Low, gentle (voice or speech). Gentleness of articulation.

A تهواش tahwāsh, (pl. تهاوش tahāwish and تهاويش tahāwīsh) A multitude, mob. A tumult.

P ته و بالا tah u bālā, Above and below, up and down. Topsy-turvy. Commotion, perturbation, restlessness.

A تهوّد tahawwud, (v. n. 5 of هاد for هود) Being converted to repentance. Returning to duty. Embracing Judaism. Articulating gently. Seeking reconciliation with one's kindred. Good conduct.

A تهوّر tahawwur, (v. n. 5 of هار for هور) Being ruined, fallen down. Plunging inconsiderately into any business. Being gone, the greater part (of night). Seizing and overpowering (as hot and mortal winds). Rashness. Military ardour, impetus.

A تهوّش tahawwush, (v. n. 5 of هاش for هوش) Being mixed. Assembling.

A تهوّع tahawwuʻ, A vomiting by force.

A تهوّك tahawwuk, (v. n. 5 of هاك for هوك) Being astonished, stupefied. Falling into difficulties from inattention. Falling down, being ruined.

A تهوّل tahawwul, (v. n. 5 of هال for هول) Placing near a camel the resemblance of a wolf, to induce her to take a liking to another's foal. Looking (at the flock) with an evil eye. Adorning one's person.

A تهوّم tahawwum, Nodding (of a drowsy man).

A تهويت tahwīt, A calling aloud, hooting.

A تهويد tahwīd, (v. n. 2 of هاد for هود) Singing with a soft voice. Answering one another (the جنّ jinn). Singing with taste and execution to the neglect of other things. Eating the bunch of a camel. Walking gently. Intoxicating (wine). Sleeping. Proselyting to Judaism. Gentleness of articulation. Low, gentle (voice or speech).

A تهوير tahwīr, A throwing down, prostrating.

A تهويز tahwīz, (v. n. 2 of هوز) Dying.

A تهويش tahwīsh, (v. n. 2 of هاش for هوش) Being mixed together (as men) in a tumultuous manner. Driving soil about in different directions (wind). Confounding, complicating.

A تهويع tahwīʻ, (v. n. 2 of هاع for هوع) Making (one) return by vomit (what he had eaten).

A تهويك tahwīk, The act of digging.

A تهويل tahwīl, (v. n. 2 of هال for هول) Terrifying. Making (a thing) become ugly and frightful. Adorning herself (a woman). A solemn oath made (among the Pagan Arabians) before a sacred fire called هولة hawlat, into which they privately threw a kind of salt, which, by making a sudden explosion, surprised and frightened the person sworn, and sometimes detected perjury. (pl. تهاويل *tahāwīl*) Any thing which terrifies, astonishes, or dazzles the eyes. A hobgoblin. Defamation, detraction.

A تهويم *tahwīm*, The nodding (of a sleepy man).

A تهوين *tahwīn*, (v. n. 2 of هان for هون) Making light and easy. Despising.

P تهي *tihī*, *tahī*, or *tuhī*, Empty, void, vacant. نان تهی *nāni tihī*, Dry bread. ميان تهي *miyān-tihī*, Hollow. *Tihī*, Name of a city.

A تهي *tihī*, (fem. from ذا *zā*) She. This, that.

A تهيّات *tahīyāt*, (pl. of تهيّة) Preparations.

A تهيّب *tahayyub*, A fearing, a being afraid.

P تهی پاي *tahī-pāy*, Barefoot.

A تهيّة *tahīyat*, Preparation, arrangement.

A تهيّث *tahayyus*, A giving, bestowing.

A تهيّج *tahayyuj*, (v. n. 5 of هاج for هيج) Being raised (as dust or anger).

P تهي چشم *tihī-chashm*, Greedy, covetous.

P تهی دست *tihī-dast*, Poor. Avaricious.

P تهيدن *tih* or *tahīdan*, To become empty, void.

P تهی دو *tihī-dav*, Idle, sauntering about.

A تهيّر *tahayyur*, A falling in ruins.

P تهي رأي *tihī-raʼy*, Unable to advise.

P تهي رفتن *tihī raftan*, To travel alone: to go empty-handed, or without information. To lose one's way. To go on a fruitless errand.

P تهي رو *tihī rav*, Deviating from the road.

P تهي روي *tihī-ravī*, Deviation. A journey.

P تهي شكم *tihī-shikam*, Empty-bellied.

A تهيّض *tahayyuz*, (v. n. 5 of هاض for هيض) Being broken again before consolidated (a bone which had been fractured and set).

A تهيّع *tahayyuʻ*, A being expanded.

A تهيعر *tahayʻur*, (v. n. 2 of هيعر Q) Being restless, unable to remain quiet in one place.

A تهيّف *tahayyuf*, (v. n. 5 of هاف for هيف) Being blown on by the hot drying wind هيف *hayf*.

P تهيگاه *tihī-gāh*, The hypochondria, the slender part of the body under the short ribs.

A تهيّل *tahayyul*, A being poured out, flowing.

A تهيم *tahīm*, Suspected.

A تهيّم *tahayyum*, A studied, elegant walk.

P تهي مغز *tihī-maghz*, Empty-brained.

P تهي ميان *tihī-miyān*, Hollow.

A تهيّؤ *tahayyuʼ*, (v. n. 5 of هيأ) Preparing for. Being right, straight, easy, feasible, in one's power.

P تهی و تهك *tahī u tahak*, Empty. Naked.

A تهييء *tahyīʼ*, A directing properly, amending.

A تهييب *tahyīb*, A making awful, venerable.

A تهيئة *tahyiʼat*, A directing properly, amending.

A تهييت *tahyīt*, A calling to any one.

A تهييج *tahyīj*, (v. n. 2 of هاج for هيج) Exciting, provoking, stimulating. Withering, drying.

A تهييخ *tahyīkh*, (v. n. 2 of هاخ for هيخ) Putting fat (into pottage). Exciting (a goat) to copulate.

A تهييد *tahyīd*, (v. n. 2 of هاد for هيد) Repulsing, prohibiting, checking. Putting in motion, stirring. Frightening. Amending, correcting, restoring. Oppressing the spirits. Rebuking. Making haste.

A تهييغ *tahyīgh*, (v. n. 2 of هيغ not in use) Watering plentifully (the earth with rain). Dressing (paste) with fat.

A تهييك *tahyīk*, A making haste. Digging.

A تهييل *tahyīl*, (v. n. 2 of هال for هيل) Pouring, causing to run over (earth or sand).

A تهييئ *tahyīʼ*, A setting in order.

P تي *tī*, (for تهي *tihī* or *tahī*) Empty, vacant.

A تي *tī*, (fem. from ذا *zā*) She. This.

A تيّا *tayyā*, (dim. of تا *tā*) The little she.

A تيّاح *tayyāh*, (A horse) going sideways with a sprightly air.

P تيّار *tayyār*, Ready, prepared. تيّار كردن *tayyār kardan*, To make ready, prepare.

A تيّار *tayyār*, A wave, billow, surge. (A vein) pouring forth blood. Astonished. Puffed up with pride, disdainful.

P تيّاري *tayyārī*, Readiness, preparation.

A تيّاز *tayyāz*, Thick, short, compact. Strong. A dwarf. A sower.

A تياس *tiyās*, (v. n. 3 of تيس) Repelling. Managing. Assaulting one another.

A تيّاس *tayyās*, Keeper or trainer of he-goats.

A التيّاسان *at tayyāsāni*, Name of two stars.

A تياسر *tayāsur*, (v. n. 6 of يسر) Playing at dice, or drawing lots together. Dividing into portions the joints of a slaughtered camel. Being mutually easy (يسير *yasīr*). Going to the left (يسار *yasār*).

A تياقة *tiyākat*, (v. n. of تاق for توق) Desiring, favouring. Wishing, longing. Being anxious to accomplish. Being light. Compassionating.

A تيّاك *tayyāk*, (dim. of تاك *tāka*) The little she or that.

A تيأم *tayʼam*, A twin-brother.

A تيامن *tayāmun*, (v. n. 6 of يمن) Going to the right (يمين *yamīn*). Arriving in Yaman.

P تيان *tiyān*, A large cauldron.

A تيّان *tayyān*, A dealer in figs.

A تيّانك *tayyānika*, (dim. of تانك *tānika*) Those little two.

A تيّاه *tayyāh*, Proud, haughty. One who loses his way and wanders about.

A تياهير *tayāhīr*, (or تياهر) (pl. of تيهور *tayhūr*, q. v.).

P تيب *tīb*, Astonished, confounded. Hasty, impatient, restless. *Teb*, (for سيب *seb*) An apple.

P تيبا *tībā*, (in zand and Pāzand) A doe.

P تيباش *tibāsh*, Wink, amorous glance. Deceit.

P تيب وشيب *tīb u shīb*, Astonied, confounded.

A تيبيس *taybīs*, A drying, placing to dry.

A تيتاء *taytāʼ*, *tītāʼ*, or تئتاء *tiʼtāʼ*, One who experiences an effusion before coition.

P تيتال *tītāl*, Deceit, flattery.

P تيتالي *tītālī*, Deceitful, insincere.

P تي تي *tī tī*, Gingerbread-figures for the amusement of children. A bird's call. The wives of the kings of Gīlān. Quickly.

A تيتيم *taytīm*, A making of orphans.

A تيتين *taytīn*, (v. n. 2 of يتن) Bringing forth with the feet foremost (a female).

P تيج *tīj*, Raw silk. Picked cotton. The flue of cotton. An arrow. Twisted, squeezed.

A تيجان *tījān*, (pl. of تاج) Crowns, diadems.

A تيح *tayh*, A being pre-determined. Staggering.

A تيّحان *tayyahān* or *tayyihān*, Talking about what concerns him not. (A horse) going sideways with a sprightly air.

A تيخ *taykh*, A striking with a مِتّيخة *mittīkhat*.

P تيخ *tekh*, Any thing sharp, pointed.

A تيد *tayd*, Lenity, softness, gentleness. تيدك *taydaka*, Gently you! go softly!

P تيداكي *tīdākī*, Jewish, Hebrew.

A تيديع *taydīʻ*, A dyeing with saffron.

A تئر *tiʼar*, (pl. of تارة *tārat*) Times, turns, many times, frequently.

P تير *tīr*, An arrow. The river Tigris (from its rapidity). The planet Mercury. A bullet, musket-ball, cannon-ball. Lightning with loud thunder. Quicksilver. Splendour. Pomp, grandeur. The beam of a house in which the joists are fixed; also a perpendicular pillar rising from the main beam, which supports the roof. A scale-beam. A rolling-pin. A measuring yard. An oblique piece of wood with which they press the oil from olives. A machine with which they squeeze the cotton from the pods. A ploughshare. The mast or yard of a ship. Name of an angel, the guardian of cattle. Security. The choicest species of any genus. Power, strength. Thread. Hair. The spring, beginning of summer, fourth month of the Persian year when the sun is in Cancer, and thirteenth day of every month. Autumn. The blossoms and incipient fruit of the palm-tree. The narcissus. Hem or border of a shirt or other garment. Any kind of flounce tacked to robes, &c. Fine linen, cambric, lawn. A certain bird resembling a peahen. A storm, tempest. Anger. Lot, portion. A desert, plain. A sort of serpent. Rank, degree. Any thing equal to another in bulk or quality. Generosity. Politeness, humanity. Narrow, confined. Turbid, dark. تير افكندن *tīr afkandan*, To revile, to abuse. تير انداختن *tīr andākhtan*, To shoot with bow and arrow. تير بازوي چرخ *tīri bāzūyi charkh*, The planet Mercury. تير بدخشان *tīri badakhshān*, A two-headed arrow. An excellent arrow. تير بندوق *tīri bundūk*, A musket-ball. تير تتماج *tīri tutmāj*, A rolling-pin. تير تخش *tīri takhsh*, A meteor. A rocket. تير تظلم *tīri tazallum*, The groans of the oppressed. تير تيزپر *tīri tez-par*, A swift arrow. تير چرخ *tīri charkh*, A rocket or shell. The planet Mercury. تير خاكي *tīrikhākī*, A light, small-headed arrow. تير خانه *tīri khāna*, The main beam of a house.

سحر *tīri sahar*, Daybreak. A sigh. A curse, imprecation. تیر سقف *tīri sakf*, The main beam in the roof. تیر قرعة *tīri kurʻa*, Arrows for drawing lots. تیر فلك *tīri falak*, The planet Mercury. تیر کشتي *tīri kishtī*, The mast or rudder of a ship. تیر گردون *tīri gardūn*, The sun. Mercury. Providential dispensations. تیر محنت *tīri mihnat*, The arrow of affliction. تیر نان *tīri nān*, A baker's rolling-pin. تیر ناوك *tīri nāwuk*, An arrow discharged through a tube. تیر یکدست *tīri yakdast*, A handful of arrows thrown at once. تیر هوائي *tīri hawāʼī*, A rocket.

A تیر *tīr*, Pride, haughtiness. The main beam of a house. A desert, a wilderness. *Tiyur*, A bird resembling a peahen.

P تیراژه *tīrāja*, The rainbow.

P تیراست *tīrāst*, (in Pehlevi) Ten. One or three hundred.

P تیرانداز *tīr-andāz*, An archer.

P تیراندازي *tīr-andāzī*, Archery.

P تیراه *tīrāh*, Name of a certain bird with beautiful plumage.

A تیرب *tayrab*, (or تیراب) Earth, soil.

P تیرباران *tīr-bārān*, A shower of arrows. A punishment in which the culprit is shot with arrows. تیرباران سحر *tīr-bārāni sahar*, A sigh, groan. تیرباران کردن *tīr-bārān kardan*, To let fly a shower of arrows.

P تیربند *tīr-band*, A girdle with a pocket in it, worn by couriers, and with little bells hung to it.

P تیرپرتاب *tīr-partāb*, Bow-shot distance.

P تیرخورده *tīr-khwurda*, Hit by an arrow.

P تیردان *tīrdān*, A quiver.

P تیررس *tīr-ras*, Bow-shot distance.

P تیرست *tīrist*, Three hundred.

P تیرك *tīrak*, (dim. of تیر *tīr*) A small arrow. The bubbles of a boiling pot. Steam. A throbbing pain. تیرك زدن *tīrak zadan*, To cast up bubbles (a boiling pot).

P تیرکش *tīr-kash*, A quiver. An embrasure.

P تیرگان *tīrgān*, The 13th day of the month *Tīr*; also a festival which the ancient Persians used to observe on that day, in commemoration of peace established between Minuchihr and Afrāsyāb.

P تیرگر *tīrgar*, An arrow-maker.

P تیرگري *tīrgarī*, Arrow-making.

P تیرگي *tīragī*, Darkness, obscurity. Gloom.

P تیرم *tīram* or *tīrum*, A great lady, matron.

P تیرمار *tīr-mār*, A viper. Viper's teeth.

P تیرماه *tīr-māh*, The first summer-month.

P تیرماهي *tīr-māhī*, Summer. Autumnal. A sort of grape. A carrot. A kind of medicine.

P تیرنشانگي *tīr-nishāngī*, A place for military exercise.

P تیرنشانه *tīr-nishāna*, A butt for archers.

P تیروان *tīrwān*, (for تیردان *tīrdān*) A quiver.

P تیره *tīra*, Turbid, muddy. Obscure, dark. Sad, sorrowful. شب تیره *shabi tīra*, A dark night. تیره شدن *tīra shudan*, To be dark. To become muddy or turbid.

P تیره چهره *tīra-chihra*, Beclouded-countenanced.

P تیره خاکدان *tīra-khākdān*, The world.

P تیره دست *tīra-dast*, Black-handed. World.

P تیره دل *tīra-dil*, Ignorant, dark, stolid.

P تیره رنگ *tīra-rang*, Muddy-coloured. A bay horse.

P تیره روزگار *tīra-rozgār*, Unfortunate.

P تیره ضمیر *tīra-zamīr*, Cloudy-minded.

P تیره کامل *tīra-kāmil*, The moon.

P تیره گل *tīra-gil*, Muddy water: feculent, dreggy.

P تیره گون *tīra-gūn*, Muddy, turbid.

P تیره لگام *tīra-ligām*, A part of the bridle, the throat-piece. A ring suspended from a horse's neck (in Persia).

P تیريّ راست *tīriy-rāst*, A note in music.

P تیریز *terīz*, Gore of a shift. A bird's wing.

A تنز *tarīz*, Strong-nerved, brawny (ass).

A تیز *tayz*, (v. n. of تاز for تیز) Piercing and trembling in the mark (an arrow). Contending for victory or superiority.

P تیز *tez*, Sharp, cutting, acute, pointed. Bold, impetuous, vehement. Swift. Tart, acrid. تیز شدن *tez shudan*, To be sharp. To be stimulated. To be inflamed with rage. تیز کردن *tez kardan*, To sharpen, to give an edge. To animate to battle. تیز کردن دندان *tez kardani dandān*, To sharpen the teeth, to have a longing desire for. تیز گردیدن *tez gardīdan*, To fly in a rage. تیغ تیز *teghi tez*, A keen-edged sword. خنجر تیز *khanjari tez*, A sharp dagger. *Tīz*, A fart. تیز دادن *tīz dādan*, To let a fart. To express contempt for, to break wind at.

A تیّز *tiyazz*, Strongly planked.

P تیز آب *tez-āb*, Aquafortis.

A تیزان *tayazān*, (v. n. of تاز) Dying.

P تیزبال *tez-bāl*, Swift-winged.

P تیزبصر *tez-basar*, Sharp-sighted.

P تیزبین *tez-bīn*, Sharp-sighted.

P تیزبینائي *tez-bīnāʼī*, Sharp-sighted.

P تیزپا *tez-pā*, Swift-footed.

P تیزپر *tez-par*, Swift of wing.

P تیزپروازي *tez-parwāzī*, Swiftness of flight.

P تیزتاز *tez-tāz*, Swift (courser).

P تیزتاي *tez-tāy*, Keen edge (of a sword).

P تیزچشم *tez-chashm*, Quick-sighted.

P تیزچنگ *tez-chang*, Griping. Brave.

P تیزچنگي *tez-changī*, Tightness of grasp, sharpness of claw.

P تیزدست *tez-dast*, Clever-handed. Strong.

P تیزدستي *tez-dastī*, Manual dexterity.

P تیزدل *tez-dil*, Bold of heart.

P تیزرو *tez-rav*, Swift-paced, rapid.

P تیززبان *tez-zabān*, Glib-tongued, eloquent.

P تیزشهوت *tez-shahwat*, Hot, lascivious, lustful.

P تیزطبع *tez-tabʻ*, Of an acute genius.

P تیزطبیعت *tez-tabīʻat*, Impatient, choleric.

P تیزفهم *tez-fahm*, Of quick understanding.

P تیزك *tezak*, Somewhat sharp. Water-cresses. *Tīzak*, A contemptuous noise with the mouth. تیزك دادن *tīzak dādan*, To make such a noise.

P تیزکار *tez-kār*, Active. Immediately.

P تیزکام *tez-kām*, One who quickly obtains the object of desire.

P تیزگام *tez-gām*, Swift of foot. A fleet horse.

P تیزگردیدن *tez gardīdan*, To become angry.

P تیزمزاج *tez-mizāj*, Hot, choleric.

P تیزمغز *tez-maghz*, Hasty, touchy, peevish.

P تیزنا *tez-nā*, The prominent part of the edge of a sword, which does the work. A horse's gambrel.

P تیزناخن *tez-nākhun*, Sharp-clawed, rapacious.

P تیزناي *tez-nāy*, Edge of a sword or hatchet.

P تیزویر *tez-wīr*, Acute, quick ingenious.

P تیزهوش *tez-hosh*, Sharp, intelligent.

P تیزي *tezī*, Sharpness. Pungency. Ardour, impetuosity. Tip, point. Arabic. An Arabian steed. Ginger. تیزيء بیني *tezīʼi bīnī*, The tip of the nose. تیزيء دریافت *tezīʼi daryāft*, Sharpness of apprehension.

P تیزي باخرز *tezī bākharz*, A note in music.

P تیزیدن *tezīdan*, To make haste. To be angry. *Tīzīdan*, To break wind upwards or downwards.

P تیزي راست *tezī rāst*, Name of a musical mode.

P تیژ *tīj*, The green sward of a sown field. A declivity. Rumbling of the belly, breaking wind.

P تیژه *tīja*, A beam, joist. An exhalation (in Arabic called *sarāb*) made by the sun in the deserts, resembling a sea.

A تیس *tays*, (pl. تیوس *tuyūs*, اتیاس *atyās*, تیسة *tiyasat*, and متیوساء *matyūsāʼ*) A he-goat (especially one old and rank). *Tayas*, The characteristics of a he-goat (as horns). The resemblance of the female-goat to the male in that particular.

A تیساء *taysāʼ*, Long-horned (she-goat).

A تیسة *tiyasat*, (pl. of تیس *tays*) He-goats.

A تیسّر *tayassur*, (v. n. 5 of یسر) Being easy, happily despatched (business). Being prepared, arranged. Being chilly (the day).

A تیسور *taysūr*, The movement of the feet (of horses). حسن التیسور *hasanu't taysūr*, Moving well (the feet). Fat (beast).

A تیسوسیّة *taysūsīyat*, Goatishness. Unpleasant and offensive manners.

P تیسه *tīsa*, A certain bird like a pigeon.

A تیسيُ *tīsaʼ*, A particle of contempt, used when a thing is rejected as false or trifling. One whom every body reviles or makes game of.

A تیسي جعار *tīsī jaʻārī*, A particle of contempt, used when any thing is rejected as false or trifling. تیسي جعار *tīsī jaʻārin*, A hyena.

A تیسیّة *taysīyat*, Goatishness: offensiveness.

A تیسیر *taysīr*, (v. n. 2 of یسر) Rendering easy, facilitating. Favouring, assisting. Teeming, being prolific, and yielding much milk (flocks). Having flocks or herds which bring forth with ease. The movement of the feet of horses.

P تيشه *tīsha*, A hatchet, axe, adze. A mattock, pick. A halbert, battle-axe. تيشه برپاىٔ خود زدن *tīsha bar pāyi khwud zadan*, To mar one's own work. تيشه بسوي خود زدن *tīsha ba sūyi khwud zadan*, To grasp, to be greedy. تيشهٔ فرهاد تيز كردن *tīshayi farhād tez kardan*, To fall in love in earnest.

P تيشه كار *tīsha-kār*, A ditcher, delver.

A تيصيص *taysīs*, (v. n. 2 of يصّ not in use) Opening the eyes (a whelp). Putting forth herbage (ground), or flowers (a plant). Making an assault (upon people).

A تيضيض *tayzīz*, The peeping (of a whelp).

A تيع *tayaʿ*, (*tayaʿ* or تيعان *tayaʿān*) (v. n. of تيع for تاع) Issuing forth (vomit). Flowing, being fluid. Going away, making haste. Infesting the road, robbing. Taking. Dipping bread in butter.

A تيّع *tayyiʿ*, (or تيّعان *tayyaʿān*) Swift to do any thing bad.

A تيعة *tīʿat*, A herd or flock, of forty or under, out of which one is due for religious purposes.

A تيعيط *tayʿīt*, (v. n. 2 of يعط not in use) Crying, "the wolf." Giving warning of the approach of an enemy.

P تيغ *tegh*, A sword, cimeter, glaive, faulchion. A knife. A razor. A lancet. An awl. A ray of the sun. A moonbeam. Point of a spear. Peak of a mountain. Any thing erect and lofty. Ridge of a house. Bridge of the nose. Lightning. Brightness. Heat. Flame. Wavy appearance on a sword-blade. تيغ آبدار *teghi āb-dār*, A sword with a Damascus blade. تيغ آتشبار *teghi ātish-bār*, A flaming sword. تيغ آفتاب *teghi āftāb*, The sun's rays. تيغ افراسياب *teghi afrāsyāb*, The reflection of the sun's rays from a vessel of crystal. تيغ الماس گون *teghi almās-gūn*, A sword shining like a diamond. تيغ بيجاده گون *teghi bījāda-gūn*, Blood-stained sword. تيغ بي دريغ *teghi bī diregh*, A remorseless cimeter. تيغ خوشهٔ جو *teghi khoshayi jaw*, Beard or awn of an ear of barley. تيغ خورشيد *teghi khwurshed*, A sun-beam. Sunrise. تيغ دو دستي *teghi du dastī*, A two-handed sword. Giving or taking a large quantity. Hard fighting. تيغ زنان و جنگ كنان *tegh-zanān u jang-kunān*, Striking and fighting with swords. تيغ ستم *teghi sitam*, The sword of oppression. تيغ سحر *teghi sahar*, Break of day. Morning-prayer. A sigh of grief. تيغ شدن *tegh shudan*, To be opposite, or face to face. تيغ عثمانيان *teghi ʿusmāniyān*, The Ottoman sword. تيغ گوشتين *teghi goshtīn*, (Sword of flesh) The tongue. تيغ كوه *teghi koh*, The peak of a mountain. تيغ نطق *teghi nuth*, An eloquent tongue.

A تيغار *tīghār*, A water-pot. A wound discharging blood copiously.

P تيغ افروز *tegh-afroz*, Polishing swords. A sword-cutler.

P تيغال *tīghāl*, The lair of a wild beast. A nest. Honey-dew found on certain trees.

P تيغ بند *tegh-band*, (Sword-girding) Esquire.

P تيغ دار *tegh-dār*, A sword-bearer. Brilliant.

P تيغ زن *tegh-zan*, A swordsman. Name of the thirteenth day of the month according to the æra of Yazdajird. تيغ زن آسمان *tegh-zani āsmān*, Sunrise. The sun. The planet Mars.

P تيغ كش *tegh-kash*, A swordsman.

P تيغه *tegha*, Blade of a sword or knife.

P تيغه باز *tegha-bāz*, A sword-player.

P تيف *tīf*, Rubbish of sticks or thorns.

A تيفاق *tayfāk* or *tīfāk*, Opposite, over against. *Tīfāk*, A time when any thing happens or takes its date. A convenient season.

A تئِفّة *taʾiffat*, Time, season.

A تيفّع *tayaffuʿ*, The climbing (of a hill).

P تيف گنج *tīf ganj*, (or تيفاگنج *tīfāganj*) Name of a note in music.

A تئِق *taʾik*, Hasty, passionate (opposed to مئِق *maʾik*). Sharp, brisk. Malignant. Sprightly (horse).

A تيّقان *tayyikān*, Impetuous (man).

A تيقظ *tayakkuz*, (v. n. 5 of يقظ) Being excited, roused, awakened. Vigilance. Lucubration.

A تيقّن *tayakkun*, A knowing for certain, prying.

A تيقور *taykūr*, Modest, grave, prudent.

A تيقيظ *taykīz*, (v. n. 2 of يقظ) Rousing.

A تيك *tayk*, The being a fool. *Tīka*, (for تلك *tilka*, fem. of ذالك *zālika*) She. That. ها تيك *hā tīka*, There she is! behold her!

P تيكوز *tīkoz*, Sour milk dried.

P تيل *tīl*, A speck, spot, mole.

P تيلا *taylā*, A speckled beetle. *Tīlā*, A reel around which yarn is wound.

P تيلماچي *tīlmāchī*, An interpreter.

P تيليك *tīlīk*, A garment with short sleeves.

A تيم *taym*, (v. n. of تام for تيم) Enslaving (as love). A servant. Name of a tribe.

A تئم *tiʾm*, A twin-brother.

P تيم *tīm*, A large caravansera.

P تيما *tīmā*, A desert.

A تيماء *taymāʾ*, A desert, solitude, plain. Name of a place south of Syria. التيماء *at taymāʾ*, Gemini.

P تيماج *tīmāj*, Butt for arrows. Goat's leather.

P تيمار *tīmār*, Defence, custody, preservation, guardianship. Care, attendance on the sick. Sympathy. Thought, meditation. Consideration, attention. A military pension. تيمار كردن *tīmār kardan*, To curry or groom (a horse). تيمار داشتن *tīmār dāshtan*, To attend, manage.

P تيماردار *tīmār-dār*, A manager of property.

P تيمارداري *tīmār-dārī*, Attendance, care of.

P تيمارداشت *tīmār-dāsht*, Grooming of horses.

P تيماره *tīmāra*, Thought, care. Sympathy.

P تيماس *tīmās*, A grove, forest, wild, uncultivated country. A brake. A reed-bed.

P تيماو *tīmāv*, Stupidity. Stolidity, inactivity of the reasoning powers.

A تئِمة *tiʾmat*, (or تيمة *tīmat*) A sheep of a superior kind, never allowed to go with the rest, but milked at home, and only killed in scarce seasons. A sheep which makes a flock exceed the number of forty. An amulet worn by children.

P تيمچه *tīmcha*, A small caravansera.

P تيمز *taymuz*, (in the Tartar dialect) Iron.

P تيمسار *temsār*, Honour, worship, majesty.

A تيمّم *tayammum*, (v. n. 5 of يمّ) Intending, proposing, or searching for any thing. Purifying or rubbing the hands, face, and other parts of the body with sand or dust (agreeable to the Mussulmān law), where water cannot be got, before performing religious duties.

A تيمّن *tayammun*, (v. n. 5 of يمن) Considering as fortunate. Relating, belonging to Yaman or Arabia Felix. Invoking a blessing. Placing a corpse in a tomb on the right side. Success. Death. تبرّكا و تيمّنا *tabarrukan wa tayammunan*, In a happy hour, under the auspices of God and fortune.

P تيمناك *tīmnāk*, Condoling. Assisting.

A تيمني *taymanīy*, Southern Arabia Felix.

P تيمور *tīmūr*, A proper name. تيمورلنگ *tīmūr lang*, Tīmūr the lame, the famous Tamerlane.

P تيموز *taymūz*, (in Tartar) Iron.

P تيموك *tīmūk*, Austerity, sternness.

A تيميم *taymīm*, (v. n. 2 of يمّ) Intending. Picking out an individual with the intent of spearing him. Teaching another, or assisting a sick person to rub his hands or face with sand, by way of ablution before prayer.

A تيمين *taymīn*, (v. n. 2 of يمن) Arriving in Yaman (Arabia Felix). Taking any one to the right. Blessing another, praying for his prosperity.

P تين *tīn*, (in zand and Pāzand) A fig.

A تين *tīn*, A fig. تين احمر *tīni ahmar*, (or احمق *ahmak*) The wild fig.

P تينا *tīnā*, (in zand and Pāzand) Clay.

A تيناء *tīnāʾ*, (for سينا *sīnā*) Mount Sinai.

P تيناب *tīnāb*, (equiv. to بيناب) A vision.

A تينان *tīnān*, A wolf. Likeness.

A تينة *tīnat*, One fig. Podex.

P تينه *tīna*, Spittle.

P تيو *tev*, Strength, power. That is to say.

P تيواز *tīwāz*, Unjust, unlawful gain.

P تيواي *tīwāy*, A plunging inconsiderately into.

P تيور *tayūr*, A bird resembling a peahen.

P تيورك *tīvrak*, Envy, jealousy.

A تيوس *tuyūs*, (pl. of تيس *tays*) He-goats.

P تيوسول *tīvsūl*, Joy at another's misfortune.

A تيّوع *tayyūʿ*, Any plant yielding a hot, excoriating milky juice, as scammony, sea-lettuce, &c.

A تيويّ *tayvīy*, Ending in تاء *tāʾ* (verses).

A تيه *tayh* or *tīh*, A desert, a deserted country. *Tayh*, *tīh*, or (تيهان *tayahān*) (v. n. of تيه for تاه)

Being proud. Being lofty and overhanging (a palace). Straying, being lost. Wandering like a lunatic or bewildered person. *Tīh*, Pride, haughtiness, vain boasting. (pl. اتياه *atyāh* and اتاويه *atāwīh*) A desert, where people wander bewildered. التيه *at tīh*, The desert of the Israelites.

A تيهاء (ارض *arz*) *tayhā,*, A desert land.

A تيهان *tayhān*, One who wanders bewildered.

A تيّهان *tayya* or *tayyihān*, Proud, haughty.

P تيهو *tīhū*, A bird smaller than a partridge, a quail. A ditch, a hole full of stagnant water.

A تيهور *tayhūr*, (pl. تياهير *tayāhīr* and تياهر *tayāhir*) An extensive plain. A desert replete with danger. Hill and dale. A proud, bewildered man. A billow, surge. A sandbank eaten into by a river. Sand which has flown down. Low-lying ground.

A تيئم *tay,am*, A twin brother.

A تيييّة *tayyiyat*, A writing the letter ي *yā*.

ث

ث *sā*, called ثاي مثلثه *sā,i musallasa*, Trebly dotted, or ثاى تخذ *sā,i sakhiz*, The fourth letter of the Arabic alphabet (never used in words of Persian origin). In arithmetic it expresses 500. The legitimate power of this letter appears to be that of *th* in the English word *think;* but in the mouth of a Turk, Syrian, Egyptian, Persian, and native of Hindūstān, it is either pronounced like an س *s* lisped, or not to be distinguished from that character. In a few instances it is pronounced like *t*, as in the word ثمين *samīn*, (pronounced *tamīn* or *thamīn*) Precious, which might otherwise, in conversation, be confounded with سمين *samīn*, Fat.

A ثاء *sā,*, Name of the letter ث. The Persians call this letter *se*.

A ثآدة *sa,ādat*, Fatness, plumpness.

A ثآليل *sa,ālīl*, (pl. of ثؤلول *su,lūl*) Nipples, teats, dugs. Warts.

A ثاب *sāba*, (fut. يثوب *yasūbu*) He returned.

A ثأب *sa,b*, (v. n. of ثئب) Being negligent, lazy, slothful. Yawning, gaping. Being torpid, as one asleep. *Sa,ab*, A gaping. Name of a tree.

A ثابّة *sābbat*, (for شابّة) Any young female.

A ثابت *sābit*, Firm, fixed, stable, constant, immoveable, invariable. Proved, confirmed, certain. Of vigorous intellect. Rigid, stiff from disease. Steady-paced. غير ثابت *ghayr sābit*, Uncertain. P ثابت كردن *sābit kardan*, To confirm, establish, render durable. To prove (by witnesses).

A ثابتة *sābitat*, (fem.) Firm. A fixed star. بروج ثابته *burūji sābita*, The signs Taurus, Leo, Aquarius, and Scorpio.

A ثابت قدم *sābit-ḳadam*, Steady. Resolute.

A ثابت قدمى *sābit-ḳadamī*, Firmness.

A ثابق *sābiḳ*, Overflowing. Profusely liberal.

A ثأثأة *sa,sa,at*, (v. n. of ثأثأ Q) Satisfying (camels) with water. Preventing (them) from drinking. Drinking enough (camels). Thirsting. Driving away. Removing one from his place. Detaining, imprisoning. Resting quiet. Extinguishing (a fire). Calling (a he-goat).

A ثأج *sa,j*, The bleating (of sheep or goats).

A ثأد *sa,ad* (v. n. of ثئد) Being affected with cold. A shameful thing. Unripe dates softening. A soft plant, easy to eat. An inconvenient place. *Sa,ad* or *sa,d*, Dew. Cold. Earth.

A ثأداء *sa,dā,*, A servant-maid. A foolish girl. ابن ثأداء *ibn sa,dā,* or *sa,adā,*, Weak, impotent.

A ثأدة *sa,ūdat*, Fatness.

A ثأدة *sa,dat*, Fleshy (woman).

A ثادق *sādiḳ*, Flowing, fluent, fluid. Raining (cloud). Name of a horse.

A ثأر *sa,r*, (v. n. of ثأر) Taking revenge, retaliating, killing one for the murder of another. (pl. اثآر *as,ār*, آثار *āsār*, and ثؤور *su,ūr*) Blood for blood. A homicide for whose blood inquisition is made. Inquisition for blood. One who appeases the avenger of blood. لاثأرت فلانًا يداه *lā sa,arat fulānan yadāhu*, Both of so-and-so's hands were useless to him. P اخذ ثأر كردن *akhzi sa,r kardan*, To take revenge.

A ياثارات زيد *yā sārāti zayd*, O slayers of Zayd!

A ثارّة *sārrat*, A talkative woman.

A ثأط *sa,t*, (pl. of ثأطة *sa,tat*) Certain stinging insects. Black muds. *Sa,at*, (v. n. of ثئط) Stinking (meat). Being troubled with a rheum or cold.

A ثأطاء *sa,tā,*, (equivalent to ثأداء *sa,dā,*) A foolish girl. An epithet of a maid-servant.

A ثأطة *sa,tat*, (pl. ثأط *sa,t*) Thin black mud. A certain insect which stings severely. ثأطة مدّت بماء *sa,tat muddat bi mā,in*, Mud augmented by water (spoken of an excessively stupid fellow).

A ثاعة *sāʻat*, A vomiting. A vomit.

A ثاغي *sāghī*, One who abuses, reviles, or accuses of something bad.

A ثاغم *sāghim*, White, a whitish colour.

A ثاغي *sāghī*, Bleating, a bleater. ما في الدار ثاغ ولا راغ *mā fi'd dār sāghin wa lā rāghin*, There is nothing in the house, there is no bleating and no braying. ما له ثاغية ولا راغية *mā lahu sāghiyat wa lā rāghiyat*, He has neither sheep nor camel.

A ثافل *sāfil*, Sediment, that which subsides. Excrement, feculent matter.

SY ثافيسا *sāfīsā*, Gum of mountain-rue.

A ثاقب *sāḳib*, Whatever is burning. Glittering (star). The planet Saturn. Penetrating. A mendicant. (A camel) abounding in milk. بالفكر الثاقب *bi'l fikri's sāḳib*, Of penetrating judgment.

A ثاقل *sāḳil*, (pl. ثواقل *sawāḳil*) Heavy, of a proper weight (money). Overloaded (stomach). Weighed down with disease.

A ثاكل *sākil*, Deprived of a friend; bereaved.

A ثالبة الشوي *sālibatu'sh shawā'*, (fem.) Chapped in the feet.

A ثالث *sālis*, Third. An arbitrator, umpire. ثالث بالخير *sālis bi'l khayri*, An unprejudiced person. ثالث ثلاثة *sālisu salāsatin*, Third of three. قائل بثالث ثلاثة *ḳā,ilun bi sālisi salāsatin*, A Trinitarian. P ثالث كردن *sālis kardan*, To arbitrate.

A ثالثا *sālisan*, In the third place.

A ثالثة *sālisat*, (fem.) Third. An arbitress, mediatrix. A third; *i.e.* A sixtieth of a second of time.

P ثالث نامه *sālis-nāma*, A deed of award.

A ثالثون *sālisūna*, The thirtieth.

P ثالثي *sālisī*, Arbitration, mediation.

A ثالج *sālij*, Cold, frigid, gelid as snow.

G ثالسقيس *sālaskis*, Seed of wild rue.

A ثأللة *sa,lalat*, A being affected with warts.

A ثالوث *sālūs*, A Trinity in the Godhead.

A ثالي *sālī*, (for ثالث *sālis*) Third.

A ثامر *sāmir*, (A tree) bearing fruit. Pulse, pease. The flower of wild sorrel.

A ثامل *sāmil*, An old rusty sword. A delightful residence.

A ثامن *sāmin*, The eighth.

A ثامنا *sāminan*, In the eighth place, eighthly.

A ثاني *sānī*, Who or what turns or bends. Second. Double. ثاني الاثنين *sānī'l isnayni*, One of two. في ثاني يوم *fī sānī yawm*, On the second day, on the morrow. ثاني واحد *sānī wāhidin*, The second; making two. ثاني الحال *sānī'l hāl*, Henceforward; in future. ثاني عطف *sānī ʻitfin*, Turning the side, *i.e.* Proud.

A ثانيا *sāniyan*, Secondly, in the second place.

A ثانية *sāniyat*, (fem. of ثاني *sānī*) Second. A sheep whose neck is bent, though not from disease. (pl. ثواني *sawānī*) A second, the 60th part of a minute.

A ثأو *sa,w*, Thinness, weakness, imbecility.

A ثأوة *sa,wat*, A lean old sheep. A fold for cattle. A little, the remainder of a deal.

A ثاوي *sāwī*, One who alights at a place or who makes a long stay.

A ثاويّ *sāwiy*, Belonging to the letter ث *sā*. (A poem) the verses of which end in that letter.

A ثأهة *sa,hat*, The uvula. The gum.

A ثاهت *sāhat*, The throat. The wind-pipe. The pericardium.

A ثأي *sa,y*, (v. n. of ثأي) Being broken, burst (as stitching). *Sa,y* or *sa,a'*, Mischief, the perpetration of any thing bad. A killing, or wounding. *Sa,a'*, Scars of wounds.

A ثائب *sā,ib*, Wind blowing fresh before rain. (A sea) swelling and dashing upon the beach. Water which collects again in a place.

A ثاية *sāyat*, A fold for cattle. A heap of stones set up for way-marks.

A ثائجة *sā,ijat*, (pl. ثائجات *sā,ijāt* and ثوائج *sawā,ij*) Lowing (cattle), bleating (sheep).

A ثائر *sā,ir*, Anger, malevolence, vindictiveness. ثار ثائره *sāra sā,iruhu*, His anger was roused. One who rages for the revenge of a murdered friend. ثائر الرأس *sā-iru'r ra-s*, Having the hair full of dust.

A ثب *sib*, (in the Himyar dialect) Sit down.

A ثبّ *sabb*, (v. n. of ثبّ) Sitting firmly; being able to do (something). Being completed.

A ثبات *sabāt*, (v. n. of ثبت) Being firm. Permanency, durability, firmness, stability, fixity, immobility. Perseverance, constancy. Proof. P ثبات پاي كردن *sabāti pāy* (or قدم *kadam*) *kardan*, To keep one's footing, remain constant. ثبات ورزيدن *sabāt warzīdan*, To persevere. A *Sibāt*, (v. n. 3 of ثبت) Knowing certainly. A belt for fastening a camel's saddle or a woman's veil. *Subāt*, A disease disabling one from moving. (pl. of ثبة *subat*) Herds, flocks, troops.

A ثباتة *sabātat*, (v. n. of ثبت) Possessing strength of mind and prudence. Being vigorous, invincible.

A ثبار *sibār*, (v. n. 3 of ثبر) Persevering, being assiduous. هو علىٰ ثبار الامر *huwa ʿala' sibāri'l amr*, He is on the point of accomplishing the business.

A ثباط *sibāt*, Fools, drivellers. Languid.

A ثبان *sibān*, (v. n. of ثبن) Putting any thing in a packet, and carrying it before one. Gathering up in front the waistband of one's breeches. Folding and hemming a garment. A bag, basket, or skirts of garments in which they gather dates.

A ثبة *subat*, The middle of a pond or cistern. (pl. ثبات *subāt* and ثبون *subūn*) A herd, flock (especially scattered), a body of (of ten or eleven horsemen). A crowd, troop, body.

A ثبت *sabt*, Firm, resolute. A brave cavalier. ثبت الغدر *sabtu'l ghadar*, Perseveringly malignant. One who keeps not silence a moment in wrangling. P ثبت كردن *sabt kardan*, To fix. A *Sabat*, Stedfastness (in battle). Argument, proof. A trusty man.

A ثبثبة *sabsabat*, A sitting firmly.

A ثبج *sabaj*, (pl. اثباج *asbāj*) The middle. The greater part of (a heap of sand). The back between the shoulder-blades. The breast of the bird called قطا *katā*. Indistinctness in speaking or writing. A kind of bird. Name of a king of Yaman.

A ثبجاء *sabjā-*, Large-bellied (woman).

A ثبجارة *sibjārat*, A channel made by water running from a spout.

A ثبجة *sabajat*, Mean between good and bad.

A ثبر *sabr*, (v. n. of ثبر) Checking, restraining, prohibiting, driving away. Cursing. Receding. Ebbing (the sea. Disappointing, baulking. *Sabar*, (v. n. of ثبر) Opening itself (a wound).

A ثبرة *sabrat*, Plain, level, soft ground. Earth resembling quicklime. A furrow, trench, ditch. *Subrat*, A heap of corn on the threshing-floor unweighed and unmeasured.

A ثبط *sabt*, (v. n. of ثبط) Hindering (from business). Standing, stopping, pausing over (any thing). Swelling (the lip). *Sabat*, (v. n. of ثبط) Being languid, torpid. Swelling (the lip). *Sabit*, (pl. اثباط *asbāt* and ثباط *sibāt*) Foolish, stupid. Languid, torpid (man or horse). Weak.

A ثبق *sabk*, (v. n. of ثبق) Flowing quick (water, or tears). Being abundant (water in a river). Shedding tears fast (the eyes).

A ثبل *subl* and *sabal*, Remains at the bottom of a vase.

A ثبن *sabn*, (v. n. of ثبن) Putting any thing in a packet and carrying it before him. Folding up and hemming a garment. Gathering up in front the waistband of one's breeches. *Suban*, (pl. of ثبنة *subnat*) Bags or baskets for gathering dates.

A ثبنة *subnat*, (pl. ثبن *suban*) A bag, basket, or skirt of a garment, in which they gather dates.

A ثبوت *subūt*, (v. n. of ثبت) Being firm. Proving by evidence. Firmness. بعد الثبوت *baʿda's subūt*, After proof.

A ثبوتة *subūtat*, A being unshaken: firmness.

A ثبور *subūr*, (v. n. of ثبر) Ruining, destroying. Ruin, perdition. Alas! woe!

A ثبون *subūn*, (pl. of ثبة *subat*) Bodies (of men).

A ثبي *saby*, (v. n. of ثبي) Collecting.

A ثبيت *sabīt*, Fixed; brave (horseman).

A ثبيتة *subaytat*, A woman's name.

A ثبين *sabīn*, That part of a garment which being held up before is used in carrying dates, &c.

A ثتّ *satt*, A fissure in stone. See عذيوط.

A ثتم *satm*, (v. n. of ثتم) Bursting, marring (a seam or stitch). Casting forth what is in the belly.

A ثتن *satan*, (v. n. of ثتن) Stinking (meat). Being soft (gum). *Satin*, Soft (gum).

A ثتوت *sutūt*, (pl. of ثتّ) Fissures in land.

A ثتيٰ *sata'*, Date-skins. Refuse of rotten dates. Straw, or chaff, with which they stuff sacks.

A ثجّ *sajj*, (v. n. of ثجّ) Flowing plentifully. Pouring out. The flowing of the blood of a victim.

A ثجّاج *sajjāj*, Rain falling in torrents.

A ثجّة *sajjat*, (pl. ثجّات *sajjāt*) A pleasant garden or mead, with fish-ponds, &c.

A ثجر *sajr*, (v. n. of ثجر) Mixing ripe dates with the refuse of unripe ones. Pouring out (water). *Sajr* or *sajir*, Broad and thick. *Sujar*, Scattered multitudes. Arrows with large broad heads.

A ثجرة *sujrat*, The middle or broadest part of a valley or of a river. The throat, breast. A valley, hollow. Hair on a camel's upper lip. A detached group of plants. A scattered company. The part where the upper portion of the bowels is collected.

A ثجل *sajal*, (v. n. of ثجل) Having a flagging, loose belly, swelling round the hypochondria.

A ثجلاء *sajlā-*, (fem. of اثجل *asjal*) Large-bellied (woman). Capacious (wallet).

A ثجم *sajm*, (v. n. of ثجم) Raining heavily. *Sajm* or *sajam*, Hasty retreat or departure.

A ثجن *sajn* or *sajan*, A road over rough ground.

A ثجو *sajw*, A being silent, speechless.

A ثجوج *sujūj*, (v. n. of ثجّ) Flowing (water).

A ثجيج *sajīj*, (v. n. of ثجّ) Flowing (water). Water flowing (from a height).

A ثجيجة *sajījat*, Butter adhering to the churn.

A ثجير *sajīr*, Dregs subsiding or expressed.

A ثحثاح *sahsāh*, An expeditious nocturnal journey in search of water.

A ثحثحة *sahsahat*, A hoarse sound in the throat.

A ثحف *sihf* and *sahif*, (pl. اثحاف *as-hāf*) The tripe of cattle (where the dung collects).

A ثخانة *sakhānat*, A being hard and thick.

A ثخرط *sikhrit*, Name of a plant.

A ثخن *sikhan*, (v. n. of ثخن) Being hard and thick. The diameter of a planet's orbit.

A ثخونة *sukhūnat*, Hardness and thickness.

A ثخين *sakhīn*, Thick. Hard. Firm (in mind and judgment. ثخين السلاح *sakhīnu's silāh*, A heavy-armed man.

A ثدّاء *suddā-*, Name of a plant about whose root fungi grow.

A ثدام *sidām*, A strainer; any cloth (put over the mouth of a vessel for that purpose).

A ثدغ *sadgh*, A breaking (the head).

A ثدق *sadk*, (v. n. of ثدق) Flowing, falling in torrents (rain or a river). Sending (horsemen). Ripping up (a sheep's belly).

A ثدقم *sidkim*, A stammerer, a stutterer.

A ثدم *sadm*, A stammerer, a stutterer. Thick, fat. Dull, stupid.

A ثدن *sadan*, (v. n. of ثدن) Stinking (meat). Being fat and heavy-bodied. *Sadin*, Corpulent. Heavy. One who labours under any bodily defect.

A ثدي *sady* or *sidy*, (pl. اثدي *asdī*, ثديّ *sudīy* or *sidīy*) The breast (in man and woman). تجوع الحرّة و لا تأكل ثدييها *tajūʿu'l hurratu wa lā taʾkulu sadyayhā*, The woman of a generous spirit will famish, but will not eat her own breasts (will not condescend to suckle for hire). *Sada'*, (v. n. of ثدي) Having a large breast. Largeness of breasts.

A ثديّ *sudīy* or *sidīy*, (pl. of ثدي) Breasts.

A ثدياء *sadyā-*, Large-bosomed (woman).

A ثديّة *sudayyat*, A case in which a horseman carries gut and feathers (for mending his bow and arrows).

A ثرّ *sarr*, (v. n. of ثرّ) Separating, scattering, dispersing. Abounding in milk (cattle), in water (a spring). (A horse) going a great pace. Large, open. A wound pouring forth blood copiously. Talkative. A cloud charged with rain. (fem. ثرّة *sarrat*) (pl. ثرور *surūr* and ثرار *sirār*) Overflowing (fountain).

A ثراء *sarā-*, (v. n. of ثرا for ثرو) Becoming numerous (people), abundant (riches). Being superior in numbers (one tribe to another). Making numerous. Possessing much wealth. Being content, having enough. Rejoicing, being glad. Opulence, abundance.

A ثراب *sirāb*, Tails, or the fat thereof.

A ثرائم *sarātim*, Remains (of meat) in a dish.

A ثرار *sirār*, (pl. of ثرّ) Places abounding in water.

A ثرارة *sarārat*, (v. n. of ثرّ) Jetting out water (a fountain). Abounding in milk, and having a large orifice (cattle).

A ثرّارة *sarrārat*, An overflowing fountain.

A ثرب *sarb*, (v. n. of ثرب Blaming, reproaching loudly, upbraiding. Taking off (a sick person's) clothes. (pl. ثروب *surūb*, اثرب *asrub*, اثارب *asārib*, and ثربات *sarabāt*) The thin caul of fat covering the intestines of animals, the omentum. (pl. of ثربة *sarbat*) Tails, or the fat thereof.

A ثرباء *sarbās*, Fat (ewe).

A ثربات *sarabāt*, The fingers.

A ثربة *sarbat*, (pl. ثرب *sarb* and ثراب *sirāb*) A tail, or the fat of it.

A ثربي *sarbīy*, Pertaining to the omentum.

A ثرّة *sarrat*, (fem. of ثرّ) A woman who pours forth a torrent of words. (A camel or sheep) having a large orifice to her teat, and abounding in milk.

A ثرتم *surtum*, (pl. ثراتم *sarātim*) Remains of meat (in a dish).

A ثرثار *sarsār*, Talkative, chattering, blabbing, talker of nonsense, dotard. Name of a river in Mesopotamia, between Sinjār and Takrīt.

A ثرثارة *sarsārat*, An overflowing fountain. A talkative woman.

A ثرثرة *sarsarat*, (v. n. of ثرثر Q) Talking much and idly. Eating largely of a variety of meats. Scattering, dispersing.

A ثرثورة *sursūrat*, An overflowing fountain.

A ثرد *sard*, (v. n. of ثرد) Crumbling (bread). Bruising (the testicles) instead of castrating. Dipping (a garment) in dye. Slaughtering (cattle) without touching the jugular vein. Slight rain. Name of an herb. *Sarad*, A fissure, crack in the lips.

A ثردة *surdat*, Crumbled bread.

A ثرط *sarata*, (fut. يثرط *yasrutu* or *yasritu*) He rebuked. He despised.

A ثرط *sart*, Liquid dung (of a camel). Shoemaker's glue. Folly, stupidity.

A ثرطلة *sartalat*, (v. n. of ثرطل Q) Being loose, flagging. Drawing the train of one's garment along the ground.

A ثرطمة *sartamat*, (v. n. of ثرطم Q) Looking on the ground (without pride or anger). Being as fat as he will be (a wether).

A ثرطئة *sirtiʼat*, Heavy, short (man or woman).

A ثرع *sariʻa*, (fut. يثرع *yasraʻu*) He came uninvited to a feast.

A ثرعط *surʻut*, (or ثرعطط *suruʻtut*) Thin clay; also ثرعطة *surʻutat*, (ثرعطط *suruʻtut*, ثرعططة *suruʻtutat*, or ثرعطيطة *suraʻtītat*) Thin broth.

A ثرعلة *surʻulat*, Feathers in a cock's neck.

A ثرغ *sargh*, (v. n. of ثرغ) Having a large mouth (an urn). (pl. ثروغ *surūgh*) The interstice between the cross-bars at the mouth of a bucket.

A ثرغامة *sirghāmat*, A wife. A woman.

A ثرقبيّة *surkubīyat*, An Egyptian linen.

A ثرم *sarm*, (v. n. of ثرم) Striking any one on the mouth, so that the teeth fall out in consequence. Knocking out a tooth. *Saram*, (v. n. of ثرم) Having a tooth knocked out.

A ثرماء *sarmās*, Broken-toothed (woman).

A ثرمان *sarmān*, A shrub which camels like.

A ثرمدة *sarmadat*, (v. n. of ثرمد Q) Cooking (meat) carelessly, or not enough; soiling (it) with ashes. Name of a bitter plant.

A ثرمط *sirmit*, A large ewe, making a crashing noise whilst eating. *Suramit*, (or ثرمطة *surmutat*) Thin mud or clay.

A ثرمطة *sarmatat*, (v. n. of ثرمط Q) Abounding with soft and watery mud or clay (land). Eating with noise (a sheep).

A ثرمل *surmul*, Name of a certain animal. ام ثرمل *umm surmul*, The hyena.

A ثرملة *sarmalat*, (v. n. of ثرمل Q) Voiding excrement. Eating ill-dressed meat. Serving up hastily for a guest, victuals not sufficiently cooked, or dirtied with ashes. Eating in a slovenly manner, smearing the beard or fingers. Doing (any work) carelessly. *Surmulat*, A bitch-fox. A fox. The groove between the nose and mouth. The remains of any thing in a vessel.

A ثرن *sarn*, The injuring a companion.

A ثرنطى *saranta'*, Heavy-bodied (man). A great fool.

A ثرواء *sarwās*, (fem. of اثري *asra'*) Wealthy.

A ثروان *sarwān*, Opulent, rich, wealthy. Copious, plentiful. *Sarawāni*, (du. of ثري *sara'*) Land and flocks.

A ثروب *surūb*, (pl. of ثرب) Cauls of fat. Deaths.

A ثروة *sarwat*, A night on which the moon and Pleiades are in conjunction. Number, multitude.

A ثرودة *sarūdat*, Crumbled, grated, or sliced bread for putting amongst milk or broth.

A ثرور *sarūr*, (A camel) abounding in milk. *Surūr*, (v. n. of ثرّ) Jetting out water (a fountain), abounding in milk (cattle). Flowing fountains.

A ثرورة *surūrat*, (v. n. of ثرّ) Flowing. Pouring forth (as a fountain). Abounding in milk, and having a large orifice in the teat (cattle).

A ثروغ *surūgh*, (pl. of ثرغ *sargh*) The interstices between the cross-bars at the mouth of buckets.

A ثروي *sarwa'*, (fem. of ثروان *sarwān*) Opulent.

A ثري *sara'*, (v. n. of ثري) Being moist (the ground); from being dry and hard becoming soft. (pl. اثراء *asrās*) Moisture. Moist dust, not uniting. Dust, earth. Ashes of the grave. Sweat. Goods, riches. تحت الثري *tahta's sara'*, Under ground. *Sarī*, Content, rich enough.

A ثريّ *sarīy*, Rich. Much wealth. Moist.

A ثرياء *saryās*, Moist earth.

A ثريّا *surayya'*, (dim. of ثروي *sarwa'*) Rich in a moderate degree. A brilliant gem. The pleiades (the third lunar mansion). (met.) Well-set teeth. Name of a woman. Name of a well in Mecca, and of certain buildings in Baghdād. سدّة ثريّا مقام *suddaʼi surayya'-makām*, A throne exalted as the Pleiades. عاتق الثريّا *ʻātiku's surayya'*, The interscapulium of the Pleiades; معصم الثريّا *miʻsamu's surayya'*, The wrist of the Pleiades; منكب الثريّا *mankibu's surayya'*, The shoulder of the Pleiades: names of stars.

A ثرياطة *siryātat*, Mud, clay mixed with water.

A ثريان *saryān*, Wet, moist. *Sarayāni*, (dual) The hair of the pubes, and the fur of a garment. The moisture of rain, and the moisture already within the earth.

A ثريد *sarīd*, A pellicle floating on the surface of wine. *Sarīd*, (and ثريدة *sarīdat*) (pl. ثرائد *sarāʼid*) Crumbled, grated, or sliced bread for putting among milk, or broth, and under meat. P ثريد كردن *sarīd kardan*, To steep bread in wine.

A ثشّ *sashsh*, The squeezing of wind out of a leathern bottle.

A ثطّ *satt*, (v. n. of ثطّ) Being thin of hair (on the beard or eyebrows). Being heavy-bellied. Voiding thin dung. (pl. اثطاط *astāt*, ثطّ *sutt*, ثطّان *suttān*, ثطاط *sitāt*, and ثططة *sitatat*) Thin-bearded, or thin-eyebrowed. Heavy-bellied. Dung. ثطّ الحاجبين *sattu'l hājibayn*, Thin-eyebrowed. *Sutt*, (pl. of ثطّ *satt*) Thin-bearded.

A ثطّاء *sattās*, A woman having no hips (*i.e.* who cannot sit at home nor attend to work). A spider or other stinging insect.

A ثطأة *sutʼat*, A kind of insect.

A ثطاط *sitāt*, (pl. of ثطّ *satt*) Thin-bearded men.

A ثطاطة *satātat*, (v. n. of ثطّ) Having a thin beard. Being heavy-bellied.

A ثطاع *sutāʻ*, Rheum, catarrh, snivel.

A ثطاعيّ *sutāʻīy*, Troubled with a rheum.

A ثطّان *suttān*, (pl. of ثطّ) Thin-bearded (men).

A ثطط *satat*, (v. n. of ثطّ) Having a thin beard. Being heavy-bellied.

A ثططة *sitatat*, (pl. of ثطّ *satt*) Thin-bearded.

A ثطع *satʻ*, (v. n. of ثطع) Being polluted by the filth of the body. Appearing clear.

A ثطعمة *satʻamat*, Superiority to one's fellows (in speaking).

A ثطف *sataf*, Enjoyment of delicacies and luxuries of all kinds. A plentiful year. Affluence.

A ثطوطة *sutūtat*, (v. n. of ثطّ) Having a thin beard. Being heavy-bellied.

A ثطي *saty*, Madness. *Satī*, Foolish, insane. *Suta'*, Spiders.

A ثعّ *saʻʻa*, (fut. يثعّ *yasiʻʻu*) He vomited.

A ثعابيب *saʻābīb*, Pure flowing water. فوه يجري ثعابيب *fūhu yajrī saʻābīb*, His mouth runs with clear spittle in strings.

A ثعابين *saɛābīn*, (pl. of ثعبان *suɛbān*) Long bulky serpents. رئيس الثعابين *raɛīsu's saɛābīn*, The basilisk or cockatrice.

A ثعارير *saɛārīr*, A kind of asparagus. A fissure in the nose.

A ثعال *suɛāl*, A bitch-fox.

A ثعالب *saɛālib*, (pl. of ثعلب *saɛlab*) Foxes.

A ثعالة *suɛālat*, A bitch-fox. Nightshade. Dry grass, hay, forage. A name for a fox (as reynard).

A ثعالي *saɛāli*, (for ثعالب *saɛālib*) Foxes.

A ثعامة *suɛāmat*, A shameless adulteress.

A ثعب *saɛb*, (v. n. of ثعب) Setting a running. Shedding (blood or tears). (pl. ثعبان *suɛbān*) A channel through which water runs. *Saɛb* or *saɛab*, Flowing (water). *Suɛab*, (pl. of ثعبة *suɛbat* and *suɛabat*) Green-headed lizards.

A ثعبان *suɛbān*, (pl. ثعابين *saɛābīn*) A large male serpent, a dragon, or cockatrice. (pl. of ثعب *saɛb*) Channels (in a valley).

A ثعبة *suɛbat* or *suɛabat*, (pl. ثعب *suɛab*) A venomous lizard having a green head. A mouse. A dormouse. Name of a tree.

A ثعثع *saɛsaɛ*, A pearl or its shell. Scarlet wool. ثع ثع *suɛ suɛ*, A command to spread through the country in the cause of God.

A ثعثعة *saɛsaɛat*, Speech of a stammerer.

A ثعج *saɛaj*, A crowd of travellers.

A ثعجرة *saɛjarat*, A pouring out.

A ثعد *saɛd*, Sour moist dates. Soft (earth). Fresh (pot-herb). ثعد معد *saɛd maɛd*, Fresh and ripe (dates). لا ثعد له ولا معد *lā saɛda lahu wa lā maɛd*, He has neither little nor much.

A ثعر *saɛr*, *suɛr*, and *saɛar*, A deleterious juice, exuding from the root of the plant سمر *samur*. *Saɛar*, Many warts.

A ثعران *suɛrāni*, (and ثعروران *suɛrūrāni*) Two warts on a horse's sheath; and the udder of a ewe.

A ثعررة *saɛrarat*, (v. n. of ثعرر Q) Being cleft.

A ثعرور *suɛrūr*, A short man. A wart. The plant طرثوث *tursūs* and the point of it. The fruit of the herb ذؤنون *zuɛnūn*. The root of the sea-onion. A small cucumber.

A ثعط *saɛat*, (v. n. of ثعط) Stinking (meat or water). Falling in pieces (a rotten hide). Swelling and cracking (the lip). *Saɛit*, Corrupted, putrid (meat).

A ثعطة *saɛitat*, An addle egg.

A ثعل *suɛl* or *saɛal*, A superfluous tooth growing out before or behind another. *Suɛl*, *saɛl*, and *saɛal*, (pl. ثعول *suɛūl*) An excrescence on the udders of cattle resembling a dug. *Suɛl*, A kind of insect to be found in putrid leathern bottles. Ignoble, despicable. *Saɛal*, (v. n. of ثعل) Growing out before and behind the others (a tooth). Name of a certain family in the Arabian tribe of Tayy.

A ثعلاء *saɛlāɛ*, (fem. of اثعل *asɛal*) Superfluous-toothed, or irregular-toothed (gum).

A ثعلب *saɛlab*, (pl. ثعالب *saɛālib* or ثعالي *saɛāli*) A fox. The upper extremity of a spear-staff upon which the head is fixed. A gutter or sink in an area. The mouth of the aqueduct which feeds ponds or cisterns. The root of a palm-shoot. داء الثعلب *dāɛu's saɛlab*, Baldness (Alopetia). عنب الثعلب *ɛinabu's saɛlab*, Nightshade. ثعلب مصري *saɛlabi misrī*, Salep.

A ثعلبان *suɛlubān*, A dog-fox. ذو ثعلبان *zū suɛlubān*, A kind of disease.

A ثعلبة *saɛlabat*, A bitch-fox. Rump-bone. Buttocks. Name of a man; and tribe, and king.

A ثعلبيّة *saɛlabīyat*, A horse's pace resembling the trot of a dog.

A ثعلة *saɛlat*, A wart upon the udder.

A ثعلول *suɛlūl*, A superfluous tooth. Passionate, angry. A sheep (which may be milked from three or four dugs).

A ثعو *saɛw*, Soft, unripe dates.

A ثعوب *suɛūb*, Gall, bile, bitterness.

A ثعول *saɛūl*, (An army) encumbered (with baggage). (Cattle) having excrescences upon the udders resembling dugs. *Suɛūl* (pl. of ثعل *suɛl*) Excrescences on the udders of cattle.

A ثعيجر *suɛayjir*, (dim. of مثعنجر *musɛanjar*) The middle of the sea.

A ثعيط *saɛīt*, Moveable sands blown about.

A ثغ *sugh*, An idol.

A ثغاء *sughāɛ*, (v. n. of ثغا for ثغو) Bleating. The bleating of sheep, goats, or deer; the cries of animals in labour. The fissures in the lips of cows, sheep, or other animals which part the hoof.

A ثغاب *sighāb*, (pl. of ثغب *saghb*) Cold, limpid streams, flowing in deep and shady glens.

A ثغارير *saghārīr*, A small melon beautifully streaked with red and yellow. In Egypt and Syria, where it grows, it is used like a nosegay, on account of its beauty and fragrance. (pl. of ثغرور *sughrūr*) Warts, excrescences (on a horse's sheath).

A ثغام *saghām*, (pl. اثغماء *asghimāɛ*) A certain mountain-plant resembling the anise.

A ثغب *saghb*, (v. n. of ثغب) Digging. Piercing. Slaughtering. *Saghb* or *saghab*, (pl. ثغاب *sighāb*, اثغاب *asghāb*, ثغبان *sighbān* or *sughbān*) Pure cold water gliding in the bottom of a valley. *Saghab*, (v. n. of ثغب) Perishing. A reservoir of cool water in a shady part of a mountain. The melting of ice in the shady part of a mountain.

A ثغبان *sighbān* or *sughbān*, (pl. of ثغب *saghab*) Lakes of cold water in the shady parts of a mountain. Meltings of ice.

A ثغثاغ *saghsāgh* (or ثغثاغ الكلام *saghsāghu'l kalām*) A stammerer.

A ثغثغ *saghsagh*, A stammerer, a stutterer.

A ثغثغة *saghsaghat*, (v. n. of ثغثغ Q) Stammering. Trembling, chattering unintelligibly. The bite of an infant before it has got teeth. Incoherent speech. Search, scrutiny.

A ثغر *saghr*, (v. n. of ثغر) Notching. Being chipped (the edge of an earthen vessel). Being notched (a sword). Breaking (any one's front teeth). Closing (a chink or breach). *Saghar* or *saghr*, (pl. ثغور *sughūr*) The fore-teeth. The mouth. A set of teeth. A large opening, fissure, or gap in a mountain; a narrow pass between hills, bordering on a hostile country. A tree bearing white blossoms. The best grass. *Sughar*, (pl. of ثغرة *sughrat*) Throats. Fissures, chinks, gaps.

A ثغرب *sighrab*, Yellowish teeth: small teeth.

A ثغرة *sughrat*, (pl. ثغر *sughar*) The pit of the stomach or the throat (the place where they slaughter camels). A fissure, gap, opening. A tract of country. A plain, level way.

A ثغرور *sughrūr*, Confines of a hostile country.

A ثغم *saghim*, A hunting dog.

A ثغور *sughūr*, (pl. of ثغر *saghar*) Passes, straits, frontiers. Front teeth. Scattered, dispersed.

A ثغية *saghyat*, Hunger. Desert, empty place.

A ثفا *safaɛ*, A kind of wild cat.

A ثفّاء *suffāɛ*, Mustard. Mustard-seed. Nose-smart (a plant).

A ثفاجة مفاجة *safājat mafājat*, Very foolish.

A ثفاريق *safārīk*, (pl. of ثفروق *sufrūk*) Grape or date-stalks.

A ثفافيد *safāfīd*, Whitish clouds, the one overtopping another. Linings of garments. A kind of garment. Concealed things (as being the subordinates or linings to others).

A ثفال *safāl*, Slow-paced (camel). *Sifāl*, (v. n. 3 of ثفل) Sitting, conversing with. Whatever is placed under to receive the flour. A water-pot with a spout. *Sifāl* or *sufāl*, The lower mill-stone.

A ثفة *sifat*, A making a trivet for a kettle.

A ثفج *safj*, (v. n. of ثفج) Being foolish.

A ثفر *safr* or *sufr*, Vulva aut vagina feræ. *Safar* or *safr*, A horse's crupper.

A ثفرقة *safrakat*, The not turning sour (of milk).

A ثفروق *sufrūk*, (pl. ثفاريق *safārīk*) The stalk of a date, or the hollow place of the fruit to which it is joined.

A ثفل *safl*, (v. n. of ثفل) Scattering at once. Keeping a hand-mill off the ground by spreading something under it. *Sufl*, Dregs, sediment, caput mortuum. Corn. Pulse. Any thing spread under a hand-mill to receive the flour. *Safal*, Slow-paced (camel). *Safil*, One who eats corn, pulse, or sediment.

A ثفن *safn*, (v. n. of ثفن) Following, coming behind. Pushing, thrusting away. Striking with the callous parts (a camel). *Safan*, (v. n. of ثفن) Becoming hard (the hand). A soreness on a camel's knees and breast. *Sufun*, The sewed sides of a purse, scrip, or bag.

A ثفنة *sifnat*, The handle of a date-hamper.

Safinat, (pl. ثفن *sufun*) The callous part of a camel, upon which he reclines, viz. the breast, knees, and corresponding joints in the hind-legs. (Hence, the word ذو الثفنات *zū's safināt* is metaphorically applied to one whose breasts, hands, and knees are become callous, from his zealous mode of performing his prostrations at prayer). The groin of a camel. The joining of the thigh and leg in a horse. The lower hem or border of a robe. A number. A crowd. A camel striking with her knee whilst being milked.

A ثفوة *sufwat*, A saucer or small dish.

A ثفي *safy*, (v. n. of ثفي) Driving away.

A ثق *sik*, (imp. of وثق *wasaka*) Trust thou.

A ثقاب *sikāb*, Chips, straw, stubble, fuel.

A ثقابة *sakābat*, (v. n. of ثقب) Being very red. Yielding milk plentifully (a camel). Being kindled; burning (a fire). Glittering (a star). Being fragrant, pungent (an odour). Penetrating, obtaining, being generally received and observed (as an opinion, saying, or command).

A ثقات *sikāt*, (pl. of ثقة *sikat*, root وثق) Trusty friends. The companions (of Muhammad).

A ثقاف *sakāf*, (A woman) of an excellent genius. *Sikāf*, (v. n. 3 of ثقف) Disputing (for superiority of genius). Litigation. Fencing. (pl. ثقف *sukuf*) A wooden instrument for straightening spears. A figure in the geomancy or enchantment called الرمل *ar raml*, resembling ⚍.

A ثقافة *sakāfat*, A being quick, acute, intelligent.

A ثقال *sakāl*, Heavy. Grave. Large-hipped (woman). Quiet, modest, retiring. Slow (camel). *Sikāl*, (pl. of ثقيل *sakīl*) Heavy; grave. Morose, unamiable. Quiet. Slow, sluggish. Oppressed with indisposition, sleep, or guilt. *Sukāl*, Heavy. Men shunned by society.

A ثقالة *sakālat*, (v. n. of ثقل) Being heavy. Becoming weighed down. Being pregnant (a woman). Being slow, sluggish. Being dull of hearing (the ear). Being full of sap (the stalk of a thistle). P با ثقالت *bā sakālat*, Gravely. Morosely, unwillingly, importunately.

A ثقب *sakāba*, (fut. يثقب *yaskubu*) He bored.

A ثقب *sakb*, (v. n. of ثقب) Perforating. Flying high (a bird). (pl. اثقب *askub* and ثقوب *sukūb*) A hole, perforation. P ثقب كردن *sakb kardan*, To bore a hole. A *Sukub*, (pl. of ثقاب *sikāb*) Chips for fuel. *Sukab* or *sukb*, (pl. of ثقبة *sukbat*) Holes.

A ثقبة *sukbat*, A hole.

A ثقة *sikat*, (v. n. of وثق) Trusting, confiding, relying upon. Confidence. Trusty, worthy of confidence. A trusty friend, one to be relied on.

A ثقثقة *saksakat*, A talking folly.

A ثقف *sakf*, (v. n. of ثقف) Conquering (by address, ingenuity, or cunning). Finding, hitting upon, perceiving. Taking, receiving, getting possession of. *Sakf* or *sakaf*, (v. n. of ثقف) Being quick, acute, intelligent. *Sakf*, *sikf*, *sakif*, and *sakuf*, Intelligent, ingenious, acute, active.

A ثقفيّ *sakafīy*, Of the tribe of ثقيف *sakīf*.

A ثقل *sakl*, (v. n. of ثقل) Feeling the weight of (any thing) by holding it (in the hand). Preponderating. *Sikl*, (pl. اثقال *askāl*) A burden, load, weight. *Sukl*, (pl. of ثقيل *sakīl*) Heavy. *Sakal*, (v. n. of ثقل) Being weighed down by disease or sleep. (pl. اثقال *askāl*) Baggage for the road. Followers, family, domestics. Every thing of superior value and carefully preserved. الثقلان *as sakalāni*, Men and demons. The Kur'ān and the family of Muhammad. رسول الثقلين *rasūlu's sakalayni*, The prophet of men and demons (Muhammad). *Sikal*, (v. n. of ثقل) Being heavy. Weight. Gravity, heaviness.

A ثقلاء *sukalā*, Men shunned by society.

A ثقلة *saklat* or *sakalat*, Heaviness. Indigestion. *Saklat*, Languor, lassitude, torpor, dulness. *Sakilat*, *sikalat*, or *sakalat*, Baggage, luggage.

A ثقوب *sakūb*, (pl. ثقب *sukub*) Fuel. *Sukūb*, (v. n. of ثقب) Being kindled (a fire). Shining (a star). Diffusing itself (an aromatic smell). Prevailing, being observed (an aphorism or command). Abounding in milk (a camel). (pl. of ثقب *sakb*) Holes, perforations.

A ثقوة *sukwat*, (pl. ثقوات) An earthen dish.

A ثقيب *sakīb*, Milch (camel). Very red.

A ثقيف *sakīf*, Very sour. Acute, intelligent (man). Name of the father of a tribe. ابو ثقيف *abū sakīf*, (Father acid) Vinegar.

A ثقّيف *sikkīf*, Very acid. Intelligent, acute.

A ثقيل *sakīl*, Heavy. Indigestible. Morose, saturnine, phlegmatic. Lazy, dull, inactive. Oppressed with indigestion, sleep, disease, or guilt. قول ثقيل *kawli sakīl*, A hard saying. يوم ثقيل *yawmi sakīl*, A heavy day. The day of judgment.

A ثك *sakk*, A flowing (of water) on the ground.

A ثكثكة *saksakat*, (v. n. of ثكثك Q) Being foolish. Being of a bad disposition. A foolish woman.

A ثكل *sukl* or *sakal*, Bereavement. Death.

A ثكلان *saklān*, Bereaved, deprived.

A ثكلانة *saklānat*, Bereaved (woman).

A ثكلي *sakla'*, Bereaved (woman).

A ثكم *sakm*, (v. n. of ثكم) Following footsteps. *Sakm* or *sakam*, (v. n. of ثكم) Persisting, persevering. Stopping, remaining, dwelling. *Sakam*, A road-guide. The middle of the road or of a multitude. *Sukam*, A guide, conductor.

A ثكن *sakan*, The middle of a road. Name of a mountain. *Sukan*, (pl. of ثكنة *suknat*).

A ثكنة *suknat*, (pl. ثكن *sukan*) A flock of birds). A necklace of pearls or other gems. An ornament of coloured wool hung round a camel's neck. A tomb. A pit in which fire is lighted (for cooking). Any hole dug of a size just sufficient to hold what is put into it. Zeal in religion, true or erroneous. A place where soldiers rally round a standard; also where no standard is. A standard, an ensign.

A ثكول *sakūl*, Bereaved (mother). Trackless.

A ثلّ *sall*, (v. n. of ثلّ) Pouring (earth into a well). Fetching up mud out of a well. Pouring out (money). Moving (a heap of soil or sand). Breaking (a heap) on one side. Destroying. Pulling down (a house). Perishing. Subverting (a throne or tent). Ruining. Voiding excrement (a solid-hoofed animal).

A ثلاب *silāb*, (pl. of ثلب) Defects, blemishes.

A ثلاث *salās*, Three (females). *Silās*, The third. *Sulās*, Three and three; in threes. ذو ثلاث *zū sulāsin*, The rope with which they fasten the woman's litters on camels.

A ثلاثاء *sal* or *sulāsā*, Third day, Tuesday.

A ثلاثاوات *salāsāwāt*, (pl. of ثلاثاء) Tuesdays.

A ثلاثة *salāsat*, Three (males). ذو ثلاثة اركان *zū salāsat arkānin*, Firm. P ثلاثة غساله *salāsaï ghusāla*, Three cups of wine taken on an empty stomach, for purging out corrupt humours.

A ثلاث مائة *salāsu miatin*, Three hundred.

A ثلاثون *salāsūna*, (oblique ثلاثين) Thirty.

A ثلاثيّ *sulāsīy*, A three-letter Arabic root.

A ثلاثيّة *sulāsīyat*, The prince of princes, or lord of lords; (it implies the second man in the kingdom, next in dignity to the sovereign, as the vazīr, the governor of a province, and the like).

A ثلّاج *sallāj*, A seller of snow or ice.

A ثلاجيّ *sulājīy*, Bright as snow (blade).

A ثلال *salāl*, Destruction. *Silāl*, (pl. of ثلّة *sallat*) Flocks of sheep.

A ثلب *salb*, (v. n. of ثلب) Reproaching. Injuring. Repulsing. Overturning. Breaking, knapping. *Silb*, (pl. اثلاب *aslāb* and ثلبة *silabat*) A camel toothless and rat-tailed (from age). An old wolf. An old man. (pl. ثلاب *silāb*) A defect, blemish, vice. *Silb* or *salib*, A man reproached with vices. *Salab*, (v. n. of ثلب) Being wrinkled, puckered. Being dirty and filthy. Being notched, broken. A griping (of the belly). Filth. *Salib*, A spear broken at the extremity. *Sulub*, (pl. of ثلوب *salūb*) Those who reproach much with vices.

A ثلبة *silbat*, Toothless and rat-tailed (she-camel). *Silabat*, (pl. of ثلب *silb*) Worn-out camels. Old men.

A ثلّة *sallat*, (pl. ثلل *silal* and ثلال *silāl*) A large flock (of sheep, or mixed with goats). A notch, crack, or chink. Wool. Wool mixed with goats' or camels' hair. (pl. ثلل *sulal*) Mud thrown out of a well. Much money. A kind of tower affording shade in a desert. Watering places for camels at intervals of two days. *Sillat*, (pl. ثلل *silal*) Death, destruction. *Sullat*, A crowd of people. Much money.

A ثلث *sals*, (v. n. of ثلث) Taking a third. Becoming a third. Making the thirtieth. Tying three teats of a camel. Ploughing land thrice. Twisting a rope of three threads. *Sils*, The third day's watering (of a palm-tree). The third colt (of a camel). *Suls* or *sulus*, A third.

A ثلثال *salsāl*, A kind of salt, bitter plant.

A ثلثان *salisān* and *salasān*, Nightshade. *Sulusāni*, Two-thirds.

A ثلثل *sulsul*, Destruction, ruin.

A ثلثلان *sulsu* or *silsilān*, Nightshade. Dry hay.

A ثلثلة *salsalat*, (v. n. of ثلثل Q) Breaking down (a heap of sand) on one side.

A ثلثوث *salasūs*, (A camel) filling three pails with milk; having three dugs dried up and milked at the fourth, or which has a teat cut off and is milked by three.

A ثلثون *salāsūna*, (oblique ثلثين) Thirty.

A ثلثي *sulusī*, Name of a hand-writing, or engrossing used in diplomas or letters patent.

A ثلج *salj*, (v. n. of ثلج) Snowing. Rejoicing. Steeping in water. (pl. ثلوج *sulūj*) Snow. ماء ثلج *māʼun saljun*, Gelid water. P ثلج چيني *salji chīnī*, China-snow, a soft white stone used as a collyrium. A *Salaj*, A being cheerful and quiet. *Salij*, Cold.

A ثلجيّ *saljīy*, A vender of snow.

A ثلخ *salkh*, (v. n. of ثلخ) Scouring in the spring (an ox). *Salakh*, A being smeared, daubed over.

A ثلد *sald*, A voiding thin dung (by an elephant).

A ثلط *salt*, (v. n. of ثلط) Voiding liquid dung, scouring (a bull, camel, sheep, boy). Bedaubing, pelting with the same. Thin dung (of an elephant).

A ثلع *salɛ*, (or ثلغ) A breaking the head.

A ثلل *salal*, (v. n. of ثلّ) Perishing. Destroying. Destruction. A shedding of the teeth. *Silal*, (pl. of ثلّة *sallat*) Flocks of sheep. (pl. of ثلّة *sillat*) Deaths. *Sulal*, (pl. of ثلّة *sallat*) Particles of earth brought out of a well. Deaths.

A ثلم *salm*, (v. n. of ثلم) Breaking, notching, nicking the edge (of a sword or an earthen vessel. *Salam*, A breach (in the bank of a river). *Sulam*, (pl. of ثلمة *sulmat*) Notches (in a sword).

A ثلمة *sulmat*, (pl. ثلم *sulam*) A fissure, crack, breach, nick, notch, indent.

A ثلمط *salmat* (or ثلموط *sulmūt*) Thin mud.

A ثلمطة *salmatat*, A being loose and flaccid.

A ثلوب *salūb*, (pl. ثلب *sulub*) One who reproaches much with vices.

A ثلوث *salūs*, (A camel) filling three pails with milk; having three dugs dried up and milked at the fourth, or which has a teat cut off and is milked by three.

A ثلوج *sulūj*, (v. n. of ثلج) Being quiet, cheerful. (pl. of ثلج *salj*) Snows.

A ثلّي *sulla'*, Fallen greatness, departed glory.

A ثليب *salīb*, Forage. Dark-coloured hay, of two years old. A certain kind of plant.

A ثليث *salīs*, A third part.

A ثليّث *sulayyis*, A little trio.

A ثليل *salīl*, The noise of water poured out.

A ثمّ *samm*, (v. n. of ثمّ) Treading, trampling on. Adjusting, adapting. Restoring, repairing with ثمام *sumām*. Wiping (the hands) with the grass ثمام *sumām* or with earth. Tearing up grass by the root with her mouth (a sheep). Devouring voraciously (meat) of every sort and of all qualities. Collecting things of all kinds good or bad, heaping up and carrying off (herbage). Sweeping the house. *Summ*, Utensils, bottles, cups. *Samma*, In that place; there. من ثمّ *min samma*, Thenceforward. Therefore. Hence. *Summa*, (or ثمّت *summat*) And, then, therefore, after, since. ظهر الاوّل ثمّ الثاني *zahara'l awwalu summa's sānī*, The first appeared, and then the second.

A ثمأ *samaʼa*, (fut. يثمأ *yasmaʼu*) He fed with fat meat. He dipped (mushrooms) in sauce. He broke (the head). He crumbled (bread) small. He stained (with privet). He voided what was in the belly.

A ثماد *simād*. See ثمد *samd*.

A ثمار *samār*, Fruit. Various kinds of wealth. *Simār* or *samār*, (pl. of ثمر *samar*) Fruits, products.

A ثمال *simāl*, An assistant, one who manages the affairs or redresses the wrongs of his friend and family. *Sumāl*, Deadly poison. (pl. of ثمالة *sumālat*) Froths.

A ثمالة *sumālat*, The remains of any thing. (pl. ثمال *sumāl*) Froth.

A ثمام *sumām*, A kind of plant, used for the removal of a white speck from the eye, and for the covering of houses. علي طرف الثمام *ɛala' tarafi's sumām*, On the tip of the *sumām* (spoken of any thing within easy reach).

A ثمانون *samānūna*, (oblique ثمانين) Eighty.

A ثماني *samānī*, Eight (women). A sort of plant.

A ثمانية *samāniyat*, Eight (males).

A ثماني عشرة *samānī ɛashrata*, Eighteen.

A ثمانين *samānīna*, Eighty. The city of Noah.

A ثمانينيّ *samānīnīy*, Of the city of Samānīn.

A ثمائل *samāʼil*, (pl. of ثميلة *samīlat*) Grains. Fried barleys. Dates in baskets.

A ثمّة *sammat*, There. *Simmat*, An old man. *Summat*, A handful of grass.

A ثمثام *samsām*, One who breaks a thing whilst taking it up.

A ثمثم *samsam*, A hunting-dog.

A ثمثمة *samsamat*, (v. n. of ثمثم Q) Covering the head of any vessel. Being badly done (work). Bending, trembling, when striking (a sword). Staying behind. Hanging (a milk-bottle) to a post that the milk may drop out.

A ثمج *samj*, Mixture, confusion.

A ثمد *samd*, (v. n. of ثمد) Impoverishing (a man) by incessant begging. Draining (a man) by excessive venery (women). Waxing fat. *Samd* or *samad*, A small quantity of water cut off from every source (whence it could be increased); the remains of water in a bottle; water which appears in winter and disappears in summer.

A ثمر *samr*, (v. n. of ثمر) Bearing fruit (a tree). Gathering fruit for cattle. Growing rich. *Samar*, (pl. ثمار *simār*, *samār*, ثمر *sumur*, and اثمار *asmār*) Fruit. Profit, advantage. Various kinds of wealth. Gold. Silver. Knots at the ends of a lash. *Samir*, Great quantities of fruits or goods. *Sumur*, (pl. of ثمر *samar*) Riches.

A ثمراء *samrāʼ*, A tree. Fruit-bearing (tree). Fruitful (soil). (pl. of ثمرة *samarat*) Fruits.

A ثمرة *samarat*, One fruit. One fruit-tree. Profit, advantage. Recompense. Progeny, offspring. A knot at the extremity of a lash. The tip of the tongue. Sincerity, honesty in making a bargain. The skin of the head. *Samirat*, Sweetness. ما بنفسي لك ثمرة *mā bi nafsī laka samirat*, There is nothing in me agreeable to thee.

A ثمط *samt*, Thin mud, or very thin dough.

A ثمطلة *samtalat*, (v. n. of ثمطل Q) Becoming relaxed, flaccid, and pendulous.

A ثمعد *samɛad*, Beautiful of face.

A ثمغ *samgh*, (v. n. of ثمغ) Mixing white (silk) with black. Dyeing well, ingraining (cloth). Anointing (the head); tinging frequently (the head with privet), dipping the head among (it). Breaking (the head). Certain funds which the Khalīf Omar left in Madīna for pious uses.

A ثمغة *samghat*, The top of a mountain.

A ثمل *saml*, (v. n. of ثمل) Giving to eat and drink. Eating before drinking. Managing (people's) affairs. Redressing the wrongs of (one's people). A delay, a stay. *Saml* or *samal*, The conveniences and luxuries of life. *Suml*, A little intellect or prudence. *Samal*, (v. n. of ثمل) Getting drunk. Drunkenness. A staying, a commorancy. A shadow, shade. (pl. of ثملة *samalat*) Menstruous cloths. *Samil*, Drunk. Inclined to, in love with. *Sumal*, (pl. of ثملة *sumlat*) Grains. Fried barleys. Dates in baskets.

A ثملة *sumlat* or *samlat*, (pl. ثمل *sumal*) Grains. Fried barley. Dates, one half of which are in (the basket), and the other half above. A little water remaining at the bottom of a cistern or a vessel. *Sumlat*, A little intellect or prudence. *Sumlat* or *samalat*, Mud at the bottom of a well. A lock of wool made use of in anointing a camel (for the scab). *Samalat*, Water remaining at the bottom of a vessel. (pl. ثمل *samal*) A menstruous cloth. Dates remaining at the bottom of a basket.

A ثملطة *samlatat*, Laxity, flaccidity.

A ثمم *sumum*, (pl. of ثموم *samūm*) Sheep which tear up grass by the roots.

A ثمن *samn*, (v. n. of ثمن) Taking the eighth

part of a man's effects. Being the eighth person, or making up the number eight. *Simn*, The eighth day from a camel's drinking. An eight days' thirst of a camel. *Sumn* or *sumun*, (pl. اثمان *asmān*) An eighth. *Saman*, (pl. اثمان *asmān*, اثمن *asmun*, and اثمنة *asminat*) Price, value. ثمن قليل *samani kalīl*, A small price.

G ثمنش *samnush*, A shrub, briar, bramble.

A ثموت *samūt*. See عذيوط *ʿizyawt*.

A ثمود *samūd* or *sumūd*, The old Arabians, to whom they say the prophet صالح *sālih* was sent.

A ثمول *sumūl*, Stay.

A ثموم *samūm*, (pl. ثمم *sumum*) (A sheep) tearing up grass with her mouth.

A ثمير *samīr*, (or ثميرة *samīrat*) Butter swimming in the milk, or sticking to the sides of the churn. Butter-milk. ابن ثمير *ibn samīr*, A moonlight night.

A ثميرة *samīrat*, Fruitful (soil).

A ثميغة *samīghat*, Liquid food mixed with the fat of meat. Moist ground. A wound in the fleshy part of the head.

A ثميل *samīl*, A composition of cream or sour milk with bread. A place containing water. Waters remaining in cisterns.

A ثميلة *samīlat*, (pl. ثمائل *samāʾil*) Water remaining in a vessel. A residue, remainder. That part of the belly where the remains of meat and drink lodge. Dates, of which one-half are in the basket and the other half above. A grain or berry. Fried barley. A building wherein are beds, couches, and household furniture. A stone structure for holding water. Name of a bird.

A ثميمة *samīmat*, Covered (head of a vessel).

A ثمين *samīn*, (pl. اثمان *asmān*) Valuable, precious. An eighth part. درّ ثمين *durri samīn*, A precious pearl.

A ثُمَيِّنة *sumayyinat*, (dim. of ثمانية) Eight.

A ثمينية *sumayniyat*, (dim. of ثمانية) Eight.

A ثنّ *sinn*, Dry hay stacked. Blackish wood.

A ثناء *sanāʾ*, Salutation, congratulation; a wishing joy, a returning of thanks. Praise, eulogium. Blame, disparagement. P ثنا كردن *sanā kardan*, To congratulate, pray for. A *Sināʾ*, A fetter, cow-band for cattle. A rope made of goat's hair or wool. Melody, song. ثناء الدار *sināʾu'd dār*, The court or quadrangle of a house. (pl. of ثنيّ *saniy*) (Camels) shedding their front teeth. *Sunāʾ*, In twos; two and two.

A ثناء ثناء *sunāʾ sunāʾ*, Two and two.

P ثنا خوان *sanā-khwān*, (or ثنا كار *sanā-kār*) An orator, one who praises or pronounces eulogium.

P ثنا خواني *sanā-khwānī*, Returning of thanks.

P ثنا كاري *sanā-kārī*, An oration, prayer.

P ثناگري *sanāgarī*, Praise, eulogy.

P ثنا گوي *sanā-gūy*, Praising; an encomiast.

A ثنان *sinān*, Many and entangled plants.

A ثنايا *sanāya'*, (pl. of ثنيّة *saniyat*) The front-teeth. Arduous undertakings. طلّاع الثنايا *tallāʿu's sanāya'*, One who aspires to great things.

A ثناية *sināyat*, A rope of goat's hair or wool.

A ثنائيّ *sunāʾiy*, Biliteral (word).

A ثُنّة *sunnat*, (pl. ثنن *sunan*) The fetlock of a horse. The abdomen. Pubes.

A ثنت *sanat*, (v. n. of ثنت) Stinking (meat). Being flaccid and bloody (the lip). *Sanit*, Stinking (meat). Flaccid and bloody (lip).

A ثنتان *sintān*, (for اثنتان *isnatāni*, fem. of اثنان *isnāni*) Two.

A ثنتان ثنتان *sintāni sintāni*, Two and two.

A ثنتاية *sintāyat*, Obscene, ill-disposed, bad-tempered (man).

A ثنتل *santal*, A rotten egg. *Sintil*, Short.

A ثنتلة *santalat*, (v. n. of ثنتل Q) Becoming squalid after being neat. A rotten egg.

A ثنجارة *sinjārat*, A channel made by water.

A ثندؤة *sunduʾat*, (ثندوة *sunduwat* or *sanduwat*) The protuberance of flesh upon the chest of a man; also the nipple (in women called ثدي *sady*).

A ثنط *sant*, A fissure, chink.

A ثنطب *suntub*, A cage-maker's knife.

P ثنگ *sang*, Book of the impostor Mānī.

A ثنن *sunan*, (pl. of ثنّة *sunnat*) Long hairs on the fetlock of a horse.

A ثنوي *sanwa'*, An exception. The head and feet of a slaughtered camel.

A ثنويّ *sanawiy*, One who holds the doctrine of the two principles, one of the sect of the Magi.

A ثنويّة *sanawiyat*, The sect of the Magi (which asserts the doctrine of the two principles).

A ثني *sany*, (v. n. of ثني) Bending. Folding. Doubling. Repeating. Averting, turning aside. Becoming added, being second. Tying (a camel) with the rope عقال *ʿikāl*. Ploughing ground twice. *Siny*, (pl. اثناء *asnāʾ*) The coiling of a serpent or rope, the winding of a river. A plait, a fold. A bend in a sheep's neck, but not from disease. The second colt of a camel. A second child. A woman or camel bringing forth a second time. An hour (of the night). *Siny*, *suna'*, or *sina'*, (pl. ثنية *sinyat*) The lieutenant or substitute of a king; a chief magistrate. *Sina'*, Any thing doubled, any action repeated. لا ثني في الصدقة *lā sina' fi's sadakat*, Tithes are not to be demanded twice (in one year). (pl. اثناء *asnāʾ*) Monday, as the second day of the week. (A camel) having twice brought forth. Secondary, inferior to another in dignity or virtue.

A ثنيّ *saniy*, (pl. ثنيان *sunyān* and ثناء *sināʾ*) Shedding the first teeth (hence implying the time when it happens to different animals, as six years for a camel, 4 for a horse, and 3 for an ox or ram).

A ثنيا *sunya'*, An exception. The head and feet of a slaughtered camel.

A ثنيان *sunyān*, (pl. ثنية *sinyat*) Secondary, next in rank, or the substitute of a prince. The head of a family. Second in dignity, authority, or excellence. Deficient in understanding. Perverse (judgment). (pl. of ثنيّ *saniy*) (Camels) which shed their front teeth.

A ثنية *sinyat*, (pl. of ثنيان *sunyān*) Secondaries. The most despicable.

A ثنيّة *saniyat*, (fem. of ثنيّ *saniy*) (A she-camel) shedding the front teeth. (pl. ثنايا *sanāya'*) One of the four front teeth. The declivity of a mountain; also the road by it, or to the summit. A narrow pass. A mountain. An arduous, difficult undertaking. An exception, any thing excepted. A palm-tree not allowed to be sold. Witnesses for God, whom He bids the lightning spare. Praise, eulogium. Blame, disparagement.

A ثواء *sawāʾ*, A remaining, dwelling in a place.

A ثواب *sawāb*, Recompense, reward, premium. Punishment for evil. A good work (as worthy of reward). Honey. A bee. A crowd, multitude. Name of a man who, in discharge of a vow made by his wife, on his return from a military expedition, submitted to be led to Mecca with a ring through his nose: hence the adage, اطوع من ثواب *atwaʿ min sawāb*, More obedient than Sawāb.

A ثوّاب *sawwāb*, A vender of garments, a slop-seller. One who has charge of a bather's garments.

A ثوابة *sawābat*, A work.

A ثوابت *sawābit*, (pl. of ثابتة) Fixed stars.

A ثؤاج *suʾāj*, The bleat of a sheep or goat.

A ثوار *siwār*, A leaping, rushing upon.

A ثوّار *sawwār*, A herdsman.

A ثوّارة *sawwārat*, The fundament or intestines of a horse.

A ثؤاط *suʾāt*, Rheum, a cold.

A ثواقب *sawākib*, (pl. of ثاقبة *sākibat*) Bright, twinkling stars.

A ثواقل *sawākil*, (pl. of ثاقل *sākil*) (Monies) of good weight.

A ثوّالة *sawwālat*, A swarm of locusts.

A ثوالث *sawālis*, Of the third generation. The third scruple (amongst astronomers).

A ثوّام *sawwām*, A seller of garlic (ثوم *sūm*).

A ثواني *sawānī*, (pl. of ثانية *sāniyat*) Seconds.

A ثواثج *sawāʾij*, (pl. of ثائجة *sāʾijat*) Bleating (sheep), lowing (kine).

A ثوب *sawb*, (v. n. of ثاب for ثوب) Returning. Being or becoming filled (a well, vase, or cistern). (pl. اثوب *aswub*, اثؤب *asʾub*, اثواب *aswāb*, and ثياب *siyāb*) A robe, vest, garment. The heart. Works, actions. Clientage, protection. A work. ثوب الماء *sawbu'l māʾ*, The secundine; whatever comes along with the fœtus.

A ثؤوب *suʾub*, (v. n. of ثاب for ثوب) Returning. Assembling. Being filled, or nearly so (a well). Collecting after having flowed off (water).

A ثؤباء *suʾbāʾ*, Yawning. *Suʾabāʾ*, Lazy, torpid.

A ثوبان *sawabān*, A recovering (of health).

A ثوباه لله *li'llāh sawbāhu*, May God abundantly reward him!

A ثوة *sawwat* or *sūwat*, A low heap of stones or cairn in the desert to serve as a direction-post. *Sūwat*, (pl. ثوي *suwa'*) Household furniture. A piece of cloth put under the churning-bottle on the ground. A bit of cloth wrapped round the churn-stick to prevent it tearing the leathern churning-bottle.

A ثوج *sawj*, A kind of basket made of palm-leaves, for carrying earth and lime.

A ثوخ *sawkh*, (v. n. of ثاخ for ثوخ) Sinking into any thing soft (the finger).

A ثور *sawr*, (pl. اثوار *aswār*, ثيار *siyār*, ثورة *siwarat*, ثيرة *siyarat*, *sīrat*, and ثيران *sīrān*) A bull. Taurus, the Zodiacal sign. A prince, lord, master. The ruddiness of twilight. A whiteness at the root of the nails. (pl. اثوار *aswār* and ثورة *siwarat*) A large piece of the coagulated milk called اقط *akit*. Green scum upon standing water; weeds growing in pools; any thing floating on water. A fool. Frenzy, madness. A mountain near Mecca, in which is a cave, celebrated in the Kur'ān. Name of a man, the father of a tribe. عين الثور *ɛaynu's sawr*, The bull's eye (name of a very brilliant star). (v. n. of ثار for ثور) Being raised (dust), excited (tumult). Breaking out (pimples). Appearing (blood). Rushing, springing upon. Rising up from the dust (locusts or the bird قطا *hatā*).

A ثؤر *suɛur*, (pl. of ثأر *saɛr*) Homicides for whose blood inquisition is made.

A ثوران *sawarān*, (v. n. of ثار for ثور) Springing up, assaulting. Breaking out (pimples). Appearing (blood). Being raised (dust, or a tumult).

A ثورة *sawrat*, A great number of men. Much wealth. Vehemence of the passions. *Siwarat*, (pl. of ثور *sawr*) Bulls. Large pieces of coagulated milk.

A ثؤرة *suɛrat*, (v. n. of ثأر) Taking revenge, retaliating, killing one for the murder of another. Delighting in revenge. *Suɛrat* or *suɛurat*, A thirst for revenge or retaliation.

A ثؤرور *suɛrūr*, An assistant to a police-officer, a peon. An unpaid militia-man.

A ثوع *sawɛ*, (v. n. of ثاع for ثوع) Flowing (as water). *Suwaɛ*, A mountain-tree, always green, having a large trunk, and branches resembling the turpentine-tree, but useless.

A ثول *sawl*, (v. n. of ثال for ثول) Being foolish, displaying madness, shewing a want of firmness. Pouring out the contents of a vessel. A camel's pizzle or sheath. A male bee. A swarm or hive. A tree of a bitter salsuginous species. *Sawal* (v. n. of ثال for ثول) Having the staggers (a sheep). A torpor in the limbs of a sheep; also a vertigo or staggers to which they, as well as goats, are sometimes subject, making them to fly from the flock. *Sūl*, (pl. of اثول *aswal*) Sheep or goats affected by a vertigo. Foolish, insane. Lazy, slow.

A ثولاء *sawlāɛ*, (fem. of اثول *aswal*) A ewe or she-goat distempered as above. Mad. Lazy.

A ثؤلول *suɛlūl*, (pl. ثآليل) A nipple. A wart.

A ثوم *sūm*, Garlic. ثوم الحية *sūmu'l hayyat*, Mountain-garlic (because spotted like a serpent).

L ثومالا *sūmālā*, (Thymelæa) Spurge-laurel.

A ثومة *sūmat*, A single clove of garlic. The pomel of a sword. *Siwamat*, Name of a tree, bearing no fruit, and more fragrant than myrtle.

A ثومتين *sawmatīn*, Spleenwort.

G ثومس *sūmus*, Thyme.

A ثؤوب *suɛūb*, (v. n. of ثاب for ثوب) Returning. Being, becoming full (well, vase, cistern).

A ثوور *suwūr*, (or ثؤور *suɛūr*) (v. n. of ثار for ثور) Being raised, flying (dust). Being excited (a tumult). Springing up in a rage to assail (a man); attacking. Breaking out (small-pox or other eruptions). Appearing (blood). Coming out, shaking themselves from the dust (locusts).

A ثؤورة *suɛūrat*, Hatred, desire of retaliation.

A ثوهد *sawhad*, A plump, jolly boy.

A ثوي *suwa'*, (pl. of ثوة) Household utensils.

A ثوي *sawīy*, (pl. اثوياء *aswiyāɛ*) A guest, stranger. A captive. A house prepared for a stranger. *Suwīy*, (v. n. of ثوي) Abiding a long time at a place. Alighting. Dying. Being interred. A piece of cloth wrapt round the churn-stick, to prevent it tearing the leathern churning bottle.

A ثويب *suwayb*, A work.

A ثويبة *suwaybat*, Name of the foster-mother of Muhammad.

A ثوية *sawīyat*, A place, a spot. A heap of stones, about the size of a man seated, raised as a sign-post in the desert. A woman. A sheep-cote, fold.

A ثويلة *sawīlat*, A heap of herbs. A miscellaneous assembly of men. A multitude of scattered houses.

A ثوينا *suwayna'*, Flour which the baker sprinkles under his leaven.

A ثهات *sahāt*, (v. n. of ثهت) Vociferating.

A ثهت *suhat*, Vociferation, making a noise.

A ثهثهة *sahsahat*, The melting (of snow).

A ثهل *sahal*, A being spread on the ground.

A ثهلل (ضلال بن *zalālu'bnu*) *sahlala*, *suhlala*, or *suhlula*, A lying, trifling, idle fellow.

A ثهمد *sahmad*, A large, fat woman.

A ثهود *sahwad*, A plump boy near puberty.

A ثياب *siyāb*, (pl. of ثوب *sawb*) Garments, robes, vestments, clothes, dresses.

A ثيابي *siyābīy*, One who takes care of (the) clothes (of the bathers in a bagnio).

A ثيار *siyār*, (pl. of ثور *sawr*) Bulls.

A ثيب *sayyib*, A woman who departs from her husband after having but once conversed with him. (The term is also applied to a man by way of reproach). A man and woman come together for the first time, depucelated. ولد الثيبين *waladu's sayyibayni*, A son born under such circumstances.

A ثية *sīyat*, A sheep-cote.

A ثيتل *saytal*, An aged he-mountain-goat. A mountain-ox, or the species. A fat, jolly man, supposed to have some good about him. Impotent.

A ثيخ *saykh*, (v. n. of ثاخ for ثيخ) Sinking into any soft substance (the finger).

A ثئد *saɛid*, Moist (place). Affected by cold.

A ثئدة *saɛidat*, Full and fleshy (thigh).

A ثير *sīr*, A coating of the eye.

A ثيران *sīrān* or ثيرة *sīrat*, (pl. of ثور) Bulls.

A ثيل *sīl*, (pl. of اثيل *asyal*) Large-sheathed (animals). *Sīl* or *sayl*, The sheath or penis of an animal. *Sīl*, (or ثيل *sayyil*) A certain plant. A kind of artichoke.

A ثيموم *saymūm*, An herb resembling wheat.

A ثين *sīn*, The place in the sea where they fish for pearls. The instruments with which, or the place where, they pierce them.

A ثيوبة *suyūbat*, Widowhood.

ج

ج *jīm*, called جيم ابجد *jīmi abjad*, جيم عربي *jīmi ɛarabī*, or جيم تازي *jīmi tāzī*, The sixth letter of the Persian and Arabic alphabets; and the character for three in arithmetic. It represents Tuesday and Cancer in astronomical books, and is also the contraction of the sixth lunar month, called جمادي الآخر *jamādi'l ākhir*. This letter is sometimes interchangeable with ت *te*, چ *che*, ز *zayn*, ژ *je*, ش *shīn*, گاف *gāf*, and ي *ye*; and has the power that is given by us to the letter *j* in *James*.

P جا *jā*, A place. Stead, room. جا گرفتن *jā giriftan*, To take hold, find a place. بجاي فلان *ba jāyi fulān*, In lieu of such a one. جا بجا *jā ba jā*, From place to place. Here and there. Scatteredly. بجا آمدن *ba jā āmadan*, To come to its place, to come to pass. To return to its former state.

A جئاء *jiɛāɛ*, (or جئاءة *jiɛāɛat*) A cover (of leather or wicker work) for a kettle.

A جاء *jāɛa* (fut. يجيء *yajiɛu*) He came. جاء بالاولاد *jāɛa bi awlād*, He came by, he begat children.

A جأجاء *jaɛjāɛ*, Coming, approaching, on the way.

A جأب *jaɛb*, (v. n. of جأب) Acquiring wealth. Selling red earth or clay. (pl. جؤوب *juɛūb*) A strong ass, wild or tame. Red clay or earth. The navel. Thick, robust. جأب الصبر *jaɛbu's sabr*, Hardy, patient.

A جأبة *jaɛbat*, (fem.) Thick, strong. Fierce. The hypochondria or short ribs. جأبة المدري *jaɛbatu'l midra'*, or جابة المدري *jābatu'l midra'*, A doe whose horns begin to shoot forth (which are then thick). جأبة البطن *jaɛbatu'l batn*, The abdomen.

A جابة *jābat*, An answer. Obedience. Power.

A جابذ *jābiz*, Drawing, attracting.

A جابر *jābir*, A setter of broken bones; a repairer of any thing broken. A proper name. ابو جابر *abū jābir*, (or جابر بن حبّة *jābiru'bn habbat*) Bread (as the staff of life).

A جابرة *jābirat*, The city of Madīna.

A جائزة *jaʼzazat*, (v. n. of جأز Q) Fleeing away. Study, effort, exertion. Flight.

A جابزة *jābizat*, Flight. Endeavour, purpose.

P جابق *jābak*, The lash of a whip.

P جابلسا *jābulsā*, (A جابلص *jābalas*) The west. Name of a city in the west, beyond which there is no habitation.

P جابلقا *jābulkā*, (or جابلق *jābalak*, The east. Name of another city, the limits of the world towards the east. (These are only to be met with in fabulous authors.)

P جابلوس *jāblūs*, Flatterer, coaxer, wheedler. جابلوس كردن *jāblūs kardan*, To flatter, to fawn.

P جابلوسي *jāblūsī*, Flattery, adulation.

A جابه *jābih*, (Any bird or beast) which meets one, and whose encounter is considered ominous.

A جابي *jābī*, (for جابئ *jābiʼ*) A locust.

A جابي *jābī*, Revenue-collector, tithe-gatherer.

A جابية *jābiyat*, (pl. جوابي *jawābī*) A large stone reservoir for watering camels. A crowd. Name of a village in the vicinity of Damascus.

P جابيدن *jābidan*, To be lazy, cowardly, frightened. To be loth, unwilling. To be vexed, to repent. To be broken.

P جاپوربا *jāpūrbā*, A city in Turkistān.

P جاپوز *jāpūz*, Name of a city in Turkistān.

H جات *jāt*, Name of a Hindū tribe.

P جاتاغ *jātāgh*, Bit of wood on a tent-pole.

P جاتن *jātan*, (in zand and Pāzand) God.

P جاتونتن *jātūnitan*, (in zand and Pāz.) To come.

A جأث *jaʼs*, (v. n. of جأث) Being heavily laden, or travelling as if overloaded (a camel). Relating news. *Jaʼas*, (v. n. of جئث) Being slow in rising or carrying a burden.

A جأّث *jaʼʼās*, Bad-tempered.

P جاثليق *jāsalīk*, A prelate, doctor, or Christian priest, in Muhammadan countries. The chief is the بطريق *bitrīk*, in Antioch. Below him the جاثليق *jāsalīk*; next to him the مطران *matrān*; then the اسقف *uskuff*; afterwards the قسّيس *hissīs*; and last, the شمّاس *shammās*.

A جاثم *jāsim*, Unconscious and motionless. Seated, squatting.

A جاثوم *jāsūm*, The nightmare. A sleeper, one who indulges in bed, and sets not out with his fellow-travellers.

A جاثي *jāsī*, (pl. جثيّ *jusiy* or *jisiy*) A kneeler. جاثي علي ركبتيه *jāsī ʻala' rukbatayhi*, Kneeling on both his knees.

A جاثية *jāsiyat*, A chapter in the Kur'ān.

A جأجاء *jaʼjāʼ*, Rout, flight, dispersion.

A جاجة *jājat*, A glass bead, a small necklace.

P جاجرم *jājarm*, Name of a city.

P جاجرمينه *jājarmīna*, Name of a fountain which dries at sunrise and is replenished at sunset.

P جاجم *jājim*, A fine bedding or carpet.

A جآجئ *jaʼājiʼ*, (pl. of جؤجؤ *juʼjuʼ*) Breasts. Ships' bows.

A جاح *jāh*, A veil, a covering.

A جاحد *jāhid*, Any one denying or obstinately resisting. A denier, opponent.

A جاحر *jāhir*, Left behind, unable to overtake.

A جاحظ *jāhiz*, (pl. جحّظ *juhhaz*) One who has prominent eyes. Prominent (eye).

A جاحظتان *jāhizatāni*, Pupils of the eyes.

A جاحم *jāhim*, Hottest part of a battle. Staring (man). A very hot place. Glowing (coal). Death.

A جاحمة *jāhimat*, Fixed, staring (eye).

A جاحي *jāhī*, Clever. Able at prayer.

A جاخر *jākhir*, A wide valley.

P جاخسوك *jākhsūk*, A sickle.

A جاد *jāda*, (fut. يجود *yajūdu*) He was liberal.

A جاد *jād*, (or ابو جاد *abū jād*) Vain.

A جاد *jādin*, (with tanwīn, for جادي *jādī*) One who asks or begs as a gift.

A جادّ *jādd*, Diligent, industrious, laborious, striving. Serious, in earnest. Rapid (nocturnal journey in search of water).

P جاداد *jā-dād*, Place, employment. Assets.

P جا دادن *jā dādan*, To give an appointment. To protect.

A جادب *jādib*, False. A liar. A railer, accuser.

A جادّة *jāddat*, (usually pronounced as if written جاده *jāda*) (pl. جوادّ *jawādd*) A highway, a straight or beaten path. The middle of the road. جادۀ عدل *jādaʼi ʻadl*, The due administration of justice.

A جادس *jādis*, Obliterated (trace). Untilled land. Any thing firm and hard.

A جادسة *jādisat*, (pl. جوادس *jawādis*) Unploughed, uncultivated land.

A جادف *jādif*, (pl. جوادف *jawādif*) A wild buck which takes short steps.

A جادل *jādil*, A wrangler. Robust (youth) arrived at puberty. A camel's colt able to follow the dam.

P جادنگو *jādango*, (or جادنگوي *jādangoy*) (in old Persian) One who embezzles property entrusted to him for pious uses.

P جادو *jādū*, Juggling, conjuration, magic. The eye of a mistress. Black. جادو كردن *jādū kardan*, To bewitch. زلف جادو *zulfi jādū*, Black hair.

P جادو خيالي *jādū-khayālī*, Spectre, illusion.

P جادو سخن *jādū-sukhan*, A poet. Eloquence.

P جادو كنا *jādū-kunā*, A practiser of magic.

P جادوگر *jādūgar*, A juggler, conjurer.

P جادوگري *jādūgarī*, Magic, conjuration.

P جادوئي *jādūʼī*, Necromancy, witchcraft.

A جادي *jādī*, (pl. جداة *judāt*) One who begs as a gift. Saffron. Wine.

A جادياء *jādiyāʼ*, Saffron.

A جأذ *jaʼz*, A drinking, swilling, guzzling.

A جاذب *jāzib*, A puller, plucker. Drawing (plaster). Alluring; attractive. An allurer. (pl. جواذب *jawāzib*) A camel giving little milk.

A جاذبة *jāzibat*, Attractive. A camel giving little milk. Attraction, charm, allurement; grace, beauty, loveliness.

A جآذر *jaʼāzir*, (pl. of جؤذر) Wild calves.

A جاذل *jāzil*, (pl. جذلان *juzlān*) What stands erect and firm (an elevated place or thing). (poetically) Cheerful. (A leathern bottle) which turns the flavour of milk.

P جاذو *jāzū*, A wizard, necromancer.

A جاذي *jāzī*, (pl. جذاء *jizāʼ*) One who stands on tiptoe. Short in the arm.

A جاذية *jāziyat*, (fem. of جاذي *jāzī*) Standing on tiptoe. Short-armed. (Sheep) giving little milk soon after the birth.

A جأر *jaʼr*, (v. n. of جأر) Lowing (an ox). Groaning in prayer. Asking with a loud voice. Being long (grass). Producing such herbage. Copious rain. Luxuriant herbage. A corpulent man. *Jaʼar*, (v. n. of جئر) Suffering a choking sensation in the chest.

A جار *jāra*, (fut. يجور *yajūru*) He was unjust.

A جار *jār*, (pl. جيران *jīrān*, جيرة *jīrat*, and اجوار *ajwār*) Neighbouring. A neighbour. A near or adjacent inn or halting-place. One who implores protection, a refugee. One taken under protection from oppression. A partner in trade. Bound by oath. An assistant. One who protects against oppression. A husband. (The) nakedness (of a wife). The arse. جار الجنب *jāru'l junub*, Neighbours. جار النهر *jāru'n nahr*, Name of a water-plant. P جار با وفا *jāri bā wafā*, A faithful friend.

A جأّر *jaʼʼār*, A corpulent man.

A جارّ *jārr*, Who or what draws, drags, or attracts. حرف جارّ *harfi jārr*, A particle which gives (to a noun) a termination in *kasra*. سيل جارّ الضبع *saylun jārru'z zabuʻa*, A swollen torrent that draws a hyena (from his den).

A جارات *jārāt*, Female neighbours.

A جارة *jārat*, A wife. A female neighbour. The arse. Tyrants, oppressors, unrighteous judges. (for اجارة *ijārat*) (v. n. 4 of جار for جور) Protecting, shielding from oppression. See بنانج *banānj*.

A جارّة *jārrat*, Camels led by the halter. The way leading to the watering place.

A جارح *jārih*, Who or what wounds.

A جارحة *jārihat*, (pl. جوارح *jawārih*) A rapacious animal. A member of the body.

A جارز *jāriz*, One who coughs violently. A barren woman. A severe cough.

A جارزة *jārizat*, (pl. جوارز *jawāriz*) Hard, dry ground surrounded by sand. Level ground.

A جارش *jārish*, (pl. جرّاش) A sinner, criminal

A جارف *jārif*, A destructive murrain, a general mortality. A certain grievous pestilence which raged in the time of Ibn Zabīr. A scavenger. Trouble, calamity.

P جارگون *jārgūn*, Envelope of nutmeg, mace.

A جارم *jārim*, (pl. جرّم *jurram* or جرّام *jurrām*) One who gathers in the produce of the palm-tree. Delinquent. بنو جارم *banū jārim*, Name of a tribe.

A جارن *jārin*, A serpent's brood. An old obliterated path. Clothes old and threadbare.

P جاروب *jā-rob*, A besom, broom, brush. A sweeper. جاروب از مژگان کردن *jā-rob az mujgān kardan*, To behold. To worship.

P جاروب زن *jārob-zan*, (or کش *kash*) A sweeper, inferior servant. A sweeper of a mosque or mausoleum (a situation both lucrative and honourable).

P جاروب کشي *jārob-kashī*, Sweeping. جاروب کشي کردن *jārob-kashī kardan*, To sweep.

A جارود *jārūd*, Very dry (season). Unfortunate, unlucky.

A جاروديّة *jārūdīyat*, Name of a sect.

A جارور *jārūr*, A stream formed by waters flowing from high grounds during excessive rains or the melting of ice.

A جاروس *jārūs*, A glutton.

A جاروف *jārūf*, Lecherous. Sprightly. Unfortunate. A glutton. Sweeping (torrent).

A جاري *jārī*, Who or what runs, or flows; proceeds, passes, happens, or becomes. Current. ماء جاري *māʼi jārī*, (P آب جاري *ābi jārī*) Running water. P جاري بودن *jārī būdan*, To flow, to run. To occur, happen, become.

A جارية *jāriyat*, (fem.) (pl. جواري *jawārī*) Flowing, running. Happening. A ship. The sun. A girl, servant, female slave, wench. A boon, favour from the hand of God.

A جأز *jaʼz*, A stifling sensation in the breast from rage, thirst, or suffocation when under water. *Jaʼaz*, (v. n. of جئز) Being affected by that sensation.

A جاز *jāza*, (fut. يجوز *yajūzu*) He passed by.

A جازح *jāzih*, A giver. Great (gift).

A جازر *jāzir*, A camel-butcher.

A جازع *jāziʻ*, The prop of a vine or a palm-tree. A prop. Impatient, querulous.

A جازم *jāzim*, (pl. جوازم *jawāzim*) Who or what deprives a consonant of its vowel, so rendering it quiescent; gezmating. A resolver, concluder. Conclusive. A camel sated with drink: full (bottle)

A جازئ *jāziʼ*, (A doe) which satisfies thirst with grass. جازئك من رجل *jāziʼuka min raju-lin*, That man will suffice you.

A جازي *jāzī*, (or with tanwīn جاز *jāzin*) Who or what suffices. Sufficient. Value, equivalent.

A جازئة *jāziʼat*, (pl. جوازي) A wild beast.

A جازية *jāziyat*, Recompense, compensation.

P جاست *jāst*, A wine-press.

A جاسد *jāsid*, Dry (blood) adhering to the body.

A جاسر *jāsir*, Bold, hardy, daring.

A جاسع *jāsiʻ*, Distant (journey).

A P جاسوس *jāsūs*, (pl. جواسيس *jawāsīs*) A spy. The white poppy.

P جاسوسي *jāsūsī*, Spying, secret intelligence, espionage. جاسوسي كردن *jāsūsī kardan*, To play the spy. To seek intelligence.

A جاسوسيّة *jāsūsīyat*, Duty of a spy, espionage.

P جاسونتن *jāsūnitan*, (in zand and Pāz.) To hold.

A جاسئ *jāsiʼ*, Hard and rough.

A جاسي *jāsī*, Hard, cruel, inhuman. Obstinate (tumour).

A جاسياء *jāsiyāʼ*, Hardness, roughness.

A جأش *jaʼsh*, (v. n. of جأش) Being inclined towards. Being disturbed; palpitating, drooping, fainting (the heart from grief or terror). (pl. جؤوش *juʼūsh*) Heart, mind, soul. رابط الجأش *rābitu ʼl jaʼsh*, Intrepid, firm, bold, steady.

P جاش *jāsh*, A heap of winnowed wheat (on the threshing-floor). A granary. (an affix implying distribution) Two parts, three parts.

A جاشر *jāshir*, (pl. جشّار *jushshār*) One who abides in the fields with his camels.

A جاشريّة *jāshirīyat*, Mid-day. Dawn. A sort of food. A morning draught, of camel's milk only.

A جأظ *jaʼz*, (v. n. of جأظ) Being oppressed with heavy, unwholesome water.

A جاعة *jāʻat*, Hungry, famished (persons).

A جاعرة *jāʻirat*, The anus. Dung of wild birds or beasts. جاعرتان *jāʻiratāni*, Buttocks of ass, horse, or man.

A جاعف *jāʻif*, (A torrent) that sweeps all away.

A ابن جاع قمله *ibnu jāʻa kamluhu*, The son of him whose louse was hungry (a low nickname of a certain sorry fellow).

A جاعل *jāʻil*, Who or what puts or places. A maker, framer, fixer, doer. A giver.

A جاعية *jāʻiyat*, Foolish (woman).

P جاغر *jāghar*, A bird's crop.

P جاغسوك *jāghsūk*, A sickle.

A جأف *jaʼf*, (v. n. of جأف) Throwing prostrate. Uprooting (a tree). Terrifying. *Jaʼaf*, (v. n. of جئف) Being terrified. Being hungry.

P جاف *jāf*, Wandering, travelling (fond of variety, not contented with one thing). A harlot.

A جأّف *jaʼʼāf*, A caller: vociferous.

A جافّ *jāff*, Withering, drying: dry, husky.

A جافجاف *jāfjāf*, A harlot.

A جافر *jāfir*, Languid from much covering.

A جافل *jāfil*, Disturbed (in body or mind). Dishevelled (hair). Displaced, removed.

A جافلة *jāfilat*, (A wind) blowing strong.

A جافي *jāfī*, Injurious, vexatious. Cruel, savage, unfeeling, unjust. Uncomfortable (bed).

P جاكشو *jāksho*, A grain resembling a lentil.

P جاكونتن *jākūnitan*, (in zand) To bring.

P جاكي *jākī*, Wood whence tooth-picks are made.

P جاگرم *jā-garm*, A warm place. Stability. Repose. Observation, contemplation.

P جاگزين *jā-guzīn*, Choosing a residence.

P جاگير *jā-gīr*, Holding, occupying a place. An assignment of the government-share of the produce of a large tract of country to an individual. A possession in land granted either in perpetuity or for life, as a reward for services or as a fee. جاگير تن *jā-gīri tan* or جاگير ذات *jā-gīri zāt*, Assignment of land for personal support. جاگير حشم *jā-gīri hashm*, Lands granted for the support of troops. جاگير سر *jā-gīri sar*, An assignment of land for the support of an establishment of officers and servants.

P جاگير دار *jāgīr-dār*, A holder of a jāgīr.

A جأل *jaʼala*, (fut. يجأل *yajʼalu*) He went and came. He gathered (wool). (Wool) was collected.

P جال *jāl*, The tooth-pick tree. Net, snare, gin.

A جال *jāl*, A wall, parapet, or fence to a well. The interior of a well from the top to the bottom. Sea-side. Side of a mountain.

A جال *jāl*, Forged, counterfeit.

A جألال *jaʼlāl*, Fear, dread.

A جألان *jaʼalān*, A limping, a walking lame.

A جالب *jālib*, Who or what attracts or draws. An author, mover, exciter, causer. A merchant who travels from country to country (with slaves, cattle, cloths, or other merchandise). (pl. جوالب *jawālib* or جلّب *jullab*) Healing (wound). جالب القلوب *jālibu ʼl kulūb*, Attracter, ravisher of hearts.

A جالّة *jāllat*, (by some جالة *jālat*) (pl. جوالّ *jawāll*) People which have left their home; exiled.

A جالس *jālis*, (pl. جلوس *julūs*) Sitting, seated, sedentary. One who comes into a high country. A companion, chum. جالس بنود *jālisi bunūd*, A camp-follower.

P جالسگر *jālisgar*, Waving, swinging, walking with a pompous air.

P جالش *jālish*, Coition. Venereous.

P جالشگر *jālishgar*, Addicted to venery. One who waves, swings, or walks with a pompous air.

A جالع *jāliʻ*, Impudent, immodest, obscene. Unveiled (woman). Conspicuous, resplendent.

A جالعة *jāliʻat*, Immodest (woman).

A جالف *jālif*, Who or what pulls up, tears out, breaks, cuts, or unbarks. (A blow) grazing the skin, but not going deep. A fatal, deadly season.

P جالندر *jālandar*, A church, chapel, shrine. Name of a district in Somnāth.

A جالوت *jālūt*, Goliah.

P جاله *jāla*, A raft made of leathern bottles.

P جالي *jālī*, The tooth-pick tree.

A جالي *jālī*, Detergent. Shining. Polished. Evident.

A جالية *jāliyat*, Exiles. Tributaries. Tribute exacted from tributaries.

P جاليز *jālīz*, A kitchen-garden. A melon-ground. A meadow.

P جاليسر *jālesar*, Jellasore in Orissa.

A P جالينوس *jālīnūs*, Galen the physician.

P جام *jām*, A cup, chalice, goblet, bowl. Glass, particularly when coloured and used in the windows of baths. A looking-glass, a mirror. Name of a district in Khurāsān. جام بورك *jāmi būrak*, A dish of macaroni. جام پراز شير و مي *jāmi pur az shīr u may*, A goblet of milk and wine. The lip of a mistress. Elegant poetry. جام جم *jāmi jam*, (or جام جمشيد *jāmi jamshed*) The cup or mirror of Jam, Solomon, or Alexander; which, according to the Eastern fabulists, represented the whole world (whence it is also called جام جهان نما *jāmi jahān-namā* or جام گيتي نما *jāmi gītī-namā*, A mirror shewing the universe; and, metaphorically, a pharos, or light-house, particularly that of Alexandria). جام بلور *jāmi billawr*, A crystal glass. A crystal coach-glass. جام زيبقي *jāmi zībakī*, A crystal goblet. جام سحر *jāmi sahar*, The sun. جام سيم *jāmi sīm*, A silver goblet. The chin of a mistress. جام شهرياري *jāmi shahr-yārī*, A royal goblet. جام شير *jāmi shīr*, A teat yielding milk. A bed of canes. جام گوهر *jāmi gohar*, A crystal cup. (met.) The lip of one's mistress. جام ملك شرق *jāmi maliki shark*, The sun's disk. جام هلالي *jāmi hilālī*, An oblong dish, resembling a ship; a tureen; also a drinking cup. جام بر سنگ زدن *jām bar sang zadan*, To dash the goblet in pieces (met.) To leave off wine.

A جام *jām*, (pl. اجؤم *ajʼum*, اجوام *ajwām*, جامات *jāmāt*, and جوم *jawm*) A silver cup. A glass.

A جامّ *jāmm*, Much, abundant, inexhaustible. Rested, refreshed, recruited (horse).

A جامات *jāmāt*, (pl. of جام) Silver cups, goblets.

P جاماسب *jāmāsb*, (جاماسف *jāmāsf*, جاماس *jāmās*, or جامات *jāmāt*) The son of the prophet Daniel, celebrated in the East as a skilful physician. جاماسب نامه *jāmāsb-nāma*, Name of a book written by him, a copy of which Castellus says he had in his possession.

P جامتونتن *jāmtūnitan*, (in zand) To arrive.

A جامح *jāmih*, Stubborn, vicious (horse).

A جامخ *jāmikh*, (pl. جمّخ) Proud, boastful.

P جامخانه *jām-khāna*, A room with mirrors.

A جامد *jāmid*, (pl. جمد *jamad*) Concrete, congealed. Consistent, solid. Rigid, stiff. Styptic. (in gram.) Underived, primitive (noun). A noun or verb from which another cannot be derived. Inanimate, unorganic (as fossils). Fat. A boundary. ماء جامد *māʼi jāmid*, Dead or stagnant water. جامد العين *jāmidu'l ʻayn*, Tearless, dry-eyed (man). جامد الكف *jāmidu'l kaff*, Close-fisted, stingy, parsimonious. جامد المال *jāmidu'l māl*, Dead stock (opposed to ذائب المال *zāʼibu'l māl*, Live stock).

P جامدار *jāma-dār*, A keeper of a wardrobe. A musqueteer.

P جامدارخانه *jāmadār-khāna*, A wardrobe.

P جامداري *jāma-dārī*, Protection, defence.

P جامدان *jāmadān*, Wardrobe, clothes-bag.

P جامداني *jāmdānī*, A species of fine cotton cloth with spots or flowers wove in the loom.

A جامس *jāmis*, (for جامد *jāmid*) Frozen (water). A plant that has lost its freshness.

A جامسة *jāmisat*, (A stone) fixed in its place.

P جامسه *jāmisa*, The Egyptian bean.

A جامع *jāmiʻ*, Who or what collects, comprehends, assembles, unites, or joins. A collector. All, whole, universal. A great mosque, temple, duomo, or cathedral, where the prayer called خطبه *khutba* is repeated on Fridays. An ass in foal of her first colt. A beast adapted for a pack-saddle or a saddle. A camel failing to breed the fore and side teeth. A proper name. (pl. جمع *jumʻ*) A large cauldron. جامع بين المشتقّين *jāmiʻu bayna'l mushtakkīna*, Uniting those who had been separated. جامع علوم الاوّلين و الآخرين *jāmiʻu ʻulūmi'l awwalīn wa'l ākhirīn*, Comprising the learning of the ancients and the moderns. ذات جامع الكمالات *zāti jāmiʻi'l kamālāt*, Containing the essence of all perfection. دعاء جامع *duʻāʼi jāmiʻ*, An universal prayer, in which is included whatever the supplicant wishes for, in this world and the next. جامع الجار *jāmiʻu'l jār*, Name of a certain coasting-place for the people of Madīna. جامع العلوم *jāmiʻu'l ʻulūm*, An encyclopædia.

A جامعان *jāmiʻāni*, equiv. to الحلّة المزيديّة *al hillatu'l mazīdīyat*.

A جامعة *jāmiʻat*, (pl. جوامع *jawāmiʻ*) A large cauldron. A pillory (as comprehending the neck and the hands). A necklace, chain, collar.

A جامعيّة *jāmiʻiyat*, Universality, generality.

P جامغول *jāmghol*, A bastard: an arch rogue.

P جامكان *jām-kān*, (جامكن *jāma-kan* or جامگاه *jām-gāh*) A wardrobe in baths, where people undress.

A جامكيّة *jāmakīyat*, (P جامگي) A gift. A salary.

P جامگك *jāmagak*, A little garment.

P جامگي *jāmagī* or *jāmgī*, A piece of cotton cloth, sufficient for a garment. A salary, stipend, wages, daily allowance of provisions. Victuals, livelihood. A gun-match. Sediment.

P جامگي خوار *jāmagī-khwār*, A stipendiary. A servant. A wine-drinker.

P جامگي دار *jāmagī-dār*, A matchlock-man.

A جامل *jāmil*, A troop of camels with their owners and keepers. A large part of a tribe. (pl. of جمل *jamal*) Full-grown camels.

P جامنونتن *jāmnūnitan*, (in zand) To speak.

P جاموار *jāmawār*, (or جامواري *jāmawārī*) Fit or intended to be made up into a garment.

P جاموتله *jāmūtala*, An orator, a speaker.

A جامور *jāmūr*, Pith of the palm-tree.

A جاموس *jāmūs*, (pl. جواميس *jawāmīs*) (from P گاوميش *gāo-mesh*) A buffalo.

P جامه *jāma*, A garment, robe, vest, gown, coat. Stuff for a dress, but not yet made up. A bed, couch, sofa. Cotton, linen cloth. A wrapper. A patch. A half-burnt fire-brand. A poker. A poem of any kind (exceeding nine verses). Eulogium, panegyric. History. Power, dignity. Protection. Stipend, salary. (for جام *jam*) A cup, goblet, flagon with a long crooked neck. جامهٔ آخرت *jāmaʼi ākhirat*, A winding-sheet. جامه بر قدش تنگ آمد *jāma bar kadash tang āmad*, His vest became tight upon his body, *i.e.* He swelled with rage. جامهٔ خواب *jāmaʼi khwāb*, Bed-clothes. جامهٔ خورشيد *jāmaʼi khwurshed*, Leaf of a tree. Dust, or a cloud, or whatever obscures the sun. The earth. Pupil of the eye. The human body. جامه در آنجا نهاد *jāma dar ānjā nihād*, He there left his clothes, *i.e.* He died in that place. جامه در نيل زد *jāma dar nīl zad*, He threw his garments into the Nile, *i.e.* He put on mourning. جامه دريدن *jāma darīdan*, To tear or rend one's garment. (met.) To make a violent exertion. To joke, jest. جامهٔ سحر *jāmaʼi sahar*, The sun. The east wind. جامهٔ عيد *jāmaʼi ʻīd*, Holiday-clothes. A scarlet vest. Blossoms, flowers. جامهٔ غوك *jāmaʼi ghok*, A green film seen to float on stagnant water. A rivulet. A pond. جامهٔ فتحي *jāmaʼi fathī*, A fine silken robe. جامه فوطه كردن *jāma fūta kardan*, To tear one's clothes into strips. جامه قبا كردن *jāma kabā kardan*, To let out a secret. جامهٔ قطران *jāmaʼi katrān*, Garments of pitch, *i.e.* Mourning. جامهٔ ماتم *jāmaʼi mātam*, Mourning-habiliments. جامهٔ مرده *jāmaʼi murda*, Grave-clothes. جامهٔ نخچواني *jāmaʼi nakhchuwānī*, Scarlet. جامهٔ نوم *jāmaʼi navam*, My new garment.

P جامه باف *jāma-bāf*, A weaver.

P جامه بافي *jāma-bāfī*, The art of weaving.

P جامه بر *jāma-bur*, A pair of scissors; shears.

P جامه پوش *jāma-posh*, Clothed, clad, dressed.

P جامه خانه *jāma-khāna*, Wardrobe, press.

P جامه دان *jāmadān*, A portmanteau. A chest of drawers, clothes-chest, wardrobe.

P جامه دران *jāma-darān*, Garment-rending.

P جامه زيب *jāma-zīb*, Becoming one's dress.

P جامه شوي *jāma-shūy*, Washer of clothes.

P جامه فروش *jāma-farosh*, A slopseller.

P جامه وار *jāmawār*, Fit to make clothes from. A flowered sheet or shawl. A kind of chintz.

P جامي *jāmī*, Name of a celebrated Persian poet, native of Jām, and a Sūfī.

A جاميّ *jāmīy*, Native of Jām in Nīsābūr.

P جان *jān*, Soul, vital spirit, mind. Self. Life. Wind. The mouth. Arms. The father of demons. Name of a race said to have inhabited the world before Adam. جان بدستارچه دادن *jān ba dastārcha dādan*, To tender one's life. To advance money. جان بر دميدن *jān bar damīdan*, To restore to life. جان بر شكرانه دادن *jān bar shukrāna dādan*, To advance money. اي جان پدر *ay jāni pidar*, O soul of (thy) father! O my dear son!

جان پريان *jāni pariyān*, Wine. جان تسليم كردن *jān taslīm kardan*, To give up the ghost, to die. جان تو ؤ جان او *jāni tu u jāni u*, His life is as dear to him as thine to thee. (It implies also) Unanimity. جان جماش *jāni jamāsh*, Wine. جان جهان *jāni jahān*, Life of the world. جان حيوان *jāni hayawān*, Milk. Butter-milk. Butter. Flesh. Honey. جان خود فروختن *jāni khwud farokhtan*, To sell one's life, *i.e.* to expose one's self to danger. جان دادن *jān dādan*, To resign one's life. To kill one's self. جان داشتن *jān dāshtan*, To wish, desire, aspire after, to have an ambition for, to endeavour with eagerness. جان در آستين داشتن *jān dar āstīn dāshtan*, To risk one's life. جان در ميان *jān dar miyān*, Though one's life be at stake. جان زمين *jāni zamīn*, Herbage, flowers, and fruits. جان سپردن *jān sipurdan*, To resign one's breath. جان عالم *jāni ɛālam*, Life of the world, *i.e.* Muhammad. جان كردن *jān kardan*, To be in the agony of death. جان كندن *jān kandan*, To labour hard. To die.

A جانّ *jānn*, (pl. جنّان *jinnān*) A demon, the devil. A kind of large snake, with black eyes, harmless, and allowed to go about the houses in the East. (pl. of جنّ *jinn*) Demons. ابو جانّ *abū jānn*, Father of demons.

P جان آزار *jān-āzār*, Inhuman, tyrannical.

P جان آزاري *jān-āzārī*, Cruelty, tyranny.

P جان آفرين *jān-āfirīn*, Creator of the soul.

P جان افزا *jān-afzā*, Soul-reviving.

P جانان *jānān*, (pl. of جان *jān*) Souls. Handsome, lovely. A mistress, sweetheart.

P جانانه *jānāna*, A beloved object.

P جان آور *jān-āwar*, Alive (spoken chiefly of winged animals). An imprudent, injudicious man.

P جان آهني *jān-āhanī*, Iron-hearted; merciless, cruel. Brave.

A جأنب *jaɛnab*, Short and fat (man or horse).

A جانب *jānib*, (pl. جوانب *jawānib*) A part, side. (pl. جنّاب *junnāb*) Strange, foreign. A foreigner. Shunned, despised, scorned. Distant between the feet (a horse). غليظ الجانب *ghalīzu'l jānib*, Rough, coarse-mannered. لين الجانب *līnu'l jānib*, Amiableness of manners. الجانب الغربيّ *al jānibu'l gharbiy*, The western side of Mount Sinai (where God appeared to Moses).

P جانباز *jān-bāz*, Playing with life, *i.e.* exposing one's self to danger; venturesome. A rope-dancer, tumbler, or other person who follows a dangerous calling. A horse-dealer.

P جانبازي *jān-bāzī*, Intrepidity. A swing. A slack rope.

A جانبة *jānibat*, A side.

P جانبخش *jān-bakhsh*, Life-bestowing. Soul-refreshing. God. The forgiver of a capital crime.

P جان بخشي *jān-bakhshī*, Animation. Vivification. The pardon of a capital offence.

P جانبدار *jānib-dār*, Partial. A supporter, a second. An advocate, a defender.

P جانبداري *jānib-dārī*, Partiality. Support.

P جان بر *jān-bar*, One who escapes with life. جان بر شدن *jān-bar shudan*, To escape with life.

P جان بر ميان *jān bar miyān*, Ready, prepared. One in expectation of death.

P جان بن جان *jān bin jān*, The name of an imaginary being, who makes a great figure in Eastern fabulous tradition. He is supposed to have been the monarch of that race of creatures called by the Arabians "Jānn" or "Jinn," (by the Persians "Jānniyān" or "Jinniyān,") and also of the Paris or Fairies, both of whom inhabited the earth before Adam's creation, but were then banished to a corner of the world called Jinnistān, for disobedience to the Supreme Being.

A جانبيّ *jānibīy*, Collateral. Foreign.

P جانبيدن *jāmbīdan*, To dislike, nauseate.

A جانبين *jānibayn*, Both parts, each side.

P جان جان *jān-jān*, God. The Great Spirit. Bread. The scrapings of the pot.

A جانح *jānih*, Inclining, inclined. A sinner.

A جانحة *jānihat*, The lower front rib.

P جاندار *jān-dār*, Animated, having a soul. Powerful, active. A daily stipend. A guardian, preserver of life. An executioner. A sword-bearer.

P جان دارو *jān-dārū*, Theriac. Opium.

P جانداري *jān-dārī*, Life, animation.

P جاندانه *jān-dāna*, The bregma of the skull, which, in an infant, is soft and moving.

P جاندر *jān-dar*, Animated. An executioner.

P جان دهي *jān-dihī*, Opposition, resistance. A sacrifice or surrender of life. Death.

P جان ربا *jān-rubā*, Soul-ravishing. Killing.

P جان رهائي *jān-rahāɛī*, A saving of one's life.

P جان سپار *jān-sipār*, Exposing one's self. Resigning one's self into the hands of another (an epithet of a lover). Devoted.

P جانسپاري *jān-sipārī*, Exposure of life. Death.

P جانستان *jān-satān*, Soul-ravishing. Alluring. Killing, murdering.

P جانستاني *jān-satānī*, Allurement. Murder.

P جانسوز *jān-soz*, Soul-inflaming: beloved object.

A جانش *jānish*, Near, adjacent (place).

P جانشكر *jān-shikar*, A hunter (of wild beasts). The angel of death. A mistress. Nervous language.

P جان شكري *jān-shikarī*, Place of execution.

P جان شيران *jān-shīrān*, (or جان شيرين *jān-shīrīn*) Sweet life! Life itself.

P جانشين *jā-nishīn*, A lieutenant, locum tenens. A successor. An associate.

P جان فرسا *jān-farsā*, Wearing out life, displeasing, disgusting, irksome.

P جان فزا *jān-fazā*, (or جان فزاي *jān-fazāy*) Enlarging, refreshing the soul. Cheering, welcome to the spirits. The water of life. The 23d day of the month in the year of Yazdagird.

P جان فشان *jān-fishān*, Ready to sacrifice one's life; zealous.

P جان فشاني *jān-fishānī*, Hard labour. Extreme diligence. A waste of life in another's service.

A جانق *jānik*, A hurler of stones from a balista.

T جانقي *jānkī*, A council, consultation.

P جان كاه *jān-kāh*, Soul-exhausting. Pathetic. Afflicting.

P جانكش *jān-kash*, Quarrelsome, contumacious.

P جان كن *jān-kan*, Soul-harrowing.

P جانگاه *jān-gāh*, Dangerous. چاه جانگاه *chāhi jān-gāh*, A dangerous pit. A labyrinth.

P جانگداز *jān-gudāz*, Soul-melting, weakening, consuming.

P جانگذار *jān-guzār*, Penetrating the mind or the heart. نالۀ جانگذار *nālaɛi jān-guzār*, A heart-breaking sigh.

P جان گزا *jān-gazā*, Deadly (poison), noxious (beasts). Any thing prejudicial to life.

P جانگي *jānagī*, Name of a country.

P جانگير *jān-gīr*, The angel of death.

P جان نثار *jān-nisār*, Scattering life: devoted.

P جانوار *jānwār*, (or جانور *jānwar*) Living, quick. An animal. An animalcule. A fierce beast. A wild boar. A bird.

P جانورك *jānwarak*, Small animal, animalcule.

P جانوسار *jānūsār*, Name of the courtier who killed Dārā (Darius Codomannus) the last king of the Kayāniyān dynasty.

P جانوسپار *jānūspār*, Name of a learned Magi.

P جانونتن *jānūnitan*, (in zand) To be, exist.

P جانه *jāna*, The vital spirit. The young of any animal. The pith of a tree. Arms, armour. An island. The cheek. اسب جانه *asb-jāna*, A foal, horse's colt. گاو جانه *gāw-jāna*, A calf.

P جانه دار *jāna-dār*, A daily pension. Food which preserves life. A preserver, guardian. One who has the charge of instruments of war.

P جاني *jānī*, Soul. Cordial. اي برادر جاني *ay birādari jānī*, O dear brother!

A جاني *jānī*, (pl. جناة *junāt*, جنّاء *junnāɛ*, and اجناء *ajnāɛ*) A gatherer. Sinning; a sinner.

P جاني دشمن *jānī-dushman*, An enemy desirous of one's life.

A جأو *jaɛw*, (v. n. of جأي) Sewing, mending (a garment). Guarding, tending (a flock). Covering, concealing, veiling. Confining. Keeping in (spittle). Wiping. Patching.

P جاو *jāw*, (in the idiom of Turkistān) A place.

A جأواء *jaɛwāɛ*, (fem. of اجأي *ajɛaɛ*) Dark chesnut (mare). Dark-coloured (crowd or troop, from their bucklers).

P جاودانه *jāwadāna*, Eternal.

A جاوان *jāwān*, A tribe in Kurdistān.

P جاوانيدن *jāwānīdan*, To hawk, spit. To chatter (as birds terrified). To be perpetual, eternal.

P جاود *jāwid*, Eternal, perpetual.

P جاودان *jāwidān*, (or جاوداني *jāwidānī*) Eternally, for ever. Eternal, everlasting. Next world.

P جاودان خرد *jāwidān-khirad*, Name of a book on practical science composed by Hoshang.

P جاودان سراي *jāwidān-sarāy*, Paradise.

P جاودانه *jāwidāna*, Eternal.

P جاور *jāwar*, State, condition. جاور كردن *jāwar kardan*, To change. چه جاور داري *chi jāwar dārī*, How are you? how do you do?

P جاورد *jāward*, (or جاوزد) White-thorn.

P جاورس *jāwars*, Millet.

A جاوشير *jāwshīr*, (from P گاوشير *gāw-shīr*) The opoponax-tree.

P جاوه *jāwa*, The interior of the mouth. Name of a stinging insect. The island of Java.

P جاويد *jāwīd*, Eternal. Eternity.

P جاويدان *jāwīdān*, Eternal, perpetual.

P جاويدان خرد *jāwīdān-khirad*, (Eternal wisdom) The title of a book, whose author is said to have been Hoshang, second king of Persia.

P جاويدانه *jāwīdāna*, Eternal.

P جاويداني *jāwīdānī*, Eternity.

P جاويد طراز *jawīd-tirāz*, Eternity-adorning.

P جاويدن *jāwīdan*, To scream (like birds). To hawk, spit.

P جاويزن *jāwīzan*, A stone found in the gall-bladder of an ox.

P جاه *jāh*, Place, rank, office. Dignity, grandeur, magnificence. Honour, reputation. Fortune, prosperity. The world. ذو جاه *zū jāh*, Dignified, exalted. عالي جاه *ālī-jāh*, Exalted in dignity.

A جاهبا *jāhiban*, Publicly, openly.

A جاهة *jāhat*, Dignity, power.

A جاهد *jāhid*, Desirous of eating, hungry. Studious, diligent, industrious, active. A seeker. A warrior in defence of religion against infidels.

P جاهدار *jāh-dār*, A holder of a public station.

A جاهشة *jāhishat*, A crowd of men.

A جاهض *jāhiz*, Penetrating, keen, acute. High (camel's) bunch.

A جاهضة *jāhizat*, (pl. جواهض *jawāhiz*) A yearling colt (of an ass or a mare).

P جاهك *jāhak*, The breast-bone next the throat.

A جاهل *jāhil*, (pl. جهل *juhl*, *juhul*, جهّل *juhhal*, جهّال *juhhāl*, جهلاء *juhalāʼ*, اجهال *ajhāl*, and جهلة *jahalat*) Ignorant. Barbarous. An idiot. A lion. هو جاهل منه *huwa jāhil minhu*, He is ignorant of that.

A جاهلي *jāhilī*, Ignorance. Paganism.

A جاهليّ *jāhiliy*, A pagan Arab, who lived in heathenism prior to the appearance of Muhammad.

A جاهليّة *jāhiliyat*, Ignorance. Paganism, heathen darkness (as prevailing in Arabia before the time of Muhammad). الجاهلية الجهلاء *al jāhiliyatu'l jahlāʼ*, The grossest ignorance or Paganism.

P جاه و جلال *jāh u jalāl*, Dignity, grandeur.

A جاهي *jāhī*, Ruined, dilapidated (house).

A جاهيا *jāhiyan*, Publicly, openly.

A جاي *jaʼaʼ*, (fut. يجاي *yajʼaʼ*) He bit.

A جاي *jaʼy*, (v. n. of جاي) Biting, fixing the teeth. Retaining, holding, containing (as a jar, water). Keeping in one's slaver. Mending (a garment). Being of a chesnut-colour (a horse). A dark-bay colour.

P جاي *jāy*, A place. An abode. Name of a flower. جاىْ اشتباه نيست *jāʼi ishtibāh nīst*, There is no room for doubt. جاىْ اعتراض *jāʼi iʻtirāz*, The place or time of opposition. جاىْ ضرور *jāʼi zarūr*, The necessary. جاىْ نماز *jāʼi namāz*, A carpet to kneel on at prayers.

P جاي باش *jāy-bāsh*, A mansion, house, palace.

A الجائب العين *al jāʼibu'l ʻayn*, A lion.

A جائبة *jāʼibat*, (pl. جوائب *jawāʼib*) News which spreads from country to country.

A جائحة *jāʼihat*, (pl. جوائح *jawāʼih*) Damage, injury, corruption, calamity; any thing destroying cattle (as old age, or the malignity of the air).

A جائد *jāʼid*, (pl. جود *jawd*) Plentiful (rain). Beneficent, liberal.

P جاي داد *jāy-dād*, An assignment in land (for the maintenance of an establishment of troops). Assets, fund, source.

P جاي داشتن *jāy dāshtan*, To be probable. To happen.

A جائر *jāʼir*, (pl. جورة *jawarat*, جارة *jārat*, and جائرون *jāʼirūn*) One who deviates from the right way. Unjust, cruel, tyrannical. Heat in the breast (from drought, hunger, or anger). Acidity in the mouth or stomach, heartburn (from eating any thing (fat). A sycophant. Many, much.

P جاي روب *jāy-rob*, A besom.

A جائز *jāʼiz*, Passing, current. One who passes by thirsty. Lawful, legal, allowable, warrantable, authorized, permitted, tolerated. Metaphorical. Indifferent. (pl. اجوز *ajwuz*, اجوزة *ajwizat*, جوزان *jūzān*, جيزان *jīzān*, and جوائز *jawāʼiz*) The beam of a house (as passing from side to side). A garden. P جائز كه *jāʼiz ki*, It is possible that. جائز داشتن *jāʼiz dāshtan*, To allow, to hold lawful.

A جائزة *jāʼizat*, Benignity. (pl. جوائز *jawāʼiz*) A gift, a present. One draught of water. The place at a well where the waterer stands.

A جائزه *jāʼiza*, Examination, review. Trial, proof, confirmation. Signature. Muster.

A جائشة *jāʼishat*, The mind, spirit, soul.

A جائع *jāʼiʻ*, (pl. جياع *jiyāʻ* and جوّع *juwwaʻ*) Starving, hungry, famishing. جائعة الوشاح *jāʼiʻatu'l wishāh*, Slender-waisted (female).

A جائف *jāʼif*, Penetrating (blow). A penetrater. Name of several places in Arabia.

A جائفة *jāʼifat*, A stab, a deep wound penetrating to the belly. (pl. جوائف *jawāʼif*) A low hill.

P جايكه *jāy ki*, Where, the place that.

P جايگاه *jāy-gāh*, A habitation, dwelling. Any place where a thing stands, or wherein it is contained. A birth-place. جايگاه غربا *jāy-gāhi ghurabā*, A hospice for travellers, a caravansera, inn. جايگاه لطيف *jāy-gāhi latīf*, A pleasant dwelling. جايگاه موي *jāy-gāhi moy* or *mūy*, Edge of eyelid.

P جاي گرفتگي *jāy-giriftagī*, Residence, stay.

P جايگير *jāy-gīr*, Possessing, occupying a place, fixing a habitation, making a settlement. Efficacious. جايگير شدن *jāy-gīr shudan*, To be respectable, venerable. To be in an exalted station.

A جائل *jāʼil*, Moving, loose (girdle, ring).

A جائلة *jāʼilat*, An affair on which one is engaged.

P جاي مانده *jāy-mānda*, Remaining in a place; incapable, impotent.

P جاي مند *jāymand*, Lazy, idle, unemployed.

P جاي نشست *jāy-nishast*, Station, situation.

P جاي نشين *jāy-nishīn*, A successor, locum tenens. An officer of government appointed to inspect the conduct of a governor.

A جائيْ *jāyiʼ*, Coming, approaching; on the road; ready to arrive. A comer.

P جاي *jāye*, One place. A kind of flower. بجاي *ba jāye*, Wherever.

A جائية *jāʼiyat*, Pus, matter. Blood.

P جاييدن *jāyīdan*, To take up a fixed abode.

A جبّ *jabb*, (v. n. of جبّ) Castrating. Fructifying the female palm-tree. Overcoming (by address or bravery). Excelling in beauty. *Jubb*, (pl. اجباب *ajbāb*, جباب *jibāb*, and جببة *jibabat*) A well (especially a deep one, without a parapet or cover). Name of a place whence giraffes are procured. A large water-bottle made of a double skin. An interior. جبّ يوسف *jubb yūsuf*, Joseph's well, twelve miles from Tiberias.

A جبء *jabʼ*, (pl. اجبؤ *ajbuʼ*, جباة *jibaʼat*, *jabʼat*, and جبا *jabaʼ*) A kind of mushroom. A hillock. A hollow place in which water collects.

A جبا *jabʼ*, (v. n. of جبا) Abhorring. Abstaining. Remaining behind, far distant. Lying hid. Selling red earth. Bending the neck. Crawling out (a serpent from his hole). Being dull (the eyesight), blunt (the edge of a sword). *Jabaʼ*, (pl. of جبء *jabʼ*) Mushrooms. High grounds. Hollow places wherein water collects.

A جبا *jabaʼ*, (pl. اجباء *ajbāʼ*) A cistern. Earth round about a well. The brink of a well, the place where the drawer stands. A going a-head of a herd of camels a day before, and getting water ready for them. Yes, very well. *Jabaʼ*, *jibaʼ*, or *jubaʼ*, (v. n. of جبا for جبو) Collecting water in a cistern. *Jibaʼ*, Water collected in a cistern.

P جبا *jibā*, Tribute, revenue.

A جبّاء *jabbāʼ*, (fem. of اجبّ *ajabb*) Bunchless (she-camel). Meagre-hipped, flat-breasted (woman). The point of a cow's horn. *Jubbāʼ*, A kind of arrow. Cowardly, dastardly.

A جبّاءة *jubbāsat*, A woman whose appearance pleases not.

A جباب *jabāb*, Dearth, a sore famine. *Jibāb*, (v. n. of جبّ) Castrating. Overcoming. Excelling. (v. n. 3 of جبّ) Boasting, exaggerating (about food or beauty). (pl. of جبّ *jubb*) Wells. (pl. of جبّة *jubbat*) Cotton waistcoats. *Jubāb*, A fluid resembling froth, swimming on the surface of camel's milk. Scarcity. Blood shed with impunity.

A جبّاب *jabbāb*, A maker or vender of the waistcoat or doublet جبّة *jubbat*.

P جبابت *jibābat*, Collection of revenue.

A جبابرة *jabābirat*, (pl. of جبّار) Tyrants: giants.

A جبابيّ *jibābiy*, Seller of the doublet جبّة *jubbat*.

A جبابير *jabābīr*, (pl. of جبّارة) Fat she-camels.

A جبابين *jabābīn*, (pl. of جبّان *jabbān*) Cheesemongers. Cemeteries.

A جبأة *jabsat*, A shoemaker's table or board on which he cuts his leather. The termination of the short ribs in the umbilical or mammillary region (of a camel). *Jibasat*, (pl. of جبء *jabs*) Mushrooms. Hillocks, rising grounds. Hollow places where water collects.

A جباجب *jabājib*, The mountains or streets of Mecca. A place for slaughtering sacrifices at Mina. Stout and fat she-camels. (pl. of جُجبة *jubjubat*) Bits of minced meat, partly dressed, dried, or larded with fat. Dirt-baskets. *Jubājib*, Much water.

A جباذ *jabāz*, Death. An intention which draws one towards any thing.

A جبار *jabār*, The area of a plain. *Jibār*, (pl. of جبارة *jibārat*) Bracelets. Splints. *Jubār*, A shedding of blood with impunity. A war without retaliation. Vain, false, frivolous. Free, quit, clear. A current. Any thing spoiled or destroyed. *Jubār* or *jibār*, The old name for Tuesday.

A جبّار *jabbār*, Great. Strong. Powerful. Omnipotent (a title of God). Proud, haughty, who admits of no superior. A tyrant, oppressor. A giant. Tall. A heart an entire stranger to pity. One who puts to death unjustly. Orion. *Jabbār* or *jubbār*, A tall palm-tree.

A جبارة *jibārat*, (v. n. of جبر) Setting (a broken bone). Repairing the broken fortunes of a friend. A bracelet. Splints bound round a broken bone.

A جبّارة *jabbārat*, (pl. جبابير) A fat she-camel.

A جبّاري *jabbārī*, Tyranny, despotic sway.

A جبّاش *jabbāsh*, A shaver.

A جبّاع *jubbāɛ*, A woman inelegant in walk or dress. Short (man or woman). A short arrow without a head.

A جبّاعة *jabbāɛat*, The fundament. *Jubbāɛat*, A woman ungraceful in walk and dress.

A جبال *jibāl*, The body. (pl. of جبل *jabal*) Mountains. جبال و تلال *jibāl u tilāl*, Mountains and hills. جبال شاهقة, Lofty mountains.

A جبان *jabān*, (pl. جبناء *jubanās*) Pusillanimous, fearful, abject; a coward. جبان الكلب *jabānu'l kalb*, Exceedingly generous.

A جبّان *jabbān*, (pl. جبابين *jabābīn*) A seller of cheese. A coward. Dastardly. A cemetery. A desert. High level ground. A rich meadow. A place where festivals are held in a desert.

A جبانة *jabānat*, (v. n. of جبن) Being cowardly and dastardly. Cowardly (woman).

A جبّانة *jabbānat*, A desert. High level ground. A rich meadow. A burying-place, a cemetery. (fem. of جبّان *jabbān*) A cheesemonger.

A جبانيّة *jabānīyat*, Cowardice.

A جباوة *jibāwat*, (v. n. of جبا for جبو) Drawing (water into a cistern). Collecting (tribute). Water collected for watering camels.

A جباه *jibāh*, (pl. of جبهة *jabhat*) Foreheads.

A جبأي *jubsa'*, Large-breasted (woman).

A جبايا *jabāya'*, Clean wells dug and stuck with branches of the vine.

A جباية *jibāyat*, (v. n. of جبي) Collecting (tribute, or water into a reservoir).

A جبائر *jabāsir*, (pl. of جبيرة) Splints, bandages.

A جبب *jabab*, The cutting off a camel's bunch, or the wounding of it by the pack-saddle. White upon a horse's legs as far as the knees or houghs. The knee of a quadruped. *Jubab*, (pl. of جبّة *jubbat*) Cotton waistcoats, doublets.

P جب باج *jub-bāj*, A royal robe worn on certain state-occasions.

A جببة *jibabat*, (pl. of جبّ *jubb*) Wells.

A جبة *jibat*, (v. n. of وجب) Being necessary. Behoving to do or suffer. Being ratified (sale), made over (purchase).

A جبّة *jubbat*, (pl. جبب *jubab* and جباب *jibāb*) A waistcoat or doublet with cotton quilted between the outside and lining. The hollow part of the head of a spear (into which they fix the staff). The wrist. The joint of the fore-foot (of a camel or horse). The bone surrounding the eye, the eyebrow. Armour, mail. The upper part of the hoof, the coronet. The middle of a house. White on the fore and hind leg of a horse.

A جبت *jibt*, An idol. A false deity. A magician, a soothsayer. A worthless man. Magic. Soothsaying.

A جبج *jabj*, (v. n. of جبج) Waxing fat after having been lean.

A جبجاب *jabjāb*, Much water.

A جبجب *jabjab*, Level ground.

A جبجبة *jabjabat*, A travelling, journeying. A stone in the water, whose upper part appears above the surface. *Jubjubat* or *jabjabat*, (pl. جباجب *jabājib*) Tripe (stuffed with minced meat and fat). A piece of a camel's hide cut round and filled with meat. *Jubjubat*, A leathern basket used for carrying away earth or mud. A drum.

A جبجبي *jubjubīy*, A tripe-seller.

A جبجبيّة *jubjubīyat*, A dish of tripe.

A جبح *jabh*, (v. n. of جبح) Throwing dice. *Jabh*, *jibh*, or *jubh*, (pl. اجبح *ajbuh* and اجباح *ajbāh*) A bee-hive.

A جبخ *jabkh*, (v. n. of جبخ) Throwing dice, or shaking them in the hand.

A جبذ *jabz*, A drawing, a pulling.

A جبذة *jabzat*, (v. n. of جبذ) Drawing (a bow). *Jabazat*, The pith of a palm-tree with roughness in it.

A جبر *jabr*, (v. n. of جبر) Setting, uniting firmly (a broken bone). Repairing the broken fortune (of a friend). Being set (a broken bone). Forcing against the will. Wholeness, soundness. Predestination, irreversible decree. A king. A slave. A man. An intrepid hero. A youth. A splint laid on a broken bone. Reduction of dislocations and fractures. Reduction of parts to a whole or fractions to integers in arithmetic. الجبر *al jabr*, (or جبر و مقابلة *jabr u mukābala*) Algebra. P جبر كردن *jabr kardan*, To force, compel, to use violence. A جبر نقصان *jabri nuksān*, Making good a deficiency (as if two horses are to be given to two persons, one to each: if they are not equally good, the saddle and bridle are then given with the worst).

A جبرا *jabran*, (P جبرانه) By force, oppressively.

A جبراعل *jabrāsil*, (or جبراعيل) Gabriel.

A جبرال *jibrāl*, Gabriel.

P جبر آهنگ *jibr-āhang*, Name of a certain thorn. Wild sesame.

A جبرائل *jibrāsil*, (or جبرائيل) Gabriel.

A جبرعل *jabrasil*, جبرعلّ *jabrasill*, or جبرعيل *jabrasīl*, Gabriel.

A جبروّة *jabarūwat* or *jabrūwat*, Pride, pomp.

A جبروت *jabrūt*, Pomp, pride. *Jabarūt*, Pomp. Omnipotence. Dominion. Heaven. Unity of God. عالم جبروت *ɛālami jabarūt*, The highest heaven.

A جبروتي *jabarūta'* or *jabarūtī*, Pomp, pride.

P جبروز *jabrūz*, (or جبرور) A porcupine.

A جبري *jabrī*, Forced, compelled. Oppression.

A جبرياء *jibriyās*, Pride, haughtiness.

A جبريّات *jabrīyat*, Algebraical problems.

A جبريان *jabariyān*, (with Pers. pl.) Fatalists.

A جبريّة *jibrīyat*, *jibirīyat*, *jabarīyat*, *jabrīyat*, Pride, pomp, haughtiness. *Jabarīyat*, Name of a Muhammadan sect which denies the freedom of the human will (in contradistinction to the sect which asserts its power, and is called قدريّة *kadarīyat*).

A جبريل *jabrayl* or *jibrīl*, Gabriel.

A جبرين *jabrīn* or *jibrīn*, Gabriel.

A جبرئيل *jabrasīl*, Gabriel.

A جبز *jabz*, (v. n. of جبز) Assigning a portion of one's property. *Jibz*, Covetous. Thick, coarse. Cowardly. Mean. Weak.

A جبس *jibs*, (pl. اجباس *ajbās* and جبوس *jubūs*) A coward. Heavy, stupid. Ignoble, sordid, vile, worthless. Impudent. A bear's cub. Plaster.

P جبسين *jabsīn*, Lime.

A جبش *jabsh*, (v. n. of جبش) Shaving (hair).

P جبغوت *jab* or *jubghūt*, Cotton or wool used for quilting. An old counterpane torn in pieces.

A جبل *jabl*, (v. n. of جبل) Creating, forming, moulding, firmly setting. Being soft (iron). An opening or space between houses. A dry tree. Great of stature. *Jabl, jubul*, or *jubl*, A crowd of people. *Jibl* or *jubl*, Many, numerous, copious. حيّ جبل *hayy jibl*, A numerous tribe. *Jubl* or *jubul*, A dry tree. *Jabal*, (pl. اجبل *ajbul*, اجبال *ajbāl*, and جبال *jibāl*) A mountain. A lord, prince. Learned. A miser. A court. جبل الرأس *jabalu'r ras*, Of little sweetness of temper. جبل سوس *jabali sūs*, Mount Atlas. جبل الطارق *jabalu't tārik*, Gibraltar. جبل كريم *jabali karīm*, Mount Olympus. جبل القمر *jabalu'l kamar*, (Mountain of the moon) A mountain in Africa. جبل موسىٰ *jabal mūsa'*, (Moses' mount) Mount Sinai. ابنة الجبل *ibnatu'l jabal*, (Daughter of the mountain) A serpent. A misfortune. A bow made from the tree نبع *nabʻ*. بلاد الجبل *bilādu'l jabal*, Media (Persian Irāk). *Jabil*, Thick, gross. A spear-head of soft iron.

A جبلّ *jubull* or *jibill*, A crowd. A dry tree.

P جبلاج *jiblāj*, A big, cowardly, base fellow.

P جبلاهنگ *jiblāhang*, Wild sesame.

A جبلة *jablat*, Coarsely-made (woman). The bunch of a camel. *Jablat* or *jiblat*, Large-bunched she-camel. The skin or its surface. Coarsely-made (woman). Vice, blemish. Strength. Hardness of ground. *Jiblat*, The face or the external skin. Coarseness. A root. Texture (of a garment). *Jiblat, jablat*, or *jublat*, Form, creation, nature, disposition, temperament, constitution. *Jiblat* or *jublat*, A crowd, company, nation, people. *Jublat*, The bunch of a camel. *Jabalat*, Form, creation, nature, disposition, temperament, constitution. *Jabalat* or *jibalat*, The face or outward skin. A thick, coarse woman. Vice, blemish. Hardness of the ground.

A جبلّة *jabullat, jubullat*, or *jibillat*, A great number. *Jibillat*, Form, creation, nature, disposition, temperament, constitution. A dry tree. Offspring, creatures. A crowd, company, nation, people. *Jubullat*, Scarce, barren (year). Created beings. A root. Texture (of a garment).

P جبلك *jablak*, Roughness, hardness. A strengthening of one thing by means of another.

P جبلهنگ *jiblahang*, Wild sesame. A kind of thorn.

A جبليّ *jabaliy*, Of or belonging to a mountain, mountainous. Native of Media, or Persian Irāk.

A جبلّي *jibilliy*, Natural, original, innate, essential. امراض جبلّيه *amrāzi jibilliya*, Diseases inherent in the constitution.

A جبن *jubn* or *jubun*, (v. n. of جبن) Being cowardly. Cowardice, fear. Cheese. *Jubun*, (pl. of جبين *jabīn*) Temples; foreheads.

A جبنّ *jubunn*, Cheese.

A جبناء *jubanāʼ*, (pl. of جبين *jabīn* or جبان *jabān*) Cowards.

A جبنان *jabanān*, A coward.

A جبنة *jubnat* or *jubunnat*, A slice of cheese.

A جبنيّ *jubniy*, A cheesemonger.

A جبوء *jubūʼ*, (v. n. of جبأ) Being dazzled (as the eye). Disliking. Arising, coming on one suddenly. Selling red earth.

A جبوب *jabūb*, Hard soil. Earth's surface.

A جبوبة *jabūbat*, (pl. جبوب *jabūb*) A clod, lump of dry clay.

A جبوة *jibwat*, (v. n. of جبي) Collecting water in a cistern. Water collected in a stone reservoir for watering camels.

A جبور *jubūr*, (v. n. of جبر) Setting a broken bone. Repairing the broken fortunes (of a friend). Being set, bound up (a broken bone).

A جبّورة *jabbūrat* or جبورة *jubūrat*, Pride.

A جبوس *jabūs*, A worthless man. A vine-tendril. *Jubūs*, (pl. of جبس *jibs*) Cowards. Worthless, low fellows. Bears' cubs.

A جبه *jubh*, (v. n. of جبه) Arriving at a well and finding nothing wherewith to draw. Striking on the forehead. Driving back. Annoying, disgusting. Coming on whilst people are unprepared (winter). *Jubah*, Width and beauty of forehead.

P جبه *juba*, Inspissated juice, rob, marmalade. Name of a drug. *Juba*, (from the Ar. جبّة *jubbat*) A coat of mail, a cuirass; any kind of iron armour. An upper coat or cloak, a surtout. جبهٔ خورشيد و ماه *jubaʼi khwurshed u māh*, Day and night. جبهٔ درويش *jubaʼi darwesh*, A cloud. Night. جبهٔ هزار ميخي *jubaʼi hazār mekhī*, The starry sky. A starlight night.

A جبّه *jubbah*, A coward.

A جبهاء *jabhāʼ*, (fem. of اجبه *ajbah*) Possessed of a large or high forehead.

P جبه پوش *juba-posh*, Clad in armour. A cuirassier. دلاوران جبه پوشان *dilāwarāni juba-poshān*, Brave cuirassiers.

A جبهة *jabhat*, Forehead, front. A troop of horse. A body of men. A prince, lord, chief, head of a family. Contempt, indignant treatment. Tax-collectors. Bumbailiffs. Name of an idol. The moon. جبهة الاسد *jabhatu'l asad*, The lion's front, *i.e.* four stars forming the tenth mansion of the moon in astrology.

P جبه خانه *juba-khāna*, Armoury, arsenal.

A جبهل *jabahl*, Rude, stupid, brutal, uncivil.

P جبهه سائي *jabha-sāʼī*, Earnest entreaty. (lit. The rubbing of one's forehead on the ground).

A جبي *jaby*, (v. n. of جبي) Collecting water in a cistern. *Jiba'*, Water collected in a cistern for camels. Money collected together.

A جبّير *jibbīr*, Proud, haughty, oppressive.

A جبيرة *jabīrat*, (pl. جبائر *jabāʼir*) A bandage or splint for broken bones. A bracelet.

P جبيره *jabīra*, An assembly of men (convened for some important purpose).

A جبيز *jabīz*, Dry bread, unleavened bread.

A جبيس *jabīs*, A bear's cub. A low, base, cowardly fellow.

A جبيش *jabīsh*, Shaven privities.

A جبيل *jabīl*, A crowd of people. Ugly. A dry tree. *Jubayl*, (dim. of جبل *jabal*) A little mountain. Name of a city in Syria.

A جبيلة *jabīlat*, A tribe.

A جبين *jabīn*, (pl. اجبن *ajbun*, اجبنة *ajbinat*, and جبن *jubun*) The temple, the side of the forehead. (pl. جبناء *jubanāʼ*) Pusillanimous. P جبين سا شدن *jabīn-sā shudan*, To rub the forehead upon the ground, to make a profound reverence.

A جبينان *jabīnāni*, Sides of the forehead.

A جبيهاء *jubayhāʼ*, (dim. of جبهاء *jabhāʼ*) A little woman with a large forehead.

P جت *jat*, Name of a despised race called Jauts in Hindūstān.

A جتّ *jatt*, (for جسّ) Feeling, handling (sheep) to ascertain whether (they) be fat or the contrary.

P جتبونتن *jatbūnitan*, (in zand and Pāz.) To sit.

P جتره *jutra*, Stained, polluted.

A جثّ *jass*, (v. n. of جثّ) Cutting, amputating. Striking, putting in fear. Being frightened. Humming loud (a bee). Rooting out of the ground. *Juss*, Wax, and such parts of the bodies or wings of bees as are found amongst honey. High ground. A dead locust. Husks of fruit.

A جثا *jasa'*, (fut. يجثو *yajsū* or يجثي *yajsī*) He collected (camels) together.

A جثاء *jasāʼ*, Compensation. Power. Number, amount. *Jasāʼ* or *jusāʼ*, A person, body, figure. *Jisāʼ*, (v. n. 3 of جثي) Sitting together with the knees joined.

A جثاجث *jusājis*, Entangled (hair or plants).

A جثال *jusāl*, A lark.

A جثالة *jasālat*, (v. n. of جثل) Being thick and entangled. *Jusālat*, Fallen, scattered leaves.

A جثام *jusām*, The nightmare.

A جثّامة *jassāmat*, A sleeper, who indulges in bed, and sets not out with his fellow-travellers. A mild, gentle prince. Stupid, doltish.

A جثّة *jissat*, Misfortune, calamity. *Jussat*, (pl. جثث *jusas*) The body of any large animal. The figure of the human body (standing, sitting, or reclining). A dead carcase.

A جثجاث *jasjās*, A bitter plant found on the banks of the Nile. Entangled, bushy (hair).

A جثجثة *jasjasat*, (v. n. of جثجث Q) Darting like a chain (lightning).

A جثر *jasir*, (A place) covered with stones, sand, and salt water.

A جنط *jast*, A voiding of liquid excrement.

A جنل *jasl*, (v. n. of جنل) Carrying away (as the wind). Many. Thick, entangled (foliage or hair). (Hair) short, bushy, and black. *Jasal*, A mother. A wife.

A جثلة *jaslat*, Hair hanging over the forehead. A tree full of foliage. (pl. جثل *jasl*) A large ant.

A جثم *jasm*, (v. n. of جثم) Reclining on the breast. Remaining in a place. Large-dated (cluster). *Jasqm* or *jusam*, Corn risen above the ground. *Jusam*, One who oversleeps himself.

A جثمان *jusmān*, The body. Any thing resembling the human figure when erect (as a vapour, spectre, and the like). A form, a figure.

A جثمانية *jusmāniyat*, Corporeity, bodiliness. The thing itself; middle, heart, principal part.

A جثمة *jusmat*, A collection or heap of earth, clay, or ashes. *Jasamat*, A hillock. *Jusamat*, One who oversleeps himself. Sedentary.

A جثوّ *jusūw*, A kneeling. A standing on tiptoe.

A جثوة *jas*, *jis*, or *juswat*, A heap of stones. The body. A burning coal or billet.

A جثولة *jusūlat*, (v. n. of جثل) Being thick and entangled. Thickness, bushiness of the hair.

A جثوم *jasūm*, A sitter, squatter. Seated, lying on the breast (as a bird). *Jusūm*, (v. n. of جثم) Reclining on the breast (a bird, shepherd, or traveller). Remaining (in a place). Sticking in, inhering. Dying, perishing. Reaching to the middle (night). Having large dates (a cluster). Collecting earth, clay, or ashes. Rising erect above the ground (corn). A hillock.

P جثّه داري *jussa-dārī*, Bulkiness, corpulency.

A جثيّ *jusa'* or *jisa'*, Stones forming the enclosure of the sacred precincts of Mecca, and on which sacrifices are offered. جثي الحرام *jusa'* (or *jisa'*) *l harāmi*, Stones heaped together when flung at a sacred festival at Mecca.

A جثيّ *jusīy*, (v. n. of جثا for جثو) Kneeling. *Jusīy* or *jisīy*, (pl. of جاثي *jāsī*) Kneelers.

A جثيث *jasīs*, A young palm or sucker.

A جثيل *jasīl*, Thick, entangled (foliage or hair). (Hair) short, bushy, and black.

P ججا *jajā*, An eagle.

A جحّ *jahh*, (v. n. of جحّ) Stretching out. Eating a small shrivelled melon. *Juhh*, A small shrivelled melon. A colocynth.

A جحا *jaha'*, (fut. يجحو *yajhū*) He eradicated.

A جحاجح *jahājih*, (جحاجحة *jahājihat* or جحاجيح *jahājīh*) (pl. of جحجح *jahjah* or جحجاح *jahjāh*) Chiefs of the people.

A جحاد *jihād*, (pl. of جحد *jahid*) Thick and short (horses).

A جحّاد *jahhād*, Slow (in consummating).

A جحادريّ *juhādiriy*, Large, great.

A جحاديّ *juhādīy*, Thick, large.

A جحادية *juhādiyat*, A bottle full of milk, or a sack full of dates or corn.

A جحارب *juhārib*, Large-bodied (horse).

A جحارم *juhārim*, Bad-tempered (man).

A جحاس *jahās*, (v. n. of جحس) Fighting hand to hand. Striving, exerting one's self. *Jihās*, (v. n. 3 of جحس) Thronging, pressing (as a crowd). Preventing, obstructing.

A جحاش *jihash*, (v. n. 3 of جحش) Pushing, squeezing. Striving, labouring. (pl. of جحش *jahsh*) Asses' colts.

A جحاشر *juhāshir*, Short-ribbed (horse). Stout, firm-jointed.

A جحاشل *juhāshil*, Swift, nimble, quick.

A جحاظ *jihāz*, Socket of the eye. Ora glandis.

A جحاف *jihāf*, (v. n. 3 of جحف) Thronging. Battle. When a (leathern) bucket, striking against the side of a well, is either torn or spills the water. *Juhāf*, Death. An universal mortality sweeping off numbers. A great deluge. The flux or diarrhœa.

A جحافل *jahāfil*, (pl. of جحفل *jahfal*) Troops, crowds. (pl. of جحفلة *jahfalat*) The lips of solid-hoofed animals.

A جحال *juhāl*, Poison, venom.

A جحام *juhām*, A distemper causing a swelling in the eyes. A disease in a dog's head.

A جحّام *jahhām*, Avaricious.

A جحامر *jahāmir*, (or جحامير *jahāmir*) (pl. of جحمرش *jahmarish*) Decrepit old women.

A جحانب *juhānib*, Dwarfish.

A جحجاح *jahjāh*, (or جحجح *jahjah*) (pl. جحاجح *jahājih*) A prince, chief amongst the people. A worthless man.

A جحجبة *jahjabat*, (v. n. of جحجب Q) Destroying, exterminating (an enemy). Wavering from side to side, going to and fro.

A جحجح *juhjuh*, A large ram.

A جحجحة *jahjahat*, (v. n. of جحجح Q) Curiously prying into, using every effort to get the knowledge of. Making haste, outstripping. Dashing on the ground. Retiring from (a rival). Hindering, warding off.

A جحد *jahd*, (v. n. of جحد) Denying, disowning. Meeting with a miser. *Jahd* or *jahid*, Scanty in acts of charity. جحد المستغرق *jahdu'l mustaghrak*, An absolute negative. *Juhd*, *jahd*, or *jahad*, Little good. *Jahad*, (v. n. of جحد) Faring hard. Being barren from drought. Being stunted in (its) growth (a plant). Being scant in acts of charity. *Jahid*, (fem. جحدة *jahidat*) (pl. جحاد *jihād*) Thick set and short (horse).

A جحدب *jahdab*, A dwarf. A lion.

A جحدر *jahdar*, Short. A dwarf.

A جحدرة *jahdarat*, A throwing down.

A جحدل *jahdal* or *juhdul*, Fat, compact.

A جحدلة *jahdalat*, (v. n. of جحدل Q) Throwing prostrate. Letting out camels on hire. From being poor, becoming rich. Tying. Filling a bottle. Collecting (wealth). Bringing (camels) together.

A جحدمة *jahdamat*, Swiftness in running.

A جحر *jahr*, (v. n. of جحر) Being sunk deep in the socket (the eye). Remaining behind. Entering his hole (a lizard). Driving (a lizard) into his hole. Being far advanced towards the meridian (the sun). Being disappointed, and unvisited by the vernal showers. A deep cavern. *Juhr*, (pl. جحرة *jiharat*, أجحار *ajhār*, and جحران *juhrān*) The den or hole of an animal.

A جحراء *jahrā*, Sunk in the socket (eye).

A جحران *juhrān*, The den of a beast. The privities of a woman. اذا حاضت المرأة حرم الجحران *izā hāzati'l mar,at haruma'l juhrān* (a proverb).

A جحرب *jahrab*, Large-bodied (horse). *Jahrab* or *juhrab*, Short, thick-bodied. جحربان *juhrabāni*, Two veins about a horse's ears.

A جحرة *jahrat* or *jaharat*, A season severe and barren. *Jiharat*, (pl. of جحر *juhr*) The dens or holes of beasts or reptiles.

A جحرش *jahrash*, Thick, compact (horse).

A جحرط *jihrit*, A decrepit old woman.

A جحرم *jahram*, A man of bad disposition.

A جحرمة *jahramat*, Poverty, difficulty. Badness of temper.

A جحزط *jihzit*, A decrepit old woman.

A جحس *jahs*, (v. n. of جحس) Fighting hand to hand. Scratching, wounding with the nails. Killing. Entering. جحس ودحس *jahs u dahs*, Fraud, stratagem, cunning, art, finesse.

A جحش *jahsh*, (v. n. of جحش) Grazing the skin without making a wound, scratching. (pl. جحاش *jihāsh* and جحشان *jihshān*) The colt of a horse or ass. Thickness, coarseness. Cruelty, severity. War against infidels. Endeavour, effort. A buck, a cheveril. A name of زينب *zaynab*, called امّ المؤمنين *ummu'l mu,minīn*, Mother of believers.

A جحشان *jihshān*, (pl. of جحش) Asses' colts.

A جحشة *jahshat*, An ass's colt (a filly). Wool (which a shepherd winds on his fingers to be employed in spinning).

A جحشر *jah* or *juhshar*, Short-ribbed (horse).

A جحشل *jahshal* or *juhshul*, Swift, nimble.

A جحشم *jahsham*, A camel whose sides bulge.

A جحط *jihit*, A word for driving sheep.

A جحظ *juhhaz*, (pl. of جاحظ) Prominent-eyed.

A جحظم *jahzam*, Large-eyed.

A جحف *jahf*, (v. n. of جحف) Peeling, barking. Carrying off the ball at shinty. Kicking (any thing) away. Drawing (water) and carrying (it) away. Sweeping or removing with a shovel. Bringing out food. Collecting. Excavating, searching. Inclining. The game of bandy.

A جحفة *jahfat*, A slice of butter. A little water left in the sides of a cistern. The gripes. A game of ball; shinty or bandy. *Juhfat*, Water remaining in the sides of a cistern or well. A little pudding in a bason. A handful of victuals. A patch of ground fit for grazing on a hillock in a desert.

A جحفل *jahfal*, (pl. جحافل *jahāfil*) A large army. (A man) of great dignity. Large-sided.

A جحفلة *jahfalat*, (v. n. of جحفل Q) Throwing on the ground. Rebuking, upbraiding. Assembling an army. (pl. جحافل *jahāfil*) The lip of a solid-hoofed animal (as a horse or ass).

A جحفلتان *jahfalatāni*, Two excrescences on the fore-legs of a horse.

A جحل *jahl*, (v. n. of جحل) Throwing (one) upon the ground. Large-sided. Small camels. A large water-bottle. The queen-bee. A chameleon. (pl. جحول *juhūl* and جحلان *juhlān*) A beetle or may-bug. A large Lybian lizard.

A جحلاء *jahlā*, Large (she-camel).

A جحلان *juhlān*, (pl. of جحل *jahl*) Beetles.

A جحلمة *jahlamat*, A throwing on the ground.

A جحم *jahm*, (v. n. of جحم) Kindling (a fire). Staring. *Jaham* or *juhm*, (v. n. of جحم) Being kindled, blazing. *Juham*, A kind of bird. *Juhum*, Shameless persons. (pl. of اجحم *ajham*) Large and red-eyed.

A جحماء *jahmā*, (fem.) Large and red-eyed.

A جحمة *jahmat*, (in the Himyarit dialect) The eye. *Jahmat* or *juhmat*, Fire piled up.

A جحمرش *jahmarish*, (pl. جحامر *jahāmir*) A decrepit old woman, or ugly, hideous, disgusting. A hare having a suckling. A rough-skinned viper.

A جحمش *jahmash*, A decrepit old woman.

A جحمظة *jahmazat*, (v. n. of جحمظ Q) Binding, confining. Running with full speed. Stringing (a bow). An infant's swaddling-bands. A cord with which they tie an ox or a sheep when about to kill it. (A slave) having his hands tied to his knees (to be flogged). Pace of a dwarf.

A جحموش *juhmūsh*, An old woman.

A جحمي *jahma'*, (pl. of جحماء *jahmā*) Large and red-eyed females.

A جحن *jahn*, (v. n. of جحن) Stinting (a household) through indigence or avarice. *Jahan*, (v. n. of جحن) Being fed with unwholesome food (a child). *Jahin*, (An infant) badly nourished. A lad of slow growth. The tike. Small and weakly (plant).

A جحنب *jahnab*, (or جحنّب *jahannab*) A dwarf. Powerful, strong. Rank, dignity.

A جحنبار *jihimbār*, A sort of plant. *Jihimbār*, (*juhumbār*, جحنبارة *jihimbārat* or *juhumbārat*) A big-bellied corpulent man. A swag-bellied dwarf.

A جحنبرة *jahambarat*, A female dwarf.

A جحنة *juhnat*, A tike.

A جحنش *jahnash*, Thick.

A جحنشة *jahnashat*, (v. n. of جحنش Q) Being big (the belly of a child).

A جحنفل *jahanfal*, Thick-lipped.

A جحو *jahw*, (v. n. of جحا for جحو) Eradicating, extirpating. Stopping still. Walking, stepping. Going out.

A جحوان *jahwān*, Name of a man.

A جحوة *jahwat*, One pace or step. The face.

A جحود *juhūd*, (v. n. of جحد) Denying, disowning, disavowing. Meeting with a miser.

A جحوش *jahwash*, A boy, ere he has attained his strength.

A جحوظ *juhūz*, (v. n. of جحظ) Being large and prominent (the eye). Criticising, finding fault.

A جحوف *jahūf*, A bucket, drawing or carrying water. Crumbled or grated bread left upon a plate.

A جحول *juhūl*, (pl. of جحل *jahl*) Beetles.

A جحوم *juhūm*, A being kindled; blazing.

P جحي *juhī*, Name of a buffoon.

A جحيش *jahīsh*, A part. A side. A half. A man who keeps alone. *Juhaysh*, (dim. of جحش *jahsh*) A little ass. جحيش وحده *juhayshu wahdihi*, (A man) wedded to his own opinion.

A جحيم *jahīm*, A large hot fire, kindled in a deep place. A very hot place. Hell.

A جحيمر *juhaymir*, (dim. of جحمرش *jahmarish*) A little old woman.

A جحيناء *juhaynā*, Hope, desire, expectation.

P جخ *jakh*, Quarrelsome, contentious. Strife.

A جخ *jakh*, Bravo! well done!

A جخّخ *jakhkh*, (v. n. of جخّ) Scattering (urine). Kicking (dirt) about. Lying with (a concubine). Raising (the belly), stretching forth (the arms). Lying on the side at full length, stretched out. Moving from place to place. Gross, foolish, worthless (man). Noisome, unhealthy.

A جخابة *jakhābat*, (*jikhābat* or جخّابة *jakhkhābat*) A fool. Gross, heavy, fleshy.

P جخاجخ *jakhājakh*, A clashing of swords.

A ابو جخاد *abū juhhād*, A locust.

A جخادب *jukhādib*, (or ابو جخادب *abū jukhādib*) Large-bodied (camel, locust, or beetle). A long-legged green locust.

A جخادباء *jukhādibā*, (or جخادبي *jukhādiba'* Thick, large, bulky. A sort of locust or beetle.

A جخادبة *jukhādibat*, Thick, large, bulky. A sort of locust or beetle.

A ابو جخادبي *abū jukhādiba'*, Thick, large, bulky. A sort of locust or beetle.

A جخادر *jukhādir*, Large-bodied.

A جخاديّ *jukhādiy*, A milking-pail. Large-bodied (camel).

A جخّاف *jakhkhāf*, Proud, arrogant.

A جخب *jakhb*, Extenuated, lean, hollow.

A جخبّ *jikhabb*, A large camel. A prince, commander. Weak.

P جخج *jakhj*, (or جخش *jakhsh*) A species of bat, but as large as a kite, which suspends itself to the branches of trees, and is said to eat its own ordure. A wen on the neck without pain; a goitre.

A جخجخة *jahhjakhat*, (v. n. of جخجخ Q) Throwing prostrate. Calling out, proclaiming aloud. Calling out جخ جخ *jakh jakh*. Keeping close (one's counsel). Lying with (a girl). Entering into the greater part of any thing.

P جخجس *jakhjas*, (or جخجن *jakhijn*, *jakhjan*, or *jukhjan*) A sort of small black seed used as a salve for sore eyes.

A جخدب *jukhdab*, A lion. *Jukhdub*, A lion. A sort of locust or beetle. Thick, large, bulky.

A جخدر *jakhdar*, (or جخدريّ) Large-bodied.

A جخدف *jakhdaf*, Great, large, corpulent.

A جخدل *jakhdal* or *jukhdul*, Fat, compact.

A جخدمة *jakhdamat*, Speed in walk or work.

A جخر *jakhr*, (v. n. of جخر) Widening the mouth (of a well). *Jakhar*, (v. n. of جخر) Being wide (a well). Being empty (the belly). Becoming stale (meat); stinking about the privities (a woman). Being wide (the bottom of a well). Drinking on an empty belly, so that the water makes a rattling noise on the stomach and renders (the flock) feeble. *Jakhir*, A glutton, one soon hungry. A coward. Feeble. Lank about the thighs. Weak-brained, addle-pated. Hideous, stinking.

A جخراء *jakhrā*, Stinking, rank (woman); also wide. Narrow (eye), and dirty with flux.

P جخشيدن *jakhshīdan*, (or جخسيدن *jakhsīdan*) To be wrinkled, shrivelled, twisted, curled, complicated. To labour hard, employ every endeavour. To distinguish by a mark. To be startled, frightened suddenly (a colt).

A جخف *jakhf*, (v. n. of جخف) Being proud. Boasting, laying claim to merit when undeserved. Sleeping. Terrifying. The snore of any one asleep. Levity, inconstancy. *Jukhuf*, (pl. of جخيف *jakhīf*) Souls, spirits. Large armies. Dwarfs.

A جخفا جخفا *jakhfan jakhfan*, Boastingly.

A جخفة *jakhfat*, Dwarfish and meagre (woman).

جخنة *jukhnat*, A tike.

A جخنّة *jukhunnat*, Bad in coitu (woman).

A جخو *jakhw*, (v. n. of جخا for جخو) Turning bottom upwards (a jar). A looseness of the skin, a leanness about the thighs.

A جخواء *jakhwā*, Lean-thighed (woman).

A جخوذة *jakhwazat*, A running pace.

A جخيف *jakhīf*, (v. n. of جخف) Boasting falsely, making unjust pretensions. Sleeping. Terrifying. Proud, haughty, lofty. The snoring of any one asleep. A rumbling noise in the belly. Levity, inconstancy. (pl. جخف *jukhuf*,) Soul, spirit. A numerous army. Short, dwarfish.

A جدّ *jadda*, (fut. يجدّ *yajiddu* or *uddu*) He strove.

A جدّ *jadd*, (v. n. of جدّ) Lopping (a palm-tree), gathering its fruit. Stripping a stalk of its dates. Cutting off as much cloth as will suffice to make a garment. Being happy, fortunate. Being great in dignity and wealth. Running (a house with rain).

A جدّ *jadd*, (pl. اجداد *ajdād*, جدود *judūd*, and جدودة *judūdat*) A grandfather (paternal or maternal), an ancestor, forefather. Dignity. Grandeur. Happiness, prosperity, good fortune. Riches. Bank of a river. Happy, fortunate. The surface of the ground. جدّ صحيح *jaddi sahīh*, A paternal grandfather. جدّ فاسد *jaddi fāsid*, A maternal grandfather. P جدّ بزرگ *jaddi buzurg*, An ancestor. A *Jidd*, (v. n. of جدّ) Speaking truth. Running (a house with rain). Endeavour, study, effort, labour, industry, application, diligence, pains. Seriousness, gravity. Haste, velocity. Any thing elaborately ascertained. The bank of a river. جدّ موفور *jiddi manfūr*, A great effort. بجدّ *bi jiddin*, Plainly, clearly. عالم جدّ عالم *ʻālimun jidda ʻālimin*, One who has attained the highest point of learning. الجدّ وسيلة الجدّ *al jidd wasilatu'l jadd*, Labour is the way to wealth. *Judd*, A well in a place plenteous in forage. A well having much, also little water. An ancient well. A well on the border of a desert. Little water. A sort of fruit. A side. Fatness. Happy. The coast off Mecca.

A جدا *jada'*, Common good, free to all. Universal, general, widely-diffused (rain). The end of an age. A gift, a present.

P جدا *judā*, Separate, distinct, divided. Apart. جدا جدا *judā judā*, One by one, separately. جدا شدن *judā shudan*, To be separated. جدا كردن *judā kardan*, To part, divide, disunite, dissolve.

A جداء *jadāʼ*, A benefit, advantage. *Jidāʼ*, (pl. of جدي *jady*) Kids. *Judāʼ*, The product of any number multiplied by itself (nine being the جداء *judāʼ*, or square of three).

A جدًّا *jiddan*, Plainly, clearly. In no shape. In earnest, seriously, attentively, eagerly, exceedingly, strongly.

A جدّاء *jaddāʼ*, (fem. of اجدّ *ajadd*) Small-breasted (woman). Crop-eared (animal). (A desert) without water. (A sheep) without milk. *Jiddāʼ*, (or بجدّاء *bi jiddāʼ*) Plainly, clearly.

A جداب *jidāb*, (v. n. 3 of جدب) Experiencing (a season) destitute of provision (a camel).

A جداة *judāt*, (pl. of جادي *jādī*) Askers of gifts.

A جداجد *jadājid*, (pl. of جدجد) Crickets.

A جداد *judād* or *jidād*, Loppings of palm-trees. *Jidād*, (v. n. 3 of جدّ) Disputing a point of right. Co-operating diligently with another. (pl. of جدود *jadūd*) Fat asses.

A جدّاد *jaddād*, One who sells, or who doctors wine. *Juddād*, (from P گداد *gudād*) Worn garments. Entangled branches. Ravelled threads. Low mountains.

A جدار *jidār*, (pl. جدر *judr* and *judur*) A wall.

A جدارة *jadārat*, (v. n. of جدر) Being worthy, proper, suitable, befitting. Shooting forth (the heads of plants) as if they were pimples or pock-marks.

P جدارك *judārak*, Name of a certain game.

P جدا شدگي *judā-shudagī*, Separation, separateness, the state of being separate.

P جدا شده *judā-shuda*, Separated.

A جداع *jadāʻ*, A severe year (for cattle). *Jidāʻ*, (v. n. 3 of جدع) Reviling, abusing. Disputing, wrangling. *Judāʻ*, Pastures where the herbage is burnt up. Unwholesome fodder. Death.

A جدافاء *judāfāʼ*, (جدافي *judāfa'* or جدافاة *judāfāt*) Prey, spoil, booty.

P جداگانه *judāgāna*, Separately, apart.

A جدال *jadāl*, Unripe, green dates. *Jidāl*, (v. n. 3 of جدل) Debating, wrangling. A warm altercation, violent contest, battle, conflict. P جنگ و جدال *jang u jidāl*, War and strife. جدال كردن *jidāl kardan*, To fight, quarrel, wrangle.

A جدّال *jaddāl*, The owner or seller of a dovecote (called جديلة *jadīlat*).

A جدالة *jadālat*, Ground especially sandy. Unripe dates when green and round. Small ants furnished with feet.

A جداماة *judāmāt*, Laden with fruit (palm).

A جدامة *judāmat*, Chaff of wheat.

A جدامئ *judāmaʼ*, A sort of fruit.

A بالجدّان *bi'l jiddān*, Plainly, clearly.

P جدانك *jid* or *jadānak*, A kind of game.

A جداول *jadāwil*, (pl. of جدول *jadwal*) Brooks. Columns. Astronomical tables.

P جداوي *jadāwī*, Servants' wages, salary, pay.

A جدايا *judāya'*, (pl. of جديّة *jadiyat*) Stuffings (of camel's saddles).

A جداية *jadāyat* or *jidāyat*, A doe, roe, gazel.

A جدائد *jadāʼid*, (pl. of جدود *jadūd*) Sheep giving little milk.

A جدائل *jadāʼil*, Locks of braided hair.

P جدائي *judāʼī*, Separation, disunion, desertion. جدائي كردن *judāʼī kardan*, To separate from, desert.

P جدب *jadb*, The pith of the palm-tree.

A جدب *jadb*, (v. n. of جدب) Charging, accusing of a fault. Being barren and scarce. Sterility. A severe season. Barren (place or places).

A جدبّ *jidabb*, Sterility. A severe season.

A جدباء *jadbāʼ*, (fem. of اجدب *ajdab*) Desolate.

A جدبة *jadbat*, (fem. of جدب) Barren (place).

P جد بجد *jad ba jad*, From father to son.

A جدة *jidat*, (v. n. of وجد) Discovering, procuring, finding, recovering (any thing lost or sought for). Being rich, having enough. Being enraged, taking occasion to quarrel with, or chide (another). Money, wealth, opulence.

A جدّة *jaddat*, A grandmother (paternal or maternal). جدّهٔ صحيحه *jaddaʼi sahīha*, A paternal grandmother. جدّهٔ فاسده *jaddaʼi fāsida*, A maternal grandmother.

A جدّة *jiddat*, (v. n. of جدّ) Being new. Newness. A dog's collar. The surface of the ground. *Jiddat* or *juddat*, A rag. The bank of a river. *Juddat*, A streak on the back of an ass. (pl. جدد *judad*) A way, track, path. A mode, method, system. A sign, signal, or distinguishing mark. Name of a town situated on the Red Sea, the port of Mecca (generally pronounced Jidda); also of a maritime tract of country where the Arabians suppose Eve to have fallen when banished from Paradise; Adam, according to their belief, being thrown upon the island of Ceylon. ركب جدّة الامر *rakiba juddata'l amri*, He took the line proper to be pursued.

P جدتين *jadtīn*, Embroidered (purse, wallet).

A جدث *jadas*, (pl. اجدث *ajdus* and اجداث *ajdās*) A tomb.

A جدثة *jadsat*, The sound (of a horse's hoof or camel's foot); also that of masticating meat.

A جدجد *jadjad*, Hard and level ground. *Judjud*, (pl. جداجد *jadājid*) An insect which resembles a locust, or (according to some) a beetle, and utters a shrill noise during the night; a cricket. A large female pudendum. A pimple or sty.

A جدح *jadh*, A stirring up a draught or ptisan.

A جدد *jadad*, Hard, even ground. Fine sand. A tumour or wen on a camel's neck. The surface of the ground. *Judad*, (pl. of جدّة *juddat*) Ways, tracks, paths. *Judud*, (pl. of جديد *jadīd*) New. Pieces of cloth fresh cut from the loom.

P جدر *jadr*, A four-year-old camel.

A جدر *jadr*, (v. n. of جدر) Having the small-pox. (pl. جدر *judr*, *judur*, and جدران *judrān*) A wall. The wall surrounding the temple of Mecca. A breaking out of the small-pox. The bottom or foundation, also the side, of a wall. (pl. جدور *judūr*) Name of a herb (growing in the sand). *Jidr*, A sort of plant. *Jadar*, (v. n. of جدر) Breaking out on a man (pimples and pocks). Having a mind to put forth leaves (a vine). A swelling in the throat. A kernel in the flesh. A pimple, a pock. The mark of a bite on an ass's neck. The berry or seed of a palm-branch. *Jadar* or *judar*, (pl. اجدار *ajdār*) A wen on the body, either natural or caused by a blow or wound. *Jadir*, Worthy, suitable. *Judur* or *judr*, (pl. of جدر *jadr* and جدار *jidār*) Walls.

A جدراء *jadrāʼ*, Scabby (sheep). *Judarāʼ*, (pl. of جدير *jadīr*) Places enclosed by walls. Worthy, suitable. Pock-marked.

P جدراك *judrāk*, A kind of game.

A جدران *judrān*, (pl. of جدر *jadr*) Walls.

A جدرة *jadarat*, An unnatural excrescence on the body, a wen, a blotch. Name of an Arabian tribe, so called because they built the wall (جدار *jidār*) of the temple of Mecca.

A جدريّ *jadariy* or *judariy*, Small-pox, pits.

A جدس *jadas*, An offset of the tribe لحم *lahm*.

A جدش *jadasha*, (fut. يجدش *yajdishu*) He had a mind to take.

A جدش *jadash*, (pl. اجداش *ajdāsh*) Coarse, rough, rugged ground.

A جدع *jadʿ*, (v. n. of جدع) Mutilating in, or depriving of (ear, hand, nose, or lip). Giving unwholesome food to a child. Carrying off. Destroying. Imprisoning. *Jadaʿ*, (v. n. of جدع) Taking unwholesome aliment (an infant). Unwholesomeness of pasture. Amputation. A mutilation of the ear, hand, nose, or lip. A prison. *Jadiʿ*, Poorly fed (child).

A جدعاء *jadʿāʾ*, (fem. of اجدع *ajdaʿ*) Mutilated in the hand, &c. Name of Muhammad's camel.

A جدعا له *jadʿan lahu*, May his nose, ears, hands, and lips be cut off!

A جدعة *jadaʿat*, That which remains of an amputated nose, ear, lip, or hand; the stump.

A جدف *jadf*, (v. n. of جدف) Amputating, cutting. Snowing. Striking with both fists. Rowing (a vessel). Pausing, breaking off in his song (a camel-driver). *Jadaf*, (pl. اجداف *ajdāf*) A grave. Wine not covered up. A kind of herb found in Arabia Felix, which has the property of quenching the thirst, when masticated. Any thing thrown off drink (as froth, motes, &c.). A kind of wine.

A جدفاء *jadfāʾ*, Crop-eared (ewe).

A جدفة *jadafat*, Sounds. Clamours, mixed murmurs. The noise made in running.

P جدگاره *jadgāra*, Different roads. Contrary ways or opinions.

A جدل *jadl*, (v. n. of جدل) Twisting (a rope) tight. Throwing prostrate on the ground. Growing, increasing in strength (as a youth, fawn, or grain in the ear). The grave. *Jadl* or *jidl*, (pl. اجدال *ajdāl* and جدول *judūl*) Strong and hard penis. The hollow bones of the hands or feet. A coarse, thick bone. The limb or member of an animal. *Judl*, (pl. of جدلاء *jadlāʾ*) Strongly-woven (coats of mail). *Jadal*, Altercation, contention. Energy, ability for disputation. P جدل كردن *jadal kardan*, To dispute. To fight. A *Jadil*, Litigious, contentious, disputatious. *Judul*, (pl. of جديل *jadīl*) Bridles of twisted thongs or hair. Ladies' girdles.

A جدلاء *jadlāʾ*, (pl. جدل *judl*) Well-formed (woman or leg). Strong (coat of mail) of a firm texture. Bent-eared (ewe), curved (substance شقشقة *shikshikat*). Name of a bitch.

A جدلان *jadlān*, as ذهب على جدلانه *zahaba ʿala jadlānihi*, (or جدلائه *jadlāʾihi*) He went his way.

A جدلة *jadlat*, A pestle.

A جدلي *jadaliy*, A disputant, controvertist, polemic. Of the tribe of جديلة *jadīlat*.

A جدم *jadm*, (v. n. of جدم) Bearing fruit and withering (a palm-tree). *Jadam*, A bird resembling a sparrow with a red beak. A kind of date.

A جدمة *jadamat*, (pl. جدم *jadam*) Short-statured (man). Sheep of a bad kind. Unripe dates. Unthrashed wheat. Chaff of wheat.

A جدمل *jadmal*, A plant (stapelia dentata).

A جدن *jadan*, Sweetness or elegance of voice. Name of a dreary waste in Yaman (Arabia Felix).

A جدو *jadw*, (v. n. of جدا for جدو) Asking for, seeking some benefit.

A P جدوار *jadwār*, Zedoary.

A جدوب *jadūb*, Barren, sterile (spot), scarce (year). *Judūb*, (pl. of جدب *jadb*) Barren places.

A جدوبة *judūbat*, (v. n. of جدب) Being barren. Scarcity, dearth, sterility, barrenness.

A جدود *jadūd*, (pl. جدائد *jadāʾid*) A ewe giving little milk (but not from disease). (pl. جداد *jidād*) A fat she-ass. *Judūd*, (pl. of جدّ *jadd*) Grandfathers.

A جدودة *judūdat*, (pl. of جدّ *jadd*) Grandsires.

A جدور *judūr*, (v. n. of جدر) Having the mark of a bite on his neck (an ass). Rendering worthy. Putting forth fruit like tubercles (a tree). Shooting forth as if they were pimples or pock-marks (the heads of a plant). Blistering from labour (the hand). Building a four-square wall. Lying concealed behind a wall. (pl. of جدر *jadr*) Herbs growing in the sand.

A جدوف *judūf*, (v. n. of جدف) Flying with the wings clipped, as if turned back (a bird). Pausing, breaking off in his song (a camel-driver). Shortening his steps (a wild buck). Flying fast. Snowing, casting flakes of snow (the sky). Striking with both fists (a man).

A P جدول *jadwal* or *jidwal*, (pl. جداول *jadāwil*) A rivulet. An astronomical table. Marginal lines on the page of a book drawn with gold or silver.

A جدول *judūl*, (v. n. of جدل) Being hard. (pl. of جدل *jadl* or *jidl*) Limbs of animals.

P جدومند *jadūmand*, equiv. to مفارق *mafārik*.

A جدوي *jadwaʾ*, General rain. Common good. Gift, present. اخو جدوي *akhū jadwaʾ*, Liberal.

A جدّوي *jiddawiy*, A native of Jidda.

A جدي *jady*, (v. n. of جدي) Seeking a benefit. (pl. اجدي *ajdi*, جداء *jidāʾ*, and جديان *jidyān*) A kid. The sign Capricorn. The polar star. A lamb until it be a year old. (pl. of جدية *jadyat*) Stuffings of saddles.

A جديّ *judayyaʾ*, My little kid.

A جدّي *jaddiy*, Ancestral. *Juddiy*, Fortunate.

A جديان *jidyān*, (pl. of جدي *jady*) Kids.

A جديب *jadīb*, Severe (year). Desolate and barren (country). جديب الجناب *jadību'l janāb*, Every way distressed.

A جدية *jadyat*, (or جديّة *jadiyat*) (pl. جدي *jady* and جدايا *jadāyaʾ*) Felt-cloth pannels or dorsers for laying under saddles or beneath loads, on camels or horses. Blood flowing. Dry blood sticking to the body. A tract of country. A particle of musk. Colour of the face.

A جديد *jadīd*, New, modern, fresh. (pl. جدد *judud*) New cloth recently cut from the loom. Death. Happy, fortunate. The surface of the ground. لكلّ جديد لذة *li kulli jadīdin lazzatun*, Every novelty affords delight.

A جديدان *jadīdāni*, Night and day (ever new).

A جدير *jadīr*, (pl. جديرون *jadīrūn* and جدراء *judarāʾ*) A place surrounded with walls. Proper, fit. Worthy, suitable. Gadīra, a town in Spain.

A جديرة *jadīrat*, A stone sheep-cote. Nature.

A جديس *jadīs*, Name of a tribe (now extinct).

A جديل *jadīl*, (pl. جدل *judul*) A bridle of twisted thongs or hair. A lady's girdle (of leather, frequently adorned with jewels). Prostrate on the ground. Name of a certain stallion.

A جديلة *jadīlat*, Mode, manner, state, condition. A tract of country, a quarter. A tribe, family. Leathern drawers worn by boys and menstruous women. A pigeon-house. Name of the mother of a tribe.

A جذّ *jazz*, (v. n. of جذّ) Breaking off. Cutting up by the roots. Making haste. Breaking in pieces. (pl. اجذاذ *ajzāz*) A bit, a piece.

A جذاء *jizāʾ*, (pl. of جاذي *jāzī*) Standers on tip-toe. (pl. of جذاة *jazāt*) Roots of large trees. (pl. of جذوة *jaz, jiz*, or *juzwat*) Glowing billets.

A جذّاء *jazzāʾ*, Broken (tooth). Disconnected, broken off (friendship amongst relations).

A جذاب *jazāb*, Death. *Jizāb*, (v. n. 3 of جذب) Turning away, diverting. The medullary substance growing on the top of a palm-tree. (pl. of جاذب *jāzib*) (Camels) which yield no milk.

A جذّاب *jazzāb*, Drawing, pulling, dragging.

A جذّابة *jazzābat*, A horse-hair springe for larks.

A جذاة *jazāt*, (pl. جذاء) The root of a large tree.

A جذاذ *jazāz*, The excellence or superiority of one thing to another. *Juz, jaz*, or *jizāz*, A fragment, particle. *Juzāz*, A stone containing gold ore.

A جذاذات *juzāzāt*, Particles of gold.

A جذاذة *jazāzat*, The superiority of one thing to another. *Juzāzat*, (Gold) filings.

A جذاع *jizāʿ*, (pl. of جذع *jazaʿ*) Youths.

A جذال *jizāl*, (pl. of جذل *jizl*) The roots of very large trees. Trunks of trees (stripped of their branches), pollards.

A جذام *juzām*, The leprosy.

A جذامة *juzāmat*, Stubble (after harvest). Chaff.

P جذام خانه *juzām-khāna*, Lazaretto, pest-house.

A جذامر *juzāmir*, One who breaks a contract.

A جذامير *jazāmīr*, (pl. of جذمار *jizmār* or of جذمور *juzmūr*) Stumps remaining on a tree stripped of its branches. اخذه بجذاميره *akhazahu bi jazāmīrihi*, He took it all.

A جذّان *jazzān*, Soft stones.

A جذّانة *jazzānat*, A soft stone.

A جذب *jazb*, (v. n. of جذب) Stretching. Drawing (as a plaster or the loadstone). Overcoming in pulling. Turning away, diverting. Weaning (a colt). Giving little milk (a camel). Drawing to a close (a month). Cutting off the medullary substance on the summit of a palm-tree. Sucking in water (without using a cup or the hands). Allurement, attraction. Dryness in the mouth. Swift (march or journey). P جذب كردن *jazb kardan*, To draw, attract. جذب گياه *jazbi giyāh*, Attraction of straws. A *Jazab*, The medullary substance which grows on the summit of the palm-tree.

A جذبات *jazabāt*, Attractions, allurements. اخذ في وادي جذبات *akhaza fī wādi jazabāt*, He missed the mark, he lost his way.

A جذبّان *jizibbān*, The strap or latchet of a shoe passing between the great toe and the next to it.

A جذبة *jazbat*, Part of a long journey, distance. Disjunction, separation. One silken thread. Passion. Strong desire.

A جذّة *juzzat*, A strip of cloth, clout, rag.

A جذجذة *jazjazat*, A cutting up by the roots.

P جذر *jazr*, The square root of a number or quantity, or that which being multiplied into itself produces the given number or quantity. Thus 3 is the جذر *jazr* of 9. A camel four years old.

A جذر *jazr*, (v. n. of جذر) Cutting up by the roots. *Jazr* or *jizr*, (pl. جذور *juzūr*) Root, origin. Root of the tongue and penis. The square root of any number: as, 3 is the جذر *jazr* of 9, 11 that of 121. The veil or tapestry of the Kaaba. The nape of the neck.

A جذع *jazaʻa*, (fut. يجذع *yajzaʻu*) He kept (a horse) without food. He overcame the journey. He passed rapidly by.

A جذع *jazʻ*, (v. n. of جذع) Keeping (a horse) without food. Tying two camels with one rope. Imprisoning. Treating contemptuously. *Jizʻ*, (pl. جذوع *juzūʻ*) The trunk (of a palm-tree). Name of a man. *Jazaʻ*, (pl. جذاع *jizāʻ* and جذعان *juzʻān*) A young man. A raw recruit. The young of cattle (as a bullock, heifer, or sheep, two years old; a horse, three; a camel, five). The year that a quadruped sheds his milk-teeth. الازلم الجذع *al azlamu'l jazaʻ*, Time. Fortune. A lion. الدهر جذع *ad'dahr jazaʻ*, Time is ever young. امّ الجذع *ummu'l jazaʻ*, Misfortune.

A جذعان *juzʻān*, (pl. of جذع *jazaʻ*) Young (men or animals). Small mountains.

A جذعمة *jazʻamat*, Little. A little one.

A جذع مذع *jizaʻa mizaʻa*, In all directions.

A جذف *jazf*, (v. n. of جذف) Cutting. Flying with clipped wings (a bird). Flying fast. Taking short steps. Rowing (a boat).

A جذل *jazl*, A large root. Boughs like clusters of dates. *Jizl*, (pl. اجذال *ajzāl*, جذال *jizāl*, جذول *juzūl*, and جذولة *juzūlat*) The root of a great tree; the trunk after the branches are lopped off, a pollard. The side of a shoe. A little wealth. Boughs resembling clusters of dates. The scrubbing-post, put up near wells where camels water. The summit or projecting part of a mountain. جذل رهان *jizlu rihānin*, One who lays wagers. جذل الطعان *jizlu't tiʻān*, Name of علقمة *ʻalhamat*, an Arabian noted for his skill in the use of the spear. جذل مال *jizli māl*, A skilful manager of property. *Jazal*, (v.n. of جذل) Rejoicing. *Jazil* and جذلان *jazlān*, (pl. *juzlān*) Glad, cheerful.

A جذلان *juzlān*, (pl. of جاذل) Erect. Cheerful.

A جذلة *jazilat*, (A vine) luxuriant in branches.

A جذم *jazm*, (v. n. of جذم) Amputating, lopping, mutilating. *Jizm* or *jazm*, (pl. اجذام *ajzām*, جذوم *juzūm*) A root. دافنة الجذم *dāfinatu'l jizm*, (A cow) having teeth worn out and almost hid. *Jazam*, (v. n. of جذم) Having the hand cut off. Suffering from the leprosy or elephantiasis. *Jazim*, Swift. *Jizam*, (pl. of جذمة *jizmat*) Whips.

A جذماء *jazmāʼ*, (fem. of اجذم *ajzam*) (A woman) having the hand cut off. Amputated hand. (for مجذومة *majzūmat*) Leprous (woman).

A جذمار *jizmār*, The stump left on the trunk of a palm-tree after lopping off a branch.

A جذمان *juzmān*, Membrum virile, or its root.

A جذمة *jazmat* or *jazamat*, The place of amputation. *Jizmat*, (pl. جذم *jizam*) A scourge, whip. A piece cut off any thing. *Juzmat*, Mutilation. *Jazamat*, The medullary substance on the head of the palm-tree.

A جذمور *juzmūr*, (pl. جذامير *jazāmīr*) The stump left on the trunk of a palm-tree after lopping off a branch. Root, origin, principal. اخذه بجذموره *akhazahu bi juzmūrihi*, He took it entirely.

A جذمي *jazmaʼ*, (pl. of اجذم *ajzam*) Those whose hands have been cut off.

A جذميّ *jazamīy* or *juzamīy*, Belonging to the tribe جذيمة *jazīmat*.

A جذن *jizn*, (equiv. to جذل *jizl*) A root; origin. The trunk of a tree without branches.

A جذو *jazw*, (and جذوّ *juzūw*) (v. n. of جذا for جذو) Standing, or rising on tiptoe. Sticking to a camel's side (a tike). Carrying fat (a camel's bunch).

A جذوب *jazūb*, Attracting. Dry (camel).

A جذوة *jaz, jiz,* or *juzwat*, (pl. جذي *jizaʼ*, *juzaʼ*, and جذاء *jizāʼ*) A burning coal or billet. A thick piece of firewood.

A جذور *juzūr*, (pl. of جذر *jazr*) Roots, origins. Square roots. Napes of necks.

A جذوع *juzūʻ*, (pl. of جذع) Trunks (of palms).

A جذول *juzūl*, (v. n. of جذل) Being placed, being erect. Being firm. *Juzūl*, (and جذولة *juzūlat*) (pl. of جذل *jizl*) Lopped trunks of trees, pollards.

A جذوم *juzūm*, (pl. of جذم *jizm*) Roots.

A جذي *jazy*, (v. n. of جذي) Hindering, preventing. *Jizy*, Root, origin. *Jizaʼ* or *juzaʼ*, (pl. of جذوة *jaz, jiz,* or *juzwat*) Glowing billets.

A جذية *jizyat*, The root of a tree.

A جذيذ *jazīz*, (or جذيذة *jazīzat*) Bruised wheat, or barley-meal.

A جذيل *juzayl*, A little scrubbing-post.

A جذيم *jazīm*, Cut off, mutilated.

A جذيمة *jazīmat*, Name of an Arabian tribe.

P جر *jar*, Crack, cleft, rent, fissure; particularly in the ground. Cracked ground. *Jur*, A saddle.

A جرّ *jarr*, (v. n. of جرّ) Drawing, dragging, haling, hurrying away, pulling about. Going over her time (a woman, mare, or camel). Grazing and walking about (camels). Being mounted on a camel, and allowing her to graze. Slitting (the tongue of) a camel's colt (that he might not suck). Driving gently. Drawing upon one's self guilt. Marking the last letter of a word with the vowel كسرة *kasra* ـِـ. The base or foot of a mountain. A valley, hollow, declivity. A basket. A lizard's or fox's hole. Something made from the bough or tendon Achilles of a camel into which a woman puts meat dressed with sweet herbs, and then suspending it at the hinder part of a portmanteau it keeps in continual motion. A rope tied to the plough-gear. (pl. of جرّة *jarrat*) Water-pots.

A جرا *jaraʼ*, Female beauty, youthful bloom.

A جراء *jarāʼ* or *jirāʼ*, The bloom of youth (in the female sex. The corn or grain of a plant. *Jirāʼ*, (v. n. of جري) Running. (v. n. 3 of جري) Running or going (along with another). Consenting, agreeing. (pl. of جرو *jarw*, *jirw*, or *jurw*) Whelps. Small cucumbers or colocynths.

A جرآء *juraʼāʼ*, (pl. of جريء) Strong, brave.

A جرّاء *jarrāʼ*, A good runner; fleet, swift.

A جراءة *jarāʼat*, Boldness, bravery, hardihood.

A جراب *jirāb*, (pl. جرب *jurub*, *jurb*, and اجربة *ajribat*) A kid-leather bag, in which travellers or shepherds carry provisions. The scrotum. That space in a well between the brink and water. (pl. of جرب *jarib*) Scabby. *Jurāb*, An empty ship.

P جرابه *jarāba*, A sock.

A جرآة *jarāʼat*, (v. n. of جرؤ) Being bold, courageous. Bravery, boldness, hardihood.

A جرأة *jurʼat*, Boldness, bravery. Rashness.

A جراثيم *jarāsīm*, Earth heaped around a tree.

A جراجب *jarājib*, Large, fat (camels).

A جراجر *jarājir*, (pl. of جرجور *jurjūr*) Large, bulky camels. *Jurājir*, A loud, noisy camel that drinks much. Water which rushes with noise.

A جراجم *jarājim*, The noise of milk shaking in a bottle.

A جراجمة *jarājimat*, A people in Mesopotamia.

A جراح *jirāh*, (pl. of جراحة *jirāhat*) Wounds.

A جرّاح *jarrāh*, A surgeon.

A جراحة *jirāhat*, A wound. The pus of a sore.

P جراحت بند *jirāhat-band*, A bandage for a wound.

A جرّاحيّ *jarrāhiy*, Surgical, chirurgical.

A جراد *jarād*, A locust (m. or f.). Men. جراد البحر *jarādu'l bahr*, (Sea-locust) A shrimp.

A جرّاد *jarrād*, (pl. جرّادون *jarrādūn*) A polisher or scourer of copper vessels.

A جرادة *jarādat*, One locust. *Jurādat*, Skin. A leaf stripped off a branch.

A جرادتان *jarādatāni*, Name of two female musicians who lived at Mecca in the days of paganism.

A جرادق *jarādiḳ*, (pl. of جردقة) Cakes.

A جرادين *jarādīn*, (pl. of جردان *jurdān*) The yards of solid-hoofed quadrupeds.

A جرازين *jarāzin*, (pl. of جرذانة) Sorts of dates.

A جرار *jirār*, (v. n. 3 of جرّ) Vexing, annoying. Delaying, putting off (any one). (pl. of جرّة *jarrat*) Water-pots, earthen jugs.

A جرّار *jarrār*, Drawing (a thing) to, with, or after one. (An army) numerous, and loaded with incumbrances. A seller of water-pots or buckets. A beggar. عسکر جرّار *ɛaskari jarrār*, A numerous and warlike army. P جرّار عدوّ شکار *jarrāri ɛadūw-shikār*, Victorious soldiers. جرّار کوچه و بازار *jarrāri kūcha u bāzār*, A beggar in the streets and markets.

A جرّارة *jarrārat*, A numerous, encumbered army. A scorpion of a small species with a heavy tail, which he drags after him.

P جرّاره *jarrāra*, A large species of deadly scorpion found in Ahwāz. A ringlet of hair.

A جراز *jarāz*, Name of a plant. ذو جراز *zū jarāz*, Hard and thick. *Jurāz*, Sharp (sword). Voracious (camel).

A جرازة *jarāzat*, (v. n. of جرز) Eating quick.

P جراسك *jarāsak*, A kind of grasshopper.

G جراسيا *jarāsiyā*, A cherry.

A جرّاش *jurrāsh*, (pl. of جارش) Criminals.

A جراشة *jurāshat*, Coarsely-pounded particles.

A جراشع *jarāshiɛ*, Spacious valleys. Stunted and rugged mountains. (pl. of جرشع *jurshuɛ*) (Horses or camels) fat with inflated sides.

A جراصل *jurāṣil*, A mountain. A hollow, a valley.

A جراصية *jurāṣiyat*, Lusty. A strong camel.

A جرآض *jirɛāẓ*, Big-bellied. Thick and strong. A lion. Afflicted, sad.

A جراض *jirāẓ*, Thick and strong. A lion. *Jurāẓ*, (A camel) soft and gentle towards her colt. A thick-necked camel.

A جراضم *jurāẓim*, A glutton, gormandizer.

A جراف *juraf* or *jirāf*, A large measure for dry goods. *Jurāf*, (A flood) sweeping every thing before it. One who thrusts the hand into any thing, especially a dish, and devours greedily. Lecherous. Cheerful, sprightly.

A جرّاف *jarrāf*, A sweeper, scraper. امّ الجرّاف *ummu'l jarrāf*, A shield, a buckler. A bucket.

A جرافز *jurāfiz*, Thick, large-bodied.

A جرافس *jurāfis*, Thick and hard. A large camel. A lion breaking his prey.

A جرافش *jurāfish*, Large-sided. Large (man).

A جرافض *jurāfiẓ*, Unhealthy, noxious, noisome.

A جرافيس *jarāfīs*, (pl. of جرفاس *jirfās*) Large-bodied. Thick and hard.

A جراقة *jurāḳat*, Lean (man). ما عليه جراقة لحم *mā ɛalayhi jurāḳatu lahmin*, He has almost no flesh upon his bones.

A جراك (من *min*) *jarāka*, (or *jarrāka*) On thy account.

A جرام *jarām*, Date-stones. *Jarām* and *jirām*, The gathering of dates or grapes. *Jirām*, (pl. of جريم *jarīm*) Gathered dates. Date-stones. Large-bodied. *Jurām* or *jarām*, Dry dates. Date-stones.

A جرّام *jurrām*, A fish. (pl. of جارم *jārim*) Gatherers of dates.

A جرامة *jurāmat*, Dates or grapes which fall when being gathered. Chaff.

A جرامز *jarāmiz*, The legs and body of a quadruped. The body of a man.

A جرامض *jurāmiẓ*, Unhealthy, unwholesome.

A جرامقة *jarāmiḳat*, A kind of thorn. Name of a tribe of strangers settled at Mawṣil at the beginning of Islām.

A جراميز *jarāmīz*, (pl. of جرموز *jurmūz*) Cisterns with high sides. Small reservoirs. Small houses. Wells. Young he-wolves. The feet of a beast. Human bodies. اخذه بجراميزه *akhazahu bi jarāmīzihi*, He took all.

A جراميق *jarāmīḳ*, (pl. of جرموق) Leathern hose.

A جران *jirān*, (pl. جرن *jurun*) The fore or curved part of the neck of a camel or horse. جران العود *jirānu'l ɛawd*, Name of a certain poet.

P جرانغار *jarānghār*, The left-hand side, the second line of the left wing of an army.

A جراول *jarāwil*, (pl. of جرول) Stony grounds.

A جراهم *jurāhim*, A large-bodied robust camel. A lion. A large mountain.

A جراهية *jarāhiyat*, A high-toned voice. Noise, clamour. Important (affair). Excellent (horse).

A جراهية *jarāhiyatan*, Plainly, evidently.

A جرايا *jarāyā'*, (for جرائي *jarāɛā*) (pl. of جريئة *jarīɛat*) Lurking-places where hunters lie in wait.

A جراية *jarāyat*, A course. Bloom, female beauty. The office of attorney or deputy. Bravery, valour, courage. *Jarāyat* or *jirāyat*, Embassy, agency. *Jirāyat*, A fixed stipend, current salary. Youthfulness.

A جرائحي *jarāɛiḥīy*, A surgeon.

A جرايحية *jarāyiḥīyat*, Surgeons.

A جرائد *jarāɛid*, (pl. of جريدة) Books, tomes.

A جرائر *jarāɛir*, (pl. of جريرة) Faults, crimes.

A جرائش *jurāɛish*, Thick, large, bulky.

A جرائض *jurāɛiẓ*, (pl. *jarāɛiẓ*) Voracious, leaf-devouring (camel). Thick, fat, strong. A lion.

A جرائك (من *min*) *jarrāɛika*, (or جرائك *jarāɛika*) On thy account, for thy sake.

A جرائم *jarāɛim*, (pl. of جريمة *jarīmat*) Crimes. جرائم سابقه *jarāɛimi sābiḳa*, Past offences. والي الجرائم *wālī'l jarāɛim*, A magistrate, police-officer.

A جرائية *jarāɛiyat*, Bravery, valour, courage. Youthful bloom.

A جرب *jarb*, (v. n. of جرب) Scraping, hewing (a stone). *Jurb*, (pl. of اجرب *ajrab*) Scabby. *Jurb* or *jurub*, (pl. of جراب *jirāb*) Wallets. Insides of wells. *Jarab*, (v. n. of جرب) Being scabby. Having scabby camels. Being destroyed (a country). Scab. Rust in the scabbard of a sword. A roughness under the eyelid causing water to flow. *Jarib*, (pl. جراب *jirāb* and جرب *jurb*) Scabby.

P جرب *jurab*, The heath-cock.

A جربّ *jarabb*, Short of stature. A deceiver, flatterer, cheat.

A جرباء *jarbāɛ*, (fem. of اجرب *ajrab*) Scabby. Heaven. Barren (ground). A beautiful girl. The orbit of the sun and moon.

A جربّاء *ji* or *juribbāɛ*, The breast of a shirt.

A جربان *jarbān*, (pl. جربي *jarba'*) Scabby. *Jirbān*, The edge of a sword; a scabbard or belt. *Jurbān*, (pl. of جريب *jarīb*) Certain corn-measures.

A جرّبان *jurubbān*, The collar of a garment. The breast of a shirt. The edge of a sword. The scabbard. The belt.

A جرّبانة *jiribbānat*, Grossness, obscenity. An obscene, noisy woman.

A جربة *jirbat*, (pl. جرب *jirab*) A sown field, or one ready for sowing. A piece of leather fixed on the brink of a well to prevent the water from falling in. Land without water or grass. A tree.

A جربّة *jarabbat*, A body of strong men. A herd of asses. An expensive unproductive family.

A جربذة *jarbazat*, (or جرباذ *jirbāz*) A heavy pace, with a hanging of head (in horse or camel).

A جربز *jurbuz*, (P گربز) Arch, sly; a deceiver.

A جربزة *jarbazat*, (v. n. of جربز Q) Going. Being contracted, drawn together. Falling. Being arch, sly (like a جربز *jurbuz*).

P جربناك *jarabnāk*, Scabby, mangy.

A جربي *jarba'*, (pl. of جربان *jarbān*) Scabby, mangy. اوبار الجربي *awbāru'l jarba'*, Name of a plant, which, when dried, becomes green.

A جربياء *jirbiyāɛ*, A south-east wind. The north or its cold. A weak man.

A جرة *jurat*, Bravery, courage, valour.

A جرّة *jarrat*, (pl. جرّ *jarr* and جرار *jirār*) A water-pot. Bread baked in the ashes. A loaf. *Jirrat* or *jarrat*, (pl. اجرّة *ajirrat*) That part of food which cattle bring up when chewing the cud. The cud. A toil for taking deer, a buckstall. *Jirrat*, A mode of drawing. A company who halt and start afresh. *Jurrat*, A buckstall. A box with many holes in the bottom for drilling wheat: a drill.

A جرثلة *jarsalat*, A flinging (of earth) about.

A جرثمة *jursumat*, Root, origin.

P جرثوم *jarsūm*, Firmly rooted: of noble origin.

A جرثومة *jursūmat*, (pl. جراثيم *jarāsīm*) Root, origin. Soil collected about the root of a tree. An ant-hill. The top of the wind-pipe.

A جرثيّ *jurasīy*, A kind of grape.

A جرثئة *jarsiat*, The wind-pipe.

A جرج *jurj*, (pl. of جرجة *jurjat*) Wallets, saddle-bags. *Jaraj*, (v. n. of جرج) Moving in a circle, turning round (a wide ring upon the finger). Wavering, tottering, on account of the roughness of the ground. A high road. The middle of the road. *Jarij*, Loose (belt) which moves round.

A جرجار *jarjār*, A camel braying in the throat. A kind of fragrant herb. Roar of thunder.

A جرجارة *jarjārat*, A mill.

P جرجان *jurjān*, A province and city in Persia.

A جرجبّ *jurjubb*, The belly. Inside cavity.

A جرجبان *jurjubān*, The belly. Inside cavity.

A جرجبة *jarjabat*, An eating. A taking the contents of a vessel.

A جرجة *jurjat*, (pl. جرج *jurj*) A cloak-bag, portmanteau. بنو جرجة *banū jurjat*, The inhabitants of Mecca. *Jarajat*, A straight road. A beaten path.

A جرجر *jarjar*, An iron instrument for threshing corn. *Jirjir*, A camel which makes a loud braying noise. Rocket. *Jirjir* or *jarjar*, A vetch, bean.

P جرجر *jirjir*, A bean. The herb rocket.

A جرجرايا *jarjarāya'*, Name of a city in Arabian Irāk. A great drinker. Water which makes a loud gurgling noise.

A جرجرة *jarjarat*, (v. n. of جرجر Q) Making a gurgling noise when descending the throat (liquor). The noise made by a camel in the throat when braying; that made by liquor flowing down the gullet. Causing any one to drink so as to make a gurgling noise.

A جرجس *jirjis*, Wax. Clay used to seal with. A book. A leaf, a page. Small gnats.

A جرجمان *jurjumān*, A glutton.

A جرجمة *jarjamat*, (v. n. of جرجم Q) Drinking. Eating. Prostrating. Demolishing.

A جرجور *jurjūr*, (pl. جراجر *jarājir*) A large, bulky camel. A noble, generous camel. A crowd, a troop. Complete (hundred).

A جرجوم *jurjūm*, Saffron. Prostration.

A جرجير *jirjīr*, Rocket.

A جرجيس *jirjīs*, George, particularly St. George of England, whom the Muhammadans rank among the prophets, and confound with the prophet Elias, as the name *Khizr Elia* implies, by which they also distinguish him.

A جرح *jarh*, (v. n. of جرح) Wounding. Reviling. Confuting, convicting (a witness) of falsehood. Being disproved (testimony). Acquiring, purchasing. Receiving a wound. *Jurh*, (pl. جروح *jurūh* and اجراح *ajrāh*) A wound.

A جرحة *jurhat*, A wound.

A جرحي *jarha'*, (pl. of جريح *jarīh*) Wounded.

P جرخست *jarkhast*, A wine-press.

P جرد *jard*, A royal throne. A certain blue bird. A kingfisher. *Jarad*, Wounded.

A جرد *jard*, (v. n. of جرد) Scraping, shaving, erasing. Denuding. Making (a country) bare. Carding cotton. Eating up herbage (locusts). Being sleek (a horse). Being bare of vegetation (a country). Having excoriations, pimples, or gripes from eating locusts. Begging and receiving a denial, or gift unwillingly. A shield. Barren (spot). (pl. اجراد *ajrād*) Threadbare (garment). Remainder, residue, balance. Horses or horsemen without footmen. Penis. Vulva. *Jurd*, (pl. of اجرد *ajrad*) Horses with fine coats, sleek. Hairless (men). اهل الجنّة جرد مرد *ahlu'l jannat jurd murd*, The inhabitants of Paradise are hairless and beardless. *Jarad*, (v. n. of جرد) Being bald; baldness. Having excoriations or pimples on the body from eating locusts. An open country exhibiting no appearance of vegetation. The back. A kind of disease in a horse's leg, stringhalt. *Jarid*, Bare, barren (field). Griped (from eating locusts).

A جرداء *jardā*, (fem. of اجرد *ajrad*) Bare, barren (country). Pure, neat (wine). Hard and shining (stone). Hairless (shoe).

A جرداب *jirdāb*, (P گرد آب) Midst of the sea.

A جرداح *jirdāh*, (or جرداحة) Rising grounds.

P جردان *jardān*, A plate (for receiving contributions for the poor). A staple, hasp of a padlock.

A جردان *jurdān*, (pl. جرادين *jarādīn*) The yard (of any solid-hoofed animal).

A جردان فار *jardān-fār*, A dormouse.

A جردبان *jardabān* or *jurdubān*, One who claps his hands upon meat on a table (to prevent it from being carried off). *Jardabān*, (from P گرده بان *girdabān*) Keeper of the bread.

A جردبة *jardabat*, (v. n. of جردب Q) Eating with an insatiable appetite. Laying his left hand on the meat to prevent any one from taking it (whether he use the right hand in eating or not).

A جردبيّ *jardabiy*, A feast-hunter. One who claps his hands upon meat on a table (to prevent it from being carried off). One who eats from his right hand, and uses the left in repelling.

A جردبيل *jardabīl*, A feast-hunter.

A جردة *jardat*, A threadbare garment. *Jurdat*, Nakedness. *Juridat*, Bare, barren ground.

A جردحة *jarduhat*, A stretching out (of the neck).

A جردحل *jirdahl*, A large camel, male or female. A valley, channel.

A جردقة *jardakat*, A thin cake, cheesecake.

A جردلة *jardalat*, A threatening to fall.

A جردم *jardam*, A black locust with a green head. A great talker.

A جردمة *jardamat*, (v. n. of جردم Q) Being past sixty. Making haste. Talking much. See جردبة.

A جردون *jirdawn*, (or جرذون) Rat, field-mouse.

P جردة *jarda*, A cream-coloured horse. *Jurda*, A horse bred from an Arabian sire, but not an Arabian dam. A gelding.

A جرذ *jarz*, (v. n. of جرذ) Granulating, becoming knotty (as a sore). *Jaraz*, Any tumour about the houghs of horses or camels. A wrinkle. *Juraz*, (pl. جرذان *jirzān*) A species of the field-mouse.

A جرذان *jirzān*, (pl. of جرذ *juraz*) Field-mice. ام جرذان *ummu jirzān*, A species of date.

A جرذانة *jarzānat*, (pl. جراذين) A sort of date.

A جرذة *jarizat*, (Land) full of field-mice.

A جرذقة *jarzakat*, A thin cake.

A جرذمة *jarzamat*, A making haste.

P جررا *jarrā*, (in zand and Pāzand) A portion, a share. A stone.

P جرز *jarz*, A bustard.

A جرز *jarz*, (v. n. of جرز) Cutting off, amputating. Lopping. Striking, wounding. Killing. Eating with haste. (pl. اجراز *ajrāz*) Bare, sterile (ground), parched, having no rain. *Jirz*, (pl. جروز *jurūz* and اجراز *ajrāz*) A kind of female garment made of camel's hair; also a coarse one made of sheep-skins. *Jurz* or *juruz*, Bare, burnt-up land. (from P گرز *gurz*) (pl. اجراز *ajrāz* and جرزة *jirazat*) A mace. *Jaraz*, Parched (land). Barren year. Body, breast, or waist of a man. Flesh of a camel's back. ذو جرز *zū jaraz*, Hard and thick.

A جرزان *jurzān*, Name of a country in the Greater Armenia.

A جرزة *jarzat*, A complete extirpation. *Jurzat*, A bundle of hay or grass. *Jarazat*, Ruin, destruction. *Jirazat*, (pl. of جرز *jurz*) Iron maces.

A جرزم *jarzam* or *jirzim*, Dry bread.

P جرس *jars*, Echo. *Jaras*, A bell hanging from (a horse's) neck. A prison. جرس در گلو بستن *jaras dar gulū bastan*, To tie a bell to the throat. (met.) To sing melodiously. جرسهاى زر *jaras-hāi zar*, The stars.

A جرس *jars*, (v. n. of جرس) Licking with the tongue. Sipping, sucking (a bee). Speaking. Humming. A part of any thing. *Jars* or *jirs*, A gentle sound (as that of a bird's bill when pecking). Part of the night. *Jirs*, Root, origin. *Jurs*, (v. n. of جرس) Culling (as a bee among flowers). Speaking in a low tone. Singing. *Jaras*, (pl. اجراس *ajrās*) A bell (especially one appended to the neck of a camel or mule). Name of a dog.

A جرسام *jirsām*, Pleurisy. Deadly poison.

P جرست *jarrast*, The noise of gnashing of the teeth or tearing calico.

P جرسدار *jaras-dār*, A bellman: courier, post.

A جرسمة *jarsamat*, A fixing the eye intently.

A جرش *jarsh*, (v. n. of جرش) Combing (the head), clearing it of the dandruff. Pounding into coarse particles. Rubbing (a hide) to render it soft and supple. Scratching, rubbing. Peeling. Running slowly. The noise made by a snake quitting its slough. A part or watch of the night; the close of the night. *Jarsh*, *jursh*, *jirsh*, *jarash*, or *jurash*, Any part between the first and third part of the night. *Jurash*, Name of a district in Arabia whence they bring leather.

A جرشب *jurshub*, A dwarf, short of stature.

A جرشبة *jarshabat*, (v. n. of جرشب Q) Being lean, meagre. Falling sick, and afterwards recovering. Bending double with age (a woman). Attaining to the age of fifty (a woman), when the courses are dried up.

A جرشع *jurshuɛ*, (pl. جراشع *jarāshiɛ*) A large fat camel or horse with inflated sides. A river with a large bed. A mountain small but rugged.

P جرشفت *jarshaft*, Lampoon, pasquinade.

A جرشمة *jarshamat*, (v. n. of جرشم Q) Recovering from sickness. Beholding stedfastly. Putting on a grim, forbidding look.

A جرشيٰ *jirishsha'*, The soul. Breath.

A جرشيّ *jurashiy*, Of the town of جرش *jurash*.

A جرض *jarz*, (v. n. of جرض) Strangling. *Jaraz*, (v. n. of جرض) Having the throat obstructed by spittle almost to suffocation (from anguish or vexation). Being sad. Saliva kept in the throat from chagrin, so as to cause a partial suffocation.

A جرضم *jarzam*, A lean, tottering old man. *Jurzum*, A guttler, glutton, gormandizer.

A جرضّم *jirzamm*, A glutton. A sheep old and fat.

A جرضيٰ *jarza'*, (pl. of جريض) Afflicted, sad.

A جرط *jart*, (v. n. of جرط) Being almost choked with meat, or rage. Trouble, anguish, suffocation.

A جرع *jaraɛa*, (fut. يجرع *yajraɛu*) He sipped.

A جرع *jarɛ*, (v. n. of جرع) Drinking, gulping (water). Being twisted more than the rest (one thread of a rope). *Jaraɛ*, A collection. An overtwist in one of the threads (of a rope). *Jariɛ*, (A rope) of which one of the threads is overtwisted. *Juraɛ*, (pl. of جرعة *jurɛat*) Single draughts.

A جرعاء *jarɛā*, A sand-hill. A sandy desert. A sandy place where vegetation thrives.

A جرعب *jarɛab*, Gross, rude, stupid. Thick. A severe misfortune.

A جرعبة *jarɛabat*, A drinking (water) well.

A جرعبيل *jarɛabil*, Thick.

A جرعة *jarɛat* or *jaraɛat*, A sand-hill where vegetation thrives. Rugged ground resembling sand. A sand-hill yielding no herbage. *Jurɛat*, *jarɛat*, or *jirɛat*, (pl. جرع) One draught or gulp.

A جرعكوك *jurɛukūk*, (or جرعكيك) Thick milk.

A جرعوب *jurɛūb*, A great drinker of water. Large-bodied.

P جرعه *jurɛa*, Remains of (wine) at the bottom of a vessel.

P جرعه دان *jurɛadān*, A drinking-glass. A leathern pouch wherein travellers stow their victuals and their flask.

P جرعه ريز *jurɛa-rez*, A vessel having a spout, either for pouring any thing down a child's throat, or for pouring water on women's heads in a bath.

A جرعيب *jirɛib*, Coarse, rude, hard, stupid.

P جرغاتو *jarghātu*, (or جرغتو *jarghatū*) A cup which has a spout (to drink out of).

P جرغان *jarghān*, A cipher or character used amongst the worshippers of fire.

P جرغند *jarghand*, A sheep's haslet. A lamp. A lamp-stand.

P جرغون *jarghūn*, (or جرغول) A plantane.

A جرف *jurf*, (v. n. of جرف) Taking every thing. Digging, ploughing. Sweeping or removing (with a shovel). A plentiful year. Goods or effects, both live and dead stock. Luxuriant herbage. Dry grass or hay in which a snake is found. A mark (on a camel's thigh or body). *Jirf*, The corner of the mouth. *Jirf* or *jurf*, A place which a torrent does not take. *Jurf*, A mark on (a camel's) thigh or body. *Jurf* and *juruf*, (pl. اجراف *ajrāf* and جرفة *jirafat*) That which the current carries along with it. A bank eaten into by the stream. A precipice. *Jiraf*, (pl. of جرفة *jirfat*) Sand-hills. Crumbs of bread.

A جرفاس *jirfās*, (pl. جرافيس *jarāfis*) Thick and hard. A large camel. A lion crushing his prey.

A جرفة *jarfat*, (v. n. of جرف) Taking much, carrying off all. Sweeping, shovelling. Diversified (soil). *Jirfat*, (pl. جرف *jiraf*) Writhed sand presenting the appearance of a rope. A piece of bread. A cutting but not a separating of a bit of skin on a camel's thigh. *Jurfat* or *jarfat*, A bit of a camel's skin cut, but not detached, and left as a mark. *Jirafat*, (pl. of جرف *juruf*) Particles of earth eaten or carried away by the stream.

A جرفسة *jarfasat*, (v. n. of جرفس Q) Throwing prostrate. Taking every thing, sweeping off. Eating voraciously.

P جرك *jurk*, A desert, a plain.

P جرگه *jargah*, A circle, ring (of men or beasts).

A جرل *jaral*, (v. n. of جرل) Being rough and hard (a place). (pl. اجرال *ajrāl*) Stones. A rough hard place. *Jaril*, (pl. اجرال *ajrāl*) Stony (ground).

A جرم *jarm*, (v. n. of جرم) Cutting. Divesting, stripping (a palm-branch of its dates). Shearing (sheep). Guessing at the produce of a palm-tree. Taking, bearing off. Gaining, acquiring. Committing a crime, trespassing. (from P گرم *garm*) Warm, hot. (pl. جروم *jurūm*) A warm country. A kind of boat or barge. *Jirm*, Sound, voice. Colour. (pl. اجرام *ajrām*, جروم *jurūm*, and جرم *jurum*) A body. A globe. The throat. جرم صبح *jirmi subh*, The light of the sun. جرم قمر *jirmi kamar*, The body of the moon. *Jurm*, (pl. اجرام *ajrām* and جروم *jurūm*) Sin, crime, fault. جرم و جنايت *jurm u jināyat*, Sin and guilt. *Jaram*, (v. n. of جرم) Eating dates which fall at gathering time. لا جرم *lā jaram*, لا ذا جرم *lā zā jaram*, لا عن ذا جرم *lā ɛan zā jaram*, or لا ان ذا جرم *lā an zā jaram*, Of necessity, assuredly, unquestionably, by all means: therefore. *Jurum*, (pl. of جرم) Bodies.

P جرم *jiram*, Name of a place in Irān.

A جرّم *jurram*, (pl. of جارم) Gatherers of dates.

A جرماق *jirmāk*, Gut whipped about a bow.

A جرمان *jirmān*, A body.

A جرمة *jirmat*, (pl. جرم *jiram*) A number of men gathering dates or grapes. A herd of thirty camels. Those who guess, estimate, or appraise the produce on a palm. *Jarimat*, A crime, fault.

A جرمزة *jarmazat*, (v. n. of جرمز Q) Being drawn together. Departing. Retiring from fear, fleeing.

P جرمزه *jarmuza*, A journey.

A جرمقاني *jarmakāniy*, One of those foreigners called جرامقة *jarāmikat*, who, at the beginning of Islām, settled at Mawsil.

A جرمقيّ *jirmikiy*, A garment worn by those persons who are called جرامقة *jarāmikat*.

P جرمناك *jurmnāk*, Guilty, criminal, faulty.

P جرمناكي *jurmnākī*, Guiltiness, criminality.

A جرموز *jurmūz*, (pl. جراميز *jarāmīz*) A cistern with high sides. A small reservoir. A small house. A well. A young he-wolf. بنو جرموز *banū jurmūz*, Name of a tribe.

A جرموق *jurmūk*, (from P سرموزه *sarmūza*) (pl. جراميق *jarāmīk*) A kind of leathern hose, worn over boots to keep them clean.

P جرمه *jarma*, A white or gray horse.

A جرن *jurn*, A place where dates are dried. A stone hollowed out and used as a bason. *Jaran*, Coarse, uneven, and stony ground. *Jurun*, (pl. of جران *jirān*) The fore or curved parts of the neck in camels and horses. (pl. of جرين *jarīn*) Threshing-floors. Places where dates are dried.

A جرنبة *jarambat*, Multitude of men or asses.

A جرنبذ *jarambaz*, Thick, gross.

A جرنبذة *jarambazat*, One whose mother has a husband.

P جرنده *jiranda*, Gristle.

P جرنغار *jaranghār*, The left wing of an army.

A جرنفس *jaranfas*, Large, thick-set man.

A جرنفش *jaranfash*, Large-sided (thing). Large (man). One who has a long and thick beard.

P جرنگ *jarang* or *jiring*, Jingling or tinkling of bells. Rattling of chains. Clashing of arms.

P جرنگيدن *jarangīdan*, To jingle, tingle, rattle, make a noise like the clashing of swords or the like.

A جرؤ *jaruɛa*, (fut. يجرؤ *yajruɛu*) He was brave.

A جرو *jarw*, *jirw*, or *jurw*, (pl. اجري *ajri*, اجرياء *ajriyāɛ*, اجراء *ajrāɛ*, and جراء *jirāɛ*) The whelp of a lion or a dog. (pl. اجرؤ *ajruɛ* جراء *jirāɛ*) The young of any thing down to a small cucumber or colocynth. A capsule, a seed, or a pod. Fruit just appearing. A swelling in the bunch and throat of a camel. *Jirw*, A dwarfish she-camel.

P جرواسك *jarwāsak*, A cricket.

A جرواض *jirwāz*, Gross, thick, strong. A lion.

A جرواط *jirwāt*, Long, tall.

A جروان *jirwān*, Wine.

A جروب *jarūb*, A hewn stone.

A جروة *jirwat*, A dwarfish she-camel. القي وطن جروته *alka' jirwatahu*, He was patient. وطن عليه جروته *wattana ʿalayhi jirwatahu*, He fixed his heart upon it.

A جروح *jurūh*, (pl. of جرح *jurh*) Wounds.

A جرود *jarūd*, A threadbare garment.

A جرور *jarūr*, Stubborn (horse or camel), refusing to follow. Very deep (well). A camel that eats much. A woman that is unable to rise from her seat from torpor or some physical defect in her constitution. A camel which has gone a month, two months, or forty days over her time (a year).

A جروز *jarūz*, Voracious, eating fast (man, woman, or camel). *Jurūz*, (pl. of جرز *jirz*) Female garments made of camels' hair, or of sheep-skins of a coarser kind.

A جروس *jarūs*, Name of a country between Herāt and Ghazna.

A جرول *jarwal*, (pl. جراول *jarāwil*) Stones. A complete handful. A certain beast of prey. *Jurawil*, Stony ground.

A جرولة *jurawilat*, Stony ground.

A جروم *jurūm*, (pl. of جرم *jarm*) Warm countries, sultry regions. Boats, vessels. (pl. of جرم *jirm*) Bodies. (pl. of جرم *jurm*) Crimes, trespasses.

P جرون *jarūn*, The ancient name of the city of Ormuz in the Persian gulf.

A جرون *jurūn*, (v. n. of جرن) Grinding (corn). Being trained, exercised, accustomed to (man or beast). Applying earnestly to. Being calendered, mangled, smoothed (linen). Being polished (a coat of mail).

P جروند *jarwand*, A lamp. A candle.

A جرة *jarah*, Unripe dates on one stalk.

P جرّه *jarra*, A jar, earthen water-vessel, ewer. *Jurra*, Active, quick. Moderately-sized, neither large nor small. A common name for any male bird or beast, but particularly of a male falcon; and it is used metaphorically for a hero or brave man. Any thing small. Name of a musical instrument. Name of a village near Shīrāz.

A جرهاس *jirhās*, Corpulent. A strong lion.

A جرهام *jirhām*, (A man) keen, active, diligent in his affairs. A lion.

A جرهة *jarhat*, A side. *Jarahat*, Several unripe dates in one pod.

A جرهد *jarhad* or *jurhud*, An active traveller.

A جرهدة *jarhadat*, (v. n. of جرهد Q) Going fast. A water-pot. *Jarhadat* or *jirhadat*, Swiftness, haste, expedition in travelling.

A جرهم *jurhum*, Name of an ancient tribe.

A جري *jary*, (v. n. of جري) Flowing, running, proceeding; moving (as ships, winds, sun, moon, or planets). Declining or conjugating. Happening.

A جريّ *jariy*, (pl. اجرياء *ajriyāʾ*) An ambassador. A hired servant. Surety, bail. A substitute, representative, procurator, agent, factor, manager.

A جرّيّ *jirriy*, The sheat-fish. An eel.

A جريء *jariʾ*, (pl. اجراء *ajrāʾ*, اجرياء *ajriyāʾ*, and جرآء *juraʾāʾ*) Bold, strong, brave. The leader of the van. A lion.

A جرياء *jiriyāʾ*, Nature, course of proceeding.

A جرياض *jiryāz*, Big-bellied. Thick and strong. A lion. Afflicted, sad.

A جريال *jiryāl*, A certain red tincture. The expressed juice of safflower. Any bright colour. The redness of gold. Wine, or its colour.

A جريالة *jiryālat*, Wine, or its colour.

A جريان *jiryān*, A red tincture. Wine. *Jarayān*, (v. n. of جري) Flowing, running, proceeding. Issuing, arising, springing. Happening, becoming. Flux of (blood or urine). P فرمان قضا جريان *farmāni kazā-jarayān* (pronounced *jiryān*), Mandates flowing like fate, *i. e.* irresistible. جريان آب *jiryāni āb*, Fluor albus. جريان شكم *jiryāni shikam*, Dysentery. A جريان مذيّ *jiryāni maziy*, Fluor albus. جريان مني *jiryāni manī*, A gleet.

A جريب *jarīb*, (pl. اجربة *ajribat* and جربان *jurbān*) A corn-measure equal to four قفيز *kafīz*. As much sown ground as will produce that quantity. A certain measure of land, 144 yards. A valley. (in India) Horticultural produce (such as tobacco, chilli, turmeric, garlic, onions, &c.).

P جريب امين *jarīb-amīn*, A land-surveyor.

P جريبانه *jarībāna*, A rate imposed for defraying the charges of measurement.

P جريب كش *jarīb-kash*, A land-surveyor.

P جريب كشي *jarīb-kashī*, Land-measuring.

A جرية *jiryat*, (v. n. of جري) Running, flowing. Flux of water. Mode of flowing. Purling of a stream.

A جرّيّة *jirrīyat*, A bird's crop.

A جرّيث *jirrīs*, An eel. A turbot.

A جريج *jurayj*, (dim. of جرجة) A little sack.

A جريح *jarīh*, Wounded (man or woman).

A جريّح *jurayyih* (dim. of جريح) Slightly wounded.

A جريد *jarīd*, A palm-branch stripped of its leaves. (A tree) despoiled of its branches, leaves, and bark. A lance, spear, rod, wand. Entire (day). بلاد الجريد *bilādu'l jarīd*, Numidia (Biledulgerid), so called from the abundance of palm-trees growing there. جريد المتن *juraydu'l matn*, The middle of the back.

A جريدان *jarīdāni*, Two days or months. مذ جريدان *muz jarīdāni*, Two days or months since.

P جريد بازي كردن *jarīd bāzī kardan*, To fight in sport, or by way of exercise or discipline.

A جريدة *jarīdat*, (pl. جرائد *jarāʾid*) A branch of a palm-tree stripped of the leaves. A number of horsemen or horses (part of a larger body). A remainder, surplus (of property).

P جريده *jarīda*, An account of receipts and expenses, a cash-book. A roll, volume, register. Only, alone. A short spear. Desolate. Deprived of relations and friends. Expeditious. جريده شدن *jarīda shudan*, To be expeditious, unencumbered.

A جرير *jarīr*, (pl. اجرّة *ajirrat*) A halter, leathern rein. A headstall for a camel.

A جريرة *jarīrat*, (pl. جرائر *jarāʾir*) Fault, crime. جريرتك (من *min*) *jarīratika*, On thy account.

P جريره *jarīra*, The daughter of Pīrān Visa.

A جريريّة *jarīriyat*, Name of a sect.

A جريسة *jarīsat*, Cattle stolen in the night.

A جريش *jarīsh*, Bruised, brayed, coarsely pounded. Salt of a bad flavour. An intrepid, penetrating man who gets through and executes business. *Juraysh*, Name of an idol formerly worshipped in Arabia.

A جرئض *juraʾiz*, Large, thick, stout. A lion.

A جريض *jarīz*, Suffocation. Anguish, grief. (pl. جرضي *jarzaʾ*) Afflicted, sad.

A جريعة *jurayʿat*, (dim. of جرعة *jurʿat*) A little draught. جريعة الذقن *jurayʿatu'z zakan*, (or جريعاء الذقن *jurayʿāʾu'z zakan*) The last breath.

A جريف *jarīf*, Dry trees. Dry grass or hay. A kind of fig.

A جريم *jarīm*, (pl. جرام *jirām*) Gathered dates or grapes. Dry dates. One who gathers or collects. Date-stones. Large-bodied. Guilty. Old.

P جريمانه *jarīmāna*, Fine, penalty, forfeit.

A جريمة *jarīmat*, (pl. جرائم *jarāʾim*) A crime, fault. A fine, mulct, pecuniary punishment. A gainer, acquirer. A provider for a family. A youngest child. Large-bodied (woman).

A جرين *jarīn*, (pl. جرن *jurun*) A place where dates are dried. Ground (corn). A threshing-floor.

A جريئة *jarīʾat*, (pl. جرايا *jarāyaʾ*) A lurking-place wherein the hunter awaits his prey.

A جرّيئة *jirriʾat*, A bird's crop.

P جز *jaz*, An island. *Jiz*, Fat of a sheep's tail fried, and poured over a dish of flour. *Juz*, Besides, except, other. جز از آن *juz az ān*, Besides that.

A جزّ *jazza*, (fut. يجزّ *yajuzzu*) He cut, reaped.

A جزّ *jazz*, (v. n. of جزّ) Having dates fit for cutting (a palm-tree). Mowing, cutting, reaping, shearing, clipping. A part of the night.

A جزء *jazʾ*, (v. n. of جزأ) Having enough, being content. Being satisfied with fresh grass and requiring no water (camels). Dividing in parts. Distributing portions. Binding. Dropping one complete part of a poem. *Juzʾ* or *jazʾ*, (pl. اجزاء *ajzāʾ*) Part, portion, particle. An ingredient. A quire of paper. A section of a book (the Kur'ān, for example, being divided into thirty جزء *juzʾ*, as the psalms are with us). A metrical foot. جزء لا يتجزأ *juzʾ lā yutajazzaʾ*, An indivisible atom. كلي و جزئ *kullī u juzʾī*, (or كلّ و جزء *kull u juzʾ*) In whole and part; totally, entirely, in every part. *Juzʾ*, The female part (of slaves).

A جزاء *jazāʾ*, (v. n. of جزي) Compensating, requiting. Sufficing. Satisfying. Recompense, retribution. دار الجزاء *dāru'l jazā*, The next world. P روز جزا *rozi jazā*, The day of retribution. A *Jizā*, (v. n. 3 of جزي) Requiting. (pl. of جزية *jizyat*) Tributes, contributions levied upon Jews and Christians. Revenues accruing from the soil.

A جزاب *jazāb*, Orchis flava (a plant).

A جزأة *juzat*, The handle (of an awl or knife). A vine-prop.

A جزاجز *jazājiz*, Penes. Testicles.

P جزء خوان *juz-khwān*, One who reads the Kur'an in parts.

A جزار *jizār* or *jazār*, (v. n. of جزر) Cutting clusters of dates. The season for so doing.

A جزّار *jazzār*, A camel-butcher.

A جزارة *jizārat*, The business of a camel-butcher. *Juzārat*, The neck and feet of a slaughtered (camel), which become the slaughterer's perquisite. عبل الجزارة *ablu'l juzārat*, Strong-legged (horse).

A جزاز *jazāz* or *jizāz*, Harvest. Date-cutting. *Jizāz*, Sheep-shearing. *Juzāz*, Any thing which falls in cutting leather, paper, &c., clippings.

A جزازة *juzāzat*, (pl. جزائز *jazāiz*) Any thing which falls in reaping, shearing sheep, gathering in dates or other produce. A cut, chip, shaving. Clippings, clip.

A جزاع *juzā*, Impatient.

A جزاف *juzāf*, *jazāf*, or *jizāf*, (from P گزاف *guzāf*) Guess, conjecture in buying or in selling. Random (sale or purchase), one made without weighing or measuring. Conjectural.

A جزّاف *jazzāf*, A fisherman.

A جزافة *juzāfat*, *jazāfat*, or *jizāfat*, Guess, conjecture in buying or selling.

A جزال *jizāl* or *jazāl*, The in-gathering of ripe dates, the date-harvest. *Jizāl*, (pl. of جزل *jazl*) Billets for the fire. (pl. of جزيل *jazīl*) Great, copious.

A جزالة *jazālat*, (v. n. of جزل) Being great, solid. Being endued with an excellent understanding.

A جزاية *jizāyat*, Tax, tribute.

A جزائر *jazāir*, (pl. of جزور *jazūr*) Camels destined for slaughter. (pl. of جزيرة *jazīrat*) Islands. Peninsulas. الجزائر *al jazāir*, Barbary. Algiers. الجزائر الخالدات *al jazāiru'l khālidāt*, (or جزائر السعادة *jazāiru's saādat*) The fortunate isles, the first meridian of Ptolemy. (They are six islands in the Western ocean, off the coast of Africa, producing in abundance all sorts of fruits, flowers, herbs, and grain).

P جزائري *jazāirī*, King of Persia's body guard.

A جزائز *jazāiz*, (pl. of جزازة) Clippings, shearings.

A جزائل *jazāil*, (pl. of جزيل *jazīl*) Copious. Numerous. Eloquent. *A* A large musket, wall-piece, swivel. A rifle used with a prong or rest.

P جزائل انداز *jazāil-andāz*, Who fires a rifle.

A جزب *jizb*, Part, portion. *Juzb*, Servants.

P جزبندي *juz-bandī*, The binding of a book.

P جزبه کردن *jazaba kardan*, To enrage.

A جزّة *jazzat*, Name of a country whence Antichrist is expected to proceed. *Jizzat*, One year's wool, a year's clip. (pl. جزز *jizaz*) Wool shorn and laid up.

P جزتن *juz-tan*, (Part of the body) a limb.

P جزجز *jizjaz*, The hissing of a frying-pan.

A جزجزة *jizjizat*, A lock of pelt wool. A flock of coloured wool appended to a camel-litter.

A جزح *jazh*, (v. n. of جزح) Going about one's business. Giving liberally without consulting any one. Entering a covert (a deer). Striking a tree that the leaves may fall. Assigning part of one's property. A gift, a boon. *Jazah* or *jazih*, Quick-sighted, shrewd (boy).

P جزد *jazd*, A cricket, a grasshopper.

P جزدان *juzdān*, A portfolio.

P جزدر *jazdar*, (*jizdar*, or جزدره *jazdara*) A fried sheep's tail.

A جزر *jazr*, (v. n. of جزر) Cutting (bunches of dates). Slaughtering or skinning (a camel). Decreasing, subsiding (water). Taking honey from a hive. Reflux, ebbtide. The sea. جزر و مدّ اقدام و احجام *jazr u maddi ikdām u ihjām*, The reflux and flux of resolves, *i.e.* irresolution. *Jazar*, A fat sheep. Land from which the tide ebbs. *Jazar* or *jazir*, (from P گزر *gazar*) A carrot. جزر الراعية *jazaru'r rāiyat*, A plant (scabiosa columbaria). جزر هندي *jazari hindī*, A species of pumpkin. *Juzur*, (pl. of جزور) Camels destined for slaughter.

A جزرات *juzurāt*, (pl. of جزور *jazūr*) Camels destined for slaughter.

A جزرة *jazrat*, One sheep destined for slaughter.

P جزرس *juz-ras*, Sagacious. Frugal.

P جزرسي *juz-rasī*, Penetration. Frugality.

P جزرو *juz-rav*, A privy, a jakes.

A جزريّ *jazarīy*, Native of Mesopotamia.

A جزز *jazaz*, Wool or grass which has been cut or clipped. *Jizaz*, (pl. of جزّة *jizzat*) Wools shorn and laid up.

A جزع *jaz*, (v. n. of جزع) Crossing (a country, valley, or river). Being impatient. A wide part of a valley producing trees; or a part in which are no trees, but sandy, and used as a halting-place. High ground. *Jaz* or *jiz*, A kind of Arabian shell, black and white, compared often by the poets to the eyes. (pl. اجزاع *ajzā*) A place where a valley bends: the centre of it: a place where it breaks off abruptly. A bee-hive. *Juz*, Saffron. Certain dyeing roots. *Juz* or *jaziz*, The axis of a pulley. *Jazaz*, Lamentation, complaint, sorrow, impatience. جزع و فزع *jazaz u fazaz*, Lamentation and groans. *Jaziz* or *jazuz*, Impatient.

A جزعة *jizat* or *jazat*, A part of a flock. A portion of the night; the darkness at the two extremes. A clump of trees. A shell. *Jizat* or *juzat*, A small quantity (of wealth, water, or milk). A little water in a bottle. *Juzat*, A knife-handle

P جزغ *jizgh*, A cricket. A locust. *Jizigh*, The fat of sheeps' tails fried and poured over a dish made of flour.

P جزغال *jizghāl*, (or جزغاله) Fat, dripping.

A جزف *jazf*, (v. n. of جزف) Buying any thing rashly, at random, uncertain of weight, quantity, or quality. Taking a thing easy.

A جزفة *jizfat*, Part of a herd feeding.

P جزك *jazak*, A distemper peculiar to fowls, affecting the roots of the quills and feathers, and causing them to drop off.

P جزگير *juz-gīr*, An instrument for keeping a book open when reading or writing. A portfolio.

A جزل *jazl*, (v. n. of جزل) Cutting, paring, clipping. Galling the back. In the measure كامل *kāmil*, which is متفاعلن *mutafāilun* thrice repeated, a making of the ت *t* quiescent, and a dropping of the ا *ā*. Copious, large (present). Liberal, generous. Prudent, firm in mind. Sound, sensible, eloquent (discourse). The cooing of a dove. A kind of plant. (pl. جزال *jizāl*) Dry firewood, especially large and thick. *Jizl*, A cutting or lump of dates. *Juzl*, (pl. of اجزل *ajzal*) Galled in the back (camels). *Jazal*, (v. n. of جزل) Being galled in the back or shoulder (a beast of burden), so that the bone is laid bare. A galling of a camel's bunch caused by the saddle.

A جزلاء *jazlā*, Prudent, intelligent (woman). Sore-backed, galled (she-camel).

A جزلة *jazlat*, A prudent woman. Large-hipped (woman). Remains of a cake. A leathern milk-bottle. A date-basket made of palm-leaves. *Jizlat*, A part, segment, portion, quantity, lump (of dates).

A جزم *jazm*, (v. n. of جزم) Cutting, amputating. Breaking off. Marking a letter with *jazma* or *jazm*. Deciding, determining, concluding, resolving. Having a partial stool. Reading slowly and distinctly. Rendering necessary, or imposing any thing upon another. Giving currency to a vow or oath. Filling (a bottle). Estimating from a survey the produce of palm-trees, &c. Being pusillanimous, weak. Keeping silence. Drinking, satisfying thirst (a camel). Eating sufficiently (a man); eating once in twenty-four hours. Any thing occurring before the time. The orthographical character *jazma* ْ, which is placed over a letter in pointed books to shew that it has no vowel (see Grammar). Any thing stuffed into the matrix of a camel to induce her to like another's colt. Evenness of the characters in writing. The common Arabic character. A pen nibbed (and not slantwise, as is the case with the قلم *kalam*). P جزم و تصديق كردن *jazm u tasdīk kardan*, To confirm one's self in a resolution. A *Jizm*, A part, portion, lot.

A جزماً *jazman*, (P جزمانه) Resolutely, definitively.

A جزمازج *jazmāzaj*, Fruit of the tamarisk.

A جزمة *jazmat*, One meal (for a man), or one feed (for cattle) during the day or night. *Jizmat*, A part of any stock, separate from the rest. A herd of camels, a flock of sheep. A herd from 100 upwards, or from 10 to 20.

A جزن *jazn*, Firewood large and thick.

A جزوء *juzūʼ*, (v. n. of جزأ) Being able by green grass to do without water (camels).

A جزور *jazūr*, (pl. جزائر *jazāʼir*, جزر *juzur*, and جزرات *juzurāt*) A camel or sheep slaughtered, or destined for slaughter.

A جزوز *jazūz*, A sheep shorn, or ready for shearing. *Juzūz*, (v. n. of جزّ) Becoming dry (dates).

A جزوزة *jazūzat*, A sheep for shearing.

A جزوع *jazūʻ*, Impatient. Lamenting, querulous. *Juzūʻ*, (v. n. of جزع) Being impatient.

A جزوف *jazūf*, A pregnant animal going over her time.

A جزوي *juzwe*, A part. A little, few: a trifle.

A جزويّات *juzwīyāt*, (pl. of جزوي) Parts.

P جزة *jaza*, A circular tent.

A جزي *jizy* or *jizaʼ*, (pl. of جزية *jizyat*) Taxes.

A جزئي *juzʼi*, (or جزئى *juzʼī*) A particle, part. A little, a few. كلّي و جزئي *kullī u juzʼī*, In whole and in part, entirely.

A جزيء *jazīʼ*, Sufficient, satisfying (food).

A جزية *jizyat*, (pl. جزي *jizy*, *jizaʼ*, or جزاء *jizāʼ*) Tribute, capitation-tax (paid by Jews and Christians). Produce of the soil. خاتم الجزية *khātimu'l jizyat*, A part of the throat so called.

P جزيدن *jazīdan*, To change.

A جزير *jazīr*, (in the language of the people of Arabian Irāk) A person selected by the inhabitants of a district to do the honours and defray the expenses incidental on receiving a visit from the monarch or his representative.

A جزّير *jizzīr*, A butcher, slaughterer (of camels).

A جزيرة *jazīrat*, (pl. جزائر *jazāʼir*) An island. A peninsula. Land from which the tide recedes. الجزيرة *al jazīrat*, Mesopotamia. الجزيرة الخضراء *al jazīratu'l khazrāʼ*, Algeziras in Spain. جزيرة العرب *jazīratu'l ʻarab*, The peninsula of Arabia. جزيرة العشّاق *jazīratu'l ʻushshāk*, Synope.

A جزيريّ *jazīrīy*, Of Algeziras.

A جزيز *jazīz*, Clipped, cut, sheared, mowed.

A جزيزة *jazīzat*, A lock of wool.

A جزيعة *jazīʻat*, A part of a stock separated from the rest. *Juzayʻat*, A flock of sheep.

A جزيف *jazīf*, A fishing-net. A purchase or sale made by guess, without weighing or measuring.

A جزيل *jazīl*, (pl. جزال *jizāl*) Much, many, numerous, copious. Great. Eloquent. اجر جزيل *ajri jazīl*, A great reward.

P جزيه خانه *jizya-khāna*, A custom-house or other place where tribute is collected.

A جزئيات *juzʼiyāt*, Trifles, particles.

A جسّ *jass*, (v. n. of جسّ) Touching, handling; feeling (the pulse). Seeking, fishing for information. Looking intently at.

A جسء *jasʼ*, (v. n. of جسأ) Becoming hard (the hand). A rough skin. Frozen water, ice.

A جساء *jasʼāʼ*, (A hand) hardened by labour.

A جسأة *jusʼat*, (v. n. of جسأ) Becoming hard (the hand). Hardness of the hand.

A جساد *jisād*, Saffron. *Jusād*, A pain in the belly.

A جسارة *jasārat*, (v. n. of جسر) Daring. Excelling in vigour of mind and intrepidity. Penetrating, passing through. Crossing a desert. Building a bridge. Boldness, presumption, fool-hardiness.

A جسّاس *jassās*, Curious, inquisitive, a great searcher. A lion digging his claws into his prey.

A جسّاسة *jassāsat*, A beast living in the islands, and which spies out and brings news to Antichrist.

A جسام *jisām*, (pl. of جسيم *jasīm*) Large-bodied. *Jusām*, Large-bodied.

A جسامة *jasāmat*, A being corpulent, big-bodied.

A جسّان *jussān*, Tambourin-players, drummers.

P جسبوس *jasbos*, (or جسبوسي) Hypocrisy.

P جست *jast*, He leaped. He escaped. A leap, jump. *Just*, He sought. Search, inquiry. جست و جوي كردن *just u joy* (or جست جوي *just-joy*) *kardan*, To search diligently.

P جستان *jastān*, Leaping, springing, bounding.

P جستانيدن *jastānīdan*, To cause to leap. To cause (wind) to blow. To make (a limb) palpitate.

P جستن *jastan*, To jump, leap, bound, spring forward. To fly (as sparks). To assail. To run away. To rise or blow (as the wind). To palpitate, leap, or beat (as the heart or pulse), to shake or tremble (a limb). جستن دل *jastani dil*, Palpitation of the heart (a disease). *Justan*, To search, seek, inquire, ask for, examine, investigate. To heap up, accumulate.

P جسته *jasta*, Escaped.

A جسد *jasad*, (v. n. of جسد) Clotting or sticking to the body (blood). (pl. اجساد *ajsād* and جسود *jusūd*) The body (of men, genii, or angels). Saffron, or any thing of that colour. Blood. The calf of the children of Israel. *Jasad* or *jasid*, Congealed, coagulated blood adhering to the body.

A جسديّ *jasadīy*, Corporeal, bodily.

A جسر *jasara*, (fut. of يجسر *yajsuru*) He dared.

A جسر *jasr*, Large, strong (camel). Brave, courageous. Tall. Large, bulky. A long-bodied camel stepping rapidly over the ground. *Jasr* or *jisr*, (pl. اجسر *ajsur* and جسور *jusūr*) A bridge. *Jasr* or *jusur*, (pl. of جسور *jasūr*) Bold, brave.

A جسرب *jasrab*, Long.

A جسرة *jasrat*, Large, swift (she-camel).

A جسرو دارو *jusraw-dārū*, Galangale.

A جسع *jasʻ*, (v. n. of جسع) Throwing up (a camel chewing the cud). Vomiting.

P جسك *jask*, Trouble. Extreme enmity.

A جسم *jism*, (pl. اجسام *ajsām* and جسوم *jusūm*) A body. A mathematical solid. جسم جمادي *jismi jamādī*, Metallic body. جسم جوهري *jismi jawharī*, Constitutional parts. جسم حيواني *jismi haywānī*, Animal body. جسم مركب *jismi murakkab*, A compound body. جسم كثيف *jismi kasīf*, (The) opake body (of a planet). جسم نباتي *jismi nabātī*, Vegetable body.

A جسمان *jusmān*, A body. Habit of body. نحيف الجسمان *nahīfu'l jusmān*, Slender-bodied.

A جسمانيّ *jismānīy* or *jusmānīy*, Corporeal.

A جسمانيّة *jis* or *jusmānīyat*, Materiality.

A جسمور *jusmūr*, That part of the back or body of a man whereon any thing rests.

P جسمي *jasmī*, A triangular thorny plant.

A جسميّة *jismīyat*, Corporality, materiality.

A جسنة *jusnat*, A species of round fish possessed of antennæ like a scorpion.

A جسو *jasw*, (v. n. of جسا for جسو) Being hard. Becoming stiff and crazed in his joints (an old man). Freezing (water).

A جسوء *jusūʼ*, A becoming hard (the hand).

A جسود *jusūd*, (pl. of جسد *jasad*) Bodies.

A جسور *jasūr*, (pl. جسر *jusr* and جسور *jusūr*) Magnanimous, brave. Tall. *Jusūr*, (v. n. of جسر) Building a bridge. Passing, penetrating. Crossing a desert. Being bold. (pl. of جسر *jisr*) Bridges.

A جسوع *jusūʻ*, Tenacity, close-handedness.

A جسوم *jusūm*, (pl. of جسم *jism*) Bodies.

A جسيد *jasīd*, Congealed (blood).

A جسيس *jasīs*, A spy.

A جسيم *jasīm*, (pl. جسام *jisām*) Great (in dignity). Gross, corpulent. Sore, disastrous. High ground with water on the summit.

P جش *jash*, A kind of blue bead made of glass, in colour approaching to that of the turquoise (worn by common people in rings and necklaces, and by the children of the rich as a charm against accidents and evil eyes).

A جشّ *jashsh*, (v. n. of جشّ) Breaking, bruising, pounding. Grinding coarsely. Beating, cudgelling. Pouring forth (tears). Drawing out. Sweeping. Cleaning (a well). A rough, stony place. The middle of a desert. The waist of a quadruped. *Jushsh*, (pl. جشاش *jishāsh*) A mountain. An hour of the night. The resemblance of a lip in which there is thickness and height.

A جشء *jashʼ*, (v. n. of جشأ) Migrating. (pl. اجشاء *ajshāʼ* and جشآت *jashʼāt*) A light bow. A branch of a tree (of which such bows are made). Much, abundant.

A جشاء *jushāʼ*, A belch. A rush (of water), a sudden approach (of night).

A جشّاء *jashshāʼ*, Loud-twanging bow. Level and gravelly land (good for palm-trees).

A جشأة *jushaʼat*, A belch, ructation.

A جشآت *jashʼāt*, (pl. of جشء *jashʼ*) Light bows.

A جشار *jushār*, A cough, hoarseness.

A جشّار *jashshār*, The owner of a field (where horses pasture). Master of the horse. *Jushshār*, (pl. of جاشر *jāshir*) Those who abide in the fields with their camels.

A جشّاريّ *jashshāriy*, One who leads horses and camels to pasture and stays out all night with them.

A جشاش *jishāsh*, (pl. of جش) Mountains.

A جشّاش *jashshāsh*, A coarse grinder.

A جشامة *jashāmat*, (v. n. of جشم) Labouring hard, achieving with difficulty.

P جشان *jashān*, A yard for measuring cloth.

A جشّان *jushshān*, Middle (of a horse or desert).

A جشب *jashb*, (v. n. of جشب) Being coarse (fare). Pounding or grinding coarsely. Causing (youth) to pass away (God). Assisting, strengthening. Despising. Eating coarse fare without sauce. جشب المأكل *jashbu'l maʼkal*, One who fares hard, a coarse feeder. *Jashb* or *jashib*, Coarse fare, food without sauce. *Jushb*, Pomegranate-rind.

A جشّة *jashshat*, Brothers, brethren, relations, kinsmen servants. *Jashshat* or *jushshat*, A crowd of persons advancing together. A simultaneous rising, march, or departure. *Jushshat*, A loud noise. A hoarse sound emitted from the nostrils.

A جشجشة *jashjashat*, (v. n. of جشجش Q) Sweeping. Cleaning (a well).

A جشر *jashr*, (v. n. of جشر) Turning to grass. Remaining all night in pasture (camels). Remaining with their camels all night. Leaping (a horse). Allowing (a horse) to graze in front of the house. Leaving. *Jashar*, (v. n. of جشر) Being hard and rough (dry mud on the shore). Men who pass the night in the fields with their camels. Flocks grazing at liberty without coming home at night. Spring vegetables. A bachelor. A roughness in the breast. A thickness or hoarseness of the voice.

A جشراء *jashrāʼ*, (fem. of اجشر *ajshar*) Hoarse.

A جشرة *jushrat*, Cough, irritation in the throat.

A جشع *jashaʻ*, A fear of the loss of a friend. Cupidity, greediness. *Jashiʻ*, Desirous, longing after, greedy of (another's share).

A جشم *jashm*, (v. n. of جشم) Labouring hard. *Jasham* or *jashm*, A heavy burden. Affliction. *Jasham*, Fatness. *Jusham*, The breast and ribs. The belly. Weight. A fish. *Jushum*, Fat persons.

A جشميزج *jashmīzaj*, (from P چشميزك) Name of a medicament for the eyes.

P جشن *jashn*, A feast, social entertainment, convivial meeting. A solemn feast. جشن بزرگ *jashni buzurg*, The sixth day of the month Farwardīn. جشن پوردگان *jashni pūrdagān*, Five intercalary days added to the Persian year. *Jashan*, Fever.

A جشنة *jushnat*, (or *jushunnat*) A kind of bird.

P جشن ساز *jashn-sāz*, New year's day (of the æra Malik).

P جشني *jashnī*, Fond of feasting; epicure.

P جشو *jashw*, (pl. جشوات) A light bow.

A جشوء *jushūʼ*, (v. n. of جشأ) Being distressed (the mind), boiling from sadness or terror. Emigrating. Retching, preparing to vomit. Growing dark. Bleating (a sheep). Impending.

A جشوب *jashūb*, Short and coarse (woman).

A جشوبة *jushūbat*, (v. n. of جشب) Being coarse and homely (food, &c.). Feeding coarsely.

A جشور *jushūr*, The breaking forth (of the dawn).

P جشه *jashsha*, An oil-measure. *Jushsha*, A sleeve.

A جشيب *jashīb*, Thick. Disagreeable, offensive: coarse, homely (food, raiment). A foul feeder.

P جشير *jashīr*, A weaver.

A جشير *jashīr*, A large corn-sack. A leathern quiver. A bachelor.

P جشيره *jashīra*, A weaver. Milk-pottage.

A جشيش *jashīsh*, Barley deprived of its husk, pounded and made into balls; ptisan. Wheat coarsely ground and cooked in a pot with meat and dates.

A جشيشة *jashīshat*, Pollard, grout.

A جشيم *jashīm*, Thick, coarse.

A جصّ *jass*, (v. n. of جصّ) Groaning, crying ah! alas! *Jass* or *jiss*, (from P گچ *gach*) Plaster.

A جصاجص *jusājis*, White and level (place).

A جصّاص *jassās*, A maker or vender of mortar.

A جصّاصات *jassāsāt*, Places where plaster is made.

A جصاصة *jisāsat*, Plastering, working in plaster.

A جصيص *jasīs*, A cry, clamour, complaint.

A جصيصة *jasīsat*, A company of persons. A tumultuous noise.

A جضّ *jazz*, (v. n. of جضّ) Walking pompously. Rushing upon (any one) with a sword.

A جضد *jazd*, Hard. Quick, active, brisk.

A جضم *juzum*, A glutton.

A جضمّ *jizamm*, Thick-waisted.

A جطح *jitih*, A word used in quieting a she-goat at milking-time.

A جظّ *jazz*, (v. n. of جظّ) Propelling. Oppressing, indisposing (grief, anguish, or any thing sticking in the throat). Throwing prostrate. Being fat and short. Running fast. Coition. Corpulent.

A جظلاء *jazlāʼ*, A weak and flabby old she-camel unable to masticate.

A جعّ *jaʻʻ*, An eating mud. A hitting with mud.

A جعاب *jiʻāb*, (pl. of جعبة *jaʻbat*) Quivers.

A جعّاب *jaʻʻāb*, A quiver-maker or vender.

A جعابة *jiʻābat*, The art of making quivers.

A جعابر *jaʻābir*, (pl. of جعبر) Short and thick.

A جعابيّ *jiʻābiy*, A quiver-maker.

A جعابيب *jaʻābīb*, (pl. of جعبوب *juʻbūb*) Weak and worthless. Mean-looking.

A جعاجر *jaʻājir*, (pl. of جعجرة) Pies, pasties.

A جعاد *jiʻād*, (pl. of جعد *jaʻd*) Short, dwarfish. Curly-haired (men).

A جعادة *jaʻādat*, (v. n. of جعد) Being crisp, curly (hair). ابو جعادة *abū juʻādat*, The wolf.

A جعاديد *jaʻādīd*, A yellow substance, thick, soft, and dry. Moisture issuing from the teat of a ewe before the biestings.

A جعار *jaʻār* or امّ جعار *umm jaʻār*, A hyena. *Jiʻār*, A rope which a camel-waterer fastens to a stake and ties round his middle when going down into a well lest he should tumble in. A mark made on the thigh of a horse or ass.

A جعاسيس *jaʻāsīs*, (pl. of جعسوس) Short, vile.

A جعاف *juʻāf*, A torrent that sweeps all away.

A جعال *jiʻāl*, (pl. جعل *juʻul*) Any cloth with which they lift a boiling kettle off the fire. Hire, price. A nest or any thing in which a bird deposits her eggs.

A جعالة *jaʻālat*, A bribe. *Jaʻālat* or *jiʻālat*, (v. n. of جعل) Making. Rendering. *Jiʻālat*, A cloth used as a kettle-holder. *Juʻālat*, *jaʻālat*, or *jiʻālat*, (pl. جعائل *jaʻāʼil*) Hire, price, fare. The price of a substitute soldier.

A جعام *juʻām*, A disease incident to camels, &c., from eating young herbage.

A جعامس *juʻāmis*, One who voids ordure once.

A جعاميس *jaʻāmīs*, (pl. of جعموس *juʻmūs*) Excrements. (in the dialect of Huzayl) A palm-tree.

A جعانس *jaʻānis*, Beetles.

A جعائل *jaʻāʼil*, (pl. of جعالة *jaʻālat*) Wages.

A جعب *jaʻb*, (v. n. of جعب) Throwing prostrate. Turning, inverting. Making a quiver. A small heap of sheep dung. *Juʻb*, The abdomen.

A جعباء *jaʻbāʼ*, Large, thick (woman). Fundament. *Jiʻbāʼ*, A throwing on the ground.

A جعباءة *jiʻbāʼat*, The fundament.

A جعباة *jaʻbaʼat*, A throwing prostrate.

A جعبّاة *jiʻibbāt*, Ring of the fundament.

A جعبة *jaʻbat*, (pl. جعاب *jiʻāb*) A quiver.

A جعبر *jaʻbar*, (pl. جعابر *jaʻābir*) Short (man). Thick, shallow, and roughly hewn (wooden bowl).

A جعبرة *jaʻbarat*, (v. n. of جعبر Q) Throwing prostrate. Short, dwarfish (woman).

A جعبريّة *jaʻbariyat*, Short, ill-made (woman).

A جعبس *juʻbus*, Stupid, silly, foolish.

A جعبلة *jaʻbalat*, Haste, expedition.

A جعبوب *juʻbūb*, (pl. جعابيب *jaʻābīb*) Weak and worthless. A little mean-looking man.

A جعبوس *juʻbūs*, Stupid, mad, foolish.

P جعبه گري *jaʻbagarī*, The art of making quivers.

A جعبي *juʻba'*, (pl. جعبيات) A red ant.

A جعبّي *jiʻibba'*, (or جعباء) The fundament.

A جعبيّ *jaʻbiy*, (pl. جعبيّات) A red ant.

A جعة *jiʻat*, Beer.

A جعتبة *jaʻtabat*, Avidity, greediness.

A جعثرة *jaʻsarat*, A collecting (of goods, stuff).

A جعثل *jaʻsal*, Rough, ill-tempered. Big-bellied.

A جعثم *jiʻsim*, Roots of the صلّيان *silliyān*.

A جعثميّات *juʻsumiyāt*, Bows.

A جعثن *jiʻsin*, The root of the plant صلّيان *sil-*

liyān. Name of the sister of Farazdak.

A جعثوم *juʻsūm*, Veretrum equi crassum.

A جعجاع *jaʻjāʻ*, A confined bad-smelling place (such as a prison). A field of battle. Rough ground. A stallion-camel braying aloud. Land, earth.

A جعجرة *juʻjurrat*, (pl. جعاجر *jaʻājir*) A paste or cake (boiled and eaten with inspissated juice).

A جعجع *jaʻjaʻ*, Rough ground. A narrow rugged place. Level ground.

A جعجعة *jaʻjaʻat*, (v. n. of جعجع Q) Throwing into a dungeon. Straitening, reducing to difficulties. Making (a camel) kneel down or rise up. Sitting down uncomfortably. Exacting a debt rigorously. Sticking, slaughtering (a camel). Kneeling down (a camel). Steeping sliced bread in broth. The sound of a mill. The noise of camels collected together. اسمع جعجعة ولا اري طحنا *asmaʻu jaʻjaʻatan, wa lā ara' tihnan*, I hear the clatter of the mill, but I see no flour. (Great cry and little wool).

A جعد *jaʻd*, Crisp, curly, short hair. A ringlet, a lock of hair. Curly-headed (man), curly-haired (camel). Avaricious. Moist ground. Liberal, generous. A round face with few pretensions to beauty. Short, dwarfish. Froth, layer upon layer. جعد اليد *jaʻdu'l yad* or جعد الانامل *jaʻdu'l anāmil*, Illiberal, avaricious. جعد الاصابع *jaʻdu'l asābiʻ*, Short-fingered. جعد القفا *jaʻdu'l kafa'*, Ignoble. P جعد انگشت *jaʻdi angusht*, Avarice. جعد شتر *jaʻdi shutur*, Hairiness (of the human body). A جعد قلم *jaʻdi halam*, Clotted ink adhering to the pen. Pleasing, amiable words. Curved letters. جعد اللغام *jaʻdu'l lughām*, (A camel) the foam of whose mouth accumulates, layer upon layer. P جعد گره گیر *jaʻdi girih-gīr*, Curling ringlets. A حيس جعد *hays jaʻd*, Thick and slab (dish *hays*). خدّ جعد *khaddi jaʻd*, A cheek-bone neither small nor smooth (the opposite to اسيل *asīl*).

A جعدبة *juʻdabat*, A bubble of water. A spider's web. Biestings (in the mouth of a kid newly dropped).

A جعدة *jaʻdat*, A curl. A ewe lamb. Strong-limbed (she-camel). Curly-haired (woman). ابو جعدة *abū jaʻdat*, (Father of curly hair) The wolf.

A جعدر *jaʻdar*, Short. A dwarf.

A جعدل *jaʻdal*, Hard. Robust (camel).

P جعده *jaʻda*, A sort of drug.

A جعذريّ *jaʻzariy*, A glutton.

A جعر *jaʻr*, (v. n. of جعر) Dunging (a wild beast). (pl. جعور *juʻūr*) Dung of wild beasts and birds of prey. ابو جعران *abū jiʻrān*, A beetle. ام جعران *umm jiʻrān*, A pelican.

A جعراء *jaʻrāʻ*, The fundament. A crowd of persons. Name of a tribe.

A جعرة *juʻrat*, A mark left on the waist by the rope جعار *jiʻār*. A kind of barley large and white.

A جعرور *juʻrūr*, A worthless kind of date. A sort of insect.

A جعرّي *jiʻirra'*, The fundament. A term of reproach. A kind of boy's game.

A جعز *jaʻz*, A stifling sensation, from rage, thirst, or when under water. *Jaʻiz*, One so troubled.

A جعس *jaʻs*, (v. n. of جعس) Voiding excrement. Excrement, dung. The place where dung falls.

A جعسوس *juʻsūs*, (pl. جعاسيس *jaʻāsīs*) Short of stature, mean, contemptible.

A جعشب *jaʻshab*, Tall and thick.

A جعشم *jaʻsham*, The middle. *Juʻsham* or *juʻshum*, A thick, stout dwarf. Tall and corpulent.

A جعشوش *juʻshūsh*, Short. Long. Vile. Meagre, slim, slender.

A جعظ *jaʻz*, (v. n. of جعظ) Pushing, thrusting away. Thick-bodied. Self-important. Bad-tempered, dissatisfied with one's food.

A جعظار *jiʻzār*, A thick dwarf. A boaster.

A جعظارة *jiʻzārat*, Weak in mind. A boaster. A dwarf who adds to his stature by art.

A جعظانة *jiʻzānat*, (or جعظان) Short, dwarfish.

A جعظر *jaʻzar*, One with large swagging hips.

A جعظرة *jaʻzarat*, (v. n. of جعظر Q) Retreating, running back. The pace of a slow man.

A جعظريّ *jaʻzariy*, Thick. Rude, rough, inhuman. Voracious. A dwarf who adds to his size by art. (Hence) one who boasts of what he has not, or assumes a false consequence.

A جعف *jaʻf*, (v. n. of جعف) Cleaning out (a well). Plucking, rooting up. Throwing prostrate. A bare subsistence.

A جعفر *jaʻfar*, A little stream. A large river, or one brimful. (A camel) abounding in milk. A man's name. ابو جعفر *abū jaʻfar*, A fly.

P جعفر آباد *jaʻfar-ābād*, A place near Shīrāz.

A جعفر صادق *jaʻfari sādih*, Name of an Imām.

P جعفري *jaʻfarī*, The finest kind of gold. A kind of cupola. A sort of screen (the interstices of the frame being lozenged). Lattice-work. Name of a yellow flower. Name of a fortress.

A جعفريّة *jaʻfarīyat*, Name of a sect. Name of a quarter in Baghdād, and of a village in Egypt.

A جعفلة *jaʻfalat*, (v. n. of جعفل Q) Unhorsing any one speared. Saying جعلت فداك *juʻiltu fidāka*, For thee I devote my head.

A جعفليق *jaʻfalīk*, A big woman.

A جعفليل *jaʻfalīl*, Killed and swollen.

A جعفيّ *juʻfīy*, Name of the founder of an Arabian tribe. A water-carrier. A cup-bearer.

A جعل *jaʻala*, (fut. يجعل *yajʻalu*) He placed.

A جعل *jaʻl*, (v. n. of جعل) Causing, effecting, rendering. Constituting, appointing, instituting. Making, creating. Constructing, building. Beginning, setting about. Nominating, naming; calling, declaring. Putting, placing; laying (one thing upon another). Seeming, pretending. Fancying, supposing. Ennobling. Stipulating, bargaining. A dwarf palm-tree. A palm watered by rain, not by art. A heifer. Counterfeit, forgery. (pl. of جعلة *jaʻlat*) Young palm-shoots. Dwarfish and worthless palm-trees. *Jiʻl* or *jaʻil*, Water swarming with dead beetles. *Juʻl*, (v. n. of جعل) Making. Causing, rendering. Nominating, constituting, instituting. Beginning, setting about. Fancying, supposing. Bargaining. The hire or reward for any work. A bribe (to a governor or judge). A reward of forty dirhams, to which a person is entitled for having brought a fugitive slave from the distance of three days' journey and upwards, and delivering him up to his master. *Jaʻal*, (v. n. of جعل) Swarming with beetles. Quarrelsome, disputatious. Shortness. Fatness. *Juʻal*, (pl. جعلان *jiʻlān*) A beetle. Black and mean (man). Litigious, quarrelsome. A watcher, a keeper. حبا جعل *haba' juʻal*, A certain boy's game. *Juʻul*, (pl. of جعال *jiʻāl*) Cloths (with which boiling kettles are taken off the fire).

A جعلان *jiʻlān*, (pl. of جعل *juʻal*) Beetles.

A جعلة *jaʻlat*, (pl. جعل *jaʻl*) The young shoot of a palm-tree. A dwarf and worthless palm-tree, or one which the hand cannot reach.

A جعلي *jaʻlī*, Forged, counterfeit, artificial.

A جعم *jaʻm*, (v. n. of جعم) Keeping back. Muzzling (a camel). Wanting an appetite. *Jaʻm* or *jiʻm*, Greedy, craving. *Jaʻam*, (v. n. of جعم) Desiring greedily. Having a foul appetite (a man, camel, or dog). Wanting an appetite. Speaking thick through a wide throat. Losing all his teeth (a camel). *Jaʻim*, Destitute of appetite.

A جعماء *jaʻmāʻ*, A doating old woman. An old she-camel. The backside.

A جعمرة *jaʻmarat*, (v. n. of جعمر Q) Drawing himself together (an ass ready to rush and bite).

A جعمسة *jaʻmasat*, A voiding of excrement once.

A جعمظ *juʻmuz*, A miserly old man, gluttonous and greedy.

A جعموس *juʻmūs*, (pl. جعاميس) Dung.

A جعن *jaʻn*, Languor of body. A shrinking and flaccidity of the skin and body.

A جعنب *jaʻnab*, Short of stature. A dwarf.

A جعنظار *jiʻinzār*, Gluttonous, greedy. A corpulent glutton.

A جعنظر *jaʻanzar*, A corpulent glutton.

A جعو *jaʻw*, A heap of camel's dung piled up with the hand.

A جعودة *juʻūdat*, The being crisp or curly.

A جعور *juʻūr*, (pl. of جعر) Excrements of wild birds or beasts. امّ جعور *umm jaʻwar*, The hyena.

A جعول *jaʻwal*, A young ostrich.

A جعونة *juʻūnat*, A contraction of the skin. Languor of body. Short and fat.

A جعيلة *jaʻīlat*, (pl. جعائل *jaʻāʼil*) Hire.

P جغ *jagh*, The ebon-tree. A churn-stick. *Jugh*, A yoke for oxen.

P جغازه *jaghāza*, A certain esculent root. Bread made of millet. A red paint used by ladies. The navel of any beast. Name of a town in Persia.

P جغاله *jaghāla*, A flock of birds. Unripe fruit.

A شغب جغب *shaghib jaghib*, Tumultuous, seditious.

P جغبت *jaghbat*, Raw cotton. Quilting.

P جغبوت *jaghbūt*, A gut-pudding. Raw cotton for quilting.

P جغد *jughd*, An owl. Battlements. Hair knotted at the back of the head.

P جغر *jaghr*, A frog.

P جغرابه *jaghr-āba*, A kind of water-moss.

P جغرات *jughrāt*, (in the dialect of Samarkand) Sour, coagulated milk.

G جغرافيه *jughrāfiya*, Geography.

P جغرد *jughard*, Verdure.

P جغرسته *jaghrista*, A spinning-rope. A reed made use of by weavers to wind their thread upon.

P جغش *jaghash*, (or جغشت) A particular esculent vegetable which appears very early in spring.

P جغنوت *jaghnūt*, Cotton used in lining.

P جغنه *jaghna*, A large yellow bird.

A جف *jaff* or *juff*, A troop, body (of men). *Juff*, An old man. Any thing hollow. The half of an old leathern bottle, which they convert into a bucket. The branch, dug-up root, or envelope of the flower of a palm-tree. A sheath or case of leather. An obstruction which one perceives between one's self and an opposite object. جفّ مال *juffu mālin*, A skilful manager of property.

A جفء *jafs*, (v. n. of جفأ) Throwing down, prostrating. Oversetting (a cauldron into a dish). Casting up scum (a torrent or boiling pot). Wiping off the scum of a boiling pot, clearing away the rubbish carried down by a stream. Shutting (a door). Opening (a door). Uprooting a (potherb).

A جفاء *jafā*, (v. n. of جفا for جفو) Oppressing, treating cruelly. Taking no care (of one's property). Not staying in (its) place. Taking (the saddle off a horse's back). Cruelty, oppression, iniquity, injustice. *Jufā*, Whatever a torrent carries along with it. An empty ship. Vainly, uselessly. Scum, foam.

P جفاپيشه *jafā-pesha*, Tyrannical. A mistress.

A جفأة *jafsat*, A year in which camels are prolific.

A جفاة *jufāt*, (pl. of جافي *jāfī*) Cruel, stern, fell, hard, austere. Unjust, ungodly. Restless. Sinners.

A جفاجف *jafājif*, Form, external appearance.

P جفاجوي *jafā-joy*, One seeking to oppress.

A جفاخ *jaffākh*, Vain-glorious; a boaster.

A جفار *jifār*, Clean wells. Camels abounding in milk. Horse's middles. (pl. of جفر *jafr*) Lambs four months old. (pl. of جفرة *jufrat*) Middles, centres.

A جفاسة *jafāsat*, A suffering from indigestion.

A جفاف *jafāf*, (v. n. of جفّ) Being dried (a washed garment). *Jufāf*, Any thing dried.

A جفافة *jufāfat*, Scattered bents of hay or grass.

P جفاكار *jafā-kār*, A tormentor, oppressor.

P جفاكش *jafā-kash*, Oppressed, belaboured.

P جفاكشي *jafā-kashī*, Endurance of oppression.

P جفاكيش *jafā-kesh*, Cruel, severe: a persecutor.

A جفال *jufāl*, Whatever a torrent sweeps along with it. Froth of milk. Much wool; an entire fleece carefully picked up. Any thing characterised by abundance.

A جفالة *jufālat*, Scum, which is taken off the surface of a boiling pot, slush. Whatever a torrent sweeps along with it. A multitude, a concourse of people running away.

P جفاله *jafāla*, A flight of birds.

A جفان *jifān*, (pl. of جفنة *jafnat*) Trenchers. Noble, liberal men. Small wells.

A جفّان *juffānī*, Tribes of بكر *bakr* and تميم *tamīm*.

A جفاية *jufāyat*, An empty ship.

A جفّة *jaffat*, The noise of the motion of a cavalcade. *Jaffat* or *juffat*, A multitude, crowd of people. All. جفّة واحدة *jaffatan wāhidatan*, (They came) in one body. *Juffat*, A large bucket.

P جفت *jaft*, Crooked (old man) bent, doubled. A trellis. The roof of a house. Skin, rind. Wrinkled. Toasted. A bunch of grapes. جفت بلوط *jafti ballūt*, The inner rind of the acorn. *Juft*, A yoke. A couple, a pair, a yoke (of oxen). An even number. A fellow, a match. A mate. جفت فلك *jufti falak*, The sun and moon.

P جفتا *jaftā*, Inclined, bent, curved.

P جفت آفريد *jufat-āfarīd*, Satyrion.

P جفت ساز *juft-sāz*, One of the kinds of music.

P جفتك *jaftak*, A heron. *Juftak*, A sort of bird that is said to have but one wing; on the opposite side to which the male has a hook, and the female a ring, so that when they fly they are joined, and separate only when they are on the ground.

P جفتگي *jaftagī*, Curvature.

P جفتن *jaftan*, To turn the mind. To be inclined, bent, curved, or crooked. To prop (a vine). To grow worse and worse (an affair).

P جفته *jafta*, Bent, curved. A cupola, vault. A prop, vine-arbour. The roof of a house. A young vine-shoot. *Jufta*, The buttocks, the space between the haunches. A kick made by an animal with his two hind feet. A knot. جفته زدن *jufta zadan*, To wince.

P جفتي *juftī*, Parity, equality. Coupling, pairing; copulation. هم جفتي *ham juftī*, Conjunction, union, equality.

P جفتيدن *jaftīdan*, To bend. To prop (a vine).

A جفجف *jafjaf*, High ground, though not very steep. Low land. An extensive flat. A violent wind. Delirious, raving, doting.

A جفجفة *jafjafat*, (v. n. of جفجف Q) Collecting. Confining, retaining. Driving camels off in haste for fear of a marauding party. Urging forward a drove of cattle, so that one is riding on another. The noise of a company of horsemen travelling leisurely along.

A جفخ *jafkh*, A being haughty, boasting.

P جفر *jafr*, Doe-skin parchment for writing.

A جفر *jafr*, (v. n. of جفر) Being spacious. Growing (a lad or lamb). (pl. اجفار *ajfār*, جفار *jifār*, and جفرة *jafarat*) A lamb four months old (when it begins to ruminate). An infant when his flesh begins to swell and he eats. منهدم الجفر *munhadimu'l jafr*, Stupid, unintellectual. من جفرك *min jafarika* or *jafrika*, On thy account. *Jafar*, The art of making amulets or charms. *Jufar*, (pl. of جفرة *jufrat*) Horses' middles.

A جفرة *jafrat*, A well not filled up, or partially filled. (fem. of جفر *jafr*) A she-lamb or female child when able to eat. من جفرتك *min jafratika*, On thy account. *Jufrat*, Middle, centre, inside of the breast. A cavity. A large circumference, circuit of country. (pl. جفر *jufar* and جفار *jifār*) The belly of a horse. Name of a place in Basra, famous for a battle in the year 70. *Jafarat*, (pl. of جفر *jafr*) Lambs four months old.

P جفرسته *jafrasta*, Spinning thread. Tongs.

A جفرّي *jufurra'*, (or جفرّاء *jufurrā*) The envelope of the bud of the female palm.

A جفريّ *jafarīy*, Maker of amulets or charms.

A جفريّة *jafarīyat*, A city founded by Mutawakkil, the tenth of Abbaside khalifs; a palace there.

A جفز *jafz*, Quickness of pace.

A جفس *jifs* or *jafis*, Degenerate, weak, dull, stupid, unworthy. *Jafas*, (v. n. of جفس) Being pained at the stomach, suffering from indigestion.

A جفش *jafasha*, (fut. يجفش *yajfishu*) He gently pressed with tips of the fingers (in milking).

A جفظ *jafz*, Fulness, repletion. A ship's rope.

A جفع *jafaᶜa*, (fut. يجفع) He threw down.

A جفل *jafl*, (v. n. of جفل) Passing lightly, swiftly by. Hastening, expediting. Voiding dung (an elephant). Peeling, stripping. Picking (a bone). Shovelling away (dirt). Casting up (fish) on the shore (the sea). Driving (a cloud) about (wind). Stirring up and driving off (an ostrich). Timid (ostrich). A cloud raining water. (pl. جفول *jufūl*) A black ant. A ship. *Jifl* or *jafl*, (pl. اجفال *ajfāl*) Elephant's dung. *Jufl*, (pl. of جفول *jafūl*) Strong (winds). Large (women).

A جفلة *jaflat*, Leafy (tree). *Juflat*, One fleece.

A جفلق *jaflak*, Very fleshy (old woman).

A جفلقة *jaflakat*, Hypocrisy in walk or talk.

A جفلى *jafala'*, Promiscuously.

A جفن *jafn*, (v. n. of جفن) Serving up (a slaughtered camel) in a large dish. A vine. A sort of grape. A vine-shoot. (pl. اجفن *ajfun*, اجفان *ajfān*, and جفون *jufūn*) An eyelid. A kind of fragrant tree. A keeping of one's self from uncleanness. *Jafn* or *jifn*, The sheath (of a sword.)

A جفنة *jafnat*, (pl. جفان *jifān*) A large dish. (*Jafnat* is the largest dish: next, قصعة *kassat*,

صحفة *sihfat*, ميكلة *mikalat*; lastly صحيفة *suhayfat*). A liberal man. A small well.

A جفو *jafw*, (v. n. of جفا for جفو), Injuring, treating harshly. Wrong, injury. Cruelty, iniquity.

A جفوة *jafwat* or *jifwat*, Cruelty, iniquity, injustice, oppression.

A جفور *jufūr*, (v. n. of جفر), Becoming languid (a stallion). Being four months old and ceasing to suck (a kid). Being wide across the flanks. Becoming distended (the sides of the body). Recovering from sickness.

A جفوف *jufūf*, (v. n. of جفّ) Being dried (a garment that had been washed). Collecting, gathering together, and going off with.

A جفول *jafūl*, (pl. جفل *jufl*) Cloud-impelling (wind). Large (woman or crowd). *Jufūl*, (v. n. of جفل) Passing rapidly along (an ostrich). Driving (the clouds) along (wind). Throwing prostrate. Being disordered (hair). (pl. of جفل *jafl*) Black ants. Ships.

A جفون *jufūn*, (pl. of جفن *jafn*) Eye-lids.

A جفي *jafy*, (v. n. of جفي) Throwing prostrate.

A جفية *jifyat*, Cruelty, injustice, oppression.

A جفير *jafīr*, A quiver of leather without wood; or of wood without leather. A sheath.

A جفيس *jafīs*, Degenerated. Weak, stupid.

A جفيظ *jafīz*, Swollen (carcase).

A جفيف *jafīf*, Dry (herbage).

A جفيل *jafīl*, Green corn cut. Much wool.

A جيق *jahh*, (v. n. of جقّ) Muting (a bird).

A جقة *jikkat*, An old worn-out she-camel.

P جك *jak*, Churning. The sentence signed by the judge. The fifteenth night of the month شعبان *shaꜥbān*, called شب برات *shabi barāt*.

P جكاشه *jakāsha*, A porcupine.

P جكاك *jakāk*, Grapes of an inferior quality.

A جكجكة *jakjakat*, The ringing noise of pieces of iron falling on one another.

P جكر *jakar*, Earth.

A جكر *jakar*, The being necessitous.

A جكرة *jakrat*, A thing necessary to be done.

A جكيرة *jukayrat*, (dim. of جكرة *jakrat*) Any little matter necessary to be done.

P جكاره *jagāra*, Different ways or opinions.

P جكتيپونستن *jagtīpūnistan*, (in zand and Pāzand) To write.

P جكر *jigar*, The liver. The diaphragm. The heart. Middle of any thing. Sadness, sorrow. Pity, compassion, sympathy. Expectation. جكر خوردن *jigar khwurdan*, To grieve, be sorrowful. To toil, drudge. جكر گل *jigari gil*, Bowels of the earth, (metaph.) the grave. داروئ جكر *dārūꜣi jigar*, Medicine or cure for the liver.

P جكر آكند *jigar-āgand*, Sheep's guts stuffed.

P جكر بند *jigar-band*, The liver, lungs, and heart. A son. Any thing lean and weak.

P جكر تاب *jigar-tāb*, Diseased in the liver.

P جكر تافته *jigar-tāfta*, Deeply in love. Hectic.

P جكر تشنه *jigar-tishna*, Thirsting, longing.

P T جكرجي *jigarjī*, A seller of livers, &c.

P جكر خواره *jigar-khwāra*, A magician, sorcerer. A fabulous being. Deeply afflicted.

P جكرسا *jigar-sā*, Wearing the liver, afflictive.

P جكرسوز *jigar-soz*, Liver-inflaming, tormenting.

P جكر فسادي *jigar-fasādī*, Disease of liver.

P جكرگرم *jigar-garm*, Hectic. An ardent lover.

P جكرگوشه *jigar-gosha*, A corner, lobe of the liver. The heart. A son. جكرگوشهٔ من *jigar-goshaꜣi man*, An affectionate mode of addressing a child.

P جكرنه *jigrana*, A kind of crane.

P جكرونتن *jagrūnitan*, (in zand) To strike.

P جكري *jigarī*, Of the nature of liver (as colour); livid. عقيق جكري *ꜥakīki jigarī*, A cornelian.

P جكي جكي *jigī jigī*, A cry of fear.

P جكيجه *jagīja*, A pot for holding grease.

P جل *jal*, A lark. The inside or (according to some) the outside of the mouth. The midst of the sea. A handle, hilt, haft. Thread. *Jul*, a horse-cloth. A veil (hung before a sanctuary). جل بك *juli bak*, (or جل وزغ *juli wazagh*) A green film which floats on stagnant ponds.

A جلّ *jalla*, (fut. يجلّ *yajillu*) He was great.

A جلّ *jall*, (v. n. of جلّ) Departing, emigrating. Collecting (camel's dung). Clothing (a horse). Drawing to one's self. Great, glorious. Contemptible. *Jall* or *jull*, (pl. جلول *julūl*) The sail of a ship. A stalk of ripe corn. *Jalla*, He shone in majesty or glory, an epithet frequently alluded to in the name of God, as, الله جلّ و علىٰ *allāh jalla wa ꜥalā'*, God the glorious and most high; (synonymous to which are جلّ جلاله *jalla jalāluhu* and حقّ جلّ شانه *hakk jalla shānuhu*). *Jill*, A male camel shedding the front teeth. Stalk of corn. A gut. Coarse, rude. Great, glorious, illustrious. A carpet. Clothes, garments. *Jull*, The site of a house or tent. من جلّك *min julliha*, On thy account. *Jull* or *jall*, (pl. جلال *jilāl* and اجلال *ajlāl*) A housing, covering for a horse. A stalk of ripe corn. Principal part of a thing. جلّ عساكره *julli ꜥasākirihi*, The greater part of his army. (from P گل *gul*) A rose. A jasmine.

A جلا *jala'*, (v. n. of جلا for جلو) Being superior to, above, on the upper part. A man's name. (v. n. of جلي) Being bald on the forehead. Baldness on the forehead. A collyrium. ابن جلا *ibn jala'*, A chief. One whose business is clear.

A جلاء *jalāꜣ*, (v. n. of جلأ) Throwing down, prostrating. Casting off, flinging away. (v. n. of جلا for جلو) Leaving one's country. Driving into exile. Establishing, confirming. Scouring, cleaning, wiping, polishing. Making clear. Being clear. Banishing care. Clearing one's vision with collyrium. Smoking a palm-tree in order to collect honey. Casting aside (a garment). Any thing clear and distinct. Emigration, exile. جلاء يوم *jalāꜣu yawmin*, The clear part of a day. P جلائ وطن كردن *jalāꜣi watan kardan*, To quit one's country. *Jilāꜣ*, (v. n. of جلو) Presenting a bride to her husband adorned and unveiled. Presenting a female attendant to his bride (a bridegroom). Polishing (a sword). (v. n. 3 of جلا for جلو) Opposing, withstanding openly. A collyrium which gives a lustre and clearness to the eyes. A style or title of honour by which any one is addressed.

A جلاء *jallāꜣ*, A polisher, scourer. Detergent, detersive, cleansing.

A جلاءة *jalāꜣat*, (v. n. of جلأ) Throwing down, prostrating. Casting off, flinging away.

A جلاب *jilāb*, A wallet. A sword-case.

P جلاب *julāb*, Name of a poet.

A جلاب *jallāb*, One who draws or drags very much. One who goes about with slaves or cattle, who hawks things about from place to place.

A جلّاب *jullāb*, (from P گل آب *gul-āb*) Rose-water. Sherbet.

A جلابان *julābān*, Name of a plant.

A جلابة *jallābat*, A noisy, clamorous, raving, and bad-tempered woman.

A جلابيب *jalābīb*, (pl. of جلباب) Ladies' veils.

A جلاج *jilāj*, (pl. of جلجة) Skulls. Bubbles.

A جلاجب *julājib*, Old and bald (man).

P جلاجل *jalājil*, A horse's poitrel hung with little bells. Little bells suspended from Arabian drums. A drum. A certain melodious bird.

A جلاجل *jalājil*, (pl. of جلجل *juljul*) Bells, small globular bells hung about the heads and necks of cattle, or round the rims of Arabian drums or cymbals. *Julājil*, (An ass) braying loud and clear. Light, airy, cheerful. Any thing stirring in the mind.

A جلاح *jilāh*, (v. n. 3 of جلح) Being proud and severe towards each other. Contending with vehemence. Shewing hatred. *Julāh*, A torrent undermining and carrying off.

A جلاخ *julākh*, A river filling its bed and sweeping away all before it.

A جلاد *jilād*, (v. n. 3 of جلد) Fighting with swords. (pl. of جلد *jald*) Quick, active, brisk. (pl. of جلد *jalad*) Hard and level grounds. (pl. of جلدة *jaldat*) Camels yielding very rich milk. Large and hard palm-trees. Camels which neither breed nor give milk.

A جلّاد *jullād*, A skinner. A dealer in hides. An executioner, or whipper. Flagellant.

P جلا داده *jalā-dāda*, Polished, burnished.

A جلادة *jalādat*, (v. n. of جلد) Being hard and strong. Hardness. Activity. Bravery. انصار جلادت شعار *ansāri jalādat-shiꜥār*, Brave auxiliaries.

A جلادح *julādih*, (pl. *jalādih*) Long.

P جلا دهنده *jalā-dihinda*, A polisher, furbisher.

A جلّادي *jallādī*, Executioner's office. Cruelty.

A جلاذيّ *jalāziy*, (pl. of جلذيّ *julziy*, q.v.). *Julāziy*, Robust, thick (camel). A swift pace. A workman, an artificer. A servitor in a church; a Christian monk.

A جلاز *jilāz*, Nerves of a camel's neck (which they twist round bows, knife-handles, and the like).

A جلازة *jilāzat*, (pl. جلائز *jalāʼiz*) The nerve of a camel's neck whipt round the handle of a bow, &c.

A جلاس *jilās*, A sitting with another.

A جلاس *jullās*, (pl. of جالس *jālis*) Sitters.

A جلاعد *julāʻid*, (pl. *jalāʻid*) A strong camel.

A جلاف *julāf*, Mud, clay.

A جلافة *jalāfat*, (v. n. of جلف) Being severe, hard, unjust. Meanness.

A جلافز *julāfiz*, Hard and strong.

A جلافي *julāfiy*, Large (bucket).

A جلاقة *julāhat*, Flesh (upon the bones).

P جلاگر *jalāgar*, A book-binder. A polisher. A glass-grinder. A smoother, glazer, cloth-presser.

A جلال *jalāl*, (v. n. of جلّ) Being great, illustrious, exalted in dignity and majesty. Growing old. Being proved, tried, experienced in business. Being contemptible. Majesty, glory, dignity, greatness, power. A pretext. جاه و جلال *jāh u jalāl*, Dignity and eminence. ذو الجلال والاكرام *zū'l jalāl wa'l ikrām*, Glorious and honourable. جلال الدين *jalālu'd dīn*, (Glory of religion) name of a celebrated king of Persia, from whom the new Persian æra called جلاليّ *jalāliy* takes its name. من جلالك *min jalāliha*, From reverence or regard to you. *Jilāl*, The sail of a ship. (pl. of جلّ *jull*) Housings, horse-coverings. (pl. of جلّة *jullat*) Hampers made of palm-leaves. *Julāl*, (v. n. of جلّ) Being great and illustrious. Great, illustrious. Large, bulky. The principal part of any thing. An ass braying loud.

A جلال *jullāl*, Great, illustrious.

A جلالة *jalālat*, (v. n. of جلّ) Being great and illustrious. Growing old. Having much experience in business. *Julālat*, A large she-camel. Great, illustrious (woman).

A جلّالة *jallālat*, A cow that eats dung and spoils her milk. *Jullālat*, (fem.) Great.

A جلاليّة *jalāliyat*, Name of a sect who worship the more terrible attributes of the deity. The followers of سيّد جلال بخاريّ *sayyid jalāl bukhāriy*. A kind of pigeon.

A جلام *jilām*, (pl. of جلم *jalam*) Kids.

A جلّام *jullām*, Shaven he-goats.

A جلامة *julāmat*, Shearings of wool.

A جلامق *jalāmik*, Tartar vestments.

A جلاميد *jalāmīd*, Weight, heaviness. (pl. of جلمود *julmūd*) Rocks, large stones. Harsh men.

P جلانك *jalānak*, A certain game. A beetle.

P جلانگر *jilāngar*, A locksmith.

A جلاوزة *jalāwizat*, (pl. of جلواز *jilwāz*) Sergeants or attendants on revenue-collectors.

A جلاه *jilāh*, (pl. of جلهة) Banks of rivers.

A جلاهض *julāhiz*, Unwholesome, unhealthy.

A جلاهق *julāhik*, A musket-ball. A weaver. A reel of thread.

A جلائب *jalāʼib*, Female slaves carried about for sale.

A جلائز *jalāʼiz*, (pl. of جلازة *jilāzat*) Nerves of camel's necks twisted round the handles of bows.

A جلائف *jalāʼif*, (Years) destructive to cattle.

A جلائل *jalāʼil*, (pl. of جليل *jalīl*) Great (things). The plants ثمام *sumām*.

A جلب *jalb*, (v. n. of جلب) Drying up (blood). Healing (as a wound). Threatening mischief. Committing a crime. Collecting, convoking. Shouting to a horse. A crime. *Jalb* or *jalab*, (v. n. of جلب) Drawing, attracting. Bringing, fetching. Raising a clamour, making a hubbub. Following (a horse) behind, and driving him up. Gaining, providing for a family. Scheming, practising fraud. *Jilb*, A small camel's saddle. A saddle-cloth. The curved timbers of a camel's saddle. *Julb*, Darkness of night. *Julb* or *jilb*, A thin cloud without rain. An opposing obstacle (such as a mountain). *Jalab*, (v. n. of جلب) Assembling together. (pl. اجلاب *ajlāb*) (Cattle) driven from place to place for sale. Sounds, clamours, mixed murmurs of men and other things. A drover, cattle-dealer. A slave-dealer.

P جلب *jalab*, A courtezan. Noise, tumult, cry.

A جلّب *jullab*, (pl. of جالب) Healing (wounds).

A جلباء *julabāʼ*, (pl. of جليب *jalīb*) Slaves carried to market.

A جلباب *jilbāb*, (or جلبّاب *jilibbāb*) (pl. جلابيب *jalābīb*) A long veil, a shift, or pelisse worn by the Eastern ladies. Power, dominion.

A جلبّار *julubbār*, A sheath. Edge of a sword.

P جلباف شنگرف *julbāfi shangarf*, Red tulips. Roses.

P جلبان *julbān*, Pease.

A جلبان *jullabān*, Name of a herb.

A جلبّان *julubbān*, Pease. Beans. Chicklings. *Julubbān* or *jilibbān*, A noisy fellow.

A جلبّانة *jilibbānat* or *julubbānat*, A termagant.

A جلببة *jalbabat*, (v. n. of جلبب Q) Putting a veil called جلباب *jilbāb* on any one.

A جلبة *julbat*, The cuticle which grows over a wound when healing. Leather used for or in camels' saddles. Part of provender or of a cloud separated from the rest. A flourishing shrub. A pot-herb. A heap of stones (blocking up the way). Adversity. Scarcity. Hunger. Sour milk poured upon new milk to curdle it. A brace put round the handle of a knife. An amulet enclosed in leather. A bit of iron for mending a bowl. Iron in a camel's saddle. A place, country, district. *Jalabat*, Sounds, clamours, mixed murmurs.

A جلبح *jilbih*, A deformed little old woman. A serious mishap.

A جلبدة *jalbadat*, The neighing of horses.

A جلبز *julabiz*, Strong, robust.

A جلبصة *jalbasat*, (for خلبصة) Flight.

A جلبقة *jalbakat*, Mixed voices, noise of a mob.

A جلبنانة *jilib* or *julubnānat*, A scold, shrew.

P جلبو *jalbū*, A plant resembling mint.

P جلبوب *jalbūb*, Ivy.

P جلبهنگ *jilbahang*, Seed of a yellow flower.

A جلبيٰ *jalbaʼ*, (pl. of جليب *jalīb*) (Slaves, male or female) carried to market.

P جلبيز *jilbez*, An informer, make-bate. A halter.

A جلّة *jallat*, (v. n. of جلّ) Collecting (camels') dung. *Jillat*, (A she-camel) until she breeds the teeth بازل *bāzil*. (A male camel) shedding the front teeth. Old (man or men, camel or camels). Great personages, lords. *Jillat*, *jallat*, or *jullat*, The orbicular dung (of camels or sheep). *Jullat*, (pl. جلال *jilāl* or جلل *julal*) A date-basket (made of palm-leaves), a hamper.

A جلت *jalata*, (fut. يجلت *yajlitu*) He struck.

P جلتا *jaltā*, (in zand) The skin of man or beast.

P جلتاق *jaltāk*, Wild sorrel.

A جلج *jalaj*, (pl. of جلجة *jalajat*) Skulls. Bubbles of water.

A جلجاب *jiljāb*, (and جلجابة *jiljābat*) Old and decrepit, large and bald (man). Stout (he-camel).

A جلجال *jaljāl*, Clattering (shower).

A جلجب *jaljab*, Old, large, and bald (man).

A جلجبّ *jiljabb*, Long, tall.

A جلجة *jalajat*, (pl. جلج *jalaj* and جلاج *jilāj*) The head, the skull. A bubble of water.

P جلجل *jaljal* or *jiljal*, A bell. The bells of a tambourine. A certain melodious bird.

A جلجل *juljul*, (pl. جلاجل *jalājil*) Little bells appended to the neck (of a camel); also those which are hung round about the rim of a tambourine. Light, airy, cheerful. دارة جلجل *dāratu juljulin*, Name of a place.

A جلجلان *juljulān*, Coriander-seed. Sesame-seed. Heart-strings, innermost recesses of the heart. جلجلان حبشي *juljulāni habashī*, Seed of the black poppy. جلجلان مصري *juljulāni misrī*, A certain poisonous plant. The Egyptian lotus.

A جلجلة *jaljalat*, (v. n. of جلجل Q) Striking with the hand, touching with the fingers (cymbals, castanets, or a tambour de basque). Roaring (thunder), Neighing clearly (a horse). Putting in motion. Twisting (a cord) tight. Mixing. Menacing, threatening. The noise of little bells. A loud rumbling noise.

A جلح *jalh*, (v. n. of جلح) Cropping (as cattle the leaves of trees). Peeling. *Julh*, (pl. of اجلح *ajlah*) Bald. *Jalah*, (v.n. of جلح) Being bald on the sides of the head. Baldness.

A جلّح *jullah*, (An ox) without horns, dodded.

A جلحاء *jilhāʼ*, Land which produces nothing.

A جلحاءة *jilhāʼat*, Land which produces nothing.

A جلحاز *jilhāz*, Narrow-minded, covetous.

A جلحاظ *jilhāz*, Hairy, shaggy, and large.

A جلحان *jilhān*, Narrow-minded, covetous.

A جلحة *jalahat*, Forehead and temples, as being the part most subject to baldness.

A جلحز *jalhaz*, Narrow-minded, covetous.

A جلحطاء *jilhitā,* A country destitute of trees.

A جلحظ *jilhiz*, Large-bodied and hairy.

A جلحظاء *jilhizā,* Hard, rough ground. Large and shaggy.

A جلحمة *jalhamat*, The twisting of a rope.

A جلحمد *jaluhmad*, Thick, coarse, gross.

A جلحن *jilhan*, Avaricious, narrow-minded.

A جلخ *jalkh*, (v. n. of جلخ) Filling its bed (a river). Cutting (a piece of flesh) with a sword. Throwing prostrate. Striking the belly. Lying with. Lengthening.

A جلخاظ *jilkhāz*, Hairy and large.

A جلخدي *jalakhda'*, Useless, good for nothing.

A جلخطاء *jilkhitā,* A country destitute of trees. Hard, rugged ground.

A جلخظ *jilkhiz*, Hairy, and bulky withal.

P جلد *jald*, Quick, swift, brisk. Onanism.

A جلد *jald*, (v. n. of جلد) Striking, lashing, whipping. Forcing against the will. Biting (as a serpent). Lying with. (pl. جلدي *jalda'*) Hard, strong (man). Penis. (pl. اجلاد *ajlād*, جلاد *jilād*, and جلد *julud*) Quick, active, brisk. *Jild*, (pl. اجلاد *ajlād* and جلود *julūd*) A skin, hide, leather. Penis. A volume. *Juld*, (pl. of اجلد *ajlad*) Hard. *Jalad*, (v. n. of جلد) Being strong and active. Being covered with hoar frost (ground). Strength. Hardness. Hard level ground. Camels or sheep that neither breed nor give milk. Large camels without any mixture of small ones. *Julud*, (pl. of جلد *jald*) Quick, active, brisk. (pl. of جليد *jalīd*) Hard, strong. A sheep whose fœtus died in the birth. Skin, hide. The skin of a camel's colt (stuffed and placed before the mother, who, thinking it alive, gives milk plentifully, or suckles the young of another camel).

A جلداء *juladā,* (pl. of جليد) Hard. Active.

A بجلدان *bi jildāna*, (or جلداء *jildā,*) Plainly.

A جلدب *jaldab*, Hard. Strong.

P جلد باز *jald-bāz*, Expeditious, fleet, hasty.

P جلد بازي *jald-bāzī*, Haste, speed, despatch.

P جلد بجلد *jald ba jald*, Quickly, speedily.

A جلدة *jaldat*, (pl. جلاد *jilād*) A large hardy palm-tree which can dispense with water. A camel yielding very rich milk. (A camel) neither breeding nor giving milk. A very fat she-camel. *Jildat*, A single skin. A cuticle. *Jaladat*, Hard, level ground. A sheep whose fœtus died in the birth. Strong and active (she-camel). Lightness, activity.

P جلد قدم *jald-kadam*, Swift of foot, fleet.

P جلدگر *jildgar*, A bookbinder.

P جلد مزاج *jald-mizāj*, Hasty, precipitate.

A جلدي *jalda'*, (pl. of جلد *jald*) Strong.

P جلدي *jaldī*, Speed, haste, quickness, swiftness.

A جلذ *julz*, (pl. مناجذ *manājiz*) A mole.

A جلذاء *jilzā,* Hard, rough ground.

A جلذاءة *jilzāsat*, A particle of such earth.

A جلذيّ *julziy*, ((pl. جلاذيّ *jalāziy*) Robust, thick (camel). A swift pace. Workman, artisan. A servitor, minister in a temple or church, a monk.

A جلز *jalz*, (v. n. of جلز) Folding, enveloping, twisting round. Extending, stretching, pulling. Whipping the sinew of a camel's neck round a knife-handle. The thicker part of a whip. The semicircle on the lower part of the teeth. Expeditious travelling. The handle of a whip. A sinew wrapped round the handle of a whip.

A جلس *jals*, Remains of honey in a vessel. Hard, rough (ground, tree, or honey-comb). Compact (camel). (A woman) keeping close at home. A noble lady. High (ground). The country of نجد *najd*. The members of an assembly, congregation, or convivial meeting. A ditch, a pond. Time, season. A long arrow. Wine. A high hill. *Jils*, A companion, comrade, messmate. Dull, stupid, stammering.

A جلساء *julasā,* (pl. of جليس) Companions.

A جلسات *jalasāt*, (pl. of جلسة) Sittings.

A جلسا خطيبي *jalsā-khatībī*, The sitting down of the khatīb (preacher) between the readings of the first and second khutbah.

A جلسام *jilsām*, (equiv. to برسام) A pleurisy.

A جلسان *jullasān*, (P گلستان) A rose-garden.

A جلسة *jalsat*, A sitting, meeting; society. Posture, situation, seat, post, state, bearing. *Jilsat*, A mode of sitting. *Julasat*, Very sedentary.

A جلّستان *jullastān*, (P گلستان) A flower-garden.

A جلسد *jalsad*, (or جلّسد) Name of an idol.

A جلسيّ *jilsiy*, The iris which encircles the pupil of the eye.

A جلط *jalata*, (fut. يجلط *yajlitu*) He lied.

A جلط *jalt*, (v. n. of جلط) Drawing (a sword). Voiding excrement. Swearing; lying. Shaving (the head). Flaying (a doe).

A جلطاء *jaltā,* Loose (tooth).

A جلطة *jultat*, Thick milk.

A جلظاء *jilzā,* Hard, coarse, uncultivated (land).

A جلع *jalɛ*, (v. n. of جلع) Pulling off clothes. *Jalaɛ*, (v. n. of جلع) Being open (the mouth). Being shameless (a woman). *Jaliɛ*, One whose privities are exposed. Obscene. Inverted-lipped, open-mouthed.

A جلعاب *jalɛāb*, Long, tall.

A جلعابة *jalɛābat*, Precipitate (camel). Cruel, savage, wicked.

A جلعب *jalɛab*, (جلعباء *jaluɛbā,* or جلعبىٰ *jalaɛba'*) Cruel, savage, wicked. Precipitate and fearless (camel).

A جلعباة *jalaɛbāt*, Strong (she-camel). Decrepit.

A جلعبانة *jiliɛbānat*, A scold, a shrew.

A جلعبىٰ العين *jalaɛba' al ɛayn*, Sharp-sighted.

A جلعة *jalaɛat*, The part where the teeth are seen in laughing. *Jaliɛat*, Immodest (woman).

A جلعد *jalɛad*, Hard, firm (thing). Dwarfish (ass). Aged (woman). Name of a place.

A جلعدة *jalɛadat*, (v. n. of جلعد Q) Laying (one) prostrate at full length. Swiftness in flight.

A جلعطيط *julaɛtīt* or *jalɛatīt*, Thick milk.

A جلعلع *jalaɛlaɛ*, (*julaɛlaɛ* or *juluɛlaɛ*) An untractable camel. A hedgehog. A beetle. A hyena.

A جلعلعة *jalaɛlaɛat* or *julaɛlaɛat*, A beetle. A beetle half clay and half a living insect.

A جلعم *jalɛam*, Impudent, obscene.

A جلغ *jalgh*, A cutting (with a sword).

A جلغاء *jalghā,* Old, toothless (she-camel).

P جلغوزة *jalghoza*, A nut resembling the pistachio. جلغوزۀ هندي *jalghoza-i hindī*, A kind of wild fruit. Seed of onion.

A جلف *jalf*, (v. n. of جلف) Peeling. Striking with a sword). Plucking, tearing up, uprooting. Scraping, shovelling (mud from off any thing). *Jilf*, (pl. جلوف *julūf*) A vessel, case, repository. Any empty vessel, pot, or pan. The lower half of a broken vessel, An animal embowelled, and skinned, with the head and feet cut off. A skin bag without head or feet. (pl. اجلاف *ajlāf*) Severe, hard, unjust. A kind of bird. A male palm-tree. Coarse, dry bread. Bread without meat or fish. The edge of a loaf. *Juluf* or *julf*, Years destructive to cattle. *Jalaf*, (v. n. of جلف) Being severe, hard, unjust.

P جلف *jilf*, Silly, trifling. Fearless.

A جلفاط *jilfāt*, (or جلفاظ *jilfāz*) The caulker of a new vessel.

A جلفة *jalfat*, A bit of camel's skin cut, but not separated, and left for a mark. *Jilfat*, A bit of bread, hard and dry. A slice or piece of any thing. *Jilfat* or *jalfat*, The portion of a pen or writing reed lying between the point and the part where the first cut is made. *Julfat*, A bit of skin peeled. *Jalafat*, A kind of goat having little hair and of small value.

A جلفدة *jalfadat*, Sounds, unmusical noises.

A جلفريز *jalfarīz*, A wrinkled old woman; one having some remains of strength. A hardy old she-camel. A misfortune. Heavy.

A جلفز *jalfaz*, A she-camel hard and thick. Strong and hard.

A جلفطة *jalfatat*, The careening (of a ship).

A جلفظة *jalfazat*, The careening (of a ship).

A جلق *jalk*, (v. n. of جلق) Shaving (the head). Making conspicuous. Shooting with a balista. Laughing with wide-open mouth. Peace, friendship.

T جلق *jalk*, Mastupration, onanism. P جلق زدن *jalk zadan*, To onanise, pollute one's self.

P جلق *julk*, The thousand and eightieth part

of an hour, or $\frac{1}{25920}$th part of a night and day.

A جلّق *jillik*, A sort of grain grown in Yaman. A word used in calling to a camel. *Jillik* or *jillak*, Damascus, or the adjacent country.

A جلقة *jalakat*, The part where the teeth are visible in laughing. *Jilikat*, An old woman. A decrepit she-camel.

A جلقة *jillikat* (or جلقّة *jilikkat*) An old woman. A decrepit she-camel.

P جلك *jalak*, A small melodious bird.

P جلكارة *jalkāra*, Opposite ways or opinions.

A جلل *jalal*, A vast and momentous affair. A light and trifling concern. من جللك *min jalalika*, On thy account. *Julal*, (pl. of جلّى *julla'*) Difficult and important affairs. (pl. of جلّة *jullat*) Date-hampers made of palm-leaves.

A جلم *jalama*, (fut. يجلم *yajlimu*) He cut.

A جلم *jalm*, (v. n. of جلم) Cutting (flesh off the bones). Shaving. Shearing. *Jilm*, The tallow of sheep. *Jalam*, Shears. Any cutting instrument. (pl. جلام *jilām*) A buck. A kid. A flock, a species of sheep with long legs, and without hair (frequently met with in Tāif in Arabia). A tike. A mark made upon a camel (by burning). The moon (particularly new moon first appearing).

P جلم *jilm*, Name of a country in the Panjāb.

SY جلماثا *jalmāsā*, A cucumber.

A جلماظ *jilmāz*, Greedy, wishful, hankering after every thing.

A جلماق *jilmāk*, The sinew of a camel (which they twist round a bow to strengthen it).

A جلمان *jalamāni*, (dual) A pair of shears.

A جلمة *jalmat* or *julmat*, The entire carcase (of a slaughtered beast). *Jalamat*, (A sheep) skinned, drawn, with the head and trotters cut off.

A جلمحة *jalmahat*, A shaving the head.

A جلمد *jalmad*, A huge stone. A cow or ox. A stern man. A large herd of camels. Aged camels. Upwards of 100 sheep. *Jilmid*, A stone in water, the upper part appearing above the surface.

A جلمدة *jalmadat*, A hard, rough, severe man. Stony ground.

A جلمريز *jalmarīz*, A she-camel hard and thick.

A جلمطة *jalmatat*, A shaving (of the head).

A جلمق *jalmak*, (pl. جلامق) A tunic open in front.

A جلمقة *jalmakat*, A warping (a bow) with gut.

A جلمود *julmūd*, A great stone. Aged camels.

A جلن *jalan*, The sound of a pair of folding-doors when striking against each other (the one called جلن *jalan*, the other بلق *balak*).

A جلّنار *jullanār*, (P گلنار) Pomegranate-flowers.

A جلّناريّ *jullanāriy*, Pomegranate-coloured.

A جلنباة *jalambāt*, A fat woman.

A جلنبط *jalambat*, A lion.

A جلنبلق *jalambalak*, The noise of opening or of slamming together of large folding-doors.

A جلنجبين *julanjabīn*, (from P گل *gul* انگبين *angubīn*), Conserve of roses made with honey.

A جلنجوجة *jālanjūja*, Pennyroyal.

A جلندح *jalandah*, Heavy, unwholesome.

A جلندحة *julandahat*, Hardy (she-camel).

A جلندد *jalandad*, Mischievous, worthless.

A جلنزي *jalanza'*, Strong and coarse (camel).

A جلنسرين *julnisrīn*, (P گل نسرين) Sweet-briar.

A جلنظي *jalanza'*, Broad-shouldered.

A جلنفاة *jalanfāt*, Dry bread without meat.

A جلنفاط *jilinfāt*, The caulker of a new vessel.

A جلنفع *jalanfaꜥ*, Weak in mind, dull, stupid.

A جلنفعة *jalanfaꜥat*, Corpulent, big-bellied (she-camel); also one aged, with some remains of strength; or one whose nose has been perforated.

P جلنگ *jiling*, Jingling of chains and the like. A kind of silken stuff wrought with gold and silver or not. Stalk of cucumbers, gourds, melons, and the like. A shrimp.

A جلو *jalw*, (v. n. of جلا for جلو) Leaving a place, emigrating. Polishing, scouring, furbishing. Driving away care. Making clear. Being clear. Driving into exile.

P جلو *jalav*, A horse-bridle. A horse led for parade. *Jalū*, *jilū*, or *julū*, A roasting-spit. Brisk, saucy. Ill-tempered.

A جلواء *jalwāꜥ*, (fem. of اجلى *ajla'*) Unclouded (sky). Bald about the forehead. Wide (forehead).

A جلواح *jilwāh*, A widely-extended country.

A جلواخ *jilwākh*, A wide valley full of water.

P جلواد *jalwād*, Ill-temper, bad disposition.

A جلواذ *jilwāz*, (pl. جلاوذة *jalāwizat*) A sergeant or attendant on the collector of tribute or revenue.

P جلو آهن *jalū-āhan*, An iron spit.

A جلوبة *jalūbat*, Any thing brought from any place for sale. Male-camels. Camels employed in the transport of goods.

A جلوبق *jalawbak*, Clamorous, noisy (man).

A جلوة *jilwat*, *julwat*, or *jalwat*, (v. n. of جلا for جلو) Presenting a bride to her husband adorned and unveiled. Presenting a female servant to his bride (a bridegroom). A female servant presented by the bridegroom to the bride. The nuptial bed; also the place where the bride sits adorned and unveiled (in which situation she is seen only by her husband). Splendour. P جلوه دادن *jilwa dādan*, To dress (a bride). To adorn, adjust, polish.

P جلو چوب *jalū-chob*, A wooden spit.

P جلود *jalūd*, A city. A village.

A جلود *julūd*, (pl. of جلد) Skins, hides. Penes.

P جلودار *jalav-dār*, An attendant, a groom.

A جلودة *julūdat*, Strength, agility.

A جلوديّ *julūdiy*, A skinner, tanner, currier.

A جلوذ *jillawz*, Hard and thick.

P جلوريز *jalav-rez*, Full speed, great expedition.

P جيلوز *jalūz*, (or جلوزة *jalūza*) The pistachio-nut.

A جلوز *jillawz*, A filbert-nut. Bold. Robust.

A جلوزة *jalwazat*, Lightness, expedition.

A جلوس *julūs*, (v. n. of جلس) Sitting. Sitting down to table. Beginning of a reign, accession to the throne, coronation. (Men) sitting together. (pl. of جالس *jālis*) Sitters. جلوس سعادت مانوس *julūsi saꜥādat-maꜥnus*, The august and glorious accession. P جلوس کردن *julūs kardan*, To sit, to sit down. To ascend the throne.

A جلوسيّ *julūsiy*, Of the beginning of a reign.

A جلوط *jalūt*, Impudent (woman).

A جلوع *julūꜥ*, (v. n. of جلع) Unveiling herself. Drawing the foreskin back behind the gland (a boy).

A جلوف *julūf*, (pl. of جلف *jilf*) Magazines. Empty butts.

A جلول *julūl*, (v. n. of جلّ) Being banished, living in exile. Taking the greater part or heart (of any thing). (pl. of جلّ *jall*) Sails of ships.

A جلولاء *jalawlāꜥ*, Name of a Persian village.

P جلوند *jalwand*, A lamp, a candle.

P جلونك *jalūnak*, Melon or cucumber-stalks.

A جلوة *jilwa*, Splendour. (See جلوة *jilwat*).

P جلوه گاه *jilwa-gāh*, A bride's apartment, in which she is unveiled by her husband. The world.

P جلوه گر *jilwagar*, Manifest, conspicuous.

P جلوه گري *jilwagarī*, Conspicuity, splendour. Blandishment, loveliness.

P جلوي *jalwī*, A mincing gait. Suite.

P جلويز *jilwīz*, A bridle-rein. Picked, chosen. A sycophant, informer.

A جله *jalh*, (v. n. of جله) Carrying away (gravel). Driving or turning one back from any arduous affair. Laying open to view. Raising the turban from off the forehead. *Jalah*, (v. n. of جله) Experiencing a partial loss of hair on the forehead.

P جلّه *julla*, A fungus. A basket, canister. A ball of thread. A date-tree. A jar, drinking-vessel.

A جلهاب *jilhāb*, A low place, a valley.

A جلهة *jalhat*, (pl. جلاه *jilāh*) A large round rock. A street or quarter of a city. An encamping-place for travellers. Side of a valley. Partial baldness before. Dates dressed with milk and butter.

A جلهزة *jalhazat*, (v. n. of جلهز Q) Being silent on a subject with which one is acquainted.

A جلهم *julhum*, A large mouse.

A جلهمة *jul* or *jalhamat*, The side or course of a river or valley. Affliction. A great thing, important affair.

A جلهوم *julhūm*, A great body of men.

A جلي *jaly* (v. n. of جلي) Polishing. *Jily*, A small window in the roof of a house.

A جلّى *julla'*, (pl. جلل *julal*) An important, momentous affair. ابن الجلّى *ibnu'l jalla'*, Name of an eminent man amongst the Sūfis.

A جليّ *jaliy*, Clear, manifest, evident. Bright, shining, resplendent. Large, plain (hand-writing). Distinctly-sounded (letter). فصل جلي *fasli jalī*, A season before the commencement of the rains in which a crop of rice is cut (in India). خفي و جلي

khafī u jalī, Hidden and discovered. جليّ الصدر *jalīyu's sadr*, Most eminent, supreme.

A جلّيان *jilliyān*, Plain, manifest, clear, open.

A جليب *jalīb*, (pl. جلبى *jalba'* and جلباء *julabā'*) (A slave) carried about for sale. (pl. جلبى *jalba'* or جلائب) A woman carried about for sale.

A جليبة *jalībat*, Cattle driven about for sale.

A جليّة *jalīyat*, (fem. of جليّ *jalīy*) Clear, manifest. Lucid. True intelligence.

A جليت *jalīt*, (for جليد) Hard and active.

A جليحاء *julayhā'*, The distinctive symbol used by the tribe of غنيّ *ghunayy*.

A جليحة *jalīhat*, A shaking of a churn in order to extract the butter.

A جليد *jalīd*, (pl. جلداء *juladā'*, اجلاد *ajlād*, جلاد *jilād*, and جلد *julud*) Hard, strong. Nimble, active. Frost, hoar-frost, ice.

A جليدة *julaydat*, A pellicle, membrane.

A جلئز *jil'iz*, A dwarfish woman.

P جليز *jalīz*, A halter. A mischief-maker.

A جليز *jalīz*, Expeditious travelling.

A جليس *jalīs*, (pl. جلساء *julasā'* and جلّاس *jullās*) A companion, comrade, guest, chum. القاضي الجليس *al kāzī'l jalīs*, Name of عبد العزيز بن جبّاب *'abdu'l 'azīzu 'bnu jabbāb*.

A جليطة *jalītat*, A sword falling from the sheath.

A جليع *jalī'*, A woman who does not screen herself when lying with her husband.

A جليف *jalīf*, A kind of pulse. Peeled. Severe, hard, unjust.

A جليفة *jalīfat*, (pl. جلائف *jalā'if*, جلف *julf* or *julf*) A fatal, deadly season.

A جليل *jalīl*, Great, glorious, illustrious. The plant ثمام *sumām*, used in covering houses or fencing tents. A tale-bearer. Coarse, rough, gross. (pl. جلّة *jillat* and اجلّة *ajillat*) Old, aged, experienced. جليل القدر *jalīlu'l kadr*, High in dignity, august, illustrious. جليل الاعتبار *jalīlu'l i'tibār*, Greatly revered.

P جليل *julayl*, A horse-cloth. A covering for a camel-litter. Name of a man who kept many cats.

A جليلة *jalīlat*, (A camel) which has brought forth once. (pl. جليل *jalīl* and جلال *jilāl*) A large palm-tree laden with fruit. Illustrious (woman).

A جليه *jalīh*, Clear of gravel, sand, or grit.

A جليهة *jalīhāt*, Dates dressed with milk and butter. A place whence gravel has been removed.

P جم *jam*, Name of an ancient king of Persia, whom they confound with Solomon and Alexander the Great. A monarch, a great king. The pupil of the eye. The second of the ten intelligences. Pure, free, exempt. Essence, nature, person.

A جمّ *jamm*, (v. n. of جمّ) Resting, recruiting his strength (a jaded horse). Leaving (water) to collect. Being fleshy (a bone). Filling (a measure), augmenting its volume. Water collected, or flowing into a well. A mass of water. A heaped measure. (pl. جمام *jimām* and جموم *jumūm*) Much, abundant, inexhaustible. The larger portion of noontide. Name of an ancient king of Persia. الجمّ الغفير *al jammu'l ghafīr*, A great multitude. *Jimm*, A devil or devils. *Jumm*, A kind of shell-fish.

A جما *jama'*, (v. n. of جمي) Being angry at. A person, body, individual.

A جما *jama'* or *juma'*, The swell of the breasts, or other parts of the body. A little swelling, pimple. A stone rising above the surface of the ground. The back, surface. A quantity, measure. Motion (of an embryo). A collection.

A جمّا *jamman*, In a heap, crowd, pell-mell.

A جماء *jamā'*, (or جماءة *jamā'at*) Body, individual existence. A swelling.

A جمّاء *jammā'*, (fem. of اجمّ *ajamm*) Unadorned (woman). Smooth, bare. A helmet. (A sheep) without horns, dodded. (A woman) having round elbows, fleshy-boned.

A جماجم *jamājim*, (pl. of جمجمة *jumjumat*) Skulls. Chieftains. Tribes to which families trace their origin. Beams of ploughs.

A جماجميّ *jamājimīy*, A maker of plough-beams.

A جماح *jimāh*, (v. n. of جمح) Being restive, refractory (a horse). Running fast. Eloping from (her) husband (a woman), and going to (her) friends. Being self-opiniated. Throwing (one hock-bone against another) so as to drive (it) from (its) place.

A جمّاح *jummāh*, Soldiers flying (from battle). (pl. جماميح *jamāmīh* and جمامح *jamāmih*) A round-headed arrow with which boys learn to shoot. A knob on the top of a stick, for boys to play with. Spikes growing from the heads of withering grass.

A جماد *jamād*, A dry season. (Ground) unwatered with rain. (A camel) wanting milk. Any thing not growing or increasing, inorganic; a fossil. جماد الكفّ *jamādu'l kaff*, Frozen-handed, stingy. *Jamād* or *jimād*, A sort of garment. *Jimād*, (pl. of جمد *jumd* and *jumud*) High places. *Jamādi*, A term of reproach addressed to a miser. جمادِ له *jamādi lahu*, May ill-luck attend him!

A جمّاد *jammād*, Sharp (sword). A vender of ice.

A جمادات *jamādāt*, Minerals, fossils.

A جمادي *jumāda'*, (pl. جماديات *jumādayāt*) Name of two months (the fifth and sixth) of the Arabian year. جمادي الاوّل *jumāda'l awwal* (اولي *ūla'* or خمسة *khamsat*) Jumāda' the first. جمادي الآخر *jumāda'l āhhir*, (اخري *ukhra'* or ستّة *sittat*) Jumāda' the second. جمادي جامدة *jumada' jāmidat*, A tearless eye.

A جماديّ *jamādīy*, Inanimate, inorganic.

A جمار *jamār*, A crowd. *Jimār*, (pl. of جمرة) Small stones (thrown in the solemnities of Mecca).

A جمّار *jummār*, The pith of a palm-tree. جمّار النهر *jammāru'n nahr*, (equivalent to جار النهر *jāru'n nahr*) Name of a plant resembling the water-lily.

A جماري *jamāra'* or *jamāran*, All, the whole.

A جمّاز *jammāz*, Quick (camel). Capering (ass).

A جمّازة *jummāzat*, A woollen waistcoat. Quick travelling (she-camel).

P جمازوان *jammāzwān*, Camel-keeper or leader.

P جم اسپرم *jam-isparm*, A creeping-plant.

A جماسيّ *jumāsīy*, Cold and frosty (night).

P جماش *jamāsh*, Cheerful, sprightly. A deceiver, cheat. Deceit. Drunken. Jollity, mirth, impudence. Drunkenness, revelry, riot. Fierceness, roughness. Decorator, adorner. جماشان گل *jamāshāni gul*, Flower-gatherers.

A جماش *jimāsh*, The part between the top of a well and the parapet.

P جمّاش *jammāsh*, An amorous glance.

A جمّاش *jammāsh*, One who toys with women.

A جماظ *jimāz*, Coarse, thick, rugged, cruel.

A جماع *jimā'*, (v. n. 3 of جمع) Consenting, agreeing. Concubitus, coitus. All, universal. A multitude, sum total, whole. A large cauldron. جماع الاثم *jimā'u'l ism*, Wine.

A جمّاع *jammā'*, One who indulges much in venery. *Jummā'*, Any thing heaped and piled together. A mixed crowd of men. جمّاع الكفّ *jummā'u'l kaff*, A handful.

A جماعة *jamā'at* A crowd, troop, body. A heap, collection. A meeting, assembly, senate, mote, council, congregation. A faction.

A جمال *jamāl*, (v. n. of جمل) Being fair, comely, becoming. Elegance, beauty, grace (of body or mind). Handsomeness of nose or features. صاحب جمال *sāhibi jamāl*, Beautiful. جمالك *jamālaka*, Take care of your behaviour. جمالك ان لا تفعل كذا *jamālaka an lā taf'ala kazā*, Mind your character and do not act thus. *Jimāl*, (pl. of جمل *jamal*) Full-grown camels. *Jumāl*, Very handsome.

A جمّال *jammāl*, (pl. جمّالون *jammālūn*) A camel-owner or driver. *Jummāl*, Very handsome.

A جمالات *jam, jim,* or *jumālāt*, (pl. of جمل *jamal*) Full-grown camels.

A جمالة *jimālat*, A troop of he-camels without females. (pl. of جمل *jamal*) Full-grown camels. *Jum, jam,* or *jimālat*, A herd of she-camels without any males. A portion of a tribe. Horses. (pl. of جمل *jamal*) Full-grown camels.

A جمّالة *jammālat*, Camel-owners.

P جمالوگ *jimālūg*, Name of a famous robber.

A جماليّ *jumālīy*, Large, strong (camel or man).

A جماليّة *jumālīyat* Strong (she-camel).

A جمام *jamām*, (v. n. of جمّ) Resting (an exhausted stallion). Recruiting his strength (a jaded horse). Rest. A heaped-up measure of corn. *Jamām, jimām,* or *jumām*, (v. n. of جمّ) Filling full (a measure). *Jimām*, Fulness (of a cup of water). Tribes, the parents of families. (pl. of جمّ *jamm*) Much. (pl. of جمّة *jammat*), Reservoirs. *Jumām* or *jimām*, The spermatic lymph of a stallion collected in his loins. A heaped-up measure.

A جمّام *jammām*, A heaped-up measure.

A جماميح *jamāmīh*, (poet. جمامح *jamāmih*) (pl. of جمّاح *jummāh*) Round-headed arrows with which boys learn to shoot. Knobs on the heads of sticks with which boys play. Spikes growing from the heads of dry, withering grass.

A جماميس *jamāmīs*, A kind of mushroom.

P جمان *jumān*, A kind of wood, the exterior of which is black, and the inside of a pistachio-green.

A جمان *jumān*, A pearl. A globule of silver resembling a pearl. A belt or girdle of leather adorned with gems or beads.

A جمّان *jammān*, Heaped-up (measure).

P جمانی *jamānī*, A cup-bearer.

A جمّانيّ *jummāniy*, Long-haired (man).

A جماهير *jamāhīr*, (pl. of جمهور *jumhūr*) Republics, commonwealths. جماهير نصارا *jamāhīri nasāra'*, The Christian republics.

A جمائل *jamāʼil*, Full-grown camels.

A جمّة *jammat*, A reservoir of water. A well full and overflowing. A crowd, troop. (pl. جمم *jumam*) The hold of a ship, in which bilge-water collects. A great part of noonday. *Jammat* or *jummat*, A crowd. He who demands the pretium sanguinis for a slaughtered kinsman. *Jummat*, Hair flowing over the shoulders. The part of the head where the hair is collected or tied up, especially the forehead. The knotty parts of plants whence the flowers spring.

P جمتود *jamtūd*, Exulting in, reviewing with complacency good deeds done by one's self.

A جمثور *jumsūr*, Earth or dust heaped up.

P جمجاه *jam-jāh*, Place of assembly. Imperial.

A جمجم *jamjam*, A sort of rustic shoe.

P جمجم *jumjum*, A kind of shoe, the under part made of rags, the upper of string.

A جمجمة *jamjamat*, (v. n. of جمجم Q) Muttering. Keeping concealed in the breast. Destroying. *Jumjumat*, (pl. جمجم *jumjum* and جماجم *jamājim*) The skull. A wooden cup. The beam of a plough. A kind of measure. A well dug in a brackish place.

A جمح *jamh*, (v. n. of جمح) Being refractory, vicious (horse). Being self-opiniated. Running away (as a wife from her husband to her relations, without leave). Throwing (one huckle-bone against another). Running fast.

A جمحظة *jamhazat*, An infant's swaddling-bands. A rope for tying the legs of an animal about to be slaughtered.

A جمحل *jummahl*, The meat inside a shell.

A جمخ *jamkh*, A being proud. Pomp, pride, glory.

A جمّخ *jummakh*, (pl. of جامخ) Proud, boastful.

A جمخر *jamkhar*, Large and hollow (reed).

A جمخور *jumkhūr*, Hollow (reed, or like thing).

A جمد *jamd*, (v. n. of جمد) Freezing, congealing (water or blood). Being frozen-hearted, unfeeling, stingy. Being due, necessary. Cutting. Congealed. *Jumd*, *jumud* and *jamad* (pl. اجماد *ajmād* and جماد *jimād*) High ground. *Jamad*, Ice. Snow. (pl. of جامد *jāmid*) Congealed, consistent. Rigid. Fossils. P جمد چيني *jamadi chīnī*, Native alkaline salt.

P جمدر *jamdar*, (said to be derived from جنب *jamb*, Side, and در *dar*, Rending) A kind of weapon.

A جمر *jamr*, (v. n. of جمر) Giving (one) a live coal. Putting away. Warding off. Assembling, flocking together. Jumping in fetters (a horse). Live coals.

A جمرات *jamarāt*, (pl. of جمرة *jamrat*) Live coals. جمرات العرب Name of three tribes.

A جمرة *jamrat*, (pl. جمر *jamr* and جمرات *jamarāt*) One live coal. Gravel, or small pebbles. Heat from the ground. A troop, especially a body of 1000 horse. A tribe made up from several, or which contains 300 horsemen. A sacred solemnity or peregrination performed in the valley of Mina, near Mecca, in which they defy and throw stones at a figure representing the devil. It is performed thrice, and is جمرة الاولى *jamratu'l ūla'*, جمرة الوسطى *jamratu'l wusta'*, and جمرة العقبة *jamratu'l ʻakabat*, First, middle, and last.

P جمرة *jamra*, Vapours, warm exhalations rising out of the earth in the spring.

P جمري *jam*, *jum*, or *jimrī*, Poor, mean.

A جمز *jamz*, (v. n. of جمز) Travelling quick (a camel). Travelling (a man). Deriding, joking, sneering. *Jamz* or *jumz*, (pl. جموز *jumūz*) The remains of a cluster of dates.

A جمزاز *jumzāz*, A lump of dates or of اقط *akit*. The seed-pod or capsule of a plant.

A جمزان *jumzān*, A species of the date.

A جمزة *jumzat*, (pl. جمز *jumaz*) A lump of dates or اقط *akit*. The seed-pod or capsule of a plant.

A جمزرة *jamzarat*, (v. n. of جمزر Q) Retiring through timidity, running away.

A جمزى *jamza'*, (v. n. of جمز) Travelling quick (man or camel). *Jamaza'*, Fleet (ass, camel, or horse).

A جمزيور *jamzīwar*, A horse white on the face, belly, and two fore-legs.

P جمس *jams*, Ice.

A جمسة *jamsat*, Fire. *Jumsat*, (pl. جمس *jums*) Half-ripe dates. A dry date. A herd of camels.

A جمست *jamast*, A kind of turquoise or coarse blue gem, found near Madīna, cups of which, it is alleged, have the singular property of preventing those who drink out of them from being intoxicated, and also of causing pleasant dreams. A low illiterate man.

A جمش *jamsh*, (v. n. of جمش) Shaving (the head). Milking with the tips of the fingers. Making for a well the part called جماش *jimāsh*. Flattering, soothing; toying, playing. A low voice, soft sound. لا يسمع فلان اذنا جمشا *lā yasmaʻu fulānun uzunan jamshan*, Such an one listens not to a word of advice.

P جمش *jamash*, An eye-glance. The turn of the eye, and outstretched neck (of rapacious birds when going to seize their prey).

P جمشاسب *jamshāsb*, Solomon. Jamshed.

P جمشاك *jamshāk*, (or جمشك) A shoe.

P جمشيد *jamshed*, (Splendid king) Name of a Persian king. جمشيد ماهي *jamshedi māhī*, (or جمشيد ماهي گير *jamshedi māhī-gīr*) The sun in Pisces. Solomon. The prophet Jonas.

P جمشيدون *jamshedūn*, Solomon. Jamshed, a Persian king.

A جمص *jams*, A sort of plant.

A جمع *jamʻ*, (v. n. of جمع) Collecting, assembling, bringing together. Putting (a word) in the plural number. Joining; conjunction. A collection, congregation. (pl. جموع *jumūʻ*, A crowd, multitude. Amount, sum total, aggregate. Rental. Price, value. Name of a place (called also مزدلفة *muzdalifat*) near Mecca, so named from the great concourse of people occasionally assembled there. Bad dates. The plural number. A palm-tree which has shot out of the stone. A palm-tree loaded with fruit. The milk of any quadruped whose dugs are tied up. Red gum. جمع الثياب *jamʻu's siyāb*, A taking to wear a veil (a grown up girl). جمع الجمع *jamʻu'l jamʻ*, Plural of a plural: as, بيوتات *buyūtāt*, (p. of بيوت *buyūt* p. of بيت *bayt*) Houses; غرابين *gharābīn*, (pl. of غربان *ghirbān* pl. of غراب *ghurāb*) Crows. جمع جمع الجمع *jamʻu jamʻi'l jamʻ*, Plural of a plural of a plural: as, اعصام *aʻsām*, (pl. of عصمة *ʻasamat* which is pl. of عصم *ʻisam*, which is pl. of عصمة *ʻismat*) Collars. جمع قلت *jamʻi killat*, Plural of paucity. جمع كثرت *jamʻi kasrat*, Plural of multitude. جمع المذكر *jamʻu'l muzakkar*, Masculine plural. جمع مصحح *jamʻi musahhah*, Sound plural. جمع مكسّر *jamʻi mukassar*, Broken or irregular plural. جمع المؤنث *jamʻu'l muʼannas*, Feminine plural. يوم الجمع *yawmu'l jamʻ*, The day of judgment. The day of عرفة *ʻarafat*. ايّام جمع *ayyāmi jamʻ*, The days of منى *mina'*. جمع ابواب *jamʻi abwāb*, Rent of land in India, fixed at a subsequent period to the time of the Emperor Akbar. جمع اصل *jamʻ asl*, Original rent of land as rated in the reign of Akbar, or at some more ancient period. P جمع آمدن *jamʻ āmadan*, Coire. جمع بالدرستي *jamʻ bi'd durustī*, Revenue accruing from fines. جمع بندي *jamʻ bandī*, An account of the quantity of land and number of houses in a district. The settlement of an assessment. A rent-roll. جمع شدن *jamʻ shudan*, To be tranquil, secure. جمع طوماري *jamʻ tūmārī*, A rent-roll. A جمع كامل *jamʻ kāmil*, Revenue that has remained unaltered for many years. جمع كثير *jamʻi kasīr*, A great multitude. P جمع كردن *jamʻ kardan*, To assemble, bring together. جمع لشكر كردن *jamʻi lashkar kardan*, To muster an army. جمع مال كردن *jamɛi māl kardan*, To acquire riches. A جمع مفصّل *jamɛ mufassal*, The aggregate amount of the different sources of revenue, whether of rent or custom. جمع واصل باقي *jamɛ wāsil bākī*, An account stating the rental, collections, balances, and arrears of a district or province. P جمع و خرچ *jamɛ u kharch*, An account of receipts and disbursements, account current. A *Jumɛ*, (pl. اجماع *ajmāɛ*) A clenched fist. (pl. of جامع *jāmiɛ*) Large cauldrons. *Jumɛ, jamɛ,* or *jimɛ*, The death of a pregnant woman, or of a virgin. *Jumɛ* or *jimɛ*, The clenching of the fist. All. A virgin. Concealed, clandestine (business). *Jumaɛ*, (pl. of جمعة *jumɛat*) Fridays.

A جمعاء *jamɛāɛ*, (fem. of اجمع *ajmaɛ*) All, every, universal. Sound, whole (mare or beast of burden). Old decrepit (she-camel).

A جمعات *jumɛāt, jumuɛāt,* or *jumaɛāt*) Fridays. *Jamaɛāt*, (pl. of جمع *jamɛ*) Companies. Accounts.

A جمعة *jumɛat*, A handful. Friendship, intimacy. *Jumɛat, jumuɛat,* or *jumaɛat*, (pl. جمع *jumaɛ*) Friday, the day of worship among Muhammadans when they assemble in the great mosque.

A جمعد *jamɛad*, Stones collected or piled up.

P جمعدار *jamaɛ-dār*, A native officer of the army so called. The head of any body, as guides, harkāras, &c. (in India).

P جمعداري *jamaɛ-dārī*, Rank of Jamaɛdār.

P جمعدان *jamaɛdān*, A traveller's scrip.

A جمعر *jamɛar*, Yellow mud (just dug out).

A جمعرة *jamɛarat*, (v. n. of جمعر Q) Turning round a sphere at the end of a stick. Stones piled up high. A high and rugged hill. A high heap of stones. Endeavouring or longing to bite (an ass).

A جمعگي *jumɛagī*, The weekly allowance to schoolboys paid on a Friday; also the present then given by them to their tutor.

A جمعلة *jumɛulat*, A lump of honey or fat the size of a nut.

A جمعليل *jumaɛlīl*, An amasser, a collector.

A جمعليلة *jumaɛlīlat*, A hyena. A she-camel old and hard.

A جمعور *jumɛūr*, Great crowd, large company.

A جمعورة *jumɛūrat*, A sphere whirled round at a stick's end. A lump of the new cheese اقط *akit*.

A جمعي *jamɛī*, A total, assembly, a many.

A جمعيّة *jamɛīyat*, A collection. A collected state. Composure, tranquillity. جمعيّت خاطر *jamɛīyati khātir*, Peace of mind.

P جمعيّت خانه *jamɛīyat-khāna*, Audience-hall.

P جمعيّت گاه *jamɛīyat-gāh*, A rendezvous.

P جمگرد *jamgard*, Name of an earthly paradise mentioned in the Saddar, written by Zardusht.

A جمل *jaml*, (v. n. of جمل) Collecting. Melting (fat). *Juml*, A cable. (pl. of جمل *jamal*) Full-grown (camels). *Jamal*, A cable. *Jamal* or *jaml*, (pl. اجمال *ajmāl*, جامل *jāmil*, جمل *juml*, جمال *jimāl*, جمالة *jam, jim, jumālat*, جمالات *jam, jim, jumālāt*, جمائل *jamāɛil*, and اجامل *ajāmil*) A camel (of full growth). A palm-tree. A kind of fish, thirty cubits long, called جمل البحر *jamalu'lbahr*, The sea-camel. اتّخذ الليل جملاً *ittakhaza'l layla jamalan*, He travelled all night, or spent the night in devotion. *Jumal*, A cable. Addition. (pl. of جملة *jumlat*) Totals. *Jumul*, A crowd of people. A cable.

A جمّل *jummal*, A cable. Addition. حساب الجمّل *hisābu'l jummal*, Addition. The reckoning of the alphabet by ابجد *abjad*.

A جملاء *jamlāɛ*, Handsome, perfectly formed (animal). Handsome, perfectly formed (woman).

A جملان *jimlān*, (pl. of جميل) Species of birds.

A جملانة *jumlānat*, A nightingale.

A جملة *jumlat*, (pl. جمل *jumal*) Sum, whole, total, aggregate. A complete proposition, a sentence. Totality. جملۀ كائنات *jumlaɛi kāɛināt*, The universe, all creatures, every thing. P جملۀ لشكر *jumlaɛi lashkar*, The whole army. A بالجملة *bi'l jumla*, In substance, upon the whole. على الجملة *ɛala'l jumla*, On the whole. في الجملة *fi'l jumla*, In short, in substance. A little. من جملة *min jumla*, From, out of the whole.

A جملةً *jumlatan*, Universally, on the whole.

P جملگي *jumlagī*, Universality, totality. All.

A جمم *jamam*, (v. n. of جمّ) Having no spear (a man). Being dodded, without horns (a sheep). Being very fleshy (a woman). Being without pinnacles or battlements (a house). Being crowded. A heaped-up measure of corn.

P جمند *jamand*, (originally جايمند *jāymand*) A slow horse. Slow, weak, languid.

A جموح *jamūh*, Refractory, unmanageable (horse). Obstinate, self-willed (man). *Jumūh*, (v. n. of جمح) Being refractory (a horse). Running away (as a wife from her husband to her relations without leave). Throwing (one huckle bone at another).

A جمود *jamūd*, (An eye) unable to weep. *Jumūd*, (v. n. of جمد) Becoming frozen (water). Being cold-hearted, unfriendly, unkind.

A جموز *jumūz*, (pl. of جمز *jamz* or *jumz*) Remainders of bunches of dates.

A جموس *jumūs*, A becoming hard (said of fat).

A جموش *jamūsh*, Barren (season), destructive to vegetation. Depilatory (lime). A well leaking at the sides.

A جموع *jamūɛ*, One who collects much. Wealthy. *Jumūɛ*, (pl. of جمع *jamɛ*) Troops, crowds. Plurals. اقصى الجموع *aksa'l jumūɛ*, منتهى الجموع *muntaha'l jumūɛ* or جمع الجموع *jamɛu'l jumūɛ*, The last of plurals, the extreme boundary of the plurals, the plural of plurals: as, بيوتات *buyūtāt*, (pl. of بيوت *buyūt* which is pl. of بيت *bayt*) Houses.

A جمول *jamūl*, A melter of fat. A fat woman.

A جموم *jamūm*, (A well) full of water, and running over. A horse that runs again as soon as the first race is ended. *Jumūm*, (v. n. of جمّ) Abounding (water in a well). Flowing afresh (water after having failed). (pl. of جمّ *jamm*) Much. Drawing near, being at hand (arrival). (pl. of جمّة *jammat*) Reservoirs.

A جمهرة *jamharat*, (v. n. of جمهر Q) Collecting. Drawing the earth over a grave, but not plastering it with clay. Communicating a portion of intelligence, but suppressing the most important part. A heap of sand.

P جمهلو *jamhalū* or *jamahlū*, A kind of grain.

A جمهور *jumhūr*, (pl. جماهير *jamāhīr*) A high heap of sand. The greater or principal part (of men or things). A noble or generous woman. A republic. Grandees. All, universal. امور جمهور *umūri jumhūr*, Public, state-affairs.

A جمهوريّ *jumhūrīy*, An intoxicating wine or drink three years old. Must boiled down to a half.

A جميء *jamiɛa*, (fut. يجمأ *yajmaɛu*) He was angry.

A جميء *jama'* or *juma'*, The swell of the breasts, or any other parts of the body. A little swelling, a pimple. A stone rising above the surface of the ground. The back or surface. A quantity, measure. Motion (of an embryo).

A جمّيء *jamma'*, Overflowing (vessel). *Juma'*, A bean.

P جميتونتن *jamītūnitan*, (zand and Pāz.) To die.

A جميح *jumayh*, A man's yard.

P جميد *jamīd*, A register of the kings of India. (for جمادي *jumāda'*) The fifth Arabian month.

A جمير *jamīr*, A place of public meeting. ابنا جمير *ibnā jamīr*, Night and day. ابن جمير *ibni jamīr*, A dark night.

A جميرة *jamīrat*, A braided lock, hair twisted or plaited.

A جميز *jamīz*, The wild fig. Acute, intelligent.

A جمّيز *jummayz*, (or جمّيزي *jummayza'*) The male fig (sweet and of various kinds).

A جميش *jamīsh*, Shaven smooth, deprived of hair (privities). (A place) destitute of herbage. Depilatory (lime).

A جميع *jamīɛ*, Collected, assembled. An army. A family of Arabs mustered together. A man arrived at maturity, with his beard full grown. The milk of every animal whose teats are tied up. All, whole, universal. Crowds. A proper name.

A جميعا *jamīɛan*, In whole, altogether.

A جميل *jamīl*, Melted (fat). Beautiful, elegant. Good, fair. ابو جميل *abū jamīl*, A potherb. *Jumayl*, (or جمّيل *jummayl*) (pl. جملان *jimlān*) The nightingale (little beautiful).

A جميلانة *jumaylānat*, A nightingale.

A جميلة *jamīlat*, (fem. of جميل *jamīl*) Beautiful. Elegance. An excellent thing. A flock of wild deer or pigeons. امور جميله *umūri jamīla*, Good things. اوصاف جميله *awsāfi jamīla*, Good qualities, excellent talents.

A جميلي *jamīlīy*, A melter, vendor of melted fat.

A جميم *jamīm*, (pl. اجمّاء *ajimmāʼ*) A plant widely spreading. Much.

A جميمة *jamīmat*, The plant نصيّ *nasiy* fifteen days old, when large enough to fill a horse's mouth.

P جن *jan*, A side, part, quarter. Towards.

A جنّ *jann*, (v. n. of جنّ) Covering, veiling (darkness). Burying. Lying hid in the womb (an embryo). Being demoniacal. *Jinn*, (vulg. *jin*) A demon. An angel, spirit, genius. Concealment. Darkness. A blossom. Ardour or precipitation of youth. Beginning of any thing. A great crowd. ابو جنّ *abū jinn*, (Father of demons) A kind of large snake with black eyes, quite harmless, and allowed to go about the houses in the East. لا جنّ *lā jinna*, No concealment.

A جنا *jana'*, The fruit or other produce (of a tree). Gibbosity. (pl. اجناء *ajnāʼ*) Gold. Shells, conchæ veneris. A fresh date. Honey.

A جناء *janāʼ*, (v. n. of جنأ) Falling prostrate upon, or leaning over (any thing). (v. n. of جنيّ) Being hump-backed. Fruit gathered. *Jināʼ*, (v. n. 3 of جنأ) Falling flat upon.

A جنآء *janʼāʼ*, (fem. of اجنأ *ajnaʼ*) Hump-backed. (A sheep) whose horns bend backwards.

A جنّاء *junnāʼ*, (pl. of جاني) Gatherers. Sinners.

P جناب *janāb*, A threshold. A contract. *Janāb* or *junāb*, A saddle-cloth. The flap of a saddle. A stirrup-leather.

A جناب *janāb*, (pl. اجنبة *ajnibat*) An inner court, vestibule. A threshold. Side, margin, part, brink. Power, dignity, dominion, sovereignty. Majesty, highness, excellency. A mountain. A standard. جناب جلالت مآب *janābi jalālat-maʼāb*, Glorious and august majesty. عالي جناب *ʻālī janāb*, Of high dignity. جناب عالي *janābi ʻālī* or جناب مبارك *janābi mubārak*, Expressions used for *you* in addressing persons of high rank. *Jināb*, (v. n. of جنب) Going a great way off, retiring, shunning, avoiding. (v. n. 3 of جنب) Being at the side. Tractable, easily led (horse). A brand on the side of a camel. (pl. of جنيب *janīb*) Tractable, easily led (horses). *Junāb*, Pleurisy.

A جنّاب *junnāb*, A fellow-traveller.

A جناباء *janābāʼ*, (or جنابي *junābaʼ*) A kind of boy's game.

A جنابان *janābāni*, (du. of جناب) Both sides.

A جنابة *janābat*, (v. n. of جنب) Being a foreigner or stranger; coming amongst, or living with, strangers. Sperma. Ceremonial uncleanness. A camel sent with money to procure provisions.

A جنّابة *jannābat*, Name of a city.

A جنابذ *janābiz*, (pl. of جنبذة *jumbuzat* or *jumbazat*) Domes, cupolas.

P جنابه *junāba*, A twin.

A جناة *janāt*, Plucked, newly-gathered (fruit). *Junāt*, (pl. of جاني *jānī*) Gatherers, pluckers. Sinners.

A جنّات *jannāt*, (pl. of جنّة *jannat*) Gardens, groves. جنّات عدن *jannātu ʻadnin*, Gardens of permanent abode.

A جنائر *janāʼir*, (pl. of جنثر) Large fat camels.

A جناجن *janājin*, (pl. of جنجن) Breast-bones.

A جناح *janāh*, (pl. اجنحة *ajnihat* and اجنح *ajnuh*) Wing or pinion. A hand. The whole arm. The armpit. The side. A fin. The flap of a saddle. Wing of an army. A black ewe. A pinnacle. The soul or essence. A string of pearls. Margin, coast, edge, side. A window. Melancholy. Name of several horses. جناح النسر *janāhu'n nasr*, (Eagle's wing) A thistle, teasel. جناح بعوضة *janāhi baʻūzatin*, A gnat's wing. A very small thing. P روزنهٔ كشاده جناح *rozanaʼi kushāda-janāh*, A window having the valves, casements, or shutters open. A على جناح السفر *ʻala' janāhi safarin*, On the wing, *i.e.* point of a journey. *Junāh*, A crime, sin. A coast, margin, edge, side. Inclination.

P جناح *junāh*, Elephant's ears (a flower).

A جناحان *janāhāni*, (obl. جناحين *janāhayni*) Both wings. ركب جناحي النعامة *rakiba janāhayi'n naʻāmat*, He gave all his attention. ركبوا جناحي الطائر *rakibū janāhayhi't tāʼir*, They have left their home.

A جنادب *janādib*, Kinds of locusts.

A جنادة *junādat*, Name of an Arabian tribe; also of several reporters of traditions.

A جنادع *janādiʻ*, Subterraneous reptiles which creep into the holes of dormice, and come out when disturbed by the spade. Beginnings (particularly of evils). Cutting language. (pl. of جندعة *junduʻat*) Bubbles. ذات الجنادع, A calamity.

A جنادف *junādif*, Short and thick. Gross, corpulent, rough (man or camel). One who moves his shoulders in walking. Fat and strong-backed.

A جنادفة *junādifat*, Fat and strong-backed (she-camel). امة جنادفة *amatun junādifatun*, A free-born, noble woman.

A جنادل *junādil*, Strong and great.

A جنّار *junnār*, A plane-tree.

A جنازة *jināzat* or *janāzat*, (pl. جنائز *janāʼiz*) A corpse. A bier. The funeral solemnity and rites. Any thing which weighs heavily, and induces sadness and gloom. A sick person. A wine-bottle. رمى في جنازته *rumiya* (or طعن *tuʻina*) *fī jināzatihi*, He died.

P جنازه *jināza*, A bier.

A جناس *jinās*, The being akin, resembling.

A جناسريّة *junāsirīyat*, A kind of date-tree which is later in bearing than all others.

P جناغ *janāgh*, A contract, bargain. The breast-bone of a bird. The bow or pommel of a saddle. *Junāgh*, An outside covering of a saddle (made of a leopard's skin). A surcingle. A stirrup-leather. The flap of a saddle. A cup. A sturgeon.

A جناف *jināf*, Alienation, desertion of kindred.

A جنافيّ *junāfīy*, Cunning, crafty, wily. Proud.

A جنافير *janāfīr*, (pl. of جنفور) Ancient tombs.

P جناق *junāk*, The flap of a saddle.

P جنان *janān*, (pl. of جن *jan*) Women.

A جنان *janān*, (v. n. of جنّ) Growing dark. (pl. اجنان *ajnān*) A dark night. Darkness, obscurity. The heart, or that part of it which fears. A garment. A great crowd. A sanctuary. Women's apartments. The spirit. The fear of an object unseen. *Jinān*, (pl. of جنّة *jannat*) Gardens with trees: paradises. *Junān*, A shield. Darkness.

A جنّان *jinnān*, (pl. of جانّ *jānn*) Demons, devils.

A جنانة *junānat*, A shield.

A جنايات *jināyāt*, (pl. of جناية) Faults, sins.

A جنائب *janāʼib*, (pl. of جنيب *janīb*) Led-horses. (pl. of جنبة *janabat*) Sides. (pl. of جنوب *janūb*) South winds.

A جناية *jināyat*, (v. n. of جني) Committing a crime. Seeking to criminate. Gathering fruit. A crime, iniquity. Taxes. Extortions. P جنايت كردن *jināyat kardan*, To commit a crime.

P جنايت ستان *jināyat-satān*, A tax-gatherer.

A جنائز *janāʼiz*, (pl. of جنازة) Corpses. Biers.

A جنب *jamb*, (v. n. of جنب) Breaking on the side. Alighting as a stranger. Removing from, shunning, repelling. Longing for. Causing one to remove or shun. (pl. جنوب *junūb* and اجناب *ajnāb*) A side, part. A tract of country, coast, boundary. The greater part of any thing. An accident, battle, engagement. Contumely, reproach. جار الجنب *jāru'l jamb*, A familiar. A neighbour. ذات الجنب *zātu'l jamb*, Pleurisy. ذو الجنب *zū'l jamb*, Pleuritic. صاحب بالجنب *sāhib bi'l jamb*, A fellow-traveller. *Janab*, (v. n. of جنب) Leading at the side (a horse of state, or a captive). Halting, limping, hobbling, or leaning to a side in walking. Adhering to the side (the lungs from thirst). When in a race the rider leads a spare horse by his side, on which he may spring in case the one on which he is mounted is likely to be beaten. When the collector of the ذكاة *zakāt* alights at the border of a district, demanding the contributions to be brought to him from the remotest parts; or when the proprietor sends his flocks to a distance to escape the importunities of the collector. Led (horses). Short. (pl. of جنيب *janīb*) Led horses. *Janib*, One who keeps out of the way to avoid meeting and inviting a stranger. One who limps or leans to one side in walking. *Junub*, (pl. اجناب *ajnāb*) A stranger, foreigner, guest. One who will not allow himself to be led, refractory. Polluted man or men. جار جنب *jār junub*, A stranger in the neighbourhood.

P جنب *janab*, A city where swords are made.

A جنبار *jimbār*, (or جنّبار) A young bustard.

P جنبان *jumbān*, Trembling, shaking, stirring, moving. Melting. دوش جنبان *dosh-jumbān*, Moving or shaking the shoulders.

A جنبان *junubān*, (pl. of جنب) Polluted.

P جنبانيدن *jumbānīdan*, To cause to move, to shake, to wag. To rock (a cradle). To shake or churn (milk).

A جنبة *jambat*, A side, tract of country. A bit of skin from a camel's side. A tree becoming green after withering in the summer. A withdrawment, secession. The being a stranger. A shrub. ذو جنبة *zū jambat*, A seceder, one who withdraws from men. *Janabat*, A side, part. *Junabat*, Any thing shunned.

A جنبتور *jambatūr*, Name of the young Egyptian who was slain by Moses.

A جنبثة *jumbasat*, A black or ugly woman.

A جنبثقة *jumbaskat*, Disgusting (woman).

A جنبثنة *jumbasnat*, Black woman (in abuse).

A جنبخ *jumbukh*, Large-bodied, long and lofty. A large louse.

A جنبخة *jumbukhat*, A large louse.

P جنبد *jumbad*, A vault, arch. A caper. *Jumbid*, A rose.

A جنبذ *jumbuz*, Pomegranate-flowers. An unblown bud. A dome, or cupola.

A جنبذة *jumbuzat* or *jumbazat*, (pl. جنابذ *janābiz*) (from P گنبد *gumbad*) A vault, dome, arch.

A جنبر *jambar*, A large short-bodied camel. A young bustard.

P جنبش *jumbish*, Motion, agitation. Gesture. Work, occupation. جنبش آمدن *jumbish āmadan*, To bestir one's self. جنبش آبا *jumbishi ābā*, The motion of the planets; namely, Saturn, Jupiter, Mars, the sun, Venus, Mercury, and the moon. جنبش اوّل *jumbishi avval*, The movement of the pen upon the tablet of the Divine decrees. The first motion of the planets setting out from the sign Aries. جنبش زمين *jumbishi zamin*, An earthquake. درين جنبش *dar īn jumbish*, At this instant. جنبش كردن *jumbish kardan*, To move, creep.

A جنبقة *jumbukat*, Ugly bad-tempered woman.

A جنبل *jumbul*, A large wooden bowl.

P جنبنده *jumbanda*, Any moving thing, living creature: creeping thing, reptile: venomous insect.

A جنبيّ *jambīy*, Lateral.

S Y جنبيد *jumbīd*, Origany, marjoram.

P جنبيدن *jumbīdan*, To move, stir, shake, vibrate, swing. To beat or throb.

P جنبيده *jumbīda*, Shaking.

P جنبيه *jambiya*, A kind of arms or armour.

A جنّة *jannat*, (pl. جنان *jinān* and جنّات *jannāt*) A garden, set with trees. A grove of palm-trees. Paradise, heaven. جنّة البلاد *jannatu'l bilād*, The paradise of regions; title of Bengal. اهالىء جنّت *ahālīi jannat*, The inhabitants of paradise. بطنان الجنّة *butnānu'l jannat*, The middle of paradise.

A جنّة *jinnat*, Demons. Angels. Insanity, fury. عبد الجنّة *abdu'l jinnat*, (Slave of devils) The nightmare. *Junnat*, (pl. جنن *junan*) A covering. A shield. A kind of veil.

P جنتر *jantar*, A kind of musical instrument used in India.

P جنّت مكان *jannat-makān*, (or جنّت آشياني *jannat-āshyānī*) Placed or nestled in paradise (a mode of speaking of deceased princes.

G جنتوريه *jantūriya*, Centaury.

A جنّتيّ *jannatīy*, Paradisiacal, heavenly.

L جنتيانا *jantiyānā*, Gentian; bitter-wort.

A جنث *jins*, Race, stock, kind, sort, root.

A جنثر *jansar* or *junsur*, A large fat camel.

A جنثورة *junsūrat*, Earth or dust heaped up.

A جنثيّ *jinsīy* or *junsīy*, A best kind of iron. *Junsīy*, One who weaves coats of mail. A sword.

P جنج *janj*, The lowing of oxen.

P جنجر *junjar*, Shepherd's staff (an herb).

A جنجل *junjul*, A pot-herb like asparagus.

A جنجن *janjan* or *jinjin*, The breast-bone.

A جنجنة *jinjinat* or *janjanat*, The breast-bone.

A جنجون *junjūn*, Breast-bone. A water-wheel.

A جنح *janh*, (v. n. of جنح) Breaking or disabling a bird in the wing. Having the ribs broken from a heavy load (a camel). *Jinh*, A side, margin, shore, coast. *Junh* or *jinh*, A part or watch of the (night).

A جنحاب *jinhāb*, Short, compact, closely set.

A جنحدل *janahdal*, Short, dwarfish.

P جند *jand*, Name of a city in Turkistān.

A جند *jund*, (pl. جنود *junūd* and اجناد *ajnād*) An army, militia, body of troops, legion. Allies, auxiliaries, confederates, comrades, fellow-soldiers. A city. Genus, species. *Janad*, Rough ground. Stones resembling mud. Name of a city in Yaman.

P جنداسابور *jundāsābūr*, A city in Persia.

P جندال *jandāl*, The vulgar. A trifling fellow. A toper.

A جندب *jundub*, *jundab*, or *jindab*, A kind of locust. امّ جندب *ummu jundabin*, An accident, misfortune, calamity. Perfidy. Oppression. وقعوا في امّ جندب *wakaʻū fī ummi jundabin*, They fell into trouble.

A جندبيدست *jundbīdast*, (or جندبيدستر *jundbīdastar*) The testicles of a beaver.

A جندخ *jundukh*, A large-bodied locust.

P جندر *jandar*, Clothes, garments.

A جندرة *jandarat*, (v. n. of جندر Q) Tracing the pen over letters which are nearly obliterated. Renewing faded embroidery.

P جندر خانه *jandar-khāna*, A wardrobe.

P جندره *jandara*, The bar of a door. Two pieces of wood used for smoothing linens: a calender, mangle. Clownish, boorish, unpolished.

A جندعة *jundaʻat*, (pl. جنادع *janādiʻ*) A bubble floating on the water. The silent beginning of evil. Any noxious reptile.

P جندل *jandal*, Name of the messenger sent by Farīdūn to the king of Yaman to demand his daughter in marriage.

A جندل *jandal*, Stone. A man's name. *Jandal* or *jandil*, A stone which can be taken or lifted up. دومة الجندل *dawmatu'l jandal*, Name of a place. *Junadil*, A stony country.

A جندلة *jandalat*, (v. n. of جندل Q) Trampling, treading. *Junadilat* or *janadilat*, A stony country.

P جندوق *jandūk*, Name of a medicine.

A جنديّ *jundīy*, One soldier, a soldier.

P جندي سابور *jandī sābūr*, (in Arab. جنديسابور *jundaysābūr*) Name of a city in Persia.

A جنز *janz*, (v. n. of جنز) Covering. Gathering, collecting. A mud-hovel.

A جنزة *janzat*, Name of a town and village.

A جنس *jins*, (pl. اجناس *ajnās* and جنوس *junūs*) Genus, kind, stock, sort, mode (more comprehensive than نوع *nawʻ*, which means species). Gender. Goods, moveables, articles, things (any estate not in money). جنس الاجناس *jinsu'l ajnās*, A general species. جنس بشر *jinsi bashar*, The human race. جنس كامل *jinsi kamil*, (in commerce) An article that fetches a full price (as sugar, pān, or cotton). جنس ادنى *jinsi adnā*, Any thing that fetches a low price (as maize). اسم جنس *ismi jins*, A generic or indeterminate noun. P هر جنس *har jins*, Every kind. A *Janas*, The freezing (of water, &c.).

P جنستان *jinistān*, Fairy-land.

P جنسواري *jinswārī*, Separately. Specifically.

A جنسيّ *jinsīy*, Generic, generical.

A جنسيّة *jinsīyat*, Correspondence of kind, race, or genus, a generic state.

A جنش *jansh*, (v. n. of جنش) Being barren and destitute of provisions (a place). Being distressed (the soul in the prospect of death). Being wishful, longing for. Fearing. The emptying of a well. (Men) approaching to one another. A neighbouring place. Terror, cry, lamentation. The twilight just before daybreak. Thickness, coarseness. بئر جنشة *biʼri janishat*, A gravelly well.

L جنطيانا *jintiyānā*, The herb gentian.

A جنع *janaʻ*, Small plants.

A جنعاظ *jinʻāz*, Ill-tempered: a fool. A glutton.

A جنعاظة *jinʻāzat*, A glutton, gormandizer. Ill-tempered at meals.

A جنعدل *ja* or *junaʻdal*, Hard and strong. *Janaʻdal* or *junaʻdil*, A thick, fat, and smooth man.

A جنعظ *jinʻiz*, Coarse, rugged, gross. Mad, foolish, crazy. A greedy old man.

A جنعيظ *jinʻīz*, Short-footed. A glutton.

A جنف *janaf*, (v. n. of جنف) Deviating (from the right way). Swerving. Acting unrighteously in regard to a precept, command, will, or testament. Deviation from the truth. Unevenness, inequality in the breast-bone. *Janif*, Unjust, biased.

A جنفليق *janfalīk*, A big fat woman.

A جنفور *junfūr*, (pl. جنافير) An old tomb.

A جنق *jank*, A throwing stones from a balista.

T جنقي *janki*, A consultation, council.

P جنگ *jang*, War, battle, combat, engagement, fight, skirmish, rencounter. Brawling, squabbling, litigating. جنگِ ساختگي *jangi sākhtagī*, A sham-fight. جنگ كردن *jang kardan*, To make war, to fight. جلادتِ جنگ *jalādati jang*, The strength of the battle. دلاورِ جنگ *dil-āwari jang*, The hero of war. مهابتِ جنگ *mahābati jang*, The terror of war. *Jung*, A large ship. A camel which has never borne a load. A large white spot. Dice.

P جنگار *jang-ār*, A warrior. A crab.

P جنگ آزموده *jang-āzmūda*, A veteran in war.

P جنگانيدن *jangānīdan*, To wage war. To thirst.

P جنگ آور *jang-āwar*, A hero. Quarrelsome.

P جنگاه *jangāh*, (for جنگ گاه) Battle-field.

P جنگ بازي *jang-bāzī*, (or زرگري) Mock fight.

P جنگ جلاب *jang-jalāb*, Stratagem. A vain attempt; the washing a blackamoor white. Procrastination. An ear-ring.

P جنگجو *jang-jo*, Quarrelsome, contentious.

P جنگجوئي *jang-joʼī* or *jūʼī*, A quarrelsome, litigious turn of mind, quarrelsomeness.

P جنگل *jangal*, A wood, forest, thicket; a country overgrown with wood, reeds, or long grass; a jungle.

P جنگلاهي *janglāhī*, (or جنگلافي) A kite.

P جنگل بري *jangal-burī*, Clearing of jungles. جنگل برئ تعلقه *jangal-burīʼi taʻalluka*, A spot of ground brought into cultivation by the possessor.

P جنگلوك *jangalūk*, Lame in the hands or the feet. An invalid beginning to recover from sickness, but still unable to walk.

P جنگلي *jangalī*, Wild, untilled, jungly.

P جنگوان *janguwān*, Name of a city in India.

P جنگوك *jangūk*, Convalescent, but not yet able to walk.

P جنگي *jangī*, Brave, warlike: fighting: a fighter.

P جنگيدن *jangīdan*, To war, battle. To thirst.

P جنگيز *jingīz*, The famous Mogul conqueror Gengīz Khān. (The Tartar Khāns of Precop claim descent from this monarch.)

A جنة *jan* or *janamat*, The whole of a thing.

A جنن *janan*, (pl. اجنان *ajnān*) A grave. A winding-sheet. A corpse. *Junan*, (pl. of جنّة *junnat*) Veils. Shields. *Junun*, Madness.

A جنوء *junūʼ*, (v. n. of جنأ) Falling prostrate on, or bending down towards. Being hump-backed.

A جنواء *janwāʼ*, Hump-backed (woman). (A sheep) whose horns turn backwards.

A جنوب *janūb*, (pl. جنائب *janāʼib*) The south. The south wind which blows from that part of the heavens where Canopus rises to that part where the Pleiades rise. *Junūb*, (v. n. of جنب) Blowing (south wind). Being blown on by the south wind. (pl. of جنب *jamb*) Sides, parts.

A جنوبيّ *janūbīy*, Southern. Sultry (day).

A جنوة *januwat*, Genoa.

A جنوح *junūh*, (v. n. of جنح) Inclining, leaning. Arriving near the ground (a bird). Inclining to its setting (the sun). Causing to incline. The approach of night.

A جنود *junūd*, (pl. of جند) Troops. Chess-men.

A جنور *jannūr*, A floor where wheat or barley is trodden out.

A جنوس *junūs*, (pl. of جنس) Kinds, sorts.

A جنوف *junūf*, (v. n. of جنف) Deviating, swerving, wandering, straying: deviation from right.

A جنون *janūn*, A demon. A harmless kind of snake. *Junūn*, (v. n. of جنّ) Covering. Being dark (night). Burying. Growing luxuriant (grass). Being covered with flowers (the earth). Flying round and humming (flies). Being a demoniac, possessed of a devil. Insanity, fury, phrensy. Darkness. جنون الشباب *junūnuʼsh shabāb*, Madness, or wildness of youth. جنون الليل *junūnuʼl layl*, Darkness of night. A little darkness at nightfall.

T جنويز *janawīz*, Genoa. A Genoese.

A جنهيّ *janahīy*, Indian cane. Delicate branch.

A جني *jany*, (v. n. of جني) Gathering, plucking fruit. Authorizing to gather fruit. *Janaʼ*, Fruit newly gathered. (pl. اجناء *ajnāʼ*) Gold. A shell. A fresh date. Honey. Grass, mushrooms, &c.

A جنيّ *janīy*, Newly-plucked, fresh-gathered.

A جنّيّ *jinnīy*, Demoniacal. One demon, spirit.

A جنيب *janīb*, (pl. جنائب *janāʼib* and جنب *janab*) Led by the side. Tractable, easy to be led. An excellent kind of date. Pained in the side.

A جنيبة *janībat*, A led camel. A camel sent with money to fetch provisions. The wool of a six-year old camel. جنيبتا البعير *janībatāʼl baʻīr*, The load on both sides of a camel.

P جنيبت كش *janībat-kash*, Master of the horse. The leader of a sumpter horse or horse of state.

A جنيّة *janīyat*, A silk cloak.

A جنيس *janīs*, Homogeneous.

A جنّيس *jinnīs*, A yellowish-white fish.

A جنيص *janīs*, Dead, defunct, deceased.

A جنيع *janīʻ*, Small plants. A yellow berry.

A جنين *janīn*, (pl. اجنّة *ajinnat* and اجنن *ajnun*) An embryo, a fœtus. Concealed, buried.

A جنينة *janīnat*, A kind of cloak. Inner parlour.

P جنيور *janīwar*, The horse-hair bridge across the eternal fire, over which the Muhammadans fancy they must pass into heaven.

P جو *jaw* or *jav*, Barley, a grain of barley. The alloy of four grains of silver in ninety-six of gold. جو برهنه *javi barahna*, Barley without husk. جو آب *jaw-āb*, Barley-water. جو فروش گندم نما *jaw-faroshi gandum-namā*, One who sells barley and shows wheat; a cheat. *Jū*, A river. A yoke. *Jo* or *jū*, (in comp.) Wishing, desiring.

A جوّ *jaww*, (pl. اجواء *ajwāʼ* and جواء *jiwāʼ*) Air, sky, atmosphere; space between heaven and earth. Low ground. Width, space, openness. Interior of a house. Yamāma, a province of Arabia.

A جواء *jiwāʼ*, A sewing up of the uterus of a camel. Low ground. Wide (valley). A space between houses. (pl. اجوية *ajwiyat*), A wide valley. A leathern cover for a pot or kettle. A kind of shepherd's wallet. (pl. of جوّ *jaww*), Low grounds.

A جواب *jawāb*, (pl. اجوبة *ajwibat*) An answer, reply. Talk. A proposition. جواب خطاب *jawābi khitāb*, An answer to a question. جواب صاف *jawābi sāf*, A clear, positive answer. جواب صواب نساب *jawābi sawāb-nisāb*, A right and true answer. جواب قطعي *jawābi katʻī*, A categorical answer. P جواب كردن *jawāb kardan*, To answer. جواب ناصواب *jawābi nā sawāb*, An impertinent answer. A حاضر جواب *hāzir-jawāb*, Echo. Of ready reply.

A جوّاب *jawwāb*, (or جوّابة) A traveller.

P جواب بالا *jawāb-bālā*, Prevail your advice!

P جوابدار *jawāb-dār*, A person responsible.

P جواب ده *jawāb-dih*, Respondent. One who makes an obstinate defence: amenable, accountable.

A جواب سوال *jawāb-suwāl*, Questions and answers: talk.

A جواب سوالي *jawāb-suwālī*, Reply, rejoinder.

P جواب نامه *jawāb-nāma*, Letters of reply. A writing fixed to the winding-sheet or the breast of the deceased, which it is intended the angels Munkir and Nakīr should read, should the poor soul be too much flurried to answer their questions.

P جواب نويس *jawāb-navīs*, A writer of orders or replies.

A جوابي *jawābī*, Ponds, cisterns.

A جوابي *jawābī*, A respondent. A kind of bill of exchange, which is not paid till notice is received of the bill's having been taken up. A chorus, especially in repeating a marsā or elegy.

A جوابي سوالي *jawābī-suwālī*, A mediator, attorney, envoy.

A جواة *jawāt*, A place or trivet for a kettle or pot. The case or cover of a pot.

A جوات *jiwāt*, (v. n. 3 of جوت obsol.) Calling camels. *Juwāt*, The word used in calling camels to water; or for checking them.

A جوائي *juʼāsaʼ*, Rough tripe.

A جواحر *jawāhir*, (Reptiles) creeping into holes and corners. Those who sneak into their houses.

A جواد *jawād*, (pl. اجواد *ajwād*, اجاود *ajāwid*, جوداء *juwadāʼ*, جود *jūd*, and جودة *juwadat*) Liberal, beneficent. جواد مطلق *jawādi mutlak*, (God) the universal benefactor. (pl. جياد *jiyād*) (A horse) running swiftly. *Juwād*, Excessive thirst.

A جوادّ *jawādd*, (pl. of جادّة *jāddat*) Highways.

A جوادس *jawādis*, (pl. of جادسة *jādisat*) Unploughed, uncultivated grounds.

A جوادف *jawādif*, (pl. of جادف *jādif*) (Wild

bucks) taking short steps.

A جواذب *jawāzib*, (pl. of جاذب *jāzib*) Camels which give no milk. (pl. of جاذبة *jāzibat*) Attractive qualities, allurements.

A جوازي *jawāzī*, (Camels) swift-going, whose feet touch not the ground.

A جوار *jawār*, Water plentiful and deep. The area of a house, the space which it occupies. (for جواري *jawārī*) Ships. *Jiwār*, (v. n. 3 of جار for جور) Becoming a neighbour. Remaining constantly in the mosque (for prayer). Receiving under protection, giving security from oppression. Neighbourhood. *Juwār*, (v. n. 3 of جار for جور irregular) Becoming a neighbour.

A جؤار *ju,ār*, (v. n. of جأر) Lowing (an ox). Groaning in prayer. Imploring. A vomiting, evacuation of any kind.

P جوار *juwār*, Leave, permission.

A جوّار *jawwār*, A farmer, agriculturist.

A جوارب *jawārib*, (and جواربة *jawāribat*) (pl. of جورب *jawrab*) Nether socks, hosen.

A جواربيّ *jawāribiy*, A maker of nether socks.

A جوارح *jawāriḥ*, (pl. of جارحة *jāriḥat*) Birds and beasts of prey. Members of the body (by which a man earns his livelihood, particularly) the hands. Mares. She-asses and camels (especially young and prolific).

A جوارز *jawāriz*, (pl. of جارزة *jārizat*) Hard or dry lands under which lie strata of sand.

A جوارس *jawāris*, (pl. of جارسة *jārisat*) Bees.

A جوارش *jawārish*, (from P گوارش *guwārish*) (pl. جوارشات *jawārishāt*) Whatever is used in the dressing of meat, or assists in digestion.

A جواري *jawārī*, (pl. of جارية *jāriyat*) Ships. Female slaves, servant-girls, lasses, girls, damsels. Wandering stars or planets. جواري و غلمان *jawārī u ghilmān*, Girls and boys. Maid-servants and men-servants. جواريء منشآت *jawārī-i munsha,āt*, Ships under full sail.

P جواز *jawāz*, A mortar. *Juwāz*, (جوازة *juwāza*, or جوازان *juwāzān*) A large wooden or stone mortar for pounding grain. Oil-press, sugar-mill.

A جواز *jawāz*, (v. n. of جاز for جوز) Passing along, through, or beyond. Being allowed, permitted, lawful, or allowable. A passport. Water with which cattle or ground is watered. Permission, lawfulness, propriety. *Jiwāz*, (v. n. 3 of جاز for جوز) Transgressing, exceeding bounds, going beyond. Forgiving. *Juwāz*, Thirst.

A جوّاز *jawwāz*, A seller of nuts (جوز *jawz*).

A جوازم *jawāzim*, (pl. of جازم *jāzim*) (Camels) satiated with drink. Particles which deprive a consonant of its vowel. Full milk-bottles.

A جوازئ *jawāzi,*, Wild, desert. A wild beast.

A جوّاس *jawwās*, A spy, scout. A lion.

A جواسّ *jawāss*, Senses.

A جواسيس *jawāsīs*, (pl. of جاسوس) Spies.

A جواظ *juwāẓ*, Impatience, ennui.

A جوّاظ *jawwāẓ*, Thick, corpulent. A hinderer, preventer. One who walks with a haughty air, proud, haughty. Melancholy. A great talker, clamorous, noisy. One who accumulates and holds fast what he has got. Weak, impotent. Coarse, unfeeling. Sounds, clamours, seditious murmurs.

A جوّاظة *jawwāẓat*, Melancholy. Unsteady. Gluttonous.

A جواف *juwāf*, A kind of fish.

A جوال *jawāl*, (pl. of جول *jūl*) Herds of horses or camels. *Jiwāl*, (v. n. 3 of جال for جول) Going round about (one another in fighting). (pl. of جول *jūl*) Walls or parapets (of wells).

P جوال *juwāl*, A sack, bag. Half of a (horse) load. The human body. Deceit, fraud. Any thing open, uncovered.

A جوّال *jawwāl*, One who travels about much.

A جوالّ *jawāll*, (pl. of جالّة *jāllat*) Exiles.

A جوالب *jawālib*, (pl. of جالب *jālib*) Healing (wounds). (pl. of جالبة *jālibat*) Things attractive, conciliating, agreeable; whatever banishes grief.

A جوالة *jawālat*, The best part of any thing. *Jiwālat*, (pl. of جول *jūl*) Parapets of wells.

A جوالح *jawāliḥ*, The flying down of bulrushes and the like, gossamer.

P جوالدوز *juwāl-doz*, A large packing-needle. A sack-maker.

P جوالدوزي *juwāl-dozī*, Sack-making.

A جوالق *jawāliḳ*, (pl. of جوالق *juwāliḳ*,) Large corn-sacks. *Jiwāliḳ*, *juwālaḳ*, or *juwāliḳ*, (pl. *jawāliḳ*, جواليق *jawālīḳ*, or جوالقات) A sack.

P جوالق *juwāliḳ*, A religious tunic, a dervish's mantle of a blue colour.

A جوالقات *jawāliḳāt*, (pl. of جوالق) Sacks.

A جواليق *jawālīḳ*, (pl. of جوالق) Sacks.

P جوام *juwām*, (in zand and Pāzand) A day.

A جوامح *jawāmiḥ*, (pl. of جامح) Stubborn.

A جوامد *jawāmid*, Boundaries.

A جوامع *jawāmiʿ*, (pl. of جامع *jāmiʿ*) Comprehensive, full. Temples, mosques. (pl. of جامعة *jāmiʿat*) Pillories. Necklaces, chains, collars. Few, but most comprehensive words. جوامع الكلم *jawāmiʿu'l kalim*, Comprehending many significations: the Kur'ān.

A جوامك *jawāmik*, Gifts, salaries.

A جواميس *jawāmīs*, (pl. of جاموس) Buffaloes.

P جوان *jawān*, Young. A young man, youth, lad. A catamite. جوان خوش شكل *jawāni khush-shakl*, A youth with a fine figure. Rice.

P جوان اسپرم *jawān-isparam*, Name of an odoriferous herb of the class called ريحان الشياطين *rayḥānu'sh shayāṭīn*.

P جوانا مرگ *jawānā-marg*, Death in the flower of youth.

P جوانان *jawānān*, (pl. of جوان) Youths.

P جوانانه *jawānāna*, Manly, gallantly.

A جوانب *jawānib*, (pl. of جانب *jānib*) Parts, sides. Boundaries. اطراف و جوانب *aṭrāf u jawānib*, Surrounding or adjacent parts, environs. جوانب اربعة *jawānibi arbaʿa*, The four sides, parts, or quarters, *i. e.* the whole.

P جوانبخت *jawān-bakht*, Young. Fortunate, promising; a brave, noble, generous youth.

A جوّانة *jawwānat*, The fundament.

A جوانح *jawāniḥ*, (pl. of جانحة *jāniḥat*) The lower ribs, the ribs which meet on the breast (those which join the back-bone being called ضلوع *zulūʿ*).

T جوانغار و برانغار *juwānghār u baranghār*, The left and right wings of an army.

P جوانمرد *jawān-mard*, A young man. A generous youth. Brave, generous, manly. A master-butcher.

P جوانمردي *jawān-mardī*, Generosity, manliness.

A جوانو *jawānū*, Germander, saw-wort.

P جوانه *jawāna*, A young man. Youth.

P جوانه سال *jawāna-sāl*, Young in years.

P جواني *jawānī*, Youth. Youthful. A young man. Aniseed.

A جواني *jawānī*, (for جوانب) Sides, parts.

A جوّانيّ *jawwāniy*, Internal. An inner court.

A جواهر *jawāhir*, (pl. of جوهر *jawhar*) Ores, metals. Jewels, gems. P جواهر سخن *jawāhiri sukhan*, Chosen words, elegant phrases.

A جواهض *jawāhiẓ*, (pl. جاهضة) Yearling colts.

A جوائب *jawā,ib*, News travelling from country to country.

A جوائح *jawā,iḥ*, (pl. of جائحة) Calamities.

A جوائز *jawā,iz*, Verses or proverbs which pass current from country to country. (pl. of جائز *jā,iz*) Beams. (pl. of جائزة *jā,izat*) Gifts, rewards.

A جوائف *jawā,if*, (pl. of جائفة *jā,ifat*) Low hills. جوائف النفس *jawā,ifu'n nafs*, The innermost or deepest recesses of the soul.

A جوب *jawb*, (v. n. of جاب for جوب) Cutting. Cleaving. Splitting. Tearing. Traversing (a country). Making the collar or breast of a shirt or other garment. (pl. اجواب *ajwāb*) A shield. A shift without sleeves. A fire-grate or chafing-dish. A large leathern bucket. *Juwab*, (pl. of جوبة *jawbat*) Gaps, breaches. Openings (between mountains or clouds).

P جوبال *jūbāl*, (in zand) A wallet, sack, bag.

A جؤبة *ju,a* or *ju,ubat*, A hideous, frowning face.

A جوبة *jawbat*, (pl. جوب *juwab*) A gap, breach, interval, or opening (between mountains, clouds, or houses). A pit or hole in hard ground. A flat betwixt two countries.

P جو بجو *jaw ba jaw*, Grain by grain, a little at a time, by degrees. Piecemeal, to atoms.

P جوبه *joba*, A market-place.

A جؤة *ju,at*, A dark bay colour.

A جوّة *jawwat*, A low-lying place. *Jūwat*, Rough ground. A cavity or hollow (in a mountain or elsewhere). A yellowish, tawny, or brown colour. A patch upon a leathern bottle.

P جوترة *jawtara*, A minaret, a lofty turret.

A جُؤُث *jusus*, A being frightened.

A جوث *jaws*, Rough tripe. *Jawas*, A prominence in the upper part of the belly with a lankness below.

A جوثاء *jawsā*, (fem. of اجوث *ajwas*) (A female) as is described above. Rough tripe.

P جوج *jūj* or *jawj*, A cock's comb. A crest. A pennant, vane. *Jūj*, (In the Malay language) Draughts, backgammon.

P جوجادو *jaw-jādū*, A bitter grain like an oat.

P جوجرة *jojira*, A dirham weighing 48 grains.

P جوجگاه *jawja-gāh*, A field of battle.

P جوجم *jojam*, A branch with flowers and fruit.

P جوجن *jūjin*, (in zand and Pāzand) A drachma of 48 grains. *Jojan*, (in Hindee) A yojana or distance of 5 or 9 miles.

P جوجو *jaw-jaw*, Bit by bit, in pieces, to pieces. Name of a city famous for musk, silks, and camphor.

A جُؤجُؤ *jusjus*, (pl. جاجئ *jasāji*) The breast. A bird's breast. A ship's prow.

P جوجه *jūja*, A chicken, a poult.

A جوح *jawh*, (v. n. of جاح for جوح) Eradicating, destroying. Deviating from the way. A Syrian melon. *Jūh*, (pl. of اجوح *ajwah*) Ample, spacious.

A جوحم *jawham*, A red rose. The hundred-leaved rose.

P جوخ *jawkh*, A troop.

A جوخ *jawkh*, (v. n. of جاخ for جوخ) Carrying away the banks (a rapid stream).

P جوخان *jawkhān*, A drying-place for dates.

A جوخة *jūkhat*, A pit, hole in the ground.

A جوخي *jawkha'*, A name for handmaids.

A جُؤُد *jusud*, (v. n. of جاد for جود) Shedding tears plentifully (the eye). Being saturated with rain (a field). Being near to death or sleep.

A جود *jawd*, (v. n. of جاد for جود) Falling in abundance (rain). Shedding tears plentifully (the eye). Doing any thing excellent; praising or proclaiming the same. Assailing and overcoming one (love). Exceeding, excelling in liberality. Being near to sleep or destruction. Heavy rain. (pl. of جائد *jāid*) Copious (showers). سماء جود *samāsi jawd*, A rainy sky. *Jūd*, (v. n. of جاد for جود) Being liberal, beneficent. Liberality. A present. Hunger. (pl. of جواد *jawād*) Liberal, beneficent. (pl. of اجيد *ajyad*) Long-necked.

A جوداء *juwādās*, (pl. of جواد *jawād*) Liberal.

P جودان *jawdān*, (or جودانه *jawdāna*) A fragrant species of camphire. A kind of pomegranate having dry seeds. A bird's crop. The mark in a horse's tooth, resembling a barley-corn, indicating his age. A species of willow. مطرتان جودان *mattatāni jawdāni*, Two bountiful showers.

A جودة *jūdat* or *jawdat*, (v. n. of جاد for جود) Being good, excellent. Speaking or doing well. Ingenuity, quickness of apprehension. Excellence. A single thirst. Slumber. *Jūdat*, (v. n. of جاد for جود) Being fleet (a horse). Fleetness. *Juwadat*, (pl. of جواد *jawād*) Liberal, beneficent.

P جودر *jawdar*, A cow. A herb growing in wheat.

P جودرة *jawdara*, A herb growing amongst wheat. Name of a certain general.

A جوديّ *jūdiy* or جودي *jūdī*, Mount Ararat in Armenia (where the ark is supposed to have rested).

A جودياء *jūdiyās*, A garment, an upper cloak.

A جوذاب *jūzāb*, A dish of sugar, rice, and meat.

P جوذر *jaw-zar*, In morsels, piecemeal.

A جوذر *jawzar* or *jawzir*, The wild calf.

A جُؤذر *juszur* or *juszar*, (pl. جاذر *jasāzir*) The wild calf.

A جوذيّ *jūziy*, A garment. A short cloak.

A جوذياء *jūziyās*, A sailor's woollen jerkin.

P جور *jawr*, A bumper of wine presented to any one. One of the lines upon the famous cup of Jamshed. باده بجور داد *bāda ba jawr dād*, He plied him with wine. *Juwar*, Height, summit. Above.

A جؤر *jusar*, A copious rain.

A جور *jawr*, (v. n. of جار for جور) Going out of the way, deviating from truth. Tyrannizing over. Imploring protection. Injustice, violence, iniquity, oppression, tyranny. Severity, austerity. A tyrant, oppressor. علي جور *ala' jawr*, On a wrong road. P جور كردن *jawr kardan*, To injure. A *Jūr*, Firozābād, famed for its roses.

A جوّر *jiwarr*, Copious rain accompanied by loud thunder. Strong-voiced (camel).

A جورب *jawrab*, (pl. جواربة *jawāribat* or جوارب *jawārib*) A shoe, sandal. A stocking.

A جوربة *jawrabat*, (v. n. of جورب Q) Putting socks (on any one). A sock.

P جوربور *jūrbūr*, A pheasant. A jungle-cock.

P جور پيشه *jawr-pesha*, Oppressive. A tyrant.

A جورة *jawarat*, Tyrants, unjust judges.

A جورف *jawraf*, An ass. A male ostrich. A quick gelding. A flood that sweeps all before it.

A جورق *jawrak*, A male ostrich.

P جورة *jūra*, Equal in size, weight, colour, &c.

A جوز *jawz*, (v. n. of جاز for جوز) Passing by or beyond. The part of Arabia called Hijāz. (from P گوز *gawz*), A nut. (pl. اجواز *ajwāz*), Middle, centre, or marrow of any thing. جوز بوّا *jawzi bawwā*, (or جوز بويه *jawzi būya*), Nutmeg. جوز ثريّا *jawzi surayya'*, The middle or cluster of the Pleiades. جوز خنز *jawzi khaniz*, An unsound nut. جوز الرت *jawzu'r rat*, A saponaceous nut. جوز رومي *jawzi rūmī*, A walnut. جوز السرو *jawzu's sarv*, Fruit of the cypress-tree. جوز الطرفا *jawzu't tarfā*, The tamarisk-nut. جوز الطيب *jawzu't tīb*, A nutmeg. جوز القيّ *jawzu'l kayy*, Nux vomica. جوز الكوثل *jawzu'l kawsal*, The physic-nut. P جوز گندم *jawzi gandum*, A جوز جندم *jawzi jandum*, Sandix-gum, juniper. جوز ماثل *jawzi māsal*, The thorn-apple. جوز المرج *jawzu'l maraj*, The winter-cherry. جوز هندي *jawzi hindī*, A cocoa-nut. A walnut.

A جوزاء *jawzās*, A star, Gemini. A sheep white in the middle of the body. الجوزاء *al jawzās*, Orion.

A جوزات *jawzāt*, (pl. of جوز *jawz*) Nuts. Knots betwixt the outer and inner barks of trees.

P جوزاغند *jawz-āghand*, A peach stuffed with walnut-kernels.

P جوزاك *jawzāk*, Sorrow. Sorrowful.

A جوزان *jūzān*, (pl. of جائز *jāsiz*) Beams.

A جوزاهنج *jawzāhanj*, An Indian medicine.

P جوز بر گنبد *jawz bar gumbad*, (Throwing) a walnut upon a cupola, (a phrase employed to signify labour in vain).

A جوزة *jawzat*, One watering, or one draught of water. A single nut. A sort of grape. A sheep white in the middle of the body.

P جوزغة *jawzagha*, A cotton-pod.

A جوزق *jawzak*, A cotton-pod.

P جوزگره *jawz-girih*, A coat-button.

A جوزل *jawzal*, A young pigeon. Poison. A youth, boy. A camel that falls down from leanness.

P جوز مغز *jawz-maghz*, A walnut-kernel. Any hard substance.

P جوزن *jaw-zan*, Blight, mildew (as smiting the corn). Name of certain magicians in India, who are said to bewitch people by means of barley-corns steeped in saffron, over which certain incantatory verses have been muttered. A Brahman (*i.e.* one of the sacerdotal caste) who pours clarified butter into the fire, which he strikes with stalks of barley (as a religious rite).

P جوزهر *jawzahr*, The dragon's head and tail. The sphere of the moon. A comet.

A جوزيّ *jawziy*, A vendor of nuts.

P جوزيدن *jawzīdan*, To be sad, melancholy.

A جوزينق *jawzīnak*, Nuts and sweetmeats.

P جوزينه *jawzīna*, Sugared almonds. A syrup.

P جوژة *jūja*, A chicken. جوژۀ دوك *jūjasi dūk*, A notch in the top of the spindle.

P جوژۀ ربا *jūja-rubā*, (لوا *luwā* or *liwā*) A kite.

A جوس *jaws*, (or جوسان *jawasān*) (v. n. of جاس for جوس) Searching for with anxiety, persevering in, and repeating the search. Rummaging a house (as a thief for plunder). Catching intelligence (a spy). Going the rounds during the night (a watchman).

P جوساك *jawsāk*, Adam's apple.

P جوسبونتن *jūsbūnitan*, (zand and Pāz.) To take.

A جوسق *jawsak*, (from P كوشك *kūshk*) A lofty building, a palace. The zodiac.

P جوسك *jawsak*, A button. Adam's apple.

P جوسن *jawsan*, A cuirass made of leather.

P جوسنگ *jaw-sang*, In weight, a barley-corn.

P جوسه *jawsa*, A balcony. A kiosk, a villa.

A جوش *jawsh*, The breast. The middle of a

man. Midnight. A large section of the night, or the latter part of it. A march during the whole of the night. *Jūsh*, The breast.

P جوش *josh*, Ebullition, effervescence; agitation (of mind or body). Heat, lust. The ring of a coat of mail. The fourteenth day of the month. (in comp.) Boiling, raging. جوش خون *joshi khūn*, Ebullition of blood (a disease). جوش طوفان *joshi tūfān*, A deluge. بجوش آمدن *ba josh āmadan*, (or جوش زدن *josh zadan*) To boil, ferment, chafe, rage, be agitated (the waves of the sea).

P جوشاك *joshāk*, Heat, ebullition, agitation.

P جوشان *joshān*, Boiling, foaming (waves).

P جوشان برة *joshān-bara*, A savoury dish.

P جوشاندن *joshāndan*, (and جوشانيدن *joshānīdan*) (trans. of جوشيدن *joshīdan*) To cause to boil, to seeth. To cook.

P جوشاندة *joshānda*, A decoction.

P جوشپرة *josh-para*, A kind of food, vermicelli.

P جوشر *jawshir*, A weaver.

P جوشش *joshish*, A boiling, ebullition. Heat. A cooking, dressing. An eruption. Thrush (a disease). A violent desire.

P جوشك *jawshak* or *jūshak*, A sort of bottle made of earthenware, having a spout to it. *Jūshak*, A button-hole.

A جوشن *jawshan*, A coat of mail. The breast. Midnight.

P جوشن *joshan*, A cuirass. A crabbed look.

P جوشن پوش *joshan-posh*, A cuirassier.

A جوشنيّ *jawshaniy*, A weaver of coats of mail.

A جُوشُوش *juṣhūsh*, The breast, or the middle of it. A coarse, rude, rough man. Part (of the night). A portion (of the people).

P جوشيدن *joshīdan*, To boil. To shoot forth.

P جوشيدة *joshīda*, Boiled. جوشيدة شدن *joshīda shudan*, To be boiled, dressed, cooked.

P جوشيدة مغز *joshīda-maghz*, Passionate. Wary.

P جوشير *jaw-shīr*, Barley-gruel. A weaver.

P جوشيرة *jawshīra*, A weaver. A kind of food.

A جوظ *jawz*, (or جوظان *jawazān*) (v. n. of جاظ for جوظ) Walking proudly. Choking, suffocating.

A جوع *jawʿ*, (v. n. of جاع for جوع) Feeling hungry, famishing. Longing for, desiring. *Jūʿ*, Hunger. جوع البقر *jūʿu'l bakar*, (or جوع الكلب *jūʿu'l kalb*) Insatiable hunger, canine appetite.

A جُوَّع *juwwaʿ*, (pl. of جائع *jāʾiʿ*) Starved.

A جوعان *jawʿān*, Hungry, famished, starved.

A جوعة *jawʿat*, A being hungry, a hungry mood.

A جوعى *jawʿā*, (fem.) Hungry, famished.

P جوغ *jūgh*, A yoke.

P جوغن *jawghan*, A thrashing instrument of wood drawn by oxen.

A جوف *jawf*, (v. n. of جاف for جوف) Wounding in the belly with a spear, reaching the inside. A wide-extended plain. (pl. اجواف *ajwāf*) The belly. Interior cavity (of any thing). The tent of a revenue-collector. A third part of the night. The fifth of the six parts of the night. *Jūf*, (pl. of اجوف *ajwaf*) Hollow, concave. (in gram.) Verbs which have for their medial radical و *wāw* or ي *yā*. *Jawaf*, (v. n. of جوف) Being hollow and roomy. Amplitude, capaciousness.

A جوفاء *jawfāʾ*, (fem. of اجوف *ajwaf*) Hollow (reed or tree). Capacious (bucket). Extensive.

A جوفان *jūfān*, The yard of an ass.

A جوفر *jawfar* (equiv. to جوهر *jawhar*, q. v.).

A جوفي *jūfī*, A sort of fish.

A جوفيّ *jūfiy*, Hollow, wide, roomy within, capacious. A sort of fish.

A جوق *jawk*, A troop, a body. *Jawak*, (v. n. of جوق) Being distorted (the face). *Jawik*, One who has a down-looking distorted countenance. Distorted (face).

A جوقة *jawkat*, A crowd, multitude.

A جوق جوق *jawk jawk*, In troops.

P جوكان *jawkān*, A club of an arched form used in the Eastern game of horse shinty.

P جوكك *jūkak*, A bird like a sparrow.

P جوكوب *jaw-kob*, Bruised, coarsely ground.

P جوگان *jawgān*, Maize.

A جول *jawl*, (v. n. of جال for جول) Going round. Choosing, electing. Earth, dust. A large flock of sheep. A numerous troop. A herd of camels or horses, 30 or 40. The choicest camels. An aged mountain-goat. A sort of tree. A mountain. *Jūl*, (v. n. of جال for جول) Going round, surrounding. (pl. اجوال *ajwāl*, جوال *jiwāl*, and جوالة *jiwālat*) A wall, parapet, or fence to a well. The interior part of a well from top to bottom. Dust. The sea-side. The side of a mountain. (pl. جوال *jawāl*) A herd, flock. Wisdom, prudence. Design, purpose. A stone at the bottom of a well or river.

P جول *jūl*, A kite.

P جولان *jawlān*, Wandering up and down. Moving, springing from side to side (as combatants or competitors in amphitheatres).

A جولان *jawlān*, The commencement of cares. Dust. Gravel or dust driven about by the wind. A dusty day. Name of a mountain in Syria. *Jawalān*, (v. n. of جال for جول) Walking round. Motion, agitation. (Cattle) of the smallest and worst kind. جولان الهموم *jawalānu'l humūm*, Beginning of sorrow or cares. P جولان كنان *jawalān kunān*, Moving, leaping, springing.

P جولانگاه *jawalān-gāh*, A champ-de-mars.

P جولانگري *jawlāngarī*, A gallop, fleetness.

P جولاني *jawlānī*, Strength (of mind or body), quickness, apprehension. Fleetness.

A جولانيّ *jawlāniy*, A man) of universal usefulness. (A day) when clouds of dust are flying.

P جولاة *jūlāh*, (or جولاهة) A spider. A weaver.

P جولاهك *jūlāhak*, A little weaver; a spider.

P جولاهي *jūlāhī*, Weaving.

A جولة *jawlat*, (v. n. of جال for جول) Going round (an enemy). Being separated and dispersed, and then returning to the attack. Flying about (dust). Choosing.

P جولخ *jolakh*, A woollen cloth worn by religious mendicants.

P جولخي *jolakhī*, A mendicant clad in a jolakh.

A جولق *jawlak*, A kind of thorny tree.

P جولق *jolak* or *jawlik*, The dress of a monk.

P جولقي *jolakī* or *jawlikī*, A religious mendicant.

P جوله *jūla*, A quiver, case for bows and arrows. Beaten (wool or cotton). A porcupine. *Jūlah*, (for جولاة *jūlāh*) A weaver. A spider. *Jola*, Grass of which animals are very fond.

P جوله گاه *jola-gāh*, A field of the grass مرغ.

P جولهه *jūlaha*, A spider. A weaver.

P جوليدن *jūlīdan*, To be confused, scattered.

A جوم *jawm*, (v. n. of جام for جوم) Seeking, searching (aught, good or bad). Shepherds, whose flocks and interests are united. (pl. of جام *jām*) Goblets.

P جومست *jawmist*, A prophet of the magi.

P جون *jawn*, The Jumna, a large river in India (in Sanscrit called Yamunā). *Jawan*, A thrashing instrument drawn by oxen.

A جون *jawn*, White. Black (camel or horse). Red. Day. An herb becoming black from verdure. Name of many horses. بنو الجون *banū'l jawn*, Name of a tribe. *Jūn*, (pl. of جون *jawn*) Black. Days. *Juwan*, (pl. of جونة *jūnat*) Spice-boxes.

A جُؤَن *juʾan*, (pl. of جُؤنة *juʾnat*) Canisters covered with leather. Vases for holding spices.

A جوناء *jawnāʾ*, The sun. A cauldron.

A جونان *jawnāni*, The two ends of a bow.

A جُؤنة *juʾnat*, (pl. جُؤَن *juʾan*) A canister covered with leather, where a druggist keeps perfumes.

A جونة *jawnat*, The sun, or his disk (when setting). A butt smeared over with pitch. Red. A coal. *Jūnat*, (v. n. of جون) Being black (the face). Blackness (of a horse), pitchy blackness. (pl. جون *juwan*) A box covered with leather (for spiceries). A small mountain.

P جونك *jūnk*, A bird's bill.

A جونيّ *jūniy*, A bird resembling a grouse, called قطا *katā*. Of the tribe of جون *jawn*.

P جووان *jiwwān*, (in zand and Pāz.) A youth.

A جُؤُوب *juʾūb*, (pl. of جأب *jaʾb*) Strong asses.

A جُؤُوبة *juʾūbat*, (v. n. of جأب) Being of a crabbed, grim countenance.

A جُؤوة *juʾwat*, A dark bay colour. Rugged and black ground.

A جُؤُوث *juʾūs*, (v. n. of جئث) Being afraid.

A جووز *juwūz*, A passing by or beyond.

A جُؤُوش *juʾūsh*, (pl. of جأش) Hearts, minds.

A جوول *juwūl*, A going round, circumambulating.

A جوة *jawh*, (v. n. of جاه for جوه) Looking at, or receiving ungraciously. *Jūh*, Look, aspect, countenance. بجوه سوء bijūhi sawin, With displeasure.

P جوه jūh, A yoke.

A جوهر jawhar, (from P گوهر gawhar) (pl. جواهر jawāhir) A jewel, gem, pearl. Matter, substance, essence, staple (distinguished from accident). Any kind of mineral whence something valuable is extracted. Quicksilver. Pith, marrow. The wavy appearance on some Oriental sword-blades. Worth, excellence. Skill, knowledge, intellect. A guide, director. Brave, intrepid. محض جوهر ذات mahzi jawhari zāt, Unmixed original essence. جوهر علوي jawhari ʻulwī, Heaven. Spirit. Fire. جوهر فرد jawhari fard, An indivisible atom. A person unrivalled or unequalled.

P جوهر jūhar, When in a siege the men, feeling unable successfully to resist their assailants, destroy their wives and children and save themselves by flight (a practice which prevailed among the Rājputs in India). A place abounding in streams. جوهر كردن jūhar kardan, To sack or plunder.

A جوهرة jawharat, One gem, a single pearl.

P جوهر دار jawhar-dār, A bright, glittering, or well-tempered cimeter, possessing the blackish marks called جوهر jawhar.

P جوهر فروش jawhar-farosh, A dealer in precious stones, a vender of jewels.

A جوهريّ jawhariy, A jeweller. Substantial, essential. Name of a celebrated lexicographer, and compiler of an Arabic dictionary called صحاح saḥāh, i.e. Accurate, free from faults.

P جوهريان jawhariyān, (pl. of جوهري jawhariy) Jewellers. A sect who attribute materiality to the Deity; materialists.

P جوهي jūhī, (or جوبي) Name of a flower.

A جوي jawa', (v. n. of جوي) Continuing a long time (a disease). Being powerfully affected by love or sadness. Loathing, detesting. Stinking (water). Warmth, ardour, heat. A decay of the vitals, consumption. Heart-felt love or grief. A dark bay colour. Consumptive. Jawī, Fetid water. Unwholesome (place). Afflicted with a disease of the chest.

P جوي jawe, A grain of barley. Joy, (jūy, جو jo or jū imperative and participle of جوييدن joyīdan or جستن justan) Seek thou. Seeking, desiring, wishing, asking. دولت جوي dawlat-joy, Wishing the happiness or prosperity of another, affectionate. جهان جوي jihān-joy, Attentive to worldly affairs; a worldling. Jūy, A running stream, rivulet. A canal or gutter cut for the purposes of irrigation. A groove in the back of a sword. جوي آب jūyi ab, A running stream. جوي تاز jūyi tāz, A rapid stream, mighty torrent.

A جويّ jawiy, Disagreeable, inconvenient. Unwholesome (place). Narrow and tight in the chest, and unable to speak plainly.

P جويا joyā, Searching, inquiring, seeking. A diligent inquirer. Wishful. Name of a champion killed by Rustam (the Persian Hercules).

P جويان joyān, Seeking. Wishing, ambitious. (pl. of جوي joy) Wishers, seekers. جويان مدد joyāni madad, Petitioners, supplicants for assistance.

P جويانيدن joyānīdan, To inquire, investigate.

P جويائي joyāʼī, Search, diligent inquiry.

P جويبار jūy-bār, A great river formed by the confluence of many smaller streams. A river's bank. A place abounding in springs or running streams. جويبار بهشت jūy-bāri bihisht, The river of paradise.

A جوية jawiyat, (or جويّة jawīyat) A disagreeable, unhealthy country.

P جويچه jūycha, (or جويك jūyak) A rivulet, brook. A groove, a furrow.

A جويل jawīl, Whatever is driven about by the wind (as dust, fallen leaves, and the like).

P جوين jawīn, (or جوينه) Made of barley.

A جوين juwayn, Name of a place; also of a man.

P جوينده joyinda, Searching. An inquirer. جوينده يابنده joyinda yābinda, Who searches, finds; seek and you will find.

A جويه juwayh, (dim. of جاه jāh) A little rank, petty rank, or dignity.

P جوييدن joyīdan, To seek, search for, hunt after. Jūyīdan, To set water a flowing.

P جويينه jūyīna, Aquatic. A swan.

P جه jah, A place. Rank, office. (imper. of جستن jastan) Leap thou. (in compos.) Leaping.

P جه jih, (in zand and Pāzand) Courtezans.

A جه jahh, (v. n. of جهّ) Repelling shamefully, keeping back.

A جهابذة jahābizat, (pl. of جهبذ jihbiz) Acute, intelligent money-changers. جهابذة النقد jahābizatuʼn nakd, Money-brokers. Able critics.

A جهات jihāt, (pl. of جهة jihat) Faces, surfaces. Superficies. Goods, effects. P جهات شش jihāti shash, Six surfaces, a cube.

A جهاد jahād, Hard ground without grass. The fruit of the اراك arāk. Jihād, (v. n. 3 of جهد) Waging war (especially against infidels). Battle, combat. An exploit. Endeavour, effort. جهاد اكبر jihādi akbar, The greater warfare, war against one's own lusts. جهاد اصغر jihādi asghar, The lesser warfare, war against infidels. P مبارز جهاد پيشه mubārizi jihād-pesha, A soldier inured to war, a veteran. A جهادك ان تفعل juhādāka an tafʻala, Your utmost endeavour should be to do.

A جهار jihār, (v. n. 3 of جهر) Carrying on open hostilities. Fighting face to face. Name of an idol. جهارا jihāran or jahāran, Publicly, in open day.

A جهارة jahārat, (v. n. of جهر) Having a handsome face and a loud voice. Being loud (voice or sound). A loud voice. Elegance of form and beauty of face.

A جهاز jahāz, A camel's saddle, or the saddle-tree. Pudenda mulieris. A ship. ضرب في جهازة zaraba fī jahāzihi, He fled and did not return. Jahāz or jihāz, (pl. اجهزة ajhizat) Paraphernalia, or portion given with a daughter, effects in the disposal of a wife, whatever a bride brings to her husband's house, her trousseau. Travelling equipage. Funeral apparatus.

P جهاز شكني jahāz-shikanī, A shipwreck.

A جهازيّ jahāzīy, A sailor. A kind of cimeter.

A جهاض jahāz, The unripe fruit of the toothpick tree (called اراك arāk). Jihāz, (v. n. 3 of جهض) Keeping back, preventing. Causing to make haste.

A جهاضة jahāzat, Shrewdness, cleverness.

A جهّاضة jahhāzat, Old, decrepit (she-ass).

A جهّال juhhāl, (pl. of جاهل) Ignorant, foolish.

A جهالة jahālat, (v. n. of جهل) Being ignorant, not knowing. Feigning ignorance. Ignorance. Barbarism. Brutality.

A جهام jahām, A cloud without rain.

A جهامة jahāmat, (v. n. of جهم) Being of a harsh, austere countenance. Receiving sternly and ungraciously.

P جهان jahān or jihān, The world. An age. Worldly possessions. Any sublunary object. Leaping, bounding. اين و آن جهان in u ān jahān, This and the other world. جهان آب و گل jahāni āb u gil, The human body. The world. جهان داشتن jahān dāshtan, To possess much property. جهان فاني jahāni fānī, The perishable world. جهان قديم jahāni kadīm, Eternity. جهان كهين jihāni kihīn, A little world, i.e. man. جهان گذران jahāni guzrān, Transitory world. جهان مهين jahāni mihīn, The world, universe. امر جهانمطاع amri jahān-mutāʻ, A mandate obeyed by all the world. پرتو جهان نما partavi jahān-namā, A world-illuminating ray.

A جهان jahān, A river (formerly the Pyramus).

P جهان آراي jahān-ārāy, World-adorning. Name of the sixth month of the year of Yazdagird.

P جهان آرائي jahān-ārāʼī, World's ornament.

P جهان افروز jahān-afroz, World-enlightening.

P جهان آفرين jahān-āfirīn, Creator of the world.

P جهان آور jahān-āwar, Valiant. Learned.

P جهان بان jahānbān, Keeper or protector of the world. God Almighty. A powerful monarch.

P جهانباني jahānbānī, Government of the world. Royal.

P جهانبين jahān-bīn, Seeing or comprehending the whole world (an attribute of God). The eye. A traveller. Offspring.

P جهان پناه jahān-panāh, Asylum of the world.

P جهان پهلواني jahān-pahlawānī, Name of a post of honour to which the bravest men were formerly advanced in Persia.

A جهانة juhānat, A young handmaid.

P جهانتاب jahān-tāb, World-inflaming. The fifth month of the æra of Yazdagird.

P جهانجو jahān-jo or jū, Ambitious of subjugating the world.

P جهان جهان *jahān jahān*, Much, many.

P جهاندار *jahān-dār*, Possessor of the world. A king, an emperor. Name of a Mogul emperor, grandson of Awrangzīb.

P جهانداري *jahān-dārī*, Monarchy, empire, rule. Imperial. اسباب جهانداري *asbābi jahāndārī*, Means of acquiring rule.

P جهان ديده *jahān-dīda*, Seeing the world; knowing mankind. A traveller. جهان ديده بسيار گويد دروغ *jahān-dīda bisyār goyad durogh*, One who has seen the world tells many lies.

P جهان رواني *jahān-ravānī*, Rule of the world.

P جهان زنده *jahān-zinda*, A perennial flower.

P جهان سالار *jahān-sālār*, A powerful monarch. A general.

P جهان ستان *jahān-satān*, World-conquering.

P جهان ستاني *jahān-satānī*, Conquest of the world.

P جهان سوز *jahān-soz*, An incendiary; a tyrant.

P جهانكشا *jahān-kushā*, World-subduing.

P جهان كشائي *jahān-kushāī*, Conquest.

P جهان كي *jahān-kay*, King of the world.

P جهان گرد *jahān-gard*, A great traveller.

P جهان گير *jahān-gīr*, Seizer or conqueror of the world (the name which Salīm, the son of Sultān Akbar, adopted on succeeding his father as Emperor of Hindūstān in the year 1605). A woman's bracelet. Short breeches worn by soldiers.

P جهان گيري *jahān-gīrī*, Universal sway.

P جهان نورد *jahān-naward*, A great traveller.

P جهاني *jahānī*, Worldly. A mortal.

P جهانيان *jahāniyān*, Mortals. Worldly people.

P جهانيدن *jahānidan*, To cause to leap. To attack. To shoot.

A جهب *jahb*, A heavy dull countenance.

A جهبذ *jihbiz*, (pl. جهابذة *jahābizat*) An acute, intelligent money-changer, who knows at once good money from bad.

A جهبذة *jahbazat*, Banking, the business of a banker or money-changer.

A جهبل *jahbal*, Large-headed. Aged. Large (mountain-goat). Name of the individual who first brought the news of Muhammad's death to the people of Hazramawt.

A جهبلة *jahbalat*, An ugly woman.

A جهة *jihat* or *juhat*, Side, face, surface; form, fashion, manner, mode; reason, regard, respect. Wages. P از جهت *az jihati*, For this reason, because of. On the side of. از جهت اين كه *az jihati īn ki*, Because that. چار جهت *chār jihat*, Four sides (of a solid). Four qualities or quantities.

A جهث *jahs*, (v. n. of جهث) Moving, agitating, rendering light and airy (anger, terror, or joy).

A جهجاه *jahjāh*, Name of the man who broke Muhammad's stick on the knee of Othmān; also of one who is destined to rule the world.

P جهجهان *jahjahān*, Skipping, prancing. Hopping. Swelling, rushing (water).

A جهجهة *jahjahat*, (v. n. of جهجه Q) Shouting at a wild beast in order that he may retire.

A جهد *jahada*, (fut. يجهد *yajhadu*) He strove.

A جهد *jahd*, (v. n. of جهد) Striving, struggling, exerting one's self. Overloading (a beast). Longing for (food). Churning, fetching out butter. Trying, examining, proving. Eating much and often. Wasting, pulling down (disease). Labour, study. جهد البلاء *jahdu'l balāa*, A numerous family. Indigence. Any condition to which death is preferable. جهد جاهد *jahdi jāhid*, Intense labours or pains. جهد الايمان *jahdu'l aymān*, The most solemn of oaths. *Jahd* or *juhd*, Power, strength, vigour. *Jahad*, (v. n. of جهد) Being wretched and uncomfortable (life).

A جهر *jahr*, (v. n. of جهر) Raising the voice, speaking loud. Revealing, declaring, publishing, discovering, disclosing. Beholding, perceiving, seeing clear without a veil. Cleaning out (a well); or exhausting it; or reaching water. Being public, divulged. Visiting one in the morning unexpectedly. Magnifying, honouring. Looking at any one whose mien or comeliness is striking and overpowering. Dazzling the eyes (the sun). Appearing great and respectable; regarding as numerous (an army). Shaking (a bottle) in order to churn butter. Measuring. Guessing. Travelling incognito over a country. High and rugged ground. A year. A portion of an age. A loud voice. *Juhr*, An elegant form. A beautiful face. Face, countenance, air, mien. ما احسن جهره *mā ahsana juhrahu*, How fair his countenance is! *Jahar*, (v.n. of جهر) Being weak and unable to bear the glare of the sun (an eye). *Jahir*, Loud-voiced; a clear speaker. Comely.

A جهرا *jahran*, (P جهرانه *jahrāna*) Publicly, evidently, clearly. سرًّا و جهرا *sirran wa jahran*, Privately and publicly.

A جهراء *jahrāa*, (fem. of اجهر *ajhar*) Unable to look at the sun. Prominent (eye). Beautiful, having a slight squint. A crowd, multitude. A level country without tree or hill. The most excellent persons of a tribe. *Juharāa*, (pl. of جهير *jahīr*) Fair, handsome.

A جهراوات *jahrāwāt*, A plain outside of Shīrāz.

A جهرة *jahrat*, Open, conspicuous.

A جهرةً *jahratan*, Publicly, visibly.

A جهرم *jahram*, Name of a town in Persia.

P جهرمي *jahramī*, Native of Jahram. The celebrated musician Barbud.

A جهرمية *jahramīyat*, A kind of linen cloth (called from جهرم *jahram*, the town above-mentioned).

P جهره *jahra*, A yarn-reel.

A جهز *jahz*, (v. n. of جهز) Rushing upon (a wounded man) with intent to kill (him), giving the coup de grace, despatching.

A جهزاء *jahzāa*, High (ground). Prominent (eye).

A جهش *jahsh*, (v. n. of جهش) Raising a scream and running frightened (as a child to its mother). Preparing to weep. Running from country to country.

P جهش *jahish*, Nature. Exterior form.

A جهشان *jahashān*, (v. n. of جهش) Fearing, dreading. Running, fleeing away. Running crying (as a child to its mother).

A جهشة *jahshat*, A tear starting. A crowd.

A جهض *jahz*, (v. n. of جهض) Overcoming, conquering. Removing, carrying off. Setting at liberty, rescuing. *Jahiz*, An abortion.

A جهضم *jahzam*, Large-headed and broad-faced. Wide-chested. A lion.

A جهل *jahl*, (v. n. of جهل) Being ignorant, foolish. Feigning ignorance. Ignorance. جهل بسيط *jahli basīt*, Simple ignorance, artlessness. جهل مركب *jahli murakkab*, Complicated ignorance, confirmed error. *Juhl*, (*juhul*, or جهّل *juhhal*) (pl. of جاهل *jāhil*) Ignorant.

A جهلاء *jahlāa*, (for جاهلية *jāhilīyat*) Paganism.

A جهلاء *juhalāa*, (pl. of جهول) Very ignorant.

A جهلة *jahalat*, (pl. of جاهل *jāhil*) Fools.

A جهم *jahm*, (v. n. of جهم) Receiving sternly and ungraciously. Weak. A lion. *Jahm* and *jahim*, Austere, sour, crabbed, surly.

A جهمة *juhmat* or *jahmat*, Beginning of the latter portion of the night, or remains of its darkness. A large kettle. *Juhmat*, A troop of about 80 camels.

P جهمرز *jih-marz*, An associate of harlots.

A جهمية *jahmīyat*, Name of a sect.

P جهن *jahn*, Spirit. *Jahn* or *jihn*, Name of the son of Afrāsyāb. *Jihan*, (for جهان) The world.

A جهن *jahn*, Sourness of face. *Juhn*, A current in the sea about a bow-shot distance from land.

A جهنّام *jahannām*, *jihinnām*, or *juhannām*, Deep (well). *Juhunnām*, The familiar spirit of الاعشى *al aasha'*. Name of عمرو بن قطن *amrū 'bni katan*.

A جهنة *juhnat*, The beginning of night.

P جهنجه *jahanja*, A kind of shoe or slipper.

A جهندر *juhandar*, A species of date.

P جهندگي *jahandagī*, A cantering pace.

P جهنده *jahanda*, (A horse) going sideways and skipping along the road. Elastic.

A جهنّم *jahannam*, Hell, the infernal fire. Deep (well). اهل جهنّم *ahli jahannam*, The damned.

A جهنّمي *jahannamīy*, Infernal, hellish.

A ليلة الجهني *laylatu'l juhnīy*, The 23d night of Ramazān (esteemed fortunate for those who pray).

A جهوا *jahwa'*, Naked posteriors.

A جهواء *jahwāa*, Clear and cloudless (sky). Naked posteriors.

A جهوة *jahwat*, Naked posteriors. A hill, a hillock. A decrepit, old she-camel.

A جهود *jahūd*, Laborious, diligent.

P جهود *juhūd*, A Jew.

P جهودانه *juhūdāna*, Judaically. The ventricle of a sheep stuffed with meat and herbs. Name of a gum-bearing tree.

P جهودي *juhūdī*, One Jew. Judaism. Judaical.

A جهور *jahūr*, Loud, clear-voiced (horse). *Jahwar*, Bold, courageous.

A جهورة *juhūrat*, Loudness of voice. Comeliness.

A جهوري *jahwariy*, Handsome, comely. Loud, clear, distinct (speech or tone of voice). جهوريّ الصوت *jahwariyu's sawt*, Loud-voiced.

A جهوش *jahūsh*, Swift, flying from region to region, unable to abide in one place. *Juhūsh*, (v. n. of جهش) Raising a cry and running frightened (a child to its mother).

A جهوضة *juhūzat*, Cleverness, shrewdness.

A جهول *jahūl*, Extremely ignorant.

A جهولي *jahūlī*, Ignorance, folly.

A جهوليّة *jahūliyat*, Extreme ignorance.

A جهوم *jahūm*, Weak, silly, impotent.

A جهومة *juhūmat*, (v. n. of جهم) Having an austere, forbidding countenance.

A جهون *juhūn*, (v. n. of جهن) Approaching.

A جهوي *jahwa'*, Naked posteriors.

A جهيد *jahīd*, (A pasture) flocked to by cattle as being agreeable to them. Laborious, painstaking. Toilsome.

P جهيدن *jahīdan*, To leap, spring, dance. To gallop. To be stimulated to running or flight To recreate, divert one's self. To drop. To grow cold. To blow (as the wind).

A جهيدي *juhaydā'*, Diligence, labour.

A جهير *jahīr*, Loud-voiced, a clear speaker. Loud (speech or tone of voice). (pl. جهراء *juharā*) Beautiful in the face. Behaving with propriety, acting honourably. Unadulterated milk.

P جهيز *jahīz*, Vestments and furniture of every kind which a bride brings to her husband's house. A dowry. Minced meat.

A جهيز *jahīz*, Light, nimble, swift (horse). Quick, sudden (death).

A جهيزة *jahīzat*, A wolf. A she-wolf. A female hyena. A she-bear or her cub. Name of a certain foolish woman.

A جهيض *jahīz*, Abortive. A castling.

A جهينة *juhaynat*, Name of a large tribe.

P جي *jay*, (in zand and Pāz.) Pure. Name of a village dependent upon Ray. *Jī*, The city of Ispahān. Name of a district in the dependency of Ispahān.

A جيء *jay*, (v. n. of جاء) Arriving, happening, coming to pass. A word used in calling to eat or drink. هيء و جيء *hiy'a wa jiy'a*, Meat and drink, or the call to them.

A جئاء *ji'ā*, (pl. of جئاوة *ji'āwat*) Repositories for kettles.

A جياء *jiyā*, (v. n. 3 of جاء) Endeavouring to conquer, or vying with, by coming often. Conferring together. Agreeing coinciding. A wicker basket or a trivet for a pot or kettle.

A جيّاء *jayyā*, Approaching, about to arrive.

A جيّاب *jayyāb*, A maker of shirt-collars.

A جيأة *jay'at*, (v. n. of جاء) Coming. Pus. Blood. Mud. *Ji'at*, Arrival. A standing pool.

A جياحة *jiyāhat*, (v. n. of جاح for جوح) Destroying. Tearing up by the roots.

A جياد *jiyād*, (pl. of جيّد *jayyid*) Good, excellent. (pl. of جواد *jawād*) Swift, excellent (horses).

A جيادات *jiyādāt*, (pl. of جيّد) Good, excellent.

A جيّار *jayyār*, A heat in the stomach from thirst, hunger, or rage. Quick lime, or an unguent made with it and arsenic for pulling out hairs by the roots.

A جيّاش *jayyāsh*, A horse curvetting when pricked with a spur.

A جيّاظ *jayyāz*, (A man) who walks proudly.

A جياع *jiyā'*, (pl. of جائع) Hungry, famished.

A جيّاف *jayyāf*, A digger-up of dead bodies.

P جي افرام *jay-afrām*, Name of a prophet.

A جيأل *jay'al*, (pl. جيائل *jayā'il*) A hyena.

A جيال *jiyāl*, A going round, circumambulating.

A جيألة *jay'alat* The pus of a wound.

A جئاوة *ji'āwat* or جياوة *jiyāwat*, (pl. جئاء *ji'ā*) Any thing (made of leather) into which a pot or kettle is placed.

A جيائد *jayā'id*, (pl. of جيّد) Good, excellent.

A جيائل *jayā'il*, (pl. of جيأل *jay'al*) Hyenas.

A جيب *jayb*, (v. n. of جاب for جيب) Cutting (a shift or garment) for the purpose of making a collar or breast. A sine (in geometry). The entrance into a country. (pl. جيوب *juyūb*) The collar of a shirt. جيب افق *jaybi ufk*, The sky. ناصح الجيب *nāsihu'l jayb*, Faithful and sincere.

T جيب *jayb* or *jeb*, A pocket. جيب خاص *jaybi khās*, A privy purse.

P جيبا *jība*, (or جيپا *jīpā*) Fuel, firewood.

A جيبة *jībat*, (v. n. of جاب for جوب) Answering. Answer, response.

P جيبر *jībar*, Gardens. Paradises.

A جئة *ji'at*, A place where water collects. A patch on a shoe. A thong for sewing shoes with.

A جية *jiyat*, Stinking water. A place where fetid water collects.

A جيّة *jīyat*, Fetid water. A place where water collects. A patch on a shoe, or a thong for sewing with.

A جيتر *jaytar*, A man of a short stature.

A جيثلوط *jaysalūt*, A term of reproach invented by women and untranslated, but seeming to mean, A lying, relaxed woman, apparently coined from the roots جلط *jalata*, جثط *jasata*, and ثلط *salata*.

A جيج *jīj*, A word for calling camels to water.

A جيحل *jayhal*, A large stone. The skin of a fish from which shields are made. Large, bulky.

P A جيحون *jayhūn*, The river Jayhūn or Bactrus. P بجيحون نشستن *ba jayhūn nishastan*, To cross the Jayhūn. To weep.

A جيحوني *jayhūniy*, Belonging to the Jayhūn. Name of a river whose waters are very sweet.

A جيخ *jayhh*, (v. n. of جاخ for جيخ) Carrying away (a rapid stream).

A جيد *jīd*, (pl. اجياد *ajyād* and جيود *juyūd*) A long, slender, beautiful neck. The lower or front part of the neck, on which jewels are suspended. A kind of short shirt. (pl. of اجيد *ajyad* and جيداء *jaydā*) Long-necked. *Jayad*, The length, slenderness, and beauty of the neck.

A جيّد *jayyid*, (pl. جياد *jiyād*, جيادات *jiyādāt*, and جيائد *jayā'id*) Good, excellent. Elegant.

A جيداء *jaydā*, (fem. of اجيد) Fine-necked.

A جيدار *jaydār*, Short, dwarfish. *Jīdār*, The holm oak.

A جيدانة *jaydānat*, Fine-necked (woman).

A جيدران *jaydarān*, Short, dwarfish.

A جيدري *jaydara'*, Short, dwarfish.

A جيذر *jayzar*, The wild calf. A camel fleshy about the ends of his bones. Short (man).

A جيذرة *jayzarat*, Name of a thick black fish.

P جير *jīr*, Declivity. A kind of leather.

A جئر *ja'ir*, Corpulent (man).

A جير *jayr*, Quick lime. *Jayri, jayrin*, or *jayra*, Certainly, indeed. *Jayar*, Shortness, brevity, contemptible littleness.

A جئرّ *ji'arr*, Copious (rain).

A جيران *jīrān* or جيرة, (pl. of جائر) Neighbours.

P جيرفت *jīruft*, Name of a city in Karmānia.

A جيرون *jayrūn*, Name of a gate of Damascus.

P جيرة *jīra*, A daily allowance.

A جئز *ja'iz*, Troubled with a stifling sensation in the chest.

A جيز *jīz*, The margin of a valley. A grave. *Jīz* and *jiyaz*, (pl. of جيزة *jīzat*) Sides, tracts.

A جيزان *jīzān*, (pl. of جائز *jā'iz*) Beams.

A جيزة *jīzat*, (pl. جيز *jīz* and *jiyaz*) A side, coast. The skirt of a valley. Name of a village in Egypt situated on the bank of the Nile.

P جيز جنگ *jīz jang*, A leathern dildo.

P جيستن *jestan*, To leap. A small purse elegantly adorned.

A جيسوان *jaysuwān*, (from P گيسوان *gīsuwān*) A very choice kind of palm-tree.

A جيسور *jaysūr*, The young man slain by Moses.

A جيش *jaysh*, (pl. جيوش *juyūsh*) An army, soldiery. A legion. *Jaysh*, (or جيشان *jayashān*) (v. n. of جاش for جيش) Boiling (a pot). Raging (as the sea). Swelling, overflowing (a river). Flowing with impetuosity (as a fountain). Being greatly moved, excited, disturbed (the mind). ذات الجيش *zātu'l jaysh*, (or اولات الجيش *ūlātu'l jaysh*) Name of a valley near Madīna. *Jīsh*, Name of a long tufted plant, the head of which is filled with seeds.

A جيشة *jīshat*, A single ebullition.

P جيشگر *jayshgar*, A general. A maker of coats of mail.

A جيص *jays*, (v. n. of جاص for جيص) Swerving, turning aside. *Jīs*, A sort of game played with seven camel-dungs.

A جيض *jayz*, (v. n. of جاض for جيض) Turning away from, declining.

A جيّض *jiyazz*, (or جيضى) A haughty air or step.

A جيظان *jayazān*, (v. n. of جاظ for جيظ) Walking proudly. Walking with difficulty under a burden.

A جيعان *jayʻān*, Hungry, famished, starving.

A جيعر *jayʻar*, A hyena.

A جيعم *jayʻam*, Hungry, famishing.

P جيغت *jayghut*, Palm-tree fibres.

P جيغوت *jayghūt*, An ill-stuffed pillow, hard in the middle. Basket made of palm-leaves or fibres.

P جيغة *jīgha*, A jewel worn in the turban.

A جيف *jayf* (v. n. of جاف for جيف) Stinking (a carcase). *Jiyaf*, (pl. of جيفة *jīfat*) Carcases.

A جيفان *jīfān*, (pl. of جائف *jāʼif*) Penetrators.

A جيفة *jīfat*, (pl. جيف *jiyaf* and اجياف *ajyāf*) A carcase, corpse, which has begun to stink, carrion.

A جيفر *jayfar*, A strong lion.

A جيفل *jayfal*, The month ذو القعدة *zūʼl kaʻdat*.

P جيفه خوار *jīfa-khwār*, A feeder on carrion.

P جيك *jik*, The noise of fowls.

P جيگ جيگ *jīg jīg*, Cry of birds and beasts.

A جيل *jayl*, The side of a well, sea, or mountain. *Jīl*, (pl. اجيال *ajyāl*) A race, a nation. Greeks. Turks. *Jayal*, A hyena.

A جلال *jaʼlāl*, Terror.

P جيلان *jīlān*, The juleb-tree. Sesame.

A جيلان *jaylān*, A dusty day. Gravel or dust blown about by the wind. Dust. *Jīlān*, The country called Gīlān, to the S.-W. of the Caspian Sea.

A جيلاني *jaylāniy*, Very dusty (day).

P جيلاهنگ *jīlāhang*, A purgative Indian root.

P جيلدارو *jīl-dārū*, A wood, black without and green within.

A جيلم *jaylam*, The moon (especially new.)

A جيم *jīm*, The letter ج *jīm*. A silk robe embroidered with gold. Libidinous camels.

P جين *jīn*, Unamiable, detestable qualities.

P جيناك *jīnāk*, A place.

P جينور *jīnawar*, The bridge across hell-fire.

P جيواد *jaywād*, Chastity, continence.

A جيوب *juyūb*, (pl. of جيب *jayb*) Shirt-collars. Pockets.

A جئوة *jiʼawat*, Dearth, scarceness.

A جيود *juyūd*, (pl. of جيد) Long, graceful necks.

A جيوش *juyūsh*, (v. n. of جاش for جيش) Boiling (a pot). Raging (the sea). Flowing with impetuosity (a fountain). Swelling, overflowing (a river). Being greatly moved and excited (the mind). (pl. of جيش *jaysh*) Armies, forces, troops. امير الجيوش *amīruʼl juyūsh*, Commander of the forces.

P جيوش آهن پوش *juyūshi āhan-posh*, Troops cased in steel.

P جيوه *jīwa*, (in Ar. زيبق *zībak*) Quicksilver.

A جيه *jīh*, Look, aspect, countenance.

A جيهبوق *jayhabūk*, Mouse-dung.

A جيهر *jayhar*, A fly tainting meat.

A جيهل *jayhal*, Huge (rock). *Jayhal* (or جيهلة *jayhalat*), A stick for stirring new wine. Ignorant. A lion.

A جيهمان *jayhumān*, Saffron.

A جيهور *jayhūr*, A fly tainting meat.

A جيئة *jayʼat*, Pus, matter, blood. Mud. *Jīʼat*, A place wherein water collects. A patch on a shoe. A thong for sewing with. Arrival.

چ

چ *che*, or, as it is sometimes called, جيم فارسي *jīmi fārsī* or جيم عجمي *jīmi ʻajamī*, is the sixth letter of the Persian alphabet, and is never met with in Arabic words. Its power is that we express by *ch* in "church". A few words are indifferently spelt with چ *che* or ژ *je*; as کاچ *kāch* or کاژ *kāj*; and also with چ *che* or ش *shīn*: as, لخچه *lakhcha* or لخشه *lakhsha*. Ignorant writers are also very apt to confound it with ج *jīm*.

P چا *chā*, Tea. چادان *chādān*, A tea-pot.

P چابك *chābuk*, Quick, swift, active. Ingenious, sharp, acute. Beautiful. A horsewhip. چابك زدن *chābuk zadan*, To whip.

P چابك بازي *chābuk-bāzī*, A whipping.

P چابك خرام *chābuk-khirām*, Swift-paced.

P چابك دست *chābuk-dast*, Dexterous, adroit, light-fingered, nimble, expeditious. Beautiful.

P چابك سوار *chābuk-suwār*, A horse-breaker, jockey, rough rider. A horse-dealer. A flogger.

P چابك سواري *chābuk-suwārī*, Jockeyship.

P چابكي *chābukī*, Agility. In need of the whip.

P چابوك *chābūk*, Quick, nimble, acute.

P چاپاتي *chāpātī*, A thin, unleavened cake.

P چاپلوس *chāplos*, A flatterer. Flattery.

P چاپلوسي *chāplosī*, Flattery, adulation.

P چاپه *chāpa*, A seal, stamp, print.

P چاتو *chātū*, A halter, rope to hang felons.

P چاچ *chāch*, A heap of corn thrashed and winnowed. Name of a city in Turkistān famed for the bows made there: hence, کمان چاچي *kamāni chāchī*, Bows brought from that place, which were neither affected by heats or damps.

P چاچله *chāchala*, A rustic shoe of raw leather.

P چادر *chādir* or *chādar*, A tent, pavilion. A mantle, scarf. A veil. A sheet. A table-cloth. A cascade. چادر احرام *chādiri ihrām*, (according to some اجرام *ajrām*) Snow. چادر اژدها *chādiri ajdahā*, The four elements. چادر اجساد *chādiri ajsād*, The four elements. چادر ترسا *chādiri tarsā*, The sun. The sun's rays. Light. A blue and yellow garment. چادر خواب *chādiri khwāb*, Bed-curtains. چادر شب *chādiri shab*, Bed-sheets. چادر قلندري *chādiri kalandarī*, A sort of tent. چادر كافوري *chādiri kāfūrī*, The dawn. چادر كحلي *chādiri kuhlī*, The heavens. A dark night. چادر لاجورد *chādiri lājaward*, The azure sky. A verdant meadow. چادر يزدي *chādiri yazdī*, A kind of woman's veil.

P چار *chār*, (contracted from چهار *chahār*) Four. A potter's kiln. Able. (for چاره) Remedy, cure.

P چار ابرو *chār-abrū*, A kind of dervish who shaves his eyebrows and whiskers.

P چار آخر *chār ākhur*, (or مادر *madār*) The four elements. Four stars in the Great Bear.

P چار اخشيج *chār akhshīj*, (ارکان *arkān*, استاد *ustād*, or عنصر *ʻunsur*) The four elements.

P چار اژدها *chār ajdahā*, The four elements.

P چار اسب *chār asb*, A team of four horses.

P چار اسباب *chār asbāb*, The four faculties: viz. of attraction, retention, digestion, and repulsion. The four elements.

P چار آيينه *chār āyīna*, A kind of armour.

P چار باغ *chār bāgh*, A palace. Name of a celebrated royal garden in the environs of Ispahān.

P چار بالش *chār bālish*, (or چار بالشت *chār bālisht*) The four elements. A kind of large cushion, on which great men sit or recline. A throne. The world. چار بالش ارکان *chār bālishi arkān*, Heat, cold, dryness, and moisture.

P چار بانگ *chār bāng*, Sensible, quick, alert.

P چار برد *chār bard*, Name of a city.

P چار بند *chār band*, The world.

P چار بندي *chār bandī*, A wallet. The world.

P چار بيخ *chār bekh*, Endive-root, fennel-root, caper-root, and parsley-root. The four elements.

P چارپا *chār pā*, (چار پاي *chār pāy*, or چارپايه *chār pāya*) A quadruped. A bedstead. Castanets.

P چار پاره *chār pāra*, Four square, in four parts. A pair of castanets or virginals. The patch of a shoe.

P چار پهلو شدن *chār pahlū shudan*, (To become four square) To guttle, gormandize. To lie supine.

P چار تا *chār-tā*, (تار *tār*, or تاره *tāra*) A four-stringed lute. A drum. The four elements. The world.

P چار تكبير بر و زد *chār takbīr bar u zad*, He deserted him, he abandoned him, as if dead (a mode of expression borrowed from the four Takbīrs, or praisings of the names of God, which are repeated by way of burial service over the dead).

P چار جامه *chār jāma*, A saddle without a tree.

P چار جوبه *chār jūpa*, A window-blind.

P چار جوهر *chār jawhar*, The four elements. Name of four stars in the Great Bear.

P چار جوي فطرت *chār jūyi fitrat*, Four constitutional habits in man; viz. sanguine, choleric, phlegmatic, and melancholy.

P چار جهت *chār jihat*, Four sides: the whole.

P چار چشم *chār chashm*, Four-eyed (a dog or sheep); *i.e.* having a black spot over each eye. One who wears spectacles. A meeting, interview, eye to eye. Full of desire, anxious.

P چارحد *chār had*, East, west, north, south.

P چارخانه *chār khāna*, A large cauldron divided into four compartments. Checker-work. A kind of cloth. Any one who assumes more than his condition entitles him to.

P چارخايه *chār khāya*, (Four-testicled) Bold, brave, warlike. Addicted to women, potent in venery.

P چاردانگ *chār-dāng*, The four quarters of the globe.

P چاردوال *chār dawāl*, An ox-goad.

P چارده *chārdah*, Fourteen. The full moon.

P چاردهم *chārdahum*, Fourteenth. Full moon.

P چارديوار *chār dīwār*, Four walls. The four quarters of the world. چارديوار نفس *chār dīwāri nafs*, The body. The world.

P چارديواري *chār dīwārī*, A court-yard, area.

P چارزانو *chār zānū*, A tailor's mode of sitting.

P چارسال *chār sāl*, A space of four years. Four years old.

P چارسالگي *chār sālagī*, Space of four years.

P چارسو *chār-sū*, A square. A market-place. A cross-road, two roads crossing. Expectation.

P چارشاخ *chār shākh*, A pronged implement for winnowing grain.

P چارشانه *chār shāna*, A dwarf. Tough, hardy, fat, lusty.

P دو چارشدن *du chār shudan*, To meet another.

P چارشنبه *chār shambih*, Wednesday.

P چارضرب *chār zarb*, Sensible, shrewd (slave).

P چار ضرب زده *chār-zarb-zada*, One whose beard, mustachios, eyebrows, and eyelashes have been all cut clean away.

P چارطاق *chār tāk*, Four columns, *i. e.* a principal room on the top of Eastern houses, open in front and supported by four pillars. A kind of quadrangular tent. The elements.

P چارغ *chārugh*, A kind of rustic shoe.

P چارك *chārak*, A military commander, a general. The leader of a caravan.

P چارگامه *chār gāma*, An ambling nag. Tumultuous mirth.

P چارگوشه *chār-gosha*, Four-cornered. A throne. A bier.

P چارگوشي *chār goshī*, A four-handled ewer.

P چارگون *chār gūn*, Mace. A saddle-tree.

P چارم *chārum* or *chāram*, The fourth. چارم اصطرلاب *chārum usturlāb*, The sun. The fourth climate.

P چارمرچاره *chār marchāra*, An inn. A stage. Learned.

P چارمغز *chār maghz*, (Four-kernel) A walnut.

P چارم كتاب *chārum kitāb*, The fourth book, *i. e.* the Kur'an (the other three being the Pentateuch, Psalms and Gospels).

P چارميخ *chār mekh*, The rope upon which rope-dancers walk or tumble; also the poles by which it is stretched and supported. The wooden frame of saddles, or of pack-saddles. A cross, a gibbet. Sodomy. The four elements. چارميخ حيات *chār mekhi hayāt*, The four elements. چارميخ شدن *chār mekh shudan*, To stand bolt upright. چارميخ كردن *chār mekh kardan*, To stretch a cord for rope-dancers to dance upon. To crucify.

P چارمين *chārmīn* or *chārumīn*, Relating to four. One or four; fourth. خسرو سپهر چارمين *khusravi sipihri chārmīn*, The monarch of the fourth sphere, *i. e.* the sun.

P چارمين بام *chārmīn-bām*, Fourth heaven.

P چار نا چار *chār nā chār*, Inevitable. Of necessity, whether willing or not willing: nolens volens.

P چارو *chārū*, Plaster, mortar.

P چاروا *chārwā*, A quadruped.

P چاروادار *chārwā-dār*, One who lets out horses.

P چارو چدر *chār u chadar*, Remedy, treatment.

P چاروغ *chārūgh*, (or چاروق) A peasant's shoe.

P چاره *chāra*, Remedy, cure. Help, succour. Escape. A knavish trick, stratagem, scheme. Separation. Mode, mean, manner, method. Once. بي چاره *bī chāra*, Without remedy, incurable. Poor, miserable, destitute of help. چه چاره *chi chāra*, What remedy? what is to be done? how can it be cured? what mode is to be pursued? what would you have? چاره دادن *chāra dādan*, To apply a remedy, cure, repair, restore. كريم چاره ساز *karīmi chāra-sāz*, (God) the great Provider of remedies.

P چاره پرداز *chāra-pardāz*, One bringing or applying a remedy.

P چاره سازي *chāra-sāzī*, Application of a remedy.

P چاره كار *chāra-kār*, Applying remedies, a restorer. Aid, assistance. Means, manner.

P چاره گر *chāragar*, A knave, deceiver, cheat.

P چاره گري *chāragarī*, Remedy, cure. Roguery.

P چاره مر چاره *chāra mar chāra*, Treachery. Open, clear.

P چاريارى *chār yārī*, Name of a sect which venerates especially the four successors of Muhammad.

P چاريك *chār yak*, One of four, a fourth.

P چاز *chāz*, A frog, a paddock.

P چاش *chāsh*, A heap of winnowed corn. Lint-seed. A lunch.

P چاشت *chāsht*, (چاشتگاه *chāsht-gāh*, or چاشتگه *chāsht-gah*) The middle hour between sunrise and the meridian, at which time they generally eat what is by some called dinner, by others breakfast; also, what is then eaten, breakfast, early dinner, luncheon. A fourth of the day. چاشت دادن *chāsht dādan*, To give a breakfast.

P چاشدان *chāshdān*, A bread-basket.

P چاشكدان *chāshakdān*, A bread-basket. A lady's workbox.

P چاشني *chāshnī*, Taste. Relish. A taste by way of a sample. A specimen. Proof, trial. Quality. The first stroke or two on a drum. چاشنيء دل *chāshnīi dil*, Kind words. چاشني كردن *chāshnī kardan*, To assay (metals).

P چاشنيگير *chāshnī-gīr*, A taster to a prince, a sewer, cupbearer. A carver. (In India the term بكاول *bakāwul* is generally used.)

P چاغ *chāgh*, Time, season, an hour (or the twelfth part of every civil day). A spider.

P چاق *chāk*, Time. Health. Healthy, well.

P چاك *chāk*, A fissure, rupture, cleft, crack, rent. A bond or note of hand. Title-deeds. Day-break. The sound made by the blow of a sword. A loop-hole, fan-light. Ready, prepared. چاك كردن *chāk kardan*, To tear. چاك چاك كردن *chāk chāk kardan*, To tear in pieces. صد چاك *sad chāk*, Torn in a hundred pieces.

P چاكاچاك *chākāchāk*, Noise. Din of swords. Full of cracks, chinks, or clefts.

P چاكانيدن *chākānīdan*, To drop, distil.

P چاك پشت *chāk-pusht*, (A horse) high in the withers and rump, and depressed in the girth.

P چاك چاك *chāk chāk*, A clash of swords. Cleft.

P چاكر *chākar*, A servant: apprentice: maid.

P چاكران زمين *chākarān-zamīn*, Lands appropriated to the maintenance of public servants.

P چاكري *chākarī*, Servitude. Apprenticeship. چاكري كردن *chākarī kardan*, To serve, to do service.

P چاكسو *chāksū*, (or چاكشو *chākshū*) A small black shining grain mixed up with camphor into an ointment for the eyes.

P چاكو *chākū*, A clasp-knive, a penknife.

P چاكوچ *chākoch*, A mallet, hammer.

P چال *chāl*, Grizzled. A sorrel horse. A hole in which weavers put their feet. A hole wherein one may stand upright without being buried. A bird's nest. A wager, a stake at play. A bustard. A beautiful kind of partridge. Name of a certain water-fowl, a moorhen. Name of a town in the district of Kazwīn. چال كردن *chāl kardan*, To win, to carry off the stakes.

P چالاك *chālāk*, Ingenious. Vigilant. Quick, nimble, clever-handed. Active, smart, laborious, hard-working. Skittish. A lofty dwelling-place. A highwayman, a cut-throat.

P چالاكي *chālākī*, Alacrity, quickness, speed. Skittishness. Vigilance. Smartness, ingenuity.

P چالان *chālān*, Invoice, bill of lading. Transportation.

P چال پشت *chāl-pusht*, Swayed, hollow-backed.

P چالپوس *chālpos*, A flatterer. A muleteer.

P چالش *chālish*, Elegant gait, graceful motion. Stateliness. Coition. Manner, conduct. Battle.

P چالشگر *chālishgar*, A swinger. A warrior. Lecherous.

P چال قمار *chāl-kumār*, A stake, bet.

P چالو *chālū*, (or چاله *chāla*) A vault, a repository for grain, not more than two or three yards deep.

P چاليش *chālish*, A pompous, stately walk. War.

P چاليك *chālīk*, The game of tip-cat.

P چام *chām*, Bent, curved, twisted.

P چام چام *chām chām*, Tangled, intricate, mazy.

P چاموش *chāmosh*, A kind of shoe.

P چامه *chāma*, A poem not exceeding seventeen couplets. A word.

P چامهدان *chāmadān*, Eloquent. An orator.

P چامه گوي *chāma-goy*, Singer of odes. A poet.

P چاميدن *chāmīdan*, To make water. To blow.

P چامين *chāmīn*, Urine. Excrement.

P چانش *chānish*, A pompous walk. War.

P چانه *chāna*, The lower jaw-bone. The chin. Jaw, jabber, talk. A dropping, distilling. A lump of dough, enough to make a cake.

P چاو *chāw*, (In Tartar) Paper-money.

P چاو چاو *chāw chāw*, The chirping or noise of sparrows or other birds (especially when terrified for themselves or young by a hawk). The first relators of bad news.

P چاوچاوان *chāwchāwān*, Indirect, swerving.

P چاوش *chāwush*, A sergeant, a beadle.

P چاوك *chāwak*, A lark.

P چاوله *chāwala*, A hundred-leaved rose. Uneven, awry.

P چاولي *chāwlī*, A winnowing fan of reeds.

P چاووش *chāwūsh*, A chief, a leader.

T چاووش *chāwūsh*, A sergeant, a beadle; any officer that precedes a magistrate or great man; a herald, pursuivant, messenger. The head of a caravan.

P چاويد *chāwīd*, Chirping of sparrows.

P چاويدن *chāwīdan*, To chirp (as frightened sparrows). To cry aloud. To masticate, chew.

P چاه *chāh*, A well, pit. A dimple. چاه بابل *chāhi bābil*, The pit of Babel, *i.e.* of magicians; also the well where two fabulous angels, called Hārūt and Mārūt, are said to hang with their heads downwards. چاه پخته *chāhi pukhta*, A bricked well. چاه پست *chāhi past*, The world. چاه زنخ *chāhi zanakh*, The pit of the chin. چاه ظلماني *chāhi zulmānī*, (The dark pit) The world. The body. چاه نخشب *chāhi nakhshab*, Name of a well in Turkistān. The face of a mistress.

P چاهجو *chāh-jo*, An instrument for drawing out any thing fallen into a well.

P چاه دلو *chāh-dalv*, Aquarius. The world.

P چاهسار *chāh-sār*, A well's mouth.

P چاهك *chāhak*, A little well. A pit or dimple on the chin. چاهك ثريد *chāhaki sarīd*, A hollow in a pudding into which sauce is poured. چاهك گوش *chāhaki gosh*, The ear-hole.

P چاهكن *chāh-kan*, A digger of wells. An instrument for dragging a well.

P چاهه *chāha*, A deep ditch.

P چاهيدن *chāhīdan*, To feel cold. To chatter (as the teeth).

P چاهيوز *chāh-yūz*, An instrument for cleaning out a well. A grappling iron for drawing out any thing that has fallen into a well.

P چاي *chāy*, (equivalent to چا *chā*) Tea.

P چبتن *chabtan*, A purse.

P چبغت *chabghut*, (or چبغوت *chabghūt*) A bed. A couch. A pillow, cushion. Old faded tapestry or hangings; worn-out clothes. Quilting.

P چبلوس *chablos*, A flatterer, wheedler, deceiver.

P چبيره *chabīra*, Ready, prepared. Assembled. An assembly, congregation, meeting.

P چبّين *chabbīn* or *chubbīn*, A bread-basket.

P چپ *chap*, The left side. Discordant, inharmonious. دست چپ *dasti chap*, The left hand. چپ دادن *chap dādan*, To sew on a patch. To deceive, betray, forsake. چپ شدن *chap shudan*, To rebel, decline, turn away. چپ و راست *chap u rāst*, (lit. Left and right) Unsteadiness, carelessness, want of principle.

P چپا *chapā*, The left side. Leftward.

P چپات *chapāt*, (or چپّات) A slap on the face.

P چپاتي *chapātī*, A thin cake: a fritter.

P چپار *chapār*, Spotted, speckled, mottled.

P چپاغ *cha* or *chipāgh*, A shad, sheath, thunny.

P چپان *chapān*, (or *chuppān*) Tattered garments.

P چپ انداز *chap-andāz*, Fraud, stratagem.

P چپاني *chapānī*, (or *chappānī*) A knave. Clad in rags.

P چپانيدن *chapānīdan*, To squeeze, compress.

P چپاول *chapāwal*, An attack, a charge.

P چپچاپ *chapchāp*, A smacking kiss.

P چپچله *chapchala*, Clayey, slippery ground. A boy's slide down a slope. A swing.

P چپدار *chipdār*, (or چپدان) A boot-stocking.

P چپ دست *chap-dust*, Left-handed.

P چپر *chapar*, A circle, ring. A thong put under a seam to strengthen it. A palisade. A wooden hut.

P چپ رو *chap-rav*, Going to the left.

P چپسيدن *chapsīdan*, To adhere, stick together.

P چپسيده شدن *chapsīda shudan*, To adhere.

P چپسين *chapsīn*, Plaster, mortar.

P چپش *chapish*, A yearling kid.

P چپكن *chap-kan*, A sort of short coat.

P چپل *chapal*, Filthy, nasty, disgusting.

P چپلان *chaplān*, Hose worn over boots.

P چپلاهنگ *chaplāhang*, Bark and seed of the purging root turpethum. A lopped branch of a tree.

P چپلك *chiplak*, Indecent: defiled, polluted.

P چپلوس *chaplos*, A flatterer.

P چپله *chapla*, A blow, a box on the ear.

P چپو *chapū*, Plunder, pillage, sack.

P چپه *chapa*, A sagacious dog. An oar.

P چپّه *chappa*, (or چپّه دست) Left-handed.

P چپيدن *chapīdan*, To lean to the left side. To turn completely over.

P چپّين *chuppīn*, A wicker bread-basket.

P چتر *chatr*, An umbrella, parasol. A tent. A tuft of hair on the crown of the head. چتر آبگون *chatri āb-gūn*, (or مينا *mīnā*) The firmament. چتر روز *chatri roz*, (زرين *zarīn*, سحر *sahar*, or نور *nūr*) The sun. چتر سماوي *chatri samāwī*, (سيمابي *sīmābī* or سيمين *sīmīn*) The full moon. چتر عنبرين *chatri ʻambarīn*, Night. چتر كحلي *chatri kuhlī*, The sky. A dark cloud. چترمار *chatri mār*, A toad-stool. چترزدن *chatr zadan*, To walk on the hands with the feet in the air.

P چترمان *chatrmān*, A governor, basha.

P چتلاقوج *chatlākūj*, A certain fruit called بن *ban* or حبّة الخضراء *habbatu'l khazrā*.

P چتو *chatū*, A veil, a covering.

P چتوك *chutūk*, A sparrow.

P چچ *chuch*, (or چج *chaj*) A kind of sieve. A pronged instrument for winnowing corn.

P چچك *chachak*, A rose. *Chachak* or *chuchuk*, A lovely cheek. A mole, a spot.

P چچله *chachala*, A slippery place. A boy's slide. *Chuchula*, Lingula.

P چچو *chuchū*, A nipple.

P چخ *chakh*, Labour, attention, active exertion. War, enmity, opposition; a flying in the face of any body. A scabbard. Dross, filth.

P چخاچخ *chakhāchakh*, Clash of swords. Strife.

P چخاچخي *chakhāchakhī*, Wrangle, dispute.

P چخان *chakhān*, Squabbling. Striving.

P چخش *chakhsh*, A swelling in the throat giving no pain, a goitre.

P چخك *chakhak*, A mole, freckle. The cheek.

P چخماخ *chakhmākh*, A little bag in which soldiers carry their comb, needles, &c. A fire-steel or tinder-box. A battle-axe fastened to the saddle.

P چخماغ *chakhmāgh*, A fire-flint.

P چخيدن *chakhīdan*, To strive, endeavour. To contend, quarrel. To breathe.

P چخيده *chakhīda*, Stricken.

P چخين *cha* or *chikhīn*, Filthy, mattery, purulent.

P چدار *chidār*, Cord or silk fetters for horses.

P چدر *chadr*, A four-year old she-camel. *Chadar*, Remedy, cure. A sheet: a table-cloth: a veil.

P چدروا *chudurwā*, The aloes-plant.

P چدن *chidan*, (for چيدن) To collect, gather.

P چده *chida*, Gathered.

P چر *char*, A song. Music. *Chur*, The organ of generation.

P چرا *charā*, Pasturing, grazing. چرا كردن *charā kardan*, To pasture. *Chirā*, Why? Wherefore?

P چرابه *charāba*, Cream.

P چراجا *charā-jā*, A field for grazing.

P چراخ *charākh*, (equiv. to چراغ) A lamp.

P چراخوار *charā-khwār*, A meadow for grazing.

P چراخواره *chirākh-wāra*, A candlestick.

P چراخور *charā-khwur*, A meadow. A pasture. (An animal) grazing.

P چرازار *charāzār*, Grazing ground.

P چراسك *charāsak*, A noisy grasshopper: the corn-cricket.

P چراسيا *charāsyā*, A cherry.

P چراغ *chāragh* or *chirāgh*, A lamp. Light.

The wick of a candle. A horse's rearing. A pasture. A guide, director. A client, dependant. چراغ آسمان charāghi āsmān, (Lamp of heaven, or جهان jahān, Of the world) The sun. Moonlight. چراغ چشم charāghichashm, (Light of the eye) Offspring. چراغ سپهر charāghi sipihr, Sun, moon, and stars. چراغ سحر charāghi sahar, The sun. The morning-star. چراغ شدن charāgh shudan, To shine, be bright. To become a client. چراغ عالم افروز charāghi ʿālam-afroz, A lamp illuminating the world, i.e. A thing known to all. چراغ کشتن charāgh kushtan, To extinguish a candle. چراغ مغان chirāghi mughān, Wine.

P چراغ آخر charāgh-ākhur, Affluence, plenty.

P چراغان charāghān, Lamps: an illumination.

P چراغبانه charāgh-bāna, A lamp-stand: a candlestick.

P چراغ بره charāgh-bara, A lamp. A stand or vessel for a lamp. A horse rearing.

P چراغپا charāgh-pā, (or پایه pāya) Foot of a lamp. Portable lamp. Candlestick. A horse rearing.

P چراغ پره charāgh-para, A candle-moth.

P چراغ پرهیز charāgh-parhez, A lantern, a screen to a candle from the wind.

P T چراغچي charāghchī, A lamp-lighter.

P چراغدان charāghdān, A stand for a lamp.

P چراغك chirāghak, A little lamp: glow-worm.

P چراغكش charāgh-kush, Engaged in any shameful work that shuns the light.

P چراغ كشاني charāgh-kushānī, A dark deed.

P چراغله chirāghla, A glow-worm.

P چراغنده charāghanda, A lamp-stand.

P چراغواره charāgh-wāra, A lamp-stand. A screen to preserve a candle from the wind.

P چراغ واسه charāgh-wāsa, A moth flying round a candle.

P چراغوره charāgh-wara, A candlestick. A horse rearing. A moth flying round the candle.

P چراغي charāghī, Land bestowed for the lighting up of a Muhammadan mosque or tomb. A present made to a Mulla for offering up oblations at the tomb of a saint. Alms given to beggars who walk the street at night, as the class called Nakshbandi. A present to soothsayers.

P چراكه chirāki, Because that.

P چراگاه charā-gāh, (or گه gah) A pasture.

P چراگر charāgar, A grazer. Alone, single.

P چرام charām, (or چرامين charāmīn) A meadow, pasture, field for grazing. Forage.

P چرامانذن charāmāndan, To allow to graze.

P چران charān, (A beast) grazing. Grazers.

P چراندن charāndan, To graze.

P چرانده charānda, A shepherd.

P چرانيدن charānīdan, To cause to graze, lead to pasture.

P چرايندة charāyinda, Grazing. A grazier.

P چرائي charāʼī, Price paid for pasturage, agistment. Chirāʼī, Wherefore art thou?

P چرايدن charāyidan, Pasturing. A pasture.

P چرب charb, Fat, greasy. Viscous, glutinous. Thick, grumous. Smooth. Corpulent. Conquering, overcoming. Prevailing. A kind of water. چرب كردن charb kardan, To anoint, rub, make supple and sleek.

P چرب آخور charb-ākhwur, A full cratch.

P چرب بلا charb-bālā, Tall, handsome.

P چرب پهلو charb-pahlū, Fat. A man from whom one gains profit and advantage.

P چربتر charbtar, Better, preponderating.

P چرب دست charb-dast, One who has a nice hand at work; expert, dexterous: wise, intelligent.

P چرب دستي charb-dastī, Manual dexterity.

P چربرود charb-rūd, Fat upon the entrails.

P چرب زبان charb-zabān or چرب گو charb-go, One who has a smooth tongue to persuade, wheedle, or deceive, glib-tongued. Agreeable, conversable, entertaining. Eloquent.

P چرب زباني charb-zabānī, Persuasion, flattery.

P چرب سخني charb-sukhanī, Coaxing, flattery.

P چربش charbish, Fat, fat of broth. A neigh.

P چربش دار charbish-dār, Fat, greasy.

P چربش گرفتگي charbish-giriftagī, Greasiness.

P چربش گرفته charbish-girifta, Fat, greasy.

P چرب شيرين charb-shīrīn, Savoury food.

P چرب غذا charb-ghizā, Dainties, viands.

P چرب قامت charb-ḳāmat, Tall and elegant.

P چربك charbak, A thin cake or wafer fried in oil and given away at funeral obsequies. Cream. Thin paper for tracing drawings. Churbak, A plausible lie. Slander, evil surmise. Sarcasm, cutting irony. Jesting. Buffoonery. Shame. An enigma.

P چربناك charbnāk, Rich (milk).

P چربنزار charb-nizār, Fat and lean (meat).

P چربو charbū, Fat. Fatness. Glue. Starch.

P چرب وخشك charb u khushk, Good and bad. More or less. Liberality and avarice. Liberal and churlish.

P چربه charba, Thin paper used for tracing writing or drawing. Fatness. Cream. A spinning-wheel. A lathe.

P چربي charbī, Fat, grease: suet. Mildness, softness. Rectitude. Facility, ease: success, prosperity.

P چربي دار charbī-dār, Fat, sleek, or pursy.

P چربيدن charbīdan, To prevail, be victorious. To dip, preponderate (as a scale). To abound.

P چرته charta, (or چرده charda) Colour, hue.

P چرخ charkh, The celestial globe, sphere. Fortune. Circular motion. Every thing revolving in an orbit, as a wheel, wheeled carriage, pulley, watch-wheel, mill-wheel, water-wheel, spinning-wheel, turner's, cutler's, or other artificer's wheel. A wine-press. A reel. The circular dance of the Muhammadan dervishes. Cupola, dome. A cart. A cross-bow. A bow in a very tense state. A machine for separating cotton from the seed. Collar of a garment. A shirt. A white falcon. Name of a city in Khurāsān. چرخ آبكشي charkhi āb-kashī, A pulley for drawing water. چرخ اثير charkhi asīr, The ethereal sphere, or that of the moon. (Synonymous to which are اخضر akhzar, Green, ترسا جامه tarsā-jāma, Christian's garb, صوفي لباس sūfī-libās, Sūfīs dress, گندنا گون gandanā-gūn, Leek-colour.) چرخ اطلس charkhi atlas, The crystalline sphere (where the Muhammadans imagine the throne of God is fixed). (Also, اكبر akbar, Greatest, برين barīn, Uppermost, نهم nuhum, Ninth.) چرخ چنبري charkhi chamburī, (دولابي dolābī, and مدوّر mudawwar) Celestial sphere. چرخ دوّار charkhi dawwār, Revolving heaven. Changeable fortune. چرخ زرين كاسه charkhi zarīn-kāsa, Fourth heaven, i.e. solar sphere. چرخ سنگ دل charkhi sang-dil, First and fourth sphere, i.e. those of the moon and the sun. چرخ غلّه charkhi ghalla, A corn-cart. چرخ فلك charkhi falak, The passion-flower. چرخ كبود charkhi kabūd, (or مينا mīnā) Azure sky. چرخ كينه ساز charkhi kīna-sāz (ستمكار sitam-kār or غدّار ghaddār) Fortune, preparing misfortune, i.e. unhappy fate. چرخ مقوّس charkhi mukawwas, The celestial orb. The Zodiac.

P چرخ انداز charkh-andāz, Archer, bowman.

P چرخ ريسك charkh rīsak, Name of a noisy chirping insect; also of a bird.

P چرخ زن charkh-zan, A spinner. A dancer. A traveller.

P چرخ ساز charkh-sāz, Moving in, or forming a circle. Circular.

P چرخست charkhust or charkhast, A wine-press.

P چرخشت charkhusht, Wine, oil, or other press.

P چرخله charkhala, Succory; also its flower. A thistle.

P چرخوك charkhūk, A spinning-top.

P چرخه charkhā, A wheel of any kind. A reel. The axis of a pulley. An Arabian thorn or thistle. A nag, jade. چرخه زدن charkha zadan, To spin.

P چرخه تير charkha-tīr, An axle-tree.

P چرخه زن charkha-zan, A spinner.

P چرخي charkhī, Spherical. Celestial. Voluble. A kind of fire-works, catharine-wheel. A dumb-waiter. A pulley. Soaring in a circle. A machine for separating cotton from the seed. A silken vest. Satin. A privy.

P چرد chard, A sill. Charad, A bay colour.

P چرّد charrud, A fray, broil, battle.

P چرده charda, A bay horse. A blackish locust. Skin. When added to nouns of colour, it denotes an approach to the tint which such noun expresses: as, سياه چرده siyāh-charda, Blackish, tending to black. زرد چرده zard-charda, Yellowish, of a straw-colour, somewhat yellow.

P چرز charz, A bustard. A bird of game, whose flesh is delicate and tender. A lark.

P چرزه *charza*, Skin of the face or body.

P چرس *charas*, A prison. Confinement. Pain. The rack. A vat in which they press out the juice of grapes by treading. A field for pasture. Alms.

P چرست *charist*, Gnashing of teeth. Weakness.

P چرستیدن *charas* or *chiristīdan*, To gnash.

P چرس دان *charasdān*, A mendicant's scrip.

P چرش *charish*, Pasture. Taste, flavour.

P چرغ *chargh*, A bird of the hawk kind.

P چرغان *charghān*, A seal for public deeds, a royal signature.

P چرغند *charghand*, (or چرغنده *charghanda*) Sheep's guts filled with meat. The standish of a lamp.

P چرغنو *charghanū*, A wine-vessel. A musical instrument.

P چرغول *charghūl*, (or چرغون) Lamb's tongue.

P چرك *chark*, A bird which hangs by its claws and chirps during the night. *Chirk*, Dirt, filth. Matter. Spittle. چرك آهن *chirki āhan*, Dross of iron. چرك گوش *chirki gosh*, Ear-wax. *Charak*, A wound, sore.

P چركاب *chirk-āb*, Dirty water. Hogwash.

P چرك آلود *chirk-ālūd*, Filthy, dirty, squalid.

P چركس *charkas* or *chirkas*, A Circassian.

P چركمك *charkamak*, Name of a small bird.

P چركن *chirkin*, A running sore. Temporal goods. Nasty, dirty.

P چرك ناك *chirknāk*, Dirty, filthy.

P چرك ناكی *chirknākī*, Dirtiness, nastiness.

P چركين *chirkīn*, Nasty, filthy, slovenly. Sordid. Rusty, mouldy. Deformed, ugly, unsightly. Dung. چركين شدن *chirkīn shudan*, To be dirty, base, disfigured.

P چركيني *chirkīnī*, Dirtiness, nastiness.

P چرگر *chargar*, A musician. A singer. *Churgar*, A muftī. A priest presiding at prayer. A prophet.

P چرگه *chargah*, An immense ring made by huntsmen, converging inwards.

P چرم *charm*, Leather; skin, hide. Cow-leather, for making sandals, or soles of shoes and slippers. Coarse camel-leather. چرم شير *charmi sher*, A thong, a lash. چرم گاو *charmi gāv*, A thong, lash, scourge. *Charam*, Name of a place.

P چرمدان *charmdān*, A leathern purse or bag.

P چرمساز *charm-sāz*, Worker in leather, currier.

P چرمك *charmak*, The ball on a spindle. *Churmak*, A riddle.

P چرمگر *charmgar*, A leather-dresser, currier.

P چرم گور *charm-gūr*, A bow-string.

P چرمه *charma*, A horse. A white or grey horse. Hire of infamous boys. Leathern. A dildo.

P چرمه پولاد *charma-pūlād*, Iron-grey horse.

P چرمينه *charmīna*, Leathern. A dildo.

P چرمينه دوز *charmīna-doz*, A shoemaker.

P چرمينه فروش *charmīna-farosh*, Shoe-vender.

P چرند *charand*, Grazing. A quadruped. چرند و پرند *charand u parand*, (Grazer and flier) Beasts and birds.

P چرند آب *charand-āb*, A place in Tabrīz.

P چرندو *charandū*, Gristle. Grazing.

P چرنده *charanda*, A grazer, grazing animal. A reptile, or whatever creeps on its belly. Gristle.

P چرنگ *chiring*, The jingling or tinkling of bells. The clash of swords. Echo.

P چرنگك *charangak*, Name of a small bird.

P چرنگيدن *chiringīdan*, To jingle, tinkle, rattle.

P چروش *charwish*, Fat seen under the skin.

P چروك *charūk*, Bread. Crumbs of bread left in a wallet. *Charūk* or *charwak*, Crumbled bread. *Churūk*, A ply, fold.

P چرون *charūn*, The old name of Ormuz.

P چروند *charwand*, (or چرونده *charwanda*) A sort of lantern or case for a lamp: a lamp-stand.

P چرونده *charwanda*, Running. Going. Imploring help.

P چرويدن *charwīdan*, To seek help. To go.

P چرويده *charwīda*, Seeking aid. Running.

P چره *chura*, A beardless youth.

P چريدن *charīdan*, To graze, pasture.

P چريدني *charīdanī*, Fit for grazing, grazeable.

P چريك *charīk*, Auxiliary forces. A man sent to a zamīndār to supply forage for an army. Origin, beginning.

P چرينه *charīna*, Ventricle of a ruminant, tripe.

P چز *chaz*, An ape.

P چزد *chazd*, A noisy insect resembling a locust, abounding in hot weather, and which the poor sometimes eat. A hiss.

P چزدره *chazdara*, (or چزده *chazda*) Bits of fat or fried sheeps' tails.

P چزغ *chizgh*, A porcupine. A hedgehog.

P چزك *chizak*, A porcupine. A hedgehog.

T چزمه *chizma*, A boot, the outer part or lining.

P چزور *chizwar*, The scum of melted fat.

P چژك *chijak*, A hedgehog.

P چس *chus*, Wind that escapes without noise.

P چسان *chi sān*, How? In what manner?

P چسپان *chaspān*, Coherent, attached. Addicted. Viscous, adhesive. Meet, suitable. A kind of upper garment.

P چسپاندن *chaspāndan*, (or چسپانيدن *chaspānīdan*) To fasten, glue, fix, cause to stick.

P چسپانده *chaspānda*, Pasted or glued together.

P چسپاني *chaspānī*, Adhesiveness, viscosity.

P چسپندگي *chaspindagī*, Adhesiveness.

P چسپنده *chaspinda*, Adhesive. A snail.

P چسپيدگي *chaspīdagī*, Adhesion, attachment.

P چسپيدن *chaspīdan*, To adhere, stick. To incline, have a propensity to unite. To be affixed to the ground. To be dwarfish. To grasp any thing firmly in the hand.

P چسپيده *chaspīda*, Joined, glued, cemented, attached. Inclined, addicted to, fond of, liking.

P چست *chust*, Quick, brisk, active, fleet. Fit, suiting. Narrow, tight. Strong. Elegant, beautiful. Accumulation, a heaping up. A kind of laced shoe.

P چستا *chastā*, Tripe. The straight gut, rectum. *Chustā*, Tight, sitting well (as clothes).

P چستان *chistān*, An enigma, riddle.

P چست چالاك *chust chālāk*, Active, alert.

P چستن *chustan*, To be accumulated, heaped.

P چسته *chasta*, Harmony, harmonious sound. The skin of a horse's fundament. *Chusta*, The ventricle of a kid, rennet.

P چستي *chustī*, Agility, alertness, activity, velocity, fleetness. Narrowness.

P چسم *chasm*, Meaning, signification.

P چسنگ *chasang*, One who is without hair, and is marked with wounds and scars. A mark on the forehead.

P چش *chash*, Taste thou. (in comp.) Tasting, partaking of the flavour: as, نمكچش *namak-chash*, Salted. (for چشم *chashm*) The eye. *Chush*, A word used for making (an ass) stand still.

P چش است *chi'sh ast*, What ails him?

P چشام *chashām*, Eye-salve from a black grain.

P چشان *chashān*, A mace of iron, silver, or gold. A passage.

P چشانيدن *chashānīdan*, To cause to taste.

P چشپر *chashpar*, The track of a wild beast.

P چشت *chisht*, Name of a place.

P چشته *chashta*, A taste, whet. Breakfast.

P چشخام *chashkhām*, A remedy for sore eyes.

P چش زخ *chash-zakh*, (An abbreviation of چشم زخم *chashm-zakhm*) A misfortune attributed to witchcraft or an evil eye.

P چشش *chashish*, Taste, a tasting. A frog.

P چشفر *chashfar*, The track of wild beasts.

P چشك *chishk*, Overflowing. Prevailing over.

P چشگر *chashgar*, A taster. Frumenty.

P چشم *chashm*, The eye. Hope. An amulet or charm (particularly of holy writ) against fascination or enchantment. The individual himself (as عين *ʿayn* in Arabic). *Chashm* or *chashum*, An eye-salve composed from a black seed pulverized. چشمرا آب داد *chashmrā āb dād*, He gave his eyes water, *i.e.* He looked at an amusing sight. چشم آغليدن *chashm āghilīdan*, To dart a side-glance. چشم انداز شدن *chashm-andāz shudan*, To disregard, overlook, be unmindful of. چشم بد *chashmi bad*, An evil eye. چشم بد دور *chashmi bad dūr*, Avaunt malicious glances! چشم براه *chashm ba rāh*, Expectation. چشم براه داشتن *chashm bar rāh dāshtan*, To be looking out for, to be impatient for. چشم برزمين افگندن *chashm bar zamin afgandan*, To cast the eyes on the ground. To blush, To worship. چشم برهم زدن *chashm bar ham zadun*, To wink the eyes. چشم بلبل *chashmi bulbul*, Name of a certain stuff. چشم بي آب *chashmi bī āb*, Shamelessness, effrontery. چشم بيمار *chashmi bīmār*, An eye that looks half-closed (from modesty; an epithet of beauty). چشمش پريد chashmash parīd, His eyes twinkled or winked. چشم پشت chashmi pusht, The anus. چشم پيش گرفتن chashm pesh giriftan, To veil the eyes. To blush. چشم خروس chashmi khuros, (Cock's eye) an herb. Wine. چشم خون آلود chashmi khūn-ālūd, Eyes tinged with blood, fiery eyes, or murderous looks. چشم داشتن chashm dāshtan, To hope. To expect. چشم روز chashmi roz, The sun. چشم رسيدن chashm rasīdan, To be affected by an evil eye, bewitched. چشم روشن شدن chashm-roshan shudan, To be rejoiced. چشم زانو chashmi zānū, The knee-pan. چشم زدن chashm zadan, To make a signal with the eye. To be awake. To fear. To muse, to cogitate. To blush. The twinkling of an eye. چشم زني كردن chashm-zanī kardan, To impede, obstruct, confine. چشم سماعيل chashmi samāʻīl, A rolling eye. چشم سوزن chashmi sozan, The eye of a needle. Narrowness. چشم سياه كردن chashm siyāh kardan, To covet, hanker after. چشم سيل زن chashmi sayl-zan, A tear-shedding eye. چشم شب chashmi shab, The moon and stars. چشم شب پيماي chashmi shab-paymāy, An eye measuring the night-watches. چشم شدن chashm shudan, To become plain, open, manifest. چشم غزال chashmi ghazāl, A bumper of wine. چشم فرنگي chashmi firingī, (European eyes) Spectacles. چشم كردن chashm (or بچشم ba chashm) kardan, To wound with malignant eyes. To wink. چشم گاو chashmi gāv, Ox-eye (a plant). چشم گاوانه chashmi gāvāna, A large open eye. چشم گرم كردن chashm garm kardan, To take little sleep. چشم نمودن chashm namūdan, To reprove, reprehend. چشم و گوش شدن chashm u gosh shudan, To be all eye and ear, to give strict attention to. آهو چشم āhū-chashm, Having the eyes of a fawn or gazel; gentle, soft-eyed. *Chashum*, A medicine for weak or sore eyes.

P چشم آرو chashm-āro, A remedy or charm against sore eyes, witchcraft, or the accidents called چشم زخم chashm-zakhm.

P چشم آغل chashm-āghil, (آغول āghūl or آغيل āghīl) A glance from the corners of the eyes.

P چشم آلوس chashm-ālūs, Looking askance.

P چشم آور chashm-āwar, An amulet (suspended in gardens to preserve the fruit from malignant eyes). A wall-eyed horse.

P چشم آويز chashm-āwez, A kind of net-work made of horse-hair, worn by women as a veil. A fly-net put over a horse's head.

P چشم بند chashm-band, Fascination of eyes. A woman's veil (of fine black). A lady's slipper.

P چشم بندك chashm-bandak, Blind-man's buff. Hide and seek.

P چشم بوس chashm-bos, Kissing the eye (a friendly salute and nearly synonymous with دست بوس dast-bos, Kissing the hand).

P چشم بينا chashm-bīnā, Quick-sighted: acute.

P چشم پنام chashm-panām, An amulet worn against witchcraft, or چشم زخم chashm-zakhm. A sword-belt worn obliquely over the shoulder.

P چشم پوش chashm-posh, A winker, conniver.

P چشم پوشي chashm-poshī, A turning away of the eyes; the affecting not to see or hear (a petitioner). Connivance. چشم پوشي نمودن chashm-poshī namūdan, To connive, to wink at.

P چشم پيش chashm-pesh, Modest, bashful.

P چشم تر chashm-tar, Moist-eyed. A weeper.

P چشم چيدن chashm-chīdan, A charm for malignant eyes.

P چشم خانه chashm-khāna, Socket of the eye.

P چشم داشت chashm-dāsht, Hope, trust: desire.

P چشم دانه chashm-dāna, A certain grain used as an eye-salve.

P چشم دريده chashm-darīda, Impudent.

P چشم رسانده chashm rasānanda, One who strikes with a malignant eye.

P چشم رسيده chashm-rasīda, Viewed with a malignant eye, bewitched.

P چشم زاغ chashm-zāgh, Blue-eyed. Shameless.

P چشم زال chashm-zāl, Just, equitable.

P چشم زخم chashm-zakhm, A fatal misfortune in consequence of witchcraft.

P چشم زد chashm-zad, An amulet of glass beads to counteract the influence of malignant eyes.

P چشم زده chashm-zada, Struck, or hurt by a malignant eye. Balked, disappointed.

P چشم زن chashm-zan, A small black grain good for sore eyes.

P چشم سار chashm-sār, A fountain-head.

P چشم فسا chashm-fisā, (or چشم فساي chashm-fisāy) One who pretends to stop the effects of witchcraft (or چشم زخم chashm-zakhm) by counter-spells.

P چشمك chashmak, A small eye. A peep-hole. Spectacles. A wink. A black shining grain made up into an eye-salve. Hire. Dog's tooth (an herb). A shoe. چشمك زدن chashmak zadan, To wink, make a sign with the eye.

P چشم كردگي chashm-kardagī, Witchcraft.

P چشم كرده chashm-karda, Fascinated, wounded by a malignant eye.

P چشمك زن chashmak-zan, Winking. A wink, leer, side-glance.

P چشم گشته chashm-gashta, Squint-eyed.

P چشملان chashmalān, The eye-ball, or pupil. Black grain used as a remedy for weak eyes.

P چشم نرم chāshm-narm, A beardless boy of a family in easy circumstances.

P چشم نمائي chashm-namāʼī, Reproof.

P چشم و چراغ chashm u chirāgh, Beloved.

P چشم وهام chashm-wahām, (or چشم وهم chashm-wahm) An amulet worn against the effect of witchcraft or چشم زخم chashm-zakhm.

P چشمه chashma, A fountain, source, spring. The sun. Spectacles. Eye of a needle. سر چشمه sari chashma, A source, a spring-head. سر چشمهٔ حيوان sari chashmaʼi ḥaywān, Head of the fountain of life. چشمهٔ اخضر chashmaʼi akhzar, Fountain of immortality. Mouth of a mistress. Wine. چشمهٔ آتش chashmaʼi ātish, Fire of a smithy. The sun. چشمهٔ تدبير chashmaʼi tadbīr, The brain. A thinking mind. A prudent man. چشمهٔ ترازو chashmaʼi tarāzū, The eye in which the tongue of the scales plays. چشمهٔ تيغ chashmaʼi tegh, Lustre of a cimeter. چشمهٔ حيوان chashmaʼi ḥaywān, Fountain of life. چشمهٔ خاوري chashmaʼi khāwarī, (or خور khwur) The sun. چشمهٔ خضر chashmaʼi khizar, The fountain of life. The lip of a mistress. چشمهٔ خون chashmaʼi khūn, The heart. چشمه درماهي chashma dar māhī, The sun in Pisces. چشمهٔ روشن chashmaʼi roshan, The sun. چشمهٔ سار chashmaʼi sār, Name of a fountain in Kohistān. چشمهٔ سيماب chashmaʼi sīmāb, The sun. The moon. Day. چشمهٔ ظلمات chashmaʼi zulumāt, Fountain of darkness. چشمهٔ قيرگون chashmaʼi kīr-gūn, A night dark as pitch. چشمهٔ گرم chashmaʼi garm, The sun. چشمهٔ گلسب chashmaʼi gulasb, Name of a fountain in Khurāsān. چشمهٔ منفجر chashmaʼi munfajir, Name of one of the lunar mansions. چشمهٔ نور بخش chashmaʼi nūr-bakhsh, The sun. The water of immortality. The mouth of a mistress. چشمهٔ نوش chashmaʼi nosh, Fountain of life. Mouth of a mistress. چشمهٔ هفت اختر chashmaʼi haft akhtar, The Pleiades. چشمهٔ هور chashmaʼi hor, The sun.

P چشمها chashmhā, (pl. of چشم chashm) Eyes. چشمهاي پرده chashmhāʼi parda, Holes and chinks.

P چشمه سار chashma-sār, Abounding in springs; a fountain.

P چشميزك chashmīzak, A black shining grain resembling a pippin, with which, when pulverized, they anoint the eyes.

P چشنده chashanda, A taster. چشندهٔ شيرين و تلخي chashandaʼi shīrīn u talkhī, A taster of sweet and bitter.

P چشني chashnī, Taste, savour: trial, essay.

P چشيدن chashīdan, To taste: to experience.

P چشيدني chashīdanī, Fit to be tasted. A taste. نچشيدم چشيدني na chashīdam chashīdanī, I have not tasted a taste.

P چشيده chashīda, Tasted. Who has tasted.

P چشيره chashīra, A kind of frumenty.

P چشيشه chashīsha, White, grey.

P چشينه chashīna, White, grey.

P چطور chi-tawr, How? in what manner?

H چطه chitta, A rough daily account.

P چغ chagh, A spider. A churn-staff. A spinning-wheel. *Chigh*, A sort of screen made of split bamboo, used as blinds. *Chugh*, A yoke. A draught-ox. Ebony.

P چغاز chaghāz, A brawling, abusive woman.

P چغاله chaghāla, Unripe fruit.

P چغامه *chaghāma*, Poetry. A poem, an ode.

P چغان *chaghān*, An instrument for preparing cotton. Name of a note in music. Striving to the utmost. Industrious, diligent. Name of a city.

P چغانه *chaghāna*, Name of a note in music. A kind of staff like a sceptre, to which are fixed sundry little bells, which, by motion, make a kind of music, and are generally used as an accompaniment to other instruments. A poem. Active, industrious. Name of a water-plant.

P چغانيان *chaghāniyān*, A part of Samarkand.

P چغبت *chaghbut*,(or چغبوت *chaghbūt*) Wadding of cotton or the like for quilting or stuffing cushions. Stuffed with cotton or wool.

P چغبلغ *chaghbulugh*, Moan, cries of sorrow.

P چغتاي *chaghtāy*, Name of a Turkish nation.

P چغد *chughd*, An owl. A knot of hair tied on the back of the head. A niched battlement. *Chaghad*, A falcon's roost.

P چغداول *chaghdāwal*, (چغدل *chaghdul*, also چغدول *chaghdūl*) Rear of an army, camp-followers.

P چغر *chaghr*, A turning towards. Honour, respectful attention. Inquiry. Fear. A looking behind. *Chughr*, A frog.

P چغرشته *chaghrishta*, An oval ball of thread.

P چغرنده *chaghranda*, A fearer: timorous, timid.

P چغريدن *chaghrīdan*, To fear, suspect. To turn towards.

P چغريده *chaghrīda*, Affrighted. Feared, suspected. Honoured, esteemed.

P چغز *chaghz*, A frog. The croak of a frog. A wound whose lips being closed the foul matter is confined within it. A groan. Fear. *Chaghaz*, A very white grass growing in a tuft like a broom.

P چغزابه *chaghz-āba*, A frog. Water-moss.

P چغزانيدن *chaghzānīdan*, To croak (as a frog).

P چغز پاره *chaghz-pāra*, (*chaghaz-pāra*, or چغزواره *chaghz-wāra*, or چغزلاوه *chaghz-lāwa*). Green filth or scum floating on stagnant water.

P چغزيدن *chaghzīdan*, To fear. To suspect. To honour. To lament, to groan.

P چغك *chughuk*, A sparrow.

P چغل *chaghal*, A plait, fold, wrinkle. A leathern vessel having a spout, whence they pour water in making ablutions. *Chughal*, A coat of mail. *Chughul*, An informer.

P چغل خور *chughul-khwur*, Tale-bearer, backbiter, calumniator, slanderer.

P چغل خوري *chughul-khwurī*, Back-biting.

P چغلي *chughulī*, Tale-bearing, back-biting.

P چغمونستن *chaghmūnistan*, (in zand and Pāz.) To stand.

P چغنت *chaghnat*, (or چغنست) Wadding.

P چغند *chaghand* or *chughand*, Hair tied in a knot at the back of the head.

P چغندر *chughundur*, Rape. Beet.

P چغنه *chaghna*, A note in music. *Chughna*, A sparrow. *Chaghana*, A musical instrument.

P چغو *chughū*, An owl. A sparrow.

P چغواره *chagh-wāra*, Water-moss. A frog.

P چغوك *chughūk*, A sparrow. A water-bird.

P چغيدن *chaghīdan*, To seek, try, aspire to.

P چفاله *chafāla*, A flight of birds.

P چفت *chaft*, A saloon built of wood and supported on columns. A prop, a trellis. چفت فلك *chafti falak*, The celestial vault. *Chift*, The chain of a door. *Chuft*, Narrow. A tight garment. A beam placed to shore up a building.

P چفتك *chuf* or *chaftak*, A kind of crane.

P چفتن *chaftan*, To understand.

P چفته *chafta*, A sheep's head. A prop for a vine. A bat. A vaulted roof. Curved, bent. Injurious suspicion, malignant imputation. An equal, peer.

P چفده *chafda*, Bent, curved. A bunch of grapes. A sheep's head. Suspicion.

P چفرسته *chafrasta*, Tongs. *Chafrusta*, A reed used by weavers to wind their thread on. Raw thread.

P چفساني *chafsānī*, Viscosity, adhesiveness.

P چفسيدگي *chafsīdagī*, Adhesiveness.

P چفسيدن *chafsīdan*, To stick, to adhere. بر چفسيدن *bar chafsīdan*, To clot together, to felt.

P چفسيده *chafsīda*, Sticking, adhering.

P چفنك *chuf* or *chafnuk*, A heron, crane.

P چفود *chifūd*, (or جفود *jifūd*) A Jew.

P چق *chak*, A churn-staff. *Chik*, A Venetian blind. *Chuk*, A yoke. A draught-ox.

P چقاچاق *chakāchāk*, (or چقاچق *chakāchak*) The clashing of battle-axes.

P A چقدار *chi-kadar*, What quantity? how much?

P چقر *chakar*, A tavern.

P چقماچي *chakmāchī*, Sarcasm, scoff, jeer.

T چقماق *chakmāk*, (or چقمق) Flint, fire-steel,

T چقماقي *chakmākī*, A firelock.

P چقندر *chukundur* or *chukandar*, Beet-root.

P چقيدن *chakīdan*, To fix a spike, drive a nail. To dash, strike together, or become tumultuous. To litigate. To be deficient.

P چك *chak*, The written and signed sentence of a judge or magistrate. Title-deeds. A draught or check for a salary or pension. An obligation, deed, bond, note. A wooden mallet used in taking cotton out of the pods. A kind of wooden fork with several prongs or branches, with which they agitate corn that the wind may clear it of the chaff. A cart. The noise made in breaking a stick, striking with a sword, or in masticating a crust. The lower jaw and chin. A word. Vine-pruning. Drop. (in compos.) Dropping. چك مسافر *chaki musāfir*, A traveller's passport. *Chik*, A walnut, the kernel of which is not easily got from the shell. A drop. One side of four. An eighth part of a thing. *Chuk*, Penis. The knee.

P چكا *chakā*, A lark.

P چكاچاك *chakāchāk*, The clashing noise made by swords or maces. Drawing, a draught.

P چكاچك *chakāchak*, The clashing of swords and maces. The chattering of the teeth. *Chukāchuk*, Any thing whispered about.

P چكاد *chakād*, Top, crown of the head. Summit of a mountain. Top of the forehead. A shield.

P چكاده *chakāda*, Crown of the head. Top of the forehead. Summit of a mountain. A shield.

P چكاره *chikāra*, (چه What? كار Business) Useless.

P چكاري *chikārī*, Useless, worthless.

P چكاسه *chakāsa*, A hedgehog, urchin.

P چكاك *chakāk*, Forelocks. A conveyancer, notary-public. A borer of pearls, bead-piercer.

P چكامه *chakāma*, A poem exceeding 18 couplets.

P چكان *chakān*, (in comp.) Dropping, distilling. خون چكان *khūn-chakān*, Dropping blood. *Chikān*, What thing?

P چكانا *chakānā*, Besprinkling, wetting.

P چكاندن *chakāndan*, To drop, trickle, distil.

P چكانيدن *chakānīdan*, (from چكيدن *chakīdan*) To make drop, to let fall in drops, or trickle.

P چكاو *chakāv*, A kind of musical instrument. See چغانه *chaghāna*. A certain water-bird. A lark. Name of a note in music.

P چكاوك *chakāwak*, A lark. A note in music.

P چكاوگاه *chakāv-gāh*, (or چكاوگاه) A notch at the end of a bow into which the string goes.

P چكاوه *chakāwa*, A lark.

P چكاه *chakāh*, A mountain's top. The crown of the head.

P چكچاك *chakchāk*, The clash of swords.

P چكچك *chakchak*, The noise made by water in dropping. The chattering of the teeth from cold. The clashing of swords. *Chihchik*, The crackling noise made by the damp wick of a candle. *Chukchuk*, News spreading on every side.

P چكدان *chak-dān*, Eloquent.

P چكرنه *chikarna*, A heron, a crane.

P چكره *chakra*, Drops sprinkled about when water is poured out. A bubble. Froth.

P چكري *chukrī*, Sorrel.

P چكس *chakas*, A roost. Shame, modesty.

P چكسه *chaksa*, A perch or roost for birds. Little niceties. A bit of paper for wrapping up powders, and the like.

P چكسيدن *chakasīdan*, To blush, be confused.

P چكش *chakish*, An oozing or dropping. Liquefaction. *Chakush*, A brazier's hammer.

P چكك *chukak* or *chukuk*, A silken band or girdle. *Chukuk*, A sparrow.

P چكله *chakla*, Whatever falls from its place. A drop. A district, the jurisdiction of a Fawjdār; as the چكله *chakla* of Hūglī in Bengal.

P چكميزك *chak-mezak*, Suppression of urine, strangury. A coming away of the urine drop by drop. Unable to retain one's urine.

P چكميزك زده *chak-mezak zada*, Troubled with

strangury, when the urine comes away drop by drop.

P چکن *chakin*, (*chikin*, or چکین *chikīn*) A kind of cloth wrought with the needle in flowers and gold. Embroidery, needle-work.

P چك نامه *chak-nāma*, A roll descriptive of land-boundaries. A grant issued to individuals, authorizing them to hold alienated lands, and specifying the limits thereof.

P چکندر *chukundur*, Beet-root.

P چکندوز *chikin-doz*, An embroiderer.

P چکن دوزي *chikin-dozī*, An embroidered robe; needle-work.

P چکنویس *chak-navīs*, An actuary, a registrar.

P چکوج *chakūj*, (or چکوچ *chakūch*) An iron tool for notching mill-stones. Notching a mill-stone. A brazier's hammer.

P چك و چانه *chak u chāna*, Prating, babble.

P چکوك *chakok*, A lark. Purslain. Name of a note in music. *Chukūk*, A sparrow.

P چیکه *chaka*, Small, minute.

P چکه *chakka*, A drop.

P چکي *chakī*, The hole in which the pivot of a mill turns.

P چکیدگي *chakīdagī*, A drop. Distillation.

P چکیدن *chakīdan*, To drop, distil, trickle.

P چکیده *chakīda*, Dropped, oozed out. A mace. *Chukīda*, Sucked.

P چکیده خون *chakīda khūn*, Red wine.

P چکین *chikīn*, Name of a country.

P چگال *chagāl*, Thick, compact, and heavy.

P چگامه *chagāma*, A poem of more than eighteen couplets.

P چگّاني *chaggānī*, A kind of melon.

P چگك *chuguk*, A sparrow.

P چگل *chigil*, A city in Turkistān, famous for handsome men and expert archers. Clay, dirt.

P چگندر *chugundar*, Beet-root.

P چگوك *chagūk*, A lark. *Chugūk*, A sparrow.

P چگونگي *chigūnagī*, Nature or manner of a thing. Circumstance, matter, quality.

P چگونه *chigūna*, How? of what kind? In what manner? in what state?

P چل *chal*, An embankment, dam, weir. (imp. of چلیدن *chalīdan*) Go thou. *Chil*, Half-witted, fool. A horse white on the off fore-foot and hind stirrup-foot. (for چهل *chihal*) Forty. *Chul*, Penis.

P چلّا *chillā*, The forty days of Lent, during which the religious fraternities in the East shut themselves up in their cells or remain at home. Quarantine. The period of forty days after child-bed, during which a woman remains unclean.

P چلاس *chalūs*, Fond of tid-bits: trencherman.

P چلاك *chalāk*, A black beetle, tumble-dung.

P چلالي *chil* or *chalālī*, A woman's work-basket.

P چلان *chalān*, Current. A letter of advice from a Zamīndār to government that his rents are ready to be paid, sometimes accompanying a remittance of the amount. An invoice.

P چلانك *chalānak* or *chulānak*, A beetle. *Chulānak*, A game.

P چلاو *chulāw*, Plain boiled rice.

P چلاه *chulāh*, A weaver. A martial dance. Cymbals.

P چلبله *chulbula*, Haste, unsteadiness. A gift.

P چلپ *chalap*, Two broad plates of brass used as a musical instrument, cymbals. Noise, clamour.

P چلپاسه *chalpāsa*, A small venomous lizard.

P چلپك *chalpak*, (or چلپل *chalpal*) A cake fried in oil or butter.

P چل چراغ *chil charāgh*, Brilliant illumination.

P چلچله *chilchila*, A tortoise. A kite.

P چلساله *chil sāla*, Forty years old.

P چلش *chulush*, Name of an acid vegetable.

P چلشته خور *chalishta-khwur*, A troublesome hanger-on.

P چل صبح *chil subh*, The forty mornings employed in mixing up the clay for the formation of Adam.

P چلغوزه *chilghoza*, The cone of a fir tree; the tree itself.

P چلك *chilk*, A ladle, skimmer. The little finger. *Chulk*, A spoon. *Chaluk*, The game of tip-cat. *Chulak*, A silken-band. A ball of packthread or silk.

H چلم *chilam*, The round plate, cup, or bowl, to which is stuck the tobacco in a *hukah*, generally a thin bit of unglazed tile, and upon the contrary side of which the fire is put.

P چلم *chilum*, The fortieth.

P چل مردان *chil mardān*, The leather fixed to the vacant part of a saddle.

P چلمله *chalmala*, Gratuitous, without labour or purchase.

P چل مناره *chil manāra*, The throne of Solomon. The famous ruins which are generally regarded as the remains of Persepolis.

P چلنچو *chalanchū*, Who dirties himself; sloven.

P چلوج *chalūj* or *chulūj*, A tool for notching mill-stones.

P چلو چوب *chalū* or *chulū-chūb*, A spit.

P چلوك *chalawk*, A halter round a horse's neck.

P چلونك *chalūnak*, Melon-seed and flowers.

P چله *chilla*, A bow-string. A selvage. A quadragesimal fast, the forty days of Lent, during which the religious fraternities of the East shut themselves up in their cells, or remain at home. Forty days of winter, during which the weather is most severe. Forty days after childbirth.

P چلیپا *chalīpā*, A cross. Any thing crooked or bent. A ringlet. A triangular bit of gold or silver worn in the girdle by some Hindus. چلیپایٔ فلك *chalīpāī falak*, A cross formed by the colure's intersecting the equinoctial.

P چلیدن *chalīdan*, To walk, go, move. Worthy, fit, suitable. To champ, gnaw.

P چلیده *chalīda*, A bone-ring worn by archers on the thumb.

P چم *cham*, An easy air. A vacillating motion in walking. Gained. Prepared, arranged. Curved, crooked, bent. A lane full of windings. Eating and drinking. Signification, meaning, soul, energy. The eye. The breast. A disk made of platted reeds used to winnow corn. A large wooden ladle. Name of one quarter of the town of Yazd. A summer-garment. Sin, crime. *Chim*, A green film which floats on stagnant water. *Chum*, Boast, bluster, gasconade. A living creature. Grape-stones or husks, the residuum after the juice has been expressed. Intense cold. An eye-salve prepared from a black shining grain.

P چماچم *cham* or *chumāchum*, The forelocks.

P چماق *chumāq*, An iron mace. A wooden club with a knob on the head.

P چمان *chamān*, Walking, giving one's self haughty, swinging, or graceful airs in walking. A goblet of wine. A party of friends.

P چمانچي *chamānchī*, A vessel for holding wine, having a narrow mouth and a large belly.

P چمانه *chamāna*, A vessel made of the rind of a gourd, especially carved or chased. The cup of king Jamshed. *Chumāna*, An animal, a living being.

P چماني *chamānī*, Walking pompously. A cup-bearer.

P چمانیدن *chamānīdan*, To walk gracefully.

P چم پریشي *cham-pareshī*, Distinct, separate. Ambiguous.

P چمتاك *chamtāk*, (or چمتك) A shoe.

P چمچاخ *chamchākh*, Bent, curved, crooked.

P چمچرغه *chamchurgha*, A scourge, a lash.

P چمچم *chumchum* or *chamcham*, An easy air, a swinging gait. *Chumchum*, A cotton-shoe. An old soft shoe. A hoof.

P چمچمه *chumchuma*, The sound made by the feet in walking.

P چمچه *chumcha*, A spoon, ladle, skimmer.

T چمدك *chimdik*, A nip, a pinch.

P چمراس *chamrās*, A sign, a miracle.

P چمش *chamsh*, (for چشم *chashm*) The eye. A portly gait in walking. A small grain used as a remedy for the eyes.

P چمشاك *chamshāk*, (or چمشك) A shoe.

P چمشه *chamsha*, (equiv. to چشمه) A fountain.

P چمك *chamak*, Power, strength. Increase. Abundance. Authority, influence. Pomp, dignity.

P چمن *chaman*, An orchard, fruit-garden. A meadow, green field, verdant plain, garden plot or bed, raised border, parterre, avenue. An easy-paced horse. چمن دهر *chamani dahr*, A terrestrial abode.

P چمنا *chimnā*, A mule.

P چمناك *chamnāk*, (or چمنك) A shoe.

P چمن بند *chaman-band*, A gardener. A fountain. A youth.

P چمن پیرا *chaman-payrā*, A gardener, pruner.

P چمند *chamand*, A horse that travels slowly. An idle lazy fellow.

P چمندة *chamanda*, Stately, pompous in walking.

P چمنزار *chamanzār*, (or چمنستان *chamanistān*) Verdant meadows.

P چمن صفه *chaman-suffa*, A garden-seat.

P چموش *chamūsh*, Vicious horse. Sort of shoe.

P چمي *chamī*, Real, true, significant.

P چميدن *chamīdan*, To walk proudly, waving from side to side. To twist, turn, bend, curve. To incline the mind.

P چميدة *chamīda*, Walking easily, stately, pompously, or gracefully. Bent, curved.

P چمين *chamīn*, Urine. Excrement.

P چن *chun*, (for چون *chūn*) When.

P چناب *chināb*, A board having a circular hole through which the tent-pole passes. Name of a large river in the Panjāb.

P چناچن *chanūchan*, The whiz of an arrow.

P چنار *chanār*, Circles which women paint upon their hands and feet with privet. A plane-tree.

P چنارستان *chanāristān*, A grove of plane-trees.

P چناغ *chanāgh*, A mullet.

P چنال *chanāl*, The plantain-tree.

P چنان *chanān*, Striving. Name of a place. *Chunān*, Like that, resembling that, to such a degree, in that manner, so. (for چون نان *chūn nān*) Like bread. چنان چنين *chunān chunīn*, In this and that manner. Evasion, subterfuge.

P چنانچه *chunānchi*, According to what. As, just as. So that. When. Would it were so!

P چنانكه *chunānki*, As, as for example. Insomuch that, so that. As much as, so much as. To such a degree.

P چنانهن *chanānhan*, (or چناهن) Well done!

P چنبر *chambar*, A circle, hoop. The pit of the throat. The collar-bone. A kerchief, collar, necklace. A cover for the *chilam* of a *hukka*. A spider's web. Bondage, captivity. Revolving. چنبر چرخ *chambari charkh*, Circle of the heavens. چنبر كبود *chambari kabūd*, Nether sky. چنبر گردن *chambari gardan*, A necklace. A dog's collar. The pillory, stocks. چنبر مينا *chambari mīnā*, The sky.

P چنبك *chumbak*, Assault, leap. Magnet.

P چنبل *chumbul*, A beggar.

P چنبلي *chumbulī*, Need, lack. Mendicity.

P چنبور *cham* or *chumbūr*, A rein, halter.

P چنبه *chumba* or *chamba*, A large bar, spar, or boom. A shepherd's staff. A fuller's beetle. Grape-stalks. Morose, perverse.

P چنبيدن *chumbīdan*, To jump, leap, bound. To run away.

H چنپا *champā*, A very fragrant yellow flower.

H چنچولي *chanchūlī*, A swing, a see-saw.

P چنخ *chinkh*, One from whose eyes a gummy substance is perpetually running.

P چند *chand*, How much? how many? how long? To what length? Whither? So many. Several, some, a few, sundry. Any indefinite quantity. چند بار *chand bār*, How often? Sometimes, frequently. چند تن *chand tan*, How many persons? بچند *ba chand*, For how much? تني چند *tane chand*, Some people. Many men. چند روز *chand roz*, A few days. How many days? راه چند روزه *rāhi chand roza*, A journey of several days. چند ساله *chand sāla*, Of few years. هر چند *har chand*, (or هر چند كه *har chand ki*) Although, nevertheless, notwithstanding, however, how much soever, with all that, so much the more. Often. Every time that.

P چندا *chundā*, How much? how many? A contribution.

S چندال *chandāl*, A nightman, sweeper.

P چندان *chandān*, Many, much, numbers, more, as many as, how many soever, so much, so greatly. Some, any indefinite quantity. So, in that manner. How long? Until then. Sandal-wood. Name of a city in China. صد چندان *sad chandān*, A hundred times more. چندانچه *chandānchi*, How much soever, notwithstanding. چندانكه *chandān ki*, As oft as, as much as, as many as, as soon as, as long as. Insomuch. How much soever. Although, notwithstanding that.

T چنداول *chandāwul*, The rear of an army. Camp-followers.

P چندر *chundur*, (for چغندر) Beet-root.

P چندفند *chandfand*, Fear, dread, terror.

P چند گاه *chand gāh*, Sundry times.

P چندل *chandal*, Sandal-wood.

P چند مردة *chand marda*, Enough for many men.

P چندن *chandan*, Sandal-wood.

P چندة *chanda*, Some.

P چندي *chande*, An indefinite quantity. Some. بعد چندي *ba'd chande*, After a while.

P چندين *chandīn*, So much, so many. All these, such as these. How many?

P چنغوب *changhūb*, Quilting, wadding.

P چنك *chunak*, A bird's beak.

P چنگ *chang*, The hook for guiding an elephant. The expanded hand, the fingers somewhat hooked. The claw of a wild beast; talon of a bird. A harp, lute. Any thing crooked or bent. Crippled in the hand or foot. Name of the shop of the impostor Mānī; also his book of paintings. چنگ مريم *changi maryam*, The herb sow-bread. چنگ موزة *changi mūza*, The point or turned-up toe of a boot. با چنگ گرفتن *bā chang giriftan*, To twitch with the fingers. *Ching*, The horny beak of a bird of prey. The point of a spear. *Chung*, A kind of large ship. A word, speech, talk. A picking-up of grains.

P چنگار *chang-ār*, A crab.

P چنگال *changāl*, Fingers, claws, talons, pounces. A dish made of dates with hot bread and butter. Slender-waisted. A target.

P چنگالخواست *changāl-khwāst*, چنگالخوست *changāl-khwust*, or چنگالخوش *changāl-khwush*, Hot bread, syrup or honey, and butter. A mixture of any kind.

P چنگالي *changālī*, Hot bread dipt in butter.

P چنگ پشت *chang-pusht*, Crook-backed.

P چنگدو *changdū*, Name of a city in China.

P چنگش *chingish*, Name of a hero of Turkistān killed by Rustam.

P چنگك *changak*, A hook for an elephant.

P چنگل *changul*, Fingers, claws. A hook.

P چنگلاهي *changlāhī*, A kite.

P چنگلوك *changalok*, or (چنگوك *changūk*) A man debilitated by disease, having his hands and feet contracted, lame, maimed, mutilated; unable to walk by himself.

P چنگلة *changala*, A psaltery, a lute. Bird's claws. Bent fingers. A hook. *Chingila*, Curly hair.

P چنگوان *changwān*, Name of a city in India.

P چنگة *changa*, Name of a luxurious king.

P چنگي *changī*, A harper, lutanist. An actor.

P چنگيدن *changīdan*, To speak, act in a play.

P چنگيز *chingīz*, The Mogul king Gengīz Khān.

P چنو *chunu*, (for چون او *chūn u*) As he, like him. A request.

P چنود پل *chunūd-pul*, The bridge over hell.

P چنه *chana*, The lower jaw, the chin. *China*, Grain, bird's food.

P چنه دان *chinadān*, The crop of a bird.

P چنيدن *chinīdan*, To gather. To admonish.

P چنيدة *chinīda*, Gathered, culled, picked up.

P چنين *chunīn*, (for چون اين *chūn īn*) Thus, such, so, in this manner. Such as this. چنين بادا *chunīn bādā*, Amen, so be it!

P چو *chu*, When. Then. Thus, as, in the same manner, like, since. If so be; for as much as. *Chū*, A stick.

P چواك *chuwāk*, Flour dressed with oil and honey.

P چوب *chūb*, (by some *chob*) A log. Wood. A tree. A staff, rod, baton, stick. A drum-stick. A beam. A plough-tail. A shoot of a tree, sucker. خشك چوب *khushk-chob*, Dry wood. چوب بازيدن *chob bāzīdan*, To lance a spear or the like in sport. چوب چيني *chobi chīnī*, China root. چوب خوردن *chob khwurdan*, To devour the rod, *i.e.* to be thrashed. چوب زدن *chob zadan*, To thrash. چوب زين *chobi zīn*, A saddle-tree. A covering for a saddle. چوب سرخ *chobi surkh*, Red-wood, logwood. چوب كار *chobi kār*, A yarn-beam. چوب نان *chobi nān*, A rolling-pin. چوب نورد *chobi naward*, A weaver's beam.

P چوبا *chobā*, A stake, a post.

P چو باد بر خاستن *chu bād bar khastan*, To rise, leap, start up like the wind.

P چوبان *chobān*, A shepherd. A horsekeeper.

P چوبان سگ *chobān-sag*, A shepherd's dog.

P چوباني *chobānī*, The pastoral office.

P چوب بندي *chūb-bandī*, A scaffold.

P چوب پاره *chob-pāra*, A chip, lath, shaving, piece of wood. An instrument for levelling the earth, a harrow.

P چوب خوار *chob-khwār*, A timber-worm. Beaten, drubbed.

P چوبخوارك *chob-khwārak*, A timber-worm.

P چوب دار *chob-dār*, A mace-bearer.

P چوبدانه *chob-dāna*, Jujube-tree and fruit.

P چوب دستي *chob-dastī*, Walking-stick: goad.

P چوب ساي *chob-sāy*, A rasp.

P چوب شكاف *chob-shikāf*, Cleaving wood. A wedge.

P چوب شكن *chob-shikan*, A woodpecker.

P چوبشوي *chob-shuwī*, A fuller's beetle.

P چوبك *chūbak*, A little stick. A watchman's rattle. A stick for separating cotton from the pods. Red-wood.

P چوبكاري *chob-kārī*, A drubbing. A kind of embroidery.

P چوبك اشنان *chobak-ushnān*, Pearl-ashes, lye.

P چوبك زن *chobak-zan*, A head watchman. A drummer.

P چوبكش *chob-kash*, An instrument for cleaning cotton.

P چوبكي *chobakī*, Timber of a saddle. Patrol, nightly watch. Commander of the nocturnal guard.

P چوبكين *chūbakīn*, A wooden or iron instrument for separating cotton from its seed. A watchman.

P چوبنه *chūbina*, A heron. A bustard.

P چوبه *chūba*, A rolling-pin. A wand. A scourge. A walking-stick. A fiddle-stick. A title of Bahrām chūbīn. The white poplar. چوبهٔ شتر *chūbaï shutur*, A quilted cloth laid upon a camel's bunch to prevent the load from hurting it.

P چوبي *chobī*, چوبين *chū*, or *chobīn*, Wooden.

P چوب يساق *chob-yasāk*, A mace-bearer's staff.

P چوبين *chobīn*, (or چوبينك *chobīnak*, or چوبينه *chobīna*) A red kind of kerchief tied over the head. A bustard, a crane. A name of Bahrām chūbīn.

P چوپان *chopān*, A shepherd.

P چوپايه *chaw-pāya*, A quadruped, beast.

P چوپربازي *chawpar-bāzī*, An Indian game.

P چوپكين *chopgīn*, A stick for cleaning cotton. A little stick.

P چوپلنك *choplank*, A fillet for the head.

P چوپله *chawpala*, A covered sedan or litter.

P چوپلين *chūpalīn*, An instrument for cleaning cotton.

H چوت *chawt*, A fourth: a fourth of the revenue formerly claimed as a right by the Marhattas.

P چوتره *chawtara*, A raised square place either in a garden or before a house.

P چوجه *chūja*, A chicken.

P چوچم *chūcham*, A shoe worn by dervishes.

P چوچو *chūchū*, A sparrow.

P چوچه *chūcha*, A rolling-pin. A swan: chicken.

P چوخا *chūkhā*, A woollen garment. A monk's garb.

P چوخيدن *chokhīdan*, To stumble, fall. To come to an end. To quarrel. To labour, strive.

P چور *chor*, (or چورپور *chorpor*) A pheasant.

P چورابه *chorāba*, Water flowing from the bottom of a dam.

P چو روز *chu roz*, (As clear) as day.

P چوره *chora*, A distaff.

H چوري *chawrī*, An instrument made of the long hair of the چامر *chāmar*, or Thibet cow, used to chase away flies. *Chūrī*, A bracelet.

P چوري فروش *chūrī-farosh*, A bracelet seller.

P چوز *chūz*, Pudenda mulieris. A falcon able to catch game before he is a year old. A pheasant. A certain thorny plant.

P چوزا *chūzā*, A kite.

P چوزه *chūza*, (or چوژه *chūja*) A chick, a young bird. A notch at the end of a spindle to hold the thread. چوزهٔ ماكيان *chūzaï mākiyān*, A chicken.

P چوزه باز *chūza-bāz*, (Playing with chickens) An old woman fond of young men.

P چوزه ربا *chūza-rubā*, A kite.

P چوزه لوا *chūza-luvā* or *livā*, A kite.

P چوسيدن *chavsīdan*, To stick, adhere.

P چوشك *chūshak*, A vessel with a spout to it.

P چوشيدن *chūshīdan*, (or چوشدن) To suck.

P چوغ *chūgh*, A yoke. A trench or canal cut through gardens or meadows. A dam, weir.

P چوغري *chūgharī*, Sour milk which remains in a linen cloth after the water is strained off. A horse of a partridge colour.

P چوك *chok*, A profound inclination or genuflexion before a king. Name of a bird. Penis. Knee.

H چوك *chok*, A market-place. A daily market. A market principally for second-hand apparel.

H چوكلاه *chūhlāh*, A district under a Fawjdār.

H چوكي *chawkī*, A raised seat, chair. A guard. A place for collecting customs. A watch-house.

P چوكي دار *chawkī-dār*, The officer of a guard. A watchman.

P چوكي گلو *chawkī-gulū*, A square ornament of gold, &c., worn on the throat.

P چوكي گماشته *chawkī-gumāshta*, A subordinate custom-house officer.

P چوكي نويس *chawkī-navīs*, One who keeps account of outposts and guards.

P چوگان *chawgān*, A stick with one end bent, used in a game at ball. The game of horse-shinty. A crooked drum-stick. A stick having one end arched, to which is suspended an iron or steel ball, carried as an ensign of royalty. چوگان سنبل *chawgāni sumbul*, The ringlets of the fair. *Chūgān*, How? Time, an hour. If. Like, resembling.

P چوگانباز *chawgān-bāz*, Player at *chawgān*.

P چوگان بازي *chawgān-bāzī*, A playing at the game of horse-shinty.

P چوگاني *chawgānī*, A horse suited for playing at the game of *chawgān*. A straight hooka-pipe.

P چوگك *chūgag*, An owl: a large kind of owl.

P چول *chawl* or *chūl*, Bent. *Chol*, Penis. *Chūl*, A desert.

P چولاه *chūlāh*, A weaver. A spider.

P چوم *chūm*, Fat, tallow. The oxyacanth.

P چوماق *chomāk*, A club, an iron mace.

P چون *chūn*, How? Like, in the manner of, as. Because, forasmuch as, whereas, seeing that, since. When, after that. If. Manner, quality. چوني بيچگون *chūni bī chigūn*, Without likeness, incomparable (an epithet of the Deity). بيچون و چرا *bī chūn u chirā*, Without why or wherefore.

P چونا *chūn ā*, How do you do?

P چونان *chūnān*, So, like that. Just as if. A rolling-pin.

P چونانك *chūnānak*, After what manner: just as.

P چوناه *chūnāh*, In this manner, thus, like, so.

P چونچرا *chūn-chirā*, Wrangling, altercation.

P چونه *chūna*, A lump, a mass.

H چونه *chūnah*, Quick lime.

P چوني *chūnī*, How art thou? Quality.

P چونين *chūnīn*, Thus, in this manner, like this.

P چويگان *chūygān*, (for چوگان) A bandy, club.

P چه *cha*, an affix to form diminutives; as, باغچه *bāghcha*, Little garden, جويچه *jūycha*, Rivulet. *Chah*, (for چاه *chāh*) A well. *Chi*, Who? What? Which? In what manner or kind? Why? Since, because, seeing that. Every, all. Whether. Or. Fifteen. What! How great! چه منزل *chi manzil*, What a mansion! چه بودي *chi būdī*, Would to God! I wish it were! چه چاره *chi chāra*, What remedy? چه خوش *chi khwush*, How delightful! چه دل *chi dil*, What heart? what courage or ability? چه سان *chi sān*, (or چه نوع *chi nawa*) Of what sort? چه سگست *chi sag ast*, What dog is he? *i.e.* what can he do? چه طرف بست *chi taraf bast*, What did it avail him? *i.e.* it availed him nothing. چه فائده *chi fāida*, What advantage? for what purpose? چه گونه *chi gūna*, How? in what shape or manner? چه معني *chi maʿna'*, What is the meaning? To what end? چه برتخت مردن چه برروي خاك *chi bar takht murdan, chi bar rūyi khāk*, What matters it (or it is all the same thing) to die on a throne or on the bare ground? چه درّ چه صدف *chi durr chi sadaf*, Whether a pearl or an oyster-shell. چه شريف و چه وضيع *chi sharīf u chi wazīʿ*, As well high as low, gentle and simple.

P چها *chihā*, (pl. of چه *chi*) What things?

H چهاپه *ch'hāpa*, Stamp, seal; chop, impression.

P چهاد *chahād*, A mountain-peak. Forehead.

P چهار *chahār*, Four. A crab.

P چهار آخرسنگين *chahār ākhuri sangīn*, The four quarters of the world. The four elements.

P چهار ارکان chahār arkān, The four points of the compass. A kind of quadrangular tent.

P چهار اقران chahār akrān, The four first khalīfs.

P چهار امام chahār imām, Four religious chiefs.

P چهار امين chahār amīn, The four khalīfs, Abū bakr, Omar, Othmān, and Aliy. The four Muhammadan lawyers, Shāfiɛi, Abū Hanīfa, Mālik, and Hambal.

P چهار آينه chahār āyina, A kind of armour.

P چهار آيين chahār āyīn, A quadrangular tent. The four immediate successors of Muhammad. The four principal sects.

P چهار باف chahār bāf, A kind of rich silk.

P چهار بالش chahār bālish, (or بالشت bālisht) A royal throne (or place spread with four cushions). The four elements. The four quarters of the globe. The world. چهار بالش ارکان chahār bālishi arkān, The four khalīfs. A quadrangular tent.

P چهار بسيط chahār basīt, (حمّال hammāl, بيخ bekh, or جوهر jawhar) The four elements.

P چهار پا chahār pā, A quadruped. A bedstead.

P چهار پاره chahār pāra, Four parts; divided into, or consisting of, four parts. The quarters of shoes. A musical instrument.

P چهار پايك chahār pāyak, A kind of disease.

P چهار پايه chahār pāya, A quadruped.

P چهار پره chahār-para, Four-winged (arrow).

P چهار تاره chahār tāra, Four-stringed.

P چهار تك chahār tak, Canter, easy gallop.

P چهار تکبير زدن chahār takbīr zadan, To abandon the world. To repeat the burial service.

P چهار جوي chahār jūy, The rivers of Paradise. The elements. Name of a province in Khurāsān. چهار جوي فطرت chahār jūyi fitrat, The four elements.

P چهار چادر chahār chādar, A cloth surrounding a woman's grave. A kind of horse-cloth.

P چهار چشم شدن chahār chashm shudan, To see or look for earnestly. To meet face to face.

P چهار چمن chahār chaman, The world.

P چهار حاشيه chahār hāshiya, Having four borders; having its four edges embroidered.

P چهار خانه chahār khāna, The ventricle of a sheep; also a pudding of it stuffed with meat, rice, butter, herbs, and spiceries. Thin cakes dressed with soup; a species of macaroni.

P چهار دانگ chahār dāng, The four quarters.

P چهار در چهار chahār dar chahār, Four times four; on all sides.

P چهار دري chahār darī, The world.

P چهار دريچه chahār darīcha, The four windows (of the body), *i.e.* eye, ear, nose, and mouth.

P چهارده chahārdah, Fourteen.

P چهاردهم chahārdahum, The fourteenth.

P چهارده ماه chahārdah māh, The full moon. A mistress.

P چهارده معصوم chahārdah maɛsūm, The prophet Muhammad, his daughter, and the twelve first eminent khalīfs.

P چهار ديوار جهان chahār dīwāri jahān, The four quarters of the world. The four elements.

P چهار رکن chahār rukn, (or رئيس raɛīs) The four elements.

P چهار روزه chahār-roza, Of four days duration.

P چهار زانو chahār-zānū, A tailor's way of sitting.

P چهار زبان chahār-zabān, (Four-tongued) an incessant talker. One who does not stick to his word: a quibbler, prevaricator.

P چهار ساله chahār-sāla, Of four years. Four years old.

P چهار سو chahār-sū, A square, market-place.

P چهار سواره chahār suwāra, A place where four ways meet.

P چهار سوق chahār-sūk, A market-place.

P چهار شاخ chahār-shākh, A winnowing fan.

P چهار شنبه chahār-shambih, Wednesday.

P چهار صد chahār sad, Four hundred.

P چهار طاق chahār tāk, A kind of tent.

P چهار طاق افگن chahār tāk afgan, A bed.

P چهار علم chahār ɛalam, The four ensigns (of the faith), viz. Abū bakr, Omar, Othmān, and Aliy. The four elements.

P چهار عيال chahār ɛiyāl, The four elements.

P چهار کرگس chahār kargas, The four elements. The throne of شدّاد shaddād, or (according to others) that of کاؤس kāɛus.

P چهار گامه chahār gāma, Swift. An ambling nag.

P چهارگان chahārgān, Four and four. In fours.

P چهار گانه chahār gāna, Of four modes. Square. Fourfold.

P چهار گلخن chahār gulkhan, The four quarters of the world. The four elements.

P چهار گوشه chahār gosha, Quadrangular. A bier. A small table. A turban.

P چهار گوهر chahār gawhar, The four elements.

P چهار لنگر chahār langar, Legs of quadrupeds.

P چهارم chahārum, The fourth.

P چهار مادر chahār mādar, The four elements.

P چهار ماهه chahār māha, Of four months. Four months old.

P چهار مسکون chahār maskūn, Habitable world.

P چهار مغز chahār maghz, (Four-kernel) A walnut.

P چهارم منظر chahārum manzar, Solar sphere.

P چهار منقوطه chahār mankūta, The orbit of the Zodiacal signs.

P چهار ميخ chahār mekh, The elements. Sodomy.

P چهار نظم chahār nazm, The four elements.

P چهار وا chahār-wā, A quadruped.

P چهاروه دار chahārwa-dār, Leader of a caravan.

P چهار هفته chahār hafta, A trifling silly thing. Non-existent. چهار و هفت chahār u haft, The four (elements) and seven (planets).

P چهار يار گزين chahār yāri guzīn, Four chosen companions, viz. Abū bakr, Omar, Othmān, and Aliy.

P چهار ياري chahār yārī, Name of a sect.

P چهار يك chahār yak, One of four. A fourth.

P چهان chahān, Many. Chihān, (pl. of چه) Who?

P چه بچه chah-bacha, A cistern, a vat.

P چهر chihr, Face, visage. Original essence. A map. Small shot. شاهي ماه چهر shāhi māh-chihr, A prince beautiful as the moon.

P چهر آزاد chihr-āzād, Name of Humāy, daughter of Bahman and mother of Dārāb.

P چهر زاد chihr-zād, Name of Humāy, daughter of Bahman. Name of Isfandyār.

P چهره chihra, Face, countenance. Air, mien. Colour of the face. Original essence. A description-roll. A wheel, yarn-reel. Shot. چهرۂ آتش نما chihraɛi ātish-namā, A face flushed (with drink or anger). چهره بر افروختن chihra bar afrokhtan, To collect, assemble. چهرۂ حال chihraɛi hāl, The circumstance of the case. چهرۂ دوك chihraɛi dok, A wheel. A yarn-reel. چهره شدن chihra shudan, To be before or in the presence of, confront, be opposed to. To dispute. To prepare. چهره کشا و جلوه نما chihra-kushā u jilwa-namā, Uncovering the face, and displaying its attractions (a lady lifting up her veil). *Chuhra*, A youth, stripling, page. A beardless boy.

P چهره پرداز chihra-pardāz, A portrait-painter. The sun. چهره پرداز جهان chihra-pardāzi jahān, The world-illuminating sun.

P چهره خراش chihra-kharāsh, Face-scratching.

P چهره کشا chihra-kushā, A portrait-painter.

P چهره کشائي chihra-kushāɛī, A display.

P چهل chihal, Forty.

P چهل پاي chihal-pāy, (Forty-foot) A centipede.

P چهل تن chihal tan, Forty persons whom Moses is affirmed to have slain and brought to life again.

P چهل ته chihal tah, A coat of mail.

P چهل درم chihal diram, An ounce.

P چهل قد chihal had, A sort of armour.

P چهل قدمي chihal kadamī, A walk. A custom at the funerals of Musalmāns of stepping back forty paces from the grave, and again advancing towards it before reading the service over.

P چهلم chahlam, A sort of armour. *Chihlum*, The fortieth.

P چهل منار chihal manār, (Forty towers) A name of Persepolis.

P چهنده chahanda, Dropping, distilling, Leaping.

P چهيدن chahīdan, To drop, distil. To leap.

P چهير chahīr, Face, countenance: complexion.

P چهيره chahīra, Face, countenance. چهيره نويس chahīra-nuvīs, One who writes down a description of the countenance (an officer so called).

P چهيوز chah-yūz, An iron instrument with four hooks for pulling any thing lost out of wells or rivers. A pulley or block. A shovel, a pick-axe, a hoe.

P چي chī, Something. Who? What? Which? A Turkish affix to form words denoting the agent.

P چیانیدن *chiyānidan*, To collect. To cut up.

P چیپر *chaypur*, A highway. Name of a fort.

P چیپور *chipūr*, The iron head of a spear.

P چیپین *chaypīn*, Interval, intervening space.

P چیت *chīt*, Painted Indian, Persian, or Turkish silks, and other cloths. Chintz.

H چیتل *chītal*, A small coin, 25 of which make a دام *dām*.

H چیته *chīta*, A sort of panther with which they hunt deer. Estimate and measurement of lands.

P چیچاب *chīchāb*, Sound of the lips in kissing.

P چیچست *chīchist*, (in zand) A mountain.

P چیچك *chīchak*, The small-pox. چیچك زده *chīchak-zada*, Diseased with small-pox.

P چیچله *chīchala*, Sickness, pain.

P چیخ *chīkh*, Blear-eyed. Humour in the eye.

P چیدار *chīdār*, A shoe.

P چیدگیء ناخن *chīdagīi nākhun*, Nail-parings.

P چیدن *chīdan*, To gather, collect. To select, pick, choose. To imbibe. To swallow. To pare the nails. To pluck up (hairs). To spread a carpet. To ascend.

P چیده *chīda*, Gathered, picked. Pared (nail). The dwarf-pine. چیدهٔ ناخن *chīdai nākhun*, Nail-parings.

P چیر *chīr*, Valiant, courageous. A conqueror. A highway. Victory, mastery. A part, a portion. A bull. Name of a town.

P چیرچنگ *chīrchang*, A dildo.

P چیرگي *chīragī*, Victory, triumph. Valour, fearlessness, fortitude. Anger. Severity of language. A fault. چیرگي کردن *chīragī kardan*, To be petulant, violent.

P چیره *chīra*, Brave. Strong, powerful. Victorious. High. Pointed. Eloquent. Impudent, unpolite, rude, uncivil. Spiteful. Wise. Victory, superiority. A part, portion. End, extremity. A turban. چیره شدن *chīra shudan*, To wax valiant. To win, beat. To prevail, conquer. To prepare for.

P چیره دست *chīra-dast*, Ready-handed, skilful, succeeding in whatever one takes in hand. Strong, brave. Boldness.

P چیره دستي *chīra-dastī*, Victory.

P چیره زبان *chīra-zabān*, Eloquent. Free-spoken.

P چیره زباني *chīra-zabānī*, Eloquence.

P چیز *chīz*, A thing, any thing. Existing. Precious. Food. ناچیز *nāchīz*, Nothing. Not existing. ناچیز شدن *nāchīz shudan*, To be annihilated or defaced, to perish.

P چیزك *chīzak*, A little thing. A porcupine.

P چیز لیز *chīz līz*, Small capital, trifling concern.

P چیزو *chīzū*, A porcupine.

P چیزوگیر *chīzū-gīr*, Irritable, hot-brained.

P چیزه *chīza*, Tweezers used chiefly by the women for pulling out hairs. چیزه بوز *chīza-būz*, Cause, motive, reason. چیزه بوزگر *chīza-būzgar*, The agent in any cause.

P چیزي *chīze*, One thing. Something. A little, few, somewhat.

P چیست *chīst*, (for چه است *chi ast*) What is it? Who is? حال چیست *hāl chīst*, What's the matter? what now?

P چیستان *chīstān*, An enigma. Quality, essence, state.

P چیستي *chīstī*, What art thou?

P چیغ *chīgh*, A projecting roof, a screen before a door.

P چیغه زن *chīga-zan*, A warrior.

P چیلان *chelān*, A forest haunted by wolves. Iron rings, bridle-bits, &c. The jujube-tree.

P چیلانه *chelāna*, The jujube-tree.

P چین *chīn*, A fold, plait, wrinkle. China. چین افگندن *chīn afgandan*, To contract into wrinkles. چین بر ابرو افگندن *chīn bar abrū afgandan*, To grow old. To frown. چین کردن *chīn kardan*, To gather, collect, pull, pluck, choose. To join, unite. To reconcile, make peace. To knit the brows. *Chīn*, (in compos. from چیدن *chīdan*) Collecting. سخن چین *sukhan-chīn*, Collecting words, *i.e.* an informer. گل چین *gul-chīn*, Gathering roses. جبین پر چین *jabīni pur-chīn*, A frowning or wrinkled brow. زلف پر چین *zulfi pur-chīn*, Curling locks.

P چینا *chīnā*, (participle of چیدن) Gathering.

P چینائیدن *chīnāidan*, To bring together.

P چین حمامه *chīn-hamāma*, Cinnamon.

P چین خانه *chīn-khāna*, A cupboard for china.

P چیندره *chīndara*, A fabulous fountain, where instruments are said to be constantly playing.

P چیندن *chīndan*, Gleaning corn-fields.

P چینده *chīnda*, A collection.

P چینوار *chīnwār*, Right, straight.

P چینود *chīnawad*, The bridge over the eternal fire which the Muhammadans believe they shall be forced to cross on the day of judgment.

P چینه *chīna*, A gin, grain, or any snare by which birds are caught. A course of bricks or stone in a wall. Grain in general. چینهٔ دیوار *chīnai dīwār*, Layers of large stones, bricks, or turfs, in building walls.

P چینه دان *chīnadān*, The crop of a bird.

P چیني *chīnī*, Chinese. White sugar-candy. China-ware, porcelain; called also چیني ظروف *chīnī-zurūf*.

ح

ح *hā* or *he*, The sixth letter of the Arabic alphabet, is a strong aspirate generated deep in the throat. It is the character to represent eight in arithmetic, and Sagittarius in astronomical books. It is called حاءِ حطي *hāi hutti*, to distinguish it from هاءِ هوز *hāi hawwaz* or ه *he*; and حاءِ مهمله *hāi muhmala*, Undotted *hā* in contradistinction to حاءِ معجمه *hāi muejama* or خ *khā*. ح *hā* is written for حين *hīn*, When, or for حينئذ *hīnaizin*, Then.

A حاء *hāe* or حا *hā*, The Arabic name of the letter ح *hā*. A good man. A shrill-voiced woman. Name of a man. لا حاء ولا ساء *lā hāe wa lā sāe*, He does neither good nor harm. He is neither man nor woman. He can neither call out to sheep nor to an ass (spoken of a man a hundred years old).

A حاب *hāba*, (fut. يحوب *yahūbu*) He sinned.

A حاب *hāb*, A sin, crime.

A حابّ *hābb*, (pl. حوابّ *hawābb*) (An arrow) going beyond the mark.

A حابة *hābat*, A court-yard. A crime.

A حابس *hābis*, Astringent. A detainer.

A حابض *hābiz*, An arrow which falls before the archer.

A حابل *hābil*, One who binds with a rope. A magician. One who lays a net. Feeding on the fruit of the thorny shrub عضاة *eizāh*. A lizard feeding on the esculent herb حبلة *hublat*. A warp in the loom. Name of a country. ثار حابلهم علي نابلهم *sāra hābiluhum eala' nābilihim*, They stirred up mischief among themselves. حوّل حابله علي نابله *hawwala hābilahu eala' nābilihi*, He turned him topsy turvy.

A حابلة *hābilat*, (pl. حبلة) Pregnant (female).

A حابور *hābūr*, A meeting of a gang of rogues.

A حابول *hābūl*, A rope for climbing a palm.

A حابي *hābī*, A giver, bestower. Near. High-shouldered. (An arrow) bounding to the mark. Whatever meets, encounters, or comes across any one. A plant growing in the sand. حابي الشراسيف *hābī'sh sharāsīf*, Prominent-sided.

A حابية *hābiyat*, Ground which produces the plant حابي *hābī*.

A حاتل *hātil*, Likeness.

A حاتم *hātim*, (pl. حتوم *hutūm*) Who or what renders necessary. A judge. A black crow. A crow with red legs and beak, called also غراب البين *ghurābu'l bayn*. حاتم طائي *hātim tāī*, Name of a man celebrated among the Arabs for his liberality. اريحيّة حاتمية *arīhiyat hātimīya*, Liberality equal to that of Hātim.

A حاتمي *hātimī*, Boundless liberality.

A حاتن *hātin*, A day equally warm in the morning and evening.

A حاتي *hātī*, A great drinker.

A حاثياء *hāsiyāe*, The hole of the field-mouse, or the earth thrown up against it.

A حاج *hāja*, (fut. يحيج *yahīju*) He needed.

A حاج *hāj*, A thorny plant resembling wild asparagus from which they gather manna. (pl. of حاجة *hājat*) Things needful.

A حاجّ *hājj*, (pl. حجّاج *hujjāj*, حجيج *hajīj*, and حجّ *hujj*) A pilgrim to Mecca.

A حاجات *hājāt*, (pl. of حاجة) Necessities.

A حاجب *hājib*, (pl. حجبة *hajabat* and حجّاب *hujjāb*) A chamberlain. A margin, extreme part.

The sun's track. (pl. حواجب *hawājib*) The eyebrow. حاجب بار *hājibi bār*, The archangel Gabriel.

A حاجبي *hājibī*, Chamberlainship.

A حاجة *hājat*, (pl. حاج *hāj*, حاجات *hājāt*, حوج *hiwaj*, and حوائج *hawāij*) Necessity, need, lack. Unavoidable business. A call of nature. Hope, wish. حاجت تجوير *hājati tajwīz*, Any thing which requires investigation, as an account. P حاجت خواستن *hājat khwāstan*, To pray, state one's wants.

A حاجّة *hājjat*, (pl. حوآجّ *hawājj*) A female pilgrim to Mecca. حاجّة بيت الله *hājjat baytu'llāh*, A female pilgrim to the house of God (Mecca or Jerusalem).

P حاجت جاي *hājat-jāy*, (or گاه *gāh*) A necessary.

P حاجتمند *hājatmand*, Indigent, needy: hoping.

P حاجتمندي *hājatmandī*, Indigence.

P حاجتومند *hājatūmand*, Needy, necessitous.

A حاجج *hājij*, A pilgrim to Mecca.

A حاجر *hājir*, (pl. حجران *hujrān*) A wall. A dam, dike, causey. High ground depressed in the middle. The place where the plant رمث *rims* grows in a circular mass.

A حاجز *hājiz*, (pl. حجزة *hajazat*) Intervenient, intervening (as a curtain). A hinderer, preventer. An oppressor.

A حاجل *hājil*, One who goes by jumps or leaps, a hopper. Fettered. الحاجل *al hājil*, A crow.

A حاجلات *hājilāt*, Houghed, limping (camels).

A حاجم *hājim*, A scarifier, cupper: a barber.

A حاجور *hājūr*, A dam, dike. Illicit.

A حاجورة *hājūrat*, Blindman's buff. A game.

A حاجيّ *hājīy*, A Christian who has performed the pilgrimage to Jerusalem, or a Muhammadan that to Mecca. A pilgrim.

A حادّ *hādd*, Sharp, bitter, sour, acrid, ardent, fiery, poignant. (A woman) laying aside her ornaments when mourning the death of her husband. حادّ النظر *hāddu'n nazar*, Sharp-sighted.

A حادث *hādis*, New, just appearing. Casual.

P حادث شدن *hādis shudan*, To appear, happen.

A حادثة *hādisat*, (pl. حوادث *hawādis*) A novelty, event. An accident rendering a person ceremonially unclean. A misfortune.

A حادر *hādir*, Firm, compact-bodied (man). Full, plump (wheat). Fat and handsome (youth). Fleshy (eye). A lion.

A حادرون *hādirūna*, Persons expert in war, powerful, active, going forth equipped.

A حادور *hādūr*, A pendant, drop, ear-ring. A descent, declivity. Destruction, ruin. A cathartic.

A حادورة *hādūrat*, A flood of tears.

A حادئ *hādi'*, A defender.

A حادي *hādī*, A driver of camels. One who lets out asses and brings them to be loaded. A male ass driving the female before him.

A حادي عشر *hādiya ʿashara*, (mas.) Eleventh.

A حاذ *hāz*, Middle of a horse's back. Back of a man. Name of a plant and a tree. خفيف الحاذ *khafīfu'l hāz*, One who has little property and a small family.

A حاذان *hāzāni*, (dual of حاذ *hāz*) The backs of the thighs against which the tail strikes.

A حاذة *hāzat*, State, condition. One حاذ *hāz* tree.

A حاذر *hāzir*, Avoiding, shunning. Ready.

A حاذق *hāzik*, Cutting: sharp, acute. Tart, sour. Ingenious, skilful, clever, penetrating, excelling.

A حاذلة *hāzilat*, (An eye) red, bare of eye-lashes.

A حاذورة *hāzūrat*, Timid, cautious, wary.

A حار *hāra*, (fut. يحور *yahūru*) He returned.

A حارّ *hārr*, Warm, hot, sultry. Difficult, laborious, painful (work). Hair in the nostrils.

A حارة *hārat*, (or حارّة *hārrat*) A street. Any quarter where the houses adjoin.

A حارث *hāris*, (pl. حرّاث *hurrās*) A farmer, ploughman. ابو الحارث *abū'l hāris*, The lion.

A حارج *hārij*, A criminal, an offender.

A حارد *hārid*, (pl. حوارد *hawārid*) Passionate, warm. Separate, remote, solitary.

A حارس *hāris*, (pl. حرس *haras*, احراس *ahrās*, and حرّاس *hurrās*) A keeper. A governor, defender, guard, watchman.

A حارش *hārish*, One who scratches; a scratcher.

A حارصة *hārisat*, A blow on the head penetrating through the skin. A cloud pouring forth rain so as to break up the ground.

A حارض *hāriz*, Vicious, bad, rejected. Sick. At the point of death.

A حارضة *hārizat*, Vicious, bad. Sick.

A حارق *hārik*, Burning, ardent. The tooth of a wild beast.

A حارقة *hārikat*, Fire. (A woman) vigorous, hot, and wanton. Narrow (woman). A woman reproachful to her neighbours. Modus coeundi.

A حارقتان *hārikatāni*, (du.) Both hip-joints.

A حارك *hārik*, The withers of a horse. The interscapula of a man.

A حارم *hārim*, Name of a small city in Syria. هو بحارم عقل *huwa bihārimi ʿaklin*, He is intelligent.

A حاروق *hārūk*, Agreeable in coitu (woman).

A حاروقة *hārūkat*, Sharp (sword).

A حاريّ *hārīy*, Native of Hīrat in Mesopotamia. حاريّ دهر *hāriya dahrin*, At any time, never.

A حارية *hāriyat*, An old and dangerous viper (having only the head, soul, and venom left).

A حاز *hāza*, (fut. يحوز *yahūzu*) He collected.

A حازّ *hāzz*, An excrescence on the callous part of a camel's breast, galling and excoriating the elbow.

A حازب *hāzib*, (pl. حزب *huzb* and حوازب *hawāzib*) Severe, difficult (affair).

A حازّة *hāzzat*, (pl. حوازّ *hawāzz*) Whatever renders the mind uneasy. حزّت حازّة من كوعها *hazzat hāzzatun min kūʿihā*, A phrase denoting The people were busy about their own affairs exclusively.

A حازر *hāzir*, Sour milk or wine. An austere, crabbed countenance. Barley-meal with an unpleasant smell.

A حازق *hāzik*, Pinched by a tight shoe.

A حازقة *hāzikat*, A multitude.

A حازم *hāzim*, (pl. حزمة *hazamat*) One who pursues a right course. Wise, provident, wary, prudent.

A حازميّة *hāzamiyat*, Name of a sect.

A حازي *hāzī*, A fortune-teller, a palmister.

A حاسب *hāsib*, A reckoner. An accountant. A paymaster.

A حاسّة *hāssat*, (pl. حواسّ *hawāss*) A sense (of which there are five, viz. سمع *samʿ*, بصر *basar*, شمّ *shamm*, ذوق *zawk*, and لمس *lums*). Destroying (herbage); as cold, hail, wind, locusts, and cattle: which are called حواسّ الارض *hawāssu'l arz*, The (five) senses of the earth. ذو الحاسّة *zū'l hāssat*, Endowed with sense and feeling, sensitive. حاسّهٔ عامّه *hāssai ʿāmma*, Common sense.

A حاسد *hāsid*, (pl. حسّد *hussad*, حسّاد *hussād*, and حسدة *hasadat*) Envious. An enemy.

A حاسر *hāsir*, (pl. حسّر *hussar*) Naked, unarmed, not having helmet, mail, or shield. A stallion which turns away wearied from covering.

A حاسن *hāsin*, Beautiful, elegant. The moon.

A حاسوس *hāsūs*, A spy (in a good sense, جاسوس *jāsūs* being used in a bad one). An unlucky wight. A year of scarcity.

A حاسي الذهب *hāsi'z zuhab*, Name of an individual who used to drink out of gold.

A حاش *hāsh*, (or حاشا *hāshā*) Besides, except. God forbid! let it not be! in no shape! P حاشا كه *hāshā ki*, Heaven forbid that . . . . A حاشاكم *hāshākum* or حاشا لكم *hāshā lakum*, Saving or excepting your reverence, with submission to you.

A حاشاء *hāshā'*, Thyme.

A حاشد *hāshid*, Ready, prepared (for any thing). A loaded bunch of dates or grapes. One who is continually milking his camel.

A حاشر *hāshir*, A collector. الحاشر *al hāshir*, Muhammad.

A حاشك *hāshik*, (A palm-tree) abounding in produce. Hard (bow). (pl. حواشك *hawāshik*) Consecutive, coming one after another.

A حاشم *hāsham*, Name of the father of a tribe.

A حاشئ *hāsha'*, Let it not be! God forbid!

A حاشية *hāshiyat*, (pl. حواشي *hawāshī*) A margin, brink, edge, border. The hem of a garment. A marginal note. Men of inferior rank. Small camels. Intimate friends. Family, kindred. A tract, side, quarter. A shadow. Protection.

A حاشيتان *hāshiyatāni*, A two-year old camel, and one entering the second year.

A حاشيش *hāshīsh*, A species of euphorbium.

P حاشيه بوس *hāshiya-bos*, Kissing the skirt.

A حاصب *hāsib*, (Wind) scattering gravel or flakes of snow. A pimply eruption from a fulness of blood. (A cloud) discharging a storm of hail.

A حاصّة *hāssat*, A disease which causes the hair to fall off. Bare (relationship).

A حاصد *hāsid*, (pl. حصدة *hasadat* and حصّاد *hussād*) A reaper, mower.

A حاصر *hāsir*, Who or what blocks up. A restrainer. An astringent. A calculator, numberer. A mat. A mat-maker.

A حاصل *hāsil*, (pl. حواصل *hawāsil*) Whatever remains over and above; a residue. Appearing, manifest, clear. Produce, whatever is gathered (as corn or fruits). Profit, gain, advantage, utility. Tax, duty, due, custom, revenue. Sum, end, conclusion, result. A locker or bin in a caravansary. حاصل ضرب *hāsili zarb*, The product of multiplication. حاصل قسمت *hāsili kismat*, The quotient. حاصل الامر *hāsilu'l amr*, The short or sum of the matter. حاصل الكلام *hāsilu'l kalām*, Upon the whole. In short, briefly. حاصل مصدر *hāsili masdar*, A verbal noun. An abstract noun. P حاصل آمدن *hāsil āmadan*, To be produced. حاصل بازار *hāsili bāzār*, Market-dues, toll. حاصل شدن *hāsil shudan*, To be gained. حاصل كردن *hāsil kardan*, (or ساختن *sāktan*) To acquire, gain, collect. To indulge.

A حاصلات *hāsilāt*, Proceeds, results.

P حاصل دار *hāsil-dār*, A collector.

A حاصن *hāsin*, (pl. حواصن) A chaste woman.

A حاصنة *hāsinat*, A chaste female.

A حاضر *hāzir*, (pl. حضّر *huzzar* and حضور *huzūr*) Any one come, or who is before. Present, ready, prepared. (in gram.) The present tense. The second person. Ready money. (pl. حضّار *huzzār* and حضرة *hazarat*) An inhabitant, near neighbour or borderer: a townsman, having a settled residence. A tribe or cantonment of wandering Arabs. A large family. امر الحاضر *amru'l hāzir*, Second person of the imperative. نهي الحاضر *nahyu'l hāzir*, Second person of the prohibitive. حاضر و ناظر *hāzir u nāzir*, Present and seeing (one of the attributes of God). P حاضر شدن *hāzir shudan*, To appear before, to be present. To be prepared, ready, in order. حاضر كردن *hāzir kardan*, To prepare, make present, or ready.

A حاضرات *hāzirāt*, Commanding or imprisoning demons, &c., raising the devil.

A حاضراتي *hāzirātī*, Commanding evil spirits.

P حاضران *hāzirān*, (pl. of A حاضر) Present.

P حاضرباش *hāzir-bāsh*, Content. An attendant.

P حاضرباشي *hāzir-bāshī*, Constant attendance.

A حاضرة *hāzirat*, A city, a fixed residence. (fem.) Ready. (pl. حواضر *hawāzir*) An elephant's ear.

A حاضر جواب *hāzir-jawāb*, Ready at an answer, pert. Echo.

A حاضر جوابي *hāzir-jawābī*, A repartee.

A حاضر ضامن *hāzir-zāmin*, A surety for personal appearance.

A حاضر ضامني *hāzir-zāminī*, A bond for personal appearance.

A حاضري *hāzirī*, Presence, readiness, attendance. Audience. Muster-roll. Breakfast. Dessert. An offering made to a saint.

A حاضن *hāzin*, (pl. حضّان *huzzān*) A fondler.

A حاضنة *hāzinat*, (pl. حواضن *hawāzin*) A nurse, foster-mother. A date-tree, whose bunches have come out and quitted the flowers: also one whose stalks are short.

A حاط *hāta*, (fut. يحوط *yahūtu*) He surrounded.

A حاطب *hātib*, A collector of good and bad. حاطب ليل *hātibu laylin*, One who talks in a confused manner. One who collects wood in the night.

A حاطم *hātim*, Who or what breaks.

A حاطورة *hātūrat*, Penetrating (sword).

A حاطوم *hātūm*, (pl. حواطيم *hawātīm*) A scarce season. Any thing which promotes digestion.

A حاظب *hāzib*, Fat.

A حافّ *hāff*, Surrounding, encircling. Coarsely ground (meal). Scurfy-headed (lad). Dry (cough). One who wounds grievously with a malignant eye.

A حافان *hāfāni*, Two greenish veins under the tongue.

A حافة *hāfat*, A coast, shore, brink, bank. Necessity, adversity, affliction. An ox treading out the corn, and the farthest from the one that occupies the centre of the circular threshing floor. (pl. of حائف *hāif*) Sides, margins, edges. Unjust, unrighteous, oppressive.

A حافد *hāfid*, (pl. حفد *hafad*) A servant. An assistant, helper.

A حافر *hāfir*, A digger, excavator. (pl. حوافر *hawāfir*) A hoof, nail, claw. A foot.

A حافرة *hāfirat*, Beginning (of business), exordium (of a speech). Original form. A way. رجع علي حافرته *rajaᵹa ᵹala' hāfiratihi*, He retraced his footsteps. مردود في الحافرة *mardūd fi'l hāfirat*, Restored to (its) former condition.

A حافز *hāfiz*, A part where the corner of the mouth bends.

A حافشة *hāfishat*, (pl. حوافش) A water-course.

A حافظ *hāfiz*, (pl. حفّاظ *huffāz* and حفظة *hafazat*) A keeper, preserver, guardian. A commander, governor. One who has by heart (the whole Kur'ān, who is also styled حافظ كلام الله *hāfizu kalāmi'llāh*, A rememberer of the word of God). A perfect poet (*i.e.* one who has composed a series of odes or other poems, in classes equal to the number of letters in the alphabet; the first class rhyming with ا *alif*, the second with ب *be*, and so on, which is called a Dīwān, and gives the poet a claim to the title of Hāfiz, which has been almost exclusively enjoyed by the celebrated Anacreon of Persia, Muhammad Shamsu'd dīn. A straight open road. حافظ الاجساد *hāfizu'l ajsād*, Wild garlic. حافظ البيت *hāfizu'l bayt*, Guardian of the house. حافظ الحرمين *hāfizu'l haramayn*, Defender of the two sacred cities, *i.e.* Mecca and Madīna. حافظ العين *hāfizu'l ᵹayn*, Not overcome by sleep, able to keep his eyes open. حافظ النحل *hāfizu'n nahl*, Euphorbium. حافظان قلاع *hāfizāni kilāᵹ*, (Pers. pl. of حافظ *hāfiz*) Governors of forts.

A حافظان *hāfizāni*, Hunger and nakedness.

A حافظة *hāfizat*, Female guardian. قوت حافظه *kūwati hāfiza*, A retentive faculty, good memory.

A حافل *hāfil*, (pl. حفّل *huffal*) (An udder or a ewe) full of milk, (a channel) filled with water.

A حافلة *hāfilat*, (A camel) full of milk.

A حافي *hāfī*, (pl. حفاة *hufāt*) Barefoot. Worn in the hoof. A cāzī or judge. One who inquires minutely into another's concerns. Benevolent, kind. Joyous, glad. A proper name.

A حافيرة *hāffīrat*, A certain black fish.

A حاقّ *hākk*, Middle (of winter, a road, or the head). حاقّ الجوع *hākku'l jūᵹ*, Real hunger. حاقّ الشجاع *hākku'sh shujāᵹ*, Perfect in bravery. رجل حاقّ الرجل *rajulun hākku'r rajuli*, A thoroughly manly person.

A حاقب *hākib*, Constipated, costive.

A حاقّة *hākkat*, (pl. حواقّ *hawākk*) Sure, impending, descending (calamity). Day of judgment. رجل حاقّة الرجل *rajulun hākkatu'r rajuli*, A truly brave man. حاقّة الشجاع *hākkatu'sh shujāᵹ*, Perfect in bravery, really brave.

A حاقد *hākid*, Rancorous, malevolent.

A حاقف *hākif*, Curved, bent. (A buck) lying down on a sand-hill, with his head and feet drawn together, and being crooked.

A حاقن *hākin*, Troubled with diabetes. One suffering under a retention of urine. A new moon lying on its back with its horns vertical.

A حاقنة *hākinat*, (pl. حواقن *hawākin*) The stomach. The lower part of the belly. The hollow between the collar-bone and the tendon of the neck.

A حاقورة *hākūrat*, The fourth heaven.

A حاقول *hākūl*, A long green fish.

A حاكة *hākat*, (pl. of حائك *hāik*) Weavers.

A حاكّة *hākkat*, A tooth.

A حاكل *hākil*, Difficult and obscure.

A حاكم *hākim*, (pl. حكّام *hukkām*) A governor, commander. A judge, magistrate. A name of God.

P حاكمانه *hākimāna*, Judicially, with authority.

A حاكمة *hākimat*, A princess, lady, governess.

A حاكي *hākī*, (pl. حكاة *hukāt*) A relator, narrator, author, historian.

A حال *hāl*, (pl. احوال *ahwāl* and احولة *ahwilat*) State, situation, condition, mode, manner. An affair, thing. Time present. A wife. Milk. Prosperous circumstances. Ecstacy. Black stinking mud. Soft earth. A child's go-cart. Hot ashes. A bundle. Any thing carried on the back. The middle of a horse's back. Name of a town in Yaman. The leaves of the thorny-tree سمر *samur* shaken into a cloth. الحال *al hāl*, Now. حال علي

حال *hāl ɛala' hāl*, Time after time. على كلّ حال *ɛala' kull hāl*, In every way. في الحال *fi'l hāl*, Immediately, forthwith, anon. P حال آنكه *hāl ānki*, Whereas, seeing that, now that, even whilst that. Though, yet, however, even, although, notwithstanding. حال كردن *hāl kardan*, To be in an ecstacy.

A حالّ *hāll*, (pl. حلول *hulūl*, حلّال *hullāl*, and حلّل *hullal*) Descending. Due (debt).

A حالاً *hālan*, Now, at present.

A حالات *hālāt*, (pl. of حالة *hālat*) States, conditions. Changes, vicissitudes.

A حالب *hālib*, (pl. حلبة *halabat*) A milker. (dual حالبان *hālibāni*) A vein in the region of the root of the thigh by which the urine passes from the kidneys to the bladder.

P حال بنجين *hāl banjin*, An anticipation of the revenue by bringing part of the next year's rents to the account of the present.

A حالبيّ *hālibīy*, Name of a medicinal plant.

A حالة *hālat*, (pl. حال *hāl* and حالات *hālāt*) State, quality, condition. Posture of affairs. One of the stages of the mystical progress of the Sūfis, ecstasy. A thing. Action. A fuller's beetle. P يك حالهٔ بار *yak hālaɪ bār*, One half of a load, as much as a beast carries on one side.

A حالحاصل *hāl-hāsil*, Present produce.

A حالز *hāliz*, Narrow, close, covetous.

A حالس *hālis*, (pl. حوالس *hawālis*) A square or circle in a certain boy's game.

A حالق *hālik*, (pl. حلقة *halakat*) A shaver. Depilatory. Unfortunate. (pl. حلّق *hullak* and حوالق *hawālik*) A full udder. High (place). Lofty (mountain). A vine-tendril curling round a branch.

A حالقة *hālikat*, Unfortunate. Separation from kin. A woman who shaves off her hair in sorrow.

A حالك *hālik*, Pitch black. Dismal: unlucky.

A حالم *hālim*, A dreamer. A sleeper. Arrived at the age of puberty (حلم *hulum*). Cresses.

A حالوقة *hālūkat*, Penetrating (sword). Sharp, keen (man).

A حالوم *hālūm*, Coagulated milk.

A حالوما *hālūmā*, The plant سرخ مرد *surkh mard*.

P حالي *hāle*, Now, at this instant, at this time.

A حالي *hālī*, Sweet. One dressing or adorning himself with jewels of gold or silver.

A حاليّ *hālīy*, Belonging to the present time. New, modern. Current (coin). Now, soon. Descriptive of a state. اسم حاليّه *ismi hālīya*, The Persian participle ان *ān*: as, جويان *joyān* or *jūyān*, Seeking: a seeker.

P حاليا *hālyā*, Present.

A حالئة *hāliɪat*, A noxious serpent. A woman whose business it is to clean hides.

A حالية *hāliyat*, (fem. of حالي *hālī*) (pl. حوالي *hawālī*) Adorning herself with gold or silver jewels.

A حاليّة *hālīyat*, The present participle. Conditionality.

A حام *hām*, Son of Noah, from whom they say the Negroes are descended. جيش حام *jayshi hām*, (The host of Ham) Darkness.

A حامّة *hāmmat*, Nobles. Relations. Children. The best (of the flock). الحامّة والعامّة *al hāmmat wa'l ɛāmmat*, Nobles and commonalty.

A حامت *hāmit*, Very sweet (date).

A حامد *hāmid*, One who praises: a praiser.

A حامر *hāmir*, The owner of an ass.

A حامرة *hāmirat*, Drivers of asses.

A حامز *hāmiz*, Strong, firm. Sour, acid, acrid, pungent. حامز الفؤاد *hāmizu'l fuɪād*, Light, cheerful, brisk. Ingenious, witty.

A حامض *hāmiz*, Bitter, salt, sour, acid (vegetable). لبن حامض *labani hāmiz*, Very thick milk made sour by boiling, and addition of a strong acid. حامض الفؤاد *hāmizu'l fuɪād*, Vicious, depraved.

A حامضة *hāmizat*, (pl. حوامض *hawāmiz*) (A camel) feeding on bitter herbage.

A حامل *hāmil*, (pl. حملة *hamalat*) A porter, carrier. (pl. حوامل *hawāmil*) Pregnant. حامل اسفار *hāmili asfār*, An ass. An ignorant workman or reader. حامل متن *hāmili matn*, A commentary rehearsing, or annexed to, the text. حامل مكتوب *hāmili maktūb*, A letter-carrier. حامل وحي *hāmili wahy*, The bearer of revelation, Gabriel. ذكر حامل *zikri hāmil*, Mental prayer.

A حاملة *hāmilat*, (pl. حوامل *hawāmil*) Pregnant. Laden with fruit (a tree). A basket in which grapes are carried to the drying-house. (pl. حوامل *hawāmil*) The foot. A sinew in the arm or foot. P حامله شدن *hāmila shudan*, To become pregnant, to conceive. حامله كردن *hāmila kardan*, To render pregnant, to impregnate.

A حامي *hāmī*, Burning, hot. (pl. حماة *humāt*) A protector, defender. A he-camel emancipated from labour. A lion. حامي الحقيقة *hāmi'l hakīkat*, A defender of the truth. حامي الحميّا *hāmi'l humayya'*, The protector of a district. حامي الذّمار *hāmi'z zimār*, One who maintains his right. P حاميان روي زمين *hāmiyāni rūyi zamīn*, Protectors of the face of the earth.

A حاميّ *hāmīy*, A son of Ham: an Ethiop, negro.

A حامية *hāmiyat*, (fem. of حامي *hāmī*) (pl. حوامي *hawāmī*) A protectress. One who protects his companions. A protective body; defenders, protectors. A she-camel exempted from labour. A trivet. Stones filling a well. Name of a fountain in which the sun is said to set. على حاميتي *ɛala' hāmiyatī*, About my business, where I pleased. حاميتان *hāmiyatāni*, The right and left of a horse's hoof.

A (آل) حاميم *(āl) hā mīm*, (pl. ذوات حاميم *zawāt hā mīm*) One of the seven chapters of the Kur'ān which begin with حم.

A حانّ *hānn*, One who covets or lusts after. Greedy. One under strong emotion.

A حاناة *hānāt*, A shop. A vintner's shop.

A حانة *hānat*, (pl. حانات *hānāt*) A wine-shop.

A حانّة *hānnat*, A camel crying for her colt.

A حانث *hānis*, A false-swearer, perjurer.

A حانط *hānit*, Red leather. One who bears intense hatred. Possessed of much wheat. The fruit of the غضا *ghaza'*. حانط الصرّة *hānitu's surrat*, One who has a long and well-lined purse. احمر حانط *ahmar hānit*, Intense red.

A حانق *hānik*, Enraged.

A حانك *hānik*, (for حالك *hālik*) Very black.

A حانوت *hānūt*, A tavern. A vintner. (pl. حوانيت *hawānīt*) A shop.

A حانويّ *hānawīy*, (or حانيّ *hānīy*) A vintner. Relating to a tavern. Official.

A حانئ *hāniɪ*, Intense. احمر حانئ Intense red.

A حاني *hānī*, A sheep or wild cow in heat. Name of a town in the district of Diyār bakar celebrated for its iron-mines.

A حانية *hāniyat*, (A woman) who refuses to remarry for her children's sake. A sheep or cow greatly in heat. Wry-necked (sheep). A shop.

A حانيّة *hānīyat*, Vintners. Wine.

A حاوي *hāwī*, One who collects, contains, or comprehends. A collector. A snake-catcher.

A حاوية *hāwiyat*, (or حاوياء *hāwiyāɪ*) (pl. حواوي *hawāwī*) An entrail.

A حائب *hāɪib*, A sinner, offender, delinquent.

A حائت *hāɪit*, A great reprover or chider.

A حائج *hāɪij*, Necessary, indispensable. Name of a certain thorny tree.

A حائد *hāɪid*, One who declines or turns from. A wanderer.

A حائر *hāɪir*, Low-lying, secure, snug (place). A garden. Emaciated, lean. Fat of meat. The burial-place of Husayn son of Alīy. (pl. حوران *hūrān* and حيران *hīrān*) A conflux of water, or the place into which it runs. حائر بائر *hāɪir bāɪir*, Perishing, ruined. Astonished, stupefied.

A حائرة *hāɪirat*, (A woman or sheep) that never attains maturity. (pl. حوائر *hawāɪir*) Worthless.

A حائريّ *hāɪirīy*, A native of Hair.

A حائش *hāɪish*, A plantation of palm-trees, &c.

A حائص *hāɪis*, Impervious (she-camel).

A حائض *hāɪiz*, (pl. حيّض *huyyaz*) Menstruous.

A حائضة *hāɪizat*, (pl. حوائض *hawāɪiz*) A menstruous woman.

A حائط *hāɪit*, (pl. حيطان *hītān* and حياط *hiyāt*) Wall, inclosure, fence. A garden. طعام حائط *taɛām hāɪit*, Food which causes the belly to swell.

A حائف *hāɪif*, (pl. حافة *hāfat* or حيّف *huyyaf*) Side, margin, edge, brink. Unjust, cruel, tyrannical.

A حائك *hāɪik*, One who walks with a strut. (pl. حاكة *hākat* and حوكة *hawakat*) A weaver.

A حائكة *hāɪikat*, (pl. حوائك) A female weaver.

A حائل *hāɪil*, (pl. حيال *hiyāl*, حول *hūl*, حوّل *huwal*, and حولل *hūlal*) Who or what restrains, detains, or intervenes (as a curtain between two).

Changing colour. A female not conceiving. A female camel colt just dropped. A camel not conceiving, or one not conceiving for one, two, or several years. A palm-tree bearing one year and not another. حائل حول *hāʼilu hūlin*, (or حائل حولل *hāʼilu hūlalin*) (A camel) not conceiving for two years. ام حائل *ummi hāʼil*, A she-camel.

A حائم *hāʼim*, (pl. حوّم *hūwam*) Anxiously desirous. (A bird) skimming in circles. Thirsty.

A حائن *hāʼin*, A fool.

A حائنة *hāʼinat*, Wine. (pl. حوائن *hawāʼin*) A destructive calamity.

A حايي *hāyī*, Living. ضرب ضربةً ليس بحايي منها *zaraba zarbatan laysa bi hāyin minhā*, He struck a blow such as no one could survive.

A حب *hub*, A grape-stone.

A حبّ *habba*, (fut. يحبّ *yahibbu*) He loved. He stopped. He fatigued.

A حبّ *habb*, (pl. حبوب *hubūb* and حبّان *hubbān*) A grain, berry, seed. A pill. حبّ البان *habbu'l bān*, The ben-nut. حبّ البطم *habbu'l butm*, Turpentine-berries. حبّ بلادر *habbi balādir*, Malacca bean-seed. حبّ البلسان *habbu'l balsān*, Carpobalsam. حبّ تحاميل *habbi tahāmīl*, Suppository pills. حبّ تمرهندي *habbi tamr-hindī*, Tamarind-seed. حبّ الخردل *habbu'l khardal*, Mustard-seed. حبّ خروع *habbi kharwaʻ*, Spurge-seed. حبّ خيار *habbi khiyār*, Cucumber-seed. حبّ الذهب *habbu'z zahab*, A grain of gold. حبّ راوند *habbi rāwand*, Rhubarb-pills. حبّ الرشاد *habbu'r rashād*, Nose-smart. حبّ الزرقة *habbu'z zurkat*, Flea-bane seed. حبّ الزيبق *habbu'z zībak*, Mercurial pills. حبّ سجستاني *habbi sijistānī*, Cardamom-bean seed. حبّ السّعلة *habbu's suʻlat*, Cough-lozenges. حبّ السّلاطين *habbu's salātīn*, A purgative seed. حبّ شاهترج *habbi shāhtaraj*, Fumitory-pills. حبّ الصّفرة *habbu's safrat*, Antibilious pills. حبّ صنوبر *habbi sanawbar*, Fruit of the pine-tree. حبّ العروس *habbu'l ʻarūs*, Cubeb-seed. حبّ عزيز *habbi ʻazīz*, A berry, black without, white within, soft, juicy, and delicious. حبّ عمومي *habbi ʻamūmī*, Pills in common use. حبّ الغار *habbu'l ghār*, Laurel-berries. Bay-tree. حبّ الغمام *habbu'l ghamām*, A hailstone. حبّ الغول *habbu'l ghūl*, Fruit of the mastic-tree. حبّ الفقد *habbu'l fakad*, Seed of the agnus castus. حبّ القلت *habbu'l kilt*, A sort of vetch. حبّ قوقايا *habbi kūkāyā*, Officinal pills. حبّ كاكنج *habbi kākanj*, The winter cherry. حبّ الكلخ *habbu'l kalkh*, Ammoniac pills. حبّ لسان الكلب *habbi lisāni'l kalb*, Seeds of hound's tongue. حبّ اللهف *habbu'l lahf*, Red night-shade berries. حبّ المصطكة *habbu'l mastakat*, Mastic-pills. حبّ المعدة *habbu'l miʻdat*, Stomachic pills. حبّ المقل *habbu'l mukl*, Bdellium-pills. حبّ الملوك *habbu'l mulūk*, A cherry. حبّ النّسا *habbu'n nisā*, Anti-hysteric pills. حبّ النّيل *habbu'n nīl*, Woad. حبّ هال *habbi hāl*, Cardamoms. حبّ اليهود *habbu'l yahūd*, The winter-cherry. *Hibb*, (v. n. of حبّ) Loving. Wishing, desiring. Love, affection. The seed of any pot-herb or fragrant plant. A small plant growing among grass. An ear-ring of a single grain. (pl. احباب *ahbāb*, حبّان *hibbān*, *hubbān*, حبوب *hubūb*, حببة *hababat*, and حبّ *hubb*) A lover, friend. *Hubb*, (v. n. of حبّ) Loving. Wishing. Pleasing, being agreeable. Love. Precious, dear. (pl. احباب *ahbāb*, حببة *hibabat*, and حباب *hibāb*) A wine-jar. A grape-stone. حبّ و وداد *hubb u widād*, Love and friendship, benevolence and charity. حبّ الوطن *hubbu'l watan*, Love of country; patriotism. *Habba*, O excellent! حبّ به *habba bihi*, How dear is he to me! حبّ بفلان *hubba bi fulānin*, How amiable is such an one!

A حبأ *habaʼ*, (pl. احباء *ahbāʼ*) A royal favourite, the familiar companion of a king.

A حبا *haba'*, A cloud piled up like a mountain.

A حباء *hibāʼ*, (v. n. 3 of حبا for حبو) Shewing respect of persons, winking at. Aiding. Leaning towards. A gift. *Hibāʼ* or *hubāʼ*, A mode of sitting with the legs and thighs contracted, and a sash wrapped about them.

A حباب *habāb*, A bubble of water. Dew. A wished-for event. A large quantity of water or sand. Four pieces of wood on which they place a water-pot. *Hibāb*, (v. n. 3 of حبّ) Loving, cultivating friendship. An ear-ring of a single grain. (pl. of حبّ *hubb*) Jars. *Hubāb*, Love, friendship. Beloved. The object of one's affections or efforts. A species of serpent. Satan. A bubble. ام حباب *umm hubāb*, (Mother Bubble) The world.

A حبّاب *habbāb*, A seller of wine-jars or pots.

A حبابة *hubābat*, (pl. حباب *hubāb*) A certain small black reptile or insect.

A حبابير *habābīr*, (pl. of حبّور) Young bustards.

A حبأة *habʼat*, Black mud.

A حبّات *habbāt*, (pl. of حبّة) Corns, grains.

A حباتر *habātir*, (pl. of حبتر *habtar*) Short-bodied. Foxes. *Hubātir*, One who abandons his parents or kindred.

A حباتك *hubātik*, Small-bodied.

A حباتل *hubātil*, Small and lean.

A حباج *habāj*, A kind of tree. A vine.

A حباجر *hubājir*, Thick. A male bustard.

A حباجعيزان *habā juʻayzān*, Name of a plant.

A حباجل *hubājil*, Short, compactly built.

A حباجي *habāja'*, (Camels) swelled from eating of the plants عرفج *ʻarfaj* and ضعة *zaʻat*.

A حباحب *habāhib*, (pl. of حبحاب *habhāb*) Small, short. Swift, active.

A حباحب *hubāhib*, Name of a very avaricious man, who was afraid to light a fire, lest it should invite guests to visit him. A weak and useless fire. Sparks from a tinder-box, or of a horse-shoe striking the stones. ابو حباحب *abū hubāhib*, A glow-worm. ام حباحب *umm hubāhib*, A sort of locust.

A حبار *habār* or *hibār*, Mark, vestige, sign.

A حبارات *habārāt*, Signs, forms, vestiges.

A حبارج *habārij*, (and حباريج *habārīj*) (pl. of حبرج *hubruj*) Certain aquatic birds. *Hubārij*, (for حباري *hubāra'*) A male-bustard.

A حباري *hubāra'*, (pl. حباريات *hubārayāt*, حباري *habārī*, and حبائر *habāʼir*) A bustard.

A حبارير *habārīr*, (pl. of حبرور) Young bustards.

A حباشة *hubāshat*, (v. n. of حبش) Collecting, gaining, getting. A mixed multitude. Name of a place near Mecca, where an annual fair of eight days is held: also of another in the tribe قينقاع *kaynukāʻ*. حباشات الطّعام *hubāshātu't taʻām*, Food which is taken.

A حباشيّة *hubāshiyat*, An eagle (specially black).

A حباض *hubāz*, Weakness.

A حباط *hubāt*, A disease arising from eating too freely of the herb ذرق *zurak*.

A حباطي *habāta'*, (pl. of حبط *habit*) Griped, swollen, and constipated. *Habātī*, (pl. of حبنطي *habanta'*) Short and big-bellied.

A حباق *hubāk*, (v. n. of حبق) Farting. A fart. يا حباق *yā habāki*, An exclamation of reproach to a maid-servant.

SY حباقا *habākā*, The lot-tree.

A حباك *hibāk*, Black above a pigeon's wings. (pl. حبك *hubak* or *hubuk*) A thong whereby a pack-saddle is fastened on. (pl. حبك *hubuk*) The string of a girdle. The summit of a sandhill. A track through the same. The path of the stars. A curl on the water. A ring in a coat of mail. A curly lock of hair.

A حباكر *habākir*, (pl. of حبوكر *habawkar*) Slender men who take short steps.

A حباكريّ *hubākiriy*, Bulky, close, compact.

A حبال *hibāl*, The muscles of the legs. Roots of the penis. (pl. of حبل *habl*) Ropes. *Hubāl*, Fulness, repletion.

A حبّال *habbāl*, A rope-maker.

A حبالة *hibālat*, (pl. حبائل *habāʼil*) A net, gin. Warp of cloth. A vine-shoot.

A حبالّة *habāllat*, A fit time, a proper opportunity. Dismissal, divorce, departure. Weight. Cheerfulness.

A حبالي *habāla'*, (pl. of حبلي *hubla'*) Pregnant.

A حبّان *hibbān*, (pl. of حبّ *hibb*) Lovers, friends. *Hubbān*, (pl. of حبّ *habb*) Berries, grains, pulse.

A حبانط *habānit*, (pl. of حبنطي *habanta'*) Short and big-bellied.

A حبائب *habāʼib*, (pl. of حبيب *habīb*) Lovers. Mistresses.

A حبائر *habāʼir*, (pl. of حباري) Bustards.

A حبائس *habāʼis*, Best camels kept at home.

A حبائك *habāʼik*, Tracks in the sand.

A حبائل *habāʼil*, (pl. of حبالة *hibālat*) Nets, snares, gins. Name of a demon which tempts women: as ابليس *iblīs* is said to be the tempter of men. حبائل الشيطان *habāsilu'sh shayṭān*, Satan's nets, *i.e.* women. حبائل اللؤلو *habāsilu'l luslus*, Strings of pearls. حبائل الموت *habāsilu'l mawt*, The snares of death.

A حبب *habab* or *hibab*, A bubble of water. A large quantity of water or sand. Freshness and brilliancy of teeth. A row of teeth (like unto pearls). Spittle. *Hibab*, (pl. of حبّة *hibbat*) Seeds of plants, berries. *Hubab*, (pl. of حبّة *hubbat*) Objects of desire.

A حببة *hababat*, (pl. of حبّ *hibb*) Lovers, friends. *Hibabat*, (pl. of حبّ *hubb*) Jars.

A حبة *hubat*, (pl. حبي *huba'*) A grape-stone.

A حبّة *habbat*, (pl. حبّات *habbāt*) One berry, grain, or seed. A grain (a weight). A botch. A particle, part. Necessity, occasion. حبّة الثوم *habbatu's sūm*, A clove of garlic. حبّة الحلوة *habbatu'l halwa*, Aniseed. الحبّة الخضراء *al habbatu'l khazrās*, A kind of fruit (in Persia called بن *ban* or ون *van*). حبّة السّوداء *habbātu's sawdās*, Coriander-seed. حبّة الغمام *habbatu'l ghamām*, (المزن *al muzn* or القرّ *al hurr*) Hailstones. حبّة القلب *habbatu'l halb*, The heart's core. Heart's blood. Original sin. جابر ابن حبّة *jābir ibn habbat*, Bread. *Hibbat*, (pl. حبب *hibab*) A wild berry. *Hubbat*, (pl. حبب *hubab*) Beloved. An object of desire. Friendship. A grape-stone.

A حبتر *habtar*, (pl. حباتر *habātir*) Short of body or stature. A fox.

A حبترة *habtarat*, (v. n. of حبتر Q) Being lean and slender-bodied. Slenderness, smallness of body.

A حبتقة *habtakat*, Anguish from avarice or care.

A حبتك *habtak*, Small-bodied.

A حبتل *habtal*, Small and bare of flesh.

A حبث *habis*, A kind of serpent without a train.

A حبج *habj*, (v. n. of حبج) Appearing suddenly. Encircling. Travelling rapidly. Approaching. Going into a corner. Striking with a stick. Breaking wind either with the mouth or armpit. *Habaj*, (v. n. of حبج) Appearing. Being griped from eating of certain plants (camels). A cautery on the flank of a camel. A kind of tree. *Hibj*, A crowd of people. *Hibj* or *habj*, A place where a tribe is convened together. *Habij*, A camel griped. One who breaks wind.

A حبجة *habjat*, A single blow with a stick.

A حبجر *hibajr*, Thick. *Hubjur*, A male bustard.

A حبجى *habja'*, Camels swollen from feeding on the plants عرفج *ɛarfuj* and ضعة *zaɛat*.

A حبحاب *hubhāb*, (pl. حباحب *habāhib*) Short, mean, deformed, minute, small. Slender (man, camel).

A حبحب *habhab*, Slender (man, camel). Gentle flow of water. (pl. of حبحبة) Syrian melons.

A حبحبة *habhabat*, Lean, slender, emaciated (she-camel). A slow flux of water. Debility. Heat or kindling of fire. The driving of camels. (pl. حبحب *habhab*) The Syrian melon.

A حبحبي *habhabīy*, Slender (man or camel).

A حبّذا *habbazā*, O excellent! brave! how charming! حبّذا طالع *habbazā tāliɛ*, O what luck!

A حبر *habr*, (v. n. of حبر *habr*) Beautifying, adorning. Doing good, acting beneficently. Putting ink into an inkstand. Making glad. Remaining (the mark of a blow). Joy, gladness, cheerfulness. Yellowness of teeth. *Hibr*, Ink. Beauty, embroidery. A vestige, sign, trace. Signs of joy. Yellowness of teeth. Like, equal, resembling. *Hibr* or *habr*, (pl. احبار *ahbār* and حبور *hubūr*) A learned man, Jewish doctor. A man of probity and honour. *Hubr*, (pl. of حبير *habīr*) Speckled, dappled clouds. Striped stuffs. New garments. *Habar*, (v. n. of حبر) Making glad. Being healed of wounds, but having a scar left. Being raw (a wound); also being healed and leaving a scar. Being healed (a hand), but having a knot on the bone. Being yellow (the teeth). Abounding in grass (land). A mark, sign, vestige. Joy, cheerfulness, blitheness. *Hibar*, (pl. of حبرة *hibarat*) Striped stuffs of Yaman. *Habir*, Soft and new. *Hibir*, A yellow concretion on the teeth. *Hubur hubur*, A word used in calling a sheep to be milked.

A حبربر *habarbar*, A young bustard. A little camel. A thing, any thing. Short, dwarfish, mean.

A حبربرة *habarbarat*, A single hair. A small and contemptible woman

A حبربور *ha* or *hibarbūr*, A young bustard.

A حبرة *habrat*, (v. n. of حبر) Making glad, delighting. Song, dance, and heavenly minstrelsy. Melody, harmony. Joy, delight. *Habrat*, *hubrat*, or *hibirat*, Yellowness of the teeth. *Hubrat*, A knot in wood out of which vessels are turned. *Hi* or *habarat*, (pl. حبر *hibar*) A striped Arabian stuff.

A حبرج *hubruj*, (pl. حبارج *habārij*, and حباريج *habārīj*) A kind of water-bird.

A حبرجل *habarjal*, Thick-lipped.

A حبرش *hibrish*, Very malevolent.

A حبرقس *habarkas*, A small camel or ram.

A حبرقش *habarkash*, A small camel.

A حبرقص *habarkas*, A dwarf. One whose flesh is compact. Small camel. Young flea. Vile fellow.

A حبرقصة *habarkasat*, A dwarfish woman.

A حبركاة *habarkāt*, (fem. of حبركى) A female tike.

A حبركى *habarka'*, Men ruined or perishing. The tike (an insect). Clouds piled on clouds. Sands heaped up. Weak in the feet, small-bodied and long-backed. Thick-necked.

A حبرمة *habramat*, (v. n. of حبرم Q) Making a preserve from pomegranates.

A حبرور *hubrūr*, (pl. حبارير) A young bustard.

A حبروف *hubrūf*, Who labours to feed a family.

A حبرون *habrūn*, Hebron, the city of Abraham.

A حبري *habra'*, Hebron, the city of Abraham.

A حبري *hibrīy*, A seller of ink. *Hibarīy*, A seller of striped stuffs of Yaman called حبرة *hibarat*.

A حبريت *hibrīt*, A plain, open, downright lie.

A حبرير *hibrīr*, A young bustard.

A حبس *habs*, (v. n. of حبس) Retaining; detaining, imprisoning. Bequeathing (a horse) to pious uses (prohibiting alienation). Displaying courage in danger. Covering (a bed) with bed-clothes. A prison. A mound, dike, dam, for confining water. Courage, bravery. A high mountain. حبس اساري *habsi asāra'*, Imprisonment of captives. حبس بول *habsi bawl*, Strangury. حبس النفس *habsu'n nafas*, Suffocation. P حبس دم *habsi dam*, Retention of the breath, which some fakīrs do for a very long time. Asthma. حبس كردن *hubs kardan*, To arrest, put in prison. A *Hibs*, (pl. احباس *ahbās*) A dam for confining water (for the use of men or cattle). A pond, reservoir, tank. Water collected but receiving no augmentation. Bed-clothes. The middle girth of a camel-litter. A pin of silver fixed in the centre of an embroidered veil. *Hubs*, Any bequest for pious uses. *Hubus*, Any thing whatever dedicated to pious uses, (as the produce of a vineyard or palm-plantation). Men on foot.

A حبّس *hubbas*, Men on foot.

A حبسة *hubsat*, Silence. Self-imposed restraint. Impediment in speech. Strangury.

A حبش *habsh*, (v. n. of حبش) Collecting, gaining, getting. *Habash*, (pl. حبشان) An Abyssinian.

A حبشان *hubshān*, A species of locust. (pl. of حبش *habash*) Ethiopians.

A حبشة *habashat*, Ethiopia. Natives of Ethiopia or of Southern Arabia.

P حبشي *habashī*, Ethiopian: Ethiopic: a slave.

A حبشيّ *habashīy*, A name of two mountains.

A حبشيّة *hubshīyat*, A species of large black ant. *Habashīyat*, The plant بهمي *buhma'*, when abundant and luxuriant. *Habashīyat* or *hubshīyat*, Camels black and strong.

A حبض *habz*, (v. n. of حبض) Dying. Making (a bow-string) twang. Falling into the archer's hand (an arrow discharged carelessly or unskilfully). A low, weak noise. *Habaz*, (v. n. of حبض) Moving, beating (as an artery). Vibrating and twanging (a bow-string). Being defrauded of one's right. Moving one's self, being moved. Beating and then stopping (the heart). Falling into the hands of an archer (an arrow, when shooting carelessly or unskilfully). Being exhausted (water in a well). Failing, not happening according to wish. Motion. Noise. A weak voice. Power, strength. Remains of life.

A حبط *habt*, (v. n. of حبط) Being shed with impunity (blood). Being done in vain or without reward (work), being lost. *Habat*, (v. n. of حبط) Being cicatrized (a wound). Swelling, becoming constipated from too much, or unwholesome food (cattle). A swelling in the udder or elsewhere. A swelling from eating of the herb ذرق *zurak*. The cicatrized scar of a wound or scourge. The vestiges of a swelling that has not burst or bled. A pain in a camel's belly from unwholesome food and constipation. *Habit*, (pl. حباطي *habāta'*) Griped, constipated, and swollen from over-eating.

A حبطة *habtat*, Remains of water in a cistern.

A حبطيّ *habatiy*,, Belonging to the Arabian tribe of حبطات بني تميم *habatāt bani tamīm*.

A حبطيطة *habatītat*, Small, mean (thing).

A حبق *habk*, (v. n. of حبق) Farting. A blow with a stick, rope, or scourge. *Hibk*, A fart. *Habak*, Mint. Pennyroyal. Basil. حبق البقر *habaku'l bakar*, Camomile. حبق الترنجان *habaku't turunjān*, Baum. حبق التمساح *habaku't timsāh*, Water-mint. حبق خراساني *habaki khurāsāni*, Sorrel. حبق الراعي *habaku'r rāع*, Mugwort. الحبق الريحاني *al habaku'r rayhāniy*, Esculent bdellium of Mecca. حبق الشيوخ *habaku'sh shuyūkh*, The plant مرو *marv*. الحبق الصعتري *al habaku's saعtariy*, Sweet basil. حبق الفيل *habaku'l fīl*, Marjoram. حبق قرنفلي *habaki karanfuli*, (or كرماني *harmāni*) Sweet basil. حبق القنا *habaku'l kana'*, Marjoram. حبق الماء *habaku'l māع*, Water-mint. حبق نبطي *habaki nabti*, Basil. *Habik*, (v. n. of حبق) Farting. A fart (of camel or sheep). *Hubak*, Weak-minded.

A حبقّ *hibikk*, Long.

A حبقبق *hubukbuk*, Sweet basil (in Yaman).

A حبقة *habkat*, One fart. *Habakat*, Ignorant.

A حبقة *hibikkat*, A dwarf.

A حبقرّ *habakurr*, Hail. ابرد من حبقر *abrad min habakurr*, Colder than hail.

A حبقّى *hibikka'*, A quick journey.

A حبك *habk*, (v. n. of حبك) Weaving well (a garment). Doing any thing firmly and well. Cutting. Decapitating. Farting. Repelling, resisting, opposing. *Habak*, A vine-root. *Hubak*, (pl. of حبكة *hubkat*) Waistbands of breeches. Pack-saddle-straps. *Hubuk*, A fragment. A lock of hair. (pl. of حباك *hibāk*, Girdle-strings. Summits of sand-hills. Tracks through the same. Paths of the stars. Curls on water. Rings in coats of mail. Ringlets of hair. *Hubuk* or *hubak*, (pl. of حباك *hibāk*) Thongs wherewith pack-saddles are secured.

A حبكّ *hibakk*, Vile, abject, base, sordid. *Hubukk*, Strong, intense.

A حبكة *hubkat*, (pl. حبك *hubak*) The waistband of breeches, the fastening place of a girdle. A strap whereby a pack-saddle is made fast. *Habakat*, A vine-root. Barley-meal.

A حبكرة *habkarat*, A collecting, bringing together.

A حبكل *habkal* or *hubkul*, Short-bodied.

A حبكّى *hibikka'*, A rapid march.

A حبل *habl*, (v. n. of حبل) Laying a net for game, or catching game in a net. Binding with a rope. Making a treaty. Acting hypocritically, dissembling. (pl. احبل *ahbul*, احبال *ahbāl*, and حبول *hubūl*) A rope, cord, halter. A tendon. A vein. Sand writhed into the resemblance of a rope. Union, connection. League, confederacy, compact. Security, protection. A continued, uninterrupted work. The starting-post at a horse-race. A name of Arafat. A grape-tree. The part between the neck and shoulder. A vein in the upper part of the arm and in the back. حبل الذراع *hablu'z zirāع*, A tendon of the arm. هو علي حبل ذراعك *huwa عala' habli zirāعika*, He is nigh thee. حبل العاتق *hablu'l عātik*, A tendon of the neck. حبل المتين *hablu'l matīn*, A strong rope, *i.e.* a firm alliance. حبل المساكين *hablu'l masākīn*, White ivy. حبل الوريد *hablu'l warīd*, The jugular vein. *Hibl*, Wise, clever, intelligent. Very shrewd and skilful in the management of property. *Hibl* or *habl*, (pl. حبول *hubūl*) Evil, misfortune. *Hubl* or *hubal*, (pl. of حبلة *hublat*) Fruits of thorny trees. *Habal*, (v. n. of حبل) Conceiving, being pregnant. Being filled. Conception, pregnancy. Anger, sadness. A vine.

A حبلان *hablān* or *hublān*, (A man) filled with liquor. Angry (man).

A حبلانة *hablānat*, Angry (woman). Pregnant (woman).

A حبلاويّ *hublāwiy*, Relating to one pregnant.

A حبلبس *habalbas*, A brave man. One who moves not from his place. A lion.

A حبلة *hablat* or *habalat*, A vine-branch or shoot. *Hublat*, A necklace. An ornament for the neck. A certain esculent. (pl. حبل *hubl* or *hubal*) The fruit of any prickly tree or shrub. *Hublat* or *habalat*, A vine or a vine-root. *Habalat*, (pl. of حابلة *hābilat*) Pregnant (females). *Habalat* or *hablat*, A shoot of a palm-tree. حبل الحبلة *habalu'l habalat*, A fœtus, embryo. Unripe grapes.

A حبلّق *haballak*, Slender, small and mean sheep.

A حبلويّ *hublawiy*, Relating to one pregnant.

A حبلى *hubla'* or *hublu'*, (A woman) filled (with liquor. *Hubla'*, (pl. حبليات *hublayāt* and حبالى *habāla'*) Pregnant (woman, also all animals that have claws). Name of a certain big-bellied man.

A حبليّ *hubliy*, Belonging to pregnant women.

A حبليل *hublīl*, A certain animalcule, which can be resuscitated by the rain after it is dead.

A حبن *habn*, Rhododaphne. *Hibn*, A monkey. *Hibn*, (or حبنة *hibnat*) (pl. حبون *hubūn*) A boil, a pimple. *Habn* or *haban*, (v. n. of حبن) Being dropsical. Being filled with rage. *Haban*, Dropsy.

A حبناء *habnāع*, (fem. of احبن *ahban*) Dropsical (woman). Big-bellied (woman). A pigeon which does not lay. Fleshy (foot).

A حبنبر *habambar*, A thing, any thing.

A حبنطا *habantas*, حبنطاة *habantaعat*, or حبنطى *habanta'*, (pl. حباطي *habāti*, or حبانط *habānit*) Short. Corpulent, fat, and big-bellied.

A حبنطاة *habantāt*, A woman of a small and contemptible stature, and big-bellied.

A حبنطى *habanta'*, Big-bellied. Full of rage.

A حبو *habw*, (v. n. of حبا for حبو) Creeping along the ground on his backside (a boy). Grazing the earth, then rising, and hitting the mark (an arrow). Being unable to rise from leanness (cattle). Meeting, encountering, coming across. Scudding along (a ship). Giving, presenting. Refusing, withholding. Guarding, defending. Being near, approaching (to fifty). Being high, raised up.

A حبوّ *hubūw*, (v. n. of حبا for حبو) Approaching, drawing near. Being long and approximating to each other (cartilages of ribs). Being joined to the back-bone (ribs). Going on hands and belly.

A حبوب *hubūb*, (pl. of حبّ *habb*) Grains, berries. (pl. of حبّ *hibb*) Lovers, friends.

A حبوبات *hubūbāt*, Vegetables, pot-herbs.

A حبوة *habwat*, (v. n. of حبا for حبو) Giving, presenting. *Habwat*, *hibwat*, or *hubwat*, A gift. *Habwat* or *hubwat*, (pl. حبى *huba'*) A mode of sitting with the legs and thighs contracted, with the sash or garments wrapped round them.

A حبور *hubūr*, (v. n. of حبر) Making glad. Cheerfulness, joy. (pl. of حبر *hibr*) Yellow concretions on the teeth. (pl. of حبر *hibr* or *habr*) Learned men, Jewish doctors. Men of probity.

A حبّور *habbūr*, (pl. حبابير *habābīr*) A young bustard. *Hubbūr*, Joy, cheerfulness.

A حبورة *hubūrat*, Jewish learning, knowledge of Hebrew law.

A حبوش *hubūsh*, Negroes, Ethiopians.

A حبوض *hubūz*, (v. n. of حبض) Being exhausted (water in a well). Diminishing, decreasing. Failing, being null and void. Disappointing favourable expectations (a youth growing up).

A حبوط *hubūt*, (v. n. of حبط) Being done in vain (work) or shed with impunity (blood).

A حبوكر *habawkar*, Bulky, close and compactly built. (pl. حباكر *habākir*) A man slender and taking short steps. ام حبوكر *umm habawkar*, A kind of bird. Misfortune. *Habawkar*, (or حبوكل *habawkal*) A sandy desert, dangerous to travellers. A misfortune, a sore disaster.

A حبوكراة *habawkarāt*, Large (she-camel).

A ام حبوكران *umm habawkarān*, A sort of bird.

A حبوكري *habawkara'*, Large-bodied (camel). Misfortune. A battle-field after the close of a war. A little lad. ام حبوكري *umm habawkara'*, A sort of bird. A dreadful misfortune.

A حبول *habūl*, Evil, misfortune. *Hubūl*, (pl. of حبل *habl*) Ropes, cords, halters. (pl. of حبل *hibl*) Evils, misfortunes.

A حبون *hubūn*, (pl. of حبن *hibn* and حبنة *hibnat*) Biles, pimples.

A حبى *huba'*, (pl. of حبوة *habwat* or *hubwat*) Peculiar modes of sitting down. (pl. of حبة *hubat*) Grape-stones.

A حبيّ *habīy*, Whatever meets, encounters, or comes across one. Clouds piled on one another, resembling mountains, immediately before night-fall.

A حبيب *habīb*, (pl. احباب *ahbāb*, احبّاء *ahibbā*, and احبّة *ahibbat*) Beloved. A lover. (pl. حبائب *habāib*) A mistress. حبيب السير *habību's sayr*, A friend to travelling. ابو حبيب *abū habīb*, Roast kid. P حبيب خدا *habībi khudā*, The beloved of God, *i.e.* Muhammad. A *Hubayib*, (dim.) A little darling.

A حبيبة *habībat*, An object of desire. Madīna.

A حبية *hibyat*, A mode of sitting with the legs and thighs drawn together and tied with a sash.

A حبير *habīr*, New. Soft. A leathern-bottle. (pl. حبر *hubr*) A dappled cloud. A kind of striped, embroidered stuff. A new garment.

A حبيرك *hubayrik*, (dim. of حبركى *habarka'*) A little weak-footed, long-backed (man).

A حبيس *habīs*, Dedicated to pious uses.

A حبيش *hubaysh*, A Guinea or Numidian hen.

A حبيق *hubayk*, A bad species of date.

A حبيك *habīk*, Firmly done. Well woven.

A حبيكة *habīkat*, (pl. حبك *hubuk*) The path of the stars. (pl. حبيك *habīk*, حبائك *habāik*, and حبك *hubuk*) A curl on water, or in a lock of hair. A ring in a coat of mail. A path through a sand-hill. A row or line of hair or eggs.

A حبيل *habīl*, (or حبيل براح *habīlu barāhin*) A lion or hero fearlessly remaining in his place.

A حبين *habīn*, Dropsical. Rhododaphne.

A حبينة *hubaynat*, (or امّ حبين) A chameleon.

A حتّ *hatt*, (v. n. of حتّ) Scraping dry dirt from a garment. Falling (as leaves from the trees). Rubbing in the hand. Peeling. Ordering (a hundred lashes) to be administered. Shaving, grazing. Throwing down. Scattered dates. Aught, any thing. (pl. احتات *ahtāt*) Fleet (horse), swift (camel). A male ostrich. Noble, generous. A dead locust. *Hutt*, Fried barley bruised small.

A حتء *hats*, (v. n. of حتأ) Plaiting, twisting, puckering the border of a garment. Sewing (a coat). Tying (a knot). Propping or strengthening a wall. Striking, knocking. Marrying, lying with. Fixing the eyes stedfastly, gazing awhile, upon any object. Unsaddling (a camel), taking wares off his back.

A حتات *hatāt*, Noises, clamours. *Hutāt*, A shaving, chip, splinter. A man's name.

A حتار *hitār*, (pl. حتر *hutur*) The foreskin. An edge or hem. The circumference of the nail. The helix or circle of the ear. The head of a purse, the part which is drawn. The circumference of the haunches. The sphincter of the anus. The perinæum. The seam between the testicles. Water of the eye. A fleshy substance, like a tooth, in a camel's mouth. Rings of cord round the skirt of a tent to which the pegs are fastened.

A حتارش *hatārish*, Motions of a boy when at play.

A حتّام *hattāma*, (for حتّى ما *hatta' mā*) How long? till when?

A حتّامة *hutāmat*, Remains of meat on a table.

A حتّان *hattān*, (as, رمدة حتّان *rimdat hattān*) The smallest particle.

A حثحاث *hathāt*, Swift, hasty. Covetous.

A حثحثة *hathatat*, Speed, haste, swiftness.

A حتد *hatad*, (v. n. of حتد) Being of a pure root. *Hatid*, Of pure origin. *Hutud*, The essence or root of a thing. (pl. of حتد *hatad* and حتود *hatūd*) Eyes affected by a hard substance which corrodes the lashes and edges.

A حتر *hatr*, (v. n. of حتر) Sparing expense, being frugal. Tasting. Eating voraciously. Sewing a border on the skirt of a tent. Feeding, giving victuals. Looking sharply. Tying tight, making fast. A small matter. A dog-fox. *Hatr* or *hitr*, Land high and long. *Hitr*, A present. Any thing sewed to the lower part of a tent to keep it close to the ground. A fixing of a border to the skirt of a tent to which the pins are fastened. *Hutur*, (pl. of حتار *hitār*) Fringes, outer edges.

A حترب *hatrab*, Short.

A حترة *hatrat*, One suck (of milk). *Hutrat*, A house-warming. A small matter. (pl. احتار *ahtār*) Any thing sewed to the lower part of a tent to keep it close to the ground. The corner of the mouth. The place where the mustachios are cut.

A حترش *hitrish*, Short and small bodied.

A حترشة *hatrashat*, Sound of a locust eating.

A حترفة *hatrafat*, (v. n. of حترف Q) Removing from (its) place. A roughness and redness (in the eyes).

A حتروش *hutrūsh*, Short. Small-bodied. A smart, active lad; also one hard, strong, and lean.

A حتش *hatsh*, (v. n. of حتش) Assembling together (people). Fixing (the eye) long upon one.

A حتف *hatf*, (pl. حتوف *hutūf*) Death. مات حتف انفه *māta hatfa anfihi*, (and sometimes حتف فيه *hatfa fīhi* or حتف انفيه *hatfa anfayhi*) He died a natural death. حيّة حتفة *hayyatun hatfatun*, A deadly serpent.

A حتفل *hutful*, Remains of broth or meat in a pot. Mother or sediment of oil. Dregs of people. Dirty stuff from the uterus. Refuse of property.

A حتك *hatk*, (v. n. of حتك) Going with a quick short step. Preparing the sand for her nest (an ostrich). Smoothing, planing, shaving. Turning one's self to, tending. *Hatak*, Young ostriches.

A حتكان *hatakān*, A light, short, quick step.

A حتكّى *hitikka'*, The pace of a dwarf.

A حتل *hatl*, A gift. Similitude. The refuse (of any thing). *Hitl*, Likeness.

A حتم *hatama*, (fut. يحتم *yahtimu*) He inspired.

A حتم *hatm*, (v. n. of حتم) Rendering necessary. Doing firmly and solidly. Exercising legal authority. Passing sentence. (pl. حتوم *hutūm*) Jurisdiction. Decree. Supplement to a discourse or a fast which had been broken off. Pure, sincere.

A حتمة *hutmat*, Blackness. *Hatamat*, A flask broken into fragments. Blackness.

A حتن *hatn* or *hitn*, (pl. احتان *ahtān*) Like, equal. *Hatan*, (v. n. of حتن) Being hot (the day). Mountain-peaks.

A حتناء *hatnās*, Bald (she-camel).

A حتنال *hatnāl*, Flight, escape.

A حتنان *hatnān*, Escape, flight. *Hatnāni*, (dual) Equals (in archery, &c.).

A حتنى *hatana'*, Even, level (arrows shot and fallen). Equal, straight, parallel.

A حتو *hatw*, (v. n. of حتا for حتو) Turning in and hemming. Twisting tight (the fringe of a garment). Running hard.

A حتوت *hatūt*, A palm-tree whose dates are scattered about.

A حتود *hatūd*, An eye affected by a disease which corrodes the eyelashes and eyelids. *Hutūd*, (v. n. of حتد) Remaining (in a place). Broadways.

A حتور *hutūr*, A being frugal in one's expense.

A حتوف *hutūf*, (pl. of حتف *hatf*) Deaths. سيوف حتوف *suyūfi hutūf*, Death-giving swords. قطوف حتوف *kutūfi hutūf*, Vintages of death. كاسات حتوف *kāsāti hutūf*, Chalices of death.

A حتوم *hutūm*, (pl. of حتم *hatm*) Decrees, jurisdictions. (pl. of حاتم *hātim*) Judges.

A حتومة *hutūmat*, Acidity, bitterness.

A حتّوي *hattawīy*, Relating to حتّى *hatta'*, Until.

A حتى *hatis*, The fruit of the dwarf palm-tree deprived of its husk.

A حتى *haty*, (v. n. of حتي) Sewing. Twisting. Making firm.

A حتّى *hatta'*, To, until, even to, as far as. In order that, so that. And. Unless, except. Together with. حتّى اذا *hatta' izā*, To when. حتّى متى *hatta' mata'*, How long? till when? اكلت السّمكة حتّى رأسها *akaltu's samakata hatta' rasahā*, I ate the fish, head and all. حتّى المقدور *hatta'l makdūr*, (حتّى الامكان *hatta'l imkān* or الوسع *al wus*) To the utmost of one's power.

A حتيّ *hatīy*, The produce of the dwarf palm-tree. The husks and refuse of dates or of a date-basket. A bad kind of dry wild date. Dung collected in a heap. Flies' wings left in honey.

A حتيرة *hatīrat*, A feast on finishing a house.

A حثّ *hass*, (v. n. of حثّ) Instigating, exciting, stimulating. Rendering greedy. *Huss*, Chaff, chopped straw scattered about. Dry, hard, glittering sand. A ptisan not moistened or rendered fluid. Dry bread (without other victuals).

A حثا *hasa'*, Chaff. Husks and refuse of dates.

A حثاث *hasās* or *hisās*, Sleep. ما اكتحل حثاثا *mā iktahala hasāsan* or *hisāsan*, He slept not a wink. *Hisās*, (pl. of حثيث *hasīs*) Swift.

A حثارة *husārat*, Chaff. A bent of straw.

A حثارم *husārim*, Thick upper-lipped.

A حثافير *hasāfīr*, The end or latter part.

A حثالة *husālat*, The worst part of any thing (as the chaff of corn, the husk and refuse of dates). Tares, darnel. Sediment of melted fat.

A حثام *hisām*, (pl. of حثمة) Young horse-colts.

A حثائل *hasāʼil*, (pl. of حثيل *hisyal*) Dwarfs. Lazy, slothful.

A حثحاث *has-hās*, Swift, making haste. A constant watering without intermission.

A حثحثة *has-hasat*, (v. n. of حثحث Q) Instigating, exciting, stimulating. Putting in motion. Vibrating, flashing (lightning).

A حثحوث *hus-hūs*, Many. Swift. Incitement (to activity). A troop, squadron. An ugly she-goat.

A حثر *hasr*, A little food. Despicable. *Hasar*, (v. n. of حثر) Having a pimple or sty (the eye-lid). Being covered with blotches (the skin). Candying, granulating (honey). Being thick and ample. An unripe, sour grape. A grape-stone just appearing. Dregs, sediment, mother of oil, lees of wine. The early fruit of the اراك *arāk* tree. A kind of mushroom resembling concreted earth with sand beneath.

A حثرب *husrub*, A sort of plant found only in hard soils. Dirty water at the bottom of a kettle.

A حثربة *hasrabat*, (v. n. of حثرب Q) Being turbid, muddy (water). Having muddy water (a well). *Hisribat*, An excrescence on the upper lip.

A حثرة *hasarat*, One globule of concreted earth.

A حثرما *hasarmā*, A kind of mint.

A حثرمة *hasramat*, Thickness of lip. *Hisrimat*, The tip of the nose. The groove below the nose. The middle of the upper lip.

A حثف *hasif* or *hisf*, (another way of writing حفث *hafis* or فحث *fahis*) The rough tripe.

A حثفر *husfur*, Dregs, sediment: waste, refuse.

A حثفرة *husfurat*, Sediment, deposit at the bottom of a water-jar.

A حثفل *husful*, Remains of broth or meat in a pot. Mother or sediment of oil. Dregs of people. Dirty stuff from the uterus. Refuse of property.

A حثفلة *hasfalat*, (v. n. of حثفل Q) Drinking the remains of broth from a pot or cauldron.

A حثل *hasl*, Unwholesome pap. Bad condition, evil case. The worst part or refuse of any thing. *Hisl*, Lean, thin, slender. *Hasal*, (v. n. of حثل) Being gorbellied.

A حثلب *hislib*, (or حثلم *hislim*) Sediment of oil or ointment.

A حثلة *hislat*, A little water left in a cistern.

A حثم *hasm*, (v. n. of حثم) Giving. Rubbing: rendering soft and pliable.

A حثماء *hasmāʼ*, Remains of sand in a river's bed.

A حثمة *hasmat*, The tip or ridge of the nose. (pl. حثام *hisām*) A young horse-colt. *Hasmat* or *hasamat*, A reddish or blackish hillock. *Husmat*, That part of a water-dam through which it runs out.

A حثو *hasw*, (v. n. of حثا for حثو) Giving little. Scattering earth. Sprinkling dust upon the face of a dead relation. Flying about (dust).

A حثواء *haswāʼ*, (A place) having much earth.

A حثوة *huswat*, (pl. حثي) A portion of earth.

A حثوث *hasūs*, Spurred on. Swift. Avaricious.

A حثي *hasy*, Whatever causes a man to raise his hands (as when he is about to pour water on his head). A handful. *Hasaʼ*, (v. n. of حثي) Scattering earth. Flying about (dust). Giving a little. Sprinkled earth. Husks of dates. Chaff. Straw, particularly after it has been thrashed.

A حثيان *hasyān*, A flying about of the dust.

A حثية *hasyat*, A single handful.

A حثيث *hasīs*, (pl. حثاث *hisās*) Greedy. Spurred on. Swift.

A حثيثي *hissīsaʼ*, Impulse, stimulation.

A حثيرة *hasīrat*, A feast on finishing a house.

A حثيل *hisyal*, (pl. حثائل *hasāʼil*) Dwarfish, short. Lazy, slothful. Unwholesomely fed (suckling). A sort of mountain-tree.

A حج *hajj*, (v. n. of حج) Setting out, tending towards. Prohibiting, restraining, averting. Arriving, approaching. Probing (a wound), preparing (it) for the reception of a tent. Overcoming in argument. Going on pilgrimage to Mecca, and performing the ceremonies there. Violent opposition, dissension. اميرحج *amīri hajj*, The chief commander of the pilgrims (an office of great dignity during the splendour of the khilāfat, and generally filled by the son or declared successor of the reigning sovereign). حج فرض *hajji farz*, The pilgrimage to Mecca ordained by law. *Hijj* or *hajj*, A pilgrimage to Mecca. *Hujj*, (pl. of حاج *hājj*) Pilgrims to Mecca.

A حجا *hajaʼ*, (fut. يحجو *yahjū*) He stood still.

A حجا *hajaʼ*, Conflict, combat. (pl. احجاء *ahjāʼ*) Side, part, quarter. Bubbles of water. *Hajaʼ* or *hijaʼ*, A whispering, buzzing sound.

A حجا *hajaʼa*, (fut. يحجا *yahjaʼu*) He rejoiced. He restrained or prevented. He took refuge.

A حجاء *hajāʼ*, A whispering, buzzing sound. *Hijāʼ*, (v. n. 3 of حجا for حجو) Overcoming in any suit or question. Contending, conflicting. Propounding riddles to one another.

A حجاب *hijāb*, (v. n. of حجب) Veiling, concealing. A partition. The diaphragm. Any separating bar. Idolatry. The track, or light of the sun. (pl. حجب *hujub*) A veil, curtain. A long streak of sand. The place where a stony country breaks off. The projecting part of a mountain. Name of a mountain below the mountain قاف *kāf*. حجاب كحلي *hijābi kuhlī*, Heaven. A black cloud. Dust. P حجاب كردن *hijāb kardan*, To veil, draw a curtain, cover, hide.

A حجّاب *hujjāb*, (pl. of حاجب *hājib*) Porters, chamberlains of the king's apartments (as having charge of the door-way).

P حجابانه *hijābāna*, A concealing, hiding.

A حجابة *hijābat*, The office of chamberlain. The charge or custody of a temple.

P حجاب چشمي *hijāb-chashmī*, Sheep's-eyed.

A حجاة *hajāt*, (pl. حجي *hajaʼ*) A bubble formed on the water by rain. (pl. احجاء *ahjāʼ*) A side.

A حجاج *hajāj* or *hijāj*, (pl. احجّة *ahijjat*) The bone surrounding the eye; the eyebrow. A side. The margin of the sun's disk. *Hijāj*, (v. n. 3 of حج) Pleading a cause, bringing proofs.

A حجاج *hajjāj*, A litigious man, a squabbler. One who makes frequent pilgrimages. A tyrant, oppressor. حجّاج بن ثقفيّ ابن يوسف *hajjāju'bn sakafīy ibn yūsuf*, Name of a notorious tyrant. *Hujjāj*, (pl. of حاجّ *hājj*) Pilgrims to Mecca.

A حجار *hijār*, (pl. of حجر *hajar*) Stones.

A حجّار *hajjār*, A lapidary. A stone-mason.

A حجارة *hijārat*, (pl. of حجر *hajar*) Stones.

A حجارة ومدارة *hijārat u midārat*, Stones and clods.

A حجاز *hijāz*, (v. n. 3 of حجز) Prohibiting, taking one from another (to prevent fighting). A rope for drawing a camel's legs together. A string, wherewith one's clothes, when tucked up, are tied round the waist. A waistband. A barrier, or any thing similar, by which two things are separated. Mecca, Madīna, and the adjacent territory, Arabia Petræa. One of the principal species, modes, or styles in the Persian music, of which there are twelve; viz. بزرگ *buzurg*, بو سليك *bū salīk*, حجاز *hijāz*, حسيني *husaynī*, راست *rāst*, رهاوي *ruhāwī*, زنگوله *zangūla*, صفاهانك *sifāhānak*, عراق *ʻirāk*, عشاق *ʻushāk*, كوچك *kūchak*, and نوا *nawā*.

A حجازة *hijāzat*, A hindering, restraining.

A حجازي *hijāzīy*, A native of Hijāz.

A حجازيك *hajāzayka*, Separate, part them.

A حجاف *hujāf*, A flux, diarrhœa.

A حجال *hijāl*, (pl. of حجلة *hajalat*) Bed-chambers of brides. ربّات الحجال *rabbātu'l hijāl*, Women.

A حجّال *hajjāl*, Flash, gleam, glitter.

A حجام *hijām*, A rein, bridle, bit, muzzle.

A حجّام *hajjām*, A barber. A bleeder, cupper, scarifier, phlebotomist. A sucker.

A حجامة *hijāmat* or *hajāmat*, (v. n. of حجم) Applying the cupping-glasses, bleeding, scarifying. *Hijāmat*, The profession of a barber, which consists in shaving, cupping, pairing nails, picking ears, and the like.

A حجّامي *hajjāmī*, Profession of cupper or barber.

A حجب *hajb*, (v. n. of حجب) Veiling. Cutting off (an heir) from his portion, barring. *Hajab*, Windpipe. *Hajib*, A hillock, heap of stones. *Hujub*, (pl. of حجاب *hijāb*) Veils. Curtains.

A حجبة *hijbat*, The office of chief porter or chamberlain. *Hajabat*, The top or projecting part of the hip (in the dual حجبتان *hajabatāni*). (pl.

of حاجب *hājib*) Chamberlains, porters.

A حجبتان *hajabatāni*, Two bones above the pubes.

A حجبي *hajabīy*, A chamberlain, a porter.

A حجة *hajjat* or *hijjat*, The lobe of the ear. An ear-ring, drop, pendant. A pilgrimage to Mecca (hence حجة الله *hajjatti'llāh*, A form of swearing). *Hijjat*, (pl. حجج *hijaj*) A year. A single pilgrimage to Mecca. ذو الحجة *zū'l hijjat*, (pl. ذوات الحجة *zawātu'l hijjat*) The last month of the Arabian year (because upon the tenth day a solemn feast is celebrated at Mecca). *Hujjat*, (pl. حجج *hujaj*) Argument, proof, reason, demonstration. Decree, decision. The sentence of a judge: a legal testimonial. Pretence, excuse. Altercation, disputation. P حجت استوار *hujjati ustuwār*, The Kur'ān. حجت كردن *hujjat kardan*, To decide, pass sentence. To make use of argument or excuse.

P حجتانه *hujjatāna*, A voucher.

A حجتي *hujjatī*, A sound reasoner. A disputatious person, a sophist, wrangler.

A حجج *hijaj*, (pl. of حجة *hijjat*) Years. Pilgrimages to Mecca. Lobes of ears. *Hujaj*, (pl. of حجة *hujjat*) Proofs, demonstrations. *Hujuj*, Excavated roads. Probed wounds.

A حجحج *hajhaj*, A worthless fellow.

A حجحجة *hajhajat*, (v. n. of حجحج Q) Retiring (in battle after having made an impression). Restraining one's self from expressing the wishes of one's mind. Stopping, standing still.

A حجر *hajr*, (v. n. of حجر) Choosing a spot, erecting a tower to denote occupancy to the exclusion of others. Illicit, forbidden. Confinement, durance. A sand-hill. The socket of the eye. Genitalia. A town in Yamāmah. (pl. of حجرة *hajrat*) Courts, sides of houses. *Hajr*, *hijr*, *hujr*, (v. n. of حجر) Prohibiting, preventing, hindering, barring, interdicting. (pl. حجور *hujūr*) An embrace, the bosom. *Hajr* or *hijr*, Custody, protection. A veil, curtain. *Hijr*, Illicit, forbidden. The northern wall of the temple of Mecca. Interdiction of an action against an idiot, infant, or slave. Intellect. The skirt of the garment held up by the hand. Hem or border of a shirt. Genitalia. Propinquity, relationship. (pl. حجور *hujūr*, حجورة *hujūrat*, and احجار *ahjār*) A mare. The country of the Tamūdites. ذو حجر *zū hijr*, Intelligent. *Hujr*, Forbidden. Confinement, durance. *Hajar*, (pl. احجار *ahjār*, احجر *ahjur*, حجارة *hijārat*, and حجار *hijār*) A stone. Silver. Gold. Sand. حجر الارض *hajaru'l arz*, A misfortune, calamity. حجر ارمني *hajari armanī*, Lapis lazuli. Bole armoniac. حجر الاسود *hajaru'l aswad*, The black stone (at Mecca). حجر اسيوس *hajari asiyūs*, Saltpetre. حجر الافروج *hajaru'l afrūj*, Pumice-stone. حجر بحري *hajari bahrī*, Coral. حجر البقر *hajaru'l bakar*, A stone found in the gall-bladder of an ox. حجر البلور *hajaru'l billawr*, Crystal. حجر الدم *hajaru'd dam*, Bloodstone. حجر السمّ *hajaru's samm*, A stone discovering poison. حجر شجري *hajari shajarī*, Coral (from its branching like a tree). حجر الشياطين *hajaru'sh shayātīn*, Adamant, loadstone, diamond. حجر قبطي *hajari kibtī*, Coptic stone: a kind of fuller's earth. حجر كبريت *hajari kibrīt*, Sulphur. حجر الكزك *hajaru'l kazak*, (or كرك *kirk*) Name of a white stone found on the banks of the Indus. حجر لازورد *hajari lāziward*, Lapis lazuli. حجر المثانة *hajaru'l masānat*, Bladder-stone. حجر المسنّ *hajaru'l misann*, A whetstone. حجر مشوية *hajari mashwiya*, Lime. حجر المطر *hajaru'l matar*, A fabulous stone supposed to produce rain. حجر المقناطيس *hajaru'l miknātīs*, The loadstone. حجر النور *hajaru'n nūr*, The marcasite. حجر اليهود *hajaru'l yahūd*, Lapis Judaicus. *Hujar*, (pl. of حجرة *hujrat*) Chambers, closets. Camel's stables. *Hujur*, Flesh surrounding the nails.

P حجر *hujr*, The waistband of the drawers.

A حجرات *hajarāt*, (pl. of حجرة *hajrat*) Courts, sides of houses. *Hujrāt*, *hujarāt*, or *hujurāt*, (pl. of حجرة *hujrat*) Stables. Closets, cells. حجرات طلبه *hujarāti taluba*, Student's cells.

A حجران *hujrān* or *hijrān*, (v. n. of حجر) Hindering, preventing, barring. (pl. of حاجر *hājir*) Walls, mounds, dikes. *Hajarāni*, Gold and silver.

A حجرة *hajrat*, (pl. حجر *hajr*, حجرات *hajarāt*, and حواجر *hawājir*) A court-yard, the side of a house. A fold. الرجل اذا كثر ماله انتشرت حجرته *ar'rajulu izā kasura māluhu, intasharat hajratuhu*, When a man's stock becomes numerous, his premises become enlarged. ارض حجرة *arzun hajratun* or *hajaratun*, A very stony country. ربض حجرة *rabaza hajratan*, He lay down on one side. *Hujrat*, (pl. حجر *hujar*, حجرات *hujurāt*, *hujarāt*, and *hujrāt*) A stable (for camels). A chamber, closet, cell. حجرهٔ خاصّ, A secret apartment.

A حجروف *hujrūf*, A certain long-legged insect bigger than a pismire.

A حجريّ *hujrīy* or *hijrīy*, Truth. Honour, reputation. *Hajarīy*, Made of stone, stony.

A حجريّة *hajarīyat*, Stoniness.

A حجز *hajz*, (v. n. of حجز) Prohibiting, preventing. Interrupting, interposing, intervening. Making (a camel) lie down, and tying his fore-legs, as a farrier does when he wishes to dress his sore back). *Hijz* or *hujz*, Root, origin. Kindred, brethren. A side, margin, quarter. *Hajaz*, (v. n. of حجز) Being diseased in the intestines from thirst. Thirst caused by a pain in the bowels.

A حجزاويّ *hijzāwīy*, A native of حجزي *hijzā'*.

A حجزة *hujzat*, (pl. حجز *hujaz*) The waistband of the breeches, or the place where the waistband-string is tied. شدّة الحجزة *shiddatu'l hujzat*, Patience. ناتئ الحجزة *nātiu'l hujzat*, Bulky-waisted (considered a blemish). *Hajazat*, (pl. of حاجز *hājiz*) Hinderers, interceptors. Oppressors.

A حجزي *hijzā'*, A village near Damascus.

A حجف *hajaf*, Leathern shields. Breasts.

A حجفة *hajafat*, (pl. حجف *hajaf*) A buckler of leather. The breast.

P حجك *hajak*, A rose.

A حجل *hajl*, (v. n. of حجل) Jumping with bound feet. Hopping (a crow). *Hijl*, (pl. احجال *ahjāl*) Whiteness. *Hijl*, *hajl*, or *hijil*, A fetter, or the ring of a fetter. *Hijl*, (*hajl*, *hijil*, or حجّل *hijill*) (pl. احجال *ahjāl* and حجول *hujūl*) Any ornament for the ankle. *Hajal*, A partridge with red feet and beak. Young camels. (pl. of حجلة *hajalat*) Ornamented bridal chambers. حجل حجل *hajal hajal*, A word used in checking sheep, or in calling them to be milked. دبّي حجل *dibbī hajal*, Name of a game.

A حجلاء *hajlā'*, White-legged (sheep).

A حجلان *hajalān*, (v. n. of حجل) Jumping with bound feet, hopping. A certain bird.

A حجلة *hajalat*, A single partridge. (pl. حجل *hajal* and حجال *hijāl*) The ornamented chamber, where the bride sits. A kind of tent or canopy.

P حجله *hajla*, (or حجلهٔ دامادي *hajlai dāmādī*) A curtain drawn before the bride's chamber.

A حجلى *hijlā'*, (pl. of حجلة *hajalat*) Partridges.

A حجم *hajm*, (v. n. of حجم) Cupping, bleeding, scarifying. Sucking (the teat). Swelling (the breast). Keeping (one) back (from any thing). A sharpness or prominence (of the elbow). (pl. حجوم *hujūm*) A swelling. A rising beneath the touch. Thickness, bigness.

A حجن *hajn*, (v. n. of حجن) Bending (a stick). Drawing any thing towards one's self with a stick curved at the extremity. Hindering, turning away. *Hajan*, (v. n. of حجن) Being avaricious, parsimonious. Remaining at home. Decay from age and labour in a beast of burden. Crookedness, curvature. *Hajan* or *hajin*, A tike. *Hajin*, (Hair) hanging straight.

A حجناء *hajnā'*, (fem. of احجن *ahjan*) Crooked, curved, hooked. An ear leaning down towards the forehead.

A حجنة *hujnat*, Crookedness. The notch in the spindle into which the thread goes. *Hujnat* or *hajanat*, The leaves of the plant ثمام *sumām*.

A حجو *hajw*, (v. n. of حجا for حجو) Stopping, standing, remaining. Recognising the stallion's voice, and going to him (a she-camel). Being avaricious. Hindering. Keeping a secret. Excelling in propounding and solving enigmas. Conjecturing. Falsely claiming, though not sure of. Thinking well of any one. Driving (as the wind a ship). Sufficing, satisfying, requiting.

A حجوة *hajwat*, A man, a thinking being.

A حجوّج *hajawwaj*, A zig-zag road.

A حجور *hujūr*, (pl. of حجر *hijr*) Mares.

A حجورة *hujūrat*, (pl. of حجر *hijr*) Mares.

A حجّورة *hajjūrat*, Blindman's-buff. A game.

A حجول *hajūl*, Distant. *Hujūl*, (v. n. of حجل) Being sunk (the eye). (pl. of حجل *hijl, hajl, hijil*, and حجّل *hijill*) Ornaments for the ankles.

A حجوم *hajūm*, A drawer of blood, a cupper. One who sucks, a sucker. Pudendum muliebre. *Hujūm*, (pl. of حجم *hajm*) Swellings. The ends of bones (as the tips of the elbows).

A حجون *hajūn*, Lazy, slothful. Remote (mountain-top). Distant (military expedition).

A حجوي *hajwa'*, A riddle.

A حجئ *hajiʼa*, (fut. يحجأ *yahjaʼu*) He was tenacious of, enslaved by, or addicted to. He held fast by, he stuck close to. He rejoiced.

A حجي *haja'*, (v. n. of حجي) Being diligent, earnest, eager; addicted to. Running away. A tract of country. A whispering, buzzing sound. (pl. of حجاة *hajāt*) Bubbles of water. *Haji*, Intelligent, sensible. *Haji* or *haja'*, Worthy. *Hija'*, (pl. احجاء *ahjāʼ*) Intellect, genius; shrewdness. Quantity, space, measure. A muttering, a buzzing.

A حجيّ *hajiy*, Worthy. Intelligent. Greedy.

A حجيء *hajiʼ*, Fit, suitable, worthy. A refugee.

A حجيّا *hujayya'*, A riddle. An enigmatist.

A حجيج *hajīj*, One who has had his wound probed. One who adduces proof, argument, or demonstration. (pl. of حاجّ *hājj*) Pilgrims.

A حجير *hajīr*, Stony (ground).

A حجّيزي *hijjīza'*, (v. n. of حجز) Hindering, preventing, restraining. A mutual retreat, receding, or cessation of hostilities.

A حجيف *hajīf*, Wind in the bowels.

A حجيل *hajīl*, (A horse) white on three feet.

A حجيلاء *hujyalāʼ*, Water unreached by the sun.

A حدّ *hadd*, (v. n. of حدّ) Setting bounds. Defining. Whetting (a knife). Mourning the loss of a husband, and laying aside her ornaments (a woman). Being angry. (P *had*) (pl. حدود *hudūd*) Boundary, limit, term, verge. Definition, distinction. Discrimination. Impediment, check. A shove, push. Punishment, chastisement by sentence of a judge (especially the inflicting of eighty lashes). A goal for racers. Point of a thing: edge (of wit or of steel). Strength, fortitude. Strength (of wine). Power. Dignity. Rage, fury. A fit of anger, precipitancy. Severity, sharpness. حدّ بلوغ *haddi bulūgh*, The term of puberty, youth. حد تكليف *hadi taklīf*, The age previous to puberty (during which a lad is permitted to enter the women's apartments). حدّ مأمورة *haddi maʼmūra*, At the time or limits prescribed. P از حد بيرون *az had bīrūn*, Beyond bounds, without the limits; enormous, excessive, exorbitant. از حد گذاشتن *az had guzāshtan*, To exceed just limits, to be exorbitant. تا حدي كه *tā hade ki*, (or تا از حد كه *tā az had ki*) So that, until that. A *Hudd*, Excluded (from good), kept (from evil).

A حدأ *hadʼ*, (v. n. of حدأ) Turning. Removing. A journey. *Hadaʼ*, (v. n. of حدئ) Succouring, protecting. Sticking, cleaving to. Seeking refuge. Being incensed at. Being broken off and remaining in the sheep's belly (the secundine). Being incommoded thereby, and complaining. (pl. of حدأة *hadaʼat*) Two-headed hatchets. Axe-heads. Arrow-heads. *Hidaʼ*, (pl. of حدأة *hidaʼat*) Kites.

A حدا *hada'*, A remaining fast in a place.

A حداء *hadāʼ*, (pl. of حدأة *hadaʼat*) Two-edged hatchets. Heads of axes. Arrow-heads. *Hidāʼ*, (pl. of حدأة *hidaʼat*) Kites. *Hudāʼ* or *hidāʼ*, (v. n. of حدا for حدو) Impelling, rousing, driving, making camels to travel with alacrity by singing to them. Following (as night follows day, or as a male-ass the female).

A حدّاء *haddāʼ*, A camel-driver.

A حداب *hadāb*, A scarce season.

A حدابير *hadābīr*, (pl. of حدبار *hidbār*) Lean (camels). Bunchless camels. Barren years. Hillocks.

A حدأة *hadaʼat*, (pl. حدأ *hadaʼ* and حداء *hadāʼ*) A two-headed hatchet. An axe-head. The head of an arrow. *Hidaʼat*, (pl. حدء *hidaʼ*, حداء *hidāʼ*, and حدآن *hidʼān*) A kite. The fore part of a horse's neck.

A حدّاث *huddās*, A company of persons discoursing together.

A حداثة *hadāsat*, (v. n. of حدث) Being new, fresh, and young. Youth, tender age. *Hidāsat*, Beginning, novelty, freshness of any thing.

A حداجة *hidājat*, (pl. حدائج *hadāʼij*) A camel-litter. An instrument, utensil, apparatus.

A حداد *hidād*, (v. n. of حدّ) Mourning (the death of a husband). Abstaining from perfumes or ornaments. Mourning-habits. *Hidād* or *hudād*, (pl. of حديد *hadīd*) Sharp. Eloquent. Hard, inexorable. *Hudād*, Sharp (sword). (pl. احداء *ahiddāʼ* and احدّة *ahiddat*) Fluent (in speech), sharp (in intellect), severe (in wrath).

A حدّاد *haddād*, A smith, a worker in iron. A porter or keeper of a gate. One who sets bounds or limits, or who sets an edge. A jailor. The sea.

A حدادة *hadādat*, A woman, a wife. *Hidādat*, The trade of a blacksmith, smithcraft.

A حداد حدّيه *hadādi huddīhi*, An expression used towards one whose aspect is repulsive.

A حدادك ان تفعل *hadāduka an tafʻala*, Your great object is to do.

A حدّادي *haddādī*, Trade of a blacksmith.

A حدارة *hadārat*, Fatness, with a firmness and compact habit of body.

A حداس *hidās*, End, extremity.

A حداق *hidāk*, (pl. of حدقة) Pupils of eyes.

A حدال *hadāl*, A sort of tree. *Hudāl*, Curved at the extremity (a bow). Smooth, bare.

A حدالي *hadāla'*, (pl. of حدل *hadil*) Partial, unjust. High-shouldered.

A حدآن *hidʼān*, (pl. of حدأة *hidaʼat*) Kites.

A حدائج *hadāʼij*, (pl. of حداجة *hidājat*) Camel-litters. Loads.

A حدائد *hadāʼid*, (pl. of حديد *hadīd*) Irons. (pl. of حديدة *hadīdat*) Sharp swords.

A حدائق *hadāʼik*, (pl. of حديقة) Gardens.

A حدب *hudb*, (pl. of حدباء *hadbāʼ*) Hunch-backed (camels). Difficult affairs. *Hadab*, (v. n. of حدب) Being high. Being convex or hump-backed. Being favourably inclined, benevolent. Declining a second marriage in order to look after her children. High ground, hilliness. A heap of thistle-down. Gibbosity, a roundness of back with a corresponding concavity in the breast. A heaping up of waters. A declivity. A mark on the skin. A kind of white thistle. Severity of winter. *Hadib*, Kind, benevolent. Hump-backed. Land abounding in white thistles.

A حدباء *hadbāʼ*, Lean-hipped (camel). Hump-backed (woman). A difficult affair.

A حدبار *hidbār*, (pl. حدابير *hadābīr*) A bunchless camel. A barren year. A hillock. Lean-hipped (camel).

A حدبة *hadabat*, Gibbosity. Swelling (of liver).

A حدبد *hudabid*, Thick (milk).

A حدبدبي *hadabdaba'*, The game of leap-frog.

A حدبق *hudbuk*, Short-bodied, compact.

A حدبير *hidbīr*, Lean-hipped (camel).

A حدة *hidat*, (v. n. of وحد) Being alone, sole and unique. علي حدة *ʻala' hidatin*, Separately. Separate, distinct. على حدته *ʻala' hidatihi*, Apart, alone, by himself. من ذات حدته *min zāti hidatihi*, (على ذات حدته *ʻala' zāti hidatihi* or من ذى حدته *min zī hidatihi*) Of his own accord.

A حدّة *hiddat*, (v. n. of حدّ) Taking an edge, becoming sharp. The edge (of a sword). Passion, vehemence, impetuosity, fury. *Huddat*, Remains of water or milk in a vessel.

A حدث *hids*, One who converses with kings, a royal favourite. An entertaining story-teller. *Hadas*, A beginning, commencement, invention. A novelty. Any thing contingent or accidental. Any thing which comes out of the body and causes defilement. (pl. احداث *ahdās*) A young man. *Hadis* or *hadus*, One who speaks, relates, or describes well.

A حدثات *hadasāt*, Accidents.

A حدثان *hidsān*, Beginning, novelty, newness, first and fresh appearance. Accidents, events. Young men. Traditions. *Hudsān*, (pl. of حديث *hadīs*) Young men. Traditions.

A حدثة *hadasat*, A young woman.

A حدثيّة *hadasīyat*, Name of a sect.

A حدج *hadj*, (v. n. of حدج) Loading a camel (particularly with a litter called *hidj*, in which women travel). Loading (a man with accusations, or suspecting of cheating in a sale). Shooting at, or wounding (with an arrow). *Hidj*, (pl. حدوج *hudūj* and احداج *ahdāj*) A burden. A camel's litter in which women ride. *Hadaj*, The wild gourd. The squash. A small melon. *Hadaj* or *hudaj*, A prickle of the plant قتب *kutb* when fresh.

A حدجة *hadajat*, A kind of bird.

A حدخة *huduhhat*, Short, dwarfish (woman).

A حدد *hadad*, (v. n. of حدّ) Waxing angry. Impediment, check. A shove, push. Prohibited, forbidden (thing). Vain, foolish (pretension).

A حدر *hadr*, (v. n. of حدر) Being fat, robust, of a firm, compact habit of body. Being fleshy (the socket of the eye). Making haste. Swelling from a blow (the skin). Causing a swelling. Descending. Flowing, falling (tears). Setting or throwing down. Relaxing the bowels (medicine). Depressing, removing from office, precipitating to destruction. Sinking (a ship). Hemming, lacing, ornamenting the edge of a garment. Enclosing, embracing, comprehending. A cast of the eye. *Hadar*, (v. n. of حدر) Shedding tears (the eye). Squinting. A declivity, descent.

A حدرّ *hudurr*, Thick.

A حدراء *hadrā*, Squint-eyed (woman). Fleshy about the thighs, but lank higher up (a good quality in a horse). *Hudarās*, A descent, declivity.

A حدرة *hadrat*, A hard, compact eye, or one large and sharp-sighted. A pimple or sore inside the eyelid. *Hudrat*, A troop of camels. A multitude, concourse.

A حدرج *hadraj*, Any one (is not at home).

A حدرجان *hidrijān*, Short (man).

A حدرجة *hadrajat*, A twisting, making strong.

A حدرد *hadrad*, Short, dwarfish.

A حدرّي *hudurra'*, An eye large, hard, or keen.

A حدس *hads*, (v. n. of حدس) Thinking, conjecturing, suspecting, imagining. Giving it as one's opinion. Wandering without a guide, uncertain of the way. Going fast, making haste. Going in a steady course. Overthrowing, levelling with the ground. Mastering, overcoming in wrestling. Trampling upon, treading down. Striking on the throat (a camel). Throwing (a sheep) down to slaughter it. Making (a camel) lie down. Shooting (an arrow), throwing (a javelin). Intending, aiming at. حدس لهم بمطفئة الرّضف *hadasa lahum bi mutfiati'r razfi*, He slaughtered for them a lean sheep which extinguished the fire and was not cooked. *Hadas*, Name of a people in the time of Solomon.

A حدق *hadk*, (v. n. of حدق) Surrounding. Beholding. *Hadak*, The brinjal or egg-plant. (pl. of حدقة *hadakat*) Pupils of the eyes.

A حدقة *hadakat*, (pl. حدق *hadak*, احداق *ahdāk*, and حداق *hidāk*) The pupil of the eye.

A حدقلة *hadkalat*, A rolling the eye when looking.

A حدل *hadl*, (v. n. of حدل) Being unjust. Unjust. *Hidl*, The waistband of the breeches, or the place of tying the drawers-string. A crick in the neck. *Hadal*, (v. n. of حدل) Being partial, unjust. Having a high shoulder. Curvature, wryness. A side-glance. *Hadil*, (pl. حدالى *hadālaʼ*) Partial, unjust. High-shouldered. Wry-necked. *Hudul*, Juice of the box-thorn. Wry-necked persons.

A حدلاء *hadlā*, (A bow) crooked at the extremity. Oblique (well).

A حدلقة *hadlakat*, (v. n. of حدلق Q) Fastening the eye upon. *Hudalikat*, The eye, or the pupil. A joint of mutton.

A حدم *hadm* or *hadam*, Fierce heat of fire.

A حدمة *hadamat*, The crackling sound of a fire. A rumbling noise in the belly. *Hadimat* or *hudamat*, Quick-boiling (pot).

A حدنبدي *hadambada'*, A wonderful thing.

A حدو *hadw*, (v. n. of حدا for حدو) Impelling, rousing, driving, making (camels) travel with alacrity by singing to them. Following (as night day).

A حدواء *hadwā*, North wind (cloud-compelling).

A حدوث *hudūs*, (v. n. of حدث) Appearing, re-appearing, emerging. Being new, fresh, young. Novelty, originality, invention.

A حدوثة *hudūsat*, Youth, early age.

A حدوج *hudūj*, Camel-litters. Loads.

A حدود *hudūd*, (pl. of حدّ *hadd*) Boundaries, confines, metes, limits. Rules, definitions. *Hudūd*, (or حدود شرعيّة *hudūdi sharʻiya*) Penal laws.

A حدور *hadūr*, A declivity, descent. *Hudūr*, (v. n. of حدر) Swelling with a blow. Descending, falling down. Causing to swell from a blow.

A حدورة *hadūrat* or *hudūrat*, A flood of tears.

A حدوق *hudūk*, (v. n. of حدق) Opening the eyes, staring (a dying man). Hurting the pupil.

A حدول *hudūl*, (v. n. of حدل) Being unjust.

A حدولة *hudūlat*, Curvature at the extremity (of a bow).

A حدولق *hadawlak*, Short and compact in body.

A حدي *hida'*, (v. n. of حدي) Remaining constantly fixed in one place. حدي الدهر, Ever.

A حديّا *hudayya'*, Contention, opposition. One of the people.

A انا حدّياك *ana huddayāka*, I present myself as your antagonist, come out to meet me.

A حديبية *hudaybiyat*, Name of a well near Mecca. A sort of tree.

A حديث *hadīs*, New, newly made. حديث السنّ *hadīsu's sinn*, Of a youthful age. (pl. احاديث *ahādīs*) Event, accident, novelty. History, tradition (particularly with regard to the sayings and actions of Muhammad. حديث بالمعني *hadīs bi'l maʻna'*, A mystical saying. الحديث *al hadīs*, A word implying "See the language of the prophet."

A حدّيث *hiddīs*, Talkative (man). A agreeable talker.

A حدّيثى *hiddīsa'*, A fable, tale, narrative.

A (ابو) حديج (*abū*) *hudayj*, The stork.

A حديد *hadīd*, Contiguous, adjacent. (pl. حداد *hidād* or *hudād*, Acute, sharp, pointed. Pungent. (pl. حداد *hidād*) Fluent (in tongue), acute (in intellect), keen (in ire). (pl. حدائد *hadāʼid*) Iron. A helmet. بالحديد *bi'l hadīd*, In armour. حديد افرنج *hadīdi afranj*, Steel. معدن حديد *maʻdani hadīd*, An iron mine, iron ore.

A حديدة *hadīdat*, (pl. حدائد *hadāʼid*) Sharp (sword). A weapon, tool (as a spade or pickaxe). حديدة الحرث *hadīdatu'l hars*, A ploughshare.

P حديده *hadīda*, A machine for drawing wire.

A حديديّ *hadīdiy*, Made of iron, iron.

A حديقة *hadīkat*, (pl. حدائق *hadāʼik*) An inclosed garden. A palm-plantation.

A حديل *hidyal*, Short, dwarfish.

A حذّ *hazz*, A cutting up by the roots, a breaking off. *Huzz*, (pl. of احذّ *ahazz*) Difficult, arduous, ungrateful (affairs).

A حذاء *hizā*, (v. n. of حذا for حذو) Measuring by fitting one thing to another (as shoe to shoe). Making a shoe. Putting a shoe on any one. Scattering dirt on the face. Biting the tongue (wine). Giving. (v. n. 3 of حذا for حذو) Being over against, facing. One thing opposite another. A shoe. The hoof or sole of a horse's or a camel's foot. The vintage. Opposite, over against.

A حذّاء *hazzā*, A shoemaker. (fem. of احذّ *ahazz*) Rat-tailed (camel). Thin-plumaged (bird). Irreparable (alienation of kindred). Lightly and hastily made (oath). Slender-bodied, small-handed (woman). Swift, rapid, transient. Perfect, faultless (poem). A poem in which the *hazaz* metre occurs; *i.e.* متفاعلن *mutafāʻilun* is changed to فعلن *faʻilun*.

A حذار *hizār*, (v. n. 3 of حذر) Being cautious of each other. *Hazāri*, Beware!

A حذارمة *huzārimat*, Talkative, loquacious.

A حذاري *hazāra'*, (pl. of حذر *hazir* and *hazur*) Timid, cautious. *Hazāra'* or *hazārī*, (pl. of حذرية *hizriyat*) Hackles of cocks. High grounds.

A حذاريات *huzāriyāt*, Alarmists.

A حذافة *huzāfat*, A shaving or paring of leather. A bit of meat, a morsel, mouthful.

A حذّافة *hazzāfat*, Podex: ring of the anus.

A حذافير *hazāfīr*, (pl. of حذفور *huzfūr*) Sides, parts, extremities. (Men) ready equipped for war. اشدد حذافيرك *ushdud hazāfīraka*, Make ready.

A حذاق *hazāk* or *hizāk*, (v. n. of حذق) Learning (the Kur'ān) by heart (a boy). Being clever at any work. *Hizāk*, (pl. of حذقة *hizkat*) Parts, sections. *Hizāk* or *huzāk*, (pl. of حذقة *hizkat*) Pieces.

A حذّاق *huzzāk*, (pl. of حاذق *hāzik*) Ingenious, expert, clever.

A حذاقة *hizākat*, (v. n. of حذق) Learning (the Kur'ān) by heart. Being clever at work; quickness, sharpness. Cutting or stretching (any thing) to cut (it) with a sickle. *Huzākat*, A mouthful.

A حذاقيّ *huzākiy*, Eloquent, speaking well. A sharp knife. The colt of an ass.

A حذال *hazāl*, An ant. *Hazāl* or *huzāl*, A substance resembling blood issuing from a certain thorny plant. A sort of gum proceeding from the tree طلح *talh*. *Hizāl*, A substance like saffron in the flower of the pomegranate.

A حذالة *huzālat*, The hem or border of a shirt. A sort of red gum. Chaff, bits of broken straw.

A حذام *huzām*, Slow, sluggish, lazy.

A حذامير *hazāmīr*, All, the whole.

A حذاية *huzāyat*, A share of plunder.

A حذةً *hizatan*, Over against, facing, opposite.

A حذّة *huzzat*, A slice of meat.

A حذحاذ *hazhāz*, A quick nocturnal journey in search of water.

A حذذ *hazaz*, Mobility, a wagging of the tail. Shortness of tail. In the measure كامل *kāmil*, a dropping of a وتد مجموع *watad majmūʻ*, whereby متفاعلن *mutafāʻilun* becomes فعلن *faʻilun*.

A حذر *hazar* or *hizr*, (v. n. of حذر) Avoiding, shunning. Fearing. Caution, prudence. Fear. حذرك زيدا *hazaraka* (or حذاريك *hazārayka*) *zaydan*, Beware of Zayd. ابو حذر *abū hazar*, (Father timidity) A chameleon. P حذر كردن *hazar kardan*, To beware. A *Hazir* or *hazur*, (pl. حذاري *hazāra'*) Fearing; timorous. Cautious, wakeful, wary, heedy. *Hazari*, Beware!

A حذرف (امّ *ummu*) *hizrif*, A hyena.

A حذرفوف *hazrafūf*, (or حذرفوت *hazrafūt*) A date-stalk. A nail-paring (a thing of no value).

A حذرقّة *huzrukkat*, A stewed dish, soup.

A حذرمة *hazramat*, Loquacity, talkativeness.

A حذرّي *huzurra'*, False, vain. Falsehood.

A حذرياء *hizriyāʻ*, A rough hill.

A حذريان *hizriyān*, Very timorous or cautious.

A حذرية *hizriyat*, (pl. حذاري *hazāra'* and *hazāri*) A cock's hackles. A rough piece of land. A rough hillock.

A حذف *hazf*, (v. n. of حذف) Taking away (part of any thing, as the hair of the head or tail of an animal). Rejecting, eliding, cutting off (a syllable of a word, by apocope). Throwing or striking (with a stick). Hitting a blow (on the head with a sword), and cutting off a part. Moving the hips or shoulder (in walking). Taking short steps. Conferring a favour, making a present. Addressing in few words. Making a brief salutation. The grammatical figure apocope. *Hazaf*, Small black sheep (without tail or ears). A small species of duck. A kind of jackdaw which they eat. A blade of corn.

A حذفاء *hazfāʻ*, Little and short (ear). *Huzafāʻ*, An institution, mode of life, manners.

A حذفة *huzafat*, Short, dwarfish (woman).

A حذفرة *hazfarat*, (v. n. of حذفر Q) Filling.

A حذفور *huzfūr*, Noble, illustrious. A large meeting or congregation. *Huzfūr*, (or حذفار *hizfār*) (pl. حذافير *hazāfīr*) A side, part, or district. اخذه بحذفوره *akhazahu bi huzfūrihi*, (or بحذفاره *bi hizfārihi*) He took it all.

A حذق *hazk*, (v. n. of حذق) Cutting (a rope). Binding hard, and hurting by the violence of the pressure. Biting (as any thing acid or astringent). Being pungent, sour. *Hizk*, (v. n. of حذق) Excelling in any art. Learning (the Kur'ān) by heart. Cutting or stretching (a thing) to cut (it) with a sickle. Being pungent, sour (vinegar). Quickness, cleverness, sharpness.

A حذقة *hizkat*, (pl. حذاق *hizāk* or *huzāk*) A part, section, segment.

A حذل *hazl*, Inclination, affection, love. *Hizl*, A heavy load oppressive to the bearer. *Huzl*, The hem or border of a shirt or a veil. *Huzl*, *hizl*, or *huzal*, A root. *Huzl*, (or حذلة *huzlat*) The lower part of the female garment called نطاق *nitāk*. The lower part of the waistband of the breeches. *Hazal*, (v. n. of حذل) Being thin of lashes (the eye). A redness, swelling, or watering of the eye. A flowing of tears. A falling off of the eyelashes. A species of berry which they smoke or burn as perfume, or make bread. *Huzal*, The waistband of drawers. *Huzal* or *huzl*, Hem or border of a shirt.

A حذلاق *hizlāk*, Sharp, acute.

A حذلقة *hazlakat*, (v. n. of حذلق Q) Claiming above one's due. Making groundless pretensions to cleverness.

A حذلم *hazlam*, Short and compactly built.

A حذلمة *hazlamat*, (v. n. of حذلم Q) Walking fast, rolling on. Filling (a bottle). Grooming (a horse) well. Chipping, shaving, sharpening (a stick).

A حذلوم *huzlūm*, Light and swift.

A حذم *hazm*, (v. n. of حذم) Cutting. Making haste, despatching business, travelling expeditiously. Reading or calling quick. *Hazam*, The flight of a bird with clipped wings. *Hazim*, Keen, sharp. *Huzam*, Short of stature. One who takes short steps. *Huzum*, Swift hares. Sharp thieves.

A حذمان *hazamān*, Celerity. Slowness.

A حذمة *huzamat*, Short. Short-stepped.

A حذمر *hizmir*, Short-bodied.

A حذن *huzn*, The waistband. The corner of one's garment. A chamber, closet, cell.

A حذنّة *huzunnat*, Small-eared. Short. Mounted, ridden (young camel) till his belly becomes big and his hump disappears. حذنّتان *huzunnatāni*, The two ears. The testes. Vulvæ labra.

A حذو *hazw*, (v. n. of حذا for حذو) Measuring by fitting one thing to another (as shoe to shoe). Putting a shoe on any one. Sitting opposite. Strewing dirt on one's face. Biting the tongue (wine). Giving. *Hazwa*, Opposite.

A حذوة *hazwat*, *hizwat*, or *huzwat*, Bits of leather cut off when making shoes and collected in a heap. *Hizwat*, A share of spoil. A gift. A slice of meat. Any thing opposite. *Hizwata*, On the opposite side, over against.

A حذوق *huzūk*, Pungency (of vinegar).

A حذي *hazy*, (v. n. of حذي) Being pungent, biting the tongue (vinegar). Tearing (a hide) much. Cutting (the hand). Reviling, reproaching. *Hizy*, A sort of tree. Opposite, over against. *Haza'*, (v. n. of حذي) Suffering pain (a ewe) from the secundine being burst.

A حذيا *huzya'*, Part of booty given to another.

A حذيّا *huzayya'*, A present made on the receipt of agreeable news. A voluntary gift. A share of plunder. حذيّاك *huzayyāka*, Opposite thee.

A حذية *hizyat*, An oblong slice (of meat). جاءا حذيتين *jāʻā hizyatayni*, Both came side by side.

A حذيّة *haziyat*, A share of plunder given one.

A حذير *hazīr*, One who cautions or bids beware.

A حذيق *hazīk*, Cut (with a sickle).

A حذيم *hizyam*, Cutting, sharp (sword). Clever.

A حر *hir*, (for حرح *hirh*) (pl. احراح *ahrāh*) Vulva.

A حرّ *harr*, (v. n. of حرّ) Being hot. Boiling, making (water) hot. Cooking the pap حريرة *harīrat*. A word used in checking a camel. (pl. of حرّة *harrat*) Stony places. (pl. حرور *hurūr* and احارير *ahārīr*) Heat, warmth. *Hirr*, Pudendum mulieris. *Hurr*, (pl. احرار *ahrār* and حرار *hirār*) Free (not a slave), liberal, true (not spurious), genteelly born. A young pigeon. A swift horse. A fawn. The fœtus of a serpent. Pure, unmixed (clay or sand). A good action. A fresh date. A hawk, falcon. A part of the countenance which is exposed. The centre of a sandhill. Blackness on the outside of a horse's ears. حرّ البقل *hurru'l bakl*, Pot-herbs eaten raw. حرّ الثياب *hurru's siyāb*, Costly raiment or furniture. حرّ الدار *hurru'd dār*, The middle of a house, a court. حرّ الرمل *hurru'r raml*, Fine sand. حرّ الوجه *hurru'l wajh*, The most prominent part of the cheek. جميل حرّ *jumaylu hurrin*, Name of a bird. ساق حرّ *sāku hurrin*, A male turtle-dove. طين حرّ *tīn hurr*, Pure, unmixed, free (clay). ما هذا منك بحرّ *mā hāzā minka bi hurrin*, This is unworthy of you, it does not become you.

A حرا *hara'*, (pl. احراء *ahrāʻ*) A side, quarter. Noise, cry, sound. A deer's lair. A nest.

A حراء *hirāʻ*, Name of a mountain near Mecca.

A حراب *hirāb*, (v. n. 3 of حرب) Fighting. Opposing. (pl. of حربة *harbat*) Short spears.

A حرّابة *harrābat*, Bearers of implements of war.

A حرابث *harābis*, (pl. of حربث) Certain plants.

A حرابي *harāba'*, (pl. of حرباء *hirbāʻ*) Sun-flowers.

A حرابيّ المتن *harābiyu'l matn*, The flesh on the vertebræ of the back.

A حراة *harāt*, An open space, an area, or court. A side, a quarter. Sound, noise; the crackling of a fire, rustling of the leaves of trees. A deer's lair.

A nest. Flame, flaming heat.

A حرات *harāt*, The crackling of fire.

A حرّات *harrāt*, (pl. of حرّة *harrat*) Stony places.

A حراث *harās*, A notch at the extremity of a bow to receive the string. *Hirās*, (pl. احرثة *ahrisat*) An unfinished arrow. The lower part of a spear-head.

A حرّاث *harrās*, A farmer, ploughman. *Hurrās*, (pl. of حارث *hāris*) Farmers, ploughmen.

A حراثة *hirāsat*, Agriculture, tillage.

A حراج *hirāj*, Thick darkness. (pl. of حرج *hirj*) Toils set to catch wild beasts. (pl. of حرجة *harajat*) Troops of camels. Thickets, brakes.

A حراجف *harājif*, (pl. of حرجف) Cold blasts.

A حراجل *harājil*, (pl. of حرجل *hurjul*) Long. Swift. *Hurājil*, Long.

A حراجلة *harājilatan*, They (came in a troop).

A حراجيج *harājīj*, (pl. of حرجوج *hurjūj*) Long, fat, strong camels.

A حراد *hirād*, (v. n. 3 of حرد) Being scarce of milk (a camel), of rain (a season). (pl. of حريد *harīd*) Living far from friends.

A حراديّ *harādiy*, (pl. of حرديّ *hurdīy*) Reeds. Rushes with which houses are thatched.

A حراديد *harādīd*, Mountain-peaks.

A حرار *harār*, (v. n. of حرّ) Becoming free from being a slave. Freedom. *Hirār*, (pl. of حرّ *hurr*) Free. (pl. of حرّان *harrān*) Thirsty. (pl. of حرّة *harrat*) Stony places.

A حرارة *harārat*, (v. n. of حرّ) Being hot. Warmth, heat. Pustules breaking out from heat. حرارت ديني *harārati dīnī*, Fanaticism. حرارت طبعيّه *harārati tabʻīya*, Natural heat.

A حراز *hirāz*, (v. n. 3 of حرز) Jesting or joking in a manner bordering on reviling and abuse.

A حرازة *harāzat*, A being guarded, fortified.

A حرّاس *hurrās*, (pl. of حارس *hāris*) Keepers, guardians. The king's guards.

A حراسة *hirāsat*, (v. n. of حرس) Guarding. Custody, guardianship. حراست ملك و ملّت *hirāsati milk u millat*, The government of kingdom and people. P حراست كردن *hirāsat kardan*, To guard, preserve, govern.

A حراسن *harāsin*, A species of fish.

A حراسين *harāsīn*, Lean camels. Barren years.

A حراش *hirāsh*, (v. n. 3 of حرش) Exasperating, setting (men or dogs) by the ears. (pl. of حرش *harsh*) Signs, vestiges.

A حرّاش *harrāsh*, An old black serpent.

P حراشاءِ رومي *harāshāʼi rūmī*, Wild mustard.

A حراشين *harāshīn*, (pl. of حرشون *harashūn*) Thistles or burs sticking to the wool of a sheep.

A حرّاص *hurrās*, (pl. of حريص *haris*) Covetous, greedy, eager.

A حراض *hirāz*, (v. n. 3 of حرض) Continuing at, dwelling upon, any work. Shooting at one another with arrows unshaven and pointless.

A حرّاض *harrāz*, One who prepares ashes of alkali. A maker or burner of lime, plaster, or cement.

A حراضة *harāzat*, (v. n. of حرض) Being at the point of death (from love or sickness). Being careworn. Being weak, cowardly, slothful. Fainting from desire.

A حرّاضة *harrāzat*, An alkali or barilla-market.

A حراف *hirāf*, (v. n. 3 of حرف) Recompensing evil. Being hindered from doing anything, or cut off from all enjoyment.

A حرافة *harāfat*, Bitterness, sharpness, mordacity.

A حرافد *harāfid*, Camels of a generous breed.

A حرافذ *harāfiz*, Fine slender camels.

A حرافش *hurāfish*, A viper.

A حرافض *harāfiz*, Lean, slender, tractable camels.

A حراق *hirāk*, Coition. All-devouring (fire). Violent (shot). *Hurāk*, Fuel. Tinder. (Water) extremely salt. (A horse) full of fire, running at full speed. That by which the palm-tree is impregnated. *Hurāk* or *hirāk*, An incendiary, a mischief-maker. The agency whereby the fructifying pollen of the male palm is imparted to the female.

A حرّاق *harrāk*, Burning; a burner, incendiary. *Hurrāk*, Inflammableness. Tinder. Water extremely salt.

A حراقة *hurākat*, Tinder.

A حرّاقة *harrākat*, (pl. حرّاقات *harrākāt*) A fire-ship loaded with naptha or missile brands. A place for making charcoal, burning lime or ashes of alkali. *Hurrākat*, Sharp (sword). Tinder.

A حراقف *harākif*, Projecting hip-bones.

A حراقم *harākim*, A kind of red colouring for shoe-latchets. Red, reddish-brown (skin or wine).

A حراقيص *harākīs*, (pl. of حرقوص) Winged fleas.

A حراك *harāk*, Motion.

A حراكك *harākik*, (and حراكيك *harākīk*) (pl. of حرككة *harkakat*) The upper parts of the thigh (on which people sit). Prominent parts of buttocks (in camels and the like). Lean nags. Certain reptiles.

A حرام *harām*, (v. n. of حرم) Being unlawful. Unlawful, forbidden, prohibited. Holy, venerable, sacred. (pl. حرم *hurum*) A Nazarite clad in the garment حريم *harīm*. ابن حرام *ibn harām*, An illegitimate son, a bastard. بلاد الحرام *bilādu'l harām*, Mecca. الشهر الحرام *ash' shahru'l harām*, The sacred month Muharram. مال حرام *māl harām*, Ill-gotten wealth. مسجد الحرام *masjidu'l harām*, (or البيت الحرام *al baytu'l harām*), The temple of Mecca. حرام الله *harāmu'llāh*, So help me God! بحرام عقل *bi harāmi ʻaklin*, Intelligent, judicious, wise. P حرام كردن *harām kardan*, To make unlawful, to interdict. To prohibit or prevent from sleeping. بحرام رفتن *ba harām raftan*, To go astray, to commit adultery. A *Hirām*, (v. n. of حرم) Wanting the male (a cloven-footed beast). (pl. of حرم *hirm*) Forbidden things. (pl. of حرمى *harmaʼ*) Libidinous (sheep).

A حرامان *harāmāni*, Mecca and Madina, the two sacred cities.

P حرام توشه *harām-tosha*, A term used in abuse.

P حرام زادگي *harām-zādagī*, Illegitimacy.

P حرامزاده *harām-zāda*, Illegitimate, spurious. A bastard. A villain, thief, robber, rogue.

A حرامس *harāmis*, Severe, barren (years).

P حرام كار *harām-kār*, A fornicator, adulterer.

P حرام كاري *harām-kārī*, Any forbidden act (but especially adultery and fornication).

A حرام مال *harām-māl*, Ill-got wealth.

P حرام مغز *harām-maghz*, The spinal marrow.

A حرام موت *harām-mawt*, Suicide.

P حرام نمك *harām-namak*, Idle. Ungrateful.

A حرامى *harāmaʼ*, (pl. of حرمى) Libidinous (ewe).

A حراميّ *harāmīy*, A robber, an assassin.

A حرامين *harāmayn*, Mecca and Madina.

A حران *hirān*, The obstinacy of a restive (horse), restiffness. *Hirān* or *hurān*, (v. n. of حرن) Being obstinate and restive (a horse).

A حرّان *harrān*, Stony ground. (fem. حرّى *harraʼ*, pl. حرار *hirār*) Thirsty. Harran in Mesopotamia.

A حراوة *harāwat*, Heat. Sharpness in the taste of mustard.

A حرايا *harāyaʼ*, (pl. of حريّة *harīyat*) Worthy, fit, proper (women).

A حرائب *harāʼib*, (pl. of حريبة *harībat*) Spoils, plundered effects.

A حرائث *harāʼis*, (pl. of حريثة) Gains.

A حرائر *harāʼir*, (pl. of حرّة *hurrat*) Noble ladies. Pure sands.

A حرائز *harāʼiz*, Choice camels not to be sold.

A حرائس *harāʼis*, (pl. of حريسة *harīsat*) Sheep stolen by night.

A حرائق *harāʼik*, (pl. of حريقة) Hasty puddings.

A حرب *harb*, (pl. حروب *hurūb*) War, battle. An enemy. دار الحرب *dāru'l harb*, Hostile countries, the country of the infidels. آلت حرب *ālati harb*, Arms, weapons. حرب و قتال *harb u kitāl*, Battle and slaughter. *Harab*, (v. n. of حرب) Spoiling, plundering, reducing to poverty. Being very angry. The buds and flowers of the palm-tree. *Harib*, (pl. حربى *harbaʼ*) (A man or lion) burning with rage, furious.

P حرب *hirab*, Buds and flowers of the palm.

A حرباً *harban*, Forcibly, with an armed force.

A حرباء *hirbāʼ*, A chameleon. The rings, buttons, pins, or joints of armour, bridles, and the like. The back or heads of the vertebræ. (pl. حرابيّ *harābīy*) The sunflower. *Hurabāʼ*, (pl. of حريب) Robbed.

A حربات *hara* or *harbāt*, (pl. of حربة) Fridays.

A حرباج *hirbāj*, Thick, gross, corpulent.

P حرباناك *hirbānāk*, Full of chameleons (spot).

A حربة *harbat*, (pl. حراب *hirāb*) A hunting-spear, javelin, dart, dagger. Friday. A corruption or degeneracy of religion. Stabbing. Plunder, rapine. *Hirbat*, (pl. حربات *harabāt*) Warlike apparatus. *Hurbat*, A sack.

A حربث *hurbus*, (pl. حرابث *harābis*) A certain herb which causes the cattle that feed thereon to yield good milk.

A حربج *hurbuj*, Thick and large-bodied.

P حرب جاي *harb-jāy*, A place of combat.

A حربش *hirbish*, A rough old woman. *Hirbish*, (حربشة *hirbishat*, حربّش *hiribbish*, or حربّشة *hiribbishat*) A large venomous serpent. A viper; one that crawls with a rasping, grating noise.

A حربصة *harbasat*, The irrigating (of a field).

A حربصيصة *harbasīsat*, A woman's ornaments.

A حربطة *harbazat*, The stringing tight (of a bow).

A حربي *harba'*, (pl. of حرب *harib*) Furious. (pl. of حريب *harīb*) Robbed, plundered.

A حربيّ *harbīy*, Warlike, hostile. Near to, or bounded by an enemy's country. Sounding or calling to arms. قلاع حربيّة *kilāẕi harbīya*, Garrisons on the enemy's frontiers.

A حربيش *hirbīsh*, Rough.

A حرة *hirat*, Pudendum mulieris.

A حرّة *harrat*, (v. n. of حرّ) Being thirsty. (pl. حرّ *harr*, حرار *hirār*, حرّات *harrāt*, حرّين *hirrīn*, and احرّين *aharrīn*) A stony country. A small pimple. Thirst. Pain, torture, punishment. Gross darkness. *Hirrat*, (v. n. of حرّ) Being thirsty. Thirst, excessive drought. حرّة على قرّة *hirrat ẕala' kirrat*, Thirst on a cold day (is the most painful). *Hurrat*, (pl. حرائر *harāïr*) Free-born, noble (woman). A fine she-camel. The back of the ear where the ear-ring plays. A cloud abounding in rain. ليلة حرّة *laylatu hurratin*, The night a bride preserves her virginity. First night of the month.

A حرت *hart*, (v. n. of حرت) Rubbing hard. Being of a bad disposition. A circular segment. The noise of cattle eating.

A حرتة *hurtat*, Tickling the nose (as snuff, pepper, and the like). *Huratat*, A glutton.

A حرتك *hartak*, Small-bodied.

A حرث *hars*, (v. n. of حرث) Tilling, sowing. Ploughing. Gaining (money). Marrying four wives. Indulging much in venery. Reading (the Kur'ān) with attention and meditating upon it. Stirring the fire, making it burn. Making a notch in the end of a bow for the string. Making lean (a beast) with over-work. Tillage. (pl. حروث *hurūs*) The produce of a field. The root of an ass's yard. Reward, recompense. A woman, a wife. A beaten road. *Haris*, A lion.

A حرثة *hursat*, The space between the extremity of the penis and the place of circumcision. A notch at the extremity of a bow to receive the string.

A حرج *hirj*, (pl. احراج *ahrāj*) The shell called concha venerea, of the small white species, hung round the neck to avert the effect of malignant eyes. A dog's collar. Narrowness. Part of the deer (given to the hounds). (pl. حراج *hirāj*) A snare for a wild beast. Clothes hung over a line or spread on the ground to dry. *Haraj*, (v. n. of حرج) Being dazzled (eye). Being forbidden. Being kept from labour (a she-camel) that (she) may fatten. Narrow. A narrow place. A bier. A sin, fault, crime. Lean (he-camel). Long (she-camel). Narrowness. A camel-litter. (pl. of حرجة *harajat*) Troops of camels. Shrubberies, bushes. *Haraj* or *harij*, Narrow. (A place) impenetrable from the closeness of the trees. *Harij*, One incessantly engaged in fighting. A criminal.

A حرجات *harajāt*, (pl. of حرجة) Shrubberies.

A حرجة *hurjat*, A small bucket, urn. *Harajat*, (pl. حرج *haraj* and حراج *hirāj*) A troop of camels. A thicket, shrubbery.

A حرجف *harjaf*, (pl. حراجف) A cold blast.

A حرجل *harjal*, A troop of horses. *Hurjul*, (pl. حراجل *harājil*) Long. Swift.

A حرجلة *harjalat*, (v. n. of حرجل Q) Being long. Running right and left from skittishness. Filling up a row. A flight of locusts. A troop of horses. Pure, unmixed soil. Lameness.

A حرجمة *harjamat*, (v. n. of حرجم Q) Driving (camels) against each other. Crowding.

A حرجوان *harjuwān*, A kind of wingless locust.

A حرجوج *hurjūj*, (pl. حراجيج *harājīj*) A long, fat, and strong she-camel. A cold biting wind. A lean, lank, intelligent she-camel.

A حرح *harh*, (v. n. of حرح) Striking (a woman) on the pudendum. *Hirh*, (pl. احراح *ahrāh*) Pudendum mulieris. *Harih*, Belonging to the pudendum muliebre. A man addicted thereto, a habitual fornicator.

A حرحيّ *hirahīy*, Belonging to the vulva.

A حرد *hard*, (v. n. of حرد) Intending, proposing. Being angry. Hindering, keeping back. Perforating. Cutting off a piece. *Hard* or *harid*, Separate, solitary, remote. *Hird*, A camel's stable. (pl. حرود *hurūd*) A piece of a camel's bunch. The intestine of a camel. *Hurd*, Swift (katā birds). *Harad*, (v. n. of حرد) Being angry, enraged. Being spavined (a camel). Having a contraction of the muscles of the fore-leg caused by the tether. Oppressing, cramping, shackling (a coat of mail). Being of unequal lengths (the threads of a bow-string). *Harid*, Passionate. Shackled, hampered by a tight coat of mail.

A حرداء *hardāʼ*, (fem. of احرد *ahrad*) (A she-camel) having the tendon of the fore-foot compressed and lamed by the fetter. *Huradāʼ*, (pl. of حريد *harīd*) Separate, alone, remote from friends.

A حردان *hardān*, Angry, enraged, furious.

A حردب *hardab*, Seed of nightshade.

A حردبة *hardabat*, Lightness, agility.

A حردة *hirdat*, A camel's stable. A piece of a camel's bunch. The intestine of a camel.

A حردمة *hardamat*, Obstinacy, stubbornness.

A حردون *hirdawn*, The male Lybian lizard.

A حرديّ *hurdīy*, (or حرديّة *hurdīyat*) (pl. حراديّ *harādīy*) A reed. A girdle of rushes tied round a fence of reeds.

A حرذمة *harzamat*, (v. n. of حرذم Q) Cursing any one (God). Filling (a vessel).

A حرذون *hirzawn*, The male Lybian lizard. A salamander.

A حرز *harz*, (v. n. of حرز) Guarding, preserving, taking care of jealously. *Hirz*, A fortification, garrison-town, castle. An amulet or charm against fascination or enchantment. حرز الظهر *hirzu'z zahr*, The spine. *Haraz*, (v. n. of حرز) Being timid, cautious, scrupulous. Imminent danger, jeopardy, risk, hazard. Dignity, nobility. Any thing kept back and preserved. (pl. احراز *ahrāz*) Polished nuts, used by children at play. Any thing preserved with jealous care.

A حرزة *harazat*, (pl. حرزات *harazāt*) An excellent thing worthy of being preserved, the choicest of one's property.

A حرزقة *harzakat*, A shutting up, a confining.

A حرس *hars*, (v. n. of حرس) Guarding. Stealing. Living a long while. (pl. احرس *ahrus*) An age. *Hirs*, Guardianship, custody, protection. *Haras*, (pl. of حارس *haris*) Guards: king's guards.

A حرسم *harsam*, A corner. *Hirsim* or *hirsam*, Poison. Death.

A حرسيّ *harasīy*, One life-guard man.

A حرش *harsh*, (v. n. of حرش) Hunting the Lybian lizard (by moving the hand at his hole; when he, supposing the motion to be that of a snake, thrusts out his tail and is taken). Scratching. Lying with (a girl) on (her) back. Springing up (enmity). (pl. حراش *hirāsh*) Mark, vestige. A crowd, company. *Harash*, (v. n. of حرش) Being rough-skinned. *Harish*, Unable to sleep from hunger. *Hurush*, (pl. of حريش *harīsh*) Voracious camels.

A حرشاء *harshāʼ*, Rough (coin). Rough-skinned (snake). Unbesmeared (scab). Scabby (she-camel). Wild mustard.

A حرشاف *harshāf*, A lean and voracious locust.

A حرشة *hurshat*, Roughness. *Harashat*, (pl. حرشات *harashāt*) Any small creeping thing.

A حرشف *harshaf*, Scales of fish. Silver studs (upon armour and the like). The rings of a coat of mail. Weak persons. Old men. Footmen. An artichoke. A small bird, ostrich, or any thing small. *Hurshuf*, Rough and hard ground.

A حرشفة *harshafat*, Rough and hard ground.

A حرشون *harashūn*, (pl. حراشين *harāshīn*) A thistle, bramble, or bur, sticking to a sheep.

A حرص *hars*, (v. n. of حرص) Splitting, tearing. Peeling, skinning. A fissure. *Hirs*, (v. n. of حرص) Desiring eagerly. Avidity, avarice, cupidity, greediness. *Hurus*, Greedy, ravenous fellows.

A حرصاً *hirsan*, (P حرصانه) Greedily, eagerly.

A حرصاء *huraṣā*, (pl. of حريص *hariṣ*) Covetous, greedy, eager, earnest.

A حرصة *harṣat*, A blow on the head breaking only the skin. A falling of the milk into the pail in a scattered manner in consequence of the width of an injured teat. *Haraṣat*, The fixed, settled spot of the centre of every thing.

A حرصيان *hirṣiyān*, The inside of the skin of the belly. The interior of an elephant's hide. A red pellicle which peels off a hide after it has been stripped off.

A حرض *harz*, (v. n. of حرض) Corrupting, destroying (one's self). *Hurz* or *huruz*, The herb alkali or its ashes, with which they wash clothes. *Haraz*, (v. n. of حرض) Being at the point of death (from love or sickness). Being worn down by incessant anxiety. Being cowardly, slothful. Gathering saffron, and having the body distempered. Being unarmed, fearing to fight. Edge of a garment. Wicked (man). Blasphemous (language). Lean (camel). Unsoundness (of mind, body, or creed). Lean (from love or grief). At the point of death. Unarmed. A coward, one afraid to fight. Good for nothing. (pl. احراض *ahrāz*, حرضان *hurzān*, and حرضة *harazat*) One from whom nothing is hoped or feared. *Haraz* or *hariz*, Unsound, vitiated, depraved in body, mind, or principles. Sick. Unable to rise. *Hiraz*, (pl. of حرضة *hirzat*) Lean (men).

A حرضان *hurzān*, (pl. of حرض *haraz*) Those from whom nothing is hoped or feared.

A حرضة *hirzat*, (pl. حرض *hiraz*) Lean (man). *Hurzat*, One who throws dice for others, but is afraid to play himself. One who neither buys meat, or eats any, except at another's expense. A kind of arrow not shaved and without a head. *Harazat*, (pl. of حرض *haraz*) Those from whom nothing is hoped or feared.

A حرضيّ *hurziy*, A seller of alkali or the ashes.

A حرف *harf*, (v. n. of حرف) Changing, inverting. Scratching. Shaving smooth. Providing for (a family). Gaining. (pl. حروف *hurūf* and احرف *ahruf*) A letter of the alphabet. A particle (as an adverb, preposition, conjunction, or interjection). (pl. حرف *hiraf*) Side, edge, extremity, margin, border. The peaked summit of a mountain, a promontory. Edge (of a sword). A camel, large, lean, and raw-boned. Way, mode, manner. A channel, a stream of water. A dialect of Arabia, seven of which they say can be detected in the Kur'ān. A mode of worshipping God. حرف الاستدراك *harfu'l istidrāk*, Adversative particle. حرف الاستفتاح *harfu'l istiftāh*, Inchoative particle. حرف الاستفهام *harfu'l istifhām*, (or سؤال *suʻāl*) Particle of interrogation. حرف الاستثنا *harfu'l istisnā*, Particle of exception. حرف الاستئناف *harfu'l istiʼnāf*, (or ابتداء *ibtidāʼ*) Inchoative particle. حرف الافتراق *harfu'l iftirāk*, Particle of disjunction. حرف الايجاب *harfu'l ījāb*, Particle of affirmation or assent. حرف التأكيد *harfu't taʼkīd*, Particle of injunction or emphasis. حرف التبعيد *harfu't tabʻīd*, Particle of removal. حرف التحقيق *harfu't tahkīk*, Particle of affirmation. حرف التحضيض *harfu't tahẓīẓ*, Particle for exciting the attention. حرف التخصيص *hārfu't takhṣīṣ*, Particle of identity or specification. حرف الترجّي *harfu't tarajjī*, Optative particle. حرف الترديد *harfu't tardīd*, Particle of disjunction. حرف التشبيه *harfu't tashbīh*, Particle of similitude. حرف التشكيك *harfu't tashkīk*, Particle of doubt. حرف التعريف *harfu't taʻrīf*, (or معرفة *maʻrifat*) The definite article. حرف التعليل *harfu't taʻlīl*, Particle of cause or reason. حرف التفريق *harfu't tafrīk*, Particle of separation. حرف التفضيل *harfu't tafẓīl*, Particle of comparison. حرف التقريب *harfu't takrīb*, Particle of drawing nigh unto. حرف التمنّي *harfu't tamannī*, An optative particle. حرف التمييز *harfu't tamyīz*, Particle of discrimination. حرف التنفيس *harfu't tanfīs*, Particle of breathing-time. حرف التنكير *harfu't tankīr*, The indeterminate article. حرف التوقع *harfu't tawakkuʻ*, Particle of expectation. حرف الجزاء *harfu'l jizāʼ*, Particle of consequence. حرف الحال *harfu'l hāl*, Particle of the present. حرف الحصر *harfu'l hasr*, Particle of restriction. حرف الخطاب *harfu'l khitāb*, Particle of address. حرف الدعا *harfu'd duʻā*, Particle of invocation. حرف الردع *harfu'r radʻ*, Particle of reproach or indignation. حرف زائد *harfi zāʼid*, Expletive particle. حرف الزجر *harfu'z zajr*, Particle of reprimand. حرف ساكن *harfi sākin*, A quiescent consonant. حرف السبب *harfu's sabab*, Causative particle. حرف الشرط *harfu'sh shart*, Conditional particle. حرف صحيح *harfi sahīh*, A consonant. حرف الصلة *harfu's silat*, Particle of conjunction. حرف الطرح *harfu't tarh*, Particle of method. حرف العطف *harfu'l ʻatf*, Copulative particle. حرف علت *harfi ʻillat*, A long vowel, as ا, و, or ي. حرف الغاية *harfu'l ghāyat*, Particle of extremity. حرف المبهمات *harfu'l mubhamāt*, Demonstrative particle. حرف متحرّك *harfi mutaharrak*, A consonant inflected with a short vowel. حرف مجهول *harfi majhūl*, An obscure letter, as و in روز *roz*, A day, and ي in شير *sher*, A lion. حرف مسروق *harfi masrūk*, A letter written though not pronounced, as و in خواهش *khwāhish*, Desire, چو *chu*, Like, تو *tu*, Thou, او *u*, He, دو *du*, Two, &c. حرف معروف *harfi maʻrūf*, An open or broad letter, as ي in شير *shīr*, Milk. حرف معنوي *hārfi maʻnawī*, A postposition. حرف معيّة *harfi maʻiya*, Particle of society. حرف الندا *harfu'n nidā*, Vocative particle. حرف الندبة *harfu'n nudbat*, Particle of lamentation. حرف النفي *harfu'n nafy*, Particle of negation. حرف آخر ابجد *harfi ākhiri abjad*, The letter غ *ghayn*, which denotes 1000; hence, The nightingale. حرف بحرف *harf ba harf*, (also حرفا حرفا *harfan harfan*) Literally. علي حرف *ʻala' harfin*, In one mode. Partially. P حرف زدن *harf zadan*, To speak, converse. A *Hurf*, Cresses (or the seed). Misfortune, the making no money. حرف بابلي *hurfi bābilī*, Babylonian cresses. *Hiraf*, (pl. of حرف *harf*) Edges, margins. Mountain-peaks. (pl. of حرفة *hirfat*) Trades, arts, crafts.

P حرف آشنا *harf-āshnā*, Acquainted with one's letters, just able to read.

A حرفان *hirfān*, Misfortune, ill-luck.

P حرف انداز *harf-andāz*, Cunning, artful.

P حرف اندازي *harf-andāzī*, Cunning, artifice.

A حرفة *harfat*, (v. n. of حرف) Anointing (the eyes) with antimony. Losing a part of one's property. *Hirfat*, A trade, craft, art, business, profession. Skill, ingenuity. Cunning. A corporation, company, or body of artificers. A meal. اهل حرفت *ahli hirfat*, An artisan, trader, craftsman. *Hirfat* or *hurfat*, Misfortune, ill-luck.

P حرفت بازي *hirfat-bāzī*, Witchcraft.

A حرفذة *harfazat*, A fine slender he-camel.

A حرفش *hirfish*, A viper.

A حرفضة *hirfizat*, An excellent she-camel.

P حرفقان *harfkān*, Ratsbane.

P حرف گير *harf-gīr*, Censurer, caviller, critic.

P حرف گيري *harf-gīrī*, Cavil. Criticism.

A حرفيّ *harfīy*, Relating to, possessing the nature or property of a particle. *Hurfīy*, A dealer in cresses, or in the seed.

A حرفيّة *harfīyat*, The quality of particle.

A حرق *hark*, (v. n. of حرق) Burning. Filing. Grinding the teeth (in a rage). Rubbing one against another. *Hirk*, That by which the female palm-tree is impregnated. *Harak*, (v. n. of حرق) Having a burnt appearance from too much beating of the fuller (cloth). Dropping off (the hair). Fire, flame. That by which the fructifying property of the male palm-tree is imparted to the female. بالحرق و الغرق *bi'l harak wa'l gharak*, By fire and flood. *Harik*, Losing the hair, bald. A man whose hands and feet are cracked. (A cloud) sending out vivid lightning.

A حرقان *hurkān*, A chafing (of the thighs).

A حرقانيّ *harakāniy*, Coloured as if singed.

A حرقة *harkat* or *hurkat*, Ardour, heat. حرقة البول *harkatu'l bawl*, Chaude-pisse, clap. *Hurkat*, Flame, fire. *Hurakat*, Sharp (sword).

A حرقد *hirkid*, The root of the tongue.

A حرقدة *harkadat*, Head of the wind-pipe.

A حرقريقة *hurakrīkat*, Acute, sharp.

A حرقصة *harkasat*, (v. n. of حرقص Q) Taking short steps. Speaking gently. Talking quick and incessantly.

A حرقصی *haraksa'*, Name of an animalcule.

A حرقفة *harkafat*, (v. n. of حرقف Q) (One ass) biting (another) on the top or the projecting bone of the buttocks (which touches the seat when one sits down). The part itself.

A حرقلة *harkalat*, A manner of walking.

A حرقوة *harkuwat*, The upper part of the uvula. The hip-bone.

A حرقوص *hurkūs*, (pl. حراقيص *harākīs*) A winged flea. A crab-louse. Stone of a green date.

A حرقوف *hurkūf*, Lean nag. Certain reptile.

A حرقي *harka'*, (pl. of حريق *harīk*) Burning.

A حرك *hark*, (v. n. of حرك) Striking (a horse) on the withers. Moving. Withholding a debt. بحركه *bi harkihi*, On his account. *Harah*, (v. n. of حرك) Being impotent. *Harik*, Nimble, quick. Ingenious. Industrious.

A حركات *harakāt*, (pl. of حركة *harakat*) Motions. Vowel-points. حركات و سكنات *harakāt u sakanāt*, Proceedings. Vowels and consonants.

A حركة *harakat*, (v. n. of حرك) Moving. Motion, movement, act, action, conduct, behaviour, procedure. Misbehaviour, impropriety of conduct. Agitation. Disturbance. Prevention. A vowel. حركت مقداري *harakati mikdārī*, The expanding or shrinking motion (in bodies capable of growth or decrease). حركت وضعي *harakati wazaʿī*, The rotatory motion (of the heavenly bodies). P حركت كردن *harakat kardan*, To move, proceed, behave. To commit an improper action.

A حركتي *harakatī*, An interrupter.

A حركثة *harkasat*, Commotion.

A حرككة *harkakat*, (pl. حراكك *harākik* and حراكيك *harākīk*) The upper part of the thigh, (by others) the nether part on which one sits. The buttock (of a camel). A lean nag. A certain reptile.

A حركلة *harkalat*, (v. n. of حركل Q) Taking no game (a hunter). A pompous mode of walking. Men on foot.

A حركوك *hurkūk*, The space betwixt the shoulders of a beast, the withers.

A حرم *harm*, (v. n. of حرم) Beating at a game of hazard. *Hirm*, (v. n. of حرم) Prohibiting. (pl. حرم *hurum*) Forbidden. Unlawful. Necessary. Expedient, proper. *Hurm*, (v. n. of حرم) Being prohibited. A wife. Any thing guarded with care, or that must be kept inviolate. *Hurm* or *hirm*, The pilgrim's mantle. *Haram*, (v. n. of حرم) Being forbidden, unlawful. Being beaten at dice. Brawling, squabbling. The most sacred and most retired place of a temple or palace. The haram or women's apartments. A wife. A daughter, a ward. A right, privilege; any thing worth defending. (pl. احرام *ahrām*) The sacred enclosure at Mecca, or precincts of the temple which is called حرم الله *haramu'llāh*. الحرم *al haram*, Mecca and its temple. The precincts of Madīna. P حرم همايون *harami humāyūn*, The seraglio of a monarch. A *Harim*, (v. n. of حرم) Prohibiting. Disappointment, repulse. *Huram*, Prohibited, inviolable. (pl. of حرمة *hurmat*) Wives. *Hurum*, (v. n. of حرم) Being prohibited. Four months during which it is unlawful to fight (viz. the first, Muharram; seventh, Rajab; and two last, Zū'l kaʿdat and Zū'l hijjat. (pl. of حرم *hirm*) Forbidden things. (pl. of حرام *harām*) Clad in pilgrim's attire. (pl. of حريم *harīm*) Things which a person keeps with care.

A حرماس *hirmās*, Smooth, even. Hard (ground).

A حرمان *hirmān*, (v. n. of حرم) Prohibiting, making unlawful. Depriving of hope. Repulse, disappointment, mortification. P غبن و حرمان كردن *ghabn u hirmān kardan*, To deceive and disappoint.

A حرمان *haramāni*, (dual) The two sacred cities of Mecca and Madīna.

A حرمة *hirmat*, (v. n. of حرم) Depriving of hope, disappointing. Disappointment, ill-luck. *Hirmat* or *haramat*, Desire of copulation (in cloven-footed beasts). Disappointment, ill-luck. *Hirmat* or *harimat*, (v. n. of حرم) Prohibiting. *Hurmat*, (v. n. of حرم) Being unlawful, forbidden. Impropriety, indecorum. *Hurmat*, *huramat*, or *hurumat*, A wife. A family. A divine command. Guard, protection. Honour, reputation, chastity. Reverence, respect, veneration. Dignity commanding respect. A part, portion, lot.

A حرمّة *harammat*, Hills where nothing grows.

A حرمد *harmad* or *hirmid*, Black mud. Changed in hue or scent.

A حرمزة *harmazat*, (v. n. of حرمز Q) Cursing. Acuteness of genius, penetration.

A حرمس *hirmis*, (pl. حرامس) A barren year.

P حرم سرا *haram-sarā*, Women's apartments.

A حرمل *harmal*, Seed of wild rue.

A حرملة *harmalat*, Name of a tree which emits fire when rubbed, the milky juice of which is a good liniment for the scab. Name of many traditionists.

A حرمي *harma'*, (pl. حرام *hirām* and حرامي *harāma'*) Libidinous (ewe or cloven-footed animal). (pl. حرامي *harāma'*) Hot (bitch). حرمي والله *harma' wa'llāh*, By God!

A حرميّ *hirmīy*, Prohibitive. (A man) connected with Mecca, or the sacred enclosure of the Kaaba. *Haramīy*, (Cloth or a garment) made, or worn at Mecca.

A حرمين *haramayn*, Mecca and Madīna.

A حرن *harn*, (v. n. of حرن) Asking a fair, just price. Dividing (cotton).

A حرنانيّ *harnānīy*, Of Harran in Mesopotamia.

A حرنفش *haranfash*, Coarse, rough. Unfeeling. Large, great.

A حرنقفة *hurankifat*, Short (woman).

A حروب *hurūb*, (pl. of حرب) Battles, wars.

A حروة *harwat*, Heat in the throat, breast, or head (from anger or pain). An acrid stench. Sharpness in the flavour of mustard.

A حروث *hurūs*, (pl. of حرث *hars*) Productions of the fields; agricultural labours.

A حرود *harūd*, (A camel) yielding little milk. *Hurūd*, (v. n. of حرد) Living alone. Mountain-peaks. (pl. of حرد *hird*) Pieces of camels' bunches. Intestines of camels.

A حرور *harūr*, A warm nocturnal wind. Solar heat. Fire. Lasting heat. *Hurūr*, Heat, warmth.

A حرورة *harūrat*, Heat, ardour. Freedom.

A حروريّ *harūrīy*, One of the sect called *Harūrīyat*. Of or belonging to heat, calorific.

A حروريّة *harūrīyat*, Name of a sect. *Harūrīyat* or *hurūrīyat*, Freedom.

A حروض *hurūz*, (or حروضة *hurūzat*) (v. n. of حرض) Being ready to die (from love or grief). Being worn by long vexation. Being cowardly, inactive, slothful. Wasting from intense desire.

A حروف *hurūf*, (pl. of حرف *harf*) Letters. Characters. Points, edges, salient angles. Particles. Mountain-peaks. حروف الاستقبال *hurūfu'l istikbāl*, Future particles. حروف الاسليّة *hurūfu'l aslīyat*, Sibilant letters. حروف الاصليّة *hurūfu'l aslīyat*, Radical letters. حروف الاضافة *hurūfu'l izāfat*, Particles of annexion. حروف التصديق *hurūfu't tasdīk*, Particles of affirmation. حروف التضعيف *hurūfu't tazʿīf*, Letters of reduplication. حروف التنبية *hurūfu't tambīh*, Particles for awakening the attention. حروف الجرّ *hurūfu'l jarr*, Particles of the genitive. حروف الحلقيّة *hurūfu'l halkīyat*, Guttural letters. حروف الزوائد *hurūfu'z zawāʾid*, Servile or redundant letters. حروف الشجريّة *hurūfu'sh shajrīyat*, Palatal letters. حروف الشفهيّة *hurūfu'sh shafahīyat*, Labial letters. حروف الصحيح *hurūfu's sahīh*, Sound letters. حروف العلّة *hurūfu'l ʿillat*, Infirm letters. حروف العلل *hurūfu'l ʿilal*, Accidental letters. حروف اللثويّة *hurūfu'l liswīyat*, Gingival letters. حروف اللسانيّة *hurūfu'l lisānīyat*, Lingual letters. حروف اللهويّة *hurūfu'l lahwīyat*, Letters pronounced from the uvula. حروف الليِّنة *hurūfu'l laynīyat*, Soft letters. حروف المدّ *hurūfu'l madd*, Letters of prolongation. حروف المصدر *hurūfu'l masdar*, Particles serving for the infinitive. حروف المضارعة *hurūfu'l muzāraʿat*, Letters forming the aorist. حروف المعجم *hurūfu'l muʿjam*, The alphabet arranged in order contrary to the *abjad*. حروف معنيّ *hurūfi maʿna'*, Particles which influence the sense. حروف المقطعة *hurūfu'l muktaʿat*, Detached letters, such as occur in certain chapters of the Kur'ān. حروف الموقوفة *hurūfu'l mawkūfat*, Quiescent letters. حروف الهجاء *hurūfu'l hijāʾ*, The letters of the alphabet.

A حروق *harūk* or *hurūk*, The pollen by which the female palm-tree is fructified. Tinder. A hoof. *Hurūk*, (v. n. of حرق) Gnashing the teeth in rage.

A حرّوق *harrūk*, (or حروقاء *harūkāʾ*) Tinder.

A حروقة *harūkat*, Pottage, gruel.

A حروم *harūm*, A camel that does not bear for several years, although not barren.

A حرون *harūn*, Refractory, restive (horse). Game which does not come down from the summit of a mountain. *Hirūn*, (pl. of حر *hir*) Pudenda mulierum. *Hurūn*, (v. n. of حرن) Being stubborn, restiff, refractory (a horse). Asking a fair, just price. Dividing (cotton).

A حروني *harūnī*, Refractoriness, stubbornness.

P حرة *hira*, Nightshade.

A حري *hary*, (v. n. of حري) Being defective, diminished. Waning (the moon). *Hara'*, A court, an open space or area. Name of a mountain near Mecca. The spot where the ostrich lays her eggs. Worthy. *Harī*, (pl. احراء *ahrā*) Worthy, fit, proper.

A حرّي *harra'*, (pl. حرّان) Thirsty (woman).

A حريّ *hariy*, (pl. احرياء *ahriyā*) Worthy, fit. *Hiriy*, Belonging to the pudendum muliebre.

A حرّيّ *harriy*, (A camel) pasturing in a stony place. Relating to a stony place.

A حريب *harīb*, (pl. حربي *harba'* and حرباء *hurabā*) Spoiled, plundered. *Hurayb*, A little war.

A حريبة *harībat*, (pl. حرائب *harāib*) Effects, of which one is plundered, or on which he subsists.

A حريّة *harīyat*, (pl. حرايا) Worthy, fit (woman).

A حرّيّة *hurrīyat*, (v. n. of حرّ) Becoming free, from being a slave. Freedom, frankness. Soft, sandy soil. Nobles of the Arabians.

A حريت *harīt*, The char (a kind of fish).

A حريثة *harīsat*, (pl. حرائث *harāsis*) Gain. A she-camel worn out with labour.

A حريد *harīd*, (pl. حراد *hirād* and حرداء *huradā*) Solitary, single. Living alone, at a distance from a friend. Fish cut in slices. حيّ حريد *hayy harīd*, A tribe living alone, from pride or poverty.

A حريداء *huraydā*, A tendon compressed by the fetter.

A حرير *harīr*, Silk. Silken cloth, a silken garment. Warm, choleric.

A حريرة *harīrat*, One silken garment. A kind of pap made from milk or fat and flour. Caudle. (fem. of حرير *harīr*) Warm, choleric.

P حرير سينه *harīr-sīna*, Soft, tender-hearted.

A حريريّ *harīriy*, A silk-merchant. A thin kind of paper.

A حريز *harīz*, Guarded, strongly fortified. Highly prized. A preservative from the effects of poison.

A حريسة *harīsat*, (pl. حرائس *harāis*) A sheep stolen by night. A stone enclosure for sheep.

A حريش *harīsh*, A serpent speckled white and black. A rhinoceros. An earwig. Name of a marine animal. (pl. حرش *hurush*) Voracious (camel). A camel whose lips are cracked by browsing on thorny shrubs.

A حريشة *harīshat*, A kind of fish. Whatever is in one's hand or possession. Hawkweed.

A حريص *harīs*, (pl. حرّاص *hurrās* and حرصاء *hurasā*) Covetous, greedy, eager, earnest. Rent (garment). حريص منصب *harīsi mansib*, Ambitious of honours and appointments.

A حريصة *harīsat*, A cloud pouring forth rain so as to break up the ground.

A حريصي *harīsī*, Greediness.

A حريض *harīz*, Unable to rise.

P حريف *harīf*, A companion, messmate. An antagonist at play. حريف آب و دندان *harīfi āb u dandān*, Whatever is agreeable to one's disposition. Delicious as sweetmeats. A faithful lover. حريف گلو بر *harīfi gulū-bur*, (or حريف گلوگير *harīfi gulū-gīr*) Deceitful fortune. Pride, vanity.

A حريف *harīf*, A man (used in a contemptible sense), a fellow. An adversary in a law-suit. A rival. One with whom you do business, a partner. A fellow workman. Clever, cunning. Pleasant, facetious. Impudent, audacious.

A حرّيف *hirrīf*, Acrid, sharp, biting (to the taste).

P حريفي *harīfī*, Stratagem, fraud.

A حريق *harīk*, (pl. حرقي *harka'*) Fired, burnt. Flame, fire. Borage. Noise of gnashing of teeth. عذاب حريق *ʿazābi harīk*, The torments of hell.

A حريقة *harīkat*, (pl. حرائق *harāik*) Pottage, gruel. Heat, warmth.

A حريك *harīk*, Weak in the waist, or who totters when he walks. Impotent.

A حريم *harīm*, (v. n. of حرم) Disappointing. (pl. احرام *ahrām* and حرم *hurum*) Sacred, inviolable, unlawful to touch. A sanctuary. The sacred enclosure at Mecca. Women's apartments. Any thing that lies round about another and belongs to it. Honour, dignity. A right, privilege. A companion, partner. A place where earth is thrown out of a well. The coarse garb of a pilgrim.

A حريمة *harīmat*, (v. n. of حرم) Prohibiting. Depriving of hope, disappointing. حريمة الربّ *harīmatu'r rabb*, That which the Lord has prohibited to whom he will.

P حريم خانه *harīm-khāna*, A woman's apartment.

A حريملة *huraymilat*, A tree containing a light, soft cottony substance, used in stuffing the pillows of the wealthy.

A حرّين *hirrīn*, (pl. of حرّة *harrat*) Stony places.

A حزّ *hazz*, (v. n. of حزّ) Cutting, making an incision, notching. Excelling, exceeding (in nobility and generosity). (pl. حزوز *huzūz*) A notch, incision. Low-lying, depressed ground. Reproachful, cutting, severe in language. Time, season.

A حزء *haz*, (v. n. of حزأ) (Vapour) raising up (a thing). Collecting, driving (camels). Lying with.

A حزا *haza'*, (or حزاء *hazā*) Wild anise.

A حزّاء *hazzā*, An astrologer, palmister.

A حزاب *hizāb*, (v. n. 3 of حزب) Confederating.

A حزابة *huzābat*, A perplexing business.

A حزابي *hazābī*, (or حزابية *hazābiyat*) (pl. حزائب *hazāib*) Thick and short. (pl. of حزباءة *hizbāat*) Rough grounds.

A حزاة *hazāt*, (or حزاءة) One anise-plant.

A حزاز *hazāz*, Scales on the head. Diligent, laborious, active, bustling. A furious driver. حزاز الصخر *hazāzu's sakhr*, Lichen. *Hizāz*, (v. n. 3 of حزّ) Earnestly endeavouring after any thing, curiously prying, using every effort to get at the knowledge of a thing. شركة حزاز *shirkatu hizāzin*, Partnership wherein mutual confidence exists not.

P حزاز *huzāz*, Dry scab, ringworm.

A حزّاز *hazzāz*, Food which turns acid on the stomach. A man who drives vehemently. An active, bustling fellow. *Hazzāz* or *huzzāz*, Any thing which harasses and worries the mind.

A حزازة *hazāzat*, Scurf. Ringworm, dry scab. Indisposition of mind from anger.

A حزازيّ *hazāziy*, A violent driver. An active, bustling man.

A حزاق *hizāk*, A thick bracelet.

A حزاقا *hizākan*, Necessarily, by force.

A حزاقة *hazākat*, A multitude.

A حزاقلة *hazākilat*, The lowest (rank of men).

A حزام *hizām*, (pl. حزم *huzum*) A belt, girth, surcingle. Swaddling-bands.

A حزامة *hazāmat*, (v. n. of حزم) Being provident, firm in mind. Bringing together, adjusting. *Hizāmat*, A belt, girth, surcingle.

A حزامير *hazāmīr*, (Taking) the whole.

A حزان *hizān*, (pl. of حزن) Grieved, sad.

A حزّان *hizzān* also *huzzān*, (pl. of حزيز *hazīz*) Rough places.

A حزانة *huzānat*, A family, domestics (a source of care). The commencement of the invasion of Persia by the Arabs and of their laying claim to the houses and fields.

A حزاني *hazāna'*, (pl. of حزين *hazīn*) Sad.

A حزاور *hazāwir*, (pl. of حزورة) Hillocks.

A حزاورة *hazāwirat*, (pl. of حزورة) Hillocks.

A حزاوير *hazāwīr*, (pl. of حزوارة) Hillocks.

A حزائب *hazāib*, (pl. of حزابية *hazābiyat*) Strong and short (men).

A حزائق *hazāik*, (pl. of حزيقة *hazīkat*) Multitudes (of men or palm-trees). Parts, sections.

A حزب *hazb*, (v. n. of حزب) Happening, occurring, befalling. Pressing upon. A perplexing business. *Hizb*, (pl. احزاب *ahzāb*) A troop, legion, cohort, crew. Associates, auxiliaries, confederates. Arms, armour. Rugged, uneven ground. A part (particularly a sixtieth of the Kur'ān). حزب مشركين *hizbi mushrikīn*, Crowds, bodies, gangs of infidels. *Huzub*, (pl. of حازب *hāzib* and حزيب *hazīb*) Severe, difficult affairs.

A حزباء *hizbā*, (pl. of حزباءة *hizbāat*) Rough, uneven grounds.

A حزباءة *hizbāat*, (pl. حزابي *hazāba'*) Rugged, uneven ground.

A حزّة *hazzat*, A single incision. Time, season.

Huzzat, The waist. The waistband of the drawers. The neck. An oblong slice of meat or of a liver.

A حزحزة *hazhazat*, Indisposition from grief or fear. A transposition of soldiers when drawn up in battle-array.

A حزد *hazd*, (for حصد *hasd*) Harvest.

A حزر *hazr*, (v. n. of حزر) Guessing, estimating. Being wrinkled (the forehead).

A حزراء *hazrāʼ*, A draught of sour milk.

A حزرة *hazrat*, (pl. حزرات *hazarāt*) The best part of flocks, or any kind of wealth. Name of a certain bitter or salt tree. The bitter lot-tree.

A حزرقة *hazrakat*, A shutting up, a confining.

A حزز *hazaz*, Vehemence, violence, severity. *Hizaz*, Swaths of cut corn. *Huzuz*, (pl. of حزيز *hazīz*) Steep, rugged places.

A حزفرة *hazfarat*, (v. n. of حزفر Q) Filling. Tying up furniture or wares. Preparing, getting ready. Smooth, level ground, with stones in it. *Hizfarat*, A hard place.

A حزق *hazk*, (v. n. of حزق) Fastening with a rope. Pulling tight (a cord). Pressing, compressing, squeezing. Breaking wind. *Hizk*, A kind of vehicle resembling a small pack-saddle. *Hizh* (and حزقة *hizkat*), (pl. حزق *hizak*) A multitude, a swarm. *Hazak*, Avarice. *Hizak*, (pl. of حزيقة *hazīkat*) Multitudes (of men, birds, or palm-trees).

A حزّق *huzzak*, (pl. of حزيقة *hazīkat*) Multitudes.

A حزق *hazukk*, (or حزقة *hazukkat*) Short of stature, taking short steps. Close-fisted. Bad-tempered. *Huzukk*, (or *huzukkat*) Narrow. Short of stature, going with short steps. Weak. Big-bellied.

A حزقة *hazukat*, Narrow. Big-bellied. Dwarfish, taking short steps.

A حزّقة *huzukkat*, A kind of game. A word used by women when dandling children.

A حزقل *hizkil*, Narrow, avaricious. Ezekiel.

A حزقيل *hizkīl*, Ezekiel.

A حزك *hazk*, (v. n. of حزك) Girding (with a rope). Pressing, squeezing. Twisting hard.

A حزم *hazm*, (v. n. of حزم) Binding, fastening (a load). Girthing (a beast). Bringing together, adjusting. Being provident, vigilant, steady, firm in mind. A firm resolve. Vigilance, wariness, industry. (pl. حزوم *huzūm*) Rough and hard ground. *Hazam*, (v. n. of حزم) Having an oppression in the breast. Having something sticking in the throat. Thickness round the middle. *Huzum*, (pl. of حزام *hizām*) Girths. Swaddling-bands. (pl. of حزيم *hazīm*) Breasts, pits of chests.

A حزماء *huzamāʼ*, (pl. of حزيم *hazīm*) Provident.

A حزمة *huzmat*, An armful (of wood or corn). A bundle of paper. A truss of straw. *Hazamat*, (pl. of حازم *hāzim*) Provident, careful.

A حزمّة *huzummat*, Short, dwarfish.

A حزمر *hazmar*, A king.

A حزمرة *hazmarat*, Vigilance, foresight. Fullness. The bursting of the leek-flower.

A حزمل *hizmil*, A despicable woman.

A حزمور *huzmūr*, (Taking) the whole.

A حزمىٰ و الله *hazma' wa'llāh*, By God!

A حزن *hazn*, Rough ground. *Huzn*, (v. n. of حزن) Grieving, making sad. Being sad. *Huzn* or *hazan*, (pl. احزان *ahzān*) Grief, sadness, affliction, sorrow. عام الحزن *ʻāmu'l huzn*, The year of grief, *i.e.* of Muhammad's death, or that in which Khadīja or Abū Tālib died. *Hazan*, (v. n. of حزن) Being grieved and sad. *Hazin* or *hazun*, (pl. حزان *hizān* and حزناء *huzanāʼ*) Sad. *Huzan*, (pl. of حزنة *huznat*) Rugged mountains.

A حزناء *huzanāʼ*, (pl. of حزين) Sad, grieved.

A حزنان *haznān*, Grieved, sad.

A حزنبل *hazambal*, Short and compact of body. A foolish female. An old woman. Thick-lipped. Prominent (pudendum muliebre). A species of sweet herbs.

A حزنة *haznat*, Rugged ground. *Huznat*, (pl. حزن *huzan*) A rugged mountain.

A حزو *hazw*, (v. n. of حزا for حزو) Guessing at, measuring. Divining, presaging.

A حزوارة *hizwārat*, (pl. حزاوير) A little hill.

A حزور *hazwar*, (or حزوّر *hazawwar*, (pl. حزاورة *hazāwirat*) A lad arrived at the age of puberty, strong, and fit for service. Weak, feeble. *Huzūr*, (v. n. of حزر) Turning sour.

A حزورة *hazwarat*, (pl. حزاور *hazāwir*, حزاورة *hazāwirat*, and حزاوير *hazāwīr*) A little hill. An obedient, tractable camel.

A حزوز *huzūz*, (pl. of حزّ) Notches, incisions.

A حزوكل *hazawkal*, Short of stature, a dwarf.

A حزولق *hazawlak*, Short and compact in body.

A حزوم *huzūm*, (pl. of حزم) Hard grounds.

A حزومة *huzūmat*, (v. n. of حزم) Being vigilant, steady, firm in mind.

A حزون *hazūn*, Vicious (sheep).

A حزونة *huzūnat*, Ruggedness of ground.

A حزي *hazy*, (v. n. of حزي) Divining, auguring. Measuring, guessing at. (Vapour) raising up (any thing).

A حزيب *hazīb*, (pl. حزب) Difficult (affair).

A حزيران *hazīrān*, The Syriac month of June.

A حزيز *hazīz*, (pl. حزّان *huzzān*, *hizzān*, احزّة *ahizzat*, and حزز *huzuz*) An active, busy man. A steep rugged place.

A حزيق *hazīk*, A multitude (of men, birds, or palm-trees). (also pl. of حزيقة *hazīkat*).

A حزيقة *hazīkat*, (pl. حزائق *hazāʼik*, حزيق *hazīk*, and حزق *huzzak*) A multitude. An inclosed garden. A palm-plantation. A section, portion.

A حزيم *hazīm*, (pl. حزماء *huzamāʼ*) Provident. (pl. احزمة *ahzimat* and حزم *huzum*) The breast, pit of the chest.

A حزين *hazīn*, (pl. حزنى *hazna'* and حزناء *huzanāʼ*) Sad, afflicted, melancholy, grieved, doleful.

A حسّ *hass*, (v. n. of حسّ) (Cold) nipping (plants), or killing (locusts). Destroying, killing. Shaking off the dust. Being touched with pity or sympathy; loving. Currying (a horse). Broiling (meat) on the coals. Laying (fire upon dough). Toasting (a locust). Eradicating. Tearing from house and home. Perceiving, knowing for certain. Cunning, tact, shrewdness, skilful management. *Hiss*, (v. n. of حسّ) Being touched with pity or sympathy; loving. Perceiving, comprehending, discovering, understanding, receiving certain intelligence. Hearing the sound of one passing by, but not seeing him. A low murmuring sound. Pains following the birth. The nipping of plants by cold. Motion. A nipping cold. Sense, feeling. Sympathy. حسّ باطن *hissi bātin*, Internal sense. حسّ ظاهر *hissi zāhir*, External sense. حسّ مشترك *hissi mushtarik*, Common sense. *Hassi*, The sudden cry of pain upon touching unexpectedly any thing burning hot, or being pricked with a thorn. من حسّك و بسّك *min hassika wa bassika*, From wheresover you please.

A حسا *hasa'*, Soup, broth, pottage.

A حساء *hasāʼ*, Soup, broth, pottage. *Hisāʼ*, (pl. of حسي *hasy*, *hisy*, or *hisa'*) Hard substrata of stone or clay, on which water which has percolated through clay lodges.

P حساب *hi* or *husāb*, Business, trade, traffic.

A حساب *hisāb*, (v. n. of حسب) Reckoning. Computation, calculation. Number. Arithmetic. A numerous throng. Sufficient. عطاء حساب *ʻitāʼ hisāb*, A sufficient gift. غير حساب *ghayr hisāb*, Not reckoned. يوم الحساب *yawmu'l hisāb*, The day of reckoning. P حساب جمّل *hisābi jummal*, The reckoning by *abjad* (where عضم means 1840). حساب كردن *hisāb kardan*, To keep accounts, calculate. بي حساب *bī hisāb*, Innumerable.

A حسّاب *hassāb*, An arithmetician, an accountant. *Hussāb*, (pl. of حاسب *hāsib*) Accountants. Receivers. Paymasters. حسّاب الرمل *hussābu'r raml*, Geomancers.

A حسابة *hasābat*, (v. n. of حسب) Having good reputation. *Hisābat*, (v. n. of حسب) Computing.

A حسّابة *hassābat*, A consummate arithmetician.

P حسابدان *hisāb-dān*, An arithmetician.

P حساب كتاب *hisāb-kitāb*, Accounts.

P حساب نويس *hisāb-navīs*, An accountant.

A حسابيّ *hisābīy*, Accountable, accurate, just.

A حسّاد *hussād*, (pl. of حاسد) Envious, haters.

A حسادة *hasādat*, An envying, a wishing ill.

A حسار *hasār*, A plant like a carrot or cress.

A حساس *husās*, Malignity, depravity. A small fish which is generally dried. Small fragments of stones, or any thing else. *Hasāsi*, An interjection of regret when a lost article cannot be found.

A حسّاس *hassās*, Endued with the five senses; acute, shrewd. An animal.

A حساسين *hasāsin*, Name of a warlike nation in Kurdistān, of whom frequent mention is made in the history of the Crusades.

A حساف *husāf*, (v. n. of حسف) Reaping.

A حسافة *husāfat*, Refuse of rotten dates. Silver-filings. Anger, rage, indignation. Hatred. A little water. Remains of food. حسافة الناس *husāfatu'n nās*, The refuse of the people.

A حساكة *hasākat*, Asperity of a malevolent mind.

P حساكك *hasākik*, The small of any thing.

A حساكل *hasākil*, (pl. of حسكل) Young animals.

A حساكلة *hasākilat*, The smaller and inferior part of an army.

A حسالة *husālat*, Chaff, husks, parings. Bran. Silver or silver-filings.

A حسام *husām*, A sharp sword; also its edge. Wholly rainy (night). P حسام خون آشام *husāmi khūn-āshām*, A blood-drinking cimeter.

A حسان *hisān*, (pl. of حسن *hasan* or حسنة *hasanat*) Good, excellent. Beautiful, elegant. *Husān*, Beautiful, elegant.

A حسّان *hussān*, Very good, beautiful, elegant.

A حسّانة *hussānat*, Beautiful (woman).

A حسب *hasb*, (v. n. of حسب) Computing, calculating, counting. Burying a corpse amongst stones or in a winding-sheet. A sufficiency. Enough. حسب الاجازة *hasbu'l ijāzat*, According to license. حسب الاشارة *hasbu'l ishārat*, In conformity to the signal or hint. حسب الاضطرار *hasbu'l iztirār*, Necessarily. حسب الاقتضاء *hasbu'l iktizā*, As occasion may require. حسب الامكان *hasbu'l imkān*, As far as possible. حسب حال *hasbi hāl*, According to exigency, from the state (of affairs, &c.). حسب الحكم *hasbu'l hukm*, According to the order: a patent or order under the seal of the Vazīr. P حسب دلخواه *hasbi dil-khwāh*, Agreeably to one's desire. بر حسب فرمان سلطان *bar hasbi farmāni sultān*, According to the commands of the emperor. A حسب القدرة *hasbu'l kudrat*, To the best of one's abilities. بحسب *bi hasbi*, According to. حسبما امر الله و بلّغ الرسول *hasbumā amara'llāh wa ballagha'r rasūl*, As God commands and the prophet explains. حسب المأمور *hasbu'l maāmūr*, Agreeable to command. حسب المدّعا *hasbu'l muddaā'*, According to wish. حسب المرام *hasbu'l marām*, Agreeable to my desires. حسب المعمول *hasbu'l maamūl*, Agreeable to custom. حسب الموعود *hasbu'l mawūd*, According to promise. حسب واقعة *hasbi wākia*, According to fact. حسب الوصولي *hasbu'l wusūlī*, According to the produce: revenues to be afterwards settled according to the crop. على حسب *ala' hasbi*, In respect, on account of. هذا رجل حسبك من رجل *hāzā rajulun hasbuka mir'rajulin*, This is a man sufficient for thee without any one else. حسبك درهم *hasbuka dirhamun*, A dirhem is enough for thee. حسبما *hasbumā*, According to which. *Hasab* or *hasb*, Quantity, measure, proportion, value. Number. Way, mode, manner. *Hasab*, (v. n. of حسب) Having a good reputation. (pl. احساب *ahsāb*) Reputation, estimation. Dignity, nobility, sometimes from ancestry, sometimes not. Pedigree. Opulence. Heart, mind, soul. A good action. Religion. Numbered, counted. *Hisab*, (pl. of حسبة *hisbat*) Rewards, remunerations. Administrations.

A حسباء *husabāa*, (pl. of حسيب *hasīb*) Esteemed, valued; conspicuous for worth, dignity, or merit.

A حسبان *hisbān*, (v. n. of حسب) Reckoning, counting, supposing, esteeming, thinking. Thought, imagination, supposition, notion. *Husbān*, (v. n. of حسب) Computing, reckoning. A short arrow. Punishment. Cold. A calamity. Wickedness. A small pillow or cushion. Any thing striking terror (as lightning). Dust, smoke. A cloud. A small ant. Locusts. (pl. of حساب *hisāb*) Numbers, crowds. P دفتر حسبان *daftari husbān*, A register.

A حسبانات *husbānāt*, Calculations.

A حسبانة *husbānat*, One short arrow. A small pillow. A pismire. A thunderbolt. A cloud.

A حسبة *hisbat*, (v. n. of حسب) Reckoning. (pl. حسب *hisab*) Reward, hire, price. Administration of affairs, police. The duty or office of the Muhtasib. A mode of reckoning. Burial of a corpse among stones, or in a winding-sheet. حسبة لله *hisbatan li'llāh*, For the love of God. حسن الحسبة *hasanu'l hisbat*, Skilful in administration. *Husbat*, A whiteness of skin from disease; leprosy, baldness, scall. A mixture of red and white in the colour of a camel. A reddish whiteness in the hair of a leprous man.

A حسبلة *hasbalat*, (v. n. of حسبل Q) Saying حسبنا الله *hasbunā'llāh*, God is sufficient for us.

A حسبيّ *hasabiy*, Belonging to nobility.

A حسّة *hassat* or *hissat*, State, plight, case.

A حسحاس *has-hās*, Liberal, generous. Destructive (sword). بنو الحسحاس *banū'l has-hās*, Name of an Arabian tribe.

A حسحس *has-has*, Loss of all one's property.

A حسحسة *has-hasat*, (v. n. of حسحس Q) Laying (meat) upon the embers. Forgiving. Being pained, and complaining.

A حسد *hasad*, (v. n. of حسد) Envying, wishing ill. Envy, malevolence. Malice, emulation. حسدني الله ان كنت احسدك *hasadanī allāh in kuntu ahsuduka*, May God give me the reward of envy, if I envy thee. P حسد بردن *hasad burdan* To envy. A *Husud*, (pl. of حسود *hasūd*) Envious.

A حسّد *hussad*, (pl. of حاسد *hāsid*) Envious.

P حسد آرا *hasad-ārā*, Malevolent.

A حسدة *hasadat*, (pl. of حاسد *hāsid*) Envious.

A حسدل *hasdal*, The tike.

A حسدليّ *hasdaliy*, Insincere in friendship.

A حسر *hasr*, (v. n. of حسر) Removing (a veil). Sweeping (a house). Baring a limb. Peeling (a branch). Wearying, tiring, vexing. *Hasar*, (v. n. of حسر) Becoming fatigued. Sighing for grief.

A حسرات *hasarāt*, (pl. of حسرة *hasrat*) Sighs.

A حسرة *hasrat*, (v. n. of حسر) Sighing for grief. Grief, regret. Impatience, passion. Strong desire, emulation, ambition. Envy. حسرة الملوك *hasratu'l mulūk*, (The envy of kings) A gut-pudding stuffed with meat and rice. حسرت و ندامت *hasrat u nadāmat*, Regret and repentance. P حسرت خوردن *hasrat khwurdan*, To sigh for. حسرت داشتن *hasrat dāshtan*, To sigh after, to regret (the absence of any one), to wish anxiously to see a person.

P حسرتا *hasratā*, Oh the pity!

P حسرت انگيز *hasrat-angez*, Perplexing.

P حسرت زده *hasrat-zada*, Woebegone, sad.

A حسريٰ *hasra'*, Tired, jaded, (she-camel). (pl. of حسير *hasīr*) Tired, jaded. Dim-sighted.

A حسف *hasf*, (v. n. of حسف) Cleaning (dates), throwing away the bad ones. Driving (sheep). Moving, floating (a cloud). Crawling (a serpent). Reaping. Modus coeundi. A thorn. The noise made by a serpent in quitting its slough. *Hasaf*, (v. n. of حسف) Becoming changed in taste and colour, stinking. Being rough. Conceiving hatred, being hostile and vindictive. Being contemptible, reprobated, discarded.

A حسفة *hasfat*, Anger, rage. Enmity, hatred, A thin, flimsy cloud.

A حسفل *hasfal* or *hisfil*, Puny (children). *Hisfil*, Whatever is small and contemptible in any thing. *Hisafl*, Large-bellied.

A حسقل *hiskil*, A tiny young one.

A حسك *hasak*, (v. n. of حسك) Being rough and angry towards (any one). Conceiving hatred. Having the nose-bag full of barley hung round his head (a horse). Envy, enmity, hostility. A prickly plant which clings to the wool of sheep. Caltrops for keeping off cavalry, being made in the shape of this prickly plant. *Hasik*, Angry, inimical.

A حسكة *haskat*, Envy. Hatred. *Hasakat*, One caltrop.

A حسكك *hiskik*, A hedgehog.

A حسكل *haskal*, Any thing bad of its sort. *Hiskil*, Sparks of fire flying from red hot iron whilst hammering. (pl. حساكل *hasākil*) A small young animal.

A حسكلة *haskalat*, A slaying a young camel. *Hiskilat*, Any thing bad of its sort.

A حسكلتان *hiskilatāni*, (dual) The testicles.

A حسل *hasl*, (v. n. of حسل) Despising, holding in contempt. Descending to meanness, lowering one's self. Leaving a portion which is useless and unserviceable. Driving violently. Green fruit of the *sidr* tree. *Hisl*, (pl. احسال *ahsāl*, حسول *husūl*, حسلان *hislān*, and حسلة *hisalat*) A young Lybian lizard recently hatched. ابو الحسل *abū'l hisl*, The crocodile or Lybian lizard. سنّ الحسل *sinnu'l hisl*, Never. *Husul*, (pl. of حسيل *hasīl*) Worst parts of things.

A حسلان *hislān* or حسلة *hisalat*, (pl. of حسل *hisl*) Land-crocodiles newly hatched.

A حسم *hasm*, (v. n. of حسم) Cutting. Searing (a limb or vein) to prevent it from bleeding. Checking the progress of a disease. Forbidding, hindering, keeping back.

A حسمى *hisma'*, A plain in the desert, the mountains near to which are scarcely ever free from dust.

A حسمي *husamīy*, Very hairy (man).

A حسن *husn*, (v. n. of حسن) Being comely, fair, and handsome. (pl. محاسن *mahāsin*) Beauty. Goodness, elegance. حسن اختيار *husni ikhtiyār*, (or ارادت *irādat*) Free-will. حسن آداب *husni ādāb*, Good manners. P حسن بي نظير *husni bī nazīr*, Incomparable beauty. A حسن تدبير *husni tadbīr*, Good management, prudence. P در حسن حال *dar husni hāl*, In an excellent manner. A حسن خطاب *husni khitāb*, Eloquence. حسن خلق *husni khulk*, A good disposition. حسن رأي *husni rasy*, Prudent counsel. حسن سلوك *husni sulūk*, Upright conduct. حسن ظنّ *husni zann*, A good opinion, favourable judgment. حسن عاريتي *husni ʻāriyati*, Borrowed beauty, *i. e.* such as is supplied by antimony or ornaments. حسن عقيدت *husni ʻakīdat*, Loyalty, fidelity. حسن عهد *husni ʻahd*, Good faith. قرين حسن قبول *karīni husni kabūl*, Agreeable, acceptable. حسن معامله *husni muʻāmala*, Good correspondence. حسن يوسف *husni yūsuf*, A sponge. *Hasan*, Any thing good and fair. A certain beautiful tree. A high sand-hill. P حسن ميمندي *hasan maymundī*, Name of the vazīr of Mahmūd Sabaktagīn. A *Hasan*, (or حسن بسن *hasan basan*) (pl. حسان *hisān*) Beautiful, elegant. *Hasan* or *husun*, A bone adjoining the elbow. *Hisan*, (pl. of حسنة *hisnat*) Salient parts of mountains. *Husan*, (pl. of حسنى) Good ends or deeds.

A حسناء *hasnās*, Beautiful (woman).

A حسنات *hasanāt*, (pl. of حسنة *hasanat*) Beautiful, good. Public foundations. P حسنات كردن *hasanāt kardan*, To perform good works, build mosques, colleges, inns, hospitals.

A حسنة *hisnat*, (pl. حسن *hisan*) The salient part of a mountain. *Hasanat*, A good work, benefit. Goodness. (pl. حسنات *hasanāt* and حسان *hisān*) Beautiful (woman). حسنه و سئه *hasana u sisa*, Good and bad.

A حسنى *husna'*, (fem. of احسن *ahsan*) More or most beautiful, excellent; fairer, fairest, better, best. Paradise. Victory, or where one dies a glorious death. The Muhammadan faith. (pl. حسن *husan*) A good end. A regard to God. اسماء حسنى *asmāsi husna'*, The excellent names, *i. e.* the ninety-nine attributes of God.

A حسنيّة *hasanīyat*, Beauty, beautifulness.

P حسو *hasū*, Pap, gruel, hasty pudding. Broth.

A حسو *hasw*, (v. n. of حسا for حسو) Sipping (soup or broth). Drinking (a bird). كحسو الطير *ha haswi't tayr*, Like the sipping of a bird, brief. (pl. احسوة *ahsuwat* or احسية *ahsiyat*) Broth.

A حسوّ *hasūw*, One who sips much. Broth.

A حسوة *haswat*, One sip. *Huswat*, What is drank at one sip; a single sip.

A حسود *hasūd*, (pl. حسد *husud*) Envious. *Husūd*, (v. n. of حسد) Envying.

A حسور *husūr*, (v. n. of حسر) Becoming dim from gazing a long while (the sight). Being indisposed, pained, tired, or fatigued. Being discovered, revealed, disclosed.

A حسوس *hasūs*, Dry, burnt up, barren (year).

A حسول *husūl*, (pl. of حسل *hisl*) Young land-crocodiles.

A حسوم *husūm*, Continued unfortunate (nights). Fatigue from unsuccessful labour. Ill-luck. Diligence in work.

A حسي *hasy*, (v. n. of حسى) Perceiving, knowing. Excavating sand from any place, that the water which lodges there may be drawn out. *Hasy*, *hisy*, or *hisa'*, (pl. احساء *ahsās* and حساء *hisās*) Loose, level ground whereon water lodges. A hard substratum of stone or clay covered with sand and holding water, and as fast as one bucket of water is drawn out another collects. *Hisy*, (pl. احساء *ahsās*) Water absorbed in sandy ground, and collecting on a solid stratum of stone or clay below; also the stratum itself.

A حسّي *hassīy*, Sensual. Sensible.

P حسيب *hasīb*, Roast meat. حسيب بزغاله *hasībi buzghāla*, A gut-pudding of rice and minced meat. *Hiseb*, (A حساب *hisāb*) An account.

A حسيب *hasīb*, (pl. حسباء *husabās*) Estimated, esteemed, valued. Conspicuous for birth, dignity, or merit. A revenger or resenter of an injury. A reckoner (a name of God).

P حسيبك *hasībak*, Sheeps' chitterlings soaked in sour milk.

A حسيّة *hasīyat*, Broth, or any thing sipped.

A حسيت *hasīt*, (for حسست) I comprehend.

A حسيدة *hasīdat*, An envying, a wishing ill.

A حسير *hasīr*, (pl. حسرى *hasra'*) Tired. Sighing. Dim-sighted.

A حسيس *hasīs*, A low, obscure sound. Killed by cold (locust).

A حسيف *hasīf*, The noise made by a serpent rubbing itself in order to cast its slough. A well excavated from a rock and never drying up. رجع بحسيف نفسه *rajaʻa bi hasīfi nafsihi*, He returned without accomplishing his business.

A حسيفة *hasīfat*, Anger, rage, indignation, hatred. Whatever is thrown away as vile and despicable (as rotten dates, &c.).

A حسيك *hasīk*, Short, dwarfish. حسيك الصدر *hasīku's sadr*, Rancorous, malevolent.

A حسيكة *hasīkat*, The unfeelingness of a malevolent mind, hatred. A hedgehog. Barley given to horses.

A حسيل *hasīl*, Calves, stirks, runts. (pl. حسل *husul*) The refuse of any thing. ابو حسيل *abū husayl*, A small crocodile or Lybian lizard.

A حسيلة *hasīlat*, Bad dates, dried, macerated, and sweetened with water from sweet dates. The dregs of the people. (fem. of حسيل *hasīl*) A calf.

A حسين *hasīn*, Beautiful, elegant. *Husayn*, (dim. of حسن *hasan*) Beautiful. Good. Name of a son of the khalif Alīy.

A حسيناء *husaynās*, Name of a small-leaved tree. حسيناه ان يفعل *husaynāh an yafʻala*, The best thing for him to do.

P حسيني *husaynī*, Relating to Husayn. Any vessel made of leather. Name of a note in music.

A حشّ *hashsh*, (v. n. of حشّ) Lighting (a fire). Withering, becoming dry (a young palm-shoot). Drying up in the womb (a fœtus). Withering (the hand). Cutting or mowing (hay). Feeding with hay or dry grass; holding it out (to a horse). Giving (a camel). Feathering (an arrow). Bettering any one in his circumstances. Multiplying, augmenting one's wealth). Enclosing (game) on both sides. Going swiftly (a horse). (pl. حشان *hishshān*) A dwarf palm-tree neither watered nor tended. *Hashsh* or *hushsh*, (pl. حشّان *hishshān*) A garden. A fire. *Hashsh*, *hishsh*, or *hushsh*, (pl. حشوش *hushūsh* and حشّون *hushshūn*) A privy (as being generally in a garden). *Hishsh*, Something, anything. *Hushsh*, A fœtus drying up in the womb.

A حشأ *hashasa*, (fut. يحشأ *yahshasu*) He struck with a whip on the side or belly. He hit (with an arrow). He lighted (a fire). He had an asthma. He lay with.

A حشا *hasha'*, (v. n. of حشي) Being short-winded, pursy, and asthmatic. Being filthy and nauseous from the pellicle or greasy particles of milk (a leathern bottle). (pl. احشاء *ahshās*) Bowels, viscera, intestines. A side, quarter.

A حشاة *hashāt*, Black ground of little value.

A حشاد *hashād*, (Ground) over which water does not flow except after an abundant shower, or which flows after a very scanty shower.

A حشاش *hishāsh*, A large sack wherein fodder is put. *Hushāsh*, (and حشاشة *hushāshat*) Remains of life, last breathings of a dying man.

A حشّاش *hashshāsh*, A forager, a grass-cutter. A haymaker. *Hushshāsh*, Foragers. حشاشاك ان تفعل كذا *hushāshāka an tafʻala kazā*, Your great point is to do so.

A حشاشان *hishāshāni*, Both sides (of a thing).

A حشاف *hishāf*, (pl. of حشفة *hashafat*) Nuts, glands. Ulcers in the throat. Rocks in the sea.

A حشافة *hushāfat*, A little water.

A حشاك *hishāk*, A muzzle to prevent a calf

from sucking. *Hashshāk,* Name of a river.

A حشاكة *hashākat,* A muzzle for a kid.

A حشان *hishshān,* (pl. of حش *hashsh*) Dwarf palm-trees neither watered nor attended to. (pl. of حش *hashsh* or *hushsh*) Gardens.

A حشايا *hashāya',* (pl. of حشيّة) Stuffed couches.

A حشائش *hashāïsh,* (pl. of حشيش) Dry grasses.

A حشائشيّ *hashāïshīy,* A forager.

A حشبلة *hashbalat,* A family, household.

A حشة *hushshat,* (pl. حشش *hushash*) A large cupola, vault, or dome.

A حشحشة *hashhashat,* (v. n. of حشحش Q) Being divided, scattered. Shaking.

A حشد *hashd,* (v. n. of حشد) Assembling, bringing together. A never-failing fountain. Growing to the full (corn). Congregating, flocking together for mutual assistance. Assembling for one object. Collecting much milk in her udder (a camel). *Hashd* or *hashad,* A troop, crowd. *Hashid,* A valley which flows after abundant rain. A fountain which never dries. One who does not spare himself in labour, assistance, or wealth.

A حشر *hashr,* (v. n. of حشر) Assembling, bringing together. Sharpening, making thin, making elegant. Destroying (as a severe season). Driving, rousing, exciting. Banishing. A light feather put on an arrow. (sing. du. and pl.) Delicately-formed (ear, or hind-head between the ears). Sharp (spear). Banishment from one's country. يوم الحشر *yawmu'l hashr,* The day of resurrection. *Hushr,* Sharp (spears or arrows). *Hushr* or *hushur,* Bran. Scurf. *Hashar,* (pl. of حشرة *hasharat*) Husks. *Hashir,* Moderated-sized, well-shaped (leathern bottle). Dirty (leathern milk-bottle).

P حشر *hashar,* A congregation, concourse.

A حشرات *hasharāt,* (pl. of حشرة *hasharat*) Creeping things, animalcules, little beasts. حشرات الارض *hasharātu'l arz,* Reptiles of the earth.

A حشرة *hasharat,* (pl. حشر *hashar*) A reptile, a stinging or biting insect. Chaff, husk. The excrescences of trees (as gum). The dregs of a milk-bottle. Game, or the nicest and choicest parts thereof.

A حشرج *hashraj,* A small jug or cup. A well in a gravelly situation. A proper name. Soft stones like chalk. A hole or crevice in a mountain (through which water subsides and becomes clear).

A حشرجة *hashrajat,* (v. n. of حشرج Q) Making a rattle in the throat (a dying man, or an ass braying).

A حشرف *hashraf,* The serrated fig-tree.

P حشرگاي *hashar-gāy,* A woman of many lovers.

A حشش *hushash,* (pl. of حشّة *hushshat*) Large cupolas, vaults, or domes.

A حشط *hasht,* (v. n. of حشط) Removing from its place, taking off (cover, horse-cloth), denuding.

A حشف *hashf,* Dry bread. *Hashaf* or *hashif,* Very bad dates, or small-stoned, dry, and worthless. A dried-up udder.

A حشفة *hashafat,* (pl. حشاف *hishāf*) Glans penis. Stubble. A decrepit old woman. Dry leaven. An ulcer in the throat, quinsey. A smooth rock in the midst of a plain. A rock in the sea.

P حشفليل *hashfalīl,* The wild carrot.

A حشك *hashk,* (v. n. of حشك) Being full of milk (an udder). Being loaded with fruit (a palm-tree). Assembling, coming together (people). Pouring down rain profusely (the clouds). Being out of breath with exercise. Eating barley (a horse). Being hard (a bow). Becoming weak and whiffling (the wind). Leaving (a camel) unmilked until her udder be completely filled. *Hashak,* A rapid filling of the udder with milk; also a rapid drawing of it. Having the nose-bag full of barley tied about the head (a horse).

A حشكة *hashkat,* Small rain. *Hashakat,* A crowd, troop, body.

A حشل *hashl,* (v. n. of حشل) Despising, discarding. Whatever is vile and worthless of any thing.

A حشم *hashm,* (v. n. of حشم) Using offensive language in the hearing of another, firing him with rage. *Putting to the blush. *Hasham,* (v. n. of حشم) Being angry, enraged. (pl. احشام *ahshām*) Train, equipage, suite. Family, relations. Domestics. Seekers, inquirers. *Hushum,* Very bashful.

A حشماء *hashmās,* Neighbours. Guests.

A حشمة *hishmat,* Anger. Shame, bashfulness. Humanity. Reverence. Pomp, magnificence. *Hushmat,* A woman. Patronage. Propinquity, affinity, neighbourhood. *Hashamat,* Servants, attendants, clients, retainers, persons ready to avenge a quarrel. Pomp, equipage, magnificence.

A حشن *hashan,* (v. n. of حشن) Smelling fetidly, from being unwashed (a milk-bottle). Grime sticking to a milk-bottle.

A حشنة *hishnat,* Malevolence, hatred.

A حشو *hashw,* (v. n. of حشا for حشو) Quilting (a garment with cotton). Hurting in the viscera. Stuffing (a pillow, cushion, or bed); also whatever they are stuffed with. People of the meanest condition. Small camels. Redundant words. The intermediate feet of a hemistich. The human soul. حشو منها *hashw minhā,* Subtraction, deduction. The quantity deducted.

A حشوة *hishwat,* People of the meanest condition. Luxuriant herbage. *Hushwat* or *hishwat,* Intestines, bowels.

A حشود *hashūd,* (A camel) collecting milk soon: and which fails not to conceive at one covering.

A حشور *hashwar,* (singular of حشورة *hashwarat*) Firm-fleshed (horse having swollen sides).

A حشورة *hashwarat,* An avaricious old woman, shrewd and sagacious. A large-bellied woman. A compact-bodied mare. Swollen-sided (horse).

A حشوش *hushūsh,* (pl. of حش *hashsh, hishsh,* or *hushsh*) Necessaries, privies, ivy-bushes.

A حشوك *hashūk,* Milk collected in (a camel's) udder. A camel that soon collects milk in the udder. *Hushūk,* (v. n. of حشك) Collecting milk in the udder (a camel). Being full of rain (a cloud), of fruit (a palm). Assembling, flocking together. Being breathless with exercise. Being hard (a bow).

A حشوم *hushūm,* (v. n. of حشم) Recovering his flesh, becoming plump (a horse), after having been lean. Eating. Taking no game. Fatigue, weariness. Contraction, shrinking. Seekers, inquirers.

A حشون *hushshūn,* (pl. of حش *hushsh*) Privies.

A حشويّات *hashwīyāt,* Unmeaning, insignificant words, such as are employed merely to fill up.

A حشى *hasha',* (v. n. of حشي) Having an asthma. Breathing hard. The liver, spleen, or rough tripe. The bowels. Whatever lies between the lowest rib and the hip-bone. Asthma. A side, margin. Protection, guardianship. *Hashi,* Short-winded.

A حشيّ *hashīy,* Dry, marred, rotten at the root.

A حشياء *hashyās,* Short-winded, pursy (woman).

A حشيان *hashyān,* Short-winded, asthmatic.

A حشيب *hashīb,* A rough, coarse garment.

A حشية *hashyat,* Short-winded, pursy (woman).

A حشيّة *hashīyat,* (pl. حشايا *hashāya'*) A stuffed couch or bed. Any stuffing which gives a false prominency to the breasts or hips.

A حشيش *hashīsh,* Dry herbage, hay, or grass. The powder of the leaves of hemp, from which they prepare an inebriating electuary. An abortion. حشيش بزر القطونا *hashīshi bazri'l kitūnā,* Leaves of fleawort. حشيش خراساني *hashīshi khurāsānī,* Worm-seed. حشيش الزجاج *hashīshu'z zajāj,* A water-plant. حشيش الفرض *hashīshu'l faraz,* Perennial darnel.

A حشيشة *hashīshat,* One herb. ابو حشيشة *abū hashīshat,* The gullet of beasts which graze. حشيشة البراق *hashīshatu'l barrāk,* Name of an herb which shines at night. حشيشة الذهب *hashīshatu'z zahab,* Name of an herb which turns sheep's teeth yellow. حشيشة الريح *hashīshatu'r rīh,* Pellitory of the wall.

A حشيف *hashīf,* Old, worn-out clothes.

A حشيكة *hashīkat,* Barley given in a bag to horses.

A حشيلة *hashīlat,* A family, domestics.

A حشيم *hashīm,* Having a retinue. Feared.

A حصّ *hass,* (v. n. of حصّ) Rubbing off the hair (a helmet). Shaving the head. Receiving one's share. Giving one's share. Thinness of hair. Docked (tail). *Huss,* A pearl. (pl. حصوص *husūs*) Saffron. The plant ورس *wars.* The yellow chives of flowers. (pl. of احصّ *ahass*) Thin-haired.

A حصء *hass,* (v. n. of حصا) Quenching (thirst). Sucking till his belly is filled (an infant). Breaking wind. Eating and drinking plentifully (a camel).

A حصّاء *hassās,* (fem. of احصّ *ahass*) (A bird) thinly feathered on the wing. Clear, free from dust (wind). Barren (year). Unfortunate (woman).

A حصاب *hisāb*, The place where pilgrims fling pebbles in the valley of Mina.

A حصاة *hasāt*, (pl. حصي *hasa'* or حصيات *hasayāt*) One pebble. A stone in the bladder. Understanding, intellect. حصاة المسك *hasātu'l misk*, A particle of musk. ذو حصاة *zū hasāt*, Endowed with understanding.

A حصاد *hasād*, Harvest. P در وقت حصاد *dar wakti hasād*, In time of harvest. A *Hasād* or *hisād*, (v. n. of حصد) Reaping.

A حصّاد *hassād*, A reaper. *Hussād*, (pl. of حاصد *hāsid*) Reapers.

A حصادة *hasādat*, Cut corn. A plant which makes sheep swell. *Hasādat* or *hisādat*, Harvest-time.

A حصار *hasār* or *hisār*, A small saddle or riding-cushion. *Hisār*, (v. n. 3 of حصر) Besieging. A fortified town, a fort, castle. A fence, inclosure. P حصار استوار *hisāri ustuwār*, A strong fortification. حصار آهنين ديوار *hisāri āhanīn-dīwār*, A castle having walls like iron. حصار برين *hisāri barīn*, The highest heaven. حصار پولاد *hisāri pūlād*, A fort hard to take. A thimble. A chafing-dish. The lower heaven. حصار پيروزه *hisāri pīroza*, (also معلق *muallak*) The sky. حصار تركش *hisāri tarkash*, A quiver. Name of a fortress in the island of Malākha. حصار شادمان *hisār-shādmān*, Name of a city in Turkistān. حصار كردن *hisār kardan*, To lay siege to. حصار هزار ميخي *hisāri hazār mekhī*, Heaven. The zodiac. The eighth heaven, that of the fixed stars.

P حصار *hisār*, Name of a town in the north-west of India. Name of a note in music.

A حصّار *hassār*, Name of a sect.

P حصاري *hisārī*, A soldier in garrison. Siege, blockade. Belonging to the town of Hisār. Name of a note in music. Strongly fortified.

A حصاص *hisās*, (v. n. 3 of حصّ) Dividing any thing with another, giving him his share. *Husās*, Velocity, speed. The scab. The full speed of an ass running with ears laid down and tail erect. A fart.

A حصاصاء *husāsā*, Earth, dust.

A حصاصة *husāsat*, Gleanings of grapes.

A حصافة *hasāfat*, (v. n. of حصف) Being endued with a sound mind and judgment.

A حصالبان اخضر *hasālbān akhzar*, Rosemary.

A حصالة *husālat*, Wheat or barley remaining on the floor after the darnel and chaff have been driven away by the winnowing fan.

A حصّام *hassām*, One who breaks wind often.

A حصان *hasān*, (pl. حصانات *hasānāt* and حصن *husun*) A chaste woman. A matron. A scourge made of twisted thongs. *Hisān* or *hasān*, (pl. حصن *husun*) A beautiful, strong, entire horse.

A حصانة *hasānat*, (v. n. of حصن) Being strong and impregnable. Being chaste (a woman), keeping close at home. Chastity. Firmness, stability.

A حصانيات *hasānīyāt*, A sort of bird.

A حصائد *hasāid*, (pl. of حصيدة *hasīdat*) Harvests. حصائد الالسنة *hasāidu'l alsinat*, Sayings for which the tongue is cut out.

A حصائل *hasāil*, (pl. of حصيلة) Residues.

A حصب *hasb*, (v. n. of حصب) Throwing pebbles. Strewing with gravel. Retiring from, turning one's back upon. *Hasab*, (v. n. of حصب) Having an eruption from fulness of blood. Fuel thrown upon the fire. Twisting a bowstring off the bow. Pebbles, small stones. Fuel, chips. *Hasib*, (A place) full of gravel. (Wind) scattering gravel. Milk which froths not through cold.

A حصباء *hasbā*, Gravel, pebbles.

A حصبة *hasbat*, Stones. ليلة الحصبة *laylatu'l hasbat*, The night after ايّام التشريق *ayyāmu't tashrīk*. *Hasbat*, *hasabat*, or *hasibat*, Measles. Spotted fever. *Hasabat*, A single stone or pebble.

A حصّة *hissat*, (pl. حصص *hisas*) A lot, portion, share, part. Division. حصّهٔ خالصه *hissai khālisa*, Crown-dues. حصّهٔ وصيّت *hissai wasiyat*, A legacy, bequest.

A حصحاص *has-hās*, Swift, not languid (nocturnal journey in search of water). Earth.

A حصحص *his-his*, Earth and stones.

A حصحصة *has-hasat*, (v. n. of حصحص Q) Walking fast. Appearing, becoming manifest (truth from falsehood). Moving one thing against another so as to fit. Scratching, examining soil right and left. Sticking close to one, importuning and boring him. Fixing the knee firmly on the ground when about to rise (a loaded camel). Walking in fetters. Voiding excrement.

A حصد *hasd*, (v. n. of حصد) Reaping. Dying. *Hasad*, (v. n. of حصد) Being twisted tight (a rope). Being closely woven (a coat of mail). Corn cut down. A dried plant. Tight, close workmanship in twisting of ropes or in weaving coats of mail. *Hasid*, Firmly-twisted (rope).

A حصداء *hasdā*, (A coat of mail) of close rings. Leafy (tree), of dense foliage.

A حصدة *hasadat*, (pl. of حاصد) Reapers.

A حصر *hasr*, (v. n. of حصر) Closely besieging, blockading, straitening. Detaining, hindering, confining. Restricting. Putting on a camel a housing, or the cushion حصار *hisār*. Having the orifices of the teats narrow (a camel). Taking the whole. P حصر كردن *hasr kardan*, To surround, besiege. A *Husr*, Costiveness. *Hasar*, (v. n. of حصر) Being avaricious. Being narrow-hearted or chested. Abstaining from commerce with a woman. Keeping close a secret. Faltering, stammering, hesitating (when reading). Straitness or tightness in the chest. Covetousness. *Hasir*, One who keeps a secret; close, trusty. Avaricious. *Husur*, (pl. of حصير *hasīr*) Assemblies. Prisons. Kings. Roads. Surfaces of the ground. Rows, ranks. Mats. Sides. Narrow, tight in the chest.

A حصراء *hasrā*, Close, impervious (woman).

A حصربة *hasrabat*, Anxious tenacity, avarice.

A حصرم *hisrim*, Sour and green grapes or other fruit. A date which has not yet fallen. Close, covetous. An iron for drawing a bucket from a well. A dwarf. Fruit of the tree مظّ *mazz*. Refuse.

A حصرمة *hasramat*, (v. n. of حصرم Q) Drawing (a bow). Twisting (a rope) very tight. Stringing (a bow) very tight. Filling (a leathern bottle). Mending (a pen). Avarice.

A حصص *hasas*, Thinness of hair on the head. *Hisas*, (pl. of حصّة *hissat*) Lots, shares, portions.

A حصف *hasf*, (v. n. of حصف) Removing far off, placing at a distance. *Hasaf*, (v. n. of حصف) Having the dry scab. Ringworm, dry scab.

A حصل *hasl* or *hasal*, Unformed, immature dates. Yellow date-flowers. Darnel and whatever is driven away by the winnowing fan. *Hasal*, (v. n. of حصل) Having the cholic from eating grit (horse). Having gravel (boy). Chaff, sweepings.

A حصلب *hislib*, Earth, dust.

A حصلة *hasalat*, A single unripe date.

A حصلم *hislim*, Earth, dust.

A حصماء *hasmā*, A she-ass that farts often.

A حصن *hasn*, *hisn*, or *husn*, (v. n. of حصن) Being chaste (a woman). Female chastity. *Hisn*, (pl. حصون *husūn*, احصان *ahsān*, حصنة *hisanat*) A castle, fortification, fort. Custody. Arms, armour. Perdition, destruction. Name of twenty-one places. P حصن فيروزه *hisni fīroza*, The sky. Name of a city and fort. حصن معلق *hisni muallak*, The sky. حصن هزار ميخي *hisni hazār mekhī*, The eighth sphere. A ابو الحصن *abū'l hisn*, (Father of the fortress) A fox. حصن حصين *hisni hasīn*, An impregnable fortress. *Husn*, Chastity, modesty. *Husun*, (pl. of حصان *hasān*) Chaste (women). (pl. of حصان *hisān*) Stallions.

A حصناء *hasnā*, A modest, chaste woman.

A حصنة *hisanat*, (pl. of حصن) Forts, fortresses.

A حصو *hasw*, (v. n. of حصا for حصو) Preventing, hindering, keeping back. The cholic.

A حصور *hasūr*, Strait, tight in the chest. A camel the orifices of whose teats are narrow. Chaste, pure from all commerce with women. Castrated. Avaricious. Timid, fearful, retiring from any thing. One who keeps a secret. الحصور *al hasūr*, John the Baptist (The chaste one, or eunuch).

A حصوص *husūs*, (pl. of حصّ *huss*) Saffrons. Plants called ورس *wars*.

A حصول *husūl*, (v. n. of حصل) Remaining over. Coming forth. Existing, appearing clear. Regaining health, recovering from sickness. Produce. Collection, acquisition. Profit, gain. حصول مرام *husūli marām*, The obtaining of one's wish. P حصول پذير شدن *husūl-pazīr shudan*, To appear.

A حصوم *hasūm*, One who breaks wind much. *Husūm*, (v. n. of حصم) Breaking. Breaking wind.

A حصون *husūn*, (pl. of حصن) Forts, castles.
P حصّه بخش *hissa-bakhsh*, Distributor of lots.
P حصّه دار *hissa-dār*, A participator, partaker, sharer. حصّه داركردن *hissa-dār kardan*, To impart, communicate, distribute.
P حصّه داري *hissa-dārī*, A title to a share.
P حصّه رسد *hissa-rasad*, An equal share.
P حصّه گير *hissa-gīr*, One who takes his share.
A حصي *hasy*, (v. n. of حصي) Hitting with a pebble. *Hasa'*, (v. n. of حصي) Making an impression. Abounding in gravel (land). Number, multitude. Gravel, small stones: gravel in the kidneys.
A حصيّ *hasiy*, Of a capacious intellect. *Husīy*, (pl. of حصي *hasa'*) Pebbles, small stones.
A حصيات *hasayāt*, (pl. of حصي) Pebbles.
A حصيب *husayb*, Name of a district in Yaman famed for the beauty of its women.
A حصيد *hasīd*, Reaped. Firmly-twisted (rope). Closely-woven (coat of mail). Overthrown and utterly destroyed. Harvest, corn piled up in ricks.
A حصيدة *hasīdat*, (pl. حصائد *hasā,id*) Any thing cut; harvest. Stubble. A sown field. Low, short, dwarfish stalks which escape the sickle.
P حصير *hasīr*, A mat. A case for a musical instrument.
A حصير *hasīr*, Narrow-minded; avaricious. One who from parsimony abstains from wine. (pl. احصرة *ahsirat* and حصر *husur*) A row, rank, file. The face of the ground. A king. A prison. Strait, tight in the chest. A mat on which one sits. The side. A vein or muscle passing by the side to the belly (of a horse). An assembly. A road. Water. Glittering surface of a sword. Any thing woven. An embroidered garment dazzling to the beholder.
A حصيرة *hasīrat*, A house for storing dates in. A muscle extending along a horse's side, easily discernible when he is lean.
A حصيريّ *hasīriy*, A seller of mats.
A حصيص *hasīs*, Shaven (hair). Thin of hair about the fetlock (a horse). Number.
A حصيصة *hasīsat*, Any thing on a horse's coat.
A حصيف *hasīf*, Firmly-woven (garment). Firm, sound in judgment.
A حصيل *hasīl*, Name of a certain plant.
A حصيلة *hasīlat*, (pl. حصائل *hasā,il*) Remains, rest. A relic.
A حصيم *hasīm*, Small gravel.
A حصين *hasīn*, Fortified, guarded. Strong. A strong coat of mail. A fortification. *Husayn*, (dim. of حصن *hisn*) A little fortress. ابو الحصين *abū'l husayn*, Father of the little fortress, *i. e.* a fox.
A حصينة *hasīnat*, Strong (coat of mail).
A حضّ *hazz* or *huzz*, (v. n. of حضّ) Instigating, exciting. *Huzz*, Incitement, instigation.
A حضأ *haza,a*, (fut. يحضأ *yahza,u*) He stirred (the fire). (The fire) burned.
A حضاج *hizāj*, A leathern bottle propped up. *Huzāj*, One whose back bends in, and belly out.
A حضاجر *hazājir*, A hyena. (pl. of حضجر *hizajr*) Capacious (milk-bottles). Camels swollen from eating bitter plants.
A حضاجرة *hazājirat*, (Camels) scattered about their keeper.
A حضاجم *huzājim*, Coarse, thick-fleshed.
A حضار *hazār*, Name of a star. حضار حضار *hazāri hazāri*, Make haste! make haste! come hither! *Hazār* or *hizār*, Excellent camels, white or red. *Hizār*, (v. n. 3 of حضر) Appearing against another; pleading against, or arraigning one (before a judge). Trying to outdo in number or in strength. White camels. A kind of aromatic on a girl's cheek. A strong swift she-camel. *Huzār*, A disease incident to camels.
A حضّار *huzzār*, (pl. of حاضر *hāzir*) Those present. Spectators, auditors, assistants.
A حضارة *hazārat*, (v. n. of حضر) Being present. *Hizārat*, (v. n. of حضر) Residing habitually in towns. *Hizārat* or *hazārat*, Town residence, a fixed abode.
A حضارمة *hazārimat*, Natives of Hazramawt.
A حضان *hizān*, (v. n. of حضن) Sitting (on eggs). Having one teat longer than the other (a ewe, camel, or woman).
A حضّان *huzzān*, (pl. of حاضن *hāzin*) They who fondle in their arms, fondlers.
A حضانة *hazānat*, (v. n. of حضن) Turning one away from any thing, and claiming it for one's self. Keeping back, hindering. *Hizānat*, (v. n. of حضن) Fondling in the bosom, embracing, caressing. Sitting on eggs. Educating, bringing up.
A حضايا *hazāya'*, (pl. of حضيّة) Favourite wives.
A حضائر *hazā,ir*, (pl. of حضيرة *hazīrat*) Small bodies of men making excursions against the enemy.
A حضب *hazb*, (v. n. of حضب) Raising a fire or throwing fuel upon it. Being let down, till it falls into the well (a rope). Twisting a rope till it snaps. Becoming stuck between the pulley and the cheek (a rope). Closing the snare the instant the bird pecks the grain (a fowler). *Hazb* or *hizb*, A male serpent. The foot or side of a mountain. *Hizb* or *huzb*, (pl. احضاب *ahzāb*) The twanging sound made by a bow-string. *Hazab* or *hazb*, Fuel.
A حضج *hazj*, (v. n. of حضج) Kindling (a fire). Striking. Dipping (into water). Running, passing over. Putting into the belly what made it well nigh burst. Dashing on the ground. Striking clothes with a beetle when washing (a washerman). *Hizj* or *hazj*, Water left by camels in a trough. *Hizj*, A tract, quarter, side, part.
A حضجر *hizajr*, (pl. حضاجر *hazājir*) A large capacious milk-bottle or churn. Large-bellied. Lean, meagre-hipped. Big.
A حضجرة *hazjarat*, (v. n. of حضجر Q) Filling. *Hizajrat*, Camels scattered about, and too numerous for the keeper to count them.
A حضجم *hizjim*, Coarse, thick-fleshed.
A حضجور *huzjūr*, Large and fleshy (breast).
A حضحض *huzhuz*, A sort of plant.
A حضد *huzad* or *huzud*, Juice of the boxthorn.
A حضض *huzuz*, Juice of boxthorn.
A حضر *hazr*, Fat in the abdomen or above it. Genitalia. See also تطفيل *tatfīl*. *Huzr*, (v. n. of حضر) Running. Lifting his feet high in running (a horse). A race, a course. *Hazar*, Town-residence, a settled abode, home. Presence. اهل الحضر *ahlu'l hazar*, Townsfolk. P درحضرش *dar hazarash*, In his presence. A *Hazir*, One who does not travel. The inhabitant of a settled residence. *Hazir* or *hazur*, One who waits for the hour of people's eating, that he may be present. *Hazur*, Eloquent. Versed in the knowledge of religion and law. *Huzur*, One who goes uninvited to a convivial party.
A حضراء *hazrā,*, (A camel) eager to eat or drink.
A حضرات *hazarāt*, (pl. of حضرة *hazrat*) Presences. Majesties.
A حضربة *hazrabat*, (v. n. of حضرب Q) Bending much (a bow). Twisting tight. Cramming.
A حضرة *hazrat*, Presence. Dignity. Majesty. Dominion, power. An epithet often joined with the names of the Deity; also a title by which kings and great men are addressed, similar to majesty, highness, lordship, worship, &c. A town-residence, a settled abode. حضرة الله *hazratu'llāh*, The Lord God. حضرت عيسيٰ *hazrat ʿīsa'*, The Lord Jesus. حضرت مريم *hazrat maryam*, The Virgin Mary. P حضرت پادشاه *hazrat pādshāh*, His majesty. حضرت خدائ بي زوال *hazrat khudā,i bi zawāl*, The Lord God without end. A *Hizrat* or *huzrat*, Presence. حسن الحضرة *hasanu'l hizrat*, One who speaks well of the absent. *Hazarat*, Presence.
A حضرمة *hazramat*, (v. n. of حضرم Q) Pronouncing vowels badly. Stringing tightly a bow. Stripping the fibrous bark off a tree. Mixing.
A حضرموت *hazramawt* or *hazramūt*, Name of a province, tribe, and city in Arabia. (Gen. x. 26.)
A حضرميّ *hazramiy*, (pl. حضارمة *hazārimat*) Sharp-pointed (shoe). A native of Hazramawt in Yaman. نعل حضرميّة *naʿl hazramiyat*, A kind of sharp-toed shoe worn by those of Hazramawt.
A حضرميّة *hazramīyat*, An impediment of speech.
A حضريّ *hazariy*, Belonging to a town. A townsman. City-bred.
A حضض *hazaz*, Something, any thing. ما عنده حضض ولا بضض *mā ʿindahu hazazun wa lā bazazun*, He has nothing. *Huzaz*, (pl. of حضيض *hazīz*) The lower parts of any thing. Low grounds. *Huzuz* or *huzaz*, Juice of boxthorn. A certain plant. A medicament prepared from camel's urine.
A حضظ *huzuz*, A medicament prepared from the urine of a camel.

A حضف *hizf*, A serpent.

A حضل *hazal*, (v. n. of حضل) Being rotten at the place where the branches shoot (a palm-tree).

A حضن *hazn*, (v. n. of حضن) Fondling (an infant) in the arms. Sitting (on eggs). Turning (one away from any thing) and claiming (it) for one's self. Witholding neighbourly kindness. Keeping back (from business). *Hizn*, (pl. احضان *ahzān*) A side. The breast, the body from the armpits to the short ribs. The den of a hyena. *Hizn* or *huzn*, The base, or what surrounds a mountain. *Hazan*, Ivory. Name of a mountain in Najd.

A حضنة سوء *huznatu sawin*, Injury, oppression, or shameful defeat, and no aid against it.

A حضنيّ *hazanīy*, Very black or red (she-goats).

A حضو *hazw*, (v. n. of حضا for حضو) Stirring (the dying embers of a fire).

A حضور *huzūr*, (v. n. of حضر) Being present. Being at hand, approaching (death). Turning aside from a haunted place. Presence, appearance. Attendance. Court, government. Rest, quiet, ease. (pl. of حاضر *hāzir*) Persons present. P حضور بالا *huzūri bālā*, The exalted presence.

A حضور طلب *huzūr-talab*, Being called to the presence, summoning attendance.

P حضور نويس *huzūr-navīs*, A secretary at court who keeps copies of all firmāns, orders, and letters.

A حضوري *huzūrī*, An attendant. Privilege of paying the revenues direct to government.

A حضوض *hazūz*, Name of a mountain in the sea which serves the Arabians as a place of exile.

A حضوضاة *hazawzāt*, Vociferation of combatants.

A حضوضيٰ *hazawza'*, Distance. Fire. Name of a certain mountain in the sea used by the Arabians as a place of banishment and transportation.

A حضون *hazūn*, A sheep, camel, or woman with one teat longer than another. A man whose testicles are of unequal size. *Huzūn*, (v. n. of حضن) Sitting (on eggs).

A حضيّ *huzzīy*, A stone at a hill's foot, a boulder.

A حضئ *hazīs*, Pure white.

A حضيّة *haziyat*, (pl. حضايا *hazāya'*) A beloved wife or favourite concubine.

A حضير *hazīr*, Thick blood in a secundine. The pus of a wound. Low ground into which the overflowings of a well fall. (pl. of حضيرة *hazīrat*, q. v.).

A حضيرة *hazīrat*, (pl. حضير *hazīr* and حضائر *hazāir*) A small body of soldiers from four to nine (employed in excursions). The van of an army. Water and matter which accompany the birth. A store-room for dates.

A حضيض *hazīz*, (pl. احضّة *ahizzat* and حضض *huzuz*) The lower extremity of any thing. The foot of a mountain. Abyss. Low ground. A stone. (In astronomy) the lower apsis in an eccentric orbit (opposed to اوج *awj*). P حضيض قعر زمين *hazīzi kaṣri zamīn*, The centre of the earth.

A حضيضة *hazīzat*, What one possesses in hand.

A حضيضيٰ *hizzīza'* or *huzzīza'*, (v. n. of حضّ) Exciting, instigating.

A حطّ *hatt*, (v. n. of حطّ) Unsaddling or unloading (a horse or a camel). Unstringing (a bow). Descending from an eminence (into a hollow). Having the spleen sticking to the side from thirst (a camel). Rubbing the side to detach the spleen therefrom. Being swollen, fat, or pimpled (the face). Putting or laying down, depositing. Removing a burden. Remitting a debt. Polishing leather and drawing figures thereon with the instrument called محطّ *mihatt*. Abatement of price. Softness and delicacy of body. P حطّ كردن *hatt kardan*, To throw down, depress, precipitate. To beat down a price.

A حطأ *hatasa*, (fut. يحطأ *yahtasu*) He struck (especially on the back with the open hand). He threw prostrate. He brake wind. He turned (him) away (from his) design. (The boiling pot) cast up scum. He lay with. He voided excrement.

A حطا *hata'*, A large louse.

A حطء *hits*, The remains of water.

A حطاب *hitāb*, A pruning away of the dry wood of a vine. Loppings, prunings.

A حطّاب *hattāb*, A seller of wood. A camel feeding on dry wood.

A حطّابة *hattābat*, Woodmen. Fellers of wood.

A حطاط *hatāt*, Pimples or pustules on the face and other parts. The froth of milk. Ora glandis. *Hitāt*, (v. n. of حطّ) Pulling at the bridle, and going towards a declivity (a camel). Eating food. *Hutāt*, A stench. A small man.

A حطاطة *hatātat*, Abatement, remission. A small man. A little girl. Any thing regarded as small and trifling.

A حطام *hutām*, Any thing dry, brittle, and reduced to bits. Rubbish, trash. A scanty share of worldly goods. Any thing small, minute, paltry.

A حطّام *hattām*, A lion.

A حطامة *hutāmat*, A broken bit, a fragment.

A حطّان *hittān*, A he-goat. A man's name.

A حطائط *hutāsit*, A little man, a dwarf. A small red ant. Abatement, remission. حطائط بطائط *hutāsit butāsit*, Large and coarse (vulva).

A حطب *hatb*, (v. n. of حطب) Collecting wood. Fetching wood for another. Abounding in small wood. Striving, attempting. Whispering, tale-bearing, traducing. حطب في حبلهم *hataba fi hablihim*, He helped them. *Hatab*, Firewood. Whispering, tale-bearing. *Hatib*, Very lean, thin, and lank (like a stick).

A حطباء *hatbās*, (fem. of احطب *ahtab*) Very thin. Unfortunate.

A حطّة *hittat*, Remission of sins, taxes, or burdens. A prayer for a remission (of sins). The month of Ramazān.

A حط حط *hut hut*, Cultivate intimate union with your kindred.

A حطحطة *hathatat*, (v. n. of حطحط Q) Descending. Making haste.

A حطر *hatr*, (v. n. of حطر) Lying with. Stringing (a bow).

A حطربة *hatrabat*, (v. n. of حطرب Q) Living hard, faring meanly. Stringing (a bow) tightly. Perplexity, narrowness, straits.

A حطط *hutut*, Soft, delicate bodies. Descending degrees.

A حطل *hitl*, (pl. احطال *ahtāl*) A wolf.

A حطم *hatm*, (v. n. of حطم) Breaking (any thing dry). Being broken (through age). Breaking (a horse) down (old age). *Hatam*, A disease in a horse's legs. *Hatim*, (A horse) broken down (with age). *Hitam*, Any dry substance broken. The pellicle of an egg. *Hutam*, Unmerciful to one's cattle. A cruel shepherd. *Hutum*, (pl. of حطوم *hatūm*) Breakers.

A حطمة *hatmat*, Barrenness. The force of flowing water. *Hatmat* or *hutmat*, A barren year. Whatever promotes digestion. *Hitmat*, A broken piece. *Hutamat*, Intense fire. The first of the seven hells. A cruel shepherd. Unmerciful to one's cattle. A troop of robust camels. Aged (camel or sheep). A glutton. Name of a man.

A حطمرة *hatmarat*, (v. n. of حطمر Q) Filling. Stringing (a bow).

A حطمط *hitmit*, Small, weak, puny.

A حطميّات *hutamīyāt*, Coats of mail made by the celebrated armourer Hutamat.

A حطو *hatw*, A moving, agitating, stirring.

A حطواء *hatwās*, Red (sheep).

A حطوبة *hutūbat*, An armful of wood.

A حطوط *hatūt*, Sloping. Depressed, low-lying. Swift, excellent (camel). *Hutūt*, Abatement of price. Softness and delicacy of body.

A حطوطيٰ *hatawta'*, Light, flighty, rash.

A حطوم *hatūm*, (pl. حطم) A breaker. A lion.

A حطيب *hatīb*, Woody (place).

A حطئة *hutasat*, Short: a dwarf.

A حطيط *hatīt*, A dwarf.

A حطيطة *hatītat*, Abatement in a price.

A حطيّئة *hutayyitat*, A shipworm.

A حطيطيٰ *hittīta'*, Abatement, remission. A small man, a dwarf.

A حطيم *hatīm*, The wall surrounding the temple at Mecca on the west. Last year's herbage.

A حطّين *hittīn*, Name of a place in Syria, the burial-place of شعيب *shuṣayb* (Jethro).

A حطئ *hatīs*, (Men) of the baser sort.

A حطيئة *hutaysat*, Short of stature, contemptible.

A حظّ *hazz*, (v. n. of حظّ) Being blessed with prosperity, enjoying abundance, favours, or privileges. (pl. احظّ *ahuzz*, احاظي *ahāzī*, حظاظ *hizāz*, حظاء *hizzās*, حظّ *huzz*, حظوظ *huzūz*, and

حظوظة *huzūzat*) Good fortune, happiness. Pleasure, delight. A part, portion, chance, lot. Happy, fortunate, rich. Ill-fortune. حظ فاني *hazzi fānī*, The fading pleasures (of the world). حظ النفس *hazzu'n nafs*, One's own pleasure, whim, or caprice. حظ نفساني *hazzi nafsānī*, Sensual pleasures. *Huzz*, (pl. of حظ *hazz*) Good fortunes, successes.

A حظا *hiza'*, (or حظاء *hizāa*) (pl. of حظوة *huzwat* and *hizwat*) Dignities. Good fortunes.

A حظاء *hizāa*, (pl. of حظوة *hazwat*) Short pointless arrows.

A حظاء *hizzāa*, (pl. of حظ *hazz*) Good fortunes.

A حظاة *hazāt*, A single louse.

A حظار *hizār*, A shed for camels made of boughs to protect them from the cold. *Hizār* or *hazār*, A wall.

A حظاظ *hizāz*, (pl. of حظ) Good fortunes.

A حظال *hazzāl*, Attentive to domestic economy.

A حظالي *hazāla'*, (pl. of حظل *hazil*) (Camels) eating colocynths.

A حظايا *hazāya'*, (pl. of حظية *hazīyat*) (Women) possessed of influence and dignity. Concubines of married men.

A حظائر *hazāir*, (pl. of حظيرة *hazīrat*) Folds for camels constructed of boughs to shelter them from the cold and wind.

A حظب *hazib*, Short and big-bellied.

A حظب *hizabb*, Hasty, choleric. *Huzubb*, Short and paunchy. Hard, cruel, severe, avaricious.

A حظبة *huzubbat*, Hasty, choleric (man).

A حظبي *huzubba'*, The back or body.

A حظة *hizat*, (v. n. of حظا for حظو) Being in high favour (with the sovereign, or a wife with her husband). A portion of goods. Felicity. Dignity.

A حظر *hazr*, (v. n. of حظر) Prohibiting, interdicting, secluding. Constructing a sheep-cote. Penning a flock in the fold. Collecting, bringing together. *Hazir*, A tree from whose boughs a hovel is constructed to shelter camels from the cold. A fresh green thorn. وقع في الحظر الرطب *wakaa fi'l haziri'r ratb*, He fell into what was above his strength. اوقد في الحظر الرطب *awkada fi'l haziri'r ratb*, He acted the tale-bearer. جاء بالحظر الرطب *jāa bi'l haziri'r ratb*, He brought many men or much wealth. He brought a hateful lie.

A حظربة *hazrabat*, (v. n. of حظرب Q) Stringing (a bow) very tight. Filling, distending (a leathern bottle).

A حظظ *huzaz* or *huzuz*, A medicine prepared from camel's urine. The juice of the boxthorn.

A حظل *hazl*, (حظلان *hizlān* or *hazalān*) (v. n. of حظل) Restraining, hindering in the use of liberty, in moving or walking. *Hazal*, (v. n. of حظل) Feeding plenteously on bitter gourds (a camel). Being decayed where the branches spring (a palm-tree). Limping and changing her colour (a ewe with a diseased udder). *Hazil*, Jealous. Attentive to business; desiring from domestics an account of what provisions are delivered out to them. (pl. حظالي *hazāla'*) (A camel) eating the colocynth.

A حظلان *hizlān*, Parsimony, domestic economy. *Hazalān*, (v. n. of حظل) Checking his steps (a man in a passion). The gait of an angry man.

A حظلبة *hazlabat*, Swiftness, speed.

A حظنبي *huzumba'*, The back or body.

A حظو *hazw*, (v. n. of حظا from حظو) Walking slowly, leisurely. Good fortune.

A حظوات *hazawāt*, (pl. of حظوة) Short arrows.

A حظوب *huzūb*, A becoming fat.

A حظوة *hazwat*, A shoot or sucker. *Hazwat* or *huzwat*, (pl. حظاء *hizāa* or حظوات *hazawāt*) A small arrow without a point, used by boys. *Hizwat* or *huzwat*, (v. n. of حظا for حظو) Obtaining rank and esteem, being in high favour. Acquiring influence, prevailing. (pl. حظا *hiza'* or حظاء *hizāa*) A portion of worldly goods. Happiness. Dignity.

A حظوظ *huzūz*, (or حظوظة *huzūzat*) (pl. of حظ *hazz*) Good fortunes, successes. Portions.

A حظول *hazūl*, Attentive to domestic economy.

A حظي *haza'*, A big louse. *Hiza'*, Good luck.

A حظي *hazīy*, Fortunate. Happy. Comfortable. The eighth horse at a race.

A حظيا *huzayya'*, A slow pace.

A حظية *hazīyat*, (fem.) (pl. حظايا *hazāya'*) Fortunate. Invested with dignity, comfortable. A married man's concubine. A share, a portion. *Huzayyat*, (dim. of حظوة *hazwat*) A small arrow without a point. احدي من حظيات لقمان *ihda' min huzayyāti lukmān*, One of Lockman's small pointless arrows; spoken of one notorious for wickedness, and from whom some good emanates.

A حظيرة *hazīrat*, A hovel constructed of boughs to protect camels from the cold. A fence, enclosure. A place for drying dates in. A parapet. نكد الحظيرة *nakidu'l hazīrat*, A covetous, worthless man. حظيرة القدس *hazīratu'l huds*, The chief place in paradise.

A حظيظ *hazīz*, Favoured by fortune, happy.

A حف *haff*, (v. n. of حف) Going, turning or carrying round, surrounding. Cutting or dressing the beard and mustachios. Serving, giving attendance. Making smooth (the face) by pulling out the hairs (a woman). Weaving a garment with the instrument called حف *haff*. Urging, pressing one (want, necessity, or unavoidable business). A weaver's instrument for stretching the web when working. A vestige, trace. A white prickly fish.

A حفا *hafa'*, (v. n. of حفى) Going barefoot. Having the hoof rubbed and worn. Wear, friction of the foot or hoof. Bareness of the feet.

A حفأ *hafaa*, (fut. يحفأ *yahfau*) He threw prostrate. He tore up by the root.

A حفأ *hafaa*, The Egyptian papyrus, especially when green and growing. The root of the papyrus fresh and esculent.

A حفاء *hafāa*, (v. n. of حفي) Being barefoot. Having a worn hoof, or sore feet from walking.

A حفاة *hufāt*, (pl. of حافي *hāfī*) Barefoot.

A حفاث *huffās*, A kind of hissing, harmless snake (larger than حفث *hafis*).

A حفاثية *hafāsiyat*, Thick, large, corpulent.

A حفار *hifār*, A piece of wood in the hole of which the central pole of a tent is fixed.

A حفار *haffār*, A grave or well-digger.

A حفاسي *hafāsiy*, Thick and worthless.

A حفاصة *hufāsat*, A collection.

A حفاض *hifāz*, (pl. of حفض *hafaz*) Household goods, or camels carrying them. Hair-tents. Standard-bearers. Weak camels. Tent-columns.

A حفاظ *hifāz*, (v. n. 3 of حفظ) Persevering in. Repelling, warding off. Shame, nice sense of honour.

A حفاظ *huffāz*, (pl. of حافظ *hāfiz*) Commanders of garrisons, protectors. Rememberers. Learned in the Kur'ān.

A حفاظة *hifāzat*, Custody, care. Memory.

A حفاف *hifāf*, (v. n. of حف) Making smooth (the face) by plucking out the hairs (a woman). The side (of any thing). (pl. احفة *ahiffat*) A curling lock round a bald head. A vestige, track.

A حفاف *haffāf*, Soft flesh below the uvula.

A حفافة *hufāfat*, Stubble. Remains of straw or clover.

A حفال *hufāl*, A large collection. Milk collected.

A حفالة *hufālat*, Worthless (man or thing). Thin (mother of oil or froth of milk).

A حفالج *hafālij*, (pl. of حفلج *hafallaj*) Young camels. *Hufālij*, Bow-legged.

A حفان *haffān*, (A vessel) filled to the brim. A young ostrich or camel. A household, domestics.

A حفاوة *hafāwat*, Importunity. مارية لا حفاوة *mārubat lā hafāwat*, Necessity is not importunity. *Hafāwat* or *hifāwat*, (v. n. of حفي) Wishing well to, favouring. Exhorting forcibly. Exulting, rejoicing. Inquiring minutely into another's condition. Urging, asking with importunity. Having a worn hoof. Honouring exceedingly. Benevolence, kindness.

A حفاية *hifāyat*, (v. n. of حفي) Treating with great respect. Inquiring minutely into one's state. Exulting, rejoicing. Being barefoot. Soreness of feet, thinness of hoof.

A حفائر *hafāir*, (pl. of حفيرة) Graves. Ditches.

A حفائظ *hafāiz*, (pl. of حفيظة *hafīzat*) Feelings of zeal or anger.

A حفة *haffat*, A weaver's beam. Perfect generosity or nobility. A kind of white prickly fish. Caresses, blandishment, kindness.

A حفت *haft*, (v. n. of حفت) Destroying. Pounding. Bruising the back. *Hafit*, Tripe.

A حفث *hafis*, (*hifs*, or حفثة *hafisat*) (pl. احفاث *ahfās*) The rough tripe. A large kind of serpent.

A حف حف *haf haf*, Used in driving poultry.

A حفحفة *hafhafat*, (v. n. of حفحف Q) Being scanty (subsistence). Making a noise (the wing of a bird flying, or a beast in running).

A حفد *hafd*, (or حفدان *hafadān*) (v. n. of حفد) Making haste (in any work). Going fast (an ostrich or camel). Serving. *Hafad*, A pace slower than خبب *khabab*. (pl. of حافد *hāfid*) Servants, domestics, retinue, assistants.

A حفدان *hafadān*, A pace slower than خبب.

A حفدة *hafadat*, Companions; attendants, servants. Children. Sons-in-law. Nephews. Daughters. Grandchildren. Progeny. Painters, limners.

A حفدلس *hafadlas*, Melancholy, gloominess.

A حفر *hafr*, (v. n. of حفر) Digging, cleaning out (a well). Hollowing out. Engraving (a stone). Searching, prying into, and getting a knowledge of. Losing the milk teeth (a child). Lying with. Making lean. Knowing the extent to which a shower of rain reaches. A wide pit. Rottenness of teeth or gums. Yellowness of teeth. P حفر بئرِ اختلال کردن *hafri bi-ri ikhtilāl kardan*, To dig a pit in another's way, to injure him. A *Hafar*, (v. n. of حفر) Being hollow (the teeth). (pl. احفار *ahfār* and احافير *ahāfir*) A wide pit. Earth thrown out of an excavation. Rottenness of the teeth about the roots. A yellowness on the teeth. *Hufar*, (pl. of حفرة *hufrat*) Ditches, pits, excavations.

A حفراة *hifrāt*, (pl. حفريٰ *hifra'*) A kind of plant. A pronged instrument for winnowing wheat.

A حفرة *hufrat*, (pl. حفر *hufar*) A ditch, pit, excavation. A grave. اخطت استه الحفرة *akhtat istuhu'l hufrat*, (a homely expression signifying) He missed the mark.

A حفرد *hifrid*, A pearl-bead or other gem. Name of a plant.

A حفريٰ *hifra'*, (pl. of حفراة) Certain plants.

A حفز *hafz*, (v. n. of حفز) Pushing, shoving forward, driving up behind. Repelling, causing one to desist. Following, driving on (as night does the day). Piercing (with a spear). Lying with (a woman). *Hafaz*, End, extremity, boundary, limit, term.

A حفس *hafs*, An eating, devouring.

A حفش *hafsh*, (v. n. of حفش) Flowing or running from all quarters. Running one course after another (a horse). Going at full speed (a horse). Abrading the surface of the ground (a torrent). Peeling, unbarking. Extracting, causing to come forth. Collecting, assembling. Banishing, driving away. Flowing to one reservoir (streams). Endeavour, effort, pains. *Hifsh*, (pl. احفاش *ahfāsh*) A small house or closet. A hair-tent. The case for a spindle. Any thing worthless, as worn-out furniture, or goods of a perishable nature. A camel's bunch. Genitalia. A little box or casket. Old, cast-off vessels. A large worn-out sack. *Hafash*, (v. n. of حفش) Eating into a camel's bunch (a sore), working from the base upwards in front, the hinder part remaining sound. Manifesting love to (her) husband (a woman). Raining heavily. *Hafish*, Diseased as above mentioned (a camel).

A حفشاء *hafshā*, A she-camel, whose bunch is eaten away before, and unhurt behind.

A حفص *hafs*, (v. n. of حفص) Collecting, gathering. Throwing from the hand. (pl. احفاص *ahfās* and حفوص *hufus*) A leathern sack with which they draw earth out of wells. A lion's whelp. A name given to Omar by Muhammad. *Hafas*, The stone or kernel of the نبق *nabk* or medlar.

A حفصة *hafsat*, A female hyena. Name of Omar's daughter, and one of the wives of Muhammad (frequently called امّ المؤمنين *ummu'l mu-minīn*, Mother of the believers). امّ حفصة, A hen.

A حفصيّة *hafsiyat*, Name of a sect.

A حفض *hafz*, (v. n. of حفض) Twisting, bending. Throwing away. *Hafaz*, (pl. حفاض *hifāz* and احفاض *ahfāz*) Household furniture when prepared for removal; or a camel carrying it. A tent of hair with its poles and ropes. A standard-bearer. A weak camel. The column of a tent. يوم بيوم الحفض المجوّر *yawm bi yawmi'l hafazi'l mujawwar*, An expression used when a man meets the same treatment he formerly gave others.

A حفضج *hifzij*, (حفضاج *hifzāj*, or حفاضج *hufāzij*) Fleshy. Flagging-bellied, loose and pendulous.

A حفضجة *hafzajat*, A growing fat.

A حفظ *hifz*, (v. n. of حفظ) Preserving, guarding. Committing to memory. Feeding, tending (cattle). Custody. Memory. Care, circumspection, caution. حفظ مراتب *hifzi marātib*, Observance of etiquette, attention to the rank of persons addressed. حفظا من ايد الناس *hifzan min aydi'n nās*, For the sake of guarding from the hands of men.

A حفظة *hifzat*, Zeal (especially in defence). Anger, warmth. *Hafazat*, (pl. of حافظ *hāfiz*) Guards, garrisons, keepers. Observers, inspectors, watchmen. Angels (as inspecting and recording the actions of men).

A حفف *hafaf*, Poverty, hardship. Margin, brink, edge. Trace, footstep. Short and strong.

A حفل *hafl*, (v. n. of حفل) Being assembled (people). Collecting or flowing together (milk or water). Pouring forth rain (the sky). Filling its bed (a river). Polishing, making bright. Fearing. Turning the mind to, minding, attending to. Shedding tears copiously (the eye). Collecting, bringing together. An assembly, synod, council, congregation. Numerous (assembly). ذو حفل *zū haflin*, Studious, diligent.

A حفّل *huffal*, (pl. of حافل *hafil*) Full udders.

A حفلة *haflat*, All, the whole of. Study, diligence. *Huflat*, A synod, council, general assembly.

A حفلج *haflaj*, One who moves his body much in walking.

A حفلّج *hafallaj*, Bow-legged. (pl. حفالج *hafālij*) A young camel.

A حفلق *haflak* or *hafallak*, Enervated, foolish.

A حفلكي *hafalka'*, Weak.

A حفلّي *hafala'*, Promiscuously, indiscriminately.

A حفليج *hiflij*, Short, dwarfish.

A حفن *hafn*, (v. n. of حفن) Taking up with both hands (meal or sand). A small gift. حفن له حفنة *hafana lahu hafnatan*, He gave him a little, a handful. *Hafan*, (v. n. of حفن) Turning the feet in walking so as to kick up the dust. *Hufan*, (pl. of حفنة *hufnat*) Ditches. Handsful.

A حفنة *hufnat* or *hafnat*, (pl. حفن *hufan*) The measure of both hands. A small quantity. A mouthful, handful. A ditch, pit, well.

A حفنّج *hafannaj*, Short of stature.

A حفنجي *hafanja'*, Languishing, numb, stiff.

A حفندد *hafandad*, Rich and careful.

A حفنس *hifnis*, Impudent, obscene (woman). A man of short stature.

A حفنسا *hafansa*, Short, thick, and big-bellied.

A حفنضاج *hifinzāj*, Fleshy. Flag-bellied. Brawny.

A حفنكي *hafanka'*, Weak.

A حفو *hafw*, (v. n. of حفا for حفو) Giving. Withholding. Honouring. Shaving the whiskers.

A حفواء *hufawā*, (pl. of حفيّ *hafiy*) Knowing, intelligent. Curiously inquisitive.

A حفوة *hafwat* or *hifwat*, (v. n. of حفي) Being barefoot. Having a worn hoof (a horse). *Hufwat* or *hifwat*, Tenderness of hoof or foot.

A حفود *hufūd*, (v. n. of حفد) Going fast. Serving. Being quick and ready in obeying and serving.

A حفوص *hufūs*, (pl of حفص *hafs*) Leathern sacks used in cleaning out wells.

A حفوف *hufūf*, (v. n. of حفّ) Being awhile unoiled, uncombed, matted, and entangled (a woman's hair neglected). Having withered vegetables (ground). Being entirely lost (one's hearing). Shaving and trimming (the head and mustachios). Injuring with a malignant eye. Poverty. Hard fare. Any thing short and strong. The side of a thing.

A حفول *haful*, (A camel) full of milk. *Hifwal*, A certain tree which bears a bitterish fruit resembling a plum. *Hufūl*, (v. n. of حفل) Flowing together (milk or water). Raining plentifully. Filling its bed (a river). Weeping profusely. Polishing. Collecting, bringing together. حفول الضرع *hufūlu'z zir*, Fulness of teats; (met.) Opulence.

A حفي *hafi*, (A beast) worn in the hoof. (A man) beat in the feet.

A حفيّ *hafiy*, (pl. حفواء *hufawā*) Knowing, intelligent. One who dives to the bottom. Importunate in asking questions. One who inquires carefully into other people's affairs. Benevolent, kind. Joyful, glad.

A حفية *hifyat*, (v. n. of حفي) Being barefoot.

Tenderness of foot, thinness of hoof.

A حفيتاء *hafaytas*, A short squat man.

A حفيتر *hafaytar*, Short, dwarfish.

A حفيج *hifīj*, Short, dwarfish.

A حفيد *hafīd*, A grandson. Daughters. Children. Grandchildren.

A حفير *hafīr*, A grave, a tomb.

A حفيرة *hafīrat*, A ditch, excavation. *Hufayrat*, (dim. of حفرة *hufrat*) A little hole.

A حفيسا *hafaysas*, Short, squat, mean, base.

A حفيسي *hafaysiy*, Thick and good for little.

A حفيظ *hafīz*, A guardian, keeper. A grazier. A governor. One who has learned by heart. God.

A حفيظة *hafīzat*, (pl. حفائظ *hafāsiz*) Zeal (especially in defence). Anger. A keeping back from whatever is unlawful.

A حفيف *hafīf*, (v. n. of حفّ) Making a noise when travelling (a horse); (a bird) flying; (a tree) shaken by the wind; (a serpent) crawling. The sound of a serpent crawling forth out of its slough; also its hissing. The noise of a fire burning.

A حفيل *hafīl*, (v. n. of حفل) Collecting, flowing together (milk or water). Using diligence, straining every nerve. Studious, diligent in business. Numerous (assembly).

A بحفيلتهم *bi hafīlatihim*, All together (came).

A حفيلل *hafaylal*, A certain kind of tree.

A حقّ *hakk*, (v. n. of حقّ) Accruing, happening unto. Coming to. Being necessary. Becoming, befitting. Rendering necessary. Overcoming at law. Being sure of, knowing of a truth. Acting justly, uprightly. Discharging an obligation. Travelling in the middle of the road. Striking on the crown of the head or in the hollow at the head of the shoulder. حققت حذره حقّا *hakaktu hazrahu hakkan*, I did to him what he was avoiding.

A حقّ *hakk*, (in Persian *hak* without tashdīd) God. An attribute of God. Truth. Justice, equity. (pl. حقوق *hukūk*) A just claim, right, due. Certainty, sure proof. Law. Reason. Rectitude. Steadiness, vigilance. The Kur'ān. Muhammadism, Islām. A thing decreed. Riches, wealth, effects, possessions. Death. Litigation, altercation. The crown of the head. Name of a bird which is said to suspend itself by the claws by night and continually cry *hak hak*. A disease in a camel's lungs. Right, just, true, genuine. Necessary, expedient, fit, proper, worthy, suitable. Firm, constant. Existing, extant. الحقّ مرّ *al hakku murrun*, Truth is bitter. P حق آشنائي *haki āshnāsī*, The rights of friendship. حق بر سر *hak bar sar*, A debt, claim, obligation. A حقّ التحصيل *hakku't tahsīl*, A merited remuneration. A sixth of the actual collections made in Bahār (in India) to the person in charge of them. حق تربيت *haki tarbiyat*, Gratitude for education. حق تعالي *hakk tasāla'*, God Almighty. حق جلّ و جلال *hakk jall wa jalāl*, The Deity in all his glory. حقّ جوار *hakki jiwār*, Right of pre-emption. حق الحماية *hakku'lhimāyat*, A present for protection. حق خدمت *hakki khidmat*, Reward of service. حق خزانه *hakki khizāna*, A duty or fee of two per cent. claimed by the inferior treasurer upon all monies paid into the royal treasury. حق الرعاية *hakku'r risāyat*, Duty of respect. P حق زادگی *haki zādagī*, Birthright. A حق السعي *hakku's sasy*, Wages for labour, recompense for trouble. حق القدم *hakku'l hadam*, The reward of a messenger. Any thing set before a guest. حقّ الله *hakku'llāh*, The rights of God; punishment inflicted for religious offences. حقّ مالضامن *hakki māl-zāmin*, Interest, usury. حقّ الناس *hakku'n nās*, The rights of man; punishment for crimes against society. حق الناظرين *hakku'n nāzirīn*, Something left after a banquet for the servants or spectators. P حق نمك *haki namak*, Fidelity. حق وارثي *haki wārisī*, Right of heirship; reversion. حق وزارت *haki wizārat*, The vazīr's fees. A بالحق *bi'l hakk*, Of a truth. P بطريق حق *ba tarīki hak*, In equity. For the love of God. در حق *dar hak*, In regard to, in respect of, in right of. A عند حق *sind hakk*, At the time of. لحقّ *la hakku*, Really, truly, verily. P نا حق *nā hak*, Unjust. نا حق كردن *nā hak kardan*, To err. A *Hikk*, (v. n. of حقّ) Entering his fourth year (a camel). Going over her time (a camel in foal). (pl. حقق *hikak*, *hukuk*, and حقاق *hikāk*) A camel just entering into the fourth year (when he or she is fit for labour or breeding). A she-camel that has lost her teeth from age. Truth, certainty, positive proof. *Hukk*, The socket of the thigh-bone, or of the shoulder-blade. (pl. حقوق *hukūk*) A spider's web. (pl. of حقّة *hukkat*) Cups, bowls. Boxes.

A حقا *haka'*, (v. n. of حقا for حقو) Suffering in the side, waist, or hypochondria. Being griped from eating meat.

A حقّا *hakkan*, By God! Really, truly.

A حقاء *hakās*, Breeches. The waistband. *Hikās*, The gripes from eating meat. (pl. of حقو *hakw*) Waists. Waistbands. Rugged places elevated above torrents. Notched ends of arrows.

A حقاب *hikāb*, (pl. حقب *hukub*) A girdle ornamented with jewels (worn by the Arabian ladies). The white at the root of the nail. A white string (tied round the loins of infants, to guard them from enchantments).

A حقارة *hakārat*, (v. n. of حقر) Despising. Being despicable. *Hakārat*, *hikārat*, or *hukārat*, Vileness, baseness. Scorn, contempt, affront, disgrace. P حقارت كردن *hakārat kardan*, To despise, affront, disgrace.

A حقاف *hikāf*, Waving sand-hills.

A حقاق *hikāk*, (v. n. 3 of حقّ) Litigating, contending for one's rights. Enmity, hostility. Altercation. Small plants of the kind called عضاء *sizāh*. (pl. of حقّ *hikk*) Camels rising four years old. (pl. of حقّة *hukkat*) Bottles. Boxes. حقاق العرفط *hikāku'l surfut*, Suckers of the plant عرفط *surfut*. نزق الحقاق *naziku'l hikāk*, A disputer about trifles.

A حقّاق *hakkāk*, A box or casket-maker.

A حقال *hukāl*, A watery humour in the bowels.

A حقّاني *hakkānīy*, True, pure, disinterested. محبّت حقّانية *mahabbati hakkānīya*, (or simply حقّانيّة *hakkānīyat*) The love of God, perfect charity.

A حقائب *hakāsib*, (pl. of حقيبة) Portmanteaus.

A حقائد *hakāsid*, (pl. of حقد *hikd*) Hatreds.

A حقائف *hakāsif*, (pl. of حقف *hikf*) Winding sand-hills.

A حقائق *hakāsik*, (pl. of حقّ *hikk*) Camels rising four years old. (pl. of حقيقة *hakīkat*) Truths. علوم حقائق *sulūmi hakāsik*, Theology.

A حقائل *hakāsil*, (pl. of حقيلة *hakīlat*) Watery humours in the intestines.

A حقب *hukb* or *hukub*, (pl. احقاب *ahkāb* and احقب *ahkub*) A period of eighty years or upwards. A year. Space of time. *Hakab*, (v. n. of حقب) Having his sheath so squeezed by the hind girth as to be unable to stale (a camel). Being destitute of minerals (a mine). Being barren from want of rain (a year). The hind girth of a camel's saddle. A girdle ornamented with jewels. *Hikab*, (pl. of حقبة *hikbat*) Years. *Hukub*, (pl. of حقاب *hikāb*) Ornamented girdles.

A حقباء *hakbās*, (fem. of احقب *ahkab*) The wild ass (because white-flanked). A hillock whose lofty head shoots upwards and girded all round with earth. A tall hillock, in the middle of which there is whitish shining earth. الحقباء *al hakbās*, The milky way.

A حقبة *hikbat*, (pl. حقب *hikab* and حقوب *hukūb*) A year, a space of time. *Hukbat*, A calm. *Hakibat*, A cloak-bag, portmanteau.

P حق بين *hak-bīn*, Having a regard to justice.

P حق پرست *hak-parast*, Devoted to truth; a worshipper of God (a name which the old Persians assumed to themselves).

P حق پسند *hak-pasand*, Approving truth; just.

A حقّة *hakkat*, (v. n. of حقّ) Being necessary. Happening indubitably. Truth. Sure; descending, impending (judgment). *Hikkat*, (v. n. of حقّ) Entering on her fourth year (a camel). A she-camel rising four years old. The age of a camel fit for breeding. A just claim, right, or due. امّ حقّة *umm hikkata*, Name of a woman. *Hukkat*, (pl. حقّ *hukk*, حقوق *hukūk*, حقق *hukak*, احقاق *ahkāk*, and حقاق *hikāk*) A round box in which pearls, jewels, or electuaries or pastils are kept; a vase, cup, bowl. A spider's web. The socket of the thigh-bone or shoulder-blade. Low-lying and circular ground. A hole in the ground. *Hukkat* or *hakkat*, A misfortune. A woman.

P حق جو *hak-jo* or *jū*, Truth-seeking.

A حقحاق *hak-hāk*, A swift nocturnal journey in search of water.

A حقحقة *hak-hakat*, (v. n. of حقحق Q) Lifting his feet high when travelling (a horse). Travelling in the early part of the night. Riding one's beast till it breaks down. Hard, back-breaking riding.

A حقد *hikd*, *hakad*, or *hakd*, (v. n. of حقد) Wishing ill, hating. *Hikd*, (pl. احقاد *ahkād*, حقود *hukūd*, and حقائد *hakāʼid*) Hatred, rancour. ارباب حقد *arbābi hikd*, The malevolent. *Hakad*, (v. n. of حقد) Being withheld (rain). Yielding no ore (a mine). Being full of fat (a camel).

P حقدار *hak-dār*, Rightful owner, proprietor.

A حقر *hakr*, (v. n. of حقر) Despising, treating with contempt. Being contemptible and despicable. Contempt, slight, scorn. Vileness, baseness.

A حقرية *hukriyat*, Contempt, scorn. Vileness.

A حقز *hakz*, (v. n. of حقز) Kicking, spurning with her foot (a woman).

P حقشناس *hak-shinās*, Knowing and performing one's duty. Rendering to every one his due. Able to appreciate. Grateful.

P حقشناسي *hak-shināsī*, Gratitude. حقشناسي كردن *hak-shināsī kardan*, To appreciate.

A حقصا *haksan*, Nimbly, quickly.

A حقط *hakat*, Agility of body, motion, activity. *Hikit*, A word used in driving a horse.

A حقطان *hikittān*, (or حقطانة) Short, dwarfish.

A حقطبة *haktabat*, The cry of the pheasant.

A حقطة *haktat*, Short, light-bodied (woman).

P حق طراز *hak-tirāz*, Observing truth.

A حقف *hikf*, (pl. احقاف *ahkāf*, حقاف *hikāf*, حقوف *hukūf*, حقائف *hakāʼif*, and حقفة *hikafat*) Sand heaped up in long waving hills; also round tumuli of sand. Foot of a sand-hill, mountain, wall.

A حقفة *hikafat*, (pl. of حقف) Waving sand-hills.

A حقق *hakak*, (v. n. of حقّ) Placing his hind foot in the track made by the fore foot (a quadruped). Not sweating (a horse). *Hikak* or *hukuk*, (pl. of حقّ *hikk*) Camels rising four years old. *Hukak*, (pl. of حقّة *hukkat*) Caskets, boxes. Pots.

A حقّق *hukkak*, Sound discourse. Cloths of a firm texture.

P حق گذار *hak-guzār*, Administering justice.

P حق گذاري *hak-guzārī*, Discharge of obligation, fulfilment of duty, acknowledgment or requital of favours.

P حق گزين *hak-guzīn*, Approving justice.

P حقگوي *hak-goy*, Speaking truth. The essence of a thing. Name of a bird that hangs by a tree and vociferates all night.

A حقل *hakl*, (v. n. of حقل) Tilling, sowing (land). (Corn) in the blade. Rich arable land. *Hikl*, A camel-litter. The gripes. A watery humour in the bowels.

A حقلة *hahlat*, (v. n. of حقل) (Cattle) swallowing earth with the grass, and being thereby griped. A disease in camels. (pl. احقال *ahkāl*) The gripes in horses from eating earth. Rich arable land. *Hiklat*, Remains of milk. Refuse of dates. Whatever is wanting to complete the filling of a cup. *Hiklat*, *haklat*, or *huklat*, Clear water remaining in a cistern.

A حقلد *hiklid*, Evil, bad. Heavy, dull, torpid.

A حقلّد *hakallad*, Avaricious, stingy. Weak. A sinner, culprit. Hatred, ill-will.

A حقم *hakm*, A sort of pigeon or other bird.

A حقن *hakn*, (v. n. of حقن) Putting milk in a bottle in order to make butter. Keeping blood or urine from being spilled. Retaining, confining. Pouring fresh milk upon thick. حقن دم فلان *hakana dam fulānin*, He preserved such an one from being slain. *Huhan*, (pl. of حقنة *huknat*) Clysters.

P حق نا حق *hak nā hak*, Right or wrong.

A حقنة *haknat*, (pl. احقان *ahkān*) The cholic. *Huknat*, A clyster. P حقنه كردن *hukna kardan*, To exhibit an enema. حقنه گرفتن *hukna giriftan*, To take an injection.

A حقو *hakw*, (v. n. of حقا for حقو) Striking on the side, waist, or hypochondria. (pl. احقى *ahkī*, احقاء *ahkāʼ*, حقيّ *hukiy*, and حقاء *hikāʼ*) Breeches. The waistband or place where the drawers are tied. The waist, side, hypochondria. (pl. حقاء *hikāʼ*) A rugged place overhanging a stream. The side of a difficult and narrow pass. The notched end of an arrow. *Hikw*, Breeches.

A حقوب *hukūb*, (pl. of حقبة *hikbat*) Years. Spaces of time.

A حقوة *hakwat*, The belly-ache from eating meat. A disease in a camel's lungs. Breeches. The waistband. *Hukwat*, The gripes from eating meat.

A حقود *hakūd*, Malevolent. *Hukūd*, (pl. of حقد *hikd*) Hatreds, enmities.

A حقوف *hukūf*, (v. n. of حقف) Lying on a sand-hill, or squatting awry like a sand-hill (a doe). Crookedness. (pl. of حقف *hikf*) Winding sands.

A حقوق *hukūk*, (pl. of حقّ *hakk*) Rights, dues. Duties. Laws, statutes. (pl. of حقّ *hukk*) Spiders' webs. (pl. of حقّة *hukkat*) Cups, bowls. Boxes. حقوق الهيّة *hukūki ilāhiya*, The divine laws. حقوق سابقة *hukūki sābiha*, Old debts, former obligations.

A حقول *hukūl*, (v. n. of حقل) Swallowing earth with grass, and being griped thereby (a horse).

P حقّه *hukka*, A round box for holding jewels or drugs: a casket. A gallipot. The glass, metal, or earthen water vessels through which the fumes pass when smoking tobacco; a hookah. حقّهٔ آتش *hukkaʼi ātish*, A kind of rocket used in war. حقّهٔ بي مغز *hukkaʼi bī maghz*, A brainless, senseless, heartless man. حقّهٔ سبز *hukkaʼi sabz*, The firmament. حقّهٔ كاوس *hukkaʼi kāwus*, Name of a note in music. حقّهٔ مينا *hukkaʼi mīnā*, The sky. حقّهاى مينافام *hukkahāʼi mīnā-fām*, The celestial orbs.

P حقّه باز *hukka-bāz*, A player at cups and balls.

P حقّه بردار *hukka-bardār*, The man who prepares the hookah.

P حقّه پردازه *hukka-pardāza*, A sky-rocket.

P حقّه گر *hukkagar*, A turner of cups and balls.

A حقي *hakī*, One who hurts the side, waist, or hypochondria.

A حقيّ *hukiy*, (pl. of حقو *hakw*) Waists. Waistbands. Breeches.

A حقّي *hukkiy*, A sort of date.

A حقيبة *hakībat*, (pl. حقائب *hakāʼib*) A pad or any thing similar tied behind a saddle. A cloak-bag, portmanteau. Profound learning.

A حقّيّة *hakkīyat*, Reality, right.

A حقيدة *hakīdat*, A hating, a wishing ill.

A حقير *hakīr*, Base, contemptible. Little, small. Thin, lean. حقير الشمائل *hakīru'sh shamāʼil*, Of base qualities. حقير المقدار *hakīru'l mikdār*, Of little value. P حقير داشتن *hakīr dāshtan*, To despise.

A حقيق *hakīk*, (pl. احقّاء *ahikkāʼ*) Worthy, deserving of. بنات الحقيق *banātu'l hukayk*, A sort of date.

A حقيقة *hakīkat*, (pl. حقائق *hakāʼik*) Truth, reality. Sincerity. The real state, circumstance, or statement of a thing. Any thing which must be defended (as a standard). A speech without trope or figure. حقيقت جمع *hakīkati jamʻ*, A general statement of the public revenues. في الحقيقة *fī'l hakīkat*, In truth.

A حقيقة *hakīkatan*, Truly, certainly.

P حقيقت شناس *hakīkat-shinās*, Intelligent.

A حقيقيّ *hakīkīy*, (P حقيقى *hakīkī*) True, unfeigned, real. Accurate. Radical, essential. P برادر حقيقي *birādari hakīkī*, One's own brother.

A حقيل *hakīl*, Land not sufficiently elevated to be called mountainous. Name of a plant.

A حقيلة *hakīlat*, (pl. حقائل *hakāʼil*) A watery humour in the bowels. The refuse of rotten dates.

A حقيمان *hakīmān*, The outer angle of the eye.

A حقين *hakīn*, Retained, confined, kept in. Milk poured into thick milk to make butter.

A حك *hakk*, (v. n. of حكّ) Scratching, rubbing. Scraping, erasing. Rubbing one substance against another. Itching, requiring to be scratched (the head). ما حكّ في صدري *mā hakka fī sadrī*, It did not occur to my mind. It gave me no pleasure. حكّ له في الدبرة *hakka lahu fī'd dabarat*, He scratched his back; he coaxed him. *Hikk*, Doubt, suspicion. A powerful opponent. حكّ شرّ *hikku sharrin*, Bold in mischief.

A حكاء *hikāʼ*, (v. n. 3 of حكي) Relating, telling. Imitating, resembling, taking after, mimicking, mocking.

A حكاة *hukaʼat*, (*hukaʼat* or حكاءة *hukāʼat*) A certain reptile bigger than a lizard.

A حكاة *hukāt*, (pl. of حاكي *hākī*) Narrators.

A حكاك *hikāk*, (v. n. 3 of حكّ) Resisting,

opposing. حكاك شرّ *hikāku sharrin*, A bringer of mischief. *Hukāk*, An itching sensation, a need of scratching. Borax.

A حكّاك *hakkāk*, A jeweller. A polisher of precious stones. A borer of pearls. Itching, prurient.

A حكّاكات *hakkākāt*, Suggestions, temptations.

A حكاكة *hukākat*, Whatever falls off in polishing, filing, rasping, sawing, planing, shaving, &c. A collyrium produced by the friction of two stones.

A حكام *hikām*, A citing before a judge.

A حكّام *hukkām*, (pl. of حاكم *hākim*) Princes, lords, nobles, governors, judges, magistrates (the names of fifteen who ruled during Pagan times have been preserved). حكّام ذوي الاحترام *hukkāmi zawi'l ihtirām*, Most worshipful magistrates.

A حكامة *hakāmat*, (v. n. of حكم) Being learned, wise, philosophical. Being skilful, able to effect.

A حكايا *hakāya'*, (pl. of حكاية *hikāyat*) Stories.

A حكاية *hikāyat*, (v. n. of حكي) Telling, relating. Tying firm a knot. Being like unto, resembling. Imitating, mimicking. History, heroic romance, fable, tradition, relation, narrative. An affair. P حكايت كردن *hikāyat kardan*, To relate, narrate. To imitate, to mimic exactly.

A حكّة *hikkat*, (pl. حكك *hikak*) Itch, scab: an itching sensation that induces scratching. A kind of boy's game. رافع حكّه و جرب *rāfiʿi hikka u jarab*, Antiscorbutic.

A حكر *hakr*, (v. n. of حكر) Keeping back (grain) till a time of scarcity, regrating behaviour. A mixture of butter and honey. *Hakr* or *hukr*, A small cup or bowl. A small matter, a trifle. *Hakar*, (v. n. of حكر) Having absolute authority, being alone in any business, monopolizing. Grain laid up in store against a season of scarcity. A dispute, quarrel, litigation. Water collected together. *Hakir*, One who stores up grain against a time of scarcity, a regrater, forestaller. One who acts alone, sole in authority. *Hukar*, Things laid up against want. Corn stored up to be sold when markets rise.

A حكرة *hukrat*, Whatever is hid or laid up against a time of scarcity.

A حكش *haksh*, A collection. A contraction, wrinkling, or shrivelling. حكش عكش *hakish ʿakish*, A wrestler, one who twists and exerts himself to get the better of his adversary.

A حكك *hakak*, (v. n. of حكك) Being worn, scratched. A scratch, rub. A certain white stone like marble. The waddling pace of a dwarfish woman. *Hikak*, (pl. of حكّة *hikkat*) Itches. Scabs. *Hukuk*, Mischief-makers. Importunate (persons), urgent in the prosecution of (their) necessary affairs.

A حكل *hukl*, Any thing giving no sound (as an ant). A cutting or chafing of one leg against the other (in a horse). A shrivelling of the nerve or tendon extending from the hip to the heel in a horse. A weakness in the ankle. A name of Solomon.

A حكلة *huklat*, (v. n. of حكل) Being obscure and doubtful (speech). Being dumb, tongue-tied. Straightening (a spear). Striking with a stick.

A حكم *hakm*, (v. n. of حكم) Bridling, or putting a curb on (a horse). Restraining (a fool). *Hukm*, (v. n. of حكم) Exercising authority, commanding. Restraining from mischief. Passing sentence, giving judgment, whether to absolve or to condemn. Command, absolute power, dominion. (pl. احكام *ahkām*) An order, permission. Judgment, sentence, decree. Relation. Wisdom, knowledge. حكم بياضي *hukmi biyāzī*, A royal mandate issued with secrecy and despatch. حكم شرع *hukmi sharʿ*, A judicial decree. A decision according to law. حكم قضا *hukmi kazā*, The decree of fate. الحكم لله *al hukm li'llāh*, God is the judge, heaven must determine. P حكم كردن *hukm kardan*, To judge, decide, sentence, decree, determine, order, command, rule over, regulate. بحكم *ba hukmi*, By way of. For the sake, or purpose of. بحكم ضرورت *ba hukmi zarūrat*, Through necessity. بحكم آن كه *ba hukmi ān ki*, Forasmuch as, seeing that, by reason that, because. To the degree that. A *Hakam*, A prince. A judge. A governor, commandant. An umpire, mediator, arbitrator. An aged man. *Hikam*, (pl. of حكمة *hikmat*) Sciences. P كلام پر حكم *kalāmi pur-hikam*, Words full of wisdom.

A حكماء *hukamāʾ*, (pl. of حكيم *hakīm*) Wise men, philosophers. Doctors, physicians. حكماءِ آفاق *hukamāʾi āfāk*, The wise men of the age.

P حكم انداز *hukm-andāz*, A skilful archer.

P حكم بردار *hukm-bardār*, Executing commands. Obedient to orders.

A حكمة *hikmat*, (pl. حكم *hikam*) Wisdom, science, knowledge. A wise saying. Prophecy. Justice, equity. Mildness. The Kur'ān. The Gospel. علم حكمت *ʿilmi hikmat*, Philosophy, physic, medicine. حكمت الهى *hikmati ilāhī*, (or حكمة الله *hikmatu'llāh*) Divine mystery. By the permission of God. (This is also expressed by P حكمت خدا *hikmati khudā* and A حكمت ربّاني *hikmati rabbānī*). حكمت بالغه *hikmati bāligha*, Mature wisdom. حكمت رياضي *hikmati riyāzī*, Mathematics. حكمت عملي *hikmati ʿamalī*, Practical knowledge. حكمت طبعي *hikmati tabʿī*, Natural reason or instinct (in contradistinction to intellectual or spiritual wisdom). P در آن چه حكمتست *dar ān chi hikmatast*, What's the wit of that? A *Hakamat*, A bridle, halter. An iron ring, or other check-rein for a horse. The chin of a sheep. The fore part of the head or face. A thing, affair, business. Power, dignity, station.

P حكمت آئين *hikmat-āʾīn*, Mirror of wisdom.

A حكمتي *hikmatī*, Clever.

P حكم راني *hukm-rānī*, Sway, dominion.

P حكم كش *hukm-kash*, Obedient to orders.

P حكم گذاري *hukm-guzārī*, Empire, sovereignty.

P حكم نامه *hukm-nāma*, A written order.

A حكمي *hukmī*, Obedient to directions (applied to medicine).

A حكوف *hukūf*, Languor in work.

A حكوك *hukūk*, (pl. of حكّ *hakk*) Erasures (of books or deeds).

A حكومة *hukūmat*, Dominion, sovereignty, absolute power. Jurisdiction. A principality. The sentence of a judge.

P حكومت ران *hukūmat-rān*, Reigning power.

P حكومتگاه *hukūmat-gāh*, Seat of government, metropolis, royal residence. A province, principality. Controul.

A حكّي *hakkī*, An erasing-knife.

A حكيّ *hakīy*, Tattling, whispering (woman).

A حكيص *hakīs*, One of whom a bad opinion is entertained: suspected.

A حكيك *hakīk*, Smooth, polished (die). Pared (hoof). A horse whose hoof is pared.

A حكيم *hakīm*, (pl. حكماء *hukamāʾ*) Learned, wise, prudent, judicious. A doctor, philosopher. A physician. One who does any thing well, firmly, and effectually. Firmly joined (chain). A name of God. حكيم مطلق *hakīmi mutlak*, Omniscient.

A حكيمة *hakīmat*, (pl. حكيمات *hakīmāt*) A learned woman. A female magistrate (of whom the names of four have been preserved).

A حكيمي *hakīmī*, The practice of medicine.

A حلّ *hall*, (v. n. of حلّ) Untying, unloosing. Unfurling a sail. Descending, alighting on a journey, resting, staying, remaining with. Running. Causing one to alight and sojourn. Diluting, dissolving, discussing. Lighting, falling on (as anger). Being deserved, proper to be inflicted (punishment). Laying aside a Nazarite's vow. Putting off her weeds (a widow). Solution. Oil of sesame or rape-seed. حلّ عقده *halli ʿukda*, The untying of a knot. حلّ و ربط *hall u rabt*, Loosing and tying. P گاه حلّ گاه شدّ كردن *gāh hall gāh shadd kardan*, To tie and unloose, unloose and tie. A *Hill*, (v. n. of حلّ) Being lawful. The dissolution of an oath. A lawful thing. A butt or mark for archers. *Hill* or *hull*, The laying aside of a Nazarite's vow. One who has laid aside his Nazarite's vow. *Hull*, (pl. of احلّ *ahall*) Weak-legged (horses).

A حلء *halʾ*, (v. n. of حلأ) Pounding, braying, mixing a collyrium, and anointing the eyes. Pulling off the skin from a fleshy part (a currier); removing the dirt and filth from a hide. Throwing prostrate. Marrying a wife and going in unto her. Striking (with a sword). Giving (money). *Halaʾ*, (v. n. of حلئ) Being marred by the knife in dressing (a hide). Being covered with an eruption after illness (lips). Pustules on the lips after a fever.

A حلا *hala'*, Pounded medicines.

A حلّاء *hallāʾ*, Feeble-legged, weak (female).

A حلاءة *halāʾat*, The middle of the hind-head.

Halāsat or *hilāsat*, A place abounding with trees. *Hulāsat*, (v. n. of حلأ) Pulling off (the skin) from a fleshy part (a currier). A thin pellicle that comes from a hide in tanning. Any thing pulled off by flaying. Any thing pounded or rubbed small (especially a collyrium for the eye).

A حلاب *hilāb*, (v. n. 3 of حلب) Milking together (with another). A milking-pail. New milk.

A حلّاب *hallāb*, A milker. A day of public convocation. Name of a horse.

A حلابس *hulābis*, A brave man.

A حلاة *halāt*, An ornament (especially on the hilt and sheath of a sword).

A حلاتة *hulātat*, Whatever falls in picking wool, wool-pickings. The cleanings or after-birth.

A حلّاج *hallāj*, A dresser of cotton, one who separates it from the seed.

A حلاجة *hilājat*, The art of dressing cotton.

A حلاجي *hallājī*, The art of dressing cotton.

P حلاجي كردن *hallājī kardan*, To card or tease (cotton or wool). To abuse, revile.

A حلاحل *halāhal*, A sort of wild onion. *Hulāhil*, (pl. *halāhil*) A prince, a chief of a tribe. A man endued with bulk and valour.

A حلّاس *hallās*, A seller of coarse woollen carpets.

A حلاف *hilāf*, (v. n. 3 of حلف) Entering into an agreement and confirming it by an oath.

A حلّاف *hallāf*, One who swears much.

A حلافي *hulāfiy*, Fruitful in the plant حلف *halaf*.

A حلاق *halāk* or *halāki*, Death. *Hilāk*, Rasure, shaving. A line, row. جيّد الحلاق *jayyidu'l hilāk*, Well-shaved (poll). *Hulāk*, A sore throat. An insatiable desire for the male without conceiving.

A حلاقاً *hilākan*, In a row (tents pitched).

A حلّاق *hallāk*, A barber, a shaver.

A حلاقة *hulākat*, That which falls when clipping or shaving, especially goat's hair; pollings.

A حلاقيم *halākīm*, (pl. of حلقوم) Throats, gullets.

A حلال *halāl*, (v. n. of حلّ) Being legal, legitimate. Fulfilling the term of a Nazarite's vow. Laying aside mourning for the death of her husband, at the expiration of 110 days (during which time she is not by law allowed to marry) (a woman). Being discharged (a debt). A lawful thing. Any thing indifferent (in religion). A lawful husband or wife. One who has fulfilled the term of a Nazarite's vow. Mastic. الحلو الحلال *al hulwu'l halāl*, Words free from doubt. بالحلال *bi'l halāl*, Legitimately. P حلال شدن *halāl shudan*, To be legal, legitimate. حلال كردن *halāl kardan*, To make pure or lawful. To slaughter cattle. To give. To marry. حلالم *halālam*, My lawful (wife or husband). A *Hilāl*, (v. n. 3 of حلّ) Lighting and resting in a place. Those who alight and stay. A lawful thing. A travelling-carriage for women. Goods, furniture. (pl. of حلّة *hillat*) Groups of houses. Assemblies, places of meeting. (pl. of حلّة *hullat*) Cloaks. Striped stuffs.

A حلّال *hallāl*, A looser, solver, dissolver, or resolver. كشّاف مشكلات و حلّال معضلات *kashshāfi mushkilāt, u hallāli muszilāt*, Resolver of doubts and solver of difficulties. *Hullāl*, (pl. of حالّ *hāll*) Those who alight and stay.

P حلال خور *halāl-khwur*, An epithet applied to the lowest and vilest classes of the people, particularly such as are employed in the meanest offices, the removing of carrion and the like; so called because every thing is lawful food to them.

P حلال خوري *halāl-khwurī*, Business of sweeper.

P حلال زادگي *halāl-zādagī*, Legitimacy of birth.

P حلال زادة *halāl-zāda*, A legitimate son.

P حلال نمك *halāl-namak*, Faithful, true.

A حلالة *halāla*, A woman married again with her first divorcer, after she had been divorced from her second husband.

P حلالي *halālī*, Fresh. Legitimate. Lawfulness. Freedom.

P حلام *halām*, A lamb.

A حلّام *hillām*, (v. n. 2 of حلم) Rendering meek and tractable. Enjoining meekness. *Hullām*, A kid taken from the mother's womb. A lamb. Blood shed with impunity.

A حلّان *hullān*, A lamb or kid taken from the belly of its dam. Whatever releases from an oath. The Lybian lizard. Blood shed with impunity.

A حلاواء *halāwāa*, Middle of the hind head.

A حلاوة *halāwat*, (v. n. of حلا for حلو) Being sweet. Pleasing, affording pleasure. Receiving good. Sweetness. Sweetness in the expression of the eye. Land which produces vegetables strong and thick. *Halāwat* or *hulāwat*, (pl. حلاوي *halāwa'*) The middle of the hind head. P حلاوت بخش *halāwat-bakhsh*, Sweetening, giving sweetness.

A حلاوي *halāwa'*, Sweetmeats. (pl. of حلاوة *halāwat* or *hulāwat*) Middles of hind heads. *Hulāwa'*, (pl. *halāwa'*) Middle of the hind head. A certain small tree and thorny plant.

A حلائب *halāsib*, Crowds, congregations. Uncle's children. (pl. of حلوبة *halūbat*) Animals which are milked. (pl. of حلبة *halbat*) Race-horses brought from different stables. Heats.

A حلائل *halāsil*, (pl. of حليلة *halīlat*) Wives.

A حلب *halb*, (v. n. of حلب) Making (one) the possessor of milch camels or sheep. Squatting on the hams. Flocking together. A milking. Allowing another to milk. *Halab*, (v. n. of حلب) Being black (the hair). A milking. New milk. A voluntary contribution to the state. Aleppo in Syria. حلب العناقيد *halabu'l sanākīd*, Wine. *Hulub*, (pl. of حلوبة *halūbat*) Animals which are milked. Black (animals). Intelligent (men).

A حلّب *hullab*, A milky plant of which hinds are fond, and which is used in tanning.

A حلبانة *halbānat*, (or حلباة) A milch-camel.

A حلبب *hulbub*, Name of a certain fruit.

A حلبة *halbat*, (pl. حلائب *halāsib*) Horses assembled from different stables for running races. A race-course. A heat. A single milking. Helpers, allies, flocking from all quarters. *Hulbat*, Fenugreek. The tragacanth. Gross darkness. A troop. *Halabat*, A horse-race. (pl. of حالب *hālib*) Milkers. *Hulubat*, Food made of dates and fenugreek, given to women in labour. A troop.

A حلبتان *halbatāni*, Morning and evening.

A حلبتور *halbatūr*, The Egyptian slain by Moses.

A حلبد *hilbid*, A dwarf camel.

A حلبدة *hulabidat*, A large sheep.

A حلبس *halbas*, A lion. Addicted, affixed. *Halbas* or *hulabis*, A gallant, brave man.

A حلبسة *halbasat*, A going away.

A حلبطة *hulabitat*, A hundred or more camels. One or two hundred sheep.

P حلبلاب *haliblāb* or *hiliblāb*, Ivy.

A حلبوب *hulbūb*, Black (hair).

A حلبوت *halabūt*, A milch camel for the saddle.

A حلبوتى ركبوتى *halabūta' rakabūta'*, (A she-camel) milch and fit for the saddle.

A حلبوس *hulbūs*, Many (sheep and camels).

A حلبي *halba'*, (A she-camel) fit for the saddle.

A حلبي ركبي *halba' rakba'*, (A camel) fit for milking and for the saddle.

P حلبي *halabī*, Belonging to a milch cow.

A حلبيّ *halabiy*, Native of Aleppo.

A حلّبيّ *hullabiy*, A leathern bottle tanned with the plant حلّب *hullab*.

A حلبيب *halbīb*, A species of hermodactyls.

A حلبيس *hilbīs*, Addicted to, affixed. A lion.

A حلّة *hallat*, A large reed-basket. An inn. A street, a quarter. *Hallat* or *hillat*, Form, fashion, mode. Intent, design, aim. *Hillat*, (v. n. of حلّ) Coming to the place of sacrifice (a victim). Putting off her weeds (a widow). Alighting and staying. Those who alight at a place, guests. The mode of alighting. Weakness, languor, debility. A number of dwellings, a hundred houses. (pl. حلال *hilāl*) An assembly, congregation, place of meeting. A certain thorny tree of which camels are fond. A piece of a mat made of split reeds. *Hullat*, (pl. حلل *hulal* and حلال *hilāl*) A cloak or covering for the body. Arms.

A حلت *halt*, (v. n. of حلت) Shaving (the head). Sorting (wool). Sitting long on horseback. Paying (a debt). Giving. Whipping. Voiding excrement.

A حلتيت *hiltīt*, (or حلتيث) Assafœtida.

A حلثب *halsab*, A miser. A proper name.

A حلج *halj*, (v. n. of حلج) Carding wool or cotton, separating cotton from the seed. Travelling during the night. Striking. Breaking wind. Rolling paste in an orbicular form. Proceeding step by step. Running towards the hen with extended wings (a cock). *Huluj*, A voracious eater.

A حلجة *haljat*, An interval, distance.

A حلجز *haljaz*, Covetous, a miser.

P حلحل *halhal*, The wild onion.

A حلحلة *halhalat*, (v. n. of حلحل Q) Moving (men) from their place. Calling out *hal* to a camel.

P حلداري *hal-dārī*, A collection for marriage licences; licences.

A حلز *halz*, (v. n. of حلز) Stripping bark off (a tree). Taking the hair off (a skin). *Haliz*, Diseased, ulcerated (liver).

A حلز *hilliz*, Of a bad disposition. Covetous. Short. An owl. A sort of plant.

A حلزة *hillazat*, Name of an insect.

A حلزون *halazūn*, A snail: a sea-shell: horn-beetle.

A حلس *hals*, (v. n. of حلس) Covering (a camel) with the saddle-cloth حلس *hils*. Raining incessantly. Receiving tithe in money instead of in kind. *Hals* or *hils*, A covenant, a treaty. *Hils*, A great man. *Hils* or *halas*, (pl. احلاس *ahlās*, حلوس *hulūs*, and حلسة *hilasat*) Dorsers put under saddles to save the camels' backs. Carpets and things similar laid under rich garments or furniture. *Hils* or *halis*, Name of the fourth gaming arrow. امّ حلس *ummu hilsin*, A she-ass. حلس بيته *hilsu baytihi*, One who does not stir from his house. *Halas*, (v. n. of حلس) Cleaving, adhering to. A saddle-mark on a camel's back of a different colour from the rest of his body. *Halis*, A strong brave man. Covetous, greedy.

A حلساء *halsāʼ*, A ewe black on the back with a mixture of red.

A حلسة *hilasat*, Camels' saddle-cloths.

A حلسمّ *hilsamm*, An avaricious man.

A حلط *halt*, (v. n. of حلط) Swearing. Contending obstinately. Being angry. Being quick, hasty (in any business).

A حلف *half*, *hilf*, or *halif*, (v. n. of حلف) Swearing. *Hilf*, (pl. احلاف *ahlāf*) A compact, confederacy. Faith in keeping agreements. A religious observer of compacts. *Halaf*, Name of a plant. *Halif*, A covenant confirmed by an oath. *Huluf*, (pl. of حلفاء *halfāʼ*) Clamorous (maids).

A حلفاء *halfāʼ*, A reed on which grapes and melons are hung to dry. Shameless and noisy (girl). A certain water-plant. *Hulafāʼ*, Name of a plant. (pl. of حليف *halīf*) Associates, confederates, friends.

A حلفة *halifat*, *halafat*, or *halfat*, A single one of the plant *halaf*.

A حلفس *hilafs*, Proud, and full of flesh, whose flesh appears prominent in different parts of his body.

A حلفق *hulfuk*, Any place for resting on, a sofa.

A حلق *halk*, (v. n. of حلق) Shaving (the head). Shearing (a goat). Filling a cistern. Measuring, guessing. Hurting one in the throat. Ill-luck. Name of a medicinal tree. (pl. حلوق *hulūk* and احلاق *ahlāk*) The throat, the gullet. حروف الحلق *hurūfu'l halk*, The guttural letters ا ح خ ع غ ه. *Hilk*, The royal signet. A silver ring without the bezel. A numerous flock. *Hulk*, Bereavement of a son. *Haluk*, (v. n. of حلق) Having an excoriated pizzle from covering often (a horse or ass). Camels branded with the mark حلقة *halakat*. *Halak*, *halik*, or *hilak*, (pl. of حلقة *halkat*) Rings. Circles. عقرا حلقا *ʻakran halkan*, May God afflict (her) with a sore throat!

A حلّق *hullak*, (pl. of حالق *hālik*) Teeming udders.

A حلقات *halakāt*, (pl. of حلقة *halkat*) Rings.

P حلق افشاري *halk-afshārī*, Pressure of the throat, strangulation.

A حلقام *halkām*, Half-ripe (date).

A حلقان *hulkān* or حلقانة, Dates two-thirds ripe.

A حلقة *halkat*, (pl. حلق *halak*, *halik*, *hilak*, or حلقات *halakāt*) A ring, hoop, circle. A rope. The ring or knocker of a door; the link of a coat of mail. A mark branded on a camel. A kind of fireworks. An assembly, circle of friends. A word used to children when belching. Arms. A vessel left empty after having been full. Fulness of a cistern or something less than fulness. P حلقهٔ آبگون *halkaʼi āb-gūn*, The sky. حلقه بر در زدن *halka bar dar zadan*, (حلقه بر سندان زدن *halka bar sindān zadan*, or حلقه زدن *halka zadan*) To knock at the door. حلقه بستن *halka bastan*, To form a circle. حلقه بگوش *halka ba gosh*, (also حلقه در گوش *halka dar gosh*) Having a ring in the ear (which formerly distinguished a slave). A servant, a slave. حلقهٔ دام *halkaʼi dām*, A horse-hair snare. A kind of veil. حلقهٔ دست بند *halkaʼi dast-band*, The horizon. The earth. حلقهٔ سفره *halkaʼi sufra*, Rings sewed round a leathern table-cover. حلقهٔ سيمين *halkaʼi sīmīn*, The full moon. Ice formed on a circular cistern. حلقه كردن *halka kardan*, To bend, curve, form into a ring, loop, or link. حلقهٔ نوش *halkaʼi nosh*, The lip. The mouth. A انتزعت حلقته *intazaʻtu halkatahu*, I outstripped him. *Hilkat*, A mode of shaving. *Halakat*, (pl. of حالق *hālik*) Shavers.

P حلقچی *halkachī*, A kind of sweetmeat.

A حلقد *hilkid*, Of a bad disposition. Heavy, dull, torpid.

A حلقمة *halkamat*, The cutting (another's) throat.

A حلقنة *halkanat*, (v. n. of حلقن Q) Being two-thirds ripe (dates).

A حلقوم *hulkūm*, (pl. حلاقيم *halākīm*) The throat, gullet, windpipe.

P حلقه بگوشي *halka ba goshī*, Servitude.

P حلقه چين *halka-chīn*, A kind of sweetmeat.

P حلقه دار *halka-dār*, (An ear) having a ring, *i.e.* attentive and obedient.

P حلقه زن *halka-zan*, One who raps at the door. A schoolmaster, preceptor.

P حلقهوار *halkawār*, Like a ring.

A حلقىّ *halkīy*, Guttural. حرف حلقي *harfi halkī*, A guttural letter (of which there are six).

A حلقيّة *halkīyat*, Gutturality. *Halakīyat*, A she-ass much followed by the males, and diseased in the uterus thereby.

A حلك *halak*, (v. n. of حلك) Being very black. (pl. احلاك *ahlāk*) Blackness.

A حلكاء *halkāʼ*, A worm that burrows in the sand. *Hulkāʼ*, *halkāʼ*, *halakāʼ*, or *hulakāʼ*, A sort of covering or veil.

P حلكاري *halkārī*, Gilding.

A حلكة *hulkat*, Intense blackness. Obscurity, ambiguity. Dumbness. A certain animalcule that burrows in the sand. A sort of covering or veil.

A حلكلك *hulakhlik*, Black, pitchy.

A حلكم *halkam* or *hulkum*, Black.

A حلكمة *halkamat*, Jettiness (of a raven).

A حلكوك *hala* or *hulkūk*, (A thing) very black.

A حلكّى *hulukkaʼ*, A sort of covering or veil.

A حلل *halal*, (v. n. of حلّ) Descending, alighting. Weakness in the hough or pastern. A pain in the haunch-bones or knees. Lankness of hips. *Hulal*, (pl. of حلّة *hullat*) Cloaks. Striped Arabian garments. Habits of paradise.

A حلّل *hullal*, (pl. of حالّ *hāll*) Those who alight and stay.

A حلم *halm*, (v. n. of حلم) Picking worms out of a hide, or tikes off a camel. *Hilm*, (v. n. of حلم) Being mild, gentle, clement. (pl. احلام *ahlām* and حلوم *hulūm*) Understanding. Mildness, meekness, clemency, long-suffering. ذو الحلم *zū'l hilm*, Endued with clemency, meek. A proper name. *Hulm*, (pl. احلام *ahlām*) A dream. *Hulm* or *hulum*, (v. n. of حلم) Dreaming in sleep, seeing in sleep. Nocturnal pollution. *Halam*, (v. n. of حلم) Being corroded, fretted by worms (a hide). Being infested by tikes (a camel). The tike. *Halim*, Full of tikes (a camel). *Hulum*, A dream.

A حلماء *hulamāʼ*, (pl. of حليم *halīm*) Mild, gentle, meek, clement.

A حلمة *halamat*, (pl. حلم *halam*) A single tike; another worm which infests a hide. The nipple. Blood shed with impunity. The prickly plant سعدان *saʻdān*. Name of another plant. *Halimat*, Infested by tikes (female kid).

A حلميّة *hilmīyat*, Mildness, gentleness.

A حلو *halw*, (v. n. of حلا for حلو) Being sweet, pleasant (to the eye, mind, or taste). Receiving good. Giving something sweet. Sweetening. Decorating (a woman) with jewels. *Hilw*, A certain small implement used in weaving. *Hulw*, (v. n. of حلا for حلو) Giving something by way of recompense or douceur above the hire. Sweet. Pleasant, agreeable. *Hulw*, (or حلوّ *hulūw*) (v. n. of حلا for حلو) Giving in marriage (a daughter or sister) with a fixed dowry on condition that the husband return to the giver a certain part of the dowry.

A حلوّ *halūw*, Sweet, pleasant, agreeable.

A حلوء *halūs*, Antimony or a similar substance brayed betwixt two stones to be applied as a collyrium to the eye. A stone rubbed upon the eye to remove bleariness. *Hulūs*, (v. n. of حلأ) Rubbing one stone upon another.

A حلواء *halwās*, Any kind of sweet cake or paste made with flour. Sweetmeats. The middle of the hind head. P حلوائ بيدود *halwāsi bī dūd*, An esteemed kind of confection. حلوائ رشته *halwāsi rishta*, A kind of vermicelli.

A حلوان *hulwān*, (v. n. of حلا for حلو) Being sweet, pleasing, agreeable. Giving (a daughter or sister) in marriage on condition that the husband refund to him a certain part of the dowry. Claiming, and receiving the marriage-portion of a daughter (due on the death of her husband or in case of a divorce). Giving something above the stipulated hire. The fee of a broker. A woman's dowry; also what is given her when divorced. A present to a soothsayer. A bribe, douceur, sweetener.

A حلواني *halwānīy*, A confectioner. *Hulwānīy*, Sweet.

P حلوائي *halwāsī*, A confectioner.

A حلوب *halūb*, One who milks. A hot day that draws the sweat. (An animal) milked. *Hulūb*, (v. n. of حلب) Flocking together.

A حلوبة *halūbat*, (pl. حلائب *halāsib* and حلب *hulub*) An animal milked, milch. One milked.

A حلوة *halūwat*, (fem.) Very sweet-tempered.

A حلوج *halūj*, Flashing (cloud).

A حلوس *hulūs*, (pl. of حلس *hils*) Saddle-cloths or things put on (a camel's) back to prevent galling. Carpets laid under rich furniture.

A حلوق *hulūk*, (pl. of حلق *halk*) Throats, gullets. حلوق الارض *hulūku'l arz*, The throats of the earth; *i.e.* its rivers, valleys, and straits.

A حلوكة *hulūkat*, (v. n. of حلك) Being very black.

A حلول *hulūl*, (v. n. of حلّ) Descending, alighting, remaining, resting in a place. Lighting upon (as anger). Arriving at the place of sacrifice (a victim). Putting off her weeds (a widow). Being due (a debt). Transmigration. (pl. of حالّ *hāll*) Those who alight and stay.

A حلوليّة *halūlīyat*, Name of a sect.

A حلوم *hulūm*, (pl. of حلم *hilm*) Clemencies.

A حلوي *halwa'* Confectionery made of honey or sugar, sweetmeats. *Hulwa'*, Sweet (thing).

A حلويّات *halwīyāt* or *hulwīyāt*, Sweetmeats.

A حلي *haly*, (v. n. of حلي) Decorating (herself) with jewels and other ornaments. Pleasing to the mind or eye. An ornament of a sword, especially on the hilt or sheath. (pl. حلِيّ *hulīy*) Jewels, female metallic ornaments. P حلي آب *halyi āb*, The rippling of water. A *Hila'* or *hula'*, (pl. of حلية *hilyat* or *hulyat*) The ornaments of a sword. External forms or descriptions of a man.

A حليّ *halīy*, (pl. احلية *ahliyat*) A white thistle, hard, dry, and beginning to wither. Sweet in the mouth (a word). *Hulīy*, (pl. of حلي *haly*) Women's ornaments or trinkets.

A حليّا *hulayya'*, A kind of plant and food.

A حليب *halīb*, New milk. Sweet milk. Fresh blood. Date-wine.

A حلية *halyat*, A jewel or a woman's metallic ornament. Name of a place in Yaman abounding in lions. *Hilyat*, (pl. حلى *hula'* or *hila'*) An ornament (of a sword, especially on the hilt and sheath). The external form, bearing, or quality of a man.

A حليّة *halīyat*, A woman dressed in her ornaments. Perfectly sweet-tempered (she-camel).

A حلّيّة *hillīyat*, Lawfulness.

A حليت *halīt*, Frost, hoar-frost. Hail.

A حلّيت *hillīt*, Assafœtida.

A حليج *halīj*, Carded or dressed (cotton).

A حليجة *halījat*, Milk, in which dates have been dissolved. Butter sticking to the churn. Butter squeezed out of a leathern bottle. Cream or butter on which milk is poured.

A حليف *halīf*, (pl. حلفاء *hulafās*) A confederate, partner, conspirator. Sharp-pointed (spear). Frisky (horse). حليف افلاس *halīfi iflās*, Poor. حليف اللسان *halīfu'l lisān*, Eloquent.

A حليفة *halīfat*, Name of a place.

P حليفه *hulayfa*, Name of a medicinal seed.

A حليق *halīk*, Shaved (on the head or chin). Shaven (beard).

A حليل *halīl*, A husband. A wife. (A man or woman) alighted at a place. A lawful thing.

A حليلة *halīlat*, A wife.

A حليم *halīm*, (pl. حلماء *hulamās* and احلام *ahlām*) Mild, meek, gentle, affable, clement. A title of God. A fat animal. Fat, grease. A kind of food dressed in the Muharram. Infested with tikes.

A حليمة *halīmat*, Name of Muhammad's nurse.

A حليمو *halīmū*, Garden-sorrel.

A حم *ham*, (pl. احماء *ahmās*) A husband's or wife's father or brother. A wife's relation.

A حمّ *hamm*, (v. n. of حمّ) Making hot (water). Heating (a furnace). Kindling. Exciting, encouraging, hastening (a departure). Tending towards, designing, purposing. Determining, defining. Decreeing. Measuring. Rendering anxious. Melting the fat from a sheep's tail. That which remains (of a sheep's tail) after the fat of it has been melted away. Anxiety, care. Escape. ما له حمّ و لا سمّ *mā lahu hammun wa lā sammun*, (or *humm wa summ*) He has neither little nor much. ما لي منه حمّ *mā lī minhu hammun*, I cannot avoid it. *Humm*, (pl. حمائم *hamāsim*) The best part of any thing. Mid-day heat. A choice camel. (pl. of احمّ *ahamm*) Black. (pl. of حمّاء *hammās*) Podices.

A حمء *hams*, (v. n. of حمأ) Cleaning (a well). Mixing with black mud (water), and becoming turbid. Becoming angry. The heat of the sun. (pl. احماء *ahmās*) The father or brother of a husband or wife. A wife's relation.

A حمأ *hamas*, (v. n. of حمئ) Mixing with black and fetid mud and becoming turbid (water). Being angry. Black, thin, stinking mud.

A حما *hama'*, A husband's father or brother.

A حماء *himās*, (v. n. 3 of حمى) Prohibiting, commanding to abstain. Repelling, guarding, defending. Paying attention (to a guest). A thing guarded and inaccessible (as pasture-land). حماءً لك *himāsan laka*, Health to you! I sacrifice myself for you.

A حمّاء *hammās*, (pl. حمّ *humm*) Podex. شفة حمّاء *shafat hammās*, A black lip.

A حمأة *hamsat*, Thin, fetid, black mud. A sort of plant.

A حماة *hamāt*, A wife's or husband's mother. (pl. حموات *hamawāt*) The calf of the leg. Hamath in Syria. *Humāt*, (pl. of حامي) Protectors.

A حمات *humāt*, (pl. of حمة) Venoms. Stings.

A حماتان *hamātāni*, Two nerves in a horse's leg.

A حماحم *hamāhim*, A kind of garden-mint. *Humāhim*, Name of one of the kings of Himyar.

A حماد *hamādi*, (Interjec. of applause) Bravo!

A حمّاد *hammād*, A great and frequent praiser.

A حماديٰ *humāda'*, (pl. حماديات *humādayāt*) End. حماداك *humādāka*, Your ultimate object.

A حماذيّ *humāzīy*, Intense heat.

A حمار *himār*, (pl. احمرة *ahmirat*, حمر *humur*, حمير *hamīr*, حمور *humūr*, حمرات *humurāt*, and محموراء *mahmūrās*) A male ass. The wild ass. A board upon which swords are polished. A piece of wood in the fore part of a camel's saddle. A kind of fetter. حمار الحائط *himāru'l hāsit*, The game of leap-frog. حمار قبّان *himāri kabbān*, An insect resembling a locust without wings. حمار وحشي *himāri wahshī*, The wild ass. حمار ابن مالك *himār ibn mālik*, Name of a man who maintained a consistent profession of religion for forty years; until having lost his ten sons, who were killed by a thunder-storm whilst hunting, he apostatized from the faith, saying, I will not worship Him who hath done this to my sons: hence the proverb, أكفر من حمار *akfar min himār*, More infidel than Himār. ذو الحمار الاسود *zū'l himāri'l aswad*, Name of Ansī, a pseudoprophet.

A حمّار *hammār*, An ass-driver.

A حماران *himārāni*, (dual) Two stones placed in an upright position, across which a third is laid for drying the new cheese called اقط *akit* upon. Name of two stars in the constellation Cancer.

A حمارة *himārat*, (pl. حمائر *hamāsir*) A female ass. A large stone. Stones erected round a hunter's lurking-place. The upper part (of the foot, the instep). A piece of wood in a camel-litter. A broad stone placed over a niche in a grave.

A حمّارة *hammārat*, A sluggish beast of burden.

A mean pack-horse. Ass-drivers.

A حمارّة *hamārrat*, (poet. *hamārat*) The hottest part of the summer.

A حمارس *humāris*, Strong. Bold, dauntless, brave. A lion.

A حماريّ *himāriy*, Asinine. Shared, common to many.

A حماريّة *himāriyat*. See فريضة مشتركة.

A حمازة *hamāzat*, (v. n. of حمز) Being strong, stout, firm. Tartness, sharpness, pungency.

A حماسة *hamāsat*, Valour, bravery. Epos, epic poetry. The anthology of the ancient Arabian poets; also modern poetry (after the Arabians became mixed with strangers).

A حماش *himāsh*, (pl. of حمش) Slender (legs).

A حمّاض *hummāz*, Wild sorrel. حمّاض الاترج *hummāzu'l utrujj*, Orange-juice. حمّاض الارنب *hummāzu'l arnab*, Dodder. حمّاض الامير *hummāzu'l amīr*, A small creeping plant. حمّاض البقر *hummāzu'l bakir*, Wood-sorrel. P حمّاض بستاني *hummāzi bustānī*, (A نهريّ *nahriy*) Garden-sorrel.

A حماط *hamāt*, Dry grass, hay in which lurks a snake. (pl. of حماطة *hamātat*) Kinds of figs.

A حماطة *hamātat*, Dry herbage. A secret of the heart. The black blood of the heart. A heat or roughness of the throat. Straw of millet. (pl. حماط *hamāt*) A tree resembling the fig, most grateful to snakes. The mountain-fig; the small black fig.

A حماطيط *hamātīt*, (pl. of حمطاط *himtāt* and حمطوط *humtūt*) Worms found in grass.

A حماق *himāk*, (v. n. 3 of حمق) Joining, countenancing in folly. Foolish (persons). *Humāk* or *hamāk*, Small-pox, measles.

A حماقة *hamākat*, (v. n. of حمق) Being silly. Being flat and dull (a market). Folly, stupidity.

A حماقى *hamāka'* or *humāka'*, (pl. of احمق *ahmak*) Fools. Foolish women.

A حماقيس *hamākīs*, Misfortunes, ills.

A حمال *himāl*, (pl. حمل *humul*) A fine exacted from a people. (pl. of حمل *haml*) Fœtuses in the womb. (pl. of حمل *haml* or *himl*) Fruits of trees.

A حمّال *hammāl*, (pl. حمّالون *hammālūn*) A porter, carrier of burdens. *Himmāl*, (v. n. 2 of حمل irregularly formed) Imposing a burden.

A حمالة *hamālat*, (v. n. of حمل) Taking upon one's self, undertaking for. Shewing anger. Being mild and patient. Whatever any one undertakes for. (pl. حمل *humul*) Tribute exacted from the people. A mulct, a fine. *Himālat*, (pl. حمائل *hamāʼil*) A sword-belt. The vocation of a porter.

A حماليج *hamālīj*, (pl. of حملوج *humlūj*) Gold smiths' bellows. Cows' horns.

A حماليق *hamālīk*, (pl. of حملاق) Internal parts of the eyelashes which they anoint with antimony.

P حمام *hamām*, A warm bath.

A حمام *hamām*, A dove, a turtle: any bird with a ruff. *Himām*, (v. n. 3 of حمّ) Decreeing death. Decree. Destiny. Death. (pl. of حمّة *hummat*) Decrees. *Humām*, The camel fever. A prince, a noble. Feverish (camel).

A حمّام *hammām*, (pl. حمّامات) A warm bath.

A حماما *hamāmā*, Stone-parsley, amomum.

A حمامات *hamāmāt*, (pl. of حمام) Ringdoves.

A حمّامات *hammāmāt*, (pl. of حمّام) Warm baths.

A حمامة *hamāmat*, (pl. حمائم *hamāʼim*) One dove. The area of a palace neat and clean. A pulley. A ring on a door. The brisket of a horse. The middle of the breast. A fair woman. Choice camels or sheep. رجل الحمامة *rijlu'l hamāmat*, (Dove's foot) The herb شنجار *shinjār* (melilot).

A حمّاميّ *hammāmīy*, A bagnio-keeper, a keeper of a warm bath.

A حماية *himāyat*, (v. n. of حمي) Protecting, defending. Forbidding, debarring. Guardianship. Patronage, countenance, support, defence, protection. P حمايت دادن *himāyat dādan*, To give protection, to defend. To patronize.

P حمايتگر *himāyatgar*, Protective: a protector.

A حمائد *hamāʼid*, (pl. of حميدة *hamīdat*) Laudable actions or qualities.

A حمائر *hamāʼir*, (pl. of حمارة *himārat*) She-asses. Broad stones laid over a grave.

A حمائص *hamāʼis*, (pl. of حميصة) Stolen sheep.

A حمائل *hamāʼil*, (pl. of حمالة *himālat*) Shoulder sword-belts. A small Kur'ān suspended from the neck as a preservative. Veins in the root or skin of the penis. A necklace of flowers. P حمائل شمشير *hamāʼili shamshīr*, A sword-belt. A حمائل فلك *hamāʼili falak*, The inclination of the sphere.

P حمائلي *hamāʼilī*, A planet's elliptical motion.

A حمائم *hamāʼim*, (pl. of حمّ *humm*) Best parts of things. Mid-day heats. (pl. of حمامة *hamāmat*) Pigeons, doves. (pl. of حميمة *hamīmat*) Warm baths. Noble she-camels.

A حمة *hamat*, A species of eagle. *Humat*, (pl. حمات *humāt* and حمى *huma'*) The venom of a scorpion. A sting. Intense cold. حمة العقرب *humatu'l ʻakrab*, (Scorpion's sting) Name of a sword.

A حمّة *hammat*, A hot medicinal spring; thermal water. *Himmat*, Sweat. Death. *Hummat*, (pl. حمم *humam* and حمام *himām*) Warmth, intense heat. Fever. Blackness. A colour between chesnut and black. A scorpion's venom. حمّة الفراق *hummatu'l firāk*, The decree of Providence, death.

A حمت *hamt*, (v. n. of حمت) Being hot (the weather). Pouring out. Hot, sultry (day). Very sweet (date). *Hamat*, (v. n. of حمت) Becoming rotten (a nut). *Humut*, (pl. of حميت *hamīt*) Leathern hairless bottles (for keeping butter and honey).

A حمحام *hamhāmi*, Nothing was left.

A حمحم *himhim* or *humhum*, Very black. A kind of bird. *Humhum*, Borage. A bramble.

A حمحمة *hamhamat*, (v. n. of حمحم Q) Neighing (as a horse when he sees his fodder). Making a noise lower than neighing. The peculiar sound made by a bull at rutting time. *Himhimat* or *humhumat*, Ox-tongue (a plant).

A حمد *hamd*, (v. n. of حمد) Praising. Returning thanks to God, thankfully acknowledging his benefits. Finding a laudable country. Seeking to please, or to discharge a debt. Praise. Praised, commendable (man or country). حمد حميد اكرم *hamdi hamīdi akram*, Praise (to God) worthy of praise. لله الحمد *li'llāhi'l hamd*, (الحمد لله *al hamdu li'llāh*) Praised be God (to which they sometimes add ربّ العالمين *rabbi'l ʻālamīn*, Lord of the universe). حمداً لله *hamdan li'llāh*, By the grace or favour of God. *Hamad*, (v. n. of حمد) Being angry.

P حمدان *himdān*, (or حمدون *hamdūn*) Penis.

A حمدة *hamdat*, Commendable (woman). *Hamadat*, The crackling sound of fire. *Humadat*, A fulsome, unblushing flatterer, extremely laudatory.

A حمدلة *hamdalat*, (v. n. of حمدل Q) Pronouncing the formula الحمد لله *al hamdu li'llāh*, Praise be to God!

A حمدونة *hamdūnat*, Hārūn Arrashīd's daughter.

P حمدونه *hamdūna*, An ape, baboon.

A حمر *hamr* (v. n. of حمر) Paring (the inside of a thong), and making it supple with grease. Skinning (a sheep). Shaving (the head). Excoriation. حمر الارض *hamru'l arz*, The earthworm. *Humr*, (pl. of احمر *ahmar*) Red. Unarmed (men). (pl. of حمار *himār*) Asses. *Hamar*, (v. n. of حمر) Stinking from eating too much barley (the mouth of a horse). Burning (with rage). Becoming as stupid as an ass from repletion. *Humar*, Tamarinds. Bitumen of Judea. (pl. of حمرة *humrat*) Rednesses. *Humar* (or حمّر *hummar*) A small red-headed bird. *Humur*, (pl. of حمار *himār*) Asses. حمرالوحش *humuru'l wahsh*, Wild asses.

A حمرّ *himirr*, Violent rain. The hottest part of summer. The wickedness of man.

A حمراء *hamrāʼ*, (fem. of احمر *ahmar*) Red. New. Recent. White, fair (woman). Barbarian (not Arabian). A barren season. Mid-day heat.

A حمرات *humurāt*, (pl. of حمار *himār*) Asses.

A حمران *humrān*, (pl. of احمر) Red. Unarmed.

A حمراويّ *hamrāwiy*, Belonging to a red or fair-complexioned female (حمراء *hamrāʼ*).

A حمرة *humrat*, Redness. A kind of tree of which asses are fond. Pestilential carbuncle. Erysipelas. ذو حمرة *zū humrat*, A sweet date.

A حمّرة *hummarat*, A single bird of the species حمّر *hummar*. ابن لسان الحمّرة *ibn lisāni'l hummarat*, Name of a celebrated preacher and genealogist.

A حمردة *himridat*, The slime of a cistern.

A حمرقة *himrakat*, Wool.

A حمز *hamz*, (v. n. of حمز) Sharpening. Grasping, seizing, griping. Biting the tongue (anything bitter or sour). Acritude, bitterness of taste.

P حمز *humz*, The tamarind.

A حمزة *hamzat*, The herb rocket. Name of a brave man, uncle to Muhammad. A lion.

A حمس *hams*, (v. n. of حمس) Frying (meat). Provoking, enraging. A noise. A gentle noise of a camel's saddle. *Hums*, (pl. of احمس *ahmas*) Strong, bold, unwavering. Hard places. Barren (years). Name of the tribes Kuraysh, Kinānat, and Jadīlat (from their constancy in religion). *Hamas*, (v. n. of حمس) Being stedfast, immoveable (in the faith and in battle). (pl. of حمسة *hamasat*) Marine animals; tortoises. *Hamis*, Strong, bold, hard, firm, unblenching (in the faith and in battle).

A حمساء *hamsā*, The Kaaba. Barren (year).

A حمسة *humsat*, Honour, reputation. *Hamasat*, (pl. حمس *hamas*) A marine animal, turtle.

A حمش *hamsh*, (v. n. of حمش) Collecting, bringing together. Inflaming with rage. Driving, pursuing in anger. Being angry. Waxing fierce (evil). Slender-shanked. (pl. حماش *himāsh*) Slender (leg). *Hamsh* or *hamash*, (v. n. of حمش) Having slender legs. *Hamish* or *hamsh*, Slender (bow-string). Slender-shanked.

A حمشة *hamshat*, (v. n. of حمش) Being angry. *Himshat*, Anger, indignation. *Hamishat* or *hamshat*, Fleshless (gum).

A حمص *hams*, (v. n. of حمص) Subsiding (a swelling). Ceasing to vibrate (a swing). Easily extracting a mote from the eye. Moving to and fro (a child in a swing without any one setting it in motion). Passing off from a horse (water). *Hims*, Name of a famous town in Syria (Emessa).

A حمّص *himmas* or *himmis*, Vetchlings, chiches.

A حمصيص *hamasīs*, (or حمّصيص *hammasīs*) A sour kind of vegetable growing in sandy places.

A حمض *hamz*, (v. n. of حمض) Being acid. Feeding on a salt, bitter plant (a camel). Loathing. Desiring. (pl. حموض *humūz*) A salt, acrid, bitter plant. Sorrel. *Humuz*, (pl. of حميض *hamīz*) Lands abounding in salt and bitter herbs.

A حمضة *hamzat*, Desire. Name of a family.

A حمضمض *humuzmuz*, The herb stork-bill.

A حمضيّة *hamzīyat*, Camels feeding constantly on the bitter herbs called حمض *hamz*.

A حمضيض *hamzīz*, Wild sorrel.

A حمط *hamt*, (v. n. of حمط) Peeling.

A حمطاط *himtāt*, (pl. حماطيط *hamātīt*) A worm found in grass.

A حمطرة *hamtarat*, (v. n. of حمطر Q) Filling (a leathern bottle). Stringing (a bow).

A حمطوط *humtūt*, (pl. حماطيط *hamātīt*) A worm found in grass.

A حمطيط *hamtīt*, A certain plant. A serpent. A caterpillar. A cankerworm.

A حمظ *hamz*, The act of pressing, squeezing.

A حمظل *hamzal*, The bitter purging apple.

A حمظلة *hamzalat*, A gathering of colocynths.

A حمق *humk* or *humuk*, (v. n. of حمق) Being foolish. Foolishness, want of understanding. Wine. حمق و غباوت *humk u ghabāwat*, Folly and stupidity. *Hamak*, Fluor albus. *Hamik*, A fool. Thin-bearded. *Humuk*, (pl. of احمق *ahmak*) Fools.

A حمقاء *hamkā*, (fem. of احمق *ahmak*) Foolish. البقلة الحمقاء *al baklatu'l hamkā*, Purslain. *Humakā*, (pl. of حمق *hamik*) Blockheads, fools.

A حمقى *hamka'*, (pl. of حمق *hamik*) Fools.

A حمقيق *himkīk*, A sort of plant. *Hamakīk*, Small-pox or measles.

A حمك *hamk*, (v. n. of حمك) Going in the capacity of a guide. *Hamak*, Lice, nits. A minute thing. The young of the katā or ostrich. Root, origin, nature. The canaille. A lamb. A guide through the desert. A colt. Boys. Pismires.

A حمكة *hamakat*, Short, contemptible (woman).

A حمل *hamala*, (fut. يحمل *yahmilu*) He bare.

A حمل *haml*, (v. n. of حمل) Carrying. Being pregnant (a woman). Bearing fruit (a tree). Instigating, urging, inducing. (pl. حمال *himāl* and احمال *ahmāl*) Fruit borne in the womb, or on a tree. P حمل كردن *haml kardan*, To impose a burden, to load. To charge, impute, ascribe, accuse. وضع حمل كردن *wazʿi haml kardan*, To lay down a load. To be delivered of a child. حمل گرفتن *haml giriftan*, To conceive, to become pregnant. A *Haml* or *himl*, (pl. احمال *ahmāl*, حمول *humūl*, and حمال *himāl*) The fruit of a tree. *Himl*, (v. n. of حمل) Lifting, taking up a burden on the head or back. Sustaining. Bearing patiently. (pl. احمال *ahmāl*) A load. Baggage. *Himl* or *haml*, (pl. حمول *humūl*) A camel which bears the women's litter هودج *hawdaj*: also the litter itself. *Hamal*, (pl. حملان *humlān* and احمال *ahmāl*) A full-grown lamb. The sign Aries. A cloud fraught with rain. لسان الحمل *lisānu'l hamal*, Lamb's tongue (an herb). *Humul*, (pl. of حمالة *hamālat*) Fines exacted from the people.

A حملاج *himlāj*, The bellows of a goldsmith. A cow's horn.

A حملاق *himlāk* or *humlāk*, (pl. حماليق *hamālīk*) The inner part of the eyelash or red part of the eyelid which they anoint with collyrium. The white of the eye.

A حملان *humlān*, (v. n. of حمل) Carrying. A beast of burden employed in carrying provisions. A wash or any thing similar with which base coin is overlaid. (pl. of حمل *hamal*) Full-grown lambs.

A حملة *hamlat*, (v. n. of حمل) Making an assault. Stirring up war. An attack, charge, assault. P حمله كردن *hamla kardan*, To charge. A *Himlat*, A burden, freight, or load of goods. *Humlat* or *himlat*, A going or a transporting from place to place. *Hamalat*, (pl. of حامل *hāmil*) Carriers, bearers.

A حملجة *hamlajat*, A twisting (a rope) firmly.

A حملقة *hamlakat*, A looking stedfastly, staring.

A حملوج *humlūj*, (pl. حماليج *hamālīj*) A goldsmith's bellows. A cow's horn.

A حملوق *humlūk*, The inner part of the eyelash, which they anoint with soorma. White of the eye.

A حمليّ *hamlīy*, Categorical.

A حمم *hamam*, (v. n. of حمم) Being black. Becoming white. Being charred (a burning coal or billet). Becoming heated (water). Blackness. *Humam*, (pl. of حمّة *hummat*) Decrees. Coals. Ashes.

A حممة *humamat*, Coal.

A حمن *hamn*, The smaller species of tike.

A حمنان *hamnān*, The smaller species of tike. A certain small-stoned grape growing at Taif. A small grape-stone found between larger grape-stones.

A حمو *hamw*, Heat. *Hamū* or *hamw*, A husband's or wife's father or brother. A wife's relation. *Humaw*, The venom of a scorpion.

A حموّ *humūw*, (v. n. of حمي) Being hot (a day, or furnace, or iron).

A حموات *hamawāt*, (pl. of حماة *hamāt*) Mothers-in-law. The calves of the legs.

A حموة *hamwat*, (v. n. of حمي) Defending, guarding. *Himwat*, (v. n. of حمي) Commanding, enjoining to abstain from.

A حموّة *humūwat*, A paroxysm of pain.

A حمّوج *hammūj*, A little fawn.

A حمود *hamūd*, Praised, lauded.

A حمور *humūr*, (pl. of حمار *himār*) Asses.

A حموز لما حمزة *hamūz limā hamazahu*, One who keeps fast hold of what he has got.

A حموشة *humūshat*, Thinness, slenderness (of leg).

A حموص *humūs*, (v. n. of حمص) Subsiding (a swelling, or boiling pot). Ceasing to vibrate (a pendulum or swing). Extracting easily a mote from the eye).

A حموض *humūz*, (v. n. of حمض) Feeding on salt and bitter plants (a camel). (pl. of حمض *hamz*) Salt, bitter plants.

A حموضة *humūzat*, (v. n. of حمض) Being acid. The pulp of an orange. Acidity, acridity, bitterness.

A حمّوقة *hammūkat*, An excessive, arrant fool.

A حمول *hamūl*, A carrier. Mild, gentle. One who bears injuries with patience. *Humūl*, (pl. of حمل *haml* or *himl*) Camels which carry women in litters called هودج *hawdaj*; the litters themselves. (pl. of حمل *haml* or *himl*) Fruits of trees.

A حمولة *hamūlat*, A beast of burthen. A load. *Humūlat*, Horse or camel-loads.

A حمئ *hamiʾ*, Muddy. حمئ العين *hamiʾu'l ʿayn*, One who looks much with a malignant eye.

A حمي *hamy*, (v. n. of حمي) Protecting, defending, guarding. Forbidding, debarring. Waxing hot and angry. Becoming hot (a day, furnace, or iron nail). Heat. *Hama'*, Verily, truly, indeed. *Hima'*, (v. n. of حمي) Being hot and sweating (a horse). (pl. احماء *ahmā*) Inaccessible, forbidden. Guarded. حمي الخلافة *hima'l khilāfat*, Name of Baghdād. *Huma'*, (pl. of حمة *humat*) The poisons of scorpions' stings.

A حمّى *humma'*, (pl. حمّيات *hummayāt*) Fever.

A حميّ *hamīy*, Sick and debarred from every thing hurtful. Guarded, protected. Impatient of insult or injury. Hot, boiling, fervent. حميّ الانف *hamīyu'l anf*, Sensitive, disposed to resent an insult. *Humīy*, (v. n. of حمى) Being hot (sun or fire).

A حميّا *humayya'*, Fierceness of anger. Beginning of rage. Strength of wine, its inebriating and maddening property. The fierceness or intenseness of any thing. The flower or sprightliness of youth.

A حميّات *hummayāt*, Fevers.

A حمياطى *himyāṭa'*, A name of Muhammad.

A حمية *himyat* (v. n. of حمى) Prohibiting, forbidding, interdicting. Guarded, inaccessible thing.

A حميّة *hamīyat*, (v. n. of حمى), Defending, guarding. Modestly abstaining. A sense of honour.

A حميت *hamīt*, Extreme (rage). (pl. حمت *humut*) A small leathern bottle, or one without hair (for keeping milk in). A leathern bottle rubbed over with a coating of inspissated juice. Very sweet (date). Any thing firm and strong.

A حميحق *humayḥiḳ*, A white sort of bird.

A حميد *hamīd*, Praised. Laudable. Glorious. اوصاف حميده *awṣāfi hamīda*, Laudable qualities.

A حمير *hamīr*, A leathern strap or thong with which they fasten loads. (pl. of حمار *himār*) Asses. *Himyar*, Name of a place west of Sanāa. Name of the father of a tribe.

A حميراء *humayrā,*, Whitish (woman). Melilot. Name of Ayisha. Name of a place near Madīna.

A حميرة *hamīrat*, A thong for fastening saddles.

A حميريّ *himyarīy*, Of the tribe of Himyar.

A حميريّة *himyarīyat*, The Himyaritic Arabic.

A حميز *hamīz*, Strong, firm. حميز الفؤاد *hamīzu'l fu,ād*, Light, cheerful, brisk: ingenious, witty.

A حميس *hamīs*, Bold, brave, intrepid. Strong, vehement. An oven.

A حميسة *hamīsat*, Any thing fried.

A حميش *hamīsh*, Fat.

A حميصة *hamīṣat*, (pl. حمائص) Stolen sheep.

A حميض *hamīz*, (pl. حمض *humuz*) Land abounding in salt and bitter herbs.

A حميق *hamīḳ*, Name of a plant.

A حميقاء *humaykā,*, (or حميقى) Small-pox.

A حمّيقة *hummaykat*, An arrant fool.

A حميقيق *humaykīḳ*, A white kind of bird.

A حميل *hamīl*, Carried. A bastard. A stranger. A surety. Sticks, carried down by the stream. A child in its mother's belly when she is brought from an idolatrous country. A foundling reared by strangers. The bed of a torrent. A shoe-latchet. Black and withered (plants ثمام *sumām* and وشيج *washīj*). A slave brought young from abroad.

A حميلة *hamīlat*, Domestics, those maintained. (pl. حمائل *hamā,il*) A sword-belt, a baldrick.

A حميم *hamīm*, Warm water. Cold water. A hot-bath. The heat of summer. Summer rains, the rainy season. Afflicted with fever. Sweat. (pl. احمّاء *ahimmā,*) A relation, especially in your care.

A حميمات *humaymāt*, A live coal.

A حميمة *hamīmat*, (pl. حمائم *hamā,im*) The choicest part of property. Hot water or milk.

A حنّ *hanna*, (fut. يحنّ *yahinnu*) He pitied.

A حنّ *hann*, (v. n. of حنّ) Averting, withholding. Commiseration, tenderness, pity. *Hinn*, A certain tribe of demons. Dogs black and dumb. The meanest and feeblest of the demon race: also their dogs. A creature between a demon and a man.

A حنوء *hanu,*, (v. n. of حنأ) Being green (a spot), having thick and luxuriant herbage. Lying with.

A حناء *hanā,*, The act of bending. *Hinā,*, Lust.

A حنّاء *hinnā,*, (pl. حنآن *hun,ān*) The dyeing, colouring shrub henna (Lawsonia inermis). الحنّاء الاحمر *al hinnā,u'l ahmar*, The fruit of the wild strawberry. حنّاء الغولة *hinnā,u'l ghūlat*, Borage. حنّاء قريش *hinnā,i ḳarīsh*, Moss growing upon stones, lichen. حنّاءُ مجنون *hinnā,i majnūn*, Woad.

A حنّاءة *hinnā,at*, A well (especially clean).

A حنابج *hanābij*, Small ants. *Hunābij*, Large-bodied, fleshy.

A حنابل *hunābil*, Strong and thick (cord).

A حنابلة *hanābilat*, (pl. of حنبليّ *hambalīy*) Hambalites, followers of Ibn Hambal.

P حنا بندان *hinā-bandān*, (or حنا بندي *hinā-bandī*) A marriage-feast.

A حناتم *hanātim*, (pl. of حنتم *hantam*) Black clouds. Green-coloured water-pots.

A حناج *hināj*, (pl. of حنج *hinj*) Roots, origins.

A حنّاج *hannāj*, Effeminate, infamous.

A حناجر *hanājir*, (pl. of حنجرة *hanjarat* and حنجور *hunjūr*) Gullets.

A حناجف *hanājif*, (pl. of حنجوف *hunjūf*) Heads of the ribs joining to the back-bone.

A حناجل *hunājil*, Short and compact of body.

A حناجير *hanājīr*, (pl. of حنجور) Gullets.

A حنادج *hanādij*, (pl. of حندج) Large camels.

A حنادر *hunādir*, Sharp-sighted.

A حنادس *hanādis*, (pl. of حندس *hindis*) Dark nights. Darknesses. Three nights after those called ظلم *zulm*).

A حناديج *hanādīj*, (pl. of حندج *hunduj* or of حندوجة *hundūjat*) Oblong tracts or heaps of sand: also short ones.

A حناذ *hanāz*, The sun.

A حناط *hināṭ*, Sweet, aromatic herbs with which they perfume the dead.

A حنّاط *hannāṭ*, A seller of wheat (حنطة *hinṭat*); or of sweet herbs for the dead (حنوط *hanūṭ*).

A حناطة *hināṭat*, The art of embalming. A vending of sweet odours for the dead (حنوط *hanūṭ*). Corn-dealing, traffic in wheat (حنطة *hinṭat*).

A حنّاطيّ *hannāṭīy*, Corn-chandler, wheat-seller.

A حناظب *hanāzib*, (pl. of حنظب *hunzub* or *hunzab*) Male locusts. Beetles.

A حناق *hināḳ*, Furious passions.

A حناك *hināk*, Certain stuff with which the palate of a new-born child is rubbed. A strap, or a part of the timber of a camel's saddle. A bit of wood tied under a camel's chin to which is fastened a rope tied round the neck of the colt. (pl. of حنكة *hunkat*) Straps of a saddle.

A حناكل *hunākil*, Despicable, rude, coarse, thick. A dwarf.

A حنان *hanān*, (v. n. of حنّ) Pitying. Parental or filial affection. Pity, compassion. Sustenance. Daily bread. Abundance, blessing, prosperity. Respect, reverence. Sedateness, gravity. Tender-heartedness. Long-continued evil. حنان الله *hanānu'llāh*, God forbid! heaven forefend!

A حنآن *hun,ān*, (pl. of حنّاء *hinnā,*) Colouring or dyeing shrubs, privets, hennas.

A حنّان *hannān*, Most compassionate or affectionate (one of the epithets of God). Tenderly affected. Open, clear (way). Beating, throbbing. Twanging (bow-string). *Hinnān*, The dyeing or colouring shrub henna (Lawsonia inermis).

A حنّانة *hannānat*, A bow. A twanging bow. A widow anxious of marrying again. A woman who, with grief and lamentation, recals to mind a deceased husband.

A حنانيك *hanānayka*, (or حنانك *hanānaka*) Shew pity on me time after time.

A حنايا *hanāya'*, (pl. of حنيّة *haniyat*) Bows.

A حناية *hināyat*, (v. n. of حني) Bending, twisting. Peeling. Flexure, bending, curvature.

A حنائر *hanā,ir*, (pl. of حنيرة) Arched works.

A حنائن *hanā,in*, (pl. of حنين *hanīn* or *hinnīn*) Months of Jamādi.

A حنّائيّون *hinnā,īyūn*, (pl. of حنّائيّ *hinnā,īy*) Venders of henna.

P حنائي *hinā,ī*, Of the colour of henna.

A حنّائيّ *hinnā,īy*, A seller of henna.

A حنب *hanab*, (v. n. of حنب) Being curved or bent in the loins or pastern (a horse). Having the hind legs wide apart.

A حنبال *himbāl*, Fleshy.

A حنبالة *himbālat*, A babbler, prater. The sea.

A حنبتر *himbatr*, Vehemence, hardness, severity.

A حنبج *himbij*, A louse. *Humbuj*, Big-bodied.

A حنبر *hambar*, Short, dwarfish.

A حنبرّ *himbarr*, Assiduity. Magnitude. Hardness, force, strength.

A حنبرة *hambarat*, Excessive cold.

A حنبريت *hambarīt*, Pure (water). Sheer (falsehood). Feeble (light).

A حنبشة *hambashat*, (v. n. of حنبش Q) Leaping. Applauding, clapping. Walking. Dancing. Laughing. Playing. Talking, narrating. Receiving familiarly.

A (ابو) الحنبص (*abū'l*) *himbis*, (Father of stratagems) The fox.

A حنبصة *hambasat*, Stratagems (in war).

A حنبل *hambal*, A short, dwarfish man. Large-bellied, fleshy. A garment made of skins. A worn-out boot. The sea. Name of an eminent Muhammadan lawyer, and head of one of the four chief sects in Muhammadism. *Humbal*, The flowers of the Egyptian thorn. *Humbul*, French beans.

A حنبلة *hambalat*, (v. n. of حنبل Q) Eating French beans. Putting on a pelisse of fur.

A حنبليّ *hambaliy*, (pl. حنابلة *hanābilat*) A follower of Hambal (one of the four chief Muhammadan lawyers).

A حنبوب *humbūb*, Very black.

A حنة *hinat*, Hatred, rancour, malevolence.

A حنّة *hannat*, A wife. The froth of a camel. The affectionate longing of a camel for her colt. A woman's name (Hanna). *Hi* or *hannat*, Madness.

A حنتأ *hanta*, A dwarf.

A حنتاء *hantā*, Short, dwarfish. A dwarf.

A حنتار *hintār*, Short, dwarfish. Small.

A حنتال *huntāl*, Escape, flight.

A حنترة *hantarat*, Difficulties, straits.

A حنتف *hantaf*, Picked clean, ready for roasting (locust). Name of a man.

A حنتفر *hintafr*, Short, dwarfish.

A حنتل *huntal*, Escape, flight.

A حنتم *hantam* (pl. حناتم *hanātim*) A green bucket or water-pot. A colocynth. Black clouds.

A حنتوف *huntūf*, One who plucks his beard from the violence of a bilious attack.

A حنث *hins*, (v. n. of حنث) Swearing falsely. A sin, crime. Obedience. A bias (true or false).

A حنثر *hansar*, (or حنثريّ) Foolish. A fool.

A حنثرة *hansarat*, Straits, difficulties.

A حنثل *hansal*, Weak, feeble.

A حنج *hanj*, (v. n. of حنج) Inclining, giving a bias. Twisting a rope. Occurring (a necessary business). Necessity, necessary business. *Hinj*, (pl. حناج *hināj*) Root, origin, stock.

A حنجب *hunjub*, Dry.

A حنجد *hunjud*, A tract of sand writhed into the resemblance of a rope.

A حنجر *hanjar*, The gullet. Shepherd's staff.

A حنجرة *hanjarat*, (v. n. of حنجر Q) Slaughtering. Being deeply sunk in its socket (eye). (pl. حناجر *hanājir*) The gullet.

P حنجرة غلطان *hanjara-ghaltān*, A warbler.

A حنجريّ *hanjariy*, Guttural.

A حنجف *hanjaf*, (*hinjif, hunjuf*, or حنجفة *hunjufat*) The top of the haunch or thigh.

A حنجل *hinjal*, A large-bodied woman. Clamorous. *Hunjul*, A wild beast, especially a lion.

A حنجود *hunjūd*, The windpipe. The throat. An oblong vessel, jug, cruet, smelling-bottle.

A حنجور *hunjūr*, The gullet. A bottle wherein they preserve scented powder. A clothes-hamper.

A حنجوف *hunjūf*, (pl. حناجف *hanājif*) Head of the ribs joining to the back-bone.

A حنح *hinh*, A word used in calling to sheep.

A حنحنة *hanhanat*, (v. n. of حنحن Q) Commiserating, compassionating.

A حند *hunud*, Waters absorbed in sand.

A حنداء *handā*, A dwarf.

A حندارة *hindārat*, The pupil of the eye.

A حندج *hunduj*, Sands producing odoriferous herbs and flowers. A name. (pl. حنادج *hanādij*) An oblong tract or heap of sand; also a short one.

A حندر *hundur*, (or حندور *hundūr*) (pl. حنادر *hanādir*) The pupil of the eye. هو على حندر عينه *huwa ʿala' hunduri ʿaynihi*, (or حندورة عينه *hundūrati ʿaynihi*) He is an offence to his sight.

A حندس *hindis*, A dark night, darkness.

A حندقوق *handa*, (*hindakūk*, حندقوقى *handa* or *hindakūka'*) The lot tree. A tall foolish fellow.

A حندل *handal*, Short. A dwarf.

A حندلس *handalis*, (A camel) fleshy, flabby, and slow-paced. Excellent (camel).

A حندم *handam*, Name of a red-rooted tree.

A حندوة *hunduwat*, A cleft in a mountain.

A حندوجة *hundūjat*, (pl. حنادج *hanādij*) An oblong tract or heap of sand; also a short one.

A حندور *hindawr* The pupil of the eye.

A حندورة *hundūrat* or *hindūrat*, The pupil of the eye. *Hundūrat*, (or حنديرة *hindīrat*) The object of vision. على حندورة العين *ʿala' hundūrati'l ʿayn*, (or على حنديرة العين *ʿala' hindīrati'l ʿayn*) In full view.

A حندوقة *hundūkat*, The pupil of the eye.

A حندير *hindīr*, (or حنديرة) Pupil of the eye.

A حنديقة *hindīkat*, The pupil of the eye.

A حنذ *hanz*, (v. n. of حنذ) Roasting (a sheep by laying it on a hot stone). Scorching (the sun). Making (a horse) sweat by exercising him a heat or two, and exposing him with housing on to the sun.

A حنذة *hunzat*, Intense heat.

A حنذمان *hinzimān*, A people, nation, tribe.

A حنذيان *hinziyān*, Egregiously wicked.

A حنذيذ *hinzīz*, One who sweats profusely.

A حنر *hanr*, A bending, an arching.

A حنزاب *hinzāb*, A stout middle-sized ass, short and thick. A strong dwarf. A wild carrot. A flight of the birds قطا *katā*. A species of the katā bird. A cock.

A حنزرة *hanzarat*, A cleft in a mountain.

A حنزقر *hinzakr*, Dwarfish, despicable.

A حنزقرات *hinzakrāt*, (pl. of حنزقرة) Serpents.

A حنزقرة *hinzakrat*, Dwarfish, mean. A serpent.

A حنزقو *hinzakw*, (or حنزقوة) Dwarfish.

A حنزوب *hunzūb*, A bevy of the birds قطا *katā*. Name of a plant.

A حنس *hanas*, (v. n. of حنس) Pushing courageously into the hottest of the battle. *Hunus*, Pious, chaste (people).

A حنش *hansh*, (v. n. of حنش) Hunting (game). Bending. Driving off, averting. *Hanash*, (pl. احناش *ahnāsh*) A serpent. Any thing whose head resembles that of a serpent. A reptile. A fly, an insect. Any bird that is hunted.

A حنص *hans*, (v. n. of حنص) Dying.

A حنصأ *hinsa*, (or حنصأو *hinsaw*) Weak and small. *Hinsa*, Weak, feeble (man).

A حنصار *hinsār*, Slender and large-bellied.

A حنصال *hinsāl*, (or حنصالة) Large-bellied.

A حنضج *hinzij*, Poor, weak, feeble.

A حنضل *hanzal*, A small pond.

A حنضلة *hanzalat*, A cavity in a stone; also water collected therein.

A حنط *hant*, (v. n. of حنط) Being red (leather). Braying. An arrow. *Hanat*, (v. n. of حنط) Coming to maturity (the herb رمث *rims*). *Hinat*, (pl. of حنطة *hintat*) Wheats.

A حنطأو *hintaw*, (or حنطأوة *hintawat*) Short and big-bellied.

A حنطب *hantab*, A goat of Hijāz.

A حنطبة *hantabat*, Courage, valour. Courageous. A kind of venemous reptile.

A حنطة *hintat*, (pl. حنط *hinat*) Wheat.

A حنطريرة *hantarīrat*, A cloud.

A حنطف *hantaf*, Large-bellied.

A حنطئ *hinti*, Short and big-bellied.

A حنطيّ *hintiy*, One who eats abundance of wheat and grows fat. Swollen.

A حنطئة *hunatiat*, A broad, fat ewe.

A حنظاءة *hanzāat*, (v. n. of حنظي Q) Reviling shamefully. Talking obscenely.

A حنظاب *hinzāb*, Dwarfish, ill-tempered.

A حنظأو *hinzaw*, Short-bodied.

A حنظب *hunzab* or *hunzub*, (pl. حناظب *hanāzib*) A male locust. A beetle or similar insect.

A حنظبا *hunzuba'* or حنظباء, A beetle.

A حنظف *hanzaf*, Big-bellied.

A حنظل *hanzal*, The wild gourd, colocynth.

A حنظوب *hunzūb* Large, gross, worthless woman.

A حنظيان *hinziyān*, Wicked, obscene, indecent.

A حنف *hanf*, (v. n. of حنف) Inclining, leaning. *Hanaf*, (v. n. of حنف) Being bow-legged. Walking limpingly on the outer edges of the feet. Rectitude, uprightness in religion. Orthodoxy.

A حنفاء *hanfā*, Crooked, wry (foot). Capricious (handmaid). A chameleon. A tortoise. A sea-tortoise, turtle. A bow. A razor. A kind of tree. *Hunafā*, (pl. of حنيف *hanīf*) Orthodox believers.

A حنفس *hinfis*, Impudent (woman).

A حنفش *hinfish*, (or حنفيش *hinfish*) A viper. A large serpent with a great head, and when irritated swells and hisses.

A حنفص *hinfis*, Slender, small-bodied.

P حنفي *hanafī*, Orthodox. مذهب حنفي *mazhabi hanafī*, The true religion. (for حنيفي *hanīfī*) The sect of Hanīfah.

A حنفيّة *hanafiyat*, True religion, orthodoxy.

A حنق *hanak*, (v. n. of حنق) Being angry, indignant. (pl. حناق *hināk*) High indignation. *Hanik*, Enraged. *Hunuk*, Fat (persons).

A حنقط *hankat*, A bird like a woodcock or snipe.

A حنك *hank*, (v. n. of حنك) Putting a curb or check-rein under a horse's chin. A bridle, the chin-strap, curb, or chain. Perceiving, understanding. Confirming, or doing firmly and well. Rendering expert (age). Chewing a date (a child). Rubbing the palate of an infant with chewed date or honey (in order to induce it to suck). *Hunk* or *hink*, Experience. Firmness. *Hanak*, (v. n. of حنك) Teaching a man wisdom (trials). (pl. احناك *ahnāk*) The palate, and the under part of the mouth which is opposite to it. The beak of a crow. A heap of white and softish stones. Blackness, jettiness. A foraging party. *Hunuk*, Experienced, tried, prudent, intelligent.

A حنكة *hunkat*, Strength, firmness. Experience. (pl. حناك *hināk*) A strap or timber of a saddle. A piece of wood, one end of which is tied under a camel's chin, and the other end round the neck of her colt. *Hanakat*, High and rugged ground. *Hunukat*, Prudent, intelligent (woman).

A حنكث *hankas*, A sort of plant.

A حنكل *hankal*, Despicable, rude, coarse. A dwarf.

A حنكلة *hankalat*, (v. n. of حنكل Q) Walking heavily. Short, contemptible (woman). Black. Rough, unfeeling.

A حنمة *hanamat*, Sleep.

A حنن *hanan*, A beetle.

A حنو *hanw*, (v. n. of حنا for حنو) Bending, twisting. Making crooked and curved. Making a bow. *Hinw* or *hanw*, (pl. احناء *ahnā*, حنيّ *haniy* and *huniy*) The crooked timber of a saddle. Crookedness, curvature. The side (of a mountain). A kind of plant. Any part of the body possessed of curvature, as the bone which surrounds the eye. The chin. The ribs. A hill of waving sand.

A حنوّ *hunūw*, (v. n. of حنا for حنو) Being affectionate, loving (as a mother who for her children's sake rejects a second marriage). Wanting the ram.

A حنواء *hanwā*, (fem. of احنى) Crook-backed.

A حنوان *hinwāni*, Two curved timbers over which is laid a net for carrying corn to the stack.

A حنوة *hunwat*, A sort of odoriferous herb.

A حنود *hanūd*, (pl. حند *hunud*) Water absorbed in a sandy soil, and resting on a solid stratum below.

A حنورة *hinnawrat*, Name of an animalcule.

A حنوط *hanūt*, Sweet herbs which they are wont to sprinkle or strew over dead bodies. *Hunūt*, (v. n. of حنط) Being fit to reap (wheat). Coming to maturity (the plant رمث *rims*). Strewing sweet herbs on the dead

P حنوط فروش *hunūt-furosh*, A vender of sweet herbs for the dead.

A حنون *hanūn*, Tender towards (her) offspring, and taking a second husband that he may look after them. Howling (wind). *Hunūn*, (pl. of حنين *hanīn* or *hinnīn*) Months of Jamādī.

A حنّون *hannūn*, Privet-blossom. A blossom.

A حني *hany*, (v. n. of حنا for حنو) Bending. *Hinā'*, The dyeing shrub henna.

A حنيّ *haniy*, (pl. of حنيّة *haniyat*) Bows. *Haniy* or *huniy*, (pl. of حنو *hinw*) Crooked timbers of saddles. Curved things.

A حنياء *hanyā*, (fem. of احنى) Crooked-backed.

A حنيّة *haniyat*, (pl. حنيّ *haniy* and حنايا *hanāya'*) A bow.

A حنيث *hanīs*, Perjured, wicked.

A حنيذ *hanīz*, Hot roast meat whose dripping falls. Roasted thoroughly under heated stones (mutton). Thrown into a sweat by being exercised in the sun (a horse). Scalding (water). A kind of ointment. A perfumed lotion for the head.

A حنيرة *hanīrat*, (pl. حنائر *hanāir*) An arch, the key-stone of arched work. A bow without the string. A bow for separating cotton.

A حنيف *hanīf*, (pl. حنفاء *hunafā*) One who leans from Judaism and Christianity; any one sincere in his inclination to Islām. Whoever performs the pilgrimage to Mecca, (so proving himself of the religion of Abraham). Circumcised. An orthodox Musulmān. Firm, unshaken in his religious profession. Short, dwarfish. A shoemaker.

A حنيفة (ابو *abū*) *hanīfat*, Name of twenty learned doctors; the most celebrated of whom was نعمان بن ثابت *nuʿmān bin sābit*, One of the four chiefs of the principal Muhammadan sects.

A حنيفيّ *hanīfiy*, A kind of sword first introduced and worn by احنف *ahnaf*. (The regular form would be احنفيّ *ahnafīy*).

A حنيفيّة *hanīfiyat*, Sect of Hanifa: orthodoxy.

A حنيق *hanīk*, Enraged.

A حنيك *hanīk*, Experienced, tried, expert.

A حنيكة *hanīkat*, Heartily-feeding (horses).

A حنين *hanīn*, (v. n. of حنّ) Experiencing and exhibiting strong emotions (whether of pleasure or of pain). Making a twanging noise (a bow-string). Love, affectionate yearning. The affectionate cry of a camel to her colt. *Hanīn*, (or حنّين *hinnīn*) (pl. احنّة *ahinnat*, حنون *hunūn*, and حنائن *hanāin*) The months Jamādī, the former and latter. *Hunayn*, A certain boot-maker whose name has passed into a proverb.

A حواء *hawā*, Voice, sound, noise. *Hiwā*, (pl. احوية *ahwiyat*) A tent of wool or goat's hair. A number of those tents adjoining to one another.

A حوّاء *hawwā*, Eve the mother of mankind. (fem. of احوي *ahwa'*) Black or dusky-lipped. Reddish-black (lip). A blue colour. Name of a plant resembling the wolf in colour. A collector of serpents, a catcher of snakes (حيّة *hayyat*).

A حوّاءة *huwwāat*, Name of a pot-herb that cleaves to the ground. One who never leaves home.

A حوأب *hawab*, An open place. A wide valley. A capacious bucket. A hoof in shape like a cup. A watering-place, or the name of one.

A حوابّ *hawābb*, (pl. of حابّ *hābb*) Arrows flying wide of the mark.

A حوأبة *hawabat*, The largest milk pail or bucket.

A حواة *hawāt*, Noise, sound.

A حواتك *hawātik*, Cattle poorly fed, or that will not fatten. A young ostrich.

A حوّاج *hawājj*, (pl. of حاجّة) Female pilgrims.

A حواجب *hawājib*, (pl. of حاجب) Eye-brows.

A حواجر *hawājir*, (pl. of حجرة *hajrat*) Court-yards, sides of a house, premises.

A حواجل *hawājil* or حواجيل *hawājīl*, (pl. of حوجلة *hawjalat*) Cruets. Flasks, decanters.

A حوادث *hawādis*, Accidents, events.

P حوادث زده *hawādis-zada*, Unfortunate.

A حوادي *hawādī*, The hind legs (as following the fore-legs).

A حواذ *hiwāz*, Distance.

A حوار *hawār* or *hiwār*, A reply. *Hiwār*, Idiom, phraseology. *Huwār*, (pl. احورة *ahwirat*, حيران *hīrān*, and حوران *hūrān*) A camel's colt from the hour it is foaled until it is weaned.

A حوارد *hawārid*, (pl. of حارد) Hot, passionate.

A حواريّ *huwāra'*, The finest and whitest flour. White bread.

A حواريّ *hawārīy*, A washer of garments. A fuller. A disciple or apostle (of Jesus Christ). An assister. A staunch supporter of the prophets.

A حواريّات *hawārīyāt*, Women who reside in towns (and thus keep their complexions fair).

A حواريّون *hawārīyūn*, Apostles, particularly those of Jesus Christ.

A حوّاز *hawwāz*, An instigator. حوّاز القلوب *hawwāzu'l kulūb*, Whatever gains the ascendancy over hearts, and impels them to the commission of what they dislike. *Hūwāz*, Large beetles.

A حوازّ *hawāzz*, (pl. of حازّة *hāzzat*) Things which fill the mind with anxiety and misgivings.

A حوازب *hawāzib*, (pl. of حازب *hāzib*) Severe, difficult (affairs).

A حوّاس *hawwās*, (A watchman) who goes the rounds during the night.

A حواسّ *hawāss*, (pl. of حاسّة *hassat*) Senses. حواسّ خمسه *hawāssi khamsa*, The five senses. حواسّ برّاني *hawāssi barrānī*, The external senses. حواسّ اندروني *hawāssi andarūnī*, Internal senses.

P حواس باخته *hawās-bākhta*, Out of one's senses.

A حواسة *huwāsat*, Inquisition for blood. A mixed assembly. A hostile invasion. Relationship.

A حواسد *hawāsid*, Enviers.

A حواشة *huwāshat*, Any thing against which one takes exception, saying, حاشا الله *hāshā ll'llāh*, God forbid! Any thing whereof one is ashamed.

Relationship, kindred. The womb. Need, necessity. A criminal affair. Separation from kindred.

A حواشك *hawāshik*, Violent winds. Light winds. (Winds) blowing from different quarters.

A حواشي *hawāshī*, (pl. of حاشية *hāshiyat*) Margins, borders, hems, marginal notes or observations. Followers, attendants, domestics. Common soldiers. امراء و حواشي *umarā u hawāshī*, Princes and people, grandees and plebeians. رقيق الحواشي *rakīku'l hawāshī*, Easy (life).

A حواص *hiwās*, A stick or skewer for sewing.

A حواصب *hawāsib*, (pl. of حاصب) Violent winds.

A حواصة *hiwāsat*, A strap for fastening a girth.

A حواصل *hawāsil*, (pl. of حاصل *hāsil*) Lockers in caravansaries. (pl. of حوصلة) (Birds') crops.

A حواصن *hawāsin*, (pl. of حاصن *hāsin*) Pregnant women. Chaste women.

A حواضر *hawāzir*, (pl. of حاضرة) Ears, handles.

A حواضن *hawāzin*, (pl. of حاضنة *hāzinat*) Nurses, foster-mothers. (Trivets) sticking fast in their place.

A حوّاط *hawwāt*, Superior to.

A حواطة *huwātat*, A place for keeping grain.

A حواطيم *hawātīm*, (pl. of حاطوم *hātūm*) Barren years. Things which promote digestion.

A حوافة *huwāfat*, Leaves of clover remaining on the ground after it has been carried.

A حوافر *hawāfir*, (pl. of حافر *hāfir*) Feet, hoofs.

A حوافش *hawāfish*, (pl. of حافشة) Water-courses.

A حواقّ *hawākk*, (pl. of حاقّة *hākkat*) Sure, impending, descending (calamities).

A حواقة *huwākat*, Sweepings, rubbish.

A حواقن *hawākin*, (pl. of حاقنة *hākinat*) Stomachs. Lower parts of bellies. Hollows between collar-bones and lower parts of necks.

A حوال *hawāl*, A circle, circuit. Change, revolution. ذو حوال *zū hawāl*, Name of a king of Himyar. *Hiwāl*, (v. n. 3 of حال for حول) Wishing. Seeking. Sharpening one's look, gazing steadily. Intervenient. *Hawāla*, Round about. Over against.

A حوالب *hawālib*, Springs (of water or tears).

A حوالة *hawālat*, A turning of one river into another. Security, caution, bail, bond, note of hand. Commission, charge. Custody, deposit of property. ورقة حوالة *warakatu hawālatin*, A draft, a cheque. P حواله شدن *hawāla shudan*, To be entrusted, to be transferred. حواله كردن *hawāla kardan*, To transmit, transfer one's power to another, to empower one to demand a debt. To give in charge, recommend. To brandish. To aim, strike.

P حوال دار *hawāl-dār*, (in India) A native military officer of inferior rank, a havildār.

A حوالس *hawālis*, (pl. of حالس *hālis*) Squares or circles in a certain boys' game.

A حوالق *hawālik*, (pl. of حالق) Full udders.

P حواله گاه *hawāla-gāh*, A public walk in the environs of a city, an esplanade.

A حوالَي *hawāla'*, Round about. حواليه *hawālayhi*, Around him, round about it. Over against it. *Hawālī*, Environs, outskirts, parts adjacent. (pl. of حاليّة *haliyat* and حاليّة *hālīyat*) Women dressed in their ornaments.

A حواليّ *hawāliy*, (pl. of حوليّ *hawliy*) Yearling solid-hoofed animals. *Hawāliy* or *huwāliy*, Prolific in stratagems (حيلة *hīlat*), astute.

A حوامل *hawāmil*, (pl. of حامل *hāmil*) Pregnant. (pl. of حاملة *hāmilat*) The feet. Tendons in the arms and feet.

A حوامي *hawāmī*, Right and left sides of a hoof.

A حوامين *hawāmīn*, (pl. of حومانة *hawmānat*) Steep and rugged places.

A حواني *hawānī*, The long ribs.

A حوانيت *hawānīt*, (pl. of حانوت) Shops.

A حواول *hawāwil*, Shrewd, penetrating.

A حواوي *hawāwī*, (pl. of حاوية) Intestines.

A حوايا *hawāya'*, (pl. of حويّة *hawiyat*) Circles of stuffed cloth put over the bunches of camels to prevent the loads from hurting them. Intestines.

A حواية *hawāyat*, (v. n. of حوي) Collecting. Comprehending, embracing. Occupying. Guarding.

A حوائج *hawāij*, (pl. of حاجة *hājat*) Affairs, necessary matters.

A حوائر *hawāir*, (pl. of حائرة *hāirat*) Worthless, good for nothing.

A حوائض *hawāiz*, (pl. of حائضة) Menstruous.

A حوائك *hawāik* (pl. of حائكة) Female weavers.

A حوائم *hawāim*, Thirsty camels.

A حوائن *hawāin*, (pl. of حائنة) Sore calamities.

A حوب *hawb*, (v. n. of حاب for حوب) Calling out to camels. Sinning, offending. Father and mother, parents. A sister. A daughter. Grief, sadness. Solitariness. Species, kind, sort, form, manner. Effort, endeavour. Poverty, humility. Pain. A camel. A word used in driving he-camels. *Hawb* or *hūb*, Crime, sin, wickedness, profligacy. *Hūb*, Affliction, grief, destruction, death. Solitariness. Disease. The soul.

A حوباء *hawbā*, (pl. حوباوات *hawbāwāt*) The soul. A body (thing or person).

A حوباوات *hawbāwāt*, (pl. of حوباء) Souls.

A حوبة *hawbat*, (v. n. of حاب for حوب) Sinning. Want, necessity. State, quality. Father and mother, parents. A sister. A daughter. An infirm, helpless man. Maternal affection. Maternal kindred. Any great and important affair. *Hūbat*, A mother. A wife. A concubine. A beast of burden. A weak man. A court. A crime.

A حوّة *hūwat*, (v. n. of حوي) Being of a dark red. Brownness, duskiness of lip. Black inclining to green. Red inclining to black. The side of a valley.

A حوت *hawt*, (v. n. of حات for حوت) Flying round any thing (a bird). *Hūt*, (pl. احوات *ahwāt*, حوتة *hiwatat*, and حيتان *hītān*) A large fish. Pisces. صاحب الحوت *sāhibu'l hūt*, (Lord of the fish) Jonah. P حوت گردون *hūti gardūn*, (The fish of the firmament) The sign Pisces.

A حوتاء *hawtā*, Thick-waisted (woman).

A حوتان *hawatān*, (v. n. of حات for حوت) Flying round any thing (a bird).

A حوتة *hiwatat*, (pl. of حوت *hūt*) Fishes.

A حوتك *hawtak*, Short. Lean.

A حوتكة *hawtakat*, A dwarf's pace.

A حوتكيّ *hawtakiy*, Short. Lean. A glutton.

A حوتكيّة *hawtakiyat*, A sash which the Arabians roll round their heads or turbans, (so called from a man named حوتك *hawtak*).

A حوتل *hawtal*, A youth near puberty. A young قطا *katā* (a kind of grouse or bittern). Weak.

A حوتلة *hawtalat*, A dwarf.

A حوث *haws*, A vein or artery of the liver and its appendages. Wheresoever. There. تركهم حوثا بوثا *tarakahum hawsan bawsan*, He left them dispersed.

A حوثاء *hawsā*, The liver with its appendages. A fat woman.

A حوثرة *hawsarat*, Glans penis.

A حوثم *hawsam*, Middle-sized (man or camel).

A حوج *hawj*, (v. n. of حاج for حوج) Having occasion, being in want of. Peace, safety. حوجا لك *hawjan laka*, Peace be unto thee! *Hūj*, Poverty. *Hiwaj*, (pl. of حاجة *hājat*) Necessaries.

A حوجاء *hawjā*, Necessity. An affair, business. A doubt, scruple. Hope, desire, any thing wished for. A reply (good or bad).

A حوجلة *hawjalat*, (v. n. of حوجل Q) Having the eye sunk. *Hawjalat*, (or حوجلّة *hawjallat*) (pl. حواجل *hawājil* or حواجيل *hawājīl*) A flask, a decanter, especially one large at the bottom.

A حوجم *hawjam*, An anti-venereal plant.

A حوجمة *hawjamat*, (pl. حوجم *hawjam*) A red rose.

A حوجن *hawjan*, A red rose.

A حوحاة *hawhāt*, A calling out to goats.

A حود *hawd*, An inclining, a leaning to.

A حودل *hawdal*, A male ape.

A حودلة *hawdalat*, A hill, hillock.

A حوذ *hawz*, (v. n. of حاذ for حوذ) Driving (camels) fast. Keeping, preserving with care. Contracting, drawing in.

A حوذان *hawzān*, The water-lily.

A حوذلة *hawzalat*, A leaning on one side of a camel's hoof.

A حوذيّ *hūziy*, Urgent in pushing on his way.

A حور *hawr*, (v. n. of حار for حور) Returning. Being astonished, bewildered. Unloosing, opening the folds of a turban-sash. A reply. Something or any thing. Washing or making white (a garment). Deficiency. Depth, profundity. That which is under the turban-sash. *Hūr*, (v. n. of حار for حور) Returning. Produce (especially flour from grain, as it falls when grinding). Ruin, destruction. Diminution, decrease. (pl. of احور *ahwar* and حوراء

hawrāʼ) Beautiful-eyed. حور في محارة *hūr* (or *hawr*) *fī muhārat*, Loss upon loss (when one's affairs are becoming desperate). هو في حور و بور *huwa fī hūrin wa būrin*, He has no craft, trade, nor income. He is in error. *Hawar*, (v. n. of حور) Being extremely bright (the white and black of the eye). Being quite circular (the pupil of the eye). Extreme whiteness of the eye with intense blackness. Total blackness of the eye (as that of a doe): this word frequently expresses the beautiful black eyes of women, but never those of men, excepting sometimes in a metaphorical sense. Astonishment, amazement, bewilderment. (pl. حوران *hūrān*) A species of red leather with which they cover wicker baskets. The white poplar. The third star of the lesser Bear. (pl. احوار *ahwār*) A cow. A plant. A preparation of burnt lead with which women anoint their face. بعيد الحور *baʻīdu'l hawr*, Intelligent. Knowing, clever.

P T حور *hūr*, (or حور بهشتي *hūri bihishtī*) A virgin of paradise, black-eyed nymph, houri. رشك حورالعين *rashki hūru'l ʻayn*, The envy of the black-eyed virgins (of Paradise), *i.e.* surpassing them in beauty. P A حورالنسا *hūru'n nisā*, The most angelic of women. حور و غلمان *hūr u ghilmān*, Girls and boys of paradise.

A حوّر *hawwar*, The (white) poplar (tree). حوّر رومي *hawwari rūmī*, The black poplar. *Hūwar*, A certain mountain in Yaman, wherein is a cave where magic is learned.

A حوراء *hawrāʼ*, (fem. of احور *ahwar*) Black-eyed. A circular brand. A sea-port near Madina.

P حوراسفند *hawr-isfand*, The anemone.

A حوران *hawrān*, The southern regions of Damascus. The herb tarragon. The skin of an elephant. *Hūrān*, (pl. of حائر *hāʼir*) Places where waters stagnate. Low-lying places. Gardens. (pl. of حوار *huwār*) Sucking camel's colts. (pl. of حور *hawar*) Red leathers for covering wicker baskets.

P حورپيكر *hūr-paykar*, Angel-faced.

P حورزاد *hūr-zād*, Born of a celestial nymph.

A حورم *hawram*, Plenty of live and dead stock.

A حورور *hawarwar*, Something, any thing.

A حورورة *hawarwarat*, A fair, white woman.

P حوري *hūre*, One virgin of paradise, one black-eyed nymph, or houri.

A حوريّ *hawariy*, Red-skinned (ram).

A حوز *hawz*, (v. n. of حاز for حوز) Collecting, accumulating, acquiring. Urging vehemently forward. Driving (camels) slowly. Coming back, returning. Drawing (a bow) with all one's might. A gentle pace. A place surrounded by a mound or bank. A king. Conjugal intercourse. ليلة الحوز *laylatu'l hawz*, The first night on which camels are led forth to water.

A حوزاء *hawzāʼ*, A war which brings together all the people.

A حوزة *hawzat*, Tract, side, part; middle (of a kingdom). Sort of grape. Nature (of a man). Vulva.

A حوزل *hawzal*, (or حوزلة) Short, dwarfish.

A حوزيّ *hawziy*, Clever in driving. One who lives alone and mixes not with others. A man of sound judgment and intellect. Black.

A حوزيّة *hūziyat*, A she-camel that retires from the herd. A she-camel which has a peculiar compactness in her make and gait, and is different and superior to the rest of the herd.

A حوس *haws*, (v. n. of حاس for حوس) Searching anxiously for any thing. Sweeping the ground with one's garments. Flaying, skinning. *Hawsa*, Amidst, among. *Hūs*, Slow camels.

A حوّس *hūwas*, Adversities, or misfortunes befalling people and entering into their houses.

A حوساء *hawsāʼ*, A she-camel that eats much, and is full of life and spirit.

A حوسى *hawsaʼ*, Numerous camels.

A حوش *hawsh*, (v. n. of حاش for حوش) Beating up (game) on all sides, and driving (it) into the net. Collecting and urging forward (camels). Eating away the sides of food. A hovel constructed of boughs to protect camels from the cold. *Hūsh*, A country, desert or inhabited by demons. Wild quadrupeds. A demon (who, according to popular belief, covers cattle, and makes them fierce and untractable). حوش الفؤاد *hūshu'l fuʼād*, Keen, acute.

A حوشب *hawshab*, A crowd, a company. A hare. A calf. A dog-fox. Gaunt-bellied. Full-sided, blown out. Fetlock-joint. The pastern.

A حوشبة *hawshabat*, A crowd, a company.

A حوشكة *hawshakat*, Any thing heard in any quarter of the house.

A حوشيّ *hūshiy*, Any thing foreign or strange. Fierce, wild, untractable. One with whom nobody associates. Obscure, unintelligible. Dark (night).

A حوشيّة *hūshīyat*, Savageness, misanthropy.

A حوص *haws*, (v. n. of حاص for حوص) Joining close. Sewing up. Going round. Covering (the eyes of a falcon). طعنت في حوص امر لست منه في شيء *taʻantu fī hawsi* (or *hūsi*) *amrin lastu minhu fī shayʼin*, I laboured at a work I could not accomplish. *Hūs*, (pl. of احوص *ahwas*) Those whose eyes are narrow at the corners. *Hawas*, (v. n. of حوص) Being close at the angles (the eyes). Narrowness at the outer corners of the eyes, or in one of them.

A حوصل *hawsal*, A bird's crop. A certain voracious bird with a large crop. The very bottom of a cistern. A large-naveled sheep.

A حوصلاء *hawsalāʼ*, A bird's crop.

A حوصلة *hawsalat*, (v. n. of حوصل Q) Stuffing its craw (a bird). *Hawsalat* or *hawsallat*, (pl. حواصل *hawāsil*) The stomach, maw, or crop. The abdomen. The very bottom of a cistern. Resolution, ambition. Capacity, spirit. Endurance.

P حوصله مند *hawsalamand*, Ambitious, aspiring.

A حوض *hawz*, (v. n. of حاض for حوض) Constructing a tank. Collecting water. (pl. حياض *hiyāz* and احواض *ahwāz*) A large reservoir of water, bason of a fountain, pond, tank, vat, or cistern. The abdomen. P حوض آب *hawzi āb*, The sky. حوض آب *hawzi āb*, (or حوض ماهي *hawzi māhī*) The sign Pisces. حوض ترسا *hawzi tarsā*, A vessel in which the juice of grapes is pressed out. A حوض الحمار *hawzu'l himār*, A term of reproach. حوض كوثر *hawzi kawsar*, A reservoir of nectar in paradise. حوض نعمان *hawzi nuʻmān*, Name of a pond whose water, which was very salt, became sweet at the advent of the prophet.

P حوضچه *hawzcha*, A small reservoir, cistern.

P حوضك *hawzak*, Small reservoir. Big dish.

A حوط *hawt*, (v. n. of حاط for حوط) Keeping, preserving, taking care of. Minding, attending to. Contracting, drawing in. A bicoloured thread, black and red, strung with beads and pieces of silver, worn by women to avert malignant eyes. *Hiwat*, What is given to make up for deficiency of weight in coins.

A حوطة *hawtat*, Intelligence, prudence in business. *Hūtat*, A kind of game called دارة *dārat*.

A حوف *hawf*, Something resembling the camel-litter هودج *hawdaj*. A large leathern water-bag. A leathern girdle worn by menstruous women or children under age.

P حوفران *hawfarān*, Tarragon.

A حوفزي *hawfazaʼ*, (v. n. of حوفز Q) Holding (a child) and raising (it) on tip-toe.

A حوفلة *hawfalat*, (v. n. of حوفل Q) Swelling, enlarging itself (glans penis). Glans penis.

A حوق *hawk*, (v. n. of حاق for حوق) Sweeping. Rubbing, smoothing. Surrounding, encompassing. A great multitude. Having the stumps of lopped branches left on the stem (a palm-tree). *Hūk* or *hawk*, Margo glandis.

A حوقاء *hawkāʼ*, Large (glans penis).

A حوقة *hawkat*, A crowd scattered.

A حوقل *hawkal*, Penis.

A حوقلة *hawkalat*, (v. n. of حوقل Q) Being impotent (an old man). Pushing, thrusting, driving away. Withered (penis). A long-necked flask or decanter. A quick pace with short steps. Fatigue, weariness. Weakness. Sleep. Retrogression. A resting with the hands on the sides (as is the way of a feeble old man). See حولقة *hawlakat*.

A حوك *hawk*, (v. n. of حاك for حوك) Weaving. Arranging (a poem). Being firmly fixed in the breast. Basil royal. Parsley. Purslain.

A حوكة *hawakat*, (pl. of حائك) Weavers.

A حوكشيّة *hawkashīyat*, Camels originally bred by one حوكش *hawkash*, of the tribe مهرة *mahrat*.

A حوكل *hawkal*, Dwarfish. Covetous.

A حوكلة *hawkalat*, A mode of walking.

A حوّل *huwul*, (v. n. of حال for حول) Departing,

going towards. Receding from an agreement.

A حول *hawl*, (v. n. of حال for حول) Changing. Elapsing, passing by. Departing, turning towards. Being of one year's growth (an animal). Leaping on horseback. Intervening, hindering, preventing. Revolving (the year). Having years pass over it (a house). Being agitated, shaking, trembling, wavering. Receding, departing from (an agreement or custom). Squinting. Being altered, turned, changed (colour). Being crooked, bent (as a bow). Fraud, deceit, craft, wile, sagacity. (pl. احوال *ahwāl*, حؤول *huūl*, and حوول *huwūl*) A year. Power. لا حول و لا قوة الا بالله *lā hawla wa lā kūwata illā bi'llāh*, There is no power nor strength except in God. *Hūl*, (pl. of حائل *hāril*) Camels not conceiving in the first year. (pl. of حولة *hūlat*) Wonders. Disagreeable and iniquitous affairs. *Hawal*, The being squint-eyed. Intervenient. *Hawil*, A squinter. *Hawla*, Round, round about. Over against. *Hiwal*, Obliquity (of eye). A turn, return. Change, departure. Transportation, passage. Craft, wile, sagacity. Power. A wonder, prodigy. A trench wherein palm-trees are planted in a row. (pl. of حيلة *hīlat*) Tricks. *Huwal*, Whatever intervenes, or stands between two objects. Very sly.

A حوّل *hūwal*, Prudent, fore-sighted. Versatile, fruitful in stratagems. (pl. of حائل *hāril*) Camels which do not conceive the first year.

A حولاء *hawlā*, Squinting (eye). Squint-eyed (woman). حولاء الناقة *hiwalāu'n nākat*, An expression employed to denote fertility and abundance of water. *Hiwalā* or *huwalā*, A membrane coming along with the fœtus.

A حولان *hūlān* or *hawalān*, A wonder, prodigy.

A حولة *hawlat*, Craft, wile, sagacity. Power, strength. *Hūlat*, (pl. حول *hūl*) Very sly. Misfortune. An unpleasant or iniquitous affair. A prodigy. Astonishment, wonder. *Huwalat*, Very sly.

A حولق *hawlak*, Pain in the throat. Misfortune.

A حولقة *hawlakat*, (v. n. of حولق Q) Saying لا حول و لا قوة الا بالله *lā hawla wa lā kūwata illā bi'llāh*, Neither power nor strength except in God.

A حولل *hūlal*, A camel not conceiving in the second year. (pl. of حائل *hāril*) Camels which do not conceive the first year.

A حولول *hawalwal*, Very sly. Ugly. Swift.

A حولي *hawla'*, Very sly (man).

A حوليّ *hawliy*, (fem. حوليّة *hawliyat*) A yearling animal (of the solid-hoof species).

A حوّلي *hūwaliy*, Versatile. Prudent, clever.

A حواليه *hawlayhi*, Round him. Over against him.

A حوم *hawm*, (v. n. of حام for حوم) Going round. Skimming in circles (as a bird). A large herd of camels. *Hawm* or *hawam*, (v. n. of حام for حوم) Anxiously desiring. *Hūm*, Vertigo.

A حوّم *hūwam*, (pl. of حائم *hāim*) Anxiously desirous. Thirsty (camels).

A حومان *hawmān*, A certain wild plant. *Hawamān*, (v. n. of حام for حوم) Moving round. Skimming in circles (a bird). (pl. of حومانة *hawmānat*) Rugged places.

A حومانة *hawmānat*, (pl. حومان *hawmān* and حوامين *hawāmīn*) A rugged place. Name of a plant.

A حومة *hawmat*, The greatest quantity or power of any thing. A field of battle. A thronged street. حومة القتال *hawmatu'l kitāl*, The chief strength of the battle. *Hūmat*, Beryl.

A حومر *hūmar* or *hawmar*, A tamarind.

A حومسيس *hawmasīs*, Emaciated.

A حومل *hawmal*, A current of pure water. The first of any thing. A cloud black with rain. Name of a penurious woman, who starved a bitch, that kept watch at night, until it bit off its own tail: hence, اجوع من كلبة حومل *ajwaɛ min kalbati hawmal*, More famished than Hawmal's bitch.

A حوملة *hawmalat*, A carrying of water.

A حونس *hawannas*, Immoveable; one whom it is impossible to oppress or move from his place.

A حوور *huwūr*, The act of returning.

A حؤول *huūl*, (v. n. of حال for حول) Elapsing, passing by. Changing, turning. *Huūl*, (or حوول *huwūl*) (pl. of حول *hawl*) Years.

A حوول *huwūl*, (v. n. of حال for حول) Not conceiving for one or two years (a camel). Passing, elapsing (a year).

A حووم *huwūm*, (v. n. of حام for حوم) Anxiously desiring.

A حويٰ *hawa'*, (v. n. of حوي) Being of a black colour inclining to green, or red inclining to black.

A حوّي *hawwa'*, Eve, the first woman.

A حويّ *hawiy*, An occupant or possessor after having deserved. A small cistern. Any thing circular and coiled.

A حويّة *hawiyat*, (pl. حوايا *hawāya'*) An intestine, or the fat adhering to it. A quilted cloth put over a camel's bunch, to prevent the load from hurting it. Circumference. A small kind of bird.

P حويج *hawij*, Pot-herbs, seasonings. Sweets.

A حويجاء *huwayjā*, Necessity, want. A call of nature. Hope, wish. Scruple, doubt. A contrary and zig-zag road.

P حويجي *hawījī*, Sweetmeats.

A حويذ *hawīz*, Nimble, clever, active in business.

A حوير *hawīr*, A reply. Enmity, mutual injury.

A حويرة *hawīrat*, A reply.

A حويزاء *huwayzā*, A treasure, deposit, hoard.

A حويساء *huwaysā*, Relationship, kindred.

A حويل *hawīl*, Any thing longed for, desired. A witness. A surety. Transportation, passage, change. Aim, search, design, purpose, intention. Cleverness, quickness, sharpness.

A حويلة *hawīlat*, Craft, wile, finesse. Power.

A حويلي *hawīlī*, A house, dwelling, habitation. The districts attached to, and in the vicinity of, the capital of a province. Government-lands.

A حيّ *hayy*, (v. n. of حوي) Collecting, comprehending, embracing. Occupying. Guarding, protecting. (v. n. of حيي) Living. Being plain and open (a road). Approaching (fifty). (pl. احياء *ahyā*) Alive. A family, part of a tribe. Plain, open (road). Pudendum muliebre. Name of a tribe. حيّ العالم *hayyu'l ɛālam*, Houseleek. حيّ لا يموت *hayy lā yamūt*, Ever-living, eternal. حيّ الماء *hayyu'l mā*, Quicksilver. حيّ و قيّوم *hayy u kayyūm*, Living and immortal (epithets of the Supreme Being). لا يعرف الحيّ من اللّيّ *lā yaɛrifu'l hayy mini'llayy*, He knows not truth from falsehood. *Hayy* or *hiy*, (pl. of حياء *hayā*) Womens' privities. *Hiy*, Life. *Hayya*, Come hither! approach! حيّ فلان *hayy fulān*, Hallo! Such an one.

A حيا *haya'*, Rain. A plentiful year. Vulva.

A حياء *hayā*, (v. n. of حيي) Living. Blushing. Being plain and open (a road). Shame, penitence. Rain. Plenty. (pl. احياء *ahyā*, احيية *ahyiyat*, حيّ *hayy* and *hiy*) Vulva, uterus. قليل الحياء *kalīlu'l hayā*, Shameless, unblushing.

A حيابة *hiyābat*, The act of sinning.

A حياة (originally حيوة *hayat*), Life. Life-time. حيات ابدي *hayāti abadī*, Eternal life, salvation. P حيات تازه *hayāti tāza*, New life, (used to express recovery from severe illness, or the pleasure derived from meeting a friend).

A حيّات *hayyāt*, (pl. of حيّة *hayyat*) Serpents.

P حيات بخش *hayāt-bakhsh*, Life-giving.

A حياد *hiyād*, (v. n. 3 of حاد for حيد) Turning aside, deviating. حيدي حياد *hīdī hayādi*, Make way!

A حيّاد *hayyād*, Any thing. A sup of milk.

P حيا دار *hayā-dār*, Modest.

A حياري *hayara'* or *huyara'*, (pl. of حيران *hayrān*) Astonished, startled, amazed, dazzled.

A حيازة *hiyāzat*, (v. n. of حاز for حوز) Collecting, gathering. Accumulating. Driving.

A حياص *hiyās*, (v. n. 3 of حاص for حيص) Laying snares. Overcoming by stratagem.

A حياصة *hiyāsat*, (v. n. of حاص for حوص) Sewing together, joining. Root, origin. A girdle.

A حياض *hiyāz*, (pl. of حوض) Large reservoirs.

A حياط *hiyāt*, (pl. of حائط *hāit*) Walls.

A حياطة *hiyātat*, (v. n. of حاط for حوط) Keeping, preserving. Watching. Drawing in. Surrounding. An enclosure in which corn is kept. A vineyard surrounded by a wall. Space within the walls of towns, not allowed to be built upon, lest it might endanger the defence of the place.

A حياك *hiyāk*, The act of weaving.

A حيّاك *hayyāk*, A weaver. Strutting fellow.

A حياكة *hiyākat*, Art of weaving. Basil royal.

A حيّاكة *hayyākat*, Strutting (woman).

A حيال *hayāl*, A string tied to the hinder girth of a camel to prevent it from pressing his sheath. Opposite, over against. *Hiyāl*, (v. n. of حال for

حيل) Not conceiving (camels) though covered, or a palm-tree though fecundated. Opposite, contrary. (pl. of حائل *hāʼil*) Camels not conceiving the first year. *Hiyāla*, (or بحيال *bi hiyāli*) Near. Over against.

A حيالة *hiyālat*, A failing to conceive.

A حيام *hayām*, A desiring anxiously.

A ابو حيّان *abū hayyān*, Name of a grammarian.

A حيبة *hībat*, Maternal kindred. Want, necessity. State, quality.

A حيّة *hayyat*, (pl. حيّات *hayyāt* and حيوات *hayawāt*) A serpent (said never to die except from accident). A fertile country. Name of a constellation called the Serpent. حيّة الوادي *hayyatu'l wādī*, (Serpent of the valley) A lion. *Hayyatu'l wādī*, (حيّة الارض *hayyatu'l arz*, or حيّة الحماط *hayyatu'l hamāt*) A cunning and malignant fellow. ذو الحيّة *zū'l hayyat*, Name of a king who reigned a thousand years. سمك حيّة *samak hayyat*, An eel.

A حيتان *hītān*, (pl. of حوت *hūt*) Large fishes.

A حيث *haysa*, (*haysu*, or حيثما *haysumā*) Where. Wheresoever, to whatever place (you go I will follow). الى حيث *ila' hays*, Whither? To whatever place. بحيث *bi hays*, So that. من حيث *min hays*, Whence? From what place. Seeing that, because. حيث بيث *haysa baysa*, Scattered, dispersed.

A حيثيّة *haysīyat*, Position, locality. Ubiquity. Universality (in science). Quality. Capacity, ability, merit. A conditional proposition. Examination. ارباب حيثيت *arbābi haysīyat*, Contemplative, scientific (persons).

A حيحاء *hīhāʼ*, *hayhāʼ*, or حيحاة *hayhāt*, (v. n. of حيحي Q) Calling (goats).

A حيد *hayd*, (v. n. of حاد for حيد) Turning aside from, swerving. (pl. حيود *huyūd*, احياد *ahyād* or حيد *hiyad*) A transverse knot upon the horn of an ibex or mountain-goat. A projection from a mountain's side. A bump or inequality in a horn or mountain. Any thing much curved like a rib. The conspicuous part of any object. *Hayd* or *hīd*, Alike, similar. *Hayad*, The sticking fast of a lamb when yeaned, and not coming out easily. Food.

A حيّد *hayyid*, Startled at his own shadow (ass).

A حيدار *haydār*, Hard gravel.

A حيدان *haydān*, Gravel (thrown about by a horse). *Hayadān*, (v. n. of حيد) Turning aside from.

A حيدة *haydat*, (v. n. of حاد for حيد) Turning aside from. An evil glance.

A حيدر *haydar*, (or حيدرة *haydarat*) A lion. حيدر علي *haydar ʻalī*, First sultān of Mysore.

P حيدر آباد *haydar-ābād*, Two cities in India.

A حيدرة *haydarat*, Destruction, ruin. A lion. A name of Alīy son-in-law of Muhammad.

A حيدلان *haydalān*, Short, dwarfish.

A حيدودة *haydūdat*, A turning aside from.

A حيدى *hayada'*, (An ass) that startles at his own shadow. A pompous strut.

A حيذوان *hayzuwān*, A ring-dove, wood-pigeon.

A حير *hayr*, (v. n. of حير) Being driven to and fro. A low-lying place where water lodges. A garden. A refuge. Kerbelā. A fold for cattle. *Hayr* or *hayar*, (v. n. of حار for حير) Being astonished, confounded, disturbed. Being dazzled (the sight). في حير بير *fi hīra bīra*, (or *hīrin bīrin*) In error. Without craft, trade, or income. *Hiyar* or *hayar*, Numerous (cattle or people). حير دهر *hiyara dahrin*, At any time, ever.

A حيّر *hayyir*, A cloud or mist covering the sky.

A حيراء *hayrāʼ*, Astonished, bewildered (woman).

A حيران *hayrān*, (pl. حياري *hayāra'* or *huyāra'*) Astonished, confounded, confused, bewildered, dazzled, amazed, astounded. *Hīrān*, (pl. of حائر *hāʼir*) Places into which waters flow. Low-lying (places). Gardens. (pl. of حوار *huwār*) Young sucking camels. عقرب الحيران *ʻakrabu'l hīrān*, Intense cold, hurtful to camels' colts. *Hayarān*, (v. n. of حار for حير) Being astonished, confounded.

A حيراني *hayrānī*, Astonishment, perturbation.

A حيرة *hayrat*, (v. n. of حار for حير) Being astounded, confounded. Being dazzled (eyes). Amazement. *Hīrat*, A city in Mesopotamia. A reply.

A حيرتان *hīratāni*, (dual) Hīrat and Kūfa.

P حيرت انگيز *hayrat-angez*, Exciting wonder.

A حيرم *hayram*, An ox. A cow.

A حيرما *hayramā*, Sometimes, often.

A حيري *hayra'*, Astonished, amazed (woman).

A حيريّ *hīriy*, Native of Hīrat in Mesopotamia. حيريّ الدهر *hayrīya'd dahr*, *hīriya'd dahr*, حيري دهر *hīri* or *hīra' dahrin*, At any time, ever.

A حيز *hayz*, A vehement driving forward. A gentle driving. *Hayz*, (or حيّز *hayyiz*), (pl. احياز *ahyāz*) A place, portion, tract of ground. A courtyard, area. *Hayzi*, A word used in driving an ass.

P حيز *hīz*, A vessel used in baths, either for drinking or pouring water upon the body. A catamite.

A حيزبور *hayzabūr*, A decrepit old woman.

A حيزبون *hayzabūn*, A decrepit old woman.

A حيزوم *hayzūm*, The breast, or the middle of it. The parts round the back and belly, the heart-ribs. High and rugged ground. The steed on which the angel Gabriel is said to ride.

P حيزي *hīzī*, Sodomy.

A حيس *hays*, (v. n. of حاس for حيس), Twisting a rope. Mixing or preparing a kind of dish made from dates, butter, and coagulated milk. Food thus prepared. A bad business. *Hayas*, (v. n. of حيس) Approaching, coming near one (death).

A حيسمان *haysumān*, Thick and brown (man).

A حيش *hayash*, (v. n. of حاش for حيش) Quaking from fear. Inspiring with terror. Making haste in going. Increasing, overflowing (a river).

A حيشان *hayshān*, (fem. حيشانة *hayshānat*) One who trembles greatly and dreads suspicion.

A حيشانة *hayshānat*, Woman dreading suspicion.

A حيشة *hīshat*, Reverence. Shame. A shrinking.

A حيص *hays*, (v. n. of حاص for حيص) Turning away from, swerving. Flying, escaping, retreating. Difficulty, perplexity, straits. حيص بيص *haysa baysa*, A perplexed business, a misfortune. Perplexity, hesitation, suspense.

A حيصاء *haysāʼ*, Narrow in the vulva.

A حيصان *hayasān*, A turning aside. A fleeing.

A حيصة *haysat* (v. n. of حاص for حيص) Running away. Turning aside from, swerving.

A حيصل *haysal*, The egg-plant.

A حيض *hayz*, (v. n. of حاض for حيض) Having the courses (a woman), and on that account abstaining from prayer. Emitting a humour resembling blood (the thorny shrub سمرة *samurat*). The menstrual discharge. P حيض آوردن *hayz āwardan*, To be menstruous. A ولد الحيض *waladu'l hayz*, A term of reproach. P حيض سفيد *hayzi safed*, Semen genitale. حيض عروس رز *hayzi ʻarūsi raz*, Red wine.

A *Hiyaz*, (pl. of حيضة *hīzat*) Catamenia.

A حيّض *huyyaz*, (pl. of حائض) Menstruous.

A حيضة *hayzat*, One menstruous turn. *Hīzat*, (pl. حيض *hiyaz*) A menstruous cloth. The menses.

A حيضي *hayzī*, A wicked brat.

A حيطان *hītān*, (pl. of حائط *hāʼit*) Walls.

A حيطة *haytat* or *hītat*, Intelligence, prudence. *Hītat*, (v. n. of حاط for حوط) Guarding, keeping, preserving, minding. Drawing in. A court, palace. A barn. An enclosure. Affection, inclination. مع فلان حيطة لك *maʻ fulānin hītatun laka*, Such an one is much inclined towards thee.

A حيعلة *hayʻalat*, (v. n. of حيعل Q) Pronouncing the formula حيّ علي الصلوة *hayya ʻala's salāt*, Come to prayer! (or علي الفلاح *ʻala'l falāh*) To safety or happiness!

A حيف *hayf*, (v. n. of حاف for حيف) Practising injustice. Injustice, violence, oppression. A male owl. The edge of a stone. *Hiyaf*, (pl. of حيفة *hīfat*) Sides, quarters.

A حيّف *huyyaf*, (pl. of حائف *hāʼif*) Sides, margins, edges, brinks. Unjust, tyrannical, oppressive.

A حيفاء *hayfāʼ*, (A field) not rained on. Ah! alas!

A حيفة *hīfat*, (pl. حيف *hiyaf*) A side, edge, margin, quarter. A piece of wood used in polishing bows and arrows. A patch in mending a shirt.

A حيفس *hayfas*, Provoked to anger, irritated. *Hiyafs*, A bloated glutton. One angry or pleased at nothing. *Hiyafs*, (حيفساء *hiyafsāʼ* or حيفسيّ *hiyafsiy*) Thick, good for nothing (man).

A حيق *hayk*, (v. n. of حاق for حيق) Surrounding, girding. Lighting upon, overtaking (as affliction or a snare). Whatever befals a man as the result of his own misconduct. Penetrating (sword).

A حيقال *hīkāl*, (v. n. of حقل) Being impotent (an old man).

A حيقان *hayakān*, (v. n. of حاق for حيق) Surrounding. Penetrating (a sword). Descending, lighting upon.

A حيقة *haykat*, A certain plant like wormwood.

A حيقر *hayhar* or *haykur*, Vile, contemptible, abject, mean. Weak.

A حيقط *haykut*, (or حيقطان) A woodcock.

A حيقل *haykal*, Worthless, good for nothing.

A حيك *hayk*, (v. n. of حاك for حيك) Strutting. Sinking into the mind (a word). Cutting, penetrating (a sword or large knife).

A حيكان *hayakān*, (v. n. of حاك for حيك) Shaking his body, and walking wide (a short man). Strutting. Penetrating (a sword or a speech).

A حيكانة *haykānat*, Strutting (woman), straddling (lizard).

A حيكى *hayakā'*, Strutting (woman).

A حيل *hayl*, Power. Craft, wile, sagacity. (pl. احيال *ahyāl* and حيول *huyūl*) Water stagnating in the bed of a river. *Hiyal*, (pl. of حيلة *hīlat*) Frauds.

A حيلان *hīlān*, A thrashing-instrument.

A حيلة *haylat*, A trip or flock of goats. Stones rolled from the top of a mountain to the bottom. Craft, cunning, shrewdness. Power. *Hīlat*, (pl. حيل *hiyal*, or حيلات *hīlāt*, or *hiyalāt*) Machination, fraud, treachery, stratagem, finesse, knavery. Disguise. Art, invention, cunning, knack. Power.

P حيله كردن *hīla kardan*, (or نمودن *namūdan*) To use art, to deceive. To lay snares.

A حيلق *haylak*, Misfortune.

A حيلم *haylam*, Certain small reptiles.

A حيلولة *haylūlat*, (v. n. of حال for حول) Coming between, intervening.

P حيله باز *hīla-bāz*, (or كار) A knave, cheat.

P حيله بازي *hīla-bāzī*, Villainy, deceit.

P حيله ساز *hīla-sāz*, A cheat, deceiver.

P حيله فروش *hīla-farosh*, A dealer in deceit; a crafty fellow. Sly, malicious, crafty.

P حيله‌گر *hīlagar*, A cheat. Subtle, crafty.

P حيله‌ور *hīlawar*, A cheat, a deceiver.

P حيله‌وري *hīlawarī*, Deceit, roguery.

A حين *hayn*, (v. n. of حان for حين) Arriving (time). Perishing. Drying, withering (an ear of corn). Being near to. Destruction. Death. A sore trial. *Hīn*, (pl. احيان *ahyān* and احايين *ahāyīn*) Time, an age, forty years, seven years, half a year, two months, eve and morn, any given period of time. A fit or proper time. The hour of milking a camel. حين حيات *hīni hayāt*, Life-time.

A حينا *hīnan*, Sometimes, in some time. For a time, season, or limited period.

A حينة *haynat* or *hīnat*, A fixed period. الحينة *al hīnat*, Once in the day or night. *Hīnat*, The hour for milking. The quantity given at a milking.

A حينونة *haynūnat*, (v. n. of حان for حين) Being near (time). Proximity of season.

A حينئذ *hīnaʼizin*, Then, at that time.

A حيوات *hayawāt*, (pl. of حيّة *hayyat*) Serpents.

A حيوان *haywān*, (v. n. of حيي) Living. Life. An animal. A brute. حيوان غير ناطق *haywāni ghayr nātik*, An irrational animal, a brute. حيوان ناطق *haywāni nātik*, A rational being. *Hayawān*, A living being, an animal. Life.

A حيوانات *haywānāt*, (pl. of حيوان *haywān*) Cattle, brutes.

P حيواني *haywānī*, Brutal. Sensual.

A حيوة *hayāt* or simply حيوة *hayat*, Life. الحيوة الطيّبة *al hayātu't tayyibat*, Lawful wealth. Paradise. روح حيوت *rūhi hayāt*, The spirit of life.

P روح بخش و حيوت افزا *rūh-bakhsh u hayāt-afzā*, Giving spirits and prolonging life.

A حيّوت *hayyūt*, A male serpent.

A حيود *hayūd*, One who inclines much. *Huyūd*, (v. n. of حاد for حيد) Declining, turning from, swerving. (pl. of حيد *hayd*) Projections from the sides of mountains. Knots in the horns of mountain-goats.

A حيوص *hayūs*, Timid, frightened, fleeing (animal). *Huyūs*, (v. n. of حاص for حيص) Turning aside. Fleeing away. Retiring.

A حيوق *huyūk*, (v. n. of حاق for حيق) Surrounding. Descending on. Penetrating (a sword).

A حيول *huyūl*, A being changed, altered. (pl. of حيل *hayl*) Stagnant waters in a river's bed.

A حيويّ *hayawīy*, Serpentine. Related to the tribe of حيّ *hayy*.

A حيهل *hayhal*, (حيّهل *hayyahal* or *hayyihal*) Name of a dwarfish, salt, and leafless plant.

A حيّهل *hayyahal*, *hayyahala*, (حيّهلن *hayyahalan* or حيّهلاً *hayyahalan*) Help! come!

A حييّ *hayīy*, Bashful.

A حييّة *huyayyat*, (dim. of حيّة) A little serpent.

A حييج *huyayj*, (dim. of حاج *hāj*) Small thorny plants called حاج *hāj*.

A حييكة *huyaykat*, Short, compressed (woman).

A حييي *hayyīy*, Of the tribe of حيّ *hayy*.

خ

خ *khā*, (called خاء سخية *khāʼi sakhiya*, خاء منقوطة *khāʼi mankūta*, خاء معجمة *khāʼi muʼjama*, Dotted *khā*) The seventh letter of the Arabic alphabet, and the ninth of the Persian, expressing in arithmetic 600. Its power is generated by a gentle vibration in the throat. The sound is not familiar to the English, but is used by the Scotch in the word loch. In this edition it is represented by *kh*. In Persian it is called *khe*. It represents Tuesday in almanacks. It is interchangeable with غ *ghayn* and ه *he*, as ستيغ *sitegh* for ستيخ *sitekh*, هجير *hijīr* for خجير *khijīr*.

P خا *khā*, The shoulder. A sewer, sink. (part. of خاييدن *khāyīdan*, used in comp.) Chewing. طوطي شكرخا *tūtīʼi shakar-khā*, A sugar-eating parrot.

P خاء *khāʼ*, Crines ani.

A خاء *khāʼ*, The letter *khā*. خاء بك علينا *khāʼi bika ʼalaynā*, Come to us quickly.

P خاب *khāb*, Cast back, rejected. Sleep.

A خابّة *khābbat*, (pl. خوابّ) Affinity, kindred.

A خابث *khābis*, Impure, wicked, base, deceitful. A subtle harlot.

A خابثة *khābisat*, Wickedness, impurity.

A خابر *khābir*, Knowing, informed, certified.

A خابز *khābiz*, Possessed of bread (خبز *khubz*).

A خابس *khābis*, A lion.

A خابط *khābit*, A stumbler. خابط الليل *khābitu'l layl*, A spectre, night-walker. A person in general.

A خابل *khābil*, Demoniacal madness. Mischievous, pernicious, corrupting. The devil.

A خابن *khābin*, Intense, strong, severe. One who lays up lies in store.

A خابور *khābūr*, Name of a river in Mesopotamia. A sort of plant.

A خابئ *khābiʼ*, Unsuccessful, foiled (plot).

A خابئة *khābiʼat*, A jar (for wine, oil, &c.).

P خابيدن *khābīdan*, To trample on, tread down. To make equal, adjust. (for خوابيدن) To sleep.

P خات *khāt*, A kite.

A خاتام *khātām*, (pl. خواتيم) A seal, signet.

A خاتر *khātir*, A deceiver. Perfidious.

A خاتل *khātil*, Insidious (wolf). A deceiver, cheat. Bold.

A خاتم *khātam*, End, conclusion. The hollow at the nape of the neck. The smallest quantity of white on the foot of a quadruped. *Khātim*, Who or what seals, a sealer. The joint of a horse's limb. *Khātam* or *khātim*, (pl. خواتم *khawātim*) A ring, seal-ring, seal, or signet. The last. خاتم الانبياء *khātimu'l ambiyāʼ*, The seal of the prophets (*i. e.* the last of the prophets, Muhammad). P خاتم جم *khātami jam*, The seal of Solomon (to which many wonderful qualities have been attributed by the Muhammadans). A cabalistic charm so called (See جم and سليمان *sulaymān*). The liver. خاتم سهيل *khātami suhayl-nishān*, (or خاتم گويا *khātami goyā* or *gūyā*) The mouth of a mistress.

P خاتم بند *khātam-band*, An inlayer. A seal engraver.

P خاتم بندي *khātam-bandī*, Inlaid work. Seal-engraving.

A خاتمة *khātimat*, (pl. خواتم *khawātim*) An end, conclusion. An epilogue.

P خاتمر *khātmar* or *khātmir*, (in zand) A sister.

P خاتمه بندي *khātima-bandī*, A kind of workmanship of which they make bows. Ceiling of a roof.

A خاتمي *khātamī* or *timī*, A ring or seal-maker.

P خاتمين *khātimin*, A sister.

A خاتن *khātin*, (fem. خاتنة) A circumciser.

P خاتوله *khātūla*, Fraud, deceit, seduction. Vileness, meanness of condition. War, battle. Full.

P خاتون *khātūn*, (Ar. pl. خواتين *khawātīn*) A lady, matron. خاتون جنت *khātūni jannat*, Queen of Paradise (a title given to Fātima, daughter of

Muhammad). خاتون جهان *khātūni jahān*, The sun. خاتون خرگه سنجاب *khātūni khargah-sinjāb*, The sun and moon. خاتون خم *khātūni khum*, A jar of wine. Wine. خاتون شبستان فلك *khātūni shabistāni falak*, The sun. The moon. The planet Venus. خاتون طيّاب *khātūni tayyāb*, Mecca. خاتون عرب *khātūni ɛarab*, (or خاتون كائنات *khātūni kāɛināt*) The Kaaba, or fane at Mecca. Fātima. خاتون عنب *khātūni ɛinab*, Wine. خاتون يغما *khātūni yaghmā*, The sun.

P خاتون آباد *khātūn-ābād*, A quarter in Ispahān.

A خاتيام *khātiyām*, A seal, a seal-ring.

A خاتية *khātiyat*, An eagle.

A خاثر *khāsir*, Thick (milk). Mixed, jumbled.

A خاثرة *khāsirat*, A body, troop, company of people. (A female) slightly affected with pain.

P خاج *khāj*, The cross. The soft part of the ear.

A خاجر *khājir*, The noise of water purling at the foot of a mountain.

P خاد *khād*, A kite.

A خادر *khādir*, Seated behind a curtain. (A lion) entering his den. Confounded. Torpid, lazy.

A خادشة *khādishat*, Extremities of a thorny tree.

A خادع *khādiɛ*, (pl. خدعة *khadaɛat*) A deceiver. Capricious, variable, changeable, fluctuating. (A road) sometimes plain, sometimes disappearing. Clipt (money) less than standard. بعير خادع *baɛīrun khādiɛun*, A camel, the tendon of whose leg moves from its place when he lies down.

A خادعة *khādiɛat*, A small door within a larger one; or a small house within a larger one. Flat, dull (market).

A خادم *khādim*, (pl. خدّام *khuddām*, خدم *khadam*, and خدمة *khadamat*) A domestic servant (male or female). A slave. An eunuch. خادم الطلباء *khādimu't tulabāɛ*, A public teacher, professor (of a college). P خادم پير *khādimi pīr*, (or سپهر *sipihr*) The planet Saturn. خادم درگاه *khādimi dargāh*, A servant who has the charge of a tomb or mosque.

A خادمة *khādimat*, A female servant.

A خادميّة *khādimīyat*, Service, servitude; act of serving; condition of a servant (خادم *khādim*).

P خادة *khāda*, A straight branch. A broomstick. An oar. A coal-rake. A gibbet.

A خاذر *khāzir*, A hider. One who hides himself from the officers of justice, or from a creditor. A fugitive.

A خاذل *khāzil*, One who denies assistance to a friend. Solitary (doe). A doe staying with her young. Routed, put to flight.

P خار *khār*, What scratches. A thorn, thistle, bramble. Pile, awn, or beard of barley. The quills of a porcupine. A sting. An enemy. Full-moon. An amorous gesture or blandishment. A very hard stone. A cock's spur. Vile. Name of a town in Persia. خار آهني *khāri āhanī*, An iron spike. خار دلو كش *khāri dalv-kash*, A hook for drawing up a bucket. خار راه *khāri rāh*, Thorns in the way. خار سپهر *khāri sipihr*, A misfortune. خار سپيد *khāri saped*, White-thorn; a thorny plant. خار شتر *khāri shutur*, A plant of which camels are fond. A thistle, teasel. خار شدن *khār shudan*, To be despised. خار كردن *khār kardan*, To vilify. خار واز گونه *khāri wāz gūna*, The inverted thorn. خار نهادن *khār nihādan*, To disobey. To oppress. خار و ترنج *khār u turunj*, (Thorns and oranges, or خار و خرما *khār u khurmā*, Thorns and dates) Trouble and repose. Indigence and affluence. خار و جمال *khār u jamāl*, A species of date.

P خارا *khārā*, A very hard stone. Waved silk.

P خارا تراش *khārā-tarāsh*, A stone-cutter.

P خارا سنگ *khārā-sang*, Marble.

P خارا شكاف *khārā-shikāf*, Stone-splitting.

P خار انداز *khār-andāz*, A porcupine.

P خارانيدن *khārānīdan*, To cause to scratch.

P خار آور *khār-āwar*, Thorny: a thorny brake.

P خارائي *khārāɛī*, Extreme hardness.

A خارب *khārib*, A thief. A camel-stealer.

P خار بست *khār-bast*, A hedge of thorns. Thorns fixed on a wall.

P خاربنان *khār-bunān*, Roots of brambles.

P خارپشت *khār-pusht*, (Thorn-back) A porcupine, a hedgehog. Name of a fruit. خارپشت بزرگ *khār-pushti buzurg*, (or خارپشت تير انداز *khār-pushti tīr-andāz*) A porcupine.

A خارة *khārat*, (pl. of خيّر *khayyir*) Virtuous.

A خارج *khārij*, External. Outside. One who rebels or comes forth in a hostile manner. الي الخارج *ila'l khārij*, Without, on the outside. من الخارج *mini'l khārij*, From without. P خارج آهنگ *khārij āhang*, Discordant, repugnant. A خارج جمع *khārij jamɛ*, Alienated from the rental. Allodial lands. P خارج حيطهٔ شمار *khārij hītaɛi shumār*, Innumerable. A خارج قسمت *khārij kismat*, Indivisible. خارج مركز *khārij markaz*, Eccentric.

P خارجا *khār-jā*, A thorny place.

A خارجاً *khārijan*, Out of doors.

A خارجة *khārijat*, Name of a certain man, whose mother is called امّ خارجة *umm khārijat*, who is also mother of several tribes.

P خارجنگ *khārjang*, (or خارچه *khārcha*) Name of a thorny plant, preserved in vinegar like capers.

A خارجه *khārija*, The word at the bottom of the page, which is repeated at the beginning of the next, an asterisk, a catch-word.

A خارجيّ *khārijīy*, A pretender, outlaw. Upstart nobility. Belonging to the people called Khārijīyat.

A خارجيّة *khārijīyat*, Name of a people.

P خارچنگ *khār-chang*, A crab. Cancer.

P خارچينه *khār-chīna*, Small forceps, tweezers. The nails of the thumbs and finger with which a pinch is inflicted.

P خارچيني *khār-chīnī*, A hard substance, whence the Chinese make mirrors: also arrow-heads, a wound from which is mortal.

P خار خار *khār khār*, Scratching. Scrubbing. Disquietude, anxiety. Affliction, anguish. Love, desire; the impulse of the heart. A wound, fissure. Heat. Itch.

P خار خسك *khār-khasak*, A triangular thorn.

A خارد *khārid*, Silent from modesty.

P خاردار *khār-dār*, Thorny. Barbed. Troublesome, arduous.

A خارز *khāriz*, A leathern-bottle stitcher.

P خارزار *khārzār*, A thorny place.

P خارزد *khār-zad*, Name of a thorny shrub.

P خارستان *khāristān*, A thorny place, a brake.

P خارسر *khār-sar*, Any thing pointed. خارسر بر *khār-sar-bur*, A thorn-cutter. An instrument for cutting thorns, a bill.

P خارش *khārish*, A sore, scratch. Scab, itch, mange. Itching. Scratching. خارش كردن *khārish kardan*, To itch.

P خارش ناك *khārishnāk*, Itchy, scabby.

A خارص *khāris*, (pl. خرّاص *khurrās*) One who estimates or guesses at the fruit on a tree or the produce on the ground. Hungry and cold.

A خارط *khārit*, Purged or scoured by green food.

A خارف *khārif*, The keeper of a palm-plantation. Name of a tribe in Yaman.

A خارق *khārik*, A tearer, splitter. افراس خارقة الصفوف *afrāsi khārikatu's sufūf*, Cavalry piercing the ranks. خارق عادت *khārik ɛādat*, Contrary to custom, uncommon.

P خارك *khārak*, A little thorn. Name of an island situated in the Persian Gulf; also of a species of dates which grow there.

P خاركش *khār-kash*, A wood-cutter. A poor man who for want of an ass is obliged to carry thorns. Name of a note in music. *Khār-kush*, A kind of leathern hose worn over boots.

P خاركن *khār-kan*, A digger up of thorns. A basket for carrying them in. A bush full of thorns. A nursery-man. Name of a note in music.

A خارم *khārim*, Cold. A cold wind. A deserter. A mischief-maker.

P خارماهي *khār-māhī*, A fish-bone. A sword-fish. A sturgeon.

P خارمهك *khār mahk*, A certain mountain-herb.

P خارناك *khārnāk*, Thorny.

P خارو *khārū*, A fish-bone. A beard of corn.

P خاروار *khārwār*, Thorny: pointed as a thorn.

A خاروج *khārūj*, A kind of palm-tree.

P خاروخس *khār u khas*, Rubbish, sweepings.

A خاروف *khārūf*, A lamb.

P خارون *khārūn*, Restive. What is scratched.

P خاروه *khārwa*, A sailor.

P خاره *khāra*, A hard stone. A kind of rich waved silk. A broomstick. A broom fixed on the end of a long pole. A woman.

A خاریٔ *khāri'*, One voiding excrement.

P خاري *khārī*, Meanness. Ignominy.

P خاريدن *khārīdan*, To scratch, itch. To curry (a horse). To provoke, irritate.

P خارين *khārīn*, Restive. What is scratched.

P خاز *khāz*, Dirt of the body, garments, and the like. A kind of linen garment. A pumice-stone for rubbing the heels in the bath.

A خاز باز *khāza bāza*, (or خازباء *khāzibā*) Flies in a meadow; also their buzzing. A disease in the neck of camels or men. A name of two sorts of herbs.

A خازر *khāzir*, Extremely shrewd, subtle.

P خازغان *khāzghān*, Brass.

A خازق *khāzik*, A spear-head. Hitting the mark (arrow). خازق ورقة *khāziku warakatin*, Bold, clever, whom no one dares molest.

A خازم *khāzim*, Cold (wind).

A خازن *khāzin*, A treasurer. The guardian of paradise. The tongue.

P خازندار *khāzin-dār*, (Ar. pl. خازندارة *khāzin-dārat*) A treasurer.

P خازنه *khāzana*, A wife's sister.

P خازني *khāzanī*, Name of a famous physician.

A خازوق *khāzūk*, A stake for impaling men.

P خازه *khāza*, Mixed, kneaded. Stucco.

A خازي *khāzī*, A shamer, disgracer.

P خازغان *khājghān*, A kettle, a pipkin.

P خاسپ *khāsip*, An apple.

P خاست *khāst*, Rising. Rise.

P خاستگي *khāstagī*, Rising or swelling of dough.

P خاستن *khāstan*, To rise, arise, get up. To excite an insurrection. To set out. (for خواستن *khwāstan*) To ask, petition.

P خاسته *khāsta*, Risen. Raised up. Leavened. A riser. نو خاسته *naw-khāsta*, Newly risen. A youth whose beard begins to appear.

A خاسر *khāsir*, A loser. One who has lost his way, a wanderer. كرّة خاسرة *karratun khāsiratun*, A losing, unprofitable turn. A useless, ineffectual assault or storm.

A خاسع *khāsiɛ*, Vilest (of the people).

A خاسف *khāsif*, (pl. خسف *khusuf*) Lean. Discoloured. Light (lad). Weak after sickness. A fountain flowing into low grounds.

A خاسق *khāsik*, A spear-head. Piercing the mark (arrow).

A خاسئ *khāsi'*, A driver away (of dogs or swine). Driven away from the society of men (dog or swine). Keeping aloof from the society of men.

P خاسيدن *khāsīdan*, To wax old.

P خاش *khāsh*, Rubbish, chips, parings. A bent of hay or straw. War, battle, strife. Vehemence, impetuosity. Immoderate in love or in friendship. Quarrelsome, squabbling. Avaricious. Doting, silly. Weak, cowardly. Abject, vile. A mother-in-law. Mastication. Name of a place.

A خاشّ *khāshsh*, (pl. خشّ *khashsh*) A pedestrian.

P خاشاك *khāshāk*, Chips, leaves, sprigs, shoots, suckers, young grass, small bits of wood, shavings, parings, or refuse of any kind; also dust, motes, straws, or any thing similar which gets into the eye, or liquors. Rubbish, siftings.

P خاشجو *khāsh-jo* or *jū*, Warlike, pugnacious.

A خاشر *khāshir*, A mob. (Barley) with no meal.

A خاشع *khāshiɛ*, Humble, modest, peaceable, bowing the head. Low (place) covered with dust, uninhabited, and pathless. قف خاشع *kuffun khāshiɛun*, A low hillock, nearly level with the ground.

A خاشف *khāshif*, One who travels through a country. One who travels boldly in the night-time. One who enters into an affair. Piercing (sword).

P خاشك *khāshak*, Sticks and straws: siftings.

P خاشكدان *khāshakdān*, A shop-till. A bread-basket. A little box or basket wherein women keep any little odds and ends.

A خاش ماش *khāsh-māsh*, or *khāshī māshi*, or خاس و خماش *khās u khamāsh*) Furniture, utensils, mean, common, and of little value.

P خاش وخش *khāsh u khash*, Sticks and straws. Chips, filings. Scraps, bits of leather.

P خاشوش *khāshūsh*, A reaping-hook.

P خاشه *khāsha*, Sticks, straws, bits of dung, &c., mixed together. Envy, jealousy.

A خاشي *khāshī*, One who fears: timid, fearful.

A خاصّ *khāss*, Particular, private, special. Own, proper, peculiar. Pure, unmixed. Fine, excellent. Single. Gentle. (pl. خواصّ *khawāss*) Noble, patrician. A royal favourite. Whatever (the king) enjoys, as his own domestic or private property. Holiness. خاصّ بحر *khāss-bahr*, The royal fleet of vessels sent every year to the king. P خاصّ بردار *khāss-bardār*, A soldier whose arms are furnished by his employer. The bearer of the betel-box. A servant who in a great man's retinue carries a firelock. خاصّ پوره *khāss-pūra*, Apartment for servants. A خاصّ تعلق *khāss-taɛalluk*, Lands exclusively belonging to government, from the original proprietors having died without heirs. An imposition of a tax to defray the expense of presents made to the king. P خاصّ جا *khāss-jā*, A sanctuary. A خاصّ الخواصّ *khāssu'l khawāss*, Most highly distinguished. P خاصّ دام *khāss-dām*, A tax for providing the king's wardrobe. خاصّ زر *khāss-zar*, Fine gold. خاصّ زمين *khāss-zamīn*, Quit-rent estates. A خاصّ طلب *khāss-talab*, Retinue, suite. خاصّ كتّان *khāss-kattān*, Fine linen, muslin. P خاصّ كردن *khāss kardan*, To apply to any particular use. To consecrate, to sanctify. A خاصّ محلّ *khāss-mahall*, A private apartment. The apartments of married women. First-married wife. P خاصّ نويس *khāss-navīs*, The office where the king's accounts are recorded. خاصّ نويسي *khāss-navīsī*, A cess for presents made to the king. خاصّ و عامّ *khāss u ɛāmm*, Noble and plebeian, gentle and simple, all, every body. Private and public. A اموال خاصّة *amwāli khāssa*, Private (royal) chattels. P سراي خاصّ *sarā-i khāss*, Inner apartments.

P خاصّان *khāssān*, (pl. of A خاصّ) Men of rank.

A خاصب *khāsib*, Red-thighed (ostrich).

A خاصّة *khāssat*, (fem. of خاصّ *khāss*) Special, private. Excellent, good, pure. Charming, virtuous. Property. Peculiarity. (pl. خواصّ *khawāss*) Noble, patrician. An intimate friend. خاصّة رجال *khāssa-i rijāl*, Chiefs of the people; nobles.

A خاصّة *khāssatan*, Especially, chiefly. But, yet, still. Only, at least. Entirely, quite, however. Truly, certainly.

A خاصرة *khāsirat*, (pl. خواصر *khawāsir*) The hypochondria, waist.

P خاصگان *khāsagān*, Nobles.

P خاصگي *khāsagī*, Peculiarity, speciality; excellence, nobility. Any thing choice and precious. A king's favourite. A royal page. A treasurer.

P خاصه *khāsa*, Fine cotton cloth of a close texture, called cossaes. An intimate, confidential friend. A private secretary. The king's victuals.

A خاصي *khāsī*, A castrator, a gelder.

A خاصّيّة *khāssīyat*, Specific or peculiar property, innate quality, natural disposition, intrinsic virtue, principle.

P خاصيدن *khāsīdan*, To suppress.

A خاضب *khāzib*, A young male ostrich with reddish, green, or yellow legs, from eating certain herbage, or from a desire for the female.

A خاضع *khāziɛ*, Humble, obsequious.

A خاضل *khāzil*, Moist, dewy.

A خاط *khāt*, A tailor.

A خاطب *khātib*, (pl. خطّاب *khuttāb*) A public speaker. A preacher. One who betroths or asks in marriage. (in gram.) The second person. خاطب الانبياء *khātibu'l ambiyā*, The prophets' preacher (Jethro, father-in-law to Moses).

A خاطر *khātir*, (pl. خواطر *khawātir*) Heart, mind, soul. Conscience. Marriage. Prayer, aspiration. Affection, propensity, inclination. Whatever occurs to or passes in the mind. Account, sake. Will, choice. Memory, remembrance. A man who walks with a stately or airy gait, a strutting fellow. P خاطر آسودن *khātir āsūdan*, To satisfy, appease. خاطر آويختن *khātir āwekhtan*, To be in love. خاطر داشتن *khātir dāshtan*, To like, have a mind for. خاطر دريا مقاطر *khātiri daryā-makātir*, A comprehensive mind. خاطر عاطر *khātiri ɛātir*, Gracious mind. خاطر كردن *khātir kardan*, To reconcile, satisfy.

P خاطر آزاري *khātir-āzārī*, Displeasure.

P خاطر آزرده *khātir-āzurda*, Melancholy, sad.

P خاطر آشفته *khātir-āshufta*, Discomposed.

P خاطر پسند *khātir-pasand*, Agreeable, liked.

A خاطر جمع *khātir-jamɛ*, Collected, composed,

comforted, contented, assured, tranquil, at one's ease. Satisfactory. Content, assurance, encouragement.

A خاطر جمعي *khātir-jamʿī*, Comfort, ease.

P خاطر خواه *khātir-khwāh*, A beloved object.

A خاطر خطير *khātir khatīr*, Noble mind.

P خاطر خواه *khātir-khwāh*, Agreeable to wish.

P خاطر خوش *khātir-khwush*, Contented.

P خاطر داري *khātir-dārī*, Confidence, comfort.

P خاطر داشت *khātir-dāsht*, Complaisance.

P خاطر زاده *khātir-zāda*, Offspring of the mind.

P خاطر فريب *khātir-firīb*, Stealing the heart.

P خاطر شكشا *khātir-kushā*, Heart-breaking.

P خاطر گرفته *khātir-girifta*, Displeased.

P خاطر گير *khātir-gīr*, Heart-captivating, mind-possessing; enchaining the affections.

P خاطر مانده *khātir-mānda*, Offended. خاطر مانده كردن *khātir-mānda kardan*, To disgust.

A خاطر ملول *khātir malūl*, Heart-sick, sad.

A خاطر ناقص *khātir-nākis*, Defective mind.

P خاطر نشان *khātir-nishān*, By heart. Any mark of remembrance. An instance of memory. A memorandum-book.

P خاطر نشين *khātir-nishīn*, Fixed in the memory. Chosen, beloved. خاطر نشين ساختن *khātir nishīn sākhtan*, To reconcile to, incline towards, impress favourably, conciliate, dispose.

P خاطر نگران *khātir-nigarān*, Anxious.

P خاطر نواز *khātir-nawāz*, Affable, gracious.

P خاطر نوازي *khātir-nawāzī*, Politeness.

P خاطره *khātira*, (for A خاطر) Mind, thought, design, intention, will, resolution, purpose.

A خاطف *khātif*, (pl. خواطف *khawātif*) A seizer, snatcher. Striking, blinding (lightning). A wolf. خاطف ظله *khātifu zillihi*, A certain bird, which upon seeing its own shadow reflected, endeavours to catch it.

A خاطوف *khātūf*, Toils for catching deer.

A خاطئ *khātiʾ*, Sinning: a sinner. One who does wrong intentionally. Deviating (arrow).

A خاطئة *khātiʾat*, (v. n. 4 of خطئ) Committing a fault, making a blunder, falling into an error.

A خاف *khāf*, Very fearful, timorous.

A خافة *khāfat*, A short leathern garment (worn by those who gather honey). A leathern bag, in which honey is put. A round sheet of leather (which is used, when spread, as a table, or converted into a travelling-sack, by the contraction of purse-strings round the edges).

A خافت *khāfit*, Silent, ceasing to speak, mute, dumb. The dead. Rainless cloud. Dwarfish corn.

A خافض *khāfiz*, A depressor; hence one of the attributes of God (as depressing the proud). Easy, quiet (life). (A particle) requiring the following word to be inflected with كسر *kasr*. (A night) in which one travels commodiously. خافض السقيا *khāfizu's sukya'*, Easily watered (field). خافض الطير *khāfizu't tayr*, Submissive and obedient.

A خافضة *khāfizat*, A female circumciser of girls. Low ground.

A خافق *khāfik*, Trembling, palpitating. The horizon. ايام الخافقات *ayyāmu'l khāfikāt*, Certain days whereon the stars were favourable to the fortunes of Abū Abbās and Abū Jāfar. خافقان *khāfikāni*, (oblique case خافقين *khāfikayni*) The two horizons, the east and west.

A خافقية *khāfikīyat*, A large drinking-cup.

A خافل *khāfil*, A fugitive.

A خافور *khāfūr*, A certain plant resembling tares.

A خافي *khāfī*, (pl. خوافي *khawāfī*) Occult, concealed. A demon.

A خافياء *khāfiyāʾ*, A demon or fairy.

A خافية *khāfiyat*, (pl. خوافي *khawāfī*) A secret, concealment, secrecy. A demon (possessing a man or haunting a place). A haunted place. The shortest feather in the wing.

A خاقان *khākān*, Emperor (of China or Tartary).

P خاقاني *khākānī*, Imperial. Name of a poet.

P خاقانيان *khākāniyān*, Emperors.

P خاق باق *khāk bāk*, A slang name for the vulva.

A خاقونية *khākūniyat*, A kind of veil.

P خاك *khāk*, Earth, soil, mould, dirt, ground. The grave. Any thing of little value, or useless. Quiet, mild, peaceable, obedient, submissive, humble. Humility, lowliness. خاك با خون سرشتن *khāk bā khūn sirishtan*, To make a general massacre. خاك بودن *khāk būdan*, To be lowly and submissive. خاك بيمار *khāki bīmār*, Pure gold. خاك بي ناموسي *khāki bī nāmūsī*, Freedom, immodesty, indecency. خاك پاي *khāki pāy*, The dirt or dust of the feet. Ground beat by the feet. خاك تاريك *khāki tārīk*, The human body. خاك تنگ *khāki tang*, A grave. بخاك چسپانيدن *ba khāk chaspānīdan*, To subdue, abase, degrade. خاك خلاص *khāk khalās*, Metal reduced to a powder. خاك دامنگير *khāki dāmangīr*, Mire, adhesive clay. خاك ذليلان *khāki zalīlān*, The bodies of infidels. خاك در بودن *khāk dar būdan*, To remain in one place. خاك ديوار خوردن *khāki dīwār khwurdan*, To practise content. خاك رنگين *khāki rangīn*, Gold. Silver. A bed of flowers. Man. خاك زدن *khāk zadan*, To sweep the ground. خاك شدن *khāk shudan*, To turn to earth. To die. To be despised. خاك شفا *khāki shafā*, Earth of the plain of Karbalā worn in rosaries, &c., and greatly venerated. خاك ضعيف *khāki zaʿīf*, Man. خاك مطبق *khāki mutabbak*, (or معلق *muʿallak*) The terrestrial globe. خاك و آب *khāk u āb*, The human body. خاك و باد *khāk u bād*, Earth and air. A footboy. A courier. A slave. Obedient.

P خاكا *khākā*, A plan, sketch, draft, outline.

P خاك آلودگی *khāk-ālūdagī*, Defilement with dirt, dirtiness.

P خاك آلوده *khāk-ālūda*, Soiled, dirtied.

P خاك انداز *khāk-andāz*, A shovel. Loop-hole. A sling. Fringe or skirt of a tent. A magician.

P خاكباز *khāk-bāz*, A kind of game.

P خاك بدر *khāk ba dar*, (Dirt at the door) Grieved. Dead. Distress, poverty.

P خاك بدهن *khāk ba dahan*, May you perish! may you have dirt (or earth) in your mouth!

P خاك بر داشته *khāk bar dāshta*, Lifted from the mire.

P خاك برسر *khāk bar sar*, (Earth upon the head) Distress, poverty. Grieved. Dead.

P خاكبيز *khāk-bez*, One who sweeps the streets and sifts the dirt. A large sieve for screening gravel or lime. One who braves difficulties to gain his point. Quick-sighted, discerning, intelligent.

P خاكبيزي *khāk-bezī*, Condition of a stranger. Travel, peregrination. Street-sweeping.

P خاك توده *khāk-tūda* or *toda*, A heap of earth. A butt to shoot at.

P خاك خسبه *khāk-khusba*, Name of a bird.

P خاك خفت *khāk-khuft*, Kissing the ground.

P خاك دان *khākdān*, A place where rubbish is deposited; also a sack in which it is carried. The world. خاكدان ديو *khākdāni dev*, The world.

P خاكدل *khāk-dil*, (Earth-hearted) An unbeliever. Ignorant. Adulterous.

P خاك رند *khāk-rand*, Dust.

P خاك روب *khāk-rob*, A sweeper.

P خاكروبه *khāk-roba*, Sweepings. A dunghill.

P خاكروبه بر *khāk-roba-bar*, A sweeper.

P خاكروبه كش *khāk-roba-kash*, A sweeper.

P خاك ريز *khāk-rez*, The foot of a wall.

P خاكزاد *khāk-zād*, Earth-born.

P خاكژي *khākjī*, Name of a certain seed used as an eye-salve.

P خاكسار *khāksār*, Earth-like. Mixed with earth, covered with dust. Base, mean, low-born, abject. One who sits in the shoe-hole.

P خاكساري *khāksārī*, Vile, abject. Dirtied, overspread with dust. Humility. Meanness.

P خاكسان *khāksān*, Contemptible, wretched.

P خاكستر *khākistar*, Ashes. خاكستر شدن *khākistar shudan*, To be reduced to ashes. To be calcined. خاكستر نشين شدن *khākistar-nishīn shudan*, To sit in ashes.

P خاكستر گون *khākistar-gūn*, Ash-coloured.

P خاكستر گوني *khākistar-gūnī*, An ashy colour.

P خاكستري *khākistarī*, Ash-coloured.

P خاكش *khākash*, A rake, harrow.

P خاك شو *khāk-shū*, A person in the mint who washes the ashes to recover any particles of bullion that may have fallen. The man who prepares earth for brick-making or pottery. A certain black grain from which an eye-salve is prepared.

P خاكشور *khāk-shor*, One who prepares earth or clay for building. One who washes the earth in which gold and silver have been fused, to discover if any particles remain.

P خاكشي *khākshi*, A weight for gold. A red bramble. A small seed used as an eye-salve.

P خاك صفت *khāk-sifat*, (Earth-like) Humble.

P خاك كش *khāk-kash*, A rake, harrow.

P خاك گينه *khāk-gīna*, A white mineral earth used in smelting, refining, or casting gold or silver.

P خاك نشين *khāk-nishīn*, Sitting on the ground; humble.

P خاك نمك *khāk-namak*, Salt-soil. A salt-mine. A boy's game, in which they hide something under one of many heaps of sand, he that hits upon the right heap gaining.

P خاكه *khāka*, A plan, a sketch.

P خاكي *khākī*, Earthen, terrestrial. Shameless, base, contemptible. Name of a tribe. The constellations Taurus, Virgo, and Capricorn. خاكي كردن *khākī kardan*, To surrender, submit. To be unsteady. خاكي نهاد *khākī-nihād*, Earth-born, humble. Worthy. Humility. Worthiness.

P خاكيان *khākiyān*, Mixed with earth. Mortals, terrestrials. Abject, destitute of all spirit or honour.

P خاكين *khākīn*, Earthen.

P خاگ *khāg*, An egg.

P خاگينه *khāgīna*, A fried egg, omelet.

P خال *khāl*, A mole, freckle. An eatable bird resembling a crow. A standard. An arrow. A large black camel. A vestige. An ambassador. A fountain, spring. Irksomeness, wearisome importunity. A pair, couple. Black. خالهاي شنگرفي *khālhāyi shangarfī*, Tears of blood trickling down the cheek. خال نان *khāli nān*, Seeds sprinkled upon bread. Blisters raised on a loaf by the fire. مشكين خال *mushkīn-khāl*, Having a musky or black mole (on the face).

A خال *khāl*, (v. n. of خال for خيل) Imagining, fancying, thinking. Being proud. Limping (a horse). Haughtiness, self-importance, conceit, pride, arrogance. Proud, haughty, conceited. A mask. A cloud. The disposition of the clouds to rain when much wanted. A sort of herb. Lightning. A rainy cloud which does not disappoint. A cloud without rain. A large horse or camel. A winding-sheet. A liberal man. A man free from the ties of love. A bachelor. A detached hill. One who sticks close to a thing. A bridle. A man weak of heart or of body. A man free from suspicion. An imaginative or fanciful man. (pl. خيلان *khīlān*) A mole on the face. Soft cloth. A striped Arabian garment. A garment worn by proud, silly, vain persons. Natural aptitude. Any thing good which one imagines. The standard of an army. An excellent administrator or manager. (pl. اخوال *akhwāl*, اخولة *akhwilat*, خؤول *khuʼul*, خؤول *khūwal*, and خوولة *khuwūlat*) An uncle by the mother. A black stallion (especially a camel). A master, owner.

A خالّ *khāll*, Scattered, disbanded (army).

P خالا *khālā*, An aunt.

P خالاون *khālāwun*, Name of a medicinal seed.

A خالب *khālib*, Deceiving; a deceiver.

A خالبة *khālibat*, A lying, deceitful woman.

A خالة *khālat*, A maternal aunt. Proud (woman or women). (pl. of خائل *khāʼil*) Proud.

P خال خال *khāl khāl*, Spotted very much.

A خالد *khālid*, Eternal, perpetual. ابو خالد *abū khālid*, A dog. الجزائر الخالدات *al jazāʼiru'l khālidāt*, The fortunate isles, in the western ocean.

P خالدار *khāl-dār*, Marked with moles.

P خالري *khālarī*, Salt works.

A خالص *khāliṣ*, Pure, unsullied. Uncorrupt, genuine, unadulterated. Best. White. A friend. خالص الجنان *khāliṣu'l janān*, Sincere of heart.

A خالصاً *khāliṣan*, (P خالصانه) Purely, sincerely.

A خالصة *khāliṣat*, (v. n. of خلص) Being good, choice, excellent. Being pure, uncorrupt. Friendship. Special, peculiar. Marrow. (fem.) Pure.

A خالصه *khāliṣa*, (or خالصه شريفه *khāliṣa sharīfa*) The principal court of exchequer, where all matters touching the revenue are transacted. Land held immediately from government.

A خالع *khāliʻ*, (A man or woman) who sues for a divorce. A dry, withered tree. Bearded, come into ear (corn). An ever-green, of the tree called عضاه *ʻiẓāh*. A very ripe date. A camel unable to rise. A twisting of a quadruped's hough.

A خالعة *khāliʻat*, A woman utterly shameless.

P خال عصي *khāl ʻaṣī*, Sin, transgression.

A خالف *khālif*, A successor, follower. Who lurks in the rear. One who sits behind. The latter part. Wicked, perverse, foolish. A water-drawer. Spoiled (wine). Opposition, contrariety. خالف اهل بيته *khālifu ahli baytihi*, The last, lowest, or worst part of the family.

A خالفة *khālifat*, The same as خالف *khālif* above. Foolish. Posterity. A very refractory and perverse man or woman. (pl. خوالف *khawālif*) Tent-pole. Opposition, contrariety. اي خالفة هو *ayyu khālifatin huwa*, What man he is (I know not).

A خالق *khāliḳ*, The Creator. A worker or cutter out of leather. خالق الجنّ و الناس *khāliḳu'l jinn wa'n nās*, Creator of demons and men.

A خالقيّة *khāliḳiyat*, Creative power.

A خالم *khālim*, Equal, equiponderant.

P خالم *khālum*, A serpent.

P خالناك *khālnāk*, Covered with moles. Freckled.

P خالو *khālū*, A maternal uncle. A trumpet.

P خالولنجان *khālūlinjān*, Galangale.

A خالون *khālūn*, (pl. of خالي) Reapers, mowers.

P خاله *khāla*, A maternal aunt.

P خاله بي بي *khāla-bībī*, Barley-broth.

A خالئ *khāliʼ*, Stubborn, that will not stir.

P خالي *khālī*, A large carpet. A maternal uncle. A garment. Arched eye-brows. A banner, streamer. *Khāle*, One mole (on the face).

A خالي *khālī*, Free, vacant, empty, void. Idle, unemployed. Proud. Pure, mere, unmixed. Only. (pl. اخلاء *akhlāʼ*) Unmarried (man or woman). A bachelor. Uncultivated, uninhabited. The time past. Past, bygone. A reaper. A grass-cutter. خالي السير *khālī's sayr*, Travelling alone. P خالي شدن *khālī shudan*, To be free, exempt from; to be empty, void. خالي كردن *khālī kardan*, To evacuate. To abandon, reject, throw away.

A خالية *khāliyat*, (fem. of خالي) Unemployed. قرون خالية *ḳurūnun khāliyatun*, Past ages.

G خاليدونيون *khālīdūniyūn*, Swallow-wort.

P خاليگ *khālīg*, A servant who has care of a nobleman's table.

P خام *khām*, Raw, undressed, crude. Unripe, immature. Unburnt (brick). A badly-executed business. Inexperienced. A headstall. A leathern garment. Wine. The silken cord of a musical instrument. A bungler. A voluntary cuckold. A horse that has been long in the stable. (for خامه *khāma*) A pen. A white reed. خام كردن *khām kardan*, To cancel. To throw aside.

A خام *khām*, An untanned hide, or one partially tanned. Unwashed linen. A stallion.

A خامّ *khāmm*, Stinking flesh.

G خاماء اقطي *khāmāʼi akṭī*, Dane-wort.

G خامادريوس *khāmādaryūs*, Germander.

G خامازاقي *khāmāzāḳī*, Dwarf laurel.

P خامارواں *khāmārwān*, The Egyptian willow.

G خامالا *khāmālā*, Mezereon.

A خامالانق الذئب *khāmālānaḳu'z ziʼb*, Wolfsbane.

G خامالاون *khāmālāwan*, Mezereon. Chameleon.

P خام آمدني *khām-āmadanī*, Gross receipts.

G خاماميلن *khāmāmīlin*, Camomile.

G خاماون *khāmāwan*, Mezereon.

P خامباز *khāmbāz*, A wide-mouthed kettle.

P خام پاره *khām-pāra*, A term of abuse applied to a woman who has been cohabited with before the age of maturity.

A خامة *khāmat*, An unhealthy region. Green, succulent grass, corn, or shrub. Dried grass. The duty of a stallion.

A خامد *khāmid*, Resting. Stupid. Dead.

P خام دست *khām-dast*, Raw-handed, unaccustomed to labour. Lazy, idle, barbarous, unskilful.

P خام روئينه *khām-roʼīna*, Parchment of a drum.

A خامس *khāmis*, The fifth.

A خامساً *khāmisan*, In the fifth place, fifthly.

P خامسوز *khām-soz*, A raw hide. The leather covering a saddle. A pancake, or any thing similar roasted on the coals, or on an iron plate. Meat roasted black.

P خامسوك *khāmsūk*, (or خامسوگ *khāmsūg*) Unleavened bread.

P خامش *khāmush*, Silent. Dead. Extinguished.

A خامشة *khāmishat*, A small stream.

P خام شوب *khām-shob*, Half-washed, rinsed.

P خامشه *khāmisha*, Fumitory.

P خامشي *khāmushī*, Silence, taciturnity.

A خامص *khāmis*, Extenuated, thin-bellied.

A خامط *khāmit*, Bitter. A bitter plant. One which yields little fruit. A kind of tree called اراك *arāk* producing little fruit. Sour milk. Good milk having a pomaceous smell. Milk which, though it have lost its sweetness, retains its smell. Sweetly-smelling (leathern bottle): also a stinking one.

P خام طبع *khām-tabع*, Foolish, dull.

P خام طبعي *khām-tabعī*, Ignorance, rawness.

P خام طمع *khām-tamaع*, Of vain desires.

A خامعة *khāmiعat*, (pl. خوامع) The hyena.

P خام عقلي *khām-عaklī*, Folly, imbecility.

P خامكار *khām-kār*, Unskilful, inexperienced.

P خامكاري *khām-kārī*, Awkwardness, rawness.

P خامگك *khāmagak*, A little pen.

A خامل *khāmil*, (pl. خمل *khamal*) Mean, obscure, unknown.

P خامن *khāmin*, Mean, obscure, unknown.

P خام نوش *khām-nosh*, A drinker of new wine.

P خاموش *khāmosh*, Silent, dumb. Silence. Extinguished. Dead. A disease in horses. Hush! خاموش بودن *khāmosh būdan*, (or شدن *shudan*) To be silent, to keep silence. خاموش كردن *khāmosh kardan*, To silence. To keep silence.

P خاموشي *khāmoshī*, Taciturnity, silence.

P خاموشيدن *khāmoshīdan*, To keep silence. To be modest. To pacify. To be wrinkled. To be wearied. To wind about.

P خام وصول *khām-wusūl*, Gross produce.

P خامه *khāma*, A pen, writing reed. Ink. A heap of sand. A heap. A flagon with a long neck. A tent made of goat's hair. Any thing of one colour. خامهٔ ازل *khāmaیi azal*, The pen of the divine decrees. خامهٔ زرين *khāmaیi zarīn*, A golden pen; letters illuminated with gold. خامهٔ سحرساز *khāmaیi sihr-sāz*, An enchanting pen. خامهٔ گوهرنثار *khāmaیi gawhar-nisār*, A pearl-scattering pen, *i.e.* an elegant writer.

P خامه دان *khāmadān*, A pen-case.

P خامه زن *khāma-zan*, A bit of wood or horn for nibbing pens on.

P خامه كش *khāma-kash*, Pen-drawing. Obliterating.

P خامي *khāmī*, Rawness, immaturity. Loss. A noose. A toil for ensnaring game. A heap of sand.

A خامي *khāmī*, (for خامس *khāmis*) Fifth.

P خاميار *khāmyāz*, (or خاميازه) Gaping.

P خاميز *khāmīz*, Broth strained and left to jelly.

P خان *khān*, A caravansary, inn, place of public reception for travellers. A prince, nobleman, lord. The khān of the Tartars. A house. A hive. A family, domestics, furniture, any thing in, or belonging to, a house. A tray or table. A shopkeeper. A shop. An exchange, market, or any other place where merchants meet. خان بره *khāni bara*, The sign Aries. خان خرك *khāni kharak*, A halting-place for a caravan. خان دل *khāni dil*, The Kaaba. خان ده *khāni dih*, (or دهخان *dihkhān*) A judge of a village or small town.

A خان *khān*, A tavern. A vintner. خان التجار *khānu't tujjār*, A caravansary.

P خاناده *khānāda*, (in Gīlān) An officer who communicates the orders of the general to the army.

A خانة *khānat*, (v. n. of خان for خون) Acting perfidiously, betraying. (pl. of خائن *khāیin*, خوون *khaیūn*, and خوّان *khawwān*) Faithless, treacherous. Deceivers.

P خانج *khānj*, A hole into which boys throw nuts.

P خانچه *khāncha*, A tray, salver. A small inn.

P خان خانان *khān khānān*, Lord of lords. A prime minister.

P خاندان *khānadān*, A family; house. Household. The court, king's household. Of noble blood. The master of a family. خاندان نبوّت *khānadāni nubūwat*, The depository of the prophetical office.

P خانديس *khāndes*, A province in the Dak'han.

A خانر *khānir*, (pl. خنّر *khunnar*) A real friend.

P خانسالار *khān-sālār*, A taster of provisions.

P خانسامان *khān-sāmān*, A house-steward, whose business is to furnish and regulate the table of the great. Rich, wealthy.

P خانساماني *khān-sāmānī*, The department which generally includes every household expense.

A خانع *khāniع*, (pl. خنعة *khanaعat*) Doubtful, suspected, scandalous. An adulterer, a whoremaster, a wicked man. Submissive, abject.

P خانغرد *khān-ghard*, A summer-house.

A خانف *khānif*, Fastidious, tossing the nose. (A camel) tender-footed, and turning the feet out.

A خانق *khānik*, A strangler. A narrow pass through mountains. A narrow street, alley. خانق الذئب *khāniku'z ziیb*, Wolfsbane. خانق الكلب *khāniku'l kalb*, Dogsbane. خانق الملك *khāniku'l malik*, Gall-apple. خانق النمر *khāniku'n namr*, A species of nightshade which destroys panthers.

P خانقاه *khānakāh*, (خانقه *khānakah*, خانگاه *khānagāh*, or خانگه *khānagah*) A monastery, or religious structure, built for the Eastern sophs or dervishes. A convent, chapel. A baiting-place. خانقاه بالا *khānakāhi bālā*, Heaven.

P خانقو *khānkū*, The city of Canton.

P خانگي *khānagī*, Belonging to the house, domestic. Home-baked bread. A kind of cake. A hen. A sparrow. A prostitute.

P خانگي محال *khānagī-mahāl*, A brothel.

P خانم *khānam*, A lady.

P خانمان *khānmān*, *khānumān*, or خان و مان *khān u mān*, Household furniture. A domestic animal. Riches, and especially hereditary possessions, moveable and real. The house, family, domestics. از خانمان بركندن *az khānmān bar kandan*, To eradicate, to tear up from house and home.

P خانواده *khānwāda* or *khānuwāda*, A family, house. A great tribe, an illustrious family. Noble, of an ancient family. The mistress of a family.

P خانه *khāna*, A house, dwelling, habitation. A tent, pavilion. A spider's web. A receptacle. A socket. The square of a chess-board. A point of the table in the game of نرد *nard*. A drawer, partition, compartment. Department. The arm from the shoulder to the elbow. A field. A woman. A page of letter-paper. A heap of corn. A hillock of sand. A plasterer. Verse, poetry. در خانه *dar khāna*, At home, in the house. صاحب خانه *sāhibi khāna*, Master of the house. كتاب خانه *kitāb-khāna*, A library. خانهٔ آفت ريز *khānaیi āfat-rez*, The world. خانهٔ باد *khānaیi bād*, An airy house. The signs Gemini, Libra, and Aquarius. خانهٔ پست *khānaیi past*, Nether world. خانهٔ ترازو *khānaیi tarāzū*, The sign Libra. خانهٔ خداي *khānaیi khudāy*, The house of God, *i.e.* the Kaaba or temple at Mecca. خانهٔ راستان *khānaیi rāstān*, The Kaaba. خانه روشن كردن *khāna roshan kardan*, To come to a conclusion. خانهٔ زر *khānaیi zar*, The sun. The fourth heaven. The sign Leo. خانهٔ زرين *khānaیi zarīn*, The sun. The stars. The eighth heaven. خانهٔ زمين كند *khānaیi zamīn-kand*, A subterraneous excavation wherein men shelter themselves. خانهٔ زين *khānaیi zīn*, The seat of a saddle. خانهٔ سيل ريز *khānaیi sayl-rez*, Wine. خانهٔ شش در *khānaیi shash dar*, (Six-doored house) The world. خانهٔ شير *khānaیi shīr*, The breast. The udder. *Khānaیi sher*, The sign Leo. خانهٔ عنقا *khānaیi عankā*, Name of a note in music. خانهٔ غول *khānaیi ghūl*, The world. خانهٔ فردا *khānaیi fardā*, The future world. خانهٔ كمان *khānaیi kamān*, The curved parts of the bow between the handle and the ends (the upper being called خانهٔ بالا *khānaیi bālā*, and the lower خانهٔ شبين *khānaیi shibīn*). خانهٔ مرغ *khānaیi murgh*, A bird's nest. خانهٔ نه در *khānaیi nuh dar*, (Nine-doored house) The world. The human body.

P خانها *khānahā*, (pl. of خانه *khāna*) Houses. The squares of a chess-board.

P خانه آباد *khāna-ābād*, Flourish your house!

P خانه باز *khāna-bāz*, One who stakes his all.

P خانه بدوش *khāna ba dosh*, A traveller, pilgrim, gipsey (whose house is on his shoulder).

P خانه برانداز *khāna bar andāz*, A traveller. A wandering monk. A prodigal, spendthrift. A beloved object.

P خانه پردازي *khāna-pardāzī*, Domestic economy, attention to household matters.

P خانه پرور *khāna-parwar*, Brought up at home.

P خانه پرورد *khāna-parward*, Brought up in the house; cade, cosset.

P خانه جنگ *khāna-jang*, Quarrelsome, ready to wrangle and fight about any trifle.

P خانه جنگي *khāna-jangī*, Civil war, bickering.

P خانه خانه *khāna khāna*, Cellular.

P خانه خدا *khāna-khudā*, Master of the house. An oratory.

P خانه خراب *khāna-kharāb*, Vain, empty, lying.

P خانه دار *khāna-dār*, Frugal, economical. A housekeeper.

P خانه داري *khāna-dārī*, Housekeeping.

P خانه داماد *khāna-dāmād*, A domesticated son-in-law.

P خانه دان *khānadān*, A great tribe, family.

P خانه دوست *khāna-dost*, Fond of home (a term of abuse).

P خانه رس *khāna-ras*, Unripe fruit falling from the branch, and coming to maturity in-doors.

P خانه روبه *khāna-roba*, Sweepings of a house.

P خانه زاد *khāna-zād*, Born in the family. The child of a slave.

P خانه سوز *khāna-soz*, Disgracing one's family.

P خانه شماري *khāna-shumārī*, House-counting: a house-tax.

P خانه فروش *khāna-farosh*, Renouncing the world, solitary. خانه فروشان *khāna-faroshān*, (pl.) Pure, devout. Hermits. Loose, abandoned fellows who frequent taverns and stews.

P خانه كن *khāna-kan*, Spendthrift. Prudent.

P خانه گير *khāna-gīr*, Possessing a house. The fourth of the seven games or rounds of the game of نرد *nard*. The first is فارد *fārd*; the second, زياد *ziyād*; third, ستاره *sitāra*; fourth, خانه گير *khāna-gīr*; fifth, طويل *tawīl*; sixth, هزاران *hazārān*; seventh, منصوبه *mansūba*.

P خاني *khānī*, A fountain, pure water. A vessel wherein they cool water. A bath. Gold. Imperial rank, khānship. Name of Humāy daughter of Dārā. Name of a coin current in Turkistān.

P خانيچه *khānīcha*, A small fountain or cistern.

P خاو *khāv*, Pile of velvet. Down, soft hair.

P خاور *khāwar*, The west, but often used by the poets for the east. The sun.

P خاوران *khāwarān*, East and west. A district in Khurāsān, birth-place of the poet انوري *anwarī*.

P خاور خداي *khāwar-khudāy*, Lord of the East (a title of سلم *salm*, son of Farīdūn).

P خاوري *khāwarī*, Western. Eastern. The sun. Title of the poet انوري *anwarī*.

P خاوش *khāwush*, A cucumber kept for seed.

P خاول *khāwul*, A biting ant.

P خاولنجان *khāwalinjān*, Galangale.

P خاوند *khāwand*, A master. Superior. The west. Definite.

P خاوندگار *khāwandagār*, A lord, a master.

P خاوندي *khāwandī*, Taste. Western. Mastery, dominion.

P خاوي *khāwī*, Flavour. Delight.

A خاوي *khāwī*, Uninhabited, ruined, or fallen down. خاوي البطن *khāwī'l batn*, Empty-bellied. خاوي الوفاض *khāwī'l wifāz*, With empty purse.

A خاوية *khāwiyat*, Empty (house). Deserted (country). Hollow (palm-tree).

P خاهر *khāhar*, (for خواهر *khwāhar*) A sister.

P خاي *khāy*, Taste thou. (in compos.) Chewing, gnawing, biting. Pleasure, any thing grateful to the sense. Ground dug up, or trenched. Low-lying land.

A خائب *khāɜib*, Unsuccessful. Disappointed. Impoverished.

A خائتة *khāɜitat*, Pouncing (eagle).

A خائذ لائذ *khāɜiz lāɜiz*, Arduous (affair).

A خائر *khāɜir*, Well off. Weak, debilitated.

P خايسته *khāyista*, Masticated. Divulged. Absurdity.

P خايسك *khāyish*, A smith's hammer. Malleable. (in zand and Pāzand) A prison.

A خائص *khāɜis*, A small present, if accepted.

A خائض *khāɜiz*, One who enters, fords, wades, or passes (through water). One who exposes himself to danger. Wandering.

A خائط *khāɜit*, A tailor.

A خائف *khāɜif*, (pl. خيّف *khuyyaf*, *khīyaf*, خوّف *khuwaf*, and خوف *khawf*) Timid, fearful, pusillanimous, afraid.

P خايك *khāyak*, (or خايگ *khāyag*) A locust.

P خايگينه *khāygīna*, A fried egg.

A خائل *khāɜil*, (pl. خول *khawal*) An imaginer (especially falsely or foolishly). An administrator, manager, factor. A guardian, keeper. An attendant, servant, or handmaid. (pl. خالة *khālat*) Proud.

A خائم *khāɜim*, Deceitful. A coward.

A خائن *khāɜin*, (pl. خانة *khānat*, خونة *khawanat*, and خوّان *khuwān*) A deceiver, traitor, rebel. Faithless. خائن العين *khāɜinu'l ɛayn*, The lion.

P خائن نان و نمك *khāɜini nān u namak*, A bread and salt traitor, (met.) A domestic villain who betrays his master.

A خائنة *khāɜinat*, A deceiver, traitor. خائنة الاعين *khāɜinatu'l aɛyun*, A stolen glance.

P خاينده *khāyanda*, A masticator.

A خائني *khāɜinī*, Treachery.

P خايه *khāya*, An egg. A testicle. A eunuch. خايهٔ ابليس *khāyaɜi iblīs*, Name of a certain stone. A rogue. خايهٔ زر *khāyaɜi zar*, The sun. خايهٔ سگ *khāyaɜi sag*, Testicles of the beaver; castor. خايهٔ غلامان *khāyaɜi ghulāmān*, A sort of grape. خايه كردن *khāya kardan*, To lay eggs.

P خايه بردار *khāya-bardār*, A cringer.

P خايه ديس *khāya-dīs*, A mushroom.

P خايه ريز *khāya-rez*, A fried egg, omelet.

P خايه كشيده *khāya-kashīda*, Castrated.

P خايه كن *khāya-kun*, (A hen) laying eggs.

P خايه كنده *khāya-kanda*, A eunuch.

P خايه گير *khāya-gīr*, Venomous sort of spider.

P خايه گينه *khāya-gīna*, Fried egg, omelet.

P خايه نهادن *khāya nihādan*, Shameful crime.

P خائيدگي *khāɜidagī*, A chewing, a masticating.

P خاييدن *khāyīdan*, To chew, gnaw.

P خاييده *khāyīda*, Chewed, gnawed.

A خبّ *khabb*, (v. n. of خبّ) Going with an ambling pace (a horse). Standing with one foot alternately up (a horse). Lifting his right and left feet together (a horse). Keeping, withholding. Absconding, getting out of the way (a miser). Becoming fraudulent. Growing (as a plant). Being agitated (the sea). A wave, surge. A low hillock of sand. A plain between two rough pieces of ground abounding in mushrooms. A deceiver, fraudulent man. *Khibb*, Perfidy, fraud, treachery, dissimulation. A seducer, deceiver. The raging of the sea. *Khubb*, (pl. اخباب *akhbāb* and خبوب *khubūb*) The bark of a tree. Low ground.

A خبء *khabɜ*, (v. n. of خبأ) Concealing. Concealment. Concealed. Any thing hid. خبء السماوات *khabɜu's samāwāt*, Rain. خبء الارض *khabɜu'l arz*, A plant.

A خباء *khibāɜ*, (v. n. 3 of خبأ) Teazing by asking questions. (pl. اخبية *akhbiyat*) A rustic Arabian tent of wool or camel's hair, supported by two or by three poles. A pod, a capsule. The envelope of wheat or barley coming into ear. Certain stars disposed in a circular form. A box for ointment. (pl. اخبئة *akhbiɜat*,) A private mark made (by burning) on an excellent she-camel.

A خباب *khibāb*, The raging of the sea.

A خبّاب *khabbāb*, Name of a sword-maker.

A خبابرة *khabābirat*, The descendants of ذو جبلة بن سواد *zū jabalat bin suwād*, the father of an Arabian tribe.

A خبابريّ *khabābiriy*, One of the Khabābirat.

A خبأة *khabɜat*, A plant. *Khubaɜat*, A woman who just shews her face to men, and then withdraws or covers herself. A woman who keeps close at home.

A يا خباث *yā khabāsi*, O infamous (woman)!

A خباثة *khabāsat*, (or خباثية *khabāsiyat*) (v. n. of خبث) Being wicked. Wickedness, infamy, baseness, depravity, impurity.

A خباجاء *khabājāɜ*, Foolish. A stallion in great request.

A خباخر *khubākhir*, Loose and large-bellied.

P خباد *khubād*, A broomstick.

A خبار *khabār*, Soft and loose earth. Soil collected about the root of a palm-tree. The holes of field-mice. من تجنّب الخبار امن العثار *man tajannaba'l khabār, amina'l ɛasār*, He who avoids loose ground is safe from stumbling. *Khibār*, (v. n. 3 of خبر) Letting land to another for part of the produce. (pl. of خبراء *khabrāɜ*) Soft loose soils where the lot-tree grows.

A خبارة *khabārat*, (v. n. of خبر) Knowing, being aware of.

P خباره *khabāra*, Quick, active, intelligent.

A خباريّ *khabāra'* and *khabārī*, (pl. of خبراء

khabrā) Soft loose grounds where the lot-tree grows.

A خبّاز *khabbāz*, A baker. *Khubbāz*, (خبازيٰ *khubāza'*, خبّازة *khubbāzat*, or خبّازيٰ) Mallows.

A خبازة *khibāzat*, Business of a baker, baking.

P خبازي *khubāzī*, Mallows.

A خبّازي *khabbāzī*, Baking, business of a baker.

A خبّاس *khabbās*, Plunder, booty. A captive. Fond of game, and killing much. A lion.

A خباساء *khubāsāʼ*, Plunder, booty, spoil, prey.

A خباسة *khubāsat*, Prey, game, spoil, plunder. A place of plunder.

A خباشات *khubāshāt*, Provisions fetched from different quarters. A multitude of men from different tribes.

A خباط *khabāt*, Dust. *Khibāt*, (pl. خبط *khubut*) A long and broad mark on the thighs or face of cattle, impressed with a hot iron; also the iron with which the mark is made. Gendering, covering. *Khubāt*, Madness, demoniacal insanity.

A خبّاط *khubbāt*, A young كنعد *kanʻad* fish.

A خباع *khibāʻ*, A tent.

P خباك *khabāk*, Four roofless walls used as a stable or fold for cattle. The precincts of a mosque.

A خبال *khabāl*, (v. n. of خبل) Being mad. Withering (the hand). Fatigue, toil, trouble. A heavy burden. Deadly poison. Corruption (particularly that putrid matter supposed by the Muhammadans to flow from the damned). A family, domestics. Decrease, deficiency, damage, loss, destruction. The condition of an old well whose sides have become honey-combed and tear the leathern bucket.

A خبان *khibān*, (v. n. of خبن) Doubling and sewing up a garment to shorten it. Laying up a secret store of provisions against a scarcity.

A خبانذ *khabānid*, (pl. of خبنديٰ *khabanda'*) Full-grown (men).

P خبانيدن *khabānīdan*, To make trample on.

A خبايا *khabāya'*, (pl. of خبيئة *khabīʼat*) Secrets. Concealed things.

A ثوب خبائب *sawbi khabāʼib*, Torn garment.

A خبائث *khabāʼis*, (pl. of خبيثة *khabīsat*) Impurities, wicked things. Evil spirits. Female demons. امّ الخبائث *ummu'l khabāʼis*, Mother of mischief, *i.e.* wine. اعمال خبائث *aʻmāli khabāʼis*, Wicked or shameful actions.

A خبب *khabab*, (v. n. of خبّ) Ambling (a horse). Standing with one foot alternately up. Lifting up his right and left legs together (a horse). Speed. *Khibab*, A torn garment.

A خبّة *khabbat*, *khibbat*, or *khubbat*, A long track or stripe (of sand or of clouds). A long roller of cloth. *Khubbat*, A kind of sweet herb. A pond.

A خبت *khabt*, (pl. اخبات *akhbāt* and خبوت *khubūt*) Plain ground, large field, sandy ground.

A خبتة *khabtat*, Humility, submission.

A خبتل *khabtal*, A short woman. *Khubtul*, Foolish, hasty. An improper meddler.

A خبتلة *khabtalat*, (v. n. of خبتل Q) Being hasty and foolish, and impertinently busy.

A خبث *khubs* or *khabs*, (v. n. of خبث) Being perfidious and impure. Fornicating. *Khubs*, Malignity, malice, brutality, perfidy, malevolence. Male demons. Impurity, fornication. *Khabas*, Nastiness, impurity. Dross of metal. *Khubas*, Impure. Impurity. يا خبث *yā khubas*, O filthy fellow! O shame! O infamous! *Khubus*, (pl. of خبيث *khabīs*) Impure, wicked, malicious.

A خبثاء *khubasāʼ*, (pl. of خبيث) Impure, wicked.

A خبثة *khibsat*, Unlawful slavery, unfair servitude. Impurity and dishonesty.

A خبج *khabj*, (v. n. of خبج) Striking with a stick. Breaking wind. Lying with. *Khabij*, Foolish.

P خبجه *khabja*, Tamarind. Indian date.

A خبخاب *khabkhāb*, Looseness, flabbiness.

A خبخبة *khabkhabat*, (v. n. of خبخب Q) Doing aught in the cool. Abating, declining (heat). Hanging down (the belly). Becoming thin after being fat. Deceiving. Name of a certain tree. بقيع الخبخبة *bakīʻu'l khabkhabat*, Name of a place nigh to Madīna where these trees grow.

A خبخر *khabkhar*, Loose and big-bellied.

A خبر *khabura*, (fut. يخبر *yakhburu*) He knew, understood, was acquainted with.

A خبر *khabr*, Seed sown. A place where water lodges on a mountain. *Khabr* or *khibr*, (pl. خبور *khubūr*) A large bag or wallet. (A camel) that yields much milk. *Khibr*, (v. n. of خبر) Going partners in the cultivation of a field. The knowledge of a thing. *Khubr*, (v. n. of خبر) Knowing, understanding, being well aware of. Trying, proving. Making (food) fat and greasy. The knowledge of a thing. *Khabar*, (v. n. of خبر) Producing the lote-tree. Being loose and stony (ground). Being full of holes of the field-mouse. (pl. اخبار *akhbār* and اخابير *akhābīr*) News, advices. Report, rumour, fame, story. Prophecy, prediction. (in grammar) The predicate. خبر خضري *khabari khizarī*, Report, sudden news, guessing what is to happen. (خضر *khizar* was a prophet skilled in divination, and hence, when, from certain symptoms, the public guess at the intentions of government, &c., intelligence of such intentions is called *khabar-khizarī*). مبتدا و خبر *mubtadā u khabar*, Subject and predicate. P خبر گرفتن *khabar giriftan*, To get information, to inquire or ascertain. A *Khabir*, Soft and stony (field). The lote-tree. (Ground) producing lote-trees. *Khabir* or *khubr*, Knowing, informed, acquainted with.

A خبراء *khabrāʼ*, (pl. خباريٰ *khabāra'*, *khabārī*, خبراوات *khabrāwāt*, and خبار *khibār*) Soft, loose, stony soil producing the lote-tree. A pit where water collects at the foot of the lote-tree. A large bag or wallet.

A خبراق *khibrāk*, One who farts much.

A خبراوات *khabrāwāt*, (pl. of خبراء *khabrāʼ*) Soft, loose soils where lote-trees grow.

A خبربج *khabarbaj*, A soft delicate body.

A خبربجة *khabarbajat*, Excellence and wholesomeness of food.

A خبرة *khibrat*, (v. n. of خبر) Proving. Making (food) fat and greasy. The knowledge of a thing. Experience, experiment, trial, proof. اهل خبرت *ahli khibrat*, A maker of experiments, censor, critic. An assayer of gold or silver. *Khubrat*, The knowledge of a thing. A sheep bought, and when slaughtered, divided amongst a number of persons. Thick porridge. A portion or ration of meat or fish. Bread or meat purchased for a household. Food served up. Travelling provisions. A dish of meat sufficient for four or five persons. *Khabirat*, A soft plain where the lote-tree grows.

A خبرجل *khabarjal*, A crane.

P خبردار *khabar-dār*, Informed, apprised, certified. Aware. Careful, cautious. An informer, scout, spy. Take care! beware! خبردار شدن *khabar-dār shudan*, To be conscious, to have intelligence. To be aware of. خبردار كردن *khabar-dār kardan*, To inform, give intelligence, assure. To caution.

P خبرداري *khabar-dārī*, Care. Information.

A خبرعة *khabraʻat*, Information against any one, espionage.

A خبرقة *khabrakat*, A tearing, slitting.

P خبرگير *khabar-gīr*, Taking cognizance, attentive. A spy, informer. A protector, patron.

P خبرگيري *khabar-gīrī*, Spying, informing. Attention. Aiding, protecting. Allowance, maintenance, establishment.

P خبرنويس *khabar-navīs*, A news-writer.

A خبروع *khubrūʻ*, An informer, sycophant.

P خبره *khabra*, Solid, firm, twisted. *Khabra* or *khibra*, Reckoning. Weighing.

P خبره نامه *khibra-nāma*, A mariner's compass. A sun-dial.

A خبريّ *khabarīy*, Predicatory. An historian.

A خبز *khabz*, (v. n. of خبز) Baking. Giving bread to eat. Pawing the earth (a camel). Urging, driving vehemently. Beating. *Khabaz*, Yellow water accompanying the fœtus. Depressed, low-lying ground. *Khubz*, Bread.

A خبزة *khubzat*, One loaf. A mass of dough ready for the oven. Darkness.

P خبزدو *khabazdū*, (or خبزدوك) A beetle.

A خبزون *khabazūn*, One with a swollen face.

A خبس *khabs*, (v. n. of خبس) Taking in the hand. Defrauding. *Khibs*, A space of time between the drinking and watering of camels.

A خبش *khabsh*, (v. n. of خبش) Collecting here and there, taking.

A خبص *khabs*, (v. n. of خبص) Mixing. Cooking the dish خبيص *khabīs*.

A خبط *khabt*, (v. n. of خبط) Striking hard, or

trampling upon. Pawing the ground with the fore-foot (a camel). Striking the leaves off (a tree) with a stick. Smiting with a sword. Conferring a favour upon an unknown person. Conferring a favour without claim or previous acquaintance. Throwing one's self down upon any place to sleep. Marking a camel on the thigh. Hurting, inflicting madness (Satan). Travelling by night without direction. Rising, standing up. خبط عشواء *khabta ʻashwāʼ*, (A camel) pawing the ground when she cannot see. (met.) An imprudent, heedless, improvident man. *Khubt*, (pl. of اخبط *akhbat*) Strikers with the feet. *Khabat*, A leaf shaken from a tree. Leaves shaken from a tree, and when dried, pounded, and mixed with meal and moistened with water, are poured down a camel's throat. Leaves trodden and crushed under the feet of cattle. *Khibat*, (pl. of خبطة *khibtat*) Bands, troops. *Khubut*, (pl. of خباط *khibāt*) Long and broad marks on the face and thighs of cattle. (pl. of خبيط *khabīt*) Cisterns trampled and broken down by camels.

A خبطة *khabtat*, A rheum which occurs before the cold weather sets in. Copious rain falling gently. A small matter, a little. *Khabtat*, *khibtat*, or *khubtat*, Milk remaining in a vessel or food in a dish. *Khabtat* or *khabatat*, Remains of water in a pond or vessel. *Khibtat*, Half a cistern or half a leathern bag full of water. Milk or water reaching to a third or half a vase or cistern. Little (milk or fodder). A portion (of the night). (pl. خبط *khibat*) A number or cluster (of men or houses).

A خبطة خبطة *khibtatan khibtatan*, In parts, groups, or companies.

A خبع *khabʻ*, (v. n. of خبع) Concealing. Abiding. Entering.

A خبعة *khubaʻat*, (A woman) concealing and uncovering herself.

A خبعثن *khubaʻsin*, Fat and juicy. *Khubaʻsin*, (*khabaʻsan*, or خبعثنة *khubaʻsinat*) Bulky and strong. A lion.

A خبعجة *khabʻajat*, A short, cautious tread.

A خبق *khabk*, (v. n. of خبق) Breaking wind. Rendering one contemptible in his own sight. *Khabak*, A noise made by a woman in coitu.

A خبقّ *khibakk* or *khibikk*, Long (man or horse). Swift (horse). Jumping, springing (man).

A خبقّاء *khibikkāʼ*, Bad-dispositioned (woman).

A خبقّة *khibikkat*, A camel taking long steps.

A خبقّي *khibikka'*, Swift (horse). Impetuous (man). Quick pace of a horse (with wide steps). (A she-camel) swift and taking long steps.

P خبك *khabak*, Strangulation, suffocation.

P خبكال *kha* or *khibkāl*, Butt for archers. Hole.

A خبل *khabl*, (v. n. of خبل) Disturbing, deranging the mind (grief). Falling short of the deeds of one's father. Mutilating (the body). Imprisoning. Denying, forbidding. Hindering, preventing. Borrowing. Amputation of the hands or feet. Any thing given (to a porter) over and above the sum stipulated. (pl. خبول *khubūl*) An affection of the limbs. Hemiplegia. Syncope of the letters س *s* and ت *t* in مستفعلن *mustafʻilun* of the two kinds of verse called البسيط *al basīt* and الرجز *ar'rujaz*. *Khubl*, Mind, heart, thought. *Khubl* or *khabl*, Madness. *Khabal*, An affection of the limbs. Hemiplegia. Epilepsy. Demoniacal madness. A disease in the legs of quadrupeds. A certain bird which seems to vociferate all night the words ماتت خبل *mātat khabal*, Khabal is dead. A large leathern water-bag filled. *Khabil*, Oppressive, overwhelming (adverse fortune). Mad.

A خبن *khabn*, (v. n. of خبن) Doubling up and sewing part (of a garment) to shorten it. Laying up (a secret store of provisions) against scarce times. A poetic licence in which the metre فاعلاتن *fāʻilātun* becomes فعلاتن *faʻilātun*. *Khubn*, The space between the ear and mouth of a leathern water-bottle. *Khuban*, (pl. of خبنة *khubnat*) Armsful.

A خبنّ *khubunn*, (A man) shrunk, drawn together.

A ذو خبنات *zū khabanāt* or *khubunāt*, A deceiver. A liar. One who, if he by chance act right, defeats immediately the effect by acting wrong.

A خبنة *khubnat*, An armful. The fastening place of the drawers.

A خبنداة *khabandāt*, (pl. خبنديات *khabandayāt*) A fine full-grown girl; or one heavy-hipped. A leg full and round.

A خبندي *khabanda'*, (pl. خبانذ *khabānid*) Full, well-made (man).

A خبنفثة *khabanfasat*, The anus.

A خبو *khabw*, (or خبوّ *khubūw*) (v. n. of خبا for خبو) Being extinguished (fire, war, or anger).

A خبوب *khubūb*, (pl. of خبّ *khubb*) Barks of trees. Low grounds.

A خبوت *khubūt*, (pl. of خبت) Soft level fields.

A خبور *khabūr*, A lion. *Khubūr*, (pl. of خبر *khabr*) Large bags or bottles.

A خبورة *khubūrat*, (v. n. 4 of خبر irreg.) Informing, giving intelligence. Finding (a milch camel) to be full of milk.

A خبوس *khabūs*, Oppressive, unjust, tyrannical. (A lion) seizing, and tearing his prey.

A خبوط *khabūt*, A horse that paws the ground.

A خبوع *khubūʻ*, (v. n. of خبع) Being choked with weeping and unable to speak (a child).

A خبوق *khabūk*, A woman by whom a noise is made in coitu.

P خبوك *khabūk*, (خبوه *khabūh* or *khubūh*) Firm.

A خبول *khubūl*, Amputation of hands and feet. (pl. of خبل *khabl*) Diseases of the limbs, palsies.

A خبون *khabūn*, (as خبنته خبون *khabanathu khabūnun*) He died.

P خبوه *khabwa*, Firm, solid.

P خبه *khaba*, Strangulation, suffocation. A difficulty in breathing; a sob. خبه كردن *khaba kardan*, To strangle, suffocate.

A خبيء *khabīʼ*, Concealed. Any thing hid.

A خبيب *khabīb*, (v. n. of خبّ) Going with an ambling pace (a horse); standing with one foot alternately up. Lifting his right and left legs together (a horse). A furrow or fissure in the ground.

A خبيبة *khabībat*, A track of sand. A strip of cloth. A slice of meat. The lowest part of a valley.

A خبيئة *khabīyat*, Hidden. A treasure. A lurking-place.

A خبيت *khabīt*, Any thing despised. Impure.

A خبيث *khabīs*, (pl. خبث *khubus* and خبثاء *khubasāʼ*) Impure, wicked, base, malignant. One whose companions are impure and malignant. خبيث البطن و الفرج *khabīsu'l batn wa'l farj*, A glutton and fornicator, careless of reputation. ارواح خبيثه *arwāhi khabīsa*, Foul spirits. الشجرة الخبيثة *ash' shajaratu'l khabīsat*, The colocynth. Dodder.

A خبّيث *khibbīs*, (pl. خبّيثون *khibbīsūn*) Extremely depraved or impure.

A خبيثى *khabīsī*, Impurity. A malignant woman.

A خبّيثي *khibbīsa'*, Malice, perfidy. Impurity.

P خبيدن *khabīdan*, To chew. To trample upon, beat or wear with the feet. To be crooked. To grow old or inveterate. To seize, snatch. To roast, boil, fry. To break. To abscond. To retire.

P خبيده *khabīda*, Crooked. Strangled. *Khubīda*, Name of a thorny plant.

P خبير *khabīr* or *khibyar*, Weighed. Counted. Prepared. Twisted.

A خبير *khabīr*, Knowing, acquainted with, informed. One acquainted with God. Skilful, intelligent. A farmer. A tiller of the ground. A digger of wells. A plant, grass, herbage (as the produce of the earth). Camel's hair. The foam of a camel's mouth. Baldness.

A خبيرة *khabīrat*, A sheep purchased and slaughtered amongst a number of people. Excellent wool, the first clipping.

P خبيره *khabera*, Sum total. Arranged. Twisted. A sand-hill. خبيره شدن *khabera shudan*, To arm one's self. To muster.

A خبيز *khabīz*, The purple mallow. Baked bread. Crumbled, grated, or sliced bread put among milk, broth, or under meat.

P خبّيز *khubbayz*, Mallows.

P خبيزه *khabīza*, Ivy. A winding, twisting. Coiled together. خبيزه شدن *khabīza shudan*, To arm one's self.

A خبيسة *khabīsat*, Plunder, booty.

A خبيص *khabīs*, A kind of sweetmeat made of dates and butter.

A خبيط *khabīt*, A horse that paws the ground. (pl. خبط *khubut*) A cistern or reservoir pawed down by the feet of camels. Thick milk; or churned milk on which fresh milk is poured.

P خبين *khubīn*, (or خپين) A wooden dish.

P خبيوره *khabyūra*, A sum total. A sand-hill.

P خبيوه *khabīwa*, A sum total. A sand-hill.

A خبيئة *khabīʼat*, A thing hid. Secrecy.

P خپ *khap*, Silent. Hush!

P خپاره *khapāra*, Active, nimble, dexterous.

P خپاك *khapāk*, A fold for cattle.

P خپچه *khap* or *khipcha*, A straight branch.

P خپك *khapak*, A large loaf. Strangulation. Vexation.

P خپه *khapa*, Strangulation, suffocation. خپه كردن *khapa kardan*, To strangle, to suffocate.

P خپيدن *khapīdan*, To be crooked.

P خپيده *khapīda*, Bent.

A خت *khatt*, A home-thrust.

A ختء *khatʼ*, A hindering, keeping back.

P ختا *khatā*, Name of a city in China.

P ختار *khatār* or *khutār*, Weeding (a garden).

A ختّار *khattār*, Great deceiver, arrant knave.

A ختارش *khatārish*, Motions of an infant.

A ختاع *khitāʻ*, A glove, a gauntlet.

A ختّال *khattāl*, One whose air is stately.

A ختام *khatām*, (v. n. of ختم) Sealing. *Khitām*, Wax or clay, with which any thing is sealed. The end of any thing. (pl. ختم *khutum*) The joint of (a horse's) limbs.

A ختان *khitān*, A convivial meeting on account of a marriage or a circumcision. The place of circumcision in a boy. Circumcision. سنّت ختان *sunnati khitān*, The rite of circumcision-feasts.

A ختّان *khattān*, A circumciser.

A ختانة *khitānat*, The profession of a circumciser. Circumcision.

A ختّاني *khattānī*, Business of a circumciser.

A ختائع *khatāʼiʻ*, (pl. of ختيعة) Thumb-stalls.

A ختت *khatat*, Languor, enervation of body.

A ختر *khatr*, (v. n. of ختر) Deceiving perfidiously. Being wicked, depraved, corrupt. Perfidy, deceit, fraud. *Khatar*, A stupor caused by medicine or poison.

A خترية *khatrabat*, A cutting in pieces or portions.

A خترشة *khatrashat*, Noise of a locust eating.

A خترفة *khatrafat*, A striking. Cutting, paring.

A خترق *khutrak*, Wormwood of Pontus. A kind of mugwort.

A خترمة *khatramat*, A keeping silence from fear.

A ختع *khatʻ*, (v. n. of ختع) Travelling. Going right in the dark (a guide with travellers). Attacking, rushing upon. Fleeing. Making haste. Limping (a hyena). Walking close after the female (a camel). Clearing off (the vapour سراب *sarāb*). *Khutaʻ*, A female hyena. *Khutaʻ* or *khatiʻ*, Skilful (guide).

A ختعة *khutaʻat*, A female leopard.

A ختعرة *khatʻarat*, A vanishing, disappearing.

P ختفرج *khatafraj*, Purslain.

P ختك *khatak*, A daily allowance, supplied by the people to the governor's table.

P ختل *khatl*, Deceiving. Name of a district in Badakhshān whence excellent horses are procured. Seed of fleawort.

A ختل *khatl*, (or ختلان *khatalān*) (v. n. of ختل) Deceiving, circumventing. Seizing by stratagem (as the wolf his prey). *Khitl*, A covering. The form or lurking-place of a hare.

A ختّل *khuttal*, A city in Transoxania.

P ختلان *khatlān*, A district in Badakhshān.

P ختلاني *khatlānī*, (or ختلي *khatlī*) Belonging to ختلان *khatlān*. An excellent horse bred there.

A ختلعة *khatlaʻat*, (v. n. of ختلع Q) Appearing, becoming manifest. Going forth to the desert.

A ختلمة *khatlamat*, A taking clandestinely.

A ختليّ *khatliy*, A horse bred in Khatl. A rogue.

A ختم *khatm*, (v. n. of ختم) Sealing. Concluding. Finishing, reading the entire Kur'ān. Covering the inside of the hive with the finest wax (a bee). Giving the first watering to corn. Honey. The mouths of beehives. ختم الله عواقبه بالخير *khatama'llāh ʻawākibahu bi'l khayr*, May God end his days in happiness! P ختم شدن *khatm shudan*, To be stamped or sealed. A *Khatam*, Sealing-wax. Sealed clay. End. A seal, seal-ring. *Khutum*, (pl. of ختام *khitām*) Joints of horses' limbs.

A ختمات *khatamāt*, (pl. of ختم *khatam*) Terminations, ends. ختمات قرآن *khatamāti kur'ān*, Recitations of the whole Kur'ān (for the souls of the dead, or in any other act of devotion).

A ختمة *khatmat*, A sealing. An epilogue.

A ختن *khatn*, (v. n. of ختن) Circumcising (a male). Cutting. Diminishing. Acting unjustly. *Khatan*, (pl. اختان *akhtān*) The nearest male relation to a woman (as father or brother). A son-in-law. A circumcision-feast.

P ختن *khutan*, Tartary; also a certain district of that country.

P ختنبر *khatambar*, A miser who complains of poverty. A trifling vain fellow, who boasts of wealth and affects distinctions which he has not.

A ختنة *khutnat*, Circumcision. Circumcision-fees. P ختنه كردن *khutna kardan*, To circumcise. ختنه نا كرده *khutna nā karda*, Uncircumcised. A *Khatanat*, A wife's mother.

A ختو *khatw*, (v. n. of ختا for ختو) Becoming broken with grief or indisposition, becoming humbled. Restraining or prohibiting. Twisting or plaiting the fringe of one's clothes by way of ornament.

P ختو *khutū*, A reed. The horn of a rhinoceros. The tooth or bone of a viper. A Chinese bird, of whose bones they make handles to knives, which, being dipt into any victuals suspected to be poisoned, are said to have the very singular virtue of immediately discovering it.

P ختوانه *khatwāna*, Garb of a religious beggar.

P ختور *khatūr*, A reed, a cane.

A ختور *khatūr*, A deceiver. Perfidious. *Khutūr*, Deceit, fraud, perfidy.

A ختوع *khatūʻ*, Skilful (guide). *Khutūʻ*, (v. n. of ختع) Travelling. Going right in the dark (a guide with travellers). Attacking, rushing upon. Fleeing. Making haste. Limping (a hyena). Walking close after the female (a camel). Clearing off (the vapour سراب *sarāb*).

A ختول *khatūl*, Insidious, perfidious.

A ختون *khutūn*, Relationship on the wife's side.

A ختونة *khutūnat*, Relationship on the side of the wife. The taking of a wife.

A ختيت *khatīt*, Base, vile. Deficient.

A ختير *khatīr* or *khittīr*, A deceiver: treacherous.

P ختيره *khatīra*, A shepherd's double scrip.

A ختيع *khatīʻ*, Calamity, misfortune, trouble.

A ختيعة *khatīʻat*, An archer's thumb-stall.

A ختين *khatīn*, Circumcised.

A خثّ *khuss*, Any rubbish carried down or left dry by a stream. Dry pond-weed.

A خثار *khusār*, Remains of food upon a table.

A خثارة *khasārat*, (v. n. of خثر) Being thick (milk). *Khusārat*, Remains, leavings, residuum.

A خثارم *khusārim*, One who forbodes evil. Thick-lipped.

A خثّة *khussat* or *khassat*, A handful of sticks, a faggot. *Khussat*, Dung and mud mixed together to anoint the teats of a camel.

A خثر *khasr*, (v. n. of خثر) Becoming thick (milk). Being confounded, disturbed (mind). Being mixed (folk). *Khasar*, (v. n. of خثر) Remaining in a rural abode, and not going out with the others in quest of provisions. Being ashamed.

A خثراء *khasrāʼ*, (or خثري *khasra'*) (Men) mixed together.

A خثران *khasarān*, Thickness of milk.

A خثرمة *khasramat*, Unskilfulness at work. *Khisrimat*, A keeping silence from fear.

A خثعلة *khasʻalat*, A walking slowly.

A خثعم *khasʻam*, A lion. A certain mountain.

A خثعمة *khasʻamat*, Reddish (she-goat). Staining the body with blood (applied particularly when people, entering into any important agreement, kill and eat together some animal, and, mixing sweet herbs with the blood, dip their hands into it by way of solemn confirmation).

A خثلة *khaslat*, Big-bellied (woman). *Khaslat* or *khasalat*, (pl. خثلات *khaslāt* and *khasalāt*) The lower part of the belly between the navel and the pubes, the abdomen.

A خثلمة *khaslamat*, Mixture. A taking of any thing clandestinely.

A خثم *khasm*, (v. n. of خثم) Bruising the nose. *Khasam*, (v. n. of خثم) Having the top of the ear and nose broad. Being flat (a pickaxe). Being closed (orifices of camel's teats). Thickness of nose or top of ear. *Khasim*, Thick-nosed, or eared.

A خثماء *khasmāʼ*, Round-hoofed and narrow-soled (she-camel).

A خثمة *khusmat*, Shortness in a bull's nose.

A خثو *khasw*, The lower part of a belly relaxed.

A خثواء *khaswāʼ*, Relaxed in the lower part of the belly (woman).

A خثور *khusūr*, (or خثورة *khusūrat*) (v. n. of خثر) Becoming thick (milk). Thickness, consistency of any liquid: cream.

A خثورة *khusūrat*, (v. n. of خثر) Remaining with his tribe, and not going out with others for provisions.

A خثي *khasy*, (v. n. of خثي) Dunging (an ox or elephant). *Khisy*, (pl. اخثاء *akhsāʼ*, خثي *khasiy*, or *khusiy*) Dung (of an ox or elephant).

A خثيم *khasīm*, Broad and prominent (vulva).

A خج *khajj*, (v. n. of خج) Driving. Cleaving. Voiding dung. Being twisted. Striking the foot on the ground. Raising a dust. Coition.

A خجء *khajʼ*, (v. n. of خجأ) Striking. Coming on (night). Lying with. Entering (a house) secretly.

A خجاة *khajāt*, (pl. خجى *khajaʼ*) Dirt, filth; sordidness, meanness. Sordid, filthy.

A خجأة *khujaʼat*, A man addicted to venery. A woman greedy of venery. Corpulent, heavy, stupid.

A خجاجة *khajjājat*, Stupid (man).

P خجاره *khajāra* or *khujāra*, A little. Weak. Buffoonery.

A خجاف *khijāf*, (pl. of خجيف) Thin, slender.

A خجالة *khijālat*, (v. n. of خجل) Being ashamed, confounded. Shame, bashfulness, modesty.

P خجاليدن *khijālīdan*, To embrace, encircle.

A خجام *khijām*, Wide (woman).

P خجاو *khujāv*, A voice, a sound.

P خجت *khajt* or *khujt*, Concupiscence.

P خجج *khajaj*, A bird's crop.

A خجخاجة *khajkhājat*, Stupid (man).

A خجخجة *khajkhajat*, (v. n. of خجخج Q) Blowing hard (wind). Lying hid. Concealing one's thoughts. Shrugging from fear. Walking fast. Coition.

A خجر *khajar*, The smell of the nether parts.

A خجرّ *khijirr*, (pl. خجرون *khijirrūn*) Voracious. Cowardly.

P خجستگي *khujastagī*, Auspiciousness.

P خجسته *khujasta*, Happy, fortunate, auspicious, blessed. A flower yellow without and black within. A woman's name.

P خجسته اختر *khujasta-akhtar*, Happy-starred.

P خجسته پي *khujasta-pay*, Happy arrival.

P خجسته راي *khujasta-rasy*, Name of a vazir.

P خجسته فرجام *khujasta-farjām*, Having happy conclusion: happily-terminating, ending well.

P خجش *khajsh*, (or خجچ *khajch* or *khujch*) A swelling in the throat.

A خجف *khajf*, Lightness. Levity. Pride.

P خجك *khajak*, A hole made with the point of the finger or a stick. A pearl in the eye. A dot, speck, or spot. A flea-bite.

P خجك دار *khajak-dār*, Spotted, speckled.

A خجل *khajal*, (v. n. of خجل) Being modest, bashful, ashamed, confounded, silent, and motionless. Getting into the mud and remaining astonished (a camel). Being over-loaded. Growing long and luxuriantly (a plant). Being intricate and perplexing (an affair). Being insolent, purse-proud, and incapable of bearing prosperity. Languor, torpor, laziness. Corruption, perversion. A number of slits in the lower part of a shirt. *Khajil*, Modest, bashful. (A valley) luxuriant with herbage. Worn out (garment) when long and wide. Long (grass). Loosely sitting on a horse (housing).

A خجلة *khajlat*, Bashfulness.

P خجلت كش *khajlat-kash*, Very bashful.

A خجلية *khajiliyat*, Shame, shamefacedness.

P خجند *khujand*, Mallows. Fortunate. Name of a town in Turkistān.

P خجو *khujū*, A lark.

A خجواء *khajwāʼ*, Wide (woman).

A خجوج *khajūj*, A violent wind, a whirlwind.

A خجوجاة *khajawjāt*, A whirlwind. Perpetually blowing (wind).

A خجوجي *khajawjaʼ*, (or خجوجاء *khajawjāʼ*) Long-footed, long-legged. Tall, large-boned, and cowardly.

P خجوله *khijawla*, A blister on hand or foot.

P خجوليدن *khijūlīdan*, To embrace.

A خجوم *khajūm*, Wide (woman).

A خجي *khajy*, (v. n. of خجي) Kicking up the dirt in walking. *Khajaʼ*, (pl. of خجاة *khajāt*) Sordid, filthy. Filths, meannesses.

P خجيدن *khajīdan*, To assemble, to meet.

P خجير *khijīr* or *khujīr*, Handsome, comely.

A خجيف *khajīf*, Lightness, levity. Pride. (pl. خجاف *khijāf*) Thin, slender.

P خچكول *khachkūl*, A beggar.

P خخ خخ *khakh khakh*, Study, labour, or endeavour thou. Well done! bravo! A pulsation.

A خدّ *khadd*, (v. n. of خدّ) Cutting furrows, trenching. (pl. اخدّة *akhiddat*, خداد *khidād* and خدّان *khiddān*) A road. A furrow in the ground. A rivulet. A crowd, company. The exterior surface of a camel-litter. An impression. (pl. خدود *khudūd*) A cheek. خدّ العذراء *khaddu'l ʻazrāʼ*, (The maidens' cheek) The anemone. The city of Kufa.

A خدا *khadaʼ*, Horse-worms, bots.

P خدا *khudā*, (from خود *khwud*, Self, and آي *āy*, Coming) God. Master, owner. حضرت خداي بي زوال *hazrat khudāsi bī zawāl*, The Almighty God without end.

P خدا آگاه *khudā-āgāh*, Knowing God.

A خدّاب *khaddāb*, A liar, an imposter.

P خدا برد *khudā-burd*, Whither bound?

P خدا بنده *khudā-banda*, Name of a Persian king.

P خدا پرستي *khudā-parastī*, Divine worship.

P خدا ترس *khudā-tars*, God-fearing, godly.

A خداج *khidāj*, (v. n. of خدج) Casting her foal (a camel). Imperfect (work or prayer).

P خدا جو *khudā-jo* or *jū*, Seeking God.

P خدا حافظ *khudā-hāfiz*, God preserve you!

P خدا خوان *khudā-khwān*, The fore-finger (because they hold it up when confessing their faith).

A خداد *khidād*, A mark burned on the cheek. (pl. of خدّ *khadd*) Furrows, trenches.

P خدا داد *khudā-dād*, (Deodatus) granted by God; a proper name. Name of the state governed by Tippoo Sultān, late sovereign of Mysore. Name of the founder of a sect.

P خدا داني *khudā-dānī*, Knowledge of God.

A خدار *khadār*, Name of a shrub.

P خدارا *khudārā*, For God's sake.

A خدارة *khadārat*, Modesty, chastity.

A خدارن *khadārin*, (pl. of خدرنق) Malespiders.

A خداري *khudāriy*, Black (hair); dark (night); black (camel).

A خدارية *khudāriyat*, An eagle.

A خداش *khidāsh*, (v. n. 3 of خدش) Excoriating. Scratching, wounding with the nails. ابو الخداش *abū'l khidāsh*, (Father of scratching) A cat.

P خدا شناس *khudā-shināsh*, God-knowing.

A خداع *khidāʻ*, (v. n. 3 of خدع) Deceiving, studying to circumvent. Abandoning, forsaking. Preventing, withholding. Fraud, deceit, perfidy.

A خدّاع *khaddāʻ*, An egregious impostor. (A year) producing little grain, and disappointing.

A خدافر *khadāfir*, Old threadbare garments.

P خدا فروشان *khudā-firoshān*, Hypocrites.

A خدافل *khadāfil*, Old, worn, every-day clothes.

A خدال *khidāl*, (pl. of خدلة *khadlat*) Fleshy, fat (legs or women).

A خدالة *khadālat*, Plumpness of arm and leg.

A خدام *khidām*, (pl. of خدمة *khadamat*) Circles of leather. Leathern ornaments worn on the ankle.

A خدّام *khaddām*, Expert in serving. *Khuddām*, (pl. of خادم *khādim*) Ministers, domestics, servants.

P خدا مشرب *khudā-mashrab*, Pious, godly.

A خدان *khidān*, A being friendly to.

A خدّان *khiddān*, (pl. of خدّ) Furrows, trenches.

P خدا نخواسته *khudā na khwāsta*, God forbid!

P خداوان *khudāwān*, The fore-finger.

P خداور *khudāwar*, Lord, possessor, prince.

P خداوند *khudāwand*, A king, prince. A lord, master. A possessor, man of great authority. خداوند مال *khudāwandi māl*, Possessor of riches. خداوند خانه *khudāwandi khāna*, The master of the house. خداوند نعمت *khudāwandi niʻmat*, (lit. Beneficent master) A form of address to superiors. Rich.

P خداوند زاد *khudāwand-zād*, A prince.

P خداوندگار *khudāwandigār*, Creator of the world. The Lord, author and perfecter of every thing. A king, a great man.

P خداوندگاري *khudāwandigārī*, A sovereignty,

principality. Royal, regal, imperial, princely.

P خداوندي *khudāwandī*, Ownership, lordship.

P خدا همّتي *khudā-himmatī*, Religious zeal.

P خداي *khud-āy*, (Self-existent) God.

P خدايا *khudāyā*, O God!

P خداي بر تو *khudāy bar tu*, A form of administering an oath.

P خدايتعالى *khudāy taʿālā'*, Most high God.

A خدائع *khadāʾiʿ*, (pl. of خديعة) Frauds, deceits.

P خدايگان *khudāyagān*, A great lord. Happy.

P خدايگاني *khudāyagānī*, Great, lordly.

P خدائى *khudāʾī*, Godship, divinity. Divine. An object of worship. The honour due to God.

P خدائيان *khudāʾiyān*, Followers of Khudādād.

P خدائي رحم *khudāʾī rahm*, A kind of food given to the poor in completion of a vow.

P خدائي فروشان *khudāʾī-firoshān*, Hypocrites.

A خدب *khadb*, (v. n. of خدب) Striking (with a sword), cutting through the skin and flesh. Striking on the head. Biting (as a serpent). Lying, deceiving. A plentiful milking. *Khadab*, Tallness and stupidity. Haste, precipitation *Khadib*, Tall and slim. A fool. Cutting, dividing; decisive.

A خدبّ *khidabb*, An old man. Large (ostrich). Strong-backed (camel).

A خدباء *khadbāʾ*, Tall, foolish (woman). A blow on the belly or concavity. (A spear) which makes a wide wound. A coat of mail soft and roomy.

A خدبة *khadibat*, A spear which makes a wide wound. وادي خدبات *wādī khadibāt*, Destruction. A departure from one's purpose.

A خدّة *khuddat*, A cheek. (pl. خدد) A furrow.

A خدد *khudad*, (pl. of خدّة) Furrows, trenches.

A خدخد *khudhkhud* or *khudakhid*, A sort of insect.

A خدر *khadr*, (v. n. of خدر) Remaining behind and being separated from the bevy (a hind), and being bewildered. Sitting behind the veil or curtain (as women in the east, concealed from the view of men). Abiding in a place. *Khidr*, (pl. خدور *khudūr*, اخدار *akhdār*, and اخادير *akhādīr*) A veil, curtain, behind which women sit. The back or interior of a house. A piece of wood on a camel's saddle covered with housing. A lurking-place, lion's den. *Khadar*, (v. n. of خدر) Being benumbed (the limbs). Torpor of the limbs. Rain. Dark (place). Intenseness, severity (of heat or cold). A weakness or heaviness in the eye caused by a mote. Sluggishness. Dark (night). *Khadar* or *khidar*, The darkness of night. *Khadir*, Wet (day). Benumbed. Dark (night). *Khadur*, Dark (night).

A خدرة *khudrat*, Thick darkness. A certain she-ass. *Khadirat*, An unripe date fallen from the tree.

A خدرعة *khadraʿat*, A making haste.

P خدرك *khadrak*, A burning coal or billet.

A خدرنق *khadarnak*, (pl. خدارن *khadārin*) A large spider. Large (penis).

A خدرنى *khadarnaʾ*, A spider.

P خدره *khadra* or *khudra*, A spark. Bit, scrap.

A خدريّ *khudrīy*, Black (ass); dark (place); black (cloud).

A خدش *khadsh*, (v. n. of خدش) Excoriating, scratching with the nails. (pl. خدوش *khudūsh*) Vestige, mark, scratch. *Khadish*, Alarm.

A خدشه *khadsha*, Fear, alarm. Danger. Doubt, question. Apprehension, solicitude.

A خدع *khadʿ* or *khidʿ*, (v. n. of خدع) Deceiving, circumventing, leading astray, insidiously injuring. Entering into a hiding-place, withdrawing (into a den). Not meeting with a ready sale (merchandize), being flat (a market). Folding, doubling up. Withholding, being parsimonious. Being discordant, contrarious. Being deeply sunk in the socket (the eye). Setting (the sun). Drying in the mouth (spittle). Being scanty (rain). Being small (stock or property). افعال خدع و بدع *afʿāli khadʿ u badʿ*, Acts of fraud and innovation. *Khadaʿ*, Wily (dragon). *Khadiʿ*, A deceiver, beguiler. Sly (lizard). *Khuduʿ*, (pl. of خدوع *khadūʿ*) Very deceitful.

A خدعة *khudʿat*, One easily cheated, a gull, a dupe. The means by which a person is imposed upon. Fraud, imposture. الحرب خدعة *al harbu khudʿatun*, (*khadʿatun*, *khidʿatun*, or *khudaʿatun*) War is fraud, *i.e.* stratagem is necessary in war. *Khadaʿat*, (pl. of خادع *khādiʿ*) Deceivers. *Khudaʿat*, A deceiver. Time. Fortune. Name of a tribe.

A خدعونة *khadʿūnat*, A slice of a gourd.

P خدعگر *khudʿagar*, An impostor.

A خدف *khadf*, (v. n. of خدف) Cutting out (a garment). Walking fast, with short quick steps. Enjoying the luxuries of life. Snowing. A rudder, a helm. *Khidaf*, (pl. of خدفة *khidfat*) Rents in shifts.

A خدفلة *khadfalat*, A putting on an old shirt.

P خدك *khadak*, A bridge. *Khudak*, A magistrate.

A خدل *khadl*, Plump, full, fleshy. *Khadal*, Plumpness in the arms and legs.

A خدلاء *khadlāʾ*, (خدلّجة *khadallajat*, or خدلم *khidlim*) A woman plump in the arms and legs.

A خدلة *khadlat*, A small grape-stone. *Khadlat* or *khidlat*, (pl. خدال *khidāl*) Plump-legged (woman). Small-boned and fleshy-limbed (woman). *Khadlat* or *khudlat*, The stem of the صاب *sāb* tree.

A خدم *khadam*, (pl. of خادم *khādim*) Servants, domestics. *Khidam*, (pl. of خدمة *khadamat*) Circles of leather. Ornaments worn on the ankle.

A خدماء *khadmāʾ*, White-legged (ewe).

A خدمة *khadmat*, An hour of the day or night. *Khidmat* or *khadmat*, (v. n. of خدم) Serving. *Khidmat*, Service, employment, office, ministry. خدمة باقى *khidmat bākī*, The service remains (in my heart), *i.e.* I shall never be unmindful of the favour. *Khudmat*, Whiteness of (a sheep's) legs. *Khadamat*, (pl. خدم *khidam* and خدام *khidām*) A lady's bracelet, also an ornament for the ankle, made of leather, and adorned with gold, silver, or jewels. A circle or congregation of men. The leg. A strap which ties a leathern shoe on a camel's foot. (pl. of خادم *khādim*) Servants, domestics. *Khidamat*, A thong.

P خدمتكار *khidmatgār*, A serving-man.

P خدمتگاري *khidmatgārī*, Service, ministry.

P خدمتگذار *khidmat-guzār*, A servant. Forward, obliging, ready to serve.

P خدمتگر *khidmatgar*, A servant.

P خدمت گزاري *khidmat-guzārī*, Ministry.

A خدمتي *khidmatī*, A magnificent present, such as is presented to great men.

A خدن *khidn*, (pl. اخدان *akhdān*) A friend. A girl, servant. A lover. Loved.

A خدنة *khudanat*, A friend to mankind.

A خدنّق *khadannak*, A big spider. A large penis.

P خدنگ *khadang*, The white poplar, a tree from which they make arrows and saddle-trees. A bow or arrow made of it. A hedgehog. A crab.

P خدو *khudū*, Spittle. خدو انداختن *khudū andākhtan*, To spit, to spawl.

A خدوج *khadūj*, A camel producing an abortion.

A خدود *khudūd*, (pl. of خدّ *khadd*) Cheeks.

A خدور *khudūr*, (pl. of خدر *khidr*) Curtains.

A خدوش *khadūsh*, A fly. A flea. *Khudūsh*, (pl. of خدش *khadsh*) Scratches, marks.

A خدوع *khadūʿ*, (pl. خدع *khuduʿ*) Capricious (camel), allowing her milk to flow, and then withholding it. (A road) in some parts plain and in others disappearing. Very deceitful.

P خدوك *khudūk* or *khadūk*, Weariness, irksomeness, vexation, plague. Anger, indignation. Envy. Shame, contempt.

A خدولة *khudūlat*, Plumpness of arm and leg.

A خدوم *khadūm*, A servant (male or female).

A خدي *khady*, (or خديان *khadayān*) (v. n. of خدي) Travelling fast (a camel). The running of an ass from his tethering post to the place where he rolls himself, going in a kind of trot. *Khadā'*, Horse-worms, bots.

A خديج *khadīj*, An abortion (of a camel). A camel producing an abortion.

A خديجة *khadījat*, Muhammad's first wife.

P خدير *khadīr*, Beauty, goodness, amiableness.

A خديرة *khadīrat*, A modest, retired woman.

P خديش *khadesh* or *khudesh*, A king. A mighty man. A householder. The mistress of a family.

A خديعة *khadīʿat*, (v. n. of خدع) Deceiving. Fraud, deceit, trick, cheat. A kind of food (or wheat) amongst the Arabians.

A خدين *khadīn*, A friend. Loved. A lover.

P خديو *khidīv*, A king, great prince, sovereign. A benevolent, excellent man. Master, possessor, rich man. A friend. خديو هند *khidīvi hind*, The king of India.

P خديور *khidīvar*, A prince. Phœnix of the age.

P خديه *khidya*, Annexed, added, joined.

A خذ *khuz*, (imper. of اخذ *akhaza*) Take thou.

A خذء *khazʼ*, A being humble and submissive.

A خذأ *khazaʼ*, Weakness of soul.

A خذا *khazaʼ*, (v. n. of خذي) Being flaccid at the root, and falling forwards (an ear).

P خذا *khuzā*, God. Master.

A خذاء *khazāʼ*, (v. n. of خذأ) Being humble and submissive. Lightness of hearing.

A خذارق *khuzārik*, A purgative salt water.

A خذاريف *khazārīf*, (pl. of خذروف *khuzrūf*, q.v.). Pieces, fragments. خذاريف الهودج *khazārifu'l hawdaj*, Timbers with which a camel-litter is made quadrangular.

A خذارم *khazārīm*, Rags, bits of cloth.

A خذاق *khazzāk*, A kind of fish (cuttle-fish ?).

A خذامة *khuzāmat*, A slice, cut, morsel.

A خذانية *khuzāniyat*, Large and strong (camel).

A خذاوية *khuzāwiyat*, Light of hearing (ear).

A خذراف *khizrāf*, A certain salt, bitter plant.

A خذراق *khizrāk*, One with a fit of purging.

A خذرة *khuzrat*, Any thing fastened to the end of a string, which boys whirl round with velocity, and cause to make a hissing or whizzing sound.

A خذرفة *khazrafat*, (v. n. of خذرف Q) Walking fast. Knocking the pebbles about (a fast-going camel). Filling (a vase). Whetting (a sword). Mutilating in the extremities. A piece of a garment.

A خذرقة *khazrakat*, A voiding of dung.

A خذرنق *khazarnak*, A large spider or penis.

A خذروف *khuzrūf*, (pl. خذاريف *khazārīf*) Any thing fastened to the end of a string, which boys whirl round with velocity, and cause to make a hissing or whizzing noise. Swift of foot. A troop of camels. A camel separated from the herd. Flashing lightning. Kneaded clay with which children play. Any thing scattered from the rest.

A خذع *khazʻ*, (v. n. of خذع) Cutting, mincing, hashing, hacking.

A خذعبة *khazʻabat*, The act of cutting.

A خذعل *khizʻil*, A foolish woman. Leathern drawers worn by menstruous women and girls.

A خذعلة *khazʻalat*, (v. n. of خذعل Q) Walking in a certain way. Slicing (a melon) very small.

A خذع مذع *khizaʻa mizaʻa*, Dispersed, scattered.

A خذعوبة *khuzʻūbat*, A segment, a slice.

A خذعولة *khuzʻūlat*, Slice of gourd or cucumber.

A خذف *khazf*, (v. n. of خذف) Throwing (a pebble or date-stone taken up between the thumb and fore-finger).

A خذفان *khazafān*, A certain camel's pace.

A خذق *khazk*, (v. n. of خذق) Muting (a bird). Voiding turbid matter (the cuttle fish). Egging, spurring, goading forward (a beast). Dung.

A خذل *khazl*, (and خذلان *khizlān*) (v. n. of خذل) Disappointing, withholding assistance. Remaining behind the herd (a doe). Staying with her young (a beast).

A خذلان *khizlān*, Weakness. Abandonment, desertion, failure.

A خذلب *khizlib*, An old, relaxed she-camel.

A خذلبة *khazlabat*, A weak, languid pace.

A خذلة *khuzalat*, A deserter of friends. خذلة و اشقياء *khuzalat u ashkiyāʼ*, Robbers and tramps.

A خذلمة *khazlamat*, A walking fast.

A خذم *khazm*, (v. n. of خذم) Cutting. Striking with his talons (a hawk). Being broken, cut off. Being drunken. *Khazam*, (v. n. of خذم) Going fast. *Khazim*, Swift (horse). Sharp (sword). (pl. خذمون *khazimūn*) Liberal.

A خذماء *khazmāʼ*, Slit-eared crosswise (sheep).

A خذمة *khazmat*, A mark on a camel. An hour.

A خذنتان *khuzunnatāni*, (dual) The lips of the pudendum The testicles. The ears.

A خذنفرة *khazanfarat*, A woman speaking through the nose.

A خذو *khazw*, (v. n. of خذا for خذو) Being loose, flabby, pendulous. Being compact (flesh).

A خذوء *khuzūʼ*, (v. n. of خذأ) Humbling one's self, submitting to (another).

A خذواء *khazwāʼ*, Flagging-eared (she-ass). Light of hearing (ear). Flabby (ear).

A خذوف *khazūf*, (A she-ass) going fast and scattering gravel; also very fat, the navel almost touching the ground.

P خذوك *khazūk* or *khuzūk*, Anger. A threat. Terror inspired from threats. Passionate.

A خذول *khazūl*, (A doe) remaining behind the rest. A mare seized with the pains of labour and not stirring from the place.

A خذوم *khazūm*, (An ostrich) going swiftly. Sharp (sword).

A خذي *khazaʼ*, (v. n. of خذي) Being loose, or hanging down. Being humble-minded, subdued.

A خذيّ *khuzayy*, (Little flap-ear) An ass.

A خذيذ *khazīz*, The running of a sore with matter.

A خذيعة *khazīʻat*, A dish of hashed meat.

A خذيم *khazīm*, Cut off. Drunken.

P خذيو *khiziw*, A great prince. Name of God.

P خر *khar*, An ass. A stupid fool. Black viscous clay. Sediment. The bridge of a violin. (imp. of خريدن *kharīdan*) Buy thou. The commonest, ugliest, largest, or coarsest of its kind (as with us the word "horse" occurs in certain compounds, as horse-laugh, horse-play, horse-chesnut): as, خرسنگ *khar-sang*, A rough stone. خرامرود *khar-amrūd*, An ill-flavoured pear. خرتنبور *khari tambūr*, The peg of a guitar. خردشتي *khari dashtī*, The wild ass. خرعيسي *khari ʻīsa*, The ass of Jesus. (met.) A solitary hermit. خربا تشديد *khari bā tashdīd*, Doubly an ass, very stupid. *Khir*, (imp. of خريدن *khirīdan*) Buy thou. *Khur*, The sun. Convenient, proper, worthy.

P خر *khir*, (in zand and Pāzand) Happiness, cheerfulness. A pleasant condition.

P خرّ *kharr*, Black mud.

A خرّ *kharr*, (v. n. of خرّ) Falling. Falling down in worship. A fall from a height. A fissure, crack. An impetuous rush from an unknown place. Death. *Khurr*, The hole in the mill through which the corn drops. A round serpent. The root of the ear. (pl. خررة *khirarat*) A channel worn by a torrent.

A خرء *kharʼ*, (v. n. of خرئ) Voiding excrement. *Khurʼ*, (pl. خروء *khurūʼ* and خرآن *khurʼān*) Dung, excrement, turd.

P خرا *khirā*, (part. of خريدن *khirīdan*) Buying.

A خراء *khirāʼ*, Dung, excrement.

A خراءة *kharāʼat*, (v. n. of خرئ) Abhorring, detesting. *Kharāʼat* or *khirāʼat*, (v. n. of خرئ) Going to stool, voiding excrement.

P خراب *kharāb*, Deserted. Overcome by wine.

A خراب *kharāb*, (v. n. of خرب) Being ruined and desolate. (pl. اخربة *akhribat* and خرب *khirab*) Ruin, desolation. Destroyed, deserted, depopulated, spoiled. Debauched. Reprobate. Noxious, vicious. Indecent. Miserable. P خراب شدن *kharāb shudan*, To be spoilt, ruined, or desolate. خراب كردن *kharāb kardan*, To spoil, ruin, mar, corrupt, blight, taint. A *Khirāb*, (pl. of خرب *kharab*) Male bustards. Inverted hairs on the crown of the human head or flank of a horse.

A خرّاب *khurrāb*, (pl. of خارب *khārib*) Thieves, camel-stealers.

P خرابابه *khurābāba*, Water strained, or oozing through any dike, bank, or mound.

P خرابات *kharābāt*, A tavern. A gaming-house. A brothel.

A خرابات *kharābāt*, (pl. of خرابة) Devastations.

P خراباتي *kharābātī*, A haunter of taverns, &c.

A خراب باطن *kharāb-bātin*, Evil disposition.

A خرابة *kharābat*, Devastation. A ruin. P دزد خرابه نشين *duzdi kharāba-nishīn*, A robber skulking among the ruins. A *Khirābat* or *kharābat*, (v. n. of خرب) Stealing (camels). *Khurābat*, A rope made of the fibres of the palm-tree. A slate or slab with a hole bored in it. A needle's eye. The fissure of the anus.

A خرّابة *kharrābat* or *khurrābat*, A needle's eye. The fissure of the posteriors. *Khirrābat*, A side of the nose. *Khurrābat*, (pl. of خارب *khārib*) Camel-stealers.

P خراب خسته *kharāb-khasta*, Ruined.

A خرابل *kharābil*, (pl. of خرنبل *kharambal*) Silly women. Decrepit old women.

P خرابه *kharāba*, Desolate, waste. *Khurāba*, Water leaking from a cistern. A small stream drawn from a larger one for purposes of irrigation. A draught of water. Name of a root.

P خرابها *kharābahā*, Ruins.

A خرابي *kharābī*, Ruin, desolation. Depravity, corruption, mischief. Debased.

A خراة *kharāt*, Name of a star.

A خراتان *kharātāni*, Two stars so named: they are زبرة الاسد *zubratu'l asad*.

P خراتگين *kharātagīn*, A kind of armour.

P خراتين *kharātīn*, Earth-worms.

A خراج *kharāj* or *khurāj*, (pl. اخرجة *akhrijat*) Tribute, tax, revenue. Capitation-tax. P خراج سر *kharāji sar*, Poll-tax. A خراج مال *kharāji māl*, Tax upon effects. خراج مصر *kharāji misr*, Sugar. Sugar-candy. A kiss. *Khurāj*, An eruption, pimple, sore, blotch. An issue. *Kharāji*, Bring out. A word used in the game خريج *kharīj*.

A خرّاج *kharrāj*, Ingenious, crafty.

P خراج گذار *kharāj-guzār*, Tributary.

A خراجة *kharāja*, Leading word in a sentence.

A خراجي *kharājī*, (Land) subject to taxation.

P خراخر *kharākhar*, Snoring. The noise of one being throttled.

P خراد *kharād*, A kite. *Kharād* or *kharrād*, Name of a certain king. خرّاد مهر *kharrād-mihr*, Name of a fire-temple.

A خراد *kharād*, A lathe. See خراط.

A خراديل *kharādīl*, Chopped small (meat).

A خرار *khirār*, (pl. of خرّارة *kharrārat*) Certain birds larger than صرد *surad*.

A خرّار *kharrār*, Murmuring, noisy (stream).

A خرارت *kharārit*, (pl. of خرّيت *khirrīt*) Skilful road-guides.

A خرّارة *kharrārat*, A piece of wood fastened to the end of a string, and making a noise when whirled round. (pl. خرار *khirār*) A sort of bird.

A خرارق *kharārik*, (pl. of خرّق) Kinds of sparrows.

P خرارة *kharāra*, A sob. Noise of a waterfall.

A خرّاز *kharrāz*, A cobbler.

A خرازة *khirāzat*, A stitching with an awl.

P خرازة *kharāza*, Membrum virile.

P خراس *khar-ās*, An ass-mill. خراس خراب *kharāsi kharāb*, (or خراس خسيسان *kharāsi khasīsān*) The firmament.

A خرّاس *kharrās*, A maker or seller of jars.

P خراسان *khurāsān*, An extensive and noble country, the ancient Bactriana, lying to the north of the river Jayhūn. Name of a note in music.

P خراساني *khurāsānī*, Of Khurāsān. The sun.

A خراسانيّ *khurāsāniy*, Native of Khurāsān.

P خراستر *kharāstar*, Noxious reptiles.

A خراسيّ *khurāsiy*, A native of Khurāsān.

P خراش *kharāsh*, Any thing torn, destroyed, and useless. Rotten fruit. Excoriated, torn. Fallen, abject, rejected. (in compos.) Piercing, scratching, tearing (with the nails or thorns). دل خراش *dil-kharāsh*, Heart-piercing.

A خراش *khirāsh*, An oblong mark or brand made upon camels. كلب خراش *kalbi khirāsh*, A dog excited and ready to fight. *Khurāsh*, A scar.

P خراشانيدن *kharāshānīdan*, To make scratch.

A خراشة *khurāshat*, A scale or filing (of iron). A small debt.

P خراشش *kharāshish*, A scratch.

A خراشع *kharāshiع*, (pl. of خرشعة *kharshaعat*) Small mountain-peaks.

A خراشيّ *kharāshiy*, Thick saliva or phlegm.

P خراشيدگي *kharāshīdagī*, A scratching, tearing or grazing. A scratch or slight wound.

P خراشيدن *kharāshīdan*, To scratch, to lacerate, irritate. To shave, smooth.

A خرّاص *kharrās*, (pl. خرّاصون *kharrāsūn*) A liar. *Khurrās*, (pl. of خارص *khāris*) They who estimate the fruit on trees, or growing crops.

A خراصة *khirāsat*, Emendation, restoration.

A خراط *khirāt*, (v. n. of خرط) Being stubborn and unmanageable (a horse). *Khurāt*, (*kharāt*, or خرّاط *khurrāt*) A pulpy substance issuing from the root of the papyrus.

A خرّاط *kharrāt*, A turner.

A خراطة *khirātat*, Art of turning, turnery.

A خراطم *khurātim*, An elderly woman.

A خراطي *kharātī*, A turner. Turned in a lathe.

A خراطی *khurāta'*, A pulp oozing from the root of the papyrus.

A خرّاطي *kharrātī*, Business of a turner; turning.

A خراطيم *kharātīm*, (pl. of خرطوم *khurtūm*) Noses, snouts. Trunks of elephants. Chiefs of the people. Wines.

A خراطين *kharātīn*, Earth-worms.

A خراع *khurāع*, The raging humour of a she-camel. A fracture in the back of a she-camel by which she is not able to rise.

A خراعة *kharāعat*, (v. n. of خرع) Being lax and flabby. Looseness, wickedness, frowardness, unruliness. Liberty, immunity.

A خرّاعة *khurrāعat*, The smell of the she-camel.

A خراف *kharāf* or *khirāf*, (v. n. of خرف) Gathering fruit in autumn. The season of gathering fruit.

A خرافات *khurāfāt*, (pl. of خرافة *khurāfat*) Fables, stories, romances, ludicrous sayings, farrago, nonsense, mythological stuff.

A خرافة *khurāfat*, A fable, an entertaining tale. Mythology. Name of a man supposed to be possessed of an evil spirit, and accustomed to tell of strange things he had seen. Autumnal fruit.

A خرافج *khurāfaj*, Affluence, comfort.

A خرّاق *khurrāḳ*, (pl. of خرق *khirk*) Extremely liberal. Handsome youths of a generous disposition.

A خراقة *kharāḳat*, Ignorance, unskilfulness.

P خراك كردن *kharāk* (or خرّاك *kharrāk*) *kardan*, To snore. To rattle in the throat when strangling.

P خرام *khirām*, Good news, joyful tidings. Joy, gladness. A waving, walking, easy air. Handsome, comely. A beautiful woman. Hospitality. خوشخرام *khwush-khirām*, Walking elegantly. موزون خرام رفتن *mawzūn khirām raftan*, To walk with a measured step, with gravity and dignity.

A خرّام *khurrām*, Persons bold in wickedness.

P خرامان *khirāmān*, Walking pompously.

P خرامانيدن *khirāmānīdan*, To cause to strut.

A خرامة *kharāmat*, Insolence and licentiousness.

P خرامقان *kharāmakān*, A fragrant plant.

A خرامل *kharāmil*, Old, worn, every-day clothes.

P خرامندة *khirāmanda*, A pompous or stately walker. A graceful walker. Airy, jaunty.

P خراميدگي *khirāmīdagī*, A stately or graceful carriage. Airiness, jauntiness.

P خراميدن *khirāmīdan*, To walk gracefully. To strut, to go with a jaunty air.

P خرامين *khirāmīn*, A kind of provender.

A خرآن *khursān*, (pl. of خرء) Excrements.

P خران *kharān*, (pl. of خر *khar*) Asses. خران گور *kharāni gūr* or *gor*, Wild asses. *Khirān* or *khirrān*, Obedient.

P خرانبار *khar-ambār*, A meeting on business. A number of men assembled at the house of one. Tumult, contention, discord. A culprit who is made to ride on an ass through the city.

A خرانف *kharānif*, (pl. of خرنفة *khirnifat*) Fruits of the tree عضاه *ʿizāh*. *Khurānif*, Long, tall.

A خرانق *kharānik*, (pl. of خرنق *khirnik*) Leverets. Tanks.

P خرانيدن *khirānīdan*, To cause to buy.

P خراهن *kharāhin* or *han*, A kind of provender.

P خراهين *kharāhīn*, Earth-worm. Mawworm.

A خرائب *kharāsib*, (pl. of خربة) Desolate places.

A خرائد *kharāsid*, (pl. of خريدة) Modest virgins.

A خرائط *kharāsit*, (pl. of خريطة) Purses. Pods.

A خرائف *kharāsif*, (pl. of خروفة *kharūfat* and خريفة *kharīfat*) Palm-trees whose produce is estimated by guess (generally in the 6th or 7th month).

A خرائق *kharāsik*, (pl. of خريق *kharik*) Winds blowing continuously. Wells whose parapets above the water have been broken.

A خرب *kharb*, (v. n. of خرب) Striking the socket of the hip-bone. Piercing, perforating. Splitting, tearing. Turning robber. Laying waste, demolishing, razing. Stealing (camels). A needle's eye. A round hole. *Kharb* or *khurb*, The fissure of the posteriors. *Khurb*, The edge of a sand-hill. Degeneracy in religion. The socket of the hip-bone. A round hole. *Kharab*, (v. n. of خرب) Lying waste, ruined, uncultivated. Being pierced, bored (as an ear). Degeneracy in religion. A male bustard. (pl. اخراب *akhrāb*, خراب *khirāb*, and خربان *khirbān*) A male bustard. The inverted hair on the flank of a quadruped, or on the crown of the human head. *Kharib*, (pl. of خربة *kharibat*) Desolate (places). A projection of a mountain. A trench or channel. *Khirab*, (pl. of خراب *kharāb*) Ruins, desolations. (pl. of خربة *khirbat*) Desolate places. *Khurab*, (pl. of خربة *khurbat*) Wallet-handles.

A خرباء *kharbās*, Slit (ear). Pierced in the ear (a she-goat).

A خربات *kharibāt*, (pl. of خربة) Desolate places.

P خربازان *khar-bāzān*, A game like leap-frog.

A خرباش *khirbāsh*, Confusion. Large (fungus).

A خرباق *khirbāk*, A tall and large woman. A quick walker. A fast pace. Farting. A proper name.

P خربان *kharbān*, An ass-driver or owner.

A خربان *khirbān*, (pl. of خرب) Male bustards.

A خربّان *khiribbān*, Pusillanimous. A coward.

A خربة *kharbat*, (pl. خربات *kharabāt*) A sieve. *Kharbat* or *khurbat*, A hole made in the ear. The fissure of the posteriors. *Khirbat*, (pl. خرب *khirab*) A desolate place. The form or bearing of a destroyer, thief, or camel-stealer. *Khurbat*, A wallet-handle. A shepherd's wallet. A round hole. The eye of a needle. Degeneracy in religion. *Kharabat*, A blemish, flaw, defect. A vulnerable part. Baseness, vileness. *Kharibat*, (pl. خربات *kharibāt*, خرب *kharib*, and خرائب *kharāib*) A ruined, desolate place.

A خربد *khurabid*, Thick, clotted, sour milk.

P خربز *khar-buz*, A water-melon. A plant resembling the herb alkali.

A خربز *khirbiz*, A melon, a pumpkin.

P خربزه *kharbuza*, A water-melon. خربزهٔ روباه *kharbuzaī rūbāh*, The bitter purging-apple. خربزهٔ هندي *kharbuzaī hindī*, The squash. خربزهٔ ابو جهل *kharbuzaī abū jahl*, The colocynth.

P خربزه فروش *kharbuza-farosh*, A melon-seller.

A خربسيس *kharbasīs*, Hard (land). Something.

A خربشة *kharbashat*, A spoiling (of a book).

A خربصة *kharbasat*, (v. n. of خربص Q) Lighting upon a pasture, and falling to with greediness. Carrying away money received. A young woman, handsome and accomplished. Discrimination.

A خربصيص *kharbasīs*, Particles glittering amongst sand. A small lean camel. An ear-ring. A gold knob. A kind of grain.

A خربصيصة *kharbasīsat*, Something. A glass bead.

P خربط *khar-bat*, A fat goose. An idiot. Stupid. A wild man, a hairy demon resembling the human form. Dishonest.

P خربطه *khar-bata*, A goose. Facetious, one who promotes laughter.

A خربق *kharbak*, (Pers. *kharbuk*) Hellebore (which is of two kinds, white and black). P خربق سپيد *kharbuki saped*, White hellebore. خربق سياه *kharbuki siyāh*, The black poplar. *Khirbik*, A place where water rises.

A خربقة *kharbakat*, (v. n. of خربق Q) Rending, slitting (a garment). Cutting (any thing) piecemeal. Cracking. Spoiling (one's work). Calling out to goats. A quick pace.

A خربقين *kharbakayn*, The two hellebores.

P خربله *kharbala*, A water-wheel. A chest, closet.

P خربنده *khar-banda*, An ass-owner, muleteer. The game of leap-frog.

P خربواز *kharbiwāz* (or خربيواز *kharbewāz*) A large bat.

P خربور *khar* or *khurbūr*, A large bat. An owl.

P خربوزه *kharbūza*, A water-melon.

P خربه *kharaba*, Desolate, laid waste.

A خربيل *khirbīl*, Name of a certain believing man of the family of Pharaoh.

P خرپشته *khar-pushta*, (Ass's back) A sharp roof. A tomb (from its shape). Any thing elevated in the centre and sloping downwards at each end (called likewise ماهي پشت *māhī-pusht*, Fish-back). A tent. A breast-plate.

P خرپشه *khar-pasha*, A fly, a gadfly.

P خرپور *kharpūr*, A large bat.

P خرپي *khar-pay*, The tendon Achilles.

A خرت *khart*, (v. n. of خرت Boring, perforating, drilling. Travelling over a country, the roads of which are not dangerous. *Khart* or *khurt*, (pl. خروت *khurūt* or اخرات *akhrāt*) The eye of a needle, or in the head of an axe. A hole. The orifice of the ear. A small rib. Swift (wolf). *Khurt* or *khurat*, The breast-button of harness.

A خرتة *khurtat*, A single ring or buckle for fastening on breast-harness.

P خرتك *khartak*, Glass beads for amulets.

P خرتنگ *khartang*, A village near Samarkand.

P خرتوت *khar-tūt*, A large, insipid mulberry.

A خرثاء *kharsās*, A woman loose-fleshed, and large round the hypochondria or short ribs. *Khirsās*, A reddish ant.

A خرثمة *kharsamat* or *kharsimat*, The fore part or toe of a shoe.

A خرثيّ *khursīy*, Utensils of the meanest sort. Spoil, booty.

A خرج *kharj* or *khurj*, (pl. اخراج *akhrāj*, اخاريج *akhārīj*, and اخرجة *akhrijat*) Revenue, tribute, tax, duty. Outgo, charge. Expense, cost. A cloud just appearing. خرج عيال *kharji ʿiyāl*, Family-expenses. خرج قليل *kharji kalīl*, Parsimony, frugality. وافر خرج *wāfir kharj*, Great expense. وكيل خرج *wakīli kharj*, A steward, a maitre-d'hotel. P خرج كردن *kharj kardan*, To expend. To go or rush out. خرج يراغ *kharji yarāgh*, Horse-apparatus. A *Khurj*, (pl. خرجة *khirajat*) A cloak-bag, portmanteau, wallet, saddle-bags. *Kharaj*, A mixture of black and white. *Khuruj*, (pl. of خراوج *kharūj*) Long-necked horses. Camels lying apart from the others.

A خرجاء *kharjās*, (fem. of اخرج *akhraj*) Black and white. White-legged (ewe). Name of a station between Mecca and Basra, remarkable for its black and white stones.

A خرجة *khirajat*, (pl. of خرج *khurj*) Wallets, saddle-bags. *Khurajat*, One who goes much in and out of doors.

P خرجسته *kharjasta*, War, strife. A republic.

P خرجل *kharjal*, A sort of bird. A locust without wings.

P خرجي *kharjī*, Travelling-expenses.

P خرجين *khurjīn*, (or خرجينه *khurjīna*) A portmanteau, saddle-bags.

P خرچاره *kharchāra*, An ass's head placed upon a pole in a garden, to guard it, as they suppose, from malignant eyes.

P خرچال *kharchāl*, A blue-coloured water-fowl. A bustard.

P خرچلوك *kharchalūk*, Name of a herb (the use of which increases women's milk).

P خرچنگ *khar-chang*, A crab. Cancer. A kind of herb.

P خرچه *kharcha*, A marginal note.

P خرچينه *khurchīna*, The comb of a bird.

A خرخار *kharkhār*, Flowing water.

P خرخاوند *khar khāwind*, Master, owner, possessor (spoken contemptuously).

P خرخجيون *khurkhujevan*, The nightmare.

P خرخر *kharkhar*, A doubling. Doubled. A cupola. An upper parlour. *Khar khur* or *khur khar*, The purring of a cat. Snoring. A noise in the throat, caused by strangulation. خرخر نمودن *kharkhar namūdan*, To snore.

A خرخر *kharkhar*, The noise made by the wings of an eagle. *Khirkhir*, (A camel) abounding in milk. Soft, delicate (man).

A خرخرا *kharkharā*, Snoring.

A خرخرة *kharkharat*, (v. n. of خرخر Q) Snoring. Rattling (one strangled). The purring of a cat or of a leopard.

P خرخره *kharkhara*, A curry-comb. خرخره كردن *kharkhara kardan*, To curry (a horse).

A خرخريّ *khirkhirīy*, (or خرخريّة *khirkhirīyat*) Weak, feeble, spindle (shank).

P خرخسه *kharkhasa*, A bird tied as a lure.

P خرخشت *kharkhusht*, A wine-press.

P خرخشه *kharkhisha*, A tumult, a crowd. A boxing-match. A dispute, quarrel, wrangling without cause. A dispute regarding boundaries. Anxiety, agitation, mental distress. A decoy.

A خرخوب *khurkhūb*, A camel giving milk plentifully, but soon ceasing.

A خرخور *kharkhūr*, A camel yielding abundance of milk. (A man) delicate in his clothing and diet.

P خرخيار *khar-khiyār*, Cucumber: ass-radish.

P خرخيز *kharkhīz*, (or خرخير *kharkhīr*) Name of a city in Khatāy; also of a stuff.

P خرد *khard* or *kharrad*, Black viscous clay. A muddy place. *Khurd*, Minute, little, small. Young. *Khirad*, Understanding, judgment, intellect, wisdom. خرد خرده بين *khiradi khurda-bīn*, A quick genius, a mind seeing minute objects. بي خرد *bī khirad*, Uninformed. دندانهاي خرد *dandānhāyi khirad*, Wisdom-teeth.

A خرد *kharad*, (v. n. of خرد) Being bashful; keeping silence, or speaking in a low tone from modesty. A long silence. *Khurud* or *khurrad*, (pl. of خريد *kharīd* and خريدة *kharīdat*) Modest women. Virgins.

P خرداد *khur-dād*, (Light-giving) Name of the third Persian month; also of the sixth day of the month. Name of an angel.

A خردازي *khardāziy*, Wine.

P خرد پرور *khirad-parwar*, Fostering wisdom.

P خرد پسند *khirad-pasand*, Commendable.

P خردتر *khurdtar*, Smaller.

P خرد خام *khurd-khām*, Being ground small. Trituration.

P خرد خان *khurd-khān*, Dispersed, scattered.

P خرد دست *khurd-dast*, The wrist. Fraud. A cut-purse. A kind of children's play of joining hands, and other manœuvres.

P خردر *khardar*, A kite.

P خر در گله *khar dar gala*, An independent tribe. A republic.

P خرد سال *khurd-sāl*, A youth of tender years. خرد سال و بزرگ منش *khurd-sāl u buzurg-manish*, In years a youth, in judgment an old man.

P خرد سوز *khirad-soz*, Consuming the understanding or reason (grief, study, love, or beauty). Name of a fire-temple.

P خردشتي *khar-dashtī*, The wild ass.

A خردق *khardak*, Broth.

P خردك *khurdak*, Well-bred. Clever.

P خردكيشي *khirad-keshī*, Practice of wisdom.

P خرد گاه *khurd-gāh*, A small tent enclosed within a larger one. That part of a camel's breast which touches the ground when he lies down. The pastern of a quadruped.

P خردگي *khurdagī*, Diminution by wear.

A خردل *khardal*, Mustard. Mustard-seed.

P خردل *khar-dil*, (Ass-hearted) Cowardly, base.

A خردلة *khardalat*, (v. n. of خردل Q) Chopping small (meat). Eating the best part of food. Being greatly shaken (a palm-tree), and having large unripe dates remaining upon it.

P خردما *khurdamā*, A bird with a sweet voice.

P خرد مرد *khurd murd*, Trifles, minutiæ.

P خردمند *khiradmand*, Wise, sensible.

P خردمندان *khiradmandān*, The wise.

P خردمندانه *khiradmandāna*, Wisely.

P خردمندي *khiradmandī*, Wisdom, prudence.

P خرد منشي *khirad-manishī*, Prudence.

P خردوات *khurdawāt*, Small wares, trifles.

P خرد و مرد *khurd u murd*, The under side of a carpet or covering. Any thing small, trifling, insignificant, or easy.

P خردومند *khiradūmand*, Wise.

P خرده *khurda*, Small, fine, minute. Any thing small. Crumbs. A chip. The teeth. That part of (a horse's leg round which the fetter passes). Quickness, smartness of wit. Criticism. Fault, blemish. A thorn. The rainbow. A spark of fire. The fifth chapter of the Zand. خردمند خرده شناس *khiradmandi khurda-shinās*, A man of the most acute understanding. خردهٔ الماس *khurdaʼi almās*, Diamond-filings. خردهٔ دست *khurdaʼi dast*, The wrist. A cut-purse. خردهٔ سماط *khurdaʼi sumāt*, Crumbs fallen from the table. خردهٔ كافور *khurdaʼi kāfūr*, (Crumbs of camphor) The stars. خردهٔ كندر *khurdaʼi kundur*, Particles of frankincense. خردهٔ مينا *khurdaʼi mīnā*, Brayed glass. Wine.

P خردها *khurdahā*, Fractions. Small things.

P خرده بين *khurda-bīn*, Acute. Critical.

P خرده بيني *khurda-bīnī*, Subtilty of genius.

P خرده دان *khurda-dān*, Sagacious. A critic.

P خرده فروش *khurda-farosh*, A vender of small wares, a piece-broker.

P خرده گاه *khurda-gāh*, The part round which the fetter passes, the pastern (of a horse). That part of a camel's breast that touches the ground when he lies down. خرده گاه ساق *khurda-gāhi sāk*, The thinnest part of the leg: shank, or cannon-bone.

P خرده گير *khurda-gīr*, Fault-seeking; caviller.

P خرده مرده *khurda-murda*, In pieces. Topsy-turvy.

P خردهي *khurdahī*, A kind of bird.

P خردي *khurdī*, Smallness. Infancy.

P خرديكك *khurdīkak*, Less, smaller.

P خردين *khurdīn*, The smallest, most minute. انگشت خردين *angushti khurdīn*, The little finger.

A خرذلة *kharzalat*, A cutting (of meat) small.

P خرذمند *khirazmand*, Wise, learned.

A خررة *khirarat*, Channels worn by torrents.

A خرز *kharz*, (v. n. of خرز) Sewing (leather) pierced with an awl, stitching. Uniting closely (the planks of a vessel). *Kharaz*, Small pearls, glass beads, coq-de-perle, or things similar (especially such as are hung round the neck to avert malignant eyes). خرز الظهر *kharazu'z zahr*, Joints in the back-bone. *Khuraz*, (pl. of خرزة *khurzat*) Stitch-holes (in a shoe or leathern bottle).

A خرزات *kharazāt*, (pl. of خرزة *kharazat*) Shells. خرزات الملك *kharazātu'l malik*, Pearls or other gems in the royal crown (to which one is added for every year the king reigns).

A خرزافة *khirzāfat*, One who sits ungracefully in an assembly. One who talks much. Light, feeble, and relaxed.

P خرزان *kharzān*, The first day of the Persian year, *i.e.* the vernal equinox. See روز *roz*.

A خرزة *khurzat*, (pl. خرز *khuraz*) A stitch, a hole made with an awl. *Kharazat*, A single shell. A gem, a jewel. A pearl, a glass-bead, or any thing that is strung. Name of a plant set thick with berries from the top to the bottom. خرزة البقر *kharazatu'l bakar*, A stone growing in an ox's gall.

P خرزدان *kharazdān* or *kharizdān*, Name of a wrestler of Turkistān.

P خرزده *khar-zada*, A beetle. Name of a flying insect which bites the nostrils of cattle.

A خرزفة *kharzafat*, A walking tremulously.

P خرزه *kharza*, A yard long and stout.

P خرزهره *khar-zahra*, A poisonous shrub or fruit. The colocynth (as being poisonous to asses, dogs, and other animals). Rododaphne. A venomous earth-worm about the size of the finger, and of a blackish red colour.

P خرزي *kharazī*, (A خرزيّ *kharaziy*) A seller of beads or small-wares.

P خرزين *khar-zīn*, (Ass-saddle) A shelf. A sort of wooden horse for hanging saddles and bridles upon. A bench for reclining upon. A pack-saddle.

A خرس *khars*, (pl. خروس *khurūs*) A wine-jar. *Khirs*, A wine-jar. *Khurs*, Meats prepared on the birth of a child. (pl. of اخرس *akhras*) Dumb. *Kharas*, (v. n. of خرس) Drinking out of a wine-jar. Being dumb. Dumbness. *Kharis*, Sleepless at night.

P خرس *khirs*, A bear. A rough fellow.

A خرساء *kharsāʼ*, (fem. of اخرس *akhras*) Dumb (woman). Still, noiseless (squadron). A misfortune, calamity. Thunderless (cloud).

A خرسان *khursān*, (pl. of اخرس *akhras*) Dumb persons. Natives of Khurāsān.

P خرس بازي *khirs-bāzī*, Romp, bear's play.

A خرسة *khursat*, Food prepared for a woman in childbed. A woman in childbed.

P خرست *kharast*, Filled with drink, drunk.

P خرستان *khuristān*, A grove of palm-trees.

P خرسته *khirista*, A leech.

P خرسك *khirsak*, A little bear. A quilted coverlet. A game like blindman's-buff; hot-cockles.

P خرس گياه *khirs-giyāh*, Name of a herb.

P خرسلاه *khar-salāh*, A muleteer. One who lets out asses on hire.

P خرسله *kharsala*, A kind of medicine.

P خرس ماده *khirs-māda*, A she-bear.

P خرس ناك *khirsnāk*, (A place) full of bears.

P خرسند *khursand*, Content, satisfied, pleased.

P خرسنده *khursanda*, Contented.

P خرسندي *khursandī*, Content, pleasure, mirth, contentment, satisfaction. Tranquillity.

P خرسنگ *khar-sang*, A large rough stone. Heaps of gravel (rendering a road disagreeable to travel on). Obstacle, stumbling-block. A rival.

A خرسنيّ *khurasaniy*, A native of Khurāsān.

A خرسع *khursaʻ*, Dumb, not braying (camel).

A خرسيّ *khursiy*, Belonging to Khurāsān.

A خرش *kharsh*, (v. n. of خرش) Scratching, tearing. Searching for, or procuring victuals for one's family. Drawing (a camel) towards one with the crooked stick مخراش *mikhrāsh*. *Kharsh* or *kharish*, Sleepless (man). *Kharash*, (pl. خروش *khurūsh*) The worst part of household furniture.

P خرش *kharash*, A wild ass. *Kharish*, A butt for ridicule. *Khurush*, Cry, uproar. Rubbish of sticks or thorns.

P خرشا *khurshā*, or خرشاد *khurshād*, (in zand and Pāzand) The sun.

A خرشاء *khirshā*, Spittle. Foam. Dust. A snake's slough. The outer shell of a broken egg. A pellicle formed upon the surface of milk. Any thing empty and blown out. Phlegm.

A خرشاف *khirshāf*, Rugged, uneven ground.

A خرشب *khurshub*, Tall, thick, and fat. Rough, coercive.

A خرشبة *kharshabat*, A working carelessly.

A خرشة *kharashat*, A fly.

P خرشته *kharashta*, Any airy kind of walking with a vacillating gait. *Kharishta*, An arched roof. A kind of armour.

A خرشع *kharshaꜥ*, (pl. of خرشعة *kharshaꜥat*) Small mountain-peaks.

A خرشعة *kharshaꜥat*, (pl. خرشع *kharshaꜥ* and خراشع *kharāshiꜥ*) A small mountain-peak.

A خرشفة *kharshafat*, Rugged, clayey ground. Motion. Confusion in speech.

A خرشمّة *khirshammat*, Hard and rugged soil.

A خرشوم *khurshūm*, A promontory beetling over a valley. A large mountain. Thick hard soil.

P خرشه *kharasha*, Enmities, tumults. A causeless quarrel. Anxiety. Scratched.

P خرشيد *khur-shed*, The sun. Sunshine.

P خرشين *kharshīn*, An airy, swinging mode of walking: oscillation, vibration. Name of a tribe of Afghāns, who claim descent from Muhammad.

A خرص *khars*, (v. n. of خرص) Obstructing (the course of a river). Guessing by the eye the produce of palm-trees. Guess, conjecture. A lie. Branch of a palm without leaves. *Khars*, *khirs*, or *khurs*, A cane-spear, especially the head of it. *Khirs*, The estimated or guessed produce of a field. Strong, firm-sided (camel). A slender spear. A basket. A wallet. *Khirs* and *khurs*, (pl. خرصان *khirsān*) A gold or silver ring. A branch of a palm without leaves. A bit of wood used as plug to a leathern bottle. *Khurs*, A branch. A wallet. ما يملك خرصاً *mā yamliku khursan*, He possesses nothing. *Kharas*, (v. n. of خرص) Enduring hunger and cold. *Kharis*, Hungry and cold. *Khuras*, *khurus*, or *khurs*, (pl. اخراص *akhrās*) A stick with which they take honey from the hive.

A خرصان *khirsān*, (pl. of خرص *khirs* or *khurs*) Rings of gold or silver. Leafless palm-branches.

A خرصة *khursat*, Indulgence, leave, permission (to depart). A portion of water. Food given to women in childbirth.

A خرصيان *khirsiyān*, (Another mode of writing حرصيان *hirsiyān*).

A خرط *khart*, (v. n. of خرط) Unbarking. Smoothing, especially in a turner's lathe. Stripping a branch of its leaves, or a cluster of the grapes, by drawing the hand from one end to the other. Making any thing long and taper. Lying with. Purging (a cathartic medicine). Letting (a bucket) into a well. Turning (camels) loose to pasture. Allowing (one's servant) to annoy people. Letting loose (a falcon) after game. Breaking wind. *Khirt*, Milk coagulating in the udders of sheep from disease. A male partridge. *Khurt*, (pl. of خروط *kharūt*) Unmanageable (horses). *Kharat*, A disease in a camel, in which the milk comes away in a clotted state, or mixed with yellow water, caused by a malignant eye or by the camel lying in a damp place.

A خرطال *khartāl*, Oats.

P خرطال *khirtāl*, A kind of purse made of an ox's skin, or the skin of a camel's neck, and filled with gold or silver.

P خرطبع *khar-tabꜥ*, Stupid. Stubborn.

A خرطم *khurtum*, The nose. Snout, proboscis.

A خرطمان *khurtumān*, Long.

A خرطمانيّ *khurtumāniy*, Large-nosed (man).

A خرطمة *khartamat*, (v. n. of خرطم Q) Striking on the nose or snout, or making it awry.

A خرطوم *khurtūm*, (pl. خراطيم *kharātīm*) The proboscis (of an elephant). A snout. The nose. Wine that speedily intoxicates or which runs before the grapes have been trodden.

A خرطيط *khirtīt*, A moth with painted wings.

A خرع *kharꜥ*, (v. n. of خرع) Cleaving, splitting. Being lax and flabby. *Kharaꜥ*, (v. n. of خرع) Being broken. Being weak (the root of a palm-branch). Perishing. Languor, flabbiness. Laxity of the joints. Astonishment. A mark in a sheep's ear, made by two slits, so that the ear being divided into three parts, the middle one hangs down. *Khariꜥ*, Languid, flabby. Weak.

A خرعب *kharꜥab*, A branch, young, tall, vigorous and flexible. Tall and full of flesh. See also خرعوب *khurꜥūb*.

A خرعوب *khurꜥūb*, (and خرعوبة *khurꜥūbat*), A beautiful girl, delicate, plump, with a fair complexion, small bones, and smooth skin. Long and flexible (branch). *Khurꜥūb*, Long and large (camel), and which yields abundance of milk.

P خرغول *khar-ghūl*, The plantain-tree. A plant called ass's ear. Seed of fleawort.

P خرغوله *kharghūla*, The plantain-tree.

P خرغون *kharġūn*, Name of a city.

A خرف *kharf*, (v. n. of خرف) Gathering fruit (in autumn). Picking for any one. *Kharaf*, (v. n. of خرف) Doting. Being greedy of autumnal fruit. The dotage of old people. A species of bad, sour date. *Kharif*, An old dotard. *Khuruf*, The season of gathering fruit, autumn.

P خرف *khirf*, Purslain. *Khirif*, Languid, weak (neither seeing, hearing, nor knowing what he does).

A خرفان *kharfān*, An old dotard. *Khirfān*, (pl. of خروف *kharūf*) Lambs.

A خرفة *khurfat*, Autumnal fruit. *Khurafat*, A fable, an agreeable, merry tale.

P خرفتن *kharif* or *ruftan*, To murmur: to snore.

A خرفج *khurfaj*, (and خرفيج *khirfīj*) Affluence, comfort. *Khurafij*, Fat.

A خرفجة *kharfajat*, A taking much of a thing.

A خرفع *khirfiꜥ*, Carded cotton. *Khurfuꜥ*, Fruit of the ꜥushar tree. Carded cotton. Cotton rotten in the pods.

P خرفق *kharfah*, Seed of wild rue.

A خرفق *kharfak*, A kind of cress.

A خرفقة *kharfakat*, (v. n. of خرفق Q) Skulking (a suspicious person), cleaving to the ground.

P خرفه *khurfa*, Purslain.

A خرفى *kharfa'*, Pease.

A خرفى *kharifī*, Dotage.

A خرفيّ *khar*, *khir*, *kharafiy*, Autumnal (fruit).

A خرفيج *khirfīj*, Fresh, tender, soft, delicate.

A خرق *khark*, (v. n. of خرق) Tearing (a garment). Coming with, bringing. Framing a lie, lying. Crossing a desert. A fissure, round hole. A passage. The vest or tunic of a mendicant or religious man. (pl. خروق *khurūk*) A widely-extended plain swept by the wind, a desert. A shrub resembling the costus. خرق عادت *kharki ꜥādat*, Contrary to nature, a miracle. *Khirk*, (pl. اخراق *akhrāk*, خرّاق *khurrāk*, and خروق *khurūk*) Extremely liberal, or ingeniously so. A handsome youth of a noble disposition. *Khurk*, Inexpertness, unskilfulness. Folly, stupidity. Asperity, unfeelingness (of heart). (pl. of اخرق *akhrak* and خرقاء *kharkā*) Inexpert, clumsy, unskilful. *Kharak*, (v. n. of خرق) Being struck with astonishment. Being frightened and staring. Keeping close at home, not quitting the house. Being unskilful, ignorant, and foolish. Sweating and being unable to rise (a fawn). Being unable to fly (a bird). Asperity, unfeelingness of heart. Inexpertness, unskilfulness. Stupefaction (from shame or fear). *Kharik*, Fearful, bashful. Ashes. A fawn weak on the legs. *Kharik* or *kharuk*, Ignorant, unskilful. *Khirak*, (pl. of خرقة *khirkat*) Clouts, rags, patches. *Khuruk*, (pl. of خريق *kharik*) Level grounds, sprouting fields.

A خرّق *khurrak*, (pl. خوارق) A sort of sparrow.

A خرقاء *kharkā*, (fem. of اخرق *akhrak*) Inexpert, unskilful. Untidy, slovenly. A slattern. Unsettled, open to discussion (question). (A sheep) bored in the ear. Violent (wind). A desert, a widely-extended plain swept by the wind. Name of the woman who used to sweep Muhammad's mosque. A she-camel which does not tread evenly. لا تعدم الخرقاء علة *lā taꜥdamu'l kharkā ꜥillatan*, The slattern is never at a loss for an excuse.

A خرقة *khirkat*, A garment made of shreds and patches; a religious habit. (pl. خرق *khirak*) A patch, rag. A piece of a locust. خرقة الحائض *khirkatu'l hāiz*, A menstruous cloth. P خرقه انداختن *khirka andākhtan*, (met.) To confess a fault. To surrender. To be lost in extacy. خرقه

خرقه ساختن *khirka sākhtan*, To rend in pieces. A *Khurkat*, Folly, stupidity, ignorance. *Kharikat*, Timid, bashful (woman).

P خرقطان *kharkatān*, Dodder.

A خرقلة *kharkalat*, (v. n. of خرقل Q) Shooting deliberately, transfixing with an arrow.

P خرقه پوشان *khirka-poshān*, (Clad in shreds and patches) Religious mendicants, dervishes.

P خرقه دوز *khirka-doz*, A botcher. Poor.

P خرقي *kharkī*, A grain of which bread is made.

A خرقيّ *khirkīy*, Name of several Imāms and reporters of traditions or sayings of Muhammad.

P خرك *kharak*, A little ass. A reptile which has the fore-legs long and the hinder ones short. The septum of the nose, that which divides the nostrils. The bridge of a musical instrument. A child's go-cart. A three-legged stool. A plank whereon culprits are made to lie to receive castigation. The rack. An instrument for separating the seed from the cotton. A chopping or sawing-block. A kind of date. An unripe date. An instrument for stocking or pecking a wall. Hot coals, embers. Name of a village near Shīrāz. A breast, nipple.

P خركبوتر *khar-kabūtar*, A wood-pigeon.

P خركرّه *khar-kurra*, An ass's colt.

P خرك زمين *kharak* (or *raki*) *zamīn*, Reptiles.

P خركس *khar-kus*, Idle babbler, silly fellow.

P خركش *kharkush*, A shoe, slipper, galoshe, patten, or clog, worn above boots, to keep them clean when walking. (Ass-killing) A multiped insect resembling a beetle, met with in cemeteries.

P خركمان *khar-kamān*, A large bow. A machine for stringing bows. A spring-gun set in gardens. An arduous and unprofitable concern. Durance, detention in any painful, toilsome, or ruinous business.

P خركوف *khar-kūf*, A kind of large owl.

P خرگاه *khargāh*, A tent, pavilion, tabernacle. A wide, spacious place of residence. A cottage or moveable Turkomān hut or tent, formed by flexible poles, and covered with felt-cloth. خرگاه خضر *khargāhi khuzr*, (سبز *sabz*, or مينا *mīnā*) The sky. خرگاه فلك اشتباه *khargāhi falak-ishtibāh*, A pavilion high as heaven. خرگاه ماه *khargāhi māh*, A halo round the moon. A mole on the cheek.

P خرگر *khargar*, A halo round the moon.

P خرگز *khar-gaz*, A large wasp, hornet. The parading of a culprit mounted on an ass.

P خرگواز *khar-gawāz* or *guwāz*, An ox-goad.

P خرگور *khar-gūr* or *gor*, (or خرگوره *khar-gūra* or *gora*) The onager or wild ass.

P خرگوش *khar-gosh*, (Ass-ear) A hare. *Khar-gosh* (or خرگوشك *khar-goshak*) Lamb's tongue (a plant).

P خرگوشك *khargoshak*, A leveret.

P خرگه *khar-gah*, A large tent: a spacious place. خرگه ازرق *khar-gahi azrak*, (The azure tent) The sky. خرگه ماه *khar-gahi māh*, A halo round the moon.

A خرم *kharm*, (v. n. of خرم) Bursting (sewing). Cutting off. Piercing the septum of the nose. Receding. Diminishing, withholding. (in poetry) The elision of ف *fe*, in فعولن *faᶑūlun*, and of م *mīm* in مفاعلتن *mufāᶑalatun*. *Kharm* or *khurm*, The brow or projecting summit of a mountain. *Kharam*, (v. n. of خرم) Being pierced in the septum of the nose.

P خرم *khurm*, Vapours, exhalations. Name of a certain plain, where there is a mountain that answers any question put to it.

P خرّم *khurram*, Cheerful, smiling, glad. A pleasant, delightful place. Name of the tenth solar month; also of the eighth day of every solar month.

P خرما *khurmā*, A date. خرماىٔ ابو جهل *khurmāi abū jahl*, A sort of date. خرماىٔ هندي *khurmāi hindī*, A tamarind.

A خرماء *kharmāᶏ*, (fem. of اخرم *akhram*) Slit-eared crosswise (she-goat). Pierced (ear). High ground sloping into a hollow. Precipitous (hill).

P خرما بن *khurmā-bun*, A palm-tree. The pith or marrow of the palm-tree.

P خرمادان *khurmādān*, A store-room for dates.

P خرماستان *khurmāstān*, A grove of palms.

A خرمان *khurmān*, A lie, a falsehood.

A خرمة *kharamat*, The part of the nose which is pierced, the septum.

A خرّمة *khurramat*, A kind of pulse or bean.

P خرّم روز *khurram-roz*, The 8th day of every solar month. A celebrated festival formerly held on the 8th day of the month دي *day*.

A خرمس *khirmis*, A dark night.

P خرمست *khar-mast*, Stupid, obstinate. Athletic.

A خرمشة *kharmashat*, (v. n. of خرمش Q) Spoiling (a work). Obliterating (writing).

P خرّم فضا *khurram-fazā*, The sky.

P خرمك *kharmak* or *khurmak*, See خرمهره.

P خرّمگاه *khurram* (or *khuram*) *gāh*, A grass-plot.

P خرمگس *khar-magas*, A gad, ass, or meat-fly.

P خرّمگه *khurram* (or *khuram*) *gah*, A large tent.

P خرمل *kharmul*, A large, tasteless pear.

A خرمل *khirmil*, A foolish woman. A decrepit old woman. A multitude of men.

P خرمن *khir* or *kharman*, The harvest. Reaped corn, but unthrashed, and piled up in a large circular stack. A halo round the moon. A parhelion or mock sun. خرمن گدا *khirmani gadā*, A heap of corn gleaned. خرمن ماه *khirmani māh*, A halo round the moon. A mole on the cheek.

P خرمنج *khar-munj*, A gadfly. A paralytic. A certain colour in a horse.

P خرمن سوخته *khirman-sokhta*, A bankrupt.

P خرمن كوب *khirman-kob*, A corn-thrasher.

P خرمن كوبي *khirman-kobī*, Corn-thrashing. گاوان خرمن كوبي *gāwāni khirman-kobī*, Oxen for treading out the corn.

P خرمن گاه *kharman-gāh*, A thrashing-floor.

P خرمن گدا *khirman-gadā*, Harvest-beggar.

P خرمن گراي *khirman-girāy*, Avaricious.

P خرّم و خندان *khurram u khandān*, Cheerful and laughing.

P خرموش *khar-mosh*, A large mouse or rat.

P خرمهره *khar-muhra*, Any little stone marked with points by nature or art, small shells, coq-de-perle, or glass beads, fastened round the neck or arms of children, as fancied protection against malignant eyes; also beads of glass, with which they ornament bridles and harness. A trumpet. A pearl in the eye.

P خرّمي *khurramī*, Gladness, cheerfulness, pleasantness. A set of voluptuaries, the sect of Bābak.

A خرّميّة *khurramīyat*, Name of a sect which maintains the doctrine of the metempsychosis.

A خرنابة *khirnābat*, The side of the nose.

P خرناي *khar-nāy*, (Throat of an ass) A brazen trumpet. Name of a note in music.

P خرنبار *kharambār*, (or خرنباز *kharambāz*) The ceremony of leading a criminal through the street, mounted upon an ass. A meeting, concourse, crowd,

P خرنباش *kharambāsh*, Name of a medicinal plant. *Khurambāsh*, The medicinal plant مرو *marv*.

A خرنبل *kharambal*, (pl. خرابل *kharābil*) A silly woman. A decrepit old woman.

P خرنجاس *khirnajās*, Name of a wrestler.

P خرند *kharand*, An herb used in washing. A low garden-wall. The parapet of a gallery.

P خرنده *kharanda*, A purchaser.

A خرنف *khirnif*, Cotton. A milch camel. The fruit of the thorny shrub عضاه *ᶑizāh*.

A خرنفة *kharnafat*, (v. n. of خرنف Q) Striking (with a sword). *Khirnifat*, (pl. خرانف *kharānif*) The fruit of the thorny shrub عضاه *ᶑizāh*.

A خرنق *khirnik*, (pl. خرانق *kharānik*) A leveret. An artificial pond. Name of a poetess.

A خرنقة *kharnakat*, (v. n. of خرنق Q) Having lumps on her sides as big as leverets (a she-camel).

P خرنوب *kharnūb* or *khurnūb*, Bean-pods, carobs. The locust-tree, bread of St. John or of the prodigal son. خرنوب نبطي *kharnūbi nabatī*, Capers. خرنوب هندي *kharnūbi hindī*, Cassia fistularis.

A خرنوص *khirnaws*, A young pig, a porker.

A خرنوف *khurnūf*, Pudendum muliebre.

P خرو *khirū* or *khurū*, Garden-mallows. *Khurū*, (for خروس *khuros*) A cock.

A خروء *khurūᶏ*, (pl. of خرء *khurᶏ*) Excrements.

A خروءة *khurūᶏat*, A voiding of excrement.

P خروار *kharwār*, An ass-load. The measure of a hundred Tabrīz maunds.

A خروب *khurūb*, (v. n. of خرب) Stealing (camels). (pl. of خربة *khurbat*) Wallet-handles.

A خرّوب *kharrūb*, See خرنوب *kharnūb*.

A خروة *khurwat*, The eye of an axe's head.

A خروت *khurūt*, (pl. of خرت) Eyes of needles.

A خروج *kharūj*, One who departs from, who goes out of. (pl. خرج *khuruj*) Long-necked (horse).

A camel lying apart from the others. *Khurūj*, (v. n. of خرج) Going out, issuing. Rushing, sallying forth in a hostile manner. Disobeying. An exception from a general rule. Egress. Exodus. Excretion. Defection, rebellion. The day of resurrection. (in poetry) the ا *alif* which follows وصل *wasl* (or صلة *silat*), as, for example, in زويلها *zawīluhā*, where ل *lām* is called the روي *rawiy*, ه *he* the وصل *wasl*, and ا *alif* the خروج *khurūj*.

P خروج *khuroj*, (for خروش) A loud cry.

P خروچ *khuroch* (for خروس *khuros*) A cock.

A خرود *kharūd*, Very modest (woman).

P خرودارو *kharū-dārū*, A species of herb.

A خرور *kharūr*, (A woman) whose privities are very watery. *Khurūr*, (v. n. of خرّ) Falling. Falling down (in an act of adoration). A fall from a height. The purring of a cat or of a leopard.

A خروز *khurūz*, Marks (as bits of pearl, &c.) on an ell or yard dividing it into half, quarter, &c. Seams between the planks or timbers of a ship, through which the water leaks.

P خروزان *khurozān*, Name of a wrestler.

A خروس *kharūs*, (A woman) conceiving for the first time. A woman in childbed. One who has little milk flowing from the nipple. *Khurūs*, (pl. of خرس *khars* or *khirs*) Earthen wine-jars.

P خروس *khuros*, A dunghill cock. A ball, a dance. The Greek chorus. A slave to his passions. خروسان طاوس دم *khurosāni tāwus-dum*, Goblets of wine. خروس كنگرهٔ عقل *khurosi kingirasi ʿaql*, The breath. Weighed, measured words.

P خروسك *khurosak*, A cockerel. A red animalcule found in baths. Lingula vulvæ. The fore-skin.

P خروسه *khurosa*, Lingula vulvæ. The fore-skin.

P خروش *khurosh*, A loud cry. A lamentation, crying O! making an exclamation, sighing.

A خروش *khurūsh*, (pl. of خرش *kharash*) The worst parts of household furniture.

P خروشانيدن *khuroshānīdan*, To raise a tumult.

P خروشيدن *khuroshīdan*, To cry aloud, shout.

A خروط *kharūt*, (pl. خرط *khurt*) Unmanageable (horse) that pulls the reins out of the rider's hands. Headstrong (man), who will have his own way. Whorish (woman).

A خروع *kharūʿ*, An adultress. Soft-bodied (woman). *Khirwaʿ*, The plant called Palma Christi. Any withered plant. *Khurūʿ*, (v. n. of خرع) Being relaxed, lax and flabby.

A خروف *kharūf*, (pl. اخرفة *akhrifat* or خرفان) A lamb. A colt six months old, or till a year old.

A خروفة *kharūfat*, A palm-tree whose fruit any one engages to gather.

P خروك *kharūk*, Name of a herb which increases women's milk. *Khurwak*, A beetle.

A خرومانة *kharūmānat*, A sort of weed found amongst cotton.

A خروق *kharūk*, A cold violent wind. *Khurūk*, (v. n. of خرق) Keeping close at home, not quitting the house. Holes. (pl. of خرق *khark*) Deserts. Widely-extended plains swept by the winds. (pl. of خرق *khirk*) Extremely liberal. Handsome youths of a generous disposition. (pl. of خريق *kharīk*) Winds blowing continually. Wells whose parapets as far as down to the water have been broken.

P خروه *khuroh*, A bird's comb. A cock.

P خروهك *khurohak*, Coral.

P خروهه *khuroha*, The comb of a bird. A lure, call, or decoy used in catching birds. Lingula vulvæ.

P خرويله *kharwela*, A shout, loud cry.

P خره *khara*, A heap. Lees of wine, sediment. Mud sticking to the bottom of a cistern. Assault, attack, throng, medley. خرهٔ چوب *kharasi chob*, Scaffolding. A wooden frame for turning an arch upon. Beams for supporting the roof of a house. خرهٔ خشت *kharasi khisht*, A pile of bricks. An oil-press. خرهٔ سنگ *kharasi sang*, A heap of stones, a cairn. *Khara*, (or خرّه *kharra*) Grains of sesame remaining in the hair-cloth after the oil has been expressed, which they give to the poor; residuum, caput mortuum. *Kharuh* or *khura*, Divine illumination, the light of reason. Light. A district or division of the Persian empire, of which there were five. *Khura*, The white ant. A disease which causes the hair to fall off, or which destroys the nose and lips. *Khurih*, Divine illumination, light of reason. *Khuruh*, A cock. Wild beasts.

P خرّه *khurra*, The noise of one being suffocated. A snore. خرّهٔ اردشير *khurrasi ardshīr*, One of the five divisions of Persia. Name of a city.

P خرهك *khuruhak*, Coral.

P خري *kharī*, Stupidity, the property of an ass. *Khirī*, Name of a yellow flower. Unlucky, inauspicious. A gallery, portico, verandah.

A خرّي *khurrīy*, The hole in the mill through which the corn falls.

A خرّيان *khirriyān*, A coward.

A خرّيت *khirrīt*, (pl. خرارت *kharārit*) An intelligent, skilful guide.

A خريج *kharīj*, A game where they cry خراج خراج *kharāji kharāji*, *i.e.* Tell what is in my hand.

A خرّيج *khirrīj*, A scholar, instructed in learning.

P خريد *kharīd*, He bought. Purchase. خريد و فروخت *kharīd u farokht*, Buying and selling, traffic.

A خريد *kharīd*, (and خريدة *kharīdat*) (pl. خرائد *kharāsid*, خرد *khurud*, and خرّد *khurrad*) An unblemished virgin, a modest woman, silent or speaking in a low and gentle voice. An unbored pearl. *Kharīd*, A low voice (an indication of modesty).

P خريدار *kharīdār*, A buyer.

P خريدارگير *kharīdār-gīr*, A marketable article.

P خريداري *kharīdārī*, Purchase.

A خريدة *kharīdat*, A pearl not perforated.

P خريدگي *kharīdagī*, A purchase.

P خريدن *kharīdan* or *khirīdan*, To buy. باز خريدن *bāz kharīdan*, To re-purchase. To buy off.

P خريده *kharīda*, Purchased, bought. The child of a purchased slave. An immature virgin.

A خرير *kharīr*, The murmuring of running water. Snoring. The sound (of wind), or of an eagle when flying. (pl. اخرّة *akhirrat*) A beaten track between two hills.

P خريش *kharīsh*, A butt for ridicule. A laugh. *Kharesh*, Scratch thou. A scratch. Thin parings that fall from leather in the currying. The dressing of leather. (in compos.) Scratching. *Khirīsh*, A lady, matron. *Khurīsh*, A king. The master or mistress of a family.

P خريشيدن *khareshīdan*, To scratch, tear, bite, pull, crop, or break with the teeth.

A خريص *kharīs*, The point or head of a spear. Hungry and cold. Cold water. Water lodged about the root of a palm-tree. Filled, full. A large cistern or reservoir. The bank of a river. An island in the sea. A gulf, bight, or bay.

A خريضة *kharīzat*, (or خريصة *kharīsat*) A beautiful girl, full of health and animal spirits.

A خريطة *kharītat*, (pl. خرائط *kharāsit*) A purse. A small bag. A letter-bag, mail. A wallet. A reticule. A letter. A pod. A volume.

A خرّيطى *khurrayta'*, Bitter weeping. A pulp oozing from the root of the papyrus.

A خريطي *kharītīy*, A wallet-maker.

A خريع *kharīʿ*, Flaccid, withered, flabby. Pendulous (camel's lip). A bad woman, an adulteress. Raging (she-camel). Soft, pliant of body. Weak.

A خرّيع *khirrīʿ*, Saffron in the flower.

A خريعة *kharīʿat*, An adulteress. Soft (woman).

A خريف *kharīf*, The first crop in the year (in India), consisting chiefly of rice. Gathered (dates). Autumn. Harvest. Autumnal rain. Fall of the leaf. Weak, doting. A canal, trench. A year.

A خريفة *kharīfat*, A palm-tree, whose fruit any one undertakes to gather. In the planting of a palm-tree, a digging out the hard clay, and putting sand in the place.

P خريفي *kharīfī*, The autumnal harvest. Grown in harvest.

A خريق *kharīk*, (pl. خرق *khuruk*) Level ground on which there is vegetation. A cold, violent wind. (pl. خرائق *kharāsik* and خروق *khurūk*) A soft, gentle wind, or one blowing continually. A well whose parapet has been broken down. A womb injured by the fœtus, and not conceiving in consequence. Shallow (canal amongst trees). The extremity of a valley opening out.

A خرّيق *khirrīk*, Very liberal. Ingeniously liberal. A handsome youth of a noble disposition.

A خريم *kharīm*, Licentious, insolent.

P خز *khaz*, A bump outside the thigh. Crawling on the hams like boys.

A خزّ *khazz*, (v. n. of خزّ) Stabbing, transfixing

(with a dart). Fencing (a wall) with thorns. Silk, raw or spun. (pl. خزوز *khuzūz*) Silken stuff. The beaver. The fine hair of the beaver.

A خزا *khaza'*, A falling into trouble or disgrace.

P خزاخز *khazākhaz*, Creeping, crawling.

A خزاخز *khuzākhiz*, Strong, robust.

A خزاز *khazāz*, (or خزازي *khazāza'*) A mountain upon which the Arabians were wont to kindle a fire the night they undertook an expedition.

A خزّاز *khazzāz*, A raw-silk merchant.

A خزاع *khuzāʿ*, Death.

A خزاعة *khuzāʿat*, A section, segment. An off-set from the tribe of ازد *azd*.

A خزّاف *khazzāf*, A seller of earthenware, or coarse crockery.

A يا خزاق *yā khazāki*, A term of reproach.

A خزام *khizām*, A nose-ring worn by women. (pl. of خزامة *khizāmat*) Hair-rings.

A خزّام *khazzām*, A maker or a vender of ropes made of the fibrous bark of trees.

P خزاما *khazāmā*, A plant promoting pregnancy.

A خزامة *khizāmat*, (pl. خزائم *khazāʾim*) A ring made of hair, put through a camel's nose, to which the bridle is tied. A thong for tying a shoe-latchet.

A خزامى *khuzāma'*, A wild fragant herb, with a long stalk, small leaves, and red flower.

A سوق الخزّامين *sūhu'l khazzāmīn*, Name of a bazaar in Madīna.

P خزان *khazān*, Creeping. Autumn. The sear and yellow leaf. The tenth day of every month. Name of the eighth month of the æra of Jalālu'd dīn. باد خزان *bādi khazān* or *khizān*, The autumnal wind, which blows during the fall of the leaves.

A خزّان *khazzān*, A hoarder. The tongue. Rotten (date), and black at the core. *Khizzān*, (pl. of خزز *khuzaz*) Male hares. *Khuzzān*, (pl. of خازن *khāzin*) Treasurers.

A خزانة *khizānat*, (pl. خزائن *khazāʾin*) A treasury, treasure, magazine, granary, repository. Public revenue. The chamber of a gun. Office of treasurer. The heart. خزانهٔ حمّام *khizānaʾi hammām*, The reservoir of a bath. خزانة السلاح *khizānatu's silāh*, An armoury. خزانهٔ عامره *khizānaʾi ʿāmira*, The imperial treasury.

T خزانچى *khazānchī*, Treasurer, cash-keeper.

P خزانه دار *khizāna-dār*, A gun with a chamber.

A خزايا *khazāya'*, (pl. of خزيان) Ashamed.

A خزاية *khazāyat*, A blushing: shame, ignominy.

A خزائم *khazāʾim*, (pl. of خزامة *khizāmat*) Nose-rings for camels. (pl. of خزومة *khazūmat*) Cows.

A خزائن *khazāʾin*, (pl. of خزانة *khizānat*) Treasuries. Treasures. Divine secrets. P خزائن بي گران *khazāʾini bī girān*, Immense treasures.

A خزب *khazab*, (v. n. of خزب) Swelling, being fat. Having a swollen udder, and thence a contraction of the teats and a deficiency of milk (a camel). A flower-pot or earthen vessel. *Khazib*, Soft (flesh). A camel or sheep with a swollen udder. Fat, bloated.

A خزباء *khazbās*, (or خزبة *khazibat*) (A she-camel) swollen in the udder or troubled with warts.

A خزباز *khizbāz*, (or خزباء *khizbās*) Flies in a meadow, also their humming. A disease in the neck of camels or men. A cat. Name of two sorts of herbs.

A خزبيل *khizbīl*, A foolish or an old woman.

A خزخز *khuzkhuz*, Thick in the muscle. *Khuzakhiz*, Strong, robust.

P خزدوك *khazdūk*, An insect like a beetle.

A خزر *khazr*, (v. n. of خزر) Running away. Being shrewd, clever, deep, crafty, and malicious. A side-glance. *Khuzr*, (pl. of اخزر *akhzar*) Small-eyed, purblind. *Khazar*, (v. n. of خزر) Looking through half-shut eyes, or with one eye only. Narrowness, smallness, or weakness of the eye. Name of a nation near the Caspian Sea, whence it is called بحر الخزر *bahru'l khazar*. Fat broth.

P خزر *khazar*, (or خزران *khazrān*) Name of a district in Turkistān. Name of a province in Gīlān.

A خزرانق *khuzrānik*, White garment or garments.

A خزربة *khazrabat*, Confusion, indistinct combination of words.

A خزرة *khazrat* or *khuzarat*, A pain in the vertebræ of the back, lumbago.

A خزرج *khazraj*, The wind. The south-wind. A lion. Name of a tribe.

A خزرجة *khazrajat*, Limping, halting (of a sheep).

P خزرك *khazruk*, Cowardice.

A خزرنق *khazarnak*, A large male spider.

P خزروان *khazarwān*, The Caspian Sea. Name of a country. Name of a warrior; also of a demon.

A خزريّ *khazarīy*, A turban made of silken stuff unravelled and rewoven.

A خزز *khuzaz*, (pl. خزّان *khizzān* and اخزّة *akhizzat*) A male hare.

A خزع *khazʿ*, (v. n. of خزع) Rescinding, restraining, preventing. Impeding, detaining. Cutting. Distributing. Separating from associates.

A خزعال *khazʿāl*, A limping, halting, lameness. A name of Gabriel.

A خزعالة *khuzʿālat*, Jest, play, sport.

A خزعبل *khuzaʿbal*, New and strange stories. *Khuzaʿbil*, Any thing false, vain, and trifling.

A خزعبلة *khuzaʿbalat*, Wonder, admiration. A marvellous thing.

A خزعبيل *khuzaʿbīl*, False, vain, trifling thing.

A خزعبيلة *khuzaʿbīlat*, A jest, laughable tale.

A خزعة *khazʿat*, Lameness in one foot. *Khizʿat*, A piece of meat. *Khuzaʿat*, One who restrains or detains another (from any thing good).

A خزعل *khazʿal*, A hyena.

A خزعلة *khazʿalat*, A limping, a halting gait.

A خزف *khazf*, (v. n. of خزف) Swinging the arms in walking. *Khazaf*, (v. n. of خزف) Drawing. Earthenware, crockery.

P خزف ريزة *khazaf-reza*, A potsherd.

A خزفيّ *khazafīy*, A potter. A seller of pottery.

A خزق *khazk*, (v. n. of خزق) Reaching the mark (an arrow). Transfixing (with a spear). Reviling, reproaching. Voiding dung (a bird). Ploughing the ground with her hoof (a camel).

A خزك *khazk* A quarrelling, wrangling: strife.

A خزل *khazl*, (v. n. of خزل) Cutting. Hindering, keeping back. The rejection of the letter ا and the quiescence of the ت in the prosodial foot متفاعلن *mutafāʿilun*. *Khazal*, (v. n. of خزل) Walking heavily. Having a broken back.

A خزلبة *khazlabat*, A quick, sharp cut.

A خزلة *khuzlat*, A dropping of the ا, and a becoming quiescent of the ت in the foot متفاعلن *mutafāʿilun*. A fracture in the back. *Khuzalat*, One who restrains another (from doing as he wants).

A خزم *khazm*, (v. n. of خزم) Perforating the bridge of the (camel's) nose, and passing a ring through it. Spitting locusts, running them through. Boring the nostrils. Piercing. An addition at the beginning of a verse, and not taken into the account in scanning. This pleonastic word may consist of one, two, three, or four letters: as,

اشدد حيازيمك للموت
ushdud hayāzīmaka li'l mawti,
فانّ الموت لاقيك
fa inna'l mawta lākīka;
ولا تجزع من الموت
wa lā tajzaʿ mini'l mawti,
اذا حلّ يناديك
izā halla yunādīka.

In scanning, no account is taken of اشدد *ushdud*. *Khazam*, A tree, of whose bark ropes are made.

A خزمة *khazamat*, Leaves of the wild palm-tree.

A خزمى *khuzma'*, Perforated in the nose (camels).

P خزميان *khazmiyān*, Beaver's testicles.

A خزن *khazn*, (v. n. of خزن) Laying up in a storehouse or treasury. Keeping (a secret). Stinking (meat). *Khazan*, (v. n. of خزن) Stinking (meat).

A خزنة *khazanat*, (pl. of خازن) Treasurers.

P خزند *khazand*, An herb used in washing.

P خزنده *khazinda*, Creeping. Reptiles.

A خزنزر *khazanzar*, Cross-grained, bad-tempered.

A خزو *khazw*, (v. n. of خزا for خزو) Subduing, reducing to order or discipline (men), breaking or exercising (horses), rendering obedient. Preventing, diverting from a project. Opposing (an enemy). Slitting a young camel's tongue.

A خزوز *khuzūz*, (pl. of خزّ) Coarse silken stuffs.

A خزوق *khazūk*, A camel impressing or grooving the ground with the sole of her foot.

A خزوك *khazūk*, A beetle, a tumble-dung.

P خزومة *khazūmat*, (pl. خزائم *khazāʾim* and خزوم *khazūm*) A cow (particularly one old and dwarfish).

A خزون *khuzūn*, (v. n. of خزن) Stinking (meat).

P خزة *khaza*, Rudder of a ship. A paddle, oar.

P خزهره *khazahra*, Asses' bane (an herb).

A خزي *khazy*, (v. n. of خزي) Disgracing. *Khizy*, (v. n. of خزي) Being base, abject, afflicted, disgraced. Ignominy, shameful notoriety. *Khaza'*, (v. n. of خزي) Blushing. Falling into trouble. Acquiring infamous notoriety.

A خزيان *khazyān*, (pl. خزايا) Blushing, modest.

A خزيبة *khuzaybat*, A gold-mine.

A خزية *khazyat* or *khizyat*, Affliction.

P خزيدن *khazīdan*, To creep. To slide along the ground on one's hams (like a child).

P خزيده *khazīda*, Concealing, lying hid.

P خزير *khazīr*, Ashes beneath which are latent sparks. Fire.

A خزير *khazīr*, (or خزيرة) Any kind of broth.

A خزيز *khazīz*, Brambles set as wall-fences.

A خزيفة *khuzayfat*, A bit of broken ware, a sherd.

A خزين *khazīn*, Bad, stinking (meat).

P خزينه *khazīna*, A treasury; magazine. Tribute.

P خزينه دار *khazīna-dār*, Treasurer: robe-keeper.

A خزيي *khazya'*, Blushing, modest (woman).

P خس *khas*, Bad, wicked. Mean. A rustic, mountaineer. Name of a tribe of mountaineers, inhabiting between India and Tartary. A miser. A weed. Rubbish of sticks or thorns. A chip of wood. A kind of large white crane. An animalcule that runs on the surface of water. خس بدهن گرفتن *khas ba dahan giriftan*, To be weak. To sue for protection. خس و خاشاك *khas u khāshāk*, Rubbish, sticks and straws. *Khus*, A mother-in-law.

A خسّ *khass*, (v. n. of خسّ) Rendering mean and vile. Lettuce. خسّ الحمار *khassu'l himār*, Melilot; bugloss.

A خسء *khas*, (v. n. of خسأ) Driving away (a dog). Being driven away (a dog). Being dim and weak (the sight).

A خسا *khasa'*, (pl. اخاسي *akhāsī* irregular) Unequal, odd numbers. خسا او زكا *khasan aw zakan*, Odd and even (a kind of game).

A خساء *khisā*, (v. n. 3 of خسأ) Pelting each other with stones.

A خسار *khasār*, (or خسارة *khasārat*) (v. n. of خسر) Sustaining a loss. Perishing. Straying from the road. Fraud, perfidy. Sordidness, baseness.

P خسارت و غارت كردن *khasārat u ghārat kardan*, To ravage and plunder.

P خساره *khisāra*, The clearing of a garden or vineyard of weeds. *Khisāra* or *khasāra*, The act of lopping superfluous branches.

A خساس *khisās*, Changing, circulating things. (pl. of خسيس *khasīs*) Small, paltry, trifling.

A خساسة *khasāsat*, (v. n. of خسّ) Being close-fisted, covetous, mean, ignoble, low-born. Parsimony. Meanness. *Khusāsat*, A horse-race. Any thing with which a horse plays. A little wealth.

A خسّاق *khassāk*, A liar.

A خسال *khisāl*, (pl. of خسيل *khasīl*) Mean. Worst, vilest.

A خسّال *khussāl*, Vile, abject (men).

A خسالة *khusālat*, Silver, or silver filings. Chaff, husks, parings.

P خسان *khasān*, (pl. of خس) Mean persons.

A خسّان *khussān*, Certain stars which never set (as the polar star, Bear, &c.).

P خساندن *khasāndan*, To grind, to triturate.

P خسانده *khisānda*, An infusion (in medicine).

P خسانيدن *khasānīdan*, To wound with the teeth.

A خسائل *khasā'il*, (pl. of خسيل) Worst. Mean.

P خسائيدن *khasā'idan*, To chew. To eat.

P خسپانيدن *khaspānīdan*, To cause to kick or trample upon. To cause to extinguish. *Khuspānīdan*, To cause to lie down; to cause to rest or sleep.

P خسپش *khuspish*, A lying down: rest, sleep.

P خسپنجا *khuspan-jā*, A bed, a couch.

P خس پوش *khas-posh*, Covered over with thorns. Varnishing over, giving a false colouring to.

P خسپي *khuspī*, The planet Jupiter.

P خسپيدن *khaspīdan*, To beat with the feet, trample, kick. To extinguish. *Khuspīdan*, To lie down, to sleep.

A خسّة *khissat*, (v. n. of خسّ) Being mean, base, and despicable. Vileness, meanness: avarice.

P خست *khast*, He wounded. Colour. Utility. Desire, violent itching (of a sick person). A reptile, an insect. *Khust*, Rest, repose. A sleeve.

P خستانه *khastāna*, The patched garment of a religious mendicant.

P خستر *khastar*, Reptiles, noxious insects.

P خستگي *khastagī*, Wound: sickness: fatigue.

P خستن *khastan*, To wound, pierce. To prick. To be indisposed, sick, ail. To be wounded, broken, split. To make an attack. To cut in pieces. To fear.

P خستو *khastū*, The stone of fruit. *Khustū*, Confessing. A noxious animal. Name of a Chinese grandee.

P خستوان *khustuwān*, Those who confess.

P خستوانه *khastuwāna*, (*khustuwāna*, or خستونه *khustūna*) A patched woollen or camelot garment, worn by fakīrs, dervīshes, and other religious mendicants (especially ragged).

P خسته *khasta*, Wounded. Sick, infirm. Fruit-stone. Ground prepared for sowing. Excited, roused. خسته حال بودن *khasta-hāl būdan*, To be in a bad situation, to be afflicted. *Khusta*, The foundation of a wall.

P خسته بند *khasta-band*, A bandage, roller for fractured limbs. A plaster. One who binds up broken bones.

P خسته دل *khasta-dil*, Sick at heart.

P خسته مزاج *khasta-mizāj*, Weak, sickly.

P خس خس *khas khas*, A sweet-scented root of a sort of grass, of which tatties are made.

A خسر *khasr*, Loss, damage. *Khasr*, *khusr*, *khasar*, or *khusur*, (v. n. of خسر) Losing, sustaining a loss. Losing the way. *Khusr*, (v. n. of خسر) Losing, missing. Damage, loss, detriment.

P خسر *khasar*, Ice. *Khusur*, A father-in-law. A mother-in-law.

A خسران *khusrān*, (v. n. of خسر) Suffering loss, losing. Missing the way. Perishing. Damage, detriment. Perfidy.

P خسرپوره *khusarpūra*, A wife's brother.

P خسرو *khusrav*, *khusraw*, or *khusrau*, A great king. A celebrated Persian king. A royal surname in Persia. خسرو اختران *khusravi akhtarān*, The sun. خسرو اقليم چهارم *khusrawi iklīmi chahārum* or خسرو انجم *khusrawi anjum*, The sun. خسرو خاور *khusravi khāwar*, The sun, the monarch of the west. خسرو هشتم بهشت *khusravi hashtum bihisht*, Title of Muhammad. *Khusurū*, A father or mother-in-law.

P خسروانه *khusrawāna*, Kingly. Like Khusraw.

P خسرواني *khusrawānī*, Any thing grand, elegant, or regal. A kind of song of rythmical prose in honour of king Khusraw. A species of old money (coined by king Khusraw).

A خسروانيّ *khusrawānīy*, A sort of wine. A kind of cloth.

P خسرو خواجه *khusraw-khwāja*, Father-in-law.

P خسرو دارو *khusraw-dārū*, Galangale.

P خسرو نشان *khusraw-nishān*, A maker of kings. Possessed of the marks of royalty. Imperial signet.

P خسروي *khusrawī*, Belonging to a king. Royal. Imperial. Monarchy. A sort of brandy.

P خسره *khusra*, A mother-in-law. A father-in-law.

P خسرينه *khusrīna*, A father-in-law.

A خسف *khasf*, (v. n. of خسف) Keeping (a horse) without provender. Treating with indignity or contempt, forcing one to do what he dislikes. Digging in a rock a well which runs perpetually. Causing to be absent, hiding. Recovering, rising up from sickness. Abounding in milk (a camel), but soon stopping in the winter. Making (her) so (God). Being lessened, diminished. A defect, imperfection, bad quality. A place where water issues from a well. A cloud rising in the west. علي الخسف *ʿala'l khasf*, (He took it) upon an empty stomach. بات الخسف *bāta'l khasfa*, He passed the night famishing. شربنا علي الخسف *sharibnā ʿala'l khasf*, We drank without eating. *Khasf* or *khusf*, Depth of water in the ground. A walnut. *Khisf*, Risen up fraught with rain (cloud). دع الامر بخسف *daʿi'l amr bi khusfin*, Leave the matter as it is. *Khusuf*, (pl. of خاسف *khāsif*) Lean, emaciated. Weak after sickness. Discoloured. Light, nimble (lads). (pl. of خسوف *khasūf* and خسيف) Wells dug in rocks springing continually.

P خسف *khasaf*, A walnut.

A خسق *khask*, (v. n. of خسق) Penetrating, hitting the mark (an arrow). Ploughing the ground with her hoof (a she-camel).

P خسق *khasak*, Saffron in the flower.

A خسقات *khasakāt*, Fairness at one time, and unfairness at another, in dealing. ذو خسقات *zū khasakāt*, One who bids for a thing, differs, and breaks off, and then offers again.

P خسك *khisk*, Bastard saffron. *Khush*, Time. Delay, repose. *Khasak*, (dim. of خس *khas*) Chips, sticks, rubbish. A triangular, prickly herb. A caltrop against cavalry.

P خسكانان *khashūnān*, Strict investigation, diligent search.

P خسكدانه *khasak-dāna*, Seed of safflower.

A خسل *khasl*, (v. n. of خسل) Rejecting, banishing. Clearing, freeing from what is useless.

A خسّل *khussal*, Vile, abject (men).

P خسم *khism*, A wound, a sore.

P خسنده *khasanda*, Insects (as flies, gnats, &c.).

A خسوء *khusūs*, (v. n. of خسأ) Being dull and weak (the sight). Being driven out from the society of men (dogs and swine). Driving away (a dog).

P خس وخاش *khasu khāsh*, Bits of cloth. Twigs.

P خسودن *khusūdan*, To reap. To praise.

P خسور *khusūr*, A father-in-law. A mother-in-law. Harvest.

P خسوردن *khusūrdan*, To reap. To enter. To salute.

P خسوره *khusūra*, Husband's or wife's father.

A خسوف *khasūf*, (pl. اخسفة *akhsifat* and خسف *khusuf*) A well dug in a rock, which springs perpetually. *Khusūf*, (v. n. of خسف) Thrusting inward (the eye), blinding. Being sunk (or lying concealed) under ground. Sinking inwards (the eye). Tearing, cutting. Being torn. Undergoing an eclipse (the moon). Cutting. An eclipse.

A خسوق *khasūk*, A camel that furrows the ground with the sole of her foot.

P خسى *khasī*, Baseness, vileness, meanness.

A خسيّ *khasīy*, A woollen cloak, garment, or tent.

A خسيج *khasīj*, A woollen tent or garment.

P خسيدن *khasīdan*, To chew. To grow old.

A خسير *khasīr*, Suffering damage. Straying from the road.

A خسيس *khasīs*, (pl. خساس *khisās*) Low, base, ignoble. Trifling, paltry. Avaricious, sordid, penurious. نفس خسيس *nafsi khasīs*, A mean soul.

A خسيسة *khasīsat*, Meanness, despicableness, avarice. Teeth projecting beyond the fore teeth in a camel (when about six years old).

A خسيعة *khasīʿat*, The vilest of the people.

A خسيف *khasīf*, Blinded (eye). A well dug in a rock and springing perpetually. (A camel) abounding in milk, but soon ceasing to give it in winter. Risen up fraught with rain (cloud).

A خسيل *khasīl*, (pl. خسائل *khasāsil* and خسال *khisāl*) Most vile, worst. Mean, base.

A خسيئ *khasīs*, The worst kind of wool.

P خش *khash*, The arm-pit. Running fast. *Khash* or *khush*, Husband's or wife's mother. *Khush*, (for خشك *khushk*) Dry.

A خش *khush*, (from P خوش *khwush*) Good.

A خش *khashsh*, (v. n. of خش) Passing a wooden ring through (a camel's) nose. Interfering, entering, or descending (in any thing). Hating. Blaming, accusing privately. Pouring forth a little rain (a cloud). A little rain. A fissure, cleft, split. A camel with a wooden ring in his nose. Rough. Black. (pl. of خاشّ *khāshsh*) Men on foot. *Khushsh*, A hillock of sand.

A خشا *khusha'*, Black growing corn. *Khasha'* or *khisha'*, (v. n. of خشي) Fearing.

A خشاء *khashās*, Hard ground without grass. *Khishās*, (v. n. 3 of خشي) Being afraid of each other, vying with one another in fearing (two men).

A خشّاء *khashshās*, Gravel and clay ground. A bee or hornet's nest. *Khishshās*, A scarecrow. *Khushshās*, A bone projecting behind the ear.

A خشاب *khashāb*, Land flooded by the least rain.

A خشّاب *khashshāb*, A seller of wood.

A خشاة *khashāt*, (v. n. of خشي) Fearing.

P خشاده *khushāda*, A prepared sown field.

A خشار *khushār*, (or خشارة *khushārat*) The refuse of any thing; as fragments of meat, or crumbs. The dregs of mankind. Barley destitute of meal.

A خشارم *khushārim*, Sounds. Thick (nose).

A خشاش *kha*, *khi*, or *khushāsh*, Insects flying or creeping. Sparrows. A sharp, bold fellow. *Khishāsh*, A wooden ring on a camel's nose, to which the reins are fastened; (if copper it is called برة *burat*; if hair, خزامة *khizāmat*). A sack. Wrath, rage. A side. A mountain-serpent very venomous. Birds or reptiles without brain (or the means of annoyance). *Khushāsh*, Bad, corrupt, naught. A raging stallion-camel.

A خشاف *khishāf*, (v. n. 3 of خشف) Driving (camels) all night. Emitting a sound (an arrow). Making haste to break a compact.

A خشّاف *khashshāf*, A man's name. امّ خشّاف *umm khashshāf*, A calamity. *Khushshāf*, A bat.

A خشافة *khashāfat*, (v. n. of خشف) Leading people rapidly on (a guide in the night).

A خشام *khushām*, (v. n. of خشم) Failing, giving way, losing their powers (the olfactory nerves). Large (nose or mountain). A lion.

A خشّام *khashshām*, Large-nosed (man).

P خشامن *kha* or *khushāman*, A mother-in-law.

A خشان *khishān*, (v. n. 3 of خشن) Behaving roughly towards. (pl. of خشن) Rough, coarse.

A خشانة *khashānat*, A being rough; roughness.

P خشانيدن *khashānīdan*, To bite, to wound with the teeth.

P خشاوه *khishāwa*, A clearing of land of the stones and weeds, and a preparing of it for cultivation. Pruning and lopping of trees.

P خشاي *khushāy*, (for خوش آي) Welcome.

A خشايا *khashāya'*, (pl. of خشياء) Timid (women).

A خشائب *khashāsib*, (pl. of خشيب *khashīb*) Roughly-hewn (bows and arrows).

A خشب *khashb*, (v. n. of خشب) Mixing (one thing with another). Polishing (a sword). Forging (a sword) in a rough, unfurbished state. Choosing, picking. Hewing out roughly (a bow or arrow). Writing off-hand (a poem). *Khishb*, as قشب خشب *kishb khishb*, Good for nothing. *Khushb*, (pl. of خشب *khashab*) Timbers. *Khashab*, (pl. خشب *khashab*, *khushub*, *khushb*, and خشبان *khushbān*) Wood, timber. Lean, scraggy cattle. *Khashib*, Rough, thick, raw-boned, and hard. Coarse (fare). *Khushub*, (pl. of خشب *khashab*) Timbers. (pl. of خشيب *khashīb*) Roughly-hewn (bows and arrows).

A خشباء *khashbās*, (fem. of اخشب *akhshab*) Rough. Wooden. Detestable, abominable. Dry.

A خشبان *khushbān*, Rugged, craggy mountains, not large or small. (pl. of خشب *khashab*) Timbers.

A خشبة *khashabat*, A stick.

A خشبل *khashball*, A hard hillock.

A خشبيّة *khashabīyat*, Name of a tribe.

P خشپخته *khish-pukhta*, (for خشت پخته *khishti pukhta*) A burnt brick.

P خشت *khisht*, A javelin, dart, spear, halberd, pole-axe. A brick. A kind of sweetmeat. The twelfth chapter of the Zand. خشت پخته *khishti pukhta*, A burnt brick. خشت زر *khishti zar*, An ingot of gold. The sun. خشت زدن *khisht zadan*, To make brick.

P خشتامن *kha* or *khushtāman*, A mother-in-law.

P خشت پز *khisht-paz*, A brick-maker.

P خشت تابه *khisht-tāba*, A brick-kiln.

P خشتچه *khishtcha*, A square piece of cloth put under the arm-pit of a shirt. The knee-pan.

P خشت خشت *khisht khisht*, The rattling of paper; the rustling of new clothes.

P خشتره *khishtara*, A gusset. A brick-maker.

P خشت زن *khisht-zan*, A lancer: brick-maker.

P خشترة *khishtja*, A sort of cloth (so called from its texture).

A خشتق *khashtak*, Flax. Silk. A gusset under the armpit of a garment.

P خشتك *khishtak*, A small brick. A gusset. The knee-pan. خشتك زر *khishtaki zar*, The sun.

P خشتگر *khishtgar*, A brick-maker.

P خشتنشار *khashtanshār*, A water-bird.

P خشتوك *kha* or *khushtūk*, Bastard, thief, rogue.

P خشته *khashta*, Poor, moneyless.

P خشجان *khashjān*, The four elements.

A خشخاش *khashkhāsh*, Poppy. A troop of men in armour. شير خشخاش *shīri khashkhāsh*, Poppy-juice, opium. خشخاش كردن *khashkhāsh kardan*, To break in pieces.

A خشخشة *khashkhashat*, (v. n. of خشخش Q) Making a noise (hard bodies clashing together). The noise made by such collision. Entering into.

P خش خشت *khish khisht*, The rattling of paper, the rustling of new garments.

A خشر *khashr*, (v. n. of خشر) Cleaning from rubbish. Leaving orts upon the table. Being disgustingly greedy. *Khashar*, (v. n. of خشر) Fleeing, running away (a coward).

A خشربة *khashrabat*, A doing (any thing) loosely and carelessly.

P خشرم *khashram*, The knocker of a door.

A خشرم *khashram*, (pl. خشارمة *khashārimat*) Bees and wasps: also their nests or swarms. The queen bee. Soft stones for making plaster. A rugged hill composed of pebbles. The soft cartilaginous parts of the nose in the head. *Khushrum*, Voices, noises. Thick (nose).

A خشرمة *khashramat*, An eating with noise.

A خشسبرم *khashasbaram*, Basil royal.

A خشش *khashash*, A little fawn.

A خششاء *khushashāʼ*, Lump behind a horse's ear.

A خششاوان *khushashāwāni*, (dual) Two bones behind the ear.

A خشع *khushaع*, (pl. of خشعة *khushعat*) Low hills. Bits of rugged ground.

A خشّع *khushshaع*, (pl. of خاشع) Modest, quiet.

A خشعة *khishعat*, A child cut out of its mother's belly. *Khushعat*, (pl. خشع *khushaع*) A low hill. A bit of rough ground.

A خشف *khashf*, (v.n. of خشف) Moving gently; also the noise caused by such motion; a low voice, a sound (as that of the feet among half-frozen snow, or the crawling of serpents). Breaking (the head with a stone). Travelling quickly. Sounding. Bringing forth (a woman). Baseness, meanness of spirit. *Khashf* or *khushf*, Wool of no value. *Khashf*, *khishf*, or *khushf*, A young hind. A sort of green fly. *Khushf*, (pl. of اخشف *akhshaf*) Mangy all over. *Khashaf*, (v. n. of خشف) Walking badly by reason of the mange. Snow lightly frozen. Thin ice. *Khushaf*, A sort of green fly.

A خشّف *khushshaf*, (pl. of خشوف *khashūf* and خشيف *khashīf*) (Camels) travelling by night.

A خشفان *khashafān*, (v. n. of خشف) Travelling through a country. Journeying by night. Being absent. Being bold in the night. Meddling in. Freezing (water). Becoming intense (cold).

A خشفة *khashfat*, Sound (of reptiles, serpents, frozen snow, and the like). A hyena's voice. Rugged ground become soft. Movement. *Khashafat*, Movement. A gentle noise. *Khishafat*, (pl. of خشف *khishf* or *khushf*) Young fawns.

P خشك *khushk*, Dry, withered. Pure, mere, genuine. Avaricious, tenacious. خشك آوردن *khushk āwardan*, To keep silence from bad temper, dislike, or aversion. خشك باختن *khushk bākhtan*, To play for nothing. To play away all one's property. خشك جنبانيدن *khushk jumbānīdan*, To move about without motive or advantage. خشك و تر *khushk u tar*, Dry and moist. Day and night. Bad and good. *Khashak*, A mountain.

P خشكاب *khashkāb*, Hindering; a hinderer.

P خشك ابزار *khushk-abzār*, Dry sweet herbs.

P خشك آخور *khushk-ākhwur*, (Dry or empty stall) A barren year. Penury. A miser.

P خشكار *khushkār*, Coarse, unsifted flour, full of bran. A fried egg.

P خشك افزار *khushk-afzār*, Condiments. Pulse, lentils, beans, and the like.

P خشكامار *khushkāmār*, Diligent inquiry. Estimate, calculation. Dropsy. A receiving of the whole of what is due.

P خشك امار *khushk-amār*, Dropsy.

P خشكانج *khushkānij*, Dry in body.

P خشك اندام *khushk-andām*, Lean, meagre, dry.

P خشك انگبين *khushk-angubīn*, Dry honey.

P خشكانيدن *khushkānīdan*, To cause to dry.

P خشك اوزار *khushk-awzār*, Dry condiments.

P خشك بازه *khushk-bāza*, Tree-loppings: bark.

P خشك پشت *khushk-pusht*, A tortoise.

P خشك پي *khushk-pay*, Unlucky, ill-omened.

P خشك تر *khushk-tar*, Melancholy; fool, idiot.

P خشكجان *khushk-jān*, (Dry soul) Ignorant, unskilful. Lukewarm, indifferent to the claims of love or friendship.

P خشك جنبان *khushk-jumbān*, Idly busy.

P خشكجهان *khushk-jahān*, An age barren in distinguished men.

P خشك چشم *khushk-chashm*, Tearless, dry-eyed.

P خشك خار *khushk-khār*, A caltrop.

P خشك دامن *khushk-dāman*, Pure, chaste, virtuous (the contrary of تردامن *tar-dāman*).

P خشك دست *khushk-dast*, Avaricious.

P خشك دماغ *khushk-dimāgh*, Grievous.

P خشك دماغي *khushk-dimāghī*, Grief.

P خشك دهان *khushk-dahān*, (Dry-mouthed) Fasting. A tyrant, oppressor.

P خشكرنده *khushk-randa*, The dry scab.

P خشك ريش *khushk-resh*, A dry scab or wound. Subtilty, fraud, stratagem, deceit, falsehood. A vain excuse.

P خشك ريشه *khushk-resha*, Crust of a wound. An excuse.

P خشكسار *khushk-sār*, Arid land far from water.

P خشك سال *khushk-sāl*, A year of drought, a general dearth. Scarcity. خشك سال آفت *khushk-sāli āfat*, The present evil world.

P خشكسالي *khushk-sālī*, Drought: dry season.

P خشك سر *khushk-sar*, Addle-pated. A babbler. Irascible. Melancholy.

P خشك شانه *khushk-shāna*, Proud, haughty.

P خشك عنان *khushk-عinān*, Unmanageable.

P خشكفا *khushk-fā*, Unfermented bread.

P خشك گردن *khushk-gardan*, Stiff-necked.

P خشكمازو *khushk-māzū*, (or خشكمازه *khushk-māza*) Withered or broken branch. Bark of a tree.

P خشكمانا *khushk-mānā*, Any thing cold eaten after meat, to moderate the heat of the stomach.

P خشك مغز *khushk-maghz*, Testy. A fool.

P خشك مغزي *khushk-maghzī*, Rage. Folly.

P خشك نان *khushk-nān*, Dry bread, biscuit.

P خشك نانه *khushk-nāna*, Bread eaten without meat or condiment.

P خشكناي *khushk-nāy*, The throat. The windpipe. The gullet.

P خشكوا *khushk-wā*, Unleavened bread.

P خشكه *khushka*, Boiled rice without butter. Flour not sifted.

P خشكي *khushkī*, Dryness. Scarcity occasioned by drought. Dry land. By land (in opposition to تري *tarī*, by water). Horse-dung dried, used instead of straw as litter. Dry, arid.

P خشكيدن *khushkīdan*, To dry up.

A خشل *khashl*, (v. n. of خشل) Rejecting as worthless. Refuse, offal. An eggshell. A certain plant, yellow, red, and green. *Khashl* or *khashal*, The dry fruit (also the stone) of the dwarf palm. The top of a woman's cloak; also her bracelets, and the rings or ornaments of her ankles. *Khashal*, (v. n. of خشل) Being worn out (a vest). Bad, corrupt, naught.

P خشل *khashal*, Bdellium, an Arabian gum.

A خشلة *khashlat* or *khashalat*, A single dry fruit or stone of the dwarf palm.

A خشل فشل *khashil fashil*, Weak.

A خشم *khashm*, (v. n. of خشم) Striking, hurting, or breaking the bridge of the nose. Failing, giving way (the olfactory nerves). Intoxicating. Having a wide nose. *Khasham*, (v. n. of خشم) Having no smell (a nose). Stinking (meat). Having a wide nose. A defective sense of smelling.

P خشم *khishm* or *khashm*, Anger, passion, rage, indignation, fury. خشم گرفتن *khishm giriftan*, To become angry. بخشم آوردن *ba khishm āwardan*, To provoke, make angry.

A خشماء *khashmāʼ*, (fem. of اخشم *akhsham*) Defective in the sense of smelling.

P خشماغيل *khishmāghīl*, Angry glance: squint.

P خشم آلود *khishm-ālūd*, Tainted with anger.

A خشمة *khushmat*, Ebriety from fumes of wine.

P خشمگين *khishm-gīn*, Full of rage, angry.

P خشمگيني *khishm-gīnī*, Angriness, anger.

P خشمن *khishmin*, Angry.

P خشمناك *khishmnāk*, Passionate, furious.

P خشمناكي *khishmnākī*, Anger, angriness.

P خشمه *khashma*, Travelling utensils.

A خشن *khashn*, (v. n. of خشن) Being rough. *Khushn*, (pl. of اخشن *akhshan*) Rough. Armed (legions). *Khashin*, (pl. خشان *khishān*) Rough, coarse, thick. خشن الجانب *khashinu'l jānib*, (A man) of rough, unpolished manners.

P خشن *khishn*, A kind of falcon. *Khashan*, A kind of grass from which coarse garments are made. خشن پوشيدن *khashan poshīdan*, To wear a rough garment. To play the hypocrite.

A خشناء *khashnā,*, (fem.) Rough. A certain green herb, rough to the touch, smooth in the mouth, adhesive like purslain. Lean (she-camel). Heavily-armed (legion).

A خشنام *khushnām*, (P خوش نام) Proper name.

P خشنان *khushnān*, Happy, prosperous.

P خشن باراني *khashn-bārānī*, The sky: a cloud.

A خشنة *khushnat*, (v. n. of خشن) Being rough. Asperity, roughness.

P خشنجه *khashanja*, A gusset, gore of a shift.

P خشن خانه *khashan-khāna*, A house constructed of reeds; also a house, the doors and windows of which are lined with the roots of a certain grass (Andropogon muricatum), which being kept continually sprinkled, a circulation of cool air is thereby maintained within; tatties.

P خشند *khushnud*, (for خشنود) Content.

P خشنسار *khashansār*, (*khushansār*, or خشنشار *khashanshār*) A kind of white-headed aquatic bird.

A خشنفل *khashanfal*, The privities of a woman.

P خشنگ *khashang*, A scar. Bald. Baldness.

P خشنو *khushnū* or *khashnū*, Content, pleased.

P خشنود *khushnūd*, Content, pleased, happy.

P خشنودي *khushnūdī*, Contentment, satisfaction, resignation, acquiescence. Reconciliation.

P خشني *khushnī*, An unchaste woman, harlot.

A خشو *khashw*, A small, bad date. *Khashw*, (or خشوّ *khushūw*) (v. n. of خشا for خشو) Producing small bad dates (a palm-tree).

P خشو *khushū*, A mother-in-law.

P خشوانه *khushwāna*, Wool, spun and wound.

P خش و خاش *khash u khāsh*, Trifles. Chips, scraps, rubbish.

P خشود *khashūd*, The pruning of young shoots.

P خشودن *khush* or *khashūdan*, To prune a tree.

A خشوع *khushūʻ*, (v. n. of خشع) Being humble. Being quiet, modest. Lowering the voice, casting down the eyes. Setting (a star). Spitting out viscous saliva. Disappearing all but a very little (a camel's bunch). Humility, submission.

A خشوف *khashūf*, (A man) who travels through a country. (A camel) travelling by night. (A man) traversing a country boldly by night. Piercing (sword). One who enters or meddles in an affair. *Khushūf*, (v. n. of خشف) Entering into any business. Travelling through a country.

P خشوك *kha* or *khushūk*, A bastard, miscreant.

A خشوم *khushūm*, (v. n. of خشم) Having a broad, flat nose.

A خشونة *khushūnat*, (v. n. of خشن) Being rough. Roughness, ruggedness. Asperity, severity. Rigidness, fierceness. Indignation, disdain.

P خشي *khashī*, Very white. Ash-coloured.

A خشي *khashy* or *khishy*, (v. n. of خشي) Fearing, dreading. *Khashī*, Timid.

A خشيّ *khashīy*, A dried herb.

A خشياء *khashyā,*, (fem. of خشيان *khashyān*) (pl. خشايا *khashāya'*) Timid (woman).

A خشيان *khashyān*, Timid, fearful. *Khashayān*, (v. n. of خشي) Fearing. Fear.

A خشيب *khashīb*, (pl. خشب *khushub* and خشائب *khashā,ib*) Rough-hewn. Rough, unfurbished (arrow or sword). Polished. Thick, hard, raw-boned (camel). Tall. Bad, vile. Picked, selected.

A خشيبة *khashībat*, Nature, temper.

A خشيبيّ *khashībīy*, Tall, thick, hard, raw-boned.

A خشية *khashyat*, (v. n. of خشي) Fearing. Knowing. Abhorring, hating, objecting to. Fear, terror, awe, dread.

P خشيج *khashīj*, Opposed, opposite. An element.

P خشيجان *khashījān*, Contraries. Elements.

P خشيش *khashīsh*, Victory, superiority.

A خشيش *khushaysh*, A little fawn.

A خشيشاء *khushayshā,*, A lump behind the ear.

P خشيشار *khashīshār*, Name of an aquatic bird.

P خشيشه *khishīsha*, A bird that frequents gardens in spring.

P خشيشي *khashīshī*, A kind of garment.

A خشيف *khashīf*, Snow. Thin ice. (A guide) travelling boldly in the night. (A man) who travels through a country. A meddler in any business. Dry (saffron). Sharp (sword).

A خشيل *khashīl*, Dry leaves or pieces of wood carried away by a torrent.

P خشين *khashīn*, Of the colour of ashes, of a darkish white; of a black and blue. Blue. A falcon with a black back.

P خشين پند *khashīn-pand*, A kite.

P خشينسار *khashīnsār*, Name of an aquatic bird with a black back and white spot on the head.

P خشينه *khashīna*, Of a black colour inclining to blue. A species of falcon. A kind of water-fowl. Ash-coloured.

A خصّ *khass*, (v. n. of خصّ) Marking especially, distinguishing peculiarly. *Khiss*, Deficient, defective. *Khuss*, (pl. خصاص *khisās*, خصوص *khusūs* and اخصاص *akhsās*) A house of reeds. A tavern. Good wine. A house or portico roofed with shingle.

A خصاء *khisā,*, A castrating: orchotomy.

A خصاب *khisāb*, A loaded palm-tree.

A خصار *khisār*, (v. n. 3 of خصر) Taking (a companion) by the hand, and walking together. Walking by the side. Going different ways and meeting at the same place. Breeches, trowsers.

A خصاص *khasās*, (or خصاصة *khasāsat*) Poverty. A hole, gap, chink, crevice. The space between the feet of a trivet. *Khisās*, (pl. of خصّ *khuss*) Houses of reeds. Taverns.

A خصاصاء *khasāsā,*, Poverty. A gap, chink.

A خصاصة *khusāsat*, (pl. خصاص *khusās*) The gleanings on a vine. A small quantity, some.

A خصاف *khisāf*, (v. n. of خصف) Casting her young in the ninth month (a camel). (pl. of خصفة *khasafat*) Baskets for dates made of palm-leaves. Coarse garments. Name of a celebrated stallion, which the owner castrated when a certain prince had sent to beg the loan of him; hence, the saying, اجرأ من خاصي خصاف *ajra, min khāsī khisāf*, More daring (or defying) than the gelder of Khisāf.

A خصّاف *khassāf*, A liar. A shoe-maker.

A خصال *khisāl*, (v. n. of خصل) Conquering at darting. Cutting away (a piece) of meat. (pl. of خصلة *khaslat*) Good manners, habits, properties, or qualities. خصال حميده *khisāli hamīda*, Praiseworthy virtues.

A خصالة *khusālat*, Chaff, refuse, sweepings.

A خصام *khisām*, (v. n. 3 of خصم) Litigating.

A خصّان *khissān* or *khussān*, Grandees, nobles, patrician orders. Royal favourites.

A خصائص *khasā,is*, Properties.

A خصائل *khasā,il*, (pl. of خصيلة *khasīlat*) Large joints of meat. Manners, customs, usages: morals.

A خصب *khasb*, A palm-branch. A fruitful palm-tree. *Khisb*, (v. n. of خصب) Being very plentiful (the year); possessing in rich abundance the comforts of life. Circulating (as sap). Fruitfulness. Plenty. Plentiful (year). Fruitful (country). *Khusb*, (pl. اخصاب *akhsāb*) A side. A white mountain-snake. *Khasib*, Fruitful (country).

A خصبة *khasbat* or *khisbat*, (Earth or a tree) fruitful in produce.

A خصر *khasr*, (pl. خصور *khusūr*) The middle, the waist. The under part of the sole of the foot, that which does not touch the ground. A road between the highest and lowest part of a sand-hill. The space between the root of the notch of an arrow and the feather. A place where Arabian tents are pitched. *Khasar*, Coldness, chillness. *Khasir*, Cold (water).

A خصرة *khusrat*, Shortness.

A خصص *khasas*, (v. n. of خصّ) Being poor.

A خصف *khasf*, (v. n. of خصف) Doubling and sewing together (a sole). Covering (the body with leaves). A shoe or slipper made of several folds, layers, or lamina. *Khasaf*, (pl. of خصفة *khasafat*) Date-baskets of palm-leaves. Coarse garments.

A خصفة *khasfat*, One fold or layer of shoe-leather. *Khusfat*, A stitch. A hole made with the point of an awl. *Khasafat*, (pl. خصف *khasaf* and خصاف *khisāf*) A basket for dates, made of palm-leaves. A very coarse garment.

P خصل *khasl*, A stipulation or condition at archery. A stake at play. A stake upon seven at the game of نرد *nard*. See كعبتين *kaʻbatayn*.

A خصل *khasl*, (v. n. of خصل) Conquering at shooting or darting; also the prize gained by the winner. Cutting off (a piece) of meat. Hitting the mark (an arrow) or falling by the side of it. A throw of the discus. *Khusal*, Entangled branches hanging down. Locks of hair.

A خصلة *khaslat*, (v. n. of خصل) Hitting the mark (an arrow) or falling by the side of it. (pl. خصال *khiṣāl*) Quality, property. Temper, humour, disposition, nature, habit, custom. An excellent work. A worthless thing. *Khaslat* or *khuslat*, A cluster of grapes. A thorny stick. *Khaslat* or *khasalat*, The extremity of a limber twig. Flexible branches of the tree عرفط *ʿurfut*. *Khuslat*, Entangled hair. A cluster of grapes. A lock of hair. A little hair. A joint of meat.

A خصم *khasm*, (v. n. of خصم) Overcoming at law. (pl. خصوم *khusūm*) An enemy, antagonist, adversary at law or game. P خصم يك چشم *khasmi yak chashm*, The devil. Antichrist. The heart. The sky. A *Khusm*, (pl. اخصام *akhsām* and خصوم *khusūm*) Side, margin. The corner of a sack or portmanteau. *Khasam*, A husband. *Khasim*, (pl. خصمون) Engaged in a law-suit or altercation.

T خصم *khism*, A friend, relation. An owner.

A خصماء *khusamāʾ*, (pl. of خصيم) Antagonists.

A خصمان *khusmān*, (pl. of خصم *khasm* or خصيم *khasīm*) The opposite parties in a law-suit. Antagonists, adversaries. خصمان سفلي *khusmāni suflī*, The elements.

P خصمانه *khasmāna*, Inimically. Housewifery.

A خصمة *khasmat*, An amulet or preservative which a man puts on when going forth to battle or to appear in the presence of a king.

P خصمكش *khasm-kush*, The slayer of a foe.

P خصمكشي *khasm-kushī*, Slaughter of a foe.

A خصم والي *khasam-wālī*, A woman whose husband is living.

A خصن *khusun*, (pl. of خصين) Small axes.

A خصور *khusūr*, (pl. of خصر *khasr*) Middles, waists. The hollows of the soles of the feet not touching the ground. Roads between the highest and lowest parts of sand-hills. Spaces beneath the roots of notches and the feathers of arrows. Places where Arabs' tents are pitched.

A خصوص *khusūs*, (v. n. of خصّ) Marking especially, distinguishing peculiarly. A thing, business, particular. Name of a place in Kufa, where jars were made. Name of several places. (pl. of خصّ *khuss*) Houses of reeds. Taverns. على الخصوص *ʿala'l khusūs*, Chiefly, especially.

A خصوصا *khusūsan*, (or خصوصيًّا *khusūsīyan*) (P خصوصانه) Particularly, especially, chiefly.

A خصوصيّات *khusūsiyāt*, Peculiarities.

A خصوصية *khasūsiyat* or *khusūsiyat*, (v. n. of خصّ) Being peculiar to. Doing for, or bestowing upon, peculiarly, and specially. Marking especially, distinguishing peculiarly.

A خصوصيّة *khusūsīyat*, Particularity, speciality, singularity. Attachment, intimate friendship.

A خصوف *khasūf*, (A camel) casting an abortion in the ninth month; (according to others) foaling in the thirteenth month.

A خصوم *khusūm*, (pl. of خصم *khasm*) Enemies, rivals. Roots. Mouths of rivers.

A خصومات *khusūmāt*, (pl. of خصومة) Law-suits.

A خصومة *khusūmat*, (v. n. 3 of خصم) Trying to overcome at law. Litigation, a law-suit. Altercation. P اظهار خصومت كردن *izhāri khusūmat kardan*, To declare war, to denounce hostilities.

A خصي *khusy* or *khisy*, A testicle. *Khasī*, One who has a pain in the testicles. *Khusa'*, (pl. of خصية *khusyat*) Testicles.

A خصيّ *khasīy*, (pl. خصية *khisyat* and خصيان *khisyān*) An eunuch. A gelded animal. Poetry destitute of erotic sentiments, castrated.

A خصّيّ *khussīy*, (A jar) made at خصوص *khusūs*.

A خصيان *khisyān*, (pl. of خصيّ) Eunuchs.

A خصيان *khusyāni*, The two follicles of the scrotum. Two testicles.

A خصيب *khasīb*, Rich, affluent (man). Cultivated, inhabited. ابو خصيب *abū khasīb*, Flesh.

A خصية *khisyat*, (pl. of خصيّ *khasīy*) Castrated. Eunuchs. *Khisyat* or *khusyat*, (pl. خصى *khusa'*) A testicle. *Khusyat*, An ear-ring, drop. خصية البحر *khusyatu'l bahr*, Castoreum. خصية الثعلب *khusyatu's saʿlab*, Satyrion. خصية الكلب *khusyatu'l kalb*, (Dog's stones) Ragwort.

A خصّيّة *khussīyat*, (v. n. of خصّ) Marking especially, distinguishing peculiarly.

A خصيتان *khusyatāni*, (dual) The testicles.

A خصيريّ *khusayrīy*, One who cuts off superfluities. An abridger, an epitomist.

A خصيص *khasīs*, Peculiar, private.

A خصيصّة *khusayssat*, (dim. of خاصّة *khāssat*) Minor nobles. Squireens.

A خصّيصي *khissīsa'*, (or خصّيصاء *khissīsāʾ*) (v. n. of خصّ) Marking especially, distinguishing.

A خصيف *khasīf*, Well-made (shoe). Of a sound judgment. (fem. خصيفة *khasīfat*) Black and white, or of any two colours. (A legion) of the colour of iron, *i.e.* in armour. New milk mixed with old. Ashes.

P خصي كرده *khasī-karda*, Gelded, castrated.

A خصيل *khasīl*, Beaten at play. The tail.

A خصيلة *khasīlat*, (pl. خصيل *khasīl* and خصائل *khasāʾil*) A piece of meat, particularly the coarse joints, as the thighs, shoulder, or leg. Any muscle thickly clothed with flesh. A little hair.

A خصيم *khasīm*, (pl. خصماء *khusamāʾ* and خصمان *khusmān*) Litigating, opposing; an opponent.

A خصين *khasīn*, (pl. خصن *khusun* and اخصن *akhsun*) A small axe.

A خضا *khaza'*, A bruising of any thing moist.

A خضاب *khizāb*, (v. n. of خضب) Tinging (the nails or hair with privet, saffron, or indigo). Tincture, colouring matter. A dye for the hair.

A خضاخض *khuzākhiz*, (A place) abounding with wood and water. Fat, large-bellied (man or camel). An east wind. A wind blowing between east and west.

A خضاخضة *khuzākhizat*, Fat, large-bellied.

A خضاد *khazād*, A soft tree without prickles. A sort of tree. A pain in the limbs.

A خضار *khazār*, Milk thinned with water. Herbs sprouting. Greens.

A خضّار *khuzzār*, A kind of bird.

A خضارب *khuzārib*, A pond or river whose water is in a violent commotion.

A خضارة *khuzārat*, Greenness. The sea.

A خضارع *khuzāriʿ*, Avaricious.

A خضارم *khazārim*, (pl. of خضرم *khizrim*) (Things) large and copious. (Men) extremely generous. *Khuzārim*, A gentle prince.

A خضارمة *khazārimat*, (pl. of خضرميّ *khizrimīy*) Strangers, persons of Persian origin. Certain people of foreign origin located themselves in various parts of Arabia at the beginning of Islām. Those who settled in Basrah were called اساورة *asāwirat*; those in Kūfa, احامرة *ahāmirat*; those in Syria, خضارمة *khazārimat*; those in Mesopotamia, جراجمة *jarājimat*; those in Yaman, ابناء *abnāʾ*; and those in Mawsil, جرامقة *jarāmikat*.

A خضّاري *khuzzāra'*, Name of a herb.

A خضاريّ *khuzārīy*, Name of a bird. Naval.

A خضاض *khazāz*, Writing ink. The meaner kind of women's apparel or ornaments. A collar or neck-ornament for a cat or doe. The pillory. A foolish man. *Khizāz*, Ink.

A خضاضة *khazāzat*, A foolish man.

A خضاع *khizāʿ*, A speaking gently (to women).

A خضاف *khizāf*, (v. n. of خضف) Eating (meat). Breaking wind. يا خضاف *yā khazāfi*, O slut!

A خضّاف *khazzāf*, One who breaks wind much.

A خضّام *khazzām*, Sharp (sword).

A خضامة *khuzāmat*, Any thing eaten with distended cheeks.

A خضب *khazb*, (v. n. of خضب) Tinging (the nails or hair with cypress or saffron). Growing green (a palm-tree). Shooting, budding (herbage). Herbage, vegetation refreshed by rain. Incipient foliage. (pl. خضوب) Greenness of a palm-tree.

A خضبة *khuzabat*, (A woman) who paints (herself) excessively, and dyes (her) hair.

A خضخاض *khazkhāz*, A liniment of tar.

A خضخض *khuzkhuz* or *khuzakhiz*, Fat, large-bellied (man or camel).

A خضخضة *khazkhazat*, (v. n. of خضخض Q) Ploughing. Turning topsy-turvy. Stirring about water, meal, &c. Polluting one's self.

A خضد *khazd*, (v. n. of خضد) Bending (the branch of a tree). Cutting. Trimming a tree. Breaking (a green stick) without its being apparent. Bending another's neck (a camel). Eating much; or something moist (as a cucumber). *Khazad*, Branches recently broken, or new cuttings of a tree. The shrivelling of fruits. A pain in the limbs.

Weakness in a plant. *Khazid*, Unable to rise.

A خضر *khazr*, (v. n. of خضر) Cutting (a palm-tree). *Khizr* or *khizar*, Name of a prophet, who, according to Oriental tradition, was vazīr and general to an ancient king of Persia, called Alexander, or Kaykobad (not Alexander of Macedon). They say that he discovered and drank of the fountain of life, and that in consequence he will not die till the last trumpet. He is by some confounded with the prophet Elias, and, which is somewhat singular, likewise with St. George of England, whom they call Khizr Elias, imagining that the same soul animated both by transmigration. P خضرراه گرديدن *khizri rāh gardīdan*, To guide, to lead the way. A *Khuzr*, Name of a certain tribe renowned for archery. (pl. of خضرة *khuzrat*) Greennesses. خضر المناكب *khuzru'l manākib*, Possessed of the comforts of life in abundance (persons). *Khazar*, (v. n. of خضر) Being green. Greenness. Softness, flexibility. A green palm-branch stripped of its leaves. *Khazir*, Green, verdant. Fresh. A verdant, pleasant spot. A kind of tree which becomes green after withering in the summer. *Khuzar*, (pl. of خضرة *khuzrat*) Greens, fresh pot-herbs.

A خضراء *khazrā*, (fem. of اخضر *akhzar*) Green. Heaven. Greenness. A multitude, great mass of people. Large troop, squadron, battalion. A bucket which has become green by use. Tame, gentle (pigeon). Leeks and onions. Apples and pears. خضراء الدمن *khazrāu'd dimn*, A comely woman, but of a low family.

A خضراوات *khazrāwāt*, (pl. of خضراء *khazrā*) Leeks and onions. Apples and pears.

A خضربة *khazrabat*, Commotion of water.

A خضرة *khuzrat*, (pl. خضر *khuzar* and *khuzr*) Greenness, verdure. Softness, flexibility. دائم الخضرة *dāimu'l khuzrat*, Evergreen. *Khazirat*, Green (branch, corn, or pot-herb). A name of Khaybar.

A خضرفة *khazrafat*, Decrepitude of an old woman, and flabbiness of skin.

A خضرم *khizrim*, (pl. خضارم *khazārim*, خضارمة *khazārimat*, and خضرمون *khizrimūn*) Overflowing (sea, or well). Any thing large or copious. A gentle prince: a generous man. *Khuzarim*, Sweet or sweetened water. A young (Lybian) lizard or crocodile.

A خضرا مضرا *khizran mizran* or *khaziran maziran*, With impunity (his blood was shed). Without paying (he took it). Fresh and green (he gathered it). هو لك خضرا مضرا *huwa laka khizran mizran*, It is yours and welcome.

A خضرمي *khizrimīy*, (pl. خضارمة *khazārimat*) One of a foreign nation that inhabited Syria at the beginning of Islām.

A خضرية *khuzriyat*, A kind of palm that produces a delicious date.

A خضريج *khizrīj*, A melon-ground, cucumber-bed, garden of pumpkins or gourds.

A خضض *khazaz*, Small beads and other ornaments, with which girls in Arabia adorn their wrists. Different kinds of food.

A خضع *khuzu'*, (pl. of خاضع *khāzi'* and خضوع *khazū'*) Humble, submissive, obsequious.

A خضعاء *khaz'ā*, (fem. of اخضع *akhza'*) Humble, obsequious.

A خضعبة *khaz'abat*, Weakness. Fat and weak (woman).

A خضعة *khaz'at*, The sound of a scourge. *Khuza'at*, Submissive to every one. A tyrannizer over equals. A palm-tree from a date-stone.

A خضف *khazf*, (v. n. of خضف) Breaking wind. Eating meat. *Khuzaf*, A small or large melon.

A خضل *khazl* or *khazal*, A pure pearl. Coq-de-perle, beads, or other inferior female ornaments. *Khazal*, (v. n. of خضل) Being moist. *Khazil*, Moist. Tender (plant). Roast meat from which fat drips.

A خضلاف *khizlāf*, A wild palm. Bdellium-tree.

A خضلة *khuzullat*, Affluence, the pleasures of life. A wife. A delicate modest woman. The rainbow. يوم خضلة *yawmu khuzullatin*, A pleasant day.

A خضلفة *khazlafat*, A small crop of dates.

A خضم *khazm*, (v. n. of خضم) Eating with the mouth full, chewing, cutting with the grinders, especially any thing soft, as cucumbers. Giving away a portion of one's property. Breaking wind.

A خضم *khuzzam*, A great assembly of men.

A خضم *khizamm*, A lord, a great and generous man. The sea. A plump horse. A great assembly of men. A sharp sword. A whetstone.

A خضمان *khuzummān*, The collar, opening, or breast of a shirt.

A خضمة *khazmat*, An amulet or preservative which a person wears. *Khuzamat*, A great eater.

A خضمة *khuzummat*, The thicker part of the arm next to the elbow. Middle. Flower of one's people. The most important part of any business.

A خضن *khazn*, (v. n. of خضن) Rushing upon, attacking (a she-camel), and biting (her) body.

A خضوب *khazūb*, Herbage or vegetation refreshed and made green by rain. First rudiments of foliage. *Khuzūb*, (v. n. of خضب) Being green. (pl. of خضب *khazb*) Greennesses of palm-trees.

A خضور *khazūr*, Green, flourishing.

A خضوع *khazū'*, (pl. خضع *khuzu'*) Humble, submissive, obsequious. A woman from whose inside a rumbling noise is heard to proceed. *Khuzū'*, (v. n. of خضع) Being humble, submissive. Being quiescent, motionless. Stilling, quieting. Setting (as a star). Travelling at a smart pace. Inviting to any thing bad. Causing one to stoop (old age). Submission, humility, respect, veneration.

A خضوف *khazūf*, One who breaks wind in presence of others.

A خضيب *khazīb*, Stained, dyed, imbued. الكفّ الخضيب *al kaffu'l khazīb*, The name of a star, at the zenith of which the Muhammadans believe every prayer to be favourably heard.

A خضير *khazīr*, Green, flourishing.

A خضيراء *khuzayrā*, Name of a bird.

A خضيرة *khazīrat*, A flourishing palm-tree, whose dates fall off when half ripe.

A خضيض *khazīz*, Ground abounding in loose earth moistened by the rain.

A خضيعة *khazī'at*, The rumbling of (a horse's) belly. The noise of a torrent.

A خضيلة *khazīlat*, Pleasant garden, verdant mead.

A خضيمة *khazīmat*, Wheat softened by boiling. Soft soil. Green, tender plants.

A خطّ *khatt*, (v. n. of خطّ) Drawing lines in the sand. Drawing a line, marking out the foundations of a house. Writing. Delineating, painting. Eating little. Occupying a place for the first time. Copulating after a certain fashion. Hindering, preventing, keeping back. (in Persian خط *khat*) (pl. خطوط *khutūt* and اخطاط *akhtāt*) A line, stripe, lineament. Down upon the cheek. The beard. Mustachios. A figure drawn on the sand by conjurors when making their incantations. A character. A letter, note, epistle, hand-writing. A street, road, highway. A faint path over soft land. Modus cœundi. Name of a place in Yamāmah. The coast of Bahrayn. Any coast. P خط آزادي *khati āzādī*, A deed of manumission. خط از خون نوشتن *khat az khūn navishtan*, To implore help in a great emergency. خط ازرق *khati azrak*, A black line. The fourth line on the cup of Jamshed. خط استوا *khati istiwā*, The equator. خط اشك *khati ashk*, The fifth line on the cup of Jamshed. A خط اوّل *khati awwal*, The letter ا *alif*. The throne of God. Mecca. خط باطل *khati bātil*, Sin, wickedness. P خط بجهان كشيدن *khat ba jahān kashīdan*, To renounce the world. خط بر سر كشيدن *khat bar sar kashīdan*, To disgrace. A خط بصرة *khati basra*, The third line on the cup of Jamshed. خط بطلان *khati butlān*, (or خط خطا *khati khatā*, خط نسخ *khati naskh*, P خط بيزاري *khati bīzārī*) Cancelling, scoring out. خط بغداد *khati baghdād*, The second line on the cup of Jamshed. P خط تيغ *khati tegh*, A gash with a sabre. A خط جدي *khati jady*, The tropic of Capricorn. خط جلي *khati jalī*, A stout, plain written character. خط جور *khati jawr*, The first line on the cup of Jamshed. حسن خط *husni khat*, (or P خوش خط *khwush-khat*) Beautiful writing. An elegant mustachio. خط خفي *khati khafī*, A thin character. P خط راه *khati rāh*, A passport. خط سبز *khati sabz*, First appearance of a beard. An anonymous epistle. A black line. A خط سرطان *khati saratān*, The tropic of Cancer. P خط سودائي *khati sawdāī*, An interest-bond. خط سياه *khati siyāh*, (or خط شب *khati shab*) A black line. The fourth line on the cup of Jamshed. A خط شريف *khati sharīf*, (or P خط همايون سعادت مقرون *khati humāyūni saʿādat-makrūn*) Royal letters, diplomas, mandates, signed or superscribed by the sovereign's own hand. P خط شمشير بند *khati shamshīr-band*, An appalling letter. A خط ضامني *khati zāminī*, A security-bond. A خط عمود *khati ʿamūd*, A perpendicular line. A خط غلامي *khati ghulāmī*, A contract for servitude, indentures. P خط فرودينه *khati farodīna*, (or مزوّر *muzawwar*) The seventh line on the cup of Jamshed. A خط قاطع *khati kātiʿ*, A secant. P خط كاسه گر *khati kāsagar*, The sixth line on the cup of Jamshed. خط كردار *khati kirdār*, The register of the divine decrees. خط كشيدن *khat kashīdan*, To draw a line or lines. To draw a line through a word. To erase, obliterate. A خط متوازي *khati mutawāzī*, A parallel line. خط محدود *khati mahdūd*, A definite line. خط غير محدود *khati ghayr mahdūd*, An indefinite line. خط محور *khati mihwar*, A longitudinal line. خط مختلف *khati mukhtalif*, An unequal line. خط مستدير *khati mustadīr*, A circular line. خط مستقيم *khati mustakīm*, (P درست *durust*) A right line. خط مشرق و مغرب *khati mashrik u maghrib*, A longitudinal line. خط مشكين *khati mushkīn*, A mole upon the cheek. خط معوّج *khati muʿawwaj*, A curved line. خط مقياس *khati mikyās*, A graduated line. خط ملاقي *khati mulākī*, A tangent. خط منحني *khati munhanī*, A curved line. خط نسخ *khati nashk*, A kind of writing invented by ابن مقلة *ibn muklat*. خط نصف النهار *khati nisfu'n nahār*, A meridional line. The equatorial line. خط وتر *khati watar*, A diagonal line. خط و كتابت *khat u kitābat*, Epistolary correspondence. *Khatt* or *khitt*, Name of a port in Bahrayn. *Khitt*, Land not moistened by rain. Land occupied for the first time. *Khutt*, One of the mountains at Mecca called اخشبان *akhshabāni*. The residence of a family, or part of a tribe. A highway.

A خطء *khatʾ*, An error, blunder. *Khitʾ*, (and خطأة *khitʾat*) (v. n. of خطئ) Sinning, offending. Erring in matters in religion. *Khitʾ*, A sin, crime, purposely committed.

A خطأ *khataʾ*, (or خطاء *khatāʾ*) A fault, error, miss, inadvertency, trespass, blunder, crime unintentionally committed. A misfortune. صواب و خطا *sawāb u khatā*, Right and wrong.

A خطا *khata'*, An error, blunder. *Khuta'*, (pl. of خطوة *khutwat*) Steps.

A خطاء *khitāʾ*, (pl. of خطوة *khatwat*) Steps.

A خطّاء *khattāʾ*, One perpetually blundering.

A خطاب *khitāb*, A discourse. Correspondence by letter. Title, address. The second person singular. فصل الخطاب *faslu'l khitāb*, A judicial sentence founded on conclusive testimony and oath. The phrase امّا بعد *ammā baʿd* at the beginning of letters, after the preamble. خطاب و جواب *khitāb u jawāb*, Conversation, question and answer. P خطاب كردن *khitāb kardan*, To speak. To say, talk.

A خطّاب *khattāb*, One employed in contracting a marriage, a match-maker. Eloquent. *Khuttāb*, (pl. of خاطب *khātib*) Public speakers. Those who betroth or ask in marriage, suitors.

A خطاباً *khitāban*, Directly to the point.

A خطابة *khatābat*, The act of preaching.

P خطا بخش *khatā-bakhsh*, Sin-forgiving.

A خطابي *khitābī*, Verbal, by speech.

A خطّابيّة *khattābiyat*, A heretical sect, originating with ابو الخطّاب *abū'l khattāb*.

P خطاپوش *khatā-posh*, Sin-covering, merciful.

A خطار *khitār*, (v. n. 3 of خطر) Putting at risk. Throwing one's self in the way of danger. (pl. of خطر *khatar*) Dangers. Bets, stakes, wagers.

A خطّار *khattār*, Tremulous (spear); also he who brandishes it. (A camel) which whisks his tail. A sling: a balista or catapulta. A lion. A man having his hand raised or hurt. A dealer in perfumes. An aromatic unguent.

A خطارب *khutārib*, One who tells lies of another.

A خطّارة *khattārat*, A fold or stable for camels.

A خطّاط *khattāt*, A fine writer, penman, caligraphist. خطّاط البلاد *khattātu'l bilād*, A geographer. A خطاط البلادي *khattātu'l bilādī*, Geography.

A خطاطيف *khatātīf*, (pl. of خطّاف *khuttāf*) Swallows. Hooks, crooked irons, cramps. خطاطيف السباع *khatātīfu's sibāʿ*, Claws of wild beasts. بقلة الخطاطيف *baklatu'l khatātīf*, Swallow-wort.

A خطّاف *khattāf*, A ravisher. Satan. *Khuttāf*, (pl. خطاطيف *khatātīf*), A swallow. A hook; a crooked iron (particularly on each side of a pulley, through which goes the axis), a grapple.

P خطاكار *khatā-kār*, (or گر *gar*) A sinner, criminal.

A خطّال *khattāl*, Parsimonious in housekeeping.

A خطّالة *khattālat*, An immodest woman, or one suspected to be so.

A خطام *khitām*, (v. n. of خطم) Suspending a bow by the string. (pl. خطم *khutum*) A halter. A bridle. A mark on the nose or across the face of beasts of burden. Suspended by the string (a bow). A bowstring.

A خطّام *khattām*, Musk which fills the olfactory vessels with its fragrance.

P خط آور *khat-āwar*, A beard beginning to appear. A youth whose beard and mustachios begin to appear.

A خطاي *khatāy*, Khatāy, a large country in Scythia or Tartary beyond mount Imaus. Northern China.

A خطايا *khatāya'*, (pl. of خطيئة *khatiʾat* or خطيّة *khatiyat*) Sins. Faults, errors.

A خطائط *khatāʾit*, (pl. of خطيطة) Lands not watered by rain (lying between others which are).

A خطائي *khatāʾī*, (pl. of خطيئة *khatiʾat*) Sins.

A خطب *khatb*, (v. n. of خطب) Asking in marriage, betrothing. (pl. خطوب *khutūb*) A thing, work, affair, matter. ما خطبك *mā khatbuka*, How (or what) do you do? عظم الخطب *ʿazuma'l khatb*, The affair became serious. *Khitb*, Betrothed (man or woman). *Khitb* or *khutb*, The word used by the betrothing party amongst the Arabians in contracting of marrigaes, and to which the betrothed party replies نكح *nik-h*, if consent be given. *Khutab*, (pl. of خطبة *khutbat*) Sermons.

A خطباء *khatbāʾ*, (fem. of اخطب *akhtab*) (A she-ass) striped with black down her back. Brown-streaked (gourd). (A hand) losing the colour with which it has been tinged. *Khutabāʾ*, (pl. of خاطب *khātib* or خطيب *khatib*) Preachers.

A خطبان *khutbān* or *khitbān*, Gourds marked with brown streaks. *Khutbān*, A sort of asparagus. The brown leaf of a certain thorn.

A خطبانيّ *khutbāniy*, Intensely brown.

A خطبة *khitbat*, (v. n. of خطب) Asking (a woman) in marriage (for a son), betrothing. (A woman) asked in marriage. *Khutbat*, (v. n. of خطب) Preaching. (pl. خطب *khutab*) An oration delivered every Friday, after the forenoon-service, in the principal Muhammadan mosques (in which they praise God, bless Muhammad and his descendants, and pray for the king). This was generally pronounced formerly by the reigning Khalīf or the heir apparent. A speech, harangue. Betrothed (woman). A dusky red and yellow colour, browness.

A خطّة *khittat*, (pl. خطط *khitat*) A boundary or foundation-line of a house. A country, territory, region, city. Land occupied for the first time. A street. A habitation. P خطّهٔ پر بهجت *khittaʾi pur bahjat*, A place full of delight. A *Khuttat*, A line. A game in use among the Arabs. An office, function. An affair (especially one of importance). Design, aim, enterprise, endeavour. A history. Name for a sorry she-goat. Ignorance.

A خط خط *khut khut*, A word used in commanding one to attack suddenly with a spear.

A خطخطة *khatkhatat*, (v. n. of خطخط Q) Inclining from side to side through languor. Scattering, squirting (urine).

P خط دار *khat-dār*, Having stripes, striped.

A خطر *khatr*, (v.n. of خطر) Vibrating, brandishing (a sword or spear), striking (with them). Trembling (a lance). Swinging the arms in walking. Lashing (his) sides with (his) tail (a stallion). A number of camels, from 40 to 1000. A pompous, stately, also a graceful, walker. A certain large measure for dry goods or liquids. A large, heavy, low-hanging cloud. Nobility, dignity. *Khatr* or *khitr*, Dung or urine adhering to the thigh of a camel. *Khitr*, A species of dyeing herb; indigo, woad. A branch. Thin, watery milk. (pl. اخطار *akhtār*) Many camels. *Khutr*, (pl. of خطير *khatīr*) Nobles. *Khatar*, (v. n. of خطر) Being in danger. Laying wagers at horse-racing or archery. Throwing the die of uncertainty. Selling what one has not (as a bird in the bush). A large, heavy, low-hanging cloud. Imminent danger, jeopardy. Dignity, nobility, court-favour. Risk, hazard. Misfortune. Like, equal. (pl. خطار *khitār* and خطر *khutur*) A bet, stake, wager. P خطر جان *khatari jān*, The hazard of life. A هٰذا خطر لهٰذا *hāzā khatar li hāzā*, This is equal in value to that. *Khatir*, Great, high in authority. Hazardous, perilous. *Khutur*, (pl. of خطر *khatar*) Bets, stakes, wagers.

P خطر *khatar*, Woad, indigo.

A خطرات الوسمي *khatarātu'l wasmīy*, Parts of a meadow beginning to wither.

A خطران *khatarān*, (v. n. of خطر) Lashing (the sides) with the tail (a stallion). Brandishing (a spear). Walking tremulously. A trembling step.

P خطرايه *khatrāya*, A kind of dervish's mantle.

A خطرب *khutrub*, One who tells lies of another.

A خطربة *khatrabat*, (v. n. of خطرب Q) Telling lies of any one. Living hardly, faring meanly. Narrowness, straits.

A خطرة *khatrat*, A species of grass. A scar or brand on a camel. Touch of the devil. لعب الخطرة *laʻibu'l khatrat*, Shaking a wreath, with which they playfully strike each other when dancing.

A خطرةً *khatratan*, Sometimes, now and then.

A خطرفة *khatrafat*, (v. n. of خطرف Q) Walking fast, taking wide steps. Striking (with a sword). Being loose-skinned (a woman).

P خطرناك *khatarnāk*, Dangerous, perilous.

P خطرناكي *khatarnākī*, Danger, jeopardy, peril.

A خطروف *khutrūf*, Swift, wide-stepping.

A خطريف *khitrīf*, Swift-paced.

A خطط *khitat*, (pl. of خطّة *khittat*) Land marked out for building upon. Streets. Habitations. *Khutat*, (pl. of خطّة *khuttat*) Lines. Affairs. Designs.

A خطف *khatf*, (v. n. of خطف) Seizing, snatching, carrying off. *Khutf*, Possibility of cure.

A خطفان *khatafān*, A travelling fast.

A خطفة *khatfat*, A limb or joint cut off (by a butcher), or torn away by a wild beast.

A خطفىٰ *khatafa'*, A rapid pace.

P خطكش *khat-kash*, A ruler (to draw lines).

P خطگذار *khat-guzār*, A scribe. A javelin-man.

A خطل *khutl*, (pl. of اخطل *akhtal*) Bangle-eared (sheep or dogs). *Khatal*, (v. n. of خطل) Speaking much nonsense. Being bent, distorted. Walking with a swinging motion. Levity of conversation, obscenity. Length and limberness (in a man, bow, or spear). Obscenity, or occasion for suspicion in a woman. Lightness. Quickness. *Khatil*, Long and waving (spear). A foolish man. A munificent man, one who gives freely and readily. Piercing quickly. (An arrow) missing the mark. (A garment) sweeping the ground. The edge of a tent. A gin or rope. (A man) having rough, hard hands. A talker of much nonsense. Hard and rough (clothes or body).

A خطلاء *khatlā*, (fem. of اخطل *akhtal*) Pendulous (ear). Coarse and flabby-breasted (woman). Flap-eared (ewe or bitch).

A خطلبة *khatlabat*, Verboseness and confusion in speech.

A خطم *khatm*, (v. n. of خطم) Smiting on the nose. Haltering (a camel or horse). Suspending (a bow by the string). Preventing one from speaking. Sewing the edges of leather called اديم *adīm*. Bringing under by words. Beak (of a bird), snout (of an animal). A nose, ness. A weighty matter. *Khutum*, (pl. of خطام *khitām*) Halters. Marks on the nose and face of beasts of burden.

A خطمة *khutmat*, The summit of a mountain.

A خطمىّ *khatmīy* or *khitmīy*, Marsh-mallows.

A خطو *khatw*, A stepping, a proceeding.

A خطوات *khutwāt*, (pl. of خطوة *khutwat*) Steps, paces. *Khatawāt* (pl. of خطوة *khatwat*) Steps.

A خطوب *khutūb*, (pl. of خطب *khatb*) Things, affairs, causes. Heavy calamities, severe misfortunes.

A خطوة *khatwat* (v. n. of خطو) Stepping. (pl. خطوات *khatawāt* and خطاء *khitā*) A single step. *Khutwat* or *khatwat*, (pl. خطوات *khutwāt*, *khutawāt*, *khutuwāt*, and خطىٰ *khuta'*) The space between the feet in stepping; a step, a pace.

A خطور *khutūr*, (v. n. of خطر) Entering, occurring, or recurring to the mind.

A خطورة *khutūrat*, (v. n. of خطر) Being elevated in dignity and high in favour.

A خطوط *khutūt*, (pl. of خطّ *khatt*) Lines, streaks. Letters, epistles. Handwritings, manuscripts. خطوط شعاعيّة *khutūti shiʻāʻiya*, Radial lines, sun's rays.

A خطوطىّ *khutūtīy*, Linear (demonstration).

A خطّة اوّل *khittasi awwal*, (or خطّة كلّ *khittasi kull*) The throne of God.

A خطىٰ *khuta'*, (pl. of خطوة *khutwat*) Steps. Spaces between the feet, when stepping out.

A خطّىّ *khattīy*, (A spear) grown at, or brought from, خط *khatt*.

A خطيب *khatīb*, A preacher. A reader of prayers at a mosque. An able orator. خطيب الهى *khatībi ilāhī*, A revealer of secrets. One engaged in rehearsing the praises of God. A reader of the Kur'ān. A professor of belief in the unity of God. خطيب الانبياء *khatību'l ambiyā*, Jethro, Moses' father-in-law. خطيب فلك *khatībi falak*, Jupiter.

A خطّيب *khittīb*, Betrothed (man).

A خطّيبة *khittībat*, Betrothed (woman).

A خطيبي *khatībī*, Preaching. P خطيبي كردن *khatībī kardan*, To preach.

A خطّيبىٰ *khittība'*, (v. n. of خطب) Betrothing (a woman). Betrothed (woman).

A خطيئة *khatīsat*, (or خطيّة *khatīyat* (pl. خطايا *khatāya'* or خطائي *khatāsī*) A sin, fault, crime. A little of any thing.

A خطير *khatīr*, (v. n. of خطر) Lashing the sides with the tail (a stallion). Pitch. (pl. خطر *khutr*) Great, honourable, dignified (man). High, lofty. A camel's halter, a rope. Dangerous, hazardous. Alike, equal. Gossamer floating in the air on a hot day. Darkness (of night). A threat. Cheerfulness, liveliness. امر خطير *amri khatīr*, An important, doubtful, or dangerous affair. خاطر خطير *khātiri khatīr*, A penetrating, comprehensive mind.

A خطيط *khatīt*, Snoring: a snore.

A خطيطة *khatītat*, (pl. خطائط *khatāsit*) Ground not watered by rain (though situated between others which are), or only partially rained upon.

A خطيف *khatīf*, Swift (dromedary). A martin.

A خطيفة *khatīfat*, A kind of milk-pottage.

A خطيئة *khatīsat*, (pl. خطايا *khatāya'*) A sin, fault, crime purposely committed. A little, some.

A خظ *khazz*, (v. n. of خظّ) Being unnerved and swaggy (man).

A خظاء *khazā*, Compactness (of flesh).

A خظا بظا *khazaʼ bazaʼ*, Firm, compact (flesh).

A خظرفة *khazrafat*, (v. n. of خظرف Q) Walking with wide steps (a camel).

A خظوّ *khuzūw*, Firmness, compactness (of flesh).

A خظوان *khazawān*, One who gains flesh, or grows plump.

A خظي بظي *khazī bazī*, (fem. خظية بظية *khaziyat baziyat*) Firm-fleshed.

A خع *khaʻʻ*, (v. n. of خعّ) Making a rattle in the throat when out of breath in running (a cheeta).

A خعخع *khuʻkhuʻ*, Name of a medicinal plant.

P خف *khaf* or *khuf*, Tinder. The fire-emitting tree مرخ *markh*.

A خفّ *khaff*, (v. n. of خفّ) Crying, barking (a hyena). Obeying. Departing in haste. Sprightly (horse). *Khiff*, (v. n. of خفّ) Being light. Light (of weight or morals), undignified. Nimble, dexterous. A small number of people. *Khuff*, (pl. خفاف *khifāf*) A boot. The sole of the human foot. (pl. اخفاف *akhfāf*) The foot of a camel or ostrich. An aged camel. Rough, coarse earth.

A خفء *khafs*, (v. n. of خفأ) Tearing up. Striking to the ground. Taking to pieces (house, tent). Cutting open (a leathern bottle) and laying it on a cistern that the earth may not imbibe the water of it.

A خفا *khafa'*, A secret.

A خفاء *khafā*, (v. n. of خفىٰ) Being concealed. The concealment of a trace. Rough ground. برح الخفاء *bariha'l khafā*, The secret escaped, the cat got out of the bag. *Khifā*, (pl. اخفية *akhfiyat*) A veil, cover, wrapper. A curtain. A thing concealed.

A خفات *khufāt*, A dying suddenly.

A خفائل *khafāsil*, (pl. of خفشل *khafsal*) Weak in mind or body. *Khufāsil*, Weak in body or mind.

A خفاجل *khufājil*, Tongue-tied.

P خفاچه *khafācha*, (or خفّاچه *khaffācha*) A certain banditti of plundering Arabs.

A خفاخف *khafākhif*, (pl. of خفخوف *khuf-*

khūf) Male hyenas, making hideous yells.

A خفادد *khafādid*, (or خفاديد *khafādīd*) (pl. of خفيدد *khafaydad*) Swift. Young ostriches.

A خفارة *khafārat*, Extreme bashfulness. Reward of labour, hire. Whatever preserves palm-trees from corruption. *Kha, khi*, or *khufārat*, Protection, safeguard: price of patronage or protection.

A خفاش *khuffāsh*, (pl. خفافيش) A bat.

A خفاضة *khafāzat*, The leading (of an easy life).

A خفاف *khifāf*, (pl. of خف *khuff*) Boots. (pl. of خفيف *khafīf*) Light. *Khufāf*, Light (of conduct or weight), undignified. Nimble, agile.

A خفاف *khaffāf*, A boot-maker or vender.

A خفافيش *khafāfīsh*, (pl. of خفاش) Bats.

A خفاق *khifāk*, (pl. of خفق *khafik* or *khufak*) Gaunt-bellied (horses).

A خفاق *khaffāk*, Broad-footed before.

A خفاقة *khaffākat*, Lank (woman). Podex.

A خفان *khaffān*, A vessel filled to the brim. Household, domestics. A young ostrich.

P خفانيدن *khafānīdan*, To make (a needle) prick.

A خفايا *khafāya'*, (pl. of خفي *khafīy*) Secrets.

A خفاير *khafāsir*, Very bashful (women).

A خفة *khiffat* or *khaffat*, (v. n. of خف) Being light (in weight or in dignity). Lightness, levity. Agility, nimbleness. Insult.

A خفت *khaft*, (v. n. of خفت) Speaking in a whisper. A whispering speech. *Khaft* or *khuft*, Rue.

A خفتار *khaftār*, The title of the king of Mesopotamia or Ethiopia.

P خفتان *khaftān*, A vest worn under armour.

P خفتانيدن *khuftānīdan*, To cause to roll. To cause to sleep. To render (the limbs) torpid.

P خفتك *khuftak*, The night-mare. A heron.

P خفتكي *khuftagī*, A lying down.

P خفتن *khuftan*, To sleep. To lie down. To sleep (as the limbs) from a stoppage of the circulation of blood. To be blunt (the edge of a sword). To become thick; congeal, clot. To kiss. نماز خفتن *namāzi khuftan*, The prayer before going to sleep.

P خفتنجا *khuftan-jā*, A bed. A bed-chamber.

P خفتني *khuftanī*, Fit to be lain upon.

P خفتو *khuftū*, The night-mare.

P خفت و خيز *khuft u khez*, Slowness. A deliberate progress. Agitation, commotion. Restlessness, inconstancy. Coition.

P خفته *khufta*, Sleeping, asleep. Extended on the ground. Curved, bent. Buried. Thick (milk). The game of tipcat. خفته دويدن *khufta dawīdan*, To run swiftly.

P خفتيدن *khuftīdan*, To roll, wallow. To be asleep. To kneel. To kiss each other. To become thick and clotted (milk).

A خفثل *khafsal*, (pl. خفائل *khafāsil*) Weak in mind and body.

P خفج *khafj* or *khafaj*, The nightmare. *Khafaj*, Wild mustard.

A خفج *khafj*, (v. n. of خفج) Copulating. Complaining of a pain in the leg from fatigue. *Khafuj*, (v. n. of خفج) Having a tremor in the fore-legs before raising them up from the ground (a camel). A kind of disease in a camel. A whitish kind of plant growing in the spring.

P خفجا *khafajā*, The night-mare.

P خفجه *khafja*, A tree bearing a red fruit.

P خفچاق *khafchāk*, Noble. Name of a desert in Turkistān. Nomade Tartars.

P خفچه *khafcha*, An ingot of gold or silver. Flowing ringlets. A straight branch shooting up.

A خفخافة *khafkhāfat*, (A woman) speaking through the nose.

A خفخفة *khafkhafat*, The noise made by a hyena or dog whilst devouring their food. The rustling of new clothes.

A خفخوف *khufkhūf*, A bird clapping its wings.

A خفد *khafd*, (*khafad*, or خفدان *khafadān*) (v. n. of خفد) Going fast (an ostrich).

P خفدان *khafdān*, A garment worn in battle.

A خفدد *khufdud*, (or خفدود *khufdūd*) A bat. Another winged animal.

P خفده *khafda*, Bent, curved, crooked.

A خفر *khafr*, (v. n. of خفر) Protecting, patronizing. Guarding. Guiding. *Khafar*, (v. n. of خفر) Being very bashful. Excessive modesty. Failing to afford protection, breaking a promise, betraying. *Khafir*, Bashful (woman).

A خفرة *khufrat*, Patronage, protection. *Khafirat*, Bashful (woman). *Khufarat*, A protector.

P خفرج *khafraj* or *khafarj*, Purslain.

A خفرجة *khafrajat*, Delicate fare, good cheer.

P خفرق *khafrak*, A word used in abuse.

P خفرنج *khafranj*, The nightmare.

A خفرنج *khafarnaj*, Soft, tender, delicate.

P خفزدو *khafazdū*, (or خفزدوك) A beetle.

A خفس *khafs*, (v. n. of خفس) Deriding, ridiculing. Overthrowing, demolishing. Speaking obscenely. Eating little. Conquering at wrestling. Putting much or little water in wine.

A خفش *khafsh*, (v. n. of خفش) Throwing. *Khafash*, (v. n. of خفش) Being weak, feeble. Being small (the front of a camel's bunch), compact, and elongated. Smallness of the eye, weakness of sight (such as see in the night not in the day, and in a dull not a clear medium).

A خفشاء *khafshās*, (fem. of اخفش *akhfash*) Small-eyed, weak-sighted. Small-bunched (she-camel). Seeing more clearly by night than by day.

A خفض *khafz*, (v. n. of خفض) Abasing (the proud). Lowering (the voice). Dropping (the wings to him), *i.e.* yielding. Putting the vowel *kasra* (ـِ) under the last letter of the oblique case (called likewise جر *jarr*). Doing with ease. Living easily, quietly, agreeably. Abiding in a place. Circumcising (a girl). A low tone, a whisper. A gentle pace. Quiet, tranquillity.

A خفع *khafȝ*, (v. n. of خفع) Being giddy (from hunger, or other cause). Striking (with a sword). The motion of a veil or a curtain. *Khafaȝ*, (or خفعان *khafaȝān*) Looseness in the joints.

A خفق *khafk*, (v. n. of خفق) Palpitating (the heart), trembling, waving (a flag). Floating, undulating (the vapour سراب *sarāb*). Nodding the head when sleeping. Vibrating (lightning). Completely burying (the yard in the matrix). Making a whistling noise (the wind). Creaking (as shoes). Flying (a bird). Tapping with any thing broad (as a slipper or the flat of a sword). *Khafik* or *khufak*, (pl. خفاق *khifāk*) Slender-bodied (horse).

A خفقان *khafakān*, (v. n. of خفق) Palpitating, trembling, waving, floating (flag or the heart). A palpitation of the heart.

A خفقاني *khafakānīy*, Subject to palpitation.

A خفقة *khifkat*, Any thing flat with which one is beaten. A level, bare plain, over which the vapour سراب *sarāb* floats. *Khafikat* or *khufakat*, Gaunt-bellied (horse).

A خفن *khafn*, Laxness of belly.

P خفنج *khafanj*, Profit, advantage. Pleasure, delight. Blandishment, coquetry. *Khufunj*, Monuments, especially of martyrs.

A خفنجل *khafanjal*, Overloaded at the stomach. One who walks slowly, with distorted legs. One who turns in his toes.

A خفنجى *khafanja'*, Needy, short of money. Weak and unprofitable.

P خفندن *khafandan*, To sprinkle. To cough, breathe hard.

P خفنديدن *khafandīdan*, To be suffocated.

A خفنشل *khafanshal*, One who walks slowly with distorted legs, with his toes in and heels out.

A خفو *khafw*, or خفو *khufūw*, (v. n. of خفا for خفو) Flashing (lightning). Appearing, being manifest. Lightning which flashes from the side of a cloud, and diffusing itself widely; (when it glances slightly it is called وميض *wamīz*, and when it darts perpendicularly it is named عقيقة *ȝakīkat*).

A خفوة *khifwat*, A secret.

A خفوة *khifwatan*, Surreptitiously, clandestinely.

A خفوت *khafūt*, A lean woman, one who looks deformed in comparison with others. *Khufūt*, (v. n. of خفت) Being subdued (tone). Ceasing to speak, becoming mute.

A خفود *khafūd*, (A camel) casting an abortion.

A خفور *khufūr*, (v. n. of خفر) Failing to afford protection, breaking a promise, betraying.

A خفوش *khafūsh*, Bread made from millet.

A خفوف *khufūf*, (v. n. of خف) Being little and few. Walking fast.

A خفوف *khaffūf*, A hyena.

A خفوق *khafūk*, Farting (camel). *Khufūk*, (v. n. of خفق) Setting (a star). Being almost past (the night). Flying (a bird). Farting (a camel). Shaking the head of any one who is nodding through sleepiness. Lankness of belly in a horse.

P خفه *khafa*, A cough. Suffocation, strangling. Sneezing. خفه كردن *khafa kardan*, To strangle. *Khufa*, A cough.

A خفي *khafy*, (v. n. of خفي) Hiding, concealing. Making manifest. Drawing out, causing to come forth. Driving out of their holes (mice).

A خفيّ *khafiy*, (pl. خفايا *khafāya'*) Clandestine, concealed. Fine, thin writing (opposed to جليّ *jaliy*). Slightly sounded (letter ن *nūn*). The voice and footmarks. *Khufiy*, (v. n. of خفي) Hiding, concealing. Making manifest. Drawing out, causing to come forth. Driving (mice) out of their holes.

A خفيّان *khafiyāni*, Voice and step of a woman.

A خفية *khifyat* or *khufyat*, (v. n. of خفي) Concealing one's self. Concealment. في خفية *fī khufyatin*, Secretly, clandestinely.

A خفيّة *khafiyat*, (pl. خفايا *khafāya'*) Any thing hidden. Maniacal madness. A thicket, brake. A well which has been often dug (the waters having sunk). Name of a place abounding with lions.

A خفيج *khafīj*, Swollen with water, and weak in the leg.

A خفيدد *khafaydad*, (pl. خفادد *khafādid*, خفاديد *khafādīd*, and خفيددات *khafaydadāt*) Swift. A nimble ostrich.

P خفيدن *khafīdan*, To breathe, breathe hard, pant. To cough. To sneeze. *Khufīdan*, To cough.

P خفيدة *khafīda*, Strangled, suffocated. Sneezing. *Khufīda*, Troubled with a cough. Known, published, blazoned abroad, celebrated.

A خفير *khafīr*, A protector, guardian, keeper. Protected, sheltered, secure. Very bashful (woman). Toll paid for protection of the roads.

A خفيس *khafīs*, Much-diluted (wine).

A خفيف *khafīf*, (pl. خفاف *khifāf*, اخفاف *akhfāf*, and اخفّاء *akhiffā*) Light (of weight). Undignified, immoral, weak in understanding. Nimble, dexterous. Lightly sounded (letter ن). A species of verse formed upon the measure فاعلاتن مستفعلن فاعلاتن *fāʿilātun mustafʿilun fāʿilātun* six times.

P خفيف آواز *khafīf-āwāz*, Babbling, a babbler.

A خفيفي دائرة *khafīfī dāʾira*, Centre of a circle.

A خفيق *khafīk*, Murmuring of the wind.

A خفيه محال *khufya-mahāl*, Lands hid from government.

P خفيه نويس *khufya-navīs*, (also خفيه نگار *khufya-nigār*) A writer of secret intelligence, employed by government.

A خقّ *khakk*, (pl. اخقاق *akhkāk* and خقوق *khukūk*) A fissure in the ground in which one may hide himself. *Khukk*, A pond or other reservoir full of cracks (from the drying up of the water).

A خقخاقة *khakhkākat*, A woman whose فرج *farj* makes a noise from leanness.

A خقان *khakān*, A king of the Turks.

A خق خق *khuk khuk*, Put ear-rings on the girl.

A خقنة *khukunat*, (pl. of خقان *khakān*) Turkish emperors.

A خقوق *khakūk*, (A horse) making a noise with his sheath. A she-ass with a wide anus. *Khukūk*, (pl. of خقّ *khakk*) Fissures, cracks in the ground.

A خقيق *khakīk*, (v. n. of خقّ) Making a noise from leanness (sheath of a beast). Murmuring, simmering (a pot over the fire). Creaking.

P خكاو *khakāv*, Name of a country.

P خكشك *khakushk*, An earthen painted jar, in which the Persians put sweetmeats, &c., and present them to their friends at the festival of نو روز *naw roz*, or new-year's day. These jars are also used as children's play-things.

P خكيدن *khakīdan*, To trample under foot.

P خگاو *khagāv*, Name of a country.

P خل *khal*, Arrival. *Khil* or *khul*, Snot. *Khul*, Bent, curved, crooked. Mad. Ashes. The fundament.

A خلّ *khall*, (v. n. of خلّ) Being diminished, extenuated, lean. Becoming poor. Being peculiar and private. Slitting the tongue of a young camel to prevent its sucking. Turning (camels) out to feed on the sweet herbage خلّة *khullat*. Pinning (clothes) with a skewer. Perforating, boring, passing quite through. A track through sand. (A serpent) creeping (over the sand). A worn garment. A rent in a garment. Thinly-plumaged (bird). A vein in the neck, and back. A camel entering into the second year. Fat. Lean. Weak (man). A salt and bitter plant. (pl. اخلّ *akhull* and خلال *khilāl*) Vinegar. Evil, wickedness. A weasel. (pl. of خلّة *khallat*) Sour, pricked wines. ما له خل ولا خمر *mā lahu khallun wa lā khamrun*, He has neither vinegar nor wine, *i. e.* any thing. ما هو بخل ولا خمر *mā huwa bi khallin wa lā khamrin*, He is neither vinegar nor wine; there is neither harm nor good about him. *Khill*, Intimate friendship. Poor, in want. *Khill* or *khull*, (pl. اخلال *akhlāl*) A friend, particularly a sincere and intimate one.

A خلأ *khalā*, (or خلاء *khilā*) (v. n. of خلأ) Being unmanageable (a she-camel), lying down without a cause. Leaving one thing and taking to another.

A خلا *khala'*, (خلا عن *khala' ʿan* or ما خلا *mā khala'*) Besides, except. خلا ان *khala' an* Saving, unless that. *Khala'*, (or خلاة *khalāt*) Green forage.

A خلاء *khalā*, (v. n. of خلا for خلو) Being vacant, deserted (a place). Being free, clear of. Loosing, letting go. Granting a private interview, retiring to consult in private. Departing, receding, abstaining from. Lighting upon a solitary place. Passing by (time). Jesting, ridiculing. Free, clear of. A privy. Empty, solitary (place). انا منك خلاء *ana minka khalā*, I am independent of thee.

P خلاب *khalāb*, Mud. Water mixed with mud. A miry, slippery place. Soft earth or mire into which the feet sink.

A خلاب *khilāb*, A deceiving, stealing the wits.

A خلّاب *khallāb*, A deceiver, liar, claw-back.

A خلابة *khilābat*, (v. n. of خلب) Deceiving with words, disappointing. Tongs, forceps.

A خلّابة *khallābat*, A deceitful, lying woman.

P خلابر *khalābar*, (or خلابش *khalābash*) A boarded servant.

A خلابس *khalābis*, A dispersed multitude. Vain. *Khulābis*, Artful, fine-spun, vain discourse. A lie.

A خلابيس *khalābīs*, Vain, false. A lie, fabulous tradition, romance. Separated (from the flock). Scattered, dispersed. An affair without method or arrangement. Worthless men.

A خلاة *khalāt*, A fresh and tender plant.

A خلاج *khilāj*, (v. n. 3 of خلج) Affecting with anxiety. A sort of striped garment.

P خلاجاي *khalā-jāy*, A privy.

A خلاخل *khalākhil*, (pl. of خلخل) Ankle-rings.

A خلاخيل *khalākhīl*, (pl. of خلخال) Ankle-rings.

A خلّار *khullār*, Name of a place in Persia renowned for its honey.

A خلّاس *khallās*, A robber, plunderer, snatcher.

A خلاسيّ *khilāsiy*, A mulatto boy. A fowl of a cross breed.

A خلاسيّة *khalāsiyat*, A woman half-gray.

P خلاش *khalāsh* or *khilāsh*, Tumult, strife. *Khilāsh*, Muddy water. A miry place.

P خلاشمه *khilāshma*, A disease from indigestion. A sore throat.

P خلاشه *khalāsha*, A rudder. A stick used as a dentifrice. Rubbish of sticks or thorns.

P خلاشي *khalāshī*, A mariner, a sailor.

A خلاص *khalās*, Liberation, release, deliverance. Redemption. Liberty. Health. P خلاص شدن *khalās shudan*, To be rescued. خلاص كردن *khalās kardan*, To set at liberty. A *Khilās*, (v. n. 3 of خلص) Acting sincerely or candidly (towards another). Safety, health. Gold or silver refined in the fire. Inspissated juice of the date. Clarified butter. The best and purest part of any thing. The secundine.

A خلّاص *khallās*, A saviour, deliverer. *Khullās*, A chink, crevice, flaw.

A خلاصة *khulāsat*, The purest and best part or substance of any thing. Abstract, conclusion, inference, moral. *Khulāsat* or *khilāsat*, Purified or clarified butter. The essence of a thing.

P خلاصگان *khulāsagān*, (pl. of A خلاصه *khulāsa*) Choice, pure, selectest.

A خلاصي *khalāsī*, Freedom, liberation, escape, redemption, discharge. Sailor. Native artilleryman.

P خلاط *khilāt*, The capital of lesser Armenia.

A خلاط *khilāt*, (v. n. 3 of خلط) Intermixing, intermingling. Involving in distress. Being perplexed in mind, losing one's wits. A miscellaneous herding of men, camels, or sheep. Coition.

A خلاطة *khalātat*, Folly, stupidity.

A خلاع *khulāʿ*, Epilepsy.

A خلاعة *khalāʿat*, (v. n. of خلع) Putting forth leaves and flourishing (the tree called عضاة *ʿizāh*). Casting off all regard for one's parents. Being discarded by relations. Unruliness, disorderliness.

P خلاف *khalāf*, A willow, an osier.

A خلاف *khilāf*, (v. n. 3 of خلف) Opposing, contradicting, rebelling against. Counteracting. Visiting (a woman) in the absence of her husband or her master. Accompanying, keeping close to. Contradiction, opposition. Contrariety, reverse. Lie, falsehood (as opposed to truth). A sleeve. A kind of willow or osier. خلاف انها *khilāfi inhā*, A false relation, lie, fiction. خلاف حق *khilāfi hakk*, Contrary to truth or justice. Iniquitously. خلاف شرع شريف *khilāfi sharʿi sharīf*, Against law and justice. خلاف صلح وصلاح *khilāfi sulh u salāh*, Repugnant to the spirit of the peace. خلاف طبيعت *khilāfi tabīʿat*, Against nature, contrary to custom. خلاف عقل *khilāfi ʿakl*, Contrary to reason. خلاف قياس *khilāfi kiyās*, Ungrammatical. خلاف معتاد *khilāfi muʿtād*, Contrary to ordinary practice. خلاف نفس الامر *khilāfi nafsu'l amr*, Against the soul of the thing, *i. e.* contrary to truth. من خلاف *min khilāfi*, From the opposite side.

A خلافا *khilāfan*, In contradiction, in opposition.

A خلاف *khallāf*, Quarrelsome, contentious.

A خلافة *khalāfat*, (v. n. of خلف) Being foolish. Degenerating from the qualities of one's father. Supplying another's place. Vice, defect, blemish. Folly, stupidity. *Khilāfat*, (v. n. of خلف) Following, coming behind. Succeeding, supplying another's place. Appointing (one) to supply another's place. Compensating, making amends. Califate, vicegerency, lieutenancy. Imperial dignity.

P خلاف ورز *khilāf-warz*, Contradictious.

P خلاف ورزي *khilāf-warzī*, Opposition, contradiction, contradictiousness.

A خلاق *khalāk*, A plenteous portion of good fortune or happiness. لا خلاق له في الآخرة *lā khalāka lahu fi'l ākhirat*, No portion for him in the next life. *Khilāk*, (v. n. 3 of خلق) Shewing kindness or good will (to any one). A species of aromatic.

A خلاق *khallāk*, Creating, forming well. The Creator. خلاق كائنات *khallāki kāʾināt*, Creator of the universe. خلاق عجائب عالم *khallāki ʿajāʾibi ʿālam*, Creator of the wonders of the world.

A خلاقة *khalākat*, (v. n. of خلق) Being smooth. Being worthy, fit, suitable. Being of an excellent disposition (a woman). Smoothness.

A خلال *khalāl*, Sour dates. *Khilāl* or *khalāl*, (v. n. 3 of خل) Shewing affection, cultivating friendship. *Khilāl*, (pl. اخلة *akhillat*) A toothpick, or any thing similar, as a wooden bodkin, skewer, pin, or peg. A skewer passed through the tongue of a young camel to prevent him from sucking. Shreds of meat sticking between the teeth. A space or interval between two things. A chink, fissure, opening. (pl. of خل *khall*) Vinegars. Tracks through sands. (pl. of خلة *khallat*) Qualities, properties. (pl. of خلة *khillat*) Rich sword-sheaths. (pl. of خلة *khullat*) Friendships. (pl. of خلل *khalal*) Infirmities. Distractions of mind. Dispersions. Interstices, intervals. خلال الدار *khilālu'd dār*, The precincts of a dwelling, spaces or alleys between the outhouses. ذو الخلال *zū'l khilāl*, Abū bakr, so called because, after having given away all his substance, he was under the necessity of pinning his dress with skewers. هو خلالهم *huwa khilāluhum* or *khalāluhum*, He is amongst them. *Khulāl*, Ripe dates sought amongst unripe ones. A tartness or a turning sour of any thing sweet.

P خلال *khilāl*, A toothpick. خلال كردن *khilāl kardan*, To leave off eating. خلال ماموني *khilāli māmūnī*, Sweet rush, from which toothpicks are made.

A خلال *khallāl*, A vinegar-merchant.

A خلالة *khal*, *khil*, or *khulālat*, Sincere friendship, candour, sincerity. *Khulālat*, Bits of meat picked from between the teeth. Ripe dates sought amongst unripe ones.

P خلالدان *khilāldān*, A tooth-pick case.

P خلالوش *khalālūsh*, (or خلاكوش *khalākūsh*) Multitude, tumult: hubbub, uproar, riot, sedition.

A خلا ملا *khalā malā*, Unfeigned friendship.

A خلاميس *khalāmīs*, (pl. of خلموس *khulmūs*) Pasturing cattle for four days, and watering them morning and evening at different places.

P خلان *khalān*, Mud at the bottom of a cistern.

A خلان *khullān*, (pl. of خليل) Intimate friends.

A خلانج *khalānij*, (pl. of خلنج *khalanj*) Trees from which arrows or trenchers are made.

P خلانوش *khalānūsh*, Tumult, contention. The clamour of a mob. The water-lily. A medicine.

P خلانيدن *khalānīdan*, To insert, to thrust or stick in, to fix, infix.

P خلاوة *khalāwat*, Free, quit, clear.

P خلاوش *khalāwush*, Busy hum, noise, tumult.

P خلاوة *kha* or *khilāwa*, Astonished. Clamour.

A خلاوي *khalāwī*, (pl. of خلوة) Closets.

A خلايا *khalāya'*, (pl. of خلية) Ships. Beehives.

A خلائف *khalāʾif*, (pl. of خليفة *khalīfat*) Vicegerents, califs. Pregnant camels.

A خلائق *khalāʾik*, (pl. of خليقة *khalīkat*) Natures, tempers, dispositions. Creatures, men, peoples. Summits of hills adapted for retaining showers.

P خلائق پناه *khalāʾik-panāh*, Asylum of men.

A خلائل *khalāʾil*, (pl. of خليلة *khalīlat*) Sincere and intimate female friends.

A خلب *khalb*, (v. n. of خلب) Seizing with the talons. Wounding with the nails, clawing, scratching, tearing. Biting. Deceiving, cajoling. *Khilb*, A nail, claw, talon. The pericardium. The envelope of the liver. The diaphragm. A radish. A vine-leaf. (pl. خلباء *khulabāʾ*) A man fond of women. خلب النساء *khilbu'n nisāʾ*, A favourite of women. *Khulb* or *khulub*, Fibres of the palm-tree, of which they make ropes. A rope made of the same. Heart or pith of the palm-tree. Clay, black and stiff. *Khalab*, (v. n. of خلب) Being foolish.

P خلب *khilb*, Snot. *Khulb*, A powder for the eyes. *Khalab*, A reed not yet wrought into a pen.

A خلب *khullab*, Clouds without rain. برق خلب *barki khullab*, Lightning when not followed by rain, (proverbially) a vain-promiser.

A خلباء *khalbāʾ*, Foolish (woman). خلباء النساء *khilbāʾu'n nisāʾ*, Beloved by women. *Khulabāʾ*, (pl. of خلب *khilb*) Men fond of women.

G خلباي *khalbāy*, Galbanum, benzoin.

A خلبة *khalibat*, A female deceiver.

A خلبسة *khalbasat*, A flattering.

A خلبصة *khalbasat*, A running away.

A خلبن *khalban*, Foolish or thin (woman).

A خلبوب *khalabūb*, (com. gen.) A deceiver.

A خلبوت *khulabūt*, A liar, deceiver, cajoler.

A خلبوص *khalabūs*, A bird less than a sparrow.

A خلة *khallat*, (pl. خلال *khilāl*) Nature, property, quality (good or bad). Poverty. (pl. خل *khall*) Sour, pricked wine, or wine losing its flavour without becoming tart. A quantity of vinegar. A detached heap of sand. A male or female camel entered into the second year. Light (woman). A small hole, chink, gap. Space, interval. Need, poverty. A vacancy caused by a person's death. الخلة تدعو الى السلة *al khallat tadʿū ila's sallat*, Poverty prompts to thieving. *Khillat*, (pl. خلل *khilal* and خلال *khilāl*) A rich sword-sheath of leather adorned with jewels and gold. A camel's sinew whipt round the horns of a bow. A bow-case. Bits of meat picked from between the teeth. Sincere friendship. A sincere friend or friends (male or female). *Khullat*, (pl. خلال *khilāl*) Friendship sound and sincere. A friend. A plant of which camels are fond. (pl. خلل *khulal*) A certain thorny tree. The habitat of the plant عرفج *ʿurfuj*. Any plant which has an agreeable flavour. A country not producing salt and bitter plants. خلت مخصوصه *khullati makhsūsa*, Most intimate friendship.

A خلج *khalj*, (v. n. of خلج) Drawing away, carrying off. Tearing up, removing forcibly. Weaning. Moving, shaking; brandishing and piercing with a spear. Making a signal by a wink of the eye. Engrossing, occupying (care). Coition. *Khalaj*, The aching of the bones from excessive labour, lassitude. Corruption, fault, blemish. *Khuluj*, (pl. of خليج *khalīj*) Small ships. Bays, gulfs. Docks. Canals leading from the main stream. Wooden platters. Name of a people in Arabia. People of uncertain origin. Quakers, tremblers, shakers.

A خلج *khilijj*, Remote, distant.

P خلجان *khalajān*, Love, desire. Inclination, propensity. Name of a village adjacent to Shīrāz.

A خلجان *khalajān*, (v. n. of خلج) Throbbing, beating (a limb); winking, twinkling (the eye). Occurring to the mind. Going about the earth like a madman. Agitation, commotion, anxiety. Curiosity. P خلجان شدن *khalajān shudan*, To tremble, to be agitated.

A خلجم *khaljam*, Long, large, corpulent.

P خلچ *khalach*, A horde of Turkomāns.

P خلچه *khulcha*, A stick with a curved head.

P خلخ *khallukh*, A large city in Khatāy remarkable for the comeliness of its inhabitants. Fragrant.

P خلخال *khalkhāl*, Name of a large city between Gīlān and Kazwīn. An ankle-ring. خلخال زر *khalkhāli zar*, (or خلخال فلك *khalkhāli falak*) The sun.

A خلخال *khalkhāl*, (pl. خلاخيل *khalākhīl*) The ring (of gold or silver) worn by the Arabian ladies round their ankles. Fine thin cloth.

A خلخان *khalkhān*, Name of an herb from which potash is made, found near Balkh.

A خلخل *khalkhal*, Fine thin cloths. *Khalkhal* or *khulkhal*, (pl. خلاخل *khalākhil*) An ankle-ring (of gold or silver).

A خلخلة *khalkhalat*, The stripping of a bone.

A خلد *khuld*, (v. n. of خلد) Abiding. Having a green old age. Eternity, perpetuity. Paradise, everlasting bliss. A green old age. A kind of lark. (pl. خلدة *khiladat*) An ear-ring. A bracelet. *Khuld* or *khald*, (pl. مناجذ *manājiz*) A mole. *Khalad*, Mind, heart, thoughts. (pl. of خلدة *khaladat*) Ear-rings. Bracelets.

A خلّد *khallad*, (in prayer) May he cause to endure for ever! خلّد الله خلافته *khallada' llāh khilāfatahu*, May God perpetuate his empire!

A خلدة *khuldat*, One mole. *Khaladat*, An ear-ring. A bracelet. *Khiladat*, (pl. of خلد *khuld*) Ear-rings. Bracelets.

A خلد مكاني *khuld-makānī*, Exalted to heaven.

P خلر *khular* or *khullar*, Pease. Beans.

A خلس *khals*, (v. n. of خلس) Seizing, drawing away, carrying off. Ripe hay, at the roots of which green herbage is sprouting up. *Khuls*, (pl. of خلساء *khalsāɛ* and خلاسيّة *khalāsiyat*) (Women) half-gray.

A خلساء *khalsāɛ*, Half-gray (woman).

A خلسة *khulsat*, Rapine, plunder. A mixture of herbage, partly dry, partly green.

P خلش *khalish*, A wounding. The sinking (of a thorn) into the flesh. Stop, interruption. Solicitude, suspicion.

P خلشك *khalushk*, The feet of long drawers. See خكشك *khakushk*. *Khulushk*, Spittle.

A خلص *khils*, (pl. خلصاء *khulasāɛ* and خلصان *khulsān*) A sincere friend. *Khalas*, (v. n. of خلص) Being handsome and agreeable (the bones within the flesh, and especially those of the hands and feet). A kind of sweet-smelling, berry-bearing parasite.

A خلّص *khullas*, (pl. of خالص) Pure, sincere.

A خلصاء *khalsāɛ*, A place in a desert where there is a fountain. *Khulasāɛ*, (pl. of خلص *khils*) Friends.

A خلصا الشنّة *khalsā'sh shannat*, A strap sewed over the seams of a leathern bottle. Pure water that leaks through the sutures of a leathern bottle.

A خلصان *khulsān*, A friend. (pl. of خلص) Friends.

A خلصة *khalasat*, A certain idol once worshipped in Arabia, in the temple of ذو الخلصة *zū'l khalasat*.

A خلط *khalt*, (v. n. of خلط) Mixing. Confusion, mixture. P خلط شدن *khalt shudan*, To be mixed. To be astonished. خلط كردن *khalt kardan*, To mix, blend, confound. A *Khalt*, *khalit*, or *khulut*, One who mixes in society, who flatters and caresses people, and makes his women and goods common property. *Khilt*, (pl. اخلاط *akhlāt*) A mixture, miscellany. Dirt. A humour, of which there are four in the human body. Chyme. A man of mean or mixed origin. Dates of different sorts mixed together. A fool. خلط فاسد *khilti fāsid*, Canker of a sore. *Khilt* or *khilit*, A bow or arrow, which, from the curved nature of the wood, cannot be made straight. *Khalit*, A fool. *Khulut*, (or خلطاء *khulatāɛ*) (pl. of خليط *khalīt*) Mixed, blended. Partners. Neighbours.

A خلطة *khiltat*, A woman who mixes with men. Society, company, intercourse. *Khultat*, Partnership.

A خلطيّ *khiltīy*, Relating to any of the humours of the body (as phlegm, choler, melancholy, &c.).

A خلطين *khaltīn*, Water, wherein dates or raisins have been steeped, until they ferment and an intoxicating liquid is formed.

A خلع *khalɛ*, (v. n. of خلع) Drawing out (slowly). Pulling off (clothes or shoes). Deposing, removing from office. Repudiating a wife, when desired by herself from an aversion to her husband (on which account she resigns all settlements, and the presents made to her at marriage, which, had the divorce taken place at his motion, must have been kept by or delivered to her). Disinheriting a son and turning him out of doors. Putting forth the beard (an ear of corn). Putting forth leaves (the tree عضاه *ɛizāh*). Waxing strong, exhibiting signs of virility (a youth). Investing with a robe of honour. Meat dressed with sweet herbs; also flesh dried in the air, and cooked with fat. *Khulɛ*, Divorcement. *Khilaɛ*, (pl. of خلعة *khilɛat*) Robes of honour, with which princes invest those they mean to dignify.

A خلعاء *khalɛāɛ*, A hyena. *Khulaɛāɛ*, (pl. of خليع *khalīɛ*) Dissolute (youths), outcasts.

A خلعة *khilɛat*, The most valuable part of one's estate or effects. (pl. خلع *khilaɛ*) A robe of honour with which princes confer dignity upon subjects, a khelaut. خلعت فاخره *khilɛati fākhira*, A royal robe, a caftan. *Khulɛat*, A divorce granted at the request of the wife. The best part of one's property.

A خلعلع *khalaɛlaɛ*, A female hyena.

A خلف *khalf*, (v. n. of خلف) Coming, after or behind, succeeding (as day to day, or as people to people). Piecing or mending a garment. Drawing water. A successor. Offspring, progeny. The latter or hinder part. The back. Posterity, generation after generation. A wicked saying. A camel's stable. A place where dates are dried. Compensation, retribution, reward. A vicious son. A worthless fellow. Absent (tribe); or after being absent, now present. A worn-out leathern milk-bottle. The head of a razor. A large one-headed hatchet. The head or edge of an axe. (pl. خلوف *khulūf*) A short rib. هو خلف صدق من ابيه *huwa khalfu* (or *khalafu*) *sidkin min abīhi*, He occupies the place of his father. خلفه *khalfahu*, Behind him, after him. *Khilf*, A camel's dug, or the tip of it. The hinder dug. A short rib. Diverse, different, discordant. Litigious, quarrelsome. A draught of water, what is drawn at once. Summer-herbage. ذات خلفين *zātu khilfayn* or *khalfayn*, (pl. ذوات الخلفين *zawātu'l khilfayn*) A hatchet. ولدت الشاة خلفين *waladati'sh shāt khilfayn*, The sheep brought forth a male one year and a female the next. *Khulf*, Breach of promise. (pl. of خليف *khalīf*, q.v.). *Khalaf*, (v. n. of خلف) Succeeding to the place of another. Being pregnant (a camel). Being difficult and disastrous. Leaning to one side occasioned by a distorted limb (a camel). Being left-handed or squint-eyed. A successor. Posterity, descendants. Any thing left behind. An heir, favourite son. A pupil, an apprentice. (pl. of خليف *khalīf*, q. v.). *Khalif*, Pregnant camels. *Khuluf*, (pl. of خليف *khalīf*, q. v.).

A خلفا *khalafan*, Successively. خلفا بعد سلف *khalafan baɛda* (or عن *ɛan*) *salafin*, Successively, uninterruptedly.

A خلفاء *khulafāɛ* (pl. of خليفة *khalīfat*) Vicars, substitutes, lieutenants, khalifs. Emperors, kings, princes. خلفاء عثمانيّه *khulafāɛi ɛusmānīya*, Turkish emperors. الخلفاء الراشدون *al khulafāɛu'r rāshidūn*, The four lawful khalifs, *i. e.* Abūbakr, Omar, Othmān, and Alīy, the immediate successors of Muhammad. (The Persians do not acknowledge the three first, being of the sect of Alīy).

A خلفات *khalifāt*, Pregnant camels.

A خلفان *khilfāni*, Two persons, one tall and the other short, or one white and the other black.

A خلفة *khalfat*, (v. n. of خلف) Mending (a shift). *Khilfat*, (v. n. of خلف) Opposing. Succeeding. A succession. A succedaneum, substitute, one thing following another. The vicissitude of day and night. Opposition, contrariety. Offspring of different sexes. Plants growing up after others are withered. Autumn or summer herbs or fruits succeeding those of the spring. Fruits of two colours, *i. e.* green and ripe upon the same tree. Something tender and green put forth by a vine after the grape is black. That which bursts forth from a tree at the commencement of cold weather. Food remaining between the teeth. A patch. A drawing of water. Any thing suspended behind a rider. A leading of a camel to water after the people are gone away. Diverse, discordant, various. A flux in which various humours are ejected. A frequent visiting of the water-closet. A union of two colours. A place for drawing water. *Khulfat*, Vice, fault, blemish. Folly, stupidity. Opposition. (pl. خلف *khulaf*) Loss of appetite from sickness. A piecing of a garment. *Khulfat* or *khalfat*, (pl. خلف *khulaf*) The last taste of food. *Khalifat*, A pregnant camel. خلفة جدود *khalifatun jadūdun*, A she-ass.

A خلفتان *khilfatāni*, Two persons, one tall and the other short, or one black and the other white.

A خلفف *khulfuf*, Foolish (man or woman). ام خلفف *umm khulfuf* or *khulfaf*, A sore calamity.

A خلففة *khulfufat*, Foolish (woman).

A خلفنة *khilafnat* or خلفناة *khilafnāt*, Repugnance, pertinacity, opposition. Exceedingly perverse and contradictory.

P خلفه *khulfa*, Purslane.

A خلفى *khalafī*, Successive.

A خلق *khalk*, (v. n. of خلق) Measuring accurately, defining the dimensions (of leather before it is cut). Producing, creating. Feigning, inventing (a lie). Straightening (a stick). Smoothing, polishing (an oration). Created things, creatures. Creation, production. People, nation, folk, populace. The world. Some one. Much, many. خلق الله *khalku'llāh*, God's creatures. P خلق آتشين *khalki ātishīn*, Devils. خلق چهاريار *khalki chahār yār*, An appellation which the Turks give unto themselves. A خلق عالم *khalki ɛālam*, Mortals, people. خلق عدالت *khalki ɛadālat*, An appellation which the Persians give themselves. P خلق كردن *khalk kardan*, To create. A *Khulk* or *khuluk*, (pl. اخلاق *akhlāk*) Nature, quality, property, custom, manner (generally in a good sense). Disposition, temper. Religion. Humanity. Politeness. Fortitude. P خلق آتشين *khulki ātishīn*, Anger, rage, fury. A *Khalak*, (v. n. of خلق) Being threadbare (a garment); made smooth (the side of a horse, by rubbing off the hair). Being smooth (a stone). (pl. خلقان *khulkān*) Worn-out clothes. Freedom from a crack or flaw in a stone. *Khalik*, Of an excellent disposition.

A خلّق *khullak*, Preternaturally strait (woman).

A خلقاء *khalkā*, (fem. of اخلق *akhlak*) (A stone) smooth, equal, free from fissure or flaw. The side (of a camel). The interior (of a cavern). The smoothest part of the forehead. Free from cracks (a camel's hoof). Impervious woman.

P خلق آزار *khalk-āzār*, Man-oppressing.

A خلقان *khulkān*, (pl. of خلق *khulk*) Threadbare garments. P خلقان فروش *khulkān-farosh*, A seller of old wares.

A خلقة *khalkat*, (v. n. of خلق) Measuring accurately, defining (leather before cutting it). *Khilkat*, Creation. Exterior form, shape. *Khulkat*, Creation. Disposition, turn of mind. *Khalakat* or *khalikat*, (A cloud) disposed to rain.

A خلقةً *khilkatan*, Naturally, as formed or created.

A خلقىّ *khalkīy*, Natural.

A خلقيّة *khalkīyat*, Creation.

A خلل *khalal*, (v. n. of خلّ) Being marred, thrown into confusion (business), by fault or negligence. (pl. خلال *khilāl*) Rupture, breach, gap, interruption, chink, flaw, or leak. Defeat, danger. Change for the worse. Disturbance, disorder of the spirits, infirmity, weakness. Division, dispersion. خلل دماغ *khalali dimāgh*, A disturbed brain, madness, melancholy. هو خللهم *huwa khalaluhum*, He is amongst them. *Khilal*, (pl. of خلّة *khillat*) Rich sword-sheaths. Shreds of meat picked from between the teeth. *Khulal*, (pl. of خلّة *khullat*) Thorny plants (of a pleasant flavour).

P خلل انداز *khalal-andāz*, Introducing confusion.

P خلم *khilm*, Anger, indignation. Adhesive mud. *Khilm* or *khulm*, Snot. خلم دادن *khilm dādan*, To run with snot. *Khulum*, Name of one of the dependencies of Balkh, on the confines of Badakhshān, and called ده فرعون *dihi firɛawn*, Pharoah's village.

A خلم *khilm* (pl. اخلام *akhlām* and خلماء *khulamās*) A friend, a companion. The covert of a deer. A bone. The tallow upon a sheep's entrails.

A خلمة *khilmat*, Camels feeding plenteously.

P خلمده *khilm-dih*, Snotty (nose).

A خلموس *khulmūs*, (pl. خلاميس *khalāmīs*) Pasturing cattle four days and nights, and driving them to water morning and evening at different places.

P خلمه *khulma*, Head of a mace or club.

P خلميدن *khilmīdan*, To blow the nose. To be angry.

P خلن *khulin*, A snotty-nosed fellow.

A خلنبوس *khalambūs*, Marcasite; a fire-flint.

P خلنج *khalanj* or *khilanj*, Bi-coloured. Piebald. *Khilanj*, A black pigeon with mottled wings. *Khilinj*, Torpor of the limbs. A pinching with the nails.

A خلنج *khalanj*, (pl. خلانج *khalānij*) A tree from which they make beams or wooden bowls.

A خلنجان *khalanjān*, The root galangale.

P خلندر *khalandar*, Origany, a root.

P خلنده *khalanda*, Penetrating, wounding.

P خلنگ *khalang*, Bi-coloured, piebald. *Khilang*, Pinching the skin with the nails.

A خلو *khilw*, (pl. اخلاء *akhlās*) Vacant, at leisure, free. Empty.

P خلو *khulū*, A large, well-formed damascene plum. Name of a mountain.

A خلوّ *khulūw*, (v. n. of خلا for خلو) Being empty, vacant, deserted (a place). Being free, clear of. Going away, receding, abstaining. Lighting on a solitary place. Granting a private interview, retiring to consult in private. Loosing, letting go. Ridiculing, laughing at. Freedom. Besides, except.

A حلوء *khalūs*, Stubborn (camel) that will not quit her place. *Khulūs*, (v. n. of خلأ) Being obstinate (a she-camel), lying down and not stirring from (her) place. Not stirring from (one's) place.

P خلواج *khalwāj*, A carnivorous bird; a kite.

A خلوب *khalūb*, A deceitful, lying woman.

A خلوة *khalwat*, (v. n. of خلا for خلو) Granting a private interview, retiring to consult in private. Laughing at, jeering. Retirement, solitude, privacy. (pl. خلاوي *khalāwī*) A closet, private apartment. A private audience. خلوت صحيح *khalwati sahīh*, Complete retirement, where is no legal or natural impediment to the commission of the carnal act of marriage. P خلوت كردن *khalwat kardan*, To retire. To evacuate. To dismiss. A *Khilwat*, Free, at leisure (woman).

P خلوتخانه *khalwat-khāna*, (or خلوتسرا *khalwat-sarā*) The women's apartment, or any other private apartment. An oratory, place for private prayer.

P خلوت دوست *khalwat-dost*, Fond of privacy.

P خلوتگاه *khalwat-gāh*, (or خلوتگه *khalwat-gah*) A solitary place, one of retirement and seclusion.

P خلوت گزين *khalwat-guzīn*, A solitaire.

P خلوتنشين *khalwat-nishīn*, Sitting in solitude.

P خلوتي *khalwatī*, Solitary; a solitaire. Name of the poet Ismail Jamālu'd dīn.

A خلوج *khalūj*, Scattered clouds full of rain. A she-camel losing her milk when her sucking colt is taken away. Swift-paced (camel). *Khulūj*, (v. n. of خلج) Flying about (the eye).

A خلود *khulūd*, (v. n. of خلد) Being perpetual, enduring. Having a green old age. Eternity. Duration. A fresh and vigorous old age.

A خلوص *khulūs*, (v. n. of خلص) Being good, choice, excellent, pure, unmixed. Reaching to, arriving at. Sediment of butter when clarified. Purity, sincerity, candour, integrity. Friendship.

A خلوصات *khulūsāt*, Purities. Extracts.

A خلوصيّة *khulūsiyat*, Purity, candour, honesty.

A خلوط *khalūt*, Mixing. A mixer, mingler.

A خلوف *khulūf*, (v. n. of خلف) Remaining behind. Succeeding, coming behind. Taking hold of behind. Supplying the place of, making amends. Ascending a mountain. Fixing a pole in the hinder part of a tent. Drawing or drinking water. Becoming very offensive (the breath from fasting). Turning (as milk or wine). Being corrupted by vice. Being silly. Degenerating from the qualities of one's father. Repairing a garment. Discarding an old garment and taking a new one. حيّ خلوف *hayy khulūf*, Arabs absent from their dwelling-place, not one remaining behind. Present after having been absent. (pl. of خلف *khilf*) The short ribs.

A خلوفة *khulūfat*, (v. n. of خلف) Becoming very offensive (the breath from fasting). Turning (milk or wine). Becoming corrupted by vice (a man). Ascending a mountain. Taking hold behind. Supplying the place, making amends. Fixing a pole in the hinder part of a tent.

A خلوق *khalūk*, A kind of aromatic.

A خلوقة *khulūkat*, (v. n. of خلق) Being worn threadbare (a garment). Creation.

P خلوگردة *khulū-gurda*, A kind of large plum.

A خلول *khulūl*, The being diminished, lean.

A خلولة *khulūlat*, Amity.

P خلوتيا *khulotiyā*, Common to all. Melancholy, gloom. Shameless, barefaced. Mad.

P خلوة *khulwa*, Disgraced, infamous.

P خله *khala*, A helm or rudder. An oar. Any sharp, piercing thing (as a needle or awl). Void, empty. Lost. Trifles, silly discourse. Any thing that goes off by degrees. Wind in the bowels causing acute pain. A writing signed by a judge, confirming any mercantile transaction. خلهٔ چشم *khalaₛi chashm*, Dirt in the eyes. *Khula*, A helm. An oar.

P خلّه *khulla*, Snot.

P خله چوب *khala-chob*, A rudder. An oar.

A خلي *khaly*, (v. n. of خلى) Cutting, mowing. Giving grass to cattle. Pulling up. Putting a bit in a horse's mouth. Drawing the bit. Putting fuel under a boiling pot, or throwing meat into it. Putting barley into a horse's nose-bag. *Khala'*, (pl. اخلاء *akhlāₛ*) Fresh, tender (plant). Any pot-herb plucked up.

A خليّ *khaliy*, (pl. خليّون *khaliyūn* and اخلياء *akhliyāₛ*) Free, unbound. At leisure. Owing nothing, clear of. Void of care. A bachelor. A bee-hive. A jar for keeping honey in. The lower part of the trunk of a tree.

A خلّي *khulliy*, (A camel) feeding on sweet herbs.

A خلّيبي *khillība'*, A woman that steals the heart, a deceiver, cajoler.

A خلية *khaliyat*, (pl. خلايا *khalāya'*) A large ship (as being free from the impulse of oars). A bee-hive. A jar for keeping honey in. The lower part of a tree. (fem. of خليّ *khaliy*) A camel taking a liking for another's colt. A camel allowed to go free and unfettered for milking. The divorcing of a wife (in the following manner): انت خليّة مني *anti khaliyat minnī*, Thou art at liberty from me.

A خلّيت *khillīt*, Name of a fort in Taymā.

P خليته *khalīta*, A purse, a linen bag.

A خليج *khalīj*, (pl. خلج *khuluj*) Bay, frith, gulf. A bason, or dock. A river or its banks. The canal which they open for the discharge of the Nile, when it swells too high. A small ship. A wooden plate. A rope. A trembler, shaker. One of obscure origin.

A خليجم *khulayjam*, Long, large, corpulent.

P خليدگي *khalīdagī*, Puncture (of a needle).

P خليدن *khalīdan*, To prick. To pierce into the flesh (a needle or thorn) causing pain thereby. To sting (as a scorpion). To sew.

P خليدة *khalīda*, Punctured, pricked. Stung. A puncture.

P خليس *khalīs*, A mixture of two things, as of dry and fresh grass, rubies and pearls. A beard of two colours.

A خليس *khalīs*, Half gray. A white man whose white is mixed with black. Ripe hay, at the roots of which herbage is sprouting. A withered plant.

A خلّيسى *khillīsa'*, A seizing, carrying off.

P خليش *khalīsh*, A tumult, a crowd. Yielding, adhesive mud.

A خليص *khulays*, Any thing white.

A خليط *khalīt*, (pl. خلط *khulut* and خلطاء *khulatāₛ*) Mixed. A mixed crowd. A partner, a co-partner. One who has a right in common to a road or watering-place. A husband. A first cousin. A neighbour. A mixer. Any mixture (as corn and chaff, clay and straw, hay and grass, or sweet and sour milk, fat and butter). Date-wine, or date-wine and raisin-wine mingled together.

A خليطة *khalītat*, A mixture of camels' and sheep's milk, or that of sheep and goats.

A خليطهٔ طوفان *khalītaₛi tūfān*, An exciter of disturbance, a calumniator, wicked person.

A خلّيطى *khillīta'*, A mixer. *Khullayta'*, (or خليطى *khulayta'*) Confusion, disorder, a perplexed business. A mob, miscellaneous company.

A خليع *khalīₑ*, Wicked (youth, and therefore deserted by his friends). A hunter. A worn-out garment. A blank arrow, of those formerly employed in sortilege. A wolf. An antagonist at play. A demon, called also Ghūl, supposed to feed on dead bodies. خليع العذار *khalīₑu'l ₑizār*, Simple, free from every kind of accession or encumbrance (as a face without a beard, a camel without a halter, or a road without a barrier). Unmanageable, ungovernable. *Khalyaₑ*, A wolf. A fool.

A خليف *khalīf*, (pl. خلف *khuluf*, *khalaf*, and *khulf*) A road or valley between two mountains. Any place through which water flows; a canal. A road. Milk after the biestings. An arrow. Sharp. A garment torn in the middle and united at both ends. A camel the second day after foaling. A woman whose hair hangs down behind. The part under the armpit of a camel.

A خليفة *khalīfat*, (pl. خلائف *khalāₛif* and خلفاء *khulafāₛ*) A successor. A lieutenant, vicegerent, deputy. An emperor, sovereign. This was the title (calif) given to the Muhammadan sovereigns or successors of their prophet; to which was annexed the most absolute authority both in religious and civil government. خليفة الله *khalīfatu'llāh*, The vicegerent of God, *i.e.* Adam. P خليفهٔ زمين *khalīfaₛi zamīn*, Emperor of the world, *i.e.* the reigning king.

A خلّيفة *khillīfat*, Extremely contradictory and perverse (man, woman, or people).

A خلّيفي *khillīfa'*, Deputyship: succession: imperial power.

A خليق *khalīk*, Worthy, fit, suitable. Well-proportioned. Disposed. Habituated, accustomed. *Khulayk*, (dim. of خلق) Somewhat worn (garment).

A خليقاء *khulaykāₛ*, The tip of a horse's nose. The interior part (of a cavern). The smoothest part of the forehead.

A خليقة *khalīkat*, (pl. خلائق *khalāₛik*) Nature, disposition. A creature (man or animal). Newly-dug (well). (A cloud) disposed to rain. خليقة الله *khalīkatu'llāh*, God's creatures.

A خليل *khalīl*, (pl. اخلّاء *akhillāₛ* and خلّان *khullān*) A sincere and intimate friend. خليل الله *khalīlu'llāh*, (or الخليل *al khalīl*) The friend of God, *i.e.* Abraham. The town Hebron, where the tomb of Abraham is venerated. The heart. The nose. Perforated, bored. Lean. Indigent.

A خليلان *khalīlān*, Name of a famous singer.

A خليلة *khalīlat*, (pl. خليلات *khalīlāt*, خلائل *khalāₛil*) Friendship. A sincere female friend.

P خليميدن *khilīmīdan*, To blow the nose.

A خليواج *khalīwāj*, A kite.

P خم *kham*, Crooked, bent, twisted, curled, curved. A curl, knot, ringlet. Crookedness, curvature, convexity. A ply, fold. A row, rank. A house for the winter-season. Flight. That part of a noose which encircles the neck; also the eye or ring through which the rope runs to form or draw tight the noose. A convex or sharp roof (en dos d'âne). خم اندر خم *kham andar kham*, Twist within twist; curling locks. خم دادن *kham dādan*, To bend. To give an inclination. To repel. To resist. خم زدن *kham zadan*, To flee away. خم كردن *kham kardan*, To bend, crook. To twist, curl. خم گرفتن *kham giriftan*, To be bent. *Khim*, A painful wound. Pus, matter. Nature, disposition. Snot. خم چشم *khimi chashm*, Dirt in the eye. *Khum*, A jar, large vessel. An alembic, still. A trumpet. A cymbal. A drum. Silence. An arch, dome, vaulted roof. Silent. خم آهن گون *khumi āhan-gūn*, (or خم لازورد *khumi lāzuward*) The firmament. رويينه خم *royīna-khum*, A brazen drum. بخم در شدن *ba khum dar shudan*, To sit in a jar; importing, to watch, contemplate, observe.

A خمّ *khamm*, (v. n. of خمّ) Stinking (as meat). Contracting an unpleasant smell (a milk-bottle). Cleaning out (a well or a house). Milking (a camel). Cutting. Congratulating. Wishing joy. Weeping sorely. Being confined in a coop (a hen). Stale (dressed victuals). *Khimm*, An empty garden. *Khumm*, A crib or hutch for fowls. Name of a place. (pl. خممة *khimamat*) A pit in the ground wherein are laid ashes for young lambs to lie on. A hamper for hens to lay in.

A خماجر *khumājir*, Brackish water. Coiled.

A خماح *khumāh*, A plant found in Yaman.

P خما خسرو *khamā khusrav*, A note in music.

A خمار *khimār*, (v. n. 3 of خمر) Hiding one's self, lurking. Residing constantly (at a place). Selling a free man as a slave. Mixing with, interfering in. Being near one another. Altering, disturbing (the mind). Bringing on a dizziness in the head (disease). (pl. اخمرة *akhmirat*, خمر *khumur* and *khumr*) A woman's veil or head-dress. A veil or covering in general. ما شمّ خمارك *mā shamma khimāraka*, What has befallen you? *Khumār*, Headache, crop-sickness after drinking. The pain or headache of a fever. A languishing appearance of the eyes, the effect of love, drowsiness, or drinking. *Khamār* or *khumār*, A great crowd.

P خمار *khumār*, Crop-sickness after drinking. Name of a city in Khatā.

A خمّار *khammār*, A vintner, a wine-merchant.

P خمار آلود *khumār-ālūd*, Intoxicating (eyes).

P خمارخانه *khumār-khāna*, A tavern.

P خمارناك *khumārnāk*, Dim (eye).

A جاءُوا خماس *jā'ū khumāsa*, They came in fives.

A خماسيّ *khumāsīy*, A word of five letters. A boy of five spans. Belonging to, or consisting of five.

P خماش *khamāsh*, (or خماشه *khamāsha*) Shavings, parings, rubbish.

A خماشات *khumāshāt*, Old hatreds, grudges.

A خماشة *khumāshat*, A wound or any injury for which there is no fixed punishment.

A خماص *khimās*, (pl. خميص *khamīs*) Lank-bellied. Famished.

A خماصة *khamāsat*, Lankness of belly.

A خمّاط *khammāt*, A roaster of meat.

A خماع *khumāʿ*, A limping, halting pace.

A خمال *khumāl*, A limping gait, or a disease the cause of it. A sincere friend.

A خمالات *khimālāt*, (pl. of خملة) Secrets.

A خماليّ *khumālīy*, A sincere friend.

G خماليون *khamāliyūn*, A kind of mezereon. Hellebore.

A خماما *khamāmā*, The elder-tree.

A خمامة *khimāmat*, A decayed feather amidst plumage. *Khumāmat*, Sweepings or filth of a house; mud taken out of a well. Offal or crumbs which one eats from motives of piety, that nothing be lost.

P خمان *khamān*, (equivalent to كمان *kamān*) A bow. Bending. Bent, curved.

A خمان *khumān*, The elder-tree.

A خمّان *khammān*, A limber spear. Dregs of the people. *Khimmān* or *khummān*, Dregs of the people. Mean furniture. A worthless, useless tree.

P خمانا *khamānā*, A rival. Emulous.

P خمانائي *khamānāʾī*, Similitude.

P خمانيدن *khamānīdan*, To bend. To be bent, curved, twisted. To distort the mouth, make mouths at, ridicule. To mimic another's words or motions.

P خماهان *khumāhān*, (or خماهن *khumāhan*) A kind of hard stone, which when brayed and dissolved in water makes a reddle.

P خماهن *khumāhan*, A species of black shells inclining to red.

A خمائص *khamāʾis*, (pl. of خميصة *khamīsat*) Lank-bellied (women).

A خمائل *khamāʾil*, (pl. of خميلة *khamīlat*) Soft sands producing trees. Low-lying grounds rich in vegetation. Trees growing thickly together.

P خمب *khumb*, A large jar. A trumpet.

P خم بخم *kham ba kham*, Coiled up together.

P خمبره *khum-bara*, A small jar. A rocket. Name of a bird.

A خمج *khamaj*, (v. n. of خمج) Stinking from long stagnation (water). Weakness. Perversion (of the mind), corruption (of religion). Rottenness (of dates), taint (of meat). *Khamij*, Depraved in morals. Languid.

P خمجاج *khamjāj*, A large painted globular glass vessel. A purse. A travelling bag for combs and tinder-boxes.

A خمجة *khamijat*, (A she-camel) abstaining from water through disease.

A خمجر *khamjar*, (or *khumajir*) Brackish water, which none but cattle will drink.

A خمجرير *khamjarīr*, Bitter. Brackish water.

A خمجريرة *khamjarīrat*, A disturbance.

A خمجليلة *khamjalīlat*, A tumult.

P خمچه *khumcha*, A small wine-jar.

P خمخانه *khum-khāna*, A wine-vault: tavern.

A خمخم *khimkhim*, A thorny plant. A full udder. *Khumkhum*, A certain marine animalcule.

P خمخم *khumkhum*, A red bramble.

A خمخمة *khamkhamat*, (v. n. of خمخم Q) Speaking through the nose, muttering (from pride). Devouring ungracefully, so as to make a noise.

A خمد *khamd*, (v. n. of خمد) Becoming low (fire). Allowing (fire) to get low.

P خم دار *kham-dār*, Twisted, curled, bent.

P خمدان *khumdān*, A repository for jars. A wine-vault. A potter's kiln.

P خمده *khamda*, Curved, bent. Asleep.

A خمر *khamr*, (v. n. of خمر) Covering, hiding, suppressing (evidence). Fermenting, leavening. Allowing (dough) to leaven. Feeling ashamed, blushing. Clouding the reason (fermented liquor). Drinking wine. Wine. A grape. خمر الحمار *khamru'l himār*, A species of soap-ashes. *Khimr*, Malevolence, hatred. Inexperienced, unversed. *Khumr* or *khumur*, (pl. of خمار *khimār*) Women's veils or coifs. *Khamar*, (v. n. of خمر) Lying hid. Being sewed a second time. Being concealed (news). Change, alteration. Any thing which obstructs the view (as a veil, mountain, valley, ditch, roof, crowd, heap of sand, or clump of trees). A great crowd. Name of a mountain at Jerusalem. جاءنا على خمر *jāʾanā ʿala' khamarin*, He came to us privately. ما هو بخلّ ولا خمر *mā huwa bi khallin wa lā khamrin*, He is neither vinegar nor wine (neither bad nor good). *Khamir*, (A place) abounding in wine. Crop-sick from ebriety. One who experiences a similar sensation on the approach of death.

A خمّر *khimirr*, A woman's veil.

A خمرة *khamrat*, Wine. A great multitude. خمرة صرف *khamratun sirfun*, Pure, neat, undiluted wine. *Khimrat*, A pod, hull, husk. A mode of covering the head with a veil. جاءنا على خمرة *jāʾanā ʿala' khimratin*, He came upon us secretly or unexpectedly. العوان لا تعلّم الخمرة *al ʿawānu lā tuʿallamu'l khimrata*, The middle-aged matron wants no teaching how to put on a veil. *Khumrat*, A cosmetic for the face. Wine dregs or lees. A small wine-jar, or vessel in which perfumes, oil, or sweetmeats are preserved. A feverish headache. Headache or crop-sickness after hard drinking. Leaven. A small mat of palm-leaves, on which they kneel, or prostrate themselves at prayer. The herb ورس *wars*. *Khumrat* or *khamarat*, Odour or fumes affecting the head. *Khamarat*, A great multitude. *Kha*, *khi*, or *khumarat*, Fragrance, a grateful smell.

P خمرخانه *khamr-khāna*, Wine-house, tavern.

P خمرفروش *khamr-farosh*, A vintner.

A خمرمحال *khamr-mahāl*, Places at which arrack and spirituous liquors are sold; also a branch of revenue arising from the sale of arrack and other spirituous liquors.

P خمره *khumra*, A small wine-jar. A bomb.

A خمريّ *khamrīy*, Red, porphyry-hued. Vinous.

A خمس *khams*, (v. n. of خمس) Taking (from the people) a fifth of their property by way of tax. Making five (by going into a company of four people). (fem.) Five. The hand. *Khims*, A watering of camels every fifth day. Camels thus watered. Name of a certain king of Yaman; also a striped stuff, of which he is said to have been the inventor. فلاة خمس *falātun khims*, A desert whose water lies so far off as only to allow cattle to drink on the fifth day. *Khums* or *khumus*, A fifth.

A خمسة *khamsat*, (masc.) Five. خمسة مسترقة *khamsat mustarihat*, Five supplementary days added unto the Persian year.

P خمستان *khumistān*, A cellar in which wine-jars are stowed. A potter's kiln.

A خمسون *khamsūn*, (obl. خمسين *khamsīn*) Fifty. عيد الخمسين *ʿīdu'l khamsīn*, Feast of Pentecost.

A خمش *khamsh*, (v. n. of خمش) Scratching (the face) with the nails. Giving a box on the ear. Mutilating in a limb.

P خمش *khamush*, Silent. Broke in.

A خمشتر *khamashtar*, Base, mean, avaricious.

A خمص *khams*, (v. n. of خمص) Emaciating (hunger). *Khums*, Going down (as the swelling of a wound). *Khamas*, (v. n. of خمص) Falling away (the belly). Being slender-waisted (man).

A خمصان *khumsān*, One who has the hollow of his foot slender. *Khumsān* or *khamasān*, Extenuated (in the belly).

A خمصة *khamsat*, Hunger. A small tract of soft beaten ground.

A خمط *khamt*, (v. n. of خمط) Roasting (meat, but not thoroughly). Skinning and roasting (a kid). Putting (milk) into a leathern bottle. Being well-flavoured (milk). Stinking. Any thing bitter or sour (especially a tree yielding but little fruit, as the اراك *arāk*). Any poisonous tree. Good milk of an apple-flavour. Milk, which, though it have lost its sweetness, has a good odour. Sour milk. *Khamat*, (v. n. of خمط) Being well-flavoured (milk); also stinking. Swelling with pride or anger. *Khamit*, Tempestuous (sea).

A خمطة *khamtat*, The odour of vine-flowers. Wine which has acquired a perfume; or acid with a certain odour. Apple-flavoured (milk). *Khamtat* or *khamatat*, The odour (of milk) when sweet or otherwise. *Kham* or *khamitat*, Fragrant (land).

A خمطرير *khamtarīr*, Brackish water.

A خمع *khamʻ*, (or خمعان *khamaʻān*) (v. n. of خمع) Limping (a hyena). *Khimʻ*, A wolf: a robber.

P خمك *khumak*, The noise made in clapping the hands. Beating time in music.

P خمّك *khummak*, The noise made in clapping the hands. Beating time in music. A small jar or pot. A drum with a brazen rim.

P خمكده *khum-kada*, A wine-house, tavern.

P خم گر *khumgar*, A maker or seller of wine-jars.

P خمگشته *kham-gashta*, Crooked.

P خمگوش *kham-gosh*, (or خمگوشه *kham-gosha*) The horns or extremes of a bow.

P خمل *khaml*, Wild saffron, dogsbane.

A خمل *khaml*, (v. n. of خمل) Putting (unripe dates) into a jar for a night or two. A kind of fish. The eyelids. A carpet with a long pile. The villous part (of tripe). Pile, plush (of velvet and the like). A cushion placed upon a saddle. The plumage of an ostrich. *Khiml* or *khuml*, A sincere friend. *Khamal*, (pl. of خامل *khāmil*) Obscure, unknown, contemptible.

A خملة *khamlat*, Trees growing close and intertwining their branches. A place thick of trees. The plumage of an ostrich. *Khamlat* or *khimlat*, Camelot, silk and camel's hair; also all silk or velvet, especially pily and plushy. *Khimlat*, A secret. Ignominy. The inner spirit. لئيم الخملة *la-ʼīmu'l khimlat*, Inwardly base.

A خممة *khimamat*, (pl. of خمّ *khumm*) Pits containing ashes for young lambs to lie in. Hampers for hens to lay in.

P خم مهره *khum-muhra*, A musical shell, conch.

A خمن *khamn*, (v. n. of خمن) Conjecturing, guessing. *Khaman*, A stink.

P خمناك *khimnāk*, Sick, diseased.

A خمنشر *khamanshar*, Base, vile, despicable.

A خمو *khamw*, Thickness and hardness (of milk).

A خمود *khumūd*, (v. n. of خمد) Abating, going out (flame or fire). Being assuaged, abated (fever). Being cooled, quieted (in mind). Fainting, dying.

A خمّود *khammūd*, Any place where fire is covered up and preserved.

A خمور *khamūr*, Leaven. *Khumūr*, Wines.

P خموش *khamosh*, Silent, taciturn. Dumb. Tame, broke in. The extinguishing of a candle.

A خموش *khamūsh*, Gnats. *Khumūsh*, (v. n. of خمش) Scratching with the nails.

P خموشيدن *khamoshīdan*, To keep silence.

A خموص *khumūs*, The subsiding (of a swelling).

A خموط *khumūt*, (v. n. of خمط) Being well-flavoured (milk). Stinking.

A خموع *khamūʻ*, A whore. *Khumūʻ*, A limping.

A خمول *khumūl*, (v. n. of خمل) Being, or rendering one's self mean, despicable, or of little note. Being obscure, dull, indistinct (sound). Obscurity, contempt. P نشسته بكنج خمول *nishasta ba kunji khumūl*, Seated in the nook of obscurity.

A خموم *khumūm*, (v. n. of خمّ) Becoming stale (dressed victuals).

P خمي *khamī*, Crookedness, curvature. خمي زانو *khamīʼi zānū*, The inner bend of the knee.

P خميازه *khamyāza*, Yawning, stretching.

A خميت *khamīt*, Thick, gross, plump, fat.

P خميدگي *khamīdagī*, Curvature, crookedness. A limping, halting pace.

P خميدن *khamīdan*, To be crooked. To limp, halt. *Khimīdan*, To blow the nose.

P خميده *khamīda*, Crooked, curved, bent.

A خمير *khamīr*, Dough, leaven, or any thing put into a mass of paste to ferment it. Leavened.

A خمّير *khimmīr*, An habitual drunkard.

A خميرة *khamīrat*, Leaven.

P خميرمايه *khamīr-māya*, Leaven.

P خميره *khamīra*, Dough. Conserve of roses or violets.

A خميس *khamīs*, A fifth. Any thing consisting of five parts (especially an army composed of van, centre, rear, and two wings). A garment or piece of cloth of five cubits; also a spear of those dimensions. A crowd, company, clan. يوم الخميس *yawmu'l khamīs*, (pl. اخمساء *akhmisāʼ* and اخمسة *akhmisat*) Fifth day, Thursday.

A خميص *khamīs*, (pl. خماص *khimās*) Extenuated in the belly. Famished.

A خميصة *khamīsat*, (pl. خمائص *khamāʼis*) A black garment four-square. Black hair. Lank-bellied (woman).

A خميط *khamīt*, Sour milk. Roasted meat, especially when skinned (when the hair only is singed off it is then called سميط *samīt*).

A خميل *khamīl*, Soft meat. Thick clouds. Pily, plushy (garments).

A خميلة *khamīlat*, (pl. خمائل *khamāʼil*) Soft sand producing trees. Low-lying ground rich in vegetation. The plumage of an ostrich. Soft cloth of the silk, velvet, satin, or camelot kinds.

A خميم *khamīm*, Praised. Heavy-spirited. Milk newly-drawn.

P خمينه *khamīna*, Heavy, continued, and unseasonable rain.

P خن *khan*, (for خانه *khāna*) A house. The hold of a ship. باد خن *bād-khan*, A summer-house. گلخن *gul-khan*, The furnace of a bath.

A خنّ *khann*, (v. n. of خنّ) Lopping (branches). Seizing (property). Emptying (a basket), taking out one thing after another. Being admitted to the sacred rights and privileges of a people. *Khinn*, A ship in ballast. *Khunn*, (pl. of اخنّ *akhann*) Persons who speak through the nose.

A خنء *khanʼ*, (v. n. of خنأ) Cutting (the trunk of a palm-tree).

A خنا *khanaʼ*, Calamities of fortune.

A خناب *khanāb* or *khinnāb*, Long, foolish, and going as if loose-jointed. *Khinnāb*, Thick-nosed.

A خنابة *khanābat*, Infamy, wickedness.

A خنّابة *khinnābat* or *khunnābat*, The side of the nose. *Khinnābat*, (or خنّأبة *khinnaʼbat*) A large tip of the nose.

A خنابث *khunābis*, Despicable. Deceitful.

A خنابس *khunābis*, (pl. خنابس *khanābis*) Squat, dwarfish. Extremely dark (night). Of a disagreeable aspect. Ancient. Solid, strong. A lion.

A خنابسون *khunābisūn*, Short, dwarfish men.

A خناث *khināś*, (pl. of خنث *khunś*) Folds. خناث الدلو *khināsu'd dalw*, The parts by which water comes out of a (leathern) bucket. (pl. of خنثى *khunsa'*) Scrats. يا خناث *yā khanāsi*, O shameful (woman)!

A خناثة *khunāsat*, A rank old catamite.

A خناثى *khanāsa'*, (pl. of خنثى) Hermaphrodites.

A خناثير *khanāsīr*, Misfortunes, evils. Household utensils.

A خناجر *khanājir*, (pl. of خنجور *khunjūr*) Milch camels. (A pl. of P خنجر *khanjar*) Daggers, hangers.

A خنادر *khanādir*, (pl. of خندريس) Old wines.

A خنادق *khanādik*, (pl. of خندق *khandak*) Fosses, moats, ditches.

P خناده *khanāda*, (in Gīlān) An officer who communicates the general's orders to the army.

A خناذيذ *khanāzīz*, (pl. of خنذيذ *khinzīz*) Excellent horses (stallions or geldings). Prominent mountain-tops. Lords, courteous heads of families.

A خناز *khanāz*, Stinking (woman).

A خنّاز *khunnāz*, A lizard. Jews who keep meat till it stinks.

A خنازير *khanāzīr*, (pl. of خنزير *khinzīr*) Pigs, hogs, swine. Swellings, wens in the neck.

A خنّاس *khannās*, The devil. A wicked man.

A خناسرة *khanāsirat*, (pl. of خنسر *khansar* or خنسريّ *khansarīy*) Wanderers in the path of error and destruction. Weak, perfidious (persons).

A خنّاسيّ *khannāsīy*, Diabolical, devilish.

A خناسير *khanāsīr*, Destruction. Urine of mountain-goats voided upon the corn or trees. Deviation from the road. Perfidy, over-reaching. The lowest or weakest of men. Sordidness, baseness.

A خناصر *khanāsir*, (pl. of خنصر) Little fingers.

A خناصرة *khunāsirat*, Name of a city in Syria.

A خناطيط *khanātīt*, Scattered crowds.

A خناطيل *khanātīl*, (pl. of خنطولة *khuntūlat*) Herds of camels or oxen. Scattered (camels). Parts of clouds. Viscous, stringy saliva.

A خناعة *khunāʿat*, The founder of a tribe.

A خناف *khināf*, (v. n. of خنف) Striking her breast with her hand (a woman). Twisting the nose (a camel) when finding the reins painful. Having the fore-feet tender and weak, and turning them outward (a camel). Cutting up (an orange).

A خنافج *khunāfij*, Very fleshy.

A خنافس *khanāfis* or خنافيس *khanāfīs*, Beetles, May-bugs. *Khunāfis*, A lion.

A خناق *khināk*, A halter with which any living creature is strangled. The throat. *Khunāk*, That place of the throat where they usually strangle. Quinsey, inflammation in the throat. Strangulation. Palpitation of the heart.

A خنّاق *khannāk*, A hangman.

A خناقة *khunākat*, Quinsey.

A خناقية *khunākiyat*, A disease affecting the crops of birds and thropples of horses.

P خناك *khunāk*, The quinsey.

P خنام *khunām*, (or خنّام *khunnām*) A disease to which horses, asses, and mules are subject.

A خنان *khanān*, The pleasures of life. *Khinān*, Circumcision. *Khunān*, A rheum at the nose (in camels). A disease in the throat or eye of birds.

A خنانيص *khanānīs*, (pl. of خنّوص) Young pigs.

A خنب *khimb*, (pl. اخناب *akhnāb*) The back parts of the joints of the legs and thighs, the hams. *Khanab*, (v. n. of خنب) Being out of joint and weak (the foot). Being lame. Perishing. Suffering from a cold in the head. A running at the nose.

A خنّب *khinnab*, Long, foolish, and going as if loose in the joints.

P خنب *khumb*, An earthen vessel (for holding wine or water). *Khanab* or *khamb*, An arched building, cupola, or portico.

A ذو خنبات *zū khunubāt* or *khanabāt*, A liar. One who, if he by chance acts right, defeats immediately the effect by acting wrong.

P خنبان *khumbān*, Moving, shaking, wagging.

P خنبانيدن *khambānīdan*, To mock, mimic.

A خنبة *khambat*, Corruption, villainy, mischief. *Khanibat*, (A girl) having a beautiful cast with the eye, and a sweet voice; lovely, fascinating. (A doe) having the neck bent back, and remaining fixed in one place.

A خنبث *khumbus*, Impure, base, malignant.

A خنبجة *khumbajat*, (from P خنبه *khumba*) A large vessel of earth or wood hollowed and incrusted with clay (in which they lay up corn). *Khumbujat*, A small jar.

P خنبره *khum-bara*, A small earthen pot. خنبرهٔ دودناك *khumbara-i dūdnāk*, The sky. *Khumbura*, A water-pot having a small mouth.

A خنبس *khambas*, A dwarf, a short man.

A خنبسة *khambasat*, (v. n. of خنبس Q) Dividing (spoil). The gait (of a lion).

A خنبش *kham* or *khimbash*, Who moves much.

A خنبع *khumbuʿ*, Fruit in its envelope.

A خنبعة *khumbuʿat*, A small veil. The space between the mustachios. The upper lip. A little protuberance in the middle of the upper lip.

A خنبق *khumbuk*, Avaricious, closefisted.

P خنبك *khumbak*, A small jar or other vessel. The noise made by a horse when drinking. Mocking, ridiculing. The rim of a drum. Striking one hand against the other in beating time in music. The dress of a dervish. *Khumbuk*, Name of a village in Badakhshān.

A خنبوص *khumbūs*, Sparks from flint and steel.

P خنبه *khamba*, A vine-arbour, trellis. A gallery. *Khumba*, A large vessel (in which they lay up corn) of earth or wood hollowed, and crusted over with clay. A dome.

P خنبيدن *khambīdan*, To be celebrated. To be bent. *Khumbīdan*, To leap, spring. To beat time.

P خنبيده *khambīda*, Celebrated, notorious.

P خنپور *khampūr* or *khumpūr*, The bridge across the eternal fire. *Khumpūr*, The resurrection. A sower.

A خنّة *khunnat*, A sound made through the nose. The foreskin.

P خنت *khant* or *khanat*, Lightning, gleam, coruscation. The celestial orb. A brazen pot.

A خنتار *khintār*, (or خنتور) Excessive hunger.

A خنتب *khuntab* or *khuntub*, An uncircumcised clitoris. Weak, impotent. Short, dwarfish.

A خنتعة *khuntuʿat*, A bitch-fox, a vixen.

A خنتف *khuntuf*, Rue.

A خنث *khans*, (v. n. of خنث) Bending outwards (a leathern bottle) at the orifice, in order to drink therefrom commodiously. Deriding. *Khins*, A dispersed crowd. The inner part of the cheek nearest to the grinders. *Khuns*, (pl. خناث *khinās*) A ply, fold. *Khanas*, (v. n. of خنث) Being flexible, flaccid. *Khanis*, Flexible, pliant. يا خنث *yā khunas*, O shameful (man)!

A خنثبة *khansabat*, *khunsabat*, *khinsabat*, and *khunsubat*, A good camel full of milk.

A خنثر *khunsar*, (*khanasir*, *khansar*, *khinsir*, or *khunsur*) Rubbish and filth left where men have been encamped.

A خنثعبة *khinsaʿbat*, (*khansaʿbat*, or *khunsaʿbat*) A camel yielding plenty of milk.

A خنثعة *khunsuʿat*, A bitch-fox, vixen.

A خنثل *khansal*, Weak. Flabby woman.

A خنثى *khunsa'*, Asphodel. (pl. خناثى *khanāsa'*, *khanāsī*, and خناث *khināṣ*) A hermaphrodite.

P خنج *khanj*, Lost. Vain, unprofitable. Interest, profit, gain, advantage. The pleasures and comforts of life, delight, festivity, song, dance, mirth. A leer, amorous glance. *Khanj khanj*, Breathing hard through the nose. *Khunj*, An owl. Name of a country in Persia.

P خنجده *khanjda*, Flesh-glue. *Khunjada*, Reddle. Venery. *Khunjida*, A butterfly.

P خنجر *khanjar*, A dagger, poniard, hanger. A sword. خنجرزر *khanjari zar*, (or خنجر زرافشان *khanjari zar-afshān*) Sunrise. A morning-beam. خنجر سيم *khanjari sīm*, A morning-beam. خنجر صبح *khanjari subh*, Sunrise. The morning-breeze. خنجر فلك *khanjari falak*, A morning-ray. Sunrise.

A خنجر *khanjar* or *khinjar*, A large knife, hanger. *Khanjar*, A milch camel.

A خنجرة *khanjarat*, A camel abounding in milk.

A خنجري *khanjarī*, A mode of printing or staining silk (گلبدن *gulbadan*). A small tambourin.

A خنجريّ *khanjarīy*, An ugly-bearded man.

A خنجرير *khanjarīr*, Salt-water.

A خنجف *khanjaf*, A camel full of milk.

P خنجك *khanjak*, A triangular thorn. Coriander-seed. A kind of grain. *Khinjak*, An esculent berry from the tree ون *van*. *Khunjak*, Wormwood of Pontus.

A خنجل *khinjil*, A foolish woman. A corpulent woman. A clamorous and obscene woman.

A خنجلة *khanjalat*, A marrying a silly woman.

A خنجور *khunjūr*, A camel full of milk.

A خنجورة *khunjūrat*, A camel abounding in milk. Large (she-camel).

P خنجه *khunja* or *khanja*, Breathing hard through the nose.

P خنجيده *khanjīda*, A balsam. *Khunjīda*, A butterfly.

P خنجير *khanjīr* or *khinjīr*, Any smell, the exhalation of fried bones, boiling oil, or melted fat, or an extinguished lamp. The point of a spear. Sharp, rough, acrid.

A خنخنة *khankhanat*, A muttering nasally.

P خند *khand*, (in compos.) Laughing, smiling. A laugher. ريش خند *rīsh-khand*, A flatterer. ريش خندي *rīsh-khandī*, Flattery, adulation. شكر خند *shakar-khand*, Sweetly-smiling.

P خنداخند *khand-ā-khand*, A continual and hearty laugher.

P خندان *khandān*, Laughing. Blooming, blossoming. Bloom, blossom.

P خندانيدن *khandānīdan*, To cause to laugh.

To laugh.

A خندب *khundub*, A bad-dispositioned man.

A خندبان *khundubān*, Fleshy, corpulent.

P خند خريش *khand-kharīsh*, Derision, mockery.

P خندخند *khandakhand*, A continued and hearty laugher.

G خندروس *khandarūs*, Frumenty.

A خندريس *khandarīs*, (pl. خنادر *khanādir*) Old wine. Old wheat.

G خندريلي *khandarīlī*, A kind of succory.

P خندستان *khandastān*, Vexation. Jeer, taunt, raillery. Ludicrous entertainment. A playhouse. The lip of a mistress.

P خندستاني *khandastānī*, The lip of a mistress.

A خندع *khundaʻ*, A kind of locust. *Khunduʻ*, A frog. Intrinsically vile.

A خندف *khindif*, Name of a tribe.

A خندفة *khandafat*, (v. n. of خندف Q) Turning the toes out with a strut. Making haste.

P خندگي *khandagī*, Laughter.

A خندلة *khandalat*, Fulness of body.

A خندلس *khandalis*, (or خندليس *khandalīs*) A fat and flabby she-camel.

P خند و تند *khand u tand*, Ruined, topsy-turvy.

A خندوف *khundūf*, A proud, strutting fellow.

P خنده *khanda*, Laughing. A laugh. Laughter. خندۀ جام *khanda-i jām*, (or خندۀ مي *khanda-i may*) The smile of the bowl. خندۀ زمين *khanda-i zamīn*, Verdure and flowers. خنده آور و مسرّت انگيز *khanda-āwar u masarrat-angez*, Promoting laughter and exciting mirth, *i.e.* a facetious man. در خنده شدن *dar khanda shudan*, To laugh.

P خنده خريش *khanda-kharīsh*, A laughing-stock, jeer. Laughter. A jeerer. A flatterer.

P خنده ريش *khanda-rīsh*, A laughing-stock. خنده ريش كردن *khanda-rīsh kardan*, To flatter, cajole. To ridicule.

P خنديدن *khandīdan*, To laugh.

A خنذاة *khanzāt*, (v. n. of خنذي Q) Talking obscenely. A wicked saying.

A خنذع *khunzuʻ*, Intrinsically vile.

A خنذق *khanzak*, (P كنده *kanda*) A ditch round fortified towns, gardens, or fields; a fosse, moat.

A خنذقة *khanzakat*, The digging of a ditch.

A خنذوة *khunzuwat*, The peak of a mountain.

A خنذيان *khinziyān*, Obscene, foul-tongued.

A خنذيذ *khinzīz*, (pl. خناذيذ *khanāzīz*) The highest peak of a mountain. An excellent stone-horse. A gelding. A brave, invincible warrior. A mild, affable nobleman. An excellent poet. An eloquent orator. Obscene in talk. One thoroughly versed in the annals and poetry of the Arabians. Long, tall. Liberal, generous. A hurricane.

A خنّر *khunnar*, (pl. of خانر) Sincere friends.

A خنز *khanaz*, (v. n. of خنز) Becoming stale, stinking (meat). *Khanaz* or *khaniz*, Stinking, corrupted.

A خنزاب *khinzāb*, Bold in villainy.

A خنزب *khanzab*, Satan. Bold in villainy.

A خنزجة *khanzajat*, Pride, haughtiness.

A خنزرة *khanzarat*, A pointed instrument to break stones with. Thickness.

A خنزوان *khanzawān*, A boar. A male-ape. *Khunzuwān*, (خنزوانة *khunzuwānat*, خنزوانيّة *khunzuwāniyat*, and خنزوة *khunzuwat*) Pride. ذو خنزوانات *zū khunzuwānāt*, Proud.

A خنزوب *khunzūb*, Bold in wickedness.

A خنزير *khinzīr*, (pl. خنازير *khanāzīr*) A boar, hog, pig. P خنزير خسته حال *khinzīri khasta-hāl*, A wounded boar. A شحم الخنزير *shahmu'l khinzīr*, Hog's lard.

A خنزيرة *khinzīrat*, (fem. of خنزير) A sow.

P خنزيري *khinzīrī*, Hoggish. A hog-stie, piggery.

A خنس *khans*, (v. n. of خنس) Returning, retiring, receding, remaining behind, withdrawing. Concealing. Keeping back, hindering. Seizing hold of the thumb. Whispering any thing bad of some one absent. *Khuns*, (pl. of اخنس *akhnas* and خنساء *khansā*) Ape-nosed. Cows. *Khanas*, (v. n. of خنس) Having a turned-up nose. *Khunus*, Deer and their haunts. Cows.

A خنّس *khunnas*, Stars, planets (especially Venus and Mercury).

A خنساء *khansā*, (fem. of اخنس *akhnas*) Pug-nosed (woman). A wild cow. Name of a poetess.

P خنسار *khansār*, Name of an aquatic animal.

P خنستان *khunistān*, Fortunate, happy.

A خنسر *khansar*, (or خنسريّ *khansariy*) (pl. خناسرة *khanāsirat*) One who frequents the ways of error, the road to perdition. *Khinsar*, Low, mean, base. A misfortune, a calamity.

A خنسير *khinsīr*, Worthless, base, vile.

P خنشا *khunshā*, (خنشان *khunshān* or *khinshān*) Happy, fortunate.

A خنشفير *khanshafīr*, A heavy calamity.

A خنشل *khanshal*, A swift camel, thick and hard.

A خنشلة *khanshalat*, A tottering (from age).

A خنشليل *khanshalīl*, A swift, thick, and hard camel. Swift, fleet, expeditious.

A خنشوش *khanshūsh*, The residue of property. Some camels.

A خنصر *khinsir* or *khinsar*, (pl. خناصر *khanāsir*) The little (or middle) finger. The little toe.

A خنصيص *khinsīs*, A young tiger.

A خنضاب *khinzāb*, Pulp of the wild date.

A خنضبة *khunzubat*, Fat (woman).

A خنضرف *khanzarif*, A jolly, corpulent, full-breasted woman.

A خنط *khant*, (v. n. of خنط) Pressing heavily, weighing down the spirits.

A خنطثة *khantasat*, (v. n. of خنطث Q) Walking with a proud step or haughty air.

A خنطرف *khantarif*, Decrepit, tottering, woman.

A خنطل *khantal*, A misfortune. A dealer in perfumes. A flight of locusts.

A خنطليلة *khantalīlat*, A herd of camels or of oxen. Part of a cloud.

A خنطول *khuntūl*, A long horn or yard.

A خنطولة *khantūlat*, Part of a cloud. *Khuntūlat*, (pl. خناطيل *khanātīl*) A herd of camels or oxen.

A خنطير *khintīr*, A wrinkled hag.

A خنظأة *khanzaʼat*, A talking obscenely.

A خنظاة *khanzāt*, (v. n. of خنظي Q) Defaming, disparaging, slandering. Mocking, laughing at. Spoiling, damaging. Impelling, exciting.

A خنظبة *khunzubat*, A sort of reptile.

A خنظرف *khanzarif*, A decrepit woman.

A خنظوة *khunzuwat*, Summit of a mountain.

A خنظيان *khinziyān*, Obscene, impudent.

A خنع *khanʻ*, (v. n. of خنع) Whoring. Talking with the ladies. Being wicked. Softness. *Khunuʻ*, Submissive, abject men. (pl. of خنعة *khanʻat*) Doubts, suspicions, scandals.

A خنعابة *khinʻābat*, A mean, vile, contemptible fellow. Lightness, levity.

A خنعب *khanʻab*, Long hair.

A خنعبة *khunʻubat*, Any thing protuberant and pendulous from the upper lip. The groove which separates the mustachios.

A خنعة *khanʻat*, (pl. خنع *khunuʻ*) Doubt, suspicion, scandal. Adultery. An empty place. *Khanaʻat*, (pl. of خانع *khāniʻ*) Doubtful, suspicious. Submissive, abject.

A خنعس *khanʻas*, A hyena.

A خنف *khanf*, (v. n. of خنف) Cutting (an orange). Striking (her) breast (a woman). *Khanaf*, A contraction in one side of the breast or back. *Khunuf*, Vestiges, impressions. (pl. of خنوف *khanūf*) Weak in the feet, and turning them outwards. (pl. of خنيف *khanīf*) Coarse linen cloths. Roads.

A خنفة *khanfat* or *khinfat*, A shameful business. *Khanafat* or *khinafat*, A slice of an orange.

A خنفثة *khunfusat*, A certain small animal.

P خنفج *khinfij*, A black grain mixed up into an eye-salve.

A خنفج *khunfuj*, Very fleshy.

A خنفس *khunfas*, (*khinfis*, or خنفساء *khunfusā*) A beetle. يوم الخنفس *yawmu'l khanfas*, A certain memorable day with the Arabs.

A خنفسة *khanfasat*, (v. n. of خنفس Q) Departing, turning away from, abhorring. *Khunfasat* or *khunfusat*, A beetle. *Khunfasat* or *khunafisat*, A camel content with the poorest pasture.

P خنفشار *khanfashār*, A large species of duck.

A خنفع *khunfuʻ*, Foolish, silly, stupid.

A خنفقيق *khanfakīk*, Calamity, evil, misfortune. A spirited, lively woman. Very swift (she-camel).

A خنق *khanik*, (v. n. of خنق) Strangling. Strangled. *Khunuk*, Narrow (intervals), small (chinks or crannies).

P خنك *khunuk*, Good, excellent, well. Happy. Cold. Cool, temperate. Ease, facility. Self. A kinsman. آب خنك *ābi khunuk*, Cold water. هوائ خنك *hawā-i khunuk*, Fresh or temperate air.

P خنكا *khunkā*, O how happy! how good!

P خنكار *khunkār*, An emperor.

P خنك جان *khunuk-jān*, Of a cold soul or temperament. Chaste. Vindictive.

P خنك هوا *khunuk-hawā*, Salubrious, fresh.

P خنكي *khunukī*, Temperature, coldness. Prosperity. خنكىء دهن *khunukī-i dahan*, Coldness or sweetness of the mouth. خنكىء هوا *khunukī-i hawā*, Temperature of the air, somewhat cooled.

P خنگ *khang*, Depravity. *Khing*, White. Gray. White raiment. A bowstring. A gray horse. خنگ راهوار *khingi rāhwār*, An ambling nag. خنگ زر *khingi zar*, The sun. خنگ شب آهنگ *khingi shab-āhang*, The moon. Break of day. A piebald horse. The quadruped on which Muhammad is said to have gone to heaven on the night of معراج *mi'rāj*. *Khung*, An angle, corner. Deeply in love. Intense love.

P خنگا *khingā*, An athletic clown. Able-bodied.

P خنگال *khingāl*, A perforated mark to shoot at.

P خنگ بت *khing-but*, (Gray image) Name of one of two huge idols in Bāmiān. The other is called سرخ بت *surkh but*, Red image.

P خنگ بيد *khing-bīd*, A thorn. White thorn.

P خنگ زيور *khing-ziwar*, A piebald horse.

P خنگسار *khing-sār*, Gray-headed. Saltpetre.

P خنگل *khangal*, A kind of armour.

P خنگو *khingū*, A sort of dodder.

P خنگ و لوك *khing u lūk*, Weak, unskilful.

A خنمة *khanamat*, A difficulty of breathing in blowing the nose.

A خننة *khunanat*, A large aged bull.

A خنو *khanw*, A being obscene in speech.

A خنوة *khanwat*, A chink, crack in a small house. Human excrement.

A خنّوت *khinnawt*, A kind of marine animal. Ignorant, stupid. An active, restless fellow, who does not sleep upon a mattrass.

A خنوخ *khanūkh*, The prophet Enoch.

P خنور *khanūr*, A sower, cultivator. *Khanūr*, *khunūr*, or خنّور *khunnūr*, Household utensils, as pots, pans, knives, or hatchets. An earthen vessel for keeping money in. Two packs thrown across a horse, between which the rider is seated. Tillage.

A خنوّر *khanawwar* or خنّور *khinnawr*, The world. امّ خنّور *ummu khannūrin* or *khinnawrin*, A hyena. A cow. Prosperity. Adversity. The fundament. Egypt. Basrah. *Khannūr* or *khanawwar*, A reed, of which they make arrows. Any soft or withered plant. Prosperity, favour, comforts.

A خنوز *khunūz*, (v. n. of خنز) Stinking, becoming stale (meat).

A خنّوز *khannūz*, A hyena. The rear rank.

A خنوس *khunūs*, (v. n. of خنس) Staying behind. Lying hid. Setting, withdrawing (stars). Concealing. Keeping back, hindering. Seizing hold of the thumb. Traducing the absent.

A خنّوس *khinnaws*, A lion.

A خنّوص *khinnaws*, (pl. خنانيص *khanānīs*) A porkling. Any young animal.

A خنّوصة *khinnawsat*, A young tiger. A palm-tree within hand's reach.

A خنوع *khanū'*, A deceiver, a promise-breaker. *Khunū'*, Submission, humility.

A خنوف *khanūf*, (pl. خنف *khunuf*) Weak-footed, turning outwards (camel). *Khunūf*, Anger.

A خني *khany*, (v. n. of خني) Cutting (the trunk of a palm-tree). *Khana'* (v. n. of خنى) Ruining, destroying. Abounding in herbage (a place). Being full of eggs (a locust). Speaking obscenely. Bearing hard upon one (fortune). The injuries of time. *Khanī*, Obscene talk.

P خنيا *khunyā*, Modulation, melody, song.

P خنياگر *khunyāgar*, A musician, singer, bard, minstrel. خنياگر فلك *khunyāgari falak*, Venus.

P خنياگري *khunyāgarī*, Minstrelsy.

A خنية *khaniyat*, Obscene talk.

A خنيثة *khunaysat*, An old catamite.

P خنيد *khanīd*, The ringing noise made by a goblet. Fame, celebrity. *Khinīd*, Sucked. *Khunīd*, Approbation. Approved, acceptable.

P خنيدن *khanīdan*, To twist. To echo. To obtain celebrity. *Khinīdan*, To suck.

P خنيده *khanīda*, Sound, echo. Celebrated. A skilful musician. Agreeable, chosen, approved. *Khinīda*, Sucked. *Khunīda*, Celebrated, praised by every one.

A خنيز *khanīz*, Unleavened bread broken into pieces (upon which they pour liquor).

A خنيف *khanīf*, (pl. خنف *khunuf*) The worst flax. Coarse hempen cloth. A road. The part under the armpit or oxter of a camel. Cheerfulness, sprightliness. Abounding in milk (camel).

A خنيق *khanīk*, Strangled.

P خنيك *khunīk*, A gray dervish's garment.

A خنين *khanīn*, A sound resembling laughing or crying through the nose.

P خنيور *khanewar* or *khunewar*, A narrow bridge across the infernal fire. A cultivator, sower. The general resurrection.

P خو *khav*, Ivy. Tares, darnel. The palm of the hand. The sole of a beast's foot. Any parasitical plant. A plank upon which masons, plasterers, or painters stand when at work. A framework for turning an arch upon. A plucking up. A lopping away of branches. The fundament of a horse. A handful. *Khū*, (*khu* or *kho*) Habit, nature, custom.

A خوّ *khaww*, Hunger. A wide river or valley. *Khūw*, Honey.

P خوا *khawā*, Flesh, meat. *Khiwā*, Taste, flavour, relish, delight. *Khuwā*, Food enough for a day.

A خوا *khawa'*, Emptiness of belly from hunger. A hemorrhage.

A خواء *khawā'*, (v. n. of خوي) Falling down and being deserted (a house). Being empty and clinging (the belly). Failing to strike fire. A hemorrhage from the nose. The space between the fore and hind legs of a horse. Space between any two things. Empty.

P خواب *khwāb*, Sleep. A dream. Nocturnal pollution. Pile, plush. خواب جاويد *khwābi jāwīd*, Eternal sleep, death. خواب خرگوش *khwābi khargosh*, A hare's sleep, (met.) negligence, inadvertency. Feigned negligence. خواب ديدن *khwāb dīdan*, To see in sleep, *i. e.* To dream. To be polluted. بخواب رفتن *ba khwāb raftan*, To go to sleep. خواب سبك *khwābi sabuk*, A light slumber. خواب شدن *khwāb shudan*, To sleep, to be asleep. در خواب شدن *dar khwāb shudan*, To be in bed, to be asleep. To sleep standing, to be stupid. خواب كردن *khwāb kardan*, To sleep, to take a nap. خواب نوشين *khwābi noshīn*, Sweet, sound sleep. خواب و خور *khwāb u khwur*, Bed and board.

A خوابّ *khawābb*, (pl. of خابّة) Kindreds.

P خواب آلود *khwāb-ālūd*, Stained or drowned in sleep, sleepy.

P خواب آلودگي *khwāb-ālūdagī*, Drowsiness.

P خوابانيدن *khwābānīdan*, To cause or put one to sleep. To cause to kneel. To tump or cover with earth (unripe fruits) in order to mellow them. To oppress, beat down. To thicken (milk).

P خواب بينا *khwāb-bīnā*, Dreaming: a dreamer.

P خواب پريشان *khwāb-pareshān*, Horrid dream.

P خواب جامه *khwāb-jāma*, A sleeping-dress.

P خوابخانه *khwāb-khāna*, (خوابگاه *khwāb-gāh*, or خوابگه *khwāb-gah*) A bed, couch. A chamber, dormitory. خوابگاه غول *khwāb-gāhi ghūl*, The world.

P خواب خيال *khwāb-khiyāl*, A spectre, phantom.

P خواب دار *khwāb-dār*, Pily, plushy (velvet, &c.).

P خواب ديده *khwāb-dīda*, Dreaming. Polluted.

P خواب رفتگي *khwāb-raftagī*, Torpor, numbness.

P خواب رفته *khwāb-rafta*, Torpid, asleep (limb).

P خوابستان *khwābistān*, A dormitory.

P خواب گذار *khwāb-guzār*, Somnolent.

P خواب نا ديده *khwāb nā dīda*, Under puberty.

P خوابناك *khwābnāk*, Sleepy, drowsy. Pily, plushy (velvet or silk).

P خوابنوش *khwāb-nosh*, Sleeping.

P خوابنوشي *khwāb-noshī*, A doze, a nap.

P خوابنيدن *khwābanīdan*, To put one to sleep.

P خوابه *khwāba*, as همخوابه *ham-khwāba*, A bedfellow.

A خوابي *khawābī*, (pl. of خابئة) Jars (for wine).

P خوابيدگي *khwābīdagī*, Negligence.

P خوابيدن *khwābīdan*, To lie down. To sleep. To kneel.

P خوابيده *khwābīda*, Asleep. Dormant.

A خوات *khawāt*, (v. n. of خات for خوت) Pouncing upon (his) prey (an eagle). Impairing, diminishing. Breaking an agreement. Noise of a flying bird of mighty wing, of thunder, or a torrent.

A خوّات *khawwāt*, An intrepid man. One who eats every hour, but little at a time.

A خواتم *khawātim*, (or خواتيم *khawātīm*) (pl. of خاتم *khātam*, *khātim*, ختام *khutām*, خاتام *khātām* and خيتام *khaytām*) Seals. Conclusions, endings.

A خواتين *khawātīn*, (pl. of P خاتون) Ladies.

P خواجگان *khwājagān*, Masters.

P خواجگی *khwājagī*, A wealthy merchant. Chiefship, mastership.

P خواجه *khwāja*, A man of distinction. A rich merchant. A doctor, professor, teacher, preceptor, schoolmaster: a pedant. Lord, master, owner. The master of a family. A bird's comb. A venerable old man. Heart, soul. An eunuch. خواجهٔ اختران *khwājasi akhtarān*, (Lord of the stars) The planet Jupiter. The sun. خواجهٔ بعث و نشر *khwājasi bas u nashr*, Lord of the resurrection, *i.e.* Muhammad. خواجهٔ چرخ ازرق *khwājasi charkhi azrak*, The sun. خواجهٔ سپهر *khwājasi sipihr*, The sun. خواجه سه ياران *khwāja sih yārān*, Name of a place of recreation close to Kābul. خواجه سرا *khwāja-sarā*, A domestic. A eunuch. خواجهٔ فلك *khwājasi falak*, The sun. Jupiter. خواجه كردن *khwāja kardan*, To castrate. خواجه گياه *khwāja giyāh*, Name of a shrub. خواجه مسّاح *khwāja massāh*, Muhammad.

P خواجه بار *khwāja-bār*, Enough to support life.

P خواجه تاش *khwāja-tāsh*, A fellow-servant. The master of a family. A scholar, school-fellow.

P خواجيدن *khwājīdan* or *khuwājīdan*, To see badly from an infirmity in the eyes. To water, to be hot (the eye).

A خواذ *khiwāz*, (v. n. 3 of خوذ not in use) Dissenting from, resisting. Consenting to, agreeing. A flying fever, the fits of which are uncertain in point of time.

P خوار *khwār*, Contemptible, abject. Poor, distressed, abandoned, friendless, wretched. Few, small, little. Easy. Soft, tender. Erect, straight. Name of a place near Ray. (in comp.) Eating or drinking. خوار داشتن *khwār dāshtan*, To hold in contempt, despise. مفت خوار *muft-khwār*, Eating for nothing, *i.e.* a parasite. *Khuwār*, Victuals.

A خوار *khuwār*, The lowing of oxen, bleating of sheep, goats, or fallow-deer. The whiz of an arrow.

A خوّار *khawwār*, (pl. خور *khūr*) Weak, soft (man or wood). Sensitive (camel). Slender (spear). Low or sloping (ground). A fire-steel. A skilful genealogist. خوّار العنان *khawwāru'l ɛinān*, Obedient to the rein and going well (horse).

P خوار بار *khwār-bār*, Food. Provisions carried from town to town. A small competency. Taste, relish. A place near Ray. A district belonging to Bokhārā.

P خواربار آرنده *khwārbār-āranda*, A purveyor.

P خواربار كش *khwārbār-kash*, A transporter of provisions.

A خوّارة *khawwārat*, Hips, buttocks. A palm-tree bearing abundantly. (pl. خور *khūr*) (A camel) abounding in milk.

A خوارج *khawārij*, (pl. of خارجيّ *khārijīy*) Heretics, schismatics. Those who rebelled against Alīy. Strangers (of a different religion). Rebels. خوارج المال *khawāriju'l māl*, Mares, she-asses, and handmaids. خرجت خوارجه *kharajat khawārijuhu*, His generosity or nobility appeared. He proceeded for the settling of his affairs.

P خوار خوري *khwār-khwurī*, Base treatment.

P خواردن *khwārdan*, To eat. To drink.

P خوارزم *khuwārazm* or *khwārazm*, Khorasmia, the ancient Chorasmu, lying along the banks of the great river Oxus or Jayhūn, and extending to the Caspian Sea; part of it belonging to Irān (Persia), and part to Tūrān (Parthia).

P خوارزمي *khwārazmī*, A Khorasmian. Thin slices of paste.

A خوارق *khawārik*, (pl. of خارق *khārik*) Penetrating, tearing (spears). Miracles, unusual things.

P خوار كار *khwār-kār*, An oppressor. A scorner.

P خوار كاره *khwār-kāra*, A reviler.

P خوار كاري *khwār-kārī*, Reproach. A reviler.

P خوارمندي *khwārmandī*, Humility; abjectness.

P خوارنيدن *khwāranīdan*, To give to eat and drink.

P خوار و زار *khwār u zār*, Abject and distressed.

P خواره *khwāra*, Stipend, every-day allowance. Victuals. *Khuwāra*, Established order. Mode, manner. Strengthening food. A frame for turning an arch upon. A scaffold.

P خواري *khwārī*, Baseness, meanness. Distress. خواري كردن *khwārī kardan*, To revile. To injure. خواري نمودن *khwārī namūdan*, To abase one's self.

P خواري خوار *khwārī-khwār*, Reviled, abused.

A خوارين *khawārīn*, (pl. of خوران *khawrān*) Fundaments of animals.

P خواز *khawāz*, A goad. A clothes-horse.

P خوازنده *khwāzanda*, A bride.

P خوازه *khwāza*, A triumphal arch. A vine-arbour. A plank on which masons or plasterers stand when at work: a scaffold. The inner apartment, alcove, or bower, surrounded with tapestry, where the royal bride awaits the arrival of her husband. A benediction. Praise, applause. Desire, wish. *Khawāza*, An arch, bower, or alcove decorated with flowers, under which the bride awaits the arrival of her husband.

P خواس *khwās*, A petitioner. *Khawās*, Fear.

P خواست *khwāst*, Petition, request, begging, solicitation, desire, wish. Will. He desired or asked. A beaten road. An island. Gold. Riches. Furniture. خواست خدا *khwāsti khudā*, The will of God.

P خواستار *khwāstār*, A petitioner, asker. Those whose son and daughter have married together.

P خواستاري *khwāstārī*, Wedlock.

P خواستران *khwāstarān*, Small worms.

P خواستگار *khwāstgār*, Petitioner, candidate.

P خواستگاري *khwāstgārī*, Request, wish. A matrimonial suit. خواستگاري نمودن *khwāstgārī namūdan*, (or كردن *kardan*) To betroth.

P خواستن *khwāstan*, To desire, wish, demand require, need, petition, beg, or pray. To will, to want. To wed. To mean, intend. عذر خواستن *ɛuzr khwāstan*, To beg pardon.

P خواسته *khwāsta*, Desired, wished, willed, wanted. Meant, intended. Wedded. Meaning, signification. Riches, possessions. The needful for travelling, requisites for carrying on war.

P خواسه *khwāsa*, A scarecrow (in a field).

A خوّاص *khawwāṣ*, A vender of palm-leaves (خوص *khūṣ*); one who covers baskets with them.

A خواصّ *khawāṣṣ*, (pl. of خاصّة *khāṣṣat*) Properties, qualities. Virtues. Attributes (of deity). Grandees, ministers of state, royal favourites, or domestics; attendants on the king's person. خواصّ و عوامّ *khawāṣṣ u ɛawāmm*, Noble and ignoble, the whole people.

A خواصر *khawāṣir*, (pl. of خاصرة *khāṣirat*) Waists.

A خواصي *khawāṣī*, The place where one sits behind a great man upon an elephant.

A خوّاض *khawwāz*, One who plunges into or encounters. Whatever recurs to the mind.

A خواطر *khawāṭir*, (pl. of خاطر) Thoughts, minds.

A خواطف *khawāṭif*, (pl. of خاطف) Lightnings.

A خواطئ *khawāṭiʼ*, (pl. of خاطئ *khāṭiʼ*) Delinquents. (Arrows) which deviate from the mark. مع الخواطئ سهم صائب *maɛ al khawāṭiʼ sahm ṣāʼib*, With the (many) arrows that miss one that hits (said of any one, who, though often blundering, is occasionally right).

A خواع *khuwāɛ*, Stupor, astonishment. A noise made through the nose.

A خواعة *khuwāɛat*, Phlegm. Mucus.

A خواف *khawāf*, Tumult, murmur, noise.

A خوافق *khawāfik*, The four cardinal points.

A خوافي *khawāfī*, (pl. of خافي *khāfī*) Demons. (pl of خافية *khāfiyat*) Secrets. The shortest feathers of the wing (the ten nearest the body). The branches of a palm-tree nearest to the pith.

A خواقين *khawākīn*, (pl. of خاقان *khākān*) Emperors, kings. سلاطين زمان و خواقين دوران *salāṭīni zamān u khawākīni dawrān*, The kings of the times and monarchs of the age, *i.e.* The reigning princes.

P خواگ *khwāg*, A hen. An egg: a fried egg.

P خوال *khwāl* or *khuwāl*, Lamp-black. Food.

A خوالد *khawālid*, Trevets. The base and solid parts of a rock. Huge stones or mountains which resist the violence of the winds.

P خوالستان *khwālistān*, An inkstand.

P خوالسته *khwālista*, Silk put into an inkstand.

An ink-horn.

A خوالف *khawālif*, (pl. of خالفة *khālifat*) Tent-poles. Women. Grounds which bear late. ايّ الخوالف هو *ayyu'l khawālif huwa*, What manner of person he is (I know not).

A خوالق *khawālik*, Smooth mountains.

P خوالگر *khwālgar*, A cook: a sewer, table-decker.

P خوالنجان *khwālinjān*, (or خوالنجن) Galangale.

P خوالي *khwālī* or *khiwālī*, Food. A river's bed. A kitchen. Beautiful, adorned. Congratulated.

P خواليدن *khwālīdan*, To spread, expand, strew. To taste. *Khawālīdan*, To come. To eat. To sleep.

P خواليگر *khwāligar* or *khiwāligar*, A cook. A sewer, a table-decker.

P خوامزة *khwā-maza*, A competency.

A خوامس *khawāmis*, Camels drinking on the fifth day.

A خوامش *khawāmish*, (pl. of خامشة) Rills.

A خوامع *khawāmiع*, (pl. of خامعة) Hyenas.

P خوان *khwān*, A table, covered table, and the meat upon it. A spacious tray. Household furniture. Rubbish of sticks and straws. Weeds, tares. (in compos.) Reading: a reader. Asking, begging. A chanter. A crier, invoker, inviter. خوان دل *khwāni dil*, The temple at Mecca. خوان يغما *khwāni yaghmā*, A public feast to which all are invited, an open table. انگشت الله خوان *angushti allāh-khwān*, The finger that appeals to God, namely, The fore-finger. ذكر خوان *zikr-khwān*, A praiser of God. خوش خوان *khwush-khwān*, Reading well.

A خوان *khiwān* or *khuwān*, (pl. اخونة *akhwinat* and خون *khūn*) A dinner-table.

A خوّان *khawwān*, A deceiver, traitor. A lion. P خوّان مظلمه كار *khawwāni mazlama-kār*, A villain, cruel betrayer. A *Khawwān* or *khuwān*, (pl. اخونة *akhwinat*, خون *khawn* and *khūn*) Name of the third month with the Pagan Arabians. *Khuwān*, (pl. of خائن *khāʼin*) Faithless, perfidious. Traitors.

P خوانا *khwānā* or *khūnā*, Legible.

P خوان پايه *khwān-pāya*, A table-cloth.

P خوانپوش *khwān-posh*, Coverlid of a tray.

A خوّانة *khawwānat*, The backside.

P خوانچه *khwāncha*, A tray, a salver. خوانچهٔ زر *khwānchaʼi zar*, (or سپهر *sipihr*) The sun.

P خواندگي *khwāndagī*, Reading, recital. Invocation. Calling. Adoption.

P خواندن *khwāndan* or *khūndan*, To read, to recite. To invite, invoke, convoke, call. To sing, to chaunt. To decipher.

P خواندني *khwāndanī* or *khūndanī*, What ought to be read: a سي پاره *sī pāra*, or a portion (a thirtieth) of the Kur'ān appointed for daily reading.

P خوانده *khwānda*, Read. Sung. Called, invited. Knowing how to read and write. نا خوانده *nā khwānda*, Unable to read: unread.

P خوانسار *khwān-sār*, A sewer, table-decker.

P خوانسالار *khwān-sālār*, A table-decker. A cook.

P خوانسامان *khwān-sāmān*, A house-steward.

A خوانق *khawānik*, (pl. of P خانقاه) Monasteries.

P خوان كرم *khwān-karam*, Open house, or table.

P خوانگر *khwāngar*, A cook. A table-decker.

P خوانندگي *khwānan* or *khūnandagī*, Singing.

P خواننده *khwānanda* or *khūnanda*, A reader. A crier or convoker. A caller. A singer. A student.

P خوانيدن *khwānīdan* or *khūnīdan*, To read. To make read. To call, convene. To sing.

A خوانيق *khawānīk*, Quinseys.

A خوانين *khawānīn*, (pl. of خان *khān*) Lords.

P خواو *khwāv*, (equiv. to خواب *khwāb*) Sleep.

P خواه *khwāh*, Wishing, desiring, needing, wanting, requiring, calling for. Desire, petition. Either, or, whether. ترقيخواه *tarakkī-khwāh*, Wishing increase. خاطر خواه *khātir-khwāh*, The desire of one's heart. دولت خواه *dawlat-khwāh*, Wishing prosperity, benevolent, kind. مرمّت خواه *maram-mat-khwāh*, Needing repair (a house). خواه مخواه *khwāh ma khwāh*, Willing or no. Certainly, positively, at all events. خواه و نا خواه *khwāh u nā khwāh*, Nolens volens, against the inclination.

P خواهان *khwāhān*, Willing, desiring: petitioners.

P خواهاني *khwāhānī*, Wish, desire, longing for.

P خواهانيدن *khwāhānīdan*, To wish. To ask. To cause to petition. To cause to wish, will, want.

P خواهر *khwāhar*, A sister. خواهر پدر *khwāhari pidar*, Aunt, father's sister. خواهر شوي *khwāhari shūy*, Husband's sister. خواهر مادر *khwāhari mādar*, Maternal aunt.

P خواهران *khwāharān*, Sisters. خواهران سهيل *khwāharāni suhayl*, Two stars, called by the Arabs اختا سهيل *ukhtā suhayl*.

P خواهر اندر *khwāhar-andar*, A half-sister.

P خواهر خوانده *khwāhar-khwānda*, (or خواهر گير *khwāhar-gīr*) An adopted sister.

P خواهر زاده *khwāhar-zāda*, Sister's son.

P خواهش *khwāhish*, Will, wish, inclination. Petition, suit. Riches. Intercession, advocacy. خواهش الهي *khwāhishi ilāhī*, The divine will.

P خواهش گر *khwāhishgar*, Intercessor, advocate.

P خواهش گري *khwāhishgarī*, Intercession.

P خواهل *khwāhil*, *khūhil*, *khuwāhil*, Crooked, curved. A shoemaker's strap, with which he binds the last to his knee; also the piece of wood upon which it is bound.

P خواهنده *khwāhanda*, One who asks, wills, wants, or wishes: a beggar, petitioner.

P خواهه *khwāha*, A petition. Desire, intent.

P خواهيدن *khwāhīdan*, To petition, intercede. To will, want.

P خواي *khwāy*, Taste, flavour: pleasure, delight.

A خواية *khawāyat*, (v. n. of خوي) Falling and becoming deserted (a house). Seizing, carrying off. Being reduced and fallen in (a woman who has recently brought forth). The hollow part of a spear-head into which the staff is inserted. Large within (man). Swift, light (horse). Swiftness in a horse. Width or space inside a packsaddle.

A خوب *khawb*, A being reduced to poverty.

P خوب *khūb*, Good. Beautiful, elegant, pleasant, graceful, lovely, amiable, charming, excellent, or gracious. Beautifully, excellently. Firm, strong. خوب صورت و پاك سيرت *khūb-sūrat u pāk-sīrat*, Elegant in form and pure in mind.

P خوبار *khūb-ār*, Convenient and inconvenient. Carrying any thing to be eaten. Provisions transported from place to place.

P خو باز كردن *kho bāz kardan*, To quit a habit.

P خوبان *khūbān*, (pl.) The fair. The good.

P خوباني *khūbānī*, Apricots stuffed with almonds.

P خوب آواز *khūb-āwāz*, Charming-voiced.

A خوبة *khawbat*, Ground without rain (between fields that have rain); likewise without herbage; barren. Hunger.

P خوبتر *khūbtar*, Better. More beautiful.

P خوبترين *khūbtarīn*, Best, fairest.

P خوب رائحه *khūb-rāʼiha*, Pleasant-scented.

P خوب رو *khūb-rū*, (or روي *rūy*) Lovely-faced.

P خوب رويان *khūb-rūyān*, (plur.) The fair.

P خوب روئي *khūb-rūʼī*, Comeliness of face.

P خوبكلا *khūbkalā*, (or خوبكلان *khūbkalān*) Name of a seed of a cooling quality.

P خوب منظر *khūb-manzar*, Handsome, fair.

P خوبي *khūbī*, Goodness, excellence. Beauty.

P خوپخين *khūpkhīn*, The substance called mummy, whether human or mineral.

P خوپذير *khu* or *kho-pazīr*, Accustomed to.

P خوپله *khwapla*, Foolish, ignorant.

A خوّة *khuwat*, Adversity. Waste ground.

A خوت *khawt*, (v. n. of خات for خوت) Pouncing on his prey (a falcon). Breaking a promise. Diminishing, lessening (provisions). Seizing, carrying off. Impairing. Growing old. Driving, impelling, pursuing.

A خوتع *khawtaع*, A skilful guide. A leveret. A sort of yellow fly found in grass. Cupidity. Vile, base, ignoble.

A خوتعة *khawtaعat*, A dwarf. A man's name.

A خوتل *khawtal*, Elegant, graceful, witty.

A خوتلى *khawtalā*, A clandestine step behind a curtain, or behind whatever else conceals a person from view.

A خوث *khawas*, (v. n. of خاث for خوث) Having a flabby, pendulous belly. Being filled, satiated. Familiarity, intimacy.

A خوثاء *khawsāʼ*, Swag-bellied (woman). A tender virgin.

A خوثع *khawsaع*, Base, vile, ignoble.

P خوچ *khoch*, The comb or the crest of a bird. Cock's-comb (a flower). Tuft of a helmet. Peak of a house. A red silk neckcloth. A fighting ram.

P خوچه *khocha*, The comb of a cock, crest of a bird. The flower called cock's-comb.

P خوچیدن *khochīdan*, To see badly from weakness in the eyes. To water, to be hard, dry, and hot (the eyes).

A خوخ *khawkh*, A peach.

A خوخاء *khawkhāʼ*, (fem. خوخاءة *khawkhāʼat*) (pl. خوخاؤون *khawkhāʼūna*) Foolish.

P خوخ اقرع *khokh akraʻ*, Indian leaf.

A خوخة *khawkhat*, A window, skylight, little window. The backside. A space between two houses, unenclosed by a door. A kind of green garment. (pl. خوخ *khawkh*) A peach.

P خوخو *khawkhaw*, (in zand and Pāzand) Rite, custom. A sword. Power, strength. A branch. A bricklayer's scaffold.

A خود *khawd*, (pl. خودات *khawdāt* or خود *khūd*) A beautiful young girl.

P خود *khūd*, A helmet. خود خروچ *khūdi khuroch*, (or خروه *khuroh*) A cock's comb. The anemone. *Khwud*, Self. Himself, herself, itself. But. خود اختیاري *khwud-ikhtiyārī*, Self-controul, self-government, self-possession. خود آراي *khwud-ārāy*, Pride, arrogance, conceit; display of one's own merits. خود بخود *khwud ba khwud*, Of himself, spontaneously. خود بدولت *khwud ba dawlat*, You, your worship. Sir. خود بسوز *khwud ba soz*, Name of a fire-temple in Azarbayjān. خود بهائي *khwud-bahāʼī*, Vanity. خود بین *khwud-bīn*, Seeing himself, *i.e.* Proud, self-conceited. خود بیني *khwud-bīnī*, Arrogance, presumption. خود پرست *khwud-parast*, A worshipper or admirer of himself. خود پرستي *khwud-parastī*, Self-conceit. Selfishness. خود پسند *khwud-pasand*, Self-approved, vain, conceited, opiniated. خود پسندي *khwud-pasandī*, Self-complacency. خود پیرائي *khwud-perāʼī*, Ostentation. خود ثنا *khwud-sanā*, A boaster. An egotist. خود حکم *khwud-hukm*, Obstinate. خود خو *khwud-kho*, Uneducated, undisciplined. Capricious. خود خواه *khwud-khwāh*, Selfish. خود دار *khwud-dār*, Content. Patient. Master of one's self. خود راي *khwud-rāy*, Self-opiniated. A fantastical, capricious humourist. خود رائي *khwud-rāʼī*, Self-conceitedness. خود رخصتي *khwud-rukhsatī*, Leaving a service of one's own accord, in which case it is customary to deduct something from wages. خود رسته *khwud-rusta*, Self-grown, wild, spontaneous. خود رنگ *khwud-rang*, Preserving the natural colour, unchanged; also yellowish colour. خود رو *khwud-rū*, With her own face, *i.e.* unpainted, adorned with native beauty. *Khwud-ro*, Spontaneous, self-growing, unplanted. خود روي *khwud-rūy*, Ill-disciplined. Spontaneous growth. خود روئي *khwud-roʼī*, Spontaneous growth. خود ستائي *khwud-sitāʼī*, Self-applause, vain-boasting. خود سر *khwud-sar*, Bold, fearless. Self-opiniated, obstinate, whimsical. Headstrong. خود سوز *khwud-soz*, Name of a fire-temple in Azarbayjān. خود غرض *khwud-gharaz*, Self-interested. خود غلط *khwud-ghalat*, Wrong-headed. خود فروش *khwud-farosh*, Selling himself, *i.e.* boasting, vaunting. خود کاره *khwud-kāra*, Acting for one's self, trusting to none. خود کاشت *khwud-kāsht*, Cultivation of one's own soil. خود کاشته *khwud-kāshta*, Self-cultivated (*i.e.* by the farmer himself). خود کام *khwud-kām*, Self-will. Living like a libertine, following his own fancy; arrogant. خود کامه *khwud-kāma*, Self-willed, opiniated. Gaining the object of one's desires. Growing spontaneously. خود کامي *khwud-kāmī*, Self-interestedness; wilfulness. خود کرده *khwud-karda*, Done of himself. خود نما *khwud-namā*, Vain, arrogant. Growing spontaneously. خود نمائي *khwud-namāʼī*, Ostentation. *Khwud* is sometimes affixed to pronouns: as, من خود *man khwud*, I myself (ego ipse). بخودي خود *ba khwudī khwud*, Of one's self, of one's own accord.

P خود ساز *khūd-sāz*, A maker of helmets.

P خود سازي *khūd-sāzī*, Helmet-making.

P خودستان *khwadistān* or *khwudustān*, Vine-shoots which are eaten young.

P خوده *khūda*, An arch, a vault. Truth.

P خودها *khwudhā*, Selves.

P خودي *khwudī*, Selfishness, conceit, egotism.

P خوديسوز *khwudī-soz*, A fire-temple in Azarbayjān.

A خوذ *khuwaz*, (pl. of خوذة *khūzat*) Helmets.

A خوذان *khawzān*, Servants, domestics. ذهب في خوذان الخامل *zahaba fī khawzāni'l khāmil*, He was ranked in a low grade of society.

A خوذة *khūzat*, A helmet. Headache.

A خور *khawr*, (v. n. of خار for خور) Striking or piercing (an animal, especially about the podex). A valley, low ground. A bay, gulf. Mouth of a river; an estuary, frith. *Khūr*, Women suspected of vice. (pl. of خوّارة *khawwārat*) (Camels) full of milk. *Khawar*, Weakness.

A خؤر *khuʼūr*, A becoming weak and languid.

P خور *khwur*, Despicable, contemptible, abject, mean, vile, base, infamous. Worthy, proper, agreeable to. The east. A partner, consort. Light, radiance. The sun. Name of an angel. The eleventh day of every solar month. Food sufficient for the support of life. Meat. Flavour, relish, taste. A chameleon. A palace, villa. The famous palace of Khawarnak. خور و حقیر داشتن *khwur u hakīr dāshtan*, To render despicable and hapless. (in compos.) Eating or consuming; as, مردم خور *mardum-khwur*, Devouring men, *i.e.* a fierce warrior. میراث خور *mīrās-khwur*, Inheriting.

P خورا *khwurā*, Worthy, suitable. Few provisions. Eating, voracious. A gangrene, cancer.

P خوراب *khwur-āb*, Impure water. A cataract. The dam of a sluice. An itch for drinking.

P خورابه *khwur-āba*, A little stream brought from a larger river for the purposes of cultivation. Water to drink. A farmer furnished with all the means and appliances of cultivation. A little water oozing through an embankment.

P خوراك *khwurāk*, Food, victuals, provisions. Daily bread, eatables. One meal. One dose of medicine. (in India) A kind of batta given by villagers to peons sent to collect the circar-duties.

P خوراكي *khwurākī*, Daily allowance of food or money to purchase it, subsistence-money.

A خوران *khawrān*, (pl. خورانات *khawrānāt* or خوارين *khawārīn*) The podex of quadrupeds.

P خوران *khwurān*, Name of one of the champions of Kay Khusrav son of Siyāvash. Eating, devouring. Voracious, gluttonous.

A خورانات *khawrānāt*, Fundaments.

P خوراندن *khwurāndan*, To eat or drink.

P خوراهه *khūrāha* or *khwarāha*, A cock's comb.

P خوراي *khwurāy*, A few provisions. Arranged. Elegant.

P خوربار *khwur-bār*, Serving up a repast. A hamper of provisions. Suitable and unsuitable.

P خورپاره *khwur-pāra*, Bits, fragments, orts.

P خورپرست *khwur-parast*, A sun-worshipper. The sunflower.

A خورة *khūrat*, Best, choicest of any thing.

P خورچین *khwur-chīn*, A portmanteau, wallet. خورچین کردن *khwur-chīn kardan*, To glean, lease.

P خورخجیون *khwurkhajīwan*, Nightmare.

P خورد *khwurd*, Little, small, minute, petty, tiny. Short. Suitable, proper. A meeting. A public address. Meat, victuals. Eating. He did eat. He met. He brake in pieces. پشهٔ خورد *pashaʼi khwurd*, A little gnat. شیر خورد *shīri khwurd*, Skim-milk. خورد کردن *khwurd kardan*, To bruise small. خورد مرد *khwurd murd*, Minutiæ of any kind. خورد و خواب *khwurd u khwāb*, One who does nothing except eat, drink, and sleep. خورد و کلان *khwurd u kalān*, (or خورد و بزرگ *khwurd u buzurg*) Small and great, all.

P خورداد *khwur-dād*, Name of the third month.

P خوردار *khwur-dār*, A boarded domestic.

P خوردتر *khwurdtar*, Smaller, younger.

P خورد سال *khwurd-sāl*, Of tender years.

P خورد سالان *khwurd-sālān*, Young ones.

P خوردستان *khwardustān*, (also خوردوستان *khwardūstān*) Yong vine-shoots which are eaten for their freshness. Any young shoot.

P خوردگان *khwurdagān*, Juniors, inferiors.

P خوردگي *khwurdagī*, Corrosion. A draught. An eating or drinking.

P خورد محل *khwurd-mahal*, The apartments of the concubines of great men.

P خوردن *khwurdan*, To eat. To gnaw. To drink. To bit. To nip. To strike. To devour, destroy. To take. To grate. To suffer. شیر خوردن *shīr khwurdan*, To drink milk. غم خوردن *gham khwurdan*, To devour sorrow, to be afflicted. سوگند خوردن *sawgand khwurdan*, To swallow an oath, to swear. عذاب خوردن *ʿazāb khwurdan*, To suffer torment. خوف خوردن *khawf khwurdan*, To fear. بازي خوردن *bāzī khwurdan*, To be gulled, cheated, hoaxed; to swallow a gudgeon.

P خوردني *khwurdanī*, Fit to be eaten, edible, esculent. Provisions, victuals, food. A repast. A beverage. سبزيء خوردني *sabzī-i khwurdanī*, An esculent vegetable; greens.

P خورده *khwurda*, Eaten. Devoured, corroded. Eating. A spark. Quickness, acuteness. A bit, scrap. A crumb. A speck. A fault. That part of a (horse's) leg which is enclosed in the fetter. Minute, slender. درد خورده *dard-khwurda*, Affected with pain. خنزير تير خورده *khinzīri tīr-khwurda*, A boar wounded by a dart. خوردهٔ انبان *khwurda-i ambān*, Crumbs in a wallet. خورده كردن *khwurda kardan*, To change money.

P خورده اديم *khwurda-adīm*, An acorn for tanning leather.

P خورده بين *khwurda-bīn*, Caviller. Microscopic.

P خورده بيني *khwurda-bīnī*, Criticism. Cavil. Microscopy.

P خورده پز *khwurda-paz*, A cook.

P خورده خوان *khwurda-khwān*, A small table.

P خورده دان *khwurda-dān*, Critical.

P خورده فروش *khwurda-farosh*, A huckster.

P خورده كاري *khwurda-kārī*, Liable to criticism.

P خورده گير *khwurda-gīr*, A criticiser, critic.

P خورده مرده *khwurda murda*, Minute objects.

P خوردي *khwurdī*, Broth, juicy meats. Eatables. Smallness, littleness.

P خوردي پز *khwurdī-paz*, A cook, broth-maker.

P خوردي فروش *khwurdī-farosh*, A broth-seller.

G خورز *khwuraz*, Greek dance or chorus.

P خورزي *khwurzī*, (or خورزينه) Barn, granary.

P خورسار *khwursār*, (or خورستار) A refectory.

P خورستان *khwuristān*, A pantry, larder, buttery. Name of a country in Persia.

P خورسند *khwursand*, Contented, happy.

P خورسندي *khwursandī*, Gladness: content.

P خورش *khwurish*, Eating and drinking; food. A father-in-law. خورش و پوشش *khwurish u poshish*, Food and raiment. خورش دستاس *khwurishi dast-ās*, A handful of wheat which the miller throws into the hopper.

P خورشيد *khwur-shed*, (or خورشاد *khwur-shād*) The sun. The animal spirit. Name of the mistress of Jamshed. خورشيد جهانتاب *khwur-shedi jahān-tāb*, The sun illuminating the world.

P خورشيد پرستان *khwurshed-parastān*, Worshippers of the sun.

P خورشيد پيكر *khwurshed-paykar*, Handsome.

P خورشيد سواران *khwurshed-suwārān*, Early-risers. Christian monks. Those who ride in the heat of the day. The favourites of a king. Angels.

P خورشيدن *khwurshīdan*, To collect. To suit. To happen agreeably. To carry one's victuals. To crack (lips with heat).

P خورصلا *khwur-salā*, A store, barn, cellar.

A خورم *khawram*, A stone full of clefts.

P خوّرم *khwurram*, Joyful, pleasant.

P خورماه *khwur-māh*, Name of a summer month.

A خورمة *khawramat*, Soft part of the nose.

P خورمك *khwarmak*, (or خوّرمك *khwarramak*) Shells worn as amulets.

P خورمهر *khwur-mihr*, Name of Solomon's sword.

P خورند *khwarand*, Worthy, suitable, proper. The twelfth day of every solar month.

P خورنده *khwuranda*, An eater. One who obtains the property of another fairly or dishonourably. A family, domestics, household.

A خورنق *khawarnak*, The palace built by نعمان بن منذر *nuʿmān bin munzir* for King Bahrām in Babylonia, and alluded to often to imply any magnificent edifice.

P خورنگاه *khwarangāh*, (or خورنگه *khwarangah*) Bahrām's palace. A portico.

P خورنه *khawarna*, The palace of Bahrām.

P خور و پوش *khwur u posh*, Food and raiment.

P خوره *khwara*, Any thing that eats or corrodes (as rust, moth, leprosy, or gangrene). Divine illumination, the light of reason. A division of the Persian empire, of which there formerly were five: namely, خورهٔ اردشير *khwara-i ārdshīr*, خورهٔ اصطخر *khwara-i istakhr*, خورهٔ داراب *khwara-i dārāb*, خورهٔ شاپور *khwara-i shāpūr*, and خورهٔ قباد *khwara-i kubād*. *Khawra*, The plant called خرزهره *khar-zahra*. Trodden. *Khūra*, A corn-sack.

P خورهگ *khwurhag*, Shells suspended from children's necks.

A خوريٰ *khūra'*, Good and pleasing (woman). (A man) abounding in good things.

P خوري *khwurī*, Baseness. A kind of cloth.

P خورياد *khwuryād*, A peasant, clown, lout.

P خوريادي *khwuryādī*, Rusticity, rudeness.

P خوريدن *khwurīdan*, To invite to nuptials.

A خوز *khawz*, Enmity, hostility.

P خوز *khūz*, Sugar-cane. The country called Khūzistān (anciently Susiana), the capital of which is Shūstar. Inhabitants of خوزستان *khūzistān*, the ancient Susiana, between Persia and Babylonia.

P خوزان *khūzān*, Name of a celebrated Persian hero. Name of a city.

A خوزب *khawzab*, A swelling of (a camel's) udder.

P خوزدوك *khawazdūk*, An insect resembling a black-beetle. The scolopendra.

P خوزده *khūzda*, A beetle, a chafer.

P خوزر *khūzar*, Name of a tree.

A خوزري *khawzara'*, The gait of one whose joints are out.

P خوزستان *khūzistān*, Susiana. A sugar-plantation. Sugar-growing country. Sugar-manufactory.

A خوزع *khawzaʿ*, An old woman.

A خوزقة *khawzakat*, The act of impaling.

A خوزلیٰ *khawzala'*, A slow, tottering pace.

P خوزم *khwazam*, A fog. *Khawzam*, Carpenter.

A خوزمة *khawzamat*, (in Hudaylish) A cow.

P خوزه *khawza*, Trampled upon, ruined. *Khūza* and *khwuza*, A triumphal arch. The inner apartment where the royal bride awaits the arrival of her husband.

A خوزهرج *khawzahraj*, (the Arab. of خرزهره *khar-zahra*) Asses'bane (a certain poisonous plant).

P خوزي *khūzī*, Pounded, beaten (meat). A native of خوز *khūz*.

P خوزي خوار *khūzī-khwār*, A contented cuckold. An eater of pounded meat.

P خوزيدن *khūzidan*, To call to a marriage.

P خوژه *khūja*, A cock's comb. Chitterlings.

A خوس *khaws*, (v. n. of خاس for خوس) Deceiving. Stinking (carrion). Breaking a promise, disappointing. Being flat and unsaleable. *Khūs*, Fraud, deceit.

P خوس *khwus*, A brother-in-law.

P خوسانيدن *khūsānīdan*, To desire, wish. To excite desire. *Khosānīdan*, To cause to moisten.

P خوست *khwust*, A melon. Rubbed. Wearied, tired. *Khost* or *khwast*, An island. A beaten road.

P خوستار *khwastār*, A petitioner, candidate.

P خوستن *khwastan* or *khūstan*, To ask.

P خوسته *khwasta*, Dug up, extirpated. Fetid.

P خوسره *khūsra*, A husband's or wife's brother.

P خوسه *khosa*, A scarecrow in fields or gardens. خوسه شدن *khosa shudan*, To be in heat (a bitch).

P خوسيدن *khūsīdan*, To dry up, shrivel. To be wrinkled. To be moist. To flow from the eyes (humour). To collect.

A خوش *khawsh*, The hypochondria, the waist under the ribs. A stab. Matrimony. Conjugal intercourse. A taking, seizure. A scattering of earth into a vessel.

P خوش *khwush*, (by some *khwash*) Good, sweet, excellent, beautiful, fair, charming, pleasant, delightful, agreeable, cheerful, amiable, lovely, delicate, tender, kind, gentle, humane, mild, meek, elegant. Healthy, wholesome, temperate. Happy, well, pleased. Willingly. خوش اسپرم *khwush isparam*, The shrub basil royal. خوش اطوار *khwush-atwār*, Well-bred. خوش الحان *khwush-alhān*, (or خوش آواز *khwush-āwāz*) With a sweet voice. خوش امّا *khwush ammā*, Very well, be it so. But. خوش آمد *khwush-āmad*, Flattery. Welcome. Gratification. اورا خوش آمد *urā khwush āmad*, It is agreeable to him. خوش آمد گو *khwush-āmad-go* or *gū*, A flatterer. خوش آمدن *khwush āmadan*, To please, become agreeable. To succeed well. To agree with (as meat or drink). To be welcome. خوش آمدي *khwush-āmadī*, Flattery. Assenting. You are welcome. خوش آمد كاري *khwush-āmad-kārī*, Content, satisfaction. خوش انگشت *khwush-angusht*, (Good-fingered) A skilful player on an instrument. خوش آهنگ *khwush-āhang*, Having a melodious voice. خوش آيند *khwush-āyand*, Flattering (endearments). Grateful, wholesome, amiable, agreeable, pleasing, charming. خوش آيندگي *khwush-āyandagī*, Spruceness, neatness, elegance, ornament. Pleasingness, agreeableness. خوش آينده *khwush-āyanda*, Amiable, agreeable to all. Elegant, neat, spruce. Grateful, agreeable. Wholesome. ملاطفات خوش آينده *mulātafāti khwush-āyanda*, Flattering caresses, blandishments. خوش باش *khwush-bāsh*, Free to stay or to depart. Lands granted to favourites at low rents on condition of serving the government when called upon. Independent. خوش بو *khwush-bū* or *bo*, Sweet-smelling. Perfume. خوش بو دار *khwush-bo-dār*, Fragrant, aromatic. خوش بوي *khwush-boy*, Fragrant, odoriferous. خوشبوي ناك *khwush-būynāk* or *boynāk*, Well-flavoured, savoury (boiling pot). خوش پوزي *khwush-pozī*, A kiss. خوش پوشاك *khwush-poshāk*, Well-dressed. خوش پيچ *khwush-pech*, Intelligent, wise. A distinguished gentleman. خوشتامن *khwush-tāman*, A mother-in-law. خوش تراش *khwush-tarāsh*, Of a good shape, graceful. خوش تقرير *khwush-takrīr*, Eloquent. خوش حال *khwush-hāl*, Happy, fortunate, in pleasant circumstances. خوش حالي *khwush-hālī*, A pleasant condition. خوش حركت *khwush-harakat*, One who acts with propriety, or who does good actions. خوش خاطر *khwush-khātir*, A cheerful mind, a gladsome heart. خوش خال *khwush-khāl*, A mistress, sweetheart. خوش خبري *khwush-khabarī*, Exhilarating news. خوش خرام *khwush-khirām*, One who walks elegantly. خوش خريد *khwush-kharīd*, Paying in ready money, buying in a private sale. خوش خصال *khwush-khisāl*, (and خوش خوي *khwush-khoy*) Of an excellent disposition. Well-bred. Affable. خوش خط *khwush-khat*, Elegant writing. A handsome youth. خوش خلق *khwush-khalk*, Affable. خوش خلقي *khwush-khalkī*, Affability. خوش خوار *khwush-khwār*, A good liver, one who lives well. خوش خوان *khwush-khwān*, Singing delightfully, melodious. خوش خوراك *khwush-khwurāk*, One who lives well. خوش خواهش *khwush-khwāhish*, Vehement desire. خوش خور *khwush-khwur*, A fortunate petition. Subacid. خوش خوئي *khwush-khuī* or *khoī*, Goodness of temper. خوش دامن *khwush-dāman*, Mother-in-law. خوش دل *khwush-dil*, Cheerful, contented, gay. خوش دلي *khwush-dilī*, Cheerfulness, gaiety. خوش دم *khwush-dam*, A sweet breath. Fine air. خوش دماغ *khwush-dimāgh*, Pleasant, mirthful. خوش ذائقه *khwush-zāïka*, Well-flavoured, savoury. خوش راه *khwush-rāh*, A good roadster. خوش رفتار *khwush-raftār*, Graceful in walking. Proceeding properly. سرو خوش رفتار *sarvi khwush-raftār*, A sweetly-waving cypress. قلم خوش رفتار *kalami khwush-raftār*, A good pen which moves easily. نگار خوش رفتار *nigāri khwush-raftār*, A beautiful woman walking gracefully; also of good conduct. خوش رنگ *khwush-rang*, Of a lively colour. خوش رو *khwush-rav*, Pleasant-paced. *Khwush-rū*, Beautiful. خوش روز *khwush-roz*, A holiday. خوش زبان *khwush-zabān*, Speaking well, having a sweet or clear voice. Plausible. خوش ساي *khwush-sāy*, The box-tree. خوش مسخره *khwush-sakhra*, A pleasant, humorous fellow. اي مادر خوش سير *ay mādari khwush-siyar*, O mother, of excellent virtues! or, O most virtuous mother! خوش شدن *khwush shudan*, To be well. To be in good health. خوش صورت *khwush-sūrat*, Handsome-faced. خوش طبع *khwush-tabع*, Jocular, good-natured. تمثيلات خوش طبع *tamsīlāti khwush-tabع*, Apologues of an entertaining nature. خوش طبعي *khwush-tabعī*, Pleasantry, mirth. خوش عنان *khwush-عinān*, (A horse) of an agreeable pace, gentle. خوش قطع *khwush-katع*, Well-shaped, nicely cut out. خوش كردن *khwush kardan*, To cure. To benefit. To do good. To rejoice. خوش كنار *khwush-kanār*, A beloved object. خوش گام *khwush-gām*, Well-paced. خوش گريستن *khwush giristan*, To weep abundantly. خوش گفتاري *khwush-guftārī*, Eloquence. خوش گو *khwush-go*, Eloquent. Melodious. شربت خوشگوار *sharbati khwush-guwār*, A pleasant beverage, easy of digestion. خوش لحن *khwush-lahn*, Melodious. مطرب خوش لهجه *mutribi khwush-lahja*, A musician having a tuneful voice. خوش مزگي *khwush-mazagī*, Pleasantness of flavour. خوش مزه *khwush-maza*, Agreeable to the palate, well-flavoured, delicious. خوش معامله *khwush-muعāmala*, An upright dealer. خوش منش *khwush-manish*, Having a good heart (ethically), or excellent spirits (physically). Satiety, glut, languor. خوش منشي *khwush-manishī*, Joke, pleasantry, sprightliness, cheerfulness, joyousness. خوش منظر *khwush-manzar*, Of a goodly aspect. خوشنشين *khwush-nishīn*, Sitting easily, having room enough. A new comer. A stranger. خوش نشيني *khwush-nishīnī*, A royal guard for which lands are assigned. خوشنظر *khwush-nazar*, Sociable, familiar. A species of red, yellow, and white rose. خوش نمك *khwush-namak*, Well-salted. Witty. A beloved object. خوش نواز *khwush-nawāz*, A musician. Name of the governor of the city of هيتال *haytāl*. خوش نويس *khwush-navīs*, A caligraphist. خوش نويسي *khwush-navīsī*, Caligraphy. خوش و خورم *khwush u khwurram*, Happy and cheerful. خوش وقت *khwush-waht*, In happy circumstances. خوش هوا *khwush-hawā*, A pleasant air. *Khwash*, A husband's or a wife's mother. A kiss. (for خويش *khwesh*) Self. *Khosh*, (for خشك *khushk*) Dry. (for خوشه *khosha*) A bunch of grapes.

P خوش آب *khosh-āb*, *khwush-āb*, or *khwash-āb*, Fresh, juicy, full of water. Water in which grapes, figs, prunes, or dried apricots are boiled together. Fresh, tender pot-herbs. Moist. Waving. Clear, pellucid. A pearl, a jewel.

P خوشاب دندان *khwushāb-dandān*, One who has clean and brilliant teeth.

P خوش آبي *khwush-ābī*, Freshness.

P خوشا خوشا *khwushā khwushā* or *khwashā khwashā*, Very well!

P خوشاد *khwushād*, A clearing of a garden.

P خوشامن *khwashāman*, Husband's or wife's mother.

A خوشان *kharwshān*, A species of orach.

P خوشاي *khoshāy*, Cluster of grapes: ear of corn.

P خوشت *khwusht*, Stark naked.

P خوشتر *khwushtar*, Sweeter, pleasanter.

P خوشترك *khwushtarak*, Somewhat pleasanter.

P خوشچه *khwushcha*, Good (girl). Prettily.

P خوشكه آرد *khwushka-ārd*, Flour not bolted.

P خوشنما *khwush-namā*, Of good appearance. Elegant, specious. Neat, pretty.

P خوشنود *khwushnūd*, Content. Pleased.

P خوشنودي *khwushnūdī*, Mirth. Contentment.

P خوشه *khosha*, A cluster or bunch of grapes or dates. An ear of corn. The constellation Virgo. Name of a bird. Gleaning. The rainbow. Separately. خوشهٔ چرخ *khoshaï charkh*, The constellation Virgo. خوشه چين *khosha-chīn*, Gathering grapes, reaping or gleaning corn. A plagiary. خوشه درگلو آوردن *khosha dar gulū āwardan*, To be coming into ear. *Khwasha*, Husband's or wife's father.

P خوشي *khwushī*, Happiness, cheerfulness, gaiety, pleasure, enjoyment, delight. Consolation, comfort, diversion. Voluntariness. Goodness, excellence, benignity. خوشي نمودن *khwushī namūdan*, To display excellence or benignity. درخوشي *dar khwushī*, In pleasantry. *Khoshī*, Name of a bird.

P خوشي بخش *khwushī-bakhsh*, Affording delight.

P خوشيدن *khoshīdan*, To grow dry. To collect, contract. To wrinkle, shrivel, chap (as the lips). To burn, fry, parch. To bring in or lay up provisions. To be busy. To love. To congratulate a stranger. To happen well, to succeed. To jest, play, represent in the manner of theatrical entertainments or public spectacles.

P خوشيده *khoshīda*, Dried. Dry.

A خوص *khūs*, Leaves of palm-trees, of cocoa-nuts, and the like (whether woven or not). *Khawas*, (v.n. of خوص) Being sunk in the head (the eye).

A خوصاء *khawsāء*, (fem. of اخوص *akhwas*) A sheep with one eye white, and the other black. A hot wind, hurting the sight. A deep well. A high hill of sand. Intensely hot (noon-day).

A خوصة *khūsat*, A leaf (of a palm or cocoa-nut).

A خوض *khawz*, (v.n. of خاض for خوض) Entering, wading, fording, or crossing a river. Plunging (into danger), entering precipitately (into business). Resolving, purposing, deliberating, taking counsel. Stirring (wine) with a stick. Acting inhumanly, piercing with a sword and turning it in the wound. Making (one) ford a river.

A خوضة *khawzat*, A pearl.

A خوط *khūt*, (pl. خيطان *khītān* and اخواط *akhwāt*) A limber twig. A corpulent man, yet handsome and active.

A خوطانة *khūtānat*, (also خوطانية *khūtāniyat*) Long and slender like a twig (man or woman).

A خوع *khawʻ*, Name of a whitish-coloured mountain. The winding of a river, the bend of a valley. A field producing the plant رمث *rims*.

A خوعلة *khawʻalat*, (v. n. of خوعل Q) Concealing one's self on account of suspicion.

A خوعم *khawʻam*, A fool.

A خوف *khawf*, (v. n. of خاف for خوف) Fearing. Surpassing in timidity. Knowing for certain. Fear, dread, terror. Murder. Red leather, cut into straps. Timid, fearful (persons). P خوف خدا *khawfi khudā*, The fear of God. A *Khūf*, (pl. of اخيف *akhyaf*) Wall-eyed (men).

A خوّف *khūwaf*, (pl. of خائف *khāʼif*) Timid.

A خوفع *khawfaʻ*, Sad, silent, melancholy. Silent, and drowsy.

P خوفناك *khawfnāk*, Terrified, timid, timorous. Frightful, terrifying.

A خوق *khawk*, (v. n. of خاق for خوق) Putting on ear-rings (a girl). Making the noise خاق باق *khāk bāk*. A ring for the ear or nose. *Khūk*, The sheath of a horse. *Khawak*, Spaciousness, roominess. The scab.

A خوقاء *khawkāʼ*, (fem. of اخوق *akhwak*) Wide, deep, extensive. Scabby (camel). Foolish (woman).

P خوك *khūk* or *khok*, A pig. Scrofula. خوك دريا *khūki daryā*, (or خوك ماهي *khūki māhī*) (Sea-hog or Fish-hog) A porpoise.

P خوك بان *khūkbān*, A swineherd.

P خوك بچه *khūk-bacha*, A young pig, a porkling.

P خوكردگي *khu-kardagī*, Habitude, practice.

P خوكرده *khu-karda*, Habituated, accustomed to.

P خوكيزه *khūkīza*, A large duck, a goose.

P خوگ *khūg*, A hog. *Khawag*, A servant.

P خوگر *khugar* or *khogar*, Accustomed to, habituated. Sociable, familiar. خوگر شدن *khogar shudan*, To be used to. To become tame.

P خوگرفتگي *khu-giriftagī*, Familiarity, habitude.

P خوگرفته *khu-girifta*, Accustomed, habituated.

P خو گير *khu-gīr*, *khū-gīr*, or *kho-gīr*, The stuffing of a saddle. A pad. A pack-saddle. خو گير دوز *kho-gīr-doz*, A saddle-maker.

A خول *khawl*, (v. n. of خال for خول) Keeping, preserving. Turning one's attention to the proper management of an estate. *Khawal*, The bit of a bridle. Wealth in servants and handmaids. (pl. of خائل *khāʼil*), Servants, domestics (male and female), followers. Shepherds. (pl. of خوليّ *khawlīy*) Excellent managers.

P خول *khol*, A lark. A kite. A white woodcock. *Khawal*, Lean. A white woodcock.

A خؤول *khuʼul*, (pl. of خال) Maternal uncles.

A خوّل *khūwal*, (pl. of خال *khāl*) Maternal uncles.

P خولان *khawalān*, Buckthorn. A كحل الخولان *kuhlu'l khawlān*, Juice of the box-thorn.

A خؤولة *khuʼulat*, Relationship by the mother's side. (pl. of خال *khāl*) Maternal uncles.

A خولة *khawlat*, A female deer, doe.

A خولع *khawlaʻ*, Terror, sudden fear. A wolf. A wild man of the woods. A skilful guide. An unlucky gambler. A wicked, dissolute youth. A fool.

P خوللو *khūlalū*, Cummin-seed.

P خولنجان *khūlanjān*, The herb galangale.

P خوله *khawla*, A quiver. A lamp. *Khola*, Empty.

A خوليّ *khawlīy*, (pl. خول *khawal*) A good manager. An able shepherd. The keeper of a garden.

P خوليا *khūliyā*, Common to the use of all.

A خون *khawn*, (v. n. of خان for خون) Being perfidious, deceitful, breaking a promise, betraying a trust. Languor of countenance. *Khawn* or *khūn*, (pl. of خوّان *khawwān* or *khūwān*) Third months. *Khūn*, (pl. of خوان *khiwān* or *khuwān*) Tables.

P خون *khwun*, (for خوان *khwān*) A table. Food. *Khūn*, Blood. Bloody. Killing. A shedder of blood. Selfishness. Pride. A table. Reading. Singing. خون آشام *khūn-āshām*, Blood-thirsty, ferocious, cruel. خون بط *khūni bat*, (جام *jām*, or رز *raz*) Red wine. خون جبال *khūni jibāl*, Rubies, cornelians. خون جگر *khūni jigar*, (or دل *dil*) Deep affliction. خون جهان *khūni jahān*, A ruddiness in the sky. خون حيوان *khūni haywān*, Milk, butter, or honey. خون خروس *khūni khuros*, Red wine. خون خم *khūni khum*, (or قربان *harbān*) Wine. خون دل خاك *khūni dili khāk*, Flowers. Rubies. خون دل بناخن آوردن *khūni dil ba nākhun āwardan*, (or رسيدن *rasīdan*) To tear the breast, to cry bitterly. خون ريختن *khūn rekhtan*, To shed blood. خون ساده *khūni sāda*, Pure blood. خون سياوش *khūni siyāwush*, Dragon's blood. خون سياوشان *khūni siyāwushān*, Dragon's blood. Brazilian wood. The fruit of a tree growing in Hazramawt. A sort of gum produced in Abyssinia. Grape-wine. A ruddiness in the sky. خون شدن *khūn shudan*, To perish. خون كبوتر *khūni kabūtar*, Wine. خون كردن *khūn kardan*, To kill, murder. *Khon*, A house, hotel, palace, mansion.

P خوناب *khūn-āb*, (and خونابه *khūnāba*) Bloody water. Blood, a torrent of blood. Tears of blood. Vermilion. Breathing hard. خوناب چشيدن *khūn-āb chashīdan*, To die.

P خون آلود *khūn-ālūd*, (or آلوده) Blood-stained.

P خونبار *khūn-bār*, Shedding (or raining) blood (generally spoken of the eyes of a lover).

P خونبها *khūn-bahā*, A fine for blood-shedding.

A خونة *khawanat*, (pl. of خائن) Rogues, traitors.

P خونجده *khūnjada*, Gum for closing wounds.

P خونجك *khwanjak*, Coriander-seed. A kind of corn.

P خونجيده *khūnjīda*, A kind of eye-salve.

P خونچك *khūnchak*, Fruit of mastic. Trefoil.

P خونچكان *khūn-chakān*, Blood-dropping.

P خونچه *khwuncha*, A small table, like a tea-board; a tray. Meats sent from a marriage-feast to an absent friend.

P خونچين *khūn-chīn*, (Blood-gathering) A bituminous liquor of the consistence of wax, found in tombs wherein embalmed bodies have lain.

P خون خرابه *khūn-kharāba*, Bloody work.

P خونخوار *khūn-khwār*, (or خونخواره *khūn-khwāra*, Devouring blood, cruel, blood-thirsty, murderous, destructive.

P خون خوارگي *khūn-khwāragī*, Murder, destruction. Ferocity, blood-thirstiness.

P خونخواري *khūn-khwārī*, Blood-shedding, blood-thirstiness. Sorrow.

P خوند *khwand*, Lord, prince. Sharp, brisk.

P خون دست *khwun-dast*, A sort of table.

P خوندكار *khwund-kār*, The Turkish emperor. A king, lord

P خوندن *khūndan*, To read.

P خونريز *khūn-rez*, Blood-shedding, blood-thirsty. An executioner. An amorous glance.

P خونريزي *khūn-rezī*, Blood-shedding.

P خونش *khūnish*, Reading. Intercession.

P خونفشان *khūn-fishān*, Blood-shedding, cruel.

P خونكار *khūn-kār*, A killer. A king (as having the power of sentencing to death; hence used as a title of the grand Turk).

P خونگر *khwungar*, A tanner, currier. A cook.

P خونگرفتار *khūn-giriftār*, Dull, stupid.

P خون گرفته *khūn-girifta*, Whose blood is taken, condemned to die, at the point of death.

P خوننده *khūnanda*, (for خواننده *khwānanda*) A reader. A singer, musician. A crier.

P خونه *khūna*, A rolling-pin, a roller.

P خوني *khūnī*, Bloody. A murderer.

P خونيان *khūnyān*, An assassin, cut-throat.

P خونين *khūnīn*, Bloody, bloody-coloured.

A خؤور *khuʼūr*, Weakness.

A خؤورة *khuʼūrat*, Debility.

A خؤولة *khuʼūlat*, The relation of a maternal uncle. (pl. of خال *khāl*) Maternal uncles.

A خؤون *khaʼūn*, Perfidious, treacherous.

P خوه *khawh*, Sweat. *Khoh*, Tares, darnel. A sister. *Khawa*, Strangulation, suffocation. Strangled. A servant. A narrow pass between two hills.

P خوها *khūhā*, (for خواها *khwāhā*) Wishing.

P خوهانيدن *khūhānīdan*, To cause to beg.

P خوهد *khwahad*, (for خواهد) He wills.

P خوهر *khūhar*, (for خواهر *khwāhar*) A sister.

P خوهش *khwahish*, Petition, entreaty.

P خوهل *khohal* or *khwahl*, Crooked, bent. A crooked-legged animal. A shoe-stretcher.

A خيازر *khayāzir*, (pl. of خيزران) Canes, rattans.

P خيازنه *khayāzana*, A wife's sister.

A خياشيم *khayāshīm*, (pl. of خيشوم *khayshūm*) Roots of noses. Gristly parts about the upper extremity of the nose and the brain; veins inside the nose. The projecting parts of mountains.

A خياض *khiyāz*, (v. n. of خاض for خوض) Entering, wading, fording (a river). Plunging (into business or danger). Making one ford a river. Stirring (wine) with a stick. Acting inhumanly towards a wounded man.

A خياط *khiyāt*, A needle. A passage, a way, path, track. حتّى يلج الجمل في سمّ الخياط *hatta' yalija'l jamal fī sammi'l khiyāt*, Until a camel enter into the eye of a needle.

A خيّاط *khayyāt*, A tailor.

A خياطة *khiyātat*, Art of sewing: tailoring.

A خيال *khayāl*, (pl. اخيلة *akhyilat*) A phantom, ghost, spectre, apparition, vision. Imagination, fancy, sentiment, idea. Meditation, reflection. The exterior form, appearance, aspect. The resemblance of a man, with which they frighten birds, a malkin or scarecrow. Name of a plant. Name of Lebid's horse. خيال باطل *khayāli bātil*, A foolish imagination. P خيال بستن *khayāl bastan*, To imagine, fancy, dream of. خيال پختن *khayāl pukhtan*, To desire, hanker after. خيال خام *khayāli khām*, A vain imagination, ridiculous idea. A خيال حافظه *khayāli hāfiza*, The retentive faculty, memory. قوت خيال *kūwati khayāl*, The powers of the imagination. خيال خلافت *khayāli khilāfat*, Ambition. ورق الخيال *waraku'l khayāl*, The inebriating leaf bang. P خيال كردن *khayāl kardan*, To imagine. A *Khiyāl*, (v. n. of خال for خول) Turning one's attention to the proper management of an estate.

A خيّال *khayyāl*, A horseman, cavalier.

A خيلاء *khuyalā*, Arrogance, pride.

A خيالات *khayālāt*, (pl. of خيالة *khayālat*) Phantoms, imaginations. P خيالات بي معني *khayālāti bī maʿna'*, Absurd ideas. A خيالات لا طائل *khayālāti lā tāʾil*, Ill-grounded expectations.

P خيال پرست *khayāl-parast*, A bard. A visionary. A lover.

A خيالة *khayālat*, (pl. اخيلة *akhyilat*) A phantom, spectre. The external form of a thing. Imagination, fancy.

A خيّالة *khayyālat*, Troop of horses, or horsemen.

A خياليّ *khayālīy*, Imaginary, ideal, capricious.

A خيام *khiyām*, (v. n. of خيم) Having recourse to fraud. Lifting the feet. Fearing, acting cowardly. (pl. of خيمة *khaymat*) Tents, pavilions.

A خيانة *khiyānat*, (v. n. of خان for خون) Deceiving. Violating an agreement. Perfidy, treason, disloyalty. Dishonesty, embezzlement. Rape. P خيانت كردن *khiyānat kardan*, To betray.

P خيانت پيشه *khiyānat-pesha*, Perfidious.

P خيانتگر *khiyānatgar*, A traitor.

P خويشتن بين *khweshtan-bīn*, Self-important.

P خويشتن بيني *khweshtan-bīnī*, Self-importance.

P خويشتن دار *khweshtan-dār*, Abstinent, keeping clear of evil. Feeding well, loving ease, and taking care of one's self.

P خويشتن داري *khweshtan-dārī*, Self-preservation.

P خويشتن ستائي *khweshtan-sitāʾī*, Self-commendation.

P خويشتن شناسي *khweshtan-shināsī*, Conceit.

P خويش قرابات *khwesh-kurābāt*, Relations.

P خويشكار *khwesh-kār*, A farmer, husbandman.

P خويشي *khweshī*, Relationship, consanguinity.

A خويصّة *khuwayssat*, (dim. of خاصّة *khāssat*) The minor nobility, squirearchy, gentry.

P خويگر *khoygar*, Habits, customs, manners.

P خوي گير *khway-gīr*, A saddle-cloth which imbibes the sweat. *Khoy-gīr*, Familiar, sociable.

A خويل *khuwayl*, (dim. of خال) A little mole.

P خويله *khwayla*, Foolish, ignorant (employed chiefly in abuse).

P خوي ناد *khwuynād*, An earth-worm.

P خويوز *khūyūz*, A bat.

P خويه *khūya*, A shovel. An oar.

P خوييدن *khwayīdan*, To sweat. To be collected. To live.

P خه *khah*, Ridicule, derision. خه خه *khah khah*, (or خهي خهي *khahī khahī*) Well done!

P خهر *khuhr*, Native soil, residence, abode.

P خهل *khahl*, *khuhl*, (or خهله *khahla*) Crooked. *Khuhal*, A last for stretching shoes.

P خي *khī*, A bottle, skin, bag.

A خيّ *khayy*, (v. n. of خوي) Falling, trembling in ruins, and being deserted (a house). Setting (a star) without being followed by rain. Intention, aim, design.

A خيّاب *khayyāb*, (A flint) not striking fire. خيّاب بن هيّاب *khayyābu' bnu hayyābin*, Loss.

P خيابان *khiyābān*, A parterre, flower-bed.

A خيابة *khayābat*, Desperation, hopelessness.

A خيار *khiyār*, The citrul. The resemblance of a cucumber. Any thing choice, excellent. The choicest part of one's property. The better classes of society. (pl. of خير *khayr*) Good, abounding in good things. (pl. of خيّر *khayyir*) Good, religious men. خيار الشرط *khiyāru'sh shart*, Optional condition. انت بالخيار *anta bi'l khiyār*, It is you to choose, the option rests with you.

A خيارة *khiyārat*, Any thing soever exquisite.

P خيار چنبر *khiyār-chambar*, (or شنبر *shambar*) Cassia fistularis.

P خياردان *khiyārdān*, A cucumber-bed. An avenue of trees.

P خيارزار *khiyārzār*, A cucumber-bed.

P خيارزه *khiyārza*, A small cucumber. خيارزهٔ سپند *khiyārzaʾi sipand*, Wild cucumber.

A خياري *khayārī*, A kind of violet.

P خوهلگي *khwahlagī*, Crookedness, curvature.

P خوهله *khwahla*, Crooked, bent.

P خوهن *khūhan*, Oil-vender or presser. A funnel.

A خوي *khawy*, (v. n. of خوي) Being reduced, fallen in, or collapsed (a woman who has recently brought forth). *Khawa'*, (v. n. of خوي) Being reduced, fallen in (a woman who has recently brought forth). Being empty (the belly), and collapsing with hunger. Failing to emit fire (the stick زند *zand*). Seizing, snatching, carrying off. A hemorrhage from the nose.

P خوي *khway*, Sweat. Filth, rubbish. A sown field, a meadow, herbage just sprouting above the ground. A saddle-cloth, or dorsers below the saddle. A helmet. Rust. Mildew. خوي آوردن *khway āwardan*, To sweat. To make sweat. خوي كردن *khway kardan*, To sweat. *Khoy*, Manner, custom, mode, humour, habit, nature, disposition, temper, principles. خوي آتشناك *khoyi ātishnāk*, A fiery temper. خوي كردن *khoy kardan*, (also خوي گرفتن *khoy giriftan*) To contract a habit. بد خوي *bad-khoy*, Of a bad temper. خوش خوي *khwush-khoy*, Of an amiable disposition. *Khawī*, Spittle, *Khawe*, A helmet.

A خويّ *khawīy*, Firm, fixed. A tract of level ground between two hills. Soft ground. *Khuwīy*, (v. n. of خوي) Being ruined, fallen, deserted (house).

A خويّة *khawīyat*, Food prepared for a woman in childbed. *Khawiyat*, *khuwīyat*, or خويّاء *khawīyā*, The space between a ewe's udder and matrix.

P خويت *khoyat*, *khuyat*, or *khūyat*, Thy temper.

P خوي چين *khway-chīn*, (or خوي خورد *khway-khwurd*) A shirt, sock, or under waistcoat (as imbibing the sweat).

P خوي خوره *khway-khwura*, A saddle-cloth, and the flaps of a saddle between the horse's sides and the legs of a rider.

P خوي خوي *khway-khoy*, Funk. Shame.

A خويخية *khuwaykhiyat*, Calamity, trouble.

P خويد *khawīd*, *khiwīd*, or *khwayd*, A sown field. Green corn, wheat or barley not yet in ear.

P خوي درد *khwe-dard*, A whitlow.

A خويدع *khuwaydiʿ*, A moving away from its place of the tendon of a (camel's) leg, lying down.

P خويدك *khwaydak*, A kind of melon.

P خويدن *khawīdan*, To chew the cud. To sell corn in the ear.

P خويسه *khawesa*, Disputing, contention.

P خويش *khwesh*, Self, himself. Body. Existence, presence. A plough. A species of linen cloth. A kinsman. (for خوش *khwush*) Good, well, pleasant.

P خويشان *khweshān*, (pl. of خويش) Relations.

P خويشاوند *khweshāwand*, A kinsman.

P خويشاوندي *khweshāwandī*, Consanguinity.

P خويشتن *khweshtan*, One's self: self. خويشتنرا آراستن *khweshtanrā ārāstan*, To adorn one's self.

P خیاوار *khiyāwār*, (or خیاور *khiyāwar*) Labour.

P خیاییدن *khayāyīdan*, To chew.

A خیبة *khaybat*, (v. n. of خاب for خیب) Being disappointed, baulked, frustrated. Being unbelieving and ungrateful. Disappointment. Hopelessness. الهیبة خیبة *al haybat khaybat*, Fear is despair. خیبة له *khaybatun lahu*, Ill luck to him!

A خیبر *khaybar*, A fort near Madīna.

P خیبرستان *khaybar-satān*, The calif Aliy.

A خیبريّ *khaybariy*, A native of Khaybar. A black serpent.

A خیت *khayt*, (v. n. of خات for خیت) Diminishing, impairing, lessening, seizing (any one's property). The causing a sound, exclamation.

P خیتال *khītāl*, A lie. A joke, jest, pleasantry. Temperament, habit, natural constitution.

A خیتام *khaytām*, A seal-ring: a seal, signet.

A خیتروع *khaytarūʻ*, A restless woman.

A خیتعور *khaytaʻūr*, Any thing that soon disappears. The semblance of water called سراب *sarāb*. Filaments in the air in hot weather, gossamer. The world. Any thing suddenly attacking a man, and destroying or depriving him of his senses; death, calamity. The imaginary demon, called also Ghūl, which is said to devour both man and beast. A lion. A wolf. A little animal that moveth constantly on the surface of water. A woman of a bad disposition. Satan. A departure to a distance.

P خیچ *khwech*, A ploughshare.

P خید *khīd*, Wheat or barley in the blade.

A خیدب *khaydab*, A straight open road.

A خیدبة *khaydabat*, Former habits, opinions, or pursuits: as, اقبل الی خیدبتك *akbil ila' khaydabatika*, Return to your old affairs.

A خیدع *khaydaʻ*, A deceiver, a knave. A sly wolf. Wrong, misleading (road). A vapour floating over the plain. An imaginary sylvan demon of different shapes and colours, supposed to devour men and animals.

P خیدن *khīdan*, To be bent or curved. To tease, to card (wool or cotton).

P خیده *khīda*, Curved, crooked. Carded.

A خیذع *khayzaʻ*, Vice, fault, defect, blemish.

A خیر *khayr*, (v. n. of خار for خیر) Being kind, favourable to. Being well off, enriched in goods. Excelling (others), especially in what is good. (pl. اخیار *akhyār* and خیار *khiyār*) One who abounds in good things. Good. Goods, riches. (pl. خیور *khuyūr*) Good. Any desirable moral quality. Better, best. Handsome, comely. Well, happy. خیر البریه *khayru'l barīya*, The best of men, *i.e.* Muhammad. خیر بوّاء *khayr-bawwāʼ*, Common cardamoms. خیر الثیاب *khayru's siyāb*, A fine whitish linen. خیر مطلق *khayri mutlak*, The chief good, summum bonum. خیر و شرّ *khayr u sharr*, Good and bad. خیر و عافیت *khayr u ʻāfiyat*, Wealth and health. خیر امور اوسطها *khayru umūrin awsatuhā*, In the medium is virtue. ابنیهٔ خیرة *abniya-i khayra*, General goods, public edifices. P خیر دعا گفتن *khayr-duʻā guftan*, To salute, congratulate, bless. A ما خیر *mā khayra*, How excellent! *Khīr*, Liberality, nobility. Root, origin. Form, figure. *Khiyar*, (v. n. of خار for خیر) Preferring, choosing, selecting.

P خیر *khīr*, A darkness in the eye, a mote or dust playing before it. The herb ox-eye. Astonished, bewildered. Bare-faced, impudent, dissolute, insolent. Brave. Vain, useless, trifling, absurd. Causeless.

A خیّر *khayyir*, (pl. خارة) A good, religious man.

A خیرات *khayrāt*, (pl. of خیرة *khayrat*) Good things. Good works, charities. Sacred edifices, charitable foundations. Land given in charity, principally to Musulmāns; it is by custom hereditary and alienable.

A خیراتي *khayrātī*, Intended for charitable purposes, given (or to be given) or received in charity.

A خیر اثر *khayr-asar*, Excellent, edifying.

P خیر اندیش *khayr-andesh*, A well-wisher.

P خیر اندیشی *khayr-andeshī*, Well-wishing.

P خیر باد *khayrbād*, Farewell. May he prosper!

P خیر بوا *khīr buwā*, Lesser cardamoms.

A خیرة *khayrat*, A good thing, any thing excellent of whatever species. The best (of men). *Khayrat* or *khiyarat*, Good, pleasing (woman). *Khīrat*, The favour or blessing of God. علی خیرة الله *ʻala' khīrati'llāh*, With the blessing of God. *Khīrat* or *khiyarat*, (v. n. of خار for خیر) Preferring, choosing, selecting. Any thing choice, exquisite. Election, choice. خیرة الله *khīrat* (or *khiyarat*) *allāh*, Muhammad. *Khiyarat*, A choice woman. Good: chosen, selected.

A خیّرة *khayyirat*, A good and religious woman. The city of Madīna.

P خیرخواه *khayr khwāh*, Well-wisher: kind.

P خیر خیر *khīr khīr*, Idle, futile words. Dark. Groundless. Sprightly, saucy.

P خیرسر *khīr-sar*, Vain. Shameless. A trifler.

P خیرگاه *khayr-gāh*, The interior (of a house).

P خیرگي *khīragī*, Malevolence, malignity. Obscurity, dimness.

P خیرو *khīrū*, Ox-eye. Mallow-flower.

P خیره *khīra*, Malevolent, malignant, quarrelsome, moody, contumacious, froward, perverse, obstinate, headstrong, unwilling to hearken. Impudent, shameless, dissolute. Brave, daring. Astonished, confounded. Broken down, helpless. Dazzled, fatigued. Dark, cloudy. Causeless, groundless. Clear, manifest. Torpid, sleeping (limb). Vacant, indolent, idle. Much, many. Stupor, astonishment. A mote or dust playing before the eye. The herb ox-eye. خیره چشم رفتن *khīra-chashm raftan*, To walk with half-shut eyes, careless and inattentive to surrounding objects. خیره کردن *khīra kardan*, To dazzle.

P خیره درای *khīra-darāy*, Simple, silly.

P خیره دست *khīra-dast*, Refractory, stubborn, headstrong. Awkward, slow, unskilful. Unlucky.

P خیره روي *khīra-rūy*, Shameless.

P خیره سر *khīra-sar*, Stupid, blundering; silly.

P خیره کش *khīra-kush*, Fearless. Tyrannical. An oppressor of the weak. One who puts to death without a cause. A beloved object.

P خیره کوش *khīra-kosh*, Crazy. A lover.

A خیريٰ *khayra'* or *khīra'*, Abounding in good things. *Khīra'*, Good, pleasing (woman).

P خیري *khīrī*, A portico, a balcony. An apartment on the top of a house from whence any object is viewed. Red colour. Mallows. Name of a certain flower of which there are several species; one black, called خیريء خطائی *khīrī-i khatāʼī*; another violet, called خیريء میردیني *khīrī-i mīrdīnī*, or هفت رنگ *haft-rang*, Seven-coloured: another, red and white, which is wild, and called خیريء خزامي *khīrī-i khazāmī*: and another yellow, called خیريء شیرازي *khīrī-i shīrāzī* or همیشه بهار *hamesha-bahār*.

A خیريّة *khayrīyat*, Welfare, safety.

P خیز *khez*, Impatient, pettish. The wantonness of the female pigeon. A spring, leap. Assault, shock, brunt. A wave. (in comp.) Awaking, exciting. Rising; a riser. Leaping, bounding, capering. سحر خیز *sahar-khez*, An early riser. شب خیز *shab-khez*, Rising in the night, leading sleepless nights. فتنه خیز *fitna-khez*, Exciting a tumult.

P خیز آب *khez-āb*, A wave, surge, billow.

P خیزان *khezān*, Rising, leaping. A wave. A root running far and wide. افتان و خیزان *uftān u khezān*, Falling and rising.

A خیزب *khayzab*, Soft, tender (flesh).

A خیزبان *khayzabān*, Soft, tender (flesh). A young ostrich.

A خیزبة *khayzabat*, A piece of flesh.

A خیزران *khayzurān*, (pl. خیازر *khayāzir*) A reed, cane, rattan. The root of the cypress. A certain Indian tree with long roots. Any limber stick. Spears. Oar. Rudder. Name of a house at Mecca. خیزران بلدي *khayzurāni baladī*, Wild myrtle.

A خیزرانة *khayzurānat*, A rudder, helm.

A خیزريٰ *khayzara'*, (or خیزلیٰ) The gait of one who walks as if his limbs were out of joint.

A خیزقة *khayzakat*, A sort of pot-herb.

P خیز گیر *khez-gīr*, (or خیزه گیر *kheza-gīr*) Rise and catch (children's game, somewhat like blindman's buff). A pigeon intoxicated with love.

A خیزل *khayzal*, (or خیزلیٰ *khayzala'*) A heavy, sluggish pace.

P خیزنده *khezanda*, Rising, leaping. Sliding. A boy's game of sliding from high ground. A sledge.

P خیزوان *khīzwān*, Name of a country.

A خیزور *khayzūr*, A reed, cane, rattan.

P خیزیدن *khezīdan*, To rise, leap. To totter, slide. To go softly. To creep on all fours.

A خیس *khays*, (v. n. of خاس for خیس) Exhaling a disagreeable smell, stinking, corrupting, being putrid (carcase). Being neglected, despised (meat upon a table, as not fresh). Being flat (a market). Violating a treaty, breaking a promise. Being fixed (to a place). Grief, trouble. Sin, crime, error. A lie. *Khīs*, (pl. اخياس *akhyās*) A thick forest, den (of a lion). Thick, entangled reeds. Milk flowing copiously. A good thing. *Khiyas*, (pl. of خيسة *khīsat*) Lions' dens.

P خيس *khīs*, A coarse linen counterpane.

A خيسان *khayasān*, (v. n. of خاس for خيس) Neglecting, dissolving, breaking (an engagement).

P خيسانيدن *khīsānīdan*, (or خيسابيدن *khīsāyīdan*) To cause to moisten. To mix. To creep forward (as a child).

A خيسة *khīsat*, (pl. خيس *khiyas*) A lion's den.

A خيسرى *khaysara'*, Destruction. Error. Perfidy. Sordidness, baseness.

A خيسرى *khaysarīy*, Losing the way. Suffering loss.

A خيسفان *khaysafān* or *khaysufān*, A worthless date. A palm that bears little, and whose dates spoil.

A خيسفوج *khaysafūj*, Cotton-seed. Rotten wood, particularly of the عشر *ɛushar*. A rudder.

A خيسفوجة *khaysafūjat*, The rudder of a ship.

A خيسق *khaysak*, Deep (well or grave).

P خيسنده *khīsinda*, Moistening. A cold infusion.

P خيسه *khīsa*, A coarse coverlet or garment.

P خيسيدن *khīsīdan*, To moisten, dissolve, or mix (an electuary). To knead a mass of paste with hands or feet. To chew. To start back (as a horse). To dread, to be terrified.

A خيش *khaysh*, (pl. اخياش *akhyāsh* and خيوش *khuyūsh*) Coarse linen cloth of an open texture, canvas. A mean, contemptible man. خيش العمل *khayshu'l ɛamal*, Expeditious in business.

P خيش *khesh*, A sort of linen cloth. Wadded, lined (garment). A yoke. A ploughshare. A ploughbeam. خيش مصر *kheshi misr*, Egyptian linen. بن خيش *buni kesh*, The plough-tail or handle.

P خيشاوه *khīshāwa*, Land prepared for sowing.

P خيشخانه *khesh-khāna*, A kind of tent constructed of reeds or linen cloth. A tent with tatties to exclude the heat. A linen shirt or shift. Pure gold.

P خيشفوج *khayshafūj*, Cotton-seed.

A خيشوم *khayshūm*, (pl. خياشيم *khayāshīm*) The nose. The bridge and the interior of the nose: the root of the nose. The olfactory region. A promontory, the projection of a mountain.

A خيشى *khayshīy*, Maker of the canvas *khaysh*.

A خيص *khays*, (v. n. of خاص for خيص) Being few. Small (thing) either given or received. *Khayas*, Inequality of the eyes, one being larger.

A خيصاء *khaysās*, (fem. of اخيص *akhyas*) (A she-goat) having one horn erect, the other close to the head. Having an inequality in the size of the eyes. Large and weak (woman).

A خيصان *khaysān*, Little (money).

A خيصى *khaysa'*, Any thing or people separated, scattered. A small quantity (of herbage).

A خيّض *khayyiz*, (A sword) made of male and female iron.

A خيضعة *khayzaɛat*, A helmet. A diversity of sounds. A clashing of swords. Shouts of war. Dust. A battle-field.

A خيضف *khayzaf*, One who breaks wind in the presence of others.

A خيط *khayt*, (v. n. of خاط for خيط) Sewing. Gliding swiftly upon sand (a serpent). (pl. خيطان *khītān*) A herd of ostriches. A swarm of locusts. (pl. اخياط *akhyāt*, خيوط *khuyūt*, and خيوطة *khuyūtat*) A thread, string, twine. A small rope. A herd of ostriches. A swarm of locusts. الخيط الاسود *al khaytu'l aswad*, The black thread, *i. e.* the darkness of the night, or the first appearance of twilight. الخيط الابيض *al khaytu'l abyaz*, The white thread, *i. e.* the dawn when diffused all around. خيط الرقبة *khaytu'r rakabat*, Spinal marrow. خيط باطل *khayti bātil*, Threads of vanity (*i. e.* an exhalation in warm weather, like threads of cobwebs floating in the air; also, rays of light, resembling threads, passing through crevices in window-shutters into a dark place). *Khīt*, A herd of ostriches. A swarm of locusts. *Khayat*, Length of neck.

A خيطاء *khaytās*, Long-necked (she-ostrich).

A خيطان *khītān*, (pl. of خوط *khūt*) Limber twigs. (pl. of خيط) Herds of ostriches: swarms of locusts.

A خيطة *khaytat*, (v. n. of خاط for خيط) Passing quickly, and at once. One thread. A pole, pin. (in the dialect of Hudayl) A slender rope made of the bark of a tree. A woollen jerkin.

A خيطف *khaytaf*, Swift-going (dromedary).

A خيطفى *khaytafa'*, A rapid pace.

A خيطل *khaytal*, A cat. A dog.

A خيطى *khayta'*, A herd of ostriches. A swarm of locusts.

A خيعامة *khayɛāmat*, A nobody, worthless man. An infamous catamite.

A خيعرة *khayɛarat*, Levity, poverty, and barrenness of mind.

A خيعل *khayɛal*, A sleeveless shift. A garment of skin. A garment open at the sides. A woman's shift open on one side. Wicked (youth), and therefore deserted by his friends. A wolf. A hobgoblin.

A خيعلة *khayɛalat*, (v. n. of خيعل Q) Putting (upon another) a sleeveless shirt or shift.

A خيف *khayf*, (v. n. of خاف for خيف) Fearing. Terror, fear. The declivity, the lower part of a mountain. Higher ground, whence water flows. A camel's sheath. The skin of a camel's udder. A side, tract, quarter. الخيف *al khayf*, A temple on the declivity of mount Mina near Mecca. *Khīf*, (pl. of خيفة *khīfat*) Fears. (pl. of اخيف *akhyaf*) Wall-eyed (men or horses). Wide-sheathed (camels). *Khayaf*, (v. n. of خيف) Being wall-eyed (a horse). A variety in the colour of the eyes (the one being blue and the other black), wall-eyedness. Roominess in the sheath of a camel.

A خيّف *khīyaf* or *khuyyaf*, (pl. of خائف *khāsif*) Timid, fearful.

A خيفاء *khayfās*, (fem. of اخيف *akhyaf*) Wall-eyed (woman). (pl. خيفاوات *khayfāwāt*) (A camel) having a large, loose bag, but destitute of milk. A composition, in which the words occur with and without diacritical points alternately.

A خيفان *khayfān*, Locusts diversified with white, yellow, or green; or whose wings are not yet formed. Excellent, swift (horse). A multitude of men. Name of a mountain-herb.

A خيفة *khayfat*, A knife. The den or haunt of a lion. *Khīfat*, (v. n. of خاف for خوف) Fearing. (pl. خيف *khīf*) Terror, fear.

A خيفق *khayfak*, Very swift (young ostrich, camel, or horse). A woman with long, small-boned legs, and taking long steps. An accident, misfortune. A prodigy. A widely-extended plain.

A خيفقان *khayfakān*, Name of a certain homicide, who, whilst fleeing from the avenger of blood, met his own cousin; who, to aid him in his flight, gave him one of his camels and half his travelling-provisions; in return for which the ungrateful wretch slew him, and took the remaining camel and provisions: hence, to express base ingratitude, ظلم ظلم الخيفقان *zalama zulma'l khayfakān*, He has perpetrated the villainy of Khayfakān.

A خيفقين *khayfakin*, Very swift (camel or ostrich). A misfortune. The noise of a horse's trot.

A خيقم *khaykam*, A particular kind of noise.

P خيك *khīk*, A leathern bottle, bag. A hide. Spoils of animals (as their skins).

P خيكچه *khīkcha*, (dim. of خيك *khīk*) A small bag of Russia leather, holding about 20 English pints of water, which the Persian cavalry tie under the horse's belly or hang at his side.

P خيك دوز *khīk-doz*, A stitcher of bottles.

P خيكله *khaykala*, Name of an herb.

P خيكاب *khīg-āb*, A leathern water-bottle.

P خيل *khayl*, A body of men, a troop. Followers. An encampment, body, tribe. *Khīl*, Snot.

A خيل *khayl*, (v. n. of خال for خيل) Imagining, thinking. Supposing, entertaining a vain notion. Being proud. Halting, limping. Eating frequently of rue. Proud, self-important. Assafœtida. Rue. (pl. اخيال *akhyāl* and خيول *khuyūl*) Horses. Horsemen, cavalry. Thick, squat (camels or horses). A black stallion. A horse-bridle. A possessor, owner. A military standard. A hillock. Not disposed for love, unmarried. Liberal. Beyond suspicion, of an excellent disposition. Suspicion, doubt. Name of a flowering shrub found in Najd. A place without a companion or friend. Weak in mind and body. Attentive, assiduous. A good steward or administrator. A winding-sheet. *Khīl*, (v. n. of خال for خيل) Imagining, supposing. Assafœtida. Rue. (pl. of اخيل *akhyal*) Persons who have many moles on the face. Green magpies. *Khayal*, Arrogance, pride.

A خيلاء *khaylāʼ*, (A woman) marked with many moles (a great beauty). *Khuyalāʼ*, Arrogance, pride.

A خيلان *khīlān*, (pl. of خال *khāl*) Moles on the body. *Khayalān*, (v. n. of خال for خيل) Thinking, entertaining a vain or false notion. Being proud.

A خيلة *khaylat* or *khīlat*, (v. n. of خال for خيل) Thinking, fancying. *Khayalat*, Arrogance, pride.

P خيلتاش *khayltāsh*, A fellow-soldier, comrade. A general.

P خيلخانه *khayl-khāna*, An illustrious family.

A خيلع *khaylaʻ*, Terror, sudden fear. A wolf. An imaginary sylvan demon. A shift without sleeves.

P خيلو *khīlū*, Mallows.

A خيلولة *khaylūlat*, (v. n. of خال for خيل) Imagining, fancying. Being proud. Pride.

P خيلي *khaylī*, Many, very much. Very long.

A خيم *khaym*, (v. n. of خام for خيم) Lifting (the feet). Fearing, acting the coward. Having recourse to fraud. *Khaym*, *khayam*, or *khiyam*, (pl. of خيمة *khaymat*) Tents. *Khīm*, The glittering surface of a sword. Nature, innate property.

P خيم *khīm*, Nature, disposition. A bad disposition. Excrement of the eye, snot, spittle, vomit, scrapings of the intestines. A wound. A large sack, woven from cotton-thread. A fool, a madman.

A خيمان *khayamān*, (v. n. of خام for خيم) Having recourse to fraud. Fearing, acting the coward.

A خيمة *khaymat* or *khīmat*, (pl. خيمات *khaymāt*, خيام *khiyām*, خيم *khaym*, *khiyam*, and *khayam*) A tent, tabernacle, circular pavilion. Any hut framed of trunks and branches of trees. خيمهٔ ازرق *khīmaʼi azrak*, The sky. خيمه بصحرا بردن *khīma ba sahrā burdan*, To be absent or invisible. To be public or exposed to view. خيمه در خرابي زدن *khīma dar kharābī zadan*, To be fearless or shameless. خيمه زدن *khīma zadan*, To pitch one's tent, to alight. To lead an army. To stand erect. To be vain and proud. خيمهٔ دهر *khīmaʼi dahr*, (روحانيان *rūhāniyān*, زنگاري *zangārī*, or كبود *kabūd*) The sky.

A خيمع *khaymaʻ*, An adultress.

P خيمناكان *khīmnākān*, Wounded (men).

P خيمه دوز *khīma-doz*, A tent-maker.

P خيمه زن *khayma-zan*, A pitcher of tents, an officer who has the direction of encampments.

P خيمه سرا *khīma-sarā*, The sky.

P خيمه گاه *khīma-gāh*, A camp.

A خيمي *khaymīy*, A tent-maker.

P خينا *khīnā*, Sweet voice, song, modulation.

P خيناگر *khīnāgar*, A musician, minstrel.

P خينور *khīnawar*, The bridge across hell-fire.

P خينيدن *khīnīdan*, To adorn, to decorate.

P خيو *khayū* or *khīv*, Spittle, saliva.

A خيوت *khuyūt*, Making a noise, exclamation.

A خيور *khuyūr*, (pl. of خير *khayr*) Goods, good things. Desirable moral qualities.

A خيوش *khuyūsh*, Coarse, flimsy linens.

A خيوشة *khuyūshat*, Subtilty. Minuteness.

A خيوط *khuyūt*, (or خيوطة *khuyūtat*) (pl. of خيط *khayt*) Threads, twines, strings.

P خيوق *khīwak*, A country in Persia.

A خيول *khuyūl*, (pl. of خيل) Horses. Troops.

A خيوم *khuyūm*, (v. n. of خام for خيم) Fearing, acting the coward. Using fraud. Lifting the feet.

A خيومة *khuyūmat*, The act of fearing.

A خيهفعي *khayahfaʻaʼ*, (or خيهفعاء *khayahfaʻāʼ*) A mongrel whelp, from a dog and a she-wolf.

A خييّة *khuyayyat*, A small letter خاء *khāʼ*.

A خييل *khuyayl*, (dim. of خال *khāl*) A little mole or freckle.

د

د *dāl*, (called دال ابجد *dāli abjad*, دال غير منقوطة *dāli ghayr mankūta*, or دال مهمله *dāli muhmala*, Undotted *dāl*) The eighth letter of the Arabic and tenth of the Persian alphabets, denoting 4 in arithmetic, and the fourth day in the week, or Wednesday; also the planet Mercury in the Ephemerides, and the sign Leo in the Zodiac. It corresponds to the letter *d*, by which it is represented in this edition. It is sometimes interchangeable with ت *te*, ذ *ze*, or ز *ze*: as, خات *khat* for خاد *khād*, آدر *ādar* for آذر *āzar*, ديزار *dīzār* for ديدار *dīdār*.

P دا *dā*, The groundwork of a building.

A دأ *daʼ*, (imp. of ودأ *wadaʼ*) Leave, let alone.

دأني *daʼnī*, Let me go, leave me alone.

A داء *dāʼ*, (v. n. of دأ for دوأ) Being sick. (pl. ادواء *adwāʼ*) Disease, sickness. Sick, indisposed. داء الاسد *dāʼu'l asad*, The lion's disease, *i.e.* any thing corrosive. داء الثعلب *dāʼu's saʻlab*, The fox's disease, *i.e.* scald, loss of hair. داء الحيّة *dāʼu'l hayyat*, The serpent's disease, *i.e.* a disease in the head causing the skin and hair to fall off. داء الذئب *dāʼu'z ziʼb*, The wolf's disease, *i.e.* hunger. داء الفيل *dāʼu'l fīl*, Elephantiasis. داء الكلب *dāʼu'l kalb*, Canine madness, hydrophobia. به داء الظبي *bihi dāʼu'z zaby*, He has the disease of the gazelle (a beautiful kind of deer), *i.e.* he is faultless; that creature being supposed to have no distemper.

A داًليك *daʼālīk*, (pl. of دؤلوك *duʼlūk*) Important affairs. Alternately. A walking on tip-toe.

A دأليل *daʼālīl*, (pl. of دؤلول *duʼlūl*) Calamities. Confusions.

A دءائث *daʼāʼis*, Roots, origins.

A دأب *daʼb*, (or *daʼab*, (v. n. of دأب) Striving, exerting one's self. Being fatigued. Thrusting violently forward. Custom, habit, manner, mode. Condition, state, situation. دأب صحبت *daʼbi suhbat*, Good manners, civilization. دأب قديم *daʼbi kadīm*, Ancient custom.

P داب *dāb*, Magnificence, pomp; ostentation.

P دابا *dābā*, (in zand and Pāzand) Gold.

P داباهانتن *dābāhānitan*, (in zand) To laugh.

P داباهانيده *dābāhānīda*, Laughing.

A دابّة *dābbat*, (pl. دوابّ *dawābb*) Whatever creeps upon the earth, a reptile. A beast of burden. A saddle-horse, a nag, hack, cob. دابّة الارض *dābbatu'l arz*, The second beast mentioned in the Apocalypse (which, according to a Muhammadan notion, is to come forth from Mecca).

A دابر *dābir*, A follower. The end, extreme part, remains, last. An arrow passing through the mark. An unlucky drawing of a gaming arrow. A building on marshy ground, which totters from the elasticity of the foundation. The arch or vault of a building. Root, origin. مات كدابر *māta kadābir*, He neglected his friend's business. امس الدابر *amsaʼd dābir*, Yesterday.

A دابرة *dābirat*, The latter part, extremity (of a sand-hill). The tendon of the foot. A horny substance growing inside a horse's leg. A bird's spur. The heel. Flight in battle. The art of tripping up the heels in wrestling. Unlucky (woman). The point of the fetlock.

P دابشليم *dābishlīm*, Name of a dynasty that reigned in Somanāt. It is said to signify Great King in the language of India.

A دابق *dābik*, Name of a town.

A دبل دابل *dibli dābil*, A severe calamity.

A دابوغ *dābūgh*, A water-melon.

A دابوق *dābūk*, Birdlime.

P دابونتن *dābūnitan*, (in zand and Pāz.) To give.

P داپرزه *dāparza*, A swallow.

P داتوبر *dātū-bar*, Administering justice, just.

P داتوره *dātūra*, The thorn-apple.

A دآث *daʼās*, (pl. of دأثاء) Handmaids.

A دأث *daʼs*, (v. n. of دأث) Eating. Dirtying, defiling. Filth. Heaviness. *Diʼs*, Implacable hatred.

A دأثاء *daʼsāʼ* or *daʼasāʼ*, A female servant, handmaid. ابن دأثاء *ibn daʼsāʼ*, Foolish, silly.

A داثر *dāsir*, Dirty (garment). Rusty (sword). Perishing. Lost. Inattentive, negligent, forgetful.

P داج *dāj*, Darkness, obscurity. A dark night.

A داجّ *dājj*, Those who go softly. Companions, associates, helpers. Those who let out on hire asses, camels, &c. Partners in trade. Traders. هؤلاء الداجّ و ليسوا بالحاجّ *haʼulāʼu'd dāj wa laysū bi'l hājj*, Those (are) traders, and are not pilgrims.

A داجة *dājat*, The followers of an army, or those who go on pilgrimage to Mecca. Minutiæ, trifles. حاجة داجة *hājat dājat*, Minutiæ, trifles.

A داجن *dājin*, (pl. دواجن *dawājin*) Tame, domestic, cade (animal). Water-drawing (camel).

Incessantly raining (cloud).

A داجنة *dājinat*, A tame sheep or pigeon. An incessant gentle rain overspreading a whole country. Rainy clouds piled one upon another.

A داجي *dājī*, Dark. Humble, obscure (life). Exuberant (benefit).

A داجية *dājiyat*, (pl. دواجي *dawājī*) Dark (night). Ample (wealth), easy (circumstances).

P داچك *dāchak*, An ear-ring.

A داح *dāh*, A painted toy or plaything for children. A platted bracelet. A kind of sweet herb. Ornamental figures on garments or on the body. Streaks on a bull. الدنيا داحة *ad dunya' dāhat*, The world is a pageant (or garish toy).

A داحر *dāhir*, One who thrusts back, or rejects.

A داحس *dāhis*, An abscess at the end of the fingers, a whitlow. Name of a celebrated horse.

A داحق *dāhik*, (pl. داحقون *dāhikūn*) (A camel) whose uterus falls after birth. Passionate. Silly. (pl. دواحق) A sort of thick yellow date.

A داحوس *dāhūs*, An imposthume under the nail, a whitlow.

A داحول *dāhūl*, (pl. دواحيل *dawāhīl*) A trap for wild asses, a buckstall.

A داحوم *dāhūm*, A net for catching foxes.

A داحي *dāhī*, (God) who spreads abroad.

P داختن *dākhtan*, To know.

A داخل *dākhil*, Who or what enters, penetrates, or arrives. Accruing (profit). Inner, internal. The interior. من داخل *min dākhil*, From within. داخل الحب *dākhilu'l hubb*, Sincere love. (according to some) Purity within the jar. داخل السرّ *dākhilu's sirr*, In the secret, a confidant. P داخل شدن *dākhil shudan*, To belong, to be referred to.

P داخل *dākhul*, A king's court.

A داخلة *dākhilat*, (pl. دواخل *dawākhil*) Low (ground). Custom, fashion, habit, rule. Intention, purpose, mind, heart. The part of the breeches which touches the body on the right side.

A داخله *dākhila*, Receipt for goods or money.

A داخلي *dākhilī*, Contained, belonging to.

P داخم *dākhim*, Sustenance, daily bread.

P داخول *dākhol*, A kind of seat or bench at the entrance of a palace. Figures set up at the corners of fields to frighten wild beasts into the toils. A scarecrow. A king's court.

P داخيدن *dākhīdan*, To open the eyes, to stare. To separate, divide one thing from another.

P داد *dād*, He gave. A gift. Justice, equity. Redress of grievances. Complaint, lamentation (under oppression). Measure. A part, portion. Revenge. A ringworm. Life. Age. A year. داد خدا *dādi khudā*, Gift of God. داد خواستن *dād khwāstan*, To demand redress. داد دادن *dād dādan*, To administer justice, to decide a cause. داد دل *dādi dil*, Heart's desire. داد ستاندن *dād satāndan*, To take vengeance. داد كردن *dād kardan*, To do justice, decide a law-suit, adjudge. داد و فرياد كردن *dād u firyād kardan*, To implore justice, to call aloud for vengeance. عدل و داد *ʿadl u dād*, Equity and justice.

P دادا *dādā*, A female servant, particularly an old one who has attended upon any one from her youth. A bandmaid.

A داداء *dādāʾ*, (pl. دآدئ *daʾādiʾ*) The latter part of the month. The night of the 25th, 26th, 27th, 28th, or 29th of the month. The three last nights of the moon. A wide channel of a river.

A دأدأة *daʾdaʾat*, (v. n. of دأدأ Q) Galloping at full speed (a camel). Following the traces of any one. Urging forward at full speed. Being present. Stirring (a thing). Stilling (a thing). Covering (a thing). The noise of a stone thrown into a torrent; also that of the rocking of a cradle. A throng, press. ليلة دأدأ *laylatun daʾdaʾ*, (دأدأة *daʾdaʾat* or دأدأءة *daʾdaʾat*) A dark, moonless night.

P دادار *dādār*, (for داد آور *dād-āwar*) Distributor of justice. One of the epithets of God.

P داد استاد *dād istād*, داد ستد *dād sitad*, or داد ستاد *dād sitād*, Giving and taking, buying and selling; commerce.

P داد آفريد *dād-āfarīd*, (or داد آفرين *dād-āfarīn*) Name of God. Name of a note in music.

P داداله *dādāla*, The handle of the bat at the game of hockey.

P دادان *dādān*, A title of the kings of Persia, from كيومرث *kayūmars* to گشتاسپ *gushtāsp*.

P داد بازي *dād-bāzī*, A game played with dice.

P داد بخش *dād-bakhsh*, Justice-dispensing.

P داد پرس *dād-purs*, Demanding justice.

P داد پرسي *dād-pursī*, A demand for justice.

A دادة *dādat*, An elderly female servant.

P داد خواه *dād-khwāh*, A petitioner for justice.

P داد خواهي *dād-khwāhī*, Requisition of justice.

A دأددة *daʾdadat*, (v. n. of دأدد Q) Playing.

P داد ده *dād-dih*, Distributing justice (name of God). The fourteenth day of the month, according to the æra of Yazdagird.

P داد دهش *dād-dihish*, Munificence: a present.

P داد دهي *dād-dihī*, Administration of justice.

P دادر *dādar* or *dir*, Brother, dear friend. God.

P داد راست *dād-rāst*, Just, upright.

P دادر اندر *dādar-andar*, A brother uterine.

P داد رسي *dād-rasī*, Redress, retributive justice.

P دادرند *dādarand*, An elder brother.

P دادستان *dādistān*, Being a partner. Being contented and satisfied. *Dād-satān*, An avenger. A king. A judicial decree.

P داد سخن *dād-sukhan*, Appreciation of a speech.

P داد طلب *dād-talab*, Seeking justice.

P داد فرماي *dād-farmāy*, God. A just king.

P دادك *dādak*, A lord chief justice. *Dāduk*, An old servant. An officer of justice.

P داد گاه *dād-gāh*, A judgment-seat. A sepulchral monument.

P دادگر *dādgar*, An administrator of justice. A superintendant of the markets, who puts a price upon provisions. Name of a certain feast. God Omnipotent. A just king.

P دادگري *dādgarī*, Administration of justice.

P داد گستر *dād-gustar*, Just. God. The heart.

P داد گير *dād-gīr*, Just. An avenger. Custom.

P دادن *dādan*, To give. To command. To play the whore. جواب باز دادن *jawāb bāz dādan*, To give a reply.

P دادند *dādand*, An elder brother.

P دادندر *dādandar*, A uterine brother.

P دادني *dādanī*, Worthy to be given. A present. Place of gifts, *i.e.* where presents must be offered. Advance of money for work or goods.

P دادو *dādū*, An aged servant. One who has served from his youth. A tutor. A youth.

P دادور *dādwar*, A name of God.

P داد و ستد *dād u sitad*, Giving and taking, lending or borrowing.

P دادوند *dādwand*, Equal, even, just.

P داده *dāda*, Given, delivered. Giving. تاب داده *tāb-dāda*, Inflamed. جزا داده *jazā-dāda*, Rewarded, requited, or chastised according to desert. داده آمدن *dāda āmadan*, To be given.

A دآدئ *daʾādiʾ*, (pl. of دأداء *daʾdāʾ*, ديداء *didāʾ*, or دؤدؤ *duʾduʾ*) The latter parts of a month, the three or four last days of the moon.

P دادي *dādī*, Name of a small bitter grain.

P داذر *dāzar*, A brother. A friend. God.

P داذر اندر *dāzar-andar*, A uterine brother.

A داذيّ *dāziy*, A certain beverage in use among reprobate fellows.

P دار *dār*, A gallows, gibbet. A beam. The roofing of a house. A tree, stake. Wood. Rope-dancing; also the rope on which they perform. A die for coining money. Long pepper. Name of a city in Malwa, or central India. Name of God. (in comp.) Holding, possessing, keeping: a keeper. Possessor, lord, master. آبدار *āb-dār*, Watery. Waving. A water-keeper. Resplendent. Fresh. پيشاني دار *peshānī-dār*, Having a front; impudent, obstinate. حصّه دار *hissa-dār*, A partaker, partner. ريش دار *rīsh-dār*, Having a beard. عمل دار *ʿamal-dār*, A tax-gatherer. گوشت دار *gosht-dār*, Fleshy. مالدار *māl-dār*, Opulent. وام دار *wām-dār*, A debtor. دار دادن *dār dādan*, To impale. دار شيشعان *dār shīshaʿān*, An aromatic bark of a prickly tree.

A دار *dār*, (pl. ادؤر *adʾur*, آدر *ādur*, ادور *adwur*, ديار *diyār*, ديارة *diyārat*, ديارات *diyārāt*, ديران *dīrān*, دوران *dūrān*, دورات *dūrāt*, ادوار *adwār*, and ادورة *adwirat*) A house, dwelling, mansion, habitation, inhabited place. A city. A tribe. A camp. Paradise. (poet.) Fire. Hell. Name of an idol. دار الادب *dāru'l adab*, A seat of learning, university. دار الامان *dāru'l amān*, House of safety. A country in which there is peace. دار الحرب *dāru'l harb*, An enemy's country. دار السلام *dāru's salām*, The mansion of peace. Paradise. The Ottoman Porte. Baghdād. Damascus. دار السلطنة *dāru's sultanat*, (دار الخلافة *dāru'l khilāfat*, دار السعادة *dāru's saɛādat*, or دار الملك *dāru'l milk*) Royal residence, metropolis. دار الخلافة آدم *dāru'l khilāfati ādam*, (or دار الخلافة پدر *dāru'l khilāfati pidar*) The world. دار سرور *dāri surūr*, (House of joy) Paradise. دار الشفاء *dāru'sh shifā*, (دار المرض *dāru'l maraz*, or دار المرضى *dāru'l marza'*) An hospital, infirmary. دار الضرب *dāru'z zarb*, (or ذهب *zahab*) The mint. دار الضيافة *dāru'z ziyāfat*, Banqueting-house. دار العيار *dāru'l ɛiyār*, Assay-office. دار القضا *dāru'l kazā*, Judgment-seat, tribunal of justice. دار الكتب *dāru'l kutub*, A library. دار غرور *dāri ghurūr*, (House of delusion) The world. دار غرور و محنت *dāri ghurūr u mihnat*, The dwelling of pride and wretchedness, i. e. The world (called also دار ابتلا *dāri ibtilā*, House of temptation; دار البوار *dāru'l bawār*, Dwelling of perdition (likewise hell); دار الحزن *dāru'l huzn*, Valley of tears, or house of sorrow; دار فنا *dāri fanā*, The frail house; and دار شش در *dāri shush dar*, House with six doors. دار البقا *dāru'l bakā*, Life eternal: synonymous to which are, دار الاخرة *dāru'l akhirat*, The last home; دار الخلد *dāru'l khuld*, House of eternity; دار القرار *dāru'l karār*, House of permanency; and دار اليقين *dāru'l yakīn*, Sure abode. دار نعيم *dāri naɛīm*, Mansion of glory, Paradise. الدار *ad'dār*, Madīna. الداران *ad'dārāni*, (or الدارين *ad'dārayn*) The present and future life.

A دارّ *dārr*, Bright, shining (lamp). Giving much milk (camel). Milky (plant). Frequently paid (tribute).

P دارا *dārā*, Holding fast. A possessor. God. Darius, son of Dārāb. The Darii, kings of Persia. A sovereign. Lees, sediment. دارائ روم *dārāi rūm*, Alexander the Great.

P داراب *dārāb*, Pomp, pride. The noise of combatants. A supporter, protector, preserver. Name of the eldest daughter of Bahman. Name of the eighth king of the Kayānian dynasty.

A دارابزين *dārābzīn*, A settee, settle, sofa.

P دارات *dārāt*, Magnificence, pomp, state.

A دارات *dārāt*, (pl. of دارة *dārat*) Houses. Circular places.

P داراد *dārād*, A name of God.

P دارادار كردن *dārādār kardan*, To abide, be firm, fixed, permanent. دارادار نمودن *dār-ā-dār namūdan*, To delay, defer, put off.

P دار آفرين *dār-āfrīn*, Any thing upon which one leans. A screen, lattice. Name of a drug. A person in whom one reposes confidence. An epithet of God. A raised bench, a sofa.

P دارانيدن *dārānīdan*, To cause to hold.

P داراي *dārāy*, A keeper, a supporter. God. Lord of the species. A king.

P دارائ گونه *dārāi gūna*, Lord of the species.

P دارائي *dārāī*, Belonging to Darius. Sovereignty. A red silken stuff (when waved خارا *khārā*).

A دارب *dārib*, Accustomed to hunt, trained.

P داربا *dār-bā*, Necessary, needful.

P دارباز *dār-bāz*, A rope-dancer.

P داربام *dār-bām*, The principal beam for the support of a roof.

A داربة *dāribat*, Clever woman. Female drummer.

P داربر *dār-bur*, A woodpecker.

P داربزين *dār-bazīn*, A screen or lattice-work in front of a door. A thing on which one leans.

P داربوي *dār-būy*, Odoriferous wood, aloes.

P دارپرنيان *dār-parniyān*, Brazil-wood.

P دارپرة *dār-para*, (or دارپژ) A chaffinch.

P دارپژة *dār-paja*, A linnet, a goldfinch.

A دارة *dārat*, (pl. دارات *dārāt* and دور *dūr*) A house. A halo round the moon. A circular place. A round heap of sand. Whatever encompasses a thing, a circle, a circumference. Land lying betwixt mountains. An Arabian tribe. Misfortune. The word دارة *dārat* is prefixed to more than a hundred places in Arabia, for which room cannot be found here: as, دارة جلجل *dāratu juljulin*, &c.

A دارج *dārij*, Moved by the wind (dust), and obliterating the vestiges of habitations. (An infant) beginning to walk.

P دارچوب *dārchob* or *chūb*, A three-legged piece of wood on which they hang clothes, a clothes-horse.

P دارچيني *dār-chīnī*, (A صيني) Cinnamon.

P دارخال *dār-khāl*, A branch, sucker, sapling. A tree not grafted.

P دارد *dārd*, A name of God.

P داردار كردن *dārdār kardan*, To remain firm.

P داردان *dārdān*, A nursery-ground.

P داردست *dār-dust*, Nightshade.

P دارزرد *dār-zard*, Turmeric.

A دارس *dāris*, Menstruous (woman). Obliterated, illegible (book), effaced (foot-step).

P دارسنب *dār-sumb*, A wimble, gimblet. A woodpecker.

P دارسنج *dār-sanj*, The world.

P دارش *dārish*, Retention, custody, guardianship, protection.

A دارش *dārish*, A black hide or leather.

A دارع *dāriɛ*, Armed with a coat of mail.

P دارفرين *dār-farīn*, A platform on which they place cushions to sit on, particularly at shop-doors.

P دارفلفل *dār-filfil*, Long pepper.

A داركة *dārikat*, The understanding.

P داركدو *dār-kadū*, A post whence they suspend cups of gold as marks and prizes for archers, who shoot riding full speed.

P داركوب *dār-kob*, A woodpecker.

P داركيسة *dār-kīsa*, A follicle, a pod.

P داركوش *dār gosh*, Preserve, take care of.

A دارم *dārim*, One who goes with short steps. Who smooths the nails. A kind of tree.

A دارمة *dārimat*, A hedge-hog.

P دارمدار *dār-madār*, Adjustment of a dispute.

P دارمك *dārmak*, A kind of fragrant grass.

P دارموش *dār-mūsh*, Arsenic.

P دارندگي *dārandagī*, Possession, tenure, holding.

P دارندة *dāranda*, Having, holding. Keeper, possessor. A bearer, carrier, messenger. دارندۀ فرمان عاليشان *dārandai farmāni ɛāli-shān*, Bearer or messenger of the king's orders. دارندگان مكتوب *dārandagāni maktūb*, Letter-carriers.

P دارنگ *dāring*, A butcher's tray.

P دارنمك *dār-namak*, A woodpecker.

P دارنهال *dār-nihāl*, Logwood.

P دارني *dārinī*, Name of a place in India abounding in idol-temples.

P دارو *dārū*, A medicine, drug. A remedy. Oxymel. A preparation of vinegar and honey. Spirituous liquors. Gunpowder. An inferior order of priests (amongst the fire-worshippers). A good man. داروي بندق *dārūyi bunduk*, Gunpowder. داروي بيهوش *dārūyi bīhosh*, A maddening draught. داروي چشم *dārūyi chashm*, An eye-salve, collyrium. داروي ديگ شكسته *dārūyi degi shikāsta*, A composition of sand and blood for mending broken pots and pans. داروي ريختني *dārūyi rekhtanī*, An injection, clyster. داروي گرم *dārūyi garm*, Hot spices, cloves, cinnamon.

P داروبرد *dār u bard*, Power, strength. Pomp, pride, strut. Battle, conflict. An arch, dome, cupola.

P دارودار *dārū-dār*, A foolish talker. One who doubles his stakes at play.

P دارودان *dārūdān*, A medicine-chest.

P داروشناسي *dārū-shināsī*, Pharmacy.

P داروغگي *dāroghagī*, A superintendency.

P داروغه *dārogha*, Head man of an office, prefect of a town or village, overseer, or superintendant of any department.

P دارو فروش *dārū-farosh*, A vender of medicines, apothecary, pharmacopolist.

P داروفروشي *dārū-faroshī*, Trade of an apothecary.

P دارو كننده *dārū-kunanda*, A medical man.

P داروكوب *dārū-kob*, One who brays medicines in a mortar. A mortar in which drugs are pounded. *Dār u kob*, (Hold and beat) Pomp, pride.

P دار و گير *dār u gīr*, Hold and take. Tumult, bustle, conflict: noise of combatants. Pomp, pride.

P دارة *dāra*, A scythe, sickle. A circle. A halo round the moon. A stipend, salary.

A دارهات الدهر *dārihātu'd dahr*, The assaults of fortune.

P داري *dārī*, Thou hast or holdest. Superintendant of the public granaries. A court, palace.

A bell in the Christian churches in the East, for summoning the people to worship. A certain measure of wheat.

A داري *dārī*, Conscious.

A دارِي *dāris*, Troubled with buboes.

A داريّ *dāriy*, One who keeps close at home. Delicate, enjoying the luxuries of life. (A camel) remaining in the fold after the others have gone. Some one, any one. The seaman who directs the sails. Belonging to the town of دارين *dārīn*. Musk, brought from Dārīn. A seller of perfumes.

A داريّة *dārīyat*, A man who stays at home.

A دارين *dārayn*, The present and future life. *Dārīn*, A sea-port in that part of Arabia called بحرين *bahrayn*, an emporium for Indian spices.

P داريونان *dār-yūnān*, Name of a medicine.

P داز *dāz*, Beards (of corn). Bones (of fish). A plasterer. Plaster. A plastered wall. A building.

P دازر *dāzar*, A builder. An epithet of God.

P دازه *dāza*, A perch, hen-roost. A word.

P داژ *dāj*, Sweepings: those of a barn.

P داس *dās*, A sickle, reaping-hook. A long-handled bill, used as a weapon of war. Destruction. Potters' earth. A beard of corn. A fish-bone. A noose, toil, snare. Rue. A pot, pan. داس رز *dāsi raz*, A vine-dresser's hook. داس زرين *dāsi zarīn*, The new moon. داس ودلوس *dās u dalūs*, Broken in pieces, destroyed. Foolish, base. Prunings, trifles, rubbish.

P داسار *dāsār*, (or داستار) A crier, broker.

P داستان *dāstān*, History. A theme, fable, romance, tale, story, news. Notoriety. Snares, ambush.

P داستخاله *dāstkhāla*, (داستغاله *dāstghāla*, داستكاله *dāstkāla*, داسخاله *dāskhāla*, داسغاله *dāsghāla*, داسكاله *dāskāla*, داسگاله *dāsgāla*, or داسگله *dāsgala*) A small sickle, pruning, or weeding-hook. A lopping-instrument. A hooked stick for pulling down branches. A mistress.

P داس درو *dās-dirav*, A sickle. Harvest.

A داسرة *dāsirat*, Swift (she-camel).

A داسم *dāsim*, A friend, companion in travail.

P داسه *dāsa*, A sickle. A beard of corn.

A داسي *dāsī*, Impure, unholy.

P داش *dāsh*, A potter's furnace. A repository for ashes. A present. (added to a noun), A companion, as خواجه داش *khwāja-dāsh*, (or سبق داش *sabak-dāsh*) A school-fellow.

P داشاب *dāshāb*, A present, free gift.

P داشاد *dāshād*, A donative. Remuneration, amends. A kiln. Cheerfulness, glee. An apothecary, perfumer.

P داشت *dāsht*, He had, he held. A bringing up, breeding, taking care of, patronage. The grooming of a horse. Service. A potter's furnace. A present. داشت نيكو يافته *dāshti nekū-yāfta*, Well-groomed (horse).

P داشتن *dāshtan*, To have. To hold. To possess. To profess, maintain. To treat. To owe. بر داشتن *bar dāshtan*, To exalt, raise up. To bear, carry. برپاي داشتن *bar pāy dāshtan*, To erect, to place upright.

P داشته *dāshta*, Had, holden. Old, worn out. دشمني داشته شدن *dushmanī dāshta shudan*, To be held in abhorrence.

P داشخار *dāsh-khār*, (or داشخال) Dross of iron.

P داشن *dāshan*, A present, free gift. Wages, recompence. A largess in money or clothing distributed amongst the poor by the ancient kings of Persia on certain days of public rejoicing.

A داشن *dāshin*, A new house, not yet inhabited. A new garment, not yet worn.

A دأص *daʿas*, (v. n. of دئص) Exulting, rejoicing, being petulant, insolent with joy. Being fat and well-liking (cattle).

A داصة *dāsat*, (pl. of دائص) Robbers, pirates.

A دأض *daʿaz*, Fatness. Fulness.

A دأظ *daʿz*, (v. n. of دأظ) Suffocating, strangling. Filling (a bottle). Being fat. Squeezing matter from a sore. Angering, insulting.

A داعب *dāʿib*, A player, a jester. Water muddy in its current.

A داع داع *dāʿi dāʿi*, Used in calling to sheep.

A داعر *dāʿir*, Impure. A whoremonger. Worm-eaten and worthless wood. Name of a certain camel of an illustrious race.

A داعرة *dāʿirat*, Impure, wicked, depraved (woman). (pl. مداعر *madāʿir* or مداعير *madāʿīr*) An unfruitful palm-tree.

A داعريّة *dāʿirīyat*, Camels descended from داعر *dāʿir*, A celebrated sire.

A داعك *dāʿik*, Foolish, silly.

A داعكة *dāʿikat*, Foolish. Fool-hardy (woman).

A داعل *dāʿil*, Who or what flees away.

A داعي *dāʿī*, Who or what invites or stimulates (others) to any thing. An author, cause. Affectionate (servant), wishing well, invoking blessings. The muezzin who calls to prayer. Who or what urges the necessity of any thing. An orator. A plaintiff. داعي الله *dāʿī allāh*, Muhammad. *Dāʿī*, (or داعية *dāʿiyat*) Remains (of milk in the udder).

A داعية *dāʿiyat*, The neighing of a war-horse. Petition, desire. Claim, pretension. Necessity, fatality. Cause, reason. Purpose, intention, resolution.

P داغ *dāgh*, A mark. Scar, spot, freckle. A blemish. Cautery. A spot upon a garment, iron-mould. A mountain. Name of a poet. داغ بلندان *dāghi balandān*, A mark made upon the forehead by frequent prostrations. داغ شدن *dāgh shudan*, To be scarred. To acquire celebrity. To be old and worn. داغ كردن *dāgh kardan*, To mark. داغ گازران *dāghi gāzurān*, A mark made on linens sent to be bleached, that they may not be changed. An indelible mark.

P داغ بررو *dāgh bar rū*, Mark of servitude.

P داغدار *dāgh-dār*, Spotted, striped: a slave.

A داغر *dāghir*, Abject. ذهب صاغرا وداغرا *zahaba sāghiran wa dāghiran*, He became abject and despicable.

P داغسر *dāgh-sar*, Bald. Name of a sweetly-singing bird. A cock-sparrow.

A داغصة *dāghisat*, Knee-pan. Pure water.

A داغلة *dāghilat*, A secret grudge. Those who narrowly watch the faults and failings of others.

A داغم *dāghim*, A black, swarthy man.

P داغ نه *dāgh-nih*, Shaming, disgracing, branding.

P داغول *dāghol*, A cheat, knave, impostor.

P داغولي *dāgholī*, Knavery, fraud, imposture. Bastardy. Name of a spy.

P داغي *dāghī*, Spotted, stained. داغي شدن *dāghī shudan*, To bear a mark. To acquire notoriety. To wax old, wear out.

P داغينه *dāghīna*, Old, used, worn out. The hot iron with which they perform the cautery.

A دافّة *dāffat*, An army gradually approaching the enemy.

A دافر *dāfir*, Stinking.

A دافع *dāfiʿ*, One who drives back, averts, or hinders. A protector. (A camel or a sheep) having biestings in the udder before bringing forth.

A دافعة *dāfiʿat*, (pl. دوافع *dawāfiʿ*) (A camel or a sheep) having biestings in the udder before bringing forth. A river, a running stream. Low ground. Repellent. قوّت دافعه *kūwati dāfiʿa*, The repelling power, or that of expulsion.

A دافق *dāfik*, (Water) poured out.

A دافناء *dāfināʾ*, The arcana (of business).

A دافنة *dāfinat*, (A cow) whose teeth are worn down with age.

A دافه *dāfih*, (for هادف) A stranger, traveller.

A داقّ *dākk*, (pl. دققة *dakakat*) One who knocks, a knocker. One who pries into or publishes the failings of Musulmāns.

A داقع *dākiʿ* Poor, abject. One who pursues trifles.

A داكس *dākis*, (for كادس *kādis*) An omen or portent drawn from sneezing, &c.

A دأل *daʿl*, Fraud. A wolf. A kind of weasel. *Daʿl*, (*daʿal* or دألي *daʿalaʾ*) (v. n. of دأل) Going slow (as being heavy laden). A short, quick, and lively step. *Daʿal*, (or دألان *daʿalān*) Deceiving.

P دال *dāl*, A large black eagle. A huge fish. Thick and fat (woman). (for دار *dār*) Hold. دال مينوفر *dāli mīnūfar*, One chapter of the one-and-twenty composing the Zand.

A دال *dāl*, Name of the letter د. Crooked, curved. (pl. of دالة *dālat*) Fames, celebrities, publicities.

A دالّ *dāll*, Who or what indicates, points out, directs, shews, signifies, denotes, or implies. Significant, indicatory, expressive, typical.

P دالابه *dālāba*, (Pickets) on guard.

P دالان *dālān*, (or دالانه *dālāna*) A hall, vestibule. A covered way.

A دألان daʼalān, A jackal. A sort of gait.

A دالب dālib, A live coal, firebrand.

P دالبزة dālbuza, A yellow-hammer (a small bird).

P دالبوز dālbūz, (دالبوزة dālbūza, or دالپوزة dālpūza) A kind of swallow.

P دال پرنيان dāl parniyān, Brazilian wood.

P دال پره dāl para, A chaffinch.

A دالة dālat, (v. n. of دال for دول) Becoming public, famous, notorious. (pl. دال dāl) Fame.

A دالّة dāllat, An amorous blandishment. Bravery, boldness, gallantry.

A دالج dālij, One who pours water from a well into a cistern. One who carries milk in a pail.

A دالح dālih, (pl. دلّح dullah and دوالح dawālih) (A cloud) full of rain.

A دالخ dālikh, (pl. دالخون dālikhūna) Enjoying a plenteous year.

P دال خال dāl-khāl, A shrub transplanted.

A دالع dāliʻ, (Foolish) in the highest degree. Useless, profitless (affair).

A دالف dālif, (pl. دلّف dullaf and دلف duluf) Heavy laden, going slow. (An arrow) falling near the mark, and then bounding off to a distance.

A دالق dālik, (A sword) easily drawn or dropping out of the sheath. Fiercely-rushing (troop).

P دال من dāl-man, A black eagle.

A دالولاء dālūlāʼ, Affected disdain in a woman.

A داله dālih, (or دالهة) Weak in mind.

A دألى daʼalaʼ, A weak kind of gait. A running pace with short steps. The pace of a joyous person.

A دالي dālī, (pl. دلاة dulāt) One who draws up water in a bucket.

A دالية dāliyat, (pl. دوالي dawālī) A water-wheel turned by oxen. Ground watered by such wheels. A vine. A thing made of palm-leaves tied on the tops of the palm-branches.

A دأم daʼm, (v. n. of دأم) Shoring up (a wall). A veil, covering.

P دام dām, A snare, trap, gin, or net. Creeping things. A winged thing. Every kind of quadruped that is not rapacious, a deer, roe, gazelle. Worldly illusions. The fortieth part of a rupee. دام گشتن dām gashtan, To spread a net. To cheat, gull. To escape from a snare.

A دام dāma, (in prayer) May it endure for ever! دام فضله dāma fazluhu, May his virtues be perpetual! دام عزّه dāma ʻizzuhu, May his glory be eternal! (and in the feminine) دامت معاليه dāmat maʻālīku, May his excellency live for ever!

A دأماء daʼmāʼ, (or داماء dāmāʼ) The sea.

A دأماء daʼmāʼ, (or دامّاء dāmmāʼ) (pl. دوامّ dawāmm) The hole of a shrew; earth scraped out of it. The sea.

P داماد dāmād, A son-in-law. A father-in-law. Husband of the king's sister. A near ally.

P دامادي dāmādī, Affinity, the relation of a son-in-law. دامادي كردن dāmādī kardan, To contract an alliance, to marry.

P دامان dāmān, Skirt, hem: foot of a mountain.

P دامانيدن dāmānīdan, To cause to ventilate.

P دامباك dāmbāk, Name of a king, who, according to Eastern belief reigned over the Anteadamites. These beings were supposed to have had flat heads, for which reason they are called by the Persians Nīm-sar (half-heads).

A دامج dāmij, Dark (night). Strong (man).

A دامخ dāmikh, Temperate (night).

P دامداري dām-dārī, The laying of nets. A branch of revenue arising from bird-catchers, players, and musicians.

A دامس dāmis, Dark (night).

P دام طرازان dām-tirāzān, Hunters. Fowlers. Contrivers, schemers. Cheats, knaves, impostors.

A دامع dāmiʻ, Wet with dew (earth.

A دامعة dāmiʻat, (A wound or fracture in the skull) letting blood flow (if the blood only appear or drop, the wound is then called دامية dāmiyat).

P دامغان dāmaghān, Name of the metropolis of a province of Persia called قومس kūms.

A دامغة dāmighat, A wound in the head penetrating the brain. Ten kinds of wounds may be received on the head with a different fine for each: viz. قاشرة kāshirat (or حارصة hārisat), باضعة bāziʻat, دامية dāmiyat, متلاحمة mutalāhimat, سمحاق simhāk, موضحة mūzihat, هاشمة hāshimat, منقلة munakhilat, آمّة āmmat, and دامغة dāmighat. (Some insert دامعة dāmiʻat between باضعة bāziʻat and دامية dāmiyat). Long hard flowers shooting forth from the medullary substance of the palm-tree, and which, if not taken away, destroy it. An iron plate on the back of a saddle. A cross-stick (from which is suspended a leathern bottle).

P دامغول dām-ghol, Scrofulous humour; swelling in the glands, wen. A sylvan demon.

A دامق dāmik, Bad, worthless.

P دامك dāmak, A rabbit, hare, or any small animal not carnivorous. A sort of veil for the head.

P دام كشي dām-kashī, The spreading of a net. Cheating, gulling. Escape from a snare.

A دامكة dāmikat, (pl. دوامك) A misfortune.

P دامگاه ديو dām-gāhi dīv, (ستور sutūr, or گرگ gurg) The world.

P دامن dāman, A skirt, tail, hem, border. The sheet (of a sail on ship-board). The foot or skirt of a mountain. دامن برافشاندن dāman bar afshāndan, To travel, to migrate. To abandon, turn away from. دامن چاك بودن دختر dāman chāk būdani dukhtar, The marriage of a daughter. دامن خشك dāmani khushk, Want of probity and piety. دامن خورشيد dāmani khwurshed, The fourth heaven. The light of the sun. دامن بدندان گرفتن dāman ba dandān giriftan, To humble one's self, to submit. To be weak. To flee away. دامن درپاي افتادن dāman dar pāy uftādan, To be disturbed and to run away. دامن درچيدن dāman dar chīdan, To draw in the skirt, (met.) To relinquish. دامن درريختن dāman dar rekhtan, To disgrace. دامن دركشيدن dāman dar kashīdan, To draw in the skirt, to turn away from, shun, quit, avoid. دامن درميان كردن dāman dar miyān kardan, To tuck up the garments, to prepare to do any thing. دامن باغي گرفتن dāmani bāghe giriftan, To seize the skirt of a garden, *i.e.* to court retirement. دامن كوه dāmani koh, The skirt of a mountain.

P دامن بوس dāman-bos, Kissing the skirt.

P دامن دار dāman-dār, Wide (cloth). Skirted.

P دامن كشان dāman-kashān, Sweeping the ground proudly.

P دامن گير dāman-gīr, Seizing the skirt, *i.e.* attaching one's self to a patron. Supplicating justice. Silencing, quieting. A refuser, denier.

P دامن گيري dāman-gīrī, Attachment, friendship. An applying for justice, arraignment.

P دامني dāmanī, A woman's veil or mantle. *Dāminī*, A scrap of the shroud kept by the relations of the deceased. A saddle-cloth, furniture, housings. An ornament worn on the forehead.

P دامود dāmūd, The forgiveness of a fault.

P داموز dāmwaz, A mattock or snow-shovel. A kind of basket carried on the shoulders by a pole passed through two handles, for removing dung.

A داموس dāmūs, A hunter's lurking-place.

P داموغ dāmūgh, Complaint, cry for help.

A داموغ dāmūgh, One who breaks the head and reaches the brain.

A داموغة dāmūghat, (A stone) which fractures the skull and injures the brain.

A داموق dāmūk, Hot, sultry (day).

P دامي dāmī, A sportsman, hunter, fowler.

A دامي dāmī, Bleeding, bloody. دامي الشفة dāmi 'sh shafat, (Bleeding-lipped) Poor.

A دامياء dāmiyāʼ, A good thing, a blessing.

P داميار dām-yār, A huntsman. A fisher's net.

A دامية dāmiyat, A contusion or wound on the head in which the blood appears, but does not flow. See دامعة dāmiʻat.

P داميدن dāmīdan, To fan, ventilate, winnow (grain). To carry away (as wind the dust). To mix boiling liquor that it may not overflow. To appear, become known. To be equal to a thing. To mount. To tear up.

P دان dān, (for دانه dāna) Grain. (an affix denoting) What holds or contains any thing: as, a vessel, sheath, purse. آبدن ābdān, A pond, cistern, bath, or reservoir of water. آتش دان ātish dān, A fire-hearth. بول دان bawldān, A urinal. شمع دان shamaʻdān, A candlestick. قلم دان kalamdān, A pen-case. مي دان maydān, A tun, pipe, butt. (impera. of دانستن dānistan) Know thou. (in compos.) Knowing, intelligent: as, قدر دان kadar-dān, Knowing the quality (of persons). نكته

دان *nukta-dān*, Subtile, penetrating.

P دانا *dānā*, Learned. A learned man. A name of God. داناۓ ایران *dānāʼi īrān*, The wise man of Irān, *i.e.* Jāmāsb, the astrologer. داناۓ روم *dānāʼi rūm*, The wise man of Greece, *i.e.* Plato. داناۓ طوس *dānāʼi tūs*, An epithet of Firdawsī and of خواجه نصیر *khwāja nasīr*.

A داناج *dānāj*, (from P دانا *dānā*) Learned.

P دانا دل *dānā-dil*, Wise-hearted.

A دانال *dānāl*, Daniel.

P دانانیدن *dānānīdan*, (tr. of دانستن) To inform.

P دانایان *dānāyān*, Men of wisdom. Sages.

P دانایانه *dānāyāna*, Learnedly. Learned.

P دانائي *dānāʼī*, Learning, knowledge, wisdom. دانائي زید *dānāʼiyi zayd*, The wisdom of Zayd.

A دانج *dānij*, (Dust) raised by the wind.

A دانج ابروج *dānaj-abruwaj*, Name of a grain. دانج وبر *dānaji wabar*, Name of a bitter yellow seed.

P دانجه *dānja*, (or دانژه *dānja*) A lentil.

P داند *dānad*, It is possible. He is able.

P دانست *dānist*, Knowledge. Opinion.

P دانستگي *dānistagī*, Knowledge.

P دانستن *dānistan*, To know. To acknowledge. To consider, to regard.

P دانسته *dānista*, Known. Having known. Wittingly. دانسته شدن *dānista shudan*, To become known.

P دانش *dānish*, Science, knowledge, learning. اهل دانش *ahli dānish*, A man of letters, a learned man. Learned.

P دانش آرا *dānish-ārā*, Knowledge-embellishing.

P دانش افزا *dānish-afzā*, Knowledge-increasing.

P دانش آموز *dānish-āmoz*, Wisdom-teacher.

P دانش پذیر *dānish-pazīr*, Fond of knowledge.

P دانش پرور *dānish-parwar*, Fostering science.

P دانش پژوه *dānish-pijūh*, Seeking knowledge.

P دانش پناه *dānish-panāh*, Asylum of wisdom.

P دانش کوتاه *dānish-kotāh*, Short-witted.

P دانشگر *dānishgar*, (or دانشمند *dānishmand*) Learned, skilful, scientific, wise, intelligent.

P دانشمندي *dānishmandī*, Wisdom, sense.

P دانش نامه *dānish-nāma*, Book of wisdom.

P دانشور *dānishwar*, A learned man.

P دانشوري *dānishwarī*, Wisdom, learning.

P دانشومند *dānishūmand*, Wise, learned.

P دانشي *dānishī*, A learned or wise man.

A دانع *dāniʻ*, Covetous. Voracious, hungry. Lowering one's self. Without judgment, silly, stupid.

A دانق *dānah*, (*dānik*, or داناق *dānāk*) (pl. دوانیق *dawānīh*) The sixth part of a dram, or two carats; also a small silver coin. *Dānih*, Lean. Abject, contemptible. Foolish. Thievish.

P دانك *dānk*, The fourth part of a dram. (according to some) The fourth part of a مثقال *miskāl*. *Dānak*, A small grain. The fourth part of a dram. A sixth of any thing. دانك ده *dānaki dih*, The sixth part of a village. شش دانك *shash dānak*, The whole manor. *Dānuh*, A particular kind of food sent by the parents of an infant, upon the first appearance of its teeth, round to the houses of their friends and relations.

P دانگانه *dāngāna*, A contribution made by travellers or others for their common expenses. Necessaries, implements; ingredients.

P دانگو *dāngū*, A kind of grain. A kind of pottage made of seven sorts of grain or pulse.

P دانندگی *dānindagī*, Knowledge.

P داننده *dāninda*, Knowing, wise. He who knows. دانندهٔ معقول *dānindaʼi maʻkūl*, An original or natural genius. دانندهٔ منقول *dānindaʼi mankūl*, A copyist.

P دانوش *dānūsh*, Name of the person who sold ʻazrā, the mistress of Wāmik. A kidnapper.

P دانه *dāna*, Grain. A berry. Stone of fruit, seed of grain or fruit. A pimple. Grain or bait scattered for catching birds. A cannon-ball. Knowledge, science, learning. Learned. دانهٔ انگور *dānaʼi angūr*, A grape, grape-stone. دانه آوردن *dāna āwardan*, To bring forth grain, to go to seed. دانه چیدن *dāna chīdan*, To pick up grain. To beg. To make obeisance. دانه بستن *dāna bastan*, To form the stone (as a grape). دانه دانه شدن *dāna dāna shudan*, To be scattered piecemeal. دانهٔ دل *dānaʼi dil*, The heart's core. Original sin. دانهٔ سبز *dānaʼi sabz*, Seed of the pine. دانهٔ سیر *dānaʼi sīr*, A clove of garlic. دانهٔ علي *dānaʼi ʻamalī*, Artificial pearls. دانه کردن *dāna kardan*, To scatter. سه دانه *sih dāna*, Three grains, three pieces.

P دانه دار *dāna-dār*, Granulated. Of a granulated appearance. Containing grain.

P دانه دان *dānadān*, A garner. Sown land. A nursery-ground. Scattered, dispersed.

P دانه زن *dāna-zan*, A sort of juggler.

P دانه فشان *dāna-fishān*, A sower of grains.

P دانه کیش *dāna-kesh*, A kind of embroidered neckcloth, worn in cold weather over the cloak.

P دانه گانه *dāna-gāna*, Necessaries, furniture, worldly goods.

A داني *dānī*, Approaching. Near, within reach (fruit on the tree). Low, vile. داني النسب *dānī'n nasab*, Nearly related.

A دانئ *dāniʼ*, Vile. Impure, dishonest.

A دانیال *dāniyāl*, Daniel.

P دانیدن *dānīdan*, To know. To roll round.

P دانیزه *dānīza*, (or دانیژه *dānīja*) A lentil.

A داأو *daʼw*, (v.n. of دأي) Lurking: circumventing.

P داو *dāv*, A wheel. A reel. Expense, disbursement. A stroke or move at play. The prize in archery. A stratum of a wall. A mud-wall. A claim. Abuse. Increasing a stake at play, which being restricted to nine times at two at a time after the first, limits the highest stake to seventeen. داو بهفت *dāv ba haft*, The concluding move at the game of tables. The seventeen prostrations at prayer. داو نیافتن *dāv nayāftan*, To sit ill (as a painting or embroidery).

A داو *dāw*, A kind of ship.

A داود *dāwud*, David.

A داودي *dāwudīy*, Name of a shrub which bears a flower like camomile. A kind of armour.

P داور *dāwar*, (for دادور *dādwar*) God. A just prince, governor, regent, ruler, judge, administrator, or arbiter. Remedy. Medicine. An opponent, adversary. داور آسمان *dāwari āsmān*, Lord of heaven, God. داور اعظم *dāwari aʻzam*, God, the Supreme Judge. داور دوران *dāwari dawrān*, Monarch of the world. سلطان داور *sultāni dāwar*, The reigning prince.

P داوردان *dāwardān*, A village near Wāsit.

P داورستان *dāwaristān*, A tribunal of justice.

P داوري *dāwarī*, Empire, sovereignty, dominion. Administration of justice. Sentence of a judge. Litigation. Quarrel, dispute. A complaint made before a judge. داوري خوردن *dāwarī khwurdan*, To submit to judgment, to suffer punishment. داوري کردن *dāwarī kardan*, To judge, to exercise a jurisdiction. داوري خانه *dāwarī-khāna*, A tribunal, seat of justice, judgment-hall.

A داوود *dāwūd*, David.

A داوودي *dāwūdīy*, David-like. دروع داوودیّه *durūʻi dāwūdiya*, Coats of mail such as were manufactured by David.

A داوي *dāwī*, Creamy (milk). Much (meat).

A داويّة *dāwiyat*, (or داوية *dāwiyat*) A desert.

P داه *dāh*, Ten. Base, ignoble, cowardly, worthless, degenerate. A maid-servant. Any servant. A boy. A forward, immodest woman. Service, attendance. An old man. داه فراشي *dāhi firāshī*, A kept mistress.

P داها *dāhā*, Caverns, mountain-hollows.

A داهر *dāhir*, Ever, at any time, never. A name for an Arabian.

A داهرة الطول *dāhiratu't tūl*, Very tall (woman).

A داهفة *dāhifat*, A foreigner. Tired camels.

P داهل *dāhil*, (*dāhul* or داهول *dāhūl*) A buck-stall. Figures set up at the corners of fields to frighten beasts into toils. A scare-crow.

A داهل *dāhil*, Confounded, amazed.

P داهم *dāhim*, A crown or diadem set with gems. A throne. A royal pavilion.

A داهن *dāhin*, Anointed (beard).

P داهول *dāhūl*, A diadem set with gems.

A داهي *dāhī*, (pl. دهاة *duhāt* and دهون *duhūn*) Ingenious, penetrating. Sly, subtle, cunning, shrewd. الداهي *ad' dāhī*, The lion.

A داهیة *dāhiyat*, (pl. دواهي *dawāhī*) Danger. Accident, misfortune, calamity. Extremely subtle or sagacious. داهیة دهواء *dāhiyatun dahwāʼ*, (دهیاء *dahyāʼ*, or دهویّة *duhwīyat*) A dreadful calamity.

P داهیم *dāhīm*, Plumaged diadem. Dominion.

A دأي *daʼy*, (v. n. of دأي) Lurking (as a wolf

to seize a gazelle). Circumventing. *Daʼy,* (دوي *duʼiy* or *diʼiy*) The vertebræ of the back or betwixt the shoulders. The gristly parts of the breast, or where the ribs meet. (pl. of داية *daʼyat*) Withers of horses.

P داي *dāy,* A stratum of a mud wall.

A دايات *daʼyāt,* The (six) scapulary ribs.

A دايات *dāyāt,* (pl. of داية *dāyat*) Nurses.

A دائب *dāʼib,* Diligent, laborious. Fatigued.

A دائبان *dāʼibāni,* (dual) Night and day.

A داية *daʼyat,* (pl. داي *daʼy*) The joints or back part of a horse's neck (next to the saddle). ابن داية *ibn daʼyat,* The crow (as pecking at the sores there).

A داية *dāyat,* (from P دايه *dāya*) A nurse.

A دآئث *daʼāʼis,* Origins, roots.

A دائحة *dāʼihat,* A large spreading tree.

A دائخ *dāʼikh,* Dark (night). Overcome. Sick.

A دائر *dāʼir,* Who or what revolves. Who or what forms a circle, or encircles. Round. دائر و سائر *dāʼir u sāʼir,* Going the circuit (judges); absolute, invested with authority. P دائر شدن *dāʼir shudan,* To depend upon, belong or relate to.

A دائرة *dāʼirat,* (pl. دوائر *dawāʼir*) A circle, circumference, circuit, periphery, compass, orbit, cycle. A circle or genus of Arabian poetry. A tambourine. A spiral lock of hair on the head or mustachio. The spur of a bird. A fatal period, bad fortune. Flight from battle. The groove in the upper lip under the nose. A monastery. P دائرهٔ دور *dāʼiraʼi dawr,* دائرهٔ دوران *dāʼiraʼi dawrān,* دائرهٔ دير پاي *dāʼiraʼi der-pāy,* The firmament. دائرهٔ گرد *dāʼiraʼi gird,* The sun. دائرهٔ هندي *dāʼiraʼi hindī,* A sun-dial.

P دائره كش *dāʼira-kash,* A pair of compasses.

A دائس *dāʼis,* A trampler. A thrashing-floor. A thrasher.

A دائش *dāʼish,* A Christian.

A دائص *dāʼis,* (pl. داصة *dāsat*) A thief, robber, pirate. A sheriff's officer. One who sneaks or prowls about.

A دائق *dāʼik,* (also مائق دائق *māʼik dāʼik*) Foolish, silly. دائق مائق *dāʼik māʼik,* Cheap (utensils), worthless (chattels).

P دايگان *dāyagān,* (pl. of دايه *dāya*) Nurses.

P دايگي *dāyagī,* The office of nurse, nursing. دايگي كردن *dāyagī kardan,* To nurse.

A دائم *dāʼim,* Permanent, perpetual, eternal, perennial. Always, continual, unintermitted. At rest. Quiescent (shadow). Stagnant (water). حمّي دائم *humma' dāʼim,* An unintermitting fever. دائم الايّام *dāʼimu'l ayyām,* Perpetual, always. دائم الخمر *dāʼimu'l khamr,* A sot. دائم المرض *dāʼimu'l maraz,* Eternally sick.

A دائما *dāʼiman,* Continually, for ever.

A دائمة *dāʼimat,* (fem. of دائم *dāʼim*) Eternal.

A دائميّة *dāʼimiyat,* Eternity. Perpetuity.

A دائن *dāʼin,* A debtor. A creditor.

P دايه *dāya,* A nurse, foster-mother. A midwife. دايهٔ شوهر پسر *dāyaʼi shawhar-pisar,* The earth.

P دايه گري *dāyagarī,* Nursing. Midwifery.

A داءِ *dāʼi,* (fem. دائية *dāʼiyat*) Sick, indisposed.

A دائي *dāʼiy,* Sick, indisposed.

P دب *dab,* Charge, custody.

A دبّ *dabb,* (v. n. of دبّ) Creeping, crawling (as a serpent). Advancing, stealing upon (as wine in the head, disease in the body, rottenness in cloth). Circulating (slander). Going slowly (an old man leaning on a stick). Small hairs upon the face. Being just (people). اكذب من دبّ ودرج *akzabu man dabba wa daraja,* The biggest liar that now walks or ever did walk (the earth). *Dibb,* A slow, creeping pace. *Dubb,* State, condition, constitution, manner, custom, mode, property, quality. (pl. ادباب *adbāb* and دببة *dibabat*) A bear. The constellation of the Bear. دبّ اكبر *dubbi akbar,* The greater Bear. دبّ اصغر *dubbi asghar,* The lesser Bear. من شبّ الي دبّ *min shubbin ila' dubbin,* From youth to old age.

A دبأ *dabaʼa,* (fut. يدبأ *yadbaʼu*) He was quiet. He smote (with a stick).

A دبا *daba',* A small locust. An ant. A slow gentle pace.

P دبّا *dabbā,* (or دبا *dubā*) A gourd.

A دبّاء *dabbāʼ,* (A woman) who has small hairs on her face. Hairy (she-camel). *Dubbāʼ,* A gourd.

A دبّاءة *dubbāʼat,* A single gourd.

P دباب *da* or *dubāb,* Name of a fragrant plant.

A دباب *dabābi,* The sound with which they call the hyena. *Dibāb,* (pl. of دبّة *dabbat*) Bottles made of raw skins. Sand-hills. Gourds.

A دبّابة *dabbābat,* An engine of war, under cover of which beseiging soldiers approach a town; a wheeling hovel.

A دبابيج *dabābīj,* (pl. of ديباج) Brocades.

A دبابيذ *dabābīz,* (pl. of دبّوذ *dubbūz*) Cloths of a double warp, of different colours.

A دبابيس *dabābīs,* (pl. of دبّوس) Clubs, maces.

A دبأة *dabʼat,* Flight.

A دبّاج *dabbāj,* A vender of brocades.

A دبّاخ *dubbākh,* A kind of game.

A دبادب *dubādib,* Corpulent, loud-voiced.

A دبا دبا *duba' duba',* In swarms like locusts.

A دبار *dabār,* Destruction. *Dibār,* (v. n. 3 of دبر) Being inimical, carrying on hostilities. Dying. Part of a sown field. Battles, engagements. Flights, routs, dispersions. Rivulets, trenches cut in sown fields in order to water them. لا يعرف قبالاً من دبار *lā yaʼrafu kibālan min dibārin,* See دبير *dabīr.* *Dibār* or *dubār,* Wednesday. The night of Wednesday. دباراً *dibāran,* (Coming to prayer) after the proper time.

A دبارة *dibārat,* One part of a field.

A دبّاس *dabbās,* A maker of the honey دبس *dibs.*

A دباساء *dibāsāʼ* or *dabāsāʼ,* Female locusts.

A دباسي *dabāsī,* (pl. of دبسي *dubsa'* or دبسيّ *dubsīy*) Stock-doves.

A دباغ *dibāgh,* (v. n. of دبغ) Tanning. Dyeing green. Any thing with which hides are tanned.

A دبّاغ *dabbāgh,* A tanner, a currier.

A دباغة *dibāghat,* (v. n. of دبغ) Tanning. Dyeing green. The art of tanning. P جاي دباغت *jāyi dibāghat,* A tan-yard, tannery. دباغت كردن *dibāghat kardan,* To tan.

P دباغت يافته *dibāghat-yāfta,* Tanned. دباغت نا يافته *dibāghat nā yāfta,* Untanned.

P دبّاغ خانه *dabbāgh-khāna,* A tannery, barkary.

P دباق *dibāk,* Shoemakers' paste.

A دباكة *dubākat,* The stump of a lopped branch remaining on the trunk (of a palm-tree).

P دبال *dabāl,* (or دباله *dabāla*) An orange.

A دبال *dubāl,* Dung, manure.

A دبب *dabab,* Hairiness. Small yellow hairs on the face. A calf just brought forth.

A دببان *dababān,* Hairiness, down. Mass of hair.

A دببة *dabibat,* A woman who has small hairs on her face. *Dibabat,* (pl. of دبّ *dubb*) Bears.

A دبّة *dabbat,* (pl. دباب *dibāb*) A vessel made of raw skins in the form of a jar or large bottle, in which merchants carry butter and oil. A sand-hill or heap. Plain ground, level sands. One hair upon the face. A glass goblet. A gourd. *Dabbat* or *dibbat,* One movement (of a creeping animal). A gentle mode of walking. A creeping movement. خفيّ الدبّة *khafīyu'd dibbat,* Stealing upon one by surprise. *Dubbat,* State, condition. Creed, faith. A she-bear. دبّة كبري *dubba kubra',* Ursa Major.

A دبج *dabj,* Painting; a picture; a map, plan.

A دبخس *dubbakhs,* Naturally large. A lion.

P دبداب *dabdāb,* Pomp, pride, state, dignity.

A دبداب *dabdāb,* A drum.

A دبدب *dabdab,* Pace of a long-legged ant.

A دبدبة *dabdabat,* The noise of a horse's shoe upon stones. Sour, coagulated milk on which fresh milk is poured. *Dabdabat,* (or دبدبي *dabdaba'*) Very thick milk.

P دبدبه *dabdaba,* A great noise; the noise of a drum. Pomp, state, magnificence.

A دبر *dabr,* (v. n. of دبر) Passing through the mark (an arrow). Growing old (man). Relating, citing on the authority of another after his decease. Carrying off (any thing). Turning the back, fleeing. Shifting, veering to the west (wind). A field (particularly that part where the ploughing cattle are turned, when they have some cut grass thrown to them. That which comes behind another, a successor. Death. Great riches. A mountain. Sleep of every hour. Grief, melancholy. (pl. ادبر *adbur* and دبور *dubūr*) A bee. A swarm of bees or hornets. A young locust. A rock in the sea covered with water, but sometimes dry. *Dibr,* Great riches. A bee. A young locust. *Dubr* or *dubur,* (pl. ادبار

adbār) The back. The backside. End, conclusion (of an affair), close (of a month). The corner of a house. من دبر *min dubr*, In the rear, behind. عتق العبد عن دبر *ʿitḳu'l ʿabdi ʿan dubri*, Manumission of a servant after the death of his master. *Dabar*, (v. n. of دبر) Being galled (backs of cattle). (pl. of دبرة *dabarat*) Warbles, ulcers on the saddle-part of a horse's back. *Dabir*, Galled in the back. *Dubura*, In the rear, after. عن دبر *ʿan duburin*, After death.

A دبران *dabarān*, (or الدبران *ad' dabarān*) A mansion of the moon, *i.e.* The hyades or five stars in Taurus, particularly the brightest, commonly called Aldebarān, or the Bull's Eye; the fourth lunar mansion.

A دبرة *dabrat*, One part of a sown field. Low ground sown. The latter part. Flight in battle, defeat, discomfit. Adverse fortune. *Dibrat*, The opposite of قبلة *kiblat*. ما له قبلة و لا دبرة *mā lahu ḳiblatun wa lā dibratun*, He does not look straight to his business. *Dabarat*, Flight in battle. A breadth of sown land. (pl. دبر *dabar* and ادبار *adbār*) A sore on a horse's back.

P دبره *dabara*, Unripe corn cut for cattle.

A دبريّ *dabariy* or *dabriy*, Late (prayer). Coming too late (as advice or recollection after opportunity is passed).

A دبريًّا *dabariyan* or *duburiyan*, After the proper time. After any one's death. Preposterously.

P دبز *dabz*, Thick, coarse (as cloth).

A دبس *dabs*, Any thing black. *Dibs* or *dabs*, A multitude of men. *Dibs* or *dibis*, Honey made by bees or flowing from dates. Date-syrup seethed over the fire. *Dubs*, (pl. of ادبس *adbas*) (Birds) of a reddish black. *Dubas*, Clouds threatening rain.

P دبستان *dabistān*, A school (for writing).

P دبستاني *dabistānī*, A pupil at such a school.

A دبسيّ *dubsiy*, A very black bird with a melodious voice, a wood-pigeon. A queest.

A دبش *dabsh*, An unbarking, peeling. A consuming, an eating up. *Dabash*, The meaner household utensils.

A دبص *dabas*, (v. n. of دبص) Growing fat.

A دبغ *dabgh*, (v. n. of دبغ) Tanning (a hide). Dying (a garment) green. *Dibgh*, (or دبغة *dibghat*) Any thing with which hides are tanned.

A دبغة *dabghat*, A single tanning of a hide.

A دبق *dibk*, Birdlime. *Dabak*, (v. n. of دبق) Adhering firmly. Being excited against, and never quitting afterwards. Name of a town in Egypt.

A دبقيّ *dabakiy*, Cloth of Dabak in Egypt.

A دبكل *dabkhal*, One who has a thick and equal skin. Deformed, hideous, stinking. امّ دبكل *umm dabkhal*, The hyena.

A دبكلة *dabkalat*, (v. n. of دبكل Q) Driving (sheep) together, gathering up stragglers.

A دبل *dabl*, (v. n. of دبل) Dunging (land). Dressing, improving, correcting (any thing). Driving or collecting together into a heap. Making up (meat) into balls. Striking (one) repeatedly with a stick. (pl. دبول *dubūl*) Plague, pestilential bubo. A brook, rill. *Dibl*, (pl. دبول *dubūl*) Calamity, ruin. Bereavement. دبل دابل *diblun dābilun*, A heavy misfortune. *Dubl*, A young or little ass. *Dubal*, Adversity. Bereaved (mother). *Dubal* or *dubul*, (pl. of دبلة *dublat*) Large mouthsful. Holes in axe-heads. *Dubul*, (pl. of دبيل *dabīl*) Trees called غضا *ghazā* growing in abundance.

A دبلة *dublat* or *dablat*, An imposthume (especially internal). *Dublat*, (pl. دبل *dubul* and *dubal*) A large globular mouthful, or any thing of that shape, as gums or confections. The hole of an axe.

P دبله *dubla*, Sugared almonds.

A دبليس *dablīs*, A ring worn by Moorish women.

A دبن *dibn*, A sheep-fold.

A دبنة *dubnat*, A large mouthful.

A دبوب *dabūb*, A stab which causes the blood to flow. A wound from which the blood streams copiously. Any thing fat. One who secretly injures by detraction. A deep cavern.

P دبودار *dubūdār*, A kind of juniper-tree.

A دبوز *dabūz*, (or دبّوز *dubbūz*) (from P دو پود *du pūd*) Cloth of a double warp, of different colours.

A دبور *dabūr*, The west wind (which blows generally towards night). *Dubūr*, (v. n. of دبر) Waxing old (man). Passing through the mark (an arrow). (pl. of دبر *dabr*) Swarms of bees or wasps.

A دبّور *dabbūr*, Habit. Sort, kind, sect, party.

P دبوس *dabūs*, A club or iron-headed mace used by cavalry. A sceptre. A place in a boat or ship; the cuddy. Name of a small city between Samarkand and Bokhārā.

A دبوس *dabūs*, Fine dates preserved in butter.

A دبّوس *dabbūs*, (pl. دبابيس) An iron mace.

P دبوس تير *dabūs-tīr*, An iron arrow with a large round head.

P دبوسك *dabūsak*, Mallows.

P دبوسه *dabūsa*, A part of a ship, the cuddy.

A دبوغ *dabūgh*, (Rain) softening the earth.

A دبّوق *dabbūk*, Name of a certain game.

A دبوقاء *dabūkāʼ*, Birdlime. Human excrement. Any thing viscous.

A دبّوقة *dabbūkat*, Plaited, braided locks.

P دبوقه *dabūka*, A bagpipe.

P دبوكي *dabūkī*, The herb turnsole. Mallows.

A دبول *dabūl*, (A woman) bereaved of her son. Misfortune, calamity. *Dubūl*, (v. n. of دبل) Dressing, trimming, correcting. Dunging (land). Oppressing (calamity). (pl. of دبل *dabl*) Brooks. Plagues. (pl. of دبل *dibl*) Calamities. Bereavements.

P دبه *daba*, Ruptured. Rupture.

A دبه *dabah*, A sandy place. A good way.

P دبّه *dubba* or *dubba*, A leathern vessel (for wine). A phial. دبّه درپاي فيل افگندن *dabba dar pāʼi fīl afgandan*, To flee from the face of a foe without fighting. To stir up sedition. دبّهٔ برنجين *dabbaʼi birinjīn*, A copper vessel. An hour-glass. دبّهٔ عوريا *dabbaʼi ʿūriyā*, A certain plant from whose root an electuary is prepared.

P دبه خايه *daba-khāya*, Ruptured.

A دبي *daba'*, A pismire. Small locusts before their wings grow. Name of a certain fair held amongst the Arabs. مال كالدبي *māl ka'd daba'*, Much wealth, many cattle (like to which are دبي دبيّ *daba' dubayyin*, or دبي دبيّين *dabyu dubayyayni*.

A دبّيّ *dibbiy* or *dubbiy*, None, no one.

P دبيب *dabīb*, A soft, easily-bruised thing.

A دبيب *dabīb*, (v. n. of دبّ) Crawling (as a serpent). Going slow (an old man, leaning on a staff). Stealing upon (a foe). Circulating (as slander). Gaining ground (disease). Creeping (as wine into the head, or rottenness into cloth).

A دبيّة *dabīyat*, Flight.

A دبّيج *dibbīj*, (or دبّيج) Nobody, none (at home).

A دبّي حجل *dibbī hajal*, A kind of game.

P دبيد *dabūd*, An electuary, medicine.

A دبيدح *dubaydah*, (as بدبيدح *bi dubaydaha*) Vainly, foolishly.

P دبير *dabīr*, A writer, secretary, notary: a writing-master. دبير صاحب التدبير *dabīri sāhibu't tadbīr*, An excellent writer. دبير فلك *dabīri falak*, (or دبير انجم *dabīri anjum*) The planet Mercury.

A دبير *dabīr*, A thread drawn out in spinning. Any thing which is drawn from one. A losing arrow at games of hazard. The upper part of the ear. Flax. لا يعرف قبيلا من دبير *lā yaʿraf kabīlan min dabīrin*, He cannot distinguish what is before from what is behind; what is advancing to, or receding from, him; or he knows not the pedigree of his mother from that of his father. عرف قبيله من دبيره *ʿarafa kabīlahumin dabīrihi*, He distinguished his rebellion from his obedience.

P دبيرستان *dabīristān* or *dibīristān*, A school (for writing). A record-office.

P دبيش *dabīsh*, An eruption from disease.

A دبيغ *dabīgh*, Tanned (leathern bottle).

A دبيق *dabīk*, Name of a city.

A دبيقيّ *dabīkiy*, Made at Dabik (stuff).

P دبيل *dabīl*, Name of a city in Armenia.

A دبيل *dabīl*, (pl. دبل *dubul*) The tree called غضا *ghazā* growing plentifully. Scattered leaves of the tree ارطى *arta'*. Low ground. دبل دبيل *dibli dabīl*, A heavy calamity, painful bereavement.

A دبيلة *dubaylat*, Adversity, calamity. An imposthume (especially internal).

P دپ *dap*, A drum with one skin.

P دپايه *dapāya*, A school.

P دپنگ *dapang*, A firm-fleshed boy.

P دپوچه *dapūcha*, A leech, blood-sucker.

A دثّ *dass*, Slight rain. A contortion of the body. A side. An opinion, a conjectural report.

A pain-giving blow. A push, a thrust. A near shot from behind one's clothes.

A دثء dasـ, (v. n. of دثأ) Bringing forth in hot weather (sheep).

A دثاث disās, Slight rain.

A دثّاث dassās, A killer of birds with a sling.

A دثار disār, An upper garment (opposed to شعار shiʿār, which means an under garment).

A دثئيّ dasaـiy, Rain falling after the heats of summer. The yeaning of sheep in the summer.

A دثّة dussat, A slight defluxion or rheum.

A دثر dasr, Copious, abundant. Plenty (of riches). *Disr*, A skilful manager of his property. *Dasar*, Filth, dirt, nastiness.

A دثط dast, (v. n. of دثط) Cutting open (an ulcer or boil), and letting out the contents thereof.

A دثع dasʿ, (v. n. of دثع) Trampling upon, treading down. Plain, level ground.

A دثق dask, A pouring out of water.

A دثنة dasnat, Little water.

A دثور dasūr, Slothful, somnolent, slow. Vile, obscure, never mentioned. *Dusūr*, (v. n. of دثر) Being obliterated, effaced, worn out. Being dirty (a garment). Contracting rust (a sword). Clothing itself with leaves (a tree). Oblivion, forgetfulness.

A دثمة dasmat, A mouse.

P دج duj, Any thing in which syrup, new wine, or dates is mixed, and adheres to the hands and feet.

A دجّ dajj, (v. n. of دجّ) Running with rain (a house). Trading. Letting (a curtain) fall. The jungle-hen.

A دجا dujaʾ, (or دجًا dujan) Darkness of the night. (pl. of دجية dujyat) Darknesses. The lurking-places of hunters.

A دجات dujāt, (pl. of دجة) Shirt-buttons.

A دجاج dajāj, A hen. الدجاج البرّي ad dajāju'l barriy, The jungle-hen. دجاج هندي dajāj hindī, A turkey. دجاج قرنبيط dajāj karnabīt, A woodcock.

A دجاجة dajājat, (pl. دجائج dajāـij) A hen. A cock. A family, domestics. A clew or hank of thread. *Dijājat* or *dujājat*, A cock. A hen.

A اسود دجاجيّ asmadu dujājiy, Extremely black, pitchy, dark.

A دجار dijār, (v. n. 3 of دجر) Fleeing away.

A دجاري dajāraʾ, (pl. of دجران dajrān) Astonished. Cheerful and saucy.

A دجال dajāl, Dung.

A دجّال dajjāl, A large company of travellers. Antichrist. One-eyed. False, lying. An impostor. Gold. The glittering of a sword.

A دجالة dujālat, Liquid pitch.

A دجّالة dajjālat, A large caravan.

A دجان dijān, (pl. of دجن dajn) Clouded skies.

A دجّانة dajjānat, Laden with wares (a camel).

A دجائج dajāـij, (pl. of دجاجة dajājat) Hens.

A دجة dujat, (pl. دجات dujāt and دجي dujaʾ) A button, stud, or clasp (especially for the breast or collar of a garment). The two first fingers and thumb, with which one takes up a mouthful.

A دجّة dujjat, Intense darkness.

A دجج dujuj, Intense darkness. Black mountains.

A دججان dajajān, (v. n. of دجّ) Loosing a veil, letting a curtain drop. A sucking child toddling after its mother.

A دجداج dajdāj, Dark.

A اسود دجدج (aswadu) dujduj, Black as pitch.

A دجدجة dajdajat, (v. n. of دجدج Q) Calling fowls together by saying دجّ دجّ dajji dajji. Being dark (the night).

A دجر dajr, The beam of a plough. *Dajr, dijr, dujr*, or *dujur*, A Turkish or French bean. *Dujr*, A machine in which grain is put for sowing, having an iron instrument at the bottom which scatters it, a drill. *Dajar*, (v. n. of دجر) Being astonished, confounded. Being tumultuous, cheerful, and saucy. Drunkenness. *Dajir*, Astonished. Cheerful, saucy.

P دجر dajir, A kind of pulse, or French bean.

A دجران dajrān, (pl. دجاري dajāraʾ and دجري dājraʾ) Astonished. Cheerful and saucy. *Dijrān*, A stick fixed for propping a vine.

A دجري dajraʾ, (pl. of دجران dajrān) Astonished. Cheerful, saucy.

A دجل dajl, (v. n. of دجل) Besmearing (a camel) with pitch (against the scab). Giving a false colouring. Deceiving. Lying. Burning. Copulating. Traversing every part of a country.

A دجلة dijlat or dajlat, The river Tigris.

A دجم dajm, (v. n. of دجم) Being dark. Being sad. Sort, mode, form, species. *Dijam*, (pl. of دجمة dijmat) Friends. Companions. Acquaintances. Customs, modes, usages. *Dujam*, (pl. of دجمة dujmat) Darknesses. The pangs of love.

A دجمة dujmat, A word. *Dijmat*, (pl. دجم dijam) Friend, companion, acquaintance. *Dujmat*, (pl. دجم dujam) Darkness. Pangs of love. A word.

A دجن dajn, (v. n. of دجن) Being dark, cloudy (day). (pl. ادجان adjān, دجان dijān, and دجن dujun) A cloudy sky. Much rain. Darkness. يوم دجن yawmu dajnin or yawmun dajnun, يوم دجنة yawmu dujunatin or yawmun dujunatun, A dark, cloudy day. *Dujan*, (pl. of دجنة dujnat) Darknesses. *Dujun*, (pl of دجن dajn) Clouded skies.

A دجنّ dujunn or dijinn, (pl. دجن dujn) Darkness. A dark, overspreading mist; mistiness.

A دجناء dajnāـ, Ugly, black (she-camel). *Dajnāـ* or *dujnāـ*, The clay of which Adam was formed.

A دجنات dujanāt, (pl. of دجنة) Darknesses.

A دجنة dujnat, (pl. دجن dujan and دجنات dujanāt) An ugly black colour (of a camel). Darkness. *Dujunat*, Darkness. Density of overspreading clouds, mistiness.

A دجنّة dujunnat or dijinnat, (pl. دجن dujn) Darkness. A dark, overspreading mist. يوم دجنّة yawmu dujunnatin, A dark day.

A دجني dijnaʾ and dujnaʾ, The kind of earth of which, they say, Adam was created.

A دجو dajw, Darkness (of the night).

A دجوّ dujūw, (v. n. of دجا for دجو) Being dark (night). Covering and enveloping every thing. Copulating. Being long and reaching to the ground (a garment). Being bushy and entangled (hair).

A دجواء dajwāـ, (A she-goat) with tangled hair.

A دجوب dajūb, A vessel. A purse, a bag.

A دجوجة dajūjat, (or دجوجاة dajawjāt) (A she-camel) stretched on the ground and covered with dust.

A دجوجيّ dajūjiy, Very dark.

A دجوجيّة dajūjiyat, Black (she-camel).

A دجون dajūn, Gentle, tame. Water-drawing (camel). *Dujūn*, (v. n. of دجن) Remaining, staying. Being cloudy (day). Being tame and cade. Darkness.

A دجونة dajūnat, Trained to watering ground.

A دجي dujaʾ, Darkness. (pl. of دجة dujat) Shirt-buttons. (pl. of دجية dujyat) The lurking-places of hunters.

A دجية dujyat, (pl. دجي dujaʾ) Darkness (of night). A hunter's lurking-place.

A دجيج dajīj, (v. n. of دجّ) Walking slowly. Creeping. Trading. Loosing down a veil.

A دجيل dujayl, Pitch. A branch of the Tigris.

P دچار duchār, A sudden meeting of two persons.

A دحّ dahh, (v. n. of دحّ) Concealing, burying. Copulating. Striking on the back of the head.

A دحاء dihāـ, (pl. of دحية) Generals, leaders.

A دحاب duhāb, (v. n. of دحب) Driving, impelling, thrusting. Going in (unto one's maid).

A دحاحيس dahāhīs, (pl. of دحّاس dahhās) Insects lying under ground.

A دحادح duhādih, Short-bodied, dwarfish.

A دحارج dahārij, (pl. of مدحرج) Revolvers.

A دحاس dihās, (A house) full of people.

A دحّاس dahhās, dihhās, or duhhās, (pl. دحاحيس dahāhīs) A yellow under-ground insect, which boys put amongst gins to catch sparrows.

A دحاض dihāz, (pl. of دحض) Slippery (places).

A دحاق dihāk, The falling of the uterus after birth (causing the mother's death).

A دحال dihāl, (v. n. 3 of دحل) Deceiving. Lying in wait. Throwing down in wrestling. Outbidding at a sale. Injuring, oppressing. Telling a fiction and concealing the truth. Keeping back, hindering. Refusal, denial. (pl. of دحل dahl and duhl) Holes in the ground, narrow at top, wide below.

A دحامس dahāmis, Dark, moonless nights. Three nights after those called ظلم zulm. *Duhāmis*, A dark brown fat man. Strong, strenuous.

A دحامل duhāmil, Proud. Coarse and compact.

A دحب dahb, (v. n. of دحب) Driving, impelling, thrusting. Lying with. Approaching.

A دحباة dahbaـat, A lying with.

A دحبة *duhabat*, Many cattle.

A دحبّة *dahabbat*, Any thing near.

A دحث *dahs*, Elegant in narrative.

A دحج *dahj*, (v. n. of دحج) Dragging along on the ground. Lying with.

A دحجاب *dihjāb*, (or دحجبان *duhjubān*) High ground (especially rough and rocky).

A دحداح *dahdāh*, (or دحداحة) Short-bodied.

A دح دح *dah dah* or *dihi dihi*, Words imposing silence, when one is going to blab or confess.

A دحدح *dahdah*, (or دحدحة) Short-bodied.

A دحدرة *dahdarat* (v. n. of دحدر Q) Rolling.

A دحر *dahr*, (v. n. of دحر) Driving off. Thrusting back. Putting to a distance.

A دحراج *dihrāj*, A turning, tumbling, revolving.

A دحرجة *dahrajat*, Turning, tumbling, revolving.

A دحروجة *duhrūjat*, Dung rolled into a round ball by a beetle.

A دحس *dahs*, (v. n. of دحس) Promoting discord. Introducing the hand between the skin and the peritoneum of a sheep, in order to get the hide off. Concealing (mischief) so as not to be discovered. Concealing. Filling (a vessel). Filling (an ear of corn). Kicking. Corn in full ear.

A دحسم *duhsum*, (دحسمان *duhsumān*, and دحسمانيّ *duhsumāniy*) Very brown. Very fat and firm. دحسمان الامر *duhsumānu'l amr*, A confounder, disturber, or perplexer of the business.

A دحص *dahs*, (v. n. of دحص) Struggling (a slaughtered ox). Examining.

A دحض *dahz*, (v. n. of دحض) Kicking (slaughtered beeves). Examining. Slipping, sliding. Disappearing (the sun). *Dahz* and *dahaz*, (pl. دحاض *dihāz*) A slippery place.

A دحق *dahk*, (v. n. of دحق) Driving to a distance. Not caring for, discarding. Casting forth, not holding seed. Bringing forth. Being unable to reach (the hand). The falling of the uterus after birth, causing the death of the mother.

A دحقبة *dahkabat*, A pushing violently forward.

A دحقلة *dahkalat*, (v. n. of دحقل Q) Swelling.

A دحقوم *duhkūm*, Large-bodied.

A دحل *dahl*, (v. n. of دحل) Digging the sides, or enlarging a well. Retiring to a distance, fearing, shunning, hiding one's self. Descending into a hole narrow at top and wide at bottom. Retiring to one side of the house. *Dahl* or *duhl*, (pl. ادحل *adhul*, ادحال *adhāl*, دحول *duhūl*, and دحلان *duhlān*) A hole in the ground, narrow at top and wide at bottom. A cavity, hollow dug for collecting water. A place in a tent, into which a woman retires when a stranger enters. *Dahal*, (v. n. of دحل) Being wealthy (in cattle). Using fraud in the sale of goods, bidding without intending to purchase, in order to raise the price to another. Being exceedingly cunning and roguish. Being dwarfish and swag-bellied. *Dahil*, An impostor, rogue. Very rich. One who bids against another to enhance the price (especially in a sly, roguish manner). A flatterer. Big-bellied, flag-bellied.

A دحلاء *dahlās*, A well with a narrow mouth.

A دحلان *duhlān*, Hollows in the ground.

A دحلة *dahlat* or *duhlat*, A well.

A دحلطة *dahlatat*, A talking confusedly.

A دحلمة *dahlamat*, (v. n. of دحلم Q) Throwing down from a mountain or into a well.

A دحم *dahm*, (v. n. of دحم) Pushing away with violence. Lying with. *Dihm*, Root, origin.

A دحًّا محًّا *dahhan mahhan* (is equivalent to دحها محها *dahhā mahhā*).

A دحمرة *dahmarat*, The filling (a leathern bottle).

A دحمس *dahmas*, A thing black. A vinegar-bottle. Brown and fat (man). Dark. *Dihmis*, Dark. *Dihmis* or *duhmus*, Any thing black.

A دحمسان *duhmusān*, Foolish. *Duhmusān*, (or دحمسانيّ *duhmusāniy*) Very brown, fat and compact.

A دحملة *dahmalat*, (v. n. of دحمل Q) Rolling on the ground. Throwing prostrate and trampling upon. Lean, loose-skinned (female). Plump, firm-fleshed (female).

A دحمور *duhmūr*, Name of a small reptile.

A دحموق *duhmūk*, Large-bellied or bodied.

A دحن *dahn*, Taciturn and inwardly wicked. *Dahan*, (v. n. of دحن) Being big-bellied and dwarfish. *Dahin*, A dwarf, prominent-bellied. Wily, wicked, treacherous.

A دحنّة *dihannat*, High land. *Dihannat* or *dihinnat*, A big-bellied dwarf.

A دحندح *dihindih*, A game. A kind of insect.

A دحو *dahw*, (v. n. of دحا for دحو) Spreading abroad the earth (God). Throwing his legs all about when running (a horse). Driving, thrusting. Causing (gravel) to fly about (rain). Having a large swagging belly. Lying with (a woman). Using nuts as marbles (a boy).

A دحوح *dahūh*, A big woman, or she-camel.

A دحور *dahūr*, One who repels, rejects, reproves. *Duhūr*, (v. n. of دحر) Driving off, thrusting back, rejecting, reprobating.

A دحوض *dahūz*, A slippery place. *Duhūz*, (v. n. of دحض) Being groundless (an argument).

A دحوق *dahūk*, (A camel) having a falling of the matrix after the birth. Sparkling-eyed (woman).

A دحول *dahūl*, Widened (well, or channel of a river). (A camel) retiring to a distance from the rest. *Duhūl*, (pl. of دحل *dahl*) Holes, caves narrow at top and wide at bottom.

A دحونّة *dihwannat*, A big-bellied dwarf.

A دحي *dahy*, (v. n. of دحي) Expanding. Spreading. Driving (camels).

A دحية *dahyat*, A she-monkey. *Dihyat*, A head, general, leader. *Dihyat* or *dahyat*, Name of a man whose form the Muhammadans believe the angel Gabriel to have assumed when he appeared to their prophet. He was of the tribe of كلب *kalb*, and one of the handsomest of men.

A دحيدحة *duhaydihat*, Short-bodied; a dwarf.

A دحيق *dahīk*, Driven to a distance. Weak-sighted (eye).

P دخ *dakh*, A throng, company. The choicest and purest part. Good, well. *Dukh*, (for دختر *dukhtar*) A daughter. A reed of which mats are woven, or on which melons are hung. A falling star.

A دخّ *dakhkh* or *dukhkh*, Smoke.

A دخا *dukha'*, Darkness.

A دخابش *dukhābish*, Large-bellied (man).

A دخاخيل *dakhākhīl*, Hedge-sparrows.

A دخادخ *dukhādikh*, A dwarf.

A دخاريص *dakhārīs*, (pl. of دخريص *dikhrīs*) Gores of shifts.

A دخاس *dikhās*, Many. (A coat of mail) wrought with close ringlets.

A دخال *dikhāl*, Mind, intention. Bringing (a camel) which had just drunk back again to the well, and introducing (him) between two others that he may drink again. The insertion or articulation of one joint into another. Religious habit, custom. *Di* or *dukhāl*, Pendulous hair on a horse's forehead.

A دخّال *dakhkhāl*, One who enters, interferes, or meddles much in business, a meddler, busybody. دخّال الاذن *dakhkhālu'l uzn*, An earwig.

A دخاليل *dakhālīl*, Hedge-sparrows.

A دخامس *dukhāmis*, Black and thick.

A دخان *dukhān*, (or دخّان *dukhkhān*) (pl. ادخنة *adkhinat*, دواخن *dawākhin*, and دواخين *dawākhīn*) Smoke. Tobacco, or the fumes. ابنا دخان *abnā dukhān*, Wealthy and unemployed (tribe or family).

P دخان نوشان *dukhān-noshān*, Tobacco smokers.

A دخانيّ *dukhāniy*, Smoky, smoke-coloured.

A دخبش *dakhbash*, Large-bellied (man).

P دخت *dukht*, A daughter. A virgin. Ability, strength. Contempt and hatred. دخت كردن *dukht kardan*, To detest. دخت اندر *dukht-andar*, A sister uterine.

P دختر *dukhtar*, A daughter. A girl. A virgin. Power, strength. دختر آفتاب *dukhtari āftāb*, (or دختر خم *dukhtari khum*) Red wine. دختر پاك اختر *dukhtari pāk-akhtar*, (or دختر پاكيزه جوهر *dukhtari pākīza-jawhar*) Daughter of a happy planet, *i.e.* a lady of family, a nobleman's daughter. دختر رز *dukhtari raz*, Wine. A grape. A grape-stone. دختر روزگار *dukhtari rozgār*, Worldly events. دختر عمران *dukhtari ʿimrān*, Name of the mother of Jesus (a confounding of Miriam, the daughter of Amram and sister of Moses, with the Virgin Mary). دختران نعش *dukhtarāni naʿsh*, The constellation of the Bear.

P دختر خانه *dukhtar-khāna*, A brothel.

P دخترزن *dukhtar-zan*, A daughter-in-law.

P دخترك *dukhtarak*, A little girl. An orphan, or girl educated by others than her parents. A lathe for turning boxes.

P دخترگي dukhtaragī, Virginity.

P دخترو dukhtar (u not sounded), A little girl.

P دختره dukhtara, Virginity. A seal.

P دختري dukhtarī, Maidenhead, virginity. A seal. دختري بردن dukhtarī burdan, (or ستدن sitadan) To deflower.

P دخترينه dukhtarina, (or دختينه dukhtīna) A young girl of a marriageable age.

P دخت زاي dukht-zāy, Bearing only girls.

P دختن dukhtan, To sew. To gain. To milk.

P دختندر dukhtandar, A daughter-in-law.

A دخخ dakhakh, Blackness, darkness.

A دخداخ dakhdākh, Name of an insect.

A,P دخدار dakhdār, (P تخت دار takht-dār) A cloth (white or black) with which they covered the throne of the old kings of Persia. Gold.

A دخدبة dakhda or dikhdibat, Firm-fleshed (girl).

A دخدخ dukhdukh, (or دخ دخ) A word imposing silence, with a mixture of contempt. A dwarf.

A دخدخة dakhdakhat, (v. n. of دخدخ Q) Humbling, making vile. Tiring. Being tired. Restraining, prohibiting, averting. Taking short, quick steps.

A دخدرة dakhdarat, The gilding (an ear-ring).

A دخر dukhr, Littleness, vileness, pitifulness.

A دخرص dikhris, Penetrating, knowing.

A دخرصة dakhrasat, A declaring openly.

A دخريص dikhrīs, The gore of a shift; a piece put in to enlarge a garment.

A دخز dakhz, Hard and strong. Coition.

A دخس dakhs, The sticking of any thing, or its being concealed, in the ground. A corpulent, thin-skinned man. A bear's cub. *Dakhas*, (v. n. of دخس) Having a swelling about the root of the hoof (a horse). A distemper affecting the hoofs of cattle. *Dukhas*, A porpoise.

P دخش dakhsh, The commencement (of any business). Commerce. Gloomy, dark.

A دخش dakhash, (v. n. of دخش) Being fleshy.

A دخّش dukhkhash, A kind of fish.

P دخشم dakhsham, An old trading connexion.

A دخشم dakhsham or dukhshum, Thick, corpulent. Black.

A دخشن dukhshun, Thick, corpulent. The state of being hump-backed; gibbosity.

A دخض dakhz, (v. n. of دخض) Voiding dung (a boy or wild beast). Dung (of wild beasts or boys).

A دخل dakhl, (v. n. of دخل) Entering. Intruding (as a stranger). Doubt, suspicion. Intrusion, interference. Disorder of mind or body. Disease, blemish. Vice. Enmity, hatred. Return, profit, advantage (from an estate). P دخل كردن dakhl kardan, To take possession of. دخل و دست درازي كردن dakhl u dast-darāzī kardan, To enter and seize by violence. دخل و خرج dakhl u kharch, Receipt and disbursement. A *Dakhl* or *dikhl*, Mind, intention. Custom, mode, institute. *Dakhal*, (v. n. of دخل) Labouring under any intrinsic defect (body, mind, or estate). Being spoiled, marred (the interior of any thing). A certain kind of disease. A tree with thick entangled branches. Vice, failing. Disorder of mind or body. A blemished reputation. Fraud, trick. Doubt, suspicion. A proselyte. One who is reckoned amongst those to whom he does not belong.

A دخّل dukhkhal, The secret intentions of the mind. Rule, custom, habit. Herbage growing amongst the roots of trees. Whatever lies between the sinews, or grows between the ظهران zuhrān and بطنان butnān of a feather. Thick, compact in body. (pl. دخاخيل dakhākhīl) An earth-coloured bird.

A دخلاء dukhalāʼ, (pl. of دخيل dakhīl) Intimate friends. Those who enter.

A دخلة dakhlat, The interior, or best (of any thing). Name of a village fruitful in dates. A beehive. *Dakhlat*, *dikhlat*, or *dukhlat*, Law, rule, regulation: intent, purpose, habit, mind, heart. *Dikhlat*, A blending of several colours. *Dukhlat*, A secret.

A دخّلة dukhkhalat, Firmness of flesh.

P دخل دان dakhldān, A money-till.

A دخلل dikhlil, Fat or flesh lying within flesh. *Dikhlal* or *dukhlul*, Intimate, familiar. *Dukhlal*, Sincere, affectionate. *Dukhlal* or *dukhlul*, The interior of any thing. The concealed thoughts of the heart; intention, purpose. Name of a small bird. Law, rule, canon.

A دخلي dakhlī, Admission, entrance.

P دخم dakhm, A tomb.

A دخم dakhm, A pushing away. Coition.

P دخماس dakhmās, Name of a weight.

A دخمرة dakhmarat, (v. n. of دخمر Q) Filling (a leathern bottle). Covering, veiling, hiding.

A دخمسة dakhmasat, (v. n. of دخمس Q) Keeping one's thoughts to one's self, not allowing any one to know them. Fraud. A rogue, a cheat.

P دخمه dakhma, A coffin. A tomb. A circular stone-building in the form of a cylinder, on the flat surface of which the fire-worshippers lay the bodies of their dead. A substance resembling lights, which protrudes from the mouth of a male camel when stung with desire. دخمهٔ زندنيان dakhma-i zindaniyān, (or دخمهٔ فيروزه dakhma-i fīroza) The sky, heaven.

A دخن dakhn, (v. n. of دخن) Smoking, sending forth smoke. *Dukhn*, Millet. *Dakhan*, (v. n. of دخن) Sending forth much smoke (a fire of green wood). Being smoked (victuals). Being smoky, tending to black. Being evil (the disposition). Malignity of temper. Hatred, secret grudge. Taint of mind or character. The glittering of a sword. A smoky colour. Smoke. *Dakhin*, Malignant, depraved.

A دخناء dakhnāʼ, Smoky-coloured (ewe). *Dukhnāʼ*, A species of sparrow.

A دخنان dakhnān, Warm (day). *Dukhnān*, A sort of sparrow.

A دخنانة dakhnānat, Dark, foggy (night).

A دخنة dukhnat, (v. n. of دخن) Being smoky, tending to black. A smoky colour. Any aromatic put in the fire, in order to fumigate; perfume, incense. ابو دخنة abū dukhnat, (Father of smokiness) Name of a bird. P دخنه كردن dukhna kardan, To fumigate.

A دخنس dakhnas, Robust, fleshy.

P دخنه جا dukhna-jā, A censer.

A دخور dukhūr, A being little, vile, pitiful.

A دخوص dakhūs, Plump, fat (girl). *Dukhūs*, (v. n. of دخص) Being fat and plump (a girl).

A دخول dukhūl, (v. n. of دخل) Entering. Entrance, access. Income, revenue. Quarrels, enmities.

A دخون dukhūn, (v. n. of دخن) Smoking, emitting smoke. Being raised in columns like smoke (dust). Being smoky-coloured (a horse or plant).

A دخى dakhaʼ, Darkness.

A دخياء dakhyāʼ, Dark (night).

A دخيس dakhīs, A joint in the pastern of a horse; also a little bone in a horse's foot (the frog). The fleshy part of the hand. Compact and plentiful flesh. Many, numerous. Numerous (hills of sand). Much (forage). Many (utensils).

A دخيل dakhīl, Interior, inner. Admitted, allowed entrance. Intimate, familiar. Sincere (love). A friend, confidant. A proselyte. A foreign word adopted into the Arabic. Intention, purpose, mind, heart. Rule, habit, custom. Articulation of the joints. A horse having forage exclusively for himself. (in poetry) The letter introduced between the letter of the رويّ rawiy and the ا alif of the تأسيس taʼsīs. داء دخيل dāʼ dakhīl, An internal malady.

A دخيلاء dakhīlāʼ or dukhaylāʼ, A sort of game.

A دخيلة dakhīlat, (دخيلاء dukhaylāʼ, or دخّيلي dukhkhaylaʼ), The arcana of business. Intention, purpose, religious habit, mind, heart. A secret of the mind. Canon, rule.

A دخيليّ dakhīliy, In-door; cade, cosset.

A دخيليات dukhayliyāt, Name of a certain game.

P دد dad, A rapacious animal, a beast of prey. A forest abounding in game.

A دد dad, Play.

A ددّ dadd, A portion of time. *Dadd*, (or دداً dadan) Play, any thing ludicrous.

P ددا dadā, Play.

A ددان dadān, Poor. Useless, unprofitable. A blunt, also a sharp, sword.

A ددد dadad, Play. Any thing ludicrous. *Dadīd*, Playful.

A P ددن dadan, Play. A ludicrous thing. Dice.

P ددناك dadnāk, Full of wild beasts.

P دده dada, A beast of prey. A calender monk.

P در dar, In, into, within, among. On, upon, above. Of, concerning, about. By, for. Because of. Near, hard by, at. To, as far as, according to.

Before, in presence of. Against. With. Under. At length. After. So much. Out, out of doors. در آنجا *dar ān jā*, There, in that place. در آمدن *dar āmadan*, To come in, enter. در آمدن از خواب *dar āmadan az khwāb*, To awake out of sleep. در آن روز *dar ān roz*, Upon that day. در این میان *dar in miyān*, In the mean time, during this interval. در ترقّي *dar tarakkī*, On the increase, in the ascendant. در خط رفت *dar khat raft*, (or در خط شد *dar khat shud*) He was distressed, afflicted, altered with grief. در دست شدن *dar dast shudan*, To come to blows. در دويم *dar duyam*, In the second place. چهار فرسخ در چهار فرسخ *chahār farsakh dar chahār farsakh*, Four leagues by four leagues; four leagues square. هفت در هفت *haft dar haft*, Seven by seven; forty-nine. *Dar*, A door, gate, passage, door-way or gate-way. A chapter (of the Zand). A subject, topic. Way, manner, method. Genus, sort, kind. Turn, step, degree. A kind of wild bird. A gnat. A blackberry. A valley. A mountain-pass. The foot, also summit, of a mountain. در آسمان *dari āsmān*, The milky way. در بدر *dar ba dar*, From door to door. در بسته كردن *dar basta kardan*, To shut the door. (imperative of دريدن *darīdan*) Tear thou. (in composition) Tearing: as, پرده در *parda-dar*, Veil-tearing: dishonouring.

A درّ *darr*, (v. n. of درّ) Emitting milk copiously (a camel), or rain (the sky). Flowing plentifully in rays (as milk from the dug, rain, or urine). Flowing (sweat). Being often paid or large (tribute). Recovering its beauty after illness (the face). Being thick and entangled (herbage). Being brisk (a market). Being soft and smooth. Milk. Soul, spirit, self. Goodness, elegance. Goods, riches. Plunder, spoil, booty. لله درّه *li'llāh darruhu*, How bountiful has God been to him! how richly has God endowed him! or, Praise be to God for having so richly endowed him! لا درّ درّه *lā darra darruhu*, Bad luck to him! *Durr*, (in Persian *dur*) A pearl. (pl. of درّة *durrat*) Pearls. P در خوش آب *duri khwush-āb*, A pearl of a fine water. در شهوار *duri shahwār*, A fine, large royal pearl. در نا سفته *duri nā sufta*, A virgin-pearl, *i.e.* not perforated. An unblemished maid. درّ يتيم *durri yatīm*, (or يكدانه *yak dāna*) A rare, inestimable pearl. Muhammad. در يكتا *duri yaktā*, A rare, inestimable pearl. A درّ مفصّل *durri mufassal*, Separate pearls, *i.e.* the gamut, or musical scale, as follows:

ا ل م ر	*a*	*la mi re*	A la mi re
ب ف پ م	*be*	*fa pe mi*	B fa be mi
ج ص ف د	*je*	*so fa do*	C sol fa ut
د ل ص ر	*dāl*	*le so re*	D la sol re
ه ل م	*he*	*la mi*	E la mi
و ف د	*wāw*	*fa do*	F fa ut
ز ص ر د	*ze*	*so re do*	G sol re ut

A درء *dar*ₔ, (v. n. of درأ) Driving away. Being impelled forward, and carried off (a torrent). Suffering from a pestilential disease, particularly a swelling in the back (a camel). Spreading out (any thing). Coming by surprise. Going out suddenly. Shining, blazing (fire). Inclination, bias. Crookedness, curvature. A cane or spear. جاء السيل درءا *jāₔa'ₔ sayl darₔan* or *durₔan*, The torrent came rushing in consequence of rain fallen in some unknown quarter (opposed to ظهرا *zahran*, which means in one's own country).

P درا *dar ā*, Enter. A bell. Pendent. Necessary.

A درّاء *darrāₔ*, (A camel) abounding in milk.

A دراب *dirāb*, (pl. of درب *darb*) Entrances to palm-plantations. Large doors.

A درابة *durābat*, Courage in business or war.

A درابج *durābij*, Pompous, walking proudly.

A درابزين *darābazīn*, Screen-work, lattice-work.

A درابس *durābis*, Thick, strong (camel).

P در آب فرو شدن *dar āb furo shudan*, To sink in the water. To be annihilated, lost.

A درابنة *darābinat*, (pl. of Per. sing. دربان *darbān*) Porters, doorkeepers.

A درأة *darₔat*, (v. n. of درأ) Repelling, driving off. Being impelled onwards (a torrent). Coming by surprise. Going out suddenly. Shining, blazing (fire). Spreading out (any thing). Suffering from a pestilential disease, especially a swelling in the back (a camel).

A درّات *durrāt*, (pl. of درّة *durrat*) Pearls.

A درّاج *darrāj*, A whisperer, who malignantly reports what he hears. A hedgehog. *Durrāj*, (pl. دراريج *darārīj*) The francolin, a kind of partridge.

A درّاجة *darrājat*, A three-legged machine moving on wheels, by which children are taught to walk, a child's go-cart. An engine of war, under cover of which soldiers approach a town; a wheeling hovel.

P درّاجناك *durrājnāk*, A country abounding in pheasants or red-legged partridges.

P درّاجه *durrāja*, A long upper garment or cloak, worn in Persia when they go abroad.

A درادح *darādih*, (pl. of دردحة *dirdihat*) Women as broad as long.

A درادر *darādir*, (pl. of دردر) Sockets of teeth.

A درادق *darādik*, Infants.

P درّادوزا *darrādūzā*, Experienced, skilful, witty.

A درّار *durrār*, (pl. of دارّ) (Camels) very milch.

A درّارة *darrārat*, A woman's spindle.

P داره *darāra*, A contented cuckold, a pimp.

A دراري *darāriₔ*, (pl. of دريء *dirriₔ*) Bright sparkling stars.

A دراريج *darārīj*, (pl. of درّاج *durrāj*) Red-legged partridges, francolins.

A دراريع *darārīɛ*, (pl. of درّاعة *durrāɛat*) Woollen garments open in front.

P دراز *darāz*, Long. دور و دراز *dūr u darāz*, Far and long, at large, diffusedly. دراز كردن *darāz kardan*, To lengthen. To extend, prolong. To delay. دراز كشيدن *darāz kashīdan*, To extend, prolong. اردشير دراز دست *ardshīri darāz-dast*, Ardeshir with long hands (Artaxerxes Longimanus, king of Persia). دراز آهنگ *darāz-āhang*, Tedious winding-up of business.

P درازا *darāzā*, Length.

P دراز باد *darāz bād*, May it long continue!

P دراز خانه *darāz-khāna*, Long-bodied (horse).

P دراز خوان *darāz-khwān*, A table-cloth, napkin.

P دراز دست *darāz-dast*, Rapacious.

P دراز دستي *darāz-dastī*, Oppression, extortion.

P دراز دم *darāz-dum*, A dog, ape: scorpion.

P دراز دنبال *darāz-dumbāl*, Ox: cow: buffalo.

P دراز رود *darāz-rūd*, A river in Turkistān.

P دراز ريش *darāz-rīsh*, Long-bearded.

P دراز زبان *darāz-zabān*, (Long-tongued) Fluent. Clamorous, brawling.

P دراز زباني *darāz-zabānī*, Length of tongue, fluency. Clamour, brawl.

P دراز سفره *darāz-sufra*, A table-cloth.

P دراز شدگي *darāz-shudagī*, Prolongation.

P دراز شمشير *darāz-shamshīr*, Able swordsman.

P دراز عمر *darāz-ɛumr*, Long-lived.

P دراز قد *darāz-kad*, Tall, of a high stature.

P دراز كار *darāz-kār*, One who attempts things too great for him. An empty boaster, braggart.

P دراز گردن *darāz-gardan*, Long-necked.

P دراز گوش *darāz-gosh*, An ass. A hare.

P دراز نا *darāz-nā*, Length. Oblong.

P دراز نفس *darāz-nafas*, Long-winded, prolix.

P درازه *darāza*, Long. A long thread.

P درازي *darāzī*, Length. درازي عمر *darāzīₔi ɛumr*, Length of life.

P درازينه *darāzīna*, Lengthwise.

A دراس *dirās*, A treading out of corn.

A دراسة *dirāsat*, A studying, a reading.

P دراستادن *darāstādan*, To begin, to attack.

P در آستين كردن *dar āstīn kardan*, To use one's own discretion, to feel one's own power.

P دراسج *darāsaj*, Ivy, bindweed.

A درّاعة *durrāɛat*, (pl. دراريع *darārīɛ*) An upper garment for men or women, of cotton or coarse wool. A soldier's cloak, cuirass, corslet.

A دراعيّ *darāɛiy*, (pl. of درعيّة *dirɛiyat*) (Arrow-heads) piercing a cuirass.

P در افتادن *dar uftādan*, To fall on: quarrel.

P درافشان *dur-afshān*, Pearl-scattering: eloquent.

A درافص *durāfis*, Large and corpulent.

A دراق *dirāk*, (pl. of درقة *darakat*) Shields made of solid leather.

A درّاق *darrāk*, Treacle. Wine.

SY دراقن *durākin*, A peach.

P درّاقن *durrākin*, A delicious white peach.

G دراقيطس *darākītus*, The plant elephant's ear.

A دراك *dirāk*, (v. n. 3 of درك) Following one another. Overtaking, coming up to, seizing. Comprehending, understanding. *Darāki*, Take thou.

A درّاك *darrāk*, Intelligent, penetrating.

A درّاكة *darrākat*, The understanding.

A درّام *darrām*, An ugly walker. A hedge-hog.

A درامة *darāmat*, (v. n. of درم) Taking short and quick steps (a hedgehog).

A درّامة *darrāmat*, A hare. A hedgehog. (A woman) short in stature and ungraceful in walking.

A درامج *durāmij*, Walking haughtily.

P در آمد *dar āmad*, Entrance. Income. در آمد بر آمد *dar āmad bar āmad*, Ingress and egress. Receipt and disbursement, incomings and outgoings.

P در آمدگي *dar āmadagī*, A turning inwards.

P در آمدن *dar āmadan*, To come in, enter. To happen, to arrive. To fall on the face. در دل آمدن *dar dil āmadan*, To come into one's heart, to occur to the mind.

P در آميختگي *dar āmekhtagī*, Mixture, confusion.

P در آميختن *dar āmekhtan*, To associate.

A دران *darān*, A fox. *Dirān*, (pl. of درن *darin*) Dirty and worn-out (clothes). Beneficent (hands).

P در انبار كردن *dar ambār kardan*, To store up.

A درانة *durānat*, A withered herb.

A درانج *durānij*, One who walks haughtily.

P در آنجا *dar ān jā*, In that place.

P در آنچه *dar ānchi*, In that which.

P در انداختن *dar andākhtan*, To throw in.

P در اندازي *dar andāzī*, Malice, enmity.

A درانس *durānis*, Strong, bulky (man or camel).

P درانك *darānak*, Name of a sea said to be the abode of angels.

P در انگشت آوردن *dar angusht āwardan*, To reckon, count, calculate.

A درآنيّ *darsāniy*, Extremely white (salt).

P درّاني *durrānī*, Name of a tribe of Pat'hāns, inhabiting the country about Kandahār. They are said to have got this name from wearing pearls in the ear. They are also called Abdālīs.

P درانيدن *darānīdan*, To tear, or cause to tear.

A درانيك *darānīk*, (pl. of درنوك) Fringed rugs.

P در آوردن *dar āwardan*, To introduce, bring in. برگ در آوردن *barg dar āwardan*, To put forth leaf.

P در آويختن *dar āwekhtan*, To suspend, hang. To provoke, or be provoked. To contend (in words or blows).

A دراويش *darāwīsh*, (pl. of درويش) Dervishes.

A دراهس *darāhis*, Misfortunes, adversities. *Durāhis*, Very fleshy. Strong, firm.

A دراهم *darāhim*, (pl. of درهم *dirham*) Dirhems.

A دراهيم *darāhīm*, (pl. of درهام) Dirhems.

P در آي *dar āy*, Come in. Coming in. Entering. Speak thou. Commencing a discourse. The beginning or exordium of an oration. Conversation. A blacksmith's hammer. A bell.

A دراية *dirāyat*, (v. n. of دري) Knowing. Using fraud and finesse. Knowledge, science. Quality, property, manner, habit, constitution, temperament, disposition. Boldness. عقل و درايت *ʻakl u dirāyat*, Judgment and science.

P درايش *darāyish*, The making an impression.

P در آينده *dar āyanda*, Entering: who enters.

P دراينده *darāyanda*, A speaker, talker.

P درائيدن *darā-īdan*, To speak, call aloud, utter. هرزه (or هذيان *hazayān*) درائيدن *harza* (or هذيان *hazayān*) *darāīdan*, To prate, rave, dote, talk nonsense.

P در آيينه نقش پري ديدن *dar āyīna nakshi parī dīdan*, To look at wine in a crystal goblet. To view the face of the cupbearer in a mirror.

A درب *darb*, (pl. دراب *dirāb*) A difficult pass through mountains. A narrow street, road, lane, alley. The entrance to a palm-plantation. A place where dates are dried in the sun. A large gate. Custom, way. *Darab*, (v. n. of درب) Being accustomed, exercised. Being greedy. A defile leading into those parts of Asia Minor called Roum.

A دربّ *durubb*, Name of a yellow fish.

P دربا *darbā*, Necessary. Attentively engaged.

A درباء *dirbāʼ*, (v. n. of دربي Q) Throwing.

A درباة *darbāt*, The act of throwing down.

P در باختن *dar bākhtan*, To play. To buy and sell. To give away. To lend.

P دربار *darbār*, A house, dwelling. A court, area. The court or levee of a prince: an audience-chamber. دربار كمان رفتن *dar bāri kamān raftan*, To draw a bow.

P دربار خرچ *darbār-kharch*, A kind of extra tax levied by Zamīndārs in some parts of the northern circars of India.

P در بارة *dar bāra*, In behalf, respecting.

P در باري *dar bāre*, Once, at one time, or turn. *Darbārī*, A courtier, an attendant at a darbār.

A درباس *dirbās*, A lion. A biting dog.

P در باقي شدن *dar bākī shudan*, To be complete, to leave no residue. در باقي كردن *dar bākī kardan*, To complete. To quit.

P دربان *darbān*, A porter, warder. دربان فلك *darbāni falak*, Porter of the firmament, *i. e.* the sun.

P درباني *darbānī*, The office of porter. درباني نمودن *darbānī namūdan*, To act as porter or warder.

A دربانيّة *darabānīyat*, A species of small high-backed beeves with little hoofs and thin hides.

P در باي *dar bāy*, Suitableness, propriety.

P در بايد *dar bāyad*, Requisite.

P در بايست *dar bāyist*, It behoveth, it is meet. Meet, suitable, becoming. Mode, manner.

P در بايستن *dar bāyistan*, To be meet, right.

A دربة *durbat*, (v. n. of درب) Being accustomed, used to. Custom. Being greedy. Intrepidity (in war or business). The bunch of a species of bull. *Daribat*, (A falcon) trained to hunt.

A دربجة *darbajat*, (v. n. of دربج Q) Becoming soft (what was hard). Going slowly from love to her colt (a camel).

P دربچه *dar-bacha*, A small door in a larger.

A دربحة *darbahat*, (v. n. of دربح Q) Running rapidly by from fear. Bending, stooping, submitting.

A دربخة *darbakhat*, (v. n. of دربخ Q) Stooping, crouching to the male, bennetting (a pigeon). Bending forwards and lowering the head (a man).

P در بدر *dar ba dar*, From door to door: door by door. A beggar, vagrant, with no fixed residence. Adjacent.

P در بر *dar bar*, Above. On, or in the breast.

P در برابر *dar bar-ā-bar*, Breast to breast, even.

P در بردن *dar burdan*, To bring, carry in, insert.

P دربزين *darbazīn*, Parapet or lattice-screen.

A دربساك *darbasāk*, A fort near Antioch.

P در بستن *dar bastan*, To tie, to bind.

P در بسته *dar basta*, Bound, tied, fastened. Mute, dumb, silent. A bar, bolt. A stutterer, stammerer.

A دربصة *darbasat*, A keeping silence through fear.

A دربلة *darbalat*, A kind of pace. A sort of drum.

P دربند *dar-band*, The bar of a door. A barrier. A narrow and difficult pass through mountains. A road dangerous on account of banditti. Name of a fortress on the Caspian Sea at the foot of Mount Caucasus. An arm of the sea. A place where there is good wine. A ferryman. Bound, fettered. A captive. در بند كردن *dar band kardan*, To bind, make prisoner. To shut the door.

A دربوب *darabūb*, Obedient, submissive, tame.

P دربي *darbī*, A bit, fragment, rag.

P در پاي افگندن *dar pāy afgandan*, To let alone, to leave free or vacant.

P در پائ چراغ كمر بستن *dar pāsi charāgh kamar bastan*, To gird one's self at the foot of the lamp (a form, amongst the Kalandars, of admitting a member into their fraternity, which is done at the tomb of one of their chiefs).

P در پرده *dar parda*, Behind the curtain, within the veil; unrevealed, hidden.

P درپريش *dar parīsh*, A beggar, vagrant. A long-necked vessel, gugglet. A cup, goblet. A burnt brick.

P در پس *dar pas*, Behind, after. در پس زانو نشستن *dar pasi zānū nishastan*, To watch. To think.

P درپش *dirapsh*, (for درفش) An awl, bodkin.

P در پشم كشيدن *dar pashm kashīdan*, To hide.

P در پوست افتادن *dar post uftādan*, To traduce.

P درپه *darpa*, A patch, fragment, bit. *Darpih*, Forgiveness, connivance. Invisible, vanished.

P در پي *dar pay*, Behind, in the rear. Necessary. *Darpī*, A patch on a garment. درپي نهادن *darpī nihādan*, To put on a patch. درپي پذيرفتن *darpī pazīruftan*, To be patched, to admit a patch.

P درپيچ *dar pech*, A screen or partition within the outer door of a house (to prevent further entrance).

P در پيچان *dar pechān*, Intricate, perplexed.

P در پيچيدن *dar pechīdan*, To fold, involve.

P در پيش *dar pesh*, Before, in front, near. در پيش آمدن *dar pesh āmadan*, To come before, oppose, obstruct, confront. در پيش گرفتن *dar pesh giriftan*, To take before. To admit, suffer.

P درپي كننده *dar pay kunanda*, A follower.

P درپين *darpen*, A patch on a garment; bit, rag.

P درپي نهاده *darpī nihāda*, Patched (garment).

P درپيوستن *dar paywastan*, To join, to unite.

A درّة *darrat*, A flow of milk. *Dirrat*, Briskness of market. Plenty of milk. A copious effusion of rain. A copious flow of milk. Blood. A bull's pizzle or other scourge. A little twisted ferula with which they strike one another sportively when dancing. Roundness of the limbs, and adaptation for running. *Durrat*, (pl. درّ *durr*, درر *durar*, and درّات *durrāt*) A large pearl. درّة التاج *durratu't tāj*, The largest pearl in a royal crown.

P درتاج *dartāj*, The herb turnsol.

A درثع *darsaع*, An aged camel.

P درج *darj*, A manuscript illuminated with figures. A closet, a place for writing.

A درج *darj*, (v. n. of درج) Passing by. Going on one's way. Keeping on the path (literally or figuratively). Ascending steps. Continuing to eat the flesh of the woodcock. Sweeping violently over gravel (wind). (pl. دروج *durūj*) Paper, or any thing pliable upon which they write. A volume.

P درج كردن *darj kardan*, To fold. To pass by. To collect, comprehend, contain, preserve. A *Durj*, (pl. درجة *dirajat* and ادراج *adrāj*) A little casket in which they deposit gems of gold. An open case for a woman's spindle. P درج تنگ *durji tang*, (or درج در *durji dur*) The mouth of a mistress. درج دهقان *durji dihkān*, Historical records. Words regarded, or otherwise. A *Daraj*, A mediator. A book in which they write. A way, a path. (pl. of درجة *darajat*) Steps, stairs. Rounds of ladders. *Duraj*, (pl. of درجة *durjat*) Clouts.

A درّج *durraj*, Perplexing affairs.

A درجات *darajāt*, (pl. of درجة *darajat*) Steps, ladders, stairs for ascending.

A درجان *darajān*, (v. n. of درج) Walking, going. Passing along. Becoming extinct (a family). Dying without issue. Exceeding a year, and not foaling (a camel). Folding (a letter or cloth).

A درجة *durjat*, *darajat*, or *durajat*, The step of a stair, round of a ladder. *Durjat*, (pl. درج *duraj*) A casket. A clout, which they stuff into the matrix of a camel, her eyes being blindfolded, and her ears stopped up. After some days it is taken out, when she, imagining herself to have been in foal, readily takes a liking for another camel's colt who has been rubbed all over with the cloth. A medicated clout thrust into the diseased matrix of a camel. *Darajat*, Gradation, degree, rank, station, dignity. A staircase. Action (of a play). A place in Paradise. An astronomical degree. درجۀ شرف *darajai sharaf*, The altitude at which the sun enters the fifteenth degree of Aries. *Dirajat*, A menstruous cloth. (pl. of درج *durj*) Cases for spindles. *Durajat*, Name of a bird about the size of a partridge.

A درّجة *durajjat*, The step of a stair, the round of a ladder.

A درجرج *durujruj*, Name of a little animal of a dark red, whose flesh is poisonous.

A درجع *durjuع*, Pulse, food for oxen.

A درجلة *darjalat*, (v. n. of درجل Q) Whipping (a bow) with gut. The gut or thong itself.

A درجنة *darjanat*, (v. n. of درجن Q) Having an affection for her colt, after an aversion (a camel).

P درجوال كردن *dar juwāl kardan*, To cheat.

A درح *darh*, (v. n. of درح) Driving away. *Darah*, (v. n. of درح) Being decrepit. *Darih*, Superannuated (camel).

A درحابة *dirhābat*, Short, corpulent (man).

P درحال *dar hāl*, On the spot, at the instant.

A درحاية *dirhāyat*, Short, fat, pot-bellied.

P درحساب گرفتن *dar hisāb giriftan*, To sum up, calculate. To call to account, blame, reprove.

P درحضور *dar huzūr*, In the presence. Ready.

P درحقّ او *dar hakki u*, With regard to, in respect of him, her, or it.

P درحقيقت *dar hakīkat*, In truth, in reality.

P درخ *dirakh*, (for درخت) A tree. A beam.

P درخاستن *dar khāstan*, To erect: put, place.

P درخال *darkhāl*, A sucker, a young tree.

A درخبيل *durakhbīl*, Misfortune, calamity.

A درخبين *durakhbīn*, Misfortune, calamity. A man who walks feebly and languidly.

P درخت *dirakht*, A tree, plant, bush, or shrub. A beam. A column. A mast. A gibbet. درخت انگور *dirakhti angūr*, A vine. درخت بادام *dirakhti bādām*, An almond-tree. درخت چهاربيخ *dirakhti chahār bekh*, The world. درخت خانه *dirakhti khāna*, A joist, beam, rafter. درخت خرما *dirakhti khurmā*, A palm-tree. درخت مريم *dirakhti maryam*, A palm-tree. درخت وقواق *dirakhti wakwāk*, A certain tree whose fruit resembles the human head.

P درختان *dirakhtān*, Trees. Abounding in trees.

P درختستان *dirakhtistān*, Planted with trees.

P درخت سنب *dirakht-sumb*, A woodlouse. A woodpecker. An auger, gimlet.

P درخت سنبه *dirakht-sumba*, An auger, wimble. A woodworm. A woodpecker. A bird's beak.

P درختك *dirakhtak*, A low, dwarf tree, a shrub. درختك دانا *dirakhtaki dānā*, (The knowing tree) Name of a tree which turns with the sun: turnsol.

P درخت كاو *dirakht-kāv*, Tree-uprooting.

P درختناك *dirakhtnāk*, Full of trees, woody.

P درختنه سنبه *dirakhtna-sumba*, A wood-pecker.

P درخستن *dar khastan*, To impress, mark, or stamp. To pierce, transfix.

P درخش *darakhsh*, Lightning. *Darukhsh*, Worthy, suitable. Desire. *Durukhsh*, Lightning. Flash, glitter. Flashing. Name of a fire-temple in Kurdistān, and of a town in Kohistān. *Durukhsh* or *durakhsh*, Splendour, light, gleam.

P درخشان *durukhshān*, Shining, flashing.

P درخشانيدن *durukhshānīdan*, To make to gleam, glitter, or flash.

P درخشش جاي *durakhshish-jāy*, The East.

P درخشندگي *durukhshandagī*, Lustre.

P درخشنده *durukhshanda*, Shining, resplendent.

P درخشي *durakhshī*, Sun-rise.

P درخشيدن *durukhshīdan*, To shine, to flash.

P درخط شدن *dar khat shudan*, To alter. To be afflicted. To become restless and lose one's senses.

P درخف *durkhuf*, A black bee.

A درخملة *durkhamlat*, A miracle, prodigy. A ridiculous thing. Whatever causes surprise or mirth.

A درخميل *durakhmīl*, (or درخمين *durakhmīn*) A calamity, misfortune. Slow, dull, doltish.

P درخواست *darkhwāst*, Petition, request, application, appeal. A proposal, tender.

P درخواستن *darkhwāstan*, To desire, request.

P درخواه *darkhwāh*, Deprecation, petition, proposal. A beggar.

P درخور *darkhwar*, Suitable, proper, becoming. In food or opulence. درخورتن *darkhwar tan*, According or agreeable to his powers, quality, or rank.

P در خورد *dar khward*, Proper, suitable.

P در خوردار *dar khwar-dār*, Any one in the enjoyment of a long and happy life.

P در خوردن *dar khwardan*, To be suitable or proper. To agree.

P درخوش *dar khwash*, Love, desire.

P درد *dard*, Pain, ache, smart, trouble, disease, grief, affliction, pang, torment. Pity, sympathy, compassion. A trumpet. درد بند انگشت *dardi bandi angusht*, Gout in the hand. درد بند شتالنگ *dardi bandi shitalang*, (or پاي *pāy*) Gout in the foot. درد السبات *dardu's subāt*, Lethargy. درد رسانيدن *dard rasānīdan*, To inflict pain. درد زه *dardi zih*, The pangs of labour. درد سر *dardi sar*, Headache, megrim. Trouble, vexation. درد سر گرفته *dardi sar girifta*, Troubled with a headache. درد شديد *dardi shadīd*, Agony. درد شكم *dardi shikam*, Pain in the belly, cholic, gripes. درد فرزندي *dardi farzandī*, Parental affection. درد كردن *dard kardan*, To give pain. درد گرفتن *dard giriftan*, To ache. درد مفاصل *dardi mafāsil*, Rheumatism. درد ناخن *dardi nākhun*, A whitlow. درد يافتن *dard yāftan*, To suffer pain. اهل درد *ahli dard*, Pained with love or grief. بدرد آمدن *ba dard āmadan*, To be in pain. *Durd*, Dregs, lees, sediment, tartar of wine, mother of oil. *Dirad*, Ringworm.

A درد *darad*, A shedding of the teeth.

P دردا *dardā*, Alas! Oh! What a pity!

A درداء *dardāء*, Toothless, aged (woman).

P درداب *dardāb*, A small odoriferous melon.

A درداب *dardāb*, The sound of a drum.

P دردار *dardār*, A large and shady kind of tree. *Dar-dār*, A porter. *Dard-ār*, Pain-producing.

A دردار *dardār*, Sound of a drum. A kind of tree.

P درد آشنايان *dard-āshnāyān*, Inured to pain.

A درداق *dardāk*, A small shop. Trodden and level ground.

G درداقس *durdākis*, The upper joint which joins the head to the neck.

P درد آگين *dard-āgīn*, Full of pain, aching.

P درد آلود *dard-ālūd*, Painful.

P دردام *durdām*, An anchoret, a beadsman.

A (ابو) دردان *(abū) dardān*, A cricket.

P درد انگيز *dard-angez*, Pitiable, exciting pity.

P دردانه *dur-dāna*, A single pearl. دردانهٔ نار *dur-dānaʼi nār*, A drop of blood.

A دردب *dardab*, (A woman) going and coming in the night.

A دردبة *dardabat*, (v. n. of دردب Q) Being accustomed, trained to. Running and looking back (one afraid). Submitting to, cowering.

A دردبيّ *dardabiy*, A drummer.

A دردبيس *dardabīs*, Misfortune, calamity. An old man. An old woman. A kind of glass bead used as an amulet.

A دردجة *dardajat*, Concord, friendship, affection. Maternal love in a camel.

A دردح *dirdih*, (pl. درادح *darādih*) Greedily addicted. An old woman. A decrepit old man. A camel toothless through age.

A دردحة *dirdihat*, (pl. درادح *darādih*) A squat woman, broad as long. An old toothless she-camel.

P درد خوار *durd-khwār*, Poor, humble. Earth.

P در در *dar dar*, In the door, at the door.

A دردر *durdur*, (pl. درادر *darādir*) That part of the gums where the teeth grow, the socket. Sharp points of a boy's teeth. اعييتني باشر فكيف بدردر *aʼyaytanī bi ushurin fa kayfa bi durdurin*, Thou hast wearied me (by rejecting my counsels) when young (when thy teeth were sharp); how (canst thou relish them now) thou art old and toothless.

A دردرة *dardarat*, (v. n. of دردر Q) Eating, munching unripe dates (a lad).

P دردرون *dar darūn*, In, within.

A دردرّي *dardarraʼ*, One with oblong testicles.

P درد زده *dard-zada*, Pained, sick.

P دردست *dar dast*, In hand. In readiness. در دست دادن *dar dast dādan*, To give up, betray.

P دردشت *dari dasht*, A quarter in Ispahān.

P درد شريك *dard-sharīk*, Sympathetical.

A دردق *dardak*, (pl. درادق *darādik*) Infants. Camels' colts, or the young of other things. A measure of wine.

P درد كش *durd-kash*, A toper, tippler, sot who drains the very dregs.

P درد كن *dard-kun*, Painful, causing pain.

P درد گير *dard-gīr*, Pained, receiving pain.

P درد گين *dard-gīn*, Painful. Sprained.

A دردم *dirdim*, A woman who goes and comes in the night. An aged she-camel.

P دردمانيدن *dar damānīdan*, To cause to blow.

P دردمن *dardman*, (for دردمند) Sick.

P دردمند *dardmand*, In pain. Sick in body or mind. Poor, miserable, afflicted. Compassionate, sympathizing. *Dar damand*, They blow or breathe.

P دردمندي *dardmandī*, Pain, affliction. Pity.

P دردمه *dardma*, The planets Saturn, Jupiter, Mars, Venus, and Mercury. The sun and moon.

P در دميدن *dar damīdan*, To blow, to inflate.

P دردناك *dardnāk*, Sick, afflicted. In pain, painful. Sprained.

P دردوخت *dar dokht*, Accusation. Rumour.

P دردوختن *dar dokhtan*, To sew. To accuse.

A دردور *durdūr*, A whirlpool.

P درده *durda*, Sediment, lees, dregs.

P دردي *dardī*, Pain. A trumpet. *Durdī*, Dregs.

A درديّ *durdiy*, Sediment, dregs.

P دردي ناك *durdīnāk*, Full of sediment, dreggy.

A درر *darar*, Camels giving much milk. The front of a house conspicuous to the eye. A place whence or whither the wind blows. A right direction (on the road). The middle (of a road). *Dirar*, (pl. of درّة *dirrat*) Heavy showers. *Durar*, (pl. of درّة *durrat*) Pearls. White teeth.

A دُرّر *durrar*, (pl. of دارّ *dārr*) (Camels) which yield much milk.

P درر بار *durar-bār*, Raining pearls, *i.e.* elegant.

P در ربودن *dar rubūdan*, To seize. To ravish.

P در رسيدن *dar rasīdan*, To arrive. To happen. To overtake.

P در رفتن *dar raftan*, To go in, enter, penetrate. در بهم رفتن *dar baham raftan*, To twist together, to weave like the meshes of a net.

P در ريختن *dur rekhtan*, (To scatter pearls) To shed tears. To speak eloquently.

P A درز *darz*, A joint, the joining of the skull, a suture, a seam. A rent in a garment which has been sewed up. Young girls. *Daraz*, Mustachios.

A درز *darz*, (v.n. of درز) Enjoying the pleasures of life. The conveniences and luxuries of life.

P در زاده *dar zāda*, A mill-dam. A sluice by which they bring water to the mill. The chest into which the flour falls.

P در زبان داشتن *dar zabān dāshtan*, To defame.

A درزة *darzat*, (as اولاد درزة *awlād darzat*) Low people, rabble. Tailors. Weavers.

P در زدن *dar zadan*, To strike. چنگ درزدن *chang dar zadan*, To fix the nails, claws, or talons in any thing. چنگ درزده بكسي *chang dar zada ba kase*, Having the hands locked with another in fight.

P درز كردن *darz kardan*, To be divulged.

P درزمان *darazmān*, A thread drawn through a needle. *Dar zamān*, In the time. Instantly. در زمان جاهليّت *dar zamāni jāhiliyat*, In the time of paganism (before the coming of Muhammad).

P درزن *dar-zan*, A knocker of a door. A needle.

P در زنا *dar zanā*, Dipping, steeping, dyeing.

P در زنجير *dar zanjīr*, In chains.

P درزند *dar zand*, Place of carnage: butchery.

P درزه *darza*, A heap of sand or rubbish. A rent in a garment which has been sewed. A girl, daughter.

P درزي *darzī*, A tailor.

A درزي *durzī*, The nation of the Druzes.

P در زير *dar zer* or *dar zīr*, Under, beneath.

P درزيگري *darzīgarī*, The business of a tailor; sewing, stitching. درزيگري كردن *darzīgarī kardan*, To sew, to do the work of a tailor.

A درس *dars*, (v. n. of درس) Being worn (a garment). Wearing out. Reading, digesting (a book). Treading or thrashing out corn. Becoming very scabby and pitched (a camel). Lying with a girl. Being menstruous. A hidden path, the traces almost defaced. Remains of scab in a camel. A camel's tail. A lecture. Exercise, study. P درس گفتن *dars guftan*, To instruct. درس عام دادن *darsi ʼām dādan*, To give public lectures. A *Dirs*, (pl. ادراس *adrās* and درسان *dirsān*) A threadbare garment. A camel's tail.

P در ساختن *dar sākhtan*, To league, ally with, join. To do with, to be satisfied or content.

P درسار *dar-sār*, (or درساره) An antechamber. An outer wall. A curtain hung before a door.

A درسان *dirsān*, (pl. of درس) Threadbare clothes.

P درسپردن *dar sipurdan*, To surrender, give in.

A درسة *dursat*, Exercise, study.

P درست *durust*, Entire, complete, perfect, whole, well, safe, sound. Straight, even. Firm. Accurate, correct. Gold or silver. Coin of the best standard. Health. درست شدن *durust shudan*, To be repaired or mended. درست كردن *durust kardan*, To check.

P درستان *darastān*, (or درستاران *darastārān*) Any gratuity over and above the stipulated wages.

P درست پيمان *durust-paymān*, Promise-keeping.

P درست تن *durust-tan*, Healthy in body.

P درست خوان *durust-khwān*, A correct reader.

P درست دينار *durust-dīnār*, Good money.

P درست كردار *durust-kirdār*, Of upright conduct.

P درست گمان *durust-gumān*, A staunch believer.

P درست گو *durust-go* or *gū*, Truth-speaking.

P درستگي *durustagī*, Soundness, healthiness.

P درسته *darasta*, Pardon, forgiveness.

P درستي *durustī*, Entireness, soundness. Propriety, amendment, adjustment, reform. Seriousness, gravity. بدرستي *ba durustī*, In truth.

P درسي *dursatī* or *dursitī*, (درشي *durshatī* or *durshitī*) Name of the daughter of Nawshīrvān.

P درس خوان *dars-khwān*, A student. Any one who reads to another.

P درس وران *dars-warān*, Elementary lectures.

P درسه *darsa*, Forgiveness.

P درش *darsh*, A stable, a stall. A tether for horses. *Darash*, A long kind of cucumber.

A درشة *durshat*, Necessity. Litigation.

P درشت *durusht*, Rough, hard, thick. Fierce, fell, morose, stern, oppressive. Rugged, unequal.

Notched (sword). Disproportionate. Hairy.

P درشت پسند *durusht-pasand*, Dull, stupid.

P درشت خوار *durusht-khwār*, Who fares hard.

P درشت گوش *durusht-gosh*, Dull of hearing.

P درشته *darashta*, Forgiveness, remission of sin.

P درشتي *durushtī*, Roughness. Severity, fierceness. Violence. درشتي كردن *durushtī kardan*, To treat with harshness.

P درشدن *dar shudan*, To be in. To enter. بكاري درشدن *ba kāre dar shudan*, To be engaged in certain business.

P در شكر بيزي بودن *dar shakar-bezī būdan*, To weep, to be shedding tears. To rejoice.

P درشكستگي *dar shikastagī*, Abatement, subsidence.

P درشكستن *dar shikastan*, To turn in, fold, double. To subside, abate.

P درشورانيدن *dar shorānīdan*, To move, stir.

P درشي *darashī*, A kind of long thin cucumber.

A درص *dars*, (v. n. of درص) Losing (her) teeth through old age (a she-camel). *Dars* or *dirs*, (pl. درصة *dirasat*, ادراص *adrās*, درصان *dirsān*, دروص *durūs*, and ادرص *adrus*) The young of mice, moles, hares, cats, or porcupines. *Dirs*, The abortion of an ass. *Daras*, (v. n. of درص) Having the teeth broken with age.

A درصاء *darsāʾ*, (A she-camel) whose teeth are broken with age.

A درصان *dirsān*, (or درصة *dirasat*) (pl. of درص) Young mice, kittens, leverets, or moles.

P درصورت *dar sūrat*, In case. In appearance.

A درع *darʿ*, (v. n. of درع) Stripping the skin from off a sheep's neck, without breaking any joint. *Dirʿ*, (pl. ادرع *adruʿ*, ادراع *adrāʿ*, and دروع *durūʿ*) Armour, whether of iron, leather, or mail. (pl. ادراع *adrāʿ*) A woman's shift, smicket, or smock. الدرع الحصينة *ad' dirʿu'l hasīnat*, The city of Madīna. *Durʿ* or *duraʿ*, Part of the medullary substance of the palm-tree covered over with the fibrous integument called ليف *līf*. *Durʿ* or *duraʿ*, (pl. of درعاء *darʿāʾ*) Black-headed (animals). (Three) nights when the moon rises with the dawn. *Daraʿ*, Whiteness on the brisket of sheep, with blackness of the thighs. *Dariʿ*, Tender (herbage). *Duraʿ*, Three nights after ايّام البيض *ayyāmu'l bīz*, viz. the 16th, 17th, and 18th of the month.

A درعاء *darʿāʾ*, (fem. of ادرع *adraʿ*) (An animal) white, with a black head. White-breasted, black-legged (ewe). (A night) on which the moon rises with the dawn.

P درع باف *dirʿ-bāf*, A weaver of coats of mail.

A درعة *durʿat*, A state in which the pasturage round a watering-place has been eaten bare. درعة النخل *durʿatu'n nakhl*, The pith of a palm-tree concealed under the fibrous integument.

A درّعة *durraʿat*, (or *duraʿat*) A cuirass, corslet.

A درعث *darʿas*, Aged and heavy (camel).

P درعرق شدن *dar ʿarak shudan*, To be in a sweat, to funk. To blush.

P درعقب *dar ʿakab*, Immediately after, behind.

A درعم *dirʿim*, Any thing rude, rustic, or of the worst kind. Obscene. A worthless fellow.

P درعهده *dar ʿuhda*, Due, promised, necessary.

A درعيّة *dirʿiyat*, (pl. دراعيّ *darāʿiy*) (A dart) piercing a cuirass.

P درغ *dargh*, A dam, wear, mound.

P درغال *darghāl*, Security, rest, tranquillity. Quiescent, at rest.

P درغاله *darghāla*, Narrow mountain-passes.

P درغان *darghān*, A city near Samarkand.

P درغست *dar ghast*, Vain, foolish, absurd.

P در غلبكن *dar-ghalbkan*, *dar-ghulbakan*, or در غلبكين *dar-ghulbakīn*, A door with a wicket, hatch, or lattice.

P درغم *dar-gham*, Name of a note in music, (so called from its power of expelling grief from the mind). A place remarkable for excellent wine.

P درغمي *darghamī*, Wine produced at Dargham.

P درغيش *darghīsh*, Many, much, copious. A kind of apricot.

A درف *darf*, A shade. A strong-hold, patronage, protection, guard. Any person to whom one flies for protection. Side, cause, party.

A درفاس *dirfās*, A large camel. A corpulent man. A large lion.

A درفس *dirafs*, Large camel. Corpulent man. Silk, silken stuff. A great standard.

A درفسة *darfasat*, (v. n. of درفس Q) Riding a large camel. Carrying a large standard (درفس).

P درفش *dirafsh*, A cobbler's awl. A standard, ensign, colours, banner. Lightning. Light, splendour. Any thing glittering, shining, or flashing. A sash wrapped round the head when going to battle. درفش كاوان *dirafshi kāwān*, (or كاويان *kāwiyān*) The standard of Farīdūn.

P درفشان *dirafshān*, Shining. Trembling.

P درفشانيدن *dirafshānīdan*, To cause to shine.

P درفش زده *dirafsh-zada*, Stitched.

P درفشه *durufsha*, A sword.

P درفشي *dirafshī*, Acquirement of celebrity.

P درفشيدن *dirafshīdan*, To shine. To tremble.

P درفنجك *darfanjak*, The nightmare.

A درق *dark*, Any thing hard. *Darak*, (pl. of درقة *darakat*) Bucklers of leather.

A درقاء *darkāʾ*, A cloud.

A درقة *darakat*, (pl. درق *darak*, ادراق *adrāk*, and دراق *dirāk*) A shield or buckler of solid leather. A wicket.

A درقع *durkuʿ*, A water-drawing camel.

A درقعة *darkaʿat*, (v. n. of درقع Q) Going fast. Fleeing through fear. Grazing heartily (sheep).

P درقفا *dar kafā*, Behind, close behind.

A درقل *dirakl*, An Armenian garment. A man who walks with grace and dignity.

A درقلة *darkalat*, (v. n. of درقل Q) Passing hastily by. Listening, attending to, obeying. Going with wide steps. Leaping. Walking proudly. *Diraklat*, A boy's game. Haughty, airy, stately.

A درقم *dirkim*, Lame. Useless, worthless. Falling. A name of Antichrist.

A درقوع *durkūʿ*, Pusillanimous, timid.

P درقه *darka*, A shield. A coat of mail.

A درك *dark*, (v. n. of درك) Prosecuting without intermission. Overtaking, reaching to. Any possible contingency. كفيل بالدرك *kafīl bi'd dark*, Bail for what may happen. *Dark* or *darak*, (pl. ادراك *adrāk*) The lowest part or depth. The pit (of hell). Punishment. A rope's end tacked on to the main rope of a bucket that it may not be rotted by the water. *Darak*, (v. n. of درك) Arriving at, overtaking.

P درك *darak*, A napkin, a handkerchief, a towel.

A دركات *darakāt*, (pl. of دركة) Steps for descending. Lowest degrees. The deepest pits of hell.

P دركار *dar kār*, In use, in operation. Necessary, useful. In requisition, required, wanted, desired.

P دركاله *darkāla*, Ice. An icicle.

A دركة *dirkat*, A loop at the horn of a bow. A piece added to a short rein. *Darakat*, (pl. دركات *darakāt*) A descending step, lowest degree.

P دركردن *dar kardan*, To place within, drive into, cause to enter. To insert. To patch.

P دركشاده *dar-kushāda*, Open-doored.

P دركشيدگي *dar kashīdagī*, A drawing in, contraction.

P دركشيدن *dar kashīdan*, To draw in, inhale. To taste. To drink. To erase. To restore. A thread, string, twine.

A دركلة *diraklat* or *dirkilat*, A kind of play.

P دركنار *dar kanār*, Upon the side, brink, bank, margin, edge. Asunder, apart. In the arms, bosom, or embrace.

P دركندن *dar kandan*, To dig.

P دركون *darkūn*, A saddle-strap, by which any thing is fastened to the side of the horse. The higher lintel of a doorway. A large high raised place for sitting.

P درگاه *dar-gāh*, The king's court. A port, portal, gate, door. The lower threshold. A court before a palace or great house. A large bench or place for reclining upon. A mosque. درگاه الهي *dar-gāhi ilāhī*, The court of heaven. درگاه معلّى *dar-gāhi muʿalla'*, The sublime court, or port.

P درگذشتن *dar guzashtan*, To pass beyond, outstrip. To advance. To abstain, cease. To die. از حد درگذشتن *az had dar guzashtan*, To exceed bounds or measure, to go beyond due limits.

P درگر *durgar*, A carpenter.

P درگردانيدن *dar gardānīdan*, To roll, to toss.

P درگرفتن *dar giriftan*, To kindle. To make an impression, take effect. To occupy, fill, overspread.

P درگسلان *dar gusilān*, Dragging or breaking off.

P درگشتن *dar gashtan*, To decline.

P درگلاله *dargulāla*, Ice. An icicle.

P درگه *dar-gah*, (for درگاه *dar-gāh*) A court.

P درلك *dirlik*, (or درليك) A short-sleeved jerkin.

A درم *darm*, (*daram*, or *darim*) (v. n. of درم) Going with short quick steps (a hedgehog). Going very gently (a horse). *Durm*, (pl. of ادرم *adram*) Fleshy on the arms, legs, or thighs. *Daram*, (v. n. of درم) Having the ankles or elbows so fleshy that no protuberance is seen in the calves of the legs. Losing the teeth. Dropping out (teeth). *Darim*, Name of a tree; also of a man.

P درم *diram*, Money, specie. A silver coin generally in value about twopence sterling. A fish-scale. A white rose. درم خريده *diram-kharīda*, Purchased with money. A slave. درم شرعي *dirami shar'ī*, Three māshas and four grains of silver.

A درماء *darmā*, A kind of bitter herb. A hare. (fem. of ادرم *adram*) Fleshy upon the arms, wrists, and ankle-bones.

P درمار ضحاكی كشيدن *dar māri zahhākī kashīdan*, To put in fetters.

P درمان *darmān*, Medicine, remedy. Weak.

A درمان *daramān*, (v. n. of درم) Taking short, quick steps (a hedgehog).

P درماندگي *darmāndagī*, Misery, distress, misfortune, want, penury. Impotency, helplessness. Paralysis. درماندگيء سخن *dar māndagī-i sukhan*, A stuttering, stammering.

P درماندن *darmāndan*, To be unfortunate, destitute. To stick fast, to despair. To boggle, stammer.

P درمانده *dar mānda*, Distressed. Helpless.

P درمان كنا *darmān-kunā*, Healing; a healer.

A درمة *darmat*, A hare. *Darimat*, Soft, easy, lying close (waistcoat).

P درمدار *diram-dār*, Monied. Scaly (fish).

P درم دزد *diram-duzd*, A beetle, tumble-dung.

A درمسة *darmasat*, A being silent. Hiding.

P درمسرا *diram-sarā*, A mint.

P درمسنگ *diram-sang*, Weighing a drachma.

P درمشت *dar musht*, In hand, under controul.

A درمق *darmak*, Very white flour.

A درمك *darmak*, Fine flour, or bread made of it. Soft sand or earth.

A درمكة *darmakat*, (v. n. of درمك Q) Running, skipping, taking short steps, passing by. Smoothing (a building). (Camels) breaking (a cistern and drinking from it).

P درم گزين *diram-guzīn*, A money-changer.

P درمل *durmul*, Grain not arrived at maturity, but which, when toasted, is eaten.

P درمنده *darmanda*, Abandoned, destitute.

P درمنه *dirmana*, Wormwood, hyssop.

A درموك *durmūk*, A coarse kind of carpet.

P درميان *dar miyān*, In the middle. In the midst, among, between, before, in view. Pledged, staked. Final, last. An interval.

P درمياني *dar miyānī*, Midmost. A mediator.

P درميدن *darmīdan*, To bark. To blow.

P درن *darn*, A leech.

A درن *daran*, (v. n. of درن) Being dirty (hands or garments). Being worn (hands), *i. e.* beneficent. Filth. Mother-country. Root, origin. امّ درن *ummi daran*, The world. الدرن *ad' daran*, Mount Atlas in Mauritania. *Darin*, (pl. دران *dirān*) Dirty, worn-out (garment). درن اليدين *darinu'l yadayn*, One whose hands are soiled and worn, *i. e.* incessantly employed in acts of beneficence.

A درنة *darinat*, (fem.) Beneficent (hand).

A درناس *dirnās*, A lion.

P درند *darand*, Form, fashion, mode, manner, quality. Like, resembling.

P درنده *daranda*, What rends or tears; a tearer, render. Rapacious, fierce.

P درنزد *dar nazd*, Near, with, among.

P درنشاندگي *dar nishāndagī*, A grafting.

P درنشاندن *dar nishāndan*, To insert, graft.

P درنشستني *dar nishastanī*, Fit for riding.

P درنفس *dar nafas*, In a breath, in a moment.

A درنفقا *daranfahan*, Hastily, quickly.

A درنك *dirnik*, A carpet with a long pile.

P درنگ *dirang*, Delay, hesitation, tardiness. Clog, hindrance. Tinkling of a bell. The noise made in breaking glass or china. Permanency. Eternity. Time. Peace. Sadness, affliction. Destruction. (in comp.) Slow, tedious, retarding. درنگ كردن *dirang kardan*, To delay, protract.

P درنگي *dirangī*, Tardy. Lateness, tardiness.

P درنگيدن *dirangīdan*, To delay, stay. To be tardy. To remain constant. To rest.

P درنوردن *dar nawardan*, To travel.

P درنورد نهادن *dar naward nihādan*, To fold together. To conceal. To obliterate.

P درنورديدن *dar nawardīdan*, To fold together.

P درنوشتگي *dar nawashtagī*, A folding inwards.

P درنوشتن *dar nawashtan*, To fold up, double, turn inwards.

A درنوف *durnūf*, A large corpulent camel.

A درنوك *durnūk*, A sort of garment. A sort of fringed carpet.

P درنه *dirna*, A bright sword.

A درنيك *dirnīk*, A sort of carpet without pile.

P درو *dar u*, In him, in it. *Dirav*, Harvest. درو كردن *dirav kardan*, To reap. اهل درو *ahli dirav*, Harvest-people. وقت درو *wakti dirav*, Reaping-season. *Dirav*, *durav*, *dirū*, or *durū*, Reap thou. *Durū*, Harvest. دروزدن *durū zadan*, To reap, mow.

A درؤ *durū*, (v. n. of درأ) Entering, or going out on a sudden. Blazing (a fire), glittering (a star). Cracks in the road.

P دروا *darwā*, Head-downwards. Inverted. Raised, cocked. The angels Hārūt and Mārūt. Necessary, needed. Astonished, amazed, dizzy. دروا شدن *darwā shudan*, To stand erect, to be cocked. دروا كردن *darwā kardan*, To erect, raise, toss. سر دروا داشتن *sar darwā dāshtan*, To hold the head erect. *Durwā*, True. Name of the kings of India.

P درواخ *darwākh*, Recovering from illness, convalescence. Strong, firm. Courageous, brave. Right, true. Sure. Courage, bravery. Severity, grossness. Sureness, certainty. Vice, blemish, disgrace.

P دروار *darwār*, Necessary. Dizzy, bewildered.

P درواز *dar-wāz*, Large gates, or doors of a city, palace, or fortress (always open). A square, market-place. Mendicity.

P دروازبان *darwāzbān*, A porter. A warden, keeper, guard of mountain-passes, gates, and the like.

P دروازه *darwāza*, A door. A gate. A square, market-place, or exchange where merchants meet, and mendicants beg; (hence) Begging. A pass through mountains. Lintel of a door. ازدروازه بدر رفتن *az darwāza ba dar raftan*, To perish, fail. دروازهٔ گوش *darwāza-i gosh*, The ear-hole. دروازهٔ نوش *darwāza-i nosh*, The mouth. دروازهٔ هزارگام *darwāza-i hazār gām*, A mile-stone.

P دروازي *dar-wāzī*, Warden, keeper of a city.

P درواژ *darwāj*, Inverted, with head downwards. Necessary. Astonished. Necessity, suitableness.

P درواس *darwās*, Name of a weight. Door-post.

A درواس *dirwās*, A big-headed dog, bandog. Thick-necked. Great, large. A tractable camel. Bold. A lion.

A درواسج *darwāsaj*, The parts of the flaps of a saddle projecting beyond the bow.

A درواقع *dar wāki'*, In fact, verily.

P درواكرده *darwā-karda*, Upraised (curtain).

P دروان *darwān*, A porter, doorkeeper.

A دروان *darwān*, The mongrel cub of a hyena and she-wolf.

P دروانه *darwāna*, A trap-door to a roof.

P درواه *darwāh*, Topsy-turvy. Giddy. Necessary, suitable.

P درواي *darwāy*, Raised, erected. درواي شدن *darwāy shudan*, To stand, to be erect, or cocked.

P دروايست *darwāyist*, Necessary. Becoming. Harmony, agreement. Accord, consent. Inverted, topsy-turvy.

A دروب *darūb*, Obsequious, tractable. *Durūb*, (pl. of درب *darb*) Passes through mountains. Narrow streets.

P دروبست *darobast*, Entirely, totally, all.

G دروبطارس *darūbitāris*, Fern upon oak-trees.

A دروج *darūj*, Rapid (wind), swift (arrow). *Durūj*, (v. n. of درج) Walking, going. Passing by. Dying without issue. Becoming extinct (a family). Exceeding a year and not foaling (a camel). Folding (a letter or cloth). (pl. of درج) Papers or things capable of being folded, wherein they write, volumes.

P درود *durod*, Timber, a plank. *Durūd*, Harvest. Benediction, mercy. Prayer. Praise, thanksgiving. Name of the last of the five intercalary days added to the Persian year. درود كردن *durūd kardan*, To salute. To bless. To bid farewell. درود بي انجام *durūdi bī anjām*, Endless salutations.

P درود كار *durod-kār*, (or درودگر) A carpenter.

P درودگري *durodgarī*, Carpentry.

P درودن *durūdan*, To reap, mow, cut down.

A درور *darūr*, (A camel or camels) giving much milk. *Durūr*, (v. n. of در) Streaming in rays (milk or rain). Lying on the nail and turning round (an arrow). Being brisk (a market). Being soft and smooth. Shining clear, giving light (a lantern).

A دروز *durūz*, (pl. of درز *darz*) Joinings of the skull, sutures. دروز الثوب *durūzu's sawb*, Seams of a garment. بنات الدروز *banātu'd durūz*, Lice, nits.

A دروس *durūs*, (v. n. of درس) Being obliterated (traces of a building). Effacing. Being menstruous. (pl. of درس *dars*) Lectures, studies.

P دروش *dirawsh*, An awl. A banner. A sash wrapped round the head in battle. The lobe of the ear. Lightning, splendour. *Durūsh*, The wound or impression made by a cautery or surgical instrument. *Durosh* or *darosh*, A lancet. *Dirawish*, Mowing, reaping.

A دروص *darūṣ*, Swift (she-camel). *Durūṣ*, (pl. of درص *dars* and *dirs*) Young mice or moles.

A دروع *durūʻ*, (pl. of درع *dirʻ*) Coats of mail.

P دروغ *durogh*, A lie, falsehood. دروغ بافتن *durogh bāftan*, (and دروغ بستن بركسي *durogh bastan bar kase*) To feign a lie, and pass it upon any one.

P دروغ گوي *durogh-goy*, (دروغگر *duroghgar*, or دروغ زن *durogh-zan*) A liar.

P دروغ گوئي *durogh-gūʼī* or *goʼī*, False-speaking.

G دروقينون *darūkīnūn*, Dragon-wort.

P دروك *durūk*, Planks, scantlings.

P دروگر *diravgar*, Reaper. *Durogar*, Carpenter.

A دروم *darūm*, A short woman who walks badly or ungracefully. Who comes and goes in the night.

A درومس *darawmas*, A serpent.

P درون *darūn*, Within. Interior, intimate. Heart. Bowels. A festival. Name of a city in Khurāsān. درون و بيرون *darūn u bīrūn*, Internal and external. Within and without. *Durūn*, A corn-measure. A form of prayer used by the fire-worshippers.

P درون پرور *darūn-parwar*, Generous, brave, noble-hearted. A warrior in defence of religion. A winner of hearts.

A درونج *darūnaj*, Doronicum, leopard's bane.

P دروند *darwand*, A bolt. A hook. Name of a medicine. Name of a wrestler. *Durwand*, (in zand and Pāzand) Wicked, perverse, heretical.

P درون دار *darūn-dār*, Malevolent, grudging.

P دروندة *dirawanda*, A reaper, mower.

P درون رويه *darūn-rūya*, Inwards, inside-facing.

P درونستان *darūnistān*, A temple, golden shrine.

P درونك *darūnak*, (Dronicum) Leopard's bane.

P درون نشينان *darūn-nishīnān*, (Those sitting within) Solitary persons. Hermits.

P درونة *darona*, Dronicum (a herb). The inside, belly. The rainbow. The bow of a cotton-dresser. *Durūna*, The bow of a cotton-dresser. The rainbow.

P دروني *darūnī*, Internal, interior, intrinsic. Intimate, confidential. The inside.

P دروي *dar way*, In him or it.

P درويدن *dirawīdan*, To mow, reap, cut.

P درويدة *dirawīda*, Reaped, mowed.

P دريوزة *darwīza*, (or دريوژة *darwīja*) The practice of begging, mendicity.

P درويش *darvesh* or *darwesh*, Poor, indigent. A dervīsh, monk. درويش سلطان دل *darweshi sultān-dil*, The poor man with the heart of an emperor, *i.e.* Muhammad.

P درويشانة *darweshāna*, Like a pauper or monk.

P درويشي *darweshī*, Poverty. A religious life.

A درة *darh*, (v. n. of درة) Repelling evil, averting, preventing. Protecting. Rising, ascending. Rushing upon, assaulting.

P درة *dara*, A valley (especially between hills through which a stream flows). The stomach of beasts which ruminate. درۀ آسمان *daraʼi āsmān*, The milky way. درة كردن *dara kardan*, To yawn.

P دزّة *darra*, A valley especially between hills (through which a stream flows). The stomach of beasts which chew the cud. Name of a district in Badakhshān. درّۀ آسمان *darraʼi āsmān*, The milky way. *Durra*, A scourge made of twisted thongs with which offenders are punished, or a drum is beaten. Proof, demonstration.

P درها *darhā*, (pl. of در *dar*) Gates, ports, doors. Ways, means. *Durhā*, Pearls. درهاي بيضا *durhāʼi bayzā*, White pearls. Stars. Lightning.

P درهام *darhām*, Current coin. *Dirhām*, (pl. دراهيم *darāhīm*) A farthing, a coin.

A درهرهة *darahrahat*, A twinkling star. A knife with a crooked point.

P درهشتة *darhishta*, A gift: beneficence, liberality.

P درهم *darham*, (from در *dar*, In, and هم *ham*, Together) Intricate, confused, entangled, intermixed, intertwined, distorted, embroiled. Afflicted. درهم نشستن *darham nishastan*, To thicken, become gross (as darkness). روي درهم كشيدن *rūy darham kashīdan*, To contract the face into wrinkles, to frown.

A درهم *dirham* or *dirhim*, (pl. دراهم *darāhim*) Money. A silver coin. A drachm, or drachma. A weight of forty-eight grains. درهم بغلي *dirhami baghlī*, Name of a gold coin as large as the palm of the hand. درهم و دينار *dirham u dīnār*, Money, gold and silver coin. *Dirham*, An enclosed garden.

P درهم افتادة *dar ham uftāda*, Ruined, fallen into chaos and confusion.

P درهم برهم *darham barham*, Confused.

P درهم پيوستگي *darham paywastagī*, Intermixture, interlacement.

P درهم پيوستة *darham paywasta*, Intermixed, interlaced, intertwined.

A درهمة *darhamat*, (v. n. of درهم Q) Producing leaves which bear a likeness to a dirham (mallows).

P درهم كشيدگي *darham kashīdagī*, A shrivelling, shrinking, puckering: corrugation.

P درهمه جا *dar hama jā*, In every place.

P درهو *darhū*, A kind of wicket through which they roll a ball.

P درهوا *dar hawā*, In the air, suspended.

A درهوس *dirhaws*, Strong, firm, stable.

A دري *dary*, (v. n. of دري) Decoying (game). Scratching the head with a comb of horn. *Dary*, *diry*, and دريّ *duriy*, (v. n. of دري) Knowing. Using fraud and finesse.

P دري *darī*, One of the three surviving dialects of the seven anciently spoken in Persia. Some say it prevailed chiefly in بلخ *balkh*, بخارا *bukhārā*, and بدخشان *badakhshān*. It is called the language of the court and of paradise. كبك دري *kabgi darī*, A kind of graceful stepped, musical-voiced partridge.

A دريء *dirriʼ* or *durriʼ*, A sparkling star.

A درّيّ *darrīy*, *dirrīy*, or *durrīy*, A sparkling star glittering like a gem. *Durrīy*, (v. n. of درأ) Glittering (a star). The glancing of a bright sword.

P دريا *daryā*, A sea, ocean. A river. (in the language of mysticism) Pure, uncreated, divine essence. درياي ابيض *daryāʼi abyaz*, The White Sea. درياي اخضر *daryāʼi akhzar*, The Indian Ocean. The sky. درياي اسود *daryāʼi aswad*, The Black Sea. درياي بصرة *daryāʼi basra*, The sea of Basrah. (met.) A large cup filled with wine. درياي بينهايت *daryāʼi bī nihāyat*, The boundless deep. درياي چين *daryāʼi chīn*, The sea of China. درياي حاملة *daryāʼi hāmila*, (or سائلة *sāʼila*) A sea abounding in pearls. Wine. درياي خزر *daryāʼi khazar*, The Caspian Sea. درياي خون *daryāʼi khūn*, An ocean of blood. درياي روم *daryāʼi rūm*, The Mediterranean Sea. درياي عقلي *daryāʼi ʻaklī*, The sea of intelligence which surrounds the throne of God. درياي عمّان *daryāʼi ʻummān*, The Persian Gulf. درياي قلزم *daryāʼi kulzum*, The Red Sea. درياي قير *daryāʼi kīr*, A sea of pitch, *i.e.* A dark night. An inkstand full of ink. درياي لعل *daryāʼi laʻl*, (A sea of ruby) A cup filled with wine. درياي محيط *daryāʼi muhīt*, The ocean. درياي مغرب *daryāʼi maghrib*, The Western Ocean. درياي نيل *daryāʼi nīl*, The river Nile. درياي هند *daryāʼi hind*, The Indian Ocean. دريا و صحرا *daryā u sahrā*, Sea and land. بدريا دادن *ba daryā dādan*, To wash. To drive off. To withdraw a glance.

P درياب *daryāb*, Know. Knowing. A sea.

P دريابار *daryā-bār*, Raining like a deluge. The ocean. A sea-port. Abounding in rivers.

P دريابانيدن *daryābānīdan*, To make understand.

P دريابند *daryā-band*, A port, haven: dock-yard.

P دريابندة *daryābanda*, Intelligent.

P دريابيدن *daryābīdan*, To hang, suspend.

P درياچه *daryācha*, A lake, pool, mere.

P دريا دل *daryā-dil*, Bountiful as the sea.

A درياس *diryās*, A lion.

P دريا شكسته *daryā-shikasta*, A sea-breach.

P دريافت *dar yāft*, Perception, understanding, knowledge. Attainment, acquisition. Discovery, inquiry, investigation. دريافت كردن *daryāft kardan*, To discern.

P دريافتگر *daryāftgar*, A discerner.

P دريافتن *daryāftan*, To understand, know, perceive, find out, comprehend, experience, be acquainted with. To accomplish, arrive at, overtake. To help, assist.

A درياق *diryāk*, *daryāk*, (درياقة *diryākat*, or *daryākat*) Treacle. Wine.

P درياك *diryāk*, Treacle: the bezoar: opium.

P درياكش *daryā-kash*, (or نوش *nosh*) An insatiable drunkard, one who could ingurgitate a sea.

P دريا كف *daryā-kaf*, Bounteous as the ocean.

P دريا گوش *daryā-gosh*, (Sea-ear) A shell.

A دريان *diryān* or *darayān*, (v.n. of دري) Knowing. Deceiving, decoying, or surprising a wild beast by lying concealed. Using fraud and finesse.

P دريا نوال *daryā-nawāl*, Bounteous as the sea.

P دريانوالي *daryā-nawālī*, Excessive liberality.

P دريانورد *daryā-naward*, A voyager.

P درياوگان *daryāwagān*, World (sea and land).

P دريائي *daryāʼī*, Marine, maritime.

A دريّة *daryat* or *diryat*, (v. n. of دري) Knowing. Decoying or surprising (a wild beast, by lying concealed). Using fraud and finesse.

A درّيج *dirrīj*, A drum, or any thing similar.

P دريچان *darechān*, An astronomical method or rule, according to which the constellations are divided into three classes.

P دريچه *darīcha*, A window. A small hole for the admission of light. A wicket. A mould in which goldsmiths cast gold and silver.

A دريد *durayd*, (dim. of ادرد *adrad*) Somewhat toothless. A man's name, or a nickname.

P دريدگي *darīdagī*, Rent, tear, laceration.

P دريدن *darīdan*, To tear, rend, lacerate. To cut out (cloth). To lay open. To subtract. To be loosed. To be torn. *Durīdan*, To reap, mow.

P دريده *darīda*, Torn. دريده شدن *darīda shudan*, To be torn. چشم دريده *chashm-darīda*, Shameless. دريده دهن *darīda-dahan*, Plain-spoken, open-mouthed. *Durīda*, Reaped.

A درير *darīr*, (v. n. of درّ) Going lightly, or galloping hard (a horse). Compact and well-proportioned. Bright, shining (lamp). Fleet, swift (horse).

A دريس *darīs*, Worn out. A threadbare garment. A camel's tail.

P دريس *dirīs*, A kind of play.

A دريص *durays*, (dim.) A very little mouse.

A دريع *durayʻ*, (or دريعة) A little cuirass.

P دريغ *diregh* or *duregh*, Denial. Refusal. Repugnance, disinclination. Sorrow, vexation, grief, anguish. Regret, sorrow for past offences. A sigh. Omission, failure. Slow, slack. Difficult, troublesome. (A particle of pity and regret) Ah! alas! دريغ آمدن *diregh āmadan*, To sigh. To fear. دريغ خوردن *diregh khwurdan*, To sigh, devour sighs, grieve. دريغ داشتن *diregh dāshtan*, To withhold, keep back, refuse, spare. دريغ كردن *diregh kardan*, To deny, refuse, withhold, reject. To lament, pity, regret.

P دريغا *diregha*, Ah! alas! well-a-day!

A دريكة *darīkat*, Prey, game pursued.

P دريك سو *dar yak sū*, In one part.

P دريگان *daregān*, Certain astronomical figures.

A دريم *darīm*, A robust, lusty, or soft youth.

P دريمنه *darīmana*, Wormwood of Pontus.

P درين *darīn*, (for در اين) In this. درين اثنا *dar īn asnā*, In the meantime. درين جنبش *dar īn jumbish*, At this moment. درين ما بين *dar īn mā bayn*, In this interval. درين ولا *dar īn walā*, Now. درين هنگامة *dar īn hangāma*, The world.

A درين *darīn*, Worn garment. A withered herb. Dry forage broken small. امّ درين *ummi darīn*, Barren ground.

P دريواس *darewās*, The four door-posts. The bar of a door. The four sides, circuit, or circumference.

P دريوز *dar-yūz*, (also دريوزه *dar-yūza*) Begging, beggary, asking. A charitable collection.

P دريوش *daryūsh*, A religious mendicant.

A دريئة *darīʼat*, (or دريّة *darīyat*) A ring at which they dart the javelin. A camel or any thing behind which the hunter conceals himself from his prey.

P دز *daz*, A gallery, balcony. *Diz*, A fortress, castle, or city.

P دزار *daz-ār*, (or دژار *daj-ār*) A builder.

P دز افتا *diz aftā*, A fort built by Shāpūr.

P دزد *duzd*, A thief, robber, assassin.

P دزدار *diz-dār*, Governor of a castle or fort.

P دزد افشار *duzd-afshār*, (or افشره *afshara*) An abettor of thieves. A thief. A nest of rogues.

P دزدان *duzdān*, (pl. of دزد *duzd*) Thieves.

P دزدانيدن *duzdānīdan*, To cause to rob.

P دزددان *duzddān*, A hole in a wall, into which the bolt or bar shoots, a staple. Stocks, pillory.

P دزدمه *dazdama*, A planet.

P دزدناك *duzdnāk*, Infested by robbers.

P دزدي *duzdī*, Robbery, theft. دزدي كردن *duzdī kardan*, To filch, steal.

P دزديدگي *duzdīdagī*, Theft, thievery, stealing, larceny. دزديدگيء نگاه *duzdīdagīʼi nigāh*, The stealing of a glance.

P دزديدن *duzdīdan*, To rob, thieve, steal.

P دزديده *duzdīda*, Stolen, purloined, pilfered. A furtive glance. By stealth, clandestinely. دزديده بودن *duzdīda būdan*, To be stolen. پنجهٔ دزديده *panjaʼi duzdīda*, Five intercalary days added to the Persian year.

A دزر *dazr*, A pushing, thrusting, driving away.

P دزغاله *diz-ghāla*, (or دژغاله) A citadel: a tower.

P دزك *dazak*, A towel, napkin, handkerchief.

P دزگاه *daz-gāh*, (vulg.) for دستگاه *dast-gāh*, q.v.

P دزگاه دار *dazgāh-dār*, A banker.

P دزمار *duzmār*, Name of a place famous for its lead or for a mine of lapis lazuli.

P دزنديس *dizandīs*, Alike, resembling. Apparent, manifest. As before. Immediately, forthwith.

P دزهرج *dizharj*, *dizhurj*, or *dizharaj*, Jerusalem. An idol-temple.

P دژ *daj*, A gallery, balcony. *Dij* or *daj*, A fortress. Ugly, bad. Wicked. Bad-tempered. Anger. Adhesion. A father. *Duj*, Wicked, wickedness. Number.

P دژا آهنگ *dujā-āhang*, Bad-tempered.

P دژ آباد *dij-ābād*, Passionate. Formidable.

P دژاگام *dijāgām*, Chaste, abstemious: a eunuch.

P دژاگامه *dijāgāma* or *dajāgāma*, Angry, moody. Ill-natured. Chaste, abstemious. A eunuch.

P دژاگاه *dijāgāh*, (or دژاگه *dijāgah*) Passionate, blustering, grumbling, spleenful, moody, ill-tempered, angry, cruel. The commander of a fortress. An executioner.

P دژ آلود *dij-ālūd*, Passionate. Peevish.

P دژ آلون *dij-ālūn*, Injustice, violence. Alas!

P دژانگاه *dijāngāh*, Angry, passionate.

P دژآهنج *dij-āhanj*, Surly. A small-pointed spear.

P دژ آهنگ *dij-āhang*, A small-pointed arrow. Ruthless. دژاهنگ افراسياب *dijāhangi afrāsyāb*, A cave in which Afrāsyāb took refuge.

P دژ برد *dij* or *daj-burd*, Irascible, scowling.

P دژ برو *daj-burū*, Frowning, scowling; grim.

P دژپراز *dij* (or *daj*) *parāz*, (or براز *barāz*) Fierce, cruel, bloody. Wrathful, bad-tempered. Ugly. Crude, raw. A caviller.

P دژ پسند *daj-pasand*, Temperate, chaste.

P دژپه *dijpih* or *dajpih*, A gland, bubo: scrofula.

P دژ پيه *dij-pīh*, (دژ پيهه *dij-pīha*, or دژپه *dajpah*) A kernel in the flesh.

P دژخم *dij-khim*, Ill-tempered. An executioner.

P دژخي *dij-khay* or *daj-khī*, A jailer. Angry.

P دژخيم *dij-khīm* or *daj-khīm*, Malignant. Ill-tempered. An executioner. A jailer. A keeper. The governor of a fort. Ugly. Avaricious, close-fisted.

P دژك *dijik* or *dajik*, A knot on a rope. *Dujuk*, A blister upon the hand or foot. A knot.

P دژكاك *dijkāk* or *dajkāk*, A carrion-bird.

P دژكام *dij-kām*, (or دژكامه *dij-kāma*) Irascible, angry. Abstemious, chaste, sober. A eunuch. Aged.

P دژگاه *dij-gāh*, Angry: malignant. An executioner.

P دژگوار *daj-guwār*, Meat hard of digestion.

P دژگير *duj-gīr*, Acid.

P دژله *dijla*, (for دجله *dijla*) The Tigris.

P دژم *dijam*, Drunken, cropsick. Melancholy, dejected, sad, downcast, disturbed, distracted, sick.

Thoughtful, anxious. Black, dark.

P دژمان *dij-mān*, Regret, vexation.

P دژمنش *dij-manish*, Wearied, tired, displeased, sated, cloyed, loathing, averse. Aversion, dislike.

P دژن *dujan*, *dijan*, or *dujn*, Acid, pungent.

P دژند *dijand*, Acid, tart. Passionate, testy, sharp, hasty.

P دژواخ *dajwākh*, Thickness, coarseness, grossness. Convalescence.

P دژوان *dajrān* or *dijrān*, A sigh. Regret, grief.

P دژوند *dijwand*, Wicked. Irreligious.

P دژه *daja* or *dija*, Angry, passionate.

P دژهخت *dijhukht*, (دژهخت گنگ *dijhukhti gang*, دژهرج *dijharj*, or *dijhurj*) Jerusalem. An idol-temple.

P دژه گیر *daja-gīr*, An instrument of iron, with which they scrape a kneading-trough.

P دژهم *dujham*, Kernels behind the ears, or under the arm-pits.

P دژهوست گنگ *dijhūst gang*, Jerusalem.

P دس *das*, (in composition) Like, resembling. That. (for دست *dast*) The hand. *Dus*, Burnt clay.

A دسّ *dass*, (v. n. of دسّ) Hiding (one thing under another). Burying in the ground. Suborning. Besmearing (a camel) with pitch, especially the softer places in the skin. P دسّ کردن *dass kardan*, To suppress.

A دساتج *dasātij*, (pl. of دستجة *dastajat*) Armsful.

A دساتیر *dasātīr*, (pl. of دستور *dustūr*) Copies, models, exemplars.

A دساتین *dasātīn*, (pl. of دستان *dastān*) Pegs (of a guitar).

A دسار *disār*, (pl. دسر *dusr* and *dusur*) A fibre of the trunk of the palm-tree, used in the place of oakum in caulking ships.

A دسّاس *dassās*, A noxious kind of serpent.

A دسّاسة *dassāsat*, An earth-worm. A deaf serpent living under ground. A white mushroom resembling an egg.

A دسافى *dusāfa'* (pl. of دسفان *dusfān*) Pimps.

A دسافین *dasāfīn*, (pl. of دسفان *disfān*) Pimps.

A دساکر *dasākir*, (pl. of دسکرة *daskarat*) Villages on mountains. Hermits' cells. Wine-houses kept by foreigners in Arabia. Palaces surrounded by other houses. Plain, level grounds.

A دسام *disām*, A spigot, plug, cork, or any thing by which orifices are stopped up (of bottles, pipes, wounds, or ears).

A دسّة *dussat*, A game among the Arabians (something is hid in a heap of earth, which being then divided into smaller heaps, he who discovers that which contains it, gains).

P دست *dast*, The hand. The hand including the arm to the elbow. A cubit, an ell. The forefeet (of any quadruped). A handle. A term applied to hawks or falcons (as راس *rās*, Head, is to horses; and زنجیر *zanjīr*, Chain, to elephants). The chief seat of precedency given to the most honoured guest. A cushion upon which they sit. A prime-minister. Power, strength. Pre-excellence, superiority, victory. Advantage, emolument, profit. A successful opportunity. Rule, method, manner. Time, turn, occasion. End, termination, limit, boundary. Trade, art, profession, labour. A game at dice. Equal, par. Any thing complete (as a suit of clothes or armour; a house and its offices). (in India) The actual collections (as opposed to *sist*, the assessment). از دست *az dast*, Off hand, immediately. بدست آوردن *ba dast āwardan*, To gain, acquire, obtain, procure. در دست دادن *dar dast dādan*, To betray. زیر دست بودن *zīr dast būdan*, To be in subjection. دست از جان شستن *dast az jān shustan*, To wash one's hands of life; to despair. دست از سر گرفتن *dast az sar giriftan*, To shew no mercy. To pay no respect to. دست افتادن *dast uftādan*, To obtain, learn, find; find out. دست افشاندن *dast afshāndan*, To dance. To display, publish. To abandon. دست آمدن *dast āmadan*, To be fluxed. دست امر *dasti amr*, (also وزارت *wizārat*) The function of a prime-minister. دست انداختن *dast andākhtan*, To swim. دست ببرد *dast ba burd*, He prevailed, excelled, or conquered. دست بدندان کندن *dast ba dandān kandan*, To be vexed, sorry. دست بر آوردن *dast bar āwardan*, To supplicate, entreat for. To come off victorious. To pretend to. To bring up. دست بردار شدن *dast bardār shudan*, To refrain, desist, remit. دست بر داشت شدن *dast bar dāsht shudan*, To be dismissed. دست بر دست نشستن *dast bar dast nishastan*, To sit down helpless. دست بر دل شدن *dast bar dil shudan*, To pine or consume away with envy. دست بر دل نهادن *dast bar dil nihādan*, To give a flat denial to one's inclinations. دست بردن *dast burdan*, To carry off. دست بر دهان بردن *dast bar dahān burdan*, To sigh, grieve, repent. دست بر سر شدن *dast bar sar shudan*, To make obeisance. دست بر کفش نهادن *dast bar kafsh nihādan*, To worship, do homage. دست بزیر زنخ ستون کردن *dast ba zīri zanakh sutūn kardan*, To be pensive or melancholy. دست بیع شدن *dast bayɛ shudan*, To resign one's self. دست پس *dasti pas*, The end of any business. Stakes given to the winners at dice. A low seat, a throne. دست پسین *dasti pasīn*, The last throw at dice. دست پیراهن *dasti pīrāhan*, A sleeve. دست پیش داشتن *dast pesh dāshtan*, To stand with the hands crossed before another. To supplicate, to beg. To hinder, to refuse. دست چپ *dasti chap*, The left hand. دست خطر *dasti khatar*, A move or throw, on which heavy stakes are depending. A high and perilous station. دست خون *dasti khūn* or *dast-khūn*, The last move at chess. A game in which the vanquished party stakes his limbs. A throne for which the possessor has waded through seas of blood. دست دادن *dast dādan*, To give the hand. To assist. To humour, favour one's wishes. To come to pass. To strike a bargain. To rest. To happen. To succeed. دست داشتن *dast dāshtan*, To delay, defer. To execrate, curse. دست در آستین داشتن *dast dar āstīn dāshtan*, To be out of employ. دست در آستین کردن *dast dar āstīn kardan*, To hinder from work. To fight, to quarrel. دست در گلو کردن *dast dar gulū kardan*, To disgrace. دست راست *dasti rāst*, The right hand. A prime-minister. دست شستن *dast shustan*, To wash the hands. To abandon. To despair. دست صلیب کردن *dast salīb kardan*, To stand with the arms crossed upon the breast. دست فشاندن *dast fishāndan*, To dance. To expose, divulge. To leave. دست کشیدن *dast kashīdan*, To touch, to stroke with the hand. To stretch forth the hand. To withhold, hinder. To leave off working. دست کفچه کردن *dast kafcha kardan*, To beg. دست کندن *dast kandan*, To grieve, be sorry for. دست گزیدن *dast gazīdan*, To regret, sorrow for. *Dast guzīdan*, To choose or aspire after the highest place. دست گشادن *dast gushādan*, To open the hand, to exercise liberality. دست موسى *dasti mūsa'*, The sun. دست و پا بسته *dast u pā basta*, Bound hand and foot. دست و پا زدن *dast u pā zadan*, To beg with importunity. To give up the ghost. دست یافتن *dast yāftan*, To take occasion, find an opportunity. To get possession of, conquer, subject. *Dist*, A span. A trident, harpoon, fishing-spear, fizgig.

A دست *dast*, A plain, desert. The chief seat of precedency given to the most honoured guest.

P دستا *dastā*, A barber. A towel, a napkin. A sash wrapped round the turban.

P دست ابرنجن *dast-abranjan*, A bracelet.

P دستاد *dastād*, Many, much. Very.

P دستادست *dast-ā-dast*, From hand to hand. A ready-money bargain. The two wings of an army. A struggle.

P دستار *dastār*, The sash or fine muslin cloth wrapt round the turban. A handkerchief, napkin. A towel. An apron. دستار خوان *dastāri khwān*, A table-cloth.

P دستاران *dastārān*, Drink-money. Money paid before work is done.

P دستار بست *dastār-bast*, A fine linen turban.

P دستار بند *dastār-band*, A servant who makes up the turban. دستار بندان *dastār-bandān*, (Wearers of turbans) Chiefs, nobles, learned men, doctors, judges, lawyers. Dervishes.

P دستارچه *dastārcha*, A small turban or sash. A handkerchief. A towel. A pennant, bandrol. دستارچه ساختن *dastārcha sākhtan*, To present an offering. Studying to conciliate.

P دستار خوان *dastār-khwān*, A table-cloth. A long table. Victuals carried home by the guests from an entertainment.

P دستارسر dastār-sar, A turban. A shroud.

P دست ارنجن dast-aranjan, A bracelet.

P دستارو dastārū, A bracelet.

P دستارة dast-arra, A hand-saw.

P دست آس dast-ās, A hand-mill. A large mortar. دست آس كردن dast-ās kardan, To grind.

P دستاسنگ dastā-sang, A sling.

P دستاش dastāsh, A faggot, a bundle.

P دست افراز dast-afrāz, A tool, implement.

P دست افشان dast-afshān, Dancing; dancer.

P دست افگن dast-afgan, Occupied. Weak. A servant.

P دستاگرد dastāgard, The handle of a saw.

P دست آموز dast-āmoz, Accustomed to the hand, tame, gentle, tractable. A bird trained to hunt. Skilful, dexterous, handy.

P دستان dastān, History, romance, fable. Song, melody, trill, shake. Foolish, idle talk. Fraud, imposture, stratagem. Name of a magician: and of a place in Samarkand. Name of Zāl, father of Rustam. (pl. of دست dast) Hands. هزار دستان hazār-dastān, The nightingale.

A دستان dastān, A key, pin, or peg, of a musical instrument.

P دست انبويه dast-amboya or ambūya, (دستنبوي dast-amboy or ambūy) Any thing odoriferous (particularly a species of small melon or apple, which is carried in the hand on account of its delightful perfume).

P دست انداز dast-andāz, A dancer. A swimmer. A cut-purse. An archer. An oppressor. Transgression, trespass, infringement. Rapine, plunder. One who goes side by side with another.

P دستان زن dastān-zan, A magician, impostor. A story-teller. One who touches the keys or chords of a musical instrument.

P دستانزند dastān-zand, The father of Rustam.

P دستان سراي dastān-sarāy, A chanticleer.

P دستانه dastāna, An agricultural tool. A whip. A glove.

P دست اورنجن dast-awranjan, A bracelet.

P دست اوزار dast-avzār, A tool.

P دست آويز dast āvez, A small present (such as an inferior carries to a great man, that he may not go empty-handed). A voucher, document, signature, note of hand, or bond. A title-deed.

P دستاهنگ dast-āhang, An agricultural tool.

P دست با پادشاه dast bā pādshāh, Hand (*i. e.* the being on an equality) with the king.

P دستباز dast-bāz, Active, dexterous. One who makes away with all he has. Clever at chess.

P دستبانه dast-bāna, A glove. A bracelet.

P دست بدست dast ba dast, From hand to hand. Joined hands. Expeditious. Ready-money.

P دست برجن dast-barjan, A bracelet.

P دستبرد dast-burd, Pre-excellence, superiority, advantage, victory (at play, in war or law).

P دست بردهان dast bar dahān, Eating.

P دست برسر dast bar sar, Grief, lamentation.

P دست برنجن dast-baranjan, A bracelet.

P دست بسته dast-basta, Close-fisted, avaricious. Engaged in prayer.

P دست بقبضه dast ba kabza, Hand to the hilt, sword in hand, ready for battle.

P دست بقچه dast-bukcha, Wrapper of a bundle.

P دستبند dast-band, Swathes for the hands. A dance where they take hands. A bracelet. دست بند حنا dast-bandi hinā, Remains of henna adhering to the hands.

P دستبوس dast-bos, (or بوسي) Kissing of hands.

P دست بويه dast-būya or boya, A kind of melon.

P دست پاك dast-pāk, Poverty. Chaste. Religious. A towel.

P دست پخت dast-pukht, Prepared, brought up, or cooked by the hand.

P دست پناه dast-panāh, A glove. Tongs.

P دست پيش dast-pesh, A suppliant, beggar.

P دست پيمان dast-paymān, An agreement ratified by all striking hands. Furniture which a bridegroom sends to the house of the bride. A dowry.

P دست تنگ dast-tang, Indigent, poor.

P دست تنگي dast-tangī, Poverty.

A دستجة dastajat, (from P دسته dasta) (pl. دساتج dasātij) An armful.

P دست چالاك dast-chālāk, Light-fingered: a thief.

P دست چالاكي dast-chālākī, Lightness of finger. Stealth. A civil war, duel.

P دست چمك dast chamak, Power, authority.

P دست چوب dast-chob, Walking-stick, club.

P دستخر dust-khar, Reproach, reviling.

P دستخط dast-khat, Hand-writing, signature.

P دستخوان dast-khwān, A long table-cloth, napkin. A pinafore.

P دست خوش dast-khwash, Buffoonery. A towel. Weak, under command. Easily procured.

P دستدرازي dast-darāzī, Violence, oppression.

P دستر dastar, (or دسترة dastara) A hand-saw. A small sickle.

P دست رس dast-ras, Within one's power, whatever one is equal to. Fruit, which one can reach with the hand. Aid, assistance. Arriving, obtaining. Able. Greatness, power, ability. Order, arrangement. دست رس كردن dast-ras kardan, To assist. To follow, to arrive.

P دست رسي dast-rasī, Ability.

P دست رنج dast-ranj, A hand-saw. Money, what is gained by labour. Trade, craft, skill, handiwork. Hire, wages. Trouble, labour, exertion.

P دست ريس dast-res, Spun, or twisted thread.

P دست زده dast-zada, Struck with the fist. Rubbed with the hands. Seized, conquered. Sifted.

P دست زن dast-zan, Vexed. A dancer: singer.

P دستزيگ dast-zīg, A mason's rule.

P دست سنگ dast-sang, A sling.

P دست سوزه dast-soza, A betrothed woman.

P دست شانه dast-shāna, A kind of comb, with which the threads of silk are kept separated when twisting them into ropes.

P دست شستني dast shustanī, Whatever is employed for washing with: any lotion with an infusion of marsh-mallows or myrtle-leaves.

P دست شفا dast-shifā, An epithet of a physician who is successful in restoring his patients to health (one who has healing in his hand).

P دست شكسته dast-shikasta, (Broken-handed) Unable to procure a livelihood, and ignorant of every trade, art, or profession.

P دست شكن dast-shikan, Bruising the hand. A curling lock.

P دست شوي dast-shūy, A wash-hand bason, or the water in which the hands are washed. Washing the hands. Potash.

P دست فال dast-fāl, Handsel.

P دست فرسود dast-farsūd, Worn by the hand.

P دست فرنجن dast-faranjan, A bracelet.

P دست فروش dast-farosh, A hawker, a retailer.

P دست فروشي dast-faroshī, Pedlery.

P دستقاله dast-kāla, A reaping-hook.

P دست قدرت dast-kudrat, Power, ability.

P دست قلم dast-kalam, Amputated in the hand. A writer.

P دستك dastak, A little hand. A plough-handle. A spindle. A clapping of hands. A pass, passport, permit, licence. A summons or order to appear. A commission. A rap at the door. دستك سوار dastak-suwār or دستك پياده dastak-piyāda, One sent by an Amil to receive rents.

P دستكار dast-kār, Wrought, manufactured. An artificer, handicraftsman, one who lives by the work of his hands. Dexterous, expert, expeditious. A hand-bill. A royal order stuck on a wall, or cut on stone. دستكار فلان dast-kāri fulān, The handiwork of such an one.

P دستكاري dast-kārī, An art, trade. Handicraft, dexterity.

P دستكاله dast-kāla, A reaping-sickle.

P دستك زن dastak-zan, One who beats time in music. A dancer, musician, singer. Penitent, sorry, vexed, in a pet.

P دستكش dast-kash, A led horse. A guide of the blind. Reward of labour. A weak bow for practising. Weak, oppressed. A captive. A beggar. Firm. A falconer. A young hound. A horse's colt.

P دست كشاد dast-kushād, Liberality.

P دست كشي dast-kashī, Touch, gentle friction. Begging, mendicity.

P دست كشيده dast-kashīda, Possessed, claimed, occupied.

P دست كله dast-kala, Fetters for a horse. Like.

P دست كوتاه *dast kotāh*, Weak, unsuccessful.

P دستكي *dastakī*, An ornament for the hands. A falconer's glove. A pocket-book, tweezer-case.

P دستگاه *dast-gāh*, A weaver's shop. A workhouse of any kind: a laboratory. Any manufacturing instrument, a loom. Utensils. A merchant's counter. Understanding. Wealth. Excellence. Learning. Wisdom. Power, strength, ability. دستگاه وجود *dast-gāhi wujūd*, The sense of hearing, seeing, touching, taste, and smell. Imagination. Thought. Memory. Common sense. بارگاه معدلت دستگاه *bār-gāhi maꜥdalat-dastgāh*, The tribunal of justice. پادشاه عالم پناه و شهنشاه سعادت دستگاه *pādshāhi ꜥālam-panāh u shahanshāhi saꜥādat-dastgāh*, The king, asylum of the world, and the monarch of the tribunal of felicity, *i.e.* the most potent and most august emperor. سپاه ظفر دستگاه *sipāhi zafar-dastgāh*, A victorious army.

P دست گذار *dast-guzār*, Assistant, helper, ally.

P دست گزين *dast-guzīn*, Choosing for one's self the chief seat. Any thing which is the object of one's choice. A led horse.

P دستگه *dast-gah*, Understanding, intellect, science, knowledge. دستگه ديرپاي *dast-gahi dīr-pāy*, The heavens. The world. Durable riches.

P دستگي *dastagī*, The world. Time. Fortune. A friend. An ally, helper. A falconer's glove.

P دستگير *dast-gīr*, Taking the hand. An assistant, patron, protector. A saint. Imprisoned. Taking prisoner.

P دستگيرا *dast-gīrā*, O (my) protector!

P دستگيري *dast-gīrī*, Assistance, aid, help. Defence, patronage, protection. Imprisonment.

P دستلاف *dast-lāf*, Handsel.

P دستمال *dast-māl*, Rubbing the hands. A towel. A handkerchief. A kettle-holder. Easy. Smooth. Bare. A prisoner. Wealth.

P دست مالچه *dast-mālcha*, A small towel.

P دستمايه *dast-māya*, Stock in trade. Source.

P دست مرد *dast-mard*, A friend, helper, ally.

P دست مردي *dast-mardī*, Intercession, help.

P دست مزد *dast-muzd*, Wages: recompence.

P دست موزه *dast-mūza*, A tool. A present.

P دستنبد *dastambad* or *bud*, A kind of dance.

P دستنبو *dastambū* or *dastambo*, (دستنبويه *dastambūya* or *dastamboya*) Perfume.

P دستنجن *dastanjan*, A glove, gauntlet.

P دست نشان *dast-nishān*, Appointed to a work. Obedient.

P دست نماز *dast-namāz*, Ablution before prayer.

P دستوار *dastwār*, A walking-stick. A shepherd's crook. Any thing a span long. An assistant, ally. A wound. A bracelet.

P دستواره *dastawāra* or *dastwāra*, Any thing a span long. Any thing capable of being taken in the hand. A walking-staff.

P دستوان *dastuwān* or *dastwān*, A gauntlet. A glove. A bracelet. A servant who takes care of the clothes of bathers.

P دستوانه *dastwāna*, A bracelet. A gauntlet. A falconer's glove. The chief seat of precedency.

P دستور *dastūr*, Leave, permission, licence, dismission, conge. A prime-minister, vazīr, senator, counsellor of state. A confidential person. A model, exemplar, rule, basis, foundation, canon, original of a book, record, formula, or any writing of authority to which people have recourse. Custom, mode, manner, fashion. Constitution, privilege. A customary fee, tax, or per centage. Fulfilment of a promise. A bolt, bar. A large log laid across a ship as ballast. A high priest of the fire-worshippers. A powerful man. دستور العمل *dastūru'l ꜥamal*, A model, rule, regulation. دستور مكرم *dastūri mukarram*, An illustrious counsellor.

A دستور *dustūr*, (pl. دساتير *dasātīr*) A note or common-place book. A senator, grandee. A pillar. A canon, copy, exemplar, model.

A دستورات *dastūrāt*, Perquisites or per centage allowed to a zamīndār on the collection of his lands.

P دست ورجن *dast-warjan*, A bracelet.

P دستورشاه *dastūr-shāh*, A royal diadem.

P دستورنجن *dast-waranjan*, A bracelet.

P دستوره *dast-wara*, A hand-saw. Earnings.

P دستوري *dastūrī*, Perquisites paid unto servants by one who sells to their master, fees. Leave. Custom. Any thing thrown in, or placed upon another (as if one should buy a pound of sugar, and an apple should be put on the top).

P دستوم *dastūm*, Recollection, memory, reflexion.

P دستون *dustūn*, The dung of animals.

P دسته *dasta*, A handle, helve, haft. A handful: a handful of reaped corn or flowers, a shock, a nosegay. A hank or skein of silk or thread, clew. A lock of hair. A pestle. The neck of a guitar or violin. A quire of paper. A friend, assistant, ally. An assemblage of people. A bundle consisting of twenty-four arrows. A division of an army, brigade. A swathe for binding a sheaf of corn. Impudent, audacious. Impudence, audacity, rudeness. importunity; fault, offence. دستهٔ دستاس *dastaꜥi dast-ās*, The handle of a hand-mill. دستهٔ ريسمان *dastaꜥi rīsmān*, A reel for winding thread upon. دستهٔ كارد *dastaꜥi kārd*, A knife-handle. دستهٔ كاغذ *dastaꜥi kāghiz*, A quire of paper. A bundle of letters. دستهٔ گل *dastaꜥi gul*, (or گل دسته *gul-dasta*) A nosegay. The sun. *Dusta*, A stone.

P دسته چلك *dasta-chilik*, A bat for trap-ball.

P دسته چوب *dasta-chob*, A staff. Importunity.

P دسته دار *dasta-dār*, Commander of a brigade.

P دسته دسته *dasta-dasta*, By handsful.

P دستي *dastī*, A torch or link carried in the hand. Any vessel which may be lifted by the hand. An earthen bottle, pot, cruise, drinking-cup with two handles. A large open vessel for washing clothes or dressing skins. Assistance. پيش دستي كردن *pesh dastī kardan*, To make haste, finish soon.

P دست ياب *dast-yāb*, Opportunity, occasion. Procurable. دست ياب شدن *dast-yāb shudan*, To find, to have found occasion. دست ياب گرديدن *dast-yāb gardīdan*, To be acquired.

P دست يابي *dast-yābī*, Controul: prefecture.

P دستيار *dast-yār*, Assistant, helper, minister.

P دستياره *dast-yāra*, A gold or silver bracelet.

P دستياري *dast-yārī*, Aid, assistance. Defence.

P دست يافت *dast-yāft*, Victory. Opportunity.

P دست يافته *dast-yāfta*, Successful.

P دستيانه *dast-yāna*, A gauntlet. A bracelet. A scourge. A fiddle-stick. A letter, scroll. Letters patent. A necklace.

P دستيج *dastīj*, A handle.

A دستيج *dastīj*, (from P دستي *dastī*) Any vessel which can be lifted up by the hand.

P دستيجك *dastījak*, A little vessel.

A دستينج *dastīnaj*, A lightning-cloud.

P دستينه *dastīna*, (A دستينج *dastīnaj*) Any female ornament for the wrists, of gems, gold, or silver. Gloves. A handle, a haft. The neck of a guitar. Any thing written at the bottom of a letter (as signature, date, or postscript). An autograph. A royal diploma or charter, an edict or decree of a judge.

P دسخط *das-khat*, (for دست خط *dast-khat*) A signature. دسخط خاص *das-khati khās*, A sign manual, a royal signature.

A دسر *dasr*, (v. n. of دسر) Driving, thrusting. Piercing with a spear. Copulating. Thrusting in the fibres of a palm-tree as oakum. Caulking a ship, or fastening it with nails. *Dusr*, (pl. of دسراء *dasrāꜥ*) Ships. *Dusr* or *dusur*, (pl. of دسار *disār*) Fibres of the palm-tree used in caulking ships.

A دسراء *dasrāꜥ*, (pl. دسر *dusr*) A ship (so called because the prow pushes back the water).

A دسس *dusus*, Outrageous armpit-stenches. Hypocritical intruders.

A دسع *dasꜥ*, (v. n. of دسع) Giving, presenting. Throwing up (as beasts when chewing the cud), vomiting, expelling. Filling. Stopping up a hole at once. Pushing, thrusting, warding off. The sinking of the veins in the flesh.

A دسفان *disfān*, (pl. دسافين *dasāfīn*) A pimp. A spy. *Dusfān*, Leading, conduct: panderism. (pl. دسافي *dusāfāꜥ*) A go-between, a pimp.

A دسفة *dusfat*, Leading, conduct, convoy, guidance. Panderism.

A دسق *dasaḳ*, Fulness of a pond, even to overflowing. The clearness of water in a reservoir.

A دسكرة *daskarat*, (pl. دساكرة *dasākirat*) A town or castle on the summit of a mountain, whether inhabited or deserted. A place of Christian worship. The cell of a hermit on a hill. A village. Houses of foreigners in Arabia (the natives not being permitted to keep them) in which they sell wine, and provide various amusements for their guests. A palace or superb building surrounded by other houses. Plain, level ground.

P دسكره *daskara*, A town. A castle on a hill. A litter for transporting the sick. Name of a town in Persian Irāk.

A دسم *dasm*, (v. n. of دسم) Corking, closing (a bottle, the ear, or a wound). Shutting (a door). Copulating. Anointing (a camel) with pitch. Watering (the ground) gently (rain). Being effaced, obliterated (vestiges). The verge of any business. *Dusm*, Dirty (garments). *Dasam*, (v. n. of دسم) Being fat (meat). Being dirty, reechy. Being of an ash-colour. Fat, grease. Nastiness, filth. *Dasim*, Fat, greasy.

A دسماء *dasmā*, (fem.) Ash-coloured, blackish.

A دسمة *dusmat*, (v. n. of دسم) Being of an ash-colour. A mean, ignoble man. Ash-colour. Any thing used for plugging a torn leathern-bottle. *Dasamat*, A single small ant. An atom.

P دسمر *dasmar*, A kind of fattening pulse.

P دسمو *dasmū*, A French bean.

P دسمه *dasma*, A sort of pulse.

A دسوة *daswat*, The being impure. A hiding of one's self, a lurking.

P دسورده *daswarda*, A rolling-pin.

P دسوك *dusūk* or *dasūk*, A small stick, wand.

A دسوم *dusūm*, (v. n. of دسم) Being obliterated (vestiges). (pl. of دسم *dasm*) Bits of fat or grease.

A دسومة *dusūmat*, Dirtiness, filthiness.

P دسه *dasa*, Thread which remains on the loom after the weaver has cut off what has been woven.

A دسي *dasy*, (v. n. of دسي) Being impure, unholy. *Dasa'*, (v. n. of دسي) Being small or few.

A دسيس *dasīs*, The concealing of a stratagem. Treachery. A spy, secret intelligencer. Roasted, toasted. An incurable stench of the arm-pits.

A دسّيسي *dissīsa'*, Concealment.

A دسيع *dasīʿ*, The place where the neck joins the shoulder.

A دسيعة *dasīʿat*, (v. n. of دسع) Driving, expelling, pushing, thrusting. Giving. Chewing the cud. Nature, disposition. A donative. A platter, trencher, dish. A table magnificently covered. Strength, power. A city on a hill. ضخم الدسيعة *zakhmu'd dasīʿat*, Liberal.

A دسيم *dasīm*, Much remembered.

P دسين *dasīn*, (and دسينه) A jar, large vessel.

P دش *dash*, Ostentation. A handsome figure. Resembling. *Dush*, Evil, bad, ugly (in such words as دشمن *dushman*, دشنام *dushnām*, &c.)

A دشش *dashsh*, A journey, march. A preparing of the wheaten broth called دشيشة *dashīshat*.

P دشبل *dushbil*, (or دشپيل *dushpīl*) A kernel growing in the flesh, scrofula.

P دشت *dasht*, A desert, plain without water. A burial-ground. A chess-board. Dry musk. Name of a tract of country in Khurāsān. Name of a town in Azarbayjān. دشت قبچاق *dashti kipchāk*, The desert of Kipchāk in Tartary. دشت استبرق *dashti istabrak*, A verdant desert. *Dusht*, Foul, shameful, ugly, bad.

P دشتان *dashtān*, A menstruous woman.

P دشتبان *dashtubān*, A watch set over sown fields to drive away wild beasts.

P دشخوار *dusht-khwār*, Difficult, arduous.

P دشت سواران *dasht-suwārān*, Those who lead a roving life in the desert. The open country of Arabia. A cemetery.

P دشت سوران *dasht-suwarān*, The inhabitants of the desert.

P دشتنام *dusht-nām*, Abuse, reproach.

P دشتي *dashtī*, Wild. *Dushtī*, A leech.

P دشتياد *dusht-yād*, Slander, secret whispering.

P دشتيبان *dashtībān*, A watch set over sown fields. Name of several places in Persia; also of a place in Turkistān.

P دشخوار *dushkhwār*, Dangerous, difficult. Heavy, severe. Indisposed. Sorrow. Heavily.

P دشخوار پسند *dushkhwār-pasand*, Approving difficulties.

P دشخوارگر *dushkhwārgar*, Mountainous, hilly.

P دشخواري *dushkhwārī*, Difficulty, trouble. Danger. دشخواري نمودن *dushkhwārī namūdan*, To give pain.

P دشخيم *dushkhīm*, Abuse, reproach, reviling.

P دشسته *dishista*, Perceived, felt.

P دشك *dashk*, *dishk*, or *dushk*, A silken thread drawn through a needle.

P دشكي *dushkī*, Thread wound about a spindle.

P دشم *disham*, An awl. *Dishum*, Afternoon, evening-prayer.

P دشمان *dushmān*, (for دشمن) An enemy.

A دشمة *dushmat*, Worthless, good for nothing.

P دشمر *dashmar*, A kind of pulse for cattle.

P دشمن *dushman*, An enemy, foe, adversary. دشمن جاني *dushmani jānī*, A mortal enemy. دشمن ذاتي *dushmani zātī*, A natural foe. دشمن قوي *dushmani kawī*, A powerful foe. دشمن داشتن *dushman dāshtan*, To hate, to hold as an enemy.

P دشمناگي *dushmanāgī*, Enmity.

P دشمنايگي *dushmanāyagī*, Enmity.

P دشمن دار *dushman-dār*, A hater.

P دشمن داشته *dushman-dāshta*, Hated.

P دشمن داشته شده *dushman-dāshta-shuda*, Hated, held in aversion.

P دشمن شكني *dushman-shikanī*, Slaughter of foes, discomfiture of an enemy.

P دشمن كام *dushman-kām*, Calamity (foe's wish).

P دشمنگير *dushman-gīr*, Taking an enemy.

P دشمني *dushmanī*, Enmity, hatred, detestation. دشمني كردن *dushmanī kardan*, To hate.

P دشمه *dashma*, Name of a wrestler of Irān.

P دشمير *dashmīr*, Contrary. The elements.

P دشن *dashn*, Handsel.

A دشن *dashn*, The act of giving, presenting.

P دشناد *dushnād*, Many, much.

P دشنام *dush-nām*, Ill name, abuse, reproach, taunt, invective. دشنام دادن *dush-nām dādan*, To give a bad name, vilify. دشنام داده شده *dushnām-dāda shuda*, Reproached, reviled, cursed.

P دشنام دهنده *dushnām-dihinda*, Fore-finger.

P دشنام يافته *dushnām-yāfta*, Abused, reviled.

A دشناويّ *dashnāwiy*, Native of Dashna.

P دشنگ *dashang*, The husk of a date. A branch whereon dates are growing. Name of a city in Khatāy. A dam of wicker-work. A silken thread.

P دشنگي *dashangī*, Time, fortune: the world.

P دشنه *dashna*, A dagger, poniard, chiefly worn by the men of Lār. A sword, cimeter. A narrow knife-blade. دشنهٔ صبح *dashnaʾi subh*, A morning ray.

P دشنه كارد *dashna-kārd*, A dagger, poniard.

A دشنيٰ *dashna'*, A place in Upper Egypt.

A دشو *dashw*, (v. n. of دشا for دشو) Plunging into the thick of the fight.

P دشوار *dushwār*, Difficult, hard, troublesome, arduous. A hilly, mountainous country. ديار دشوار گذار *diyāri dushwār-guzār*, A difficult pass. قلعهٔ دشوارگير *kalʿaʾi dushwār-gīr*, An impregnable fortress.

P دشوار پسند *dushwār-pasand*, Fond of knots.

P دشوار خو *dushwār-khu*, Bad-tempered.

P دشوارزاي *dushwār-zāy*, Producing with pain.

P دشوارگر *dushwārgar*, Hilly: a mountain.

P دشواري *dushwārī*, Difficulty. دشواريهاي راه *dushwārīhāʾi rāh*, Difficulties of the road.

A دشوة *dashwat*, An entering boldly into a fight.

A دشيشة *dashīshat*, Wheaten broth.

P دشيشگه *dashīsh-gah*, (or دشيشك) Night.

A دصّ *dass*, (v. n. of دصّ) Waiting on, serving.

A دصدصة *dasdasat*, The shaking (of a sieve).

A دصق *dask*, (v. n. of دصق) Breaking (glass or any thing brittle).

A دضّ *dazz*, (v. n. of دضّ) Serving efficiently and properly.

A دظّ *dazz*, Ejectment, expulsion. A tearing. Doubt, suspicion.

A دع *daʿ*, Meddle not, let alone. Take care, mind you do not slip.

A دعّ *daʿʿ*, A driving with vehemence.

A دعاء *duʿā*, (v. n. of دعا for دعو) Calling, calling to. Naming. Invoking, praying (God). Imploring a blessing. Imprecating. Driving, urging forward. Inflicting any thing disagreeable. Leaving milk in the udder. Invitation. (pl. ادعية *adʿiyat*) Invocation, prayer. Salutation, congratulation, benediction. Imprecation. الدعا *ad' duʿā*, (or والدعا *wa'd duʿā*) Adieu. P بد دعا *bad-duʿā*, A curse. A جماعت دعا *jamāʿat-duʿā*, Public prayer.

خير دعا *khayr-duʻā*, A benediction. سورة الدعاء *sūratu'd duʻāʼ*, The first chapter of the Kur'ān, namely, the chapter of prayer. دعاي خير *duʻāʼi khayr*, A benediction. دعاي دولت *duʻāʼi dawlat*, Praying for one's prosperity, a benediction. P دعاي عافيت كردن *duʻāʼi ʻāfiyat kardan*, To wish health, salute, bless, congratulate. دعا گفتن *duʻā guftan*, To bid adieu.

A دعّاءة *daʻʻāʼat*, The forefinger, index.

A دعاب *diʻāb*, The act of playing with.

A دعّاب *daʻʻāb*, A jester.

A دعابة *duʻābat*, (v. n. of دعب) Playing. Playfulness, jest. Folly, insanity. A black-winged ant.

A دعّابة *daʻʻābat*, A jester.

A دعاة *duʻāt*, (pl. of داعي) Those who pray.

A دعات *duʻāt*, Invocations, prayers.

A دعاث *diʻās*, (pl. of دعث *diʻs*) Hatreds.

A دعادع *daʻādiʻ*, A watery herb (with which cattle are fed in summer-time).

A دعّار *duʻʻār*, (pl. of داعر) Whoremongers.

A دعارة *daʻārat* or *diʻārat*, Wickedness, dishonesty. Whoredom. دعارة الحبّ *daʻāratu'l hubb*, Unchaste love.

A دعارّة *daʻārrat*, Badness of disposition.

A دعاع *daʻāʻ*, Young domestics. *Duʻāʻ*, Palm-trees planted separately. A black two-winged ant.

A دعّاع *daʻʻāʻ*, A gatherer of the seeds of دعاعة *duʻāʻat*, with which they make bread.

A دعاعة *duʻāʻat*, A single black two-winged ant. A kind of black seed whereof they make bread.

P دعاگوي *duʻā-gūy* or *goy*, A preacher. Wishing well, benevolent. A supplicant. A public dancing girl.

P دعا گوئي *duʻā-goʼī* or *gūʼī*, Invocation of a blessing.

A دعام *diʻām*, (pl. دعائم *daʻāʼim*) A pillar, column. A vine-prop. The support of a family.

A دعامة *daʻāmat*, A condition, agreement, stipulation. *Diʻāmat*, (pl. دعائم *daʻāʼim*) A pillar, prop. The support or chief of a family. Two cheek-pieces of a pulley which support the axle. A pronoun in the nominative case interposed between the subject of a proposition and the predicate: as, زيد هو المنطلق *zayd huwa'l muntalik*, Zayd, he is the one with an open countenance. 1 Kings xviii. 39.

A دعاميص *daʻāmīs* (pl. of دعموص *duʻmūs*) Tadpoles. Royal favourites, whence infants are called دعاميص الجنّة *daʻāmīsu'l jannat*, The favourites of heaven.

A دعانة *daʻānat*, Carelessness, recklessness about what one says or does.

A دعاوة *daʻāwat* or *diʻāwat*, Pretension, especially a false claim to relationship.

A دعاوي *daʻāwī*, (pl. of دعوي *daʻwaʼ*) Claims, causes, pretensions. Changes, vicissitudes.

A دعائم *daʻāʼim*, (pl. of دعمة *diʻmat*, دعام *diʻām*, and دعامة *diʻāmat*) Columns (of houses), props (of vines). اقامت دعائم شرع شريف *ikāmati daʻāʼimi sharʻi sharīf*, The establishment of the articles of law and justice.

A دعب *daʻb*, (v. n. of دعب) Driving, thrusting. Copulating. Playing, jesting. *Daʻib*, A jester.

A دعبب *duʻbub*, A jest. Fruit of nightshade. A singer. A youth fat and soft-skinned. A jester.

A دعبع *daʻbaʻ*, Sounds uttered by a sucking child.

A دعبل *diʻbil*, A robust camel. Frog's spawn. A thief.

A دعبلة *daʻbalat*, A strong she-camel. A thief.

A دعبوب *duʻbūb*, A black-winged ant. A species of black grain. A kind of black esculent root. A dark night. An open, beaten track. A contemptible dwarf. A fool, butt for ridicule, A castrato, catamite. Brisk. A long-bodied horse.

A دعبوث *duʻbūs*, Suspected of something bad. Dishonest. One who allows himself to be abused contrary to nature.

A دعبوس *duʻbūs*, Mad, insane, foolish.

A دعبيّة *duʻbiyat*, A strong wind.

A دعة *daʻat*, Quiet, tranquillity. Easy circumstances. صاحب الدعة *sāhibu'd daʻat*, Meek. اهل الدعة *ahlu'd daʻat*, The meek.

A دعت *daʻt*, A driving, a thrusting.

A دعث *daʻs*, (v. n. of دعث) Beating small (the ground) with hands and feet. Being seized with a shivering (at the access of a fever). The commencement of a disease. *Diʻs*, Remains of water. (pl. ادعاث *adʻās*, and دعاث *diʻās*) Hatred, rancour, malevolence.

A دعثر *daʻsar*, Foolish. *Diʻasr*, Strong (camel) breaking down and demolishing every thing.

A دعثرة *daʻsarat*, A breaking, demolishing.

A دعثور *duʻsūr*, A pond or reservoir ill-constructed, full of chinks. Abundance of good things.

A دعج *daʻaj*, (v. n. of دعج) Being large and very black (eye).

A دعجاء *daʻjāʼ*, Fury, madness. Black-eyed (woman). The twenty-eighth day of the moon.

A دعجة *duʻjat*, Largeness and blackness (of eye).

A دعد *daʻd*, A name for a chameleon. (pl. دعود *duʻūd*, دعدات, or ادعد *adʻud*) Name of a woman.

A دعداع *daʻdāʻ*, A dwarf. Slow, uneven steps.

A دعدع *daʻdaʻ*, Ground bare of herbage.

A دعدع *duʻduʻ*, A word for calling to sheep.

A دعدعة *daʻdaʻat*, (v. n. of دعدع Q) Going slow, or shamblingly. Filling (a dish). Shaking (a measure) to make (it) hold more. Calling to, or checking cattle. Calling to any one about to fall, bidding him take care.

A دعر *duʻr*, A wood-worm. مالك بن دعر *māliku'bnu duʻrin*, Name of the individual who drew Joseph out of the pit. *Daʻar*, (v. n. of دعر) Being depraved. Being wicked, impure, whoring. Smoking, though not blazing (wood). Emitting no fire (a flint). *Daʻir*, Worm-eaten wood, which extinguishes before it is well lighted. *Daʻir*, *daʻar*, or *duʻar*, Bad (wood), smoking not flaming.

A دعربة *daʻrabat*, A pledge for plighted faith. Hardness, difficulty. A mulct for any injury (as manslaughter).

A دعرة *duʻrat*, A woodlouse, a worm which destroys wood. *Daʻarat*, Wickedness, whoredom.

A دعرم *diʻrim*, Worthless, short, mean. A camel drinking last.

A دعرمة *daʻramat*, (v. n. of دعرم Q) Walking with short, quick steps.

A دعرور *duʻrūr*, Vile, abject, worthless.

A دعز *daʻz*, A pushing, thrusting, driving away. Coition.

A دعس *daʻs*, (v. n. of دعس) Filling full (any vessel) by cramming. Treading down, trampling under foot. Piercing (with a spear). Putting the hand between the upper and under skin in flaying a sheep. Copulating. (A road) distinguished by many marks. A mark, sign, impression. *Diʻs*, Cotton. A circular sand-hill.

A دعسبة *daʻsabat*, A kind of dancing pace.

A دعسجة *daʻsajat*, A going fast.

A دعسرة *daʻsarat*, Lightness, swiftness.

A دعسقة *daʻsakat*, (v. n. of دعسق Q) Rushing upon. Walking hard. Advancing. Retreating. Driving away altogether. (Camels) breaking down (a cistern). Having a straight face (a camel).

A دعسقة *duʻsukhat*, Long (night).

A دعسوقة *daʻsūhat*, A kind of beetle.

A دعشوقة *duʻshūkat*, A kind of beetle. A nickname for a woman or girl of short stature.

A دعص *daʻs*, (v. n. of دعص) Killing. Giving a kick with the foot. *Diʻs* and دعصة *diʻsat*, (pl. دعص *diʻas* and ادعاص *adʻās*) A circular heap or hillock of sand. *Diʻas*, (pl. of دعصة *diʻsat*) Round heaps of sand.

A دعصاء *daʻsāʼ*, Level, smooth ground. Land exposed to the sun, and burnt up.

A دعصة *diʻsat*, (pl. دعص *diʻas*) A round heap of sand. *Diʻasat*, (pl. of دعص *diʻs*) Round heaps of sand.

A دعظ *daʻz*, A putting in of the whole.

A دعظاية *diʻzāyat*, Corpulent and short, or long.

A دعفس *diʻfis*, Camels which wait until the others have drunk, to drink what they have left.

A دعفسة *diʻfisat*, Slim, slender (woman).

A دعفقة *daʻfakat*, Folly, madness.

A دعق *daʻk*, (v. n. of دعق) Beating (a path). Trampling, treading down a cistern (camels). Urging to the gallop. Sending forth a plundering party. Putting to flight. Terrifying. Beaten (track).

A دعقة *daʻkat*, A herd of camels. One fall or plump of rain.

A دعك *daʻk*, (v. n. of دعك) Rubbing, softening, or smoothing (a garment) by wear. Appeasing (an enemy). Rubbing (leather). Rolling upon the ground, permitting to tumble about. *Daȥah,* (v. n. of دعك) Being silly and foolish. Madness, folly. *Daȥik,* Litigious, quarrelsome. Squabbling. *Duȥak,* Weak. A beetle. Name of a bird.

A دعكانة *diȥkānat,* Corpulent, fleshy.

A دعكاية *diȥkāyat,* Fleshy and tall (man or woman). Short, dwarfish.

A دعكة *duȥkat,* The best and most beaten part of the road. A herd or troop of camels.

A دعكسة *daȥkasat,* (v. n. of دعكس Q) Dancing with joined hands in the manner of the Magi.

A دعكلة *daȥkalat,* (v. n. of دعكل Q) Beating a path with the feet.

A دعكن *daȥkan,* Soft. Good-tempered. A tractable beast of burden.

A دعكنة *daȥkanat* or *diȥkanat,* A plump, firm she-camel.

A دعكنة *diȥkannat,* Thick, coarse (vulva).

A دعل *daȥal,* Deception, fraud.

A دعلج *daȥlaj,* Full sacks. Different kinds of cloths, or garments. Plants twisting round one another. A saunterer about without necessity and doing nothing. Tracks of people going to and fro. A glutton. A handsome, delicately-formed youth. Darkness. A wolf. An ass. A camel that does not move onwards when driven. Name of a horse. Name of a tribe.

A دعلجة *daȥlajat,* (v. n. of دعلج Q) Moving backwards and forwards. Collecting (water) into a reservoir. Receiving much. Turning. Darkness.

A دعلقة *daȥlakat,* (v. n. of دعلق Q) Being the worst of any thing. Going far. Following, prosecuting, pursuing. Vileness, meanness.

A دعم *daȥm,* (v. n. of دعم) Supporting any thing falling. Straightening a crooked column. Copulating. A troop. *Daȥam,* Firmness, stamina. لا دعم به *lā daȥama bihi,* He is enervated. *Diȥam,* (pl. of دعمة *diȥmat*) Columns. Props (of vines).

A دعمة *diȥmat,* A pillar, column: vine-prop.

A دعمصة *daȥmasat,* (v. n. of دعمص Q) Abounding in tadpoles (water).

A دعمظة *daȥmazat,* (v. n. of دعمظ Q) Putting in (the whole of any thing).

A دعموص *duȥmūs,* (pl. دعاميص *daȥāmīs*) A black animalcule bred in dry ponds, a tadpole. Name of a whoremonger who was metamorphosed into a tadpole. A royal favourite. Acute, penetrating.

A دعموظ *duȥmūz,* Bad-tempered, ill-natured.

A دعميّ *duȥmiy,* A carpenter. The middle or best of a road. Any thing solidly supported. White on the brisket (a horse).

A دعن *daȥn,* Branches of the palm-tree slightly joined together, on which they spread the dates. *Daȥin,* Naturally depraved. Badly fed.

A دعنّ *diȥann,* A careless, impudent, saucy fellow.

A دعنّة *diȥannat,* (pl. of دعنّ) Careless fellows.

A دعنكر *daȥankar,* (or دعنكران *daȥankarān*) One who acts basely or oppressively to another.

A دعوا *daȥwa',* (for دعوى *daȥwa'*) Law-suit.

A دعوة *daȥwat,* (v. n. of دعا for دعو) Inviting to a feast. Swearing. A prayer. Invitation, call. Petition, request, entreaty. A citing before a judge. An assembly, a convivial meeting. Assumption. Priority of claim to be heard. A proselyting to the Muhammadan faith. P دعوت نمودن *daȥwat namūdan,* To invite, to call. A *Daȥwat* or *diȥwat,* Pretension, claim to relationship (true or false). *Daȥwat* or *duȥwat,* An invitation to a feast.

A دعود *duȥūd,* (pl. of دعد) Names of women.

A دعوس *daȥūs,* Very bold, warlike.

A دعوى *daȥwa',* (v. n. of دعا for دعو) Invoking, praying (God). Pretension, claim, demand. The subject of ambition, the thing desired or contended for. A law-suit. Excuse. Events, changes, or vicissitudes of fortune. P دعواي برابري كردن *daȥwā-i bar-ā-bari kardan,* To pretend or claim equality.

A دعويّ *duȥwiy,* Any one. ما دعويّ بالدار *mā duȥwiyun bi'd dār,* There is nobody at home (or who can be made to answer).

P دعوي دار *daȥwa'-dār,* A plaintiff, claimant.

P دعوىگي *daȥwagi,* Supplication.

A دعيّ *daȥiy,* (pl. ادعياء *adȥiyā*) A spurious child, bastard. An adopted son. One about whose pedigree suspicion is entertained.

A دعيمص *duȥaymis,* Intelligent, clever. دعيمص الرمل *duȥaymisu'r raml,* Name of a certain clever black slave.

P دغ *dagh,* (for داغ *dāgh*) Mark, stigma. Bald. One whose beard, mustachios, eye-brows, and eye-lashes have been cut off. Ground where nothing grows. بيابان دغ *biyābāni dagh,* A barren desert.

P دغا *daghā,* Imposture, deceit, treachery. Seduction, adulation. Vicious. False, insincere. A bastard. Base money. Sediment, dregs. Rubbish, sticks and straws. دغا نمودن *daghā namūdan,* To deceive, circumvent.

P دغا باز *daghā-bāz,* An impostor, cheat, traitor. Fraudulent.

P دغا بازي *daghā-bāzī,* Fraud.

P دغا پيشه *daghā-pesha,* Sly, artful, cunning.

A دغال *dighāl,* (pl. of دغل *daghal*) Vices, depravities, taints.

A دغام *dughām,* A disease in the throat.

A دغامر *daghāmir,* Sharp, clever. Bold, brave.

A دغاول *daghāwil,* Misfortunes.

A دغبجة *daghbajat,* (v. n. of دغبج Q) Driving to water every day. Giving one's self up to pleasure.

A دغت *daght,* (v. n. of دغت) Strangling.

A دغثر *daghsar,* Foolish; a fool.

P دغد *dughd,* A bride.

P دغدار *dagh-dār,* Branded. Blemished. A slave. *Dughdār,* A falcon.

A دغدغة *daghdaghat,* (v. n. of دغدغ Q) Tickling under the arm-pit or sole of the foot. Stinging (with severe words). Titillation.

P دغدغك *daghdaghak,* Titillation.

P دغدغه *daghdagha,* Fear, confusion of mind. An inclination for any thing. *Dighdigha,* Tickling under the arm-pits.

P دغدو *dughdū,* Name of a bird weighing about fifty pounds, the dodo (now extinct). *Dughdū,* (or دغدويه *dughdūya*) Name of Zardusht's mother.

A دغر *daghr,* (v. n. of دغر) Invading or attacking (an enemy). Entering (a house) forcibly or uninvited. Thrusting away. Mixing. Strangling, throttling. Raising the uvula of a new-born infant. Suckling insufficiently (a child), so that it receives little nourishment from it. *Daghar,* (v. n. of دغر) Rushing in headlong without pause or hesitation. Rubbing the black stone at Mecca, either with the lip or hand. A bad disposition.

A دغرة *daghrat,* A seizing, carrying off forcibly.

A دغرور *dughrūr,* Shameful, indecent.

A دغرى *daghra',* Giddy boldness. Repulse. *Daghra', daghara',* دغراء *daghrā,* or دغرا *daghran,* (Rushing on an enemy) regardless of military order.

P دغسر *dagh-sar,* Bald-headed.

A دغش *daghsh,* (v. n. of دغش) Assailing, attacking. Entering into (the darkness of the night). *Daghash,* Darkness.

A دغص *daghas,* (v. n. of دغص) Being full (of meat or of rage). Over-eating till he cannot chew the cud (a camel).

A دغصان *daghsān,* Full of rage, furious.

A دغف *daghf,* A taking much and often.

A دغفاء *daghfā,* A word used in practising enchantment and sorcery.

A دغفر *daghfar,* A large lion.

A دغفصة *daghfasat,* Fatness, corpulency.

A دغفق *daghfak,* Fruitful (year): easy (life).

A دغفقة *daghfakat,* (v. n. of دغفق Q) Pouring forth (water) copiously. Being heavy at first (rain).

A دغفل *daghfal,* A young elephant or wolf. Fruitful (year). Comfortable (life). Thick (plumage). Name of a man.

A دغل *daghl,* (v. n. of دغل) Doubting, suspecting. *Daghal,* (pl. ادغال *adghāl* and دغال *dighāl*) Depravation, corruption, damage, spoil. A forest, thicket, wood, grove. Luxuriant, entangled herbage. A lurking-place, or dreaded ambush. *Daghil,* Retired (place) where snares are laid.

P دغل *daghal,* Blemish, defect. Fraud, deceit, villainy. Base coin. Thorns for heating a bath. Lees, dregs. An impostor, villain. A cut-purse. A blockhead. Lazy, indolent. False, insincere. دغل خاكدان *daghali khākdān,* The world. The human body. خانه دغل *khāna-daghal,* One who disgraces his house.

P دغل دري *daghal-dari,* A slanderer: hypocrite.

P دغل دوست *daghal-dost,* A pretended friend.

P دغل زن *daghal-zan,* A fornicator, adulterer.

A coiner or adulterer of money. A perfidious villain.

A دغلي *daghlī*, Treacherous.

P دغلي *daghalī*, Fraud. Treachery, villainy. Bastardy. دغلي نمودن *daghalī namūdan*, To cozen.

A دغم *daghm*, (v. n. of دغم) Breaking the inner part, also laying flat the nose. Covering (a vessel). Enfeebling, benumbing (heat or cold). *Dughm*, White. *Dagham*, (or دغمة *dughmat*) Blackness in the face and lip of cattle, the body whitish.

A دغماء *daghmā‚*, (fem. of ادغم *adgham*) (A sheep) having the two ears and under the chin black. Black about the muzzle (mare).

A دغمان *dughmān*, also *daghmān*, Black with bigness. Black men.

A دغمرة *daghmarat*, Confusion, mixture. Stubborn depravity, vice, blemish.

A دغمريّ *daghmariy* or *dughmuriy*, Mixed. Bad (temper).

A دغمشة *daghmashat*, A travelling fast.

A دغمور *dughmūr*, Depraved, vile, ignoble.

A دغناس *daghnās*, A small bird with a black ring round its neck, and red stripes along its back.

A دغنّة *dughunnat*, Darkness, cloudiness. Clouds piled up. Dark clouds without rain.

A دغنجة *daghnajat*, Corpulency in woman. A mode of walking with short steps. A going backwards and forwards. The flocking of camels to water.

A دغوة *daghwat*, A depraved and inconstant disposition.

A دغور *dughūr*, (v. n. of دغر) Entering.

A دغوشة *daghwashat*, A mixing tumultuously.

P دغول *daghūl*, A cheat, impostor. A bastard.

A دغون *dughūn*, (v. n. of دغن) Being cloudy.

P دغوي *dagh* or *daghuway*, Name of a forest.

A دغية *daghyat*, A depraved disposition.

A دغيلة *daghīlat*, Depravation, damage, spoil. A forest, thicket.

P دف *daf*, A single drum (*i.e.* with only one skin), a cymbal tambour de basque.—(It is of Arabian original, and introduced by the Saracens into Spain). دف زدن *daf zadan*, To beat the tambour, *i.e.* to want, ask, beg.

A دفّ *daff*, (v. n. of دفّ) Marching slowly or stealing upon (an enemy). Flapping the wings. Scattering (by ventilation), winnowing. Eradicating. The side, the surface of a thing. A gentle (camel's) pace. The side of a hill facing one. The creaking noise of a shoe. A drum. Sprightly (horse). *Duff*, (pl. دفوف *dufūf*) A drum.

A دفء *dif‚*, (pl. ادفاء *adfā‚*) Heat, warmth. Disagreeableness. Stupe, warm stuff of wool or camel's hair. Whatever a camel or sheep yields (as young ones, milk, wool, or hair). The warmest corner in an apartment. A present, a gift.

A دفا *daft'*, Crookedness in the back or horns.

A دفأ *dafa‚*, (v. n. of دفئ) Cherishing, warming, putting on a warm garment. Warmth. Fruit gathered. Disagreeableness. A tent.

A دفاء *daf‚ā‚*, (A woman) warmly clad.

A دفاء *difā‚*, Warm clothing.

A دفاءة *dafā‚at*, (v. n. of دفئ) Putting on warm clothing. Being warm (the night). Heat, warmth.

A دفاءة *dafa‚at*, Great warmth.

A دفاتر *dafātir*, (pl. of دفتر *daftar*) Books, registers. Volumes.

A دفادف *dafādif*, (pl. of دفدفة *dafdafat*) Sides of mountains.

A دفار *dafār*, A maid, wench. The world. امّ دفار *ummi dafārin*, Mother of stink, *i.e.* the world. يا دفار *yā dafār*, O stinking! (to sluttish maids).

A دفاع *difāع*, (v. n. 3 of دفع) Spurning, driving away. A proper name for a certain kind of sheep or wild cow.

A دفّاع *daffāع*, One who repels with violence. One who defends his right. One who throws away a bone out of a dish that its place may be supplied by meat. *Duffāع*, A great current of water, a billow, surge, wave.

A دفاف *difāf*, (v. n. 3 of دفّ) Despatching (a wounded man).

A دفّاف *daffāf*, Drummers, players on the دفّ.

A دفاق *difāk*, Fast-going (camel). Fleet (mare). *Dufāk*, Mighty torrent, filling its bed. Fleet (camel).

A دفآن *daf‚ān*, Clad in warm clothing.

A دفان *difān*, A concealed well or pit. (pl. دفن *dufun*) Partly filled (well).

A دفائي *daf‚a'*, (A woman) living in a tent.

A دفائن *dafā‚in*, (pl. of دفينة) Concealed, kept close (women). Things buried or hidden. Treasures.

A دفئيّ *dafa‚iy*, Rain at the end of spring.

A دفّة *daffat*, A page. Either side of any thing. دفّتا الكتاب *daffatā'l kitāb*, The two boards of a book, or any thing similar, between which a volume is contained; the two skins (of a drum); the two sides or flaps (of a saddle).

P A دفتر *daftar*, (pl. دفاتر *dafātir*) A book, record, register, journal. A roll, list, catalogue, inventory, account-book, index. A bundle of papers or written documents tied together in a cloth. دفتر ابواب التحويل *daftari abwābu't tahwīl*, Register of household expenses. دفتر ابواب المال *daftari abwābu'l māl*, Register of the public revenues. دفتر اعمال *daftari aعmāl*, Book of life. P دفتر كردن *daftar kardan*, To enrol, put down in a list, make an inventory. دفترا گاو خورد *daftarrā gāw khwurd*, The accounts are settled. دفتر موقوفات *daftari mawkūfāt*, Chamber of accounts.

P دفتر بند *daftar-band*, A filer of records. An office-keeper. A bookbinder.

P دفتر خانه *daftar-khāna*, A public office where they keep the archives, with a particular register of the royal pensions and donations. The record-office. An office, counting-house.

P دفتردار *daftar-dār*, High treasurer, intendant of the finances, chancellor of the exchequer. Keeper of records.

P دفتر نويس *daftar-navīs*, A clerk, registrar.

P دفتري *daftarī*, An office-keeper.

P دفته *dafta*, (or دفتين) A weaver's comb.

P دفتي *daftī*, (or دفتين *daftīn*) Pasteboard.

A دفدفة *dafdafat*, (v. n. of دفدف Q) Making haste. Moving her wings and feet in flying (a pigeon). (pl. دفادف *dafādif*) A side of sloping ground.

A دفر *dafr*, (v. n. of دفر) Stinking. Smiting the breast. Stink. امّ دفر *ummu dafrin*, The world. Calamity. دفرا له *dafran lahu*, Fye upon him! *Dafar*, The breeding of worms in meat from putrefaction. Stink. Contemptibleness. *Dafir*, Stinking.

A دفراء *dafrā‚*, Stinking (woman). Rusty-armed (squadron).

A دفرة *dafirat*, Stinking, sluttish (maid).

P دفزك *dafzak*, Thick, gross, fat.

P دف ساز *daf-sāz*, A drummer.

A دفص *dafs*, Smoothness, bareness. Glitter.

A دفض *dafz*, (v. n. of دفض) Breaking.

A دفطسة *daftasat*, Loss of one's cattle.

A دفع *dafع*, (v. n. of دفع) Pushing, thrusting, driving away, beating off, parrying, repelling, averting, warding off. Giving, delivering. Repulse. P دفع انداختن *dafع andākhtan*, To drive off, postpone. دفع غم كردن *dafعi gham kardan*, To drive off care. A دفع عطش *dafعi عatash*, Slaking thirst. دفع الوقت *dafعu'l wakt*, Postponing, deferring, putting off. *Dufaع*, (pl. of دفعة *dufعat*) Floods.

A دفعات *dafaعāt*, (pl. of دفعة) Times, instants.

A دفعة *dafعat*, A race, a beat. One time, once. A moment, instant. دفعة *dafعatan*, Suddenly. دفعة واحدة *dafعatan wāhidatan*, All at once, at one stroke; for this time. دفعه بدفعه *dafعa ba dafعa*, From time to time, repeatedly. *Dufعat*, (pl. دفع *dufaع*) A rush or gush of water. A plump of rain. Water poured out of a pail at once.

P دفع دار *dafaع-dār*, A subaltern officer of cavalry. A head peon.

A دفعي *dafعe*, Then, immediately. Again.

A دفغ *dafgh*, Straw or chaff of millet.

A دفق *dafk*, (v. n. of دفق) Pouring out (water). Letting out the vital spirit. Killing. Shedding at once (the contents of a water-pot). Being poured out, flowing. *Dafak*, (v. n. of دفق) Projecting, and being near falling out (teeth). Swift (horse).

A دفق *difakh* or *difikh*, Swift (horse).

A دفقة *dufkatan*, At once.

A دفقّة *difakkat*, Swift (mare).

A دفقى *difakka'*, Swiftness. Swift and high-blooded (mare). Swift, excellent (she-camel) but having no colts. *Difikka'*, Swift (camel). Generous (mare). A walking first on one side, and then on the other. Swiftness.

P دفك *dafak*, A butt or mark for archers.

A دفل *difl*, Pitch (melted or dry). A certain

poisonous plant called in Persian خرزهره *khar-zahra*.

A دفلي *difla'*, A certain poisonous plant, in Persian called خرزهره *khar-zahra*.

A دفن *dafana*, (fut. يدفن *yadfinu*) He buried.

A دفن *dafn*, (v. n. of دفن) Hiding under ground, interring, burying. Running off. Going where there is no occasion. Obscure, unknown. P دفن نمودن *dafn namūdan*, To bury. A *Difn*, Latent (disease). *Dufun*, (pl. of دفان *difān*) Places filled up. (pl. of دفين *dafīn*) Partly filled (wells).

A دفناء *dufanā˒*, (pl. of دفين) Covered. دفناء الامر *dafinā˒u'l amr*, The middle of any business.

A دفناس *difnās*, Mad. Covetous. A mean man or woman. A negligent shepherd, who sleeps and suffers the camels to graze where they like.

A دفنس *difnis*, A large-sized woman. A foolish, crazy woman. A low, paltry, crazy fellow.

P دفنوك *dafnūk* or *dafanūk*, A saddle-cloth of silk intermixed with gold.

A دفني *dafna'*, (pl. of دفينة) Secluded (women).

A دفني *dafanīy*, A kind of striped garment.

A دفؤ *dafu˒a*, (fut. يدفؤ *yadfu˒u*) He put on warm clothing.

A دفو *dafw*, The killing a wounded man.

A دفواء *dafwā˒*, (fem. of ادفي *adfa'*) Long-horned (goat). Long-necked and handsome (she-camel). Hook-beaked (eagle). A large tree.

A دفوع *dafū˓*, A propeller, driver: an instrument by which any thing may be driven forward: a cannon. *Dufū˓*, (pl. of دفعة *daf˓at*) Times, moments.

A دفوف *dafūf*, (An eagle) which approaches the ground when darting after its falling prey. *Dufūf*, (pl. of دف *duff* or *daff*) Tabours, tabrets.

A دفوفي *dufūfiy*, A maker or seller of drums.

A دفوق *dafūk*, Swift, high-blooded (mare). *Dufūk*, (v. n. of دفق) Being poured out at once.

A دفون *dafūn*, (A woman) keeping company with men. A she-camel accustomed to get amongst the males at drinking-time. (A run-away slave) hiding himself: any one who conceals himself.

A دفئ *dafi˒a*, (fut. يدفأ *yadfa˒u*) He warmed, or cherished. He put on warm clothing.

A دفي *dafy*, The despatching of a wounded man.

A دفئ *dafi˒*, Clad in warm raiment.

A دفيّ *dafīy*, Warm, genial (day, night, place, or garment).

A دفئة *dafi˒at*, A warm country.

A دفيف *dafīf*, (v. n. of دف) Marching slowly or stealing upon (an enemy). Skimming along a little above the ground (a bird). Fluttering (a dove). A gentle camel's pace.

A دفين *dafīn*, (pl. ادفان *adfān* and دفناء *dufanā˒*) Hid, buried under ground. Interred. Latent (disease). Partly-filled (well). A concealed well or pit. Retired, secluded (woman).

A دفينة *dafīnat*, (pl. دفني *dafna'* and دفائن *dafā˒in*) Retired (woman). (pl. دفائن *dafā˒in*) Hidden, buried treasure.

A دفئيّ *dafa˒iy*, Rain at the end of spring. Any young animal brought forth at that season.

A دفيئة *dafi˒at*, A warm country.

A دفئيّة *dafa˒iyat*, Provisions laid up before summer. Any thing produced before summer.

P دق *dak*, A coarse dervish's garment. Begging, mendicity. A bald head. A kind of costly stuff. Contradiction, opposition. دق زدن *dak zadan*, To beg. دق گرفتن *dak giriftan*, To reproach, vilify.

A دقّ *dakk*, (v. n. of دقّ) Bruising, pounding small, braying (in a mortar). Battering (the walls of a city). Shewing, disclosing. P دق باب كردن *dakk bāb kardan*, To knock at the gate. دق و لق كردن *dak u lak kardan*, To make a brawling noise. A *Dikk*, Subtile, minute, slender. Fret. A subtile disease, a hectic fever. دق الحطب *dikku'l hatab*, Small wood, chips. اخذت دقه و جله *akhaztu dikkahu wa jillahu*, I took it little and big.

A دقارير *dakārīr*, (pl. of دقرارة *dikrārat*, q. v.). Lies, slanders.

A دقاريس *dakārīs*, Foxes.

A دقاع *dakā˓* or *dukā˓*, Earth, dust.

A دقاق *dikāk*, Chips, laths. (pl. of دقيق *dakīk*) Minute, fine. *Dukāk*, Laths, chips. Minute, small. A crumb. A particle.

A دقّاق *dakkāk*, A mealman. A fuller.

A دقّاقة *dakkākat*, A pestle for bruising rice.

A دقّاقي *dakkākī*, Fulling. P دقاقي كردن *dakkākī kardan*, To thump, pound. To full.

A دقال *dikāl*, (pl. of دقلة *dakalat* or *dakilat*) Lean, small-boned (sheep).

A دقائق *dakā˒ik*, (pl. of دقيقة *dakīkat*) Subtilties, smaller particulars, minutiæ. Minutes, moments. Meals, flours.

A دقّة *dikkat*, (v. n. of دقّ) Being fine, minute (as dust or flour). Slenderness. Exility. Avarice, meanness. Littleness. A subtile or minute thing. Abstrusity. Difficulty. Punctuality, accuracy. *Dukkat*, (pl. دقق *dukak*) Small dust carried away by the wind. Pounded salt or seasoning. Elegance, comeliness, beauty. An ornament worn by the people of Mecca. Name of a certain madman.

P دقّت پسند *dikkat-pasand*, Liking subtilties.

P دقّ دار *dikk-dār*, Troublesome, teasing.

P دقّ داري *dikk-dārī*, Trouble, vexation.

A دقداق *dakdāk*, Small sand-hills piled up.

A دقدان *dakdān*, A fire-place, a stove for boiling a kettle.

A دقدقة *dakdakat*, The sound of a horse's feet striking the stones. Confused noise of men.

A دقر *dakr*, A garden full of flowers and plants. *Dakar*, (v. n. of دقر) Being filled with food. Being watered and full of flowers (a place). Being luxuriant (herbage). Vomiting from repletion.

A دقرار *dikrār*, Sailors' short trowsers.

A دقرارة *dikrārat*, (pl. دقارير *dakārīr*) Misfortune, evil. A whisperer, calumniator. Contradiction, opposition. Detraction, slander. Sailors' breeches. Quarrel, grudge. Foul language. An evil habit. Short, dwarfish.

A دقران *dukrān*, (pl. of دقرانة) Vine-props.

A دقرة *dakrat*, A garden of flowers and plants.

A دقرور *dukrūr*, Sailors' short trowsers.

A دقرورة *dukrūrat*, (pl. دقارير *dakārīr*) Opposition, contradiction. Trowsers.

A دقري *dakara'*, A garden of flowers and plants.

A دقسة *duksat*, Millet. *Duksat* or *daksat*, An animalcule.

A دقش *daksh*, equivalent to نقش *naksh*, q. v.

A دقشة *dakshat*, Name of a bird, and of an animalcule, both spotted with black and white.

G دقطامانون *daktāmānūn*, Wild mint.

A دقع *daka˓*, (v. n. of دقع) Being contented though indigent, bearing the trials of life without complaining. Fretting under poverty. Cleaving to the ground. Sucking too much milk (a camel's colt).

A دقعاء *dak˓ā˒*, Earth, dust. Ground without herbage. The worst kind of millet.

A دقعم *dik˓im*, Earth, dust.

A دقف *dakf*, (pl. دقوف *dukūf*) A strong unnatural propensity.

A دقفانة *dukfānat*, A catamite, a pathic.

A دقق *dukak*, (pl. of دقّة *dukkat*) Dusts.

A دققة *dakakat*, (pl. of داقّ *dākk*) Those who publish the faults of Musulmāns: cavillers, hypercritics.

A دقل *dakl*, (v. n. of دقل) Hindering, prohibiting. Striking (on the nose, mouth, chin, or neck). Weakness of body. *Dakal*, Colour with which they tinge the face, beard, palms of the hands, or nails. The worst kind of dates. A palm-tree loaded with fruit. The mast of a ship.

A دقلة *dakalat* or *dakilat*, (pl. دقال *dikāl*) Slender-shanked, extenuated (sheep).

A دقم *dakm*, (v. n. of دقم) Breaking the front teeth by a sudden blow. Striking on the breast. Entering into any thing (the wind). Affliction, sadness (from debt or any other cause). *Daham*, (v. n. of دقم) Losing the front teeth. Damage, loss.

A دقمّ *dikamm*, Ample, wide. *Dikimm*, A person having broken teeth.

A دقماق *dukmāk*, A shad-fish.

A دقمة *dakimat*, A sheep or camel whose jaw hangs down from decrepitude.

A دقمس *dikams*, Silk, white silk.

A دقن *dakn*, (v. n. of دقن) Striking on the beard, bearding. Hindering.

A دقوان *dakwān*, (fem. دقوي *dakwa'*) (A camel's colt) drinking too much milk.

A دقوس *dukūs*, (v. n. of دقس) Going throughout (a country). Entering into the ground (a stake). Filling (a well). Charging in an enemy's rear.

A دقوع *dakū˓*, A camel pawing the ground

much with his fore-feet (as if exploring).

A دقوف dukūf, A strong unnatural propensity.

A دقوق dakūk, A kind of collyrium.

A دقوقة dakūkat, Oxen and asses that tread out the corn.

A دقول dukūl, Absence. Entrance.

P دق و لق dak u lak, Dry. Empty. An extensive uncultivated plain. A bald head.

A دقى daka', (v. n. of دقي) Drinking much milk and becoming disordered (a camel's colt). Daki, Disordered in the belly from drinking too much milk (a camel's colt).

A دقيرة dakīrat, A garden of flowers and plants.

A دقيق dakīk, (pl. دقاق dikāk) Subtile, minute, abstruse. Fine. Slim, slender. Trifling, little worth. Flour. سؤال دقيق suāli dakīk, A subtle question.

A دقيقة dakīkat, (fem.) Subtile. A trifle, any thing that almost escapes observation. A sheep. (pl. دقائق dakāik) A minute, a moment of time. The sixtieth part of an astronomical degree.

P دقيقه ياب dakīka-yāb, Discovering subtilties.

A دقيلة dakīlat, Lean, slender (ewe).

A دقيوس dakyūs, The emperor Decius, who is said to have erected a place of worship over the cave of the seven sleepers.

P دك dak, A part, portion. Measure, decree. A beggar. Beggary. Strengthened, firm, fortified, strong. Blow, collision, shock, or bruise. The head. A bald head. A barren mountain. A desert without vegetation. Hard ground. A leafless tree. Foundation of a wall. دك زدن dak zadan, To beg. Dik, A word used in calling a cock.

A دكّ dakk, (v. n. of دكّ) Bruising, braying, grinding. Sweeping. Ruining, demolishing, levelling with the ground. Weakening any one (disease). Being reduced by disease. Smoothing, levelling inequalities in the ground. Filling with earth (a well). (pl. دكاك dikāk) Level sand. A hillock. (pl. دكوك dukūk) A level place. Dukk, (pl. دككة dikakat) A low hill. Strong and bulky. (pl. of ادكّ adakk) Broad-backed (horses).

A دكأ dakaa, (fut. يدكأ yadkau) He repelled.

A دكّاء dakkā, Broad-backed (mare). Plain-backed, bunchless (she-camel). A hillock, a flat heap of earth or clay.

A دكادك dakādik, (and دكاديك dakādīk) (pl. of دكدك dakdak, dikdak, or دكداك dakdāk) Sands heaped up but not high.

A دكاس dukās, Drowsiness, sleepiness.

A دكاع dukāʻ, A disease incident to the chest of camels and horses.

A دكاك dikāk, (pl. of دكّ dakk) Level sands.

A دكاكين dakākīn, (pl. of دكّان dukkān) Shops.

A دكالى dakāla' or dukāla', A name of Satan.

P دكان dukān, A shop. A work-shop. Moss or soft excrescences upon trees. Fuel.

A دكّان dukkān, A bench or counter for sitting upon. (pl. دكاكين dakākīn) A shop.

P دكانچه dukāncha, A little shop. A bench or counter in front of a shop for exposing goods.

P دكاندار dukān-dār, A shop-keeper.

P دكان داري dukān-dārī, Shop-keeping. Assertion, persuasion, flattery.

A دكّاوات dakkāwāt, (pl. of دكّاء dakkā) Plain-backed (she-camels).

A دكة dikat, A being fat and greasy.

A دكّة dakkat, (pl. دكك dikak) A bench, counter for sitting upon. Level sand.

P دكچي dukchī, A ball of thread on the spindle.

A دكداك dakdāk, (pl. دكاديك dakādīk) Sand piled up and level, or sticking close to the ground. Rugged ground.

A دكدك dakdak or dikdak, (pl. دكادك dakādik) Sand heaped up and level, or which sticks close to the ground. Rugged ground.

A دكر dikr, A game among the Ethiopians.

P دك زده dak-zada, One who has shaved off his beard, whiskers, eyebrows, and eyelashes.

A دكس daks, A sprinkling of dust upon the face of any one. Dakas, Accumulation, a heaping up.

A دكك dakak, The evenness of a camel's back. Dikak, (pl. of دكّة dakkat) Benches.

A دككة dikakat, (pl. of دكّ dukk) Low hills.

A دكل dakl, (v. n. of دكل) Collecting, compressing, and kneading with the hand (clay). Trampling.

P دكل dakal, One whose beard is not yet grown, and whose hands and feet are large and coarse.

P دكلان duklān, A cotton-spinning instrument.

A دكلة daklat, A bit of, or remains of the herb صلّيان silliyān. Dakalat, Thin, clay. (People) paying no obedience to the mandates of their prince.

A دكم dakm, (v. n. of دكم) Pushing (on the breast) and thrusting away. Striking any thing hard upon another.

A دكن dakn, (v. n. of دكن) Placing, putting (utensil above utensil, or furniture upon furniture). Dakan, (v. n. of دكن) Inclining to black.

P دكن dakan, Highest point of a mountain.

A دكناء daknā, (fem. of ادكن adkan) Inclining to black. Meat or pudding thickly sprinkled with herbs or spiceries.

A دكنة duknat, A colour verging to black.

P دكنيا dakniyā, (in zand and Pāz.) A palm-tree.

P دكنيان dakaniyān, The people of the Deccan.

P دك و ديم dak u dīm, Head and face.

A دكوك dukūk, (pl. of دكّ) Level places.

P دك و لك dak u lak, Dry. Empty. A desert. A bald head.

A دكه dak-h, A breathing (in one's face).

P دكه duka, (in zand and Pāzand) A prison.

P دكه dakka, A mountain-goat.

P دكهن dak-han, The south. The southern part of the peninsula of Hindūstān, the Deccan.

P دكيا dakyā, (zand and Pāz.) I may become pure.

A دكيشة dakīshat, A crowd, troop, body.

A دكيك dakīk, The whole, the entire (year).

A دكيناء dukaynā, Name of a creeping insect.

P دگر digar, Another. Again, anew. Any more, any longer. Evening-tide. دگر بار digar bār, Another time. دگر باره digar bāra, At another time. دگر روز digar roz, Yesterday. دگرشب digar shab, The other night. دگر شدن digar shudan, To alter, become changed. دگرگون digar gūn, Changed, altered, varied: inverted. دگرگونه digar-gūna, Altered, changed. دگر نماز digar namāz, Evening-prayer.

P دگل dagal, A youth capricious, proud, and perverse. One whose feet are large and coarse. Roguery, deceit. Base coin.

P دگمه dugma, A coat-button.

P دل dil, The heart, mind, soul. Marrow. Pith of a tree. Trunk of a tree. The centre. The eye. An enigma. با جان و دل bā jān u dil, With soul and heart. دل آسمان dili āsmān, Mid-heaven. A star. The earth. دل بدل dil ba dil, Mutual love, interchange of hearts. دل خاك dili khāk, Heart of the earth. The grave. An ox. A fish. Prophets. Holy men of God. دل دادن dil dādan, To inspire with courage, to hearten. دل روز dili roz, Mid-day. The sun. دل شب dili shab, Midnight, دل صيد شدن dil sayd shudan, To be caught in the trammels of love. دل طاق كردن dil tāk kardan, To call off the affections from surrounding objects. دل گرفتن dil giriftan, To be sick, nauseate, have heart-burn. دل گرم كردن dil garm kardan, To be in love. دل نمودن dil namūdan, To shew humanity. دل و جان dil u jān, Heart and soul. Tooth and nail. دل و جاني dil u jānī, Heartily. دل و دماغ dil u damāgh, Ambition, pride, stateliness. صاحب دل sāhib-dil, A generous, brave, noble-hearted man. بي دل bī dil, Without a heart: inhuman, cowardly. Dul, An abscess in the bowels produced by constipation.

A دلّ dalla, (fut. يدلّ yadullu) He directed.

A دلّ dall, (v.n. of دلّ) Guiding, directing. Looking with affected anger (as lovers). Looking and speaking amorously. Affected disdain in a woman. Behaviour, good conduct. Aspect, exterior form. (from P دل dil) The heart.

A دلاء dilā, (v. n. 3 of دلا for دلو) Behaving to another with kindness. ((pl. of دلو dalw) Buckets.

A دلاة dalāt, (pl. دلى dala') A small urn. Dulāt, (pl. of دالي dāli) Bucket-drawers.

A دلاث dilās, Swift (camel).

A دلاثم dulāsim, Going swiftly.

A دلاخ dilākh, (pl. of dulākh) Large-hipped (women). Dulākh, (pl. دلاخ) Large-hipped (woman).

A دلادل dalādil, (pl. of دلدل duldul) Porcupines.

P دل آرا dil-ārā, Beloved: a sweetheart.

P دل آرام dil-ārām, Quieting the mind, heart-approving. A lovely woman, sweetheart. Any thing admired or wished for. كنيز دل آرام kanīzi *dil-ārām*, A charming girl.

P دلازار *dil-āzār*, Heart-tormenting, cruel. رقيب دلازار *rakībi dil-āzār*, A cruel rival.

P دلاسا *dil-āsā*, Mind-assuaging, soothing. Encouragement.

P دلاسائي *dil-āsāʼī*, Consolation, encouragement. دلاسائي كردن *dil-āsāʼī kardan*, To console.

P دلاشوب *dil-āshūb*, A tree whose seed is good for the dropsy.

A دلاص *dilāṣ*, Shining. A bright coat of mail, or coats of mail. (pl. of دلص *dalis*) Those who stumble or slip about much. (pl. of دلصة *dalisat*) Level grounds.

A دلّاص *dallāṣ*, Smooth (ground). Bald and smooth (she-camel).

A دلاصة *dalāṣat*, Brightness (of a coat of mail).

A دلاظ *dilāẓ*, Struggle, conflict, wrestling.

A دلاع *dulāʻ*, The Indian melon.

A دلّاع *dullāʻ*, A kind of sea-shell.

A دلاعة *dulāʻat*, An apple half-ripe, inclining to be sweet.

A دلاعس *dulāʻis*, A she-camel thick and sluggish. Obedient, tractable (camel). A masculine and disobedient woman.

A دلّاك *dallāk*, A waiter at baths. A barber.

A دلاكة *dulākat*, What is milked before the first فيقة. (The فيقة *fīkat* is the milk collected in the udder between two milkings.)

P دلاگاه *dil-āgāh*, Prudent. Vigilant, provident. شاه دلاگاه *shāhi dil-āgāh*, A wise king.

P دلال *dalāl* or *dilāl*, An amorous glance; coquetry, ogling. The eye. The eyebrow.

A دلال *dalāl*, Affected disdain in a woman. A catamite.

A دلّال *dallāl*, An auctioneer. A broker. A road-guide. A crier. A dissembler.

A دلالة *dalālat*, Direction, guide, mark, indication, expression. Demonstration, argument. *Dalālat* or *dilālat*, Brokerage, the auctioneer's allowance. Money paid to a guide. *Dalālat*, *dilālat*, or *dulālat*, (v. n. of دلّ) Guiding, conducting, directing, pointing out. Indicating, denoting.

A دلّالة *dallālat*, A procuress. Delilah.

P دلّاله *dallāla*, A female guide, a bawd.

A دلّالي *dallālī*, Brokerage.

A دلام *dalām*, Black. Blackness.

P دلام *dilām*, A short spear.

A دلامث *dulāmis*, Swift.

A دلامز *dalāmiz*, (pl. of دلمز *dulamiz* and دلامز *dulāmiz*) Robust. Long-sighted. *Dulāmiz*, (pl. دلامز *dalāmiz*) The devil. Strong, powerful. Acute, penetrating. Shining-bodied.

A دلامزة *dulāmizat*, Vile, rascally (robbers).

A دلامس *dulāmis*, Evil, misfortune. Very dark.

A دلامص *dulāmiṣ*, Smooth, polished (gold).

A دلانع *dalāniʻ*, (pl. of دلنع) Smooth, level (roads).

P دل انگيزان *dil-angezān*, A musical note.

P دلاور *dil-āwar*, Bold, warlike, brave.

P دلاوري *dil-āwarī*, Valour, bravery.

P دلاويز *dil-āwez*, Heart-ravishing, suspending the soul (with delight). Fragrant.

A دلاهث *dulāhis*, A lion. A strong man.

A دلائل *dalāʼil*, (pl. of دليل *dalīl*) Arguments, demonstrations, indications.

P دلب *dulb*, A plane-tree.

P دل باخته *dil-bākhta*, Timid, cowardly.

P دلباز *dil-bāz*, Eloquent: verbose. A juggler.

P دلبازي *dil-bāzī*, Rashness.

A دلبة *dulbat*, Blackness. A single plane-tree.

A دلبحة *dalbahat*, (v. n. of دلبح Q) Bending (the back) and putting forward the head.

P دلبر *dil-bar*, Heart-ravishing. A lovely woman, a sweetheart.

P دلبري *dil-barī*, Captivation of the heart.

P دلبستگي *dil-bastagī*, Attachment, friendship, love. Anguish.

P دلبسته *dil-basta*, In love, earnest. Afflicted. Addicted.

P دلبند *dil-band*, Attractive, lovely. A beloved child. The bowels.

A دلبوث *dalabūs*, A species of lily.

P دل بيدار *dil-bīdār*, Whose heart is awake.

P دلپذير *dil-pazīr*, Grateful to the soul. Agreeable. Amiable. Soothing. Acceptable. Good.

P دلپسند *dil-pasand*, Agreeable, pleasing, engaging. Esteemed.

P دل پيشه *dil-pesha*, Silence.

A دلّة *dallat*, Amorous affectation.

P دلتنگ *dil-tang*, Distressed, sad, mournful.

A دلث *dulus*, (pl. of دلاث) Swift (camels).

A دلثاء *dalsāʼ*, A weak, drooping she-camel.

A دلثة *dulsat*, A crowd, band, troop.

A دلثع *dalsaʻ*, A perfectly level road through an even or uneven country. *Dalsaʻ* or *dilsiʻ*, Very fleshy about the gums. Greedy, gluttonous. *Dilsaʻ*, Stinking, filthy. One whose lip is inverted.

A دلثم *dalsam* or *dulasim*, Swift, fleet.

A دلج *dalaj*, The journey made during the first watch of the night.

A دلجان *dalajān*, Swarms of locusts.

A دلجة *daljat* or *duljat*, A journey performed during the early part of the light. دلجة الضبع *daljatu'z zabuʻ*, (The hyena's journey) Midnight.

P دلجو *dil-jū* or *jo*, Agreeable, desirable.

P دلجوئي *dil-jūʼī* or *joʼī*, Comfort, satisfaction.

P دل چسپ *dil-chasp*, Beloved, pleasant.

P دل چلي *dil-chalī*, Bravery, resolution.

P دل چور *dil-chor*, Inattentive. Timid.

A دلح *dalh*, (v. n. of دلح) Going with short steps (one overloaded). *Dulah*, A horse that sweats much. *Duluh* (pl. of دلوح *dalūh*) and دلّح *dullah*, (pl. of دالح *dālih*) (Clouds) fraught with rain.

A دلخ *dalakh*, A being fat. *Dalikh*, Fat (camel).

A دلّخ *dullakh*, Fat (camels).

A دلخة *dulakhat*, Large-hipped (woman).

P دلخراش *dil-kharāsh*, Horrible, heart-rending.

P دلخسته *dil-khasta*, Afflicted, love-sick.

A دلخمّ *dilhhamm*, Heavy, weighty. A severe distemper. A light, easy, and long sleep. A camel of great bulk.

P دلخواسته *dil-khwāsta*, Heart's desire.

P دلخواه *dil-khwāh*, What one likes or longs for, heart's desire. A beloved object. A wager, stake.

P دلخوش *dil-khwush*, Contented, cheerful, glad.

P دلخوشي *dil-khwushī*, Joy, glee, cheerfulness. دلخوشي كردن *dil-khwushī kardan*, To console, cheer.

P دلخون *dil-khūn*, Desirous, wistful. Deserted.

P دلداده *dil-dāda*, Who has given his heart.

P دلدار *dil-dār*, Heart-holding. A mistress, lover. دلدار پري رخسار *dil-dāri parī-rukhsār*, A lovely woman with the cheeks of an angel (or fairy).

P دلداري *dil-dārī*, Demonstrations of love. Comfort, consolation.

A دلدال *daldāl*, Agitation, particularly in walk. *Daldāl* or *duldāl*, Uncertain, hesitating between two. *Dildāl*, (v. n. of دلدل Q) Shaking the head and limbs in walking. Travelling.

A دلدع *dulduʻ*, Name of a plant useful against the bite of a snake and bloody flux.

P دلدل *duldul*, Name of Aliy's mule. (pl. دلادل *dalādil*) A porcupine. An important business. قوم دلدل *kawmun duldulun*, Irresolute, unsteady people. *Dildil*, A groan.

A دلدلة *daldalat*, (v. n. of دلدل Q) Shaking the head and limbs in walking. Travelling.

P دل دل كنان *dil dil kunān*, Sighing. Irresolute.

P دلدوز *dil-doz*, Heart-piercing.

A دلدول *duldūl*, A large hedgehog.

P دلده *dil-dih*, Hearty, earnest, zealous.

P دلدهي *dil-dihī*, Heartiness, earnestness.

P دلربا *dil-rubā*, (or دلرباي *dil-rubāy*) Heart-ravishing. A beloved object.

P دل رفته *dil-rafta*, Heartless, faint-hearted.

P دلريش *dil-resh*, Heart-wounded. A lover.

A دلس *dalas*, (pl. ادلاس *adlās*) Darkness. Darkness within darkness. Vegetation, growth at the end of summer. Deceit, fraud, fallacy.

P دلساز *dil-sāz*, Pleasing the heart.

P دلسازي *dil-sāzī*, Ardour.

A دلسة *dulsat*, Darkness.

P دلستان *dil-satān*, Heart-stealing, ravishing.

P دلسرد *dil-sard*, Cold-hearted.

P دل سوخته *dil-sokhta*, Afflicted.

P دلسوز *dil-soz*, Heart-burning, heart-inflaming. A sweetheart. Affecting, moving. Compassionate, benevolent.

P دل سوزي *dil-sozī*, Compassion.

P دلشاد *dil-shād*, Happy, contented, glad. Gladness. A gift. Resolution.

P دل شدگي *dil-shudagī*, Stupidity, insanity.

P دلشده *dil-shuda*, Bereft of reason. In love.

P دلشكستگي *dil-shikastagī*, Broken-heartedness.

P دلشكسته *dil-shikasta*, Heart-broken.

P دلشگفته *dil-shigufta*, Of expanded heart.

A دلص *dalas*, (v. n. of دلص) Losing her teeth (an old camel). *Dalis*, (pl. دلاص *dilās*) A man who stumbles or trips much. Bald or shaved on the head. (A camel) without hair. Level ground.

A دلصاء *dalsā*, Bald or shaven-headed (woman). Aged (she-camel), losing her teeth. (A she-ass) clothing herself with a new coat.

A دلصة *dalisat*, Level ground. Light (soil).

A دلطم *dilatm*, A strong man or camel.

A دلظ *dilazz*, One who drives violently.

A دلظ *dalz*, (v. n. of دلظ) Striking on the breast. Passing quickly by, running.

A دلظم *dalzam*, *dilzim*, *dilazm*, or دلظمّ *dilzamm*, A she-camel worn out with age. *Dilazm*, A strong camel. A rough man.

A دلظي *dalaza'*, One from whom another retreats in battle, as being unequal to him.

A دلع *dal'*, (v. n. of دلع) Lolling out the tongue. Hanging out of the mouth (the tongue). *Dula'*, A large sort of hedgehog.

A دلعاث *dil'ās*, A strong, tractable camel.

A دلعاس *dil'ās*, A fat, lazy camel. Obedient, tractable (camel).

A دلعب *dil'ab*, A large fat camel.

A دلعة *dul'at*, The vein of the penis. A horn. A female rupture.

A دلعث *dal'as* or *dila's*, A strong docile camel.

A دلعثي *dal'asa'*, Thick.

A دلعس *dal'as* or *dila's*, A corpulent, lazy, enervated camel.

A دلعك *dal'ak*, A fat relaxed she-camel.

A دلعوث *dil'aws*, Thick.

A دلعوس *dil'aws*, A corpulent, lazy, enervated camel. A wilful woman disobedient to her husband. (A camel) bold in travelling at night and untractable.

A دلعيس *dil'īs*, A bulky, lazy camel.

A دلغماظ *dilighmāz*, Greedy. Slanderous.

A دلف *dalf* or *dalaf*, (v. n. of دلف) Going with a slow step (an old man). Rising with a load (a camel). Going before (a troop or battalion). *Dilf*, Bold, brave, warlike. *Dulf*, (pl. of دلوف *dalūf*) Swift-flying eagles. *Duluf*, (A she-camel) rising with a load.

A دلف *dullaf* or *duluf*, (pl. of دالف *dālif*) Arrows falling near of the mark and then bounding to a distance. Heavy-laden, going slow.

A دلفاق *dilfāk*, A clear, open road.

A دلفان *dalafān*, (v. n. of دلف) Going with a slow step (an old man). Going before (a troop).

P دلفروز *dil-furoz*, Heart-cheering, delightful.

P دلفريب *dil-firīb*, Heart-alluring, charming.

P دلفريبي *dil-firībī*, Attraction, loveliness.

A دلفق *dalfak*, A clear, open road.

P دلفگار *dil-figār*, Melancholy, splenetic, mournful, thoughtful, pensive. An epithet of a lover.

P دلفگاري *dil-figārī*, Melancholy, spleen.

P A دلفين *dulfīn*, The dolphin; which, according to old Persian writers, is ever attentive to the saving of men when in danger of drowning.

P دلق *dalk*, Bad, naught, worthless.

A دلق *dalk*, (v. n. of دلق *dalk*) Drawing (a sword). *Dalak*, A hay-weasel. (from P دله *dala*) A dervīsh's habit. *Dalik*, (A sword) easily drawn or dropping out of the sheath. *Duluk*, (A troop) rushing impetuously.

A دلقاء *dalkā*, (A sword) which easily drops from its sheath. (A camel) whose teeth are broken with age.

P دلق پوش *dalak-posh*, Clad in shreds and patches; a dervīsh, a hermit.

A دلقم *dilkim*, An old woman. An aged camel with broken teeth.

P دل قوي *dil kawī*, Confidence.

A دلك *dalk*, (v. n. of دلك) Rubbing (any thing). Giving a smart rub or shrewd brush, teaching experience (fortune). *Dalak*, Smoothness. Weakness. *Duluk*, (pl. of دليك *dalīk*) Men versed in business.

A دلكة *dulakat*, Name of an animalcule.

P دلكش *dil-kash*, Heart-attracting, amiable. Chosen, approved of, beloved. Delicious; pleasant. خوب و دلكش *khūb u dil-kash*, Beautiful and attractive.

P دل كشاي *dil-kushāy*, Exhilarating, rejoicing. A sweetheart. در باغ دلكشاي *dar bāghi dil-kushāy*, In a pleasant garden.

P دلكور *dil-kūr*, Blind-hearted.

P دل گداز *dil-gudāz*, Heart-melting.

P دلگر *dalgar*, Meat sticking to a pot-bottom.

P دل گران *dil-girān*, Heavy-hearted: displeased.

P دل گراني *dil-girānī*, Displeasure. Heaviness.

P دلگرم *dil-garm*, Warm-hearted, brave, full of desire, animated.

P دل گرمي *dil-garmī*, Friendship, warmth.

P دلگير *dil-gīr*, Seizing the heart, terrifying, filling with horror or anguish. Abhorring. Melancholy, sad, afflicted, low-spirited, grieved. Soothing, conciliating.

P دلگيري *dil-gīrī*, Aversion, horror, indignation. Affliction. دلگيريء هوا *dil-gīrīi hawā*, Miasma.

A دلم *dulm*, (pl. of ادلم *adlam*) Black (men or asses). *Dalam*, (v. n. of دلم) Being very black. Hanging (the lip). Pendulousness of lip. A thing like a serpent found in Hijāz. A kind of dove. *Dulam*, An elephant. *Dulum*, A pimple, florid ulceration of the skin.

A دلماء *dalmās*, The thirtieth night of the moon (as being quite dark).

P دلماب *dilmāb*, Milk thickened by boiling, and eaten with honey or sugar.

P دلمانده *dil-mānda*, Sorrowful, indisposed.

A دلمث *dulamis*, Swift.

P دل مردگي *dil-murdagī*, Slowness or deadness of heart, dulness of comprehension.

P دل مرده *dil-murda*, Dead-hearted.

A دلمز *dilamz*, Very rough. *Dulamiz*, Strong, firm, robust. Long-sighted, acute, penetrating. Shining.

A دلمزان *dulamizān*, A youth fat and foolish.

A دلمس *dilmis*, Misfortune. *Dulamis*, Very dark. Misfortune.

P دل مشغولي *dil-mashghūlī*, Heart-ache, anxiety.

A دلمص *dulamis*, Smooth, polished, shining (gold). Bald in front (head).

A دلمظ *dilmiz*, An old she-camel.

P دلمك *dulmak*, A tarantula. *Dalamak*, New cheese.

P دلمل *dulmul*, Unripe grain. Vetches or pulse in the pod.

P دلمه *dulma*, A tarantula. *Dalama*, New cheese.

P دلنشين *dil-nishīn*, Agreeable, pleasing. A heart at ease.

A دلنظي *dalanza'*, (fem. دلنظاة *dalanzāt*) Hard, strong. A thick, fat, or swift camel.

A دلنع *dalanna'*, (pl. دلانع *dalāni'*) Smooth, level (road).

A دلنفقا *dalanfakan*, Swiftly.

P دلنگ *dalang*, An embankment of twigs, earth, and stones. A short spear. A hoe, mattock, pick-axe. The spathe in which dates are enveloped. *Dalang* or *dilang*, Suspended.

P دلنگان *dalingān*, Hung, suspended.

P دل نگراني *dil-nigarānī*, Sorrow.

P دلنمودگي *dil-namūdagī*, Display of the heart.

P دلنواز *dil-nawāz*, Soothing: gracious. A mistress.

P دلنوازه *dil-nawāza*, Blandishment. دلنوازه كردن *dil-nawāza kardan*, To soothe, caress, flatter.

P دل نه *dil-nih*, One who fixes his heart.

P دل نهاد *dil-nihād*, Attention.

P دل نهي *dil-nihī*, Fixedness of heart.

A دلنيس *dalnīs*, A shell-fish found in Egypt.

A دلو *dalw*, (v. n. of دلا for دلو) Letting down (a bucket) into a well. Drawing (water). Asking in the name of another, employing a mediator. Driving (a camel) slowly. Treating benevolently. (pl. ادلي *adlī*, دلاء *dilā*, دليّ *duliy*, and دلي *dala'*) A bucket, urn. The sign Aquarius. The hopper of a mill. A mark burnt upon camels. A calamity, evil. The fifth heaven formed of gold.

P دلوا *dalwā*, Pendulous, inverted. Astonished.

P دلوار *dilwār* or دلور *dilwar*, Bold, courageous.

A دلوج *dulūj*, (v. n. of دلج) Drawing water from a well and pouring it into the cistern or trough. Emptying a milk-pail.

A دلوح *dalūh*, (pl. دلح) (A cloud) big with rain.

A دلوخ *dalūkh*, A loaded palm-tree. (pl. دلّخ *dullakh* and دوالخ *dawālikh*) Fat (camel).

A دلّوص *dillaws*, Moveable, not fixed.

A دلوع *dalū'*, A she-camel that takes the lead or outstrips all the rest. *Dulū'*, (v. n. of دلع) Hanging (tongue from the mouth). Lolling the tongue.

A دلوف *dalūf*, (pl. دلف *dulf*) A swift eagle.

A دلوق *dalūḳ*, (pl. دلق *duluḳ*) (A sword) easily drawn or dropping from its sheath. A firmly-built horse, and swift-paced. (A troop) rushing with impetuosity. A camel whose grinders are broken by age (so that he cannot contain his spittle).

A دلوك *dalūk*, Any thing with which the body is rubbed (as oil or odours). *Dulūk*, (v. n. of دلك) Sloping westward, setting (the sun).

A دلولة *dulūlat*, (v. n. of دلّ) Pointing out the road, directing.

A دلوه *dalūh*, (A camel) consoled or indifferent about the loss of her colt.

A دله *dalh*, (v. n. of دله) Being consoled, forgetting one's griefs. Having no regard for her colt (a camel). Blood shed with impunity. *Dalh*, *dalah*, or دلوه *dulūh*, (v. n. of دله) Becoming insane, distracted (from grief or love). *Daluh*, Frantic, distracted (camel).

P دله *dala*, A weasel, fitchet, or stote. A coarse dervish's habit. A sly, deceitful woman, a coquette. *Dila*, The heart.

P دلّه *dalla*, The ermine. Fraud, treachery. False, insincere. A whirlwind.

A دلها *dalhan*, With impunity.

A دلهاث *dilhās*, A lion. A strong, bold man.

A دلهام *dilhām*, A bold man. A lion.

A دلهث *dalhas*, A lion.

A دلهثة *dalhasat*, (v. n. of دلهث Q) Going fast. Outstripping, taking the lead.

P دلهرا *dilhirā* or *harā*, Name of a king of India.

A دلهم *dalham*, Dark. A wolf. The male قطا *katā*. Insane, distracted with love.

A دلهمس *dalahmas*, A lion. Bold, brave. Swift, penetrating. An obscure, difficult affair. A very dark night. A large, strong, hard man.

A دليٰ *dala'*, (pl. of دلو *dalw*) Buckets.

P دلي *dilī*, Belonging to the heart. Hearty. Cardiac. *Dilī*, (or دلّي *dillī*) The city of Delhi.

A دلّيٰ *dullā'*, A highway, clear road.

A دليّ *duliy*, (pl. of دلو *dalw*) Buckets.

A دليّة *dulayyat*, A small bucket.

A دليث *dalīs*, A walking with short steps.

P دليده *dalīda*, Coarsely-ground (grain).

P دلير *dilīr*, Brave, intrepid. Audacious, fearless, insolent, bold. دلير گردانيدن *dilīr gardānīdan*, To impeach, indict, arraign. To convict.

P دليرانه *dilīrāna*, Heroically. Insolently.

P دليري *dilīrī*, Valour, courage. Hardihood.

A دليص *dalīṣ*, Smooth, bright (thing). Flashing, bright. Brightness (of gold).

A دليظ *dalīẓ*, One who drives people from the king's gate.

A دليع *dalīʿ*, A spacious and level road.

A دليف *dalīf*, (v. n. of دلف) Going with a slow step (an old man). Going before (a troop). A slow pace. The step of an old man.

P دليك *dalīk*, Seed of roses.

A دليك *dalīk*, Dust blown about by the wind. Fruit of a red mountain-rose tree. (pl. دلك *duluk*) A man versed in business. A dish made of fresh butter and dates.

A دليل *dalīl*, (pl. ادلّة *adillat*) A guide, director. (pl. دلائل *dalāʾil*) Argument, proof, test, demonstration. A urinal. A road. A syllogism. دليل برهاني *dalīli burhānī*, A convincing argument or proof. P دليل روشن *dalīli roshan*, A clear proof. A دليل قاطع *dalīli kātiʿ*, A decisive proof. P دليل گرفتن *dalīl giriftan*, To infer, deduce.

A دليلي *dalīlī*, Argumentative: a good arguer.

A دلّيليٰ *dillīla'*, Guidance, direction. Accurate knowledge in a guide. A road-guide.

A دليمزان *dulaymizān*, A youth fat and foolish.

P دم *dam*, Breath. Air. Life. Scent, smell, fume. Breath of an oven. The mouth of the stove of a hot-bath. Bellows. Goldsmiths' bellows. The stewing over a slow fire. Hot, fiery, fervid. Pride, haughtiness. Ambition. Fraud. Black blood. Cheerfulness, pleasure, recreation. Society (as breathing together). A groan, sigh, exclamation, fy! Time, season, hour, moment. Poetical metre. Incantatory verses. A draught of water. Edge (of a sword). Point (of a spear). A fish-bone. An apparition. A crow, raven. The mouth. دم آب *dami āb*, A little water, a draught. دم بدم آب خوردن *dam ba dam āb khwurdan*, To sip up water. دم تسليم *dami taslīm*, Silence. Resignation, obedience. دم خرّم *dami khurram*, A day of festivity. دم خوردن *dam khwurdan*, To be cheated. To rest, repose. دم دادن *dam dādan*, To deceive. دم زدن *dam zadan*, To breathe. To keep silence. To hesitate. To leave. To escape. To boast, pretend unto. To sprinkle. دم سرد *dami sard*, A cold sigh. A sigh of despair. دم عيسيٰ *dami ʿīsa'*, The breath of Jesus, whereby he resuscitated the dead. دم كشيدن *dam kashīdan*, To breathe. To gasp. To be idle or unemployed. دم گرفتن *dam giriftan*, To retain the breath. To confine the air. To be suffocated. To keep silence. To wait, halt. To quit. To become putrid from the unwholesomeness or stagnation of the air. To be corrupted (in mind or body). دم نقد *dami nakd*, Ready (as dinner). دم نيم سوز *dami nīm-soz*, (or دم سنجابي *dami sinjābī*) The sigh of one in pain. خوش دم *khwush-dam*, Happy, glad, delighted. هر دم *har dam*, Every moment, continually. هر دم كه *har dam ki*, As often as. هر دم تازه *har dam tāza*, Ever fresh, ever verdant. دم وا پسين *dami wā pasīn*, The last breath. *Dum*, The tail. End, extremity. A rudder. Dry dung used as fuel. A felon, sore. دم گاو *dumi gāv*, An ox's tail. A scourge, lash. A brazen trumpet. دم گرگ *dumi gurg*, Name of a constellation. Twilight or false dawn.

A دم *dam* (originally دمي *damay*), (dual دمان *damāni* or دميان *damayāni*) (pl. دماء *dimāʾ* or دميّ *dumiy*) Blood. Life. A cat. دم الثعبان *damu's saʿbān*, (or دم الاخوين *damu'l akhawayn*) Dragon's blood. دم الغزال *damu'l ghazāl*, Name of a pot-herb. سفك دم *safki dam*, A shedding of blood. سيل دم *sayli dam*, A bloody flux.

A دمّ *damm*, (v. n. of دمّ) Plastering (a house). Pitching or caulking (a ship). Anointing or tinging the exterior of the eyes. Dyeing (a garment, especially red). Tormenting greatly. Breaking the head. Beating. Prostrating. Grinding, crushing. Destroying. Levelling the ground. Leaping on a mare. Spreading soil over a mushroom. Overloading. Covering its hole with earth (a shrew-mouse). Name of an herb. Blood. نبات دمّ *nabātu damm*, Name of a certain plant. *Dimm*, Rupture.

P دما *damā*, Breath. *Dimā*, (in zand and Pāz.) The channel of a river. Temperament, constitution.

A دما *dama'*, (v. n. of دمي) Emitting blood. Being stained with gore.

A دماء *dimāʾ*, (pl. of دم) Streams of blood, lives.

P دمابر *damā-bur*, Asthmatic, short-breathed.

P دم آبي *dam-ābī*, One draught of water.

A دماث *dimās*, pl. of دمث, Soft sandy grounds.

A دماثة *damāsat*, Softness, easiness.

A دماثر *dumāsir*, Level ground. Fleshy camel.

A دماج *dimāj* and *dumāj*, A clandestine, (according to others) a firm, solid (peace).

A دماحس *dumāhis*, A lion.

A دماحل *dumāhil*, Compact, closely set.

A دماخ *dumākh*, A kind of Arabian game.

P دمادم *dam-ā-dam*, Now and then, frequently, from time to time. *Dum-ā-dum*, Step by step.

A دمادم *damādim*, Little hills of easy ascent. *Dumādim*, A species of medicinal herb of two kinds, red and scarlet.

P دمار *damār*, The necessaries of life. Breath. Smoke. Revenge. Perdition. A fixed residence.

A دمار *damār*, (v. n. of دمر) Destroying. Perishing, disappearing. Ruin, destruction, perdition. *Dimār*, (v. n. 3 of دمر) Watching all night.

A دمارة *damārat*, (v. n. of دمر) Destroying.

A دماس *dimās*, A covering.

A دماشق *dumāshik*, Swift (man or camel).

A دماع *dimāʿ*, A scar, a mark. A mark of tears remaining on the cheek from the eye to the nose. *Dumāʿ*, A sort of plant.

A دمّاع *dammāʿ*, (The earth) moistened by dew. A mizzling day. *Dummāʿ*, Tears flowing either from disease or age. Tears distilling from vines in the spring. The membrane which is taken off an infant's head when brought forth.

P دماغ *damāgh*, The palate. Pride, haughtiness, consequential airs.

A دماغ *dimāgh*, (pl. ادمغة *admighat*) The brain. امّ الدماغ *ummu'd dimāgh*, Mother of the brain, the membrane called the dura and pia mater.

P دماغ داري *dimāgh-dārī*, Madness.

P دماغي *damāghī*, Vain, frivolous, proud.

A دمال *damāl*, Decaying (buds, flowers, and incipient fruit (of dates). Rubbish thrown up by the sea. Earth and dung trodden down by cattle. Dung. Fruit, old, rotten, and black.

P دمال *dumāl* or *dummāl*, A sore bile. A tail.

A دمالص *dumālis*, Resplendent.

A دمالق *dumālik*, Round and smooth (stone). Shaven. Wide (cranny).

A دماليج *damālīj*, Hard grounds. (pl. of دملوج *dumlūj*) Bracelets, armlets. Amulets.

A دمام *dimām*, A liniment with which they anoint the brows and eyelids of infants. Any tincture. A waterless cloud. (pl. of دميم *damīm*) Short and deformed.

A دمّام *dammām*, A mender of old kettles.

A دمامة *damāmat*, (v. n. of دمّ) Being ugly. Doing mischief, injuring. Ugliness,

P دمامه *damāma*, A small drum or trumpet.

A دماميس *damāmīs*, (pl. of ديماس *dīmās*) Dens of wild beasts. Dark dungeons. Baths.

A دماميل *damāmīl*, (pl. of دمّل) Boils, pimples.

P دمان *damān*, Swift, making haste. Powerful, strong, terrible. A powerful assault. Time, season. Shouts (of joy or anger). Haste. Women. Cries for help. پيل دمان *pīlī damān*, A terror-striking elephant.

A دمان *damān*, Rottenness of the palm-tree, with cracks and blackness. Dung. Ashes. One who manures the ground.

P دمانك *damānak*, A blunderbuss, carbine.

P دمان كش *damān-kash*, Time, season, space.

P دماور *dam-āwar*, Asthmatic.

P دماوند *damāwand*, Name of a mountain near Hamadān: also of a city near the same.

P دم آهنج *dam-āhanj*, Short-winded, pursy.

A دمائم *damāim*, (pl. of دميمة *damīmat*) Short and contemptible (women).

P دمايه *dumāya*, The cream of milk.

P دمب *dumb*, The tail.

P دم باز *dam-bāz*, Coaxer, wheedler, deceiver.

P دم بازي *dam-bāzī*, Flattery, adulation, deceit.

P دمبال *dumbāl*, A tail. A man's back. دمبال چشم *dumbāli chashm*, The corner of the eye.

P دمبدم *dam ba dam*, From moment to moment, every moment, now and then, frequently.

P دم بريده *dum-burīda*, Docked.

P دمبسته *dam-basta*, Breathless. Amazed.

P دمبند *dam-band*, An alembic.

P دمپ *dump*, The tail.

P دم پخت *dam-pukht*, A kind of pilaw.

P دم پلنگ *dum-palang*, An active soldier.

A دمة *damat*, Blood, or any particle of it.

A دمّة *dimmat*, A ball of camel's dung. A louse. An ant. A cat. A cow. Sick cattle. Short and deformed. *Dummat*, A kind of game. Manner, way, mode. The hole of the field-mouse; also earth scraped out of it.

P دمتك *dumtak*, A water-wagtail.

A دمث *damas*, (v. n. of دمث) Being soft and level (a sandy place). *Damis*, (pl. دماث *dimās*) A soft sandy place. Good-tempered.

A دمثر *dimasr* or *dumasir*, Fat, fleshy (camel).

A دمثرة *damsarat*, Fatness, fleshiness, corpulency.

A دمج *damj*, A twisted lock. *Dimj*, A friend.

P دمچار *dam-chār*, Exhalation of any thing odoriferous. Appearance of colour. Smoke, and its smell.

P دمچام *damchām*, Smoke. Smell of smoke.

P دمچه *dumcha*, A small tail (of a bird), the rump; peacock's train. A fly-flap of horse's tails. A little stalk. A wicker basket. Sweepings. Trefoil.

P دمچي *dumchī*, A crupper.

A دمحسي *dumhusīy*, Black (man). Robust.

A دمحق *damhak*, Thick milk. *Dumhuk*, A box in which they keep medicines, particularly of the olfactory kind, a snuff-box.

A دمحقة *damhakat*, A soaking (of linen) in branny water, that it may appear to possess a strong texture.

A دمحلة *damhalat*, (v. n. of دمحل Q) Rolling, causing to roll. *Dumahilat*, A fat and fair woman.

A دمحمح *damahmah*, A strong, compactly-built man. Round, gathered in a heap.

A دمحوق *dumhūk*, Big-bodied. A snuff-box.

A دمخ *damkh*, (v. n. of دمخ) Being high, lofty. Breaking (the head). Name of a mountain.

A دمخخة *damkhakhat*, A walking slowly, heavily.

P دمخنيوس *damkhanīwas*, Name of the merchant who stole عذرا *ẓazrā*.

P دمدار *dam-dār*, Elastic. *Dum-dār*, Tailed, possessing a tail. Holding the tail, coming behind. The rear-guard, camp-followers. An agreement, condition. ستارهٔ دمدار *sitārasi dum-dār*, A comet.

A دمدامة *damdāmat*, (pl. دمدام *damdām*) A root resembling a carrot.

P دم دراز *dum-darāz*, Long-tailed.

A دمدم *dimdim*, Dry forage. Silliyān-roots.

A دمدمة *damdamat*, (v. n. of دمدم Q) Fixing, uniting unto the ground. Giving one up to destruction (God). Grinding, destroying. Being angry with, inveighing against. Anger, rage.

P دمدمه *damdama*, Tumult, disturbance, clamour. Fame, rumour, renown. Fraud, deceit. A drum. A mound, eminence, raised battery.

P دمدميا *damdamyā*, (in zand and Pāz.) The sea.

A دمراء *damrāẓ*, (A sheep) giving little milk. A bold assailant (female or otherwise).

A دمرغ *dumarigh*, Very red (man).

A دمّرغيّ *dummarghaʼ*, Extreme, very (white).

A دمس *dams*, (v. n. of دمس) Suppressing (news). Burying, interring. Covering (a hide) in order to strip off the hair. Reconciling. Copulating. A person, body, individual. *Dums*, Serious, important affairs. *Damas*, Hidden, concealed. *Dumus*, (pl. of دموس *damūs*) Those who cover or bury skins to get off the hair.

P دمساز *dam-sāz*, A friend, confidant, companion, or consort. Agreeing, consenting. Harmonious, singing, reciting together. نغمهٔ دمساز *naghmasi dam-sāz*, Musical harmony.

P دمسازي *dam-sāzī*, Intimacy, confidence.

P دمسان *dam-sān*, A confidant. Agreeing.

P دمسنجه *dumsinja*, A kind of swallow or swift. A bird, which when once on the ground is said to be unable to rise.

P دمسه *dimsa*, White silk.

P دمسيجه *dumsīja*, or دمسيچه A wag-tail.

A دمش *damash*, Palpitation, excitement produced by heat or medicine.

P دمش *damish*, A breathing, blowing. Assault. Boast. Eruption, efflorescence.

A دمشق *damshak*, *dimashk*, or *dimshik*, Swift of foot. دمشق اليدين *damshaku'l yadayn*, Dexterous, expeditious. *Dimashk* or *dimishk*, Damascus.

A دمشقة *damshakat*, A despatching, expediting.

P دمشقي *dimashkī* or *dimshikī*, Of Damascus.

P دم شناس *dam-shinās*, A skilful physician.

A دمص *dams*, Haste (as that of a bitch in whelping, or of a hen in laying an egg). *Dims*, Any layer of stones in a well except the nethermost (this being called رهص *rihs*). *Damas*, (v. n. of دمص) Having the eyebrows thin at the outer extremity, and thick at the inner. Having little hair.

A دمصاء *damsāẓ*, Thin-eyebrowed (woman).

A دمع *damẓ*, (v. n. of دمع) Weeping. (pl. دموع *dumūẓ*) A tear. دمع داوُد *damẓu dāud*, (David's tears) A certain medicine. *Dumẓ* or *dumuẓ*, A burnt mark on the lachrymal duct. *Damaẓ*, (v. n. of دمع) Shedding tears (the eye). *Dumuẓ*, Traces of tears on the cheek.

A دمعان *damẓān*, Overflowing (cup).

A دمعة *damẓat*, A tear-drop. Gum. A disease in the eye. دمعة العشّاق *damẓatu'l ẓushshāk*, Woad. دمعة الشجر *damẓatu'sh shajar*, Ivy. دمعة الكرم *damẓatu'l karm*, Tears which drop from a vine in the spring. *Damiẓat*, (A woman) prone to weep.

A دمعق *dimaẓk*, White silk.

A دمغ *damgh*, (v. n. of دمغ) Wounding, piercing to the brain. Injuring the brain, giving a coup-de-soleil (the sun).

P دم غازه *dum-ghāza*, Root of the tail.

P دمغزه *dum-ghaza*, The tail, the rump.

A دمق *damak*, Snow and wind. Theft.

A دمقة *damakat*, A blacksmith's bellows.

A دمقس *dimaks*, (دمقاس *dimkās*, دمقص *dimaks*, or دمقاص *dimkās*) Silk (especially white), raw silk. A silken or a linen garment.

A دمك *damk*, (v. n. of دمك) Running fast (a hare). Twisting (a rope). Grinding. Ascending (the sun). Mounting the female (a camel). *Dumuk*, (pl. of دموك *damūk*) Windlasses, pulleys.

P دم كرده *dam-karda*, Inflated.

A دمكمك *damakmak*, Strong, firm. A mill which turns rapidly and grinds well.

P دم گاوه *dum-gāwa*, A lash. Brazen trumpet.

P دمگاه *dam-gāh*, A smith's forge: a furnace.

P دم گرفته *dam-girifta*, Putrid, rotten (hide).

P دمگه *dam-gah*, A forge. Stove of a bath.

P دمگير *dum-gīr*, Suffocating, stifling, choking.

A دمل *daml*, (v. n. of دمل) Manuring land. Reconciling (men). Healing (a wound). Effecting a cure (medicine). Benignity. *Dumal*, (pl. دملان *dimlān*) A pimple, a boil.

A دمّل *dummal*, (pl. دماميل *damāmīl*) A swelling, bile, felon, boil.

P دم لابه *dum-lāba*, (Tail-wag) A dog.

A دملاج *dimlāj*, (or دملجة *dumlajat*) The finishing, completing, or perfecting of a thing.

A دملان *dimlān*, (pl. of دمل *dumal*) Pimples, boils. *Damalān*, (v. n. of دمل) Manuring (land). Reconciling (men).

A دملج *dumlaj*, *dumluj*, or ملوج *dumlūj*, (pl. دماليج *damālīj*) A bracelet worn above the elbow; an amulet fastened round that part as a charm against fascination.

A دملحة *damlahat*, (v. n. of دملح Q) Rolling, turning round. *Dumluhat*, A female fat and juicy.

A دملص *dumalis*, Shining, resplendent.

A دملق *dumalik*, Round and smooth (stone).

A دملقة *damlakat*, A making round and smooth.

A دملكة *damlakat*, A making round and smooth.

A دملوج *dumlūj*, (pl. دماليج *damālīj*) A smooth stone. Furniture. A load or burden.

A دملوق *dumlūk*, Round and smooth (stone). A certain plant smaller than عرجون *ʿurjūn*, and growing in sand or in gardens.

A دملوك *dumlūk*, Smooth and round (stone).

A دمم *dimam*, Glue. Any thing for closing chinks. Blood. (pl. of دمّة *dimmat*) Pellets of camel's dung. *Dumam*, (pl. of دمّة *dummat*) Holes of field-mice.

A دمماء *dumamāʾ*, The hole of the field-mouse.

A دممة *dumamat*, The hole of a field-mouse; also earth excavated from it.

A دمن *damn*, (v. n. of دمن) Dunging, manuring (land). Harbouring a grudge. Rottenness of a palm-tree, with blackness. *Dimn*, The pill-like dung of cattle. Dung caked together. A manager of property, a steward. خضراء الدمن *khazrāʾu'd dimn*, A man of an engaging exterior, but of a devilish temper. (pl. of دمنة *dimnat*) Traces of people. Old grudges. *Daman*, (v. n. of دمن) Harbouring a grudge (against another). *Diman*, (pl. of دمنة *dimnat*) Old grudges. Marks left by people.

P دمن *daman*, A skirt. Damayanti, bride of Nala (whose adventures form an episode in the great Sanskrit epic poem Mahābhārata). *Diman*, Give me.

A دمنة *dimnat*, (pl. دمن *dimn* or *diman*) A dung-hill. A place near a house. The marks left on the ground where a number of people have been sitting. A manager of property, a steward. Malevolence, old grudge, thirst for revenge.

P دمندان *damandān*, Fire. Hell.

P دمنده *damanda*, Blowing; hissing. Crying for help.

P دمنه *damna*, Name of the jackal that figures conspicuously in the Anvāri suhayli. The blast-hole of an oven or furnace. *Dimna*, A fox. A jackal. A shrewd, cunning fellow.

P دمنه داني *damna dānī*, Rags for closing chinks in an oven.

A دمو *damaw*, Blood.

A دموج *dumūj*, (v. n. of دمج) Being inserted, adhering firmly. Running fast with short steps (a hare).

P دمور *damūr*, A low, gentle voice. Name of a kinsman of Afrāsyāb.

A دمور *dumūr*, (v. n. of دمر) Intruding impudently without leave. Destroying. Perishing, disappearing. An evil assault.

A دموس *damūs*, (pl. دمس *dumus*) One who buries a skin in order to take off the hair. *Dumūs*, (v. n. of دمس) Being thick (darkness). Being defaced (vestiges).

A دموع *dumūʿ*, (pl. of دمع *damʿ*) Tears. بحار من دموع *bihār min dumūʿ*, Oceans of tears.

A دموق *damūk*, Worthless. *Dumūk*, (v. n. of دمق) Entering abruptly, without leave. Creeping into his lurking-place (a hunter). Breaking the teeth. Inserting one thing into another.

A دموك *damūk*, (pl. دمك *dumuk*) A windlass, pulley, mill-wheel, any thing having a rapid motion. Swiftly borne along (hare or wheel). *Dumūk*, (v. n. of دمك) Twisting (a rope). Becoming smooth. Running swiftly (a hare).

A دمّون *dammūn*, Ugly, filthy.

A دمويّ *damawiy*, Bloody. Plethoric.

P دمه *dama*, Wind and snow. An icicle. An eolipile. A pair of bellows. Asthma. دمهٔ آهنگران *damaʾi āhangarān*, Blacksmiths' bellows. دمهٔ زرگر *damaʾi zargar*, A goldsmith's bellows.

A دمه *damah*, The scorching reflection from sands. A certain game.

A دمهكر *damahkar*, (from P دمه گير) Suffocating.

A دميٰ *damaʾ*, (v. n. of دمي) Bleeding. Being bloody. *Damī*, Bloody. *Dumaʾ*, (pl. of دمية *dumyat*) Idols.

P دمي *damī*, A kind of hookah for smoking.

A دميّ *damiy*, Bloody. *Dumayy*, A small quantity of blood. *Dumiy*, (v. n. of دمي) Bleeding. Being bloody. (pl. of دم *dam*) Bloods. Lives.

P دميا *damyā*, (in zand and Pāzand) Blood.

A دمياط *dimyāt*, Damietta in Egypt.

P دمياطي *dimyātī*, A kind of cotton cloth; dimity.

A دميان *damayāni*, (du. of دم *dam*) Two bloods.

A دمية *dumyat*, (pl. دميٰ *dumaʾ*) An idol, image, statue (of marble). احسن من الدمية *ahsan mini'd dumyat*, More lovely than a statue.

A دميث *damīs*, (or دميث بليث *damīs balīs*) Easy, good-tempered.

A دمّيجة *dummayjat*, Fond of much sleep. Fixed at home.

P دميدگي *damīdagī*, A breaking out, an eruption on the body, efflorescence, pimple. The diffusion of odours.

P دميدن *damīdan*, To blow (with the breath, or as the wind). To breathe. To fill one's self with wind. To blow, blossom (as flowers). To appear (as the dawn). To break out in pimples or swellings (the body). To assault. To boast.

P دميده *damīda*, Blowing. Blown, blossomed. Sprouting. Stretched out. The dawn.

A دميس *damīs*, Hidden, concealed.

A دميغ *damīgh*, Foolish. Wounded in the brain (دماغ *dimāgh*) by a fracture. دميغ الشيطان *damīghu'sh shaytān*, The nickname of a certain man.

A دميق *damīk*, Inserted, thrust in.

P دميقي *dimīkī*, Silk woven as a bed-tick.

P دميك *damyak*, Name of a village near Ghaznin. *Damīk*, Land. A boundary, land-mark.

A دميك *damīk*, Complete (mouth). Snow.

A دميم *damīm*, (pl. دمام *dimām*) Short of stature, squat, deformed: contemptible, base. Bedaubed, in order to close up chinks (a pot).

A دميمة *damīmat*, (pl. دمائم *damāʾim* and دمام *dimām*) Contemptible, mean, base (woman).

A دمّيني *dummaynaʾ*, The field-mouse's nest.

P دن *dan*, Shouts and cries of joy. Going with a gay and joyous air.

A دنّ *dann*, (v. n. of دنّ) Buzzing (a fly). Muttering unintelligibly. (pl. دنان *dinān*) A very large oblong wine-vessel, partly fixed in the ground.

A دنا *danaʾ*, (v. n. of دنو) Being vile, mean.

A دناٴ *danaʾ*, (v. n. of دنئ) Being hump-backed. Gibbosity. A hunch.

A دناء *dunaʾāʾ*, (pl. of دنيء *daniʾ*) Mean, small, trifling. Vicious, licentious, careless of reputation.

A دنّاء *dannāʾ*, Crook-backed, hollow-breasted, depressed in the neck (female).

A دناءة *danāʾat*, (v. n. of دنا) Being bad, mean, base, abject, careless of censure. Baseness, worthlessness, meanness.

A دناج *dināj*, Establishment, confirmation.

A دنادن *danādin*, The lower parts of shifts. The folds of a garment.

A دناسة *danāsat*, A being dirtied, sullied, nasty.

A دناعة *danāʿat*, (v. n. of دنع) Being impatient for food (a child). Hungering. Coveting. Lowering one's self. Being vile, abject.

A دنافس *dunāfis*, Of a bad disposition.

A دنّامة *dinnāmat*, Short (woman). An emmet.

P دنان *danān*, Walking quick with joy. Boiling with rage.

A دنان *dinān*, (pl. of دنّ *dann*) Wine-jars.

A دنانير *danānīr*, (pl. of دينار) Dinārs, ducats.

A دناوة *danāwat*, (v. n. of دنو) Approaching. Affinity, propinquity, relationship. Nearness.

A دنأي *dan‿a'*, Hump-backed (woman).

A دنايا *danāya'*, (pl. of دنيّة) Vile things: vices.

A دناية *dināyat*, A being mean and vile.

P دنب *dumb*, A tail.

A دنّب *dinnab*, (or دنّبة) Short. A dwarf.

P دنبال *dambāl*, A buffoon, jester. Pleasantry, waggery. *Dumbāl*, Tail, rump. Latter part. Desire. Vestige, trace. The shaft of an arrow. After. دنبال چشم *dumbāli chashm*, Outer corner of the eye. دنبال كشتي *dumbāli kashtī*, Stern of a ship. بدنبال آمدن *ba dumbāl āmadan*, To follow.

P دنباله *dumbāla*, The tail. A felon. The outer corner of the eye. The shank of a sword or knife. The rudder of a ship. The hinder part of a saddle. After, behind. دنبالۀ تازيانه *dumbāla‿i tāziyāna*, The end of a whip or lash. دنبالۀ ميوه *dumbāla‿i mīwa*, Stalk of fruits. ستارۀ دنباله دار *sitāra‿i dumbāla-dār*, A comet (a star having a tail).

P دنباور *dumb-āwar*, Tailed. Rear of an army.

P دنباوند *dambāwand*, Name of a mountain.

A دنبح *dumbuh*, Bad-dispositioned (man).

P دنبر *dambar*, Name of a city in India.

P دنبره *dumbara*, A guitar.

P دنب غزه *dumb-ghaza*, The tail-bone.

P دنبك *dumbak*, A bagpipe.

P دنبل *dambal*, Mockery. Any thing ludicrous. A sort of wooden drum. *Dumbal*, Imposthume, bubo.

P دنبوقه *dumbūka*, Flowing hair. The end of a turban-sash hanging down.

P دنبه *dumba*, The tail, also the fat of a sheep's tail. دنبه دادن *dumba dādan*, To put one off his guard. To deceive. دنبه نهادن *dumba nihādan*, To play tricks upon, to deceive.

P دنبه بره *dumba-bara*, (Lamb's tail, often contracted into دنبره *dumbara*) A guitar.

P دنبه گداز *dumba-gudāz*, A pan in which a sheep's tail is fried. A species of sorcery by a sheep's tail stuck with needles suspended in an old tomb, and exposed to the heat of a burning lamp. As the fat melted, so the object of persecution was believed to pine away.

A دنّة *dinnat*, A certain insect like an ant.

A دنج *dunuj*, (pl. of داناج) Wise, learned.

A دنح *dinh*, The Epiphany.

A دنحبة *danhabat*, Perfidy, treason, disloyalty.

A دنحس *danhas*, Strong, corpulent, fleshy.

A دنخان *danakhān*, A slow pace under a load.

P دند *dand*, A rib. Poor, in want of food. A race of beggars, whose practice is to stab and wound their bodies if their applications are not presently attended to. (See شاخشانه *shākhshāna*). A weaver's teethed instrument. Name of a purgative seed: also of a certain herb. Any thing styptic or astringent. Stupid, silly, ignorant. Bold, fearless, wilful. Unconscionable. A thief. (for دندان *dandān*) A tooth. *Dund*, A kind of bee.

P دندا *dandā*, Lost. Middle of a mountain.

P دندان *dandān*, A tooth. Desire, greediness. Hope, wish, expectance. ارّۀ مار دندان *arra‿i mār-dandān*, A saw made of serpents' teeth. دندان از ترش كردن *dandān az tursh kardan*, To set the teeth on edge. دندان آسيا *dandāni āsyā*, A grinder. دندان بخون بردن *dandān ba khūn burdan*, To bite. دندان بزهر خائيدن *dandān ba zahar khā‿idan*, To hate, be severe. دندان بكام خود بردن *dandān ba kāmi khwud burdan*, To be gratified. دندان تيز كردن *dandān tez kardan*, To sharpen the teeth; to covet, to long for. To taste. To foster enmity. دندان حوت *dandāni hūt*, Gentle rain. A tear. دندان خنده *dandāni khanda*, The laughing tooth (namely the fore-teeth, as they appear when one laughs). دندان داشتن *dandān dāshtan*, To endeavour, to strive tooth and nail. To hope, to wait for. To cherish hatred. دندان زدن *dandān zadan*, To strip. To contend, dispute for equality. To adhere, stick. To cherish enmity. دندان سپيد كردن *dandān saped kardan*, To make the teeth white. To laugh, smile. To fear. To be weak, to submit unto. دندان شير *dandāni shīr*, The milk-teeth. دندان طمع *dandāni tama‿*, Severity, hatred. دندان فرو بردن *dandān faro burdan*, To dislike. To be in a rage. To labour hard, persevere. دندان فرو گذاشتن *dandān faro guzāshtan*, To strive, make great exertion. To hope, expect, wait for. To hate. دندان فيل *dandāni fīl*, Elephant's tusks; ivory. دندان كردن *dandān kardan*, To forbid, prohibit. To turn away from. To straiten, oppress. دندان كليد *dandāni kalīd*, The wards of a key. دندان كندن *dandān kandan*, To pull out the teeth, *i.e.* To suppress desire. دندان گوساله *dandāni gosāla*, A bone-headed arrow. دندان گير *dandāni gīr*, The biting or fore-tooth. دندان مصري *dandāni misrī*, A kind of sweetmeat. دندان ناب *dandāni nāb*, A canine tooth. دندان نمودن *dandān namūdan*, To shew the teeth. To laugh, be pleased. To ridicule. To terrify. To fear. To cry aloud. دندان نهادن *dandān nihādan*, To covet. دندان نيشتر *dandāni nishtar*, A canine tooth.

A دندان *dindān*, A muttering tone of voice.

P دندان آپريز *dandān-āprīz* (آپريش *āprīsh*, اپريز *aprīz*, اپريش *aprīsh*, آفريز *āfrīz*, or آفريش *āfrīsh*) A tooth-pick.

P دندان پريز *dandān-parīz*, (or دندان پريش *dandān-parīsh*) A tooth-pick.

P دندان تيز *dandān-tez*, Sharp-toothed. Cruel, iniquitous. Envious.

P دندان ريخته *dandān-rekhta*, One who has lost or shed his teeth, toothless, edentated.

P دندان سا *dandān-sā*, Purslain.

P دندان فريز *dandān-farīz*, (or فريش *farīsh*) A tooth-pick.

P دندان كاو *dandān-kāv*, A tooth-pick.

P دندان كنان *dandān-kanān*, Suppressing desire. Restlessness. Ignominy, shame. Lamentation, groan. *Dandān-kunān*, Disgracing, despising. Groaning.

P دندان گير *dandān-gīr*, Stupefying or benumbing the teeth (any thing acid). Biting (horse).

P دندان مال *dandān-māl*, A dentifrice.

P دندان مز *dandān-maz*, Dessert after dinner.

P دندان مزد *dandān-muzd*, Money and other things distributed to the poor at a time of feasting.

P دندان نماي *dandān-namāy*, Shewing the teeth, grinning either in anger or in weak spite.

P دندانه *dandāna*, A tooth. Teeth of a saw or comb. Wards of a lock. A battlement, embrasure. Notched, indented.

P دندانه دار *dandāna-dār*, Teethed, notched.

P دندانيدن *dandānīdan*, To gnaw.

P دندش *dandish*, A muttering to one's self in anger or in joy. Enigmatical discourse. Prayers addressed in a low tone of voice.

A دندك *dunduk*, A he-goat shaking with fat.

A دندم *dindim*, A plant black with age.

A دندن *dandan*, A plant black with age. *Dindin*, The root of the صلّيان *silliyān*.

A دندنة *dandanat*, (v. n. of دندن Q) Moving about to and fro. Muttering unintelligibly. Buzzing (flies). Humming (wasps). A plant black with age. Root of the صلّيان *silliyān*.

P دندنه *dandana*, Muttering to one's self.

P دنده *danda*, A rib.

P دنديدن *dandīdan*, To mutter to one's self in anger. To boil with rage.

A دنس *danas*, (v. n. of دنس) Being dirty, soiled, sullied, tarnished. Dirt, filth. Rust. *Danis*, (pl. ادناس *adnās* and مدانيس *madānīs*) Dirty, filthy, sullied.

A دنع *dana‿*, (v. n. of دنع) Being impatient for food (a child). Hungering. Longing for, coveting. Lowering one's self. Being vile, abject. Baseness, meanness. Offal which the camel-butcher throws away. Vileness. Dregs of the people. *Dani‿*, Foolish, destitute of judgment. Greedy. Vile, worthless. Hungry.

A دنغ *danigh*, (pl. دنغة *danaghat*) Worthless.

A دنف *danaf*, (v. n. of دنف) Approaching. Suffering under severe illness. Being about to set (the sun). Being yellow. Severe and continued illness. *Danaf* or *danif*, (fem. دنفة *danifat*) One suffering under severe and protracted illness.

A دنفاس *dinfās*. See دفناس *difnās*.

A دنفخ *danfakh*, Thick and corpulent.

A دنفس *dinfis*, Foolish (woman).

A دنفشة *danfashat*, A looking on the ground.

A دنفصة *dinfisat*, Name of a certain animalcule. Slender (woman).

A دنق *dank*, Sebestens.

A دنقالة dunkālat, Dongola, capital of Nubia.

A دنقة danḳat or danaḳat, Tares, darnel.

A دنقر danḳar, Nitre, saltpetre.

A دنقرة danḳarat, (v. n. of دنقر Q) Pursuing minute objects. The pace of horses of the worst kind.

A دنقريّ dan or dinkiriy, A dwarf: a sorry nag.

A دنقسة danḳasat, (v. n. of دنقس Q) Stirring up dissensions. Lowering the head, or looking downwards through humility.

A دنقشة danḳashat, (v. n. of دنقش Q) Looking on the ground. Exciting mischief, or dissension.

P دنقه danḳa, Tares. Name of a black grain.

P دنكس dan-kas, Unmanly, worthless, mean.

A دنكسة dankasat, (v. n. of دنكس Q) Keeping close at home, unmindful of the claims of society.

A دنكلة dankalat, The sea-gull, sea-mew.

P دنگ dang, Astonished, confounded. Stupid. Ignorant. Half a (horse) load. The noise made by the collision of two stones. The traces of a pair of compasses. *Ding*, A wooden instrument with iron teeth, used in separating rice from the chaff. A machine for making powder.

P دنگادنگ dang-ā-dang, Equipoised, equal, exact. Knee to knee, intimately connected. Equally.

P دنگاله dangāla, An icicle.

P دنگداله dangdāla or dangadāla, An icicle.

P دنگ کوب ding-kob, Separating rice from the chaff.

P دنگل dangal, Sitting knee to knee. *Dangil*, A cuckold, privy to a wife's infidelity. Foolish. Disproportioned, awkward.

P دنگي dingī, A separater of rice from chaff.

A دنمة dinnamat, Short (woman). A small ant. An atom.

A دنن danan, (v. n. of دنّ) Having a stooping neck, short fore-feet, with curved back (quadruped).

A دنوّ dunūw, (v. n. of دنو) Approaching, drawing near. Propinquity. The lowest degree of baseness.

A دنوءة dunūʼat, (v. n. of دنأ) Being mean, base, abject, wicked. Being careless of censure.

P دنواش dinwāsh, The man who sold عذرا ʻazrā.

A دنوح dunūḥ, The being lowly, humble.

A دنوع dunūʻ, (v. n. of دنع) Being impatient for food (a child). Hungering. Coveting. Lowering one's self. Being vile, abject.

A دنوق danūḳ, A frugal person, one economical in domestic expenditure. *Dunūḳ*, (v. n. of دنق) Giving attention to minute objects; numbering with care, reckoning to a farthing (دانق dānaḳ). Being sunk in the socket (the eye). Being brown and emaciated from fatigue or sickness (the face).

P دنه dana, Cheerfulness. Shouts of joy. Song. Sauciness, petulance, insolence. Pride, presumption. Worldly possessions. Name of a woman. دنه گرفتن dana giriftan, To take fire, to fall in a passion. To be proud, take much state. To presume.

P دنه گرفته dana-girifta, Proud, insolent, ungrateful for divine favours. Exceeding bounds in mirth. A fast runner.

P دني danī, Alacrity, mirth, cheerfulness.

A دنىً duna', (pl. of دنيا dunya') Worlds. Worldly possessions.

A دنيّ daniy, Near, neighbouring. *Daniy*, (or دنيء danīʼ) (pl. ادناء adnāʼ or دناء dunaʼāʼ) Vicious, contemptible, licentious, careless of reputation. Small, mean, trifling, paltry, base. ادنىٰ دنيّ adna' daniyin or danna', The first thing. P چرخ دني پرور charkhi danī-parwar, Fortune, the nurse of villains.

A دنيا dunya', (pl. دنىً duna') The world. Worldly goods (either from their nearness to us, or from their fading nature). People. (fem. of ادنىٰ adna') Nearest. دنيا و دين dunya' u dīn, Country and religion. الدنيا الدنيّة ad'dunya'd daniyat, The worthless world. Worldly goods. الحيوة الدنيا al hayātu'd dunya', The present life. السماء الدنيا as samāʼu'd dunya', or سماء الدنيا samāʼu'd dunya', Lower sky.

A دنيا dinyan or dunyan, In close relationship.

P دنيا پرست dunya'-parast, A Mammonist.

P دنيادار dunya'-dār, Worldly-minded, worldly.

P دنياداري dunya'-dārī, Economy. Mammon.

A دنياويّ dunyawiy, Of the world, worldly.

A دنية dinyatan, Very closely related.

A دنيّة daniyat, Vice, blemish, defect, imperfection. The high cap of a Cāzi (from its resemblance to the wine-jar called دنّ dann).

A دنّيّة danniyat, A high cap worn by judges, from its resemblance to a wine-jar (دنّ dann).

P دنيدن danīdan, To walk with pomposity. To boil with rage. To run with alacrity and joy.

P دنيده danīda, Gone or going with a pompous, jaunty, or cheerful gait.

A دنيع danīʻ, (or دنيعة danīʻat) Foolish, without judgment. Worthless.

A دنيق danīḳ, One who eats privately, lest a guest should surprise him.

A دنيلس danīlas, A kind of shell.

A دنين danīn, (v. n. of دنّ) Muttering. Humming, buzzing (a fly). A word spoken in a low, unintelligible voice. A plant black with age.

A دنيويّ dunyawiy, Worldly, secular. مال دنيوي māli dunyawī, Worldly goods. دنيوي و اخروي dunyawī u ukhrawī, Of this and next world.

P دنيي dunyī, The world.

A دنييّ dunyiy, Worldly.

A دنيئة danīʼat, Vice, blemish, defect.

P دو dav, (from دويدن dawīdan or dawīdan) Running. نيك دو nek-dav, Running well.

P دو du, (in India do) Two.

A دوّ daww, A desert, extended plain.

A دوء daws, (v. n. of دوأ) Being sick, ailing.

A دواء dawāʼ, diwāʼ, or duwāʼ, (pl. ادوية adwiyat) A medicine, remedy. A sweating draught for a horse. A fattening medicine for a woman. Any fattening herb. P دواي زهر dawāʼi zahr, An antidote to poison. A *Diwāʼ*, (v. n. 3 of دوي) Giving medicine. Curing a disease, remedying.

P دوآب do-āb, Name of a province in Hindūstān, lying between the rivers Ganges and Jumna.

A دوابّ dawābb, (pl. of دابّة dābbat) Cattle, beasts. Reptiles, creeping things.

A دوابة duwābat, A pellicle.

A دوابل dawābil, (pl. of دوبل dawbal) Young pigs. Boars. Swine. راعي الدوابل rāʻi'd dawābil, A swineherd.

A دواة dawāt, (pl. دوىً dawa', دويّ duwiy, or diwiy) An ink-stand. Rind of a colocynth or melon: the skin of a grape.

P دوات dawāt, An ink-holder. A pen-case. دوات سياهي dawāti siyāhī, An inkstand.

P دوات آر dawāt-ār, Keeper of the seals.

P دو آتش du ātish, The lips of a mistress.

P دو آتشه du ātisha, Double distilled. شراب دو آتشه sharābi du ātisha, Double-distilled liquor, *i. e.* very strong.

P دواج dawāj, A bed-quilt. A sheet.

A دوّاج dūwāj, A scarf or upper garment. A blanket or coverlet.

A دواجن dawājin, (pl. of داجن) Tame, cade.

A دواحق dawāhiḳ, (pl. of داحق) Yellow dates.

A دواحيل dawāhīl, (pl. of داحول) Onager-traps.

A دواخس dawākhis, The feet of a cauldron (because buried in the ashes).

A دواخل dawākhil, (pl. of داخلة dākhilat) Low (grounds). (pl. of دوخلة dawkhalat) Baskets made of palm-leaves.

A دواخن dawākhin, Chimneys. *Dawākhin* and دواخين dawākhīn, (pl. of دخان dukhān and dukhkhān) Smokes.

A دواد duwād, Small worms. The ring-worm. A swift man.

A دوادم duwādim, Tears of the Egyptian thorn.

P دوادو dav-ā-dav, Running incessantly, or in every direction. A messenger. Any one constantly employed in running of errands.

A دوار dawār or duwār, Giddiness, vertigo, whirl. The temple of Mecca, from the circular inclosure of pillars. Name of an idol. *Diwār*, (v. n. 3 of دور for دار) Going about (with another). Adjusting, setting to rights, administering well. Watching any one to see how he will manage a business.

A دوّار dawwār, Moving in a circle, revolving, rotary. Versatile. P چرخ دوّار charkhi dawwār, The revolving heavens. A *Dawwār* or *dūwar*, The temple of Mecca. Name of an idol.

A دوّارة dawwārat, Any thing round and immoveable. A halo about the moon. Compasses. A spiral lock of hair on the head or mustachios. The roundest part of the head. The groove in the upper lip under the nose. The part of a sheep's belly which holds the intestines. *Dūwārat*, Any thing round and moveable. A circular tumulus of sand.

The roundest part of the head. A sheep's paunch.

A دوارج *dawārij*, The feet (of horses).

A دوارس *dawāris*, (pl. of دارس *dāris*) Effaced (vestiges).

P دواري *dawārī*, A gold coin of five drachms.

A دوّاريّ *dawwāriy*, Rotary. Versatile, variable. Time. Fortune. شكل دوّاري *shakli dawwārī*, A circular figure.

P دوازدگانه *duwāzdagāna*, Twelve.

P دوازده *duwāzdah*, Twelve. دوازده جوسق *duwāzdah jawsak* (or ميل *mīl*), The twelve signs of the Zodiac.

P دوازدهم *duwāzdahum*, The twelfth.

P دوازدهي *duwazdahe*, A dozen.

A دوّاس *dawwās*, A lion. Strong, bold, courageous. Sagacious, subtile.

P دو اسبه *du asba*, A post-boy, messenger. A post-master. A soldier who has two horses found him. Quick, expeditious. Haste, expedition.

A دواسة *duwāsat*, A crowd of men.

A دوّاسة *dawwāsat*, The nose.

A دواسر *duwāsir*, Thick, firm (camel).

P دو اسطرلاب *du usturlāb*, The sun and moon.

P دو آشيانه *du āshyāna*, A kind of tent.

A دواعي *dawāʿī*, Vicissitudes of fortune.

A دواغص *dawāghis*, (pl. of داغصة *dāghisat*) Knee-pans. Pure waters.

A دوافع *dawāfiʿ*, (pl. of دافعة *dāfiʿat*) Expellers, repellents. Low, falling grounds.

A دواقة *dawāḳat*, The being mad or foolish.

P دوال *duwāl*, A stirrup-leather. A skin, hide. An emerald. Fraud, deceit. A glittering sword. دوال شمشير *duwāli shamshīr*, A leathern sword-belt. دوال نعلين *duwāli naʿlayn*, A shoe-latchet, or any thing for fastening shoes. دوال گشادن *duwāl gushādan*, To fly.

A دوالب *dawālib*, Water-wheels.

P دوال باز *duwāl-bāz*, A knave, cheat: a cut-purse.

P دوال پاي *duwāl-pāy*, (Leather-leg) Slender and limber-legged man. Name of a people in India, who, according to Castellus, have legs thin and ductile, like leathern straps: they pretend to be lame, and importune travellers to carry them on their backs; which proves fatal to such whose compassion induces them to comply; as the villains twist their legs round their necks and instantly strangle them. A thug. A bug-bear.

A دوالح *dawāliḥ*, (pl. of دالح) Rainy (clouds).

A دوالخ *dawālikh*, Fat (camels).

P دوالك *duwālak*, A little strap. A leathern strap used in a game at dice. A black Indian slave. A species of moss.

P دوالك بازي *duwālak-bāzī*, Cheating, deceit.

P دواله *duwāla*, A kind of sweet-smelling drug. *Du* or *dawāla*, A leather strap used in a game at dice.

P دوالى *dawālī*, One who uses sleight of hand, a juggler: cheat, deceiver. A kind of fragrant creeper.

A دوالي *dawālī*, A species of blackish grapes. Unripe dates hung up to become fit for eating. A distemper incident to the human foot and leg, originating in varicose veins.

A دواليّ *dawāliy*, A grape grown at Tāyf.

A دواليب *dawālīb*, (pl. of دولاب *dūlāb*) Wheels. Wheels for drawing water.

A دواليك *dawālayk*, Alternately. *Dawālīk*, التحفز في المشي *at' tahaffuz fi'l mashy*.

A دوام *dawām*, (v. n. of دام for دوم) Persisting, persevering in. Continuing, lasting. Perpetuity, duration. على الدوام *ʿala'd dawām*, Continually, assiduously. *Duwām*, Vertigo, giddiness.

A دوامّ *dawāmm*, (pl. of دأماء *daʾmāʾ*) Holes of field-mice.

A دوّامة *duwwāmat*, (pl. دوّام *duwwām*) A boy's top, or whirligig, which he either throws from his hand, or whips on the ground. A whirlpool.

A دوامك *dawāmik*, (pl. of دامكة) Ills, evils.

A دواميس *dawāmīs* (pl. of دودمس *dūdamis*, q.v.).

P دوان *dawān*, Running, walking fast.

P دو اني *do anī*, A coin, the 8th of a gold mohur.

P دوانيدن *dawānīdan*, To cause to run.

A دوانيق *dawānīḳ*, (pl. of دانق *dānik*) Weights of two carats.

A دواوين *dawāwīn*, (pl. of ديوان *dīwān*) Muster-rolls. Public records. Account-books.

A دواهي *dawāhī*, (pl. of داهية) Sore calamities.

A دوايات *dawāyāt*, (pl. of دواة) Ink-stands.

A دواية *duwāyat*, A greenish colour of the teeth. *Duwāyat* or *dirāyat*, The scum of broth or of milk, also a pellicle formed on the surface of the same.

A دوائح *dawāʾiḥ*, (pl. of دائحة *dāʾihat*) Large spreading (trees).

A دوائر *dawāʾir*, (pl. of دائرة *dāʾirat*) Circles.

A دوائس *dawāʾis*, Men trampling on each other. A threshing-floor. Cattle treading out corn. (Horses) following at the heels of one another.

A دوائم *dawāʾim*, (pl. of دائم *dāʾim*) Perpetual, uninterrupted.

A دوائيّ *dawāʾiy*, Medicinal, medical.

A دوب *dawb*, (or دؤوب *duʾub*) (v. n. of دأب) Striving, using diligence. Labouring, becoming fatigued. Travelling hard.

P دو بارو *do bārū*, Name of a game.

P دو باروح *du bārūh*, Nightshade.

P دو باره *do* or *du bāra*, Twice. Double-distilled.

P دو باز *do bāz*, A kind of pigeon. A child's kite.

P دو بازو *do bāzū*, A rustic instrument.

P H دو باشي *du bāshī*, An interpreter.

P دو بال *du bāl*, A strap for fastening on a saddle. Leather. An emerald. Fraud, deceit. A glittering sword.

P دو بالا *du bālā*, Excessive.

P دو بخشه *du bakhsha*, Double.

P دو بد *du bud*, (or دو بود *du būd*) A kind of cloth.

P دو بدو *du ba du*, Two together, without a third.

P دو برا *du burā*, (in zand and Pāz.) A sword.

P دو برابر *du barābar*, Double, equal to two.

P دو برادران *du birādarān*, Two bright stars in the lesser bear. Name of a certain rapacious bird.

P دو برجي *du burjī*, A secret visit of one woman to another.

A دوبل *dawbal*, (pl. دوابل *dawābil*) A small ass. The wild ass of Khatay, small in body. A young pig. A boar. A fox. A wolf, black and white. Name of a poet.

P دوبل *dūbal*, Insincere, unfaithful.

P دو بند *du band*, A double embankment.

P دو بيتي *du baytī*, A poem consisting of four hemistichs, a tetrastich. دو بيتي خواندن *du baytī khwāndan*, To read.

P دو پا *du pā*, A small worm found chiefly in oak-trees (quercus coccifera or kermes oak), and which imparts to cloth a beautiful red colour.

P دو پادشاه قهّار *du pādshāhi kahhār*, (Two mighty kings) Night and day.

P دو پاره *do pāra*, Halved.

P دو پايه *do pāya*, Two-legged, biped. Man.

H دو پتّه *do patta*, (Two breadths) A sheet of cloth thrown loosely over the shoulders.

P دو پخچه *do pakhcha*, A clew of thread. Name of a bird.

P دو پروانه *du parwāna*, Night and day.

P دو پلكا *do palkā*, (Having two eyelids) A kind of pigeon. A kind of stone for a ring.

P دو پوده *du pūda*, Cloth, woven in streaks or stripes of two colours.

P دو پوست *du post*, Two (leaves) pasted.

P دو پيازه *du* or *do piyāza*, A rich fricassee made with butter, turmeric, onions, garlic, and various spices; a dish without gravy.

P دو پيكر *du paykar*, Gemini. A two-edged axe.

P دو تا *du tā*, Double, doubled. Bent, curved. Bending the body. Fine cloth. دو تا شدن *du tā shudan*, To be bent or doubled. دو تا كعبتين *du tā kaʿbatayn*, Night and day.

P دو تا شدگي *du tā shudagī*, An overlapping or folding over.

P دو تا شده *du tā shuda*, Overlapped. Folded.

P دو تاه *du tāh*, Double, doubled. دوتاه كردن *du tāh kardan*, To fold, to double.

P دو تاي *du tāy*, A two-stringed harp.

P دو تن *du tan*, Two persons. Double.

P دو تو *du taw* (or ته *tah*), Double. A meeting.

P دو تهي *do tahī*, (Two-plied) Cloths lined.

A دوثة *dawsat*, Flight from battle.

A دوثيّ *dusiy*, A cuckold.

A دوج *dawj*, A serving, a waiting upon.

P دوج *dūj*, Name of an herb.

P دو جا *du jā*, (Two places) Squint-eyed.

P دوجان *dojān*, The jugular vein.

P دو جنيبت *du janībat*, Night and day.

P دو جهان *du jahān*, This world and the next.

P دو چار *du chār*, Twice four. A sudden and unexpected meeting, encounter, or interview. دو چارزدن *du chār zadan*, To meet. To converse. To dispute, to fight. دو چار کردن *du chār kardan*, To meet one another on the road.

P دو چشم چار شدن *du chashm chār shudan*, The sudden, unexpected encounter of two persons.

P دو چشمه *du chashma*, The sun and moon. Night and day. The pupils of the eyes.

P دو چله *du challa*, A roof sloping two ways.

P دو چند *do* (or *du*) *chand*, Twice, double.

P دو چندان *du chandān*, Twice as much.

P دو چوبه *do* (or *du*) *choba*, Two-poled (tent).

P دو چهار *du chahār*, A sudden, unexpected meeting or interview.

A دوح *dawh*, (v. n. of داح for دوح) Swagging (the belly). Being large (a tree). (pl. of دوحة *dawhat*) Large trees.

A دوحة *dawhat*, (pl. دوح *dawh*) A large tree. The trunk of a tree. A grove, nursery, orchard.

P دو حجرهٔ خواب *du hujrasi khwāb*, Two eyes.

P دو حرف *du harf*, Two letters, *i.e.* ك *kāf* and ن *nūn*, signifying كن *kun*, Be thou.

P دو حورلقا *du hūri likā*, Reason and soul.

A دوخ *dawkh*, (v. n. of داخ for دوخ) Being base and abject. Subduing, subjugating.

P دوخ *dūkh*, Bald. A barren place. A head bald in front. Leafless branch. A smooth face. A rocket. A reed, from which mats are woven, and on which grapes and melons are hung to dry.

P دو خاتون *du khātūn*, (or دو خاتون بينش *du khātūni binish*) Pupils of the eyes. Sun and moon.

P دو خادم حبشی و رومی *du khādimi habashī u rūmī*, Night and day.

A دوخة *dawkhat*, Sickness, indisposition.

P دوخت *dokht*, A virgin. Power. Sewing, stitch. دوخت کردن *dokht kardan*, To hate, despise, loathe.

P دوخترة *dokhtara*, A daughter. A virgin.

P دوختن *dokhtan*, To sew. To pay, perform. To gain, acquire, collect. To fix, fasten. To milk. To plaster.

P دوخته *dokhta*, Stitched, sewed, closed. Milked. Payed, performed. Gained. Plastered.

P دوخ چکاد *dūkh chakād*, A head bald in front. Bald-headed.

A دوخلة *dawkhalat*, (or دوخلّة *dawkhallat*) A basket made of palm-leaves.

P دو خمّه *do khamma*, A bent hookah-pipe.

P دو خواهر *du khwāhar*, Name of two stars.

P دو خيط ملوّن *du khayti mulawwan*, The twilight or false dawn, and break of day.

A دود *dawd*, (v. n. of داد for دود) Breeding worms (bread or meat). *Dūd*, (pl. ديدان *dīdān*) A worm. دود الحرير *dūdu'l harīr*, (or دود القز *dūdu'l kazz*) A silk-worm. دود القرمز *dūdu'l kirmiz*, Kermes, or coccus ilicis, an insect full of red-dish juice, which is used in dyeing red: hence, crimson. Cochineal.

P دود *dūd*, Smoke. Vapour. Breath. Anguish, sadness. دود دل *dūdi dil*, (or دود دم *dūdi dam*) A sigh. دود آه *dūdi āh*, The exhalation of a sigh. دود بر آوردن *dūd bar āwardan*, To eradicate. دود کردن *dūd kardan*, To emit smoke. To fumigate. پر دود *pur dūd*, Full of smoke.

A دوداة *dawdāat*, (or دوداة *dawdāt*) The murmuring noise of a number of men and cattle. A swing.

A دوداة *dawdāt*, Motion of a swing.

P دودافكن *dūd-afkan*, A kind of magician.

P دود آلود *dūd-ālūd*, Smoked, perfumed. Name of a town and river in India.

P دوداله *dūdāla*, The game of tipcat.

P دو دامي *do dāmī*, Flowered muslin, the flowers worked with a needle.

P دود آهنج *dūd-āhanj*, (or آهنگ *āhang*) Chimney of a kitchen or bath. An earthen pot placed over a lamp to gather smoke for making lamp-black.

A دودة *dūdat*, One worm.

A دودح *dawdah*, Short-bodied.

A دودحة *dawdahat*, Fatness.

P دود خانه *dūd-khāna*, House, family, race.

P دود خوار *dūd-khwār*, (Smoke-eater) A moth flying round the candle. A chimney. A smoker of tobacco.

P دودر *dūdar*, Coat-buttons (or the shanks). Buckle of a belt. Twisted (chain, rope, or loop).

A دودري *dawdara'*, A short-bodied girl.

P دو دري *du darī*, The world.

A دوّري *dawdarra'*, One who goes or comes without occasion.

P دو دستي *du dastī*, Of two hands' length. A hard-fought battle. A blow on the back with both hands in order to hasten any one. A sort of ewer.

P دود كش *dūd-kash*, A vent for smoke, chimney.

P دود گرفتگي *dūd-giriftagī*, Smokiness.

P دود گرفته *dūd-girifta*, Smoked, smoky.

P دود گند *dūd-gand*, Exhaling fragrance.

P دود گنده *dūd-ganda*, Smelling of smoke.

P دود گين *dūd-gīn*, (Filled with smoke) The tunnel of a chimney. Smoky.

P دو دل *du dil*, (Two-hearted) Uncertain, irresolute, wavering. A hypocrite.

P دودله *dūdala*, also *dūdila*, The game of tipcat. *Du dila*, Wavering, doubtful, in suspense, uncertain, irresolute. Absent in mind. One who is constantly changing his creed.

P دودله شدگي *du dila shudagī*, Double-heartedness, irresolution, uncertainty.

A دودم *duwadim*, The tears or red gum of the Egyptian thorn سمرة *samurat*.

P دودمان *dūdmān*, A great tribe, family, illustrious house. Generation, race. Fragrance. Name of a place near Shīrāz.

A دودمس *dūdamis*, (pl. دودمسات *dūdamisāt* and دواميس *dawāmīs*) A kind of serpent with an inflated neck which burns whatever it breathes upon.

A دودن *duwadin*, Dragon's blood.

P دو دو *du du*, Two and two. Sound of a pipe.

A دؤدؤ *dusdus*, (pl. دآدئ *dasādis*) The latter end of a month. The night of the 25th, 26th, 27th, 28th, or 29th of the month: last nights of the moon.

P دوده *dawda*, A circle. *Dūda*, Round cottages. A tribe, family. People. A chimney. An eldest son. Soot, lamp-black, with which they make ink.

P دود هنج *dūd-hanj*, (or دودهنگ *dūd-hang*) A chimney. A pot for collecting smoke.

P دور *dawr*, Time, age. A revolution, period of years. The world, fortune. The repetition of a lesson. A cup handed round by the guests. Intelligence which spies transmit to the court of their sovereign. دور چرخ *dawri charkh*, (or دور گردون *dawri gardūn*) Motions of the heavens. A دور زمان *dawri zamān*, Revolution of ages. دور قمري *dawri kamarī*, The lunar cycle (at the commencement of which Adam was created). دور الكرة *dawru'l kurat*, A spherical motion. P دور كردن *dawr kardan*, To encircle, surround. To turn about, revolve. To muffle or wrap round. دور گوشمال *dawri gosh-māl*, Times of sedition or oppression. Days of calamity, distress, or poverty. A دور مدام *dawri mudām*, Perpetual motion. دور مجري *dawri mijjarī*, The moon's orbit. ربح دور شرعي *ribhi dawri sharsī*, Legal usury. جور دور *jawri dawr*, Injuries of fortune. P *Dūr*, Remote, distant. Absent. Far off. دور از كار *dūr az kār*, Far from the purpose: in opposition to, contrary to the inclination. دور از ما *dūr az mā*, Far from us. دورادور مدّعا *dūr-ā-dūr muddasa'*, A tedious, diffusive discourse. دور شدن *dūr shudan*, To be distant, absent. دور كردن *dūr kardan*, To remove, avert, send away, banish. دور و دراز *dūr u darāz*, Far and long. Prolixly, at full length. دور و نزديك *dūr u nazdīk*, Far and near. از دور *az dūr*, From afar.

A دور *dawr*, (v. n. of دار for دور) Going round, moving in a circle, being turned about. A species of argument, reasoning in a circle. Circle, circuit, circumference. A turn. *Dūr*, (pl. of دارة *dārat*) Houses. Arabian tribes. *Dawra*, About, around.

A دورات *dūrāt*, (pl. of دار) Houses, mansions.

P دورادور *dūrādūr*, Very distant.

P دور آسران *dūr-āsarān*, Name of a king of the magicians.

P دوراغ *dūrāgh*, Sour milk, upon which new milk is poured.

P دوران *dawrān*, A revolution, period, circle, cycle. Time, an age. Fortune, vicissitude. Rolling round. دوران سر *dawrāni sar*, A swimming in the head. دوران خداي *dawrān-khudāy*, A whoremonger. *Dūrān*, A pipe.

A دوران *dūrān*, (pl. of دار *dār*) Houses, habitations. *Dawarān*, (v. n. of دار for دور) Moving round, revolving. Vertigo.

P دور انداختني *dūr andākhtanī*, Fit only to be thrown away, refuse.

P دور اندر *dūr-andar*, Deep (goblet or well).

P دور انديش *dūr-andesh*, Far-sighted, penetrating. Anticipative.

P دور انديشه *dūr-andesha*, Foresight.

P دور انديشي *dūr-andeshī*, Far-sightedness. Anticipation.

P دوران سرون *dūrān sarūn*, Name of a king of the magicians.

P دوراني *dawrānī*, Temporal, secular.

P دوراي *dūrāy*, A flute, a psaltery.

P دور باد *dūr bād*, God forbid! Far be it!

P دور باش *dūr bāsh*, A staff, a walking-stick. A club, mace, bludgeon, pole, or baton, with which they keep the mob from pressing too close in public solemnities. A battle-axe (usually fixed to the saddle). The commander of a caravan. A sigh. Have a care! stand back! give way! keep off, at a distance!

P دور بر آمدن *dūr bar āmadan*, To be wretched.

P دوربل *dūrbal*, Faithless, insincere, untrue.

P دوربين *dūr-bīn*, One who sees at a distance; far-sighted. A telescope. Provident, penetrating, perspicuous, ingenious, intelligent, judicious. عقل دوربين *ʻakli dūr-bīn*, A solid judgment.

P دوربيني *dūr-bīnī*, Far-sightedness.

P دورپار *dūr-pār*, God forbid! (female phrase).

A دورة *dawrat*, An epicycle. A revolution.

P دورتر *dūrtar*, More remote, furthest.

P دورخولي *dūr-khūlī*, A wild kind of lily.

P دو رخي *du rukhī*, A kind of bow.

P دور دراز *dūr darāz*, Far, distant.

P دوردست *dūr-dast*, Distant, out of reach.

P دوردستي *dūr-dastī*, Remoteness, out of reach.

A دور دور *dawr dawr*, Prosperity.

P دورس *dūras*, Hellebore.

P دورفرو *dūr-firo*, (or دورفرود) Deep. Very low.

A دورق *dawrah*, A water-pot with handles. A kind of wine-measure.

P دوركرده *dūr-karda*, Removed, taken away.

P دورگيران *dawr-gīrān*, Kings. Wine-drinkers.

A دورم *dawram*, A youth, short and bad walker.

P دورنج *dawranj*, Name of a medicinal herb.

P دورنگ *dawrang*, A sort of medicinal plant. *Du rang*, Of two colours, piebald, bi-coloured. Double-faced, hypocrite, deceitful man. The world.

P دور نگاه *dūr-nigāh*, Long-sighted, seeing far.

P دورنگي *du rangī*, The property of possessing two colours. Of two colours. Capriciousness. Hypocrisy. Capricious.

P دو رو *du rū*, Two-faced, *i.e.* a deceitful villain, hypocrite. Inconstant. A kind of rose, red without and white within. Name of a small brass coin.

P دو روزۀ عمر *du rozaʼi ʻumr*, A short life.

P دوروزي *dūrūzī*, Health, soundness of body.

P دورونه *dorūna*, A bow for cotton. The rainbow.

P دو رويه *do* (or *du*) *rūya*, Double, two-faced.

P دوروني *du rūʼī*, Hypocrisy, double-facedness.

P دورة *dawra*, A curling lock. A wine-measure. *Dūra*, A small measure, such as a vial or flask.

P دوري *dūrī*, Distance: absence, separation. A hypocrite. دوري نمودن *dūrī namūdan*, To shew aversion, to be distant and shy.

A دوريّ *dūriy*, Any one, somebody.

P دوريسه *dūrīsa*, A handkerchief (of muslin) with a downy pile, fringed at the borders. A fringed carpet or counterpane.

P دوريشه *dūrīsha*, The same: linen cloth.

P دوز *doz*, Stork's dung. (in comp.) Sewing. پينه دوز *pīna-doz*, A botcher. زردوز *zar-doz*, An embroiderer in gold.

P دوزاي *dūzāy*, (or دوژاي) A pipe, flute.

P دو زبان *du zabān*, Double-tongued. A pen. A hypocrite.

P دو زباني *du zabānī*, Double-tonguedness.

P دوزخ *dozakh*, Hell. Evil company. Jealousy. Trouble, affliction. The belly. اهل دوزخ *ahli dozakh*, The inhabitants of hell, the damned. كفّار دوزخ قرار *kuffāri dozakh-karār*, The infidels devoted to hell, infernal firebrands.

P دوزخ بان *dozakhbān*, Keeper of the infernal pit.

P دوزخي *dozakhī*, Infernal. A glutton.

P دوزك *dawzak*, Any thing large and light.

P دوزندگي *dozandagī*, Needlework.

P دو زنگي و رومي *du zangī u rūmī*, Night and day. Youth and old age.

P دوزنه *dozana*, (or دوژنه) Sting of an insect.

P دوزه *doza*, A kind of prickly plant. Gum lac, a kind of wax for fastening handles on knives.

P دوزيدن *dozīdan*, (equivalent to دوختن *dokhtan*, but rarely used) To sew, stitch. To be used to.

P دو زيره *du zīra*, A kind of rice.

P دوزينه *dozīna*, Bee's sting, gnat's trunk.

P دوژ *doj*, Filth. Tincture of lac. Stork's dung. A proboscis.

P دوژنه *dojana*, A bee. A gnat. A sting.

P دوژه *dūja*, A kind of thorn. A knot in wood.

P دوژينه *dojīna*, The sting of an insect.

A دوس *daws*, (v. n. of داس for دوس) Beating with the feet (the ground), trampling clay. Treading out (corn). Thrashing, drubbing. Indulging much in venery. Polishing (a sword). Baseness, meanness. *Dūs*, Furbishers, polishers.

P دوس *daws* or *dawas*, Water for strengthening the stomach, in which red-hot iron has been cooled. *Dūs*, Plaster.

P دوسانيدن *dosānīdan*, To fasten, glue, cement.

A دوسة *dawsat*, A thrashing.

P دوست *dost*, A friend. A lover. A mistress, sweetheart. (for دو است *du ast*) Are two. دوست داشتن *dost dāshtan*, To like, love, be fond of, esteem as a friend.

P دوستار *dostār*, A friend. A lover. Lovingly.

P دوستانه *dostāna*, Friendly, affectionately.

P دوستاني *dostānī*, Friendly, affectionate.

P دوست بين *dost-bīn*, The twenty-second day of the month, of the æra of Jalālu'd dīn.

P دوست دار *dost-dār*, A friend: lover. Lovingly.

P دوست داري *dost-dārī*, Friendship. Love.

P دوستر *dostar*, Dearer, preferable.

P دوستكام *dost-kām*, A lover, friend. A sweetheart. A cup of wine which a lover drinks to his mistress's health. Any business which succeeds to the wishes of one's friends.

P دوستكامي *dostkāmī*, Prosperity (friend's wish).

P دوستكان *dost-kān*, Loved: a lover. A goblet.

P دوستكاني *dost-kānī*, Wine drank at an entertainment, or with a mistress or friend; a large draught, full bumper drank to the health of a lady or friend. A cup, glass, or wine-vessel.

P دوستگان *dostgān*, Beloved. A mistress.

P دوستگانه *dostgāna*, A toast to a mistress.

P دوستگين *dost-gīn*, Clammy, ropish substance.

P دوستنبه *dostamba*, Folded (flower). Manifold.

P دوستي *dostī*, Friendship. Love, affection. دوستي داشتن *dostī dāshtan*, (or كردن *kardan*) To contract or cultivate friendship.

A دوسر *dawsar*, A strong lion. A huge camel. A thick, stout horse. Penis crassus. Any thing ancient. Tares, darnel. A sort of plant whose grain is called ماش *māsh*. Name of a legion which belonged to نعمان بن المنذر *nuʻmān bini'l munzir*.

P دوسر *dūsar*, Oats. Tares. Two heads. دوسر دهليز *du sari dihlīz*, The four elements. The five senses. دوسر قنديل *du sari kindīl*, The seven planets. Any glittering star. The firmament.

P دوسراني *dawsarānī*, Large, thick.

A دوسرانيّ *dawsarāniy*, Thick, strong, hard.

A دوسرة *dawsarat*, Any thing chewed. A large, swift she-camel. The root of the two jaws.

A دوسريّ *dawsariy*, Thick, strong, hard.

A دوسك *dawsak*, A lion.

P دوسگر *dosgar*, (or دوشگر) A plasterer.

P دوسنبه *du samba*, Folded together: doubled.

P دوسند *dosand*, Adhesion. Curvature.

P دوسنده *dosanda* or *dosinda*, Sticking, adhesive. Curved, bent. Mixed, pounded. Adhesive mud.

P دوسنگ *du sang*, Two stones; namely, the mountains Safā and Marwat, near Mecca.

P دوسوي *du suwī*, Parting of braided hair.

P دو سه *du sih*, Two or three. دو سه قنديل *du sih kindīl*, (Two or three candles) The stars. دو سه ويران ده *du sih wayrān dih*, The seven climes.

P دوسيدگي *dosīdagī*, A cleaving, sticking.

P دوسيدن *dosīdan*, To plaster, incrust, bedaub. To glue, cement, stick together. To adhere, cleave close to. To collapse. To arrive. To incline, bend. To be benumbed in the limbs. To shake up and down, or backwards and forwards. To move forward. To apprehend.

P دوش *dosh,* The shoulder. Last night. A dream. A kind of lac with which they fasten knife-handles; solder for metals. Foolish, stupid. Right over against. (imperative of دوشيدن *doshīdan,* (or دوختن *dokhtan*) To milk). دوش بر زدن *dosh bar zadan,* To shrug the shoulders for joy. دوش كردن *dosh kardan,* To dream. To occur, meet, fall plump upon. *Davish,* A running.

A دوش *dawash,* (v. n. of دوش) Being clouded, sunk, squint, or injured by disease (the eye). Dim-sightedness.

P دوشا *doshā,* Milch. Spunged upon.

A دوشاء *dawshāɛ,* (fem. of ادوش *adwash*) Dim-sighted, squinting, or hurt in the eye from disease.

P دوشاب *dosh-āb,* Syrup of grapes or dates. Any thing upon which milk is poured. Milch.

P دوشابگر *doshābgar,* A maker of syrups.

P دو شاخ *du shākh,* The pillory. A gold-wrought girdle.

P دو شاخه *du shākha,* Bifurcated. The pillory.

P دوشانيدن *doshānīdan,* To milk. To cause to milk.

P دو شاهين *du shāhīn,* The handle of a pair of scales. The constellations of the Eagle and Lyre.

P دو شده بند *du shuda-band,* An imperial historiographer.

A دوشق *dawshak,* A house neither large nor small. Large (house). Big (camel).

P دوشك *dūshak,* A kid. A cat. A carpet. Bedding. A quilt.

P دوشكن *dosh-kan,* A short garment hanging from the shoulders.

A دوشلة *dawshalat,* Glans penis.

P دوشمال *dosh-māl,* A towel used by butchers.

P دو شنبه *du shambih,* Monday.

P دوشنده *doshanda,* A milker.

P دوشنه *doshana,* A milk-pail.

P دوشوار *dūshwār,* (for دشوار) Difficult.

P دوشوان *doshwān,* A breast-plate, stomacher.

P دوشه *dosha,* A milking-pan or pail.

A دوشية *dawshiyat,* Name of a sect.

P دوشيدن *doshīdan,* To milk. To take.

P دوشيدني *doshīdanī,* Fit to be milked, milch.

P دوشيده *doshīda,* Milked. Any milkable animal: milch. A woman with large breasts. Twins.

P دوشيزگي *doshīzagī,* Virginity, maidenhead. دوشيزگي بردن *doshīzagī burdan,* To deflower.

P دوشيزه *doshīza,* A virgin. دوشيزگان جنّت *doshīzagāni jannat,* Virgins of paradise.

P دوشينه *doshīna,* Last night's. A shoulder-load.

P دوشينه شب *doshīna-shab,* Yesternight.

A دوص *daws,* Water thick and black in which a blacksmith has cooled his heated iron; and which is said to be strengthening to the stomach.

P دو صحن *du sahn,* (Two dishes) Earth and sky.

P دو صد *du sad,* Two hundred.

A دوصر *dawsar,* A kind of herb, tares.

P دو طرفي *du tarfī,* Mutual; on both sides.

P دو طفل پسنديده *du tifli pasandīda,* (نور *nūr,* or هندو *hindū*) The pupils of the eyes.

P دو طوطي *du tūtī,* (Two parrots) The lips of a mistress.

A دوطيرة *dawtīrat,* A rudder, a helm.

A دوع *dawɛ,* (v. n. of داع for دوع) Running, tripping, going with haste. *Dūɛ,* (pl. دوع *duwaɛ*) A small red fish.

P دو علوي *du ɛulwī,* Saturn and Jupiter.

A دوغ *dawgh,* (v. n. of داغ for دوغ) Being general, prevailing (sickness). Damaging, destroying (as cold). Being cheap (food). Reposing.

P دوغ *dogh,* Churned sour milk, whey, butter-milk. A reed. Name of a medicine. دوغ زدن *dogh zadan,* To churn.

P دوغ آبا *dogh-ābā,* Food prepared with milk.

P دوغبا *dogh-bā,* Butter-milk dried.

A دوغة *dawghat,* An epidemy. Cold. Folly.

P دوغو *doghū,* Sediment of butter or oil.

P دوغوا *dogh-wā,* Meat dressed with sour milk.

P دوغه *dogha,* (or دوغينه) A strainer for purifying oil or butter. Dregs of oil or melted butter.

A دوف *dawf,* (v. n. of داف for دوف) Moistening. Mixing. Braying musk.

A دوفان *dūfān,* The nightmare.

A دوفص *dawfas,* An onion.

A دوق *dawk* or *dūk,* (v. n. of داق for دوق) Being insane, mad. Being emaciated (cattle). Being satiated and leaving the mother (a colt). Nauseating the food (cattle). Tasting.

A دوقانيّة *dawkāniyat,* (or دوقة *dawkat*) Corruption, spoil, damage. Madness, folly.

A دوقة *dawkat,* The being mad or foolish.

A دوقرة *dawkarat,* Low-lying grounds between mountains destitute of vegetation.

P دو قرص گرم و سرد *du kursi garm u sard,* The sun and moon.

A دوقعة *dawkaɛat,* An abject condition. Poverty. Hunger.

A دوقل *dawkal,* Penis. A ship's mast.

A دوقلة *dawkalat,* (v. n. of دوقل Q) Taking and eating food. Lying with. Dangling and striking the back of the thighs (testes). Thick (glans).

P دوقو *dūkū,* (or دوقوس) Seed of wild carrot.

A دوك *dawk,* (v. n. of داك for دوك) Pounding small (colours). Falling into confusion and perplexity. Falling sick. Plunging into water. Burying in sand. Lying with.

P دوك *dūk,* A woman's spindle.

P دو كارد *du kārd,* Scissors, shears. Smoked. A blow upon the chest. دو كارد فريز *du kārdi firez,* A pair of shears.

P دوكاك *du kāk,* The pupils of the eyes.

P دوكان *dūkān,* A shop. دوكان چيدن *dūkān chīdan,* To shut up shop. دوكان مي فروش *dukāni may-farosh,* A wine-tavern, vintner's shop.

P دوكان داري *dūkān-dārī,* Shop-keeping. Flattery.

P دوكاني *dūkānī,* Shop-keeping: a shop-keeper.

A دوكة *dawkat* or *dūkat,* A brawl, quarrel, mob. Evil. An Indian palm-tree.

P دوك تراش *dūk-tarāsh,* A spindle-maker.

P دوكجي *dūkjī,* A ball of thread.

P دوكچه *dūkcha,* The woof, or the thing round which it is wound. A spindle.

P دوكدان *dūkdān,* A spindle-case.

P دوكريس *dūk-rīs,* Sewing with cotton thread.

P دوكريسه *dūk-rīsa,* A whirl put upon a spindle, to give it a circular motion.

A دوكس *dawkas,* A lion. Many flocks. Entangled, intricate, folded together. لمعة دوكس *lumaɛat dawkas,* Part of a plant withered or curled up.

P دوكسي *du kasī,* Two persons; fit for two.

P دو كعبتين *du kaɛbatayn,* The sun and moon.

P دو كله دار *du kulah-dār,* The sun and moon. Day and night. Two powerful kings.

P دو كونه *du kūna,* The two hips.

P دو كوهانه *du kohāna,* Double-humped (camel)

P دوگان *dugān,* In twos, two and two. Double.

P دو گانه *du gāna,* Two, double, a pair, twins. Binary. Of two sorts. Two genuflexions in prayers. دوگانه زادن *dugāna zādan,* To bring forth twins.

P دوگانه زاينده *dugāna zāyanda,* Twin-bearing (female).

P دو گاو پير *du gāvi pīr,* The sign Taurus and an ox. Night and day.

P دو گاو پيشه *du gāv-pesha,* Day and night.

P دو گاهواره *du gāhwāra,* Heaven and earth.

P دو گوشمال *du gosh-māl,* Troublous times. A serious disaster.

P دو گوشي *du goshī,* A turban with two ends hanging down. A two-handed ewer.

P دو گونه *du gūna,* Both cheeks.

P دوگوهر *du gawhar,* Spirit and understanding.

A دول *dawl,* (v. n. of دال for دول) Changing (as fortune). Revolving. Being worn out (a garment). Becoming public, notorious (any thing). Swagging, hanging loose (the belly). Fortune, vicissitude. State, condition. A pitcher, pail, bucket. *Dawal,* An arrow shot backward and forward. Ancestral glory. *Du, di,* or *dawal,* (pl. of دولة *daw* and *dūlat*) Periods. Successes. Riches.

P دول *dol,* A bucket, milk-pail, pitcher. The hopper of a mill. The sign Aquarius. A deceitful, shameless person. Base, ignoble. The mast of a ship. A purse. *Duwal,* The bark of the olive-tree.

P دولا *dolā,* A pitcher, ewer: a water-bucket.

A دولاب *dawlāb* or *dūlāb,* (pl. دواليب *dawālīb*) A water-wheel.

P دولاب *dol-āb,* A wheel, especially for raising water to overflow fields. A machine in the walls of monasteries, hospitals, or lazarettos, into which people on the outside put victuals or other necessaries, (also children,) and then, turning it upon its axis, leave them to be carried off by those within. A storehouse, pantry, buttery, locker. A labyrinth. Trick, fraud, machination. A drum. A ditch. Profit. Commerce. Hard usage. دولاب مينا *dolābi mīnā*, The sky.

P دولابه *dolāba*, A water-wheel. A pantry.

A دولات *dūlāt*, (pl. of دولة) Vicissitudes, changes.

P دولانه *dūlāna*, A fruit like a red apple.

P دو لاي *du lāy*, Double, two-fold.

P دولبند *dol-band*, A turban, or the sash.

P دولبند و بست *dawl-band u bast*, The rent-roll of a district, drawn out at the beginning of a year, shewing the sum expected to be realized.

A دولة *dawlat*, (v. n. of دال for دول) Going round each other in battle. Being, loose, relaxed (the belly). Victory, conquest. Fortune, prosperity. Happiness, felicity, wealth. Empire, monarchy, dominion, power. Reign. Dynasty. The accomplishment of one's wishes, as respects the present and the next world. Happy stroke of fortune. Freedom from a wife or debt. Revolution of time. A bird's crop. A thing resembling a bag or purse with a narrow mouth. A substance resembling lights that comes forth from the mouth of a stallion camel in heat. The side of the belly. P دولت تيز *dawlati tez*, Speedy good-fortune. A دولت دنيا *dawlati dunya'*, Worldly felicity. دولت عثمانيّه *dawlati ʿusmānīya*, The Ottoman empire. دولت عظمىٰ *dawlati ʿuzma'*, The mighty empire. دولت عاليّه *dawlati ʿaliya*, The high imperial house (of Timūr). صاحب دولت *sāhib-dawlat*, Possessed of, or enjoying happiness (a title equivalent to My Lord or Sir). *Dūlat*, (pl. دول *duwal*, *dawal*, *diwal*, دولات *duwalāt* or *dūlāt*) Change of time, fortune, or happiness. Riches. Felicity in the next life. A circuit. *Duwalat*, Misfortune, adversity.

P دولت بر انداز *dawlat bar andāz*, Government-subverting, revolutionary.

P دولت پناه *dawlat-panāh*, Asylum of empire.

P دولتخانه *dawlat-khāna*, A palace. A house. Your house. دولتخانۀ خاص *dawlat-khānaʾi khās*, The king's palace.

P دولت خدا *dawlat-khudā*, Wealthy, powerful.

P دولت خدائی *dawlat-khudāʾī* or *dawlati khudāʾī*, Riches, prosperity, happiness. One whose bounty is overflowing.

P دولت خواه *dawlat-khwāh*, Well-wisher: I, me.

P دولت خواهي *dawlat-khwāhī*, Good-will.

P دولت سرا *dawlat-sarā*, A palace; your house.

P دولتمدار *dawlat-madār*, Abode of felicity.

P دولتمند *dawlatmand*, Rich, fortunate, happy. A rich man. Cause, occasion, effect.

P دولتي *dawlatī*, Rich, fortunate, prosperous, happy. Prosperity.

P دولت ياب *dawlat-yāb*, Prosperous, fortunate.

A دولج *dawlaj*, A subterraneous dwelling. A wild beast's den.

P دولچه *dolcha*, A leathern bucket.

P دولخجه *dūlakhja*, A ball of thread. Name of a bird.

A دولسيّ *dawlasiy*, Subservient, subsidiary.

A دولع *dawlīʿ*, An open, level road.

A دولعة *dawlaʿat*, A kind of marine shell which, on being brought near the fire, sends forth a substance resembling a finger-nail.

P دولميان *dol-miyān*, A purse. A letter-bag.

P دو لو *du lū*, Doubled, folded, lined.

A دؤلوك *duʾlūk*, (pl. دآليك *daʾālīk*) An important, serious business.

A دؤلول *duʾlūl*, (pl. دآليل) Calamity. Confusion.

P دوله *dawla*, A whirlwind, hurricane. A cup. A circle. A ringlet. *Dūla*, A circle. An ascent, steep. Fraud, trick. A sigh, groan, howl. The belly. A stupid, conceited fellow. A whirlwind. A lizard. Earth, dust. *Dawala*, A goblet.

A دولىٰ *dūla'*, A misfortune.

P دولي *dawalī*, Fraud, deceit.

A دوم *dawm*, (v. n. of دام for دوم) Continuing, lasting. Being still and stagnant. Reposing. Being filled (a bucket). Perennial. Perpetuity. Quiescent (shadow). A dwarf palm-tree; the lote, any large thick tree.

P دوم *duwum*, Second. The ring-finger. Inferior.

P دوّم *duwwum*, The second.

A دوماء *dawmāʾ* or دومان *dawamān*, The circular career of a bird.

A دوماً دوماً *dawman dawman*, Incessantly raining.

A دومة *dawmat*, A drunken woman. A testicle. Name of a certain woman who sold wine. دومة الجندل *dū* or *dawmatu'l jandal*, Name of a fort.

P دو مرجان *du marjān*, The lips of a mistress.

A دو مرّيخ ذرب فعل *du mirrīkhi zarb-fiʿl*, (or دو مرّيخ زحل سيما *du mirrīkhi zuhal-sīmā*) Two rings of a chain.

A دومص *dawmas*, An iron helmet.

P دو مغز *du maghz*, (Two kernel) An almond.

A دوملة *dawmalat*, A making peace, reconciling.

P دو منزل *du manzil*, This world and the next.

P دو موي *du mūy*, A man half gray-headed.

P دو مويه *du mūya*, Beginning to grow gray.

P دومي *duwumī*, The second.

P دو ميخ *du mekh*, The two poles.

P دومين *duwumīn*, The second.

P دو ميناي طرب *du mīnāʾi tarab*, A cup of wine.

A دون *dawn*, (v. n. of دان for دون) Being low, vile, contemptible, or weak. *Dūn*, Base, mean, inferior, ignoble, despicable. Little, few, small. Noble, excellent. A mandate. A threat. دهر دون *dahri dūn*, The vile world. *Dūna*, (or من دون *min dūna*) Below, under, on this side, short of, inferior to, less than, exclusively of. Near, nearer. Above. Beside. Before. Behind, after.

P دو نان گرم و سرد *du nāni garm u sard*, (دو نان رنگين *du nāni rangīn* or دو نان فلك *du nāni falak*) The two loaves, hot and cold, two coloured loaves, or two loaves of the sky, *i.e.* the sun and moon.

P دوندگي *dawindagī*, A running, a racing.

P دونده *dawanda*, Running; a racer.

A دونك *dūnak*, Take (it). دونكه *dūnakahu*, Take it, seize it.

P دونگي *dūngī*, A pinnace, smack, dingy.

P دون نواز *dūn-nawāz*, A patron of the base.

P دونه *dūna*, A decoy bird by a net. A basket of leaves. دونه تركي *dūna tarkī*, A kind of aniseed.

P دون همّت *dūn-himmat*, Base. Ungrateful.

P دون همّتي *dūn-himmatī*, Low-mindedness.

P دوني *dūnī*, A long swift vessel. Negligence.

A دوني *dūnī*, Baseness, inferiority.

A دونيج *dūnīj*, A swift sailing yacht.

P دونيم *du nīm*, Two halves. Divided in two.

A دووق *duwūk* or دووقة *duwūkat*, (v. n. of داق for دوق) Being crazed.

P دووم *duwūm* or *dawūm*, A gum-bearing tree.

A دوويّ *dawawiy*, Any, any one.

P دووير *du wer*, A writer. A schoolmaster, teacher of languages.

A دوه *dawh* or *dūh*, A word used in calling cattle home, or camels to water on the fifth day.

P دو هاروت كافر *du hārūti kāfir*, The fascinating eyes or pendent ringlets of a mistress.

P دو همزاد *du hamzād*, Twins.

P دو هندوي طفل *du hinduyi tifl*, (or چشم *chashm*) The pupils of the eyes.

A دوىٰ *dawa'*, (v. n. of دوي) Ailing. Being heart-sick. Being full of rancour. Dying of an internal disease. Disease. Ailing inwardly, decayed. Foolish (man). Apparently lifeless. (pl. of دواة) Ink-stands. *Dawī*, Having an internal complaint. A fool. One who remains in a place.

P دوي *dawī*, A cheat, deceiver, knave. *Duwī*, Two and two.

A دويّ *duwiy*, Any thing, any person. A singing noise in the ear. The humming or murmur (of bees, birds, or wind). *Duwiy* or *diwiy*, (pl. of دواة *dawāt*) Ink-stands. *Duwiy*, Any one. A desert.

A دوّيّ *dawwiy*, Any person.

A دويات *dawayāt*, (pl. of دواة) Ink-stands.

A دويبّة *duwaybbat*, (dim. of دابّة) A little beast.

A دوية *dawiyat*, Indisposed (woman). *Dawiyat* or *duwiyat*, An unhealthy country.

A دوّية *dawwiyat*, A desert. The order of the Knights Templars. *Dawiyat* or *duwiyat*, Unhealthy (country).

P دويت *dawet*, An inkholder or pen-case.

P دويت آشور *dawet-āshūr*, Stick for mixing ink.

A دويد *duwayd*, (dim. of دود) A little worm.

P دويدار *dawe-dār*, One who carries an ink-stand.

P دويدگي *dawīdagī*, A running.

P دويدن *dawīdan*, To run. To make haste to serve. To flow. To spring up, be carried high.

A دويرة *duwayrat*, (dim. of دارة) A small house. A little halo round the moon. Name of a place.

P دويرة *dawīra*, A leathern strap used at dice.

A دويسة *duwaysat*, A crowd of men.

P دويست *duwist*, Two hundred. دويست درم شرعي *duwist dirami sharʻī*, Fifty-four tolas, five māshas and two grains.

P دو يك *du yak*, The last breath.

A دويل *dawīl*, Dry; or annual or biennial (plant, particularly the نصيّ *nasiy*).

P دويل *duwel*, Fraud, cheat, trick. Coarse silk from a cocoon, in which 2 silk-worms were enclosed.

P دويم *duyum*, (or دويمين *duyumīn*) The second. A deputy.

A دوين *duwayn*, (dim. of دون *dūn*) A little below.

A دويهية *duwayhīyat*, An awful calamity.

P دوئي *duī*, Duality.

P ده *dah*, Ten. Displeasure. Annoyance, trouble. Curses, imprecations. Commanding what is right, and forbidding what is wrong. ده چند *dah chand*, Ten-fold, ten times. ده در دنيا ستر در آخرت *dah* (for *dih*?) *dar dunyaʼ*, *sattar* (perhaps for ستان *satān*) *dar ākhirat*, Give in this world, and receive in the next, or perhaps, 10 in this world, 100 in the next (a benediction used by mendicants). ده درم شرعي *dah dirami sharʻī*, Two tolas, eight māshas, and ten grains and a half. *Dih*, A town, village. (imp. of دادن *dādan*) Give thou. (in comp.) A giver. دهي ويران *dihi werān*, The world. The human body. *Duh*, (for دم *dum*) A tail.

A الّا ده فلا ده *illā dahin falā dahin*, Now or never.

P دها *dahā*, The ten days of the Muharram. The models of the tombs of Hasan and Husayn, or the model of a building containing the tombs, which are carried about in procession during those ten days. On the tenth day the tombs are buried, or in some places thrown into water; the building, if made of cheap materials, shares the same fate; if costly it is carried back and deposited in the Dargāh or Karbalā.

A دهاء *dahāʼ*, (v. n. of دهي) Being subtle, penetrating. Ingenuity, shrewdness, soundness of judgment, sagacity.

A دهاءة *dahāʼat*, (v. n. of دهي) Being sagacious, subtle, cunning, astute.

A دهاة *duhāt*, (pl. of داهي or دهي) Ingenious, sly.

P دهات *dihāt*, Villages. The country.

A دهادة *dahādih*, (pl. of دهداه) Small camels.

P دهاده *dih-ā-dih*, From every part, from all quarters. From place to place.

P دهار *dahār*, A grotto, cavern, cleft in a mountain. Excellence. Learning, wisdom. A clamour, a cry for help.

A دهار *dihār*, (v. n. 3 of دهر) Bargaining for a long period (دهر *dahr*, as شهار *shihār* signifies Agreeing by the month, شهر *shahr*).

A دهارس *dahāris*, (or دهاريس *dahārīs*) (pl. of دهرس *dahras*) Misfortunes, calamities, adversities.

A دهارير *dahārīr*, The commencement of past time. دهور دهارير *duhūr dahārīr*, Times of adversity and times of tranquillity.

P دهاز *dahāz*, (or دهاژ *dahāj*) Clamour, noise. A grotto, cavern. *Dihāz*, Former site of a village. Cleft of a mountain.

A دهاس *dahās*, Soft soil free from sand. Large-hipped (woman).

A دهّاس *dahhās*, Easy, gentle (man).

A دهاسة *dahāsat*, Gentleness, easiness of temper.

A دهاع *dahāʻi*, Used in calling to kids.

A دهاق *dihāk*, Full (cup), or cup after cup. Much (water). Shot out (seminal fluid).

A دهاقنة *dahākinat*, (or دهاقين *dahākīn*) (pl. of دهقان *dihkān* or *duhkān*) Chief men of Persian villages. Industrious.

P ده آك *dah āk*, Ten vices. Name of the tyrant Zahhāk, who was notorious for ten defects of body or mind, viz. Ugliness of feature, shortness of stature, excessive pride, indecency, gluttony, scurrility, cruelty, precipitance, falsehood, and cowardice.

P دهاك *dahāk*, Places of tens in arithmetic.

A دهالك *dahālik*, Black hills in Arabia.

A دهاليز *dahālīz*, (pl. of دهليز *dihlīz*) Vestibules. Places where stagnant waters lie. ابناء الدهاليز *abnāʼu'd dahālīz*, Foundlings, exposed children.

A دهام *duhām*, Black. A stallion-camel.

A دهامج *duhāmij*, A double-bunched camel. Going fast with short steps. Large, bulky. Plain, soft.

A دهامق *duhāmik*, Soft earth.

A دهامنة *dahāminat*, (pl. of دهمن) Kings of Persia.

P دهان *dahān* or *dihān*, The mouth. An orifice. دهان پشت *dahāni pusht*, Anus. دهان ضيغم *dahāni zaygham*, The first point in the constellation Leo.

A دهان *dihān*, (v. n. of دهن) Having little milk (a camel). Red leather shining with oil. A slippery place. (pl. of دهن *duhn*) Oils, ointments, unguents. Gentle rains, moistening only the surface of the ground.

A دهّان *dahhān*, One who makes or presses oil.

P دهان بند *dahān-band*, A mouth-veil: a muzzle.

A دهانة *dahānat*, (v. n. of دهن) Having little milk (a camel).

A دهانج *duhānij*, Going fast with short steps. Large, bulky.

P دهان دره *dahān-dara*, Yawning: one who yawns. A narrow pass between mountains.

P دهانه *dahāna*, Any thing which resembles the mouth. The mouth of a river. The opening of a valley. The bit of a bridle. A weaver's instrument. Any thing with which the edge of a knife or hatchet is covered for the safety of carriage. Rust of brass; verdigris. A precious stone of a greenish colour, melochites, malachite.

P دهانيدن *dah* or *dihānīdan*, To cause to give.

A دهب *dahb*, An army put to flight.

P ده باش *dih-bāsh*, Tame, domestic.

A دهبرّج *dahbarraj*, (P ده پرّه) Ten-feathered.

P ده بست *dah bist*, Ten or twenty.

A دهبل *dahbal*, A kind of bird.

A دهبلة *dahbalat*, (v. n. of دهبل Q) Making up large gobbets, in order to eat more than the others.

P ده پانزده داري *dah pānzdah dārī*, Ornament.

P ده پنجي *dah-panjī*, Bad money, false coin.

P ده تاس *dah tās*, A wooden shoe.

A دهث *dahs*, A thrusting, a driving away.

A دهثم *dahsam*, A strong camel. A soft, simple man. *Dahsam*, (or دهثمة) Level soft ground.

P ده چند *dah chand*, Ten times as much.

P ده چندگي *dah chandagī*, Ten-fold. A word with which they return a salutation.

P دهچه *dihcha*, Husbandmen, peasantry.

P ده حواس *dah hawās*, The five external and the five internal senses.

P دهخان *dih-khān*, (ده خدا *dih-khudā*, or ده دار *dih-dār*) Lord or headman of a village.

P ده ختني *dah khatanī*, The ten fingers.

A دهداء *dihdāʼ*, (or دهداة *dahdāt*) (v. n. of دهدأ Q) Rolling (a stone). Heaping (things) together, topsy-turvy.

P ده دادن *dah dādan*, Reviling any one by holding up the ten fingers to his face. Contradicting. Hating, detesting.

P ده دار *dih-dār*, Headman of village or township.

A دهداع *dahdāʻ*, Used in calling kids.

A دهداق *dahdāk* or *dihdāk*, (v. n. of دهدق Q) Breaking (bones). Mincing (meat). Rising and tumbling about in the cauldron (boiling meat). *Dahdāk*, A horse-laugh. A horse's pace with wide steps. The boiling of a pot.

A دهداه *dahdāh*, (pl. دهاده *dahādih*) A small camel. A dwarf. ايّ الدهداه *ayyu'd dahdāh*, Who he is (I know not).

A دهدرّ *duhdurr*, (and دهدرّين *duhdurrayn*) A trifling, futile thing. A lie. دهدرّ بن سعد القين *duhdurru'bnu saʻdu'l kayn*, A liar.

A دهدعة *dahdaʻat*, A calling to kids.

A دهدقة *dahdakat*, (v. n. of دهدق Q) Breaking (bones). Cutting, hashing (meat). Rising and tumbling about in a boiling cauldron (meat).

P ده دله *dah dila*, (Of ten hearts) Fickle, faithless. One who is perpetually changing his creed. Brave, courageous.

A دهدمة *dahdamat*, (v. n. of دهدم Q) Overthrowing, destroying. Piling things one upon another, pell-mell.

A دهدموز *dahdamūz*, A glutton.

A دهدن *dahdan*, People.

A دهدنّ *duhdunn*, Vain (discourse). A lie.

A دهدوّة *duhdūwat*, (دهدوه *duhdūh*, دهدية *duhdiyat*, or دهديّة *duhdīyat*) A little ball of dry dung carried by a beetle.

P ده ده *dah dah*, (or ده دهي) Pure gold.

A دهدهان *duhdu* or *dahdahān*, A herd of camels.

A دهدهة *dahdahat*, (v. n. of دهده Q) Rolling (a stone). Heaping up (especially in disorder). A troop of above 100 camels.

A دهر *dahr*, (v. n. of دهر) Befalling, happening to. (pl. ادهر *adhur* and دهور *duhūr*) Time, a year, age, thousand years, eternity. The end, last. Extremity. Fortune. Adverse fortune. Victory, superiority. God. Will. Danger. Custom, habit, mode, manner. Care, solicitude. The world. Atheism. دهر داهر *dahri dāhir*, Adverse fortune. فى اوّل الدهر *fī awwali'd dahr*, Now long ago. ما ذاك بدهر *mā zāka bi dahr*, That is not usual. ما دهري بكذا *mā dahrī bi kazā*, I do not care for that. دهر الداهرين *dahra'd dāhirīn*, At no time (will I do that). دهر دهارير *dahri dahārīr*, Severe times, adversity. دهور دهر دهارير *duhūri dahri dahārīr*, Past time. Past misfortunes. P دهر كاسه گردان *dahri kāsa-gardān*, This lower world. A *Dahar*, An age, a lengthened period, a thousand years.

A دهرا *dahran*, Perpetually.

A دهرجة *dahrajat*, Swift pace.

A دهرس *dahras*, (pl. دهارس *dahāris*) Misfortune. Agility, sprightliness.

P دهرگه *dah raga*, Strong, muscular, brave. Experienced in business. Zealous. A bastard.

P دهر نكوهي *dahr-nikūhī*, A blaming of fortune.

P دهره *dahra*, A reaping-sickle. A pruning-hook. A farrier's instrument for paring horses' hoofs. A small two-edged, sickle-formed, sharp dagger. دهرهٔ صبح *dahra-i subh*, Morning-light.

A دهريّ *dahriy*, Secular, temporal, worldly. Impious, atheistical. *Da* or *duhriy*, One who maintains the eternity of matter. *Duhriy*, Aged, old.

P دهريش *dah rīsh*, (Ten beards) A thick beard.

A دهس *dahs*, A plant not yet of a green colour. Soft soil without sand, dust, or clay. *Duhs*, Soft sands. *Dahas*, A reddish black.

A دهساء *dahsā*, (fem. of ادهس *adhas*) Red inclining to black (ground, or goat). Gentle, mild. Large-hipped.

P ده سال *dah sāl*, Ten years. The planets (a term of science). A large wave.

A دهسة *duhsat*, A reddish black.

P دهستان *dahistān*, A town in Tabaristān.

A دهسمة *dahsamat*, (v. n. of دهسم Q) Hiding.

A دهش *dahsh*, (v. n. of دهش) Striking with consternation. *Dahash*, (v. n. of دهش) Being greatly amazed, and astonished. *Dahish*, Astonished, amazed, confounded, bewildered.

P دهش *dihish*, A gift, alms. Liberality.

A دهشة *dahshat*, Amazement, wonder. Strangeness. Fear.

P دهشت *dahasht*, Union, unanimity, resemblance. Singularity.

P دهشت انگيز *dahshat-angez*, Horrible.

P دهشت ناك *dahshatnāk*, Alarming.

P دهشته *dihishta*, A free gift, an alms.

A دهشرة *dahsharat*, (v. n. of دهشر Q) Doing any thing expeditiously. A large she-camel.

A دهع *dahꜥ*, (v. n. of دهع) Calling to kids.

A دهف *dahf*, The taking in a large quantity.

A دهفشة *dahfashat*, Deception, fraud. Soft, amorous, polite conversation with ladies.

A دهق *dahk*, (v. n. of دهق) Breaking or cutting. Filling (a cup). Emptying (a vase) with violence. Sousing, or pressing down with a shock. Striking. Torturing, putting on the rack. Giving away (part of one's property). *Dahak*, Torture, the rack.

A دهقان *dihkān* or *duhkān*, (from P ده خان *dih-khān*) (pl. دهاقنة *dahākinat* and دهاقين *dahākīn*) Chief man or magistrate of a village, prince or head of the farmers (among the Persians). A husbandman, cultivator. Expert in the management of affairs, industrious. A merchant.

P دهقان *dihkān*, A minstrel, bard. دهقان پير *dihkāni pīr*, Old wine. دهقان خلد *dihkāni khuld*, The porter of Paradise named Rizwān. Muhammad.

P دهقان نورد *dihkān-naward*, Register, history.

P دهقاني *dah* or *dihkānī*, Tillage, husbandry.

A دهقانيّة *dihkāniyat*, Husbandry.

A دهقة *dahkat*, (The chief) part of wealth.

A دهقلة *dahkalat*, (v. n. of دهقل Q) Straightening and tightening (a skin), and shaving off the hair.

A دهقنة *dahkanat*, (v. n. of دهقن Q) Appointing to the office of دهقان *dihkān*. The magistracy of a village. Farming business. Shrewdness.

A دهقوع *duhkūꜥ*, The cravings of hunger.

A دهك *dahk*, (v. n. of دهك) Breaking, bruising. Grinding. Wearing down, trampling (the ground). Copulating. *Duhuk*, (pl. of دهوك *dahūk*) Instruments with which any thing may be broken to pieces. Breakers, grinders.

P دهك *dihak*, dim. of ده *dih*, A small village.

P ده كان ده كان *dah kān dah kān*, In tens.

P دهكاني *dahkānī*, Agriculture. A sown field.

A دهكث *dahkas*, A dwarf, short-bodied.

A دهكل *dahkal*, Adversity, sore calamity.

A دهكلة *dahkalat*, (v. n. of دهكل Q) Treading (the ground). A confused noise of men riding a race.

A دهكم *dahkam*, An old man, decrepit.

P ده كيا *dih-kiyā*, A certain fruit cooked with meat. Chief man or magistrate of a village.

P دهگان *dihgān*, A farmer, sower. A historian. A village.

P دهگاني *dahgānī*, A certain gold coin. *Dihgānī*, Tillage, husbandry.

P دهگر *dihgar*, A villager.

P ده گزي *dah-gazī*, Of ten cubits' length.

A دهل *dahl*, An hour, moment. A little thing.

P دهل *duhul* A drum, tabor. دهل زدن *duhul zadan*, To beat a drum. دهل يك رويه *duhuli yak rūya*, A single drum. دهل دو رويه *duhuli du rūya*, A double drum.

A دهلاث *dihlās*, A strong man.

A دهلب *dahlab*, Heavy. Disagreeable and shunned by society. Name of a poet.

P دهل باز *duhul-bāz*, A drummer. A small brass drum fastened to the saddle when hawking, and struck whilst the falcon is on the wing, to animate him to hunt for and kill his prey.

P دهل دريده *duhul-darīda*, Disgraced.

P دهل زن *duhul-zan* or نواز *nawāz*, A drummer.

A دهلقة *dahlakat*, A rubbing the hair off a skin.

A دهلك *dahlak*, An island in the Red Sea.

A دهلويّ *dihlawiy* (or دهليّ *dihliy*) Of Delhi.

P دهله *dahla*, A thorny plant. A bridge.

P دهلي *dihlī*, The city of Delhi.

A P دهليز *dihlīz*, (pl. دهاليز *dahālīz*) A vestibule, place between two gates, or between the outer gate and the house. A portico, outward court, gallery, piazza, or place for walking. A corner of the house. A cavity inside the heart. A privy. A place wherein water collects.

P دهليزي *dahlīzī*, Rumours, vague reports.

A دهم *dahm*, (v. n. of دهم) Coming suddenly, rushing upon. (pl. دهوم *duhūm*) A multitude, large army. A person, body, creature of God. A serious affair. Evil, misfortune. A laurel. ايّ الدهم هو *ayyu'd dahmi huwa*, Of what people is he? *Duhm*, Three moonless nights in the month.

P دهم *dahum*, (or دهمى *dahumī*) The tenth.

A دهماء *dahmā*, (fem. of ادهم *adham*) Black (mare) with a greenish and white mixture. (A garden) rank and of a dark green. Old and blackish. Quite red (sheep). The face of a man. A pot or kettle, old and black. A crowd. The common people. A large number. A kind of broad-leafed herb with which they tan hides. The last night of the moon.

A دهماص *dihmās*, Firm, solid (workmanship).

P ثني دهمان *sinyu duhmān*, Evening-prayers.

A دهمة *duhmat*, Blackness.

A دهمثة *dahmasat*, Soft ground.

A دهمج *dahmaj*, Large, bulky. Plain, soft.

A دهمجة *dahmajat*, (v. n. of دهمج Q) Going slow, as if the feet were tied. Making haste with a short step (a camel). Adding fictitious circumstances to news.

P دهمرده *dah marda*, A company of ten men. A captain over ten men. ده مرده گوي *dah marda-goy* or *gūy*, Extremely loquacious.

A دهمسة *dahmasat*, The last night of the lunar month. Power, vigour. An assaulting or springing upon one another. A communicating of secrets to one another.

P دهمست *dahmast*, The laurel.

P ده مسكن ادريس *dihi maskini idrīs*, The heaven of amber.

A دهمقة *dahmakat*, (v. n. of دهمق Q) Breaking, cutting. Softening (a bow-string). Making (meat) sweet and tender. Not preparing or cooking (it) well. Speaking elegantly.

A دهمن *dahman*, (pl. دهامنة *dahāminat*) A title of the kings of Persia.

A دهموث *duhmūs*, Liberal.

A دهن *dahn*, (v. n. of دهن) Anointing, oiling. Playing the hypocrite. Bruising, beating (with a stick). Slightly moistening the face of the earth (rain). Slight rain. *Dihn*, A tree fatal to wild beasts. *Duhn*, (pl. دهان *dihān* and ادهان *adhān*) Oil, ointment, unguent. Slight rain. Name of a tribe. *Dahin*, Fat. Anointed.

P دهن *dahan*, The mouth. Orifice; also covering of a vessel. Bit of a bridle. آب دهن *ābi dahan*, Spittle. دهن تير *dahani tīr*, Notch of an arrow. دهن شمشير *dahani shamshīr*, Edge of a cimeter. دهن كشاي غيبت كردن *dahan-kushāyi ghibat kardan*, To open the mouth of detraction.

A دهناء *dahnāʼ*, A field. A reddish herb. An extensive desert without water. Name of a place; also of a woman.

P دهناد *dahnād*, Order, series, arrangement.

A دهناوي *dahnāwīy*, Belonging to دهناء *dahnāʼ*.

P دهن بسته *dahan-basta*, Muzzled.

P دهن بند *dahan-band*, The covering of the mouth. A woman's veil. A muzzle.

A دهنة *dahnat*, (v. n. of دهن) Anointing. *Duhnat*, A portion of ointment. Odour, perfume. طيّب الدهنة *tayyibu'd duhnat*, Fragrant, scented.

A دهنج *dahnaj*, *dahanaj*, or *duhanij*, A gem resembling an emerald.

A دهنجة *dahnajat*. See دهمجة *dahmajat*.

P دهن دره *dahan-dara*, Yawning, gaping.

P دهن دريده *dahan-darīda*, A vain babbler. Shameless.

P دهندگی *dihandagī*, A giving: liberality.

P دهنده *dihanda* or *dihinda*, A giver. (A woman) giving or prostituting (herself).

A دهنقة *dahnakat*. See دهمقة *dahmakat*.

P دهنه *dahnuh*, Ornament, decoration. Diminution, depreciation. Any two things of equal value. Ninety (ten nines). *Dahana*, An orifice. A fissure. The jaws. A notch. دهنهٔ لگام *dahanaʼi ligām*, The bit of a bridle. Jasper. A precious stone of a thick greenish colour, melochites.

A دهنية *duhnīyat*, Fatness: ointment: unctuosity.

P دهنيم *dah-nīm*, An old coin. Tax of 5 per cent.

A دهو *dahw*, (v. n. of دها for دهو) Occurring, happening, befalling. A certain day whereon a memorable battle was fought.

P دهو *dihū*, A mountain (called also Rohūn, and by the Portuguese Pico d'Adam) in the island of Ceylon, where the Persians believe Adam lived, when banished from Paradise.

A دهواء *dahwāʼ*, as داهية دهواء *dāhiyatun dahwāʼ*, A great misfortune or calamity. *Duhawāʼ*, (pl. of دهيّ *dahīy*) Intelligent, clever, shrewd.

P ده و دار *dih u dār*, (or دهٔ و گير *dih u gīr*) Give and take. Tumult, conflict, noise of combatants. Pomp, pride.

A دهور *duhūr*, (pl. of دهر *dahr*) Ages, times.

A دهورة *dahwarat*, (v. n. of دهور Q) Gathering. Throwing into a gorge between two mountains. Pronouncing full and open one word after another. Overturning, destroying (a wall). Making up large mouthsful. Voiding liquid stools.

A دهوريّ *dahwarīy*, Strong-bodied (man).

A دهوس *dahūs*, (or الدهوس *ad' dahūs*) A lion.

A دهوك *dahūk*, (pl. دهك *duhuk*) An instrument for breaking any thing. A breaker, grinder.

A دهوم *duhūm*, (pl. of دهم) Large armies.

P دهون *dahūn*, Recital from memory. Memory. ازدهون خواندن *az dahūn khwāndan*, To say by heart.

A دهون *duhūn*, (pl. of دهي *dahī*) Ingenious, clever, shrewd.

A دهويّة *duhwīyat*, as داهية دهويّة *dāhiyatun duhwīyatun*, A great calamity or misfortune.

P دهها *dahhā*, The ten first days of the month Muharram. Tens. *Dihhā*, Villages.

P ده هزار *dah hazār*, (or ده هزاران *dah hazārān*) The fourth game at نرد *nard*. Ten thousand.

P ده هفت *dah haft*, Name of an ancient coin.

A دهي *dahy*, (v. n. of دهي) Being shrewd, subtle, or ingenious. Imputing to any one great shrewdness, calling him a very clever fellow. Disgracing, dishonouring. Overtaking with calamity. Ingenuity, subtlety. Soundness of judgment, sagacity. Fraud, craftiness. *Dahī*, (pl. دهون *dahūn*) Ingenious, sagacious. Subtle, sly, cunning.

A دهيّ *dahīy*, (pl. ادهية *adhiyat* and دهواء *duhawāʼ*) Intelligent.

P دهيد *dihīd*, (imp. دادن) Give ye. Strike ye.

A دهيدهان *duhaydihān*, A herd of small camels.

A دهير *dahīr*, Ever, at any time. دهر دهير *dahri dahīr*, Adverse fortune.

P دهيك *dah yak*, A tenth part, one out of ten. دهيك كردن *dah yak kardan*, To decimate. ده يك گيرنده *dah yak gīranda*, A tithe-taker.

P دهيم *dihīm*, The crown of the kings of Persia.

A دهيم *duhaym*, Foolish. Misfortune, evil, calamity. A monster. امّ الدهيم *ummu'd duhaym*, A misfortune.

A دهيماء *duhaymāʼ*, A misfortune.

A دهين *dahīn*, Anointed. Milkless (camel).

P ده يوپد *dah yopad*, Enjoining what is right, and forbidding what is wrong.

P ده يوده *dah yoda*, Ten, ten units.

P دي *day*, Name of an angel presiding over the affairs of the month دي *day*, and of the tenth day of every month. Name of the tenth month of the solar year. Winter, or the first month of it, December. *Dī*, Yester: as, ديروز *dī-roz*, Yesterday. ديشب *dī-shab*, Yesternight.

A ديابوذ *dayābūz* or ديابيذ *dayābīz*, (pl. of ديبوذ *daybūz*) Cloths of a double warp.

A ديابيج *dayābīj*, (pl. of ديباج) Brocades.

A ديات *diyāt*, (pl. of دية) Mulcts for homicide.

A دياثة *diyāsat*, Softness, versatility of tongue.

A دياجي *dayājī*, (pl. of ديجاة) Darknesses.

A دياجير *dayājīr*, (pl. of ديجور) Darknesses.

A ديار *diyār*, (pl. of دار *dār*) Houses, mansions. (pl. of ديرة *dayrat*) Circuits, countries, regions, districts. ديار بكر *diyār-bakr*, The country called anciently Mesopotamia.

A ديّار *dayyār*, Any one. The head of a convent. ما في الدار ديّار *mā fī'd 'dāri dayyārun*, There is nobody in the house.

A ديارات *diyārāt*, (or ديارة *diyārat*) (pl. of دار *dār*) Houses. Towns.

A دياس *diyās*, (and دياسة *diyāsat*) (v. n. of داس for دوس) Treading, trampling upon. Treading out (corn). Conquering (a country). Polishing (a sword).

A ديّاس *dayyās*, A thrasher of corn.

A ديّاص *dayyāṣ*, One against whom nothing can be said or done. Fat.

A ديّاصة *dayyāṣat*, A fat and short woman.

A دياف *diyāf*, Name of a village in Syria or Mesopotamia renowned for camels and swords.

Aديافيّ *diyāfīy*, Stout and strong (camel).

A دياميس *dayāmīs*, (pl. of ديماس) Dungeons.

A دياميم *dayāmīm*, (pl. of ديمومة) Deserts.

A ديّان *dayyān*, A requiter of good and evil; hence an epithet of God. Computing, settling accounts with another. A manager. A conqueror, subduer. A judge, umpire, administrator. Religious.

A ديانة *diyānat*, (v. n. of دان for دين) Embracing, adhering to religion. Acting uprightly. Conscience, honesty, justice, piety, virtue, integrity. ارباب ديانت *arbābi diyānat*, Religious persons. اهل ديانت *ahli diyānat*, Religious.

P ديانت دار *diyānat-dār*, Just, honest, pious.

P ديانوش *dayānosh*, The man who sold عذرا.

A دياوين *dayāwīn*, (pl. of ديوان *dīwān*) Muster-rolls. Poems.

P ديب *dīb*, Name of a sea-port in India.

P ديبا *dībā*, Brocade. The eye of a mistress. The tenth of the month. ديباي معلم *dībāʼi muʻallam*, Embroidered cloth.

P ديبا باف *dībā-bāf*, A brocade-manufacturer.

A ديباج *dībāj*, (pl. ديابيج *dayābīj*, or دبابيج *dabābīj*) A vest of brocade, or cloth of gold, with a rich edging. Frontispiece of a book.

A ديباجتان *dībājatāni*, Cheeks. Hips.

P ديباجه *dībāja*, (or ديباچه *dībācha*) The preface, exordium, or preamble to a book (as being generally written in an ornamented stile, and adorned with gilding and other decorations). A cheek.

P ديباجي *dībājī*, A vesture of gold cloth. A weaver of brocade.

P دي بادين *day bādīn*, God. Name of angel.

The twenty-third day of the month.

P ديبازر daybāzar, The eighth day of the month. The angel who presided over this day. Sleepy.

P ديبار dībār, Nuptials: a banquet, feast.

P ديبال پور dībāl pūr, A place in the Panjab.

P ديباوند debāwand, Name of Tahmūras.

P ديباه dībāh, (or ديبه dībah) Gold tissue. ديبه خسروي dībahi khusravī, Khusraw's third treasure.

P ديبدار debdār, The Indian pine, devadāru.

P ديبدين daybadīn, God. Name of an angel. The twenty-third day of every solar month.

P دي بمهر day ba mihr, God. Name of an angel. The fifteenth day of every solar month.

A ديبوب daybūb, One who secretly injures by detraction. A pander to his own wife.

P ديبود day-būd, A double-bordered garment.

A ديبوذ daybūz, (from P دو پود du pūd) (pl. ديابوذ dayābūz or ديابيذ dayābīz) A garment with a double border.

A دية diyat, (v. n. of ودي) Paying a mulct or compensation for manslaughter. Bringing near. Preparing to stale or cover (a horse). Voiding something after having made water. (pl. ديات diyāt) An expiatory mulct for murder or homicide, a fine, damages.

A دئثان diʼsān, (or ديثاني dayasānīy) Asleep, unconscious, motionless. The nightmare.

A ديج dayj, A going slowly or creepingly.

A ديجاة dayjāt, (pl. دياجي) Thick darkness.

A ديجان dayajān, (v. n. of داج for ديج) Going slowly, creeping along. Small wreaths; also fringes or other ornaments round the edges of any thing. The foot of a locust. A large part of a swarm of locusts. A small household.

A ديجوج dayjūj, Dark, obscure.

P A ديجور dayjūr, Earth, dust. Darkness, obscurity. The night of conjunction of sun and moon. A dark night without moonlight. Dark. Dust-coloured. Much dry herbage. P شب ديجور shabi dayjūr, A very dark night.

A ديحان dayhān, A locust.

A ديحس dayhas, Much.

A ديخ dīkh, (pl. ديخة diyakhat) A bunch of dates.

A ديخس daykhas, Luxuriant, matted (fodder).

A ديد dayd, Play.

P ديد dīd, (pret. of ديدن dīdan) He saw. Sight. The eye. بديد آوردن ba dīd āwardan, To produce, to bring to sight.

P ديدا daydā, Lost, missing.

A دئداء diʼdāʼ, (v. n. of دأدأ Q) Galloping at full speed. Urging forward. Following the steps of any one. Stirring (a thing). Stilling (a thing). Covering (a thing). (pl. دآدئ daʼādiʼ) The latter end of the month. The night of the 25th, 26th, 27th, 28th, or 29th of the month. The last three nights of the moon.

P ديدار dīdār, Sight, vision, look. The eye. Face, countenance, cheek. Appearance. Interview. Manifest, exposed to view.

P ديداري dīdārī, Worthy of being seen, fair.

A ديدان daydān, Manner, custom. Play. Dīdān, (pl. of دود dūd) Worms. ديدان الامعاء dīdānu'l amʻāʼ, Intestinal worms.

A ديدب daydab, The wild ass. Daydab, (or ديدبان daydabān) (from P dīdbān) A watch, guard, observer. The vanguard.

P ديد بازي dīd-bāzī, Looking about one: taking the air.

P ديدبان dīdbān, A watch, guard. One who keeps a look-out from a mountain, or a ship's mast.

P ديدباني dīdbānī, Observation, watching.

A ديدبون daydabūn, Play, pastime, diversion. A game played by the Arabians.

A ديدجان daydajān, A camel bearing furniture or wares.

P ديددان daydadān, Custom, manner, usage.

P ديدگان dīdagān, (pl. of ديده) Spies, scouts.

P ديدگاه dīd-gāh, A prospect.

A ديدن daydan, Custom, habit.

P ديدن dīdan, To see, look, observe. To perceive, feel. بلند ديدن baland dīdan, To look high, to exalt one's self. پست ديدن past dīdan, To look low, to abase one's self.

P ديدني dīdanī, Fit to be seen.

P ديدوار dīdawār, Perspicuous, visible.

P ديدوان dīdwān, A watch.

P ديدواني dīdwānī, An inspector of boats.

P ديد و ديد dīd u dīd, An interview.

P ديده dīda, Seen. The eye. The sight. The pupil of the eye. A wanton, impudent eye. Impudence. Any place within ken. A watch-tower. A spy. A sentinel. One who has seen. ديده بر دوختن dīda bar dokhtan, To close the eyes. ديدۀ بصيرت dīdaʼi basīrat, The eye of prudence, foresight. ديدۀ پشت dīdaʼi pusht, Anus. ديدۀ حق بين dīdaʼi hak-bīn, A just, penetrating eye. ديدۀ كافوري dīdaʼi kāfūrī, Blind. ديدۀ گاو dīdaʼi gāv, Ox-eye (a plant). The star called the Bull's-eye. A kind of armour. A sort of grape. امور ديده umūr-dīda, Who has seen things, i.e. expert in business. جهان ديده jahān-dīda, One who has seen the world, has travelled and learnt experience.

P ديده باز dīda-bāz, Throwing the eyes round.

P ديده بان dīdabān, (or ديده دار dīda-dār) A watch, sentinel. ديده بان چهارم dīdabāni chahārum, The sun. ديده بان كبود حصار dīdabāni kabūd-hisār, The planet Saturn. Any one of the planets. ديده بانان عالم dīdabānāni ʻālam, The seven planets, i.e. Saturn, Jupiter, Mars, the sun, Venus, Mercury, and the moon. ديده بان فلك dīdabāni falak, The sun. The planet Saturn. ديده چون تخت جوهري dīda chūn takhti jawharī, A blue eye. A blind eye.

P ديده براه dīda ba rāh, On the look out.

P ديده پوش dīda-posh, Veiling the eyes.

P ديده دار dīda-dār, A sentinel, watch.

P ديده ريزي dīda-rezī, A fatiguing the eye.

P ديده سخت dīda-sakht, Shameless, barefaced.

P ديده گاه dīda-gāh, (or گه gah) A place whence observation is made, the station of a spy or sentinel.

P ديده وار dīdawār, (or ديده ور dīdawar) Perspicuous, quicksighted. An inspector. A sentinel.

P ديده وان dīdawān, The sight (of a gun).

P ديده ودانسته dīda u dānista, Seen and known. Knowingly, wittingly, purposely.

P ديده ور dīdawar, A seer, a looker.

P ديدوري dīdawarī, Sharpness of sight.

A دي دي day day, (for يا يديّ yā yadayya') O my hand!

A دير dayr, (pl. اديار adyār) A monastery, convent. P ديرتنگ dayri tang, The world. ديرسپنجي dayri sipanjī, (رند سوز rind-soz, or مكافات mukāfāt) The present world. ديرمغان dayri mughān, A temple of the Magi. A tavern. ديرمينا dayri mīnā, The sky. A رأس الدير rasu'd dayr, The superior of a convent or monastery: an abbot.

P دير dīr, (by some der) Slowly, tardily. Late, after. A while ago. A long while. Old, antique. ديررو dīr-rav, Slow-paced. ديرشدن dīr shudan, To be at a great distance. To die. ديرغضب dīr-ghazab, Slow to anger; gentle, mild. ديرمردگان dīr-murdagān, (pl.) Long since dead. ديرواداشتن dīr vā dāshtan, To keep long open; to protract.

P ديرآ dīr-ā, Slow in coming.

A ديران dīrān, (pl. of دار) Houses, habitations.

P ديرانه dīrāna, A long time.

A ديرانيّ dayrānīy, The head of a convent.

P ديربار dīr-bār, Long. Very remote.

P ديرباز dīr-bāz, The world. Long, tall. Long ago.

P ديرپا dīr-pā, Slow-paced. A centipede. A scorpion. Always, constant, durable.

P دير پاي dīr-pāy, Firm, steady. A spider. Old, decrepit. A man of a good constitution, who does not soon grow old.

P ديرپائي dīr-pāʼī, Durability, firmness.

P دير پروازي dīr-parwāzī, Flying heavily, slow.

A ديرة dayrat, A circular heap of sand. (pl. ديار diyār) A circuit.

P ديردارنده dīr-dāranda, A procrastinator.

P ديرداشت dīr-dāsht, Delay (of payment).

P ديررنج dīr-ranj, Slow to anger, forbearing.

P ديرزي dīr zī, Live long. Name of the 27th day of the month.

P ديرك dīrak, A weevil. A moth.

P ديركشاي dīr-kushāy, Difficult to open (lock).

P ديرگاه dīr-gāh, Always.

P ديرگوار dīr-guwār, Slow of digestion.

P ديرماندگي dīr-māndagī, Oldness, staleness.

P ديرمايه dīr māya, Bile.

P ديرند dīrand, Time, an age. Fortune. A long space of time. An amulet.

P دیرنده *dīranda*, One slow to act. Time, an age.

P دیروز *dī-roz*, Yesterday.

P دیر وقت *dīr waḳt*, Much time.

P دیره *dīra* or *dera*, A house, habitation, tent.

A P دیري *dayrī*, An age, a length of time.

P دیري *dīrī*, Late, slow. Slowness, lateness.

P دیریدن *dīridan*, To rend asunder.

P دیرین *dīrīn*, Old, ancient, of times past.

P دیرینگی *dīrīnagī*, Antiquity. Perpetuity.

P دیرینه *dīrīna*, Ancient, old. Long, continual. Wise. Cunning. بندۂ دیرینه *bandaʼi dīrīna*, An old servant. عهدۂ دیرینه *ʻuhdaʼi dīrīna*, An ancient covenant.

P دیرینه روز *dīrīna-roz*, Of a great age.

P دیرینه سال *dīrīna-sāl*, A decrepit old man.

P دیز *dez*, Colour. Ash-colour. An ash-colour with which certain animals are striped from the head to the tail. A black colour. A citadel. A sort of cooking-pot. A kind of eye-salve. A hair-sieve. شبدیز *shab-dez*, Khusraw's famous horse.

A دیزج *dayzaj*, (from P دیزه *deza*) A bay horse. A horse striped black from the withers to the tail.

P دیزندان *dīzandān*, The feet of a boiler. A trivet.

P دیزو *dīzū*, A small clay or copper vessel.

P دیزه *deza*, A horse or mule of an ash-colour. Colour. A dark colour. A horse, mule, or ass marked with a black stripe extending from the head to the tail. A fortress.

A دیس *days*, A nipple, dug. A bulrush. *Dīs* and *diyas*, (pl. of دیسة *dīsat*) Thick forests.

P دیس *des*, (placed after words) Like; as ماه دیس *māh-des*, Like the moon. (in Hindūstān) A country, province. A day.

P دیسال *dī-sāl*, The past year.

A دیسة *dīsat*, pl. دیس *dīs* or *diyas*, Thick forest.

P دیستانه *dīstāna*, A woman in her courses.

A دیسع *daysaʻ*, Thick (she-camel): one that chews the cud much.

A دیسق *daysaḳ*, A table of silver, also a table in the form of a bason. A particular kind of vessel. A woman's ornaments of bright silver. The clear appearance of vapour on a plain. A cistern full of water. Whiteness. Beauty. A long road. A bull. An old man.

A دیسکی *daysakaʼ*, A herd of ostriches, or cattle.

A دیسم *daysam*, Cock's comb (an herb). A whelp bred from a wolf and a bitch, or a fox and a bitch. A leveret. A fox. A friend, a companion in travail. A bear's cub. Blackness. Young bees.

A دیسمة *daysamat*, A small ant. An atom.

P دیسمه *dīsama*, A wave.

P دیسه *dīsa*, A person.

P دیش *desh*, Give to him. Give that. A gift.

A دیش *dīsh*, A dunghill-cock. Name of a man.

A دیصان *dayaṣān*, (v. n. of داص for دیص) Bending, inclining. Being crooked. Withdrawing, going away privately. Retiring or flying in battle. Stealing. Being cheerful, brisk. Being moved backwards and forwards with the hand (a gland in the body). Becoming basely degenerate after having been distinguished for honour.

A دیضّی *diyizzaʼ* Haughty air, jaunty step.

P دیف رخش *dīf-rakhsh*, A note in music.

A دیفق *dayfaḳ*, Fast-going (she-camel).

A دیق *dayḳ*, A causing to bend or decline.

A دیقوع *dayḳūʻ*, Fierce, cephalalgic (hunger).

A دیك *dīk*, (pl. دیوك *duyūk*, ادیاك *adyāk*, دیکة *diyakat*) A cock. A hen. Kind, gracious, compassionate. The spring. A trivet. Trivets. The lump behind a horse's ear. دیك دیك *dīk dīk*, Words used in calling fowls. دیك الجن *dīku'l jinn*, An insect found in meadows. دیك هندي *dīki hindī*, A turkey. دیك الکرم *dīku'l karm*, (Cock of the vine) The hoopoo.

A دیکة *dīkat*, A hen. *Diyakat*, (pl. of دیك *dīk*) Cocks.

A دیکس *daykas* or *diyaks*, Many sheep or cattle.

A دیکساء *diyaksāʼ*, *day*, or *dīkasāʼ*, A large flock.

P دیگ *dīg*, Yesterday. *Deg*, A pot, kettle, cauldron. A large cannon or mortar. Meat in the pot. A bird's crop. دیگ سفالین *degi sifālīn*, An earthen pot. دیگ مسین *degi misīn*, A copper kettle. دیگ بر دیگ *deg bar deg*, Pot upon pot (as piled up in kitchens). Arsenic.

P دیگ افزار *deg-afzār*, (or دیگ اوزار *deg-avzār*) Pot-herbs, roots, fruits, or any produce of the garden with which meat is seasoned. A pot, large or small, in which they are cooked. A pot-lid.

P دیگ انداز *deg-andāz*, A cook.

P دیگانه *dīgāna*, A tortoise. A hedgehog.

P دیگ بند *deg-band*, A scullion.

P دیگپاي *deg-pāy*, A trivet, the foot of a pot.

P دیگپایه *deg-pāya*, A trivet. A star in Lyra.

P دیگ پخت *deg-pukht*, Cooked in a pot.

P دیگچه *degcha*, A pot, a small cauldron.

P دیگدان *degdān*, A trivet, tripod, pot-hook. A fire-place, hearth.

P دیگدان سرد *degdān-sard*, (Cold-pot) A miser.

P دیگر *dīgar*, Another, other, more. The rest. Over again. Near. Besides, further, moreover. Again. Some. Any more, any longer. Hitherto. Afternoon, evening. نمازدیگر *namāzi dīgar*, Evening-prayer.

P دیگر بار *dīgar bār*, Another time.

P دیگر روز *dīgar roz*, The other day: yesterday.

P دیگر سال *dīgar sāl*, Next year: the future.

P دیگر شب *dīgar shab*, Last night.

P دیگر گون *dīgar gūn*, Altered. دیگر گون شدن *dīgar gūn shudan*, To change, be disturbed, ruined.

P دیگر گوني *dīgar gūnī*, Change, alteration.

P دیگري *dīgarī*, A tax on trees and the like.

P دیگشب *dīgshab*, (for دیگر شب) Last night.

P دیگ گیر *deg-gīr*, A cloth wherewith a pot is taken off the fire, a kettle-holder.

P دیگینه *degīna*, (Meat) dressed in a pot. *Dīgīna*, Of yesterday.

A دئل *duʼil* or *duʼul*, A jackal. An animal resembling a weasel. *Duʼil*, Name of a tribe.

P دیل *dīl*, A dot. The heart. A fold, cote.

P دیلپایه *dīl-pāya*, Stuffed with almonds.

A دیلم *daylam*, A misfortune. A crowd. A male woodcock. The katā or grouse. Enemies. A puddle at a cistern where camels kneel to drink, and where ants and tikes swarm. The سلام *salām* tree.

P دیلم *delam*, Name of a city in Gīlān.

P دیلمان *delamān*, Name of a city in Gīlān.

P دیلمك *delmak*, A venomous spider.

A دیلمي *daylamīy*, Native of Daylam or Delam.

A دیم *daym*, (v. n. of دام for دیم) Raining gently and incessantly. *Diyam*, (pl. of دیمة *dīmat*) Incessant but gentle rains, without thunder or lightning.

P دیم *dīm*, Face, countenance, cheek. Leather.

A دیما دیما *dīman dīman*, Incessantly (raining).

A دیماس *daymās* or *dīmās*, (pl. دیامیس *dayāmīs* or دمامیس *damāmīs*) A dark dungeon. A den. A bath. A dungeon belonging to Hajjāj.

P دیماطي *dīmāṭī*, A kind of stone found in the sea. A sort of hot vapour.

P دیماوند *dīmāwand*, A mountain in Persia.

A دیمة *dīmat*, (pl. دیم *diyam*, دیوم *duyūm*, and دیمات *diyamāt* or *dīmāt*) An incessant gentle rain (for several days, at least eight hours each day, and unaccompanied by wind, thunder, or lightning).

P دیمر *dīmar*, Face, countenance, cheek.

A دیمري *daymurīy*, Sharp, keen; one who sticks close and asks favours from everybody.

A دیموم *daymūm*, Spacious plain; arid desert.

A دیمومة *daymūmat*, (v. n. of دام for دوم) Persevering, continuing in, lasting. (pl. دیامیم *dayāmīm*) A desert without water. A spacious plain. Perpetuity, continuance.

A دیموند *dīmawand*, The mountain Damāwand.

P دیمه *dayma*, Light. Corn. *Dīma*, Face, cheek.

P دیمهاج *dīmhāj*, (in Gīlān) Bugloss, borage.

P دیمیاد *dīmyād*, Pride, vain-glory, vanity.

P دیمین *daymīn*, The game of tip-cat.

A دین *dayn*, (v. n. of دان for دین) Borrowing, asking in loan. Lending. Requiting. Repaying. Being obedient, serving. (pl. ادین *adyun*, دیون *duyūn*, and دینة *dīnat*) Debt, payable with interest at a fixed period (قرض *karz* expressing an indefinite time). Death. Any thing not present. علیه دین *ʻalayhi dayn*, He is a debtor. له دین *daynun lahu*, He is a creditor. باع بدین *bāʻa bi dayn*, He sold upon credit, or he gave a delay for payment. اعطاه دینا *aʻṭāhu daynan*, He gave it upon credit. اخذه دینا *akhazahu daynan*, He took it upon credit. P دین کردن *dayn kardan*, To contract debt. دین دادني *dayn dādanī*, Having much debt to pay. A *Dīn*, (v. n. of دان for دین) Submitting to, obeying, serving. Embracing the religion of Muhammad, called Islām. Becoming owner or possessor. Bringing under by force, forcing against one's will. Taming, rendering obedient, breaking in. Degrading. Being great and powerful. Rebelling. Being contemptible and abject. Disobeying. Possessing. Repaying, requiting, benefiting. Being attacked by disease. Faith, religion, worship. A belief or profession of the unity of God. Obedience to God. Religious abstinence. Custom, rite. Institution, regulation. Condition, state. Judgment, decree. Disease. Empire, government, dominion. Victory, conquest, predominance, superiority. An emperor, king, sovereign. Submission. Retribution, repayment. Destiny. Disobedience. Computation, numbering. Slight incessant rains. Rains which often visit one place. Debtors. كما تدين تدان *hamā tadīn tudān*, As thou judgest thou wilt be judged. دين متين *dīni matīn*, Firm faith. دين و دولت *dīn u dawlat*, Religion and country, church and state. P بي دين *bī dīn*, Faithless, impious, irreligious.

P دين *dīn*, This (compounded of the preposition ب *ba*, and اين *īn*): as, بدين قدر *badīn hadar*, In this quantity or proportion. Name of the 24th day of the month.

A دَيّن *dayyin*, Religious.

P دينا *dīnā*, Dinah, daughter of Jacob. A judicial decree. A judge.

A دينار *dīnār*, (originally دنّار *dinnār*) Money. A dīnār, ducat. The weight of a drachm and a half. Complete. Seed of dodder. Name of a large bird. الدينار البيضاء *ad' dīnāru'l bayzās*, The sun. P دينار سرخ *dīnāri surkh*, Gold coin.

P دينار اشمر *dīnār-ushmur*, (or شمر *shumur*) A banker, a money-changer.

P ديناروية *dīnārūya*, Wild anise.

P ديناري *dīnārī*, A kind of silk. Red wine.

A دينارِيّ *dīnāriy*, Name of a horse.

P دين پرست *dīn-parast*, Religious. A fire-worshipper.

P دينپرور *dīn-parwar*, A king, a monarch, defender of the faith.

P دينپروري *dīn-parwarī*, Defence or cherishing of the faith: monarchy, dominion.

P دين پژوه *dīn-pijūh*, (*pujūh*, or پژه *pujuh*) Name of the fifteenth day of the month.

P دين پناه *dīn-panāh*, Support or prop of religion. A sovereign, defender of the faith.

P دينپناهي *dīn-panāhī*, Defence of the faith. The office or duty of him who supports or defends the faith. Royal dignity.

A دينة *dīnat*, Incessant, gentle rains. Obedience. Debt payable at a fixed period. (pl. of دين *dayn*) Debts. Deaths.

P دين تمسّكي *dayn-tamassukī*, A bond, note.

P ديندار *dayn-dār*, A debtor. *Dīn-dār*, Pious.

P دينداري *dīn-dārī*, Constancy in religion.

P دين روز *dīn-roz*, The 24th day of the month.

P دينور *dīnūr* or *dīnwar*, Religious, faithful. *Dīnavar*, Name of a large city in Persian Irāk.

A دينونة *daynūnat*, Judgment.

P دينه *dīna*, Yesterday.

A دينِيّ *dīniy*, (fem. دينيّة *dīniyat*) Religious.

P ديو *dīv*, by some *dev*, A devil, demon, genius, spirit, ghost, hobgoblin. A sort of woollen armour. A horse. Anger, passion, force, violence. Brave. Losing the way, deviating, led astray. Perverse. ديو دين *devi dīn*, Satan. ديو سپيد *devi saped*, Satan transformed into an angel of light. Name of a celebrated champion slain by Rustam. ديو شبينه *devi shabīna*, The nightmare. ديو شهوت *devi shahwat*, The demon of lust.

P ديو آباد *dev-ābād*, Possessed by the devil, a demoniac.

P ديوار *dīwār*, A wall. A species of juniper yielding milk. ديوار بيني *dīwāri bīnī*, The septum of the nose. ديوار حصار *dīwāri hisār*, Walls of a fortress. ديوار گلين *dīwāri gilin*, A mud-wall. A dam. در و ديوار *dar u dīwār*, Gates and walls.

P ديوارچه *dīwārcha*, A low wall, a screen.

P ديوارگر *dīwārgar*, A builder, plasterer.

P ديوارو *devārū*, The pine, or devadāru.

P ديوارة *dīwāra*, A raised rim.

P ديو اسپست *dev ispist*, The lote-tree.

P ديو استنبه *dev-istamba*, A rough man.

P ديوال *dīwāl*, (equiv. to ديوار *dīwār*) A wall.

P ديواله *dīwāla*, A bankrupt.

P ديوالي *dīwālī*, Bankruptcy. A Hindū festival.

A ديوان *daywān*, (P *dīwān*) (pl. دواوين *dawāwīn* and دياوين *dayāwīn*) A royal court. Tribunal of justice or revenue. A council of state, senate, or dīvān. A title given to a collector-general of the public revenues of a province or district; and the servants of the East-India Company in Bengal usually distinguish the principal native civil officer acting under them by this appellation. This word is sometimes used to express the bags in which the Kāzī's records are kept. An account-book. A muster-roll, or military pay-book. A recueil, or miscellaneous collection from different authors. A complete series of odes or other poems by one author, running through the whole alphabet; the rhymes of the first class terminating in ا *alif*, the second in ب *be*, the third in ت *te*, &c., also the collection of the works of one author in prose, as well as verse, especially after he is dead. (See حافظ *hāfiz*). Many authors have completed Dīwāns: as Ghassānī, Sā'utī, and Zamrānī, among the Arabians; and Hāfiz and Jāmī among the Persians. —The Caliphs of the house of Abbas constituted a dīvān (called ديوان المظالم *dīwānu'l mazālim*, The court of oppression), which took cognizance of all the acts of tyranny of the great men throughout the empire. The Caliphs themselves for some time presided in it; but in the reign of Muktadir (about the beginning of the tenth century) a woman, according to some historians, discharged the office of president. ديوان اعلى *dīwāni aʿla'*, A prime-minister, a vazīr. ديوان خاصّ *dīwāni khāss*, A privy-council chamber. ديوان خالصه *dīwāni khālisa*, The accountant-general of the king's revenue. P ديوان داشتن *dīwān dāshtan*, To hold a council. A ديوان عام *dīwāni ʿām*, A public hall of audience. P ديوان عرض لشكر *dīwāni ʿarzi lashkar*, A court for military petitions. ديوان هايون *dīwāni humāyūn*, The august or imperial court. A رأس الديوان *rāʾsu'd dīwān*, President of the council, chancellor.

P ديوان *devān*, (pl. of ديو *dev*) Demons.

T ديوان بيگي *dīwān-begī*, An officer of state.

P T ديوانچي *dīwānchī*, A cabinet-minister.

P ديوان خانه *dīwān-khāna*, A tribunal, office. A hall of audience. The dīwān's office or court.

P ديوانسي *dīwānsī*, Inordinate desire.

P ديوانگي *dīwānagī* or *devānagī*, Insanity.

P ديوانه *dīwāna* or *devāna*, Foolish, insane. Mad, furious. ديوانهٔ خدا *dīwānaʾi khudā*, Inspired by the deity, in a heavenly ecstacy.

P ديوانه دو *dīwāna* or *devāna-dav*, Running, or behaving like a madman.

P ديوانه سگ *dīwāna* or *devāna-sag*, A mad dog.

P ديواني *dīwānī*, Belonging to a court. A courtier. A poet laureat. The office or jurisdiction of a dīwān, or superintendant of the administration of civil justice.

P ديو آورد *dev-āward*, A pine. A brazen cup.

P ديو باد *dev-bād*, The devil's wind, *i.e.* a whirlwind. A fleet horse. A swift camel or dromedary. Madness, phrenzy.

P ديو بخوريده *dev ba khwurida*, Possessed of the devil. Epileptic.

P ديو بند *dev-band*, Name of the 16th day of the month. Name of Tahmūras. Name of a drug.

P ديو پا *dev-pā*, (or ديو پاي *dev-pāy*) A spider (devil-footed). The lote-tree.

A ديّوث *dayyūs*, A contented cuckold.

A ديّوثي *dayyūsī*, Cuckoldom.

P ديو جامه *dev-jāma*, A garment of skin with the hairy part outside. A lion's skin wherewith warriors clothe themselves.

P ديو جان *dev-jān*, Hard-hearted. An old man.

P ديوچه *devcha*, A weevil, a moth. A woodworm. A leech. A carrot. ديوچه خورده *devcha-khwurda*, Moth-eaten, worm-eaten.

P ديو خار *dev-khār*, A juniper: pine: bramble.

P ديو دار *dev-dār*, A demoniac. A juniper.

P ديو دارو *dev-dārū*, The Indian pine.

P ديو دال *dev-dāl*, The white poplar-tree. Ignorance. Brave.

P ديو دست *dev-dast*, (Devil-handed) Clever.

P ديو دل *dev-dil*, Courageous. Cruel, fell.

P ديو دلي *dev-dilī*, Stout-heartedness, valour.

P ديو دولت *dev-dawlat*, Enjoying a short-lived prosperity (like that of the devil).

P ديو ديد *dev-dīd*, (or ديده) Mad, crazy, frantic.

P ديوديس *devdes*, (Devil-like) Thick and deformed. Crafty, fraudulent.

P ديور *dīwar*, The master of the house.

A ديّور *dayyūr*, Any one.

P ديو رخش *dev-rakhsh*, Name of a note in music.

P ديو زاي *dev-zāy*, Fierce, choleric. Afflicted.

P ديو سار *dev-sār*, Like a devil. Bad-tempered. Ill-favoured. An evil-worker. A place abounding in demons. Clad in a rough garment.

P ديو سالار *dev-sālār*, Evil-doer, devil's factor.

P ديو سبلت *dev-siblat*, A salt and bitter plant.

P ديو سپست *dev-supust*, The lote-tree.

P ديو ستان *dev-satān*, A demoniac. *Devistān*, A desert, the habitation of demons. A whirlwind.

P ديوستنبه *devistamba*, An ill-bred man.

P ديو سوار *dev-suwār*, A bold horseman.

P ديوسه *dīv-sah*, A sort of garment.

P ديو غول *dev-ghūl*, A sylvan demon. A wen.

P ديو غولي *dev-ghūlī*, A gland, kernel, wen.

P ديو فرسا *dev-farsā*, (or ديو فرساي *dev-farsāy*) Having eruptions on the lips from frightful dreams.

P ديوك *devak* or *devuk*, A weevil. A moth. The white ant. A leech. An unmarried woman, a young married lady, a daughter-in-law.

A ديوك *duyūk*, (pl. of ديك *dīk*) Cocks.

P ديوكردار *dev-kirdār*, An evil-doer.

P ديو كلوچ *dev-kulūch*, An epileptic boy.

P ديو كلوخ *dev-kulūkh*, Large clods turned up.

P ديوكمان *dev-kamān*, A big (deuce of a) bow.

P ديو گندم *dev-gandum*, A kind of wheat with two grains in one ear. A large ear without grain.

P ديو گير *dev-gīr*, Catching a devil. Possessed by a devil. Name of the city of Dawlat-ābād in India.

P ديوگيري *dev-gīrī*, A silk stuff made at Devgīr.

P ديولاخ *devlākh*, Inhabited by demons, *i.e.* a desert, uncultivated region.

P ديولاك *dīvlāk*, A desolate spot.

A ديوم *duyūm*, (pl. of ديمة *dīmat*) Incessant gentle rains without thunder and lightning.

A ديّوم *dayyūm*, Perpetual, lasting, enduring.

P ديو مرد *dev-mard*, Wild man, monster, satyr.

P ديو مردم *dev-mardum*, Mischievous: a satyr.

P ديو مشنگ *dev-mashang*, A kind of grain.

A ديون *duyūn*, (pl. of دين *dayn*) Debts.

P ديوند *dīwand*, A kind of drug.

P ديوه *dīwa*, A silk-worm. Mushrooms. A leech.

P ديو هفت در *devi haft dar*, The seven climates.

P ديو هفت سر *devi haft sar*, Night. The globe.

P ديوي *devī*, Gigantic, demoniacal. Devilishness. ديوي كردن *devī kardan*, (or نمودن *namūdan*) To play the devil, to act like the devil.

P ديويت شور *dewet-shor*, An instrument for mixing ink.

P ديه *dīh*, (or ديهه *dīha*) A town, village.

P ديهبان *dīhbān*, The chief of a village.

P ديهمد *dīhamad*, The 15th day of the month.

P ديهمك *dīhmak*, The same. The 5th day.

P ديهور *dīhūr*, Heaven.

P ديهول *dehūl*, A crown inlaid with gems.

P ديهي *dīhī*, A peasant, villager.

P ديهيم *dayhīm*, A crown or diadem adorned with jewels, worn by the kings of Persia. A throne.

A ديّ *daʻy*, (pl. of دأية *daʻyat*) The joints or back part of a horse's neck (next to the saddle).

A ديّ *dayyiʻ*, (fem. ديّئة) Sick, indisposed.

P ديير *dayīmir*, The 16th day of the month.

ذ

ذ *zāl*, (called ذال منقوطه *zāli mankūta* or ذال معجمه *zāli muʻjama*, Dotted *zāl*) The ninth letter of the Arabic alphabet, denoting in arithmetic 700. In the almanacks it is used as a contraction for the last month of the Arabian year, ذو الحجّة *zū'l hijjat*: as ذا *zā* is the character used for ذو القعدة *zū'l kaʻdat*, The penultimate month. The letter ذ is used by the tribe ربيعة *rabīʻat* where د is used by the other tribes. Scarcely more than one or two words in the Persian language begin with this letter, though it is occasionally found in the middle of a Persian word; as in پذيرفتن *pazīruftan*, گذاشتن *guzāshtan*, گذشتن *guzashtan*, and the like. In the middle of words it is sometimes confounded with د *dāl*: as, پذر *pizar* and پدر *pidar*, A father. But, according to some respectable authorities, it is more correct to write ذ *zāl* (not د *dāl*) whenever that letter follows a quiescent ا *alif*, و *wāw*, and ي *ye*. The words شاد *shād*, نمودن *namūdan*, شنيد *shanīd*, افتادن *uftādan*, بودن *būdan*, and a host of others in common use, ought, therefore, to be written شاذ *shāz*, نموذن *namūzan*, شنيذ *shanīz*, افتاذن *uftāzan*, بوذن *būzan*, in accordance with the rule laid down in the following stanza:

آنانكه بفارسي سخن ميرانند
ānān ki ba fārsī sukhan mī rānand,
در معرض دال ذال را بنشانند
dar maʻrazi dāl zālrā bi nishānand.
ما قبل وي ار ساكن جز واي بود
mā kabli way ar sākin juz wāy buvad.
دال است وگرنه ذال معجم خوانند
dāl ast: wa garna, zāli muʻjam khwānand.

ذ *zāl* may also be written for د *dāl* when following any letter not quiescent, except ا *alif*, و *wāw*, and ي *ye*. It would be equally correct, therefore, to write بذ *baz* for بد *bad*, Bad, vicious. Its legitimate sound was, perhaps, somewhat like *th* in "that," but the Persians make but little, if any, difference between it and ز *zā*.

A ذا *zā*, He, this. Who, what, which. (accus. of ذو *zū*) A lord, master, endowed with. ذا اربعة اضلاع *zā arbaʻat azlāʻ*, Four-sided, a square.

A ذأابة *zaʻābat*, (v. n. of ذؤب) Resembling a wolf (ذئب *ziʻb*) in cunning and villainy.

A ذآنين *zaʻānīn*, (pl. of ذؤنون) Sorts of herbs.

A ذأب *zaʻb*, (v. n. of ذأب) Collecting, assembling. Sounding. Thrusting. Driving. Making a small saddle for a camel's bunch. Terrifying. Adorning the forehead (of a boy) with forelocks. Despising. Making haste in going or travelling. Contempt, blame. A loud and a strong voice. (A bucket) moving quickly up and down.

A ذاب *zāb*, Vice, fault, blemish.

A ذابّ *zābb*, Unable to stand still and quiet.

A ذابح *zābih*, A sacrificer, cutter. A butcher, slayer, slaughterer. A mark impressed on the throat crossways. Hair growing between the throat and sticking place. سعد الذابح *saʻdu'z zābih*, Two bright stars in the left horn of Capricorn, forming the twenty-second lunar mansion.

A ذابر *zābir*, One who learns properly. Learned.

A ذابل *zābil*, (pl. ذبل *zubul* and ذبّل *zubbal*) Flexible, limber (reed). A spear. Withered (leaf).

A ذأت *zaʻt*, (v. n. of ذأت) Strangling so that the tongue is forced out of the mouth. (for ذات *zāt*) (fem. of ذو *zū*) Possessed of, mistress of.

A ذات *zāt*, (fem. of ذو *zū*) (pl. اولات *ulāt* and ذوات *zawāt*) Possessed of or endowed with. (fem. of ذا *zā*) She, this. Soul, essence, substance, nature, body, person. Tribe, caste, sort. Generation, genus, species. Foot, rank and file (opposed to horse). Act, deed. ذات البين *zātu'l bayn*, Concord, friendship, union. ذات التلافيف *zātu't talāfīf*, The smaller intestines. P اصلاح ذات البين كردن *islāhi zātu'l bayn kardan*, To reconcile parties. A ذات الجنب *zātu'l jamb*, Pleurisy. ذات حمل *zāt hamlin*, Pregnant. ذات الرقاع *zātu'r rikāʻ*, A kind of bibliomancy. ذات الرية *zātu'r riyat*, Inflammation in the lungs. ذات شريف *zāti sharīf*, An excellent mind. A noble personage. ذات الصدر *zātu's sadr*, An inflammation in the chest. A collecting of matter in the chest. ذات الصدور *zātu's sudūr*, Whatever revolves in the breast. ذات الكمالات *zātu'l kamālāt*, Possessed of all perfections. ذات مال *zāti māl*, Opulence. ذات مكرم صفات *zāti mukarram-sifāt*, Endowed with excellent qualities. ذات يوم *zāt yawm*, On a certain day. اسم ذات *ismi zāt*, A noun substantive. بالذات *bi'z zāt*, He himself, in person. في ذاته *fī zātihi*, In itself, in person. من ذات نفسه *min zāt nafsihi* Of his own accord.

A ذاتيّ *zātiy*, Personal. Essential, substantial, natural, original. Real. قوّت ذاتيّه *kūwati zātiya*, Natural vigour.

A ذأج *zaʻj*, (v. n. of ذأج) Drinking (water) with avidity. Sipping (water). Tearing (a leathern bottle). Slaughtering.

A ذاجّ *zājj*, One just come off a journey.

A ذاجل *zājil*, Unjust, tyrannical.

A ذاخر *zākhir*, Fat. One who lays up a store.

A ذادة *zādat*, (pl. of ذائد *zāʼid*) Repellers, defenders of their rights.

A ذاذاء *zaʼzāʼ*, (and ذأذأة *zaʼzāʼat*) A reproof, a chiding. A vacillating motion in walking.

A ذأذأة *zaʼzaʼat*, A vacillating motion in walking.

A ذاذيّ *zāẕiy*, A long-cluster bearing plant.

A ذأر *zaʼr*, (v. n. of ذأر) Besmearing a camel's teats with dung to prevent the colt from sucking. *Zaʼar*, (v. n. of ذئر) Being seized with terror and fleeing away. Disdaining, abhorring, loathing, and turning away from. Being angry. Being accustomed, used, addicted to. Being refractory (a wife).

A ذارع *zāriʻ*, (pl. ذوارع *zawāriʻ*) A small wine-bottle made of the leg-skin of an animal. One who measures by the yard or ell (ذراع *zirāʻ*). اولاد ذارع *awlad zāriʻin*, Dogs and asses.

A ذاريات *zāriyāt*, Quick-scattering (winds).

A ذأط *zaʼt*, (or ذأطة *zaʼtat*) (v. n. of ذأط) Strangling (so that the tongue is forced out of the mouth). Slaughtering. Filling (a vase). Being filled.

A ذاعر *zāʻir*, Timid, timorous, afraid.

A ذاعط *zāʻit*, Swift, speedy (death).

A ذاغية *zāghiyat*, Foolish, froward (female).

A ذأف *zaʼf*, Sudden death.

A ذأفان *zaʼfān*, (v. n. of ذأف) Dying suddenly. Sudden and deadly (poison). Death.

A ذاقنة *zāḳinat*, (pl. ذواقن *zawāḳin*) The top of the throat or gullet; pomum Adami. The sticking place in cattle. The collar-bone. The abdomen.

A ذاك *zāka*, He, that. ذاك الآن *zāka'l ān*, (or ذاك الوقت *zāka'l waḳt*) Then, at that time.

A ذاكر *zākir*, A rememberer. A praiser of God.

A ذاكرة *zākirat*, The faculty of remembering, the retentive memory.

A ذاكي *zākī*, Strong-scented, diffusive (musk).

A ذاكية *zākiyat*, Fragrant (musk).

P ذال *zāl*, A cock's comb.

A ذال *zāl*, Name of the letter ذ.

A ذأل *zaʼal*, A going lightly and airily along.

A ذألان *zaʼlān* or *zuʼlān*, A wolf. A jackal. *Zaʼalān*, (v.n. of ذأل) Going swiftly and airily along. (pl. ذآليل *zaʼālīl*) The pace of a wolf or jackal.

A ذالغ *zāligh*, (A man) grinning hideously. Useless, profitless (business).

A ذالك *zālika*, That.

A ذآليل *zaʼālīl*, (pl. of ذألان *zaʼalān*) Paces of wolves and jackals.

A ذأم *zaʼm*, (v. n. of ذأم) Blaming, reproaching. Despising. Driving away. Bringing under.

A ذام *zām*, (v. n. of ذام for ذيم) Reproaching, charging with a fault. Esteeming as vile. Vice, blemish.

A ذأمة *zaʼmat*, One word (I did not hear).

A ذامر *zāmir*, Angry, furious, threatening.

A ذامي *zāmī*, Game hit with a shot.

A ذان *zān*, Vice, fault, defect, blemish.

A ذان *zāni*, (dual of ذا *zā*) These two males.

A ذانب *zānib*, A follower: one of the tail.

A ذانك *zān* or *zānniha*, (du. of ذاك) Those two.

A ذا نون *zā nūn*, (Lord of the fish) Jonah.

A ذآنين *zaʼānīn*, (pl. of ذؤنون) Sorts of herbs.

A ذأو *zaʼw*, (v. n. of ذأو) Driving (camels) with violence. Marrying a wife and going in unto her. Withering (grass).

A ذأوة *zaʼwat*, Emaciated (cattle).

A ذاوي *zāwī*, Withered (herb), dried (fruit).

A ذاهب *zāhib*, Who or what goes away or departs, passes by, precedes, or disappears. الطويل الذاهب *at tawīlu'z zāhib*, Very long, passing tall.

A ذاهبة *zāhibat*, (pl. ذواهب) Travelling (camel).

A ذاهفة *zāhifat*, Tired, jaded (camels).

A ذاهل *zāhil*, Careless, inattentive, negligent.

A ذأي *zaʼy*, (v. n. of ذأي) Driving (camels) with violence. Lying with. Withering (grass).

A ذائب *zāʼib*, Melting. Fusible. ذائب المال *zāʼibu'lmāl*, Live stock, *i.e.* slaves and cattle (in contradistinction to جامد المال *jāmidu'lmāl*, Dead stock).

A ذائد *zāʼid*, (pl. ذوّد *zūwad*, ذوّاد *zūwād*, and ذادة *zādat*) One who drives away. A repeller. One who defends his right.

A ذائر *zāʼir*, Disobedient (wife). Bold.

A ذائق *zāʼiḳ*, One who tastes, a taster.

A ذائقة *zāʼiḳat*, Sense of tasting, palate: taste.

A ذائك *zāʼik*, That.

A ذائل *zāʼil*, Long-tailed (horse). Long (coat of mail) with thin and light rings. Small and light (ring of a coat of mail).

A ذائلة *zāʼilat*, Long-tailed (mare). Long and light-ringed (coat of mail).

A ذبّ *zabb*, (v. n. of ذبّ) Driving away, keeping off, repelling. Defending. Having but little remaining (the day). Becoming lean, withering, drying up (with heat), losing colour (a man). Gadding to and fro. A wild bull, (called also ذبّ الرياد *zabbu'r riyād*, because always roaming after the females). A man who visits and courts the women. (pl. of ذباب *zubāb*) Flies. Bees.

A ذباب *zubāb*, (pl. اذبّة *azibbat*, ذبّان *zibbān*, and ذبّ *zubb*) A fly. A bee. The image in the eye (because always moving). A black speck in the pupil of the eye of a horse. A little well. Madness. Ill-luck. The point of a sword. The thin edge of a sword. Erysipelas. The thinner part of the ear. Evil. Early blossoms of the shrub hinna.

A ذبّاب *zabbāb*, A keeper, defender, protector of women. One who keeps everybody away from his harem. A little well.

A ذبابة *zubābat*, One fly. One bee. Remainder of any thing, balance of a debt.

A ذبّابة *zabbābat*, Withered and hanging (lip).

A ذبابيّ *zubābīy*, A swelling of the arachnoid tunic of the eye from a wound or other accident.

A ذبأة *zabʼat*, A slender, graceful, lively girl.

A ذباح *zabāh*, (v. n. of ذبح) Splitting, cleaving. Slaughtering, sticking. Sacrificing. Strangling. Tapping (a barrel). Beginning to cover the lower part of the chin (beard). *Zibāh*, A sore throat. Suffocating blood. *Zubāh*, A suffocating disease in the throat. A deadly plant. *Zubāh* or *zubbāh*, Cracks on the tips of the fingers, or under the toes.

A ذباذب *zabāzib*, Penis. Flounces or other things hung round a girdle by way of ornament.

A ذبار *zibār*, (pl. of ذبر *zabr*) Books written in the Himyarit, or old Arabic character, on palm-leaves. Sheets of paper.

A ذبارة *zibārat*, (v. n. of ذبر) Learning (news). Looking keenly. Fastening well. Committing (poetry) to memory and reciting (it) well.

A ذبال *zubāl*, An ulcer in the side, reaching the intestines. (pl. of ذبالة *zubālat*) Wicks of candles.

A ذبالة *zubālat* or *zubbālat*, A candle-wick.

A ذبّان *zibbān*, (pl. of ذباب) Flies. Bees.

A ذبائح *zabāʼih*, (pl. of ذبيحة) Sacrifices.

A ذبب *zabab*, A drying up (of the lip).

A ذبح *zabaha*, (fut. يذبح *yazbahu*) He slew.

A ذبح *zabh*, (v. n. of ذبح) Cleaving, splitting. Slaughtering, slaying, cutting the throat. Sacrificing. Strangling. Tapping (a barrel). Appearing below the chin (the beard), leaving the upper part uncovered. Purifying, making lawful (the use of any thing). *Zibh*, Any animal sacrificed. *Zubah* or *zibah*, A species of mushroom. *Zubah*, A wild carrot, or other plant, of which ostriches are fond. Another sort of plant.

A ذبحة *zibahat*, *zibhat*, *zubhat*, or *zubahat*, A pain in the throat. Blood, choking and killing.

A ذبذب *zabzab*, Penis. A little well.

A ذبذبة *zabzabat*, (pl. ذباذب *zabāzib*) Motion, the waving of any thing in the air. The tongue. Penis. A testicle. Harm, injury, hurt. Custody or protection (of women, or a neighbourhood). An ornament hung on a camel-litter.

A ذبر *zabr*, (v. n. of ذبر) Writing. Marking (letters) with points, dotting. Manuscript. Silent and quick reading. (pl. ذبار *zibār*) A book in the Himyarit, or old Arabic character, written on palm-leaves. A sheet of paper. Wisdom, knowledge. Speech, language. A mountain. *Zabar*, (v. n. of ذبر) Being angry. *Zabir*, (A book) easy to read.

A ذبل *zabl*, (v. n. of ذبل) Languishing, withering (a plant). Becoming extenuated or weak. Becoming dry (the skin). Losing flesh (a horse). Voiding dung (a sheep). The shell of a tortoise, of which they make combs, &c. Tortoiseshell-bracelets. *Zibl*, Bereavement. *Zubul*, (pl. of ذابل *zābil*) Limber (reeds). Spears.

A ذبّل *zubbal*, (pl. of ذابل) Limber (reeds). Spears.

A ذبلاء *zablāʼ*, Dry-lipped (woman).

A ذبلة *zablat*, A scorching, withering blast. One ball of dung. *Zublat*, The withering or chapping of the lips from thirst.

A ذبنة *zubnat*, The withering or chapping of the lips from thirst.

A ذبوب *zubūb*, (v. n. of ذبّ) Pining away (the body), withering (a plant), shrivelling from thirst (lip), drying from heat (pond), losing (his) colour (a man). Having but little remaining (the day).

A ذبول *zubūl*, (v. n. of ذبل) Withering (a plant). Becoming dry (the skin). Losing flesh (a horse).

A ذبّي *zibbīy*, A serjeant attendant on a collector.

A ذبيان *zubyān* or *zibyān*, Name of an Arabian tribe, whence sprang النابغة *an'nābighat* the poet.

A ذبيب *zabīb*, (v. n. of ذبّ) Shrivelling from thirst (the lip).

A ذبيح *zabīh*, Sacrificed, slaughtered. A sacrifice. The victim about to be offered. الذبيح *az' zabīh*, The sacrifice, *i.e.* Ishmael, son of Abraham, progenitor of the Arabians.

A ذبيحة *zabīhat*, (pl. ذبائح *zabāʼih*) An animal destined to be offered in sacrifice. A pain in the throat, quinsey. Blood which suffocates.

A ذبيل *zabīl*, Sore, grievous (bereavement). ذبلاً ذبيلاً *zablan zabīlan*, May God destroy him!

A ذجّ *zajj*, A drinking. A coming off a journey.

A ذجل *zajl*, Iniquity, tyranny.

A ذحّ *zahh*, A slap with the palm of the hand. Contusion, pounding. A fissure. Coition.

A ذحج *zahj*, (v. n. of ذحج) Stripping off the bark, scratching. Carrying (any thing) before (it) from place to place (the wind).

A ذحذح *zuhzuh*, (or ذحذاح) Short, big-bellied.

A ذحذحة *zahzahat*, (v. n. of ذحذح Q) Walking with short, quick steps. Driving (dust) about (wind).

A ذحل *zahl*, (pl. اذحال *azhāl* or ذحول *zuhūl*) Revenge, or the thirst for it, reprisals. Enmity, hatred.

A ذحلطة *zahlatat*, A talking confusedly.

A ذحلمة *zahlamat*, (v. n. of ذحلم Q) Slaying, slaughtering. Collecting, bringing together.

A ذحم *zahm*, (v. n. of ذحم) Blaming, reproaching. Despising. Driving away.

A ذحملة *zahmalat*, (v. n. of ذحمل Q) Rolling.

A ذحول *zuhūl*, (pl. of ذحل) Revenges: hates.

A ذخائر *zakhāʼir*, (pl. of ذخيرة) Provisions, stores.

A ذخذاخ *zakhzākh*, An examiner, scrutineer. Cautious, ever on one's guard, avoiding greatly.

A ذخذخان *zakhzakhān*, Eloquent.

A ذخر *zukhr*, (v. n. of ذخر) Laying up a treasure. (pl. اذخار *azkhār*) Provision or treasure laid up in store for future use: a hoard.

A ذخو *zakhw*, (v. n. of ذخا for ذخو) Driving (camels) with violence. Lying with (a woman).

A ذخي *zakhy*, (v. n. of ذخي) Beating (wool) with a rod. Making haste. Smiting one whilst unprotected (wind).

A ذخيرة *zakhīrat*, (pl. ذخائر *zakhāʼir*) A treasure, a hoard. Store, provision.

P ذخيره خانه *zakhīra-khāna*, A granary.

A ذر *zar*, (imper. of وذر) Leave thou, let alone.

A ذرّ *zarr*, (v. n. of ذرّ) Pounding small, crumbling (salt). Sprinkling, scattering, strewing. Throwing pounded salt or pulverized drugs into the eye. Wrinkling, shrivelling. Rising (the sun). Springing up (herbage). Whitening (the fore part of the head). A small ant (of which a hundred are equal to one barley-corn). An atom.

A ذرء *zarʼ*, (v. n. of ذرأ) Creating, procreating, multiplying. Scattering. Blundering, speaking unadvisedly (the mouth). Sowing. Somewhat (of good). Any thing which intervenes or separates two parties. ذرء النار *zarʼu'n nār*, The progeny of hell, those doomed to damnation. *Zaraʼ*, (v. n. of ذرئ) Turning gray on the forehead. Turning gray (the hair).

A ذرا *zara'*, An asylum, place of safety. Tears shed. Any thing scattered by the wind.

A ذرآء *zarʼāʼ*, (fem. of اذرأ *azraʼ*) Gray about the forehead. Black-bodied and dapple-eared (mare or she-goat).

A ذراب *zurāb*, Poison.

A ذرابة *zarābat*, (v. n. of ذرب) Being incurable (a disease). A disorder of the stomach.

A ذرأة *zarʼat* and *zurʼat*, Hoariness on the forehead. Extreme whiteness of salt.

A ذراح *zarāh*, Thin, watery milk. *Zurāh*, (or ذرّاح *zurrāh*) (pl. ذراريح *zarārīh*) A Spanish fly, cantharides.

A ذرار *zarār*, (v. n. of ذرّ) Turning away the face in anger. Being vicious (camel). *Zirār*, Malignancy (of a man in anger), anger, aversion, a turning away of the face. (v. n. 3 of ذرّ) Being vicious (a camel).

A ذرارة *zurārat*, Particles, flying or scattered about, of any thing grinding or pounding.

A ذراريّ *zarārīy*, (pl. of ذرّيّة *zurrīyat*) Progenies, offsprings, seeds.

A ذراريح *zarārīh*, (pl. of ذرحرح *zurahrah*) Spanish flies, cantharides.

A ذراع *zarāʻ* or *zirāʻ*, (A woman) who spins expeditiously. *Zirāʻ*, (v. n. 3 of ذرع) Selling by the yard. Mixing. (pl. اذرع *azruʻ* and ذرعان *zurʻān*) The arm from the elbow to the tip of the middle finger. The fore-leg (of a horse) above the pastern. A yard, a cubit. A mark impressed on the leg of a camel. The part of a spear from the middle to the point. Disposition. Power. حبل الذراع *hablu'z zirāʻ*, A vein extending through the arm to the hand. على حبل الذراع *ʻala' habli'z zirāʻ*, Ready. واسع الذراع *wāsiʻu'z zirāʻ*, Of a generous disposition. ضاق بالامر ذراعه *zāka bi'l amr zirāʻuhu*, His arm was unequal to the business. الذراع *az'zirāʻ*, (or ذراع الاسد *zirāʻu'l asad*) Two bright stars in the head of Gemini, denoting the seventh mansion of the moon. اولاد ذراع *awlādu zirāʻin*, Dogs and asses.

A ذرّاع *zarrāʻ*, A male-camel that strikes the female with his fore-leg to make her lie down. A maker of coats of mail. A small wine-bottle made of the leg-skin of an animal (ذراع *zirāʻ*).

A ذرآنيّ *zarʼ* or *zaraʼāniy*, Very white (salt).

A ذراوة *zurāwat*, Refuse in winnowing corn. Any part of a plant, dry, broken, and carried away by the wind,

A ذرائع *zarāʼiʻ*, (pl. of ذريعة *zarīʻat*) Hunters' lurking-places.

A ذرب *zarb*, (v. n. of ذرب) Sharpening. A shoemaker's paring knife. *Zirb*, A kernel in the neck. A disease of the liver. *Zurb*, (pl. of ذرب *zarib*) Sharp-tongued. *Zarab*, (v. n. of ذرب) Being sharp, acute. Being incurable (a disease). A disorder of the stomach. An incurable disease. Corruption (of a wound), or the extension of it, or an ichorous discharge. Rust. A healthy state of the stomach. (pl. اذراب *azrāb*) Obscenity in conversation, ribaldry. *Zarib*, (pl. ذرب *zurb*) Acute. Sharp-tongued, noisy. *Zirab*, (pl. of ذربة *zirbat*) Glands, swellings, kernels.

A ذربان *zarabāni*, (du.) Evil and opposition.

A ذربة *zirbat*, Clamorous (woman). Perfidy, treachery. (pl. ذرب *zirab*) A kernel in the neck.

A ذربي *zaraba'*, Defect, blemish. Misfortune.

A ذربيّ *zarabīy*, A misfortune, calamity.

A ذربيّا *zarabayya'*, Misfortune, calamity.

A ذرة *zurat*, A species of millet.

A ذرّة *zarrat*, An atom, particle. A single small ant. A mote in the sun-beams. P ذرّهٔ آتش *zarraʼi ātish*, A spark of fire. A ذرّه قدر *zarra-kadar*, As much as an atom, just nothing.

A ذرح *zarh*, (v. n. of ذرح) Poisoning (food) with cantharides. Strewing, scattering to the wind. *Zarah*, A kind of tree whereof they make saddles.

A ذرّح *zurrah*, (ذرحرح *zurahrah*, *zuruhruh*, ذرّحرح *zurruhruh*, or ذرحوح *zurhūh*) (pl. ذراريح *zarārīh*) A Spanish fly, used to raise blisters.

P ذرخش *zarakhsh*, Thunder. Lightning.

A ذرذار *zarzār*, Talkative.

A ذرذرة *zarzarat*, A scattering (of grains or salt).

A ذرز *zaraz*, (v. n. of ذرز) Possessing the conveniences and luxuries of life.

A ذرطاة *zartāt*, An ungraceful mode of eating.

P ذرع *zarʻ*, The border of a sown field.

A ذرع *zarʻ*, (v. n. of ذرع) Measuring with a cubit. Putting the foot on a camel's fore-leg in order to mount. Interceding. Being wearied with travelling (the legs). Seizing violently (a fit of vomiting). Preceding, going before. Drinking out of the bottle called ذراع *zirāʻ*. Strangling from behind by means of the arm. Strength, power. Habit, temper, disposition. ضعيف الذرع *zaʻīfu'z zarʻ*, Impotent, weak. واسع الذرع *wāsiʻu'z zarʻ*, Of an enlarged, generous disposition. *Zaraʻ*, Desire, concupiscence. Hope. Any thing behind which a hunter lurks. (pl. ذرعان *zirعān*) The calf of the wild cow. *Zariع*, Slanderous-tongued. One who travels night and day. Sociable, agreeable.

A ذرعات *zariعāt*, (pl. fem.) Swift (she-camels), taking long steps, moving their arms freely.

A ذرعان *zirعān*, (pl. of ذرع *zaraع*) Wild calves *Zurعān*, (pl. of ذراع *zirāع*) Arms.

A ذرعة *zurعat*, A cause, mode, motive, occasion. A present.

A ذرعم *zirعim*, Worthless. Foul-mouthed.

A ذرعمط *zuraعmit*, Thick milk. Wishful.

A ذرف *zarf*, (v. n. of ذرف) Shedding tears. Flowing (tears).

A ذرفان *zarfān* or *zarafān*, (v. n. of ذرف) Shedding tears. Flowing (tears). *Zarafān*, A feeble pace.

A ذرق *zark*, (v. n. of ذرق) Muting (a bird). Dung of birds. *Zurk* or *zurak*, Clover. *Zurak*, The lote-tree.

A ذرقطة *zarkatat*, A speaking, pronouncing.

A ذرم *zarm*, (v. n. of ذرم) Miscarrying.

A ذرملة *zarmalat*, (v. n. of ذرمل Q) Voiding (excrement). Setting before a guest bread hastily baked upon the ashes.

A ذرنوح *zurnūh*, A Spanish fly.

A ذرو *zarw*, (v. n. of ذرا for ذرو) Passing rapidly, going with fleetness. Winnowing. Carrying off, scattering dust (the wind). Falling down. Breaking. Breaking off in the middle of a sentence. Flying about (dust). A part of speech.

A ذروبة *zurūbat*, Disorder of the stomach.

A ذروة *zirwat* or *zurwat*, (pl. ذري *zura'*) The summit or pinnacle. The top of a camel's bunch. The summit of a mountain. Great wealth.

A ذروح *zarūh*, (*zarrūh*, or *zurrūh*) A Spanish fly.

A ذرور *zarūr*, (pl. اذرّة *azirrat*) Any thing pounded small and sprinkled (as salt or drugs). A kind of perfume. *Zurūr*, (v. n. of ذرّ) Rising (the sun). Springing up (grass).

A ذروع *zarūع*, A horse or camel that travels nimbly with long steps.

A ذروف *zurūf*, (v. n. of ذرف) Flowing (tears). Shedding (tears).

P ذرّهوار *zarrawār*, (or ذرّه صفت *zarra-sifat*) Humble, lowly, like a mere atom.

A ذري *zary*, (v. n. of ذري) Scattering dust (the wind). Winnowing. *Zura'*, Things scattered by the wind. (pl. of ذروة *zirwat* or *zurwat*) Summits.

A ذرّي *zarrīy*, Highly-tempered (sword); also its glittering surface.

A ذري *zarīء*, Sown (field).

A ذرياطة *ziryātat*, Land of one kind of soil.

A ذريب *ziryab*, A yellow fever. A yellow flower or blossom.

A ذريبّا *zarayabba'*, Defect, blemish, disgrace.

A ذرّيّة *zurriyat*, *zarriyat*, or *zirriyat*, (pl. ذراري *zarārīy*) Progeny, offspring, children, descendants, race, stock, seed. Women.

A ذريح *zarīh*, (pl. of ذريحة) Spanish flies.

A ذرّيح *zirrīh*, (pl. ذراريح) A Spanish fly.

A ذريحة *zarīhat*, A ridge of mountains stretching far away. A Spanish fly.

A ذريحي *(ahmar) zarīhīy*, (احمر) Deep red, purple.

A ذريرة *zarīrat*, A certain perfume. Any drug pounded small and sprinkled. A pellicle floating on the surface of wine.

A ذريرح *zurayrah*, A small Spanish fly.

P ذريس *zarīs*, A kind of partridge.

A ذريع *zarīع*, An intercessor. A medium. Swift. Ample, vast. (A horse or camel) going lightly with long steps. Wide-spread mortality. قتل ذريع *katli zarīع*, Sudden death, killing at once.

A ذريعة *zarīعat*, A cause, mode, motive, occasion, conjuncture, subject. A medium, means. A present. Any thing behind which a hunter lurks.

A ذريف *zarīf*, (v. n. of ذرف) Flowing (tears). Shedding (tears). Shed (tear.

A ذشّ *zashsh*, (v. n. of ذشّ) Travelling fast.

A ذعاذع *zaعāziع*, Crowds. Scattered. Worthless palm-trees.

A ذعّار *zaععār*, Fear-inspiring, terrifying.

A ذعاريرالانف *zaعārīru'l anf*, That which issues from the nose like milk. تفرّقوا ذعارير *tafarrakū zaعārīra*, They were scattered about through fear.

A ذعاعة *zaعāعat*, (pl. ذعاع *zaعāع*) A troop, body. A worthless palm-tree. A herd, flock. *Zaعāعat* or *zuعāعat*, The space between two palm-trees.

A ذعاف *zaعāf*, (v. n. of ذعف) Dying. *Zuعāf*, (pl. ذعف *zuعuf*) A deadly poison. موت ذعاف *mawti zuعāf*, Instant death.

A ذعاق *zuعāk*, Mortal (disease). Salt, hard, muddy, undrinkable water.

A ذعاليب *zaعālīb*, A threadbare garment.

A ذعبان *zuعbān*, A young wolf.

A ذعت *zaعt*, (v. n. of ذعت) Strangling violently. Rubbing in the dirt. Driving violently.

A ذعج *zaعj*, (v. n. of ذعج) Impelling forcibly. Lying with.

A ذعذاع *zuعzūع*, Publisher of secrets, tell-tale.

A ذعذعة *zaعzaعat*, (v. n. of ذعذع Q) Dispersing abroad, squandering (wealth). Disclosing (a secret), publishing news. Shaking a tree (wind).

A ذعر *zaعr*, (v. n. of ذعر) Terrifying. *Zuعr*, Terror. *Zaعar*, Stupefaction, amazement. *Zuعar*, Any thing formidable or terrific.

A ذعراء *zaعrāء*, The fundament.

A ذعرة *zuعrat*, Anus. *Zuعarat*, A wag-tail.

A ذعري *zuعrīy*, Scarce, barren (year).

A ذعط *zaعt*, A slaughtering with despatch.

A ذعف *zaعf*, (v. n. of ذعف) Giving poison to drink, poisoning. A deadly poison. ذعف اللعاب *zaعfu'l luعāb*, (A serpent) whose bite is instant death. *Zaعf* or *zaعaf*, (v. n. of ذعف) Dying. *Zuعuf*, (pl. of ذعاف *zuعāf*) Poisons.

A ذعفان *zaعafān*, Death.

A ذعق *zaعk*, (v. n. of ذعق) Crying out. Alarming, frightening.

A ذعل *zaعal*, Confession of a fact before denied.

A ذعلبة *ziعlibat*, An ostrich. A light, trifling business. The hem of a garment. A bit of cloth.

A ذعلفة *zaعlafat*, (v. n. of ذعلف Q) Destroying.

A ذعلوب *zuعlūb*, (pl. ذعاليب *zaعālīb*) A bit of cloth. The hem of a garment. An old garment.

A ذعلوق *zuعlūk*, A leek or scallion. A word used in calling sheep to be milked. Hot-headed, light-spirited (lad). A small kind of bird. A sort of mushroom. Light and narrow-mouthed (sheep).

A ذعمطة *zaعmatat*, (v. n. of ذعمط Q)) Slaughtering quickly. An unchaste or obscene woman.

A ذعن *zaعan*, The act of obeying, submitting.

A ذعور *zaعūr*, Frightened, trembling. Foul language. (A camel) running off when her udder is touched. A woman that dreads being suspected.

A ذعوط *zaعwat*, Speedy (death).

A ذغّ *zaghgh*, (v. n. of ذغّ) Lying with.

A ذغمور *zughmūr*, Obstinately malevolent.

A ذفّ *zaff*, (v. n. of ذفّ) Going quick, making haste. Running to dispatch a wounded man. Carrying off (people) quickly (pestilence). Being easy, feasible, in one's power. Sheep. The creaking noise of a shoe in walking. *Zuff*, A little water.

A ذفاري *zafāra'*, (and ذفاريّ *zafārīy*) (pl. of ذفري *zifra'*) Protuberant parts of the head behind the ears in camels.

A ذفاريق *zafārīk*, (pl. of ذفروق) Date-stalks.

A ذفاف *zafāf* or *zifāf*, (v. n. of ذفّ) Running to dispatch a wounded man. *Zifāf*, (v. n. of ذفّ) Going quick, making haste. Carrying off (people) quickly (pestilence). Being easy, feasible, in one's power. A place where a thing may be suspended. *Zifāf* or *zafāf*, Any thing. *Zifāf* or *zufāf*, (pl. ذفف *zufuf*) Venom instantly mortal. A little water. *Zufāf*, Quick. خفاف ذفاف Quick and ready.

A ذفذفة *zafzafat*, (v. n. of ذفذف Q) Hasting to slay a wounded man. Walking stately, strutting.

A ذفر *zafar*, (v. n. of ذفر) Emitting a smell. Perfume, a strong smell, an acrid scent (good or bad). The spermatic lymph of a stallion. The smell of the armpits. *Zafir*, Fragrant (musk). Stinking abominably, rank, fetid (armpit). Pungent.

A ذفرّ *zifirr* or *zifarr*, Strong and hard. A camel, behind whose ear the bump ذفري *zifra'* is large. A tall, active youth. Large, bulky.

A ذفراء *zafrāء*, (fem. of اذفر *azfar*) Fragrant, of an acrid smell. Wild rue. An army ill-smelled (from rusty armour).

A ذفرة *zafarat*, A strong acrid scent. Stench of armpits. *Zafirat*, Name of a plant. Fragrant grove.

A ذفرّة *zifirrat*, Excellent (she-camel). Strong (ass). A she-camel, big-bumped behind the ear.

A ذفروق *zufrūk*, (pl. ذفاريق) A date-stalk.

A ذفري *zifra'*, (pl. ذفريات *zifrayāt* and ذفاري

zafāra') A protuberance of skull behind the ears of a camel, and which sweats.

A ذفط *zaft*, (v. n. of ذفط) Treading (as a bird), lining (as a goat). Muting (a fly).

A ذفطسة *zaftasat*, A wasting of one's property.

A ذفف *zafuf*, (v. n. of ذفّ) Making haste to despatch a wounded man. *Zufuf* (pl. of ذفاف *zifāf* and *zufāf*) Poisons instantly mortal.

P ذفكر *zafkar*, Seed of mountain-parsley.

A ذفل *zifl* or *zafl*, Thin liquid pitch.

A ذفوط *zafūt*, Weak.

A ذفيف *zafīf*, Swift, hastening. Deadly (pest). خفيف ذفيف *khafīf zafīf*, Quick and ready.

A ذفيفة *zafīfat*, Short and hasty (prayer as that offered up by a man on a journey).

A ذقّاحة *zukhāhat*, A false accuser, or one who suspects falsely.

A ذقذاق *zakzāk*, Rapid in utterance, fluent and voluble in speech.

A ذقط *zakt* or *zukt*, (v. n. of ذقط) Gendering (as birds or goats). Voiding excrement (a fly). *Zakit*, Enraged. *Zukat*, (pl. ذقطان *ziktān*) A little fly.

A ذقطان *zaktān*, Enraged, irascible. *Ziktān*, (pl. of ذقط *zukat*) Little flies.

A ذقطة *zukatat*, Wicked, unclean (man).

A ذقن *zakn*, (v. n. of ذقن) Chucking under the chin. Resting the chin (upon the hand or a staff). Losing, missing. *Zikn*, An old man, decrepit and under-hung. The chin. *Zakan*, (v. n. of ذقن) Being sewed obliquely (a leathern bucket). (pl. اذقان *azkān*) The chin. The beard. A dimple.

A ذقناء *zaknā'*, (pl. ذقن *zukn*) Long-chinned (woman). One whose pudendum is oblique. A she-camel whose load leans on one side.

A ذقواء *zakwā'*, Flaccid-eared and nosed (mare).

A ذقون *zakūn*, A leathern bucket obliquely sewed. A camel hanging her jib. A water-pot whose spout is awry.

A ذقيط *zakīt*, Wicked, unclean (man).

A ذكا *zakā'*, (v. n. of ذكي) Flaming (fire). Diffusing itself (the smell of musk). A flaming fire.

A ذكاء *zakā'*, (v. n. of ذكا) Being quick, penetrating, judicious. Burning, flaming (fire). Slaughtering. A live coal. Vivacity, acuteness of genius, penetration. (Advanced) age. *Zukā'*, The sun. ابن ذكاء *ibn zukā'*, Child of the sun, *i. e.* The dawn.

A ذكاة *zakāt*, The act of slaughtering.

A ذكار *zikār*, (pl. of ذكر *zakar*) Males.

A ذكارة *zikārat*, (pl. of ذكر *zakar*) Males.

A ذكّارة *zukkārat*, The male palm-tree.

A ذكاوة *zakāwat*, Brightness of genius, wit.

A ذكاوين *zakāwīn*, (pl. of ذكوانة) Small saddles.

A ذكذكة *zakzakat*, Vivacity, life, spirits.

A ذكر *zakr*, (v. n. of ذكر) Striking on the penis. *Zikr*, (v. n. of ذكر) Remembering. Keeping in mind, retaining. Engaging in exercises of devotion. Repeating the names, attributes, and praises of God. Asking (a woman) in marriage, or opposing (her) betrothing. Preserving one's right, remembering it, and not suffering it to be lost. Remembrance, commemoration. Memory. Mention. The Kur'ān. The Pentateuch. The Gospel. Any book wherein the doctrines of religion are distinctly laid down. Strong, bold, refractory (man). Hard and copious rain. A strong, pithy, sententious saying. ذكر الحق *zikru'l hakk*, The sentence of a judge written and signed. Praise. Fame. Nobility. اهل الذكر *ahlu'z zikr*, Jews and Christians. ذكر جميل *zikri jamīl*, (or ذكر بالخير *zikri bi'l khayr*) Honourable mention, favourable recommendation. ذكر جزء ارادة كل *zikri juz' irādasi kull*, The rhetorical figure synecdoche (by which a part is taken for the whole). ذكر حال و ارادهٔ محل *zikri hāl u irādasi mahall*, The figure metonymy (where the matter is put for the materiate). سابق الذكر *sābiku'z zikr*, Aforementioned. ذكر الله العزيز و عنده مفاتيح الغيب برزق من يشاء بغير حساب *zikru'llāhi'l ʻaziz, wa ʻindahu mafātīhu'l ghayb, yarzaku man yashā' bi ghayr hisāb*, Praise to the glorious God, with whom are the keys of every secret, who enricheth him whom he pleaseth beyond computation (words which are sometimes written at the top of diplomas and other royal deeds, where they often, however, substitute the single word هو *huwa*, He, *i. e.* God). P ذكر خدا *zikri khudā*, The praising of God. ذكر نام خدا *zikri nāmi khudā*, An invoking of the name of God. ذكر كردن *zikr kardan*, To mention, to commemorate. To praise, to sing the praises of God. A *Zukr*, Mental remembrance. An edge: as, ذو ذكر *zū zukr*, A sharp-edged sword. *Zakar*, (pl. ذكور *zukūr*, ذكورة *zukūrat*, ذكار *zikār*, ذكارة *zikārat*, ذكران *zukrān*, and ذكرة *zikarat*) Male, masculine. Male iron, steel. An excellent sword of high-tempered steel. (pl. ذكور *zukūr* and مذاكير *mazākīr*) Penis. *Zakir* or *zakur*, One who retains in memory, gets, or recites by heart.

P ذكر *zakar*, Peony, or ass-rose.

A ذكران *zukrān*, (pl. of ذكر *zakar*) Males.

A ذكرة *zakrat*, Masculine (woman). *Zikrat*, Males, male children. *Zukrat*, Masculine ardour, male energy. Mention, fame, rumour. An edge. Sharpness. A piece of steel on the head of an axe. *Zikarat*, (pl. of ذكر *zakar*) Males.

A ذكرى *zikra'* Remembrance. An admonition (if remembered). Repentance, turning from sin.

A ذكو *zakw*, A burning, a flaming.

A ذكوان *zakwān*, (pl. ذكاوين) A small saddle.

A ذكوة *zakwat*, (v. n. of ذكا for ذكو) Cutting the throat, butchering. Whatever makes a fire burn. A live coal. Name of a place abounding in lions.

P ذكور *zakūr*, Endued with a retentive memory. *Zukūr*, Damascus-steel.

A ذكور *zukūr*, (pl. of ذكر *zakar*) Males. Male organs. Strong, coarse (vegetables).

A ذكورة *zukūrat*, Essence, purity, freedom from all admixture. (pl. of ذكر *zakar*) Males.

A ذكوريّة *zukūriyat*, Masculineness.

A ذكيّ *zakiy*, (pl. اذكياء *azkiyā'*) Acute. Fiery, flaming. Slaughtered. Strong, diffusive musk.

A ذكية *zakyat* or *zukyat*, Fuel. Whatever makes a fire burn.

A ذكيّة *zakiyat*, Strong, diffusive (musk).

A ذكير *zakīr*, Male iron, steel. *Zakīr*, (or ذكّير *zikkīr*) Endued with a good memory.

A ذلّ *zalla*, (fut. يذلّ *yazillu*) He was vile.

A ذلّ *zill*, (v. n. of ذلّ) Being submissive, easy, compliant. Benignity, benevolence, compassion. Gentleness (of a horse). Softness of temper. (pl. اذلال *azlāl*) A course, a current, way, mode, manner, custom, usage. ذلّ الطريق *zillu't tarīk*, An easy, beaten road. *Zull*, Gentleness, softness of temper, submission. Benignity, benevolence, compassion. *Zull*, (or ذلّة *zillat*) (v. n. of ذلّ) Being abject, vile. Baseness, meanness of spirit.

A ذلّاح *zullāh*, Milk diluted with water.

A ذلاذل *zalāzil*, (pl. of ذلذل *zulzul*) The lower parts of shifts. The meanest of men.

A ذلاقة *zalākat*, (v. n. of ذلق) Being sharp, ready, glib (the tongue). Readiness of speech, volubility.

A ذلال *zilāl*, (pl. of ذليل) Base, abject: submissive.

A ذلالة *zalālat* or *zulālat*, (v. n. of ذلّ) Being abject, obsequious. Baseness.

A ذلّان *zullān*, Abject, vile. Kept under.

A ذلّة *zillat*, Baseness of spirit. Insult.

A ذلج *zalj*, A sipping, a gulping (of water).

A ذلذل *zalzul*, (*zulazil*, *zulzul*, or *zilzil*) The lower part of a shift, or any garment, toward the feet.

A ذلذلات *zulzulāt*, The meanest of men.

A ذلذلة *zalzalat*, *zulazilat*, or *zilzilat*, The lower part of a long shirt.

A ذلغ *zalgh*, (v. n. of ذلغ) Larding (meat), or eating it. Lying with. *Zalagh*, (v. n. of ذلغ) Being inverted (the lip).

A ذلف *zulf*, (pl. of ذلفاء *zalfā'*) Small, ape-nosed (women). *Zalaf*, (v. n. of ذلف) Having a small, flat nose. Smallness and flatness of nose. Being straight (a sword).

A ذلفاء *zalfā'*, (fem. of اذلف *azlaf*) Small-nosed, ape-nosed (woman). A woman's name.

A ذلق *zalk*, (v. n. of ذلق) Being quick, sharp, glib, ready at speech (the tongue). Whetting (a sword). Weakening one (poison or fasting). Voiding dung (a bird). Point or tip (of the tongue). The place in a pulley where the axle turns. A sharp and ready tongue. Readiness of speech, volubility. حروف الذلق *hurūfu'z zalk*, Those letters which are pronounced with the tip of the tongue and the lips, viz. ب ر ف ل م ن. *Zulk*, (pl. of اذلق *azlak*) Sharp, pointed, edged. Oratorical (speakers). *Zalak*, (v. n. of ذلق) Being moveable or restless. Being voluble, sharp, glib (tongue).

Burning bright (a lamp). Leaving rough hard sand for moister quarters (a lizard). Dying of thirst. Motion, mobility. *Zalik*, Eloquent, sharp, glib (tongue). Eloquent (orator). *Zulak*, Sharp and ready (tongue). *Zuluk*, Ready (tongue).

A ذلقة *zalkat* or *zalakat*, Point or sharp edge. *Zalikat*, An eloquent woman.

A ذلك *zālik* or *zālika*, That.

A ذلل *zulul*, (pl. of ذلول) Tractable (horses).

A ذلم *zulam*, A shallow river's mouth.

A ذلول *zalūl*, (pl. ذلل *zulul*, and اذلة *azillat*) Obedient (horse). Subject to the authority of another. Gentle, tractable. Free from thunder and lightning (cloud).

A ذلولى *zalūla'*, Obsequious, humble (man).

A ذلولي *zalūliy*, (pl. ذلوليّون *zalūliyūn*) Soft, easy, good-tempered, tame, gentle.

A ذلى *zaly*, A gathering (of dates).

A ذليذلات *zulayzilāt*, The meanest of men.

A ذليق *zalīk*, Sharp and voluble (tongue). Eloquent (orator).

A ذليقة *zalīkat*, An eloquent woman.

A ذليل *zalīl*, (pl. ذلال *zilāl*, اذلاء *azillāa*, and اذلة *azillat*) Abject, mean, contemptible, trifling. Gentle, submissive.

A ذم *zamm*, (v. n. of ذمّ) Reproaching. Being snotty (a kid's nose). Blame, disapprobation, reproach. The debit side of an account. *Zamm* or *zimm*, Blamed. Blameable. *Zimm*, Quite spent and emaciated. Perishing. Nuptials. A treaty or agreement tending to bestow security; patronage, protection. A festival. Confederates.

A ذمأ *zamaa*, (fut. يذمأ *yazmaau*) It was difficult and troublesome.

A ذماء *zimāa*, (v. n. of ذمي) Being stout-hearted, manifesting strength of heart. Shaking. The dying palpitation of a slaughtered animal. Remains of life, strength of heart. Motion. الضب اطول شيء ذماء *az zabb atwal shayain zimāan*, The lizard is the longest of any thing in dying.

A ذمار *zimār*, Any thing that ought to be kept with care (as reputation). The great name or reputation of ancestors. حامي الذمار *hāmi'z zimār*, The defender of his rights.

A ذمارة *zamārat*, Courage, bravery in the defence of those under one's protection.

A ذمام *zimām*, (pl. اذمّة *azimmat*) Protection. Honour, reputation. Right, justice, claim, what is due. (pl. of ذمّة *zammat* and ذميمة *zamīmat*) Wells with little water; also abounding with water.

A ذمّام *zammūm*, An accuser, slanderer, blamer.

A ذمامة *zamāmat* or *zimāmat*, A security for life and property. A covenant ensuring protection. *Zumāmat*, Remains, residue.

A ذمائر *zumāair*, Misfortune, calamity.

A ذمائم *zamāaim*, (pl. of ذميمة *zamīmat*) Misdeeds. Base qualities.

A ذمّة *zammat*, (pl. ذمام *zimām*) A well with little water; also abounding. *Zimmat*, A deed whereby one is taken under protection. A warrant for the security of life and property. Protection. Subjection, vassalage. Furnished with a covenant or promise. A feast. A nuptial entertainment. Trust, charge. اهل الذمّة *ahlu'z zimmat*, Tributary, tributaries. Jews, Christians, or fire-worshippers. A client. برات ذمّة *barāti zimmat*, A safe-conduct, pass, or warrant of security. قضى بذمّته *kaza' bi zimm* or *zammatihi*, He conferred benefits on him, so as to save him from contempt.

A ذمت *zamt*, (v. n. of ذمت) Being changed, altered, troubled. Becoming emaciated with age.

A ذمحلة *zamhalat*, A rolling.

A ذمخ *zamakh* or *zimakh*, A kind of fruit.

A ذمذمة *zamzamat*, A giving little.

A ذمر *zamr*, (v. n. of ذمر) Exciting, stimulating (to fight). Roaring (as a lion). Reproaching, blaming. Terrifying, threatening. *Zimr*, Misfortune, calamity. *Zimr* or *zamir*, (pl. اذمار *azmār*) An intrepid man, particularly in defence of those under his protection. Intelligent, wise, sagacious.

A ذمّر *zimirr*, Bold, brave.

A ذمرة *zamirat*, Sound, noise, voice.

A ذمط *zamt*, (v. n. of ذمط) Slaughtering. *Zamit*, (Meat) which descends easily.

A ذمطة *zumatat*, A man quick of apprehension, skilful, clever. A great eater.

A ذمل *zaml*, (ذملان *zamalān*, and ذميل *zamīl*) (v. n. of ذمل) Going fast with a long easy step.

A ذمّل *zummal*, (pl. of ذمول *zamūl*) (She-camels) waving from side to side.

A ذملق *zamallak*, One who speaks soothingly. Quick, smart. Eloquent. Keen (sword). Light.

A ذملّقاني *zamallakāniy*, One who speaks fast.

A ذملقة *zamlakat*, Blandishments, politeness.

A ذملّقي *zamallakiy*, Eloquent.

A ذمم *zimam*, (pl. of ذمّة) Clientships. Covenants.

A ذمول *zamūl*, (pl. ذمّل *zummal*) (A camel) waving from side to side. *Zamūl*, (v. n. of ذمل) Going fast with a long easy step.

A ذموم *zamūm*, One who blames, reproaches, or disparages greatly. *Zumūm*, Vices, defects.

A ذمه *zamah*, (v. n. of ذمه) Being intense (heat). Being oppressed with heat (a man). The scorching reflexion from sands. A kind of game.

A ذمي *zamy*, (v. n. of ذمي) Struggling in the agony of death (a slaughtered beast). *Zama'*, Stink.

A ذمّي *zimmiy*, One tolerated by the Muhamdan law, on paying an annual poll-tax. A client, tributary, subject. A Christian or Jew.

A ذمياط *zimyāt*, Damietta in Egypt.

A ذميان *zamayān*, (v. n. of ذمى) Hastening. Hurting, injuring. Being exalted. Remaining over, being left.

A ذمير *zamīr*, Handsome, beautiful. A brave man who protects his dependants.

A ذميل *zamīl*, A long, easy pace. Jaded.

A ذميلة *zamīlat*, Vicious, faulty (woman).

A ذميم *zamīm*, Blamed, blameable. Loathsome, unwholesome water. Eruptions on the face from heat. Snot. A well containing little or much water. Urine. Mucus at the point of a goat's pizzle, or milk at the tip of a sheep's teat. Dew on a tree, by dust converted into mud. White on a kid's nose.

A ذميمة *zamīmat*, Paralysis.

A ذنّ *zann*, (v. n. of ذنّ) Languishing. Perishing. Begging.

A ذنّاء *zannāa*, Snotty-nosed (woman): also one who suffers from a continuous menstrual flux.

A ذناب *zināb*, (v. n. 3 of ذنب) Being near delivery (a mare). (pl. ذنائب *zanāaib*) A place through which water flows between two higher grounds. The tail. Extremity of any thing. A rope with which they confine a camel's tail, to prevent his switching it round his rider. (pl. of ذنوب *zanūb*) Long-tailed (horses). Portions. Buckets. Evil days.

A ذنابة *zunābat* or *zinābat*, End of time, or of an age. The lower part of a valley through which water runs. Water flowing down the declivity of a mountain, or by cascades, from garden to garden. *Zinābat*, The surface or beaten part of a road. Propinquity, affinity, relationship. *Zunābat*, The toe of a shoe. A follower.

A ذنابي *zunāba'*, A tail or train, particularly that of a bird, Snot running from a camel's nose.

A ذناذن *zanāzin*, Lower parts (of shirts).

A ذنان *zunān*, (or ذناني) Thin, running snot.

A ذنانة *zunūnat*, Weak, perishing remains. Remains of a debt or obligation. Necessity. Long-tailed horses. Buckets. Evil days.

A ذنائب *zanāaib*, (pl. of ذناب *zanāb* and *zināb*) Places through which water flows. Tails. (pl. of ذنوب *zanūb*) Portions.

A ذنب *zamb*, (v. n. of ذنب) Following closely. Keeping close to the tail of another. (pl. ذنوب *zunūb*) A crime, sin, fault. *Zanab*, (pl. اذناب *aznāb*) A tail. (in astronomy) Tail of the dragon, descending node. Long. ذنب الثعلب *zanabu's saɛlab*, Fox-tail (a plant). ذنب الخيل *zanabu'l khayl*, A certain plant. ذنب السبع *zanabu's sabuɛ*, Lion's tail (a plant). ذنب العين *zanabu'l ɛayn*, The outer angle of the eye. ذنب الفار *zanabu'l fār*, Ribwort. ذنب الفرس *zanabu'l faras*, Name of a star. ضرب بذنبه *zaraba bi zanabihi*, He stopped; he was firm. ركب ذنب البعير *rakiba zanaba'l baɛīr*, He mounted on the camel's tail, i.e. he contented himself with a humble fortune. ركب ذنب الريح *rakiba zanaba'r rīh*, He rode upon the tail of the wind, *i.e.* he got so far a-head of them that they could not overtake him.

A ذنبات *zanabāt*, The rabble, tag-rag.

A ذنبان *zanabān,* Name of a plant like millet.
A ذنبب *zumbub,* A wild bull.
A ذنبة *zanabat,* The lower part of a valley through which the water flows. End of time.
A ذنبّي *zunubba',* (or ذنبي *zimbīy*) A tail.
A ذنذن *zinzin* or *zunzun,* (pl. ذناذن *zanāzin*) The lower part of a shirt or other garment.
A ذنن *zanan,* (v. n. of ذنّ) Being snotty.
A ذنوب *zanūb,* (pl. اذنبة *aznibat,* ذنائب *zanāib,* and ذناب *zināb*) Long-tailed (horse). A portion, lot, good or bad fortune. The grave. A bucket (full or not full of water). A long evil day. The lower muscle of the loins. Flesh of buttocks. *Zunūb,* (pl. of ذنب *zamb*) Crimes, sins, trespasses.
A ذنوبات *zunūbāt,* (pl. of ذنوب) Sins, crimes.
A ذنوبان *zanūbāni,* (dual) The loins.
A ذنيباء *zunaybāʼ,* A grain found amongst wheat; tares, darnel.
A ذنيبّي *zunaybīy,* A kind of striped stuff.
A ذنين *zanīn,* The running of snot. Snivel.
A ذو *zū,* (pl. ذوون *zawūn*) A lord, master. Having, possessed of, endowed with. Who, which. The kings of Arabia Felix, because they all had ذو *zū* prefixed to their name: as, ذو جدن *zū jadan,* ذو رعين *zū ruʻayn,* &c. (for الذي *allazī*) Who. ذو الالسنة *zū'l alsinat,* Linguists. Preachers, admonishers. ذو الف اوراق *zū alf awrāk,* The plant millefoil. ذو الجلال *zū'l jalāl,* Majestic, possessed of dignity, glorious. Prodigious, wonderful. ذو الحاسة *zū'l hāssat,* Possessed of feeling. ذو الحجّة *zū'l hijjat,* The twelfth Arabian month. ذو الحركة *zū'l harakat,* Possessed of motion. ذو الحوت *zū'l hūt,* (Lord of the fish) The prophet Jonah. ذو الحيوة *zū'l hayāt,* Having life. ذو ذوابه *zū zuwāba,* (Tailed) A comet. ذو الفقار *zū'l fakār,* Name of the famous two-edged sword of Aliy, which Muhammad reported he had from the angel Gabriel. ذو فنون *zū funūn,* Learned. ذو القدر *zū'l kadr,* Powerful. ذو القربي *zū'l kurba',* A kinsman. ذو القرنين *zū'l karnayn,* Bicornous; Alexander the Great. ذو القعدة *zū'l kaʻdat,* The eleventh Arabian month. ذو لونين *zū lawnayn,* Bi-coloured. ذو المتن *zū'l matn,* An epithet of God. ذو وجهتين *zū wijhatayn,* (Two-faced) Bearing a double meaning.
A ذوا *zuwā,* (du. of ذو *zū*) Two lords.
A ذؤابة *zuʼābat,* (pl. ذوائب *zawāʼib*) The forelocks dangling over the brow. The highest dignity or nobility. That part of the upper leather of a shoe which touches the ground. A skin hung over the back part of a camel's saddle.
A ذوابل *zawābil,* (pl. of ذابل *zābil*) Lances.
A ذواة *zawāt,* The husk or rind of wheat, grapes, or melons.
A ذوات *zawāt,* (pl. of ذات *zāt*) Ladies, mistresses of. ذوات الاربع *zawātu'l arbaʻ,* Quadrupeds. ذوات السموم *zawātu's sumūm,* Venomous (insects or reptiles).

A ذواتا *zawātā,* (du. of ذاة *zāt,* fem.) Those two.
A ذوّاد *zawwād,* A defender of his right. *Zuwād,* (pl. of ذائد *zāʼid*) Repellers. Defenders of their rights.
A ذوارع *zawāriʻ,* (pl. of ذارع *zāriʻ*) Small bottles made of the leg-skins of animals.
A ذؤاف *zuʼāf,* Sudden death. Quick poison.
A ذواق *zawāk,* (v. n. of ذاق for ذوق) Tasting. Examining. Drawing a bow-string to try the tension of the bow. Any thing tasted.
A ذوّاق *zawwāk,* A taster. Afflicted, sad.
A ذواقن *zawākin,* (pl. of ذاقنة *zākinat*) Lower parts of the throat and belly.
A ذؤالة *zuʼālat,* (pl. ذئلان or ذؤلان) A wolf.
A ذواهب *zawāhib,* (pl. of ذاهبة *zāhibat*) Travellers: birds migrating from a cold to a warm climate.
A ذوائب *zawāʼib,* (pl. of ذؤابة *zuʼābat*) Forelocks. Tresses.
A ذوب *zawb,* The purest honey. *Zawb,* (or ذوبان *zawabān*) (v. n. of ذاب for ذوب) Becoming liquid, melting. Waxing hotter (the sun). Becoming foolish after having been sensible. Being legally due. Eating honey constantly. ما ذاب في يدي منه خير *mā zāba fī yadī minhu khayrun,* No good has flowed into my hand from him.
A ذؤبان *zuʼbān,* (pl. of ذئب *ziʼb*) Wolves; also wild dogs. Arabs or religious mendicants who live like wolves by plundering.
A ذوبان *zūbān,* Hair on camel's or horse's neck.
A ذوبة *zawbat,* Remains of property.
A ذوج *zawj,* (v. n. of ذاج for ذوج) Drinking. A beverage, a draught.
A ذؤج *zaʼuj,* Intense (red).
A ذوح *zawh,* (v. n. of ذاح for ذوح) Collecting, driving (cattle). Moving with a hard pace or trot.
A ذود *zawd,* (v. n. of ذاد for ذود) Repelling, driving, thrusting (camels). (pl. اذواد *azwād*) A number of camels from 3 to 10: or 15, 20 or 30; or from 2 to 9 she-camels. الذود الي الذود *az zawd ila'z zawd,* Camels in a place by two's.
A ذوّد *zūwad,* (pl. of ذائد *zāʼid*) Repellers, thrusters. Defenders of their rights.
A ذوذح *zawzah,* Impotent. See تيتاء *taytāʼ.*
A ذوذخ *zawzakh,* Impotent. See عذيوط *ʻizyawt.*
A ذور *zawr,* (v. n. of ذار for ذور) Frightening. *Zuwar,* (pl. of ذورة *zūrat*) The parts of birds' crops in which the water lodges.
P ذوراق *zawrāk,* A kind of barley-gruel.
A ذورة *zūrat,* Earth, soil, dust. (pl. ذور *zuwar*) The fore part of a bird's crop, where the water lodges.
A ذورور *zawarwar,* Something, any thing.
P ذوش *zosh,* Bad-tempered, severe.
A ذوط *zawt,* (v. n. of ذاط for ذوط) Strangling violently till the tongue protrudes.
A ذوطة *zawtat,* A yellow-backed spider.
A ذوع *zawʻ,* (v. n. of ذاع for ذوع) Needing, wanting. Extirpating.

A ذوف *zawf,* (v. n. of ذاف for ذوف) Going with short and straddling steps.
A ذؤفان *zuʼfān,* (or ذوفان *zūfān*) Deadly poison.
A ذوق *zawk,* (v. n. of ذاق for ذوق) Tasting, trying, examining. Drawing a bow-string to try the tension of a bow. Taste. Delight, joy, pleasure. اهل ذوق *ahli zawk,* A voluptuary. ذوق لا يعبّر *zawk lā yuʻabbar,* Inexpressible pleasure. بذوق *bi zawk,* With pleasure, willingly, delightfully.
A ذوقان *zawakān,* (v. n. of ذاق for ذوق) Tasting. Trying, examining.
A ذؤلان *zuʼlān,* A jackal. A wolf. (pl. of ذؤالة *zuʼālat*) Wolves.
A ذولق *zawlak,* The tip (of the tongue). The point (of a spear).
A ذولقيّة *zawlakīyat,* Lingual (letters, ل ر ن).
A ذوو *zawū,* (nom. pl. of ذو *zū*) Lords, possessors.
A ذؤوب *zaʼūb,* Fat (camel).
A احمر ذؤوج *ahmar zaʼūj,* Bright red.
A ذؤنون *zuʼnūn,* (pl. ذءانين) A sort of pot-herb.
A ذوويّ *zawawīy,* Related to ذو *zū,* Lord.
A ذوي *zaway,* (obliq. of ذوا *zawā,* du. mas. of ذو *zū*) Two possessors. من ذوي عدل *min zaway ʻadlin,* From two persons endued with justice. *Zawī,* (oblique of ذوو *zawū,* pl. of ذو *zū*) Lords, masters, possessors. سلاطين ذوي الاقتدار *salātini zawī'l iktidār,* Powerful princes. ذوي الاحترام *zawī'l ihtirām,* Most honoured. ذوي الاعتبار *zawī'l iʻtibār,* In the highest esteem. ذوي الاكرام *zawī'l ikrām,* Held in veneration. ذوي العقول *zawī'l ʻukūl,* Rational. *Ziwa',* Little sheep.
A ذويّ *zuwīy,* (v. n. of ذوي) Withering (a herb).
A ذويل *zawīl,* Dry (plant).
A ذويلة *zuwaylat,* (dim. of ذال *zāl*) A little ذ.
A ذه *zih* or *zihi,* (fem. of ذا *zā*) This.
A ذهّ *zahh,* Acuteness of genius.
A ذهاب *zahāb,* (v. n. of ذهب) Going, walking, or passing by, proceeding. Passing into use. Going, being shed (blood). A current form of speech. A departure. *Zihāb,* (pl. of ذهب *zahab*) Yolks of eggs. Dry measures in Yaman (Arabia Felix). (pl. of ذهبة *zihbat*) Light rains.
A ذهب *zahab,* (v. n. of ذهب) Having the eyes dazzled at the glare of gold, or on entering suddenly into a glittering mine. (pl. اذهاب *azhāb,* ذهوب *zuhūb,* and ذهبان *zuhbān*) Gold. (pl. ذهاب *zihāb* and اذهاب *azhāb*) The yolk of an egg.
A ذهبان *zuhbān,* (pl. of ذهب) Particles of gold.
A ذهبة *zihbat,* (pl. ذهاب *zihāb*) Light rain, or a copious shower. *Zahabat,* A particle of gold.
A ذهبيّ *zahabīy,* Golden.
A ذهبيّون *zahabīyūn,* Name of a company of reporters of Muhammadan traditions.
A ذهر *zahar,* (v. n. of ذهر) Having black teeth.
A ذهل *zahl,* (v. n. of ذهل) Forgetting, leaving carelessly, abandoning. Ease, quiet, no wish for society. That part of the night when people

are already refreshed with sleep. *Zuhl*, Part of the night. Name of the tree بشام *bashām*.

A ذهلول *zuhlūl*, A generous, noble horse.

A ذهن *zihn* or *zahan*, (v. n. of ذهن) Excelling in genius. Causing to forget, drawing off the attention, employing, occupying. (pl. اذهان *azhān*) Understanding, memory, genius. *Zihn*, Ability, strength. Fat, grease.

A ذهنيّ *zahaniy*, Mental.

A ذهو *zahw*, A being proud.

A ذهوب *zahūb*, One who departs. *Zuhūb*, (v. n. of ذهب) Going, walking, passing by. (pl. of ذهب *zahab*) Golds.

A ذهول *zuhūl*, (v. n. of ذهل) Forgetting, neglecting, leaving. Ease, quiet, no wish for society.

A ذهولة *zuhūlat*, Carelessness, inadvertency.

A ذهيب *zahīb*, Gilded.

A ذهين *zahīn*, Sagacious, ingenious. Powerful.

A ذي *zī*, (fem. of ذا *zā*) This. (oblique case of ذو *zū*) A lord, endowed, possessed of. ذي بال *zī bāl*, Powerful, brave. ذي جاه *zī jāh*, Appointed to a place of honour. ذي الجلال *zi'l jalāl*, Endowed with magnificence (one of the epithets of God). ذي الحجّة *zi'l hijjat*, The last month of the Arabian year. ذي حقّ *zī hakk*, A legal or just claimant. ذي روح *zī rūh*, Rational. ذي شان *zī shān*, Conspicuous for dignity. ذي القعدة *zi'l kaʿdat*, The penultimate month of the Muhammadan year. ذي قيمة *zī kīmat*, Precious. P ذي هوش *zī hosh*, Sensible. ذي يال و بال *zī yāl u bāl*, Endowed with strength and courage. A جاء من ذي نفسه *jāʾa min zī nafsihi*, He came of his own accord.

A ذيّا *zayyā*, (dim. of ذا *zā*) The little this.

A ذئاب *ziʾāb*, (pl. of ذئب) Wolves: wild dogs.

G ذيابيطس *ziyābītas*, Diabetes.

A ذياج *ziyāj*, Pot-companionship, intimacy.

A ذياد *ziyād*, (v. n. of ذاد for ذود) Driving (camels).

A ذئار *ziʾār*, (or ذيار *ziyār*) Fresh camels' dung and earth, with which they anoint dugs to wean colts.

A ذيّاك *zayyāka*, (dim. of ذاك) The little that.

A ذيّال *zayyāl*, Long-tailed (horse). Tall of stature. (A man) sweeping round with a train and walking proudly. ذيّال الذنب *zayyālu'z zanab*, Dragging the tail on the ground. ابو ذيّال *abū zayyāl*, (Father Long-tail) An ox.

A ذيّالة *zayyālat*, A threaded needle.

A ذيّالك *zayyālika*, (dim. of ذلك *zālika*) The little he or that.

A ذيّان *zayyān*, (dim. of ذا *zā*) The little this.

A ذيّائك *zayyāʾika*, (dim. of ذائك *zāʾika*) The little that.

A ذيب *zayb*, (equiv. to عيب *ʿayb*) Vice.

A ذئب *ziʾb* or ذيب *zīb*, (pl. اذئب *azʾub*, ذئاب *ziʾāb*, and ذؤبان *zuʾbān*) A wolf. A wild dog. A cottage, a hut. داء الذئب *dāʾu'z ziʾb*, The wolf's disease, *i.e.* hunger.

A ذئبان *ziʾbān*, Camels' hair on the neck or lip. *Ziʾbāni*, Two stars betwixt the عوائذ *ʿawāʾiz* and فرقدان *farkadān*.

A ذيبان *zībān*, Hairs on camel's or horse's necks.

A ذئبة *ziʾbat*, A disease in the throats of camels. The vacant space under the pommel of a saddle: something there which hurts the withers of a horse. Ringlets overhanging the forehead. A she-wolf.

A ذيّة *zayyata zayyata*, (ذيت ذيت *zayta zayta*, or ذيّاء *zayyāʾ*) So and so, thus, in this manner.

A ذيج *zayj* or *zīj*, A draught, beverage.

A ذيخ *zīkh*, (pl. ذيوخ *zuyūkh*, اذياخ *azyākh*, ذيخة *ziyakhat*) A hairy male hyena. Bold, brave. A wolf. A fine stallion. A cluster of dates. A reddish star. Pride.

A ذيخة *zīkhat*, A hairy female hyena. *Ziyakhat*, (pl. of ذيخ *zīkh*) Male hyenas; wolves. Horses.

A ذئر *zaʾir*, Enraged. Bold. Refractory (wife).

A ذير *zayr*, (v. n. of ذار for ذير) Disliking, detesting, disapproving.

A ذئرة *zaʾirat*, Odious, disagreeable, disapproved. Severity. The violence or brunt of war.

A ذيرة *zīrat*, Fresh dung mixed with earth.

A ذيع *zayʿ*, (ذيعان *zayaʿān*, ذيوع *zuyūʿ*, or ذيعوعة *zayʿūʿat*) (v. n. of ذاع for ذيع) Being published (news), divulged (a secret).

A ذئفان *ziʾfān*, (ذيفان *zīfān*, *zayfān*, or *zayafān*) Venom, poison.

A ذيل *zayl*, (v. n. of ذال for ذيل) Sweeping (the ground) with a train, strutting. Cocking the tail. Having a long tail. Being lowly, or mean (condition). Being despised (a thing). Laying aside one's gravity. Being meagre (a woman). Being impudent and saucy. (pl. اذيال *azyāl*, ذيول *zuyūl*, or اذيل *azyul*) The last, hinder, or supplementary part of any thing; as the appendix to a book, the lappet or train to a robe, the long tail of a beast, especially the lower extremity (as of a lion or a bull). Traces in the sand left by the wind or the train of a garment. The lower margin of a book where the notes are usually put. Appendix, postscript. ذيل ذائل *zaylun zāʾilun*, Ignominy, shame, vileness, meanness.

A ذئلان *ziʾlān*, (pl. of ذؤالة *zuʾālat*) Wolves.

A ذيم *zaym*, (v. n. of ذام for ذيم) Accusing, reproaching, treating opprobriously. *Zaym* or *zīm*, Blame, reproach.

A ذيمريّ *zaymuriy*, Sharp, keen, acute, clever, who says or does something astonishing. Difficult to be understood.

A ذين *zīn* or *zayn*, Defect, vice, blemish.

A ذيوخ *zuyūkh*, (pl. of ذيخ) Male hyenas. Wolves.

A ذيوع *zuyūʿ*, (v. n. of ذاع for ذيع) Becoming divulged (news).

A ذيول *zuyūl*, (pl. of ذيل *zayl*) Long tails. Skirts. Trains.

A ذيويّ *zayawiy*, Relating to so and so.

A ذيّه ذيّه *zayyah zayyah*, So and so.

ر

ر *re* or *rā*, (called راى قرشت *rāʾi karashat*, راىٔ غير منقوطه *rāʾi ghayr mankūta*, or راىٔ مهمله *rāʾi muhmala*, Undotted ر) The tenth letter of the Arabic alphabet, and the twelfth of the Persian. In arithmetic it expresses 200; in almanacks it is the astronomical character for the moon; and in dates it denotes the month ربيع الآخر *rabiʿu'l ākhir*. This letter is interchangeable with د *dāl*, ز *ze*, ژ *je*, ل *lām*, and ن *nūn*.

P را *rā*, An inseparable particle added to Persian nouns, generally serving to denote the oblique cases. It marks the accusative when the word is used definitely: as, گلرا چيد *gulrā chīd*, He gathered *the* rose. It may occasionally be construed by the particle *to*, the English sign of the dative: as, چون قضاي الهى نزول يابد ديدهٔ بصيرترا نه روشني ماند *chūn kazāʾi ilāhī nuzūl yābad, dīdaʾi basīratrā na roshanī mānad*, When the decree of heaven is accomplishing, no light remains *to* the eye of understanding. ما همه مردنرا پيدا شده ايم *mā hama murdanrā paydā shuda īm* (or *em*) We were all born *to* die. By the word *for*: as, خدارا يك نظر اي سرو آزاد *khudārā yak nazar ay sarvi āzād*, *For* God's sake, one look, O waving cypress! درد عاشقرا دواىٔ بهتر از معشوق نيست *dardi ʿāshikrā davāʾi bihtar az maʿshūk nīst*, There is no remedy *for* a lover's pain better than his beloved. هزار روپيهرا اسبي خريدم *hazār rūpiyarā asbe kharīdam*, I bought a horse *for* a thousand rupees. It denotes possession, in such sentence as this: اورا ده رأس اسپ بود *urā dah raʾsi asp būd*, He had, or possessed ten head of horses. It also denotes, With. By reason of. After: as, اندك وقتيرا *andak waktērā*, After a short time. If را *rā* occurs sometimes with a genitive signification, it is but seldom, and without good authority; and in the best authors it is often omitted, and frequently redundant. *Rā*, contracted from the Arabic رأي *raʾy*, signifies, Seeing: as, روشن را *roshan-rā*, Seeing light, *i.e.* penetrating, wise. وزراىٔ نيك را *wuzarāʾi nek-rā*, Prudent vazirs or counsellors.

A راء *rāʾ*, The Arabic name of the letter ر. The shrub Palma Christi. Froth of the sea. A large tike.

A رءّاء *raʾʾāʾ*, One who sees much or well; judicious, intelligent.

A رءّاب *raʾʾāb*, A mender of broken vessels.

A رآبيل *raʾābīl*, (pl. of رئبال or ريبال) Lions.

A رءّاس *raʾʾās*, A vender of heads of cattle.

A رأفة *raʾāfat*, A pitying. Mercy, clemency.

A رأب *raʾb*, (v. n. of رأب) Shooting forth after being cropped (the earth). Mending a broken (cup). Making up differences. Repairing any thing. (pl. رئاب ri,āb) A herd of seventy camels. A great chieftain; a portly lord. A crack or chink in a vessel.

A راب rāb, Quantity. Worth, value, price.

A رابّ rābb, A step-father.

A رابّة rābbat, A step-mother.

A رابج rābij, Quenched, assuaged (thirst).

A رابح rābih, Gainful, lucrative, profitable (trade). A gainer. (pl. ربح rabah) A camel's colt.

A رابحة rābihat, Lucrative, profitable (business).

A رابد rābid, A hoarder, preserver. A treasurer.

A رابض rābiz, An inhabitant, a resident.

A رابضان rābizāni, Turks and Ethiopians.

A رابضة rābizat, Vile, contemptible. Any thing struck or wounded by a malignant eye. Unable to speak except on trivial subjects. Certain angels said to have come down to earth with Adam, and to bring those who have erred into the right way.

A رابط rābit, A binder, strengthener. Encamped on an enemy's frontier. A monk who renounces the world. A philosopher. Large, ample (soul). A mark of connexion. رابط الجاش rābitu'l jāsh, Intrepid, firm, brave.

A رابطة rābitat, (pl. روابط rawābit) A chain, ligature, any thing binding, connecting, or regulating. The catch-word, placed at the corner of a page under the last line, and repeated at the top of the page which follows. A troop maintaining its post. A large army. P رابطهٔ آشنائي rābita,i āshnā,i, The cement of friendship.

A رابع rābiɛ, Fourth. Athirst, and drinking every fourth day (camel). Quartan (fever). Stedfast.

A رابعاً rābiɛan, In the fourth place, fourthly.

A رابغ rābigh, Agreeable (life). Luxuriant in herbage (spring). Employed agreeably and successfully about any thing. Name of a valley.

A رآبل ra,ābil, pl. of رئبال ri,bāl, Lions. Wolves. Only sons.

A رأبلة ra,balat, (v. n. of رأبل Q) Walking softly or pompously. Wiliness, subtlety, malice.

A رابلتان rābilatāni, (dual of رابلة rābilat) The pulpy, fleshy part of both thighs.

A رابن rābin, The part of the leg on which the gaiters or leggings (called ران rān) are put.

P رابو rābū, A kind of flower.

A رابي rābi, Who or what ascends. Conspicuous. Intense, increasing, additional.

A رابية rābiyat, High ground. Increasing, excessive, intense.

A رآبيل ra,ābil, pl. of رئبال ri,bāl, Lions. Wolves. Only sons. Heroes.

A رأة ra,at, (v. n. of رأي) Seeing. Thinking.

A رأت ra,t or رات rāt, (pl. روات ruwāt) Straw (تبن tibn). (According to some) A fig (تين tīn).

P راتب rātib, A lot, or portion of the necessaries of life.

A راتب rātib, Firm, constant, fixed. Daily allowance of food (to animals, particularly to dogs and elephants): rations.

P A راتبه rātiba, A salary, stipend, pay, ration.

P راتبه خور rātiba-khwur, A pensioner.

A راتج rātij, Name of a certain castle or fort.

A راتخ rātikh, Thin (clay or paste).

A راتع rātiɛ, (pl. رتاع ritāɛ, رتع rutuɛ, رتّع ruttaɛ, and رتوع rutūɛ) Feeding plentifully (camel). Expatiating, ranging at large, walking.

A راتق rātik, (pl. رتقة ratakat) A closer of a breach. راتق فاتق rātik fātik, Who shuts and opens.

A راتلة rātilat, Short-bodied, dwarfish (woman).

A راتم rātim, Fixed, resident, abiding.

A راتي rāti, Learned. A man of erudition. A doctor of divinity.

A P راتيانج rātiyānaj, (or راتيانه rātiyāna) Resin.

A راتين rātīn, Resin.

P راتينج rātīnaj, Resin of the pine-tree.

A راثع rāsiɛ, Covetous, full of greedy desire. A man who is content with an insignificant present. One who keeps mean or wicked company, to indulge genius or whim.

A راجبة rājibat, (pl. رواجب rawājib) The first joint of the finger. The windpipe of an ass.

A راجح rājih, Excelling. Preponderating, dipping scale. (pl. رجح rujuh) Big-hipped (woman).

A راجز rājiz, A composer of the verse رجز rajaz.

A راجس rājis, Thundering (cloud). One who throws the stone مرجاس mirjās into a well.

A راجع rājiɛ, Returning, retrograde. Looking towards, referring, relative, belonging to. A bird which leaves the flock. A woman whose husband being dead, returns to her friends. (pl. رواجع rawājiɛ) (A camel) giving false symptoms of pregnancy.

A راجعة rājiɛat, A she-camel bought with the proceeds of the sale of another camel. A pond or ditch where water stagnates.

A راجف rājif, A trembling fever, ague.

A راجفة rājifat, The first blast of the trumpet at the resurrection.

A راجل rājil, (pl. رجال rijāl, رجّالة rajjālat, رجّال rujjāl, رجّالى rujjāla', رجالى rajāla', rujāla', رجلة rajlat or rijlat, and رجلى rajla') A pedestrian. A vigorous walker. One who treads firmly. A camel left at liberty with her colt, her teats not tied.

A راجلة rājilat, A ram with the shepherd's wallet.

A راجم rājim, Obscene. A hurler of stones.

A راجن rājin, Accustomed to any place or thing. Tame, domestic, cade, cosset.

P راجه rāja, A Hindu rajā.

A راجي rāji, A hoper, asker, interceder. A client.

P راح rāh, Name of a note in music. راح روح rāhi rūh, Name of one of the notes of the barbud.

A راح rāh, (v. n. of راح for روح) Being near attaining an object, and enjoying satisfaction. Wine. A windy day. (pl. of راحة rāhat) The palms of the hands. Level grounds yielding abundantly. راح ريحاني rāhi rayhānī, Sweet-smelling wine.

A راحات rāhāt, (pl. of راحة) Palms of hands.

A راحة rāhat, (v. n. of راح for روح) Being nimble, ready at any act of kindness (the hand). Being kept apart as a stallion (a horse). Putting forth its leaves (a tree). Receiving kindness. Resting. Quiet, repose, ease, tranquillity, rest. A spouse. A court, an area. The fold of a garment. Level ground producing abundantly. (pl. راح rāh and راحات rāhāt) The palm of the hand. راحة الكلب rāhatu'l kalb, Name of a plant. بيت الراحة baytu'r rāhat, (House of ease) A privy. تركته على انقى من الراحة taraktuhu ɛala' anka' mini'r rāhat, I left him without any thing.

A راحل rāhil, (pl. رحّل ruhhal) A traveller. The head or a leader of a travelling party, who gives the order for starting.

A راحلة rāhilat, A company travelling together, a caravan. (pl. رواحل rawāhil) A camel or other beast of burden. A dromedary.

A راحم rāhim, One who pities, pardons, and compassionates. (A sheep) with a swollen uterus.

A راحول rāhūl, A camel's saddle.

A راحولات rāhūlāt, An embroidered saddle.

A راحيل rāhīl, Rachel, the wife of Jacob.

P راخ rākh, Sadness, sorrow. Conjecture.

A راخم rākhim, (A hen) sitting on eggs.

A راخي rākhi, Blest with life's comforts.

A رأد ra,d, (v. n. of رأد) Blazing, shining forth (forenoon). A girl, a beautiful lass. رأد الارض ra,du'l arz, A desert spot. رأد الضحى ra,du'z zuha', The midway hour between sunrise and noon.

P راد rād, Liberal, munificent. Bold. Intelligent. Eloquent. A story-teller. A wall. A granary. راد خانه rādi khāna, The walls of a house.

A راد rād, One going or sent in quest of forage.

A رادّ rādd, Bring back. A restorer. A repeller, a refuter.

P راد بو rād bū, bo, بوي būy or boy, Aloe-wood.

A رأدة ra,dat, A handsome girl.

A رادة rādat, (A woman) gadding to and fro among neighbours. Gentle (wind). (pl. of رائد rā,id) Foragers.

A رادّة rāddat, Return, reversion. Profit, advantage, emolument, utility. A cross-bar in the fore part of a carriage, the splinter-bar.

A رادع rādiɛ, A prohibiter, impeder, hinderer. (A garment) perfumed with odoriferous unguents.

A رادعة rādiɛat, A tunic shining with unguents or saffron.

A رادف rādif, Who or what comes after.

A رادفة rādifat, The second blast of the trump at the resurrection. A more distressing matter than a former one. See راجفة rājifat. (pl. روادف rawādif) A shoot growing from the trunk of a palm-tree. Streaks of fat in the body.

P راد منش rād-manish, Liberal, munificent.

A رادن *rādin*, Saffron.

A رادني (احمر *aḥmari*) *rādinīy*, Yellowish red.

A رادوف *rādūf*, (pl. روادیف *rawādīf*) Fat, grease, tallow. Name of a man.

A رادي *rādī*, Corrupt, naught. الرادي, A lion.

A رائم *rāzim*, Milch (camel). A sheep whose milk flows abundantly.

A راذنات *rāzināt*, Many villages.

A رار *rār*, Thin marrow corrupted and black.

A رأرأ *rasras*, A man who has a piercing gaze, and who rolls about the pupil of his eye.

A رأرأة *rasrasat*, (v. n. of رأرأ Q) Turning the eyes. Looking stedfastly at. Shining, flashing (a cloud or vapour). Wagging her tail (a hind). Viewing (herself) in a glass (a woman). Twinkling with (her) eyes (a woman). Calling a sheep by saying أر أر *ar ar*. *Rasrasat*, (رأرأ *rasras*, or رأراء *rasrās*) A woman who twinkles her eyes.

P راز *rāz*, A secret, a mystery. Colour. A porcupine. A hornet. A plasterer of walls. Name of a village. Name of a prince. راز دادن *rāz dādan*, To dye. راز دل آب *rāzi dil-āb*, The moisture, coldness, or virtue of water, which is the cause of vegetation. Water of jewels. A shadow, a reflected image. Vegetation. راز زمین *rāzi zamīn*, Plants, flowers. راز نهان *rāzi nihān*, A profound secret. Rain. The sex of a child in the womb. The place of one's death. Future events. Food for the morrow. راز نهان خاك *rāz nihāni khāk*, Plants gradually evolved from the earth. راز نهفته *rāzi nihufta*, A hidden secret. راز دل زمانه *rāzi dil zamāna*, The sun.

A راز *rāz*, (pl. رازة *rāzat*) An architect, master-builder. (Gabriel is said to have been the راز *rāz* of Noah's ark).

P رازبان *rāzbān*, A confidant. One whose office is to present petitions to the king. A privy counsellor.

P راز پنهاني *rāz-pinhānī*, A profound secret.

A رازح *rāziḥ*, (pl. رزح *ruzzaḥ*) Decaying, consuming away (camel).

P رازدار *rāz-dār*, Trusty, faithful, who keeps a secret. A mason.

P رازداري *rāz-dārī*, Keeping a secret: secrecy.

P رازدان *rāz-dān*, Acquainted with secrets or mysteries. رازدان اسرار نا شنیده *rāz-dāni asrāri nā shanīda*, The penetrator into unheard mysteries (Muhammad).

A رازق *rāziḳ*, Giver of the necessaries of life.

P رازقي *rāziḳī*, A sort of grape. Linseed. The white lily.

A رازقي *rāziḳīy*, Weak. A species of oblong grape.

A رازقية *rāziḳīyat*, A kind of white linen. A kind of wine.

P رازکش *rāz-kash*, A betrayer of secrets.

P راز گاه *rāz-gāh*, Repository of secrets.

A رازم *rāzim*, (pl. رزام *rizām*) A she-camel unable to rise from leanness. A she-camel making a murmuring noise in the throat over her young one.

P راز نیاز *rāz-niyāz*, Lovers' secrets, prattle.

P رازه *rāza*, A secret.

A رازي *rāzīy*, Inhabitant of the city of Ray.

P رازیام *rāzyām*, Fennel, anise.

A رازیانج *rāziyānaj*, Fennel.

P رازیانه *rāziyāna*, Fennel. رازیانهٔ رومی, Anise.

P راژ *rāj*, A heap of corn threshed or trodden out.

A رأس *rass*, (v. n. of رأس) Wounding in the head. (pl. أرؤس *arsus*, رؤس *rusus*, and رؤوس *rusūs*) Head, top. A prince, chieftain. A powerful and influential community. End, close. رأس آية *rassu āyatin*, The end of a verse. على رأس ستين *ʿala' rassi sittīn*, At the end of sixty (years he died). رأس الجبل *rassu'l jabal*, A mountain-top. A cloud covering it. رأس الجدي *rassu'l jady*, The winter solstice. رأس العين *rassu'l ʿayn*, Callirhoe in Mesopotamia. رأس السرطان *rassu's saraṭān*, The summer solstice. رأس الشيطان *rassu'sh shayṭān*, (Devil's head) Name of a plant. رأس فقط *rass faḳaṭ*, A horse of a middling breed. رأس الكفر *rassu'l kufr*, (The head of impiety) Antichrist. Satan. P رأس كلان *rass kalān*, A horse of a high breed. A رأس المال *rassu'l māl*, A capital, principal sum or fund. P صد رأس اسپ *sad rass asp*, A hundred head of horses. A مسقط الرأس *maskiṭu'r rass*, One's native place. بيت رأس *bayt rass*, Name of a place in Syria renowned for wine. بالرأس و العين *bi'r rass wa'l ʿayn*, With head and eye: most willingly. رميت منك في الرأس *rumītu minka fi'r rass*, Your opinion of me is bad.

P راس *rās*, Way, road. (for راسو) A weasel.

A رأساء *rassās*, (pl. رآسي *rasāsa'*) Black-headed and white-bodied (ewe).

A راسب *rāsib*, Firm, immoveable. Mild, meek. Intelligent. Tame and fat (animal). Sediment.

P راست *rāst*, Right, true. Good, just, sincere, upright. Straight, even, level. Right (opposed to left). Actually, certainly, surely, truly. Name of a note in music. دست راست *dasti rāst*, The right hand. راست شدن *rāst shudan*, To be clear, justified. راست کردن *rāst kardan*, To prepare, fashion, arrange, make ready. To level. To collate, confront (books). تار ساز راست کردن *tāri sāz rāst kardan*, To tune a stringed instrument. راست که *rāst ki*, Straight that, soon as, or ever.

P راستا *rāstā*, Right. True. Straight. A road. براستا *ba rāstā*, Opposite, over against.

P راستاد *rāstād*, Stipend, salary. A pension.

P راستان *rāstān*, (pl. of راست) Right, true, just.

P راست باز *rāst-bāz*, Faithful, trustworthy.

P راست بازي *rāst-bāzī*, Fidelity, integrity.

P راست بود *rāst-būd*, (Really existing) God.

P راست بین *rāst-bīn*, Impartial, seeing right.

P راست خانه *rāst-khāna*, Most conscientious.

P راست خدیو *rāst-khidīv*, An epithet of God.

P راست روشن *rāst-rawshan*, The vazīr of Bahrām Gūr, a practiser of gross injustice.

P راست ساز *rāst-sāz*, Attuned, in tune, strung.

P راستکار *rāst-kār*, One who acts justly, does right, or performs well. Just, pious. A master of any art, an artificer.

P راست کردار *rāst-kirdār*, A fair dealer.

P راست مزه *rāst-maza*, Well-flavoured.

P راست معامله *rāst-muʿāmala*, One whose actions are fair and good.

P راست نما *rāst-namā*, Appearing upright.

P راسته *rāsta*, Dexterous, right-handed. Upright, just, true. A market-place. A level road.

P راسته بندي *rāsta-bandī*, Road-making or repairing.

P راستي *rāstī*, Rectitude, justice, fidelity, loyalty. Truth, veracity. Straightness. The state or condition of being the right: dextrality. عین راستي *ʿayni rāstī*, Truth itself. راستي و درستي *rāstī u durustī*, Honesty and fidelity.

P راستین *rāstīn*, True, real. State of the case.

P راستینه *rāstīna*, True, real.

P راسخ *rāsikh*, A mountain with a large base. A bell-wether, the leader of a flock, a ram, he-goat. Learned, well versed in. *Rāsukh*, Antimony.

A راسخ *rāsikh*, Firm, solid, durable, constant, rooted. علمای راسخ *ʿulamāsi rāsikh*, Learned, classical authors. راسخ الارکان *rāsikhu'l arkān*, (راسخ البنیان *rāsikhu'l bunyān*, or راسخ الاساس *rāsikhu'l asās*) Firm, well founded, immoveable. ارکان دولت راسخ البنیان *arkāni dawlati rāsikhu'l bunyān*, The pillars of his firm-established empire, *i.e.* the ministers of state.

P راسخت *rāsukht*, Antimony, from a mixture of which, with galls, a kind of oil is expressed by a hot iron, with which the ladies anoint the hair of their eyelids and brows, not only to give them a beautiful black, but to smooth away excrescences.

A راسلان *rāsilāni*, The two shoulders, or veins in the shoulders. The pulpy parts of the thighs.

A راسم *rāsim*, One who seals, marks, writes, or delineates. Water flowing in spiral windings.

P راسن *rasan*, Elecampane. Juniper.

P راسو *rāsū*, A weasel.

A راسوم *rāsūm*, A kind of wooden seal, with which they mark jars of wine, &c.

A رآسي *rasāsa'*, (pl. of رأساء *rassās*) White sheep with black heads and faces.

A راسي *rāsī*, Firm, immoveable (mountain or cauldron). Anchored, fast-moored (ship).

A راسیة *rāsiyat*, (pl. رواسي) Firm (mountain).

P راش *rāsh*, A heap of winnowed corn.

A راش *rāsh*, A feather. Slender and tremulous (spear). ذو راش *zū rāsh*, Hairy-eared and faced.

A رأش *rasash*, Weak-loined (camel). Hairy-eared (camel). Weak (spear).

A راشح *rāshiḥ*, A colt able to follow the dam. (pl. رواشح *rawāshiḥ*) A reptile of any kind. Foot of a hill wet with dew. Sweat exuding from a stone.

A راشد *rāshid*, A follower of the right path. Orthodox, faithful, pious. خلفاءُ راشدين *khulafāʼi rāshidīn*, The Commanders of the Faithful, *i.e.* the Arabian caliphs; but more particularly applied to Muhammad's four immediate successors. امّ راشد *umm rāshid*, A mouse.

A راشق *rāshiḳ*, An archer. A thrower of the javelin. Penetrating (look). Mark-hitting (arrow).

A راشن *rāshin*, One who goes uninvited to a feast. A present or small gratuity given by a master to a journeyman over and above his wages. A dweller. Fixed, resident.

A راشوم *rāshūm*, A wooden seal for grain.

A راشي *rāshī*, A briber.

A راصد *rāṣid*, An observer, watcher (of stars or roads). (An assassin, robber, or informer) lying in wait. A lion.

A راضب *rāẓib*, Gentle, continued rain. A species of the tree called سدر *sidr*, or lote-tree.

A راضبة *rāẓibat*, One tree of the lote species.

A راضة *rāẓat*, (pl. of رائض) Horse-breakers.

A راضع *rāẓiʻ*, (pl. رضّع *ruẓẓaʻ* and رضّاع *ruẓẓāʻ*) A suckling. A miser, who sucks his own cattle to avoid being overheard and importuned for milk.

A راضعة *rāẓiʻat*, (pl. رواضع) A milk-tooth.

A راضي *rāẓī*, (pl. رضاة *ruẓāt*) Content, satisfied, pleased, willing, acquiescent. Pleasing, pleasant, agreeable. P راضي شدن *rāẓī shudan*, To be content, consent, acquiesce, permit, condescend, approve. راضي كردن *rāẓī kardan*, To satisfy, content.

P راضي برضا *rāẓī ba riẓā*, God willing.

P راضي نامه *rāẓī-nāma*, A deed acknowledging one to be satisfied for a debt, assault, and the like. An agreement, a consent in writing. Reconciliation. Resignation. راضيا بلا اجبار *rāẓiyan bilā ijbār*, Consenting without compulsion.

A راطب *rāṭib*, Humid, moist.

A راطم *rāṭim*, Necessarily of, inseparable.

G راطيني *rāṭīnī*, Resin.

A راعب *rāʻib*, One who applies the magic amulet called رعب *raʻb*. One who speaks with a cadence or rhythm.

A راعبيّ *rāʻibīy*, (fem. راعبيّة) A kind of pigeon

A راعج *rāʻij*, A shepherd.

A راعد *rāʻid*, (and راعدة *rāʻidat*) Thundering (cloud). صلف تحت الراعدة *ṣalif taḥta'r rāʻidat*, A fellow that has no good in him.

A راعسة *rāʻisat*, Sprightly (she-camel).

A راعف *rāʻif*, Excelling in swiftness (a horse), gaining a race. The tip of the nose. A promontory. Troubled with a hemorrhage (رعاف *ruʻāf*).

A راعل *rāʻil*, The male palm-tree, or that which either bears no fruit, or bad fruit.

A راعوثة *rāʻūṡat*, (or راعوفة *rāʻūfat*) A stone seat near a well for those who drink; also a stone at the bottom for him to stand on who cleans it out.

A راعي *rāʻī*, (pl. رعاة *ruʻāt*, رعيان *ruʻyān*, رعاء *ruʻāʼ*, and رِعاء *riʻāʼ*) Feeding, grazing. Guarding. A shepherd, pastor. A guardian, protector. A prince, governor. راعي البستان *rāʻī'l bustān*, (Devourer of the garden) A sort of locust.

A راعية *rāʻiyat*, A shepherdess. A flock. Beginning of hoariness. راعية الاتن *rāʻiyatu'l utun*, A species of locust. راعية الخيل *rāʻiyatu'l khayl*, Name of a bird. راعية الشيب *rāʻiyatu'sh shayb*, Beginning of hoariness.

P راعيل *rāʻīl*, Name of Zulaykhā.

P راغ *rāgh*, The lower part of a mountain. A pleasant verdant meadow. A villa, summer-house. باغ و راغ *bāgh u rāgh*, Gardens and villas.

A راغب *rāghib*, Willing, wishing, desirous, curious. A disciple submitting to the directions of his spiritual guide. راغب جهاد *rāghibi jihād*, Desirous of war.

A راغم داغم *rāghim dāghim*, Unwillingly. راغم الانف *rāghimu'l anf*, One whose nose has been rubbed in the dirt. Against the will, unwilling.

A راغي *rāghī*, Braying (camel). Some, any one.

A راغية *rāghiyat*, A she-camel.

A رأف *raʼf*, Wine. Merciful, compassionate. *Raʼaf*, (v. n. of رأف) Being greatly moved with pity. Compassion, clemency.

P راف *rāf*, Mace, envelope of the nutmeg.

A راف *rāf*, Wine.

A رافّ *rāff*, A preserver.

A رأفة *raʼfat*, (v. n. of رأف) Pitying. Commiseration, pity, compassion, clemency, grace, favour (more of tenderness than رحمة *raḥmat*).

A رافخ *rāfikh*, Happy, comfortable (life).

P رافد *rāfid*, The Euphrates.

A رافد *rāfid*, An assistant. A giver. *Rāfid*, (or رافدة *rāfidat*) (pl. روافد *rawāfid*) A rafter.

A الرافدان *ar'rāfidāni*, Tigris and Euphrates.

A رافز *rāfiz*, (Beating) pulse or artery.

P رافس *rāfas*, Name of an astronomer.

A رافض *rāfiẓ*, A thrower (of javelins or stones). Camels pasturing freely.

A رافضة *rāfiẓat*, (pl. روافض *rawāfiẓ*) A body of soldiers who deserted their commander and turned back again. A portion of the sect of the Shīites or followers of Alīy, who, after vowing, renounced their allegiance to Zayd, son of Alīy, son of Husayn.

A رافضيّ *rāfiẓīy*, One of the aforementioned sect.

A رافع *rāfiʻ*, One who raises or exalts; or who brings near or adduces. Who or what puts a noun into the nominative case. A plaintiff. Flashing (lightning). (A camel) having biestings in her udder. Name of 35 of Muhammad's companions.

A رافغ *rāfigh*, (pl. روافغ) Comfortable (life).

A رافقة *rāfiḳat*, Name of a town on the Euphrates built by Al Mansūr, now called رقّة *raḳḳat*.

A رافنة *rāfinat*, (A woman) who walks airily.

P رافونه *rāfūna*, Mint.

P رافه *rāfa*, An herb resembling garlic.

A رافه *rāfih*, One who lives in tranquillity. Merciful, compassionate. (A camel) having as much fodder and water as he likes.

A رافهة *rāfihat*, (pl. روافه *rawāfih*) Convenient (night for travelling).

A راقب *rāḳib*, An observer, watcher. A rival.

A راقد *rāḳid*, (pl. رقود *ruḳūd* and رقّد *ruḳḳad*) Lying, laid; asleep, sleeping.

A راقز *rāḳiz*, Beating (vein or artery).

A راقص *rāḳiṣ*, A leaper. A dancer.

A راقم *rāḳim*, A writer. راقم الحروف *rāḳimu'l ḥurūf*, The writer of the letters, *i. e.* of these presents, of this letter.

A راقنة *rāḳinat*, Handsome. Coloured, stained with henna (woman).

A راقود *rāḳūd*, (pl. رواقيد *rawāḳīd*) A large oblong wine-vessel, pitched within. A kind of small fish. A kind of measure.

A راقول *rāḳūl*, A rope for climbing palm-trees.

A راقي *rāḳī*, (or راقية *rāḳiyat*) An enchanter.

P راك *rāk*, A horned, and fighting ram. A cup, goblet. A thread. (in zand and Pāz.) A way, road.

P راكاره *rākāra*, An immodest woman, harlot.

A راكب *rākib*, (pl. ركّاب *rukkāb*, ركبان *rukbān*, ركوب *rukūb*, ركبة *rikabat*, and ركب *rakb*) One riding (on a camel); a rider. Sailing. A disease in the back incident to sheep. The summit of a mountain. *Rākib*, (or راكبة *rākibat*) A palm-branch hanging pendulous from the top, but not touching the ground.

A راكد *rākid*, Quiet, fixed, still, stagnant (water). Evenly balanced, still (scales). مياه راكدة *miyāhun rākidatun*, Still, stagnant waters.

A راكس *rākis*, An ox in the middle of a thrashing-floor, round which the others turn when treading out the grain. A conductor.

A راكض *rākiẓ*, Galloping (horse).

A راكع *rākiʻ*, One who bows the head, who evinces humility and lowliness.

A راكن *rākin*, One who leans.

A راكوب *rākūb*, (or راكوبة *rākūbat*) A palm-branch hanging pendulous.

A رأل *raʼl*, (fem. رألة *raʼlat*) (pl. ارؤل *arʼul*, رئلان *riʼlān*, رئال *riʼāl*, and رئالة *riʼālat*) A young ostrich, or one a year old.

A رأم *raʼm*, (v. n. of رأم) Loving. Sticking close to (her colt). Mending (a dish). Healing (a wound). Fastening with glue. Making solder. Trimming (an arrow). Twisting hard (a rope). The skin of a sucking camel's colt stuffed with straw, and placed before the dam, which she supposing to be alive, is induced to give her milk plentifully, or suckles another's colt.

P رام *rām*, Obedient, obsequious. Tame, domestic. Happy, cheerful. Industrious. Shrewd. Alacrity. Affluence, plenty. Name of the inventor of the lute. The twenty-first day of the month. Name of the angel who presides over that day. Going, passing by, penetrating. (for آرام *ārām*) Quiet, repose. رام كردن *rām kardan*, To tame, render obedient, break in. با او رام گرفت *bā u rām girift*, He became familiar with him.

A رام *rām*, A kind of tree.

P رام آردشير *rām ārdshīr*, Name of a city.

P رام برزين *rām-barzīn*, Name of a fire-temple; and of a wrestler.

A رأمة *ra,mat*, Shells considered as philters for conciliating love.

A رامة *rāmat*, Ramah, Samuel's abode.

P رامتين *rāmitīn*, Name of a famous musician.

A رامج *rāmij*, A decoy bird or an owl tied by the leg to decoy falcons.

A رامح *rāmih*, One who is armed or who pierces with a spear. Horned (bull). السماك الرامح *as' simāku 'r rāmih*, Name of a large star between the legs of Bootes.

P رامر *rāmar* or *rāmir*, Name of a city famous for its earthenware.

A رامز *rāmiz*, One who makes signs.

A رامسات *rāmisāt*, Winds obliterating traces, filling up wells, or scattering earth.

P رامش *rāmish*, Cheerfulness, singing for joy. Rest. Counsel, advice. A singer, musician.

P رامشت *rāmisht*, Rest, repose. The fourth of the five intercalary days added to the Persian year.

P رامش جان *rāmishi jān*, (or رامشخوار *rāmish-khwār*) Name of a note in music.

P رامشك *rāmishk*, Rest, repose.

P رامشگر *rāmishgar* A singer. A musician.

P رامشگري *rāmishgarī*, Vocal and instrumental music. Talk.

P رامشي *rāmishī*, A musician. A singer.

P رامشين *rāmishīn*, A musician.

A رامع *rāmiʿ*, Who moves the head up and down.

A رامق *rāmih*, One who looks slightly or glances at. (pl. رمق *rumuk*) Who beholds with envy. A decoy bird, which the fowler places in order to lure the hawk. Indigent, afflicted. رامق الامر *rāmiku'l amr*, One who manages business improperly.

P رامك *rāmak*, Name of a certain anti-dysenteric medicine.

A رامك *rāmak* or *rāmik*, A black composition which they mix up with musk. *Rāmik*, Stable, permanent. Infirm, worn out (man), who cannot stir from his place.

P رام گير *rām-gīr*, Fleeing away.

P رامناد *rāminād*, Obedient, submissive. Subtle.

P رامندي *rāmandī*, An ancient dialect of the Persian language.

P رامني *rāmnī*, An island in India, whence comes camphire.

P راموز *rāmūz*, A ship-master, seaman.

A راموز *rāmūz*, The sea. Race, stock, root; type, exemplar, model, specimen.

A راموس *rāmūs*, A sepulchre, grave.

P رامهرمز *rām-hurmuz*, A city in Kohistān.

P رامي *rāmī*, Name of the inventor of the lute.

A رامي *rāmī*, (pl. رماة *rumāt*) An archer, shooter, thrower, hurler (of javelins, or stones). The sign Sagittarius. A jester, scoffer. رامي الصيد *rāmī s' sayd*, A hunter, a shooter at game.

A رامىّ *rāmiy*, Native of Rām-hurmuz.

P رامياد *rām-yād*, Obedient. Name of the twenty-eighth day of the month.

P راميار *rām-yār*, A shepherd.

P راميتن *rāmetan*, A town near Bokhārā.

P رامين *rāmīn*, (or رامينه *rāmīna*) Name of the lover of ويس *Wīs*.

P ران *rān*, The thigh. Assafœtida. (in compos. from راندن *rāndan*) Driving. Expelling. Exiling. سخن ران *sukhun-rān*, Speaking. Lengthening out a discourse. A speaker. قلبه ران *kulba-rān*, Driving plough. كامران *kām-rān*, Enjoying one's desires. ران افشردن *rān afshurdan*, To animate, excite. To spur a horse. ران گشادن *rān gushādan*, To mount a horse. To travel. To alight. To expose a fault. To be naked.

A ران *rān*, Gaiters, leggings. Name of a region bordering on Azarbayjān.

A رأن *ra,n*, (v. n. of رأن) Listening to, approving. Rendering weak and foolish, stultifying.

P رانا *rānā*, A pomegranate. A Hindu rāja.

A رانّة *rānnat*, A woman that makes a noise in her throat when crying.

P رانج *rānaj*, A cocoa-nut.

A رانج *rānij*, A walnut. A smooth black date.

P راندگان *rāndagān*, (pl. of رانده) Exiles.

P راندگي *rāndagī*, A driving. Expulsion.

P راندن *rāndan*, To drive, drive away; to banish, expel. To purge. To force. To pursue. To incline (to a colour). To move off. اسپ راندن *asp rāndan*, To drive or urge forward a horse.

P رانده *rānda*, Expelled, exiled, driven away; rejected, outcast.

P رانش *rānish*, Expulsion, removal. Denial.

A رانع *rāniʿ*, Playing; playful.

A رانفة *rānifat*, (pl. روانف *rawānif*) The lower part of the buttock when standing. The lower extremity of the gristle of the nose, or the pellicle which covers it. The ball of the thumb. The thinner part of the liver. The border of a sleeve. The lower flap of a tent which is fastened to the ground.

P رانه *rāna*, An herb like garlic, eaten toasted. Drawers. A Hindu rāja. A cocoa-nut.

P راني *rānī*, A (Hindu) queen or princess.

A راني *rānī*, One who looks incessantly at.

P رانين *rānīn*, Breeches, drawers: greaves.

P راوچه *rāwcha*, A sort of grape.

P راود *rāwad*, A verdant flowery hill and dale. Muddiness.

P راورا *rāwrā*, (or اورا *ra,awrā*) A hedgehog. A porcupine.

A راوق *rāwuk*, A strainer. An earthen wine-vessel. A large vessel from which (wine) is strained off into smaller ones. A goblet.

P راوك *rāwak*, Purest and best (of a thing).

A راؤل *rā,ul*, Growth of a horse's teeth. Spittle or foam of a horse's mouth.

P راوماده *rāw*, *rāvi*, or *rāvumāda*, Assafœtida.

P راوند *rāwand*, A line upon which they hang clothes or bunches of grapes. Rhubarb. Name of a city in Persia near Ispahān. راوند چيني *rāwandi chīnī*, China rhubarb. راوند خراساني *rāwandi khurāsānī*, Rhubarb of Khurāsān which is given to beasts.

P راوندان *rāwandān*, Name of a fort near Aleppo.

A راووق *rāwūk*, A strainer. An earthen wine-vessel.

A راؤول *rā,ūl*, Spittle (of horses). A redundant tooth in man or horse.

A راوي *rāwī*, (pl. رواة *ruwāt*) One who relates the words of another, who alleges that he said so and so. An historian, a narrator, teller. One who has the superintendence and management of horses. Who or what assuages thirst. Well and at one's ease.

A راويّ *rāwiy*, Belonging to a standard.

A راويان *rāwiyān*, (with P. pl.) Historians.

A راوية *rāwiyat*, A water-carrying camel, or horse; also the large leathern bottle in which it is contained. A traveller's leathern provision-bag. A relater of another's words.

P راويد *rawīd*, The herb clary.

P راويز *rāwīz*, A thorn which camels like.

P راه *rāh*, Way, road, path, passage. Pattern, rule. Custom, fashion. Intellect, mind. A word. The inward part. A musical tone. A time, turn. An Indian prince. راه آب *rāhi āb*, An aqueduct, canal, conduit, water-course. راه آفتاب *rāhi āftāb*, The sun's path, the ecliptic. راه افتادن *rāh uftādan*, To fall in with a gang of thieves. To receive damage. راه بردن *rāh burdan*, To travel. To find. To separate. راه بريدن *rāh burīdan*, To travel. راه بسر بردن *rāh ba sar burdan*, To reach the termination of one's journey. To complete. راه پيمودن *rāh paymūdan*, To measure the road, to travel. راه جامه دران *rāhi jāma-darān*, Name of a note in music (so called because the auditors tore their garments on hearing it). راه حاجيان *rāhi hājiyān*, The road of the pilgrims; likewise the milky way. راه خارکش *rāhi khār-kash*, (or خار كن *khār-kan*) Name of a note in music. راه خسرواني *rāhi khusrawānī*, Name of a note in music. راه خفته *rāhi khufta*, A long, level, tedious way. راه خوابيده *rahi khwābīda*, (also روشن *roshan*) An open, main road. راه دادن *rāh dādan*, To admit. راه ديدن *rāh dīdan*, To keep aloof, wait the event. راه روح *rāhi rūh*, Name of a note in music. راه زدن *rāh zadan*, To rob on the highway. راه شبديز *rāhi shabdez*, Name of a note in music. راه عدم *rāhi ʿadam*, Death. راه غل *rāhi ghul*, Name of a note in music. راه غول *rāhi ghūl*, The world. راه غول دار *rāhi ghūl-dār*, Time, fortune. راه فنا *rāhi fanā*, Sicknesses, calamities. راه قطع كردن *rāh katʿ kardan*, To proceed, travel. راه قلندر *rāhi kalandar*, Abandonment of the world. Name of a note in music. راه كاهكشان *rāhi kāh-kashān*, The milky way. راه گرفتن *rāh giriftan*, To stop the way. خط راه *khati rāh*, A passport.

P راه انجام *rāh-anjām*, Travelling-apparatus. A messenger, courier, postman. A horse, mule, &c.

P راه آورده *rāh-āwarda*, (or راه آور *rāh-āwar*) A present, especially brought by one to another from a distance, or by an ambassador to his sovereign, from the prince to whom he had been sent.

A راهب *rāhib*, (pl. رهبان *ruhbān*) A Christian monk. A lion.

P راهبان *rāhbān*, A road-guard. A traveller. A robber. *Rāhibān*, (Pers. pl. of A راهب) Monks.

A راهبة *rāhibat*, A fearful state. A nun.

P راهبر *rāh-bar*, A road-guide. راه بري نمودن *rāh-bari namūdan*, To guide, show the way. To persuade, convert.

P راهبند *rāh-band*, A highway-robber. A road-patrol. A toll-gatherer.

P راه خرچ *rāh-kharch*, Road-charges.

P راهدار *rāh-dār*, (Occupying the road) One who suddenly attacks, binds, or murders travellers, a robber, bandit. A road-patrol. One who has charge of the public roads. A road-toll gatherer.

P راهداري *rāh-dārī*, A branch of revenue collected from travellers for protection afforded. A passport to be excused tolls.

P راهدان *rāh-dān*, A road-guide.

P راه دراز *rāh-darāz*, Great distance, long way.

P راه راست *rāh-rāst*, A straight road.

P راهرو *rāh-rav*, A traveller. راه روان *rāh-ravān*, Holy men, devotees, keeping watch by night.

P راه روش *rāh-ravish*, Manners, ways, customs.

P راهزن *rāh-zan*, A highway-robber. A musician. A singer.

P راهزني *rāh-zanī*, Highway-robbery.

A راهشان *rāhishāni*, Two veins in the fore-legs of a horse.

P راهشاه *rāh-shāh*, Main road. Great traveller.

A راهطاء *rāhitāʾ*, A hole through which the jerboa throws up the earth.

P راهگان *rāhgān*, Any thing picked up upon the road. Gratis, without labour or purchase. In vain.

P راهگذار *rāh-guzār*, (or راهگذر *rāh-guzar*) A passage, channel, ferry, or pass through mountains. The gullet. A traveller. A road-guide.

P راه گستر *rāh-gustar*, A beast whereon one may ride. Pleasant-paced (horses, mules, or camels).

P راه گير *rāh-gīr*, A traveller, wayfarer.

P راهن *rāhan*, The cornel-tree. *Rāhin*, Name of an herb or root given to horses in medicine.

A راهن *rāhin*, Firm, stable. Perennial. Prepared, set in order, arranged. Lean. A mortgager.

P راهنامه *rāh-nāma*, A road-book, map, chart.

A راهنة *rāhinat*, The navel or umbilical region (of a horse). Wine.

P راه نشين *rāh-nishīn*, A way-side beggar. A messenger. A post, express.

P راهنما *rāh-namā*, (راهنماي *rāh-namāy*, or راهنمون *rāh-namūn*), Shewing the way; a guide.

P راه نمائي *rāh-namāʾī*, A shewing of the way.

P راه نموني *rāh-namūnī*, Guidance, direction.

P راه نورد *rāh-naward*, A riding-horse. A postman. A messenger. A foot-traveller. A beggar. Houseless.

P راهوار *rāhwār*, A quick, easy, ambling-paced horse, a good roadster.

P راهواره *rāhwāra*, A present from a distance.

P راهواري *rāhwārī*, An ambling pace.

P راهوان *rāhwān*, Guard of the road, watch over enemies or thieves. A toll-gatherer.

P راه ور *rāhwar*, An easy, ambling nag.

A راهون *rāhūn*, Name of an India mountain in Ceylon, on which Adam is said to have fallen.

P راهوي *rāhuwī*, Name of a note in music.

P راهها *rāhhā*, (pl. of راه *rāh*) Roads, ways.

P راهي *rāhī*, A thin biscuit. A traveller.

A راهي *rāhī*, Tranquil, comfortable (life). Lasting, durable, constantly supplied (victuals).

A راهية *rāhiyat*, (Gently flying) a bee. Wine.

A رأى *raʾa*, (fut. يري *yara* for يرأي) He saw.

A رأي *raʾy*, (v. n. of رأي) Seeing. Thinking, judging. Consulting. Planting a standard. Striking fire. Emitting fire (the stick zand). Hurting in the lungs. (pl. آراء *ārāʾ*, ارآء *arʾāʾ*, اري *ary*, ريّ *rayy*, *riy*, and رئيّ *raʾiy*) Knowledge, wisdom. Idea. Opinion, belief, view, judgment, counsel. Form, aspect. Whatever delights the eye (as worldly things). Good pleasure. رأي ثاقب *raʾyi sākib*, Prudent counsel. رأي فاسد *raʾyi fāsid*, Bad advice. اصحاب الرأي *as-hābu'r raʾy*, Speculatists, theorists, metaphysicians. Logicians. جعلته رأي عينك *jaʿaltuhu raʾya ʿaynika*, I placed it in sight of your eye. P رأي يك شدن *raʾy yak shudan*, To be of one mind, to conspire together. رأي زدن *raʾy zadan*, To propose, form a plan, consult. رأي كردن *raʾy kardan*, To deliberate, determine. رءي *ruʾa'*, (pl. of رؤيا *ruʾya'*) Dreams, visions.

P راي *rāy*, Opinion, counsel. Meditation, deliberation. A road, path. A rāja or Hindū prince.

A راي *rāy*, (pl. of of راية *rāyat*) Small flags.

A رايات *rāyāt*, (pl. of راية *rāyat*) Banners. A camp. رايات ظفر آيات *rāyāti zafar-āyāt*, Victorious standards.

P رايانيدن *rāyānīdan*, To lead out, or forth.

A رائب *rāʾib*, Thickened (milk). Disordered in the intellect. Weary, heavy-laden. Intricate, confused, and muddled (business). Turgid, torpid from satiety or too much sleep. A liar.

A رأية *raʾyat*, (v. n. of رأي) Seeing. Thinking, judging. A standard, ensign, banner, flag, colours. رأية الاخفاق *raʾyatu'l ikhfāk*, The standard of indigence. رأيت بيضاء *raʾyati bayzāʾ*, The white flag (of good success). P رأيت كاوبان *raʾyati kāwiyān*, The standard of Farīdūn.

A راية *rāyat*, (pl. رايات *rāyāt* and راي *rāy*) A standard, flag. A collar or ring put round the neck of a runaway lad.

P رايت *rāyat*, A short spear.

A رائج *rāʾij*, Vendible. Customary, current, usual, common. رائج الوقت *rāʾiju'l wakt*, Fashion or custom of the times.

P راي چنپا *rāy champā*, Name of a certain fragrant flower found only in India.

A رائح *rāʾih*, (pl. روح *rawah*) Who comes home at even. رائح و جائي *rāʾih u jāʾī*, Goer and comer.

A رائحة *rāʾihat*, (v. n. of راح for روح) Coming home in the evening (camels). (pl. روائح *rawāʾih*) Odour, fragrance, perfume. A stink. Blood. Evening rain. Any thing. P خوب رائحه *khūb-rāʾiha*, Pleasant smelling.

A رائد *rāʾid*, (pl. روّاد *ruwwād* and رادة *rādat*) One who goes or is sent a foraging. A seeker. A forager. A pastor. A leader. The handle of a hand-mill. رائد الضحى *rāʾidu'z zuha'*, The blaze of the forenoon. رائد العين *rāʾidu'l ʿayn*, A mote in the eye, causing it to twinkle.

A رائدة *rāʾidat*, A woman who gads to and fro amongst her neighbours. A soft, gentle breeze.

P راي رايان *rāyrāyān*, The first officer of the Dīwān who has charge of the crown-lands.

A رائرة *rāʾirat*, Marrow in the knee.

P راي زن *rāy-zan*, A person whom one consults.

A رائس *rāʾis*, A governor. Master (of the dogs).

A رائش *rāʾish*, One who fits wings to an arrow. A broker employed to conciliate the favour of a judge by presents. A feathered arrow.

A رائض *rāʾiz*, (pl. راضة *rāzat* and روّاض *ruwwāz*) A breaker of horses. Clever at any thing.

A رائطة *rāʾitat*, A thin, light garment. A woman's name.

A رائع *rāʾiʿ*, Redundant, increasing. Returning. Happening agreeably. Swift (horse). (pl. ارواع *arwāʿ*) Handsome, winning, engaging.

A رائغ *rāʾigh*, One who steals away, retires privately, or flees. Crooked (road). Cunning as a fox. (A man) lurking for a fox; (a fox) deceiving a man.

A رائف *rāʾif*, Merciful, gracious, propitious.

A رائق *rāʾik*, Fasting. Pure, genuine. Water taken early upon an empty stomach. Dry bread. Empty-handed. Addle, unfruitful (cod). (pl. روقة *rūkat*) Beautiful, lovely. Wonderful (beauty).

P رايكا *rāyikā*, Beloved, wished for, desired.

P رايگان *rāygān*, Any thing picked up on the

road. Gratis, gratuitous, without labour or purchase. In vain. ریگاه رفته raygān-rafta, Shed with impunity (blood).

A رائل rāʼil, Whatever falls in drops: flowing (horse's spittle). A redundant tooth.

A رائم rāʼim, Fond of her colt (a she-camel).

A رائمة rāʼimat, A cade sheep which licks a passenger's clothes. Fond of her colt (she-camel).

P رایه rāya, An ulcer on the heads of children.

A رائي rāʼi, A beholder, a seer.

A رايي rāyiy, (or رائي rāʼiy) Pertaining to a flag.

A ربّ rabb, (v. n. of ربّ) Being lord. Ruling, governing. Collecting, bringing together. Completing, finishing. Keeping up in good order. Educating, bringing up. Possessing, owning. Creating. Yeaning (a ewe). Sweetening a leathern bottle with inspissated juice. Rendering (oil) sweet and pleasant. Increasing. Stopping, resting in one place. Cleaving unto. (pl. ارباب arbāb and ربوب rubūb) A lord, master, possessor, proprietor; and with the article ال al applied exclusively to God. A supporter, maintainer. An elder brother. A king. Creator. God. ربّی rabbī, My lord! یا ربّ yā rabb, O lord! ربّ العزة rabbu'l ʻizzat, (or ربّ عزّت rabbi ʻizzat) Lord of glory. ربّ العالمین rabbu'l ʻālamīn, Lord of the universe. ربّ الارباب rabbu'l arbāb, Lord of lords. ربّ العباد rabbu'l ʻibād, God, the protector of his servants. ربّ الدار rabbu'd dār, Master of the house. Rubb, (v. n. of ربّ) Sweetening a leathern bottle with inspissated juice. (pl. رباب ribāb) Decoction of the juice of citrons and other fruits, for seasoning victuals; inspissated juice, rob. Sediment of butter. The month Jamādi the first. ربّ السوس rubbu's sūs, Extract of liquorice. Rubba or ruba, rabba or raba, rubu or rub, A few, some. Many. Often, frequently. Sometimes, now and then. Perhaps.

A ربأ rabʼ, (v. n. of ربأ) Keeping watch, becoming a spy or scout. Going up to a height, in order to take a view. Appearing from a height, impending. Being high, exalted, lifted up. Lifting, raising, elevating. Amending, correcting, adjusting. Carrying off. Amassing all kinds of provisions. Going slowly, heavily. ما ربأت ربأه mā rabaʼtu rabʼahu, I knew him not, or cared not about him.

A ربا riba', Profit on goods. Usury. Buying on credit.

P ربا rubā, (in compos. from ربودن rubūdan) Robbing, stealing, carrying off by violence. آهن ربا āhan-rubā, The magnet. سامان ربا sāmān-rubā, Robbing the understanding, rendering insane. دلربا dil-rubā, Ravishing the heart (a mistress).

P ربّا rubbā, (in zand and Pāzand) Great. Shining, flashing.

A رباء rubāʼ, (v. n. of ربو) Being multiplied, augmented. Ascending high ground. Being reared, growing up. Conferring a favour. Abounding towards. Excess. Length. Much wealth, many effects. Ribāʼ, (v. n. 3 of ربأ) Watching, observing. Being aware of, fearing.

A رباءة rabāʼat, A hillock, rising ground.

A رباب rabāb, A white cloud. A rebeck. Ribāb, (v. n. of ربّ) Being near her time (a ewe). Five Arabian tribes confederate together. A covenant. Tithes, tenths. (pl. of ربّة ribbat) Great numbers. Certain plants. (pl. of ربّ rubb) Inspissated juices. Rubāb, (pl. of ربّي rubba') Ewes which have lately yeaned.

P رباب rubāb, A four-stringed instrument in the form of a short-necked guitar, but having a surface of parchment instead of wood.

A ربابة ribābat, A covenant, treaty. Lordship, deity, divinity. Rule, dominion. A quiver, in which are contained the arrows used in drawing lots; a heap or handful of these arrows; also the string which binds them, or a glove which the man who draws them, wears.

A ربابنة rabābinat, (pl. of ربّان) Ship-masters.

A ربابيّ rabābiy, A performer on the rebeck. Name of مندود بن عبد الله mandūd bin ʻabd allāh, A skilful performer on this instrument.

A رباة rabʼat, A triangular water-vessel made of four skins.

A رباة rabāt, A hill, hillock, heap.

P ربات ribāt, (for رباط ribāt) An inn.

A رباجة rabājat, Dulness of intellect, stupidity.

A رباجيّ rabājiy, Foolish, stupid. Stiff, dry soil, lying between cultivated and desert ground.

A رباجية rabājiyat, Stupid, foolish (woman).

A رباح rabāh, Gain, profit. Name of a certain cup-bearer. A kind of cat, the civet-cat. Ribāh, (pl. of ربح rabah) Camel's colts.

A رباحيّ rabāhiy, A sort of camphor.

A ربّاح rubbāh, A male-ape. A kid. A camel's colt small and slender. زبّ ربّاح zubb rubbāh, A kind of date.

A رباخ rabākh, The act of fainting in coition.

P ربا خور ribā-khwur, An usurer.

A ربّاد rabbād, A worker in, builder of clay.

A رباذ ribāz, (pl. of ربذة ribzat or rabazat) Clews of wool or tow dipped in pitch, with which they besmear scabby camels.

A ربازية rabāziyat, Evil, malignity.

A ربارب rabārib, (pl. of ربرب rabrab) Herds of wild oxen.

A ربازة rabāzat, (v. n. of ربز) Becoming clever. Being full of fat (a ram).

A ربّاض rubbāz, A lion couchant. A recliner.

A رباط ribāt, (v. n. 3 of ربط) Equipping a horse for a holy war. Taking up a station on the confines of an enemy's country. Persevering in, sticking close to. A firm structure, public edifice for lodging travellers, caravansera, inn. A station upon an enemy's frontier. A troop of horse (five or more), armed for war. Five and upwards of horses tied up. The heart. (pl. ربط rubut) A rope with which they bind cattle, or the mouth of a leathern bottle.

A رباطات ribātāt, (pl. of رباط) Solid edifices.

A رباطة ribātat, (v. n. of ربط) Plucking up spirit. Enduing the mind with patience and stedfastness.

A رباع rabāʻ, Mode, manner. State, situation, condition (especially a good one). A bullock, heifer, or sheep four years old. Ribāʻ, (v. n. 3 of ربع) Assisting in lifting up or placing a load. Hiring or engaging with any one for the spring-season. (pl. of ربع rabʻ) Spring-mansions. (pl. of ربع rubaʻ) Camels' colts dropt in the spring. (pl. of ربيع rabīʻ) Spring-seasons. (pl. of رباعي rabāʻī) Sheep which shed their fore-teeth called رباعية rabāʻiyat. Rubāʻ, The number of four. Fours at dice. Consisting of four equal parts. In fours.

A رباعا rubāʻan, By fours, in companies of four.

A ربّاع rabbāʻ, One who deals much in spring-mansions, who buys and sells them.

A رباعة rabāʻat or ribāʻat, Mode, manner, state, situation (especially a good one). A way, a road. Religion, sect. A tribe, family, house. Ribāʻat, A kind of sword-belt. The office of a porter.

A رباعي rabāʻī, (fem. رباعية rabāʻiyat) (pl. ربع rubʻ, rubuʻ, rubaʻ, ارباع arbāʻ, and رباعيات rabāʻiyāt) An animal that has shed his tooth called رباعية rabāʻiyat, i.e. that which is between the two fore-teeth and the canine (which happens to sheep and goats when four years old; to horses and black cattle at five; and to camels at seven).

A رباعيّ rubāʻiy, A four-letter word. A verse of four hemistichs, a tetrastich.

A رباعيات rubāʻiyāt, Tetrastics.

A رباعية rabāʻiyat, (pl. رباعيات rabāʻiyāt) A tooth growing between the front teeth and the canine tooth. (They are four).

A رباغة rabāghat, Abundance, plenty.

A رباق ribāk, (pl. of ربقة ribkat) Halters with loops, nooses, or lassoes.

A ربالة rabālat, Fulness of flesh, fleshiness.

A ربّان rubbān, (pl. ربابنة rabābinat) The master of a ship. Rubbān or rabbān, All, every. The first. A crowd.

A ربّانيّ rabbāniy, Divine, godly. A doctor of divinity, a rabbi. Rubbāniy, The master of a ship.

P ربانیدن rubānīdan, To cause to rob.

A رباوة ra, ri, or rubāwat, A hill, a hillock.

P رباه rubāh, A fox.

A ربايا rabāya', (pl. of ربيئة rabīʼat) Scouts.

A ربائب rabāʼib, (pl. of ربيبة rabībat) Step-daughters. Nurses.

A ربائث rabāʼis, (pl. of ربيثة rabīsat and of ربّيثى ribbīsa') Obstacles.

P ربایندگی rubāyandagī, Robbery, seizure.

P رباینده rubāyanda, A robber, plunderer.

P ربائي rubāʼī, (in compos.) A plundering.

P ربايدن *rubāyīdan*, To cause to seize or steal. To seize, rob.

A ربب *rabab*, Plenty of good water.

A ربة *rubat*, Ten thousand drachmas.

A ربّة *rabbat*, A lady, a female possessor. A Kaaba which belonged to مذحج *mazhij* and لات *lāt*. A large mansion. *Ribbat*, A sort of herb. The carob-tree. The month of Jamādi the second and of Zū'l kaȥdat. *Ribbat* or *rubbat*, (pl. اربّة *aribbat*) A great number. A myriad. *Rubbat*, Abundance of the comforts of life, affluence. Inspissated juice.

A ربت *rabt*, (v. n. of ربت) Educating, bringing up. *Rabat*, (v. n. of ربت) Being obscure and unintelligible (speech). Obscurity, unintelligibility.

A ربّت *rubbata* or *rubata*, *rabbata* or *rabata*, Perhaps. Now and then, sometimes. Often.

A ربّتما *rubbatamā*, *rubatamā*, *rabbatamā*, or *rabatamā*, Sometimes, often.

A ربث *rabs*, A hindering, a letting.

A ربج *rabj*, Small and light money.

A ربح *ribh*, (v. n. of ربح) Gaining. Gain. *Rabah*, Profit in trade, interest, usury. (pl. of رابح *rābih*) Camels' colts. Fat. (pl. رباح *ribāh*) A camel's colt. Camels or horses exposed to sale. *Rubah*, A bird resembling a crow. A camel's colt. A kid. A certain animal from which camphor is procured.

A ربحل *ribahl*, Well-shaped in the body. Tall and lusty. High in rank.

A ربحلة *ribahlat*, Tall, lusty, and well-made (girl).

P ربحي *ribhī*, Whatever is gained by usury.

A ربخ *rabakh*, (v. n. of ربخ) Travelling with difficulty through sand (a camel).

A ربد *rubd*, (v. n. of ربد) Keeping back, detaining, imprisoning. *Rabd* or *rabad*, Thin clay or mud. *Rubd*, (pl. of اربد *arbad*) Ostriches of a dust-colour. *Rubad*, The lustre or undulary surface of a Damascus sword-blade.

A ربداء *rabdāʼ*, (fem. of اربد *arbad*) Dust-coloured (female ostrich). (A she-goat) black, with red spots. Great (misfortune). A prodigious, unheard-of thing.

A ربدة *rubdat*, A colour inclining to that of dust or ashes.

A ربذ *rabz*, (v. n. of ربذ) Being dexterous, nimble in the manipulation of unfeathered arrows. *Rabiz*, Light of foot. (A gum) bare of flesh. ربذ العنان *rabizu'l ȥinān*, One who runs away alone. *Ribaz*, (pl. of ربذة *ribzat* and *rabazat*) Tufts of tow dipped in pitch, with which they besmear camels for the scab. Cloths for polishing plate. Woollen tufts of different colours hung round the necks of horses or camels by way of ornament. Menstruous cloths. Stopples of bottles. Worthless men. Strings at the handles of whips. Severities.

A ربذاء *rabzāʼ*, Name of a woman. ابو الربذاء *abū'r rabzāʼ*, A nickname among the Arabians.

A ذو ربذات *zū rabizāt*, One who blunders much in speaking.

A ربذانيّ *rabazāniy*, An idle talker, prattler.

A ربذة *ribzat* and *rabazat*, (pl. ربذ *ribaz* and رباذ *ribāz*) A handful of wool or tow dipped in pitch, with which they besmear camels for the scab. Any cloth employed in cleansing jewels, plate, or dishes. *Ribzat*, A worthless man. A crowd of men. The stopple of a bottle. A woollen tuft hung to the ear of a camel. A menstruous cloth. Filth. *Rabazat*, A string at the handle of a whip or scourge. Vehemence, severity.

A ربذيّ *rabazaʼ*, A scourge. A string, cord.

A ربرب *rabrab*, A herd of wild oxen.

SY ربرق *rabrak*, Nightshade.

P ربرونتن *rabrūnitan*, (in zand and Pāz.) To die.

P ربزبا *rabzubā*, (in zand and Pāzand) The sun.

A ربس *rabs*, (v. n. of ربس) Striking with the hand. Filling (a leathern bottle). *Ribs*, Misfortune. *Rubs*, (pl. of ربساء *rabsāʼ*) Great calamities.

A ربساء *rabsāʼ*, A great calamity.

A ربسة *rabasat*, A dirty, sordid woman.

A ربش *rabash*, White on the nails of youths.

A ربشاء *rabshāʼ*, (fem. of اربش *arbash*) Various or changing-coloured. Abundant in grass (land).

A ربشة *rubshat*, A change or variety of colour.

A ربص *rabs*, An expecting, waiting for.

A ربصة *rubsat*, Expectation, waiting. The time allowed for a wife to live in her husband's house, after which she may leave him if he fails to perform conjugal duty. Variety in colour.

A ربض *rabz*, (v. n. of ربض) Taking refuge. Giving refuge. Lying down (as a sheep, cow, dog, or horse) with the fore feet tucked under them. *Rabz*, *rubz*, *rabaz*, or *rubuz*, A wife, a mother, or a sister. *Ribz*, A crowd, troop. *Rubz*, The centre of any thing. A group of thorny trees. The foundation of an edifice. That part of any thing which touches, or is nearest to, the ground. (pl. of ربوض *rabūz*) Large, thick (trees or chains). *Rabaz*, (pl. ارباض *arbāz*) Family, kindred, wealth, or house to which one resorts for quiet and comfort. The walls of a town. The sides or circumference of any thing. A sheepcote. A side, tract, quarter. Domestics. The ropes which fasten the saddle under a camel's belly. A kind of surcingle. The intestines (the heart excepted). A habitation, house. Food sufficient for one. Milk sufficient for a meal. منك ربضك وان كان سمارا *minka rabazuka, wa in kāna samāran*, Home is home, though ever so homely. *Rubuz*, An indolent man who neglects necessary business.

A ربضة *rabzat* or *ribzat*, (v. n. of ربض) Lying down (a sheep, dog, or lion). Resting securely. *Ribzat*, A place of slaughter, where many have been killed at once. A carcase, trunk, body, figure. A crowd. The mode in which a sheep lies down. ربضة ارنب *ribzatu arnabin*, A hare's body squatting in her form. *Rubzat*, A slice of pudding. A maker of it. *Rubazat*, Cut, wounded, slain. Laid prostrate. A maker of a pudding.

A ربط *rabt*, (v. n. of ربط) Binding, tying. Connexion, friendship. Practice, habit, use. Construction (in grammar). P ربط كردن *rabt kardan*, To bind, strengthen, fasten. To discipline, govern, hold in subjection. A *Rubut*, (pl. of رباط *ribāt*) Ropes, cords, thongs.

A ربع *rabȥ*, (v. n. of ربع) Platting a four-fold cord. Drinking every fourth day (a camel). Completing with one's self the number four, forty, or forty-four. Receiving a fourth part of booty. Taking a fourth of people's property. Seizing any one (a quartan fever). Passing the spring. Lifting up a stone with the hands as a trial of strength. Raising up a load with another man, either by a pole placed under, or with linked hands. Abounding in herbage. Being watered by vernal rain. Inclining, being favourably disposed towards. Refraining, abstaining from, doing less than one is equal to. Roaming at large, grazing where they please (camels). Doing just as he likes (a man), using water as he chooses. Reposing, remaining quiet in a place. Standing, stopping. Waiting, expecting. Restraining, confining. (pl. رباع *ribāȥ*, ربوع *rubūȥ*, اربع *arbuȥ*, and ارباع *arbāȥ*) A house, a spring-mansion. A mansion, inn, or halting-place for travellers. (A man) of middle stature. A bier, a coffin. Soul, spirit, self. A crowd, troop, body. *Ribȥ*, The watering of camels on the fourth day. The attack of a quartan fever. A quartan ague. *Rubȥ*, *rubuȥ*, or *rubaȥ*, (pl. of رباعي *rabāȥī*) Sheep who have lost the teeth رباعية *rabāȥiyat*). *Rubȥ* or *rubuȥ*, A fourth part. ربع دائره *rubȥi dāʼira*, An astronomical quadrant. ربع مسكون *rubȥi maskūn*, An inhabited quarter of the world. *Rabiȥ*, Mode, manner, state, condition (especially a good one). *Rubaȥ*, (pl. رباع *ribāȥ* and ارباع *arbāȥ*) A young camel colted in the spring. ما له هبع ولا ربع *mā lahu hubaȥ wa lā rubaȥ*, He has no stock foaled in autumn or in spring. *Rubaȥa*, In fours. *Rubuȥ*, (pl. of ربيع *rabīȥ*) Fourths.

A ربعات *rabȥāt* or *rabaȥāt*, (pl. of ربعة *rabȥat*) Square-bodied men or women. *Rabaȥāt* or *rabiȥāt*, Mansions, halting-places, inns. *Rabaȥāt*, *rabiȥāt*, and *ribaȥāt*, Mode, manner, a good state.

A ربعان *ribȥān*, (pl. of رباعي *rubāȥī*) Sheep which have lost the teeth رباعية *rabāȥiyat*.

A ربعة *rabȥat*, (pl. ربعات *rabȥāt* and *rabaȥāt*) A middle-sized woman. *Rabȥat* or *rabaȥat*, Square-bodied (man or woman), *i.e.* of a middle stature. A box for spiceries. A casket in which they deposit the Kur'ān in sections, to be read at stated times. *Rabaȥat*, The space between the legs of a cauldron. A particular pace. *Ribaȥat*, Mode, manner, station, condition (especially a good one).

A ربعيّ *ribȥiy*, Vernal. Born in the spring. Born

in his father's old age (a son). *Rabaʻiy*, Related to the tribe of ربيعة *rabīʻat*.

A ربعيّة *ribʻiyat*, Provisions for winter.

A ربغ *rabgh*, (v. n. of ربغ) Living delicately, enjoying the luxuries of life. A draught which satisfies thirst. Fine earth or sand. *Rabagh*, The happiness or conveniences of life. The newness or first and fresh appearance (of any thing). *Rabigh*, A lewd, impudent fellow.

A ربق *rabk*, (v. n. of ربق) Haltering a camel. Entangling, embroiling in any business. *Rabk* or *ribk*, (v. n. of ربق) Tying. Drawing (the head) in a noose. *Ribk*, A rope with many loops or nooses for tying lambs or kids. *Ribak*, (pl. of ربقة *ribkat*) Halters.

A ربقة *ribkat* or *rabkat*, (pl. ربق *ribak*, ارباق *arbāk*, and رباق *ribāk*) A halter, a rope with a loop or noose. A yoke. حلّ ربقته *halla ribkatahu*, He unloosed his yoke, *i.e.* dispelled his grief.

A ربك *rabk*, (v. n. of ربك) Throwing into the mire. Mixing up crumbled bread with broth. Preparing the dish ربيكة *rabīkat*. *Rabak*, (v. n. of ربك) Being troubled, confused. *Rabik*, Weak, silly, idle. *Rubak*, Confused in business.

A ربكّ *ribakk*, Confused in business.

A ربل *rabl* (v. n. of ربل) Increasing, being numerous (people). Having much wealth, many cattle, or many children. Producing trees in leaf, or verdant grass in autumn (the earth). (pl. ربول *rubūl*) A sort of tree producing leaves in autumn by the coolness of the nights without rain. After-grass, eddish. *Ribl*, Fleshy (man). *Rabal*, A very green herb, an antidote to a viper's bite. *Rabil*, Fat, fleshy.

P ربل *ribl*, Southernwood.

A ربلة *rablat* or *rabalat*, The interior part of the thigh, the swell of flesh round those parts, and also of the breasts. *Rabilat*, Fleshy (woman). Thin about the thighs (woman).

A ربم *rabam*, Thick, entangled herbage.

A ربّما *rubbamā*, *rubamā*, *rabbamā*, or *rabamā*, Sometimes, often.

A ربّنا *rabbanā*, O our Lord!

A ربو *rabw*, (v. n. of ربا for ربو) Being increased, multiplied. Being reared, growing up amongst. Climbing (a hill), being on the top of. Pouring water upon fried barley-meal سويق *sawīk*, so that it swells. Labouring under an asthma, breathing hard. Swelling, puffing (as a horse with running or from fright). Taking usury. A hill, tumulus, heap. Increase, augmentation. An asthma. (pl. ارباء *arbāʼ*) A crowd, body.

A ربوّ *rubūw*, (v. n. of ربا for ربو) Being reared, brought up (amongst). Being multiplied, augmented. Climbing (a hill), ascending to the summit.

A ربواء *ribwāʼ*, Usury.

A ربوب *rabūb*, A step-son, wife's son. *Rubūb*, (pl. of ربّ *rabb*) Lords. (pl. of ربّ *rubb*) Syrups.

A ربوبيّ *rabūbīy*, Divine, theological (learning).

A ربوبيّة *rubūbiyat*, Dominion, supreme power. Deity, divinity.

A ربوة *ribwat*, *rabwat*, or *rubwat*, A hill, rising ground, heap. *Ribwat*, Ten thousand drachmas.

P ربوت *rabūt*, A hoopoo, a puet.

A ربوخ *rabūkh*, Subject to faint in coition.

P ربوخه *rabūkha*, Sensual delights.

A ربود *rubūd*, (v. n. of ربد) Standing still, staying, abiding. Imprisoning.

P ربودگي *rubūdagī*, Spoliation, plunder, robbery.

P ربودن *rubūdan*, To rob, seize, carry off.

P ربوده *rubūda*, Seized, plundered, robbed.

P ربوده عقل *rubūda-ʻakl*, Robbed of one's senses.

P ربوسه *rubūsa*, (ربوشه *rubūsha*, and *rabūsha*) (originally رو پوشه *rū-posha*) A veil for the head.

A ربوض *rabūz*, (pl. ربض *rubuz*) Large, thick (tree or chain). Wide (shirt or coat of mail). Populous (village). *Rubūz*, (v. n. of ربض) Repairing (as a sheep to the fold, a dog to his kennel, a lion to his lair). Abiding in a place. Desisting from blissoming (a ram). Covering the earth (night). Lying down with the feet tucked under them (dogs, sheep, horses, or cattle). Lying down over his prey (a lion), or a champion over his prostrate foe. Resting securely.

A ربوع *rubūʻ*, (pl. of ربع *rabʻ*) Vernal mansions.

A ربول *rubūl*, (pl. of ربل *rabl*) Trees which clothe themselves afresh about autumn.

P ربوله *rabūla*, A kind of artichoke.

P ربون *rabūn*, Money advanced on goods which is returned if they should be damaged. Earnest. Drink-money. Handsel. Profit. A prisoner.

A ربون *rabūn*, Earnest-money.

A ربيّ *rubaʼ*, (pl. of ربية *rubyat*) Certain insects.

A ربّي *rabbī*, My lord! *Rubba'*, (pl. رباب *rubāb*) Beneficence. The comforts of life. A necessary business. A firm knot. (A sheep, goat, or camel) which lately brought forth, or is near the birth, or when its young one is dead. The months Jamādi the first and the last.

A ربيّ *rabiy*, (v. n. of ربي) Growing up, being educated (amongst them).

A ربّيّ *ribbīy*, (pl. ربّيّون *ribbīyūn*) A myriad. *Rubbīy*, A vender of the inspissated juice ربّ *rubb*.

A ربيب *rabīb*, A step-son, a wife's son. A step-father. Brought up, reared, protected. Possessed, in the power of another. Confederated. A king.

A ربيبة *rabībat*, (pl. ربائب *rabāʼib*) A step-daughter. A ewe fed in doors for the sake of her milk. A nurse, foster-mother.

A ربية *rubyat*, Usury. A kind of insect. A cat.

A ربيث *rabīs*, Hindered, let, prevented.

SY ربيثا *rabīsa'*, A kind of small fish.

A ربيثة *rabīsat*, (or ربّيثى *ribbīsa'*) (pl. ربائث *rabāʼis*) Impediment, let, hinderance; whatever prevents (especially prayer or a good action).

A ربيخ *rabīkh*, Large and flabby (man). A thick and large camel's saddle.

A ربيد *rabīd*, Dates piled up, sprinkled with water.

P ربيد *rubayd*, Confection, preserve, pickle.

A ربيدة *rabīdat*, A repository, a book-case in which documents are kept.

P ربيدن *rubīdan*, To seize, rob, plunder.

A ربيز *rabīz*, Compact, fat, and large-tailed (ram). Ingenious, subtle, witty. Elegant, pretty. Great, eminent in one's own department (of science, &c.)

A ربيس *rabīs*, Full of flesh. Brave, strenuous. Beaten, struck. Injured in his property or otherwise, plagued with a murrain in his flocks. Misfortune. Unfortunate. A bunch, a cluster. Much (wealth). *Rubays*, (امّ الربيس *ummu'r rubays*) A viper, a large serpent.

A ربّيس السامرة *ribbīsu's sāmirat*, The president of those who hold nocturnal conversations; the chief of romancers.

A ربيض *rabīz*, A flock with the shepherd reclining; also the place where they recline. The place where the intestines are collected.

A ربيط *rabīt*, Bound, fixed, tied, fastened. Constant, firm, intrepid. Devout. A hermit. A philosopher retired from the world. Dry dates steeped in water. ربيط الجاش *rabītu'l jāsh*, Brave (man), never running away.

A ربيطة *rabītat*, (Horses) equipped for battle.

A ربيع *rabīʻ*, (pl. اربعاء *arbiʻāʼ*, اربعة *arbiʻat*, and رباع *ribāʻ*) The spring. Spring-grass. The spring-harvest, or grain cut in the spring, as wheat, pease, and the like. The beginning of autumn. Vernal showers. A rivulet. Two spring months called ربيع الاوّل *rabīʻu'l awwal*, The first Rabī, *i.e.* the third month of the Muhammadan year, and ربيع الآخر *rabīʻu'l ākhir*, The last Rabī, *i.e.* the fourth month. (pl. ربع *rubuʻ*) A fourth. ربيع رابع *rabīʻun rābiʻun*, A plenteous spring-harvest. ابو الربيع *abū'r rabīʻ*, (Father of the spring) The hoopoo or puet. P باران ربيع *bārāni rabīʻ*, Vernal rains.

A ربيعان *rabīʻāni*, (du. of ربيع *rabīʻ*) The two months called Rabī. The two seasons, each consisting of two months, first spring and second spring.

A ربيعة *rabīʻat*, A stone lifted or dragged as a trial of strength. An iron helmet. Provisions brought from a distance at the beginning of winter. A kitchen or flower-garden. A wallet. A dish wherein perfumes are laid. Name of the father of a tribe.

A ربيعيّ *rabīʻīy*, Produced in, or belonging to, the spring, vernal.

A ربيق *rubayk*, (امّ الربيق) Misfortune.

A ربيقة *rabīkat*, Tied by the neck (a lamb or kid). Snared (game).

A ربيك *rabīk*, A kind of soup made of dates, butter, and cheese; and sometimes flour and barley-meal. Confounded, puzzled, pothered in an affair.

A ربيكة *rabīkat*, A kind of soup made of dates,

butter, and cheese; and sometimes of flour and barley-meal. Butter and milk. Water mixed with clay.

A ربيل *rabīl*, A robber who goes plundering alone.

A ربّيل *ribbīl*, Name of an individual who did good service at the battle of Ḳādisiya.

A ربيلة *rabīlat*, Plumpness. Ease, tranquillity. Wealth, comforts of life.

A ربّيون *ribbīyūn*, (pl. of ربّي *ribbīy*) Many thousands, myriads.

A ربيئة *rabīʼat*, (pl. ربايا *rabāya'*) A scout, spy.

P ربد *rapad*, (or رپود *rapūd*) Name of an intoxicating herb.

P رت *rat*, Naked. *Rut*, Hollow, empty. Poor, indigent. All. Paper.

A رتّ *ratt*, (v. n. of رتّ) Stammering. Speaking rapidly and unintelligibly. (pl. رتّان *ruttān* and رتوت *rutūt*) A chief, prince, governor. (pl. رتوت *rutūt*) A hog.

A رتّاء *rattāʼ*, (fem. of ارتّ *aratt*) A stammerer.

A رتاج *ritāj*, A great door with a smaller one in it. A name of Mecca. ناقة رتاج الصلا *nāḳatun ritāju's sala'*, A firm-fleshed she-camel.

A رتاجة *ritājat*, (pl. رتائج *ratāʼij*) A rock.

A رتاع *ritāɛ*, (v. n. of رتع) Roaming in rich pastures. Ranging at large. (pl. of راتع *rātiɛ*) (Camels) feeding plentifully.

A رتاق *ritāḳ*, Two garments sewed together.

A رتام *ritām*, (or رتائم *ratāʼim*) (pl. of رتيمة *ratīmat*) Threads tied round the finger to remind one of any thing. *Rutām*, Any thing broken or pounded.

A رتامي *rutāmā'*, (Men) sick from eating broom.

A رتان *ratʼān*, A gentle laugh, smile. A canter.

A رتّان *ruttān*, (pl. of رتّ) Chiefs, governors.

A رتائج *ratāʼij*, (pl. of رتاجة) Rocks, stones.

A رتب *ratab*, A being poured out. The space between the third and fourth finger, or between the third and the middle finger. A compression of the four fingers. Affliction, adversity, indigence. Coarse fare. Rocks of unequal height close together. High ground. *Rutab*, (pl. of رتبة *rutbat*) Steps. Degrees of rank.

A رتباء *ratbāʼ*, A she-camel that walks erect, and travels all night.

A رتبة *rutbat*, A degree, a step. A high place whereon a vidette is posted. Dignity, grandeur. Rank, office. رتبهٔ عليا *rutbaʼi ɛulya'*, The highest degree or step. P عيسيٰ رتبگان *ɛīsa'-rutbagān*, Followers of Jesus. Jesuits.

A رتبيل *ratbal*, Short, dwarfish.

A رتّة *ruttat*, Hesitation in speaking.

A رتج *ratj*, (v. n. of رتج) Shutting (a door). *Ritj*, Wealth locked up. An impervious row of palm-trees. A blind alley. *Rataj*, (v. n. of رتج) Stammering (in speech). A great door with a small one in it. A name of Mecca.

A رتجان *ratajān*, The creeping (of a child).

A رتخ *ratkh*, (v. n. of رتخ) Being thin and soft (mud). Remaining still. Falling back, hanging back, shrinking from. A slight scarification. *Ratikh*, Adhering to a fissure in the skin (a tike).

A رتخة *ratakhat*, Clay mixed with water.

A رترة *ratratat*, (v. n. of رترت Q) Stammering in pronouncing the letter ت *te*.

A رتع *ratɛ*, (v. n. of رتع) Roving in wide, rich pastures (sheep). *Rutuɛ* and رتّع *ruttaɛ*, (pl. of راتع *rātiɛ*) (Camels) pasturing freely and plentifully.

A رتعة *ratɛat* or *rataɛat*, Amplitude, plenty, abundance, luxuriance of pasture. القيد و الرتعة *al ḳayd wa'r ratɛat*, Serfdom with plenty of food.

A رتق *ratḳ*, (v. n. of رتق) Shutting, filling, sewing up, closing. Closed. رتق و فتق *ratḳ u fatḳ*, Shutting and opening. *Ruthḳ*, (pl. of رتقاء *ratḳāʼ*) Impervious (women). *Rataḳ*, A narrowness of female organs to such a degree as only to allow a passage for the urine. (pl. of رتقة *rataḳat*) Steps.

A رتقاء *ratḳāʼ*, Close, impervious (woman). Impregnable (city).

A رتقة *rataḳat*, (pl. رتق *rataḳ*) A step. (pl. of راتق *rātiḳ*) Closers of breaches.

A رتك *ratak*, (*ratk*, or رتكان *ratakān*) (v. n. of رتك) Going with a short, quick step (a camel).

P رتك *rutak*, Wild mint.

A رتل *ratal*, A discourse pronounced with a clear, melodious voice. Smoothness, cleanness, regularity, whiteness (of teeth). A neat and regular arrangement of any thing. *Ratal*, Coldness, freshness (of water). *Ratil*, Smooth, white-teethed (man), or one whose teeth are conspicuous. Cold and fresh (water). Teeth even, white, and fresh.

A رتم *ratm*, (v. n. of رتم) Breaking. Pounding small. Bruising (the nose). Growing up, being educated (amongst others). Being sick from eating broom. Browsing broom (goats). Speaking. Broken-nosed (man). (pl. of رتمة *ratmat*). *Ratam*, Furze or broom. A traveller's wallet stuffed with provisions. A whisper. Extreme modesty. (A husband's) twisting together of two branches of a broom-bush when going abroad, which if found upon his return in the state he left them, he remained perfectly satisfied of the fidelity of his wife. A highway.

A رتماء *ratmāʼ*, (A she-camel) fond of broom. (A she-camel) carrying a full provision-bag.

A رتمة *ratmat*, (pl. رتم *rutm*) A thread rolled round the finger to bring to mind any thing. *Ratamat*, A sprig of broom.

A رتن *ratn*, A mixing of dough with lard.

A رتو *ratw*, (v. n. of رتا for رتو) Setting forward, stepping, proceeding. Loosing, opening (a bottle). Fastening. Strengthening (the mind). Drawing up gently (a bucket). Drawing to one's self, hugging. Nodding.

A رتوّ *rutuʼ*, (v. n. of رتأ) Drawing (a knot) tight. Strangling (an animal). Standing still. Being dismissed, going away. ما رتأ كبده بطعام *mā rataʼa kabiduhu bi taɛāmin*, He ate not wherewith to satisfy his hunger.

A رتوّ *rutūw*, (v. n. of رتا for رتو) Nodding. Stepping, proceeding. Drawing to one's self, hugging.

A رتوب *rutūb*, (v. n. of رتب) Being firm, solid, motionless. Being in a valley.

A رتوة *ratwat*, One step. An eminence. A brief space of time. See دعوة *daɛwat* and فطرة *fitrat*. Bow-shot. As far as the eye can ken; a mile.

A رتوت *rutūt*, (v. n. of رتّ) Stammering, having an impediment in the speech. (pl. of رتّ *ratt*) Princes. Governors. Hogs, swine.

A رتوع *rutūɛ*, (v. n. of رتع) Pasturing at discretion (cattle). (pl. of راتع *rātiɛ*) (Camels) pasturing freely and plentifully.

A رتوق *rutūḳ*, Glory. Nobility, dignity.

P رته *rata*, An Indian filbert-nut.

A رتّى *rutta'*, A stammering woman.

P رتيبانج *ritībānaj*, A kind of sea-crab. A sort of medicinal stone.

A رتيلاء *rutaylāʼ*, (or رتيلا *rutayla'*) (pl. رتيلاوات *rutaylāwāt*) Certain kinds of insects whose bite is venomous. A certain herb good for the bite of this insect and for the sting of a scorpion.

A رتيم *ratīm*, Broken-nosed (man). Broken, bruised (nose). Slow travelling.

A رتيمة *ratīmat*, (pl. رتائم *ratāʼim* and رتام *ritām*) A thread wound round the finger as a reminder. A twisted branch of broom. (See رتم *ratam*).

A رثّ *rass*, (pl. رثاث *risās*) Worn, torn. Ragged clothes. Shabby furniture. رثّ الهيئة *rassu'l hiʼat*, Ragged, squalid (man).

A رثأ *rasʼ*, (v. n. of رثأ) Milking new milk upon sour milk in order that it may coagulate. Coagulating (milk), making (it) sour. Preparing (for a company) the coagulated milk رثيئة *rasīʼat*. Mixing, confounding together. Becoming lame from a disease in the shoulder (a camel). Lamenting or praising a deceased person in verse or in a funeral oration. Striking. Being calmed (anger). Sterility of intellect, folly. *Rusʼ*, A mixture of black and white spots.

A رثآء *rasʼāʼ*, Black and white (ewe).

A رثاء *risāʼ*, (v. n. of رثي) Praising (the dead) in a funeral oration, weeping and wailing over him (hired mourners).

A رثّاءة *rassāʼat*, A hired female mourner.

A رثأة *rasʼat*, Lameness in a camel's shoulder.

A رثاث *risās*, (pl. of رثّة *rissat*) Old, shabby moveables.

A رثاثة *rasāsat*, (v. n. of رثّ) Being dirty, squalid, unsightly, ragged, going to pieces. Raggedness.

A رثام *risām*, (pl. of رثمة) Gentle rains.

A رثان *rasān*, Rain following rain.

A رثاية *risāyat*, (v. n. of رثي) Remembering or repeating the sayings of another. Lamenting or praising a deceased person in verse or in a funeral oration. Being tenderly affected. Condoling. A funeral oration.

A رثّاية *rassāyat*, A hired female mourner.

A رثة *risat*, (v. n. of ورث) Inheriting.

A رثّة *rissat*, (pl. رثث *risas*) Ragged furniture. Foolish woman. The vulgar.

A رثد *rasd*, (v. n. of رثد) Laying (furniture or wares) side by side, or one upon another. Delaying. Waiting, expecting. *Rasad*, (v. n. of رثد) Being dark and turbid. The meanest, lowest of men. Household utensils arranged side by side. (pl. of رثدة *rasadat*) Weak men.

A رثدة *risdat* or رثد *risd*, (pl. رثد *risad*) A crowd of men standing. *Rasadat*, (pl. رثد) A weak man.

A رثع *rasaɛ*, (v. n. of رثع) Being very greedy and covetous. Avidity, greediness. *Rasiɛ*, (pl. رثعون *rasiɛūn*) Covetous, full of desire. One who receives a present for any bad act. One who keeps mean or wicked company to indulge a whim.

A رثغ *rasagh*, A speaking thick, a lisping.

A رثم *rasm*, (v. n. of رثم) Bruising and making bloody (the nose or mouth). Anointing (the nose with an odoriferous unguent). *Rasam*, (v. n. of رثم) Being white-lipped. Whiteness on a horse's upper lip. *Rasim*, White-lipped (horse).

A رثماء *rasmāɛ*, (fem. of ارثم *arsam*) White-lipped (mare). (A ewe) having the tip of the nose black and the rest white.

A رثمة *rasmat*, A side of a loaf. *Rasmat* or *rasamat*, (pl. رثام *risām*) Small rain. *Rusmat*, Whiteness on a horse's upper lip.

A رثو *rasw*, (v. n. of رثا for رثو) Praising (the dead) in a funeral oration. Recollecting, recalling to mind the sayings of another. New and sour milk mixed together.

A رثوثة *rusūsat*, Raggedness, going to pieces.

A رثوط *rusūt*, A remaining fixed (to a seat).

A رثي *rasy*, (v. n. of رثي) Becoming tenderly affected, commiserating. Weeping, mourning. Praising (the deceased) in a funeral sermon, crying over him (hired mourners), condoling. Remembering (the words of another).

A رثية *rasyat*, (and رثيّة *rasiyat*) A stiffness in the knees, joints, or feet from distemper or age. Folly.

A رثيث *rasīs*, Worn, gone to pieces. Covered with wounds, and expiring.

A رثيد *rasīd*, Laid one upon another; also side by side. Any thing so placed.

A رثيم *rasīm*, Bruised and bloody-nosed.

A رثيمة *rasīmat*, A mouse.

A رثيئة *rasīɛat*, New and sour milk mixed together. Sterility of intellect, folly.

A رجّ *rajj*, (v. n. of رجّ) Shaking, making quake. Being shaken; trembling. Imprisoning, confining. Constructing a gate.

A رجا *raja'*, (fut. يرجو *yarjū*) He hoped.

A رجا *raja'*, (pl. ارجاء *arjāɛ*) A side, border (of a well). Hope.

A رجاء *rajāɛ*, (v. n. of رجا for رجو) Hoping. Fearing. Hope. Fear. A side, border. Prayer.

A رجّاء *rajjāɛ*, Large-bunched (she-camel).

A رجاءة *rajāɛat*, Hope.

A رجاب *rijāb*, (pl. of رجب) Months Rajab.

A رجاة *rajāt*, Hope.

A رجاج *rajāj*, Lean (sheep or goats). Weak, languid (men or camels).

A رجاح *rajāh*, (pl. رجح) Large-hipped (woman).

A رجاحة *rajāhat*, Excellence, superiority.

A رجّاحة *rujjāhat*, A swing, a see-saw.

A رجاد *rajād*, A carrying of corn from the field.

A رجّاد *rajjād*, One who carries corn from the field into the barn, or piles it into stacks.

A رجازة *rijāzat*, Any thing put into a scale to make even weight, a make-weight. The cloth in which stones are put, to form an equilibrium in the camel's litter, called هودج *hawdaj*. A vehicle resembling a howdah, but smaller. Tufts of wool or hair hung round those vehicles as an ornament.

A رجّاس *rajjās*, Thundering (cloud). Braying (camel). The sea.

A رجاسة *rajāsat*, (v. n. of رجس) Perpetrating a shameful deed and defiling one's self thereby.

A رجاع *rijāɛ*, (v. n. of رجع) Returning, as a bird of passage from a warm to a cold climate. Giving false signs of pregnancy (a she-camel or ass). (v. n. 3 of رجع) Repeating, doing any thing over again (with another). Returning from one journey to begin another. (pl. ارجعة *arjiɛat* and رجع *rujuɛ*) A camel's halter. (pl. of رجع *rajɛ*) Ditches or low places where waters stagnate.

P رجاف *rajāf*, The beat of a drum.

A رجّاف *rajjāf*, The day of the resurrection. The sea. An airy, jaunty manner in walking.

A رجال *rijāl*, (pl. of رجل *rajul* and *rajl*) Men. (pl. of راجل *rājil*) Men on foot. Infantry. (pl. of رجلى *rajla'*) Pedestrian (women). رجال الدما *rijālu'd dama'*, Bloody men, men of blood. رجال الغيب *rijālu'l ghayb*, An invisible being, moving in a circular orbit round the world. P ارسال رجال كردن *irsāli rijāl kardan*, To despatch a body of men.

A رجّال *rajjāl*, Name of a certain apostate. *Rujjāl*, (pl. of راجل *rājil* and رجل *rajil*) Pedestrians.

A رجالات *rijālāt*, (pl. of رجال *rijāl*) Men.

A رجّالة *rajjālat*, (pl. of راجل *rājil* and رجل *rajil*) Men on foot.

A رجالى *rajāla'*, (pl. of رجل *rajul*, *rajil*, and *rajal*) Men whose hair is partly crisp and partly lank. *Rajāla'* and رجّالى *rujjāla'*, (pl. of راجل *rājil* and رجل *rajil*) Footmen, infantry. (pl. of رجلى *rajla'*) Women on foot. *Rujāla'*, (pl. of رجيل *rajīl*) Vigorous walkers.

A رجام *rijām*, A grave-stone, a monument. A stone tied to a rope and let down into a well to ascertain whether there be water in it; also a stone tied to a bucket, that it may descend faster. (pl. of رجمة *rujmat*) Sepulchral monuments, tomb-stones.

A رجامان *rijāmāni*, Two posts over a well, to which a pulley is fixed for drawing water.

P رجّان *rajjān*, Name of a place in Persia, called also ارّجان *arrajān*.

P رجّاني *rajjāni*, A native of رجّان *rajjān*.

A رجاوة *rajāwat*, (v. n. of رجا for رجو) Hoping. Fearing. Hope.

A رجائع *rajāɛiɛ*, (pl. of رجيع *rajīɛ*) (Horses or camels) returning fatigued from a journey.

A رجب *rajb*, (v. n. of رجب) Fearing. Being ashamed. Worshipping, revering. Abusing, reviling. Growing out alone (a branch). *Rujb*, The space between the ribs and thorax. *Rajab*, (v. n. of رجب) Worshipping, revering. Fearing, betraying shame. (pl. ارجاب *arjāb*, رجوب *rujūb*, رجاب *rijāb*, and رجبات *rajabāt*) The seventh month of the Muhammadan year. *Rujab*, (pl. of رجبة *rujbat*) Props of trees. Toils for taking wolves.

A رجبات *rajabāt*, (pl. of رجب) Months of Rajab.

A رجبان *rajabāni*, (dual) The seventh and eighth months, *i.e.* Rajab and Shaabān.

A رجبة *rujbat*, (pl. رجب *rujab*) The prop of a tree overloaded with fruit. A snare for catching wolves. (pl. رواجب *rawājib*) The first joint of the finger. The windpipe of an ass.

A رجبيّة *rujabīyat*, (and رجّبيّة *rujjabīyat*) A propped palm-tree.

A رجح *rujuh*, (pl. of راجح *rājih* and رجاح *rajāh*) Large-hipped (women). Dishes filled with crumbled bread or meat. Battalions with a heavy train.

A رجحان *rujhān*, (v. n. of رجح) Inclining, preponderating, drawing (a scale). *Rajahān*, (v. n. of رجح) Dipping, preponderating, drawing (a scale). Excelling, surpassing. Excellence, superiority.

A رجد *rajd*, A trembling, a being terrified.

A رجراج *rajrāj*, Tremulous. Quicksilver.

A رجراجة *rajrājat*, (A woman) shaking from corpulency. (A multitude) agitated to and fro, yet making no progressive motion on account of their crowding.

A رجرج *rujruj*, A species of plant.

A رجرجة *rajrajat*, (v. n. of رجرج Q) Being agitated, trembling. Being wearied. *Rijrijat*, A small quantity of muddy water in the bottom of a cistern. A large body (of men) in battle. Spittle. A man without judgment.

A رجز *rajz*, (v. n. of رجز) Making or repeating the verses called *rajaz*. *Rijz* or *rujz*, Pain, torment. Impurity, uncleanness. Satanical suggestions. Plague, pestilence. An idol. Idolatry, polytheism. *Rajaz*, A species of verse, the measure of which is مستفعلن *mustafɛilun* six times repeated. A disease in the buttocks of a camel.

A رجزاء *rajzāɛ*, A she-camel diseased with رجز

A رجس *raj́s*, (v. n. of رجس) Thundering loudly. Braying (a camel). Keeping back, restraining. Sounding the depth of water. Being in violent commotion (clouds). *Rijs*, Uncleanness. Torment, punishment. An infamous action deserving of chastisement. Any thing regarded as filthy and abominable. Sin, iniquity. Rage. Suspicion, doubt. *Rajas*, (v. n. of رجس) Perpetrating a shameful deed, and defiling one's self. *Rajas* or *rajis*, Impurity.

A رجع *rajȝ*, (v. n. of رجع) Bringing back, restoring. Turning, converting, changing. Profiting, benefiting, turning to account. Agreeing with, doing good (food). Returning from one journey and setting out on another. Selling a camel and buying another with the proceeds. Being restored to health. Ambling, bringing his fore-feet back (a horse). A pace. The lines marked upon the face with a needle's point, which they rub over with indigo or with cyprus. The dung of a dog or of wild beasts. Utility, profit. A reply to a letter. (pl. رجاع *rijāȝ*, رجعان *rijȝān*, or *rujȝān*) A ditch: any place where water stagnates, or place into which a torrent disgorges itself and passes through. Dung. Pestilence. The top of a hill. Rain after rain. Water. Vernal verdure. The lower part of the shoulder. *Rijȝ*, (A camel) returning from a journey. *Rujuȝ*, (pl. of رجيع *rajīȝ*) (Beasts) returning from a journey. (pl. of رجاع *rijāȝ*) Camels' halters.

A رجعان *rijȝān*, (pl. of رجع *rajȝ*) Waters stagnant, pent up, or regorged; also the places where they stagnate. *Rujȝān*, (v. n. of رجع) Returning. The answer to a letter. (pl. of رجع *rajȝ*) Ditches. Rains after rains. Profits. Pestilences. Tops of hills.

A رجعة *rajȝat* or *rijȝat*, (v. n. of رجع) Returning to earth after death. Receiving again a divorced wife. An answer to a letter. The doctrine of the metempsychosis or transmigration of souls. *Rijȝat*, The refuse of camels or goods brought home unsold from a market. A camel purchased with the proceeds of the sale of another. *Rujȝat*, An answer to a letter.

A رجعى *rujȝa'*, A reply to a letter.

P رجغك *rajghak*, A belch.

A رجف *rajf*, (v. n. of رجف) Moving, causing to move. Being greatly shaken (the earth). Preparing for battle. Thundering with reverberation. Tremor. An earthquake.

A رجفان *rajafān*, (v. n. of رجف) Trembling dreadfully (the earth). Moving. Thundering with reverberation. Tremor, violent agitation.

A رجفة *rajfat*, Agitation. An earthquake.

P رجك *rajak*, A belch.

A رجل *rajl*, (v. n. of رجل) Tying the foot. Striking on the foot. Hanging up by the feet (a sheep). Leaping, springing upon. Bringing forth a child with the feet foremost. Sucking as the young of animals the dam. Turning (a dam) loose with (her) colt. A man. A pedestrian. (pl. of راجل *rājil*) Footmen, infantry. *Rijl*, (v. n. of رجل) Having a pain in the foot. (pl. ارجل *arjul*, رجلات *rijalāt*, and *rijilāt*) The foot; or from the root of the thigh to the foot. The hinder foot of a quadruped. Time, an age. (pl. ارجال *arjāl*) A part or portion (as of a flask of wine or oil). A bay of the sea. A numerous body, as of locusts. Destruction. Breeches of a single fold. A portion, lot. Sleepy (man). White paper. Indigence, misfortune: torment. Human excrement. Time, life-time. A misanthrope who shuns society. An army. Precedence, priority. The lower end of a bow when shooting (the upper end being called يد *yad*, Hand). Either end of an arrow. رجل البحر *rijlu'l bahr*, A river; a frith or arm (literally, a foot) of the sea. رجل الجراد *rijlu'l jarād*, A sort of orach. رجل الحمامة *rijlu'l hamāmat*, Ox-tongue. رجل الدجاجة *rijlu'd dajājat*, Camomile. رجل الطائر *rijlu't tāsir*, A certain mark burnt on a camel; also the iron with which it is made. رجل الغراب *rijlu'l ghurāb*, Crow's foot. A sort of machine fastened to a camel's udder to prevent the colt from sucking. *Rajal*, (v. n. of رجل) Being on foot and remaining so. Having one foot marked white (a horse). Having a large foot (a man). Being partly curled and partly straight (a head of hair). Turning a dam loose with her colt that he may suck at pleasure. Turned loose among others (a horse). Lambs or kids turned loose with the dam. Hair partly curled and partly lank. *Rajil*, A head of hair partly curled, partly sleek. (pl. رجّالة *rajjālat*, رجّال *rujjāl*, رجّالى *rujjāla'*, رجالى *rajāla'*, *rijāla'*, رجلة *rijlat*, *rajlat*, ارجلة *arjilat*, اراجل *arājil*, and اراجيل *arājīl*) A man on foot. A camel's colt left loose with the dam. *Rajul*, (pl. رجال *rijāl*, رجالات *rijālāt* رجلة *rijlat*, *rijalat*, مرجل *marjal*, اراجل *arājil*, and رجلة *rajlat*) A man. A man of intrepidity. A man on foot. Potent in venery. Hair partly curled and partly sleek. *Rajul*, *rajil*, or *rajal*, (pl. ارجال *arjāl* and رجالى *rajāla'*) A man whose hair is partly curled and partly lank. *Rijal*, (pl. of رجلة *rijlat*) Water-pipes, conduits.

A رجلاء *rajlās*, (fem. of ارجل *arjal*) (A mare or sheep) with one foot white. Rough, stony (ground).

A رجلان *rajlān*, (pl. رجلى *rajla'*) A person on foot. *Rijlāni*, Two feet. The two thighs of the breeches. *Rujlān*, (pl. of رجيل *rajīl*) Foot-soldiers.

A رجلة *rajlat*, Firmness of tread in walking. Purslain. (pl. of رجل *rajul*) Men. (pl. of رجل *rajil* and راجل *rājil*) People on foot. *Rijlat*, (v. n. of رجل) Having a pain in the foot. A place where the plant عرفج *ȝarfaj* grows. Firmness of tread in walking. (pl. رجل *rijal*) A water-course from stony to level ground. Purslain. Persons on foot. احمق من رجلة *ahmak mir rijlatin* or *rajlatin*, More insipid than purslain. *Rijlat* or *rijalat*, (pl. of رجل *rajul*) Men. *Rujlat*, (v. n. of رجل) Being marked with white on the foot (a horse). Manliness. Vigour in walking. *Rajilat*, Horses turned loose among others. *Rajulat*, Masculine (woman).

P رجله *rajla*, Purslain.

A رجلى *rajla'*, A rough, stony road. (pl. رجال *rijāl* and رجالى *rajāla'*) Pedestrian (woman). (pl. of رجلان *rajlān* and راجل *rājil*) Men on foot.

A رجلى *rajaliy*, An excellent runner.

A رجلية *rujlīyat*, Manliness, virility.

A رجليون *rijlīyūn*, Pedestrians.

A رجم *rajm*, (v. n. of رجم) Stoning to death, killing. Pelting with stones. Passing by swiftly and impetuously. Putting up a sepulchral monument. Speaking by conjecture. Desertion. Persecution, banishment. Detestation, reproach, contumely, execration. (pl. رجوم *rujūm*) Any thing thrown. Opinion. Vice, fault, blemish. Conjecture. A friend, pot-companion. *Rajm* or *rajam*, A brother. *Rajam*, A tomb, grave. A well, pit, ditch, trench. A furnace. Brethren. *Rujam*, (pl. of رجمة *rujmat*) Stones piled up over a grave. *Rujum*, Flying stars. Lights or torches with which they drive away evil spirits. Sepulchral monuments.

A رجمة *rajmat* or *rujmat*, A grave. *Rujmat*, The den of a hyena (which is oft a tomb). (pl. رجم *rujam*) A tumulus of stones over a grave, a monument. A prop for the branches of a good palm-tree.

A رجن *rajn*, (v. n. of رجن) Keeping (a horse) in the stable, and bringing (him) down by poor provender. Being so kept back (a horse).

A رجو *rajw*, (or رجوّ *rujūw*) (v. n. of رجا for رجو) Hoping. Fearing. Hope.

A رجوب *rujūb*, (v. n. of رجب) Revering, venerating. (pl. of رجب *rajab*) Months Rajab.

A رجوة *rajwat*, Hope. Fear.

A رجوح *rujūh*, (v. n. of رجح) Dipping, preponderating (a scale).

A رجوس *rajūs*, Thundering (sky). Braying (camel). Violently dashing (sea). One who throws a stone called مرجاس *mirjās* into a well in order to raise the mud.

A رجوع *rujūȝ*, (v. n. of رجع) Returning. Bringing back, restoring. Returning from a colder to a warmer climate (a bird). Bandying mutual accusations. Succeeding well. Benefiting. A return. Proof. A referring. Reference. An answer to a letter. P رجوع فرمودن *rujūȝ farmūdan*, To refer, appeal, bring a suit into court.

A رجوعام *rajūȝām*, Rehoboam, son of Solomon.

A رجوعة *rajūȝat*, An answer to a letter.

A رجوف *rujūf*, (v. n. of رجف) Trembling greatly, being violently shaken (the earth). Moving.

A رجوليّة *ru* or *rajūlīyat*, Manliness, virility.

A رجوم *rujūm*, (pl. of رجم *rajm*) Things thrown.

A رجون *rujūn*, (v. n. of رجن) Abiding in, tarrying at, or being used to (a place). Being kept in the stable and brought down by poor provender. Blushing (for any one).

A رجه *rajh*, (v.n. of رجه) Seizing and holding firmly. Moving and growing (a lad).

P رجه *raja*, A clothes-line. A row.

A رجي *rajiya*, (fut. يرجى *yarja'*) He ceased from speaking, he was interrupted.

A رجيّة *rajīyat*, A thing hoped for.

A رجيح *rajīh*, Excellent, surpassing.

A رجيع *rajīʿ*, (pl. رجائع *rajāʾiʿ*) (A horse or camel) returning fatigued from a journey and immediately despatched upon another. What returns from market unsold. Cold victuals dressed a second time; a rifacciamento. Untwisted, and again twisted (rope). An answer. Excrements of wild beasts. An old striped garment. The remains of food which cattle bring up when chewing the cud. Any thing returned, restored, or rejected. A pool of stagnant water. The bridle, or the middle of the bit, which presses upon the tongue. Sweat. A lean camel. Big-bellied from excess of food. A palm-tree.

A رجيعة *rajīʿat*, (pl. رجائع *rajāʾiʿ*) A camel bought with the price of one sold. A she-camel returned from a journey, and immediately despatched on another.

A رجيف *rajīf*, A trembling. A moving.

A رجيل *rajīl*, (pl. رجالي *rujāla'*) (A man) vigorous, stout in walking. Standing upon one foot. Whole, unworn in the hoof (a horse). Worn down by riding and not sweating (horse). Very distant in one extreme from the other (a place). Hard. Extempore (speech). *Rujayl*, (dim. of رجل *rajul*) A little man, a manikin.

A رجيلاء *rujaylāʾ*, Name of certain pedestrians.

A رجيلاءً *rujaylāʾan*, One after another (the ewes were delivered of lambs).

A رجيم *rajīm*, Overwhelmed with stones. Devoted to destruction, execrable (devil).

A رجين *rajīn*, Deadly poison.

A رجينة *rajīnat*, Resin, gum. A crowd, troop.

P رچال *richāl*, A confection.

P رچك *rachuk*, Eructation.

A رحا *raha'*, A mill-stone.

A رحاب *rihāb*, (pl. of رحبة *rahbat* or *rahabat*) Spacious areas. *Ruhāb*, Large, open (place). Wide, capacious (caldron or woman).

A رحابة *rahābat*, A being spacious, commodious.

A رحاض *ruhāz*, A flowing of sweat in a fever.

A رحاق *ruhāk*, Pure, good, generous (wine).

A رحال *rihāl*, (pl. of رحل *rahl*) Small camels' saddles. Carpets from Hira in Mesopotamia.

A رحّال *rahhāl*, Skilful in riding camels. A maker of camels' saddles. One who travels to and fro.

A رحالة *rihālat*, (pl. رحائل *rahāʾil*) A saddle made of leather, without any wood in it.

A رحالة *rihāla*, A word for calling a sheep.

A رحامة *rahāmat*, (v. n. of رحم) Having a disease in the uterus, and being thereby rendered unable to receive the male (a camel).

A رحامس *ruhāmis*, Bold, brave, courageous.

A رحائب *rahāʾib*, Wide plains, or confines.

A رحائل *rahāʾil*, Leathern saddles.

A رحب *rahb*, Spacious (place). Wide (in the chest). *Rahb*, *rahab*, رحبات *rahbāt*, or *rahabāt*, (pl. of رحبة *rahabat*) Spacious areas, or other places for walking. *Ruhb*, (v. n. of رحب) Being large, spacious. Being commodious.

A رحبة *rahbat* also *rahabat*, (pl. رحاب *rihāb*, رحب *rahab* or *rahb*, رحبات *rahabāt* or *rahbāt*) A spacious area (of a temple or other place). A widely-extended piece of verdant ground. A valley, to every part of which the water flows. The broad side of fruits adhering to the branch.

A رحبتان *rahbatāni*, Two bones joining the armpits at the top of the ribs, or against which the elbows strike, or the place where the heart beats.

A رحبي *ruhba'*, The broadest rib of the breast. A mark impressed on a camel's side.

A رحّة *rahhat*, A coiled up serpent.

A رحح *rahah*, Breadth of a horse's hoof (reckoned a beauty unless flat). *Ruhuh*, Wide dishes.

A رحراح *rahrāh*, (رحرح *rahrah*, or رحرحان *rahrahān*) Broad, large.

A رحرحة *rahrahat*, (v. n. of رحرح Q) Failing to reach the bottom of a thing. Speaking darkly and unintelligibly. Concealing, keeping secret.

A رحض *rahz*, (v. n. of رحض) Washing (either hands or clothes). An old worn out leathern bottle or wallet.

A رحضاء *ruhazāʾ*, A sweat after the paroxysm of a fever, or so as actually to bathe the skin.

P رحل *rahl*, A reading-stick, a support for a book. The eyebrow of a mistress.

A رحل *rahl*, (v. n. of رحل) Saddling (a camel). Bearing (any inconvenience) patiently. Departing, travelling. A mansion, a resting-place. (pl. ارحل *arhul* and رحال *rihāl*) A small camel's saddle. Household furniture, especially what is carried on a journey.

A رحّل *ruhhal*, (pl. of راحل *rāhil*) Travellers.

A رحلاء *rahlāʾ*, (fem. of ارحل *arhal*) (A sheep) white on the back, the rest black; or vice versâ.

A رحلة *rihlat*, (v. n. of رحل) Travelling, departing, migrating. The mode of fixing a camel's saddle. Journey, departure (particularly of camels). ذو رحلة *zū rihlat* or *ruhlat*, (A camel) fit for travelling. Death. P رحلت شهزاده از دار فنا *rihlati shah-zāda az dāri fanā*, The departure of the prince from this frail world. رحلت كردن *rihlat kardan*, To depart, travel. To die. A *Ruhlat*, Fitness for making a journey. The side or direction to which one is travelling. One journey. انتم رحلتي *antum ruhlatī*, Ye are those towards whom I am travelling, you are the object of my journey.

A رحم *rahm* or *raham*, (v. n. of رحم) Having a diseased womb. *Rihm*, (v. n. of رحم) Pitying, regarding with compassion. Commiseration, sympathy. *Rihm* or *rahim*, (pl. ارحام *arhām*) The womb. Kin, relationship. Affection of near relatives. صلة رحم *silaʾi rahim*, A union of kindred, a meeting of friends. قطع رحم *katʿi rahim*, A desertion, cutting, or alienation of kinsfolk. *Ruhm* or *ruhum*, Mercy. امّ رحم *ummu ruhmin*, (or ام الرحم *ummu'r ruhmi*, Mother of compassion, *i. e.* Mecca.

A رحماء *rahmāʾ*, (or رحوم *rahūm*) (A camel) suffering from a disease in the uterus after foaling, which proves fatal to her.

A رحمان *rahmān*, Merciful, compassionate (God).

P رحماني *rahmānī*, Divine.

A رحمة *rahmat*, A gift of the divine mercy. A prophetical gift. Rain. A woman's name. *Rahmat* or *rahamat*, Pity, compassion, commiseration. Pardon, forgiveness. P رحمت كردن *rahmat kardan*, To pity, commiserate.

A رحمن *rahmān*, (for رحمان *rahmān*) Merciful.

A رحموت *rahamūt*, Pity, commiseration. رهبوت خير من رحموت *rahabūt khayr min rahamūt*, Better be feared than pitied: it is more desirable to be an object of dread than of pity.

A رحمى *ruhma'*, Mercy, pity. Forgiveness.

A رحو *rahw*, (v. n. of رحا for رحو) Building (a mill). Turning (a mill). Coiling itself (a serpent).

A رحول *rahūl*, (or رحولة *rahūlat*) A strong, able, travelling beast.

A رحوم *rahūm*, Diseased in the uterus.

A رحويّ *rahawīy*, Rotatory (motion).

A رحي *rahy*, (v. n. of رحي) Building, also turning (a mill). Twisting itself spirally (a serpent). *Raha'*, (pl. ارحي *arhī*, ارحاء *arhāʾ*, ارحي *arhiy*, رحيّ *rahīy*, *ruhīy*, and ارحية *arhiyat*) A millstone, mill. The breast, the callous part on which a camel reclines. The hoof of a camel or elephant. Spinage. A back tooth. An independent tribe. A chief of the people. A body of domestics. A field of battle. A number of camels crowding upon one another. A round cloud. A piece of high ground about a mile square, to which the water never rises. رحى اليد *raha'l yad*, A hand-mill.

A رحيان *rahayāni*, (du.) Two hand-mills.

A رحيب *rahīb*, Wide (place). Broad-chested. A glutton.

A رحيّة *rahīyat*, A snake coiled up.

A رحيض *rahīz*, Washed.

A رحيق *rahīk*, The best wine. Pure, clear, generous (wine). A kind of perfume.

A رحيل *rahīl*, A journey. Saddled (camel). A camel fit for the road. *Ruhayl*, (dim. of رحل *rahl*) A little travelling furniture.

A رحيم *rahīm*, Merciful, compassionate. Pitied.

P رخ *rakh*, A sigh. Grief, anguish, sorrow. Disease. The sound of a musical instrument. A cleft, chink, notch, fissure. *Rukh*, A cheek. The face, countenance. A side, point, quarter. The rook or tower at chess. A knight-errant. A head-stall for a horse. A rhinoceros. Name of a certain bird of mighty wing (perhaps the condor, but most probably fabulous). A beast resembling a camel, but very fierce. The skin of the throat of a certain water-fowl. A reed, rush, or flag whence mats are made. A crown formerly worn by the kings of Persia. افرازرخ *afrāzi rukh*, The protuberant part of the cheek. رخ آوردن *rukh āwardan*, To come. رخ دادن *rukh dādan*, To countenance.

A رخّ *rakhkh*, (v. n. of رخّ) Treading, trampling on. Mingling (wine). *Rukhkh*, (pl. رخخة *rikhakhat*) The castle at chess. Name of a monstrous bird, which is said to have powers sufficient to carry off a live rhinoceros. A soft and withered herb.

A رخا *rakha'*, Looseness, softness, weakness.

A رخاء *rakhāṣ*, Affluence, the conveniences and pleasures of life. *Rakhāṣ* or *rukhāṣ*, (v. n. of رخو) Being loose, soft, flabby, relaxed. *Rikhāṣ*, (v. n. 3 of رخو) Making soft, loose, and relaxed. *Rukhāṣ*, A gentle breeze.

A رخّاء *rakhkhāṣ*, (pl. رخاخيّ *rakhākhīy*) Soft ground, or ground swelled and yielding to the pressure of the feet.

A رخاخ *rakhākh*, (v. n. of رخّ) Treading upon. Mixing (wine). Easy (life). Soft, open (ground).

A رخاخيّ *rakhākhīy*, (pl. of رخّاء *rakhkhāṣ*) Soft grounds yielding to the tread.

A رخاص *rukhāṣ*, A woman's name.

A رخاصة *rakhāṣat*, (v. n. of رخص) Being low-priced, cheap (provisions). Being remiss. Being tender, delicate of body.

A رخاف *rikhāf*, (pl. of رخف *rakhf*) Thin butters. (pl. of رخفة *rukhfat*) Pumice-stones.

A رخافة *rakhāfat*, Thinness, wateriness (of paste).

A رخال *rikhāl* or *rukhāl*, (pl. of رخل *rikhl*, *rakhil*, and رخلة *rikhlat*) Ewe-lambs.

A رخام *rukhām*, Marble, alabaster. P رخام سفيد *rukhāmi safed*, White marble.

A رخامة *rakhāmat*, (v. n. of رخم) Being soft, gentle (speech). Being softly spoken (a young girl). *Rikhāmat*, A heavy stone. *Rukhāmat*, A sun-dial. A sort of plant.

A رخامي *rukhāma'*, Gentle breeze. Kind of tree.

P رخامي *rukhāmī*, Any thing made of marble. Fine silken stuff interwoven with gold threads. A species of thorn.

A رخاميّ *rukhāmīy*, Made of marble.

P رخانگ *rakhāng*, The country of Arracan.

A رخاوة *rakhāwat* or *rukhāwat*, (v. n. of رخو) Being loose, soft, flabby.

A رخائص *rakhāṣis*, (pl. of رخصة *rakhṣat*) Soft, flexible (fingers).

P رخبين *rikhbīn*, Sour milk. Butter-milk, or any thing dressed with it. A dish made of sour and fresh milk with flour. New cheese.

P رخبينه *rukhbīna*, Made from sour milk. Turpentine.

P رخت *rakht*, Goods and chattels, apparatus. Wearing apparel. Traps. Rich furniture, tapestry, housings, harness. A horse. A ray or beam of the sun or moon. Sadness, grief. Right, true. A meal for one man. رخت افگندن *rakht afgandan*, To stop still. To be weak. رخت بربستن *rakht bar bastan*, To set off upon a journey. To die. رخت بصحرا كشيدن *rakht ba sahrā kashīdan*, To die. رخت خانه *rakhti khāna*, Household furniture. رخت خورشيد و ماه *rakhti khwurshed u māh*, The sun's rays, and the beams of the moon. رخت سفر *rakhti safar*, Travelling apparatus. رخت سلامي *rakhti salāmī*, A dress put on when going to court. رخت عروس *rakhti ʿarūs*, Whatever the bride carries from her parent's to her husband's house. رخت و متاع *rakht u matāʿ*, Articles pertaining to personal estate. رخت هستي *rakhti hastī*, Reason, understanding. رخت هستي بصحراى نيستي بردن *rakhti hastī ba sahrāi nīstī burdan*, To deprive of life or reason.

P رخت كش *rakht-kash*, A beast of burden.

P رخت مال *rakht-māl*, A kind of mangle for smoothing linen.

P رخته *rakhta*, Wounded, sick, diseased.

P رخج *rakhj* or *rakhaj*, Sordid, base, angry, bad-tempered. *Rukhj*, Name of a place in بست *bust*.

A رخخة *rikhakhat*, (pl. of رخّ) Castles at chess.

A رخراخ *rakhrākh*, (or رخرخ) Thin mud.

P رخ ربا *rukh-rubā*, Name of a rapacious bird.

P رخسار *rukhsār*, The cheek. The face, countenance. پري رخسار *parī-rukhsār*, Fairy-faced, beautiful as an angel.

P رخساره *rukhsāra*, Cheek, face, complexion, mien.

P رخش *rakhsh*, Lightning. The rainbow. Reflection of light. A mixture of red and white. A face marked with moles. A mottled or partridge-coloured horse. Swift. A horse. Name of the horse of the celebrated Rustam. Happy, fortunate, prosperous. Joyful. Commencement. Happiness, prosperity. رخش بهار *rakhshi bahār*, Vernal breezes or clouds. *Rukhsh*, A whitening beard. A ray of light, a flash. The sun.

P رخشا *rakhshā*, (*rukhshā*, and رخشان *rukhshān*) Shining, flashing.

A رخشة *rakhshat*, Motion, agitation.

P رخشگر *rakhshgar*, One who sings for hire with instruments.

P رخشندگي *rakhshandagī*, Flash, shine, lustre.

P رخشيدن *rakhshīdan*, To shine, flash. To boast.

A رخص *rakhṣ*, Soft, flexible. Tender, delicately brought up. *Rukhṣ*, (v. n. of رخص) Being cheap; lowness of price, cheapness. Indulgence.

A رخصة *rakhṣat*, (pl. رخائص *rakhāṣis*) Delicate (finger). *Rukhṣat*, A turn at drinking or at giving drink. *Rukhṣat* or *rukhuṣat*, Indulgence, unbounded license, remissness, connivance. Facility. Leave, permission to depart; dismissal, discharge. P رخصت خواستن *rukhṣat khwāstan*, To desire permission to depart. رخصت دادن *rukhṣat dādan*, To dismiss. رخصت كردن *rukhṣat kardan*, To dismiss, suffer to depart. رخصت گرفتن *rukhṣat giriftan*, To take leave.

P رخصتانه *rukhṣatāna*, A present made on dismissing a person.

P رخصت فرما *rukhṣat-farmā*, Granting leave.

A رخصتي *rukhṣatī*, A thing given at parting.

A رخف *rakhf*, (v. n. of رخف) Being soft, thin, watery (paste). (pl. رخاف *rikhāf*) Thin butter. Soft, thin, watery paste. A sort of dye. *Rakhaf*, (v. n. of رخف) Being thin and watery (paste). Thinness and wateriness (of paste).

A رخفة *rakhfat*, Fresh, thin butter. Thin mud. (pl. رخاف *rikhāf*) A pumice-stone. صار الماء رخفة *sāru'l māṣ rakhfatan*, The water became thin mud. *Rakhfat*, *rukhfat*, or *rakhafat*, Thinness and wateriness of paste. *Rakhafat*, Thin clay.

P رخ فروز *rakh-firoz*, A female ornament for the wrist. *Rukh-firoz*, The 7th day of the month.

P رخگيره *rakh-gīra*, A bracelet of gold, silver, &c.

A رخل *rikhl* or *rakhil*, (pl. ارخل *arkhul*, رخال *rikhāl*, *rukhāl*, رخلان *rikhlān*, رخلة *rakhalat* and *rikhlat*) A ewe-lamb.

A رخلان *rikhlān*, (pl. of رخل *rikhl* and رخلة *rikhlat*) Ewe-lambs.

A رخلة *rikhlat*, A ewe-lamb. *Rikhlat* or *rakhalat*, (pl. of رخل *rikhl*) Ewe-lambs.

A رخم *rakhm*, (v. n. of رخم) Playing, toying with, caressing. Softening. Being soft and delicate (speech). Sitting (as a hen upon her eggs). *Rakham*, A bird shaped like a vulture, of the size of a raven; a pelican. Thick milk. Favour, affection. Softness, gentleness. *Rukhum*, A small quantity of biestings.

A رخماء *rakhmāṣ*, (fem. of ارخم *arkham*) White-headed, black-bodied (ewe).

A رخمة *rakhamat*, (v. n. of رخم) Sitting (as a hen upon eggs). Love, mercy. A single pelican. A certain bird which feeds on carrion.

P رخمه *rakhma*, A carrion-eating bird.

P رخنه *rakhna*, A breach in a wall, a fracture, notch (in a sword or knife), hole, crack, chink. A window. رخنه در ديوار آوردن *rakhna dar dīwār āwardan*, To quit a religious life. رخنه زده زبان *rakhna-zada zabān*, Cursed by all. *Rukhna*, Paper.

P رخنه دار *rakhna-dār*, Notched, cracked.

A رخو *rakhw*, *rikhw*, or *rukhw*, Soft, loose, relaxed. *Rikhw* or *rukhw*, Looseness, flabbiness.

A رخوة *rikhwat*, (v. n. of رخو) Being loose, soft, flabby. Easy-paced (horse). حروف رخوة *hurūfu rikhwatin*, The soft letters, viz., شثّص, خظّ, خش, هز, فذّ ضغث. *Rikhwat* or *rukhwat*, Looseness.

A رخود *rikhwadd*, (fem. رخودة *rikhwaddat*) Small-boned and fleshy. Delicate-bodied.

A رخودة *rakhwadat*, Delicacy. Softness. Tenderness. Luxuriance in produce. Affluence, ease, comfort, happiness.

A رخوصة *rukhūsat*, (v. n. of رخص) Being low-priced. Being easy, remiss. Being delicate of body.

A رخوفة *rukhūfat*, Thinness, wateriness (of paste).

A رخيّ *rakhīy*, Blest with the conveniences of life. Wide, ample. رخيّ البال *rakhīyu'l bāl*, In easy, affluent circumstances.

A رخيخ *rakhīkh*, Soft (clay).

P رخيدن *rakhīdan*, To pant, puff, breathe hard.

A رخيص *rakhīs*, Soft (garment). Easy and sudden (death). Low-priced, cheap, reasonable.

A رخيفة *rakhīfat*, (pl. رخاف *rikhāf*) A soft and loose lump of paste. Thin butter.

A رخيم *rakhīm*, Easy, gentle (language). Softly spoken (girl).

A رخيمة *rakhīmat*, Soft and gentle spoken (girl).

P رخين *rakhīn*, A goad. Whey. A churn.

P رخينه *rakhīna*, Resin of the pine-tree.

P رد *rad*, Intelligent, skilful, learned, philosophic. Bold, strong, brave. A high priest of the Magi.

A ردّ *radd*, (v. n. of ردّ) Driving, casting, bringing, or sending back. Turning back. Disproving, disallowing, imputing to error. Refusing, rejecting. Refuting. Rendering, restoring. Vomiting. Repulse, rejection, refutation. Repeal, abrogation. Restitution to its pristine condition. Bad, worthless. Reprobate, rejected (as bad money). An impediment in speech. ردّ بدل *radd badl*, Argument, discussion, altercation. ردّ جواب *raddi jawāb*, A reply, rejoinder. ردّ السلام *raddu's salām*, (also ردّ سلام *raddi salām*) A re-salutation, the return of a salute. ردّ العجز علىٰ الصدر *raddu'l ʿajzi ʿala's sadr*, The antistrophe, repeating at the end of a verse the same word with which it begins, or beginning another with the word which terminated the preceding; a kind of rondeau. ردّ كلام *raddi kalām*, Refutation, reply. ردّ و قبول *radd u kabūl*, Refusal and acceptance. ردّ و قدح *radd u kadh*, Argument, discourse, dispute. P ردّ كردن *radd kardan*, To return. To resist, repulse. To cancel, erase, rescind. A *Ridd*, A prop, support.

A ردء *rid'*, A companion. An ally, helper. Assistance, aid. Matter. A heavy load, an equipoise.

A ردأ *rada'a*, (fut. يردأ *yarda'u*) He aided and strengthened. He propped up (a wall). He hit with a stone. He paid attention (to his camels), he looked well (after them).

A رداء *ridā'*, A cloak or mantle. A sword. A bow. Intelligence. Ignorance. Ornament, honour. Disgrace, infamy. Debt. A lady's girdle (of leather) adorned with jewels. خفيف الرداء *khafīfu'r ridā'*, Having few domestics; or little debt. غمر الرداء *ghamru'r ridā'*, Liberal. رداءُ نيل *ridā'i nīl*, (A black cloak) Night.

A رداءة *radā'at*, (v. n. of ردأ) Being naught, bad, worthless. Badness, worthlessness.

A رداة *radāt*, (pl. ردي *rada'*) A hard stone, rock. *Ridāt*, A cloak, a mantle.

A رداح *radāh*, (pl. ردح *ruduh*) Large-hipped (woman). Large-rumped (ram). A large dish. Wide (plain). A spacious grove. An army encumbered with numbers, and proceeding slowly. Rich, fruitful. Great and dangerous (insurrection). Overloaded (camel).

A رداحة *radāhat*, The den of a hyena.

A رداد *ra* or *ridād*, A repulse, loathing. *Ridād*, (v. n. 3 of ردّ) Repelling. Resisting, opposing.

A ردّاد *raddād*, A setter of broken bones.

A رداع *ridāʿ*, Clay and water, mud. *Rudāʿ*, Indisposition. A relapse. Remains of perfumed unguent on the body.

A رداعة *ridāʿat*, An enclosure, into which they decoy wolves and hyenas.

A رداغ *ridāgh*, (pl. of ردغة) Thick muds.

A رداف *ridāf*, The place where a second person sits on horseback. (pl. of رديف *radīf*) Those who ride behind another.

A ردافة *ridāfat*, The rank next to the king (amongst the Pagan Arabians). He who enjoyed it sat on the right of the prince; acted as his regent, when he was upon any expedition; and received the fourth part of the plunder.

A ردافي *rudāfa'*, Mutual assistants (when one drops or is fatigued, another filling his place). Singers to camels. (pl. of رديف *radīf*) Those who sit behind others on horseback. جاءوا ردافي *jā'ū rudāfa'*, They came one behind another.

A ردام *rudām*, (v. n. of ردم) Breaking wind. A fart. A worthless fellow.

P ردان *radān*, (pl. of رد) Expert, knowing, wise.

A رداه *ridāh*, (pl. of ردهة *radhat*) Cavities on hills or among rocks where water stagnates.

A ردب *radb*, An impervious, impassable road, that has no outlet.

A ردّة *raddat*, Deformity (in which there is some trace of beauty). *Riddat*, (v. n. of ردّ) Repelling. Drinking a second time (a camel). Disproving. Apostacy. A swelling of the udder, abundance of milk before the birth. Echo. A receding of the chin. اهل الردّة *ahlu'r riddat*, Apostates.

A ردج *radaj*, Excrements of a lamb or foal newly dropt (before they have tasted any thing).

A ردجان *radajān*, (v. n. of ردج) Creeping, advancing slowly.

A ردح *radh*, (v. n. of ردح) Enlarging (a tent). Plastering a wall, especially round the bottom of a house. Effecting his object (a man). Being established in a husband's good graces. Slight pain. *Radah*, A long time. *Ruduh*, (pl. of رداح *radāh*) Heavy-hipped (women). Large dishes. Serious seditions.

A ردحان *radhān*, A long time.

A ردحة *rudhat*, The curtain in the back part of the house or tent before the sleeping apartments. A piece let in to enlarge a tent. Liberty, opportunity.

A ردحيّ *rudhīy*, A greengrocer.

A ردخ *radkh*, The breaking of any thing hollow. *Radakh*, Thin clay.

A ردد *rudud*, Deformed, ugly man.

A ردس *rads*, (v. n. of ردس) Hitting with a stone. Breaking, crushing, pounding small. Battering (a wall). Thumping, levelling (ground). Going away with, carrying off.

A ردع *radaʿa*, (fut. يردع *yardaʿu*) He hindered.

A ردع *radʿ*, (v. n. of ردع) Driving away. Prohibiting, hindering. Lying with. Tinging, staining. Changing colour. Striking a spear upon the ground, in order to fix the head firmer. Opening the breast of a garment. Marks of blood, saffron, or ointment upon the body. The neck. Saffron. P ردع كردن *radʿ kardan*, To repel. A ركب ردعه *rakiba radʿahu*, He fell on his face in his own blood. *Rudʿ*, Black-breasted and white-bodied (sheep).

A ردعاء *radʿā'*, Black-breasted, white-bodied ewe.

A ردعل *ridaʿl*, Little children.

A ردغ *radgh* and *radagh*, (pl. of ردغة *radghat* and *radaghat*) Thick clays. *Radigh*, Muddy (spot).

A ردغة *radghat* or *radaghat*, (pl. ردغ *radgh*, *radagh*, or رداغ *ridāgh*) Mud, clay mixed with water. ردغة الخبال *radghatu'l* or *radaghatu'l khabāl*, The sweat which the Muhammadans suppose to pour from the damned.

A ردف *radf*, (v. n. of ردف) Coming after. Succeeding (one employment to another). *Ridf*, (pl. ارداف *ardāf*) Any person mounted behind another; or thing following or placed behind another. He who sits at the right hand of the king, and drinks after him and follows him when he goes to war, his henchman. The buttocks of a horse (as the place on which the second person sits). A sailor in the stern of a vessel. A rival. Name of a star in the breast of the Swan. (In poetry) One of the infirm letters, ا, و, or ي, when immediately preceding the رويّ *rawīy*, or final letter of the rhyme: as in قتال *kitāl*, غروب *ghurūb*, مبين *mubīn*. *Radaf*, Any person or thing following or placed behind another.

A الردفان *ar'ridfāni*, Day and night (as following each other). Two sailors seated in the stern of the vessel.

A ردفي *radfa'*, Lambs dropped in autumn.

A ردق *radak*, Excrements of a lamb or foal newly dropt (before they have tasted any thing).

P ردكا *radkā*, (in zand and Pāz.) Straight. True.

A ردم *radama*, (fut. يردم *yardimu*) He closed.

A ردم *radm*, (v. n. of ردم) Shutting, closing up (a gap). Bolting (a door). Mending, patching (a garment). Being stationary (a cloud). Continuing without intermission (the watering of cattle or a fever). Breaking wind. Flowing. Becoming green again (a tree). (pl. ردوم rudūm) A stopple. Any wall, mound, or barrier (particularly that between Gog and Magog). Part of a wall tumbled down. Any thing worthless. A worthless fellow. A voice or sound. The twang of a bowstring. A fart. *Rudum*, (pl. of رديم radīm) Worn, torn, or mended (clothes).

A ردمة *ridmat*, Shreds of meat sticking between the teeth. Dates left at the bottom of a hamper.

A ردن *radn*, (v. n. of ردن) Arranging or piling one over another (merchandize or household utensils. Emitting smoke. The noise of arms clashing against each other. *Rudn*, (pl. اردان ardān) A gusset or the arm-hole of a sleeve. Spears made in Bahrayn. *Radan*, (v. n. of ردن) Spinning thread. Being shrivelled (skin). Spun silk. A child's caul.

P ردنجو *radan-jo*, A moth.

A ردوس *radūs*, A repeller. A flinger of stones.

A ردوم *rudūm*, (pl. of ردم) Bungs, stopples.

A رده *radh*, (v. n. of رده) Smiting (with a stone). Building a large (house). Obtaining rule (over others) by valour, liberality, &c. (pl. of ردهة radhat) Cavities in hills or rocks, where water lodges. *Radah*, (pl. of ردهة radhat) Hills rugged with rocks. *Radih*, Hard, immoveable, unsubdued (man).

P رده *rada*, A line, rule, series, a row of stones, course of bricks. A thrashing instrument.

A ردّه *ruddah*, (pl. of ردهة radhat) Cavities in rocks, where rain-water stagnates.

A ردهة *radhat*, (pl. ره radh, رداه ridāh, or ردّه ruddah) A cavity upon hills or in rocks, wherein water stagnates. A large mansion, a palace. A rock in water. Snow-water. A garment coarse and threadbare. (pl. رده radah) A hill rough with rocks.

A ردئ *radiʼ*, (pl. ارداء ardāʼ) Bad, naught.

A ردي *rady*, (or رديان radayān) (v. n. of ردي) Striking the ground with the feet (a horse on the trot). Scampering to the stable. Hopping (a little boy or a crow). Hopping on one leg. Going away. *Rady*, (v. n. of ردي) Hitting any thing with a stone to break it. Throwing a stone. Increasing, becoming numerous. Falling into a well, or from a mountain. Exceeding (fifty). *Rada'*, (v. n. of ردي) Perishing. Destruction. (pl. of رداة radāt) Large stones. *Radī*, Corrupt, perishing, ruinous.

A ردّي *raddī*, Rejected. Rejected things.

A ردّي *rudda'*, A divorced woman returning to her father's house.

A رديّ *radiy*, Bad, naught, worthless.

A رديء *radīʼ*, (pl. اردئاء ardiʼāʼ) Bad, naught.

A ردية *ridyat*, A mode of wearing a cloak or upper garment. هو حسن الردية *huwa hasanu'r ridyat*, He has an elegant way of wearing his cloak. *Radiyat*, (fem. of ردي radī) Perishing, ruinous.

A رديها *rudayhan*, A long time.

A رديد *radīd*, (A cloud) pouring out water.

A ردّيدي *riddīda'*, (v. n. of ردّ) Returning, driving back. Restitution.

A ردّيس *riddīs*, A great thrower of stones. A man who repels.

A رديع *radīʻ*, (A spear) losing the head.

A رديغ *radīgh*, A fool. One who frequently floors his fellows.

A رديف *radīf*, (pl. ردافى rudāfa') One who rides behind another on the same horse. A star near the Eagle. A star which rises when the one opposite sets. One who seeks to join himself to the fortunate party at games of hazard with arrows. رديف سرطان *radīfi saratān*, The sign Leo.

A رديم *radīm*, (pl. ردم rudum) Worn, torn, or mended (garment).

A رديمة *radīmat*, (pl. ردم rudum) The edges of two garments sewed together.

A رديني *rudaynīy*, A straight spear (so named from ردينة rudaynat, the wife of the famous spear-maker سمهر samhar).

A رذّ *razz*, (v. n. of رذ) Raining small rain, misling (the sky).

A رذاة *ruzāt*, Lean, worn out (camels).

A رذاذ *razāz*, Small, misling, gentle rain; dew.

A رذال *ruzāl*, (and رذالة ruzālat) The worst left after the best is taken. *Ruzāl*, (pl. ارذلة arzilat) Vile (man). (pl. of رذل razl) Vile, ignoble.

A رذالة *razālat*, (v. n. of رذل) Being vile and base. Baseness, meanness. Avarice.

A رذالي *ruzāla'*, Vile, ignoble, base (persons).

A رذام *ruzām*, A palm-shoot ready for planting. A worthless fellow. A vessel full to overflowing.

A رذاوة *razāwat*, (v. n. of رذي) Becoming worn down with fatigue.

A رذايا *razāya'*, (pl. of رذيّة) Worn-out (camels).

A رذائل *razāʼil*, (pl. of رذيلة razīlat) Mean, worthless things. امّ الرذائل *ummu'r razāʼil*, Mother of baseness, *i.e.* ignorance (in opposition to امّ الفضائل *ummu'l fazāʼil*, Mother of excellence, *i.e.* science).

A رذل *razl*, (v. n. of رذل) Despising, discarding. Rendering vile and despicable. (pl. ارذال arzāl, رذول ruzūl, and رذّال ruzzāl) Mean, base.

A رذلاء *ruzalāʼ*, (pl. of رذيل) Vile, ignoble, base.

A رذم *razm*, (v. n. of رذم) Flowing, overflowing (any vessel). Running (the nose). Palm-shoots ready for planting. A worthless fellow. Full to overflowing. *Razam*, (v. n. of رذم) Being brimfull, running over (a vessel). A dispersed body of men. Threadbare garments. صار بعد الخزّ في رذم *sāra baʻda'l khazz fī razam*, After (being dressed in) silk he has become (clothed) in threadbare garments. *Razam* or *ruzum*, (pl. of رذوم razūm) Overflowing (vessels). *Ruzum*, (pl. of رذوم razūm) Flowing, fluid (substances).

A رذمان *razamān*, (v. n. of رذم) Running (the nose). A small body of men.

A رذول *ruzūl*, (pl. of رذل) Mean, worthless.

A رذولة *ruzūlat*, The being mean, base, niggardly.

A رذوم *razūm*, Flowing, fluid. (pl. رذم razam and ruzum) Overflowing (vessel). (A bone) full of marrow.

A رذومة *ruzūmat*, The pace of a loaded horse.

A رذيّ *raziy*, (pl. رذاة ruzāt) Extenuated, worn down with fatigue, weak, feeble.

A رذيّة *raziyat*, (pl. رذايا razāya') Worn out and lean with fatigue (a she-camel).

A رذيل *razīl*, (pl. رذلاء ruzalāʼ or رذالي ruzāla') Mean, vile, worthless, ignoble.

A رذيلة *razīlat*, A mean, worthless thing. Vileness, worthlessness (the opposite of فضيلة *fazīlat*).

Pررا *rarā*, (in zand and Pāzand) The ear.

P رز *raz*, A vineyard. A vine. A grape. A deadly poison. A dyer. Colour. A battle. A castle. *Riz*, Scattering.

A رزّ *razz*, (v. n. of رز) Thrusting her tail into the ground to deposit her eggs (a locust). Raining with noise, or making a noise (the heavens). Making an iron eye to a door for receiving the bolt. Piercing with a spear. Fixing, fitting one thing into another. *Rizz*, An indistinct sound of any thing at a distance. Distant rolling of thunder. Wind in the bowels. The muttering of a stallion-camel. *Ruzz*, Rice.

A رزء *ruzʼ*, (v. n. of رزأ) Overtaking (as misfortune), injuring, impairing, diminishing (a man's substance). Receiving benefit. Diminishing, lessening. (pl. ارزاء arzāʼ) A misfortune, calamity, disaster.

A رزاح *razāh*, (v. n. of رزح) Dying from fatigue or leanness (a camel). Being wearied, worn out, indisposed.

A رزاحي *razāha'*, Decaying (camels).

A رزاز *razāz*, (for رصاص rasās) Lead.

A رزاز *razzāz*, A seller of rice (رز ruzz).

A رزاغ *rizāgh*, (pl. of رزغة razaghat) Clays.

A رزّاق *razzāk*, An attribute of God, as the provider of the necessaries of life, the giver of daily bread.

A رزاقيّ *razākiy*, Wine.

A رزام *rizām*, (v. n. 3 of رزم) Doing one thing immediately after another, as eating hastily mouthfuls of different kinds of victuals. Pasturing in two fields alternately (a camel). Offering up thanks to God after a meal or between every mouthful. Remaining long at home. A severe man. (pl. of رازم rāzim) Camels unable to rise from leanness. *Ruzām*, (v. n. of رزم) Being unable to rise or to move.

A رزان *razān*, (A woman) modestly behaved in a public company. *Rizān*, (pl. of رزن razn) High grounds in the middle of an overflowed valley. (pl. of رزن rizn) Pools, ponds.

A رزانة *razānat*, (v. n. of رزن) Being heavy (in weight); being grave, modest, sedate. Modesty, sedateness, gravity.

A رزايا *razāya'*, (pl. of رزئة raziʼat) Afflictions.

A رزب *razb*, (v. n. of رزب) Firmly adhering, without moving.

P رزبان *razbān*, The dresser of a vineyard.

P رزبر *raz-bur*, A vine pruning-hook.

A رزّة *razzat*, The hole into which a bolt shoots.

A رزح *razh*, (v. n. of رزح) Spearing through.

A رزّح *ruzzah*, (or رزحى *razha'*) (Camels) pining away.

A رزخ *razkh*, A blow with a ferule at the end of a spear.

P رزد *razd*, A glutton.

A رزداق *ruzdāk*, A canton, village, market-town.

A P رزدق *razdak*, A row, a line.

P رزده *razda*, Tired, knocked up. Hindered.

A رزرزة *razrazat*, (v. n. of رزرز Q) Moving, shaking. Equalizing a load.

A رزغ *razagh*, (v. n. of رزغ) Sticking fast in the mire, or in any difficulty. (pl. of رزغة *razaghat*) Clays. *Razigh*, Stuck in the mud, or in any difficulty.

A رزغة *razaghat*, (pl. رزغ *razagh*) Clay.

A رزف *razf*, (v. n. of رزف) Braying aloud.

A رزفات *razafāt*, Environs, suburbs.

A رزق *razk*, (v. n. of رزق) Bestowing what is necessary for the support of life. Returning thanks. *Razk* or *rizk*, A giving, bestowing. The conferring of an advantage or benefit. *Rizk*, (pl. ارزاق *arzāk*) Riches, good fortune, acquired wealth, that whereby any one is profited. A pension, stipend, subsistence-money, rations. Support, daily bread. A present. Rain. رزق معلوم *rizki maɛlūm*, Daily bread, destiny. رزق الله *rizku'llāh*, A proper name.

A رزقات الجند *razakātu'ljund*, Soldiers' rations.

A رزقة *razkat*, (pl. رزقات *razakāt*) One gift, pension, or allowance. A single ration.

P رزم *razm*, War, battle, combat. A chump, a log for cooking. رزم كردن *razm kardan*, To fight. *Razam*, (from رزيدن *razīdan*) I stain.

A رزم *razm*, (v. n. of رزم) Drawing together (a sack). Dying. Taking. Eating once. Bringing forth (a mother). Overthrowing (a rival) and sitting upon him. *Razam* or *rizam*, (pl. of رزمة *razmat* or *rizmat*) Bundles of clothes, bales. *Ruzam*, Standing firm on the ground (as an elephant). A lion.

A رزما رزما *razman razman*, Little by little.

P رزم آزما *razm-āzmā*, Skilled in war, warlike.

A رزمة *razmat*, (v. n. of رزم) Becoming cold (winter). An eating once. *Razmat* or *rizmat*, A bundle of clothes. A violent blow. اكل الرزمة *akala'r razmata*, He ate once a-day. *Razamat*, The murmuring of a she-camel in the throat without opening her mouth. An ineffectual threat. The roaring of wild beasts.

P رزم گاه *razm-gāh*, (or گه *gah*) A battle-field.

P رزمگير *razm-gīr*, Name of the 15th of the month.

P رزم يوز *razm-yūz*, Seeking war, pugnacious.

A رزن *razn*, (v. n. of رزن) Balancing any thing in the hand to try its weight. Abiding, staying. (pl. رزون *ruzūn* and رزان *rizān*) High ground in the middle of an overflowed valley. *Rizn*, A tract of land. A margin, side, border. (pl. رزان *rizān*) A place where water stagnates.

A رزنة *riznat*, (pl. رزان *rizān*) Any place where water stagnates, a pond.

P رزنده *razanda*, A stainer, a dyer.

P رزوان *razwān*, The keeper of a vineyard.

A رزوح *ruzūh*, (v. n. of رزح) Falling away and dying (a camel). Being tired, worn out, indisposed.

A رزوف *razūf*, Long-legged, wide-stepping.

A رزوم *ruzūm*, (v. n. of رزم) Being unable to rise or move from leanness (a camel). Bundling up (any thing). Receiving. Kneeling. Dying. Bringing forth. Excelling (one's) fellows.

A رزون *ruzūn*, (pl. of رزن *razn*) High grounds in the middle of an overflowed valley.

P رزه *raza*, A stretched line over which clothes are hung. Nightshade. A ring or staple.

A رزي *razy*, (v. n. of رزي) Accepting kindness.

A رزّي *ruzziy*, A seller of rice.

A رزيح *razīh*, Lean (camel).

P رزيدن *razīdan*, To dye, tinge, stain, colour.

P رزيده *razīda*, Stained, dyed.

A رزيز *razīz*, A dyeing herb.

A رزيزى *rizzīza'*, An indistinct sound (as of distant thunder). A rumbling in the belly.

A رزيف *razīf*, (v. n. of رزف) Going fast (a she-camel). Approaching, advancing. Murmuring or braying inwardly (a camel). Haste from fright.

A رزيم *razīm*, The roaring of a lion.

P رزين *razīn*, Firm, solid, strong.

A رزين *razīn*, Modest, grave, patient. Weighty, heavy, ponderous. ابو رزين *abū razīn*, A sweetmeat.

A رزيئة *razīɛat*, (pl. رزايا *razāya'*) Affliction, misfortune, disaster.

P رژ *raj*, Indignation, rage, chiding.

P رژد *rajad*, Voracious, devouring.

P رژم *rajam*, War, battle.

P رژه *raja*, A stretched rope on which they hang clothes to dry. A mason's rule. Edging, border.

P رس *ras*, (in compos. from رسيدن *rasīdan*) Arriving. Happening. Touching. Ripe. A vine. A glutton. A corrupter, destroyer, mischief-maker. A rope, cable. A necklace. A neckcloth. Smelted ore. Hard, firm, strong. دست رس *dast-ras*, Whatever comes to hand. فرياد رس *firyād-ras*, One whom lamentation reaches, *i. e.* A protector, rescuer. نيم رس *nīm-ras*, Half-ripe. *Ris*, Spin thou. *Rus*, A glutton. Hard, firm, steady. Yellow-bodied (man).

A رسّ *rass*, (v. n. of رسّ) Digging (a well or grave). Burying. Hiding, secreting. Making peace, reconciling. Exciting discord. Seeing. Saying (to one's self). Thrusting her tail into the ground to deposit her eggs (a locust). Inquiring into and learning the affairs of another. First attack (of a fever or love). The beginning of a thing. A well (constructed with stones, &c.). (in poetry) The vowel of the letter which follows or precedes the ا *alif* of تأسيس *taɛsīs*, or inflecting the letter with *fatha* before the تأسيس *taɛsīs*. Name of a certain well in which the people of ثمود *samūd* imprisoned one of their prophets until he died: hence their name, اهل الرس *ahlu'r rass*.

P رسا *rasā*, Arriving, attaining. Quick of apprehension, skilful, capable, clever. Much, many.

A رسابة *rasābat*, Sediment (of water).

A رساتيق *rasātīk*, (pl. of رستاق *rustāk*) Many villages. Villagers.

A رساطون *rasātūn*, Wine (a Greek word).

A رساعة *risāɛat*, (pl. رسائع *rasāɛiɛ*) A small twisted thong at the lower end of a sword-belt.

A رساغ *risāgh*, (v. n. 3 of رسغ) Catching (an adversary) by the wrist or ankle (in wrestling). A rope fastening the pastern of a horse to a stake, to prevent his running off, a heel-rope.

A رسال *risāl*, A camel's feet.

A رسالة *rasālat*, (v. n. of رسل) Going with an easy pace (a camel). *Risālat* or *rasālat*, A mission, legation. The gift of prophecy. A letter, mandate of a judge, summons in writing, or any thing sent. A little tract, a small work. A prophet. A troop of horse. امّ رسالة *ummu risālata*, Pity, mercy.

P حضرت رساله پناه *hazrati risāla-panāh*, The dignity of the prophetic asylum (Muhammad).

P رسالت مآب *risālat-maɛāb*, Seat or depository of prophecy (Muhammad).

P رساله دار *risāla-dār*, The commander of a risāla, or body of horse.

P رساله داري *risāla-dārī*, Command of a troop.

P رسّام *rassām*, Name of an armourer, and engraver.

A رسّام *rassām*, A designer, describer, delineator.

P رسان *rasān*, (in compos.) Bringing. Producing. سلام سلامت رسان *salāmi salāmat-rasān*, A salutation, wishing health. مژده رسان *mujda-rasān*, A bearer of joyful news.

P رسانه *rasāna*, Grief, regret, lamentation.

P رسانيدن *rasānīdan*, To cause to arrive. To bring to bear. To convey, carry and deliver. To pay.

A رسائع *rasāɛiɛ*, (pl. of رساعة *risāɛat*) Small twisted strings at the lower parts of sword-belts.

A رسائل *rasāɛil*, (pl. of رسالة *risālat* or *rasālat*) Epistles, missives. Tracts. Messages.

P رسائي *rasāɛī*, Access, entrance. Wisdom, quickness of apprehension, cleverness, skill, talent, ability. Propriety, fitness, perfection.

A رسب *rasab*, Piercing (sword). *Rusab*, The sword of Muhammad. Meek, patient, intelligent.

A رسّة *rassat*, A strong beam or a ship's mast. *Russat*, A hat, cap, or bonnet.

P رست *rast*, He escaped. Liberty. One who has the victory over his passions. Free, secure.

Firm, steady. A row, rank. A portico, gallery, verandah. The ground. *Rust,* He grew. Growth, increase. Victory, superiority. Ground. A sort of hard ground. Hearty, courageous. Solid, not hollow. Strengthened, firmly bound. Strong, firm.

P رستاخيز *rastā-khez,* Day of the resurrection.

P رستاد *rastād,* A stipend, a salary.

P رستار *rastār,* Safety, deliverance. Liberated, set free, safe. Benevolent. *Rustār,* A countryman, peasant, villager.

A P رستاق *rustāk* or *rastāk,* (pl. رساتيق *rasātīk*) A village, market-town, encampment of tents or huts. A villager. The commander of a file of men, a corporal.

P رستاك *rastāk,* A young shoot, sapling.

P رستانيدن *rustānīdan,* To cause to grow.

P رستخيز *rastakhez,* The day of resurrection. *Rustakhez,* Newly sprung up.

P رستگار *rastagār,* Safe, free, escaped. Bountiful.

P رستگاري *rastagārī,* Safety, escape. Bounty.

P رستگان *rastagān,* (pl. of رسته) Free, escaped.

P رستم *rustam,* Rustam the son of Zāl, the most renowned hero among the Persians; to whom the great men of the East are equally proud to be compared, as those of Europe are to Hercules, Alexander, and Cæsar.

P رستمدار *rustam-dār,* Name of a province in Māzandarān.

P رستم دستان *rustam-dastān,* The celebrated hero Rustam. One who takes precedency in eating.

P رستم ركاب *rustam-rikāb,* Brave, valiant.

P رستمون *rustamūn,* An assembled multitude.

P رستمين *rustamīn,* Grass just springing up.

P رستن *rastan,* To be liberated, to escape. To let go. *Ristan,* To spin. To buzz. *Rustan,* To grow, come forth, appear.

P رستني *rustanī,* What grows: a vegetable. The time when, or the place where, any thing grows.

P رسته *rasta,* Delivered, rescued, saved. Escaped, free. A row, a line of merchant's warehouses; also a market so built, with regular ranges of shops, full of goods. Rule, institute, custom, manner, fashion. Pure without and within. *Ristah,* Spun. *Rusta,* Grown. Whatever increases in size. A kind of sweetmeat. A market-town. رستهٔ خاك *rustaʼi khāk,* All existing things.

P رسته گار *rastagār,* Liberated, escaped.

P رستهگاري *rastagārī,* Escape. Remission of sins.

P رستهم *rustahm,* Rustam, the Persian Hercules.

P رستي *rastī,* Escape, deliverance. *Rustī,* Daily bread, maintenance, allowance. Undressed meat. Sweetmeats. Bravery, courage, firmness, vigour. Victory, superiority. Rest, repose, leisure.

A رسح *rus-h,* (pl. of ارسح *arsah* and رسحاء *ras-hāʼ*) Lank about the hips and thighs. *Rasah,* Slenderness, leanness in the hips or thighs.

A رسحاء *ras-hāʼ,* (pl. رسح *rus-h*) Meagre-hipped, mis-shapen (woman).

P رسد *rasad,* A store of grain laid in for an army, a supply of provisions. A share. Worthy of. Arriving. Entering into.

P رسداق *rusdāk,* A habitation in a village or encampment of huts. The commander of a file of men.

A رسداق *rusdāk,* A canton comprising many market-towns.

P رسدي *rasadī,* Grain. A moiety.

A رسرسة *rasrasat,* (v. n. of رسرس Q) Being strong and able to rise with his load (a camel kneeling).

P رسش *rasish,* Approach, arrival. Accident, occurrence.

A رسع *rasʻ,* (v. n. of رسع) Being glued together (the eye), either from disease or otherwise. Putting an amulet on the hand or foot of a child to avert the influence of malignant eyes. Being relaxed and useless (the joints of the foot). *Rasaʻ,* (v. n. of رسع) Having a complaint in the eyelid, whereby the lashes appear as if glued together. A complaint in the eyelashes.

A رسعاء *rasʻāʼ,* (fem. of ارسع *arsaʻ*) Diseased in the eyelids.

A رسعني *rasʻanīy,* Native of رأس عين *raʼsʻayn.*

A رسغ *rusugh* or *rusgh,* (pl. ارساغ *arsāgh* and ارسغ *arsugh*) The slender part which in quadrupeds extends from the fetlock-joint to the hoof; the pastern. The wrist or ankle-joint in man. *Rasagh,* A weakness and torpor in the feet of a camel.

A رسف *rasf,* (or رسفان *rasafān*) (v. n. of رسف) Walking as if in fetters.

A رسل *rasl,* (v. n. of رسل) Having the hair hanging down. Going softly and gently. A gentle pace. Loose, flowing (hair). Easy-paced (camel). *Risl,* Ease, convenience. Slowness, sedateness, gravity. Milk. The upper part of a horse's fore-leg, the part connected with the shoulder. على رسلك *ʻala' risliha* or *rasliha,* At your own conveniency. *Rusl* or *rusul,* (pl. of رسول *rasūl*) Messengers. Ambassadors. Apostles. Angels. رسل رسائل *rusuli rasāʼil,* Epistolary correspondence. *Rasal,* (v. n. of رسل) Going gently. Flowing (hair). (pl. ارسال *arsāl*) A herd of camels, flock of sheep. *Rusul,* A young girl who does not yet veil herself.

A رسلاء *rusalāʼ,* (pl. of رسيل *rasīl*) Those who send, or are sent; also those to whom sent.

A رسلة *raslat,* Hairy-legged (woman). Easy-paced (she-camel). Sluggishness. *Rislat* or *raslat,* Convenience, ease. Slowness, gravity.

P رسم *rasm,* A law, canon, rule, regulation, precept, habit, custom, mode, manner, usage. A mark. A scar. A waiting-servant. رسم قسمت *rasmi kismat,* The right of a judge to decide the partition of an inheritance.

A رسم *rasm,* (v. n. of رسم) Marking out, drawing, writing. Prescribing, ordering, commanding. Preserving vestiges sticking in the ground. Obliterating the vestiges of a house (rain). Concealing one's self under ground. Sketch, outline. (pl. ارسم *arsum* رسوم *rusūm*) The trace or vestige of a house on the ground or sand. Slight remains, an indistinct vestige. A model. An injunction, precept. A well concealed under ground. The superscription of a coin. A thing which gives a polish to gold coin. A large wooden seal with which corn in the granary is stamped. A game among children, the laws of which are, that one puts a question to another, who is obliged to reply in words which do not contain either of the three letters ر *rā,* س *sīn,* or م *mīm,* which compose the word رسم *rasm.* If one of these should be found in his answer, he is condemned as a penalty to imitate the voice of any animal that may be directed by the questioner. رسم الخط *rasmu'l khatt,* Orthography, prescribed form of writing. P رسم كردن *rasm kardan,* To design, to delineate. A *Rasam,* An elegant air in walking.

P رسمان *rismān,* (for ريسمان *rīsmān*) A thread.

P رسمو *rasmū,* A bee.

P رسمي *rasmī,* Belonging to writing, or designing. Ritual. Usual, customary. Middling, second sort. Destined for the king's use. A pensioner. A domestic. One hired by the day, month, or year. واو رسمي *vāvi rasmī,* Quiescent or silent و, *i.e.* when written and scarcely pronounced: as, in خواستن *khwāstan* (not *khawā* or *khuwāstan*) To be willing.

A رسميات *rasmiyāt,* Rules, usages.

A رسن *rasn,* (v. n. of رسن) Tying with a rope; haltering. *Rasan,* (pl. ارسان *arsān* and ارسن *arsun*) A halter. خليع الرسن *khalīʻu'r rasan,* Wild, lawless, dissolute.

P رسن *rasan,* A rope, string, cord, thread. رسن كشتي *rasani kishtī,* A hawser. رسن لنگر *rasani langar,* A ship's cable.

P رسنباز *rasam-bāz,* A tumbler, rope-dancer.

P رسن تاب *rasan-tāb,* (or رسنگر) A rope-maker.

P رسنواد *rasnawād,* (in zand) A spear, lance.

A رسو *rasw,* (v. n. of رسا for رسو) Being firm, immoveable. Standing fast (a mountain). Lying at anchor (a ship). Coming to the male, and standing quiet. Maintaining one's ground in battle. Reconciling, making peace. Purposing to fast. Telling any thing on the authority of another, or quoting his own words. Relating part of a story.

A رسوّ *rusūw,* (v. n. of رسا for رسو) Being firm, immoveable. Maintaining one's ground (in battle). Lying at anchor (a ship). Leaping on the female.

P رسوا *ruswā,* (and رسواي *ruswāy*) Dishonoured, disgraced, infamous, ignominious. Open, notorious. Accused. One held up to public view, as an example to deter. رسواي كردن *ruswāy kardan,* To disgrace.

P رسوائي *ruswāʼī,* Ignominy, dishonour.

A رسوب *rasūb,* Sharp, piercing (sword). Glans penis. *Rusūb,* (v. n. of رسب) Sinking to the bottom (in water): precipitating (as sediment).

A رسوبيّ *rasūbiy*, Sedimentary. A precipitate.

A رسوة *raswat*, A bracelet of beads or shells.

A رسوخ *rusūkh*, (v. n. of رسخ) Being firm, solid, constant. Becoming dry (a pond). Sinking into the ground and reaching the moisture below the surface (rain). Firmness, constancy. Stability, solidity. صاحب رسوخ *sāhib rusūkh*, Endued with constancy. رسوخ و اشتداد *rusūkh u ishtidād*, Firmness and strength.

A رسوخيّة *rusūkhīyat*, Firmness, constancy, steady friendship.

P رسوران *raswarān*, (for سرو روان *sarvi rawan*) A cypress. Moving gracefully like a cypress (epithet of a mistress).

A رسوع *rusūʿ*, Small twisted thongs in the middle of a bow.

A رسول *rasūl*, (pl. ارسل *arsul*, رسل *rusul*, *rusl*, and رسلاء *rusalāʾ*) Sent. A letter, message, news. An ambassador, legate, missionary, apostle, or prophet. An associate or playmate (in archery, &c.). الرسول *ar' rasūl*, The prophet, *i.e.* Muhammad. The angel Gabriel.

A رسولي *rasūlī*, A mission.

A رسوم *rasūm*, One who remains a night and day on a journey. One who travels day and night. (A she-camel) leaving traces of footmarks in the ground. *Rusūm*, (pl. of رسم *rasm*) Vestiges. Traces of habitations left upon the sand. Inscriptions, written laws, canons, customs. Dues, taxes, usages, established fees: allowances. Postage of letters. رسوم سزاولي *rusūmi sazāwalī*, A free gift to a Sazawwal for his support. رسوم عرفيّة *rusūmi ʿurfīya*, Custom, tribute exacted by a lord of a manor.

P رسوم دار *rusūm-dār*, One who holds a particular perquisite.

A رسيّ *risa'*, (pl. of رسوة *raswat*) Bracelets.

A رسيّ *russa'*, Rain falling in large drops. A mountain.

A رسيّ *rasiy*, Constant, immoveable (either in good or evil). The middle pole of a tent.

P رسيد *rasīd*, He arrived. A youth. An acknowledgment of arrival or receiving; a receipt.

P رسيدگي *rasīdagī*, Arrival at maturity, puberty, or perfection. Ripeness. The attainment of an end or object.

P رسيدن *rasīdan*, To arrive, attain. To be accomplished, perfected, finished. To ripen, mature, mellow. To be cooked. To rub, cut, or chafe. To lie with a woman. رسيدن خبر موت شهزاده بشاه *rasīdani khabari mawti shāh-zāda ba shāh*, The arrival of the news of the death of the prince to the king. *Risīdan*, To spin.

P رسيده *rasīda*, Arrived. Mature, ripe: of age.

A رسيس *rasīs*, The beginning of love or of a fever. Any thing solid. Intelligent, sensible, shrewd. Rumour, false or uncertain news.

A رسيغ *rasīgh*, Plentiful, happy (life). Abundant (food).

A رسيف *rasīf*, A walking as if in fetters.

A رسيل *rasīl*, (pl. رسلاء *rusalāʾ*) One who sends or is sent. A letter, news, or message. One who returns the arrow when shooting or throwing. A stallion. Spacious. Delicate, elegant. Sweet water.

A رسيلي *rusaylā'*, Name of a small animal.

A رسيم *rasīm*, (v. n. of رسم) Leaving marks on the ground. A camel's gait.

P رسين *rasīn*, (in zand and Pāzand) A spear.

P رش *rash*, Uneven, hilly ground. A cubit. A fathom. Quicksilver. A kind of rich silken stuff. A sort of dark-coloured date. A species of fig. The semblance of water floating over a plain. The 11th day of the Persian month. Name of the angel which presides over that day. *Rish*, The beard. A wound. *Rush*, An angry roll of the eye.

A رشّ *rashsh*, (v.n. of رشّ) Sprinkling with a little water. Raining gently, misling. Flowing softly, dropping, trickling, (water, blood, or tears). A pain-giving blow. (pl. رشاش *rishāsh*) Little rain.

A رشء *rashʾ*, (v. n. of رشأ) Bringing forth (a hind). Lying with a woman.

A رشأ *rashaʾ*, (pl. ارشاء *arshāʾ*) A fawn beginning to walk. A herb growing in clefts of sand-hills.

A رشاء *rashāʾ*, A rope. *Rishāʾ*, (v.n.3 of رشا for رشو) Assisting. Endeavouring to conciliate, soothing by presents. Conniving at. (pl. ارشية *arshiyat*) A rope. The rope of a bucket. The tail of a serpent. The stalk of a cucumber, gourd, or colocynth. A cluster of small stars, called بطن الحوت *batnu'l hūt*, as resembling a fish, in the navel of which is the 28th mansion of the moon.

A رشاة *rashāt*, (pl. رشا) Name of a plant.

A رشّاح *rashshāh*, One who sweats.

A رشاد *rashād*, (v.n. of رشد) Pursuing a straight course. The right way, the road to salvation. Victory, triumph. Garden-cresses. رشاد الماء *rashādu'l māʾ*, Water-cress. حبّ الرشاد *habbu'r rashād*, Cresses, or the seed. (pl. of رشادة *rashādat*) Stones. اصحاب رشاد *as-hābi rashād*, The faithful.

A رشادة *rashādat*, Justice. Exercise of authority. Severity tempered with clemency. A stone which fills the hand.

A رشاش *rashāsh*, A sprinkling of water, a trickling of blood or tears. *Rishāsh*, (pl. of رشّ *rashsh*) Drops of water.

A رشاقة *rashāhat*, A being of an elegant shape.

A رشانة *rashānat*, (v. n. of رشن) Going uninvited to a feast. Entering without leave.

A رشبة *rushbat*, The shell of a cocoa-nut, used as a spoon.

P رشت *rasht*, Very dry, friable, crumbling to pieces. Earth, dust. Sweepings. Lime. A wall ready to fall. Name of a city in Gīlān. *Risht*, Nature, disposition. Spinning. *Rusht*, Bright, lucid, glittering. Old and ruinous, threatening to fall. Any thing beginning to perish from age. Name of a famous alchymist.

P رشتاك *rashtāk*, A shoot, a sapling.

P رشتن *rishtan*, To spin, to twist. *Rushtan*, To colour, dye.

P رشته *rishta*, Thread, line, rope. A fringe, lace. A row, file, train. The dracunculus or Guinea-worm, a disease common to the inhabitants of لار *lār*. Relationship, connexion, kin. A kind of sweetmeat. Slices of paste put amongst soup, &c., a kind of macaroni. رشتهٔ باران *rishtaʾi bārān*, Rain falling in an unbroken stream. رشتهٔ تب *rishtaʾi tab*, Any charm applied to the arm of one in a fever. رشتهٔ خاك *rishtaʾi khāk*, Man and other animals. رشتهٔ دراز دادن *rishtaʾi darāz dādan*, To give a long line, *i. e.* to afford opportunity. رشتهٔ دندان *rishtaʾi dandān*, A row of teeth. رشتهٔ قطائف *rishtaʾi katāʾif*, A kind of sweetmeat. رشتهٔ ضحاك *rishtaʾi zahāk*, Rain. A long space of time. رشتهٔ نگنده *rishtaʾi niganda*, Thread for sewing counterpanes. *Rushta*, Coloured, dyed.

P رشته دار *rishta-dār*, A dependant, relation.

P رشته كش *rishta-kash*, Drawing thread. Reducing to order.

P رشتي *rashtī*, Sweepings of dust, dirt, or rubbish. Meanness. Humility. A sweeper. A besom. Of the town of Rasht.

A رشح *rashh*, (v. n. of رشح) Sweating. Flowing, distilling, trickling, dropping. Giving, bestowing. Bounding (as a deer). *Rashah*, Sweat.

A رشحة *rash-hat*, A dropping, dripping, distilling. Sweat.

A رشد *rushd*, (v. n. of رشد) Following the right way, being guided in the proper path. Rectitude. A strict and unflinching observance of what is right. The way of salvation. سنّ رشد *sinni rushd*, The age of discretion. *Rashad*, (v. n. of رشد) Pursuing a straight course. A straight road, a right way.

A رشدة *rashdat* or *rishdat*, A lawfully begotten son. هو لرشدة *huwa li rishdatin*, He is a legitimate child.

A رشدي *rashadaʾ*, Inquiry after the right way.

A رشراش *rashrāsh*, Dry and soft bread. A soft bone. Roasting meat whence the fat drops.

A رشرش *rashrash*, Dry and soft bread.

A رشرشة *rashrashat*, (v. n. of رشرش Q) Being soft (a bone). Softness. Being competent to grapple with a person of whom one is afraid.

A رشف *rashf*, (v. n. of رشف) Sipping, sucking. Emptying entirely the contents of a vessel. الرشف انقع *ar'rashfu ankaʿ*, Sipping is the most efficacious quencher of thirst. *Rashaf*, (v. n. of رشف) Drawing in (water) with the extremity of the lips, sipping. The surface water which (a horse) sucks up. A little water left in a cistern.

A رشق *rashk*, (v. n. of رشق) Hitting (with an

arrow). *Rashh* or *rishh*, The sound made by a pen in scribbling. *Rishh*, Archery. Any thing about which a wager is laid or stakes deposited. A side or direction in which an arrow is shot. A certain mode of shooting. *Rashak*, Rapidly-shooting (bow). (pl. of رشيق *rashīk*) Of elegant stature.

P رشك *rashk*, Envy, jealousy. Pride, haughtiness, self-admiration. Jealous. Nits. رشك بردن *rashk burdan*, (or خوردن *khwurdan*) To envy, be jealous. بي رشك *bī rashk*, A contented cuckold. *Rishk*, Nits. Erect, upright. A man with a large beard. Dirt, filth, pus, matter. *Rushk*, A scorpion.

A رشك *rishk*, One with a large beard. A marker for those who shoot for a wager. A thick beard.

P رشك آور *rashk-āwar*, (or خور) Jealous.

P رشكن *rashkin*, Jealous, envious. Proud.

P رشكناك *rashknāk* or *rishknāk*, Full of nits or eggs of lice, nitty.

P رشكين *rashkīn*, Jealous. St. Anthony's fire.

A رشم *rashm*, (v.n. of رشم) Writing. Marking. Sealing grain. Rain. *Rasham*, (v.n. of رشم) Getting a keener edge to the appetite by smelling the flavour of meat. Any black or conspicuous mark on the face (of a hyena). The marks of rain upon the ground. The first sprouting of a plant above the earth. Rain.

A رشماء *rashmāʼ*, Marked on the face (hyena).

P رشميز *rashmīz*, A worm that destroys wood.

P رشن *rashn*, Name of the eighteenth day of the Persian month. Name of an angel. A little hill. A bite, a sting.

A رشن *rashn*, (v. n. of رشن) Coming uninvited to a feast. Thrusting his muzzle into a pot (a dog). *Rashn* or *rashan*, The mouth of a river. A time, turn, or rotation (in drinking).

P رشنواد *rashnawād*, Name of the commander of the armies of Humāy, daughter of Bahman.

P رشني *rashnī*, A sweeper of the streets.

A رشو *rashw*, (v. n. of رشا for رشو) Corrupting with presents (a judge or governor) to gain a cause.

A رشوة *rashwat*, *rishwat*, or *rushwat*, (pl. رشى *rushaʼ*, *rishaʼ*, رشوات *rishawāt*, or *rishwāt*) A gift for corrupting a judge, bribery, simony. A bribe. Manure.

P رشوت خور *rishwat-khwur*, A taker of bribes.

A رشوتي *rishwatī*, One who accepts bribes.

A رشوف *rashūf*, (A woman) with a sweet and delicate mouth and a dry فرج *farj*. (A camel) cropping with the lips.

A رشون *rushūn*, (v. n. of رشن) Thrusting his chops into a pot (a dog). (Flocks) feeding.

A رشي *rashaʼ*, (pl. of رشاة *rashāt*) Certain plants. *Rishaʼ* or *rushaʼ*, (pl. of رشوة *rishwat* or *rushwat*) Bribes.

A رشيح *rashīh*, Sweat. The leakings of a leathern bottle. Name of a plant.

A رشيد *rashīd*, A director, conductor, guide. Sagacious, intelligent, wise, guided aright. One of the attributes of God, as he who guides aright. Rosetta in Egypt. هارون الرشيد *hārūn ar`rashīd*, Name of the fifth caliph of the house of Al Abbās, contemporary with Charlemagne.

A رشيدة *rashīdat*, Rosetta, a town in Egypt.

P رشيدن *rashīdan*, To pour out, spill, shed.

P رشيده *rashīda*, Fringe of a turban-sash.

A رشيديّة *rashīdiyat*, Name of a sect. (from P رشته *rishta*) Slices of paste in soup.

A رشيف *rashīf*, A sipping, a sucking.

A رشيق *rashīk*, (pl. رشق *rashak*) Of an elegant stature. Rapidly-shooting (bow).

P رشينه *rashīna*, Resin.

A رصّ *rass*, (v. n. of رصّ) Cementing, glueing, cramping, joining. Placing her eggs in order with her beak (a hen).

A رصّاء *rassāʼ*, (fem. of ارصّ *arass*) A thigh sitting close to the other.

A رصاد *risād*, (pl. of رصدة) Single showers.

A رصّاد *rassād*, A patrol. A collector of toll. An astronomer. A mathematician. An observatory.

A رصاص *rasās*, (vulg. *risās*) Lead; of which there are two kinds, black and white. The former is called اسربّ *usrubb* and ابّار *abbār*, and in India, شيشه *shīsha*. The latter is called قلعي *kalʻiy* and قصدير *kasdīr*, Tin.

A رصّاص *rassās*, A seller of tin or lead. A tinman.

A رصّاصة *rassāsat*, A miser. Curbstones closely joined round a running fountain.

A رصاع *rasāʻ*, A lying with. Venery.

A رصّاع *rassāʻ*, Frequent in venery.

A رصاغ *risāgh*, The tether of a horse.

A رصاف *risāf*, (pl. رصف *rusuf*) The bones of the side. (pl. of رصفة *rasafat*) Raw, beaten sinews whipped round a bow or the head of an arrow. (pl. of رصيف *rasīf*) Horses' sinews.

A رصافة *rasāfat*, (v. n. of رصف) Being firm and solid. Firmness, solidity. *Rusāfat*, A raw macerated sinew of a camel's neck bound round the head of an arrow.

A رصانة *rasānat*, A being strong, firm, fixed.

A رصائع *rasāʼiʻ*, (pl. of رصيعة *rasīʻat*) Bosses on the hilts of swords. Twisted chains whereby a sword is hung to the belt.

A رصب *rasab*, The space between the roots of the fore and middle fingers.

A رصح *rasah*, Closeness of the thighs. Leanness of buttocks.

A رصحاء *ras-hāʼ*, (fem. of ارصح *arsah*) Close-hipped and lank-thighed (woman).

A رصخ *rashh*, A being firm, unmoved, unshaken.

A رصد *rasd* or *rasad*, (v. n. of رصد) Watching (the road or the stars). *Rasad*, (pl. ارصاد *arsād*) A road-watcher. Little (corn or rain). A watcher, or watchers (male or female).

P رصد بند *rasad-band*, A fixer of astronomical tables.

A رصدة *rasdat*, (pl. رصاد *risād*) One fall of rain. *Rusdat*, A pit dug to catch a lion. A silver or brass ring by which a sword hangs to the belt.

P رصد خانه *rasad-khāna*, An observatory.

P رصدگاه *rasad-gāh*, An observatory. A king's court. The receipt of custom, the office where the cultivators pay their rents. رصدگاه دهر *rasad-gāhi dahr*, The world. رصدگاه خاكي *rasad-gah khākī*, The world. The human body.

A رصدي *rasadiy*, A keeper of the road. A toll-gatherer.

A رصراصة *rasrāsat*, Curb-stones fixed about a running fountain in hard ground.

A رصرصة *rasrasat*, (v. n. of رصرص Q) Firmly uniting, cramping (a building). Remaining fixed in one place.

A رصع *rasʻ*, (v.n. of رصع) Striking with the hand. Bruising between two stones. Abiding in a place. Entering deep into a wounded man (the point of a spear). Stabbing deeply. *Rasaʻ*, (v. n. of رصع) Having meagre thighs. Adhering to any thing (perfumes). Adhering firmly. Young palm-trees.

A رصعاء *rasʻāʼ*, (fem. of ارصع) Meagre-hipped.

A رصغ *rusgh*, Pastern in animals; wrist in man.

A رصف *rasf*, (v. n. of رصف) Joining together stones in pavements, or the feet in prayer). Agreeing, being suitable. Whipping the head of an arrow about with a bruised sinew. *Rasaf*, Water descending from a mountain amongst stones. Stones laid upon and adhering to others.

A رصفاء *rasfāʼ*, Narrow, impervious (woman).

A رصفة *rasafat*, (pl. رصاف *risāf*) A fresh moist sinew, beaten, and whipped about the head of an arrow. One stone laid upon and adhering to others.

A رصم *rasam*, An entrance into a narrow pass through hills.

A رصن *rasn*, (v. n. of رصن) Performing, finishing. Overcoming; acquiring any difficult science. Reproaching.

A رصو *rasw*, (v. n. of رصا for رصو) Doing any thing firmly and properly.

A رصوخ *rusūkh*, (for رسوخ *rusūkh*, q. v.).

A رصود *rasūd*, (A she-camel) waiting till others have done drinking and then taking their place.

A رصوف *rasūf*, Narrow, strait (woman).

A رصوفة *rusūfat*, A sinew moistened, beaten, and whipped round the head of an arrow.

A رصيد *rasīd*, (A dog or beast) lying in wait.

A رصيص *rasīs*, Eggs placed one upon another. A veil which covers the face, the eyes only seen.

A رصيع *rasīʻ*, A clasp for keeping a book shut.

A رصيعة *rasīʻat*, (pl. رصائع *rasāʼiʻ*) A knot or boss upon bridles, sword-hilts, or belts (adorned with gems). A ring on a sword or saddle. The part of a horse's back where the ribs meet. A gem set. Wheat bruised, boiled, and cooked with butter.

A رصيف *rasīf*, Solid (business). Firm (answer). One who works side by side with another doing exactly the same amount of labour as he does. (pl. رصاف *risāf*) The sinew of a horse.

A رصين *rasīn*, Firm, solid, fixed, fortified. Sick, pained. Benevolent. Attentive to the necessities of a friend. رصينا الفرس *rasīnā'l faras*, Two bones that join the two edges of the knee-pan of a horse. رصين الجوف *rasīnu'l jawf*, Pained in the belly.

A رض *raz*, (for رضي الله عنه *raziya'llāh ʿanhu*) May God be pleased with him!

A رضّ *razz*, (v. n. of رضّ) Striking, beating. Bruising, breaking (in large pieces). Dates stoned and macerated in milk.

A رضا *riza'*, Content, satisfaction, good pleasure.

A رضاء *rizās*, (v. n. 3 of رضي) Endeavouring to please, contending who shall please most. Being pleased and satisfied with each other. Consent, agreement, acquiescence, good pleasure.

A رضاب *ruzāb*, Saliva, spittle sucked with the lips. A particle of musk, snow, or hail. A dewdrop on a tree. The froth of honey.

A رضاة *ruzāt*, (pl. of راضي *rāzī*) Content, satisfied, pleased, acquiescing.

P رضا جوئي *rizā-joī*, An effort to please.

A رضارض *razāriz*, Camels turned to graze.

A رضاض *ruzāz*, A fragment broken off.

A رضاع *razāʿ* or *rizāʿ*, (v. n. of رضع) Sucking (the mother). Asking. *Rizāʿ*, (v. n. 3 of رضع) Delivering (a child) to a wet nurse. Sucking a pregnant mother. Having a foster-brother.

A رضّاع *razzāʿ*, A suckling. A miser, worthless fellow. *Ruzzāʿ*, (pl. of راضع *rāziʿ*) Sucklings.

A رضاعة *razāʿat*, (v. n. of رضع) Being sordid, avaricious. The west wind. A south-west wind. اخو من الرضاعة *akhū mini'r razāʿat*, A foster-brother. *Razāʿat* or *rizāʿat*, (v. n. of رضع) Sucking (the mother).

A رضام *rizām*, (pl. of رضمة *razmat*) Large stones for building. *Ruzām*, A kind of plant. Little herbage, or a little of any thing.

P رضامند *rizāmand*, Consenting, permitting.

P رضامندي *rizāmandī*, Consent, permission.

P رضائي *razāī*, A cover for the head in winter.

A رضب *razb*, (v. n. of رضب) Distilling gently (rain). Lying down (a sheep). Sucking (saliva) wantonly. *Razab*, A species of the tree سدر *sidr*.

A رضح *razh*, (v. n. of رضح) Breaking (pebbles or date-stones). نوى الرضح *nawa'r razhi*, Scattered bits of pounded date-stones. *Ruzh*, Broken date-stones. Bits of pounded substances.

A رضخ *razkh*, (v. n. of رضخ) Bruising, crushing small stones. Dashing to the ground. Preparing to butt (a he-goat). Giving a small present. A small present. Uncertain, not credited news.

A رضد *razd*, (v. n. of رضد) Laying (goods) side by side. *Razad*, Piled up (wares).

A رضراض *razrāz*, Gravel, pebbles; also a road paved with them. Fleshy, corpulent (man). The buttocks of a horse shaking with fat. Small rain.

A رضرض *razraz*, Gravel, small pebbles.

A رضرضة *razrazat*, A breaking, a pounding.

A رضع *razʿ*, (v. n. of رضع) Asking for milk or for any thing. *Razʿ*, *razaʿ*, or *raziʿ*, (v. n. of رضع) Sucking (the mother). *Rizʿ*, Trees on which camels feed. *Razaʿ*, Any thing sucked. *Razaʿ*, *raziʿ*, or *rizaʿ*, Small palm-trees. *Razaʿ* or *raziʿ*, Avarice. *Raziʿ*, Any thing sucked. (pl. رضع *ruzuʿ*) A suckling.

A رضّع *ruzzaʿ*, (pl. of راضع *rāziʿ*) Sucklings.

A رضعاء *ruzaʿās*, (pl. of رضيع *raziʿ*) Sucklings. Foster-brothers.

A رضف *razf*, (v. n. of رضف) Burning, branding, roasting, or boiling with a hot stone. Voiding dung. Folding a pillow. A hot stone thrown into milk, in order to warm it; also one with which they cauterize animals. Bones in the knee resembling fingers compressed. (In a horse they are situated between the كراع *kurāʿ* (Shin) and ذراع *zirāʿ* (Arm). مطفئة الرضف *mutfiʼatu'r razf*, (Quenching the hot stone) A piece of fat or a serpent gliding over it. A severe misfortune. *Razaf*, Hot stones thrown into milk to warm it.

A رضفات العرب *razafātu'l ʿarab*, Four Arabian tribes; namely, شيبان *shaybān*, تغلب *taghlib*, بهراء *bahrās*, and اياد *iyād*.

A رضفة *razfat* or *razafat*, A single knee-bone. *Razafat*, A brand made with a hot stone.

A رضم *razm*, (v. n. of رضم) Going with a slow step (an old man). Ploughing. Striking (the ground with any thing). Throwing one's self upon the ground. Laying stones (in building or paving). Lying still (a bird). Erecting, building. Loitering at home. *Razm* or *razam*, (pl. of رضمة *razmat*) Large stones for building.

A رضمان *razmān*, Slow-paced (camel). *Razamān*, A short-stepped pace.

A رضمة *razamat*, A large stone (for building). *Ruzamat*, Still, quiet (bird).

A رضو *razw*, (v. n. of رضي) Conquering, excelling (in pleasing).

A رضوان *rizwān* or *ruzwān*, (v. n. of رضى) Accepting, acquiescing; being pleased, gratified. Receiving as an associate, approving of. *Rizwān*, Complacency. Approbation. A blessing, benediction. Paradise. Name of the porter or gardener of paradise. رضوان الله عليهم اجمعين *rizwānu'llāh ʿalayhim ajmaʿīn*, May the blessing of God be upon them all!

P رضوان كدة *rizwan-kada*, The heaven of amber.

P رضواني *rizwānī*, Belonging to paradise.

A رضوة *rizwat*, Good pleasure.

A رضوعة *razūʿat*, Giving suck, milch (sheep).

A رضى *razī*, (pl. رضون *razūn*) Content, pleased, satisfied. *Riza'*, Agreeable, approved, acceptable, laudable. A surety, sponsor, bail. A lover, a friend. *Riza'* or *ruza'*, (v. n. of رضي) Acquiescing, being pleased and gratified. Receiving one as a partner. رضى الله عنه *raziya'llāh ʿanhu*, God reward him!

A رضيّ *raziy*, (pl. ارضياء *arziyās*) Quiet, easy, gentle. Content, pleased.

A رضيح *razīh*, Crushed (date-stone).

A رضيد *razīd*, Piled up (wares).

A رضيض *razīz*, Broken (into coarse lumps).

A رضيع *raziʿ*, An infant, a suckling. A foster-brother. Worthless. A miser.

A رضيف *razīf*, (Milk) boiled by a hot stone.

A رضيم *razīm*, Firmly-built, built of stone.

A رضيّم *ruzayyim*, A sort of bird.

A رطء *ruts*, Foolish, silly (women).

A رطأ *ratasa*, (fut. يرطأ *yartasu*) He lay with. He voided excrement. He rendered discontented.

A رطأ *ratas*, Folly, stupidity.

A رطاء *ritās*, (pl. of رطئ *ratiy*) Foolish, stupid.

A رطاء *ratsās*, Foolish, stupid (woman).

A رطاءات *ratsāsāt*, Foolish, silly (women).

A يا رطاب *yā ratābi*, O flabby! (a taunt to a woman). *Ritāb*, (pl. of رطبة *ratbat*) Fresh grasses.

A رطابة *ratābat*, A being fresh, moist, tender.

A رطازات *rutāzāt*, Fables, idle stories.

A رطاط *ritāt*, (pl. of رطيط *ratīt*) Sounds, clamours. Follies, inadvertencies. Fools.

A رطام *rutām*, Close confinement.

A رطانة *ratānat*, Companies of camels with their masters. *Ratānat* or *ritānat*, (v. n. of رطن) Speaking any language, not Arabic.

A رطائط *ratāsit*, (pl. of رطيط *ratīt*) Clamours, shouts. Fools.

A رطب *ratb*, (v. n. of رطب) Feeding (a horse) on fresh clover. Giving (people) fresh dates to eat. Being moist and fresh (a date). Living on fresh and moist dates. Fresh. Tender (youth). Moist. Delicate (boy), resembling a girl. لؤلؤ رطب *luslus ratb*, Brilliant pearls, (figuratively) White teeth. *Rutb* or *rutub*, Green herbage or trees. Much grass, many trees. *Ratab*, (v. n. of رطب) Speaking out right or wrong, saying what is pleasing or displeasing. *Rutab*, (pl. ارطاب *artāb*) A ripe date.

A رطبة *ratbat*, (pl. رطاب *ritāb*) Green plants (especially medicinal). A tender, delicate girl. Loud, distinct (fart). *Rutabat*, A single fresh and moist date.

A رطراط *ratrāt*, Water left by camels in a cistern.

A رط رط *rut rut*, Words used in bidding one pretend to be a fool.

A رطز *rataz*, Weak, insipid (verse): weak (hair).

A رطزات *ratazāt*, Fables, foolish tales.

A رطس *rats*, A slap with the palm of the hand.

A رطع *ratas*, (v. n. of رطع) Lying with. Rheum, or any thing similar.

A رطل *ratl,* (v. n. of رطل) Running. Weighing in the hand. Soft, gentle. Relaxed in the joints. Slender (youth). One near the age of puberty. One whose bones are not strong. Languid old man. Mad, crazy. A fool. Equity, justice. *Ratl* or *ritl,* (pl. ارطال *artāl*) A pound of twelve ounces. Light (horse).

P رطل *ritl,* A cup of wine.

P رطل زن *ratl-zan,* A weigher of provisions.

P رطل كشان *ritl-kashān,* Presenting the bowl with delight and pleasure.

A رطم *ratm,* (v. n. of رطم) Throwing (into any business), inextricably. Shutting up, confining. Dunging (an animal). Copulating.

A رطمة *rutmat,* Perplexed, intricate business.

A رطو *ratw,* (v. n. of رطا for رطو) Copulating. Being foolish.

A رطوب *rutūb,* (v. n. of رطب) Giving (a horse) fresh clover to eat.

A رطوبة *rutūbat,* (v. n. of رطب) Being moist, soft, fresh, tender. Moisture, juiciness.

A رطول *rutūl,* (v. n. of رطل) Running, making haste. Weighing in the hand.

A رطوم *ratūm,* Mad, foolish, crazy. Strait, close, impervious (female).

A رطون *ratūn,* Companies of camels with their owners.

A رطي *raty,* A copulating. A becoming foolish.

A رطي *ratīy,* (pl. رطاء *ritāʼ*) Mad, foolish, silly.

A رطيب *ratīb,* Moist, humid, fresh. (pl. رطاب *ritāb*) Ripe (date).

A رطيط *ratīt,* (pl. رطاط *ritāt* and رطائط *ratāʼit*) Mad, crazy. Tumult, uproar. Folly.

P رطينا *ratīnā,* A medicament for the eyes.

A رطينا *rutaynā',* (or رطيني *rutaynā'*) Unintelligible discourse.

A رطيئة *ratīʼat,* (fem. of رطيء *ratīʼ*) Silly.

A رعّ *raʻʻ,* Tranquillity, quiet, rest.

A رعاء *riʻāʼ* or *ruʻāʼ,* (pl. of راعي *rāʻī*) Shepherds. Guardians.

A رعّاب *raʻʻāb,* One who applies the magical charm رعب. One who speaks with a rhythm.

A رعابيل *raʻābīl,* Torn, worn garment.

A رعاة *ruʻāt* (pl. of راعي) Shepherds: keepers.

A رعاث *riʻās,* (pl. of رعثة *raʻsat*) Ear-rings.

A رعّاد *raʻʻād,* Thundering (cloud). Talkative (man). The torpedo, or benumbing fish.

A رعاديد *raʻādīd,* Delicate women. Tremulous.

A رعارع *raʻāriʻ,* (pl. of رعراع) Handsome lads.

A رعّاس *raʻʻās,* Tremulous (spear).

A رعاع *raʻāʻ,* Vile, upstart, and young cowards. رعاع رعايا *raʻāʻi raʻāya',* The worst of subjects.

A رعاعة *raʻāʻat,* A she-ostrich. Silly, stupid.

A رعاف *ruʻāf,* (v. n. of رعف) Emitting blood from the nose. Blood from the nose. A hemorrhage.

A رعاقيّ *ruʻāfiy,* One who gives liberally.

A رعاق *ruʻāk,* A rumbling inside a horse's belly when trotting, or of his yard within the sheath.

A رعال *riʻāl,* (pl. of رعلة *raʻlat*) Tall palm-trees. Troops, crowds. *Ruʻāl,* Whatever flows from the nose, snot.

A رعالة *raʻālat,* Madness, folly, stupidity.

A رعام *raʻām,* Sharpness of sight. *Ruʻām,* (v. n. of رعم) Being lean (sheep). Observing. Watching the setting sun. Having a running at the nose. (pl. ارعمة *arʻimat*) Snot running from the nose of a sheep, diseased or otherwise.

A رعامة *ruʻāmat,* Name of a tree.

A رعامى *ruʻāma',* Name of a tree. An enlargement of the liver.

A رعان *riʻān,* (pl. of رعن *raʻn*) Prominent parts of mountains; noses, nesses.

A رعاوي *ru* or *raʻāwa',* Camels feeding near home.

A رعاوية *raʻāwiyat,* A herd (especially of camels, marked with the royal signet).

A رعايا *raʻāya'* (pl. of رعيّة *raʻiyat*) Herds of camels. Subjects, peasants, the lower order of people of all kinds, under-tenants, ryots, cultivators.

A رعاية *riʻāyat,* (v. n. of رعي) Ruling, governing. Guarding, protecting. Looking after, tending. Feeding, grazing (cattle). Receiving affably, giving presents to inferiors. Paying attention. The office of shepherd, ruler, or pastor. Observation, respect, honour. Treatment. Kindness, favour. Patronage, encouragement. Remission, indulgence, favour. Pity. رعايت فرمودن *riʻāyat farmūdan,* To observe. P رعايت كردن *riʻāyat kardan,* To honour, revere, cultivate, pay attention to, take care of, guard, regulate. To observe, fulfil. To give a present to an inferior.

A رعايةً *riʻāyatan,* In honour of, from regard to.

A رعايتي *riʻāyatī,* A favoured person.

A رعب *raʻb,* (v. n. of رعب) Terrifying, scaring. Filling (a lake). Breaking the hole in the top of an arrow wherein they fix the point. Cooing, mourning aloud (a dove). Cutting (a camel's bunch). An amulet or magic charm. Threats with which the Arabians animate one another when going to battle. *Ruʻb,* (pl. رعبة *riʻabat*) A hole in the top of an arrow in which the head is fixed. *Ruʻb* or *ruʻub,* (v. n. of رعب) Frighting. Fear, terror, trepidation. *Raʻab,* (v. n. of رعب) Fearing, trembling. *Raʻib,* Name of a country whence come the doves called راعبيّة *rāʻibīyat.*

A رعبب *ruʻbab,* Root of the date-blossom.

A رعبة *riʻabat,* (pl. of رعب *ruʻb*) Holes in the tops of arrows or spear-staves.

A رعبل *raʻbal,* Clad in worn-out raiment (a woman). Foolish (woman). A mother. A man's name.

A رعبلة *raʻbalat,* (v. n. of رعبل Q) Mincing (meat). Tearing (a garment). Dividing, breaking in pieces. Marrying a silly woman. (Wind) unsteady, whiffling. *Riʻbalat,* (pl. رعابيل *raʻābīl*) Worn-out (garment). (A woman) clad in tatters. Silly (woman), or one whose flesh hangs loose.

A رعبليب *raʻbalīb,* A mild, soft, and gentle woman. One who tears whatever he can.

A رعبليل *raʻbalīl,* Unsteady or whiffling wind.

A رعبوب *ruʻbūb,* Weak, cowardly. Tall and full of flesh. Of a delicate, graceful form.

A رعبوبة *ruʻbūbat,* A slice of a camel's bunch. The root of the blossom of the date. *Ruʻbūbat,* (رعبوب *ruʻbūb* and رعبيب *riʻbīb*) (A girl) tall and graceful, fair and delicate. Light, unsteady.

A رعبولة *ruʻbūlat,* A torn or worn garment.

A رعة *riʻat,* Abstinence from every thing deemed unlawful. A victim destined for sacrifice at Mecca. Elegance of form. Ugliness of aspect. Condition.

A رعث *raʻs,* (v. n. of رعث) Biting (a snake) and taking away a little. *Raʻas* and *raʻs,* A woollen tassel suspended from a camel-litter. Whiteness of the points of the slit ears of a goat.

A رعثاء *raʻsāʼ,* An oblong grape. (A sheep) having two bits hanging down under the ears.

A رعثة *raʻsat* or *raʻasat,* (pl. رعاث *riʻās*) An ear-ring. The hairy plumage under the neck of a cock. The comb or wattles of a cock. A cup made from the palm-tree. *Ruʻsat,* A lock of dyed wool suspended from a camel-litter.

A رعج *raʻj,* (v. n. of رعج) Flashing in quick succession (lightning). Rendering affluent. Disturbing, disquieting. *Raʻaj,* (v. n. of رعج) Being very numerous (herds or children).

A رعد *raʻd,* (v. n. of رعد) Thundering. Dressing, decorating herself (a woman). Striking with terror, fulminating. Thunder: or its presiding angel. ذات رعد *zātu raʻd,* War.

P رعد انداز *raʻd-andāz,* Ordnance. A cannoneer.

A رعدة *ruʻdat* or *riʻdat,* A tremour. Stiffness.

A رعديد *riʻdīd,* (or رعديدة *riʻdīdat*) A delicate woman. Trembling, timid, cowardly. Gruel with honey in it.

A رعراع *raʻrāʻ,* Pusillanimous. A long reed or pen.

A رعرع *raʻraʻ,* (*ruʻruʻ* also رعراع *raʻrāʻ* (pl. رعارع *raʻāriʻ*) A tall, well-made, handsome youth.

A رعرعة *raʻraʻat,* (v. n. of رعرع Q) (God) causing to grow. Waving and shining on the surface of the ground (water). Breaking, exercising, or training (a horse).

A رعز *raʻz,* (v. n. of رعز) Lying with.

A رعس *raʻs,* (v. n. of رعس) Trembling, shaking. Scattering. Walking slowly (from fatigue and weakness).

A رعسان *raʻasān,* Shaking of the head with age.

A رعش *raʻsh* or *raʻash,* (v. n. of رعش) Trembling. *Raʻish,* Rushing to kill. One who hastens to confer a favour. Fearful, timorous, faint-hearted.

A رعشاء *raʻshāʼ,* (A she-camel) going quick and trembling. Swift (ostrich).

A رعشان *raʻshān,* Shaking of the head with age.

A رعشة *raʻshat,* A shaking, tremor. Palsy.

A رعشن raʿshan, Tremulous (man or camel). A coward. Swift (ostrich or camel).

P رعشه دار raʿsha-dār, Tremulous. Paralytic.

P رعشناك raʿshanāk, Tremulous. Aspen-like.

A رعشيش riʿshīsh, Timorous, cowardly. Rushing to kill. One who hastens to confer a favour.

A رعص raʿs, (v. n. of رعص) Shaking, disturbing, dragging, setting in motion.

A رعظ raʿz, (v. n. of رعظ) Making a hole in the top of an arrow wherein to fix the point. Breaking that hole. *Ruʿz*, (pl. ارعاظ arʿāz) A hole in the top of an arrow or spear-staff, in which they fix the point. *Raʿaz*, A breaking of the hole in the top of an arrow wherein the point is fixed. *Raʿiz*, (An arrow) broken at that hole.

A رعف raʿf, (v. n. of رعف) Bleeding at the nose. Taking the lead, outstripping, winning a race (a horse). Causing a horse's hoof to be stained with blood (pebbles). Entering (a door). *Raʿaf*, (v. n. of رعف) Flowing (blood).

A رعل raʿl, (v. n. of رعل) Piercing through and through with a spear, or cutting with a sword. A promontory or projecting part of a mountain. Garments (of a man). *Riʿl*, The male palm-tree. *Ruʿl*, (pl. of رعلاء raʿlāʾ) Camels or sheep of whom part of the ear hangs down. *Raʿal*, (v. n. of رعل) Being foolish, half-witted.

A رعلّ raʿalla, Perhaps.

A رعلاء raʿlāʾ, A camel or sheep, part of whose slit ear hangs down. Long-eared (sheep).

A رعلة raʿlat, (pl. ارعال arʿāl, اراعيل arāʿīl, and رعال riʿāl) A body from 20 to 25; the advanced part of a larger number. Domestics (especially numerous). A great company, many. A small herd of horses. A herd of cattle. The female ostrich. The first appearance of branches or leaves. A tall palm-tree; also one bearing bad dates. The foreskin. The edge or sharp part of any thing. Part of a camel's ear hanging down. ابو رعلة abū riʿlat, The wolf. *Ruʿlat*, A chaplet of myrtle and other odoriferous herbs.

A رعلول ruʿlūl, Dracunculus hortensis.

A رعم raʿm, (v. n. of رعم) Having a running at the nose (a sheep). Watching the setting sun. *Riʿm*, Fat, grease. امّ رعم ummu riʿmin, A hyena.

A رعن raʿn, (v. n. of رعن) Causing to languish with heat (the sun), giving the headache. A coup de soleil. (pl. رعون ruʿūn and رعان riʿān) The most prominent part of a mountain, a ness. A long mountain. *Raʿan*, (v. n. of رعن) Being relaxed, languid; foolish. Relaxation, languor. *Ruʿun*, Girls.

A رعنّ raʿanna, Perhaps.

P رعنا raʿnā, Beautiful, delicate, tender, lovely, amiable, admirable. Moving gracefully, graceful. A foolish admirer of himself. Free from care. گل رعنا guli raʿnā, A beautiful rose. رعنائ صاحب بربط raʿnāʾi sāhib barbat, The planet Venus.

A رعناء raʿnāʾ, (fem. of ارعن arʿan) Silly, foolish. The city of Basrah. A kind of grape.

P رعنائي raʿnāʾī, Graceful gait. Beauty, loveliness, grace.

A رعو raʿw, riʿw, or ruʿw, Care, attention; the avoidance of what is bad.

A رعوة raʿwat or riʿwat, (v. n. of رعي) Abstaining from evil. *Raʿ, riʿ*, or *ruʿwat*, Avoidance of what is bad. Any thing about which one cares.

A رعود ruʿūd, (pl. of رعد raʿd) Thunders.

A رعوس raʿūs, (A camel) shaking her head with age or glee. Throwing the feet about nimbly. Drowsy, nodding. Tremulous (lance).

A رعوش raʿūsh, (A she-camel) shaking the head with age.

A رعوف ruʿūf, Slight rains.

A رعويّ raʿwaīy, Ill-dressed (roast meat).

A رعوم raʿūm, Very lean. Blackness of ink. Rheumy (sheep). Soul, spirit, self. *Ruʿūm*, Tender, delicate (woman).

A رعون raʿūn, Moving, moveable. Strong. Rough. Darkness of night. *Ruʿūn*, (pl. of رعن raʿn) Prominent parts of mountains, noses, nesses.

A رعونة ruʿūnat, (v. n. of رعن) Being relaxed and languid. Being foolish. Adorning one's self. Laxity. Decoration.

A رعوي raʿwāʾ or ruʿwāʾ, Care, custody, guardianship. Any thing that one cares for.

A رعي raʿy, (v. n. of رعي) Pasturing, feeding (as cattle). Tending flocks (a shepherd). Guarding. Observing (the stars) set. Abstaining from. رعي الحمام raʿyu'l hamām, Valerian. *Riʿy*, (pl. ارعاء arʿāʾ) Pasture, forage.

A رعيّ raʿīy, Pastured. Guided. Guarded.

A رعيا ruʿyāʾ, Any thing about which one is careful. Care, custody, guardianship.

A رعيان ruʿyān, (pl. of راعي rāʿī) Shepherds, pastors. Guardians.

A رعيب raʿīb, Fearing, terrified. Dropping fat. Large and full (camel's bunch).

A رعية riʿyat, Hard, stony ground. What is fed upon. Management, tendance (of camels).

A رعيّة raʿīyat, (pl. رعايا raʿāyāʾ) A herd of grazing camels. People, subjects. A subject, peasant, plebeian, generally a husbandman and manufacturer. An under-tenant, tenant of the soil, renter, ryot. Any thing that requires to be taken care of. P سلطان رعيّت پرور sultāni raʿīyat-parwar, A prince, the nourisher of his people.

P رعيّت دار raʿīyat-dār, A governor, a ruler.

P رعيّت داري raʿīyat-dārī, Government, rule. رعيّت داري کردن raʿīyat-dārī kardan, To administer government.

P رعيّت واري raʿīyatwārī, By individuals, individually. The ryotwary system.

A رعيتي raʿīyatī, Subjection. Tenancy. Land farmed out, tenanted, and cultivated on the spot.

A رعيداء ruʿaydāʾ, Refuse, chaff.

A رعيس raʿīs, (A camel) waggling in pace, or whose fore-leg is tied to his hind-leg.

A رعيظ raʿīz, (An arrow) broken at the head.

A رعيف raʿīf, A cloud in advance of others.

A رعيق raʿīk, (v. n. of رعق) Making a noise (the belly). The rumbling noise of a horse's belly when trotting, or of his yard within the sheath.

A رعيل raʿīl, A small body of horse.

A رعين raʿīn, A small body of horse. See رعون raʿūn. *Ruʿayn*, Name of a fort. ذو رعين zū ruʿayn, Name of a king.

P رغ rugh, Belching, eructation.

A رغاء rughāʾ, (v. n. of رغا for رغو) Crying (as an infant). Roaring or braying (as a hyena, camel, or ostrich). Frothing (milk).

A رغّاء raghghāʾ, A kind of bird.

A رغاب raghāb, Soft ground. Land not flooded, except after heavy rains. Extensive and level ground. *Righāb*, (pl. of رغيب raghīb) Camels abounding in milk and very serviceable.

A رغابي rughābaʾ, Enlargement of the liver.

A رغاث rughās, (Land) not flooded, except after heavy rains.

A رغال raghāl, A handmaid. ابو رغال abū righāl, Name of the man who served as guide to ابرهة abrahat, صاحب الفيل sāhibu'l fīl.

A رغام raghām, Soil. Soft soil, or soil mixed with sand. *Rughām*, Snot of sheep.

A رغامة rughāmat, Any thing wished for.

A رغامي rughāmaʾ, Enlargement of the liver. The air-tube of the lungs, the windpipe. The nose. A kind of plant.

A رغاوة ri or rughāwat, Froth (of milk).

A رغائب raghāʾib, (pl. of رغيبة raghībat) Things longed for. Much riches. Large presents.

A رغاية ri or rughāyat, Froth (of milk).

A رغب raghb, rughb, or raghab, (v. n. of رغب) Wanting, wishing, desiring, longing for. Disliking. Turning away from, loathing. Imploring. رغب بنفسه عنه raghiba bi nafsihi ʿanhu, He preferred himself to him, he esteemed himself above him. *Rughb*, (v. n. of رغب) Having a spacious paunch. Gormandizing. *Rughb* or *rughub*, (v. n. of رغب) Having a spacious channel (a river). Strong desire, avidity, voracity. Capaciousness. Softness. *Rughub*, Capacious. Land not flooded, except after heavy rains.

A رغباء raghbāʾ, (or رغبان raghabān) (v. n. of رغب) Supplicating, beseeching.

A رغبانة rughbānat, A knot on the lower part of the shoe-string.

A رغبة raghbat, (v. n. of رغب) Wishing, desiring, longing for, hankering after. Turning away from, being sated with. Esteeming, preferring. Estimation, preference, favour, pleasure. *Raghabat* or *rughbat*, (v. n. of رغب) Imploring, beseeching.

A رغبوب raghbūb, Greedy (man).

A رغبوت raghabūt, A wish, desire, longing for. Wishful, desirous, greedy (man).

A رغبوتا raghabūta', (or رغبوتي raghabūta') (v. n. of رغب) Supplicating, beseeching.

A رغبي ra or rughba', A supplicating, entreating.

P رغث raghs, Pomegranate-flowers.

A رغث raghs, (v. n. of رغث) Sucking (the mother). Stabbing repeatedly. Complaining of a pain in the udder. Being interrogated so frequently as to be exhausted.

A رغثاء rughasās, Root of the udder. Lacteal ducts, milky veins.

A رغد raghd or raghad, (v. n. of رغد) Being easy and comfortable (life). Easy, comfortable (life). Raghad, (Men or women) leading a comfortable life.

A رغرغة raghraghat, (v. n. of رغرغ Q) Living very comfortably. Drinking his fill every day (a camel). Confining (camels) to a pasturage of حمض hamz. Watering (camels) one day in the morning and another day in the evening. Watering them insufficiently. Finding the plant حمض hamz near a watering-place (a camel). Concealing. Ease, or comfort of life.

P رغزه raghza, A kind of woollen cloth.

A رغس raghs, (v. n. of رغس) Endowing plentifully with the good things of this life, enriching (God). Affluence, increase, riches, goods. (pl. ارغاس arghās) A benefit, boon, blessing.

A رغش raghsh, (v. n. of رغش) Stirring up evil.

A رغف raghf, (v. n. of رغف) Forming into balls (paste or clay). Giving (a camel) seeds and flour made up into flat cakes. Rughuf, (pl. of رغيف raghīf) Round flat cakes, cracknels.

A رغفان rughfān, Flat round cakes, cracknels.

A رغل raghl, (v. n. of رغل) Sucking (as a kid the dam). Grain when just formed in the ear. A fulness of grains in an ear of corn. Rughl, (pl. ارغال arghāl) The plant orage.

A رغلاء raghlās, Slit-eared (she-camel).

A رغلة raghlat, (v. n. of رغل) Sucking (as a kid its dam or another). A small animal (as a lamb or kid). Rughlat, The foreskin.

A رغم raghm, (v. n. of رغم) Displeasing; doing a thing contrary to the will of another. Raghm, righm, and rughm, (v. n. of رغم) Abhorring, disliking, hating, detesting, nauseating. Being soiled, dirtied. Being unable to obtain justice. Being compelled, subjected, forced against one's will. Stripping the bark off a tree. Disgust, antipathy, ill-will. Violence, severity, force, constraint. Contempt. Vileness, slavishness, meanness. Bark, skin, peel. Earth, dust. A being soiled with dirt. علي رغمه ȝala' raghmihi, Against his will. رغما عن انفه raghman ȝan anfihi, Against his will

A رغماء raghmās, (A sheep) which has a white speck upon the nose, or of a different colour from the rest of the body.

A رغن raghn, (v. n. of رغن) Listening favourably to any thing. Eating and drinking freely, having plenty. Wishing eagerly, hankering after. Inclining, leaning to.

A رغن raghanna, Perhaps. رغني raghanni, (or رغنني raghannanī) Perhaps I, haply I.

A رغنة raghnat, Level and soft ground.

P رغند raghand, Noise of beasts of prey.

A رغو raghūw, (A she-camel) which brays much.

A رغوان raghwān, A name given to a certain eloquent man.

A رغوة raghwat, A rock, a huge stone. Ragh, righ, or rughwat, (pl. رغي rugha') Froth of milk.

A رغوث raghūs, Giving suck, milch.

A رغول raghūl, A sheep giving suck promiscuously. One who seizes and eats any thing.

P رغوه raghwa, A sparrow with a red head.

A رغي rugha', (pl. of رغوة raghwat, righwat, or rughwat) Froths.

A رغيب raghīb, Desired, esteemed. A great eater, a glutton. Greedy, covetous. (pl. رغاب righāb) (A camel) abounding in milk, and very serviceable. Large-paunched (man); capacious (bottle or cistern). Deep and wide (river). Long-stepping (horse). Broad and glittering (sword).

A رغيبة raghībat, (pl. رغائب raghāȝib) A thing desired. Much wealth, a large present. Big-bellied.

A رغيد raghīd, Free, easy, comfortable (life).

SY رغيدا raghīdā, Tares, darnel.

A رغيداء rughaydās. See رعيداء ruȝaydās.

A رغيدة raghīdat, Hasty pudding.

A رغيغة raghīghat, An easy life. A sip of caudle.

A رغيف raghīf, (pl. ارغفة arghifat, رغف rughuf, رغفان rughfān, and تراغيف tarāghīf) A thin round flat cake, paste, or wafer. A cracknel.

A رغيفي raghīfīy, Belonging to a cake.

P رغين raghīn, Over-alls, spatterdashes. Fair.

P رف raf, A seat, bench, or settle at a house-door. A moulding, tablet, or basement about four inches in height from the floor, serving as an ornament to a room, or as a shelf.

A رف raff, (v. n. of رف) Eating much. Kissing (a woman) with the tips of the lips. Sucking, sipping. Sucking milk (as a colt). Defending, preserving. Favouring, serving, doing good to. Honouring. Shining, glittering (colour). Flashing but not spreading (lightning). Winking or twinkling with the eye. Expanding her wings when about to alight (a bird). Rejoicing, being glad. Sewing any thing to a garment, in order to lengthen it. Surrounding. Drinking milk daily. Being attacked by fever every day. (pl. رفوف rufūf) A broad shelf whereon is laid the most valuable articles of a house: such as bowls of china or silver. Large camels. A flock (of sheep), herd (of oxen). A sheep-cote, hovel, or any place for cattle. A high heap of sand. Saliva. A soft garment of cloth. A mode of eating by sheep or camels. Glancing of lightning. A daily allowance of milk. A daily attack of fever. Corn brought from a distance. Riff, Large camels. A daily draught. اخذته الحمي رفا akhazathu'l humma' raffan, The ague seizes him daily. Ruff, Straw, chaff, bits of straw.

A رفء rafs, (v. n. of رفا) Mending a garment, darning, drawing together. Cementing broken frendship. Quieting, pacifying. Hawling up to the shore (a ship).

A رفاء rifās, (v. n. of رفأ) Giving rest. Conciliating, making peace between two parties. Agreeing, being suitable. Adhering, sticking together. (v. n. 3 of رفأ) Behaving mildly, shewing respect, acting kindly. (v. n. 3 of رفا for رفو) Agreeing. Healing (as a wound). Being united, soldered. Concord, peace, tranquillity. بالرفاء والبنين bi'r rifās wa'l banīn, With concord and children (a form of congratulating newly-married people).

A رفاء raffās, A mender, darner, fine-drawer.

A رفات rufāt, Any thing broken or pounded. A fragment, a broken bit. A carious bone.

A رفادة rifādat, A bandage for dressing a wound. A stuffed saddle-cloth, or cushion. A symbol, passed among the Pagan Arabians of the Kuraysh tribe for the purchase of corn and grapes, of which they made wine for those who celebrated the solemnities of the Kaaba or temple at Mecca.

A رفارف rafārif, (pl. of رفرف) Arches of a house.

A رفاس rifās, (v. n. of رفس) Striking with the feet. Tying (a camel) by the foot. A rope for tying a camel's feet.

A رفاش raffāsh, One who turns corn with a shovel from the floor to the man who measures it.

A رفاض rifāz, Different and contrary ways. Rufāz, A fragment or piece torn off any thing. رفاض الحطب rufāzu'l hatab, Small bits of wood.

A رفاضة raffāzat, One who pastures scattered camels. People whose herds feed on widely-scattered forage.

A رفاع rafāȝ, Abundance of corn in a field. Rafāȝ or rifāȝ, The carrying of the cut-down corn into the thrashing-floor. ايام الرفاع ayyāmu'r rafāȝ, The season when this is done, or when it is trodden out. Rifāȝ, (v. n. 3 of رفع) Citing before a judge, accusing. Sparing, leaving alive.

A رفاع raffāȝ, One who raises or carries high.

A رفاعة rafāȝat, (v. n. of رفع) Raising the voice. Rafāȝat, rifāȝat, and rufāȝat, An elevation, clearness or loudness of voice. Rifāȝat, A name of 23 companions of Muhammad. Rifāȝat or rufāȝat, The quilting of the petticoats to give a prominence to the hips. A rope fastened to a fetter or chain round the ancle, and held by the person chained, to raise it, and prevent its hurting the leg.

A رفاغ rifāgh, (pl. of رفغ) Level, soft lands.

A رفاغة *rafāghat*, (v. n. of رفغ) Abounding in comforts (life).

A رفاغية *rafāghiyat*, An elegant style of living, ease, pleasure.

A رفاق *rifāk*, (v. n. 3 of رفق) Accompanying (on a journey). Aiding. A rope for tying a camel's leg above the knee. (pl. of رفقة *rafkat*, *rifkat*, or *rufkat*) Companies.

A رفاقة *rafākat*, (v. n. of رفق) Being companions, fellow-travellers. Benignity. Society, companionship, friendship. *Rufākat*, A company of fellow-travellers.

P رفاگر *rafāgar*, A fine-drawer. (The raffagars of India will repair a rent in a piece of the finest muslin, so that the joining cannot easily be discovered).

A رفال *rafāl*, Long and flowing (head of hair). *Rifāl*, Any thing tied over the sheath of a he-goat to prevent him from gendering.

P رفان *rafān*, Saffron. An intercessor.

A رفان *rifān*, Small, misling rain.

A رفانينة *rufānīnat*, Delightfulness of life.

A رفاهة *rafāhat*, (v. n. of رفه) Being easy and comfortable (life). *Rafāhat*, (or رفاهية *rafāhiyat*) Repose, quiet, tranquillity, content. Affluence, enjoyment of life.

A رفة *rifat*, Verdant (plant). *Rufat*, A fig. Dry straw.

A رفّة *raffat*, A drinking of milk once. *Ruffat*, Straw, chaff. A solid meal.

P رفت *raft*, He went. A going, travelling. رفت سلطان *rafti sultān*, The journey of the emperor. *Ruft*, He swept. رفت و روب *ruft u rob*, A broom. A sweeping.

A رفت *raft*, (v. n. of رفت) Breaking, pounding. Being bruised, broken. Being cut off. *Rufat*, A breaker, bruiser. Straw, litter.

P رفتار *raftār*, Gait, pace, (elegant) air in walking. Walking, going, moving off. (for گرفتار *giriftār*) A prisoner. خوش رفتار *khwush-raftār*, A graceful walker. رفتار نا هموار *raftāri nā hamwār*, An inelegant walker, or way of walking. A shameful manner of proceeding.

P رفت گذشت *raft-guzasht*, Past.

P رفتگی *raftagī*, Departure: loss. رفتگيء خون *raftagīi khūn*, Loss of blood. رفتگيء شنوائي *raftagīi shinawāī*, Loss of hearing.

P رفتن *raftan*, To walk, go, proceed, depart, pass along, travel. To elapse, glide by. To die. To arise. رفتن شکم *raftani shikam*, Diarrhœa. *Ruftan*, To sweep. To clean the teeth with a toothpick.

P رفتن روب *ruftan-rob*, A broom, besom.

P رفتنگاه آب *raftan-gāhi āb*, An aqueduct.

P رفته *rafta*, Gone, passed. Defunct. رفته رفته *rafta-rafta*, Step by step, by degrees, gradually, in process of time. *Rufta*, Swept. Sweepings. رفته روب *rufta-rob*, A besom.

A رفث *rafs*, (v. n. of رفث) Being obscene. *Rafas*, (v. n. of رفث) Being obscene. Obscenity, ribaldry (by a woman during coition). Coition.

A رفد *rafada*, (fut. يرفد *yarfidu*) He gave.

A رفد *rafd*, (v. n. of رفد) Making or tying on a رفادة *rifādat*, q. v.). Giving, presenting. Assisting. A large goblet. A stuffed saddle-cloth or pad. *Rifd*, A present, a gift. Aid. *Rifd* or *rafd*, A large cup. هريق رفده *hurīka rifduhu*, His cup was spilled, *i. e.* he died.

A رفراف *rafrāf*, An ostrich. The bird called خاطف ظلّه *khātif zillihi*.

A رفرف *rafraf*, A broad shelf whereon are laid the costliest articles in a house. A bed of verdure, green plot. A tent made of goat's hair. Any gracefully-pendant tree. Green cloth, of which they make counterpanes and other bed furniture; a bed, a bed-tick. A pillow, cushion, floor-cloth. The lower flaps of a tent. Any superfluous part of a counterpane hanging down and doubled up. The sides of a coat of mail, with the skirts depending from them. Any thing fixed to the helmet, and falling down over the back. Hanging branches of the lote-tree. Fine brocade. A window. An arch. A caruncle. A certain sea-fish. A kind of tree growing in Yaman.

A رفرفة *rafrafat*, (v. n. of رفرف Q) Spreading out and fluttering its wings (a bird) when desirous of pouncing on his prey, or of alighting.

A رفز *rafz*, (v. n. of رفز) Striking. Beating, throbbing (as an artery).

A رفس *rafs*, (v. n. of رفس) Striking or shaking (any thing) with the feet. Tying up a (camel's) foot.

A رفسة *rafsat*, A kick on the breast.

P رفش *rafsh*, (for درفش *dirafsh*) An awl.

A رفش *rafsh*, (v. n. of رفش) Living luxuriously, eating and drinking riotously. Instigating, stimulating. Pounding, thumping, bruising, braying. الرفش و القفش *ar' rafsh wa'l kafsh*, Good eating and venery. *Rafsh* or *rufsh*, A shovel. من الرفش الي العرش *mini'r rafsh ila'l ɛarsh*, From the spade to the throne (said of one suddenly or greatly promoted). *Rafash*, (v. n. of رفش) Having a large ear. Being large (the ear).

A رفصة *rufsat*, A suitable opportunity, time, turn (an inversion of فرصة *fursat*).

A رفض *rafz* or *rafaz*, (v. n. of رفض) Leaving, abandoning, abdicating. Leaving (camels) to graze at liberty. Displaying its clusters (a palm-tree) the spathe having fallen off. Throwing, shooting. Being wide (a valley). A small quantity of water. (pl. ارفاض *arfāz*) (Camels) feeding at liberty with their keeper. *Rafaz*, A little water remaining in a leathern bottle. Many ostriches divided into bodies. (Camels) feeding at liberty.

A رفضة *rufazat*, One who takes hold, and immediately lets go. One who allows a herd of camels, brought together, soon to separate.

A رفع *rafaɛa*, (fut. يرفع *yarfaɛu*) He raised.

A رفع *rafɛ*, (v. n. of رفع) Lifting, raising, elevating. Taking off, removing. Taking away (the meal being ended). Ascending to higher ground. Putting the vowel point ـُ *u* over a letter. Deposing, laying aside. Leaving off, giving over. Finishing, completing. Carrying a matter before the prefect. Settling, deciding, clearing up. Redressing. Praising. Rescuing from evil. Carrying in the harvest to the barn or thrashing-floor. Going expeditiously (a camel). Making (a camel) travel fast. Zamma, the short vowel ـُ *u* at the end of a word (in nouns answering to the nominative case). رفع دفع *rafɛ dafɛ*, Deciding, settling, finishing. رفع شرّ *rafɛi sharr*, Settling a quarrel, deciding a difference, getting rid of a dispute. P رفع لوا کردن *rafɛi liwā kardan*, To erect the standard. رفع نقاب کردن *rafɛi nikāb kardan*, To uncover, to withdraw the veil. دفع و رفع کردن *dafɛ u rafɛ kardan*, To take away, remove.

A رفعان *rufɛān*, (v. n. of رفع) Carrying (any thing) before a judge in a judicial capacity.

A رفعة *rifɛat*, (v. n. of رفع) Being elevated, raised, exalted, noble, or high-priced. Elevation, exaltation, promotion. Altitude. Highness, eminence, magnificence, sublimity.

A رفعيّة *rafɛiyat*, Presentation.

A رفغ *rafgh*, Affluence. Plenty. Fruitfulness. Soft earth or food. Unfruitful, barren (place). (pl. ارفاغ *arfāgh*) Common people, rabble. (pl. ارفغ *arfugh*) The lowest and worst part of a valley. A tract, district, or border of a country. (pl. رفاغ *rifāgh*) Soft level ground. A district of many soils, or one abounding in soil. Soft, thin lime or mortar. A narrow-mouthed bottle. A middling sort of bottle (neither good nor bad). *Rafgh* or *rufgh*, (pl. ارفاغ *arfāgh* and رفوغ *rufūgh*) Dirt of the nails, groins, or arm-pits. The inner part of the arm-pit or groin; the groin, or any part where dirt collects. *Rufgh*, Affluence, plenty.

A رفغاء *rafghāɛ*, Slender-thighed (woman); also one impervious, or deep-groined.

A رفغنية *rufaghniyat*, Affluence, plenty.

A رفف *rafaf*, Thinness, fineness.

A رفق *rafk*, (v. n. of رفق) Tying together (a camel's) fore-legs immediately beneath the shoulder to prevent him from running away. Being useful, profitable. Striking the elbow. *Rifk*, (v. n. of رفق) Being benevolent, kind, or easy. Assisting. Benignity, benevolence. Courtesy, favour. Profit, advantage. Assistance, aid. بالرفق *bi'r rifk*, Easily, without inconvenience, gently. *Rafak*, (v. n. of رفق) Having the elbow distorted (a camel). (Desire) easily satisfied. (Water) easily drawn, (pasture) very accessible. A jutting out of the elbow. A disease in the udder or orifice of the teat from unskilful milking. *Rafak* and *rifak*, (pl. of رفقة *rufkat*) Societies, fellowships. *Rufah,* (pl. of رفقة *rafkat, rifkat,* and *rufkat*) Companies of fellow-travellers. Societies.

A رفقاء *rafkās,* (fem. of ارفق *arfak*) (A she-camel) with a distorted elbow; also one the orifice of whose teat is obstructed. *Rufahās,* (pl. of رفيق *rafik*) Companions in travel, fellow-travellers.

A رفقة *rafkat, rifkat,* or *rufkat,* (pl. رفاق *rifāk,* رفق *rufak,* and ارفاق *arfāk*) A company of fellow-travellers. (pl. رفق *rifak, rufak, rafak*) Society, fellowship. *Rufkat,* (pl. of رفيق *rafik*) Companions. *Rafakat,* A twist of the elbow. *Rafikat,* A camel, the orifice of whose teat is closed.

A رفل *rafl,* (v. n. of رفل) Being ignorant, unskilful, unlearned, negligent (in dress). Filling (a well) with water. *Rafl* or *rafal,* (v. n. of رفل) Being awkward and clumsy in putting on dress, or in doing any thing. *Rafl* (or رفلان *rafalān*), (v. n. of رفل) Dragging the garments along the ground, swinging the arms and walking fastidiously but ungracefully. *Rifl,* The train or skirt of a garment. *Rafal,* The deepest part of a well. *Rafal rafal,* Used in calling sheep to be milked. *Rafil,* One who sweeps the ground with his clothes pompously but ungracefully. The train or skirt of a garment. A fool. Untidy, awkward, clumsy.

A رفل *rifall,* Long, trailing, loose (garments). Long-tailed (horse). Loose-skinned (camel). Fleshy, corpulent.

A رفلاء *raflās,* Slatternly, awkward (woman).

A رفلة *rafilat,* An agreeable life. A woman whose train sweeps gracefully. A foolish woman. *Rafilat* or *rifilat,* Ugly (woman).

A رفن *rafn,* An egg.

A رفن *rifann,* (for رفل) Long-tailed (horse).

A رفنه *rafana,* (for عارفانه *ʿārifāna*) A symbol.

A رفو *rafw,* (v. n. of رفو for رفا) Mending (a garment). Calming, allaying, pacifying, appeasing.

P رفو *rafo,* Sewing close, counterpoint, darning, fine-drawing.

A رفواء *rafwās,* (fem. of ارفى *arfa'*) Large-eared.

A رفوث *rufūs,* Ribaldry (in a woman). Coition. Any thing obscene said or done before a woman.

A رفوج *rafūj,* The root of a palm-branch.

A رفوخ *rufūkh,* Calamities, misfortunes.

A رفود *rafūd,* (A camel) filling the dish *rafd* at one milking.

A رفوش *rufūsh,* The being wide, ample, extended.

P رفوشه *rafūsha,* Sin, transgression. Pleasantry, jocularity, humour. Discovery, tracing, tracking. Palmistry.

A رفوض *rufūz,* (v. n. of رفض) Pasturing alone (a scattered herd of camels). Bodies, sects. A tract of land abandoned, and claimed by nobody. Widely-scattered forage.

A رفوغ *rufūgh,* (pl. of رفغ *rafgh*) Groins, armpits, or those parts where dirt collects.

A رفوف *rufūf,* (pl. of رفّ *raff*) Broad shelves whereon are laid the choicest articles in a house.

P رفوگر *rafogar,* A fine-drawer, darner. A sewer of counterpoint. A tailor. A patch for mending.

P رفون *rafūn,* Saffron. Cyprus.

A رفه *rafh, rifh,* (or رفوه *rufūh*) (v. n. of رفه) Living quietly and comfortably. Drinking daily their fill (camels). *Rafh* or *rufūh,* (v. n. of رفه) Being filled with provender and water. *Rifh,* Small palm-trees. Ease, comfort. *Rufah,* Straw.

P رفه *rafa,* The Pleiades.

A رفهان *rafahān,* One who lives comfortably.

A رفهة *rafahat,* Pity, compassion, mercy.

A رفهنية *rufahniyat,* The conveniences of life.

P رفيده *rafīda,* Old clouts sewed together, whereon bread is laid to be baked in the oven.

A رفيص *rafīs,* A pot-companion, partaker, an associate. One whose cattle drink at the same time as those of a neighbour.

A رفيض *rafīz,* Rejected, thrown away. Sweat. Broken (spear). Camels allowed to pasture freely.

A رفيع *rafīʿ,* High, sublime. Noble, eminent, exalted. Loud-voiced. بنيان رفيع الاركان *bunyāni rafīʿu'l arkān,* A building with lofty pillars. مكان رفيع *makāni rafīʿ,* A high place. رفيع الدرجات *rafīʿu'd darajāt,* Of eminent degree. رفيع الشان *rafīʿu'sh shān,* Of exalted dignity. رفيع القدر *rafīʿu'l kadr,* (or رفيع المقدار *rafīʿu'l mikdār*) Of high estimation. Eminent in power.

A رفيعة *rafīʿat,* High. Noble (woman). What is told of another. Any matter carried before a prefect. جبال رفيعه وتلال منيعه *jibāli rafīʿa u tilāli manīʿa,* High mountains and inaccessible rocks.

A رفيغ *rafīgh,* Easy, comfortable (life).

A رفيف *rafīf,* (v. n. of رفّ) Shining (colour). Swelling with sap (herbage). (A tree) glittering with dew. The ceiling of a house. Plenty of provender. Thin, fine (garment). A lily. A window or opening for receiving light. ذات الرفيف *zātu'r rafīf,* Ships moored side by side across a river or creek so as to afford a passage for kings, princes, or governors of provinces: a bridge of boats.

A رفيق *rafīk,* (pl. رفقاء *rufakās* and رفقة *rufkat*) A friend, companion, colleague, accomplice, associate, assistant, partner, ally. A fellow-traveller. Skilful, active, industrious. Kind, friendly. رفيق جهاد *rafīki jihād,* A fellow-soldier. P رفيق و همراه شدن *rafīk u ham-rāh shudan,* To keep company, to associate with.

A P رفيقي *rafīkī,* Society, companionship.

A رفيه *rafīh,* One who lives agreeably.

P رق *rik,* Tortoise-shell.

A رق *rakk,* Thin. Parchment, vellum. A sheet of paper, book, volume (that especially in which the recording angels are supposed to register the actions of men). (pl. رقوق *rukūk*) A large tortoise or turtle. P رق سپهر *rakki sipihr,* The expanse of heaven. A *Rikk,* Servitude. Possession, dominion, property, right. Soft level ground. Leaves and tender branches of trees easily cropt by cattle. A certain thorny plant. Parchment, vellum. A sheet of white paper. Thin. Compassionate, affectionate. *Rukk* or *rakk,* Shallow water extending over a great surface. Soft level ground.

A رقا *raks,* (v. n. of رقا) Drying up, becoming dry (tears). Being promoted (perspiration). Exciting discord. Establishing peace. Ascending (a staircase or ladder).

A رقاء *rakās,* Corruption, depravity, mischief.

A رقاء *rakkās,* One who uses enchantments and sorceries (رقية *rukyat*), an enchanter, wizard.

A رقاب *rikāb,* (v. n. 3 of رقب) Guarding. (pl. of رقبة *rakabat*) Necks. Purchased (slaves).

A رقابة *rakābat,* (v. n. of رقب) Waiting, expecting. Putting a chain round the neck.

A رقابة *rakkābat,* One who has the care of the baggage of travellers during their absence. A mean, low, worthless fellow.

A رقاحة *rakāhat,* Gain, profit. Trade.

A رقاحيّ *rakāhīy,* A merchant, factor: steward.

A رقاد *rukād,* Sleep (especially a long slumber in the night).

P رقارق *rakārāk,* Noise of quadrupeds' legs.

A رقارق *rukārik,* Shallow water widely extended. Thin vapour. A bright sword.

A رقاش *rakāsh,* A serpent. *Rakāshi,* A proper name for women.

A رقاص *rakkās,* A dancer, jumper, tumbler. A letter-carrier.

A رقّاصة *rakkāsat,* Ground producing nothing (though watered by rain). A kind of game.

A رقاصي *rakkāsī,* Dancing.

A رقاع *rikāʿ,* (pl. of رقعة *rukʿat*) Bits of cloth, patches. Short letters, notes.

A رقاعة *rakāʿat,* Foolishness. *Rikāʿat,* (v. n. of رقع) Doting, being imbecile. Alacrity to fight.

A رقاعيّ *rikāʿīy,* A kind of handwriting.

A رقاق *rakāk,* Warm, hot (day). Soft level ground, beneath which lies a harder stratum. A desert. *Rakāk* or *rukāk,* Land from which the water has retired. *Rikāk,* (pl. of رقيق *rakīk*) Slaves. (pl. of رقاقة *rukākat*) Thin cakes. (pl. of رقّة *rakkat*) Tracts of land liable to be flooded. *Rukāk,* (v. n. of رق) Going gently and feebly; also going fast. A kind of round cake, a pancake, fritter, cheese-cake. Slow, leisurely (camel's pace). Thin.

A رقاق *rukkāk,* Thin.

A رقاقة *rakākat,* Thinness. *Rukākat,* (pl. رقاق *rikāk*) A thin cake.

A رقال *rikāl,* (pl. of رقلة) Tall palm-trees.

A رقان *rikān,* Saffron. Privet.

P رقانه *rikāna,* A page of a sheet of paper.

A رقائق *rakāʾik,* (pl. of رقيقة) Subtilties.

A رقائم *rakāʾim,* (pl. of رقيم *rakīm*) Books.

A رقب *rakab*, Thickness of neck. (pl. of رقبة *rakabat*) Necks, or lower parts of them. Purchased slaves. *Rukub*, (pl. of رقيب *rakīb*) Serpents of a malignant species.

A رقباء *rukabāʼ*, (pl. of رقيب *rakīb*) Watchers.

A رقبات *rakabāt*, (pl. of رقبة *rakabat*) Necks. Purchased slaves. رقبات واملاك *rakabāt u amlāk*, Slaves and possessions.

A رقبان *rikbān*, (v. n. of رقب) Watching, expecting. Throwing a chain on any one's neck. *Rakabān*, (or رقباني *rakabāniy*) Thick-necked.

A رقبة *rakbat*, (v. n. of رقب) Expecting, watching. *Rikbat*, (v. n. of رقب) Expecting, watching, guarding, preserving. Putting a chain on the neck. Heed, vigilance. Space, interval, division. Remote kindred. Fear. Bereavement, the want or loss of offspring. ورث مالاً عن رقبة *warisa mālan ɛan rikbatin*, He inherited property from his relations (not from his father). *Rukbat*, A pit for catching leopards. *Rakabat*, (pl. رقاب *rikāb*, رقب *rakab*, ارقب *arkub*, and رقبات *rakabāt*) The neck, or the lower part of it. The essence of any thing. A slave purchased with money.

A رقبه *rakba*, Enclosure, esplanade, environs.

A رقبى *rukbaʼ*, (v. n. of رقب) Giving any thing to another, to remain his property if he survives the donor, if not, to return; also the thing so given (of the nature of a tontine). A house or land which becomes alternately the property of the survivor.

A رقة *rikat*, The first sprouting of the plants نصيّ *nasiy* and صلّيان *silliyān*. Green with summer-rain (ground). (pl. رقون *rikūn*) Stamped coins, moneys.

A رقّة *rakkat*, (v. n. of رقّ) Being thin. (pl. رقاق *rikāk*) A tract of land, by the side of a river, which is fertilized by inundations. Name of a city on the Euphrates. *Rikkat*, (v. n. of رقّ) Being thin. Being affectionate, compassionate. Being ashamed. Thinness, subtleness. Pity, condolence, benevolence. Sympathy, compassion, tenderness, weeping. Modesty. صاحب رقّت قلب *sāhibi rikkati kalb*, Tender-hearted.

A رقد *rakada*, (fut. يرقد *yarkudu*) He slept.

A رقد *rakd*, (v. n. of رقد) Sleeping. Lying with. Sleep. Mountain whence they hew mill-stones.

A رقّد *rukkad*, Sleepers.

A رقدان *rakadān*, Exultation, a leaping or frisking for joy.

A رقدة *rakdat*, One slumber. رقدة من حرّ *rakdat min harr*, Heat of ten days' duration. *Rukadat*, Addicted to sleep.

A رقراق *rakrāk*, The undulating shining surface of the vapour of the desert. A bright sword. Name of a sword.

A رقراقة *rakrākat*, A woman whose face appears as if water were running over it.

A رقرقان *rukrukān*, Moving, trembling (vapour over a plain).

A رقرقة *rakrakat*, (v. n. of رقرق Q) Pouring out (water or broth), thinly spreading (it) over a large surface. Shaking (a gugglet of water). Watering, becoming watery (the eye).

A رقز *rakz*, (v. n. of رقز) Beating, throbbing (an artery). Dancing.

A رقش *raksh*, (v. n. of رقش) Painting figures of two or more colours. *Ruksh*, (pl. of ارقش *arkash* and رقشاء *rakshāʼ*) Speckled, spotted.

A رقشاء *rakshāʼ*, (A female serpent) marked with black and white spots. A canker-worm. A substance resembling lights protruding from a camel's mouth at rutting time.

A رقص *raks*, (v. n. of رقص) Shining, glittering (as vapour). Fermenting (as wine). Ambling (a camel). Dancing. Leaping. A caper. A dance, a ball. رقصت الخمرفي رؤسهم *rakasati'l khamr fī rususihim*, The wine danced in their heads, *i. e.* made them drunk. P رقص پهلو *raksi pahlū*, A rolling from side to side. Rest, repose. رقص روباه *raksi rūbāh*, A sham negligence. رقص كردن *raks kardan*, To dance, to caper. رقص ملا *raksi mallā*, Lascivious motions. A *Rakas*, (or رقصان *rakasān*) The ambling (of a camel), capering (of a man).

P رقص كنان *raks-kunān*, Dancing, capering.

P رقصيدن *raksīdan*, To dance.

A رقطاء *raktāʼ*, (fem. of ارقط *arkat*) A she-leopard spotted black and white. Speckled (hen). Dangerous (sedition). Oily, buttery (pudding). An epistle, or literary composition, artificially arranged, wherein the letters occur with and without diacritical points alternately.

A رقطة *ruktat*, Variegation by white and black spots. A branch of the plant عرفج *ɛarfaj* getting into leaf.

A رقع *rakɛ*, (v. n. of رقع) Patching a garment (mending by sewing being called رفأ *rafʼ*). Repairing (a well which threatens dilapidation). Piercing an enemy with a spear (especially at a distance). Hitting the mark (with an arrow). Catching in one of the hands, when eating, what falls from the mouth. Upbraiding, gibing, satirizing. Making haste. The seventh heaven. A husband. *Rukaɛ*, (pl. of رقعة *rukaɛat*) Certain large trees.

P رقعا *rakɛā*, A medicinal wood found near the Caspian Sea.

A رقعاء *rakɛāʼ*, (fem. of ارقع *arkaɛ*) Marked with white on the side (a sheep). Insane, foolish (woman). Destitute of hips (woman).

A رقعة *rakɛat*, The sound of an arrow piercing the mark. *Rukɛat*, A letter, or the postscript. (pl. رقاع *rikāɛ*) A short letter or note. A letter written to a king by any one not a vazīr (letters from them being named تلخيص *talkhīs*). A bit of cloth for mending a garment, a patch. A sheet of paper upon which any thing is written. A target of pasteboard. All medicinal applications made to fractured limbs. A chess-board. Territory. Beginning of a battle. P رقعهٔ بلند نيلگون *rukɛaʼi baland-nīlgūn* or رقعهٔ غبرا *rukɛaʼi ghabrā*, The sky. رقعهٔ پشت نيلگون *rukɛaʼi pusht-nīlgūn*, (or ادكن *adkan*) The earth. رقعه دوختن *rukɛa dokhtan*, To patch. رقعهٔ شطرنج *rukɛaʼi shatranj*, A chess-board. رقعهٔ كژدم *rukɛaʼi kajdum*, See سپندارمذ *sipandārmuz*. رقعهٔ مهماني *rukɛaʼi mihmānī*, A note of invitation to a feast.

A *Rukaɛat*, (pl. رقع *rukaɛ*) A large tree resembling the plane in the trunk, with fruit like the fig, and the leaf of a gourd.

P رقعه *rakɛa*, Any herb useful for setting a fractured limb. Name of a certain medicinal wood.

P رقعه وار *rukɛawār*, Letter-paper. Painted.

A رقق *rakak*, Soft, plain ground (without sand) under which there is a harder stratum; soft soil overflowed. Slenderness (of a bone). Scarcity (of money). Debility.

A رقل *rakl*, (pl. of رقلة) Tall palm-trees.

A رقلة *raklat*, (pl. رقل *rakl* and رقال *rikāl*) A tall palm-tree.

A رقم *rakm*, (v. n. of رقم) Marking with orthographical points. Writing. Sealing. Rendering distinct. Weaving a garment in stripes. Marking (a piece of cloth or a garment) with the price. The price-mark. Notation. A kind of striped or embroidered garment. A misfortune. A writing. Much. *Rakam*, Name of a day amongst the Arabs. Name of a place in Madīna where arrows are made. *Rakam* or *rakim*, Much. A misfortune. بنت الرقم *bintu'r rakim*, Adversity, misfortune.

P رقم *rakam*, Notation. Description. Arithmetic. A writing. A sign. Manner, mode, kind, method. Class, sort. A royal edict. Written, marked. اهل رقم *ahli rakam*, Skilled in arithmetic. علم رقم *ɛilmi rakam*, The science of arithmetic. قلم سعادت رقم *kalami saɛādat-rakam*, Writing well, a felicitous pen. رقم اوّل *rakami awwal*, The throne of God. رقم كردن *rakam kardan*, To write, fold up, seal and despatch a letter. To assort.

A رقماء *rakmāʼ*, A place where one cannot stand.

P رقم پذير *rakam-pazīr*, Committed to writing.

A رقمة *rakmat*, A pleasant flowery garden or meadow. Mallows. The side of a river. Any part in a valley where water is collected. *Rakamat*, Name of a plant.

A رقمتان *rakmatāni*, The interior horny parts of the legs of horses, or asses, which have no hair. Two substances resembling claws on the fore-feet of sheep. Two marks on the edge of the thigh of an ass. The two sides of the buttocks of a quadruped.

P رقمزده *rakam-zada*, Written, put on paper.

P رقمكش *rakam-kash*, Impressing characters, drawing lines. Erasing, obliterating.

A رقميّات *rakamīyāt*, Arrows made at Rakam.

A رقن *rakan*, A pelican's egg.

A رقو *rakw*, Heaped up. A round sand-hill.

A رقوء *rakūs*, Any thing applied to staunch a bleeding. An atonement or expiatory offering for the shedding of blood. *Rukūs*, (v. n. of رقأ) Drying up, becoming dry (tears). Being promoted (perspiration).

A رقوب *rakūb*, (v. n. of رقب) Waiting, expecting. A woman having no children, or losing those she had. A wife looking for the death of her husband on account of the inheritance. A camel which cannot get near the well for the crowd. امّ الرقوب *ummu'r rakūb*, Misfortune. *Rukūb*, (v. n. of رقب) Waiting, expecting. Putting a halter round the neck.

A رقوة *rakwat*, A heap of sand.

A رقود *rukūd*, Sleep. Sleepers.

A رقوف *rukūf*, (v. n. of رقف) Trembling, shaking, shivering.

A رقوق *rukūk*, (pl. of رقّ) Large tortoises.

A رقوم *rukūm*, (pl. of رقم *rakm*) Characters.

A P رقون *rakūn* or *rukūn*, Saffron. Privet.

P رقّه *rakka*, Name of a city on the bank of the Euphrates (now in ruins).

A رقي *raky*, (v. n. of رقي) Mounting (a ladder). Enchanting, fascinating. Securing against fascination by talismanic charms. *Ruka'*, (pl. of رقية *rukyat*) Enchantments. Amulets against witchcraft.

A رقّيٰ *rukka'*, Thin or liquid fat, or lard.

A رقيّ *rukīy*, (v. n. of رقي) Enchanting, fascinating. Securing against fascination by talismanic charms. Ascending.

A رقيب *rakīb*, A guardian, preserver. A watcher, keeper. الرقيب *ar'rakīb*, God (the preserver). One who watches the motions of another (as a rival or spy). A rival, competitor. A father's brother's son. One star opposite to another star, and setting when it rises (from observations upon which they prognosticate rain or fair weather). The third arrow at a kind of game of chance. (pl. رقيبات *rakībāt* and رقب *rukub*) A serpent of a malignant species. The survivor of brothers, relations, or partners.

A رقيبات *rakībāt*, (pl. of رقيب *rakīb*) Serpents of a malignant species.

P رقيبان *rakībān*, (Pers. pl. of Arab. رقيب *rakīb*) Keepers. رقيبان هفت بام *rakībāni haft bām*, The seven planets.

A رقية *rukyat*, (v. n. of رقي) Enchanting, bewitching. Arming with a talismanic amulet, or written charm, against sorcery. Superstition. (pl. رقيٰ *ruka'*) Magical incantation, sorcery. An amulet.

A رقيّة *rukayyat*, A daughter of Muhammad.

A رقيّة *rikkīyat*, Servitude.

A رقيش *rukaysh*, (dim. of ارقش *arkash*) Slightly speckled with black and white spots.

A رقيع *rakīʿ*, Foolish, defective in understanding. (pl. ارقعة *arkiʿat*) The lower heavens, the expanse of sky, firmament.

A رقيق *rakīk*, Thin (paper). Fine. Soft. Subtle, minute. Tender, delicate. Slender. Benign. Gentle, compassionate. Vile. (pl. رقاق *rikāk*) A servant, slave. رقيق البدن *rakīku'l badan*, Slender-bodied. رقيق الحاشية *rakīku'l hāshiyat*, One who keeps a small establishment. سلطان رقيق القلب *sultāni rakīku'l kalb*, A prince of a compassionate heart.

A رقيقان *rakīkāni*, (dual) The testicles. The two veins in the neck to which the cupping-glass is applied. The sides of the nostrils. The parts between the hypochondria and the groin.

A رقيقة *rakīkat*, A bond-woman.

A رقيم *rakīm*, (pl. رقائم *rakāsim*) A book; especially that which records the history of the Seven Sleepers; their dog and village, with the mountain and cave in which they slept. An inkstand. A tablet. Wise, sensible.

A رقيمة *rakīmat*, A chaste, prudent woman.

P رقيمه *rakīma*, A letter, epistle, note. رقيمهٔ اوّل *rakīmasi avval*, The throne of God. The letter ا *alif*.

A رقين *rakīn*, Money, coin; a dirhem.

P رك *rak*, A grumbling through discontent, or anger. A row, a line. (in zand and Pāzand) Thou.

A رك *rakk*, (v. n. of رك) Being weak, or extenuated. Chaining by the neck. Accusing. Placing (one thing upon another), laying a sin upon any one. Passing the hand over the tail of a sheep, to ascertain if it be fat or not. Pressing, squeezing, feeling. Lying with. *Rakk* or *rikk*, (pl. اركاك *arkāk* and ركاك *rikāk*) Small rain. ارض رك *arzun rikkun*, Ground wet with small rain.

A ركاء *rakās*, An echo. *Rakās*, (or ركّاء *rakkās*) The screech or hooting of an owl. *Rikās*, (pl. of ركوة *rak*, *rik*, or *rukwat*) Small barks or skiffs. Cloths put under wine presses. Rimæ mulierum.

P ركاب *rikāb*, A cup, a goblet, tall and eight-sided. A procession, cavalcade. A riding-horse, nag.

A ركاب *rikāb*, (pl. ركب *rukub*) A stirrup. A ship. (pl. ركابات *rikābāt*, ركب *rukub*, and ركائب *rakāsib*) A camel for the saddle or for burdens (though راحلة *rāhilat* is generally, in this sense, used for the singular). ركاب السحاب *rikābu's sahāb*, Winds. P ركاب گردان شدن *rikāb-gardān shudan*, To get on horseback. To assault. ركاب همايونه *rikābi humāyūna*, To the imperial stirrup, *i.e.* referred or presented to the king (expressed also by ركاب گردون جناب *rikābi gardūn-janāb*).

A ركّاب *rakkāb*, A rider on a camel. An attempter. *Rukkāb*, (pl. of راكب) Riders on camels. Sailors.

A ركابات *rikābāt* (pl. of ركاب *rikāb*) Camels for the saddle or for burdens.

A ركّابة *rakkābat*, A palm-branch hanging pendulous, but not touching the ground.

P ركاب خانه *rikāb-khāna*, A pantry; buttery.

P ركابدار *rikāb-dār*, A cup-bearer. A pantry-man, a butler. A stirrup-holder: an attendant, courier, groom. One who has charge of the saddle-room.

P ركاب دوال *rikāb-duvāl*, A stirrup-leather.

P ركابي *rikābi*, A small dish, plate, or saucer. A cup, a goblet. A cup-bearer. A led horse for parade. A sword carried on a horse's side. A kind of rupee current in Lucknow.

A ركابيّ *rikābīy*, A kind of Damascus oil carried on camels. One who holds the stirrup, that his master may mount.

P ركابي مذهب *rikābī-mazhab*, Parasitical.

A ركاز *rikāz*, (pl. ركائز *rakāsiz*) Fossils (especially the more valuable). Treasures buried in the earth (particularly from remote ages). A piece or mass of gold or silver (from the mine).

A ركاس *rikās*, The rope which fastens the camel's halter to his leg, to keep his head down.

A ركاسة *rakāsat* or *rikāsat*, A stake or peg driven into the ground for tethering cattle.

P ركاسه *rukāsa*, (or ركاشه) A porcupine.

A ركاض *rikāz*, The act of riding a race with.

A ركاك *rikāk*, (pl. of رك *rakk*, *rikk*, and ركيكة *rakīkat*) Small rains. (pl. of ركيك *rakīk*) Thin. Weak, silly. Weak-voiced. *Rukāk*, (and ركاكة *rukākat*) (A man) worthless and weak in mind. One who neglects wife and friends, and is despised by them in return.

A ركاكة *rakākat*, (v. n. of رك) Being thin, weak. Being weak-minded. Accusing of a crime. Placing (one thing upon another). Copulating. Squeezing. Imbecility of understanding. Meanness. A voluntary cuckold. Accusation. Weak, silly (woman).

A ركّال *rakkāl*, A vender of leeks (ركل *rakl*).

A ركام *ra* or *rukām*, Clouds or sands heaped up. A throng. قطيع ركام *katīʿ rukām*, A large herd.

P ركان *rakān*, Mutterers from anger.

A ركانة *rakānat*, (v. n. of ركن) Being firm, constant, steady, grave.

A ركايا *rakāya'*, (pl. of ركيّة *rakīyat*) Clean wells.

A ركائب *rakāsib*, (pl. of ركاب *rikāb*) Camels for the saddle or for burdens.

A ركائز *rakāsiz*, (pl. of ركاز *rikāz*) Fossils (especially the more valuable). Treasures buried in the earth (particularly from remote ages). Lumps of gold and silver from the mine.

A ركائل بن آدم *rukāsil bini ādam*, Rukayl the son of Adam, according to Eastern opinion, and younger brother to Seth.

A ركب *rakiba*, (fut. يركب *yarkabu*) He rode.

A ركب *rakb*, (v. n. of ركب) Striking on the knee. Seizing one by the hair, and striking his forehead with one's knee. A mouse. (pl. اركب *arkub* and ركوب *rukūb*) About a dozen of people on camels or horses travelling together, a cavalcade. (pl. of راكب *rākib*) Riders on camels. *Rakab*, (v. n. of ركب) Having a large knee. (pl. اركاب *arkāb* and اراكيب *arākīb*) Locus ubi exoritur pubes (proprie in muliere, et ipsa muljebria). *Rukab*, (pl. of ركبة *rukbat*) Knees. Elbows. *Rukub*, (pl. of ركاب *rikāb*) Stirrups. Camels for the saddle or for burdens. (pl. of ركيب *rakīb*) Sown fields. Canals cut through sown fields. Palms or vines planted between two walls or hedges.

A ركباة *rakbāt*, (A she-camel) for the saddle.

A ركبان *rukbān*, (pl. of راكب *rākib*) Riders on camels. ركبان السنبل *rukbānu's sumbul*, Beards of wheat first protruding from the ear. *Rakabāni*, (dual) The roots of the thighs, the groins.

A ركبانة *rakbānat*, (A she-camel) for the saddle. (A she-camel) well broke in.

A ركبة *rakbat*, (A she-camel) well-adapted for the saddle, quiet and gentle. *Rikbat*, A particular mode of riding. *Rukbat*, (pl. ركب *rukab*) The knee. The elbow. Root of the herb صلّيان *silliyān* after it has been cut. *Rakabat*, A body of travellers mounted on camels (less than ركب *rakb*). *Rikabat*, (pl. of راكب *rākib*) Riders on camels.

A ركبوت *rakabūt* or ركبوتیٰ *rakabūta'*, (A she-camel) fit for the saddle, or one quiet and gentle.

A ركح *rakaha*, (fut. يركح *yarkahu*) He leaned.

A ركح *ruk-h*, (pl. ركوح *rukūh* and اركاح *arkāh*) The base, side, angle, or projection of a mountain. (pl. اركاح *arkāh*) A foundation. The middle area of a house. The back premises of a house.

A ركحاء *rak-hāʼ*, Hard, high, rough ground.

A ركحة *ruk-hat*, An area, square, quadrangle, court of a house. Remains (of caudle or bread-pudding) in a dish.

A ركداء *rakdāʼ*, Silent, inaudible (serpent).

P ركده *rakda*, A small leathern bottle. A wash-hand bason. A cup in the form of a ship, with which the poor draw water.

A ركراكة *rakrākat*, Large-hipped (woman).

A ركركة *rakrakat*, Imbecility, weakness.

A ركز *rakz*, (v. n. of ركز) Sticking (a spear) into the ground. (God) fixing in the earth (gold or silver mines). Beating (an artery). *Rikz*, A low sound. An intelligent, liberal man. Sense, feeling.

A ركزة *rakzat* or *rikzat*, A palm-branch torn from the trunk. *Rikzat*, Firmness, steadiness of intellect. A large bit of gold or silver mineral.

A ركس *raks*, (v. n. of ركس) Inverting, placing the last first. Throwing down. Tying the rope ركاس *rikās*. *Riks*, Filth, impurity. Many men.

A ركض *rakz*, (v. n. of ركض) Moving the feet; striking them against the ground, kicking (as a camel). Making (a horse) go faster by spurring or hitting him with the heels. Driving. Fluttering the wings (a bird). Running away.

A ركضة *rakzat*, Motion, impulse, concussion.

A ركع *rukkaʻ*, (pl. of راكع) Hanging the head.

A ركعة *rakʻat*, A sacred inclination of the head, so that the palms of the hands rest upon the knees (in prayer). ركع المصلّي ركعة و ركعتين وثلاث ركعات *rakaʻa'l musallī rakʻatan, wa rakʻatayni, wa salāsa rakaʻāt*. *Rukʻat*, (pl. ركع *rukaʻ*) Low hollow ground.

A ركل *rakl*, (v. n. of ركل) Striking a horse with the heel, to make him gallop. A leek.

A ركلة *ruklat*, A bundle of herbs.

A ركم *rakama*, (fut. يركم *yarkumu*) He heaped.

A ركم *rakm*, (v. n. of ركم) Heaping, piling up, accumulating. *Rakam*, Clouds heaped together.

A ركمة *rukmat*, Clay heaped up in one place.

A ركن *rakn*, A mouse. The jerboa. A mole. *Rukn*, (pl. اركان *arkān*, (pl. of pl. اراكين *arākīn*) A pillar, prop, especially that side on which any thing is supported. The feet of a verse. A member of the body. Aid, support, guard, protection. Grandeur, dignity. A momentous affair. The black stone of the Kaaba at Mecca. ركن الدولة *ruknu'd dawlat*, (or ركن سلطنت *rukni sultanat*) A nobleman (as a pillar of the state).

P ركناباد *ruknābād*, A small stream of the finest water near the city of Shīrāz. It is equally celebrated by the poets of Persia as the waters of Helicon are by those of Greece.

P ركنى *ruknī*, Gold refined. Ruknābād.

A ركو *rakw*, (v. n. of ركا for ركو) Adapting, amending. Fastening, drawing tight, strengthening. Digging. Staying, stopping, abiding, tarrying. Keeping back, putting behind, hindering. Accusing, disparaging, defaming, charging with a crime. Doubling (a camel's load).

P ركو *rukū* or *raku*, A piece of old cloth, rag.

A ركوات *rakawāt*, Small leathern bottles.

A ركوب *rakūb*, Any one mounted. A camel for riding. Any beast or vehicle upon which people ride. (A road) worn down by riding. *Rukūb*, (v. n. of ركب) Mounting, sitting, riding (a horse or chariot). Perpetrating, committing (a crime). Attempting, engaging in. (pl. of راكب *rākib*) Riders on camels. (pl. of ركب *rakb*) Small companies of men riding on camels.

A ركوبة *rakūbat*, A horse or a camel for riding (حمولة *hamūlat* implying a beast of burden). A she-camel fit for riding upon. A gentle she-camel.

A ركوة *rakwat*, (pl. ركاء *rikāʼ* and ركوات *rakawāt*) A water-vessel, a small bottle. *Rakwat*, *rikwat*, or *rukwat*, (pl. ركيّ *rukīy*, ركايا *rakāya'*, or ركوات *rakawāt*) A small bark or skiff. A cloth, or scarce, used in straining grapes or any thing similar. Rima mulieris. صارت القوس ركوة *sārati'l kawsu rakwatan*, The bow shoots backward (applied to any perverse business).

P ركوتا *rakūtā*, (in zand and Pāzand) Wise.

A ركوح *rukūh*, (v. n. of ركح) Leaning, inclining. Resting, reposing. Turning back. (pl. of ركح *ruk-h*) Extremities, promontories of mountains.

A ركود *rakūd*, Full (dish). (A camel) always abounding in milk. *Rukūd*, (v. n. of ركد) Being still, calm (wind or water); at anchor (a ship); quiet or slothful (people); in equipoise (a balance); in his zenith (the sun). ركود الصلوٰة *rukūdu's salāt*, Repose or tranquillity of posture after having made the sacred inclinations of the head in prayer.

A ركوسيّة *rakūsīyat*, Name of a sect between Christians and Sabeans (who worship the stars).

A ركوض *rakūz*, Far-shooting (bow).

A ركوع *rukūʻ*, (v. n. of ركع) Bowing the head in humility and reverence; also from age, or in prayer, so that the palms of the hands touch the knees. From being wealthy becoming poor.

P ركوگ *rakūg*, Patches for mending garments. A tent which has no patches about it. ركوگ حيض *rakūgi hayz*, A menstruous cloth.

P ركوگر *rakūgar*, A patcher, botcher.

P ركوم *rakūm*, (in zand and Pāzand) Ye, you.

A ركون *rukūn*, (v. n. of ركن) Reclining, leaning. Being quiet.

A ركونة *rukūnat*, (v. n. of ركن) Being firm, constant, grave, steady.

A ركّیٰ *rukka'*, Fat easily melted.

A ركيّ *rakīy*, Weak, infirm. (pl. of ركيّة) Wells.

A ركيب *rakīb*, Engrafted. Mounted, set (as a stone in a ring). One person carried along or riding with another. (pl. ركب *rukub*) Planted in a row (palm-trees). A piece of ground in cultivation, having a raised border round it. A cut or gutter through a sown field. Palms, vines, or corn planted between two walls or hedges. A sown field. نخل ركيب *nakhl rakīb*, Palm-trees planted in a row along the side of a rivulet.

P ركيبي *rakībī*, A plate, a dish.

A ركيّة *rakīyat*, (pl. ركيّ *rakīy* and ركايا *rakāya'*) A well, especially a clean one.

P ركيدن *rakīdan*, To mutter in anger.

A ركيك *rakīk*, (pl. ركاك *rikāk*) Thin, slender, minute. Subtile, fine, flimsy. Weak, silly. Vile. Worthless, a despiser of, and despised by, wife and friends. ركيك العلم *rakīku'l ʻilm*, Possessed of little learning or knowledge.

A ركيكة *rakīkat*, (pl. ركاك *rikāk*) Small rain. ارض ركيكة *arz rakīkat*, Land wet with fine rain.

A ركيزة *rakīzat*, (pl. ركائز *rakāʼiz*) Fossils, precious minerals. A particular mark or character in geomancy.

A ركين *rakīn*, Grave, steady, quiet, tranquil (man). Firm, strong, solid. (A mountain) having projecting sides, lofty spurs or buttresses. ركن ركين *rukni rakīn*, A strong pillar. *Rukayn*, A mouse. A mole. The jerboa.

P رگ *rag*, A vein. Lineage, race, stock. Muttering from rage. A slight dash (of water into wine). رگ بسمل خاريدن *ragi bismil khāridan*, To commit an act which costs one's life. رگ تن خاستن *ragi tan khāstan*, To swell with rage. رگ جان *ragi jān*, An artery. The jugular vein. رگ زدن *rag zadan*, To bleed, to breathe a vein. رگ گردن *ragi gardan*, Pride. بد رگ *bad-rag*, An evil-thinking man.

P رگال rugāl, A live coal.

P رگ باز گرفتن rag bāz giriftan, (or رگ خوابانیدن rag khwābānīdan) To be slow, remiss.

P رگبند rag-band, A bandage for bleeding.

P رگدار rag-dār, Veined. Slightly dashed with water (wine). Cloth in which the threads are uneven, so that some appear like veins. A wicked brat.

P رگ ریشه rag-resha, Veins and fibres. Every thing, all.

P رگ زده rag-zada, Bled, blooded.

P رگ زن rag-zan, A phlebotomist, bleeder.

P رگو rugo, (rigo, رگوک rugok, رگوي rigoy, or رگوه rigoh) A sheet. Fine linen, muslin. Linen rags. Any clout, patch, or piece of old cloth.

P رگیدن ragidan, To grumble from sadness. To mutter with rage.

P رم ram, A herd of cattle. An assemblage of people. Terror. Flight. رم خوردن ram khwurdan, To be scared. Ram or rum, Flesh about the mouth. Rim, Pus, matter. Rum, Hair about the privities.

A رمّ ramm, (v. n. of رمّ) Mending, repairing (a house). Restoring, setting to rights. Cropping with the lips shoots of trees (a cow). Devouring. Any thing. Flight, escape. ما له حمّ ولا رمّ mā lahu hamm wa lā ramm, He has nothing. ما لي منه حمّ ولا رمّ mā lī minhu hamm (or humm) wa lā ramm (or rumm), I have no help for it. Rimm, (v. n. of رمّ) Being carious and rotten (a bone). Earth. Marrow. Great riches, or large flocks. Straw or sticks on the surface of water, or on the ground. Moisture. Rumm, Flight. Mental disquietude. Repair of a house.

A رمء rams, (v. n. of رمأ) Remaining, dwelling, resting, reposing. Increasing (above 100). Thinking or believing to be true.

A رماء ramās, Usury. Increase. Excess. Rimās, (v. n. 3 of رمي) Contending or assaulting with missile weapons.

A رمّاء rammās, White (sheep).

A رماة rumāt, (pl. of رامي rāmi) Throwers, hurlers. Shooters. Archers. Revilers.

A رماث rimās, (pl. of رمث ramas) Rafts for crossing rivers.

A رمّاثة rammāsat, A wild heifer.

A رماج ramāj, The spaces between the joints of a cane-spear.

A رماح rimāh, (pl. of رمح rumh) Spears. رماح الجنّ rimāhu'l jinn, The plague. رماح العقرب rimāhu'l ʻakrab, The tail of a scorpion. اخذت الابل رماحها akhazati'l iblu rimāhahā, The camels became fat; or abounded in milk, in which state they restrain their owner, as it were, from slaughtering them.

A رمّاح rammāh, A maker of spears. A thrower or jouster with spears.

A رماحة rimāhat, The art of making spears. Poverty, indigence, want.

A رمّاحة rammāhat, Strong, far-shooting (bow).

A رماحس rumāhis, Bold, strong. A lion.

A رماد ramād, Ashes. Lye.

A رمادة ramādat, Destruction of cattle by hail or frost. عام الرمادة ʻāmu'r ramādat, The 18th year of the Hijra (remarkably fatal to men and cattle).

P رمارم ramāram, Opposite. Diverse. Of different colours. Successive, following, pursuing.

A رمّاز rammāz, One who speaks mysteriously, or by signs. A propounder of riddles.

A رمازة ramāzat, (v. n. of رمز) Being moveable, volatile. Being grave, modest. Being prudent, intelligent. Being noble, venerable, honourable.

A رمّازة rammāzat, Winking, beckoning (courtesan). The podex. An army (from its fluctuating multitude). Any thing fat in the knee-pan.

P رماس ramās, Mastic.

A رماضة ramāzat, (v. n. of رمض) Sharpening (a spear's point) between two stones. Sharpness.

A رماع rumāʻ, (v. n. of رمع) Suffering from the lumbago. Lumbago. Paleness of (a woman's) face from a pain in the back.

A رمّاعة rammāʻat, The two bones on the upper part of the head (which are tender and moist in infants). Podex. كذبت رمّاعته kazabat rammāʻatuhu, He broke wind.

A رماق ramāk or rimāk, Just enough to support life; a small competency, a bare subsistence. Rimāk, (v. n. 3 of رمق) Having little life remaining, being neither dead nor alive. Doing business ill. Acting hypocritically. Looking askance with hate. (pl. of رمق ramak) Flocks of sheep.

A رماك rimāk, (pl. of رمكة) Sorry jades.

A رمال rimāl, (pl. of رمل raml) Sands. Shores, margins. امّ رمال ummu rimāl, A hyena. Rumāl, A flimsily-woven mat. Rumāl or rimāl, Palm-leaves woven into a rope or the like. The woof or weft in a piece of cloth.

A رمّال rammāl, A geomancer, soothsayer, prophet, conjurer, fortune-teller.

A رمام rimām, Old, rotten (rope). (pl. of رمّة rimmat) Rotten bones. (pl. of رمّة rummat) Pieces of an old decayed rope. Rumām, Rotten, carious.

A رمامة rumāmat, Sufficiency to support life.

P رمان ramān, Timid, fugitive.

A رمّان rummān, A pomegranate. رمّان الانهار rummānu'l anhār, The herb all-heal. رمّان السعالي rummānu's suʻālā', White poppy. رمّان الخشخاش rummānu'l khashkhāsh, Poppy-heads.

A رمّانة rummānat, One pomegranate. A weight for scales. The rough tripe of beasts.

A رمّاني rummāniy, A seller of pomegranates. Resembling a pomegranate. Ruby-coloured.

A رمّانية rummāniyat, A dish dressed with the seeds and juice of pomegranates.

P رمانیدن ramānīdan, To terrify, fright, scare.

A رمايا ramāya', (pl. of رميّ ramiy) Small parts of clouds. Clouds raining large drops.

A رماية rimāyat, (v. n. of رمي) Shooting an arrow.

A رمائم ramāʼim, (pl. of رميم) Rotten (bones).

A رمّة rimmat, (v. n. of رمّ) Becoming putrid, rotten, worn. (pl. رمم rimam and رمام rimām) A carious bone. A ship-worm. Moist ground. Marrow. A winged pismire. A piece of a rope. Rummat, (pl. رمم rumam and رمام rimām) Part of an old rotten rope. A rope tied round the neck of an animal. Rotten, decayed bones. شيء برمّته shaysun bi rummatihi, The (whole) thing without any reserve (as it were, rope and all). Rummat or rumat, The forehead.

A رمث rams, (v. n. of رمث) Adapting. Repairing, restoring, mending. Stroking, wiping with the hand. Rims, A species of forage eaten by camels; also a tree. (A man) clothed in ragged garments. Weak in the back. Ramas, (v. n. of رمث) Eating of the plant رمث rims, and suffering from it (a camel). Being confused, mixed. (pl. رماث rimās) A raft or float. Remains of milk in the udder. Excess, redundance, superfluity. Any thing from which a leathern bottle is suspended for churning milk.

A رمثة ramisat, (رمثى ramsa', and رماثي ramāsa') (A she-camel) pained by the plant رمث rims.

A رمج ramj, (v. n. of رمج) Muting (a bird). Rimj, Bird's evacuations.

A رمح ramh, (v. n. of رمح) Piercing (with a spear). Kicking (a horse). Throwing up the gravel with the feet. Flashing (lightning). Rumh, (pl. ارماح armāh and رماح rimāh) A spear, lance. Poverty. A star in the knee of Bootes.

A رمخ rimkh, Thick, entangled trees. Rimakh and rumakh, (pl. of رمخة rimakhat) Unripe dates.

P رمخ ramakh, The last breath.

A رمخاء ramkhāʼ, Greedy of eating the thick and entangled trees رمخ rimkh (a sheep).

A رمخة rumkhat, (pl. رمخ rumakh), or rimakhat (pl. رمخ rimakh), An unripe date.

A رمد ramd, (v. n. of رمد) Perishing by hail or frost (cattle). Rumd, A gnat. (pl. of ارمد armad) Ash-coloured. Ramad, A disorder in the eyes, or a swelling in the tunica conjunctiva: ophthalmia. Ramid, Blear-eyed. Stinking (water).

A رمداء ramdāʼ, An ostrich (as ash-coloured).

A رمدة حتّان rimdat hattān, The smallest remnant. Ramidat, A sore eye.

A رمدد rimdid, rimdad, (and رمديد rimdīd) Destructive, deadly. Perishing. Impalpable (ashes).

A رمدداء rimdidāʼ, Ashes.

A رمرام ramrām, A sort of tree. Spring-grass.

A رمرمة ramramat, A moving the lips in talking.

A رمز ramz, (v. n. of رمز) Intimating, hinting by moving the lips, knitting the brows, lolling the tongue, or by waving the hand. Bounding (as a deer). Instigating. Filling (a water-bottle). Shaking, being unable to walk from weight and fatness. Transferring (a flock of sheep) from the hand of a negligent shepherd to the care of one more watchful. An enigmatical discourse or writing, mystery, ambiguous expression. A subtle distinction or mark. Abbreviation of words by ciphers, a cipher. P رمز كردن *ramz kardan*, To beckon, wink, nod. To accuse. A *Ramz, ramaz*, or *rumz*, (pl. رموز *rumūz*) A nod, wink, sign, signal (with the lip, eye, eyebrow, mouth, hand, or tongue). An enigma. *Rumz*, (Camels) in excellent condition, plump, healthy.

A رمزان *ramazān*, (v. n. of رمز) Bounding (as a deer). Instigating. Filling (a water-bottle).

A رمزة *ramzat*, A single nod, slight wink.

P رمزشناس *ramz-shinās*, Knowing signs.

P رمزك *ramjak*, Sin: a slip, fall: a cast, fling.

P رمس *rams*, The grave.

A رمس *rams*, (v. n. of رمس) Covering with earth and levelling. Burying. Concealing, suppressing (news). Throwing a stone. Hitting (with an arrow). Plunging the head in water. (pl. ارماس *armās* or رموس *rumūs*) A grave, tomb, or its dust.

A رمش *ramsh*, (v. n. of رمش) Throwing or striking (with a stone). Feeding poorly (a flock). Stroking with the hand. Taking with the tips of the fingers. A bundle of sweet or fragrant herbs. *Ramash*, Luxuriance of herbage. Hairiness about the ears. Curling of the hair. Whiteness on the nails of young men. Redness of the eyelids, with a running humour.

P رمش *ramish*, Change. Terror, fear.

A رمشاء *ramshās*, (fem. of ارمش *armash*) Fruitful (ground). Barren. Hairy-eared. Sore-eyed.

A رمص *rams*, (v. n. of رمص) Repairing a misfortune (God). Binding up what has been broken. Making peace (between persons). Voiding excrement (a hen). Bringing forth (a wild beast). Acquiring, earning. *Ramas*, (v. n. of رمص) Being dirty (the eye). White sordes collected in the inner corner of the eye. Dry sordes (when wet it is called غمص *ghamas*).

A رمصاء *ramsās*, (fem. of ارمص) Dirty-eyed.

A رمض *ramz*, (v. n. of رمض) Splitting (a sheep) and roasting it in the skin upon a hot stone covered with ashes. Pasturing (flocks) on scorching ground. Sharpening (the point of a spear) between two stones. *Ramaz*, (v. n. of رمض) Being hot from the influence of the sun (a day, stones, or sand). Grazing in the sun and becoming diseased in the liver (a sheep).

A رمضاء *ramzās* or *ramazās*, Hot from the sun, scorching (ground).

A رمضان *ramazān*, (pl. رمضانات *ramazānāt*, رمضانون *ramazānūn*, ارمضة *armizat*, ارمض *armuz*, or ارمضاء *armizās*) The ninth month of the Muhammadan year. God, as the pardoner, and likewise the consumer, of sinners.

A رمضة *ramizat*, A woman chafed in the thighs.

A رمضيٌ *ramaza'*, (Rain or clouds) at the end of summer.

A رمط *ramt*, (v. n. of رمط) Reproaching, reviling. *Ramt*, (more correctly رهطة *rahtat*) A place where lofty thorny trees are thickly set.

P رمظان *ramzān*, Name of a fire-worshipper.

A رمع *ramę*, (or رمعان *ramaęān*) (v. n. of رمع) Making haste. *Ramaę*, (or رمعان *ramaęān*) (v. n. of رمع) Tossing (the nose) in anger. Being pale in the face from a complaint in the vulva (a woman). Beckoning (with the hand). Moving or breaking (the head). Bringing forth (a child). Flowing (tears). Lumbago. Paleness of face from a pain in the back.

A رمعة *rumęat*, A part, portion, piece.

A رمغ *ramgh*, Rubbing (leather) with the hand.

A رمق *ramk*, (v. n. of رمق) Looking or glancing at. *Ramak*, (pl. ارماق *armāk*) The last breath, the departing spirit. What is barely sufficient to keep body and soul together. (from P رمه *rama*) (pl. رماق *rimāk*) A flock of sheep. *Ramik*, Expiring (life). A bare subsistence, just enough to keep body and soul together. *Rumuk*, (pl. of رموق *ramūk* and رامق *rāmik*) Poor, distressed (scarcely able to live). Envious.

A رمّق *rummak*, Weak, flaccid.

A رمقة *rumkat*, A bare maintenance.

P رمك *ramak*, (for رمه *rama*) A herd, flock.

A رمك *ramak*, (pl. of رمكة) Brood mares. Jades.

A رمكاء *ramkās*, Of the colour of ashes.

A رمكات *ramakāt*, (pl. of رمكة) Brood mares.

A رمكة *rumkat*, The ash-colour of old camels. *Ramakat*, (pl. رمك *ramak*, ارماك *armāk*, or رماك *rimāk*) A breeding mare or jade. Weak (man).

P رمگا *ramgā*, (in zand and Pāzand) Mares.

P رمگان *ram* or *rumgān*, Hair on the pubes.

A رمل *raml*, (v. n. of رمل) Making (mats), or any thing of a flimsy texture. Covering (the ground) with mats, and adorning them with gems, or any thing similar. Making the back of a sofa with platted palm-leaves. Adorning (a sofa or throne) with gems, &c. Putting (meat) into sand to preserve (it). Tinging, besmearing with blood. (pl. رمال *rimāl* and ارمل *armul*) Sand. *Ramal*, (v. n. of رمل) Running, going fast, between running and walking. Geomancy, called by the Arabians علم الرمل *ęilmu'r ramal*. Augmentation, increase, excess. (pl. ارمال *armāl*) Little rain. A species of Arabian metre. Lines on the feet of the wild cow different in colour from the rest. *Rumal*, (pl. of رملة *rumlat*) Black lines.

A رملاء *ramlās*, (fem. of ارمل *armal*) Black-footed (sheep). Rainless (year).

A رملان *ramalān*, (v. n. of رمل) Running.

A رملة *ramlat*, One heap of sand. Name of a place in Palestine. A woman's name. *Rumlat*, (pl. رمل *rumal* and ارمال *armāl*) A black line.

A رملي *ramlīy*, A geomancer.

A رمم *rimam*, Rotten (rope). (pl. of رمّة *rimmat*) Carious bones. *Rumam*, (pl. of رمّة *rummat*) Parts of old rotten ropes. *Rumum*, Sharp, shrewd lasses.

P رمن *raman*, (in zand) All, the whole.

P رمندة *ramanda*, Wild, terrified, timid.

A رمو *rumūs*, (v. n. of رما) Remaining, dwelling. Resting, reposing. Increasing (above 100). Thinking or believing to be true.

P رموان *ram* or *ramawān*, A shepherd. Flocks.

A رموح *ramūh*, Apt to kick, wincing (horse).

A رموز *rumūz*, (pl. of رمز *ramz*) Signs, signals, winks, nods. Abbreviations. Enigmas.

P رموزدان *rumūz-dān*, Skilled in mysteries.

A رموس *rumūs*, (pl. of رمس *rams*) Graves.

A رموص *ramūs*, (A hen) voiding excrement.

A رموق *ramūk*, (pl. رمق *rumuk*) Poor, distressed, and scarcely able to live. Envious.

P رموك *rumūk*, Stay, sojourn, commorancy.

A رموك *rumūk*, (v. n. of رمك) Abiding (in any place). Being permanent. Keeping close to the water (a camel).

P رمون *ramūn*, Earnest-money. Money paid in advance, to be returned if the goods turn not out well.

P رمه *rama*, A herd, flock, bevy, covey. A company, troop, body. All. The Pleiades.

A رمىٰ *rama'*, (fut. يرمي *yarmī*) He threw.

A رمي *ramy*, (v. n. of رمي) Flinging. Throwing (from the hand), darting (a javelin). Shooting, hitting. Voiding excrement. Hitting the mark. Exceeding, increasing (above fifty). Assisting, rendering superior, favouring, benefiting. Railing at, reproaching, vilifying. رمي احجار *ramyi ahjār*, A throwing of stones. *Rima'*, The sound of a stone thrown.

A رميّ *ramīy*, (pl. ارماء *armās*, ارمية *armiyat*, and رمايا *ramāya'*) Stricken. Small parts of clouds. Clouds falling in large heat-drops.

A رمّيا *rimmiya'*, A sharp contest in shooting.

A رمّيّا *rimmīya'*, A hurling at each other.

P رميار *ram-yār*, A shepherd, keeper of flocks.

A رمية *ramyat*, One throw. One bow-shot. دون رمية حجر *dūn ramyati hajar*, Within a stone's throw. رمية من غير رام *ramyat min ghayr rāmin*, A shot without a shooter (said of any sudden, unlooked-for event).

A رميّة *ramīyat*, (fem. of رمي *ramīy*) Game which is aimed at or killed by a throw or a shot.

A رميح *rumayh*, (dim. of رمح *rumh*) A little spear. Veretrum. ذو الرميح *zū'r rumayh*, A species of long-footed mole. رميح ابي سعد *rumayhi abi saęd*, A staff on which an old man leans.

P رميدگي *ramīdagī*, Terror, flight. Aversion.

P رميدن *ramīdan*, To be afraid, terrified, seized with horror; to be disturbed, agitated; to fly in terror, to shun from aversion. To frighten.

P رميدة *ramīda*, Horror-struck, disturbed, afflicted. Offended, indignant, having an antipathy. رميدة و آرميدة *ramīda u āramīda*, Moveables and immoveables. رنجيدة و رميدة كردن *ranjīda u ramīda hardan*, To molest, vex, injure.

A رميز *ramīz*, Moveable, volatile. Grave, modest. Prudent, intelligent. Radical. Noble, venerable. Honoured, esteemed. Narrow-minded, covetous. Many. *Rumayz*, A stick, staff.

A رميس *ramīs*, Concealed, suppressed (news). Buried (man).

A رميصاء *rumaysā*, Name of a certain woman.

A رميض *ramīz*, Sharpened. A sharp knife.

A رميم *ramīm*, (v. n. of رمّ) Waxing old, putrefying. Putrid, carious, corrupted, worn. محيي عظام رميم *muhyiẓi ezāmi ramīm*, Restoring life to corrupted bones (applied to Jesus Christ).

A رنّ *rann*, (v. n. of رنّ) Giving ear, listening.

A رنا *ranw*, (v. n. of رنا) Beholding, looking at. Coming. Being slow, sluggish (in walking).

A رنا *rana'*, A spectacle, any thing admired for its beauty. An object steadily gazed upon. A steady gaze at any object.

A رناء *runāe*, A sound, especially musical. Joy, emotion, dancing.

A رنّاء *rannāe*, A gazer or admirer of the fair sex.

P رنب *rumb*, رنبة *ru* or *ramba*, Hair of the pubes.

A رنّة *rannat*, (v. n. of رنّ) Crying, vociferating. Sound. A noise when crying, in the throat.

P رنج *ranj*, Trouble. Grief, affliction, sadness. Toil. Pain of the body. Anguish of mind. Remorse. Cholic, gripes. Injury, offence, molestation, anger. Powder. (in comp.) Vexing. (equiv. to رنگ *rang*) Colour. رنج باريك *ranji bārik*, Hectic fever. رنج بردن *ranj burdan*, To suffer distress. رنج كردن *ranj hardan*, To lament.

P رنجال *ranjāl*, Food.

P رنجانيدن *ranjānīdan*, To molest, annoy, occasion vexation. To cause to labour and toil.

P رنجبر *ranj-bar*, An artificer, mechanic.

P رنج دان *ranjdān*, A priming-flask or horn.

P رنجش *ranjish*, Indignation, offence. Grief, affliction, toil.

P رنجك *ranjak*, The touch-hole of fire-arms. The priming-pan.

P رنجن *ranjan*, A soft belly well purged.

P رنجور *ranjūr*, Sick, infirm. Afflicted, grieved, sorrowful. عشّاق رنجور *eushshāki ranjūr*, Distressed lovers.

P رنجوردار *ranjūr-dār*, Attendant on the sick.

P رنجوري *ranjūrī*, Sickness. Anguish.

P رنجه *ranja*, Pain. Grief. An affected air. Sad, vexed, afflicted. رنجه داشتن *ranja dāshtan*, To grieve, be distressed.

P رنجيدگي *ranjīdagī*, Affliction, sadness.

P رنجيدن *ranjīdan*, To be sad, melancholy, vexed; to fret. To be angry, enraged, filled with indignation. To carve, grave.

P رنجيدة *ranjīda*, Vexed, exasperated, indignant. رنجيدة و رميدة كردن *ranjīda u ramīda hardan*, To irritate. To molest, disturb, interrupt.

P رنجين *ranjīn*, A ploughshare.

A رنح *ranh*, A giddiness in the head. A piece of the brain of the shape of a sparrow.

A رنخ *rankh*, A languishing. A being obscure.

P رند *rand*, A word, saying. Any thing fragrant. Agreeable, easy of digestion. Dust. Theft, plunder. Any thing rough, tart, and astringent (as the rind of a pomegranate). Laurel. Myrtle. A chip, shaving. A carpenter's plane. *Rind*, Sagacious, shrewd. A knave, rogue. A sufi. Dissolute. A drunkard, debauchee. One whose exterior is liable to censure, but who at heart is sound. A wanderer, traveller. An insolent, reckless, fearnought fellow. رند دهل دريدة *rindi duhul-darīda*, One who has erred. رندان خاك بيز *rindāni khāk-bez*, Penetrating, discerning, shrewd (persons). *Rund*, The rice-bird.

A رند *rand*, Laurel. Wood of aloes. Myrtle. A sort of hamper made of platted palm-leaves.

P رندانيدن *randānīdan*, To cause to carve, engrave, plane, scrape, or rasp.

P رندش *randish*, Sculpture. Rasure. Chips, filings. Scrapings, planings, raspings.

P رندك *rindak*, An arch lad, waggish boy.

P رندة *randa*, A joiner's plane. Shavings. A certain fattening herb. A grater, rasper. A sort of black leather made from goat's skin. Great, large.

P رندي *randī*, A polishing, a planing. Sawdust. *Rindī*, A draught, drink. Trick, fraud.

P رنديدن *randīdan*, To polish, smooth; chip or hew with a hatchet. To scrape, rasp, grate, plane. To walk pompously. To grow.

P رنديدة *randīda*, Polished: planed: scraped.

A رنز *runz*, Rice.

A رنف *ranf* or *ranaf*, A kind of forest-willow.

A رنق *rank*, *ranak*, or *ranik*, Turbid (water). *Rank* or *ranak*, (v. n. of رنق) Being muddy (water). *Ranik*, Full of trouble (life).

A رنقاء *rankāe*, (A bird) sitting upon eggs. Barren, unproductive ground.

A رنقاوات *rankāwāt*, Barren grounds.

P رنگ *rang*, Colour, hue. Paint, stain, dye. Stratagem, fraud, imposture; insincerity, perfidy, disloyalty. Playfulness, innocent delusion or frolic, ridicule. Pleasure. Kind, sort, state, condition. Manner, method, order, form, habit, usage, custom. Modesty, bashfulness. Dishonour, reproach. A blemish. Indignation with a mixture of shame. Grief, pain, affliction. Spirit, soul. Comeliness, neatness, grace, elegance. Goodness. Health, happy circumstances. Gold. Wealth, substance. A small capital. Profit, utility. Hope, desire, expectation of advantage. A game at dice. Money gotten at games of hazard. A theft of gold or silver. Power, strength. Lot, portion, share. A lord, master, possessor. A black spot or mole. Blood. Small globular bells hung round the rims of Arabian drums. An old patched garment. Squint-eyed. A wild mountain-goat. A wild ox, or beast in general. A fine he-camel kept for stock. Like, resembling. Corrupt, bad. Growing herbage. رنگ آزادان *rangi āzādān*, The habits of generous men. رنگ از آسمان تراشيدن *rang az āsmān tarāshīdan*, To attempt impossibilities, to labour in vain. رنگ از ديوار تراشيدن *rang az dīwār tarāshīdan*, To be bold, impudent, shrewd, clever, or witty. رنگ آوردن *rang āwardan*, (or بر آوردن *bar āwardan*) To blush. To colour up with indignation. رنگ برگان *rangi bargān*, A soft stone for making glass. رنگ ربيع *rangi rabīe*, Vernal tints. رنگ ريختن *rang rekhtan*, To lay the foundation of a building. رنگ شه باز *rangi shah-bāz*, Darkness. رنگ شدن *rang shudan*, To colour, to blush. رنگ كردن *rang hardan*, To colour, paint, tinge. رنگ ماتم *rangi mātam*, Blackness. Sable. رنگ محل *rang-mahal*, An apartment dedicated to voluptuous enjoyment. رنگ و بوي *rang u boy*, Majesty, power. Aptitude, capacity. رنگ هوا *rangi hawā*, Darkness. گل رنگ *gul-rang*, Rose-coloured.

P رنگارنگ *rang-ā-rang*, Various-coloured. Of different sorts.

P رنگ آميز *rang-āmez*, Mixing colour. Possessing colour, painted, dyed, stained. Conversant with many subjects. Fickle, inconstant. Painting. Stratagem.

P رنگ آور *rang-āwar*, Coloured. Deceitful, fraudulent, knavish. Shame-faced. Pompous in diction, one who values himself on flowery language.

P رنگاني *rangānī*, The price paid for dyeing. A certain space of time during which a cloth is dyed.

P رنگ بالا *rang-bālā*, Bright-coloured (rose).

P رنگ برنگ *rang ba rang*, Various.

P رنگ بست *rang-bast*, A fixed, fast colour.

P رنگ رز *rang-raz*, A dyer. رنگ رز گلگون *rang-razi gulgūn*, A vintner.

P رنگرزان *rang-razān*, Autumn.

P رنگ رش *rang-rash*, Silk-merchant or spinner.

P رنگروتا *ringarūtā*, (in zand) An elephant.

P رنگ روش *rang-rosh*, A silk-merchant. A cheat, deceiver.

P رنگ ريز *rang-rez*, A dyer.

P رنگ زدة *rang-zada*, Tinged, coloured, dyed.

P رنگساز *rang-sāz*, A painter. A dyer.

P رنگ فروش *rang-farosh*, A dyer. A silk-merchant. A cheat.

P رنگ لاك *rang-lāk*, A dyeing tincture.

P رنگ لكا *rang-lukā*, Tincture of lac.

P رنگيدن *rangīdan*, To grow, increase.

P رنگين *rangīn*, Coloured, tinctured, painted, of many colours. Allegorical, figurative, metaphorical, elegant, flowery.

P رنگينا *rangīnā*, (or رنگينان) A red peach.

P رنگين كمان *rangīn-kamān*, The rainbow.

A رنم *ranam*, (v. n. of رنم) Sounding, singing. Sound, voice. *Runum*, Skilful female singers.

A رنمة *ranamat*, A musical voice; melody, rhythm. A kind of slender plant.

A رنن *ranan*, A thing that makes a noise in the water in hot weather.

A رنوّ *ranūw*, An incessant gazer and admirer of the ladies. One who gazes incessantly at any object, and listens to any thing with intense delight. *Runūw*, (v. n. of رنا for رنو) Looking at incessantly. Listening attentively. Dancing for joy. Any thing ludicrous which employs the mind. Victory.

A رنوة *ranwat*, (pl. رنوات) A piece of flesh.

A رنوخ *runūkh*, A being weak and contemptible.

P رنود *ranwad*, Absence.

P رنوس *runūs*, A sort of stone, which, when made into a ring, banishes care from the wearer's mind.

A رنوع *runūع*, (v. n. of رنع) Changing (colour). Being flaggy and slender. Shaking off flies from the head (a horse). Playing.

A رنوق *runūk*, (v. n. of رنق) Being muddy.

A رنوناة *ranawnāt*, (A thing) remaining always in one place. (pl. of رنونيات *ranawnayāt*) A drinking-cup in continual use.

A رنّي *runna'*, Name of the sixth month (named also جمادي الآخرة *jumāda'lākhirat*). الرنّي *ar'runna'*, People, all mankind.

A رنيم *ranīm*, A song, catch, glee, mirth, jubilee.

A رنين *ranīn*, (v. n. of رنّ) Twanging (as a bow-string). Vociferating, crying out, hooting. Listening to. Ringing, resounding, echoing.

P رو *rav*, A sigh, groan. (imp. of رفتن *raftan*), Go thou; (also the contracted form of رونده *rawanda*), Who goes. پيش رو *pesh-rav*, One who precedes, or goes before. *Rū*, Face, countenance. Aspect, appearance. Sake, cause, reason. Hypocrisy. Colour, pretence. Hope, expectation. Wish. Manifestation. Search, investigation. (in comp.) Having a face, like: as, پري رو *parī-rū*, Fairy-faced. رو دادن *rū dādan*, To appear. چه رو داده است *chi rū dāda ast*, What appearance has it given? *i. e.* how has it happened or succeeded?

P روا *rawā*, (part. of رفتن *raftan*) Going. Current (coin). Lawful, right. Equitable, reasonable. Admissable, allowable. Tolerated. Worthy, proper, suitable. Pleasant, agreeable. Obtaining one's desire. روا بودن *rawā būdan*, To be worthy. رواست *rawāst*, It is proper, it ought to be so. روا داشتن *rawā dāshtan*, To judge right, commend, approve, allow. روا شدن *rawā shudan*, To be lawful. روا كردن *rawā kardan*, To approve. To adjust. *Rivā*, Fruitfulness, plenty.

A رواء *rawā'*, Sweet, wholesome (water). The well Zamzam. *Riwā'*, (pl. اروية *arwiyat*) A rope for fastening loads. (pl. of راوي *rāwī*) Those who quench their thirst with water. *Ruwā'*, Face, countenance. Elegance of look. Pleasantness of prospect.

A رؤاء *ru'ā'*, Agreeableness of aspect.

A روابط *rawābit*, (pl. of رابطة) Connexions.

A روابع *rawābiع*, (Camels) which are watered on the fourth day.

A روابي *rawābī*, (pl. of رابية) High hills.

A رواة *ruwāt*, (pl. of راوي *rāwī*) Historians, narrators, tellers, relaters, reporters. Those who drink sufficient, or quench their thirst with water.

A روات *ruwāt*, (pl. of رأت *ra't*) Straws.

A رواتب *rawātib*, (pl. of راتبة *rātibat*) Stipends, salaries, appointments, dues.

A رواج *rawāj*, (v. n. of راج for روج) Being vendible, in great demand, or selling well (goods) (كساد *kasād* implying a difficulty of sale). Being current, circulating freely (money). A facility in buying or selling. Blowing from different quarters (wind). Use, custom, practice, fashion. Customary, current. P رواج شدن *rawāj shudan*, To become current, obtain, prevail.

A روّاج *rawwāj*, One who goes round a well without being able to get at it for the crowd.

A رواجب *rawājib*, (pl. of راجبة *rājibat* and رجبة *rujbat*) Finger-joints. Asses' windpipes.

A رواجع *rawājiع*, (pl. of راجع *rājiع*) (Asses or camels) which give false signs of pregnancy. Birds of passage returning from a cold to a warm climate.

A رواح *rawāh*, (v. n. of راح for روح) Going, coming, or doing any thing at sun-set. Walking, going (at any hour). Being on the point of accomplishing (a thing). The afternoon, the evening. Ease, quiet, repose. *Riwāh*, (v. n. 3 of راح for روح) Doing (two things) alternately. Standing first on one foot, then on another.

P روا حال *rawā hāl*, Immediately. Swift.

A رواحة *rawāhat*, Ease, quiet, repose, tranquillity. Joy on account of the certainty of a thing.

A رواحل *rawāhil*, (pl. of راحلة) Camels of burden.

P رواد *rawād* or *ruwād*, A place full of hills, risings, pasture, and water. The green bank of a river. A muddy stream.

A رواد *riwād*, (v. n. 3 of راد for رود) Asking, requiring, begging, soliciting. Diverting from, hindering. Wish, desire.

A روّاد *rūwād*, (pl. of رائد *rā'id*) Foragers.

P روا دار *rawā-dār*, An approver, chooser, consenter. Judging right. Lawful, true, just, proper, fit.

A روادة *ruwādat*, (A woman) who gads to and fro amongst her neighbours.

A روادف *rawādif*, (pl. of رادفة *rādifat*) Additions, supplements. Shoots, sprouts growing from the trunks of palm-trees. Ducts of fat in the hinder part of a camel's bunch.

A روادق *rawāzik*, (pl. of روذق *rawzak*) Stripped (skins). Kids scalded ready for roasting. Meats cooked and mingled with seasoning.

A رواذك *rawāzik*, Small camels or sheep.

P روار *rawār*, A jailer, a turnkey.

P روارو *rav-ā-rav*, Proceeding, travelling, following quick. *Rū-ā-rū*, Face to face.

P رواز *rawāz*, A jailer, a turnkey.

P روازاري *rawāzārī*, Metaphorical, figurative.

A روازن *rawāzin*, (pl. of روزن) Windows.

P رواس *rawās*, Water-cresses. *Riwās*, Sorrel.

A روّاس *rawwās*, A dresser and seller of heads of cattle.

A رواسي *rawāsī*, (pl. of راسية) Firm (mountains).

A رؤاسيّ *ru'āsiy*, Large-headed.

A روّاسيّ *rawwāsiy*, A seller of heads of cattle.

A رواسيم *rawāsīm*, Books of the Pagan Arabs.

A رواش *rawāsh*, (for رواج *rawāj*) Vendible.

A رواشح *rawāshih*, Exudations (from chinks in a rock). An excrescence resembling a teat on a sheep's udder. (pl. of راشح *rāshih*) Reptiles. Bases of hills wet with dew.

A رُوّاض *rūwāz*, (pl. of رائض) Breakers of colts.

A رواضع *rawāziع*, (pl. of راضعة) Milk-teeth.

A رواع *ruwāع*, (v. n. of راع for روع) Succeeding well, benefiting. رواع الفؤاد *ruwāع'l fu'ād*, (or رواعة الفؤاد *ruwāعatu'l fu'ād*) Acute, sagacious, sly (she-camel).

A رواعد *rawāعid*, (pl. of راعدة *rāعidat*) Thundering (skies). ذات الرواعد *zāt* or ذوات *zawātu'r rawāعid*, Misfortune, calamity.

A رواعف *rawāعif*, Spears (bloody, victorious).

A رواعي *rawāعī*, Beginning (of hoariness).

A رواغ *rawāgh*, Flight, retreat, a turning aside. A kind of trot.

A روّاغ *rawwāgh*, Inclining. A fox.

A رواغة *riwāghat*, A theatre for wrestlers.

A روافد *rawāfid*, Beams for a roof, rafters.

A روافض *rawāfiz*, The followers of the sect of Aliy, denominated Shiites (so called from their forsaking Zayd Ibn Aliy Ibnu'l Husayn). Heretics. Soldiers, or any people who desert their chiefs.

A روافغ *rawāfigh*, (pl. of رافغ) Comfortable (lives).

A روافه *rawāfih*, (pl. of رافهة *rāfihat*) Easy night-journeys. Camels that daily drink their fill.

P رواق *rawāk*, Purified, filtered, strained.

A رواق *riwāk* or *ruwāk*, (pl. اروقة *arwikat* and روق *rūk*) A house resembling a tent. A portico; an apartment open before, either at the top of the house or projecting before it, in the manner of a balcony, for the advantage of air or prospect. A tent of goat's hair. A house or caravansary for travellers. The king's court or tent; hall of audience, tribunal of justice. That part of the roof projecting beyond the wall, the eaves. The eyebrow. The beginning of a part of the night. A horned ewe. P رواق بي ستون *riwāki bi sitūn*, The heavens. رواق سيم گون *riwāki sīm-gūn*, The sky. رواق منظر چشم *riwāki manzari chashm*, The pupil of the eye.

P رواقي *rawāķī*, Purification, straining, filtration.

A رواقيّ *riwāķiy*, (from رواق *riwāķ*, A portico) A stoic, a frequenter of the stoa, or porch.

A رواقيد *rawāķīd*, Large wine-vessels.

A رواكب *rawākib*, Folds or layers of fat in the fore-part of a camel's bunch (those in the hinder part being called روادف *rawādif*).

A رواكيب *rawākīb*, Shoots growing out of the stems of palm-trees.

P رواگ *rawāg*, A saloon open in front.

A رؤال *ruwāl*, Growth of teeth (in a horse). Spittle or foam of a horse's mouth.

A روال *ruwāl*, Spittle, saliva (of a horse). A redundant tooth.

A رؤام *ruwām*, Saliva, spittle.

A روام *ruwām*, Foam of a camel's mouth.

A روامس *rawāmis*, Winds effacing vestiges, filling up wells, or scattering earth. Night-birds; also beasts roaming at night.

P روان *rawān*, Life, soul, spirit. The reasonable soul. The heart. (part. of رويدن *rawīdan* or رفتن *raftan*) Going, passing. Brisk, active (sale). Mounted, riding. Running. Flowing, fluid. Lawful, proper. Text. Reading. Forthwith, immediately, quickly. آب روان *ābi rawān*, Running water. تخت روان *takhti rawān*, A palanquin, litter, travelling couch, sedan-chair (borne by two horses or mules). نقد روان *nakdi rawān*, Current coin. روان آمدن *rawān āmadan*, To flow. روان شدن *rawān shudan*, To go, flow, pass, run. روان كردن *rawān kardan*, To make current. To despatch. To spill. روان كرد كشتي را *rawān kard kishtīrā*, He navigated the vessel. سخن روان *sukhan-rawān*, Eloquent.

P روانان *rawānān*, (pl. of روان) Souls, spirits.

P روان آورد *rawān-āward*, Wise, learned.

P روان بخش *rawān-bakhsh*, The Holy Spirit.

P روان بد *rawān-bud*, All-pervading spirit.

P روانتر *rawāntar*, More current.

P روان خواه *rawān-khwāh*, A wandering beggar.

A روانف *rawānif*, (pl. of رانفة *rānifat*) The lower parts of the buttocks when standing.

A روانق *rawānik*, (pl. of رونقة) Muddy waters.

P روان كرد *rawān-kird*, Power. The kingdom of heaven.

P روانگي *rawānagī*, A running, a flowing, flux. A passing, a travelling. پيوسته روانگي بول *paywasta rawānagīi bawl*, Diabetes.

P روانه *rawāna*, Going, running, passing, flowing. Prepared. Despatched, departed. Travelling. A custom-house passport, pass, or permit. Fortune, prosperity. روانهٔ راه كردن *rawānaʼi rāh kardan*, To prosecute a journey.

P رواني *rawānī*, A course. Effusion. Briskness of market. Currency. رواني دادن *rawānī dādan*, To despatch, cause to be received, make any thing have its full weight (as a mandate), or value (as goods). روانيِ آب *rawānīʼi āb*, The flowing of water. روانيِ شكم *rawānīʼi shikam*, A flux, diarrhœa.

P روانيدن *rawānīdan*, To make current, cause to be received, despatch. To behove, be necessary. To be vendible, current (goods or money). *Ruwānīdan*, To cause to grow.

P رواوه *rawāwa*, A musical instrument called رباب *rabāb*.

P رواه *rawāh*, Food for prisoners.

A رواهش *rawāhish*, Veins outside the hand, or in the fore-legs of a horse.

A رواهص *rawāhis*, Stones fixed in a row; also such as hurt the feet of horses.

A رواية *riwāyat*, (v. n. of روي) Drawing water, and presenting it (to a friend). Fastening a water-bag on a camel. Relating the words of another. Twisting a rope. A history, narrative, relation, tale, story, tradition, report, fiction. روايت صحيح *riwāyati sahīh*, Indubitable report (a law treatise). روايت مشهور *riwāyati mashhūr*, Celebrated reports. ضعيف الرواية *zaʼīfu'r riwāyat*, One whose report of Muhammadan traditions is feeble, and of little weight and authority.

A روائح *rawāʼih*, (pl. of رائحة *rāʼihat*) Odours, perfumes. Delightful breezes. Evening rains.

A روائس *rawāʼis*, Upper parts of valleys. The advanced portion of a cloud.

P روايش *rawāyish*, A facility in disposing of goods. Precious commodities (as easily sold).

A روائم *rawāʼim*, Trivets.

P روائي *rawāʼī*, A passing along, by, or through. Currency, circulation. Briskness of markets. Fulfilment, success, completion. Suitableness, worthiness. Elegance. Figurative, allegorical. روائي دادن *rawāʼī dādan*, To give currency. روائي يافتن *rawāʼī yāftan*, To obtain currency, to circulate.

A روب *rawb*, (v. n. of راب for روب) Being thick (milk). Being confounded, bewildered, disordered in the intellect. Being torpid from sleep or repletion. Mixing. Giving any one thickened milk. Being wearied with travelling. Lying. Being near perishing. Thickened (milk). Milk that has been churned. لا شوب ولا روب في البيع و الشراء *lā shawba wa lā rawba fi'l bayʼ wa'sh shirāʼ*, No fraud nor mixing in selling and buying. راب دمه *rāba damuhu*, His blood thickened (he was at the point of death).

A رؤوب *ruʼūb*, (v. n. of رؤب) Being confounded, bewildered. Being torpid (from sleep or repletion). Being wearied with travelling. Lying. Being disordered in the intellect.

P روب *rob*, (from رفتن *ruftan*) Sweep. (in comp.) Sweeping. روب كردن *rob kardan*, To sweep. خاك روب *khāk-rob*, A besom. خانه روب *khāna-rob*, Sweeping the house.

P روبا *rūbā*, Fox-grapes. Nightshade.

P روبارو *rū bā rū*, Face to face, opposite. Comparatively. روبارو كردن *rū bā rū kardan*, To compare, confront, collate.

A روبان *rawbān*, Turgid, torpid from satiety or too much sleep. Disturbed in mind.

P روبان *robān*, Sweeping. One who sweeps.

P روبانيدن *robānīdan*, To cause to sweep. To clean the teeth.

P روباه *rūbāh*, A fox. روباه پر *rūbāhi par*, The flying fox. روباه تركي *rūbāhi turkī*, A porcupine. روباه دريائي *rūbāhi daryāʼī*, A beaver. روباه زرد *rūbāhi zard*, The sun.

P روباه بازي *rūbāh-bāzī*, Fox-play, stratagem, subtlety. روباه بازي كردن *rūbāh-bāzī kardan*, To play the fox, to act with wiliness.

P روباه بچه *rūbāh-bachcha*, A fox's cub.

P روباه تربك *rūbāh-turbak*, Foxgrapes. Nightshade.

P روباه ماده *rūbāh-māda*, A bitch-fox, a vixen.

P روباهي *rūbāhī*, Foxship, vulpine cunning.

A روبة *rawbat* or *rūbat*, A ferment, or preparation of sour milk, put amongst new milk to make it coagulate. Remains of milk. The seminal lymph of a stallion. A part of the night. A piece of meat. Necessity, any thing necessary to be done. A crowd of business. Slowness, torpor. Poverty. The medlar-tree. Forceps for drawing game from its den. Ground producing excellent plants. The means of living, or of accomplishing and bringing to pass.

A رؤبة *ruʼbat*, (pl. رئاب *riʼāb*) Solder for mending broken vessels.

A روبج *rawbaj*, Small and light money.

P رو براه *rū ba rāh*, Fit for business, adjusted, prepared. Reformed, returned from an erroneous course. رو براه شدن *rū ba rāh shudan*, To begin or proceed on a journey, to pass along.

P رو برو *rū ba rū*, Face to face, in front of. Presence. رو برو محاربه كردن *rū ba rū muhāraba kardan*, To fight front to front.

A روبع *rawbaʼ*, Weak. Short. Base, contemptible.

A روبعة *rawbaʼat*, Short, dwarfish. A shortness of the hough or tendon Achilles. A disease incident to young camels.

P روبكار *rū ba kār*, Approaching, at hand, about to be, in agitation. Ready for business, intent upon.

P روبكاري *rū ba kārī*, Proceeding (of a cause). A warrant.

P روبند *rū-band*, A lady's veil or mask.

P روبه *rūbah*, A fox.

P روبهانه *rūbahāna*, Fox-like, crafty, wily.

P روبهك *rūbahak*, A young fox, a fox's cub.

P روبيان *rūbiyān*, A shrimp.

P روبيدن *robīdan*, To wipe, sweep, dust.

P روپاك *rū-pāk*, A woman's veil. A hand kerchief. A towel.

P روپوش *rū-posh*, A veil covering the whole

face, especially a virgin bride's of red silk. Concealed, disappearing out of sight. روپوش شدن *rū-posh shudan*, To abscond.

H روپیه *rūpiya*, A rupee.

A روث *raws*, (v. n. of راث for روث) Dunging (a horse). Bedaubing (with dung). (pl. of روثة *rawsat*) Ordures. Tips of noses.

A روثة *rawsat*, (pl. روث *raws* and ارواث *arwās*) Dung. Tip of the nose. Chaff remaining in a sieve. The top of the handle of a sword, which, when grasped, touches the little finger.

P روج *roj*, A day. Unripe grapes.

A روجيل *rūjayl*, (irreg. dim. of رجل *rajul*, A man) A little man, a manikin.

P روچك *rūchak*, The 15th of the month Shaʻbān.

P روچه *rawcha* or *rūcha*, Unripe dates.

A روح *rawh*, (v. n. of راح for روح) Visiting in the afternoon. Coming in the wind. Beating any one (the wind). Destroying. Uprooting. Quiet. Mercy, clemency. Assistance. Justice. Riches, good fortune. A pleasant, refreshing wind. Agreeable (day). روح بال *rawhi bāl*, Heart-ease. *Rūh*, (pl. ارواح *arwāh*) The soul, incorporeal spirit. The breath of God. Revelation. Quicksilver. Love. Divine command. Prophecy. The work of prophecy. The Kur'ān. Jesus Christ. An angel in the form of a man with an angelic body. The angel Gabriel (whom the Muhammadans call likewise الروح الامين *ar' rūhu'l amīn*, The faithful spirit, and الروح القدس *ar' rūhu'l kudus*, (or روح قدسي *rūhi kudsī*) The holy spirit; Muhammad being named simply الروح *ar' rūh*). روح اعظم *rūhi aʻzam*, The supreme spirit. روح الله *rūhu'llāh*, The spirit of God, the Holy Ghost (but with the Muhammadans, as above, Jesus Christ, and the angel Gabriel). روح الهي *rūhi ilāhī*, The divine spirit. روح توتيا *rūhi tūtiyā*, Mercury. A sort of pewter. روح حيوتي *rūhi hayātī*, The vital spirit. روح حيواني *rūhi haywānī*, Animal spirit. P روح روان *rūhi rawān*, A living soul. روح طبيعي *rūhi tabīʻī*, The animal spirit. روح مبارك *rūhi mubārak*, A blessed soul. روح معادن *rūhi maʻādin*, Mineral spirit. روح مكرم *rūhi mukarram*, The angel Gabriel. روح نباتي *rūhi nabātī*, Vegetable spirit. *Rawah*, A turning out of the feet (less than فحج *fahaj*). Scattered (birds) returning in the evening (to their nests).

P روح *rūh*, Name of a note in music.

A روحاء *rawhās*, (fem. of اروح) Shallow (dish).

P روح آسوده *rūh-āsūda*, Dead, whose soul rests.

P روح افزا *rūh-afzā*, Increasing the spirits, prolonging life.

A روحاني *rawhānīy*, Good, agreeable, clean and pure (place). *Rūhānīy*, (pl. روحانيون *rūhāniyūn*) Spiritual. Holy, contemplative. Quicksilver. An angel. A fairy.

A روحانية *rūhānīyat*, Spirituality, sanctity.

A روحة *rawhat*, Quiet, repose, ease, tranquillity. Joy. Agreeable (night).

P روخ *rūkh*, The intestines. Bald. Mangy. Name of a plant.

P روخ چكاد *rūkh-chakād*, Bald-headed (man).

A رود *rawd*, (v. n. of راد for رود) Seeking. Going in quest of forage and water. Going and coming, moving to and fro. Soft, gentle (breeze). *Rūd*, A slow, easy pace. علي رود Softly! gently!

A رؤد *rusd*, (pl. ارآد *arsād*) A beautiful young woman. The root of the beard.

P رود *rūd*, (by some *rod*) A river, torrent, flowing water. The Oxus. Intestines, gut. The string of a musical instrument. A bow-string. Song, cheerfulness, jovial conversation, convivial mirth. Vocal or instrumental music. A son or daughter. A beautiful brunette. A comely and amiable youth. A plucked bird. A sheep stripped of its wool. رود خيزان *rūdi khezān*, A torrent. رود مصر *rūdi misr*, The river of Egypt, the Nile.

P رودا *rodā*, A bow-string. A gut. A branch.

P رودابه *rūdāba*, Name of the mother of Rustam. Name of a fort.

P روداد *rū-dād*, An account of circumstances, narrative, statement of a case.

P رو دادن *rū dādan*, To happen.

P رودار *rū-dār*, A man of rank or dignity.

P روداري *rū-dārī*, Rank, dignity. Flattery.

A رودان *rawadān*, (v. n. of راد for رود) Gadding up and down amongst neighbours (a woman).

P رود آور *rūd-āwar*, A river's bed. A river.

P رود آورد *rūd-āward*, Branches of trees, straws, &c., carried down by a stream.

P رودبار *rūd-bār*, A large river. A river in a valley, a channel formed by the torrent; a place where many streams run. The bank of a river. Name of a country, and of a city.

A رؤدة *rusdat*, Gentleness, slowness. *Rus* or *rasudat*, A handsome girl. *Rasudat*, Root of the beard.

P رودجامه *rūd-jāma*, A lute.

P رودچكاد *rūd-chakād*, Bald (man), bare.

P رودخانه *rūd-khāna*, A river's bed or channel.

P رودزن *rūd-zan*, A harper. رودزن فلك *rūd-zani falak*, (Minstrel of the sky) The planet Venus.

P رود زم *rūd jam*, Name of a river.

A رودس *rūdis*, The island of Rhodes.

P رودساز *rūd-sāz*, A musician.

A رودك *rawdak*, Comely, blooming (youth).

P رودك *rūdak*, A rivulet. A small musical instrument. *Rodak*, Name of an animal found in Tartary, of whose skin fur-garments are made.

A رودكة *rawdakat*, (v. n. of رودك Q) Beautifying. Small camels or sheep.

P رود كشف *rūd-kashf*, Name of a note in music.

P رودگان *rūdagān*, (pl. of روده) Intestines.

P رودگانها *rūdagānhā*, Bowels, viscera, intestines.

P رودگاني *rūdagānī*, Bowels. *Rūdagāne*, One gut.

P رودگر *rūdgar*, A musician. A maker of fiddle-strings.

P رودلاخ *rūdlākh*, A place abounding in rivers.

P رودن *rūdan*, (or رودنگ *rūdang*) Madder.

A رودنة *rawdanat*, A being wearied.

P روده *rūda*, A gut, an intestine. The string of an instrument. The fundament of a quadruped. Any thing steeped in hot water. A river. روده بين *rūda-bīn*, Inspecting the entrails, *i.e.* a diviner, augur. روده كردن *rūda kardan*, To pour hot water (amongst flour when baking; or to take feathers off birds by scalding).

P روده كرده *rūda-karda*, Stripped of its feathers (a bird), or of its wool (a lamb).

P رودين *rūdīn*, Pertaining to a river.

A روذة *rawzat*, (v. n. of راذ for روذ) Moving to and fro, going and coming.

A روذس *rūzis*, The island of Rhodes.

A روذق *rawzak*, (pl. رواذق *rawāzik*) Stripped, flayed (skin). A kid ready for roasting, the hair having been scalded off. Meat cooked and mixed with pot-herbs and other seasonings.

A روذكة *rawzakat*, (pl. رواذك *rawāzik*) A small camel or sheep.

A روذمة *rawzamat*, A pace of a Tartar horse.

A روذنة *rawzanat*, The being wearied.

P رورمنا *rormanā*, (in zand) A pomegranate.

A روز *rawz*, (v. n. of راز for روز) Assaying, proving. Examining, considering, pondering. Weighing any thing heavy. Residing on one's estate and improving it. Wishing for and begging a thing.

P روز *roz*, A day. روز اميد و بيم *rozi umed u bīm*, The day of hope and fear, *i.e.* the day of judgment. (Synonymous to which are the following words employed with روز *roz*, Day: باز *bāz* خواست *khwāst*, Investigation; پسين *pasīn*, Final; جزا *jazā*, Retribution; داد *dād*, Justice; درنگ *dirang*, Delay; شمار *shumār*, Reckoning; قيامت *kiyāmat*, Resurrection; مظالم *mazālim*, Grievances; and محشر *mahshar*, General assembly). Daytime. The sun. The face. Good fortune. Opportunity. The vernal equinox. Power, strength. Courage. Open, manifest, clear, evident. در روز فيروز مسرّت اندوز *dar rozi fīrozi masarrat-andoz*, In a happy hour, on a day of victory and joy. روز استفتاح *rozi istiftāh*, A happy day. روزبازار *rozi bāzār*, Market-day. A brisk market. The resurrection. روز با عيش *roz bā ʻaysh*, Good day (to you). روز بيگاه *rozi bīgāh*, An hour or two before sun-set. روز تاب *rozi tāb*, A hot day. روز تحويل *rozi tahwīl*, The day after the sun enters a sign of the zodiac. روز تنگ *rozi tang*, The day of battle. روز جك *rozi jak*, (or چك *chak*) The 15th of the month Shaʻbān. روز جواني *rozi jawānī*, The season of youth. روز جشن *rozi jashn*, A festival. روز حسين *rozi husayn*, The day after the death of Husayn. روز خوش *rozi khwush*, The season of youth. روز ساختن *roz sākhtan*, To be ashamed. روز سياه *rozisiyāh*, (or سيه *siyah*) A day of mourning, trouble, or vexation. روز عزلت *rozi ɛuzlat*, A day of retirement, *i.e.* a fast-day. روز عيد *rozi ɛīd*, A festival-day. روز فراخ *rozi farākh*, Day-break. روز كشش *rozi kushish*, A day of slaughter. روز كوشش *rozi koshish*, Day of battle. روزگذراندن *roz guzrāndan*, To flatter, time-serve; to benefit. روز مهر *rozi mihr*, Sunday. روز ميدان *rozi maydān*, Day of battle. روز ننگ و نام *rozi nang u nām*, A day of battle, strife, or contention. A day of mirth and festivity. روز ننگ و نبرد *rozi nang u nabard*, A day of battle. روز و شب *roz u shab*, Day and night. روز هرمزد *rozi hurmuzd*, Thursday. نوروز *nawroz*, New year's day; the vernal equinox.

P روز افزاي *roz-afzāy*, Increasing the days; name of the fourth month in the æra of Yazdagird.

P روز افزون *roz-afzūn*, Increasing daily (in glory), a royal title, implying august, fortunate. A benediction, friendly congratulation. Alms.

P روز افكن *roz-afkan*, A tertian ague. The sun.

P روزان *rozān*, Days. روزان و شبان *rozān u shabān*, Days and nights.

P روزانه *rozāna*, Daily. Daily pay, pension.

P روز بازي *roz-bāzī*, Time. Fortune.

P روزبان *rozbān*, A porter, especially at the royal gates. A footman, mace-bearer. A protector, patron. An executioner.

P روز بروز *roz ba roz*, Day after day, from day to day, every day.

P روز به *roz bih*, Fortunate days, happy times. Improving daily.

P روز پيكر *roz-paykar*, Upright, honest, sincere. Enlightened.

P روز خسپ *roz-khusp*, Lazy, idle, inattentive.

P روز خسپ شبخيز *roz-khuspi shab-khez*, A pretended devotee. A night-robber.

P روز خون *roz-khūn*, An unexpected assault by robbers in the daytime.

P روز دار *roz-dār*, A day-labourer.

P روز ديده *roz-dīda*, Aged, having seen days.

P روزرانه *rozrāna*, A market-town. An exile.

P روزرخ *roz-rukh*, Clearness, freshness, ruddiness of face.

P روز روز *roz roz*, From day to day, daily.

P روزكور *roz-kūr*, Purblind, not seeing by day.

P روزگار *rozgār*, The world. Fortune. Time, season, an age. Vanity. Wind, air. Slaughter. Service, employ, situation. Occasion. Earning. روزگار پيغمبر *rozgāri paygham-bar*, The time of the apostle. روزگار بردن *rozgār burdan*, To pass one's time. To live. روزگار گذشتن *rozgār guzashtan*, To subsist, live. روزگار ديده *rozgār-dīda*, One who has seen the world, experienced.

P روزگار رفتگان *rozgār-raftagān*, Unfortunates.

P روزگاري *rozgārī*, Worldly. Vain. Aerial. One who earns. *Rozgāre*, Some time.

P روزگانه *rozgāna*, Pay, pension. Fore part of the head.

P روزگذار *roz-guzār*, Sufficient for the day.

P روزگرد *roz-gard*, (Turning the day) The sun.

P روزگردك *roz-gardak*, The sunflower.

P روزمرة *roz-marra*, Daily conversation, common discourse. Daily allowance. Always, daily.

P روزمه *roz-mah*, Date, day of the month.

P روز ميان *roz miyān*, The third day, every other day.

P روزن *rawzan* or *rozan*, A window. An aperture in the middle of the house for allowing the smoke to escape, a louvre-window. (in fortification) A loophole, an embrasure.

P روزنامچه *roz-nāmcha*, (or روزنامه *roz-nāma*) A book of the day, *i.e.* An ephemeris, calendar, almanack; a journal of daily transactions or expense; a daily account-book or journal; a daily list, account, or report.

A روزنة *rawzanat*, A window.

P روزندن *rūzandan*, To increase. To ooze.

P روزنك سر *rawzanak-sar*, The soft part of the head. *Rūzank-sar*, The hoopoo.

P روزنه *rawzana*, A window, or any hole in the wall for receiving light. (in fortification) A loophole.

P روزنه سر *rūzana-sar*, The hoopoo.

P روزة *roza*, Fasting. A fast. A fast-day. Daily allowance. Any thing additional over the hose سرموزة *sar-mūza*. روزة خوردن *roza khwurdan*, To avoid keeping fast. روزة داشتن *roza dāshtan*, To fast. روزهٔ عزلت *rozaɪ ɛuzlat*, A fast of 24 hours. روزة كشودن *roza kushūdan*, To breakfast (especially in the month of Ramazān, when it is not permitted till the evening). روزهٔ مريم *rozaɪ maryam*, Silence. Death.

P روزة دار *roza-dār*, Who fasts or keeps Lent.

P روزة راة *roza-rāh*, A day's journey.

P روزة كشا *roza-kushā*, Breakfasting.

P روزة كشائي *roza-kushāɪī*, Breakfast.

P روزي *rozī*, Fortune, lot, portion. Goods, chattels. Monthly wages. Provision, daily food. Sustenance. Activity. *Roze*, One day. A certain day. روزي چند *roze chand*, Several days.

P روزي افزاي *rozī-afzāy*, Name of the fourth month according to the æra of Yazdagird.

P روزيانه *roziyāna*, Daily. Daily allowance. A journal, pension or pay-book. An ephemeris.

P روزي خواران *rozī-khwārān*, Living creatures.

P روزيدن *rozīdan*, To sweat out. To increase.

P روزي ده *rozī-dih*, (or روزي رسان *rozī-rasān*) Giver of daily bread (an epithet of God).

P روزي كناد *rozi kunād*, God prosper (him)!

P روزينه *rozīna*, Daily pay, a pension. A daily allowance granted to Brahmans, fakeers, poor or infirm persons, to be enjoyed during their lifetime.

P روزينه دار *rozīna-dār*, One who receives a daily allowance.

A روس *raws*, (v. n. of راس for روس) Walking with a haughty air. Carrying off (as a torrent does rubbish). Saying, doing, or making good. Eating much. روس سوء *rawsu sūɪin*, A wicked man.

P روس *ros*, Russia. A fox. An elk. Walking pompously. Outstripping, leaving behind.

A رؤس *ruɪus*, (pl. of رأس *raɪs*) Heads. Chiefs, princes, leaders. رؤس جبال *ruɪusi jibāl*, Mountain-tops. رؤس مرائس *ruɪus marāɪis*, Strong heads.

A رؤّس *rūwas*, A horse that bites the heads of the others in running, or that keeps ahead in fleetness. (A camel) lean except about the head.

A رؤساء *ruɪasāɪ*, (pl. of رئيس) Princes, nobles.

P رو ساختن *rū sākhtan*, To blush, be ashamed.

P روس انگرده *ros-angurda*, Foxgrapes.

A روسب *rawsab*, Misfortune.

P روسپي *rūspī*, A courtesan. A cuckold.

P روسپي بارگي *rūspī-bāragī*, Whoredom.

P روسپي بارة *rūspī-bāra*, A whoremonger.

P روسپي زادة *rūspī-zāda*, Son of a whore.

P روستا *rostā*, (or روستاي *rostāy*) A market-town, village, cantonment of Turkomān huts. A market-place. Any inhabited place, cultivated country, with towns and villages. An inhabitant of such a place. An assemblage, concourse of people. A corn-field. بي روستاي عيد *bī rostāy ɛīd*, Mirth, festivity without noise or rusticity.

P روستاخيز *rūstā-khez*, Day of the resurrection.

P روستار *rūstār* or *rostār*, A villager.

P روستا زادة *rūstā-zāda* or *rostā-zāda*, Village-born. A peasant, a rustic.

P روستائي *rūstāɪī* or *rostāɪī*, A villager. A country-life, rural life.

P روستخيز *rūstakhez*, The day of judgment.

P روستم *rūstam*, The Persian Hercules.

A روسختج *rūsakhtaj*, Antimony.

A روسم *rawsam*, A mark, a vestige. A seal for marking wine-casks. A large wooden seal with which corn in the granary is stamped. Any thing which gives a polish to gold coin. An institute, ordinance, canon. A misfortune.

P روسي *rosī*, A little. A cup of wine. A hero. A Russian. A kind of stuff.

P روسياه *rū-siyāh*, Black (in face, mind, or name). Criminal. Unfortunate, mean, abject. An Ethiopian, a black Arabian.

P روسياهي *rū-siyāhī*, Blackness of face. Disgrace. Sin, criminality.

A روش *rawsh*, (v. n. of راش for روش) Eating much: also little. Enfeebling in the loins (disease).

P روش *rosh*, Wicked, bad-tempered, inhuman. A command. (for روشن *roshan*) Light, splendid. *Ravish*, Motion, going, coming. Walking, outstripping, passing by. Way, mode, manner. Order, proceeding, custom, institution, rite, law, rule, regulation. Avenue, walk, path, way, passage. روش احمد داشتن *ravishi ahmad dāshtan*, To keep the precepts of Muhammad, or the laudable way.

A روّش *rawwash*, Hairy. Hairy about the ears and face (man).

P روشان *roshān*, Light, clear, luminous.

P روشانه *roshāna*, A proper name, Roxana.

A روشم *rawsham*, An engraved block of wood with which they seal wheat in the granary.

A روشن *rawshan*, A window.

P روشن *roshan*, Light, splendid, luminous, bright, serene, resplendent. Clear, evident, manifest, conspicuous. Illustrious, celebrated. Neither thick nor thin, moderate. روشن کردن *roshan kardan*, To clear. گلو روشن کردن *gulū roshan kardan*, To clear the throat. وزير روشن ضمير *wazīri roshan-zamīr*, A vazīr of an enlightened genius. روشن راي *roshan-rāy*, Of a serene mind (a sister of Aurangzeb).

P روشنا *roshanā*, Light, splendour. A marcasite or fire-stone. *Roshan* or *roshanā*, was the name of one of the queens of Alexander the Great, called by the Greeks Roxana.

P روشناس *rū-shināṣ*, Conspicuous, celebrated, honourable, respectable. An acquaintance, one whose face is known, a cap-acquaintance. روشناسان *rū-shināsān*, Chiefs (of a kingdom or city). Stars.

P روشناسي *rū-shināsī*, Acquaintance.

P روشنائي *roshanāī*, Luminous, affording light. Light. The marcasite or fire-stone. Splendour. Ink. An eye-salve.

P روشن بصر *roshan-basar*, Clear-sighted.

P روشنچراغ *roshan-chirāgh*, A note in music.

P روشندان *rawshandān*, A window-frame. *Roshandān*, A skylight. A lamp.

P روشن دل *roshan-dil*, Of an enlightened mind.

P روشن دماغ *roshan-damāgh*, Snuff.

P روشن قياس *roshan-kiyās*, Sagacious, acute.

P روشنك *roshank*, Name of the wife of Alexander. A certain drug. A torch-bearer.

P روشنگر *roshangar*, A polisher, furbisher.

P روشني *roshanī*, Light. Law. A trace. Bright steel. روشنيء صبح *roshanīi subh*, Light of morn.

P روشنيگاه *roshanī-gāh*, A lightsome place.

A روص *raws*, (v. n. of راص for روص) From being a fool, becoming wise.

A روض *rawz*, A quantity of water, half a leathern bottle full. (pl. of روضة *rawzat*) Kitchen or flower-gardens. Meadows, meads, lawns.

A روضات *rawzāt*, (pl. of روضة) Gardens: meads.

A روضة *rawzat*, (pl. روض *rawz*, رياض *riyāz*, and ريضان *rīzān*) A kitchen or flower-garden. A meadow, pleasant place, lawn. Paradise. The tomb of a learned or pious man, a mausoleum. Water just covering the bottom of a lake or cistern. A place in sand or grass where water lodges. Half a leathern bottle full. Water collected in trenches.

P روضهٔ باغ رفيع *rawzaï bāghi rafīʿ*, The gardens of paradise. A روضهٔ تركيب *rawzaï tarkīb*, The human body. P روضهٔ خوب *rawzaï khūb*, Heaven, paradise. روضهٔ دوزخ بار *rawzaï dozakh-bār*, A bright, flaming sword. A روضهٔ رضوان *rawzaï rizwān*, The garden of paradise. P روضهٔ فيروزه رنگ *rawzaï fīroza-rang*, The sky.

P روضه رنگ *rawza-rang*, Of a green colour.

A روط *rawt*, (v. n. of راط for روط) Fleeing unto the hills (a wild beast). (from P رود *rod*) A river.

A روطة *rūtat*, Name of a town in Spain.

A روع *rawʿ*, (v. n. of راع for روع) Pleasing. Astonishing, surprising. Serving, benefiting. Terrifying. Fearing. Terror. *Rūʿ*, The heart (as the seat of fear). The understanding. *Rawaʿ*, Beauty. Astonishment, surprise.

A روعاء *rawʿāʾ*, (fem. of اروع *arwaʿ*) Handsome and engaging. Cunning, sly (mare or camel).

A روعة *rawʿat*, (v. n. of راع for روع) Terrifying. Fearing. Pleasing. Serving, benefiting. Dread, terror, alarm, fear. Somewhat of comeliness: grace.

A روعي جعار *rūʿī jaʿāri*, A word of contempt.

A روغ *rawgh*, (or روغان *rawaghān*) (v. n. of راغ for روغ) Lying in wait for a fox (a man). Deceiving a man (a fox). Being cunning as a fox. Stealing off privately, skulking. Trotting (a fox). Turning towards, seeking a pretext against. Turning aside from, swerving. Inclining to.

P روغ *rūgh*, An eructation, a belch.

P روغن *rawghan*, Oil. Butter. Clarified butter, ghee. Fat, grease. روغن بيدانجير *rawghani bīd-anjīr*, Castor-oil. روغن تلخ *rawghani talkh*, Common oil, expressed from rape or mustard-seed. روغن خالص *rawghani khālis*, Pure butter. روغن خود *rawghani khwud*, One's religious opinions. روغن خوش *rawghani khwush*, Sesame-oil. روغن داغ *rawghani dāgh*, Melted butter. روغن زرد *rawghani zard*, Butter. روغن زيت *rawghani zayt*, Olive-oil. روغن ساده *rawghani sāda*, Melted butter. روغن ستور *rawghani sutūr*, Animal-grease. روغن سبز *rawghani sabz*, Oil of roses. روغن سياه *rawghani siyāh*, Oil. روغن كنجد *rawghani kunjad*, Oil of sesame (a kind of grain). روغن گاو *rawghani gāw*, Ghee. روغن گلاب *rawghani gulāb*, Oil of roses. Ambergris. روغن گوشت *rawghani gosht*, Fat of meat. روغن مصري *rawghani misrī*, Oil of balsam. روغن مغز *rawghani maghz*, (Brain-oil) Intellect, judgment.

P روغناس *roghnās*, Madder.

P روغن دار *rawghan-dār*, (Meat) dressed with oil.

P روغندان *rawghandān*, An oil-bottle. An unguent-box.

P روغن رفته *rawghan-rafta*, (Whose oil is spent) One whose years and prosperity are ended.

P روغن زبان *rawghan-zabān*, Oily-tongued.

P روغن زباني *rawghan-zabānī*, Cajolery.

P روغن فروش *rawghan-farosh*, A vender of oil. A seller of butter.

P روغن كده *rawghan-kada*, An oil-mill.

P روغنگر *rawghangar*, A butter-maker or seller. An oil-presser.

P روغنگري *rawghangarī*, Oil-making.

P روغني *rawghanī*, A kind of sweetmeat dressed with butter. Any thing fried in butter. Greasy, oily. An oil-presser. A seller of butter.

P روغنين *rawghanīn*, Fried in butter.

P روغنينه *rawghanīna*, Bread baked with butter.

A روف *rawf*, (v. n. of راف for روف) Resting. Forgiving. Shewing pity and compassion. Kindness, benevolence. Rest.

A رؤف *raʾuf*, God. Merciful, benign.

P روف *rūf*, (in Samarkand) Seed of fleawort.

P روفانيدن *rūfānīdan*, To clean the teeth.

A روفة *rawfat*, Mercy, benevolence.

P روفتن *rūftan*, To sweep, to wipe, to rub.

A روق *rawk*, (v. n. of راق for روق) Being clear, bright (wine). Giving pleasure, striking with admiration, appearing beautiful. Being pleased. Excelling in (beauty, goodness, &c.). (pl. ارواق *arwāk*) The horn of an ox or sheep. A part of the night. The bottom part, the lower story of a house. The flower of youth. The first or best part of any thing. Life, age. A handsome horse that pleases the beholder. A vail. A curtain before a door. A portico. A tent of goat's hair. A hunter's lurking-place. A hero that is unassailable. Design, purpose. Action. A lord. Clear, pure (water). Pleasing, agreeable. Surprise, admiration, pleasure. Expiring breath. A crowd. Sincere friendship. Augmentation, addition, increase. Substitute, equivalent. A body, a carcase. Name of a village in جرجان *jurjān*. روق الفرس *rawku'l faras*, A lance couched by a cavalier between the ears of his horse (forming a kind of portico). اكل روقه *akala rawkahu*, He has eaten his youth, *i.e.* he is stricken in years. داهية ذات روقين *dāhiyatun zāt rawkayn*, A heavy calamity. *Rūk*, (pl. of اروق *arwak*) Those whose front upper teeth overhang the lower. (pl. of روق *rawk*) Porticoes. Handsome youths. (pl. of رواق *riwāk* or *ruwāk*) Tents of goats' hair. Porticoes. *Rawak*, The projection of the front upper beyond the under teeth.

A روقاء *rawkāʾ*, A horned ewe.

A روقة *rawkat*, Surpassing beauty. *Rūkat*, Handsome, lovely (boy or girl). Any thing little. Any thing fine and fair. (pl. of رائق *rāʾik*) Handsome (boys).

A روكاء *rawkāʾ*, The screech of an owl.

A روكة *rawkat*, A wave. The hoot of an owl.

P روكش *rawkash*, The world. Time, age. *Rūkash*, Any thing whose exterior and interior differ.

P روگاه *rū-gāh*, The upper or best side of a garment. The frontispiece of a book. The hem of a garment. A leader.

P روگردان *rū-gardān*, Face-averted, disobedient.

P روگردانيدن *rū gardānīdan*, To desert.

P روم *rawm*, The bdellium-tree. *Rom*, Hair of

the pubes. *Rūm*, (for روي من *rūyi man*) My face.

A روم *rawm*, (v. n. of رام for روم) Seeking, anxiously desiring. Moving clandestinely, slily, softly. The lobe of the ear. *Rūm*, The lobe of the ear, in which they put rings. Greece, Rome, the Roman empire, Roumelia, Europe, the whole Turkish empire. A Roman. بحر الروم *bahru'r rūm*, The Mediterranean Sea. بلاد روم *bilādi rūm*, The cities, kingdoms, or empire of Greece, or of Europe in general. روم و حبش *rūm u habash*, (metaph.) Night and day. The world.

A رؤم *rasum*, Tame (sheep). Fond of her colt.

P رومال *rū-māl*, (Wiping the face) A handkerchief, towel, napkin, sudary.

P رومالي *rūmālī*, A kind of pigeon. A mode of exercising the arms, by turning the mugdars (clubs used as dumb bells) over the head. A sodomite. A handkerchief worn about the head.

A روماني *rumāniy*, Of a ruby-colour.

P رومائي *rūmāsī*, Roman.

A رومة *rūmat*, Glue.

P رومنا *romnā*, (in zand) The pomegranate.

P رومه *roma*, Hair about the pubes, or body.

P رومي *rūmī*, Roman, Greek, Turkish. A kind of garment. Colour. رومي و زنگي *rūmī u zangī*, Greek and Ethiopian, (metaph.) Night and day.

A رومي *rūmiy*, Greek. The sail of an empty ship.

P روميان *rūmiyān*, (pl. of رومي) Romans: Greeks.

P روميانه *rūmiyāna*, Grecian, Greek fashion.

P رومي بچگان *rūmī-bachagān*, Tears.

A رومية *rūmiyat*, The city of Rome.

A روميّة *rūmiyat*, The city of Rome. Grecian or Roman (lady). Romania or Greece, Turkey. روميّة صغري وارمنيّة كبري *rūmiyasi sughra' wa armaniyasi kubra'*, Asia Minor and Armenia Major.

P رومي خوي *rūmī-khoy*, Fickle, like a Greek.

P رومي زن رعنا *rūmī zan rasnā*, The sun.

P رومينا *rūmīnā*, Polished, cleaned, brightened.

A رون *rawn*, The extremity of a sown field. *Rūn*, (pl. روون *rusūn*) Adversity, rigour, severity.

P رون *rūn*, Cause, reason. *Rawan*, Trial, proof.

A رون *risun*, (pl. of رئة *risat*) Lungs.

P روناس *ronās*, Madder, a red-dyeing root.

A رونة *rūnat*, The greatest part of a thing.

P رونج *rawanj* or *riwanj*, Sheep's chitterlings stuffed with meat and rice.

P رونجو *rawanjo*, A wood-worm.

A روند *riwand*, Rhubarb.

P روندگي *rawandagī*, Rapidity of motion.

P رونده *rūnda*, Fluid, liquid. Thin, soft. Grain fried, and ground with a hand-mill. *Rawanda*, A goer, traveller, passenger. Prepared to go. A custom-house permit. آينده و رونده *āyanda su rawanda*, A comer and goer, traveller. روندگان عالم *rawandagāni sālam*, The planets; namely, Saturn, Jupiter, Mars, sun, Venus, Mercury, and moon.

A روندي *riwandiy*, A seller of rhubarb.

A رونق *rawnak*, Beauty, elegance, grace, splendour, brightness, ornament. رونق السيف *rawnaku's sayf*, The glittering surface of a sword.

A رونقة *rawnakat*, (pl. روانق *rawānik*) Disturbed, discoloured by mud (water).

P رونما *rū-namā*, Shewing the face, appearing. A present made to a bride when she unveils herself.

P رونياس *roniyās*, Madder.

A رؤوب *rusūb*, (v. n. of راب for روب) Becoming thick (milk).

A رووح *ruwūh*, (v.n. of راح for روح) Being at the point of attaining (an object) and feeling satisfaction.

A رؤودة *rasūdat*, A handsome girl. The root of the beard. *Rusūdat*, Gentleness, slowness.

A رؤوس *rasūs*, (A camel) fat only in the head. *Rusūs*, (pl. of رأس *rass*) Heads. Chiefs. علي رؤوس الاشهاد *sala' rusūsi'l ash-hād*, In the presence of witnesses.

A رؤوش *rasūsh*, Weak, feeble in the loins (man). Hairy about the face and ears.

A رؤوف *rasūf*, Compassionate.

A رؤوم *rasūm*, A cade sheep that licks a passenger's garments. Fond of her colt (a she-camel).

A روون *ruwūn*, (pl. of رون) Adversities, distresses.

A روه *rawh*, (v. n. of راه for روه) Being driven over the ground (water).

P روه *rūh*, Good behaviour, purity, sanctity.

P روهبان *rūhbān*, A monk, ascetic, devotee.

P روهن *rohan*, (روهنا *rohinā*, روهينا *rohīnā*, روهني *rohinī*, روهيني *rohīnī*, or روهينيا *rohīniyā*) The finest Indian steel, of which the most excellent swords are made; also the swords made of that steel.

P روهنده *rūhanda*, A flourishing, thriving crop.

P روي *ravī* or *rawī*, A journey, progress. *Rūy*, (often pronounced *rū*) The face, air, mien, aspect, countenance. Surface, appearance, semblance. Edge (of a sword). Hypocrisy. Doubt. Hope. Investigation, or incitement to make inquiry. Path, way. Cause, reason. از چه روي *az chi rūy*, On what account? روي بازگونه داشتن *rūy bāz gūna dāshtan*, To deviate from the right way. در روي آفتاب *dar rūyi āftāb*, Exposed or opposite to the sun. روي آن نداشت *rūyi ān na dāsht*, He had not the face for that, he durst not do it. روي آوردن *rūy āwardan*, To turn the face. روي بردن *rūy burdan*, To turn one's self, to look behind. روي بقا *rūyi bakā*, Solid, steady. Health, soundness. The path of blessedness. روي پاي *rūyi pāy*, The face of the foot, *i.e.* the upper part. The lower part or hollow of the hand. روي تعارف *rūyi tasāruf*, The power of discovering hidden things. روي خاندان *rūyi khāndān*, A most illustrious house. روي دادن *rūy dādan*, To appear, happen, occur. روي داشتن *rūy dāshtan*, To dare. To support, to sustain. To regard, esteem. To tend towards. روي دست *rūyi dast*, A certain manœuvre in wrestling. The back of the hand. روي دل كشادن *rūyi dil kushādan*, To open the heart. روي دل نمودن *rūyi dil namūdan*, To be generous, liberal. روي ديدن *rūy dīdan*, To favour, be partial to. روي زمين *rūyi zamīn*, Surface of the ground. روي كار *rūyi kār*, The front. Near. روي كردن *rūy kardan*, To turn the face or attention. روي كمان *rūyi kamān*, The face of a bow, that part furthest from the archer when he shoots. روي گلگون *rūyi gul-gūn*, A rosy complexion. روي نسل آدم *rūyi nasli ādam*, The noblest of men. Prophets. Rest, repose. روي نمودن *rūy namūdan*, To happen, come to pass. To occur to the mind. To shew the road. بروي يكديگر بيرون آمدن *ba rūyi yakdīgar bīrūn āmadan*, To come forth against one another (in battle). *Roy*, Brass, روي صفر *roy sufr*, Name of a mixed metal.

A روي *riwa'*, (v. n. of روي) Drinking enough. Being green and succulent (a tree). Sweet, wholesome water, by which the thirst may be quenched. Abundance, plentifulness.

A رؤي *rusa'*, (pl. of رؤيا *rusya'*) Visions, dreams. *Rusy*, Intense darkness.

A رويّ *rawiy*, The last letter of a distich, in which all the verses in the same poem terminate. If this letter be ل *lām*, the poem is called قصيدة لاميّة *kasidat lāmiyat*, A poem ending in ل *lām*. (Water) sweet and quenching the thirst. A cloud pouring forth rain in large drops. A full draught. *Rawiy*, The countenance, looks. Elegance of look.

A رؤيّ *rusiy*, A handsome countenance. Elegance of looks.

P رويا *royā*, Growing. Any thing which grows.

A رؤيا *rusya'*, (pl. رؤي *rusa'*) A vision, dream. Intense darkness.

A رؤياء *rusyās*, (pl. رؤي *rusa'*) A dream, vision. تعبير رويا *tasbīri rūyā*, The interpretation of a dream. P رويا ديدن *rūyā dīdan*, To dream.

P رويا روي *rūy-ā-rūy*, Face to face.

A رؤيان *rusyān*, (v.n. of رأي) Seeing, perceiving.

P رويانيدن *royānīdan*, To cause to grow. To produce, bring forth. To excite, stimulate.

A رويبضة *ruwaybizat*, (dim. of رابضة *rābizat*) Mean, contemptible (man).

P روي بند *rūy-band*, A lady's veil.

P روي پوش *rūy-posh*, A lady's veil. Gilded, plated. Any thing whose inside and outside differ.

A رؤية *rusyat*, (v. n. of رأي) Seeing. Thinking, considering. Knowledge, opinion. Sight, vision. Consideration. بغير رؤية *bi ghayr rusyat*, Inconsiderately.

A رويّة *rawiyat*, Careful consideration of any thing. Necessity, any thing necessary to the completion of another; balance of a debt; remainder.

A رويجل *ruwayjil*, (dim. of رجل *rajul* irregularly formed) A little man, a manikin.

A رويحة *rawīhat*, Convenience, ease. Repose. Joy arising from attaining an object.

A رويد *ruwayd*, (dim. of رود *rūd*) A gentle pace. Gentle driving. رويدك *ruwaydak*, Go thou softly. رويدك عمراً *ruwaydaka ɛamran*, Let Amr alone, softly with Amr! رويدكني *ruwaydakanī*, Softly with me! رويدكماني *ruwaydakumānī*, Softly with me, both of you! رويدكموني *ruwaydahumūnī*, Softly with me, all of you! رويدكنني *ruwaydakunnanī*, Softly with me, ye women! ساروا سيرا رويدا *sārū sayran ruwaydan*, They travelled at an easy pace. رويدا *ruwaydan*, Slowly, by degrees.

A رويداء *ruwaydāɛ*, (رويديّة *ruwaydīyat*, or رويدية *ruwaydiyat*) (v. n. 4 of راد for رود) Assisting, favouring. Driving gently. Being benevolent, kind, easy. Going gently.

P روي داد *rūy-dād*, Occurrence, accident. A statement of facts.

P روي داري *rūy-dārī*, Regard, countenance.

P روي دست *rūy-dast*, A trick in wrestling.

P روي دل *rūy-dil*, Affable, smiling.

P رويدن *rawī* or *rawīdan*, To go, travel, walk.

P رويز *rawīz*, Opinion. رويز غالب *rawīzi ghālib*, The prevailing opinion.

P روي زرد *rūy-zard*, Pale-faced, ashamed.

A رويزيّ *ruwayziy*, A mantle or scarf.

P روي سخت *rūy-sakht*, A liniment for tinging the hair and eye-brows black.

P رويش *rūyash*, His, her, or its face.

P روي شناخته *rūy-shinākhta*, (or روي شناس *rūy-shinās*) Conspicuous, respectable.

P روي شناسان *rūy-shināsān*, Acquaintances.

P رويشند *rawīshand*, (in zand and Pāzand) A shield. The head.

P روي شويه *rūy-shūya*, A wash or cosmetic lotion for the face.

A رويغة *ruwayghat*, Stratagem, trick, artifice.

A رويفع *ruwayfiɛ*, Muhammad's servant.

P روي گر *roygar*, A coppersmith, brazier.

P رويمال *rūy-māl*, Wiping the face. A handkerchief, napkin, sudary.

P روبناز *roy-nāz*, (or روبناس) Madder.

P روين *royan*, Madder. *Royin*, Brazen.

P رويندة *royanda*, Growing: what grows.

P روينگ *royang*, Madder.

P روينه *roy-nih*, A tinman, tinker. One who tins brass pots. Any thing made of or overlaid with brass. A red dye. *Rūy-nih*, A veil for the face.

P رويوانه *rūywāna*, A veil, a curtain.

P رويه *rūya*, Facing, towards. Mode, manner. Behaviour. يك رويه *yak rūya*, Single-faced. دو رويه *du rūya*, Double-faced.

A رويئة *rawīɛat*, Careful consideration, mature deliberation.

P روئيدگي *roɛīdagī*, Vegetation, growth.

P روئيدن *roɛīdan*, To grow, increase.

P روئيدنگاه *roɛīdan-gāh*, A place of growth.

P روئيدني *roɛīdanī*, Whatever grows; vegetables.

P روئيده *roɛīda*, Grown up, produced.

P روبين *royīn*, Brazen. Bell-metal. Red, of a red tincture, paint used for the face. Name of a champion of Irān; of a son of Afrāsyāb: of the son of Pirān Visa: also of a country.

P روبين تن *royīn-tan*, (Brazen-body) Name of Isfandyār. Displaced, dismissed. The stomach.

P روبين تني *royīn-tanī*, Dismissal. Abdication.

P روبين چنگ *royīn-chang*, Brazen-clawed.

P روبين خم *royīn-khum*, A brazen drum.

P روبين دژ *royīn-dij*, A brazen drum. Name of a fortress.

P روبين ساز *royīn-sāz*, A coppersmith.

P روبينه تن *royīna-tan*, (Brazen body) Name of Isfandyār. The stomach.

P روبينه خم *royīna-khum*, A brazen drum.

P روبينه مال *royīna-māl*, A noise with the mouth.

P روبينه ناي *royīna-nāy*, A brazen trumpet.

P ره *rah*, A road. Law, rule, custom. Time, turn. A whole, total. Melody. Intellect, genius. (imper. of رستن *rastan*) Escape thou. ره افتادن *rah uftādan*, To attack, rob, plunder. To befal. ره بردن *rah burdan*, To find the road. ره جامه دران *rahi jāma-darān*, Name of one of the notes of the lute (perhaps very thrilling or doleful). ره هوان رفتن *rahi hawān raftan*, To go the way of, or to choose poverty. *Ruh*, A religious life, sanctity.

A ره *rah*, See thou. (for رحمة الله عليه *rahmatu'llāh ɛalayhi*) The mercy of God be upon him!

A رهّ *rahh*, Wide and shallow (dish).

P رها *rahā*, Liberation, escape. Liberated. رها كردن *rahā kardan*, To set free, discharge, dismiss, quit, leave, discard, abandon. رها يافتن *rahā yāftan*, To escape, to be preserved.

A رهاء *rahāɛ*, Wide (woman). A large district. *Rihāɛ*, (v. n. 3 of رها for رهو) Drawing near, approaching. Consenting. (pl. of رهو *rahw*) Aqueducts. الرهاء *ar' ruhāɛ*, Edessa.

A رهاب *rahāb*, (pl. of رهابة *rahābat*) Breast-bones. *Rihāb*, (pl. of رهب *rahb*) Sharp points of spears or arrows.

A رهابة *ruhābat*, (*rahābat*, رهّابة *ruhhābat*, or *rahhābat*) The breast-bone.

A رهابنة *rahābinat*, (رهابين *rahābīn*, or رهبانون *ruhbānūn*) (pl. of رهبان *ruhbān*) Christian monks.

P رهاد *rahād*, A water-course. A traveller. A note in music.

A رهادة *rahādat*, Softness, tenderness.

P رهادن *rahādan*, To set free.

A رهادن *rahādin*, (pl. of رهدن *rahdan*, *rihdun*, *ruhdan*, رهدنة *ruhdunnat*, and رهدون *ruhdūn*) Birds resembling sparrows.

A رهاص *rihās*, (v. n. 3 of رهص) Watching an opportunity of arresting a debtor.

A رهّاص *rahhās*, One who prepares clay or mortar for building. A builder of mud walls.

A رهاط *rihāt*, Household furniture. (pl. ارهطة *arhitat*) A skin whence thongs are cut. (pl. of رهط *raht*) Skins whence thongs are cut.

A رهافة *rahāfat*, (v. n. of رهف) Being thi.

A رهاق *ruhāk* or *rihāk*, About (a hundred).

A رهام *rahām*, Lean flocks. *Rihām*, (pl. of رهمة *rihmat*) Small, gentle (rains). *Ruhām*, Numerous, copious. A great number. Timid (bird, in opposition to a falcon or similar hunting-bird).

P رهام *ruhām*, One of the twelve champions.

A رهان *rihān*, (v. n. 3 of رهن) Betting at a horse-race. (pl. of رهن *rahn*) Pawns, pledges.

P ره انجام *rah-anjām*, A complete travelling-apparatus. A horse. A courier, messenger. ره انجام روحاني *rah-anjāmi rūhānī*, The animal whereon Muhammad is said to have ridden to heaven on the night called معراج *miɛrāj*. A quiet, tranquil soul.

P رهانيدن *rahānīdan*, To set at liberty, let out of the hand (a horse or bird). To snatch away.

P رهاو *rahāv*, A traveller by water. An aqueduct, a canal.

P ره آور *rah-āwar*, A traveller. *Rah-āwar*, (or ره آورد *rah-āward*) An elegant present (brought on returning from a journey).

P رهاوي *rahāwī*, Name of a note in music.

A رهاويّ *ruhāwiy*, Of the city of رهاء (Edessa).

P رهايش *rahāyish*, Freedom, escape, liberation.

A رهائن *rahāɛin*, (pl. of رهينة) Pledges, hostages.

P رهائي *rahāɛī*, Dismission, liberation, deliverance. Divorce. Acquittal, discharge, freedom, release, escape, relief. رهائي دادن *rahāɛī dādan*, To give liberty or escape, to release. رهائي يافتن *rahāɛī yāftan*, To obtain deliverance, to escape.

P رهائي بخش *rahāɛī bakhsh*, Giver of liberty.

P رهائي جا *rahāɛī-jā*, A place of escape or deliverance, a refuge.

A رهب *rahb*, (pl. رهاب *rihāb*) The sharp point of spear or arrow. A lean she-camel. A tall camel. *Rahab*, A sleeve. *Rahab*, *rahb*, *ruhb*, (رهبان *ruhbān* or *rahabān*) (v. n. of رهب) Fearing, revering.

A رهباء *rahbāɛ* or *ruhbāɛ*, Fear.

P رهبان *rahbān*, One who guards the way. *Ruhbān*, Pious (said to be derived from ره *ruh*, Sanctity, and بان *bān*, an affix denoting Keeper).

A رهبان *ruhbān*, (pl. رهابين *rahābīn*, رهابنة *rahābinat*, and رهبانون *ruhbānūn*) A monk. (pl. of راهب *rāhib*) Monks, Christian priests.

P رهبان خانه *ruhbān-khāna*, A monastery.

A رهبانيّة *rahbānīyat* or *ruhbānīyat*, A monastic life, monkery, monkish practices, such as self-castration, wearing of chains round the neck, or putting on of sackcloth. لا رهبانيّة في الاسلام *lā rahbānīyata fi'l islām*, There is no monasticism in Islām.

A رهبة *rahbat*, (v. n. of رهب) Fearing. Embracing a monastic life. Monkery, monachism.

P رهبر *rah-bar*, A way-guide, escort. Demonstration, proof. لشكر ظفر رهبر *lashkari zafar-rahbar*, A victorious army, an army guided to victory.

P رهبري *rah-barī*, Guidance, direction, leading.

رهبري كردن *rahbarī kardan*, To guide.

A رهبل *rahbal*, Unintelligible speech.

A رهبلة *rahbalat*, A particular kind of pace.

A رهبوت *rahabūt*, (or رهبوتى *rahabūta'*) Fear.

A رهبى *rahba'* or *ruhba'*, Fear.

A رهج *rahj* or *rahaj*, Dust. Tumult. Rainless clouds.

A رهجوج *rahjūj*, Soft, delicate.

A رهجيج *rihjīj*, Weak. Soft, delicate.

A رهد *rahd* or *rahad*, A rubbing violently.

P رهدار *rah-dār*, Toll-collector. Highwayman.

A رهدل *rahdal*, Weak, silly, foolish. *Rahdal*, *rihdil*, or *ruhdul*, A kind of bird.

A رهدن *rahdan*, *rihdan*, or *ruhdan*, (pl. رهادن *rahādin*) Pusillanimous, base. Foolish. A kind of Mecca-sparrow.

A رهدنة *rahdanat*, Delay. Detention, let, hindrance. A turning round, going in a circle. *Rahdanat* or *ruhdunnat*, A kind of Mecca-sparrow.

A رهدون *ruhdūn*, A Mecca-sparrow. A liar.

A رهراه *rahrāh*, Wide and shallow (dish). *Rahrāh*, (or رهروه *ruhrūh*) Soft, white (body).

P رهرو *rah-rav*, A traveller: follower: sectary.

P رهروان *rah-ravān*, (pl. of رهرو *rah-rav*) Travellers. رهروان ازل *rah-ravāni azal*, Religious students. رهروان راه اخرت *rah-ravāni rāhi akhirat*, Travellers in the right road to heaven. رهروان سحر *rah-rawāni sahar*, Those who watch and pray during the night. رهروان طريقت *rah-ravāni tarīkat*, Followers of any order. The four elements. رهروان گردون *rah-ravāni gardūn*, The planets.

P ره روي *rah-ravī*, Gait, march, pace, walk.

A رهره *rahrah*, Soft and white (body). Wide and shallow (dish).

A رهرهة *rahrahat*, (v. n. of رهره Q) Spreading (a table) from liberality. A softness, whiteness, and beauty of the colour of the body.

A رهز *rahz*, (or رهزان *rahazān*) (v. n. of رهز) Moving one's self, wriggling. Motion, agitation.

P رهزن *rah-zan*, A highway-robber.

P رهزني *rah-zanī*, Highway-robbery. رهزني كردن *rah-zanī kardan*, To rob on the highway.

A رهس *rahs*, (v. n. of رهس) Trampling, treading violently under foot.

P ره شاه *rah-shāh*, A main road, royal road.

A رهشة *ruhshat*, (or رهشوشة *ruhshūshat*) Liberality accompanied with modesty.

A رهشوش *ruhshūsh*, Liberal and modest. Abounding in milk (a camel).

P رهشه *rahsha*, Sesame-flour mixed up with honey and milk.

P رهشي *rahshī*, Sesame-meal.

A رهص *rahs*, (v. n. of رهص) Pressing, squeezing. Dunning continually (a creditor). Laying the first row of stones in a wall, building (a wall) with mud. Vehement pressure; a hard bite. Reproof. Incitement to haste. *Rihs*, The lowest row of stones in a wall. A mass of clay or mortar for building. *Rahas*, (v. n. of رهص) Being lamed in the frog by a stone (a horse).

A رهصة *rahsat*, The friction or wearing away of a hoof by a stone.

A رهط *raht*, (v. n. of رهط) Devouring voraciously by large mouthsful. (pl. ارهط *arhut*, اراهط *arāhit*, ارهاط *arhāt*, and اراهيط *arāhīt*) A family or tribe of men (without women) under ten. (pl. رهاط *rihāt*) A kind of petticoat of leather reaching to the knees, worn by girls and sometimes by women (the rest of the body naked) slashed at the sides and bottom for the conveniency of walking. An enemy. ذووا رهط *zawū rahtin*, Assembled together. *Rahat*, A family or tribe of men (without women) under ten.

A رهطاء *ruhatā*, (or رهطة *ruhatat*) The hole through which the jerboa throws up the earth.

A رهطى *rahta'*, Name of a bird.

A رهف *rahf*, (v. n. of رهف) Whetting (a sword). *Rahaf*, (v. n. of رهف) Being thin.

A رهق *rahak*, (v. n. of رهق) Approaching, following, entering, being near. Touching. Adhering. Keeping close behind so as nearly to tread on the heels. Covering, darkening. Hastening. Lying. Overspreading. Madness, levity, folly, ignorance. Haste, velocity. Iniquity, oppression. Transgression of the law. The commission of a forbidden act. Compulsion to attempt what is beyond one's power.

A رهقى *rahaka'*, Quickness of pace.

A رهك *rahk*, (v. n. of رهك) Grinding coarsely betwixt two stones, bruising, braying hard. Fatiguing by excessive venery. Staying in one place. A good work.

A رهكة *rahkat*, Weakness. *Rahakat*, A weak she-camel. *Rahakat* or *ruhakat*, A worthless fellow.

P ره كشاي *rah-kushāy*, Opening a road.

P رهگذار *rah-guzār*, A pass, passage, road, the meeting of two or more roads. A traveller. A guard, patrole, watch.

P رهگذر *rah-guzar*, A traveller. An accident, event.

P رهگذري *rah-guzarī*, A pass, a passage. A meeting of two or more roads.

P ره گشاي *rah-gushāy*, Name of the 17th day of the month according to the æra of Yazdagird.

P ره گوي *rah-goy* or *gūy*, A singer, musician.

P ره گير *rah-gīr*, A traveller.

A رهل *rahal*, (v. n. of رهل) Shaking, being loose and flabby (flesh). Swelling, being inflated (without disease). Yellow water accompanying the fœtus. *Rahil*, Loose, soft, and tremulous (flesh). *Rihal*, A thin cloud.

A رهمان *rahamān*, A swinging from side to side in the pace of a camel.

A رهمة *rihmat*, (pl. رهم *riham* and رهام *rihām*) Gentle rain, small and incessant.

A رهمج *rahmaj*, Large, spacious.

A رهمسة *rahmasat*, (v. n. of رهمس Q) Concealing. Meditating an oblique (injury).

A رهن *rahn*, (v. n. of رهن) Pledging, giving in pawn, depositing. Tying (the tongue). Being firm, established, and perennial. Establishing, fixing, rendering perpetual. (pl. رهان *rihān*, رهون *ruhūn*, رهن *ruhun*, and رهين *rahīn*) A pledge, pawn. A hostage. رهن مال *rihnu mālin*, A steward of an estate. *Ruhun*, (pl. of رهن *rahn*) Pledges.

A رهنامج *rahnāmaj*, (from P رهنامه *rah-nāma*) A mariner's chart. A road-book.

P ره نشين *rah-nishīn*, A way-side beggar. A houseless traveller. A postman, courier. A highway-robber. A toll-collector.

P رهنما *rah-namā*, A guide, pilot, escort. هادىء حق و رهنماي سبل *hādīi hak u rah-namāyi subul*, The guide to truth, and the director to the way of righteousness (an epithet of Muhammad). رهنماي لشكر *rah-namāyi lashkar*, An army-guide. بي رهنما *bī rah-namā*, Without a guide.

P رهنماي *rah-namāy*, A road-guide.

P رهنمائي *rah-namāī*, Conduct, guidance.

P رهنمون *rah-namūn*, A guide, pilot, escort.

P رهنموني *rah-namūnī*, Guidance, escort.

P ره نورد *rah-naward*, A horse. Swift of foot (man or beast). Any person or thing which rolls along the road. A beggar.

A رهو *rahw*, (v. n. of رها for رهو) Going softly. Standing, sitting, or going wide, straddling. Being kind and easy. Becoming calm (the sea). Rest. A calm. (pl. رهاء *rihā*) An aqueduct to a town. A furrow, ditch, canal, pipe, or any water-course. High ground. Low ground in which water collects. A crowd of men. A kind of bird, a crane. The expansion of a bird's wings. The space between the legs when straddling. A way round a market, by the sides of which sit the venders of commodities. A woman wide and roomy.

P رهو *ruhū*, Custom, rite, law, institute. Trace, mark, vestige. *Ruhū* or *rahū*, Name of a mountain in Ceylon, upon which Adam is said to have alighted when turned out of Paradise.

P رهوا *rahwā*, A swift, ambling horse.

A رهواج *rahwāj*, Easy-going (horse).

A رهوار *rahwār*, An ambling, easy-going nag, a high-blooded horse, a roadster. سمند رهوار *samandi rahwār*, A swift horse.

P رهواري *rahwārī*, The easy pace of a horse.

A رهوة *rahwat*, High ground. Low ground where water collects. Gutters, kennels, water-courses.

A رهوج *rahūj*, Weak, tender, soft.

A رهوجة *rahwajat*, Easy pace of a horse.

A رهودية *rahwadiyat*, Favour, kindness. Gentleness, softness. Assistance, aid.

P رهور *rahwar*, A traveller. An easy-going nag.

A رهوس *rahwas*, A glutton.

A رهوق *rahūk*, Swift, wide-stepped (she-camel).

A رهوك *rahwak*, Fat (kid or doe). Delicate (youth).

A رهوكة *rahwakat*, (v. n. of رهوك Q) Being moved. Walking with a rolling pace, shaking. A laxity in the joints from walking.

A رهوم *rahūm*, Lean (sheep). (A man) who forms an opinion without proper inquiry. Weak in one's actions and opinions.

A رهون *ruhūn*, (v. n. of رهن) Being lean. Being firm, fixed, lasting. (pl. of رهن *rahn*) Pledges.

A رهوي *rahwa'*, Wide, roomy (woman).

P رهي *rahī*, A slave. This person. A traveller.

P رهياب *rah-yāb*, One who discovers a way, or a new mode of doing any thing.

A رهياة *rahyaʼat*, (v. n. of رهيا Q) Being weak in mind or counsel. Being languid, debilitated, impotent. Planning any work and setting about it in earnest. Putting on a load without tying it fast. Being driven about and threatening rain (a cloud). Weakness. Delay, hesitation, slowness. The load on one side (of a horse) hanging lower than the other. Watering of the eyes (from age or study).

A رهيّة *rahīyat*, Wheat in the ear rubbed between the hands, bruised and boiled with milk.

A رهيدة *rahīdat*, A soft, delicate girl. Bruised wheat and milk.

P رهيدن *rahīdan*, To escape, be liberated.

P رهيده *rahīda*, Dismissed, set free, escaping.

A رهيش *rahīsh*, (A camel) having little flesh on the back. Spare of flesh. Weak, slack, slender. A thin sword or spear-head, a light arrow. A slender bow, the string of which strikes against the middle in shooting. Earth that will not adhere together. A (horse's) cutting of one foot with the other in travelling. A camel giving plenty of milk.

A رهيشة *rahīshat*, A camel giving plenty of milk.

A رهيص *rahīs*, Hurt in the feet by the stones and limping (a horse). A hoof so injured. Savage, cruel (lion). A man's surname.

A رهيط *ruhayt*, (dim. of رهط *raht*) A few men.

A رهيف *rahīf*, Thin-edged (sword) and sharp in the middle of the curvature.

A رهيق *rahīk*, Wine.

A رهيك *rahīk*, Ground or bruised small.

P رهين *rahīn*, Pledged. A hostage. Dependence, connection.

A رهين *rahīn*, (pl. رهائن *rahāʼin*) Pledged, pawned, given as a hostage: a pledge. (pl. of رهن *rahn*) Pledges. P رهين دادن *rahīn dādan*, To pawn. رهين گرفتن *rahīn giriftan*, To take a pledge.

A رهينة *rahīnat*, (pl. رهائن *rahāʼin*) Any thing given in pledge.

P ري *ray*, The capital of Persian Irāk.

A ريّ *rayy*, (v. n. of روي) Watering, sprinkling, drawing water, presenting it or drinking to a friend. Tying on a load. *Rayy* or *rīy*, (v. n. of روي) Satisfying thirst. Being green and succulent (a tree). Greenness and succulence of a tree. Easy circumstances. Whatever pleases the eye. (pl. of رأي *raʼy*) Opinions, views, doctrines. *Rīy*, A handsome countenance or appearance.

A ريء *riʼ*, Sight, vision.

A ريّا *rayya'*, (fem. of ريّان *rayyān*) (A woman) quenching thirst. An agreeable smell.

A رياء *riyāʼ*, (v. n. 3 of رأي) Acting with dissimulation. Studying to be seen by men. Fearing. Hypocrisy. Dissimulation, subterfuge, evasion, affectation. Quantity. رياء الف *riyāʼ alfin*, A hundred apparently. بيوت رياء *buyūti riyāʼ*, Opposite houses, or other buildings. قوم رياء *kawmi riyāʼ*, Antagonists, men facing one another.

A رئاب *riʼāb*, (pl. of رأب *raʼb*) Herds of camels. Great chieftains. Cracks or chinks in pots. (pl. of رؤبة *ruʼbat*) Solders and such like things for mending broken dishes.

A ريّاب *rayyāb*, Alarming, fearful, inauspicious.

A رئات *riʼāt*, (pl. of رئة *riʼat*) The lungs.

A رياح *rayāh*, Wine. *Rayāh* or *riyāh*, Afternoon. *Riyāh*, (pl. of ريح *rīh*) Winds. Odours.

A رياحة *riyāhat*, (v. n. of راح for روح) Being at the point of accomplishing an object, and rejoicing thereat.

A رياحين *riyāhīn*, (pl. of ريحان *rayhān*) Odoriferous herbs. Hyacinths.

A رياد *riyād*, (v. n. of راد for رود) Seeking. Going in quest of forage and water. The to and fro motion of a camel when pasturing.

A ريازة *riyāzat*, The profession of an architect or master-builder (راز *rāz*).

A رئاس *riʼās*, The hilt, or a ring of silver or iron on the head of the hilt of a sword. A sword-belt. Beginning (of business).

A رئاسة *riʼāsat*, (v. n. of رأس) Governing, ruling. Government, dominion, headship, command.

A رياش *rayāsh*, Hairy about the face and ears (she-camel). *Riyāsh*, A splendid vest painted and ornamented. Plenty of provisions, abundance of wealth. (pl. of ريش *rīsh*) Feathers.

A ريّاش *rayyāsh*, One who feathers arrows.

A رياض *riyāz*, (v. n. of راض for روض) Training, or breaking in (a colt). (v. n. 3 of راض for روض) Striving to conciliate, coaxing, soothing. (pl. of روضة *rawzat*) Gardens. P رشك رياض ارم *rashki riyāzi iram*, The envy of the garden of Iram.

A رياضة *riyāzat*, (v. n. of راض for روض) Breaking in (a colt). Teaching, training. Discipline. Exercise. Abstinence, mortifying the flesh, austerity. اهل رياضت *ahli riyāzat*, Abstemious, austere.

P رياضت كيش *riyāzat-kesh*, Ascetical, sober.

P رياضت يافته *riyāzat-yāfta*, Trained, broke in. رياضت نا يافته *riyāzat-nā yāfta*, Not broke in, untrained.

A رياضيّ *riyāzīy*, Disciplinary. علوم رياضيه *ʻulūmi* (or فنون *funūni*) *riyāzīya*, Mathematics, the exact sciences.

A رياط *riyāt*, (pl. of ريطة *raytat*) Veils of one piece of cloth.

A رياع *riyāʻ*, (pl. of ريعة) High grounds, hills.

A رياغ *riyāgh*, Fruitfulness, plenty.

A رياغة *riyāghat*, A place for wrestling.

P رياكار *riyā-kār*, A hypocrite.

A رئال *riʼāl*, (pl. of رأل *raʼl*) Young ostriches. Name of certain stars.

A ريال *riyāl*, (v. n. of رال for ريل) Slavering (an infant). Spittle, saliva.

A رئالة *riʼālat*, (pl. of رأل) Young ostriches.

A ريّان *rayyān*, (pl. رواء *riwāʼ*) One whose thirst is quenched. The beginning of youth. Full of juice. Florid, flourishing. جبل الريّان *jabalu'r rayyān*, Name of a mountain in Tayy which never ceases flowing with water.

A ريانق *rayānik*, (pl. of رونقة) Muddy waters.

A P رياني *riyāʼī*, A hypocrite, sophist.

A ريب *rayb*, (v. n. of راب for ريب) Doubting, suspecting. Offending, scandalizing. Adverse fortune. Danger. Doubt, suspicion, scandal. Necessity, bad fortune, danger. ريب المنون *raybu'l manūn*, Adversity, fatal misfortune, death. P بي ريب و ريا *bī rayb u riyā*, Without dissimulation and hypocrisy; undisguised.

P ريباج *ribāj*, Sorrel. A graff-stock.

P ريباس *rebās*, A sour herb, sorrel, rhapontic.

A ريباس *rībās*, Name of a plant good for small-pox, measles, and plague.

A رئبال *riʼbāl*, (pl. رآبل *raʼābil* and رآبيل *raʼābīl*) A lion. Infirm old man. A long twining herb. Rapacious (wolf). Villainous (robber). An only son.

A ريبة *rībat*, (v. n. of راب for ريب) Offending, scandalizing. Doubt. Opinion. Suspicion. Scandal. اهل الريبة *ahlu'r rībat*, People of doubtful or disreputable character. بيت الريبة *baytu'r rībat*, A tavern: a gaming-house: a brothel.

P ريبد *raybad*, Name of a plain celebrated as the scene of the combat of the twelve champions. See دوازده رخ *duwāzda rukh*.

A ريبل *raybal*, Fleshy (woman or she-camel).

A رية *riyat*, (v. n. of وري) Being kindled (a fire). Emitting sparks of fire (the stick زند *zand*). Tinder, or any thing which catches fire.

A رئة *riʼat*, (pl. رئات *riʼāt* and رئون *riʼūn*) The lungs. ذات الرئة *zātu'r riʼat*, An inflammation in the lungs, peripneumony.

A ريّة *rayyat*, A filling with water, watering. (A fountain) abounding in water. Abundance. *Rīyat*, Sight, perception, knowledge. A fountain abounding in water.

P ريتانج *rītānaj*, Resin.

P ريته *rīta*, The dyeing fruit of an Indian tree.

P ريتيانج *rītiyānaj*, A kind of sea-crab.

A ريث *rays*, (v. n. of راث for ريث) Delaying, hesitating. Coming slowly or late (news).

Quantity, space, measure.

A ريّث *rayyis*, Slow, tardy, dull.

A ريثما *raysamā*, So long as, as soon as. Whilst.

P ريچاله *rīchāla*, (or ريچار *rīchār*) A confection, electuary, preserved fruits. Any thing made from sheep's milk.

A ريح *rīh*, (v. n. of راح) Being windy (the day). Striking any thing (wind). Feeling the wind, and beginning to bud (a tree). (pl. ارواح *arwāh*, ارياح *aryāh*, رياح *riyāh*, and ريح *riyah*) Wind. Odour, smell, exhalation. Victory, superiority. Power. Happiness, prosperity. Assistance. Good, excellent, pure (thing). Pity, compassion. ريح جنوبي *rīhi janūbī*, The south wind. ريح الحدب *rīhu'l hadab*, Wind in the back, or a wound or sore appearing in the neck. ريح طيبه *rīhi tayyiba*, Fragrance. *Riyah*, (pl. of ريح *rīh*) Winds.

A ريّح *rayyih*, Pleasantly windy (day). Fragrant, sweet-smelling.

A ريحان *rayhān*, The support of life. A son. Offspring. A kind of writing. A hyacinth. An odoriferous herb, as sweet basil: also the leaf or tip of it. P ريحان تاتاري *rayhāni tātārī*, Handsome, well-looking. ريحان داود *rayhāni dāwud*, Chickweed. ريحان زرد *rayhāni zard*, The sun's rays. A ريحان الشيوخ *rayhānu'sh shuyūkh*, Name of a flower. سبحان الله و ريحانه *subhāna'llāh wa rayhānahū*, Imploring a subsistence from God.

A ريحانة *rayhānat*, A sort of odoriferous herb. A handful of basil.

A ريحة *rīhat*, Wind.

A ريّحة *rayyihat*, (or ريحة *rīhat*) A plant germinating at the root of the thorny shrub عضاه *i-zāh*, remaining from last year. Grass which grows from the coolness of the night without rain.

A ريحي *rīhī*, Windy, flatulent.

A ريخ *raykh*, (v. n. of راخ for ريخ) Being loose, remiss, relaxed, fatigued. Straddling, being wide between the thighs. Having a prolapsus ani. Prolapsus ani.

P ريخ *rīkh*, Thin excrement in a diarrhœa. ريخ زدن *rīkh zadan*, To have liquid stools.

P ريخبين *rekhbīn*, A dark-coloured acid preparation of sheep's milk and flour. Dry grass. The Euphrates.

P ريختگي *rekhtagī*, Effusion.

P ريختن *rekhtan*, To pour, infuse, diffuse. To cast, melt. To scatter, disperse, break in pieces. To flow.

P ريختنگاه آب در دريا *rekhtangāhi āb dar daryā*, An estuary, frith, mouth of a river.

P ريختني *rekhtanī*, A scattering, dispersion. Capable of being poured in or injected. Any thing thrown about on festive occasions (as money, flowers, &c.).

P ريخته *rekhta*, Poured. Cast or founded. Scattered. A syrup or medicinal preparation from sugar. An egg beat and fried. Mortar, plaster. A sort of language formed of the Persian and Hindustānī mixed, in which many poems have been written. A stone-house.

P ريخته گر *rekhtagar*, A melter of brass or copper, one who makes any kind of fusile works.

P ريخر *rikhar*, The bezoar-stone.

P ريخن *rikhin*, Troubled with diarrhœa, loose.

P ريخيز *rikhīz*, A plough-tail. A ploughshare.

A ريد *rayd*, (pl. ريود *ruyūd*) The salient angle of a mountain. *Rīd*, Wish, desire.

A رئد *ri*,*d*, Equal in age, wealth, or manners. Narrow, tight. A slip, a shoot.

A ريدة *raydat*, (or ريدانة) Soft-blowing (wind).

P ريدك *raydak* or *rīdak*, A servant boy. A beardless youth.

P ريدكان *rīdakān*, Little boys.

P ريدن *rīdan*, To ease nature, to stool. To be stupefied.

A ريذجان *rayzajān*, A camel that carries merchant's wares. A camel's load of merchandize.

A رير *rayr*, (v. n. of رار for رير) Having a plenteous year. Slaver running from a child's mouth. *Rayr* or *rīr*, Thin marrow, corrupted and black.

A ريرق *rayrah*, (or ريزق *rayzah*) Nightshade.

P ريز *rez*, An egg beat together. Bruised small, minute. A little boy. A cheesecake made with yolks of eggs and saffron. Any thing fusile or friable. A small thing, crumbled or reduced to powder. Affluence, wealth. A cup, goblet, bowl. Will, desire, concupiscence. A drop left at the bottom of a cup. Mercy. (in compos. from ريختن *rekhtan*, or ريزيدن *rezīdan*), Pouring, scattering. اشك ريز *ashk-rez*, Shedding tears. خون ريز *khūn-rez*, A shedder of blood. شكر ريز *shakar-rez*, Dropping sugar. عرق ريز *ʿarak-rez*, Sweating. گهر ريز *guhar-rez*, Strewing jewels. هلاهل ريز *halāhil-rez*, Scattering poison or venom.

P ريزاب *rezāb*, Dirty water that runs off from baths, wash-houses, &c.

P ريزان *rezān*, (or ريزا *rezā*) Scattering, pouring. Raining (cloud or sky). Melting, casting. Poured, fusile. Conveniences, affluence. Desire, wish. ريزان شدن *rezān shudan*, To be pouring. To be poured. باد خزان و صرصر ريزان *bādi khizān u sarsari rezān*, The autumnal wind, boisterous, and scattering (the leaves of the trees).

P ريزاندن *rezāndan*, To pour.

P ريز ريز *rez rez*, Bit by bit. Drop by drop.

P ريزش *rezish*, Fusion, pouring. A flowing in small quantities, a scattering. A running at the nose.

P ريزفين *rīzfīn*, The jujube. A wooden shovel.

P ريزگي *rezagī*, A scrap, bit. Small coin (as four-rupee pieces).

P ريز مريز *rez ma rez*, A lean, lank fellow. A species of small cucumber.

P ريزناك *reznāk*, Friable, crumbled small.

P ريزنان *reznān* or *rezanān*, Bar of a door.

P ريزندگي *rezandagī*, A copious effusion.

P ريزه *reza*, Broken small. Very minute (animal, vegetable, or mineral). A crumb. An egg beaten up and fried. A scrap, piece, bit, orts. Small coin. A kind of cock. Children employed in mason-work, and who receive one-half, or a third, of a man's pay. The young of any animal. پيل ريزه *pīl-reza*, A young elephant. ريزهٔ سيمين *rezasi sīmīn*, The stars. ريزه شدن *reza shudan*, To be broken or pounded small.

P ريزه خط *reza-khat*, Fine-striped, thin-lined.

P ريزه خور *reza-khwur*, An eater of fragments or orts. A gleaner.

P ريزه ريزه *reza reza*, Scraps, pieces: in bits.

P ريزه ريزه كرده *reza reza karda*, Broken in small pieces.

P ريزه كار *reza-kār*, Neat, nice. Shrewd, clever.

P ريزه كاري *reza-kārī*, Neatness, gracefulness, elegance. Shrewdness, cleverness.

P ريزي *rezī*, An overflowing. Mercy, clemency. ريزي بريز *rezī bi rez*, Shew mercy. Pour a draught.

P ريزيدن *rezīdan*, To be dissolved, broken in pieces. To be scattered, bruised, melted. To pour, diffuse, scatter. To rot. To be wearied, disgusted.

P ريزيده *rezīda*, Dispersed, melted. Fallen in pieces. Rotten. Displeased. The herb cyprus.

P ريزين *rezīn*, Most minute.

P ريژ *rīj*, Desire, concupiscence. Hilly ground.

P ريژك *rījak*, Transgression. A slip, fall.

A ريس *rays*, (v. n. of راس for ريس) Holding fast. Overcoming. Being raised above the people. *Rays*, (or ريسان *rayasān*) (v. n. of راس for ريس) Being proud, walking with a haughty air.

A رئس *ra*,*is*, A head, chief, principal, president, commander. A citizen. The captain of a ship. A pilot. Wounded in the head (رأس *ra*,*s*).

P ريس *rīs*, (in compos.) Spinning. Scattering. One who uses diligence. Buzzing. A design, a pattern for embroidery. Anger. Force, violence. A vaulted edifice of Khusraw Parwez. باريك ريس *bārīk-rīs*, Sighing. *Res*, Thick broth. Spinning.

A ريّس *rayyis*, A head, chief, chieftain.

P ريسانيدن *rīsānīdan*, To excite to diligence. To make spin.

P ريستن *rīstan*, To buzz. To use diligence. To scatter. To weep, to mourn for the dead. To sigh. To descend (into a well or the sea). To evacuate fæces. *Rīstan* or *restan*, To spin, to twist.

P ريسمان *rīsmān*, A rope, thread, twine, string, cord. ريسمان كشتي *rīsmāni kishtī*, A cable, hawser.

P ريسنده *rīsanda*, A spinner.

P ريسي *resī*, A sort of grape.

P ريسيدن *rīsīdan*, To spin, twist. To cry aloud, lament. To be diligent. To buzz. To scatter. To void excrement.

A ريش *raysh*, (v. n. of راش for ريش) Fitting and gluing feathers (to arrows). Collecting wealth and furniture. Giving meat and drink and clothing to a friend. Leafy herbage. *Rīsh*, (pl. ارياش *aryāsh* and رياش *riyāsh*) A feather. A splendid vest painted and adorned. Plenty of provisions, much wealth, the conveniences of life. ذات الريش *zātu'r rīsh*, A plant resembling southernwood. مائة بريشها *mi,at bi rīshihā*, A hundred complete. *Rayash*, Abundance of hair in the ears and about the face. *Rayish*, Leafy, feathery (herbage).

P ريش *resh*, A wound, sore, pimple, scar; pus, matter. Thick pottage made of bruised wheat boiled to a consistency. (in comp.) Wounded or wounding. دلريش *dil-resh*, Wounded in the heart. *Rīsh*, The beard. Wool. A tunic, cloak, or loose upper garment; also, a dress, suit of clothes for festive occasions. Violence, atrocity, fury, indignation. A leaf of the palm-tree. ريش بر آوردن *rīsh bar āwardan*, To become bearded. ريش بز *rīshi buz*, Goat's beard, an herb. ريش در دست كسي دادن *rīsh dar dasti kase dādan*, To give one's beard, *i. e.* to entrust one's affairs to any one. ريش قاضي *rīshi kāzī*, A linen strainer; also the corner of it trickling with wine. ريش كندن *rīsh kandan*, To labour in vain. ريش گاو *rīshi gāv*, The beard of a cow (a proverbial saying when a man does any thing mean, as unworthy of his beard). The halter of a cow. A fool. Covetous, greedy.

A ريِّش *rayyish*, Leafy, feathery (herbage).

P ريشائيل *rīshā,īl*, Having a long beard.

P ريش بچه *rīsh-bacha*, The beard under the lips. A small beard.

P ريش برآمده *resh bar āmada*, Ulcerated.

A ريشة *rīshat*, A single feather.

P ريشتاب *rīsh-tāb*, A curling beard.

P ريشتن *rīshtan*, To be diligent. To buzz. To spin. To set at liberty, to absolve.

P ريشته *rīshta*, Any thing twisted (as a match, candle-wick, or linstock). Slices of paste put in soup, macaroni.

P ريشخند *rīsh-khand*, Adulation, flattery, fulsome compliments. Ridicule. Hope, desire. Laughing, risible. A flatterer, a sycophant. An ass. ريش خند كردن *rīsh-khand kardan*, To ridicule, to deride.

P ريشخندي *rīsh-khandī*, Risibility. A laughing-stock. A proverbial saying when one does a thing unworthy of his beard.

P ريش خوك *resh-khūk*, Scrofula, king's evil.

P ريش ساز *resh-sāz*, A physician, surgeon.

P ريش سفيد *rīsh-safed*, An old man, a grey-beard. A head, a chief.

P ريش سياه *rīsh-siyāh*, A young man, black-beard.

P ريشم *resham* or *rīsham*, Silk.

P ريشمال *rīsh-māl*, A contented cuckold.

P ريشمالي *rīsh-mālī*, Cuckoldom.

P ريشمان *rīshmān*, (or ريشماني) Silken.

P ريشمي *rīshmī*, (or ريشينه) Silken.

P ريشناك *reshnāk*, Sore.

P ريشه *rīsha*, A fringe. Threads suspended. A fibre. Stringiness of a mangoe. The fibres of the palm-tree. A tendril. The eye-lids. Hair on the human body. Any thing twisted (a match, candle-wick, or linstock). The parts of a tree which are under the ground. Name of a disease. ريشهٔ سبحانيّه *rīsha,i subhāniya*, A monk's cowl. *Resha*, A wound.

P ريشه دار *resha-dār*, Wounded.

P ريشه وار *rīshawār*, Fibrous.

P ريشيدن *rīshīdan*, To pour out. To melt. To scatter.

P ريشيده *rīshīda*, Silk interwoven or fringed with points of different colours. The fringe of a turban-sash. Coloured. Painted and embroidered China silk. Shining, luminous. *Reshīda*, Wounded.

A ريِّض *rayyiz*, (A horse or camel) not thoroughly broke in. A tyro, novice. Gentle, tractable. Unmanageable.

A ريضان *rīzān*, (pl. of روضة) Gardens. Meads.

A ريضة *rīzat*, A place in which water collects.

A ريطة *raytat*, (pl. ريط *rayt* and رياط *riyāt*) A veil of one piece of cloth. A thin, light garment.

A ريع *rayع*, (v. n. of ريع) Being torn, falling in pieces. Increasing, growing, augmenting. Waxing strong (wheat). Returning, reverting. Coming out well and augmented (bread from the oven, or meat from the pot). Redundancy, residue, superfluity, leavings. Utility, profit. The undulating motion of the vapour سراب *sarāb*. Fear, terror. The first and best part of any thing. Width of sleeve of a coat of mail. The ends of a shift's sleeves. Clearness and brightness of that part of the forenoon called ضحي *zuhā'*. Answer, reply. *Rīع*, A tower. A monastery or cloister with a belfry. A dove-cote. A high hill. *Rīع* or *rayع*, High ground, a hill. A way, an open path between mountains.

A ريعان *rayعān*, The first or best part (of any thing). The flower (of youth).

A ريعانة *rayعānat*, A camel giving much milk.

A ريعة *rīعat*, Abstinence from any thing deemed unlawful, a scrupulous dread of doing wrong. A crowd closely packed. (pl. رياع *riyāع*) High ground.

P ريعناك *rayعnāk*, Fertile, productive (ground).

P ريغ *rīgh*, Hate. *Regh*, Skirts of a mountain.

A ريغ *rīgh*, Dust. Earth. Fugacity.

P ريغال *rīghāl*, A cup, a goblet.

P ريغل *rīghal*, Thin, dry, lean.

A ريف *rayf*, (v. n. of راف for ريف) Coming to the kind of country called *Rīf*. Grazing that kind of land (cattle). *Rīf*, (pl. ارياف *aryāf*) A cultivated country, a sown field or pasture luxuriant in produce. Land which lies contiguous to water, verdant, and rich in agricultural produce. Abundance of meat and drink.

A رئف *ra,if*, Merciful, benign, benevolent.

A ريِّف *rayyif*, (A field) rich in produce.

A ريفيّة *rīfiyat*, A cultivated plain (the opposite to برّيّة *barriyat*, A desert).

A ريق *rayk*, (v. n. of راق for ريق) Shining on the ground like water, and appearing to flow (vapours). Coming in small quantity (rain). Being poured out (water). The first and best of a thing. The first part (of youth). Glitter. Water. Dry bread. False, vain. *Rīk*, (pl. ارياق *aryāk*) Spittle, water running from the mouth in the morning. Strength. The last breath. علي ريق *عala' rīkin*, With a morning stomach, *i.e.* empty. على ريق نفسي *عala' rīki nafsī*, Whilst I was yet fasting.

A ريِّق *rayyik*, Fasting. The first and best part (of rain, youth, &c.). Handsome-shaped (horse).

A ريقة *rīkat*, Spittle.

P ريك *rīk*, Bravo! well done! fortunate!

P ريكا *rīkā*, Loved. A beloved object.

P ريكاسه *rekāsa*, (or ريكاشه *rekāsha*) A hedge-hog. A porcupine.

A ريكة *riyakat*, The lobe of a horse's liver.

P ريكن *rīkan*, (or ريگن *rīgan*) An impostor, villain. Malevolent. Polluted. Addicted to magic.

P ريگ *reg*, Sand, gravel, dust. A kind of gold-coloured dust, with which they sprinkle writings. An atom. Fortune, luck. Fortunate! well done! ريگ روان *regi rawān*, Moving sand.

P ريگ پشته *reg-pushta*, A hill or heap of sand.

P ريگ توده *reg-toda*, A sandhill.

P ريگدان *regdān*, A sand-box.

P ريگ ريگ *reg reg*, To atoms.

P ريگ زاده *reg-zāda*, (Sand-bred) The skink.

P ريگزار *regzār*, (or ريگستان) A sandy region.

P ريگماهي *reg-māhī*, (Sand-fish) A skink.

P ريگناك *regnāk*, Sandy.

A ريل *rayl*, The slavering (of an infant).

A رئلان *ri,lān*, (pl. of رأل) Young ostriches.

P ريلو *rīlū*, Ashes of which they make soap.

A ريم *raym*, (v. n. of رام for ريم) Departing. Deserting, abandoning. Desisting, ceasing. Departure. Distance. A small package laid on the top between the loads on a beast of burden. A grave. The middle of a grave. Redundancy, excess. Increase. Any thing redundant or remaining over (especially after distributing the joints of a slaughtered camel; also the part given to the butcher). A long hour. The evening (till dark). A leaning to one side of a camel's load. The joining of the sides or lips of a wound. A step, stair, or round of a ladder. A milk-white doe. Small mountains.

P ريم *rīm*, Pus, matter, humour, rheum. Dregs, mother of oil, lees of wine. Dross of metal. The poplar; an Egyptian tree. ريم آهن *rīmi āhan*, The dross of iron (left in the furnace, or which flies off in hammering). ريم گوش *rīmi gosh*, Ear-wax. ريم كردن *rīm kardan*, To suppurate.

A رئم *ri,m*, (pl. ارآم *ar,ām* and آرام *ārām*) A milk-white doe. *Ru,im*, The buttocks, backside.

P ريما *rīmā*, An unicorn, rhinoceros.

P ريماز *rīmāz*, (or ريمز) A kind of light garment.

A رئمان *risman*, (v. n. of رأم) Loving affectionately, being addicted, or having a propensity to. Healing (a wound). Twisting hard (rope). Holding or taking up ashes (the trivets of a pot).

A ريمان *rayamān*, A closing up of the lips of a healing wound.

P ريم آهنج *rīm-āhanj*, (P ريم آهنگ *rīm-āhang*) Root of the plantain.

SY ريمسعت *rīmasat*, Galangale.

P ريمن *rayman*, A cheat, villain. *Rīman*, An impostor, villain. Impure, filthy. Addicted to magic. A guide to evil. Satan. A horse. A son. *Rīmin*, A running sore.

P ريمناك *rīmnāk*, Corrupt, mattery. Suppurative (wound or sore). Sloughy. Filthy, nasty. Impure, polluted. Puffy, turgid.

P ريمناكي *rimnākī*, Filthiness, nastiness, dirtiness. Slough of a sore or wound.

P ريمه *rīma*, Dirt in the corners of the eyes and about the eyelashes.

A رين *rayn*, (v. n. of ران for رين) Conquering, overcoming, prevailing. Making (advances in wickedness). Being confounded, disturbed, perplexed. Falling into inextricable difficulty. Being contaminated, impure. Dirt, filth. Rust.

A رينة *raynat*, Wine.

P ريو *rev*, Fraud, deceit, stratagem. Name of the son of كاوس *kāwus*.

P ريواج *rewāj*, Sorrel.

P ريواز *riwāz*, Justice, equity: order, method.

P ريواس *rewās*, Sorrel. Fraud, hypocrisy.

P ريوجام *rivjām*, Sobriety, chastity.

A ريوح *rayūh*, Agreeably-blowing (day).

P ريود *riwad*, A plant with which animals are intoxicated.

A ريود *ruyūd*, (pl. of ريد *rayd*) Projections of mountains.

A ريوض *rayūz*, (A horse, camel, or boy) not trained, awkward. Tame, gentle. Untractable.

A ريوق *ruyūk*, A giving up of the ghost.

A ريّوق *rayyūk*, The best of any thing. Fasting.

P ري و قاف *ri u kāf*, Trifles. Light talk. An argument.

A رئون *risūn*, (pl. of رئة *risat*) Lungs.

A ريون *ruyūn*, (v. n. of ران for رين) Conquering, overcoming, prevailing. Being contaminated, impure. Being confounded, disturbed.

P ريونجو *rewanjū*, (or ريونجه) A timber-worm.

P ريوند *riwand*, Rhubarb. ريوند چيني *riwandi chīnī*, China rhubarb.

P ريونيز *revnīz*, Name of the son of Kay Kāwus.

P ريوه *reva*, A hillock or high bank. Deceit, fraud, incantation. Name of the son of Kay Kāwus.

P ريويدن *riwīdan*, To be absolved, dismissed.

P ريويج *riwīj*, Sorrel.

P ريويز *riwīz*, Fraud, treachery, machination, imposture. Sorrel.

P ريه *rayh*, (v. n. of راه for ريه) Coming and going, appearing and disappearing (vapour, mirage).

P ريه *rih*, Brackish soil. Depression: despair.

P ريهانيدن *rīhānīdan*, To make desolate.

A ريهقان *rayhukān*, Saffron.

P ريهه *rīha*, A king, prince, emperor.

P ريهيدن *rihīdan*, To fall, roll down (as loose earth or sand from a height). To flow murmuringly (as water from a cistern). To be diffused or poured out. To putrefy.

P ريهيده *rihīda*, Fallen. Rotten, putrid. Infirm.

A رئّي *rasiy*, (pl. of رأي *rasy*) Opinions, views, counsels. Doctrines. *Rasiy* or *risiy*, A genie, demon, or spirit that is seen and loved. The object seen (as cloth exposed to sale). A large serpent. رئّي من الجنّ *rasiy mini'l jinn*, Touch of the devil.

A رئيس *rasis*, A head, chief. A master, captain. Wounded in the head (sheep). الاعضاء الرئيسة *al aszāsu'r rasisat*, The principal members, viz. The heart, brain, liver, and testes.

A رئّيس *rissis*, One who becomes a great chief.

P رئينه خم *ruyīna-khum*, A brazen drum.

ز

ز *zā* or *ze*, (called زائ هوّز *zāsi hawwaz*, زائ منقوطة *zāsi mankūta*, زائ معجمة *zāsi musjama*, Dotted *zā*) The eleventh letter of the Arabic alphabet, and the thirteenth of the Persian, denoting seven in arithmetic, Saturday in the almanacks, and the sign Scorpion in the zodiac. The letter ز *ze* is sometimes changed for ج *jīm*; as, سوج *soj* for سوز *soz*: for چ *che*; as, پچشك *pichishk* for پزشك *pizishk*: for غ *ghayn*; as, گريغ *guregh* for گريز *gurez*: for س *sīn*; as, اياس *ayās* for اياز *ayāz*. The power of ز *ze* is exactly that of the English z.

P ز *za*, (or زا *zā*) (for زاد *zād*) Born. *Zi*, (contracted for از *az*) From. Than. Off. زمن *zi man* (for ازمن *az man*) From, than, me.

A زا *zā*, (or زاء *zās*) (pl. ازواء *azwās*) The letter ز, so called by the Arabs. A glutton.

A زاء *zāsa*, (fut. يزوؤ *yazūsu*) (Fortune) turned.

A زآبيب *zasābib*, Flasks, glass-bottles.

P زاب *zāb*, Quality, property. A fountain. The eye. Name of the tenth king of Persia, of the Peshdādian dynasty.

A زأب *zasb*, (v. n. of زأب) Lifting up and going off with what one can carry. Driving (a camel). Turning. Drinking with a gulp.

P زابا *zābā*, (in zand and Pāzand) Pure gold.

A زأبج *zasbaj*, All, the whole. اخذه بزأبجه *akhkazahu bi zasbajihi*, He took the whole of it.

A زأبر *zasbar*, All, the whole. بزأبره *bi zasbarihi*, All of it, without any remainder.

A زأبرة *zasbarat*, (v. n. of زأبر Q) Being shagged and nappy (cloth). Stripping (cloth) of the nap.

P زابغر *zābghur*, (or زابگر *zābgur*) Puffing the cheek and striking it so that the wind may escape with noise.

A زأبل *zasbal*, (*zasbil*, زابل *zābal*, or *zābil*) Short, dwarfish.

P زابل *zābul*, Name of a country, and of a people. Name of a note in music.

P زابلستان *zābulistān*, Kābul, Ghaznīn, &c.

A زابن *zābin*, A life-guardsman, serjeant, tipstaff, beadle. A demon who drives the damned into the infernal pit.

A زابنة *zābinat*, A hillock diverging from a valley.

A زابوقة *zābūkat*, A corner of a house. An angular lurking-place in a house. A place near Basrah, where the battle of the camel was fought.

A زابيان *zābiyāni*, (or زابان *zābāni*) Name of two rivers below the Euphrates.

P زابيدن *zābīdan*, To be endowed with, or described by, any particular quality.

A زات *zāta*, (fut. يزيت *yazītu*) He fed with oil.

A زأت *zast*, (v. n. of زأت) Putting in a passion, filling with rage.

P زاج *zāj*, A woman in childbed, until the eighth day. Copperas, vitriol, shoemaker's black. معدن زاج *masdani zāj*, Mineral of vitriol. زاج ابيض *zāji abyaz*, (or زاج سفيد *zāji safed*) Alum. زاج احمر *zāji ahmar*, Sory. زاج اصفر *zāji asfar*, Vitriol. زاج عراقي *zāji sirākī*, Green vitriol. زاج كبود *zāji kabūd*, Blue vitriol.

A زأج *zasj*, (v. n. of زأج) Breeding a quarrel.

A زاج *zāj*, Copperas, shoemaker's black.

A زاجر *zājir*, Prohibitive, who or what hinders. One who excites and stirs up. A threatener, rebuker. ابو زاجر *abū zājir*, A crow.

A زاجرات *zājirāt*, Divinations. Rebukes. The angels which preside over the winds and clouds.

P زاج سور *zāj-sūr*, A feast on the birth of a child.

A زاجل *zājal*, (or زأجل *zasjal*) The tread of a male ostrich. The lymph of a stallion. Whatever runs from the fundament of a she-ostrich during the period of incubation. A ferule at the foot of a spear. A short spear. A mark on the neck (of camels). *Zājil*, One who makes a loud noise, a chanter. حمام الزاجل *hamāmu'z zājil*, A carrier-pigeon. *Zājil* or *zājal*, (pl. زواجل *zawājil*) A piece of wood at the end of a rope for fastening the mouth of a leathern bottle or bag. Commander of an army.

P زاجور *zājūr*, (for زاجسور *zāj-sūr*) A feast made on the third day after the birth of a child.

A زاجي *zājī*, Contemptible. Little, small.

A زاجيّ *zājiy*, Ready, expeditious. Obtaining easily. Black, of the colour of vitriol or ebony.

P زاچه *zācha*, A woman in childbed until seven days are past.

A زاحف *zāhif*, (pl. زواحف *zawāhif*) Dragging the legs, fatigued (a camel). Falling short of the mark (an arrow), but rebounding from the ground and hitting it. One who creeps on his backside.

A زاحفة *zāhifat*, (pl. زواحف *zawāhif*) A she-camel that drops her legs from fatigue.

A زاخر *zākhir*, Full, swelling (sea), surgy (main). Noble (root). High nobility. Joyous, cheerful.

A زاخف *zākhif*, Vain-glorious, arrogant.

P زاخل *zākhil*, The infernal tree زقّوم *zakkūm*, the fruit of which is said to be the heads of devils.

P زاخورش *zā-khwurish*, A woman, a little eater.

P زاد *zād*, (3d. pers. pret. of زادن *zādan*) He was born. Birth. Age. A son. A foal. Orthodox, a follower of the Sunna. (for آزاد *āzād*) Free. زاد خاطر *zādi khātir*, (Offspring of the thoughts) poetry. آدمي زاد *ādami-zād*, A man, born of man. پري زاد *parī-zād*, Born of an angel or fairy, (met.) beautiful woman; (hence the daughter of Darius, called Parysatis by the Greeks). بزاد بر آمده *ba zād bar āmada*, Of an advanced age. مادر زاد *mādar-zād*, Stark naked, as born from the mother. زاد بر زاد *zād bar zād*, Generation upon generation.

A زأد *zaʼd*, (v. n. of زأد) Terrifying.

A زاد *zād*, (also زاد و زوادة *zād u zawāda*) Travelling-provisions, victuals, vivres. P زاد راه *zādi rāh*, Provisions for the way. زاد بر زاد *zād bar zād*, Provisions on provisions. A خير الزاد التقوي *khayru'z zādi't takwa'*, The best provision for the journey is piety (a saying of Muhammad).

A زاد الله *zāda'llāh*, May God increase (it)!

P زاد بوم *zād-būm*, The mother-country.

P زاد خر *zād-khur* or زاد خور *zād-khwur*, Old.

P زاد خو *zād-khu* or *zād-kho*, Decrepit.

P زاد خواست *zād-khwāst*, (or زاد خوست *zād-khwust*) Of full age, but not grown in proportion. An old man. A man of a thin, meagre, debilitated figure. One who spends all he possesses.

P زاد سرو *zād-sarv*, The fir-tree, the cypress.

P زاد شم *zād sham*, Name of Afrāsyāb's father.

P زادغر *zād-ghar*, A bastard. A scoundrel.

P زادگي *zādagi*, Birth.

P زاد مرد *zād-mard*, Free. Valiant. Generous.

P زادن *zādan*, To bring forth. To be born.

P زاد و بود *zād u būd*, Goods and chattels.

P زادوس *zādūs*, (or زادوش) The planet Mercury.

P زادة *zāda*, Born. A son. Offspring. زادۀ خاطر *zādasi khātir*, (Offspring of the mind) Prose or verse. Voice. Action. زادۀ دهن *zādasi dahan*, (Offspring of the mouth) A word. زادۀ شش روزه *zādasi shash roza*, (Offspring of six days) Heaven and earth. Living creatures. زادۀ طبع *zādasi tabʻ*, Original composition. زادۀ مرّيخ *zādasi mirrīkh*, The offspring of Mars, *i. e.* iron. اصل زادة *asl-zāda*, Nobly born. حرام زادة *harām-zāda*, Illegitimate. A scoundrel. حلال زادة *halāl-zāda*, A lawful son. شاه زادة *shāh-zāda*, (or شهزادة *shah-zāda*) A king's son, a prince.

P زادة خوست *zāda khwust*, A decrepit old man.

A زاذ *zāz*, A species of date.

A زاذان (بنات *banātu*) *zāzān*, Asses.

A زأر *zaʼr*, (v. n. of زأر) Growling inwardly (a lion). Braying inwardly (a stallion-camel).

A زار *zāra*, (fut. يزور *yazūru*) He visited.

P زار *zār*, A groan, plaint, lamentation. Weeping, crying. Desire. Groaning, afflicted. Weak, thin. Contemptible. A crowd, multitude. Vain. (An affix denoting) A place where any thing grows. گل زار *gulzār*, A rose-garden. لاله زار *lālazār*, A bed of tulips.

P زاراغنگ *zārāghang*, Hard soil. Sandy soil.

A زأرة *zaʼrat*, A place where canes grow.

A زارة *zārat*, A herd of camels. The crop or craw.

A زارّة *zārrat*, A blue or red fly infesting camels.

P زارتشت *zārtusht*, (or زارتهشت) Zoroaster.

P زارج *zārij*, Barberries. Name of a prince.

P زار خوار *zār-khwār*, One who desires. Afflicted.

P زار خور *zār-khwur*, (A lad) who eats little, and thrives not. Desirous. Roguish, dishonest. One who uses equivocal language.

P زار خورش *zār-khwurish*, Abstemious woman.

P زاردشت *zārdusht*, (or زاردهشت) Zoroaster.

P زار زار *zār-zār*, Great lamentation.

A زارع *zāriʻ*, (pl. زرّاع *zurrāʻ*) A sower. One who causes to grow. اولاد زارع *awlādu zāriʻ*, Dogs.

P زارغنگ *zār-ghang*, Hard and sandy land.

P زارة *zāra*, Contemptible, abject. Plaint, moan. A cry for help. Meanness. Vehement desire.

P زارهشت *zāruhsht*, Zoroaster.

P زاري *zārī*, Lamentation, plaint. Cry for help.

A زاري *zārī*, A chider, disparager, censurer, accuser, traducer. One who irritates.

P زاريانة *zāriyāna*, Cause, motive, reason. Whatever occasions weeping and lamentation.

P زاريدن *zārīdan*, To groan, cry. To afflict, vex.

A زأزأة *zaʼzaʼat*, (v. n. of زأزأ Q) Moving, disturbing. Terrifying, putting in bodily fear. Shaking his head, wings, and tail in walking (an ostrich).

P زازال *zāzāl*, Name of a small black bird which cannot rise from the ground.

P زازل *zāzal*, A colander, strainer.

A زازية *zāziyat*, Rough ground. A small hill.

P زاژ *zāj*, Sweepings of a thrashing-floor.

P زاست *zāst*, Name of a country.

P زاستر *z'āstar*, (contracted from زانسوتر *z'ān sūtar*) (Go or sit) a little farther off! Separate. Increase, excess.

P زاستن *zāstan*, To bear, bring forth a child.

A زاعب *zāʻib*, One who travels through various countries (as a guide). The point of a spear. Name of a man, and of a country.

A زاعبي *zāʻibiy*, Name of a kind of spear.

A زاعة *zāʻat*, Life-guards. The forlorn hope, the vanguard.

A زاعر *zāʻir*, Of a bad disposition. A gipsey.

A زاعط *zāʻit*, Sure, violent, and speedy (death).

P زاغ *zāgh*, A crow, raven, rook. A sort of pigeon. The internal bend of a bow near the extremities. Vitriol. Sedition, mutiny. Bias, inclination. Name of a note in music. A name for a created being. زاغ آبي *zāghi ābī*, (Water-crow) A coot. زاغ پاسرخ *zāghi pā-surkh*, A certain delicately-flavoured bird.

A زاغ *zāgh*, (pl. زيغان) A small, whitish crow.

P زاغ پا *zāgh-pā*, (Crow-foot, black-leg) Reproach, reproof, taunt, contumely.

A زاغة *zāghat*, (pl. of زاغي *zāghī*) Wanderers from the truth.

P زاغج *zāghij*, A crow, a rook.

P زاغ چشم *zāgh-chashm*, Blue-eyed.

P زاغچند *zāghchand*, A fortress in Turkistān.

P زاغچه *zāghcha*, A small crow, a daw.

P زاغ دل *zāgh-dil*, Hard-hearted.

P زاغر *zāghar* or *zāghur*, A bird's crop.

P زاغ زبان *zāgh-zabān*, (Crow-tongue) A man whose curses prevail. A term implying excellence in a horse.

P زاغنول *zāgh-nol*, A mattock. A battle-axe.

P زاغوك *zāghūk*, A ball for a balista.

P زاغونه *zāghūna*, The socket of a candlestick. A reed used by weavers to wind their thread upon.

A زاغي *zāghī*, One who declines (from truth).

A زاغية *zāghiyat*, A modest woman obedient to her husband. A whore, lascivious woman.

P زاغيچه *zāghīcha*, A small crow, a daw.

A زأف *zaʼf*, (v. n. of زأف) Commanding or causing to make haste. A sudden or speedy death.

A زافرة *zāfirat*, A crowd, assembly. Companions, friends, allies, assistants. A troop, squadron, battalion. A great lord. A bow. That part of the arrow below the feathers, or within two-thirds of the point. (pl. زوافر *zawāfir*) A prop or buttress.

A زافنة *zāfinat*, A lame she-camel. A woman sufficient for a man. A dancing-woman.

P زافه *zāfa*, A kind of stinking herb. A hedgehog.

P زاق *zāk*, The young of any thing. Vitriol. A black tincture. زاق و زيق *zāk u zīk*, Children. Noise, uproar.

P زاقدان *zākdān*, The womb, matrix.

A زاقي *zākī*, (pl. زواقي *zawākī*) Vociferating, hooting, hallooing, crowing.

A زأكان *zaʼakān*, A pompous, stately gait.

A زاكي *zākī*, Pure. Strong, growing (lad).

P زاگ *zāg*, Vitriol. Alum. Shoemaker's black. Blacking for boots and shoes. Copperas.

P زاگاب *zāg-āb*, Vitriol-water, writing-ink.

A زال *zāla*, (fut. يزول *yazūlu*) He displaced.

P زال *zāl*, Name of a famous Persian prince, father to the still more celebrated hero Rustam. An old man. An old woman. Decrepit. Grey-headed. A year. زال بد افعال *zāli bad-afʻāl*, (زال رعنا) *zāli raʻnā*, زال سفيد رو *zāli safed-rū*, or زال سفيد ابرو *zāli safed-abrū*, زال عقيم *zāli ʻakīm*, or زال مستحاضه *zāli mustahāza*) The world. زال پیر *zāli pīr*, A very decrepit old man. زال زر *zāl zar*, Zāl, father of Rustam. زال سر سفید سیه دل *zāli sar-safedi siyah-dil*, The world. Ruthless, unmerciful. زال کوز پشت *zāli kūz-pusht*, The sky. زال موسیه *zāli mūsiya*, The world. A musical instrument.

A زالّ *zāll*, (Money) below standard-weight.

P زال ابرو *zāl-abrū*, The sky. New moon.

A زالج *zālij*, Gliding from the bow (arrow). One who escapes from dangers or whirlpools. One who gulps (liquor).

P زال دستان *zāl-dastān*, Father of Rustam.

P زال کوفه *zāl-kūfa*, Name of an old woman.

P زالو *zālū*, A leech. A quick-falling rain.

A زالوج *zālūj*, Swift. Long ridge of mountains.

P زالوك *zālūk*, A ball for a balista.

A زأم *zaʼm*, (v. n. of زأم) Dying suddenly. Eating and drinking voraciously. Terrifying. Bringing on a tremor (severe cold). Speaking in ambiguous language. A loud cry. Necessity. Wind. A sufficiency of food. *Zaʼam*, (v. n. of زئم) Being exceedingly frightened. Crying aloud.

A زام *zām*, A fourth part of the day, a watch. A fourth part. زامان *zāmāni*, Two watches, half a day.

A زامّ *zāmm*, (pl. زمّم *zummam*) A tyer, binder. One who raises the head. Proud: silent from pride.

A زأمة *zaʼmat*, (v.n.of زأم) Bawling out to. Guttling and swilling. Standing stock still. Dying. A loud, sonorous, or strained voice. Speech. A word of doubtful meaning, a double entendre. A sufficiency of food. Necessity, unavoidable business. Wind, air.

A زامة *zāmat*, A body, sect, company.

A زأمج *zaʼmaj*, The entire. بزأمجهم *bi zaʼmajihim*, All of them (men). بزأمجه *bi zaʼmajihi*, The whole.

A زامح *zāmih*, A sore, felon, bile.

A زامخ *zāmikh*, (pl. زمّخ *zummakh*) Proud, lofty. Full, overflowing (measure).

A زامر *zāmir*, (rarely used) A piper.

A زامرة *zāmirat*, A female piper.

A زامل *zāmil*, Any person or thing which follows, a follower. (A horse or camel) going in a curvetting pace from sprightliness.

A زاملة *zāmilat*, A camel loaded with provisions, household furniture, and the like.

P زامهران *zāmahrān*, A sort of antidote.

P زامیاد *zāmyād* Name of the 28th day of the Persian month; and of its presiding angel.

P زامیج *zāmīj*, A small city in Turkistān.

P زامیم *zāmīm*, Name of a mighty river.

P زامین *zāmīn*, A small city near Samarkand.

P زان *z'ān*, (for از آن *az ān*) From that. زان پس *z'ān pas*, Afterwards. زان سپس *z'ān sipas*, After that. زانکه *z'ān ki* for that cause.

A زان *zān*, A tree, for making bows and arrows.

A زأنبى *zaʼnaba'*, A slow gait in walking.

A زانة *zānat*, Indigestion, dyspepsy.

P زانسوتر *z'ān sūtar*, (or زانستر) A little further.

A زانكي *zānikīy*, One who teases, thwarts, or harasses his relations.

P زانگه *z'ān gah*, From that time, since.

P زانما *z'ān mā*, From thence to us-ward.

P زانو *zānū*, The knee. The lap. A bow, obeisance. Worship. سر زانو *sari zānū*, The knee-pan. زانو بزانو *zānū ba zānū*, Knee to knee. زانو رصدگاه کردن *zānū rasad-gāh kardan*, To sit and muse in a pensive mood. To watch. زانو زدن *zānū zadan*, To kneel. زانوی کاه *zānūyi kāh*, A truss of straw.

P زانو زده *zānū-zada*, Sitting on the knees.

P زانه *zāna*, A noisy winged insect in baths.

A زاني *zānī*, (pl. زناة *zunāt*) A whoremonger.

A زانية *zāniyat*, (pl. زواني) An adultress, whore.

P زانیج *zānīj*, One's native country.

P زاو *zāv*, A mason. A plasterer. A master of any craft. Athletic, powerful. A cleft, chink. A narrow mountain-pass. A brickbat.

P زاودش *zāwdush*, The planet Mercury.

P زاور *zāwar*, A servant. Power, strength. Boldness. Health and safety. Huge, mighty, powerful. Alive, well. Gall. A dark colour. Black-coloured water (a disease). The planet Venus. A saddle-horse. An assistant. A companion. Bad-tempered. Covetous. Impossible.

A زاورة *zāwirat* or *zāwurat*, The crop, craw, maw.

P زاورس *zāwars*, (or زاوس) The planet Venus.

P زاور فرتاش *zāwar-fartāsh*, Whose existence is impossible.

P زاوش *zāwush*, The planet Jupiter.

A زأوق *zaʼuk*, Quicksilver.

P زاول *zāwul*, Name of a country in Persia; also of a people; of a note in music; and of an ancient Persian dialect now obsolete.

P زاولانه *zāwlāna*, A fetter, chain. Curly hair. Gold-dust.

P زاولستان *zāwulistān*, A country in Persia.

P زاووش *zāwūsh*, Mercury. Jupiter (planets).

A زاووق *zāʼūk*, Quicksilver.

P زاوه *zāwa*, Name of a town in Khurāsān.

A زاوية *zāwiyat*, (pl. زوايا *zawāyā'*) A corner, angle. A cell, monastery, convent, cloister, hermitage. زاويهٔ حادّه *zāwiyaʼi hādda*, An acute angle. زاويهٔ قائمه *zāwiyaʼi kāʼima*, A right angle. زاويهٔ مجسّمه *zāwiyaʼi mujassima*, A solid angle. زاويهٔ منفرجه *zāwiyaʼi munfarija*, An obtuse angle.

P زاویل *zāwīl*, An architect. A worker in clay.

A زاهد *zāhid*, Religious, devout, abstinent, continent, content. A monk, hermit. P زاهد خشك *zāhidi khushk*, A rigid monk. A hypocrite, dissembler. زاهد کوه *zāhidi koh*, The sun.

P زاهدانه *zāhidāna*, Religiously, like a monk.

A زاهدي *zāhidī*, Continence, a monkish life, piety. A sort of date.

A زاهر *zāhir*, Shining. Florid, vivid. Lucid, clear, plain.

P زاهري *zāhirī*, Odour, fragrance. Clearness.

A زاهرية *zāhirīyat*, A stately air in walking. Name of a certain unfathomable spring in Callirhoe.

A زاهق *zāhik*, (pl. زهق *zuhk* and *zuhuk*) Put to flight, routed, going away, vanishing. Perishing, expiring. An arrow which does not hit the mark, but passes beyond. Fat, full of marrow (an animal, or bone). Exceeding lean. Dry. Strong, rapid (current).

A زاهل *zāhil*, Tranquil, quiet, secure.

A زاهي *zāhī*, (A camel) which does not feed on the bitter herb حمض *hamz*. What shines, glitters, or pleases the eye.

A زأي *zaʼy*, The being proud and haughty.

P زاي *zāy*, (in composition) Bringing forth.

A زاي *zāy*, (pl. ازوي *azwī* and ازيي *azyī*) Name of the letter ز *zayn*.

P زایچه *zāycha*, A horoscope.

A زائد *zāʼid*, Exceeding. Redundant, excrescent, superfluous, ascititious, additional, accessory. A servile letter. زائد الوصف *zāʼidu'l wasf*, Beyond description, indescribable.

A زائدة *zāʼidat*, Any thing necessary or additional. زائدة الكبد *zāʼidatu'l kabid*, The lobe of the liver. الزائدة العظمىٰ *az zāʼidatu'l ʿuzma'*, The thigh-bone of a wild beast. The point of the nipple.

P زایدن *zāydan*, (for زائیدن *zāʼīdan*) To be born. To beget.

A زائر *zāʼir*, Roaring (lion). (pl. زائرون *zāʼirūn*, زوّار *zuwār* and زوّر *zuwar*) A visitor.

P زایش *zāyish*, Increase, augmentation. Production, produce.

A زائغون *zāʼighūn*, Wanderers from the way.

A زائف *zāʼif*, Clipt money. A lion.

P زایگر *zāygar*, Bearing a child. Fruitful.

A زائل *zāʼil*, Defective, deficient, failing, perishing, vanishing, transitory, fleeting, frail. Any thing moveable or animated. ليل زائل النجوم *layli zāʼilu'n nujūm*, A starless night. P زائل شدن *zāʼil shudan*, To perish, fail. زائل کردن *zāʼil kardan*, To destroy, cancel, obliterate.

A زائلة *zāʼilat*, Any thing possessed of motion or animation.

A زائن *zāʼin*, Dressed, adorned (woman).

P زاینده *zāyanda*, Bringing forth. A mother.

P زائیدگي *zāʼīdagī*, Child-birth.

P زائیدن *zāʼīdan*, To bring forth (a child). To originate, appear, come forth.

P زائیده *zāʼīda*, Procreated, generated, born.

P زب *zab*, Easy. Unbought, gratis. Straight.

A زبّ *zabba*, (fut. يزبّ *yazibbu*) (The camel) was very hairy. (The sun) was near setting. (The corners of his mouth) frothed.

A زبّ *zabb*, (v. n. of زبّ) Filling (a water-pot). Foaming. *Zubb*, The beard or the fore-part of it. The nose. (pl. ازبّ *azubb*, ازباب *azbāb*, and زببة *zababat*) The privy member of a man.

P زبّا *zubbā*, The daughter of a king of Hīra.

A زبّاء *zabbāʼ*, (fem. of ازبّ *azabb*) Hairy (she-camel). (Ground) luxuriant in grain or herbage. The fundament. A sore calamity.

A زباب *zabāb*, A field-mouse, a mole. Blind. Ignorant. A messenger, courier. A calumniator.

A زبّاب *zabbāb*, A seller of raisins or currants.

A زبأة *zabʼat*, Rage, anger, passion.

A زباد *zabād*, Civet, the perfume of the civet cat, *i.e.* the scraped-off filth collected under its tail.

A زبّاد *zubbād*, A thing of no value. Name of an herb. زبّاد اللبن *zubbādu'l laban*, Worthless milk.

A زبّادي *zubbādaʼ* or *zubādaʼ*, Name of an herb.

A زبادية *zabādiyat*, (properly ربادية *rabādiyat*) Evil, wickedness.

A زباريق *zabārīk*, The convulsions and paleness (of death).

A زبازاء *zabāzāʼ*, (or زبازاة) Short-bodied (woman).

A زبازية *zabāziyat*, Dissension, evil.

A زبال *zibāl*, An ant or bee's mouthful. *Zibāl* or *zubāl*, Any thing small or trifling.

A زبّال *zabbāl*, One who draws dung.

A زبالة *zubālat*, Any thing.

P زبان *zabān* or *zubān*, The tongue. Language, dialect, idiom, speech. The tongue or the shank of a button. A flame. Leave, permission. زبان آوردن *zabān āwardan*, To speak, tell, say, declare. زبان بر ديوار ماليدن *zabān bar dīwār mālīdan*, To rub the tongue on the wall, meaning to be resigned and content. زبان بره *zabāni bara*, (Lamb's tongue) The plantain. The plant hare's ear. زبان بريدن *zabān burīdan*, To silence. To make a present, to bribe. زبان بستن *zabān bastan*, To keep silence. To silence. زبان بيزبان *zabāni bī zabān*, The dumb tongue (of brutes). Dumb expression. A pen. زبان بي سر *zabāni bī sar*, Trifling, futile, impertinent discourse. زبان پارسي *zabāni pārsī*, (or فارسي *fārsī*) The Persian language, as spoken in Fārs or Persia Proper. زبان پهلوي *zabāni pahlavī*, The Pahlavī or ancient tongue, in which are written the Zand and other books of the Magi or worshippers of fire. زبان تر كردن *zabān tar kardan*, To speak. To wet one's whistle. زبان حال *zabāni hāl*, Language expressed by one's condition, situation, or by signs (in contradistinction to language of the tongue, and which is called زبان قال *zabāni kāl*). زبان دادن *zabān dādan*, To promise, agree, stipulate. To give permission. زبان در كشيدن *zabān dar kashīdan*, To keep in one's tongue. زبان دري *zabāni darī*, A purer dialect of the Persian, spoken at court. زبان زدن *zabān zadan*, To speak. زبان زرگري *zabāni zargarī*, An enigmatical kind of language. زبان ستدن *zabān sitadan*, To put to silence. زبان طوطي *zabāni tūtī*, (Parrot's tongue) Name of an herb. زبان گشادن *zabān gushādan*, To speak, utter. To revile. زبان كوفتن *zabān koftan*, To stammer, stutter. زبان گاو *zabāni gāo* or *gāv*, Borage. The point of a spear. زبان گرفتن *zabān giriftan*, To stammer. To know the state of an adversary's affairs. زبان گنجشك *zabāni gunjishk*, (Sparrow's tongue) Seed of the ash-tree. زبان لگام *zabāni ligām*, The tongue of the bridle. A ring on the bridle under the chin. زبان مغز دار *zabāni maghz-dār*, Profound speech. An eloquent tongue. زبان يافتن *zabān yāftan*, To obtain leave. بي زبان *bī zabān*, Dumb, speechless.

A زبان *zabān*, Refractory, contumacious. *Zubān*, The sixteenth mansion of the moon.

P زبان افگن *zubān-afgan*, Vomiting flames.

P زبان آور *zabān-āwar*, Eloquent. A backbiter.

P زبان آوري *zabān-āwarī*, Eloquence, fluency.

P زبان بر *zubān-bur*, (Tongue-cutting) A silencing argument. Hush-money.

P زبان بران *zubān-burān*, Satirist, lampooner.

P زبان بريده *zabān-burīda*, Silenced.

P زبان بند *zubān-band*, Fascination, as tying up the tongue. A fascinator.

P زبان بندي *zabān-bandī*, Deposition of a witness.

P زبان تران *zubān-tarān*, A satirist: railer: reviler.

P زبانخواه *zabān-khwāh*, A beggar.

P زباندان *zabān-dān*, A linguist. An interpreter. A poet. A scholar, a pupil.

P زباندراز *zabān-darāz*, Extending the tongue, *i.e.* speaking much and malevolently, abusive.

P زبان درازي *zabān-darāzī*, Loquacity. Obloquy, censure. زبان درازي كردن *zabān darāzī kardan*, To scold.

P زبان ران *zabān-rān*, Eloquent. Prolix, talkative. A story-teller.

P زبان راني *zubān-rānī*, Conversation. Talk.

P زبانزد *zabān-zad*, Talked about. Every-day talk.

P زبان زدگي *zubān-zadagī*, Mention.

P زبان زده *zubān-zada*, Spoken of, talked about.

P زبان فريب *zubān-firīb*, (or فريفته *firifta*) A liar.

P زبان فريفته *zubān-firifta*, A liar. Deceived.

P زبانگر *zabāngar*, Any thing which bites the tongue. Milk formed into butter.

P زبان گرفته *zabān-girifta*, Dumb, tongue-tied.

P زبان گز *zubān-gaz*, Acrid, tart, pungent.

P زبان گويا *zabān-goyā*, Eloquent speaker.

P زبانگير *zabān-gīr*, A tongue-taker, *i.e.* taking a prisoner to gain information. A spy. Whatever bites the tongue.

P زبانه *zabāna* or *zubāna*, Flame. The shank of a button. The tongue of a balance. Lingula pudendi. زبانه زدن *zabāna zadan*, To flame, blaze.

A زباني *zabānī*, A life-guard man. An infernal guard (*i. e.* a devil who is supposed to toss the damned into the flames).

A زبانيان *zubāniyānī*, The two claws (of a scorpion). Two bright stars, the scales of Libra, and the sixteenth mansion of the moon.

A زبانية *zabāniyat*, (pl. of زبنية *zibniyat*) Guards. Strong, stubborn, rebellious (jinns or men).

A زبب *zabab*, (v. n. of زبّ) Being hairy. Hairiness. The long hairs about a camel's face.

A زببة *zababat*, pl. of زبّ *zubb*, Membra virilia.

A زبتل *zabtal*, Short, dwarfish.

A زبد *zabd*, (v. n. of زبد) Churning. Feeding with cream or fresh butter. Giving. A little money. A small present. *Zubd*, Cream. Fresh butter. *Zabad*, Froth (of the sea), foam (of a camel), scum or dross (of silver). زبد البحر *zabadu'l bahr*, Cuttle-fish bone. زبد القصبة *zabadu'l kasabat*, An efflorescence which appears at the root of a cane. زبد القمر *zabadu'l kamar*, The moon-stone. *Zubad*, (pl. of زبدة *zubdat*) Creams.

A زبدان *zubdān*, Cream.

A زبدة *zubdat*, Cream of milk, best of any thing. Devonshire cream. Marrow. Butter. The middle. Chosen. زبدهٔ اركان *zubdaʼi arkān*, The best part of the creation. زبدهٔ ولاة الانام *zubdaʼi wulāti'l anām*, The cream of the rulers of men (Muhammad).

A زبديّ *zubdiy*, Creamy.

A زبر *zabr*, (v. n. of زبر) Writing. Hindering, keeping back, driving off. Understanding. Building, constructing (a well). Flowing profusely. Flinging stones. Laying the foundations of an edifice one upon another. Scolding, reproving, speaking harshly. Discourse, talk. Patience. Stones. Strong. اخذه بزبره *akhazahu bi zabrihi*, He took it all. *Zibr*, (pl. زبور *zubūr*) A book. *Zabar*, All, the whole. *Zubar* or *zubur*, (pl. of زبرة *zubrat*) Bits of iron. *Zubur*, (pl. of زبور *zabūr*) Books.

P زبر *zabar*, Above, upon, high, superior. The Persian term for the short vowel ـَـ *fat'ha*, because placed over a letter. A baker's trough. از زبر *az zabar*, From above. Aloft, over-head. زبر پرچين *zabari pur-chīn*, Thorns stuck on the top of a wall. *Zibar*, A shield. (for از بر *az bar*) By heart.

A زبّر *zibbir*, Strong, very powerful.

A زبراء *zabrāʼ*, (fem. of ازبر *azbar*) Wide between the shoulders. Name of a girl proverbially choleric.

P زبر آب *zabar-āb*, A film on stagnant water.

P زبرپوش *zabar-posh*, An upper garment. A quilted coverlet.

A زبرة *zabrat*, Writing. *Zubrat*, (pl. زبر *zubur* and *zubar*) A splinter or piece of iron. A bit. The space between the shoulders. The shoulder of a man or a lion. The hair of a lion's mane. The eleventh mansion of the moon. An anvil.

P زبر تنگ *zabar-tang*, A surcingle, girth.

A زبرج *zibrij*, An ornamented various-coloured garment; also a decoration of jewels, or any thing similar. Gold. Thin ruddy clouds, with a mixture of white.

P A زبرجد *zabarjad*, An emerald. A topaz.

P زبرجدي *zabarjadī*, Of the colour of the emerald or topaz.

A زبردج *zabardaj*, An emerald. A topaz.

P زبردست *zabar-dast*, Athletic, vigorous. Overbearing, tyrannical, harsh, oppressive, violent. Superior. The upper part, higher side.

P زبردستي *zabar-dasti*, Oppression, tyranny, severity, harshness, violence. Superiority, upper-handedness.

P زبرفوف *zabar-fūf*, Abuse, curse, execration.

A الزبرقان *az'zibrikān*, The moon. Thin-bearded. Name of a man.

A زبرقة *zabrakat*, (v. n. of زبرق Q) Dyeing (a garment) red or yellow.

P زبر گلوید *zabar-gilwīd*, A cauldron.

P زبرم *zibarm*, Memory, recollection.

P زبرة *zubara*, A bar of iron.

P زبري *zabarī*, Violence, oppression.

P زبرين *zabarīn*, Higher, upper. Of, or belonging to, the word زبر *zabar*, Above. Superior.

A زبزب *zabzab*, A kind of ship. Name of an animal of the size of a little dog, whose fur is good against gout and rheumatism.

A زبزبة *zabzabat*, (v. n. of زبزب Q) Being angry. Being routed in battle.

A زبط *zabt*, (v. n. of زبط) Quacking (a duck).

A P زبطانة *zabtānat*, (or P زبطانه *zabtāna*) A long hollow tube, through which they shoot small birds with pellets forced out by the breath.

P زبطانه *zabtāna*, The top of a saw, by which the handle is fixed.

A زبعبق *zabaʿbak*, (or زبعباق *zibiʿbāk*) Of a bad disposition.

A زبعبك *zabaʿbak*, (or زبعبكي *zabaʿbakiy*) Wicked, bold, wholly regardless of what is said to him.

A زبعر *zabʿar*, A species of the plant مرو *marv*. *Zabʿar* or *zibʿar*, Name of a fragrant herb.

A زبعراة *zibaʿrāt*, Thick and hairy (ear). Bad-tempered, cross (woman).

A زبعري *zibaʿra'*, Ill-disposed. Hairy about the eyebrows or jaws (a man or camel). A certain tree which grows in Hijāz. A female crocodile. A certain beast which is said to carry an elephant on his horn. *Zibaʿra'* or *zabaʿra'*, Gross, thick.

A زبعريّ *zabʿariy*, A species of the plant مرو *marv*. *Zibaʿriy*, A kind of arrow with long feathers.

A زبغ *zabagh*, Beginning, or novelty (of any thing). A sum, whole, total. An attack, assault.

P زبغر *zabghur*, (or زبگر *zabgur*) Filling the cheeks with wind, and then making a sound by striking them.

A زبغر *zibghar*, An odoriferous herb.

A زبق *zabk*, (v. n. of زبق) Plucking (the beard). Mixing. Restraining, keeping back.

A زبل *zabl*, (v. n. of زبل) Manuring (land), dunging (a crop). *Zibl*, Dung. *Zubul*, (pl. of زبيل *zabīl*) Baskets.

A زبلان *zublān*, (pl. of زبيل *zabīl*) Baskets.

A زبلة *zublat*, A mouthful. *Zabalat*, A trifle.

P زبلدان *zibldān*, A dunghill, a mixen.

P زبلوق *zablūk*, A term of reproach.

A زبن *zabn*, (v. n. of زبن) Beating off, driving away. Striking with the knee when being milked (a camel). Selling fruit on the tree by guess for dates received by measure. One who drives violently. Separate, detached (dwelling-house). *Zibn*, Need, necessity. *Zaban*, Stuff of the size of a room (as a curtain hung before a lady's chamber). A side, a quarter.

A زبنّ *zubunn*, One who pushes away violently.

A زبنة *zubunnat*, The fore-leg of a camel.

A زبنتر *zabantar*, Short, contemptible, dwarfish. Ugly. Calamity, misfortune.

A زبنتري *zabantara'*, Calamity, misfortune.

A زبنية *zibniyat*, (pl. زبانية *zabāniyat*) A life-guard man. A devil who is supposed to throw the damned into the flames. Strong, severe. Stubborn, rebellious, (jinn or man).

A زبوبر *zabawbar*, All, the whole.

P زبوخه *zabūkha*, Venereal pleasures.

P زبوده *za* or *zubūda*, Carelessness. A scallion.

A زبور *zabūr*, (pl. زبر *zubur*) Writing. A book. Word of God. Psalms of David. *Zubūr*, (pl. of زبر *zibr*) Books.

P زبورخوان *zabūr-khwān*, A psalm-singer.

P زبوز *zabūz*, A whirlpool.

A زبول *zubūl*, (v. n. of زبل) Dunging (land).

P زبول يافته *zubūl-yāfta*, Renovated by manure.

P زبون *zabūn*, Weak, infirm, helpless. Vile. Of the worst kind, spoilt, bad. Irksome. Conquered, made captive. Willing. Greedy. Complaining. The earnest paid upon purchase. A purchase, in which the purchaser buys with avidity.

A زبون *zabūn*, (A battle) wherein the combatants crowd upon one another. (A she-camel) kicking her milker. Negligent, imprudent. A dupe. Weak in mind. A fellow. A well with some remains of water at the bottom.

A زبّون *zabbūn*, Pride.

P زبون بافته *zabūn-bāfta*, Of a flimsy texture.

A زبّونة *zabbūnat*, Pride, arrogance. Rebellion, stubbornness. *Zabbūnat* or *zubbūnat*, Whatever defends the side. The neck.

P زبونكش *zabūn-kush*, A persecutor of the weak.

P زبوني *zabūnī*, Infirmity, indisposition, weakness. Vileness.

P زبهر *zibhar*, Disgust at filial undutifulness.

A زبهمة *zabhamat*, Haste, expedition, an expeditious mode of walking. A wheeled carriage.

P زبهيده *zabhīda*, Fallen, dropped.

A زبي *zaby*, (v. n. of زبي) Carrying. Lying in wait with mischievous intent. Driving forward. Calling, inviting. *Zuba'*, (pl. of زبية *zubyat*) High grounds where water does not reach.

A زبيب *zabīb*, Currants, sun-raisins: dried figs or dates. Foam. The poison of a serpent. زبيب الجبل *zabību'l jabal*, A small raisin or currant which expels phlegm, and removes an impediment in the speech. *Zubayb*, (dim. of زبّ *zubb*) A boy's cock.

A زبيبة *zabībat*, One raisin. An ulcer growing on the hand.

A زبيبتان *zabībatāni*, Two black spots above the eyes of a serpent and of a dog. Saliva at the corners of the lips after speaking much. The two corners of a serpent's mouth.

A زبيبيّ *zabībiy*, A seller of raisins or currants. Wine made from raisins steeped without boiling.

A زبيبيّة *zabībiyat*, Name of a quarter in Bagdād.

A زبية *zubyat* or *zabyat*, (pl. زبي *zuba'*) High ground, where water does not reach. A pit dug for a lion (generally on high ground).

A زبيدة *zubaydat*, The wife of Hārūn Arrashīd.

A زبير *zabīr*, Adversity, misfortune. The mountain on which God spoke to Moses. Thin, fetid, black mud. A writing. The ear.

P زبير *zibīr*, Memory, recollection: by heart.

A زبيط *zabīt*, (v. n. of زبط) Quacking (a duck).

A زبيع *zabīʿ*, Enraged, pouring forth invective.

A زبيق *zabīk*, Plucked (beard).

A زبيل *zabīl*, Dung. *Zabīl*, (or زبّيل *zibbīl*) (pl. زبل *zubul* and زبلان *zublān*) A dried and hollow pumpkin, gourd, or calabash, in which women keep their cotton. A basket, a wallet.

A زبّين *zibbīn*, One who expels or retains excrement and urine against his will.

P زپ *zap*, Straight, right, true.

P زپر *zipar*, A shield.

P زپره *zapara*, Quicksilver.

P زت *zat*, Naked.

A زتّ *zatt*, (v. n. of زتّ) Dressing (a bride).

A زتوخ *zutūkh*, (v. n. of زتخ) Adhering (a tike).

P زج *zaj*, Name of a yellow bird. *Zuj*, A bone-headed arrow. A very short arrow. Dried curds.

A زجّ *zajj*, (v. n. of زجّ) Striking with the ferule (of a spear). Throwing. Running (an ostrich). *Zujj*, (pl. زجج *zijaj* and زججة *zijajat*) The tip of the elbow. The point of an arrow. The cramp-iron or ferule of a spear. (pl. of ازجّ *azajj*) (Men) with long, thin eyebrows. Long-striding ostriches.

A زجاء *zajāʾ*, (v. n. of زجا for زجو) Being easy, successful, happening fortunately. Being ready, expeditiously collected (revenue). Being broken off (laughter).

A زجّاء *zajjāʾ*, (fem. of ازجّ *azajj*) Possessed of long and thin eyebrows. (A female ostrich) going with long strides.

A زجاج *zijāj*, The canine teeth of a stallion. (pl. of زجّ *zujj*) The ferules of spears. Tips of elbows. Points of arrows. *Zujāj*, *zijāj*, or *zajāj*, Glass.

A زجّاج *zajjāj*, A glass-manufacturer.

A زجاجة *zujājat*, A bit of glass. A cup, a glass.

P زجاجهٔ مي ناب *zujāja-i may-i nāb*, A glass of pure wine.

A زجاجيّ *zajājiy*, A vender of glass. *Zujājiy*, Made of glass. A glass-maker. قصر زجاجي *kasri zujājī*, A building of glass, a crystal palace.

P زجال *zajāl*, A spider.

A حمام الزجال *hamāmu'z zajāl*, A carrier-pigeon.

A زجبة *zujbat*, One word (is not heard).

A زجج *zajaj*, Length and thinness of eyebrows. *Zujuj*, Quiet, tame, domestic asses. Short spears furnished with heads.

A زججة *zijajat*, (pl. of زجّ *zujj*) The tips of the elbows. The ferules of spears. Points of arrows.

A زجح *zajh*, An excoriating, a scratching.

A زجر *zajr* or *zajar*, (pl. زجور *zujūr*) Divination, augury from the flight of birds. A large kind of fish. زجر و منع الهی *zajr u manʿi ilāhī*, The divine prohibition or chastisement. *Zajr*, (v. n. of زجر) Hindering, prohibiting. Checking, chiding. Crying out, calling (to cattle) to move onward. Driving up, urging forward. Casting her foal (a camel). Conjecturing, divining, auguring, observing the flight of birds. Force, violence. Threat. Punishment.

A زجل *zajl*, (v. n. of زجل) Throwing. Shooting, hitting. Striking with the ferule of a spear. Injecting. Pushing, thrusting, driving away. Sending (a carrier-pigeon) anywhere. Bringing forth. *Zajal*, (v. n. of زجل) Playing. Singing with taste, chanting. Sounds, clamours, mixed murmurs. *Zajil*, (A cloud) reverberating with the noise of thunder. One who raises his voice, a chanter. A house or tent, through which the wind whistles. *Zujal*, (pl. of زجلة *zujlat*) Crowds. Parts, portions.

A زجلاء *zajlāʾ*, Swift (she-camel or ostrich).

A زجلة *zaj* or *zujlat*, The voice of men. A crowd. *Zujlat*, A part, portion: a single drop or particle. The skin between the eyes. State, condition.

A زجم *zajm*, (v. n. of زجم) Muttering inarticulately. Listening to what is said low, in a whisper.

A زجّم *zujjam*, A kind of bird.

A زجمة *zajmat*, The moisture that comes out with a new-born infant. *Zajmat* or *zujmat*, A mutter, whisper. A word. Somewhat.

P زجمول *zajmūl*, Flax-seed.

A زجن *zajn*, (v.n. of زجن) Delaying, being slow. Displacing. Short, dwarfish (man).

A زجنة *zajnat*, A word. A whisper.

A زجنجل *zujanjal*, A polished mirror.

A زجو *zajw*, (v.n. of زجا for زجو) Driving, thrusting away. *Zajw*, (or زجوّ *zujūw*) (v. n. of زجا for زجو) Being easy, successful, happening fortunately. Being readily and expeditiously collected (tribute). Being broken off (laughter).

A زجور *zajūr*, (A she-camel) which one recognises by the eyes and not by the nose. (A camel) which does not give her milk until she be chidden. A camel that smells another's colt and refuses to give her milk. *Zujūr*, (pl. of زجر *zajr* or *zajar*) Divinations. Huge fishes.

A زجول *zajul*, Long, distant (mountain-steep).

A زجوم *zajūm*, (A bow) which makes a low, obscure twang. Madness. Bad-tempered (camel): one that will not take a liking to another's foal.

P زجه *zaja* (or زچه *zacha*) A woman who has recently brought forth (so called until the fortieth day after her delivery).

P زچگی *zachagī*, Child-birth.

A زحّ *zahh*, (v. n. of زحّ) Removing (from its place). Impelling, repelling. Driving away. Drawing quickly.

A زحار *zihār*, (v. n. 3 of زحر) Being inimical, hostile. *Zuhār*, A certain disease incident to camels. *Zuhār*, (or زحارة *zuhārat*) A looseness in the belly, dysentery, with griping and discharge of blood. Hard breathing attended with groans.

A زحّار *zahhār*, One who sighs and breathes hard.

A زحاف *zihāf*, (in prosody) A dropping of one letter between two others.

A زحالة *zuhālat*, A certain animal that enters its hole tail foremost. A man who travels not. A woman who keeps aloof from all kinds of work.

A زحالف *zahālif*, Small reptiles resembling ants. *Zahālif*, (or زحاليف *zahālīf*) (pl. of زحلوفة *zuhlūfat*) The marks of boys sliding from high grounds.

A زحاليق *zahālīk*, (pl. of زحلوقة) Boys' slides.

A زحام *zihām*, (v. n. of زحم) Pressing (people in a crowd). A crowd. كثير الزحام *kasīru'z zihām*, Very crowding.

A زحاميك *zahāmīk*, (pl. of زحموك) Dodders.

A زحر *zahr*, (v.n. of زحر) Breathing hard, groaning (a woman in labour). Groaning when asked for any thing (a miser). Wounding the head with a spear. *Zuhar*, A miser.

A زحران *zahrān*, A miser.

A زحرة *zahrat*, A single throe.

A زحزاح *zahzāh*, Remote, far distant.

A زحزح *zahzah*, Absence, distance.

A زحزحة *zahzahat*, (v.n. of زحزح Q) Separating, detaching. Driving away, putting to a distance.

A زحف *zahf*, An army marching against the enemy. *Zahf* or *zahaf*, (v. n. of زحف) Proceeding, advancing gradually. Creeping forward (as a child on the ground). Dragging the limbs from fatigue (a camel). Skimming along or grazing the ground until it has reached the mark (an arrow that had fallen short).

A زحفان *zahafān*, A proceeding, or advancing gradually.

A زحفة *zuhafat*, One who does not travel through countries. نار الزحفتين *nāru'z zahfatayn*, A fire made of the plant شيح *shīh* and of the الاء *alāʾ* (both of which kindle rapidly).

A زحك *zahk*, (v. n. of زحك) Being tired (a camel). Stopping in one place. Approaching. Going to a distance.

A زحل *zahl*, (v. n. of زحل) Departing. Being wearied, lagging behind on a journey. A loiterer behind. *Zahil*, One who departs and goes away. *Zuhal*, The planet Saturn. One who fails in, or gives up his work. Black-lead. غلام زحل *ghulāmu zuhal*, Name of Abū Kāsim the astronomer.

A زحلّ *zihall*, A camel which pushes the others away from the cistern that he may drink himself.

A زحلفة *zahlafat*, (v. n. of زحلف Q) Rolling. Giving a thousand. Thrusting, driving away. Talking fast. Filling (a vessel).

A زحلق *zihlik*, Violent, boisterous (wind).

A زحلقة *zahlakat*, (v. n. of زحلق Q) Turning, tumbling, revolving.

A زحلكة *zahlakat*, (v. n. of زحلك Q) Rolling.

A زحلوط *zuhlūt*, Avaricious, base, abject.

A زحلوفة *zuhlūfat*, (or زحلوقة *zuhlūkat*) (pl. زحالف *zahālif*, زحاليف *zahālīf*, زحاليق *zahālīk*) The marks left by a boy sliding from high ground, a boy's slide. An insect somewhat like an ant.

A زحلوقة *zuhlūkat*, The grave. A plank laid athwart another in the game of see-saw.

A زحلوكة *zuhlūkat*, (pl. زحاليك *zahālīk*) A boy's slide down a slope.

A زحلول *zuhlūl*, A narrow, slippery place.

A زحليل *zihlīl*, One who retires, and remains behind. A narrow and slippery place. Swift, quick.

A زحم *zahm*, (v. n. of زحم) Pressing, squeezing (as in a crowd). A crowd, throng. امّ الزحم *ummu'z zahm* or *zuhm*, Mecca (on account of the crowds of pilgrims).

A زحمة *zahmat*, (v. n. of زحم) Squeezing, pressing (as a dense throng). The pangs of child-birth. A crowd, bustle, throng. Disquietude, indisposition of body or mind; pain, trouble, disease. زحمت فرنگ *zahmati farang*, The French disease. P زحمت دادن *zahmat dādan*, To incommode, molest, annoy, torment.

P زحمت كش *zahmat-kash*, Afflicted.

A زحمرة *zahmarat*, (v. n. of زحمر Q) Filling (a leathern bottle).

A زحموك *zuhmūk*, (pl. زحاميك) Dodder.

A زحن *zahn*, (v. n. of زحن) Proceeding slowly. Moving (from its place). *Zahn* or *zuhan*, Short.

A زحنة *zahnat*, Intense heat. A caravan with its luggage and followers. *Zuhnat*, A bend in a valley. *Zuhanat*, Short, dwarfish (woman).

A زحنففة *zahanfafat*, One whose two heel-tendons knock against each other. One who crawls on the ground.

A زحنقف *zahankaf*, One who hitches along on his bottom. One whose heels strike against each other in walking.

A زحوب *zuhūb*, (v. n. of زحب) Approaching.

A زحوف *zahūf*, (A she-camel) which drags the limbs from fatigue. *Zuhūf*, (v. n. of زحف) Proceeding, advancing gradually. Creeping forward (as a little boy on his bum). Dragging the limbs from fatigue (a camel).

A زحوك *zuhūk*, (v. n. of زحك) Being jaded.

A زحول *zahūl*, A camel that will not leave the cistern without drinking, although beaten. Long and distant (mountain-steep). *Zuhūl*, (v.n.of زحل) Declining, retiring to a distance.

A زحير *zahīr*, (v. n. of زحر) Groaning, or breathing hard. A looseness in the belly. Hard breathing. A twisting of the guts, with griping and discharge of blood, dysentery.

A زحيل *zahīl*, One who departs and goes away.

P زخ *zakh*, A groan. Tinkling of a bell. A wart. The driving in of a stake. (for زخم *zakhm*) A wound.

A زخّ *zakhkh*, (v. n. of زخّ) Throwing down. Lying with (a woman). Causing to fall into a hole. Discharging urine. Rushing upon, assaulting. Becoming angry, taking fire. Travelling at a cruel pace (a camel-driver). Blazing, flashing (fire).

A زخار *zikhār*, (v. n. 3 of زخر) Boasting, glorying (against another).

A زخّار *zakhkhār*, Full, and swelling (sea).

A زخارف *zakhārif*, Channels for water in grooves, furrows, or gutters. Ships. Four-footed insects flying on the surface of the water. Worldly pomps and pageants.

P زخاره *zakhāra*, (or زختاره) A branch.

A زخاريّ *zakhāriy*, (A place) full of luxuriant herbage. *Zukhāriy*, Luxuriant (plant). *Zukhāriy* or *zakhāriy*, The blossom of a plant. Greenness and freshness of herbage.

A زخباء *zakhbā*, Patient, hardy (she-camel).

A زخّة *zakhkhat*, Rage. Malevolence, envy. A woman. *Zukhkhat*, Small sheep.

A زخر *zakhr*, (v. n. of زخر) Filling. Rising en masse (a people). Overflowing (a channel): swelling (the sea): boiling furiously (a pot): raging (war). Scattering to the winds. Glorying in one's wealth. Growing luxuriantly (a plant). Exhilarating. Making (cattle) fat and well-liking (grass).

A زخرط *zikhrit*, The snot or slaver of sheep or camels. A sort of plant.

A زخرف *zukhruf*, Gold. Painting, gilding. Beauty, elegance, ornament. A speech embellished with fine imagery and romantic fiction. Different genera of plants.

A زخرفة *zakhrafat*, (v. n. of زخرف Q) Arranging (a discourse). Adorning with paint or gilding.

A زخروط *zukhrūt*, Old and decrepit (camel).

P زخره *zakhra*, Spectator at games of hazard.

A زخريّ *zukhriy*, Long, tall.

A زخريط *zikhrit*, The snot and slaver of sheep or camels. A sort of plant.

A زخزبّ *zukhzubb*, Strong and firm in flesh.

A زخزخة *zakhzakhat*, The act of lying with.

A زخف *zakhf*, A being vain-glorious, proud.

A زخلوط *zukhlūt*, A low, worthless fellow.

P زخم *zakhm*, A wound, scar, sore, cut, blow: a fracture. Sickness. زخم بريان *zakhmi biryān*, A kind of pilaw. زخم خوردن *zakhm khwurdan*, To be wounded. زخم سهمناك *zakhmi sahamnāk*, An envenomed, mortal wound. زخم ناخن *zakhmi nākhun*, A scratch with the nails. Astronomical lines. چشم زخم *chashm-zakhm*, A wound with the eye, a fascinating look.

A زخم *zakhm*, (v. n. of زخم) Forcing, driving furiously. Stinking (flesh). *Zakham*, (v. n. of زخم) Stinking (especially the flesh of wild-beasts). *Zakhim*, Stinking, offensive, fetid.

A زخماء *zakhmā*, Stinking (woman).

A زخمة *zakhamat*, The stink of wild-beasts' flesh.

P زخم خورده *zakhm-khwurda*, Wounded. خنزير زخم خورده *khinzīri zakhm-khwurda*, Wounded hog.

P زخمدار *zakhm-dār*, Wounded, struck.

P زخمرس *zakhm-ras*, Wounding, piercing.

P زخمكاري *zakhm-kārī*, A blow, mortal wound.

P زخمناك *zakhmnāk*, Wounded, struck.

P زخمه *zakhma*, The bow (of a violin, &c.).

P زخمي *zakhmī*, Wounded.

P زخناره *zakhnāra*, The branch of a tree.

P زخود *zi khwud*, Of itself. زخود شدن *zi khwud shudan*, To be out of one's senses.

A زخور *zukhūr*, (v. n. of زخر) Being full, overflowing (a channel). Swelling, raging (the sea). Growing luxuriantly (a plant). Boiling furiously (a pot), raging (war). Rising en masse (a people). Filling. Glorying in one's possessions. Exhilarating. Rendering (cattle) fat and comely (grass). Scattering to the winds. *Zakhwar*, Luxuriant (plant).

A زخوريّ *zakhwariy*, Tumid, turgid, pompous (speech). Luxuriant (plant).

A زخومة *zakhūmat*, Stinking (woman).

P زخون *zakhūn*, Pride, conceit.

A زخيخ *zakhīkh*, (v.n. of زخّ) Flaring (a fire).

A زخيف *zakhīf*, The being vain-glorious, proud.

P زد *zad*, (pret. of زدن *zadan*) He struck. A stroke, blow. Battle, conflict, combat. زد و خورد *zad u khwurd*, Battle conflict. زد و كوب *zad u kob*, Beating and thumping. Battle.

P زدا *zidā*, (in compos.) Cleaning, wiping, scouring off (rust). Dissipating, dispelling. ظلمت زدا *zulmat-zidā*, Dispelling darkness (Muhammad). غم زدا *gham-zidā*, Driving away grief. غم زدا و مسرّت افزا *gham-zidā u masarrat-afzā*, Dispelling care and augmenting joy. Pleasant, delightful.

P زدانيدن *zadānīdan*, To cause to strike.

P زداي *zidāy*, (in compos. from زدودن *zidūdān*) Wiping, cleaning, scouring.

P زداينده *zidāyanda*, A polisher, furbisher.

P زداييدن *zidāyīdan*, To scour, cleanse.

A زدب *zidb*, (pl. ازداب) Portion, share, lot.

A زدر *zadr*, (v. n. of زدر) Returning.

P زدر *zadar*, Over. *Zidar*, Worthy, deserving.

A زدع *zadʻ*, (v. n. of زدع) Lying with.

A زدق *zidk*, (for صدق *sidk*) Truth, veracity.

P زدگي *zadagī*, Percussion. A blow.

P زدن *zadan*, To strike, beat, dash against, flap. To touch. To sound, blow. To play on an instrument. To verge, tend, incline towards. To forge (a sword). To accentuate. To eat. To lie with. بوسه زدن *bosa zadan*, To kiss. بهم زدن *ba ham zadan*, To strike together, to dash against one another. تپانچه زدن *tapāncha zadan*, To give a smack on the face. جراحت زدن *jarāhat zadan*, To wound. سر در سنگ زدن *sar dar sang zadan*, To strike one's head against a stone; *i.e.* to blunder, to lie. دف زدن *daf zadan*, To beat a drum. شانه بر يال اسب زدن *shāna bar yāli asb zadan*, To comb the mane of a horse. گل بر سر زدن *gul bar sar zadan*, To put roses on the head. لاف زدن *lāf zadan*, To boast. مثل زدن *masal zadan*, To propound parables, relate fables. مشت زدن *musht zadan*, To bruise with the fist. ناله زدن *nāla zadan*, To groan, sigh, lament. ندا زدن *nidā zadan*, (or صلا زدن *salā zadan*) To proclaim. ني زدن *nay zadan*, To sound a pipe, blow a flute. بسرخي زند *ba surkhī zanad*, It inclines towards red.

A زدو *zadw*, (v. n. of زدا for زدو) Playing at a game with nuts, rolling them into a hole. Aiming at or hitting (the goal). Stretching out the hand (towards any object).

P زدوار *zadwār*, Zedoary.

P زدودن *zidūdan*, To polish, clean, scour, furbish. To clear the country of mutiny or sedition. To wipe sadness from the mind. To pluck, gather.

P زدوده *zidūda*, Polished, cleaned, brightened.

P زدونتن *zadūnitan*, (in zand and Pāz.) To buy.

P زده *zada*, Stricken, smitten. Affected, or afflicted with any disease. Accentuated (as the final syllable of بوده *būda*, رسيدن *rasīdan*, &c.). Masticated, eaten. Published abroad. Old, worn out. Cut down, lopped off. Clipped, trimmed. Adorned, set off. Forged (sword). A cart, dray. An order, row, series. A line (in writing). زده بودن *zada būdan*, To be possessed of a devil. زده شدن *zada shudan*, To be beaten. پازده *pā-zada*, Struck or beat down with the feet. سودا زده *sawdā-zada*, Sad, melancholy, hypochondriacal. محبّت زده *mahabbat-zada*, Smitten with love.

P زر *zar*, Gold. Money, riches, wealth. An old man or woman. An old man, grey and ruddy. زر اصل *zari asl*, A principal sum. Pure gold. زر اندودن *zar andūdan*, To gild. To acquire money. زر تلي *zari talī*, Pure gold. زر جعفري *zari jaʻfarī*, The purest kind of gold. زر خالص *zari khālis*, Fine gold. زر خشك *zari khushk*, Pure gold. زر ده پنجي *zari dah panjī*, Gold debased by alloy in the proportion of one half. زر دست افشار *zari dast-afshār*, Gold reduced to a soft state, and capable of being wrought by the hand. زر ده دهي *zari dah dahī*, Gold without any alloy. زر ده ششي *zari dah shashī*, Gold, two-fifths of which is alloy. زر ده مهي *zari dah mahī*, The finest gold. زرده

نهي *zari dah nuhī*, Gold, a tenth whereof is alloy. زر ده هشتي *zari dah hashtī*, Gold, a fifth whereof is alloy. زر ده هفتي *zari dah haftī*, Gold, three-tenths of which is alloy. زر ركني *zar ruknī*, Pure gold. زر رومال *zari rū-māl*, Gilded (copper). زر ساده *zari sāda*, Pure, unwrought gold. زر ساو *zari sāw*, Pure gold, of the full standard. A particle or filing of gold (which falls off when working). زر سرخ *zari surkh*, Gold. Pure gold of a red colour. Gold coin. Name of a suit in cards. زر سفيد *zari safed*, Silver. A suit in cards. زر شش سري *zari shash sarī*, Pure gold. زر طلا *zari tilā*, Fine ductile gold for gilding. زر طلي *zari talī*, Pure gold. زر قلب *zari kalb*, Base coin. زر گل *zari gul*, The yellow stamina of a rose. زر مذاب *zari muzāb*, Melted gold. زر مسكوك *zari maskūk*, Gold coin. زر مصري *zari misrī*, Pure gold. زر مشت افشار *zari musht-afshār*, A soft kind of gold which might be moulded into any shape. زر مغربي *zari maghribī*, Purest gold. The sun. زر موجود *zari mawjūd*, Ready money. زر ناخني *zari nākhunī*, The purest gold, on which the finger nail leaves an impression. زر نقد *zari nakd*, Ready money. زر و سيم *zar u sīm*, Gold and silver. زال زر *zāl-zar*, Name of Rustam's father.

A زرّ *zarr*, (v. n. of زرّ) Buttoning (a garment). Plucking, twitching. Chasing away, pursuing. Biting. Stabbing. Shutting close the eyes. Being heated, inflamed (the eye). Collecting violently. Shaking (furniture). Waxing strong (the intellect). Oppressing a rival. Getting understanding, after lacking wisdom. *Zirr*, (pl. ازرار *azrār* and زرور *zurūr*) A coat-button. A bird's egg. The edge of a sword. The knob of the hip. A bone like a half-nut, in which the lizard's head turns. A socket in general. The socket of the shoulder. A piece of wood into which the top of the tent-pole is fixed. Skilled in pasturing camels. The stay or support of any thing. A small bone under the heart acting as a support. زرّ الدين *zirru'd dīn*, The stay of religion. زرّ مال *zirru mālin*, Skilful in the management of camels. زرّ الورد *zirru'l ward*, A rose-bud. The button or knob which remains after the leaves of the rose are shed.

P زراب *zarāb*, Gold-water. Wine. A mountain near Baghdād.

P زراب ريز *zarāb-rez*, Shedding blood. Perspiring.

A زرابي *zarābiy*, (pl. of زربيّ *zirbīy* or *zurbīy*) Couches, pillows, or carpets for sitting on. (pl. of زربيّة *zirbīyat* and *zurbīyat*) Fountains, jet-d'eaux.

P زراتشت *zarātusht*, Zoroaster (the author of the religion of the Magi).

P زراج *zarāj*, The barberry and its tree.

P زراچه *zarācha*, An Ethiopian wrestler.

A زرّاح *zurrāh*, Quick in motion.

A زراد *zirād*, A rope fastened round a camel's neck, to prevent him from bringing up his food when chewing the cud and throwing it on his rider. A scourge or piece of stick, with which they strike one another playfully when dancing.

A زرّاد *zarrād*, A maker of coats of mail with iron rings (زرد *zarad*).

P زرّاد خانه *zarrād-khāna*, Armourer's shop.

P زرادشت *zarādusht*, Zoroaster.

P زرادهشت *zarāduhsht*, Zoroaster.

A زرار *zurār*, Of a quick, sprightly genius.

A زرارة *zurārat*, Any thing thrown against a wall and sticking there.

A زراريق *zarārīk*, (pl. of زرّق *zurrak*) Hawks. White falcons.

A زرازر *zurāzir*, Sharp, quick, sprightly.

A زرازرة *zarāzirat*, (pl. of زرزار *zirzār*) Commanders of ten thousand men.

P زراسب *zar asb*, Name of a son of طوس *tūs*.

P زراسگ *zarāsag*, (or زراسنگ *zarāsang*) A kind of dust like gold with which they sprinkle writings.

A زراط *zirāt*, (for سراط *sirāt*) A way, path.

A زراع *zirāɛ*, (v. n. 3 of زرع) Giving a field to sow, and furnishing the seed.

A زرّاع *zarrāɛ*, A sower, farmer. *Zurrāɛ*, (pl. of زارع *zāriɛ*) Sowers.

A زراعة *zirāɛat*, Agriculture, husbandry, tillage. Sowing, cultivation. P زراعت كردن *zirāɛat kardan*, To cultivate.

P زراغش *zarāghash*, Hard and sandy ground.

P زراغن *zarāghan*, A sob, hiccough. *Zarāghan* or زراغنك *zarāghank*, Hard, sandy ground.

P زراف *zarāf*, A giraffe.

A زرّاف *zarrāf*, A cameleopard.

A زرّافات *zarrāfāt*, A kind of watering machine.

A زرافة *zarāfat* or زرّافة *zarrāfat*, A body of men (about ten). *Zarāfat* or *zurāfat*, (pl. زرافى *zurāfa'*) A cameleopard, a giraffe. *Zurāfat*, A great liar.

A زرافى *zurāfa'*, (pl. of زرافة) Cameleopards.

P زرافين *zurāfīn*, A bar, a bolt. The ring of a door-post for fastening a door.

A زرّاق *zarrāk*, A hypocrite, sycophant, rogue.

P زرّاقانه *zarrākāna*, Hypocritically.

P زراك *zarāk*, The barberry.

P زرآلو *zar-ālū* (or زرآلود *zar-ālūd*) A plum.

A زراميم *zarāmīm*, Contracted within itself.

P زرانداز *zar-andāz*, A hooka-carpet.

P زراندرزر *zar andar zar*, Profusely gilded.

P زراندود *zar-andūd*, (or اندوده *andūda*) Gilded.

P زراندودن *zar andūdan*, To gild.

A زراوح *zarāwih*, (pl. of زروحة *zarwahat*) Low, wide spread hills.

P زراوشان *zirāwishān*, A species of violet.

A زراوند *zarāwand*, Aristolochy, birthwort.

P زراوه *zarāwa*, Name of a champion of Irān.

P زراه *zarāh*, Sea. زراه اكفوده The Caspian.

A زراهمة *zurāhimat*, An unblemished maid. A fat young woman.

A زرائب *zarāɛib*, (pl. of زريبة *zarībat*) Folds, enclosures for cattle. Dens of wild beasts. Lurking-places of hunters.

A زراية *zirāyat*, (v. n. of زري) Chiding, reproving. Defaming.

P زرايو *zirāyū*, A woman's veil.

A زرب *zarb*, (v. n. of زرب) Flowing. *Zarb* or *zirb*, (pl. زروب *zurūb*) A sheep-fold. A place of entrance. *Zirb*, A canal.

A زرباب *zirbāb*, Gold; or its glitter. Yellow.

P زرباف *zar-bāf*, (or زربافته *zar-bāfta*) Brocade, cloth of gold.

P زربان *zarbān*, Old, decrepit. Abraham.

A زربة (عين *ɛayn*) *zarbat* (or زربى *zarba'*), Name of a city in Cilicia.

P زربفت *zar-baft*, Brocade, cloth of gold.

P زربق *zarbak*, Name of a town in Khurāsān; also of a river in the same province, called likewise نهر مرغاب *nahri murghāb*.

A زربون *zarbūn*, A kind of fish, a perch. *Zurbūn* or *zarabūn*, A kind of shoe or slipper.

A زربيّ *zirbīy* or *zurbīy*, A couch, bed, cushion. (A plant) turning yellow in summer.

P زربياو *zarbayāw*, Melted silver.

A زربيّة *zar, zir,* or *zurbīyat*, A fountain. An ornamented couch. See شادروان *shād-rawān*.

P زرپرست *zar-parast*, A mammonist.

P زرپزي *zar-pazī*, The smelting of gold.

P زرپيكردرخش *zar-paykar durukhsh*, The sun. The planet Jupiter.

A زرة *zirat*, (v. n. of وزر) Committing a crime, sinning. Fatness.

A زرّة *zirrat*, The mark of a bite. The fat of camels.

A زرت *zart*, (v. n. of زرت) Strangling.

P زرتاري *zar-tārī*, Cloth of gold tissue.

P زرتشت *zartusht*, Supreme intelligence. Divine light. The rational soul. The first created. The planet Mercury. A truth-speaker. Zoroaster.

P زرتگ *zartag*, Juice of safflower.

A زرج *zarj*, (v. n. of زرج) Striking with the lower end of a spear. A tumult, noise of horses.

P زرجامي *zarjāmī*, A kind of grape.

A زرجنة *zarjanat*, A dividing of property amongst sundry people, one taking the house, another the land. Fraud, cheating, trickery.

P زرجول *zarjūl*, (زرچول *zarchūl* or زرخول *zarkhūl*) A game, in which a small stick is struck forward by a larger one, tipcat, hockey.

A زرجون *zarjūn* or *zarajūn*, A vine. The shoot of a vine or palm-tree. Wine. Pure rain-water standing in the hollow of a stone. *Zarjūn*, (for P زرگون *zar-gūn*) Of a gold-colour. Any thing which dyes of a red or gold-colour.

A زرجينة *zarjīnat*, A vine.

P زرچ *zarich*, A partridge.

P زرچوبه *zar-choba*, Turmeric.

A زرح *zarh*, (v. n. of زرح) Breaking the head.

Zarah, (v.n. of زرح) Removing from place to place.

P زرخرید *zar-kharīd*, Purchased (as a slave).

P زرخیز *zar-khez*, Rich, yielding gold, auriferous.

P زرد *zard*, Yellow, saffron-coloured; pale, pallid, wan. Saffron. A species of date. زرد زمین *zardi zamīn*, A skirret, parsnip. زرد و سرخ *zard u surkh*, (Yellow and red) Ashamed, bashful, alarmed, timid.

A زرد *zard*, (v.n. of زرد) Strangling, throttling, squeezing (the throat). Swallowing (a mouthful). Making a coat of mail; linking together the iron rings of a coat of mail. *Zarad*, (pl. ازراد *azrād*) A coat of mail. *Zarid*, Quick at swallowing.

P زرداب *zardāb*, Safflower-water. Bile. The pus or yellow matter running from a wound. Saffron-coloured wine.

P زرد آبریز *zardāb-rez*, Bad-tempered, passionate. A bad-temper. Freeing the heart from anger. One who sheds blood.

P زردار *zar-dār*, A monied man, wealthy, rich.

P زردالو *zard-ālū*, A small apricot.

P زردان *zardān*, Name of a leader of the Magi.

A زردان *zaradān*, Vulva.

P زردانیه *zardāniya*, The sect of Zardān.

P زرداهنگ *zardāhang*, A sandy place. Firm.

A زردبة *zardabat*, The act of strangling.

P زردپور *zard-pūr*, A beech-coloured horse.

P زردجت *zardajt*, Zoroaster.

P زردچرده *zard-charda*, Inclining to yellow.

P زردچکو *zard-chakū*, Name of a yellow bird.

P زردچوب *zard-chob*, Yellow wood. Turmeric.

P زردچول *zard-chūl*, Steel, hard iron.

P زردچوه *zard-chūh*, Inclining to yellow.

P زردچهره *zard-chihra*, Inclining to yellow. A boy or girl smoothfaced and comely. A bearded old woman.

P زرد خانه *zarad-khāna*, An armoury.

P زردخایه *zard-khāya*, The yolk of an egg.

P زردخو *zard-khav*, Name of a plant found in gardens, yielding a yellow fragrant blossom.

P زرد رخ *zard-rukh*, Turning colour from fear.

P زرد رنگ *zard-rang*, Yellow. Bashful.

P زردرو *zard-rū*, (or روي *rūy*) Bashful. The sun.

P زرد روئي *zard-rūī*, Bashfulness.

P زردسا *zard-sū*, A piece of gold unstamped.

P زردست *zardust*, Zoroaster.

P زردسته *zar-dasta*, A club, a mace.

P زردسر *zard-sar*, A fire-worshipper. Name of a little yellow-headed bird.

P زردشت *zardusht*, Zoroaster. Abraham.

P زردفام *zard-fām*, Yellowish.

P زرد قواره *zard-kawāra*, The sun.

P زردك *zardak*, Yellowish. A carrot. Juice of the safflower. Name of an animal whose flesh is very delicious. Any undyed stuff (as nankeen). زردك دشتي *zardaki dashtī*, (or زردك ريگي *zardaki regī*) Wild carrot.

P زردکف *zard-kaf*, (Yellow hand) The sun.

P زردگوش *zard-gosh*, Malignant. A hypocrite. A flatterer.

P زردگي *zardagī*, A deep yellow colour.

P زردم *zardam*, (or زردمه *zardama*) Victuals hastily prepared for a journey.

A زردمة *zardamat*, (v. n. of زردم Q) Swallowing. Strangling, squeezing the throat. The throat, gullet. The head of the asper artery.

P زردمن *zardaman*, Wind-pipe. A kind of bird.

P زردو *zar-dū*, A smelter of gold.

P زردوز *zar-doz*, An embroiderer. Embroidered.

P زردوزي *zar-dozī*, Embroidery.

P زردوست *zar-dost*, Fond of gold; a miser.

P زرده *zarda*, Rice dressed with honey and saffron. Inclining to yellow. Bile. A bilious habit. Jaundice. The yolk of an egg. Smut. A carrot. A parsnip. Name of a mountain containing gold. A dun-coloured horse. زردهٔ کامران *zardaï kāmrān*, The sun. Day. *Zar-dih*, Gold-giving.

P زرده چاو *zarda-chāv*, Yellow wood.

P زرده چوب *zarda-chob*, Wood with which they dye yellow. The larger species of swallow-wort. A kind of paste.

P زرده رسیده *zarda-rasīda*, Jaundiced.

P زردهشت *zarduhsht*, Zoroaster. Name of a sage descended from Zoroaster. Abraham.

P زردي *zardī*, Yellowness. Yolk of an egg. Jaundice. Smut, mildew. A circle round the sun. زردي زرد *zardī zard*, Very yellow.

A زرر *zarar*, (v. n. of زرّ) Oppressing, or seeking to gain advantage over. Getting understanding after lacking wisdom.

P زررشته *zar-rishta*, A gold thread.

P زررشته‌گر *zar-rishtagar*, A gold-thread maker.

P زررکني *zar ruknī*, Pure gold.

A زرزار *zarzār*, Of a quick and sprightly genius. *Zirzār*, (pl. زرازرة *zarāzirat*) Commander of 10,000.

A زرزر *zurzur*, A starling, a stare.

A زرزرة *zarzarat*, (v. n. of زرزر Q) Singing (a starling). Continuing long at meals. Abiding.

A زرزور *zurzūr*, (pl. زرازير) A narrow vehicle. A starling. Skilful in the management of property.

P زرزوره *zarzūra*, A kind of spider.

A زرزوريّ *zarzūrīy*, Spotted, speckled (like a stare). *Zurzūrīy*, A kind of mule.

P زرسا *zar-sā*, A crucible. Melted gold. Like gold. Particles of gold.

P زرسان *zarsān*, Like gold. A gold thread. A bit of gold.

P زرساوه *zar-sāwa*, Gold-filings.

P زرساي *zar-sāy*, A manufacturer of gold thread, a goldbeater, a preparer of gold for painting. A crucible. Like gold.

P زرسود *zar-sūd*, Turmeric.

P زرشك *zirishk*, Barberries. A certain fragrant flower.

P زرشناس *zar-shinās*, A banker, goldsmith, or money-changer, as skilled in gold.

A زرط *zart*, A swallowing (of a mouthful).

A زرع *zarꜥ*, (v. n. of زرع) Sowing, scattering seed. From being poor, growing rich. Producing, making to grow. Strengthening. (pl. زروع *zurūꜥ*) Seed sown. Seed-time. A sown field. A child. *Zarꜥ* or *zurꜥ*, An ear of corn.

A زرعة *zurꜥat*, Seed. Corn. *Zurꜥat*, *zarꜥat*, *zirꜥat* or *zaraꜥat*, A spot of land for sowing.

A زرعونيّ *zarꜥūnīy*, A certain kind of electuary.

A زرغب *zarghab*, Back-leather of horse or ass.

P زرغنج *zarghunj*, Name of a stinking herb brought from China.

A زرف *zarf*, (v. n. of زرف) Breaking out afresh (a healing wound). Making haste (in walking). Leaping, skipping, advancing towards. Talking much. *Zaraf*, (v. n. of زرف) Breaking out afresh (a healing wound).

P زرفان *zarfān*, A decrepit old man. The patriarch Abraham.

P زرفشان *zar-fishān*, Scattering gold. Name of the 9th of the month of the æra of Yazdagird.

A زرفنة *zarfanat*, (v. n. of زرفن Q) Marking (the temples) with the figure of a ring. Curling the hair around the temples.

P زرفين *zurfīn*, A bolt or ring of a door.

P زرق *zark*, Hypocrisy, fraud. Detraction. Pretending to abstinence. زرق برق *zark bark*, Shining, splendid clothes. زرق و برق *zark u bark*, Magnificence, pomp, royal grandeur.

A زرق *zark*, (v. n. of زرق) Turning towards any object (the eye), so that scarce any thing but the white appears. Brandishing or hurling (a javelin). Moving back (the burden or saddle of a horse or camel). Muting (a bird). *Zurk*, Spear-heads. (pl. of ازرق *azrak*) Blue-eyed. Blind. *Zurk* or *zarak*, White upon the hoof of a horse; also on a bone, but not going quite round. Length of hair round about the hoofs. Hills of sand in the desert. *Zarak* (v. n. of زرق) Being blue or grey (the eye). Blueness. Blindness.

A زرّق *zurrak*, (pl. زراريق *zarārīk*) A white falcon, sparrow-hawk, merlin. Whiteness on the forehead of a horse.

A زرقاء *zarkās*, (fem. of ازرق *azrak*) Blue or grey-eyed. Wine. Name of a quick-sighted woman, who could see a distance of three days' journey.

A زرقة *zarkat*, A shell used as an amulet. *Zurkat*, A blue or grey colour. Blueness or greyness of the eyes. Seed of the fleabane.

P زرقطونا *zir-kitūnā*, Seed of fleawort. Turmeric.

A زرقفة *zarkafat*, The being nimble, expeditious.

P زرق فروش *zark-farosh*, A hypocrite.

A زرقلة *zarkalat*, (v. n. of زرقل Q) Discharging a debt. Plucking up (hair).

P زرقم *zurkum*, Very blue or grey.

SY زرقون *zarkūn*, Vermilion.

P زرك *zarak*, Gold-leaf. *Zirik*, The barberry and its tree.

A زرك *zarak*, The being of a depraved temper.

P زركار *zar-kār*, Any thing golden or gilded.

P زركش *zar-kash*, A gold-wire drawer. Embroidered or covered with gold thread.

A زركشة *zarkashat*, A sewing with gold.

P زركوب *zar-kob*, A goldbeater.

P زركوفت *zar-koft*, Plated with gold.

P زركوه *zar-koh*, Name of a rock in the midst of the Sea of Omān, dangerous to ships.

P زرگر *zargar*, A goldsmith. زرگر چرخ The sun.

P زرگري *zargarī*, Business of a goldsmith. A kind of dialect.

P زرگنج *zargunj*, Name of a stinking herb brought from China. A large earthen vessel.

P زرگون *zar-gūn*, Of the colour of gold.

P زرگيا *zar-giyā*, Name of an Indian golden-coloured herb.

P زرم *zarm*, Tears. A shedding of tears.

A زرم *zarm*, (v. n. of زرم) Cutting. Interrupting (urine). Stopping, suspending (tears or words). Bringing forth (a mother). Caution, prudence, fear. *Zaram*, (v. n. of زرم) Being interrupted (urine or tears). Being constipated, having hard, dry dung in the rectum (a dog or cat). Sticking in the throat (a word). Bringing forth (a mother). Being stingy, penurious. *Zarim*, In narrow circumstances. Avaricious, mean, vile. Unsettled in a place.

P زرمان *zarmān*, A decrepit old man. Abraham.

A زرمانقة *zurmānikat*, A sleeveless garment or tunic of wool or camel's hair.

A زرموج *zurmūj*, A shoe, a slipper.

P زرمچه *zar-mahcha*, A golden or gilded moon, or crescent, at the point of a banner or spear.

P زرنا *zurnā*, A trumpet, a hautbois.

P زرناپا *zurnāpā*, (or زرنپا) A cameleopard.

A زرنب *zarnab*, Name of an odoriferous plant. Saffron. The dung of a wild beast. Vulva.

P زرنباد *zurumbād*, (زرنبا *zurumbā*, or زرنباهه *zurumbāha*) Zedoary, a Chinese root.

P زرنبلج *zarambulj*, Sorrel. A red currant.

P زرنج *zirinj*, Gum of a tree.

P زرند *zarand*, Hell. Name of a hard barren tree.

P زرنشان *zar-nishān*, Figures of gold inlaid in steel (as in swords). Gilded. Set in gold.

A زرنقة *zarnakat*, (v.n.of زرنق Q) Buying (any article) at a high price to be paid at a future fixed time, and in the mean time selling (it) again at a lower price by the hands of the original vendor, or by any other person. Enveloping any one in clothes. Concealing. Debt. Increase. Redundance. Perfect beauty. A drawing of water with the machine called زرنوق *zurnūk*. A fixing of this machine at a well. Money paid in advance.

P زرنك *zaranh*, Magnificence, grandeur.

P زرنگ *zarang*, The barberry. New. A troop of horses. Yellow wood. Safflower-water. Mustard-seed. Yellow clay used in colouring. The peak of a mountain. Hell. Name of a large and hard tree. Name of a city, the government seat of Sīstān. *Zurang*, A troop of horses.

P زرنگار *zar-nigār*, Gilded. Inlaid with gold.

A زرنوق *zurnūk*, A rivulet, a stream.

A زرنوقان *zurnūkāni* or *zarnūkāni*, Two perpendicular beams at the mouth of a well, supporting another transversely placed, to which the bucket-pulley is fixed.

A زرنوك *zurnūk*, The winch of a hand-mill.

P زرني *zurnī*, (زرنيخ *zirnīkh*, or زرنيق *zirnīk* or *zarnīk*) Arsenic.

A زرنيلج *zarnīluj*, (from P زرنيله) Sorrel.

P زرو *zarū*, A leech. A kind of powder or salve with which the eyes are anointed. Hardness in the hand or foot.

P زرواس *zarwās*, Liberality, munificence.

P زروان بزرگ *zarwāni buzurg*, Abraham.

A زروب *zurūb*, (pl. of زرب *zarb*) Folds for cattle. Lurking-places (of hunters).

A زروح *zarwah*, A low wide-spread hill.

A زروحة *zarwahat*, A low wide-spread hill.

P زرود *zarūd*, A desert.

A زرور *zurūr*, (pl. of زرّ *zirr*) Coat-buttons.

A زروع *zurūʻ*, (pl. of زرع *zarʻ*) Sown fields. Seeds sown. Children.

P زروغ *zarūgh* or *zurūgh*, A belch.

A زروف *zarūf*, Swift, fleet (she-camel).

P زروك *zarūk*, Name of a medicinal herb. *Zurūk*, A leech.

P زره *zirih*, A coat of mail. Name of a kinsman of Afrāsyāb. Name of a province in Sīstān. زره كلاه *zirih-kulāh*, A helmet, with a texture of iron rings hanging down as a defence for the neck. زره پوش *zirih-posh*, Clothed in mail or any other military garment.

P زرهانتن *zarhānitan*, (in zand) To bring forth.

P زره پيچ *zarah-pech*, (in zand and Pāz.) Winter.

P زرهتشت *zarahtusht*, (or زرهدشت *zaruh-dusht*) Zoroaster.

P زره خود *zirih-khūd*, The lining of a helmet.

P زره دار *zirih-dār*, Clad in mail.

P زره گر *zirihgar*, A maker of coats of mail.

P زره مو *zirih-mū* or *mo*, One whose hair forms a sort of covering (resembling a coat of mail).

P زره ور *zirihwar*, Clad in mail.

P زرهون *zarhūn*, The patriarch Abraham.

A زري *zary*, (or زريان *zuryān*) (v. n. of زري) Chiding, censuring. Being angry against. Defaming.

A زريّ *zariy*, Middle-sized (leathern bottle).

A زريبة *zarībat*, A fold, pen, enclosure for cattle. The den or haunt of wild beasts. The lurking-place of a hunter.

P زريتونتن *zarītūnitan*, (in zand and Pāzand) To cultivate the ground.

P زرير *zarīr* or *zirīr*, A yellow-dyeing wood. Bile. Jaundice. Name of the brother of Gushtasp.

A زرير *zarīr*, (v. n. of زرّ) Being hot, red, and inflamed (the eye). Of a quick and sprightly genius.

SY زريرا *zarīrā*, Purslane.

P زريره *zarīra*, Wormwood.

A زريز *zarīz*, Active, nimble, light. Pure, clean. Prudent, intelligent.

A زريع *zarīʻ*, Fit for sowing.

A زرّيع *zirrīʻ*, Whatever is produced annually from the shedding of the seed at harvest-time.

A زريعة *zarīʻat*, Seed sown. A seed-plot. Cause.

A زريف *zarīf*, A going slowly, leisurely.

A زريق *zūrayh*, A kind of bird. بنو زريق *banū zurayh*, Name of those allies of Muhammad who are designated by the title of انصار *ansār*.

A زريقاء *zurayhāʼ*, Bread crumbled or sliced into milk or fat. An animal resembling a cat.

P زريقان *zirīkān*, Tenacious, avaricious.

A زريقي *zurayhīy*, Name of a poet.

P زريك *zirīk*, The barberry (a thorn).

P زرين *zarīn* (or زرّين *zarrīn*) Golden. مرغ زرّين بال *murghi zarrīn-bāl*, The bird with golden wings, *i. e.* The sun. زرين ترنج *zarīn-turunj*, The sun. زرين درخت *zarīn-dirakht*, The orange-tree. زرين صدف *zarīn-sadaf*, (or زرين كاسه *zarīn-kāsa*) The sun. زرين عذار *zarīn-ʻizār*, Yellow, pale-faced. زرّين قدح *zarrīn-hadah*, A white and yellow narcissus. زرّين كلاه *zarrīn-kulāh*, The gold tiara, *i. e.* The chamberlain or keeper of the palace, who wears a golden cap. The sun. زرين گاو *zarīn-gāv*, A drinking-cup made in the shape of an ox. زرين نرگسه *zarīn-nargisa*, The stars.

A زرّين *zarrīn*, A certain white bird.

P زرّينه *zarrīna*, Golden. شهنشين زرّينه طاق *shah-nishīni zarrīna-tāh*, A portico supported by golden pillars.

P زرين هماي *zarīn-humāy*, The sun.

P زريو *zarīv*, Gravity, sedateness, temperance.

P زريون *zar-yūn*, (Gold colour) The anemone. Green and pleasant. Yellow.

P زريوند *zarewand*, Name of a wrestler.

P زريوه *zarīwa*, A trance, ecstacy.

A ززّ *zazz*, A tapping gently on the neck.

P ززرونه تربا *zazrūna-tirbā*, (in zand) A hen.

P زژه *zaja*, A clothes-line.

P زست *zust*, Strong, violent, vehement, irascible, harsh, passionate. Sharp, acid, pungent. Clear.

P زستن *zistan*, To live. To excoriate. To rob.

P زش *zash*, What is the matter? *Zush*, Dew.

P زشار *zishār*, A press for squeezing juice.

P زشت *zasht*, Sight, seeing. *Zisht*, Hideous, ugly, rough, rude, austere, obscene, filthy. A race.

P زشتار *zishtār*, Obscene, a bawdy talker.

P زشت خو *zisht-khu* or *kho*, Bad-tempered.

P زشت خوئي *zisht-khoʼī*, Badness of temper.

P زشت ديدار *zisht-dīdār*, Of hideous aspect.

P زشت روي zisht-rūy, Ugly-faced.

P زشت روئي zisht-rūī, Ugliness of face.

P زشت گوي risht-gūy, An obscene speaker.

P زشتن zushtan, To unbark, skin, peel, strip.

P زشتي zishtī, Ugliness. زشتي و نكوئي zishtī u nikūī, Good and evil. Sadness and joy. Poverty and riches.

P زشتياد zisht-yād, Detraction, back-biting.

P زشي zashi, (or زشّي) What is the matter?

A زطّ zatt, (v. n. of زطّ) Buzzing softly (flies). Zutt, Name of a people in India, the Jauts (?).

A زطّيّ zuttīy, Of the above-mentioned nation.

A زطّيّة zuttīyat, A cross. A triangular piece of gold or silver worn in the girdle by a people in India called زطّ zutt.

A زعابل zaʻābil, (pl. of زعبل zaʻbal) Foolish mothers. Boys digesting badly their victuals.

A زعّار zuʻʻār, (pl. of زاعر) Wicked. Gipsies.

A زعارة zaʻārat, (or زعارّة zaʻārrat) Badness of temper.

A زعازع zaʻāziʻ, Adversities, tribulations. Zuʻāziʻ, A hurricane.

A زعاف zuʻāf, A sudden death. (Poison) hastening death.

A زعافر zaʻāfir, (pl. of زعفران) Saffrons.

A زعافير zaʻāfīr, (pl. of زعفران) Saffrons.

A زعاق zuʻāk, Thick, brackish, undrinkable (water). Fugaciousness. Fugitive (wild goat).

A زعّاق zaʻʻāk, Swift (horse).

A زعاقة zaʻākat, (v. n. of زعق) Being thick, brackish, and undrinkable (water).

A زعاقيق zaʻākīk, Young partridges.

A زعاكك zaʻākik, (or زعاكيك zaʻākīk) (pl. of زعكوك zuʻkūk) Fat (camels). Short, mean-looking.

A زعال ziʻāl, (v. n. 3 of زعل) Rendering brisk and lively. Shoving from its place.

A زعامة zaʻāmat, (v. n. of زعم) Answering (for another), being surety. Becoming prince or leader. Weapons. Armour. Magnificence. The best part of wealth. The largest portion of an inheritance. A chieftain's share of spoil. Dominion, authority, nobility. A cow. Ziʻāmat, A seigniory or fief bestowed for military services.

A زعّامة zaʻʻāmat, A cow.

A زعانف zaʻānif, (pl. of زعنفة ziʻnifat) Dressed goat-skins with the feet hanging to them. Detached portions of tribes. Lower parts of torn garments. Misfortunes. Fins of fishes.

A زعب zaʻb, (v. n. of زعب) Driving away, or thrusting back. Giving (money). Taking up, carrying off (a full vessel). Filling (a vase or valley). Dividing, sharing among themselves. Cutting. Lying with. Being filled (a river). Moving heavily (a loaded camel). Ziʻb, A little money. Zuʻb, (pl. of زعبوب zuʻbūb) Short-bodied, mean of stature.

A زعبة zuʻbat or zaʻbat, A little property.

A زعبج zaʻbaj also ziʻbij, A thin white cloud. Any beautiful object. The olive.

A زعبريّ zaʻbarīy, A kind of arrow.

A زعبقة zaʻbakat, A separating, a scattering.

A زعبل zaʻbal, A mother. A foolish woman. A boy who digests badly his victuals, and whose belly is large and neck thin. A viper. A chameleon. The cotton-tree.

A زعبلة zaʻbalat, (v. n. of زعبل Q) Making a handsome present. One who has a slender neck with a corpulent body.

A زعبوب zuʻbūb, Short and mean of stature.

A زعج zaʻj, (v. n. of زعج) Disturbing, moving (from its place). Taking from any one's hand. Banishing, driving away. Crying aloud, shouting. Zaʻaj, Disquietude, agitation, commotion.

A زعجة zaʻjat, A noise.

A زعجلة zaʻjalat, Badness of temper, narrowness of disposition.

A زعر zaʻr, Coition. Bare, barren (place). Zaʻr, or zaʻar, (v. n. of زعر) Being thin and dishevelled (hair). Being thin-haired. Zaʻar, Thinness of hair. Zaʻir, Thin of hair. Dishevelled (hair). Bare, barren (spot). A man of a bad disposition.

A زعراء zaʻrāʼ, Thin-haired (girl). A kind of peach. Name of a place.

A زعرة zuʻarat, A kind of bird which always appears frightened.

A زعرف zaʻraf, Abounding in water (sea).

A زعرور zuʻrūr, Of a bad disposition. A medlar.

A زعزاع zaʻzāʻ, Stormy, boisterous (wind).

A زعزاعة zaʻzāʻat, A large troop of horse.

A زعزع zaʻzaʻ, Stormy (wind). Tottering (pace).

A زعزعان zaʻzaʻān, Stormy, boisterous (wind).

A زعزعة zaʻzaʻat, (v. n. of زعزع Q) Shaking a tree (wind). Any violent shaking.

A زعزف zaʻzaf, Abounding in water (sea).

A زعط zaʻt, (v. n. of زعط) Strangling. Braying.

A زعف zaʻf, (v. n. of زعف) Killing on the spot.

P A زعفران zaʻfarān, (pl. زعافر zaʻāfir or زعافير zaʻāfīr) Saffron. Rust of iron.

A زعفرانيّ zaʻfarānīy, Dressed with saffron. Saffron-coloured.

A زعفرة zaʻfarat, A tinging with saffron.

P زعفري zaʻfarī, Yellow, saffron-coloured.

A زعفوق zuʻfūk, Of a bad disposition.

A زعق zaʻk, (v. n. of زعق) Calling out, terrifying. Driving (cattle). Over-salting (the pot or meat). Making (the dust) fly (wind). Stinging (a scorpion). Zaʻak, (v. n. of زعق) Being timid at night, starting with fear. Being brisk, cheerful, leaping with joy. Zaʻik, Timorous. Brisk, cheerful.

A زعقوقة zuʻkūkat, A young partridge.

A زعكة zaʻkat, Delay.

A زعكوك zuʻkūk, (pl. زعاكك zaʻākik and زعاكيك zaʻākīk) Short, mean-looking. Fat (camel).

A زعل zaʻal, (v. n. of زعل) Being brisk, cheerful. Leaping, galloping without a rider (a horse). Alacrity. Zaʻil, Brisk. One writhing from hunger.

A زعلة zaʻlat, (A mother) which brings forth every other year. A female ostrich.

A زعلجة zaʻlajat, Depravity, evil disposition.

A زعلوق zuʻlūk, Brisk, cheerful. Name of a plant.

A زعلول zuʻlūl, Light, active (man).

A زعم zaʻm, ziʻm, or zuʻm, (v. n. of زعم) Thinking, supposing, imagining, presuming, or speaking from belief. Pretending, assuming, asserting without sufficient warrant. Answering for another, becoming surety or sponsor. Becoming chief, prince, or leader. Becoming well-flavoured (milk). An opinion, notion. Vanity. Truth. A lie. Zaʻam, (v. n. of زعم) Coveting, hankering after. Zaʻim, (Roast meat) full of dripping.

A زعماء zuʻamāʼ, (pl. of زعيم zaʻīm) Feudal chiefs, barons. Princes, leaders. Sureties. Spokesmen.

A زعموم zuʻmūm, A stammerer.

A زعميّ zuʻmīy, A liar. A speaker of truth.

A زعن zaʻn, (v. n. of زعن) Inclining.

A زعنفة zaʻnafat, (v. n. of زعنف Q) Dressing, bedecking (a bride). Ziʻnafat, (pl. زعانف zaʻānif) Short of stature, dwarfish. Ignoble, mean, worthless. A piece of a garment, or the lower part torn and playing loose. Part of any thing, as the fore or hind legs of a dressed skin. A company of persons not derived from one common stock. Part of a tribe detached from the rest. A small tribe uniting itself to a larger. A misfortune.

A زعو zaʻw, (v. n. of زعا for زعو) Acting justly.

A زعوف zuʻūf, Dangerous places.

A زعوفة zaʻūfat, A stone left at the bottom of a well when it is excavated, for the person who cleans out the well to stand upon.

A زعوم zaʻūm, (A ewe or a camel) of which a doubt is entertained whether she be fat or not. A stammerer. Full of fat. Destitute of fat. Zuʻūm, A hesitation in speech.

A زعيب zaʻīb, (v. n. of زعب) Croaking (a raven). The humming of a bee.

A زعيق zaʻīk, Terrified.

A زعيم zaʻīm, (pl. زعماء zuʻamāʼ) A boaster, pretending to what he has no right. A surety, sponsor. A spokesman. A prince, leader. A feudal chief.

P زغ zagh, (for زاغ zāgh) A crow.

A زغّ zughgh, Stench of a negro's arm-pits.

A زغابة zughābat, Fine hair, down. Any thing very small.

A زغابي zughābaʼ, Fine hair, down.

A زغاد zaghghād, Full and swelling (river).

A زغادب zughādib, Much froth. Rude, rough, deformed of visage. Blubber-lipped.

P زغار zaghār, Brackish ground. A loud cry. A cry for help. A sort of food. Millet or rice-bread. Nightshade. Wet ground. Rusty. Mouldy. A burning coal. Uneasiness. Any thing coloured.

A زغار zughār, Earth-worms.

P زغارچه zaghārcha, A certain sweet herb.

P زغار غس zaghār ghas, Small strips of fur wherewith the natives of some parts of the East garnish the skirts of their clothing.

P زغار كرم zaghār-kirm, An earthworm.

P زغارو zaghārav or zaghārū, A brothel, stew.

P زغاره zaghāra, Paint for the face. Bread made of millet. Millet. *Zughāra*, A live coal.

A زغاريت zaghārīt, Shrillcries of women's joy.

P زغاريدن zaghārīdan, To cry aloud.

P زغازه zaghāza, Bread made from millet.

P زغاس zaghās, Uneasiness arising from love.

P زغاك zaghāk, A vine-branch.

P زغال zughāl, A live coal. Cornel-tree or fruit.

P زغاو zaghāv, A courtesan. A brothel.

A زغاوة zughāwat, A certain negro race.

A زغب zaghab, (v. n. of زغب) Having yellow hair or down (young birds): also such as appears upon the head of an old man after his hair becomes thin. The beginning of any thing. Down. Small hairs. *Zughab*, White and black (mountain). Ash-coloured (camel).

A زغبب zughbub, A dwarf. A miser.

A زغبة zughbat, A small animal like a mouse.

A زغبج zaghbaj, The fruit of the wild olive, like the small lote fruit, green; afterwards white, then black, and then becomes sweet with a slight acidity, and is used in cookery.

A زغبد zaghbad, Cream; fresh butter. Froth.

P زغبر zaghbar, Name of a fragrant herb.

A زغبر zaghbar, A collection. *Zaghbar* or *zaghbur*, The nap or pile of new cloth. *Zaghbar*, or *zighbar*, The tree مرو marw with delicate foliage.

A زغبرة zaghbarat, (v. n. of زغبر Q) Being new and shaggy (cloth).

A زغبور zughbūr, A kind of wild beast.

A زغد zaghd, (v. n. of زغد) Braying loudly (a camel). Forcing butter out of a leathern bottle by pressure. Irritating by abusive language. Squeezing the throat. Life, pleasure, luxury.

A زغدب zaghdab, A loud braying noise. Fat, grease. Much froth.

A زغدبة zaghdabat, Anger. The importunity of a beggar.

P زغده zaghda, Name of a bird.

A زغر zaghr, (v. n. of زغر) Overflowing (as the river Tigris). Forcing, constraining, taking away by violence. A multitude, plenty. Excess, redundancy.

P زغر zaghar, Trouble. Soft ground. Any thing coloured. Name of a fountain. A sort of food. *Za* or *zughar*, Name of Lot's daughter; also of a tribe.

A زغرب zaghrab, Copious (urine); flowing plentifully (well): deep (sea). Many, full, abundant.

A زغربة zaghrabat, A well abounding in water. Laughter.

A زغربي zaghrabiy, Deep (sea).

A زغرتة zaghratat, (v. n. of زغرت Q) Uttering the shrill cries of joy زغاريت zaghārīt (women).

A زغردة zaghradat, Inward bray of a camel.

P زغرغاش zagharghāsh, (زغراش zaghrāsh, or زغريماش zaghrīmāsh) Scrapings of leather which the currier throws away. Thongs cut from a hide.

A زغرف zaghraf, Full (sea).

P زغره zaghara, The best pieces of leather for sewing round the edges of garments for shewing to buyers as musters or samples.

A زغريّ zughrīy or zaghrīy, The fruit or produce of a valley. A kind of date.

A زغزغ zaghzagh, Light, active (man).

P زغزغ zughzugh, A dwarf. A child. A small bucket. A species of bird.

A زغزغة zaghzaghat, Weakness of speech. Irony, ridicule, mockery. Concealment. An endeavour to untie the mouth of a bottle.

A زغزغيّة zaghzaghīyat, A dish of flour and butter. *Zughzughīyat*, Name of a barbarous nation. A barbarous idiom.

A زغزف zaghzaf, Full (sea).

A زغف zaghf, (v. n. of زغف) Stabbing. Pouring forth rain and covering the face of the heavens (a cloud). Being abundant (the water of a well). Embellishing with fiction (a narrative). A cloud which has poured forth its contents. A stab. *Zaghf* or *zaghaf*, (pl. of زغفة zaghfat and zaghafat) Slight coats of mail. *Zaghaf*, Thin pieces of wood, also the extreme slender branches of trees.

A زغفة zaghfat or zaghafat, (pl. زغف zaghf, zaghaf, ازغاف azghāf, and زغوف zughūf) A slight coat of mail of slender rings, closely, firmly woven.

A زغفل zaghfal, Name of a tree.

A زغفلة zaghfalat, (v. n. of زغفل Q) Telling a lie. Setting fire to the tree called زغفل zaghfal.

P زغگك zaghagak, A sob, hiccup.

A زغل zaghl, (v. n. of زغل) Ejecting at one dash, squirting out (saliva). Sucking the (dam). Spirting out urine (a she-camel).

A زغلة zughlat, A quantity of urine made at one time; also of milk poured from a bottle. A little. Liquid squirted from the mouth. The fundament.

A زغلجة zaghlajat, Badness of temper, moroseness.

A زغلمة zaghlamat or zughlamat, Doubt, opinion, persuasion. Malevolence, hatred: a secret grudge.

A زغلول zughlūl, Light, active. An infant.

P زغم zugham, Force, violence, injury.

A زغمل zughmul, Hatred, a secret grudge.

P زغن zaghan, A kite. A black sparrow.

P زغنار zughnār, Madder, a dyeing root.

P زغند zaghand, The cries of a wild beast, especially of a panther. A spring, bound. A sally. Flight, levity.

P زغنگ zaghang, Hiccup. A wink, glance. A moment.

P زغنگيدن zaghangīdan, To sob, to sigh.

A زغو zaghw, (v. n. of زغا for زغو) Crying (a child). Dealing with justice and equity.

P زغوته zaghūta, A reed used by weavers to wind their thread upon. Raw silk wrapped round the spindle.

A زغوف zughūf, (pl. of زغفة zaghfat or zaghafat) Slight, also wide coats of mail.

A زغول zaghūl, Greedy of suck, (camels or sheep).

A زغوم zaghūm, (or زغموم) A stammerer.

A زغى zugha', Stench from negroes.

A زغيد zaghīd, (Butter) forced out by squeezing the bottle.

P زغيده zaghīda, Expressed (juice).

P زغير zaghīr, Linseed. A kind of food.

A زغيم zughaym, A kind of bird.

A زفّ zaff, (or زفاف zifāf) (v. n. of زفّ) Conducting (a bride) home to her husband's house (which is generally done with music and much pomp). Blowing (wind). Going with a quick pace (an ostrich or man). Gleaming (lightning). Expanding the wings; letting itself down gently (a bird). *Ziff*, Young ostrich-feathers, or those of any bird whilst yet small.

P زفاف zifāf, The marriage-night.

P زفاك zafāk, A rainy cloud.

P زفان zufān, (equiv. to زبان zubān) The tongue.

P زفانه zafāna, Flame. Tongue of a balance.

A زفّانى ziffānīy, Quick, speedy. Thick-plumaged (male-ostrich).

A زفّة zaffat, A bird's throwing itself once on the ground. A time, turn, once. *Zuffat*, A multitude, troop, crowd.

P زفت zaft, Thick, gross, rude, coarse. Fat. Full, heaped up. Acid, tart, pungent. *Zift*, Pitch. Black. *Zuft*, Of a bad disposition, crabbed, quarrelsome. Avaricious. Astringent, styptic.

A زفت zaft, (v. n. of زفت) Waxing hot, becoming angry. Driving away, pushing forcibly. Pouring (a story) into the ear. A fatiguing, wearying, jading. A filling. A hindering. *Zift*, Pitch, resin.

P زفتى ziftī, Pitchy. *Zuftī*, Covetousness.

A زفد zafd, (v. n. of زفد) Filling. Stuffing (a horse with barley).

P زفر zafr or zafar, A jaw-bone. The mouth. A corner of the mouth. Filth.

A زفر zafr, (v. n. of زفر) Making a noise in the throat (a man, or an ass beginning to bray). Crackling (a fire). Carrying (a load). Drawing water. *Zifr*, Travelling equipage. A burden. A bottle (in which they carry oil or milk). An assembly, crowd, body. *Zufr*, (pl. of ازفر azfar) Large-sided (horses). *Zafar*, Any thing for propping a tree. Any thing fat, from which they abstain in rigid fasts. *Zufar*, A lord. A powerful, strong, brave man. A lion. The sea. A river brimful. An abundant gift. Strong, able to carry burdens. A large camel. A troop, squadron, battalion.

P زفرافيدن zafrāfīdan, To eat much. To sneeze.

A زفرة *zafrat,* The middle of any thing (as of the body of a horse). *Zafrat* or *zufrat,* (v. n. of زفر) Sighing, crying out. A deep-fetched breath. Possessed of breath; an animal.

P زفرفيدن *zafrafīdan,* To eat little. To threaten to sneeze without doing it.

P زفره *zafra* or *zufra,* Victory or gain at play; sitting down to game. The mouth. The chin.

P زفرين *zufrīn,* An iron ring for holding the bolt or chain of a door.

A زفزف *zafzaf,* (زفزاف *zafzāf,* and زفزافة *zafzāfat*) A wind blowing violently for a long time. Light, active. An ostrich.

A زفزفة *zafzafat,* (v. n. of زفزف Q) Blowing violently (the wind); whistling through the grass. Expanding the wings, letting itself down (a bird). Trembling, quaking. The noise made by the motion of a cavalcade.

A زفف *zafaf,* Closeness of plumage.

A زفقة *zufkat,* A mouthful.

A زفقلة *zafkalat,* Haste, expedition.

A زفن *zafn,* (v. n. of زفن) Dancing. Leaping. Dandling (an infant). Dancing and playing with arms. *Zifn,* A shade, awning, or canopy spread above the roof, to keep off the spray of the sea or heat. Branches of palm-trees stripped of the leaves, woven into a kind of open lattice or mat-work.

P زفني *zifnī,* A certain black medicinal stone.

P زفو *zufu,* The tongue.

A زفوف *zafūf,* An ostrich. *Zufūf,* (v. n. of زف) Going with a quick pace (an ostrich or a man).

A زفون *zafūn,* A she-camel kicking her milker. Lame (she-camel).

P زفونيا *zafūniyā,* A thorny shrub.

A زفي *zafy,* (v. n. of زفي) Driving, carrying away (as wind). Exalting, raising any thing (vapour). Resounding (a bow). Stretching out the wings, running, and frightening a person (ostriches).

A زفيان *zafyān,* Swift (camel). Swift-shooting (bow). *Zafayān,* (v. n. of زفي) Carrying away (the wind). Resounding (a bow). Raising any thing (vapour). (A camel) going quick. (A bow) shooting an arrow with rapidity. A dwarfish woman.

A زفير *zafīr,* (v. n. of زفر) Beginning to bray (an ass). The beginning or sending forth the bray of an ass. (The conclusion or drawing in of his voice is called شهيق *shahīk*). A flame of fire. A calamity.

P زفيزف *zafīzaf,* The red jujube-tree.

A زفيف *zafīf,* (v. n. of زف) Going fast (an ostrich or a man). Expanding the wings, letting itself down (a bird). Thick-plumaged (male ostrich). A quick pace. Quick. Speedy.

A زقّ *zakk,* (v. n. of زقّ) Feeding her young (a bird). Muting. *Zikk,* (pl. ازقاق *azkāk,* زقاق *zikāk,* زقّاق *zukkāk,* or زقّان *zukkān*) A skin used as a bottle (for wine). *Zukk,* (pl. زققة *zakakat*) Wine.

A زقا *zakā',* A certain tree with small leaves.

A زقاء *zakā,* or *zukā,* (v. n. of زقا for زقو) Crowing (a cock). Shrieking (an owl). Echoing. Returning the crow (as cock to cock).

A زقاطة *zakātat,* A seed or grain of the plant زلم.

A زقاع *zuhā',* (v. n. of زقع) Breaking wind violently (an ass). Crowing (a cock).

A زقاق *zakāk,* One who drinks at table, having meat in his mouth. *Zukāk,* (pl. زقّان *zukkān* and ازقّة *azikkat*) A street, alley, lane, square, market-place. A space between a row of palm-trees. بحر الزقاق *bahru'z zukāk,* The straits of Gibraltar. *Zikāk,* (pl. of زقّ *zikk*) Wine-bottles.

A زقّاق *zakkāk,* Maker or seller of leathern bottles. *Zukkāk,* (pl. of زقّ *zikk*) Leathern wine-bottles.

A زقاقي *zukākīy,* Belonging to a street: vulgar.

A زقّيع *zakākī',* Young partridges.

A زقّان *zukkān,* (pl. of زقّ *zikk*) Leathern wine-bottles. (pl. of زقاق *zukāk*) Streets.

A زقب *zakb,* (v. n. of زقب) Forcing any one to enter into a cave or a hole. Entering it. *Zakab,* Near. من زقب *min zakabin,* From near, from a short distance. *Zakab* or *zukub,* A narrow road.

A زقبة *zakabat,* (pl. زقب) A very narrow lane.

A زقّة *zukkat,* Name of a small bird.

A زقح *zak-h,* The chattering of apes.

A زقر *zakr,* (for صقر *sakr*) A kind of hawk. *Zakar,* (for صقر *sakar*) Hell.

A زقزاق *zikzāk,* The dandling of an infant.

A زقزاقة *zakzākat,* Lightly-stepping (female).

A زقزق *zikzik,* A sort of ant.

A زقزقة *zakzakat,* (v. n. of زقزق Q) Dandling an infant. Feeding her young (a bird). Voiding excrement (a bird). Lightness, agility. A gentle laugh. A certain note of a dog. The chirping of the birds at dawn of day.

A زقع *zak',* (v. n. of زقع) Crowing (a cock). Breaking wind loudly (an ass).

A زقف *zakf,* (v. n. of زقف) Snatching any thing greedily (as a starving person does victuals).

A زقفة *zukfat,* A mouthful. Any thing taken with the hand.

A زققة *zakakat,* Ring-doves. (pl. of زقّ) Wines.

A زقل *zukl,* Robbers.

A زقم *zakm,* (v. n. of زقم) Eating a kind of food called زقّوم *zakkūm.* Eating, swallowing.

A زقمة *zukmat,* Plague, pestilence.

A زقن *zakn,* A carrying, lifting, loading.

A زقو *zakw,* (v. n. of زقا for زقو) Crowing, hooting. Answering (as the echo, or cock to cock).

A زقّوم *zakkūm,* An infernal tree (mentioned in the Kur'ān), the fruit of which is supposed to be the heads of devils. A thorny tree, whose fruit is sweet and styptic, and from whose stone oil is extracted. A kind of wild plant, whose flower resembles the jasmine. The tree of which scammony is the gum. Fresh dates and cream. The food of the infernals.

P زقّه *zakka,* A grain with which a bird feeds her young. A kind of medicine which the midwife pours down the throat of a new-born babe.

A زقي *zaky,* (v. n. of زقي) Crowing (a cock), hooting (an owl). Answering (as echo, or cocks).

A زقية *zakyat,* Clamour, shriek, cry. *Zukyat,* A heap (of money, &c.).

A زقّية *zakkīyat* or *zukkīyat,* A mode of shaving the head.

A زقيلة *zakīlat,* A narrow street.

P زك *zak,* A black tincture, vitriol. *Zuk,* Muttering to one's self. High. (in zand and Pāz.) That.

A زك *zakk,* (v. n. of زك) Taking short steps. Trotting (a hen). Running. Voiding dung. Filling (a leathern bottle). Lean, emaciated. *Zukk,* The young of the ringdove.

A زكء *zak,* (v. n. of زكأ) Paying quickly, readily, and before the appointed day, with ready money. Taking refuge with. Leaning against, propping one's self up by. Lying with. Dropping her young between her feet (a camel).

A زكا *zaka',* A pair. خسا او زكا *khasan aw zakan,* Odd or even.

A زكأ *zuka,* (زكأة *zuka,at,* or زكاء *zukā,*) A rich man who pays with ready money or before the day.

A زكاء *zakā,* (v. n. of زكي) Growing, increasing. Living comfortably. Being thirsty. Agreeing with, being proper, becoming, befitting. Being pure, pious, just. Purity, piety.

P زكاب *zakāb,* Ink. Spittle. *Zukāb,* Aloes.

A زكاة *zakāt,* Alms. Purity, purification (the Muhammadan law recommending it to every person to give to the poor, or for other religious uses, a certain portion of their possessions, by way of purifying or giving a blessing to the rest). A fortieth.

A زكأة نكأة *zuka,at nuka,at,* One who pays a debt without delay.

P زكاره *zakāra,* Quarrelsome, litigious.

A زكازك *zukāzik,* Reproached, despised.

P زكاسه *zukāsa,* (or زكاشه *zukāsha*) A hedgehog. A porcupine.

A زكام *zukām,* Defluxion, rheum. A cold.

P زكان *zakān* or *zukān,* Murmuring, growling.

A زكانة *zakānat,* (or زكانية) Whatever one finds out by conjecture or guessing. A correct guess.

A زكاوة *zakāwat,* Purity, probity, innocence. Ingenuousness. Quickness of parts, ingenuity.

A زكب *zakb* or *zakab,* (v. n. of زكب) Marrying or lying with. Filling. Being delivered of a child at once, without pain. Fulness.

A زكبة *zukbat,* A fœtus. Male seed. الأم زكبة *al,amu zukbatin,* The basest thing.

A زكّة *zikkat,* Arms. *Zukkat,* Rage. Sadness.

A زكت *zakt,* (v. n. of زكت) Filling (a bottle).

A زكر *zakr,* (v. n. of زكر) Filling. *Zukar,* (pl. of زكرة *zukrat*) Small leathern sacks for carrying oil or wine in.

A زكرة *zukrat,* A small skin for wine or vinegar.

A زكري *zakarī*, (زكريّ *zakariy*, زكريّا *zakariya'*, or زكرياء *zakariyāʼ*) Zacharias.

A زكري *zakriy* or *zakariy*, Very red (she-goat, doe, or fawn).

A زكرياوان *zakariyāwāni*, (dual of زكرياء *zakariyāʼ*) Two Zachariases.

A زكرياوي *zakariyāwiy*, Belonging to Zacharias.

A زكزاكة *zakzākat*, Large-buttocked (woman).

A زكزكة *zakzakat*, A taking of short steps.

P زكش *zakish*, Styptic, astringent.

A زكك *zakak*, (v. n. of زكّ) Taking short steps.

A زكم *zakm*, (v. n. of زكم) Casting out (seed). Filling (a bottle).

A زكمة *zukmat*, A defluxion, rheum. A cold. Youngest son or colt. A rude, unpolished man.

A زكن *zakn*, A guess, suspicion. *Zakan*, (v. n. of زكن) Knowing, understanding, perceiving, conjecturing. Thinking, imagining, suspecting. *Zakin*, A physiognomist. *Zukan*, One who preserves or holds fast. A vigilant guard.

P زكنج *zukanj*, A large dish or trencher.

P زكند *zukand*, A large earthen dish.

A زكوّ *zukūw*, (v. n. of زكا for زكو) Growing, increasing. Waxing strong (a plant). Being fruitful. Becoming, fitting. Living comfortably. Being pure, pious, just.

A زكوة *zakāt*, Alms. Best and purest part.

P زكور *zakūr*, A miser. A robber.

A زكى *zaka'*, An even number, a pair.

A زكيّ *zakiy*, (pl. ازكياء *azkiyāʼ*) Pure, virtuous, just, pious, chaste. Rich, abounding in wealth. One who gives the prescribed portion of his wealth to the poor. Ingenious, quick. Strong, growing (lad).

P زكيا *zakiyā*, (in zand and Pāzand) A knife.

A زكيبة *zakībat*, A kind of Egyptian sack.

P زكيد *zakīd*, Wearied, tired out, displeased.

P زكيدن *zakīdan* or *zukīdan*, To mutter to one's self in a rage.

A زكيك *zakīk*, (v. n. of زكّ) Walking with short steps. Walking gracefully (a woodcock). A walk with contracted steps.

P زگال *zugāl*, Charcoal.

P زگالاب *zugāl-āb*, (or زگاله *zugāla*) Ink. A mole on the body.

A زلّ *zalla*, (fut. يزلّ *yazillu*) He slided.

A زلّ *zall*, (v. n. of زلّ) Slipping, sliding, falling. Blundering. Passing away (life). *Zull*, Slippery (place).

A زلّاء *zallāʼ*, (fem. of ازلّ *azall*) (A woman or a she-wolf) light and lank in the hips and thighs. (A bow) from which the arrow slips off suddenly.

A زلابية *zalābiyat*, A thin pancake.

A زلّات *zallāt*, (pl. of زلّة *zallat*) Errors, slips. زلّات و خطايا *zallāt u khatāya'*, Faults and sins.

A زلاج *zilāj*, A bar, a bolt, or latch of a door, which is opened by the hand (مغلاق *mighlāk* implying a lock that requires a key).

A زلازل *zalāzil*, Afflictions, misfortunes. (pl. of زلزلة *zalzalat*) Tremblings, tremors. Earthquakes.

A زلاقة *zalākat*, The buttocks of an animal. A slippery place.

A زلال *zulāl*, Pure, limpid, wholesome water. Humidity of lips. A yellow-spotted worm of a finger's length, bred in the snow, which swells in cold water. زلال خضر *zulāli khizr*, The water of life. P زلال چشمهٔ مهر و محبّت *zulāl chashmaʼi mihr u mahabbat*, The pure water of the fountain of benevolence and love.

A زلالل *zulālil*, Pure, limpid, wholesome (water).

A زلاليّ *zalāliy*, (pl. of زلّيّة *zilliyat*) Coverlets of woollen, without a pile, neither striped nor painted.

A زلب *zalab*, (v. n. of زلب) Cleaving to its mother (an infant).

A زلبة *zulbat*, White ivy. An arrow.

A زلّة *zallat*, A slip, fall (in the mud, or on the ice). An error, blunder, mistake, sin, fault. Whatever one carries away from the table of a friend. Matrimony, nuptials. *Zallat* or *zullat*, An act. A benefit, a kindness. *Zillat*, Smooth, shining stones. *Zullat*, Slippery (place). Anguish of spirits. Asthma, difficulty of breathing.

A زلج *zalj*, (v. n. of زلج) Being borne lightly over the surface of the ground (as on ice, or frozen snow). Barring or bolting (a door). *Zalj* or *zalaj*, A slip, slide, tumble. A slippery place. *Zuluj*, Smooth stones.

A زلجان *zalajān*, Advance, progressive motion.

A زلجب *zaljab*, One who slips or falls.

A زلجى *zaluja'*, Swift (she-camel).

A زلح *zalh*, (v. n. of زلح) Tasting. Vanity. Vain, fruitless, unsuccessful. *Zuluh*, Large dishes.

A زلحفة *zalhafat*, (v. n. of زلحف Q) Driving to a distance. A heavy calamity.

A زلحلح *zalahlah*, Light of body. Shallow (channel of a river).

A زلحلحة *zalahlahat*, Thin, broad (cake). Wide (shallow dish).

A زلحم *zulham*, A Morocco cloak and hood.

A زلخ *zalkh*, (v. n. of زلخ) Striking with the ferule of a spear. A slippery declivity. Any interval not exceeding a bow-shot. *Zalakh*, (v. n. of زلخ) Waxing fat. *Zala* or *zalikh*, A slippery place.

A زلخان *zal* or *zalakhān*, Progress, advance.

A زلّخة *zullakhat*, A slippery declivity, down which boys slide. The lumbago (a disease in the loins). A pain between the shoulders. The mark left by a boy sliding down a declivity.

A زلدبة *zaldabat*, The swallowing (of a gobbet).

A زلز *zalaz*, (v. n. of زلز) Tottering, staggering. Being restless. *Zalaz* or *zaliz*, A road by which any one comes. Household furniture; goods, stuff.

A زلزاء *zalzāʼ*, A thing, business, affair.

A زلزال *zalzāl*, Tremor. *Zilzāl*, (v. n. of زلزل Q) Causing (the earth) to tremble (God). An earthquake.

A زلزة *zalzat*, A light, giddy female, gadding about from house to house, a gossip.

A زلزل *zalzul*, Name of a celebrated harper. *Zalzil*, Household furniture, effects. *Zulzul*, An expert tambourine-player.

A زلزلة *zalzalat*, (v. n. of زلزل Q) (God) making (the earth) to tremble. An earthquake.

A زلزول *zulzūl*, Light, smart. Ingenious, clever, witty. Lightness, agility. Battle, fight. Evil.

A زلط *zalt*, A quick pace.

A زلع *zalʻ*, (v. n. of زلع) Seizing by stratagem. Burning one's foot at the fire. *Zalaʻ*, (v. n. of زلع) Having chapt feet; also hands, if on the outside (any fissure on the palms being expressed by كلع *kalaʻ*). Being corrupted, in a bad state (a wound). A crack or chap on the hands or feet.

A زلعة *zalaʻat*, A nasty, raw wound.

P زلف *zalf*, Part of the night. *Zulf*, A curling lock, ringlet, tuft, head of hair. An aigrette. زلف بستن *zulf bastan*, To discover herself (as a mistress to her lover). زلف پريشان *zulfi pareshān*, Dishevelled, scattered locks. زلف تابدار *zulfi tāb-dār*, Curling ringlets. زلف خطا *zulfi khatā*, Fault, transgression. زلف دراز *zulfi darāz*, Long locks. زلف زمين *zulfi zamīn*, Night. The clay from which man was formed. زلف عنبرين *zulfi ʻambarīn*, Perfumed (with ambergris) locks. زلف و خال *zulf u khāl*, Ornaments of gold and jewels wherewith a bride is decorated on her wedding-night.

A زلف *zalf*, (v. n. of زلف) Proceeding, preceding. *Zilf*, A garden or meadow. *Zalaf*, Procedure, progress, step. Nearness, propinquity. A full cistern. A step, stair, ladder. (pl. of زلفة *zalafat*) Full cisterns. *Zulaf*, (pl. of زلفة *zulfat*) First parts of the night. *Zuluf*, The first part of the night.

A زلفات *zulafāt*, (pl. of زلفة *zulfat*) First parts of the night.

A زلفة *zulfat*, (pl. زلف *zulaf*, زلفات *zulfāt*, *zulufāt* and *zulafāt*) Nearness, propinquity. Edge, margin. A stage, a halting-place. The first part or watch of the night. A plate or dish. *Zalafat*, (pl. زلف *zalaf*) Any constructed work filled with water (as a cistern, well, pond, or ditch). A green bottle or bowl. A shell, mother-of-pearl. A smooth stone. Hard, uneven (ground). Swept (ground). A hill, soft, sandy, and level. A plate or large dish. A woman, or her face.

P زلفنجانه *zulfinjāna*, A sword, dagger, or knife, made of silver, or with a silver hilt. Name of an ancient king.

P زلفه *zalfa*, A narrow dark place or alley.

A زلفى *zulfa'*, Nearness, approach. A step, rank, post, station. The first part of the night. A stage, halting-place.

P زلفيدن *zalfīdan*, To slide, stumble. To fall upon ice.

P زلفين *zulfīn*, A bar, bolt, ring of a door.

A زلق *zalk*, (v. n. of زلق) Moving from its place, putting to a distance. Retiring, departing. Shaving (the head). Sliding, falling in a slippery place. Causing to slide. The buttocks of beasts. *Zalak*, (v. n. of زلق) Slipping, sliding. Being melancholy and moped in a place, and retiring from it. A slippery place. زلق الامعاء *zalaku'l amᶊāᵴ*, Diarrhœa. زلق الكلية *zalaku'l kulyat*, Diabetes. *Zalak* or *zalik*, The buttocks of a beast. *Zalik*, A slippery place. Soon angry. Cui sperma effluit ante congressum.

A زلقة *zalkat*, A slippery place. A fall. زلقهٔ قدم *zalkaᵢi kadam*, A slip of the foot. *Zalakat*, A bright smooth stone. A woman.

A زلقوم *zulkūm*, The jaws, throat, gullet.

P زلك *zalak*, A live coal, a fire-brand.

P زلگ *zalug*, A leech.

A زلل *zalal*, (v. n. of زل) Stumbling, falling. Erring, blundering. Being lank-hipped. Being deficient in weight, less than standard (money). A fall. Slippery (place).

A زلم *zalm*, (v. n. of زلم) Filling (a reservoir). Giving little (in a present). Committing an error, blundering. Cutting (the nose). Like, similar, resembling. *Zalam*, A kind of flowerless, seedless plant. *Zalam* or *zulam*, (pl. ازلام *azlām*) An arrow without wings or points, used by the Pagan Arabians in gaming. A divided hoof (of oxen); also what grows behind it. A domestic animal, resembling a cat, with a very short tail.

A زلماء *zalmāᵴ*, (fem. of ازلم *azlam*) (A goat) having an excrescence under the chin. Slit-eared (ewe or she-camel). A mountain-goat. A female hawk or falcon.

A زلمة *zalmat*, *zulmat*, *zalamat*, or *zulamat*, Right, true. Really, truly, in fact. هو العبد زلمة *huwa'l ᶊabdu zalmatan*, He has the very cut and figure of a slave. *Zalamat*, A small excrescence under the throat of a goat.

A زلنباع *zilimbāᶊ*, A man diffusive in speech.

A زلنبور *zalambūr*, One of the five sons of the devil, who, according to eastern belief, sow discord between husband and wife.

A زلنفح *zalanfah*, Perverse in disposition.

A زلنقطة *zulunkutat*, A dwarfish woman. Penis.

P زلو *zalū*, A leech.

A زلوج *zalūj*, Swift, quick. A steep declivity reaching far. (An arrow) which falls out of the hand from slipperiness.

A زلوغ *zulūgh*, (v.n.of زلغ) Rising (sun). Flaming up (fire).

A زلوف *zalūf*, High (mountain-cliff). A long, tedious mountain-path.

A زلوق *zalūk*, Extensive, long (ridge of a mountain). Swift (she-camel).

P زلوك *zalūk*, A leech.

A زلول *zalūl*, Deficient, light (money). Pure, limpid, wholesome water. *Zulūl*, (v. n. of زل) Being deficient, light (money). Slipping, sliding. Falling in the mire. Blundering. Passing rapidly by.

A زله *zalh*, The odoriferous flower sweet basil. The stone at the mouth of a well, where the person stands who draws water. Astonishment. *Zalah*, Solicitude, mental distraction from grief or anxiety.

P زلّه *zalla*, Victuals carried home by the guests from an entertainment. *Zalla* or *zilla*, A kind of cricket which hums very loud in summer.

A زلهب *zalhab*, Thin-bearded and light of flesh.

P زليبيا *zalībiyā*, A sort of fritter or pancake.

A زلّية *zilliyat*, (pl. زلالي *zalālīy*) A coverlet of woollen, without a pile, neither striped nor painted.

A زليج *zalīj*, (v. n. of زلج) Being carried lightly over the surface of the ground. Barring (a gate). Swift (camel).

P زليخا *zulayhhā*, The wife of Potiphar, whose passion for Joseph is much celebrated in the East, particularly in the elegant Persian poems by Nazāmī and Jāmī.

A زليطة *zalītat*, A mouthful of pap.

P زليف *zalīf*, Fear, dread.

A زليف *zalīf*, A proceder from place to place.

P زليفن *zalīfan* or *zilīfan*, Causing to fear. Terror, fear, dread. A threat. Hatred, revenge. A bow for separating cotton from the seed.

A زليق *zalīk*, (A fœtus) slipping from the belly.

A زليق *zullayk*, A smooth peach, a nectarine.

P زليل *zalīl*, A hiccough, a belch.

A زليل *zalīl*, (v. n. of زل) Slipping, falling (in the mud). Blundering (in speech). Passing rapidly by. Pure, limpid, wholesome water. A dish made of starch, honey, and water.

A زلّيلاء *zillīlāᵴ*, (v. n. of زل) Slipping, sliding. Blundering in speech. Lapsus linguæ.

A زلّيلى *zillīlā'*, (v. n. of زل) Slipping. Blundering in speech. Slip, stumble, trip: error, blunder.

A زليم *zalīm*, (An arrow, also a staff) smooth, straight, justly formed, and of a proper size.

P زم *zam*, Cold. A biting wind. A wound. A child slavering. One whose lips are turned out in speaking. A cheek, jaw. A torch, match. A tent, suppository. Gently, slowly, softly. Name of a river, and of a city. The well Zamzam at Mecca.

A زمّ *zamm*, (v.n.of زمّ) Binding, fastening (with transverse thongs). Bridling, reining, haltering. Carrying (the head) high, tossing up (the nose), being haughty, supercilious. Raising (his) head when in pain (a camel). Going before others. Seizing (as a wolf a sheep). Speaking. Filling (a bottle).

P زما *zi mā*, (for از ما *az mā*) From, than us.

A زمانة *zamātat*, A being modest, grave, sedate.

A زماجر *zamājir*, (or زماجير *zamājīr*) (pl. of زمجرة *zamjarat*) Flutes. Whores.

A زمّاح *zummāh*, Name of a bird that carries off children from their cradles.

A زماخريّ *zumākhhirīy*, Tall and hollow.

A زمار *zimār*, The voice of an ostrich. (pl. of زمير *zamīr*) Short, dwarfish.

A زمّار *zammār*, A flute-player, flutist, piper.

A زمارة *zimārat*, Skill in playing on the pipe or flute. A piping or playing on the pipe or flute.

A زمّارة *zammārat*, A flute, pipe. A harlot. A log tied to a dog's neck to prevent him entering into a vineyard to eat the grapes. An iron pin between the two rings of an iron collar. كسب الزمّارة *kasbu'z zammārat*, The gains of a whore.

P زماروغ *za* or *zumārūgh*, A toadstool, fungus.

A زمازم *zumāzim*, Plenteous (water). The famous well Zamzam at Mecca.

A زمازير *zamāzīr*, Shrivelled, wrinkled (flesh).

A زماع *zamāᶊ* or *zimāᶊ*, Despatch. Diligence, promptitude. Boldness. *Zimāᶊ*, (pl. of زمعة *zamaᶊat*) Excrescences on the back of the hoofs of cloven-footed animals.

A زمّاعة *zammāᶊat*, The backside.

A زمال *zamāl* or *zimāl*, (v. n. of زمل) Running with a limp on one side. *Zimāl*, (v. n. of زمل) Travelling unequally loaded (a beast). Limping (a camel). Curvetting from sprightliness (a camel). Causing (one) to follow, or ride behind on the crupper. (pl. زمل *zumul* and ازملة *azmilat*) Lameness of a camel. The wrapper of a wallet.

A زمّال *zummāl*, Cowardly, slothful, weak.

A زمّالة *zummālat*, Weak, cowardly, timid.

A زمالق *zumālik*, Effusive before coition.

A زمام *zimām*, (pl. ازمّة *azimmat*) A halter fastened to the ring of a camel's nose, a rein. That whereby a thing is bound or fastened. زمام اختيار *zimāmi ikhtiyār*, The reins of self-controul.

A زمّام *zummām*, High (grass).

P زمان *zamān*, Death.

A زمان *zamān*, (pl. ازمان *azmān*, ازمنة *azminat*, ازمن *azmun*) Time, season. An age. Tense. A season of the year; of which, like the people of India, they reckon six, each of two months' duration; viz. ربيع الاوّل *rabīᶊu' awwal*, صيف *sayf*, قيظ *kayz*, ربيع الثاني *rabīᶊu's sānī*, خريف *kharīf*, and شتاء *shitāᵴ*. The world. Fortune, chance, fate, destiny. Heaven. P زمان پيشين *zamāni peshīn*, Former time. زمان و زمين *zamān u zamīn*, The universe. پادشاه زمان *pādshāhi zamān*, King of the world, monarch for the time being.

A زمانا *zamānan*, Sometimes, in good time.

A زمانة *zamānat*, (v. n. of زمن) Being worn out with age or labour (a beast). Love. A distemper amongst cattle arising from weakness in the limbs.

A زمان زمان *zamān zamān*, Time after time.

P زمانه *zamāna*, Time. Fortune. The world. Revolutions of the heavens. زمانهٔ حال *zamānaᵢi hāl*, The present time.

P زمانه ساز *zamāna-sāz*, A time-server, turn-coat.

P زمانه سازي *zamāna-sāzī*, Time-serving. Hypocrisy. Necessity.

P زمانه موافق *zamāna-muwāfik*, Well-timed.

P زماني *zamānī*, Temporal. Worldly. Frail.

A زمانيّ *zamānīy*, Relating to time, temporal.

P زمانيان *zamāniyān*, People of the world.

A زمانئذ *zamāna*ʾ*izin*, Then, at that time.

P زمانيكه *zamāne ki*, When, at the time that.

A زماورد *zumāward*, A dish of eggs and meat.

P زماهن *zam-āhan*, Hard, unmalleable iron. Labour in vain. Sordid, mean, doing good to none.

A زمّت *zummat*, Name of a bird of various hues.

P زمترا *zamatrā*, (in zand and Pāz.) Ridicule.

P زمج *zamj*, Vitriol. Gum. زمج بلّور *zamji billawr*, Alum.

A زمج *zamj*, (v. n. of زمج) Filling (a bottle). Stirring up strife. Entering without leave. *Zamaj*, (v. n. of زمج) Being angry. Anger. *Zamij*, Angry.

A زمّج *zummaj*, Name of a bird, of the eagle-kind.

A زمجّة *zimijjat*, The beak of an ostrich.

A زمجر *zamjar*, (pl. زماجر *zamājir* and زماجير *zamājīr*) A small arrow. A long, hollow reed. *Zimajr*, A shout, noise, clamour.

A زمجرة *zamjarat*, (v. n. of زمجر Q) Roaring (a lion). Shout, noise, clamour. (pl. زماجر *zamājir*) A flute, pipe. A whore.

P زمجي *zimjī*, The rump of a bird.

A زمجّى *zimijja'*, The rump of a bird.

A زمجيل *zimjīl*, A leopard.

P زمچ *zamch*, Vitriol, a black dyeing colour. زمچ بلور *zamchi bilawr*, Alum. *Zimch*, A hawk, falcon.

P زمچك *zamchak*, A winged insect.

A زمّح *zummah* Ignoble, beggarly. Short and contemptible. Black and deformed.

P زمحن *zimahn*, (or زمحنة *zimahnat*) Of an evil disposition. Avaricious.

A زمخ *zamkh*, (v. n. of زمخ) Being proud and haughty. *Zamakh*, A long rugged declivity.

A زمّخ *zummakh*, (pl. of زامخ) High-nosed, haughty.

P زمخت *zumukht* or *zamukht*, Styptic, astringent. Sugar-cane. A very hard knot. A miser. Harsh, severe. Improper, untoward.

A زمخر *zamkhar*, A kind of arrow. A long and slender reed. A flute, a pipe. Thick and entangled (trees). Hollow, soft and succulent (plant).

A زمخرة *zamkharat*, (v. n. of زمخر Q) Being violent (noise). Being angry and yelling (a pard). Shooting forth (grass). A courtesan, whore.

A زمخريّ *zamkhariy*, Thin-legged (ostrich). Tall and hollow (said of any thing).

P زمخشر *zamakhshar*, A city in Khwārazm.

P زمخك *zamukhk* or *zumukhk*, Mean, avaricious. Styptic, astringent. Hard knot.

A زمخير *zimkhīr*, Something, any thing.

A زمر *zamr*, (v. n. of زمر) Performing on a flute, or hautboy. Filling (a bottle). Publishing (a story). Instigating, setting one against another. *Zamar*, (v. n. of زمر) Being thin-haired and of a dastardly mind (a man). *Zamir*, Thin-haired (man). Handsome-faced. Cowardly, dastardly. *Zumar*, (pl. of زمرة *zumrat*) Crowds of people, troops, families.

A زمرّ *zimirr*, Strong, vehement.

A زمران *zamarān*, (v. n. of زمر) Being frightened and running away (a roe).

A زمرة *zumrat*, (pl. زمر *zumar*) A multitude, troop, group, a dispersed crowd. زمرهٔ ملك *zumra*ʾ*i malak*, A legion of angels.

A زمرّد *zumurrud* An emerald.

A زمرّديّ *zumurrudīy*, P زمرّدين *zumurrudīn*, Emerald-coloured.

A زمرّذ *zumurruz*, An emerald.

P زمرونتن *zamrūnitan*, (in zand and Pāz.) To sing.

A زمزرة *zumzarat*, (v. n. of زمزر Q) Shaking (a vessel nearly full) that it may be thoroughly filled.

P زمزم *zamzam*, The fourteenth chapter of the Zand. Gently. A low whispering, buzzing sound made by the fire-worshippers. زمزم افشاندن *zamzam afshāndan*, To cry.

A زمزم *zamzam*, A famous well at Mecca, called Hagar's well. Plenteous (water). Long-necked (camel). P زمزم آتش فشان *zamzami ātish-fishān*, (or رسن *rasan*) The sun. A *Zimzim*, A herd of camels six years old. *Zumazim*, The well Zamzam.

A زمزمة *zamzamat*, (v. n. of زمزم) Q) Rolling, pealing (thunder). Murmuring, muttering (as the Magi at their ablution, or at meals). A whispering, buzzing sound. A lion's roar. A concert. Conviviality. *Zimzimat*, A group, company of people, or camels: fifty camels. A company of demons or wild beasts. A herd of camels without young ones.

P زمزمه *zamzama*, A musical manner of reading, a chant. A low, murmuring noise made by the fire-worshippers when performing their ablutions, or at meal-time. Soft whispering, flattering speech. Name of a chapter of the Zand.

P زمزمه پيراي *zamzama-payrāy*, Singing.

P زمزمه گويان *zamzama-goyān* or *gūyān*, Singers, chanters. Cooing (turtles).

P زمزميدن *zamzamīdan*, To eat much. To sneeze softly.

A زمزوم *zumzūm*, Choicest (camels). A hundred (camels). Worst (men).

A زمزيم *zimzīm*, A herd of camels six years old.

P زمستان *zamistān*, Winter. Wisdom, science.

P زمستاني *zamistānī*, Wintry, winterly, brumal.

A زمع *zamɛ*, (v. n. of زمع) Making haste, using diligence. Applying diligently to and persevering in. *Zamaɛ*, (v. n. of زمع) Being confounded, astonished, panic-stricken. Consternation, fear, amazement. The lowest, meanest of mankind. The fetlock of a horse. The spur of a cock. An excrescence on the fingers, or a redundant finger. A narrow or languid stream. Quick, clever, active, vigorous (in business). Tremor, ague. (pl. of زمعة *zamaɛat*) Substances growing behind the hoofs of cloven-footed animals. Bearing spurs of fruit-trees. *Zamiɛ*, One who, when angry, sheds tears or urine.

A زمّع *zummaɛ*, A stingless wasp, a drone. Slow.

A زمعاء *zumaɛāʾ*, (pl. of زميع) Bold, enterprising.

A زمعان *zamaɛān*, (v. n. of زمع) Being slow in progress. Lightness, swiftness. A slow pace.

A زمعة *zumɛat*, A bit of a plant. *Zamaɛat*, Any thing growing on the back of the hoof of a cloven-footed animal. Hair hanging at the back of the foot of a sheep, doe, or hare. The spur of a cock. The bearing spur of a vine. The hinder part of the foot of a hare. (pl. ازماع *azmāɛ*) A small stream winding through a valley. Low ground.

A زمعيّ *zamɛīy*, Mean, low, paltry. Hasty, choleric. A very shrewd, cunning fellow.

A زمق *zamk*, (v. n. of زمق) Pulling out hairs. Unlocking, opening a lock.

A زمقة *zamakat*, Any thing, aught.

A زمك *zamk*, (v. n. of زمك) Exciting against any one, putting him in a passion. Filling (a bottle). *Zamak*, The rump, also the tail of a bird. Anger.

A زمكّ *zimikk*, The tail of a bird.

A زمكة *zamakat*, Hasty, choleric. Foolish. Dwarfish.

A زمكّى *zimikka'*, Rump, also tail of a bird.

P زمكان *zam* or *zumgān*, Hair about the pubes.

A زمل *zaml*, (v. n. of زمل) Going as it were in a limping pace from sprightliness. Making (any one) ride behind one's self, or putting (him) on the opposite side. Going at the heels of another. *Ziml*, One who rides behind another. A load. Half a sack full. *Zimal*, (*zumal*, or زمّل *zummal*) Pusillanimous, languid. The fruit of a tree.

A زملان *zamalān*, (v. n. of زمل) Going as it were of a limping pace from sprightliness.

A زملة *zimlat*, Luxuriant pith of the palm-tree. Small palm-trees or shoots joined together. A palm-shoot out of hand's reach. *Zumlat*, A crowd. A company of travellers. *Zamalat*, A family. Many.

A زملق *zumalik*, (or زمّلق *zummalik*) Cui sperma effluit ante congressum (same as زمالق).

A زمم *zamam*, Intent, design. Manifest. Equal, even, just. Moderate. Opposite to, corresponding with. Near.

A زمّم *zammam*, The well Zamzam at Mecca. *Zummam*, (pl of زامّ *zāmm*) Proud, high, haughty.

A زمن *zaman*, (v. n. of زمن) Being afflicted by age or labour (a beast of burden). Time, season. An age. *Zamin*, Tried, afflicted. Impaired in constitution by disease, afflicted with a chronic disease. Galled in the back. A heap of dung.

A زمنة *zumnat*, (v. n. of زمن) Being injured by time or age. Being hurt in the back (a beast of burden). *Zamanat*, Time.

P زمنج *zamnaj*, A cylindrical stone or roller, with which they smooth the clay roofs of houses. *Zimunj*, One of two rapacious birds called دو برادران

du birādarān, Two brothers; because if one is over-matched by the animal he attacks, he is aided by his companion.

A زمنى *zamna'*, (pl. of زمن *zamin* and زمين *zamīn*) Injured by age, time, or a wound in the back.

P زمو *zamū* or *zumū*, Mud, whether moist or dry. *Zumū*, A roof formed of timber and clay, or earth; also the earth so used.

A زموخ *zamūkh*, Long and rugged (declivity).

P زمودن *zamūdan*, To embroider. To paint.

P زموده *zamūda*, Painted. Embroidery. *Zumūda*, A swing or see-saw.

A زمور *zamūr*, A handsome youth.

A زموع *zamūʿ*, Swift, hasty. Light, brisk (woman). A hare that takes short light steps, that she may not be tracked.

A زموم *zamūm*, Quicksilver. *Zumūm*, (v. n. of زمّ) Being filled (a bottle).

A زمه *zamh*, (v. n. of زمه) Scorching any one (the sun). *Zamah*, (v. n. of زمه) Being oppressed with heat. Being intense (heat). Intense heat.

P زمه *zama*, Rock-alum. Vitriol. Black dye.

A زمهرة *zamharat*, (v. n. of زمهر Q) Reddening with anger (the eye).

P زمهرير *zam-harīr*, (Making cold) Name of an intensely cold quarter from which the wind blows.

A زمهرير *zamharīr*, Intense cold. The moon.

P زمى *zamī*, (for زمين *zamīn*) The earth.

P زمياد *zamiyād* or *zamyād*, Name of the angel who guards the Hūris. The 28th of the month.

A زميت *zamīt*, Grave, modest, mild, patient.

A زمّيت *zimmīt*, Exceedingly grave or modest.

P زميدار *zamī-dār*, (for زميندار *zamīn-dār*) An officer under the Mughal government of Hindūstān, who (as the term imports) had charge of the land, and whose duty was to collect the revenues of the district entrusted to his superintendence, for which he was allowed a certain per centage.

P زميدن *zamīdan*, To chew. To scream.

A زمير *zamīr*, (v. n. of زمر) Piping, playing on the flute or flageolet. Good (singing). (pl. زمار *zimār*) Short, dwarfish. A handsome youth.

A زمّير *zimmīr*, A kind of fish.

A زميع *zamīʿ*, (pl. زمعاء *zumaʿāʾ*) Ready, diligent. Swift, hasty. Bold, enterprising. Sagacious, prudent.

A زميق *zamīk*, Plucked (beard).

A زميل *zamīl*, One who sits or rides behind another. A fellow-traveller on business. *Zumayl*, (also زميّل *zimyall*) Cowardly, slothful.

A زمّيل *zummayl* or *zimmīl*, Cowardly, slothful.

A زميلة *zumaylat* or *zummaylat*, Weak, cowardly.

P زمين *zamīn*, Earth, ground. Land, soil. A region, country. The pavement at the bottom of a pond or cistern. The ground of a picture. زمين افتاده *zamīni uftāda*, Land which has lain fallow for a time. زمين آئمّه *zamīni āʾimma*, Lands granted for the support of priests. زمين تابستاني *zamīni tābistānī*, Land which yields only summer-crops. زمين توفير *zamīni tawfīr*, Land thrown in unto the tenant over and above what is specified in the lease. H زمين جلي *zamīni jalī*, Land which can only be cultivated during the rainy season. P زمين چاهي *zamīni chāhī*, Land irrigated from a well. زمين خسته *zamīni khasta*, Land ploughed or trodden. زمين را ساية شدن *zamīn rā sāya shudan*, Humility, depression. زمين بدندان گرفتن *zamīn ba dandān giriftan*, (To bite the ground) To manifest weakness and humility. زمين زمستاني *zamīni zamistānī*, Ground yielding only winter-crops. زمين مرده *zamīni murda*, Waste ground. زمين و زمان *zamīn u zamān*, Place and time. The universe. علم زمين *ʿilmi zamīn*, The science of geometry.

A زمين *zamin* (pl. زمنى *zamna'*) Afflicted, worn down by age or labour (a beast of burden). *Zumayn*, (dim. of زمان *zamān*) A little time. ذات الزمين *zāta'z zumayn*, A little while ago.

P زمين بوس *zamīn-bos*, Kissing the ground. Making a very low bow.

P زمين پيماي *zamīn-paymāy*, (or زمين جسته *zamīn-justa*) A land-measurer. A traveller.

P زميندار *zamīn-dār*. See زميدار *zamī-dār*.

P زميندارى *zamīn-dārī*, The office of a zamīndār. The country or jurisdiction of a zamīndār.

P زمين دوز *zamīn-doz*, A kind of tent.

P زمين زاده *zamīn-zāda*, Earth-born. Man. Muhammad.

P زمين كنده *zamīn-kanda*, A yam (root).

P زمين كوب *zamīn-kob*, A horse, camel, &c.

P زمين گير *zamīn-gīr*, A paralytic.

P زمين لرزه *zamīn-larza*, An earthquake.

P زمين نيكو *zamīn-nekū*, Good soil.

P زميني *zamīnī*, Earthy. Subterraneous house.

P زن *zan*, A woman. A lady. A bride, a wife. Effeminate, timid, cowardly. One who assumes a bold and animated air in walking. زن باردار *zani bār-dār*, A pregnant woman. زن بردن *zan burdan*, (or زن خواستن *zan khwāstan*, also زن كردن *zan kardan*) To espouse a woman, to marry. زن بمزد *zan ba muzd*, A harlot. زن پسر *zani pisar*, A son's wife. زن پيرايه *zani payrāya*, A tire-woman. زن دود افكن *zani dūd-afkan*, An enchantress. A dark night. زن كوچهٔ باستان *zani kūchaʾi bāsitān*, The world. زن مردانه *zani mardāna*, A vixen, virago. زن و شوي *zan u shūy*, Husband and wife. زن و فرزند *zan u farzand*, Wife and children. مرد و زن *mard u zan*, Male and female. Man and wife. *Zan*, (in composition from زدن *zadan*) Striking, beating. تيغ زن *tegh-zan*, A swordsman. خشت زن *khisht-zan*, A brick-maker. راه زن *rāh-zan*, Infesting the way, *i.e.* a robber. طبل زن *tabl-zan*, A drummer. ناي زن *nāy-zan*, A flute-player. *Zun*, Tares.

A زنّ *zann*, (v. n. of زنّ) Shrinking, shrivelling (a sinew). Suspecting. *Zinn*, Oats. A small, round, green pulse.

A زنء *zanʾ*, (v. n. of زنأ) Ascending (a mountain). Skipping, leaping for joy. Approaching (to fifty). Drawing near. Adhering, sticking close to the ground. Making haste. Strangling. Fleeing to. Decreasing, diminishing (as a shadow). Suffering from a strangury.

P زنا *zanā*, (from زدن *zadan*) Beating, striking.

A زنا *zina'*, (in the Hijāz dialect) Fornication.

A زناء *zanāʾ*, Short, compact (man or shadow). One who suppresses his urine. *Zināʾ*, (v. n. of زني) Fornicating. Calling (any one) a bastard. (v. n. 3 of زني) Committing fornication. Adultery, fornication. P فرزند زنا *farzandi zinā*, A bastard. A ولد زنا *waladi zinā*, A bastard. A fire-fly.

A زنّاء *zannāʾ*, A whoremonger, fornicator.

A زنّاءة *zannāʾat*, A she-ape.

A زناءيّ *zināʾiy*, A whoremonger.

A زنابير *zanābīr*, (pl. of زنبور) Wasps. Hornets.

A زنابيل *zanābīl*, (pl. of زنبيل *zimbīl*) Baskets.

A زناة *zunāt*, (pl. of زاني *zānī*) Adulterers.

A زناج *zināj*, Compensation, retribution.

P زنّاج *zunnāj*, Stuffed chitterlings. Paste doubled, between which are put fruits, meat, and the like, a kind of puff.

A زناد *zinād*, (pl. of زند *zand*) Instruments for striking fire.

A زنادقة *zanādikat*, (or زناديق *zanādīk*) (pl. of زنديق *zindīk*) Sadducees. Infidels. Atheists. Fire-worshippers.

A زنّار *zunnār*, (or زنّارة *zunnārat*) (pl. زنانير *zanānīr*) A belt (particularly a cord worn round the middle by the Eastern Christians and Jews; and also by the Persian Magi. The Brahmanical thread. A priest's gown. (metaph.) The ringlets of a mistress. P زنّار ساغر *zunnāri sāghar*, The bubbles of a goblet of wine. The ring left by wine in a goblet. A ارباب زنّار و ناقوس *arbābi zunnār u nākūs*, Those who use girdles and bells, *i.e.* Christians.

P زنّاردار *zunnār-dār*, Belted. A Brahman.

P زنا شوهري *zanā-shawharī*, Wedlock.

P زناشوئي *zanā-shūʾī*, Wedlock. زناشوئي كردن *zanāshūʾī kardan*, To toy with a spouse. عقد زناشوئي بستن *ʿakdi zanāshūʾī bastan*, To tie the marriage-knot.

A زناط *zināt*, (v. n. of زنط) Pressing, thronging. A throng, press, crowd.

A زناطرة *zanātirat*, Turbulent fellows.

A زناق *zināk*, A necklace, any ornament for the neck. *Zunāk*, Any thing put round the nose of a horse, to hold him steady, when shoeing or bleeding; also a ring on the bridle under his chin. Tetters or tethers, with which they bind the feet.

P زناكار *zinā-kār*, An adulterer, whoremonger.

P زناكاري *zinā-kārī*, Fornication, whoredom.

A زنام *zunām*, Name of a flutist. Misfortune.

P زنان *zanān*, (pl. of زن *zan*) Women. زنان خوانده *zanāni khwānda*, The women who conduct the bride to her husband. Women who, being invited, may visit the women's apartments. Beating. تيغ زنان *tegh-zanān*, Swordsmen.

A زنان *zanān*, Short (shadow).

P زنانه *zanāna*, Women's apartments. Feminine. Womanly.

A زناني *zunāna'*, Snot from a camel's nose.

A زناني *zanāniy*, Sufficient for himself (man).

P زنانيدن *zanānīdan*, To bring to life again.

A زنانير *zanānīr*, Pebbles, gravel. Small flies, gnats. (pl. of زنّار *zunnār* and زنارة) Belts, girdles.

A زناويّ *zināwiy*, A whoremonger, wencher.

P زنايانيدن *zināyānīdan*, To neigh, or to make a horse neigh. To cause (a dog or a wolf) to howl.

A زنب *zanab*, (v. n. of زنب) Being fat.

A زنبار *zimbār*, A wasp. A hornet. A tree resembling the plane. The fig called حلوانيّ *hulwāniy*.

P زنباره *zam-bāra*, A whoremonger, wencher.

A زنباع *zimbāع*, The edge of the hoof or shoe.

A زنباق *zambāk*, Name of a hot, biting vegetable, which gives a headache.

P زنبان *zambān*, Anise.

P زنبر *zambar*, A vessel in which they carry earth or clay. A leathern bag for drawing water. A certain warlike instrument. A litter. The barberry. A cuckold. A mean rascal who will endure to be scouted. A whoremonger, rake. *Zumbar* or *zumbur*, A kind of soft cloth with a long pile. *Zumbur*, Inflating the cheeks and striking them so that the wind escapes with noise.

A زنبر *zambar*, A lion. *Zumbur*, Little, small. Witty, quick at repartee.

P زنبرك *zamburak*, A cross-bow.

P زنبري *zambarī*, A kind of ship.

A زنبريّ *zambariy*, Thick, heavy. Large (ship).

A زنبريّة *zambariyat*, A kind of ship.

P زنبغول *zambaghūl*, (or زنبغل *zumbaghal*) Filling the cheeks with wind, which escapes with noise when the cheeks are struck.

A زنبق *zambak*, Oil of jasmine. A flute, a pipe. امّ زنبق *umm zambak*, Wine.

P زنبل *zambal*, A leathern basket in which dirt and rubbish is removed. The barberry.

P زن بمزد *zan ba muzd*, A pimp, a pander.

P زنبور *zambūr*, A bee. زنبور خر *zambūri khar*, A wasp. زنبور عسل *zambūri ‘asal*, A bee.

A زنبور *zumbūr*, (pl. زنابير *zanābīr*) A bee. A hornet. Light. Witty, ingenious, smart, quick at repartee. An ass able to carry burdens. A large mouse. A tree resembling the plane. A sort of fig.

A زنبورة *zumbūrat*, A hornet.

T زنبورچي *zambūrchī*, A fusileer.

P زنبور خانه *zambūr-khāna*, A bee's nest. The person of a holy man, full of divine grace. Vindictive.

P زنبور زرد *zambūr-zard*, A wasp.

P زنبور سرخ *zambūr-surkh*, A hornet. Live coal.

P زنبورك *zambūrak*, A cross-bow. A small cannon. A camel-swivel. A kind of very sharp weapon.

P زنبور كافر *zambūr-kāfir*, A sort of wasp.

P زنبوره *zambūra*, A black bee. A small gun. A particular kind of arrow-head, and of military arms. A kind of guitar made from two gourds (in India). A concourse of people.

A زنبوع *zumbūع*, The fruit of such trees as the orange, citron, &c., which always have fruit on them.

P زنبه *zamba*, White rose. Pubes. Quicksilver.

P زنبير *zambīr*, A two-handled basket, a pannier of palm-leaves.

A زنبير *zimbīr*, A tree resembling the plane-tree. The حلوانيّ *hulwāniy* fig.

P زنبيل *zambīl* or *zimbīl*, A basket made of palm-leaves. A dried and hollow gourd or calabash wherein women keep their cotton. A wallet. زنبيل در آب افگن *zambīl dar āb afgan*, Throw the basket into the water, *i.e.* give up the business.

P زنبيل باف *zambīl-bāf*, A basket-weaver.

P زنبيل ساز *zambīl-sāz*, A basket-maker.

P زنبيله *zambīla*, A thimble-case. A wardrobe.

P زنپاره *zam-pāra*, An adulterer, fornicator.

P زنپان *zumpān*, The herb or seed anise.

P زن پدر *zam-pidar*, A step-mother.

A زنة *zinat*, (v. n. of وزن) Weighing. A weight. A proper mode. The measure of a word. A just proportion. *Zinata*, Opposite, over against.

A زنّة *zinnat*, Bad-tasted (wheat). ابو زنّة *abū zinnat* or *zannat*, A male ape.

A زنترة *zantarat*, Difficulty, straits.

A زنتو *zantū*, (or زنتور *zantūr*) A dulcimer, or quadrangular instrument, strung with brass wires, and struck with two small rods.

P زنج *zanj*, Plaint, lamentation. Crying, weeping. Derision, mockery, jest, joke. A knot upon a tree. *Zinj*, Two brass orbs, which when struck together make a kind of music or accompaniment to other instruments. Gum. Heart-beating. Quicksilver. Alum. *Zunj*, Gum. The chin.

A زنج *zanj* or *zinj*, (pl. زنوج *zunūj*) An Ethiop. A drum. *Zanaj*, Thirst contracting the intestines.

P زنجاب *zinjāb*, (for سنجاب) Pontic mouse.

P زنجابي *zinjābī*, Mouse-coloured.

A زنجار *zinjār*, Rust, verdigris. زنجار الحديد *zinjāru'l hadīd*, Rust of iron.

A زنجب *zunjab*, (or زنجبان) A belt, girdle.

A زنجبة *zanjabat*, A cushion, or pad wherewith women shew a false prominency round the hips.

A زنجبيل *zanjabīl*, Ginger. Wine, especially that which the Muhammadans suppose to be in heaven; the fountain of paradise. زنجبيل الشام *zanjabīlu'sh shām*, Elecampane. Juniper. زنجبيل العجم *zanjabīlu'l ‘ajam*, Root of the assafœtida. زنجبيل الكلاب *zanjabīlu'l kilāb*, Dog's bane.

A زنجبيلة *zanjabīlat*, A certain herb called also فتائل الرهبان *fatā'ilu'r ruhbān*.

A زنجرة *zanjarat*, (v. n. of زنجر Q) Putting the thumb-nail to that of the fore-finger (saying, I don't care that for you).

P زنجرف *zinjarf*, Red-lead, vermilion.

P زنجرو *zanjurū* or *zunjurū*, Flesh-glue. Name of an herb.

P زنجره *zanjara*, An insect which makes a noise in the night, a cricket.

P زنجستان *zanjistān*, Zanguebar, in Africa.

P زنجف *zinjaf*, A stuff, half-silk, wherewith the fringes or edges of garments are lined. Edging.

A زنجفر *zunjufr*, Red lead, vermilion, cinnabar.

P زنجفره *zinjifra*, (or زنجفر *zinjafr*) Red lead.

A زنجفيل *zanjafīl*, (for زنجبيل) Ginger.

P زن جلب *zan-jalab*, A pander to his own wife.

P زن جلبي *zan-jalabī*, Panderism to one's own wife. زن جلبي نمودن *zan-jalabī namūdan*, To pimp.

P زنجور *zanjūr*, A chain. A harrow. A ball on the top of a tower.

A زنجور *zunjūr*, A kind of fish.

P زنجه *zanja*, Gripes. Plaint, wail. Concatenation.

A زنجيّ *zanjiy*, (P *zanjī*) Of the region of Zanj.

P زنجير *zinjīr* or *zanjīr*, A chain. A ball fixed on the top of a tower. A harrow. A ploughshare, coulter. A term applied to elephants; as سر *sar*, Head, to horses; and نفر *nafar*, Troop, to camels. در زنجير كردن *dar zinjīr kardan*, To put in chains.

A زنجير *zinjīr*, Smack of the fingers. White specks on the nails of boys.

A زنجيرة *zanjīrat*, Name of a fortress in Mesopotamia. *Zinjīrat*, White specks on the nails of boys.

P زنجيرك *zanjīrak*, (dimin. of زنجير *zanjīr*) A small chain. Strokes excellently formed in writing or in sculpture.

P زنجيري *zanjīrī*, (pl. زنجيريان) Mad, insane.

A زنجيل *zinjīl*, (A man) weak in body.

P زنچك *zanchak*, A loose woman, a whore.

P زنچه *zancha*, A common whore.

A زنح *zanh*, (v. n. of زنح) Praising. Driving. Squeezing. Making a hard bargain. *Zunuh*, Equals in any quality admitting of comparison. Those who make a requital for good or evil.

A زنخ *zankh*, (v. n. of زنخ) Raising his head (a lamb) when sucking (from suffocation or dryness in the throat). *Zanakh*, (v. n. of زنخ) Being rancid, stinking (oil or meat). *Zanikh*, Rancid, stinking (oil or ointment).

P زنخ *zanakh*, The chin, or pit in the chin. A word, discourse, conversation. Idle, unmeaning talk, chat. Boast, brag. زنخ بر خون زدن *zanakh bar khūn zadan*, To blush. زنخ زدن *zanakh zadan*, To wag the chin, *i.e.* To talk, to tell stories. To talk idly, prate, boast, vapour.

A زنخة *zanikhat*, (Camels) whose bellies are shrunk from thirst.

P زنخدان *zanakhdān*, The chin, the lower jaw.

چاه زنخدان *chāhi zanakhdān*, The dimple in the chin.

A زنخرة *zankharat*, Breathing from the nostrils.

P زنخك *zunukhk*, A kind of astringent diet.

P زن خواسته *zan-khwāsta*, Married (man).

P زند *zand*, The book of Zardusht. The books of the patriarch Abraham. A fire-steel. The myrtle-tree. Name of a champion of Tūrān. Great. زند رزم *zand-razm*, A great battle. *Zind*, (in zand and Pāzand) The soul.

A زند *zand*, (v. n. of زند) Filling. (pl. ازناد *aznād*, ازند *aznud*, and زناد *zinād*) An instrument for striking fire (the Arabians make use chiefly of one piece of wood rubbed hard or struck upon another concavely formed, which by the collision emit sparks of fire. The upper piece of wood in rubbing (زند *zand*) is usually the wood عفار *ʿafār*, and the lower piece (زندة *zandat*) is of the tree مرخ *markh*. A certain thorny tree. The elbow, the smaller and interior bone of which is called الزند الاعلى *az' zandu'l aʿla'*, and the other الزند الاسفل *az' zandu'l asfal*. *Zanad*, (v. n. of زند) Thirsting. A clout stuffed into the matrix of a camel to induce her to take a liking to another's colt.

P زنداستا *zand astā*, Title of the book of Zardusht or Zoroaster.

A زندان *zandāni*, (dual of زند *zand*) The two pieces of wood for producing fire. The two bones of the elbow. طويل الزندين *tawīlu'z zandayn*, One, the bones of whose arms are long.

P زندان *zindān*, A prison, jail; pound, pin-fold. زندان سكندار *zindāni sikandar*, The city of Yazd. Darkness. زندان برجيس *zindāni birjīs*, (likewise زندان مشتري *zindāni mushtarī*) The sign Virgo. زندان خاموشان *zindāni khāmoshān*, The grave. زندان كردن *zindān kardan*, To put in prison. زندان نا مسجون *zindāni nā masjūn*, The fish which swallowed Jonah. زندان نيّرين *zindāni nayyirayn*, (Prison of the two luminaries) The head and tail of the dragon (the author of eclipses).

P زندانبان *zindānbān*, A jailer.

P زندانباني *zindānbānī*, The office of jailer. زندانباني كردن *zindānbānī kardan*, To keep a jail, to act as jailer.

P زنداني *zindānī*, Of a prison. A prisoner.

P زند آور *zand-āwar*, Allowed by the Zand. Free-born. Lawful.

P زنداوستا *zand avastā*, Title of the book of Zoroaster. The first chapter of the same book.

P زندبار *zandbār*, Harmless animal, as a sheep.

P زند باف *zand-bāf*, A priest of the Magi. The nightingale. A ring-dove.

A زندبيل *zandabīl*, (from P زنده فيل *zanda-fīl*) A large elephant.

P زند پيچي *zand pechī*, Coarse cloth.

A زندة *zandat*, An excavated piece of wood placed beneath another (in which are received the sparks of fire produced by friction).

P زند خوان *zand-khwān*, A chanter or reader of the Zand. A priest of the Magi. A nightingale. A ring-dove. Any melodious bird.

P زندران *zindrān*, A nightingale.

P زندرود *zandarūd*, Name of a note of the guitar. Name of a river which runs through Ispahān from west to east.

P زندستان *zandastān*, (or زندستا *zandastā*) The book of Zardusht or Zoroaster.

P زندش *zandish*, Salutation, benediction.

A زندق *zandak*, Exceedingly covetous.

A زندقة *zandakat*, Impiety, heresy. A belief in the two principles of light and darkness.

A زندقيّ *zandakīy*, Exceedingly covetous.

P زندگان *zindagān*, (pl. of زنده) The living.

P زندگاني *zindagānī*, Life. Sustenance, food. زندگاني دادن *zindagānī dādan*, To give life (a mode of expressing death). زندگاني دوم *zindagānīʼi duwum*, The next life. زندگاني كردن *zindagānī kardan*, To live.

P زندگي *zindagī*, Life.

P زند لاف *zand-lāf*, (زندوان *zandwān*, or زندواف *zand-wāf*) A priest of the Magi. A nightingale. A ring-dove.

A زندنيجيّ *zandanījīy*, Cloth from the town of زند *zand* in Bukhārā.

P زندوست *zandavast*, (or زندوستا *zandavastā*) Title of the book of Zoroaster. *Zan-dost*, Fond of women. A whoremonger.

A زندوق *zundūk*, A chest.

P زندونديد *zandwandīd*, The eighth chapter of the book of Zoroaster.

P زنده *zanda*, Immense. Horrible. A fire-steel. *Zinda*, Alive, living. Life. A match, or any thing similar catching fire. Poor, needy. Great, huge, terrible. Proud, haughty. Name of a river which flows through Ispahān. Name of a celebrated wrestler of Tūrān. زنده داشتن *zinda dāshtan*, To keep alive. To be watchful. زنده ساختن *zinda sākhtan*, (or زنده گردانيدن *zinda gardānīdan*) To give or restore to life. زنده كردن خاك *zinda kardan khāk*, To resuscitate. To cause to grow. زنده گشتن *zinda gashtan*, To revive.

P زنده پيل *zanda-pīl*, A male elephant. A large elephant. A title of Shaykh Ahmad Jāmī.

P زنده دار *zinda-dār*, Keeping alive. Wakeful. زنده داران شب *zinda-dārāni shab*, Those who pass sleepless nights, or keep vigils.

P زنده دل *zinda-dil*, Live-hearted, *i. e.* pious.

P زنده ران *zanda-rān*, A nightingale.

P زنده رزم *zanda-razm*, Name of a champion killed by Rustam.

P زنده رود *zanda-rūd*, A great river. Name of a river which flows through Ispahān.

P زنده ساز *zinda-sāz*, One who brings to life.

P زندگاني *zindagānī*, Life. Sustenance.

P زندگي *zindagī*, Life.

P زندواف *zandawāf*, The nightingale.

P زنديدن *zinadīdan*, To be impregnated.

A زنديق *zindīk*, (pl. زنادقة *zanādikat* and زناديق *zanādīk*) Impious. An atheist. A fire-worshipper. One who maintains the doctrine of the principles of light and darkness. A disbeliever in a future state.

A زنديقي *zindīkī*, Impiety, heresy.

P زنديك *zandīk*, A fire-worshipper.

P زنسان *'zinsān*, (for از اين سان) On this wise.

P زن سيرتان *zan-sīratān*, Pathics.

P زنشت *zinisht*, Sight, vision.

P زنشوي *zan-shūy*, A concubine. A man who keeps a mistress.

A زنف *zanaf*, (v. n. of زنف) Being angry.

A زنفجة *zanfajat*, A misfortune, calamity.

P زن فعل سبز چادر *zan-fiʿli sabz-chādar*, The world. Misfortune. Melancholy. A catamite.

A زنفل (امّ *ummu*) *zanfala*, An evil.

A زنفلة *zanfalat* (v. n. of زنفل Q), (or زنقلة *zankalat*, (v. n. of زنقل Q) Walking as if overburdened. Making haste.

A زنفليجة *zinfīlajat*, (زنفليجة *zanfalījat*, or زنفالجة *zinfālajat*) (from P زنبيله *zambīla*) A repository for clothes, a wardrobe.

A زنق *zank*, (v. n. of زنق) Putting a ring encased in leather as a chin-rein on a horse. Keeping (domestics) at short allowance (either from avarice or poverty). Binding the four feet (of a mule). *Zanak*, (pl. زنوق *zunūk*) The part athwart which the chin-strap passes on a horse. The point of the head of an arrow. *Zunuk*, Matured intellects.

A زنقة *zanakat*, A narrow street, or a narrow space between rows of palm-trees. ذو الزنقة *zū'z zanakat*, A trapezoid.

A زنقلة *zankalat*, A walking as if overloaded.

P زنقه *zanaka*, A dark, narrow street.

A زنقير *zinkīr*, A nail-paring. The pellicle which covers the date. Somewhat, a trifle. A mere nothing.

P زنك *zanak*, A little woman. The sun's rays.

P زنك آباد *zank-ābād*, A quarter in Baghdād.

P زنكاري با خويش *zan-kārī bā khwesh*, Cohabitation with one near of kin, incest.

P زنكباري *zankbārī*, Turpentine.

A زنكة *zanakat*, The lobe of the liver.

P زنگ *zang*, Rays of the sun. Light of the moon. Rust. A clapping of the hands. Clear water. Wine. Gumminess in the corners of the eyes. The testicles. Strong and sharp. Hot, burning. A bell carried by couriers and calendar-monks. Ethiopia. زنگ گرفتن *zang giriftan*, To gather rust. زنگ هوا *zangi hawā*, Darkness.

P زنگار *zangār*, Verdigris, rust. زنگار معدني *zangāri maʿdanī*, Green vitriol.

P زنگاري *zangārī*, Verdure.

P زنگان *zangān*, Name of a city between Kazwīn and Tabrīz.

P زنگانه *zangāna*, Name of a river. Name of

a note in music.

P زنگانه رود *zangāna-rūd*, Name of a musical instrument. Name of a river.

P زنگاهن *zangāhan*, Iron-filings prepared in a certain manner.

P زنگبار *zangbār*, Blue vitriol. Ink. A bell. A coat-button. Zanguebar. Name of a fabulous island in India.

P زنگباري *zangbārī*, Turpentine of fir. Native of Zanguebar.

P زنگدان *zangdān*, Bells tied to women's feet.

P زنگ زداينده *zang-zidāyanda*, One who rubs off rust.

P زنگ گرفته *zang-girifta*, Grown rusty.

P زنگل *zangul*, A bell, a rattle.

P زنگله *zangala*, A note in music. A bell which women and letter-carriers tie to their feet. A rattle, small globular bells hung round the rims of tambourins. A grand warlike kind of music. A coat-button. Name of a champion of Turkistān. زنگلۀ روز *zangala-i roz*, (or زنگلۀ زر *zangala-i zar*) The sun. *Zingila*, Part of a large bunch of grapes.

P زنگوله *zangūla*, A rattle. Name of a note in music. Name of a champion of Tūrān.

P زنگه *'zangah*, (for از آن گه *az ān gah*) From that time. *Zanga*, Name of a country; and wrestler.

P زنگي *zangī*, Egyptian, Ethiop, Moor, Negro. A savage. A fool. Name of the founder of a dynasty.

P زنگيار *zangyār*, A little bell. A coat-button.

P زنگي دارو *zangī-dārū*, Leaves of spleenwort.

P زنگي مزاج *zangī-mizāj*, Of Ethiopian temperament, *i.e.* Habitually cheerful (merry as a Greek).

A زنم *zanam*, An excrescence behind the hoofs of goats. *Zanim*, (A noble camel) the lobe of whose ear being slit is allowed to hang down.

A زنماء *zanmā*, (fem. of ازنم *aznam*) Slit-eared.

A زنمة *zanmat*, *zunmat*, *zanamat*, or *zunamat*, Stature of a man. Really and truly. *Zanamat*, The slit part of the ear (which is allowed to hang down in the superior species of camels). A sort of herb. Incipient foliage.

P زنمتان *zanamtān*, An excrescence like a teat on a goat's neck.

A زنمتان *zanamatāni*, *zanmatāni*, (dual) An excrescence (of which there are two) like a teat on a goat's neck. زنمتا الاذن *zanamatā'l uzn*, The two little prominences in the ears. زنمتا الفوق *zanamatā'l fūḳ*, Points on each side the notch of an arrow.

P زن مرد *zan-mard*, Matrimony, nuptials.

P زنمرده *zan-marda*, A man-woman, virago.

P زن مريد *zan-murīd*, Hen-pecked.

A زنن *zanan*, Scanty (water). Uncertain (well), doubtful whether it contains water or not.

P زنند *'zanand*, Decked, dizened. Ornament.

P زننده *zananda*, (from زدن *zadan*) A striker.

P زنو *zanū*, A ship-worm. A leech.

A زنوّ *zunūw*, The state of being narrow.

A زنوء *zunū*, (v.n. of زنأ) Ascending, climbing (a mountain). Drawing near. Taking refuge, fleeing for protection. Being narrow. Decreasing, contracting (a shadow). Making haste. Adhering, sticking close to the ground. Skipping, leaping for joy. Labouring under a suppression of urine.

A زنوبر *zanawbar*, All, the whole.

A زنوج *zunūj*, (pl. of زنج *zanj*) Ethiopians.

A زنوح *zanūḥ*, A swift she-camel.

A زنوخ *zunūkh*, (v. n. of زنخ) Raising his head (a lamb) when sucking, from suffocation or dryness in the throat. Speaking imperiously; haughtiness.

P زنودن *zinūdan* or *zunūdan*, To neigh. To howl. To sleep or slumber.

P زنور *zanūr*, Stalk of a bunch of dates. A leech.

A زنور *zunūr*, (v.n. of زنر) Filling. Girding with a zone (زنّار *zunnār*).

A زنوق *zunūḳ*, (pl. of زنق *zanaḳ*) The points of arrow-heads.

A زنون *zunūn*, (v. n. of زنّ) Shrinking, shrivelling, contracting (a sinew). Suspecting.

A زنويّ *zanawīy* or *zinawīy*, A fornicator, an adulterer. *Zinawīy*, Relating to weight or measure.

P زنويه *zanoya*, The howling of dogs. A continued moan.

P زنويدن *zanoyīdan*, To howl. To neigh.

P زنهار *zinhār*, Security. A deposit, trust. Asylum, refuge. Protection, defence, patronage. A league, covenant. Faith, religion. Knowledge. Wariness, consciousness, notice. Grief, vexation. Complaint. Fear, dread. Ridicule, banter, vexation. Abstinence, continence, avoidance. Haste, speed. Delay, suspension. Take care! beware! By all means, verily, truly, assuredly. Alas!

P زنهارخوار *zinhār-khwār*, A truce-breaker. *Zinhār-khwār*, (or زنهارخواه *zinhār-khwāh*) A refugee.

P زنهارداده *zinhār-dāda*, Taken under protection.

P زنهاردار *zinhār-dār*, One who gives protection or quarter, delay or respite.

P زنهاري *zinhārī*, One who makes a compact. One who seeks protection. Subject, tributary, under protection. A betaking of one's self to a refuge.

P زنهاريدن *zinhārīdan*, To be reconciled, to make peace. To grant security, afford protection. To raise complaints against. To render chaste, abstemious. To hasten, excite to diligence. To teach, instruct in any science. To alarm, terrify.

A زنهرة *zanharat*, A looking most intently.

P زني *zanī*, State of a wife: marriage. Womanhood. بزني آوردن *ba zanī āwardan*, To wed a wife.

A زني *zina'*, (v. n. of زني) Fornicating.

A زنّي *zanna'*, Narrow (case, sheath, &c.).

A زنّي *zanīy*, Small (leathern bottle). *Zinīy*, Relating to weight or measure (زنة *zinat*).

P زنيان *zinyān*, Aniseed sprinkled on a loaf and baked with it.

A زنية *zanyat*, A single act of fornication. ابن زنية *ibnu zanyatin*, Born of fornication. *Zinyat*, A mode of committing fornication. الزنية *az'zinyat*, The youngest son. ابن زنية *ibn zinyat*, A bastard. بنو زنية *banū zinyat*, Name of a tribe. لزنية *li zinyatin*, Not in earnest, thoughtlessly, at random.

P زنير *zanīr*, Wise, learned, intelligent.

A زنير *zunnayr*, A girdle, zone, belt; sash.

A زنيق *zanīḳ*, Firm, settled, fixed.

P زنيله *zanīla*, A sheath, a needle-case.

A زنيم *zanīm*, A worthless fellow, son of a whore. Superfluous; added or adhering to any thing. (A man) intruding into a society, tribe, or family, with which he has no connexion. (A goat) having a substance growing behind the hoof. (A camel) having slit ears, and part hanging down. Excellent (sheep).

A زنين *zanīn*, One who labours under a suppression of urine. One who voids excrement and urine at the same instant.

P زو *zaw*, The sea. Name of the son of Tahmāsb. *'Zu*, (for از او *az u*) From him. *Zū*, (for زود *zūd*) Quick, nimble. Quickly. Haste, despatch.

A زوّ *zaww*, Predestination, fate. Two fellows, a couple. Name of a large ship built by Al Mutawakkil.

A زوء *zaw*, (v. n. of زوأ) Turning, changing, upsetting (the vicissitudes of fortune). Produce, proceeds. Whatever happens or proceeds from any thing.

A زؤاب *zu-āb*, Vicissitude, change.

A زوابع *zawābi'*, (pl. of زوبعة) Hurricanes.

A زوآت *zaw-āt*, Vicissitude, change.

A زواج *ziwāj*, Wedlock.

A زواجر *zawājir*, (pl. of زاجرة *zājirat*) Prohibitions, forbidden things. زواجر شرعي *zawājiri shar'ī*, Prohibitions by the law. زواجر مخالفات و منتبهات آفات *zawājiri mukhālafāt u muntabihāti āfāt*, Prohibitions of adversity and admonitions of affliction.

A زواجل *zawājil*, (pl. of زاجل *zājil*) Pieces of wood at the end of a rope for fastening the mouths of leathern bottles or bags.

A زؤاجل *zu-ājil*, (A man) weak in body.

A زواح *zawāḥ*, A going away, departure.

A زواحف *zawāḥif*, (pl. of زاحفة *zāḥifat*) (She-camels) dragging the legs, fatigued.

P زواده *zawāda*, Provision for a journey.

P زوار *zawār*, An under jailer. A servant. An attendant on the sick. A decrepit old woman. A shrill voice. Alive. Name of the brother of Rustam.

A زوار *ziwār*, (pl. ازورة *azwirat*) Any thing forming a stay or protection. A strap between the poitrel and hind girth (of a camel). *Zuwār*, A visit.

A زؤار *zu-ār*, The inward growl (of a lion).

A زوّار *zawwār*, A visitor. A stranger, pilgrim. *Zūwār*, (pl. of زائر *zā-ir*) Visitors.

A زوارة *ziwārat*, (v. n. of زار for زور) Visiting. Telling lies.

A زوارق *zawārik*, (pl. of P زورق *zawrak*) Boats.

P زواره *zawāra*, An under jailer. A servant.

The brother of Rustam. A city in Persian Irāk.

P زواريدن zuwārīdan, To be old or thready.

A زوازي zawāzī, (pl. of زيزاءة) Small hills.

A زوازئة zuwāzīʼat, (or زوازية zuwāziyat) Capacious (cauldron). Short and thick (man or men).

P زواغار zawāghār, A species of small bird. A solemn feast-day of the fire-worshippers. Name of a priest of the Magi.

A زؤاف zuʼāf, Acceleration, quick motion. Sudden or hastened death by poison.

A زوافر zawāfir, (Maid-servants) who carry leathern bottles on their backs. (pl. of زافرة zāfirat) Helpers, assistants. Pillars, supports, buttresses.

A زوّاق zawwāk, A painter.

A زواقي zawākī, (pl. of زاقية zākiyat) Crowing cocks. اثقل من الزواقي askal mini'z zawākī, Heavier (more grievous) than the cocks (whose crowings was the signal for breaking up the conversations held by moonlight amongst the Arabians).

A زواقيل zawākīl, Robbers. زواقيل العمامة zawākīlu'l ʻimāmat, Hairs peeping under the turban.

A زوّاك zawwāk, Any part of a journey performed. One who wags his shoulders in walking.

A زوال zawāl, (v. n. of زال for زول) Departing. Leaving. Advancing (the day). Declining (as the sun from the meridian). Being removed from its place. Defect, deficiency, failure. Misery, humiliation. زوال شكّ zawāli shakk, Removal or solution of a doubt. زوال شمس zawāli shams, The going down of the sun, sundown. زال زواله zāla zawālahu, (or ازال الله زواله azāla'llāh zawālahu) May God destroy him! P بي زوال bī zawāl, Unfailing; faultless. زوال كردن zawāl kardan, To decline, decay. A Ziwāl, (v. n. 3 of زال for زول) Remedying, curing. Wishing, desiring, seeking, asking.

P زوال zuwāl, A live coal, firebrand.

A زوّال zawwāl, One who goes with a swinging motion. A part of a road or journey.

P زوال پذير zawāl-pazīr, Transitory, fading.

P زواله zawāla, A large globular mass of leaven prepared for baking; any thing of a similar globular form; as a ball, either for play, or for a cross-bow or sling. A three-pronged instrument for sifting flour.

A زؤام zuʼām, Sudden and violent death.

A زؤامي zuʼāma', Battle, conflict, carnage.

P زوان zawān, A kind of drug. (for زبان zabān) The tongue. Zuwān, (for زبان zubān) The tongue. A flame.

A زوان zawān, (ziwān, zuwān, زؤان zuʼān, zawʼān, and ziwʼān) Tares, darnel.

P زوان بره zawān-bara, Lamb's tongue (an herb). Fleawort. A sheet of paper.

P زوانش zuwānish A star. Good fortune.

P زوانه zawāna, The tongue of a balance. Flame. Za or zuwāna, Cotton or silk put into an ink-horn.

A زواني zawānī, (pl. of زانية zāniyat) Whores.

P زواووق zawāwūk, Quicksilver.

P زواه ziwāh, Meat given to prisoners, prison-diet. A ball for a cross-bow, made of clay, of the bigness of a filbert.

A زوايا zawāya', (pl. of زاوية) Corners, angles.

A زوائد zawāʼid, (pl. of زائدة zāʼidat) Superfluities, redundancies. Excrescences growing at the back of the hoofs of cloven-footed animals. Lumps at the back of a saddle. (in gram.) Servile letters, or letters of increase. ذو زوائد zū zawāʼid, A roaring, roaming lion, with long teeth and nails.

A زوائديّ zawāʼidīy, One who has something superfluous about him, particularly a third testicle. Name of a man.

A زوائل zawāʼil, Women. Stars. Prey, game.

A زوب zawb, (v. n. of زاب for زوب) Flowing (water). Taking flight.

P زوبا zūbā, (in zand) A highway-robber.

P زوباشي zūbāshī, (T صوباشي) A president.

P زوباغ zūbāgh, Name of the man who is said to have introduced the practice of sodomy.

A زوبر zawbar, All, whole. The whole. Zawbar or zūbur, The shag or nap of cloth. شيء بزوبره shayʼun bi zawbarihi, The entire thing without any residue. رجع بزوبره rajaʻa bi zawbarihi, He returned unsuccessful.

A زوبرا zawbara', Evil, calamity, misfortune.

A زوبرة zawbarat, Nappiness, shagginess.

A زوبعة zawbaʻat, A marriageable girl. Name of a demon. ابو زوبعة abū zawbaʻat, (or امّ زوبعة umm zawbaʻat) A typhon, tornado, or hurricane whirling dust aloft in the shape of columns.

P زوبيوه zūbīwa, The ferrule of a battle-axe.

P زوپه zūpa, (in zand and Pāz.) A loan, debt.

P زوپين zūpīn, A short two-pronged spear, javelin, trident, fizgig. Musical, poetical. Name of the son of Kāwus.

P زوت zūt, for از و ترا az u turā, From him to thee.

P زوتر zūtar, (for زودتر) Quicker, sooner.

A زوج zawj, (v. n. of زاج for زوج) Stirring up strife, setting by the ears. A pair, couple. An even number. (pl. ازواج azwāj and زوجة ziwajat) A spouse, husband, wife. A covering to the hawda or camel-litter. A certain colour in the brocade called ديباج dībāj. Equal, alike. Joined, attached. Nearest unto. زوج او فرد zawj aw fard, Even or odd. زوج الزوج zawju'z zawj, Any number capable of being continually divided by two until the last number be unity (as eight). زوج الزوج و الفرد zawju'z zawj wa'l fard, Any number which, continually divided by two, has its first quotient an even number and its last an odd one (as twelve).

A زوجات zawjāt, (pl. of زوجة zawjat) Spouses, wives. زوجات عالي درجات عصمت صفات zawjāti ʻālī darajāti ʻismat-sifāt, Spouses of a high rank, and chaste.

A زوجان zawjāni, (dual of زوج zawj) Spouses, husband and wife. A pair (of doves, or spurs). A couple, male and female.

A زوجة zawjat, A wife, spouse. Ziwajat, (pl. of زوج zawj) Spouses, husbands and wives.

A زوجيّ zawjīy, Matrimonial. Married.

P زوج يا فرد zawj yā fard, Odd or even.

A زوح zawh, A scattering; also an assembling of camels. Removal, distance, separation, departure.

P زوخ zūhh, A wart.

A زود zawd, (v. n. of زاد for زود) Preparing provisions (زاد zād) for a journey.

P زود zūd, Swift, quick. Early, soon. Quickly.

A زؤد zuʼd or zuʼud, Terror, fright, fear.

P زودازود zūd-ā-zūd, Quickly, readily.

P زود آشنا zūd-āshnā, Soon intimate.

P زود اشنا zūd-ashnā, Sacred offerings made by the Parsis at the fire-temples.

P زود انداز zūd-andāz, An impromptu.

P زودتر zūdtar, Quicker, more speedily.

P زود جور zūd jūr, The game of tipcat.

P زود خشم zūd-khishm, Pettish, touchy.

P زود خيز zūd-khez, Obedient. A domestic.

P زود رو zūd-rav, A swift traveller.

P زود زن zūd-zan, A quick striker.

P زود زود zūd zūd, Quick! quick! Make haste!

P زود سير zūd-ser, Soon satisfied or filled.

P زود فهم zūd-fahm, Of quick apprehension.

P زود فهمي zūd-fahmī, Quickness of intellect.

P زودكشاي zūd-kushāy, Soon opened (a lock).

P زود مست zūd-mast, Easily intoxicated.

P زود نقد zūd-nahd, Wealthy, ready-monied.

P زود هشيار zūd-hushyār, Actively prudent.

P زودي zūdī, Celerity, quickness, speed.

A زور zawr, (v. n. of زار for زور) Visiting. Approaching (a man or place) respectfully. Going on pilgrimage. Putting the strap زوار ziwār on a camel. The upper part of the breast. The breast-bone. A straight palm-branch without leaves. The understanding. A lord. A chief, a leader. A dream, a vision by night. Resolution, determination. A stone which a well-digger meets with, and, being unable to break it, places it on the outside. (for جور jawr) Iniquity, injustice, tyranny. Zūr, A lie, falsehood. Idolatry. The giving of companions to God (in allusion to the Trinity, which the Muhammadans do not acknowledge). A false deity, idol. A leader, chief. A choir of singers, musical concert. Power, force. Understanding, prudence. Opinion, counsel. Vain. A trifle. Taste of meat, agreeable flavour. Softness and cleanness of a garment. Feasts of the Jews and Christians. A certain river which falls into the Tigris. (pl. of ازور azwar) Armies. ما له زور و لا صيّور mā lahu zūr wa lā sayyūr, He has no purpose and no plan. Zawar, Inclination. An inequality or obliquity in the two prominences of a horse's breast. A looking askance.

P زور zūr or zor, Strength, power, vigour. Violence, strong effort, force. Weight. زور كردن zor *kardan*, To force. To use violence. بزور گرفتن *ba zor giriftan*, To seize by force. با هزار زور و زار *bā hazār zor u zār*, Amidst a thousand difficulties. ساعد پر زور *sāʻidi pur zor*, A strong arm. *Zawar*, (for زبر *zabar*) Above. (for زفر *zafar*) The jaw.

A زوّر *ziwwar*, A chief. *Zūwar*, (pl. of زائر *zāʼir*) Visitors.

A زورّ *ziwarr*, Hard, firm. A hard place. A camel equipped for a journey. A chief.

A زوراء *zawrāʼ*, Deep (well). Distant (lands). A cup, bowl, or silver vessel. A bow. The market-place of Madīna. Baghdād, also the bend of the river Tigris which washes its walls.

P زور آزما *zor-āzmā*, An athletic wrestler.

P زورانه *zawrāna*, Chains for the feet, fetters.

P زورانيدن *zorānīdan*, To be wearied, annoyed.

P زور آور *zor-āwar*, Strong. A strong man.

P زور آوري *zor-āwarī*, Violence. Strength.

P زور باز *zor-bāz*, Strong, robust.

A زورة *zawrat*, One visit. Distance. Keen she-camel which looks from the outer corner of her eye.

P زوردين *zawardīn*, The month of the vernal equinox, beginning the Persian year.

P زورفين *zūrfīn*, An iron ring, staple, hasp.

P زورق *zawrak*, A ship, boat, gondola, bark, yawl, skiff. The prow of a boat whereby she is moored. A sort of cowl worn by dervishes. زورق زرّين *zawraki zarrīn*, The sun. زورق سيمين *zawraki sīmīn*, The silver skiff, *i.e.* the new moon.

P زورقي *zawrakī*, A kind of monk's cowl.

A زورقيّ *zawrakiy*, The bone of the heel.

P زور كار *zor-kār*, Arduous. Doing violence.

P زور گوي *zūr-goy* or *zūr-gūy*, A liar.

P زورمند *zormand*, Robust, powerful, strong.

P زورمندي *zormandī*, Power, courage.

P زورنيم *zawarnīm*, A patch upon a garment; also a gore or piece inserted to enlarge it.

P زور و دم *zor u dam*, Power, strength. Pride.

P زوروين *zawarwīn*, (or زورين *zawarīn* for زبرين *zabarīn*) Superior, above, sublime, very high.

P زوره *zawra*, The vertebræ of the back. An elegant oration.

P زوري *zorī*, Power, strength.

P زوريدن *zorīdan*, To loathe. To commit violence, to force. *Zawarīdan*, To raise high.

P زوز *zūz*, Reproach, reproof.

A زوزاءة *zawzāʼat*, Haste, expedition.

A زوزاة *zawzāt*, (v. n. of زوزي Q) Going with short steps and an erect back. Despising. Driving away.

P زوزك *zawzak*, The seed of hog's bean. Name of an herb.

A زوزكة *zawzakat*, (v. n. of زوزك Q) Moving the hips and sides in walking (a woman). (A woman) who takes the lead.

P زوزن *zozan*, Name of a country. Name of a king. *Zūzin*, A weight of forty-eight grains.

P زوزني *zūznī*, (in zand and Pāz.) The knee.

P زوزو *zu zu*, (for از او از او *az u az u*) From him. *Zū zū*, (for زود زود *zūd zūd*) Quick, quick!

P زوزه *zūza*, Weeping, wailing, lamentation.

A زوزيّ *zawazzaʼ*, Short of stature. A boaster. Quick, sagacious.

A زوزية *zuwaziyat*, (or زُوَزِئة *zuwaziʼat*) Large (cauldron).

P زوژ *zūj*, Wound, stab (with sword or tongue).

A زوش *zūsh* or *zawsh*, A knavish servant.

P زوش *zosh*, Vehement, violent, hard-hearted, wicked, unmannerly. Sharp, acrid. Potent, brave. *Zawash* or *zavush*, The planet Jupiter.

P زوشيدن *zūshidan*, To drop, distil. To involve in trouble.

A زوع *zawʻ*, (v. n. of زاع for زوع) Bending, causing to incline. Separating from the muscles (flesh). Cutting a slice (of a melon) for any one. Drawing. Snatching. Jogging (a camel's reins that he may quicken his pace). *Zūʻ* or *zuwaʻ*, A spider.

A زوعة *zawʻat*, One slice (of a melon). *Zūʻat*, (pl. زوع *zuwaʻ*) Part of a plant beginning to wither. Compact flesh. A light, brisk, active man.

A زوغ *zawgh*, (v. n. of زاغ for زوغ) Deviating, inclining. Causing to deviate or incline. Drawing, or pulling on (a camel) by the rein.

P زوغ *zogh*, A river.

P زوغار *zūghār*, Name of a certain high-priest of the Magi or fire-worshippers. Name of a country.

A زوغان *zawaghān*, (v. n. of زاغ for زوغ) Transgressing bounds in talking. Deviating, inclining. Causing to deviate or incline.

A زوف *zawf*, (v. n. of زاف for زوف) Spreading out the wings and tail, and sweeping the ground with it (a pigeon). Walking with relaxed limbs.

A زوفا *zūfaʼ*, (also زوفائ يابس *zūfāʼi yābis*) Hyssop. Grease in wool. زوفاى رطب *zūfāʼi ratb*, A filthy substance found on the tails of the Armenian sheep, said to be owing to their feeding on a milky kind of grass which is very heating.

P زوفرا *zūfurā*, Wild anise. Name of a bird.

P زوفرين *zūfrīn* or زوفلين *zūflīn*, A hasp, staple.

A زوفي *zūfaʼ*, Hyssop. See زوفا *zūfaʼ*.

A زوق *zuwak*, (in Madīna dialect) Quicksilver.

A زوقلة *zawkalat*, (v. n. of زوقل Q) Letting fall the ends of the turban.

A زوك *zawk*, (or زوكان *zawkān*) The strut of a crow. The shaking of the shoulders in walking.

A زوكان *zawakān*, A swinging or strut in walking.

A زول *zawl*, (v. n. of زال for زول) Putting to a distance, removing, displacing. (pl. ازوال *azwāl*) Elegant, ingenious, clever, witty (youth). Liberal, generous. Strong, strenuous, intrepid. Wonderful. An astonishing thing. A misfortune, trial. A person, individual. Pudenda viri. A bird of prey, a hawk. *Zawal*, (or زولان *zawalān*) (v. n. of زال for زول) Departing, failing: declining (sun from the meridian).

P زول *zūl*, A large cup. *Zawal*, Turnsole. The herb clary.

P زولابي *zūlābī*, Name of Abū Muslim's spy.

A زوّلات *zuwalāt*, Witty, clever (lasses).

P زولانه *zawlāna*, Fetters, tethers. Curly hair.

P زول زده *zūl-zada*, Goat's thorn.

A زولع *zawlaʻ*, One whose heels are cracked.

P زولفين *zūlfīn*, A hasp or staple on a chest.

P زوله *zūla*, A lash.

A زوم *zawm*, A delicate dish made from milk.

A زوم *zuʼūm*, (v. n. of زأم) Dying suddenly. Eating voraciously.

A زومان *zūmān*, A tribe of Kurds or Turkomāns.

A زومح *zawmah*, Short, mean; black and ugly.

A زومر *zawmar*, A handsome youth.

A زوملة *zawmalat*, (v. n. of زومل Q) Driving (a loaded camel or ass). ابن زوملة *ibnu zawmalat*, The son of a handmaid. هو ابن زوملتها *huwa ibnu zawmalatihā*, He knows that.

P زون *zūn*, A part, portion, share.

A زون *zūn* or *zawn*, A dwarf. *Zūn*, An idol. A place wherein idols are set up.

A زونّ *ziwann*, Short, mean-looking.

A زونة *zūnat*, Ornament, decoration. An intelligent, sensible woman.

A زونّة *ziwannat*, Short, mean (woman).

P زونج *zawanj*, *zawinj*, or *ziwanj*, A sausage, a meat-pudding.

P زونزك *zawanzak*, Hump-backed, of a contemptible appearance.

A زونزك *zawanzak*, Short, mean-looking man. Proud, haughty, and carrying himself above his rank or fortune.

A زونزي *zawanzaʼ*, Short of stature. A boaster. Quick, sagacious.

A زونك *zawnak*, A woman who takes the lead, or gets precedency.

A زونّك *zawannak*, Short, mean-looking. One who carries himself above his rank or fortune.

A زونكل *zawankal*, Short, dwarfish.

P زونگ *zawang*, Hump-backed. Despicable.

P زونگل *zawangal*, Hump-backed. Despicable. *Zawangul*, A little bell. Name of a note in music.

P زوني *zūnī*, The knee.

A زؤورة *zuʼūrat*, The crop or craw of a bird.

A زؤول *zuʼūl*, (v. n. of زال for زول) Departing, failing. Declining (the sun from the meridian).

A باب زويلة *bāb zuwaylat*, Name of a gate in Cairo.

P زوهمند *zohmand* or *zohamand*, Trees or grass full-grown.

P زوهيدن *zūhīdan*, To drop, distil, trickle.

A زوي *zawy*, (v. n. of زوي) Concealing. Collecting, seizing, grasping. Putting to a distance.

P زويج *zawīj*, A sausage. Minced meat.

P زويدن *zawīdan*, To be above, high. To sigh.

A زوير *zuwayr*, A prince, chief, leader.

P زويره *zawīra*, A whirlwind, hurricane.

A زويزي *zuwayzaʼ*, Short, compressed.

A زويل *zawīl*, (v. n. of زال for زول) Departing from one's place, being no more. Declining (the sun from the meridian). Motion. A side.

A زوم *zawīm*, Collected, assembled.

P زه *za*, Penis. *Zah*, A place where water boils up and comes forth. *Zah* or *zih*, A bowstring. Bringing forth, child-birth. Offspring of men (or of cattle). Male seed. Dropping, distilling, or exudation of water. The running of a sore. A parapet round a well. Any thing twisted or drawn through a hole (as gold or silver-thread). Lace, a welt, fringe, purfle, border, hem, or other ornament of gold or silk round the edge or collar of a garment. Bravo! well done! Good, excellent. زه برزدن *zih bar zadan*, To sew on a border. زه كردن *zih kardan*, To string (a bow). بي زه *bī zah*, Barren. *Zih*, Reward, remuneration.

A زهاء *zahā*, A beautiful plant, or its flower. *Zuhā*, A yellow, unripe date. Number. زهاء عشرين *zuhā ɛishrīna*, Twenty.

P زهاب *zah-āb*, The oozing of water through a tank or bank of a river. A place where water springs either from the ground or from a rock. Deep water. *Zahāb* or *zihāb*, A running fountain.

P زهابناك *zahābnāk*, Watery, verdant (ground), full of land-springs.

A زهاة *zuhāt*, The number (of one hundred).

A زهّاد *zuhhād*, (pl. of زاهد *zāhid*) Religious, abstinent men, monks.

A زهادة *zahādat*, (v. n. of زهد) Not hankering after, abstaining from, putting away (worldly things). Being devout, religious. A religious life.

A زهّادة *zahhādat*, Religious, abstinent men.

P زهار *zahār*, A bladder. Lower part of the belly. موي زهار *mūyi zahār*, The hair about those parts.

A زهارة *zahārat*, A being white and beautiful.

P زهارتنگ *zahār-tang*, The back girth of a camel.

P زهاز *zahāz*, A noise, clamour. A cry for help.

A زهازج *zahāzij*, (pl. of زهزج *zahzaj*) The howlings of demons.

P زهازه *zih-ā-zih*, Bravo! well done.

A زهاق *zuhāk* or *zihāk*, Quantity, number.

A زهالق *zahālik*, Asses straight-backed from fat.

A زهاليق *zahālīk*, (pl. of زهلوق *zuhlūk*) Fat, equal, and smooth.

P زهانيدن *zahānīdan*, To cause to open. To enable one to win at backgammon. To throw down.

A زهب *zihb*, (or زهبة *zuhbat*) Part of wealth.

P زه بند *zih-band*, An ornament for a lady's neck.

P زه خيار *zih-khiyār*, A kind of collar. Early cucumbers.

A زهد *zahd*, (v. n. of زهد) Guessing the produce (of palm-trees). A small quantity. *Zuhd*, (v. n. of زهد) Abstaining from, treating with indifference (the things of this world). Being given to religious exercises. Continence. Devotion. زهد الاكل *zuhdu'l akl*, Abstinence from food, sobriety. *Zahad*, Whatever portion of one's property is consecrated to God.

P زهدان *zahdān* or *zihdān*, The womb. افتادن زهدان *uftādani zihdān*, Lapsus uteri. زهدان نهادن *zihdān nihādan*, To knock under, to acknowledge one's inferiority.

A زهدم *zahdam*, A falcon. A young hawk. A lion.

P زه ديده *zih-dīda*, Impudent, wanton-eyed.

P زهر *zahr*, Poison, venom. Anger, indignation. Sadness. زهر خون ريختن *zahri khūn rekhtan*, To vent one's spleen. زهر زمين *zahri zamīn*, The cypress. The colocynth. زهر زير نگين *zahr zīri nigīn*, Poison kept in a ring against an evil day. زهر سبز *zahri sabz*, Vitriol. زهر كردن *zahr kardan*, To poison or embitter (life). زهر گوش *zahri gosh*, Ear-wax. زهر مينا *zahri mīnā*, A bitter draught. زهر هلاهل *zahri hulāhil*, (or زهر قاتل *zahri kātil*) Deadly venom, mortal poison. *Zi har*, (for از هر *az har*) From every, from each.

A زهر *zahr*, A flower, particularly a yellow one. (pl. of زهرة *zahrat*) Flowers, especially yellow ones. زهر الحجر *zahru'l hajar*, Lichen, or efflorescence upon stone. *Zihr*, A necessary thing, need, occasion. *Zuhr*, (pl. of ازهر *azhar*) Bright (stars). *Zahar*, (v. n. of زهر) Being white and beautiful.

A زهراء *zahrā*, (fem. of ازهر *azhar*) White, splendid, clear, serene, bright, shining, beautiful, flourishing, blooming. The wild cow. A bright evening cloud. Name of Fātima, daughter of Muhammad. زهرۀ زهرا *zahra-i zahrā*, The most lovely Venus.

P زهر آب *zahr-āb*, Dirty, stagnant, or envenomed water. Rennet for curdling cheese. Water in which fruits have been macerated, their bitterness being left behind. An aquatic herb. زهر آب اجل *zahr-ābi ajal*, The cup of death.

P زهراب *zahrāb* or *zuhrāb*, The nightingale.

P زهرابي *zahrābī*, The nightingale. *Zuhrābī*, A bright sword of the finest steel.

P زهر آلود *zahr-ālūd*, Poisoned, envenomed.

A زهراوان *zahrāwānī*, The two brilliant chapters, that of بقرة *bakurat*, and آل عمران *ālu ɛimrān*.

P زهراوي *zahrāwī*, Name of a physician.

P زهربا *zahr-bā*, A kind of deadly poison.

P زهرباد *zahr-bād*, The quinsey.

A زهرة *zahrat* or *zaharat*, (pl. زهر *zahr*, ازهار *azhār*, and ازاهير *azāhīr*) A flower (especially a yellow one). The freshness and bloom of a plant. The beauty and goodliness (of the world). زهرة الملح *zahratu'l milh*, A kind of plant. زهرة النحاس *zahratu'n nuhās*, The efflorescence of molten brass. *Zuhrat*, Whiteness, beauty. *Zuharat* or *zuhrat*, The planet Venus. A flower, blossom.

P زهر خند *zahr-khand*, A forced smile, grin.

P زهردار *zahr-dār*, Infected. Poisoned. Poisonous, venomous. خنجر زهردار *khanjari zahr-dār*, A poisoned dagger.

P زهر دارو *zahr-dārū*, An antidote against poison. Bezoar.

P زهرگيا *zahr-giyā*, A kind of poisonous plant.

P زهرمهره *zahr-muhra*, The bezoar-stone.

P زهرناك *zahrnāk*, (or زهرور) Venomous.

P زهره *zahra*, Boldness, spirit. Power, vigour. The gall-bladder, bile. زهرۀ شب *zahra-i shab*, A light by night. زهرۀ ميغ *zahra-i megh*, Drops of rain. *Zuhra*, The planet Venus.

P زهره تراك *zahra-tirāk*, Broken in heart.

P زهره خنده *zahra-khanda*, Smile of contempt.

P زهره رخان *zuhra-rukhān*, Handsome persons, with countenances like Venus.

P زهره نوا *zuhra-nawā*, Musical as Venus.

P زهزاد *zih-zād*, Offspring, progeny.

A زهزاق *zahzāk*, The dandling of an infant.

A زهزاه *zahzāh*, Proud, and of repulsive aspect.

A زهزج *zahzaj*, (pl. زهازج *zahāzij*) The howling or hissing of a demon in the wilderness.

A زهزفة *zahzafat*, (v. n. of زهزف Q) Rendering (a saying) current. Making (a thing) unsaleable.

A زهزقة *zahzakat*, (v. n. of زهزق Q) Dandling (an infant). Laughing immoderately.

A زهزمة *zahzamat*, A short, quick step in travelling. See also زمزمة *zamzamat*.

P زهش *zahish*, Emanation. Copulation. *Zihish*, A fountain, water-spring. Praise, approbation.

P زهشت *zihisht*, Breath.

A زهف *zahaf*, (v. n. of زهف) Being light, active, swift. Carrying any thing (wind). Lightness, agility, leaping.

A زهق *zahk*, (v. n. of زهق) Going out, expiring. Outstripping, taking the lead. *Zuhk* and *zuhuk*, (pl. of زاهق *zāhik*) Put to flight, routed. *Zahak*, Low, level ground. *Zahik*, Light, moveable.

A زهقي *zahaka'*, Fleet (horse), passing the rest.

P زهك *zahk* or *zihk*, The first milk of a cow after calving.

A زهك *zahk*, (v. n. of زهك) Blowing hard, sweeping the ground (wind). Grinding, pounding small.

P زه كرده *zih-karda*, Strung (bow).

P زهكوني *zih-kūnī*, A kick on the backside.

P زه گير *zih-gīr*, A ring, generally of bone, worn by archers on the thumb, to save it from being cut by the bowstring. The womb.

A زهل *zahl*, Separation, or a receding from evil. *Zahal*, (v. n. of زهل) Being smooth. Being white. Baldness. Whiteness. *Zahil*, Sound (tree).

A زهلب *zahlab*, One who has a thin beard.

A زهلجة *zahlajat*, Affability. Dissimulation.

P زهلخا *zih-lakhā*, (or زهلخاد *zih-lakhād*) Any ornament sewed upon boots or shoes.

A زهلفة *zahlafat*, A causing to penetrate.

A زهلق *zihlik*, A lamp. A violent gale. Active, nimble (man).

A زهلقة *zahlakat*, (v. n. of زهلق Q) Making white (a garment). Walking at a nimble pace.

A زهلقي *zahlaka'*, Cui sperma effluit ante congressum. Name of a celebrated horse.

A زهلوق *zuhlūḳ*, (pl. زهاليق *zahālīḳ*) Fat, equal, and smooth.

A زهلول *zuhlūl*, Smooth, bare (place).

A زهم *zahm*, (v. n. of زهم) Being full of marrow (a bone). Hindering, preventing. Talking much against. *Zuhm*, Fat, grease. Civet. A stink. *Zaham*, (v. n. of زهم) Being fat, greasy (handed). Stinking. Being oppressed with indigestion. *Zahim*, Greasy, besmeared with fat. Stinking. زهق زهم *zahuḳ zahim*, Fat and greasy.

A زهمان *zahmān*, Oppressed with indigestion. *Zahmān* or *zuhmān*, Name of a dog.

A زهمة *zuhmat*, The smell of fat and stinking meat.

P زهمت *zihmat*, Stinking meat or fish.

A زهمق *zahmaḳ*, Short and firm of body.

A زهمقة *zahmaḳat*, Smell (of body or armpit).

A زهملة *zahmalat*, (v. n. of زهمل Q) Placing one thing on another.

P زهمن *zahman*, Name of a house in Ray, under which the owner found a large treasure.

P زهناك *zahnāk*, Possessed of progeny. *Zihnāk*, One who begets noble offspring.

P زهنجه *zihanja*, Discipline: vehemence, asperity.

A زهنعة *zahnaʿat*, A dressing, decking (a girl).

A زهو *zahw*, (v. n. of زها for زهو) Growing yellow or red (an unripe date). Being tall (a palm-tree). Growing up, becoming a young man. Sparkling, appearing beautiful, giving pleasure. Being vain and proud. Rendering proud. Being near yeaning (a sheep). Going all the night or day without water (a camel). Blowing (the wind). Travelling a night or two after having been watered (camels). Making (them) travel so. Going in search of pasture after drinking. Lighting a lamp. Making (a sword) gleam. Striking with a stick. Measuring or guessing at (a hundred pounds). Shaking a tree (wind). Driving. Shewing or raising higher (vapour or smoke). Undervaluing, despising. Elegance. A lovely countenance. A beautiful plant or its flower. Pride, vain-glory, vanity. A lie. *Zahw* or زهوّ *zahūw*, A yellow, unripe date. *Zuhw*, (in Arabia Petrea) The colour of a ripening date. Ripening (date).

P زهو *zahū*, Ear-wax.

A زهور *zuhūr*, (v. n. of زهر) Shining (as a lamp, the moon, or a face).

P زه و زاد *zih u zād*, Offspring, wife and children.

A زهوطة *zahwaṭat*, (v. n. of زهوط Q) Eating large mouthfuls. A great mouthful.

A زهوف *zuhūf*, (v. n. of زهف) Being submissive, humble, abject, or vile. Being near death. Telling a lie. Perishing.

A زهوق *zahūḳ*, A deep well. A high but open way between mountains. Vain, foolish. Perishing. *Zuhūḳ*, (v. n. of زهق) Going away, departing. Perishing. Expiring, vanishing, coming to nothing. Being vain, to no purpose. Being compact in the bone (marrow). Being filled (a bone with marrow). Passing beyond the mark and not hitting (an arrow). Outstripping (a horse).

A زهومة *zuhūmat*, (v. n. of زهم) Being fat, greasy, and stinking (meat).

A زهي *zihi*, O excellent! bravo! Alas! زهي روي *zihi rūy*, O what a face! زهي سعادت *zihi saʿādat*, O what happiness!

A زهي *zuha'*, Fashion, splendour (of the world).

A زهيد *zahīd*, Abstinent, abstemious, temperate. Few, little, small. Narrow (stream). زهيد الاكل *zahīdu'l akl*, Eating sparingly. وادي زهيد *wādi zahīd*, A channel which holds but little water.

P زهيدن *zahīdan*, To flow, trickle, drop, fall. To gain at backgammon. *Zihīdan*, To bring forth.

A زهير *zahīr*, Reduced by sickness, thin. Sad, melancholy, low-spirited. *Zuhayr*, Name of a celebrated Arabian poet.

A زهيرية *zuhayrīyat*, Name of a tribe.

P زي *zay*, Life. Sustenance. *Zi*, (imperat. and part. of زيستن *zīstan*) Live thou. Living. Life. Provisions. Measure, bounds. A side, quarter, track, coast, shore. Towards, near. (equivalent to زهي *zihi*) Wonderful! O charming! زي سپاهان *zi sipāhān*, Towards Ispāhān.

A زيّ *zayy*, (v. n. of زوي) Concealing (a secret from a friend, or property from an heir). Putting to a distance. Collecting. Seizing, grasping. Closing the eyelids. *Zayy* or *zay*, (pl. ازياء *azyā*) The letter ز. *Ziy*, (pl. ازياء *azyā*) Dress, garb, habit, costume. A form, external appearance. ايّاكم و زيّ العجم *īyākum wa ziya'l ʿajam*, Beware of (imitating or adopting) the dress of foreigners!

A زيّات *zayyāt*, An oil-merchant.

P زياد *ziyād*, Increase, augmentation. One of the games at نرد *nard*. May he live long! A false witness. Name of a fortress in لار *lār*. زياد شدن *ziyād shudan*, To be increased.

A زيادة *ziyādat*, Augmentation, increase, surplus, addition, redundancy. An excrescence. More, too much, excessively. Luxuriant. (in grammar) Introducing a new letter into a word. زيادة الكبد *ziyādatu'l kabid*, The lobe of the liver. حروف الزيادة *hurūfu'z ziyādat*, Servile letters or incrementals, comprised in the technical words اليوم تنساه *al yawma tansāhu*, To-day thou wilt forget it, or in امان و تسهيل *amāna wa tas-hīl*. P زياده از *ziyāda az*, More than. زياده شدن *ziyāda shudan*, To grow, abound. زياده كردن *ziyāda kardan*, To augment, add, amplify. To overcharge.

A زيادتي *ziyādatī*, Abundance, surplus. Superfluous, redundant.

P زياده جو *ziyāda-jo* or *jū*, Avaricious.

P زياده سر *ziyāda-sar*, One who has a high opinion of himself. One who engages in an enterprise which he is unable to finish.

P زياده سري *ziyāda-sarī*, Vanity, conceit.

P زياده طلبي *ziyāda-talbī*, Inordinate desire.

P زيادگي *ziyādagī*, Augmentation, increase.

A زيار *ziyār*, Any thing which furnishes protection or support. A bow.

A زيارة *ziyārat*, (v. n. of زار for زور) Visiting. A visit. A pilgrimage. A bow.

P زيارت گاه *ziyārat-gāh*, A place of pilgrimage.

P زيارت نامه *ziyārat-nāma*, A passport for religious visitation.

A زيازي *zayāzī*, (pl. of زيزاءة *zīzāʾat*) Small hills. Birds' feathers Edges of feathers.

A زيازية *ziyāziyat*, A wheel.

A زئاط *ziʾāt*, A talking much and loud. A small bell hung to the neck of a horse.

A زياط *ziyāṭ*, Vociferation. Altercation.

A زيّاط *zayyāṭ*, Clamorous, noisy.

A زياف *ziyāf*, (pl. of زيف) Clipt or base coins.

A زيّاف *zayyāf*, A lion.

A زيال *ziyāl*, (v. n. 3 of زال for زيل) Departing from, abandoning. Declining (as the sun from the meridian). Advancing (the day).

A زيان *zayān*, Beautiful (moon). *Ziyān*, Ornament, dress, decoration.

P زيان *ziyān*, (part. of زيستن *zīstan*) Living. Damage, detriment, deficiency, prejudice, injury, fraud. زيان كردن *ziyān kardan*, كشيدن *kashīdan*, or يافتن *yāftan*) To suffer loss. در زيان افگندن *dar ziyān afgandan*, To defraud.

P زيان آور *ziyān-āwar*, Injurious, detrimental.

P زيان آوري *ziyān-āwarī*, Injury, damage.

P زياندار *ziyān-dār*, Noxious, hurtful.

P زياندن *ziyāndan*, To bring to life.

P زيان رسيده *ziyān-rasīda*, Injured, damaged. Defrauded.

P زيان زده *ziyān-zada*, Suffering loss (in trade).

P زيانكار *ziyān-kār*, (or زيانگر *ziyāngar*) A destroyer. Noxious, hurtful, destructive.

P زيانكاري *ziyān-kārī*, Injury. Sin.

P زياني *ziyāne*, A loss, damage, perdition.

P زيانيدن *ziyānīdan*, To reanimate, resuscitate.

A زيائد *zayāʾid*, Redundancies, excrescencies.

P زيب *zīb*, (in India *zeb*) Ornament, elegance, beauty. Lovely, graceful. زيب و تر *zīb u tar*, Decked. Fresh. زيب و زينت *zīb u zīnat*, Elegance and beauty.

P زيبا *zībā*, Beautiful, elegant. Adorned, arranged. Consistent. چه زيبا *chi zībā*, How beautiful! how appropriate! how pertinent! how well!

P زيبا خو *zībā-khu* or *kho*, Of good disposition.

P زيبا رو *zībā-rū*, Handsome-faced.

P زيبال *zībāl*, Fleet, swift (horse, mule, camel).

P زيبان *zībān*, Beautiful, elegant. Decked.

P زيبايش *zībāyish*, Decoration.

P زيبائي *zībāī*, Beauty, gracefulness.

P زيبد *zībad*, It is worthy, it becomes, behoves. Fit, proper, becoming.

A زئبر *ziʾbar* or *ziʾbur*, The nap, pile, or shag upon cloth. The down upon fruit.

P زبر *zibur*, A vessel made of coarse cloth for removing rubbish. A counterpane of camel's hair.

P زيبق *zībak*, *zībik*, or زئبق *ziʼbak*, Quicksilver. زيبق كردن *zībak kardan*, To destroy. زيبق مجزا *zībaki mujazzā*, Drops of rain. Tears.

A زيبقي *zībakiy*, Of, belonging to quicksilver.

A زئبل *ziʼbil*, (or زيبل) Calamity, misfortune.

P زيبن *zī* or *zayban*, Who abandons the world.

P زيبندگي *zībandagī*, Adornment, decoration.

P زيبنده *zībanda*, Adorned, elegant, beautiful. سرو زيبنده خرام *sarvi zībanda-khirām*, A gracefully-waving cypress (epithet of a mistress).

P زيبيدن *zībīdan*, To adorn. To become, suit.

A زيت *zayt*, (v. n. of زات for زيت) Dressing (meat) with oil. Giving (people) oil in their condiment. Olive-oil. زيت بني اسرائيل *zayti banī isrāʼīl*, Lapis Judaicus.

P زيتار *zaytār*, Mother or dregs of oil.

A زيتون *zaytūn*, An olive-tree.

A زيتونة *zaytūnat*, A single olive. The olive-tree. جبل الزيتونة *jabalu'z zaytūnat*, Mount of Olives. مدينة الزيتونة *madīnatu'z zaytūnat*, City of Olives, *i. e.* Athens.

P زيتوني *zaytūnī*, An olive-garden. روغن زيتوني *rawghani zaytūnī*, Olive-oil.

A زيتونيّ *zaytūniy*, Oily.

P زيج *zīj*, A mason's rule or line. Astronomical tables. Palpitation of the heart. Ridicule, derision. A boot. A coat of mail. Name of a certain instrument of war.

A زيج *zīj*, (from Persian) A mason's rule. (pl. زيجات *zījāt*) Astronomical tables.

P زيجك *zījak* (or زيجك) The intestines of a lamb stuffed with mince meat, rice, &c., and dressed.

A زئجيل *ziʼjīl*, (A man) weak in body.

P زيچ *zīch*, A drawing out. Active, expert, dexterous. A delicious sort of grape. Ridicule, jest, buffoonery, fun. A boot. Lace used in embroidery.

A زيح *zayh*, (or زيحان *zayahān*) (v. n. of زاح for زيح) Being distant, absent.

A زيحلة *zayhalat*, An arrogant strut.

A زئنّة *zihannat*, Slow, dilatory in attending to a call of necessity.

A زيخ *zaykh*, (or زيخان *zayakhān*) (v. n. of زاخ for زيخ) Tyrannizing. Removing to a distance. Going on one side.

P زيخ *zīkh*, Palpitation (from joy or fear).

A زيد *zayd*, (v. n. of زاد for زيد) Being augmented. Increasing, augmenting, adding. Exceeding. Waxing greater, overflowing. A fictitious name (as John Nokes or Thomas Stiles with us). *Zida*, It is increased; and optatively, زيد قدره *zida kadruhu*, May his fortune or rank be advanced! (applied to a man in an inferior office or style of life; to those of a superior station they use زيد مجده *zida majduhu*, May his glory increase! to a kāzī or judge they say زيد فضله *zida fazluhu*, May his learning or excellence be exalted! and to those in a religious line, زيد تقواه *zida takwahu*, May his piety be promoted!) *Zayd*, *zīd*, or *zayad*, Increase, augmentation, addition.

A زيدان *zaydān*, Increase, augmentation. ابو زيدان *abū zaydān* or *abū zīdān*, Name of a medicine.

P زيدك *zīdak*, Name of a handsome young slave.

A زيديّ *zaydīy*, Name of a sect in Yaman.

A زيديّة *zaydīyat*, Name of a sect.

A زئر *zaʼir*, Roaring (lion). An enemy.

P زير *zīr*, (in India *zer*) Under, below, beneath. Lower. The character of the short vowel *i*, called by the Arabians كسرة *kasra* (ـِ). Any thing dressed under meat when roasting (as rice). Covered, concealed. Great, large. The smallest string of a lute, guitar, &c. A yellow-dyeing wood. A linen summer-garment. زير تراب *zīri turāb*, Under ground. A subterraneous granary. زير زبان گفتن *zīri zabān guftan*, To speak in an under tone. زير و بالا *zīr u bālā*, Below and above, topsy turvy. Sodomy. Sin. زير و بالا گفتن *zīr u bālā guftan*, To say whatever comes uppermost, to talk at random. زير و زار *zīr u zār*, A low plaintive tone of voice. زير و زبر *zīr u zabar*, Below and above. The vowels kasra and fat'ha. زير و زبر شدگي *zīr u zabar shudagī*, The condition of being topsy turvy. زير و زبر شده *zīr u zabar shuda*, Topsy turvy. زير و زبر كردن *zīr u zabar kardan*, To turn upside down, to destroy. از زير *az zīr*, Below, from under. در زير *dar zīr*, Under part, at the bottom.

A زير *zīr*, (pl. ازوار *azwār*, زيرة *ziyarat*, and ازيار *azyār*) One who delights in the company of women. The smallest string of a lute. A lute-string, thick or fine. The acutest tone of an instrument. A large ewer. Linen, flax. An oblong wine-jar lined with pitch. Habit, custom. A button.

A زيّر *zayyir*, Angry.

P زيرا *zīrā*, Because, on account of, since. Any thing placed under. زيراكه *zīrā ki*, Because that.

P زير از ميانه *zīr az miyāna*, Weak, infirm. Vile.

P زيرافكن *zīr-afkan*, (or زير افگند *zīr-afgand*) A small carpet, a rug. Bedding. Name of a note in music (called كوچك *kūchak*, Small).

P زيراك *zīrāk*, for زيراكه *zīrā ki*, Because that.

P زير انداز *zer-andāz*, The cloth which is spread under a hookah.

P زيرانيدن *zīrānīdan*, To cause to sigh. To bring down from a high to a low place.

P زيربا *zīr-bā*, Broth or spoon-meat.

P زير بار *zer bār*, Embarrassed, overburdened with expense or borne down with oppression.

P زيرباري *zer-bārī*, Wretchedness.

P زيربر *zīr-bur*, A cut-purse. A false friend.

P زير بريان *zer-biryān*, A kind of dish.

P زير بزرگان *zer-buzurgān*, A note in music.

P زيربند *zer-band*, A martingal. A girth. A whip, a lash.

P زير پا *zīr pā*, (or زير پاي *zīr pāy*) Subject, tributary. زير پاي كشيدن *zīr pāy kashīdan*, To induce any one to confess.

P زيرپوش *zīr-posh*, An under garment.

A زيرة *zīrat*, A bit of linen or flax. A segment. A section, portion. Visiting clothes, or the mode of paying visits. *Ziyarat*, (pl. of زير *zīr*) Men fond of female society.

P زيرتر *zīrtar*, Lower.

P زير تنگ *zīr tang*, A girth. The sun.

P زير جامه *zīr jāma*, An under garment.

P زير چاق *zīr chāk*, A weak bow. Extremely obedient.

P زير چوب *zīr-chob*, Under the rod.

P زير خرد *zīr khurd*, Name of a note in music.

P زيردست *zīr-dast*, A vassal. A handmaid.

P زيرفان *zīrfān*, The moon.

P زيرفون *zīrfūn*, The barren jujube-tree.

P زيرفين *zīrfīn*, A bolt, bar, latch of a door.

P زيرقان *zīrkān*, Name of a month of the æra of Yazdagird.

P زيرك *zayrak* or *zīrak*, Ingenious, intelligent, prudent, penetrating, sagacious, smart, quick in understanding or at manual labour. Steel possessing a wavy appearance called جوهر *jawhar*.

P زيرك سار *zīrak-sār*, Sagacious, intelligent.

P زيركي *zīrakī*, Ingenuity, sagacity, quickness.

P زيرگاه *zer-gāh*, A chair, a seat.

P زير مشق *zīr mashk*, Any thing placed under a sheet of paper that one may write commodiously.

P زير ميانه *zīr-miyāna*, Middling, below par.

P زيروا *zīr-wā*, A kind of broth or spoon-meat.

P زيره *zīra*, Cumin-seed. زيرهٔ رومي *zīraʼi rūmī*, Caraway-seed.

P زيره با *zīra-bā*, A dish made of the flesh of birds, with cumin-seed and vinegar.

P زيريدن *zīrīdan*, To be under or below. To bring down from a high to a low place. To sigh, sob.

P زيرين *zīrīn*, Inner. Inferior, lower. Infernal. Of or belonging to the word زير *zīr*.

P زيريان *zīriyān*, Vinegar, in which onions have been steeped.

P زيز *zīz*, Sleet. A cricket.

A زيزاء *zayzāʼ* and *zīzāʼ*, Rough ground. The extremities of feathers. A small hill.

A زيزاءة *zīzāʼat*, (or زيزاة *zīzāt*) (pl. زيازي *zayāzī*) A small hill.

A زيزفون *zayzafūn*, A swift she-camel.

P زيزك *zīzak*, The oxyacanth-fruit.

A زيزم *zīzam*, An inarticulate voice, the whispering of demons.

A زيزيٰ *zayzaʼ*, Rough ground. A small hill.

A زي زي *zī zī*, The cries of the *jins*.

P زيژ *zīj*, Snow.

P زيس *zīs*, Side, part, tract, quarter, coast.

P زيست *zīst*, Life, existence.

P زيستن *zīstan*, To survive, live. باكس زيستن *bā kas zīstan*, To associate, live with any one.

P زيش *zīsh*, A pipe, a little tube.

A زيط *zayt*, A vociferating.

A زيعر *zayɛar*, Poor, possessed of little.

A زيغ *zaygh*, (v. n. of زاغ for زيغ) Inclining. Deviating (from the right way). Declining from the meridian (sun). Becoming dim (eye). Doubt.

P زيغ *zīgh*, A mat. Any carpeting or cushions. Renewal of friendship or love. Joy, peace of mind.

P زيغال *zīghāl*, A cup, goblet.

A زيغان *zīghān*, (pl. of زاغ *zāgh*) Small crows inclining to white. *Zayaghān*, (v. n. of زاغ for زيغ) Inclining. Declining from the meridian (the sun). Becoming dim (the sight).

P زيغن *zīghan*, Any thing hard.

A زيغنون *zīghanūn*, Name of a city.

A زيغوغة *zayghūghat*, (v. n. of زاغ for زيغ) Inclining. Declining from the meridian (the sun). Becoming dim (the sight).

A زيف *zayf*, (v. n. of زاف for زيف) Hastening. Being bad or clipt (money). Leaning to one side (a camel). Strutting. Carrying the head erect and sweeping the ground in circles with the tail (a male pigeon when courting the female). The coping of a wall. Pinnacles, battlements. Steps, stairs. (pl. زياف *ziyāf* or ازياف *azyāf*) Clipt, base (coin).

P زيف *zīf*, Sin. Churlishness. Inhuman. Pitch.

A زيّف *zayyif*, Whatever passes with difficulty from hand to hand (as base money).

A زيفان *zayafān*, (v. n. of زاف for زيف) Being bad or clipt (money). Leaning to one side (a camel). Carrying the head erect and sweeping the ground in circles (a pigeon). Strutting.

A زيفة *zayfat*, One pinnacle. One step.

A زيفن *ziyafn*, Long and strong.

A زيفنّ *zīfann*, Long and strong.

P زيفنون *zīfnūn*, Name of the city in which عذرا *ɛazrā* dwelt.

A زيق *zīk*, The collar of a shirt. زيق الشيطان *zīku'sh shaytān*, The devil's thread, *i. e.* Gossamer, cobweb filaments floating in the air in hot weather.

P زيكا *zeka*, (in zand and Pāzand) Wind.

P زيكاسه *zīkāsa*, (or زيكاشه) A hedgehog.

A زيكان *zayakān*, A haughty gait, strut.

P زيگ *zīg*, A mason's rule. Astronomical tables. Threads by which embroiderers are guided in their work. A bird about the size of a sparrow. Name of a tribe.

P زيگر *zīgar*, (Boys) striking with the hand the cheeks when full of wind.

A زيل *zayl*, (v. n. of زال for زيل) Removing (from its place). Separating, distinguishing. Dividing into portions. Leaving off, ceasing. ما زلت افعله *mā ziltu afɛaluhu*, (and sometimes زلت افعله *ziltu afɛaluhu*) I have not ceased to do it. *Zayal*, Width between the thighs.

A زيلع *zaylaɛ*, A sort of shell, concha veneris.

P زيلو *zelū* or *zaylū*, A kind of woollen blanket worn by the poor.

P زيلوچه *zelūcha*, A small woollen garment.

A زيلولة *zaylūlat*, (v. n. of زال for زول) Taking up their quarters at their own place (companies travelling in camel-litters), and afterwards leaving it.

A زيم *zaym*, (v. n. of زام for زيم) Bidding any one hold his peace. Quitting one's place. *Ziyam*, Scattered sheep, goats, or mice. Cut meat scattered about. Name of a horse.

A زئم *ziɛm*, The eye. Reputation. *Zaɛim*, Much frightened.

A زيمة *zīmat*, A herd of camels from 3 to 15.

P زيمله *zaymula*, A vessel for carrying fruit and vegetables in.

P زيمور *zīmūr*, The disclosure of a secret.

P زين *zayn*, One who has bid farewell to the pleasures of the world. *Zīn*, A saddle. زين بر گاو نهادن *zīn bar gāv nihādan*, To prepare for a journey. To travel. زين بر گرگ نهادن *zīn bar gurg nihādan*, To saddle the wolf (to bell the cat). زين بستن *zīn bastan*, To saddle. زين زرين *zīni zarīn*, The sun. (for از اين *az īn*) From this. Hence, because. زين پس *zīn pas*, (or زين سپس *zīn sipas*) From henceforth, henceforward. زين ميان *zīn miyān*) By this medium, hence.

A زين *zayn*, (v. n. of زان for زين) Adorning, decking. (pl. ازيان *azyān*) An ornament, an honour. The comb of a cock.

A زينابة *zīnābat*, A small kind of fish.

P زين افراز *zīn-afrāz*, Horse-armour for battle.

P زينان *zīnān*, Those present. (or زينيان *zīnayān*) Caraway-seeds.

A زينب *zaynab*, Name of a handsome and fragrant tree. Name of a Jewess who poisoned Muhammad. A woman's name. A coward, dastard.

P زين پوش *zīn-posh*, The ornamental covering of a saddle.

A زينة *zīnat*, Ornament, decoration, dress, beauty, elegance. Grass, verdure. Clothes to cover one's nakedness. يوم الزينة *yawmu'z zīnat*, A rejoicing or gala-day, festival. The day on which the waters of the Nile are let out.

P زين ساز *zīn-sāz*, A saddle, saddle-maker.

P زين سازي *zīn-sāzī*, Business of a saddler.

P زين كوده *zīn-kūda*, (زين كوه *zīn-koh*, or زين كوهه *zīn-koha*) The bow of a saddle.

P زينگر *zīngar*, A saddler.

P زينو *zīnū*, A woollen garment of the poor.

P زينه *zīna*, A ladder, step, stair.

P زينهار *zīnhār*, Take care! Defence, protection. A league, a covenant. Fear. A complaint. Haste. Wariness, notice. Alas! زينهار دادن *zīnhār dādan*, To protect, shield from oppression.

P زينهار خوار *zīnhār-khwār*, A truce-breaker.

P زينهار خواه *zīnhār-khwāh*, Seeking protection. Tributary.

P زينهاري *zīnhārī*, Under protection. A coming under protection. Agreed, bound by covenant.

A زئني *ziɛnīy*, Short (dog).

P زينيان *zīnyān*, Caraway-seeds.

P زيو *zīv*, A ship-worm. Deceit, fraud.

P زيوار *zīwār*, A street in a town or village. *Zevār*, Equality, similitude, uniformity, straightness.

P زيوان *zīwān*, A kind of tare or darnel growing amongst wheat, having a black grain, which causes inebriety and madness.

A زيوح *zuyūh* or *ziyūh*, (v. n. of زاح for زيح) Being far off, going away.

P زيودن *ziyūdan*, To slumber agreeably.

P زيور *zīwar* or *zewar*, An ornament of gems, gold, or silver.

A زيوف *zuyūf*, (v. n. of زاف for زيف) Being clipt, light, base (money). Clipping or adulterating (money). Overleaping (a wall). Inclining to its setting (the sun).

P زيولج *zīvlaj*, A woodcock.

P زيونجو *zīwanjo*, A ship-worm.

P زييدن *ziyīdan*, To suit, become, befit. To be adorned.

A زئير *zaɛīr*, A lion's roar. Roaring (lion).

P زيين *zayīn*, (in zand and Pāzand) Long, tall. *Ziyīn*, A partisan. Partial.

ژ

ژ *je*, (called زاىٔ عجمي *zāɛi ɛajamī* or زاىٔ فارسي *zāɛi fārsī*) The fourteenth letter of the Persian alphabet. It is often confounded with ز, and occasionally changed for ج or ر. Its power is that of *s* in "treasure" or of *z* in "azure." In this edition it is represented by *j*, with two dots over it to distinguish it from ج.

P ژابيژ *jābīj*, Southernwood. Sap which exudes from green wood laid on the fire. Sparks of fire.

P ژاژ *jāj*, A kind of camel's thistle. A kind of wormwood. A sort of artichoke. Any plant not growing from seed. Heath or broom for kindling a fire. Sweepings of a thrashing-floor. Circumference of the mouth. Dung. The door of a thrashing-floor surrounded with a low wall for keeping the cattle out. Idle, trifling, or insipid speech. ژاژ خاي *jāj-khāy*, A trifler. One who speaks obscenely.

P ژاژ خور *jāj-khwur*, The same. Any beast chewing the cud.

P ژاژومك *jājūmak*, A pulse, French bean.

P ژاژه *jāja*, A sort of thistle. Trifling speech.

P ژاژيدن *jājīdan*, To chew the cud. To howl.

P ژاغر *jāghar*, The crop of a bird.

P ژافه *jāfa*, A kind of fetid herb. A hedgehog.

P ژالكه *jālka*, Name of a plant.

P ژاله *jāla*, (or ژال *jāl*) Dew, hoar-frost. Hail.

Vernal showers. An air-blown bag or bladder for swimming with; a log used as a raft for crossing a stream. ژالهٔ نرگس *jāla-i nargis*, Tears. ژاله باریدن *jāla bārīdan*, To hail.

P ژاو *jāv*, The purest or best of any thing.

P ژاوا *jāwā*, Chewing the cud. Howling.

P ژاویدن *jāwīdan*, To ruminate. To howl.

P ژبون *jubūn*, Advantage, gain (when unlawful).

P ژح *jah*, A groan. The shrill cry of wild beasts.

P ژخ *jakh*, A groan, plaint. The shrill cry of wild beasts. A wart. Troublesome. Disquieted, weary. *Jukh*, A wart.

P ژخار *jikhār*, A noise, cry. Hardness.

P ژخش *jakhsh*, Lightning. The rainbow. A ray.

P ژد *jad*, Gum, the tears of a plant.

P ژدن *jidan*, To darn. To sew, stitch. To notch a millstone.

P ژدوار *jadwār* or *judwār*, Zedoary.

P ژراغن *jarāghan*, A sandy place.

P ژراغنگ *jarāghang*, Sandy soil. *Jurāghang*, Land full of flints, and cracking from drought.

P ژرد *jard*, Gluttony. Fulness. A glutton.

P ژرف *jarf*, Deep. High. Deep search, strict examination. Acute, penetrating (man). Great. Much, copious. A long and tedious story. A ditch, a pit. A narrow-mouthed vessel. دریای ژرف *daryā-i jarf*, The deep sea, the bottomless ocean.

P ژرفا *jarfā*, Depth.

P ژرف بین *jarf-bīn*, (or نگاه) Deep-sighted.

P ژرفی *jarfī*, Depth. Sagacity, penetration. Penetrating, sagacious, deep-sighted.

P ژروار *jarwār*, Zedoary.

P ژره *jara*, A line for hanging clothes on.

P ژغار *jaghār*, Rust. Mouldiness. A cry, clamour, fearful noise. Hardness, roughness. A colouring herb.

P ژغاره *jaghāra*, Bread of millet. The navel of an ox, or of any animal. Paint for the face. Complaint, lamentation, clamour.

P ژغال *jaghāl*, Bread of millet. *Jughāl*, A live coal. The cornel-tree or fruit.

P ژغاله *jaghāla*, The navel of an ox. Bread of millet. Red paint for the face.

P ژغاو *jaghāv*, A brothel, stew. A whore.

P ژغژغ *jaghjagh*, Going backwards and forwards. Labouring. A gnashing of the teeth, from cold or from rage. The noise made by nuts or by almonds shaken together in a bag; also that made in masticating food.

P ژغل *jaghal*, *jughal*, and *jughul*, A live coal.

P ژغند *jaghand*, The cries of a wild beast when taken in a net. A bell. Hardness.

P ژف *jaf*, Wet, moist.

P ژفت *jaft*, Lean. Thick, corpulent.

P ژفره *jafra*, Victory at play. *Jufra*, Environs of the mouth.

P ژفك *jafk*, Gumminess at the eyes. Snot.

P ژفك آب *jafk-āb*, (or ژفگاب *jafgāb*) Dirt collected in the corner of the eyes.

P ژفیده *jafīda*, Moistened, macerated.

P ژك *juk* or *jak*, An inward murmur from anger or vexation. One who murmurs inwardly. A traveller.

P ژكاره *jakāra*, Quarrelsome, squabbling, disobedient, contumacious, stubborn.

P ژكاژ *jakāj*, A species of iron mallet, sharp at one end, a mattock. A small mirror. Peevishness, frowardness, obstinacy.

P ژكاسه *jakāsa*, (or ژكاشه *jakāsha*) A hedgehog.

P ژكاك *jakāk*, A bird which feeds on carrion. *Jukāk*, Coal.

P ژكال *jukāl*, (or ژگال *jugāl*) A live coal, brand.

P ژكان *jakān* or *jukān*, Murmuring inwardly. Wretched. Disturbed.

P ژكس *jakas*, May God avert! fly we to God.

P ژكفر *jakfar*, Very patient, meek, mild.

P ژكفری *jakfarī*, Patience.

P ژكور *jakūr*, A miser. A freebooter, robber.

P ژكید *jakīd*, Fatigued.

P ژكیدن *jakīdan* or *jukīdan*, To mutter to one's self in a rage.

P ژگان *jigān*, Helpless, powerless, moneyless.

P ژم *jam*, A midwife.

P ژم آورده *jam-āwarda*, Senior wife, matron.

P ژمو *jamū*, Borax. *Jamū*, (or ژمولوغ *jamūlūgh*) A cylindrical stone or roller wherewith they smooth the clay roofs of houses.

P ژن *jan*, Base, deformed.

P ژنبر *jambir*, A basket for removing rubbish.

P ژند *jand*, A garment worn out and torn. A piece. A patch. A fire-steel. The Zand, or book of Zartusht.

P ژند ژند *jand jand*, In pieces, piecemeal.

P ژنده *janda*, Old, worn out. Rent. Cut up into strips. Pure. A patched garment. Huge, horrible. A bit, piece, patch. *Jinda*, An old patched garment. Huge, horrible.

P ژنده پوش *janda-posh*, Clothed in rags.

P ژنده پیل *janda-pīl*, A large elephant. A furious elephant.

P ژنكدان *jankdān*, A bell which women tie to their feet.

P ژنكه *janka*, Blight, mildew.

P ژنگ *jang*, Rust. Mould, blight. Night. The sun, sunbeams. A patch upon a garment. The book of the impostor Mānī. A wrinkle on the skin. ژنگ بسته *jang-basta*, (ژنگ پذیر *jang-pazīr*, ژنگ خورده *jang-khwurda*, also ژنگ گرفته *jang-girifta*) Rusty. Sick, ailing. *Jing*, A drop of rain.

P ژنگار *jangār*, Rust. Verdigrise. Mould. شمشیر ژنگار گرفته *shamshīri jangār-girifta*, A rusty sword.

P ژنگاری *jangārī*, Of the colour of verdigrise, sea-green. Rusty.

P ژنگدان *jangdān*, (or ژنگدن *jangdan*) Rust. Small globular bells hung round the rims of Arabian drums.

P ژنگله *jangala*, A cloven foot (as in oxen or deer). *Jungula*, The stop of an organ.

P ژنگلیچه *jangulīcha*, An open-mouthed bell.

P ژنگه *janga*, Blight, mildew, smut.

P ژنه *jana*, Sting of insects: point of a needle.

P ژنیان *jinyān*, Anise.

P ژوار *juwār*, An under jailer.

P ژواغار *jawāghār*, (or ژواگر *jawāgar*) A solemn festival among the fire-worshippers. Name of one of their priests. Name of the chiefs of the idol-worshippers.

P ژوپین *jopīn*, A sort of spear, or demi-lance.

P ژورك *jawrak*, Name of a small red bird.

P ژوژ *jūj*, (or ژوژه) A porcupine, hedgehog.

P ژوشیدن *jūshīdan*, To distil, drop. To be troublesome, to involve in difficulties.

P ژوغار *jūghār*, A kind of bird.

P ژول *jūl*, A lark, or any bird pecking up the seeds after sowing. Sadness, grief, agitation of mind. *Jol*, A fold, ply, wrinkle, inequality.

P ژوله *jūla*, A lark.

P ژولیدن *jolīdan*, To become intricate or mixed. To grow gray (hair). To change colour or shrink with the morning cold. To fall as dew. To blow as wind. To be scattered or dishevelled.

P ژولیده *jolīda*, Entangled, mixed. Rubbed with the hand. Dishevelled.

P ژولیده موی *jolīda-moy*, One who has entangled or dishevelled hair.

P ژومیده *jūmīda*, A field sown and watered.

P ژون *jūn*, A kind of bird. An idol, false god.

P ژوهیدن *johīdan*, To distil, drop, trickle (as rain from the eaves).

P ژوهیده *johīda*, Watered (garden).

P ژه *ja*, (equiv. to چه *cha*) An affix of diminution.

P ژی *jī*, A reservoir, cistern, ditch. Elegant apparel. Name of a village near Isfahān.

P ژیان *jiyān*, Formidable, terrible, rapacious, fierce, angry. A savage beast. A scorpion. A wood. شیر ژیان *sheri jiyān*, A fierce lion.

P ژیر *jīr*, A cistern, reservoir.

P ژیره *jīra*, Cumin-seed.

P ژیز *jīz*, A man. A wrestler, champion.

P ژیژ *jīj*, Carrion. Filthy, impure.

P ژیغال *jīghāl*, A large cup.

P ژیك *jīk*, Drops of rain. A porcupine.

P ژیگ *jīg* A friend, companion. Drops of rain.

P ژین *jīn*, A friend, companion, associate.

P ژینان *jīnān*, Anise.

P ژیوه *jīwa*, Quicksilver, mercury.

س

س *sīn*, (called سین غیر منقوطه *sīni ghayr*

mankūta, سين مهملة *sīni mukmala,* Undotted *sīn*) The twelfth letter of the Arabic alphabet, and the fifteenth in the Persian. In arithmetic it denotes 60, and in almanacks is the character for the sun in his sixth aspect: it likewise, in abbreviatures, stands for السلام *as'salām,* Peace. Prefixed to a verb in the aorist it limits it to a future signification. This letter is sometimes interchangeable for ت *te,* ج *jīm,* ح *hā,* ز *zayn,* ش *shīn,* ص *sād,* ه *he,* and ي *ye*: as, تينا *tīnā* or سينا *sīnā*; بر مجيدن *bar majīdan* or بر مسيدن *bar masīdan*; ويه *wayh* or ويس *ways*; زرنا *zurnā* or سرنا *surnā*; پابوش *pā-bosh* or پابوس *pā-bos*; بساق *busāk* or بصاق *busāk*; آماه *āmāh* or آماس *āmās*; خامي *khāmī* or خامس *khāmis.* Its power is that of the English *s* in *sun.*

P سا *sā,* Tribute, revenue. A kind of rich silk. (in composition, from سابيدن *sāyīdan*) Rubbing. جهبه سا *jahba-sā,* (or جبين سا *jabīn-sā*) Rubbing the forehead (on the ground), *i.e.* making a profound reverence. (When affixed to a word) Like: as, عنبر سا *ʿambar-sā,* Resembling ambergris.

A ساء *sāʾa,* (fut. يسوء *yasūʾu*) He did evil.

A ساءة *sāʾat,* The horn of a bow.

A سأّر *saʾʾār,* One who leaves orts.

A سآفة *saʾāfat,* (v. n. of سوف) Suffering from distemper (cattle).

A سآم *saʾām,* A being wearied or disgusted.

A سآمة *saʾāmat,* (v. n. of سئم) Being wearied. Weariness, disgust.

A سأب *saʾb,* (v. n. of سأب) Strangling, suffocating. Stretching, widening (a leathern bottle). Quenching the thirst. (pl. سؤب *suʾub*) A bottle (of a large size); a leathern case in which they put it. *Saʾab,* (v. n. of سئب) Being saturated with water.

A سابّ *sābb,* A curser, reviler.

A ساباط *sābāt,* (pl. ساباطات *sābātāt* and سوابيط *sawābīt*) A covered passage connecting two houses.

A سابح *sābih,* (pl. سبّاح *subbāh*) A swimmer. (pl. سوابح *sawābih*) Swift-going (horse).

A سابحات *sābihāt,* Spirits of the faithful (*i. e.* of Muhammadans). Ships. Stars, planets.

A سابريّ *sābiriy,* Cloth of the finest and most excellent kind. A coat of mail of the best texture formed of small compact rings. The best species of dates. عرض سابريّ *ʿarzi sābiriy,* The offering for sale of any valuable commodity that needs no puffing, like the cloth *sābiriy.*

P سابزج *sābizaj,* (or سابزك) A mandrake.

A سابع *sābiʿ,* (pl. سبعة *sabaʿat*) Seventh.

A سابعا *sābiʿan,* In the seventh place, seventhly.

A سابغ *sābigh,* Complete, ample, full, profuse; long (tail, buttocks, &c.). Long-pizzled. Neck-armour (a texture of rings hanging from the helmet).

A سابغة *sābighat,* A long coat of mail covering the whole body.

A سابق *sābik,* (pl. سبّق *subbak*) Past, preceding, going or gone before, former, by-gone. Before in point of time. Swift (horse) that takes the lead and wins the race. A predecessor. A conqueror. One who surpasses. Before-mentioned. زمان سابق *zamāni sābik,* Time past. سابق الانعام *sābiku'l inʿām,* An ancient benefactor.

A سابقا *sābikan,* Before, in time past, formerly.

A سابقات *sābikāt,* Angels (as excelling others).

A سابقة *sābikat,* (fem. of سابق *sābik*) The past. Ancient right or custom. Pre-excellence, precedence, superiority. A remarkable progress (in any thing). Friendship. سابقهٔ لطف و عنايت *sābikaʾi lutf u ʿināyat,* Past favours and assistances. سابقه معرفت *sābiha-maʿrifat,* Old acquaintance.

P سابقه سالار *sābika-sālār,* A leader. Muhammad.

A سابقين *sābikīn,* (pl. obliq.) Predecessors.

A سابل *sābil,* Pouring (rain).

A سابلة *sābilat,* Beaten paths. Travellers (especially going different ways). Goers and comers.

P سابوته *sābūta,* (in zand) An old woman.

P سابود *sābūd,* A circle round the moon. A swing. Ivy. A green film on the surface of stagnant water. A certain manœuvre in wrestling.

P سابودانه *sābū-dāna,* Sago.

P سابور *sābūr,* Name of a province in Persia. Name of a city in the aforesaid province. Name of a city in Khūzistān. (from P شاه پور *shāh-pūr*) Sapor (called also ذو الاكتاف *zū'l aktāf*) son of Ardshīr, and king of Persia.

A سابورا *sābūrā,* One of the five cities which were overthrown in the time of Lot.

P سابوره *sābūra,* A hermaphrodite. A sodomite.

P سابوس *sābūs,* Seed of fleawort.

A سابوط *sābūt,* Name of a marine animal.

A سابياء *sābiyāʾ,* (pl. سوابي *sawābī*) The membrane enclosing the child in the womb, or which covers the nose of a young camel when born. The breeding of cattle (particularly when prolific). Prolific (sheep). Numerous herds. Camels kept for breeding. The earth about the hole of the field-mouse.

P سابيزج *sābīzaj,* (or سابيزك) A mandrake.

A سأة *saʾat,* The horn of a bow.

A سأت *saʾt,* (v. n. of سأت) Strangling, suffocating. *Saʾat,* A side of the throat. سأتان *saʾatāni,* (dual) The two sides of the throat.

P سات *sāt,* Sleep.

A سات *sātt,* The sixth.

A ساتر *sātir,* A concealer, coverer, hider.

P ساتگن *sātgin,* (ساتگني *sātginī,* ساتگي *sātgī,* ساتگين *sātgīn,* or ساتگيني *sātgīnī*) A large bumper-glass of wine drank to any one's health.

P ساتگين *sātgīn,* A beloved object.

P ساتل *sātil,* A plant like a dry mushroom.

A ساتل *sātil,* Consequent, coherent (as rolling tears or pearls on a string).

A ساتور *sātūr,* Name of one of the magicians, who believed in Moses.

A ساتي *sātī,* The sixth.

P ساج *sāj,* A certain kind of bird. An iron plate for baking bread upon. The teak-tree.

A ساج *sāj,* (pl. سيجان *sījān*) A green or a black sash rolled round the head and hanging down behind. The teak-tree.

A ساجب *sājib* (pl. سواجب *sawājib*) A dried up leathern bottle.

A ساجد *sājid,* (pl. سجّد *sujjad*) Prostrate in adoration. One who bends forward his head in adoration. An adorer.

A ساجدة *sājidat,* Weak, dull, dim (eye). (A palm-tree) bending under the weight of its fruit.

A ساجر *sājir,* A place filled by a flux of water.

A ساجسيّ *sājisiy,* White and high-bred (ram).

A ساجع *sājiʿ,* (One) speaking rythmically. A long-bodied camel: also one which calls to her colt in a modulated tone of voice. A handsome, well-formed face. (equiv. to قاصد *kāsid*) Resolving, aiming at. One who goes straight.

A ساجعة *sājiʿat,* (pl. سواجع *sawājiʿ*) Cooing (turtle-dove).

A ساجم *sājim,* (pl. سواجم) Flowing (tear).

A ساجور *sājūr,* (P ساچور *sāchūr*) A dog's collar; or a piece of wood suspended to it, to prevent his running away, gnawing the cord with which he is led, or entering a vineyard to eat the grapes.

A ساجول *sājūl,* A (wicker) cover of a flask.

A ساجوم *sājūm,* A kind of seasoning or sauce. A certain colour.

A ساجي *sājī,* Calm, tranquil (sea or eye). Dark (night), concealing the stars.

P ساچك *sāchak,* A rite observed at nuptials.

P ساچي *sāchī,* White.

A ساح *sāh,* (pl. of ساحة *sāhat*) Courts, inner parts of buildings. Shores, tracts of country.

A ساحّ *sāhh,* Fat (sheep).

A ساحات *sāhāt,* (pl. of ساحة) Shores. Areas.

A ساحب *sāhib,* One who proudly sweeps the ground (with the robe of a garment).

A ساحة *sāhat,* (pl. ساح *sāh,* سوح *sawh,* and ساحات *sāhāt*) A court, quadrangle, the inner part of a building. An opening or space between houses. A shore, coast, or tract of country. ساحت طوبيٰ *sāhati tūbaʾ* Paradise.

A ساحّة *sāhhat,* (pl. سحاح *sihāh* and سحاح *suhāh*) Very fat (sheep).

A ساحر *sāhir,* An enchanter, magician, necromancer, fascinater, sorcerer. A wise man.

A ساحرة *sāhirat,* An enchantress, sorceress.

A ساحري *sāhirī,* Enchantment, magic, sorcery.

A ساحق *sāhik,* One who brays: a bruiser.

A ساحل *sāhil,* Beach, shore, coast. Phœnicia.

A ساحي *sāhī,* A lizard feeding on the سحاء.

A ساحية *sāhiyat,* A violent rain, water sweeping all before it.

P ساخ *sākh,* A series, train. Well adapted, adjusted. Collected, accumulated. Expedited.

P ساخت sākht, Make, construction, fabric, manufacture. Furniture, apparatus, gear. Pretence. A stirrup-leather. The girth or surcingle of a horse, together with his armour, covered on both sides with felt cloth. A cord for fastening on a load. ساخت آماج sākhti āmāj, Plough-gear.

P ساختگي sākhtagī, Make, formation. Effort, machination. Design (in contradistinction to what is natural). Hypocrisy. Furniture, gearing.

P ساختن sākhtan, To make, form, fashion, prepare, perform, build, construct, manufacture. To feign, counterfeit. To compose. To adapt, adjust, polish, furbish. To be content to do, to manage (with).

P ساخته sākhta, Made, formed. Counterfeited, false. Surreptitious. Apt, adjusted. A flatterer.

P ساخته رنگ sākhta-rang, Consenting, agreeing, consonant.

P ساخته روزگار sākhta-rozgar, Prudent, experienced in worldly matters.

P ساخته لگام sākhta-ligām, Headstrong, stubborn, obstinate.

A ساخر sākhir, A jeerer, mocker, derider.

A ساخط sākhit, Angry, indignant.

P ساخن sākhin, Mortar mixed with sand. The living soul.

A ساخن sākhin, (fem. ساخنة) Warm (day).

A سأد saɛd or saɛad, (v. n. of سأد) Strangling. Saɛad, (v. n. of سئد) Bursting, growing raw (a wound). Drinking.

P ساد sād, Pure, unmixed. Plain, simple, unadorned. Smooth, even. Rubbed, worn out. A new garment not rumpled or creased. A desert, open champaign. A boar. A doctor, learned man. ساد شدن sād shudan, (or بودن būdan) To have the dysentery. ساد كردن sād kardan, To purify. To castrate, cut all clean away.

A سادات sādāt, (pl. of سيّد sayyid) Princes, lords (especially the descendants of Muhammad). سيّد سادات sayyidi sādāt, Lord of lords, *i.e.* Muhammad.

P ساداك sādāk, A stove, especially the back part where the fire is lighted.

SY ساد آوران sād āwarān, A gum found in the roots of walnut-trees.

P ساداوران sādāwarān, Gall-apple.

A سادة sādat, (pl. of سائد sāɛid) Lords.

A سادّة sāddat, An eye which, although open, does not see clearly. An eye entirely white and sightless. Old, decrepit (she-camel). Forelocks dangling over the brow.

P سادج sādaj, Indian spikenard.

A سادج sādij, Unfermented. Unmixed, simple. Sincere.

A سادح sādih, Abounding in produce. One living in cheapness and plenty.

A سادحة sādihat, A thick, dark cloud.

A سادر sādir, Careless, indifferent about what one does. Astonished, stupefied. Blinded by the heat. Sullen, cross, perverse.

A سادس sādis, (fem. سادسة sādisat) Sixth.

A سادسا sādisan, In the sixth place, sixthly.

P سادسايه sād-sāya, A level place.

P سادك sādik, A species of nightingale.

P سادگي sādagī, Smoothness. Plainness, absence of ornament. Equality, evenness. Artlessness, simplicity, openness. Purity.

A سادم sādim, Penitent, contrite, sorrowful.

A سادن sādin, (pl. سدنة sadanat) Keeper of the fane of Mecca, or an idol-temple. A porter.

P ساده sāda, Smooth, even, plain. Erased, without writing or impression. Pure, unmixed, simple. Open, sincere. Artless, unadorned (speech). An open champaign. A pure white garment for the summer. Beardless. White. Stupid. A feast kept by the Persians at the winter solstice. Indian spikenard. P ساده كردن sāda kardan, To purify. To castrate. (for ايستاده īstāda) Standing.

P ساده دشت sāda-dasht, The heaven above the starry firmament. The crystalline sphere.

P ساده دل sāda-dil, Simple-hearted. Artless, simple. Stupid. A simpleton.

P ساده دلي sāda-dilī, Simple-heartedness.

P ساده رو sāda-rū, Smooth-faced, beardless.

P ساده زنخ sāda-zanakh, Beardless.

P ساده سپهر sāda sipihr, The crystalline sphere.

P ساده شده sāda-shuda, A dysentery.

P ساده طوري sāda-tawrī, Gentleness. Simplicity. Stupidity.

P ساده كار sāda-kār, A kind of goldsmith.

P ساده كرده sāda-karda, A eunuch.

P ساده لوح sāda-lawh, A rasa tabula. Simple, and unblemished. Pure in heart. A simpleton.

P ساده مرد sāda-mard, A simple, ignorant man.

P ساده وضعي sāda-wazɛī, Artlessness, simplicity. Stupidity.

A سادي sādī, (A camel) pasturing without a keeper. (for سادس sādis) The sixth.

A سادج sāzaj, (from P ساده sāda) Indian spikenard. A plant that grows on the surface of the water, having leaves and branches, but no roots. سادج هندي sāzaji hindī, Indian leaf.

P سادجه sāzaja, Simple, plain, clear.

A سأر saɛr, (v. n. of سأر) Leaving remains of food. Saɛar, (v. n. of سئر) Remaining.

P سار sār, A starling. A camel. Pain, affliction, grief, trouble. A place, spot. A hollow reed. A milestone. A wine-press. A title by which the princes in Georgia were formerly addressed. A czar. High, tall. (for سر sar) The head. Top, summit. Having many inequalities (ground). سار سبز sāri sabz, A green starling. چشمسار chashm-sār, A well's mouth. سبكسار sabuk-sār, Light-headed. نگون سار nigūn-sār, Head downwards. گاو سار gāw-sār, The mace of Rustam which bore the figure of a bull's head. Placed after nouns it denotes plenty, magnitude, similitude, or possession: as, شاخسار shākhsār, Full of branches, branchy. رخسار ruhksār, A large, beautiful cheek. سنگسار sangsār, Stony. كوهسار kohsār, Mountainous. عنبرسار ɛambarsār, Full of ambergris; name of a place whence the finest comes. شاه سار shāhsār, Like a king. ديو سار devsār, Like a demon. سگ سار sagsār, Like a dog, doglike (in disposition. شرمسار sharmsār, Possessed of shame, ashamed.

A سار sār, Remainder of a thing, all, the whole.

A سارّ sarr, Who or what makes glad.

P سارا sārā, Pure, excellent. Undefiled. Sarah, Abraham's wife. زرسارا zar sārā, The purest gold. عنبر سارا ɛambar-sārā, The most odoriferous ambergris. مشك سارا mushk-sārā, The finest musk.

P ساران sārān, The head. Heads. Upper part (opposed to پايان pāyān). Name of a town in Irāk.

A سارب sārib, A wanderer at large. Apparent, conspicuous.

P ساربان sārbān, A prince. A camel-driver. شتران بي ساربان shuturāni bī sārbān, Camels without a leader.

P ساربوغ sārbūgh, A commander.

A سارة sārat, Sarah, a woman's name.

A سارّة sārrat, Exhilarating (woman), who makes cheerful. اخبار سارّة akhbāri sārra, Joyful tidings.

P سارج sāraj, (or سارچه sārcha) A sweet-singing bird, a kind of starling.

A سارح sārih, (fem. سارحة) (Cattle) pasturing freely (whence the proverb لا له سارحة و لا رائحة lā lahu sārihat wa lā rāɛihat, He has no cattle nor effects, he is very poor).

P سارخك sārkhak, sārkhk, or sārikhk, A gnat. Sārikhk, The sting of a gnat.

P سارخكدار sārkhak-dār, A large shady tree, called the gnat-tree.

P سارشك sārashk, A gnat.

P سارشك دار sārashk-dār, The gnat-tree.

A سارق sārik, A thief. سارق اليد sāriku'l yad, Weak-handed.

A سارقة sārikat, (pl. سوارق sawārik) A female thief. A large cauldron. A pillory. Name of a place on the way to Mecca.

P سارك sārak, A starling.

P سارنج sāranj, A small black bird.

P سارنگ sārang, A small black bird.

P سارو sāro, Name of a black bird in India. Sārū, Plaster or mortar mixed with sand.

P ساروان sārwān, A camel-driver.

P ساروج sārūj, Plaster or mortar mixed up with sand. Lime mingled with ashes. Quick-lime; also ointment, made of it and arsenic, for pulling out hairs. Name of a bird in India of a black colour.

A سارواء sārūrāɛ, Joy, cheerfulness.

P ساروك sārūk, A kind of talking-bird.

P سارونه sārūna, A vine-branch.

P سارة *sāra*, Posts or stones for shewing the way, placed at the distance of a parasang or league. A starling. The sash of a turban. A dress worn by the women of the Deccan, consisting of a scarf passed round the waist and brought upon the head. A kind of striped stuff brought from India. A veil, covering. A bribe. Sarah.

P ساري *sārī*, A starling. A milestone. The common dress of Hindū women of all classes, consisting of a sheet of cloth worn round the body, and passing over the head and shoulders like a hood. A sort of dress worn by women in the Deccan. Name of a city in Māzandarān.

A ساري *sārī*, Passing, penetrating, pervading, flowing. Infecting, contagious. Noble. Chief. A cloud risen in the night. A lion.

P ساريان *sāriyān*, A city in Georgia.

A سارية *sāriyat*, (pl. سواري *sawārī*) A column. A ship's mast. A night-cloud.

P ساريخ *sārikh*, A whip made of chains.

P ساز *sāz*, A musical instrument. Concord, harmony. Arms, apparatus, accoutrements, harness, furniture. Preparations (for nuptials, journey, or any important business). A feast, banquet. Gain, advantage. Patience, meekness. Fraud, deceit, trick. Like, equal to. Just as, in the manner of. Worthy. (for سامان *sāmān*) Intellect, reason. ساز راه *sāzi rāh*, Travelling apparatus. ساز كار *sāzi kār*, A workman's tools. ساز كردن *sāz kardan*, To tune (an instrument). To prepare necessaries for war, a journey, or domestic use. ساز نوروز *sāzi naw-roz*, The feast of new-year's day. Name of a note in music. سوز و ساز *soz u sāz*, Words and sound, vocal and instrumental music. ساز و سلب *sāz u salab*, Apparatus, armour. Spoils. نا ساز *nā sāz*, Mad, crazy. (in compos. from ساختن *sākhtan*) Preparing, making, effecting. زنده ساز *zinda-sāz*, Resuscitating. فلك سحرساز *falaki sihr-sāz*, The enchantress Fortune. منشيان سحرساز *munshiyāni sihr-sāz*, Writers scattering fascination (*i.e.* enchanting by their elegance).

P سازاك *sāzāk*, A porch, portico, vestibule.

P سازباز *sāz-bāz*, Trim, dressy. Ornament.

P سازدار *sāz-dār*, One who disposes properly.

P سازش *sāzish*, Make, contrivance, artifice, invention. Combination, collusion, confederacy.

P سازق *sāzak*, A resinous pine, which, when split, burns like a torch.

P سازك *sāzak*, A melodious bird. A vestibule.

P سازكار *sāz-kār*, (or گار *gār*) Consonant, concordant, in accordance. Agreeing. A musical instrument. A poet, actor; any one who invents or feigns. A hypocrite. One who arranges, adjusts, disposes suitably, or equalizes. سازكار شدن *sāz-kār shudan*, To be consonant, suit, agree.

P سازكاري *sāz-kārī*, Agreement. Concord, harmony. Peace. Equalization, adjustment.

P سازگاري *sāz-gārī*, Agreement, harmony.

P سازگري *sāzgarī*, A sort of musical air.

P سازمند *sāzmand*, Arranged properly, disposed.

P سازندگي *sāzandagī*, A musical performance.

P سازنده *sāzanda*, Effective, effectual. A player on musical instruments. An arranger, one who composes, adjusts, pacifies. A maker, performer. A comedian. سازنده و خواننده *sāzanda u khwānanda*, Instrumental and vocal.

P سازو *sāzū*, A rope or cable made of the fibrous bark of the palm-tree.

P سازوار *sāzwār*, Agreeing, suitable.

P سازواري *sāzwārī*, Conformity, harmony, agreement, resemblance. Aid, help, assistance.

P سازو باز *sāzū-bāz*, A rope-dancer.

P سازور *sāzwar*, Neatly finished, prepared. Proper, suitable. Worthy. Furnished with arms or furniture; accoutred.

P ساز و ساخت *sāz u sākht*, Furniture, apparatus.

P سازيدن *sāzīdan*, To arm. To prepare. To agree, be fit, proper, worthy. To search for by groping.

P سازيراق *sāz-yarāk*, Warlike instruments, furniture, baggage.

P ساس *sās*, A certain insect of the flea-species, or louse-species, but larger (a bug?). A mother-in-law. Pleasant, elegant, graceful. Neat, clean. Poor. Name of an old family in Persia.

A ساس *sās*, (v. n. of سيس) Being affected by the weevil (corn). A black corrosion of the teeth. A corroded tooth.

A سأسأة *sa,sa,at*, (or سأسآء *sa,sā,*) (v. n. of سأسأ Q) Calling (an ass) to water. Chiding (an ass), driving (him) to water.

A ساساة *sāsāt*, (v.n.of ساسي Q) Reproaching, reviling, disgracing.

SY ساسار كشت *sāsār kisht*, Seed of nettle.

SY ساساليوس *sāsāliyūs*, Assafœtida.

P ساسان *sāsān*, Solitary, recluse. A beggar. Name of the father of اردشير بابك *ardshīr bābak*, founder of the dynasty of the Sāsānides, who reigned in Persia from A.D. 202 till 636; when Yazdagird, the last of the race, was overpowered by the Arabians. (pl. of ساس *sās*) Poor, indigent.

A ساسب *sāsab*, Name of a tree from which arrows are made.

A ساسة *sāsat*, (pl. of سائس *sā,is*) Governors. Guardians. Horsekeepers, grooms.

P ساستا *sāstā*, Name of a certain demon.

P ساسر *sāsar*, A starling. *Sāsur*, A hollow reed used for writing.

A سأسم *sa,sam*, The ebony-tree. A tree from which bows are made.

P ساسم *sāsim*, Anise.

P ساسو *sāsū*, Name of a man.

P ساسي *sāsī*, Poor, indigent: a beggar. Beggary.

A ساسية *sāsiyat*, A red skull-cap worn by Morocco women.

A ساطح *sātih*, (God) who expands (the earth).

A ساطر *sātir*, A butcher. A satellite.

A ساطرون *sātirūn*, Name of a king of Persia.

G ساطريون *sātiryūn*, The herb rag-wort.

A ساطع *sātiɛ*, Raised up. Diffused, spread. Bright, clear, evident. ساطع النور *sātiɛu'n nūr*, Resplendent. براهين ساطعة *barāhīni sātiɛa*, Clear proofs, evident prodigies.

A ساطل *sātil*, Raised, flying about (dust). Name of a medicinal plant.

A ساطن *sātin*, Impure, wicked, base, malicious.

A ساطور *sātūr*, A butcher's large knife.

A ساطي *sātī*, Long-stepping (horse) that carries his tail high; also vicious, striking or biting other horses. (A stallion-camel) raging and running out of the herd. Long.

A ساع *sāɛ*, (or ساعات *sāɛāt*) (pl. of ساعة *sāɛat*) Hours. Moments. Times present.

A ساعاتي *sāɛātiy*, A watch or clock-maker.

A ساعة *sāɛat*, (pl. ساعات *sāɛāt* and ساع *sāɛ*) An hour. A little while. A watch or clock. The time present, a moment. Those who are perishing. الساعة *as' sāɛat*, The hour of the resurrection. ساعت بساعت *sāɛat ba sāɛat*, From hour to hour. ساعت زماني *sāɛati zamānī*, An astronomical hour. ساعة سوءاء *sāɛatun sawɛā,*, Unfortunate times. من ساعته *min sāɛatihi*, Immediately, forthwith, on the spot. ساعة *sāɛatan*, For a little while. P ساعتي نيك *sāɛate nek*, A good while.

A ساعتئذ *sāɛata,izin*, Then, at that time.

A ساعد *sāɛid*, (pl. سواعد *sawāɛid*) The arm from the wrist to the elbow, the fore-arm. ساعد الطير *sāɛidu't tayr*, The wing of a bird.

A ساعدة *sāɛidat*, A lion. Beam of a pulley.

A ساعل *sāɛil*, The throat. Coughing (camel).

A ساعور *sāɛūr*, A furnace, stove. A fire. The leader of the Christians in the medical art.

A ساعورة *sāɛūrat*, Fire.

A ساعي *sāɛī*, (pl. سعاة *suɛāt*) One who endeavours, attempts, or strives after: studious, diligent, laborious: earnest, eager. A gainer, acquirer. A messenger, courier. One who exercises jurisdiction or authority, a governor. A collector of tithes and other revenues. A calumniator, whisperer. A chief amongst Jews and Christians. One who throws work upon another. ساعي بالفساد *sāɛī bi'l fasād*, A labourer in iniquity, a malignant defamer.

P ساغ *sāgh*, A bird resembling a starling. A thatched house. Burnt brick.

A ساغب *sāghib*, (pl. سغاب *sighāb*) Hungry, famished, and tired.

A ساغد *sāghid*, (A colt) filled with milk.

P ساغر *sāghar*, A cup, goblet, bowl, tumbler.

P ساغري *sāgharī*, Back-leather of a horse or ass.

A ساغية *sāghiyat*, A delicious draught.

A سأف *sa,f*, (v. n. of سأف) Being cracked about the nails (the hand). Being chapped (the lip). Being peeled and divided into fibres (the palm-tree). *Saʻaf*, (v. n. of سعف) Being cracked (the hand). Palm-branches. Hair (of a wolf), bristles. A cuckoo.

A ساف *sāf*, A row of stones in a wall. Wind raising the dust. (pl. of سافة *sāfat*).

A سأفة *saʼāfat*, (v. n. of سؤف) Having one's cattle suffering from distemper.

A سافة *sāfat*, (pl. ساف *sāf*) Land lying between hard ground and sand.

A سافر *sāfir*, A traveller. (pl. سفرة *safarat*) A writer. One who interposes to reconcile two parties. (pl. سوافر *sawāfir*) (A woman) with face unveiled. A horse having little flesh upon him.

A سافرة *sāfirat*, A body of travellers. Name of a western nation.

A سافك *sāfik*, A pourer, shedder. A sword.

A سافل *sāfil*, Lower part. Mean, low, vile.

A سافلة *sāfilat*, The lower part of the body. The lower half of a spear.

A سافنة *sāfinat*, (pl. سوافن *sawāfin*) (Wind) which raises the dust.

P سافوت *sāfūt*, A shrill noise produced by blowing forcibly on the ends of the two fore-fingers put into the mouth.

A سافي *sāfī*, A violent, sweeping wind. Dust carried away by the wind.

A سافياء *sāfiyāʼ*, Dust, or the wind raising it.

P سافيسك *sāfīsak*, A small melon. Perfume.

A سافين *sāfin*, An artery in the back.

A ساق *sāka*, (fut. يسوق *yasūku*) He drove.

A سأق *saʼk*, (pl. سؤوق *suʼūk*) A leg.

A ساق *sāk*, (pl. سوق *sūk*, سيقان *sīkān*, and أسؤق *asʼuk*) The leg from the ankle to the knee, the shank. The trunk, shaft, or bole of a tree: the stem or stalk of an herb. One mode, order, sex, or species: as, ولدت بنين علي ساق *waladat banīna ʻalaʼ sākin*, She brought forth many children of the same sex (all boys). Vehemence, severity. Gravity, weight. Affliction, pain, torment. A male pigeon. ساق حرّ *sāku hurrin*, The male turtle-dove. ساق عروس *sāki ʻarūs*, Bride's leg, a sort of bread so called. ساق الميزان *sāku'l mīzān*, The scale or bason of a balance. يكشف عن ساق *yukshafu ʻan sākin*, Afflictions shall cease. التفت الساق بالساق *iltafafati's sāk bi's sāk*, A phrase expressive of the last anguish of this world and the first of the next. P تشمير ساق كردن *tashmīri sāk kardan*, To uncover the legs, *i. e.* to tuck up the clothes, or prepare to do any thing with vigour.

A ساقان *sākāni*, (du.) Legs (of man, trousers, &c.).

A ساقب *sākib*, Near. Far off.

A ساقة *sākat*, The rear of an army. The stirrup-leather. Drivers of camels.

A ساقط *sākit*, (pl. سقّاط *sukkāt*) Falling, failing, lagging. Fearing. Contemptible, vile. Mutilated. مرض ساقط *marazi sākit*, Falling sickness.

A ساقطة *sākitat*, (fem.) (pl. سواقط *sawākit* سقطى *sakta'*) Low in price, quality, or estimation. Pathless, bare (spot). Fallen (leaf).

A ساقور *sākūr*, Heat. A heated iron for branding.

A ساقي *sākī*, (pl. سقيّ *sukiy*, سقاة *sukāt*, also سقّي *sukka'*) A water-carrier. A cup-bearer, page.

P ساقيء روحانيان *sākīʼi rūhāniyān*, Adam. Gabriel. Satan. ساقيء شب *sākīʼi shab*, The moon. The dawn. An aged instructor, guide. ساقيان لحجة *sākiyāni lahja*, Musicians, singers.

A ساقية *sākiyat*, (pl. سواقي *sawākī*) A river, canal, trench, cut, gutter.

P ساقيگر *sākīgar*, A cup-bearer.

P ساقيگري *sākīgarī*, Office of cup-bearer.

P ساك *sāk*, Ignorance. Weakness of understanding. Defect, deficiency. The transmigration of the soul two degrees descending, *i. e.* from a human to a vegetable body.

A ساكب *sākib*, Flowing (blood, tears, or water). Aquarius.

A ساكت *sākit*, Silent, quiet. Silence.

A ساكر *sākir*, Quiet, silent, still (night).

A ساكع *sākiʻ*, Foreign, strange, far from home.

A ساكف *sākif*, The lintel of a door.

A ساكن *sākin*, Quiet, peaceable, sedate. Firm, fixed, still. A consonant not followed or inflected by a vowel (as بائ ساكن *bāʼi sākin*, *i. e.* ب *bā* quiescent in شبخانه *shab-khāna*. An inhabitant. A demon. ساكن الطبع *sākinu't tabʻ*, Of a gentle disposition, affable, peaceable. P ساكن شدن *sākin shudan*, To inhabit, dwell. To rest, remain. ساكن كردن *sākin kardan*, To mitigate, pacify. ساكنان خاك *sākināni khāk*, Dwellers on the earth. ساكنان سدرة *sākināni sidra*, Angels. ساكنان گردون *sākināni gardūn*, The stars. Angels.

A ساكنة *sākinat*, Quiet. A female inhabitant.

A ساكوت *sākūt*, A silent man.

A ساكوتة *sākūtat*, Silence. Silent, taciturn.

P ساكيز *sākīz*, A cushion, pad, or rug to lie on.

H ساگوان *sāgwān*, Teak-wood.

H ساگون *sāgūn*, An Indian tree whose leaves are compared to elephants' ears.

A سأل *saʼala*, (fut. يسأل *yasʼalu*) He asked.

P سال *sāl*, A year. A ship. A timber-tree used in ship-building. سال آينده *sāli āyanda*, The coming year, next year. سال حال *sāli hāl*, The present or current year. سال شمسي *sāli shumsī*, Solar year. سال قمري *sāli kamarī*, (or سال مه *sāli mah*) Lunar year, consisting of 354 days. سال سال *sāl sāl*, (سال بسال *sāl ba sāl* or سال در سال *sāl dar sāl*) From year to year. سال ديگر *sāli dīgar*, Next year, the year to come. Another year. سال قحط *sāli kaht*, A year barren for want of rain. سال گذشته *sāli guzashta*, Last year.

A سالّ *sāll*, (pl. سلّان *sullān* and سوالّ *sawāll*) A widely-extending valley producing the trees سلم *salam* and سمر *samur*.

P سالار *sālār*, Old, aged. A prince, chieftain, leader, general, commander, vicegerent, viceroy, lord-lieutenant, judge, or any person in high office. سالار بيت الحرام *sālāri baytu'l harām*, Muhammad. سالار جنگ *sālāri jang*, A leader in war (one of the titles given by Eastern princes to their nobles). سالار خوان *sālāri khwān*, A table-decker, sewer. سالار قافلة *sālāri kāfila*, Chief of a caravan, leader of a troop. سالار قوم *sālāri kawm*, A leader of the people, a general.

P سال افزون *sāl-afzūn*, Increasing the year. The twelfth month of the æra of Yazdagird.

G سالامندرا *sālāmandirā*, A salamander.

P سالانه *sālāna*, Yearly.

A سالب *sālib*, A seizer, spoiler, plunderer, ravisher. (pl. سوالب *sawālib*) Delivered of an abortion.

P سالبر *sāl-bar*, A tree bearing every other year.

A سالبة *sāliba*, (in logic) A negative proposition.

P سالبية *sālbiyah*, Sage (an herb).

A سآلة *saʼālat*, (or سألة *saʼlat*) (v. n. of سأل) Asking, begging, praying.

A سالح *sālih*, Armed. An armed man. Scouring from eating green herbage (camel).

P سال حاصل *sāl-hāsil*, Yearly produce.

A سالخ *sālikh*, (The scab) excoriating a camel. A snake which has cast her slough. A black serpent. اسود سالخ *aswadu sālikh*, A black serpent. اسودان سالخ *aswadāni sālikh*, Two black serpents. اساود سالخة *asāwidu sālikhat*, Black serpents.

P سالخداه *sāl-khidāh* or *sāl-khudāh*, Fortunate. (in astrology) Lord of the ascendant.

P سال خورد *sāl-khwurd*, (سالخورده *sal-khwurda*, and سالدار *sāl-dār*) Aged; and, synonymous with سالديده *sāl-dīda*, One who has seen many years: an old man. پيران سالديده *pīrāni sāl-dīda*, Old men laden with years.

A سالغ *sāligh*, (A cow or sheep) exceeding six years, having their teeth dropt out. (Afterwards she is called سالغ سنة *sālighu sanatin*, سالغ سنتين *sālighu sanatayn*, and so on).

A سالف *sālif*, Preceding, going before, passing by. Past, by-gone. A predecessor. سالف الذكر *sālifu'z zikr*, Above-mentioned.

A سالفة *sālifat*, By-gone days. The neck of a horse or the fore-part of it. The front of the neck.

A سالقة *sālikat*, Loud, shrill-voiced (woman), when in distress, or who strikes her face. A snake that casts his slough several times a year.

A سالك *sālik*, A traveller. A devotee. P سالكان عرش *sālikāni ʻarsh*, Angels. Holy men.

P سالگاني *sāligānī*, Life, age. Annual pension. Anniversary.

P سال گردش *sāl-gardish*, Beginning the new-year from the accession of the king.

P سال گره *sāl-girih*, Birth-day, on the anniversary of which a knot is annually added on a string kept for this purpose.

P سال گشت *sāl-gasht*, Old, in years.

P سالگي *sālagī*, Age, years old.

A سالم *sālim*, Safe, free, entire, sound, perfect. (in gram.) A sound or regular verb, *i.e.* not having for either of its radicals an ا, و, or ي, or the second radical letter similar to the third. Verse, wherein there is no dropping or elision of any letter.

A سالما *sāliman*, Freely, safely, securely.

P سال ماه *sāl-māh*, Date of the year and month. Continually, perpetually.

A سالمة *sālimat*, The herb sage.

P سالمه *sāl-mah*, Date. Continually, perpetually.

P سالنج *sālanj*, Name of a small black bird.

P سالوس *sālūs*, A deceiver, flatterer, hypocrite.

P سالوسي *sālūsī*, Fraud, deceit, subterfuge.

P سالوك *sālūk*, A highway-robber. Courteous.

P ساله *sāla*, Age, years, the age of animals (when added to numerals, however, it is applicable as well to human beings as to brutes). The rear-guard of an army. شش ساله *shash-sāla*, Six years old (horse, ass, or camel). پير صد ساله *pīri sad sāla*, An aged man a hundred years old.

P سالها *sālha*, (pl. of سال *sāl*) Years. For many years. سالهاي دراز *sālhāyi darāz*, Length of years.

P سالي *sāle*, A year, a certain year. سالي چند *sāle chand*, Several years. سالي حال *sāle hāl*, The present year. *Sālī*, Old, aged. Used.

P ساليان *sāliyān*, Every day. One year. Years. Life. Annual, an annual pension. Name of a place.

P ساليانه *sāliyāna*, Life, age. An annual pension. ساليانه كردن *sāliyāna kardan*, To bargain by the year.

P ساليانى *sāliyānī*, Annual. An annual stipend.

G ساليون *sālyūn*, Parsley. Seed of mountain-parsley.

A سأم *sa*,*ām*, (v. n. of سئم) Being wearied.

A سأم *sa*,*m*, Death. *Sa*,*m* or *sa*,*am*, (v. n. of سئم) Being wearied.

P سام *sām*, The rainbow. A swelling. A disease. Fire. Death. Destruction. سرسام *sar-sām*, A swelling in the head. سام سوار *sām-suwār*, Riding on the rainbow (a metaphorical figure for a horseman whose motions are as rapid as the wind). سام نريمان *sām narīmān*, A celebrated hero in old Persian romance, father to زال زر *zāl zar*, and grandfather to رستم *rustam*. He was named also دل سنگين *dil-sangīn*, Heart of stone, in allusion to which Suhaylī, speaking of the fierceness of Sulaymān, says that the fire of his rage would have melted the brazen body of Isfandiyār, and changed the stony heart of Sām to a heart of flesh.

A سام *sām*, Shem, son of Noah. Gold and silver; also veins of those metals running through stones. A hole where water lodges. A cane, rattan.

A سامّ *sāmm*, Distressingly hot and pestilentially windy (day). Venomous, baneful, infectious. Peculiar, proper. سامّ ابرص *sāmm abras*, A large and venomous kind of lizard.

P ساماخچه *sāmākhcha*, Bodice, stays, corset.

P سامافچه *sāmāfcha*, A bodice: shift: short vest.

P ساماكچه *sāmākcha* or ساماكي *sāmākī*, A bodice.

P سامان *sāmān*, Household furniture, baggage, articles. Instrument, tools, apparatus. Order, arrangement, disposition. Preparation. Foundation of a house. A boundary, limit, place where any sign or mark is placed, to separate one field from another, a balk. A side, quarter. End, scope, aim. A butt for archers. Measure, quantity, proportion. Currency. Patience, quiet. Rest, pause. Cessation, conclusion. Continence, chastity. Opulence. A good disposition, probity. Understanding, reason, intellect. Power, strength. An assembly, company: people met together. A whetstone. Custom, habit. A city, town. Seasonable, pat. Proper time. Facilitated, rendered easy, feasible. Uncertain. Name of the father of a dynasty of kings called سامانيه *sāmāniya*. سامان جنگي *sāmāni jangī*, Warlike apparatus. بي سر و سامان *bī sar u sāmān*, Immense, boundless. Stupefied, brainless. Destitute, indigent. Endless, applied to affairs.

A سآمة *sa*,*āmat*, (v. n. of سئم) Being wearied.

A سأمة *sa*,*mat*, A being wearied or disgusted. The feeling of irksomeness.

A سامة *sāmat*, (pl. سيم *siyam*) An excavation down to a well. (pl. سام *sām*) A vein in a mountain different from the rest. Gold. Silver, or veins of the same in stone. A cane. A rattan. A hole wherein water lodges.

A سامّة *sāmmat*, (fem.) Poisonous. Familiar. Special. An intimate friend. A patrician. The aristocracy. Death.

A سامح *sāmih*, Liberal. Affable, gentle.

A سامد *sāmid*, One who carries the head haughtily. A good-tempered, jolly fellow. A singer.

P سامر *sāmir*, Name of a place noted for the manufacture of stuffs.

A سامر *sāmir*, (pl. سمّار *summār*) One who converses at night, by moonlight: the place where such conversations are held: the people assembled.

A سامرة *sāmirat*, Samaritans. Those who hold nocturnal conversations by moonlight.

A سامريّ *sāmirīy*, Name of a magician said to have been contemporary with Moses, and to have made a speaking calf. Samaritan.

A سامرّيّ *sāmarrīy*, Native of Surmanrā.

A سامريّة *sāmarīyat*, Samaria.

A سامط *sāmit*, Milk turning sour. Bread baked without salt.

A سامع *sāmiʻ*, Who hears; a hearer: obedient.

A سامعة *sāmiʻat*, (fem.) Hearing. The ear. قوّت سامعه *kūwati sāmiʻa*, The sense of hearing.

A سامغان *sāmighānī*, (du.) The sides of the mouth.

A سامق *sāmik*, Tall and long.

A سامك *sāmik*, High, raised, elevated, lofty.

P سام كيس *sām-kīs*, Great, noble.

A سامل *sāmil*, A composer of differences: a peace-maker. Studious of living with propriety.

A سامن *sāmin*, Fat, plump. Rich in butter.

P سامندر *sāmandar*, (or سامندل) A salamander.

A سامور *sāmūr*, Adamant.

A سامونا *sāmūnā*, A weight of three carats or one-eighth of an ounce.

P سامه *sāma*, A covenant. An oath. A loan. An asylum, place of safety. Particularly, especially, chiefly. A banner. A snare. Friends.

A سامه *sāmih*, (pl. سمّه *summah*) One who runs without fatigue. Astonished.

A سامي *sāmī*, Sublime, exalted. (pl. سوامي *sawāmī*) Stallions which carry their heads high. (pl. سماة *sumāt*) A hunter.

P ساميز *sāmīz*, A whetstone.

P سان *sān*, Law, custom, rule, fashion. Habit, disposition. Form, figure, semblance. Apparatus, furniture, utensils. Honour, reputation, respect, fame, dignity, rank. Cause, reason, manner. End, conclusion. A kind of military garment, either for one's self, horse, or elephant. A bit, piece. A share, portion. A whetstone. A file, rasp. Review of an army. Shewing one's self off in a comely manner. Name of a town in the district of Balkh. Equal, like. (Added to nouns it implies similitude, resemblance) شمع سان *shamaʻsān*, Like a candle.

A سانح *sānih*, (A bird) which turns the right side to a man, and passing from his left to the right (considered as a good omen). Happy, fortunate.

P سانح شدن *sānih shudan*, To appear, be evident.

A سانحة *sānihat*, Revelation (in augury).

P ساندوس *sāndūs*, The river Indus.

P سان سان *sān sān*, In parts, pieces, portions.

A سانعة *sāniʻat*, Handsome (she-camel).

P سانقه *sānika*, Maiden's hair. Dragon's blood.

P سانگير *sān-gīr*, A proper arrangement. A natural temper. Adorned. A simple man.

P ساننج *sānanj*, A kind of melodious bird, small and black.

A ساني *sānī*, Water-drawing (camel).

A سانية *sāniyat*, A large bucket with the apparatus. (pl. سواني *sawānī*) A female camel trained to water ground.

A سأو *sa*,*w*, (v. n. of سأا) Extending far (one's anxiety). Doing evil to. Running. Stretching (a garment) till it tears. Sowing dissensions. Propensity, desire, inclination, intention, purpose. A place to which one has been accustomed, home.

P ساو *sāv*, Tribute (especially of oxen, paid by enemies who have submitted). A bit of gold. Filings. Pure gold. Bought gold. A crucible. A part, portion. A steel for sharpening a sword or knife. A prickly stick about which silkworms entwine themselves when about to spin, or used as firewood. (in comp.) Filing, cutting with a saw.

ساو آهن *sāvi āhan*, Filings of iron.

P ساوا *sāwā*, (or ساواي) Gold or silver-filing.

A ساوة *sāwat*, Name of a place.

P ساود *sāwad*, The garment fits the body tight.

P ساوري *sāwarī*, Tax, tribute.

P ساوزيدن *sāwazīdan*, To rub gently.

P ساوند *sāwand*, Rhyme, measure.

P ساوو *sāwū*, Tribute.

P ساوة *sāwa*, A bit or filing of pure gold. A crucible. Name of a wrestler of Tūrān. Name of a city in Irāk.

P ساويدن *sāwīdan*, To file. To polish, furbish. To saw. To bruise, bray small. To anoint. To understand, reason. To dissolve in water. To strain off. To handle.

P ساويدة *sāwīda*, Brayed small. Filed.

P ساويز *sāwīz*, Of good morals or temper.

P ساويس *sāwīs*, Any thing of great value. Carded cotton, with which a garment is lined. A garment wadded with a cotton lining, worn in battle. A woman's basket for cotton.

P ساوين *sāwīn*, A basket for holding cotton prepared for spinning. ساوين پنبه *sāwīni pamba*, Baskets of cotton.

A ساهر *sāhir*, Waking. ليل ساهر *laylun sāhirun*, A sleepless night.

A ساهرة *sāhirat*, The earth, or its surface. White ground, *i.e.* not beaten with the feet. Hell. A running fountain. An extensive desert without water. A country which God will make new on the day of the resurrection. Syria. The sheath into which they imagine that the moon enters when eclipsed.

A ساهرية *sāhiriyat*, Name of a perfume, in the preparation of which vigilance is indispensable.

A ساهف *sāhif*, Thirsty, especially when mortally wounded. Perishing. Pale, pallid.

A ساهك *sāhik*, A disease of the eyes; also an itching in the eyes. Violent (wind).

A ساهمة *sāhimat*, An extenuated camel.

P ساهور *sāhūr*, Name of a mountain which yields stone of the hardest kind.

A ساهور *sāhūr*, The moon; also the sheath into which (according to the belief of the vulgar Arabs) she enters when eclipsed. Moonlight. The moon's orbit. A halo round the moon. The shadow of the earth. Watching, wakefulness. Abundance. The last nine days of the moon. The root of the eye. The surface of the earth.

P ساهويه *sāhūya*, Name of a celebrated interpreter of dreams.

A ساهي *sāhī*, Negligent, careless. Stupefied.

P ساي *sāy*, (from سودن *sūdan* used in comp.) Filing, polishing, rubbing. A delicate sort of stuff. نگين ساي *nigīn-sāy*, A polisher of rings or gems, an engraver. زلف مشك ساي *zulfi mushk-sāy*, A ringlet scented with musk.

A سأي *sa*y*, (v. n. of سأي) Stretching (a garment) until it tears. Sowing dissensions.

P سايانيدن *sāyānīdan*, To cause to rub or anoint.

A سائب *sā*ib*, Flowing, current, fluid.

P سايبان *sāyabān*, A canopy, umbrella, parasol. A shade formed by foliage or by any other projection. A tent, pavilion. سايبان اخضر *sāyabāni akhzar*, The sky. سايبان سيمابي *sāyabāni simābī*, The false dawn. سايبان ظلماني *sāyabāni zulmānī*, The false dawn. A dark night.

A سائبة *sā*ibat*, (pl. سيّب *suyyab*) Set at liberty, as a slave; or as a she-camel in obedience to a vow, or in consequence of having been delivered of ten female colts, when she immediately receives a dispensation from all further labour. انت سائبة *anti sā*ibat*, Thou art free (formula of manumission).

A ساية *sāyat*, Evenness, equality. ضرب لي ساية *zaraba lī sāyatan*, He directed a word to me.

A سائح *sā*ih*, Devout, fasting in the mosque. A traveller.

P سايد *sāyad*, Dross of iron.

A سائد *sā*id*, (pl. سادة *sādat* and سيائد *sayā*id*) A lord, prince by birth (inferior to سيّد *sayyid*).

A سائر *sā*ir*, A walker, goer, traveller, wanderer. Current (story, habit, &c.). Remainder, rest (though often employed to signify the whole). A tax on personal property. Land-customs.

A سائرة *sā*irat*, A crowd of travellers going along the same road.

A سائر جهات *sā*ir jihāt*, A tax on boats; inland toll. All kinds of taxation besides the land-rent (a term used chiefly in India).

A سائس *sā*is*, (pl. سياس *siyās* and ساسة *sāsat*) A governor, manager. A guardian. A master of horse, horse-keeper, equerry, groom. A trainer or breaker in. An executioner. A black corrosion of the teeth. A corroded tooth. P سائس پنجم رواق *sā*isi panjum rivāk*, The planet Mars.

P سائسخانه *sā*is-khāna*, A beast of burden.

A سائسي *sā*isī*, The business of a groom.

P سايش *sāyish*, Friction, polish. An anointing.

A سائع *sā*i*, Lost, missing. Neglected, useless. ضائع سائع *zā*i* sā*i*, Straying, strayed.

A سائغ *sā*igh*, (or سائغ لائغ *sā*igh lā*igh*) (Wine or food) flowing gently down the throat.

A سائف *sā*if*, A possessor of a sword. A striker with a sword. A sword-bearer. Armed with a sword.

A سائفة *sā*ifat*, (pl. سوائف *sawā*if*) Fine sand at the base of a hillock. Land lying between hard ground and sand. A long slice of meat.

A سائق *sā*ik*, (pl. سوّاق *suwwāk*) A stimulator, instigator, impeller, driver. A coachman, postilion.

P سايكي *sāykī*, A drinking-cup. A crow, raven.

P سايگي *sāyagī*, A shade. Shadiness.

A سائل *sā*il*, An asker, interrogator, questioner, proponent. A beggar. Flowing, fluid, liquid.

A سائلة *sā*ilat*, A blaze extending from a horse's forehead to his nose.

P سائل كف *sā*il kaf*, A beggar.

A سائم *sā*im*, (pl. سوائم *sawā*im*) (A horse) going to pasture.

A سائمة *sā*imat*, (pl. سوائم *sawā*im*) Camels, goats, and the like, which subsist during the greater part of the year upon pasture.

P سايندة *sāyanda*, A grinder.

P سايوان *sāyawān*, A shade. Dust of floors.

P سايوس *sāyūs*, Seed of fleawort.

P سايه *sāya*, A shade, shadow. An apparition. A wicked spirit. Name of a demon. Protection. A petticoat. Wickedness, lewdness. سايه افكندن *sāya afkandan*, To travel towards. سايهٔ ربّ النعيم *sāya*i rabbu'n na*īm*, A caliph. سايهٔ حمايت *sāya*i himāyat*, Shadow of protection. سايهٔ خدا *sāya*i khudā*, Shadow of God. سايهٔ ركاب *sāya*i rikāb*, Protection. Followers. سايهٔ قشور *sāya*i kushūr*, Shadow of a tree. سايه گستردن *sāya gustardan*, To conceal. To shew favour. To bind. To speak ill of. سايه و نور *sāya u nūr*, Shadow of a tree. Night and day. سايهٔ يزدان *sāya*i yazdān*, Shadow of God, *i.e.* A mighty monarch.

P سايه بان *sāyabān*, An umbrella: a parasol.

P سايه برك *sāya-burak*, (or سايه برگ *sāya-burag*) Name of a soporiferous plant.

P سايه پرست *sāya-parast*, Loving darkness. A whoremonger.

P سايه پرستي *sāya-parastī*, Wickedness, lewdness.

P سايه پرور *sāya-parwar*, Educated in the shade, or at home; soft, delicate, knowing little of the world. Any thing eaten with bread. A parasite, trencher-fly.

P سايه پرورد *sāya-parward*, Quiet, at rest. A receiver of favours.

P سايه پروردگان خم *sāya-parwardagāni khum*, Grape-stones thrown into a wine-jar.

P سايه پسند *sāya-pasand*, Fond of shade, quiet.

P سايه پسندي *sāya-pasandī*, Fondness for shade.

P سايه پوش *sāya-posh*, A parasol. An arbour.

P سايه خزك *sāya-khazak*, A certain plant eaten with bread.

P سايه خوش *sāya-khwush*, The elm, as shady.

P سايه دار *sāya-dār*, Shady, umbrageous. A protector. A demoniac. سرو سايه دار *sarvi sāya-dār*, The shady cypress.

P سايه داشت *sāya-dāsht*, Shady. Possessed of a spirit.

P سايه رو *sāya-rav*, A watch. A night-robber.

P سايه زده *sāya-zada*, Shady. A demoniac.

P سايه شكن *sāya-shikan*, Breaking a shade, *i.e.* a destroyer of false religion. A reformer, illuminator. A polisher, furbisher. Light, luminous.

P سايه گاه *sāya-gāh*, A shady place, tent, bower.

P سايه گستر *sāya-gustar*, Shade-diffusing, shady.

P سايه گير *sāya-gīr*, Shaded, catching shade.

P سايه ناك *sāyanāk*, Shady, overcast.

P سايه نشين *sāya-nishīn*, One who has seen few troubles, who has sat in the shade.

P سائيدن *sāīdan*, To grind. To rub, wear. To gnash the teeth. To smooth, polish. To anoint. To dissolve. To draw. To strain off. To understand.

P سائيده *sāīda*, Ground. Polished. Worn.

A سبّ *sabb*, (v.n. of سبّ) Cutting, clipping. Wounding. Stabbing in the backside. Reviling, reproaching, cursing. Imputing error. Execration, reproach. *Sabb* or *sibb*, Very reproachful and abusive. *Sibb*, (pl. سبوب *subūb*) A turban; fillet, sash, or female head-dress. Fine linen-cloth. A rope. A stake. A reviler.

A سبا *saba'*, (fut. يسبي *yasbī*) He took prisoner.

A سبأ *sabɛ*, (v. n. of سبأ) Buying wine. Passing any thing slightly and inattentively. Being fearless and indifferent in regard to an oath. Skinning. Flagellating. Burning, scorching. Taking by the hand, shaking hands. A snake's slough. *Sabɛ* or سبا *saba'*, A country in Arabia Felix, where they suppose بلقيس *bilkīs*, queen of Sheba to have reigned. Name of Ibn Yashjub bin Yaɛrab bin Kahtān, from whom the tribes derive their origin.

A سبا *saba'*, Name of a tribe in Yaman. Wood, timber drifted by a current from country to country. تفرّقوا ايدي سبا *tafarrakū aydī saba'*, (or ايادي سبا *ayādī saba'*) They were dispersed everywhere, like the Sabeans (or sons of Sabā after the submersion of their country).

A سباء *sabāɛ*, (v. n. of سبأ) Purchasing (wine). Burning (a skin). Flagellating. Skinning. Taking by the hand, shaking hands. Wood, timber carried by a current from country to country. *Sibāɛ*, (v. n. of سبي) Purchasing and carrying wine from country to country. Making a slave, taking prisoner. (A woman) stealing the heart (of a man). Wine bought.

A سبّاء *sabbāɛ*, A vender of wine.

A سباب *sibāb*, A reviling, an abusing.

A سبّاب العراقيب *sabbābu'l ɛarākib*, A sword.

A سبّابة *sabbābat*, The fore-finger, the index. The second toe. P انگشت سبّابه *angushti sabbāba*, The fore-finger.

A سبّابتان *sabbābatāni*, Thumb and index.

A سبابجة *sabābijat*, Name of a people from Scinde, who dwelt at Basrah, acting as prison-keepers.

A سبأة *subɛat*, A long journey.

A سبات *subāt*, Rest, sleep. A light sleep. A doze. Commencement of sleep in the head. Lethargy. Time, fortune. A very subtle man. ابنا سبات *ibnā subāt*, Night and day.

A سبّاج *sabbāj*, A seller of small shells, &c.

A سبّاح *sabbāh*, (pl. سبّاحون *sabbāhūn*) A swimmer. *Subbāh*, (pl. of سابح *sābih*) Swimmers.

A سباحة *sibāhat*, (v. n. of سبح) Swimming. Natation. اهل سباحت *ahli sibāhat*, Skilful swimmer.

A سبّاحة *sabbāhat*, The fore-finger.

A سباخ *sibākh*, (pl. of سبخة) Saltish grounds.

A سبادح *sabādih*, (Persons) short of victuals.

A سبادرة *sabādirat*, Unemployed, idle fellows. Partners in any vain amusement.

P سباده *subāda*, The smyris, with which they cut glass and stones for seals.

P سبار *sabār*, Household furniture. A wine-press. A large trough into which the grapes are thrown, and pressed with the feet. A ploughshare. A furrow. A field.

A سبار *sibār*, A surgeon's probe.

P سباروك *sabārūk*, A pigeon.

P سباره *sabāra*, A stone for making whetstones.

P سباري *sibārī*, A stalk of corn.

P سباريت *sabārīt*, (or سباري *sabārī*) (pl. of سبروت *subrūt*) Waste grounds. Beardless boys. ارض سباريت *arzsabārīt*, Waste, uncultivated land.

P سباريدن *sabārīdan*, To be cleft (ground).

A سبارينا *sabārīnā*, Sarsaparilla.

A سباسب *sabāsib*, A desert country. السباسب *as'sabāsib*, The feast of palms. بلد سباسب *balad sabāsib*, A widely-spread town. يوم السباسب *yawmu's sabāsib*, A certain festival of the Pagan Arabs.

A سباط *sabāt*, A fever. *Subāt*, A Syro-Macedonian month (February).

A سباطة *sabātat*, (v. n. of سبط) Being lank (the hair). *Subātat*, Rubbish, sweepings (of a house). Abundance, plenty; amplitude. سباطة المطر *subātatu'l matar*, Abundance of rain.

A سباطر *subātir*, A long-necked bird. Tall.

A سباع *sibāɛ*, (v. n. 3 of سبع) Indulging in venery. Making a boast, priding one's self on this matter. Obscene talk, ribaldry. Reproaching, cursing each other. (pl. of سبع *sabuɛ*) Lions, beasts, or birds of prey.

A سباعيّ *subāɛīy*, Complete, entire, unmutilated (in the body). Fierce. Large and long (camel). (in grammar). Consisting of seven letters.

P سباغ *sibāgh*, Meat, or aught eaten with bread.

A سباق *sibāk*, (v. n. 3 of سبق) Endeavouring to get the lead (in running), trying to outstrip. Precedence. A race. سباق البازي *sibāku'l bāzī*, A hawk's leash.

A سبّاق *sabbāk*, One who takes the lead, and gets far a head. *Subbāk*, (pl. of سابق *sābik*) Predecessors. Conquerors.

A سبّاك *sabbāk*, A melter, smelter.

P سباكي *sabākī*, The smelting of gold and silver. A coiner.

P سبال *sibāl*, A whisker.

A سبال *sibāl*, (pl. of سبلة *sabalat*) Whiskers.

A سبالة *sibālat*, Whiskers.

A سبانت *sabānit* (pl. of سبنتى *sabanta'*) Bold, brave men. Leopards.

A سباند *sabānid*, (pl. of سبندي *sabanda'*) Bold men or animals. Leopards. Tall, long.

A سباندة *sabānidat*, (pl. of سبندي) Bold men or animals, especially leopards. Idlers, triflers.

A سباه *sabāh*, A man who has lost his wits or his way. *Subāh*, A trance.

A سبايا *sabāya'*, (pl. of سبيّ *sabīy*) Captives.

A سبائب *sabāɛib*, (pl. of سبيب *sabīb*) Manes, forelocks. (pl. of سبيبة) Linen vests or cloths.

A سبائيّة *sabāɛīyat*, Name of a sect of hypershīyas who ascribe divinity to Alīy.

A سبائخ *sabāɛikh*, (pl. of سبيخة *sabīkhat*) Particles which fall from carded cotton, or bird's feathers.

A سبائك *sabāɛik*, (pl. of سبيكة *sabīkat*) Bars, ingots of gold or silver.

P سبائل *sabāɛil*, The capital of Kandahār.

A سبب *sabab*, (pl. اسباب *asbāb*) Cause, occasion, reason, motive, argument, mean, medium, instrument. A rope. Connexion of relationship, affinity. A tract or quarter of the heavens or earth. A way. A gate. A banner. Household furniture, exclusive of hangings or apparel. Life. (in prosody) A foot consisting of two letters, whereof the first is always inflected with a vowel, and the last either marked with a vowel or quiescent. If the final be quiescent, the foot is then called light: as, من *man*, بل *bal*, لا *lā*. If both consonants are inflected, the foot is then heavy: as, له *lahu*.

A سببة *subabat*, A railer, reviler.

A سببيّة *sababiyat*, A cause, causation, handle.

A سبّة *sabbat*, A portion of time. Several days of heat, cold, or sense and intelligence. منذ سبّة *munzu sabbatin*, For some time. Podex. *Sibbat*, The fore-finger. *Subbat*, Reproach, slander, disgrace, injury, villainy. A man whom all revile.

A سبت *sabt*, (v. n. of سبت) Observing the Jewish sabbath, sabbatizing. Allowing the hair to fall in braids. Cutting. Rest, quiet, repose. (pl. اسبت *asbut* and سبوت *subūt*) The sabbath. A swoon. Stupor, astonishment. A shaving of the head. A drowsy, somnolent man. An extremely subtle man. A fleet, generous horse. A section, a cutting. Time. A while. Fortune. A bold, impudent boy. Brave, courageous. A quick pace of a camel. اصحاب السبت *as-hābu's sabt*, Sabbatarians. Jews. ما رأينا الشمس سبتا *mā raɛaynā'sh shamsa sabtan*, We have not seen the sun for a week (or for some time). *Sibt*, Tanned ox-leather (especially with Egyptian thorns). *Subt* or *sabt*, A kind of mallow.

A سبّت *sibbitt*, Aniseed.

A سبتاء *sabtāɛ*, (A woman) whose ears are wide, whether long or short. A desert.

A سبتان *sibtān*, A fool.

A سبتة *sabtat*, Ceuta in Africa. A long portion of time, a while. A herd of goats.

A سبتل *subtul*, A pot-herb seed.

A سبتيّة *sibtīyat*, A shoe made of neat's leather.

A سبج *sabaj*, (from P شبه) Small black shells.

A سبجة *subjat*, A blackish garment or carpet. A sleeveless vest. Breast of a shirt. Gore of a shift.

A سبح *sabaha*, (fut. يسبح *yasbahu*) He swam.

A سبح *sabh*, (v. n. of سبح) Swimming. Going and coming. Travelling far. Labouring to support life; occupation. Liberty, leisure; rest, repose, sleep. Digging, excavating. Talking much. *Subah*, (pl. of سبحة *subhat*) Rosaries.

A سباحا *subahā*, (pl. of سبوح *sabūh*) Swimmers.

A سبحات *subuhāt*, Glory (of God). Oratories.

A سبحان *subhān*, (v. n. of سبح) Praising, glorifying (God). Exclaiming سبحان الله *subhāna'llāh*. The soul, heart. Swiftness in yielding obedience to the divine commands. سبحان الله *subhāna'llāh*, Far be it from God (to have a wife or son)! سبحان من كذا *subhān min kazā*, O wonderful! strange! حق سبحانه و تعالى *hakk subhānahu wa taʻāla'*, God the most holy and most high.

A سبحانيّ *subhāniy*, Divine.

A سبحة *sabhat*, Garments made of skins. *Sabhat* or *subhat*, Majesty, glory (of God). *Subhat*, (pl. سبح *subah*) A rosary, chaplet (for repeating prayers). Worship. Any indifferent act of Muhammadan worship not prescribed in the Kur'ān or Sunna: prayers of supererogation. سبحهٔ بلور *subhaʻi bilawr*, Stars (a rosary of crystal).

A سبحل *sibahl*, (or سبحلل *sabahlal*) Thick, bulky (camel, lizard, girl, or bucket).

A سبحلة *sabhalat*, (v. n. of سبحل Q) Repeating the words سبحان الله *subhāna'llāh*, God be praised!

A سبحنة *sabhanat*, (v. n. of سبحن Q) Pronouncing the formula سبحان الله *subhāna'llāh*, God be praised! Be it far from God! Wondering.

P سبحه دار *subha-dār*, Worshipper, beadsman.

A سبحيّ *subhiy* or *sabhiy*, Of, relating, pertaining to a rosary or chaplet of beads.

A سبخ *sabhh*, A retiring to a distance. Rest. Deep sleep.

P سبخ *sibahh*, Salt. Wit, animation.

A سبخة *sabkhat*, *sabakhat*, or *sabikhat*, (pl. سباخ *sibāhh*) Saltish ground. Weeds floating on the surface of stagnant water.

A سبد *sabd*, (v. n. of سبد) Shaking (the bead). *Sibd*, (pl. اسباد *asbād*) A wolf. A cunning fellow, an adroit thief. *Sabad*, A little hair. ما له لبد و لا سبد *mā lahu labadun wa lā sabadun*, He has nothing. *Sabid*, Remains of herbage. *Subad*, (pl. سبدان *sibdān*) The hair of the pubes. A kind of cloth used to preserve the water in a tank from becoming muddy. Ill luck. A certain bird with soft plumage. Name of a place near Mecca. Rizām bin Māzin (a man's name).

P سبد *sabad* or *sabud*, A basket.

P سبد چين *sabad-chīn*, Gleanings of fruits.

A سبدة *sabazat*, (from P سبد *sabad*) A kind of basket holding fifteen صاع *sāʻ*.

A سبر *sabr*, (v. n. of سبر) Probing (a wound). Examining (any business) to the bottom. A lion. *Sabr* or *sibr*, A beauteous form, mode, or manner. Origin, root. Colour. Beauty. حسن الحبر والسبر *hasanu'l hibr wa's sibr*, Very beautiful and lovely. *Sibr*, Hostility, reproach. *Subar*, A kind of bird.

A سبرات *sibrāt*, Poor, indigent.

A سبرة *sabrat*, (pl. سبرات *sabarāt*) A cold morning. *Subrat*, A sort of bird.

A سبرت *sabrat*, Name of a market in Tripoli. *Subrut*, Poor, indigent.

A سبرتة *sabratat*, A being contented.

A سبرجة *sabrajat*, (v. n. of سبرج Q) Hiding, wrapping up, making obscure, mystifying.

A سبردة *sabradat*, (v. n. of سبرد Q) Shaving. Casting a hairless fœtus (a camel).

A سبروت *subrūt*, (pl. سباريت *sabārīt* and سباري *sabārī*) Poor, indigent. Barren, waste, uncultivated ground. Mean, contemptible. Little (wealth). Beardless (youth).

A سبرور *subrūr*, Poor. Barren (land).

A سبريت *sibrīt*, (pl. سباريت) Poor, indigent.

P سبز *sabz*, Green, verdant, fresh. Black, dark, opaque. Grass. A sword, dagger, or breast-plate of a blueish hue. سبز بودن *sabz būdan*, To continue in full bloom, green and flourishing. سبز بهار *sabzi bahār*, Name of a note in music. سبز دو تاي *sabzi du tāy*, Night.

P سبز آب *sabz-āb*, A green thing on water.

P سبز آخر *sabz-ākhur*, (or سبز آخور *sabz-ākhwur*) A stable full of fresh grass. The sky.

P سبزارنگ *sabzā-rang*, Of a green colour.

P سبز آشيانه *sabz āshyāna*, (سبز ايوان *sabz aywān*, or سبز باديان *sabz bādyān*) The sky.

P سبز اندر سبز *sabz andar sabz*, Name of the ninth musical note of the barbud.

P سبز باغ *sabz-bāgh*, The human body. The sky.

P سبز بال *sabz-bāl*, (or بالي *bālī*) A sort of grape.

P سبز بستان *sabz-bustān*, A grass-plot, green.

P سبز پا *sabz-pā*, (or سبز پاي *sabz-pāy*) One who brings ill luck with him (Black-foot).

P سبز پري *sabz-parī*, The verdant spring.

P سبز پوش *sabz-posh*, Clothed in green. A tree in full leaf. Dressed in mourning. Angels. Saints, religious persons. A dyer. A currier. سبز پوشان باغ بهشت *sabz-poshāni bāghi bihisht*, The hūris. سبز پوشان فلك *sabz-poshāni falak*, Angels.

P سبز خانه *sabz-khāna*, A house of mourning. A cemetery.

P سبز خنگ *sabz-khing*, A bay horse. The sky. سبز خنگ منحوس *sabz-khingi manhūs*, The world. Fortune.

P سبز خوان *sabz-khwān*, The sky.

P سبز دانه *sabz-dāna*, Green (corn), just in ear, before the grain is formed. Seed of turpentine.

P سبز دايه *sabz-dāya*, A violet.

P سبز در سبز *sabzi dar sabz*, Name of a note.

P سبز ده *sabz dih*, The sky.

P سبز رنگ *sabz-rang*, Green. Black.

P سبز روشن *sabz-roshan*, A kind of pigeon.

P سبززار *sabzzār*, Of a greenish colour.

P سبز زاغ *sabz-zāgh*, The world. The sky.

P سبز طاق *sabz-tāk*, The sky.

P سبز طاوس *sabz-tāʻus*, The sky.

P سبز طشت *sabz tasht*, The sky.

P سبز فام *sabz-fām*, Of a greenish colour.

P سبز فرش *sabz-farsh*, The sky.

P سبز قبا *sabz-kubā*, Name of a bird (called also سبزك *sabzak*) of a yellowish green. Another species of bird. An inebriating draught made of hemp-leaves and opium.

P سبز قدم *sabz-kadam*, Unfortunate, unlucky.

P سبزك *sabzak*, Green, fresh, flourishing. A flagon. Maslock. Name of a bird (coracias).

P سبز كارگاه *sabz-kār-gāh*, (or سبز كوشك *sabz-kūshk*) The sky.

P سبز كالك *sabz-kūlak*, An unripe melon.

P سبز گرا *sabz-girā*, Name of a bird.

P سبز گلشن *sabz-gulshan*, The sky.

P سبز مال *sabz-māl*, A kind of grape.

P سبز منظره *sabz-manzara*, The sky.

P سبز ميدان *sabz-maydān*, The sky.

P سبز نان *sabz-nān*, Green or mouldy bread.

P سبزنگ *sabzang*, Mouldy, musty.

A سبزوات *sabzawāt*, (pl. of P سبزه) Greens.

P سبزوار *sabzwār*, Name of a country in Persian Irāk; also of a town there. *Sabzawār*, Name of a town in Khurāsān.

P سبزه *sabza*, A green herb, a pot-herb. Verdure. An incipient beard. Bloom. A green stone worn in the ear as an ornament. سبزهٔ بهار *sabzaʻi bahār*, Name of a note in music. سبزهٔ نورس *sabzaʻi naw-ras*, A sprouting or incipient beard.

P سبزه آب *sabza-āb*, Thick stinking water.

P سبزه اندر سبزه *sabza andar sabza*, Name of a note in music.

P سبزه دانه *sabza-dāna*, A violet.

P سبزه زار *sabza-zār*, A verdant mead. Wicked.

P سبزي *sabzī*, Verdure, greenness. Any esculent vegetable. Pleasantness, freshness. Spirituous liquor. A wine-vessel. A mistress of a dark colour. Profit.

P سبزي فروش *sabzī-farosh*, A seller of greens.

A سبسب *sabsab*, An extensive desert. A desert country. بلد سبسب *balad sabsab*, A widely-extended city.

A سبسبة *sabsabat*, (v. n. of سبسب Q) Voiding (urine). Causing to flow.

A سبسطيّة *sabsatiyat*, Name of a town in Palestine, where Zachariah and St. John were buried.

A سبط *sabt*, (v. n. of سبط) Being lank (the hair). Lank hair. سبط الجسم *sabtu'l jism*, Of a fine stature or handsome figure. سبط اليدين *sabtu'l yadayn*, Liberal. مطر سبط *matarun sabtun*, Pouring rain. *Sibt*, (pl. اسباط *asbāt*) A son's son, progeny, family. A tribe (of Israelites). *Sabat*, (v. n. of سبط) Having smooth, lank hair. Lank hair. (pl. اسباط *asbāt*) The herb نصيّ *nasiy* when green (an excellent pasture. It is called حليّ *ha-*

ly when dry). Any tree growing from one root, and having many branches. *Sabit*, Of a good stature, straight, tall. Lank hair. سبط الشعر *sabitu'sh shaʿr*, Lank-haired (man). سبط اليدين *sabitu'l yadayn*, Liberal.

A السبطان *as'sabtāni*, (du.) Hasan and Husayn, sons of Alīy, and grandsons of Muhammad.

A سبطانة *sabatānat*, A hollow tube from which they shoot little birds with balls of clay propelled by the breath. A cane, spear, or javelin. A bird.

A سبطة *sabatat*, A single plant نصيّ *nasīy*.

A سبطر *sibatr*, Sharp, clever, witty. (A lion) stretching himself to make a spring. One whose arrow flies far. Tall, easy, and good-natured.

A سبطرات *sibatrāt*, (Camels) stretched upon the ground.

A سبطرة *sabtarat*, An obeying orders carefully.

A سبع *sabʿ*, (v. n. of سبع) Becoming the seventh, making up the number seven. Taking a seventh part. Twisting a rope of seven plaits. Railing at, insulting. Falling foul of, or biting. Shooting at, or scaring (the wolf). Carrying off a sheep, making havock amongst the flock (a wolf). Stealing. (fem.) Seven. A lion. A great and important affair. The place of the general resurrection. سبع الارض *sabʿu'l arz*, Maiden's hair (a plant). سبع سيّارة *sabʿ sayyāra*, The seven planets. سبع الشعر *sabʿu'sh shaʿr*, Dodder of thyme. سبع الوان *sabʿ alwān*, Seven kinds of food. The seven stories of the heavens; also of the earth. السبع المثاني *as'sabʿu'l masānī*, The first chapter of the Kur'ān (as consisting of seven verses), or the seven long chapters from بقرة *bakrat* to توبة *tawbat*. يوم السبع *yawmu's sabʿ*, A certain holiday amongst the Pagan Arabs. احدي من سبع *ihda' min sabʿ*, One of seven (a name for any dire calamity). *Sibʿ*, An interval of seven days between the times of a camel's drinking. *Subʿ*, The seventh part. *Sabuʿ*, *sabaʿ*, or *sabʿ*, (pl. اسبع *asbuʿ* and سباع *sibāʿ*) A savage beast. A lion. Name of a constellation.

A سبعار *sibʿār*, (or سبعرة *sabʿarat*) The alacrity of a she-camel when briskly tossing her head and whisking her tail.

A سبعان *sabʿāni*, (dual) The two sevens, *i.e.* the seven heavens and the seven earths.

A سبعة *sabʿat*, (according to some *sabaʿat*) (masc.) Seven. سبعةُ سيّارة *sabʿa-i sayyāra*, The seven planets. وزن سبعة *wazn sabʿat*, A weight of seven مثقال *mishkāl*. *Sabʿat* or *sabuʿat*, A lioness.

A سبعطري *sabaʿtara'*, A long slim fellow.

A سبعلل *sabaʿlal*, Thick, bulky (man). Bold, impudent, fearless.

A سبعمائة *sabʿa miʾat*, Seven hundred.

A سبعون *sabʿūna*, (obliq. سبعين) Seventy.

A سبعي *sabuʿīy*, Fierce, ferocious, fell, ferine.

A سبعية *sabuʿīyat*, Fierceness, cruelty, wildness.

P سبغ *sabagh*, Fine, precious, pure, clean. Beautiful, elegant, graceful, lovely. A rapacious animal. A palace having many windows of glass. A house painted with a number of figures. A large loaf or cake toasted on the coals or under the ashes. *Subugh*, The roof of a house. A honeycomb. A reed.

A سبغ *subugh*, Clad in a coat of mail, covering the entire body.

P سبغانه *sabghāna*, Earnest. *Subghāna*, Tall.

A سبغة *subghat*, Ease, affluence, abundance of the enjoyments of life.

A سبغللاً *sabaghlalan*, Naked and unarmed.

P سبفانه *sabfāna*, Cup, bowl. *Subfāna*, Tall.

A سبق *sabk*, (v. n. of سبق) Going before, taking the lead, preceding, excelling, outstripping, surpassing. Coming in first at a horse-race. Overcoming. Aggression. ما سبق *mā sabaka*, The above-mentioned. *Sabak*, A lecture, lesson. (pl. اسباق *asbāk*) A bet, stake (at a horse-race, or in shooting at a mark). P سبق بردن *sabak burdan*, To surpass, overcome, take the lead, carry precedency. To do much. سبق گفتن *sabak guftan*, To say a lesson.

A سبّق *subbak*, (pl. of سابق *sābik*) By-gone, past.

A سبقان *sibhāni*, Two contending (especially at a horse-race).

A سبقة *subkat*, A wager, a stake.

P سبقتاش *sabak-tāsh*, A fellow-student.

A سبك *sabk*, A melting, casting, pouring.

P سبك *sabuk*, Light (not heavy). Light-footed, expeditious, active. Undignified, degrading, unsteady. Shallow. Independent. Haste, despatch. سبك شدن *sabuk shudan*, To be light. To be smoothed. To be alleviated. To be despised. سبك گرفتن *sabuk giriftan*, To despise. To hold light. *Sibik*, Name of a bird which flies towards the sun. *Subik*, Soft. Weak. Softness, weakness.

P سبكاد *sabkād*, Summit of a mountain. The crown of the head.

P سبكبار *subuk-bār*, Of a light weight, ready to rise and travel. Lightly loaded, unencumbered. Jocund, blithe, free from care.

P سبك پاي *sabuk-pāy*, Light of foot. A postman. A post-horse. A courier. Inconstant.

P سبك پر *sabuk-par*, Swift-winged.

P سبكتگين *sabuktigīn*, Name of a brave general (and the father of Sultān Mahmūd, founder of the dynasty of the Ghaznawīds, who flourished in the beginning of the eleventh century; and hence any man distinguished for intrepidity). A precious thing. A divorced woman returning to her husband, and cohabiting with him without a remarriage (reckoned infamous); an adulteress, a whore.

P سبكچه *sabukcha*, Somewhat light.

P سبكخرد *sabuk-khirad*, Flighty, injudicious.

P سبك خيز *sabuk-khez*, Vigilant, quick, brisk, active. A rivulet (as rising rapidly).

P سبكداد *sabuk-dād*, Active, nimble, clever.

P سبكدار *sabuk-dār*, A postman. A letter-bag.

P سبكدارو *sabuk-dārū*, Any medicine which soon operates. A physician who administers pleasant medicines to his patient.

P سبك داشت *sabuk-dāsht*, Contempt.

P سبك دست *sabuk-dast*, Expert, dexterous.

P سبك دستي *sabuk-dastī*, Quickness, dexterity.

P سبك رفتار *sabuk-raftār*, Swift-paced.

P سبك رو *sabuk-rav*, Who travels quickly.

P سبك روح *sabuk-rūh*, Merry, jovial, jolly.

P سبك سار *sabuk-sār*, Light-headed. Contemptible. Helpless. Unsteady, undignified. Hasty. A fool. Alone, independent.

P سبك ساران *sabuk-sārān*, Worldly persons.

P سبك سايه *sabuk-sāya*, Fleeting, transient.

P سبكسر *sabuk-sar*, Light-headed. Sober.

P سبك سران *sabuk-sarān*, Poor, low persons.

P سبك سنگ *sabuk-sang*, Light, undignified.

P سبك سير *sabuk-ser*, Soon satisfied.

P سبك عنان *sabuk-ʿinān*, Swift. Tractable.

P سبك لقا *sabuk-likā*, Frank, open, prepossessing. Prompt, obedient.

P سبكمايه *sabuk-māya*, Cheap. Ignorant.

P سبك مزاج *sabuk-mizāj*, (or سبك مغز *sabuk-maghz*) Weak. Fickle, inconstant, irresolute.

P سبكي *sabukī*, Lightness, levity. Littleness. Weakness of mind. Insult.

A سبل *subl*, An ear of corn, or an ear well filled with grain. Inclined. *Sabal*, Rain (especially before it has touched the ground). The nose. Execration, reproach, contumely. A spear. A long garment. An ear of corn. A disease or a web in the eye. Name of an excellent horse. سبل من رماح *sabalun mir' rimāhin*, Bit of a spear (long or short). *Subul*, (pl. of سبيل *sabīl*) Ways. Modes of life.

A سبلاء *sablāʾ*, Long-lashed (eye).

P سبلان *sabalān*, A mountain near Ardebil.

A سبلانيّ *sabalānīy*, Long-mustachioed (man).

A سبلة *sablat* or *sabalat*, (pl. سبال *sibāl*) Whiskers, mustachios. Hair in a camel's nostrils. Garments, robes. P سبلت سست كردن *sablat sust kardan*, To weaken or distress. A *Sublat*, Widely-extended rain. *Sabalat*, Thinness of a (camel's) skin. The pit of the chest, the sticking place (in camels). نشر سبلته *nashara sabalatahu*, He came in a menacing mood. *Sabalat* or *sublat*, A waving ear of corn. *Sabilat*, Long, pendulous (testicle).

P سبلت *siblit* or *sibilt*, Glue.

A سبنتيٰ *sabanta'*, (pl. سبانت *sabānit*) Bold (man or beast). A leopard.

P سبنج *sibunj*, The beam of a plough.

A سبنجونة *sabanjūnat*, A fur pelisse of fox-skin (said to be derived from P آسمان گون *āsmān-gūn*).

A سبنداة *sabandāt*, Bold. Long, tall.

A سبنديٰ *sabanda'*, (pl. سباند *sabānid* and سباندة *sabānidat*) Bold (man or beast). A leopard. A kind of silken stuff adorned with figures of oranges.

A سبنيّة *sabanīyat*, Black trousers for females (from سبن *saban*, A district of Baghdād).

P سبو *sabo*, A cup, ewer, jar, glass, pitcher, pot. سبو شكستن *sabo shikastan*, To break the cup (of hope), to despair. To spill wine: or to forbid its use.

A سبوب *subūb*, (pl. of سبّ *sibb*) Ropes. Sashes, or female head-dresses.

A سبوت *subūt*, (pl. of سبت *sabt*) Sabbaths.

P سبوچه *sabocha*, A little pitcher, jar, or ewer.

A سبوح *sabūh*, (pl. سبحاء *subahāʼ*) A swimmer. A pleasant-paced horse.

A سبّوح *subbūh* or *sabbūh*, Holy (epithet of God).

A سبوحة *sabūhat*, Mecca. The valley of Arafāt.

A سبّورة *sabbūrat*, A tablet, slate for writing on, the writing of which may be afterwards effaced.

P سبوره *sabūra*, A catamite.

P سبوس *sabos* or *subos*, Bran, chaff. Scurf.

P سبوسه *sabosa*, Dandriff, scurf. Bran. Sawdust. A weevil. Froth.

P سبوسه ناك *subosanāk*, Scaly, scurfy (head).

A سبوط *subūt*, (or سبوطة *subūtat*) (v. n. of سبط) Being lank (hair).

A سبوع *subūʻ*, A week.

A سبوعا *subūʻan*, Seven times.

A سبوغ *subūgh*, (v. n. of سبغ) Being ample, profuse, complete (benefit). Being long, reaching the ground. Inclining to and arriving at (one's home).

A سبولة *sabūlat* or *subulat*, A head of hair. An ear of corn full of grains.

A سبه *sabah*, Dotage.

A سبهلل *sabahlal*, Idle. جاءنا سبهللا *jāʼanā sabahlalan*, He came to us, being idle; or self-important and careless. الضلال بن السبهلل *az zalālu 'bnu's sabahlal*, False, vain, trifling.

A سبي *saby*, (v. n. of سبي) Making a captive, taking prisoner. (A woman) stealing the heart (of a man). Purchasing and carrying wine from one country to another. Digging until water is reached. Making a stranger. (God) leading to a great distance. (pl. سبيّ *sibiy*) Whatever is carried to a distance. Women (either because they steal the hearts of men, or because they are made captive and possessed). *Siby*, The slough of a snake.

A سبيّ *sabiy*, (pl. سبايا *sabāya'*) A captive, a prisoner. Drift wood, timber carried by a stream from place to place. A snake's slough.

A سبيب *sabīb*, (pl. سبائب *sabāʼib*) A reviler. Hair hanging over the forehead of a horse; the mane; the tail. A handful of hair. Entangled hair.

A سبيبة *sabībat*, (pl. سبائب *sabāʼib*) A linen vest or cloth. Hair hanging over the forehead of a horse. The mane. The tail. A handful or bunch of hair. A clump of the thorny trees عضاة *ʻizāt*.

A سبّيبا *sibbība'*, A railing, reproaching, cursing.

A سبيئة *sabīʼat*, Wine.

A سبيّة *sabīyat*, Wine carried from one country to another. A female captive. A pearl brought up by a diver.

P سبيج *sabīj*, A shirt without sleeves. A black woollen garment.

A سبيجة *sabījat*, A sleeveless shirt. A black vest.

A سبيخ *sabīkh*, (pl. سبائخ *sabāʼikh*) Any thing which falls from carded cotton, or birds' feathers. Bowed cotton folded up for spinning. Deep sleep.

A سبيخة *sabīkhat*, A piece of cotton spread out, whereon any medicament is laid. Deep sleep.

A سبيطر *sabaytar*, Tall. A long-necked bird.

A سبيع *sabīʻ*, A seventh. Name of a family.

A سبيكة *sabīkat*, (pl. سبائك *sabāʼik*) A mass, ingot, bar, or lamina of gold or silver. P سيمين سبيكه *sīmīn-sabīka*, A bar or ingot of silver.

A سبيل *sabīl*, (pl. سبل *subul*) A way, road, path. A straight and right road. A mode, manner, means. Opportunity of attacking an enemy. Means of effecting a reconciliation. Conjunction, link, bond of union. Necessity. Water distributed to thirsty travellers during the first ten days of the Muharram. Way of escape. ابن السبيل *ibnu's sabīl*, Son of the way, *i. e.* a traveller. Any one who is left behind on the road, through the death, fatigue, or sickness of his beast. ابناء سبيل *abnāʼi sabīl*, Wayfaring men. في سبيل الله *fī sabīl allāh*, In the way of God, *i. e.* for the love of God, for sacred uses. A war against infidels. سبيل الضلال *sabīlu'z zalāl*, The way of error. P سبيل كردن *sabīl kardan*, To prepare, arrange, put in order.

P سبيل *sibīl*, Whiskers, mustachios.

A سبيلان *sabīlāni*, (Two ways) Fore and aft.

A سبيلة *sabīlat*, A way, road, path.

P سبيوش *sibyūsh*, Seed of fleawort.

A سبيئ *sabīʼ*, A snake's slough.

A سبيئة *sabīʼat*, A female captive. Wine.

P سپا *sipā*, A tripod. Three-legged (stool).

P سپار *sipār*, A wine-press. A large trough into which the grapes are thrown, and pressed with the feet. (in compos.) Committing, resigning, recommending, giving in charge. *Sipār* or *supār*, Household furniture. A vessel in general, especially one in which grapes are carried from place to place. *Supār*, A ploughshare.

P سپاردن *sipārdan* or *supārdan*, To resign.

P سپارده *sipārda*, Committed to.

P سپارش *sipārish*, Recommendation, delegation, commission, charge. Intercession. سپارش كردن *sipārish kardan*, To recommend to the care of another, to consign. To command.

P سپارنده *sipāranda*, A betrayer, traitor.

P سپاروك *sapārūk*, A pigeon.

P سپاره *sapāra*, A whetstone. *Sipāra*, (from سي *sī*, Thirty, and پاره *pāra*, A portion) A chapter, or rather a thirtieth part of the Kur'ān.

P سپاري *sipārī*, The stalk of corn. An ear of corn or barley. *Supārī*, The areca-nut.

P سپاريدن *sipārīdan*, To delegate, empower, commit, charge. To finish, complete. To pursue, or perform (a voyage).

P سپاس *sipās*, Praise, thanksgiving. Kindness, grace, favour. Consent, approval. Prayer.

P سپاس دار *sipās-dār*, Grateful, thankful.

P سپاس داري *sipās-dārī*, Gratitude, thanksgiving. سپاس داري كردن, To return thanks.

P سپاس گذاري *sipās-guzārī*, A thanksgiving.

P سپاسه *sipāsa*, Gratitude, thanksgiving. Kindness, humanity. An obligation, a favour by which one is bound to gratitude.

P سپاسي *sipāsī*, A beggar.

P سپاسيان *sipāsiyān*, Beggars. Those to whom the first apostle of Persia was sent.

P سپاسيدن *sipāsīdan*, To praise (God) for benefits received. To implore assistance, grace, or favour.

P سپاغ *sipāgh*, A thatched house. Meat eaten with bread.

P سپاناج *sipānāj* or سپاناخ *sipānākh*, Spinage.

P سپاوه *sipāva*, Magnificence, pomp, power.

P سپاه *sipāh* or *supāh*, An army, a militia. Soldiers, cavalry. سپاه شدن *sipāh shudan*, To muster. سپاه كردن *sipāh kardan*, To go a warfaring. سپاه مور شمار *sipāhi mor-shumār*, An army numerous as pismires. پادشاه انجم سپاه *pādshāhi anjum-sipāh*, A king with an army equalling the stars in number.

P سپاهان *sipāhān*, (pl. of سپاه) Soldiers. Ispāhān.

P سپاهسالار *sipāh-sālār*, General of an army.

P سپاهگري *sipāhgarī*, The military profession.

P سپاهي *sipāhī*, Military, belonging to an army. A horseman, cavalier. A military tenant, lord, feudal chief of a town or village. *Sipāhe*, One soldier, sepoy.

P سپاهيان *sipāhiyān*, (pl. of سپاهي) Soldiers.

P سپايه *si-pāya*, A tripod, trevet. A horse-militia. سپايهٔ هوائي *si-pāyaʼi hawāʼī*, (The airy tripod) the constellation called the Eagle.

P سپتاك *siptāk*, White paint for the face.

P سپتان *siptān*, Liquorice-root.

P سپختن *supukhtan*, To drive (as a nail into a wall, or a stake into the ground). To stab.

P سپد *sapad*, A basket. A grain. A grass. A little. *Sipad*, The earth. Name of an angel. Name of the 12th solar month. The 5th of the month. Rue.

P سپد چين *sapad-chīn*, Grapes remaining after the vintage.

P سپد دار *sapad-dār*, A basket-bearer.

P سپدگر *sapadgar*, A basket-maker.

P سپر *sipar*, A shield, buckler, target. Travelling, treading upon. (A mill) having three sails. سپر آتشين *sipari ātishīn*, The sun. سپر سياه *sipari-siyāh*, The sun. سپر شنگرفي *sipari shangarfī*, The sun. سپر گاو *sipari gāw*, A buckler made of the hide of a buffalo. سپر انداخت *sipar andākht*, (سپر افكند *sipar afkand*, also سپر برآب افكند *sipar bar āb afkand*) He threw away his shield, *i. e.*

he surrendered, was conquered, laid down his arms.

P سپرانيدن *sipurānīdan*, To cause, allow, or command to be trodden under foot.

P سپرد *sipurd* or *supurd*, Charge, keeping, care, trust. Solitude. Contentment. Patience. Long-suffering. Submission, humility. Perseverance in a right course. A being trodden. Fatigue from travelling. The conclusion of a song.

P سپر دادة *sipar-dāda*, Mace.

P سپردار *sipar-dār*, A shield-bearer.

P سپرداري *sipar-dārī*, Protecting, shielding.

P سپردگي *sipurdagī*, A treading, a trampling.

P سپردن *sipardan*, To fold up, wrap together. *Sipardan* or *sapardan*, To travel. *Sipurdan*, To give in charge, entrust, consign, make over to. To betray. To supply, to strengthen. To cause to arrive. To sit solitary. To lay up. To be humble, content, resigned. To trample. To be trampled.

P سپردني *sipurdanī*, Fit to be entrusted.

P سپردة *saparda* or *siparda*, Trampled. Travelled. Folded.

P سپرز *supurz*, The spleen, the milt.

P سپرز رنگ *supurz-rang*, Spleen-coloured.

P سپرش *siparish*, A skirt. A handkerchief, veil.

P سپرغم *spargham* or *sipragham*, Sweet basil. Marjoram.

P سپرك *siprak* or *siparak*, A herb which, boiled, dyes yellow. *Siparak*, A little shield. The measles.

P سپرگي *sipar* or *sapragī*, Pain, grief, affliction.

P سپرلوس *siparlos*, A king's palace.

P سپرم *siporsiparam*, Sweet basil. Always young.

P سپرنگ *siparang*, A city near Samarkand.

P سپرة *sipra*, Vitriol. A kind of game.

P سپرهم *siparham*, Sweet basil.

P سپري *siparī*, Any thing brought to a conclusion. Trampled under foot. Annihilated. A broad-headed arrow. Complete, perfect. A herb producing seed. سپري شدن *siparī shudan*, To be finished, ended, exhausted, annihilated. سپري گردانيدن *siparī gardānīdan*, To close, finish, annihilate, exterminate. سپري كردن *siparī kardan*, To exhaust.

P سپريدن *siparīdan*, To finish, perfect.

P سپريس *sipres*, A race-ground.

P سپريغ *saprīgh*, A full bunch of grapes or dates. A straight road. *Saprīgh* or *suparīgh*, Ears of wheat, especially those left after reaping. A full bunch of grapes, still hard, or beginning to form.

P سپريگ *siprīg*, Trefoil. Yellow-dying wood.

P سپزگي *sipazgī*, Affliction, sadness, sorrow.

P سپس *sipas*, Behind, at the back, after. The backside. زان سپس *'zān sipas*, After that. زين سپس *'zīn sipas*, After this. *Supus*, A louse. سپس جستن *supus justan*, To louse, to hunt for lice. بيضۀ سپس *bayzaᵢi supus*, The egg of a louse, a nit.

P سپسار *sipsār*, A broker.

P سپسا رفتن *sipasā raftan*, To retreat.

P سپسايگي *sipasāyagī*, Retrogression, motion back. سپسايگي رفتن *sipasāyagī raftan*, To retreat.

P سپست *sapist*, A stink. Nasty, dirty, stinking. Any fattening herb, especially trefoil. *Supust*, Trefoil, clover. Offensive, stinking (as the smell of fish, damp clothes, pitch, copper vessels).

P سپستان *sipistān*, Sebestens.

P سپستر *sipastar*, Posterior, farther back.

P سپستزار *supustzār*, A clover-field.

P سپستة *sapista*, A fetid smell.

P سپس جستگي *supus-justagī*, Search for lice.

P سپس رفتگيء بيني *sipas raftagiᵢi bīnī*, A turning up or cocking of the nose.

P سپس رو *sipas-rav*, A follower.

P سپسين *sipasīn*, Hindermost.

P سپش *sipush*, Seed of fleawort.

P سپغ *supugh*, The roof of a house. A honeycomb. A reed.

P سپك *siph*, A yellow blight on corn.

P سپكاد *siphād*, Crown of head: mountain-top.

P سپل *sapal*, Foot of a camel or elephant.

P سپنج *sipanj*, A place where one halts or rests for a few days; hence metaphorically, The world. A lodge for those who watch fields. A stranger, a guest. Any thing easily corrupted, a perishable commodity. Any thing borrowed or lent. A place abounding in grass and water. Fifteen (سه *sih*, Three, and پنج *panj*, Five). سپنج كعبتين *sipanji kaᶜbatayn*, Thirty chessmen or table-men at the game of نرد *nard*, or tables.

P سپنجاب *sipanjāb*, Name of a country.

P سپنج خانه *sipanj-khāna*, Hired house: world.

P سپنجي *sipanjī*, Borrowed: transient, fleeting.

P سپند *sipand*, Wild rue (of which and its seeds they prepare a fumigation against malignant eyes). Name of a mountain.

P سپندار *sipandār*, The stay of the sun in Pisces. A candle. Name of the son of Gushtāsp.

P سپندارمذ *sipandārmuz*, The twelfth month of the Persian year (February), so called from an angel supposed to preside over the earth. The earth.

P سپند آسا *sipand-āsā*, Brisk, quick.

P سپندان *sa* or *sipandān*, The seed of wild rue. Mustard. Nasturtium. سپندان تلخ *sipandāni talkh*, The bitter seed of a certain herb. Plantane. Cresses. سپندان خرد *sipandāni khurd*, Mustard-seed. سپندان سرخ *sipandāni surkh*, Cresses. سپندان گنده *sipandāni ganda*, Rue.

P سپندسوز *sipand-soz*, Who fumigates with rue.

P سپندوز *sipandoz*, A piece of wood having a round hole in it, fixed on the top of a tent-pole.

P سپندين *sipandīn*, Seed of wild rue. Mustard.

P سپنگور *sapangūr*, Nightshade.

P سپوخ *sipokh*, A point, puncture, poke.

P سپوختن *sipokhtan* or *sapokhtan*, To prick, pierce, transfix, thrust, poke. To thrust one thing violently into another. To draw forth one thing from another. To throw down. To cause to fall into a hole.

P سپوختة *sipokhta* or *sapokhta*, Thrust violently in, poked. Drawn forth.

P سپوز *sipoz*, A puncture. Extraction. Insertion. (in comp.) Pricking. Drawing out. Fixing in.

P سپوزگار *sipozgār*, Dilatory, tedious, negligent.

P سپوزيدن *supozīdan*, To prick, pierce, thrust.

P سپه *sipah* or *supah*, Army, soldiery, cavalry.

P سپهابد *sipahā-bad*, A commander, general.

P سپهبد *sipah-bud*, (or بدة *buda*) An emperor, general, lord, chief. A title of the kings of Tabaristān.

P سپهبدان *sipahbudān*, Name of a musical note.

P سپه دار *sipah-dār*, Commander of an army.

P سپهداري *sipah-dārī*, Command of an army.

P سپهر *sipihr*, The heavens, sky, sphere, celestial globe. Fortune. The world. Time. The sun. سپهر اعظم *sipihri aᶜzam*, (or سپهر پوشيدة *sipihri poshīda*) The heaven of heavens. سپهر برين *sipihri barīn*, The ninth or highest heaven. سپهر بوقلمون *sipihri būkalamūn*, The varying sky. سپهر دولابي *sipihri dūlābī*, (or سپهر زنگاري *sipihri zangārī*) The sky. سپهر هشتم *sipihri hashtum*, The eighth sphere, *i.e.* the Zodiac.

P سپهرار *sipihrār*, The sphere of fire.

P سپهر آفرين *sipihr-āfirīn*, God, the creator.

P سپهرم *sipahram*, Name of a wrestler of Tūrān.

P سپهرة بند *sipihra-band*, A magician.

P سپهسالار *sipah-sālār*, Commander-in-chief.

P سپه سالاري *sipah-sālārī*, Command of an army.

P سپهكش *sipah-kash*, (Army-leading) A general.

P سپيتاك *sa* or *sipetāk*, White paint for the face.

P سپيچه *supecha*, *sipecha*, or *sapecha*, A pellicle floating on the surface of vinegar.

P سپيخ *sapīkh*, The haunt of a wild beast. A hunter's retreat.

P سپيد *saped*, White. Name of a fort, of a demon, and of a river. سپيد شدن *saped shudan*, To be clear, evident, known. سپيد و سياه *saped u siyāh*, White and black. Day and night. Good and bad. Arabians and Persians. All creatures.

P سپيدا *sapedā*, Ceruse, white-lead.

P سپيداب *sapedāb*, White-lead. A sort of food.

P سپيداج *sapedāj*, Ceruse, white-lead.

P سپيدار *sapedār*, The white poplar. A willow.

P سپيدان *sipīdān*, A fort built by Jamshed.

P سپيدبا *saped-bā*, Meat, onions, butter, olives, and dry cheese (mixed without spices or seasoning).

P سپيد بالا *saped-bālā*, First dawn of day.

P سپيد بام *saped-bām*, A whitish colour.

P سپيد بر *saped-bar*, The summer.

P سپيد برگ *saped-barg*, Beet, spinage.

P سپيد پا *saped-pā*, (White-foot) One who brings good luck.

P سپيد پر *saped-par*, (White-wing) A gnat.

P سپيد پوست *saped-post*, White-skinned. Tin.

P سپيد پوش *saped-posh*, Clothed in white. The white poplar.

P سپيد پهنا *saped-pahnā*, Second or true dawn.

P سپيد تاك *saped-tāk*, A shrub used in tanning, galangale.

P سپيد جامگان *saped-jāmagān*, Clad in white. Fire-worshippers (pl. of سپيد جامه *saped-jāma*).

P سپيد خار *saped-khār*, A kind of thistle.

P سپيد خوار *saped-khwār*, An animal which devours dead bodies.

P سپيد دار *saped-dār*, A willow.

P سپيد دان *sapeddān*, Mustard.

P سپيد دست *saped-dast*, Liberal, munificent. Happy, fortunate, blest. Moses (leprous-handed).

P سپيد دم *saped-dum*, A white-tailed pigeon. A kind of plant.

P سپيد رو *saped-rav*, An excellent falcon. *Saped-rū*, Complete. Excellent, behaving with propriety. A beetle.

P سپيد رود *saped-rūd*, A river in Azarbayjān.

P سپيد روي *saped-rūy*, Tin. Fortunate. Bright-faced. Red-faced.

P سپيد فام *saped-fām*, Whitish-coloured.

P سپيد كار *saped-kār*, Honest, upright. Liberal.

P سپيدگي *sapedagī*, Whitish. White fard.

P سپيد مرد *saped mard*, A flower like the anemone.

P سپيد مو *saped-mū* or *mo*, Grey-haired.

P سپيد موئي *saped-mūī*, Grey-hairedness.

P سپيد مهره *saped muhra*, A tube, a post-boy's horn; a shell which they sound as a trumpet. Small shells, conchulæ veneris.

P سپيد نامه *saped-nāma*, Of fair character.

P سپيد وا *saped-wā*, A dish made of sour milk.

P سپيده *sapeda*, Whiteness. The white of an eye. The dawn. The white of an egg. سپيدهٔ زنان *sapeda-i zanān*, Ladies' white, *i.e.* a white fard.

P سپيده بالا *sapeda-bālā*, The false dawn.

P سپيده دم *sapeda-dam*, The dawn. *Sapeda-dum*, Name of a plant resembling the anemone.

P سپيدي *sapedī*, Whiteness, purity. A white substance cast forth by a female in want of the male. سپيديء خايهء مرغ *sapedī-i khāya-i murgh*, The white of an egg.

P سپي ديو *sape-dev*, (for ديو سپيد *devi saped*) Name of a demon killed by Rustam.

P سپيرك *sapīrak*, (or سپيرو *sapīrū*) A red-winged insect found in baths.

P سپيل *sapīl*, The shrill cries of birds.

A ستّ *satt*, Foul language. A vice, blemish, stain. *Sitt*, (originally سدس *sids*) Six (females). ستّ عشرة *sitta ʿashrata*, Sixteen (males).

P ستا *satā*, A commentary on the Zand. *Sitā*, Praise, benediction. A kind of canopy. A three-stringed instrument. Triple, three-thread. The third game of nard. Name of a musical note. Three goblets of wine for cleansing the stomach. (in compos.) A praiser, flatterer. خود ستا *khwud-sitā*, A self-praiser. *Sutā*, A comment on the Zand.

A ستا *sata'*, Kindness, favour, benefit.

A ستاع *sitāʿ*, A playing at a romping game in which they kick each other on the backside.

P ستاخ *sitākh*, A branch of a tree twining about another. A young branch shooting from another.

P ستادن *satādan*, To take away, to carry off. *Sitādan*, To take, to carry away. To stand, stay.

P ستاده *sitāda*, Taken, carried away. Placed, deposited. Stood, standing.

P ستاذاب *sitāz-āb*, The trickling of water. The spirting up of water.

P ستار *satār*, A star. A mosquito-curtain. *Sitār*, A three-stringed guitar. A rising star.

A ستار *sitār*, (pl. ستر *sutur*) A veil, covering.

A ستّار *sattār*, The keeper of the curtain, the porter at the royal doorway. (An attribute of God) covering: as, ستّار العيوب *sattāru'l ʿuyūb*, Hiding sins (casting a veil of mercy over them).

P ستار باز *sitār-bāz*, A player on the guitar.

A ستارة *sitārat*, (pl. ستائر *satāʾir*) A covering. Protection. A skin over the nail. A palisade.

P ستارچه *sitārcha*, A little star. A spark.

P ستارگان *sitāragān*, (pl. of ستاره) Stars.

P ستاره *satāra*, A mosquito-curtain. A sort of canopy. A star. A rule for drawing right lines. *Sitāra*, A star. Horoscope, nativity. Fortune, felicity. A spark. A geometrical rule by which right lines are drawn. Form, pattern. A kind of guitar with three strings. The third game at نرد *nard*. A kind of fire-work. A kind of canopy or awning. A banner. A threshold. Quicksilver. Name of a city in India. ستارهٔ بام *sitāra-i bām*, The morning star. ستارهٔ دمدار *sitāra-i dum-dār*, (or دنباله دار *dumbāla-dār*) A comet. ستارهٔ زمين *sitāra-i zamīn*, Talc, lapis specularis. ستارهٔ قلندران *sitāra-i kalandarān*, The sun. ستاره شمردن *sitāra shumurdan*, To count the stars. To lie awake.

P ستاره پيشاني *sitāra-peshānī*, Having a star on the forehead (reckoned a blemish in a horse).

P ستاره دان *sitāra-dān*, An astrologer.

P ستاره سوختگي *sitāra-sokhtagī*, Bad luck.

P ستاره سوخته *sitāra-sokhta*, Ill-fated.

P ستاره شمر *sitāra-shumur*, An astrologer.

P ستاره شناس *sitāra-shinās*, An astrologer.

A ستّاريّ *sattāriy*, Belonging to a coverer.

P ستاشتن *sitāshtan*, To take, seize, ravish.

P ستاغ *sitāgh*, Barren. A colt not yet saddled. A horse. A horn. Tamarisk. An abortion. A camel giving much milk. The buttocks.

P ستافند *sitāfand*, A portico. A stage, theatre.

P ستاك *sitāk*, Young tree, shoot, sucker, tendril.

A ستال *sitāl*, A following in succession.

A ستالة *sutālat*, Worst left after the best is gone.

P ستام *sitām*, The ornamented part of a saddle. The nail of a horse-shoe. A cymbal. A kettle-drum. Ornaments of gold or silver (especially horse-furniture). A threshold.

P ستان *satān*, (in compos.) Seizing, taking, occupying: as, باج ستان *bāj-satān*, Receiving toll or duty. دلستان *dil-satān*, Ravishing the heart. شاه كشورستان *shāhi kishwar-satān*, A monarch, conquering kingdoms. *Sitān*, Reclining, sleeping or lying on the back. Impatient, weak, feeble. ستان افگندن *sitān afgandan*, To throw flat upon the back. (for آستان *āstān*) A threshold. *Stān*, when preceded by a quiescent letter, and *istān*, when preceded by a moveable one, is an affix denoting "place:" as, خرماستان *khurmāstān*, A palm-grove, بوستان *bostān*, A fruit-garden, گلستان *gulistān*, A flower-garden.

P ستانا *satānā*, Receiving.

P ستاندن *satāndan*, To take. To take a wife.

P ستانده *satānda*, Seized. Carried off.

P ستانند *satānand*, They take. An edifice supported by pillars. ستانند و دهند *satānand u dihand*, They take and give.

P ستانه *sitāna* A threshold. Tears (of the vine); also the bud or eye. A wound from a malignant eye.

P ستانيدن *satānīdan*, To take, to seize.

P ستاوند *sa* or *sutāwand*, A portico. A balcony, a lofty veranda supported by a single pillar.

P ستاوه *satāwa* or *sitāwa*, Fraud, deceit.

P ستاويز *satāwez*, Eaves. A portico. *Sitāwez*, A market-place, shambles. A piece of timber with hooks on which they hang meat in the markets. The bench of a magistrate.

P ستاوين *satāwīn*, A pillared room. Shambles.

P ستاه *sitāh*, A star. Base silver. Name of a note in music.

A ستاهيّ *sutāhiy*, (pl. ستهان *suthān*) One who has large posteriors. Fond of large buttocks.

A ستائر *satāʾir*, (pl. of ستارة *sitārat*) Veils, coverings. Palisades.

P ستايش *sitāyish*, Praise, encomium, benediction, returning thanks. Glory. An enigma. ستايش كردن *sitāyish kardan*, (or دادن *dādan*) To glorify God, to return thanks.

P ستايشگاه *sitāyish-gāh*, The place of praise, *i. e.* the last verse of a Persian ode; called also شاه بيت *shāh-bayt*, The royal distich; in which the poet, without the least imputation of vanity, generally addresses himself in the highest strain of self-approbation.

P ستاينده *sitāyanda*, A praiser, panegyrist.

P ستاييدن *sitāyīdan*, To praise. To call.

A ستب *satb*, Fatigued (pace); creeping.

P ستبر *sitabr*, Thick, coarse. Hard, stiff.

P ستبر ناي *sitabr-nāy*, Thickness, coarseness. A large size.

P ستبري *sitabrī*, Thickness. ستبريء آواز *sitabrī-i āwāz*, Hoarseness, gruffness of voice.

A ستّة *sittat*, Six (males). ستّة ضروريّة *sittat zarūriyat*, Six necessary things, by physicians called non-naturals: namely, air, meat and drink, bodily motion and rest, spiritual movement and repose, sleep and waking, excretion and retention.

P ستخر *sitakhr*, A pond, cistern. Name of a fort.

P ستخسه *sitakhsa*, A sieve.

P ستخوان *sutukhwān*, A bone. Stone of fruit.

P ستخيز *satkhez*, The resurrection.

P ستدن *sitadan*, To take, seize, carry off.

P ستده *sitada*, Received, taken. Placed.

A ستر *satara*, (fut. يستر *yasturu*) He veiled.

A ستر *satr*, (v.n. of ستر) Covering, veiling, concealing. Suppressing, restraining, keeping back. *Sitr*, (pl. ستور *sutūr* and استار *astār*) A veil, covering. Fear, shame, modesty. Work, labour. *Satar*, A shield, buckler. *Sutur*, (pl. of ستار *sitār*) Veils.

P ستر *satar*, A mule. *Sutur*, Shaving. A knife, razor. موي ستر *mūy* or *moy-sutur*, A barber.

P سترب *sitrab*, A satrap (obsolete).

P ستربانگ *suturbāng* or *suturbānag*, A starling. A wagtail.

A سترة *sutrat*, Any thing which covers or defends, as a veil, awning, shield, wall, and the like.

P ستردن *si* or *suturdan*, To shave, scrape, pare, pull out hairs. To erase, cancel, abolish, cut off.

P سترده *suturda*, Shaved, erased. Cut off.

P سترده پا *suturdā-pa*, One whose feet are cut off.

P ستر سا *satar-sā*, Sense, feeling.

P ستر سائي *satarsāī*, Obvious to sight or sense.

P ستركا *satarkā*, A sort of gum.

P ستركش *suturkish*, Uneasiness. Greatness.

P سترگ *saturg*, *siturg*, or *suturg*, Impudent. Quarrelsome, passionate. Large, and able-bodied. Rough, rugged. انگشت سترگ *angushti suturg*, The large finger, *i.e.* the thumb.

P سترنگ *satrang*, The mandrake. Chess.

P ستروك *satrūk*, An idle, prating fellow, addicted to thieving. Quarrelsome, contentious. Passionate, bad-tempered. Indigent. Idle: useless.

P سترون *satarwan* or *suturwan*, (Mule-like) Barren. A woman who has only borne one son.

P ستره *sutura* or *suturra*, A razor. The hire of a house.

P ستزيدن *sitizīdan*, To importune, urge. To contend. To be stubborn, headstrong, tyrannical.

A ستل *satl*, (v. n. of ستل) Following in close succession (men, tears, or pearls). *Satal*, (pl. ستلان *sitlān* or *sutlān*) An eagle. Followers.

P ستل *satal*, Injury, hurt. *Sital*, A pond, reservoir. *Sutul*, Wheat (in the ear) scarcely ripe, scorched, and bruised (which they eat some days before harvest, in order to taste the first-fruits).

A ستلان *sit* or *sutlān*, (pl. of ستل *satal*) Eagles.

P ستم *sitam*, Tyranny, oppression, injustice, extortion, distress, injury, violence, affliction, threatening, vexation. A heavy misfortune. Seeing or knowing. Deliberately, designedly, purposely. ستم كردن *sitam kardan*, To oppress.

P ستم آباد *sitam-ābād*, Land of oppression: world.

P ستم آميز *sitam-āmez*, Tyrannical, cruel.

A ستمائة *sitta-miₐat*, Six hundred.

P ستم پرور *sitam-parwar*, An oppressor. One who connives at or patronizes oppression.

P ستم ديده *sitam-dīda*, (pl. ديدگان) Oppressed.

P ستم رسيدگان *sitam-rasīdagān*, The oppressed.

P ستمكار *sitam-kār*, A tyrant, oppressor.

P ستم كش *sitam-kash*, Oppression-enduring.

P ستمكشيده *sitam-kashīda*, Oppressed.

P ستم كيش *sitam-kesh*, An oppressor.

P ستمگر *sitamgar*, Cruel, oppressive. A tyrant.

P ستمگري *sitamgarī*, Tyranny, oppression.

P ستمي *sitamī*, Tyranny, injury.

P ستميدن *sitamīdan*, To oppress. To be headstrong.

P ستن آوند *sutun-āwand* or *situn-āvand*, A portico or veranda supported by a single column.

P ستنبر *sitambar*, Name of an herb like mint.

P ستنبه *sitamba*, Strong, robust, powerful, bold. The night-mare. Any hideous or terrifying form. Contumacious, litigious, unwilling to listen.

P ستنج *satanj* or *sitanj*, Provisions stored up. *Sitanj*, A thrashing instrument.

P ستنخيز *satankhez*, Day of the resurrection.

A ستو *satw*, A making haste.

P ستو *sito*, Triple. A three-stringed guitar. Base (money).

P ستوا *satwā*, A female statue in Bāmyān.

P ستوار *sut*, *sutuwār*, or ستوان *sutwān*, Strong, firm. Faithful, trustworthy. Trust, credit, belief.

P ستودان *satūdān* or *sutūdān*, A gravestone. A cemetery. A circular stone building whereon the fire-worshippers lay the bodies of the dead.

P ستودگي *sutūdagī*, Praise, glorification.

P ستودن *sitūdan*, properly *sutūdan*, To praise.

P ستوده *sitūda*, Praised, celebrated, blessed, glorified. Laudable, praiseworthy. ستوده كردن *sitūda kardan*, To praise, to glorify God. ستوده اخلاق *sitūda-akhlāk*, Of an excellent disposition. ستوده صفات *sitūda-sifāt*, Of laudable qualities.

P ستوده مال *sitūda-maₐāl*, In a happy state.

P ستور *sutūr*, An animal; a quadruped, cattle, beast of burden. A horse, mule, or ass.

A ستور *sutūr*, (pl. of ستر *sitr*) Veils, coverings.

P ستوراب *sutūr-āb*, The falling down of water, or humours, into the feet of horses: a capellet.

P ستوربان *sutūrbān*, (or ستوروان *sutūrwān*) A groom, driver, herdsman of horses. A wagtail.

P ستوردان *sutūrdān*, A stall: stable. *Sutūr-dān*, Master of the horse, equerry, groom.

P ستوردن *sitūrdan* or *sutūrdan*, To shave, scrape, pull out hairs.

P ستوره *sutūra*, (or ستوري *sutūrī*) A razor. A yellowish bee.

P ستوسر *satūsar*, (or ستوسه *satūsa*) A sneeze.

A ستّوق *sattūk* or *suttūk*, False (money), base coin washed over with silver.

P ستول *sutul*, Wheat (in the ear) unripe, parched, and bruised (eaten some days before harvest).

P ستوم *sitūm*, The plant papyrus.

P ستون *sutūn*, A pillar, column, prop, or beam. ستون سفينه *sutūni safīna*, Mast of a ship. پايۀ ستون *pāyaₑi sutūn*, The pedestal of a column.

A ستّون *sittūn*, (oblique ستّين *sittīn*) Sixty.

P ستونه *sitūna*, An assault, attack, onset. Flight. A wave, billow, surge. *Sutūna*, A pivot.

P ستوه *sutūh*, Fear, dread, veneration. Distress, affliction, uneasiness, indigence. Stupefied, astonished. Sad, melancholy, indigent, helpless. Weak, tired, feeble-minded.

P ستوهيدن *sutūhīdan*, To loathe, to shun. To repent. To vex.

A سته *sath*, (v.n. of سته) Following. Striking or kicking the arse. *Sath*, *satah*, or *sith*, (pl. استاه *astāh*) The backside, bum, buttocks. *Satah*, (v.n. of سته) Having large buttocks. The rump-bone. Largeness of bum. *Satih*, Pertaining to the bum or buttocks. Anal. Large-buttocked. Fond of a large bum. A sodomite. *Sutuh*, (pl. of استه *astah*) Large about the posteriors.

P سته *sata* or *satta*, Any thing kept all night. Vinegar.. A grape. *Sita*, Weak, vexed. *Sitih*, Weak. Contention, litigation. *Sutuh*, Sad, melancholy, afflicted.

P ستها *satahā*, (in zand and Pāz.) The world.

A ستهاء *sat-hāₐ*, Large backsided (woman).

A ستهان *sut-hān*, (pl. of ستاهيّ *sutāhīy*) Large about the buttocks.

A ستهم *sut-hum*, Large-buttocked (man). One fond of large buttocks.

P ستهنده *sitihanda*, Importunate. Contentious.

P ستهي *sitihī*, Contentious, quarrelsome.

A ستهيّ *satahīy*, Belonging to the backside, anal. One who is always behind, who hangs an arse.

P ستهيدن *sitihīdan*, To contend. To warble. To make a noise, to kick up a row. To injure.

P ستي *satī*, A spear-head; also the iron ferule at the end of a spear or staff. *Satī* or *sattī*, Iron, steel.

A ستّي *sittī*, (corrupt. of سيّدتي *sayyidatī* or *sidatī*) My lady! madam! A lady. The Virgin Mary.

P ستيا *satyā*, (in zand and Pāz.) The world.

A ستيتة *sutaytat*, A name given to a company of female reporters of Muhammadan traditions.

P ستيخ *sitekh*, Any thing tall, straight, or flat. The sharp peak of a mountain. Tallness, straightness.

P ستيخ گوش *sitekh-gosh*, Pointed-eared, who or what pricks his ears.

A ستير *satīr*, One who hides another's fault. (fem. ستيرة *satīrat*) Covered, concealed. Honest, modest, chaste, abstaining from what is unlawful.

P ستير *siter*, A weight of 6½ drachms. A fortieth part of a من *man*.

A ستّير *sittīr* or *sattīr*, One who veils himself.

P ستيز *sitez*, Emulation, strife, contention, litigation. Battle, war, conflict, combat. Rebellion. Levity, temerity, rashness. Anger, hatred. Obstinacy, stubbornness. Discordance. Obstinate, perverse, stubborn. ستيز كردن *sitez kardan*, To contend, dispute, fight, squabble. آهنگ ستيز *āhangi sitez*, Preparations for battle. ميدان ستيز *maydāni sitez*, A field of battle.

P ستيزگر *sitezgar*, Obstinate, litigious.

P ستيزندگي *sitezandagī*, Contention, strife.

P ستيزنده *sitezinda*, Quarrelsome, litigious.

P ستيزه *siteza*, Broil, dispute, squabble, strife. Hostility, enmity. Tyranny. Violence. ستيزه كردن *siteza kardan*, To contend, quarrel.

P ستيزه خو *siteza-kho* or *khu*, Quarrelsome.

P ستيزه روي *siteza-rūy*, Ugly. Contentious.

P ستيزه كار *siteza-kār*, Quarrelsome.

P ستيزيدن *sitezīdan*, To contend, compete, go to law, be obstinate, perverse. To injure, oppress.

P ستيژه *siteja*, A weaver's shuttle. A selvage.

P ستيغ *sitegh*, Straight and tall (spear or column). A lofty peak. The sky. Contention, dispute.

P ستيم *sitem*, Blood mixed with water. Pus and matter in a sore. A wound, a sore affected by cold, and swollen. Corrupt blood.

A ستّين *sittīn*, (obliq. of ستّون *sittūn*) Sixty.

P ستيهش *sitehish*, (or ستيهندگي *sitehindagī*) A squabble, brawl, loud strife.

A ستيهيّ *sutayhīy*, One who habitually hangs an arse, or lags behind.

P ستيهيدگي *sitehīdagī*, Contention, litigation.

P ستيهيدن *sitehīdan*, To contend, quarrel, wrangle, brawl. To disobey. To be severe, unjust, cruel.

P سج *saj*, The cheek. *Suj*, The buttocks.

A سجّ *sajj*, (v.n.of سجّ) Being soft and thin excrement. Incrusting or bedaubing (a wall) with clay.

A سجا *saja'*, (fut. يسجو *yasjū*) He reposed.

P سجا *sajā*, Lettering or inscription of a book.

A سجاج *sajāj*, Thin, watery milk.

A سجاجيد *sajājid*, (pl. of سجّادة *sujjādat*) Carpets, rugs, or hassocks for prayer.

A سجاح *sajāh*, Name of a pretended prophetess cotemporary with Musaylimat the impostor. *Sijāh*, Opposite. *Sujāh*, Air, atmosphere.

A سجاحة *sajāhat*, (v. n. of سجح) Being smooth and equal (the cheek), being of a moderate length and not too plump.

A سجّاد *sajjād*, One who bows in adoration.

A سجّادة *sujjādat*, (pl. سجاجيد *sajājīd*) A carpet or mat on which the Muhammadans prostrate themselves when at prayer. The place of adoration, the mosque, or altar. The mark made on the forehead by prostration. P سجّادهٔ نان *sujjadaʼi nān*, A tablecloth. سجّاده نشين *sujjāda-nishīn*, Sitting upon the carpet (applied to the Muhammadan priests when saying prayers). سجّاده نشين محراب *sujjāda-nishīni mihrāb*, A priest at the altar.

A سجّاعة *sajjāʻat*, One who speaks rhythmically.

P سجاف *sajāf*, A curtain hung before a door. Fringe, edging. *Sijāf*, A veil, curtain.

P سجاكند *sajākand*, Armed, accoutred.

A سجال *sijāl*, (v. n. 3 of سجل) Contending with another, emulating, in running or in drawing water. (pl. of سجل *sajl*) Large udders. Water-buckets. Liberal men. الحرب سجال *al harb sijāl*, War resembles buckets (sometimes one belligerent party being in the ascendant, sometimes the other).

A سجالة *sajālat*, Length and pendulosity (of the scrotum or of a camel's udder).

P سجام *sajām*, Intense cold.

A سجام *sijām*, The flowing (of tears).

A سجّان *sajjān*, Keeper of a prison, jailer.

P سجانيدن *sa* or *sijānīdan*, To cool a thing.

P سجانيده *sajānīda*, Changed, altered by the influence of cold, cooled, chilled.

P سجاهر *sajāhar*, Equal, like, resembling.

A سجايا *sajāya'*, (pl. of سجيّة) Dispositions.

A سجائن *sajāʼin*, (pl. of سجينة *sajīnat*) Incarcerated, imprisoned (women).

A سجب *sajb*, (pl. *sujb*) An old leathern bottle.

A سجّة *sajjat*, Thin, watery milk. *Sujjat*, (also السجّة *as' sajjat*) Name of an idol.

A سجج *sujuj*, Flat roofs of houses plastered with clay. Pure souls or essences.

A سجح *sajh*, (v. n. of سجح) Being smooth, equal (cheek), of a moderate length, and not too plump. Cooing (a dove). Speaking ambiguously. *Sujh*, Smoothness. A highway, straight road. Size, measure. بيوت على سجح واحد *buyūt ʻala' sujhin* (or *sujuhin*) *wāhidin*, Houses upon one plan or size. *Sajah*, Beauty, symmetry. A scratch. *Sujuh*, Soft and smooth.

A سجحاء *sajhāʼ*, A she-camel, full-proportioned, and long-backed.

A سجيّة *suj* or *sajhat*, Nature, temperament.

P سجد *sajad*, Intense cold. Name of a river.

A سجد *sajad*, A swelling (of the foot).

A سجّد *sujjad*, (pl. of ساجد *sājid*) Worshippers.

A سجداء *sajdāʼ*, (fem. of اسجد *asjad*) Troubled with a swollen foot.

A سجدة *sij* or *sajdat*, Adoration, an inclination or prostration, the forehead touching the ground.

P سجده گاه *sajda* or *sijda-gāh*, Place of adoration: a church, mosque, temple, altar, and the like.

A سجر *sajr*, (v. n. of سجر) Heating a furnace or oven. Filling with water (a river). Lengthening her affectionate cry to her colt (a camel). Tying a log of wood to a dog's neck. Pouring (water) down the throat. *Sajar*, (v. n. of سجر) Having a bloodshot eye. *Sujar*, (pl. of سجرة *sujrat*) Little pits, wells, which by the aid of rain are filled.

A سجراء *sajrāʼ*, (fem. of اسجر *asjar*) One, the white of whose eye is bloodshot. An eye thus affected. *Sujarāʼ*, (pl. of سجير) Intimate friends.

A سجرة *sujrat*, (pl. سجر *sujar*) A little pit, which, by the aid of rain-water, becomes filled. A red tinge on the white of the eye.

A سجز *sajz* or *sijz*, The country of Sijistān.

A سجزيّ *sajziy* or *sijziy*, Native of Sijistān.

A سجس *sajas*, (v.n. of سجس) Being corrupted, changed, turbid (water). A crowd, tumult. *Sajis*, Muddy (water).

P سجستان *sijistān*, A kingdom to the east of Persia (the ancient Drangiana).

A سجسج *sajsaj*, Temperate (air). Neither cold nor hot (day). Neither hard nor soft (land). A temperate situation.

A سجع *sajʻ*, (v. n. of سجع) Speaking rhythmically. Cooing (a dove). Crying (a she-camel). Intending, proposing, aiming at. (pl. اسجاع *asjāʻ*) Rhyme, metre, cadence, poetry. Any thing written or recited in rhythm. The cooing of turtles.

A سجّع *sujjaʻ*, (pl. of سجوع) Cooing (turtles).

P سجع گو *sajʻ-go* or *gū*, A rhymer.

A سجف *sajf*, (v. n. of سجف) Letting fall a curtain before a tent-door. A curtain in two parts hanging before a door. Any door before which a curtain with an opening is hung. *Sajf* or *sijf*, (pl. سجوف *sujūf* and اسجاف *asjāf*) A veil, curtain. *Sajaf*, Slenderness of waist, lankness of belly.

A سجفة *sujfat*, An hour of the night.

P سجك *sajuk*, A sigh, sob. Hiccough. Buttermilk mingled with milk.

A سجل *sajl*, (v. n. of سجل) Throwing down from above. Pouring out (water). Reading (a chapter of the Kur'ān) continuously. (pl. سجال *sijāl* and سجول *sujūl*) A large water-bucket filled. A bucket-full. A large udder. A liberal man. *Sijl* or *sijill*, A register, the record of a court of judicature, the decree of a judge, the minute or attestation of a notary. Table of laws, public acts. A schedule. P سجل كردن *sijil kardan*, To seal. A *Sujl*, (pl. of سجلاء *sajlāʼ*) Swaggy-uddered (camels).

A سجلّ *sijill*, A scribe. A notary. A man. Name of Muhammad's scribe. Name of a king.

A سجلاء *sajlāʼ*, (pl. سجل *sujl*) Large-hipped (woman). (A camel) having a long, swaggy udder.

A سجلّات *sijillāt*, (pl. of سجلّ) Judges' decrees.

A سجلّاط *sijillāt*, Jasmine. The covering, awning, or canopy over the هودج *hawdaj* or camel-litter, in which the Eastern ladies travel. A fine painted or figured linen cloth.

G سجلّاطس *sijillātus*, A kind of carpet.

A سجلماسة *sijilmāsat*, Sijilmāsa a city of Morocco.

A سجم *sajm*, (v. n. of سجم) Delaying, procrastinating. Pouring down (tears or rain). *Sajam*, Water flowing. A tear. The leaf of the willow.

A سجمان *sajamān*, (v. n. of سجم) Shedding, letting drop. Flowing (tears).

A سجن *sajn*, (v.n. of سجن) Imprisoning. Brooding over care, keeping it to one's self. *Sijn*, (pl. سجون *sujūn*) A prison, dungeon; durance.

P سجن *sajan*, Intense cold.

A سجناء *sujanāʼ*, (or سجنى *sajna'*) (pl. of سجين

sujin) Imprisoned, incarcerated.

A سجنجل *sajanjal*, A mirror. Gold. Ingots of silver. Saffron. Spectacles. Pure, clear.

A سجوّ *sujūw*, (v. n. of سجا for سجو) Overspreading. Being quiescent. Continuing. Prolonging (as a she-camel her cry).

A سجواء *sajwā*, Steady (eye, woman, or camel when milking).

A سجود *sujūd*, (v. n. of سجد) Adoring. Bowing, stooping as an act of reverence. Standing erect. An act of adoration, an inclination or prostration with the forehead touching the ground.

A سجور *sajūr*, Chips with which they heat ovens or furnaces. *Sujūr*, (v. n. of سجر) Lengthening her affectionate cry to her colt (a she-camel).

A سجوريّ *sajwariy*, A light, active man. A fool.

G سجوس *sajūs*, The bog-rush.

A سجوع *sajū*, (pl. سجّع) Cooing (turtle-dove).

A سجوف *sujūf*, (pl. of سجف) Veils, curtains.

A سجول *sajūl*, Overflowing (fountain). *Sujūl*, (pl. of سجل *sajl*) Large water-buckets. Large udders. Liberal men.

A سجوم *sajūm*, A camel straddling to be milked. (An eye) shedding (tears). (A cloud) pouring (rain). *Sujūm*, (v. n. of سجم) Flowing (tears). Shedding.

A سجون *sujūn*, (pl. of سجن) Prisons, dungeons.

A سجيّ *sajiy*, A companion, friend.

A سجيّة *sajiyat*, (pl. سجايا *sajāya'*) Disposition, temper, nature, habit, constitution.

A سجيح *sajīh*, Soft and smooth. A highway.

A سجيحة *sajīhat*, Nature, disposition, habit. Symmetry, proportion, measure.

P سجيدن *sajīdan*, To be very cold.

A سجير *sajīr*, (pl. سجراء) A sincere friend.

A سجيس *sajīs*, Muddy, dirty (water). سجيس الاوجس *sajīsa'l awjasi*, (سجيس عجيس *sajīsa ajīsin* or سجيس الليالي *sajīsa'l layālī*) Never.

P سجيف *sajīf*, A bow-string. Notch in a bow.

A سجيل *sajīl*, A large bucket. Long, swaggy (cod, udder). Portion, lot. Hard, strong: intense.

P سجّيل *sijjīl*, Hard stones; bricks made from these stones, and hardened (according to Eastern belief) in hell-fire, upon which are inscribed the names of men, with a catalogue of their sins (said to be derived from سنگ *sang*, A stone, and گل *gil*, Clay). See also سجّين *sijjīn*.

A سجيلة *sajīlat*, A large water-bucket.

A سجين *sajīn*, (pl. سجناء *sujanā* or سجنى *sajna'*) Imprisoned, incarcerated: a prisoner. Hard, violent (blow).

A سجّين *sijjīn*, One always a bachelor. Continued, continual, and violent (blow). Firm. A dreadful prison; the seventh hell, the lowest and most horrible of the fatal dungeons; also the infernal registers, in which the crimes of infidels and reprobates are engrossed by demons. Publication, publicity. A bason round the foot of a palm-tree.

A سجينة *sajīnat*, (pl. سجائن *sajāin* and سجنى *sajna'*) Incarcerated, imprisoned (woman).

P سچك *sachuk*, Oxygal mingled with milk and anise. Hiccough.

A سحّ *sahh*, (v. n. of سح) Pouring out or causing to flow (tears, waters, or words). Flowing. Striking, whipping. Waxing very fat. *Sahh* or *suhh*, Dry dates scattered.

A سحا *saha'*, (pl. of سحاة *sahāt*) Skins, barks. Bats. Tracts. Court-yards.

A سحاء *sihā*, (pl. اسحية *as-hiyat*) The band of a book. A thorny tree with a white flower, from which the bees extract exquisite honey.

A سحّاء *sahhā*, A maker of, or worker with, shovels. One who scrapes the roads, a scavenger. A gardener who, with his spade or rake, keeps his flower-beds neat. A hot wind. Rainy (cloud or sky).

A سحاءة *sahāat*, A thin membrane which incloses the brain. *Sihāat*, A part of a cloud. Any thing scratched or scraped off (as the flue of paper). The band of a book.

A سحاب *sahāb*, Quicksilver. (pl. of سحابة) Clouds. سحاب البحر *sahābu'l bahr*, Sponge. سحاب صاعقه‌دار

P *sahābi sāika-dār*, Thunder-clouds.

A سحابة *sahābat*, (pl. سحب *suhub* and سحائب *sahāib*) A (thin) cloud. The whole of the day. *Suhābat*, Water remaining in a pond.

A سحاة *sahāt*, A bat, night-bird. The skin or bark of any thing. Any thing peeled, scratched, or scraped off (as the flue of paper). A tract, coast, shore. A court-yard, area, quadrangle. A certain thorny tree.

A سحّاج *sahhāj*, (A camel) pawing the ground.

A سحاح *sahāh*, Air, atmosphere. *Sihāh*, (pl. of ساحة *sāhhat*) Fat (sheep). *Sihāh* or *suhāh*, Fat (sheep). A flock.

A سحّاح *sahhāh*, Pouring, raining (cloud). *Suhāh*, (pl. of ساحة *sāhhat*) Fat (sheep).

A سحّاحة *sahhāhat*, Flowing with tears (eye).

A سحادل *suhādil*, The penis.

A سحادلان *suhādilāni*, Testes.

A سحار *sihār*, A certain fattening pot-herb.

A سحّار *sahhār*, An enchanter, magician, necromancer, fascinator. A very early riser.

A سحارة *suhārat*, The lungs and windpipe of a sheep (which the butcher tears out).

A سحّارة *sahhārat*, A female enchanter, a witch. A child's plaything.

A سحّاريّ *sahhāriy*, Magic. Magical.

A سحاف *sihāf*, A dysentery. Bits of fat. *Suhāf*, Consumption.

A سحّاق *sahhāk*, A rubber, grinder.

A سحّاقة *sahhākat*, Large woman with swagging breasts. Quæ confrictu libidinem alterius explet.

A سحال *sihāl*, (v. n. of سحل) Reviling, blaming, reproving. (v. n. 3 of سحل) Getting ashore. A bridle, bit, snaffle. A wooden muzzle to prevent a kid from sucking. *Suhāl*, (v. n. of سحل) Braying (a mule). A braying noise.

A سحالة *suhālat*, Filings of gold or silver. Husks of wheat, barley, &c. The dregs of mankind.

A سحام *suhām*, Blackness.

A سحامة *sahāmat*, Name of a company of reporters of Muhammadan traditions.

A سحائب *sahāib*, (pl. of سحابة) Clouds.

A سحاية *sahāyat*, (pl. اسحية *as-hiyat*) Any thing peeled or scraped off, a membrane. *Sihāyat*, A thin membrane which encloses the brain. A part of a cloud. Any thing peeled or scraped off, a membrane.

A سحائف *sahāif*, Bits of fat cut from the back.

A سحب *sahb*, (v. n. of سحب) Dragging on the ground (the train of a garment). Eating or drinking to excess; intemperance. Spreading. Flowing. *Suhub*, (pl. of سحابة *sahābat*) Clouds.

A سحبان *sahbān*, Water left in a bottle. A man that sweeps off every thing that comes near him. سحبان بن وائل *sahbān bin wāil*, Name of a man whose eloquence was unrivalled.

A سحباني *sahbānī*, Extremely eloquent.

A سحبة *suhbat*, A veil, covering. Remains of water in a pond.

A سحبل *sahbal*, (also سبحلل *sabahlal*) Large (lizard, bucket, bottle, or belly). Wide (channel).

A سحبلة *sahbalat*, Pendulous, loose (testicle).

A سحت *saht*, (v. n. of سحت) Eradicating. Pulling fat from the flesh. Scraping flesh from off a bone. Making unlawful gain. Being vile and illicit (trade). Intense cold. A threadbare garment. Blood that may be shed, or property plundered, with impunity. A desert of fine, light soil. *Suht* or *suhut*, (pl. اسحات *as-hāt*) Unlawful (gain). *Suht*, (Wealth) dissipated or carried off.

A سحتاء *sahtā*, Land which yields no pasture.

A سحتب *sahtab*, Bold, fearless.

A سحتوت *suhtūt*, A threadbare garment. A plain consisting of light, soft soil. A thin ptisan.

A سحتيّ *suhtiy*, A threadbare garment.

A سحتيت *sihtīt*, A ptisan with very little fat.

A سحج *sahj*, (v. n. of سحج) Excoriating. Scratching, tearing (the face in a frenzy of despair). Opening the hair upon the skin of the head before combing it. Making haste. A horse's pace short of full speed. A disease in the bowels.

A سحجلة *sahjalat*, (v. n. of سحجل Q) Rubbing, polishing, furbishing.

A سحدد *suhdud*, Very refractory, rebellious.

A سحر *sahr*, (v. n. of سحر) Deceiving. Retiring to a distance. Setting out or doing any thing at daybreak. A scar remaining on the back of a camel. (pl. اسحار *as-hār* and سحور *suhūr*) Lungs, lights. انتفخ سحره *intafakha sahruhu*, He overstepped his bounds. He played the coward. انقطع منه سحري *inhatasa minhu sahrī*, I despaired of him. *Sihr*, (v. n. of سحر) Enchanting, bewitching.

Occupying, amusing, engaging the attention. Deceiving. Quieting. Knowing, understanding perfectly. Going to a distance. Magic, enchantment, fascination, witchcraft, sorcery, necromancy. Any subtlety or trick whereby a person may be deceived. علم سحر *ʻilmi siḥr*, The art of magic, necromancy. سحر بنان *siḥri banān*, Magic of the fingers, *i. e.* elegant penmanship. سحر حلال *siḥri ḥalāl*, Legitimate enchantment, *i. e.* poetry. A poetic licence. Name of a book. سحر الكلام *siḥru'l kalām*, Magic of oratory. P سحر كردن *siḥr kardan*, To enchant, charm, fascinate. A *Suḥr*, (pl. اسحار *as-ḥār*) Lungs, lights. The heart. *Saḥar*, (pl. اسحار *as-ḥār*) Twilight, dawn. White spread over black. The edge of any thing. Lights, lungs. علي السحر *ʻala's saḥar*, Towards morning. P هنگام سحر *hangāmi saḥar*, The time of dawn..

P سحرآميز *siḥr-āmez*, Fascinating.

P سحرباز *siḥr-bāz*, An enchanter, sorcerer.

P سحربازي *siḥr-bāzī*, Magic.

P سحربنان *siḥr-banān*, (Magic-fingered) An elegant penman.

A سحرة *suḥrat*, The morning, the early dawn. A gap, opening, or gulf in stony ground. *Saḥarat*, (pl. of ساحر *sāḥir*) Magicians.

P سحرخيز *saḥar-khez*, An early riser.

P سحرزده *siḥr-zada*, Bewitched, fascinated.

P سحرساز *siḥr-sāz*, An enchanter.

P سحرگار *siḥrgār*, A magician.

P سحرگاري *siḥrgārī*, Magic.

P سحرگاه *saḥar-gāh*, Morning, dawn. To-morrow.

P سحرور *saḥrūr*, A species of wild bird.

P سحري *saḥre*, One morning, on a certain morning. *Saḥrī*, Morning, matutinal.

A سحريّ *saḥariy*, (or سحريّة *saḥariyat*) A little before dawn.

A سحريا *saḥaraya'*, (or سحراً *saḥran*) Very early.

A سحساح *saḥsāḥ*, Rain falling in torrents.

A سحساحة *saḥsāḥat*, Overflowing (fountain).

A سحسح *saḥsaḥ*, A quadrangle, court, square, area. Heavy rain.

A سحسحة *saḥsaḥat*, An area; a court-yard.

A سحط *saḥt*, (v. n. of سحط) Slaughtering expeditiously, at one blow. Diluting (wine) with water. Turning a lamb loose with its dam. Choking one (food).

A سحف *saḥf*, (v. n. of سحف) Shaving (the head), extirpating (hairs). Taking (the flesh) from a bone, or (fat) from the flesh or skin of the back. Burning. Eating any thing. Driving away (as wind the clouds). Grazing where they like (camels).

A سحفة *saḥfat*, (pl. سحف *suḥuf* and سحاف *siḥāf*) The fat of the back adhering to the skin. The noise of milk being milked into the pail.

A سحفتان *saḥfātani*, (dual) The two sides of hair between the under lip and the chin.

A سحفنية *suḥafniyat*, Shaven, polled. A shaveling.

A سحق *saḥḳ*, (v. n. of سحق) Breaking, tearing, rubbing, bruising, pulverizing. Softening (any thing hard). Cracking (a louse). Wearing out (clothes). Effacing vestiges (wind). Running slowly. Shaving the head. Letting fall tears (the eye). Trotting hard (a horse). An old, worn garment. A thin cloud. P سحق كردن *saḥḳ kardan*, To pound, bruise, grind, triturate. A *Suḥḳ* or *suḥuḳ*, (v. n. of سحق) Being far, remote. Removing to a distance. Being tall (a palm-tree). Distance. (pl. of سحوق *saḥūḳ*) Long-bodied (asses). (Palm-trees) long in the trunk. سحقاً له *suḥḳan lahū*, May he be far off!

A سحك *saḥk*, (v. n. of سحك) Rubbing. Reducing to pieces.

A سحكوك *suḥ* or *saḥakūk*, Very black (hair).

A سحل *saḥl*, (v. n. of سحل) Counting out and paying down (a sum of money). Shedding tears (the eye). Giving one (so many lashes). Reviling, abusing. Filing. Peeling. Braying (an ass). Smoothing, polishing, planing, shaving, scraping, brushing (as wind the ground). Plaiting a rope with a single twist. (pl. أسحال *as-ḥāl*, سحول *suḥūl*, and سحل *suḥul*) A species of white cotton cloth. Cloth or rope made of single threads. Ready money. *Suḥul*, (pl. of سحل *saḥl*) White cotton cloths.

A سحلال *saḥlāl*, Gorbellied.

A سحلة *suḥalat*, A young hare, leveret.

A سحلوت *suḥlūt*, A slut who minds nothing.

A سحم *saḥam*, Blackness. Iron. Name of a tree. *Suḥum*, Blacksmith's hammers.

A سحماء *saḥmāʼ*, Name of a tree. Podex.

A سحمة *suḥmat*, Blackness.

A سحن *saḥn*, (v. n. of سحن) Breaking (a stone). Making (a board or stick) smooth and shining by rubbing. يوم سحن *yawmu saḥnin*, A day of general assembly. *Siḥn*, Protection, guardianship.

A سحنة *saḥnat*, *saḥanat*, (or سحناء *saḥnāʼ*) External form. A smooth softness of the skin. Colour.

A سحنفية *suḥanfiyat*, A man whose poll is shaven.

A سحو *saḥw*, (v. n. of سحا for سحو) Pulling off, unbarking, excoriating. Shaving, scraping. Covering or binding a book with the membrane of the papyrus or linden-tree.

A سحوج *saḥūj*, A woman who swears much and breaks her oath.

A سحوح *suḥūḥ*, A pouring out. A flowing.

A سحور *saḥūr*, The meal which the Muhammadans make a little before dawn during the month of Ramazān to enable them to fast till night. *Suḥūr*, (pl. of سحر *saḥr*) Lights of beasts.

A سحوف *saḥūf*, (A camel) fat about the back. (A camel) which has long teats with a small orifice. (A camel) that drags her legs after her. Thin of wool about the belly (a sheep). (A shower) which sweeps the surface of the ground. The noise of a mill; or of milk being drawn into a pail. A bucket which empties a well.

A سحوق *saḥūḳ*, (pl. سحق *suḥḳ*) Long-bodied (ass). Tall-stemmed (palm-tree).

A سحوقة *suḥūḳat*, (v. n. of سحق) Being old and worn out (a garment). Being tall (a palm-tree).

A سحول *saḥūl*, Name of a town in Yaman. A fuller, a bleacher. *Suḥūl*, (v. n. of سحل) Shedding tears. (pl. of سحل *saḥl*) White cotton garments.

A سحوليّ *saḥūliy*, (Cloth) manufactured at Saḥūl in Yaman.

A سحي *saḥy*, (v. n. of سحي) Pulling off, unbarking, excoriating; shaving, scraping with spade or shovel. Shaving (the head). Sweeping away. Stirring embers. Covering or binding a book with the membrane of the papyrus or linden-tree.

A سحيت *saḥīt*, Dissipated wealth.

A سحير *saḥīr*, Pained in the belly. Big-bellied (horse). *Suḥayr*, (or *suḥayran*) In the morning.

A سحيف *saḥīf*, Noise (of a mill).

A سحيفة *saḥīfat*, (pl. سحائف *saḥāʼif*) A leaf of fat covering the short ribs. Fat cut from the back. Heavy rain sweeping the ground. The noise of a mill. The noise of milking into a pail.

A سحيق *saḥīḳ*, Very remote. Far-fetched, quaint. A medicinal powder. A medical drink, a ptisan.

A سحيقة *saḥīḳat*, A very heavy rain, sweeping things before it.

A سحيل *saḥīl*, (v. n. of سحل) Braying (a mule). Reviling, blaming. A single thread; also cloth or a rope made of such threads (not of several twisted together). A braying noise in the chest of an ass.

SY سحيلس *saḥīlis*, A sort of fragrant plant.

A سحيم *suḥaym*, A leathern bottle.

P سخ *saḳh*, Dirt, filth, impurity. *Suḳh*, Good, happy, auspicious. Happiness, goodness.

A سخّ *saḳhḳh*, (v. n. of سخّ) Thrusting the tail into the ground (a locust when laying eggs). Penetrating deep (in digging), going far on a journey. *Suḳhḳh*, (a foreign word) A weight of 24 منّ *mann*.

A سخا *saḳha'*, (v. n. of سخي) Being liberal, munificent. Limping (a camel). Lameness in a camel's shoulder. Name of a town in Egypt.

A سخاء *saḳhāʼ*, (v. n. of سخي) Being liberal, munificent. Leaving, dismissing. Liberality, generosity. P شاه سخا گستر *shāhi saḳhā-gustar*, A king diffusing liberality.

A سخّاء *saḳhḳhāʼ*, (pl. سخاخيّ) Ground soft and swelling, and yielding easily to the tread.

A سخاءة *saḳhāʼat*, (pl. سخاء) A certain pot-herb.

A سخاب *siḳhāb*, (pl. سخب *suḳhub*) An ornament for the neck, consisting of beads, fragrant berries, or odoriferous substances (without jewels).

A سخّاب *saḳhḳhāb*, Noisy, vociferous.

A سخاخ *saḳhāḳh*, Soft earth clear of sand.

A سخاخيّ *saḳhāḳhiy*, (pl. of سخّاء) Grounds soft and swelling, and yielding easily to the tread.

A سخاخين *saḳhāḳhīn*, (pl. of سخّين *siḳhḳhīn*) Spades. *Suḳhāḳhīn*, Hot (water). Heat in the eyes from tears of sorrow.

A سخاسخ *sakhāsikh*, Soft soil, free from sand.

A سخافة *sakhāfat*, (v. n. of سخف) Being thin and slender. Being weak in the mind, of a slender understanding. Leanness. A relaxation of the solids.

P سخال *sikhāl*, Enmity, hatred. Contrariety. Stubbornness, obstinacy. Violence, tyranny. Opiniated, self-willed.

A سخال *sikhāl*, (pl. of سخلة *sakhlat*) Lambs recently dropt.

A سخّال *sukhkhāl*, Weak and base (men).

A سخالة *sukhālat*, Refuse of any thing (as chaff). The choicest part of any thing, carefully picked.

A سخام *sukhām*, Blackness of a cauldron. Coal. Black (hair). Wine which goes smoothly down the throat. Soft plumage under the feathers. Soft, satiny (garment). سخام المس *sukhāmu'l mass*, Soft to the touch (clothes, plumage, cotton, or hair).

A سخامة *sukhāmat*, Podex.

A سخاميّ *sukhāmīy*, (or سخاميّة *sukhāmīyat*) Wine which goes smoothly down the throat.

A سخانة *sakhānat*, Heat, hotness (of water).

A سخاوة *sakhāwat*, (v. n. of سخي) Being liberal, munificent. Leaving, letting alone, having nothing to do with. Liberality, munificence.

A سخاوج *sakhāwij*, A country without water, and having no landmarks to guide travellers.

A سخاوي *sakhāwa'* or *sakhāwī*, (pl. of سخواء *sakhwāʼ*) Large districts of soft soil.

A سخاويّ *sakhāwīy*, (A district) consisting of soft soil. Native of Sakha in Egypt.

A سخاويّة *sakhāwīyat*, (pl. سخاويّ *sakhāwīy*) Widely-extended and level ground.

A سخايا *sakhāya'*, (pl. of سخيّة) Liberal (women).

A سخائم *sakhāʼim*, (pl. of سخيمة) Hatreds, grudges.

A سخب *sakhab*, Loud voice. *Sukhub*, (pl. of سخاب *sikhāb*) Ornaments for the neck, of beads, berries, or odoriferous substances.

A سخبر *sakhbar*, A species of thorny plant like the odoriferous cane. ركب السخبر *rakiba's sakhbara*, He deceived, he acted perfidiously.

P سخت *sakht*, Hard, strong, firm, secure, solid, vehement, intense, violent. Austere, harsh, severe, stern. Cruel, painful, arduous, difficult. Stubborn. Tight. Adhesive. Obstinate. Stingy, sordid. Base. Afflicted, disturbed, wretched, unfortunate. Abundant, copious. Weighed. A balance. Thick, coarse. Intensely, extremely, very much, sorely, exceedingly, vehemently, arduously. سخت آمدن *sakht āmadan*, To grudge; refuse; be unwilling. To be oppressed. سخت بستن *sakht bastan*, To bind tightly. سخت كردن *sakht kardan*, To harden. سخت گرفتن *sakht giriftan*, To seize or hold firmly. To oppress. سخت و نرم نمودن *sakht u narm namūdan*, To appear hard and soft, vary, threaten and soothe by turns, tamper with.

A سخت *sakht*, Strong, vehement. *Sukht*, The contents which issue from the bowels of hoofed animals before they have yet eaten any thing.

P سخت انداز *sakht-andāz*, An archer.

P سختانه *sakhtāna*, Harsh, unkind language.

P سخت آويز *sakht-āwez*, Fast suspended.

P سخت بازو *sakht-bāzū*, Strong in the arm, powerful, able to protect.

P سخت باف *sakht-bāf*, Of coarse texture.

P سخت بانگ *sakht-bāng*, Loud-voiced.

P سخت بنياد *sakht-bunyād*, Of solid structure.

P سخت خوردگي *sakht-khwurdagī*, Voracity.

P سخت روي *sakht-rūy*, Of an austere, indignant countenance.

P سخت روئي *sakht-rūʼī*, Austerity. Disdain. Indignation.

P سخت زبان *sakht-zabān*, Scurrilous.

P سخت زباني *sakht-zabānī*, Railing.

P سخت ساق *sakht-sāk*, Steady, constant.

P سخت سفيد *sakht-safed*, Very white.

P سخت سياه *sakht-siyāh*, Intensely black.

P سخت گوشت *sakht-gosht*, Brawny.

P سختگي *sakhtagī*, Hardness.

P سخت گير *sakht-gīr*, Holding fast (hound).

P سخت لگام *sakht-ligām*, Hard-mouthed.

P سختن *sakhtan* or *sukhtan*, To weigh. To draw. To be twisted. To turn or render hard. To winter.

P سختو *sukhtū*, Intestines of a bird. Sheep's tripe stuffed with minced meat and rice. Penis.

P سخته *sakhta* or *sukhta*, Weighed. Arranged. Money.

P سختي *sakhtī*, Hardness, harshness, asperity. Obduracy. Severity. Intensity of application. Stinginess. Adversity, indigence, distress, evil, calamity.

A P سختيان *sakhtiyān* or *sikhtiyān*, Goats' leather, morocco. *Sikhtiyān*, Name of a city.

A سختيت *sikhtīt*, Strong, vehement. Barley broth (without fat). Dust whirled in the air. Fine white flour.

P سختيدن *sukhtīdan*, To weigh.

P سختي كشيده *sakhtī-kashīda*, Distressed.

P سخج *sikhaj*, (or سخچ *sikhach*) Asthma.

A سخد *sakhd*, Warm, hot, sultry. Swelling, puffiness. *Sukhd*, Water. A yellow liquid which accompanies the birth.

A سخدود *sukhdūd*, Acute, intelligent (man).

A سخر *sakhr*, (v. n. of سخر) Enjoying a favourable breeze (a ship), sailing prosperously. *Sakhr*, *sakhar*, *sukhr*, or *sukhur*, (v. n. of سخر) Ridiculing.

A سخّر *sukhkhar*, A certain kind of pot-herb found in Khurāsān.

A سخرة *sukhrat*, (v. n. of سخر) Ridiculing, laughing at. A ridiculous fellow, butt for satire, laughing-stock. One compelled to labour. Obedient, tractable, submissive. *Sukharat*, A mocker, sneerer, laugher.

P سخره *sukhra*, Whatever is done gratis, either from courtesy or compulsion. A ship, or cattle, pressed into the king's service without freight or hire. A post-horse. Weak, wretched. سخره گرفتن *sukhra giriftan*, To take by force, to press.

A سخريّ *sikhrīy* or *sukhrīy*, (v. n. of سخر) Proposing to any one, or compelling him against his will. Overcoming by force. Obedient, tractable, submissive. A laughing-stock. Derision. *Sukhrīy*, (v. n. of سخر) Regarding as ignorant, light, trifling.

A سخريّة *sukhrīyat*, Derision. Play, merriment.

P سخش *sakhsh*, Old. Lightning. A stumble.

A سخط *sukht* or *sakhat*, (v. n. of سخط) Waxing hot, being angry. *Sukht*, *sakhat*, or *sukhut*, Indignation, disdain: dislike, displeasure. Divine displeasure, and its effect (as transformation into a stone).

A سخف *sakhf*, Indigence, straitened circumstances. *Sakhf* or *sukhf*, Imbecility of intellect, deficiency of judgment. Leanness of body from hunger. *Sukhf*, (v. n. of سخف) Being broken, torn, burst, or split (a leathern-bottle).

A سخفة *sakhfat* or *sukhfat*, Leanness produced by hunger. *Sukhfat*, Mental imbecility.

A سخل *sakhl*, (v. n. of سخل) Cleaning, sifting. Taking fraudulently. (pl. of سخلة *sakhlat*) Young lambs or kids.

A سخّل *sukhkhal*, Weak, infirm (men). (People) of the lowest rank. (in the dialect of Madina) Dates with soft stones. Any thing incomplete.

P سخلات *sakhlāt*, The jessamine.

A سخلان *sukhlān*, (pl. of سخلة *sakhlat*) Lambs or kids just dropped.

A سخلة *sakhlat*, (pl. سخل *sakhl*, سخال *sikhāl*, سخلان *sukhlān*, or سخلة *sikhalat*) A lamb or kid just dropped, or till they have past the fourth month.

A سخم *sakham*, Blackness.

A سخماء *sakhmāʼ*, (fem.) Black. Stony and soft ground intermixed.

A سخمة *sukhmat*, Hate, malevolence: blackness.

A سخن *sakhn*, Heat, fever. Inflammation of the eyes from weeping. *Sakhn* or *sakhan*, (v. n. of سخن) Being hot and inflamed with weeping (the eyes). *Sukhn*, Warm, hot (day, or water). *Sakhan* or *sukhun*, (v. n. of سخن) Being hot (water). *Sukhun*, Hot (day).

P سخن *sukhun*, *sukhan*, *sakhan*, or *sakhun*, A word, vocable, speech, saying, discourse. Will, pleasure. A thing, business, affair. Somewhat. در سخن آمدن *dar sukhan āmadan*, To begin a speech, conversation. سخن جور *sukhani jawr*, Harsh, unkind words. سخن داشتن *sukhan dāshtan*, To converse with, to have influence with. سخن دل فروش *sukhuni dil-farosh*, Kind words. Salutary advice. سخن زمانه *sukhani zamāna*, Calumny (as being the talk of the world). سخن زمهرير *sukhuni zamharīr*, Cold, insipid, unimpressive language. سخن شيرين *sakhuni shīrīn*, Sweet words. سخن غيبي *sukhani ghaybī*, Foretelling, predicting. Second sight. سخن گفتن *sukhanguftan*, To speak. سخن مفزا *sakhun ma fazā*, Lengthen not your discourse; have done with long speeches. سخن ميان تهي *sakhuni miyān-tihī*, (or بي مغز *bī maghz*) Empty, unmeaning words. سخن نافرجام *sukhuni nā farjām*, Trifling, impertinent words.

P سخن آرا *sakhun-ārā*, Adorning discourse; eloquent. Silence.

P سخن آرائي *sukhan-ārāī*, Eloquence.

P سخن آفرين *sakhun-āfirīn*, Eloquent. A liar.

A سخنان *sakh, sukh*, or *sakhanān*, Warm (day).

A سخنانة *sakh, sukh*, or *sakhanānat*, Hot (night).

P سخن پرداز *sukhun-pardāz*, Fluent orator.

P سخن پرور *sukhan-parwar*, A poet, author.

P سخن پيوند *sukhun-paywand*, A poet.

A سخنة *sakhnat, sikhnat, sukhnat*, or *sakhanat*, Heat, warmth. Inflammation of the eyes, or hot tears (from crying with vexation; weeping for joy being called cold tears). *Sukhnat*, (v. n. of سخن) Being hot (water).

P سخن چين *sukhan-chīn*, An informer, tale-bearer, calumniator.

P سخن چيني *sukhan-chīnī*, Detraction, slander.

P سخن خوره *sukhun-khwura*, (or سخن خوارة *sukhun-khwāra*) Severe of speech. Impudent.

P سخندان *sukhun-dān*, Eloquent: a poet.

P سخن داني *sakhun-dānī*, Eloquence. Philology.

P سخن ران *sukhun-rān*, Lengthening a discourse, prolix. An orator, rhetorician.

P سخنراني *sukhun-rānī*, Eloquence, elocution, rhetoric. Random, rambling talk.

P سخن روان *sukhun-ravān*, Eloquent.

P سخن زن *sukhun-zan*, A poet. A liar. Intelligent.

P سخن ساز *sukhan-sāz*, Who makes words to suit his purpose: a deceiver, a cheat, knave.

P سخن سازي *sukhan-sāzī*, Defamation.

P سخنسرا *sukhun-sarā*, A modulator or arranger of words. An orator, excellent writer.

P سخن سنج *sukhan-sanj*, Weigher of words. Prudent. A poet.

P سخنشناس *sukhun-shinās*, Eloquent.

P سخن فروش *sukhan-farosh*, A flatterer. A poet.

P سخن فهم *sukhan-fahm*, Intelligent, quick.

P سخن فهمي *sukhan-fahmī*, Intelligence.

P سخن كوتاه *sukhan kotāh*, Summarily.

P سخنگذار *sukhun-guzār*, A ready speaker, a persuasive orator. A porter (at a gate).

P سخن گو *sukhun-go* or *gū*, Eloquent

P سخن گوئي *sakhun-goī* or *gūī*, Rhetoric.

P سخن نا شنو *sukhan-nā shinav*, Inattentive.

P سخن نا شنوي *sakhun-nā shinavī*, Heedlessness, inattention.

P سخنور *sukhanwar*, Eloquent.

P سخنوري *sukhanwarī*, Eloquence, rhetoric.

A سخو *sakhw*, (v. n. of سخي) Being liberal. (v. n. of سخا for سخو) Lighting a fire under a cauldron. Resting, becoming quiescent.

A سخواء *sakhwāī*, (pl. سخاوي *sakhāwa'* and *sakhāwī*, A field of soft earth. Level ground. *Sukhawāī*, (pl. of سخي *sakhīy*) Liberal, generous.

A سخوة *sukhūwat*, A being liberal.

A سخود *sakhwad*, Soft, delicate (youth).

P سخون *sakhūn*, A word, a speech.

A سخون *sakhūn*, Warm (soup). *Sukhūn*, (v. n. of سخن) Weeping; being hot with crying (eyes).

A سخونة *sukhūnat*, (v. n. of سخن) Being warm (water). Being hot or inflamed with crying (eyes).

A سخي *sakhy*, (v. n. of سخي) Lighting a fire under a cauldron. Resting, becoming quiescent. *Sakha'*, A lameness in a camel's shoulder. *Sakhī*, Limping (camel).

A سخي *sakhīy*, (pl. اسخياء *askhiyāī* and سخواء *sukhawāī*) Liberal, generous. Lame-shouldered.

A سخية *sakhiyat*, (pl. سخيات *sakhiyāt* and سخايا *sakhāya'*) Liberal (woman).

A سخيت *sakhīt*, Strong, vehement, rough.

P سخير *sakhīr*, Name of a bitter drug.

A سخيف *sakhīf*, Weak in understanding, light, flighty, hasty. Thin, flimsy, of a thin texture.

A سخيلة *sukhaylat*, A kid.

A سخيمة *sakhīmat*, (pl. سخائم *sakhāim*) Hatred, ill-will, malevolence. Impurity, ordure.

A سخين *sakhīn*, Painful (blow). Hot in the eyes, from tears of sorrow. Hot (water).

A سخّين *sikhkhīn*, (pl. سخاخين) A spade. A butcher's knife. A plough-handle. Hot (water).

A سخينة *sakhīnat*, A kind of gruel. A name given by way of reproach to Kuraysh, amongst whom this dish was much in use. A testicle.

P سد *sad*, A hundred.

A سدّ *sadd*, (v. n. of سدّ) Stopping up, closing, filling (a hole or chink), blocking (the way), shutting (a gate). Impeding, obstructing. Strengthening, repairing, refitting. Silencing. (pl. اسدّة *asiddat*) Any bodily defect, obstructing a natural action (as blindness, deafness, impotency, and the like). Any thing made of twigs consisting of several layers or stages. *Sadd* or *sudd*, An obstruction, any thing blocking up, barring, or preventing a passage, as a mountain, barrier, fortification, mound, bank, wall, rampart, or ditch. A garrison on an enemy's frontier. (*Sudd* is used to imply a natural barrier, and *sadd* an artificial one). P سدّ باب كردن *saddi bāb kardan*, To lock or to bolt a door. سدّ سكندر *saddi sikandar*, Alexander's rampart. سدّ راه *saddi rāh*, An obstruction of the road. A سدّ رمق *saddi ramak*, A bare subsistence. The last remains of life; the agonies of death. سدّ ياجوج و ماجوج *saddi yaījūj u maījūj*, The wall of Gog and of Magog. *Sidd*, Right, well-directed (word). *Sudd*, A mountain. A bar. A shadow. A river. Whatever fills, occupies, or holds. (pl. سدود *sudūd*) A black cloud. (pl. سددة *sidadat*) A channel full of rocks, obstructing the flux of the water. جراد سدّ *jarādun suddun*, Swarms of locusts choking up the sky.

A سداء *sadāī*, A green, unripe date.

A سداب *sadāb*, (or سدابة) The herb rue.

P سداب *sudāb*, Rue. Power, strength.

A سداة *sadāt*, (pl. اسدية *asdiyat*) The warp. The damp of the night.

A سدّاج *saddāj*, A liar.

A سداجة *sadājat*, Simplicity.

A سداد *sadād*, (v. n. of سدّ) Being right and well directed; hitting the mark. Rectitude, straightforwardness in word or action. The way of truth or of salvation. Prosperity, happiness. Firmness. Name of a bow. *Sadād* or *sidād*, A cork, stopple. Whatever obstructs or fills up; a stop-gap. Sufficient for the necessities of life. *Sidād*, Milk concreting in the teat of a camel. *Sudād*, An obstruction in the nose.

A سدار *sidār*, A sort of vail or curtain.

A سدارة *sadārat*, A being stupefied.

A سداس سداس *sudāsa sudāsa*, In sixes.

A سداسيّ *sudāsīy*, (A garment) of six yards. Six-year-old (sheep). A word consisting of six letters.

A سدافة *sidāfat*, A veil, curtain.

A سدام *sidām*, Widely-spread (waters).

A سدان *sadān*, A vail, curtain.

A سدانة *sidānat* or *sadānat*, (v. n. of سدن) Serving the Kaaba or an idol-temple. Acting as doorkeeper, porter, or warder. *Sidānat*, The custody or charge of a temple.

P سدانية *sadāniya*, A village in Balkh.

P سداهرا *sadāhrā*, A bird found only in Lahore.

A سدائل *sadāil*, (pl. of سديل *sadīl*) Awnings or canopies placed over camel-litters.

P سد پايه *sad-pāya*, A centipede.

A سدّة *saddat*, Obstruction, obstacle. A strait, frith. *Suddat*, (pl. سدد *sudad*) A porch, vestibule, door-way. An obstruction in the nose, coryza. سدّة سعادت *suddaīi saīādat*, The court of felicity (an epithet by which some Eastern princes distinguish their royal residences).

A سدج *sadj*, (v. n. of سدج) Suspecting.

A سدح *sadh*, (v. n. of سدح) Throwing down flat on the face, prostrating. Placing (a thing) on (its) side. Causing (a camel) to lie or to kneel down. Killing, slaughtering, cutting the throat. Filling (a bottle). Remaining, resting, or stopping in a place. Being beloved by her husband, and bearing many children (a woman).

A سدد *sadad*, Rectitude. *Sudad*, (pl. of سدّة *suddat*) Doors, porches, vestibules. Obstructions in the nose, coryzæ. *Sudud*, Eyes which see not.

A سددة *sidadat*, (pl. of سدّ) Channels full of rocks, obstructing the current. Stones in a channel.

A سدر *sadr*, (v. n. of سدر) Setting (the hair) a flowing (a woman). Letting fall (a vail). *Sidr*, (pl. سدور *sudūr*) A lote-tree bearing fruit called نبق *nabk*. *Sadar*, (v. n. of سدر) Being stupefied with heat, and having the eyes dazzled (a camel). Vertigo, giddiness. Sea-sickness. *Sadir*, Stupefied, dazzled (camel). The sea. *Sidar*, (pl. of سدرة *sidrat*) Species of the lote-tree.

P سدر *sidar*, The lote-tree; a sort of plum.

A سدّر *suddar*, A kind of game.

A سدرة *sidrat*, (pl. سدرات *sidrāt*, *sidirāt*, *sidarāt*, and سدر *sidar*) One kind of the lote-tree. سدرة المنتهي *sidratu'l muntaha'*, A tree in paradise in the seventh heaven. The heavenly mansion of the angel Gabriel.

A سدرات *sid*, *sida*, or *sidirāt*, (pl. of سدرة *sidrat*) Species of the lote-tree bearing the fruit نبق *nabk*.

P سدرت قامت *sidrat-kāmat*, Tall of stature.

P سدرة نشينان *sidra-nishinān*, Angels.

A سدس *sads*, (v. n. of سدس) Demanding or taking a sixth part. Making up the number six. *Sids*, The watering of a camel on the sixth day (from the last time of drinking). *Suds* or *sudus*, (pl. اسداس *asdās*) The sixth part. سدس ثمن *sudsu sumnin*, A sixth of an eighth (a manner of expressing a forty-eighth part). (pl. of سدس *sadas* and سديس *sadīs*) Eight-year old camels. *Sadas*, The tooth of an eight-year-old camel, the one which comes before the بازل *bāzil*.

A سدع *sadeع*, (v. n. of سدع) Striking one against another. Slaughtering. Stretching out. Being oppressed by misfortune.

A سدعة *sadعat*, Adversity, calamity.

A سدغ *sudgh*. See صدغ *sudgh*.

A سدف *sadaf*, Darkness. Night. The twilight. Light. The dawn. Part of the night. A sheep called to be milked by the words *sadaf sadaf*.

A سدفة *sadfat* or *sudfat*, (in the dialect of Tamīm) Darkness. (in the dialect of Kays) Light. *Sudfat*, A door. A porch or doorway. A curtain before a door to exclude the rain.

A سدق *sadah*, A festival-night when many fires are lighted.

A سدك *sadh* or *sadah*, (v. n. of سدك) Being assiduous, adhering to. *Sadih*, Wishful, desirous, addicted to, greedy. Necessary, proper, suitable. Expeditious, ready-handed. One who stabs quickly with a spear.

P سدكام *sadkām*, Asking from necessity.

P سدكس *sadkas*, (سدكيس *sadkes*, or سدكيش *sadkesh*) The rainbow.

P سدگاه *sad-gāh*, A court, hall of audience.

A سدل *sadl*, (v. n. of سدل) Splitting, tearing. Travelling through (a country). (A woman) loosening (her garments, veil, or hair). A mode of wrapping one's self in a garment, with the hands underneath. *Sidl*, (pl. سدول *sudūl*) A string of pearls hanging down the bosom. (pl. اسدال *asdāl*, سدول *sudūl* and اسدل *asdul*) A veil, covering. *Sudl*, A veil. (pl. of اسدل *asdal*) Pendulous, floating loose. *Sadal*, The awning or covering of a camel-litter. A bend, inclination.

A سدّلي *sidilla'*, A three-roomed house.

A سدم *sadm*, (v. n. of سدم) Shutting, closing (a door). *Sadam*, (v. n. of سدم) Being penitent, contrite. Grief, repentance. A greedy desire. Libidinous (stallion). ما له هم و لا سدم الا ذاك *mā lahu hammun wa lā sadamun illā zāka*, He has no care nor anxiety but that. *Sadim*, Enraged. Libidinous (stallion). Violently in love. *Sadim*, *sadum*, *sadam*, or *sudum*, (pl. اسدام *asdām* and سدام *sidām*) Wide spread (water). *Sudum* or *sudm*, (pl. اسدام *asdām*) A concealed well (filled with earth).

A سدمان *sadmān*, Penitent, sorrowful, sad. ندمان سدمان *nadmān sadmān*, Penitent, contrite.

A سدن *sadn*, (v. n. of سدن) Serving the Kaaba, or a temple. Performing the work of a porter or door-keeper. Loosening (one's garments), letting down (a curtain). *Sadan*, (pl. اسدان *asdān*) A veil, a curtain. The curtain of a camel-litter.

A سدنة *sadanat*, (pl. of سادن *sādin*) Keepers of the temple of Mecca; also of idol-temples.

A سدود *sudūd*, (pl. of سدّ *sudd*) Black clouds.

A سدور *sudūr*, (pl. of سدر *sidr*) Lote-trees.

P سدوس *sadūs*, Indigo.

A سدوس *sadūs* or *sudūs*, A kind of green hood, mantle, cape, or coif, called طيلسان *taylasān*. *Sudūs* or *sadūs*, The smoke of burning fat, which tinges with a green colour. Indigo.

A سدوف *sudūf*, Figures which appear black in the distance.

A سدول *sudūl*, (pl. of سدل *sidl*) Strings of pearls. Veils. (pl. of سديل *sadīl*) Awnings or canopies over a camel's litter. Shades of night.

A سدوم *sadūm*, Name of the magistrate of Sodom. An oppressive ruler. Libidinous (stallion). *Sudūm*, Name of the capital of Bahrām Gūr.

A سدوميّ *sadūmiy*, A native of Sodom.

A سدويّ *sadawiy*, Grown at سديّا *sudayya'* (a pomegranate).

P سده *sada*, A flaming fire. A festival-night, on which the Persians light a number of large fires, in commemoration of the following popular tradition: In the time of Hoshang (about 800 years before the Christian æra) a monstrous dragon infesting the country, the king himself attacked him with stones, when one of them falling with prodigious force upon another, struck fire, set the herbage and surrounding trees in a blaze, and consumed the dragon in the flames. A sort of tree with a thick, smooth stem and dense foliage, called in Arabic شجرة البقّ.

A سدي *sady*, (v. n. of سدي) Stretching out the hand. Intending, proposing. Making towards. Going with long steps (a she-camel). Playing with walnuts (a boy). Beginning to ripen at the stalk (dates); becoming flaccid and pendulous (at the sheath). *Sada'*, (v. n. of سدي) Beginning to ripen at the stalk (dates). The nocturnal dew (the dew of the day being ندي *nada'*). A green, unripe date. Kindness, favour, benefit. Honey. The warp of cloth. *Sada'* or *suda'*, Turned loose to pasture without a keeper (camels). *Sadī*, (fem. سدية *sadiyat*) (Ground) wet with dew. Dewy (day). (An unripe date) soft at the bottom.

A سدّيّ *suddiy*, Name of Ismaعīl, who sold coifs in the vestibule (سدّة *suddat*) of the mosque of Kufa.

A سديّا *sudayya'*, Name of a place.

A سديح *sudīh*, Prostrate, flat on the face.

A سديد *sadīd*, Right, well-directed, salutary. ذهن سديد *zihni sadīd*, A clear judgment.

A سدير *sadīr*, Name of an edifice built by Numān bin Munzir for Bahrām Gūr. Grass.

A سديس *sadīs*, An eight-year-old camel. The tooth of an eight-year-old camel; the one which appears previous to the بازل *bāzil*. A five-year-old ox or sheep. Cloth six ells long. The sixth part. A kind of measure. سديس عجيس *sadīsun عujaysun*, Never.

A سديف *sadīf*, The fat of a camel's bunch.

A سديل *sadīl*, (pl. سدول *sudūl*, اسدل *asdul*, and سدائل *sadāil*) The awning or canopy over a camel's litter. A veil stretched across a tent or in front of a female apartment.

A سديم *sadīm*, Greatly engaged in praising God. A thin mist.

A سدين *sadīn*, Fat, grease. Blood. Wool. A veil, a curtain.

A سذاب *sazāb*, (equiv. to سداب *sadāb*) Rue.

A سذابيّ *sazābiy*, A seller of rue.

A سذانق *sazānak* or *suzānuk*, A kind of hawk.

A سذبة *suzbat*, A sheath, case, cover.

A سذق *sazah*, (from P سده *sada*) A festival-night whereon many fires are lighted.

A سذوم *sazūm*, Sodom.

P سر *sar*, Head, top, summit, point, pinnacle. The capital of a pillar. A cover, a lid. A salient angle. Any projecting part. Beginning, origin, principle. End, extremity. The most select or choicest part of any thing. A general, commander of an army. Great, large. Thought, idea, fancy. Power, strength, force. Highest, greatest, chief. Complete, perfect, entire. A veil, awning, canopy, covering. A collar, also a log of wood fastened to a mastiff's neck. A term applied to horses, as دست *dast*, Hand, is to falcons. Desire, longing, wish, intention, will. Love. Cheerfulness. Froth, foam, scum. A mystery. Atmosphere, gentle gale. A tract of country. A Turkomān shoe or sandal. Foolish. بر سر آتش *bar sari ātish*, To the fire. سراز آب *sar az āb*, A bubble of water. سراز آب بيگانه شستن *sar az ābi bīgāna shustan*, To wash one's head with a stranger's water: to find goods which have no owner. سراز پا نشناختن *sar az pā na shinākhtan*, Not to know one's head from one's feet: to be utterly confused. سرازشيشهٔ

تهی چرب کردن *sar az shīsha-i tihī charb kardan*, To anoint the head from an empty glass: to deceive. سر از قدم ساختن *sar az kadam sākhtan*, To be happy, to rejoice. سر آشنائی *sar āshnā-i*, Intimacy. سر افکندن *sar afkandan*, To hang the head, to blush. سر آمدن *sar āmadan*, To wax strong and powerful. To come to a conclusion. To accomplish. سر اندر زدن *sar andar zadan*, To conceal one's self from fear. To be in a thoughtful mood. To be bewildered. سر انگشت *sar angusht*, Tip of the finger. سر آوردن *sar āwardan*, To be finished. سر باختن *sar bākhtan*, To sport with one's life. سر با افسر *sari bā afsar*, A crowned head. سر بتیغ خاریدن *sar ba tegh khārīdan*, To decapitate. سر بر آوردن *sar bar āwardan*, To rebel. To turn away with ingratitude. سر براه *sar ba rāh*, Being in the way to execute a thing: performance, the execution of a business. سر براه کار *sar ba rāh kār*, A business conducted in partnership. The officers of government collectively. سر براه کردن *sar ba rāh kardan*, To accomplish. سر بر خط *sar bar khat*, Obedient, compliant. سر بر خلد بردن *sar bar khuld burdan*, To become eternal. To attain the object of one's desires. بسر بردن *ba sar burdan*, To pass (days or months). سر بر دنیا زدن *sar bar dunya' zadan*, To travel. سر بر زانو نشستن *sar bar zānū nishastan*, To crouch. To watch. To sit in a melancholy mood. سر بر زدن *sar bar zadan*, To shoot up (as herbage). To appear, become manifest, happen, occur. سر بر کردن *sar bar kardan*, To lift up the head. To be refractory, rebel. سر بر کمر زدن *sar bar kamar zadan*, To be mad. سر بر گرفتن *sar bar giriftan*, To awake. To travel. سر بر نهادن *sar bar nihādan*, To be silent. سر بریدن *sar burīdan*, To behead. سر بزمین *sar ba zamīn*, Profound reverence. سر بستن *sar bastan*, To form a skin or pellicle on the surface, to froth (milk or broth). سر بسینه کردن *sar ba sīna kardan*, To hang the head on the bosom (in a contemplative attitude). سر بگریبان بردن *sar ba girībān burdan*, To be thoughtful. سر بمهر *sar ba muhr*, Sealed. Veiled, concealed. سر پا زدن *sari pā zadan*, To trip, stumble. To kick. سر پستان *sari pistān*, The nipple. سر پستان سیاه کردن *sari pistān siyāh kardan*, To anoint the nipple with a black drug in order to wean the child. سر پس کشیدن *sar pas kashīdan*, To recede. سر پیچیدن *sar pechīdan*, To rebel, be disobedient. سر پیش کردن *sar pesh kardan*, To meditate, think deeply. To be covered with blushes. بسرت *ba sarat* or بسر تو *ba sari tu*, By thy head. سر تافتن *sar tāftan* or سر بر تافتن *sar bar tāftan*, To turn away the head: to be refractory, to rebel. سر تیر *sari tīr*, A learned, distinguished man. One who administers justice. سر تیغ *sar tegh*, Point of a sword. Peak of a mountain. Light. سر جغرات *sar jughrāt*, Cream. سر جفت کردن *sar juft kardan*, To whisper. سر چاه *sar chāh*, Mouth of a well. سر چشمه *sar chashma*, A fountain, a fountain-head. سر حساب شدن *sari hisāb shudan*, To take good care of, be collected. سر خاریدن *sar khārīdan*, To be desperate, lose hope. To blush. To seek excuses, procrastinate. To be unable to reply. To observe, guard, preserve. To be willing. To calm, soothe, cajole, flatter. To befriend. To cheat, defraud. سر خر *sari khar*, (Asses head) a shameless fellow; one who intrudes himself into a place where he has no business. سر خریدن *sar kharīdan*, To scratch the head. To be at one's wit's end. To be ashamed, confounded. To ransom, redeem. از سر خشم *az sar khishm*, From anger. سر خط *sar khat*, Superscription, direction of a letter; a receipt. سر خط نهادن *sar khat nihādan*, To oblige, follow. سر خم *sar khum*, The lid of a wine-jar. Name of a plant. سر خود گرفتن *sari khwud giriftan*, To follow our own way. سر خویش گرفتن *sar khwesh giriftan*, To depart. سر دادن *sar dādan*, To release, dismiss, send away. To die. To discharge fire-arms. To be bold. در سر در آمدن *dar sar dar āmadan*, To rush upon. سر در پاي نمودن *sar dar pāy namūdan*, To be helpless, disconsolate. سر در گریبان زدن *sar dar girībān zadan*, To have finished, ended. سر در نشیب کردن *sar dar nishīb kardan*, To hang down the head. To be ashamed. سر دزدیدن *sar duzdīdan*, To refuse to obey, to rebel. سر دست *sari dast*, Ready at hand. سر دست افشاندن *sari dast afshāndan*, To be in a rage. To leave, discard, renounce. To dance. سر دیوار *sari dīwār*, Top of a wall. سر ذات *sar zāt*, Per man. سر راه *sari rāh*, The high road, higher part of the road; the head of a street. سر راه داشتن *sari rāh dāshtan*, To keep a look out. To purpose travelling. سر راه گرفتن *sari rāh giriftan*, To block up a road. سر رفتن *sar raftan*, To be slain. سر رو *sari rū*, The cephalic vein in the arm. سر زانو *sari zānū*, The knee-pan. Observation, contemplation. سر زبان *sari zabān*, Tip of the tongue. سر زدن *sar zadan*, To behead. To rebuke sharply. To enter suddenly without leave. To happen. To appear. To let off, fire, shoot. سر زلف *sari zulf*, A wink, nod, amorous glance. Reproof. سر زمین *sar zamīn*, The earth. A country, region. Limits, confines. Upon the spot, the premises. سر سال *sari sāl*, Beginning of the year. سر سفره *sari sufra*, Anus. سر شاخ *sari shākh*, The projecting bones upon the forehead. سر شام *sari shām*, Evening, early in the evening. سر شاه *sari shāh*, The two projecting bones of the forehead. سر شدن *sar shudan*, To happen; to die; to be released; to obtain fire. سر شیر *sari shīr*, A skin on the surface of milk. سر صدق *sari sidk*, Faith, rectitude, truth. سر عسکر *sar ʿaskar*, General of an army, seraskier. سر فتنه *sari fitna*, An exciter of sedition. سر فرو آوردن *sar faro āwardan*, To submit. سر فرو بردن *sar faro burdan*, To be ashamed. سر کار *sar kār*, A shop, manufactory. Government. سر کردن *sar kardan*, To let off, discharge (fire-arms). To burst (a boil or wound), come to a head. سر کشیدن *sar kashīdan*, To disobey. سر کمند *sari kamand*, A cord fastened to the stable-door of princes, which serves as a sanctuary to thieves or to manslayers. سر کوه *sari koh*, Summit of a mountain. سر کوي *sari kūy*, Top or end of a street. سر گروه *sar guroh*, A chief, leader, head of a tribe. A chief of fakīrs, a provincial. سر ماهه *sari māha*, The handle of an auger. سر منزل *sari manzil*, End of a day's journey. سر مو *sari mo* or *mū*, Point of a hair. A little. سر نو *sari naw*, Beginning again, new commencement, or date. سر نهادن *sar nihādan*, To prostrate. To die. سر نیزه *sari neza*, Point of a spear. سر و برگ *sar u barg*, Apparatus. Means of subsistence. Desire, lust. سر و بن *sar u bun*, Head and root, totally. سر و پا *sar u pā*, All, the whole. An honorary dress. سر و پاچه *sar u pācha*, Sheep's head and feet dressed. سر و رو کردن *sar u rū kardan*, To be angry at, to rebuke. سر و شاخ *sar u shākh*, Head and branch, totally. *Sur*, Shoes or slippers, made in Khurāsān, of goats' hair or cotton. A kind of strong drink made from rice (perhaps arrack or beer). A florid ulceration of the skin. The swordfish. Red colour. A spout on the house-top. A sort of dance.

A سرّ *sarr*, (v. n. of سرّ) Making glad. Wishing, or expressing a wish that one may be joyful. Cutting away the navel-string of a new-born child. Doing a kindness. Wounding in the navel. Complaining of a pain in the navel. Adjusting a bit of touch-wood to a fire-steel that it may take fire. برّ سرّ *barr sarr*, One who makes glad and joyful. Good. One who does good secretly. *Sirr*, (pl. اسرار *asrār*) A secret, mystery. A sacrament. Pure, the most excellent (stock or race). Marriage, or the publication of it. The middle or heart of any thing. Root, origin. The best part of a valley. Rich land. A tomb. Fornication. Coitus. Vulva. The beginning, middle, or close of a month. Membrum virile. ولد له ثلاثة علی سرّ *wulida lahu salāsatun ʿala' sirrin*, Three boys were born to him in succession. كاتب السرّ *kātibu's sirr*, A secretary. *Sirr* or *surr*, (pl. اسرار *asrār*) A line, fold, or crease on the palm of the hand. *Surr*, (v. n. of سرّ) Making glad. (pl. اسرّة *asirrat*) The navel-string which the midwife cuts. عرفت ذاك قبل ان يقطع سرّك *ʿaraftu zāka kabl an yuktaʿ surruka*, I knew that before your navel-string was cut.

A سرء *sarʾ*, (v. n. of سرأ) Laying eggs (a locust). Being very prolific (a woman). A locust's egg. Fish-spawn. *Surūʾ*, (pl. of سروء *sarūʾ*) Locusts laying eggs.

A سرّء *surraʾ*, (pl. of سروء) Locusts laying eggs.

P سرا *sarā*, A palace, mansion. *Sirā* or *sarā*,

Singing, modulation. سرا شدن *sirā shudan*, To sing, shake, trill. بلبل دستان سرا *bulbuli dastān-sirā*, The melodious nightingale.

A سرًّا *sirrān*, Secretly, mysteriously, clandestinely. سرًّا و علانية *sirran wa ʿalāniyatan*, (or سرًّا وجهرا *sirran wa jahran*) Privately and publicly.

A سراء *sarāʾ*, (v. n. of سرو) Being generous. A tree of which bows are made, a kind of yew. *Sirāʾ*, (pl. of سروة *sirwat*) Small arrows.

A سرّاء *sarrāʾ*, (fem. of أسرّ *asarr*) Hollow (pipe). Rich (country). (A she-camel) galled in the breast. Cheerfulness. One who travels much in the night. An easy, happy condition (opposed to ضرّاء *zarrāʾ*).

A سراءة *sirāʾat*, A locust's egg.

P سرآب *sar-āb*, A fountain-head. A cut in the side of a river, whence water is drawn off by smaller channels for purposes of irrigation. Purest, best part of any thing. Non-existent. Pride, haughtiness.

A P سراب *sarāb*, A vapour resembling the sea at a distance, formed by the reflection of the sun's meridian rays upon the surface of sandy plains. The camel of بسوس *basūs*, q.v. اشأم من سراب *ashʾam min sarāb*, More disastrous than Sarāb.

P سرابار *sarā-bār*, A bundle on a horse's load.

P سراباش *sarābāsh*, An iron mace.

P سرابالا *sarā bālā*, Steep.

P سرابالاني *sarā bālānī*, (A road) up a precipice.

P سرابستان *sarābistān*, Land of delusion, *i.e.* this world. *Sarā-bustān*, A garden adjoining to a house.

P سرابن كردن *sar-ā-bun kardan*, The bend the head, point, or extremity of any thing.

P سرابيدن *sirābīdan*, To sing, to warble.

A سرابيل *sarābīl*, (pl. of سربال) Shirts, vests.

P سرابيلي *sarābīlī*, Effeminate, infamous.

P سراپا *sar-ā-pā*, (or سراپاي *sar-ā-pāy*) Totally, from head to foot, cap-a-pie. An honorary vest.

P سراپا شرارت *sar-ā-pā sharārat*, Vice all over.

P سراپرده *sarā-parda*, A curtain, especially at the door of a royal palace or pavilion. A wall of canvas surrounding a cluster of tents. سراپردهٔ جهان *sarā-pardaʾi jahān*, The sky. سراپردهٔ كحلي *surā-pardaʾi kuhlī*, The sky. A black cloud.

A سراة *sarāt*, Top, highest, or best of any thing. (pl. سروات *sarawāt*) Back of a horse. Name of a part of Arabia. The middle (of the day or road). A company of generous persons. (pl. of سريّ *sarīy*) Liberal.

A سرأة *saʾa* or *sirʾat*, A locust's egg: fish-spawn.

P سرات *sarāt*, A mountain near Yaman.

A سرّات *surrāt*, (pl. of سرّة *surrat*) Navels.

A سراج *sirāj*, (pl. سرج *suruj*) A lamp, lantern, luminary, candle. The sun. سراج الدولة *sirāju'd dawlat*, The lamp of the state. سراج الظلام *sirāju'z zalām*, The herb glasswort. سراج القطرب *sirāju'l kutrub*, The fairy's lamp; a plant which shines at night like the glow-worm.

A سرّاج *sarrāj*, A saddler: a vender of saddles. A groom. A liar.

A سراجة *sirājat*, The art of saddle-making.

P سرّاج خانه *sarrāj-khāna*, A saddler's shop.

P سراجه *sirāja*, A disease incident to horses, mules, or asses. Name of a place famous for melons.

A سراجيّ *sirājīy*, Lucid, resplendent. Belonging to a lamp or candle.

P سراچه *sarācha*, A closet, inner apartment. A cabinet. A casket within a larger case. A hen-coop without a bottom. A palace, mansion. سراچهٔ آدرنگ *sarāchaʾi ādrang*, House of vexation, *i.e.* the world. سراچهٔ آفتاب *sarāchaʾi āftāb*, A parhelion, mock sun. سراچهٔ خاك *sarāchaʾi khāk*, The world. سراچهٔ دل *sarāchaʾi dil*, Purse of the heart. سراچهٔ ضرب *sarāchaʾi zarb*, The mint. سراچهٔ كل *sarāchaʾi kul*, Throne of God. World. سراچهٔ ماه *sarāchaʾi māh*, A halo round the moon.

A سراح *sarāh*, Dismission. Divorce. في سراح و رواح *fī sarāhin wa rawāhin*, Easily, conveniently. *Sarāh* or *sirāh*, (pl. of سرحان *sirhān*) Wolves. Lions. Middles of roads.

A سراحين *sarāhīn*, (pl. of سرحان) Wolves.

P سرآخر *sar-ākhur*, (or سرآخور *sar-ākhwur*) A horse tied at the head of all the rest in a stable.

P سرآخور *sar-ākhwur*, Master of the horse.

A سراد *sarād*, Unripe, sour dates. A palm-tree, dry and withered for lack of moisture. *Sirād*, Sewing of leather and the holes made by the punctures.

P سرادار *sarā-dār*, Master of the horse. A landlord, vintner, tavern or innkeeper. An attendant at an hospital.

A سرادح *sarādih*, (pl. of سرداحة *sirdāhat*) Long and excellent she-camels.

A سرادخ *surādikh*, Dates moistened with water.

A سرادق *surādik*, (pl. سرادقات *surādikāt*) The curtain before the door of a house or tent. A cotton tent. Dust whirled up into the air, and enveloping any thing. Thick smoke.

A سرار *sarār*, The last night of the moon. The purest and best of any thing. An unripe date. The navel-string which the midwife cuts. The finest spot (in a valley). *Sirār*, (v. n. 3 of سرّ) Whispering in the ear. Telling a secret. The last night of the moon. (pl. أسرّة *asirrat*) A line on the palm of the hand, or on the forehead.

A سرارة *sarārat*, The best of any thing. The finest spot in a valley. Excellence.

P سراروي *sarārūy*, The outer cephalic vein.

A سراريّ *sarārīy*, (pl. of سرّيّة) Concubines.

P سرازير *sar-ā-zīr*, Sloping (little used).

A سراس *sirās*, (pl. of سرس or سريس) Impotent.

P سراسر *sar-ā-sar*, From beginning to end. From one end to the other, all, the whole, entirely. Walking on a green sward, or by the side of a stream. Brocade, embroidery.

P سراسري *sar-ā-sarī*, A medium, average. A summary. An ornament worn on the head.

P سراسيمگي *sarāsīmagī*, Amazement.

P سراسيمه *sarāsīma*, (from سر *sar* and آسيمه *āsīma*) Astonished, confounded, stupefied, disturbed in the brain, insane. Hesitating.

P سرآشيب *sar-āshīb*, Steep down. Declivity.

A سراط *sirāt*, A way, road. *Surāt*, Sharp (sword).

A سراطيّ *surātīy*, Sharp. Swift. A glutton.

A سراع *sirāʿ*, (pl. of سريع *sariʿ*) Swift.

A سراعة *surāʿat*, Haste speed. Quick, speedy.

P سراغ *surāgh*, Sign, mark, footstep. Inquiry. Guidance. A thing searched for, or cried publicly.

P سرآغاز *sar-āghāz*, Exordium, prelude.

P سراغوچ *sarāghoch*, (سراغوش *sarāghosh*, or سراغج *sarāghuj*) A woman's hood, cloak, veil, fillet, or head-dress. A camel's halter.

P سرافراز *sar-afrāz*, Head-exalting: glorious, eminent, distinguished. The commander of an army. A halter, head-stall. The 3d day of every month.

P سرافرازي *sar-afrāzī*, Eminence, exaltation.

P سرافسار *sar-afsār*, (or *sari afsār*) Head of the reins, *i.e.* the part held in the hand.

P سرافگندگي *sar-afgandagī*, A bow of the head.

P سر افگندني *sar-afgandanī*, Veil for the head.

P سرافگنده *sar-afganda*, Confused, abashed.

A سرافين *sarāfīn*, Seraphim.

A سرّاق *surrāk*, (pl. of سارق *sārik*) Thieves.

P سراكاري *sarākārī*, An infamous crime.

P سراكوفت *sarā-koft*, A rebuke, railing at.

P سراكون *sarākūn*, Head downwards.

P سراگوش *sarāgosh*, A woman's hood or veil.

P سرآل *sar-āl*, In continual movement (as a mill). Stupefied, bewildered.

P سراماج *sarāmāj*, (or سراماچ *sarāmāch*) A yoke. The plough-tail.

P سرآمد *sar-āmad*, Froth, scum, or whatever floats on the surface. Perfect, complete, accomplished. Master of any art, profession, or excellence. Chief.

A سرامط *surāmit*, Long-bodied (camel).

P سران *sarān*, (pl. of سر *sar*) Generals, commanders. سران چرخ *sarāni charkh*, Angels, seraphim.

P سرانجام *sar-anjām*, Conclusion, end, accomplishment. An accident, event. Issue, termination. Apparatus, utensils, furniture, materiel. Materials, ingredients, supply, provision. سرانجام خرج *sar-anjām kharch*, Revenue-charges. سرانجام كردن *sar-anjām kardan*, To supply, provide.

P سرانداز *sar-andāz*, Warlike, intrepid, undaunted, fool-hardy, blood-thirsty. Shameless. Impure. A robber. Active, nimble. A man moving his head remarkably, from disease, drunkenness, pride, or any singular habit. Confused, bashful. A fine linen or painted silk veil, which the ladies wear when they go abroad; a coif, a hood. A main beam into which the joists are framed. A rug laid at the door. A note in music, called also صوفيانه.

P سرانداه *sarāndāh*, Madagascar.

P سرانديب *sarāndīb*, (or سرانديل) Ceylon.

P سرانگشت *sar-angusht*, Tip of the finger.

P سرانگشتي *sar-angushtī*, A dish of a particular kind of meat, pease, thin paste, and the like. Privet, with which they tinge the tips of the fingers and toes.

P سراو *sarāū*, Name of a river.

A سراوة *sarāwat*, (v. n. of سرو) Being liberal. Laying eggs (a locust).

A سراوع *sarāwiʿ*, (pl. of سروعة) Small sand-hills.

P سراوند *sarāwand*, Yellow colour.

P سراويزه *sarāweza*, A linen veil or head-dress.

A سراويل *sarāwīl*, (pl. of سروال *sirwāl*, سروالة *sirwālat*, and سرويل *sirwīl*) Breeches, trousers. سراويل الطلول *sarāwīlu't tulūl*, A kind of ivy.

A سراويلات *sarāwīlāt*, Breeches, trousers.

A سراوين *sarāwīn*, Breeches, trousers.

P سرآهنگ *sar-āhang*, The vanguard: forlorn hope. A nightly watch, patrole. Song. A note in music. A tetrastic. The thickest string of a musical instrument.

P سراي *sarāy*, A house, palace, grand edifice, king's court, seraglio. An inn. سراي پادشاهي *sarāy-pādshāhī*, A royal palace. سراي بقا *sarāyi bakā*, The mansion of eternity, the other world. Synonymous to which are the following words in composition with سراي *sarāy*: جاويد *jāwīd*, Eternal; جزا *jazā*, Retribution; زاهدان *zāhidān*, Holy men; سرور *surūr*, Joy; محمود *mahmūd*, Praised; نهفت *nihuft*, Concealed; هفت پرده *haft parda*, Seven-veiled.—سراي تزوير *sarāyi tazwīr*, The house of deceit, *i.e.* this world. Equivalent to which are the following: سپنج *sipanj*, Borrowed; شرور *shurūr*, Wickedness; شش در *shash dar*, Six-doored, six-sided, cubic; فاني *fānī*, Fading.—سراي خراج *sarāyi kharāj*, The council-chamber, the place where public affairs are debated, the court. The exchequer. سراي سپنج *sarāyi sipanj*, A lodge erected for people who watch sown fields. The world. سراي سرور *sarāyi surūr*, (House of mirth) A tavern. Paradise. سراي شرور *sarāyi shurūr*, A tavern. A gaming-house. The world. Hell. سراي شمرده *sarāyi shumurda*, The exchequer. سراي هفت پرده *sarāyi haft parda*, The heavens. كاروان سراي *kārwān-sarāy*, A caravansera. (particip. of سراييدن *sarāyīdan* or *sirāyīdan*) Singing, modulating. بربط سراي *barbut-sarāy*, A performer on the barbiton (a species of Persian harp or lute). نغمه سراي *naghma-sarāy*, An excellent singer.

A سرايا *sarāyaʾ*, (pl. of سريّة *sarīyat*) Brigades. Generous (women).

P سرايان *sarāyān*, Singing, warbling. Reciting. A singer. Name of a place.

P سرايانيدن *sarāyānīdan*, To cause to sing.

A سراية *sirāyat*, (v. n. of سري) Travelling or walking by night. Passing from one thing to another. Flowing, circulating through every part. A nocturnal journey. A contagion, infection. P سرايت كردن *sirāyat kardan*, To communicate (as pestilence). رايت نصرت سرايت *rāyati nusrat-sirāyat*, The victorious banner.

P سرايچه *sarāycha*, A tent, small habitation.

A سرائح *sarāʾih*, (pl. سريحة *sarīhat*) Strips of cloth. Thongs of leather. Long tracts of blood. Narrow roads thickly planted.

P سرايدار *sarāy-dār*, A garrison-soldier, a keeper of the palace.

A سرائر *sarāʾir*, (pl. of سريرة *sarīrat*) Secrets.

P سرايش *sarāyish*, Song, melody. Conversation.

P سراينده *sarāyanda*, Singing. A singer, reciter, or chanter. سراينده مرغ *sarāyanda-murgh*, A singing-bird.

P سراييدن *sarāyīdan* or *sirāyīdan*, To sing, modulate, shake. To coo as a turtle. سراييدن بسر *sarāyīdan ba sar*, To speak by signs or nods.

A سرب *sarb*, (v. n. of سرب) Sewing stitches. A way, road. Flocks, cattle at pasture. A side, part, mode, manner. The breast. A stitch. اذهبي فلا اندہ سربك *izhabī falā andahu sarbaki*, Get thee gone! I care not for thee! (a formula of divorce before the time of Muhammad). *Sirb*, Mind, soul, heart. A herd (of deer), flight (of birds), bevy (of women). A road. A grove of palm-trees. هو آمن في سربه *huwa āminun fī sirbihi*, He is happy in his mind. واسع السرب *wāsiʿu's sirb*, Liberal-minded. *Sarab*, (v. n. of سرب) Emitting water (a leathern bottle). Water flowing (from or into a bottle). The den or haunt of a wild beast. An aqueduct, pipe, conduit. A subterraneous habitation. *Sarib*, (A leathern bottle) emitting water.

P سرب *surb*, Lead. A cavern. *Sarib*, Old, rotten, squeezed, gone to pieces.

A سرباخ *sirbākh*, An extensive desert.

P سربار *sar-bār*, A bundle on the top of a load. سربار شدن *sar-bār shudan*, To be heavy-headed, to have a pain in the head.

P سرباري *sar-bārī*, A small load placed upon a heavier. A load borne upon the head.

P سرباز *sar-bāz*, Bare-headed. Brave, resolute, fool-hardy, intrepid, risking one's own life or head. A soldier. مبارز سرباز *mubārizi sar-bāz*, (or دلاور سرباز *dilāwari sar-bāz*) An intrepid soldier.

P سربازي *sar-bāzī*, Courage, fool-hardiness.

P سرباش *sar-bāsh*, (or سرباشي *sar-bāshī*) A chief. A battle-axe. A beadle.

P سرباك *sar-bāk*, A police-officer.

A سربال *sirbāl*, A shirt, shift. Any vestment.

P سربالا *sar-bālā*, A hill, a mountain.

P سربالين *sar-bālīn*, A pillow.

P سربان *sarbān*, A small bundle laid on the top of a load. A steep precipice.

P سربانگ *sar-bāng*, A woodpecker.

A سربة *sarbat*, A short journey. A single stitch. *Surbat*, (pl. سروب *surūb*) A flock of birds, bevy of roes, herd of horses or asses, company of people from twenty to thirty. A row of vines. Curly hair from the breast to the belly. Sect, mode, rule, institute. A grove of palms. *Saribat*, Leaky (water-bottle).

A سربج *surbuj*, A tribe in Turkistān.

A سربجي *surbujīy*, Of the tribe of سربج *surbuj*.

P سربجيب *sar ba jayb*, Hanging the head upon the bosom in a contemplative attitude.

A سربخ *sarbakh*, An extensive country, where one easily wanders out of the road.

A سربخة *sarbakhat*, Agility, lightness. A noon-day walk. A slow, gradual pace.

P سربخش *sar-bakhsh*, A portion, share. Past, gone by. High-minded.

P سربر *sar-bar*, A small bundle laid on the top of a load; a surplus addition to a burden. Magnitude, altitude. All, the whole. Back of the head, nape of the neck.

P سربراه *sar ba rāh*, A performer, finisher.

P سربراهي *sar barāhī*, Execution, performance.

P سربرغ *sar-bargh*, A dam-head.

P سربزرگ *sar-buzurg*, Great, of exalted dignity.

P سربزمين *sar ba zamīn*, Head to the ground.

P سربست *sar-bast*, Difficult, obscure. Free.

P سربسته *sar-basta*, Impervious, closed at the end. Covered, concealed, veiled. Wearing a turban. Any word, contract, or promise, by which one is bound.

P سربستي *sar-bastī*, Exemption, freedom.

P سربسر *sar ba sar*, Equal. Equally. Totally.

P سرب سوخته *surb-sokhta*, Antimony, burnt lead, wherewith females tinge their eye-brows.

A سربلة *sarbalat*, (v. n. of سربل Q) Putting on (a coat or shirt). Crumbled bread soaked in broth.

P سربلند *sar-baland*, High-headed, *i.e.* eminent, glorious, excellent. A fillet for the head. سربلند كردن *sar baland kardan*, To aggrandize, exalt.

P سربلندي *sar-balandī*, Eminence, exaltation.

P سربمهر *sar ba muhr*, Sealed.

P سربند *sar-band*, A plug or stopple. A wreath or fillet for fastening the ladies' head-dress. A turban.

P سربندي *sar-bandī*, An inclosure, a park.

P سربنهادن *sar binihādan*, To be refractory, fierce, stubborn.

P سربها *sar-bahā*, Price of blood. Ransom.

P سربيله *sar-bela*, A broad arrow-head.

P سربيني *sar-bīnī*, Tip of the nose.

P سرپا زدن *sar pā zadan*, To kick.

P سرپاس *sar-pās*, A head watchman. An iron mace. A shield. An iron helmet.

P سرپاش *sar-pāsh*, One whose faculties are impaired by age. One who has seen the world. A huge mace. A column.

P سرپايان *sar-pāyān*, A helmet. A turban. A soft linen cap worn under a helmet. Rings hanging from a helmet. Breeches.

P سرپائي *sar-pāī*, Sexual intercourse, adultery.

P هرپر *sar-par*, A chief.

P سرپرده *sarparda*, Name of a note in music.

P سرپرست *sar-parast*, A servant.

P سرپره *sar-para*, Lines drawn on the sand, between which they play at dice.

P سرپز *sar-paz*, Who cooks beasts' head and feet.

P سرپست *sar-past*, Medica, a sort of trefoil.

P سرپل *sarpal*, Tripping, stumbling. *Sar pul*, (Bridge-head) Name of a place.

P سرپنجگي *sar-panjagī*, Strength of fist, violence.

P سرپنجه *sar-panja*, Nails, claws, open hand, expanded fingers. Powerful, conquering. Dauntless.

P سرپنگ *sar-pang*, A helmet.

P سرپوش *sar-posh*, A cover, lid, or stopple. A female veil or head-dress of fine linen, muslin, or silk, part of which flows down and covers the face, shoulders, and sometimes the whole body. Any concealed business. Enigmatical discourse. Hidden, veiled, concealed.

P سرپوشنه *sar-poshna*, (or سرپوشه *sar-posha*) A cover, lid. A female veil, head-dress.

P سرپوشیده *sar-poshīda*, A virgin.

P سرپهن *sar-pahan*, A man or object, whose head, top, or upper part is plain or level. Name of an herb.

P سرپیچ *sar-pech*, (or سرپیش *sar-pesh*) An ornament of gold, silver, or jewels, generally placed in front of the turban.

A سرّة *surrat*, (pl. سرّات *surrāt* and سرر *surar*) (A woman) who makes cheerful. The navel, or the place where it is cut. The middle (of a valley). The choicest part of a valley. The lowest part of a cistern, where the water lodges.

P سرتاب *sar-tāb*, Refractory.

P سرتابي *sar-tābī*, Disobedience.

P سرتاپا *sar tā pā*, (or پاي *pāy*) Head to foot.

P سرتاج *sar-tāj*, A chief.

A سرتاح *sirtāh*, A generous camel. Level and fruitful ground.

P سرتادم *sar tā dum*, From head to tail.

P سرتازیانه *sar-tāziyāna*, In a second, directly.

P سرتاسر *sar tā sar*, From end to end.

P سرتاق *sar-tāk*, A tunic worn under the upper garment.

P سرتاقدم *sar tā kadam*, Head to foot. سرتا قدم لطافت *sar tā kadam latāfat*, Grace all over.

A سرتة *surtat*, Name of a town in Spain.

P سرتخته *sar-takhta*, A steel-plate pierced with holes of different dimensions, for wire-drawing gold or silver.

P سرتراش *sar-tarāsh*, A head-shaver, barber.

P سرتراشي *sar-tarāshī*, A shaving of the head.

P سرت سبز باد *sarat sabz bād*, May you live to be gray!

P سرتماج *sar-tumāj*, A hood, coif, veil.

P سرتير *sar-tīr*, Great: wise, learned: excellent.

P سرتيز *sar-tez*, Sharp-pointed (sword, thorn, &c). Irascible. The eye-lashes of the fair.

A سرج *sarj*, (v. n. of سرج) Saddling (a horse). Platting the hair. Lying. A saddle. *Saraj*, (v. n. of سرج) Having a handsome face. Lying.

P سرجا *sar-jā*, The chief place at a feast.

A سرجج *surjaj*, Permanent, perpetual, eternal.

P سرجفت كردن *sar juft kardan*, To listen.

A سرجم *sarjam*, Long, tall.

P سرجنگ *sarjang*, (or *sari jang*) A general, chief, leader of a body of troops. A serjeant.

A سرجوج *surjūj*, Foolish.

A سرجوجة *surjūjat*, Nature, disposition, manner, mode, institution. هم علي سرجوجة واحدة *hum ʻala' surjūjatin wāhidatin*, They are of the same disposition.

P سرجوش *sar-josh*, What is taken out of a pot for tasting. Best part or cream. Effervescence.

A سرجيجة *sirjījat*, Nature, disposition, mode.

A سرجين *sirjīn*, (from P سرگين) Dung, ordure.

P سرچپ *sarchap*, Leprosy, white morphew.

P سرچشمه *sar-chashma*, A fountain-head, spring. سرچشمهٔ جان *sar-chashmaʼi jān*, Fountain of life.

P سرچكاد *sar-chakād*, Top of the forehead.

P سرچكادي *sar-chakādī*, Any thing taken gratis; as when a purchaser having bought a couple of pounds of dried raisins walks off with a handful of vetches into the bargain. (In Hindūstān it is called دستوري *dastūrī*.)

P سرچنگ *sarchang*, Labour, fatigue. A kick in the backside.

A سرح *sarh*, (v. n. of سرح) Giving leave to roam, setting free. Bringing forth what is in the breast. Letting (hair) flow loose. Gushing forth (urine). A court before a house. Excrement. Large, tall trees, especially free from thorns. Cattle going out at morn. *Sarah*, (v. n. of سرح) Going on easily with one's affairs. *Suruh*, Nimble. Swift (horse). Quiet, gentle (she-camel). A gift made without delay. An easy pace.

A سرحا *suruhan* or *sarahan*, Easily.

A سرحال *sirhāl*, A wolf.

A سرحان *sirhān*, (pl. سراح *sarāh*, *sirāh*, and سراحين *sarāhīn*) A wolf. A lion. The middle of a pond. ذنب السرحان *zanabu's sirhān*, False dawn.

A سرحة *sarhat*, A she-ass full grown and not conceiving. Tall (woman).

P سرحدّ *sar-hadd* or *sar-had*, A frontier, confine, boundary, limit. A fortress on the frontiers. سرحد نشين *sarhad-nishīn*, Living or stationed on the confines. A marcher.

P سرحلقه *sar-halka*, A chief, head of the ring.

A سرحوب *surhūb*, A long-bodied horse, going expeditiously. A jackal. A tall man. A certain blind demon inhabiting the sea. Name of ابو جارود *abū jārūd*, the founder of a sect. سرحوب سرحوب *surhūbu surhūbu*, A calling of sheep to be milked.

A سرحوحة *surhūhat*, A similarity of temper. Temper, disposition.

P سرخ *surkh*, Red. A red tincture, or red ink. سرخ زنبوران *surkhi zumbūrān*, The tips of the fingers tinged with privet. سرخ و سفيد *surkh u safed*, Gold and silver. ماهيِ سرخ *māhīʼi surkh*, A red salmon found in the Caspian and its rivers.

P سرخاب *surkhāb*, Red water, *i.e.* paint used by the ladies. Blood. Wine. Name of a river in Kābul, so called from the hue of the water. A bright bay-horse. A horse belonging to Rustam. Name of a wrestler. Name of a son of Rustam. Name of a mountain near Tabrīz. Name of a king descended from Bahrām Gūr. A sort of water-fowl, called likewise خرچال *kharchāl*.

P سرخابي *surkhābī*, A red duck. A bay-horse.

P سرخارنگ *surkhā-rang*, Inclining to red.

P سرخاره *sar-khāra*, A golden bodkin which women wear in their hair, either by way of ornament or to fasten their veil. A kind of flesh-brush made of bone. A comb.

P سرخاش *sar-khāsh*, Main beam of a house.

P سرخباد *surkh-bād*, St. Anthony's fire.

P سرخ باده *surkh-bāda*, The erysipelas.

P سرخ بال *surkh-bāl*, (Red-wing) A bird resembling a partridge, but smaller.

P سرخ بت *surkh-but* (or بد *bud*), Name of an idol of a colossal size, existing at Bāmiān in Kābul.

P سرخ بيد *surkh-bīd*, A kind of willow-tree.

P سرخپا *surkh-pā*, (or پاي *pāy*) Wood-sorrel.

P سرخ پوش *surkh-posh*, Dressed in red.

P سرختيره *surkh-tīra*, A red or bay-horse.

P سرخ چشم *surkh-chashm*, Red-eyed. Cruel. An executioner.

P سرخچه *surkhicha*, (or سرخجه) Measles.

P سرخ دانه *surkh-dāna*, Red medicinal berry.

P سرخده *surkhida*, (سرخره *surkhira*, سرخزه *surkhiza*, or سرخژه *surkhija*) Measles.

P سرخ رو *surkh-rū*, Honourable. Acquitted. Pleased, contented. سرخ روي شدن *surkh rūy shudan*, To be red in the face or overspread with blushes.

P سرخر و بن خار *sar khar u bun khār*, An ass.

P سرخ روده *surkh-rūda*, The gullet.

P سرخ روئي *surkh-rūʼī*, Honour. Acquittal.

P سرخريد *sur-kharīd*, A ransom.

P سرخزرده *surkh-zarda*, Reddish yellow horse.

P سرخس *sarkhas*, Laurel. *Sarakhs*, A medicinal wood, black without and green within, found on the shores of the Caspian. A city in Khurāsān.

P سرخست *sirkhist*, (or سرخشت) A species of white manna, dissolving in water like chalk, administered, mixed with flour, in fevers. A small sprinkling rain.

P سرخ سر *surkh-sar*, (Red-head) A red-headed sparrow. A name by which the Persians are called.

P سرخ سرك *surkh-sarak*, A red-headed bird.

P سرخ سفيد *surkh-safed*, Red and white, fair.

P سرخ سوار *surkh-suwār*, The liver.

P سرخ شبان ياهودار *surkh shabāni yāhūdār*, (in zand and Pāzand) Moses.

P سرخشك ابلق *sar-khushki ablak*, Fortune. Time. The world.

P سرخط *sar-khat*, An agreement to hire service. A bill of sale.

P سرخ عيار *surkh-ʼiyār*, Proof, assay.

P سرخك *surkhak*, (dim. of سرخ *surkh*) Reddish. Measles. The cornel-tree or fruit.

P سرخگان *surkhgān*, Measles. Buboes.

P سرخ گون *surkh-gūn*, A saul.

P سرخم *sar-khum*, A jar-lid. Name of an herb.

P سرخ مرد *surkh-mard*, Name of a red flower.

P سرخو *surkhū*, Measles.

P سرخواب *sar-khwāb*, The first sleep.

P سرخوار *sir-khwār*, Possessed of hidden treasures, skilled in mysteries. A poet.

P سرخوارة *sar-khwāra*, A comb. A golden bodkin which women wear in their hair, as an ornament or to fasten their veil.

P سرخوان *sar-khwān*, Calling out. A reader, lecturer. A singer. A precentor. *Sur-khwān*, A kind of red pigeon.

P سرخواني *sar-khwānī*, The office of a precentor. Singing. Speaking. Telling one's fortune by reading the writing on the forehead. Irony, ridicule, jesting, buffoonery.

P سرخود *sar-khwud*, One's own master.

P سرخوش *sar-khwush*, Merry-headed. Tipsy (implying the stage of cheerful liveliness, not of stupid inebriation).

P سرخوشي *sar-khwushī*, Exhilaration.

P سرخة *surkha*, Red tincture. A kind of red pigeon. The windpipe. A pimple on the eyelid, a sty. Name of the son of Afrāsyāb. Name of a place. سرخةدار *surkha-dār*, The alder-tree, as producing a red dye.

P سرخي *surkhī*, Redness. Brickdust. A red tincture. Red ink. Blood. سرخي سرخ *surkhī surkh*, Intensely red.

P سرخيچة *surkhīcha*, (سرخيزة *surkhīza* or سرخيژة *surkhīja*) The measles.

P سرخيل *sar* or *sari khayl*, A general, commander of a regiment, a troop, or a body of men. سرخيل شياطين *sar-khayli shayātīn*, Iblīs, Satan.

G سرخيوس *sarkhiyūs*, Fumitory.

P سرد *sard*, Cold. Damp. Tasteless. Disagreeable, unpleasant. Without root. Bottomless. آب سرد *ābi sard*, Cold water. گرم و سرد *garm u sard*, Hot and cold. نفس سرد *nafasi sard*, A cold sigh. سرد شدن *sard shudan*, To be cold. To die. To grow tired of.

A سرد *sard*, (v. n. of سرد) Sewing (a leathern bottle). Weaving (a coat of mail). Linking. Perforating. Persevering (in observing a fast). Pursuing (a narrative) with fluency. A coat of mail; also the mutual intertexture of the rings. The sewing of leather, and the holes made by the punctures. Any thing continued, connected, uninterrupted, adhering. السرد *as' sard*, The months Zi'l kaʼdat, Zi'l hijjah, and Muharram. *Sarad*, (v. n. of سرد) Continuing, prolonging (a fast).

A سرداب *sard-āb*, A grotto, ice-house, a cold bath, a subterranean dwelling. *Sirdāb*, An intimate friend. Rock-parsley.

A سرداب *sirdāb*, (from P) A grotto. An ice-house.

P سردآبة *sard-āba*, A grotto, ice-house. A place where water is kept cool. A subterranean dwelling. A cool summer residence. A friend. Name of a waterfall in Kazwin, and of a Spanish island.

P سردآبي *sard-ābī*, The keeper of an ice-house; also any thing belonging to it.

A سرداح *sirdāh*, A cluster of palm-flowers. (pl. سرادح *sarūdih*) A fine, fat, strong she-camel.

P سردار *sar-dār*, A general, field-marshal, officer of rank, king's lieutenant, a chief in any department. سردار مگس انگبين *sardāri magasi angubīn*, A queen-bee.

P سرّدار *sirr-dār*, A confidant.

P سردارة *sar-dāra*, Rhyme.

P سرداري *sar-dārī*, Rank of سردار, chiefship.

A سردانية *sardāniyat*, Sardinia.

P سرداوة *sardāwa*, A cavern, grot, ice-house. An open apartment for the benefit of air.

P سرد بيان *sard-bayān*, Destitute of the graces of elocution. Plain-spoken, offensive. Dull, stupid.

A سردجة *sardajat*, A turning (camels) to pasture.

A سردح *sardah*, Plain, soft ground, producing the plant نصيّ *nasīy*.

A سردحة *sardahat*, A letting camels pasture freely.

P سردر *sar-dar*, The lintel of a door.

P سر در آمدن *sar dar āmadan*, To stumble, to fall on the head.

P سردرد *sar-dard*, Headache. Trouble.

P سردردي *sar-dardī*, Vexation.

P سر در سر *sar dar sar*, From end to end.

P سر در كف *sar dar kaf*, In great danger.

P سر در گليم *sar dar gilīm*, Head on the carpet, the game of hot-cockles.

P سر در هوا *sar dar hawā*, Head in the air, *i.e.* haughty, proud, lofty. Light-headed.

P سردست *sar-dast*, The wrist. Taking with the finger-ends.

P سردستار *sar-dastār*, A turban. Turban-sash.

P سردستة *sar-dasta*, A walking-staff.

P سردستي *sar-dastī*, Forthwith, without delay. Any thing taken up hastily with the tip of the finger. Whatever is at hand. A wandering dervish's staff.

P سرد سير *sard-ser*, A cold place. A summer habitation in high grounds (opposed to گرم سير).

P سردفتر *sar-daftar*, An officer of government, clerk, accomptant. An exordium, preamble, title page. A summary, synopsis. سردفتر آفرينش *sar-daftari āfirīnish*, Muhammad.

A سردقة *sardakat*, The putting up an awning.

P سرد گوي *sard-gūy* or *goy*, Harsh-spoken, one who uses ill language or utters offensive truths.

P سردمة *sardama*, A quick, light pace.

P سردوال *sar-duwāl*, Reins: a head-stall.

P سردوان *sar-dawān*, Nodding in walking.

A سردوخ *surdūkh*, Dates moistened in water.

P سردور *sar-dawr*, A chief spy.

P سردوز *sar-doz*, A kind of head-stall.

A سردولة *sardūlat*, A walnut.

P سردة *sarda*, A drinking-cup. The president of a company of topers. A cup-bearer. A sort of melon. Any fruit which ripens early. Kind, species. *Sirda*, Late fruits of the choicest kinds, which are sent in presents. Fruits left upon the trees after the in-gathering, after-fruits.

P سردي *sardī*, Cold, coldness.

P سردين *sardīn*, (in the language of the people of the West) A kind of fish, a sardine.

A سرر *sarar*, The navel-string which the midwife cuts. The middle of any thing. Hollowness. The middle of a month. The last night of the month. A hurt on a camel's breast. *Sarar* and *surar*, (pl. اسرار *asrār*) Lines, lineaments on on the palm of the hand. *Sirar*, Dirt adhering to, or the skin of, a mushroom. Lineaments, lines, wrinkles, creases on the palm of the hand or on the forehead. (pl. اسرار *asrār* and اسارير *asārīr*) The navel-string which the midwife cuts. The last night of a month. ولد له ثلاثة على سرر *wulida lahu salāsatun ʼala' sirarin*, Three boys were born to him consecutively. *Surar*, Skins or dirt sticking on a mushroom. The last night of a month. The middle of a month. (pl. of سرّة *surrat*) Navels. *Surur*, The upper part of the stalk of a plant. *Surur* or *surar*, (pl. of سرير *sarīr*) Thrones. Litters.

P سر راست *sar* or *sari rāst*, With head erect. Any thing rightly done. A well-cut reed or pen.

P سررشتة *sar-rishta*, A rope, thread, cord, extremity of a rope. Office, employment. Connexion, affinity. Desire, intention, purpose. سررشتهٔ اميد *sar-rishta-i umed*, Thread of hope. سررشتة يافتن *sar-rishta yāftan*, To obtain a clue to.

P سرز *sarz* or *saraz*, A plasterer's trowel.

P سرزدة *sar-zada*, Depraved, ill-bred.

P سرزن *sar-zan*, Rebellious, disobedient.

P سرزنش *sar-zanish*, Reproach, reproof, reprehension, chiding, sarcasm, rebuking, railing at. سرزنش روزگار *sar-zanishi rozgār*, Fortune's frowns.

P سرزور *sar-zor*, Rebellious, disobedient.

P سرزير *sar-zer*, With the head inclined.

P سرزيرة *sar-zīra*, Name of a fragrant herb.

P سرزيغ *sar-zīgh*, Bunch of dates or grapes.

A سرس *saras*, (v. n. of سرس) Being impotent, not gendering. Being cunning, shrewd, intelligent, and knowing how to keep what he has got. Being of an evil disposition. Becoming provident and vigilant after having been ignorant and thoughtless. *Saris*, (pl. سراس *sirās*) Impotent, unable to impregnate (man or animal). Weak. Cunning, shrewd, careful of what one has gotten.

A سرساء *surasā*, (pl. of سريس *sarīs*) Impotent.

P سرساخ *sar-sākh*, Fine, smooth silk.

P سرساد *sar-sād*, Cinquefoil.

P سرسام *sar-sām*, Stupefied. Frenzy, delirium.

P سرسامه *sar-sāma*, Mad, crazy.

P سرسامي *sar-sāmī*, Stupidity. Delirious.

P سرسان *sar-sān*, Fear, dread, astonishment.

P سرسبز *sar-sabz*, Verdant, fresh. Flourishing, thriving. Prosperous, fortunate. Rich. Life. Freshness. A king.

P سرسبزي *sar-sabzī*, Verdure. Prosperity.

P سرسبك *sar-sabuk*, Light-headed, vain.

P سرستون *sar* or *sari sutūn*, Capital of a pillar.

P سرسختي *sar-sakhtī*, Carelessness, inattention, heedlessness to what is said. Harsh words.

P سرسر *sarsar*, Foolish, silly. A veil, covering. Saw-dust. Folly, madness. A lid. سرسر شير *sarsari shīr*, Cream.

A سر سر *sur sur*, (imp.) Aim at high matters!

A سرسرة *sarsarat*, (v. n. of سرسر Q) Whetting (a shoemaker's knife).

P سرسره *sar-sara*, Top of a mountain, summit.

P سرسري *sarsarī*, Folly. Feebleness of administration. Inattention to, remissness in necessary duties. Vain words spoken without reflection. Astonishment. Mean. A fool. Quick of apprehension. Swift horse. An easy business. Easily. Gratuitously, for nothing.

P سرسم *sirsim*, Water-mint.

P سرسنه *sarisna* or *sirisna*, A district in Persia.

P سرسواران *sari suwārān*, Master of the horse.

A سرسور *sursūr*, Intelligent, knowing, shrewd, sly; one who gets a quick insight into any matter. An intimate friend. The point of a spindle. سرسور مال *sursūru mālin*, An able manager of property, one skilful in the management of camels.

P سرسينه *sar-sīna*, A pit in the neck.

P سرش *sirash*, (from سه *sih*, Three, and رش *rash*, Yard) Muslin, fine linen; also a lady's veil, three yards in length, flowing from the head to the feet. *Sirish*, Glue, starch, paste. (in zand and Pāzand) Vile, bad.

P سرشاخ *sar-shākh*, Main beam of a house.

P سرشار *sar-shār*, Brim-full. Intoxicated.

P سرشب *sarshab*, A royal falcon.

P سرشت *sirisht*, Mixed. Nature, temperament, constitution, complexion, natural shape, form, or make. Understanding, intellect. The four elements. Baking, kneading. پاكيزه سرشت *pākīza-sirisht*, Of an excellent disposition.

P سرشتن *sirishtan*, To mix, knead. To create, form into shape.

P سرشته *sirishta*, Mixed. (from سر رشته *sar-rishta*) A record, account; registry-office.

P سرشته دار *sirishta-dār*, A keeper of the records of a province. The native head-officer of a cutcherry or court (in India).

P سرشستني *sar-shustanī*, A lotion for the head (as an infusion of mallow-leaves, &c.).

P سرشف *sarshaf*, Mustard-seed.

P سرشك *sirishk*, A tear. A drop. Droppings of the eaves. Flowing of a fountain. Sparks of fire. A red-flowering tree. The flying upwards of sparks of fire. Barberries. The cypress. A white rose inclining to red, which blooms summer and winter. سرشك آتش *sirishki ātish*, Sap oozing from green wood when placed upon the fire. سرشك انگبين *sirishki angubīn*, A syrup composed of honey, water, and vinegar. Date-syrup. سرشك باريدن *sirishk bāridan*, To shed tears. سرشك شور *sirishki shor*, Tears of sorrow. سرشك هوا *sirishki hawā*, (Tears of the air) Dew.

P سرشك باران *sirishk-bārān*, Rain. Small rain.

P سرشكستگی *sar-shikastagī*, Fracture of skull.

P سرشكسته *sar-shikasta*, Broken-pated.

P سرشكن *sar-shikan*, Head-breaking. A free grant of land, the rents of which are made up by an additional assessment on the residue of the lands.

P سرشكني *sar-shikanī*, Resistance. Death.

P سرشكوان *sirishkwān* or سرشكون *sirishkwan*, A curtain by which a bride is concealed on her wedding-night.

P سرشوي *sar-shūy*, A barber, shaver. A kind of white clay with which women clean their hair.

P سرشير *sar* or *sari shīr*, Cream, scum of milk.

A سرط *sarat*, (v. n. of سرط) Swallowing (any thing). *Surat*, A hard runner. A swallower of large mouthfuls.

P سرطاق *sar-tāk* or *sari tāk*, A balcony or upper summer apartment open to the front.

A سرطان *saratān*, (v. n. of سرط) Swallowing. A crab. The sign Cancer. A sore, cancer, canker. A disease incident to the feet of cattle. Swift of foot. A swallower of large mouthfuls. Bold, brave. سرطان بحري *saratāni bahrī*, A sea-crab. سرطان نهري *saratāni nahrī*, A cray-fish. سرطان رحم *saratāni rahim*, A cancer in the womb.

A سرطة *suratat*, Swift in swallowing, a bolter.

A سرطراط *siritrāt* or *saratrāt*, A dish composed of flour, honey, or dates and water.

A سرطعة *sartaʻat*, A running fast from fear.

A سرطل *sartal*, Tall and tottering.

A سرطلة *sartalat*, A tottering from disproportioned height.

A سرطم *sartam* or *sirtim*, Long. One who speaks clearly. One who has a wide swallow. *Sirtim*, A glutton. An eloquent speaker.

A سرطيط *sirtīt*, A swallower of large gobbets.

A سرع *sarʻ* or *sirʻ*, A vine-shoot. Any branch fresh and moist. A tender youth. *Saraʻ* or *siraʻ*, Haste, expedition. السرع السرع *as' siraʻu's siraʻ*, Quick, quick! *Siraʻ*, (v. n. of سرع) Making haste.

A سرعان *sarʻān*, *sirʻān*, or *surʻān*, He hastened. *Sirʻān* or *surʻān*, (pl. of سريع *sarīʻ*) Twigs of the tree called بشام *bashām*. *Surʻān*, (pl. of سريع *sarīʻ*) Quick, nimble, hasty, expeditious. *Saraʻān*, A bowstring made from the sinews of the back. *Saraʻān* or *sarʻān*, The first (of the people), principals. The best (horses), such as take the lead.

A سرعة *surʻat*, (v. n. of سرع) Doing (any thing) with despatch: haste, expedition, quickness, despatch.

P سرعت كردن *surʻat kardan*, To make haste.

A سرعة *surʻatan*, Quickly.

A سرعرع *saraʻraʻ*, A fresh, moist branch. A tender, limber youth. Tall.

P سرعسكر *sar-ʻaskar*, A general, commander of land forces; seraskier.

P سرعشر *sar-ʻashar*, A mark or marginal asterisk placed after every decade of verses in the Kur'an.

P سرعطسة آدم *sar ʻatsasi ādam*, Jesus Christ.

A سرعفة *sarʻafat*, A feeding well (an infant).

A سرعوب *surʻūb*, A weasel.

A سرعوف *surʻūf*, Tender, delicate, light of flesh. Tall, slim woman. A locust. A moth. A tall horse.

A سرغ *sargh*, (v. n. of سرغ) Eating grapes with the stalks. (pl. سروغ *surūgh*) A vine-shoot.

P سرغچ *sarghich*, A wooden bowl.

P سرغنة *sarghana*, Great, large, and incomparable. A chief. Abovementioned, aforesaid.

P سرغوت *sarghūt*, Opulence. Beneficence.

P سرغوغا *sar-ghawghā*, Ringleader of a mutiny, or tumult. Vanguard of an army.

P سرغين *sar*, *sirghīn*, (or سرغينه) A corn-pipe.

A سرف *sarf*, (v. n. of سرف) (A caterpillar) eating the leaves of trees. Feeding her young badly, giving it too much milk. *Saraf*, (v. n. of سرف) Exceeding bounds, being prodigal. Exercising one's self in any thing. Omitting, slighting, neglecting, forgetting, being ignorant of. Mistaking, blundering, doing wrong. Obscurity, dulness of intellect. Leaking through the sides of a well (water). Greediness. Excess. Habit, habitude. Nobility, dignity, rank. *Sarif*, Deficient in understanding, blunder-headed, silly; negligent, careless. *Suruf*, A white substance resembling the web of a silk-worm.

P سرف *surf*, A cough. One who coughs. Lead. *Saraf* or *suruf*, A soreness in the throat or the chest from coughing. A tickling sensation of the palate.

P سرفاك *sarfāk*, Sound, voice, clamour.

P سرفانيدن *surfānīdan*, To cough. To make (any one) cough.

A سرفة *surfat*, The white ant. A ship-worm. A caterpillar. A certain insect, which having constructed a dwelling from particles of wood, enters it and dies. اصنع من سرفة *asnaʻ min surfatin*, Better mechanician than the white ant. *Sarifat*, (A country) abounding in such vermin.

A سرفح *sarfah,* A name of the devil.

P سرفراز *sar-farāz,* Eminent, exalted; having the head raised, distinguished; proud, disobedient. Height, dignity. Name of the third day of the month of the æra of Malik.

P سرفرازي *sar-farāzī,* Grandeur, exaltation.

P سرفرو *sar-faro,* With a humble head, submissive. Humiliation.

P سرفروش *sar-farosh,* Who cooks and sells the heads of cattle. Ready to sacrifice one's life.

P سرفروشي *sar-faroshī,* Bravery, fidelity. Sacrifice of life. Sale of heads of cattle.

P سرف سرف *surf surf,* A cough. Coughing.

P سرفه *surfa,* Cough. Ship-worm. Caterpillar.

P سرفه زده *surfa-zada,* Troubled with a cough. سرفه زده گرديدن *surfa-zada gardīdan,* To be attacked by a cough.

P سرفيدن *surfīdan,* To cough.

A سرق *saraka,* (fut. يسرق *yasriku*) He stole.

A سرق *sarak,* (v. n. of سرق) Being concealed. Being weak (the joints). (from P سره *sara*) (pl. of سرقة *sarakat*) Strips of white silk. *Sarak, sarik,* or *sark,* (v. n. of سرق) Stealing. Pilfering. *Sarik,* Theft, larceny. Plagiarism.

A سرّق *surrak,* Name of a man.

A سرقات *sarikāt,* Literary thefts, plagiarisms.

A سرقة *sarkat,* Theft. *Sarakat,* A strip of white silk. *Sarakat* or *sarikat,* (v. n. of سرق) Stealing. *Sarikat,* Theft, larceny. Plagiarism. P سرقه كردن *sarika kardan,* To steal, pilfer.

A سرقةً *sarikatan,* By stealth, stealthily.

A سرقسطة *sarakustat,* Saragossa (in Spain).

A سرقع *surkuᵒ,* Sour or pricked wine.

P سرقفلي *sar-kuflī,* Fees for unlocking, exacted from a tenant on his taking possession of a house.

P سرقليان *sar-kaliyān,* The round plate to which is stuck the tobacco in a hookah, generally a thin piece of unglazed tile, and upon the contrary side of which the fire is put.

A سرقنة *sarkanat,* The dunging (of land).

P سرقوارة *sarkawāra,* A finger-nail.

P سرقوج *surkūj,* A plume of feathers, decorated with gold and jewels, with which Persian ladies and great men adorn their heads.

A سرقين *sirkīn* or *sarkīn,* Dung, manure.

P سرك *sirk,* Red and white paint for the face. *Surk,* Measles. *Sarak,* A little head. (in the dialect of Kazwīn) A boy.

A سرك *sarak,* (v. n. of سرك) Becoming thin and weak after having been strong (the body).

P سركا *sirkā,* Vinegar.

T سركاتبي *sir-kātibī,* A secretary.

P سركار *sar-kār,* A chief, superintendant, supervisor, overseer, agent. A title by way of respect given to a person present or absent. A weaver's shop. A workshop. A king's court. Government. Estate. Property. Knowledge, practice. (in India) A district comprising several pergunnahs.

P سركاري *sar-kārī,* Superintendence. Belonging to the estate or to government.

P سركب *sarkab,* Name of a famous musician.

P سركج *sar-kaj,* Curved at the head (stick).

P سركحلي *sar-kuhlī,* A black thing: dark cloud.

P سركردگي *sar-kardagī,* Chief command.

P سركرده *sar-karda,* Begun. A beginning.

P سركس *sarkas,* Name of a melodious bird.

P سركش *sar-kash,* Refractory. Proud, arrogant, contumacious. Powerful, disobedient, stubborn, rebellious, mutinous, obstinate. A wild, unbroke horse. An old acquaintance. Name of a celebrated musician. An upright or a straight man. A horse that carries his head erect. A reed prepared for writing. اسب سركش *asbi sar-kash,* A hard-mouthed, restive horse.

P سركشي *sar-kashī,* Obstinacy, mutiny.

P سركن *sarkan,* The herb orage.

P سركنگبين *sirkangubīn,* Oxymel, honey and vinegar, prescribed for the bile.

P سركوب *sar-kob,* Head-striking. Overlooking, overtopping. A machine erected to overtop a wall; a battery. A battering machine. Any eminence which commands a fortress or houses. A citadel. A superintendant. Excelling in every art. Valiant in battle. A sturdy fellow. A molester. Contumely, reproach.

P سركوبه *sar-koba,* Heavy mace. Smart reproof.

P سركوچك *sar-kūchak,* Vile, low, worthless.

A سركوك *surkūk,* Lean, emaciated (camel).

P سركه *sirka,* Vinegar. A glow-worm. A nit. سركهٔ ده ساله *sirkaᵢ dah sāla,* Vinegar ten years old; an ancient grudge. سركه فروختن *sirka farokhtan,* (To sell vinegar) To put on a sour look. سركهٔ هندي *sirkaᵢ hindī,* (India vinegar) Rice-water left till it becomes sour.

P سركه ابرو *sirka-abrū,* A crabbed fellow.

P سركه با *sirka-bā,* Hashed meat, bruised grain, and vinegar.

P سركه فشاني *sirka-fishānī,* Reproach, sarcasm.

P سركيجه *sarkīja,* Vertigo. سركيجه در آمدن *sarkīja dar āmadan,* To be seized with a giddiness (from hunger or any other cause).

P سرگذشت *sar-guzasht,* An event, accident, transaction. A recollection or relation of any past circumstance. A story. Experienced.

P سرگر *sargar* or *surgar,* A cobbler. A maker or vender of beer. *Surgar,* A kind of hedgehog.

P سرگران *sar-girān,* Having the head confused with drink, intoxicated, crop-sick. Proud, arrogant. Angry. Dissatisfied. Pierced. Head-ache, crop-sickness. A heavy club.

P سرگراني *sar-girānī,* Dissatisfaction.

P سرگردا *sar-gardā,* Vertigo, giddiness.

P سرگردان *sar-gardān,* Confounded, stupefied, amazed, astonished, distressed. Giddiness. Wandering, straying. Humbled, depressed. A vagabond.

P سرگرداني *sar-gardānī,* Amazement. Distress.

P سرگرده *sar-garda,* Astonished, stupefied.

P سرگرفته *sar-girifta,* Head-ache. Reproach. A reviler.

P سرگرم *sar-garm,* Inflamed with love. Intent upon, attentive. A wandering Muhammadan monk.

P سرگرمي *sar-garmī,* Application, attention. Love, the being in love.

P سرگره *sar-girih,* A knot on a rosary-head.

P سرگزيت *sar-gazīt,* (or گزيد *gazīd*) Tribute. Poll-tax, head-money levied on Jews and Christians.

P سرگزين *sar-gazīn,* Tribute. *Sar-guzīn,* One who picks out the best of the flock. The choicest animal thus selected.

P سرگشتگي *sar-gashtagī,* Astonishment, bewilderment.

P سرگشته *sar-gashta,* Astonished, stupefied, bewildered: dizzy, vertiginous. Wandering. Busy. Under authority. سرگشتگان باديه *sar-gashtagāni bādiya,* Wanderers in the desert.

P سرگل *sargal,* A ball for playing with.

P سرگلو *sar-gulū,* A disease in the brain (as affecting the head and throat).

P سرگله نهادن *sar gala nihādan,* To choose. To honour.

P سرگم شدن *sar gum shudan,* To be bewildered; to lose one's way, or rather, one's head.

P سرگوتا *sargūtā* or *sirgūtā,* (in zand and Pāzand) A secret. A gibbet.

P سرگوشي كردن *sar-goshī kardan,* To whisper.

P سرگيجش *sar-gījash* (or سرگيجه *gīja*), Vertigo.

P سرگيري *sar-gīrī,* Beginning of business. Putting out a lamp.

P سرگيس *sargīs,* The rainbow.

P سرگين *sargīn,* Dung, especially dried and kept for firing. سرگين انداختن *sargīn andākhtan* (or افگندن *afgandan*), To void excrement. سرگين در زمين زدن *sargīn dar zamīn zadan,* To dung land.

P سرگين پاشيده *sargīn-pāshīda,* Manured (field).

P سرگين جاي *sargīn-jāy,* A dunghill.

P سرگين دان *sargīndān,* A dunghill.

P سرگين زار *sargīnzār,* A mixen, dunghill.

P سرگين غلطان *sargīn-ghaltān,* A tumble-dung.

P سرگين گردان *sargīn-gardān,* A beetle.

P سرگين ناك *sargīnnāk,* Defiled with ordure. Dunged, manured.

G سرلاب *surlāb,* An astrolabe.

P سرلاد *sar-lād,* The top of a wall. A wall.

P سرم *sarm,* Artichoke. Cold. Wild-mustard.

A سرم *surm,* The intestine which communicates with the anus, the straight gut, the rectum. *Saram,* A pain in the fundament.

P سرما *sarmā,* Winter, cold. Cold (weather).

P سرما برد *sarmā-burd,* The blasting (of trees).

A سرما *sarman,* Used in driving away dogs.

P سرماخوردگي *sarmā-khurdagī,* Chilliness, nip.

P سرما خورده *sarma-khwurda*, Nipped by cold.

P سرما ريزگي *sarmā-rezagī*, Hoar frost.

P سرما زدگي *sarmā-zadagī*, Chill, nip, blast.

P سرما زده *sarmā-zada*, Stricken with cold.

P سرماسرد *sarmāsard*, A summer habitation (among mountains).

P سرما فزاي *sarmā-fizāy*, Name of the ninth month of the year of the æra of Malik.

P سرمامك *sar-māmak*, Game of hide and seek.

A سرمان *surmān*, A malignant sort of hornet.

P سرماهي *sar-māhī*, Heads of fish; the name given by the Persians to those whom the Greeks called Ichthyophaghi, or people who live on fish. Monthly pay.

P سرمايه *sar-māya*, The capital of a merchant, stock in trade, principal sum. Head. Fortune. Possibility, means.

P سرمايه دار *sarmāya-dār*, A monied man.

P سرمائي *sarmāī*, Wintry. Winter-clothing.

P سرمج *sarmaj*, Orage. A kind of ivy.

P سرمخار *sar ma khār*, Don't scratch your head, *i.e.* be quick.

A سرمد *sarmad*, Everlasting. A long night.

A سرمدا *sarmadan*, Eternally, for ever.

A سرمديّ *sarmadiy*, Eternal, perpetual. Divine.

A سرمديّة *sarmadiyat*, Eternity.

P سرمره *sar-mara*, A numbering by the head. سرمره كردن *sar-mara kardan*, To count by the head.

A سرّمرّيّ *surra marriy*, A native of Sur man rā.

P سرمست *sar-mast*, Very drunk, crop-sick. A camel which staggers when travelling as if drunk.

P سرمستي *sar-mastī*, Intoxication, ebriety.

P سرمش *sarmish*, Apricots stuffed with almonds.

P سرمشق *sarmashk*, A copy (for writing). سرمشقهاي طفلان مكتب *sarmashkhāyi tiflāni maktab*, Copies for boys at a writing-school.

A سرمط *sarmat*, Long-bodied (camel).

A سرمطيط *sarmatīt*, Long-bodied (camel).

A سرمق *sarmak* or *surmuk*, Orage, an herb. The herb all-heal.

P سرمك *sarmak*, Orage.

A سرّ من رأي *surra man raa'*, Name of a city or imperial residence near Baghdād.

P سرمو *sar-mo* or *mū*, A hair's point; a trifle.

P سرموتك *sarmūtak*, Commotion, noise, cry.

P سرموزه *sar-mūza*, Hose worn over boots.

P سرمه *sarma*, Orage. Galangale. *Surma*, A collyrium, with which they tinge the eyebrows and lashes, antimony, lead-ore. Name of a village in Persia. سرمهٔ خاك بين *surmai khāk-bīn*, A collyrium of Khusraw Parwez, which enabled any one whose eyes were anointed therewith to see to the distance of three feet under the ground. سرمهٔ گيتي *surmai gītī*, A dark night. ميل سرمه *mīli surma*, A style with which they apply collyrium.

P سرمه آلوده *surma-ālūda*, (or سرمه كشيده *surma-kashīda*) Anointed with surma.

P سرمه چوب *surma-chob*, A surma-style,

P سرمه دان *surmadān*, A box in which they keep surma. سرمه دان عاجي *surmadāni ājī*, An ivory surma-box. A concealed figure.

P سرمه طاش *surma-tāsh*, Antimony.

P سرمه كش *surma-kash*, One who applies the collyrium to the eye: the instrument by which it is applied. Whatever enlightens the eye. A dark night.

A سرمينيّه *sarmīniya*, A town near Aleppo.

P سرمئي *surmaī*, Of surma colour, greyish.

P سرن *saran*, The white lily.

P سرنا *surnā*, A hautbois; a clarion.

P سرناپا *surnā-pā*, A cameleopard.

P سرناچي *surnāchī*, A hautbois-player.

P سرنازن *surnā-zan*, A player on the hautbois.

P سرناس *sarnās*, An old sedate man. Manly, arrived at the age of a man. Impotent. *Sirnās*, One who has experienced the vicissitudes of fortune.

A سرناف *sirnāf*, Long, tall.

P سرنامه *sar-nāma*, Titles at the beginning of a letter, given to the person to whom it is addressed. Address, superscription, direction of a letter: as, در فلان محل بفلاني برسانند *dar fulān mahal ba fulānī bi rasānand*, May they cause (it) to reach so and so at such a place!

P سرناي *surnāy*, A trumpet, clarion, bugle.

A سرنج *saranj*, Vermilion, sandix. A kind of salve for wounds.

P سرنج *sirinj*, A cymbal. Red lead, vermilion.

P سرند *sirind*, Entangling the legs, as wrestlers to trip each other. A swing. A noose for catching prey by the foot, a lasso. A green film which floats on the surface of stagnant water. A kind of sparrow. *Sirand* or *sirind*, Ivy.

P سرنده *saranda*, An island in the sea of Omān.

A سرنديٰ *saranda'*, (fem. سرنداة *sarandāt*) Quick, active in business. Firm, well knit.

A سرنديب *sarandīb*, Ceylon.

P سرنديدن *sarandīdan*, To sit cross-legged. To water.

P سرنگ *sarang*, (in comp.) Mixing. A mixture of words. A kind of mixed silken stuff. *Saring*, Orage. *Sirang*, (سه رنگ *sih rang*) A garment of three colours. The griffin.

P سرنگون *sar-nigūn*, Head-downwards. Depressed. Vile, mean, abject. Backward. Inverted. Prone (as a quadruped). Abashed. Head over heels, a summersault. سرنگون رفتن *sar-nigūn raftan*, To retire confounded. طاس سرنگون *tāsi sar-nigūn*, A cup turned down.

P سرنگيدن *sarangīdan*, To wager. To mix in conversation. To laugh. To expand. *Sirangīdan*, To dispute. *Siringīdan*, To put on clothes.

P سرنگيل *sirangīl*, A certain kind of writing.

P سرنوبه *sar-nawba*, A head watchman.

P سرنوشت *sar-navisht*, Written on the forehead, *i.e.* Destiny, predestination, fate, fortune. The title or frontispiece of a book.

A سرنوف *surnūf*, A sparrow-hawk.

P سر نهادن *sar nihādan*, To bow the head, to kiss the ground in adoration or respect.

P سرنهين *sar-nihīn*, A furnace, oven. A pot.

P سرني *surnay*, A clarion.

A سرو *sars* or *sirs*, A locust's egg: fish-spawn.

P سرو *sarv*, The cypress-tree. سرو آزاد *sarvi āzād*, The free cypress (so called from its freedom from curvature, and its independence of all support, or from its being always green). سرو آهو *sarvi āhū*, A stag's attire. سرو بلند *sarvi baland*, The tall cypress. سرو خرامان *sarvi khirāmān*, A mistress with a graceful figure. سرو سهي *sarvi sahī*, A cypress straight and bipartite. Name of a note in music. سرو سياه *sarvi siyāh*, A juniper. سرو كاشغر *sarvi kāshghar*, The figure of a mistress. سرو كوهي *sarvi kohī*, Juniper or wild cypress. سرو ناز *sarvi nāz*, Fresh. A cypress-shoot. A cypress whose branches extend in all directions. A beautiful woman, a sweetheart. Name of a note in music. *Surū*, A horn. A lie. A goblet of wine.

A سرو *sarw*, (v. n. of سرو) Being liberal, generous. Laying eggs (a locust). Putting off (clothes). Stripping. Driving away care. A cypress. A weevil. A liberal man. Humanity, generosity, liberality. Nobility. The abode of the Himyarit Arabs. A rocky declivity. Land overhanging a valley. ابو السرو *abū's sarw*, Perfumes.

A سروء *sarūs*, (pl. سرء *surus*, rarely سرّء *surras*) A locust laying eggs.

P سروا *sarwā*, A romance, fable. A lie, false report. Bare-headed. An apartment open to the front. *Surwā*, A word.

A سرواء *surawās*, (pl. of سريّ) Liberal, generous.

A سروات *sarawāt*, (pl. of سراة *sarāt*) Backs. (pl. of سريّ *sariy*) Liberal, generous.

P سرواد *sarwād*, Poesy, ode, song. Vain, idle talk.

P سرواده *sar-wāda*, The last consonant in a verse to which all the other distichs rhyme.

P سروار *sar-wār*, A small load upon a heavier.

A سرواط *sirwāt*, A glutton.

A سروال *sirwāl*, (or سروالة *sirwālat*) (pl. سراويل *sarāwīl*) Breeches, trousers.

P سرواله *surwāla*, A bur, a kind of prickly adhesive plant.

P سروان *sarwān*, Chiefs. A camel-leader.

P سروب *sarob*, (in zand and Pāzand) A word.

A سروب *surūb*, (v. n. of سرب) Pasturing at liberty (a camel). Walking abroad, ranging at large. (pl. of سربة *surbat*) Groves of palm-trees.

A سروة *sarwat*, One cypress. *Sarwat*, *sirwat*, or *surwat*, (pl. سريٰ *sira'*) A small arrow. A short arrow with a long and broad head. *Sirwat*, A locust just hatched. When first hatched it is called سروة *sirwat*: then دبا *daba'*: then غوغاء *ghawghās*: lastly, كتفان *kutfān*.

P سروتك *sarotak* or *saravtak*, Tumult, scuffle.

A سروج *sarūj*, Name of a town near حرّان *harrān*. *Surūj*, (pl. of سرج *sarj*) Saddles.

P سروچ *saroch*, A desert in Karmānia.

P سرو چمان *sarvi chamān*, A graceful girl.

A سروح *surūh*, (v. n. of سرح) Pasturing at large (in the morning).

P سروخشت *sarūkhisht*, Good advice unheeded.

P سرود *sarwad*, Poesy, ode, song. *Surod*, A song. A word. Singing and dancing. سرود گفتن *surod guftan*, To sing.

P سرود گوي *surod-goy* or *gūy*, A singer.

P سرودن *surodan*, To sing.

P سرودي *surodī*, A singer.

P سرور *sarwar*, A sovereign, prince, lord, chief, head, leader, general. Warlike. Work, business. Name of a Muhammadan saint. سرور كائنات *sarwari kāināt*, (Chief of the world) Muhammad. سرور مجلس *sarwari majlis*, Master of a feast.

A سرور *surūr*, (v. n. of سرّ) Making glad. Joy, cheerfulness, delight, pleasure. Contentment. Tips of branches of odoriferous plants. P سرور تامّ و ذوق بي انجام *surūri tāmm u zawki bī anjām*, Perfect pleasure and endless delight.

P سرور آباد *surūr-ābād*, Abode of joy; pleasant.

P سرورسيدن *sarwarasīdan*, To be used to.

P سروري *sarvarī*, Empire, sovereignty, chiefship. A principality. Pre-excellence. *Surūrī*, Name of a poet.

A سروس *sarūs*, Name of a town in Africa.

P سروستان *sarvistān*, A place abounding with cypresses. Name of a note in music. Name of a place in Persia.

P سروستاه *sarv-sitāh*, Name of a note in music.

P سروش *surosh*, (pl. سروشها *suroshhā*) An angel. Gabriel. The seventeenth day of every solar month. سروش اعظم *suroshi azam*, Gabriel.

P سروشه *surosha*, An angel. Gabriel.

A سروعة *sarwaᶜat*, A tumulus, hillock of sand.

A سروغ *surūgh*, (pl. of سرغ) Vine-shoots.

A سروف *sarūf*, Large, powerful.

P سروقت *sar-wakt*, A retired bed-chamber, closet, cabinet. A convenient, leisure time.

P سروقد *sarv-kad*, In stature like the cypress, straight, erect.

P سروكار *sar u kār*, Affair, concern, business.

A سروكة *sarwakat*, An awkward and sluggish pace, from weakness or fatigue.

P سرول *sarwal*, Name of a city in India. *Sarūl*, Envy, malice.

A سرولة *sarwalat*, A putting into breeches.

A سرومط *sarawmat*, Long-bodied (camel). A sheep-skin in which they put a wine-bottle. A blanket or wrapper in which any thing is enveloped.

P سرون *sarūn*, A horn. سرون زدن *sarūn zadan*, To butt, to gore. *Surūn*, Buttocks.

P سروي *sarūy*, A horn. *Surūy*, Buttocks.

A سرويّ *sarawīy*, Relating to the arrow سروة.

P سرويسه *sarwesa*, The rainbow.

A سرويل *sirwīl*, (pl. سراويل) Breeches, trousers.

P سره *sara*, Current (coin). Good money (opposed to نبهره *nabahra*). Going well (horse). A narrow path between mountains. A channel in a declivity made by a torrent. Water beyond a man's depth. A rent in a banner. Root. Issue, progeny, offspring. A kind of Turkomān shoe or sandal. A web of cloth. A strip of white silk. Good, agreeable, pure, faultless.

P سرها *sarhā*, (pl. of سر *sar*) Heads.

P سرهال *sar-hāl*, Bewildered, astonished, confounded. The firmament. Continually revolving.

A سرهب *sarhab*, A glutton, a drunkard. Silly.

A سرهبة *sarhabat*, Long, corpulent (woman).

A سرهجة *sarhajat*, (v. n. of سرهج Q) Refusing. Twisting tight (a rope). Obstinacy, refractoriness.

A سرهدة *sarhadat*, (v. n. of سرهد Q) Feeding (an infant) well. Cutting a camel's bunch.

A سرهفة *sarhafat*, A feeding (an infant) well.

P سره مرد *sara-mard*, Benevolent. Clever.

P سرهنگ *sar-hang*, A general, a commander, captain, chief, champion, combatant. A boatswain. A serjeant, lictor, lifeguard-man. An overseer. A commissary. A foot-soldier. Disobedient, rebellious.

P سره وقت *sara-waht*, Leisure.

P سري *sarī*, Chiefship, rank of general. A large river. A funnel. A kind of armour for a horse's head. A palace, house. Name of a certain saint.

A سري *sary*, (v. n. of سري) Running a distance under ground (the root of a tree). Throwing baggage on the back of a beast. Casting (a garment) from one. *Sira'*, (pl. of سروة *sarwat*, *sirwat*, or *surwat*) Small arrows. *Sura'*, (v. n. of سري) Travelling by night. A nocturnal journey. Generosity, liberality. (pl. of سريّ *sarīy*) Liberal. ابن السري *ibnu's sura'*, A traveller by night.

A سرّي *surra'*, (v. n. of سرّ) Making glad.

A سريّ *sariy*, (pl. اسرية *asriyat* and سريان *suryān*) A rivulet running to a palm-plantation. (pl. اسرياء *asriyā*, سرواء *surawā*, سري *sura'*, and سراة *sarāt*) Liberal, generous. Choicest, best. سريّ سقطيّ *sariy saktiy*, A well-known saint.

A سرّيّ *sirriy*, Mysterious. *Surriy*, A native of Surr man rā.

A سرياح *siryāh*, Long. Liberal, munificent.

A سريان *suryān*, (pl. of سريّ *sariy*) Rivulets.

P سرياني *suryānī*, Syriac.

A سرية *saryat* or *suryat*, (v. n. of سري) Travelling by night. *Siryat*, A locust newly hatched. *Suryat*, A nocturnal journey.

A سريّة *sariyat*, (pl. سرايا *sarāya'*) A brigade, army, troops, any body of men from five to 300 or 400. A small round spear-head. (pl. سريّات *sariyāt* and سرايا *sarāya'*) Liberal (woman).

A سرّيّة *surrīyat*, (pl. سراري *sarāri*) A concubine, a mistress clandestinely kept.

A سريج *surayj*, A beautiful nose. Name of a certain smith or armourer.

A سريجيّ *surayjiy*, (Armour) made by Surayj.

P سريچه *saricha*, A wagtail.

A سريح *sarīh*, Naked, unsaddled, uncovered (horse). Flowing (urine). Easy, convenient.

A سريحة *sarīhat*, (pl. سرائح *sarāʾih*) A leathern thong for sewing with. A long track of blood. A narrow road thickly planted. A piece of a garment.

P سري خنور *sariyi-khanūr*, A funnel.

P سريخه *sarīkha*, A pelican.

P سريد *sarīd*, A green film which floats on the surface of stagnant ponds. A swing.

A سريد *sarīd*, A cobbler's awl.

P سرير *sarīr* or *sirīr*, The rainbow.

A سرير *sarīr*, (pl. اسرّة *asirrat* and سرر *surur* and *surar*) A throne. An ornamented sofa or couch. A kingdom. A bier (without the body). A sleeping-place. A favour, benefit. Affluence, the comforts of life. Root, basis. That part of the head next to the neck. Sand upon a hillock. The pulp of the papyrus. سرير فلك *sarīri falak*, The Great Bear. P سرير مرده *sarīri murda*, A bier. A سرير معدلت مصير *sarīri maᶜdilat-masīr*, The throne of justice. *Surayr*, Name of an anchorage in Hijāz frequented by ships from Abyssinia to Madīna.

P سرير افراز *sarīr-afrāz*, Name of a city. The cave in which Kay Khusraw disappeared.

A سريرة *sarīrat*, (pl. سرائر) A secret, mystery.

P سريري *sarīrī*, The king of Sarīr-afrāz.

A سريس *sarīs*, (pl. سرساء) Unable to beget.

P سري سواري *sarī-suwārī*, On the way, or road.

P سريش *sirīsh*, A certain herb, which, whilst green, is boiled and eaten; but when dry, is reduced to powder, and from it a paste is made for shoemakers and book-binders. Glue.

P سريش خشم *sirīsh-khishm*, One who sticks close to his enemy.

P سريشم *sirīshim*, Glue. Birdlime. سريشم ماهي *sirīshimi māhī*, Isinglass.

A سريط *surayt*, A dish made of flour, honey, and water.

A سرّيط *surrayt*, Any thing swallowed.

A سريطاء *suraytāʾ*, Hasty-pudding.

A سرّيطي *surrayta'*, Any thing swallowed. الاخذ سرّيطي و القضاء ضرّيطي *al akhz surrayta'*, *wa'l kazāʾ zurrayta'*, Borrowing and spending money is an easy affair; paying back is an irksome matter. (*Sirrīta' zirrīta'*, سرّيط ضرّيط *surrayt zurrayt*, سريط ضريط *surayt zurayt*, سريطا ضريطا *surayta' zurayta'*, are other forms.)

A سريع *sarīᶜ*, (pl. سرعان *surᶜān*) Quick, nimble, ready, swift, who makes haste. (pl. سرعان *sirᶜān* or *surᶜān*) A slender branch falling from the tree بشام *bashām*. سريع الحساب *sarīᶜu'l hisāb*, Ready in reckoning (God). سريع الزوال *sa-*

riʿu'z zawāl, Soon passing away, fading, frail. ابو سريع abū sariʿ, The plant عرفج ʿarfaj; or a fire kindled in it.

A سريعا sariʿan, Swiftly, with expedition.

A سريعة sariʿat, Name of a certain fountain.

P سريغ sarigh, A bunch of grapes.

A سريف sarif, A row of vines.

SY سريقون sarīkūn, Burnt lead.

P سرين surīn, The buttocks. سرين افكندن surīn afkandan, To sit four-square. سرين گاه surīn-gāh, The buttocks. A seat, throne.

P سزا sazā, Worthy, deserving of. Congruous, agreeing with, suitable, convenient. Retribution. Correction, condign punishment.

P سزاوار sazāwār, Worthy, deserving.

P سزاواري sazāwārī, Fitness, worthiness, suitableness, applicability. Excellence.

P سزاور sazāwar, Worthy, deserving.

P سزاول sazāwal, A monthly revenue-collector.

P سزاولي sazāwalī, Relating to a sazāwal.

P سزد sazd, White thorn. Sazad, It suits, becomes, is proper.

P سزگي sazgī, Grief, trouble, affliction, vexation.

P سزيتونتن sazītūnitan, (in zand and Pāz.) To go.

P سزيد sazīd, Worthy, deserving. Recompense, retribution. Desert, merit.

P سزيدن sazīdan, To be worthy, suit, become.

G سسالي sasālī, Assafœtida.

P سست sust, Soft, tender. Weak, feeble, impotent, relaxed, slow, dilatory, languid, lazy, idle, dronish, indolent, vain, addle. Negligent. Paralytic. Profane. باران سست barāni sust, A gentle rain.

P سست اذعان sust-iẕʿān, Weak in judgment.

P سست اندام sust-andām, Contracted in any member of the body. Impotent, unable to generate.

P سست بازو sust-bāzū, Weak in the arm.

P سست بينائي sust-bīnāʾī, Weak-sighted.

P سست پيمان sust-paymān, Unsteady to one's engagement.

P سست خوان sust-khwān, A slow reader.

P سست ريش sust-rīsh, A fool, simpleton.

P سست عنان sust-ʿinān, Loose-reined, lazy.

P سست گوش sust-gosh, Submissive.

P سست مهار sust-mahār, Inept. A fool, idiot. Obedient, tractable. Obedience.

P سستي sustī, Debility, impotence. Idleness, laziness, languor, sluggishness, remissness, slowness, slothfulness, negligence, dilatoriness, relaxation. Deliberation.

SY سسطيعون sastīʿūn, Wild anise.

SY سسغند sasghand, A kind of fragrant wood.

P سشنبه sashambih or sishambih, Tuesday.

P سصد sasad or sisad, Three hundred.

A سطأ sataʾa, (fut. يسطأ yastaʾu) He lay with.

A سطاح suttāh, Herbage or plants spreading.

G سطاخينس satākhīnus, A sort of wild leek.

G سطاريون satāriyūn, The herb ragwort.

A سطاع sitāʿ, A long mark made in a camel's neck by burning. A column. A tall, stout camel. The longest pole in a tent.

A سطام sitām, Edge of a sword. Acute (people). Stopple of a phial. A fire-poker. A bolt, bar.

P سطبر sitabr, Thick, gross, dense.

P سطبر گردن sitabr-gardan, Thick-necked.

P سطبري sitabrī, Thickness, coarseness.

G سطبوس satbūs, Pomegranate-flowers.

A سطة sitat, (v. n. of وسط) Sitting in the midst. A woman of mediocrity in character and family.

A سطح sath, (v. n. of سطح) Spreading out the earth (God). Laying (a man) on his back. Letting young lambs run with the mother. (pl. سطوح sutūh) A flat roof, platform, or terrace. A surface.

P سطح زمين sathi zamīn, The surface of the ground.

A سطّح suttah, Extensive and flat (mountains).

A سطحي sathīy, Superficial, flat.

A سطر satara, (fut. يسطر yasturu) He wrote.

A سطر satr, (v. n. of سطر) Delineating. Cutting with a sword. Writing. A kid one year old. (pl. اسطر astur, سطور sutūr, اسطار astār or اساطير asātīr) A row, line, series, rank. A writing. Satar, A line, row, writing.

G سطراك satrāk, Zedoary.

P سطر بندي satar-bandī, Ruling, writing-lines.

A سطرة sutrat, Wish, desire.

P سطركاه sitarkāh, Gum of the olive-tree.

A سطرلاب suturlāb, An astrolabe.

G سطرونيون satrūniyūn, Pearl-ashes. Saturnion?

A سطط sutut, Tyrants, oppressors.

A سطع sataʿ, (v. n. of سطع) Being raised (dust), diffusing itself (as perfume, or the dawn). Clapping (the hands). Sataʿ, (v. n. of سطع) Being long (in the neck). Length of neck. The noise of a blow, of a fall, or of clapping of hands.

A سطعاء satʿāʾ, (fem. of اسطع) Long-necked.

G سطقسات sutuksāt, The elements.

A سطل satl, A brass kettle. (pl. سطول sutūl) A vessel with one handle, used in baths, to pour water upon the bathers.

A سطم satm, (v. n. of سطم) Shutting (a door). The edge of a sword. Sutum, Roots, origins.

A سطو satw, (or سطوة satwat) (v. n. of سطا for سطو) Making an attack, assaulting, overpowering. Extracting the sperm from the matrix of a camel. Extracting a dead child from the womb (which the husband is allowed to do, in case the midwife be absent). Abounding (water). Tasting meat. Going with long steps (a horse). Being headstrong (a horse).

A سطوة satwat, Dominion, majesty, power, authority, awfulness. An assault, attack.

A سطوح sutūh, (pl. of سطح sath) Flat roofs, terraces. Surfaces, superficies.

A سطور sutūr, (pl. of سطر satr) Lines, rows.

A سطوع sutūʿ, (v. n. of سطع) Being diffused (the dawn or lightning), being scattered (odours), being raised (dust).

A سطول sutūl, (pl. of سطل) One-handled bowls.

A سطيح satīh, Expanded, lying upon the back. Killed. Slow in rising, from weakness in the feet. Name of a celebrated soothsayer. A large, and also a smaller leathern bottle or bag in which travellers carry water.

A سطيحة satīhat, A large, and also a small leathern bottle or bag in which travellers carry water. A level surface.

A سطيع satīʿ, (v. n. of سطع) Being raised (dust), diffused (odours). The dawn. Long, tall.

A سعّ suʿʿ, Tares. Bad or wild wheat.

A سعّاء saʿʿāʾ, Active in plotting and scheming.

A سعابر saʿābir, Tares, darnel.

A سعابيب saʿābīb, Rheum, phlegm, spittle, spawl, or honey hanging in threads.

A سعاة saʿāt, Controul, possession; ability for work. Suʿāt, (pl. of ساعي sāʿī) Messengers, couriers. Collectors of tithes or other revenues.

A سعاد suʿād, Name of a woman.

A سعادة saʿādat, (v. n. of سعد) Being happy, blessed. Felicity, happiness, beatitude, good fortune, prosperity. سعادت اصلي saʿādati aslī, Innate felicity. P سعادت جاويد saʿādati jāwīd, Eternal bliss. A سعادت دنيا و آخرت saʿādati dunyaʾ wa ākhirat, Happiness of this world and the next. P سعادت خانه saʿādat-khāna, Mansion of felicity, the royal palace. A سعادت مدار saʿādat-madār, Asylum of prosperity, most august. سعادت مقرون saʿādat-makrūn, United to fortune.

P سعادتمند saʿādatmand, Happy, fortunate.

P سعادتمندي saʿādatmandī, Felicity.

A سعاديّ suʿādaʾ, Galangale.

A سعار suʿār, (pl. سعران siʿrān and سعر suʿur) Fire, heat. Vehemence of hunger. Evil, mischief.

A سعاط suʿāt, A sharp, pungent, fragrant smell.

A سعال suʿāl, (v. n. of سعل) Coughing. A cough. سعال ساعل suʿāli sāʿil, A violent cough.

A سعالي saʿālī, (pl. of سعلاء siʿlāʾ or سعلاة siʿlāt) Hideous and dangerous dragons. Hobgoblins, witches. امّ السعالي ummu's saʿālī, A certain root. Suʿālaʾ, Name of a medicinal plant.

A سعانين saʿānīn, The festival of palms, held on the Sunday before Easter.

A سعاوي suʿāwī, Patient of labour in watching or travelling.

A سعاية siʿāyat, (v. n. of سعي) Accusing or informing against. Collecting tribute or taxes. Being set over others, especially for collecting tithes or other revenue. Paying a part of his wages (a slave who is working himself free). Committing whoredom (a servant-maid). Calumny, accusation. Work expected from a half-free servant.

A سعائل saʿāʾil, Long (camels).

A سعب saʿb, (v. n. of سعب) Flowing in threads

(as honey, syrup, or pitch). Any viscous substance running in this manner.

A سعبر saʻbar, (also سعبرة saʻburat) A well abounding in, or overflowing with water. Saʻbar, Much, abundant (water). Cheap.

A سعبوب suʻbūb, (pl. سعابيب saʻābīb) Rheum, spittle, or honey hanging in threads.

A سعة saʻat or siʻat, (v. n. of وسع) Being large, ample. Going fast with a wide step (a horse). Being able to perform, being equal to. Being of a noble breed. Giving facility, affording opportunity. Being capacious, roomy, holding easily, containing (as a vessel or place). Being easily held or contained. Extending (as the divine mercy to all creatures). Amplitude, capacity, wideness. Liberty. Facility, convenience, opportunity, or ability (of doing any thing). Power, ability, wealth. ذو سعة zū saʻatin, In easy circumstances. علىٰ قدر سعته ʻala' kadri saʻatihi, According to his ability. و ليسعك بيتك wa'l yasaʻka baytuka, And let your own house hold you (stay at home).

P سعتر saʻtar, A dildo, or artificial penis.

A سعتر saʻtar, Origany, marjoram.

P سعتري saʻtari, (or سعتر باز saʻtar-bāz) Lascivious (woman), one who uses a سعتر saʻtar.

A سعتريّ saʻtariy, Crafty, political. Impudent, fearless. Liberal. Brave.

A سعد saʻd, (v. n. of سعد) Being auspicious (the day). (pl. سعود suʻūd) Felicity, happiness, prosperity, a fortunate aspect of the stars, especially ten stars, of which four make the 12th, 13th, 14th, and 15th mansions of the moon. A third of an unbaked brick. Name of an idol. سعد اصغر saʻdi asghar, The planet Venus. سعد اكبر saʻdi akbar, The most fortunate of all the stars, the planet Jupiter. سعد الدين saʻdu'd dīn, The beneficent star of religion, a proper name. سعد السعود saʻdu's suʻūd, The 24th lunar mansion. اسعد ام سعيد a saʻd am suʻayd, Is it Sād or Suayd? (names of two men) Is it lucky or unlucky? ابو سعد abū saʻd, Lokman the sage. Old age, decrepitude. Suʻd, Galangale. Suʻud, A kind of date.

A سعداء suʻadāʻ, (pl. of سعيد) Happy, fortunate.

A سعدان saʻdān, A prickly plant of which camels are fond. A baboon. مرعىً ولا كالسعدان marʻan wa lā ka's saʻdān, A pasture; but not like the saʻdān. Suʻdān, (for اسعاد isʻād) Blessing. سبحانه و سعدانه subhānahu wa suʻdānahu, (God) the praised and blessed. Saʻdāni, (or السعدان as' saʻdāni) The two beneficent stars, i.e. Jupiter and Venus (نحسان nahisāni denoting the malignant planets Saturn and Mars).

A سعدانة saʻdānat, The nipple of a woman's breast. The callous part of a camel's breast on which he reclines. A kind of thorny plant. A dove. The name of a dove. (pl. سعدانات saʻdānāt) The knot on the lower part of the rope or chain which suspends the scale to the balance; a similar knot on the strings of sandals. The ring of the fundament. A hard, horny, warty substance growing in the inside of a horse's leg.

P سعدي saʻdī, A celebrated Persian poet, author of the Gulistān, Bostān, and other poems.

A سعديٰ suʻda', (fem. of اسعد asʻad) More or most happy or fortunate. Name of a woman.

P سعديا saʻdiyā, O Saadī!

A سعديك saʻdayka, Happiness attend you!

A سعدين saʻdayn, (obl. of سعدان saʻdāni) Jupiter and Venus. قران سعدين kirāni saʻdayn, Conjunction of Jupiter and Venus.

A سعر saʻr, (v. n. of سعر) Exciting, kindling (war or flame). Infecting with contagion, or causing to run. Siʻr, (pl. اسعار asʻār) Price or assize put upon provisions by the magistrate. Suʻr, Heat. Fury. Hunger, an insatiable craving for meat. The communication of contagion. Saʻir, (pl. سعريٰ saʻra') Outrageous, furious. Suʻur, Torment. Trouble, sickness. Fury. Stupidity, dulness of intellect. (pl. of سعار suʻār) Fires, flames, heats. Evils, mischiefs. (pl. of سعير saʻīr) Flaming fires.

A سعرارة siʻrārat, Aurora. Rays of the sun transmitted through a window or a crevice into any dark place. Motes playing in the sun.

A سعران siʻrān, (pl. of سعار suʻār) Fires, flames, heats. Evils, mischiefs. Siʻrān or saʻarān, A violent running.

A سعرة saʻrat, (v. n. of سعر) Going backwards and forwards when doing any thing, going about performing one's business. A slight cough. Beginning of any business; keenness with which one pursues any new undertaking.

A سعرورة suʻrūrat, The morning sun-beams entering through a crevice. The dawn.

A سعريٰ saʻra', (pl. of سعر) Furious, mad.

A سع سع suʻ suʻ, (imp.) Practice سوعاء suwaʻāʻ.

A سعسعة saʻsaʻat, (v. n. of سعسع Q) Calling (goats) by crying سع سع saʻ saʻ. Oiling the hair. A trembling of the body from old age: decrepitude; mortality, frailty. Name of a place in Syria.

A سعسلق saʻsalik, A certain root.

A سعط saʻt, (v. n. of سعط) Putting medicine or snuff up the nostrils of another. Piercing (in the breast with a spear).

A سعف saʻf, (v. n. of سعف) Furthering, finishing (any one's business). Merchandize, wares, household stuff. A mean, low fellow. Saʻaf, (v. n. of سعف) Cracking about the nails. A fissure in the nails. (pl. سعوف suʻūf) The furniture which a bride carries to her husband's house, her trousseau. Good and valuable possessions of any kind, moveable or immoveable. A distemper in camels, which makes the hair drop from the nose. A palm-branch or palm-leaf (when dried). Saʻaf or saʻf, The summit of a mountain.

A سعفاء saʻfāʻ, (fem. of اسعف asʻaf) A camel losing the hair about her muzzle.

A سعفة saʻfat, A kind of ulcer or scurf growing on the heads of infants. Saʻafat, A dry branch of a palm-tree.

A سعل saʻl, (v. n. of سعل) Being brisk, lively, sprightly. Saʻal, A bad species of dry dates, called شيص shīs.

A سعلاء siʻlāʻ, (or سعلاة siʻlāt) (pl. سَعالى saʻālī) A hideous and a dangerous species of dragon. A hobgoblin, a witch. A swift horse.

A سعلة saʻlat, A cough. Suʻlat, (v. n. of سعل) Coughing.

A سعم saʻm, (v. n. of سعم) Travelling quickly (a camel). Saʻam, The quick pace of a camel.

A سعن saʻn, Fat of meat. Wine. يوم سعن yawmu saʻnin, A day of drinking pure, unmixed wine. Suʻn, (pl. سعنة siʻanat) A large leathern bottle cut through the middle for holding wine, water, and the like. A large bowl into which they milk. A case in which a woman puts her work.

A سعنة saʻnat, Happy, fortunate, blest. Unfortunate, unblest. A little; a small thing. Suʻnat, A shade, awning, canopy. A bar across a bucket. Pendulous (upper lip of the camel). Siʻanat, (pl. of سعن suʻn) Large leathern bottles cut in two.

A سعوة siʻwat, A shameless, obscene, abandoned woman. Siʻwat, (سعواء siʻwāʻ, or سعواء suʻwāʻ) An hour, a little of the night.

A سعود suʻūd, (v. n. of سعد) Being happy, blest with good fortune. Being favourable (day), lucky, auspicious (a constellation). (pl. of سعد saʻd) Prosperities, fortunate circumstances. سعود النجوم suʻūdu'n nujūm, Ten stars: namely, سعد بلع saʻdu bulaʻa, سعد الاخبية saʻdu'l akhbiyat, سعد الذابح saʻdu'z zābih, سعد السعود saʻdu's suʻūd. (These four form the 12th, 13th, 14th, and 15th mansions of the moon); سعد ناشرة saʻdu nāshirat, سعد الملك saʻdu'l malik, سعد البهام saʻdu'l bihām, سعد الهمام saʻdu'l humām, سعد البارع saʻdu'l bāriʻ, and سعد مطر saʻdu matar. These six are not lunar mansions. Each consists of two stars apparently a cubit's distance from each other.

A سعودة suʻūdat, (v. n. of سعد) Being favourable, auspicious. Being happy. Happiness. Benign influence of the stars.

A سعوط saʻūt or suʻūt, Medicinal snuff, a sternutatory.

A سعوف suʻūf, (pl. of سعف saʻaf) Moveables, furniture which a bride carries home. Household utensils. Large flagons or bowls. Liberal principles and noble dispositions.

A سعوم saʻūm, Quick-paced (she-camel).

A سعيٰ saʻa', (fut. يسعيٰ yasʻa') He purposed.

A سعي saʻy, (v. n. of سعي) Purposing. Striving or attempting. Walking; running. Accusing; informing against. Gaining. Collecting tribute or revenue. Endeavour, purpose, design, enterprise, attempt, exertion, effort, diligence, care, labour. The age at which men begin to work.

A سعيا *saʿya'*, Isaiah (the prophet).

A سعية *saʿyat*, A name for a she-goat.

A سعيد *saʿīd*, Fortunate, happy, august. A river, brook, gentle stream. Name of several places. *Suʿayd*, A fourth of an unburnt brick.

P سعي دار *saʿy-dār*, A striver.

A سعيدة *saʿīdat*, A house to which pilgrimages were once made by the Arabs. Name of a woman.

A سعيديّ *saʿīdīy*, Relating to one happy.

A سعيديّة *saʿīdiyat*, Striped Arabian stuff.

A سعير *saʿīr*, (pl. سعر *suʿur*) A flaming fire. A flame. Name of a certain quarter in hell. Destined to the fire. اصحاب سعير *as-hābi saʿīr*, Idolaters. *Suʿayr*, Name of an Arabian idol.

A سعيط *saʿīt*, Tartar of wine. The aroma of wine, &c. The myrobalan or its balsam. Oil of mustard. A sharp pungent scent.

A سعيع *saʿīʿ*, Tares, darnel. Bad wheat.

P سغ *sagh*, An oblong arched edifice, portico, gallery, or piazza. A roof. A story. A cow's horn. Ring-worm. Excoriated skin.

A سغاب *sighāb*, (pl. of سغب *saghib*, ساغب *sāghib*, or سغبان *saghbān*) Hungry, famished.

A سغابة *saghābat*, A hungering, being famished.

A سغاديٰ *sughāda'*, Name of a plant.

P سغانه *saghāna*, A cool, subterranean dwelling.

A سغب *saghb* or *saghab*, (v. n. of سغب) Hungering, craving. Hunger. *Saghab*, Thirst. *Saghib*, (or سغبان *saghbān*) (pl. سغاب *sighāb*) Hungry, famished, and tired.

O سغبر *saghbar*, A medicinal kind of wood found on the shores of the Caspian Sea.

A سغبلة *saghbalat*, (v. n. of سغبل Q) Larding (meat), buttering bread. Anointing (the head) with oil. Being full of sores.

P سغبه *sughba*, Fat, greasy. Cheated.

A سغبيٰ *saghba'*, Hungry, famished (woman).

O سغبين *saghbīn*, A kind of gum.

A سغد سغد *saghd saghd*, or سغد مغد *saghd maghd*, A gentle rain. *Saghad*, (v. n. of سغد) Swelling.

P سغد *sughd*, Ready. Bent with age. Low-lying ground where rain-water collects. Name of a pleasant land in the province of Samarkand, called بهشت دنيا *bihishti dunya'*, Paradise of the world.

P سغدو *sughdū*, A stuffed pudding.

P سغده *saghda*, Ready, prepared.

P سغدي *sughdī*, Readiness. Meat dressed with pease and prunes; also with grapes, kernels of nuts, spiceries, and sweet herbs. A pudding or sausage stuffed (with mushrooms). One of the seven ancient dialects of Persia, now lost.

P سغديانه *saghdiyāna*, A capacious goblet, from which a full bumper is drunk to a friend's health.

A سغر *saghr*, (v. n. of سغر) Rejecting, refusing, repelling, driving away.

P سغر *sughar* or *sughur*, A porcupine.

P سغراق *saghrāk*, A flagon, a jug.

P سغرنه *sugharna*, A gray porcupine; hedgehog.

P سغري *saghrī*, The buttocks of a horse or other beast of burden; the crupper. The leather of a horse's back; also from the sides of a camel. The skin of a certain fish, shagrin. Grimness.

P سغري پوش *saghrī-posh*, Saddle-cloth, housing.

A سغسغة *saghsaghat*, (v. n. of سغسغ) Pressing (any substance) against the forehead to extract the oil therefrom. Removing any thing from its place (as a stake). Oiling (the head). Hiding under the earth. Rolling in the dust. Larding (meat).

A سغل *saghal*, (v. n. of سغل) Being small, slender, and deformed. Being badly fed, lean, and haggard. Trembling. *Saghil* or *soghl*, Small, slender, and deformed. Emaciated and wrinkled. Tremulous, tottering. Badly fed. Bad-tempered.

A سغم *saghm*, (v. n. of سغم) Lying with without consummating. *Saghim*, One badly fed.

A سغماً *saghman*, Against one's will.

P سغو *saghw* or *saghav*, The ringing noise of a large bason.

A سغوب *sughūb*, (v. n. of سغب) Hungering, suffering hunger and fatigue.

P سغود *sughūd*, The bird called قطا *katā*.

A سغير *saghīr*, A kind of medicinal root.

A سف *saf*, A particle prefixed to the aorist, giving it a future sense. See سوف *sawf*.

A سفّ *saff*, (v. n. of سفّ) Weaving, plaiting palm-leaves. Eating dry meat (a camel). Taking dry medicines. Drinking much water without quenching the thirst. The blossom of the male palm-tree. *Siff* or *suff*, A species of flying spotted serpent.

A سفاء *safā*, (v. n. of سفي) Being silly and stupid. Ceasing to flow (camels' milk). *Sifā*, Medicine, a medicament.

A سفاتج *safātij*, (pl. of سفتجة) Bills of exchange.

A سفاح *sifāh*, (v. n. 3 of سفح) Whoring.

A سفّاح *saffāh*, A shedder of blood. A giver of liberty. Liberal. Eloquent. Surname of the first caliph of the house of Abbas. A whoremonger.

A سفاد *sifād*, (v. n. of سفد) Mounting on the female, covering (applied to goats, camels, kine, wild beasts and birds).

O سفاديكوس *safādīkūs*, The wild onion.

A سفار *sifār*, (v. n. 3 of سفر) Travelling with others. Being contrary (as one wind sweeping away what another brings). Dying. Travellers. (pl. اسفرة *asfirat*, سفر *sufur*, and سفائر *safāir*) An iron or leathern curb across the nose of a camel. (In a horse it is called حكمة *hakamat*).

P سفار *sufār*, Eye of a needle. The notch of an arrow which receives the bowstring.

A سفّار *saffār*, A bookseller. *Suffār*, (pl. of سافر *sāfir*) Travellers.

A سفارة *safārat* or *sifārat*, (v. n. of سفر) Making peace (between others), acting as a mediator. *Sifārat*, Mediation. *Sufārat*, Sweepings.

A سفارج *safārij*, (pl. of سفرجل) Quinces.

A سفارش *sifārish*, Commission. Recommendation.

P سفاري *safārī*, The stalk or reed of corn.

A سفاريج *safārīj*, (pl. of سفرجل) Quinces.

A سفاسف *sufāsif*, Excessive hunger.

A سفاسق *safāsik*, (pl. سفسقة *safsakat*) Undulated surfaces of swords. Grooves or lines on the blade or back (of swords). *Sufāsik*, Any thing stretched out.

A سفاسير *safāsīr*, (or سفاسرة *safāsirat*) (pl. of سفسير *sifsīr*) Brokers.

A سفاطة *safātat*, (v. n. of سفط) Being liberal, humane, benignant. *Sufātat*, Household furniture.

A سفافيد *safāfīd*, (pl. of سفود) Roasting-spits.

A سفاقة *safākat*, (v. n. of سفق) Being closely woven (cloth). Being hard and stiff (cloth). Being bare-faced (a man).

A سفّاك *saffāk*, A shedder of blood. One whose words prevail, eloquent.

A سفال *safāl*, (v. n. of سفل) Being low. Descending from the top to the bottom. Becoming old. Lowness. *Sifāl*, (v. n. of سفل) Being low, mean, or ignorant.

P سفال *sifāl* or *sufāl*, Earthenware. A sherd. Skin of a walnut, almond, &c.

P سفال پاره *sifāl-pāra*, A pot-sherd.

A سفالة *safālat*, (v. n. of سفل) Being mean, low in rank. Meanness, baseness. *Sufālat*, The bottom. Lowness, the lower part. Sofala in the East Indies.

سفالة الريح *sufālatu'r rīh*, Under the wind.

P سفالگر *sifālgar*, A potter.

P سفاله *safāla*, Sofala (an island). A tile. *Sifāla* or *sufāla*, A sherd. A sickle.

P سفالين *sifālīn*, Made of earth. An earthen vessel, earthenware, crockery. A potter.

P سفالينه *sifālīna*, Glass or earthenware.

A سفّان *saffān*, Commander of a ship (سفينة *safīnat*). A shipwright.

P سفاناج *sifānāj*, (or سفاناخ) Spinage.

A سفانة *sifānat*, The art of ship-building.

A سفّانة *saffānat*, A pearl. Name of the daughter of Hātim Tay.

P سفاني *safānī*, Name of a plant.

A سفاه *safāh*, (v. n. of سفه) Being foolish. Drinking much without quenching thirst. Folly. *Sifāh*, (v. n. 3 of سفه) Railing at, reviling. Folly, mental imbecility. (pl. of سفيه *safīh* and سفيهة *safīhat*) Foolish. Thin, flimsy (cloths).

A سفاهة *safāhat*, (v. n. of سفه) Being sottish, unwise, light, unsteady, hasty, inconsiderate. Drinking much without quenching the thirst. Bleeding instantly (a spear-wound). Stupidity, folly, insolence; buffoonery. Insipidity.

A سفاهةً *safāhatan*, Foolishly, saucily.

P سفاهن *safāhan*, A comb.

A سفائر *safā,ir*, (pl. of سفار *sifār*) Camels' curbs of iron or leather.

A سفائن *safā,in*, (pl. of سفينة *safīnat*) Ships.

A سفائه *safā,ih*, (pl. of سفيهة) Foolish (women).

A سفة *suffat*, A grain. Medicine taken dry or in powder (not in the form of an electuary). A handful of corn. A basket made from plaited palm-leaves. A fillet with which women bind their hair.

A سفت *saft*, (v. n. of سفت) Drinking a great quantity without quenching thirst. *Sift*, Pitch. *Safit*, Unwholesome meat.

P سفت *sift*, Coarse, thick, rude. The shoulder. *Suft*, Hard, stiff (linen cloth). Firm, strong. The shoulder. The upper part of a man. The eye of a needle. Bore, perforation.

P سفتانيدن *suftānīdan*, To cause to bore.

A سفتجة *saftajat*, (v. n. of سفتج Q) Giving a bill of exchange or letter of credit, paying money to receive it with interest abroad. Paying money to a person in one place, to receive it back again in one's own city. *Suftajat*, A bill of exchange or letter of credit.

P سفتجه *suftaja*, Bills of exchange, notes.

P سفتگر *suftgar*, A borer of pearls.

P سفتن *suftan*, To bore, perforate, pierce, drill. To be perforated. To exude, trickle.

P سفته *safta*, A new or fresh word or work. Any person from whom a place has been taken and another given him. The point of an arrow. Any thing having a sharp point. A bill of exchange. Earnest-money, handsel. *Sifta*, Thick, coarse, hard, firm, strong. A stiff kind of cloth. *Sufta*, Pierced, drilled, bored. A gift. News, advice. An ear-ring of gold or silver. The point of an arrow. A consignment made by a person of one country to another.

P سفته گوش *sufta-gosh*, Bored in the ears, *i.e.* a slave. Obedient, submissive.

P سفتين *siftīn*, A country in Turkistān.

P سفج *safj*, (سفچ *safch*, or سفچه *safcha*) An unripe pumpkin or gourd. A drinking cup made of the rind of a pumpkin. Must boiled down to a third part of its quantity.

A سفج *safj*, A violent blast of wind. ما اشدّ سفج هذه الريح *mā ashadda safja hāzihi'r rīh*, How violent the blast of this wind!

A سفجر *safjar*, Small (atoms). ذرّ سفجر *zarr safjar*, Emmets, pismires.

A سفح *safh*, (v. n. of سفح) Pouring, out shedding (water or blood). Flowing. (pl. سفوح *sufūh*) The foot of a mountain, at which water flows.

A سفحان *safahān*, (v. n. of سفح) Flowing (tears).

P سفد *safad*, A wicker basket. *Sifad*, Earth. Rue. Name of an angel. Name of the twelfth month. Name of the fifth day of the month.

A سفر *safr*, (v. n. of سفر) Breaking forth (light), shining (the dawn). Unveiling (her) face (a woman). Putting a curb across (a camel's nose). Making peace (between others). Sweeping (a house). Extirpating hairs. Separating. Flying swiftly (a bird). Selling the choicest sheep. Breaking up (war). A file for polishing. A traveller, or travellers. (pl. سفور *sufūr*) A mark, impression, vestige. سفر البحر *safru'l bahr*, Voyagers. *Sifr*, (pl. اسفار *asfār*) A written book, volume. A letter. A portion of the Pentateuch. *Safar*, (pl. اسفار *asfār*) A journey, voyage, travelling, setting out on a tour or warlike expedition. Remains of daylight after sunset. Whiteness, brightness (of the dawn). P سفر خشك *safari khushk*, A journey undertaken without motive or advantage. سفر دورادور *safari dūr-ā-dūr*, A very long journey. سفر شدن *safar shudan*, To be at war. To be on the road. A سفر ظفر اثر *safari zafar-asar*, A victorious war. P سفر كردن *safar kardan*, To travel. To empty, finish. سفروا پسين *safari wā pasīn*, The last journey, death. A السفر وسيلة الظفر *as' safar wasīlatu'z zafar*, Travel is productive of advantage. آلات اسباب سفر *ālāti asbābi safar*, Warlike apparatus. Preparations for a journey. في السفر و الحضر *fi's safar wa'l hazar*, Abroad and at home. P در سفر و حضر *dar safar u hazar*, In peace and war. Abroad and at home. A *Sufar*, (pl. of سفرة *sufrat*) Tables. Provisions for the way. *Sufur*, (pl. of سفار *sifār*) Camels' curbs of iron or leather.

P سفر *sufur* or *sufar*, A porcupine.

A سفراء *sufarā,s*, (pl. of سفير *safīr*) Ambassadors. Mediators, arbiters, umpires.

A سفرة *sufrat*, Travelling-provisions. A table (especially a circular one of leather, which travellers spread upon the ground; when on the road, it is contracted by strings round the edges into the form of a wallet for carrying provisions). *Safarat*, (pl. of سافر *sāfir*) Writers. Recording angels.

A سفرجل *safarjal*, (pl. سفارج *safārij*, سفاريج *safārīj*, and سفرجلات *safarjalāt*) A quince.

P سفرجل رنگ *safarjal-rang*, Quince-coloured.

A سفرقع *sufurkuʿ*, (inaccurately for سقرقع *sukurkuʿ*) Ethiopian ale.

P سفرنگ *safrang*, Commentary, explanation.

P سفرنه *safarna*, A hedgehog: a porcupine.

P سفرود *safrod*, The bird called قطا *katā*.

P سفره *sufra*, Any thing on or in which victuals are placed. The wallet of religious mendicants. Provisions prepared by men of hospitality for strangers, travellers, and the poor. Heaven. Earth. سفرۀ آرد *sufra,i ārd*, A cloth laid on the ground to receive the flour as it comes out of the mill. سفرۀ فصاحت *sufra,i fasāhat*, An eloquent tongue. Compositions. سفره نهادن *sufra nihādan*, To lay a table.

P سفره چي *sufrachī*, A table-decker, sewer.

P سفره دام *sufra-dām*, A large fishing-net.

P سفره نشين *sufra-nishīn*, A guest at table.

P سفري *safarī*, Travelling provisions. سفري آم *safarī ām*, A guava (Psydium pyriterum).

P سفسار *sifsār*, A broker. A money-changer.

A سفساف *safsāf*, Corrupt, bad, sorry. A contemptible business. Any thing bad. Bad hair. Fine flour which flies about.

A سفسفة *safsafat*, (v. n. of سفسف Q) Sifting (meal). Doing carelessly. Lines on a sword-blade.

A سفسقة *safsakat*, (v. n. of سفسق Q) Muting (a bird). *Safsakat* or *sifsikat*, (pl. سفاسق *safāsik*) The glittering surface of a sword, or lines on the blade, or a long groove on the back.

A سفسوقة *safsūkat*, A highway, straight road. *Sufsūkat*, Resemblance. See سفسيقة *sifsīkat*.

A سفسير *sifsīr*, (pl. سفاسير *safāsīr* and سفاسرة *safāsirat*) A broker. A superintendant, a manager. A servant. A courier, messenger, or follower. A camel-keeper. Ingenious, clever, master of his art. A brave man. One conversant with voices; also with ironmongery. An armful of green fodder.

A سفسيقة *sifsīkat*, The glittering surface of a sword; lines on the blade; long groove on the back.

A سفط *saft*, (v. n. of سفط) Being liberal, humane. *Safat*, (pl. اسفاط *asfāt*) The crust upon the skin of a fish. A case, casket, box, basket, or sack.

A سفع *safʿ*, (v. n. of سفع) Flapping the wings (a bird). Buffeting, striking, flogging. Tormenting. Appearing despicable and contemptible. Catching one by the forelock, and dragging him by it. Marking any thing. Scorching (as the sun, hot wind, or fire) and changing the hue of the face. A garment. *Sufʿ*, Colocynth-seeds. (pl. of سفعاء *sufʿās*) Trivets. Black (women) inclining to red. *Safaʿ*, A blackish colour in the cheeks of a fatigued, emaciated woman.

A سفعاء *safʿās*, (fem. of اسفع *asfaʿ*) A pigeon marked with reddish black on the neck. A trivet.

A سفعة *safʿat*, (v. n. of سفع) Being mad, furious, possessed with the devil. A malignant eye. A change of colour. *Sufʿat*, Blackness, with a mixture of red. Seed of the colocynth. Discoloured remains of dung, ashes, and rubbish in a place where people have encamped.

A سفق *safk*, (v. n. of سفق) Setting (a door) wide open. Shutting (a door) close. Buffeting, slapping (the face).

A سفقة *safkat*, A bargain struck by shaking hands. A shake of the hand in a bargain.

A سفك *safk*, (v. n. of سفك) Shedding. Using many words, being diffuse in speech. Effusion. سفك دم *safki dam*, Effusion of blood.

A سفكة *sufkat*, A wink, a glance.

A سفل *safl*, also *sufl*, (v. n. of سفل) Being low in rank or station, plebeian, mean, or ignorant. Meanness of origin. Depression. Lowness. السفلان

as' siflāni, Venus and Mercury (as inferior planets).

A سفلة *siflat*, Lowness. *Safilat*, The feet of camels. *Safilat* or *siflat*, The common people, the canaille. The noise of a rabble.

A سفلّج *safallaj*, Long, tall.

P سفله *sifla*, (from Ar.) (pl. سفلگان *siflagān*) Low, base, ignoble. Avaricious, stingy. Envious.

P سفله دان *sifladān*, A plate to throw scraps on.

A سفلى *sufla'*, (fem. of اسفل) Lower, lowest.

P سفلى *sufī*, An iron pot with open mouth.

A سفليّ *sufliy*, Inferior, lower. Mean. Infernal. علوي و سفلي *ɛulwī u suflī*, High and low. عناصر سفليّه *ɛanāsiri sufliya*, The inferior elements.

P سفليدن *siflīdan*, To whistle; to break wind. To blow a flute. To compress. To pierce. *Suflīdan*, To cough, sneeze.

A سفن *safn*, (v. n. of سفن) Peeling, shaving, scraping, planing, filing. Sweeping. Whirling up the dust (the wind). *Safan*, A hatchet, plane, stone, file, rough skin or sand-paper, or any thing used in smoothing or polishing an unfinished arrow. The skin of the Lybian lizard used as sand-paper, or of a crocodile with which they cover the hilts of swords. *Sufun*, (pl. of سفينة *safīnat*) Ships.

A سفنّج *safannaj*, A swift ostrich. A certain bird that jumps much.

A سفنجة *safnajat*, A paying promptly.

P سفنجه *safanja*, Rest, quiet. A water-melon.

P سفند *sifand*, Wild rue or the seed.

P سفندارمذ *sifandārmuz*, Earth. Name of an angel. The sign Pisces. Name of the twelfth month. The fifth day of the month.

A سفنق *sufnuk*, A mackerel.

A سفو *safw*, A running or flying swiftly.

A سفواء *safwās*, (fem. of اسفى *asfa'*) Swift (mule).

A سفوح *sufūh*, (v. n. of سفح) Spilling (water or blood). Shedding (tears). Flowing. (pl. of سفح *safh*) Bases of mountains (about which water flows). Smooth rocks.

A سفّود *saffūd*, (pl. سفافيد *safāfīd*) A roasting-spit. A poker for the fire.

A سفور *sufūr*, (pl. of سفر) Marks, vestiges.

A سفّور *saffūr*, A kind of very prickly fish.

A سفّورة *saffūrat*, A tablet for writing on, the writing of which may afterwards be effaced.

A سفوف *safūf*, (A medicine) taken simply, (not mixed, in opposition to an electuary); powder. A pomegranate-seed.

A سفوفات *safūfāt*, Medicinal powders.

A سفوك *safūk*, The soul, self. A liar.

A سفول *sufūl*, (v. n. of سفل) Being low. Descending from top to bottom. Waxing old. Lowness.

A سفون *safūn*, (pl. سوافين *sawāfīn*) Sweeping (wind). *Sufūn*, (pl. of سفينة *safīnat*) Ships.

A سفه *safh*, (v. n. of سفه) Overcoming in railing. *Safh*, *sifh*, or *sufh*, (v. n. of سفه) Instigating to acts of folly. Destroying. Flowing fast and drying up (blood from a wound). Drinking much without quenching the thirst. *Sifh*, (v. n. of سفه) Charging with folly. *Safah*, (v. n. of سفه) Being foolish. Being light, unsteady, rash. Drinking much without quenching thirst. Bleeding instantly (a spear-wound). Folly, stupidity, imprudence, rashness, caprice, inconstancy. *Safah* or *safh*, (v. n. of سفه) Being busily employed. Forgetting, neglecting to take (one's share).

A سفّه *suffah*, (pl. of سفيهة) Foolish (women).

A سفهاء *sufahās*, (pl. of سفيه *safīh*) Fools, madmen, idiots, simpletons, blockheads.

A سفي *safy*, (v. n. of سفى) Scattering, carrying away dust (wind). *Safa'*, (v. n. of سفي) Being stupid and silly. Being cracked (the hand). A certain thorny plant of the kind called بهمى *buhma'*. Earth or dust (especially dug from a grave or well). Thinness of hair on the forehead of a horse. Leanness. Any thorny tree. The beards of corn.

A سفيّ *safīy*, A violent wind. Light, silly (man). A cloud.

A سفياء *safyās*, (fem. of اسفى *asfa'*) (A mare) which has thin scattered hairs on the forehead. Swift (mule).

A سفيح *safīh*, The eighth arrow at lots (which is unlucky). A coarse garment. A sack.

A سفيحان *safīhāni*, Two sacks like saddle-bags.

P سفيد *safed*, White, fair. Clear, evident, manifest. بحر سفيد *bahri safed*, The White Sea, *i. e.* the Mediterranean. سفيد داشتن *safed dāshtan*, To long after, love. سفيد شد *safed shud*, It became clear, evident.

P سفيدا *safedā*, White-lead.

P سفيداج *safedāj*, (or سفيد آب *safed-āb*) A white wash used by ladies.

P سفيدار *safedār*, The white poplar: aspen.

P سفيد اسفند *safed isfand*, White mustard.

P سفيدالچه *safedālcha*, A kind of shawl.

P سفيد آهو *safed-āhū*, (White doe) A mistress captivating the heart.

P سفيد با *safed-bā*, A kind of white soup made with curds, to which they add meat and spinage.

P سفيد بري *safed-barī*, (Yellow leaf) Autumn.

P سفيد پر *safed-par*, (White-wing) A large gnat.

P سفيد تاك *safed-tāk*, Galangale.

P سفيدتر *safedtar*, Whiter.

P سفيدترين *safedtarīn*, Whitest.

P سفيد خار *safed-khār*, White-thorn: a bramble.

P سفيد روح *safed-rūh*, Mercury, quicksilver. A mixture of copper and tin.

P سفيد ريش *safed-rīsh*, A gray-beard, old man.

P سفيد زد *safed-zad*, A mixed metal.

P سفيدك *safedak*, Somewhat white, whitish.

P سفيد كار *safed-kār*, A good (white) action.

P سفيدكاسه *safed-kāsa*, Generous, liberal.

P سفيدگر *safedgar*, A tinman, whitesmith.

P سفيد مهره *safed-muhra*, A small white shell of the kind called concha veneris, or mother-of-pearl.

P سفيدن *sufīdan*, To bore, to pierce.

P سفيده *safeda*, Chalk, whiting.

A سفير *safīr*, A dry and fallen leaf carried by the wind. (pl. سفراء *sufarās*) An ambassador, internuncio. A mediator, arbiter. A broker.

P سفّير *saffīr*, A sapphire.

A سفيرة *safīrat*, A collar, necklace, or chain of gold or silver.

A سفيرج *sufayrij*, (dim. of سفرجل *safarjal*) A small quince.

A سفيط *safīt*, Liberal, benign, humane. Low, mean, worthless. An unripe date fallen from the tree.

A سفيف *safīf*, (v. n. of سفّ) Passing, skimming along above the surface of the ground (a bird). Weaving, plaiting (palm-leaves). A name of Iblis. The girth of a camel's saddle. Name of a plant.

A سفيفة *safīfat*, Any thing made of the leaves of palm-trees (as a mat).

A سفيق *safīk*, Hard, firm (cloth). Bare-faced.

A سفيقة *safīkat*, A thin piece of wood, long and broad, around which mats are wrapped. A long thin wick of gold, silver, or any thing similar.

A سفيك *sufīk*, Poured out, overflowing; shed.

A سفين *safīn*, (pl. of سفينة *safīnat*) Ships.

A سفينة *safīnat*, (pl. سفائن *safāïn*, سفن *sufun*, سفين *safīn* and سفون *sufūn*) A ship, vessel, bark, boat. Of an oblong form (a book). A blank book, common-place book. سفينهٔ نوح, Noah's ark.

A سفيه *safīh*, (pl. سفهاء *sufahās* and سفاه *sifāh*) Foolish, silly, stupid, idiotic. Insane, ignorant, imprudent. Impertinent, impudent, insolent, petulant, saucy, licentious, extravagant. Thin, open, flimsy (cloth). Shaking, flapping (rein).

A سفيهة *safīhat*, (pl. سفيهات *safīhāt*, سفائه *safāïh*, سفّه *suffah*, and سفاه *sifāh*) Foolish (woman). (A camel) which shakes the rein.

A سفيهي *safīhī*, Madness, stupidity, insolence.

A سقّ *sakh*, (v. n. of سقّ) Muting (a bird).

A سقاء *sikās*, (pl. اسقية *askiyat*, اسقيات *askiyāt*, and اساقي *asākī*) A leathern bottle for water or milk, made from the skin of a two-year-old sheep.

A سقّاء *sakkās*, (pl. سقّاؤن *sakkāūn*) Carrier or vender of water. Cup-bearer. سقّاي نيل *sakkāi nīl*, A cloud. P مرغ سقّا *murghi sakkā*, A pelican.

A سقّاءة *sakkāsat*, A female cup-bearer, or water-carrier.

A سقاب *sikāb*, A piece of cotton which an afflicted woman was accustomed to stain with her blood and wear upon her head, leaving one end of it to appear from under her hood that all who saw it might know her to be in affliction. (pl. of سقب *sakb*) Young male camels.

A سقاة *sukāt*, (pl. of ساقي *sākī*) Water-carriers. Cup-bearers.

A سقّار *sakkār*, (pl. سقّارون *sakkārūn*) An impious wretch; one who pours forth curses on those undeserving of them. A liar.

A سقاط *sakāt*, A sword cutting through any thing so as to fall to the ground, or to cut into a second object. *Sikāt*, (v. n. 3 of سقط) Being languid, fainting in the course (a horse). Causing to fall. Reciting any thing (as verses) alternately with another. A fall, trip, stumble. A blunder, mistake in arithmetic, writing, &c. Dates purchased in Yamāmah. Unripe dates fallen from the tree. The lower parts of tents or birds' wings. *Sukāt*, Any thing fallen. The lowest of the people.

A سقّاط *sakkāt*, A broker, dealer in small wares, a pedlar. A sword so cutting any thing as to fall through to the ground. *Sukkāt*, (pl. of ساقط *sākit*) Contemptible, vile.

A سقاطة *sukātat*, Any thing fallen; droppings.

A سقاع *sikāʿ*, The rein-ring in a camel's nose. A garment of shreds and patches; the habit of a religious mendicant. A kind of veil.

A سقّال *sakkāl*, A polisher, a furbisher.

A سقالبة *sakālibat*, (pl. of سقلبيّ) Sclavonians.

A سقام *sakām*, (also سقامة *sakāmat*) Sickness. *Sikām*, (pl. of سقيم *sakīm*) Sick, ailing.

A سقاية *sikāyat*, A cup, drinking-vessel. *Sikāyat* or *sukāyat*, The place in the belly where water in the dropsy collects. A place for drinking water, a watering-place. A drinking-vessel. A measure, particularly for water or wine. Grape-wine which, in the days of Paganism, Kuraysh used to furnish the pilgrims to Mecca.

A سقّاية *sakkāyat*, A female water-carrier, or cup-bearer.

A سقائف *sakāʾif*, (pl. of سقيفة) Planks; decks.

A سقب *sakb*, (pl. اسقب *askub*, سقاب *sikāb*, سقوب *sukūb*, and سقبان *sukbān*) The male foal of a camel. (pl. سقبان *sikbān*) The pole of a tent. Long. *Sakab*, (v. n. of سقب) Being near; nearness. Near.

A سقبان *sikbān*, (pl. of سقب *sakb*) Tent-poles. *Sukbān*, (pl. of سقب *sakb*) Young he camels.

A سقبة *sakbat*, A female ass-colt.

A سقت *sakt* or *sakat*, (v. n. of سقت) Being unfortunate. *Sakit*, Unfortunate, unblest.

A سقح *sakah*, Baldness of the forehead.

A سقحة *sakahat*, A bald place on the forehead.

A سقدة *suhdat*, (pl. سقد *sukad*) A certain red bird the size of a sparrow.

A سقدد *sukdud*, A lean, attenuated horse.

A سقر *sakr*, The heat of the sun, or inconvenience of it. Juice flowing from the date-tree. Panderism to one's own wife. A falcon. *Sakar*, Hell. A mountain at Mecca. نار سقر *nāri sakar*, Hell-fire.

A سقراط *sukrāt*, Socrates. Wise, learned.

P سقراطيون *sukrātiyūn*, Mushrooms, funguses.

P سقراق *sakrāk*, A jug, a pitcher.

A سقرة *sakrat*, The intense heat of the sun.

A سقرقع *sukurkaʿ*, (P سكركه *sukurka*) Ethiopian ale. An inebriating draught made from millet.

A سقرلات *sakirlāt*, Warm woollen cloth, purpet.

A سق سق *sak sak* or *sik sik*, Used in driving bulls.

A سقسقة *saksakat*, (v. n. of سقسق Q) Muting (a bird). Reciting verses alternately.

A سقط *sakt*, Snow. Dew. Vile, contemptible. *Sakt* or *sikt*, The lower part or edge nearest the earth (of clouds, tents, or wings of birds). *Sakt*, *sikt*, or *suht*, Sparks struck from a steel. A place where sands terminate. The name of a dīwān or poem of above 3000 distichs, so named by the author (ابو العلي *abū'l ʿula'*), because struck off in the fire of his youth. An abortion. *Sakat*, An error, failure, fault, erratum, blunder, mistake (in computation, writing, or speaking). Disgrace, ignominy. A weak, low, base, contemptible fellow. (pl. اسقاط *askāt*) Any thing of a base or useless nature. Small wares or damaged goods. Whatever drops from a height, and is dashed to pieces, bruised, or scattered in the fall. Maimed, mutilated. P سقط شدن *sakat shudan*, To die. (applied to animals) To miscarry, to cast their young.

P سقط *sakat*, An error, mistake. Excrement.

P سقط گفتن *sakat guftan*, To revile, to abuse.

A سقطان *siktāni*, (dual) The two wings (of an ostrich). The first and last parts (of the night).

A سقطة *saktat*, (pl. سقاط *sikāt*) A fall, slip, stumble, false step. Detriment.

A سقطري *sukutra'*, (or سقطراء *sukutrāʾ*) The island of Socotra, from whence they procure aloes and dragon's blood.

A سقطريّ *siktiriy*, Expert in distinguishing good money from bad.

P سقط فروش *sakat-farosh*, A pedlar.

A سقطم *siktim*, A mouse.

A سقطى *sakta'*, (pl. of ساقطة *sākitat*) Low, little worth.

A سقطيّ *sakatiy*, A dealer in old furniture or in small wares: a pedlar.

P سقطى نامه *sakti-nāma*, A casualty-list of horses that have died in the cavalry.

A سقع *sakʿ*, (v. n. of سقع) Striking a hard body. Eating food from one side of it. Going away (no one knows whither). Crowing (a cock). *Sukʿ*, A shore, coast, tract. The environs of a well.

A سقعاء *sakʿāʾ*, (fem. of اسقع *askaʿ*) White-headed (bird or mare).

A سقعطري *sakaʿtara'*, (or سقعطريّ *sakaʿtariy*) Very long-bodied (man or camel). *Sakaʿtara'*, Large and strong.

A سقف *sakf*, (v. n. of سقف) Covering in, roofing (a house). (pl. سقف *suhuf* and سقوف *sukūf*) A roof. Raftering of a house, ceiling. The sky. Long and dangling (beard). سقف ايوان *sakfi aywān*, The world. P سقف خانه *sakfi khāna*, Roof of a house, ceiling. سقف نيم خانه *sakfi nīm-khāna*, A vaulted roof. The sky. A *Sukf*, A bishop. *Sakaf*, Length, with curvature (as in the ostrich). *Sukuf*, (pl. of سقيف *sakīf*) Roofs.

P سقف *sukuf*, (for اسقف *uskuf*) A bishop.

A سقّف *sukuff*, A bishop.

A سقفاء *sakfāʾ*, (fem. of اسقف *askaf*) Long and crooked, bent in consequence of the length. Long-necked (ostrich).

A سقفان *suhfān*, Roofs: floors, stories.

A سقفي *sakfī*, A beam, rafter.

A سقق *sukuk*, Whisperers, slanderers.

A سقل *sakl*, Polish. *Sukl*, The hypochondria or body under the short ribs. *Sahil*, Thin-waisted (man). Lean-buttocked (horse).

P سقلاب *saklāb*, A beaver. Sclavonia.

P سقلّات *sakallāt*, Scarlet cloth.

A سقلاط *siklāt*, (for سجلاط *sijlāt*) Jasmine. The covering, awning, or canopy over the camel-litter in which the Eastern ladies travel. A fine painted or figured cloth.

P سقلاطون *saklātūn*, (سقلاطين *saklātīn* or سقلاطا *saklātā*) Scarlet cloth.

A سقلبة *saklabat*, A casting on the ground.

A سقلبيّ *saklabīy*, (pl. سقالبة) A Sclavonian.

A سقم *sakam* or *sukm*, (v. n. of سقم) Being indisposed. Sickness.

G سقمونيا *sukmūniya'* or *sakmūniya'*, (سقمونياء *sukmūniyāʾ* or *sakmūniyāʾ*) Scammony. Soap.

A سقمى *sakma'*, (pl. of سقيم) Sick, infirm.

P سقن *sakan*, Juice of dates.

A سقنطار *sikintār*, A good judge of coin.

G سقنقور *sakankūr*, (or سقنقس *sakankus*) A species of newt or spawn of the crocodile burrowing in the sand (when held in the hand it is said to be a stimulative to venery).

A سقوب *sukūb*, (v. n. of سقب) Being near. (pl. of سقب *sakb*) Male fœtuses of camels just born. The feet of a camel.

G سقورديون *sakūrdiyūn*, Water-germander.

A سقوط *sakūt*, Falling, fallen. *Suhūt*, (v. n. of سقط) Falling. Being delivered, dropping (a colt). Setting (a star). Committing an error in writing or speaking. Coming on (heat); also going off. Alighting, tarrying with. A fall, slip, tumble.

A سقوطرة *sukūtarat*, The island of Socotra, whence they bring aloes and dragon's blood.

A سقوف *sukūf*, (pl. of سقف) Roofs of houses.

A سقى *saka'*, (fut. يسقي *yaskī*) He watered.

A سقي *saky*, (v. n. of سقي) Watering. Sending rain. Presenting liquor unto. Drinking to another. Having the dropsy; or a yellow water in the belly at the delivery. Traducing, slandering, inveighing against the absent. A draught. P سقي كردن *saky kardan*, To water (as plants). A *Siky*, (pl. اسقية *askiyat*) Water either for drinking or watering ground. Yellowish water in the belly. A skin containing yellow water which comes out at the delivery. Watered, irrigated. *Siky* or *saky*, Water collected in the belly.

A سقّى *sukka'*, (pl. of ساقي *sāķī*) Water-carriers. Cup-bearers.

A سقيّ *sakīy*, (pl. اسقية *askiyat*) A cloud pouring down great drops of rain. A palm-tree. Papyrus. Portions of water. *Sukīy*, (pl. of ساقي *sāķī*) Water-carriers, drawers of water.

A سقيا *sukya'*, A shower.

A سقيدة *sukaydat*, (pl. سقيدات *sukaydāt*) A red bird of the size of a sparrow.

SY سقي رغلا *sakī raghlā*, The herb polypody.

G سقيروس *sakīrūs*, A hard swelling, scirrhus.

A سقيط *sakīt*, (pl. سقطى *sakta'*) Snow. Ice. Hoar frost. Dew. Hail. Deficient in intellect.

A سقيطة *sakītat*, A mean or base woman. Deficient in intellect.

A سقيف *sakīf*, (pl. سقف *sukuf*) A roof.

A سقيفة *sakīfat*, (pl. سقائف *sakā,if*) A broad plank, a slab. A broad stone, shingle, or plank used for roofing. The deck of a ship. A high bench for reclining upon, before the doors or under the porticos. Splinters for tying round broken bones. A camel's rib. Part of the bone of a camel's head.

A سقّيفى *sikkīfa'*, Episcopacy, office of a bishop.

A سقيم *sakīm*, (pl. سقام *sikām*) Sick, infirm, ailing. Poor, weak (excuse).

P سك *sik*, Vinegar. *Suk*, Sadness. The musk gall-apple.

A سكّ *sakk*, (v. n. of سكّ) Overlaying (a door) with broad iron plates, or studding it with huge nails, by way of security. Fastening tight, making firm. Eradicating the ear. Having the orifice of the ear small. Digging. Casting forth the contents of its belly (an ostrich). Straight, upright (edifice). A narrow-mouthed well. (pl. سكاك *sikāk* and سكوك *sukūk*) A nail. An iron fastening. A coat of mail formed of close rings. *Sukk*, A certain aromatic composition formed into pastils. The expressed juice of the myrobolan. A narrow-mouthed well. A scorpion's hole. A spider's den. Baseness, sordidness. Narrow (coat of mail). Closed up (road). (pl. of اسكّ *asakk*) Small-eared. Deaf.

A سكاء *sikā,*, A begging with importunity.

A سكّاء *sakkā,*, (fem. of اسكّ *asakk*) Small-eared (woman), or destitute of ears. Small (ear) or one with a small orifice. Narrow (coat of mail).

P سكاب *sukāb*, Musk-water.

A سكابيج *sakābīj*, (pl. of سكباج *sikbāj*) Dishes of meat, wheat, flour, and vinegar.

A سكات *sukāt*, (v. n. of سكت) Being silent. Becoming calm (anger). Dying. Silence, or whatever causes it. A silent, lurking serpent, not perceived till he bites. End, completion, termination. على سكات امر *ʻala' sukāti amrin*, On the point of accomplishing an object.

A سكاتة *sukātat*, Whatever puts to silence.

P سكاچه *sukācha*, The nightmare. A porcupine. Litigious, quarrelsome.

P سكاد *sakād*, Mountain-top. Crown of head.

P سكار *sakār*, *sikār*, or *sukār*, Bread of the finest flour baked with butter and sugar, usually given in presents on new-year's day. Thin paste, between the folds of which they put plums or apples, making a kind of puff. Charcoal. A live coal. A firebrand. سكارآهنج *sakār-āhanj*, A hook with which they draw the bread from the oven and meat from the pot. سكاروا *sukār-wā*, Bread baked upon the coals or under the ashes.

A سكّار *sakkār*, A maker or vender of date-wine, mead, and the like, called سكر *sakar*.

P سكارچه *sakārcha*, Foolish, ignorant.

P سكارو *sakārū*, Mouldy. *Sukārū*, A cake made of fine flour, milk, butter, and sugar. Bread baked or meat roasted on the ashes.

A سكارى *sa* or *sukāra'*, (pl. of سكران) Drunk.

A سكاريج *sakārīj*, (pl. of سكرجة) Platters.

P سكاسته *sukāsta*, (سكاسه *sukāsa*, سكاشته *sukāshta*, or سكاشه *sukāsha*) A porcupine, hedgehog.

A سكاسك *sakāsik*, A tribe in Yaman.

A سكّاف *sakkāf*, A boot or shoemaker.

A سكافة *sikāfat*, Trade of a shoemaker.

P سكافره *sukāfara*, (or سكافه) Bow of a violin.

A سكاك *sikāk*, A row or line (of houses or tents). (pl. of سكّ *sakk* and of سكّي *sakīy*) Nails. *Sukāk*, The air reaching to the confines of the sky. The atmosphere. The feathered part of an arrow.

A سكّاك *sakkāk*, A cutler.

A سكاكا *sikākan*, In a row.

A سكاكة *sukākat*, Air, atmosphere, sky, heaven. Wedded to one's own opinion. Small-eared.

A سكاكي *sakkākī*, Business of a cutler: cutlery.

A سكاكين *sakākīn*, (pl. of سكين) Knives.

A سكاكيني *sakkākīnīy*, A cutler.

P سكال *sikāl*, Thought. Who wishes or inquires after. A speaker. Conversation.

P سكالش *sikālish*, Thought, reflection. Intention, purpose, wish.

P سكالو *sukālū*, (or سكاليو *sukāliyū*) Bread or meat dressed upon the coals.

P سكاله *sukāla*, Dung (of dogs).

P سكاليدن *sikālīdan*, To think. To suspect. To speak. To wish. To write.

A سكّان *sakkān*, A cutler, knifemaker. *Sukkān*, A rudder, helm. (pl. of ساكن *sākin*) Inhabitants.

P سكّان فرشي *sukkāni farshī*, All creatures.

A سكانة *sakānat*, A being or a becoming poor.

P سكاهن *sikāhan*, A black tincture composed of the rind of pomegranates, vinegar, iron, and other ingredients, used chiefly by shoemakers.

A سكب *sakb*, (v. n. of سكب) Pouring out (water). Falling incessantly in big drops (rain). Calling the hour of prayer (the muezzin). Flowing, current. Quick-going (horse). A sort of garment. A tall man. Light, brisk, joyous. A necessary or important business. A continued rain. *Sakb* or *sakab*, Name of the first horse possessed by Muhammad. Brass. Lead. *Sakab*, Name of an odoriferous tree. The anemone. The scales of the head.

P سكبا *sik-bā*, (or A سكباج *sikbāj*) (pl. سكابيج *sakābīj*) A dish made of meat, wheat-flour, and vinegar. سكباج البقر *sikbāju'l bakar*, A dish made of beef thus prepared.

A سكبة *sakbat*, A kind of veil or net worn on the head. A membrane in which the fœtus is enveloped. *Sakabat*, A single odoriferous tree. Scales on the head.

P سكبه *sakba*, Mixture of oil and buttermilk.

A سكبينج *sakbīnaj*, (from P سكبينه *sakbīna*) Sagapenon, a medicinal herb; also gum Arabic.

A سكّة *sikkat*, A ploughshare. A mattock, pick-axe or shovel. An avenue between two rows of palm-trees. A wide and straight street. Possibility, the favourable moment for the accomplishment of a thing. A die for coins. A stamp.

A سكت *sakt*, (v. n. of سكت) Keeping silence. Dying. Subsiding (anger). Silence. Silent, yet able to speak well when occasion requires. A pause between two shakes without taking breath.

A سكتة *saktat*, Silence. An apoplexy. A trance. A pause. *Suktat*, Any thing imposing silence. Fruit, or play-things (as pacifying children). The remains of any thing in a vessel.

P سكتيان *saktiyān*, Leather.

A سكّيت *sikkīt*, Silent, taciturn, reserved.

P سكج *sakij*, Dried currants.

P سكخانه *sik-khāna*, A wine-shop, tavern.

A سكر *sakara*, (fut. يسكر *yaskiru*) He shut.

A سكر *sakr*, (v. n. of سكر) Filling. Damming up (a river). Stopping (the menstruous flow). Enchanting, fascinating. A certain herb that may be eaten raw. Drunk. *Sakr*, *sakar*, *sukr*, or *sukur*, (v. n. of سكر) Being drunk. *Sikr*, (pl. سكور *sukūr*) A mound or dike for confining water. A high bank of a river. *Sukr*, Drunkenness. Wine, or whatever intoxicates. *Sakar*, Any inebriating or forbidden drink, especially wine from dates or the inebriating plant كشوث *kushūs*. Vinegar. Food, victuals. Fulness, repletion. Rage, anger. A secret grudge. *Sakir*, Often drunk.

P سكر *sukar*, A saucer. A hedgehog: porcupine.

A سكّر *sukkar*, Sugar. An excellent sort of date. A delicious kind of grape. سكّر العشر *sukkaru'l ʻushar*, A kind of dew collecting on the tree *ʻushar*, and which resembles particles of salt. سكّر محرّر *sukkar muharrar*, Sugar-candy.

A سكرات *sakarāt*, Agony, fainting. سكرات موت *sakarāti mawt*, The agony of death.

A سكران *sakrān*, (fem. سكرانة *sakrānat*) (pl. سكارى *sakāra'*, *sukāra'*, or سكرى *sakra'*) Drunk. *Sakarān*, (v. n. of سكر) Being drunk. Subsiding, becoming calm (wind).

A سکرانیّة *sakrāniyat*, Intoxication.

P سکرپین *sukkar-pīn*, Marchpane.

A سکرة *sakrat*, Drunken (woman). A missing or losing one's way: error. Drunkenness. The agony of death, or the depths of woe. *Sakarat*, Tares or darnel. *Sakirat*, Drunken (woman).

A سکّرة *sukkarat*, A lump of sugar.

A سکرّجة *sukurrujat*, (pl. سکاریج *sakārīj*) A platter, a saucer.

P سکرچه *sukracha*, A saucer. A measure.

P سکرفانیدن *sikarfānīdan*, To commit a crime. To fold together. To be haughty, insolent. To pour out drink.

P سکرفنده *sakarfanda*, Tripping, stumbling.

P سکرفیدن *sakarfīdan*, To stumble (a horse).

A سکرکة *sukurkat*, Drink made from millet, used in Abyssinia; a kind of ale or beer.

P سکره *suk*, *suka*, or *sukkara*, An earthen dish.

A سکری *sakra'*, (fem. of سکران *sakrān*) Drunken (woman). (pl. of سکران *sakrān*) Drunkards.

A سکّریّ *sukkariy*, Made of sugar: saccharine.

P سکّرین *sukkarīn*, (Made) of sugar, sugared.

P سکز *sakiz*, Mastic. *Sikiz*, A carpenter's hatchet.

P سکزه *sikiza*, Contention, combat.

P سکزی *sakzī*, One of the seven dialects of Persia now lost.

P سکستن *sukustan*, To be broken or torn up.

P سکسک *suksuk*, Swift (horse). A horse going quick with a jolting trot. The noise made with the feet. Rough ground. A tree, the fire of which will burn for a week.

A سکسکة *saksakat*, Weakness. Fortitude.

P سکسکی *suksukī*, Palpitation of the heart.

A سکسکیّ *saksakiy*, Of the tribe of سکاسک.

A سکع *sakeʻ*, (v. n. of سکع) Taking (any place) for one's abode and residence. *Sakeʻ* or *sakaʻ*, (v. n. of سکع) Going no one knows whither, wandering about in sadness and astonishment. *Sakiʻ*, Foreign, strange. *Sukaʻ*, Astonished, bewildered, stupefied.

A سکف *sakaf*, (v. n. of سکف) Making the foot of a door, or that part which revolves in a socket in the threshold or lintel, and performs the function of a hinge.

A سکک *sakak*, Smallness of the ear sticking close to the head. Smallness of the orifice of the ear. Deafness, a stoppage in the ears. *Sikak*, (pl. of سکّة *sikkat*) Ploughshares. Wide streets.

A سکل *sikl*, (or سکلة *sikalat*) (pl. اسکال *askāl*) Name of a large black fish.

A سکم *sakm*, (v. n. of سکم) Going with short, fatigued, slow steps.

A سکن *sakn*, (pl. of ساکن *sākin*) Inhabitants, the people of a house. (pl. اسکان *askān*) Victuals, viands, aliment. *Sakan*, A dwelling. Residence, stay. Domestic comforts, as wife or children. Fire. Repose, rest, quiet. A blessing. Pity, compassion.

A سکنة *saknat*, Name of a disease. *Suknat*, Any thing used for soothing or quieting a child. The remains of any thing in a vessel. *Sakanat*, (pl. of ساکن *sākin*) Inhabitants, citizens. سکنهٔ صحرا *sakana-i sahrā*, Inhabitants of the desert. Trees, grass, and the like. سکنهٔ عالم *sakana-i ʻālam*, Inhabitants of the world, creatures. سکنهٔ کانون *sakana-i kānūn*, Charcoal. *Sakinat*, (pl. سکنات *sakināt*) A habitation. That part of the head which joins the neck. Straightness, upright posture.

P سکنج *saknaj*, A kind of bitumen brought from Syria. *Sahunj* or *sukunj*, A fetid smell from the mouth. One who has a fetid breath. *Sikunj*, A cough. Shaving, scraping. A bite, a sting.

A سکنجبین *sikanjabīn*, (P سکنگبین) Oxymel.

P سکنجیدن *sikinjīdan*, To cough. To take up with the tips of the fingers. To nip, pinch. To bite, to sting. To smooth, to scrape.

P سکند *sikand*, Venery.

P سکندر *sikandar*, Alexander. Two princes of this name are much celebrated in the East, both distinguished by the title of ذو القرنین *zū'l harnayn*, Having two horns (of the world), implying that they conquered the globe from east to west; the first supposed to be one of the most ancient kings; the other, Alexander of Macedon, whom they call also Bin Filikus (son of Philip), and Rūmī (the Grecian). Hanging the head (a quadruped whose fore-legs are short). Standing on the head (a mountebank's trick). سکندر خوردن *sikandar khwurdan*, To trip, stumble.

P سکندری خور *sikandarī-khwur*, Apt to stumble.

P سکندری خوردن *sikandarī khwurdan*, To trip, to stumble.

P سکندریّه *sikandarīya*, Alexandria.

P سکنگبین *sikangubīn*, Oxymel.

P سکنه *sihana*, A wimble, auger, gimlet.

A سکنیٰ *sukna'*, A residence, habitation.

P سکو *sako* or *suko*, A sofa, settle, bench, garden-seat. *Sikū*, A wooden fork with several prongs or branches, with which they agitate corn, that the wind may clear it of the chaff. A broom, besom.

P سکوا *sik-wā*, A dish of vinegar, meat, and flour.

P سکوان *sahwān*, Name of a city in India.

A سکوب *sakūb*, Fluent (blood, water, and the like). *Sukūb*, (v. n. of سکب) Flowing (blood).

P سکوبا *sukūbā*, A bishop, presbyter. Name of the founder of a Christian convent.

A سکوت *sakūt*, Quiet, silent, taciturn (man). *Sukūt*, Silence, quietness.

A سکور *sakūr*, Frequently drunk. *Sukūr*, (v. n. of سکر) Becoming calm (wind after a storm). (pl. of سکر *sikr*) Mounds or dams for confining water.

P سکوره *sukūra*, An earthen dish.

P سکوشاک *sukūshāk*, Lightning, thunderbolt.

A سکوک *sakūk*, A narrow-mouthed well. *Sukūk*, (pl. of سک *sakk*) Nails.

A سکون *sukūn*, (v. n. of سکن) Being still, quiet, fixed. Inhabiting, occupying, dwelling. Having no vowel (a consonant). Being poor, needy, feeble, or miserable. Dying. Tranquillity, rest, quiet. Cessation. Residence, dwelling. Firmness, constancy.

P سکون و جنبش *sukūn u jumbish*, Rest and motion.

A سکونة *sukūnat*, Dwelling, habitation, residence. سکونت ورزیدن *sukūnat warzīdan*, To dwell.

P سکوهنج *suhohanj*, A triangular thorny plant. A stick, straw.

P سکوی *sahwī*, A sofa, bench, garden-seat.

P سکوینه *sahwīna*, A sort of gum.

P سکه *sikka*, (from A سکّة *sikkat*) A die for coining. Rule, law, regulation. Dress, costume. سکه زدن *sikka zadan* (or کردن *kardan*), To coin, mint. سکهٔ نو بهار *sikka-i naw-bahār*, Vernal blossoms.

P سکه خانه *sikka-khāna*, A mint.

P سکه دار *sikka-dār*, Having power of coining, *i.e.* an independent sovereign.

P سکه روپیه *sikka-rūpiya*, A rupee of full weight.

P سکه زن *sikka-zan*, Coiner, master of the mint.

A سکّیٰ *sakka'*, An iron fastening. A nail.

A سکّیّ *sakkiy*, A nail. A die for coining. A coat of mail formed of close rings. *Sikkiy*, Coined, stamped, minted (money). A dīnār.

A سکیب *sakīb*, Flowing, current (water).

A سکیت *sukayt*, (or سکّیت *sukkayt*) Silent, taciturn. The last horse in running a race (especially the tenth).

A سکّیت *sikkīt*, Silent, reserved.

A سکّیر *sikkīr*, Very drunken, always drunk.

A سکیران *suhayrān*, (pl. سکیرانون *suhayrānūn*) Drunkish, a little drunk. (dim. of سکران *sakrān*).

P سکیز *sikīz*, Malignant, wild, fierce, vicious. A young unbroke horse. A kicker, jumper. A kick. A blacksmith's forge, furnace.

P سکیزان *sikīzān*, Cantering, or kicking (horse).

P سکیزه *sikīza*, Kicking (horse). A gallop, canter. A broil, a quarrel.

P سکیزیدن *sikīzīdan*, To gallop. To be obstinate, refractory, vicious, to spring or prance backwards and forwards. To kick. To tread (as a cock).

P سکیله *sakela*, A sort of iron. Hiccough.

A سکین *suhayn*, A swift ass.

A سکّین *sikkīn*, (pl. سکاکین) A knife.

A سکینة *sakīnat*, Tranquillity of mind. Repose. A violent wind. The gracious presence of God dwelling amongst them. A living creature with the face of a man, and the remainder of its form thin as air: according to some, with the head of a cat like an emerald or sapphire. *Sukaynat*, A she-ass. Name of the gnat that entered the nostril of Nimrod and caused his death. Name of the daughter of Husayn and grand-daughter of Alīy, to whom is referred the طرّة سکینیّة *turrat sukayniyat*, or Sukayni ringlet.

A سکّینة *sikkīnat*, A knife. Quiet, repose.

P سگ *sag*, A dog. سگ آبگیر *sagi āb-gīr*, A

water-lizard. سگ ابلق *sagi ablah*, (Spotted dog) Time, fortune. سگ بوزينه *sagi būzīna*, A dog whereon a mountebank's monkey rides. سگ دريا *sagi daryā*, An otter. سگ ديوانه‌وار *sagi dīwāna-wār*, Like a mad dog, rabid.

P سگ آب *sagi āb*, (or سگ آبي) A beaver.

P سگابي *sagābī*, The castor or beaver.

P سگال *sigāl*, Thought. Hatred, enmity. A word, saying. Calumny. A speaker. A singer. نيك سگال *nek-sigāl*, Benevolent. بد سگال *bad-sigāl*, Malevolent. دشمن بد سگال *dushmani bad-sigāl*, A malignant enemy. *Sugāl*, A board.

P سگالش *sigālish*, Thought. Controversy, litigation, altercation. Enmity. Evil-speaking.

P سگاله *sagāla* or *sugāla*, Dung of dogs.

P سگاليدن *sigālīdan*, To think. To speak traducingly of the absent, meditate mischief, resolve to injure. To deceive. To speak. To warble, sing.

P سگاليده *sigālīda*, Thoughtful.

P سگان *sagān*, (pl. of سگ *sag*) Dogs. سگان آز *sagāni āz*, Greedy, worldly-minded people. سگان خيمهٔ دنيا *sagāni khaymaʼi dunya'*, Worldlings.

P سگ انگور *sag-angūr*, Dogs' grape, nightshade.

P سگان ماده *sagān-māda*, (pl. of سگ ماده *sag-māda*) Bitches.

P سگانه *sigāna*, Triple, of three kinds. Name of a village in Ghaznīn.

P سگاوند *sagāwand*, Name of a mountain said to abound in dogs.

P سگبان *sagbān*, A dog-keeper.

P سگ بچه *sag-bacha*, A whelp, a pup.

P سگبستك *sag* or *sagibastah*, A sagacious dog.

P سگ بوزينه *sag-būzīna*, A dog with a monkey mounted on his back.

P سگبه *sagba*, A dish made of butter and milk.

P سگ پستان *sag-pistān*, Sebestens.

P سگ پوي *sag-pūy*, Sound of feet in walking.

P سگ تازي *sagi tāzī*, A greyhound.

P سگ جان *sag-jān*, Dog-souled, malignant.

P سگ جگر *sag-jigar*, Cruel, inhuman.

P سگچه *sagcha*, A little dog. A sagacious dog.

P سگ چهرها *sag-chihrahā*, Crabbed (people).

P سگ دل *sag-dil*, Dog-hearted, fierce.

P سگدندان *sag-dandān*, A canine tooth.

P سگ دوي *sag-davī*, A fruitless running about.

P سگ ديوانه *sagi dīwāna*, A mad dog.

P سگر *sugur*, A porcupine.

P سگرنه *sugurna*, (or سگزنه) A porcupine.

P سگز *sigz*, A mountain in Zābulistān.

P سگ زاده *sag-zāda*, A son of a bitch.

P سگزن *sagzan*, A sort of sharp-pointed arrow. A broad-headed, pointless arrow, with which boys learn to shoot.

P سگزه *sagza*, A sob. A sharp-pointed arrow.

P سگزي *sigzī*, A certain people residing near the mountain *Sigz*.

P سگزيدن *sigzīdan*, To commit a crime. To be folded.

P سگسار *sagsār*, Dog-like. A species of imaginary monster, with the head of a dog, the yellow face of a dragon, the hair of a goat, the ears of an elephant, and blue eyes. Avaricious. Worldly-minded. A parasite.

P سگستان *sigistān*, A fruit like a plum. Sijistān.

P سگسر *sag-sar*, Dog-headed.

P سگسنبويه *sagsambūya*, Seed of cinquefoil.

P سگ شكاري *sagi shikārī*, A hunting-dog.

P سگك *sagah*, A little dog. A species of bur or prickly grass. A kind of grappling iron.

P سگ كش *sag-kush*, Dog-willow.

P سگ كن *sag-kan*, The mandrake.

P سگل *sagl*, A kind of plant.

P سگلاب *saglāb*, (or سگلابي *saglābī*) A beaver.

P سگلابيدن *saglābīdan*, To bark (as a dog).

P سگلاو *saglāv*, (or سگلاوي *saglāwī*) A beaver.

P سگليدن *saglīdan*, To sigh, sob. To belch.

P سگم *sagam*, A cricket.

P سگ ماده *sag-māda*, A bitch.

P سگ منش *sag-manish*, Churlish, currish.

P سگنجه *saganja*, Hail.

P سگنگور *sagangūr*, (for سگ انگور) Nightshade.

P سگي *sigī*, Wine.

P سگي خانه *sigī-khāna*, A tavern.

P سگيله *sagīla*, A sigh, sob. A belch.

P سل *sal*, A raft. A ship. *Sil*, Consumption.

A سل *sal*, (imp. of سأل) Ask thou!

A سلّ *salla*, (fut. يسلّ *yasullu*) He drew forth.

A سلّ *sall*, (v. n. of سلّ) Drawing one thing out of another (especially a sword from the scabbard). Withdrawing privately, purloining. Losing the teeth. Horse-stealing. A man deprived of his teeth. (pl. سلال *silāl*) A canister covered with leather in which victuals are kept. *Sill* or *sull*, Consumption, ulceration of the lungs. A hectic fever.

P سلّ *sull*, The lungs.

A سلء *sals*, (v. n. of سلأ) Melting, clarifying, heating (butter). Taking off prickles (from a palm-tree). Expressing (oil of sesame). Paying ready money quickly. Striking, scourging.

P سلا *salā*, Song. Name of a singer.

A سلا *sala'*, (v. n. of سلي) Being delivered of the afterbirth (a ewe). (pl. اسلاء *aslā*) The membrane enveloping the fœtus in the womb, the secundine. سلا جمل *sala' jamalin*, The secundine of a he-camel (either an impossibility, or a difficult and troublesome affair).

A سلاء *silās*, (pl. اسلئة *aslisat*) Melted butter.

A سلاء *sullās*, (pl. of سلاءة *sullāsat*) Prickles on palms. A sort of bird. A kind of spear resembling the prickles on a palm-tree.

A سلاءة *sullāsat*, (pl. سلاء *sullās*) A prickle on a palm-tree.

A سلاب *silāb*, A black mourning-habit.

A سلابة *sallābat*, A spoiler, male or female.

P سلات *salāt*, Name of a famous musician.

A سلاتة *sulātat*, (Meat) scraped or licked from off the fingers. Any thing removed or taken away (as water from the sides of a cup).

P سلاجت *salājit*, A species of storax.

A سلاجقة *salājihat*, The Seljukian dynasty.

A سلاجم *salājim*, (pl. of سلجم *saljam*) Arrows with a long head or point. Long camels. *Sulājim*, Long (camel). Old and strong (camel).

A سلاح *silāh*, (pl. اسلحة *aslihat*) Arms (especially sword, mace, and stringless bow). P پرسلاح *pur-silāh*, Fully armed. A *Sulāh*, Dung, excrement.

A سلاح *sallāh*, Who voids much excrement.

A سلاحة *sulāhat*, The urine of the mountain-goat, which in stony places becomes congealed.

P سلاح خانه *silāh-khāna*, An arsenal, armoury.

P سلاح دار *silāh-dār*, A sword-bearer, esquire.

P سلاح شور *silāh-shor*, A fencing-master. An armourer. A breaker or trainer of horses.

A سلاحف *salāhif*, (pl. of سلحفا *sulahfa'*, سلحفاء *sulahfās*, and سلحفية *sulahfiyat*) Tortoises.

P سلاحه *salāha*, The urine of a mountain-goat, black and viscous like pitch, which they gather from the rocks.

A سلاحي *silāhī*, A sword or armour-bearer.

A سلاخ *sallākh*, A skinner, a flayer.

A سلاخة *salākhat*, Insipidness, want of flavour. *Sulākhat*, Flayings, skinnings.

A سلاخد *salākhid*, (pl. of سلخد *sillakhd* and سلخداة *salakhdāt*) Strong she-camels.

P سلارس *salāras*, Liquid storax.

A سلاس *sulās*, Weakness of mind. Insanity, loss of intellect.

A سلاسة *salāsat*, Easiness, simplicity. Facility, ductility. Gentleness. Perspicuity, clearness.

A سلاسل *salāsil*, (pl. of سلسلة *silsilat*, or سلسل *silsil*) Lightnings darting to a great distance. Clouds linked together like a chain. Sands adhering together, not easily moved. The lines of a book. *Sulāsil*, Limpid water flowing down the throat. Mellow wine.

A سلاط *silāt*, A cloth for holding straw. (pl. of سلطة *siltat*) Long and slender arrows. (pl. of سلط *salit*) Points of spears not swelling in the middle.

A سلاطة *salātat*, (v. n. of سلط) Having a sharp, piercing tongue. Being long-handed, rapacious, and oppressive. Sovereignty, power, authority. Fluency of tongue.

A سلاطح *sulātih*, Broad. Name of a valley.

A سلاطين *salātīn*, (pl. of سلطان *sultān*) Kings, princes, emperors, sovereigns, potentates. P سلاطين با تمكين *salātīni bā tamkīn*, Mighty potentates.

A سلاع *silāş*, (pl. of سلعة) Fractures, cuts.

A سلاف *sulāf*, Juice which flows from the grapes before pressure. Wine. Whatever comes through the pores of the skin. The van of an army.

A سلاف *sullāf*, (pl. of سلف *salaf*) Predecessors,

leaders of the people. Ancestors.

A سلافة *sulāfat*, The first juice pressed from any thing. Wine.

A سلاق *sulāk*, A tubercle on the tongue. An excoriation or consumption of the teeth about the roots. Efflorescence or pimples on the body. A hard substance on the eye-lid corroding the lashes and edges. The feast of Ascension.

A سلّاق *sallāk*, Clear, shrill-voiced; a rhetorician, sublime orator. *Sullāk*, A certain Christian festival.

A سلاقع *salākiɛ*, (pl. of سلقع *salkaɛ*) Rugged, desert grounds.

A سلاقم *sulākim*, A lion.

P سلاك *salāk*, An ingot of gold or of silver. Hire, rent.

A سلال *silāl*, (pl. of سلّ *sall* or سلّة *sallat*) Canisters covered with leather. Canisters or wardrobes wherein victuals or clothes are kept. *Sulāl*, Hectic fever, consumption, ulceration of the lungs.

A سلّال *sallāl*, A maker of wicker baskets. A cattle-stealer.

A سلالة *sulālat*, Whatever is extracted from any thing. A fœtus. Human seed. A running, gleet, strangury. Stock, posterity. The purest part of any thing.

A سلالم *salālim*, (or سلاليم *salālīm*) (pl. of سلّم *sullam*) Steps, ladders, stairs.

A سلاليج *salālīj*, Tall plane-trees.

A سلام *salām*, (v. n. of سلم) Saluting, wishing health or peace. Submitting, surrendering. Being secure from harm. A salutation, greeting. Peace, safety, security from harm. A kind of tree. Freedom from vice or blemish. Compassion; hence one of the attributes of God. A man bit by a serpent. دار السلام *dāru's salām*, Paradise. مدينة السلام *madīnatu's salām*, The city of peace, *i.e.* Baghdād. نهر السلام *nahru's salām*, The river of peace, *i.e.* the river Tigris. سلام الله *salāmu'llāh*, The peace of God. P سلام سلامت انجام و پيام مودّت اختتام *salāmi salāmat-anjām, wa payāmi mawaddat-ikhtitām*, Affectionate salutations and demonstrations of friendship. A السلام عليكم *as' salām ɛalaykum*, Peace be with you. May God preserve you! والسلام *wa's salām*, And (so) farewell, adieu. P سلام كردن *salām kardan*, To salute. A ابو سلام *abū salām*, The mandrake. *Silām*, A kind of tree. (pl. of سلم *salm*) One-handled buckets. (pl. of سلم *silm*) Those who cultivate peace and friendship. (pl. of سلمة *salamat* or *salimat*), Stones.

A سلّام *sallām*, Solomon the son of David. David.

A سلامان *salāmān*, Name of a tree.

A سلامة *salāmat*, (v. n. of سلم) Being secure from danger, escaping from harm. Salvation, safety, peace, rest, repose, immunity, liberty, integrity, soundness, recovery, health.

A سلّامة *sallāmat*, A woman's name.

P سلامت رو *salāmat-rav*, An economist.

P سلامت روي *salāmat-ravī*, Economy.

P سلامت كوچه *salāmat-kūcha*, A military entrenchment.

A سلامتي *salāmatī*, Safety.

A سلامج *salāmij*, (pl. of سلمج *salmaj*) Long, slender arrow-heads.

A سلامى *salāma'*, The south wind. *Sulāma'*, (pl. سلاميات *sulāmiyāt*) The bones of the fingers. A bone in the sole of a camel's foot.

P سلامي *salāmī*, A salute of cannon. A present on being introduced to a superior. Earnest-money; a free gift from a farmer to government on taking lands, and from the same to the Zamīndār to build his house. سلامي خانه باري *salāmī khāna bārī*, A present from the farmer to his landlord to enable him to build his house.

A سلاميّ *salāmiy*, A native of مدينة السلام *madīnatu's salām, i.e.* Baghdād.

A سلّان *sullān*, (pl. of سالّ *sāll*) Widely-extended valleys producing the trees *salam* and *samur*.

A سلاهبة *salāhibat*, (pl. of سلهب) Long, tall.

A سلائب *salāïb*, (pl. of سلوب *salūb* or سليب *salīb*) (Women or camels) delivered of abortions.

A سلائط *salāït*, Large cakes.

A سلائق *salāïk*, Foot or hoof-marks on a road.

A سلب *salb*, (v. n. of سلب) Putting on mourning clothes. A quick pace. Haste, expedition. Name of a certain tree. Deprivation. Negation, denial, rejection. سلب جزئي *salbi juzā*, A special negation. سلب كلي *salbi kullī*, A general negation. *Salb* or *salab*, (v. n. of سلب) Spoiling, seizing by force. *Silb*, The beam of a plough. *Sulb*, Delivered of an abortion (woman or camel). *Salab*, (pl. اسلاب *aslāb*) Rapine, plunder. The hide, feet, and paunch of an animal slain in sacrifice. The bark of an Arabian tree, of which they make ropes. The bark of a reed. Name of a certain tall tree. A rapid pace. Seized, carried off. P سلب فرشته داشتن *salabi firishta dāshtan*, To be clothed in green. A *Salib*, Protracted, extended, long (spear). Light, nimble. سلب القوائم *salibu'l kawāïm*, Nimble-footed, swift. سلب اليدين *salibu'l yadayn*, Ready-handed, expert. *Sulub*, (pl. of سلاب *silāb*) Mourning-clothes. (pl. of سليب *salīb*) Delivered of abortions.

A سلبة *sulbat*, Bareness, nakedness, nudity.

A سلبوب *salabūb*, A spoiler (male or female).

A سلبى *salba'*, (pl. of سليب) Bereft of senses.

A سلبيّ *salbiy*, Negative.

A سلّة *sallat* or *sillat*, (pl. سلال *silāl* and اسلال *aslāl*) Theft. The drawing of a sword. A canister or wardrobe in which provisions or clothes are kept. A woman who has lost her teeth. A crack or flaw in a cistern. The pace or speed of a horse. Ulceration of the lungs, consumption. A sewing with a double thong. A return of broken-windedness in a horse after it had been concealed.

A سلت *salt*, (v. n. of سلت) Shaving (the head). Cutting. Cutting clean off (the nose) with a sword. Voiding excrement. Striking, flogging. Drawing out (an intestine). Rejecting, throwing off marks of the dye of henna from the hand. Wiping, scraping (a dish) with the fingers. Removing the pellicle from off the blood of the victim بدنة *badanat* till the blood is visible. *Sult*, A kind of barley without husks, or a bitter sort of barley.

A سلتاء *saltāɛ*, (fem. of اسلت *aslat*) One whose nose has been cut clean off. (A woman) negligent of herself, not colouring her hair or nails with حناء.

A سلتة *saltatan*, Suddenly, unexpectedly. ذهب عنّي فلتة و سلتة *zahaba ɛannī faltatan wa saltatan*, He went from me suddenly, I know not whither.

A سلتم *saltam*, Any thing. *Siltim*, A misfortune. A demon, supposed to haunt woods in a human shape. Toothless (camel), and deprived of the lower lip. A scarce year. A small thing, any thing.

A سلتين *siltīn*, A palm-tree, around whose foot a bason has been dug that may hold the water.

A سلج *salj*, (v. n. of سلج) Having a looseness from eating the herb سلّج *sullaj* (camels). Sucking the dam (a camel's colt). Swallowing (a mouthful). A present, gift. *Sulaj*, A shell-fish, oyster.

A سلّج *sullaj*, A species of herb, on which camels pasture.

A سلجان *salajān*, (v. n. of سلج) Swallowing (a mouthful). الاكل سلجان و القضاء ليّان *al akl salajān, wa'l kazāɛ layyān*, To spend borrowed money is easy; to repay it is the difficulty.

A سلجان *sillijān*, The gullet, throat. *Sullajān*, A sort of herb whereon camels pasture.

A سلجلج *sa* or *sulajlaj*, Savoury, nice (food).

A سلجم *saljam*, (pl. سلاجم *salājim*) Long, tall. Thick (beard). Long-jawed (head). Old (well) full of water. A turnip. Old and strong (camel).

P سلجن *saljan*, Bitter words. Shamelessness, effrontery.

A سلجن *sillajn*, Biscuit.

P سلجوق *saljūk*, (or سلجق *saljuk*) Name of the founder of the Seljukian dynasty in Persia.

A سلجوقي *saljūkiy*, Seljukian.

A سلح *salh*, (v. n. of سلح) Voiding excrement. Furnishing with a sword, arming with a bow. Dung. *Sulh*, Inspissated juice, with which they season leathern bottles. *Salah*, Rain-water collected in ponds. *Silah*, Arms (sword, club, and stringless bow). *Sulah*, (pl. سلحان *silhān*) A young partridge.

A سلحان *silhān*, (pl. of سلح *sulah*) Young partridges. *Sulhān*, Arms, (particularly a sword, club, and stringless bow).

P سلح خانه *silah-khāna*, An armoury, arsenal.

P سلحدار *silah-dār*, Armour-bearer, esquire.

P سلح شور *silah-shor*, A horseman that displays the throwing of the javelin, vaulting, and other dexterity on horseback. A champion, a gladiator. A horse-breaker.

A سلحفا *sulahfa'*, (سلحفاء *sulahfās*, سلحفاة *silahfāt*, *sulahfāt*, سلحفية *sulahfiyat*, or سلحفي *sulahfa'*) (pl. سلاحف *salāhif*) A tortoise.

A سلحوت *sulhūt*, An indecent woman who cares for nothing.

A سلخ *salkh*, (v. n. of سلخ) Skinning, flaying (an animal). Peeling (bark). Taking off (a shift or smock). Drawing towards a close, finishing (the month). Spending (the month), drawing towards the close of it. Becoming green after withering (a plant). (God) drawing forth (day from night). Quitting its slough (a snake). Committing a literary theft, clothing the ideas of an author in new language. Digging down until water is found. The end of a month. Day of the moon. A goat's skin. The skin of a serpent. That which is stripped off a sheep. دار السلخ *dāru's salkh*, A slaughter-house. P سلخ كردن *salkh kardan*, To flay, skin. To discharge fire-arms. A *Salakh*, Thread on a spindle.

A سلّخ *sullakh*, (or سلّخة *sullakhat*) (pl. of سالخ *sālikh*) Black serpents.

A سلخب *salkhab*, One who stammers much.

P سلخ خانه *salkh-khāna*, A slaughter-house.

A سلّخد *sillakhd*, (and سلخداة *salakhdāt*) (pl. سلاخد *salākhid*) A strong she-camel.

A سلّخف *sillakhf*, Light, giddy, confused.

A سلدانيون *saldāniyūn*, A certain tree which resembles the willow.

A سلس *sals*, A thread upon which they string beads, with necklaces of which the servant-girls adorn their necks. An ear-ring. *Salas*, (v. n. of سلس) Losing its branches (a palm-tree). Being rotten and worm-eaten (wood). Gentleness, docility. Easiness. A diabetes. *Salis*, Easy, docile, gentle (horse). Submissive, obedient (man). Afflicted with a diabetes.

A سلسال *salsāl*, Limpid water flowing down the throat, waving like a chain.

A سلسبيل *salsabīl*, Name of a fountain in Paradise. Mellow wine. Milk in which is no roughness.

A سلسة *salisat*, A kind of plant or thistle.

A سلسل *salsal*, Limpid water flowing down the throat. Water flowing like a chain. Mellow wine. Lightning when darting like a chain.

A سلسلة *salsalat*, (v. n. of سلسل Q) Pouring (water). Tasting (food). Connecting with a chain. Union, connexion. A long slice of a camel's bunch. *Silsilat*, A chain. A series, suite, concatenation, succession, line, descent, inheritance, genealogy, family, progeny. An unbroken tradition. (pl. سلاسل *salāsil*) Lightning, when darting along like a chain. A concatenation of clouds. A long slice of a camel's bunch. A red reptile that cleaves to the ground.

P سلسله *silsila*, A chain.

P سلسله پيوند *silsila-paywand*, Link-connecting.

P سلسله جنبان *silsila-jumbān*, (Shaking the chain) A cause, means. A pledge.

P سلسيس *salsīs*, A sort of stone.

P سلش *salish*, (in zand and Pāzand) Bad.

A سلط *salt*, Vehement, sharp. Long-tongued. A long tongue. *Sult*, Delegation, appointment to any post of authority or charge. *Salit*, (pl. سلاط *silāt*) Point of a spear not swelling in the middle. *Silat*, (pl. of سلطة *siltat*) Long and slender arrows.

A سلطات *salitāt*, Sharp hoofs (of a horse).

A سلطان *sultān*, (pl. سلاطين *salātīn*) Victorious, ruling over. A monarch, sovereign, prince, potentate, emperor. A queen, lady, princess. Absolute power, despotic authority, sovereignty, dominion. Convincing proof. Power, virtue, efficacy (applied to any thing). The boiling of blood. (pl. of سليط *salīt*) Oils of olive or sesame. P سلطان كامران *sultāni kām-rān*, A powerful sovereign, despot. A سلطان كثير الاحسان *sultāni kasīru'l ihsān*, A prince of unbounded clemency. P سلطان گيتي ممالك ستان *sultāni gītī mamālik-satān*, A king subduing the universal world. سلطان مكرمت آشيان *sultāni makramat-āshyān*, A potentate, the nest of liberality. سلطان اختران *sultāni akhtarān*, The sun. سلطان درويشان *sultāni darweshān*, Muhammad. A سلطان الدم *sultānu'd dam*, The avenger of blood. سلطان عهد *sultāni ʿahd*, The reigning monarch. سلطان فلك *sultāni falak*, (Lord of the firmament) The sun. P سلطان يك سوارهٔ گردون *sultāni yak suwāra-i gardūn*, The sun. *Sulutān*, Absolute power.

A سلطانة *salatānat* or *silitānat*, Sharp, long-tongued, clamorous woman.

P سلطاني *sultānī*, (A سلطانيّ *sultāniy*) Belonging to a prince or sovereign. Royal, imperial, princely. A kind of broad-cloth. A sultanine (a gold coin about nine shillings); also another of ten aspres (about three farthings each). A fine sort of peach. Dominion, principality.

A سلطة *siltat*, (pl. سلط *silat* and سلاط *silāt*) A long and slender arrow. A sheet for holding hay or straw. *Sultat*, Power, delegated authority.

A سلطحة *saltahat*, Broad, wide (girl).

A سلطقي *saltakī*, A kind of dervish's garment.

A سلطنة *saltanat*, (v. n. of سلطن Q) Making emperor. *Sultanat*, Power, authority, magnificence, majesty. An empire, kingdom, principality.

A سلطوع *sultūʿ*, A smooth, bare mountain.

A سلطيط *siltīt*, Big-bellied. Commissioned.

A سلع *salʿ*, (pl. سلوع *sulūʿ*) A fissure, crack, chink, gap; a chap (in the feet). A cleft in a mountain. *Silʿ*, (pl. اسلاع *aslāʿ* and سلوع *sulūʿ*) A similitude, a simile. Alike, equal. A cleft in a mountain. *Sulʿ*, (pl. of اسلع *aslaʿ*) Cracked in the feet. Leprous. *Salaʿ*, (v. n. of سلع) Having cracks in the feet. Being leprous. The leprosy. A disordered state of body. A certain bitter tree or noxious plant. Poison, bane. A crack in the feet. A sort of aloe. Fractures in the skull. *Silaʿ*, (pl. of سلعة *silʿat*) Tumours, wens. Wares.

A سلعاف *silʿāf*, Pointed stakes erected round trees for killing wild beasts.

A سلعام *silʿām*, One who has a wide throat, large belly, and long nose. Long-snouted (wolf).

A ابو سلعامة *abū silʿāmat*, (Father Long-snout) The wolf.

A سلعة *salʿat*, or *salaʿat*, (pl. سلعات *salʿāt* and سلاع *silāʿ*) A fracture, contusion, or cut. *Silʿat*, (*salʿat*, *salaʿat*, or *silaʿat*) A tumour, an excrescence on the body moveable by the touch (as a wen, goitre, kernel, blotch, or a scrofulous swelling, varying in size from a vetch to a melon). Coagulated blood. *Silʿat*, (pl. سلع *silaʿ*) Merchandise, goods, wares. Household furniture.

A سلعف *sillaʿf* (or سلعفّ *silʿaff*) Nodding, shaking the head, staggering, tottering. Proud.

A سلعفة *salʿafat*, The act of swallowing.

A سلعنة *salʿanat*, A running furiously.

A سلغ *salgh*, (v. n. of سلغ) Breaking (the head). *Salagh*, The toughness of old meat, which boiling cannot make tender.

A سلغاف *silghāf*, (for سلعاف *silʿāf*) Pointed stakes fixed round trees for killing wild beasts.

A سلّغد *sillaghd*, (or سلغدّ *silghadd*) A glutton, a drunkard. A fool. A languid, also a passionate man. A wolf. Bright bay (horse). A horse with a chesnut mane and tail.

P سلغر *salghar*, Name of the father of Seljūk shāh.

A سلغزة *salghazat*, A running at full speed.

A سلغف *salghaf*, Robust, full grown, firm of body. A fat ox.

A سلّغف *sillaghf*, Disturbed, confused, giddy.

A سلغفة *salghafat*, The act of swallowing.

A سلف *salf*, (v. n. of سلف) Levelling (the ground). Harrowing a field for sowing. Smoothing with a trowel. (pl. اسلف *asluf* and سلوف *sulūf*) A large wallet. Leather not sufficiently dressed. *Silf*, The husband of a wife's sister. *Sulf*, A woman forty-five years old. (pl. of سلوف *salūf*) Swift (horses). Long (arrow-heads). *Salaf*, (v. n. of سلف) Passing, going by. Preceding. Smearing (a leathern bottle). (pl. سلّاف *sullāf* and اسلاف *aslāf*) A predecessor, ancestor, or (pl.) predecessors. A precedent. Any one who goes before to make any requisite preparations. Money paid down, or before it is due, for goods to be afterwards delivered. Money lent without interest. Any good action. A son dead, and gone before. A purse. *Salif*, Thin of trees (a country). The husband of of a wife's sister. *Salif* or *silf*, (pl. اسلاف *aslāf*) The skin. The husband of a wife's sister. *Sulaf*, (pl. سلفان *silfān* or *sulfān*) A young partridge. (pl. of سلفة *sulfat*) Whets before dinner. Boot-linings. Parts of a sown field levelled.

P سلف *sulf*, A cough.

A سلفان *silfān* or *sulfān*, (pl. of سلف *sulaf*) Young partridges. *Silfāni*, (dual of سلف *silf*) Two men married to two sisters.

P سلفانیدن *sulfānīdan*, To cause to cough.

A سلفة *silfat*, The relationship of two women married to two brothers. A brother's wife. *Silfat* or *silafat*, A woman's name. *Sulfat*, (pl. سلف *sulaf*) Breakfast, or any thing eaten as a whet before dinner. Food prepared and reserved for an expected guest. Thin leather, with which they line boots. Part of a sown field made level. جاوا سلفة *jāū sulfatan*, They came in a train, one after another.

A سلفتان *silfatāni*, Two women married to two brothers. Two men married to two sisters.

A سلفع *salfaʿ*, Bold, intrepid, strenuous. One who has a large breast or chest. A woman of a bad disposition, immodest, noisy, scolding. A swift she-camel. Name of a bitch.

A سلفعة *salfaʿat*, A woman of a bad disposition, immodest, noisy, and a scold.

A سلفون *salifūn*, (plur.) Preceding. Kindred.

P سلفه *sulfa*, A cough.

P سلفیدن *sulfīdan*, To sneeze, cough. To insert, place upon.

A سلق *salk*, (v. n. of سلق) Excoriating, cutting the skin (with a lash). Stripping (meat from a bone). Scalding off the hair. Parboiling eggs or pot-herbs. Throwing down upon the back, laying prostrate. Lying with a girl supine. Nipping (as cold a plant). Leaving marks upon a road (the feet of men or hoofs of quadrupeds). Raising a clamour. Running and shouting. Tormenting another (particularly with opprobrious language). Anointing, greasing, smearing all over with pitch. Passing a stick through the handles of two sacks for the conveniency of carriage. Bringing together the two handles of a wallet. A scar left upon the back of a beast of burden, or the mark of the girths. Beet. *Silk*, (pl. سلقان *sulkān*) A flux of water: also the channel by which it flows. The herb beet. A wolf. (pl. of سلقة *silkat*) She-wolves. سلق الماء *silku'l māʾ* and سلق البرّ *silku'l barr*, Names of two plants. *Sulk*, (pl. of سلق *silak* and سليق *salīk*) Leaves and branches fallen. Honeys. Sides of roads. *Salak*, The mark upon a beast of burden, left by the tying of the girths; also the scar of a wound. Footmarks left on the ground. (pl. سلقان *sulkān*) Light, good soil, level ground. *Silak*, (pl. سلق *sulk*) Whatever falls from a tree, particularly leaves and branches. Withered thorns. Honey. A road-side. *Suluk*, A large leathern sack.

A سلقاء *silkāʾ*, (v. n. of سلقی Q) Throwing flat on the back, laying prostrate. Piercing, stabbing.

A سلقاة *salkāt*, A sort of wen (or a modus coeundi) upon the back.

A سلقامة *silkāmat*, A she-wolf.

A سلقان *silkān*, (pl. of سلق *silk*) Wolves. *Silkān* or *sulkān*, (pl. of سلقة *salkat*) Good soils, level grounds. (pl. of سلقة *silkat*) Noisy, impudent women. *Sulkān*, (pl. of سلق *silk*) Streams of water, or the channels by which they flow. Wolves. (pl. of سلق *salak*) Level grounds.

A سلقة *salkat*, (pl. اسلاق *aslāk*, سلقان *silkān* or *sulkān*) Good soil, level ground. *Silkat*, (pl. سلقان *silkān* and *sulkān*) A clamorous, abandoned woman. (pl. سلق *silk*) A she-wolf.

A سلقد *silkid*, Slender-bodied, lean (horse).

A سلقدة *salkadat*, A making (a horse) lean.

A سلقع *salkaʿ*, A male ostrich. (pl. سلاقع *salākiʿ*) Rugged ground. A desert. بلقع سلقع *balkaʿ salkaʿ*, A barren desert.

A سلقلق *salaklak*, A woman troubled with piles.

A سلقلقة *salaklakat*, A shrew, termagant.

A سلقم *salkam*, A lion. A camel with a strong jawbone and a long nose.

A سلقمة *salkamat*, A gnashing of the teeth. Whatever excites suspicion, or makes one doubt.

P سلقیس *salkīs*, A city built by Zū'l karnayn.

A سلك *salk*, (v. n. of سلك) Thrusting in, threading. Walking, treading. Causing any one to tread or walk through. *Silk*, A thread. What comes away from a camel before the biestings. A series, train, connexion. A road. سلك جواهر *silki jawāhir*, (or سلك لآلي *silki laʾālī*) A string of pearls. A handsome row of teeth. سلك دور قمر *silki dawri kamar*, The world. Fortune. Night and day. *Sulak*, (pl. سلكان *silkān*) A young kata or partridge.

P سلك *salk*, *silk*, or *sulk*, A canal, mill-dam, or stream which drives the wheel. *Silak*, Pease. Vetches.

A سلكان *silkān*, (pl. of سلك) Young partridges.

A سلكة *silkat*, (pl. سلك *silk*, اسلاك *aslāk*, and سلوك *sulūk*) Sewing thread. *Sulakat*, A young female partridge.

P سلكك *silkak*, A small canal or mill-dam.

A سلكوت *sulkūt* or *salakūt*, Name of a bird.

A سلكی *sulka'*, A direct thrust or stab. A straightforward business.

P سلم *salm*, The eldest son of Farīdūn. *Salm* or *silam*, Tables on which boys learn to write.

A سلم *salm*, (v. n. of سلم) Tanning (leather) with the bark of a tree called salam. Completing the making of a bucket. Peace. Safety. The bite of a serpent. (pl. اسلم *aslum* and سلام *silām*) A one-handled bucket. *Silm*, (v. n. of سلم) Saluting. Paying in advance. Health, safety. Peace. The Muhammadan religion. (pl. سلام *silām* and اسلام *aslām*) One who cultivates peace and friendship. *Salam*, The payment of ready money for goods to be delivered at an after-period. Surrender, submission, delivery. Captivity. A captive. Salutation, greeting. (pl. اسلام *aslām*) A kind of thorny plant.

A سلّم *sullam*, (pl. سلاليم *salālīm* and سلالم *salālim*) A ladder, staircase. Stirrups of leather (used when riding camels). Certain stars below العانة *al ʿānat*, to the right. A means or occasion of uniting with, or procuring. *Sallama*, May (He) preserve!

A سلماء *sulamāʾ*, (pl. of سليم *salīm*) Safe from danger, sound: free from hurt or harm.

A ابو سلمان *abū salmān*, A beetle.

A سلمة *salamat*, One tree called سلم *salam*. Name of a man. امّ سلمة *ummu salamat*, One of Muhammad's wives. *Salimat*, (pl. سلام *silām*) A stone. A woman who has delicate hands and feet.

A سلمج *salmaj*, A long slender arrow-head.

P سلمك *salmak*, One of the six musical styles.

P سلمه *salma*, A vegetable used in tanning.

A سلمی *salma'*, The south wind. White lizards. Name of a woman, of a tribe, and of a mountain. A kind of plant. ابو سلمی *abū salma'*, A sun-flower. A chameleon. ابو سلمی *abū sulma'*, Name of a man.

P سلنج *silunj*, An ulcer on the lip. Cracked in the lips.

A سلنطاع *silintāʿ*, A tall man. A babbler, prater.

A سلنطح *salantah*, A large, wide, extensive plain.

A سلنطع *salantaʿ*, A tall man.

A سلنقاع *silinkāʿ*, Flashing lightning.

A سلو *salw* or سلوّ *sulūw*, (v. n. of سلا for سلو) Being tranquil, contented, or relieved from anxiety, care or sorrow. Forgetting.

A سلواة *salwāt*, A single quail.

A سلوان *salwān*, (v. n. of سلا for سلو) Forgetting. A shell, amulet, or charm. *Sulwān*, A remedy for love or grief (especially water poured from a kind of shell, and drank to one's health as a supposed charm for removing all sorrow from the mind; also water poured upon earth taken from the grave of a dead man, which they imagine to be a cure for love). A medicine which the physicians call مفرّح *mufarrih* (exhilarating). Name of a fountain at Jerusalem, the pool of Siloam.

A سلوانة *sulwānat*, Honey. *Sulwānat* or *salwānāt*, A kind of shells, amulets, or charms.

A سلوب *salūb*, (pl. سلائب *salāʾib* and سلب *sulub*) Liable to abortions (camel or woman).

A سلوة *salwat* or *sulwat*, A remedy for grief or for love. Tranquillity, cheerfulness, comfort, solace, content. Conveniences of life, prosperity. سلوت و سرور *salwat u surūr*, Contentment and cheerfulness.

P سلّور *sillūr*, An eel.

A سلوطة *salūtat*, (v. n. of سلط) Having a sharp tongue. Being long (the tongue). Being long-handed, rapacious and oppressive. Dominion, power.

A سلوع *sulūʿ*, (pl. of سلع *salʿ*) Fissures, cracks in the feet. (pl. of سلع *silʿ*) Clefts in mountains. Similes, similitudes.

A سلوغ *sulūgh*, (v. n. of سلغ) Shedding the teeth after the sixth year (oxen or sheep). Breeding those teeth which are called ناب *nāb*.

A سلوف *salūf*, (pl. سلف *sulf*) The first of a herd (of camels) that rushes to water. Long head (of an arrow or spear). Swift (horse). *Sulūf*, (v.

n.of سلف) Passing, preceding. (pl.of سلف *salf*) Large wallets. Undressed leathers.

A سلوق *salūk*, Nature, genius. Name of a town in Arabia Felix, whence coats of mail manufactured there are called سلوقي *salūkīy*; also name of a town famous for dogs, which are also called *salūkīy*.

A سلوقية *salūkīyat*, That part of a ship in which the master sits: the captain's cabin.

A سلوك *sulūk*, (v. n. of سلك) Proceeding, going by the way. Navigating. Threading. A journey, way, road. Institution, mode, manner, rule. Usage, treatment. Intercourse. (pl. of سلكة *silkat*) Sewing threads. P سلوك كردن *sulūk kardan*, To travel. To follow any rule or institution.

A سلوى *salwa'*, Honey. Quails. The little bittern. Solace of any kind.

P سلّه *salla*, A wicker, or snake-catcher's basket.

A سلهابة *silhābat*, (or سلهاب) Bold (woman).

A سلهب *salhab*, (pl. سلاهبة *salāhibat*) Long, tall (horse or man). Thick, and long-boned (horse).

P سلّه باف *salla-bāf*, (or گر) A basket-maker.

A سلهبة *salhabat*, Tall and large-boned (horse). Large-bodied (woman).

A سلهج *salhaj*, Long, tall.

A سلهم *salham*, Slim and long. Weak through sickness. *Silhim*, Name of a man.

A سلى *sala'*, (pl. اسلاء *aslāa*) The secundine which envelopes the fœtus. The caul of a camel's colt. *Sila'*, (v. n. of سلي) Being contented, tranquil, relieved from anxiety. Forgetting. Melting butter.

A سلياء *salyāa*, (A camel or sheep) freed from the after-birth: also one whose secundine remains in the belly.

A سليب *salīb*, (pl. سلبى *salba'*) Stripped of fruit or foliage (a tree). Robbed of one's senses. Bark, of which ropes are made. (pl. سلب *sulub*) (A woman or camel) delivered of an abortion.

A سليج *salīj*, Savoury and agreeable (food).

A سليجة *salījat*, A large kind of tree, from which doors are made.

P سليح *salīh*, Warlike apparatus. *Silīh*, An armed man. A general. The van of an army.

A سليخة *salīkhat*, (P سليخه *salīkha*) A certain perfume. A child; offspring. Benzoin or balsam of the Bān-tree before it is prepared. The part of the رمث *rims* which is not eaten. Cassia of Arabia.

A سليخ مليخ *salīkh malīkh*, One who copulates vigorously without impregnating. Destitute of food. Insipid (meat).

P سليس *salīs*, Easy, plain, familiar, simple, not abstruse. A sort of stone. سليس نويس *salīs-nawīs*, Writing a plain hand.

P سليش *salīsh*, (in zand and Pāzand) Bad.

A سليط *salīt*, Vehement. Sharp. Long-tongued. Eloquent. A long tongue. (pl. سلطان *sultān*) Olive-oil. Oil of sesame. Any oil from seed.

A سليطة *salītat*, A clamorous, brawling woman.

P سليطةُ بازار *salītaɪ bāzār*, A common whore.

A سليف *salīf*, Passed, gone by. A predecessor.

A سليق *salīk*, (pl. سلق *sulk*) Whatever falls from a tree; leaves or branches. Withered thorns. Honey. A road-side.

A سليقة *salīkat*, Boiled pot-herbs. Millet pounded and dressed with condiment. New cheese mixed with the herb طرائيث *tarāsis*. The place where the straps come out (of the saddle). The mark upon a beast of burden, left by the tying of the girths. The mark of a horse's hoof on the road. Nature, genius, good disposition, knack. Way, custom, knowledge, dexterity, address. بالسليقة *bi's salīkat*, (He talks) naturally (not from learning). P سليقةُ گفتگو *salīkaɪ guftgū*, Polite conversation. A سليقةُ مجلس *salīkaɪ majlis*, Good breeding, manners of society.

A سليقه شعار *salīka-shiʿār*, Of good disposition.

P سليك *salīk*, Name of one of the twelve musical styles.

A سليل *salīl*, A new-born infant. A little boy. (pl. سلان *sullān*) A wide-extended valley, producing the tree called السلم *as' salam* and السمر *as' samur*. The spinal marrow. The middle of a valley, through which water flows. Drawn (sword). A male-camel fœtus just extracted from the mother. A horse colt. A fœtus born without a secundine or caul. The brain of a horse. Pure wine or other beverage. A camel's bunch.

A سليلة *salīlat*, A lock of wool or cotton held in the hand when spinning. A daughter. A long muscle in the loins. A long kind of fish.

A سليم *salīm*, (pl. سلماء *sulamāa*) Entire, free from flaw or stain; perfect, sound, healthy, wholesome. Pacific, affable. Mild (medicine). Tame. Bitten by a serpent. Cured in the last extremity. That part of a hoof between the امعر *amʿar* and the صحن *sahn*. سليم الادراك *salīmu'l idrāk*, Of a good understanding. سليم الطبع *salīmu't tabʿ*, Affable, mild. سليم القلب *salīmu'l kalb*, Sincere, mild, gentle-hearted. P سليم دل *salīm-dil*, Weak, ignorant, simple-hearted.

A سليمان *sulaymān*, Solomon. خاتم سليمان *khātami sulaymān*, (or P مهر سليمان *muhri sulaymān*) The seal of Solomon. The knot of Solomon, being two triangles interbraced. سليمان زمان *sulaymāni zamān*, The Solomon or oracle of his age.

P سليماني *sulaymānī*, Belonging to Solomon. A kind of white date. An onyx.

A سم *sim* or *sam*, (for اسم *ism*) A name.

P سم *sum*, A hoof, foot. A cavern, grotto. سم افكندن *sum afkandan*, To limp.

A سمّ *samm*, (v. n. of سمّ) Presenting poison. Poisoning (victuals), infecting with venom. Making special. Intending, proposing. Amending, correcting. Stopping up, corking close. Penetrating deep, investigating, probing, looking to the end. Being particular, special, and peculiar. Reconciling. A refuge, asylum. Aim, object, intention. A fox. (pl. سموم *sumūm* and سمام *simām*) A small hole. The nose, ear, or mouth. Poison, venom. Two veins in the nose of a horse. Mother-of-pearl. A sea-shell. سمّ ابرص *sammu abrasa*, A large and venomous kind of lizard. سمّ الحاجة *sammu'l hājat*, Object, aim. سمّ الحمار *sammu'l himār*, Rhododaphne. سمّ الخياط *sammu'l khiyāt*, The eye of a needle. سمّ ساعة *sammu sāʿatin*, Instant poison. سمّ السمك *sammu's samak*, A poisonous milky grass bearing a yellow flower, when thrown into a pond it makes fishes drunk. سمّ الفار *sammu'l fār*, Ratsbane. Realgar. سمّ قاتل *sammi kātil*, Deadly poison. ذات السمّ *zātu's samm*, A venomous animal. ما له سمّ ولا حمّ غيرك *mā lahu samm wa lā hamm* (or *summ wa lā humm*) *ghayraka*, He has none beside thee. *Simm*, A small hole. Poison. Mother-of-pearl. *Summ*, The orifice of the ear. The eye of a needle. A shell called concha veneris or mother-of-pearl. Poison. A refuge. A fox.

A سما *sima'*, *sama'*, or *suma'*, A name. Heaven.

A سماء *samāa*, (pl. اسمية *asmiyat*, سماوات *samāwāt*, سميّ *sumīy*, and سمى *suma'*) Heaven, sky. A cloud. A roof, canopy. A projection or shade over a door, a portico. Surface, superficies. Rain. A good shower. Eminence, dignity. A horse; also his back. باب السماء *bābu's samāa*, The milky way. ماء السماء *māu's samāa*, Name of a woman. *Simāa*, (v. n. 3 of سمى) Comparing or disputing as to height; boasting against: opposing, contending.

A سماة *samāt* or *simāt*, A sign, mark, note, index. *Sumāt*, (pl. of سامى *sāmī*) Hunters.

A سمات *simāt*, (pl. of سمة) Marks by burning.

A سماج *simāj*, (pl. of سمج *samj*, *samij*, and سميج *samīj*) Hideous, foul, ugly.

A سماجة *samājat*, (v. n. of سمج) Being deformed, filthy, ugly. Deformity, shamefulness, turpitude. Adulteration.

A سماح *samāh* or *simāh*, (v. n. of سمح) Being beneficent, liberal, humane. *Simāh*, (v. n. 3 of سمح) Using lenity (with any one). Pardoning. Houses made of dressed skins. (pl. of سمحة *samhat*) Beneficent, liberal (women).

A سماحة *samāhat*, (v. n. of سمح) Being benevolent, liberal. Beneficence. ارباب سماحت *arbābi samāhat*, Generous people. P سماحت پيشه *samāhat-pesha*, Liberal, courteous, affable.

A سماحيق *samāhīk*, Thin bits of skin in fat about the intestines. سماحيق السماء *samāhīku's samāa*, Transparent clouds in the sky.

A سماخ *simākh*, The ear. Orifice of the ear.

P سماخچه *samākhcha*, (or سماچه *samācha*) A stomacher, bodice, or corslet worn by women.

A سماد *samād*, Dung and ashes mixed.

A سمادير *samādīr*, Weakness of sight. Any confused object appearing before the eyes when drunk, giddy, or fainting. Somnolency, drowsiness.

A سمّار *summār*, (pl. of سامر *sāmir*) Those who hold nocturnal conversations by moonlight.

P سماروغ *samārūgh*, (or سماروخ *samārūkh*) A white mushroom resembling an egg. Salsuginous, unproductive ground.

P سماروغزار *samārūghzār*, A mushroom-bed.

P سماروغناك *samārūghnāk*, Full of mushrooms.

P سماروك *samārūk*, A pigeon.

P سماري *sumārī*, A ship.

A سماسرة *samāsirat*, (pl. of سمسار *simsār*) Brokers. Mediators.

A سماسم *samāsim*, A kind of bird. (pl. of سمسمة *simsimat*) Red ants. *Sumāsim*, A fox. Light, nimble, active.

A سماط *simāt*, (pl. سمط *sumut*) An order, series, row. The space between the centre and extreme part of a valley. سماط الطعام *simātu't taʿām*, A row of guests. *Sumāt*, (pl. اسمطة *asmitat*) A table covered with victuals. P خوردۀ سماط *khwurdaʾi sumāt*, The remains (of dinner).

A سماطان *simātāni*, Two rows (of trees or men).

P سماطين *samātīn*, A carpet, coarse cloth. A room hung round with mirrors.

A سماع *samāʿ*, (v. n. of سمع) Hearing, listening to. Accepting, taking well. A hearing, listening. Fame, reputation, a good report. Ecstacy occasioned by hearing singing, particularly in dervishes when hearing hymns. A song, dance (especially one of a circular figure performed by the dervishes). The sense of hearing. (in grammar) Prescription, authority, usage. ذو سماع *zū samāʿ*, Of good report. *Sumāʿi*, Hear thou.

A سمّاع *sammāʿ*, A listener, a hearer.

A سماعة *samāʿat*, A hearing, an audience. *Samāʿat*, (or سمّاعة *sammāʿat*) Hearing (ear).

P سماع خانه *samāʿ-khāna*, A house for song or dance (particularly where the dervishes perform).

A سماعيّ *samāʿiy*, Belonging to a dance or a song. A quick air, an allegro. Whatever has been heard. Traditional, oral. Founded on custom. (in grammar) Irregular, arbitrary, prescriptive.

A سماعية *samāʿiyat*, A hearing, a listening to.

P سماعيلي *samāʿīlī*, Sacrifice, oblation. Name of a sect which worships the organ of generation.

A سماق *sumāk*, Mere, pure. A sheer lie.

A سمّاق *summāk*, (or سماقيل *samākīl*) Sumach.

A سمّاقيّ *summākiy*, A vender of sumach.

A سمّاقية *summākiyat*, Dressed with sumach.

P سماك *simāk*, A road well guarded.

A سماك *simāk*, (pl. سمك *sumuk*) That upon which any thing is supported or raised. The part of the breast next the collar-bone. (pl. of سمك *samak*, Fishes. (also السماكان *as' simākāni*) Name of two stars, called likewise the feet of the lion, viz. السماك الاعزل *as' simāku'l aʿzal*, Spica virginis (being the fourteenth mansion of the moon; and السماك الرامح *as' simāku'r rāmih*, Arcturus.

A سمّاك *sammāk*, A fishmonger.

P سمّاك *summāk*, Sumach.

P سماكار *samākār*, (also سماكاره *samākāra*) A waiter at a tavern. A servant.

P سماكچه *samākcha*, A bodice, corset, stomacher.

A سمأل *samʾal*, A shadow.

A سمال *samāl*, A worm in water. *Simāl*, (pl. of سملة *samalat* or *sumlat*) Remains of waters in cisterns or wells.

A سمّال *sammāl*, One who knocks another's eye out, or who gouges. A kind of tree.

A سمالج *sumālij*, Sweet milk.

A سمالخ *sumālikh*, Coagulated milk.

A سمالخيّ *sumālikhiy*, Insipid (meat or milk). Milk put into a leathern bottle and buried in the ground, that it may turn thick.

A سمالق *samālik*, (pl. of سملق) Level grounds.

P سم آلود *sam-ālūd*, Envenomed.

A سمام *samām*, A kind of swallow. Light and active. A swift she-camel. *Simām*, A small-bodied wolf. (pl. of سمّ *samm*) Mouths, ears, and noses (of men). Small holes. Venoms, poisons.

A سمامة *samāmat*, The person, figure, or body of a man. A favourite ring on the neck of a horse. Visible remains of a ruined tenement. A banner. Aspect, countenance. A kind of bird. The blossoms of a palm-tree. A swift she-camel.

P سمان *samān*, (for آسمان *āsmān*) Heaven. The 27th of the month. *Simān*, Name of a city.

A سمان *simān*, (pl. of سمين *samīn*) Fat.

A سمّان *sammān*, A seller of butter. A kind of wash or dye. A kind of plant. *Sammāni*, Two veins in the cartilaginous parts of the nose of a horse or ass.

A سماناة *sumānāt*, A single quail.

A سمانة *samānat*, (v. n. of سمن) Becoming fat.

A سمانجونيّ *samānjūniy*, A sapphire.

P سمانه *samāna*, A quail. A roof.

A سماني *sumānaʾ*, A quail.

A سماوات *samāwāt*, (pl. of سماء) The heavens.

A سماوة *samāwat*, (v. n. of سما for سمو) Being rampant among the females, and leaping upon them (a stallion). Any thing standing or projecting upright. A roof. A projection or shade over a door, a portico. A model, figure, form, or mould. Name of a place between Kūfa and Syria.

A سماويّ *samāwiy*, Heavenly. Sky-coloured, cerulean, azure.

A سماهج *sumāhij*, Insipid, not sweet (milk).

P سماهيج *samāhīj*, Name of an island.

A سمائم *samāʾim*, (pl. of سموم *samūm*) Hot, pestilential winds, simooms. The dog-days.

A سمائي *samāʾī*, (pl. of سماء) The heavens.

A سمائيّ *samāʾiy*, Celestial.

P سمباده *sumbāda*, A polishing-stone: adamant.

A سمبل *sumbul*, (for سنبل) Spikenard. Hyacinth.

P سمپار *sumpār*, (or سمپاره) A hard sort of stone used in sharpening and polishing swords or knives.

A سمة *simat*, (v. n. of وسم) Branding with a hot iron. A mark made (by burning); a brand.

A سمّة *summat*, (pl. سمم *sumam*) A mat of palm-leaves, or any sort of carpet laid under a tree to receive the fallen fruit. Kindred, relationship. *Summat* or *simmat*, The fundament.

A سمت *samt*, (v. n. of سمت) Travelling. Groping along. Seeking, making for. Guessing the way. Preparing a discourse, getting ready an opinion. A way, road, path; a part, tract, country, quarter. Towards. The right way, the path of probity. سمت الرأس *samtu'r raʾs*, The zenith, the vertical point of the heavens. السمت *as' samt*, The azimuth. ما احسن سمته *mā ahsana samtuhu*, With what propriety he conducts himself!

P سمتراش *sum-tirāsh*, An instrument for paring horses' hoofs.

P سمتگر *samtgar*, Partial. A partisan.

P سمتگري *samtgarī*, Partiality.

A سمتيّ *samtiy*, One who arranges his thoughts, and discourses with propriety.

P سمج *samj* or *sumj*, Any subterraneous passage, mine, or burrow. A common sewer. A cavern, a grot, the resort of the destitute, or a fold for sheep. *Simij*, Secrets.

A سمج *samj*, Rich milk of a disagreeable flavour. *Samj* or *samij*, (pl. سماج *simāj*) Deformed, ugly, hideous, stinking, offensive.

A سمجرة *samjarat*, (v. n. of سمجر Q) Making (milk) very watery.

P سمچه *sumcha*, A subterraneous passage. A sheep-cote.

A سمح *samh*, (v. n. of سمح) Being beneficent, liberal. (pl. سمحاء *sumahāʾ* and مسامیح *masāmīh*) Beneficent, liberal: easy, humane. Unknotty (wood).

A سمحاء *sumahāʾ*, (pl. of سمح) Beneficent, liberal.

A سمحاج *simhāj*, Long-backed (mare or she-ass).

A سمحاق *simhāk*, The pericranium, or a wound touching that membrane.

A سمحة *samhat*, (pl. سماح *simāh*) Beneficent (woman). A single display of liberality and beneficence. An even and flexible bow. An easy creed, one which imposes but few restrictions.

A سمحج *samhaj*, Long-backed (mare or she-ass). Slender-waisted. Thick-fleshed (mare). A long bow.

A سمحجة *samhajat*, Length.

A سمحوج *sumhūj*, Tall of stature, and of a hostile countenance.

A سمحوق *sumhūk*, A tall palm-tree.

A سمخ *samkh*, (v. n. of سمخ) Wounding in the ear-hole. Beginning to shoot out (corn).

A سمخة *simkhat*, A mode of hearing. حسن السمخة *hasanu's simkhat*, One who hears to good purpose, remembering all he hears.

A سمد *samd*, Perpetual.

A سمداً *samdan*, In perpetuity.

P سمدار sum-dār, Solid-hoofed (animal).

P سمّدار samm-dār, Noxious, poisonous.

A سمدور sumdūr, A monarch (dazzling beholders' eyes). Dimness of sight. A tunic of the eye.

A سمر samr, (v. n. of سمر) Fixing with nails or pins, nailing. Holding an evening conversation by moonlight. Knocking out an eye, gouging. Diluting milk with water. Discharging an arrow. Cropping herbage (flocks). Drinking wine. Sumr, (pl. of اسمر asmar) Tawny. Spears. Samar, Evening conversations (such as the Arabians hold sitting around their tents). Night. Darkness. The shadow of the moon. Moonlight. Time. لا السمر و لا القمر lā as' samar wa lā al kamar, Neither in the dark nor by moonlight, i. e. never. Samur, Thorny trees growing in the desert.

P سمر samar, A weaver's brush. Name of a king, the founder of the city of Samarcand.

P سمّر sammar, A weaver's brush.

A سمّر summar, (pl. of سامر sāmir) Those who hold nocturnal conversations.

A سمراء samrā‚, (fem. of اسمر asmar) Of a tawny colour, olivaster, brunette. Wheat. Wheaten flour not separated from the bran. A leathern milk-pail.

A سمرات samurāt, (pl. of سمرة) Thorny shrubs.

P سمراد samrād, Imagination, thought, fancy.

A سمرة sumrat, (v. n. of سمر) Being of a tawny colour. A yellowish, tawny, or brown colour, the colour of wheat; a shade between black and white. Samarat, Samaritans. Samurat, (pl. سمر samur, سمرات samurāt, and اسمر asmur) Egyptian thorn.

A سمرّج samarraj, (or سمرّجة samarrajat) Tribute received at three instalments; or the day when paid (from P سه sih, Three, and مرّة marra, Time).

A سمرجة samrajat, (v. n. of سمرج Q) Giving. سمرج له samrij lahu, Give to him.

A سمرطال samartāl, (or سمرطول samartūl) Tall and tottering.

P سمرقند samarkand Name of a famous city and kingdom in higher Asia.

P سمرقندي samarkandī, An inhabitant of, or one belonging to, Samarcand. Hollow friendship, insincere professions of goodwill. A beam, rafter. A bar, bolt; a measuring pole or perch.

P سمرکند samarkand, A large city in Turkistān.

A سمرمرة samarmarat, A demon of the woods.

A سمروت sumrūt, Long, tall.

A سمرود sumrūd, Long.

A سمريّ samariy, One who relates stories at the nocturnal conversations سمر samar. Samuriy, (A camel) feeding on the Egyptian thorn سمر samur.

A P سمسار simsār, (pl. سماسرة samāsirat) A broker. A mediator, reconciler of friends. A possessor of a thing, or one who is the supporter and establisher of it. سمسار الارض simsāru'l arz, One who is conversant with earthly matters.

A سمسام samsām, Swift, nimble (man).

A سمسرة samsarat, (v. n. of سمسر Q) Knowing the states or ways (of the earth). Brokerage.

A سمسق samsak, simsik, sumsuk, or sumsak, Jessamine. Sweet-marjoram.

A سمسم samsam, A fox. A small-bodied wolf. Simsim, The grain sesame. A kind of serpent. Sumsum, A red ant. Light, active (man).

A سمسمان sumsumān, Swift, nimble (man).

A سمسمانيّ sumsumānīy, Light, nimble, active.

A سمسمة samsamat, The running of a fox. Simsimat, (pl. سماسم) A red ant. Light, active (man).

A سمط samt, (v. n. of سمط) Scalding the hair off (a kid) before roasting (it). Suspending (any thing). Sharpening (a knife). Light, active (fellow). Simt, (pl. سموط sumūt) A thread upon which beads are strung, as a necklace or ornament for the neck (especially when long and hanging down the bosom). A strap hanging from the saddle with which burdens are fastened. The harness on the crupper of a horse. Sand writhed into the resemblance of a rope. Nimble, agile, light. A huntsman. Crafty, cunning. A part of the sash of the turban hanging over the breast or shoulders. Thin, plain garment (not quilted or stuffed). بنو السمط banū's simt, Name of a Christian community. Sumt, A woollen garment. Sumut, A camel not branded. Simple, single, without lining (shoe). (pl. of سماط simāt) Rows, series.

A سمطيّ simtīy, (Verses) the third and fourth hemistichs of which end with the same rhyme, the following distichs having a different termination.

A سمع samiʻa, (fut. يسمع yasmaʻu) He heard.

A سمع samʻ, (v. n. of سمع) Hearing. Listening unto. (pl. اسماع asmāʻ, اسمع asmuʻ, اسامع asāmiʻ) The hearing. The ear. Whatever strikes the ear, or is heard. Fame, a good report. امّ السمع ummu's samʻ, (Mother of hearing) The brain. هو بين سمع الارض و بصرها huwa bayna samʻi'l arzi wa basarihā, He is somewhere or other, heaven knows where. سمعا و طاعة samʻan wa tāʻatan, Willing, obeying a word or sign, shewing that one is ready. Most willingly. سمعا و لا بلغا samʻan wa lā balghan, (or simʻan wa lā bilghan) It is heard, but let it not be confirmed (a mode of expression when any disagreeable news is reported). سمعك الىّ samʻaka ilayya', Listen thou unto me. Simʻ, The mongrel whelp of a he-wolf and a she-hyena. A hearing. Fame, good reputation. One of good report. ذهب سمعه في الناس zahaba simʻuhu fi'n nās, His fame was diffused among the people. Sumuʻ, (pl. of سموع samūʻ) Hearing (ears).

A سمّع summaʻ, Light, active. The animal called غول ghūl.

A سمعا samʻan, Within hearing.

A سمعاء sumaʻā‚, (pl. of سميع samīʻ) Hearers.

A سمعان simʻān, Simeon, Simon.

A سمعة samʻat, A single hearing. Samʻat, samaʻat, or samiʻat, Hearing (ear). Simʻat, A mode of hearing. Sumʻat, Sound. Fame. Dissimulation, hypocrisy. فعله رياء و سمعة faʻalahu riyā‚an wa samʻatan, (sumʻatan, or samaʻatan) He did it that it may be seen and heard.

A سمعج samʻaj, Milk, thick and sweet.

A سمعمع samaʻmaʻ, Small-headed. Small-bearded. Light, active. Extremely subtle. A wolf. Tall and slender (man). A woman who, in the presence of others, is sour and scowling, but in their absence is noisy and clamorous.

A سمعنة simʻanat, A listening woman.

A سمعنّة simʻannat, simʻinnat, sumʻunnat, (or سمعنة simʻanat) A woman who upon hearing any thing judges it to be a false report.

A سمعيّ samʻīy, Oral, traditional.

A سمغد simaghd, Tall. Strong on his pins. Foolish, proud, arrogant.

A سمك samk, (v. n. of سمك) Exalting, raising, bearing up, elevating, lifting up. Being high, lofty, and lifted up. Ascending. The roof of a house. Height, depth, profundity. Stature. Samak, (pl. سماك simāk and سموك sumūk) A fish. The sign Pisces. A fish on which the earth is supposed to rest; hence, از سمك تا سما az samak tā samā, From the abyss to heaven. Sumuk, (pl. of سماك simāk) The supports of any thing.

P سمك samuk, Vain-glory, arrogant pretensions. Vain, silly, foolish.

P سمكار simkār, A city in Badakhshān.

A سمكة samakat, A fish. The sign Pisces.

A سمل saml, (v. n. of سمل) Blinding, knocking out an eye. Reconciling differences. Cleaning a well or vessel. Bringing up a small quantity of water or mud (a bucket). Samal, (pl. of سملة samalat or sumlat) Small quantities of water. Samal or samil, An old tattered garment.

A سمّلاج simmilāj, A Christian festival.

A سملاخ samlākh, Thistles, called also نصيّ nasiy. Simlākh, Ear-wax. The orifice of the ear.

A سملان sumlān, Remains or dregs (of wine).

A سملة sumlat, Tears forced by extreme hunger (and making the eyes dim). Samalat, An old, worn garment. Samalat or sumlat, (pl. سمل samal or سمال simāl, سمول sumūl, and اسمال asmāl) The remains of water in a cistern or well. A little water. Thin, fetid, black mud.

A سملج samlaj, One with a yard round and long.

A سملّج samallaj, Light, nimble. A well-formed slender arrow. Sweet milk. Forage.

A سملجة samlajat, A sipping, drinking gradually.

A سملّع samallaʻ, A wolf.

A سملق samlak, (pl. سمالق) Smooth, level ground.

A سملكة samlakat, (v. n. of سملك Q) Making up a long and a round mouthful.

A سملوخ sumlūkh, Ear-wax. The orifice of the ear. Twigs torn from the plant نصيّ nasiy.

A سمم *sumam*, (pl. of سمّة *summat*) Mats of palm-leaves laid under trees to receive the fruit as it falls. Kindreds, relationships.

A سمن *samn*, (v. n. of سمن) Dressing or preserving (meat) with butter. Giving butter or fat meat to eat. (pl. اسمن *asmun*, سمون *sumūn* and سمنان *sumnān*) Butter. Fat. *Siman*, (v.n.of سمن) Being fat. Fatness.

P سمن *saman* or *suman*, Trefoil. A certain white fragrant flower. (for یاسمین *yāsmīn*) Jessamine.

P سمنار *simnār*, Name of a famous architect.

P سمناك *samnāk*, Liberality, generosity.

A سمنان *sumnān*, (pl. of سمن *samn*) Butters.

P سمن بر *saman-bar*, Jessamine-bosomed.

A سمنة *sumnat*, A fattening medicine for women (especially grains of a shrub resembling pepper). Summer herbage.

P سمند *samand*, Dun or cream (colour of a horse). An arrow.

P سمند اسلار *samand aslār*, Name of an animal whose look was said to be fatal.

P سمندر *samandar*, *samandir*, or *samandur*, (سمندل *samandal*, سمندور *samandūr*, سمندوك *samandūk*, سمندول *samandūl*, or سمندون *samandūn*) (said to be derived from سام *sām*, Fire, and اندرون *andarūn*, Within) A salamander.

P سمنزار *samanzār*, A jessamine-garden.

P سمنسا *samansā*, Jessamine-like. Fair.

P سمنگان *samangān* or *samungān*, Name of a city in Ahwāz.

P سمنو *samanū*, A kind of sweet macaroni. *Sumanū*, Macaroni-soup.

A سمنون *samnūn*, Name of an austere monk.

A سمنية *sumaniyat*, Name of a sect of Hindoos who profess to believe in the metempsychosis.

P سمو *sumū*, Wild cresses.

A سمّو *sumūw*, (v. n. of سما for سمو) Being high, elevated. Raising, lifting up. Towering aloft, becoming conspicuous. Going out a hunting. Height, sublimity, dignity.

A سموات *samawāt*, Heavens, skies.

A سموال *samawwal*, Name of a bird. A shadow. Flies found on the surface of vinegar. Rapid (nocturnal journey for water).

P سموت *samūt*, Saddle-straps.

A سموت *sumūt*, (pl. of سمت *samt*) Ways.

A سموح *samūḥ*, Beneficent, affable. Liberal. *Sumūḥ*, Liberality, beneficence. Affability.

A سموحة *sumūḥat*, Liberality. Clemency.

A سمود *sumūd*, (v. n. of سمد) Swelling with anger; carrying the head high from pride. Being studious, attentive, exerting one's self. Being high, elevated in dignity. Being idle, lazy. Travelling at a smart pace (camels). Standing astonished, being lost in bewilderment. Giving attention to play, amusement, or trifles. Grief. Joy.

A سمور *samūr*, Swift (she-camel). *Sumūr*, (v. n. of سمر) Holding a conversation by moon-light.

A سمّور *sammūr*, The Scythian weasel or marten, the sable; also the fine skin or fur of that animal. P سمّور سیه *sammūri siyah*, Night.

P سموسه *samosa*, A kind of small pastry of minced meat of a triangular form. A pie. A shawl or handkerchief, doubled diagonally, to throw over the shoulders.

A سموط *sumūt*, (v.n.of سمط) Being silent. Losing its sweetness, or beginning to turn (milk). (pl. of سمط *simt*) Threads whereon beads are strung. Straps hanging from the saddle, wherewith burdens are fastened.

A سموع *samūʻ*, (pl. سمع *sumuʻ*) Hearing (ear).

A سموق *samūk*, Sumach. *Sumūk*, (v. n. of سمق) Being high and tall. Growing high (a pot-herb).

A سموك *sumūk*, (v. n. of سمك) Being high, elevated. (pl. of سمك *samak*) Fishes.

A سمول *samūl*, Old and worn (garment). *Sumūl*, (v. n. of سمل) Waxing old (a garment). (pl. of سملة *samalat*) Waters left at the bottom of cisterns.

A سموّل *samawwal*, A wide tract of light land.

A سمولة *samwalat*, (v. n. of سمول Q) Breeding flies (vinegar). *Sumūlat*, (v. n. of سمل) Waxing old (a garment).

A سموم *samūm*, (pl. سمائم *samāʼim*) A sultry, pestilential, destructive wind, blowing by day, and sometimes at night: simoom. *Sumūm*, (pl. of سمّ *samm*) Mouths, noses, and ears. Poisons. Small holes.

A سمون *sumūn*, (pl. of سمن *samn*) Butters.

A سموه *sumūh*, (v. n. of سمه) Being astonished, thunder-struck. Running unfatigued (horse).

A سمويّ *samawiy* or *simawiy*, Nominal.

A سمويل *samwīl*, A sort of bird. Name of a country. The angel Gabriel.

P سمه *sima*, A weaver's brush. Concealed, hidden. A green-coloured weed floating on stagnant water. A spatula with which weavers put the glue upon their thread.

A سمّه *summah*, (pl. of سامه *sāmih*) (Horses) running without being fatigued. Astonished (men). Pasturing freely (camels). Vain, futile, trifling things.

A سمّهاء *summahāʼ*, Air, atmosphere.

A سمهاث *sumhās*, Red wheat.

A سمهاج *simhāj*, A falsehood, lie.

A سمّهة *summahat*, Palm-leaves twisted and made up in the form of a table-cloth.

A سمهج *samhaj*, (or سمهجیج *samhajīj*) Milk mixed with water. Sweet butter or fat.

A سمهجة *samhajat*, (v. n. of سمهج Q) Adorning with fiction (a speech). Adulterating money. Giving currency, circulating. Sending, despatching. Making haste. Twisting tight. Swearing outrageously.

A سمهد *samhad*, Any thing hard and dry.

A سمهدد *samahdad*, A fat, bulky camel.

A سمهدر *samahdar*, Plump (young man). Large extensive (city). Far, remote (country where one strays). Penis.

A سمهرة *samharat*, (v. n. of سمهر Q) Growing without multiplying itself (seed sown).

A سمهريّ *samhariy*, A straight, hard spear (from سمهر *samhar*, A famous spear-maker).

A سمهريّة *samhariyat*, A stiff, dry cane or reed.

A سمّهی *summahaʼ*, A lie. Follies, trifles. The atmosphere, air. Scattered, wandering (camels). Atoms playing in the sun during the heat of the day.

A سمي *samy*, (v. n. of سمي) Going a hunting. *Simaʼ*, A name. *Sumaʼ*, A good name, good report.

A سميّ *samīy*, Of the same name, synonymous. Resembling another, worthy of being called by the same name. A name-sake. High. *Sumayy*, (dim. of سم *sim*) A little name. *Sumīy*, (or سمی *sumaʼ*) (pl. of سماء *samāʼ*) Rains. Heavens.

A سمّيّة *sammīyat*, Poisonousness, venomousness, banefulness.

P سميج *samīj*, The lurking-place of a hunter. The haunt of a large wild beast.

A سميج *samīj*, (pl. سماج *simāj*) Deformed, ugly. Fat, bad-tasted.

A سميح *sumayh*, (or سميّح *sumayyih*) (dim. of سمح *samh*) Somewhat beneficent. Somewhat easy.

P A سميد *samīd*, (or سميذ *samīz*) White bread.

A سميدر *samaydar*, A salamander.

A سميدع *samaydaʻ*, Any illustrious and liberal personage, whose house is much frequented. A hero. A wolf. A sword. Light, active in business.

P سميدن *samīdan*, To smell, scent, emit perfume.

A سمير *samīr*, Time, age. Evening entertainments, nocturnal conversations; the places, especially among the Arabian tents, where these conversations are held; also the subject. ابنا سمير *ibnā samīr*, Night and day. لا افعله ما سمر السمير *lā afʻaluhu mā samara's samīr*, (or ابن سمير *ibnu samīrin*, or ابنا سمير *ibnā samīrin*, or ما اسمر *mā asmara*) I will not do it so long as night and day succeed each other. *Samīr*, (or سمّير *simmīr*) Fond of such entertainments or nocturnal conversations.

P سميرا *samīrā*, A cupping-horn. *Sumayrā*, Name of a famous woman, called مهین بانو *mihīn bānū*.

P سميرم *samīram*, Name of a place between Irāk and Persia, whence they bring water which, wherever carried, is followed by a small black bird that devours the locusts.

P سميره *samīra*, A line drawn. Written.

A سميريّة *sumayrīyat*, A kind of ship.

P سميز *samīz*, An invocation, a prayer.

A سميساط *sumaysāt*, Name of a place on the bank of the Euphrates.

A سميط *samīt*, Verse, the third and fourth hemistichs of which end with the same rhyme, the following distichs having a different termination. A kid ready for roasting, the hair being taken off by warm water. Any thing macerated or scalded in warm water (as hair or feathers from animals). (pl. اسماط *asmāt*) Simple, single (as a garment without lining, or a shoe with one sole). Nimble, active (man). *Samīt* or *sumayt*, A regularly-built brick building.

A سميع *samīʿ*, A hearer. Hearing (ear). One who makes others hear. One of the titles of God. A lion hearing a noise from afar. امّ السميع *ummu's samīʿ*, The brain.

A سميعة *samīʿat*, Hearing (ear).

A سميق *samīk*, A part of the yoke which incloses the ox's neck,

A سميكاء *sumaykāʾ*, A small fish which they dry.

A سميل *samīl*, Old and worn-out (garment). Remains of water in a cistern.

A سمين *samīn*, (pl. سمان *simān*) Fat, full, plump. Buttered, greasy.

A سمينة *samīnat*, Fat, loamy ground, free from stones. *Sumaynat*, Name of a place.

A سمّينة *summaynat*, Name of an idolatrous sect.

P سمينه *samīna*, A thin, delicate sort of stuff.

A سميهاء *sumayhāʾ*, (or سمّيهاء *summayhāʾ*) A lie. Vanities, trifles.

A سميهى *sumayhaʾ*, (or سمّيهى *summayhaʾ*) A lie. Vain follies, trifles. The atmosphere, external air. Atoms playing in the sun during the hottest part of the day. ذهبت ابله السمّيهى *zahabat ibluhu's summayhaʾ*, His camels dispersed themselves in all directions. مشت هٰذه الامة السمّيهى *mashat hāzihi'l amatu's summayhaʾ*, This damsel walked with a mincing or pompous air.

P سن *san*, Colour. Sort, species. Rule, law, custom, usage. A spear. Ivy. Like.

A سنّ *sann*, (v. n. of سنّ) Forming, shaping. Polishing, sharpening, whetting, giving an edge to (a sword). Cleaning, rubbing (the teeth). Breaking the teeth. Walking in any road, path, or mode of life. Making plain and clear. Letting fall gently on the ground (sand), and making it heap up. Fixing the head upon a spear. Pouring (water) softly on the face. Making clay into earthenware. Piercing with the point of a spear. Exciting a relish for. Biting with the teeth. Being eaten bare (herbage). Putting a coat of mail upon another. Sending flocks to pasture; feeding camels well, making them look clean and sleek. Driving (camels) fast. Mounting the female lying down (a camel). *Sinn*, (pl. اسنان *asnān*, اسنّة *asinnat*, and اسنّ *asunn*) A tooth. (Advanced) age. The teeth of a sickle. A clove of garlick. Period of life. A horn. The nib of a pen. Coeval. The protuberance of a bone beyond a plain surface, the sharpness of the dorsal vertebræ. Greedy eating. A wild bull. كم سنّك *kam sinnuka*, What is thine age? هو سنّه *huwa sinnuhu*, He is of the same age as he. ذو السنّ *zū's sinn*, One who has a redundant tooth. وقع في سنّ رأسه *wakaʿa fī sinni raʾsihi*, He obtained the summit of his wishes. سنّ الحسل *sinna'l hisl*, Never (literally the tooth of the crocodile, because it never sheds its teeth).

P سنا *sanā*, Name of a tree from which toothpicks are made.

A سنا *sanaʾ*, Light, splendour, brightness, flashing (of lightning). Senna (the drug). A kind of silk.

A سناء *sanāʾ*, Elevation, height, altitude, eminence. Senna. *Sināʾ*, (v. n. 3 of سنا for سنو) Agreeing (with one) by the year. Satisfying. Soothing, making happy, acting kindly, humanely. Giving annually. Bearing fruit every other year (a palm-tree).

A سناب *sanāb*, Great, enormous wickedness. *Sināb*, Long-bodied.

A سنّابة *sinnābat*, Long-bodied.

A سنابك *sanābik*, (pl. of سنبك *sumbuk*) Foreparts of horses' hoofs.

A سنابل *sanābil*, (pl. of سنبلة) Ears of corn.

A سناج *sināj*, The mark left upon a wall by the smoke of a lamp. Any stain made by somewhat of a different colour. A lamp.

A سناح *sināh*, (v. n. 3 of سنح) Coming on the left of the hunter (game).

A سناخة *sanākhat*, Scrapings of skins, or any species of filth. A bad smell. Indications of tanning.

P سناد *sanād*, Much, abundant.

A سناد *sinād*, (v. n. 3 of سند) Assisting, helping, compensating, requiting. In verse, when the antepenult of one hemistich is pointed with a vowel different from the antepenult of the other; as when داد *dād* is made to rhyme with دود *dūd* or دید *dīd*. A strong she-camel. A huge animal; a rhinoceros.

A سنادين *sanādīn*, (pl. of سندان *sandān*) Anvils.

P سنار *sanār*, A lover. *Sanār* or *sinār*, A seaport. A dock or bed of mud, where ships are moored. The smyris. *Sunār*, A daughter-in-law.

A سنّار *sunnār*, (pl. سنانير *sanānīr*) A cat.

A سناسن *sanāsin*, (pl. of سنسن *sinsin*) The paddles of a wheel for drawing water. The projecting parts or processes of the vertebræ in the back.

A سناط *sināt* or *sunāt*, (pl. سنط *sunut* and اسناط *asnāt*) Beardless (though of ripe years). Bearded about the chin, though not on the cheek.

A سناطة *sanātat*, (v. n. of سنط) Being beardless or having a thin beard.

A سناعة *sanāʿat*, (v. n. of سنع) Being beautiful, graceful, excellent, proper.

A سناف *sināf*, (pl. صنف *sunuf*) The poitrel or breast-harness of a camel. A girth tied to steady the breast-harness when a camel is lank-bellied.

A سنام *sanām*, (pl. اسنمة *asnimat*) A camel's bunch. High ground. A promontory. The centre of the earth. A support, pillar, or fundamental part. جمل السنامين *jamalu's sanāmayn*, The double-bunched or Bactrian camel.

P سنا مكي *sanā makkī*, The senna of Mecca.

A سنان *sinān*, (v. n. 3 of سنّ) Following, pursuing the female (a camel). (pl. اسنّة *asinnat*) A spear. The iron head of a spear. The point of an arrow or needle. A whetstone. P سنان جان ستان *sinānī jān-satān*, A spear ravishing the life, giving a mortal wound.

A سنانير *sanānīr*, (pl. of سنّور *sinnawr* and سنّار *sunnār*) Cats.

A سنانيق *sanānīk*, (pl. of سنّيق *sunnayk*) Houses plastered with lime.

P سناو *sanāv*, Filings. Much.

A سناة *sināh*, (v. n. 3 of سنه) Agreeing with any one by the year. Giving annually. Bearing fruit every other year (a palm-tree).

A سنايا *sanāyaʾ*, Noble (man).

A سناية *sināyat*, The whole, all. اخذه بسنايته *akhazahu bi sināyatihi*, He took the whole of it.

A سنائع *sanāʾiʿ*, (pl. of سنيعة *sanīʿat*) Roads leading over mountains.

A سنائن *sanāʾin*, (pl. of سنينة *sanīnat*) High and extensive sands. Winds. (The horses came) in one and the same manner.

P سنب *sumb*, A subterraneous dwelling, into which the poor retreat, and which serves as a fold for sheep. The hoof of a beast. The foot. A wimble, auger, gimlet. Perforation. (in compos.) Boring, perforating (from the verb سفتن *suftan*).

A سنب *sanib*, (pl. سنوب *sunūb*) A horse running well.

A سنباء *sambāʾ*, The fundament.

P سنبات *sambāt*, (*sumbat*, or سنبوت *sambūt*) An apparition. Magic, illusion.

A سنبات *sambāt*, The fundament. *Sambāt* or *simbāt*, Badness of temper, pettishness, irascibility. *Simbāt*, Extremely wicked, abounding in evil.

P سنباد *sambād*, Thought, reflection. Name of a magician.

A سنبادج *sumbādaj*, (or سنباذج *sumbāzaj*) (P سنباده *sumbāda*) The smyris, with which they cut glass: emery. A stone for sharpening and polishing swords, and for cleaning teeth.

P سنبالو *sambālo*, An ape.

P سنبانيدن *sumbānīdan*, To cause to bore. To cause to prop.

A سنبة *sambat* or *simbat*, Badness of temper, pettishness. *Sambat*, (or سنبتة *sambatat*) A space of time, a while.

A سنبر *sambar*, Wise, very intelligent, clever.

A سنبريت *sambarīt*, Bad-tempered.

A سنبس *simbis*, Quick, making haste.

A سنبسة *sambasat*, A making haste.

P سنبك *sumbuk*, A small ship.

A سنبك *sumbuk*, (pl. سنابك *sanābik*) A mode of running. The fore part of a horse's hoof. Anterior, prior to. A side. The side of an ornamented sword-hilt. The two strings by which a veil is tied on. The beginning of a shower. The crest of a helmet. Rough ground of little value. على سنبك *ʿala' sumbuki*, In the time of.

A P سنبل *sumbul*, A flower (especially of an odoriferous plant). The hyacinth. Spikenard, to which the hair of a mistress is compared. An ear of corn. The sign Virgo. سنبل برخط *sumbul bar khat*, A mole on a beautiful face. سنبل تر *sumbuli tar*, A ringlet. سنبل خطائي *sumbuli khatāī*, Angelica. سنبل رومى *sumbuli rūmī*, Celtic nard. سنبل العصافير *sumbulu'l ɛasāfīr*, Indian spikenard. سنبل هندي *sumbuli hindī*, The spikenard.

A سنبلانيّ *sumbulānīy*, Long and wide (shirt).

A سنبلة *sambalat*, (v. n. of سنبل Q) Coming into ear (corn). Drawing (a garment) from before or behind. The thorny shrub عضاة *ɛizāh*. *Sumbulat*, (pl. سنابل *sanābil*) An ear of corn. The sign Virgo. P سنبلهٔ زر *sumbula-i zar*, A chafing-dish.

P سنبل هوا *sumbul-hawā*, A cloudy sky.

A سنبوت *sanabūt*, Angry, irascible.

P سنبوسك *sambūsak*, A pie.

P سنبوسه *sambūsa*, A kind of triangular pasty, a pie. A square mantle which women wear doubled into a triangular form. Any thing triangular.

A سنبوق *sumbūk*, A small boat, pinnace.

A سنبول *sumbūl*, An ear of corn.

P سنبه *sumba*, Ceiling of a room. A black bee or grape. Once, for this time. An instrument for notching a millstone. An auger. Deceived.

P سنبهاري *sambahārī*, Mint.

P سنبيدن *sumbīdan*, To bore, perforate. To lean upon, to be propped. To deceive, cheat. To tread under foot.

A سنة *sanat*, (pl. سنون *sinūn*, سنهات *sanahāt*, and سنوات *sanawāt*) A year. Dearth. Barren, unfruitful (ground). The year is divided into six seasons, each season consisting of two months; namely, 1. الربيع الاوّل *ar' rabīɛu'l awwal*, 2. صيف *sayf*, 3. قيظ *kayz*, 4. الربيع الثاني *ār' rabīɛu's sānī*, 5. خريف *kharīf*, 6. شتاء *shitā-*. سنة سنواء *sanatun sanwā-*, A calamitous year. سنة بسنة *sanat bi sanat*, From year to year, every year. سنهٔ هجره *sana-i hijra*, The year of the Hijrah (or Muhammadan æra, commencing the 15th of July, 622. See تاريخ *ta-rīkh*). سنة ثمان و ثمانين و الف *sanat samān wa samānīn wa alf*, The year of the Hijra 1088 (A. D. 1677). *Sinat*, Carelessness, negligence, inadvertency. Indolence. Beginning of sleep, slumber. سنة الفناء *sinatu'l fanā-*, The sleep of death.

A سنّة *sannat*, A she-bear. A female cheeta. *Sinnat*, A double-headed hatchet. Money, specie, coin. The nib of a pen. A coulter or ploughshare. A clove of garlic. *Sunnat*, Nature, habit, custom, manner, institution, regulation, or mode of living. Form, surface. The face, countenance; the contour of the face. Countenance, forehead. Both sides of the forehead. Torment, punishment. The Madina date. Circumcision. The law of God, the divine commands and prohibitions. The Sunna, or the traditions of Muhammad, which, by the orthodox Muslims, are considered as a supplement to the Kur'ān, and of nearly equal authority. These are rejected however by the Shiites, or sect of Alīy. سنّت و جماعت *sunnat u jamāɛat*, The followers of the four first caliphs. اهل سنّت *ahli sunnat*, The circumcised, the Turks and others who acknowledge the Sunna. P سنّت كردن *sunnat kardan*, To circumcise.

A سنت *sanit*, (pl. سنتون *sanitūn*) Worthless.

A سنتب *suntub*, Of a bad disposition.

A سنتبة *santabat*, A confirmed vice. A strong wardrobe.

A سنتة *sanitat*, Unproductive (land).

A سنتون *sanitūn*, (pl. of سنت *sanit*) Worthless.

A سنتى *sante*, Instead, stead.

P سنج *sanj*, Weight. Measure. A conch-shell. A cymbal. (in compos.) Weighing. سخن سنج *sukhun-sanj*, A weigher of words, *i.e.* an orator. نغمه سنج *naghma-sanj*, (or ترانه سنج *tarāna-sanj*) A measurer of sounds, *i.e.* a musician. *Sinj*, Elected, chosen. A choice. A cymbal. Little bells suspended from Arabian drums. Oxygal put into sweet milk, which sours and curdles it. Vermilion. A young shoot. Monks' rhubarb. *Sunj*, Buttocks.

A سنج *sanj*, (v. n. of سنج) Smoking, discolouring. *Sunuj*, The red jujube-plant.

P سنجاب *sinjāb*, Ermine, the pontic mouse, the grey squirrel. Verdure. Night. Name of a country.

P سنجابي *sinjābī*, Grey, russet.

A سنجار *sanjār* or *sinjār*, A fort near Mūsul.

P سنجاف *sanjāf*, Edging. A border of a garment.

P سنجانيدن *sanjānīdan*, To cause to weigh.

A سنجة *sanjat*, (from P سنجه *sanja*) A balance, scales, a stone used for this purpose. *Sunjat*, (pl. سنج *sunj*) Variegation by black and white spots.

P سنجد *sinjid*, The jujube-tree and fruit.

P سنجد بوي *sinjid-boy* or *būy*, A kind of rose.

P سنجر *sanjar*, A prince, emperor, king. Name of a celebrated monarch. Name of a hunting bird. Ecstasied, enraptured.

P سنجرستان *sanjaristān*, A monastery built for the sufis or dervishes.

A سنجسبويه *sanjisbūya*, (P سنگسبويه *sangisboya*) Cinquefoil.

P سنجق *sanjak*, A flag, banner. A cornet. A pin. *Sanjak* or *sanjuk*, A waistband, girdle, belt.

A سنجلاط *sinjilāt*, A kind of sweet flower.

P سنجوق *sanjūk*, A flag. A girdle.

P سنجه *sanja*, A balance, scales. A weight. An equipoise, or make-weight. Name of a demon. Name of a country.

P سنجيد *sinjīd*, The jujube-tree.

P سنجيدگي *sanjīdagī*, Gravity, weight.

P سنجيدن *sanjīdan*, To weigh. *Sinjīdan*, To prepare.

P سنجيده *sanjīda*, Weighed. Weighty, grave. Tried, proved. *Sinjīda*, Prepared, set in order.

A سنح *sanh* or *sunh*, (v. n. of سنح) Being open, clear, manifest, occurring, presenting itself. Being easy to one (poetry). Bringing out, drawing forth. Overtaking (with mischief), hurting. Speaking. Turning (any one) from his design. *Sunh*, A good omen, happiness succeeding misfortune. The middle of a road.

A سنحان *sinhān*, Name of a district in Yaman.

A سنحنح *sanahnah*, Sleepless, lying awake.

P سنخ *sanhh*, Dirt, filth, nastiness. Salt.

A سنخ *sinkh*, (pl. سنوخ *sunūkh* and اسناخ *asnākh*) The root of a tooth, the stump. The paroxysm of a fever. Cause, source, origin. *Sanakh*, (v. n. of سنخ) Turning, becoming rotten, rancid, or tainted. Rankness. Abounding (in food). Eating much food. *Sanikh*, Infected with an epidemic disorder (a place).

A سنخة *sankhat* or *sanakhat*, A noxious smell (as in houses which have been long shut up).

A سنختان *sunkhatāni*, Two statures or fathoms.

P سنخج *sanakhj*, (*sinakhj*, or سنخچ *sanakhch*) An asthma, shortness of breath.

P سند *sind*, India, particularly the western regions on the river Sind or Indus. Suppositious, spurious, of an unknown father or mother. A bastard, a foundling. *Sanad*, The seal or signature of a judge. A royal ordinance, mandate, or decree. A patent, grant, document, warrant, any royal deed of appointment under which another acts. An order, a written authority for holding either land or office.

A سند *sind*, Sind. India. (pl. of سنديّ *sindīy*) Natives of Sind. *Sanad*, A prop, any thing upon which another leans, or by which it is supported. A vine-arbour. A part of a mountain facing one; also its steep or its acclivity. Relation, connexion. The authority of a writer. (pl. اسناد *asnād*) A striped stuff.

P سند آب *sind-āb*, The river Indus.

A سنداب *sinda-b*, Hard, strong (camel).

P سنداره *sandāra* or *sindāra*, A foundling.

A سندان *sandān*, (pl. سنادين *sanādīn*) An anvil. *Sindān*, Large and powerful (man or wolf).

P سندان *sindān*, An anvil. The iron on which the knocker of a door strikes.

A سندانة *sindānat*, A she-ass.

A سنداو *sinda-w*, (or سنداوة *sinda-wat*, pl. سنداوون *sinda-wūna*) Agile, nimble. Bold, intrepid. Short. Thin-bodied, with a large head. A jolt-headed fellow. A she-wolf.

P سندباد *sindbād*, A book on practical science.

P سندر *sandar*, A gum resembling amber.

A سندرة *sandarat*, Celerity. A tree, of which they make bows and arrows. Name of a woman who sold wheat and gave full measure.

A P سندروس *sandaros*, (or سندره *sandara*) Gum of the red juniper, sandaracha, red arsenic.

P سندره *sindira* or *sandara*, A bastard.

A سندريّ *sandarīy*, Strong and long. Bold. A

lion. One who hastens, accelerates, or stimulates. Active, nimble, expeditious. A sort of bird. Having thick, heavy eyes. Good, elegant, excellent. Bad, worthless. A white arrow or one made from the tree سندرة *sandarat*. A blue spear-head. A strong bow and strung. A certain large measure. Name of a poet.

A سندس *sundus*, Brocade, silk wrought with gold or silver.

A سندسيّ *sundusiy*, Made of brocade.

P سندكيش *sindkesh*, The rainbow. A vapour exhaled by the heat of the sun, representing the sea at a distance: the mirage.

P سندل *sandal*, A sandal, a kind of slipper. Sandal-wood. A fool, idiot. A small boat employed in carrying fresh water and victuals to ships lying at a distance from shore, a bumboat.

P سندلك *sandalak*, (or سندله *sandala*) A small shoe or slipper.

P سندلي *sandalī*, A bench whereon shoes are left.

P سندنه *sandana*, A kind of bird. Steps of a stair.

A سندوق *sundūk*, A chest.

P سنده *sanda*, An anvil. Fetid excrement. *Sunda*, Fetid excrement.

P سندهان *sindihān*, Wood of aloes. A species of steatites.

P سندي *sanadī*, Held by written deeds.

A سنديّ *sindīy*, A native of Sind. Indian.

P سنديان *sindiyān*, A kind of oak. Natives of Sind.

A سنر *sanar*, Obstinacy, stubbornness.

P سنز *suniz*, Caraway-seeds.

P سنسان *sansān* or سنسن, Inelegant language.

A سنسق *sansak*, A dwarf myrtle.

A سنسن *sinsin*, (pl. سناسن *sanāsin*) Thirst. Head or projection of the ribs; protuberant part or process of the vertebræ of the back. Top of a pulley. A paddle on a water-wheel.

P سنسور *sansūr*, Trunk of elephant or gnat.

P سنسه *sunsa*, A black bee. A black grape.

A سنط *sint*, The wrist, wrist-joint. *Sanat*, A kind of thorn, acacia. *Sunut*, (pl. of سناط *sināt*, *sunāt*, سنوط *sanūt*, or سنوطيّ) Beardless youths.

A سنطاب *sintāb*, A blacksmith's hammer.

A سنطاح *sintāh*, A camel wide in the vulva.

A سنطالة *suntālat*, A light, easy step. A hanging of the head.

A سنطبة *santabat*, Perpetual uneasiness (of life). Tallness with staggering and tottering.

A سنطلة *santalat*, Length, longitude.

A سنطليل *santalīl*, Long.

A سنطير *santīr*, A spinnet, harpsichord.

A سنع *sinꜥ*, (pl. سنعة *sinaꜥat* and اسناع *asnāꜥ*) The ankle or pastern-joint. The wrist-joint. *Sanaꜥ*, Beauty, comeliness.

A سنعاء *sanꜥāꜥ*, An uncircumcised girl.

A سنعبة *sunꜥubat*, A weasel. The caruncle in the middle of the upper lip.

A سنعبق *sanaꜥbak*, Name of a fetid plant.

A سنعة *sinaꜥat*, (pl. of سنع *sinꜥ*) Ankle or pastern-joints. Wrist-joints. Joints connecting the fingers and wrist.

A سنعيف *sinnaꜥf*, Light, giddy, confused.

A سنغما *sinnaghman*, Against one's will.

A سنف *sanf*, (v. n. of سنف) Girthing (a camel) with the strap called سناف *sināf*. Taking the lead of others (a she-camel). *Sinf*, The leaf of a tree called مرخ *markh*, from which the Arabians strike fire. The pod or envelope of fruit. A crowd. A part, portion, sort, species. Tares, darnel. *Sunf* or *sunuf*, (pl. of سنيف *sanīf*) Clothes thrown over the shoulders of camels. *Sunuf*, (pl. of سناف *sināf*) Poitrels or breast-harness for camels to steady the loads.

A سنفة *sinfat*, One pea-shell or bean-pod. A branch stripped of its leaves. A leaf. *Sinafat*, (pl. of سنف *sinf*, pl. of سنفة *sinfat*) Pods, capsules.

A سنفتان *sunfatāni* or *sanfatāni*, The two upright posts of a pulley.

A سنق *sanak*, (v. n. of سنق) Having the stomach overloaded with milk (a camel's colt).

P سنقر *sunkur*, A falcon that hunts well.

P سنقره *sunkura*, A sort of bird, whose flesh is said to be poisonous.

A سنقطار *siniktār*, An experienced judge of good and bad money.

A سنك *sunuk*, Clear, open roads.

P سنگ *sang*, A stone. A rock. A weight. A cannon-ball. Gravity, authority, dignity. Value, worth, price. Equality. سنگ آتش *sangi ātish*, Marcasite-stone. سنگ احمر *sangi ahmar*, A red poisonous stone. سنگ اسکاف *sangi iskāf*, A shoemaker's lapstone. سنگ آسيا *sangi āsyā*, A millstone. سنگ آسيان *sangi āsyān*, A whetstone, hone. سنگ آهن کش يا آهن ربا *sangi āhan-kash yā āhan-rubā*, The stone attracting iron, or seizing, *i.e.* the loadstone or magnet. سنگ بر شيشه زدن *sang bar shīsha zadan*, To break the goblet to pieces, *i.e.* to leave off drinking wine. سنگ برگان *sangi bargān*, A soft stone used by glass-makers. سنگ بصري *sangi basrī*, The Basrah-stone. Tutty. سنگ بلور *sangi bulūr* or *bilawr*, Crystal. سنگ پرستوك *sangi parastūk*, Swallow-stone. سنگ ترازو *sangi tarāzū*, A stone, any thing similar used in weighing. سنگ تراشيده *sangi tarāshīda*, A hewn or squared stone. سنگ توتيا *sangi tūtiyā*, The stone tutty. سنگ جراحت *sangi jarāhat*, A species of steatites. سنگ جهودان *sangi juhūdān*, Lapis Judaicus. سنگ خاره *sangi khāra*, A hard stone. سنگ خروس *sangi khuros*, A stone found in the side of a cock, good for medicinal purposes. سنگ در آستين *sang dar āstīn*, Cruel, injurious, persecuting. سنگ در قنديل زدن *sang dar kindīl zadan*, To darken. سنگ در موزه *sang dar mūza*, (Stone in one's boot) Of slow motion. سنگ در موزه افتادن *sang dar mūza uftādan*, To be distressed, irresolute. سنگ راه *sangi rāh*, Impediment. سنگ راه شدن *sang rāh shudan*, To be forbidden. سنگ رعد *sangi raꜥd*, A stone ball (for a cross-bow). A stone-roller for making smooth the flat roofs of houses. سنگ روشنائي *sangi roshnāī*, Marcasite-stone. سنگ زخم *sangi zakhm*, Ivory-stone. سنگ سليمان *sangi sulaymān*, An onyx, agate. سنگ سماق *sangi sumāk*, Porphyry. سنگ سودا *sangi sawdā*, Pumice-stone. سنگ سياه *sangi siyāh*, The black stone at Mecca. سنگ سياه سوخته *sangi siyāh sokhta*, Pumice-stone. سنگ سياه کردن *sang siyāh kardan*, To slay, destroy. سنگ شجري *sangi shajarī*, Coral and its roots. سنگ فال *sangi fāl*, A stone of divination. سنگ قالي *sangi kālī*, A stone placed on the edge of a counterpane or carpet to prevent the wind from entering and blowing it up. سنگ قبطي *sangi kibtī*, Fullers' earth. سنگ قمر *sangi kamar*, Moonstone. سنگ قناعت *sangi kanāꜥat*, Stone of contentment, *i.e.* a stone strapped tight to the belly to deaden the pangs of hunger. سنگ گردان *sangi gardān*, A millstone. سنگ گردانيدن *sang gardānīdan*, To petrify. سنگ گشتن *sang gashtan*, To be petrified. سنگ ماهي *sangi māhī*, A hard white stone found in the head of a fish. سنگ مثانه *sangi masāna*, Stone in the bladder. سنگ مرمر *sangi marmar*, Marble. سنگ مغني *sangi maghnī*, A soft stone used by glassmakers. سنگ مقناطيس *sangi miknātīs*, The loadstone. سنگ موسیٰ *sangi mūsa'*, A black stone so called, a kind of coal. سنگ نمك *sangi namak*, Native salt, rock salt. سنگ و سبو *sang u sabū*, Servitude. سنگ ياسم *sangi yāsim*, A kind of fullers' earth. سنگ يشم *sangi yasham*, A kind of jasper or agate.

P سنگار *sangār*, A fellow-traveller; ships sailing together.

P سنگ آسا *sang-āsā*, (Like a stone) Firm, solid, immoveable.

P سنگاش *sangāsh*, Envy, hatred.

P سنگ اشکن *sang-ishkan*, A sort of date. Corn, grain.

P سنگ اشکنك *sang-ishkank*, A kind of date.

P سنگ انداز *sang-andāz*, A loophole in a fortress. A slinger. A tippler, sot. Pleasure. Thirst. A holiday celebrated at the end of Shaabān.

P سنگ اندازي *sang-andāzī*, A throwing of stones, lapidation. سنگ اندازي کردن *sang-andāzī kardan*, To throw stones.

P سنگانه *sangāna*, A red-headed sparrow.

P سنگبار *sang-bār*, Raining stones. Stony place.

P سنگباري *sang-bārī*, A hurling of stones.

P سنگبر *sang-bar*, Stony place. Fellow-traveller.

P سنگبسته *sang-basta*, A grape hardened ripe.

P سنگ بوم *sang-būm*, A stony country.

P سنگپستان *sang-pistān*, Sebestens.

P سنگ پشت *sang-pusht*, A tortoise: a turtle.

P سنگپوست *sang-post*, (Stone-skin) A tortoise.

P سنگتراش *sang-tirāsh*, A stone-cutter: mason.

P سنگتره *sang tara*, A kind of orange.

P سنگ توده *sang-toda*, A heap of stones, a cairn.

P سنگ تول *sang-tawl*, Equal in weight.

P سنگ جان *sang-jān*, (or سنگ دل *sang-dil*) Cruel, merciless, having a heart of stone.

P سنگ جوش *sang-josh*, Boiled by a hot stone.

P سنگچه *sangcha*, A hailstone, hail.

P سنگ خارا *sang-khārā*, (also سنگ خاره *sang-khāra*) A kind of hard stone. Ruggedness of temper. Avarice.

P سنگ خوار *sang-khwār*, (also سنگخور *sang-khwur*) A bittern. An ostrich; also a species of eagle (as swallowing stones). The bird called katā.

P سنگخوارك *sang-khwārak*, (or سنگخواره *sang-khwāra*) A hard pebble. A bird called قطا *katā*.

P سنگخورك *sang-khwurak*, (also سنگخوارج *sang-khwāraj*) A little gravel-eating bird called قطاة *katāt*.

P سنگدان *sangdān*, Crop of a bird, gizzard.

P سنگ دانه *sang-dāna*, The gizzard of a bird. A kind of grain. A potter. A potter's workhouse. A place of idols. An idol-maker.

P سنگدوله *sungdūla* or *dola*, A whirlwind.

P سنگر *sangur*, A porcupine. Intrenchment.

P سنگرف *singarf*, Cinnabar.

P سنگرك *sangurk* or *sangrak*, Hail. The whirl of a spindle.

P سنگ ريز *sang-rez*, Flinging stones.

P سنگ ريزه *sang-reza*, Gravel. A bulse of diamonds, or what a merchant carries about him for sale. A kind of soup.

P سنگريزه ناك *sang-rezanāk*, Gravelly (spot).

P سنگ زن *sang-zan*, A light pair of scales. A make-weight.

P سنگسار *sangsār*, Stony. A stoning. A slinger. Firmness, stability. Transmigration. سنگسار كردن *sangsār kardan*, To stone to death.

P سنگساري *sangsārī*, A stoning to death.

P سنگسبويه *sangisboya*, Cinquefoil. The plant crab's eyes, which, infused in vinegar, they use for the leprosy.

P سنگست *sangast*, Name of a place.

P سنگستان *sangistān*, A stony country.

P سنگ سرمه *sang-surma*, Native antimony.

P سنگ شكن *sang-shikan*, Fruits of the earth, corn, grain. A sort of date.

P سنگشوئي *sang-shūī*, Washing (rice) before dressing, washing the gravel out of it.

P سنگ فسان *sang-fisān*, A whetstone.

P سنگك *sangak*, A little stone, a pebble. Hail. A sort of bread baked on a stone. A kind of small and black grain. A sort of bird.

P سنگلاخ *sanglākh*, A stony place: rocky, stony.

P سنگله *sangula*, Vetch or millet-bread.

P سنگم *sangam*, Intimate union, junction. A fellow-traveller. *Sangum*, A certain winged animal. An insect resembling a beetle found in baths.

P سنگمبر *sangam-bar*, A fellow-traveller. Union.

P سنگناك *sangnāk*, Stony (place).

P سنگوان *sangwān*, Name of a fortress in Persia.

P سنگور *sangūr*, A basket in which they carry about and sell beer. A whirl on the top of a spindle. Name of a bird.

P سنگوك *sangok*, A whirl fixed on a spindle.

P سنگول *sangūl*, Necessaries, requisites.

P سنگويه *sangūya*, A strong fort in India.

P سنگه *sanga*, A hedgehog. Hail.

P سنگي *sangī*, Stony. Heavy. Hard. Weight.

P سنگ يده *sang-yada*, A stone growing in animals' bodies.

P سنگين *sangīn*, Heavy, weighty. Stony. Hard, firm, solid. Obstinate. A bayonet. Name of a fort.

P سنگين خوار *sangīn-khwār*, A small gravel-eating bird. A bittern. An ostrich.

P سنگين سار *sangīn-sār*, A starling.

P سنگيني *sangīnī*, Weight, heaviness. A load. Solidity. Nightmare. Offensiveness, disagreeableness, unpleasantness.

P سنلخ *sanlakh*, A short-sleeved garment.

A سنم *sanam*, (v.n. of سنم) Having a high bunch (a camel). Being high and hunchbacked. *Sanim*, High-bunched (camel). (Water) flowing over convex ground. High, lifted up, flowering plant.

A سنم *sunnam*, A cow.

A سنّمار *sinimmār*, A robber. One who does not sleep by night. The moon. An architect. Name of a celebrated architect, who was cast headlong from the top of the famous palace خورنق *khawarnak*, which he had built by order of نعمان *nuemān*, king of Arabia, lest he should erect a similar or superior edifice for any other person: hence, جزاء سنمار *jazāi sinimmār*, Sinimmar's requital.

A سنمة *sanamat*, The top (of a plant). A flower, blossom.

A سنن *sanan*, Galloping (camels). *Sanan* or *sunan*, Road, way, path. Rule, mode, manner. *Sanan*, *sinan*, *sunan*, or *sunun*, Surface of a road. *Sunan*, (pl. of سنّة *sunnat*) The laws, sayings, or doings of Muhammad.

A سنو *sanw*, The opening (of a door).

A سنوّ *sunūw*, (v. n. of سنا for سنو) Watering ground, carrying water on camels for that purpose. Rising high (a flame). Shining (lightning).

A سنواء *sanwāi*, Barren, scarce (year).

A سنوات *sanawāt*, (pl. of سنة *sanat*) Years. *A* A rupee which has been current more than one year. Old coin current at a depreciated rate after a certain number of years.

A سنوت *sanūt*, Angry, irascible. A liar.

A سنوت *sannūt* or *sinnawt*, Cummin. Anise. Fennel. Honey. Cream. Cheese. A sort of date. Inspissated juice.

A سنوح *sunūh*, (v. n. of سنح) Happening, occurring, presenting itself. Being easy to one (poetry). Manifesting, exposing, declaring. Bringing out, drawing forth. Overtaking (with mischief), injuring, hurting. (Game) turning the right side to a man, and passing from his left to the right (which is considered as a good omen). Turning (one) away (from his design).

A سنوخ *sunūkh*, (v. n. of سنخ) Being firm, solid in knowledge. Firmness, constancy. (pl. of سنخ *sinkh*) Roots of teeth.

P سنود *sanūd*, The exercise of the mind upon a difficult subject.

A سنود *sunūd*, (v. n. of سند) Being propped, leaning upon or against. Climbing (a mountain). Approaching (to fifty). Striking the buttocks right and left (a camel's tail).

G سنوديق *sinūdik*, Relating to a synod.

A سنور *sinnawr*, (pl. سنانير *sanānīr*) A prince, chief, master of a family. A cat. Vertebræ of the neck. Root of the tail.

A سنوّر *sanawwar*, Armour, arms, a complete equipment. A leathern coat of mail.

P سنوس *sunūs*, Name of a tree and herb.

A سنوط *sanūt*, (or سنوطي *sanūta'*) (pl. سنط *sunut* and اسناط *asnūt*) Beardless. Name of a certain medicine.

A سنوع *sunūع*, (v. n. of سنع) Being beautiful, excellent, graceful.

A سنوف *sanūf*, A horse that shakes the saddle backwards.

A سنون *sanūn*, A dentifrice, a stick used for that purpose. *Sinūn* or *sunūn*, (pl. of سنة *sanat*) Years. Unfruitful (grounds).

A سنويّ *sanawīy*, Annual. آثار سنويّه *āsāri sanawīya*, Chronicles, annals, annual registers.

A سنه *sanh*, (v. n. of سنه) Bearing no fruit for many years (a palm-tree). *Sanih*, Mould, mustiness. Musty, mouldy (bread). (Wheat) several years old.

P سنه *sanah*, An execration, imprecation, malediction, curse. Robust, strong. A species of hard iron, which, when hot, absorbs water. A bramble. *Sunuh*, A daughter-in-law.

A سنهاء *sanhāi*, (fem. of اسنه *asnah*) Old, ancient, of long continuance. A palm-tree bearing every second year.

A سنهات *sanahāt*, (pl. of سنة *sanat*) Years.

P سنهار *sunhār*, A daughter-in-law.

A سني *sany*, (v. n. of سني) Watering the ground (a camel or a cloud). Blazing high (a fire). Shining, flashing (lightning). Drawing water for themselves (people). Opening (a door). *Sina'*, (v. n. of سني) Becoming tall. Being employed in drawing water (a beast).

P سني *sanay*, Iron, steel. *Sinī*, A large shallow bason or voider, of silver, wood, or brass, in which they carry dishes of meat to and from table; also in which they bake pies in the oven. Dross of iron.

P سنّي *sunni*, A delicious fish found in Multān.

A سنيّ *saniy*, High, lofty, exalted. Sublime, grand. Precious, costly. سنّت سنيّه *sunnati saniya*, The holy law.

A سنّي *sunniy*, Lawful. An orthodox Muhammadan, or one who receives the traditionary portion of the Muhammadan law (سنّة *sunnat*); which was not, like the Kur'ān, committed to writing by Muhammad, but preserved from his lips by his immediate disciples, or founded on the authority of his actions. One who reveres equally the four successors of Muhammad; and hence also called چهار ياري *chahār yārī*.

A سنيبيت *sunaybit*, A moment, a little while.

A سنيّة *sunayyat*, A little year: a bad year. السنيّات البيض *as' sunayyātu'l bīz*, Certain years disastrous to the people of Madīna.

A سنيت *sanīt*, Barren (year).

A سنيج *sanīj*, A lamp.

A سنيح *sanīh*, (Game) which turns the right side to a man, and passes from his left to the right. A pearl or thread not yet strung. Women's gear.

A سنيد *sanīd*, Spurious; a bastard.

P سنيز *sunīz*, Caraway-seed.

P سنيژه *sanīja*, A weaver's reed or shuttle. Thread beyond the width of the piece in the loom and not woven.

A سنيع *sanīʻ*, Excellent, beautiful.

A سنيعة *sanīʻat*, Handsome (female) having smooth joints and an elegant conformation of the bones. (pl. سنائع *sanāʼiʻ*) A road leading over a mountain.

A سنيف *sanīf*, (pl. سنف *sunf* or *sunuf*) A bit of rug placed on the shoulders of a camel. The border of a carpet or rug.

A سنّيق *sunnayk*, Certain stars in the milky way. (pl. سنّيقات *sunnaykāt* and سنانيق *sanānīk*) (A house) plastered with lime.

A سنين *sanīn*, Sharp, acute, whetted. Fragments which fly from stones when hewing: iron-filings. Coeval. Ground eaten bare of herbage or plants. Of, to, from years. سنين و شهور *sanīn u shuhūr*, For years and months.

A سنينة *sanīnat*, (pl. سنائن *sanāʼin*) Wind. Coeval. High and extensive sands. *Sunaynat*, (dim. of سنّ *sinn*) A little tooth.

P سو *saw*, Name of a fountain in Tūs. *Sū*, A side, part, quarter. Towards. Water. Light. Splendour. As, like as. (for سود *sūd*) Emolument, profit. آن سو *ān sū*, That part, there, thither. اين سو *īn sū*, This side, here, hither. سوي باغ *sūyi bāgh*, Towards the garden. سو بسو *sū ba sū*, From this side to that, here and there. سو پس *sū pas*, Afterwards. سوي خود تيشه زند *sūyi khwud tīsha zanad*, He draws the water to his own mill.

A سو *saw*, (in grammar) A particle prefixed to the aorist to give it a future sense. See سوف *sawf*.

A سوء *saws*, (v.n. of ساء) Grieving, saddening. Displeasing, disgusting. Doing evil. رجل سوء *rajulu sawsin*, (or رجل السوء *rajulu's saws*) A bad man. *Sūs*, Leprosy. A disgrace, vice, stain. Evil. Every kind of misfortune. A weakness in the eye. Fire. Hell. Perfidy, treachery. سوء حال *sūsi hāl*, A bad plight. سوء الحساب *sūsu'l hisāb*, A bad reckoning, no remission of sins. سوء ظنّ *sūsi zann*, An evil thought, ill-grounded suspicion, false idea, rash judgment. سوء عمل *sūsi ʻamal*, A villainous action. صحبت سوء القرين *suhbati sūsi'l karīn*, The society of a bad companion. دائرة السوء *dāsiratu's sūs*, Rout, dispersion. Evil. دابّة سوء *dābbatu sūsin*, A sorry brute (as a dog or an ass).

A سواء *sawās*, (v.n. of ساء) Acting wrong. Displeasing. Disgusting. Grieving, saddening. Being bad, vicious, depraved, corrupt. The conveniences of life, enjoyment. Indecency of behaviour. The thirteenth or fourteenth night of a lunar month. The summit of a mountain. Equality. The middle. Mediocrity. The middle (of the day). Straight, level. Other, another. Beside, except. (pl. اسواء *aswās*, سواسية *sawāsiyat*, سواسي *sawāsī*, and سواسوة *sawāsiwat*) Equal, of one sort, all alike, one and the same. سواه *sawāhu*, Beside him. سواء الرأس *sawāsu'r ras*, Top of the head. علي سواء *ʻala' sawās*, Equally. ايّام سواء *ayyāmu sawās*, Complete, entire days. *Siwās*, (v. n. 3 of سوي) Being equal to, a match for. Like.

A سوءاء *sawsās*, (or سوآء *sawsās*) (fem. of اسوأ *aswas*) Ugly, deformed, ill-favoured, offensive. Whoredom. Indecency. A bad quality.

A سواءان *sawāsāni*, (du. of سواء) Two equals.

A سواءة *sawāsat*, (v.n. of ساء) Displeasing, disgusting, grieving, saddening. *Suwāsat*, A name.

P سواب *sawāb*, A straining, a squeezing out.

A سوابح *sawābih*, (pl. of سابحة) Horses.

A سوابغ *sawābigh*, Roomy coats of mail.

A سوابق *sawābik*, (pl. of سابقة *sābikat*) Past events. Swift horses. سوابق محبّت *sawābiki mahabbat*, Old acquaintance, ancient friendship.

A سوابي *sawābī*, (pl. of سابياء) Secundines.

A سوابيط *sawābīt*, (pl. of ساباط *sābāt*) Covered passages, corridors between two houses.

A سوأة *sawsat*, Deformity, nastiness. Whoredom. Indecency. Secret parts. Any thing abominable. A bad quality.

A سواج *suwāj*, A moving slowly.

A سواجب *sawājib*, (pl. of ساجب *sājib*) Dried, shrivelled leathern bottles.

A سواجع *sawājiʻ*, (pl. of ساجعة) Cooing (turtles).

A سواجم *sawājim*, (pl. of ساجم) Flowing (tears).

A سوّاح *sawwāh*, A traveller.

A سواحل *sawāhil*, (pl. of ساحل) Coasts.

A سواخ *suwākh*, Soft earth in which the feet sink.

A سواخر *sawākhir*, (Ships) sailing with a fine favourable gale.

A سوّاخي *sūwākha'*, Soft, yielding earth.

A سواخية *suwākhiyat*, Much clay.

P سواد *sawād*, Lees of wine. Circuit, circumference. Dung, manure. سواد پيشاني *sawādi peshānī*, The appearance of the countenance.

A سواد *sawād*, Blackness. A black colour. The heart's core. The figure of a man at a distance (because he then appears black). Sable raiment, mourning habiliments. A rough draft. Reading. Ability. Great riches. Villages. The common people. A multitude of people. A great number. A date. The towns or villages in the Babylonian or Arabian Irāk (as those in Khurāsān are called رستاق *rustāk*, and in Arabia Felix مخالف *makhālif*). سواد اعظم *sawādi aʻzam*, Any large city. Mecca. سواد البطن *sawādu'l batn*, The liver. سواد صرف *sawād sirf*, Gross darkness. سواد العين *sawādu'l ʻayn*, A beloved mistress. سواد القلب *sawādu'l kalb*, Love. The black or interior part of the heart. Original sin. اصحاب السواد *as-hābu's sawād*, Melancholy people. *Siwād*, (v. n. 3 of ساد for سود) Whispering in the ear. Voice, noise. *Suwād*, Paleness of face. Greenness in the nail. A disease incident to cattle. A whisper in the ear.

A سُؤاد *susād*, A distemper produced by drinking brackish water.

A سوادي *sawādī*, Long-stepped (she-camels).

A سواديّ *sawādiy*, A resident in a town.

A سواديّة *sawādiyat*, A sparrow.

A سوار *siwār*, (v. n. 3 of سار for سور) Assailing, springing on another, seizing by the head. *Siwār* or *suwār*, (pl. اسورة *aswirat*, اساور *asāwir*, اساورة *asāwirat*, سور *sūr*, and سُوُور *susūr*) A bracelet. ذات سوار *zāt siwār*, A female wearing a bracelet. *Suwār*, Strength (of wine): sharpness of a thing.

P سوار *suwār*, A cavalier, horseman, rider, trooper. A Persian chief (as being skilful in horsemanship and archery). Embarked in a ship, going on board. سوار سيستان *suwāri sīstān*, Rustam Zāl. سوار شدن *suwār shudan*, To be mounted. سوار رفتن *suwār raftan*, To go mounted, ride. سوار و پياده *suwār u piyāda*, Horse and foot, cavalry and infantry. آب سواران *āb-suwārān*, Water-horsemen, *i.e.* bubbles.

A سوّار *sawwār*, One who leaps upon or otherwise assaults his pot-companions and friends. One into whose head wine rapidly mounts and intoxicates. (A discourse) which takes effect in the head. A lion. Name of a tribe.

P سواران *suwārān*, (pl. of سوار *suwār*) Horsemen.

P سواران آب *suwārāni āb*, Bubbles. Waves.

P سوارپا *suwār-pā*, An active walker.

A سوارق *sawārik*, (pl. of سارقة *sārikat*) Female thieves. Large cauldrons. Pillories. Wings on the bolts of a door, wards.

P سوارك آب *suwāraki āb*, A bubble. A wave.

P سواركار *suwār-kār*, A good rider, jockey.

P سوارکاري *suwār-kārī*, Good riding, jockeyship. Cavalry. A trooper. Drunk, tipsy.

P سوارگان *suwāragān*, (pl. of سواره) Troopers.

P سوارون *sawārūn*, A small seed used in making an eye-salve.

P سواره *suwāra*, Mounted on horseback. A horseman. A trooper. Papyrus. Sweepings.

A سواري *sawārī*, (pl. of سارية *sāriyat*) Beams. Columns. Night-clouds.

P سواري *suwārī*, The manege, art of horsemanship. Riding. Equipage, suite. اسب سواري *asbi suwārī*, A saddle-horse. شتر سواري *shuturi suwārī*, A camel for the saddle.

A سواس *sawās*, A kind of tree which emits fire. *Suwās*, A disease incident to the neck of a horse.

A سواسوة *sawāsiwat*, (pl. of سواء *sawā*) Equals.

A سواسي *sawāsī*, (pl. of سواء *sawā*) Equal.

A سواسية *sawāsiyat*, (pl. of سواء *sawā*) Equal.

A سوّاط *sawwāt*, A whipper of criminals.

A سواع *suwā'*, The first watch of the night. Rest, repose. Any short space of time. Any thing voided after making water; also مذي *mazy*. *Suwā'* or *sawā'*, Name of an ancient Arabian idol. See سوعاء.

A سواعد *sawā'id*, (pl. of ساعد *sā'id*) The arms. Channels, through which streams flow from rising grounds to rivers or the sea. The ducts in the bones, through which the marrow runs.

A سواغ *siwāgh*, That whereby ease is given to any pain in the throat by putting down any thing sticking in it. *Suwāgh*, (v. n. of ساغ for سوغ) Going easily down the throat (wine or victuals).

A سواف *sawāf*, (v.n. of ساف for سوف) Perishing. A cucumber. *Siwāf*, (v.n.3 of ساف for سوف) Whispering in the ear. Lying with. *Suwāf*, (*sawāf*, or سؤاف *su'āf*) A disease, a mortal distemper, death widely spread (especially of cattle).

A سوافح *sawāfih*, (pl. of سافح) Flowing (tears).

A سوافر *sawāfir*, (pl. of سافرة *sāfirat*) Women with unveiled faces.

A سوافع *sawāfi'*, Scorching (blasts of wind). Scorchings of the face.

A سوافك *sawāfik*, Blood-shedding swords.

A سوافل *sawāfil*, Lower parts of the body.

A سوافن *sawāfin*, Ground-sweeping winds.

A سوافين *sawāfīn*, (pl. of سفون *safūn*) Ground-sweeping winds.

A سوّاق *sawwāk*, A cattle-driver. *Suwāk*, Long-legged. Any plant growing on a stem. The buds of a palm-tree when become a span long. (pl. of سائق *sā'ik*) Drivers.

A سواقط *sawākit*, Visitors to Yamāmah to purchase dates. Low mountains. (pl. of ساقطة *sākitat*) Things fallen, as leaves, &c.

A سواقي *sawākī*, (pl. of ساقية *sākiyat*) Trenches cut in sown fields to water them.

A سواك *siwāk*, (v. n. 3 of ساك for سوك) Rubbing (the teeth with a certain wood). Going tremblingly (emaciated cattle). (pl. سوك *suwuk*) A dentifrice. *Suwāk*, A soft, gentle pace.

P سواك *suwāk*, Smut, blight upon corn.

A سواكن *sawākin*, An island in the Red Sea.

A سؤال *su'āl*, (v. n. of سأل) Asking, begging. Praying for. A question, petition, interrogation, demand, request. A proposition. سؤال و جواب *su'āl u jawāb*, Question and answer, dialogue. P سؤال كردن *su'āl kardan*, To ask questions, interrogate.

A سؤّال *su''āl*, Beggars.

A سوالّ *sawāll*, (pl. of سالّ *sāll*) Wide valleys producing the trees سلم *salam* and سمر *samur*.

A سوالب *sawālib*, (pl. of سالب *sālib*) Delivered of an abortion. (pl. of سالبة) Seizers, spoilers.

A سوالخ *sawālikh*, (pl. of سالخ) Black serpents.

A سوالف *sawālif*, (pl. of سالفة *sālifat*) Past events. سوالف ايّام *sawālifi ayyām*, Past times.

A سوالي *suwālī*, A questioner. He who sings the marsiya.

A سوام *sawām*, (Cattle) going to pasture. A cavity below a horse's eye. *Suwām*, (v. n. of سام for سوم) Bidding against, raising the price upon another. Name of a bird.

A سوامّ ابرص *sawāmm abras*, (or simply سوامّ *sawāmm*) (pl. of سامّ ابرص *sāmm abras*) Certain large poisonous lizards.

A سوامد الليل *sawāmidu'l layl*, Constant night journeys.

A سوامي *sawāmī*, (pl. of سامي *sāmī*) (Horses) which carry their heads erect.

A سوانح *sawānih*, Accidents, occurrences, events.

P سوانح نگار *sawānih-nigār*, A news-writer.

A سواني *sawānī*, (pl. of سانية *sāniyat*) Camels used to irrigate. سير السواني سفر لا ينقطع *sayru's sawānī safar lā yankati'*, The going to and fro of water-drawing camels is a journey that never ends.

A سواهم *sawāhim*, Over-fatigued (camels).

A سوأى *sū'a'*, Deformed (woman). Fire. Hell. Torment. Evil (opposed to حسنى *husna'*, Good).

A سوايا *sawāya'*, (pl. of سويّ *sawiy*) Equal, even. Well-proportioned. (pl. of سويّة *sawīyat*) Straw-stuffed pack-saddles.

A سواية *sawāyat*, (v. n. of ساء) Disliking, being indisposed. Afflicting, grieving, saddening. Being vicious, wicked.

A سوائف *sawā'if*, (pl. of سائفة *sā'ifat*) Fine sands at the bottom of hillocks.

A سوائم *sawā'im*, Flocks, herds feeding.

A سوائية *sawā'iyat*, (v. n. of ساء) Doing ill. Afflicting, grieving, saddening.

P سوب *sūb*, Water.

A سؤب *su'ub*, (pl. of سأب) Leathern bottles.

A سؤبان مال *su'bānu mālin*, A steward or manager of an estate, or of a herd of camels.

A سوبة *sūbat*, A long journey.

P سوبدي *sūbdī*, A starling.

P سوبرا *sūbarā*, (in zand) Hope, hopefulness.

P سوبسو *sū ba sū*, From side to side: side by side.

P سوبهار *sūbahār*, An ancient temple in Ghaznīn.

A سوبية *sūbīyat*, Wine made from wheat.

P سوپ *sūp*, Water.

P سوپاري *sūpārī*, The areca-nut.

P سوپس *sū pas*, Afterwards.

A سؤة *su'at*, The horn of a bow.

P سوتام *sūtām*, Little, small: deficient: few. Bad.

P سوتر *sūtar*, Farther, beyond.

P سوته بردار *sota-bardār*, A mace-bearer.

A سوج *sanj*, (or سوجان) A going slowly.

P سوج *soj*, (for سوز *soz*) A burning.

A سوجان *sawjān*, A going and coming.

A سوجر *sawjar*, An osier. A willow.

A سوجرة *sawjarat*, (v. n. of سوجر Q) Tying the log ساجور *sājūr* to a dog's neck.

P سوجرونتن *sūjarūnitan*, (in zand) To bring.

P سوجش *sojish*, (for سوزش *sozish*) A burning.

A سوجل *sawjal*, (or سوجلة *sawjalat*) The (wicker) cover of a flask.

P سوچه *sūcha*, A gore, gusset. A fool. In love.

A سوح *sawh*, (pl. of ساحة *sāhat*) Fields. *Sūh*, (pl. of ساحة *sāhat*) Courts. Shores, coasts.

A سوحر *sawhar*, An osier. A willow.

A سوحق *sawhak*, Long.

A سوخ *sawkh*, (or سوخان *sawakhān*) (v. n. of ساخ for سوخ) Sinking in the mud. Yielding to the feet (soft earth).

P سوخ *sūkh*, An onion. A city in Turkistān.

P سوخت *sokht*, Burnt. A revoke at cards.

P سوخت تيره *sokht-tīra*, Bay, chesnut horse.

P سوختگي *sokhtagī*, Combustion: a burn. The burnt wick or snuff of a candle. Vexation, heart-burning. سوختگي از آب گرم *sokhtagī az ābi garm*, A scald from hot water.

P سوختن *sokhtan*, To burn, to be inflamed. To set on fire.

P سوخته *sokhta*, Burnt. Diseased in the liver. A slow match. Weighed. Overtaken by troubles. Dross. Dregs, lees. Tinder. Drunk. Name of one of the treasures of Khusraw. A student.

P سوخته جان *sokhta-jān*, Consumed, pained.

A سود *sawd*, (v. n. of ساد for سود) Drinking water, on which there is a yellow tinge. The even surface of a mountain-side. Black stones or gravel. The stony bottom of a mountain (especially black). *Sūd*, A being prince or chief. Dominion. (pl. of أسود *aswad*) Black, or excessively dark. Illustrious, powerful. سود الاكباد *sūdu'l akbād*, (Black-livered) Enemies. سود البطون *sūdu'l butūn*, Extenuated cattle. ايّام السود *ayyāmu's sūd*, Dark, disastrous days. *Sawad*, (v. n. of سود) Being afflicted with the disease سواد *suwād*.

P سود *sūd*, Gain, lucre, emolument, advantage, profit. Interest, usury. A feast, festive conversation. Acquainted with every art. سود خوردن *sūd khwurdan*, To exact usury. سود داشتن *sūd dāsh-*

tan, To derive profit. To avail. سود مايه *sūdi māya*, Profit on capital stock. (3d pers. sing. pret. of سودن *sūdan*, To rub) مى بايد سود *mī bāyad sūd*, It is proper to rub. *Sawad*, A wicker basket.

P سودا *sawdā*, Melancholy, spleen. Love. Ambition, desire, strong inclination. Trade, traffic, marketing. Gain, profit, emolument.

A سوداء *sawdāʼ*, (fem. of اسود *aswad*) Black. A beaten footpath. Old and rotten. A large black female serpent. The heart's core. Original sin. Melancholy. A mania. Madness. Atrabilis. An evil word. حبّة السوداء *ḥabbatu's sawdāʼ*, Coriander. ما ردّ علىّ سوداء و لا بيضاء *mā radda ʻalayya' sawdāʼ wa lā bayzāʼ*, He did not answer me either black or white, *i.e.* bad or good.

P سودابه *sūdāba*, The wife of Kay Kāwus.

P سوداپرست *sawdā-parast*, Sensual: ambitious.

P سوداجاي *sawdā-jāy*, A place of brisk trade.

P سودار *sawdār*, A general, commander.

P سودا زده *sawdā-zada*, Mopish, melancholy.

P سودا سلف *sawdā saluf*, Traffic, barter.

P سوداگر *sawdāgar*, A merchant. Melancholic.

P سوداگري *sawdāgarī*, Trade, commerce.

P سودان *sawdān*, A sort of nightingale.

A سودان *sūdān*, Negroes, blacks. Ethiopians.

A سوداني *sūdānīy*, Ethiopic, black.

P سود آور *sūd-āwar*, Profitable. A merchant.

P سوداوه *sūdāwa*, The wife of Kay Kāwus.

A سوداوي *sawdāwīy*, Melancholy, dejected, atrabilarious. سوداويّ المزاج *sawdāwīyu'l mizāj*, Of a melancholy temperament. An atrabilarian.

P سودائى *sawdāʼī*, Melancholy, black bile.

A سودة *sawdat*, Part of the stony bottom of a mountain (especially black). A woman's name.

A سؤدة *suʼdat*, Remains of youth or strength.

P سود خور *sūd-khwur*, An usurer: a publican.

A سودد *sūdad*, A principality, dominion.

A سؤدد *suʼdud*, Principality, dominion.

A سودق *sawdak*, A kind of falcon. A bracelet.

P سودگي *sūdagī*, Wear and tear, friction.

A سودل *sawdal*, Mustachios.

A سودلة *sawdalat*, The having long mustachios.

P سودمند *sūdmand*, Useful, fruitful, gainful, salutary, profitable, advantageous.

P سودمندي *sūdmandī*, Profit, gain, advantage.

P سودن *sūdan*, To rub, wear, tear, consume, break. To dissolve, steep in water. To handle, stroke. To anoint, besmear, incrust, bedaub. To transfix, pierce.

P سوده *sūda*, Rubbed, worn, triturated. Melted, dissolved, effaced. Powder.

P سودي *sūdī*, Money borrowed at interest.

A سوذانق *sūzānik*, *sawzānik*, or *sūzānah*, A kind of hawk.

A سوذق *sawzak*, A bracelet. The heart. *Sawzak* or *sūzah*, A kind of hawk. The ring of a fetter.

A سوذقيّ *sawzakīy*, Brisk, cheerful. Prudent, cautious. Sly, deceitful.

A سوذنيق *saw* or *sūzanik*, A kind of falcon.

A سور *sawr*, (v. n. of سار for سور) Climbing (a wall). Mounting and circulating in the head (wine). Assaulting, rushing at any one, aiming at (his head). *Sūr*, (v. n. of سور) Mounting to the head (wine). (pl. اسوار *aswār* and سيران *sīrān*) A wall of a city, a rampart. Noble camels. (pl. of سوار *siwār*) Bracelets. (pl. of سورة *sūrat*) Lofty edifices. Chapters of the Kur'ān. *Suwar*, (pl. of سورة *sūrat*) Structures, especially lofty. Rows of stones in a wall. Chapters of the Kur'ān.

P سور *sūr*, Nuptials. A banquet, feast, entertainment. Redundant, exceeding. Excuse, plea. Ash-colour. Red colour. Red wine. A horse, ass, or mule marked with a stripe from the withers to the tail. Name of a bird. Name of a city. A name by which some of the Afghāns are distinguished.

A سؤر *suʼr*, (pl. اسآر *asʼār*) Remains, leavings. سؤر الاسد *suʼru'l asad*, Name of ابو خابئة *abū khābiʼat*, the Kūfite, seized by a lion and left alive.

P سورا *sūrā*, Name of a city.

A سورات *sūrāt*, (pl. of سورة *sūrat*) Sūras or chapters of the Kur'ān.

P سوراخ *sūrākh*, A hole, orifice, passage. سوراخ بيني *sūrākhi bīnī*, The nostril. سوراخ سوز *sūrākhi soz*, Touchhole of fire-arms. سوراخ مقعد *sūrākhi maḳʻad*, (or كون *kūn*) The hole of the fundament.

P سوراخ دار *sūrākh-dār*, Perforated, drilled, full of holes. Worm-eaten.

P سوراخ سنب *sūrākh-sumb*, A wimble, auger. An instrument for tapping horses' navels.

P سوراخ كرده *sūrākh-karda*, Bored, drilled.

P سوراخ كن *sūrākh-kan*, A wimble, gimlet, borer.

P سوران *sūrān*, A starling.

A سورة *sawrat*, An assault, attack. Strength (of wine); violence (of a fever, especially when affecting the head). Power or despotism (of a sovereign). Severity of cold. Sign, trace, vestige. Height (of glory). *Sūrat*, (pl. سور *sūr* and *suwar*) A chapter of the Kur'ān (of which there are 114). A structure (especially lofty). One row of stones in a wall. Dignity, exaltation: nobility. Mark, sign.

A سؤرة *suʼrat*, Remains of the vigour of youth. (for سورة *sūrat*) A chapter of the Kur'ān.

P سورت *sūrat*, City and province of Surat.

P سورج *sūraj*, A sort of foam of the sea.

P سورستان *sūristān*, Syria.

P سورغون *sūrghūn*, The red saul.

P سورميدن *sūrmīdan*, To blow a trumpet.

P سورن *sūran*, An assault, irruption, war-whoop.

P سورنا *sūr-nā*, A multitude of people, convivial meeting. *Sūr-nā*, (or سورناي *sūr-nāy*) A trumpet, a clarion blown on feast-days.

P سورنجان *sūrinjān*, Wild saffron, dog's-bane.

P سوري *sūrī*, A beautiful red rose of an odoriferous and exhilarating flavour. Vitriol, red copperas. Mirth. A kind of arrow or javelin. Belonging to the city of Sūr. *Sure*, One marriage.

A سورية *sūriyat*, Syria.

P سوريوس *sūriyūs*, Name of Nimrod.

P سوز *soz*, Burning. Inflammation, heat. A burning fever. Heart-burning, ardour. Affection. Disturbed in mind. The cautery. A stanza of a marsiya or elegiac poem. سوز برادري *sozi birādarī*, Fraternal affection. پر سوز *pur-soz*, Full of heat.

P سوزا *sozā*, Burning violently, giving excruciating pain. A bile, felon. ريش سوزا *reshi sozā*, A smarting wound.

P سوزار *sozār*, Flame. A setting on fire.

P سوزاك *sozāk*, An inflamed ulcer, a pimple. Burning. Gonorrhœa, chaude-pisse.

P سوزان *sozān*, Burning, inflaming. Ardent, fervent. آتش سوزان *ātishi sozān*, A flaming fire.

P سوزاني *sozānī*, Heat.

P سوزانيدن *sozānīdan*, To set on fire.

P سوزش *sozish*, Burning, conflagration. A chafing or fretting. Solicitude, vexation.

P سوزگداز *soz-gudāz*, Burning and melting. An impassioned style in poetry.

P سوزم *sozam*, Sour milk falling in clots.

P سوزن *sozan*, A needle. Pricker (of a gun).

P سوزناك *soznāk*, Burning, ardent. Plaintive.

P سوزندان *sozandān*, (سوزندار *sozan-dār*, or سوزنيام *sozan-yām*) A needle-case.

P سوزندگي *sozindagī*, A conflagration.

P سوزنده *sozanda*, Burning, kindling: a burner.

P سوزن فروش *sozan-farosh*, A needle-vender.

P سوزنگر *sozangar*, A needle-maker.

P سوزني *sozanī*, Quilting. A kind of ornamented carpet. A small throne; seat of state.

P سوز و ساز *soz u sāz*, Inflamed with passion, love, or grief. Anguish of mind.

P سوزه *soza*, (or سوژه *soja*) The head-band or fastening of the breeches. A bit of cloth (especially quadrangular, put under the armpits of shirts). Elevation of mind, dignity, pride. Name of a plant resembling spinage.

P سوزي *sozī*, A conflagration.

P سوزيان *sūziyān*, (from سود *sūd*, Profit, and زيان *ziyān*, Loss) Advantage. Good and bad. Open and secret. Money, wealth, capital, goods, and chattels. A present. A secret. Sympathetic.

P سوزيدن *sozīdan*, To burn. To be burnt.

P سوس *sūs*, Liquorice. An ointment used by women from the fat of the سوسمار *sūsmār*. Name of a town of Khūzistān, where the tomb of the prophet Daniel is venerated. Hay, clover. A moth.

A سوس *sūs*, Nature, disposition. Root, origin. Moth, weevil, tike, or other similar worms. Liquorice. *Sawas*, (v. n. of سوس) Being injured by moths (wool), by weevils (corn), by tikes (sheep). Being troubled by the disease *sawas* (a horse). A disease in the buttocks of a horse.

P سوسبار *sūsibār*, (or سوسبا *sūsibā*) (in zand

and Pāzand) A horse.

P سوسپند *suspand*, A kind of milky grass.

A سوسة *sūsat*, One weevil. The city Suza.

P سوس زده *sūs-zada*, Worm-eaten, moth-eaten.

P سوسك *susk*, An insect resembling a beetle, mostly found in baths. *Sūsak*, A bird resembling a partridge, but smaller.

P سوسمار *sūsmār*, A species of green lizard, with the head of a serpent, which burrows in the ground like a mole. (It is bulkier than a weasel, and its grease women eat and anoint themselves with, to augment their fatness.) An alligator. A porpoise.

A سوسن *sawsan*, The lily.

P سوسن *sūsan*, A lily, of which there are four sorts; viz. سوسن آزاد *sūsani āzād*, The white; سوسن ازرق *sūsani azrak*, The blue; سوسن خطائي *sūsani khatāī*, The yellow; and سوسن آسمانگوني *sūsani āsmān-gūnī*, Yellow, white, and blue. The fir-tree. سوسن و سير *sūsan u sīr*, (Lily and garlic) Any two things incongruous.

P سوسنه *sūsana*, A lily.

P سوسني *sūsanī*, Lilied. A blueish colour.

P سوسه *sūsa*, A weevil.

P سوسيى *sūsī*, A cloth of silk and cotton.

A سوصنا *sūsannā*, Susanna.

A سوط *sawt*, (v. n. of ساط for سوط) Flogging, lashing. Mixing, stirring up liquids. (pl. سياط *siyāt* and اسواط *aswāt*) A scourge, bull's pizzle, cat-o'-nine-tails. The part lashed; the pain, smart. A share, portion. Violence, severity. A place where water collects. Remains in a well. An affair, business. سوط باطل *sawtu bātilin*, Moles playing in a sunbeam darting through a window.

A سوطان *sawatān*, (v. n. of ساط for سوط) Palpitating, beating, leaping (the heart).

A سوطرة *sawtarat*, (v. n. of سوطر Q) Presiding as inspector, being appointed or set over.

A سوع *sawaʿ*, (v. n. of سوع) Being turned loose and allowed to pasture freely without a keeper (a herd or flock). A side. A portion of time, a third of the night. The still part of night.

A سوعاء (ساعة *sāʿat*) *sawʿāʾ*, Adverse fortune.

A سوعاء *suwaʿāʾ*, A seminal effusion. A preparation for staling or covering (in an ass).

A سوغ *sawgh*, (v. n. of ساغ for سوغ) Going easily down the throat (wine or victuals). Being lawful, allowed, permitted. Swallowing easily. Sinking under the feet (soft earth). Running and waxing strong (a she-camel). One born immediately after another, as a next brother.

P سوغات *sawghāt*, A magnificent present, particularly of different articles, made to kings or grandees, or sent by friends to friends. A curiosity.

A سوغان *sawaghān*, (v. n. of ساغ for سوغ) Going easily down the throat (wine or victuals).

A سوغة *sawghat*, One born immediately after another, as a next brother.

P سوغه *sawgha*, A fixed sum paid to the accountants by soldiers out of their monthly pay.

A سوف *sawf*, (v. n. of ساف for سوف) Discovering by the smell. Being patient. Approaching land lying between hard ground and sand. Perishing, being destroyed by disease (cattle). A particle giving to the verb a future sense, and implying, A promise, threat, or wish. A wish, desire, hope. Patience. A philosopher. يقتات السوف *yaktātu's sawf*, He feeds on hope. *Sūf* and *suwaf*, (pl. of سوفة *sūfat*) Lands, grounds.

G سوف *sūf*, Wisdom.

P سوفار *sūfār*, (or سوفال *sūfāl*) The notch in the arrow which receives the string. A small perforation. The eye of a needle. An earthen vessel. سوفار سوزن *sūfāri sozan*, A needle's eye.

P سوفان *sūfān*, Tinder.

P سوفانه *sūfāna*, The eye of a needle. The notch of an arrow.

A سوفة *sūfat*, (pl. سوف *sūf* and *suwaf*) Earth, ground. Land lying between hard ground and sand.

P سوفته *sūfta*, Deceit, fraud. A weevil.

P سوفچه *sūfcha*, A part of melted gold and silver. Excrement or gum of the eyes. Sticks and straws.

P سوفرا *sūfarā*, Name of Kaykubād's vazīr.

G سوفسطائية *sūfistāʾiya*, A sophister.

P سوفي *sūfī*, Wise.

A سوق *sawk*, (v. n. of ساق for سوق) Driving on, stimulating, impelling, urging, pushing forward, sending. Carrying off, despatching, sending (a marriage portion to a bride). Hurting the leg. Being at the point of death. *Sūk*, A market, public square, forum. A combat, scuffle, boxing-match, (pl. of ساق *sāk*) Legs. سوق البز *sūku'l bazz*, A cloth-hall. سوق الدجاج *sūku'd dajāj*, A poultry-market. سوق الحرب *sūku'l harb*, The fiercest part of a battle-field. اهل سوق *ahli sūk*, People at market. *Sawak*, (v. n. of سوق) Having a handsome leg. Length and elegance of legs. *Suwak*, (pl. of سوقة *sūkat*) Subjects.

A سوقاء *sawkāʾ*, (fem. of اسوق *aswak*) Long and handsome-legged.

P سوقات *sawkāt*, (for سوغات) A present.

A سوقة *sūkat*, (pl. سوق *suwak*) Subjects, plebeians, lowest of the people. A species of the plant طرثوث *tursūs*. A concourse of people at market.

A سوقعة *sawkaʿat*, A hollow in a pudding, into which they pour sauce. The part of a turban-sash, veil, or cloak, which touches the head and becomes soonest dirty. The edge, side, or corner of a thing.

A سوقم *sawkam*, The scammony-tree.

A سوقي *sūkīy*, Belonging to a market, market.

A سوك *sawk*, (v. n. of ساك for سوك) Rubbing (the teeth with a dentifrice). Rubbing or stroking. *Suwuk*, (pl. of سواك *siwāk*) Dentrifices.

P سوك *sok*, An ear of corn. A beard of corn. Thin-bearded.

P سوكك *sūkak*, Blight, smut, mildew.

P سوكه *sūka*, A hole. Anus. Vulva.

P سوگ *sog*, Grief, sorrow, affliction, mourning.

P سوگا *sogā*, Very sad, in deep distress.

P سوگدار *sog-dār*, Dressed in mourning.

P سوگل *sūgal*, Blight, smut, mildew.

P سوگند *sawgand*, An oath, swearing. سوگند خوردن *sawgand khwurdan*, (or سوگند ياد كردن *sawgand yād kardan*) To take an oath, to swear. سوگند دادن *sawgand dādan*, To administer an oath. سوگند دروغ *sawgandi durogh*, A false oath.

P سوگند اسوگندي *sawgand-ā-sawgandī*, Mutual asseveration.

P سوگند خوار *sawgand-khwār*, A swearer.

P سوگوار *sogwār*, Mournful, afflicted. عندليب سوگوار *ʿandalībi sogwār*, The mournful nightingale.

P سوگواري *sogwārī*, Mourning.

P سوگي *sogī*, Afflicted, mournful.

P سوگيانه *sogyāna*, Mourning-clothes.

P سوگيدن *sogīdan*, To weep, mourn. To cough.

A سؤل *suʾl*, (or سول *sūl*) Any thing which is the subject of inquiry.

P سول *sūl*, An aqueduct, canal. *Sūl* or *suwal*, The sole of the foot of a camel, a sheep, or a goat. An ash-coloured stripe, verging to black, from the withers to the tail of a horse, ass, or mule.

A سول *sūl*, (pl. of اسول *aswal*) Flag-bellied. Low (clouds). *Sawal*, (v. n. of سول) Being swag-bellied.

A سولاء *sawlāʾ*, (fem. of اسول *aswal*) Flag-bellied (woman). Large (bucket).

P سولاخ *sūlākh*, (for سوراخ *sūrākh*) A hole.

P سولان *sawalān*, Juice of the buckthorn. Roof of a house. Heights, eminences. Name of a mountain near Ardabīl, in every age the abode of pious men.

A سولة *sawlat*, A looseness, pendulousness, or swagging in the belly. A pigeon-house. *Sūlat*, A question. *Suwalat*, Very inquisitive.

A سؤلة *suʾlat*, (or سولة *sūlat*) A subject of inquiry. *Suʾalat*, A very inquisitive man.

A سولع *sawlaʿ*, The bitter aloe.

P سولك *sūlak*, Mildew, smut.

P سوله *sola*, A hole, anus; vulva. A home-born slave. A cry. The yell of a dog.

P سوليدن *sūlīdan*, To weep, mourn. To cough.

A سوم *sawm*, (v. n. of سام for سوم) Estimating, fixing a price. Bidding, offering a price. Bidding against, raising the price upon another. Compelling to any thing. Making one an overseer or manager. Treating with indignity or contempt. Veering (as the wind), and then blowing constantly. Hovering over any thing (a bird). Pasturing, going to pasture. Price.

P سوم *siwum*, Third.

P سومان *sūmān*, A little, somewhat.

A سومة *sūmat*, A distinguishing mark worn in battle. A sign, mark made upon cattle. A price. Valuation, appraisement.

A سوملة *sawmalat*, A small cup.

P سومنات *somanāt* or *somnāt*, Name of an idol-temple in Guzerat, destroyed by Mahmūd Ghaznavī.

P سومندر *somandar*, A salamander.

P سومه *sūma*, Dust, filings. A mark for archers. A banner. The image or stamp on coin.

A سون *sawn*, Swagging, pendulousness of belly.

P سون *sūn*, A side, a part. Like, resembling. *Sawan*, Praise.

P سونانك *sonānk*, Snoring. Breathing hard from running.

P سونچ *sūnich*, (also سونچه *sūncha*) A quadrangular patch of cloth put under the armpits of shirts.

P سونخ *sūnakh*, Name of a city.

P سونش *sūnish*, Any fragment that falls in filing or polishing, filings.

G سونوخوش *sūnokhwush*, A continued fever.

P سونيز *sawnīz*, Coriander.

A سووخ *suwūkh*, (v. n. of ساخ for سوخ) Yielding to the feet (soft earth).

A سوؤر *suʼūr*, (pl. of سوار *siwār*) Bracelets.

A سوور *suwūr*, (v. n. of سار for سور) Assaulting, leaping upon, aiming at, or striking. Mounting to the head (wine).

A سوؤق *suʼūk*, (pl. of ساق *sāk*) Legs.

A سؤوم *saʼūm*, Languid, sated, wearied.

P سوهان *sūhān*, (or سوهن *sūhan*) A file for iron or wood. سوهان كردن *sūhān kardan*, To file.

P سوهان كار *sūhān-kār*, Worker with a file, filer.

A سوهق *sawhak*, Full of moisture (trunk of a tree, &c.). A liar.

A سوهقة *sawhakat*, A canal, conduit, water-pipe.

P سوهن *sūhan*, A file. A whetstone.

P سوهه *sūha*, An anvil. Filings.

A سوىٰ *sawa'*, Intention, design. *Siwa'* or *suwa'*, Middling, ordinary. Equal, straight. Alike. A mean, medium, middle, mediocrity. Other, another. Beside, except. Equality, straightness. لا يسوي شيا *la yaswa' shayan*, (It) is worth nothing. مكان سوىٰ *mqhānun siwa'*, A place marked by signs or traces. سوىٰ عليّ *siwa' ʻalayya'*, It is all the same to me. *Suwa'*, Straight, even (road).

P سوي *suwī*, A side, part, quarter. Towards. سوي بالا *suwī bālā*, Upwards. سوي پا ديدن *suwī pā dīdan*, To look towards the feet; to be bashful. در آن سوي *dar ān suwī*, On that side.

A سويّ *sawīy*, (pl. سوايا *sawāya'*) Equal, proportioned. Even, level. Right, alike, parallel. Entire. سويّ الخلق *sawīyu'l khulk*, Even-tempered.

A سويّة *sawīyat*, (fem. of سويّ *sawīy*) Equal. Equality, uniformity, straightness, evenness. (pl. سوايا *sawāya'*) A kind of pack-saddle stuffed with hair, straw, or herbage. علي السويّة *ʻala's sawīyat*, (or بالسويّة *bi's sawīyat*) Equally, uniformly. *Suwayyat*, Name of a woman.

P سويد *sawīd*, A ploughshare.

A سويد *suwayd*, (dim. of اسود *aswad*) Inclining to black, blackish. امّ سويد *umm suwayd*, The anus.

A سويداء *suwaydāʼ*, Blackish (woman). Coriander. سويداء القلب *suwaydāʼu'l kalb*, (or سويداء بال *suwaydāʼi bāl*) The heart's core. Original sin.

P سويدان *suwaydān*, A burying-ground.

P سويرغال *sūyarghāl*, A royal robe or present. A territory, town, or village granted by the king in feudal tenure.

P سوي زن *suwī zan*, A needle.

P سويس *suwes*, Ignorance. Carelessness.

A سويس *suwīs*, Suez on the Arabian gulf.

P سويست *suwest*, Ignorance. Inadvertency.

P سويسه *suwesa*, The rainbow.

P سويشم *suwīshim*, A green stone. An agate.

A سويط *suwīt*, Mixed (flocks or other property).

A سويطاء *suwaytāʼ*, Broth containing a large proportion of onions, pulse, &c.

A سويعة *suwayʻat*, (dim. of ساعة *sāʻat*) A short hour, a brief space of time.

P سوي غامش *sūy ghāmish*, The tuning of musical instruments. Compliments, flattery paid.

A سويق *suwīk*, (pl. اسوقة *aswikat*) The meal of wheat, barley, or vetches pounded small and fried. Barley deprived of its husks, pounded and made into balls, ptisan. Wine.

A سويل *suwīl*, Equal.

P سوين *suwīn*, Household utensils, as pots, kettles, cups, and saucers.

A سويوخة *suwaywikhat*, (dim. of سواخي *suwākha'*) A little softish earth, in which the feet sink.

A سه *sah* or *suh*, Buttocks, hips, podex.

P سه *sih*, Three. سه فرزند اخشيجان *sih farzandi akhshījān*, Animals, vegetables, and minerals.

A سها *suha'*, An obscure star in the Lesser Bear.

A سهاء *sihāʼ*, (pl. of سهو *sahw*) Stillnesses. Kindnesses. (pl. of سهوة *sahwat*, q.v.)

A سهاد *suhād*, Inability of sleeping, wakefulness.

A سهار *suhār*, Wakefulness, watching.

A سهّار *sahhār*, Watchful, a watcher.

P سه اسبه *sih asba*, Haste. Swift, expeditious.

A سهاف *suhāf*, A disease in which the thirst cannot be quenched.

A سهّاك *sahhāk*, Eloquent, rapid in utterance.

A سهالة *sahālat*, A being easy or soft.

P سهاله *suhāla*, Filings of gold or silver.

A سهام *sahām*, The scorching of the wind. Cobwebs or gossamer playing in the sun during the hottest part of the day. Summer-heat. A change, alteration. *Sihām*, (pl. of سهم *sahm*) Lots, chances. Arrows, either for shooting or drawing lots *Suhām*, (v. n. of سهم) Being lean, extenuated, emaciated. Changing colour, turning pale. Leanness. A disease incident to camels.

A سهّام *sahhām*, An archer.

P سه انگشت *sih angusht*, (or سه شاخ *sih shākh*) A three-pronged fork with which they turn corn.

A سهاوة *sahāwat*, Easiness, smoothness of pace.

P سه ايوان دماغ *sih aywāni dimāgh*, The three chambers of the brain, which are the seats of reflection, imagination, and memory.

A سهب *sahb*, A wide-extended plain or desert. A salt-marsh. A taking, seizing. A horse going with long steps, or at full gallop. *Suhb*, (pl. سهوب *suhūb*) A pathless desert or tract. Level ground.

A سهبة *sahbat*, Deep (well).

A سهبرة *sahbarat*, Name of a well.

P سه برگه *sih barga*, (Three leaf) Trefoil.

A سهبل *sahbal*, Bold, brave.

P سه بندي *sih bandī*, A soldier employed in collecting revenue. An establishment of peons, &c. مدام سه بندي *mudām-sihbandī*, A fixed establishment. هنگامه سه بندي *hangāma-sihbandī*, A temporary establishment.

P سه پاي *sih pāy*, A tripod. A high three-legged stool, used in mosques when lighting the lamps.

P سه پايه *sih pāya*, A tripod. سه پايهٔ هوائي *sih pāyaʼi hawāʼī*, The airy tripod, *i.e.* the Eagle (a constellation).

P سه پرك *sih parak*, (or سه پره *sih para*) Lines drawn on sand for playing at dice.

P سه پهر *sih pahar*, The third watch. Afternoon.

P سه پهلو *sih pahlū*, Trilateral.

P سه تا *sih tā*, Threefold. Three-stringed.

P سه تار *sih-tār*, (or سه تاره *sih tāra*) A guitar. The Great Bear.

A سهج *sahj*, (v. n. of سهج) Pounding (spices). Travelling all night. Sweeping clean (as wind the ground). Blowing hard.

P سه جاده *sihjāda*, (Three ways) Length, breadth, and thickness. Truth, law, and religious rites.

A سهجرة *sahjarat*, A running as if frightened.

P سه چند *sih chand*, Thrice as much.

P سه خوان *sih khwān*, A Trinitarian, Christian.

P سه خواهران *sih khwāharān*, (or سه دختر *sih dukhtar*) Three stars in the Great Bear.

A سهد *sahd*, Beautiful, elegant. *Suhd*, Watchfulness, sleeplessness. *Sahad*, (v. n. of سهد) Waking. Being unable to sleep. *Suhud*, One who sleeps little: vigilant, quick, sharp.

A سهدة *sahdat*, A thing worthy of credence. *Suhdat*, Watching, inability to sleep.

A سهدر *sahdar*, Far-distant (country).

P سه درك *sih darak*, Lines drawn upon the sand for playing at games of hazard.

P سه دوري *sih dūrī*, The three distances, *i.e.* length, breadth, and thickness.

P سه دير *sih dayr*, (Three cupola) Name of an oratory built for Bahrām gūr Numān bin Munzir.

P سهر *sihr*, An ox. A cow.

A سهر *sahar*, (v. n. of سهر) Watching, remaining awake. Wakefulness, watching.

P سهراب *suhrāb*, Name of the son of Rustam Zāl.

A سهران *sahrān*, Watching.

A سهرة *suharat*, Sleepless, wide-awake.

P سه رنگ *sih rang*, Three-coloured. A silk.
P سه روح *sih rūh*, Animals, vegetables, minerals.
P سه رود *sih rūd*, Three-stringed (guitar).
P سه روز *sih roz*, Three days.
P سه روزه *sih roza*, Of three days continuance.
A سهريز *suhrīz* or *sihrīz*, A sort of date.
P سه ساله *sih sāla*, Three-yearly, triennial.
P سهستن *sahastan*, To fear, to dread.
P سه سنبر *sih sambar*, Water-mint.
P سه سنبل *sih sumbul*, Mother of thyme.
P سه شاخ *sih shākh*, (Three branches) Animals, vegetables, and minerals.
P سه شنبه *sih shambih*, Tuesday.
P سه علم *sih ɛilm*, Three sciences, theological, natural, and mathematical.
P سه غرفهٔ مغز *sih ghurfa-i maghz* (or دماغ *dimāgh*) The three chambers of the brain, *i.e.* of reflection, imagination, and memory.

A سهف *sahf*, (v. n. of سهف) Weltering in blood, and writhing (a murdered man). The scales of a fish. *Sahaf*, (v. n. of سهف) Being extremely thirsty. Intense thirst.

P سه فرزند *sih farzand*, (or سه نتاج *sih nitāj*) (Three children) The three kingdoms of nature, animal, vegetable, and mineral.

A سهك *sahk*, (v. n. of سهك) Blowing with violence (wind). Sweeping the dust from the ground (wind). Rubbing. Wearing. Crushing, crumbling. *Sahak*, (v. n. of سهك) Smelling fetidly (meat or sweat). The smell of fish. The rust of iron. *Sahik*, Fetid (from the smell of fish or rust).

A سهكة *sahkat* or *suhakat*, The smell of rust of iron. Stink of fish or tainted meat.

P سه كنجه *sih kunja*, Triangular. A triangle.
P سه كوهك *sih kūhak*, A twig. A triangular thorny plant.
P سه كان *sih gān*, Triple.
P سه گانه *sih gāna*, A drinking-cup. Triple.
P سه گل *sih gul*, A sort of mulberry; a blackberry.
P سه گنبدان *sih gumbadān*, Name of a fortress.
P سه گوشه *sih gosha*, A triangle: thistle: caltrop.
P سه گوهر *sih gohar*, Three substances, *i. e.* animals, vegetables, and minerals.

A سهل *sahl*, (pl. سهول *suhūl*) A plain, level country, soft soil. Sandy-bedded (river). A crow. Easy (tempered). Easy, soft. One who has little flesh on his cheeks. سهل الخدّين *sahlu'l khaddayn*, Smooth-cheeked. *Sahil*, A soft-bedded river. Easy, soft. Sandy (soil).

A سهلة *sahlat*, Soft, plain ground. *Sihlat*, Large sand (especially what comes from the bladder in gravelly complaints). Soil carried down by water, detrita. Sand (especially large and coarse). *Sahilat*, (A country) abounding in soft soil.

P سهل گو *sahl-go*, A soft or easy speaker.

A سهليّ *sahliy*, Growing on a sandy plain. *Suhliy*, Soft. Feeding on a plain (cattle).

P سهم *sahm* or *sahim*, Terror, dread.

A سهم *sahm*, (v. n. of سهم) Beating (another) at casting lots. (pl. سهام *sihām*) An arrow either for shooting or for drawing lots. Name of a constellation. A transverse beam (of a house). (pl. سهمان *suhmān* and سهمة *suhmat*) A portion, lot. A measure of six cubits. A stone at the mouth of a trap for catching lions, which falls and keeps them in. The segment of a circle. A versed sine. سهم الرامى *sahmu'r rāmī*, Name of a star. سهم الغيب *sahmu'l ghayb*, The invisible arrow, the fatal shaft, fate, death. سهم قضا *sahmi kazā*, The arrow of destiny. *Suhum*, Radial lines, rays of the sun. Thirst. Intense heat. Intellectual men, philosophers.

A سهمان *suhmān*, (pl. of سهم) Lots, portions.

P سه ماه *sih māh*, The three mathematical dimensions, length, breadth, and thickness.

P سه ماهه *sih māha*, Of three months' duration.

A سهمة *suhmat*, Kindred, relationship. A lot, portion. Propinquity. (pl. of سهم *sahm*) Lots, portions.

P سهمگين *sahmgīn*, Formidable, fearful, awful.
P سهمناك *sahimnāk*, Horrible. Frightened.
P سهميدن *sahmīdan*, To dread, to fear.
P سهند *sahand*, A mountain in Azarbayjān.

A سهنساه *sihinsāh* or *sihunsāh*, At the end of every thing; as, افعل ذلك سهنساه *afɛalu zālika sihinsāh*, I will do that after every thing else.

P سه نوبت *sih nawbat*, Childhood, manhood, and old age. Prayer at dawn, sunrise, and noon. The three times a-day that music was played before the royal palace (a practice established by Alexander, and increased to five times by Sanjar).

A سهو *sahw*, (v. n. of سها for سهو) Forgetting. Blundering through inattention. Neglecting, omitting, leaving undone. Not reaching the mark. Conceiving, although menstruous (a woman). Easy, smooth-going (camel). An error, fault, mistake, blunder, inadvertency. Omission. (pl. سهاء *sihāʼ*) Modesty, humility, gentleness, lenity, quietness. Sport, play, pastime. Easy. Cold, limpid water. سهو الانسان من اللسان *sahwu'l insān mini'l lisān*, (A proverb) A man's fall is caused by the tongue. سهو قلم *sahwi kalam*, A slip of the pen, an error in writing. سهو كاتب *sahwi kātib*, An error of the copyist. P سهو كردن *sahw kardan*, To make a mistake, blunder, neglect.

A سهوّ *suhūw*, (v.n. of سها for سهو) Forgetting. Blundering through inattention. Neglecting, omitting, leaving undone.

A سهوا *sahwan*, Inadvertently, erroneously.

A سهواء *sahwāʼ*, An hour, part of the night, especially the first watch. Name of a horse.

A سهوان *sahwān*, Careless, negligent.

A سهوب *suhūb*, (pl. of سهب *suhb*) Widely-extended deserts. سهوب الفلاة *suhūbu'l falāt*, Trackless parts of a desert.

A سهوة *sahwat*, (pl. سهاء *sihāʼ*) A reposing bench raised before the door of an Arabian house. A rock, a huge hard stone. A flexible bow. A small warehouse or cellar. A clay vessel in which grain is kept. A small window, hole, or niche in a wall, especially where any thing is placed. A tent or canopy. A veil or awning in front of a house. Three or four pieces of wood joined together, upon which any thing is laid, a rack. (A she-camel) which goes gently and smoothly.

A سهوج *sahūj* or *sahwaj*, Violent (wind).

A سهود *sahwad* or *sahūd*, Fresh, tender (youth), tall and strong. *Suhūd*, Wakefulness.

A سهوق *sahwak*, A liar. Full of sap and moisture (trunk of a tree). Long-legged. Storm, squall.

A سهوّق *sahawwak*, A taker of long strides.

A سهوك *sahūk*, Violent wind, storm. An eagle. *Suhūk*, (v. n. of سهك) Running lightly (a horse).

A سهوكة *sahwakat*, (v.n. of سهوك Q) Affecting badly, destroying. Driving (an animal) gently. *Suhūkat*, The stink of a man sweating.

A سهول *sahūl*, Aperient, laxative, cathartic. *Suhūl*, (pl. of سهل *sahl*) Plains. Light soils.

A سهولة *suhūlat*, (v.n. of سهل) Being soft and level (ground). Being easy. Facility, ease, easiness. Smoothness, softness of ground, plainness.

A سهوم *sahūm*, Austere, stern, grim. An eagle. *Suhūm*, (v.n. of سهم) Being lean. Turning pale. Grimness, crabbedness, austerity.

P سهى *sahī*, Erect (cypress). Fresh, young.
A سهيٰ *suha'*, A small star in the Lesser Bear.
A سهيب *sahyab*, Deep (well).
P سهيت *sahīt*, A lofty edifice.
P سه يك *sih yak*, A third.
A سهيكة *sahīkat*, A sort of food.

P A سهيل *suhayl*, The star Canopus. سهيل عرب *suhayli ɛarab*, Name of a celebrated Arab.

A سهيلة *suhaylat*, Name of a proverbial liar.
P سهيلى *suhaylī*, Relating to Canopus.
P سهيم *sahīm*, A partner. Equal, even.

P سى *say*, A stone. *Sī*, Thirty. سى و دو *sī u du*, Thirty-two (implying the teeth).

A سى *say*, (in grammar) A particle prefixed to the aorist, and giving it a future signification.

A سىّ *sayy*, A desert. *Siy*, The conveniences of life, enjoyments. A desert. Like. Even, level.

A سىء *sayʼ* or *sīʼ*, Milk in the udder, or flowing out without being milked.

A سىّء *sayyiʼ*, Bad, wicked. سىّء الاختيار *sayyiʼu'l* (or سىء *sayʼu'l*) *ikhtiyār*, One who makes a bad choice.

P سيا *sayā*, Senna. *Siyā*, Black.
A سياب *sayāb*, *sayyāb*, or *suyyāb*, An unripe date.
P سياب *siyāb*, Ornament. Life. Adorn thou.
A سيابة *sayābat*, Wine. One unripe date.
P سيابيدن *siyābīdan*, To adorn, array, prepare.
P سيا پوش *siyā-posh*, A public situation. Testimony taken by a judge.

A سيات *siyāt*, (pl. of سية *siyat*) Horns of a bow, or the notches into which the strings go.

A سيّآت *sayyi-āt*, (pl. of سيّئة) Sins, crimes.

A سياج *siyāj*, A thorn-hedge, fence. A wall.

A سيّاح *sayyāh*, A traveller. A pilgrim.

A سياحة *siyāhat*, (v.n. of ساح for سيح) Travelling, going on pilgrimage. Moving, turning (as a shadow). Flowing on the surface of the ground (water). A journey, voyage. A pilgrimage.

A سياخ *siyākh*, Workers in clay.

A سيادة *siyādat*, Dominion, rule, sovereignty. Relationship to Muhammad by regular descent from Fātima. (Such persons are called Sayyids).

P سيار *siyār*, A press for wine, cider, or oil. Bread of barley, beans, and millet. Household furniture.

A سيّار *sayyār*, One who wanders, walks much, or takes the air for amusement. A body of travellers. A planet.

A سيّارة *sayyārat*, (fem. of سيّار *sayyār*) (A woman) who walks much. A body of travellers, a caravan. A planet or planets.

P سياري *siyārī*, Galangale; sweet cane.

P سياس *siyās*, Tale-bearing.

A سياس *siyās*, (pl. of سائس *sā,is*) Grooms.

A سيّاس *sayyās*, Who guards or governs well.

A سياسة *siyāsat*, (v. n. of ساس for سوس) Ruling, governing, managing. Keeping within due bounds and limits. Chastising, punishing. Government, administration of justice. Administration. Public punishment, torture. Chastisement, torment, pang, agony. P سياست جاني *siyāsati jānī*, Capital punishment. A سياست شرعيّه *siyāsati sharʻiya*, Legal punishment. P سياست كردن *siyāsat kardan*, To govern. To punish with infamy, torture. سياست مدن *siyāsati mudun*, The art of government, civic economy. سياست نمودن *siyāsat namūdan*, To punish, chastise.

P سياستگاه *siyāsat-gāh*, Place of execution.

P سياسر *sayāsar*, A starling. *Siyāsar*, A pen ready cut.

A سياسي *sayāsī*, (pl. of سيساء *sīsā,*) The ligatures of the vertebræ or joints of the back. The withers of horses.

A سياسي *siyāsiy*, Politico-economic, relating to the science of government.

A سياط *siyāt*, The stalks of leeks with their زماليق *zamālīk* upon them. Name of a celebrated singer. (pl. of سوط *sawt*) Scourges.

A سياع *sayāʻ* or *siyāʻ*, Clay mixed with straw for plastering walls. *Sayāʻ*, The frankincense tree, or a tree resembling it. Grease rubbed on a leathern bottle to make it water-tight.

A سيّاف *sayyāf*, Armed, begirt, or striking with a sword, a swordsman. A gladiator. A possessor of a sword. An executioner. A sword-cutler.

A سيّافة *sayyāfat*, (pl. of سيّاف *sayyāf*) Sword-cutlers. Possessors of swords.

A سيافي *sayāfī*, (pl. of سيف) Shores, strands.

A سياق *siyāk*, (v. n. of ساق for سوق) Hurting the leg. Being at the point of death. Sending (a marriage portion to a bride). A dowry.

A سياقة *siyākat*, (v.n. of ساق for سوق) Driving, stimulating, urging onward. Driving in one fashion. Leading away. Numeration by the Arabic alphabet.

A سياقلة *sayākilat*, (pl. of سيقل) Polishers.

P سياكاسه *siyā-kāsa*, A prisoner. A miser.

P سياكيز *siyākīz*, Coarse woollen cloth.

P سيال *sayāl*, Jasmine (either white or yellow).

A سيال *siyāl*, (pl. of سيالة *sayālat*) Certain tall, thorny, and milky plants. Tall سمر *samur* trees.

A سيّال *sayyāl*, Current, rapid, flowing like a torrent. (A cloud) pouring forth much rain. A species of large fish. ياقوت سيّال *yākūti sayyāl*, A brilliant ruby.

A سيالة *sayālat*, (pl. سيال *siyāl*) Name of a tall, thorny, milky plant. A tall سمر *samur* plant.

A سيّالة *sayyālat*, A torrent.

P سيالخ *sayālikh*, A kind of prickle: a caltrop.

P سيام *siyām*, The kingdom of Siam. *Siyām* or *sayām*, Name of a mountain near Samarkand.

P سي ام *sī um*, The thirtieth.

P سيامك *siyāmak*, Solitary, alone, lonely. The son of Kayūmars; also one of the twelve champions.

P سيان *sayān*, Ivy.

A سيان *siyānī*, Two (things) alike.

P سياوخش *siyāwakhsh*, Intellectual delights. Name of the son of Kay Kāwus.

P سياوخش آباد *siyāwakhsh-ābād*, (or سياوخش گرد *siyāwakhsh-gird*) Name of a city in Tūrān.

P سياوش *siyāwush* or *siyāwash*, Name of the father of Cyrus (he is the same as سياوخش *siyāvakhsh*). A kind of red duck. خون سياوشان *khūni siyāwushān*, Dragon's blood.

P سياوش آباد *siyāwush-ābād*, (or سياوش گرد *siyāwush-gird*) Name of a city in Tūrān.

P سياه *siyāh*, Black. Bad, unhappy, unlucky. Drunk. An Arabian or Ethiopian slave. The fourth line on the cup of Jamshed. Name of a horse of Isfandiyār. The fourteenth chapter of the Zand. سياه و سفيد فرق كردن *siyāh u safed fark kardan*, To distinguish black from white. To read a book.

P سياهان *siyāhān*, (pl.) Arabians. Ethiopians.

P سياه بادام *siyāh-bādām*, (Black-almond) The eye of a mistress.

P سياه بخت *siyāh-bakht*, Unlucky, hapless.

P سياهبختي *siyāh-bakhtī*, Ill-luck, misfortune.

P سياه بويه *siyāh-boya*, The black and odoriferous coriander.

P سياه بيد *siyāh-bīd*, A kind of willow.

P سياه پستان *siyāh-pistān*, (Unlucky-breast) A woman who loses every child whom she suckles.

P سياه پوش *siyāh-posh*, Clothed in sable. A mourner. A groom. A life-guardsman, serjeant, or officer who clears the way for a great man. Master of the hall of audience. The nightly watch. A keeper of wild beasts.

P سياه پير *siyāh-pīr*, Late in growing old, favoured with a green old age.

P سياه جام *siyāh-jām*, Blackish, dark-coloured.

P سياه چرده *siyāh-charda*, (or سياه چرته *siyāh-charta*) Dark brown. اسب سياه چرده *asbi siyāh-charda*, A dark brown horse.

P سياه چشم *siyāh-chashm*, Black-eyed; unkind.

P سياهچه *siyāhcha*, Blackish brown. A sort of doe.

P سياه خانه *siyāh-khāna*, A haunted or ill-fated house. A prison. A weather-beaten tent. سياه خانهٔ وحشت *siyāh-khāna,i wahshat*, The world. The grave. (Dark house of dreariness.)

P سياه دارو *siyāh-dārū*, A kind of wild vine.

P سياه دانه *siyāh-dāna*, Coriander-seed.

P سياه دست *siyāh-dast*, (Black-handed) Avaricious, stingy, vile.

P سياه دل *siyāh-dil*, Black-hearted.

P سياه دلي *siyāh-dilī*, Malevolence.

P سياه رو *siyāh-rū*, A criminal (from the custom of blacking their faces). Unlucky, disgraced.

P سياه روز *siyāh-roz*, Unhappy. Misfortune.

P سياه زبان *siyāh-zabān*, Foul-mouthed.

P سياه سفيد *siyāh-safed*, Ash-coloured.

P سياه فام *siyāh-fām*, Black-coloured.

P سياه كار *siyāh-kār* (or كرد *kard*), Wicked.

P سياه كاري *siyāh-kārī*, (Black art) Wickedness, lewdness. Oppression. Roguery, deceit.

P سياه كاسه *siyāh-kāsa*, Black-cup, *i.e.* miser.

P سياه گليم *siyāh-gilīm*, Unfortunate.

P سياه گوش *siyāh-gosh*, Black ear, an animal of the panther kind, wherewith they hunt deer: lynx.

P سياه گون *siyāh-gūn*, Black-coloured.

P سياه گوني *siyāh-gūnī*, Blackness of colour.

P سياه مست *siyāh-mast*, Dead-drunk.

P سياه نامه *siyāh-nāma*, A worthless wretch.

P سياهويه *siyāhwiya*, Coriander-seed.

P سياهه *siyāha*, Blackness. An account-book. A written account. A list, inventory. A whore. سياههٔ چشم *siyāha,i chashm*, The black of the eye.

P سياهي *siyāhī*, Blackness. Darkness. Shade. Ink. A tincture for dyeing the beard black. A black servant. سياهي ء نوشتن *siyāhī,i nawishtan*, (or سياهي ء دوات *siyāhī,i dawāt*) Writing-ink.

P سياهي دان *siyāhīdān*, An inkstand.

P سياهي ده *siyāhī-dih*, One who puts another to the blush. Imparting strength. Opposing, resisting.

A سيائد *sayā,id*, (pl. of سائد) Princes, lords.

A سيائق *sayā,ik*, (pl. of سيّقة *sayyikat*) Hunters' ambushes.

A سيب *sayb*, (v. n. of ساب for سيب) Flowing (water). Running or walking fast. Going where they please (cattle). (pl. سيوب *suyūb*) A present. Favour, benefit. An oar. The hair of a horse's tail. A horse's mane. *Sīb*, A place where water flows. The course of a stream.

P سيب *seb,* An apple. The hair on a horse's forehead and tail. سيب غبغب *sebi ghabghab,* The chin. سيب كوهي *sebi kohī,* A crab-apple. *Sīb,* Confounded, astonished, amazed. Bewilderment. سيب و تيب *sīb u tīb,* Confounded, astonished, bewildered. Bewilderment.

A سيّب *suyyab,* (pl. of سائبة *sāʼibat*) Set at liberty (as slaves or she-camels which have been delivered of ten female colts).

P سيب زار *sebzār,* An apple-orchard.

P سيب فروش *seb-farosh,* A costermonger.

A سيبنة *sībannat,* A bird found in Egypt.

P سيبوس *saybūs,* (or سيبوسن) Fleawort-seed.

P سيبويه *seboyah,* (from سيب *seb* and بويه *boya*) The perfume of an apple. *Sībawayh,* Name of عمرو بن عثمان *ʼamr bin ʼusmān,* a native of Shirāz, and a very celebrated Arabic grammarian.

I سيبيا *sībiyā,* Cuttle-fish, sepia.

P سيپارة *sī pāra,* One portion of the thirty into which the Kurʼān has been divided (like the psalms with us: from سي *sī,* Thirty, and پارة *pāra,* Piece, division, section).

P سيپوس *saypūs,* Lint-seed.

A سئة *siʼat,* The horn of a bow.

A سية *siyat,* Equality. Like. (pl. سيات *siyāt*) The horn of a bow, or the notch into which the string goes.

P سيج *sayj,* (or سيچ *saych,* Currants. *Sīj* or *sīch,* Trouble. Preparation, order.

A سيجان *sījān,* (pl. of ساج *sāj*) Indian plantains, teak-trees. Green sashes rolled round the head, and hanging down behind.

P سيچغنه *sīchughana* or *sīchaghana,* A sparrow-hawk. A red-headed sparrow.

P سيچيدن *sīchīdan,* To prepare, equip, arm, fit out (one's self or another). To weigh.

A سيح *sayh,* (v. n. of ساح for سيح) Flowing over the surface of the earth (water). Travelling, going on a pilgrimage. Moving about (a shadow). Pasturing about freely (cattle). Running water. A striped garment.

A سيحان *sayahān,* (v. n. of ساح for سيح) Flowing on the surface of the ground (water). Travelling, going on pilgrimage.

A سيحف *sayhaf, siyahf,* or *sīhaf,* Broad or long (spear-head).

A سيحفانيّ *sayhafānīy,* Long-bearded.

A سيحفيّ *sayhafīy,* Eloquent. Long-bearded.

A سيحوج *sayhūj,* An ass running under full speed.

P سيحون *sayhūn,* The river Jaxartes.

A سيخ *saykh,* (and سيخان *sayakhān*) (v. n. of ساخ for سيخ) Sinking, subsiding into any thing soft.

P سيخ *sīkh,* A roasting-spit. A wooden skewer used in fastening the mouth of a sack. Any thing like a nipple (especially a machine of leather, which, in Persia, they fill with milk to give to sucking infants instead of the teat). The top of a small flagon. A furrow made by the plough. A drinking-cup. An iron instrument with which they stuff pack-saddles. A sort of yoke for carrying burdens.

P سيخ پر *sīkh-par,* (Spit-feather) Unfledged.

P سيخچه *sīkhcha,* A little spit, spike, skewer.

P سيخدار *sīkh-dār,* The holm-tree.

P سيخك *sīkhak,* A small spit: a spike. Small bits of roast meat.

P سيخگاه يافتن *sīkh-gāh yāftan,* To discover the weak side or vulnerable part.

P سيخور *sīkhūr,* (or سيخول) A porcupine.

A سئد *saʼid,* Festering (wound).

A سيد *sīd,* A wolf. A lion.

A سيّد *sayyid,* (pl. سادة *sādat* and سيائد *sayāʼid*) A lord, prince. The title of the chiefs of the family of Muhammad, descended from his daughter Fātima by Alīy. Generous, liberal. Wise, learned. Meek, mild. An aged goat. السيّد *as' sayyid,* St. John the Baptist. سيّد الابرار *sayyidu'l abrār,* Chief of the righteous. سيّد الانام *sayyidu'l anām,* Prince of mankind and of all living creatures, *i. e.* Muhammad (who is likewise called سيّد الآفاق *sayyidu'l āfāk,* Lord of the universe). سيّد الانبياء *sayyidu'l ambiyāʼ,* (or سيّد المرسلين *sayyidu'l mursalīn*) First of the prophets, or head of the apostles. سيّد البشر *sayyidu'l bashar,* Prince of mortals. *Siyad,* An aged goat.

A سيدارة *sīdārat,* A cloth worn by women to prevent their head-dress from being soiled by the unguent or pomatum of their hair. A fillet or wreath for fastening a lady's head-dress.

A سيداق *saydāk,* A kind of tree, the ashes of which are used in bleaching.

A السيّدان *as' sayyidāni,* (dual) Hasan and Husayn, the sons of Alīy by Fātima.

A سيدانة *sīdānat,* A wolf.

A سيّدة *sayyidat,* (pronounced سيده *sayda*) A lady, a princess, especially the wife or daughter of a Sayyid or a descendant of Alīy. سيّدة المخدّرات *sayyidatu'l mukhaddarāt,* The princess or chief of chaste virgins (a title given to sultānas and women of rank). سيّدة نساء العالمين *sayyidatu nisāʼi'l ʼālamīn,* Princess of womankind, *i. e.* Fātima.

A P سيد خانه *sed-khāna,* (corruption of صحّت خانه *sihhat-khāna*) A necessary, privy.

P سيدره *sī dara,* A kind of game.

A سيدودة *saydūdat,* (v. n. of ساد for سود) Being chief (of a tribe), reigning over, governing.

P سيدي *saydī,* A cricket, a kind of locust.

A سيّدي *sayyidī* or *sīdī,* My lord.

A سيديّ *saydīy,* Relating to a chief, lordly.

A سيذاق *sayzāk,* A hawk.

A سيذقان *sayza* or *sayzukān,* A kind of hawk.

A سيذنوق *sayzanūk,* A kind of falcon.

A سيذونيق *sayzūnīk,* A large kind of hawk.

A سير *sayr,* (v. n. of سار for سير) Walking, perambulating, amusing one's self. Living (with others). Causing one to go. Obtaining, becoming established (as a custom). Striking with a strap or leathern thong. Happening, coming to pass. A journey. March, pace. A spectacle, show, an agreeable prospect, or any similar amusement. (pl. سيور *suyūr*) An oblong strip of leather, thong. A shoe-latchet. Acts and deeds. P سير رفتن *sayr raftan,* To walk, to go to see any thing. To behold with delight. سير كردن *sayr kardan,* To walk or travel for amusement. سير نمودن *sayr namūdan,* To travel. سير و شكار *sayr u shikār,* The sports of the field. A *Siyar,* (pl. of سيرة *sīrat*) Virtues, morals, qualities, dispositions, acts, deeds. P شه نيكو سير *shahi nekū-siyar,* A king of noble qualities.

P سير *ser,* Full, satiated, sated, tired. A weight of 15 miskāls. Name of a city. سير آمدن *ser āmadan,* To be tired, disgusted. To be full and independent. سير شدن *ser shudan,* To be full, independent. To repose. سير كردن *ser kardan,* To fill, saturate. *Sīr,* Garlic. Water-mint.

A سيراء *siyarāʼ,* A silk yellow-striped vest. Pure gold. A sort of plant. A crust adhering to a date-stone. The pericardium. A leafless palm-branch.

P سيراب *serāb,* Moist, wet, humid, full of water, succulent, fresh, juicy. Blooming. سيراب كردن *serāb kardan,* To quench the thirst. سيراب گشتن *serāb gashtan,* To be completely watered (as cattle), to have the thirst quenched. To be saturated with water, or irriguous.

P سيرابه *sīrāba,* Food made of curds and garlic.

P سيرابي *serābī,* Aquatic, humid. Freshness. Satiety, repletion (from drinking water).

P سيراچه *sīrācha,* An inclosure for a tent.

P سيراف *sīrāf,* Name of a city that formerly existed on the Persian gulf.

A سيران *sayrān,* A walk for recreation: diversion, pleasure. *Sīrān,* (pl. of سور *sūr*) City-walls.

P سيرانگاه *sayrān-gāh,* A place of recreation.

P سيراوه *sīrāwa,* A dish of milk and oxygal.

P سير پنير *sīr-panīr,* A dish of garlic and cheese.

A سيرة *sayrat,* A mode of walking. A blow with a leathern strap or thong. *Sīrat,* (pl. سير *siyar*) A motion, going. Act, deed. Form, disposition, temperament, nature, morals, qualities. Institution, regulation, mode of living. A driving. Provisions, victuals. *Suyarat,* One who walks much.

P سير سور *sīr-sūr,* (Feast of garlic) Name of the 14th day of the month, on which they eat garlic, send their lads to school, or bind them to some trade.

P سيرش *sīrash,* A veil; a puckered female head-dress or veil of the finest cloth, particularly such as are worn by brides, of a crimson colour.

P سيرغ *serigh,* A cluster of grapes.

P سيرفروش *sīr-farosh,* A seller of garlic.

P سيركوب *sīr-kob,* A mortar wherein garlic is pounded.

P سیرگاه *sayr-gāh*, A passage, pass, thoroughfare. A place of recreation. A theatre.

P سیرم *sīram*, Raw deer-skins cut into thongs, used in sewing saddles. A hawk's leash. The shoemaker's strap which binds the last to his knee.

P سیرمان *sīrmān*, A ruby. Embroidered silk.

P سیرمو *sīrmū*, Mountain-garlic.

P سیرنگ *sīrang*, Thirty colours. The simurgh or عنقا *ʿankā*. Any thing impossible, or which the mind cannot grasp. The unsearchable God.

P سیرو *sīro*, A porcupine: a hedgehog.

A سیرورة *sayrūrat*, A walking, a perambulating.

P سیرون *serūn*, Cold of a moderate degree.

P سیرة *sayra*, A certain melodious little bird.

P سیری *serī*, Fulness, repletion, satiety.

P سیرین *sīrīn*, Dressed with garlic (سیر *sīr*).

P سیرینگاه *sīrīn-gāh*, A royal throne.

P سیز *sez*, Sharp, strong, vehement.

P سیزده *sezdah*, Thirteen.

P سیزدهم *sezdahum*, The thirteenth.

P سیزگی *sezagī*, Hardness, violence, suffering.

P سیس *sīs*, Freckles upon the face or other parts of the body. Leaping and jumping. A swift horse. A wine-vessel.

A سیساء *sīsāʼ*, (pl. سیاسی *sayāsī*) Ligatures of the vertebræ or joints of the back. Withers of a horse. The back of an ass. A limit, boundary.

A سیساءة *sīsāʼat*, Ground soft and trodden down.

A سیساب *saysāb*, Name of a tree.

P سیسارون *sīsārūn*, The stem of the coriander. A certain water-plant with leaves so large that they make cups of them.

P سیسالك *sīsālak*, (or سیسالنگ) The wagtail.

G سیسالیوس *sīsāliyūs*, Assafœtida.

A سیسب *saysab*, Name of a tree, from which arrows are made.

A سیسبان *saysabān*, A kind of grape. *Saysabān*, (or سیسبی *saysaba'*) Name of a tree.

P سیسبان *sīsabān*, Seed of cinquefoil.

P سی ستارۀ پاك *sī sitāraʼi pāk*, The thirty teeth.

P سیستان *sīstān*, Sijistān (the ancient Drangiana), a country lying to the eastward of Fārsistān, or Persia Proper. The famous Rustam held this country as a fief under the kings of Persia.

P سیستن *sīstan*, To leap, bound. To flee away.

P سیسخانه *says-khāna*, Baggage-horses employed in war.

P سیسرك *sīsirk*, A weevil.

P سیسرو *sīsarū*, A weevil. Wall-lice.

P سیسك *sīsak*, A weevil. A sort of pulse.

G سیسنبر *sīsambar*, (or سیسنبرون *sīsambarūn*) Water-mint. Mother of thyme.

A سیطرة *saytarat*, (v. n. of سیطر Q) Presiding as inspector. Being appointed, set over. Prevailing, overcoming.

A سیطل *saytal*, A vessel with one handle. A one-handled bowl used in baths. A tall man.

A سیع *sayʿ*, (v. n. of ساع for سیع) Flowing (water or wine). Pasturing freely without a keeper. Water that flows along the surface of the ground.

A سیعاء *sīʿāʼ*, (or *siyaʿāʼ*) Part of the night.

A سیغ *saygh*, (v. n. of ساغ for سوغ) Swallowing with ease. Born immediately after another, as a next brother.

P سیغ *sīgh*, Beautiful, excellent. Body of men, band of soldiers, crowd. A house with many windows.

A سیّغ *sayyigh*, (or سیّغ لیّغ *sayyigh layyigh*) Sweet (water), which easily flows down the throat.

P سیغر *sīghur*, A porcupine.

P سیغود *sayghūd*, Humility, submission.

P سیغور *sayghūr*, Nobleness of mind, mental energy, ambition.

A سیف *sayf*, (v. n. of ساف for سیف) Striking with a sword. Being cracked about the nails (the hand). (pl. اسیاف *asyāf*, سیوف *suyūf*, اسیف *asyuf*, and مسیفة *masīfat*) A sword, cimeter, falchion, sabre (for which, according to the Kāmus, there are upwards of a thousand names). The hair of a horse's tail. The sword-fish. سیف الغراب *sayfu'l ghurāb*, The crow's sword, a name for the plant دلبوث *dalabūs*. *Sīf*, (pl. اسیاف *asyāf*) A bank, margin, coast, shore, strand, beach (applied particularly to the southern coast of Arabia). The sword-fish. A fibrous excrescence at the roots of the palm-branches. السیف الطویل *as' sīfu't tawīl*, The long coast, *i.e.* The coast of Barbary.

A سئف *saʼif*, Cracked (nail or hand).

A سیفان *sayfān*, (fem. سیفانة *sayfānat*) Long and slender; shaped like a sword.

A H سیف بان *sayf-bān*, A rocket with a sword attached to it.

A سیفة *sīfat*, Distance. The advanced guard, a reconnoitering party.

P سیف زبان *sayf-zabān*, (Sword-tongued) One whose curses prevail.

A سیفنّة *sīfannat*, Name of a bird in Egypt that eats all the leaves of the tree it alights upon.

P سیفور *sayfūr*, Silken stuff of great value.

A سیفی *sayfī*, Cursing.

A سیّق *sayyik*, A rainless cloud wind-driven.

A سیقان *sīkān*, (pl. of ساق *sāk*) Legs, shanks.

A سیّقة *sayyikat*, Whatever an enemy carries off (as cattle, women, or slaves). (pl. سیائق *sayāʼik*) A hunter's lurking place.

A سیقل *sayhal*, (pl. سیاقلة *sayākilat*) A polisher, a furbisher. See صیقل *sayhal*.

P سیك *sīk*, A blight upon corn, mildew, rust, smut. *Si yak*, A third.

A سیكب *saykab*, Flowing, current (water).

P سیكبا *sīk-bā*, A sort of acid broth.

P سیكران *sīkrān*, Black henbane-seed.

A سیكران *saykurān*, Name of an evergreen plant, whose seed is eaten.

P سیك زده *sīk-zada*, Blighted, smutty (corn).

A سیكف *saykaf*, A shoemaker.

P سیكك *sīkak*, A weevil. Mildew.

P سیكل *sīkal*, A blight upon corn.

A سیكم *saykam*, Short-stepping from fatigue.

P سیكی *sīkī*, White-wine vinegar. Wine. New wine boiled down to a third. A goblet of wine.

A سیل *sayl*, (v. n. of سال for سیل) Flowing. Winding in a serpentine form from the forehead to the nose (the blaze on a horse's face). Flowing (water). (pl. سیول *suyūl*) A torrent, current, flux, flood. ماء سیل *māʼ sayl*, Running water. P سیل آب *sayli āb*, A flux of water. A سیل دم *sayli dam*, A torrent of blood. P سیل سیف كردن *sayli sayf kardan*, To invade a country, to fall upon it like a torrent, sword in hand.

P سیلاب *saylāb*, An inundation. سیلاب زعفران *saylābi zaʿfarān*, Flowing blood. Tears.

P سیلابكند *saylāb-kand*, A gulley.

P سیلان *saylān*, Ceylon. *Selān*, Syrup of dates.

A سیلان *sīlān*, That part of a sword or knife which is fixed in the handle, the shank. *Sayalān*, (v. n. of سال for سیل) Flowing. A running.

P سیلانچه *sīlāncha*, A cook.

P سیلانه *sīlāna*, The jujube-tree and fruit.

P سیل آورد *sayl-award*, Brought by a torrent.

A سیلة *sīlat*, A flux of water.

P سی لحن *sī lahn*, Thirty musical notes, tones, or keys (making nearly four octaves), arranged in the following order, and named by the celebrated Persian musician Bārbud:—1. آرایش خورشید *ārāyishi khwurshed* (called also آرایش جهان *ārāyishi jahān*); 2. آیین جمشید *āyīni jamshed*; 3. اورنگی *awrangī*; 4. باغ شیرین *bāghi shīrīn*; 5. تخت طاقدیسی *takhti tāḳdīsī*; 6. حقّۀ كاوس *hukkaʼi kāwus*; 7. راه روح *rāhi rūh*; 8. رامش جان *rāmishi jān* (or رامش جهان *rāmishi jahān*); 9. سبز در سبز *sabz dar sabz*; 10. سروستان *sarwistān*; 11. سرو سهی *sarvi sahī*; 12. شادروان مروارید *shādurwāni marwārīd*; 13. شبدیز *shabdez*; 14. شب فرخ *shabi farkh*; 15. قفل رومی *hufli rūmī*; 16. گنج باد آورد *ganji bād-āward*; 17. گنج گاو *ganji gāv* (or گنج كاوس *ganji kāwus*); 18. گنج سوخته *ganji sokhta*; 19. كین ایرج *kīni īraj*; 20. كین سیاوش *kīni siyāwush*; 21. ماه بركوهان *māhi bar-kūhān*; 22. مشك دانه *mushk-dāna*; 23. مروای نیك *murwāyi nīk*; 24. مشك مالی *mushk-mālī*; 25. مهربانی *mihrbānī* (or مهرگانی *mihrgānī*); 26. ناقوسی *nākūsī*; 27. نوبهاری *naw-bahārī*; 28. نوشین باده *noshīn-bāda*; 29. نیم روز *nīm-roz*; 30. نخچیرگانی *nakhchīrgānī*.

P سیلخیز *sayl-khez*, A torrent. Streaming (eye).

A سیلق *saylak*, Swift (woman).

P سیلك *sīlak* or *sīluk*, A weevil. Mildew.

P سیلگاه *sayl-gāh*, The world.

P سیله *sela*, A herd, drove, or flock. A slap.

P سیلی *sīlī*, A blow upon the nape of the neck with the open hand edgewise (as in killing a rabbit). A musical stringed instrument. سيلي خوردن *sīlī khwurdan*, To receive a blow on the nape of the neck. سيلي زدن *sīlī zadan*, To give such a blow.

P سيلي خوارة *sīlī-khwāra*, Often buffetted.

P سيلي زدة *sīlī-zada*, Cuffed, buffetted.

P سيلي زنندة *sīlī-zananda*, Giver of cuffs, blows.

P سيم *saym*, The neck-yoke of oxen. *Sīm*, Silver. A sort of fish. A wink, nod, sign. Name of a river. سيم سوختة *sīmi sokhta*, Burnt silver. Pure silver. سيم سية *sīmi siyah*, Bad silver, base coin. سيم گاورس دار *sīmi gāwirs-dār*, Moon and stars. سيم ماهي *sīmi māhī*, Scale of a fish. سيم مجبول *sīmi majbūl*, (or سيم مجعول *sīmi majʿūl*) The eye. سيم مذاب *sīmi muzāb*, (Molten silver) Pure water. Pure wine. *Siyum*, The third.

A سئم *saʾim*, Wearied, disgusted.

A سيم *siyam*, (pl. of سامة *sāmat*) Excavations down to wells.

P سيما *sīmā*, Face, forehead, countenance, aspect. Resemblance, similitude. Colour of the face or body. سما سيما *samā-sīmā*, Heavenly-faced. ملك سيما *malak-sīmā*, Having the face of an angel.

A سيما *sīmaʾ*, A mark. *Sīmā* or *siyamā*, Especially, chiefly, principally. Like.

A سيماء *sīmāʾ*, A sign, note.

P سيماب *sīmāb*, Quicksilver, mercury. Malevolent, shameless. سيماب آتشين *sīmābi ātishīn*, (Fiery quicksilver) The sun. سيماب شدن *sīmāb shudan*, To be unsteady, run away, elude pursuit.

P سيماب بار *sīmāb-bār*, Weeping.

P سيماب پا *sīmāb-pā*, A runaway, truant.

P سيماب چشمة *sīmāb-chashma*, A tear.

P سيماب در گوش *sīm-āb dar gosh*, (Quicksilver in the ear) Deaf. Deafness.

P سيماب دل *sīmāb-dil*, Chicken-hearted.

P سيمابي *sīmābī*, Colour of quicksilver.

P سيمازة *sīmāza*, A stone for polishing swords.

P سيماك *sīmāk*, Name of a certain youth.

P سيم اندود *sīm-andūd*, Plated with silver.

P سيم آهنگ *sīm-āhang*, A wild cucumber.

P سيمبر *sīm-bar*, With a bosom like silver. Young. An inn. A palace-gate. سيم برشدن *sīm-bar shudan*, To be young.

P سيمبراسوار *sīmbar-aswār*, (in Gīlān) Arabian guards who attend the door of kings.

P سيم پالا *sīm-pālā*, Silver in a lump ready for being coined. A crucible. A smelter of silver.

P سيم پرست *sīm-parast*, Venal, selfish.

A سيمة *sīmat*, Valuation, appraisement. A bidding, price. A mark made upon cattle. Guise, habit. Pasture, pasturing.

P سيمتاج *sīmtāj*, Avarice, stinginess.

P سيمتن *sīm-tan*, With body fair as silver. زن سيم تن *zani sīm-tan*, A lovely woman silver-hued.

P سيمراخ *sīmrākh*, Asking any thing of God.

P سيمرغ *sīmurgh*, A fabulous bird, often mentioned in Eastern romance, the griffin (see عنقا *ʿanḳā*). *Sīmurgh* signifies literally (Of the size of) thirty birds; it sometimes also denotes the eagle. Name of a learned man from whom زال *zāl* became accomplished. سيمرغ آتشين *sīmurghi ātishīn*, (The fiery Sīmurgh) The sun.

P سيم سياه *sīm-siyāh*, Missletoe.

P سيم كش *sīm-kash*, A gold or silver wire-drawer. One who draws to himself all he can get. *Sīm-kush*, Extravagant, profuse. Eager in the pursuit of wealth; close-fisted, avaricious.

P سيم گل *sīm-gil*, A wash for walls or roofs.

P سيمگون *sīm-gūn*, Silver-coloured. A star.

P سيمناد *sīmnād*, A chapter, section.

P سيمود *saymūd*, (or سيمور) A silken garment.

P سي مهرة ماة صيام *sī muhraʾi māhi siyām*, The thirty days of the month Ramazān.

P سيمه سار *sīma-sār*, Astonished, confounded.

P سيمي *siyumī*, The third.

P سيميا *sīmyā*, Enchantment, fascination, natural magic, *i. e.* charms of mind or person; also poesy and rhetoric.

A سيمياء *sīmiyāʾ*, A mark, a sign.

P سيميازة *sīmyāza*, A stone for polishing swords.

P سيميار *sīm-yār*, One who converses by signs.

P سيمين *sīmīn*, Of silver, silverized, overlaid or incrusted with silver. Fair, delicate. Thirtieth. ساغر سيمين *sāghari sīmīn*, A silver goblet.

P سيمين بدن *sīmīn-badan*, With a silver form.

P سيمين صولجان *sīmīn-sawlajān*, The new moon.

P سيمين فوارة *sīmīn-fawāra*, The moon.

P سيمين نان *sīmīn-nān*, (Silver loaf) Full moon.

P سين *sīn*, A man who hems and haws very much. Alchymy. China. Name of a village near Ispahān. Muhammad. (for سينة *sīna*) The breast. سين دوخت *sīn-dokht*, Avaricious, vile, depraved. Name of a female ancestor of Rustam.

A سين *sīn*, The letter س. A ringlet, lock.

P سينا *sīnā*, A borer, perforator. The breast. Name of the father of ابو علي بن سينا *abū ʿalīy bin sīnā*. (The celebrated physician Avicenna).

A سيناء *sīnāʾ*, Small stones, gravel. *Sīnāʾ* or *saynāʾ*, (or طور سيناء *ṭūri sīnāʾ*) Mount Sinai.

P سينبر *sīmbar*, Turnsole. Water-mint.

A سينة *sīnat*, A tooth.

P سينج *siyanj*, A furrow. A ploughshare.

P سينجر *sayanjur*, A lighted coal. A spark.

P سينة *sīna*, The bosom, breast. A teat, a dug. The prow or stem of a ship. Taunt, contumely, satire. سينهٔ كشتي *sīnaʾi kashtī*, The prow of a ship. سينة سپر كردن *sīna sipar kardan*, To stand in the foremost ranks without flinching. سينة كردن *sīna kardan*, To strike the ground (as an arrow); to bound up again, and fall elsewhere. To boast, swagger. سينة گشادن *sīna gushādan*, To be happy. سينة كشيدن *sīna kashīdan*, To put forth strength. داروي سينة *dārūyi sīna*, A pectoral medicine.

P سينة باز *sīna-bāz*, Piebald. Name of a bird.

P سينة بستة *sīna-basta*, Locked up in the heart or breast, in petto; a secret.

P سينة بند *sīna-band*, (or سينة پوش *sīna posh*) Poitrel of a horse. A stomacher, stays, bodice.

P سينة چاك *sīna-chāk*, Having the bosom torn, *i. e.* grieved.

P سينة ريش *sīna-resh*, Wounded at heart.

P سينة زنان و ماتم كنان *sīna-zanān u mātam-kunān*, Beating the breast and clothed in mourning.

P سينة زور *sīna-zor*, Robust, proud of strength.

P سينة زوري *sīna-zorī*, Strength: pride of strength.

P سينة گذار *sīna-guzār*, Piercing the breast.

A سيني *saynaʾ*, Mount Sinai.

P سيني *sīnī*, A salver, tray, round table of gold, silver, brass, or copper. Dross of iron. Name of a certain ore. Painted tiles on walls or baths. A loan.

A سينية *sīniyat*, (pl. سينين) A sort of tree.

A سينين *sīnīn*, Name of a tree. طور سينين *ṭūru sīnīna*, Mount Sinai.

P سيو *sev*, (for سيب *seb*) An apple.

P سيوار تير *sewār-tīr*, Name of a note in music.

A سيواس *sīwās*, Name of a city.

P سيواي *siwāy*, Beside, except. سيواي وصول *siwāyi wuṣūl*, Surplus, balance of annual collection.

A سيوب *suyūb*, Hidden (treasures or mines). (pl. of سيب *sayb*) Gifts.

A سيوح *suyūḥ*, A travelling, going on pilgrimage.

P سيوختة *siyūkhta*, A species of soft plant growing in water and used for tinder.

P سي و دو *sī u du*, The thirty and two (teeth).

P سيور *sīwar*, A myriad, ten thousand.

A سيور *suyūr*, (pl. of سير *sayr*) Straps, thongs.

A سيوري *suyūrīy*, Maker of thongs or straps.

P سيورغال *suyūrghāl*, A fief, a feudal tenure. Charity-lands.

P سيورغاميشي *suyūrghāmishī*, Good-will, favour, beneficence.

P سيوس *suyūs*, Name of a tree.

A سيوط *suyūṭ*, A village in Upper Egypt.

A سيوع *suyūʿ*, (v. n. of ساع for سيع) Flowing (water or wine). Pasturing freely without a keeper.

A سيوف *suyūf*, (pl. of سيف *sayf*) Swords.

A سيول *suyūl*, (pl. of سيل *sayl*) Floods.

P سيوم *siwum*, (or سيومين *siwumīn*) Third.

A سيوي *siyawīy*, Of the notch of a bow.

P سيويست *saywist*, Carelessness, inattention.

P سية *siyah*, Black. Unlucky, disastrous. Drunk. An Arab. An Ethiopian slave. The horse of Isfandiyār. One of the books of the Zand. One of the seven lines on the cup of Jamshed. سية پوش *siyah-posh*, Clad in mourning. A life-guardsman. A nightly watch. A keeper of wild beasts. سية پوشان *siyah-poshān*, The name of a country where all are said to wear black. P سية درون *siyah-darūn*, Black within, *i. e.* having a malignant heart.

P سية بادام *siyah-bādām*, The eye of a mistress.

P سية پستان *siyah-pistān* (or بوستان *bostān*),

A woman who loses every suckling.

A سیهج *sayhaj*, Violent (wind).

P سیه چرده *siyah-charda*, Blackish.

P سیه خانه *siyah-khāna*, A black tent. A prison. An unlucky house. سیه خانهٔ آبنوسی *siyah-khānaꜥi ābnūsī*, An ebony flute.

P سیه دست *siyah-dast*, (Black-hand) Covetous.

P سیه دل *siyah-dil*, Black-hearted, malevolent.

P سیه رو *siyah-rū*, (Black-faced) Covered with shame, infamous, wicked.

P سیه روز *siyah-roz*, Unfortunate, afflicted, sad.

P سیه روئی *siyah-rūꜥī*, Infamy, ignominy.

P سیه سار *siyah-sār*, A crocodile.

P سیه سر *siyah-sar*, (Black-head) Man. A pen.

P سیه سنبل *siyah-sumbul*, Water-mint.

P سیه فام *siyah-fām*, Inclining to black. Black.

P سیه قند *siyah-kand*, Molasses.

A سیهك *sayhak*, Violent (wind). Dust swept along by a violent wind.

P سیه کار *siyah-kār* (or کرد *kard*), A scoundrel, prevaricator, sinner. A coward.

P سیه کاری *siyah-kārī*, Sinfulness.

P سیه کاسه *siyah-kāsa*, A miser. One who murders his guests.

P سیه گلیم *siyah-gilīm*, Unfortunate, afflicted, poverty-stricken.

P سیه گوش *siyah-gosh*, The lion's provider.

P سیه مغز *siyah-maghz*, Gloomy, dumpish.

P سیه مو *siyah-mū* or *mo*, Black-haired.

P سیه موئی *siyah-mūꜥī* or *moꜥī*, Blackness of hair.

P سیه نامگی *siyah-nāmagī*, Wickedness.

P سیه نامه *siyah-nāma*, Wicked. Adulterous; a vile wretch, a blackguard.

A سیهوج *sayhūj*, (or سیهوك) Violent wind.

P سیهه *sīha*, A harlot.

A سیّئة *sayyiꜥat*, Sin, wickedness, crime. Evil. Barrenness, scarcity. Torment.

P سییس *sayīs*, A horse-keeper, a syce.

A سئیم *saꜥim*, Wearied, disgusted.

P سیینج *sīyanj*, A furrow. A ploughshare.

ش

ش *shīn*, (called شین منقوطه *shīni manḳūṭa* or شین معجمه *shīni muꜥjama*, Dotted *shīn*) The thirteenth letter of the Arabic alphabet, and the sixteenth of the Persian. It denotes 300 in arithmetic, and is the abbreviature for شمال *shamāl*, The north. ش *ash*, In Persian, signifies, His, her, it, to him, her, it (when affixed to a noun, pronoun, verb, or particle): as, برادرش *birādarash*, His brother; نیش *nayash*, His reed; فرزانگیش *farzānagiyash*, His knowledge; دادش *dādash*, He gave to him; کش *kash*, Which to him (was sent); منش *manash*, I unto her (gave); بیندازش *biyandāzash*, Throw to him. ش *ish*, when added to the imperatives of certain verbs, forms abstract nouns: as, دانش *dānish*, Knowledge, from دان *dān*, Know; بینش *bīnish*, Sight, from بین *bīn*, See. In Arabic, by a peculiar idiom, ش *shi* is substituted for ك *ki*, the affixed pronoun of the second person singular feminine: as, تعالي الى مولاش ينادیش *taꜥālī ila' mawlāshi, yunādīshi*, (O handmaid!) come to thy lord: he calleth thee. This letter is interchangeable with چ ,ج ,خ ,ز ,س, and ص; and has the power of *sh* in English orthography.

P شا *shā*, (for شاد *shād*) Joyful, glad. (for جا *jā*) A place.

A شأ *shaꜥ*, Used in checking or chiding, pshaw!

A شاء *shāꜥa*, (fut. یشوء *yashūꜥu*) He went before. He grieved, he rendered sad. He was pleased with, he rejoiced in. (fut. یشوء *yashūꜥu* or یشیئ *yashīꜥu*) He gave pleasure. ان شاء الله *in shāꜥa 'llāh*, God willing.

A شاء *shāꜥ*, A sheep. (pl. of شاة *shāt*) Sheep. Wild oxen. Women.

P شاب *shāb*, Alum. شاب رومي *shābi rūmī*, White pepper.

A شابّ *shābb*, (pl. شباب *shabāb* and شبّان *shubbān*, اشباب *ashbāb* and شببة *shababat*) A young man (especially from 24 to 40). (A sheep or ox) in the prime of age.

P شاباش *shābāsh*, (for شاد باش *shād bāsh*) Bravo! excellent! Money thrown about at marriages, or given to singers.

P شاباشي *shābāshī*, Praise, applause.

P A شابانك *shābānak*, (and شابانج *shābānaj*) A species of hard Egyptian wood.

A شابّة *shābbat*, ((pl. شوابّ) A young woman.

A شابرالمیزان *shābiru'l mīzān*, A thief.

P شابران *shāburān* or *shābarān*, Name of a seaport in Persia.

P شابرن *shāburan*, Native steel.

A شابع *shābiꜥ*, (in poetry) Full, sated.

A شابك *shābik*, Cross and intricate (road). (A lion) whose teeth lock one within another.

A شابل *shābil*, A lion with close-set teeth. (A boy) tenderly and indulgently brought up.

A شابلوط *shābalūṭ*, Oil of cinnamon, stacte.

A شابن *shābin*, Soft, delicate, juicy (youth).

P شابود *shābwad*, A halo round the moon.

P شابوراك *shābūrāk*, (شابوران *shābūrān*, شابورق *shābūrak*, شابورقان *shābūrakān*, شابورگان *shābūragān*, شابورن *shāburan*, or شابرن *shāburan*) A species of hard iron or native steel.

P شابورد *shābward*, A halo round the moon.

P شابهار *shābahār*, An idol-temple in Kābul.

A شآبیب *shaꜥābīb*, (pl. of شؤبوب *shuꜥbūb*) Showers. Tears.

P شابیزج *shābīzaj*, (or شابیزك) The mandrake.

P شاپور *shāpūr*, King of Persia, called by the Romans Sapores. This prince defeated and took prisoner the emperor Valerian. Several other kings of Persia have borne the same name. Name of a painter and match-maker between Khusraw and Shīrīn. شاپور ذو الاکتاف *shāpūr zū'l aktāf*, Shāpūr of the shoulder-blades (so called from his taking out the shoulder-blades of a number of Arab prisoners he made, and afterwards releasing them).

A شاة *shāt*, (for شاهة *shākat*) (pl. شاء *shāꜥ*, شیاه *shiyāh*, شواه *shiwāh*, اشاوه *ashāwih*, شوي *shawa'*, شیه *shīh*, *shayh*, شیّه *shayyih*, and شواهي *shawāha'*) A sheep. A wether. A goat. A deer. An ostrich. The wild ass. A wild cow. A woman. Certain small stars. الشاة *ash'shāt*, The sheep-species.

A شتاتاة *shatāt*, Winter.

P شاتل *shātil*, Name of a medicinal plant.

A شاتم *shātim*, One who rejoices in another's misfortunes. One who treats with contumely. Grossly opprobrious.

A شاتن *shātin*, A weaver.

P شاتو *shātū*, A ladder, staircase.

A شاتي *shātī*, Cold, wintry (day).

A شأج *shaꜥj*, A making sad, vexing.

A شاجب *shājib*, Perishing, dying. (A crow) which croaks very loudly. Sad, grieved, melancholy. A delirious doting fellow who talks nonsense.

A شاجر *shājir*, (pl. شواجر *shawājir*) Whatever hinders or keeps back. Adversity, calamity.

A شاجن *shājin*, Melancholy, sad.

A شاجنة *shājinat*, (pl. شواجن *shawājin*) A road through a valley. A valley abounding with trees.

A شاحب *shāhib*, Lean. Changing colour.

A شاحم *shāhim*, A seller of tallow. One who gives fat or lard (شحم *shahm*) to eat.

A شاحن *shāhin*, Filled, full: freighted (ship).

A شاحیة *shāhiyat*, (pl. شواحي *shawāhī*) Gaping, yawning (horse).

P شاخ *shākh*, A branch, bough, shoot, sucker, twig. A horn, antler. The arm, from the tip of the finger to the shoulder. The leg, from the groin to the foot. The spur of a cock. A small cut from a main stream. A gusset, gore. A goblet, drinking-horn. The main beam in the roof of a house. A rib. A bit, piece. The forehead. Civet: the civet-cat. Spices, perfumes. A scent-box; a horn wherein they keep civet. Smooth, lank hair. Full-grown. Wine mixed with rose-water. شاخ انگور *shākhi angūr*, Name of a medicine or simple. A young shoot, tendril of a vine. شاخ آهو *shākhi āhū*, A buck's attire. A bow. A false promise. شاخ بر آوردن *shākh bar āwardan*, To colour up. شاخ بر دیوار *shākh bar dīwār*, Conceited, arrogant, proud. شاخ برشاخ *shākh bar shākh*, Far, distant, long. Various. شاخ بشاخ *shākh ba shākh*, From branch to branch. شاخ درشاخ *shākh dar shākh*, Various-coloured, of different sorts. Far and wide. Weeping, lamentation. شاخ دمیدني *shākhi damīdanī*, A trumpet. شاخ زدن *shākh zadan*, To butt or push with the horns. To sound a trumpet or horn. شاخ زرّين *shākhi zarrīn*, A yellow pen. شاخ زعفران *shākhi zaʿfarān*, (lit. A twig of saffron) One who esteems too highly his own deserts. Any thing strange and rare. شاخ سمن *shākhi saman*, Stature of a mistress. شاخ شاخ *shākh shākh*, In branches. In pieces, broken in various places, full of fissures. The song or note of the nightingale. شاخ غزال *shākhi ghazāl*, A bow. The new moon. شاخ كردن *shākh kardan*, To cup. شاخ گوزن در هوا *shākhi gawazn dar hawā*, The new moon. شاخ گيسو *shākhi gīsū*, A ringlet of hair.

P شاخابه *shākhāba*, A small cut from a main stream. An arm of the sea.

A شاخب *shākhib*, Spurting out (blood).

A شاخة *shākhat*, Moderate, temperate, equal.

P شاخچة *shākhcha*, A small branch, twig.

P شاخچه بندي *shākhcha-bandī*, Scandal, slander. Increase.

P شاخدار *shākh-dār*, Branched. Horned. A cuckold, cornuto. Pure, unadulterated. Conceited.

P شاخ ريزة *shākh-reza*, Loppings of branches.

P شاخسار *shākhsār*, Full of branches. A place abounding in trees. The extremity of a branch. A plate of steel perforated with many holes for drawing gold or silver-wire.

P شاخست *shākhast*, Victuals, provisions.

P شاخشانه *shākh-shāna*, Name of a certain description of mendicants, so called from the circumstance of their carrying in one hand a ram's horn and in the other a ram's shoulder-blade, with which they make a grating noise before the door of any one from whom they seek relief. If their application be not forthwith attended to, they begin to lacerate their bodies with knives, or (with a view to excite greater horror) they put the knives into the hands of their own children. Intimidation, threat.

P شاخ شكستة *shākh-shikasta*, Broken-horned.

A شاخص *shākhis*, One whose eyes are fixed and looking up. (An arrow) flying above the mark. High, prominent. Going, travelling; a traveller.

P شاخك *shākhak*, Melilot.

P شاخل *shākhil* or *shākhul*, A sort of grain.

P شاخنگور *shākhangūr*, Name of a medicine. A vine-tendril.

P شاخور *shākhūr*, (or شاخورة) A kiln, furnace.

P شاخول *shākhūl*, Cytisus Cajan (a grain).

P شاخة *shākha*, A branch. A horn. A cup in the shape of a horn. Wine mixed with rose-water.

P شاخي *shākhī*, A winnowing-fork.

P شاد *shād*, Cheerful, exulting. Glad, happy. Much. Full. Wine. Light, a ray, gleam. شاد شدن *shād shudan*, To be joyful.

A شادّ *shādd*, One who fastens, makes secure, or closes up. A comptroller, director, governor.

P شادآب *shād-āb*, Full of water. Moist, humid, fresh, succulent, pleasant. Fresh pasture.

P شاد آبي *shād-ābī*, Freshness, moisture.

P شاد اسپرم *shād-isparam*, Basil royal.

P شادان *shādān*, Cheerful, glad. A dancing girl.

P شادانج *shādānaj*, Blood-stone.

P شادانك *shādānah*, Inebriating hemp-seed.

P شادباد *shād-bād*, Name of a note in music.

P شادباش *shād-bāsh*, Excellent! well done! Name of the twenty-sixth day of the month according to the æra of Malik.

P شاد بهر *shād-bahr*, A happy situation. Name of a damsel.

A شادح *shādih*, Copious, abundant (pasturage).

P شادخ *shādakh*, The old name of Nīshābūr.

A شادخ *shādikh*, A youth. Deviating from a purpose or design. Small, young, fresh, and moist.

A شادخة *shādikhat*, A blaze upon the forehead of a horse or other animal, reaching to the nose.

P شاد خو *shād-kho*, Cheerful, joyous, glad.

P شاد خواب *shād-khwāb*, Refreshing sleep.

P شاد خوار *shād-khwār*, (شاد خوارة *shād-khwāra* or شاد خور *shād-khwur*) Fortunate, well off. Voluptuous. A dancing girl. An adultress, strumpet. One who drinks wine without scruple. One who passes his life without care or trouble; happy, cheerful.

P شاد خواست *shād-khwāst*, Vehement desire.

P شاد دل *shād-dil*, Cheerful, gay-hearted.

P شادران *shādurān*, A sort of iron which absorbs water. Name of a port in Shirwān.

P شادروان *shādurwān*, (or شادربان *shādurbān*) A large veil, curtain, or tapestry suspended before the gate of a royal palace. A richly-figured carpet. A foundation. A kind of moveable Turkomān house, variously ornamented. A parhelion or circle round the sun or moon. Name of a note in music. A cornice. Eaves, projecting roof. شادروان خاك *shādurwāni khāk*, The earth. شادروان مرواريد *shādurwāni marwārīd*, Name of the twelfth tune of the Bārbud.

P شاد كار *shād-kār*, Gratuitous service.

P شاد كام *shād-kām*, Rejoicing, triumphing, exulting, joyous, happy, contented. Name of the brother of Farīdūn.

P شادكامة *shād-kāma*, A tumult. شادكامة كردن *shād-kāma kardan*, To rejoice at another's trouble.

P شادكامي *shād-kāmī*, Gladness, happiness, delight, content.

P شادگونه *shād-gūna*, A mattress for sleeping on. Any thing upon which one leans; a resting-place: a sofa. A coat of mail stuffed. A female singer or performer.

P شادمار *shād-mār*, Many serpents. A huge serpent.

P شادمان *shādmān*, Cheerful, joyful, pleased.

P شادمانه *shādmāna*, A rejoicing or jubilee (especially on the public entry of a king or other festivity). The cultivation or improvement of any place. Joyfully. شادمانه شدن *shādmāna shudan*, To be joyful and glad.

P شادماني *shādmānī*, Gladness, joy, pleasure, delight. شادماني كردن *shādmānī kardan*, To rejoice.

A شادن *shādin*, A young deer, a fawn become independent of its dam.

P شادناك *shādnāk*, Cheerful, blithe, joyous.

P شادنه *shādna*, (A شادنج *shādanaj*) A kind of stone shaped like a lentil, and used medicinally for the eyes. (It is called حجرالدم *hajaru'd dam*, حجر الطور *hajaru't tūr*, and حجر هندي *hajari hindī*.)

P شادوان *shādwān*, Cheerfulness, mirth. Eaves. A canopy over the head of a king or great man when giving audience in the open air. A veil, a piece of tapestry. An artificial fountain.

P شادورد *shādward*, A circle round the moon. A royal throne. A bed, couch, dormitory. A carpet. Name of the seventh of Khusraw's treasures. Name of a note in music.

P شادة *shāda*, Glad. Wine. Much water.

P شادهكام *shādakām*, The country of delight, the name of a province in the kingdom of جنستان *jinnistān* or Fairy-land, much celebrated in Eastern romance, the capital of which is called جواهر آباد *jawāhir-ābād*, City of jewels.

P شادي *shādī*, Gladness, festivity, joy, rejoicing. A wedding. An ape. Name of a certain boy.

A شادي *shādī*, A singer. A reciter of verses. A driver. One who has learned a part of morals or good breeding. In pursuit of some aim or object.

P شادياخ *shādyākh*, The city of Nīshābūr.

P شاديانة *shādyāna*, A band: a music gallery.

P شاديچة *shādīcha*, A counterpane, coverlet.

P شاديدن *shādīdan*, To rejoice, to triumph.

P شادي مبارك *shādī mubārak*, Congratulations on marriage, or on the birth of a child.

P شادي مرگ *shādī-marg*, An easy death. Death from joy. Dying easily or from joy.

P شادية *shādaya*, A medicine for the eyes.

P شاديها *shādīhā*, (pl. of شادي *shādī*) Rejoicings.

P شاذ *shāz*, Glad.

A شاذّ *shāzz*, (pl. شواذّ *shawāzz*) Divided from the rest. Uncommon, rare, miraculous, wonderful. Irregular. Seldom.

A شاذب *shāzib*, Absent from one's country: solitary, forlorn, hopeless.

A شاذكونة *shāzakūnat*, Certain coarse clothes made in Yaman.

A شاذنج *shāzanaj*, Hemp-seed.

P شاذنة *shāzana*, A sort of fragile stone of a blackish red colour, employed medicinally.

P شاذي *shāzī*, Gladness.

P شار *shār*, A city. Adulteration, debasement. A jackal. A very fine sort of muslin, from which veils and lanterns are made. A certain black bird that talks like a parrot. A lofty edifice. Dancing. A fall of water, an outpouring of wine; the gentle noise made thereby. A whirlpool, eddy. A wide, open road. A title of the princes of غرجستان *ghur-*

jistān; also of the kings of Ethiopia. آب شار *āb-shār*, A waterfall.

A شارب *shārib*, (pl. شرب *sharb* and شروب *shurūb*) A drinker. Weakness, languor. (pl. شوارب *shawārib*) A whisker, a mustachio.

A شاربان *shāribāni*, (dual) Two projecting points on the hilt of a sword.

A شاربة *shāribat*, People who dwell near a river.

A شارة *shārat*, A form, figure. A garment, apparel, dress, costume. Beauty, ornament. Fatness. Name of a town in Spain.

P شارج *shāraj*, An isle in the Persian Gulf.

A شارح *shāriḥ*, A commentator, expositor, explainer. A guard over sown fields (against birds).

A شارخ *shārikh*, (pl. شرخ *sharkh*) A youth.

A شارد *shārid*, (pl. شرد *sharad*) Flying, fugitive (camel). (A song) flying all over the country, fugitive (poetry).

P شاردة *shārda*, Sardinia.

P شارسان *shārsān*, A country having many cities. A large city, castle.

P شارستان *shāristān*, A city. A villa surrounded by gardens. A country abounding in towns. Name of a book written by Farzāna Bahrām.

P شارشك *shārashk*, A bird resembling a partridge, but smaller. A rebeck, a parchment violin.

A شارع *shāriʻ*, Any one going into water. (Fishes) swimming out of deep into shallow water, and raising their heads. One who makes manifest. One entering upon business. A beginner. Learned both theoretically and practically, a teacher, tutor. Situated upon the highway (a house). A highway, a straight road. Near, adjacent. P شارع پهنا *shāriʻi pahnā*, A broad street or road. Any thing near. A شارع عام *shāriʻi ʻām*, A public road. غير شارع *ghayr shāriʻ*, Uncertain of, or wandering from, the road.

A شارعة *shāriʻat*, (pl. شوارع *shawāriʻ*) Levelled, pointed (spear). Setting (star).

A شارف *shārif*, (pl. شرّف *shurraf*) Noble; also one that is soon to be ennobled. An aged she-camel. An old arrow. A wine-jar, a tun. (pl. شرف *shuruf*) A trial, temptation.

A شارفة *shārifat*, (pl. شوارف *shawārif*, شرف *shuruf*, شرّف *shurraf*, and شروف *shurūf*) Aged and decrepit (she-camel).

A شارق *shāriḳ*, (pl. شرق *shurḳ*) (The sun) rising and shining. The eastern side. Name of an idol. P شارق شدن *shāriḳ shudan*, To rise (as the sun).

P شارك *shārak*, A species of talking-bird. A grackle. A nightingale.

P شاركار *shār-kār*, Idle, sluggish. Any gratis work which one is compelled to perform.

A شارم *shārim*, An arrow which grazes the side of the mark.

P شارمار *shār-mār*, A large kind of serpent.

P شارو *shārū*, A certain talking-bird: a grackle.

P شاروان *shārwān*, A large curtain. A canopy.

P شارود *shārūd*, A halo round the moon.

P شاروف *shārof*, (from جاروب *jārob*) A besom.

A شاروق *shārūḳ*, Plaster, mortar. Ashes mixed.

P شارويه *shārūya*, The son of Khusraw Parwez.

P شاره *shāra*, A large turban or wreath for the head. A veil. The muslin cover of a lantern.

A شاري *shārī*, (pl. شراة *shurāt*) Quarrelsome, contentious. A sect of schismatics.

P شاريدن *shārīdan*, To flow (as rivers) with a great noise. To pour, trickle, urine. To be guilty.

A شآريز *shaʼārīz*, (pl. of شيراز *shīrāz*) Strained and solid oxygals.

A شأز *shaʼz*, (v. n. of شأز) Lying with. *Shaʼaz*, (v. n. of شئز) Being hard and rocky (a place). Being moveable, restless, unsteady, and timid. A stony or rocky place.

A شازب *shāzib*, (pl. شزّب *shuzzab* and شوازب *shawāzib*) Lean, gaunt (horse). Rough (way).

A شأزة *shaʼzat*, Fat (horses).

A شأس *shaʼs*, The road between Khaybar and Madīna. (pl. شئيس *shaʼīs* and شؤس *shuʼs*) A rough, hard, and gravelly place. *Shaʼas*, (v. n. of شئس) Being hard and rough.

P شاس *shās*, Bad-tempered: dishonest: wicked.

A شاسّ *shāss*, Thin, lean, extenuated.

A شاسب *shāsib*, (pl. شسب *shusb*) Meagre, shrivelled, dry (horse).

P شاسپرم *shāsparam*, Basil royal.

P شاست *shāst*, A bustard.

A شاسع *shāsiʻ*, (pl. شسع *shusʻ*) Distant, separate. Spacious. One who has the fastenings of the shoes (شسع *shisʻ*) burst.

A شاسف *shāsif*, Lean, gaunt, dry (horse). Dried (leathern bottle).

A شاسئ *shāsiʼ*, Coarse, rough, hard. Cruel.

P شاش *shāsh*, Vicious. Contrary. Urine. Name of a city in Turkistān, whence come excellent bows.

A شاش *shāsh*, A turban-sash.

A شأشأ *shaʼshaʼ*, A word used in calling an ass to drink, or in driving an ass or flock of sheep.

A شأشاء *shaʼshāʼ*, (v. n. of شأشأ Q) Calling out to an ass or flock of sheep, شأشأ *shaʼshaʼ* or شؤشؤ *shuʼshuʼ*. Failing to receive the pollen of the male, not being fructified (a female palm-tree). A species of very bad sour date. A tall palm-tree.

A شأشأة *shaʼshaʼat*, A calling an ass.

P شاشدان *shāshdān*, The bladder. An urinal. A poplar.

P شاشدن *shāshidan*, To make water, urine.

P شاشك *shāshak*, A four-stringed instrument. Name of a note in music. A bird resembling a partridge, but smaller. An animal resembling an ape.

P شاشنگ *shāshang*, A four-stringed instrument. A small sort of partridge.

P شاشو *shāshū*, Name of a medicinal herb. One who habitually makes water in his clothes.

P شاشوله *shāshūla*, The loose end of a turban.

P شاشه *shāsha*, Urine. Exudation.

P شاشه‌دان *shāshadān*, The bladder. An urinal.

A شاشيّ *shāshīy*, Of شاش *shāsh* in Turkistān.

A شاشية *shāshiyat*, (pl. شواشي *shawāshī*) (in Morocco) A little turban.

P شاشيدن *shāshīdan*, To make water. To pour, trickle, exude, be wet. To be fit, proper.

A شاصب *shāṣib*, (A life) oppressed with penury. Lean, attenuated (horse).

A شاصر *shāṣir*, (pl. اشصار *ashṣār*) A young deer butting with the horns.

A شاصرة *shāṣirat*, A net, gin, trap, snare.

A شاصلاء *shāṣulāʼ*, (or شاصلّي) Name of an herb.

A شاصونة *shāṣūnat*, An earthen vessel.

A شاصي *shāṣī*, (One) viewing intently the sky. Swollen (corpse), whose arms and legs stand out.

A شاصية *shāṣiyat*, Distended (leathern bottle).

A شاطّ *shāṭṭ*, Of a tall straight shape or figure. Distant. شاطّي *shāṭṭī*, Acting unjustly by me.

A شاطب *shāṭib*, Crooked (road).

A شاطبة *shāṭibat*, (pl. شواطب *shawāṭib*) A woman who cuts leather into slips after having accurately measured it. Name of a city in Spain.

A شاطّة *shāṭṭat*, Tall, upright (girl).

P شاطر *shāṭir*, A courier, messenger, footman.

A شاطر *shāṭir*, (pl. شطّار *shuṭṭār*) One who teases, thwarts, and harasses his relations. Arch, cunning, sly, naughty, roguish. Shameless, impudent, forward, saucy. Prodigal (son). Bold, intrepid. Clever. A chess-player. Rogues.

G شاطريون *shāṭaryūn*, Satyrion.

A شاطف *shāṭif*, Doing no execution (arrow).

A شاطل *shāṭil*, Name of a solvent medicine.

A شاطن *shāṭin*, Wicked, bad-tempered criminal.

A شاطئ *shāṭiʼ*, (pl. شواطئ *shawāṭiʼ* and شطآن *shuṭʼān*) The bank of a river. The sea-shore.

A شاع *shāʻ*, Undistributed (portion). The urine of a female in want of the male, or of one that has taken the male. Scattered (camel's urine).

A شاعبان *shāʻibāni*, The two shoulders.

A شاعة *shāʻat*, A wife. Published, spread, news.

A شاعر *shāʻir*, (pl. شعراء *shuʻarāʼ*) A poet. (An eminent poet is called خنذيذ *khinẕīẕ*. The rank below is شاعر *shāʻir*: below him, شويعر *shuwayʻir*: below him, شعرور *shuʻrūr*; and below him, متشاعر *mutashāʻir*.)

A شاعرة *shāʻirat*, A poetess.

A شاعری *shāʻirī*, The art of poetry.

A شاعل *shāʻil*, One kindling a fire. Partly white on the tail and forelocks (a horse). Bright, luminous. One who has a predatory troop scattered about. Possessed of اشعال *ishʻāl*, (a woman).

A شاعي *shāʻī*, Far distant. Undistributed lot.

A شاغر *shāghir*, Deserted, none being left to govern or to defend (a country).

A شاغران *shāghirān*, The place where the navel-string is cut.

A شاغل *shāghil*, Who or what calls off the attention. One who occupies and keeps employed. شغل شاغل *shugli shāghil*, A work demanding much attention.

P شاغوله *shāghūla*, The loose end of a turban.

A شاغية *shāghiyat*, Redundant, distorted (tooth).

P شاف *shāf*, A suppository or clyster.

A شاف *sha*ʼ*f*, (v. n. of شنف) Hating. Irritating, enraging. Being terrified. Dreading the influence of an evil eye. Directing a disliked, disgusting person to another. Cracking about the nails (the hand). The corruption of a wound that refuses to heal. *Sha*ʼ*af*, (v. n. of شئف) Being afflicted with an ulcer called شأفة *sha*ʼ*fat*.

A شاف *shāf*, A diseased and incurable condition (of a wound).

A شافانج *shāfānaj*, A kind of hard Egyptian wood.

A شآفة *sha*ʼ*āfat*, (v. n. of شئف) Hating. Irritating, enraging. Being terrified. Dreading the influence of an evil eye. Directing a disliked or disgusting person to another. Cracking about the nails (the hand).

A شأفة *sha*ʼ*fat*, An ulcer on the lower part of the foot from a burn, which they cauterize. Root. (pl. of شائف *shā*ʼ*if*) Haters, enemies.

P شافتن *shāftan*, To swim. To grow old. To break. To burst. To crumble to dust, be worn.

A شافر *shāfir*, Ora rimæ muliebris.

A شافع *shāfiʻ*, An advocate, intercessor. A patron. One who makes an even number. A ram or goat which always begets twins. A camel or sheep big with young, and followed by their young.

A شافعة *shāfiʻat*, (An eye) seeing double.

A شافعي *shāfiʻiy*, Name of the Imām ابو عبد الله محمد بن ادريس *abūʻabdu'llāh muhammad bin idris*, one of the chiefs of the four principal sects of the Muhammadan religion. A follower of Shāfiʻiy.

A شافعية *shāfiʻiyat*, Sect of شافعي *shāfiʻiy*.

P شافعي مذهب *shāfiʻī-mazhab*, A Shāfite.

A شافن *shāfin*, Jealous (man), who looks askance or with half-shut eyes.

P شافه *shāfa*, Cotton dipped in medicine, and applied to the eyes. A bougie, pessary, suppository.

A شافه *shāfih*, Thirsty.

A شافي *shāfī*, Healing, salutary. Distinct, clear. True. جواب شافي *jawābi shāfī*, Categorical answer.

A شاق *shākk*, Difficult, troublesome, disgusting, perplexing, toilsome, wearisome.

P شاقل *shāķul*, A mason's plummet: a pendulum.

A شاقول *shāķūl*, An instrument for ploughing used at Basrah. Penis. A bricklayer's plummet.

A شاقي *shāķī*, (pl. شواقي *shawāķī*) Tall, lofty (mountain). A salient point of a mountain. Miserable. Criminal.

P شاك *shāk*, A shoot, twig. A he-goat. Tumid, swelling. One-footed, monoped. A bandage of linen, with which women truss their breasts, a stomacher, corslet.

A شاك *shāk*, Clad in armour. Armed with pointed weapons, &c.

A شاكّ *shākk*, (pl. شكّاك *shukkāk*) Armed. Arrayed in armour. One who draws a bow or pierces with a spear. Prickly.

P شاكار *shākār*, A gratuitous work (especially when one is compelled to work for nothing). A scholar, apprentice. A boy, servant, groom.

A شاكة *shākat*, (v. n. of شاك for شوك) Falling amongst, or walking in thorns. Thorny, prickly.

A شاكّة *shākkat*, A swelling in the throat.

P شاكر *shākar*, Work done for nothing.

A شاكر *shākir*, (One who) celebrates, praises, or gives thanks. Grateful. A hired servant. P شاكر شدن *shākir shudan*, To return thanks, be thankful.

P شاكرباه *shākirbāh*, One compelled to keep horses for the public service. Service, attendance on a judge or magistrate.

A شاكرة *shākirat*, A sack, bag, purse.

A شاكري *shākiriy*, (from P چاكر *chākir*) A hired servant, apprentice, journeyman.

A شاكل *shākil*, Likeness. A road.

A شاكلة *shākilat*, Form, figure. A whiteness between the ear and the temples or cheeks. The haunch, hypochondria (of a quadruped). A tract, side, quarter. Design, intention. Way, manner, mode, rule, opinion, creed.

P شاكلول *shāklūl*, A blabbler. A glutton.

P شاكله *shākala*, A strawberry.

P شاكمند *shākmand*, A covering or blanket of goats' hair.

S شاكموني *shākmūnī*, A name of Budd'ha.

P شاكورد *shākward*, A halo round the moon. A dormitory. A royal throne. The seventh treasure of Khusraw. Name of a note in music.

A شاكي *shākī*, Equipped with arms. Lamenting, querulous. A complainer. One slightly ailing. A backbiter. A lion.

P شاگرد *shāgird*, A scholar, student, apprentice. A disciple, pupil. A boy, servant, groom. A copier of records. شاگرد رشيد *shāgirdi rashīd*, A complete, apt scholar.

P شاگردانه *shāgirdāna*, A scholar, apprentice, or a servant. Presents made to children at the time of نشره *nushra*. The fee given by a scholar to his teacher. An extra gratuity over and above wages due: drink-money. Alms.

P شاگرد پيشه *shāgird-pesha*, A menial. Retinue.

P شاگردي *shāgirdī*, A gratuity over and above wages due. Alms. A scholar, student, apprentice. Apprenticeship. Learning, study.

P شال *shāl*, A shawl or mantle, made of very fine wool of a species of goat common in Tibet. A coarse mantle of wool and goats' hair, worn by dervīshes. A small carpet. White hair-cloth, horse-cloth, or housing. شال تنگ *shāli tang*, A girth. شال كشتن *shāl kushtan*, To strangle with a shawl (mode of execution). شال كهنه داشتن *shāli kuhna dāshtan*, To wear an old shawl, *i.e.* be very poor.

A شالج *shālij* or *shālaj*, Half a قفيز *kafīz*.

P شالخ *shālikh*, Salah, son of Arphaxad, and grandfather of Abraham.

P شال دار *shāl-dār*, Stamped to imitate shawl.

P شالده *shālda*, The foundation of a wall.

A شالم *shālam*, Tares.

P شالنگ *shālang*, One taken in the stead of another. The nimble pace of a courier. Woollen padding sewn under a carpet. A horse-cloth.

P شالنگي *shālangī*, A rope-maker. A spinner of materials for tent-making.

P شال نمد *shāl-namad*, Housing of goats' hair.

P شالهنگ *shālhang*, A pledge. Quarrel, broil. Fraud, deceit. Obstinacy, stubbornness, disobedience.

P شالي *shālī*, Rice in the husk. شالي آبي *shālīʼi ābī*, A kind of wild rice.

P شالي پايه *shālī-pāya*, A rice-field.

P شالي زار *shālīzār*, A rice-field, rice-ground.

P شام *shām*, Evening. Supper. شام دادن *shām dādan*, To give a supper. شام شكستن *shām shikastan*, To breakfast in the evening. شام غربت *shāmi ghurbat*, The supper of a poor, destitute traveller. شام كردن *shām kardan*, To sup. نماز شام *namāzi shām*, Evening-prayer, vespers.

A شأم *sha*ʼ*m*, (v. n. of شأم) Being unlucky. Rendering so, bringing ill luck. Name of several cities in Syria. Syria.

A شام *shām*, (pl. of شامة *shāmat*) Black moles or marks. Syria and its capital Damascus. شام شريف *shāmi sharīf*, The noble city of Damascus.

A شامّ *shāmm*, Smelling. A smeller.

P شاماخ *shāmākh*, A kind of millet. *Shāmākh*, (or شاماخچه *shāmākhcha*) A bandage with which women truss their breasts.

P شامار *shāmār*, (or شاماز *shāmāz*) Name of a place, the abode of many fire-worshippers.

P شاماك *shāmāk*, A short female garment, reaching to the middle of the leg; also an under shirt, worn in hot weather, or in violent exercise, to prevent the perspiration from staining the other clothes. A short working garment. A bandage for the breasts.

P شاماكچه *shāmākcha*, A stomacher. A bandage for trussing the breasts. A short shift or inner garment. A sleeveless shirt, tunic, or vest. A cloak.

P شاماكه *shāmāka*, Hard pitch.

A شآمة *sha*ʼ*āmat*, A being unfortunate, unlucky.

A شأمة *sha*ʼ*mat*, The left side. Adversity, misfortune, shame. Disaster, disgrace. الشأمة *ash' sha*ʼ*mat*, Syria and the capital Damascus.

A شامة *shāmat*, (pl. شام *shām* and شامات *shāmāt*) A black spot or mole. A mark, sign. A black she-camel. A lunar spot. ما له شامة و لا زهراء *mā lahu shāmat wa lā zahrā*ʼ, He has no camels, either black or white.

A شامّة *shāmmat*, Smelling (woman). The nose. قوّت شامّه *kūwati shāmma*, The olfactory sense. يا ابن شامّة الوذرة *yā ibnu shāmmati'l wazrat*, A coarse and obscene term of reproach.

A شامت *shāmit*, A rejoicer at another's loss.

A شامخ *shāmikh*, (pl. شمّخ *shummakh*) High, lifted up. Lofty, proud. جبل شامخ *jabali shāmikh*, A high mountain, towering to the sky.

A شامز *shāmiz*, (pl. شوامز *shawāmiz*) Pregnant (camel), or shewing signs of it. Fructified (palm-tree). A scorpion.

P شامر *shāmir*, A veil, covering for the head.

A شامر *shāmir*, (and شامرة *shāmirat*) A sheep or camel whose udder sticks close to the belly. Sticking close to the roots of the teeth (gums).

P شامس *shāmis*, (or شاموس *shāmūs*) The Greek island of Samos. Samian earth, resembling talc, which if touched with the tongue adheres to it; also a kind of viscous earth, white or black, that dissolves in water.

A شامس *shāmis*, (pl. شمس *shums* and شوامس *shawāmis*) (A horse) apt to throw his rider.

A شامط *shāmit*, A pot capable of containing an entire sheep with the condiments.

P شامك *shāmak*, A vest reaching to the waist.

P شامكچه *shāmakcha*, A short garment reaching to the waist. A linen bandage with which women truss their breasts.

P شامگاه *shām-gāh*, Evening-tide.

A شأمل *shaʼmal*, The north.

A شامل *shāmil*, Who or what extends itself, touches all round, surrounds, comprehends, contains, communicates with. Included, concerned in, connected with. Universal. United, confederate.

P شامه *shāma*, A woman's veil. A lord, master. Supper. Any thing lying. A black thing. Darkness. A falcon's hood. A place. A seat. A comb. The elbow.

P شامي *shāmī*, Supper. Of the evening.

A شأمي *shaʼmīy*, (شآمي *shaʼāmī*, or شآمّي *shaʼāmīy*) A Syrian, Syriac. The Syrian side of Sanaa (opposed to يماني *yamānīy*). A citizen of Damascus.

P شاميانه *shāmyāna*, A parasol, umbrella, canopy.

A شآمية *shaʼāmiyat*, Syrian (woman).

A شامئة *shāmiʼat*, Syrian (woman).

A شامية *shāmiyat*, The people of Syria.

P شان *shān*, A bee-hive. Virgin honey. A large loaf of fine flower, such as they give in presents on new-year's-day. A mandate. Science. An enigma. A shoemaker's last. Fear. Respect, regard. Natural disposition, habit. A white Indian dress. A whetstone. (for ايشان *eshān*) They. جامهٔ شان *jāmaʼi shān*, Their garment. اسب شان *asbi shān*, Their horse.

A شأن *shaʼn*, (v. n. of شأن) Doing, minding, or looking after (one's business). Doing a service, rendering a benefit. Destroying, laying waste. Certifying, informing. Proposing. (pl. شؤون *shuʼūn* and شئان *shiʼān*) Thing, affair, business. Nature, constitution, habit, desire, disposition. A vein of soil in mountains producing palms and other trees. (pl. اشؤن *ashʼun* and شؤن *shuʼun*) Lachrymal ducts. Conjunction of the sutures of the head. شان شريف *shāni sharīf*, A noble condition.

A شأنان *shaʼnāni*, (dual) Two veins from the head to the eyes.

A شانب *shānib*, One who has clean teeth and a sweet breath. Cold (day).

P شاندار *shān-dār*, A man of quality or rank.

P شاندان *shāndān* or *shānadān*, A comb-case.

P شاندن *shāndan*, To comb. To mark. To lay (the dust).

P شانزده *shānzdah*, Sixteen.

P شانزدهم *shānzdahum*, The sixteenth.

A شانف *shānif*, A hater, despiser, averse: one who turns away his face. شانف عنّا بانفه *shānifun ʻannā bi anfihi*, Hanging us at his nose, *i.e.* despising us.

P شانك *shānak*, The crop of a bird.

P شانوان *shānawān*, A comb-case.

P شانه *shāna*, A comb. A crest. A hay or corn-fork. A honey-comb. A bee-hive. The shoulder-blade. Speed. Leaping, bounding. A desert. شانهٔ اسب *shānaʼi asb*, (or شانهٔ ستورخار *shānaʼi sutūr-khār*) A curry-comb. شانه در ريش زدن *shāna dar rīsh zadan*, To be prepared. شانهٔ دست *shānaʼi dast*, A lint, wool, or cotton-card. شانه زدن *shāna zadan*, To comb. شانهٔ كرپاس *shānaʼi karpās*, A weaver's instrument. شانه كردن *shāna kardan*, To comb. To curry.

P شانه دان *shānadān*, A comb-case.

P شانه زن *shāna-zan*, A comber.

P شانه ساز *shāna-sāz*, A comb-maker.

P شانه سر *shāna-sar*, (or شانه سرك *shāna-sarak*) (Crest-head) The hoopoo or puet.

P شانه كاري *shāna-kārī*, Quarrel, dispute, contest.

P شانه نا كرده *shāna nā karda*, Uncombed.

P شانه هيد *shāna-hīd*, A hay or corn-fork.

P شاني *shānī*, Name of a coin formerly current.

A شانئ *shāniʼ*, (pl. شنّاء *shunnāʼ*) A hater (of man or woman), an evil-wisher.

P شانيدن *shānīdan*, To comb. To card.

A شأو *shaʼw*, (v. n. of شأا for شأو) Preceding, outstripping. Astonishing, surprising. Excelling. Walking fast. Raking mud (out of a well). A boundary, term, goal, end, extremity. Clay, rubbish, soil drawn out of a well. A camel's halter. Camel's dung. A basket.

P شاوار *shāwār*, Choice; fit for a king.

P شاوران *shāwarān*, A city in Shirwān.

P شاوزد *shāwazd*, A kind of white thorn.

P شاوغر *shāwghar*, A brazen trumpet. Name of a country in Turkistān.

P شاوني *shāwinī*, Covering of a cradle.

P شاوور *shāwūr*, A confidant of خسرو پرويز *khusraw parwez*, king of Persia, who went to the court of Heraclius, emperor of Greece, and dropt the picture of his prince in the sight of the princess شيرين *shīrīn*, the emperor's daughter, in consequence of which she fell in love with him (see پرويز *parwez*). A pimp. Shāpūr, king of Persia.

A شاوي *shāwī*, A roaster of meat. *Shāwī*, (or شاويّ *shāwīy*) Of or belonging unto sheep, ovine. Rich in sheep.

A شاوية *shāwiyat*, Dry and withering (palm-branch). Worst part, refuse.

P شاه *shāh*, A king, sovereign, emperor, monarch, prince. The king at chess. A bridegroom. A son-in-law. A title assumed by fakirs. A wide, main road. A sort of garment used in India. Root, origin. Name of an animal. Of noble blood. Great, excellent in any degree. شاه آفاق گرد *shāhi āfāk-gird*, Alexander Zū'l Karnayn. شاه داد *shāhi dād*, The just king. شاه خواندن *shāh khwāndan*, To adduce cogent arguments. شاه زاول *shāhi zāwul*, Name of Mahmūd Sabuktigīn. شاه زنگ *shāhi zang*, Night. شاه عاليجاه *shāhi ʻālī-jāh*, A king of exalted dignity. شاه گوهران *shāhi gawharān*, A certain precious stone which belonged to Khusraw Parvīz, and which, on being cast into the sea, attracted to itself a number of other precious stones. شاه مربّع نشين *shāhi murabbaʻ-nishīn*, The Kaaba. شاه مردان *shāhi mardān*, King of valour, Aliy. شاه نيم روز *shāhi nīm-roz*, A title of the governor of Sīstān. The following words, with many others, are employed with شاه *shāh*, King, as epithets of the sun: شاه انجم *shāhi anjum*, King of the stars; خاور *khāwar*, Of east or west; خرگاه مينا *khargāhi mīnā*, Of the azure pavilion; سيّارات *sayyārāt*, Of the planets; گردون *gardūn*, Of the firmament; مشرق *mashrik*, Of the east; نيمروز *nīm-roz*, Of midday; يك اسپه *yak aspa*, Of one horse.

A شاه *shāh*, Sharp-sighted.

P شاها *shāhā*, (vocative case) O king!

P شاهاب *shāhāb*, A red colour. Red juice of the flower of the كاجيره *kājīra*.

P شاه آباد *shāh-ābād*, A district of south Bahār.

P شاه اسپرم *shāh-isparam*, (شاه اسپرهم *shāh-isparham*, شاه اسفرهم *shāh-isfarham*, شاه پرم *shāh-param* or *shāh-parum*, شاه اسپرغم *shāh-ispargham*, شاه سپرغم *shāh-sipargham*, شاه سپرم *shāh-siparam*, شاه سپرهم *shāh-siparham*, شاه سفرغم *shāh-sifargham*, or شاه سفرم *shāh-sifaram*) Basil-royal.

P شاه افسر *shāh-afsar*, Melilot.

P شاه آلو *shāh-ālū*, A sort of plum.

P شاهان *shāhān*, (pl. of شاه *shāh*) Kings.

P شاه انجير *shāh-anjīr*, A small but delicious fig.

P شاهانه *shāhāna*, Royal. Splendid, magnificent. Royally. A dress worn by a bridegroom.

A شاهب *shāhib*, Ash-coloured, of a dusky white.

P شاهباز *shāh-bāz*, A royal falcon. The longest

feathers in a falcon's wing. Royal, generous, noble.

P شاهبال *shāh-bāl*, Longest feather in a wing.

P شاهبالا *shāh-bālā*, One who is exactly of the same age, height, and figure as the bridegroom, and who attends the bridegroom to the house of the bride.

P شاهبانج *shāh-bānaj*, A hard Egyptian tree.

P شاهبانك *shāh-bānak*, A sort of medicinal plant.

P شاه بسه *shāh-busa*, Melilot.

P شاه بلوط *shāh-balūt*, (Royal oak) A chesnut.

P شاهبندر *shāh-bandar*, The shābandar, the receiver-general of duties or tribute. The custom-house (at Dacca).

P شاهبوي *shāh-boy* or *būy*, The odour of amber or musk. Ambergris.

P شاه بيت *shāh-bayt*, The royal distich or concluding verse of the Ghazal or Eastern ode.

P شاهپر *shāh-par*, Largest feather in a wing.

P شاهپري *shāh-parī*, Amber. Musk.

P شاه تراب *shāh tarāb*, A viceroy. A king's favourite. A satrap.

P شاهترّه *shāhtarra*, (A شاهترج) Fumitory.

P شاه توت *shāh-tūt*, A large, excellent mulberry.

P شاه تير *shāh-tīr*, The king-beam, the large beam of a house.

P شاه جان *shāh-jān*, Name of the city مرو *marw*.

P شاه جهان *shāh-jahān*, Name of an emperor of Hindūstān.

P شاه چيني *shāh-chīnī*, The expressed juice of a China plant.

P شاه خوردي *shāh khwurdī*, Sweetmeats used on great days.

P شاهد *shāhid*, A beautiful woman. A handsome man. A ringlet of hair especially belonging to a mistress. Known. Things of great value. شاهد جان *shāhidi jān*, The beloved of one's soul. شاهد زربفت پوش *shāhidi zarbaft-posh*, Heaven. Day. The sun. شاهد زرد *shāhidi zard*, White wine. شاهد رخ زرد *shāhidi rukh-zard*, (شاهد روز *shāhidi roz*, شاهد زعفراني *shāhidi zaꞬfarānī*, شاهد شاه فلك *shāhidi shāhi falak*, or شاهد طغان چرخ *shāhidi tighāni charkh*) Name of the sun.

A شاهد *shāhid*, (pl. شهود *shuhūd*, شهّد *shuhhad*, شهد *shahd*, اشهاد *ash-hād*, and شواهد *shawāhid*) A witness, eye-witness, by-stander. An angel (as a witness of the actions of men). An epithet of Muhammad. Expeditious (affair). A star. The Pleiades. The tongue. Friday. A mucus which accompanies (as a witness) the new-born child. Fleetness, an excellent pace in a horse. شاهد حال *shāhidi hāl*, Witness of facts. شاهد فاستقم *shāhidi fā istakim*, (شاهد لعمرك *shāhidi liꞬumrika*, or شاهد گويندگان *shāhidi goyandagān*) An epithet of Muhammad. شاهد معتمد *shāhidi muꞬtamad*, (or شاهد عادل *shāhidi Ꞅādil*) A witness of veracity. صلوة الشاهد *salātu'sh shāhid*, Evening-prayer.

P شاه دارو *shāh-dārū*, (Sovereign remedy) A name which Jamshed gave to wine.

P شاهدان *shāh-dān*, A large, beautiful pearl.

A شاهدانج *shāhdānaj*, Hemp-seed.

P شاهدانه *shāh-dāna*, A large pearl. Hemp-seed. A cherry.

P شاهد باز *shāhid-bāz*, Whoremonger. Sodomite.

P شاهد بازي *shāhid-bāzī*, Whoredom.

P شاهد پرست *shāhid-parast*, A devoted lover.

A شاهدة *shāhidat*, The earth.

P شاه درخت *shāh-dirakht*, The royal fir.

P شاه دود *shāh-dūd*, A sort of musical instrument.

A شاهدي *shāhidī*, Testimony, evidence.

P شاه ديوار *shāh-dīwār*, A palace-wall.

A شاهر *shāhir*, One holding a drawn sword.

P شاه راه *shāh-rāh*, King's highway, main road.

P شاهرخ *shāh-rukh*, The horn of a rhinoceros. A title given to the sons of the nobility. Name of a son of Tīmūr.

P شاهرش *shāh-rash*, A fathom.

P شاهرگ *shāh-rag*, The jugular vein.

P شاه رود *shāh-rūd* or *rod*, A large river. Name of a river. The bass cord of an instrument. Name of a musical instrument.

P شاه زادگي *shāh-zādagī*, Minority of a prince. Youthful folly. Foolish pride.

P شاه زاده *shāh-zāda*, King's son; heir apparent.

P شاه زيره *shāh-zīra*, Caraway-seed.

A شاهسبرم *shāhasbaram*, (from P) Sweet basil.

P شاه سوار *shāh-suwār*, An excellent horseman.

P شاه صيني *shāh-sīnī*, The expressed juice of a plant, brought from China, good for the headache.

P شاه عالم *shāh-Ꞅālam*, One of the Great Moguls.

P شاه غرجكان *shāh-gharjikān*, A royal habit of fine muslin.

A شاهق *shāhik*, High, lofty (mountain or edifice). An artery. A high or throbbing vein. ذو شاهق *zū shāhik*, One not greatly enraged.

P شاه قام *shāh-kām*, A term used at chess by the vanquished.

P شاهكار *shāh-kār*, (King's work) A gratuitous work, which one is compelled to do. Any thing great, pure, and magnificent.

P شاه كال *shāh-kāl*, Squint-eyed.

P شاه گام *shāh-gām*, Pleasant-paced (horse). A particular pace of a horse, the royal pace.

P شاهگان *shāhgān*, (or شاهگانه *shāhgāna*) Any thing great and noble. A royal treasure. A species of verse.

P شاه گردي *shāh-girdī*, Captivity, subjection.

P شاه گوهران *shāh-gawharān*, A jewel of the first magnitude and purest ray. A single pearl filling its shell.

P شاه گهر *shāh-guhar*, Ancestor of kings.

P شاه لوچ *shāh-lūj*, A sort of plum.

P شاه لوك *shāh-lūk*, A large yellow plum.

P شاه مات *shāh māt*, Checkmate at chess.

P شاهمانند *shāhmānd*, Resembling a king. Royal.

P شاه مهره *shāh-muhra*, A precious stone, said to be found in a serpent's mouth or a dragon's head.

P شاهن *shāhan* or *shāhin*, A shepherd's pipe. *Shāhin*, The beam of a balance. An excellent falcon.

P شاه نام *shāh-nām*, A sort of musical instrument. Name of a city in Shirwān.

P شاه نامه *shāh-nāma*, A history of kings. The royal book, the title of a poetical and most romantic history of the ancient Persian monarchs, by Firdawsi, who is justly considered as the Homer of the East.

P شاهناي *shāh-nāy*, A military trumpet.

P شاهندن *shāhandan*, To be honest, sincere; to act uprightly.

P شاهنده *shāhanda*, Pious, honest, upright. Excellent, blest.

P شاهنشاه *shāhanshāh*, (شاهنشه *shāhanshah*, or شهنشاه *shahanshāh*) (a contraction of شاهان شاه *shāhān-shāh*) King of kings, lord of lords. شاهنشاه زندواستا *shāhanshāhi zandwāstā*, (or شاهنشاه فلك *shāhanshāhi falak*) The sun.

P شاهنشاهي *shāhanshāhī*, Imperial dignity, monarchy. Royal, imperial, princely, monarchial.

P شاهنشين *shāh-nishīn*, The seat of the king, *i.e.* a gallery or balcony projecting from the palace, where the king shews himself to his people. A balcony, gallery, portico, or similar projection. A costly carpet.

P شاهو *shāhū*, Large, excellent, royal (pearl).

P شاهوار *shāhwār*, Royal, noble; like a king, fit for a king, befitting a king. A fine royal pearl.

P شاهورد *shāhward*, A halo round the moon. A royal throne. A dormitory. The seventh treasure of Khusraw. Name of a note in music.

P شاهوش *shāhwash*, A maiden, virgin. Royal.

P شاهول *shāhūl*, A plumb-line. A pendulum.

P شاهه *shāha*, A turret raised above a house for the benefit of air. Name of a city in هاماوران.

P شاهي *shāhī*, Royal. Imperial dignity, dominion, sovereignty, royalty. The followers of the sect of Aliy. Name of a poet. Name of a coin. A sort of sweetmeat, made of starch and white of egg.

A شاهي *shāhī*, Sharp-sighted.

A شاهيّ *shāhiy*, Of or belonging to sheep, ovine. One who keeps sheep.

A شاهية *shāhiyat*, A hawk.

P شاهيدن *shāhīdan*, To be honest, upright, righteous, sincere, pious. To reign, to exercise kingly authority.

P شاهيده *shāhīda*, Pious, chaste, upright.

A شاهين *shāhīn*, (pl. شواهن *shawāhin* and شواهين *shawāhīn*) A royal white falcon. The beam of scales. A place to recline. The tongue of a balance.

P شاي *shāy*, God.

P شايار *shāyār*, Gratuitous work which one is compelled to do.

P شايان *shāyān*, Legal, lawful, allowed, permitted. Worthy, suitable. Agreeable. Possible, contingent. Gratuitous but forced work.

P شايانيدن *shāyānīdan*, To cause to comb.

A شائب *shāꜣib*, A mixer. Grey-haired.

A شائبة *shāꜣibat*, (pl. شوائب *shawāꜣib*) An impure thing. Suspicion, doubt. A calamity. Mixture.

A شائح *shāꜣih*, Diligent. Jealous. Hard-breathing (horse). One who goes gently.

P شايد *shāyad*, Let it be. It is agreeable, suitable, worthy, proper. May be, perhaps, perchance, possibly, probably. Probability.

A سائس *shāꜣis*, Hard.

P شايستانيدن *shāyistānīdan*, To cause to suit, to render useful.

P شايستگي *shāyistagī*, Aptitude, suitability, conveniency. Propriety, fitness. Affability.

P شايستن *shāyistan*, To become, suit, agree. To be worth. To assist. To be destroyed. To be necessary.

P شايسته *shāyista*, Worthy, honourable. Legal, unobjectionable. Suitable, decent, useful. Well-bred, polite. شايسته بود *shāyista-būd*, (or شايسته هستي *shāyista hastī*) Whose existence is necessary, *i.e.* self-existent.

P شايسته مزاج *shāyista-mizāj*, Affable, mild.

A شائع *shāꜣiꜥ*, Divulged, published, promulgated. Diffused. Celebrated. Distressed. Undistributed (portion).

A شائف *shāꜣif*, (pl. شافة) A hater, enemy.

A شائق *shāꜣik*, Loved. A beloved object, one which excites desire. Desirable.

A شائك *shāꜣik*, Thorny, prickly. Clothed in armour; armed with sharp weapons.

P شاي كليو *shāy kalīv*, Name of a Persian prophet.

P شايكه *shāyika*, A certain thorn which bears the gum عنزروت *ꜥanzarūt*.

P شايگان *shāygān*, (for شاهگان *shāhgān*) Any thing worthy of a king or great man. Large, immense (particularly a royal treasury). Name of one of Khusraw's treasures. Opened, displayed. Wide, spacious. Repeated, reiterated. Worthy, suitable, befitting. Any thing which one is compelled to do gratuitously for the king. Verse that ends in ان *ān*, and is of two classes. The first, which is called شايگان خفي *shāygāni khafī*, is ان *ān* at the end of words denoting the agent: as, گريان *giryān*, Weeping; a weeper: خندان *khandān*, Laughing; a laugher. Words of this class are not allowed to rhyme with such words as زمان *zamān*, Time, or كمان *kamān*, A bow. In like manner, ين *īn*, forming adjectives of relationship in such words as آتشين *ātishīn*, Fiery, سيمين *sīmīn*, Silvery, may not rhyme with such words as زمين *zamīn*, Earth, or كمين *kamīn*, Ambush. The second class, which is called شايگان جلي *shāygāni jalī*, is ان *ān* at the end of words in the plural: as, ياران *yārān*, دوستان *dostān*, Friends. Such words may not rhyme with a noun in the singular: as, فلان *fulān*, So-and-so. The occurrence of these terminations more than once in the Ghazal or Kasīda is forbidden.

P شايگينه *shāyigīna*, (or شايگيني) Small, cheap.

A شائل *shāꜣil*, (pl. شوّل *shūwal*, شيّل *shuyyal*, *shiyal*, and شوال *shiwāl*) Milkless (camel). (A camel) that, by cocking her tail, shews she is pregnant. A lifter, a carrier.

A شائلة *shāꜣilat*, (pl. شول *shawl* and اشوال *ashwāl*) (A camel) whose dugs are wrinkled for want of milk. A camel seven months after foaling. A flock of sheep.

A شائم *shāꜣim*, Unlucky, ominous. One who brings ill-luck upon others.

P شايورد *shāyward*, A halo round the moon. Name of the seventh treasure of Khusraw; also of a note in music.

P شايه *shāya*, Fruit.

A شائه *shāꜣih*, Sharp-sighted. A lynx.

P شائي *shāꜣī*, A worshipper of God.

A شائيّ *shāꜣiy*, Belonging to a sheep, ovine.

P شاييدن *shāyīdan*, To become, suit, agree. To be worthy. To be useful and necessary.

P شب *shab*, Night. Darkness. شب اندر روز *shab andar roz*, (Night within day) A silken stuff of a mixed colour (pepper and salt, thunder and lightning). شب برات *shab barāt*, The 14th night of Shaꜥbān. شب پيمودن *shab paymūdan*, To measure the night, *i.e.* to remain awake all night. شب تاريك *shabi tārīk*, An obscure night. شب تيغ *shabi tegh*, The tenth night of the month Muharram. شب چك *shabi chak*, The 15th night of Shaabān. شب در ميان دادن *shab dar miyān dādan*, To become security for a night, or for a longer time. شب ديجور *shabi dayjūr*, A dark night. شب زنگي *shābi zangī*, A dark night. شب سده *shabi sada*, Name of the 10th night of the month بهمن *bahman*. شب شبه گون *shabi shaba-gūn*, A dark night. شب شدن *shab shudan*, To terminate (the season of youth). شب طاق *shabi tāk*, The 19th, 20th, 21st, and 22d nights of Ramazān. شب ظلمت اندود *shabi zulmat-andūd*, A night veiled in darkness. شب عنبرين *shabi ꜥambarīn*, (or شب گيسو فشان *shabi gīsū-fishān*) A dark night. شب فرّخ *shabi farrukh*, The fourteenth note of the barbut. شب قدر *shabi kadar*, (or A ليلة القدر *laylatu'l kadar*) The night of power, *i.e.* the 27th of the month Ramazān. شب كائنات *shabi kāꜣināt*, The world. شب گذشته *shabi guzashta*, Last night. شب ماه *shābi māh*, Light night, moonlight. شب مسري *shabi masra'*, The night of Muhammad's pretended ascent to heaven. شب وروز *shab u roz*, Night and day. شب يلدا *shabi yaldā*, Longest winter-night. در شب *dar shab*, In the night, at night.

A شبّ *shabb*, (v. n. of شبّ) Kindling (a flame or war). Being on fire. Raising up (any thing). Being determined, predestinated, appointed. Height, elevation. A certain disease. Alum. *Shibb*, A young wild ox. من شبّ الى دبّ *mish' shubba ila' dubba*, From youth to old age.

A شبا *shaba'*, Water-moss. A scorpion's sting.

P شباب *shabāb*, Name of a note in music. *Shibāb*, A cherry.

A شباب *shabāb*, (v. n. of شبّ) Growing up, becoming a young man. Youth, the prime of life, from thirty to forty. Beginning of any thing. عنفوان شباب *ꜥunfuwāni shabāb*, Flower of youth. (pl. of شابّ *shābb*) Youths. *Shibāb*, (v. n. of شبّ) Lifting up both the fore-feet when curvetting (a horse). Showing more brilliancy (colour). Whatever is used in lighting a fire. Joyousness, cheerfulness. A lifting up of the hands.

A شبابانك *shabābānak*, An Egyptian tree.

A شبابيث *shabābīs*, (pl. of شبّاث *shabbās*, and شبّوث *shabbūs*) Pot-hooks.

A شبابيط *shabābīt*, (pl. of شبوط *shabūt*, شبّوط *shabbūt*, or *shubbūt*) Fishes with narrow tails, broad bodies, and small jowls.

A شبابيك *shabābīk*, (pl. of شبّاك *shubbāk*) Nets. (pl. of شبّاكة *shubbākat*) Lattices.

A شبأة *shabꜣat*, The tongue or bolt of a lock.

A شباة *shabāt*, (pl. شبيٰ *shaba'* and شبوات *shabawāt*) The end or point of any thing (particularly of a scorpion's sting). A scorpion as soon as born. A yellow kind of scorpion. A horse pulling at the rein; or one that rears. The side of the toe of a shoe.

A شبات *shubāt*, (for شباط *shubāt*) February.

A شبّاث *shabbās*, (pl. شبابيث) A pot-hook.

A شباحة *shabāhat*, (v. n. of شبح) Being broad in the arm. Extending, stretching itself (a chameleon).

A شبادع *shabādiꜥ*, (pl. of شبدع *shibdaꜥ* and *shibdiꜥ*) Misfortunes, calamities. (pl. of شبدعة *shibdiꜥat*) Scorpions.

A شبارق *shabārik*, (A garment) torn in pieces. (Meat) cut in bits and cooked. A crowd. *Shabārik* or *shubārik*, Name of a tall tree (of which they make amulets to hang round the necks of horses, as a preservative against the fascination of malignant eyes). Pieces. *Shubārik*, Torn (garment). Inner breeches, drawers.

P شباروز *shab-ā-roz*, Night and day. Always.

P شباروزي *shab-ā-rozī*, The civil day, twenty-four hours. باران شباروزي *bārāni shab-ā-rozī*, Twenty-four hours rain.

P شباره *shabāra*, A woman running about at night. A bat.

A شباريق *shabārīk*, Pieces. Torn (garment).

P شباشب *shab-ā-shab*, Night by night. Quick.

A شباص *shibās*, Name of a flying fish.

A شباط *shubāt*, The Syriac month of February.

A شباع *shibāꜥ*, (pl. of شبعان) Full, satiated.

A شباعة *shabāꜥat*, (v. n. of شبع) Having a capacious understanding. *Shubāꜥat*, Leavings after the appetite is satisfied. The well Zamzam.

P شب افروز *shab-afroz*, Illuminating the night. *i.e.* the moon, a candle, a glow-worm, and the like. The 10th month of the æra of Malik.

A شباك *shibāk*, Many wells adjoining together. (pl. of شبكة *shabakat*) Nets.

A شبّاك *shubbāk*, (pl. شبابيك *shabābīk*) A net. A lattice. A kind of plant. Network, whether of leather or matting. An iron grating.

A شبّاكة *shubbākat*, Network. A lattice.

A شبال *shibāl*, (pl. of شبل *shibl*) Whelps.

P شبالنگ *shabālang*, Chace, game.

A شبام *shabām*, A certain plant. *Shibām*, A piece of wood put into the mouth of a kid to prevent him from sucking: a gag. A string for tying on a woman's veil. Name of a city and tribe.

P شبان *shabān*, A bat. (pl. of شب *shab*) Nights. *Shabān* or *shubān*, A shepherd, pastor. شبان وادي ايمن *shabāni wādi-i ayman*, The shepherd of the happy valley, *i.e.* Moses.

A شبّان *shubbān*, (pl. of شابّ) Young men.

P شب انبوي *shab-ambūy*, Winter gilly-flower.

P شبانروزي *shabān-rozī*, Night and day. The civil day, twenty-four hours.

P شبان فريب *shabān-firīb*, (فريبك *firībak*, or فريوك *firīwak*) The shepherd-mocker or deceiver, a kind of bird with a shrill pipe.

P شبانكاره *shabānkāra*, Name of a district in Persia, and of a village near Tūs.

P شبانكاري *shabānkārī*, A nation.

P شبانگاه *shabān-gāh*, Evening. A lodging-place. A fold. *Sha* or *shubān-gāh*, A shepherd's cabin.

P شبانگاهي *shabān-gāhī*, Belonging to the evening. طعام شبانگاهي *taʿāmi shabān-gāhī*, The evening meal, supper.

P شب انگيز *shab-angez*, Henbane. A bat.

P شبانور *shabānūr* or *shabānvar*, A bat.

P شبانه *shabāna*, Nocturnal. Supper. Night-clothes. Night-wages. Last night's (bread or wine). Muddled, tipsy. Wine taken at night. A guardian, keeper. *Shabāna* or *shubāna*, A shepherd.

P شبانه روز *shabāna-roz*, The civil day, consisting of twenty-four hours.

P شباني *shabānī*, Pastoral charge, pastorate: the office of shepherd. A coin weighing 7 drachms. داه شباني كننده *dāhi shabānī kunanda*, A shepherdess.

A شبانيّ *shubāniy*, Red-faced and red-whiskered.

P شب آوا *shab-āwā*, Crying out at night. A nocturnal cry.

P شباويز *shabāwez*, Name of a bird which is said to suspend itself by the claws, and cry حق حق *hak hak* all night, till the blood drops from his mouth.

A شباه *shabāh* or *shubāh*, A seed like cress-seed.

A شباهة *shabāhat*, Similarity, resemblance.

P شباهنگ *shabāhang*, The morning-star. Dawn. The dog-star. The nightingale. A cote. The teeth of a mistress.

P شباهنگام *shabā-hangām*, Night-time.

A شبائب *shabāʾib*, (pl. of شبّة) Young girls.

A شبائح *shabāʾih*, Broad timbers in the camel's saddle قتب *katab*.

A شبب *shabab*, A sheep or ox in the prime of age.

P شب باره *shab-bāra*, A strumpet. A bat.

P شب باز *shab-bāz*, Who plays by night, particularly a puppet-man. One who reads the Kur'ān by night. A bat.

P شب بازه *shab-bāza*, A bat. A strumpet.

P شب بازي *shab-bāzī*, Tricks by night.

P شب باش *shab-bāsh*, A night-lodger.

P شب باشي *shab-bāshī*, Nightly lodging.

A شببة *shababat*, (pl. of شابّ *shābb*) Youths.

P شب بخير *shab ba khayr*, Good night, salutation at night.

P شب بو *shab-bo*, Polyanthus tuberosa.

P شب بوزه *shab-būza*, A bat.

P شب بوي *shab-boy*, The yellow violet. A fragrant forest-flower resembling camomile.

P شب بيدار *shab-bīdār*, Waking or watching all night, sleepless.

P شبپره *shab-para*, (or شبپرك *shab-parak*) A bat.

P شبپور *shab-pūr*, A bat.

P شب پوش *shab-posh*, Night-covering, *i.e.* Quilts, counterpanes, blankets, bedding of any kind. A woman's veil.

P شب پوي *shab-pūy*, The noise of the feet in walking gently.

P شب پيماي *shab-paymāy*, (Measuring the night) Sleepless. Sick. A lover.

A شبّة *shabbat*, A young girl.

P شبت *shibit*, (or A *shibitt*) Anise. *Shibt*, A hall.

P شب تاب *shab-tāb*, (Night-light) The moon. A candle. A black cat, from her eyes shining remarkably in the night. A fire-fly. A gem. كرم شب تاب *kirmi shab-tāb*, A fire-fly, a glow-worm.

P شب تاز *shab-tāz*, An attack by night.

P شب تك *shab-tak*, A sort of game.

A شبث *shabas*, (pl. شبثان *shibsān*) A spider. A multiped venomous insect. *Shabis*, Attached strongly to one's friends. Adhering, having the hands locked (combatants).

A شبثّ *shibiss*, Aniseed.

A شبثان *shibsān*, (pl. of شبث) Multiped insects.

A شبثة *shubasat*, Attached strongly to friends.

A شبج *shabaj*, A lofty gate or gates.

P شب جا *shab-jā*, A lodging place for the night.

P شبچراغ *shab-chirāgh*, (Night-lamp) A carbuncle, a brilliant gem. A glow-worm. A fire-fly.

P شبچراغك *shab-chirāghak*, A glow-worm.

P شبچره *shab-chara*, Dried fruits eaten at night. A nightly grazing of cattle.

P شبچك *shabchak*, (or شبچه *shabcha*) A festival-night in the month Shaabān or Zū'l Kaada.

A شبح *shabh*, (v. n. of شبح) Splitting, cleaving. Stretching out a skin between pegs. Extending the hand in supplication. Standing erect in the presence of another. Resembling, being like. Lying outstretched on a branch (a chameleon). Broad in the arm. *Shabh* or *shabah*, (pl. اشباح *ashbāh* and شبوح *shubūh*) An object indistinctly seen at a distance; form, figure. The body. A lofty gate or door. شبح الذراعين *shabhu'z zirāʿayn*, Broad-armed (man).

A شبحان *shabhān*, Long.

A شبحتان *shabahatāni*, (dual) Two sticks used in the game of منقلة *minkala*.

A شبخ *shabkh*, The noise made by milk in milking.

P شبخانه *shab-khāna*, A bed-chamber. A haram. A closet into which one retires at night for exercises of devotion.

P شب خوابي *shab-khwābī*, Night-clothes.

P شبخوان *shab-khwān*, The nightingale.

P شب خوش *shab-khwush*, Good night.

P شبخون *shab-khūn*, A night-assault. A nocturnal journey.

P شب خوني *shab-khūnī*, Robbery by night.

P شبخيز *shab-khez*, One who rises to pray or who watches in the night.

P شب خيزك *shab-khīzak*, Water-cresses.

P شبخيزي *shab-khezī*, A rising in the night.

A شبدع *shibdaʿ* or *shibdiʿ*, (pl. شبادع) Misfortune, calamity. *Shibdiʿ*, The tongue. A scorpion.

A شبدعة *shibdiʿat*, (pl. شبادع) A scorpion.

P شبديز *shab-dez*, (Night-colour) A horse of a dark rusty colour. A noble, generous steed. Name of a famous horse that belonged to Khusraw. Name of a modulation in music. شبديز نقره خنگ *shab-dezi nuhra-khing*, Heaven. Night. Day. Time. Fortune. The world.

P شبديگ *shab-deg*, (Night-pot) A dish composed of meat and turnips dressed all night on the fire.

A شبذارة *shibzārat*, Extremely jealous (man).

A شبذر *shabzar*, Clover.

P شبذير *shabzīr*, A name of God.

A شبر *shabr*, (v. n. of شبر) Measuring with the span. Giving. Tearing lengthwise. The hire for prostitution. What is paid for the loan of a stallion. Marriage. Conjugal rights. A dower. *Shabr* or *shibr*, Life. The sperm of a stallion. *Shabr* or *shabar*, (v. n. of شبر) Giving money or a sword. Asking, wishing. A gift. *Shibr*, (pl. اشبار *ashbār*) The space between the tip of the thumb and that of the little finger, a span. قبال الشبر *kibālu'sh shibr*, A serpent. قصير الشبر *kasīru'sh shibr*, Of a compact body. Short, dwarfish. *Shabar*, (v. n. of شبر) Being insolent, petulant, ungrateful to the Supreme Being, returning no thanks for prosperity. A gift. Goods, riches. An oblation: the sacrifice of the mass. An offering made by one Christian to another. Solid bodies. Powers, virtues. The Gospel.

P شبر *shibr*, A man's name. *Shabar*, A flame.

A شبراق *shibrāk*, (v. n. of شبرق Q) Tearing (a garment). Cutting (meat) into pieces. Torn in pieces (a garment). Intensity.

A شبربص *shabarbas*, A small camel.

A شبرذاة *shabarzāt*, Swift (she-camel).

A شبرزة *shabarzat*, Velocity.

A شبرزي *shabarza'*, Swift (camel).

P شبرغان *shaburghān*, The ancient name of the city of Balkh. A town near Balkh.

A شبرق *shabrak*, Torn in pieces (a garment). *Shibrik*, A species of thorn. A kitten.

A شبرقة *shabrakat*, (v.n. of شبرق Q) Running with wide and quick steps (a horse). Tearing (as a hawk his prey). Cutting in pieces.

P شبرم *shibram*, Spurge, sea-lettuce, tythimallus.

A شبرم *shubrum*, A kind of pulse. Tythimallus, a thorn. Covetous. *Shubrum* or *shabram*, Short.

A شبرمة *shubrumat*, A queen-cat. Scattered portions of a thread or rope.

P شبرنگ *shab-rang*, Obscure, black, clothed in sable. A dark bay or iron-gray horse. Name of a flower. A species of stone which burns like coal. Name of the horse of Siyāwush.

P شبرو *shab-rav*, One who travels in the night. A night-watch. A holy man. اسب شبرو *asbi shab-rav*, A swift horse, going well in the night.

P شب روي *shab-ravī*, A travelling in the night.

A شبري *shabra'*, A name common to fifty-three places in Egypt.

A شبزق *shabzak*, Touched by the devil, affected by Satanic influence.

P شب زنده دار *shab-zinda-dār*, Vigilant during night. Keeping, or who keeps the night alive.

P شب زنده داري *shab-zinda-dārī*, A keeping of vigils.

P شبست *shibist*, A monster; terror-striking.

P شبستان *shabistān*, A bed. A bed-chamber, dormitory. A king's bed-chamber. A closet where one says nightly prayers.

P شبستاني *shabistānī*, Night-clothes.

P شبسده *shab-sada*, The Epiphany. A bat.

A شبشبة *shabshabat*, A completing, finishing.

A شبص *shabas*, Roughness. Thickness and entanglement of thorns on a tree.

P شبطباط *shabitbāt*, Shepherd's-staff (an herb).

A شبع *shabaع*, Fulness, satiety. *Shibع* or *shibaع*, Enough to satisfy for once. *Shibaع*, (v. n. of شبع) Being satiated, sated, disgusted. Approaching to satiety. Being disgusted with repetition. Satiety.

A شبعان *shabعān*, Full, satiate.

P شب عبا *shab-عabā*, A dark night.

A شبعة *shubعat*, Enough to satisfy for once.

A شبعي *shabعa'*, (fem. of شبعان *shabعān*) Full, satiate. Plump (woman). شبعي الخلخال *shabعa'l khalkhāl*, (or شبعي السوار *shabعa's siwār*) A fat woman, especially when her ankle-rings and bracelets are too small for her.

P شبغا *shabghā*, (شبغار *shabghār*, شبغاره *shabghāra*, شبغاز *shabghāz*, شبغازه *shabghāza*, or شبغاو *shabghāw*) A night-fold for cattle.

P شب غريب *shab-gharīb*, Cakes and sweets distributed at a grave on the night after interment.

A شبق *shabak*, (v.n. of شبق) Burning with lust. Nauseating (food). Lust. *Shabik*, Libidinous, lewd.

A شبك *shabk*, (v.n. of شبك) Mixing. Inserting, infixing. *Shabak*, Teeth (of a comb). (pl. of شبكة *shabakat*) Nets.

P شبك *shibk*, A whirl on a spindle.

A شبكة *shubkat*, Family-connexion, affinity, relationship. *Shabakat*, (pl. شبك *shabak* and شباك *shibāk*) A fishing-net. A network veil. A lattice. Many wells adjoining each other. Wells clean and open. A country abounding in wells. The holes of a field-mouse (like network for number).

A شبكرة *shabkarat*, (from P شبكور) Purblindness.

P شبكلاه *shab-kulāh*, A night-cap. A black cap.

P شبكن *shab-kun*, Undertaking a nocturnal expedition, making an assault in the night. The cricket. Morning, dawn. شبكن زدن *shab-kun zadan*, To travel in the night.

P شبكند *shabkand*, A bird's nest.

P شبكور *shab-kūr*, Purblind at night.

P شبكوري *shab-kūrī*, Purblindness at night.

P شبكوك *shab-kūk*, (شبكوكا *shab-kūkā*, or شبكوكه *shab-kūka*) A species of mendicity, in which the mendicant at night-time takes up his post on the summit of a tree or a hillock, and from thence calls out to each individual in the village by name to come and administer to his relief.

P شبگاه *shab-gāh*, (A night-place) for sheep. Night-time.

P شبگرد *shab-gard*, The night-patrol, a watchman. The moon.

P شبگردي *shab-gardī*, A watching at night.

P شبگز *shab-gaz*, A flea (biting by night).

P شبگو *shab-go* or *gū*, Chief of the night-patrol. A singer.

P شبگون *shab-gūn*, The colour of night, *i.e.* black. A carbuncle, gem. شبگون عيار *shab-gūni عayār*, The sky. شب شبگون *shabi shab-gūn*, A very dark night.

P شبگونتن *shabgūnitan*, (in zand) To leave.

P شبگير *shab-gīr*, One who passes a sleepless night. A cricket, a nightingale, or any animal which sings at night. A certain bird that sings plaintively at daybreak. Travelling after midnight and before sunrise. A servant who works or travels in the night-time. The morning. Attacking by night. A nocturnal assault.

A شبل *shibl*, (pl. اشبال *ashbāl*, اشبل *ashbul*, شبول *shubūl*, and شبال *shibāl*) The whelp of a lion when able to hunt, or other beast of prey.

P شبلانيدن *shablānīdan*, To make adhere, unite.

A شبم *shabm*, (v. n. of شبم) Putting the stick شبم *shibamm* into (a kid's) mouth, gagging (him). *Shabam*, (v.n. of شبم) Being cold (water). Cold. *Shabim*, Cold (water or morning). Cold from want of food. Death. Poison.

A شبم *shibamm*, A piece of wood put into a kid's mouth crosswise to prevent him from sucking.

P شب مانده *shab-mānda*, Yesterday's (victuals), stale (bread).

A شبمة *shabimat*, Fat (cow).

A شبن *shabn*, (v. n. of شبن) Being soft and full of animal juices (a youth). Drawing near.

P شبنك *shabnak*, Name of a boy's game.

P شبنم *shab-nam*, (Night-moisture) Dew. A very fine species of muslin.

P شبنم صفت *shabnam-sifat*, Like dew.

P شبنيه *shabniha*, Treasure buried under ground.

P شب نياسودان *shab nayāsūdān*, (Those who rest not at night) Lovers. Thieves.

A شبو *shubūw*, (v. n. of شبا for شبو) Being high and lofty. Being bright and shining after an alteration for the worse (the face). Rearing on his hind-legs (a horse). Kindling (a fire).

A شبوات *shabawāt*, (pl. of شباة) Sharp points.

A شبوب *shabūb*, Any thing fresh and vigorous. Whatever is used in lighting a fire. A sheep or wild ox in his prime. One who does a thing well. Whatever imparts strength or beauty. A horse whose hind-feet outstep his fore-feet. *Shubūb*, (v. n. of شب) Lifting up both feet when curvetting (a horse). Kindling (a flame or war). Giving more life or brilliancy (to colour). Burning, being kindled.

P شبوبك *shabūbak*, The hoopoo.

A شبوة *shabwat*, (v. n. of شبا for شبو) Being high and lofty. A newly-hatched scorpion. A scorpion's sting. A nickname for a scorpion, as اسامة *usāmat* is for a lion. A foul-mouthed woman.

A شبّوث *shabbūs*, (pl. شبابيث) A pot-hook.

A شبوح *shubūh*, (pl. of شبح *shabah*) Bodies.

P شبور *shabūr*, A sort of musical instrument.

A P شبّور *shabbūr*, A brazen trumpet.

A شبوط *shabūt*, (شبّوط *shabbūt* or *shubbūt*) A kind of shad-fish.

P شبوقه *shubūka*, The elder-tree.

A شبول *shubūl*, (v. n. of شبل) Growing. Being delicately brought up. (pl. of شبل *shibl*) Whelps of lions or other beasts.

A شبه *shibh* or *shibah*, (pl. اشباه *ashbāh*) Like. (pl. اشباه *ashbāh*) Brass. شبه عمد *shibhi عamd*, Manslaughter. كوز شبه *kūzi shibh* or *shabah*, A copper vessel. *Shabah*, (pl. اشباه *ashbāh*) A kind of large tree. Made of brass, brazen. A kind of thorny plant bearing a scarlet blossom. (pl. مشابه *mashābih* and مشابيه *mashābīh*) Likeness, similitude, image, resemblance. *Shubah*, (pl. of شبهة *shubhat*) Doubts. Intricacies, obscure points.

P شبه *shaba*, A kind of soft black stone, a sort of coal. Agate, jet, black coral, black shells, or glass beads. A tree resembling the myrtle. يك شبه *yak shaba*, Space of one night, one night's.

A شبهان *shabahān* or *shubuhān*, Name of a thorny plant. A kind of wild thyme. A plant smaller than wheat, with which a composition is made for closing up chinks in houses and curing pains in the eyes.

A شبهة *shubhat*, (pl. شبهات *shubhāt*) Doubt, scruple, ambiguity, suspicion. An obscure, doubtful point. Intricacy. Resemblance, similitude. P دفع شبهه كردن *dafiʻ shubha kardan*, (or شبهه زائل كردن *shubha zāʼil kardan*) To remove all doubt.

P شبهر *shabhar*, The beak of the چرغ *chargh*, (a sort of hawk).

P شبهم *shabham*, A porcupine.

P شبهنگام *shab-hangām*, Night-time. At night.

A شبهي *shibhīy*, Brazen.

P شبي *shabe*, A certain night. *Shabī*, Nightly, belonging to the night. A night-shirt.

P شبيار *shab-yār*, A soporific electuary, a night-potion (a night-friend). Aloes.

P شبياره *shab-yāra*, New wine, must.

P شب يازه *shab-yāza*, A bat.

A شبيب *shabīb*, (v. n. of شبّ) Shewing more brilliancy (colour). Lifting up the fore-feet when curvetting (a horse), capering. Rearing (horse).

A شبيبة *shabībat*, (v. n. of شبّ) Attaining to puberty. Youth.

P شبيبي *shabībī*, A narcotic root. The inebriating hemp-seed also bears this name.

A شبيبيّة *shabībiyat*, Youth, youthful age.

P شبيخون *shabī-khūn*, A night-attack, surprise.

P شبيدن *shabīdan*, To turn aside, sit down in a place, perch (as a bird). To rest anywhere at night. To hang any thing to the head, or to tie round the loins.

A شبيع *shabīʻ*, Many. Hairy (rope). شبيع الغزل *shabīʻu'l ghazl*, (Cloth) of many threads, of a thick texture. شبيع العقل *shabīʻu'l ʻakl*, Of full, ample, mature intellect.

A شبيك *shubayk*, A small net.

P شبيكه *shabīka*, A net, gin, snare. Full of holes.

P شبيم *shabīm*, Running away, flight.

P شبينه *shabīna*, Nocturnal. Stale. Of last night. A bat. Grapes. Turpentine.

A شبيه *shabīh*, Alike, equal, like, resembling. A picture. شبيه بالحق *shabīh bi'l hakk*, Like the truth, probable.

P شپ *shap*, Jumping. Quick. Brilliant.

P شپاشاپ *shapāshāp*, (or شپشاپ *shapshāp*) The whiz of an arrow, or of spears.

P شپتك *shiptak*, A slap with a shoe, a kick.

P شپر *shappar*, Good, excellent.

P شپره *shapara*, (or شپرك *shaprak*) A bat.

P شپش *shapush*, *shipish*, or *shupush*, A louse.

P شپ شپ *shap shap*, Agitated, disturbed. Quick, hasty. Undignified. The whiz of an arrow. The branch of a tree.

P شپشه *shipisha*, A moth. A weevil.

P شپشين *shipishīn* or *shupushīn*, Lousy.

P شپل *shipl*, Camel's-foot (an herb). *Shipl*, (or شپلت *shiplat*) Degree, rank, dignity. The noise made by a bird's wing when flying. A loud noise.

P شپلانيدن *shaplānīdan*, To cause to adhere.

P شپليدن *shaplīdan* or *shiplīdan*, To be foolish. To act like a madman. To press, squeeze, smooth with the hand. *Shiplīdan*, To chirp, whistle.

P شپنيدن *shipnīdan*, To whistle to a horse when drinking.

P شپوختن *shipokhtan*, To give a violent shock. To sprinkle.

P شپور *shapūr*, A shad-fish.

P شپوز *shappūz*, (or شپوژ *shappūj*) A bat.

P شپوش *shap-posh*, A cap, a night-cap. A fillet worn under the head-dress. Night-clothes. A quilt, a counterpane.

P شپهٔ تير *shapaʼi tīr*, The whiz of an arrow.

P شپيختن *shipekhtan*, To sprinkle, scatter.

P شپير *shapīr*, Name of a high mountain.

P شپيل *shapīl*, Camel's-foot (an herb). *Shipel*, Pressure, squeeze. A chirp, whistle. Distress of mind, madness.

P شپيليدن *shipelīdan*, To squeeze. To play the madman. To chirp, whistle.

P شت *shat*, Money given to by-standers at the end of a game. Presence, worship, majesty.

A شتّ *shatt*, (v. n. of شتّ) Being separate, distinct, scattered. Separating, scattering. Dispersion. (pl. اشتات *ashtāt* and شتوت *shutūt*) Separate, distinct, dispersed, scattered.

A شتا *shataʼ*, Rough place. Opening of a valley.

P شتا *shitā*, One who eats nothing the whole day. (for شتاب *shitāb*) Making haste. Haste.

A شتّا *shattaʼ*, (for شتّى *shattaʼ*) Distinct, various.

A شتاء *shitāʼ*, (v. n. 3 of شتو for شتا) Agreeing (with one) for the winter. (pl. شتيّ *shutiy* and اشتية *ashtiyat*) Winter. Cold. Rain. Scarcity. (pl. of شتوة *shatwat*) Winters. وقت شتا *wakti shitā*, In the winter-time. شدّت شتا *shiddati shitā*, The severity of winter. في قلب الشتاء *fī kalbi'sh shitāʼ*, In the heart of winter, mid-winter.

P شتاب *shitāb*, Haste, speed, expedition, quickness. Quick, speedy. Quickly. (in compos.) Hastening: as, آهو شتاب *āhū-shitāb*, Hastening like a stag. بي شتاب *bī shitāb*, Slow, patient.

P شتابان *shitābān*, Any one making great haste. Hastily. شتابان روان شدن *shitābān rawān shudan*, To hurry on with great expedition.

P شتابانيدن *shitābānīdan*, To hasten, urge.

P شتاب باران *shitāb-bārān*, Wind and rain.

P شتاب باز *shitāb-bāz*, Hasty, expeditious.

P شتاب دويدگي *shitāb-dawīdagī*, Fast running.

P شتاب رو *shitāb-rav*, Swift-going, fleet.

P شتاب زدگي *shitāb-zadagī*, Haste, precipitancy, over-hastiness.

P شتاب زده *shitāb-zada*, Hasty, precipitate.

P شتاب كار *shitāb-kār*, One who makes haste. Expeditious, despatchful, diligent.

P شتاب كاري *shitāb-kārī*, Haste, despatch.

P شتابندگي *shitābandagī*, Haste.

P شتابنده *shitābanda*, Making haste, swift.

P شتابي *shitābī*, Haste, speed. Quick, hastily. شتابي كردن *shitābī kardan*, To make haste.

P شتابيدن *shitābīdan*, To make haste.

A شتات *shatāt*, (v. n. of شتّ) Being separate, distinct. Scattering, dispersing. Being dispersed, scattered. جاؤا شتات شتات *jāʼu shatāta shatāta*, They came separate and scattered.

P شتاغ *shitāgh*, Any animal which gives milk. A highway-robber. A herd.

P شتافتن *shitāftan*, To make haste.

P شتافته *shitāfta*, One who hastens. An onset.

P شتاك *shatāk*, Shoots springing from the root.

P شتالنگ *shitālang*, The ankle-bone. The heel. Sole of the foot. That part of the axletree which enters into the nave. The silken string of a musical instrument. A large clew of silk.

A شتّام *shattām*, A supercilious man.

A شتامة *shatāmat*, (v. n. of شتم) Being ugly, ill-favoured. Rejoicing at (an enemy's) distress.

P شتان *shutān*, (in zand and Pāzand) Years.

A شتّان *shattān*, (A particle having the force of a verb) They are different. شتّان ما زيد وعمرو *shattāna mā zayd wa ʻamr*, There is a difference between Zayd and Amr, they are separated. شتّان ما بينهما *shattāna mā baynahumā*, There is a great difference between them two.

P شتاه *shitāh*, A swimmer.

P شتر *shatr*, A side, corner. *Shatar*, A bird's beak. *Shutur*, A camel. شتر بي مهار *shuturi bī mahār*, Incorrigible, refractory. شتر دو كوهان *shuturi du kohān*, A dromedary. شتر سوار *shuturi suwār*, A light camel to carry expresses.

A شتر *shatr*, (v. n. of شتر) Rendering the eyelids inverted and relaxed. Cutting, chopping. Afflicting, vexing, wounding. (from P چتر *chatr*) (pl. شتور *shutūr*) An umbrella. *Shatar*, (v. n. of شتر) Being inverted, relaxed, and wide open (the eyelids). Having such eyelids (a man or the eye). Disparaging, speaking ill of. Being cut or broken off. A relaxation of the eyelid. A fissure in the upper lip. In the verse هزج *hazaj*, a shortening of مفاعيلن *mufāʻīlun* into فاعلن *fāʻilun*. *Shutar*, A worthless fellow.

P شترب *shatarb*, A tiger.

P شترباد *shutur-bād* (or بال *bāl*), A dromedary.

P شتربار *shutur-bār*, A camel's load.

P شتربان *shuturbān*, A camel-driver, or owner.

P شتر بختي *shutur-bukhtī*, A dromedary.

P شتربه *shatraba*, (mis-spelt for شنزبه *shanzaba*) Name of the ox that was instigated by the jackal Dimna to fight the lion, and perished in the contest.

P شترپا *shutur-pā* (or پاي *pāy*), Camel's-foot, an herb; turnsole, the sun-flower. Origany.

A شترة *shutrat*, Space between two fingers.

P شترخار *shutur-khār*, A thistle of which camels are fond.

P شترخو *shutur-kho*, Camel-tempered, spiteful.

P شتردل *shutur-dil*, Camel-hearted. Vindictive, spiteful. Timid, cowardly.

P شتردلي *shutur-dilī*, Cowardice, timidity.

P شتردندان *shutur-dandān*, Copperas, vitriol.

P شترزن *shutur-zan*, (Camel-striker) A large kind of spider.

P شترزهره *shutur-zahra*, Equal to a camel in courage, *i.e.* timid, cowardly.

P شترسنب *shutur-sumb*, A worm which destroys trees.

P شترسوار *shutur-suwār*, Mounted on a camel.

P شترسواري *shutur-suwārī*, (lit. Riding on a camel) Dispensing with keeping fast-days.

P شترغاز *shutur-ghāz*, A certain plant whose root is used in pickles. Root of assafœtida.

P شترغان *shutur-ghān*, Sole of a camel's foot. Butter-burr.

P شترغمزه *shutur-ghamza*, Wickedness, deceit.

P شترقطار *shutur-kitār*, A string of camels.

P شترك *shuturak*, A small camel. A wave. A man who puts himself into the shape of a camel.

P شترك بيضا *shuturak-bayzā*, A thorn of which camels are fond.

P شتركره *shutur-kurra*, A camel's colt. A wave.

P شتركش *shutur-kush*, A camel-butcher.

P شتركينه *shutur-kīna*, Bearing malice (for which the camel is remarkable).

P شترگام *shutur-gām*, A camel-step.

P شترگاو *shutur-gāw*, (also شترگاو پلنگ *shutur-gāw-palang*) A cameleopard. Name of one of the men at chess.

P شترگربه *shutur-gurba*, (Camel-cat), *i.e.* any two things which are very disproportionate, incongruous, and which have no relation to each other.

P شترگياه *shutur-giyāh*, A herb eaten by camels.

P شترماده *shutur-māda*, A she-camel.

P شترمرغ *shutur-murgh*, The ostrich.

P شترمور *shutur-mūr*, A sort of ant as big as a goat or a small calf, and said to be native of a forest in the west (literally, camel-ant).

P شترنال *shutur-nāl*, A gun carried and fired on a camel's back: a camel-swivel.

P شترنج *shatranj*, Chess. A sort of carpet. A dish composed of sundry kinds of vegetables.

P شترنگ *shatrang*, Chess. (This game is most probably of Indian origin: the word chatur anga denoting, in Sanscrit, the four members of an army; namely, elephants, horse, chariots, and infantry. A plant called مردم گياه *mardum-giyāh*, from China.

P شتروار *shutur-wār*, A camel-load.

P شتري *shuturī*, A kind of kettle-drum. A colour so called.

A شتع *shataʿ*, (v. n. of شتع) Being impatient under sickness or hunger.

A شتغ *shatgh*, (v. n. of شتغ) Trampling. Subduing. Despising, holding in contempt.

P شتفت *shitaft* or *shitift*, Height. Covering of any kind, especially the roof of a house. Furniture.

P شتكار *shat*, *shit*, or *shutkār*, Ploughing.

P شتل *shatal*, Money given to by-standers after a game is over.

P شتلم *shutulum*, Wanton, uncalled for severity, oppression. A quarrel.

A شتم *shatm*, (v. n. of شتم) Treating contumeliously, vilifying. Contumely, contempt, outrage, reproach, injury, villainy.

P شتمن *shatmin*, (in zand) The backside.

A شتن *shatn*, (v. n. of شتن) Weaving; texture. شتن الكف *shatnu'l kaff*, Hard and thick-handed.

P شتن *shatan*, (in zand and Pāzand) A city.

A شتو *shatw*, (v. n. of شتا for شتو) Wintering, passing the winter. Being very cold (winter). Suffering from scarcity in winter.

A شتوة *shatwat*, (pl. شتاء *shitāʾ*) Winter.

A شتوت *shutūt*, (pl. of شت *shatt*) Dispersed, scattered. شتوت من الناس *shutūt mini'n nās*, Different kinds of men.

A شتور *shutūr*, (pl. of شتر *shatr*, a word coined from P چتر *chatr*) Umbrellas.

A شتوم *shutūm*, (pl. of شتم *shatm*) Reproaches, injuries, outrages, oppressions. P اوضاع شتوم آميز *awzāʿi shutūm-āmez*, Acts mixed with contumely.

A شتون *shatūn*, A weaver. *Shutūn*, Soft, cloths.

A شتوي *shatwiy* or *shatawiy*, Wintry, brumal. Winter-rain.

P شته *shata*, Weak, sick. *Shata* or *shitta*, A grape. Food left at night and eaten in the morning.

P شتي *shatī*, A large salver of gold, silver, or brass.

A شتّى *shattā*, Distinct, divided. Various. قوم شتّى *kawm shattā*, A miscellaneous company or crowd. اشياء شتّى *ashyāʾ shattā*, Diverse things.

A شتي *shatiy*, Winter-rain. *Shutiy*, (pl. of شتاء *shitāʾ*) Winters.

A شتية *shatiyat*, Winter.

A شتيت *shatīt*, (v. n. of شت) Scattering, dispersing. Being separate, scattered. Separate, distinct: scattered, divided. (Teeth) widely set.

A شتير *shittīr*, Abounding in wickedness and vices, of a bad disposition.

A شتيم *shatīm*, Reproached, reviled, cursed. Deformed, horrible, hideous, grim. A lion.

A شتيمة *shatīmat*, Contumely, reproach, outrage.

P شتين *shatīn*, A rope.

P شتينا *shatīnā*, (in zand and Pāz.) Laughing.

A شث *shass*, A bee. A wild nut. Bitter, odoriferous herbs, with which hides are tanned. (pl. شثاث *shisās*) A piece broken off the summit of a mountain, and standing like a pinnacle.

A شثا *shasā*, The opening of a valley.

A شثالة *shasālat*, (v. n. of شثل) Being thick and hard (the fingers).

A شثر *shisr*, (pl. شثور *shusūr*) The projection or summit of a mountain. *Shasar*, (v. n. of شثر) Becoming thick and dim from mattery humour (the eye). *Shasir*, (A spear) broken in pieces.

A شثل *shasl*, Thick-fingered (man). *Shasal*, (v. n. of شثل) Being thick (the fingers).

A شثن *shasn*, (v. n. of شثن) Being rough and thick (the palm of the hand). Swelling (a camel's lip) from browsing upon thorns. Thick, coarse, fat (in the hand or the fingers). Thick-limbed. Swollen from eating thorns (a camel's lip). Texture, weaving.

A شثور *shusūr*, (pl. of شثر *shisr*) Summits or salient points of mountains.

A شثونة *shusūnat*, (v. n. of شثن) Being thick and rough (the palm of the hand).

A شثير *shasīr*, Whatever a torrent sweeps along (as herbage, straw, chips of wood, and the like). Young saplings growing around the root of a tree.

P شج *shaj*, Hard, white, and unproductive soil.

A شج *shajj*, (v. n. of شج) Breaking (the head). Crossing (a desert). Ploughing the ocean (a ship). Diluting (wine).

A شجا *shajā*, (v. n. of شجي) Being anxious, vexed. Being pained in the throat, suffocated. Going off. Any thing which causes a pain in the throat. Chimera. Busy, occupied, employed.

A شجاءة *shajāʾat*, A being sad and sorrowful.

A شجاب *shijāb*, A three-footed piece of wood on which they hang clothes, a horse. A stopple.

A شجاج *shijāj*, (pl. of شجة *shajjat*) Wounds, fractures on the head. P شجاج بي علاج *shijāji bi ʿilāj*, Incurable wounds.

A شجاذ *shajāz*, (a corruption of مشجاذ *mishjāz*) A sling for throwing stones.

A شجار *shijār*, (v. n. 3 of شجر) Resisting, opposing, controverting Pasturing, tending cattle. A wooden bar or bolt of a door. A bit of wood put into a kid's mouth to prevent his sucking. The flooring of a house. The crooked billet with which a bucket is drawn up. The wood-work of a bed or sofa. A burnt mark on a camel. (pl. of شجر *shajr*) Chins. *Shijār* or *shajār*, (pl. شجر *shujur*) The wood-work of the hawdah. An open camel-litter.

P شجارا *shajārā*, (in zand and Pāzand) A tree.

A شجاع *shajāʿ*, *shijāʿ*, or *shujāʿ*, (pl. شجعة *shajʿat*, *shijʿat*, *shujʿat*, and *shajaʿat*) Intrepid, warlike, magnanimous. *Shijāʿ*, (pl. of شجيع *shajīʿ*) Bold, brave. *Shujāʿ* or *shijāʿ*, (pl. شجعان *shijʿān* and *shujʿān*) A species of serpent. شجاع الجوع *shujāʿu'l jūʿ*, A maw-worm in the bowels.

A شجاعة *shajāʿat*, (v. n. of شجع) Being bold, courageous, magnanimous. Fortitude, valour, intrepidity. ذو شجاعة *zū shajāʿat*, Warlike. *Shujāʿat*, *shajāʿat*, or *shijāʿat*, Brave, bold (woman).

P شجاعت شعار *shajāʿat-shiʿār*, Intrepid.

P شجام *shajām* or *shijām*, A nipping cold.

P شجانيدن *shajānīdan*, To expose to cold, to chill.

P شجانيده *shajānīda*, Affected or altered by cold.

A شجائع *shajāʾiʿ*, (pl. of شجيعة) Bold (women).

A شجب *shajb*, (v. n. of شجب) Giving a death's wound. Making sad. Employing, occupying. Dragging. Strengthening. Corking (a bottle). Wounding a deer, which stirs his legs, but is unable to move from his place. (pl. شجوب *shujūb*) Want, necessity. Grief, care, solicitude. A column. A dried leathern bottle with a few pebbles in it, by which a rattling noise is made for driving on a camel. A leathern bottle cut in two, of which one half serves as a bucket. Long. Name of the father of an Arabian tribe. *Shajab*, (v. n. of شجب) Perishing. Grief. Pain, anguish, sorrow, either from sickness or from battle. *Shajib*, Perishing, lost. Sad, grieved, melancholy. *Shujub*, Three sticks on which a shepherd hangs his implements.

A شجة *shajjat*, (pl. شجاج *shijāj*) A contusion or fracture on the skull.

A شجج *shajaj*, The scar of a wound (on the forehead). Murmuring of flowing water.

A شججى *shajaja'*, A kind of bird. A sort of crow.

P شجد *shajad*, Intense cold.

A شجذة *shajzat*, A slight shower, gentle rain.

A شجر *shajr*, (v. n. of شجر) Averting, diverting, turning from. Opening the mouth. Tying, binding. Preventing, hindering, pushing away, putting to a distance. Propping (a house with a pillar). Lifting up the branches of a tree which hang down. Twitching, jerking the bridle, making a horse open his mouth. Piercing (with a spear). Hanging (a garment) over the clothes-horse called مشجر *mishjar*. A controversy, a discordant, intricate affair. A narrow space between two places. The holding place of a pack-saddle. (pl. اشجار *ashjār*, شجور *shujūr*, and شجار *shijār*) The chin. The orifice of the mouth, or the outer corner of it. The space between the jaws. *Shajar*, (v. n. of شجر) Being many, numerous (a collection, crowd, or sum told). An intricate, embroiled, disputed business. The part between the كزين *kazzayn* of a man. The upper part of the mouth, the palate. *Shajar* or *shijar*, A tree, a plant, rising on a stem, and supporting itself. *Shajir*, Woody, abounding in trees. *Shujur*, (pl. of شجار *shijār*) Wooden bars or bolts of doors. Open camel-litters.

A شجراء *shajrās*, (fem. of اشجر *ashjar*) Abounding in trees. A tree.

A شجرة *shajarat*, One tree. Any plant. A dimple in the chin. Quantity. Form, dimension, measure. A man. شجرهٔ ابراهيم *shajaraʼi ibrāhīm*, Cinquefoil. Egyptian thorn. شجرة البراغيث *shajaratu'l barāghīs*, Hemp-agrimony. شجرة التين *shajaratu't tīn*, The tree called elephant's ears. شجرة الجن *shajaratu'l jinn*, The juniper. شجرة الحيوة *shajaratu'l hayāt*, Tree of life. The cypress. شجرة الخطاطيف *shajaratu'l khatātīf*, Turmeric. شجرة الدب *shajaratu'd dubb*, The bear's-tree. The medlar-tree. شجرة الدم *shajaratu'd dam*, Fumitory. شجرة الراهب *shajaratu'r rāhib*, A kind of tree, the oil of which is a powerful emetic. شجرهٔ رستم *shajaraʼi rustam*, Long birthwort. شجرة الزقوم *shajaratu'z zakkūm*, The infernal tree, the fruit of which is devils' heads. شجرهٔ سليمان *shajaraʼi sulaymān*, The wild apple. Name of a plant which shines at night; also name of several other plants. الشجرة الطيبة *ash' shajaratu't tayyibat*, The palm-tree. شجرة الكافور *shajaratu'l kāfūr*, Camomile. شجرة مريم *shajarat maryam*, (or شجرة الطلق *shajaratu't talk*) Sowbread. شجرهٔ موسي *shajaraʼi mūsa'*, Moses' bush, *i.e.* the bramble. ما احسن شجرة ضرع الناقة *mā ahsana shajarata zarʻi'n nākati*, How beautiful is the teat of the camel as to size, form, veins, skin, and flesh!

P شجرستان *shajaristān*, A place set with trees.

P شجر نامه *shajar-nāma*, A list of saints or holy predecessors, given to disciples (in the manner of a genealogical tree).

A شجري *shajariy*, Palatal. الحروف الشجرية *al hurūfu'sh shajarīyat*, The letters شضج.

A شجع *shajʻ*, (v. n. of شجع) Excelling in intrepidity or activity. *Shajaʻ*, Swiftness of foot in a camel. Tallness. *Shajiʻ*, Nimble, swift. Frantic (camel). *Shajiʻ* or *shijaʻ*, Intrepid, brave, warlike. *Shujuʻ*, Roots of a tree. Wooden reins. (pl. of شجيع *shajīʻ*) Bold, brave.

A شجعاء *shajʻās*, (fem. of اشجع *ashjaʻ*) Bold, swift. Active, nimble. *Shujaʻās*, (pl. of شجيع *shajīʻ*) Brave, intrepid.

A شجعان *shujʻān* or *shijʻān*, (pl. of شجيع *shajīʻ*) Brave, warlike. (pl. of شجاع *shujāʻ* or *shijāʻ*) Species of serpents.

A شجعة *shajʻat*, A camel's colt imperfectly formed when foaled. *Shajʻat*, *shijʻat*, *shujʻat*, or *shajaʻat*, (pl. of شجاع *shajāʻ*, *shujāʻ*, or *shijāʻ*) Bold, intrepid. *Shujʻat* or *shajʻat*, Weak, feeble, heartless. *Shajiʻat*, Bold, brave (woman): nimble (she-camel).

A شجعم *shajʻam*, Long, tall. The body or neck of a man. A lion.

A شجغ *shajgh*, (v. n. of شجغ) Moving the feet quickly (an animal when running).

P شجليز *shajlīz*, Intense cold.

A شجم *shajam*, Death, destruction *Shujum*, Long, tall, and withal impure, wicked, subtle (men). Long-continued misfortunes.

A شجن *shajn*, (v. n. of شجن) Detaining any one (necessary business). Making sad. (pl. شجون *shujūn*) A road (especially through a valley). *Shajan*, (v. n. of شجن) Being sad, sorrowful. (pl. شجون *shujūn*, and اشجان *ashjān*) A necessary thing. (pl. اشجان *ashjān*) Anguish, grief, sadness. Intricate (branches). Ramification. Compactly-built (camel).

P شجن *shajan*, Intense cold.

A شجنة *shajnat*, *shijnat*, or *shujnat*, Ramification. شجنة الرحم *shujnatu'r rahim*, Connection by alliance or relationship. *Shijnat*, A ripe stalk of a bunch of grapes. A fissure in a mountain. *Shijnat* or *shujnat*, Intangled roots of trees.

A شجو *shajw*, (v. n. of شجا for شجو) Falling out, quarrelling. Making sad. Setting (persons) a quarrelling. Causing to leap for joy. Affliction, anguish. Necessity.

A شجواء *shajwās*, A desert difficult to pass.

A شجوب *shajūb*, (A woman) overwhelmed with care, and well-nigh broken-hearted. *Shujūb*, (v. n. of شجب) Perishing. Destroying. Making sad. Keeping back, imprisoning. Wounding (a deer) with an arrow, so that he cannot move from the place.

A شجوجاة *shajawjāt*, Perpetually blowing (wind). A she-magpie.

A شجوجي *shajawja'*, (or شجوجاء *shajawjās*) Very tall and large-boned. Long-legged. Long-backed and short-legged. Bulky (horse). A magpie. Perpetually blowing (wind).

A شجور *shujūr*, (v. n. of شجر) Being debated, disputed, becoming an occasion of contention. (pl. of شجر *shajr*) Chins. Openings of mouths, spaces between jaws.

A شجون *shujūn*, (v. n. of شجن) Making sad. Being sad. Ways, modes. Designs, views, machinations. (pl. of شجن *shajn*) Roads, ways, especially through valleys. (pl. of شجن *shajan*) Necessary things. ذو شجون *zū shujūn*, Mixed, intermingled.

A شجي *shajī*, Anxious, vexed, sorrowful.

A شجي *shajīy*, Busy, occupied, employed. Sad, sorrowful, grieved.

A شجية *shajiyat*, Sad, melancholy (woman).

A شجيج *shajīj*, Fractured in the skull. Split (post).

A شجير *shajīr*, Abounding in trees, woody. Foreign (man or camel). A sword. An arrow used in drawing lots, not from the same tree as the others. A companion. Bad, naught.

A شجيرة *shujayrat*, A small tree, shrub, bush.

A شجيع *shajīʻ*, (pl. شجع *shujuʻ*, شجاع *shijāʻ*, شجعان *shijʻān*, *shujʻān*, or شجعاء *shujaʻās*) Bold, brave, intrepid.

A شجيعة *shajīʻat*, (pl. شجائع) Brave (woman).

P شچك *shachuk*, Hiccup. A preparation of fresh milk, sour milk, and anise.

A شح *shahh*, (v. n. of شح) Being avaricious. *Shuhh*, *shahh*, or *shihh*, Avarice. الشح المطاع *ash' shuhhu'l mutāʻ*, One whom his friend obeys in keeping back and withholding just dues.

A شحا *shaha'*, Ample, wide.

A شحاث *shahhās*, (vulg. for شحاذ *shahhāz*) A beggar. A grinder.

A شحاج *shuhāj*, (v. n. of شحج) Croaking an ill-omened note (as a crow).

A شحاج *shahhāj*, Braying (ass). The wild ass. بنات شحاج *banātu shahhāj*, Mules.

A شحاح *shahāh*, Avaricious. Ground on which water does not remain excepting in excessive rains. Ground on which it easily stagnates. Little (water). Barren. Shallow (well). A flint, a marcasite, or any similar stone which does not strike fire, being good for nothing. A camel which gives little milk. *Shiḥāḥ*, (v. n. 3 of شح) Acting covetously (towards another). (pl. of شحيح *shaḥīḥ*) Avaricious.

A شحاذ *shaḥḥāẕ*, A sturdy beggar. A grinder.

A شحاذة *shiḥāẕat*, Beggary, mendicity.

A شحارير *shaḥārīr*, (pl. of شحرور *shuḥrūr*) Certain melodious birds.

A شحاص *shiḥāṣ*, (pl. of شحص *shaḥṣ*) Sheep which yield no milk; or fat and barren.

A شحاف *shiḥāf*, (in Himyaritic) Milk.

A شحاك *shiḥāk*, A piece of wood put crosswise into a kid's mouth to prevent him from sucking.

A شحام *shaḥḥām*, A vender of fat or lard.

A شحامة *shaḥāmat*, (v. n. of شحم) Being fat; having much fat or lard.

A شحائح *shaḥāʼiḥ*, (pl. of شحيحة *shaḥīḥat*) (Camels) whose milk flows sparingly.

A شحة *shiḥḥat*, Any thing guarded with avaricious care.

A شحتلة *shaḥtalat*, A pinch (of snuff). A single plucking of hair.

A شحجان *shaḥajān*, The croak of a raven.

A شحدد *shuḥdud*, Bad-tempered.

A شحذ *shaḥẕ*, (v. n. of شحذ) Grinding, whetting (a knife). Gnawing the stomach (hunger). Driving on, urging forward with violence. Driving away, banishing. Eyeing malignantly. Peeling. Begging with importunity. Wrath.

A شحذان *shaḥaẕān*, Starved, famished, hungry, sharp-set. A hard cattle-driver. Active at work.

A شحذوف *shuḥẕūf*, Swift, impetuous (horse, &c.).

A شحر *shaḥr*, (v. n. of شحر) Opening the mouth. The aperture of the mouth. The hollow of a valley. The channel of a river. The scar remaining on a camel's back after the raw is healed. *Shaḥr* or *shiḥr*, The Arabian coast from Omān to Aden.

A شحرة *shiḥrat*, A narrow bank of a river.

A شحرور *shuḥrūr*, (pl. شحارير *shaḥārīr*) A kind of singing bird.

A شحز *shaḥz*, Marriage. Venery. Fear, a fleeing away in terror.

A شحس *shaḥs*, A certain tree resembling the wild olive, and, when very dry, used for making bows.

A شحسار *shaḥsār*, Long.

A شحشاح *shaḥshāḥ*, Avaricious. Assiduously attentive. Jealous. A strong woman. A virago.

A شحشح *shaḥshaḥ*, Swift-flying (bird). Jealous. Assiduously attentive to any thing. Eloquent, bold in speech. Ground on which water soon lies after a little rain. Ground on which water does not lie except after excessive rains. Much croaking (raven). Intrepid. Long. Avaricious. Perverse, evil-disposed. An extensive desert. *Shaḥshaḥ* or *shuḥshaḥ*, Light (ass).

A شحشحان *shaḥshaḥān*, Avaricious. Jealous. Long.

A شحشحة *shaḥshaḥat*, (v. n. of شحشح Q) Flying swiftly. Braying in the throat (a camel). Caution, prudence. The note of the bird صرد *ṣurad*.

A شحص *shaḥṣ* or *shaḥaṣ*, (pl. اشحاص *ash-ḥāṣ*, شحاص *shiḥāṣ*, شحص *shuḥṣ*, and *shaḥaṣ*) A sheep which yields no milk: or one fat and barren, which has never been blissomed.

A شحصاء *shaḥṣāʼ*, (or شحصة *shaḥaṣat*) A sheep yielding no milk, or one fat and barren; or one that has not been blissomed.

A شحط *shaḥṭ*, Dung of birds. A vine-prop. Commotion of the blood. *Shaḥaṭ* or *shaḥṭ*, (v. n. of شحط) Being distant, absent. Retiring, receding. Filling a vessel. Out-stripping, excelling in any thing. Diluting (wine or milk). Slaughtering (a camel). Being estimated beyond the value. Training, propping (a palm-shoot). Voiding dung. Stinging (a scorpion). Twittering (a bird). Cutting off (hopes). Wallowing in blood (a wounded man).

A شحطة *shaḥṭat*, A disease incident to the breasts of camels. Vestiges of a scratch on the side or thighs.

A شحف *shaḥf*, (in the dialect of Yaman) A peeling of the skin.

A شحك *shaḥk*, (v. n. of شحك) Putting the cross stick called شحاك *shiḥāk* in a kid's mouth to prevent him from sucking, gagging him.

A شحم *shaḥm*, (v. n. of شحم) Giving fat to eat. Fat, grease, lard, suet. Colocynth-pulp (from its resemblance). The delicate yellowish pulp between the seeds of the pomegranate. Pith. A mushroom. A white earth-worm. A kind of bird. A sort of game. شحم الخنزير *shaḥmu'l khinzīr*, Hog's lard. شحم كلاه *bi shaḥmi kulāhu*, In his state of joy. *Shaḥam*, (v. n. of شحم) Being fond of, or longing for, fat. Being smeared with fat (a skin). *Shaḥim*, Fond of fat, lard, or suet. Juiceless (grape).

A شحمة *shaḥmat*, A bit of fat. A kind of bird. A sort of game. شحمة الاذن *shaḥmatu'l uẕn*, The lobe of the ear. شحمة الارض *shaḥmatu'l arẓ*, A white mushroom. A kind of white worm. شحمة الحنظل *shaḥmatu'l ḥanẓal*, Pulp of the colocynth. شحمة الرمان *shaḥmatu'r rummān*, Pulp of the pomegranate. شحمة العين *shaḥmatu'l ʻayn*, The black, also the white of the eye. شحمة المرج *shaḥmatu'l marj*, Marsh-mallows.

A شحموط *shuḥmūṭ*, Long.

A شحن *shaḥn*, (v. n. of شحن) Filling (a vessel or a town with armed men), loading (a ship). Driving away. Prosecuting the chase to a distance, but not catching (dogs). *Shaḥan*, (v. n. of شحن) Hating.

A شحناء *shaḥnāʼ*, Enmity, extreme hatred.

P شحنائي *shaḥnāʼī*, Superintendence.

A شحنة *shiḥnat*, Daily allowance of forage for cattle. A body or small troop of horse. Enmity, hatred. Troops enough to controul a city, garrison.

A شحنكية *shaḥnakīyat*, Vicegerency.

P شحنگي *shaḥnagī*, The police.

P شحنه *shaḥna*, A viceroy, vicegerent, representative, lieutenant. Head of the police. A prefect. A mayor, provost. An ambassador. A peon or servant of a tax-gatherer. شحنهٔ پنجم حصار *shaḥnaʼi panjum ḥiṣār*, The planet Mars. شحنهٔ چهارم *shaḥnaʼi chahārum*, (شحنهٔ چهارم كتاب *shaḥnaʼi chahārum kitāb*, شحنهٔ درياي عشق *shaḥnaʼi daryāyi ʻishq*, or شحنهٔ غوغاي قيامت *shaḥnaʼi ghawghāyi qiyāmat*) Muhammad. شحنهٔ چهارم حصار *shaḥnaʼi chahārum ḥiṣār*, The Sun. Jesus. شحنهٔ شب *shaḥnaʼi shab*, A watchman. A house-breaker. A lover. A prisoner. شحنهٔ شب و سحر *shaḥnaʼi shab u saḥar*, The night-patrol. Muhammad. شحنهٔ نجف *shaḥnaʼi najaf*, The caliph Aliy. *Shiḥna*, The night-patrol. *Shaḥana*, The guards of a town.

A شحو *shaḥw*, (v. n. of شحا for شحو) Opening (the mouth). Being open.

A شحواء *shaḥwāʼ*, Wide (well).

A شحوب *shuḥūb*, (or شحوبة *shuḥūbat*) (v. n. of شحب) Being changed in colour (the face, from extreme hunger or from travel). Paring the surface, making smooth or level (with a spade).

A شحوة *shaḥwat*, A step, a pace. بعيد الشحوة *baʻīdu'sh shaḥwat*, Who goes with long steps.

A شحور *shaḥwar*, A kind of sweetly-singing bird.

A شحوص *shaḥūṣ*, Lean with fatigue (she-camel).

A شحوط *shuḥūṭ*, (v. n. of شحط) Being distant, absent. Retiring, receding. Outstripping. Diluting (wine or milk). Slaughtering (a camel). Stinging (a scorpion). Chirping (a bird). Being estimated above the value. Propping (a palm-shoot). Filling (a vessel). Voiding (dung). Wallowing in one's blood (a wounded man).

A شحول *shaḥwal*, Long-footed (man).

A شحوم *shuḥūm*, (pl. of شحم) Fats, suets, lards.

A شحي *shaḥy*, An opening. A being open.

SY شحيثاء *shaḥīsāʼ*, A magic or mystical word by which intricate places are opened without keys.

A شحيج *shaḥīj*, (v. n. of شحج) Croaking (a raven), braying (a mule). Growing old, and getting a hoarse note (a crow).

A شحيح *shaḥīḥ*, (pl. شحاح *shiḥāḥ*, اشحة *ashiḥhat*, and اشحاء *ashiḥḥāʼ*) Covetous, avaricious.

A شحيحة *shaḥīḥat*, (pl. شحائح *shaḥāʼiḥ*) A camel which gives little milk, stingy.

A شحير *shaḥīr*, A sort of tree.

A شحيم *shaḥīm*, Fat, greasy, suety. One who eats fat willingly.

P شخ *shakh*, Hard ground, especially on the summit or at the skirt of a mountain. Any thing hard. A mountain. The nose of a mountain, a promontory. A branch. A horn. *Shukh*, Dirt, filth.

A شخخ *shakhkhkh*, (v. n. of شخ) Snoring in sleep. The noise made by milking or making water. Urine, stale.

A شخا *shakhā'*, Saltish ground.

P شخا *shakhkhā*, The sinking of a needle or thorn into the flesh. Scratching. A tearing with the nails.

A شخاب *shikhāb*, Milk whilst being drawn, new milk. (pl. of شخبة *shukhbat*) Streams of milk.

A شخات *shikhāt*, (pl. of شخت *shakht* or *shakhat*) Thin, slender (men), but not emaciated.

P شخادان *shakhādān*, Scratching, wounding with the nails.

A شخادب *shakhādib*, (pl. of شخدب *shukhdub*) Reptiles of a certain kind.

A شخاذب *shukhāzib*, Thick and hard.

P شخار *shakhār*, Ashes of which they make soap or lye for washing; a lixivium used by fullers or dyers. Sal ammoniac, vitriol, copperas. A brick. A spot, mole. The lungs. Orage.

A شخاصة *shakhāsat*, A being large-bodied.

A شخاف *shikhāf*, (in Himyaritic) Milk.

P شخال *shakhāl*, A tearing with the nails.

A شخال *shikhāl*, (v. n. 3 of شخل) Behaving sincerely, acting with pure affection.

P شخاليدن *shakhālīdan*, To tear with the nails. To prick.

P شخانه *shakhāna*, A lixivium for dyeing, as in شخار *shakhār* above. *Shukhāna*, A meteor.

P شخانيدن *shakhānīdan*, To cause to stare. *Shukhānīdan*, To cause one to tear with the nails. To cause to leap.

P شخاي *shakhāy*, (incomp.) Scratching, tearing.

P شخاييدن *shakhāyidan*, To scratch, to wound with the nails. To be pricked.

P شخاييده *shakhāyida*, Wounded with the nails. scratched. Pricked.

A شخب *shakhb*, (v. n. of شخب) Milking. Blood. *Shakhb* or *shukhb*, Milk which streams in rays when milked. شخب في الاناء و شخب في الارض *shakhb fi'l inā wa shakhb fi'l arz*, One emulsion into the pail, and one on the ground (now a hit, and then a miss). *Shakhab*, (v. n. of شخب) Streaming in rays (as milk or blood).

A شخبة *shukhbat*, (pl. شخاب *shikhāb*) One ray of streaming milk.

A شخت *shakht* or *shakhat*, (pl. شخات *shikhāt*) Thin, slender, lean (man), but not emaciated.

A شختيت *shikhtīt*, Dust which is whirled aloft.

A شخدب *shukhdub*, (pl. شخادب *shakhādib*) A sort of reptile.

A شخر *shakhr*, (v. n. of شخر) Braying, snivelling, neighing, grunting, making a noise through the nose or throat. Ripping (the anus). Tearing his sack, and throwing the contents about (a camel). Beginning (of youth). The seat of a saddle. Any thing fallen from a mountain.

P شخرور *shakhrūr*, A black mulberry. Ashes used by bleachers.

P شخروز *shakhrūz*, A black mulberry.

A شخز *shakhz*, (v. n. of شخز) Tottering, staggering. Undergoing difficulties. Disquieting. Throwing into trouble and difficulties. Piercing with a spear. Tearing out (an eye). Setting people by the ears. Agitation, commotion. Inconvenience, trouble, labour, pains. Affliction.

A شخزب *shakhzab*, Thick and hard.

A شخس *shakhs*, (v. n. of شخس) Undergoing difficulty and trouble. Being different, diversified. Opening his mouth when yawning (an ass). Agitation, commotion. Discord, contrariety.

P شخسار *shakhsār*, Hard ground. A place abounding in trees.

P شخش *shakhsh*, A slip, trip. Any thing old and worn out. *Shakhish*, A slip, slide, trip. *Shukhash*, Name of a small, but melodious bird.

A شخش *shakhsh*, Fragments, pieces of soft stone called يرمغ *yarmaġ*.

A شخشاخ *shakhshākh*, (A boy) who makes water into the air.

P شخشار *shakhshār*, Name of a bird whitish about the head.

P شخشانيدن *shakhshānīdan*, To cause to stumble.

A شخشخة *shakhshakhat*, (v. n. of شخشخ Q) Making water in a stream (a boy). Being extended, drawn out. Lifting up his brisket when lying down (a camel). The clashing of arms, the rustling of papers or of new clothes.

P شخشيدن *shakhshīdan*, To hurt the foot against a stone. To trip, stumble, fall.

A شخص *shakhs*, (v. n. of شخص) Being bulky and corpulent. (pl. اشخص *ashkhus*, شخوص *shukhūs*, and اشخاص *ashkhās*) A person, body, individual. Any figure appearing black at a distance.

A شخصي *shakhse*, A certain one, somebody.

A شخصيّة *shakhsiyat*, Nobility. Rank. Humanity.

A شخف *shakhf*, Noise of milk being milked.

P شخكاسه *shakhkāsa*, Hoar-frost. Hail.

P شخل *shakhl*, Sound, noise, complaint. Whistling. Pecking (as a bird).

A شخل *shakhl*, (v. n. of شخل) Racking, making bright (wine). Milking (a camel). A boy, youth, friendly and sincere. A friend.

P شخلي *shakhlī*, A thorn, thorny plant.

P شخليدن *shakhlīdan*, To whistle. To inspire, breathe. To faint, wither, flag.

P شخم *shukhm*, Land ploughed and ready for sowing. شخم زدن *shukhm zadan*, To plough.

A شخم *shakham*, (v. n. of شخم) Stinking, being spoiled (meat). *Shukhum*, Those whose noses are filled with odours (good or bad).

P شخن *shakhan*, A tearing, wounding. Afflicted.

P شخنشار *shakhanshār*, Name of a water-bird of a dark colour, with a white head.

A شخوتة *shukhūtat*, A being or a becoming slender, but not meagre.

P شخود *shakhūd*, Wounded with the nails. A scratch made by the nails.

P شخودن *shakhūdan*, To vex. To scratch with the nails. To scratch the face with the nails. To be scratched. To spring upon, to assail. To assemble, be collected. To be narrow, to be in difficulty.

P شخوده *shakhūda*, Scratched, wounded by the nails or teeth.

A شخوص *shukhūs*, (v. n. of شخص) Exalting, raising one's self. Lifting (the eyes). Looking earnestly with open eyes. Departing, travelling from country to country. Going high. Passing over the mark (an arrow). Being large-bodied. Being open and swelling (a wound). Remaining wide open (the eye). Ascending, being high (a star). Being pronounced or appearing to come out of the upper part of the mouth (a word). (pl. of شخص *shakhs*) Bodies, persons.

P شخول *sha* or *shikhūl*, A whistling noise made to induce a horse to drink. A cry for help, roar, lamentation. Feebleness, languor, extenuation of body.

P شخوليدن *sha* or *shikhūlīdan*, To cry out, scold, groan, make a noise: to thunder. To neigh. To whistle. To understand imperfectly, to take in a wrong light. To scratch. To pine away, grow pale, flag, wither.

P شخوليده *shakhūlīda*, Languid, dried, withered.

A شخيت *shakhīt*, Thin and slender. *Shakhīt*, (or شخيت *shikhkhīt*) Dust whirled in the air.

A شخيخ *shakhīkh*, (v. n. of شخ) Voiding urine in a stream: squirting it to a distance. Snoring.

P شخيد *shakhīd*, Presence, worship.

P شخيدن *shakhīdan*, To slip, slide, fall down. To recover when stumbling. To stare, to fix the eyes sternly (like an angry man or bull). To grow pale, languid.

P شخيده *shakhīda*, Withered. Slipped, slidden. One who recovers himself when stumbling.

A شخير *shakhīr*, (v. n. of شخر) Making a sound through the throat or nose, snivelling. Neighing (a horse). Lifting up the saddle-cloth in order to put the saddle more forward. Laying the clusters of dates upon the branches that they may not snap. Any thing flowing or falling from a mountain.

A شخير *shikhkhīr*, One who makes a loud and frequent noise in the throat or nose.

P شخيره *shakhīra*, Ashes of which they make soap.

A شخيس *shakhīs*, Scattered, distracted, broken up.

P شخيش *shakhīsh*, Name of a melodious bird.

A شخيص *shakhīs*, Corpulent, large-bodied. A chief, a prince. Harsh speech.

A شخيف *shikhkhīf*, Thick, corpulent.

P شخيل *shakhīl*, A whistling noise made to induce a horse to drink. A cry for help.

A شخيل *shakhīl*, A youth friendly and sincere.

P شخيليدن *shakhīlīdan*, To whistle. To coax a horse to drink. To wither, become pale.

P شد *shud*, (from شدن *shudan*) It was, or became. He departed, went; he perished, ceased, died. آمد و شد كردن *āmad u shud kardan*, To come and go. To frequent.

P شدّ *shadd*, (in music) A pitching of the voice. شدّ پهلوان *shaddi pahluwān*, A shout made by wrestlers before setting to.

A شدّ *shadd*, (v. n. of شدّ) Running. Rushing (to battle), attacking. Binding, tying, girding. Strengthening, establishing, confirming, corroborating. Ascending (fire). Holding fast, firmly. Manifesting a desire. Being hard, rigid, and firm. شدّ المئزر *shaddu'l mi*ز*ar*, Tying up one's breeches (an expression denoting abstinence from venery, or preparation for labour). شدّ النهار *shaddu'n nahār*, The hottest part of the day. (pl. شدود *shudūd*) A covering for the head, worn by the higher classes in Morocco. (in gram.) The character tashdīd or sign of reduplication.

A شدا *shada'*, Remains of strength. A part. Edge, point. Heat. Battle.

A شداد *shidād*, (pl. of شديد *shadīd*) Severe. Strong, hard.

A شداقم *shudāḳim*, Large-mouthed, large about the corners of the mouth. A lion.

P شد آمد *shud-āmad*, A going and coming. Custom, usage.

A شداه *shudāh*, Astonishment, amazement, confusion of mind. Occupation, employment.

A شدائد *shadāïd*, (pl. of شديدة *shadīdat*) Adversities, troubles, tribulations, disagreeable events.

P شد بود *shud būd*, So so.

A شدّة *shaddat*, One assault, attack, or charge. *Shiddat*, (v. n. of شدّ) Being hard, vehement. Intensity, vehemence, violence, severity. Force, strength. Adversity, affliction, difficulty. Scarcity, famine.

A شدح *shadh*, (v. n. of شدح) Being fat. Having liberty, facility, or opportunity.

A شدحة *shudhat*, Liberty, opportunity, ability. Space, room, width.

A شدخ *shadkh*, (v. n. of شدخ) Breaking any thing hollow, whether dry or moist (as the head, or an apple). Hitting the مشدّخ *mushaddakh*. Treading, trampling. Appearing false and vain. Reaching from the forehead to the nose (the blaze on a horse's face). Being curved, bent, and crooked. Declining. *Shadakh*, An abortion.

A شدخاء *shadkhā*, (fem. of اشدخ *ashdakh*) (A mare) with a white streak on the forehead to the nose.

A شدخة *shadkhat*, Soft, flexible, juicy (plant).

P شدّ رغو *shadd-raghū*, Name of a musical instrument.

A شدف *shadf*, (v. n. of شدف) Cutting piecemeal. *Shadaf*, (pl. شدوف *shudūf*) A person, body, individual. Any figure appearing black at a distance. Darkness. Height, sublimity. Nobility. Joy, glee, exultation. A distortion of the cheek. *Shadif*, Tall, large. Nimble, brisk in the attack. *Shuduf*, (pl. of شدفاء *shadfā*) Wry-cheeked (women). Curved (Persian bows).

P شدف *shadaf*, A drum.

A شدفاء *shadfā*, (fem. of اشدف *ashdaf*) Leaning to a side (a she-camel) from sprightliness. Large-bodied (mare). Wry-cheeked (woman). Curved (Persian bow).

A شدفة *shudfat*, A part of the night, or of any thing. *Shudfat* or *shadfat*, Darkness.

A شدفة *shudfatan*, Piecemeal.

A شدق *shadḳ* or *shidḳ*, (pl. اشداق *ashdāḳ*) The environs of the mouth, the corner of the mouth inside the cheek. The side of a valley, brink of a river. *Shudḳ*, (pl. of اشدق *ashdaḳ*) Wide-mouthed. Eloquent. (pl. of شدقاء *shadḳā*) Eloquent female orators. *Shadaḳ*, A largeness or wideness about the corners of the mouth or chops.

A شدقاء *shadḳā*, (fem. of اشدق *ashdaḳ*) Large-mouthed. An eloquent female orator.

A شدقم *shadḳam*, Large-mouthed, wide about the corners of the mouth. A lion. Name of an excellent camel belonging to Nuعmān, son of Mundir.

A شدقميات *shadḳamīyāt*, Excellent camels.

P شدكار *shudkār*, Ground prepared for sowing. Ploughing. A person whose business it is to examine the state of the harvest. Survey. گاو شدكار *gāvi shudkār*, A ploughing-ox.

P شد كن *shud-kun*, Working upwards.

P شدكيس *shadkīs*, The rainbow.

P شدگان *shudagān*, (pl. of شده *shuda*) Those who have departed; men of former days.

P شدگي *shudagī*, A going, a departure.

A شدن *shadn*, A tree whose flower resembles the jasmine. *Shadan*, Name of a place in Arabia Felix.

P شدن *shudan*, To be. To become. To be lost or elapsed. To be doing. To go, depart, emigrate, pass. To transfer, transport. To remove, deface, erase. آلوده شدن *ālūda shudan*, To be defiled.

P شدنگاه *shudan-gāh*, A place where any thing is or happens.

P شدني *shudanī*, Possible, practicable. شدني شد *shudanī shud*, Any thing proper to be done.

A شدنيات *shadanīyāt*, Camels bred in شدن.

A شدو *shadw*, (v. n. of شدا for شدو) Urging, pressing, driving (camels). Repeating (verses) in a loud, sonorous voice. Pursuing one's aim. Learning any thing elegant or laudable from another. Comparing. Likening. A little out of a large quantity. A side.

A شدود *shudūd*, (pl. of شدّ *shadd*) Kinds of head-dresses.

A شدوف *shudūf*, (pl. of شدف *shadaf*) Figures which appear black and raised in the distance.

A شدون *shudūn*, (v. n. of شدن) Growing strong, becoming independent of the dam (a colt or fawn).

A شدونة *shidūnat*, Medina Sidonia, a city in Spain.

A شده *shadh*, (v. n. of شده) Breaking the head. Amazing, astonishing, stupefying. *Shadh*, *shudh*, or *shadah*, (v. n. of شده) Being astonished, amazed, confused. Being occupied. *Shadh* or *shudh*, Occupation, employment. *Shudh* or *shadah*, Stupor, amazement, astonishment.

P شده *shada*, A bird's bill. *Shuda*, Been, become. Lost. Escaped. Gone by. When added to another word it forms a passive participle: as, خواب شده *khwāb shuda*, Gone to sleep; بيدار شده *bīdār shuda*, Become awake; زده شده *zada shuda*, Stricken; كوفته شده *kofta shuda*, Bruised.

P شده بند *shuda-band*, Writer of facts, historian.

A شدّى *shuddā*, Adversity, trouble, hard case.

P شديار *shudyār*, (or شذيار *shuzyār*) Ground tilled and sown. Ploughing.

P شدياريدن *shudyārīdan*, To drive plough. To plough. To make ready for sowing.

A شديد *shadīd*, (pl. اشدّاء *ashiddā*) Strong, vehement, violent, intense. Vigorous. Fierce, rigorous, severe, afflicting. Barren (year). Difficult, arduous. Avaricious. Intrepid, warlike. A lion. شديد العداوة *shadīdu'l عadāwat*, Violent in enmity. شديد العقاب *shadīdu'l عiḳāb*, (God) the severe punisher of the wicked. الحروف الشديدة *al hurūfu'sh shadīdat*, The strong letters, i. e. those comprised in the technical words اجدت طبقك.

A شديدة *shadīdat*, (pl. شدائد *shadāïd*) Adversity, distress, hard fortune.

A شديدي *shadīdīy*, Relating to a difficult thing.

A شديق *shadīḳ*, The side of a valley.

A شذّ *shazz*, (v. n. of شذّ) Being solitary, separated, remaining alone. Being singular. Separating. A dog-fly.

A شذا *shaza'*, An injury, harm, annoyance. Dog-flies. Flies in general. The scab. Salt. Pungency of smell. Remains of strength. Hunger. A kind of ship. Broken pieces of wood. Name of a tree from which dentifrices are made. ضرم شذاه *zarima shazāhu*, His hunger was extreme.

A شذاة *shazāt*, One dog-fly. One ship. Acridness of smell. Remains of strength. Malicious.

A شذّاذ *shuzzāz*, People living in a tribe or family to which they do not belong. Few in number.

A شذام *shazām*, Salt. Sting of scorpion or hornet.

A شذّان *shizzān*, The lote-tree. شذّان الحصا *shazzānu'l* (or *shuzzānu'l*) *hasa'*, Pebbles scattered.

A شذائي *shazāïy*, Native of شذا *shaza'*, a town near Basrah.

A شذب *shazb*, (v. n. of شذب) Prohibiting, averting. Unbarking, peeling. Casting its branches (a tree). Cutting, pruning, lopping. *Shazab*, (pl. اشذاب *ashzāb*) A bit of dry wood or bark. Loppings or bark of trees. A bank, dam, dyke. Remains of forage. Household furniture. (pl. of شذبة *shazabat*) Branches (especially dry ones lopped off). *Shazib*, One whose veins stand out conspicuous.

A شذبة *shazabat*, One lopped branch.

A شذحوف *shuzhūf*, Swift, impetuous (horse, &c.).

A شذر *shazr*, Particles of gold from the mine, unrefined by fire. Small pearls or beads, which are usually strung. شذر مذر *shazara mazara* or *shizara mizara*, Dispersed up and down, scattered here and there.

A شذرة *shazrat*, One particle of gold.

A شذف *shazf*, An obtaining, a getting.

P شذكار *shuzkār*, Ground tilled and sown.

A شذو *shazw*, (v. n. of شذا for شذو) Injuring, hurting. Perfuming one's self with musk. Understanding (news), and afterwards causing it to be understood. Musk; also the smell or colour of it.

A شذوذ *shuzūz*, (v. n. of شذّ) Remaining alone, apart, and separate from the rest. Separating. Being separate, scattered.

A شذور *shuzūr*, (pl. of شذرة *shazrat*) Particles of gold from the mine, unrefined by fire.

P شذه *shaza*, (for شده *shada*) A bird's beak.

A شذي *shazy*, (v. n. of شذي) Knowing and giving to understand. *Shaza'*, A dog-fly.

P شر *shar*, A city. *Shir*, The sun. *Shur*, A shoe.

A شرّ *sharr*, (v. n. of شرّ) Being wicked, malignant, malevolent, perverse. Exposing to the sun or air to dry. The evil one, the devil. A fever. Poverty. Worse, worst. *Sharr* or *shurr*, (pl. شرور *shurūr*) Wickedness, depravity, malignancy. شرّ و فساد *sharr u fasād*, Wickedness and mischief. خير و شرّ *khayr u sharr*, Good and evil. *Shurr*, (v. n. of شرّ) Accusing, reproaching. Vice, turpitude, villainy. Blame, censure.

A شراء *sharāʾ*, A side, quarter, district. *Shirāʾ*, (v. n. of شري) Buying. Selling. (v. n. 3 of شري) Making a contract of purchase or sale. Striving, quarrelling, disputing. Merchandise.

A شراب *sharāb*, Wine. Any beverage. شراب اصول *sharābi usūl*, Syrup of roots. P شراب بي كيف *sharābi bī kayf*, Wine without cheerfulness, i.e. weak, that does not exhilarate. شراب گذشته *sharābi guzashta*, Flat, insipid wine. شراب نوش گوار *sharābi nosh-guwār*, Honey-wine. Wine which does not cause crop-sickness. A شراب يهود *sharābi yahūd*, Jews' wine. (metaph.) Drinking wine in secret, as the Jews do from fear of the Muhammadans. P شراب بگردان *sharāb bugardān*, Drink, pass the bowl.

A شرّاب *sharrāb*, A toper. *Shurrāb*, Drinkers.

A شرابات *sharābāt*, Syrups. Sherbets.

A شراباتيّ *sharābātiy*, A maker of sherbets.

A شرابث *shurābis*, Thick in the bands and feet (as a lion).

P شراب خانه *sharāb-khāna*, A cellar; tavern.

P شراب خوار *sharāb-khwār*, A wine-bibber.

P شرابدار *sharāb-dār*, (A شرابيّ *sharābiy*) A cup-bearer. A butler.

P شراب زده *sharāb-zada*, Sated with wine.

P شرابه *sharāba*, A goblet of wine.

A شرابي *sharābī*, A drunkard.

A شرأبيبة *shuraʾbībat*, A stretching out of the neck to gaze, a looking with out-stretched neck.

A شراة *sharāt*, The choicest portion of a flock: also the worst. *Shurāt*, (pl. of شاري *shārī*) Certain sects of schismatics (sellers of themselves).

A شراج *shirāj*, (pl. of شرج *sharaj*) Places through which water flows from high and rocky grounds into a plain. Species, modes. Troops, companies, sects.

A شرّاح *sharrāh*, A commentator.

A شراحة *shurāhat*, Name of a Hamadān woman.

P شراحي *sharāhī*, A dish of roast meat.

A شراحيل *sharāhīl*, A man's name.

P شراخي *sharākhī*, A sort of food.

A شراد *shurād* or *shirād*, (v. n. of شرد) Fleeing away, being terrified.

A شراذم *sharāzim*, Tattered garments. (pl. of شرذمة *shirzimat*) Parts. Bands. Handfuls.

A شراذيم *sharāzīm*, (pl. of شرذمة *shirzimat*) Parts. Bands. Handfuls.

A شرار *sharār*, Sparks. *Shirār*, (v. n. 3 of شرّ) Injuring, being malignant or averse. Sparks.

A شرارة *sharārat*, (v. n. of شرّ) Doing evil. A spark of fire. Wickedness, malice, depravity, villainy. P شرارهٔ كارزار *sharāraʾi kārzār*, The flame or heat of the battle. A *Shirārat*, A spark.

A شراريز *sharārīz*, (pl. of شيراز *shīrāz*) Strained and solid milks turned sour and thick.

A شراريف *sharārīf*, (pl. of شرّاف) Battlements.

A شراز *shirāz*, A contending: a being malignant.

A شرّاز *shurrāz*, The tormentors of mankind.

A شراس *shirās*, (v. n. 3 of شرس) Giving hard treatment. The best shoemakers' paste.

A شرّاس *shurrās*, Hard (ground).

A شراسة *sharāsat*, Malignity, maliciousness, evilness of nature. A voracious appetite in cattle.

A شراسي *sharāsī*, Hard (ground).

A شراسيف *sharāsīf*, (pl. of شرسوف *shursūf*) Cartilages of the ribs.

A شراشر *sharāshir*, The whole of the body. The mind, soul, affection, love. (pl. of شرشرة *sharsharat*) Burdens. The whiskings of (a horse's) tail.

A شراص *shirās*, (pl. of شرص *shirs*) Baldnesses round the temples.

A شراط *shirāt*, (v. n. 3 of شرط) Acting or making an agreement on certain conditions.

A شراع *shirāʿ*, (pl. اشرعة *ashriʿat* and شرع *shuruʿ*) The sail of a ship. The string of a bow. A spear. A tent. A canopy, an awning. The neck of a camel. (pl. of شرع *shirʿ*) Like, resembling. Bowstrings. Music-strings. *Shurāʿ*, Name of a celebrated spear-maker. A full-grown plant.

A شرّاع *sharrāʿ*, A seller of شريع *sharīʿ* linen.

A شراعة *sharāʿat*, Boldness, courage.

A شراعيّ *shurāʿiy*, Long (spear).

A شراعية *shurāʿiyat*, Long-necked (she-camel).

A شراف *shirāf*, (v. n. 3 of شرف) Ascending. Being aware of, apprised. Being near.

A شرّاف *shurrāf*, (pl. شراريف) A pinnacle.

A شرافة *sharāfat*, (v. n. of شرف) Being noble.

A شرافيّ *shurāfiy*, White raiment, or raiment procured from the part of Persia contiguous to Arabia.

A شرافية *shurāfiyat*, Long (ear). Bulky and large-eared (she-camel).

A شراك *shirāk*, (v. n. 3 of شرك) Going partners. (pl. شرك *shuruk* or اشرك *ashruk*) A shoe-strap or latchet. A quantity of fodder.

A شراكة *shirākat*, Partnership.

A شراكةً *shirākatan*, Jointly.

A شرامح *sharāmih*, (or شرامحة *sharāmihat*) (pl. of شرمح *sharmah* and شرمحي) Robust. Long.

P شرّان *sharrān*, *shirān*, or *shurrān*, (part.) Purling (as running water).

A شرّان *sharrān*, A sort of gnat. An evil, vexation.

A شرانق *sharānik* or *shurānik*, The cast-skin or slough of a serpent. Torn clothes. (pl. of شرنقة *shurnuhat*) Silk-worms' balls.

P شرّانگيز *sharr-angez*, Incendiary, breed-bate.

A شراويض *sharāwīz*, (pl. of شرواض) Fat camels.

A شراهة *sharāhat*, Gluttony, appetite.

G اهيا شراهيا *ihyan shārāhiyan*, (incorrectly for اهيا و اشراهيا *ihyan wa asharāhiyan*) Eternal.

A شرائص *sharāʾis*, (pl. of شريصة) Cheeks.

A شرائط *sharāʾit*, (pl. of شريطة *sharītat*) Conditions, compacts, agreements, capitulations, stipulations. Customary observances. Signs, marks.

A شرائع *sharāʾiʿ*, (pl. of شريعة *sharīʿat*) Ordinances. Highways.

A شرائف *sharāʾif*, (pl. of شريفة) Noble.

A شرائك *sharāʾik*, (pl. of شريكة) Partners.

A شرايين *sharāyīn*, (pl. of شريان *sharyān* or *shiryān*) Arteries, by which the pulse is felt.

P شرب *sharb*, Fine Egyptian linen.

A شرب *shariba*, (fut. يشرب *yashrabu*) He drank. He told a lie against. He was thirsty. He became weak.

A شرب *sharb*, (v. n. of شرب) Understanding, comprehending. (pl. of شارب *shārib*) Drinkers (of wine). A kind of herb. *Sharb*, *shirb*, or *shurb*, (v. n. of شرب) Drinking. Imbibing. شرب الدخان *sharbu'd duhhān*, Smoking tobacco. *Shirb*, Any thing that is drunk, drink. Water. A portion of water. The place or time of drinking water. *Shurb*, Drink, any thing drank (especially as much as is sufficient for one draught, or to satisfy thirst). A beverage. A drinking-bout. شرب شراب *shurbi sharāb*, A draught of wine. شرب و اكل *shurb u akl*, Drink and meat. ترك اكل و شرب *tarki akl u shurb*, Abstinence from meat and drink. *Sharab*, (v. n. of شرب) Thirsting. Drinking. Being weak (a camel).

A شرباً *shurban*, At a single draught.

A شربات *sharabāt*, (pl. of شربة *sharabat*) Small wells round the roots of palm-trees by which they are watered.

A شرباخ *shirbākh*, Rotten mushrooms, puffs.

A شربب *shurbub*, Compact, heaped up (plants).

A شربة *sharbat*, One drink or sip, a single draught.

Sherbet, syrup. A dose or medicine. The penetration of one colour into another. A palm-tree grown from a date-stone. شربت الماس *sharbati almās*, A glittering sword. شربت مسهل *sharbati mushil*, A cathartic or purgative medicine. *Shurbat*, A draught of water. Redness in the face. *Sharabat*, A little well or pit round the root of a tree for watering it. A furrow. Much drinking. Thirst. Intense heat. *Shurabat*, A great drinker, drunkard.

A شربّة *sharabbat*, A spot abounding in grass, but destitute of trees. Way, manner. علىٰ شربّة واحدة *ɛala' sharabbatin wāhidatin*, Dwelling upon one thing, insisting upon one topic.

P شربت *sharbat*, Wild leek.

P شربت خانه *sharbat-khāna*, A repository of medicines, a medicine-chest.

P شربت دار *sharbat-dār*, A servant who has charge of the water or wine, a butler. One who has charge of the medicine-chest.

P شربتي *sharbatī*, A goblet of wine which may be emptied at a single draught. A sort of fine linen.

A شربش *sharbash*, The scalloped or fringed edge of a garment.

A شربيل *sharbīl*, A sort of Morocco shoe.

P شربين *sharbīn*, A tree, from which flows liquid pitch. The larch. Berberis. Ditch-bur.

P شرپون *shurpūn*, Liquid pitch. Any thing very black.

A شرّة *sharrat*, Worse (woman). *Shirrat*, Greediness, cupidity. Warmth and sprightliness of youth.

A شرث *shars*, A worn slipper, old shoe. *Sharas*, (v. n. of شرث) Being cracked; also thick (the hand). Not being made straight (an arrow). *Sharis*, A sharp sword.

A شرثة *sharsat*, A worn slipper, old shoe.

A شرج *sharj*, (v. n. of شرج) Laying bricks one upon another. Mixing. Mixing raw meat with dressed meat. Collecting. Lying. Shutting a purse by drawing the strings. (pl. شراج *shirāj* and شروج *shurūj*) A place through which water flows from high rocky grounds into a plain. A purse. A troop, body. Society, partnership. A sect. A species, mode, kind, sort, manner. Colour. Oil of sesame. Resemblance, any thing like another, a pair. هما شرج واحد *humā sharjun wāhidun*, They both are of one sort. *Sharj* or *sharaj*, Habit, nature, disposition. فلا رأيهم رأيي و لا شرجهم شرجي *fa lā raɛyuhum raɛī wa lā sharjuhum sharjī*, Their opinion is not my opinion, nor their disposition my disposition. *Sharaj*, (v. n. of شرج) Having an inequality in the testicles. (pl. اشراج *ashrāj*) A crack in a bow or arch. The handle of a portmanteau. Pudenda mulieris. The milky way. Width or extent of a channel or valley. Handles.

A شرجان *sharjāni*, (dual of شرج *sharj*) Two sects or parties; two sections or parts; two different colours or kinds.

A شرجب *sharjab*, Tall, long. Noble (horse). Long-legged.

A شرجبان *shar* or *shurjabān*, A plant, with the leaves and fruit of which leather is tanned.

A شرجة *sharjat*, A hole dug and lined with a piece of leather, from which they water camels.

A شرجع *sharjaɛ*, A bier. A funeral-solemnity or rites. A square piece of wood. Long (she-camel).

A شرجعة *sharjaɛat*, (v. n. of شرجع Q) Hewing, cutting off the edges or corners, making (a piece of wood) even and level. Making oblong.

A شرح *sharh*, (v. n. of شرح) Explaining, expounding. (God) opening the heart, disposing the mind (to religion). Enlarging. Understanding, comprehending. Dissecting or carving well. Beginning. Deflowering (a virgin). Explanation, declaration, interpretation, commentary, paraphrase. Remark, observation, reason. Expression. Allowance, pay, rate. P شرح كردن *sharh kardan*, To explain. شرح و بسط *sharh u bast*, Explicitly and openly.

P شرح *sharah*, The strings or bands of a garment. A tent-rope. The milky way.

A شرحاف *shirhāf*, Broad in the instep. Broad (spear-head).

A شرحب *sharhab*, Long. A name.

A شرحبان *sharhabān*, Name of a tree.

A شرحبيل *shurahbīl*, Name of a man.

A شرحة *sharhat*, A slice of meat. A piece of doe's flesh, dry, but not cut into strips. شرحه شرحه *sharha sharha*, In pieces, piece by piece.

P شرحوار *sharhwār*, Explanatory.

A شرحوف *shurhūf*, Ready to rush (upon a foe).

A شرخ *sharkh*, (v. n. of شرخ) Cutting (as teeth the gums). Blade of a sword, unpolished and without a hilt. Point of a spear. A son born every year. An annual fœtus (especially of a camel). Beginning of any thing. Early youth. Human progeny. Root, origin. A salient point. (pl. شروخ *shurūkh*) An equal, peer. (pl. of شارخ *shārikh*) Young men.

A شرخان *sharkhāni*, Two co-equals or peers. شرخا الرحل *sharkhā'r rahl*, The fore and hinder part of a camel's saddle. شرخا الفوق *sharkhā'l fūk*, The two sides of a needle-eye or arrow-notch.

P شرخست *shirkhist*, A kind of manna, which, at certain seasons, drops upon the leaves of trees. Pottage, gruel.

A شرخوب *shurkhūb*, Joint-bones of the back.

P شرخوردن *shurkhwurdan*, To scrape, scratch.

P شرخيوه *shirkhīwa*, A drawing in of the breath, a whistling.

A شرد *sharad*, (pl. of شارد *shārid*) Fugitives, runaways. *Shurud*, (pl. of شرود *sharūd*) Run-aways.

A شرّد *shurrad*, Celebrated poems flying from mouth to mouth.

A شرداح *shirdāh*, Thick, broad-footed (man). Fleshy, flabby. Long and large (woman or camel).

A شرداخ *shirdākh*, Large, broad-footed.

P شرداغ *shirdāgh*, A short-sleeved gown.

A شرذمة *shirzimat*, (pl. شراذم *sharāzim* and شراذيم *sharāzīm*) A part. A slice. A handful of men.

A شرر *sharar*, Sparks. Malice.

A شررة *sharurat*, A spark of fire.

A شرز *sharz*, (v. n. of شرز) Cutting. Hardness, roughness. Difficulty, refractoriness. Vehemence, violence, force, strength. Destruction. Extremely strong and powerful. *Sharaz*, Pure, unmixed.

A شرزة *sharzat*, Ruin, utter destruction.

P شرزدك *shirizdak*, A medlar.

P شرزه *sharza*, Fierce, enraged, panting for revenge. Roaring, growling (lion or other wild beast). A brawler; one who puts himself in the attitude of fighting or defiance.

A شرس *shars*, (v. n. of شرس) Dragging (a camel) by the rein. Steeping or tanning (a skin). Paining (a friend) by rough, uncourteous language. Eating voraciously. *Shurs*, The scab on the lips of a camel. *Sharas* or *shirs*, Small thorny mountain-shrubs. *Sharas*, (v. n. of شرس) Feeding habitually on the thorny plant شرس *shirs*. Shewing love. Malignity, violent opposition. *Sharis*, Of a bad disposition. A voracious eater.

A شرساء *sharsāɛ*, Hard ground. Thin white cloud.

A شرسفة *sharsafat*, A bad disposition.

A شرسوف *shursūf*, (pl. شراسيف *sharāsīf*) The cartilage of the ribs, the extremities of the ribs above the belly, the short ribs. Gristle or soft bone. A calamity. The beginning of trouble. Fettered (camel), houghed in one leg.

A شرشر *sharshar*, Dripping fat (meat when roasting). *Sharshar* or *shirshir*, Name of a plant which creeps along the ground like a rope.

A شرشرة *sharsharat*, (v. n. of شرشر Q) Cutting in pieces. Biting and breaking to pieces. Biting (a serpent). Cropping herbage (cattle). Whetting (a knife) on a stone. Making water in one's clothes). (pl. شراشر *sharāshir*) Furniture, baggage. The whisking motion of a tail. *Shirshirat*, (pl. شراشر) A certain herb. A slice or segment.

A شرشق *shirshik*, A green magpie.

A شرشور *shurshūr*, A species of bird.

A شرص *shars*, (v. n. of شرص) Taking the lead (in conversation). Drawing. Cutting. The first walking of a camel's colt. Intensity, severity. Thickness. *Shirs*, (pl. شرصة *shirasat* and شراص *shirās*) Baldness round the temples. *Sharas*, An incision in a camel's nose, through which the rein-ring passes. A catching by the hip, and a throwing one down when wrestling, a cross-buttock. Roughness of ground.

A شرصة *shirasat*, (pl. of شرص *shirs*) Baldnesses of the temples.

A شرصتان *shirsatāni*, (du.) The two sides of the forehead, the temples whence the forelocks spring.

A شرط *shart*, (v. n. of شرط) Scarifying, breathing a vein. Stipulating. Suspending one thing upon another. Laying down conditions. (pl. شروط *shurūt*) A condition, agreement, compact, convention, pact, stipulation, limitation, clause, restriction, modification. Obligation, duty. (pl. اشراط *ashrāt*) Mean, low, base, vile. P شرط بستن *shart bastan*, To stipulate. To bet. شرط نمك *sharti namak*, Service, employment. بشرط ان *bi sharti an*, On condition that. A *Sharat*, (v. n. of شرط) Falling into any serious and perilous affair. (pl. اشراط *ashrāt*) A sign, mark, signal. More excellent, nobler. Any small channel that comes from one of the depth of ten cubits. The beginning of any thing. Small, vile, refuse, after the best has been taken away. *Shurat*, (pl. of شرطة *shurtat*) Life-guards. The advanced guard, forlorn hope (as being marked for destruction). Things defined or agreed upon.

A شرطان *sharatāni*, Two bright stars in the head of Aries. The first mansion of the moon.

A شرطة *shurtat*, (pl. شرط *shurat*) A life-guardsman. The advanced guard or forlorn hope. Any thing defined or stipulated. Any thing made dependent on another; condition, contingency. Helpers, friends, confederates, allies. An officer that goes before a magistrate or other great man. A peon, policeman, or beadle attendant on a police-magistrate.

A شرطونيّة *shartūnīyat*, Laying on of hands in making priests.

P شرطه *shurta*, Judge of the market. King's guards. Covered with black, clad in mourning. Propitious, favourable, agreeable. باد شرطه *bādi shurta*, A favourable wind.

P سرطي *shurtī*, A life-guardsman. Suitable, agreeable. Favourable, prosperous. A questor, paymaster. A notary.

A شرطيّ *shartīy*, Conditional. A lottery. *Shurtīy* or *shuratīy*, A life-guardsman; a lictor, serjeant, beadle. See شرطة *shurtat*.

A شرطيّة *shartīyat*, Conditionality, contingency.

A شرع *sharʿ*, (v. n. of شرع) Making or prescribing laws. Pointing out the way in which His servants should walk (God). Going or leading into the public road, having a door opening upon it (a house). Making manifest. Stripping (a hide). Raising any thing aloft. Entering the water (an animal). Beginning, setting about. Untwisting a rope and inserting the ends in the handles of a vessel. Levelling (a spear). Being levelled (a spear). What sufficeth (thee). Religion, faith, law, justice. equity. Precepts of Muhammad. Sort, mode, manner. Like, equal. An equal thing, a pair. اهل شرع *ahli sharʿ*, A judge, assessor to a judge, lawyer. شرع شريف *sharʿi sharīf*, (or شرع الله *sharʿu'llāh*) Citing one before a court of justice. *Shirʿ*, A lute-string. A shoe-latchet. *Shirʿ* or *sharʿ*, (pl. of شرعة *shirʿat*) Strings for bows or musical instruments. Things like another. *Sharaʿ*, Equal, alike. Common property. Sort, mode, manner. *Shiraʿ*, (pl. of شرعة *shirʿat*) Strings for bows or musical instruments. *Shuruʿ*, (pl. of شراع *shirāʿ*) Sails of ships.

A شرّع *shurraʿ*, (Spears) levelled at any body. (Fishes) swimming from deep into shallow water and raising their jowls. Those who enter into water. Undertakers of business.

A شرعاً *sharʿan*, Judicially, lawfully.

A شرعاف *shirʿāf* or *shurʿāf*, The skin or bark of the envelope of the flowers of the male palm-tree.

A شرعب *sharʿab*, Long.

A شرعبة *sharʿabat*, A cutting (leather) in slips.

A شرعبيّ *sharʿabīy*, A kind of striped garment. Tall and handsome.

A شرعة *shirʿat*, The law of God. A plain, straight road. Any thing like another. *Shirʿat* or *sharʿat*, (pl. شرع *shirʿ*, *sharʿ*, and *shiraʿ*) The string of a musical instrument or bow. A bird-net. *Sharaʿat*, (pl. اشراع *ashrāʿ*) A ship. A veranda, portico, or covered gallery.

P شرع نهاد *sharʿ-nihād*, Habituated to justice.

A شرعوب *shurʿūb*, Name of a plant.

A شرعوف *shurʿūf*, A certain plant, or its fruit.

A شرعي *sharʿīy*, Legal, just. Tight drawers. *Shirʿīy*, A bowstring. Like, equal.

A شرغ *shargh*, (*shirgh*, or *sharagh*) A small frog.

A شرغوف *shurghūf*, A certain plant, or its fruit. A small frog.

P شرف *sharf*, The threshold of a door.

A شرف *sharf*, (v. n. of شرف) Excelling in glory, being more noble. Constructing battlements (on an edifice). *Shurf*, Aged she-camels. *Sharaf*, (v. n. of شرف) Being high and noble. Contending about nobility. Being on the brink or point of. Eating continually camels' bunches. Being high (the shoulder), long (the ear). Nobility, dignity, honour, glory, grandeur, rank, excellence. Height, point, altitude. The honour derived from ancestors. An eminence, a high place. Bunch of a camel. A horse-race, especially of one heat (about a mile). (pl. of شريف *sharīf*) Noblemen, gentlemen (especially the descendants of Muhammad): sherriffes, sherifs. A شرف تحسين *sharafi tahsīn*, Honour of being approved. شرف خدمت *sharafi khidmat*, Honour of service. شرف ملازمت *sharafi mulāzamat*, Honour of attendance. على شرف *ʿalā' sharafin*, On a brink, edge, or point. *Shuraf*, (pl. of شرفة *shurfat*) Battlements, pinnacles. *Shuruf*, (or شرّف *shurraf*) (pl. of شارف *shārif*) Old arrows. Aged camels. Lofty buildings, with battlements or pinnacles. Trials, temptations. شرف جون *shuruf jūn*, Dark temptations.

A شرّف *shurraf*, Aged she-camels.

A شرفاء *sharfāʾ*, (fem. of اشرف *ashraf*) (pl. شرف *shuruf*) Furnished with battlements, pinnacled (edifice). Long (ear). *Shurafāʾ*, (pl. of شريف *sharīf*) Nobles, princes, the grandsons and descendants of Muhammad, sherriffes, sherifs.

A شرفات *shurafāt*, (pl. of شرفة *shurfat*) Battlements or galleries round the turrets of the mosques. *Shurufāt*, The neck (of a horse), and the part whereon any one mounted behind the rider sits.

P شرفاك *sharfāk*, (*shirfāk*, شرفالنگ *sharfālang*, *shirfālang*, شرفانگ *sharfāng*, *shirfāng*, or شرفنگ *sharfang*) A light, low sound (as of feet when walking).

P شرف بخش *sharaf-bakhsh*, Honour-giving.

A شرفة *shurfat*, (pl. شرف *shuraf*) Honour, dignity, good fortune. The battlement or highest pinnacle of a tower or wall, a cornice. The round gallery near the top of the minarets, from which the crier proclaims the hour of prayer. The best of any thing (as of cattle).

A شرفث *sharfas*, A species of milky shrub.

P شرفريز *sharaf-rez*, Scattering honours.

P شرفنج *sharfanj*, A rugged road.

P شرفه *shar* or *shirfa*, Noise of feet in walking.

P شرفياب *sharaf-yāb*, Honoured, dignified.

A شرفيّة *sharfīyat*, Nobility, high birth.

A شرق *shark*, (v.n. of شرق) Rising (as the sun). Gathering the vintage. Slitting the ear of a sheep. Producing unripe dates (a palm-tree). The east. The rising sun. A fissure. Light shining through a crevice. A bird between a kite and a hawk. A handsome woman. شرق و غرب *shark u gharb*, East and west. لحم شرق *lahm shark*, Lean meat. *Shirk*, Light transmitted through a crevice. *Shurk*, (pl. of شارق *shārik*) Rising stars. *Sharak*, (v. n. of شرق) Being slit in the ear (a sheep). Being suffocated, choked. Giving a feeble light, and being about to set (the sun). Being blood-shot (the eye). The sun. *Sharik*, (Flesh meat) without fat. *Shuruk*, (pl. of شريق *sharīk*) Handsome youths.

A شرقاء *sharkāʾ*, Slit-eared (sheep).

A شرقة *sharkat*, A sunny place. *Sharkat* or *sharikat*, The rising sun. The east. *Shurkat*, Choaking in the throat, suffocation. *Sharakat*, A mark set on a slit-eared sheep.

A شرقراق *sharakrāk* or *shirikrāk*, A green magpie.

P شرقستان *sharkistān*, The east, Asia.

A شرقيّ *sharkīy*, Oriental, eastern. Sunny, exposed to the sun.

P شرك *shark* or *shirk*, Strips of linen in which medicines are rolled up. *Shirk*, Small-pox. *Sharak*, Eruptions of the body, measles.

A شرك *shirk*, (pl. اشراك *ashrāk*) Company, society, partnership. A letting to any one a field in consideration of a half or a third of the produce. A lot, portion, share, part. Infidelity, idolatry, paganism. Dissimulation, hypocrisy. A partner. شرك بالله *shirki bi'llāh*, The giving of companions to God (in allusion to the Trinity, which the Muhammadans do not acknowledge); hence *shirk* implies also a Christian, Pagan, the worship of idols, or a plurality of deities. اهل شرك *ahli shirk*, A Christian. An idolater. *Sharah*, (v. n. of شرك) Having the latchets broken (a shoe). (pl. شرك *shuruk*) A fowler's net. A wide, open road. The middle of the road. (pl. of شركة *sharakat*) Nets. Open roads. *Shuruk*, (pl. of شرك *sharah*) Nets, fowlers' snares. (pl. of شراك *shirāk*) Roads. Shoe-straps or latchets.

A شركاء *shurakāʼ*, (pl. of شريك *sharīk*) Partners.

A شركة *shirkat*, (v. n. of شرك) Going partners. Society, company, partnership, communication, participation. شركة الشيطان *shirkatu'sh shaytān*, The malignity of Satan. *Shurkat*, Partnership. *Sharakat*, (pl. شرك *sharak*) A fowler's net.

A شركسيّ *sharkasiy*, Circassian.

A شركيّ *shurakiy*, Often and quickly repeated (slap or blow). Rapid (march).

A شرّكيّ *shurrakiy*, Rapid (march).

P شرم *sharm*, Bashfulness, modesty, shame. Pudendum. شرم داشتن *sharm dāshtan*, To blush, to be ashamed. بي شرم *bī sharm*, Shameless.

A شرم *sharm*, (v. n. of شرم) Splitting, cleaving, cutting slightly. Giving away little money. A bay, gulf. A whirlpool. Grass in great abundance. A kind of tree of which the top only is eaten. *Sharam*, A fissure in the nose.

A شرماء *sharmāʼ*, Burst, abused (woman).

P شرمانيدن *sharmānīdan*, To make blush.

A شرمح *sharmah*, Long. *Sharmah*, (or شرمحيّ *sharmahiy*, (pl. شرامح *sharāmih* and شرامحة *sharāmihat*) Robust.

A شرمّح *sharammah*, Long.

P شرم زده *sharm-zada*, Ashamed, abashed.

P شرمسار *sharmsār*, Abashed, ashamed.

P شرمساري *sharmsārī*, Bashfulness. شرمساري بردن *sharmsārī burdan*, To be ashamed.

A شرمطة *sharmatat*, (v. n. of شرمط Q) Tearing.

P شرمگاه *sharm-gāh*, The privy parts.

P شرمگين *sharmgīn*, Bashful, ashamed.

P شرمندگي *sharmindagī*, Modesty. Shame.

P شرمنده *sharmanda*, (or شرمناك *sharmnāk*) Covered with shame, confused, disconcerted.

P شرميدن *sharmīdan*, To be ashamed, to blush.

A شرن *sharn*, A being split (as a rock).

A شرناض *shirnāz*, Bulky, long-necked (camel).

A شرناف *shirnāf*, Corn with long leaves.

A شرناق *sharnāk*, A sty on the eyelid.

A شرنبث *sharambas*, Thick about the hands and feet. A lion.

A شرنبذ *sharambaz*, Thick, gross, fat.

A شرنتي *sharanta'*, A kind of bird.

A شرنفة *sharnafat*, (v. n. of شرنف Q) Cutting away the long leaves (شرناف *shirnāf*) of corn.

A شرنفح *sharanfah*, Light of foot.

A شرنقة *sharnakat*, The act of cutting.

P شرنگ *sharang*, Poison. A colocynth.

A شرنوغ *shurnūgh*, A small frog.

A شرو *sharw* or *shirw*, Honey.

P شروا *sharwā*, A lie. Vain, senseless talk.

A شرواص *shirwās*, Large, thick, and flabby.

A شرواض *shirwāz*, (pl. شراويض) Fat, soft.

A شرواط *shirwāt*, Long-bodied. A swift camel.

A شروال *shirwāl*, Drawers, trowsers.

P شروان *shirwān*, Media.

P شرواني *shirwānī*, A Mede.

A شروب *sharūb*, Water neither salt nor sweet. A she-camel longing for the male. A great drinker of water. *Shurūb*, Drinkers.

A شروج *shurūj*, (pl. of شرج *sharj*) Places through which water flows from rocky grounds into a plain.

A شروح *shurūh*, (pl. of شرح *sharh*) Explanations, commentaries. Rudiments, elements.

A شروخ *shurūkh*, (v. n. of شرخ) Growing (youth). Cutting the gum (teeth of a camel). The thorny shrub عضاه *ʻizāh*. (pl. of شرخ *sharkh*) Sword-blades unpolished and without hilts. Equals, peers. شروخ شرّخ *shurūkh shurrakh*, Perfectly equal.

A شرود *sharūd*, (pl. شرد *shurud*) One who flies away with terror; a fugitive. Fugitive (piece of poetry). *Shurūd*, (v. n. of شرد) Fleeing away.

A شرور *shurūr*, (pl. of شرّ) Iniquities, evils.

A شروط *shurūt*, Conditions, stipulations.

A شروع *shurūʻ*, (v. n. of شرع) Entering (an animal the water). Beginning, setting about (any business). Beginning, commencement; onset, attack. (Camels) entering the water. P شروع كردن *shurūʻ kardan* (or نمودن *namūdan*), To begin, make a beginning, commence.

A شروف *shurūf*, (v. n. of شرف) Being aged (a she-camel). (pl. of شارف *shārif*) Aged (camels).

A شروق *shurūk*, The rising (of the sun).

A شروم *sharūm*, Burst, abused (woman).

P شروه *sharwa*, A mode of reading or chanting.

A شرويّ *sharwa'*, Alike, resembling. لا شرويّ له *lā sharwa' lahu*, There is none like unto him.

P شروين *sharwīn*, The fort of Shirwān.

P شره *shara*, Greedy, gluttonous. Voracity. Name of a plant called in India تلسي *tulsī*.

A شره *sharah*, (v. n. of شره) Being very greedy. Desire, appetite, avidity, gluttony. P نفس شره آلود *nafsi sharah-ālūd*, A soul stained with gluttony, addicted to excess. A *Sharih*, (or شرهان *sharhān*) Gluttonous. Greedy.

A شرهفة *sharhafat*, (v. n. of شرهف Q) Feeding (an infant) well.

A شري *shary*, (v. n. of شري) Buying. Selling. Exposing to the sun to dry. Ridiculing, deriding, holding up to contempt. Exasperating, enraging. Taking on one's self to speak or fight on behalf of others. Afflicting with pimples. A colocynth. A palm-tree growing from a date-stone. *Shara'*, (v. n. of شري) Shaking to and fro (a camel's halter). Playing with the bridle in this manner (a horse). Being obstinate and stubborn (a man). Boiling with rage (a man). A pimply or florid ulceration of the skin (especially from acrid nocturnal vapours). The worst part of one's flock; also the best. A road. A mountain. (pl. اشراء *ashrāʼ*) A district, country, tract, quarter. ذو الشريّ *zū'sh shara'*, Name of an idol. *Sharī*, Exquisite. Pimpled. *Shira'*, (v. n. of شري) Buying. Selling. Flying rapidly about (mischief). Flashing repeatedly (lightning). Being angry and quarrelsome. Having a pimply eruption (the skin). Running at his utmost speed, and shaking his bridle much (a horse). (pl. اشرية *ashriyat*) A bargain.

A شرّي *shurra'*, Worse, worst (woman). Malignant, fascinating (eye).

A شريّ *sharīy*, Well-going (horse); one that takes wide steps. A horse that moves his bridle to and fro in running.

A شرّيّ *sharrīy*, The best, or worst, of cattle.

A شرياف *shiryāf*, The long, luxuriant leaves of corn which they are used to cut away.

A شريان *sharyān* or *shiryān*, A tree of which bows are made. (pl. شرايين *sharāyīn*) An artery, by which the pulse is felt.

A شريب *sharīb*, Water neither fresh nor salt: potable water. A pot-companion. One who draws water, or who waters cattle along with another.

A شرّيب *shirrīb*, Given to drink, a toper.

A شريبة *sharībat*, A sheep which, after drinking, stands in her former place that the rest may follow.

A شرية *sharyat*, One colocynth. A palm-tree grown from a date-stone.

A شريّة *sharīyat*, Rule, way, mode. Nature. (A woman) bringing forth only girls.

P شريتا *sharītā*, (in zand and Pāzand) A king.

P شريتونتن *sharītūnitan*, (in zand) To open.

A شريج *sharīj*, Like. Wood of which bows are made. Similitude, resemblance.

A شريجان *sharījāni*, (dual) Two different colours. Two striped borders on a garment.

A شريجة *sharījat*, A bow made of two pieces of wood; or of several framed together. A basket of palm-leaves, wherein they put fruits. A dove-cote made of reeds. The bruised nerve of a camel's neck, with which they fasten the wings of an arrow. A piece or part of any thing. The binding of a book.

A شريح *sharīh*, (or شريحة *sharīhat*) An oblong slice of meat. *Shurayh*, Pudendum mulieris.

A شريد *sharīd*, Separated, flying away.

P شريدن *sharīdan*, To exude, drop. To flow.

P شرّيدن *shurrīdan*, To flow, murmur (as water or any liquor poured out).

P شرير *sharīr*, Good. Beautiful.

A شرير *sharīr*, (pl. اشرار *ashrār* and اشرّاء *ashirrāʼ*) Wicked, malignant, perverse. The sea-side. A tree growing in the sea.

A شرّير *shirrīr*, (pl. شرّيرون *shirrīrūn*) A worthless scoundrel.

A شريرة *sharīrat*, A large sacking-needle.

P شري زدة *shara-zada*, Pimpled (skin).

A شريس *sharīs*, Malignity. Evilness of nature. Malignant, of a bad disposition. A lion.

A شريصة *sharīsat*, (pl. شرائص) The cheek.

A شريط *sharīt*, A rope made of the fibrous bark of a palm-tree. A dish wherein a woman's perfumes are placed. A chest of drawers.

A شريطة *sharītat*, (pl. شرائط *sharāʼit*) A condition, stipulation. A mason's rule. (A sheep or camel) having a scarified ear.

A شريع *sharīʻ*, Bold. The finest linen.

A شريعة *sharīʻat*, Law, justice, equity. The law of God. The laws of Muhammad. A plain, straight road. Any place where beasts drink. A threshold. شريعت شريفة *sharīʻati sharīfa*, The holy law. شريعت اظهر *sharīʻati azhar*, The resplendent law.

A شريف *sharīf*, (pl. شرفاء *shurafāʼ*, اشراف *ashrāf*, and شرف *sharaf*) Noble, eminent, holy. A nobleman, gentleman (especially the descendants of Muhammad); the prince or sherif of Mecca. Excellent (with regard to inanimate things). A golden Arabian ducat. شريف الوجود *sharīfu'l wujūd*, Noble person. شريف و وضيع *sharīf u wazīʻ*, Nobles and plebeians. مجلس شريف *majlisi sharīf*, A noble assembly. A tribunal. مزاج شريف *mizāji sharīf*, A noble disposition, excellent temper. How do you do? بحسب الشرع شريف *bi hasabi'sh sharʻi sharīf*, According to justice and the holy law. خلاف شرع شريف *khilāfi sharʻi sharīf*, Against religion and justice. *Shurayf*, Name of the highest mountain in Arabia.

A شريفة *sharyafat*, (v. n. of شريف Q) Cutting away the luxuriant corn-leaves. *Sharīfat*, (fem. of شريف *sharīf*) Noble. Excellent.

A شريفتان *sharīfatāni*, (dual) The eye and ear.

A شريق *sharīk*, The East. The rising sun. (pl. شرق *shurūk*) Beautiful (youth). An excellent vine. Narrow about the privities (woman); or one whose two passages have become one.

A شريك *sharīk*, (pl. اشراك *ashrāk* and شركاء *shurakāʼ*) A partner in trade, companion, associate, accomplice, school-fellow. A fellow, or companion given to God. An idol. A man's name.

A شريكة *sharīkat*, (pl. شرائك) A female partner.

A شريكي *sharīkī*, A partnership.

A شريم *sharīm*, The privities. An instrument for chipping wood, a plane. Burst, abused (woman).

P شرينه *shirīna*, (or *shirrīna*) A dry scab.

A شز *shazz*, Dry and hard.

A شزازة *shazāzat*, Hardness and dryness.

A شزب *shazb*, (v. n. of شزب) Being lean, lank, dry, attenuated (horse). Being dry and withered (a branch). Being rough (way).

A شزّب *shuzzab*, (pl. of شازب *shāzib*) Lank, gaunt-bellied (horses). Rough roads.

A شزبة *shazbat*, A bow neither old or new. Dry, attenuated (she-camel or ass). *Shuzbat*, An occasion, opportunity.

A شزر *shazr*, (v. n. of شزر) Looking askance or angrily to right or left with half-shut eyes. Hitting in the eye. Grinding from the right hand inwards. Piercing with a spear. Twisting (a rope) from the left hand, or from the outside, inwards. Vehemence, severity. Difficulty, affliction. غزل شزر *ghazlun shazrun*, Uneven spinning. *Shazar*, Aversion, a turning away of the face; pride, anger.

A شزراء *shazrāʼ*, Reddish (eye).

A شزرة *shuzrat*, A redness in the eyes.

A شزن *shazn* or *shuzun*, A cube or die for playing with. *Shazan*, (v. n. of شزن) Being hard and rough (ground). Being tired with much walking barefoot. Being active, nimble, brisk, and cheerful. A tract (of country). The side (of any thing). Hard, rough ground. Fatigue, pain from walking (especially on bare feet). A man of a severe disposition. A life of poverty or distress. Distance. Thickness, grossness. Intensity. *Shuzn* or *shuzun*, A tract (of country). The side (of any thing).

A شزنة *shaznat*, An avaricious woman. *Shuzunat*, *shazanat*, or *shuznat*, Hardness, roughness. A side, border.

A شزو *shazw*, A being high.

P شزو *shuzuv*, (in zand) A sinner, criminal.

A شزوب *shuzūb*, (v. n. of شزب) Being gaunt and dry (a horse). Being rough (a road). Being dry and withered (a branch). (pl. of شزيب *shazīb*) Untrimmed twigs.

A شزون *shuzūn*, (pl. of شزن *shazan*) Tracts of land. Sides.

A شزونة *shuzūnat*, Thickness, coarseness. Intensity. Ruggedness of ground.

A شزيب *shazīb*, (pl. شزوب *shuzūb*) A rough unlopped, untrimmed, withered branch. A bow neither old or new.

A شزيز *shazīz*, Dry and hard.

A شسّ *shass*, (pl. شساس *shisās*, شسوس *shusūs*, and شسيس *shasīs*) Hard earth. A certain herb.

A شسابة *shasābat*, A being lean and dry.

A شساس *shisās*, (pl. of شسّ *shass*) Grounds as hard as a stone.

A شسافة *shas* or *shisāfat*, A being thin and dry.

P شسب *shasb*, Lightning, flashing, glittering.

A شسب *shisb*, A bow made of slender wood. A bow neither new or old. *Shusb*, (pl. of شاسب *shāsib*) Meagre, shrivelled, dry. *Shasab*, (v. n. of شسب) Being lean, dry, wrinkled.

P شسپ *shasp*, Leaping, skipping. Absence.

P شست *shast*, A thumb-stall worn by archers. A fish-hook. A lancet. Sixty. The thumb. A girdle worn by the fire-worshippers and Hindus. The bow, also the string of a musical instrument, a fiddle-stick. A hair-ring. A woman's hips. شست نهادن *shast nihādan*, To fish, angle. *Shist*, (for نشست *nishast*) He sat down. A sitting down. A session. Aim. شست كردن *shist kardan*, To take aim. *Shust*, He washed. A lotion, washing.

P شستر *shustar*, The ancient city of Susa, famous for the manufacture of brocade.

P شستگاني *shistagānī*, Basis, foundation.

P شستگاه *shust-gāh*, Baptism. Baptismal font.

P شستگران *shastgarān*, Archers, bowmen.

P شستگي *shustagī*, Lotion, washing, ablution.

P شستم *shastum*, The sixtieth.

P شستن *shistan*, (for نشستن *nishastan*) To sit. *Shustan*, To wash. To baptize. To slack lime.

P شستنگاه *shustan-gāh*, A place for washing.

P شستني *shustanī*, A lotion.

P شست وشو *shust ushū*, Washing and cleansing.

P شسته *shusta*, Washed, cleansed, dressed, prepared. A handkerchief, towel. شسته شدن *shusta shudan*, To be baptized.

P شسته گفتگو *shusta-guft gū*, Pure language.

A شسع *shasʻ*, (v. n. of شسع) Being far distant (a mansion or halting-place). Putting strings (to a shoe). *Shisʻ*, (pl. شسوع *shusūʻ* and اشساع *ashsāʻ*) A shoe-strap or latchet. A narrow spot of ground. A side, a quarter. A little, small quantity, remains or the worst part (of flocks); also the best of them. A skilful manager of flocks. *Shusʻ*, (pl. of شاسع *shāsiʻ* and شسوع *shasūʻ*) Distant, remote. *Shasaʻ*, (v. n. of شسع) Having the fore-teeth and the canine teeth wide asunder (a horse). Having the latchet broken (a shoe). *Shisiʻ*, A shoe-string.

A شسف *shasf*, (v. n. of شسف) Bursting, splitting (an unripe date). *Shisf*, A dry crust.

A شسل *shasl*, Thick and fat (foot).

P شسن *shasn*, An oyster. Any thing capable of growth. Sugar-cane. A thorny shrub on which manna or honied dew is found. The womb.

A شسوب *shasūb*, A camel losing her colt in the winter, and giving no milk.

A شسوس *shusūs*, (v. n. of شسّ) Withering (a plant). (pl. of شسّ *shass*) Lands hard as a stone.

A شسوع *shasūʻ*, (pl. شسع *shusʻ*) Distant, remote. *Shusūʻ*, (v. n. of شسع) Being far distant (a house). (pl. of شسع *shisʻ*) Shoe-strings.

A شسوف *shusūf*, (v. n. of شسف) Being thin and dry (a horse).

A شسيب *shasīb*, A bow made of slender wood. A bow neither new nor old. A camel running dry and losing her colt.

A شسيس *shasīs*, (v. n. of شسّ) Being lean, shrivelled. (pl. of شسّ *shass*) Grounds as hard as a stone.

A شسيف *shasīf*, (Meat) which dries up. Dry (leathern bottle). Burst, split (unripe date).

P شش *shash*, Six. *Shush*, The lights. A fan. A soft, pendulous bosom. درد شش *dardi shush*,

Peripneumony.

P شش آماسيدة *shush-āmāsīda*, Timid.

P شش انداز *shash-andāz*, Throwing sixes at dice. A man who contrives to throw six balls, so that four are always in the air. A player at the game of نرد *nard*. The full moon.

P شش بانو *shash-bānū*, (شش خاتون *shash khātūn* or شش بانوي پير *shash bānūyi pīr*) The six princesses (or شش عروس *shash ʿarūs*, The six brides), *i. e.* Saturn, Jupiter, Mars, Venus, Mercury, and the moon.

P ششبندان *shash-bandān*, Six days of the month Shawāl, at the close of Ramazān, on which the Muhammadans fast. The wild vine.

P شش پا *shash-pā*, Six-footed. A worm with six feet; earwig; eft; scolopendra; beetle.

P ششپر *shash par*, A halberd, iron mace.

P شش پستان *shash-pistān*, (Six-teated) A bitch. A name of reproach for a woman. *Shush-pistān*, A pendulous-breasted woman. An old woman.

P شش پنچه *shash pancha*, A medicinal plant.

P ششت *shusht*, Vile, detestable, deformed, shameful, bad.

P ششتا *shash tā* (or تار *tār*), A kind of lute with six strings. شش تا زدن *shash tā zadan*, To play upon a six-stringed guitar. To throw sixes at dice.

P ششتازن *shash tā-zan*, One who strikes the lyre ششتا *shash tā*. One who throws sixes at dice.

P ششتر *shushtar*, Susa (famous for cloths).

P شش تره *shash tara*, Madder, a dyeing root.

P ششتم *shashtum*, The sixtieth.

P شش جهت *shash jihat*, Six-sided. A cube.

P ششجهتي *shash jihatī*, Six-sided, hexagonal.

P ششخان *shash khān*, (or شش خانه *shash khāna*) A kind of circular tent used by the Persians. A curtain at the door of a palace or pavilion.

P شش خانج *shash khānj*, A kind of a game played with walnuts filled with lead.

P ششخانه *shash khāna*, (A building) divided into six courts. Name of a musical instrument. ششخانه تفنگ *shash khāna tufang*, An arquebuss.

P شش خنج *shash khanj*, Drawers. Beardless. Nuts filled with lead, with which boys play.

P شش دانگ *shash dāng*, A dram and a half. A whisperer.

P ششدر *shash dar*, Six doors. Chess-tables. A cube, die. A point of the table at the game of نرد *nard*, from which one cannot extricate one's self. Wonderful, confounding. ششدر بازي *shash dar-bāzī*, Any game at dice. The world. Astonishment. شش در تنگ *shash dari tang*, (or شش در فنا *shash dari fanā*) The world. Shame.

P شش دره *shash dara*, A chess-board. A die. A point of the table at the game of نرد *nard*, from which one cannot extricate one's self.

P شش دري *shash darī*, A house with six doors. The world.

P شش روزكون *shash rozi kawn*, The six days of creation.

P شش روزن *shash rawzan*, The six planets. The world. A living creature.

P ششساله *shash sāla*, Six years old.

P شش سري *shash sarī*, Pure gold.

P شش سو *shash sū*, Above and below, before and behind, right and left. A hexagon. Six-sided.

P ششصد *shash sad*, Six hundred.

P شش ضرب *shash zarb*, Sixes at dice. Stakes at dice which are swept off at a throw. شش ضرب نتيجۀ خوب *shash zarbi natījaʾi khūb*, A gem. Gold. Musk. Sugar. Honey. Fruits of different sorts.

P شش طاق *shash tāk*, A kind of royal tent.

P شش طرف *shash taraf*, Six sides, *i. e.* east, west, north, south, above, beneath.

P ششعلم *shash ʿalam*, A kind of smooth carpet.

P ششقاقل *shashkākil* or *shashkākul*, Root of an Indian tree. The wild carrot.

A ششقلة *shashkalat*, (v. n. of ششقل Q) Adulterating changing; also weighing, examining (gold).

P ششك *shushk*, Excrement of the eye.

P شش كانج *shash kānaj*, A circular tent.

P ششگوشه *shash gosha*, A hexagon.

P ششم *shashum*, (ششمي *shashumī*, or ششمين *shashumīn*) Sixth.

P ششم زمين *shashum zamīn*, The sixth climate.

P شش مسكن *shash maskin*, An oyster-shell with its contents. A gold mine. A fruit-bearing tree. A shrub with manna upon it.

P شش نتيجۀ خوب *shash natījaʾi khūb*, The six excellent substances; jewels, gold, musk, sugar, honey, and sweet fruits.

P شش و پنج *shash u panj*, (Sixes and fives) Confusion, perplexity. Dice. شش و پنج بازي *shash u panj-bāzī*, Fraud, treachery. شش و پنج زنان *shash u panj-zanān*, Dice-players. Perfect, pure. One who loses his all at play.

P ششه *shasha*, (or شش يندان *shash yandān*) Six days of the month Shaabān, on which they fast.

P شش يك *shash yak*, A sixth.

A شصّ *shass*, (v. n. of شصّ) Keeping back, restraining. *Shass* or *shiss*, (pl. شصوص *shusūs*) A fish-hook. A sly thief, an expert plunderer.

A شصّاب *shassāb*, A butcher.

A شصار *shisār*, A piece of wood fastened across a camel's nose. A skewer for closing the hinder parts of a camel after foaling.

A شصاص *shisās*, (v. n. of شصّ) Having little or thick milk (a camel). Going away. Hindering. Being uncomfortable from poverty (life). Gnashing the teeth.

A شصاصاء *shasāsāʾ*, Adversity, penury, scarcity. A barren year. Haste, expedition. Any business which one cannot leave. A bad horse, camel, or vehicle.

A شصائب *shasāʾib*, (pl. of شصيبة *shasībat*) Calamities, scarcities. Bottoms of wells. Timbers of a camel's saddle.

A شصائص *shasāʾis*, (pl. of شصوص *shasūs*) (Camels) which yield little milk.

A شصب *shasb*, (v. n. of شصب) Failing to conceive, though frequently covered (a camel). Being afflicted, indigent. Being difficult (an affair). *Shasb* or *shasab*, A flaying, skinning. A scalding of the hair before roasting. Dryness. *Shisb*, (pl. اشصاب *ashsāb*) Adversity, scarcity. A lot, fortune. *Shasab*, A becoming dry. The being difficult and intricate. *Shusub*, Flayed (sheep).

P شصت *shast*, (for شست) Sixty. A hook.

P شصتم *shastum*, (for شستم) A sixtieth.

P شصت يك *shast yak*, A sixtieth.

A شصر *shasr*, (v. n. of شصر) Pricking (a thorn). Spearing. Leaping (a horse). Butting with the horns (a bull). Sewing (with wide stitches), basting. Fixing the skewer شصار *shisār* in the hole of a camel's nose. Fixing the skewer شصار *shisār* to the hinder part of a camel. *Shisr*, A skewer with which the hinder parts of a camel are kept up, after a falling of the matrix. *Shasar*, (fem. شصرة *shasarat*) (pl. اشصار *ashsār*) A young deer strong and butting with his horns. A bird less than a sparrow.

A شصص *shusus*, (A sheep) having no milk. Camels which give little milk. Scarce (years).

A شصلب *shaslab*, Robust, firm.

A شصو *shasw*, Intenseness, severity. Adversity.

A شصوّ *shusūw*, (v. n. of شصا for شصو) Being fixed on an object (the eye). Being carried high in the air (a cloud). Being filled with water and sticking out (a leathern bottle).

A شصوب *shusūb*, (v. n. of شصب) Being afflicted, indigent. Being difficult (an affair).

A شصور *shusūr*, (v. n. of شصر) Being fixed (the eye of a dying person). Being turned (the eye).

A شصوص *shasūs*, (pl. شصائص *shasāʾis*) (A camel) having little milk. A scarce (year). *Shusūs*, (v. n. of شصّ) Being scarce (season). Having little milk (a camel). Gnashing the teeth. Going away. Hindering. Being indigent. (pl. of شصّ *shass* or *shiss*) Fish-hooks. Cunning thieves.

A شصيّ *shusīy*, (v. n. of شصي) Swelling (a carcase), so that the hands and feet stand out.

A شصيب *shasīb*, A foreigner. Lot, fortune.

A شصيبة *shasībat*, (pl. شصائب *shasāʾib*) Calamity, penury. The bottom of a well.

A شصير *shasīr*, A prick from a thorn.

A شطّ *shatt*, (v. n. of شطّ) Being troublesome, oppressing. Being far distant. (pl. شطوط *shutūt* and شطّان *shuttān*) The bank of a river. The Tigris. (pl. شطوط *shutūt*) The side or half of a camel's bunch.

A شطء *shatʾ*, (v. n. of شطأ) Walking on a river's bank. Fastening on a camel's saddle. Subjugating, overpowering (a man). Lying with. Overloading (a camel). Producing branches or foliage (a tree). Being a match for a load (a man). Casting forth her young (a mother). (pl. شطوء *shutū*) A shoot, young branch. The sprouting of foliage. A blade, a leaf. The bank of a river. (pl. اشطاء *ashtā*) A sapling, sucker growing about the root of a tree.

A شطاء *shitā*, (v. n. 3 of شطأ) Walking (with another) on the opposite bank of a river.

A شطاب *shitāb*, The lining of a saddle-cloth.

A شطّاح *shattāh*, Meretricious, lewd, obscene.

A شطّاحي *shattāhī*, Shamelessness, effrontery. One who speaks contrary to the law.

A شطار *shitār*, A halving with another.

A شطّار *shuttār*, (pl. of شاطر *shātir*) Those who harass, pester, thwart, and oppose their friends. Rogues, impudent, shameless, daring fellows.

A شطارة *shatārat*, (v. n. of شطر) Troubling, opposing, teasing to distraction. Abandoning (friends). Being disobedient, perverse. Being far removed. Retiring, receding. Having one teat longer than the other (an ewe). Alacrity, activity. Sharpness.

A شطاط *shatāt* or *shitāt*, (v. n. of شطّ) Being of a well-proportioned shape. Being long. A fine shape. Distance. A brickbat.

A شطاطة *shatātat*, Distance.

A شطآن *shutān*, (pl. of شاطئ) Banks of rivers.

A شطّان *shuttān*, (pl. of شطّ) Banks of rivers.

A شطائب *shatāib*, Divers sects. Adversities.

A شطائط *shatāit*, (pl. of شطوطى *shatawta'*) Large-bunched she-camels.

A شطب *shatb*, (v. n. of شطب) Cutting (a camel's bunch). Turning away, bending. Being distant. Opening and spreading out (silk). Fresh and green (palm-branch). Tall and handsome. *Shutab* or *shutub*, (pl. of شطبة *shutbat* or *shutabat*) Long grooves on the backs or surfaces of swords.

A شطبة *shatbat*, The green branch of a palm-tree; (and from the resemblance) a sword. *Shatbat* or *shitbat*, Tall, elegant (girl). Sleek (horse). *Shutbat* or *shutabat*, (pl. شطوب *shutūb*, شطب *shutab*, and *shutub*) A long groove on the back or blade of a sword. A long strap of leather, or a long slice of a camel's bunch.

A شطّة *shattat*, Fine, well-proportioned (girl). *Shittat*, Distance.

A شطّيح *shittah*, Used in driving goats or kids.

A شطر *shatr*, (v. n. of شطر) Milking (a camel) of two teats. (pl. اشطر *ashtur* and شطور *shutūr*) The half or part of a thing. The two fore, or the two hinder teats of a camel. Sort, kind. A side, part, or tract. A hemistich (in scanning). The cæsura or pause. شطر شطره *shatara shatrahu*, He prosecuted his design. *Shutr* or *shutur*, Far distant.

A شطران *shatrān*, Half-filled (cup or vessel).

A شطرة *shitrat*, (Children) half male, half female.

P شطرنج *shatranj*, Chess (so called, according to some, from صد رنج *sad ranj* (A hundred cares), from شاه رنج *shāh-ranj* (The royal care or sorrow), or from شش رنگ *shash rang* (Six species or ranks amongst the pieces): as, شاه *shāh*, King; فرزين *farzīn*, Queen; فيل *fīl*, Elephant; فرس *faras*, Horseman or knight; رخ *rukh*, Tower or castle; and پيادگان *piyādagān*, Footmen, peons, or pawns).

P شطرنج *shitranj*, Chess.

P شطرنج باز *shatranj-bāz*, A chess-player.

P شطرنج بازي *shatranj-bāzī*, Chess. A sort of carpet.

P شطرنجي *shatranjī*, A kind of bread. A kind of carpet. A chess-player.

P شطرنجي باف *shatranjī-bāf*, Carpet-weaver.

A شطره *shatrahu*, Towards him.

A شطرى *shatra'*, (fem. of شطران *shatrān*) Half-filled (vessel).

A شطس *shats*, (v. n. of شطس) Wandering, travelling. Ingenuity, shrewdness. Adeptness in the art of fraud. *Shuts*, (or شطسة *shutsat*) Contrariety, opposition. A lie.

A شطسّي *shutasīy*, Unjust; contumacious. Extremely subtle.

A شطشاط *shatshāt*, A sort of bird.

A شطط *shatat*, (v. n. of شطّ) Exceeding just bounds. Tyrannizing over. Being unjust in one's dealings. Injustice, oppression. Excess, redundancy.

A شطع *shataʻ*, A being weak from disease.

A شطف *shatf*, (v. n. of شطف) Going away. Receding. Wandering, running about. Being distant. Washing.

A شطم *shatm*, (v. n. of شطم) Lying with.

A شطن *shatn*, (v. n. of شطن) Tying with a rope. Opposing, thwarting. Being obstinate, perverse. Opposition (hence شيطان *shaytān*, The devil). *Shatan*, (pl. اشطان *ashtān*) A long rope.

A شطوء *shutū*, (v. n. of شطأ) Putting forth suckers or foliage (a tree). (pl. of شطء *shat*) Banks of rivers. Suckers of palm-trees. Blades of corn, leaves.

A شطوب *shutūb*, (pl. of شطبة *shut* or *shutabat*) Long grooves on the backs or surfaces of swords.

A شطور *shatūr*, (A sheep) which has one teat dry, or one shorter than another. A garment of which one side is longer than the other. *Shutūr*, (v. n. of شطر) Looking at one thing with one eye, and seeming to direct the other to a different object; squinting. Having one teat longer than the other (a ewe). Abandoning friends or family. (pl. of شطر *shatr*) Parts, halves.

A شطورة *shutūrat*, (v. n. of شطر) Retiring, being far removed: abandoning friends or family.

A شطوس *shatūs*, One who, refusing to obey orders, retires somewhere alone.

A شطوط *shatūt*, (pl. شطائط *shatāit*) A she-camel having a large bunch. *Shutūt*, (v. n. of شطّ) Being distant. Being troublesome, oppressing. (pl. of شطّ *shatt*) Sides or halves of camels' bunches. Banks of rivers.

A شطوطي *shatawta'*, (pl. شطائط *shatāit*) A large-bunched camel.

A شطوف *shatūf*, Far distant (design). *Shutūf*, (v. n. of شطف) Going away. Becoming distant. Wandering, running about.

A شطون *shatūn*, Very remote (design or military expedition). Deep (well), or one wide at top, narrow at bottom, and having two ropes. *Shutūn*, (v. n. of شطن) Going. Being far distant. Entering deep into the ground firmly or loosely.

A شطيء *shita'*, (v. n. of شطي) Swelling (a corpse), so that the hands and feet stand out.

A شطيّ *shatīy*, (pl. شطيان *shityān*) A circuit: a breadth of land in tillage.

A شطياة *shatyaat*, (v. n. of شطيا Q) Being weak, irresolute, uncertain in mind or counsel.

A شطيبة *shatībat*, A long section of leather. A piece of a camel's bunch. A she-camel without milk. A stick cut lengthwise to be made into a bow.

A شطير *shatīr*, A foreigner. Far distant. A half.

A شطّير *shittīr*, Distant, foreign. A half.

A شطيط *shatīt*, (v. n. of شطّ) Committing injustice, passing an unjust sentence.

A شظّ *shazz*, (v. n. of شظّ) Being difficult. Throwing into difficulty and embarassment. Separating, driving away (people). Having a priapism. Passing a crooked billet through the handles of two sacks, in order to lay them on the back of a horse. The remaining part of a day.

A شظاظ *shazāz*, Dispersion. *Shizāz*, (pl. اشظة *ashizzat*) The billet mentioned under شظّ *shazz*. Name of a famous robber.

A شظاظا *shazāzan*, Scatteredly.

A شظاف *shazāf*, Adversity, penury. *Shizāf*, Distance. (pl. of شظف *shazf*) Straits, difficulties.

A شظافة *shazāfat*, (v. n. of شظف) Becoming hard, not being sufficiently watered (a tree).

A شظايا *shazāya'*, (pl. of شظيّة *shazīyat*) Splinters, fragments. Chips, laths.

A شظف *shazf*, (v. n. of شظف) Hindering, keeping back. Castrating (a ram) by compressing the sinews, so that the parts wither away. The castration of a ram. A split stick. Refusal, hindrance. *Shizf*, (pl. شظفة *shizafat*) A small rod or peg. Dry bread. *Shazaf*, (v. n. of شظف) Being pinched by want, distressed. Penetrating between the skin and the flesh (an arrow). Becoming hard (a tree not sufficiently watered). (pl. شظاف *shizāf*) Adversity, penury, straits. *Shazif*, A he-camel rushing in amongst the herd and doing mischief. Quarrelsome, contentious. Pinched, distressed. *Shuzuf*, Bad-tempered, wickedly disposed. A fierce combatant.

A شظفة *shazifat*, Hard ground. *Shizafat*, (pl. of شظف *shizf*) Small rods or pegs. Dry loaves.

A شظو *shazw*, A side, tract, district.

A شظي *shaza'*, (v. n. of شظى) Trembling in the small bones (called شظا *shaza'*). Being split (a stick). Branching out in many directions (nerves and sinews). Swelling (a corpse), so that the hands and feet stick out. The small bones and tendons of the elbows or knees. A stranger who joins himself to a body of men. A succession of breadths or slips of arable land extending over the whole surface which is in tillage.

A شظيّ *shazīy*, The swelling (of a dead body).

A شظيّة *shazīyat*, (pl. شظايا *shazāyaʼ*, شظيّ *shazīy*, or *shizīy*) A chip, lath, fragment, splinter. A certain part of an astrolabe. A bow. The leg-bone. *Shazīyat*, (or شظية *shizyat*) A large rock projecting from a mountain.

A شظيظ *shazīz*, Split wood. A fastened sack.

A شظيف *shazīf*, (A tree) hardening for want of watering.

A شعّ *shaعع*, (v.n. of شعّ) Scattering urine from side to side (a camel). Being scattered and dispersed. Pouring forth a host of marauders. Any thing scattered. A chariot, cart, waggon. *Shuعع*, (pl. اشعّة *ashiععat* and شعاع *shiعāع*) A sunbeam. A cobweb.

A شعاب *shiعāb*, (v. n. 3 of شعب) Removing, keeping at a distance. Dying. (pl. of شعبة *shuعbat*) Branches of trees, ramifications.

A شعّاب *shaععāb*, A mender of broken vessels, plates, or dishes.

A شعابين *shaعābīn*, (pl. of شعبان *shaعbān*) Months of Shaabān.

A شعار *shaعār*, Trees, especially thick and entangled. An under garment. Trees in smooth ground, which afford shade in summer and shelter in winter. *Shiعār*, (v. n. 3 of شعر) Contending or excelling in poetry. Lying or sleeping together in one under garment. (pl. اشعرة *ashعirat* and شعر *shuعur*) An under garment (opposed to دثار *disār*). A horse-cloth. A sign, mark, signal, parole, watchword, military password, or any symbol by which the soldiers in battle distinguish their comrades, or in travelling at night. Habit, custom. Death. Whatever is used to preserve wine. Thunder. Trees. (pl. of شعر *shaعr*) Hairs. شعار الحجّ *shiعāru'l hajj*, The rites, ceremonies, and sacrifices prescribed in the pilgrimage to Mecca. ذات كرم شعار *zāti karam-shiعār*, Adorned with nobleness or generosity. P سردار ظفر شعارم *sar-dāri zafar-shiعārum*, My victorious general.

A شعارة *shiعārat*, (pl. شعائر *shaعāʼir*) The foundation, root, or origin of the ceremonies and sacrifices prescribed in the pilgrimage to Mecca. The most important of those ceremonies, such as halting at the different stations, the procession round the Kaaba, &c. A symbol of obedience.

A شعارير *shaعārīr*, A sort of game. (pl. of شعرورة *shuعrūrat*) Small cucumbers. *Shaعārīra*, In different directions. ذهبوا شعارير بقذّان *zahabū shaعārīra bi huzzāna* (or بقندحرة *bi hindahrata*), They were scattered in all directions like flies.

A شعاع *shaعāع*, Beards of corn. A spirting of blood in rays. Thin, watery milk. A separating, a scattering. Wavering (opinion). Unsteady, distracted (camels). Confused, perplexed, scattered. *Shiعāع*, Beards of corn. (pl. of شعّ *shuعع* or شعاع *shuعāع*) Rays of the sun. *Shuعāع*, Beards of corn. Light, splendour, lustre. (pl. شعاع *shiعāع*, اشعّة *ashiععat*, and شعع *shuعuع*) A ray, sunbeam. شعاع شمس *shuعāعi shams*, Rays of the sun.

A شعاعة *shuعāعat*, A single sunbeam.

A شعاعيّ *shuعāعiy*, Radial. خطوط شعاعيّة *khutūti shuعāعīya*, Radial lines, radii.

A شعاف *shiعāf*, (pl. of شعفة *shaعafat*) Summits of mountains. Upper parts of the head. صهب الشعاف *suhbu'sh shiعāf*, Red-haired. *Shuعāf*, Madness, insanity.

A شعاليل *shaعālīl*, (Bodies of men) setting out and taking different roads.

A شعائر *shaعāʼir*, (pl. of شعارة *shiعārat* and شعيرة *shaعīrat*) Signs, symbols, sacred observances (especially such as are of divine appointment). (pl. of شعيرة *shaعīrat*) Animals sacrificed or offered. شعائر الذهب *shaعāʼiru'z zahab*, A kind of necklace in the shape of barley-corns.

A شعائل *shaعāʼil*, (pl. of شعيلة) Lighted wicks.

A شعب *shaعb*, (v. n. of شعب) Collecting together. Repairing, mending, interpolating. Turning (a horse's) head in a contrary direction to what he wants to go. Dividing, separating. Propagating. Sending (an ambassador). Longing for home. Destroying, ruining. Breaking the top branches of a tree (a camel). Occupying, employing. Appearing, being conspicuous. Leaving one's friends and going amongst strangers. A crowd. Dispersion. (pl. شعوب *shuعūb*) People, nation, large and noble tribe, distinguished by the fame of their founder. The joining or suture of the bones of the head. Corn. Distance. Distant. A fissure, a cleft. A mountain. *Shiعb*, (pl. شعاب *shiعāb*) A path through mountains. A cleft, a chasm. A mark made on camels by burning. A water-course between two hills. *Shuعb*, (pl. of اشعب *ashعab*) (Goats) having the horns distant from each other, also the hips asunder. *Shaعab*, (v. n. of شعب) Being distant. Interval; space between the shoulders or horns. *Shuعab*, (pl. of شعبة *shuعbat*) Branches, ramifications. Fingers (as branching from the hand). Barbs of arrows or fish-hooks. شعب الفرس *shuعabu'l furas*, The extremities or prominent points of a horse. *Shuعub*, (pl. of شعيب *shaعīb*) Travellers' provision-bags in two divisions. Old leathern water-bottles.

A شعبان *shaعbān*, (pl. شعبانات *shaعbānāt* and شعابين *shaعābīn*) The eighth Arabian month. غزال شعبان *ghazālu shaعbān*, Name of a little beast.

A شعبانات *shaعbānāt*, (pl. of شعبان *shaعbān*) Months of Shaabān.

A شعبة *shuعbat*, (pl. شعب *shuعab* and شعاب *shiعāb*) The branch of a tree; ramification. Derivation. The end of a branch. A part separated from the whole. Distance between branches or horns. The barb of an arrow or fish-hook. A gore or any thing similar engrafted into garments to adapt them to a shape; also a piece cemented into a broken vessel. Division, separation. A people, nation. A small water-channel, especially through sands. A large stream winding through a valley. A mountain cleft, to which birds repair. الحياء شعبة من الايمان *al hayāʼ shuعbat mini'l īmān*, Modesty is a branch of religion. الشباب شعبة من الجنون *ash' shabāb shuعbat mini'l junūn*, Youth is a branch of madness.

P شعبده *shuعbada*, Sleight of hand, juggling.

P شعبده باز *shuعbada-bāz*, A juggler, conjurer. فلك شعبده باز *falaki shuعbada-bāz*, The juggling heavens, *i.e.* the deceitful world or fortune.

A شعبذة *shaعbazat*, The act of juggling.

A شعة *shaعat*, (v. n. of وشع) Mixing.

A شعث *shuعs*, (pl. of اشعث *ashعas*) Those whose hair is dishevelled and filled with dust. Uncurried (horses). *Shaعas*, (v.n. of شعث) Being separated, scattered. Having the hair dishevelled, and the head covered with ashes. Being disordered (business). A tumult. *Shaعis*, Dishevel-haired.

A شعثاء *shaعsāʼ*, Dishevel-haired (girl). Name of a certain sect.

A شعثان *shaعsān*, Dishevelled and dusty-haired.

A شعر *shaعr*, (v. n. of شعر) Lining (a boot) with hair. Knowing. Versifying; excelling in poetry. Lying or sleeping together under one garment. (pl. اشعار *ashعār*, شعور *shuعūr*, and شعار *shiعār*) Hair (of man or any animal excepting camels and sheep). A plant, a tree. Saffron. شعر الجنّ *shaعru'l jinn*, (also شعر الغول *shaعru'l ghūl*) Maidens'-hair (a plant). P شعر مردمك *shaعri mardumak*, The eyelid. A صاحب شعر *sāhibi shaعr*, Hairy. *Shiعr*, (v. n. of شعر) Understanding, perceiving. Versifying, excelling in poetry. (pl. اشعار *ashعār*) Science; poesy, verse, metre. شعر شاعر *shiعri shāعir*, An excellent poem. علم شعر *عilmi shiعr*, The art of poetry. ليت شعري *layta shiعri*, O that I knew! *Shuعr*, A plant, a tree. Saffron. Substances like warts growing from the hoofs of sheep. (pl. of اشعر *ashعar*) Hairy. More intelligent. More happily poetical. (pl. of شعراء *shaعrāʼ*) Dreadful misfortunes. *Shaعar*, (v. n. of شعر) Knowing, perceiving, understanding. Versifying, writing poetry. Excelling in poetry. Being very hairy. Possessing slaves. Hair. *Shaعir*, Very hairy. *Shuعur*, (pl. of شعار *shiعār*) Under garments. Horse-cloths. Badges, military signals.

A شعراء *shaعrāʼ*, (fem. of اشعر *ashعar*) Hairy (sheep). Rough, disagreeable (woman or she-camel). A kind of peach. A fly infesting camels, asses, or dogs. A fur pelisse. Grassy (field). A kind of salt and bitter plant. A woody country.

A garden over-topped with trees. Sandy ground producing the plant نصيّ *nasiy*. Dreadful (misfortune). A multitude of persons. The hair of the pubes. *Shuʻarāʼ*, (pl. of شاعر *shāʻir*) Poets. Wise men, doctors. Those who charge God foolishly.

A شعران *shaʻrān*, Pasture in a salt-marsh. A species of the plant رمث *rims*, green inclining to dust-colour.

A شعرانيّ *shaʻrānīy*, Very hairy about the body.

P شعر آور *shiʻr-āwar*, Poetical. A poet.

P شعر بازي *shiʻr-bāzī*, The art of poetry.

A شعرة *shaʻrat*, One hair. Old age. A daughter. *Shiʻrat*, *shaʻrat*, or *shuʻrat*, (v. n. of شعر) Understanding, knowing, perceiving. *Shiʻrat*, Hair of the pubes, or the pubes (especially of a woman). A bit of hair. *Shaʻirat*, A sheep having hair growing betwixt the hoofs, and bleeding therefrom; or one troubled with an itching in the groin.

A شعرور *shuʻrūr*, (pl. شعارير *shaʻārīr*) An indifferent poet. A small cucumber. A fly that settles on a raw part of a camel.

A شعرورة *shuʻrūrat*, (pl. شعارير *shaʻārīr*) A small cucumber.

A شعري *shiʻra'*, *shaʻra'* or *shuʻra'*, (v. n. of شعر) Perceiving, understanding, knowing. Excelling in poetry. Being a poet. The dog-star.

A شعريّ *shiʻrīy*, Poetic.

A شعريّات *shaʻarīyāt*, The pelican's young ones.

A شعريان *shiʻrayāni*, The two dog-stars. viz. الشعريُ العبور *ash'shiʻra'l ʻabūr*, (or شعريُ اليماني *shiʻra'l yamānī*) The star Sirius, or the greater dog-star. شعريُ الغميصاء *shiʻra'l ghumaysāʼ*, (or شعريُ الشامية *shiʻra'sh shāmīyat*) The lesser dog-star.

A شعريّة *shaʻrīyat*, A kind of veil.

A شعشاع *shaʻshāʻ*, Divided, dispersed. Nimble, agile, active. Long, tall. A thin or light shadow. Handsome.

A شعشع *shaʻshaʻ*, Thin or light (shadow). Long.

A شع شع *shuʻ shuʻ*, A word enjoining contentment, patience, or resignation; also the allowing of the hair to grow long.

A شعشعان *shaʻshaʻān*, (fem. شعشعانة) Long, tall, handsome (man, woman, or camel).

A شعشعانيّ *shaʻshaʻānīy*, Long, tall, handsome.

A شعشعة *shaʻshaʻat*, (v. n. of شعشع Q) Mixing, tempering, diluting (wine with water) Making thin and long. Dipping (a cake into fat). Shining. Mixture. Splendour.

A شعصب *shaʻsab*, A decrepit old man.

A شعصبة *shaʻsabat*, A being worn with age.

A شعصور *shuʻsūr*, A wood-nut, wild walnut.

A شعع *shuʻuʻ*, (pl. of شعاع) Rays, sunbeams.

A شعف *shaʻf*, (v. n. of شعف) Seizing the heart, making sick, disordering the mind (love). Putting forth some verdure (a withered plant). Besmearing (a camel with pitch). *Shaʻaf*, (v. n. of شعف) Loving desperately, being overcome with love. Losing the hair about the eyes (a she-camel). The top of a camel's bunch. Bark of the غاف *ghāf* tree. A disease incident to camels, making the hair of the eyes fall off. (pl. of شعفة *shaʻafat*) Mountain-tops.

A شعفاء *shaʻfāʼ*, Bare about the eyes from disease (a she-camel).

A شعفات *shaʻafāt*, (pl. of شعفة) Gentle rains.

A شعفة *shaʻfat*, A gentle rain. *Shaʻafat*, (pl. شعف *shaʻaf*, شعوف *shuʻūf*, شعاف *shiʻāf*, and شعفات *shaʻafāt*) Summit of a mountain. Upper part of the heart. Gentle rain. Hair of the head, especially the forelocks.

A شعفرة *shaʻfarat*, Name of a poet.

A شعل *shaʻl*, (v. n. of شعل) Advancing far into, looking to the end of. Kindling (a fire). Light, testy (man). Bold. *Shaʻal*, (v. n. of شعل) Having white hairs in the tail or forelock. White hairs in the tail or forelocks (of a horse). *Shuʻal*, (pl. of شعلة *shuʻlat*) Flames. *Shuʻul*, (pl. of شعلة *shuʻlat*) Flames. Things set on fire. (pl. of شعيلة *shaʻīlat*) Lighted wicks.

A شعلاء *shaʻlāʼ*, (A mare) partly white (especially on the tail).

A شعلة *shuʻlat*, (pl. شعل *shuʻul* and شعول *shuʻūl*) Light, splendour, lustre, shining, flashing, coruscation. Fire, flame. Any thing on which the fire has kindled. A mixture of white on the tail or forelocks (of a horse). P شعله دار *shuʻla-dār*, شعله زن *shuʻla-zan*, and شعله ور *shuʻlawar*, Flaming, resplendent, brilliant.

A شعلّع *shaʻallaʻ*, Long, tall (man or beast).

A شعلّعة *shaʻallaʻat*, (A tree) whose branches are wide, separate, and not entangled.

A شعم *shaʻm*, A reconciling of differences.

A شعموم *shuʻmūm*, Long, tall.

A شعن *shaʻan*, Dry fallen leaves.

A شعنبة *shaʻnabat*, The horn of a ram, rising straight, and bending towards the extremity.

A شعنلع *shaʻanlaʻ*, Long, tall (man or beast).

A شعو *shaʻw*, The erection of the hairs or feathers (from terror).

A شعواء *shaʻwāʼ*, Wide-diffused, branchy (tree). Desultory (excursion against an enemy).

A شعوانة *shaʻwānat*, A mass of dishevelled hair.

A شعوب *shaʻūb*, Death. *Shuʻūb*, (pl. of شعب *shaʻb*) Assembled crowds. Dispersed bodies. Nations (especially of Pagans).

A شعوبيّة *shuʻūbīyat*, Name of a sect which places the Arabians above the Persians.

A شعوذة *shaʻwadat*, (or شعوذة) Sleight of hand.

P شعوده *shuʻvada*, Sleight of hand, juggling.

A شعوذيّ *shaʻwazīy*, A express, post-boy.

A شعور *shuʻūr*, (v. n. of شعر) Knowing. Perceiving, understanding, being aware of. Being a poet. Science, knowledge, wisdom, intelligence. (pl. of شعر *shaʻr*) Hairs. ارباب شعور *arbābi shuʻūr*, The learned.

A شعورة *shuʻūrat*, (v. n. of شعر) Perceiving, knowing, understanding.

A شعوف *shuʻūf*, (pl. of شعفة) Mountain-tops.

A شعول *shuʻūl*, (pl. of شعلة *shuʻlat*) Flames. Substances set on fire.

A شعيّ *shuʻa'*, A tress of dishevelled hair.

A شعيا *shaʻya'*, The prophet Isaiah.

A شعيب *shaʻīb*, (pl. شعب *shuʻub*) A traveller's provision-bag in two divisions. An old leathern bottle. *Shuʻayb*, Jethro, father-in-law of Moses.

A شعيبيّة *shuʻaybīyat*, Name of a sect.

A شعير *shaʻīr*, Barley. A companion, friend.

A شعيراء *shuʻayrāʼ*, A sort of tree.

A شعيرة *shaʻīrat*, One grain of barley. A round knob resembling a barley-corn, fixed on the end of a knife-handle to hold the blade fast. (pl. شعائر *shaʻāʼir*) Any animal sacrificed, or marked for a sacrifice, at Mecca. A rite, ceremony, or sacred observance performed at Mecca during the pilgrimage, regarded as an act of obedience to God. *Shuʻayrat*, (dim.) A little hair.

A شعيع *shaʻīʻ*, A chariot, cart, waggon.

A شعيفات *shuʻayfāt*, Small forelocks.

A شعيل *shaʻīl*, Partly white on the tail.

A شعيلة *shaʻīlat*, (pl. شعيل *shaʻīl* and شعل *shuʻul*) A burning lamp, match, or wick. Fire generated in heated dung.

P شغ *shagh* or *shugh*, A branch. Horn of an ox. Antlers of a stag. A drinking-horn. *Shugh*, Callousness of the hands from hard labour. A little. A quiver.

A شغّ *shughgh*, (v. n. of شغّ) Scattering his urine when staling (a camel). Separating, going different ways (people).

P شغا *sha* or *shughā*, A quiver and bow-case.

A شغا *shagha'*, (v. n. of شغا for شغو) Having the teeth uneven and distorted. The trickling of urine drop by drop.

A شغاب *shighāb*, (v. n. 3 of شغب) Injuring. Defaming. Squabbling, raising tumults.

A شغّاب *shaghghāb*, Seditious, a breedbate.

P شغاد *shaghād* or *shughād*, Name of the brother of Rustam. *Shighād*, Whatever is permitted in matters of religion.

P شغار *shaghār*, A badger, brock, kind of stinking weasel. An urchin, hedgehog. *Shighār*, Noise, uproar. Reproof.

A شغار *shaghār*, Empty. Two veins in a camel's side. Full (well or wells). *Shighār*, A combination of two persons to oppress a third. A double treaty of marriage, common among the Pagan Arabians, one man marrying the sister or daughter of another, and giving him in return his daughter or sister, in order to avoid the paying of marriage-portions. (This practice was abolished by Muhammad).

A شغّارة *shaghghārat*, A flint for striking fire.

A شغاف *shaghāf*, The place where the بلغم *balgham* is secreted. The pericardium. The heart's core. Original sin. *Shaghāf* or *shughāf*, A pain in the clitoris or pericardium. A species of distemper under the short ribs on the right side.

P شغال *shaghāl*, A jackal.

P شغالى *shaghālī*, A sort of grape.

P شغام *shaghām*, Rustam's younger brother.

A شغاميم *shaghāmīm*, (pl. of شغموم *shughmūm*) Long, tall, handsome.

P شغان *shaghān*, Honey in the comb.

P شغاه *shaghāh*, A quiver.

A شغب *shaghb*, (v. n. of شغب) Declining, turning aside, swerving from the way. *Shaghb* or *shaghab*, (v. n. of شغب) Stirring up evil (against any one). Accusation. Mischief. Contention, altercation. Sauciness. ذات شغب *zāt shaghb*, A woman who refuses the caresses of her husband; also one who longs for any thing when pregnant. *Shaghb, shaghib*, or *shighabb*, A fomenter of broils.

P شغب *shaghab*, A tumult, noise, disturbance, confusion, cries, lamentation, shrieking. Bashfulness. Politeness.

A شغبر *shaghbar*, (or شغبز *shaghbaz*) A jackal.

P شغتا *shaghtā*, A quiver.

A شغر *shaghr*, (v. n. of شغر) Lifting his legs to urine (as a dog). Striking (his) head under the teats of the female (a male camel), lifting her up and throwing her prostrate. Trampling, treading upon. Going fast. Lifting up (a woman's) leg. Leading out, expelling, ejecting. Scattering, dispersing. Being far distant from defenders (a place). Being depopulated, none being left to govern (a city). Being distant and far from help and protection. Division, separation. Distance. شغرت برجلي في الغريب *shaghartu bi rijli fi'l gharib*, I overcame the men under his protection. شغر بغر *shaghara baghara* or *shighara bighara*, (They) were dispersed) everywhere.

P شغر *Shughr*, A hedgehog. A badger. *Shaghar*, Hardness or blisters on the hands or feet from working or from walking. *Shughur*, A hedgehog.

A شغربة *shaghrabat*, (v. n. of شغرب Q) Tripping (an adversary) in wrestling.

A شغربيّة *shaghrabīyat*, A mode of tripping in wrestling.

A شغرنة *shaghranat*, (v. n. of شغرن Q) Tripping in wrestling. Handling roughly.

A شغرور *shughrūr*, Name of a plant.

A شغري *shaghra'*, A stone against which a dog lifts his leg. A horse-block formerly at Mecca.

A شغز *shaghz*, (v. n. of شغز) Stirring up strife. Tyranny, usurpation. A setting of men by the ears.

A شغزب *shaghzab*, Name of a celebrated wrestler. A man powerful, strong, and firm-fleshed.

A شغزبة *shaghzabat*, (v. n. of شغزب Q) Treating severely, handling roughly. Tripping in wrestling.

A شغزبي *shaghzaba'*, (or شغزبيّة *shaghzabīyat*) A mode of tripping in wrestling.

A شغزبيّ *shaghzabīy*, Hard, difficult, troublesome. A watering-place lying out of the road.

A حجر الشغزي *hajaru'sh shaghza'*, A horse-block that formerly stood at Mecca.

A شغشغة *shaghshaghat*, (v. n. of شغشغ Q) Working the point of a spear in a wounded man and drawing it out. Braying in a certain manner (a camel). Cooing (a turtle-dove). Moving the bit to and fro in (a horse's) mouth when breaking (him) in. Pouring water into a vessel so as not to fill it. Drinking little. Muddying a well. Haste. A carriage, cart, waggon.

A شغف *shaghf*, (v. n. of شغف) Wounding in the pericardium, or in the heart's core. *Shaghf* or *shaghaf*, The place where the بلغم *balgham* is secreted. Original sin. Heart's blood, the inner recesses of it. *Shaghaf*, (v. n. of شغف) Lodging in the heart's recesses. Bark of the غاف *ghāf* tree.

A شغفر *shaghfar*, A beautiful woman.

P شغك *shaghak*, Ignorant, silly. Cruel, unjust.

A شغل *shaghl* and *shughl*, (v. n. of شغل) Occupying, keeping employed at. Keeping employed, diverting from. *Shaghl, shughl, shaghal*, or *shughul*, (pl. اشغال *ashghāl* and شغول *shughūl*) Work, workmanship. Occupation, employment, business. شغل شاغل *shughli shāghil*, A work which occupies much. شغل القرآن *shaghlu'l kur-ān*, Acting in conformity with the precepts of the Kur'ān. *Shagil*, Employed, busy. *Shughal*, (pl. of شغلة *shaghlat*) Corn-ricks, stacks of unthrashed corn.

A شغلة *shaghlat*, (pl. شغل *shughal*) A corn-stack.

A شغم *shaghim*, Greedy, covetous.

A شغموم *shughmūm*, (pl. شغاميم *shaghāmīm*) Long, handsome, (man, woman, or camel).

A شغمومة *shughmūmat*, Tall and fair (woman).

A شغميم *shighmīm*, Tall and handsome.

A شغن *shughan*, (pl. of شغنة) Tender branches.

A شغنب *shaghnab*, (or شغنوب) A tender branch.

A شغنة *shughnat*, (pl. شغن *shughan*) A tender branch. A bundle or load of food.

A شغو *shaghw*, (v. n. of شغو) Having uneven, distorted teeth. *Shughw*, (pl. of اشغي *ashgha'* and شغواء *shaghwā*) Those whose teeth are uneven.

A شغواء *shaghwā*, (fem. of اشغي *ashgha'*) (A woman) with distorted or unequal teeth. An eagle.

A شغور *shaghūr*, A long, straddling she-camel. *Shughūr*, (v. n. of شغر) Lifting up (a woman's) leg. Lifting up (his) leg to make water (a dog).

P شغور *shughūr*, Forbidden by religion. A badger. A jackal. A cow's hide. The horn of an ox. Somewhat.

A شغوش *shaghūsh*, (*shughūsh* or شغوشيّ *shaghūshiy*) Wheat mixed with darnel.

A شغول *shughūl*, (pl. of شغل *shughl* or *shughul*) Occupations, employments.

P شغه *shagha*, A branch. A horn. Hardness, callosity, or blistering of the hands or feet. شغه بستن *shagha bastan*, To become hard and blistered (as the hands from labour, or the feet from walking).

A شغياء *shaghyā*, (A woman) who has unequal, distorted teeth.

A شغية *shaghyat*, A trickling of urine. Unevenness of teeth.

P شغيدن *shughīdan*, To be callous, blistered.

A شغير *shighghīr*, Of a bad disposition.

A شغيزة *shaghīzat*, A large packing-needle.

A شغيل *shaghīl*, Busy, employed.

P شف *shaf*, (for شب *shab*) Night. Alum.

A شفّ *shaff*, (v. n. of شفّ) Emaciating, making lean (grief or care). The latter end of a day. *Shaff* or *shiff*, (v. n. of شفّ) Gaining. Increasing. Diminishing. Gain, profit, advantage. Overplus, redundance. Decrease, detriment. Wind. (pl. شفوف *shufūf*) Transparent, thin, flimsy (cloth). *Shiff*, (v. n. of شفّ) Moving one's self, being moved.

P شفا *shafā*, Any thing lawful. Lawful, legitimate. *Shifā* or *shufā*, A quiver.

A شفا *shafa'*, (v. n. of شفي) Setting, or being about to set (the sun). (pl. اشفاء *ashfā*, شفيّ *shufīy*, and *shifīy*) The small remains (of life, of the setting sun, or of the moon upon the wane). Extremity, edge, border, side, margin, corner. شفا الدنيا *shafa'd dunya'*, The end of the world. على شفا حفرة من النار *'ala'shafa' hufratin mini'n nār*, On the edge of a gulf of fire.

A شفاء *shifā*, (v. n. of شفا for شفو) Applying a remedy, seeking to cure. Freeing (from disease), healing, curing. Setting, or being about to set (the sun). (pl. اشفية *ashfiyat* and اشافي *ashāfī*) Medicine, remedy, cure. Recovery of health, convalescence. دار الشفاء *dāru'sh shifā*, A hospital.

P شفادارو *shifā-dārū*, The bezoar-stone.

A شفار *shifār*, (pl. of شفرة *shafrat*) Large knives.

A شفارة *shafārat*, (v. n. of شفر) Having little or superficial animal passion (a woman).

A شفارج *shufārij*, A tray upon which sweetmeats in saucers or flowers are handed round to a company. A tray covered with plates and dishes. A kind of sweetmeat.

P شفاره *shifāra*, A badger, brock.

A شفاريّ *shufārīy*, (A jerboa) having hairy ears, long and broad, soft-fleshed, fat, long-legged, and not easily overtaken.

A شفاريّة *shufārīyat*, Large (ear).

P شفا ساز *shifā-sāz*, (شفا بخش *shifā-bakhsh*, or شفا رسان *shifā-rasān*) Salutary, healthful.

P شفا سازي *shifā-sāzī*, A cure.

A شفاشف *shufāshif*, Extreme thirst.

A شفاعة *shifā'at*, (v. n. of شفع) Increasing. Interceding for. Increase. Deprecation, intercession, advocacy, entreaty, recommendation. The addition of one work good to another. P شفاعت كردن *shifā'at kardan*, To intercede. شفاعت نامه *shifā'at-nāma*, An interceding, recommendatory letter.

P شفاعت كننده shifāʻat-kunanda, Intercessor.

A شفاف shifāf, (pl. of شفيف shafīf) Scorching heats and pains of intense cold.

A شفّاف shaffāf, Transparent, very thin, clear.

A شفافة shufāfat, Water at the bottom of a vessel.

A شفّافي shaffāfī, Transparency, diaphaneity.

A شفّان shaffān, Cold wind, with rain. غداة ذات شفّان ghadātun zātu shaffāni, A morning cold and windy.

P شفانه shafāna, Name of a large bird. A lark.

A شفانين shafānin, (pl. of شفنين) Pigeons.

A شفاه shifāh, (pl. of شفه shifah, شفة shafat, and شفهة shafahat) Lips.

A شفاهيّ shufāhīy, Large-lipped, thick-lipped.

A شفائر shafāʼir, Oræ vulvarum.

A شفائع shafāʼiʻ, Different kinds of grass or fodder which grows in pairs.

A شفة shafat or shifat, (originally شفهة shafhat or شفوة shafwat)(pl. شفوات shafawāt or شفاه shifāh) A lip. Work. Praise, eulogium. شفة حسنة shafat hasanat, Honourable mention. ما احسن شفة الناس عليك mā ahsana shafatu'n nās ʻalayka, How handsomely people speak of you! شفة الركيّة shafatu'r rakīyat, Margin of a well. بنت الشفة bintu'sh shafat, Daughter of the lip, i.e. a word. خفيف الشفة khafīfu'sh shafat, (Light-lipped) Importunate, urgent in one's inquiries. Taciturn, making little inquiry.

A شفّة shiffat or shaffat, (v. n. of شفّ) Increasing. Diminishing. Gaining.

P شفت shaft, Fat, greasy. Coarse, thick. Unshaved, untrimmed. Low-priced, cheap. Name of a town in Gilān famous for its china. *Shaft* or *shift*, Curved, crooked, unequal. *Shift*, A running of blood or matter. *Shuft*, A miser.

P شفتا shaftā, A quiver.

P شفتالو shaftālū, (شفتالود shaftālūd, or شفتالوج shaftāluj) A peach (rough plum). A lover's kiss.

P شفتاهج shaftāhanj, A perforated plate of steel, through which ingots of gold or silver are drawn into wire.

A شفترة shaftarat, A being separated, divided.

P شفترك shiftarah, A red bramble.

P شفترنك shafat-rang, A red peach; also a species of large apricot, with a sweet kernel, having one side red, the other white.

P شفتل shaftal, Trefoil.

P شفتلنك shaftalang, A red peach.

P شفتن shiftan, To become mad. To trickle. To scratch. To make drop.

A شفتنة shaftanat, A lying with.

P شفته shafta, A ball of thread. A couch. Beginning of sunrise. Any thing thin and delicate. *Shafta* or *shufta*, A rod with which they beat cotton before it is separated by the bow. *Shifta*, Mad, insane. Distracted with love. شفته رنك shifta-rang, Of the colour of love, i.e. a beautiful species of peach. *Shufta*, A lath.

P شفتيدن shiftīdan, To drop, run, trickle. To cause to drop. To scratch, wound.

A شفر shafr, (v. n. of شفر) Striking (oram vulvæ). *Shafr* or *shufr*, (pl. اشفار ashfār) A margin, an edge (particularly of the eyelids). Ora vulvæ. Any one, any body. ما بالدار شفر mā bi'd dār shafrun or shufrun, There is no one at home. *Shufr*, The higher side of a valley. *Shafar*, (v. n. of شفر) Being diminished, deficient.

A شفرة shafrat, (pl. شفار shifār) A large knife. A broad and sharp blade. A shoemaker's knife. The side or sharp edge of a spear-head. A servant. Any one. اصغر القوم شفرتهم asgharu'l kawm shafratuhum, The least of men is their servant. *Shafrat* or *shufrat*, Provisions sufficient. *Shafirat*, A woman whose passion is soon satisfied (in orâ vulvæ).

P شفره shafra or shufra, A large bookbinders' or shoemakers' knife.

A شفري shufrī, An excellent sort of pomegranate.

A شفز shafz, (v. n. of شفز) Striking with the sole or flat part of the foot, or with the toe.

P شفش shafsh or shufsh, The branch of a tree. A long reed, hooked at the end, used by cotton-dressers. Dry dung. A distemper incident to the fore-feet of horses from drinking too much water. A pipe, a flute.

A شفشاف shafshāf, Cold wind. Cold and rain. Slightly made (garment).

P شفشاهج shafshāhanj, (or شفشاهنك shafshāhang) A perforated plate of steel through which gold and silver wire is drawn.

P شفشاهنك shafshāhang, A carder of cotton; also his bow. (See also شاخسار shāhhsār).

P شفشف shafshaf, A crooked branch. The root of a tree.

A شفشفة shafshafat, (v. n. of شفشف Q) Emaciating (care or grief). Drying (heat or cold). Nipping (cold). Sprinkling urine. Bathing or throwing pulverized drugs into (a wound). Trembling, quaking. Being confused, perplexed (business).

A شفشليق shafshalīk, A flabby old woman.

P شفشه shifsha, The yarn-beam of a loom. Ringlets flowing about the face. An ingot of gold. *Shafsha* or *shifsha*, A cotton-dresser's rod. A branch, thin, straight, and smooth.

A شفصلة shafsalat, (v. n. of شفصل Q) Eating the fruit شفصلّى shifsilla', or plant شاصلّى shāsulla'.

A شفصلّى shifsilla', Name of a plant which entwines itself round trees; or its sesame-like berry.

A شفع shafʻ, (v. n. of شفع) Making even. Interceding, advocating. Increasing, adding one thing to another. Being in foal whilst followed by her colt (a camel). Aiding any one in injuring another. An even number, a pair. A solemn festival held at Mecca. Creatures (in pairs, male and female). *Shifʻ*, (v. n. of شفع) Being followed by her colt (a camel).

A شفعاء shufaʻāʼ, (pl. of شفيع) Intercessors.

A شفعة shufʻat, (v. n. of شفع) Wishing to add a neighbour's estate to one's possessions. Any possession coveted. Redemption. Madness, fury. حق شفعه haki shufʻa, Right of pre-emption in favour of a person whose possessions adjoin to a land offered for sale. *Shufʻat* or *shafʻat*, Two sacred inclinations of the head or genuflexions at the hour of the day called ضحى zuha'.

P شفعه گيرا shufʻa-gīrā, A redeemer, avenger.

A شفف shafaf, (v. n. of شفّ) Being thin and transparent (a garment). A small thing, a little.

A شفق shafak, (v. n. of شفق) Compassionating, pitying, condoling. (pl. اشفاق ashfāk) The crepuscle, twilight, or ruddiness in the sky, from sunset till total darkness. A day. Bad, naught. A coast, shore, tract. Fear. Pity, condolence, kindness, sympathy. The anxious wish of adviser for the good of the advised. P شفق گلگون shafaki gulgūn, The ruddy crepuscle, the roseate twilight.

A شفقان shafkān, Kindly disposed, benevolent.

A شفقة shafakat, (often pronounced *shafkat*) Compassion, pity, mercy, commiseration, clemency, indulgence, kindness. P اظهار شفقت نمودن izhāri shafkat namūdan, To commiserate. بي شفقت bī shafkat, Merciless, inhuman.

P شفقت نامه shafkat-nāma, Letter of condolence.

P شفك shafk, Any thing bad, worn out, ruinous. *Shafak*, Ignorant, unskilful, silly, stupid.

P شفل shaful, A camel's hoof.

P شفلج shaflaj, Capers.

A شفلّح shafallah, (A man) who has distended nostrils and thick lips. Wide (woman). Flabby and thick-lipped (vulva). Capers. A tree whose stem has four edges, each of which is sharp enough to cut a sheep's throat, and the fruit whereof resembles a negro's head. Split dates.

A شفلّع shafallaʻ, (erroneously written for شعلّع shaʻallaʻ) Long, tall (man or beast).

A شفلّقة shafallakat, A game, in which one strikes another down by a kick on the backside.

P شفليدن shuflīdan, To whistle (as pigeon-fanciers do when they wish to fly a pigeon, or as does a groom when he wishes a horse to drink).

A شفن shafn, (v. n. of شفن) Looking stedfastly through half-shut eyes. One who eagerly expects an inheritance. *Shafn* or *shafin*, Ingenious, intelligent, penetrating. *Shufan*, Sharp-sighted.

A شفنتر shafantar, Bald; whose hair is falling.

A شفنتري shafantara', Separated, divided.

A شفنين shif or shafnīn, A pigeon, turtle-dove.

A شفو shafw, (v. n. of شفا for شفو) Being near setting (the sun). Rising (the new moon). Appearing, being conspicuous (a person's figure).

A شفوات shafawāt, (pl. of شفة shafat) Lips.

A شفوان shafawāni, Two sides or extremities.

P شفوت shifūt, A demon in a human form.

The principle of evil, آهرمن *āhiraman*. A maniac.

P شفود *shafūd*, What is forbidden by religion.

P شفوده *shufūda*, A week.

A شفوع *shafūʿ*, (A she-camel) filling two pails at one milking.

A شفوف *shufūf*, (v. n. of شفّ) Becoming emaciated. Being thin, transparent (garment). (pl. of شفّ *shaff* and *shiff*) Thin, flimsy, transparent cloths.

A شفوق *shafūḳ*, Merciful, compassionate.

A شفون *shafūn*, One who looks askance with half-shut eyes. *Shufūn*, (v. n. of شفن) Looking stedfastly through half-shut eyes (in astonishment or in abhorrence).

A شفويّ *shafawīy*, Labial.

A شفه *shafh*, (v. n. of شفه) Detaining (one) from any business by keeping (him) employed on something else. Persevering in questioning until a person's stock of information is exhausted. Eating up, consuming, exhausting. Striking on the lip. *Shifah*, (pl. شفاه *shifāh*) A lip.

A شفهاء *shafhāʾ*, A woman whose lips close not.

A شفهة *shafahat*, The lip.

A شفهيّ *shafahīy*, Labial. حروف الشفهيّة *ḥurūfu'sh shafahīyat*, Labial letters; namely, ب *bā*, ف *fā*, and م *mīm*.

A شفيّ *shafīy*, Labial. *Shufīy* and *shifīy*, (pl. of شفا *shafā*) Small remains of life. Extremities, edges, sides, borders.

A شفير *shafīr*, Edge, margin. Extremity of a camel's lip. Upper edge of a valley. Edge of the eyelid.

A شفيرة *shafīrat*, A woman whose passion is in orâ vulvæ (شفر *shafr*), and is speedily satisfied.

A شفيع *shafīʿ*, An advocate, intercessor, patron. Possessed of a claim of pre-emption founded on the right of contiguity. شفيع الامم *shafīʿu'l umam*, Intercessor for the people. شفيع جار *shafīʿi jār*, The occupant of ground which is simply in the neighbourhood of another estate. شفيع خليط *shafīʿi khalīt*, The occupant of ground in actual contact or intermixed with another estate. شفيع العصاة في العرصات *shafīʿu'l ʿuṣāt fi'l ʿaraṣāt*, The advocate for sinners before the (heavenly) tribunal. شفيع الوري *shafīʿu'l warā*, Intercessor for men.

A شفيعا *shafīʿā*, A kind of Persian character.

A شفيف *shafīf*, (v. n. of شفّ) Gaining. Being thin, transparent (garment). Nipping (cold). A piercing cold wind accompanied with rain. The intense heat of the sun. Few, small. (pl. شفاف *shifāf*) The scorching pain of intense cold.

A شفيق *shafīḳ*, Merciful, compassionate, condoling; affectionate, benevolent. A kind and benevolent adviser, anxious for the welfare of the advised. اخ شفيق *akhi shafīḳ*, An affectionate brother.

P شفيليدن *shifīlīdan*, To express (juice). To whistle, to make a chirping noise when watering a horse. To listen.

A شفيهة *shufayhat*, (dim. of شفة) A small lip.

A شقّ *shaḳḳ*, (v. n. of شقّ) Splitting, tearing. Growing (a side-tooth). Extending through mid-sky, without going left or right (lightning). Being fixed upon any object (the eye of a dying person). Separating, scattering. Passing along, threading the streets. Being difficult, troublesome. Throwing into difficulties. Speaking clearly, enunciating distinctly. (pl. شقوق *shuḳūḳ*) A fissure, crack, crevice, slit, nick. Day-break, dawn. A half. Suspense. Split, cleft (place). شق العصا *shaḳḳa'l ʿaṣā*, He broke the stick, *i.e.* he quitted the assembly, he went about his business (he cut his stick). P شقّ كردن *shaḳḳ kardan*, To tear, split, divide. A *Shiḳḳ*, A half. As much as a horse carries on one side; the space between the two loads. A brother. A side. A sort of demon. A little. A friend. A mistress. Trouble, difficulty. شق الشعرة *shiḳḳu* (or *shaḳḳu'*) *sh shaʿrat*, Equal, even, to the splitting of a hair. هو اخي وشق نفسي *huwa akhī wa shiḳḳu nafsī*, He is my brother and half of myself. *Shuḳḳ*, (pl. of شقّاء *shaḳḳāʾ*) Wide women. Long mares.

A شقأ *shaḳʾ* (v. n. of شقأ) Growing (a front tooth). Parting (the hair without a comb). Striking (any one with a stick) at the parting of the hair. Cleaving the skull.

P شقا *shaḳā*, A quiver.

A شقا *shaḳā'*, (or شقاء *shaḳāʾ*) (v. n. of شقي) Being miserable, unhappy. Exceeding in misery, being more wretched. Misery, straits. Insolence. ارباب شقا *arbābi shaḳā*, Miserable, unfortunate people. Insolent. P گروه شقامدار *gurohi shaḳā-madār*, Swarms of villains.

A شقّاء *shaḳḳāʾ*, (fem. of اشقّ *ashaḳḳ*) Wide (woman). Long-bodied (mare).

A شقاب *shiḳāb*, (pl. of شقب *shaḳb* and *shiḳb*) Narrow passes between two mountains.

A شقاح *shiḳāḥ*, (v. n. 3 of شقح) Railing against.

A شقّاح *shuḳḳāḥ*, Name of an herb. The fundament of a bitch.

A شقاحة *shaḳāḥat*, (v. n. of شقح) Being shameful, deformed, ugly. Deformity, villainy, dishonesty, a fault, a rascally action.

A شقاحط *shaḳāḥiṭ*, (pl. of شقحطب *shaḳaḥṭab*) Rams with ugly crooked horns.

A شقاذي *shaḳāẕā'*, (pl. of شقذ *shaḳẕ, shiḳẕ*, and *shuḳaẕ*) Young chameleons.

A شقّار *shuḳḳār*, A species of fish with a long hump. (pl. of شقر *shaḳir*) Anemones.

A شقاري *shuḳārā'*, A lie. (pl. of شقر) Anemones.

A شقّاري *shuḳḳārā'*, (pl. of شقر *shaḳir*) Anemones. A kind of herb.

A شقاطب *shaḳāṭib*, (pl. of شقحطب *shaḳaḥ-ṭab*) Rams with ugly or crooked horns.

A شقاف *shiḳāf*, (pl. of شقف *shaḳaf*) Potsherds.

A شقاق *shiḳāḳ*, (v. n. 3 of شقّ) Contending, quarrelling, opposing. Discord, opposition, hostility. Rebellion. Felony. *Shuḳāḳ*, Fissures in the hands or feet. Cracks in the pasterns of horses.

P شقاقل *shaḳāḳul*, A wild carrot. A species of hartwort. A kind of small fish.

A شقاوة *shaḳāwat* or *shiḳāwat*, (v. n. of شقي) Being wretched and miserable. Misery, wretchedness, unhappiness. Insolence, sauciness. Villainy, malignity, robbery, assassination.

A شقاويّ *shiḳāwīy*, Miserable.

A شقائق *shaḳāʾiḳ*, (pl. of شقيقة *shaḳīḳat*) Fissures. Uterine sisters. شقائق النعمان *shaḳāʾiḳu'n nuʿmān*, The anemone.

A شقب *shaḳb* also *shiḳb*, (pl. شقاب *shiḳāb*, شقوب *shuḳūb*, and شقبة *shiḳabat*) A cleft in a mountain or rock; a narrow pass between two hills. A hollow where birds build their nests. Low ground on which water stagnates. *Shiḳb* or *shaḳab*, A kind of tree, with fruit resembling the lote.

A شقبان *shaḳabān*, A kind of bird.

A شقبة *shiḳabat*, (pl. of شقب *shaḳb*) Caverns. Clefts, gorges between mountains.

A شقّة *shiḳḳat*, The half, especially of any thing split or torn the long way. A chip of wood. Distance; a track followed by a traveller. A long journey. Rage. Iniquity. *Shuḳḳat*, A kind of long cloth. A garment open in front. An interval. Distance. A tract of country. شقّة الباب *shuḳ-ḳatu'l bāb*, Half a door. شقّت شاقّه *shuḳḳati shāḳ-ḳa*, A long and difficult journey. Great difficulty. *Shuḳḳat* or *shiḳḳat*, (pl. شقق *shuḳaḳ* and *shiḳaḳ*) Inconvenience, trouble, labour, pains.

A شقح *shaḳ-ḥ*, (v. n. of شقح) Breaking. Lifting the leg to make water (a dog). Daubing, dirtying. قبحا شقحا *ḳubḥan shuḳ-ḥan* or *ḳabḥan shaḳ-ḥan*, For shame! fie!

A شقحاء *shaḳ-ḥāʾ*, Froth not quite white.

A شقحة *shaḳ-ḥat*, The matrix of a bitch. *Shaḳ-ḥat* or *shuḳ-ḥat*, A reddening date. *Shuḳ-ḥat*, The dug of a bitch. A red colour mingled with white.

A شقحطب *shaḳaḥṭab*, (pl. شقاحط *shaḳāḥiṭ* or شقاطب *shaḳāṭib*) (A ram) having two or four horns.

A شقحيّ *shuḳaḥīy*, Red (gown).

P شقدار *shiḳ-dār*, A governor. An officer appointed to collect the revenue from a certain division of land. Perplexing.

P شقداري *shiḳ-dārī*, The office of shikdār. Uncertainty, perplexity.

A شقدة *shiḳdat*, An herb good for fattening.

A شقدف *shuḳduf*, A vehicle used in Hijāz.

A شقذ *shaḳẕ*, (v. n. of شقذ) Departing, going far off. ما به شقذ ولا نقذ *mā bihi shaḳẕun wa lā naḳẕun* (or *shuḳẕun nuḳẕun*), There is no blemish neither fault in him. *Shaḳẕ, shiḳẕ*, or *shuḳaẕ*, (pl. شقذان *shiḳẕān* and شقاذي *shaḳāẕā'*) A young chameleon. *Shiḳẕ*, A reptile, an insect. The chick of a bustard or katā. A wolf. *Shaḳaẕ*, (v. n. of شقذ) Being sleepless. Having a malignant, fascinating eye. Having a quick eye. ما له شقذ ولا نقذ *mā lahu shakazun wa lā nakazun*, He possesses nothing. *Shakiz*, Sleepless. Evil-eyed. A wolf.

A شقذاء *shakzā*, A hungry eagle.

A شقذان *shikzān*, Reptiles. Stinging or biting insects. Young bustards. Young katās. (pl. of شقذ *shakz*, *shikz*, and *shukaz*) Young chameleons. (pl. of شقذان *shakazān*) Chameleons. *Shakazān*, Sleepless. Malignant-eyed. Quick-sighted; (hence) a chameleon. *Shakazān* or *shikzān*, A wolf.

A شقذي *shakaza'*, A hungry eagle.

A شقر *shakr*, (v. n. of شقر) Being of a clay-coloured red or chesnut. (pl. شقور *shukūr*) Any business which demands attention, or which presses heavily on the mind. *Shakir*, (pl. شقرات *shakirāt*, شقّار *shukkār*, شقران *shakirān*, شقاري *shukkāra'*, and شقاري *shukāra'*) The anemone, tulip. *Shukar*, A cock. A lie.

A شقراء *shakrā*, Name of a mare.

A شقرات *shakirāt*, (pl. of شقر *shakir*) Anemones.

A شقراق *shakrāk* or *shikrāk*, A green magpie.

A شقرّاق *shaka* or *shikarrāk*, A green magpie.

A شقران *shikrān*, The anemone. *Shakirān*, (pl. of شقر *shakir*) The anemone, the tulip.

A شقرة *shukrat*, (v. n. of شقر) Being of a bright red. A clear shining ruddy colour. A rosy complexion in a man or woman. *Shakirat*, One anemone. Cinnabar.

G شقرديون *shakardiyūn*, Water-germander.

A شقري *shikra'*, An excellent kind of date.

A شقشقة *shakshakat*, (v. n. of شقشق Q) Twittering (a sparrow). Vociferating. Braying. *Shikshikat*, A substance resembling lights protruding from the mouth of a stallion camel in heat. ذو شقشقة *zū shikshikat*, Vehement, sonorous (orator).

A شقشقيّ *shikshikiy*, Loud (harangue).

A شقص *shiks*, A particle, part, portion, share. A good horse. A piece of ground. A little out of much. Partnership.

A شقع *shakẓ*, (v. n. of شقع) Drinking, sipping. Eyeing, viewing with a malignant eye.

A شقف *shakaf*, (pl. شقاف *shikāf*) An earthen pot, potsherd.

P شقق *shakak*, Beating time in music.

A شقق *shakak*, Length of body in a horse. *Shikak*, (pl. of شقّة *shikkat*) The halves of things split lengthwise. *Shukak* or *shikak*, (pl. of شقّة *shukkat* or *shikkat*) Long strips of cloths. Intervals. Long journeys.

A شقل *shakl*, (v. n. of شقل) Weighing (money). Having to do (with a woman).

A شقم *shakam*, A kind of date.

A شقن *shakn*, (v. n. of شقن) Doing little: diminishing. *Shakn*, *shakin*, (or قليل شقن *kalīlun shaknun*) Few, small.

A شقوء *shukūʾ*, (v. n. of شقأ) Splitting (the head). Combing (the hair). Growing (a front-tooth). Striking (any one with a stick) at the parting of the hair.

A شقوب *shukūb*, (pl. of شقب *shakb* or *shikb*) Caverns. Clefts between mountains.

A شقوة *shakwat* or *shikwat*, (v. n. of شقي) Being miserable. Wretchedness, misery, straits.

A شقور *shukūr* or *shakūr*, Any thing necessary to be done. *Shukūr*, (pl. of شقر *shakr*) Affairs which press heavily on the mind.

A شقوق *shukūk*, (pl. of شقّ *shakk*) Fissures.

A شقوقة *shakūkat*, A kind of bird.

A شقون *shukūn*, (or شقونة *shukūnat*) (v. n. of شقن) Being little (a present). Smallness of a present.

P شقه *shaka*, A hardness in the hand or foot from working or walking.

A شقّه *shukka*, (lit. a piece, from شقّ *shakk*) A royal order, a letter (especially from a superior).

P شقه بند *shaka-band*, A kind of horse-armour.

A شقي *shaky*, (v. n. of شقي) Appearing, growing (the cheek-tooth of a camel).

A شقيّ *shakiy*, Poor, miserable, wretched. Villainous. Insolent. A robber, assassin, bandit.

A شقيّة *shikiyat*, Modus cœundi.

A شقيح *shakīh*, Weak after disease. *Shakīh*, (or قبيح و شقيح *kabīh u shakīh*) Deformed.

A شقيذ *shakīz*, Sleepless. Evil-eyed.

A شقير *shukayr*, A kind of chameleon or locust.

A شقيص *shakīs*, A partner. (A horse) running swiftly. A little remaining of a great deal. A part, portion, share. Partnership.

A شقيط *shakīt*, Earthen jugs: crockery.

A شقيظ *shakīz*, Earthenware.

A شقيق *shakīk*, (pl. اشقاء *ashikkāʾ*) Split or halved. One half. A brother uterine. A strong calf.

A شقيقة *shakīkat*, (pl. شقائق *shakāʾik*) A fissure, crack, crevice, notch. One side (of the head). A uterine sister. A pass or space between two mountains producing grass. Pain seizing one half of the head and face. A kind of herb. Rain or lightning (as piercing the clouds). A kind of bird. *Shukaykat*, (dim. of *shakīkat*) A certain small bird.

A شقين *shakīn*, Few, little, small.

P شك *shak*, Doubt. Scandal. A magpie. *Shuk*, Arsenic.

A شكّ *shakk*, (v. n. of شكّ) Doubting, suspecting. Limping (a camel). Cleaving, adhering to. Having the arm adhering to the side. Covering one's self with complete (armour). Building (houses) in a line. Leaning against. Piercing (with a spear).[1] (pl. شكوك *shukūk*) Doubt, suspicion, hesitation, suspense, uncertainty. A small crack in a bone. Arsenic. *Shikk*, A covering for the horns of a bow. An upper garment. *Shukk*, Division. Schism. Difficulty, trouble. (pl. of شكوك *shakūk*) She-camels of the fat of whose bunches doubts are entertained.

A شكأ *shakʾ*, (v. n. of شكأ) Growing (the side-tooth of a camel). *Shakaʾ*, (v. n. of شكئ) Being cracked or split (nails or hoofs).

A شكاء *shakāʾ*, Sickness. *Shikāʾ*, (pl. of شكوة *shakwat*) Water-bottles or milk-bottles.

A شكاة *shakāt*, (v. n. of شكا for شكو) Complaining, telling one's misfortunes. Making sick, afflicting. Relating a state of one's maladies. Sickness. Reproach, rebuke. A disgrace, vice, blemish.

P شكار *shikār*, Prey, game. The chase, hunting. Plunder, booty, pillage, rapine, spoil. Perquisites. شكار شدن *shikār shudan*, To be taken captive, to be seized. عزم شكار كردن *ẓazmi shikār kardan*, To go a-hunting. (part. of شكاريدن *shikāridan*) Hunting, seizing. A hunter. جان شكار *jān-shikār*, Ravisher of hearts. مردم شكار *mardum-shikār*, Pursuing or seizing men.

P شكار افگن *shikār-afgan*, A hunter.

P شكار باز *shikār-bāz*, A sportsman.

P شكار بند *shikār-band*, Cords for tying game to a saddle.

P شكارستان *shikāristān*, A hunting-place, a chase.

P شكار كنان *shikār-kunān*, Hunting.

P شكار گاه *shikār-gāh*, A hunting-country.

P شكارگر *shikārgar* (or گير *gīr*), A hunter.

A شكاري *shakāra'*, Milch camels or ewes.

P شكاري *shikārī*, Any thing belonging to hunting (as dogs, hawks, or horses). A hunter, fowler. A bird or beast of prey. Game, prey. سگ شكاري *sagi shikārī*, A hunting dog, a hound.

P شكاريدن *shikāridan*, To hunt.

A شكاز *shakkāz*, One who experiences an effusion from merely talking with a woman. One to whom the like happens before coition. One who stools during coition. Outrageous when drunk.

A شكازة *shakkāzat*, One who, on seeing a lovely picture, pollutes himself.

A شكاسة *shakāsat*, Depravity of nature.

P شكاشك *shakāshak*, Noise of feet in walking.

A شكاص *shikās*, A woman whose teeth are uneven.

A شكاعة *shukāẓat*, A thorn filling a camel's mouth.

A شكاعي *shukāẓa'* or *shakāẓa'*, A kind of thorn, to which a person of an emaciated form is often likened.

P شكاف *shikāf*, A fissure, crack, slit, crevice, rupture, split, cleft in a mountain. A cavern. A hank of silk. (in comp.) Tearing, splitting, cleaving, breaking, bursting, dividing. سينه شكاف *sīna-shikāf*, Rending the breast. ناجخ تيز عمر شكاف *nājakhi tezi ẓumur-shikāf*, The sharp hatchet, cutting (the thread of) life, *i. e.* death. استاد مو شكاف *ustādi mū-shikāf*, A master of hair-splitting, *i. e.* a subtle reasoner.

P شكافانيدن *shikāfānīdan*, To cause to split.

P شكافتگي *shikāftagī*, A fracture, fissure.

P شكافتن *shikāftan*, To split, break, tear, destroy. To divide into two long strips. To mediate between buyer and seller. To be torn, lacerated, defaced, destroyed.

P شكافته *shikāfta*, Split. A box, pyx. Cholic.

P شكافش *shikāfish*, A cleaving; cleft, fissure.

P شكافه *shikāfa*, Bow of violin. A cradle.

P شكافه زن *shikāfa-zan*, A player on the violin.

P شكافيدن *shikāfīdan*, To tear lengthwise.

A شكاك *shakāk*, A quarter, side, tract. *Shikāh*, Houses built in a row.

A شكاك *shukkāk*, (pl. of شاك) Clad in armour.

A شكاكة *shakākat*, A tract of land.

P شكال *shikāl*, A cord for tying the fore-feet of an unruly mule or horse. Cunning, deceit. A jackal.

A شكال *shikāl*, (pl. شكل *shukul*) A horse-tether of goats' hair. A surcingle. A rope by which the hinder girth is fastened to the foremost to prevent its hurting the sheath of the animal. (A horse) having three legs white, the other of the colour of the body, and vice versâ.

P شكالش *shikālish*, Thought, care. Roguery.

P شكال گاه *shikāl-gāh*, The pastern of a quadruped.

P شكاله *shikāla*, A hedgehog, urchin. شكالۀ زر *shikāla-i zar*, A particle of gold.

P شكاليدن *shikālīdan*, To think. To deceive.

P شكان *shikān*, Rupture, breach. A curling lock of hair. A wrinkle, plait. A knot, tie, twist. Broken. Curly.

P شكانك *shakānak*, Crop of a bird.

A شكاوة *shakāwat*, (v. n. of شكى) Lamenting, complaining. Making sick, afflicting.

P شكاوند *shakāwand*, Name of a mountain.

P شكاونده *shikāwanda*, A digger, delver, borer.

P شكاونه *shikāwna* or *shikāwana*, A digger. One who digs up dead bodies for the grave-clothes.

A شكاه *shikāh*, (v. n. 3 of شكه) Resembling, being alike. Being near, neighbouring. Being a friend, companion, or cotemporary. Vicinity, propinquity.

A شكاية *shikāyat*, (v. n. of شكي) Lamenting, complaining, explaining the cause of any complaint or ailment. Making sick, afflicting. Impeaching, accusing. Lamentation, complaint. Accusation.

P شكايت كنان *shikāyat-kunān*, Making lamentation, querulous. شكايت گستر *shikāyat-gustar*, Habitually complaining.

A شكائر *shakā,ir*, Forelocks.

A شكائك *shakā,ik*, (pl. of شكيكة *shakīkat*) Sects, bodies, troops, bands. Ways, modes, fashions.

A شكائم *shakā,im*, (pl. of شكيمة) Bridle-bits.

A شكب *shukb*, A present. Recompense.

A شكبان *shukbān*, A net for holding grass.

P شكپا *shikpā*, Crabbed, austere.

P شكپوي *shakpūy*, The noise of one walking softly. One who walks softly. Snoring.

A شكة *shikkat*, Arms. A wedge driven between the handle and head of a hatchet to make them fast. *Shukkat*, Difficulty, trouble. A garment torn in front. Division. Schism.

A شكد *shakd*, (v. n. of شكد) Giving, presenting. *Shukd*, A present. Thanksgiving.

A شكر *shakr*, (v. n. of شكر) Producing the small leaves called شكير *shakīr* (a palm-tree). Coition. *Shakr* or *shikr*, Pudenda mulieris. *Shukr*, (v. n. of شكر) Returning thanks (to God), praising (Him) for his benefits. Rewarding, conferring favours (God). Accepting, being pleased and satisfied. Praise, thanksgiving, gratitude (to God). Recompense, reward (from God). شكر الهي *shukri ilāhī*, (P شكر ايزد *shukri ezid*, or شكر خدا *shukri khudā*) Thanks to God! God be praised! شكر نعمت *shukri niemat*, (or اداي شكر نعمت *adā,i shukri niemat*) Acknowledgment of favours (in opposition to كفر نعمت *kufri niemat*, Ingratitude). *Shakar*, (v. n. of شكر) Being full of milk (a sheep or camel). Becoming fat on little grass. Being liberal, or becoming so after having been niggardly. Producing saplings, growing around the base (a tree). *Shukur*, (pl. of شكير *shakīr*) Barks of trees. Things growing round the roots of trees.

P شكر *shakar*, Sugar. Sweet words. The lip of a mistress. A black bee. Name of a woman whom Khusraw married against the will of Shīrīn. شكر عقيق رنگ *shakari eakīk-rang*, (Cornelian-coloured sugar) The lip of a mistress. گل بشكر *gul ba shakar*, Conserve of roses. *Shikar*, The chace, game. A hunter. One who routs or puts to flight.

P شكر *shakkar*, Sugar. *Shikkar*, A porcupine.

P شكر آب *shakar-āb*, Sugar-water. A little falling out, or a coolness betwixt friends.

P شكر افشاني *shakar-afshānī*, Sweet speech.

A شكران *shukrān*, (v. n. of شكر) Returning thanks for favours received. Gratitude, acknowledgment; assent, complacency. Grateful.

P شكرانه *shukrāna*, Gratitude, thanksgiving. A fee paid by plaintiff or defendant on the cause being decided in his favour.

P شكر بادام *shakar-bādām*, Sugared almonds. Dried apricots stuffed with almonds. The eye and lip of a mistress.

P شكربار *shakar-bār*, Raining sweetness, mellifluous.

P شكر برگ *shakar-barg*, A sweetmeat made of almonds and sugar. A large pair of compasses made of sugar.

P شكر بوره *shakar-būra*, (بوزه *būza*, بيره *bīra*, or بيزه *bīza*) Cake stuffed with sugar-candy, almonds, and pistachio-nuts.

P شكر پاره *shakar-pāra*, A lump of sugar.

A شكرة *shakarat*, Abundance of milk in the udder. *Shakirat*, (pl. شكاري *shakārā'* and شكري *shakra'*) Full of milk (ewe or camel). Grass which increases the milk greatly.

P شكر چين *shakar-chīn*, Gathering sugar. One who collects whatever is thrown about at a festivity.

P شكر خار *shakar-khār*, Name of a thorny tree called غرقد *gharkad*.

P شكر خند *shakar-khand*, (or خنده *khanda*) A smiling sweetly, speaking gently with a smile of love. Gracious, delicate, attractive, charming, amiable.

P شكر خواب *shakar-khwāb*, A sweet sleep. A morning-doze.

P شكر خيز *shakar-khez*, Producing sugar.

P شكرد *shikarad*, A hunter, fowler. Remedy.

P شكردن *shikardan*, To hunt. To catch, seize. To break. To apply a remedy, to cure. *Shukurdan*, To kill. To die.

P شكرده *shakarda*, Active, quick, dexterous.

P شكرديدن *shikardīdan*, To hunt. To put to flight. To break.

P شكر ريز *shakar-rez*, Who scatters sugar. Mellifluous. A maker of sugar-confectionery. Money or other things thrown about at weddings. Presents sent from the bridegroom's house to that of the bride. Sweet or elegant language. Poetry. Singing or talking. Good-natured, jocose. Tears of joy. The lip of a mistress. شكر ريز طرب *shakar-rezi tarab*, Tears of joy.

P شكر ريزه *shakar-reza*, March-pane.

P شكر ريزي *shakar-rezī*, Sweet discourse. Tears of joy.

P شكر زخمه *shakar-zakhama*, An arrow hitting the mark.

P شكرسان *shakar-sān*, (شكر شان *shakar-shān*, or شكر شاه *shakar-shāh*) Honey in the comb.

P شكرستان *shakaristān*, A sugar-refinery. A plantation of sugar-canes.

P شكر سنگ *shakar-sang*, A stone which stops hemorrhages.

P شكرش *shakrish*, A bad name, ill-fame.

P شكر شكن *shakar-shikan*, Sweetly-spoken.

P شكر فروش *shakar-farosh*, A sugar-merchant. A mistress.

P شكرفنده *shikarfanda*, Stumbling. A horse apt to stumble.

P شكرفيدن *shi* or *shakarfīdan*, To trip, stumble.

P شكر قلم *shakar-kalam*, A sweet pen. A sort of sweetmeat.

P شكر قميش *shakar-kamīsh*, The sugar-cane.

P شكر قند *shakar-kand*, Sweet potatoes. Sugar-candy.

P شكر گذار *shukr-guzār*, Grateful, thankful.

P شكر گذاري *shukr-guzārī*, Thanksgiving.

P شكر گفتار *shakar-guftār*, Sweet-spoken.

P شكرلب *shakar-lab*, Sugar-lipped; a mistress. Hare-lipped.

P شكرنگ *shakrang*, A sort of sweetmeat.

P شكرودة *shakarwada* or *shakarvuda*, Nimble.

P شكره *shikara*, Rapacious birds trained to hunt.

P شكرهنج *shakarhanj*, A kind of thorn.

A شكري *shakra'*, A piece of fat meat. (pl. of شكرة *shakirat*) Milch (ewes or camels).

P شكري *shakarī*, A kind of Phālsa so called (Grewia asiatica).

A شكرية *shakarīyat*, The returning of camels

from spring-pasture.

P شکریدن *shikrīdan*, To hunt. To rout an enemy.

P شکرینه *shakarīna*, A confection, especially white and hard, made of the root عسلج *ʿaslaj* boiled long with wine and sugar.

A شکز *shakz*, A poking or thrusting of the finger, or the annoying of any one with the tongue. A stab, dig, penetration. Coition. *Shakz* or *shakiz*, Of a bad disposition.

A شکس *shaks*, One or two days before the new moon. *Shakis*, A miser. *Shakus* and *shakis*, (pl. شکس *shuks*) Hard and ill-tempered (man).

P شکست *shikast*, He broke. A fracture. Defeat, rout. Deficiency, loss. Shame, modesty. Dislike, antipathy. Warmth, indignation. An eating and evacuation. Broken. Impaired. Odd, uneven. شکست خوردن *shikast khwurdan* (or یافتن *yāftan*), To be defeated. شکست دادن *shikast dādan*, To defeat. شکستِ فاحش *shikasti fāhish*, A shameful defeat. دل شکست و همت پست *dil-shikast u himmat-past*, Broken-hearted and low-spirited.

P شکست خورده *shikast-khwurda*, Broken off. Defeated, routed.

P شکستگي *shikastagī*, Fracture, rupture. Grief, sadness, affliction. Infirmity, sickness. Defeat, rout. دل شکستگي *dil-shikastagī*, Broken-heartedness.

P شکست مکست *shikast mikast*, Trifles.

P شکستن *shikastan*, To break. To defeat (an enemy). To turn away the face. To be rough and severe. To eat, chew. To be broken, split, opened. To be covered with shame.

P شکست و مکست *shikast u mikast*, He broke (it) awhile ago.

P شکسته *shikasta*, Broken. Discomfited, routed. Reduced to straits. Ashamed, Penitent. Proud. Weak. Sick, wounded. The broken or current Persian hand, in which letters in India are generally written. It is a corruption of the تعليق *taʿlīk*. Name of an ancient fort in Persia. شکسته شدن *shikasta shudan*, To be broken. To be distressed. To be diminished. To become less rigid or intense.

P شکسته بال *shikasta-bāl* (or دل *dil*), Broken-hearted, distressed in mind, melancholy.

P شکسته بسته *shikasta-basta*, (Broken and tied) Fast and loose, a mixture of bad and good.

P شکسته بند *shikasta-band*, A binder of broken bones. A mender of broken vessels. A swath, bandage.

P شکسته پا *shikasta-pā*, Broken-footed, weak.

P شکسته حال *shikasta-hāl*, Indigent, distressed.

P شکسته حالي *shikasta-hālī*, Indigence, distress.

P شکسته خاطر *shikasta-khātir*, Disturbed, afflicted. Offended.

P شکسته دلان *shikasta-dilān*, The poor, wretched.

P شکسته زبان *shikasta-zabān*, A stammerer.

P شکسته گمان *shikasta-gumān*, Contrary, adverse, dissentient.

P شکسته مزاج *shikasta-mizāj*, Sick, ailing.

P شکسته وعده *shikasta-waʿda*, Faithless.

P شکست یافته *shikast-yāfta*, Routed, defeated.

P شکشك *shakshak*, Sound of feet in walking.

A شکشکة *shakshakat*, Sharp arms, or their edge.

A شکص *shakis*, Bad-tempered.

A شکع *shakʿ*, (v. n. of شکع) Tossing (up the rein). *Shakaʿ*, (v. n. of شکع) Groaning much. Being pained. Being angry. Being full of grain (ears of corn). *Shakiʿ*, In pain, unable to sleep. Avaricious, mean. Sour, crabbed. بات شکعا *bāta shakiʿan*, He passed the night in pain, unable to sleep.

P شکفت *shikaft*, A cave or grotto. Crooked. Twisted. Uneven. *Shikift*, He wondered. Any thing wonderful. Admiration, surprise. باید شکفت *bāyad shikift*, It is admirable. *Shikuft*, A prodigy. Magnificence. Dignity, authority, gravity. Opening, expanding. *Shukuft*, It expanded or flourished. A miracle. Reverence, awe, fear.

P شکفتانیدن *shikaftānīdan*, To cause to be cleft.

P شکفتن *shikaftan*, To crook, twist, make uneven. To be cleft. To exercise patience. *Shikiftan*, To look with wonder. To be amazed, surprised. *Shikuftan*, To open, expand (as a flower). To smile.

P شکفته *shikufta*, Flourishing, florid, expanded. گل شکفته *guli shikufta*, A new-blown rose.

P شکفتیدن *shikiftīdan*, To wonder, be amazed.

P شکفه *shikufa*, Blossoms of a fruit-tree.

P شکفیدن *shukfīdan*, To blow, open (as a flower).

P شکك *shakak*, A kind of guitar. A round prickly thorn. The noise made by the feet in walking.

A شکك *shikak*, (pl. of شکة *shikkat*) Arms. Wedges driven between the handles and heads of hatchets in order to make them more fast. *Shukak*, A camel of which there is a doubt if she be fat or not. *Shukuk*, (pl. of شکیکة *shakīkat*) Sects, crowds. Customs, modes, usages.

P شککال *shikhāl*, The greatest king of India.

A شکل *shakl*, (v. n. of شکل) Fettering (a horse). Girthing (a camel). Ripening partially (dates). Being intricate and dubious (an affair). Any thing suitable, becoming. Pointing (a book), inserting carefully the vowel-points indicating the cases of nouns or persons of verbs; making plain and perspicuous. (pl. اشکال *ashkāl* and شکول *shukūl*) Figure, form, shape, manner, mien, face, appearance, effigy, semblance, image, resemblance, likeness: mode, species. The graceful air of a beautiful woman. (pl. اشکال *ashkāl*) Any thing doubtful, obscure, or intricate. An ear-ring of pearls or silver. A certain yellow and red plant. A poetic license, wherein the measure فاعلاتن *fāʿilātun* becomes فعلات *faʿilātu* by dropping the second and seventh letters (thus combining the licenses of خبن *khabn* and کفّ *kaff*). شکل تربیع *shakli tarbīʿ*, A square figure. شکل دواري *shakli dawārī*, A circular figure. شکل متوازي *shakli mutawāzī*, A parallel figure. شکل المجسم *shaklu'l mujassam*, A solid body. هٰذا من هوايَ و من شکلي *hāzā min hawāya' wa min shaklī*, This is to my liking and to my taste. *Shikl*, Image, resemblance, similitude. The graceful air of a woman. *Shukl*, (pl. of اشکل *ashkal*) White with an inclination to red or black (water, ram, &c.). (pl. of شکلاء *shaklāʾ*) Reddish, blood-shot (eyes). *Shakal*, (v. n. of شکل) Being obscure, intricate. Having whitish thighs (a sheep). Being reddish (the eye). Darting amorous glances, alluring (a lovely woman). *Shukul*, (pl. of شکال *shikāl*) Horse-tethers made of goats' hair.

A شکلاء *shaklāʾ*, (fem. of اشکل *ashkal*) Reddish (eye). White-hipped (sheep). Need, necessity.

A شکلة *shuklat*, A mixture of red and black. A darkish colour of the eye with a shade of red. فیه شکلة من ابیه *fīhi shuklat min abīhi*, He bears a resemblance to his father. *Shakilat*, A coquette.

P شکل نویس *shakl-navīs*, A portrait-painter.

P شکله *shikla*, Part of a garment torn off by adhering to any thing. *Shikla* or *shakla*, A piece, segment, slice, cut.

P شکلیدن *shiklīdan*, To tear. To be torn, split. To disturb.

A شکم *shakm*, (v. n. of شکم) Biting. Recompensing, returning one present for another. Corrupting or bribing (a judge). *Shukm*, Recompense, retribution. (pl. of شکیمة *shakīmat*) Bits which the horse champs. *Shakam*, (v. n. of شکم) Hungering. *Shakim*, A lion.

P شکم *shikam*, The belly, paunch, stomach; fat tripe. شکم کف *shikami kaf*, Palm of the hand. شکم ران *shikami rān*, Inside of the thigh. شکم بآب زن *shikam ba āb zan*, Practice of villainy. Giving or taking excessively. شکم چار پهلو کردن *shikam chār pahlū kardan*, To guttle till one is ready to burst. شکم خاریدن *shikam khārīdan*, To feign, pretend. بشکم رفتن *ba shikam raftan*, To go on the belly, to crawl as an insect. باد شکم *bādi shikam*, Wind in the bowels, flatulency.

P شکم بنده *shikam-banda*, A slave to his belly, an epicure. A servant who works for his board.

P شکمبه *shikamba*, Belly, stomach, tripe.

P شکم پرست *shikam-parast*, A pamperer of his belly, an epicure, a glutton.

P شکم پرور *shikam-parwar*, A sensualist, epicure.

P شکم پیچ *shikam-pech*, A twisting of the guts.

P شکم خوار *shikam-khwār*, (or شکم خواره *shikam-khwāra*) A glutton. Hungry.

P شکم خوارگي *shikam-khwāragī*, Gluttony.

P شکم خواري *shikam-khwārī*, Hunger.

P شکمدار *shikam-dār*, Big-bellied, paunchy.

P شکم درد *shikam-dard*, Belly-ache, gripes.

P شکم دردمند *shikam-dardmand*, Griped.

P شکم ران *shikam-rān*, Purgative (medicine).

P شکم رو *shikam-rav*, A diarrhœa.

P شکم شکسته *shikam-shikasta*, A complaint from indigestion.

P شكم گرفتگي *shikam-giriftagī*, Costiveness.

P شكم گرفته *shikam-girifta*, Constipated, costive.

A شكمي *shukma'*, A reciprocal present.

P شكمي *shikamī*, Skin of the belly. Big-bellied. A glutton.

P شكن *shikan*, A fold, wrinkle, curl. Defeat, rout, and flight of an army. Turning away the face. Warmth, vehemence. Moroseness. Roughness, severity. Mildness, gentleness. Fraud, deceit, cunning. Eating. Mastication. A beating of time in music. A catch, glee, song. (in compos.) Breaking. Shrinking, shrivelling, constringing. شكن جامه *shikani jāma*, A fold in a garment. شكن زلف *shikani zulf*, A curl. شكنهاي كام *shikanhāyi kām*, The wrinkles in the roof of the mouth. دشمن شكن *dushman-shikan*, A conqueror of enemies. طاقت شكن *tākat-shikan*, Breaking the strength, rendering powerless. *Shikin* or *shakn*, Name of a country.

P شكنب *shikamb*, The belly.

P شكنب ابا *shikamb-abā*, (شكنب اوا *shikamb-awā*, or شكنب وا *shikamb-wā*) Tripe-broth.

P شكنبه *shikamba*, The tripe.

P شكنج *shikanj*, A ply, fold. The twisting or coiling of a rope. A knot. Confusion, intricacy, twisting. A red serpent. Fraud, deceit. A beating of time in music. Sound, tune, musical melody. Torture, rack. A fragment. A brickbat. An eruption of the body. *Shikunj*, A plucking, pinch.

P شكنجد *shikanjad*, A bookbinder's press.

P شكنجه *shikanja*, Pain, torture; rack; stocks. A bookbinder's press. شكنجه كردن *shikanja kardan*, To punish, to torture with the rack.

P شكنجيدن *shikanjīdan*, To put to the rack. To put in a press. To bind (a book).

P شكند *shakand* or *shikand*, Mud-worms.

P شكن دار *shikan-dār*, Wrinkled.

P شكنه *shikana*, An amorous glance. A porcupine.

A شكو *shakw*, (v. n. of شكا for شكو) Complaining. Relating a state of one's maladies. A disease. A small camel.

A شكوا *shakwa'*, A complaint. P شكوا نامه *shakwa'-nāma*, Letters of complaint or condolence.

P شكوب *shukūb*, A napkin. A turban.

A شكوة *shakwat*, (pl. شكوات *shakawāt* and شكاء *shikā*) A water or milk-bottle (made of the skin of a sucking kid).

A شكوثاء *shakūsā*, (or شكوثي *shakūsa'*) Dodder.

P شكوخ *shu* or *shikūkh*, A slip, stumble, fall.

P شكوخنده *shikūkhanda* or *shukūkhanda*, Stumbling, tripping. Alarmed.

P شكوخه *shukūkha*, A slip, tumble.

P شكوخيدگي *shukūkhīdagī*, A stumble.

P شكوخيدن *shu*, *sha*, or *shikūkhīdan*, To stumble and recover one's self. To fear, to be alarmed.

A شكور *shakūr*, Grateful. Satisfied with little, yet becoming fat (cattle). One of the names of God (as requiting the services of his servants, or being satisfied with little, and rewarding munificently). *Shukūr*, (v. n. of شكر) Returning thanks (to God), acknowledging (his) favours, praising (him) for (his) benefits.

P شكور *shukūr*, An animal which roots up and eats dead bodies.

P شكوف *shukūf*, A cleft, fissure.

P شكوفا *shukūfā*, Flourishing.

P شكوفتن *shukūftan*, To open, blow, blossom. To wonder.

P شكوفته *shukūfta*, Open, blown.

P شكوفنده *shikūfanda*, Cleaving, notching.

P شكوفه *shikūfa*, Blossom of fruit-bearing trees. Vomit. شكوفهٔ سنگ *shikūfasi sang*, A bloom which grows on certain stones, and is used medicinally.

P شكوفيدن *shukūfīdan*, To blow, bloom, flourish. To open. To notch. To break. To put to flight.

A شكوك *shakūk*, (pl. شكك *shukk*) A camel of the fatness of whose bunch a doubt is entertained on account of its hairiness. *Shukūk*, (pl. of شك *shakk*) Doubts, suspicions.

P شكول *shukūl*, Celerity, agility, promptitude.

A شكول *shukūl*, (pl. of شكل) Figures, forms.

P شكوله *shukūla*, A hard, full nut.

P شكوليدن *shukolīdan*, To disturb: mix, confound.

P شكونه *shukūna*, Inverted, turned upside down.

P شكوه *shikūh*, Fear, terror. *Shukoh*, Majesty, magnificence, dignity, grandeur, power; train, pomp, attendance. Gravity, reverence. A small town.

P شكوهانيدن *shukohānīdan*, To carry one's self with gravity.

P شكوهمند *shukohmand*, Grave.

P شكوهمندي *shukohmandī*, Decorum.

P شكوهنج *shikohanj*, A certain triangular thorn.

P شكوهندگي *shikūhandagī*, Fear. A slip, slide, fall. The stumbling or tripping of a horse. *Shukohandagī*, Magnificence, respectability, display.

P شكوهنده *shikūhanda*, Fearful, timid. *Shukohanda*, Great. Decorating, adorning. A listener.

P شكوهه *shukoha*, Beauty, gracefulness, ornament, elegance. Austerity, gravity. Magnificence. A kind of thistle.

P شكوهيدن *shikūhīdan*, To fear, to be terror-struck. *Shukohīdan*, To be grave, venerable. To be elegant. To listen and yield obedience.

P شكوهيده *shikūhīda*, Terrified. A stumbling horse. *Shukohīda*, Distinguished for gravity and stateliness. Attentive to another's words. Adorned.

A شكوي *shakwa'*, (v. n. of شكي) Lamenting, complaining. Making sick, afflicting. Complaint, lamentation. A disease.

P شكه *shikuh*, Fear. *Shukuh*, Majesty, gravity. Elegance, beauty. Ornament, decoration.

P شكهيدن *shikihīdan*, To be agitated, grieved.

A شكي *shakka'*, Name of a place in Armenia, whence they bring bridles and skins. *Shukka'*, A rough or sharp bridle.

A شكي *shakkī*, Doubtful. شكي مزاج *shakki-mizāj*, Undetermined, wavering, hesitating.

A شكي *shakiy*, Habitually complaining, querulous. Lamentable, deserving to be complained of. Complained of. Pained, indisposed. Slightly ailing.

P شكيب *shikīb*, Patience. Patient.

P شكيبا *shikībā*, Extremely patient.

P شكيبانيدن *shikībānīdan*, To exhort to patience. To render patient.

P شكيبائي *shikībāī*, Long-suffering, toleration, patience. نا شكيبائي *nā shikībāī*, Impatience.

P شكيبايدن *shikībāyidan*, To be patient, to bear patiently.

P شكيبنده *shikībanda*, Patient, long-suffering.

P شكيبيدن *shikībīdan*, To be patient.

A شكية *shakīyat*, (v. n. of شكي) Complaining, lamenting, exposing (one's circumstances). Relating (a state of one's maladies). Making sick, afflicting. Remainder, residue.

P شكير *shakīr*, A sort of peach.

A شكير *shakīr*, (pl. شكر *shukur*) Bark of a tree. The small leaves which are round palm-branches. Any thing growing round about the root of a large tree. Soft, limber twigs growing amongst others hard and dry. A vine sprung from a shoot. New grass springing up amongst that which is old and sear. A young shoot or palm-sapling. Small herbage, foliage, feathers, or hairs mixed with larger. Hairs about the neck and face. Small camels. Hairs at the root of a horse's mane.

P شكيش *shakīsh*, A sack, bag made of reeds.

A شكيص *shakīs*, Of a bad disposition.

P شكيفت *shikeft*, Wonder. Patience, endurance.

P شكيفتن *shikeftan*, To wonder. To be patient.

A شكيكة *shakīkat*, (pl. شكائك *shakāik* and شكك *shukuk*) A sect, multitude, crowd, people. Custom, way, manner, fashion. A fruit-basket. The throat, the gullet.

A شكيل *shakīl*, Well-shaped, handsome. Blood mixed with foam on the bit of a bridle.

P شكيل *shikīl*, A horse-tether of goats' hair. Fraud, deceit, stratagem. The chain by which the knife or dagger hangs to the girdle (the Persians in general stick it loose into the girdle itself). The bars or spars of wood which keep the different parts of a gate together. Name of a tree.

A شكيم *shakīm*, (v. n. of شكم) Biting. The ear or handle of a pot. (pl. of شكيمة *shakīmat*) Bridle-bits.

A شكيمة *shakīmat*, (pl. شكائم *shakāim*, شكم *shukm*, and شكيم *shakīm*) Bit of the bridle. Malice. Badness of temper. Pride. Image, resemblance. Self-preservation from oppression. A loathing, disdaining. The hunting beast called cheeta. Venom. Rust, soil, dirt. شديد الشكيمة *shadīdu'sh shakīmat*, Refractory, untractable, refusing the bit.

P شكينه *shakīna*, A large oblong jar in which grain is kept. A goad.

P شگا *shagā*, (*shugā*, or شگاه *shagāh*) A quiver.

P شگاد *shagād* or *shigād*, Rustam's brother.

P شگار *shagār*, A jackal. *Shigār*, Any thing eatable. *Shugār*, A coal.

P شگارآهنج *shigār-āhanj*, A wooden instrument with an iron hook, used by bakers in drawing any thing out of ovens.

P شگال *shagāl*, A jackal. *Shigāl*, A deep channel excavated by a torrent. Fetters for a horse. *Shugāl*, Charcoal. The cud.

P شگاله *shagāla*, All, the whole.

P شگالیو *shugālīv*, Dressed on the coals.

P شگانه *shagāna*, Bow of a violin. A cradle.

P شگاوند *shagāwand*, Name of a mountain.

P شگپوي *shagpūy*, Noise of the feet in walking.

P شگر *shi* or *shugar*, A porcupine, hedgehog.

P شگرف *shigarf* or *shagarf*, Rare, fine, good, beautiful, excellent, glorious. Great, venerable, respectable, generous. Amiable, acceptable. Strong, thick. Robust, vigorous. Boiled. Laxative, aperient. Suppurative. A good, brave, magnificent man. Wonder.

P شگفت *shigift*, Wonder, astonishment.

P شگفتگي *shiguftagī*, State of flourishing.

P شگفتن *shigiftan*, To have patience. To be amazed, astonished. *Shiguftan*, To blossom, blow.

P شگفته *shigufta*, Blossomed, blown.

P شگفته خاطر *shigufta-khātir*, Happy-minded.

P شگفته رو *shigufta-rū*, Of placid countenance.

P شگفتیدن *shigiftīdan*, To be amazed, astonied.

P شگفیدن *shigifīdan*, To be astonished.

P شگل *shigil*, A tether for a horse or a mule. A string tied round a sparrow's leg.

P شگن *shugun*, An auspicious omen.

P شگوار *shugwār*, Sad, mourning.

P شگوفتن *shigūftan*, To admire. To flourish, open, bud, expand as a flower.

P شگوفه *shigūfa*, A flower, blossom. شگوفهٔ سر کودك *shigūfa-i sari kūdak*, A disease which causes the hair or eyelashes to drop off. شگوفه کردن *shigūfa kardan*, To expand, blow, or flourish.

P شگون *shugūn*, A good omen. Augury, presage.

P شگونه *shugūna*, Inverted, topsy-turvy.

P شگونیا *shagūniyā*, A diviner, augur.

P شل *shal*, One who can take nothing in his hands, as being disjointed, paralytic, or stiff. A kind of thin, coloured leather, used in lining boots, and in giving a finish to a saddle. The thigh of a man. Name of a town in the district of Mūkān. شل دست *shali dast*, Palsied in the hands. *Shil*, A spear, javelin, halbert; trident, fizgig, harpoon. *Shil* or *shul*, A sort of quince. *Shul*, Soft, languid.

A شلّ *shall*, (v.n. of شلّ) Driving (camels). Sewing (clothes) with wide stitches, basting. Being withered, dried up (the hand). Shedding tears.

A شلا *shalā'*, A limb, member. The body.

A شلّاء *shallā*, (fem. of اشلّ *ashall*) (A woman) with a dried paralytic hand. Withered and palsied (hand). Dim-sighted, blind (eye).

A شلّافة *shallāfat*, A whore. A concubine.

A شلاق *shalāk*, Impudent, seditious. Flagellation. A stick, whip, scourge.

A شلّاق *shallāk*, A small bag, carried by beggars.

A شلال *shilāl*, Dispersed men. Drivers of camels. لا شلالِ *lā shalāli*, May thy hand not wither!

A شلّال *shallāl*, A furious driver.

A شلايا *shalāya'*, (pl. of شليّة *shaliyat*) Remains of property.

P شلايين *shalāyin*, Disgustingly importunate.

A شلبثا *shalbisā*, An electuary for curing the palsy and a distorted mouth.

P شلپوي *shalpūy*, Noise of feet in walking.

A شلّة *shullat*, Intention. The intention or object of a journey. *Shullat* or *shallat*, Remote business.

P شلتاق *shiltāk*, A dispute with one upon false grounds, accusation, litigation. A tumult.

P شلتوك *shaltok*, Rice still in the husk.

P شلته *shalta*, A mixen, dunghill.

A شلثان *shulsān*, (another mode of writing سلطان *sultān*) An emperor, sultan, soldan.

A شلجم *shaljam*, A turnip.

A شلحاء *shalhā*, (or شلحا *shalha'*) (pl. شلح *shulh*) A sharp sword.

A شلّحف *shillahf*, Tottering, weakly by nature. Thick (foot). A fat fool.

A شلخ *shalkh*, (v. n. of شلخ) Dividing by a blow of a sword. A round (of musquetry), a discharge. Root, origin. Race, stock. Sperma viri. Vulva.

A شلخب *shalkhab*, A stammerer, stutterer.

P شلخت *shalakht*, A kick on the backside.

P شلخته *shalakhta*, A kick on the backside.

A شلّخف *shillakhf*, Nodding, shaking the head, staggering, tottering.

A شلشال *shalshāl*, Urine scattered about in drops. *Shilshāl*, (v.n. of شلشل Q) Scattering urine (a boy).

A شلشل *shalshal*, (Water or blood) which falls drop by drop. *Shulshul*, Having little flesh, lean. Light, nimble, active, fit for employment. *Shulshul* or *shalshal*, Active and ready in serving others, social, friendly.

A شلشلة *shalshalat*, (v. n. of شلشل Q) Letting (water) fall drop by drop. Trickling with blood (a sword). Scattering urine about (a boy).

A شلط *shalt*, A knife. *Shilat*, (pl. of شلطة *shiltat*) Long and slender arrows.

A شلطاء *shaltā*, A knife.

A شلطة *shiltat*, A long slender arrow.

A شلغ *shalgh*, A breaking (another's skull).

P شلغم *shalgham*, A turnip, rape.

P شلغم وا *shalgham-wā*, Turnip-porridge.

P شلغه *shilgha*, (or شلقه) A corn or hay-fork.

P شلف *shalf*, A strumpet. A river in Africa.

P شلفا *shilfā*, A corn or hay-fork.

P شلفينه *shalfina* or *shulfina*, Vulva.

P شلفيه *shalfiya*, Vulva. الفيه شلفيه *alfiya shalfiya*, Name of a lascivious book.

A شلق *shalk*, The stroke given by a scourge. Laceration of the ear lengthwise. Discharge or report of a gun. Coition. P شلق کردن *shalk kardan*, To discharge fire-arms. A *Shilk* or *shalik*, A kind of small fish: an eel.

A شلقاء *shilkā*, A knife.

A شلقة *shilkat*, The eggs of the Lybian lizard. *Shalakat*, A wooden mallet. Horse-breakers.

P شلقت *shilkat*, (in Gīlān) A goose.

P شلك *shalk*, A leech. *Shilk*, Black viscous clay, in which the feet stick. *Shalak*, A young tree.

P شلکا *shalkā*, A leech. *Shilkā*, Black and adhesive mud.

P شلکك *shilkak*, A drain. A spout.

A شلل *shalal*, (v. n. of شلّ) Being withered (the hand). Driving (camels). A spot in a garment which cannot be washed out. لا شللاً *lā shalalan*, May thy hand not wither! *Shulal* or *shulul*, Active and ready in serving others, social, friendly.

P شلل گوش *shalal-gosh*, A dog with long and shaggy ears.

P شلم *shalm*, A traveller's shoe. *Shalam*, A turnip. *Shilim* or *shilm*, The tears or gum of a tree. *Shulum*, Contention, quarrel, strife. An unjust and violent seizure: oppression, tyranny.

A شلم *shalam* or *shalim*, Jerusalem.

A شلّم *shillam*, Sparks of anger.

P شلماب *shilmāb*, Barley-water. Bread grated and boiled with a little water, sugar, or honey.

P شلمابه *shalmāba* or *shalamāba*, Turnip-water. Boiled turnips.

A شلمانسر *shalmānasar*, Shalmanassar.

A شلمق *shalmak*, A very old woman.

P شلمك *shalmak*, Name of a medicine.

P شلميز *shalmīz*, Fenugreek.

P شلنگ *shalang* or *shiling*, Preparation made by runners previous to a journey or race of importance.

A شلو *shalw*, (v. n. of شلا for شلو) Going away. Carrying off. *Shilw*, (pl. اشلاء *ashlā*) A limb, member, joint of a slaughtered animal. The body.

P شلو *shilv*, Stature of the body.

P شلوار *shalwār*, also *shulwār*, Inner breeches, drawers reaching to the feet (the outer breeches are called تنبان *tumbān*), sailors' or travellers' trousers.

P شلوار بند *shalwār-band*, Fastening of breeches.

A شلوة *shilwat*, A piece, part, portion.

P شلوك *shalūk*, A leech.

A شلول *shalūl*, Active and ready in serving others; social, friendly. Aged (she-camel or woman)

A شلوم *shalūm*, Name of a certain prophet.

P شلون *shalūn*, An animal of the jackal species.

P شلوهج *shulūhaj*, (or شلوهك) A kind of thistle.

P شله *shala*, A sentence of death by the law of retaliation. *Shula*, A dish called shula pilaw. The wood or coal-storehouse in baths.

P شلّه *shalla*, An idol. A narrow way, defile. A strip of a garment. *Shalla* or *shulla*, A mixen, dunghill. *Shulla*, Vulva. A menstruous cloth.

P شلياق *shalyāk*, The constellation of the Lyre.

A شليّة *shalīyat*, (pl. شلايا *shalāya'*) Remains of cattle. A piece (of meat), portion (of the night), part (of a mountain).

A شليخ *shalīkh*, A small carpet, mat, or cushion, on which they kneel at prayer. Sound, noise, echo.

P شليخا *shalīkhā*, The companions of Jesus.

A شليك *shalīk*, Volley, discharge of fire-arms.

P شليل *shalīl*, (or شلير) A red and white peach.

A شليل *shalīl*, (pl. اشلّة *ashillat*) A garment worn under a coat of mail; also a short coat of mail under a larger. Woollen or hair-cloth, used as covering (for horses). Snot, snivel. The middle of a channel, where deepest. The marrow of the neck. The swell of flesh upon the back.

P شم *sham*, Terror, flight. The tail. Deceit, fraud, trick. Distance. Terrified, astonished, fearing. Disturbed, distracted. A subterraneous habitation. A house for the accommodation of travellers, a caravansera. A place for cattle. A nail. Name of a wrestler. (for شوم *shavam*) I am, or may be. *Shum*, Rustic or travelling shoes, coarsely made of undressed leather, and fastened to the feet with straps.

A شمّ *shamm*, (v. n. of شمّ) Smelling, scenting, Becoming proud. The sense of smell. *Shumm*, (pl. of اشمّ *ashamm*) High (mountains).

P شما *shamā*, A pastile. Naked. *Shumā*, Ye. You.

A شما *shama'*, (for شمع) Wax, wax-taper.

A شمّاء *shammā'*, (fem. of اشمّ) High-nosed.

A شمات *shamāt*, (v. n. of شمت) Rejoicing at the distress of another. *Shimāt*, (or شماتى *shamāta'*) Persons deceived by vain hopes, disappointed in their expectation.

A شماتة *shamātat*, (v. n. of شمت) Rejoicing at another's misfortunes. Clamour, noise, tumult.

A شماج *shamāj*, Any trifle (as skin or stone of grapes, thrown away when eating). Barley-bread.

P شماخ *shamākh*, A bandage for trussing the breasts. *Shamākh* or *shammākh*, Name of a wrestler.

A شماذ *shimāz*, (v. n. of شمذ) Being impregnated (a she-camel), of which she gives proof by cocking her tail. Being fecundated (a palm-tree).

A شمار *shamār*, (or شمرة *shamarat*) Fennel.

P شمار *shimār*, A kind of very hard wood, from which the handles of tools are made. Fennel. *Shumār*, Number, numeration, reckoning, computation. An equal number. Thereabouts. Ten millions. A troop, crowd, multitude. Like, resembling. Friendship, love. An incurable wound. (in comp.) Numbering, counting, numerous as. انجم شمار *anjum-shumār*, Numerous as the stars. بى شمار *bī shumār*, Innumerable. شمار روز *rozi shumār*, The day of reckoning, *i.e.* the last day. عسكر مور شمار *ʿaskari mor-shumār*, An army numerous as the ants.

P شمارا *shumārā*, You, to you.

P شمار افراز *shumār-afrāz*, A rosary.

A شمارق *shamārik*, (or شماريق *shamārīk*) Torn, cut (garment).

P شماركار *shumār-kār*, Place of the last judgment.

P شمارگاه *shumār-gāh*, A counting-house.

P شمارگير *shumār-gīr*, A numberer, accountant. Cultivating friendship.

P شمارنده *shumāranda*, A teller, numberer.

P شماره *shumāra*, Number, computation.

P شمارى *shumārī*, Counting. A rosary.

A شماريج *shamārīj*, (pl. of شمراج) Idle lies.

A شماريخ *shamārīkh*, (pl. of شمراخ and شمروخ) Clusters of dates. Summits of mountains.

P شماريدن *shumārīdan*, To number, count, tell, calculate. To be counted.

P شماريده *shumārīda*, Numbered, told.

A شمازيزة *shumāzīzat*, A timorous woman. A contraction.

A شماس *shimās*, (v. n. of شمس) Being vicious, enduring no rider, or throwing him (a horse).

A شمّاس *shammās*, (pl. شمامسة *shamāmisat*) A Christian priest or deacon; a shaveling. Name of the man who first established fire-worship.

P شماسان *shumāsān*, Name of a champion of Tūrān; also one of Irān.

P شماسيان *shamāsiyān*, Christian ministers, deacons. Followers of the fire-worshipper Shammās.

A شماشم *shamāshim*, Fresh dates remaining on the bunch.

A شماص *shumās*, Haste, expedition. جارية ذات شماص وملاص *jāriyatun zātu shimās wa milāsin*, A girl, light, delicately formed, somewhat saucy.

A شماط *shimāt*, Pot-herbs and spiceries put into victuals whilst dressing.

A شماطيط *shamātīt*, (pl. of شمطيط *shimtīt*) Scattered companies. Worn-out, tattered garments.

A شماطيطا *shamātītan*, Scatteredly.

A شمّاع *shammāʿ*, A maker of wax-candles.

P شماغنده *shamāghanda*, Stinking, fetid. A stinking woman.

P شماغيدن *shamāghīdan*, To stink.

A شمأل *shamʼal*, (or شمألّ *shamʼall*) (pl. شمائل *shamāʼil*) The north.

A شمال *shamāl*, North (wind or quarter). The left hand. *Shimāl*, (pl. اشمل *ashmul*, شمائل *shamāʼil*, and شمل *shumul*) The left hand. Left hands. A bad omen. (pl. شمالات *shimālāt*) The north wind. Swift (she-camel). A reaper's handful of corn. A mark upon a sheep's udder. (pl. شمائل *shamāʼil*) Disposition, innate quality. A bag put upon the dugs of cattle to prevent their being sucked. A sheath, cover. اصحاب يمين وشمال *as-hābi yamīn u shimāl*, Those to the right and left. P باد شمال *bādi shimāl*, (A نسيم شمال *nasīmi shimāl*) North wind, Boreas. A بلاد شمال *bilādi shimāl*, Northern region or coast. يد شمال *yadi shimāl*, The left hand. ذو الشمالين *zū'sh shimālayn*, Ambidexter.

P شمال *shimāl*, Good nature.

A شمالات *shimālāt*, (pl. of شمال *shimāl*) Northern winds or regions.

P شمال رو *shimāl-rū*, Facing the north.

P شمال نما *shimāl-namā*, Mariner's compass.

P شماله *shamāla*, A candle. A kind of rice.

A شمالىّ *shamālīy*, Northern. A cold day.

A شماليل *shamālīl*, (pl. of شملول *shumlūl*) Small quantities (of rain, men, or fruits). (A robe) made of small pieces. Scattered twigs or branchlets. ذهبوا شماليل *zahabū shamālīl*, They went away scattered, and in separate companies.

A شمّام *shammām*, (or شمّامة *shammāmat*) An odoriferous melon, of the bigness of a small colocynth, striped red, green, and yellow.

A شمّامات *shammāmāt*, Fragrant things.

A شمامسة *shamāmisat*, (pl. of شمّاس *shammās*) Christian priests or deacons.

P شمامه *shamāma*, A perfumed pastile. Naked. A musical pipe composed of unequal reeds. شمامهٔ كافور *shamāmaʼi kāfūr*, The sun. The moon. Light. The day. خامهٔ محبّت شمامه *khāmaʼi mahabbat-shamāma*, A pen perfumed with friendship.

P شمان *shamān*, Groaning. Weeping, sobbing. Terrified. Crazed. Frantic or fainting from thirst. Lamentation, loud and continued clamour. Thirst.

P شمانيدن *shamānīdan*, To disturb, perplex, confound. To deprive of sense. To be disturbed, perplexed, confounded. To lose one's senses. To fear. To faint from thirst.

P شمايان *shumāyān*, You, ye.

P شمائل *shamāʼil* or *shimāʼil*, Good qualities. خجسته شمائل *khujasta-shamāʼil*, Happy-tempered. *Shimāʼil*, A young shoot. A rivulet. A small company of persons.

A شمائل *shamāʼil*, North winds or regions. (pl. of شمال *shimāl*) Virtues, talents, abilities of mind and body. Left hands.

A شمائم *shamāʼim*, (pl. of شميمة *shamīmat*) Odours, perfumes.

A شمباء *shambāʼ*, Clean-teethed and sweet-breathed (girl).

P شمپورى *shampūrī*, Forcible, violent, compulsive, unnatural.

A شمّة *shammat*, One odour. One smell at.

P شمج *shamj* or *shammaj*, A grotto, cavern.

A شمج *shamj*, (v. n. of شمج) Sewing with long stitches, basting. Making haste. Mixing.

A شمجرة *shamjarat*, A running away in terror.

A شمجى *shamajaʼ*, Swift (she-camel).

A شمحاط *shimhāt*, (or شمحط *shamhat*) Disproportionately long.

A شمحوط *shumhūt*, Long.

A شمخ *shamkh*, (v. n. of شمخ) Being high and lofty. شمخ بانفه *shamakha bi anfihi*, He was high-nosed, *i.e.* haughty. *Shamakh*, Remote and high (design).

A شمّخ *shummakh*, (pl. of شامخ *shāmikh*) High. High-nosed, haughty.

A شمختر *shamakhtar*, (from P شوم اختر *shūm-akhtar*) Unfortunate, born under an unhappy planet. Mean, ignoble.

A شمّخر *shummakhr*, Proud, pompous.

A شمخرة *shamkharat*, Greatness, pomp, pride.

A شمّخز *shimmakhz* or *shummakhz*, Sharp-sighted. Large-sized (man or camel).

A شمّخزة *shummakhzat*, A great age.

A شمّخزيزة *shummakhzīzat*, Great age, fulness of days.

A شمذ *shamz*, (v. n. of شمذ) Being impregnated (a she-camel), and cocking her tail to give intimation of the same. Pulling up one's drawers or breeches. Being fructified (a palm-tree). Stuffing a clout into herself to prevent a prolapse of the womb (a woman).

P شمذ *shamaz*, White bread. Pale lapis lazuli.

A شمّذ *shummaz*, (pl. of شامذ *shāmiz*) (Camels) pregnant, or shewing signs of it. Fructified, fruitful palm-trees.

A شمذار *shimzār*, A swift pace.

A شمذارة *shimzārat*, Light, smart, active (lad). A swift pace.

A شمذة *shamazat*, The means of, or access to, fructification (spoken of a young female palm-tree).

A شمذر *shamzar* or *shimzar*, A swift pace.

A شمر *shamr*, (v. n. of شمر) Walking with nicety, circumspection, or with a haughty air. Going fast. Drawing (any thing) together. Pruning (the palm-tree). *Shimr*, Liberal. Alert, expeditious, expert. Penetrating, quick-sighted, examining with attention. *Shamar*, Name of a tract in Arabia containing many towns and villages. *Shimar*, Name of one of Yazīd's generals, who slew Husayn in the plains of Karbalā; and hence now means, vile, infamous.

P شمر *shamar*, A rivulet. A small tank or cistern. Any hollow place where water collects and stagnates, in a rock, at the foot of a tree, &c. A whirlpool. Cream.

A شمرّ *shimirr*, Great (misfortune).

A شمراج *shimrāj*, (pl. شماريج *shamārīj*) An idle lie.

A شمراخ *shimrākh*, (pl. شماريخ *shamārīkh*) A branch or cluster of dates or grapes. The summit of a mountain. The higher part of a cloud. A white mark from the forehead of a horse to his nose.

A شمراخيّة *shimrākhiyat*, Name of a sect.

A شمرة *shamrat* or *shumrat*, Fennel. *Shimrat*, The gait of a corrupt and mischievous man.

A شمرج *shumruj*, Cloth of a flimsy texture.

A شمرجة *shamrajat*, (v. n. of شمرج Q) Sewing badly or widely. Mixing lies in one's speech. Nursing well, rearing carefully.

A شمرخة *shamrakhat*, A cutting of date-clusters.

A شمرداة *shamardāt*, A swift she-camel.

P شمردگی *shumurdagī*, Numeration.

A شمردل *shamardal*, (or شمرذل *shamarzal*) Beautiful, swift, long, tall (camel or any other thing).

P شمردن *shumurdan*, To number, reckon, compute, count. To give. فرصت شمردن *fursat shumurdan*, To find or regard a convenient opportunity.

P شمرده *shumurda*, Numbered.

A شمردي *shamarda'*, Name of a plant or tree.

A شمرذاة *shamarzāt*, A swift she-camel.

A شمرذي *shamarza'*, Swift (camel).

A شمرس *shamras*, A species of thorn.

P شمرش *shumurish*, Clearly, distinctly. Supposing the case.

A شمرضاض *shimirzāz*, A certain kind of tree found in Mesopotamia.

A شمرطل *shamartal*, (or شمرطول *shamartūl*) Tall and tottering.

A شمروج *shumrūj*, Cloth of a flimsy texture.

A شمروخ *shumrūkh*, (pl. شماريخ *shamārīkh*) A branch or cluster of dates or grapes.

A شمري *shamarīy*, *shimirīy*, or *shumurīy*, Alert, expeditious, expert.

A شمّري *shimmarīy*, Alert, expeditious, expert.

A شمريّة *shimirīyat*, *shimarīyat*, *shumurīyat*, or *shamarīyat*, Active and expeditious (she-camel).

P شمريدن *shamrīdan*, To be terrified. To sigh or sob loudly. *Shamarīdan*, To praise.

A شمرير *shamrīr*, (in Morocco) A hat, cap.

A شمز *shamz*, A being frightened, running away.

A شمس *shams*, (v. n. of شمس) Being sun-shiny (the day). Shewing enmity. (pl. شموس *shumūs*) The sun. Gold (in chemistry). A fountain. A kind of necklace. A comb. Name of an ancient idol. شمس الدين *shamsu'd dīn*, (Sun of religion) A proper name. *Shums* or *shumus*, (pl. of شموس *shumūs*) Horses apt to throw their riders.

P شمسا *shamsā*, (in zand) Light. A ray.

A شمسات *shamasāt*, Figures of the sun.

A شمساط *shamsāt*, Name of a city.

A شمسة *shamsat*, The figure or resemblance of the sun. A statue, image, idol, painting, sculpture.

P شمسدر *shimasdar*, (in zand and Pāz.) Garlic.

A شمسل *shimsil*, An elephant.

P شمسه *shamsa*, An orange, citron. A round cake adorned with punctures. Figures or pictures wrought in silk. Little tassels affixed to a rosary.

A شمسيّ *shamsīy*, Solar. طريق شمسيّه *tarīki shamsīya*, The ecliptic, sun's course.

A شمسي قمري *shamsī kamarī*, A perquisite taken by the officers of government, being the difference between the pay for a lunar and a solar month. A monthly period of three or four days, during which the female attendants in the women's apartments have leave of absence.

P شمش *shumsh*, An ingot of gold.

P شمشاد *shamshād*, Any tall and upright tree. Marjoram. The graceful figure of a mistress. *Shimshād*, The box-tree. Marjoram. شمشاد شمائل پرست *shimshādi shamā'il-parast*, A box-tree shaken by the north wind.

P شمشار *shimshār*, Box-sprig. Mastich. Cypress.

A شمشاط *shamshāt*, Name of a place.

P شمشدر *shimashdar*, (in zand and Paz.) Garlic.

P شمشرا *shamsharā*, Mouse-ear (a fragrant plant).

A شمشقة *shimshikat*, A substance resembling lights, which protrudes from the mouth of a male camel raging with lust.

P شمشك *shimashk*, (in zand and Pāz.) Sesame.

A شمشليق *shamshalīk*, A flabby and quick-paced old woman.

P شمشور *shumshūr*, Name of a culinary plant.

P شمشير *shamshīr*, (said to be derived from شم *sham*, Claw, and شير *sher*, A lion) (*shimshīr* or *shamsher*) A sword, scimiter, sabre. A blade. The light of the morning or of the sun. شمشير آبدار *shamshīri āb-dār*, A bright or sharp sword. شمشير پهن *shamshīri pahn*, A broadsword. شمشير زدن *shamshīr zadan*, To fight or strike with a sword. شمشير صاعقه تأثير *shamshīri sā'ika-tā'sīr*, A sword penetrating like a thunderbolt. شمشير كشيدن *shamshīr kashīdan*, To draw a sabre. شمشير گوشتين *shamshīri goshtīn*, The sword of flesh, *i.e.* tongue. شمشير الملك *shamshīru'l mulk*, Sword of the empire (a proper name).

P شمشير باز *shamshīr-bāz*, A sword-player.

P شمشير بازي *shamshīr-bāzī*, Sword-playing.

P شمشير بهادر *shamsher-bahādur*, (ironically) A useless, worthless fellow.

P شمشيرزن *shamshīr-zan*, Striking with a sword; warlike, a gallant soldier.

P شمشير ساز *shamshīr-sāz*, A sword-cutler.

P شمشير سازي *shamshīr-sāzī*, Sword-making.

P شمشيرگر *shamshīrgar*, A sword-cutler.

A شمص *shams*, (v. n. of شمص) Urging on (a horse) violently. Driving gently or violently. Poking (a beast) with a stick that he may quicken his pace. Being indisposed through eating green clover (a horse). Striking (any one). *Shamas*, (v. n. of شمص) Speaking fast.

A شمصرة *shamsarat*, (v. n. of شمصر Q) Being severe, pressing hard (upon one).

A شمط *shamt*, (v. n. of شمط) Mixing (two things). Filling (a vessel). Being scattered (unripe dates). Losing its leaves (a tree). *Shamt*, *shimt* or *shamat*, Pot-herbs and spiceries put into victuals whilst dressing. *Shumt*, (pl. of اشمط *ashmat*) Half-grey. Bi-coloured. *Shamat*, (v. n. of شمط) Having hair black and grey. A mixture of black and white hairs.

A شمطاء *shamtā*, (fem. of اشمط *ashmat*) Bi-coloured. Half-grey (woman).

A شمطاط *shimtāt*, A rag. A sect, band, company.

A شمطالة *shumtālat*, A piece of fat meat.

A شمطان *shumtān*, (pl. of اشمط *ashmat*) Half-grey. Bi-coloured.

A شمطانة *shumtānat*, A date ripening on one side.

A شمطوط *shumtūt*, Long, tall. A troop, company.

A شمطيط *shimtīt*, A sect, band, company.

A شمظ *shamz*, (v. n. of شمظ) Preventing, hindering. Mixing. Taking any thing by little and little. Instigating, exciting, stimulating. Shaking softly. Mixing in a speech severities with soft words.

A شمع *shamʿ*, (v. n. of شمع) Playing, jesting. *Shamʿ* or *shamaʿ*, Wax, a wax-candle, taper; any candle. شمع الهى *shamʿi ilāhī*, (The divine candle) The Kur'ān. The Muhammadan religion. Sun and moon. P شمع زرّين لگن *shamʿi zarrīn-lagan*, The sun. شمع سحر *shamʿi sahar*, Morning-beam or false dawn. The sun. شمع شب افروز *shamʿi shab-afroz*, A night-illuminating candle. شمع صباح *shamʿi sabāh*, The sun. شمع فلك *shamʿi falak*, Sun, moon, and stars. شمع مزعفر *shamʿi muzaʿfar*, (or شمع هفت چرخ *shamʿi haft charkh*) The sun. شمع يهودي وش *shamʿi yahūdī wash*, Red wine.

A شمعة *shamʿat*, One wax-light or candle.

P شمعدان *shamʿdān*, Candlestick, chandelier.

P شمع ساز *shamʿ-sāz*, Candlemaker, chandler.

A شمعل *shamʿal*, (or شمعلة) A brisk she-camel.

A شمعلة *shamʿalat*, (v. n. of شمعل Q) Being scattered, dispersed (people). The Jews' mode of reading their Scriptures.

A شمعون *shamʿūn*, Simon. شمعون الصفا *shamʿūnu's safa'*, Simon Peter, Cephas.

A شمعيّ *shamʿiy*, Waxen. Of, belonging to, a candle or taper. A dealer in wax.

P شمعي رنگ *shamaʿi-rang*, Flame-colour.

P شمغند *shamghand*, A stinking woman. Stinking, ill-flavoured. Dirty (garment). Filth. Impurity.

P شمغندان *shamghandān*, Unseemly, stinking.

P شمغنده *shamghanda*, Fetid, stinking. Struck with fear.

P شمغنديدن *shamghandīdan*, To be bad, fetid.

P شمغيدن *shamghīdan*, To smell disagreeably.

A شمق *shamk*, (v. n. of شمق) Being brisk, frisking, playing. *Shamak*, Insane mirth.

A شمّق *shimikk*, (fem. شمّقة *shimikkat*) Long, tall.

A شمقمق *shamakmak*, Long, tall. Brisk, frisky.

A شمكور *shamkūr*, Name of a city.

P شمگير *shamgīr*, Name of a famous general.

A شمل *shaml*, (v. n. of شمل) Tying a bag over a sheep's udder to prevent the lamb from sucking. Comprehending, containing, surrounding on every side, covering. Plucking the dates from a palm-tree. Taking the left hand. Exposing (wine) to the north wind to cool. Lying with. Being universal, common, belonging to all. Understanding, capacity. A disjointed work. The north. Collection. فرّق الله شملهم *faraka'llāh shamlahum*, May God break up their confederacy! *Shaml* or *shamal*, A great crowd. *Shiml*, (*shaml*, or شمّل *shimill*) A bunch of dates or grapes; or one having little fruit. *Shamal*, (v. n. of شمل) Conceiving (a camel). Concealing a stallion camel amongst them (a herd of females). Being exposed to the north wind. Being universal, common to all. Experiencing (good or evil). The shoulder. (pl. اشمال *ashmāl*) A small quantity (of rain, men, or fruits). The north wind. *Shumul*, (pl. of شمال *shimāl*) Left hands.

P شمل *shamal*, A rustic shoe.

A شملال *shimlāl*, Swift-going (she-camel). The left hand. Equality.

A شملة *shamlat*, A garment or covering for the whole body. *Shimlat*, The mode of wholly investing the body. الشملة الصمّاء *ash'shimlatu's sammāʾ*, A peculiar style of wrapping one's self up. امّ شملة *ummu shumlat*, The world. Wine. *Shamalat*, A small quantity of dates remaining on a palm-tree. A little rain.

A شمّلة *shimillat*, Swift-going (she-camel).

A شملتين *shamlutayn*, (obliq.) A double garment.

P شملخ *shamlakh* or *shamalkh*, A turnip.

P شملغ *shamlagh*, A turnip.

A شملق *shamlak*, A very old woman.

A شمللة *shamlalat*, (v. n. of شملل Q) Being swift, expeditious. Pulling all the dates from a palm-tree.

A شملول *shumlūl*, The shoulder. (pl. شماليل *shamālīl*) A small quantity (of rain, men, or fruits).

P شمله *shamla*, The end of the turban or waist-band, sometimes tucked into the folds, and sometimes left flying loose. A kind of shawl for throwing over the shoulders or wrapping about the head. *Shumla*, A meteor.

P شمليت *shimlīt*, Fenugreek.

P شمليد *shamlīd*, (or شمليز *shamlīz*) Fenugreek. A fragrant kind of flower.

A شمليل *shimlīl*, Swift-going (she-camel).

P شمم *sha* or *shumam*, A rustic shoe *Shumam*, Flight, propensity to run away. Distance, absence.

A شمم *shamam*, The summit or height of a mountain. Straightness of nose (when aquiline it is called قنا *kanā*). Length of nose. Depression of the tip of the nose. Proximity, nearness. Distance.

P شمن *shaman*, An idolater. An idol.

P شمنان *shamanān*, (pl. of شمن *shaman*) Idolaters. One who pants from thirst or from running. A large bed or carpet.

P شمند *shamand*, Insensible. Insensibility. Health, vigour. Cry, lamentation.

P شمنده *shamanda*, A hero, brave man. Astonished, amazed. Terrified, stupefied, insensible. A giver, bestower.

A شموّ *shumūw*, A being high. Sublimity.

A شموخ *shamūkh*, Extensive (waste). *Shumūkh*, (v. n. of شمخ) Being high and lofty. Being proud.

A شموذ *shumūz*, (v. n. of شمذ) Being impregnated (a she-camel), and carrying her tail high in indication of the same. Being fecundated (a palm-tree).

A شمّور *shammūr*, The diamond.

A شموس *shamūs*, Stubborn and bad-tempered. (pl. شمس *shums* or *shumus*) (A horse) restive and apt to throw his rider. Wine. *Shumūs*, (v. n. of شمس) Being ill-tempered. Throwing his rider (a horse). (pl. of شمس *shams*) Suns.

A شموص *shamūs*, Quick, active, and joyous.

A شموع *shamūʿ*, Frolicsome, jesting (man or woman). *Shumūʿ*, (v. n. of شمع) Playing, joking. Being separated, divided, scattered. Leaving, forsaking. (pl. of شمع *shamaʿ*) Candles, wax-lights.

P شمول *shamol*, Composure, collectedness. Quiet, repose, rest.

A شمول *shamūl*, Cold wine. The north wind. *Shumūl*, (v. n. of شمل) Comprehending, containing, surrounding on all sides. Being universal, common, belonging to all. Covering. Veering to the left. Turning to the north. Comprehension, comprisal. Fellowship.

A شموم *shamūm*, Odorous, fragrant, scented.

P شمه *shama*, Milk which flows spontaneously from the udder. *Shima*, Cream. *Shima* or *shimma*, The greasy parts of milk or cheese.

P شمّه *shamma*, (from A شمّة *shammat*) Odour, perfume. Nature, habit. Custom, mode, rite. A little. An atom, particle, the smallest quantity (of perfume). A pinch of snuff.

A شمهذ *shamhaz*, Sharp. Iron. Light, active (dog) with sharp teeth.

A شمهذة *shamhazat*, (v. n. of شمهذ Q) Sharpening. Thinning (iron). Light (dogs) with sharp teeth.

P شميا *shamyā*, Heaven.

A شميت *shamīt*, Reproach. Brawl, squabble.

P شميد *shamīd*, Astonished, amazed. Stupefied (with love, grief, or surprise).

P شميدن *shamīdan*, To be confounded, lose one's wits, dread, be terror-stricken. To weep aloud, to sob. To flee in terror, to shun from aversion. To smell. To gasp from thirst.

P شميده *shamīda*, Terrified, afraid. Shunning with aversion. Parched with thirst. Panting from running or weeping. Weeping, crying. Amazed, stupefied. A furious lion.

A شميذر *shamayzar*, Active, nimble (camel, lad).

A شمّير *shimmīr*, Diligent, alert, expeditious, expert (man). Swift (camel).

P شميران *shamīrān*, The governor of Shikin.

P شميز *shamīz*, A sower. *Shumīz*, A field prepared for receiving seed.

SY شميسا *shamīsā*, Light.

A شميسة *shumaysat*, (dim. of شمس) A little sun.

A شميستان *shumaysatāni*, Name of two gardens.

A شميط *shamīt*, Mixed. Bi-coloured (wolf). Milk so well flavoured that neither its acidity or freshness can be detected. A bird whose tail is partially white. Herbage dry and green mixed together. The dawn, light and darkness. Children, half boys, half girls.

A شميطية *shamītiyat*, Name of a sect.

A شميل *shamīl*, The north.

A شميم *shamīm*, (v. n. of شمّ) Smelling, scenting. Deviating from the right way. Becoming proud. High (saddle). Elevated. Odour, perfume, fragrance. A tree, particularly a fragrant one. Odoriferous. P گل عنبر شميم *guli ʿambar-shamīm*, A rose fragrant as ambergris. A نسيم عبهر شميم *nasīmi ʿabhar-shamīm*, A jessamine-breathing gale.

A شميمة *shamīmat*, Odour, smell, stink.

A شمّيمى *shimmīmā'*, (v. n. of شمّ) Smelling.

P شن *shan*, Amorous blandishments. Hemp.

A شنّ *shann*, (v. n. of شنّ) Pouring out gently. Pouring (water into wine). Sending forth (marauding parties) in all directions. (pl. شنان *shinān*) An old, dried up, small leathern bottle.

A شنء *shanʾ*, (*shinʾ*, or *shunʾ*) (v. n. of شنأ) Hating. Becoming clear of. *Shanaʾ*, (v. n. of شنئ) Paying one (his) due. Acknowledging. Acquitting one's self, getting clear of. Drawing forth.

P شنا *shinā*, Swimming. شنا كردن *shinā kardan*, To swim.

A شنّاء *shunnāʾ*, (pl. of شانئ *shāniʾ*) Haters.

A شنآءة *shanāʾat*, (v. n. of شنأ) Hating.

P شناب *shināb*, Swimming.

A شنابث *shunābis*, A lion. Thick.

P شنابيدن *shinābīdan*, To understand.

A شنأة *shanaʾat*, (v. n. of شنأ) Acknowledging, confessing. Paying, giving.

A شناة *shunāt*, (pl. of شاني *shānī*) Haters.

A شناتر *shanātir*, (pl. of شنترة *shantarat* or *shuntarat*) Fingers. Ear-rings. ذو شناتر *zū shanātir*, Name of a king of Yaman, with a redundant finger.

P شناح *shanāh*, A raft constructed of inflated leathern bottles.

A شناح *shanāh*, A young camel. *Shanāh*, (شناحى *shanāhī*, or شناحيّ *shanāhiy*) Long, very tall (man). Fat. *Shināh*, (pl. شنح *shunuh*) A drunkard.

A شناحية *shanāhiyat*, A tall, jolly, plump girl.

A شناخ *shinākh*, A promontory, the projecting part of a mountain.

P شناخت *shinākht*, He knew. Understanding, intellect. Knowledge, acquaintance. شناخت يار *shinākhti yār*, The knowledge of a friend.

P شناختگان *shinākhtagān*, Acquaintances.

P شناختگي *shinākhtagī*, Knowledge, acquaintance, acquaintanceship.

P شناختن *shinākhtan*, To know, to be acquainted with. To acknowledge.

P شناخته *shinākhta*, Known, understood.

A شناخيب *shanākhīb*, (pl. of شنخوب *shunkhūb* and شنخوبة *shunkhūbat*) Mountain-tops.

P شنار *shanār*, The herb hyssop. *Shinār*, Swimming. Shamefulness, disgrace, dishonour. Unlucky, bad, inauspicious. The bottom of any piece of water; a port, harbour. A shallow in the sea or in a river surrounded by deep water, on which ships are liable to be wrecked. A young branch of a tree. A country laid waste and deserted.

A شنار *shanār*, Disgrace, infamy. Any affair notoriously shameful.

A شنارى *shunāraʾ*, A cat.

P شناريدن *shinārīdan*, To swim.

P شناس *shinās*, Explanation, notification. (in comp.) Knowing, understanding. نكته شناس *nukta-shinās*, Understanding the most minute points.

P شناسا *shināsā*, Comprehending, knowing.

P شناسان *shināsān*, Explanation, notification.

P شناسائي *shināsāʾī*, Acquaintance, knowledge.

P شناسندگان *shināsandagān*, The knowing ones.

P شناسيدن *shināsīdan*, To understand, know.

A شناص *shanās*, (شناصيّ *shanāsiy*, or *shunāsiy*) Tall, strong, and swift (horse).

A شناط *shināt*, (pl. شناطات *shināṭāt* and شنائط *shanāʾit*) A woman of a fine healthy rosy complexion.

A شناظ *shināz*, The summit of a mountain. Abundance and compactness of flesh.

A شناظي *shanāzī*, (pl. of شنظوة *shunzuwat* or شنظاو *shanzāw*) Sides or summits of mountains.

A شناظير *shanāzīr*, (pl. of شنظير) Bad-tempered.

A شناعة *shanāʿat*, (v. n. of شنع) Being deformed, filthy, fetid, odious, shameful. Filthiness.

A شناعيف *shanāʿīf*, (pl. of شنعاف *shinʿāf*) Tops of mountains. Tall men.

P شنافتن *shināftan*, To hear. To understand.

A شناق *shanāk*, Long, tall. *Shināk*, (v. n. of شنق) Receiving a mulct (called شنق *shanak*) for homicide. (v. n. 3 of شنق) Mixing one's flocks or effects with those of another. The string or strap which fastens the mouth of a full bottle. Long, tall (male or female). A bowstring.

A شناقصة *shanākisat*, (pl. of شنقاصيّ *shinkāsiy*) Certain kinds of troops.

P شناگر *shināgar*, A swimmer.

A شنآن *shanʾān*, (fem. شنآنة *shanʾānat*) Hated, disliked (man). Hostile, hating (man). *Shanʾān* or *shanaʾān*, (v. n. of شنأ) Hating, detesting.

A شنان *shanān*, Hated. *Shinān*, (pl. of شنّ *shann*) Old leathern bottles (which, when shrivelled up, they strike with a stick to urge forward camels). *Shunān*, Cold water. Scattered. (Water) dropping from a bottle.

P شنان *shinān*, Wild leek. *Shunān*, The herb alkali, and the ashes which are made from it, with which they wash clothes.

A شنآنة *shanʾānat*, (fem. of شنآن *shanʾān*) Hated, disliked (woman). Hostile, hating (woman).

A شنانة *shunānat*, Droppings, tricklings.

P شناو *shināw*, Swimming: a swimmer. A shoal.

P شناور *shināwar*, A swimmer. Nimble, active. دلاور شناور *dilāwari shināwar*, A bold swimmer.

P شناوري *shināwarī*, Swimming, natation. شناوري كردن *shināwarī kardan*, To swim.

P شناوش *shināwish*, Swimming, natation.

P شناويدن *shināwīdan*, To swim.

P شناه *shināh*, Swimming. A swimmer.

A شنأى *shanʾaʾ*, Hated, disliked, detested (woman). Hostile (woman).

P شناي *shināy*, Swimming.

A شنائيّ *shanaʾiy*, Belonging to the tribe of أزد شنوءة *azdu shanūʾat*.

A شنائط *shanāʾit*, (pl. of شناط *shināt*) Women of fine healthy complexions.

A شنائع *shanāʾiʿ*, (pl. of شنيعة *shanīʿat*) Shameful actions, vices, crimes, villainies.

A شنائية *shanāʾiyat*, Hated, disliked (woman). Hostile (man).

P شنابيدن *shināyīdan*, To hear.

P شنب *shamb*, A cupola, dome.

A شنب *shanab*, (v. n. of شنب) Being fresh and sweet (the mouth or teeth). Being cold (the day). Coldness, freshness, or beauty of the teeth. The edge of the teeth, as when they resemble a saw. White specks on the teeth. *Shanib*, Cold (day).

A شنباء *shambāʾ*, (fem. of اشنب *ashnab*) Sweet-breathed (girl), with fresh and white teeth. A kind of pomegranate destitute of seeds.

A شنبة *shumbat*, Coldness of the weather.

A شنبث *shambas*, A lion. *Shumbas*, Rough, hard.

A شنبثة *shambasat*, (v. n. of شنبث Q) Laying hands on. Seizing the heart, laying a fast hold (love). Attachment, affection.

P شنبد *shambid*, Saturday.

A شنبلة *shambalat*, (v. n. of شنبل Q) Kissing.

P شنبليت *shambalīt*, (شنبليد *shambalīd*, or شنبليله *shambalīla*) Fenugreek. Name of a flower.

P شنبه *shamba*, The neighing of a horse. Roaring of a lion. *Shambih*, A day. Saturday. دو شنبه *du shambih*, Monday. سه شنبه *sih shambih*, Tuesday. چهار شنبه *chahār shambih*, Wednesday. پنج شنبه *panj shambih*, Thursday. شنبهى كردن *shambihī kardan*, To keep a Sabbath, to sabbatize.

A شنّة *shannat*, An old dried up leathern bottle.

P شنت *shanat*, (in zand and Pāzand) A year.

P شنتان *shinatān*, (in zand and Pāzand) Years.

A شنترة *shantarat*, (v. n. of شنتر Q) Tearing (a garment). *Shantarat* or *shuntarat*, (pl. شناتر *shanātir*) The space between two fingers. A finger. An ear-ring.

A شنتقة *shuntukat*, A net or reticulated cane-work, wherein women keep cotton.

A شنث *shanas*, (for شثن *shasan*) (v. n. of شنث) Becoming thick (the hand; or the lip of a camel from browsing on thorns).

P شنج *shanj*, Buttocks, thighs, hips, haunches. A promontory. Hard, stony, uneven ground. *Shinj*, Buttocks. *Shunj*, A shell for glazing.

A شنج *shunj*, A shell whence they make tutty. *Shanaj*, (v. n. of شنج) Being wrinkled, shrivelled. Corrugation. A male camel. *Shanij*, (A horse) having the thigh-nerve contracted.

A شنجار *shinjār*, (from P شنكار) Melilot; bugloss.

P شنج غنج *shanj ghanj*, Buttocks, hips, haunches.

P شنجود *shanjūd*, Wounded. A wound.

P شنجودن *shanjūdan*, To wound. To scratch.

P شنجيدن *shanjīdan*, To vex. To leap. To drop.

A شنح *shunuh*, (pl. of شناح *shināh*) Drunkards.

A شنحف *shanhaf*, (or شنحف *shinnahf*) Long.

A شنخاب *shinkhāb*, A mountain-top. Shoulder-blade. Vertebræ of the back.

A شنخب *shankhab*, Long, tall.

A شنخف *shinnakhf*, Thick, corpulent. Long.

A شنخفة *shankhafat*, Pride, vain-glory, vanity.

A شنخم *shinnakhm*, Fat.

A شنخوب *shunkhūb*, (or شنخوبة *shunkhūbat*) (pl. شناخيب *shanākhīb*) A mountain-top. The shoulder-blade. The vertebræ of the back.

P شند *shand*, The beak of a bird.

P شندف *shandaf*, A military or musical drum.

A شندف *shunduf*, (A horse) tall and wry-faced.

P شندله *shundila*, Mallows.

A شنذاخ *shinzākh*, (*shunzākh*, شنذاخيّ *shunzākhīy*, شنذخ *shunzakh*, شندخ *shundākh*, or شندخة *shundukhat*) A feast gratuitously given on the finishing of a house, on returning from a journey, or on the recovery of any thing lost.

A شنذارة *shinzārat*, Jealous. Obscene. A fornicator. A scoundrel.

A شنذخ *shunzukh*, Strong, powerful. Tall. Compact in flesh. A lion. A fleet horse.

A شنذخة *shanzakhat*, (v. n. of شنذخ Q) Preparing the feast شنذاخ *shinzākh*, mentioned above.

A شنذيرة *shinzīrat*, Worthless. A fornicator. A scoundrel. Jealous. Foul-mouthed.

A شنرة *shanrat*, The walk of an honest man.

A شنزب *shanzab*, Hard, firm, rough, sharp.

P شنزبه *shanzaba*, Name of the ox mentioned in the fable of Kalila wa Dimna.

A شنزرة *shanzarat*, (v. n. of شنزر Q) Being rough. Ruggedness, asperity.

P شنش *shansh*, A long hooked reed used by cotton-dressers.

A شنشنة *shinshinat*, Nature, temper, disposition. Usage, custom. A piece of meat.

A شنصرة *shansarat*, Vehemence. Ruggedness, asperity. Affliction, adversity.

A شنصير *shinsīr*, Vehemence. Affliction, adversity. Refuge, asylum.

A شنط *shunut*, Pieces of meat dressed.

A شنطوف *shuntūf*, Summit of any thing.

A شنظاة *shanzāt*, Summit of a mountain.

A شنظب *shunzub*, Long. Of a good disposition. Any channel with water in it.

A شنظرة *shanzarat*, Reproach, reviling, contumely.

A شنظوة *shunzuwat*, (pl. شناظي *shanāzī*) The side; also the top of a hill.

A شنظورة *shunzūrat*, A piece of rock rolling from a mountain.

A شنظوف *shunzūf*, A branch.

A شنظيان *shinziyān*, Perverse, cross (woman).

A شنظير *shinzīr*, A piece of rock detaching itself from a mountain and rolling down; a boulder stone. *Shinzīr*, (and شنظيرة *shinzīrat*) Of a bad temper or villainous disposition. Obscene, wicked.

A شنظيرة *shinzīrat*, Promontory, mountain-peak.

A شنع *shanȝ*, (v. n. of شنع) Reviling, treating opprobriously. Regarding as light and contemptible. Pulling to pieces a patched garment, destroying the nap. *Shunȝ*, (v. n. of شنع) Detesting, abhorring, being disgusted and horrified. *Shaniȝ*, Odious, foul, detestable.

A شنعاء *shanȝā*, (fem. of اشنع *ashnaȝ*) Base; ugly, mis-shapen, or deformed to an extreme degree.

A شنعاب *shinȝāb*, Tall (man).

A شنعاف *shinȝāf*, (pl. شناعيف *shanāȝīf*) Top of a mountain. High mountain. Tall and weak man.

A شنعة *shunȝat*, Baseness, a horrid crime, ugliness, turpitude, brutality.

A شنّعف *shinnaȝf*, Tall, but weak and tottering.

A شنعفة *shanȝafat*, Length, tallness.

A شنّعم *shinnaȝm* A tall, corpulent man.

A شنعنع *shanaȝnaȝ*, Thin, lean, loosely built.

A شنعوف *shunȝūf*, The top or ridge of a mountain. High mountains.

P شنغ *shunugh*, A cow's horn.

A شنغاب *shinghāb*, A long slender branch. A long rope. Tall (man).

P شنغار *shunghār*, A royal falcon.

A شنغب *shunghub*, A long slender stalk. A rope. Long-bodied (animal).

A شنغرة *shangharat*, (and شنغيرة *shinghīrat*) Wickedness, badness of disposition, impudence.

A شنّغف *shinnaghf*, Staggering, loosely built.

A شنّغم *shinnaghm*, Long, tall.

A شنّغمًا *shinnaghman*, Against the will.

A شنغوب *shunghūb*, A long thin vein or stratum in the earth. A long rope or thin branch. A long and narrow strip of salt, marshy ground.

A شنغير *shinghīr*, Unchaste, impudent, foul-mouthed. Of a bad disposition.

A شنف *shanf*, (v. n. of شنف) Looking transversely or askance at any one, either in admiration, surprise, or contempt. (pl. شنوف *shunūf*) A ring for the top of the ear (those in the lobe being called قرط *kurt*). *Shanaf*, (v. n. of شنف) Hating. Disapproving, disliking. Being intelligent, knowing. Having the upper lip turned out. *Shanif*, A hater.

A شنفار *shanfār*, Light, nimble, active.

A شنفارة *shinfārat*, Agility, briskness, impetuosity (of a she-camel).

P شنفتن *shiniftan*, To hear.

A شنفرىٰ *shanfara'*, Name of a poet of the tribe of ازد *azd*, and a famous runner: hence, اعدىٰ من الشنفرىٰ *aȝda' mini'sh shanfara'*, More swift of foot (or a better runner) than Shanfara.

A شنفعة *shanfaȝat*, Length, tallness.

A شنفلة *shanfalat*, (v. n. of شنفل Q) Drawing out money to answer a demand.

A شنفيرة *shinfīrat*, Agility, briskness, impetuosity (in a she-camel). Of a bad disposition.

A شنق *shank*, (v. n. of شنق) Checking (a camel) with a bridle till the back of his head touches the front of the saddle. Fastening (the mouth of a full bottle). Tying (up a horse to a tree or to a high peg). Hanging on a gibbet. Tying (a camel) with a شناق *shināk*. Putting the cross-bar شنيق *shanīk* into a bee-hive. *Shanak*, (v. n. of شنق) Burning with desire (for any thing). Length of head. (pl. اشناق *ashnāk*) The intermediate numbers between any given two, as between 10 and 40, and between 40 and 120 (especially with regard to the proportion of cattle taxed by the Muhammadan law, from such herbs or flocks, for pious uses). A partial mulct of expiation for homicide or wounding, being rather a supplement to something before paid. Work, labour. A remainder, surplus. A rope. Equity, justice. *Shanik*, Extremely desirous.

A شنقاء *shankā*, (A bird) feeding young ones.

A شنقاب *shinkāb*, (or شنقب) A kind of bird.

P شنقار *shunkār*, A falcon.

A شنقاصيّ *shinkāsiy*, (pl. شناقصة *shanākisat*) A certain kind of military corps.

A شنقصة *shankasat*, (v. n. of شنقص Q) Getting to the bottom of any thing.

A شنّقم *shinnakm*, Little, few.

A شنقناق *shiniknāk*, The prince of demons. Calamity.

P شنكرك *shankrak*, Amorously playful. A thief. An elephant's trunk. Name of an Indian king.

P شنكزن *shankzan*, A worm which eats corn.

P شنكسه *shankasa*, Penis. A dunghill. A dirty gown.

P شنكل *shankal*, A highway-robber. A sort of grain. *Shankul*, A robber, an assassin. Name of a king of India who assisted Afrāsyāb.

P شنكله *shankala*, The fringe of a pocket-handkerchief or veil. A cluster; an ear of corn. Dirty clothes. An impure place. A stable.

P شنكليل *shankalīl*, Ginger.

P شنكور *shankūr*, The whirl of a woman's spindle. A round piece of wood on the top of a tent-pole.

P شنكوك *shankūk*, A whirl fixed on a spindle.

P شنكول *shankūl*, Saucy, Witty. Beautiful. A robber. An elephant's trunk.

P شنگ *shang*, Beautiful, delicate, handsome. Amorously playful. Lively, graceful. Lazy. A thief, robber. A cheat, knave. Pomp, pride, excess, exorbitancy. A cypress. The proboscis of an elephant. A cucumber kept for seed. *Shing*, A sort of pulse. A kind of cucumber. Goats'-beard (a plant). Name of a village. *Shung*, Name of a straight, smooth tree used for making bows.

P شنگار *shingār*, Melilot. Bugloss.

P شنگان *shingān*, Name of a country.

P شنگبیز *shangbīz*, Date-wine. Ginger.

P شنگرف *shangarf*, Cinnabar, vermilion. A slug. شنگرف زاولی *shangarfi zāwulī*, Red lead.

P شنگرک *shangurk*, A whirl on a spindle.

P شنگول *shangūl*, (or شنگوله *shangola*) Beautiful, lovely. A thief, robber. An elephant's trunk.

P شنگویر *shangvīr*, Date-wine.

P شنگویز *shangwez*, Date-wine.

P شنگه *shanga*, Penis. A menstruous cloth. A dunghill.

P شنگیار *shingyār*, A sort of cucumber.

P شنگینه *shangīna*, A stick, staff, cudgel.

P شنلك *shanlak*, An ear of corn. A bunch of grapes or dates.

P شنلوك *shanlūk*, A whirl on a spindle's top.

A شنم *shanm*, (v.n.of شنم) Scratching, tearing. Splitting. A scratch. *Shunum*, Crop-eared (persons).

A شنم *shinnam*, Sparks of anger.

P شنو *shanū*, The cypress. The wild plum or cherry-tree. A tree of which arrows are made. *Shinav* or *shunav*, Hearing, understanding.

P شنوا *shinavā*, A hearer.

P شنوار *shanwār*, (for شلوار) Inner breeches.

P شنوانیدن *shinwānīdan*, To cause to hear or understand.

P شنوائی *shanwāī*, Hearing, auscultation.

A شنوءة *shanūat* or *shunūat*, One who hates and shuns impurity. A hatred of impurity. ازد شنوءة *azdu shanūat* (or شنوّة *shanūwat*) Name of a tribe (so called from the hatred they bore amongst themselves).

A شنوّة *shanūwat*, A hatred of impurity.

P شنود *shunūd*, He heard. A hearing.

P شنودن *shunūdan* or *shinūdan*, To hear, to understand. To perceive, to snuff. To obey.

P شنوسه *shanūsa*, (شنوشه *shanūsha*, or *shinūsha*) Sneezing.

A شنوص *shunūṣ*, (v. n. of شنص) Adhering, sticking to, being assiduous. Hanging.

A شنوع *shunūع*, Ugliness, foulness, shamefulness.

A شنوف *shunūf*, (pl. of شنف *shanf*) Ear-rings.

A شنون *shanūn*, Neither fat nor lean. Hungry. Fat. Lean.

P شنونتن *shanūnitan*, (in zand and Pā.) To write.

P شنونده *shinor shinawanda*, A hearer, auditor.

P شنوه *shanwa*, Genoa.

A شنويّ *shanawīy*, Of the tribe of ازد شنوءة *azdu shanūat*. One who hates impurity.

P شنویدن *shin* or *shinawīdan*, To hear. To smell.

P شنه *shana*, A corn-fork with five prongs for winnowing. Neighing of horses. Grunting of hogs, purring of a lion; noise. Curse, malediction.

P شنّه *shanna*, The neighing of a horse.

A شنهبر *shanahbar*, (or شنهبرة) An aged woman.

P شني *shanī*, A salver of gold, silver, brass, or copper. Name of an herb, of whose fibres ropes are made. The spear at the top of an ensign-staff or banner, a demi-lance, or javelin.

A شنيّ *shanīy*, Disliked, detested, hated.

A شنيب *shanīb*, Clean-teethed, sweet-breathed.

P شنيد *shanīd*, The beak or pounces of a bird. He heard. Hearing, auscultation. The thing heard.

P شنيدن *shanīdan*, To hear, listen, attend to. To obey. To make an assault. To smell. To perceive. To collect.

P شنيده *shanīda*, Heard. Who has heard.

A شنّير *shinnīr*, Of a bad disposition, infamous, covered with disgrace.

A شنّيرة *shinnīrat*, Notoriously bad, infamous.

P شنيز *shanīz*, Ebony. A bow. *Shunīz*, Coriander.

A شنّيز *shinnīz*, Fennel-flower, or its seed.

P شنيژه *shanīja*, Fringe on the edge of cloth.

A شنيع *shanīع*, Base, shameful, odious, hateful, deformed, abominable, hideous, detestable, shocking, foul, scurrilous. اخبار شنيعه *akhbāri shanīعa*, Disagreeable news.

A شنيعة *shanīعat*, A shameful thing, turpitude.

A شنيق *shanīk*, A bastard. A cross-bar for supporting honey-combs in a hive.

A شنّيق *shinnīk*, (A youth) self-admiring, pleased with himself.

A شنيقة *shanīkat*, Flattering, coquettish (woman).

A شنين *shanīn*, Drops of water or of tears. A trickling down of water. Milk, new or old, into which water is poured.

P شو *shav* or *shū*, (imp. of شدن *shudan*) Be, exist. Be thou. (in comp). Being, existing. *Shav*, (for شب *shab*) Night. *Shū*, Wash thou. Washing. A husband. شست و شو کردن *shust u shū kardan*, To wash.

P شوا *shawā*, Existing. Deaf. *Shiwā*, A hardness or blister in the hands or feet from too much work, or over-walking. Filth on the body. A small vestibule. Anise.

A شواء *shiwāء* or *shuwāء*, Any thing roasted, especially flesh-meat.

A شوّاء *shawwāء*, A roaster (of meat).

A شواءة *shiwāءat*, A piece of roast meat.

A شوابّ *shawābb*, (pl. of شابّة *shābbat*) Youths, young men. Young women.

A شواة *shawāt*, (pl. شوي *shawa'*) The skin of the head. *Shiwāt*, A piece of roast meat.

P شوات *shawāt* or *shuwāt*, A bustard. A kind of water-fowl.

A شواجر *shawājir*, (pl. of شاجر *shājir*) Things which avert or prevent. Hardships of fortune. رماح شواجر *rimāh shawājir*, Intermingled spears.

A شواجن *shawājin*, (pl. of شاجنة *shājinat*) Roads through valleys.

A شواحي *shawāhī*, (pl. of شاحية *shāhiyat*) Gaping (horses).

P شواد *shawād* or *shuwād*, A bustard. *Shuwād*, Flame.

A شواذّ *shawāzz*, (pl. of شاذّ *shāzz*) Separate from the rest. Rare, uncommon, irregular.

P شوار *shawār* or *shuwār*, A bustard. A kind of water-fowl.

A شوار *shawār*, (v. n. of شار for شور) Riding (a horse) backwards and forwards by way of shewing him off to a buyer. Exercising, proving. Turning about (a horse or female slave). A gentle wind. A form, figure. A garment, apparel, dress, ornament. Beauty, elegance. Fatness. *Shawār*, *shiwār*, and *shuwār*, Household furniture. Apparatus for a journey. Pudendum virile et muliebre. Penis, testicles, and anus.

A شوارب *shawārib*, The channels whereby liquids pass into the stomach. Veins in the throat. (pl. of شارب *shārib*) Whiskers, mustachios. صخب الشوارب *sakhbu'sh shawārib*, Loud-braying (ass).

A شوارع *shawāriع*, (pl. of شارع *shāriع*) Highways: broadways, thoroughfares. (pl. of شارعة *shāriعat*) Levelled, pointed (spears). Setting (stars).

A شوارف *shawārif*, (pl. of شارفة *shārifat*) Old arrows. Old camels.

A شوارق *shawārik*, (pl. of شارقة) Splendours.

A شواريز *shawārīz*, (pl. of شيراز *shīrāz*) Oxygals strained and firm.

A شوازب *shawāzib*, (pl. of شازب *shāzib*) Lean (horses). Rough (roads).

A شواش *shawāsh*, Diversity, discord, dissension.

P شواش *shiwāsh*, Aniseed.

A شواصر *shawāsir*, (pl. of شاصرة) Nets, gins.

SY شواصرا *shawāsirā*, A kind of mugwort.

A شواصن *shawāsin*, (pl. of شاصونة *shāsūnat*) Earthen vessels.

A شواصي *shawāsī*, (pl. of شاصية *shāsiyat*) Distended leathern bottles.

A شواطب *shawātib*, (pl. of شاطبة *shātibat*) Women who cut leather into strips after having accurately measured it.

A شواطئ *shawātiء*, (pl. of شاطئ *shātiء* or شاطئة *shātiءat*) Sides of streams, banks of rivers.

A شواظ *shiwāz*, (v. n. 3 of شاظ for شوظ) Abusing one another, calling one another bad names. *Shiwāz* or *shuwāz*, Flame without smoke. Smoke of fire. Heat of fire, or of the sun. Excessive thirst. Exclamation, clamour.

A شواعل *shawāعil*, (pl. of شاعل *shāعil* and شاعلة *shāعilat*) Flaming, shining. Flames.

A شواعي *shawāعī*, (pl. of شاعي *shāعī*) Diffused, dispersed. جاءت الخيل شواعي *jāءati'l khayl shawāعī*, The horses came scattered, or straggling.

A شواغل *shawāghil*, (pl. of شاغلة *shāghilat*) Affairs which occupy much.

A شواقّ *shawākk*, Difficult, arduous affairs.

A شواقي *shawākī*, (pl. of شاقي) Lofty (mountains).

A شواكل *shawākil*, (pl. of شاكلة *shākilat*) Roads, ways branching off from a main road: by-lanes.

P شوال *shawāl*, Coarse loose trousers. Trade, craft, profession. A bustard. A kind of water-fowl.

A شوال *shiwāl*, (v. n. 3 of شال for شول) Elevating, lifting, raising. (pl. of شائل *shāʼil*) (Camels) milkless and in want of the male.

A شوّال *shawwāl*, (pl. شوّالات *shawwālāt* and شواويل *shawāwīl*) The tenth Muhammadan month.

A شوّالة *shawwālat*, Cock-tail (a nickname for a scorpion). Calumniating, whispering (woman).

P شوالك *shawālak*, A little bustard. A certain water-fowl with changing-coloured plumage.

A شوامت *shawāmit*, The feet of beasts.

A شوامخ *shawāmikh*, (pl. of شامخ) High mountains.

A شوامذ *shawāmiz*, Fructified (female palms).

A شوامس *shawāmis*, (pl. of شامس *shāmis*) Restive (horses), apt to throw their riders.

P شوان *shuwān*, A shepherd.

A شواني *shawānī*, Riches held with a loose hand (as though they were hated by their owner).

A شواويل *shawāwīl*, Months of Shawwāl.

A شواة *shiwāh*, (pl. of شاة) Sheep. Wild oxen.

A شواهد *shawāhid*, Witnesses, evidences.

A شواهق *shawāhik*, (pl. of شاهق *shāhik*) High mountains.

A شواهن *shawāhin*, (pl. of شاهين) Falcons.

A شواهي *shawāha'*, (pl. of شاة *shāt*) Sheep.

A شواهين *shawāhīn*, (pl. of شاهين) Falcons.

A شوايا *shawāya'*, (pl. of شويّة *shawīyat*) Remains of flocks or peoples.

A شوائب *shawāʼib*, (pl. of شائبة) Impurities.

A شواية *shi, sha*, or *shuwāyat*, Worst part or refuse. Remainder of a flock or of a people that has perished. A crust, biscuit. *Shuwāyat*, A bit of meat for roasting. A slice of roast meat. A small portion of a large quantity. An easy, light matter.

A شوائع *shawāʼiʻ*, (pl.) Scattered, diffused.

P شوائي *shawāʼī*, Deafness.

A شوب *shawb*, (v. n. of شاب for شوب) Mixing. Repelling, defending one's self moderately. Mixture, alloy. Juice of meat. Honey. A piece of cake or paste.

P شوب *shob*, A turband. A handkerchief, napkin. (from شستن *shustan*) Washing.

P شوبا *shawbā*, Gruel. Weavers' glue.

P شوبان *shobān*, A shepherd, pastor.

A شوبة *shawbat*, Deceit, fraud.

P شوبج *shūbaj*, A rolling-pin.

P شوبرگ *shūbarg*, New or made wine.

P شوبست *shobast*, (or شوپست *shopast*) An incantation, fascination. A cure.

A شوبق *shūbak*, A baker's rolling-pin.

A شؤبوب *shuʼbūb*, (pl. شابيب *shaʼābīb*) A plump of rain. The vehemence, sharpness, or severity of any thing. The intenseness of the solar heat. The sun's path. The first indications of beauty.

P شوپره *shav-para*, A bat.

A شوترة *shawtarat*, Large-buttocked (woman).

P شوتن *shūtan*, Name of a man.

A شوحط *shawhat*, A tree whence bows are made.

A شوحطة *shawhatat*, Long (mare).

P شوخ *shokh*, Cheerful, sprightly, mirthful, jovial, festive, joyous, brisk, spirited. Saucy, impertinent, petulant, insolent, bold, brazen, impudent, shameless. Whimsical, capricious, playful, mischievous. Ready (with an answer): pert. Beautiful, pleasing. A robber, highwayman. A hedgehog. Hands or feet hard from work or walking. A tree which, when one branch is lopped off, throws out several new ones. شوخ بستن *shokh bastan* (or گرفتن *giriftan*) To become hard, callous, thick, and rough from labour (the hand). *Shūkh*, Dirt, filth, impurity. Pus, matter.

P شوخ چشم *shokh-chashm*, Impudent, wanton.

P شوخ چشمي *shokh-chashmī*, Impudence.

P شوخ ديدگي *shokh-dīdagī*, Barefacedness.

P شوخ ديده *shokh-dīda*, Impudent, wanton.

A شوخط *shawkhat*, An ear of corn: bunch, cluster.

P شوخ رنگ *shokh-rang*, Of a bright colour.

P شوخ طبيعت *shokh-tabīʻat*, Naturally gay.

P شوخگن *shokhgin*, Hard, callous. *Shūkhgin*, (or شوخگين *shūkhgīn*) A running sore.

P شوخ گير *shūkh-gīr*, Sordid. A coal-rake.

P شوخگين *shokh-gīn*, Callous (hand or foot).

P شوخگيني *shokh-gīnī*, Hardness, callosity.

P شوخناك *shūkhnāk*, Sordid, nasty, filthy.

P شوخودن *shokhūdan*, To scratch. To assemble.

P شوخي *shokhī*, Jollity, mirth, petulance, impudence. *Shūkhī*, Filth, rust, rubbish.

P شوخيدن *shokhīdan*, To be jovial, cheerful. *Shūkhīdan*, To be rusty, filthy. To flatter. To vex, plague, disgust. To hide. To make haste.

P شود *shūd*, (for شد *shud*) Is, was, became, was made. A garment singed by fire. A little ant. *Shiwid*, Anise.

A شودانيق *shūdānīk*, A woodpecker.

A شودح *shawdah*, Long-bodied (she-camel).

P شودر *shūdar*, A plant like the citron.

A شودكان *shawdakān*, A hunter's net or toils. Arms (as sword, mace, and bow).

P شودن *shūdan*, To be, become. To go, depart. To die. To cease, fail. To carry off, remove. To obliterate, erase.

P شودي *shūdī*, Perfection, completion.

A شوذانق *shawzānak*, A kind of hawk.

A شوذب *shawzab*, Long, tall, and handsome. ذو الشوذب *zū'sh shawzab*, Name of a king.

A شوذح *shawzah*, A long she-camel stretched on the ground.

A شوذر *shawzar*, (from P چادر *chādar*) A veil reaching to the heels, which women put on when going out. A short shift or inner garment. A sleeveless shirt.

A شوذق *shawzak*, A bracelet.

A شوذقة *shawzakat*, (v. n. of شوذق Q) Taking hold of any thing with the fingers, like a bird of prey.

A شور *shawr*, (v. n. of شار for شور) Publishing, divulging. Taking (honey) from a hive. Becoming fat (a camel). Riding (a horse) backwards and forwards by way of shewing him to a buyer. Exercising, trying, proving, turning about (a horse or female slave). Form, figure. Beauty, elegance. Dress, ornament. Fatness. Honey gathered.

P شور *shor*, Salt, brackish. Salsuginous ground. Terror. Flight. Bad luck. Commotion, agitation. A tumult. Fluctuation (of water). Washing, cleaning. Calamity. Contention, litigation. Cry, noise, outcry. Unfortunate, unlucky. Labour, exertion. Dirty water. A brazen trumpet. Mixed, confounded. *Shawar*, (in zand and Pāzand) Full, satisfied.

A شورا *shūrā*, Agreement, convention. Mixture.

A شوراء *shuwarāʼ*, (pl. of شيّر *shayyir*) Counsellors, advisers, ministers.

P شورابه *shorāba*, Salt, brackish water.

A شوران *shaw* or *shūrān*, Saffron in the flower.

P شورانگيز *shor-angez*, Tumult-exciting.

P شورانگيزي *shor-angezī*, Sedition.

P شورانيدن *shorānīdan*, To cause to mix. To render muddy. To make mad. To give to wash.

P شوربا *shorbā*, Broth, soup, gruel. شورباي اشك *shorbāyi ashk*, Drink consisting of tears: the tears of the afflicted.

A شورباج *shūrabāj*, Soup.

P شوربخت *shor-bakht*, Unfortunate. Sordid.

P شوربوم *shor-būm*, Brackish, barren ground.

P شورپا *shor-pā*, A horse that cuts or knocks his knees together in travelling.

P شورپشت *shor-pusht*, Quarrelsome, noisy.

A شورة *shawrat*, Bashfulness. *Shūrat*, Form, figure. A bee-hive. Beauty, elegance. Clothing, dress, ornament. Fat (she-camel). Fatness. Within. Without. *Shūrat* or *shawrat*, A place where any thing is to be seen, a spectacle, a theatre.

A شورج *shawraj*, (from P شوره) A salt-marsh.

P شورچشم *shor-chashm*, Malignant-eyed.

P شورزمين *shor-zamīn*, Salt, barren land.

P شورستان *shoristān*, A marsh, salt-marsh.

P شورسلح *shor-silah*, A soldier ready armed for battle. The vanguard.

P شورش *shorish*, Confusion, mixture, tumult, rebellion, insurrection. Nausea, disgust. Salt-pits. Victuals over-salted.

P شورشار *shor-shār*, (شورشرّ *shor-sharr*, شور شرابا *shor-sharābā*, and شورشغب *shor-shaghab*) Noise, tumult, disturbance, bustle, clamour.

P شورگياه *shor-giyāh*, Salsuginous herbage.

P شورم *shoram*, A hill or mountain. Ink. A quince.

P شورمور *shor mōr*, Small ants.

P شوروا *shorwā*, (equiv. to شوربا *shorbā*) Broth.

P شوروغوغا *shor u ghawghā*, Tumult and riot.

P شورومور *shor u mor*, Weak, mean, vile, contemptible. Unlucky. Noise, tumult, confusion.

P شوره *shora*, Marshy, unfertile ground. A salt-marsh. Nitrous earth. Nitre, saltpetre. A bees' nest. Baldness. A horse-market. White leprosy. Flowing of water. Humidity. A sort of quince. *Shawra*, Shame, modesty.

P شوره زار *shorazār*, Salt, brackish (ground).

P شوره گر *shoragar*, A saltpetre-manufacturer.

P شوره گز *shora-gaz*, A kind of tamarisk.

P شوره ناك *shoranāk*, Brackish, salt (land).

A شوري *shawra'*, A certain marine plant. *Shūra'*, Counsel, consultation, deliberation, advice.

P شوريّت *shoriyat*, Salsuginousness.

P شوريدگي *shoridagī*, Confusion. Love. Madness.

P شوريدن *shoridan*, To be disturbed, perplexed, mixed, confounded. To grow mad, to play the fool. To wash.

P شوريده *shorida*, Disturbed. Mixed. Mad, frantic, desperately in love. Faint, dejected.

P شوريده بخت *shorida-bakht*, Unfortunate. Infamous.

P شوريده خاطر *shorida-khātir*, Dejected, sad.

P شوريده راه *shorida-rāh*, Heretical.

P شوريز *shawrīz* or *shorīz*, A field ready for receiving seed. A sower. Name of a drug.

A شوز *shawz*, A loving with ecstacy.

A شؤز *shuūz*, (v. n. of شئز) Being rugged, high, and hard. Being restless, unsteady, timid.

A شوزب *shawzab*, A mark, sign, impression.

A شؤزة *shuūzat*, (v. n. of شأز) Being hard and rocky (a place). Being unstable, unquiet, tottering.

A شوس *shaws*, A rubbing of the teeth; a chewing of any thing used as a dentifrice. *Shūs*, (pl. of اشوس *ashwas*) Persons looking through half-closed eyes. Bold men. Various, diversified. Dissentient. (pl. of شأس *shaas*) Stony or rocky places. *Shawas*, (v. n. of شوس) Contracting the eyelids to look more steadily; also through the outer angle from rage, pride, or contempt.

A شؤس *shuūs*, (pl. of شأس *shaas*) Rough, hard, gravelly (places).

A شوسلاء *shawsalāa*, (in Abyssinia) Venery.

P شوش *shawsh*, A branch cut from a vine. *Shūsh*, Name of a city in Khūzistān.

A شوش *shūsh*, Bold men. ابطال شوش شوش *abtāl shūsh shūsh*, Brave men disagree.

A شوشاء *shawshāa*, (or شوشاة *shawshāt*) A light swift camel.

A شوشب *shawshab*, A scorpion. An ant. A louse.

P شوشتر *shūshtar*, The capital of Khūzistān.

P شوشك *shūshak*, A violin with a large belly, long neck, and four strings. A sort of partridge.

P شوشمير *shūshmīr*, Cardamom.

P شوشو *shūshū*, Millet.

A شؤشؤ *shuashua*, A word used in calling an ass to drink, or in driving an ass or a flock of sheep. A word used in calling sheep to feed.

P شوشه *shūsha*, An ingot of gold or silver. Chips, rubbish, filth. A heap of sand. A grave-stone, a tablet. A particle, part. Gold or silver thread.

A شوص *shaws*, (v. n. of شاص for شوص) Erecting, fixing, planting. Washing, cleaning. Shifting, moving (a thing) from its place. Rubbing with the hand. Using the dentifrice سواك *siwāk*, rubbing the teeth up and down. Leaping in the womb (a fœtus). The toothache. The gripes. *Shawas*, (v. n. of شوص) Looking through one corner of the eye from pride or anger. A rubbing of the teeth.

A شوصاء *shawsāa*, An eye that appears to look out at the inner angle. A female who looks through the corner of her eye.

A شوصة *shawsat*, A puffiness of the skin above the ribs. A swelling inside the ribs. The gripes. A throbbing of an artery.

A شوصر *shawsar*, A young deer, strong and able to butt with his horns.

A شوصلة *shawsalat*, (v. n. of شوصل Q) Eating the herb شاصلّي *shāsulla'*.

A شوط *shawt*, (pl. اشواط *ashwāt*) One course or heat. A turn, a round. (pl. شياط *shiyāt*) A space between two hills, having a road for men and for water, the length whereof is about as far as a man's voice will reach. شوط باطل *shawti bātil*, Light through a hole in the wall, which appears to turn round. شوط براح *shawti barāh*, A jackal.

A شوع *shawa*, (v. n. of شوع) Being dishevelled (the hair). One born immediately after another. *Shūa*, The tamarisk tree or its fruit. A certain shrub growing on plains or mountains. (pl. of اشوع *ashwaa* and شوعاء *shawaāa*) (Men or women) whose hair is hard, coarse, and dishevelled. *Shawaa*, (v. n. of شوع) Being dishevelled, coarse, and hard (the hair). Whiteness on one of a horse's cheeks.

A شوعاء *shawaāa*, (A woman) whose hair is dishevelled, harsh, and coarse.

P شوغ *shogh*, Callousness of the hands and feet. Filth on the body or garments. Impudent, shameless.

P شوغا *shav-ghā*, A fold, pen, stable for cattle.

P شوغار *shavghār*, (or شوغاره *shav-ghāra*) A fold for cattle. *Shūghār*, Alum.

P شوغاه *shav-ghāh*, (originally شبگاه *shab-gāh*) A fold for cattle.

A شوغر *shawghar*, Strong-built, firm, hale.

A شوغرة *shawgharat*, A basket of palm-leaves.

P شوغه *shogha*, Blisters rising from hard work.

A شوف *shawf*, (v. n. of شاف for شوف) Polishing, furbishing. Anointing with pitch (a camel). Adorning (a woman). Seeing. A harrow; an implement of wood or stone for levelling ploughed ground.

A شوق *shawk*, (v. n. of شاق for شوق) Filling with desire. Exciting, inflaming one (desire, love). Rearing (a leathern bottle) against a wall. Tying a rope (to a stake). (pl. اشواق *ashwāk*) Love, desire, propension, affection, inclination. Zeal, eagerness. Alacrity, gaiety, cheerfulness. *Shūk*, (pl. of اشوق *ashwak*) Lovers. Affectionately inclined.

A شوقب *shawkab*, A tall man. A large hoof. Two timbers of a camel's saddle to which the ropes are fastened.

P شوق درست *shawk durust*, Sincere desire.

A شوق ذوق *shawkzawk*, Pleasure, gratification.

A شوقلة *shawkalat*, (v. n. of شوقل Q) Being modest, mild, gentle, grave, sedate.

A شوقيّ *shawkīy*, Loving, cheerful.

A شوقية *shawkiya*, The part of an epistle which follows the complimental address.

A شوك *shawk*, (v. n. of شاك for شوك) Wounding. Pricking as a thorn; piercing any thing with a thorn; walking over or falling amongst thorns; being pricked. Being thorny (a plant or land). Growing out (the side-teeth of a camel). Being covered with a panoply. Being intrepid in battle: appearing, being displayed (bravery). Pointing or swelling (the breasts of a girl). Armed. (pl. اشواك *ashwāk*) A thistle, thorn, prickly shrub, sting. جاء في الشوك و الشجر *jāa fi'sh shawk wa'sh shajar*, He came with an immense number. شوك مبارك *shawki mubārak*, Carduus benedictus. شجرة شوكة *shajratun shawkatun*, A thorny tree. *Shawik*, Thorny. Armed with pointed weapons. Clad in armour.

P شوك *shūk*, (in zand and Pāz.) A market-place.

A شوكاء *shawkāa*, Rough (new garment).

P شوكار *shav-kār*, (for شبكار) A night-robber.

A شوكة *shawkat*, One thorn; a sting (of a scorpion); a thorny plant. Bravery in war. The brunt of the battle-field. Slaughter of the enemy. Thorny (ground or tree). Arms and their edges. A wound. Hostile malevolence. A weaver's instrument, used for making the surface of the texture even. A certain disease and redness overspreading the body. Majesty, power, grandeur, magnificence, dignity, pomp, pride. شوكة البعير *shawkatu'l baīr*, A thistle. شوكة البيضا *shawkatu'l bayzā*, A prickly kind of shrub. شوكة الكتّان *shawkatu'l kattān*, A lump of soft clay stuck full of palm-tree prickles, and, when dried, used for clearing flax of the combings. P شوكت شاهانه *shawkati shāhāna*, Imperial majesty. شوكت مقرون *shawkat-makrūn*, Imperial, royal, glorious.

A شوكهة *shawkahat*, (pl. شوكه *shawkah*) A large door containing a smaller one within it.

P شوكران *shavkarān*, Fennel, hellebore.

P شوكك *shokak*, (or شوكل) Whirl of a spindle.

A شوكل *shawkal*, Infantry, the right and left wing. A kind of bramble. A side, quarter.

P شوكه *shūka*, A mould in which ingots are cast.

P شوگ *shūg*, Hemlock.

P شوگا *shav-gā*, (or شوگاه *shav-gāh*) (for شب گاه *shab-gāh*) A fold for cattle. Evening.

P شوگون *shūgūn*, A good omen.

A شول *shawl*, (v. n. of شال for شول) Eleva-

P شوي *shūy*, A husband. Washing. A washer. Starch, paste, size. جامه شوي *jāma-shūy*, A washer of clothes. *Shavī*, A shirt, shift. *Shiwī*, Anise. A small vestibule.

A شوي *shawa'*, Any thing light and easy. The worst part of cattle or any thing. Hands, feet, or extremities. The pericranium. The skull, cranium. A part of the body which, being wounded, proves not mortal. (pl. of شواة *shawāt*) Skins of heads. (pl. of شاة *shāt* and شاء *shāꜫ*) Sheep. Wild oxen.

A شويّ *shawīy*, Roasted (meat). A stammerer. *Shuwayy*, (dim. of شيء *shayꜫ*) A small matter.

P شويانيدن *shūyānīdan*, To cause to wash.

A شويّة *shawīyat*, (pl. شوايا *shawāya'*) The remainder of a flock or nation which has perished.

P شويت *shiwīt*, (or شويد *shiwīd*) Anise.

A شويثيّ *shuwaysīy*, A species of date.

A شويخ *shuwaykh*, (dim. of شيخ *shaykh*) A little doctor, or a little old man.

P شوي ديده *shūy-dīda*, A married woman. A widow (one who has seen a husband).

P شويست *shawīst*, Dispersion, distraction.

A شويعر *shuwayꜫir*, A petty poet, poetaster.

A شويكة *shuwaykat*, A little thorn. A kind of camel. شويكهٔ ابراهيم *shuwaykaꜫi ibrāhīm*, Eryngium, sea-holly.

P شويلا *shuwīlā*, Artemisia. A quince.

A شويلاء *shuwaylāꜫ*, Name of a medicinal herb.

P شويله *shuwīla*, A dunghill.

P شوي مال *shūy-māl*, One who starches cloths in the loom. A machine for glazing clothes.

P شويندگي *shūyandagī*, Washing. شويندگي كردن *shūyandagī kardan*, To wash. To baptize.

P شويه *shūya*, A wash, cosmetic lotion.

A شويهة *shuwayhat*, (dim. of شاة *shāt* for شاهة *shāhat*) A small sheep.

P شوييدن *shūyīdan*, To wash.

P شه *shah*, A king, sovereign prince. Check (at chess). A bridegroom. A prohibition. Full, satiated. (in comp.) Great, large, noble: as, شه زور *shah-zor*, Stout, gallant, strong, brave, heroic. شه سوار *shah-suwār*, A good rider. A jockey, horse-breaker. شه حجله *shahi hajla*, The sun. شه خاور *shahi khāwar*, The sun. شه نيمروز *shahi nīm roz*, Adam. Muhammad. Rustam. The heart. The sun. *Shuh*, Execration, reproaching with extended finger, spitting while rejecting with disdain, abhorring.

P شها *shahā*, O king! Suitable, proper.

P شهاب *shahāb*, Red juice from the flower of the plant هاجيره *hājira*.

A شهاب *shahāb*, Milk diluted with water. *Shihāb*, (pl. شهب *shuhub*, شهبان *shuhbān*, *shihbān*, and اشهب *ash-hub*) A bright star. The nocturnal fires, commonly called falling stars. A flame. A flaming fire. Prompt, active, expeditious in business. شهاب ثاقب *shihābi sākib*, A bright flame.

A شهابة *shuhābat*, Milk, two-thirds water.

P شومن *shūman* or *shūmin*, (in zand) Forelocks.

A شؤمي *shuꜫma'*, The left hand or side.

A شوميّة *shūmiyat*, Stinginess, niggardliness.

P شوميز *shawmīz*, A farmer. *Shūmīz*, A field ploughed and ready for sowing. شوميز كردن *shūmīz kardan*, To plough.

P شوميزيدن *shūmīzīdan*, To till the ground.

P شومين *shūmīn*, Spinage.

P شومي نفس *shūmīꜫi nafs*, Badness of temper.

P شون *shūn*, Gores of shifts.

A شؤون *shuꜫun*, (pl. of شأن *shaꜫn*) Lachrymal ducts. Meetings of the sutures of the cranium. شؤونك زفرة *shuꜫunuka zaꜫirat*, In your tears is the breathing of one in anger.

A شونة *shawnat*, A foolish woman. (pl. شواني *shawānī*) An armed ship, corsair, pirate. A granary.

P شوند *shawand*, (pl. شوندان *shawandān*) Cause, reason, motive.

P شوندا *shawandā*, A hearer, listener.

P شوندر *shawandar*, Beet-root; a carrot.

P شونده *shavanda*, Existing, what exists.

P شونست *shūnist*, Incantation. Remedy, cure.

P شونك *shawnik*, A horse with white legs and a black tail.

A شؤنوز *shuꜫnūz*, Coriander-seed.

P شونيج *shūnīj*, Ground prepared for sowing.

P شونيز *shūnīz*, Sesame. Coriander; pepper. Land prepared for sowing. A farmer, an agriculturist.

A شونيز *shūnīz*, Coriander-seed.

A شونيزيّة *shūnīzīyat*, The burial-place of pious men (صلحاء *sulahāꜫ*) in Baghdad.

P شونيزيه *shawnīzya*, Name of a mosque.

A شؤون *shuꜫūn*, (pl. of شأن *shaꜫn*) Affairs, things. Conditions. Veins of soil in a mountain where palms and other trees are planted.

A شوه *shawh*, (v. n. of شاه for شوه) Being ugly (the countenance). Terrifying. Hurting with an evil eye. Envying, hating. Coveting. *Shawah*, (v. n. of شاه for شوه) Being ugly (the face). Length, also shortness of neck.

P شوه *shawa*, Cause, motive, subject, matter. *Shawuh*, Agate, jet, black coral.

A شوهاء *shawhāꜫ*, (fem. of اشوه *ashwah*) Ugly-faced. Wide-mouthed, also small-mouthed (mare). Handsome and long-bodied (mare). Beautiful. Unfortunate.

A شوهب *shawhab*, An urchin, a male hedgehog.

A شوهة *shawhat*, (v. n. of شاه for شوه) Being ugly. Terrifying. Hurting with a malignant eye. Envying, hating. Coveting. *Shūhat*, Distance.

P شوهر *shawhar*, A husband.

P شوهردار *shawhar-dār*, A married woman.

P شوهره *shohira*, Ploughed land. A vine-arbour.

P شوهن *shūhan*, Sesame.

P شوهير *shawhīr*, Beholding, observation.

P شوهين *shūhīn*, Spinage.

P شوهيه *shūhīh*, Ground prepared for sowing.

ting, raising, lifting (a stone or water-pot, or a camel her tail). Being cocked (the tail). Rising (as the scales of a balance). Departing (a tribe), and leaving the place of their abode empty. Being discordant, disagreeing (words or opinions). Declining, departing, waning (greatness and power). A she-camel. A small quantity of water. Light of weight. شالت نعامته *shālat naꜫāmatuhu*, He became light, his anger subsided. He died. (pl. اشوال *ashwāl*) Remains of water in a bottle or bucket. A little wealth. Light, active (man). (pl. of شائلة *shāꜫilat*) Camels seven or eight months from the birth, whose udders are shrivelled for want of milk. *Shawil*, Serviceable, active in attendance.

P شول *shol*, Seeing, knowing. Name of a race.

A شوّل *shūwal*, (pl. of شائل *shāꜫil*) Milkless (camels) wanting the male.

P شولان *shawlān*, A halter, noose, rope.

A شولان *shawalān*, (v. n. of شال for شول) Raising, cocking her tail (a camel). Being cocked (tail).

A شولة *shawlat*, The tail of a scorpion, or the cocked up part of it. Two stars which mark the 19th mansion of the moon. A prating woman. Name of a certain foolish woman whose advice always proved disastrous to those who followed it; hence the proverb, انت شولة الناصحة *anti shawlatu'n nāsihat*, Thou art counsellor Shawlat. *Shawilat*, A nickname for a scorpion (cock-tail).

A شولقيّ *shawlaqīy*, One fond of sweets.

P شولك *shawlak*, A bird that often changes colour. *Sholah*, A swift horse. The horse of Isfandiyār. A whirl on the top of a spindle.

A شولم *shawlam*, Tares.

P شولمن *sholman*, (in zand and Pāzand) Hell.

P شوله *shawla*, A dunghill, place for rubbish. A place for drying dung for fuel in baths. A single fold of cloth. A meteor. Name of a lunar mansion.

P شولي *shūlī*, Name of a dialect of the Persian.

P شوليدن *sholīdan*, To be distracted; to be undetermined, to have a thousand thoughts.

P شوليده *sholīda*, Distracted. A ruined house. A stable.

A شؤم *shuꜫm*, (v. n. of شأم) Being ominous. Unfortunate. Ill luck. Hopeless. Black (camels).

A شوم *shūm*, Blacks. A miser, niggard. Unlucky.

P شومارمند *shūmārmand*, (in zand) Weeping.

P شومال *shū-māl*, Again. A machine for glazing clothes.

A شومة *shūmat*, Pride, haughtiness; covetousness.

P شومخ *shawmakh*, *shawmikh*, *shawmukh*, or *shūmikh*, Balm-gentle, citrago, parsley.

P شومز *shūmiz*, A field prepared for sowing.

P شومستان *shūmistān*, A fort in Turkistān.

A شوم طبع *shūm-tabꜫ*, Ill-tempered.

A شوم قدم *shūm-hadam*, Unlucky foot, bad omen.

A شومل *shawmal*, The north.

A شوم مزاج *shūm-mizāj*, Stingy.

A شهاجر *shahājir*, A sort of carrion-eating bird.

A شهاد *shahād*, Evidences, witnesses. *Shihād*, (pl. of شهد *shahd* and *shuhd*) Honey-combs.

A شهادة *shahādat*, (v. n. of شهد) Testifying, bearing witness to. Being present. Swearing. Obtaining knowledge of, knowing for a certainty. Evidence. True knowledge, certainty. Presence. Martyrdom. A testimony, attestation, witnessing, making a confession of faith: as, لا اله الا الله و محمد رسول الله *lā ilāha illa'llāh, wa muhammad rasū-lu'llāh*, There is no god but God, and Muhammad is the apostle of God. P شهادت كردن *shahādat kardan*, To give evidence, bear witness. شهادت سربسته *shahādati sar-basta*, Indubitable evidence. A عالم شهادت *ʿālami shahādat*, The visible world.

A شهار *shihār*, (v. n. 3 of شهر) Agreeing for, or giving monthly, bargaining by the month.

A شهاق *shuhāk*, (v. n. of شهق) Making a murmuring noise in the throat, as an ass before braying. Sighing, groaning, drawing the last breath.

A شهام *shahām*, A witch, hag. *Shihām*, (pl. of شهم *shahm*) Active, bold. Quick, clever, witty.

A شهامة *shahāmat*, (v. n. of شهم) Being ingenious. Being bold, courageous. Being fleet and strong (a horse). Generosity, nobleness of mind. Bravery, dauntless courage. Ingenuity, quickness of parts. Agility, swiftness.

P شهامت انديش *shahāmat-andesh*, Noble-minded, generous.

P شهانه *shahāna*, Royal. Royally, kingly.

A شهاوي *shahāwa'*, (pl. of شهوان *shahwān*, شهوي *shahwa'*, and شهواني *shahwāniy*) Greedy, eager.

A شهب *shahb*, (v. n. of شهب) Changing a person's complexion (heat or cold). Distressing cattle (a severe season). A snow-capped mountain. *Shuhb*, White predominating over black. *Shahab*, (v. n. of شهب) Being of the colour of ashes; of a mixed colour, where white predominates. A blackish colour. *Shuhub*, (pl. of شهاب *shihāb*) Flaming fires. Bright sparkling stars. Three nights of the month.

P شهبا *shahbā*, A mule of an ash-colour, inclining to black. A stubborn, biting, kicking mule.

A شهباء *shahbāʾ*, Ash-coloured (goat), verging to white. Clear and cold (night). Bright with arms (squadron). Barren (season), destitute of verdure. (A mare) in whose forelocks are hairs of different colours.

P شهباز *shah-bāz*, The noblest species of falcon. A noble, generous man. A brave soldier. An excellent youth. شهباز بلند پرواز *shah-bāzi baland-parwāz*, A high-soaring falcon.

P شهبال *shah-bāl*, Longest feather in the wing.

P شه بالا *shah-bālā*, (or شه باله *shah-bāla*) The friend of the bridegroom.

A شهبان *shuhbān* or *shihbān*, (pl. of شهاب *shihāb*) Flaming fires. *Shahabān*, A certain tree.

A شهبة *shuhbat*, An inclination more to white than black, a blackish white.

P شهبد *shahbad*, The leader of an army.

A شهبر *shahbar*, Broad, large, and thick.

A شهبرة *shahbarat*, (v. n. of شهبر Q) Being ash-coloured. Being about to weep (on account of something). An old woman with remains of strength.

P شهبري *shahbari*, Amber.

P شهبلوط *shah-balūt*, A chesnut.

P شهبندر *shah-bandar*, A custom-house. A free port. The chief custom-house officer. Head of the merchants.

P شهبيت *shah-bayt*, The last distich of the ghazal or Eastern ode; also of an epigram. شهبيت دعاى شاه *shah-bayti duʿā-i shāh*, The conclusion of the prayer for the king.

P شهپر *shah-par*, The longest feather in a wing.

P شه تار *shah-tār*, The thickest string of a lute.

A شهترج *shahtaraj*, (P شاهتره) Fumitory.

P شهتوت *shah-tūt*, A blackberry. A mulberry.

P شه جان *shah-jān*, The city of مرو *marv*.

A شهجبة *shahjabat*, A mixture, confusion, and perplexity of business.

P شهچال *shah-chāl*, A term used at chess when the king only can move.

A شهد *shahd*, (pl. شهاد *shihād*) Honey. A honey-comb. (pl. of شاهد *shāhid*) Evidences, eye-witnesses. P شهد آميز *shahd-āmez*, Sweet as honey. كلام شهد آميز *kalāmi shahd-āmez*, Words mixed with honey, eloquence. A شهد فائق *shahdi fāʾik*, Pure honey. *Shuhd*, Honey. A honey-comb. *Shahad*, (v. n. of شهد) Being present, witnessing.

A شهد *shuhhad*, (pl. of شاهد *shāhid*) Witnesses.

A شهدا *shahdan*, Before one's face.

A شهداء *shuhadāʾ*, (pl. of شهيد *shahīd*) Witnesses. Martyrs. تأريخ الشهداء *taʾrīkhu'sh shuhadāʾ*, The æra of the martyrs, *i.e.* The persecutions of Dioclesian.

P شهدآب *shahd-āb*, (or شهدابه) Hydromel.

A شهدارة *shihdārat*, Wicked, obscene, flagitious. A sower of discord, a whisperer, breedbate. Short and thick-bodied.

P شهدان *shahdān*, Name of a place, or mountain.

A شهدانج *shahdānaj*, Hemp-seed.

P شهدانه *shah-dāna*, Hemp-seed. A large pearl. The largest bead or grain in a rosary. Mastic.

A شهدة *shahdat*, The choicest honey.

A شهدر *shahdar*, A boy (especially from three to six years old). Wealthy, abounding in good things.

A شهدرة *shahdarat*, (v. n. of شهدر Q) Stirring about (a boy or girl between the age of three or six).

P شهدك *shahdak*, Pleasures sweet as honey.

P شه دو پاس *shahi du pās*, Lord of two watches, namely, Muhammad. The sun. Adam. The heart.

P شهديوار *shah-dīwār*, A high wall surrounding a palace: a royal wall.

A شهذارة *shihzārat*, Wicked, flagitious. A whisperer, a breedbate. Short and thick-bodied. One who travels in pain.

P شهر *shahr*, A city, a town.

A شهر *shahr*, (v. n. of شهر) Publishing abroad, blazoning forth. Drawing a sword and brandishing it over people's heads. The moon, the new moon. Nail-parings. (pl. اشهر *ash-hur* and شهور *shuhūr*) A month (especially lunar). Learned. P شهر خدا *shahri khudā*, The month of God, *i. e.* Rajab.

P شهر آراي *shahr-ārāy*, One whose office is to decorate a city on public and festive occasions.

P شهر آزاديه *shahr-āzādiya*, Name of a city.

P شهر آشوب *shahr-āshob*, A disturber of (the tranquillity of) the city, a mistress. A kind of verse.

P شهراه *shah-rāh*, The king's highway.

A شهرب *shahrab*, An old man. A little trench round a palm-tree.

P شهرباز *shahr-bāz*, The river Oxus.

P شهرباش *shahr-bāsh*, A citizen, townsman.

A شهربة *shahrabat*, An old woman.

P شهر بشهر *shahr ba shahr*, City by city.

P شهربند *shahr-band*, City-walls. A prison.

P شهر پناه *shahr-panāh*, Walls, fortifications, defences, or entrenchments round a town.

A شهرة *shuhrat*, (v. n. of شهر) Publishing. Being published. Renown, fame, reputation. A divulging, celebrating, or rendering illustrious. Rumour, report. Publicity, (scandalous) notoriety. A title of respect. شهرۀ آفاق *shuhra-i āfāk*, (or شهرۀ عالم *shuhra-i ʿālam*) Celebrated all over the world. P شهرۀ دروغ *shuhra-i durogh*, A false report. شهرۀ شهر شد *shuhra-i shahr shud*, It is spread over the city, it is town-talk. شهرت يافته شده *shuhrat-yāfta-shuda*, Become renowned, celebrated.

P شهرت گزين *shuhrat-guzīn*, Seeking fame.

P شهرخا *shah-rukhā*, A term used at chess.

P شهردار *shahr-dār*, A hunter, bird-catcher.

P شهر روا *shahr-ravā*, Current coin.

P شهرزور *shahr-zor*, A city near Babylon.

P شهرستان *shahristān*, A large fortified city.

P شهرسبز *shahr-sabz*, A city near Samarkand.

P شهرغريب *shahr-gharīb*, A stranger, traveller.

P شهرگ *shah-rag*, The great vein in the arm.

P شهرمند *shahrmand*, Covetous, full of desire.

P شهرناز *shahr-nāz*, The sister of Jamshed.

P شهروا *shah-ravā*, Name of a certain despotic monarch, who forced leathern money to pass current in his kingdom.

P شهرود *shah-rūd*, A mighty river. Name of a river; also of a city. The thickest cord of a musical instrument. Name of a musical instrument.

P شهروز *shah-rūz*, A great river.

P شهروزه *shuh-roza*, One who begs his bread.

P شهره *shah-rah*, A royal road, main road.

P شهره بند *shuhra-band*, Attentive only to the surface of things, shallow. Famous, well-known.

P شهري *shahri*, A citizen. شهرو شهري *shahr u shahri*, City and citizens.

P شهريار *shahr-yār*, (Friend of the city) A potent monarch, emperor, king. شهريار هفت اقليم *shahr-yāri haft iklīm*, Sovereign of the seven climates, *i.e.* The sun.

P شهرياري *shahr-yārī*, Imperial, royal, princely. Regal dignity. An empire, kingdom.

A شهريّة *shihrīyat*, Pack-horse, beast of burden.

P شهريده *shahrīda*, Disturbed, troubled, confused. Widened, flattened.

P شهرير *shahrīr*, Name of the eighth Persian month (August). The fourth day of every month, according to the æra of Jalālī'ddīn. Name of a presiding angel.

P شهريورگان *shahrīwargān*, Name of the fourth day of the month.

P شهزادگان *shah-zādagān*, (pl. of شهزاده *shahzāda*) Kings' sons, princes.

P شهزاده *shah-zāda*, A king's son, a prince. A great-nephew.

A شهزيز *shihzīz* or *shuhzīz*, A species of date.

P شهسوار *shah-suwār*, A brave cavalier, intrepid hero, valiant champion. شهسوار دشت ارزن *shah-suwāri dashti arzan*, Muhammad. شهسوار فلك *shah-suwāri falak*, The sun. شهسوار مضمار مغازي *shah-suwāri mizmāri maghāzī*, The champions and heroes of the field of battle. طبقهٔ شهسواران *tabakaʼi shah-suwārān*, The equestrian order.

A شهق *shahk*, (v. n. of شهق) Lighting upon any one (a malignant glance).

A شهقة *shahkat*, A murmuring in the throat, such as an ass makes when beginning to bray.

P شهكار *shahkār*, Sown land. Deceit, wiliness.

A شهل *shahl*, A lie. *Shahal*, (v. n. of شهل) Being of a darkish-grey colour with a shade of red (the eye). Dark grey (in the eyes) with a shade of red.

P شهلا *shahlā*, A black eye inclined to red, and having a sly, deceitful, sinister look.

A شهلاء *shahlāʼ*, Dark-grey eyed (woman). Dark-grey (eye). Any thing necessary to be done, need, necessity.

P شهلان *shahlān*, Name of a mountain and place.

A شهلة *shahlat*, (v. n. of شهل) Being of a dark-grey colour (eyes) with a shade of red (like those of a sheep). An old woman. A middle-aged and intelligent woman. *Shuhlat*, A darkish colour of the eye with a shade of red.

P شهلنگ *shahlang*, A rope-maker.

P شهله *shahla*, A bat. Very fat meat.

P شهليده *shahlīda*, Disturbed, troubled, confused. Pressed, flattened, widened.

A شهم *shahm*, (v. n. of شهم) Frightening. Calling to (a horse). Nimble, active, swift. Bold, audacious. A stone intended to act as a trap-door, placed at the entrance of a snare set for lions. (pl. شهوم *shuhūm*) Of great authority (a chief). A fleet, powerful horse. (pl. شهام *shihām*) Acute, quick, clever, witty.

P شهمات *shah-māt*, Check-mate.

A شهملة *shahmalat*, An old woman.

P شهناز *shah-nāz*, Name of a note in music.

P شهناي *shah-nāy*, A clarion, hautbois.

P شهند *shahand*, Health, welfare.

P شهنشاه *shahanshāh*, (or شهنشه *shahanshah*) King of kings, as پادشاه *pādshāh* and شاهنشاه *shāhanshāh*. شهنشاه فلك *shahanshāhi falak*, The sun.

P شهنشاهي *shahanshāhī*, Regal, monarchical.

P شهنشين *shah-nishīn*, A royal seat. A palace. A gallery, balcony.

P شه نگار *shah-nigār*, Deception, imposition.

P شهنگانه *shahangāna*, Dew. Hail.

A شهنيز *shihnīz*, Coriander-seed.

A شهوات *shahwāt* or *shahawāt*, (pl. of شهوة *shahwat*) Desires. شهوات نفسانيه *shahwāti nafsānīya*, Carnal appetites, lusts.

P شهوار *shahwār*, The most precious pearl. Befitting a king. The most excellent thing of its kind. Royal, imperial.

A شهوان *shahwān*, (or شهوانيّ *shahwānīy*) (pl. شهاوي *shahāwa'*) Desirous, greedy, sensual.

A شهوانيّة *shahwānīyat*, Lustful (woman).

A شهوة *shahwat*, (v. n. of شها for شهو) Wishing, desiring. Lusting for, hankering after. Desire, appetite, lust, lasciviousness, wantonness.

P شهوت انگيز *shahwat-angez*, Lust-exciting.

P شهوت پرست *shahwat-parast*, Slave to lust.

P شهوت مند *shahwatmand*, Lustful.

A شهود *shuhūd*, (v. n. of شهد) Being present, being an eye-witness. (pl. of شهد *shahd* and شاهد *shāhid*) Witnesses, evidences, present at the fact. Evidences of parturition, as blood, the secundine, &c. اهل شهود *ahli shuhūd*, Eye-witnesses, those who were present or assisting in any thing. Alive.

A شهور *shuhūr*, (pl. of شهر *shahr*) Months. شهور معلومات *shuhūri maʻlūmāt*, The four known or sacred months amongst the Muhammadans; viz. محرّم *muharram*, The first; رجب *rajab*, The seventh; ذو القعدة *zū'l kaʻdat*, The eleventh; and ذو الحجّة *zū'l hijjat*, The twelfth. Some, however, substitute شوّال *shawwāl*, The tenth month, for رجب *rajab*, because upon the first of that month begins the great carnival, called عيد الفطر *ʻīdu'l fitr* (Feast of breaking the fast), which immediately succeeds their Lent.

A يوم شهورة *yawmi shahwarata*, A high day observed by the tribe of بني كنانة *banī kinānat*.

A شهوق *shuhūk*, A being high, raised up.

A شهوم *shuhūm*, (v. n. of شهم) Frightening. Calling to a horse. (pl. of شهم *shahm*) Chiefs of great authority.

A شهوي *shahwa'*, (pl. شهاوي *shahāwa'*) Desirous, greedy, sensual (woman).

P شهه *shiha*, The neighing of a horse.

P شهي *shahī*, Royal. Royalty. The relationship of a son-in-law. Happy, cheerful. A kind of sweetmeat.

A شهيّ *shahīy*, Wishful, desirous. Lascivious. Desirable, delicious. اطعمهٔ شهيّه *atʻimaʼi shahīya*, Exquisite viands.

A شهيد *shahīd* or *shihīd*, (pl. شهداء *shuhadāʼ*) A witness. Faithful in testimony. Privy to every thing. A martyr. P شهيد شدن *shahīd shudan*, To be a martyr. شهيد كردن *shahīd kardan*, To martyr.

A شهيده *shahīda*, A kind of thick pottage made of bruised wheat boiled to a consistency; to which they add meat, butter, cinnamon, and aromatic herbs.

P شهيدي *shahīdī*, A whoremonger.

A شهير *shahīr*, Celebrated, famous, notorious, well-known. P شهر شهير *shahri shahīr*, A famous city.

A شهيرة *shahīrat*, Broad (woman or she-ass).

A شهيق *shahīk*, (v. n. of شهق) Making a murmuring noise in the throat, as an ass before braying. Sighing, sobbing, groaning, drawing the last breath. The last bray or drawing in of the voice of an ass (the first or sending out being زحير *zahīr*).

A شهيم *shahīm*, Prudent, ingenious.

P شهين *shahīn*, Name of a city.

P شي *shī*, A corner.

A شي *shayy*, (v. n. of شوي) Roasting (meat). Heating (water). *Shayy* or *shīy*, Stammering.

A شيء *shayʼ*, (v. n. of شيئ) Wishing, willing, desiring. (pl. اشياء *ashyāʼ*, اشياوات *ashyāwāt*, اشاوات *ashāwāt*, اشاوي *ashāwa'*, اشايا *ashāya'*, اشيايا *ashyāya'*, and اشاوه *ashāwih*) A thing, any thing, something, somewhat. (in algebra) A square number. An unknown quantity. شيء الله *shayʼu'llāh*, It is the thing or will of God; God willing, a form of salutation, especially among the dervishes. شيء محقّر *shayʼi muhakkar*, A small matter, a trifling thing. لا شي *lā shay*, Nothing. عن لا شي *ʻan lā shay*, In vain. كالشيء الذي *kash'shayʼallazī*, At that rate, according to the proportion, as that which. يا شيء *yā shayʼa*, An exclamation of astonishment.

A شياب *shiyāb*, A mixture. Water mixed with any thing.

P شيابي *shiyābī*, A dram-weight. A loan.

A شياة *shiʼat*, Will.

A شيات *shiyāt*, (pl. of شية *shiyat*) Marks.

A شياح *shiyāh*, (v. n. of شاح for شيح) Being diligent, striving (in business). Fighting. Being cautious, abstinent. Dearth, scarcity. Prudence, caution, fear. Pains, diligence.

A شياد *shiyād*, (v. n. of شاد for شيد) Calling out to. Rubbing the skin with fragrant unguent.

P شيار *shiyār* also *shayār*, Ploughed ground. Sowing. شيار كردن *shiyār kardan*, To plough.

A شيار *shiyār*, (v. n. of شار for شور) Exercising (a horse): riding him backwards and forwards by way of shewing him off to a buyer. Examining (a female slave offered for sale). Beauty, elegance. Dress, ornament. Form, figure. Fatness. (pl.

اشير *ashyur,* شير *shuyur,* and *shīr*) Saturday. Fat (camels), in good case. *Shiyār,*(or شيارة *shiyārat*) (v. n. of شار for شور) Taking (honey) from a hive.

P شياريدن *shiyāridan,* To plough. To prepare the ground for sowing. To sow. To behold.

A شياص *shiyāṣ,* Malignity of nature.

A شياط *shiyāṭ,* The smell of burnt cotton or wool. (pl. of شوط *shawṭ*) Spaces between hills wide enough to admit the passage of men and of a rivulet, and about as long as a man's voice will reach.

A شياطة *shiyāṭat,* (v. n. of شاط for شيط) Being burnt. Being absorbed in cooking (butter or oil). Perishing (a man). Having the burnt part of victuals sticking to it (a pot). Being distributed entirely (a slaughtered camel). Mixing blood, *i. e.* killing a homicide in the act of murder. Going away with impunity after shedding blood. Making haste in any work.

A شياطين *shayāṭīn,* (pl. of شيطان *shayṭān*) Devils. شياطين الفلا *shayāṭīnu'l falā',* Thirst (devils of the desert). رؤوس الشياطين *ru·ūsu'sh shayāṭīn,* (Devils' heads) Name of a plant.

A شياظمة *shayāẓimat,* (pl. of شيظمي *shayẓamīy*) Long, tall, robust (men, horses, camels).

A شياع *shiyāʿ,* (v. n. 3 of شاع for شيع) Following (another), keeping close or adhering (to one). Assisting. Calling camels which lag behind. A shepherd's pipe. Callers; or callers out to cattle that lag behind. The sound of a shepherd's pipe. *Shiyāʿ* or *shayāʿ,* Chips, firewood.

A شياف *shiyāf,* A fine collyrium or medicament for the eye.

A شياق *shiyāk,* The tying of a rope (to a post). That whereby any thing is stretched in order to be tied to another.

A شيام *shayām,* Soft, level ground. *Shi* or *shayām,* Earth, soil. *Shiyām,* (pl. شيم *shīm*) A mouse.

A شئان *shay·ān,* Long-sighted. *Shi·ān,* (pl. of شأن *sha·n*) Things, affairs, businesses. Conditions.

P شيان *shiyān,* Dragon's blood. *Shiyān* or *shayān,* A recompense, good or evil.

P شياني *shiyānī,* Name of an ancient coin.

A شياة *shiyāh,* (pl. of شاة *shāt*) Sheep.

A شياهم *shayāhim,* (pl. of شيهم *shayham*) Porcupines. Soldiers.

A شيب *shayb,* White hairs, hoariness. شيب شائب *shayb shā·ib,* Extreme hoariness. *Shīb,* (pl. of اشيب *ashyab*) White or grey-haired. Snowy mountains. Sound made by camels' lips when drinking. The thong of a whip. *Shuyub,* Grey-haired men.

P شيب *shīb* or *sheb,* A descent, declivity. The lower part, base, foundation. The anus. The end of a whip-lash. Under, below. Wet ground made uneven and rugged by the trampling of men, and afterwards hardened by the influence of the sun. Troubled in mind, distracted, bewildered. Hasty, precipitate. Weeping, lamentation, from excessive grief. The whizzing of an arrow. شيب بلا *shībi balā,* The world. شيب تيب *shīb tīb,* (or شيب و تيب *shīb u tīb*) Astonished, confounded, insane. شيب و بالا *shīb u bālā,* Heaven and earth. Giving and taking. Truth and falsehood. Hot and cold. Sodomy. شيب و فراز *shīb u farāz,* Descent and ascent.

P شيبا *shībā,* A huge serpent.

A شيباء *shaybā·,* (fem. of اشيب *ashyab*) White or grey-haired (woman). ليلة شيباء *laylatun shaybā·,* The night wherein a bride loses her virginity. The last night of the month.

P شيبا زبان *shībā-zubān* or *zabān,* Eloquent.

A شيبان *shaybān,* Cold and cloudy without rain (day). *Shaybān* or *shībān,* Name of a month; whence شيبان و ملحان *shībān wa milhān,* Two winter months extremely cold.

P شيبان *shībān,* Mixed, jumbled. Trembling.

A شيبانيّة *shaybānīyat,* Name of a sect.

P شيبانيدن *shībānīdan,* To mix up meal in water. To cause to tremble.

P شيب پالا *shīb-pālā,* A skimmer of sweets.

P شيبنده *shībanda,* Mixed. Trembling.

P شيبور *shaybūr,* (شيپور *shaypūr,* or *shīpūr*) A pipe, tube, or flute. A brazen trumpet with a large mouth used of old in battle.

P شيبيدن *shībīdan,* To be mixed. To mix. To tremble, quake.

P شيبين *shībīn,* Inferior. Lower.

P شيپوي *shaypūy,* Noise made by the feet in walking. Snoring.

A شئة *shi·at,* (v. n. of شيئ) Willing, wishing. Will, desire. Mixture of colour.

A شية *shiyat,* (v. n. of وشي) Painting, printing, staining (cloth). Being conspicuous (white hairs amongst black). Colouring (a story) with falsehoods. Reporting (any one) to the king. A mark, blemish. A mixed or unnatural colour. A colour different from that of the rest of the body. Colour (of a horse). A sheep.

A شيتان *shaytān,* A small quantity of locusts.

P شيترة *shaytura,* Fumitory.

A شيتعور *shayta·ūr,* (or شيتغور) Barley.

A شيث *shīs,* Seth, son of Adam. Name of the founder of the Kaaba.

A شيح *shayh,* (v. n. of شاح for شيح) Striving, taking pains, being active. Being extremely cautious. *Shīh,* (pl. شياح *shiyāh*) The wormwood of Pontus, which destroys worms. Striped stuff of Yaman. Cautious, timorous. Diligent. شيح ارمني *shīh-armanī,* A species of wormseed.

A شيحان *shayhān,* Jealous. Cautious, timid. *Shayhān* or *shīhān,* A horse that breathes hard in running. Long.

A شيخ *shaykh,* (pl. شيوخ *shuyūkh, shiyūkh,* اشياخ *ashyākh,* شيخة *shiyakhat, shīkhat,* شيخان *shīkhān,* مشيخة *mashyakhat, mashīkhat,* مشيوخاء *mashyūkhā·,* مشيخاء *mashyukhā·,* and مشائخ *mashā·ikh*) A venerable old man: a man of fifty and upwards. A man of authority, a chief, prelate, prior, abbot, superior of the dervishes or Muhammadan monks; doctor learned in religion and law; preacher. A sheik. A kind of tree. شيخ الاسلام *shaykhu'l islām,* Head of religion, *i. e.* high priest, mufti, patriarch. شيخ الشيوخ *shaykhu'sh shuyūkh,* Chief of the doctors. شيخ المرأة *shaykhu'l mar·at,* Head of the woman, *i. e.* a husband. شيخ المرسلين *shaykhu'l mursalīn,* The patriarch Noah. شيخ النار *shaykhu'n nār,* The old man of the fire, *i. e.* the devil. شيخ نجدي *shaykhi najdī,* The devil. *Shayakh,* (v. n. of شاخ for شيخ) Growing old. Being a sheik.

A شيخان *shīkhān,* (pl. of شيخ) Old men: doctors.

P شيخانه *shī-khāna,* The corner of a house.

A شيخة *shaykhat,* An elderly woman. A colocynth. *Shiyakhat* or *shīkhat,* (pl. of شيخ *shaykh*) Sheiks. Elders. High priests. Doctors.

A شيخوخة *shaykhūkhat,* A growing old.

A شيخوخيّة *shaykhūkhīyat,* Old age.

A شيخون *shaykhūn,* An old man; a man fifty years old and upwards.

P شيد *shayd,* Deceit, fraud, hypocrisy. *Shed,* The sun. Light. Clear, shining, bright. Fascination. Shame, modesty. Name of the son of Afrāsyāb. شيد آهرمن *shedi āhiraman,* Infernal light. Illusions.

A شيد *shayd,* (v. n. of شاد for شيد) Plastering (a wall). Making (a wall) high. Perishing. *Shīd,* Plaster, mortar.

P شيدا *shaydā,* Mad, insane, distraught, in love.

P شيداب *shīdāb,* Name of a person who instituted the worship of earth, as others pay adoration to the element of fire.

P شيد اسپهبد *shed-ispahbud,* The holy spirit.

P شيدان *shīdān,* A dining-table.

P شيد اندود *shīd-andūd,* Plastered.

P شيدانه *shīdāna,* The jujube-tree and fruit.

P شيدائي *shaydā·ī,* Insanity, distraction.

P شيدرنگ *shed-rang,* Name of a philosopher.

P شيدوش *shedosh,* The son of Gūdarz.

P شيده *sheda,* Bright, luminous. The sun. Name of the son of Afrāsyāb. *Shīda,* A horse.

A شيذارة *shīzārat,* Jealous (man).

A شيذة *shīzat,* A mode of wrapping the turban round the head.

P شيذر *shezar,* (or شيذير *shezīr*) Name of God.

A شيذق *shayzak,* (شيذقان *shayzakān,* or شيذاق *shayzāk*) A kind of hawk.

A شيذمان *shayzamān* or *shayzumān,* A wolf.

A شيذمانة *shayzumānat,* A young and swift she-camel. A kind of tree. A husband.

P شير *sher,* A lion. The sign Leo. One of the twelve champions. A tiger. شير آبي *sheri ābī,* An alligator. شير البشر *sheru'l bashar,* Muhammad. شير چرخ *sheri charhh,* (شير آسمان *sheri āsmān,* شير سپهر *sheri sipihr,* شير فلك *sheri falak,* شير

گردون *sheri gardūn*, or شیر مرغزار فلك *sheri marghzāri falak*) The constellation Leo. The sun. شیر خدا *sheri khudā*, Alīy. شیر سیستان *sheri sīstān*, The hero Rustam. شیر شادروان *sheri shādurwān*, The figure of a lion painted upon a tent. شیر شرزه *sheri sharza*, A furious lion. شیر شرزهٔ غاب *sheri sharza-i ghāb*, The caliph Alīy. شیر گنجشك *sheri gunjishk*, A rapacious bird of the kite species. شیر مگس *sheri magas*, A spider. شیران پولاد خاي *sherāni pūlād-khāy*, (Iron-eating lions) Brave warriors. Mettlesome horses. *Shīr*, Milk. شیر خام خوردن *shīri khām khwurdan*, To be imprudent, careless, inattentive. شیر خورانیدن *shīr khwurānīdan*, To suckle. شیر خوردن *shīr khwurdan*, To drink or suck milk. شیر شنجرف گون *shīri shanjarf-gūn*, Red wine. شیر مرغ *shīri murgh*, Birds' milk, *i.e.* any thing not in existence. از شیر باز کردن *az shīr bāz kardan*, To wean. از شیر باز کردگی *az shīr bāz kardagī*, Ablactation, weaning.

A شیر *shiyar*, Any plant having a stalk or stem, tree. *Shuyur* or *shīr*, (pl. of شیار *shiyār*) Saturdays.

A شیّر *shayyir*, (pl. شیار *shiyār*) Fat, in good condition. Excellent (elegy or poem). (pl. شوراء *shuwarā*) A counseller, adviser, or prime-minister. صیّر شیّر *sayyirun shayyirun*, Beautiful in form. خیّر شیّر *khayyirun shayyirun*, An able adviser.

P شیرابه *shīrāba*, Poppy, poppy-juice.

P شیراز *shīrāz*, A celebrated city in Persia, the birth-place of Sheikh Sādī, the author of the Gulistān, Bostān, &c.; whence he is likewise called Shīrāzī. Curd strained and firm; a kind of cheese. A confection, electuary, preserved fruits, or pickles.

A شیراز *shīrāz*, (or شیّراز *shiyrāz*) (pl. شواریز *shawārīz*, شراریز *sharārīz*, or شآریز *sha-ārīz*) Curd strained from the whey and firm; a sort of cheese.

P شیرازبان *shīrā-zabān*, Gentle, insinuating.

P شیرازه *shīrāza*, Sewing, working button-holes, or the back of a book.

P شیرازه بسته *shīrāza-basta*, Bound (book).

P شیرازه بندي *shīrāza-bandī*, Binding of a book.

P شیرازي *shīrāzī*, Of the city of Shīrāz.

P شیراغ *shīrāgh*, Shade, curtain in palace or tent.

P شیرافکن *sher-afgan*, Overthrowing lions.

A شیراملة *shīrāmula*, (or شیراملج *shīrāmulaj*) The myrobolan-fruit.

P شیرانداز *sher-andāz*, Strong, courageous. *Shīr-andāz*, A breast emitting milk spontaneously.

P شیرانه *sherāna*, Lion-like, brave. *Shīrāna*, A churn-stick.

P شیر آور *shīr-āwar*, Milk-giving, milch.

P شیراوزن *sher-avzan* (or اوژن *avjan*), Conqueror of lions; brave, bold, strong, courageous.

P شیراي *shīrāy*, Ebony.

P شیربا *shīr-bā*, (or شیروا *shīr-wā*) Meat or rice dressed with milk. Curds eaten with fresh milk.

P شیربچه *sher-bacha*, A lion's whelp.

P شیربخ *shīrbakh*, (or شیربخس *shīrbakhs*) An Indian root, a solvent for bile and phlegm.

P شیربخت *shīrbukht*, Oil of sesame.

P شیر بخشیر *shīr bakhshīr*, A yellow root growing in Hindūstān and Kashmīr.

P شیر برنج *shīr-birinj*, Milk dressed with rice.

P شیر بها *shīr-bahā*, (Price of milk) A present to a wet-nurse. The portion and paraphernalia of a bride; what she takes to her husband's house.

A شیرة *shayarat*, (for شجرة *shajarat*) A tree.

A شیرج *shīraj*, (from P شیره *shīra*) Oil extracted from sesame, or rape-seed.

P شیرجامه *shīr-jāma*, A cup of milk. A nipple.

P شیر خرما *shīr-khurmā*, Dates and milk.

P شیرخشت *shīr-khisht*, Manna.

P شیرخشخاش *shīr-khashkhāsh*, Opium.

P شیر خشك *shīr-khushk*, A kind of manna.

P شیرخوار *shīr-khwār* (or خور *khwur*), A suckling.

P شیرخوارگي *shīr-khwāragī*, Suckling.

P شیر خواره *shīr-khwāra*, A sucking babe.

P شیر خوردني *shīr-khwurdanī*, Milk-diet.

P شیر خورده *shīr-khwurda*, A suckling.

P شیردار *shīr-dār*, Milch, giving milk.

P شیرداغ *sher-dāgh*, A short-sleeved garment open in front.

P شیردان *shīrdān*, A milk-pan. Ventricle of sheep or kid (stuffed with meat, and dressed).

P شیردل *sher-dil*, Lion-hearted; brave.

P شیردوشه *shīr-dosha*, A milk-pail.

A شیردوغ *shīr-dogh*, New milk mixed with sour milk or meat.

P شیرده *shīr-dih*, A wet-nurse.

P شیردهي *shīr-dihī*, A giving suck.

P شیرریز *shīr-rez*, Emitting milk.

P شیرزا *shīr-zā*, Name of a fattening drug which gives an increase of milk.

P شیرزبان *shīr-zubān*, Soft, gentle in speech.

P شیرزج *shīr-zaj*, Bats' milk.

P شیرزده *shīr-zada*, A sucking child indisposed and nauseating the milk.

P شیرزق *shīrzak*, Milk of a bat.

P شیرزنه *shīr-zana*, A churn. A churn-stick.

P شیرزه *sherza*, A rapacious beast. Strength.

P شیرژیان *sher jiyān*, A furious lion. Brave.

P شیرستان *sheristān*, The region of lions.

P شیرسگ *sher-sag*, A hare-hunting dog.

P شیرسوار *sher-suwār*, The sun.

P شیرشکار *sher-shikār*, (Lion-hunter) Fierce.

P شیرشکر *shīr-shakar*, A kind of silk. Affection.

P شیرطاقي *sher-tākī*, Proud, arrogant. Timid.

P شیرغران *sher-gharān*, A fierce lion. A warrior.

P شیرك ساختن *sherak sākhtan*, (To make (one) a little lion) To inspire with courage.

P شیرکش *sher-kush*, Lion-killing. A pigeon.

P شیرکي *shīrkī*, A Chinese animal, having a yellow body and black mouth.

P شیرگرم *shīr-garm*, Milk-warm, lukewarm.

P شیرگیا *shīr-giyā*, Name of a milky herb.

P شیرگیاه *shīr-giyāh*, A species of milky grass.

P شیرگیر *sher-gīr*, (or شیرگیري *sher-gīrī*) Tipsy, half drunk. An instigator, exciter. Persevering in business. Name of the 28th day of the month.

P شیرلعاب *shīr-luꜥāb*, Honey.

P شیرمال *shīr-māl*, Bread made with milk.

P شیرمان *shermān*, (Lion-like) Warlike.

P شیرماهي *sher-māhī*, (Lion-fish) A fish of whose bones they make knife-handles. *Shīr-māhī*, (Milk-fish) Name of a delicious fish with white scales.

P شیرمایه *shīr-māya*, Rennet.

P شیرمرد *sher-mard*, (Lion-man) Bold, courageous, athletic. One who, by a course of severe discipline, has attained eminence in the divine life.

P شیرمردان *sher-mardān*, Heroes. Holy men.

P شیرمرغ *shīr-murgh*, (Milk-bird) The bat (because it suckles its young).

P شیرمست *sheri mast*, A raging lion. Brave, warlike. *Shīr-mast*, A fat lamb six months old.

P شیرناك *shernāk*, Abounding in lions (a place). *Shīrnāk*, Full of milk, milch.

P شیرنج *shīranj*, A species of black root.

P شیرنما *sher-namā*, Appearing like a lion.

P شیرني *shīr-nay* (or *shīri-nay*), Sugar-cane juice.

P شیروان *shīrwān*, A country in Persia.

P شیر و شکر *shīr u shakar*, Milk and sugar.

P شیروشلیم *shīrūshilīm*, Jerusalem.

P شیروغن *shīrawghan*, Oil of sesame.

P شیرونه *shīrūna*, An ulcer growing on the heads of children. A disease of the head or brain, madness. A disease amongst cattle.

P شیروي *sherūy*, A son of Khusrav Parvez.

P شیرویه *sherūya*, Great, honourable, dignified. Brave, valiant. Name of the son of Khusraw.

P شیره *shīra*, New or made wine. An intoxicating kind of drink. The expressed juice of any fruit except olives. Oil of sesame. A tray with a leg to stand upon. Maslock. شیرهٔ خرما *shīra-i khurmā*, Juice of dates. شیرهٔ شکر *shīra-i shakar*, Juice of sugar: molasses. شیره شراب *shīra-sharāb* (or انگور *angūr*), New wine, must.

P شیره ریوند *shīra-rewand*, Gamboge.

P شیري *sherī*, Lion-like. Ferocity. شیري نمودن *sherī namūdan* (or کردن *kardan*), To display leonine ferocity. *Shīrī*, Milky. Part of a ship.

P شیرین *shīrīn*, Sweet. Pleasant, gentle, gracious, affable. Delicate. A sweetmeat or confection. An infant at the breast. Name of a celebrated lady. بادهٔ شیرین *bāda-i shīrīn*, Sweet wine. شاهدِ شیرین جمال *shāhidi shīrīn-jamāl*, A nymph resembling Shīrīn in beauty.

P شیرین ادا *shīrīn-adā*, Singing sweetly; speaking eloquently.

P شیرین دهن *shīrīn-dahan*, Sweet-mouthed.

P شیرین زبان *shīrīn-zabān* (or گفتار *guftār*), With an enchanting tongue. Eloquent. Sweet-spoken, affable.

P شيرين زباني *shīrīn-zabānī*, Sweetness of speech. Eloquence.

P شيرين سخن *shīrīn-suhhan*, Sweetly-spoken.

P شيرين شمائل *shīrīn-shamāʼil*, Amiable.

P شيرين طبع *shīrīn-tabaʻ*, Sweet-tempered.

P شيرينك *shīrīnak*, Somewhat sweet, sweetish. A kind of eruption common to children.

P شيرين كار *shīrīn-kār*, Of gentle manners. A maker of sweetmeats.

P شيرين كاران *shīrīn-kārān*, Flatterers. Of mild dispositions. Makers and venders of sweetmeats. Jugglers, buffoons.

P شيرين گوار *shīrīn-guwār*, Easy of digestion.

P شيرينه *shīrīna*, An eruption common to children. A disease incident to cattle. Blight, mildew. A churn-stick.

P شيريني *shīrīnī*, Sweetness. A sweetmeat.

A شيز *shīz*, An Indian wood for making saucers. Ebony. The nut-tree. A bow.

A شئز *shaʼiz*, Rough, rugged, elevated (place).

A شيزي *shīza'*, A black shining wood of which they make saucers. Ebony. The nut-tree.

A شيش *shīsh*, A bad sort of date.

A شئس *shaʼis*, Hard and rugged (place).

A شيشاء *shīshāʼ*, A vile species of date.

P شيشاك *shīshāk*, A yearling lamb. A four-stringed instrument.

P شيشالنگ *shīshālang*, The wagtail.

P شيشك *shīshak*, A sheep a year old. A magpie. A small partridge. A four-stringed instrument.

P شيشله *shīshala*, Weak, languid. Paralytic. Drunk. Any thing faded, ragged, or spoilt from age. A hole in silk or linen (from friction, contusion, the gnawing of mice, or moths). Whatever is beaten or carded (as cotton, wool, or flax).

P شيشم *shīshum*, Name of a musical instrument.

P شيشو *shīshū*, A small kind of partridge. An animal resembling an ape. A descent, declivity.

P شيشه *shīsha*, Glass. A glass, bottle, flask, phial, cup, caraff, decanter; a cupping-glass. The highest heaven. شيشهٔ حجامت *shīshaʼi hijāmat*, A cupping-glass. شيشهٔ خوناب *shīshaʼi khūnāb*, The sky. شيشهٔ ماه *shīshaʼi māh*, The moon. The sky. آتشي شيشه *ātishī-shīsha*, A burning-glass.

P شيشه باز *shīsha-bāz*, A player at cups and balls. The sun.

P شيشه با فرزان *shīsha bā farzān*, White.

P شيشه شيشه *shīsha shīsha*, Flask after flask.

P شيشه گر *shīshagar*, A glass-blower.

P شيشه گردان *shīsha-gardān*, A juggler, cheat.

P شيشه گردن *shīsha-gardan*, Silly, stupid.

P شيشه محل *shīsha-mahal*, A glazed palace.

P شيشيك *shīshīk*, A kind of small partridge.

A شيص *shīs*, (or شيصاء *shīsāʼ*) A kind of very bad sour date (such as is produced when the flowers of the male palm-tree have not been sprinkled over the female). A kind of fish. Toothache. Gripes. ابو الشيص *abū'sh shīs*, Name of an Arabian poet.

A شيصبان *shaysabān*, A male ant. An ant's hole. A race of demons. The devil.

A شيط *shayt*, (and شيطوطة *shaytūtat*) (v. n. of شاط for شيط) Being burnt up, or absorbed in cooking (butter or oil). Having the burnt part of victuals sticking to it (a pot). Perishing (a man). Being distributed entirely (a slaughtered camel). Mixing bloods, *i. e.* killing a homicide in the act of murder. Going away with impunity after shedding blood. Making haste in any work.

A شيطان *shaytān*, (pl. شياطين *shayātīn*) Satan, the devil: a demon, deuce. Proud, stubborn, perverse (demon, man, animal). A serpent of a hideous appearance. A mark branded on a camel from the thigh to the hock. Vain, trifling. الشيطان عليه اللعنة *ash 'shaytān ʻalayhi'l laʻna*, Satan, on whom be the curse (of God). شيطان طائر *shaytān-tāʼir*, The devil's bird, *i. e.* the bat or the owl. شيطان الفلا *shaytānu'l fala'*, (Demon of the desert) Thirst.

A شيطاني *shaytānīy*, Diabolical, devilish.

A شيطانية *shaytānīyat*, Diabolical pride or stubbornness, diabolism, devilishness, satanism.

A شيطرج *shītaraj*, An Indian medicine very acrid and caustic.

P شيطره *shaytara*, Fumitory.

A شيطنة *shaytanat*, (v. n. of شيطن Q) Being proud, obstinate, satanic, devilish. Diabolism, diabolical pride, or malignity, devilishness.

A شيطي *shaytīy*, Dust raised into the air.

A شيظ *shayz*, (v. n. of شاظ for شيظ) Piercing the hand, penetrating the flesh (a splinter from a spear).

A شيظان *shayzān*, Harsh, cruel, fell, grim.

A شيظم *shayzam*, (pl. شياظمة *shayāzimat*) Long, tall, robust (young man, horse, or camel). A large old porcupine or hedgehog. A lion.

A شيظمي *shayzamīy*, (pl. شياظمة *shayāzimat*) Fat, robust (youth, horse, or camel). Eloquent. Swift (horse). A lion.

A شيع *shayʻ*, (v. n. of شاع for شيع) Being divulged, published. Publishing, divulging. Following, attending. Filling (a vessel). Portion of time (as one hour) following another. Born immediately after another, the next brother or sister. A follower. (pl. اشياع *ashyāʻ*) The whelp of a lion. Quantity; space; measure. Like. *Shīʻ*, A follower, a dangler after. *Shiyaʻ*, (pl. of شيعة *shīʻat*) Multitudes following one another; followers, adherents.

A شيّع *shayyiʻ*, (pl. شيعاء *shuyaʻāʼ*) A follower.

A شيعاء *shuyaʻāʼ*, (pl. of شيّع *shayyiʻ*) Followers.

A شيعان *shayaʻān*, A being divulged, published.

A شيعة *shayʻat*, A certain tree from which bees cull honey, and with which clothes are perfumed. *Shīʻat*, (pl. اشياع *ashyāʻ* and شيع *shiyaʻ*) A multitude following one another in pursuit of the same object. الشيعة *ash'shīʻat*, The sect of Alīy.

A شيّعة *shayyiʻat*, Common property, free to all.

A شيعوعة *shayʻūʻat*, (v. n. of شاع for شيع) Being divulged, published. Leaving (a portion) undivided. Following.

A شيعي *shiyaʻīy*, Of the sect of Alīy, Shīite.

A شيعية *shīʻīyat*, A following of the sect of Alīy, the being a Shīite (as opposed to a Sonnite).

A شيف *shīf*, Thorns on branches of a palm.

A شيّفان *shayyifān*, (and شيّفة *shayyifat*) Vanguard, picket, advanced post, scout, spy.

P شيفتگي *sheftagī*, Astonishment, loss of one's senses. Greediness.

P شيفتن *sheftan*, To become insane or distracted with love.

P شيفته *shefta*, Mad, enamoured. Strongly inclined. Astonished. شيفته رنگ *shefta-rang*, An apricot, a smooth peach. A kind of sweet white carrot, a parsnip, skirret.

A شيق *shīk*, A mountain; a high and inaccessible part of it. A narrow fissure in a mountain. A small white duck. A kind of fish. Glans penis. Hairs in a horse's tail. A side.

A شيّق *shayyik*, Lecherous, full of desire, longing, lascivious.

A شيقة *shīkat*, A single hair in a horse's tail. A kind of water-fowl.

P شيك *shīk*, A paralyzed hand or foot. Languid, inert.

A شيكة *shīkat*, (v. n. of شاك for شوك) Falling (amongst thorns). Pricking any one (a thorn). Pricking (any one), running a thorn into (him).

P شيكران *shaykurān*, A species of hemlock.

P شيگار *shīgār*, An order to work for nothing.

A شيّل *shuyyal* and *shiyal*, (pl. of شائل *shāʼil*) Milkless (camels) in want of the male.

P شيلان *shīlān*, A royal table or entertainment. The jujube. Growing corn. A place luxuriant in green herbs.

P شيلانه *shelāna*, The jujube.

P شيلك *shīlak*, The mouth of a musket.

A P شيلم *shaylam*, Tares or darnel (which if eaten in bread cause a slight intoxication).

A شيلم *shaylam*, Mean-looking. A miser.

P شيلونه *shaylūna*, A tortoise.

P شيله *shīla*, Rice-soup. Wormwood.

A شيم *shaym*, (v. n. of شام for شيم) Putting (one thing into another, especially a sword) into the sheath. Hiding one thing within another. Enjoying (a maiden). Drawing (a sword). Watching a thunder-cloud to discover whether it will rain. Entering into. Soiling with black spots. Having black moles on the skin. Making an accurate attack in war. Striking (a horse) with the heel to make (him) go faster. *Shīm*, (pl. of اشيم *ashyam*) Distinguished by a black mole or any other natural mark. A kind of fish. (pl. of شيام *shiyām*) Mice. *Shayam*, Soil never yet dug, remaining in its original state of hardness. *Shiyam*, (pl. of شيمة *shīmat*) Manners, habits. Soils dug up.

P شيم *shīm*, A small, spotted, scaly fish. The fish which swallowed Jonah. Sir, your worship.

A شيماء *shaymāꜣ*, Name of a woman.

A شئمة *shiꜣmat*, Habit, nature, disposition.

A شيمة *shīmat*, (pl. شيم *shiyam*) Habit, nature, disposition. Earth dug up.

A شيمذان *shaymuzān*, A wolf.

A شيمل *shaymal*, The north.

P شيمه *shema*, A kind of grape.

A شين *shayn*, (v. n. of شان for شين) Disgracing, dishonouring, degrading. Disgrace, shame. *Shīn*, The letter ش. Three hundred.

P شين *shīn*, A man addicted much to venery. (for نشين *nishīn*) Sit down.

A شيّن *shayyin*, Shameful.

P شينا *shīnā*, Swimming, natation.

P شيناب *shīnāb*, Labour, study. Swimming.

P شين خيار *shīn-khiyār*, A large cucumber kept for seed.

P شينه *shīna*, A kind of pipe.

P شينيز *shaynīz*, Coriander-seed.

A شينيز *shīnīz*, Coriander-seed.

P شيو *shev*, A declivity. Base, foundation. Below, under. Humble, low. A valley. Rice-soup. Abow.

P شيوا *shevā*, Eloquent.

P شيواد *shīwād*, A kind of water-fowl.

P شيوا زبان *shevā-zabān*, Eloquent-tongued.

P شيوان *shīwān*, Mixed, jumbled. Trembling.

P شيوانيدن *shīwānīdan*, To mix. To steep flour in water, to knead. To cause to tremble.

A شيوخ *shuyūkh* or *shiyūkh*, (pl. of شيخ *shaykh*) Aged men. Elders. Doctors. Sheikhs. Prelates.

A شيوخة *shuyūkhat*, A growing old.

A شيوخيّة *shuyūkhīyat*, Old age.

P شيوشه *shuyūsha*, An ingot of gold. The stalk of a cucumber.

A شيوط *shuyūt*, (or شيوطة *shuyūtat*) (v. n. of شاط for شيط) Being burnt up.

A شيوع *shayūꜥ*, Firewood. *Shuyūꜥ*, A being divulged, published.

A شيوم *shuyūm*, (v. n. of شام for شيم) Making an accurate attack in war.

P شيون *sheran*, Lamentation. A spear.

P شيونده *shīwanda*, Mixed. Tremulous.

A شيوه *shayūh*, Dishonest, shameful. Reproachful, opprobrious.

P شيوه *sheva*, Amorous looks, gestures, blandishments, coquetry, feigned disdain, or playfulness of lovers. The graceful movements of a lovely girl; an air of elegance, beautiful, delicate, tender. A habit, custom, natural disposition; a manner of living or acting. Skill, perfection. Business, trade, profession, art. Acquisition. A sect. Apparatus.

P شيوه باز *sheva-bāz*, (also شيوه گر *shevagar*) A lover, a male or female coquet, playing off all the pretty arts of love.

P شيوه دار *sheva-dār*, An artist, a craftsman. A tradesman. Expert, clever.

P شيوه زبان *sheva-zabān*, Sweetly-spoken: eloquent.

A شيه *shayh*, (v. n. of شاه for شيه) Accusing, reproaching, treating opprobriously. *Shīh*, (*shayh*, or شيّه *shayyih*) (pl. of شاة *shāt*) Sheep.

A شيهم *shayham*, A (male) porcupine with large quills.

A شيهمة *shayhamat*, An old woman.

P شيهه *shiha*, The neighing of a horse.

A شيّي *shayīy*, A stammerer.

A شييء *shuyayꜣ*, A little thing, a trifle.

A شيئة *shīꜣat*, Will, desire. كلّ شيء بشيئة الله تعالى *kull shayꜣ bi shīꜣat allāh taꜥāla'*, Every thing (happens) by the will of God most High.

A شئيت *shaꜣīt*, A horse apt to stumble. A horse that places his hind-feet short of his fore-feet.

A شييخ *shuyaykh* or *shiyaykh*, (dim. of شيخ *shaykh*) A little doctor, or old man.

P شييدن *shayīdan*, To arm or equip one's self.

A شييرة *shuyayrat*, (for شجيرة) A small tree.

A شئيس *shaꜣīs*, (pl. of شأس) Rough, hard places.

A شييء *shuyayꜣ*, (dim. of شيء) A little thing.

ص

ص *sād*, (called صاد غير منقوطه *sādi ghayr mankūta*, صاد مهمله *sādi muhmala*, Undotted ص) The fourteenth letter of the Arabic, and the seventeenth of the Persian alphabets. In arithmetic it expresses 90, and is the abbreviature for صفر *safar*, the second Muhammadan month. It seldom occurs in words not derived from the Arabic, and is interchangeable with ث *sā*, ج *jīm*, ز *zayn*, س *sīn*, ش *shīn*, and ع *ꜥayn*. The power of ص *sād* is that of *s* pronounced with a thick, dull, hollow sound from the roof of the mouth, not easily to be described.

A صا *sā*, (Arab. form of P چا *chā*) Tea.

A صاء *sāꜣ*, (or صاءة *sāꜣat*) The water contained in the caul which envelops the fœtus in the womb.

A صاءاة *sāꜣāt*, Water contained in the secundine.

A صاب *sāb*, A certain bitter tree. The juice of a bitter tree. Raining, rainy (cloud or sky).

A صأب *saꜣab*, (v. n. of صئب) Being troubled with nits (the head). Drinking much water (a man). Quenching (the thirst).

A صابّ *sābb*, A pourer, a diffuser.

A صابة *sābat*, Weakness of intellect. A slight touch of insanity. Misfortune, disaster.

A صابح *sābih*, Clear, plain, perspicuous.

A صابر *sābir*, Patient. One who compels, forces, or restrains. One who forcibly detains another in order to put him to death. Job. ابو صابر *abū sābir*, Salt.

A صابغ *sābigh*, Full-uddered and shining.

P صابوته *sābūta*, An old woman, or mare.

A صابون *sābūn*, Soap. صابون الشباب *sābūnu'sh shabāb*, The tree called ابو مالك *abū mālik*. صابون القاف *sābūnu'l kāf*, Soap-ashes.

A صابئون *sābiꜣūn*, (pl. of صابئ *sābiꜣ*) Sabeans, Pagans, idolaters, who change their religion.

P صابوني *sābūnī*, A mixture of almonds, honey, and sesame oil.

A صابونيّ *sābūnīy*, A soap-maker. Saponaceous.

A صابئ *sābiꜣ*, (pl. صابئون *sābiꜣūn*, صباة *subāt*) An idolater, who changes his religion, Pagan, Sabean.

A صابية *sābiyat*, The north-east wind.

A صات *sāt*, Loud-voiced (man or ass). A good report, name, or reputation.

T صاچمه *sāchma*, Small shot.

A صاح *sāh*, (for صاحب *sāhib*) A friend. يا صاح *yā sāhi*, (for يا صاحبي *yā sāhibī*) Oh my friend!

A صاحب *sāhib*, (pl. صحب *sahb* and صحبة *suhbat*) Enjoying, possessed of, or endowed with. A lord, master, great man, governor, chief. A companion, a friend. A title of courtesy, equivalent to Master, Mr., and Sir. This word is much used in composition to denote the master or possessor of any quality or thing, in some instances with, in others without kasr: as, صاحب اختيار *sāhibi ikhtiyār*, Possessed of free election or option. Pre-eminent. صاحب اعتبار *sāhibi iꜥtibār*, Esteemed, enjoying reputation. صاحب اغراض *sāhibi aghrāz*, Factious, who excites sedition or rebellion. P صاحب افسر گردون *sāhibi afsari gardūn*, Jesus Christ. A صاحب اقتدار *sāhibi iktidār*, Potent, possessed of power. صاحب امضا *sāhibi imzā*, Prime-minister, secretary of state. صاحب اهتمام *sāhibi ihtimām*, A prudent manager. صاحب البريد *sāhibu'l barīd*, A post-master. P صاحب تاب و توان *sāhibi tāb u tuwān*, Powerful. A صاحب تاج *sāhibi tāj*, A crowned head. The sun. P صاحب تاج و تخت *sāhibi tāj u takht*, Possessor of crown and throne. صاحب تخت *sāhibi takht*, Possessor of the throne; a king. A صاحب تدبير *sāhibi tadbīr*, A prudent counsellor. صاحب تصرّف *sāhibi tasarruf*, Adroit, skilful. صاحب تمكنت *sāhibi tamkanat*, Possessed of dignity. صاحب تميز *sāhibi tamyīz*, A man of discernment. صاحب جمال *sāhibi jāmal*, Beautiful, handsome. صاحب جوزا *sāhibi jawzā*, The planet Mercury. صاحب حق *sāhibi hakk*, Rightful owner. صاحب الحوت *sāhibu'l hūt*, (or صاحب النون *sāhibu'n nūn*) (Lord of the fish) Jonah. P صاحب خاطران *sāhibi khātirān*, Poets. Orators. Jocular. صاحب خانه *sāhibi khāna*, Master of the house. A صاحب خبر *sāhibi khabar*, A chamberlain, a lord in waiting. An ambassador. P صاحب خطران *sāhibi khatarān*, Kings, princes, or other illustrious personages. صاحب درد *sāhib-dard*, Pained. صاحب دل *sāhib dil*, A man of piety. A صاحب دولت *sāhib dawlat*, Wealthy. A mighty lord. صاحب ديوان *sā-*

hibi dīwān, Superintendant of the finances. The author of a set of odes. P صاحب راز *sāhibi rāz*, A confidant. A صاحب راي *sāhibi rāy*, A vazir. صاحب الرسالة *sāhibu'rrisāla*, Lord of the embassy, *i.e.* Muhammad. صاحب رصد *sāhibi rasad*, Name of a celebrated astronomer. A صاحب روايت *sāhibi riwāyat*, An able story-teller. صاحب ري *sāhib-ray*, Avicenna. صاحب الزمان *sāhibu'z zamān*, Lord of the age. صاحب سرير *sāhibi sarīr*, A king. صاحب سفران افلاك *sāhibi safarāni aflāk*, Sun, moon, and planets. صاحب سكه و خطبه *sāhibi sikka u khutba*, A king, an absolute sovereign (who has the right of coining money, and for whom public prayers are offered up in the mosques). P صاحب سنگ *sāhibi sang*, A man of gravity, power, or dignity. A slanderer, backbiter. صاحب شكوه *sāhib shukoh*, Grave, dignified, majestic. صاحب صابي *sāhibi sābī*, Jesus Christ. Name of the person who instituted the worship of the stars. صاحب صفين *sāhibi siffīn*, The caliph Alīy. A صاحب ظهور *sāhibi zuhūr*, Illustrious. A hero. صاحب عرفان *sāhibi ɛirfān*, Intelligent, wise. صاحب العصا *sāhibu'l ɛasa'*, Lord of the staff, *i.e.* Moses. صاحب عطا و نعم *sāhibi ɛatā u niɛam*, Munificent. صاحب العمود *sāhibu'l ɛamūd*, Lord of the column, *i.e.* Simeon Stilites. صاحب عنوان *sāhibi ɛunwān*, Excellent, supreme. صاحب عيار *sāhibi ɛiyār*, Shrewd, sly. صاحب عين دبران *sāhibi ɛayni dabrān*, The constellation Taurus. صاحب فراست *sāhibi firāsat*, Sagacious. A physiognomist. صاحب فراش *sāhib firāsh*, Bed-ridden. صاحب فصل الخطاب *sāhibi fasli'l khitāb*, King David. صاحب الفيل *sāhibu'l fīl*, Lord of the elephant, name of Abrahah, forty-sixth king of Yaman. صاحب قبول *sāhibi kabūl*, Agreeable. A willing receiver. صاحب قران *sāhib-kirān*, Lord of the happy conjunction. A fortunate and invincible hero. A title of Tīmūr. Muhammad. P صاحبقراني *sāhib-kirānī*, Heroic. Royal, imperial. A صاحب كتاب *sāhib kitāb*, Instructed in the Scriptures. A scripturist. An author. صاحب كرم *sāhibi karam*, Beneficent. صاحب كمال *sāhibi kamāl*, Perfect, excellent. صاحب مال *sāhib māl*, Wealthy. صاحب مجد *sāhib majd*, Glorious. صاحب محله *sāhibi mahalla*, The head man of a ward. صاحب مقام *sāhib makām*, Exalted in dignity. صاحب النار *sāhibu'n nār*, Doomed to the fire. صاحب ناموس *sāhibi nāmūs*, A lawgiver. صاحب نظر *sāhib nazar*, Clear-sighted. Pious. صاحب وجود *sāhibi wujūd*, Powerful, potent. صاحب وقوف *sāhibi wukūf*, Experienced. Privy, acquainted. P صاحب هنر *sāhib hunar*, Skilful. A صاحب يد بيضا *sāhibi yadi* (or كف *kafi*) *bayzā*, Lord of the white hand, *i.e.* Moses.

A صاحبة *sāhibat*, A lady. A wife. (pl. صواحب) A female companion. A handmaid. Possessed of.

P صاحبي *sāhibī*, A kind of striped silken stuff.

A صاحبي *sāhibī*, Rule, lordship. Kind of grape.

A صاحة *sāhat*, Ground which produces nothing.

A صاحي *sāhī*, Clear, serene (day or sky).

A صاخة *sākhat*, (pl. صاخات *sākhāt* or صاخ *sākh*) A misfortune, evil. A lump on a bone from a bite or blow.

A صاخّة *sākhkhat*, A noise which grates or stuns the ear. The day of judgment. A calamity.

A صاخد *sākhid*, A solitary palm-tree stripped of its bark. Intense (heat).

A صاخر *sākhir*, Sound from the collision of pieces of iron.

A صاخرة *sākhirat*, A kind of earthen vessel.

A صاد *sād*, The letter ص. Copper, brass, or a particular kind thereof. A brazen vessel. A cock rolling on the ground. (pl. اصياد *asyād* and اصائد *asāɛid*) A vein between the eyes of a camel. A disease in a camel causing a discharge at the nose. A camel so distempered. سورة صاد *sūraɛi sād*, The 38th chapter of the Kur'ān (to which is prefixed ص as an abbreviature for صدق *sidk*, Truth, or some such mysterious word). P صاد كردن *sād kardan*, To inscribe an account with the letter ص *sād*, implying that it has been audited.

A صادح *sādih*, Singing (bird).

A صادر *sādir*, Who or what flows, originates, emerges, springs up or out. Produced, derived, happened, arrived. (A road) leading from the water. An ancient writer. Extraordinary taxes levied on any great emergency. P صادر شدن *sādir shudan*, To proceed, emanate. A صادر وارد *sādir wārid*, Going and coming; a traveller. Sundry charges in an office of business, such as ink, paper, oil, &c. ما له صادر و لا وارد *mā lahu sādir wa lā wārid*, He possesses nothing.

A صادرة *sādirat*, A certain kind of the lote-tree. A tree in Paradise, called سدرة المنتهى *sidratu'l muntaha'*, the abode of the archangel Gabriel.

A صادع *sādiɛ*, Covering much ground (a mountain or water). Shining (dawn). كلام صادع *kalāmi sādiɛ*, An eloquent, powerful discourse.

A صادف *sādif*, Deviating, receding; who or what deviates or recedes.

A صادفة *sādifat*, (pl. صوادف *sawādif*) A camel waiting until the others have drunk.

A صادق *sādik*, True, just, sincere, ingenuous, good. A heavy blow, a stroke which tells. An epithet of Joseph, Abūbakr, and Jesus Christ. صادق القول *sādiku'l kawl*, Truth-speaking. لسان صادق البيان *lisāni sādiku'l bayān*, A tongue expressive of truth. نيت صادقة *niyati sādika*, Pure intention, good conscience. غبّ صادقة *ghibb sādikatin*, After the thing became evident. صادق الجوع *sādiku'l juɛ*, Real hunger.

A صادي *sādī*, (fem. صادية) Dry, thirsty.

A صاديّ *sādiy*, Brazen.

A صارّ *sārr*, Trees whose branches intertwine, so as to form a perpetual, continuous shade.

A صارة *sārat*, Summit (of a mountain). A place thickly set with trees. Strong musky smell.

A صارّة *sārrat*, (pl. صرائر *sarāɛir* and صوارّ *sawārr*) Any thing necessary to be done. Thirst.

A صارخ *sārikh*, One who calls for assistance. An assistant. A dunghill-cock.

A صارخة *sārikhat*, (v. n. of صرخ) Bringing help. Cries for help. Clamorous (woman).

A صارد *sārid*, Overshooting the mark (arrow).

A صارف *sārif*, A changer, an alterer. A deceiver, cheat. Prodigal, extravagant. Libidinous (bitch).

A صارفة *sārifat*, Vicissitudes of fortune.

A صارم *sārim*, (pl. صوارم *sawārim*) A sharp sword. An intrepid, expeditious man. A lion.

P صاروج *sārūj*, Plaster, mortar, cement. Quick lime. An unguent, composed of quick lime and arsenic, for extirpating hairs.

A صارور *sārūr*, (صاروراء *sārūrāɛ*, or صارورة *sārūrat*) A man neglecting to go on pilgrimage to Mecca. A bachelor.

P صاره *sāra*, The plant elephant's ears.

A صاري *sārī*, (pl. صرّاء *surrāɛ*, صراريّ *sarārīy*, and صراريّون *sarārīyūn*) A sailor. The mast or yard of a ship.

A صارية *sāriyat*, (pl. صواري *sawārī*) The main yard of a ship. A mast. A lofty column. A well of water old and stinking.

A صأصأة *saɛsaɛat*, (v. n. of صأصأ Q) Blinking, while yet unable to open his eyes (a whelp). Exclaiming. Being timid, cowardly. Dreading, being in fear of, submitting to. (A female-palm) from not being impregnated with the flowers of the male bearing bad dates without stones.

A صاصل *sāsal*, A well. Name of a plant.

A صاع *sāɛ*, Low ground. A bat for playing at horse-shinty. A place swept and then played upon. A mark left by an ostrich's breast on the ground. (pl. اصوع *aswuɛ*, اصؤع *asɛuɛ*, اصواع *aswāɛ*, and صوع *sūɛ*) A dry measure of four mudds, each mudd weighing a ritl and one-third. A drinking-cup, goblet. P صاع زر يوسف *sāɛi zari yūsuf*, The sun.

A صاعب *sāɛib*, Arable land, stony, bushy, and difficult to work.

A صاعة *sāɛat*, A place where women separate or card cotton. Low ground.

A صاعد *sāɛid*, One climbing a mountain.

A صاعداً *sāɛidan*, Upwards, above, more: as, الواحد فصاعداً *al wāhid fa sāɛidan*, One and upwards.

A صاعديّ *sāɛidiy*, Belonging to wild asses.

A صاعقة *sāɛikat*, (v. n. of صعق) Striking (any one) with lightning (heaven). Striking any one (a thunderbolt). Lightning. A thunderbolt. Death. Punishment, deadly torment. A loud noise or cry of pain. A scourge in the hand of the angel who drives the clouds.

A صاغة *sāghat*, (pl. of صائغ *sāɛigh*) Goldsmiths, silversmiths. ملح الصاغة *milhu's sāghat*, Borax.

P صاغر *sāghar*, A large drinking-cup.

A صاغر *sāghir*, (pl. صغرة *sagharat*) Contemptible, submitting slavishly to indignant treatment.

A صاغية *sāghiyat*, Those who turn towards any one in their necessities.

P صاف *sāf*, Pure, clear, sincere, candid.

A صاف *sāf*, Wool. Woolly (ram), producing wool, lanigerous. (for صائف *sāʼif*) Hot (day). (for صافي *sāfī*) Clear. Sincere. صاف الرقبة *sāfu'r raḳabat.* See صوف الرقبة *sūfu'r raḳabat.*

A صافّات صفّا *sāffāt saffan*, (Adoring angels) ranged in ranks.

A صافّة *sāffat*, (pl. صوافّ *sawāff*) Putting down the feet in a right line (a camel).

A صافح *sāfiḥ*, Dry, milkless (camel).

A صافد *sāfid*, Fettered.

P صاف دل *sāf-dil*, Simple-hearted.

P صاف دلي *sāf-dilī*, Simple-heartedness.

A صافر *sāfir*, A fifer. A hisser, whistler. Any singing bird. Any bird that does not hunt. Name of a timorous bird. A robber. Any body (at home).

P صاف ضمير *sāf-zamīr*, Pure-minded.

A صافقة *sāfiḳat*, (pl. صوافق *sawāfiḳ*) A crowd, company. Hardness, severity. An accident.

A صافن *sāfin*, (pl. صافنات *sāfināt*) (A horse) standing on three legs, and touching the ground with the tip of the fourth hoof. Who places the feet even (a man in prayer, or a sheep when milked). The saphena vein, running from the inner ankle to the great toe.

A صافنات *sāfināt*, Fleet, high-blooded horses.

A صافورا *sāfūrā*, Zipporah, the wife of Moses.

A صافي *sāfī*, Pure, clear, fine, bright, unsullied, limpid, unmixed, sincere, candid. Serene, cloudless, and cold (day). Elect. A filter or cloth, through which drinks or medicines are strained. Woolly, wool-bearing, lanigerous. Name of Adam.

P سيم صافي *sīmi safī*, Pure silver.

A صافي *sāfī*, Clearness. Purity, candour.

A صافيات *sāfiyāt*, (pl. of صافية) Pure, sincere.

A صافية *sāfiyat*, (fem. of صافي *sāfī*) Pure, clear.

P صافي دل *sāfī-dil*, Of a sincere heart.

P صافي نامه *sāfī-nāma*, A certificate, discharge.

A صاق *sāḳ*, (for ساق *sāḳ*) The leg.

A صاقرة *sāḳirat*, A descending calamity.

A صاقع *sāḳiʻ*, One who strikes upon the head. Crowing (cock). صه صاقع *sah sāḳiʻ*, Hush, you liar!

A صاقعة *sāḳiʻat*, (for صاعقة) A thunderbolt.

A صاقل *sāḳil*, (pl. صقلة *saḳalat*) A furbisher.

A صاقور *sāḳūr*, A large hammer for breaking stones. A large axe. The tongue.

A صاقورة *sāḳūrat*, The third heaven. The inside of the skull over the brain.

A صاك *saʼak*, (v. n. of صئك) Emitting a foul stench. Sticking, adhering. Congealing and sticking (blood).

A صأكة *saʼkat*, The smell of damp wood.

A صاكّة *sākkat*, (صواكّ *sawākk*) A heavy stroke or rub of fortune.

P صال *sāl*, A raft, a float.

A صال *sāl*, (v. n. of صال for صول) Being proud, unjust: assaulting.

A صالّ *sāll*, Water, which falling on the ground, penetrates it.

A صالب *sālib*, A burning fever. The loins. The back-bone.

A صآلة *saʼālat*, (v. n. of صؤل) Being fierce, untractable, especially to men (a camel).

A صألة *saʼlat*, A charge, attack.

A صالّة *sāllat*, A heavy misfortune.

A صالح *sāliḥ*, Good, apt, fit, proper, just, beneficial. A man of probity and honour. Sedate, steady. The patriarch Sāliḥ, who was sent on a mission to the Arabian tribe of ثمود *samūd*.

A صالحات *sāliḥāt*, (pl. fem.) Good works.

A صالحة *sāliḥat*, (fem. of صالح *sāliḥ*) Virtuous, chaste (woman). A virtuous action.

A صالحيّة *sāliḥiyat*, Name of a sect.

A صالخ *sālikh*, Corroding (scab).

A صالدة *sālidat*, (pl. صوالد *sawālid*) (A tooth) making a grating noise.

A صالغ *sāligh*, (pl. صلّغ *sullagh* and صوالغ *sawāligh*) A five or six-years-old sheep (when the teeth are all grown after being shed). A six-year-old ox. صالغ سنة *sālighu sanat* (or سنتين *sanatayn*), Of one or two years growth beyond سديس *sadīs*.

A صالف *sālif*, A mountain where the Pagan Arabs were used to form their solemn leagues.

A صالي *sālī*, (pl. صليّ *suliy*) One who bakes upon the fire.

A صأم *saʼm*, (v. n. of صأم) Guiding an army against. *Saʼam*, (v. n. of صئم) Drinking much water.

A صامت *sāmit*, Silent, saturnine. Irrational (especially applied to wealth in gold or silver, in contradistinction to an estate in slaves or cattle). Thick (milk). Twenty (camels). جمع صامت و ناطق *jamʻi sāmit u nātiḳ*, A collection of immoveable and moveable (effects).

SY صامر بوما *sāmir būmā*, Name of a plant called حشيشة العقرب *hashīshatu'l ʻaḳrab* (Scorpion-herb).

A صامغان *sāmighānī*, Corners of the mouth.

A صامق *sāmiḳ*, Hungry. Thirsty.

A صامل *sāmil*, Dry, withered.

A صامورة *sāmūrat*, Excessively sour or bitter.

A صانع *sāniʻ*, (pl. صنّاع *sunnāʻ*) A maker, manufacturer, artificer, artisan. صانع عالم *sāniʻi ʻālam*, The Creator of the world.

A صانق *sāniḳ*, (pl. صنقة *sanaḳat*) Firm, strong, hardy. A skilful camel-keeper.

A صاني *sānī*, Addicted to service.

A صاوي *sāwī*, (fem. صاوية *sāwiyat*) Dry.

A صاهل *sāhil*, (A camel) that paws the ground with his feet, and refrains from braying aloud through pride. A she-camel, the mother of such a camel.

ذو صاهل *zū sāhil*, Violent in making an assault.

A صاهلة *sāhilat*, (pl. صواهل *sawāhil*) A whinnying, a neighing. Buzzing of flies in grass. The sound made by a mattock, pick-axe, &c.

A صاهور *sāhūr*, The sheath into which (according to the belief of the vulgar Arabs) the moon enters when eclipsed.

A صائب *sāʼib*, Right, straight. Who or what hits the mark. Raining (sky or cloud). صائب التدبير *sāʼibu't tadbīr*, Advising right, prudent. صائب نظران *sāʼib-nazarān*, (Pers. pl.) Looking straight, considering justly.

P صايبان *sāybān*, (for صايه بان) A shade.

A صائبة *sāʼibat*, Straight-flying (arrow).

A صائت *sāʼit*, Exclaiming; a cry for help.

A صائحة *sāʼiḥat*, Wail of a mourning house.

A صائد *sāʼid*, A hunter. A fowler.

A صائر *sāʼir*, A pin at the top and heel of a door, which, revolving in a socket in the lintel and threshold, serves as a hinge. Becoming, who becomes.

A صائرة *sāʼirat*, Dry fodder, which for a while is eaten after the green.

A صائغ *sāʼigh*, (pl. صاغة *sāghat*) A goldsmith. A founder, moulder, caster, maker of castings.

A صائف *sāʼif*, Wool-bearing, lanigerous, woolly (ram). Hot (day or night). Summer-rain. One who begets children at an advanced time of life, having a vigorous old age. صيف صائف *sayfi sāʼif*, Summer-heat.

A صائفة *sāʼifat*, (pl. صوائف *sawāʼif*) Summer-provision. A summer-campaign.

A صائق *sāʼiḳ*, Adhering, adhesive.

A صائل *sāʼil*, Presumptuous, arrogant, furious.

A صائم *sāʼim*, Thirsty. (pl. صوّام *suwwām*, صيّام *suyyām*, صوّم *suwwam*, صيّم *suyyam*, *siyam*, and صيام *siyām*) One who fasts, or they who fast. One who abstains from food, talk, travelling, or venery. صائم الدهر *sāʼimu'd dahr*, Continually fasting. P صائم شدن *sāʼim shudan*, To fast.

A صائن *sāʼin*, A preserver, keeper, guardian.

A صبّ *sabb*, (v. n. of صبّ) Pouring out. Being poured out. Descending into a valley. Being smitten with love. Smitten with love, burning with desire. Flowing (water). Victuals poured out.

A صبا *sabā*, (v. n. of صبا for صبو) Blowing from the east (wind). (pl. صبوات *sabawāt* and اصباء *asbāʼ*) The zephyr, gentle gale; a refreshing wind (generally blowing from the east at the equinox). The east wind. P باد صبا *bādi sabā*, The zephyr. *Sibāʼ*, Boyishness, childishness.

A صبأ *sabʼ*, (v. n. of صبأ) Rising (a star). Coming forth (as a tooth or a nail). Putting one's fingers into the dish to take food. Being a model, pattern, exemplar. Guiding, directing (an enemy against one). Changing one's religion, *i. e.* apostatizing from Muhammadism, and turning Sabean, or worshipper of the heavenly bodies.

A صباء sabā, (v. n. of صبا for صبو) Playing with boys, acting boyishly. Feeling a juvenile affection for. Leaning towards the male (a female palm). Being silly (a boy). Boyishness. *Sibā*, (v.n.3 of صبا for صبو) Inverting (a sword) to sheath it; (a spear) to strike with it; (or the lips of a camel) to drink. Composing verses with little point or meaning. Causing (an edifice) to lean.

A صبابة *sabābat*, Love, desire (especially tender or vehement). Faintness caused by desire. A fog. لهيب صبابة *lahībi sabāba*, Ardour of love. *Subābat*, Remainder of milk or water in a vessel.

A صباة *subāt*, (pl. of صابئ *sābi*) Sabeans.

A صباح *sabāh*, Morning, dawn. To-morrow morning. Depredation (because generally committed in the morning). Name of a bird. صباح الخير *sabāhu'l khayr*, Good morning; (to which they answer) يا صباح الخير *yā sabāhu'l khayr*, O! Good day (to you also). ذا صباح *zā sabāh*, In the morning. ذو صباح *zū sabāh*, Early (man). علي الصباح *ʿala's sabāh*, Before dawn. يوم الصباح *yawmu's sabāh*, A day of plunder. لقيته صباح *lakītuhu sabāha*, (or ذا صباح *zā sabāha*) I met him in the morning. *Sibāh*, (pl. of صبيح *sabīh*) Beautiful. *Subāh* or *sabāh*, The light or flame of a candle. *Subāh*, Comely, handsome.

A صبّاح *subbāh*, Handsome, comely.

A صباحاً *sabāhan*, (also ذا صباحاً *zā sabāhan*) Early in the morning, betimes.

A صباحة *sabāhat*, (v. n. of صبح) Being handsome, beautiful, comely. Beauty, comeliness, gracefulness, handsomeness of face.

P صباح كنان *sabāh-kunān*, Those who wish good morning.

P صباح نمازي *sabāh-namāzī*, Morning-prayer.

A صباحيّ *subāhīy*, (Blood) extremely red.

A صباحيّة *subāhīyat*, Broad points (of spears).

A صباخ *sibākh*, (pl. of صبخة *sabkhat* or *sabakhat*) Saltish, salsuginous (grounds).

A صبار *sibār*, (v. n. 3 of صبر) Being patient, exercising patience towards one another. A stopple. The fruit of a bitter, salt, or sour vegetable. (pl. of صبرة *subrat*) Rough stones heaped together. (pl. of صبير *sabīr*) Hard stones. *Subār*, Tamarinds. Melancholy madness.

A صبّار *subbār*, Tamarinds. امّ صبار *ummu sabbār*, Heat. Misfortune, calamity. A destructive war.

A صبارة *sabārat*, (v.n. of صبر) Answering or being security for another. Intense winter-cold. *Sa*, *si*, or *subārat*, Stones. Fragments of iron or stones.

A صبّارة *sabbārat*, Intenseness of cold. Rough and high ground. صبّارة الشتاء *sabbāratu'sh shitā*, Intenseness of winter-cold.

A صباصب *sabāsib*, Thick, solid.

A صباغ *sibāgh*, Colour, tincture, dye. (pl. of صبغ *sibgh*) Seasonings, sauces.

A صبّاغ *sabbāgh*, A dyer, tinger, painter. A liar, one who gives a false colouring to a statement. صبّاغ اثمار *sabbāghi asmār*, (Colourer of fruits) The moon. صبّاغ تنگار *sabbāghi tangār*, The moon. صبّاغ جواهر *sabbāghi jawāhir*, Jewel-painter (epithet of the sun). دود الصبّاغين *dūdu's sabbāghīn*, Dyers' insect, kermes, crimson, cochineal.

A صباغة *sibāghat*, Art of dyeing or colouring.

A صباوة *sabāwat*, Infancy, childhood, boyhood.

A صبايا *sabāya*, (pl. of صبيّة) Girls, damsels.

A صبيب *sabab*, (v. n. of صبّ) Being violently in love, and frantic. (pl. اصباب *asbāb*) A declivity. A waterfall. Sliding sand.

A صبّة *sabbat*, (fem.) Inflamed with love. *Subbat*, A portion of the night. Remains of water or milk in a vessel. Victuals poured out. A table or tray on which victuals are placed. A little of any thing. A crowd, body. A herd of cattle, camels, or horses (from 10 to 40, or of camels below a 100).

A صبث *subs*, (v. n. of صبث) Mending or darning (a shirt).

A صبح *sabh*, (v. n. of صبح) Coming in the morning. *Subh*, (pl. اصباح *asbāh*) Morning, dawn. صبح اوّلين *subhi awwalīn*, (P صبح نخست *subhi nukhust*, A صبح كاذب *subhi kāzib*, P صبح دروغ *subhi durogh*, or A صبح ملمّع نقاب *subhi mulammaʿ nikāb*) The first or false dawn, the twilight. P صبح پسين *subhi pasīn*, (صبح راست *subhi rāst*, or A صبح صادق *subhi sādik*) The last or true dawn, break of day. صبح و مسا *subh u masā*, (or صبح و شام *subh u shām*) Morning and evening. امّ صبح *ummu subh*, Mecca. من الصبح *mini's subh*, Since morning. اتيته لصبح خامسة *ataytuhu li subhi*, (or *sibhi*) *khāmisatin*, I came to him on the morning of the fifth day. *Sabah*, (v. n. of صبح) Being of a white colour inclining to red. The flash or gleam of steel.

A صبحا *subhan*, In the morning.

A صبحاء *sabhā*, (fem. of اصبح *asbah*) Black-haired, inclining to red.

A صبحان *sabhān*, Handsome. One who drinks early in the morning. *Sabahān*, One who makes haste to drink betimes.

A صبحة *sabhat* or *subhat*, A morning-nap. *Subhat*, (v. n. of صبح) Being of a white colour mixed with red (hair). Being of a reddish black. Any amusement by which one whiles away the morning. A black colour inclining to red. الصبحة *as' subhata*, The morning, in the morning.

P صبح خيزا *subh-khezā*, (or صبح خيزيا *subh-kheziyā*) A set of thieves who arise betimes, and steal before people are awake.

P صبح دل *subh-dil*, Of an enlightened understanding. Honest, pious, pure.

P صبحدم *subh-dam*, Early in the morning.

P صبح روان *subh-ravān*, Youths. Travellers.

P صبحگاه *subh-gāh*, The morning. مهر صبحگاه صفت *mihri subhgāh-sifat*, Like the morning-sun.

P صبح نشينان *subh-nishīnān*, Early risers, holy.

A صبخة *sabkhat* or *sabakhat*, (pl. صباخ *sibākh*) Saltish, brackish, salsuginous (ground or water).

A صبر *sabr*, (v. n. of صبر) Being patient, waiting patiently. Restraining, withholding one's self or another. Compelling, forcing. Detaining forcibly and putting to death. Adhering, sticking close to. Collecting, heaping up (stores of food) without weight or measure. Giving bail or surety. Answering for, or becoming surety. Patience, toleration, endurance, resignation. The aloe. P صبر داشتن *sabr dāshtan*, To have patience, to wait, expect, suffer, bear with. صبر نمودن *sabr namūdan*, To bear up, endure, support. A الصبر مفتاح الفخر *as'sabr miftāhu'l fakhr*, Patience is the key of glory (a proverb). صبر و قرار *sabr u karār*, Patience and constancy. شهر الصبر *shahru's sabr*, The month of patience, *i. e.* of fasting. يمين الصبر *yamīnu's sabr*, A compulsory oath. صبر سمنجاني *sabri samanjānī*, The worst species of aloe. صبر عربي *sabri ʿarabī*, The small Arabian aloe. امرّ من الصبر *amarr mini's sabr*, More bitter than the aloe. *Sibr* or *subr*, (pl. اصبار *asbār*) A white cloud. A side, brink, brim, margin, lip. The entire of any thing. *Subr* or *subur*, Gravelly, but not rocky, ground. *Sabar*, Ice. Snow. Fulness to the brim. *Sabir*, The aloe. *Subar*, (pl. of صبرة *subrat*) Garners. Heaps of corn. *Subur*, (pl. of صبور *sabūr*) Patient. (pl. of صبير *sabīr*) White clouds.

A صبراً *sabran*, Patiently. حلّف صبراً *hullifa sabran*, He was forcibly detained and compelled to swear. قتل صبراً *kutila sabran*, He was forcibly detained and put to death.

A صبراء *subarā*, (pl. of صبير *sabīr*) Sponsors, sureties. Leaders, patrons. Mountains.

A صبرة *sabrat*, Mid-winter. Intense cold. Dung of cattle heaped, or adhering to the environs of a watering-place. *Subrat*, A heap of corn unweighed and unmeasured. Sifted corn. Ballast of a ship. (pl. صبار *sibār*) Rugged stones or coarse gravel heaped together. Mid-winter. اخذه صبرة *akhazahu subratan*, He received it by the heap, without weight or measure.

A صبر سقّوطري *sibr sukkūtarī*, Soccotrine aloes.

A صبصاب *sabsāb*, Thick, solid, firm. A brave, powerful, and active man. The remains of any thing poured out. Any thing gone or obliterated. خمس صبصاب *khimsi sabsāb*, An effort made to water camels on the fifth day.

A صبصب *sabsab*, Thick, solid.

A صبصبة *sabsabat*, (v. n. of صبصب Q) Dispersing an army. Pouring out. Abolishing, erasing, obliterating. Scattering, squandering (money).

A صبط *sabt*, A plough-beam.

A صبع *sabʿ*, (v. n. of صبع) Pointing the finger at one in scorn; making a signal, beckoning. Stopping with the finger part of a bottle's mouth, to prevent a thing pouring out being spilt. Examining with the finger if a hen is with egg. Pride. Proud.

A صبغ *sabgh* or *sibagh*, (v. n. of صبغ) Dyeing (cloth). Plunging or dipping (the hand in water). Baptizing. Forming a judgment (by the motion of the eye). *Sibgh*, (pl. صباغ *sibāgh*) Seasoning or sauce for victuals, especially meat or fish. (pl. اصباغ *asbāgh*) Colour, tincture, dye. Christian baptism. صبغ الثمن *sibghu's saman*, A just, fair price. انها لحديثة الصبغ *innahā la hadīsatu's sibgh*, She is the first with whom a matrimonial alliance has been formed. *Sibagh*, Colour, tincture, dye.

A صبغاء *sabghāɛ*, (fem. of اصبغ *asbagh*) A sheep or a mare white at the extremity of the tail. A certain tree growing in the sand producing white fruit: also one whose buds are green on the upper parts exposed to the sun, and white in the parts which lie in the shade.

A صبغة *sibghat*, Colour, tincture, dye. Christian baptism. Religion. The rite of circumcision. The law of God. *Subghat*, A date partly ripe.

A صبغيّ *sibghīy*, A dyer. A vender of colours.

A صبن *sabn*, (v. n. of صبن) Prohibiting, preventing, withholding. Laying the dice even in the hand before throwing. Turning away (a cup) from any one.

A صبناء *sabnāɛ*, (A hand) ready for treachery

A صبنيّ *sabnīy*, Expressed juice of senna.

A صبو *sabw*, The being childish or foolish.

A صبوّ *subūw*, (v. n. of صبا for صبو) Blowing from the east (wind). Playing with boys, behaving like a child. Having a juvenile passion. Turning the head towards the pasture (a flock). Leaning towards the male, from a distance (a female palm).

A صبوء *subūɛ*, (or صبوءة *subūɛat*) (v. n. of صبأ) Rising (a star). Coming forth (a tooth or nail). Being a model or exemplar. Changing one's religion, becoming a Sabean. Guiding, conducting an enemy against any one.

A صبوان *sub* or *sibwān*, (pl. of صبيّ *sabīy*) Boys.

A صبوب *sabūb*, Poured out. Sloping ground.

A صبوة *sabwat*, (v. n. of صبا for صبو) Being childish. Juvenile ignorance. The keenest part of a sword. (pl. of صبيّ *sabīy*) Boys. *Sabwat*, (or صبوّة *subūwat*) (v. n. of صبا for صبو) Playing with boys, behaving like a child. Having a juvenile passion.

A صبوح *sabūh*, A morning draught. Wine which is drunk in the morning. A camel milked betimes. ذا صبوح *zā sabūha*, In the morning.

A صبوحة *sabūhat*, A camel milked betimes.

A صبوحي *sabūhī*, A morning draught. P صبوحي كردن *sabūhī kardan*, To drink betimes.

A صبور *sabūr*, Patient, gentle, mild, long-suffering. Lenient towards offenders. امّ صبّور *umm sabbūr*, Heat. Misfortune, calamity. Stony ground, burned up. A destructive war.

A صبورة *sabūrat*, Taken and kept to be slain.

P صبورة *sabūra*, Obscene, impure. A catamite.

A صبوري *sabūrī*, Patience, forbearance.

A صبوغ *subūgh*, (v. n. of صبغ) Becoming distended, sleek (udder). Being long (a muscle). Pointing, directing, beckoning with the eye.

A صبيٌ *saba'* or *siba'*, (v. n. of صبا for صبو) Being childish and foolish. *Siba'*, Childhood, boyishness.

P صبي *sabī*, Senna. The herb alkali.

A صبيّ *sabīy*, (pl. اصبي *asbī*, اصبية *asbiyat*, صبوة *sabwat*, صبية *subyat* or *sibyat*, صبوان *subwān* or *sibwān*, صبيان *subyān* or *sibyān*) A boy. Boyish. An unweaned child. The keenest part of a sword. The part of the skull below the ear. The top of the foot as far as the root of the toes. Chief of the people. The side of the jaw. صبيّ العين *sabīyu'l ɛayn*, The pupil of the eye. P صبيّ غافل بي باك *sābīyi ghāfili bī bāk*, A heedless boy, without fear.

A *Subayy*, (dim. of صبيّ *sabīy*) A little boy.

A صبيان *subyān* or *sibyān*, (pl. of صبيّ) Boys.

A صبيب *sabīb*, Water poured out or spilled. Blood (especially when shed). Juice, sap, spirit. Ice. Edge or point of a sword. The finest honey. Juice of the leaves of sesame, of cypress, or other plants of a deep red colour. A substance resembling indigo or woad. A red tincture or dye. Flowers of the bastard saffron. A shrub resembling rue or senna.

A صبية *sibyat* or *subyat*, (pl. of صبيّ) Boys.

A صبيّة *sabīyat*, (pl. صبايا *sabāya*) A girl, damsel, child, or daughter. *Subayyat*, (dim. of صبية *sibyat*) Little boys.

A صبيح *sabīh*, (pl. صباح *sibāh*) Beautiful, handsome. A lovely face.

A صبيحة *sabīhat*, Morning, dawn.

A صبيخة *sabīkhat*, Any thing which falls from carded cotton or bird's feathers. صبيخة القطن *sabīkhatu'l kutn*, Cotton spread out for spinning.

A صبير *sabīr*, Patient, mild, long-suffering. (pl. صبراء *subarāɛ*) A surety, sponsor. A patron, leader, or director of people's affairs. (pl. صبر *subur*) A white cloud, curling one part above another, or a piece of a cloud falling from the rest. A mountain. A tray or table. *Sabīr*, (or صبيرة *sabīrat*) A thin, round, crisp biscuit laid under meat. ابو صبيرة *abū subayrat* Name of a bird having a red breast, with back, head, and tail black.

A صبيغ *sabīgh*, Name of a man who was accustomed to embarrass people by difficult and perplexing questions; for which offence he was banished by the caliph Omar from Madina to Basra.

A صبينة *sabyanat*, A retiring, a departing.

A صتّ *satt*, (v. n. of صتّ) Smiting with a calamity or with bitter words. Clamour, loud noise. A violent push or repulse. A squeeze. A blow with the hand. A body of men. *Sitt*, The contrary, opposite. A crowd, company.

A صتأ *satɛ*, (v. n. of صتأ) Undertaking an important business.

A صتات *sitāt*, A litigating, a contending.

A صتام *sutām*, Large, bulky (head).

A صتّة *suttat*, The contrary, opposite.

A صتت *satat*, Near. Opposite. Purpose, design, point (as, on the point of retiring).

A صتع *satɛ*, (v. n. of صتع) Prostrating. *Sataɛ*, A robust youth. A wild ass. Contortion of the neck or head of an ostrich. A hardness and gracefulness in the head.

A صتم *satm* or *satam*, (pl. *sutm*) Thick, strong (slave or camel). Complete (thing). (A man) of full age. *Sutm*, as الف صتم *alf sutm*, A thousand complete. اموال صتم *amwālun sutmun*, Perfect, complete flocks or riches. حروف الصتم *hurūfu's sutm*, All the letters excepting ب, ر, ف, ل, م, ن.

A صتمة *satmat*, Hard (stone or she-camel).

A صتو *satw*, (v. n. of صتا for صتو) Going, prancing, or hopping along.

A صته *sath*, A rendering vile, abject.

A صتّية *suttīyat*, Fine linen of Yaman. A veil of fine linen.

A صتيت *satīt*, Sound, noise, murmur. A body of men, crowd, tumult.

A صتيمة *satīmat*, A hard stone.

A صجّ *sajj*, (v. n. of صجّ) Striking one piece of iron against another.

A صجج *sujuj*, Noise of iron striking iron.

A صحّ *sahh*, (v. n. of صحّ) Being sound, entire, free from flaw, true. Recovering from sickness. *Sahh* or *sahha*, It is true. *Suhh*, Soundness, integrity, freedom from blemish. Health.

A صحاب *sihāb*, (pl. of صاحب) Companions.

A صحابة *sa* or *sihābat*, (v. n. of صحب) Associating together. (pl. of صاحب *sāhib*) Companions.

A صحابيّ *sahābīy*, (fem. صحابيّة *sahābīyat*) One of the صحاب *sihāb* or صحابة *sahābat*, i.e. Companions of Muhammad or their descendants.

A صحابيّات *sahābīyāt*, Female companions of Muhammad.

A صحاح *sahāh*, (pl. *sihāh*) Complete, perfect, sound, entire. Sound, whole, uncut (skin). Right, just, true, certain. Hard (road). Soundness, health, freedom from blemish. The title of an Arabic lexicon, compiled by جوهريّ *jawhariy*. A rough road.

A صحار *sihār*, (v. n. 3 of صحر) Doing any thing plainly, openly, and publicly. *Suhār*, Name of a town on the southern coast of Arabia. The sweat or fever of horses.

A صحاراً *sihāran*, Publicly, openly.

A صحاري *sahāra'*, (*sahāri*, or صحاريّ *sahārīy*) (pl. of صحراء *sahrāɛ*) Deserts.

A صحاصح *sahāsih*, (pl. of صحصح *sahsah*, صحصاح *sahsāh*, and صحصحان *sahsahān*) Extensive pieces of level ground. ترّهات صحاصح *turrahāti sahāsih*, Trifles, vanities, futile things.

A صحاف *sihāf*, (pl. صحف *suhuf*) A place where water collects. (pl. of صحفة *sahfat*) Platters, dishes.

A صحّاف *sahhāf*, A bookseller. A bookbinder.

A librarian.

A صحائح *sahāsih,* (pl. of صحاح *sahāh* and صحيح *sahīh*) Sound, entire, unblemished. The Thummim.

A صحائف *sahāsif,* (pl. of صحيفة *sahīfat*) Pages, leaves, books. P در صحائف سابقه *dar sahāsifi sābika,* In the preceding pages.

A صحب *sahb,* (v. n. of صحب) Skinning a slaughtered animal. (pl. of صاحب *sāhib*) Companions. صحب كرام *sahbi kirām,* The illustrious companions (*i. e.* of Muhammad).

A صحبان *suhbān,* (pl. of صاحب *sāhib*) Companions, friends, associates.

A صحبة *suhbat,* (v. n. of صحب) Associating together. Society, friendship, companionship. Companionship of Muhammad. Communion. An assembly. A fair. Conversation, discourse, intercourse. Coition. (pl. of صاحب *sāhib*) Companions. صحبة الرسول *suhbatu'r rasūl,* In company with the apostle. صحبته *suhbatuhu,* Together with him. P صحبت داشتن *suhbat dāshtan,* To associate. صحبت كردن *suhbat kardan,* To keep company, to converse with. A الصحبة مؤثرة *as'suhbat muasassirat,* Society is contagious.

P صحبت خانه *suhbat-khāna,* A privy.

P صحبت داري *suhbat-dārī,* Association.

A صحّة *sihhat,* (v. n. of صحّ) Recovering from sickness, being convalescent. Being right, straightforward (a business). Integrity, soundness, freedom from blemish. Health. صحّه و عافيه *sihha su ɛāfiya,* Health to you, your health (when drinking to another, or when he has finished his draught).

P صحّت خانه *sihhat-khāna,* A necessary.

A صحر *sahr,* (v. n. of صحر) Cooking. Giving a pain in the head (the sun). *Suhr,* Name of Lokman's sister, who met a bad requital for doing good; hence, ما لي الّا ذنب صحر *mā lī illā zambu suhr.* *Sahar,* A dusty white inclining to red. *Suhar,* (pl. of صحرة *suhrat*) Gaps, openings in the earth.

A صحراء *sahrās,* (pl. صحاري *sahāra',* *sahārī,* صحاريّ *sahāriy,* and صحراوات *sahrāwāt*) A desert, plain, barren waste. P صحراى سيم *sahrāsi sīm,* The true dawn. صحراى قدسي *sahrāsi kudsī,* Heaven.

P صحرا گرد *sahrā-gard* (or نورد *naward*), A traveller in the desert.

P صحرا نشين *sahrā-nishīn,* (Desert-sitting, desert-inhabiting) A hermit, solitary man.

A صحراوات *sahrāwāt,* (pl. of صحراء) Deserts.

A صحراويّ *sahrāwiy,* Campestrian, desert.

A صحرائى *sahrāsiy,* Wild, desert, uninhabited.

A صحرة *suhrat,* (pl. صحر *suhar*) A gap, opening, or gulf in stony ground. Of the colour of the anemone. صحرة بحرة نحرة *suhrata buhrata nuhrata,* (*sahrata bahrata nahrata,* or *sahratan bahratan nahratan*) (I saw him) openly, no object intervening. *Suharat,* A dusty colour inclining to red.

A صحصح *sahsah,* (صحصاح *sahsāh,* and صحصحان *sahsahān*) An extensive piece of level ground. *Suhsuh,* (or صحصوح *suhsūh*) One who pursues minute objects; quick, subtle, penetrating.

A صحصحة *sahsahat,* A being manifest, certain.

A صحف *suhuf,* (pl. of صحاف *sihāf*) Small places where water collects. (pl. of صحيفة *sahīfat*) Books, leaves, pages, folios. صحف ربّانيّه *suhufi rabbānīya,* The sacred (or rabbinical) writings.

A صحفة *sahfat,* (pl. صحاف *sihāf* or صحفات *sahafāt*) A plate, a dish.

A صحفيّ *sahafiy,* One who makes mistakes in reading, inaccurate. *Suhufiy,* A bookseller.

A صحل *sahal,* (v. n. of صحل) Being hoarse. A cracked voice. *Sahil,* Hoarse.

A صحماء *sahmās,* (fem. of اصحم *as-ham*) Black and yellowish. Dusty, squalid. A sort of plant.

A صحمة *suhmat,* Blackness inclining to yellow, or dust-colour inclining to black, or red to white.

A صحن *sahn,* (v. n. of صحن) Effecting a reconciliation, making up differences. Striking. Giving (something in a dish). A large cup or goblet. (pl. اصحن *as-hun*) A hollow dish or platter. A cymbal. A court, court-yard, square, area. A floor. A grass-plot. The inner part of a hoof. صحن ارم *sahni iram,* A garden. P صحن دو رنگ *sahni du rang,* The world. صحن سيم *sahni sīm,* A sheet of white paper. The moon's disk. A صحن عظيم *sahni ɛazīm* (or وسيع *wasīɛ*), The earth's surface.

A صحنا *sahna'* or *sihna',* Jelly of fish.

A صحناء *sahnās,* Interior of the ear. Fish-jelly.

A P صحناة *sahnāt,* The jelly of salted fish. *Sahnāt* or *sihnāt,* A kind of food prepared from fish.

A صحنان *sahnāni,* (dual of صحن *sahn*) Two plates which they strike one against another, making a musical accompaniment to drums and other instruments, cymbals. Magdeburg spheres.

A صحنة *suhnat,* A hollow in hard, rocky ground.

A صحو *sahw,* (v. n. of صحا for صحو) Recovering from ebriety. Leaving off childish folly and vanity. Going off (cold); departing, being dispersed (clouds). Being clear and serene (day or sky). Serenity of sky, clearness of the atmosphere. A trance. Cloudless (day or sky).

A صحور *sahūr,* White, red, kicking (she-ass).

A صحون *sahūn,* Kicking (camel).

A صحيح *sahīh,* (pl. اصحّاء *asihhās* or صحائح *sahāsih*) Complete, perfect, entire, sound. Free from blemish, pure, unbroken. Right, just, true, certain, authentic, accurate, correct. A sound verb. Certainly, truly. صحيح الخبر *sahīhu'l khabar,* An accurate historian. حرف صحيح *harfi sahīh,* A sound letter (not ا *alif,* و *wāw,* or ي *ye*). قياس صحيح الاركان *kiyāsi sahīhu'l arkān,* An argument founded on pillars; *i. e.* a syllogism. حكايةُ صحيح الروايه *hikāyasi sahīhu'r riwāya,* History faithfully related. P صحيح كردن *sahīh kardan,* To correct, amend.

A صحير *sahīr,* The braying of an ass.

A صحيراء *suhayrās,* A kind of milk.

A صحيرة *sahīrat,* Milk heated, into which butter or flour is put.

A صحيف *sahīf,* The surface of the earth. (pl. صحيف *sahīf*) The surface of the skin.

A صحيفة *sahīfat,* (pl. صحائف *sahāsif* and صحف *suhuf*) A book. A leaf, page. P صحيفهٔ تيغ سحر *sahīfasi teghi sahar,* The twilight or the false dawn. صحيفهٔ زر *sahīfasi zar,* The sun. A yellow cheek. Autumnal leaves. A *Suhayfat,* A plate, small dish (enough to satisfy one person).

A صخّ *sakhkh,* (v. n. of صخّ) Deafening with a thundering noise. Pecking a camel's back (a crow). Collision of solid and sonorous bodies. Sound of a stone when struck.

A صخاءة *sakhāsat,* Dirt, filth. A kind of vegetable or pot-herb.

A صخّاب *sakhkhāb,* (fem. صخّابة *sakhkhābat*) Clamorous. Scurrilous, foul-mouthed.

A صخب *sakhab,* (v. n. of صخب) Being noisy and clamorous. Clamour, noise, murmur, tumult. *Sakhib,* Noisy, dashing (waves). Clamorous. صخب الشوارب *sakhibu'sh shawārib,* (An ass) reiterating a sound in his throat, braying loudly.

A صخبان *sakhbān,* (pl. *sukhbān*) Clamorous, noisy, tumultuous.

A صخبة *sakhbat,* A glass-bead or shell worn as a philter or amulet. *Sakhibat,* Clamorous, noisy (woman). عين صخبة *ɛaynun sakhibatun* or *sakhbatun,* A fountain noisy and dashing.

A صخبّة *sukhubbat,* Clamorous, noisy (woman).

A صخّة *sakhkhat,* The sound of striking stones.

A صخد *sakhd,* (v. n. of صخد) Scorching (as the sun). Chattering (as the bird called صرد *surad*). Squeaking (the jerboa). *Sakhad,* (v. n. of صخد) Being intensely hot (the day).

A صخدان *sakh* or *sakhadān,* Very hot (day).

A صخر *sakhr* and *sakhar,* (pl. of صخرة *sakhrat* and *sakharat*) Rocks, huge hard stones. *Sakhir,* Rocky (place).

A صخرات *sakharāt,* (pl. of صخرة *sakhrat* or *sakharat*) Rocks, huge stones.

A صخرة *sakhrat* or *sakharat,* (pl. صخر *sakhr, sakhar,* صخور *sukhūr,* and صخرات *sakharāt*) A rock, huge hard stone.

A صخف *sakhf,* A digging with a spade.

A صخم *sakhm,* (v. n. of صخم) Scorching, burning (as the sun).

A صخماء *sakhmās,* A rocky country, part plain, part mountainous.

A صخو *sakhw,* The act of opening (a fire).

A صخوب *sakhūb,* Clamorous, noisy.

A صخود *sukhūd,* A listening, a paying attention.

A صخور *sukhūr,* (pl. of صخرة *sakhrat*) Rocks.

A صخي *sakha',* (v. n. of صخي) Being dirty (clothes). Filth. *Sakhī,* Dirty, filthy.

A صخيخ *sakhīkh,* The collision of solid and sonorous bodies. The noise of a stone when struck.

A صخير *sakhīr*, A sort of plant.

P صد *sad*, A hundred. صد چندان *sad chandān*, A hundred more or less. A hundred such. صد شاخ كردن *sad shākh kardan*, To break into a hundred pieces.

A صدّ *sadd*, (v. n. of صدّ) Prohibiting, checking, hindering, turning away. *Sadd* or *sudd*, A mountain. The side of a channel, a valley.

A صدء *sad*ʼ, (v. n. of صدأ) Clearing away rust, polishing. Rust.

A صدأ *sada*ʼ, (v. n. of صدئ) Contracting rust (iron). Being of a bay or rusty colour. Standing up and looking (a man). Slender-bodied (man), of a graceful form. Rust.

A صدا *sada*', Reverberating noise, echo. اصمّ الله صداه *asamma'llāh sadāhu*, May God silence him! صداى كوس ظفر مأنوس *sada'i kūsi zafar-maʼnūs*, The sound of the victorious kettle-drums.

A صداء *sidāʼ*, (v. n. of صدا for صدو) Dissembling. Neither refusing nor consenting. Covering, veiling. Opposing, resisting.

A صدآء *sadʼāʼ*, Rust-coloured or bay (mare). Mailed in rusty armour and stinking (troop). Name of a well of very sweet water.

A صدّاء *saddāʼ*, Name of a well of sweet water.

A صدأة *sudʼat*, A rusty colour.

A صداح *sudāh*, (v. n. of صدح) Calling out aloud, making a noise. The crowing of a hen.

A صدّاح *saddāh*, One who makes a loud noise.

A صداد *sidād*, Female dress, covering: a veil.

A صدّاد *suddād*, (pl. صدائد *sadāʼid*) A serpent. A kind of lizard. A way to water.

A صدار *sidār*, (v. n. 3 of صدر) Requiring, compelling, or urging. Breast-harness. A mark on a camel's breast. A kind of kerchief or coif, the upper part of which covers the head, and the lower part conceals the bosom and shoulders. كلّ ذات صدار خالة *kullu zāti sidārin khālatun*, Every veiled woman (ought to be regarded as) a maternal aunt.

A صدارة *sadārat*, The office of grand vazīr or prime-minister, premiership. Chief-justiceship. (pl. صدائر *sadāʼir*) Higher, advanced part of a valley.

A صداع *sudāʻ*, Headache, megrim.

A صداغ *sidāgh*, A mark burnt on the temples.

A صداغة *sadāghat*, A being weak, feeble, silly.

A صداق *sadāk* or *sidāk*, (pl. صدق *sudk* and *suduk*) A marriage-settlement; a portion which the husband engages to give to his future wife. *Sidāk*, (v. n. 3 of صدق) Cultivating friendship. Sincere and mutual friendship.

A صداقة *sadākat*, True friendship, sincerity, candour, loyalty, fidelity. P صداقت پرور *sadākat-parwar*, Educated in truth, accustomed to sincerity. صداقت كار *sadākat-kār*, (or صداقت گستر *sadākat-gustar*) Sincere, faithful. صداقت گستري *sadākat-gustarī*, Show or profession of sincerity or candour.

A صدام *sidām*, A distemper in horses' heads.

A صدّان *suddāni*, The two sides of the top of the head. The two sides of the notch of an arrow.

A صدائد *sadāʼid*, (pl. of صدّاد *suddād*) Serpents. Lizards.

A صدائر *sadāʼir*, (pl. of صدارة *sadārat* or of صديرة *sadīrat*) Higher, advanced parts of valleys.

P صدبرگ *sad-barg*, Centfoil. Name of a damsel. گل صدبرگ *guli sad-barg*, A many-leaved rose.

P صدپا *sad-pā*, A centiped.

P صدپاره *sad-pāra*, In a hundred pieces.

P صدپايه *sad-pāya*, A centiped.

P صد پيوند *sad paywand*, Shepherd's staff.

P صدتر *sad-tar*, (or صدتو *sad-to*) A hundred folds; part of the tripe or stomach so called.

A صدح *sadh*, (v. n. of صدح) Raising the voice, singing, croaking, or crowing loud (a man, crow, or cock). *Sadah*, A standard, ensign. An empty place. A hillock. A heap of stones. A kind of fruit more red than the jujube. A broad stone. (pl. صدحان *sidhān*) A black, a negro.

A صدحان *sidhān*, (pl. of صدح) Blacks, negroes.

A صدحة *sadhat*, *sudhat*, or *sadahat*, A bead or shell used as an amulet.

A صدد *sadad*, Near. Opposite. Purpose, design.

P صد در *sad dar*, Hundred doors or ways: title of one of the sacred books of the fire-worshippers.

P صددهن *sad dahan*, (Hundred-mouthed) One who first says one thing, and then another.

P صدر *sadr*, Chief seat. Prime-minister. A judge.

A صدر *sadr*, (v. n. of صدر) Returning. Leading back from watering. Wounding the breast. Rejecting, dropping the ا *alif* in the measure فاعلن *fāʻilun*. (pl. صدور *sudūr*) The breast. Proemium or exordium of a letter. A beginning. A part. The first seat of precedency. Any thing opposite or confronting. Pre-eminence. Chief. Government. The prow or bow of a ship. That part of an arrow from the middle to the point. The first foot of the first hemistich. The body of a letter or petition. صدر اعظم *sadri aʻzam*, Prime-minister. Dignity of premier. Chief seat. صدر الحقّ *sadru'l hakk*, Chief judge. صدر صدور *sadri sudūr*, Chief judge, chancellor. صدر عدالة *sadr ʻadālat*, The superior court of justice, the presidency. صدر القدم *sadru'l kadam*, The forepart of the instep; the root of the toes. بنات الصدر *banātu's sadr*, Care, solicitude. في صدر الاسلام *fī sadri'l islām*, At the commencement of Muhammadism. *Sadar*, Return from water or from pilgrimage. The fourth of the days of نحر *nahr*.

A صدرة *sudrat*, The upper part of the human breast. The thorax. A stomacher. A cassock.

P صدرنج *sad ranj*, (Hundred cares) Chess.

P صدرنشين *sadr-nishīn*, Holding the first dignity, sitting in the highest place of honour. The grand vazīr. صدرنشين مسند *sadr-nishīni masnad*, Sitting on the throne, *i.e.* the reigning king.

P صدره *sad rah*, A hundred kinds or ways.

A صدريّ *sadrīy*, Pectoral. Supreme.

P صد سال *sad sāl*, A century.

A صدع *sadʻ*, (v. n. of صدع) Cleaving (especially a hard substance). Suffering from headache. Going in the middle of the road. Asking or desiring. Distinguishing truth from falsehood. Crossing (a desert). Speaking with a loud voice. Exposing openly, uncovering, displaying, making public. Acknowledging publicly. Reaching, arriving at. Giving a right order or correct judgment. Appealing to the liberality of any one. Carrying on open hostilities, being an undisguised enemy. Being inclined to. Deterring, averting from. Herbage. (pl. صدوع *sudūʻ*) A fissure, rupture, crack in a hard substance. A company, body, troop, band. *Sadʻ* or *sadaʻ*, Light or thin of flesh. Of a middle stature, age, weight, or robustness. عليهم صدع واحد *ʻalayhim sadʻun wāhidun*, The enmity amongst them is mutual. *Sidʻ*, A crowd. A piece of any thing. *Sadaʻ*, Rust. *Sadaʻ* or *sadʻ*, Young and vigorous (mountain-goat, buck, ass, or camel). *Suduʻ*, (pl. of صديع *sadīʻ*) Dawns. New patches on old garments. Halves.

A صدعات *sadaʻāt*, Different opinions or sects. Schisms, divisions, separations.

A صدعة *sidʻat*, A herd, flock. A half of any thing split in twain.

A صدغ *sadgh*, (v. n. of صدغ) Overtaking, and walking by the side of another. Travelling or walking in company, cheek by jowl. Branding (a camel). Turning from, beating off, diverting. Crushing (a pismire). *Sudgh*, (pl. اصداغ *asdāgh*) The temple, that part of the face from the eye to the ear. The hair that flows around the temples. صدغ معقرب *sudghi muʻakrab*, Curling locks.

A صدف *sadf*, (v. n. of صدف) Declining, receding, turning away from. Diverting. *Sadaf*, (v. n. of صدف) Declining, receding from. (pl. اصداف *asdāf*) A shell, shell-fish, pearl, mother-o'-pearl, oyster. A closeness of the thighs in a horse with a straddling of the feet. The top of the shoulder-blade. Lofty (wall). A cartilaginous excrescence, in consequence of a wound on the skull. Any thing elevated. The higher part of a wall or mountain. P صدف آتشين *sadafi ātishīn*, (or صدف روز *sadafi roz*) The sun. صدف صد و چهارده عقد *sadafi sad u chahārdah ʻakd*, The Kur'ān (as consisting of 114 chapters). A صدف فلك *sadafi falak*, The highest heaven. Sun and moon. Name of a figure formed by several stars near the north pole. P صدف مشكين رنگ *sadafi mushkīn-rang*, The sky. صدف هزار بيدق *sadafi hazār baydak*, The stars. *Sadaf*, *sudaf*, *suduf*, or *saduf*, The part at which a mountain breaks off: a side or tract of it. *Sudaf*, Name of a certain beast or bird.

A صدفان *sudufāni*, The two sides of a valley or pass through mountains.

P صدف پاره *sadaf-pāra*, A piece of a shell.

A صدفة *sadafat*, A single oyster-shell.

P صدفچه *sadafcha*, A small or fine shell.

P صدف گون ساغر *sadaf-gūn sāghar*, Glass goblet.

A صدق *sadk*, (v. n. of صدق) Speaking truth. Being true, just, honest, upright. Hard and smooth (spear). Complete, perfect in number. True, sincere. Truth, veracity. *Sidk*, Truth, veracity, sincerity. Praise. A good name. Good, excellent. Vehemence, intenseness. *Sudk* or *suduk*, (pl. of صدق *sadk*, صدوق *sadūk*, and صداق *sadāk*) True. Perfect. *Sadak*, A festival-night, on which the Persians were wont formerly to light a large number of fires. (It is properly written with a س *sin*).

A صدقاء *sudakās*, (pl. of صديق *sadīk*) True, just, sincere friends.

A صدقات *sudkāt*, *sudakāt*, and *sudukāt*, (pl. of صدقة *sudkat*) Marriage-portions. *Sadakāt*, (pl. of صدقة *sadakat*) Alms. *Sadukāt*, (pl. of صدقة *sadukat*) Marriage-portions.

A صدقان *sudkān*, (pl. of صديق) Sincere friends.

A صدقة *sadkat*, Perfect (woman). *Sadakat*, Alms; that part of an estate dedicated to pious uses. *Sada*, *sadu*, *sad*, *sud*, *suda*, or *sudukat*, A woman's dowry.

P صدق ورز *sidk-warz*, Sincere, true.

A صدم *sadm*, (v. n. of صدم) Beating, bruising. Hitting, striking one hard body against another. Overtaking one (a sore misfortune). Collision.

A صدمات *sadamāt*, (pl. of صدمة *sadmat*) Blows, collisions. Adversities. صدمات آلات قتال *sadamāti ālāti kitāl*, Clashings of deadly weapons.

A صدمة *sadmat*, A baldness about the temples. Blow, collision, shock. Adversity, blow of fortune.

A صدمتان *sad* or *sidmatāni*, Both sides of the forehead.

A صدو *sadw*, A clapping of the hands.

A صدوح *sadūh*, One making a loud noise.

A صدود *sadūd*, Sly, deceitful. A certain substance rubbed on a mirror, and afterwards made into a collyrium. *Sudūd*, (v. n. of صدّ) Turning away the countenance, declining, being averse, alienated. Hindering, preventing, diverting. Aversion.

A صدور *sudūr*, (v. n. of صدر) Rising, springing, proceeding, flowing, issuing. The higher and more advanced parts of a valley. (pl. of صدر *sadr*) Breasts.

A صدوع *sudūʻ*, (v. n. of صدع) Having a strong propensity, being inclined. Declining, diverting from, preventing. Dividing (a flock) into two parts. (pl. of صدع *sadʻ*) Fissures, ruptures. Companies, troops, bands.

A صدوف *sadūf*, (A woman) turning her face towards you, and then immediately looking a contrary way. One who has a fetid breath. *Sudūf*, (v. n. of صدف) Declining, receding from.

A صدوق *sadūk*, (pl. صدق *sudk* or *suduk*) Very sincere, faithful. Who speaks the truth. The bird قطا *katā* (as being a trusty guide to water).

P صد هزار *sad hazār*, A hundred thousand.

A صدي *sada'*, (v. n. of صدي) Being thirsty. A male owl. A cricket. Echo. Expert in the management of camels. The part of the head which is the seat of hearing: brain, sensory. The vocation of a Mutasaddy. Thirst. Slim, slender (man). A human corpse. A long black fish. One time, once. Name of a certain volatile which issues from the head of one slain when it has putrefied (according to a notion of the Pagan Arabs). Expectancy, a waiting or watching for any thing. *Sadi*, Thirsty.

A صاغر صدئ *sāghiri sadis*, Obnoxious to censure or accusation.

A صدیء *sadis*, Rusty. Stained with, or smelling of the rust of iron.

A صديا *sadya'*, (fem. of صديان *sadyān*) Thirsty.

A صديان *sadyān*, Thirsty.

A صديد *sadīd*, (v. n. of صدّ) Crying out. Vociferation. Blood and matter mingled. Thin watery matter, or ichor, in a wound before it concretes into pus. Hot water become thick. Sweat.

A صدير *sudayr*, Any covering for the breast.

A صديرة *sadīrat*, (pl. صدائر *sadāsir*) The higher and more advancing part of a valley.

A صديع *sadīʻ*, (pl. صدع *suduʻ*) Any thing split in two. A half of any thing split in two. Half a garment. A new patch on an old garment. The breaking forth of the dawn. A flock. A herd of camels as far as thirty. Fresh milk become cold, with a skin on the surface. Young mountain-goat. Middle-sized. A garment worn under armour.

A صديغ *sadīgh*, An infant under seven days. Weak, feeble, puny (man).

A صديق *sadīk*, (pl. اصدقاء *asdikās*, صدقاء *sudakās*, صدقان *sudkān*, and اصادق *asādik*) A sincere friend. True, just. P صديق وفادار *sadīki wafā-dār*, A faithful friend.

A صدّيق *siddīk*, A faithful witness of the truth. Joseph. Abū bakr.

A صديّق *sudayyik*, A most sincere friend.

A صدّيقة *siddīkat*, The Virgin Mary. Ayisha, Muhammad's wife, and daughter of Abū bakr.

A صديقي *sudaykīy*, A most sincere friend.

A صدّيقيّة *siddīkīyat*, Extreme veracity.

P صديك *sad yak*, One per cent. A hundredth.

A صدئ *sadi*, Rust.

A صذوم *sazūm*, Sodom.

A صرّ *sarr*, (v. n. of صرّ) Tying the string called صرار *sirār* round the dugs of a camel. Shutting (a purse). Making a noise, crying out. Pricking his ears to listen (a horse). A bucket become loose and flabby, and to which a handle is fastened to straighten it. *Sirr*, Intensity of cold. An intense cold destroying the herbage. A yellow-hammer.

A صراء *sirās*, (v. n. of صري) Vociferating. (pl. of صراية *sarāyat*) Colocynths. Waters in which colocynths have been soaked.

A صرّاء *sarrās*, Solid (rock), returning no sound. *Surrās*, Deadly (serpent). (pl. of صاري *sārī*) Seamen.

A صراب *sirāb*, Seed sown in autumn after harvest.

A صراية *sirābat*, A colocynth inclining to yellow.

A صراة *sarāt*, Long detained (semen virile). A ewe kept for several days unmilked, that she may appear to greater advantage when exposed for sale. Name of a river in Irāk.

A صراح *sarāh* or *surāh*, Pure, unmixed. *Sirāh* or *surāh*, A speaking or performance of any thing openly, publicly. Speaking openly, disclosing what is passing in the mind. *Surāh*, A plain, open speech. Name of an Arabic dictionary, translated into Persian. A cup of neat, unmixed wine.

A صرّاح *surrāh*, A volatile resembling a locust, and which is eaten as food.

A صراحة *sarāhat*, (v. n. of صرح) Being pure, unmixed, unadulterated. Palpableness, pureness. *Sarāhatan*, Purely. Publicly, plainly, evidently.

P صراحي *surāhī*, A long-necked flask, goblet.

P صراحي بردار *surāhī-bardār*, Carrier of the flask.

A صراحية *surāhiyat*, Pure wine. Plain speech.

A صراحيّة *surāhīyat*, A drinking-vessel.

P صراحي دار *surāhī-dār*, Surāhī-shaped (pearl).

A صراخ *surākh*, A clamour, a scream.

A صرّاخ *sarrākh*, A peacock (lit. a screamer).

A صرّاخة *sarrākhat*, Noisy, clamorous (female). Name of a plant.

A صرّاد *surrād*, A thin cloud without water.

A صرادحيّ *surādahīy*, A violent blow.

A صرار *sarār*, (pl. of صرارة *sarārat*) Those who have never visited Mecca. *Sirār*, (v. n. 3 of صرّ) Forcing or detaining against the will. High ground not overflowed by water. (pl. اصرّة *asirrat*) A string with which they tie the dugs of camels to prevent the young from sucking.

A صرّار *sarrār*, Vociferating. صرّار الليل *sarrāru'l layl*, (Vociferous in the night) A cricket.

A صرارة *sarārat*, One who has not visited Mecca. A bachelor.

A صراريّ *sarārīy*, (pl. صراريّون) A seaman.

A صراصر *sarāsir*, (pl. of صرصر *sarsar*) Loud noises. Cold winds.

A صراصرة *sarāsirat*, The Nabatheans of Syria.

A صراط *sirāt*, A way, direct road. The bridge across the infernal fire. الصراط المستقيم *as 'sirātu'l mustakīm*, The right way, *i.e.* the Muhammadan religion. *Surāt*, A long sword.

A صراع *sirāʻ*, A wrestling, throwing down.

A صرّاعة *surrāʻat*, A skilful wrestler, who floors every opponent.

A صراف *sirāf*, (v. n. of صرف) Being in heat (bitch). Not mixing (wine). Accession, increase. (pl. of صريفة) Dry palm-branches. Thin cakes.

A صرّاف *sarrāf*, A banker, shroff, money-changer. One who understands the value of things in general. A grammarian. صرّاف خزان *sarrāfi khizān*,

The sun. Autumn. Autumnal winds. P صرّافانِ نقودِ معاني *sarrāfāni nukūdi maʻānī*, Those who well understand, or can give change (so to speak) in matters of recondite meaning or spiritual import.

A صرّافة *sarrāfat*, The place where bankers transact their business, a bank. The exchange.

A صرّافي *sarrāfī*, Banking, money-changing.

A صرام *sarām*, War. *Sarām* or *sirām*, Loppings of trees. The season of gathering dates. *Surām*, War. Misfortune. Milk remaining in the udder and afterwards milked. Skilful in pruning trees or in interrupting a conversation. A sharp sword.

A صرّام *sarrām*, A vendor of (صرم *sarm*) leather.

A صرامة *sarāmat*, (v. n. of صرم) Being robust, strong (man). Hardiness, courage.

A صرّان *surrān*, The mastich-tree growing in hard ground.

A صرايا *sarāya'*, (pl. of صرياء *saryā'*) (Camels) left unmilked for several days.

A صراية *sarāyat*, (pl. صراء *sirā'*) A colocynth, or the water in which it has been macerated.

A صرائح *sarā'ih*, (pl. of صريح) Pure, unmixed.

A صرائد *sarā'id*, (pl. of صريدة *sarīdat*) Sheep injured by the cold.

A صرائر *sarā'ir*, (pl. of صارّة *sārrat*) Things necessary to be done.

A صرائق *sarā'ik*, (pl. of صريقة *sarīkat*) Thin cakes baked on stones.

A صرب *sarb*, (v. n. of صرب) Preparing, collecting sour milk. Cutting. Sewing, stitching. Retaining, suppressing (urine). Not voiding for a whole day (an infant). Yielding choice grass (ground). *Sarb* or *sarab*, Milk milked upon that which has become acid. Milk stored up in a bottle for a journey. The gum of the tree طلح *talh*. A red colour. *Sirb*, Small dwellings of the Scenite Arabs. *Surb*, Milk-meats soured. *Sarab*, (v. n. of صرب) Collecting, assembling, coming together.

A صربة *sarbat*, A portion of sour milk. *Sarabat*, A bit of gum صرب *sarab*. A vegetable resembling the head of a cat in the hollow of which there is a most delicious juice. Choice grass.

A صربخة *sarbakhat*, Levity, mobility.

A صربى *sarba'*, Cattle exempted from labour, and never milked but on the arrival of strangers. See بحيرة *bahīrat*.

A صرّة *sarrat*, Noise, confusion, clamour. A crowd, tumult. Fierceness of war. Intenseness of heat or cold; extreme mental distress. Small beads or shells hung by women round their necks to secure the affections of their lovers. Austerity, grimness of visage. A sheep left unmilked in order to make an increase. *Sirrat*, Intense cold. A loud noise. *Surrat*, A purse, belt, sash in which money is tied.

A صرح *sarh*, (v. n. of صرح) Speaking openly. Shewing plainly. (pl. صروح *surūh*) A castle, lofty edifice (especially one belonging to Nebuchadnezzar). *Sarah*, Pure, choice, unmixed.

A صرحاء *surahā'*, (pl. of صريح *sarīh*) Pure, mere.

A صرحة برحة *sarhatan barhatan*, Valiantly (he sallied forth).

A صرخبة *sarkhabat*, Lightness, mobility, agility.

A صرخة *sarkhat*, (v. n. of صرخ) Crying out, bawling. Summons to prayers from the minaret.

A صرخد *sarkhad*, Wine. Name of a town.

A صرخديّ *sarkhadiy*, Belonging to the town of صرخد *sarkhad*. شراب صرخديّ *sharāb sarkhadīy*, Wine of Sarkhad.

A صرد *sard*, (v. n. of صرد) Shooting beyond the mark. Pure (water), sincere (love), plain, evident (lie). Cold. An elevated part of a mountain. A nail through the head of a spear. A large army. *Sarad*, (v. n. of صرد) Being soon sensible of cold. Cooling, changing one's mind. Passing beyond the mark or falling wide of the mark (an arrow). Being galled in the back under the saddle (a horse). Coming out in bits (butter from a churn). A large army. *Sarid*, One soon sensible of cold. Galled in the back (a horse). Milk which separates into particles, and will not coagulate. *Surad*, (pl. صردان *sirdān*) A species of black and white bird about the size of a lark, which hunts sparrows. A white mark on the back of a horse from galling.

A صرداح *sirdāh*, (or صردح) Level ground.

A صرداخ *sirdākh*, Generous, fruitful (palm-tree).

A صردان *sirdān*, (pl. of صرد *surad*) Speckled birds. *Suradāni*, Two greenish veins under the tongue.

A صردخ *sirdikh*, Great, large.

A صردغة *surdughat*, Two fleshy substances in a sheep, corresponding to the part in man called بادرة.

A صرر *sarar*, (pl. of صررة *sararat*) Corn still in the stalk; ears of corn ere the grain be formed.

A صرصر *sarsar*, A cricket. A cock. A cold boisterous wind. P صرصرِ كوه پيكر *sarsari kohi paykar*, A strong, active horse or camel. A *Sursur*, A cricket.

A صرصران *sarsarān*, A smooth kind of fish.

A صرصرانيّ *sarsarānīy*, A camel of a mixed breed, between a Bactrian and an Arabian. A large double-bunched camel. A species of sea-fish.

A صرصرة *sarsarat*, (v. n. of صرصر Q) Singing (the green woodpecker). Making a noise, crying aloud.

A صرصور *sursūr*, Large camels. A Bactrian camel. A cricket.

A صرع *sarʻ*, (v. n. of صرع) Putting folding doors to a gate. Beginning a poem with a hemistich, to the last syllable of which all the other verses in the poem must rhyme. The epilepsy. One thing opposite another. A part (of a day) either from sunrise to the noon-tide, or from thence to sunset. P صرعِ ستارگان *sarʻi sitāragān*, Falling of the stars. ذو صرعين *zū sarʻayn*, Bi-coloured: a double-dealer. A *Sarʻ* or *sirʻ*, (v. n. of صرع) Throwing down, laying prostrate. (pl. اصرع *asruʻ* and صروع *surūʻ*) A mode, species, sort, form. Like, resembling. *Sirʻ*, (pl. صروع *surūʻ*) A single thread of a rope. A wrestler. *Suruʻ*, (pl. of صروع *sarūʻ*) Great wrestlers. (pl. of صريع *sarīʻ*) Unpolished bows. Scourges.

A صرعان *sarʻāni*, (dual) Morning and evening. Two herds of camels, one going to drink when the other has done. Two states or conditions. *Sirʻāni*, Any two similar bodies. Two wrestlers.

A صرعة *sarʻat*, A throwing prostrate once. An epileptic fit. State, quality, condition. *Sirʻat*, A mode of falling. A mode of throwing down. سوء الاستمساك خير من حسن الصرعة *sū'u'l istimsāk khayr min husni's sirʻat*, Holding on awkwardly is better than falling gracefully. *Surʻat*, One whom many men throw down. *Suraʻat*, A skilful wrestler, one who throws many down.

P صرع زده *sarʻ-zada*, Struck with epilepsy.

A صرعى *sarʻa'*, Morning and evening. Posture of affairs. (pl. of صريع *sarīʻ*) Prostrate, thrown down. Epileptic. *Sirʻa'*, A posture of affairs, a disposition (to give or to refuse).

A صرف *sarf*, (v. n. of صرف) Changing, turning, converting. Averting evil (God). Driving back. Using dexterity, address, cunning. (A master) letting (boys) loose (from school). Addition to a story. Excellence, of a finer alloy (money). Gain, advantage. Repentance. Change, conversion. Vicissitude of fortune. Dexterity, cunning, finesse, stratagem. Ransom, redemption, equivalent. The orthographical or etymological parts of grammar; accidence, declension, conjugation. A work of supererogation. Just weight or measure. An ordinance of God, an indispensible religious duty. صرفِ عنان *sarfi ʻinān*, A turning the reins towards (any place). *Sirf*, Pure, neat, unmixed (wine). A red tincture, with which they dye the straps or shoe-latchets. Mere, only, alone. P صرفِ بجاده رنگ *sirfi bijāda-rang*, Saffron-coloured wine. *Suruf*, (pl. of صريفة) Dry palm-branches. Thin cakes.

P صرفان *sirfān*, Lead. A kind of date.

A صرفان *sarafān*, Lead. A fine sort of date. Death. Brass. الصرفان *as' sarfāni* or *sirfāni*, Night and day.

A صرفة *sarfat*, The twelfth mansion of the moon; a bright star in the heart of Leo. Vicissitudes of fortune. A milking of a camel in the morning, and leaving till the same hour of the following day. An unlucky bow. A magic shell.

P صرفه *sarfa*, Gain, profit. Surplus, addition, redundancy. Expense. صرفه بردن *sarfa burdan*, To take the lead. To gain, acquire.

A صرفيّ *sarfīy*, Grammatical. A grammarian. *Sarafīy*, Excellent (camel).

A صرق *sarak*, Thin, slender. *Suruk*, (pl. of صريقة *sarīkat*) Thin cakes baked on round stones.

A صرقاعة *sirkāʻat*, The end of a sling which makes a humming noise.

A صرقعة *sarkaʻat*, A smack with the fingers.

A صرم *sarm* or *surm*, (v. n. of صرم) Pruning,

lopping. Cutting clean off. Interrupting a speech. Delaying, tarrying a month. Being broken or cut off (a rope). A segment, section. Thick leather with which they sole shoes. (from P چرم charm) Leather. *Sirm*, (pl. اصرام *asrām* and اصارم *asārim*) Contiguous houses. (pl. اصرام *asrām*, اصارم *asārim*, اصاريم *asārīm*, and صرمان *surmān*) A blow. A crowd. Shod (camel's hoof). Sort, kind. *Surm*, (pl. of صرماء *sarmāʼ*) Arid deserts. Milkless (camels). *Siram*, (pl. of صرمة *sirmat*) Herds of camels.

A صرماء *sarmāʼ*, (pl. صرم *surm*) A desert without water, and remote from it. Milkless (camel).

A صرمان *surmān*, (pl. of صرم) Blows. Crowds.

A صرمة *sirmat*, (pl. صرم *siram*) Herd of camels (from 20 to 40). Part of a cloud. صرمة الصرمات *sarmatu's sarmāt*, Slow in recovery from a passion.

A صرنفح *saranfah*, Noisy, clamorous.

A صرنقح *saranhah*, Ingenious, acute, subtile, elegant. Proud and malicious. One who keeps fast hold of his property.

P صرو *sarw*, Name of a plant.

A صرو *sarw*, A looking, seeing, beholding.

A صرواح *sirwāh*, Name of a fortress in Yaman, said to have been built by the Genii for Bilkīs.

A صروة *sirwat*, A small plant.

A صروح *surūh*, Lofty edifices. Citadels.

A صروحة *surūhat*, (v. n. of صرح) Being pure, unadulterated. Pureness, freedom from admixture.

A صرود *surūd*, (pl. of P سرد *sard*) Cold regions.

A صرور *sarūr*, (صرورة *sarūrat*, and صروريّ *sarūriy*) (A man or woman) neglecting to go the pilgrimage to Mecca. A bachelor, one who does not visit the ladies.

A صروع *sarūʻ*, (pl. صرع *suruʻ*) A great wrestler. *Surūʻ*, (pl. of صرع *sarʻ*) Modes, kinds, forms, similitudes. (pl. of صرع *sirʻ*) Threads of ropes.

A صروف *sarūf*, (A camel) making a noise with the teeth. *Surūf*, (v. n. of صرف) Being in heat (a bitch). Not mixing (wine). (pl. of صرف *sarf*) Changes, vicissitudes.

A صروم *sarūm*, A sharp sword. A dexterous pruner of trees. A camel that will not approach the trough till left alone.

P صرّة *surra*, A purse full of gold or of silver. صرّهٔ جبال *surrasi jibāl*, A mine of turquoise or other precious stones (purse of the mountains).

A صري *sary*, (v. n. of صري) Breaking off, cutting off. Averting, prohibiting. Pushing, thrusting away. Retaining urine. Pounding (water). Abstaining from conjugal intercourse. Separating those that quarrel. Rescuing from danger, guarding, preserving. Ascending. Descending. Inclining, being propitious. Preceding, going before. Retiring, falling back. Remaining (an hostage). Stagnating awhile (water). *Sara'*, (v. n. of صري) Stagnating awhile, and acquiring a nasty taste (water). Remains. Milk of a bad taste. *Sara'* or *sira'*, Water corrupted by stagnating.

A صرّيٓ *sirra'*, *surra'*, *surrī*, and *sirrī*, Labour, pains, purpose. منّي صرّيٓ *minnī sirra'*, Labour is bestowed by me. *Surra'*, A sheep kept several days unmilked.

A صريّ *sariy*, Who goes in unto his father's wife.

A صرّيّ *sarriy* or *sirriy*, Money which chinks when counted out.

A صرياء *saryāʼ*, (pl. صرايا *sarāya'*) (A camel) left unmilked for several days that she may appear to greater advantage when offered for sale.

A صريب *sarīb*, (pl. صرب *surb*) Milk or milk-meats soured.

A صريح *sarīh*, (pl. صرحاء *surahāʼ* and صرائح *sarāʼih*) Clear, evident, palpable. Pure, unmixed, sheer. Milk without froth. حقّ صريح *hakki sarīh*, The undisguised truth. غلط صريح *ghalatun sarīhun*, A sheer mistake. نتيجهٔ صريح *natījasi sarīh*, An evident conclusion, undoubted consequence.

A صريحة *sarīhatan*, Purely, without mixture.

A صريخ *sarīkh*, A cry for help. One who calls for assistance. One who brings help.

A صرّيد *surrayd*, A thin, waterless cloud.

A صريدة *sarīdat*, (pl. صرائد *sarāʼid*) A sheep injured by the cold.

P صرير *sarīr*, The grating of a door, the scratching of a pen. A noise in general.

A صرير *sarīr*, (v. n. of صرّ) Making a noise, crying aloud. Grating (as a door upon the hinges). Scratching (as a pen on paper). Making a singing noise from thirst (the ear). Chirping (as a cricket). The creaking of a pulley. Current (coin). Money enclosed in a purse (صرّة *surrat*), pursed.

P صريرا *sarīrā*, The anemone.

A صريرة *sarīrat*, Noise, crash, clash, gnashing.

A صريع *sarīʻ*, (pl. صرعيٓ *sarʻa'*) Prostrate, thrown down. Epileptic. (pl. صرع *suruʻ*) A bow unpolished, made of a rough branch, or one that has withered. A scourge. A long slender branch bent to the ground, and remaining in the shade becomes supple and retains its perfume; from it dentifrices are made.

A صرّيع *sirrīʻ*, One who frequently throws down his antagonists or equals (in wrestling).

A صريف *sarīf*, (v. n. of صرف) Creaking (as a door or pulley), gnashing (teeth). Drinking neat wine. Letting (boys) out of school. The grating of a camel's teeth. Pure silver. Milk still warm from the udder, or wine fresh from the cask. A withered tree.

A صريفة *sarīfat*, (pl. صرف *suruf*, صراف *sirāf*, and صريف *sarīf*) A dry branch of a palm-tree. A thin cake.

A صريفون *sarīfūn*, Name of a place in Chaldea.

A صريفيّة *sarīfiyat*, A Chaldean wine.

A صريقة *sarīkat*, (pl. صريق *sarīk*, صرائق *sarāʼik*, and صرق *suruk*) Thin bread baked on a round stone.

A صريم *sarīm*, Cut off, pruned, lopped. A quantity of sand divided from a larger heap. A dark night, or part of it. Morning. Black ground yielding nothing. A piece of wood fastened in a kid's mouth to keep him from sucking. صريم سحر *sarīmu saharin*, Disappointed.

A صريمة *sarīmat*, Resolution, enterprise, undertaking. A place abounding in the trees ghazā and salam. A reaped field of corn. A quantity of sand divided from a large heap. Part of the night. The termination or breaking off of any business.

A صصص *sasas*, The excrement of a child.

P صطخر *sitakhr*, Istakhr in Persia.

A صطر *satr* or *satar*, (pl. اصطر *astur* and صطور *sutūr*) A line. A writing. A row (of stones). *Satar*, A yearling lamb.

A صعاء *siʻāʼ*, (pl. of صعو) Red-headed sparrows.

A صعاب *siʻāb*, (pl. of صعب *saʻb*) Difficult, arduous, hard. صعاب الامور *siʻābu'l umūr*, Difficult matters, hard points. صعاب المنطق *siʻābu'l mantik*, Subtleties of logic.

A صعابيب *saʻābīb*, (pl. of صعبوب *suʻbūb*) Hard and difficult.

A صعاتر *saʻātir*, Difficult, arduous (matters).

A صعاديّ *suʻādiy*, Tall, long (camel).

A صعاديّة *suʻādiyat*, Long-bodied (she-camel).

A صعار *siʻār*, (v. n. 3 of صعر) Turning the face awry, distorting the countenance. Turning away the face in indignation.

A صعّار *saʻʻār*, Proud, haughty, supercilious.

A صعارير *saʻārīr*, (pl. of صعرور *suʻrūr*) Concrete gums. Long and twisted gums. Substances yellow, dry, and softish issuing first from the teat. The first biestings. Fruits of trees resembling juniper. Gums in general.

A صعاصع *saʻāsiʻ*, (pl. of صعصع *suʻsuʻ*) Locust-hunting birds. *Saʻāsiʻa*, Flying in all directions.

A صعاف *siʻāf*, Certain small birds.

A صعافقة *saʻāfikat*, (or صعافيق *saʻāfīk*) (pl. of صعفق *saʻfak*, صعفوق *saʻfūk*, and صعفقيّ *saʻfakiy*) Those who go to market though they have no capital wherewith to buy any thing.

A صعاليك *saʻālīk*, (pl. of صعلوك *suʻlūk*) Poor, indigent. عروة الصعاليك *ʻurwatu's saʻālīk*, Name of a person who, with the spoil he had plundered, was a liberal friend to the poor.

A صعاية *siʻāyat*, A being small and fine.

A صعائد *saʻāʼid*, (pl. of صعود) High (places).

A صعب *saʻb*, (pl. صعاب *siʻāb*) Hard, difficult, arduous, rough, troublesome, disagreeable. Inaccessible. Disobedient, stubborn, perverse. A fierce lion.

A صعبة *saʻbat*, Refractory, perverse (woman).

A صعبر *saʻbar*, (صعنبر *saʻambar*, or صنعبر *sanaʻbar*) A kind of lote-tree.

A صعبوب *suʻbūb*, (pl. صعابيب) Hard, difficult.

A صعبور *suʻbūr*, Small-headed.

A صعت *saʻt*, Squat, square in stature. صعت الربة *saʻtu'r rubat*, Slender-waisted.

A صعتر saʻtar, Savory, origany.

A صعترة saʻtarat, (v. n. of صعتر Q) Feeding on origany (a bee). Adorning, decorating, garnishing.

A صعتري saʻtariy, One who teases, thwarts, or harasses his relations. Noble, generous. Bold, brave.

A صعد saʻad, Violent (torture). عذاب صعد ʻazābi saʻad, Extreme pain, excruciating torment. Suʻud, (pl. of صعود saʻūd) High places. (pl. of صعيد saʻīd) Surfaces of the ground.

A صعداء saʻdāʼ, Inconvenience, trouble, pain, distress. Suʻadāʼ, Deep, long-fetched breath or sigh.

A صعدات suʻudāt, (pl. of صعيد saʻīd) Surfaces of the ground. Roads.

A صعدة saʻdat, (pl. صعدات saʻadāt) A straight cane or spear. A she-ass. A tool, an implement. (pl. صعدات saʻdāt) Straight, erect (woman). بنات صعدة banātu saʻadat, Wild asses; onagers.

A صعدد suʻdud, Inconvenience, difficulty, trouble.

A صعر saʻar, (v. n. of صعر) Having a distorted face, being wry-necked. A disease in a camel producing a wry neck. Distortion of countenance (from pride or contempt). A distortion of the neck. Smallness of the head. An eating of صعارير saʻārīr.

A صعررة saʻrarat, (v. n. of صعرر Q) Making globular. Rolling up (dung) into a ball (a beetle).

A صعروب suʻrūb, Small-headed (man or beast).

A صعرور suʻrūr, (or صعرّر suʻurrur) (pl. صعارير saʻārīr) Concrete gum. Long twisted gum. A substance, yellow, thick, dry, and softish, issuing from the teat. The first biestings. The fruit of a tree resembling the juniper. Gum in general.

A صعرورة suʻrūrat, Dung rolled by a beetle.

A صعرية saʻariyat, An oblique mode of walking.

A صعصاع siʻsāʻ, A shaking. A separating.

A صعصع saʻsaʻ, Separated, dispersed. Saʻsaʻ or suʻsuʻ, (pl. صعاصع saʻāsiʻ) A certain speckled bird that hunts locusts.

A صعصعة saʻsaʻat, (v. n. of صعصع Q) Separating, dividing, moving, shaking, dispersing. Anointing with oil (the head). Name of a purgative plant. Name of the father of a tribe.

A صعط saʻt, (v. n. of صعط) Putting a cephalic medicine or snuff up the nostrils of another.

A صعف saʻf, Wine (made from honey or a fermentation of bruised grapes). (pl. صعاف siʻāf) A kind of little bird.

A صعفان saʻfān, Fond of the wine صعف saʻf.

A صعفة saʻfat, Trembling, a cold fit.

A صعفرة saʻfarat, (v. n. of صعفر Q) Putting (asses) to flight. Being bent (the neck).

A صعفصة saʻfasat, A dish made of meat, wheat-flour, and vinegar.

A صعفق saʻfak, (صعفوق saʻfūk, or صعفقي saʻfakiy) (pl. صعافقة saʻāfikat and صعافيق saʻāfīk) One who goes to market, though he has no capital wherewith to buy.

A صعفقة saʻfakat, (v. n. of صعفق Q) Being lean.

A صعفوق saʻfūk, Mean, worthless.

A صعق saʻk, (v. n. of صعق) Striking (any one) with lightning (heaven). Saʻk or saʻak, (v. n. of صعق) Fainting, swooning. Dying. Saʻak, A loud noise. Saʻik, Braying (ass). Fainted, swooned. Loud-voiced. One who, from excess of terror, expects a thunderbolt (صاعقة sāʻikat).

A صعقة saʻkat, (v. n. of صعق) Fainting, falling into a swoon. Dying. Fire which falls from heaven. A swoon. The first blast of the last trump.

A صعقر suʻkur, Eggs or row of fish.

A صعل saʻl or saʻal, Small-headed and necked (man or ostrich). Long. Bald (ass) that has lost his hair. Saʻal, (v. n. of صعل) Having a small head and slender neck. Smallness or slenderness.

A صعلاء saʻlāʼ, Small-headed and necked (woman, ostrich, or palm-tree). Bald, hairless (she-ass).

A صعلة saʻlat, (A palm-tree) whose branches are slender, crooked, and barkless. Small-headed and necked (woman, ostrich, or palm-tree).

A صعلكة saʻlakat, (v. n. of صعلك Q) Reducing one to poverty. Fattening camels (herbs). Making, raising a crust over a pudding.

A صعلوك suʻlūk, (pl. صعاليك saʻālīk) Poor, indigent. A robber.

A صعمور suʻmūr, A water-wheel, or its buckets.

A صعنب saʻnab, One who has a little head.

A صعنبة saʻnabat, (v. n. of صعنب Q) Heaping up dough or bread crumbled into broth. Raising the crust of a pie. Being drawn in, contracted.

A صعو saʻw, (pl. صعوات saʻwāt and صعاء siʻāʼ) A red-headed sparrow. A finch, goldfinch.

A صعوب suʻūb, Hard, difficult, arduous, rough, disagreeable. Disobedient, stubborn, perverse.

A صعوبة suʻūbat, (v. n. of صعب) Being difficult, intricate. Being disobedient, refractory. Difficulty, trouble. Affliction.

A صعوة saʻwat, Small-headed (she-camel). (pl. صعو saʻw and صعاء siʻāʼ) A hen-sparrow with a red head. A water-wagtail. A finch.

A صعود saʻūd, (pl. صعد suʻud and صعائد saʻāʼid) High, towering, craggy, steep. The highest, most inaccessible part of a mountain. Name of a mountain in hell. (A camel) that casts her colt, and takes a liking to her last-year's foal. Suʻūd, (v. n. of صعد) Ascending (an acclivity, ladder, or stair). Mounting, surmounting. Ascent.

A صعوداء saʻūdāʼ, The most inaccessible part of a mountain: a steep difficult of ascent, a crag.

A صعوط saʻūt, Snuff. Any cephalic medicine, taken in through the nostril.

A صعوّن siʻwann, An ostrich with a small head and slender neck.

A صعي saʻy, (v. n. of صعي) Being small and fine (the head). Piping, chirping (a chick).

A صعيد saʻīd, (pl. صعد suʻud and صعدات suʻudāt) Earth, dust on the surface of the earth. A road. The grave. Surface of the earth. Dust which the Muhammadans use for religious purification when unable to procure water. صعيد مصر saʻīdi misr, Upper Egypt (in length 15 days' journey).

A صعيدة saʻīdat, A sacrifice, offering.

A صغّ saghgh, (v. n. of صغّ) Eating much.

A صغا sagha', Inclination, bias.

A صغاب sughāb, Nits.

A صغار sighār, (pl. of صغير saghīr) Small. صغار و كبار sighār u kibār, Small and great, little and big. Sughār, Little, small.

A صغارة saghārat, (v. n. of صغر) Being small. Being mean, abject, slavish. Being younger. Inclining to its setting (the sun). Smallness (of price, worth, or dignity).

A صغانة saghānat, (P چغانه chaghāna) A staff like a sceptre, to which are fixed three cymbals, which make a kind of music. Four wooden timbrels used for the same purpose.

A صغانيان saghāniyān, A city beyond the Oxus.

A صغائر saghāʼir, (pl. of صغيرة saghīrat) Despicable things, trifles. Venial sins. Small, young girls.

A صغبلة saghbalat, (v. n. of صغبل Q) Larding (meat), buttering (bread).

G صغبين sighbīn, Sagapenon, a medicinal herb.

P صغد sughd, Name of a river and of a country in Turkistān, Sogd, Sogdiana.

A صغر saghr, (v. n. of صغر) Being younger. Sughr, (v. n. of صغر) Being mean, abject, slavish. Meanness. Injury, injustice. Saghar, (v. n. of صغر) Being little, small, abject, contemptible, mean, slavish. Sighar, (v. n. of صغر) Being small. Smallness, lightness (of body or weight). Littleness, tenderness (of age), minority. Sughar, (pl. of صغري sughra') Juniors, minors. Lesser, least.

A صغرا sughra', (for صغري sughra') (fem. of اصغر asghar) Smaller. Less, least.

A صغراء sugharāʼ, (pl. of صغير) Small, slender.

A صغران sughrān, (v. n. of صغر) Being small. Being mean, abject, slavish. Little, small.

A صغرة sighrat, Juniors, inferiors, small fry. Sagharat, (pl. of صاغر sāghir) Contemptible, submitting disgracefully.

A صغري sughra', (fem. of اصغر asghar) (pl. صغر sughar) Less, least. The minor of a syllogism.

A صغصغة saghsaghat, (v. n. of صغصغ Q) Combing and oiling (the hair). Making (hair) neither curly nor lank. Moistening (a pudding) with fat.

A صغل saghil, Small, slender, and deformed. Tremulous, tottering. Badly fed. Bad-tempered.

A صغو saghw or sighw, Inclination, leaning, proneness, bias. Saghw, (or صغوّ sughūw) (v. n. of صغا for صغو) Leaning, inclining to one side. Swerving. Declining, setting (the sun). Sighw, The hollow part of a ladle. The side of a well. The bended part of a leathern bucket.

A صغواء saghwāʼ, Sloping, declining (sun).

A صغى sighā', (or صغيّ sughīy) (v. n. of صغى) Inclining, leaning to one side. Swerving. Listening, lending (an ear). Declining, setting (the sun).

A صغير saghīr, (pl. صغار sighār and صغراء sugharā,) Small, little, inferior, junior, minor.

A صغيّر sughayyir, (dim. of صغير saghīr, Small) Very small, tiny, the smallest of the small.

A صغيرة saghīrat, (pl. صغائر) A venial sin.

A صغيري saghīrī, Smallness. Infancy.

A صفّ saff, (v. n. of صفّ) Drawing up (soldiers) in a file, placing in battle-array. Standing in a row. Placing (their) feet in a row whilst being milked (camels). Dressing (bits of meat) stuck in a row upon a skewer. Putting a seat to a saddle. Placing milk-pails in a line at milking-time. Stretching the wings (a bird). (pl. صفوف sufūf) A series, order, rank, row, file (of soldiers). P صفّ تيغ saffi tegh, The surface of a sword-blade. صفّ جنگ saffi jang, The ranks of war, battle-array. A صفّ خاصّه saffi khāssa, The distinguished order; prophets and saints. صفّ صفّ saff saff, In military order, rank and file. صفّ نعال saffi nicāl, A place where slippers are left.

P صفا safā, Purity, clearness, polish, brightness. Pleasure, recreation.

A صفا safa', Name of one of the sacred places at Mecca. (pl. of صفاة safāt) Large, smooth stones.

A صفاء safā,, (v. n. of صفا for صفو) Being serene (the sky). Abounding in milk (a camel). Purity, clearness, transparency. Pleasure, joy, festivity, delight, recreation, diversion, pastime, relaxation of mind, content, comfort, satisfaction, complacency. (pl. of صفاة safāt) Large, smooth stones. صفاءِ عقيدت safā,i ɛakīdat, Purity of faith. صفاءِ عيون و انهار safā,i ɛuyūn u anhār, Clearness of fountains and rivers. P صفا كردن safā kardan, To rejoice, enjoy pleasure. A اهل صفا ahli safā, Voluptuous. P با صفاءِ خاطر bā safā,i khātir, With cheerfulness of the mind, willingly.

A Sifā,, (v. n. 3 of صفا for صفو) Having a pure and sincere affection towards another.

P صفابخش safā-bakhsh, Delicious. Purifying.

P صفا پذير safā-pazīr, Purified, purged, racked.

A صفاة safāt, (pl. صفوات safawāt, صفا safa', صفاء safā,, اصفاء asfā,, صفيّ sufiy, and sifiy) A large, smooth stone or rock, on which nothing grows.

A صفات sifāt, (pl. of صفة sifat) Qualities. صفات الذات sifātu'z zāt, Essential attributes.

A صفاتيّة sifātīyat, Name of a sect.

A صفائيّة safā,iyat, Name of a sect.

A صفاح sifāh, A broad and ugly appearance of a horse's cheek. (pl. of صفح safh) Tracts, parts. The sides of a man. (pl. of صفح safh or sifh) The broad sides of swords or of faces.

A صفّاح suffāh, A broad, thin stone, a flagstone. A broad sword. (pl. صفّاحات suffāhāt and صفافيح safāfīh) Large-bunched (camel).

A صفّاحات suffāhāt, (pl. of صفّاح suffāh) Camels with large bunches.

A صفاد sifād, (pl. اصفاد asfād) A chain, fetter.

A صفار sufār, A hissing, whistling. A collection of yellowish water in the belly. Yellowness. A worm or serpent which gnaws the bowels of a starving man. The plant بهمى buhma' when dry. A tike. An insect in the hoof of a horse or camel. Sufār or sifār, Bits of straw sticking in the roots of a horse's teeth.

A صفّار saffār, A coppersmith.

P صف آرا saf-ārā, One who draws up in array.

A صفارة sufārat or safārat, (pl. صفار sifār) Dry and withered plants.

A صفّارة saffārat, A hollow brazen tube which they sound to decoy pigeons, and to call asses to water, a call. A child's whistle. Podex.

P صفّاريان saffāriyān, (Coppersmiths) Name of a dynasty which reigned in Persia for about half a century.

A صفاريّة sufārīyat, A bird of the sparrow kind.

A صفاريت safārīt, (pl. of صفريت) Poor, needy.

A صفا صاف safan sāf, Without trace or vestige.

A صفافيح safāfīh, (pl. of صفّاح suffāh) Large-bunched camels.

A صفاق sifāk, A thin skin or membrane beneath the skin that produces the hair. The peritonæum. (pl. of صفيق safīk) Thick, stout (stuffs, silks).

A صفّاق saffāk, A great travelling merchant.

A صفاقة safākat, (v. n. of صفق) Being stout, coarse (cloth). Being impudent. Brazen-facedness.

P صفاهان sifāhān, Metropolis of Persian Irāk.

P صفاهاني sifāhānī, A native of Isfāhān. پردهٔ صفاهاني pardaˏi sifāhānī, A species of melody peculiar to Isfāhān.

A صفايا safāya', (pl. of صفيّ safiy) (Camels) abounding in milk. The best parts (of any thing, especially of plunder).

A صفائح safā,ih, Broad swords. Flagstones. (pl. of صفيحة safīhat) Broad surfaces. Scales of fish. Planks. Panels of doors. Bones of the cranium.

A صفائق safā,ik, (pl. of صفوق safūk) Inaccessible, of difficult ascent (mountain-steeps, crags). Events, accidents. (pl. of صفيقة safīkat) Accidents.

A صفائي safā,ī, Purity, clearness.

P صف بسته saf-basta, Ranged in rank or file.

A صفة sifat, (v. n. of وصف) Describing. Inclining to be good-tempered (a colt). Quality, attribute, property (as blackness, knowledge, &c.). Form, mode, manner. Description, epithet. An adjective, or whatever qualifies a noun. Like, resembling. صفت بهيمت بشريّت ملكيّت sifati bahīmat, bashariyat, malakīyat, Properties of beast, man, (or) angel. صفت ثبوتيّه sifati sulūtīya, A substantial form, fixed quality. صفت عارضيّه sifati ɛārizīya, An accidental or moveable quality. بدر صفت badr-sifat, Like the full moon. P لاله صفت lāla-sifat, Resembling a tulip. نيكو صفت nekū-sifat, Of excellent qualities.

A صفّة suffat, (pl. صفف sufaf) A sofa, bench. A place for reclining on before the doors of Eastern houses, made of wood or stone. A dais, estrade, or floor raised a foot high. The seat of the saddle. اهل الصفّة ahlu's suffat, (Benchers) A certain community, companions of Muhammad's flight from Mecca, who, having neither friends nor calling at Madina, lived on the donations of the faithful, and lodged in the صفّه suffa of Muhammad's mosque.

A صفتّ sifitt, One who conquers or who excels. Sifitt, (صفتّان siftitān, and صفتّان siffitān) Large-bodied. Smooth, succulent, full of flesh, and compact. Strong, powerful. Cruel, oppressive.

A صفتات siftāt, Strong, athletic, fleshy, muscular.

A صفتة saftat, Victory, conquest. Excess.

A صفتيت siftīt, A powerful, athletic man. Fleshy and muscular; strongly, powerfully built.

A صفح safh, (v. n. of صفح) Turning away (the face). Leaving, quitting. Pardoning, forgiving. Looking into any business. Looking at the surface of any thing. Driving (camels beyond the well). Making broad, expanding. Striking with the broad part of a sword. Refusing a beggar. Giving to drink of any beverage soever. Smiting her hands together (a woman weeping). Reviewing or perusing one by one, or sheet by sheet. Pardon. Clemency. A tract, side, quarter, border. The lowest part of a mountain; also a smooth, level part on its side. ضربت عنه صفحا zarabtu ɛanhu safhan, I turned away my face from him. Safh or sufh, (pl. صفاح sifāh) The broadest side of a sword, or the face. The side or cheek of a man. Safah, A disproportionate breadth.

A صفحة safhat, A face. A side, page, expanse, surface. Breadth. A tract, border, quarter. P صفحهٔ تيغ سحر safhaˏi teghi sahar, First streaks of light in the morning. The sky. A صفحهٔ حال safhaˏi hāl, State of the case, face of the matter.

A صفد safd, (v. n. of صفد) Binding, fastening, fettering. Safad, (pl. اصفاد asfād) A chain, fetter. A present. Name of a city in Syria.

P صفدر saf-dar, Warlike, brave, who breaks the ranks. مرد دلاور و امير صفدر mardi dilāwar, u amīri saf-dar, A valiant man and gallant commander. مبارزان صفدر و بهادران لشكر mubārizāni saf-dar, u bahādarāni lashkar, Courageous soldiers and bold warriors.

P صفدري saf-darī, The routing of armies.

A صفر safr, (v. n. of صفر) Having a collection of yellowish water in the belly. Sifr, Copper. Gold. A cypher. Sifr, sufr, safr, safir, or sufur, (pl. اصفار asfār) Empty (house of furniture). صفر اليد sifru'l yad, Empty-handed, poor, weak. صفر صحر sifrun sihrun, Quite empty. صفر كردن sifr kardan, To empty. Sufr, Gold. Copper. آنيهٔ صفر

āniyatun sufrun, Empty vessels. *Safar*, (v. n. of صفر) Being empty, without furniture (a house). Being empty (a vessel). A distemper in the belly, which makes the face pale (as hunger, the cholic, or worms). A maw-worm; the serpent which the common Arabians suppose gnaws the bowels of a starving person. The heart. (pl. اصفار *asfār*) The second month of the Muhammadan year. Insertion of the month Muharram into Safar. Intellect, understanding. A knot, compact, league. Terror. Hunger. صفرت وطأته *safirat waṭ-atuhu*, He died.

P صفرا *safrā*, Bile. Wine. Yellow, saffron-coloured. صفرا كردن *safrā kardan*, To be angry. To avert the face. To vomit.

A صفراء *safrāʼ*, (fem. of اصفر *asfar*) Yellow, pale, pallid. Bile. Gold. A certain herb growing in a sandy plain. A bow made of the tree نبع *nabʻ*. An empty locust's egg. A locust when it has left the egg.

A صفرات *sifrāt*, (pl. of صفر *sifr*) Cyphers.

P صفراغون *safrāghūn*, A yellowish bird frequenting melon-grounds.

P صفرا كش *safrā-kush*, (Bile-killing) Breakfast.

A صفران *safarāni*, (dual of صفر *safar*) The two first months in the Muhammadan year, محرّم *muharram* and صفر *safar*.

A صفرة *safrat*, Hunger. *Safrat* or *sufrat*, Madness. A paroxysm of madness. *Sufrat*, Yellowness. Blackness. The yolk of an egg. A she-goat.

A صفرد *sifrid*, A lark. اجبن من صفرد *ajban min sifrid*, More timorous than the lark.

P صفردار *sifr-dār*, Empty. Very little.

A صفرّق *sufurruk*, A dish made of starch, honey, and water. A kind of plant.

A صفرويّ *safrawiy*, (or صفراويّ) Bilious, choleric.

A صفريّ *safariy*, Rain at the beginning of autumn. The beginning of the seasons. A lamb yeaned under the ascension of Canopus.

A صفريّة *sufriyat*, A species of date growing in Yaman, which, being dried in an unripe state, is used instead of sugar in preparing a ptisan. *Sufriyat* or *sifriyat*, Name of a sect of the Harūriyat. *Safariyat*, A plant or vegetation at the beginning of autumn. Decline of the hot season and approach of the cold. Beginning of the seasons. Lambs yeaned at the ascension of Canopus.

A صفريت *sifrīt*, (pl. صفاريت) Poor, needy.

P صف زده *saf-zada*, Formed in line or rank

P صف زن *saf-zan*, One who breaks the ranks of an enemy, brave.

P صفزني *saf-zanī*, A breaking of the enemy's ranks, bravery.

P صفشكن *saf-shikan*, A breaker of the enemy's ranks. صفشكنان رستم رسوم *saf-shikanāni rustam-rusūm*, Those who break the lines after the fashion of Rustam, *i.e.* heroic champions.

A صفصاف *sufsāf*, A willow, osier.

A صفصافة *safsāfat*, A dish composed of meat, wheaten-flour, and vinegar.

A صفصف *safsaf*, Plain, level ground. The side of a mountain. *Sufsuf*, A sparrow.

A صفصفة *safsafat*, (v. n. of صفصف Q) Travelling alone over a plain. Causing to feed on the willow صفصاف *safsāf*. A dish composed of meat, wheaten-flour, and vinegar. Chirping of a sparrow.

A صفصلّى *sifsilla'*, A sort of herb.

A صفع *safʻ*, A tapping gently on the neck.

A صفعان *safʻān*, One who takes blows patiently. One who gives a blow on the nape of the neck.

A صفغ *safgh*, (v. n. of صفغ) Taking up in the hand. Pulverizing, rubbing with the hand.

A صفف *safaf*, What is worn under a coat of mail. *Sufaf*, (pl. of صفّة *suffat*) Seats of saddles. Sofas.

A صفق *safk*, (v. n. of صفق) Flapping (as a bird its wings) and making a loud noise. Dashing, shaking, agitating (as the wind a tree). Striking the strings, sounding (a lute). Striking with a sword. Going, travelling. Clapping the hands. Taking or shaking hands (when wishing joy or striking a bargain). Suffering a prolapse of the uterus, so that the foal dies (a camel). Alighting at any one's house (a company). Turning. Filling (a cup). Opening, and likewise shutting (the eyes or a door). Pouring (water) out of one vessel into another. The side or slope (of a hill). A side, a quarter. Sale. Purchase. Water put into a new leathern bottle and turned yellow by shaking. The side (of the neck). The cheek (of a horse). The smell of tanning. A place. *Sifk*, One half of a folding-door. *Sufk*, A side, quarter. *Safak*, Water put into a new bottle and turned yellow by shaking. A side, quarter. The hinder part of the brain. *Sufuk*, (pl. of صفاق *sifāk*) Peritonœa. (pl. of صفوق *safūk*) Inaccessible (mountains). Soft, limber (bows). Smooth and lofty (rocks).

A صفقة *safkat*, (or صفقّى *sifikka'*) A bargain made by striking hands. خسارة الصفقة *khasāratu's safkat*, A losing bargain.

A صفن *safn*, A substance resembling lights, protruding from a camel's mouth when raging with lust. A table. Travelling-provisions. *Safn* or *safan*, (pl. صفنان *sufnān*) The scrotum. A leathern water-bottle. *Sufn*, A leathern water-bottle (especially for washing the face and hands before prayer). A shepherd's provision-bag. *Safan*, The pod in which the ears of corn are enveloped. A wasp's nest.

A صفنان *sufnān*, (pl. of صفن *safan*) Scrotums.

A صفنة *safnat*, A shepherd's provision-bag. A table. Travelling-provisions. A substance resembling lights, which protrudes from a camel's mouth when raging with lust.

A صفو *safw*, (v. n. of صفا for صفو) Taking the brightest part of any thing. Brightness, clearness. The purest part of any thing.

A صفوّ *sufūw*, Clearness, brightness.

A صفواء *safwāʼ*, (or صفواة *safwāt*) (pl. صفوان *safwān* or *safawān*) A smooth, equal stone.

A صفوات *safawāt*, (pl. of صفاة) Smooth stones.

A صفوان *safwān*, The second of the days of cold weather. *Safwān* or *safawān*, (pl. of صفواء *safwāʼ* or صفواة *safwāt*) Smooth and even stones. The substance called شقشقة *shikshikat*. يوم صفوان *yawmi safwān*, A clear, cloudless, and cold day.

A صفوة *saf*, *sif*, or *sufwat*, Choicest, best, purest part. صفوة الله من خلقه *safwatu'llāh min khalkihi*, Chosen by God among men (Muhammad). صفوت قلب *safwati kalb*, Purity of heart, peace of mind.

P صفوت كده *safwat-kada*, A house. A chamber. A council-chamber. The heart.

A صفوح *safūh*, Liberal; forgiving. Distant, shy, retiring (woman). *Sufūh*, (v. n. of صفح) Losing her milk, becoming dry (a camel).

A صفور *sufūr*, (v. n. of صفر) Being empty.

A صفوراء *safūrāʼ*, (صفورة *safūrat*, or صفورياء *safūriyāʼ*) Zipporah, Jethro's daughter, Moses' wife.

A صفوريّة *sufūriyat*, A sort of plant.

A صفوف *safūf*, (A camel) filling vessels placed in a row. (A camel) placing her fore-feet even when milked. *Sufūf*, (pl. of صفّ *saff*) Ranks, rows, lines.

A صفوق *safūk*, (pl. صفق *sufuk* and صفائق *safāʼik*) High and inaccessible (mountain). Supple, limber (bow). Smooth and towering (rock). A she-camel that has cast her colt, and has been induced to take a liking to her last year's foal.

A صفون *sufūn*, (v. n. of صفن) Standing on three feet (a horse), the point of the other hoof only touching the ground. Placing the feet properly (in prayer). Striking the ground.

A صفي *safī* or *sufī*, The surname of a dynasty of Persian kings (who reigned from about the year 1500 till the usurpation of Nādir Shāh in 1736), named from Ismael Safi, first monarch of this house.

A صفيّ *safiy*, (pl. اصفياء *asfiyāʼ*) Pure, clear, bright. Just, upright, sincere. Best, purest, choicest (of any thing). That part of the plunder which a general takes to himself before a division. (pl. صفايا *safāya'*) (A camel) plentiful in milk. A palm-tree laden with fruit. صفيّ الله *safiyu'llāh*, Adam, the father of mankind. *Sufiy* or *sifiy*, (pl. of صفاة *safāt*) Large, smooth stones.

A صفيّة *safiyat*, Sophia, one of Muhammad's wives. *Sufayyat*, First of the days of cold weather.

A صفيح *safīh*, The sky. The surface of any broad substance. A broad sword.

A صفيحة *safīhat*, (pl. صفائح *safāʼih*) Surface, exterior (of the skin). The broadest side of any thing (as of a sword). A thin plate. Scale (of a fish). A plank. Panel of a door. A broad sword.

A صفير *safīr*, (v. n. of صفر) Whistling; singing (a bird). Calling an ass to water by a hissing sound. Sound, clangour, hissing, blowing. A sapphire. حرف الصفير *harfu's safīr*, A sibilant letter. P صفير

زدن safīr zadan, To whistle. To hiss.

A صفيرة safīrat, A hillock or a mound of sand dividing two portions of country.

A صفيريّ safīriy, Sibilant (letter).

A صفيف safīf, Bits of meat spitted in a row for cooking. Things laid in a row to dry in the sun.

A صفيق safīk, (pl. صفاق sifāk) (A garment) of a coarse, hard texture. Impudent, unblushing (face).

A صفيقة safīkat, (pl. صفائق) An accident, event.

A صفين siffīn, A town on the Euphrates.

P صفينه safīna, The juniper.

A صق sakk, (v. n. of صقّ) Crying out (a chameleon). A nail firmly driven into a hard place.

A صقاب sikāb, (v. n. 3 of صقب) Being opposite and near. (pl. of صقب sakb) Long and somewhat slender. Camels' foals. See سقاب sikāb.

A صقار sikār, (pl. of صقر sakr) Curses, imprecations upon those who deserve them not. *Sikār*, (or صقارة) (pl. of صقر sakr) Kites, hawks, falcons.

A صقار sakkār, One who curses. A calumniator, whisperer. An infidel. A seller of syrup of dates or grapes called صقر sakr.

A بالصقاريّ والبقاريّ bi's sukāra' wa'l bukāra', With a downright lie (he came).

A صقاع sikāع, A cloth with which a woman covers her head, to keep her veil from being soiled by the unguent of her hair. The rein-ring in a camel's nose. An iron ring or other check rein for a horse. A brand on the back of a camel's head. A lady's veil. *Sukāع*, (v. n. of صقع) Crowing (a cock).

A صقال sikāl, (v. n. of صقل) Polishing (a sword). Polish, lustre. The art of managing or looking after horses. The belly.

A صقالبة sakālibat, (pl. of صقلاب siklāb) Northern nations, Sclavonians, Russians, Scythians.

A صقالة sikālat, A furbishing, polishing.

A صقب sakb, (v. n. of صقب) Striking with the fist. Giving a slap with the hand. Rearing high (an edifice). Collecting. Chattering (a bird). (pl. صقاب sikāb and صقبان sukbān) Long and somewhat slender. A young camel or fœtus. (pl. صقوب sukūb) The middle and longest pole of a tent. *Sakab*, (v. n. of صقب) Being near. Being distant. Nearness, neighbourhood. Distance. Near. الجار احقّ بصقبه al jār ahakk bi sakabihi, The neighbour has a prior right (to be the purchaser) by (reason of) his proximity.

A صقبان sukbān, (pl. of صقب sakb) Long and slender. Young camels.

A صقح suk-h, (pl. of اصقح ashah and صقحاء sakhāع) Bald (men or women). *Sakah*, (or صقحة sakahat) Baldness in front.

A صقحاء sak-hāع, (fem. of اصقح) Bald (woman).

A صقر sakr, (v. n. of صقر) Beating with a stick. Breaking (stones) with a large mattock. Burning intensely (the sun). Being exceedingly acid (milk). Kindling (a fire). (pl. اصقر ashur, صقور sukūr, صقورة sukūrat, صقار sikār, صقارة sikārat, and صقر sukr) Any bird of prey, as a hawk, kite, or falcon. Very sour milk. A circle behind the region of the liver (of which there are two). Fetid water. Panderism to one's own wife. (pl. صقور sukūr and صقار sikār) A curse, imprecation on one who does not deserve it. صقر صاقر sakrun sākirun, Sharp-sighted. *Sakr* or *sakar*, Date-honey, or from raisins. *Sukr*, (pl. of صقر sakr) Kites, hawks, birds of prey. *Sakar*, Deciduous leaves of the plants عضاه ɛizāh and عرفط ɛurfut. (for سقر sakar) Hell. صقر مقر sakir makir, A date full of honey. بالصقر و البقر bi's sukar wa'l bukar, With a downright lie.

A صقرة sakrat, Intenseness of solar heat. *Sakarat*, Water remaining at the bottom of a cistern, where dogs and foxes piss. *Sakirat*, An acute, sharp-sighted woman.

A صقع sakع, (v. n. of صقع) Striking (a bird or horse) on the middle of the head being white. Branding either on the face or head. Striking (lightning). Covering the earth (hoar frost). Throwing prostrate, dashing on the ground. Crowing (a cock). Farting loudly (an ass). Going, tending towards. Turning out of the road. A blow upon any thing dry and solid. A slap with the open hand. *Sukع*, A shore, coast, side, tract (of country). *Sakaع*, (v. n. of صقع) Turning aside from the road. Being white-headed (a horse or bird). Being struck with lightning. Falling in (a well). Languor of mind from extreme heat. *Sakiع*, Tormented with thirst.

A صقعاء sukعāع, (fem. of اصقع ashaع) White on the forehead (mare or bird). The sun.

A صقعب sakعab, Long. Creaking (door), grinding, grating (teeth).

A صقعة sukعat, Whiteness on the head of a horse.

A صقعر sukعur, Water cold; or bitter, thick, fetid.

A صقعرة sakعarat, A shouting in another's ear.

A صقعل sikaعl, Dry dates soaked in milk.

A صقعلة sakعalat, Cool (beverage).

A صقعيّ sakaعa', The beginning of the foaling-season. A camel's colt dropped at the beginning of the foaling-season.

A صقغ sukgh, (for صقع) A coast, side, tract.

A صقل sakl, (v. n. of صقل) Polishing, furbishing, making bright (a sword). Cudgelling. Making lean. Throwing on the ground. *Sukl*, The hypochondria. The side. Light, active (horse). *Sakal*, Length of the hypochondria. *Sakil*, Irregular in one's pace. (A horse) spare of flesh. (A horse) long in the hypochondria.

A صقلاب siklāb, A glutton. White and red. Strong (head). Voracious (camel). (pl. صقالبة sakālibat) A Sclavonian, Russian, Scythian.

A صقلة saklat, The hypochondria. *Sakalat*, (pl. of صاقل sākil) Polishers, furbishers, armourers.

P صقل گر sakalgar, A polisher of swords, &c.

A صقلية sikilliyat or sikliyat, Sicily.

A صقوب sukūb, (pl. of صقب) Longest tent-poles.

A صقور sukūr, (pl. of صقر sakr) Curses, imprecations on the undeserving. *Sukūr*, (and صقورة sukūrat) (pl. of صقر sakr) Birds of prey, hawks, kites.

A صقور sakkūr, A cuckold, pimp to his own wife.

A صقوف sukūf, (pl. of صقف) Roofs, ceilings.

A صقيع sakīع, (v. n. of صقع) Crowing (a cock). Hoar frost, rime. A kind of wasp.

A صقيل sakīl, Polished, furbished (sword).

A صكّ sakk, (v. n. of صكّ) Striking violently, knocking. Placing one thing on another, and making to adhere. Shutting (a door). Giving a written sentence (a judge). (from P چك chak) (pl. اصكّ asukk, صكوك sukūk, and صكاك sikāk) The written and signed sentence of a judge. صكّ المسافر sakku'l musāfir, A traveller's passport.

A صكاك sikāk, (pl. of صكّ sakk) Sentences signed by a judge. *Sukāk*, The air, atmosphere.

A صكاك sakkāk, The actuary, who writes the sentence of a judge.

A صكة sakkat, Violence of noon-day heat. A rap at a door.

A صكك sakak, A being knock-kneed.

A صكم sakm, (v. n. of صكم) Striking. Driving back, thrusting away. Falling on any one (adverse fortune). Champing (the bit), and stretching out his neck (a horse).

A صكم sukkam, Hoofs of camels.

A صكمة sakmat, A violent collision, impulse, impact, or blow with a stone.

A صكوك sukūk, (v. n. of صكّ) Being hard and firm (flesh). (pl. of صكّ sakk) Writings, deeds. Written and signed sentences of a judge.

A صكيك sakīk, (v. n. of صكك) Being knock-kneed. Weak, silly.

A صلّ sall, (v. n. of صلّ) Watering seeds mixed with earth. Clearing, straining, racking off (wine). *Sill*, (pl. اصلال aslāl) A basilisk. Like, equal; a match for. A sharp sword. Name of an herb. صلّ صفا sillu safan, Malignant to an extreme, like a serpent. صلّ اصلال silli aslāl, A basilisk of basilisks, *i.e.* a malignant, rascally scoundrel. *Sall* or *sill*, Flying and scanty (showers). *Sull*, Tainted, stinking (meat, &c.).

P صلا salā, Kindling a fire in cold weather. A proclamation either for giving food to the poor or for selling any thing.

A صلا sala', (v. n. of صلا for صلو) Becoming loose about the haunches (a mare at foaling-time). The burning of fire. Roast meat. (pl. صلوات salawāt and اصلاء aslāع) Middle of the back of a man or quadruped. Lower part of the haunch-bone. Space between the fundament and tail. Either side of a (horse's) tail. Fire, or its heat.

A صلاء salāع, (v. n. of صلي) Growing hot. *Salāع* or *silāع*, (v. n. of صلي) Enduring the heat of fire. *Silāع*, A fire. Roast meat. The burning of fire.

A صلاءة *salāʼat*, A stone on which they bray musk.

A صلاب *silāb*, (pl. of صليب) Hard, strong, firm.

P صلاب *sulāb*, An astrolabe.

A صلابة *salābat*, (v. n. of صلب) Being hard, strong, robust. Gibbetting. Firmness, hardness, induration. Severity, rigour. Majesty, dignity, awe.

P صلابه *salāba*, A stone for grinding drugs. صلابه كردن *salāba kardan*, To grind drugs.

A صلات *silāt*, (pl. of صلة *silat*) Gifts.

A صلاح *salāh*, Rectitude, probity, virtue, integrity, honour, honesty, devotion. Advisableness, propriety, fitness, a proper thing, prudent measure. Well-being. Advisable, prudent, good, right. A name of Mecca. صلاح حال *salāhi hāl*, Suitable to the time, seasonable. صلاح دولت *salāhi dawlat*, Good for the state. صلاح وقت *salāhi waḳt*, A fit, proper opportunity, a favourable time. *Silāh*, (v. n. 3 of صلح) Reconciling, making peace.

P صلاح ديد *salāh-dīd*, Advisable.

P صلاح كار *salāh-kār*, An adviser.

A صلاحيّة *salāhiyat*, Honesty, integrity, worth, virtue, goodness, chastity. Ability, fitness.

A صلاخد *sulākhid*, (pl. *salākhid*) Hard, strong (camel). Rapid and penetrating (arrow).

A صلاد *sullād*, Wood which emits no fire.

A صلادم *salādim*, (pl. of صلادم *sulādim*) Lions. Hard-hoofed.

A صلاصل *sulāsil*, Noisy (ass).

A صلاطح *sulātih*, (or صلاطح بلاطح *sulātih bulātih*) Broad.

A صلاع *silāʻ*, Summer-heat.

A صلاع *sullāʻ*, Broad, large, and hard (rock).

A صلافح *salāfih*, Money, cash.

A صلافى *salāfa'*, (pl. of صلف *salif*) Arrogant, boastful. *Salāfī*, (pl. of صلفاء *salfā*) Hard grounds.

A صلاق *sallāḳ*, Eloquent, speaking well.

A صلاقة *sulāḳat*, Water, which has long lain in a place, and become dirtied by cattle.

A صلاقيم *salāḳīm*, Heads. Teeth, especially the canine teeth of quadrupeds.

A صلال *silāl*, (pl. اصلّة *asillat*) The lining or leg of a boot. (pl. of صلّة *sallat*) Dry earths.

A صلّال *sallāl*, Clay dry and hard which emits a sound. Stinking (water).

A صلالة *silālat*, The lining or leg of a boot. *Sulālat*, Whatever falls over in pouring out water, &c.

A صلّام *sall, sill*, or *sullām*, Pulp of the lote-fruit.

A صلامة *si, sa*, or *sulāmat*, A multitude; a sect.

A صلاية *salāyat*, (pl. صليّ *suliy* or *siliy*) A stone or mortar in which they bray musk. The forehead.

A صلائف *salāʼif*, (pl. of صليفة *salifat*) Women unloved by their husbands, whom they cannot please.

A صلائق *salāʼiḳ*, Thin bread. (pl. of صليقة *salīḳat*) Meats thoroughly dressed, well-roasted.

P صلايه *silāya*, Stones on which they bray musk. صلايه كردن *silāya kardan*, To bray as with a muller.

A صلب *salb*, (v. n. of صلب) Crucifying. Gibbetting. Strengthening (a bucket) with a double cross. Roasting (meat). Burning. Extracting marrow (from bones). Becoming quotidian (an ague or fever). *Sulb*, Hard, strong, robust. Schirrous. Rude, gross, simple. Right, real. Patient of labour. Strength. Estimation, value. Dignity, modesty. Crucifixion. Burning. Teasing, fretting, vexing. *Sulb* or *salab*, (pl. اصلب *aslub*, اصلاب *aslāb*, and صلبة *silabat*) Back-bone. Loins. Hard, rocky ground. *Salab*, Marrow, fat. اصحاب الصلب *as-hābu's salab*, Those who collect bones and extract the marrow therefrom. *Sulab*, Name of a bird. *Sulub*, (pl. of صليب *salīb*) Marrows, fats.

A صلّب *sullab*, Hard, strong. A whetstone.

A صلبان *sulbān*, (pl. of صليب *salīb*) Crosses.

A صلبة *silabat*, (pl. of صلب *sulb*) Loins. Hard, rocky grounds.

A صلبوب *sulbūb*, A flute, pipe, psaltery.

A صلبيّ *sulbiy*, Proceeding from the loins, lumbar. Real, natural. P شيشهٔ صلبي *shīshaʼi sulbī*, Bladder. فرزند صلبيش *farzandi sulbiyash*, His own son. A *Salabīy*, Belonging to the cross, cruciferous.

A صلّبيّ *sullabīy*, Sharpened. A whetstone. A furbishing instrument.

A صلّبيّة *sullabīyat*, A whetstone.

A صلة *silat* also *sulat*, (v. n. of وصل) Joining, coupling. *Silat*, (v. n. of وصل) Being united by bonds or friendship. Arriving. Conjunction, connection, consanguinity, relationship, affinity, propinquity. A present. حرف صله *harfi sila*, A conjunctive particle, a preposition prefixed to a noun (as, P بحصار *ba hisār*, To the castle). صلهٔ رحم *silaʼi rahim*, A visit to, or intercourse with, kindred.

A صلّة *sallat*, Widely-spread rain. Rain (in flying showers). A cutting of grass. Ground wet with dew. The noise of a nail when struck hard. The tinkling sound of a bridle-bit. A stinking skin in a tan-pit. A dry skin before it is tanned. Forage, fodder. A shoe. (pl. صلال *silāl*) Earth hard from dryness and having no rain, though lying between two fields which have. خفّ جيّد الصلّة *khuffun jayyidu's sallat*, A boot made of the finest leather. *Sillat*, One basilisk. The noise of a nail smartly struck. *Sullat*, Remains (of water, &c.). A stink. The moisture of fresh meat.

A صلت *salt*, (pl. اصلات *aslāt*) A broad, wide front or forehead. A sharp and shining sword. An active, bustling man. A horse's leap. Prominent, projecting. Straight, even, level (race-course). *Salt* or *sult*, A large knife. *Silt*, A thief, robber.

A صلتان *salatān*, Brisk, swift (horse or ass).

A صلج *salj*, (v. n. of صلج) Smelting (silver). Rubbing (penem). Cudgelling. *Salaj*, Deafness. *Sulūj*, Good money.

A صلّج *sullaj*, A silkworm's cone, cocoon.

A صلّجة *sullajat*, A silken garment.

A صلح *silh*, Good, fair. *Sulh*, Peace, concord, reconciliation, pacification. Compact, convention, a treaty, truce. P صلح باعوض *sulh bā ʻiwaz*, Compromise. صلح كل *sulhi kul*, Perfect reconciliation, definitive treaty. Universal toleration. صلح وصلاح مستوجب الفلاح *sulh u salāhi mustawjibu'l falāh*, Peace and honesty productive of prosperity.

A صلحاً *sulhān*, Pacifically.

A صلحاء *sulahāʼ*, (pl. of صالح *sālih*) Just, pious.

P صلح آميز *sulh-āmez*, Conciliatory.

P صلح نامه *sulh-nāma*, Treaty of peace, compact.

A صلحيّ *sulhīy*, Belonging to peace. Any thing obtained in consequence of a peace, as land.

A صلخاء *salkhāʼ*, (fem. of اصلخ *aslakh*) Mangy.

A صلخام *silkhām*, Tall, strong, hardy (camel).

A صلخد *salkhad, silakhd*, صلّخد *sillakhd*, صلخاد *silkhād*, صلخدي *salakhda'*, Hardy, strong, robust (camel). (An arrow) piercing with velocity.

A صلخدم *salakhdam*, Strong (camel).

A صلّخف *sillakhf*, Baggage (for man or horse).

A صلّخفة *sillakhfat*, Broad and shallow (dish).

A صلخم *salkham*, Steep, inaccessible (mountain). *Salkham*, (or صلخمّ *silkhamm*) Strong, sharp, penetrating.

A صلخى *salkha'*, Mangy (camels).

A صلد *sald*, A smooth, shining forehead (especially if bald). (A horse) not sweating (a bad quality). *Sald* or *sild*, Hard, solid, strong, and smooth. A place where nothing grows.

A صلداء *sildāʼ*, (or صلداءة) Rough, hard ground.

A صلدام *sildām*, A lion. Strong.

A صلدة *saldat*, Milkless (camel).

A صلدح *saldah*, A large, broad stone. Large-bodied (girl).

A صلدم *sildim*, A lion. Hard-hoofed.

A صلصال *salsāl*, Clay mixed with sand, or clay not made into earthenware. Clay dry and hard which yields a sound. Noisy (ass).

A صلصل *salsal*, Forelocks of a horse. *Sulsul*, A ring-dove, a wood-pigeon. Noisy (ass). Forelocks of a horse. Water (or other liquid) remaining in a vessel or in a ditch. White in a horse's mane. A cup, small vessel. A skilful shepherd. Any white place about the brisket of a horse, where the hair has been rubbed off.

A صلصلة *salsalat*, (v. n. of صلصل Q) Sounding with a thundering or crashing noise. Rolling with a loud rattling peal (thunder). Threatening, terrifying. Killing (the commander of an army). Boasting of one's cleverness. *Salsalat* or *sulsulat*, Remains (of water or other liquid) in a vessel or a ditch. *Sulsulat*, A pigeon. A bushy head of hair.

A صلطح *saltah*, (fem. صلطحة) Thick, broad.

A صلع *sulʻ*, (pl. of اصلع *aslaʻ*) Bald-headed (men). *Salaʻ*, Baldness.

A صلّع *sullaʻ*, A broad and hard stone. A place producing no herbage.

A صلعاء *salɛās*, (fem. of اصلع *aslaɛ*) Bald (woman). Bare, producing nothing (ground). (Trees) naked by the falling of the leaves. A misfortune. Any great and notorious affair.

A صلعان *sulɛān*, (pl. of اصلع) Bald-headed.

A صلعة *salaɛat* or *sulaɛat*, A bald place.

A صلعم *salɛam*, A mysterious word (added often to the name of Muhammad) formed from the abbreviation of the following words, صلّى الله عليه و سلم *salla'llāh ɛulayhi wa sallam*, The blessing and peace of God be with him!

A صلغ *salgh*, (v. n. of صلغ) Shedding her teeth of the sixth year (a sheep). Entering on her fifth or sixth year. *Salagh*, A red hillock.

A صلّغ *sullagh*, (pl. of صالغ *sāligh*) Six-year-old (cows or sheep).

A صلغة *salghat*, A large ship. *Salaghat*, A fat seven-year-old she-camel.

A صلّغد *sillaghd*, One whose nose is red and peeled.

A صلف *salf*, A vacuum in the heart of a palm-tree. *Salaf*, (v. n. of صلف) Being unable to please her husband, though behaving properly (a woman). Speaking disagreeably, or invidiously. Commending one's self. Making false pretensions, boasting. Being tasteless and insipid (food). A year of scarcity. *Salif*, A vessel holding little water. Heavy (vessel). Insipid (food). Rainless, thundering (cloud). (pl. صلافى *salāfa'*, صلفاء *sulafās*, and صلفين *salifin*) Arrogant, boastful; a boaster.

A صلفاء *sal*, *silfās*, صلفاة *sal*, or *silfāt*, Hard land. A large, smooth stone level with the ground. *Sulafās*, (pl. of صلف *salif*) Arrogant, boastful.

A صلفة *salifat*, (pl. صلفات *salifāt* and صلائف *salāsif*) (A woman) unable to please her husband.

A صلفحة *salfahat*, A changing, turning (money).

A صلفعة *salfaɛat*, (v. n. of صلفع Q) Beheading. Shaving (the head). Becoming poor and destitute.

A صلق *salk*, (v. n. of صلق) Making a loud, grating noise. Beating (with a stick). Lying with (a girl) on (her) back. Going in and out of the water and dirtying it. Overwhelming (an enemy) with a tremendous attack. Oppressing with heat (the sun). A loud voice. *Salak*, (pl. اصلاق *aslāk* and اصالق *asālik*) Plain, level ground.

A صلقاب *silkāb*, One whose teeth or tusks whet each other.

A صلقام *silkām*, A lion.

A صلقع بلقع *salkaɛ balkaɛ*, Vacant (desert).

A صلقعة *salkaɛat*, (v. n. of صلقع Q) Cutting off, or shaving (the head). Becoming poor. Extending (the voice).

A صلقم *salkam*, One who grinds his teeth. Bulky (camel). A lion. *Silkim*, An old woman. Thick.

A صلقمة *salkamat*, A grinding (of the teeth).

A صلك *silak*, That which comes from a sheep before the biestings.

A صلم *salm*, (v. n. of صلم) Extirpating, mutilating (nose or ears). *Salam*, Strong, bold men.

A صلمة *sulmat*, A helmet. *Salamat*, Strong men. A kind of dish made from wheaten-flour.

A صلمحة *salmahat*, A shaving (of the head).

A صلمعة *salmaɛat*, (v. n. of صلمع Q) Pulling out the hairs, or shaving (the head). Making smooth. Becoming poor. Poverty, want. هو صلمعة بن قلمعة *huwa salmaɛatu 'bnu kalmaɛat*, He is unknown.

A صلنباح *silimbāh*, A kind of long slender fish.

A صلندحة *sal* or *sulandahat*, Hardy (she-camel).

A صلنفح *salanfah*, Noisy, clamorous.

A صلنقح *salankah*, Shrewd, keen. Malicious.

A صلنقع *salankaɛ*, Strong, loud (voice). Quick, keen, bold (man). Open, clear (road).

A صلنقى *salanka'*, (or صلنقاء *salankās*) Talkative.

A صلو *salw*, A striking on the middle of the back, or the lower part of the haunch-bone.

A صلوات *salawāt*, Synagogues, Jewish oratories. (pl. of صلوة *salāt*) Prayers. Benedictions, blessings. (pl. of صلا *sala'*) Middles of backs.

A صلوة *salāt*, (v. n. 2 of صلى, irregular) Praying. Being merciful (God). Pronouncing a blessing. Following the leader (a horse). Prayer. The first chapter of the Kur'ān. Compassion, mercy (from God). The divine benediction or salutation. A benediction bestowed or invoked upon an angel or apostle. Supplication for forgiveness. Adoration paid with an inclination of the head. A place of prayer, a synagogue. الصلوة الربّانية *as salātu'r rabbāniyat*, The Lord's prayer.

A صلوتة *sulūtat*, (v. n. of صلت) Having a broad, open forehead.

A صلوح *sulūh*, see صلاح *salāh*. *Sulūh*, (v. n. of صلح) Being good, excellent. Being right, fit, proper, corresponding with.

A صلوخ *salūkh*, Fatal (misfortune).

A صلود *salūd*, Slow-boiling (kettle). (A horse) not sweating. (A camel) which yields little milk. One who, through fear, ascends a mountain. Separate, single, solitary. *Sulūd*, (v. n. of صلد) Sounding when struck, yet emitting no fire (a tinder-box or any thing similar). Striking the ground when leaping (a horse). Ascending (a mountain). Being hard (ground). Shining (as a bald head). Being avaricious. Making a grating noise (teeth).

A صلودح *salawdah*, Hardy, strong.

A صلودد *salawdad*, Hard, solid, strong, smooth.

A صلور *sillawr*, An eel.

A صلوغ *sulūgh*, Fulness of growth (in a sheep).

A صلول *sulūl*, (v. n. of صلّ) Beginning to putrify (meat), to stink (water).

P صلون *salūn*, Capers.

A صلهام *silhām*, Bold. A lion.

A صلهب *salhab*, Tall (man). Large (house). *Salhab*, (or صلهبى *salahba'*) Robust, hardy (camel).

A صلهباة *salahbāt*, Robust, hard (she-camel).

A صلهبة *salhabat*, The being tall.

A صلهج *salhaj*, A large stone. A hardy she-camel.

A صلى *saly*, (v. n. of صلى) Warming before the fire. Burning by fire. Roasting (meat). Deceiving by caresses, circumventing, betraying into danger. *Sala'*, (v. n. of صلى) Becoming relaxed about the haunches (a mare at foaling-time).

A صلّى *salla'*, (pret. of 2d conj. used optatively) May He pour blessings, or be propitious!

A صلّى *suliy*, (pl. of صالي *sāli*) Those who bake upon the fire. *Suliy* or *siliy*, (v. n. of صلى) Burning. Warming before the fire, bearing its heat. (pl. of صلاية *salāyat*) Stones on which musk is rubbed.

A صلّيان *silliyān*, A species of herb.

A صليب *salib*, (pl. صلاب *silāb*) Hard, strong, firm. (pl. صلبان *sulbān*) A cross, crucifix. A standard. A hill. A cruciform brand on a camel. (pl. صلب *sulub*) Marrow, fat. Four stars behind the Eagle. صليب اكبر *salibi akbar*, (Great cross) A colure. P صليب باديروا *salibi bādi-rawā*, A window-frame. A بنو الصليب *banū's salib*, Sons of the cross, *i.e.* Christians.

P صليب خطى *salib-khatti*, A quadrangular line.

P صليب وار *salibwār*, Across, crosswise.

A صليبى *salibiy*, Belonging to the cross. Cruciferous. Cruciform. A Christian priest.

A صليجة *salijat*, An ingot of pure silver.

A صليح *salih*, Good, apt, fit, proper, just.

A صليد *salid*, Flashing. Alone, single.

A صليع *saliɛ*, Bare (mountain).

A صليعاء *sulayɛās*, The exposed privities of man or woman. Any shameful affair. A sore calamity.

A صليف *salif*, The side of the neck, the head of the vertebræ, where they join the skull. صليفان *salifāni*, The two sides of the neck. Two cross pieces of wood on a camel's saddle.

A صليق *salik*, Even, smooth, shining.

A صليقة *salikat*, (pl. صلائق *salāsik*) Meat dressed soft. A thin cake.

A صليل *salil*, (v. n. of صلّ) Sounding (iron or an empty egg-shell). Being struck and driven into any thing (a nail). Becoming dry from intense thirst (the entrails of a camel). The tingling sound of iron when struck; the rumbling of the guts when empty.

A صمّ *samm*, (v. n. of صمّ) Closing or corking (a bottle). Breaking or bruising (with a stick or stone). Dying, perishing (an echo). Emitting no sound when struck (a stone clotted with gore). Being deaf. *Simm*, A lion. A misfortune. *Summ*, (pl. of اصمّ *asamm* and صمّاء *sammās*) Deaf. صمّ بكم *summun bukmun*, Deaf (and) dumb persons. جذر الصمّ *jazru's summ*, The square root of a surd.

A صما *sams*, (v. n. of صما) Impelling, exciting, stirring up. Arising upon.

A صمّاء *sammās*, (fem. of اصمّ *asamm*) Deaf, dumb, one that can neither hear nor be heard. Hard, solid (rock), returning no echo. A surd in arithmetic. Misfortune, a calamity. A serpent of a dangerous species. A peculiar mode of putting on a species of loose upper Arabian garment, somewhat resembling the plaids worn by the highlanders of Scotland. Rough ground. Fat (she-camel). (A camel) in foal. The extremity of the small guts. صمّاء الغبر *sammāʼu'l ghabar*, A heavy misfortune.

A صمات *samāt*, Aught, any (food). علي صمات *ʻala' simāt*, Within sight or hearing. *Sumāt*, Silence. Any thing causing silence. Thirst soon returning.

A صماح *sumāh*, The stench of the arm-pits when sweating. An animal smaller than that called وبر *wabr*. Melted lard applied to a cut. *Sumāh*, (or صماحي *sumāhīy*) The cautery.

A صماخ *simākh*, The ear, organ of hearing. Orifice of the ear. A little water.

A صمّاخة *sammākhat*, Intelligence, understanding. A sharp, clever, intelligent woman.

A صماد *simād*, (v. n. 3 of صمد) Fighting with swords. A cork, stopple, or leathern strap, with which they cover the mouth of a bottle. A kerchief worn round the head.

A صمادح *sumādih*, Clear, open (road). A lion. *Sumādih*, (and صمادحيّ *sumādihīy*) Strong, hardy. Hot (day). Pure, exquisite.

A صمارح *sumārih*, Pure, unmixed, sincere.

A صماري *samāra'*, (*sumāra'*, or صماريّ *sumārīy*) Podex.

A صماريد *samārīd*, Hard grounds. Fat (sheep). Lean (sheep).

A صماصم *sumāsim*, A lion. *Sumāsim*, (or صماصمة *sumāsimat*) Bold, hardy, keen.

A صماغان *simāghāni*, The corners of the mouth.

A صماك *simāk*, (pl. صمك *sumuk*) The strickle or stick with which corn above the bushel is struck off.

A صمالخ *sumālikh*, Thick milk.

A صمالخي *sumālikhīy*, Milk put into a leathern bottle and buried in the ground that it may turn thick. Insipid (meat or milk).

A صمالك *samālik*, (pl. of صملك) Strong.

A صماليخ *samālīkh*, Tender shoots of the plants called نصيّ *nasīy*.

A صمام *samām*, A misfortune. صمام صمام *samāmi samāmi*, Be silent, pretend to be deaf. *Simām*, (and صمامة *simāmat*) The stopple of a bottle.

A صمّان *sammān*, (and صمّانة *sammānat*) Hard, stony ground on a tract of sand. *Summān*, (pl. of اصمّ *asamm*) Deaf.

A صمّة *simmat*, (pl. صمم *simam*) A male serpent. A female hedgehog. A bold man. A lion. The stopple of a bottle.

A صمت *samt*, Silence.

A صمتة *sumtat*, Silence, taciturnity. *Sumtat* or *simtat*, Any thing producing silence (as sweetmeats or the like given to children).

A صمجة *samajat*, (pl. صمج *samaj*) A lamp.

A صمح *samh*, (v. n. of صمح) Dissolving (as intense heat does the brain). Striking with a whip. Questioning in coarse and opprobrious language.

A صمحاء *simhāʼ*, Rugged ground.

A صمحمح *samahmah*, (صمحمحي *samahmahīy*, or صمحمحة *samahmahat*) A stout, thick, hardy man, firm and compact of body. Bald, or having the head shaved. Dwarfish.

A صمخ *samkh*, (v. n. of صمخ) Striking on the hollow of the ear. Smiting the face vehemently (the sun). Striking (eye or ear) with the clenched fist. *Simkh*, A dry crudity in a ewe's teat after lambing, which dropping away, the milk improves.

A صمخة *samikhat*, Soft, delicate-bodied (woman).

A صمخدد *samakhdad* or *sumakhdid*, Pure, excellent. The better sort (of mankind).

A صمد *samd*, (v. n. of صمد) Going towards, wishing to approach. Erecting, establishing, planting. Beating. Blackness of face from the heat of the sun. An elevated, rugged place. Purpose, design, intention. *Samad*, A lord, chief man, master of a family. One to whom people resort on important matters. Perpetual, eternal, stable, permanent. Sublime, high. Solid, not hollow. A man capable of enduring hunger and thirst in war. A people without art or trade to subsist by.

A صمدان *samdān*, (صمداني *samdānīy*, or صمديّ *samadīy*) Eternal. Divine.

A صمدة *samdat*, A rock immoveably fixed in the ground, even with, or raised above the surface. Barren (she-camel), one that has not borne for years.

A صمدحة *samdahat*, (v. n. of صمدح Q) Being intensely hot (the day).

A صمديّة *samadīyat*, Eternity. Sublimity. An epithet of the deity.

A صمر *samr*, (v. n. of صمر) Being avaricious. Flowing through a plain from a declivity (water). Keeping back, hindering. *Samr* or *samar*, (v. n. of صمر) Being very salt and bitter. The smell of fresh fish. Stink. *Simr*, A place where water lies still. *Sumr*, (pl. اصمار *asmār*) Lip, edge, or thickness of a vessel. Aside. *Samar*, Smell of meat or fish. *Samir*, Stinking. يدي من السمك صمرة *yadī mini's samak samirat*, My hand smells of fish.

A صمرة *samrat*, Milk destitute of sweetness.

A صمرد *simrid*, A camel abounding in, or having little milk.

A صمصام *samsām*, Bold, resolute, keen. A sword that bends not.

A صمصامة *samsāmat*, Bold, resolute, keen. *Simsāmat*, A sword which bends not.

A صمصم *samsam*, Extremely avaricious. *Simsim*, Thick (man). Short. *Simsim* or *sumasim*, Bold, hardy, keen. *Sumasim*, A lion.

A صمصمة *samsamat*, (v. n. of صمصم Q) Proceeding (on a journey or business). The cry of the female hedgehog. *Simsimat* or *samsamat*, (pl. صمصم *simsim*) The midst of the people. A crowd.

A صمع *samʻ*, (v. n. of صمع) Striking (with a stick). Passing by (people), and restraining (them) by words. *Sumʻ*, (pl. of اصمع *asmaʻ*) High, lofty. (pl. of صمعاء *samʻāʼ*) Small ears. Smooth, slender stems. Pods not yet burst. صمع الكعوب *sumʻu'l kuʻūb*, An epithet applied to dogs, because they have small ankle-bones. *Samaʻ*, (v. n. of صمع) Following one's own whim without heeding any body. Blundering in speech. Having a small ear.

A صمعاء *samʻāʼ*, Small ear set close to the head. Small-eared. A smooth, slender stem. A pod not yet burst. A tree or plant whose fruit enlarges without having yet burst the pod.

A صمعان *samʻān*, Light, elegant feathers, with which they wing arrows. *Sumʻān*, (pl. of اصمع *asmaʻ*) Elegant plumages.

A صمعر *samʻar*, Strong, stout, hardy. Rough ground. Name of a horse, and of a she-camel.

A صمعرة *samʻarat*, Hard ground. Thick skin of the head.

A صمعريّ *samʻarīy*, Strong, hardy. One against whom fascination or enchantment has no power. Base, sordid, abject. Very pure red.

A صمعريّة *samʻarīyat*, A malignant serpent.

A صمعور *sumʻūr*, Short, dwarfish. Bold, brave.

A صمعيوت *samʻayūt*, Sharp-headed.

A صمغ *samgh* or *samagh*, (pl. صموغ *sumūgh*) Gum of the tree قرظ *karaz*, called also صمغ عربي *samghi ʻarabī*, Gum Arabic. P صمغ آلو *samghi ālū*, Plum-tree gum. A صمغ بطم *samghi butm*, Gum of the turpentine-tree. صمغ القتاد *samghu'l katād*, Tragacanth-gum. صمغ المحروث *samghu'l mahrūs*, Assafœtida. *Simagh*, A dry crudity in a camel's dug after colting, which falling off, the milk improves.

A صمغان *samghān*, One whose mouth, ears, eyes, and nose distil dirt as a tree does gum. *Simghāni*, The two corners of the mouth.

A صمغة *samghat*, A clot of gum. A sore. ابو صمغة *abū simghat*, One whose mouth, eyes, ears, and nose distil dirt-like gum. *Simaghat*, A concretion in a camel's teat.

A صمغد *simaghd*, Strong, hardy.

A صمقة *samakat*, Milk that has lost its flavour. Rough (stony place).

A صمقرة *samkarat*, (v. n. of صمقر Q) Becoming exceedingly acid (milk).

A صمك *sumuk*, (pl. of صماك *simāk*) Strickles, sticks with which they strike the grain to level it with the bushel or measure.

A صمكة *samakat*, Strong (man).

A صمكمك *samakmak*, Hard, strong, and thick. Fetid. Water which trickles from the bucket and acquires a disagreeable scent.

A صمكوك *samakūk*, (or صمكيك *samakīk*) Strong, powerful, hardy, rough, coarse. Foolish, stupid (man). Prone to villainy. Thick, viscous.

A صمكيك *samkīk*, Hasty, impetuous, foolish.

A صمل *suml*, (v. n. of صمل) Striking (with a

stick). Being hard, firm. Becoming stiff (a tree) when not watered. Abstaining (from meat).

A صمل *sumull*, Strong, hardy, and square-built (man). Hard (hoof).

A صملاخ *simlākh*, Ear-wax. The inner cavity of the ear.

A صملج *samallaj*, Strong, powerful.

A صملك *samallak*, (pl. صمالك *samālik*) Strong, robust, hardy. A part cut off.

A صملوخ *sumlūkh*, Ear-wax.

A صمليل *simlīl*, Weak-bodied. Name of a plant.

A صمم *samam*, (v. n. of صمّ) Growing deaf. Deafness. A stoppage in the ears. Firm and strong. Bold, resolute, keen. *Simam*, (pl. of صمّة *simmat*) Lions. Male serpents.

A صموت *samūt*, Silent. Heavy (coat of mail), not sounding. Deep-piercing (sword). Full (honey-comb). ضربة صموت *zarbatun samūtun*, A blow which reaches the bone, and the effect of which remains there. صموت كالحوت *samūt ka'l hūt*, Mute as a fish. جارية صموت الخلخالين *jāriyatun samūtu'l khalkhālayn*, A girl with ankles so fat that the rings are silent. *Sumūt*, Silence. Silent (persons).

A صموح *samūh*, Hard (hoof).

T صمور *samūr*, Sable (fur).

A صمور *sumūr*, (v. n. of صمر) Being avaricious. Flowing through a plain from a declivity (water). Preventing, hindering.

A صموغ *sumūgh*, (pl. of صمغ *samgh*) Gums.

A صمول *sumūl*, (v. n. of صمل) Being hard and firm. Becoming stiff (a tree) when not watered. Abstaining (from food).

A صمي *samy*, (v. n. of صمي) Falling down in the place where it was struck (game). Descending, alighting upon. Driving, forcing onward.

A صميان *samayān*, (v. n. of صمي) Falling down in the place where it was struck (game). Returning, retiring, receding. Leaping, starting up. Making haste. Inversion, turning. An assault. Celerity. Bold. One who makes a sure charge.

A صمّيت *simmīt*, Silent, taciturn, saturnine.

A صميدح *samaydah*, A hot day. Strong, hardy.

A صمير *samīr*, (A man) with dry withered flesh, emitting disagreeable effluvia. *Sumayr*, Sunset.

A صميل *samīl*, Dry, withered.

A صميم *samīm*, Pure, unmixed, sincere. The bone which forms the entire support of any member. The choicest part (of any thing). The intensest (of cold or heat). The outward shell of an egg. عن صميم القلب *ʻan samīmi'l kalb*, From the bottom of the heart; cordially, affectionately.

A صميماء *sumaymāʼ*, A plant like a carrot.

A صميميّ *samīmīy*, Cordial, inward: pure, sincere.

A صنّ *sinn*, A little basket in which they carry bread. The urine of a camel which is very fetid. The first of the five days (at the end of winter) called العجوز *al ʻajūz*.

A صناء *sanāʼ*, (or صنا *sana'*) Ashes. Dirt, filth.

A صناب *sināb*, A kind of seasoning for meat made of mustard and dried grapes bruised together.

A صناب *sināb*, (or صنابة *sinābat*) Long in back and belly.

A صنابر *sanābir*, Intense cold.

A صنابيّ *sinābiy*, Of a reddish colour, mixed with white hairs, of the colour of mustard (a horse).

A صنّاج *sannāj*, A player on the صنج *sanj*.

A صنّاجة *sannājat*, A clear, moonlight night.

A صناخر *sunākhir*, A large-bodied camel. A tall and robust man.

A صناخيّة *sunākhiyat*, A large-bodied man.

A صنادل *sunādil*, Large and big-headed camel.

A صناديد *sanādīd*, (pl. of صنديد *sindīd*) Kings, princes, chiefs, generals. Troops, battalions. Misfortunes, dangers. صناديد غزاة *sanādīdi ghuzāt*, The principal commanders. حامي الصناديد *hāmī's sanādīd*, Intensely hot (day).

A صناديق *sanādīk*, (pl. of صندوق *sundūk*) Chests.

A صنار *sinār*, (or صنّار *sinnār*) (from P چنار *chanār*) The plane-tree. The head of a spindle.

A صنّارة *sannārat* or *sinnārat*, Ill-tempered and boorish. *Sinnārat*, (pl. صنانير *sanānīr*) Handle of a shield. Head of a spindle. The ear.

A صناع *sanāʻ*, (pl. صنع *sunuʻ*) Industrious, dexterous, clever, neat-handed (man or woman). A water-dam. Name of an individual, native of Emessa.

A صنّاع *sannāʻ*, Artist, artisan, handicraftsman, *Sunnāʻ*, (pl. of صانع *sāniʻ*) Workmen, operatives.

A صناعة *sināʻat*, (pl. صنائع *sanāʼiʻ*) Art, industry; profession, trade, craft.

A صنّاعة *sannāʻat*, A water-dam.

A صناعيّ *sināʻiy*, Artificial.

A صنافر *sunāfir*, Pure, unmixed.

A صنافرة *sunāfirat*, The offspring of an unknown father. The limits of the earth where bounded by the horizon.

A صناق *sanāk*, (pl. صنق *sunuk*) The stench of the arm-pits. *Sināk*, Braying deeply (a camel).

A صنان *sunān*, (pl. اصنّة *asinnat*) The smell of the arm-pits.

A صنانيت *sanānīt*, (pl. of صنّوت *sannūt*) Small baskets of palm-leaves. Coverings of glass bottles.

A صنانير *sanānīr*, (pl. of صنّارة *sinnārat*) Heads of spindles. Ears. Shield-handles.

A صناية *sināyat*, The whole. بصنايته *bisināyatihi*, With the whole of it, totally.

A صنائع *sanāʼiʻ*, (pl. of صناعة *sināʻat*) Arts, trades, crafts. Miracles. (pl. of صنيعة *saniʻat*) Acts, actions: benefits, kindnesses. صنائع ومعارف *sanāʼiʻ u maʻārif*, Arts and sciences.

A صنائعي *sanāʼiʻiy*, Working people, the operative class. A craftsman, artisan, mechanic.

A صنبر *sambar*, Thin, slender, and weak.

A صنّبر *sinnabr*, A cold wind. The second of the five days (at the end of winter) called العجوز *al ʻajūz*. *Sinnibr* or *sinnabr*, Cold, also hot (morning).

A صنبرة *sambarat*, (v. n. of صنبر Q) Being slender at the lower part, destitute of leaves, and thinly bearing fruit (a palm-tree). A rough and filthy heap of urine and ox-dung.

A صنبعة *sambaʻat*, (v. n. of صنبع Q) Shrinking back, refusing to give.

A صنبعر *simbaʻr*, Ill-tempered.

A صنبل *sumbul* or *sumbal*, Crafty, deep, shrewd.

A صنبور *sumbūr*, A cold, also a hot wind. The mouth of a syphon. A cock by which the water is drawn off from a cistern. An aqueduct, a lead or iron water-pipe, or tunnel. A solitary palm-tree. The root of a palm-tree. A palm-tree, slender at the base, bare of leaves, and bearing little fruit. A little boy. A misfortune. A man without children or brethren. Weak and contemptible.

A صنّة *sinnat*, The stench of the arm-pits, or of any nook, cranny, chink, or crevice of the body.

A صنتع *suntuʻ*, An ostrich or an ass with a hard head. One who has projecting eyebrows or cheeks. One who has a large forehead and thin hollow cheeks. An ass with a small head.

A صنتوت *suntūt*, One, unique. A part.

A صنتيت *sintīt*, A legion. A prince, commander.

A صنج *sanj*, An Arabian cymbal, or two concave disks, which, when struck together, make a tingling sound, chiefly used as an accompaniment to other instruments. A kind of man. A sort of stringed instrument. *Sunuj*, Dishes made of ebony.

A صنجة *sanjat*, A balance, scale.

A صنخ *sinkh*, (pl. اصناخ *asnākh*) Root of a tooth. *Sanikh*, (A mouth) the roots of whose teeth are bare.

A صنخاب *sinkhāb*, Large, corpulent (camel).

A صنخة *sanakhat*, Filth, nastiness.

A صنخر *sinakhr*, A fool. *Sinkhir*, Dry, unripe dates. *Sinkhir*, (*sunakhir*, or صنخر *sinnakhr*) Large (camel). Large and tall (man).

A صندح *sandah*, A broad stone.

A صندد *sindid*, A king, prince, gallant commander. Mild, gentle, noble, liberal. A projecting part of a mountain.

A صندعة *sindaʻat*, A sharp and separate part of a mountain.

A صندل *sandal*, Sandal, an odoriferous wood. A camel with a large head, thick, and strong. A four-legged stool. P صندل سفيد *sandali safed*, White sandal-wood.

A صندلانيّ *sandalānīy*, A dealer in sandal-wood. A hawker, pedlar, huckster.

A صندلة *sandalat*, (v. n. of صندل Q) Having a large head, being hard and thick (a camel or ass).

P صندل دانه *sandal-dāna*, A sort of wild rue.

P صندلي *sandalī*, Name of a city in Kashmīr.

P A صندوق *sandūk* or *sundūk*, (pl. صناديق *sanādīk*) A chest, casket, coffer, box, trunk. A cash-chest. A grave, sepulchre, tomb, mausoleum.

P صندوقچه *sandūkcha*, A small chest.

A صندوقي *sandūkī*, Box-shaped (tomb, or scabbard of a sword made in that form).

A صنديد *sindīd*, (pl. صناديد *sanādīd*) A prince, gallant commander. Violent (wind or heat). (Rain) consisting of large drops. Triumphant.

A صنط *sant* or *sanat*, A kind of thorn, acacia.

A صنطير *santīr*, A dulcimer, spinet, harpsichord.

A صنع *sanʻ*, (v. n. of صنع) Well-grooming and feeding (a horse). Name of a bird and animalcule. *Sanʻ* or *sunʻ*, (v. n. of صنع) Making, doing, preparing, creating, constructing. *Sinʻ*, (pl. اصناع *asnāʻ*) Clever-handed, delicate-handed. A roasting-spit. Dressed meat, travelling-provisions. A garment. A cistern. A turban, tiara, sash, or turban-cloth. A tailor. *Sunʻ*, (v. n. of صنع) Doing a kind action, behaving well to. Doing ill by. An act, deed. *Sanaʻ*, Glib-tongued. Clever-handed. Glib (tongue). *Sunuʻ*, Industrious, clever, dexterous (men or women).

A صنعاء *sanʻāʼ*, The metropolis of Yaman.

A صنعانيّ *sanʻānīy*, Of the city صنعاء *sanʻāʼ*.

A صنعبة *sanʻabat*, Hard, strong (she-camel).

A صنعة *sanʻat*, (v. n. of صنع) Exercising a trade. Grooming and feeding well (a horse). Profession, art, trade, craft. Work, handiwork, skill. P صنعت سخن *sanʻati sukhun*, The art of poetry.

P صنعتكار *sanʻat-kār*, A workman, a craftsman.

P صنعتگر *sanʻatgar*, An artisan, mechanic.

A صنعي *sinʻa'*, *sunʻa'*, *sanaʻa'*, or *sunuʻa'*, Industrious, clever-handed people.

A صنعيّ *sunʻīy*, Artificial, artistic.

A صنف *sanf*, Name of a place whence fragrant wood is brought. *Sanf* or *sinf*, (pl. اصناف *asnāf* and صنوف *sunūf*) Kind, sort, species. Mode, manner, form. *Sinf*, Quality, property. Mode, manner. *Sinf*, (صنفة *sinfat*, or *sanifat*) The border of a veil, whether plain or ornamented. A part, side. *Sunf*, (pl. of اصنف *asnaf*) Male-ostriches, whose legs are excoriated.

A صنفيّ *sanfīy*, An inferior species of wood used in fumigation.

A صنق *sanak*, A rank smell under the arm-pit. *Sanik*, Strong, hardy. Large, bulky. Stinking, rank. *Sunuk*, (pl. of صناق *sanāk*) Stinks of arm-pits.

A صنقة *sanakat*, Coarse, stony ground. Those who take care of camels well. *Sanikat*, Large, stout, bulky (camel).

A صنقعر *sinkaʻr*, The milky preparation called اقط *akit*. A lump of gum.

A صنم *sanam*, (pl. اصنام *asnām*) An image, idol. A beloved object, a mistress. A stink. A (slave's) strength. *Sanim*, Strong (slave).

A صنمة *sanamat*, A quill. Misfortune. *Sanimat*, (A camel) left unmilked every other time, that the milk may increase.

P صنم خانه *sanam-khāna*, An idol-temple.

A صنو *sanw*, (pl. صنوّ *sunūw*) Bad wood, stones, or a small stream between two mountains. *Sinw*, (pl. اصناء *asnāʼ* and صنوان *sinwān*) A deserted pit. A uterine brother. A son. A paternal uncle. *Sinw* or *sunw*, (du. صنوان *sinwāni*, *sanwāni*, or *sunwāni*, صنيان *sinyāni*, *sunyāni*, or *sanyāni*) From the same origin, as two brothers by the same father and mother; two streams from the same fountain-head; two trees from the same stock.

A صنوان *sinwān*, (pl. of صنو *sinw*) Uterine brothers. Sons. Paternal uncles.

A صنوبر *sanawbar*, Any cone-bearing tree; a fir. The pistachio-nut. The fruit of the ارز *arz*.

A صنّوت *sannūt*, (pl. صنانيت *sanānīt*) A small basket made of palm-leaves. The wicker cover of a flask or glass bottle.

A صنوج *sunūj*, (v. n. of صنج) Restoring (every man) to his first state. Striking with a stick. Cymbals.

A صنّور *sinnawr*, Avaricious; ill-disposed.

A صنوف *sunūf*, (pl. of صنف *sinf* or *sanf*) Different sorts or forms.

A صنهاج *sinhāj*, (or صنهاجة *sinhājat*) A slave sunk in bondage.

A صنهاجة *sinhājat*, Name of a Moorish people.

A صنيّ *sunayy*, A small pit with a little water in it, unfrequented by any one. A small quantity of water in a furrow.

A صنيع *sanīʻ*, Any work of art; operation, creation, performance, act, deed. A present, donative, gift, benefit. Meat (especially well-dressed). Polished and proved (scimiter or arrow). Clever, neat-handed. Well-groomed and fed (horse). سوء صنيع *sūʼi sanīʻ*, A villainous action.

A صنيعة *sanīʻat*, (pl. صنائع *sanāʼiʻ*) An art, action. Benefit, kindness. The person upon whom a benefit is conferred.

A صوّ *saww*, Free. Empty, hollow.

A اخذه بصواه *akhazahu bi suwāhu*, He took it by the extremities.

A صواب *sawāb*, Rectitude, justness of acting or of thinking; accuracy, reason, right way, correct mode, proper manner. A happy issue, success. سمت صواب *samti sawāb*, The path of reason. بالصواب *bi's sawāb*, Justly, properly, rightly, reasonably.

A صؤاب *suʼāb*, (pl. of صؤابة *suʼābat*) Nits.

P صواب انديش *sawāb-andesh*, Right-thinking.

A صؤابة *suʼābat*, (pl. صؤاب *suʼāb* and صئبان *siʼbān*) A young louse, a nit.

A صوّابة *suwwābat*, The better sort (of people).

P صوابديد *sawāb-dīd*, Approval, good opinion.

P صوابنما *sawāb-namā*, Showing well, appearing probable, just, or reasonable.

A صواح *suwāh*, Plaster, clay. Sweat of horses. Milk in which the water prevails. A palm-branch.

A صواحب *sawāhib*, (pl. of صاحبة *sāhibat*) Female companions. Female possessors.

A صواحبات *sawāhibāt*, (pl. of صواحب *sawāhib*, pl. of صاحبة *sāhibat*) Female companions.

A صوّاحة *suwwāhat*, Hair divided and falling down.

A صوّاخ *suwwākh*, Clay in which the feet stick.

A صوادف *sawādif*, (pl. of صادفة *sādifat*) Camels waiting until the others have drank.

A صوادي *sawādī*, Tall palm-trees. Palm-trees which grow without being watered.

A صوار *suwār* or *siwār*, (pl. صيران *sīrān*) A herd of wild oxen. (pl. اصورة *aswirat*) A little musk. A fragrant perfume.

A صوّار *sawwār*, (A sparrow) answering when called. *Suwār*, A herd of wild oxen.

A صوارّ *sawārr*, (pl. of صارّة *sārrat*) Things needful to be done.

A صواران *siwārāni*, The corners of the mouth.

A صوارف *sawārif*, (pl. of صارفة *sārifat*) Vicissitudes of fortune, accidents, events, revolutions.

A صوارم *sawārim*, (pl. of صارم) Sharp swords.

A صواري *sawārī*, (pl. of صارية *sāriyat*) Ship-masts. Lofty columns.

A صواع *suwāʻ*, (pl. صيعان *sīʻān*) A drinking-vessel. *Suwāʻ* or *siwāʻ*, A certain dry-measure.

A صواعق *sawāʻik*, (pl. of صاعقة) Thunderbolts.

A صواغ *suwāgh*, Form, shape, mould, cast.

A صوّاغ *sawwāgh*, (pl. صوّاغون *sawwāghūn*) A founder, moulder, one who casts into a form. A liar.

A صوّاف *sawwāf*, Wool-stapler: woollen-draper.

A صوافّ *sawāff*, (pl. of صافّة *sāffat*) (Camels) placing their feet in a right line.

A صوافّا *sawāffan*, Straightly, in a row.

A صوافق *sawāfik*, Events, accidents.

A صواكم *sawākim*, (pl. of صاكمة *sākimat*) Heavy strokes or rubs of fortune.

A صوالجة *sawālijat*, (pl. of صولجان *sawlajān*, q.v.).

A صوالد *sawālid*, (pl. of صالدة *sālidat*) Teeth which make a grating noise.

A صوالغ *sawāligh*, (pl. of صالغ *sāligh*) Six-year-old (sheep).

A صوام *sawām*, An arid country.

A صوّام *sawwām*, One who fasts continually. *Suwwām*, (pl. of صائم *sāʼim*) Fasters.

A صوامع *sawāmiʻ*, (pl. of صومعة *sawmaʻat*) Oratories, places of worship. Hermitages; cells.

A صوان *sa*, *si*, or *suwān*, A chest, boards between which clothes are laid. Care or management (of a horse). *Suwān*, Assuan in Nubia.

A صوّان *sawwān*, (pl. of صوّانة *sawwānat*) Hard stones. Podices.

A صوّانة *sawwānat*, (pl. صوّان *sawwān*) A species of hard stone, a rock. Podex.

A صوانيّ *sawānīy*, (pl. of صينيّة *sīniyat*) China, porcelain. Chinese vases.

A صواوين *sawāwīn*, (pl. of صيوان) Tents.

A صواهل *sawāhil*, (pl. of صاهلة *sāhilat*) Neighings. Buzzings of flies.

A صوائح *sawāʼih*, (pl. of صائحة *sāʼihat*) Noisy.

A صوائف *sawāʼif*, (pl. of صائفة *sāʼifat*) Summer-campaigns.

A صوب sawb, (v. n. of صاب for صوب) Raining, falling (rain). Pouring forth water (a cloud). Hitting the mark (an arrow). Touching or wetting (rain). Descending. Pouring out. Design, aim. Preparation. A part, side. A path, track. The right way. A gift. Effusion. Towards. Rain.

A صُوبَة suʻbat, A granary, barn, or similar place. A heap; a pile of money neither told nor weighed.

A صوبج sawbaj, (P چوبه choba) A rolling-pin.

P صوبه ṣūba, A province, such as Bengal, Bahār, &c., comprising several circārs (districts), each circār containing so many pergunnahs (or hundreds of a district, so to speak).

P صوبه دار ṣūba-dār, (or صوبدار ṣūbadār) Viceroy or governor of a province. A military officer among Indian troops, whose rank corresponds to that of captain.

P صوبه داري ṣūba-dārī, Viceroyalty. Captaincy.

A صُوَّة suwat, (pl. صويٰ suwa' or اصواء aswāʻ) High and rugged ground, though not so as to be a mountain. A heap of stones serving as a way-post. A herd of wild beasts. An irregular current of wind. Echo, reverberating sound.

A صوت sawt, (v. n. of صات for صوت) Calling out. Sounding. (pl. اصوات aswāt) A sound, voice. Clamour, noise, call for help. A good name, reputation, or good report. صوت الكلب sawtu'l kalb, The barking of a dog.

A صوتن suwatin or tan, Avaricious, close-fisted.

A صوجان sawjān, Dry, lean, or stiff in the loins. (A palm-tree) with stiff, dry branches. اي صوجان ayyi sawjān, What man (he is I know not).

A صوح sawh, (v. n. of صاح for صوح) Splitting, dividing. Sawh or sūh, A wall, or the precipitous part of a mountain resembling a wall. Base of a mountain. Bank of a river. A mountain.

A صوحان ṣūhān, Dry. A palm-tree whose branches are hard and dry.

A صوخ sawhh, (v. n. of صاخ for صوخ) Sinking into the ground and sticking fast (feet).

A صور sawr, (v. n. of صار for صور) Inclining or causing to hang down. Turning (the face) towards. Bending, making crooked or wry. Cutting, dissecting, dividing. Breaking, demolishing. (pl. صيران sīrān) Small palm-trees joined together. The side of the neck. The bank of a river. The root of a palm-tree. Crookedness, curvature. Sūr, Tyre. A trumpet, clarion, horn. (pl. of اصور aswar) Wry-necked. حملة العرش صور hamalatu'l ʻarsh sūr, The bearers of the throne (of God are) wry-necked.

P صور آه sūri āh, The cry of one in pain. صور صبح گاهي sūri subuh-gāhī, The cries of any one very early in the morning. A Sawar, (v. n. of صور) Inclining. Being wry or crooked. Siwar, suwar, or sūr, (pl. of صورة sūrat) Forms, figures. Modes.

P صوراخي sūrākhī, A long-necked flagon.

A صورة sawrat, An itching on the head. Sūrat, (pl. صور suwar, siwar, and sūr) Image, form, figure, face, effigy, visage, countenance, features, appearance, semblance, resemblance, picture, portrait. Copy, transcript, or abstract. Spectre, apparition, ghost. Mode, manner, condition, state, or quality. P صورت بستن sūrat bastan, To assume a form, to consist. To be conceivable, possible, practicable. To exist. صورت پذير كردن sūrat-pazīr kardan, To assume a shape or appearance. To succeed, be near accomplishing. A صورت حال sūrati hāl, A written statement of facts, state of the case. صورت دفتر sūrati daftar, A book of accounts; a journal, register, inventory; transcript or entry in such books. P تبديل صورت كردن tabdīli sūrat kardan, To disguise, change habits, go in masquerade, travesty, incognito.

A صورت معامله sūrati muʻāmala, Dissimulation, fiction. صورت وهمي sūrati wahmī, A spectre, hobgoblin, phantom. P در صورت dar sūrat, (or در صورتيكه dar sūrate ki) In case, provided that.

A صورة sūratan, To all appearance, apparently, ostensibly. Extrinsically, externally.

P صورت آشنا sūrat-āshnā, Slight acquaintance.

P صورت بند sūrat-band, A maker of effigies, painter, statuary. صورت بنديء تماثيل كردن sūrat-bandīi tamāsīl kardan, To form or paint images or portraits.

P صورت پرست sūrat-parast, An iconolater.

A صورت حرام sūrat harām, Plausible, whose appearance promises more than events will justify: specious, superficial. Fair without, foul within.

P صورت خانه sūrat-khāna, A picture-gallery.

P صورت گر sūratgar, A painter. A sculptor.

P صورت گري sūratgarī, A giving form, formation.

P صورتنما sūrat-namā, Apparent. صورتنما شدن sūrat-namā shudan, To appear, to seem.

A صورتي sūratī, Handsome.

P صورقون كبود surkūni kabūd, A kind of willow.

A صورنجان sūranjān, Hermodactyls.

A صوريّ sūriy, External, apparent. Pertaining unto the face. A native of Tyre. انهزام صوري inhizāmi sūrī, A feigned retreat, rout, or defeat. P پريشاني صوري pareshānīi sūrī, Alteration of countenance, disturbed external appearance. مواصلت صوري muwāsalati sūrī, Personal interview. علّت صوريّه ʻillati sūriya, Ostensible cause. متاعب صوريّه matāʻibi sūriya, Outward troubles.

A صوص sūs, Worthless, mean, avaricious. One who lives and eats alone, especially by moonlight, unseen by strangers, a curmudgeon.

A صوصلاء sawsalāʻ, Name of a plant.

A صوط sawt, The sound of falling water.

A صوطل sawtal, A wild turnip.

P صوطله sūtala, A species of beet.

A صوع sawʻ, (v. n. of صاع for صوع) Separating. Scattering. Coming (to one's fellows or others) from parts adjacent to them. Following one another. Measuring with the measure called صاع sāʻ. Inspiring with terror, frightening. Sawʻ or sūʻ, A certain dry measure of 4 mudds. Sūʻ, (pl. of صاع sāʻ and of صواع siwāʻ) A certain dry-measure. Suwaʻ, Parts of a plant beginning to wither.

A صوغ sawgh, (v. n. of صاغ for صوغ) Creating, forming, shaping, moulding, casting. Melting. Exercising the goldsmith's or founder's art. Flowing easily down the throat (wine). Framing (a lie). Subsiding (water into ground, or sauce into meat). Form, mode. Like, equal.

A صوغان sawghāni, (dual) A pair, two things uniform. Coeval, born at the same time.

A هو صوغة اخته huwa sawghatu ukhtihi, He is the image or counterpart of his sister.

A صوف sawf, (v. n. of صاف for صوف) Flying wide of the mark (an arrow). Declining, departing from one. Being turned away (the face). Sawf or sawaf, (v. n. of صوف) Being woolly, wool-bearing. Sūf, Wool, a fleece. Goats' hair. Camelot. Stuff, half silk, half worsted. صوف الرقبة sūfu'r rakabat, Nape of the neck, or hair in that place. Without reserve; gratis, gratuitously. Sawif, Woolly.

A صوف suʻuf, (v. n. of صاف for صوف) Being woolly, bearing wool. Departing, going away (evil).

A صوفانة sūfānat, A certain dwarfish and lanigerous pot-herb.

A صوفانيّ sūfāniy, Woolly, wool-bearing.

A صوفة sūfat, A flock, lock of wool. صوفة الدواة sūfatu'd dawāt, Wool, cotton put into an inkholder.

A صوفعة sawfaʻat, Top of a turban or cap.

P صوفي sūfī, Wise, intelligent. Pious, devout, spiritual. A religious man of the order of the Sūfī; hence the surname of the kings of Persia. The Sūfī is a higher order of mystic than the Kalandar or Malāmati; for although the two latter renounce the world, they still are subject to a superior; whilst the Sūfī acknowledges no spiritual head.

P صوفيان sūfiyān, Sūfīs, religious brethren.

P صوفيانه sūfiyāna, Victuals not containing flesh.

A صوفيّة sūfiyat, Sūfīism.

A صوق sawk, (v. n. of صاق for صوق) Driving. Sūk, (for سوق sūk) A market-place.

A صوقر sawkar, A large axe.

A صوقرة sawkarat, (v. n. of صوقر Q) Imitating or mimicking the cry of a bird.

A صوقرير sawkarīr, Imitation of a bird's note.

A صوقعة sawkaʻat, (v. n. of صوقع Q) Striking on the head. A cloth with which a woman covers her head to keep her veil from being soiled by the unguent of her hair. A hollow in a pudding into which sauce is poured. A place where there has been much fighting. The middle (of a bird's or horse's) head white. A turban.

A صوقيٰ sūka', Good.

A صوك sawk, (v. n. of صاك for صوك) Adhering to the body (the smell of saffron). Being imbued with the smell of saffron (a garment or the body). First. Beginning. Semen virile. اوّل صوك و بوك *awwala sawkin wa bawkin*, At first, before all things. ما به صوك و بوك *mā bihi sawkun wa bawkun*, There is no motion in him (or it).

A صول *sawl*, (v. n. of صال for صول) Being proud, insolent, perverse, unjust, furious, assaulting, attacking, rushing upon. Defining in quantity or measure.

A صوّل *sawul*, Furious, rampant, fierce (camel).

A صولان *sawalān*, (v. n. of صال for صول) Being proudly obstinate. Assaulting.

A صولب *sawlab*, Seed sown and harrowed in.

A صولة *sawlat*, (v. n. of صال for صول) Attacking, rushing upon. Defining in quantity or measure. Fury, violence, ferocity, impetuosity, rampancy (of a stallion). صولت و شجاعت *sawlat u shajāʿat*, Ferocity and valour. *Sūlat*, (Wheat) winnowed and heaped up.

A صولج *sawlaj*, Pure, unmixed. Refined silver.

A صولجان *sawlajān*, (pl. صولجة *sawālijat*) A long bat, curved at one end, with which horsemen strike the ball in the game of horse-shinty. (See چوگان *chawgān*, whence this word is coined).

A صولجة *sawlajat*, Pure, sincere, unmixed.

A صولع *sawlaʿ*, A bright spear-head.

A صوليب *sawlīb*, Seed sown and harrowed in.

A صوم *sawm*, (v. n. of صام for صوم) Fasting. Standing without provender (a horse). Ceasing from all accustomed work (as a silkworm before it casts the skin; a pulley, or any thing similar that will not turn). Keeping silence. Being still (wind). Becoming noon. Tasting (death). Muting (an ostrich). Taking shelter under the tree صوم *sawm*. A fast. A sort of ill-looking tree. One who fasts. A Christian church. Ostrich-dung. صوم و صلات *sawm u salāt* (for صلوة), Fasting and prayer.

A صوّم *suwam*, (pl. of صائم *sāim*) Fasters.

A صومان *sawmān*, (pl. صيامى) One who fasts.

A صومر *sawmar*, Wild basil.

A صومرة *sawmarat*, The herb basil.

A صومع *sawmaʿ*, A cloister, cell, hermitage.

A صومعة *sawmaʿat*, (v. n. of صومع Q) Heaping up to a point. Collecting, bringing together. A high-crowned cap, mitre, tiara. The peak or point of a pudding. (pl. صوامع *sawāmiʿ*) A cloister, an oratory. An eagle. صومعة النصاري *sawmaʿatu'n nasāra'*, A Christian's cloister.

P صومعه داران فلك *sawmaʿa-dārāni falak*, The angels who surround the throne.

P صومعه نشين *sawmaʿa-nishīn*, A monk.

A صومل *sawmal*, Name of a tree that grows in the highest part of Arabia, called عالية *ʿāliyat*.

A صوملة *sawmalat*, (v. n. of صومل Q) Having a dry skin from hunger or any other cause.

A صون *sawn*, (v. n. of صان for صون) Guarding, preserving. Laying up. Standing on the point of the foot either from pain or a defect in the foot (a horse).

A صونة *sawnat*, A dish in which are laid perfumes for a bridegroom or bride.

A صونع *sawnaʿ*, Name of a bird or animalcule.

A صوول *sawūl*, Fierce, rampant (camel). *Suʾūl*, (v. n. of صال for صول) Being insolent and overbearing. Attacking, assaulting.

A صوي *suwa'*, (pl. of صوّة *suwwat*) Mile-stones. Herds of wild beasts.

A صويّ *sawiy*, Withered (palm). *Suwiy*, (v. n. of صوي) Withering (a palm). Being strong. Drying up, losing her milk (a sheep).

A صويب *sawīb*, Right, straight, hitting the mark.

A صويت *suwayt*, (dim. of صوت) A gentle noise.

A صويرة *suwayrat*, Mogadore in Morocco.

A صويرّة *suwayrrat*, Of a narrow disposition.

A صويق *sawīk*. See سويق *sawīk*.

A صه *sah* or *sahin*, Hush! silence!

A صهاء *sihāʾ*, (pl. of صهوة *sahwat*) Springs of water flowing from rocks. Summits of mountains. Middles of horses' backs. Low grounds or caves to which stray camels are apt to repair. (v. n. 3 of صهي) Mounting on the middle of a horse's back.

A صهابجّ *suhābijj*, Reddish (hair or wool).

A صهابيّ *suhābiy*, Of a reddish colour, mixed with white (a camel). Complete, without defect. Flocks of which the proportion due for pious uses has not been paid. A man who keeps no account-book. Violent (death).

A صهابيّة *suhābīyat*, A locust.

A صهار *sihār*, A making matrimonial alliances.

A صهارة *suhārat*, Marrow. Melted fat. Pomatum. A slice of fat or lard. A chameleon.

A صهارج *suhārij*, (pl. صهاريج *sahārīj*) A cistern, bath, pond, or other reservoir.

A صهال *suhāl*, The neighing of a horse.

A صهّال *sahhāl*, A neighing horse.

P A صهام *suhām*, Name of an imaginary animal, having the body of a flame-coloured dragon, and the head of a horse with four eyes.

A صهب *suhb*, (pl. of اصهب *as-hab*) Red (camels). صهب السبال *suhbu's sibāl*, Red-whiskers, *i.e.* enemies (particularly the Greeks, who were the chief foes of the Arabians, and mostly red-haired). *Sahab*, (or صهبة *suhbat*) Red colour. A reddish colour mixed with white in camels about the belly.

A صهباء *sahbāʾ*, Reddish (she-camel). Wine, or the expressed juice of white grapes. صهباءِ نشاط افزا *sahbāʾi nashāt-afzā*, Wine raising the spirits, increasing cheerfulness.

A صهد *sahd*, (v. n. of صهد) Burning one (the sun).

A صهدان *sahadān*, Intense heat.

A صهر *sahr*, (v. n. of صهر) Melting. Dissolving, causing to melt. Hurting by its heat (the sun). Anointing the head. Hot, sultry. *Sihr*, (pl. اصهار *as-hār* and صهراء *suharāʾ*) A father-in-law. A son-in-law. A sister's husband. The grave, as being nearly related to man. Kindred, relationship. The sacredness of the married state. *Suhr*, (pl. of صهور *sahūr*) Roasters of meat. Renderers of lard.

A صهراء *suharāʾ*, (pl. of صهر *sihr*) Relations.

A صهرة *sihrat*, (pl. صهرات *sihrāt*) A mother-in-law. A wife's mother.

A صهرجة *sahrajat*, A plastering (of a cistern).

A صهريّ *sihriy*, (also صهريج *sihrīj*) (pl. صهاريج *sahārīj*) Cisterns, reservoirs.

A صهصلق *sahsalik*, Noisy (old woman). Clamour.

A صهصليق *sahsalīk*, Noisy (old woman).

A صهصهة *sahsahat*, A bidding to keep silence.

A صهطلة *sahtalat*, Laxity, looseness.

A صهل *sahal* or *sahl*, A sharp, hoarse voice.

A صهميم *sihmīm*, One who recedes not from his purpose. Unmixed (good or bad). An illustrious chief, a prince. A camel which does not bray. Of a perverse disposition, contumacious (camel). A gift to a soothsayer.

A صهوبة *suhūbat*, A reddish white in camels.

A صهوة *sahwat*, A spring of water flowing from a rock. Summit of a mountain. (pl. صهي *suha'*) A castle on a hill. (pl. صهاء *sihāʾ*) Low, hollow ground, into which stray camels are apt to get. (pl. صهوات *sahawāt* and صهاء *sihāʾ*) The middle of a horse's back, where the rider sits. The hinder part of a camel's bunch.

A صهود *sahwad*, Large-bodied, corpulent.

A صهور *sahūr*, (pl. صهر *suhr*) A roaster of meat. A melter of fat: one who renders lard.

A صهي *sahy*, (v. n. of صهي) Being moist, humid, running (wound). Being rich. *Suha'*, (pl. of صهوة *sahwat*) Castles upon hills.

A صهير *sahīr*, Melted, rendered (fat or lard).

A صهيل *sahīl*, (v. n. of صهل) Neighing. The neigh of a horse. P صهيل كردن *sahīl kardan*, To neigh.

A صهيون *sihyawn*, Zion.

A صيّاب *suyyāb*, (or صياب *suyāb*) The better sort of mankind. Root, origin.

A صيّابة *suyyābat*, A lord. *Suyyābat*, (or صيابة *suyābat*) Any thing excellent. The better sort of people. Root, origin.

A صياة *sayʾat*, (or صياءة *siyāʾat*) The matter coming from the uterus after delivery.

A صيّاجة *sayyājat*, Moonlight (night).

A صياح *siyāh*, (v. n. 3 of صاح for صيح) Calling aloud, shouting to one another. Exclamation, clamour. *Siyāh* or *suyāh*, (v. n. of صاح for صيح) Shouting. Crowing (a cock). Being tall (a palm-tree). Bursting full formed from the envelope (a cluster of dates).

A صيّاح *sayyāh*, Loud-voiced, clamorous, noisy. A kind of perfume or lotion for the head.

A صياخيد *sayākhīd*, (pl. of صيخود *saykhūd*) Intensely hot (days). Hard (stones).

A صيّاد *sayyād*, A hunter. A fowler. A fisherman. A lion. صيّاد اجل *sayyādi ajal*, The fatal hunter, *i.e.* death.

A صيادة *siyādat*, Hunting, fowling, fishing.

A صيادلة *sayādilat*, (pl. of صيدلانيّ *saydalāniy*) Natives of Saydalān.

A صيّادي *sayyādī*, Hunting, fowling, fishing, shooting. The chace; field-sports.

A صيار *siyār*, Sound of a lute. A musk-bag.

A صيّار *sayyār*, A herd of wild oxen.

A صيارة *siyārat*, A sheep-cote.

A صيارف *sayārif*, (صياريف *sayārīf*, and صيارفة *sayārifat*) (pl. of صيرف *sayraf* and صيرفيّ *sayrafiy*) Bankers. Money-changers. Jewellers.

A صياصي *sayāṣī*, (pl. of صيصة *ṣīṣat*) Cocks' spurs. Horns of cattle. Castles, fortresses.

A صياط *siyāt*, A loud, confused noise.

A صيّاغ *sayyāgh*, A goldsmith, silversmith. A founder, moulder, caster.

A صياغة *siyāghat*, The art of a goldsmith. The art of founding, casting, or moulding.

A صياقل *sayākil*, (or صياقلة *sayākilat*) (pl. of صيقل *saykal*) Furbishers, armourers.

A صيال *siyāl*, (v. n. of صال for صول) Insulting, overbearing, assaulting, attacking. *Siyāl*, (or صيالة *siyālat*) (v. n. 3 of صال for صول) Studying to insult, rivalling any one in committing an insult.

A صيام *siyām*, (v. n. of صام for صوم) Fasting. (pl. of صائم *sāʼim*) Fasters. شهر صيام *shahri siyām*, The month of fasting, *i.e.* the Ramazān.

A صيّام *suyyām*, (pl. of صائم *sāʼim*) Fasters.

A صيامي *suyāmaʼ*, (pl. of صومان) Fasters.

A صيان *siyān*, (v. n. of صان for صون) Keeping, preserving. Laying up. Standing on the point of his foot (a horse). *Si, sa*, or *suyān*, A wardrobe.

A صيانة *siyānat*, (v. n. of صان for صون) Preserving, laying up. Defence, protection, preservation. اهل الصيانة *ahlu's siyānat*, Honest, upright people. P صيانت خون و مال كردند *siyānati khūn u māl kardand*, They preserved their lives and property. صيانت كردن *siyānat kardan*, To defend, support, guard, patronize, maintain, observe. صيانت نفس *siyānati nafs*, Self-defence or preservation.

A صيب *sayb*, (or صيبوبة *saybūbat*) (v. n. of صاب for صوب) Being well-directed (arrow), hitting the mark. Reaching, attaining. *Suyub*, (pl. of صيوب *sayūb*) Arrows hitting the mark.

A صيّب *sayyib*, A cloud pouring down rain. Rain.

A صئبان *siʼbān*, (pl. of صؤابة *suʼābat*) Nits.

A صئبل *siʼbil* or *siʼbul*, A misfortune.

A صيبوبة *saybūbat*, (v. n. of صاب for صوب) Hitting the mark (an arrow).

A صيت *sīt*, Fame, good reputation. A mallet, a smith's hammer. A goldsmith. A founder, moulder. A furbisher. صيت و اشتهار *sīt u ishtihār*, Fame and reputation.

A صيّت *sayyit*, Loud-voiced (man or ass).

A صيتة *sītat*, Fame, good repute, reputation.

A صيح *sayh*, (صيحة *sayhat*, or صيحان *sayahān*) (v. n. of صاح for صيح) Shouting, crying aloud. Crowing (a cock). Being tall (palm-tree). Bursting full formed from the envelope (a cluster of dates).

A صيحانيّ *sayhāniy*, A kind of Madīna date.

A صيحة *sayhat*, An exclamation, cry, shriek. Torture, torment, anguish. Thunder.

A صيخاد *saykhād*, Hard (stone).

A صيخد *saykhad*, The sun's eye (a flower).

A صيخدون *saykhadūn*, Firmness, hardness.

A صيخود *saykhūd*, (pl. صياخيد *sayākhīd*) Intensely hot (day). Hard (stone).

A صيد *sayd*, (v. n. of صاد for صيد) Hunting. Making (any one) wry-necked. The chase. Prey, game. A net. Any thing with which they hunt. Any thing firm and strong not in the possession of any one. P صيد سمك كردن *saydi samak kardan*, To fish. صيد شدن *sayd shudan*, To be hunted, caught, snared, or entrapped. A *Sīd* or *sayad*, A distemper incident to camels, causing them to run at the nose. *Sayad*, (v. n. of صاد for صيد) Hunting. (v. n. of صيد) Being wry-necked.

A صيداء *saydāʼ*, Sidon. Rough and rocky ground. Large stones, of which they make cauldrons. A well of sweet water.

A صيداح *saydāh*, Who raises his voice: clamorous.

A صيدان *saydān*, Stone-kettles. Gold. Brass.

A صيدانة *saydānat*, The lamia of the desert, (an imaginary monster) with a woman's head. A loquacious, bad woman.

P صيد انداز *sayd-andāz* (or باز *bāz*), A sportsman.

A صيدانيّ *saydāniy*, Of Sidon, Sidonian.

A صيدح *saydah*, Who raises his voice. Clamorous. Neighing loud. Name of a camel, the property of ذو الرمة *zū'r ramat*.

A صيدق *sayduk*, Faithful, trusty. The polar star. A king.

P صيدگاه *sayd-gāh*, A forest, chace, hunting-place.

P صيدگر *saydgar*, A hunter, fowler, fisher.

A صيدلان *saydalān*, Name of a country or place.

A صيدلانيّ *saydalāniy*, (pl. صيادلة *sayādilat*) A native of Saydalān. A dealer in the perfume called صيدلة *saydalat*.

A صيدلة *saydalat*, A kind of perfume.

A صيدن *saydan*, A hyena. A king. A fox; also another burrowing animal. Coarse (garment).

A صيدنانيّ *saydanāniy*, An animal which burrows under ground. A hawker, pedlar.

A صيدنة *saydanat*, Name of a medical treatise.

A صير *sayr*, (v. n. of صار for صير) Cutting. Beginning. Becoming. Being reduced (to charcoal). Returning to quarters (a foraging party). Flocking, assembling (round water). *Sīr*, A side, quarter. A crevice in a door. Water to which they flock. Fish-jelly, or a food prepared from fish. Small fish salted, from which this food is prepared. A Jewish bishop. *Sīr* or *sayr*, End, success, conclusion. *Sīr* or *siyar*, (pl. of صيرة *sīrat*) Sheep-cotes.

A صيّر *sayyir*, Well-made, goodly (man). A company, a crowd. The grave.

A صيران *sīrān*, (pl. of صور *sawr*) Small palm-trees closely united. (pl. of صوار *sawār, suwār*, and صيار *sayār*) Herds of oxen.

A صيرة *sīrat*, (pl. صير *sīr* and *siyar*) A sheep-cote.

A صيرف *sayraf*, (or صيرفيّ *sayrafiy*) (pl. صيارف *sayārif*, صيارفة *sayārifat*, or صياريف *sayārīf*) A banker, or money-changer. A judge of money or of jewels and precious stones. A deceiver, cheat.

A صيرم *sayram*, Firm, steady-minded. A single meal taken once in twenty-four hours. Misfortune. اكل الصيرم *akala's sayram*, He ate only once in four-and-twenty hours.

A صيرورة *sayrūrat*, (v. n. of صار for صير) Being, becoming, proving. Beginning.

A صيص *says*, (v. n. of صيص) Producing bad dates (a palm-tree). *Sīs*, (صيصاء *sīsāʼ*, or صئصاء *siʼsāʼ*) Sour dates (produced by the female palm-tree when not sprinkled with the flowers of the male). Grains of the colocynth without pulp.

A صيصة *sīsat*, (or صيصية *sīsiyat*) (pl. صياصي *sayāsī*) Spur of a cock. Horn of an ox. A castle, fortification, stronghold. An instrument in a loom, which stretches equally the weft and warp. A shepherd who skilfully manages his flock. A pin with which dates are pulled off.

A صئصئ *siʼsiʼ*, (or صيصي *sīsiʼ*) Root, origin.

A صيع *sayʻ*, (v. n. of صاع for صيع) Separating, scattering. Attacking, rushing upon one another.

A صيعان *sīʻān*, (pl. of صواع *suwāʻ*) Certain dry-measures. Drinking-vessels.

A صيعريّ *sayʻariy*, Large (camel's bunch).

A صيعريّة *sayʻariyat*, A distorted, oblique pace. A mark on a she-camel's neck.

A صيّغ *sayyigh*, An inventor of fictions; a liar.

A صيغة *sīghat*, A form or mould for casting metal. A form, shape. A form of words used in marriage-ceremonies. The voice or mood of a verb; conjugation, verbal inflection. Root, stock. صيغهٔ امر *sīghaʼi amr*, The imperative mood. صيغة الماضي *sīghatu'l māzī*, The form of the past tense. صيغهٔ معروف *sīghaʼi maʻrūf*, Active voice. صيغهٔ مجهول *sīghaʼi majhūl*, Passive voice. سهام صيغة *sihāmun sīghatun*, Arrows, the make of one man.

A صيّغة *sayyighat*, Bread put amongst soup.

A صيغل *siyaghl*, Compact, impacted (dates), sticking close together. Compact, adhesive (mud).

P صيغه *sīgha*, Marriage.

A صيف *sayf*, (v. n. of صاف for صيف) Passing the summer. Going wide of the mark (an arrow). (pl. اصياف *asyāf*) Summer (*i.e.* May and June, the hotter months being called قيظ *kayz*). Summer-rains. *Sayif*, Summer-rains. *Siyaf*, (pl. of صيفة *sayfat*) Parts of summer.

A صيّف *sayyif*, Summer-rains.

A صيفة *sayfat*, (pl. صيف) Part of summer.

A صيفوفة *sayfūfat*, (v. n. of صاف for صيف)

Erring (from the mark).

A صيفيّ sayfiy, Pertaining to, or born in summer. (Offspring)begotten in old age. Summer-rain. Name of a man.

A صيق sīk, (pl. صيق siyak) Dust, especially driven about by the wind. Density of dust. Noise. Sweat. Stink from a beast. Somewhat red in the interior part of a palm-tree. (pl. صيقان sīkān) A sparrow. *Siyak*, (pl. of صيق sīk or صيقة sīkat) Particles of dust driven by the wind.

A صيقبانيّ saykabāniy, A perfumer: a druggist.

A صيقة sīkat, Dust driven about by the wind.

A صيقل saykal, (pl. صياقل sayākil and صياقلة sayākilat) A polisher, furbisher. A sword-armourer. A furbishing-instrument. P صيقل مس آفرينش saykali misi āfirīnish, The sun.

A صيقم saykam, Stinking, fetid.

A صيك sayk, (v. n. of صاك for صيك) Adhering (the smell of any perfume to the body).

A صئك sasik, Robust, strong, powerful (man).

A صيل sayl, An attack, a rushing upon.

A صئل sasil, Fierce and dangerous (camel).

A صيلة sīlat, The knot on a scourge.

A صيلخود saylakhūd, Strong (she-camel).

A صيلم saylam, A dangerous or momentous affair. Misfortune. A sword. A single meal taken once only in twenty-four hours. That by which any thing is extirpated or rooted out. وقعة صيلمة wakeat saylamat, An exterminating war.

A صئم sism, A drinking (water) copiously.

A صيّم siyam, Hard, strong, compactly-built. *Siyam* or *suyyam*, (pl. of صائم sāsim) Those who fast.

P صيمگان sīmgān, Name of a country in Persia.

A صين sīn, The empire of China.

A صينيّ sīniy, Chinese. Porcelain.

A صيوان sīwān, (pl. صواوين) A palace, tent.

A صيوب sayūb, A cloud pouring rain. (pl. صيب suyub) Right, direct, what hits the mark.

A صيود sayūd, (pl. صيد suyud or sīd) A hunter.

A صيّود sayyūd, An arrow striking the mark.

A صيّور sayyūr, Mind, intellect, prudence. Dry herbage, which is eaten for some time after green. امّ صيّور umm sayyūr, Intricate, embroiled business. *Sayyūr*, (or صيّورة sayyūrat) End, extremity.

A صئول sasūl, Fierce, rampant, and dangerous.

A صيهب sayhab, Intense heat. A sultry day. A sun-burnt place. A hard stone. A tall man. A spit.

A صيهج sayhaj, Large stone. Strong she-camel.

A صيهد sayhad, Long. The vapour called سراب sarāb. Intense heat. A desert without water. A thick yard, with an inclination to one side.

A صيهم siyahm, (or صيهمّ sīhamm) Thick, coarse, strong (man), one who carries his head high.

A صيهوج sayhūj, Smooth, shining with plaster.

A صيهود sayhūd, A desert without water. عزّ صيهود eizz sayhūd, Inaccessible glory or greatness.

A صيهورة sayhūr, A kind of earthen shelf for the reception of copper vessels, and the like.

A صيهون sayhūn, Mount Sion.

A صئيّ sasiy, (v. n. of صأي) Twittering (a young bird). *Sasiy, sisiy*, or *susiy*, The braying, grunt, or squeak of camels, hogs, rats, and scorpions.

A صئة sisat, A slight washing of the head.

A صئيل sasil, The neighing of a horse.

ض

ض zād, (called ضاد منقوطه zādi manküta or ضاد معجمه zādi muejama, Dotted ض) The fifteenth letter of the Arabic alphabet, and the eighteenth as adopted by the Persians; not radically belonging to their language. In arithmetic it expresses 800. This letter, as pronounced by the Persians, particularly in India, is very like ز z; but its true sound can only be acquired by ear from the mouth of an accurate speaker.

A ضآلة zasālat, (v. n. of ضؤل) Being small, attenuated (in body), puny. Being weak (in mind).

A ضابث zābis, Sticking, inherent.

A ضابح zābih, (pl. ضوابح zawābih) (A horse) which breathes with noise, a roarer.

A ضابط zābit, One who holds firm. Provident, prudent. A governor, commander, superior, chief, lord, master, possessor. Strong (man or camel). A lion. ضابط امور خزانه zābiti umūri khizāna, Chief-treasurer. ضابط حصار zābiti hisār, Governor of the city, commander of the garrison. ضابط الكلّ zābitu'l kull, Omnipotent (God).

A ضابطة zābitat, A list. Rule, custom, law.

A ضابع zābie, (A loaded camel or horse) going quick, extending the neck, throwing out the fore-feet.

A ضابي zābī, Hot ashes.

A ضاجّ zājj, One who raises his voice; a shouter.

A ضاجع zājie, One who reclines much from laziness: indolent, lazy, who scarcely ever quits the house. Silly, foolish. A star setting in the west. (pl. ضواجع zawājie) The bending of a river.

A ضاجعة zājieat, The mouth of a river. Many, numerous (sheep). Full (bucket), inclining, leaning.

A ضاحة zāhat, Sight, vision. The eye.

A ضاحك zāhik, Smiling, laughing. A ridiculer, laugher, derider. Flashing (cloud). A bright white stone conspicuous on a mountain.

A ضاحكة zāhikat, (pl. ضواحك zawāhik) The fore-teeth (as being conspicuous when laughing). Any one of the teeth between canine and grinders.

A ضاحي zāhī, Exterior, jutting out. Exposed to the sun, sunny.

A ضاحية zāhiyat, (pl. ضواحي zawāhī) An outer part (as the shoulder-blade). An open, exposed tract of country. (A flock) drinking in the forenoon.

A ضاحيةً zāhiyatan, Openly, publicly.

A ضاخة zākhat, (or ضاخية) A misfortune.

A ضأد zasd, (v. n. of ضأد) Setting upon, quarrelling with. Vulva.

A ضاد zād, The letter ض. The puet, hoopoo.

A ضادي zādī, (pl. ضداة zudāt) Angry. (pl. ضوادي zawādī) An irritating, exasperating expression.

A ضارّ zārr, Noxious, detrimental, hurtful.

A ضارب zārib, A beater, striker, bruiser, stamper. A coiner. A goer, traveller. Verging, lying towards. A long, rough strip of land in a level country. A wide part of a valley. (pl. ضوارب zawārib) A swimmer. A she-camel whisking her tail and travelling on. (A she-camel) striking the milker and running away. A valley planted with trees. A night overspread with darkness towards some parts of the horizon, but clear in others. A bird seeking his food. One who presides, shakes, and throws the arrows at games of chance. (Those arrows were eleven in number, without points or feathers, the first having one notch, the second two, and so progressively to seven, the last four being blanks They were much in use among the Pagan Arabs, but were prohibited by Muhammad) (Ezek. xxi. 21).

A ضاربة zāribat, A she-camel whisking her tail and travelling onwards.

A ضارع zārie, Small, weak. Humble, suppliant.

A ضارور zārūr, (or ضارورة zārūrat) Need, necessity, straits. Narrow, strait.

A ضاروراء zārūrās, Necessity, need. Dearth, scarcity. Defect, diminution. Harm, loss. Bad plight, evil case. Adversity, affliction.

A ضاري zārī, (A dog) trained to hunting. (A wound) which bleeds profusely. A bottle, in which milk being kept retains a good flavour.

A ضأز zasz or zasaz, (v. n. of ضأز) Acting unjustly, defrauding.

A ضأضأ zaszas, Noise of men, especially in battle.

A ضأضأة zaszasat, A crying, shouting in battle.

A ضأزي zasza' or zasaza', Defective (portion).

A ضأط zasat, (v. n. of ضئط) Moving the head and shoulders in walking.

A ضاعف zāeafa, (In prayer) May he double! as, ضاعف الله اقتداره zāeafa'llāh iktidārahu, May God double (or increase) his power!

A ضاعل zāeil, A robust male camel.

A ضاغب zāghib, (or ضاغث zāghis) One who hides himself to frighten boys by imitating the cries of wild beasts.

A ضاغط zāghit, A guard, observer. Appointed, set over: a collector of revenue. A lizard. An opening under the arm-pit of a camel.

A ضاغن zāghin, Stubborn (horse), that refuses to run without the whip.

A ضافط zāfit, One who makes a distant journey. One who carries merchandize for sale from city to city. A burden-bearing camel.

A ضافطة zāfitat, A burden-bearing camel. A low, base fellow. The scum of the people.

A ضافي *zāfī*, Long (garment). ضافي الرأس *zāfi'rras*, (A man) with a long and thick head of hair.

A ضأل *zasl*, A rendering contemptible, despising.

A ضال *zāl*, The wild lote-tree.

A ضالّ *zāll*, (pl. ضوالّ *zawāll*) Straying. A wanderer. Forgetful. A prevaricator.

A ضآلة *zasālat*, (v. n. of ضؤل) Being small, attenuated (the body). Being weak (the mind).

A ضالة *zālat*, Arrows and other arms.

A ضالّة *zāllat*, Wandering, lost, stray (animal).

A ضالع *zāliع*, Erring from the right way. Lame, but not so by nature.

A ضامّ *zāmm*, One who contracts, draws together.

A ضامر *zāmir*, (pl. ضمّر *zummar*) Slender, lank (camel). (A yard) flexible after emission.

A ضامز *zāmiz*, Silent. One who hangs back. One who dishonours, disparages, or disgraces.

A ضامل *zāmil*, Dry.

A ضامن *zāmin*, A surety, spousor, security, bondsman, bail. (pl. ضوامن *zawāmin*) A pregnant camel. حاضر ضامن *hāzir-zāmin*, Security for personal appearance, personal bail. مال ضامن *māl-zāmin*, Monied security, security for payment of a debt.

A ضامنة *zāminat*, (Palm-trees) comprised within the limits of a town or a village.

P ضامن دار *zāmin-dār*, A surety.

A ضامني *zāminī*, Bail. P ضامني دادن *zāminī dādan*, To give bail.

A ضامنيّة *zāminiyat*, Caution, surety, bail.

A ضأن *zasn*, (v. n. of ضأن) Separating sheep (from goats). (pl. اضان *azsān*, ضئين *zasīn*, and اضؤن *azsun*) A sheep. A wether. *Zasn* or *zasan*, (pl. of ضائن *zāsin*) Sheep. Wethers.

A ضأنة *zasnat* (or ضانة *zānat*) A camel's nose-ring when made of a sinew.

A ضانئ *zānis*, Fruitful, prolific (woman).

A ضانيّ *zāniy*, Of or belonging to a wether.

A ضانئة *zānisat*, Prolific (woman). Opulence.

A ضاوي *zāwī*, A nocturnal traveller. The morning-star. Lean and weak.

A ضاويّ *zāwiy*, Slender-bodied, puny.

A ضاويّة *zāwiyat*, Slender-bodied (girl).

A ضاهر *zāhir*, The top of a mountain. A valley.

A ضاهس *zāhis*, One who bites with his front teeth. لا اطعمه الله الّا ضاهساً و لا سقاه الّا قارساً *lā atعamahu'llāh illā zāhisan wa lā sakāhu illā kārisan*, May God give him to eat only as much vegetable as he can nibble with his front teeth, and give him to drink water with no milk in it!

A ضاهلة *zāhilat*, Small in water (a well).

A ضأي *zasy*, (v. n. of ضأي) Becoming slender.

A ضائس *zāsis*, (An herb) beginning to wither.

A ضائع *zāsiع*, (pl. ضياع *ziyāع*) Wandering, lost, perished. Vain, useless, fruitless, abortive. Addle (egg). Empty, hungry guts. Loss, damage.

A ضائق *zāsik*, Narrow, strait.

A ضائك *zāsik*, Straddling (she-camel).

A ضائم *zāsim*, Oppressing, oppressive.

A ضائن *zāsin*, (pl. ضأن *zasn*, *zasan*, and ضئين *zasīn*) Wool-bearing cattle, sheep. A wether. Languid, relaxed about the belly. Well-shaped. A little eater. Extensive and white (sand-hillocks).

A ضائنة *zāsinat*, (pl. ضوائن *zawāsin*) A ewe.

A ضبّ *zabb*, (v. n. of ضبّ) Cleaving unto the ground. Flowing, distilling, dropping (as blood from the gums, saliva from the mouth, or water). Anxiously desiring, having the mouth watering. Hating, bearing a concealed grudge. Having a pain, in breast, leg, or foot (a camel). Being silent, but making observation, and laying up for future remembrance. Milking (a camel) with the whole hand, or with the thumb and fingers. A disease in the lip causing the blood to flow. A disease in the elbow of a camel: also a swelling in the brisket or hoof. Bold, shameless. Strong, hardy. A flower of the palm-tree before it opens. (pl. اضبّ *azubb*, ضباب *zibāb*, ضبّان *zubbān*, and مضبّة *mazabbat*) A lizard of the Arabian or Lybian species, large-bodied, with a pointed tail, and much sought after for the delicious flavour of the flesh. احير من ضبّ *ahyar min zabbin*, More bewildered than a lizard (in regaining his hole). خبّ ضبّ *khabbun zabbun*, Cunning and shrewd. *Zabb* or *zibb*, Anger, hatred.

A ضبأ *zabs*, (v. n. of ضبأ) Cleaving to the ground. Throwing down (on the earth). Joining, causing to stick. Lying hid, lying in ambush. Flying, taking refuge. Coming by surprise, arriving suddenly. Being high, looking down from an eminence. Blushing, being ashamed.

A ضبّاء *zabbās*, (fem. of اضبّ *azabb*) (A she-camel) having swellings on the breast and feet.

A ضباب *zabāb*, Mist, fog. *Zabāb* or *zibāb*, Bold, shameless. Strong, hardy. *Zibāb*, An iron bar or nail in a door. (pl. of ضبّ *zabb*) Lybian lizards.

A ضبابة *zabābat*, (pl. ضباب *zabāb*) Mist, fog.

A ضباث *zabās*, A lion. *Zubās*, The soft parts under the claws of a lion.

A ضبّاث *zabbās*, (or ضباثم *zubāsim*) A lion.

A ضباثية *zubāsiyat*, A large, fleshy arm.

A ضباح *zubāh*, (v. n. of ضبح) Breathing hard (a horse in running). Litigating, quarrelling with. Changing the colour of a thing without burning it (fire or sun). Barking of a fox. Hoot of an owl.

A ضبار *zibār* or *zubār*, Books.

A ضبّار *zabbār*, Name of a dog. *Zubbār*, A tree resembling the oak.

A ضبارة *zabārat*, Compactness, strength. *Zibārat* or *zubārat*, A little faggot, bundle, packet (of sticks or papers). (pl. ضبائر *zabāsir*) A crowd, company.

A ضبارز *zubāriz*, Strengthened, firmly bound. Compact, square-built (man).

A ضبارك *zabārik*, (pl. of ضبراك *zibrāk*) Strong, large-bodied. *Zubārik*, A lion. Large, corpulent, strong-bodied. One who has a numerous household.

A ضبارم *zubārim*, (and ضبارمة *zubārimat*) A strong lion. Bold, intrepid (against foes).

A ضباضب *zubāzib*, Plump and short-bodied. Strong, hardy. Smart, active. Obscene, bold, shameless. Scurrilous.

A ضباطة *zubātat*, (v. n. of ضبط) Binding tight, seizing, grasping, holding, keeping fast.

A ضباع *zibāع*, Many stars lying below the Great Bear. (pl. of ضبع *zabع* and *zabuع*) Hyenas. (pl. of ضبعة *zabiعat*) Libidinous (she-camels).

A ضباعة *zubāعat*, Name of a woman.

A ضباعيٰ *zabāعa'*, (pl. of ضبعة *zabiعat*) Libidinous (she-camels or women).

A ضباعين *zabāعīn*, (pl. of ضبعان) Male hyenas.

A ضباغط *zabāghit*, (pl. of ضبغطيٰ *zabaghta'*) Bugbears for children.

A ضبّان *zubbān*, (pl. of ضبّ) Lybian lizards.

A ضبائر *zabāsir*, (pl. of ضبارة *zabārat* or *zibārat*) Crowds, companies.

A ضبب *zabab*, (v. n. of ضبّ) Abounding in Lybian lizards (a country). A tumour on a camel's foot. *Zabib*, A place abounding in Lybian lizards.

A ضبّة *zabbat*, The skin of the Lybian lizard rendered into butter. (pl. ضبّ *zabb* and ضباب *zibāb*) The female Lybian lizard. A broad strengthening bar of iron on a door. Blossom of the palm-tree.

A ضبث *zabs*, (v. n. of ضبث) Striking. Feeling whether or not (an animal) is fat. Taking, seizing, grasping, griping. *Zabis*, A lion.

A ضبثة *zabsat*, A brand set upon (a camel).

A ضبثم *zabsam*, A lion.

A ضبج *zabj*, A throwing one's self on the ground.

A ضبح *zabh*, (v. n. of ضبح) Breathing hard (a horse in running). Yelping, barking (a fox). Litigating, quarrelling. Changing the colour of any thing without burning it (fire or sun). The place in Arafāt from whence the foremost pilgrims rush. *Zibh*, A slight scorching. *Zibh* or *zabh*, Ashes.

A ضبحاء *zabhās*, A bow affected by the fire.

A ضبحة *zabhat*, A noise in the night.

A ضبد *zabd*, A mixing of ripe with unripe dates. *Zabad*, Anger, suppressed wrath.

A ضبر *zabr*, (v. n. of ضبر) Leaping with joined feet (a horse or a man in fetters). Laying (stones, books, or papers) in order, one upon another. A walnut-tree. The nutmeg. A wild pomegranate. A multitude rushing upon the enemy's ranks. (pl. ضبور *zubūr*) A hide stuffed with straw and wood, under cover whereof armed men approach a fortress. *Zibr*, The arm-pit. *Zabir*, A walnut-tree.

A ضبرّ *zibirr*, Capering (horse). A lion.

A ضبراك *zibrāk*, (pl. ضبارك *zabārik*) Strong, large-bodied (man or camel).

A ضبران *zabarān*, (v. n. of ضبر) Leaping with joined feet (a horse or fettered man).

A ضبرك *zibrik*, Large-thighed (woman).

A ضبز *zabz*, (v. n. of ضبز) Looking askance. *Zabiz*, (A wolf) which looks fiercely askance.

A ضبس *zabs*, (v. n. of ضبس) Pressing hard upon, harassing, or dunning (a debtor). ضبس شرّ *zibsu sharrin*, A malicious man. *Zabas*, (v. n. of ضبس) Being bad, naught. Being ill-disposed (the mind). *Zabis*, Bad-dispositioned (man). Difficult. A desperately cunning and deceitful fellow.

A ضبضب *zibzib*, Fat. Bold, brassy, scurrilous.

A ضبط *zabt*, (v. n. of ضبط) Keeping in subjection or obedience. Holding fast, preserving, guarding, defending. Managing, keeping. Tying tight, grasping firmly. Spelling, writing (a word). Being rained upon. Government, direction, administration, discipline, management, regulation, check, controul. Confiscation, sequestration, attachment. P ضبط كردن *zabt kardan*, To take possession, rule over, watch, guard, preserve, moderate, keep in the line of duty. To seize, restrain, sequestrate, confiscate, forfeit. ضبط نمودن *zabt namūdan*, To write, spell, or give the orthography. A ضبط و ربط *zabt u rabt*, Adjustment, settlement. اهل الضبط *ahlu'z zabt*, Agents. *Zabat*, Ambidextrousness.

A ضبطاء *zabtāʼ*, Ambidextrous (woman).

T ضبط بيگی *zabt-begi*, Overseer of confiscations.

A ضبطة *zabtat*, Name of a game.

A ضبطر *zibatr*, A powerful lion. Strong, firm. Thick-set, compact in body.

A ضبطي *zabti*, A confiscator. Confiscated.

A ضبع *zabɛ*, (v. n. of ضبع) Stretching out the arms in prayer; also when striking with a sword. Throwing out rapidly the fore-feet, going quick (a horse). Dividing, sharing, parcelling out. Making a portion of a road to or for any one. Tyrannizing over, injuring, oppressing. Inclining to peace. Going fast, and shaking his sides (a camel). Breathing hard, making the noise of his breath heard, roaring (a horse). (pl. اضباع *azbāɛ*) An arm, especially the fleshy part; the arm-pit. A hillock of an oblong shape and a dark colour. A swift pace. A hyena. ضبعًا لبعًا *zabɛan labɛan*, In vain. *Zabɛ*, *zibɛ*, or *zubɛ*, A tract of country, a coast. Protection. *Zubɛ* and *zubuɛ*, (pl. of ضبع *zabɛ* and *zabuɛ*) Hyenas. *Zabaɛ*, (v. n. of ضبع) Being libidinous (a female). *Zabuɛ*, (pl. اضبع *azbuɛ*, ضباع *zibāɛ*, ضبع *zubuɛ*, *zubɛ*, and مضبعة *mazbaɛat*) A female hyena. A barren year. Hunger.

A ضبعان *zibɛān*, (pl. ضباعين *zabāɛīn*) (Male) hyena. *Zabaɛān*, (v. n. of ضبع) Throwing out the fore-feet when running rapidly (a horse or camel).

A ضبعانة *zibɛānat*, (pl. ضبعانات) A female hyena.

A ضبعة *zabɛat*, A female hyena. *Zabaɛat*, Lust (in a she-camel). *Zabiɛat*, (pl. ضباع *zibāɛ* and ضباعي *zabāɛa'*) Libidinous (woman or she-camel).

A ضبعطي *zabaɛta'*, A fool. A word used to frighten children.

A ضبغطران *zabaghtarāni*, A pair of hyenas.

A ضبغطري *zabaghtara'*, Tall (man). Strong, hardy. Foolish. A bugbear for children. A scarecrow, a dudman. Any thing carried on the head and steadied by the hand. A hyena; or the female.

A ضبغطي *zabaghta'*, A bugbear for children.

A ضبن *zabn*, (v. n. of ضبن) Preventing, withholding, detaining, keeping back. *Zabn* or *zabin*, Clear, transparent water, free from sediment. *Zibn*, That part of the body between the arm-pits and short-ribs. An excavation which one despairs of making. *Zaban*, Detriment. *Zabin*, A narrow place.

A ضبنة *zabnat*, *zibnat*, *zubnat*, or *zabinat*, Domestics; those whom a person maintains. Indigent and dependent on friends.

A ضبنط *zabannat*, Strong and powerful.

A ضبنطي *zabanta'*, Strong, robust.

A ضبو *zabw*, (v. n. of ضبا for ضبو) Altering the colour of any thing: roasting (fire). Taking refuge.

A ضبوء *zubūʼ*, (v. n. of ضبأ) Cleaving to the ground. Causing to cleave (to the earth). Lying hid. Taking refuge (with any one). Coming upon one suddenly. Being high and overlooking. Blushing, being ashamed.

A ضبوب *zabūb*, A little beast that voids urine whilst running. (A ewe) narrow in the teat. *Zubūb*, (v. n. of ضبّ) Adhering to the ground. Distilling, dropping (as blood from the gums).

A ضبوث *zabūs*, A camel, concerning which doubts are entertained if she be fat or not; whose fat can be ascertained only by feeling. A lion.

A ضبور *zabūr*, A lion. *Zubūr*, (pl. of ضبر *zabr*) Hides stuffed with straw and wood, under cover of which armed men invest a citadel.

A ضبوع *zubūɛ*, (v. n. of ضبع) Throwing out the fore-feet in running (a horse or camel).

A ضبوك *zubūk*, Furrows in the ground made by the wind. Herbage sprouting. Signs of rain.

A ضبيّ *zubiy* (v. n. of ضبا for ضبو) Altering the colour of any thing, roasting (fire). Taking refuge with (any one).

A ضبيب *zabīb*, (v. n. of ضبّ) Flowing, trickling (water). Running (blood from the gums). Swelling (the gum). Anxiously desiring. The edge of a sword. (for دبيب *dabīb*) Whatever creeps on the earth.

A ضبيبة *zabībat*, Butter. A kind of syrup given to a child in a fever.

A ضبير *zabīr*, Strong, firm. Hardy. Penis.

A ضبيرة *zubayrat*, Name of a woman.

A ضبيز *zabīz*, (A wolf) looking fiercely askance. Fierce and sly (wolf).

A ضبيس *zabīs*, Of a bad disposition. Foolish, silly, weak in mind or body. A coward. Heavy, stupid. Difficult. Stubborn and refractory (horse). ضبيس شرّ *zabīsu sharrin*, A wicked man.

A ضبيطر *zabaytar*, A powerful lion.

A ضبيء *zabīʼ*, Cleaving to earth; (hence) man.

A ضتع *zutɛ*, Name of an animalcule or bird.

A ضتيريب *zutayrib*, A little agitation.

A ضجّ *zajj*, (v. n. of ضجّ) Crying out (as any one helpless or overcome). Submitting.

P ضجاج *zajāj*, Every tree which yields a scent. *Zijāj*, A kind of white gum, used in washing clothes.

A ضجاج *zajāj*, (v. n. of ضجّ) Forcing one unjustly to work. Mischief, accompanied with tumult and noise. Ivory. A sort of pearl or bead. Violence. *Zijāj*, (v. n. 3 of ضجّ) Exciting a disturbance. A kind of esculent gum. Any sort of tree whose fruit is poisonous to bird or beast.

A ضجاعم *zajāɛim*, (or ضجاعمة *zajāɛimat*) Descendants of ضجعم *zujɛum* or *zajɛam*.

A ضجّة *zajjat*, Noise, clamour of a mob.

A ضجحرة *zajharat*, (v. n. of ضجحر Q) Filling (a leathern bottle).

A ضجر *zajr*, Narrow (place). *Zajar*, (v. n. of ضجر) Being oppressed in mind, and impatient of any thing painful or irksome. Braying much whilst being milked (a camel). Sorrow, anguish, grief, vexation, distraction. *Zajir*, Afflicted, melancholy, weary, out of spirits. Restless, noisy (camel). Narrow (place).

A ضجرة *zujrat*, Sorrow, anguish, grief, vexation, weariness of spirit. Name of a bird.

A ضجع *zajɛ*, (v. n. of ضجع) Reclining, especially on the side (on a bed or the ground). Inclining to set (a star). A sort of vegetable. Any thing used (as potash) in washing clothes. A plant resembling a cucumber, only larger, and having quadrangular leaves. *Zijɛ*, Inclination, leaning, bias.

A ضجعاء *zajɛāʼ*, Many, numerous (sheep).

A ضجعة *zajɛat*, One sleep or recumbency on the side. Weakness of mind. *Zijɛat*, Sluggishness, indolence. A mode of lying down on one side. A rug or any thing similar to lie down upon. *Zujɛat*, Disease. Weakness of mind. One who is commanded to lie down much. *Zujɛat* or *zujaɛat*, One who reclines or sleeps much, sluggish. Sedentary. *Zajaɛat*, A lying or sleeping on one side.

A ضجعم *zujɛum* or *zajɛam*, Name of the father of a tribe, some of which reigned in Syria.

A ضجعيّ *zij*, (or *zujɛiy*, ضجعيّة *zij* or *zujɛiyat*) One who reclines or sleeps much, sluggish.

A ضجم *zajam*, (v. n. of ضجم) Being oblique, distorted in any member, as in the mouth, jaw, chin, or neck: also in walking. An obliquity or slant (in a well or wound).

A ضجمة *zujmat*, A certain stinking insect.

A ضجوج *zajūj*, Braying whilst milking or carrying a load (a she-camel).

A ضجور *zajūr*, Melancholy, glum, peevish, fretful. Braying (camel) whilst milking.

A ضجوع *zajūɛ*, Weak in mind. A woman disobedient to her husband. A capacious bucket. A large bottle or urn, which causes the person carrying it to lean on one side. A wide well. A camel pasturing in a corner or on one side. A cloud full of rain, and moving slowly. *Zujūʻ*, (v. n. of ضجع) Reclining, especially on the side (on bed or ground).

A ضجيج *zajīj*, (v. n. of ضجّ) Crying out (as one helpless or overcome). Clamour, noise, tumult. Fear.

A ضجيع *zajīʻ*, A bed-fellow. Hunger.

A ضحّ *zihh*, The sun. The light of the sun. Any thing exposed to the sun, or that the sun shines upon. A large plain.

A ضحاء *zahās*, (v. n. of ضحي) Going forth into the sun, apricating. Dinner or lunch. *Zihās*, (v. n. 3 of ضحا for ضحو) Coming to one in the forenoon, paying a forenoon visit. *Zuhās*, That part of the day about half-way between sunrise and mid-day. Luncheon. (pl. of ضحوة *zahwat*) Forenoons. عيد الضحاء *ʻīdu'z zuhās*, Name of a festival celebrated on the tenth of Zi'l hijja, when an animal is sacrificed in commemoration of Abraham's sacrifice of his son Ismael, according to the Muhammadans.

A ضحا ظلّه *zaha' zilluhu*, He died.

P ضحّاك *zahhāk*, Name of a king of the Peshdādian dynasty, proverbial for his cruelty.

A ضحّاك *zahhāk*, A great laugher. A ridiculer, mocker. A wide road. Middle of a road.

A ضحال *zihāl*, (pl. of ضحل) Shallow waters.

A ضحايا *zahāya'*, (pl. of ضحيّة) Sacrifices.

A ضحة *zihat* or *zahat*, (v. n. of وضح) Being clear, evident, manifest.

A ضحضاح *zahzāh*, (or ضحضح *zahzah*) Little, shallow (water). Much (water).

A ضحضحة *zahzahat*, (v. n. of ضحضح Q) Undulating (the shining vapour سراب *sarāb*). Flowing (water). Being manifest, apparent (any thing). *Zahzahat*, (ضحضح *zahzah* or *zuhzuh*) The motion of the vapour سراب *sarāb*.

A ضحك *zahk*, Fresh butter. White honey. White fore-teeth. Snow. Froth of milk. Admiration. Flowers of the palm-trees bursting from the envelope. Blossom of a tree. Middle of the road. *Zahk*, *zihk*, *zihik*, or *zahik*, (v. n. of ضحك) Laughing. Being pleased, satisfied, contented. Grinning, chattering (like an ape). Being menstruous (a hare). Flashing, shining (a cloud). *Zuhk*, (pl. of ضحوك *zahūk*) Extremely prone to laugh. *Zahak*, (v. n. of ضحك) Being menstruous (a hare). Wondering; being astonished and frightened. Flashing (a cloud). Grinning, laughing (an ape).

A ضحكة *zahkat*, One laugh. *Zuhkat*, A laughing-stock, object for ridicule or laughter. *Zuhakat*, (or ضحكّة *zuhukkat*) A satirist, mocker. A very great or immoderate laughter.

A ضحل *zahl*, (v. n. of ضحل) Being little and shallow (water). Containing little water (a pond). (pl. اضحال *azhāl*, ضحول *zuhūl*, and ضحال *zihāl*) Little or shallow water. اتان الضحل *atānu'z zahl*, A stone in the water, the upper part appearing above.

A ضحو *zahw*, (v. n. of ضحا for ضحو) Being open, clear, conspicuous (a road). Pasturing in the heat of the day. Performing the forenoon-prayer. Being affected or scorched by the sun. That part of the day about half-way between sunrise and mid-day. Luncheon. *Zahw*, (or ضحوّ *zuhūw*) (v. n. of ضحا for ضحو) Exposing one's self to the sun.

A ضحوة *zahwat*, Forenoon. Lunch, dinner.

A ضحوك *zahūk*, (pl. ضحك *zuhk*) Extremely prone to laugh. A wide, open, clear road.

A ضحول *zuhūl*, (pl. of ضحل) Shallow waters.

A ضحي *zahy*, (v. n. of ضحي) Sweating. *Zuha'*, The half-way hour between sunrise and mid-day; luncheon-time. The sun. Clearness of meaning. The forenoon-prayer.

A ضحيّ *zuhayy*, (dim. of ضحو *zahw*) A small part of the hour called ضحو *zahw*. *Zuhīy*, (v. n. of ضحا for ضحو) Exposing one's self to the sun, apricating. Being scorched by the sun.

A ضحيّا *zuhayya'*, A small portion of the mid-way hour between sunrise and noon.

A ضحياء *zahyās*, A woman free from hair on her body. (fem. of اضحي *azha'*) (A mare) white or grey. Clear and serene (night).

A ضحياة *zahyāt*, Clear, serene (sky).

A ضحيان *zahyān*, (fem. ضحيانة *zahyānat*) One who basks in the sun. Exposed to the sun. Bright (day or lamp). One who eats at mid-day.

A ضحيّة *zahīyat*, That part of the day half-way between sunrise and mid-day. (pl. ضحايا *zahāya'*) A sheep for sacrifice.

A ضخّ *zahhkh*, Tears. The shooting of water from a fountain. The squirting of urine.

A ضخّابة *zahhkhābat*, Noisy, ill-tempered woman.

A ضخامة *zakhāmat*, (v. n. of ضخم) Being great, thick, and bulky. Bulk, thickness. Corpulence.

A ضخز *zakhz*, A tearing out (of an eye).

A ضخم *zakhm*, (v. n. of ضخم) Being great, thick, and bulky. Broad, clear, open (way). Heavy (water). *Zakhm*, (*zakham*, ضخام *zukhām*) (pl. ضخام *zikhām*) (fem. ضخمة *zakhamat*) (pl. ضخمات *zakhamāt*) Thick, large, bulky, fleshy, lusty, stout. *Zikham*, (v. n. of ضخم) Being thick and bulky.

A ضخمّة *zikhammat*, (fem.) Broad, wide. Soft and delicate.

A ضخيم *zakhīm*, Large, tall, corpulent.

A ضدّ *zadd*, (v. n. of ضدّ) Filling (a bottle). Getting the better, gaining a cause (at law). Prohibiting, averting, with kindness. *Zidd*, (pl. اضداد *azdād*) The contrary, opposite (as virtue to vice). An enemy, a rival. Enemies, rivals. Resembling, alike. An assistant (as being the opposite to a foe). A company. Malice, spleen. الضدّان لا يجتمعان *az'ziddāni lā yajtamiʻāni*, Opposites never meet.

A ضدأ *zadas*, A being angry, enraged.

A ضدن *zadn*, (v. n. of ضدن) Rendering easy. Amending, correcting, restoring.

A ضدي *zada'*, A being angry.

A ضدّيّة *ziddīyat*, Contrariety, opposition.

A ضديد *zadīd*, Contrary, opposite. Like.

A ضرّ *zarra*, (fut. يضرّ *yazurru*) He injured.

A ضرّ *zarr*, (v. n. of ضرّ) Injuring, hurting, harming. Marrying a second wife, the first being still living. Loss, damage. *Zirr* or *zurr*, Matrimony, especially (in the idea of polygamy) marrying a second wife, the first being alive. ضرّ اضرار *zirru azrārin*, Extremely shrewd. *Zurr*, Injury, loss, damage. A bad condition or habit of body, leanness.

A ضرء *zars*, (v. n. of ضرأ) Hiding one's self.

A ضراء *zarās*, (v. n. of ضري) Being trained to hunt (a dog). Attempting to hide one's self. Level ground with a few trees, whither wild beasts repair. Trees in a valley thick and entangled. يمشي الضراء *yamshī'z zarās*, He walks (stealthily) among thick trees. (metaphorically) He deceives his friend. *Zirās*, (v. n. of ضري) Being trained to hunt (a dog). (pl. of ضرو *zirw*) Hunting dogs.

A ضرّاء *zarrās*, (pl. ضرّاوات *zarrāwāt*) Adversity, misfortune, affliction (opposed to سرّاء *sarrās*). Loss, waste, murrain, amongst cattle or men.

A ضراب *zirāb*, (v. n. of ضرب) Covering (as a he-camel). Whisking her tail and travelling on (a she-camel). (v. n. 3 of ضرب) Fighting, striking with a sword, fencing. Being distracted among themselves. Conquering, getting the better in striking. Carrying on trade for another on certain conditions of gain.

A ضرّاب *zarrāb*, A striker. A coiner of money.

A ضرابة *zarābat*, (v. n. of ضرب) Excelling in striking a blow (the hand).

P ضرّابخانه *zarrāb-khāna*, A mint for coining.

A ضرابية *zurābiyat*, Name of a town in Egypt.

A ضراة *zarāt*, The being greedy or addicted.

A ضرّات *zarrāt*, (pl. of ضرّة *zarrat*) Women who have a husband in common, rival wives.

A ضراح *zarāhi*, (imper.) Remove to a distance. *Zirāh*, (v. n. of ضرح) Kicking (as a horse). A kick. (v. n. 3 of ضرح) Contending in throwing the javelin. Assaulting, attacking. Approaching, drawing near. *Zurāh*, The heavenly house, situated in the fourth heaven, called also البيت المعمور *al baytu'lmaʻmūr*.

A ضرار *zirār*, (v. n. 3 of ضرّ) Hurting.

A ضرارة *zarārat*, Loss, decrease, diminution (of men or cattle). Blindness.

A ضراريّة *zarāriyat*, Name of a sect.

A ضراس *zurās*, The toothache.

A ضراسي *zarāsa'*, (pl. of ضريس *zarīs*) Hungry, famished. Wells full of water.

A ضراط *zurāt*, (v. n. of ضرط) Breaking wind aloud. A fart.

A ضرّاط *zarrāt*, One who breaks wind much. One who makes a contemptuous noise with the mouth.

A ضراطميّ *zurātimīy*, Large, thick (muliebria).

A ضراع *ziräɛ*, (v. n. 3 of ضرع) Resembling.

A ضراعة *zarāɛat*, (v. n. of ضرع) Humbling one's self, supplicating. Being weak, infirm. Humility, submission, supplication.

A ضرافط *zurāfit*, Corpulent, gorbellied.

A ضراك *zurāk*, Thick, robust. A lion. Very muscular and sinewy.

A ضراكة *zarākat*, (v. n. of ضرك) Becoming poor, unfortunate, oppressed, afflicted, blind, or foolish. Being very muscular and sinewy.

A ضرام *zirām*, Chips, brushwood, or other fuel with which a fire is lighted. Lighted wood.

A ضرامة *zirāmat*, The turpentine-tree. Chips, brushwood, or twigs on fire.

A ضراوة *zarāwat*, (v. n. of ضري) Being trained, accustomed to. Being greedy, addicted to. Hunting game (a dog). Habitude.

A ضرائب *zarāɛib*, (pl. of ضريب *zarīb*) Frosts, ices, snows, hoar-frosts. Equals. (pl. of ضريبة *zarībat*) Natures, dispositions. Whatever is taken for tribute or taxes. Cotton threads rolled into a clew.

A ضراية *zarāyat*, (v. n. of ضري) Being greedy.

A ضرائر *zarāɛir*, Necessary things. (pl. of ضرّة *zarrat*) Palms of the hands, especially the fleshy parts; also of the feet. Women who have a husband in common with others, rival wives.

A ضرائك *zarāɛik*, (pl. of ضريك *zarīk*) Blind. Poor. Oppressed, miserable. Male vultures.

P ضرب *zarb*, A porcupine.

A ضرب *zarb*, (v. n. of ضرب) Striking, drubbing, beating. Pricking. Removing, causing to go afar off. Swimming. Striking, touching (a harp). Acquiring, or studying to acquire (fame). Departing, making haste. Passing (as time). Staying, stopping, standing still. Being moved, moving. Being long. Taking, holding, or preventing. Inclining, tending, verging towards. Turning away the face. Covering (a camel). Whisking her tail and travelling (a she-camel). Multiplying (arithmetically). Making any saying proverbial. Separating. Striking or coining (money). Fixing or pitching (tents). Crouching from fear. Making clear, pointing out. Travelling, going up and down (in the way of trade or hunting). Flying in quest of prey or food (a bird). Any thing thin and delicate. White honey. Velocity, despatch. A blow, stroke. Force, violence. Multiplication (in arithmetic). The last foot of the second hemistich of a couplet (that of the first being called عروض *ɛarūz*). (pl. ضروب *zurūb* and اضرب *azrub*) Form, species, mode, ratio. Similitude: like, equal. Slight (rain). A place prepared for sowing. (A man) active, light of body, sharp, and clever. Struck, coined (money), coinage. ضرب على آذانهم *zaraba ɛala' āzānihim*, He struck upon their ears, *i.e.* he prevented them from hearing. ضرب على يد الظالم *zaraba ɛala' yadi'z zālim*, He imprisoned the culprit. ضرب مثل *zarbimasal*, A mode of expression, an idiom, phrase, proverb, parable. P ضرب خيام كردن *zarbi khiyām kardan*, To pitch tents, to encamp. ضرب دست *zarbi dast*, By force of arms, by strength of hand. ضرب كردن *zarb kardan*, To strike. To coin money. To multiply (in arithmetic). سه را در سه ضرب كردن *sihrā dar sih zarb kardan*, To multiply 3 by 3. A دار الضرب *dāru'z zarb*, The mint. ضرب الخلاء *zarbu'l khalāɛ*, (or ضرب الغائط *zarbu'l ghāɛit*) A visit to the privy. A *Zarab*, (v. n. of ضرب) Being struck with cold. Thick, white honey. *Zarib*, A striker, beater.

A ضربا *zarban*, By force, violently.

A ضرباء *zurabāɛ*, (pl. of ضريب *zarīb*) Those who throw gaming arrows.

A ضربات *zar* or *zarabāt*, (pl. of ضربة) Blows.

A ضربان *zarabān*, (v. n. of ضرب) Travelling, going up and down (in the way of trade or hunting). Being full of matter (a wound). Pulsation, the throbbing pain of a wound.

A ضربة *zarbat*, One blow.

A ضربجيّ *zarbajīy*, Base (coin).

P ضرب خانه *zarb-khāna*, The mint.

P ضربزن *zarbuzan*, A piece of artillery.

A ضربي *zarbī*, By force, violence, compulsion.

A ضرّة *zarrat*, (pl. ضرائر *zarāɛir*) The fleshy part of the foot near the toes (on which one treads). Wealth on which one relies belonging to another. A portion of wealth, camels, or sheep. A bad situation, hurt, damage, adversity, indigence. Grief, care, anguish. Loss, waste of men or cattle. A camel's teat. The whole of the udder. The root of the breast. The palm of the hand (especially the fleshy parts under the thumbs). One woman who has a husband in common with another, a rival wife. ضرّة شكري *zarrat shakra'*, A breast or an udder abounding with milk. *Zurrat*, Necessity, force, compulsion, violence.

A ضرّتان *zarratāni*, (dual) The upper and nether millstone. The buttocks or two sides of the bone. Two wives of one man.

A ضرج *zarj*, (v. n. of ضرج) Splitting. Soiling. Staining (with blood). Throwing away.

A ضرجع *zarjaɛ*, A leopard.

A ضرح *zarh*, (v. n. of ضرح) Pushing, thrusting away. Refuting. Digging (a grave). Kicking (as a horse). A skin, hide, leather. *Zarah*, Bad (man or intention).

A ضردخ *zirdikh*, Great, large.

A ضرر *zarar*, Injury, damage, detriment, loss. Distress, difficulty, straits. Narrow, tight, strait. The brink of a cavern. ذو ضرر *zū zarar*, Narrow (place). لا ضرر *lā zarar*, There's no harm. P ضرر كردن *zarar kardan*, To prejudice, demolish, hinder, ruin, injure, hurt.

A ضرز *zarz*, Evenness, absence of ruggedness.

A ضرزّ *zirizz*, Avaricious. Hard (rock). A lion.

A ضرزّة *zirizzat*, Short, deformed; base and covetous (woman).

A ضرزل *zirzil*, Penurious, sparing, very covetous.

A ضرزم *zirzim*, A viper which gives a severe bite. *Zirzim* or *zarzam*, A camel giving little milk. A she-camel beginning to grow old.

A ضرزمة *zarzamat*, (v. n. of ضرزم Q) Biting severely, digging the teeth into. A penetrating bite.

A ضرس *zars*, (v. n. of ضرس) Biting with the teeth (to try the hardness of any thing). Being severe, cruel (fortune). Making an incision in a camel's nose and inserting the nose-ring. Building with stones (a well). Silence kept during a day and night. Land in which the vegetation is scattered here and there. *Zirs*, (pl. ضروس *zurūs* and اضراس *azrās*) A tooth, grinder. Rain, small drops. A long continuance in prayer. A rough hill. A closing up of the place left for the eyes in a lady's veil. The plant شيح *shīh* and رمث *rimas* whose roots have been eaten. (pl. ضروس *zurūs*) A curb-stone placed round the edge of a well; stones with which a well is built. ضرس الحلم *zirsu'l hulm*, Wisdom-teeth. ضرس العير *zirsu'l ɛayr*, Name of the sword of Alkamat. *Zaras*, (v. n. of ضرس) Being benumbed or set on edge (the teeth). Being hard (the times). *Zaris*, Easily enraged when hungry. Of a difficult and touchy temper. Name of a horse bought by Muhammad. ضرس شرس *zaris sharis*, (A man) of a touchy disposition.

A ضرسامة *zirsāmat*, Torpid, stupid. Ignoble, mean; of a bad disposition.

A ضرضم *zarzam*, A lion. A male beast of prey.

A ضرط *zart* or *zarit*, (v. n. of ضرط) Breaking wind. *Zarat*, Thinness of the beard or eyebrows. *Zarit*, One who breaks wind.

A ضرطاء *zartāɛ*, (fem. of اضرط *azrat*) Thin about the eyebrows.

A ضرطة *zartat*, A fart.

A ضرطم *zirtim*, Large, fat in the belly.

A ضرع *zarɛ*, (v. n. of ضرع) Breaking in, taming (a horse). (pl. ضروع *zurūɛ*) The udder or dug of beasts dividing the hoof (a camel's being called خلف *khilf*). *Zirɛ*, (pl. ضروع *zurūɛ* and اضرع *azruɛ*) Similitude. Alike, equal. A single thread of a rope. *Zaraɛ*, (v. n. of ضرع) Being humble, supplicating. Infirm, weak (man or men). Small. Unable to run (colt). *Zariɛ*, Weak. Humble, suppliant.

A ضرعاء *zarɛāɛ*, Large-breasted (woman): large-teated (ewe).

A ضرعة *zaraɛat*, Humble, suppliant, mean.

A ضرعمط *zuraɛmit*, Desirous, hankering (man). Thick milk.

A ضرغاطة *zirghātat*, Black, adhesive (clay).

A ضرغام *zirghām*, (or ضرغم *zargham*) A lion.

A ضرغامة *zirghāmat*, A lion. Strong, intrepid, powerful. An excellent stallion. Strong, stiff clay.

A ضرغد *zarghad*, Name of a mountain; also

of a burial-place.

A ضرغمة *zarghamat*, The fierceness of a lion.

A ضرف *zarif*, A mountain fig-tree.

A ضرفة *zurfat*, Abundance (of wealth).

A ضرفطة *zarfatat*, A tying tight, binding fast.

A ضرفطيّ *zirifṭīy*, (or ضرفاطة *zirfātat*) Corpulent, gorbellied.

A ضركاء *zurakāʼ*, (pl. of ضريك *zarīk*) Unhappy. Blind. Poor. Eagles. Male vultures.

P ضرم *zarm*, French lavender.

A ضرم *zurm* or *zirm*, Name of a fragrant shrub, sticados, French lavender. *Zaram*, (v. n. of ضرم) Being hot (day). Being inflamed with anger. Burning and casting forth flame (a fire). Clinging with hunger (a man). Eating voraciously. *Zarim*, Rapid, fleet (horse). Hungry (man). An eaglet.

A ضرمة *zurmat*, Stoechas, sticados, or cotton-weed. *Zaramat*, A fire-brand. A live coal. Fire. ما بها نافخ ضرمة *mā bihā nāfikhu zaramatin*, There is no one to puff the fire, *i.e.* no one within.

A ضرو *zarw* or *zirw*, Juniper-berries. *Zirw*, A tree (called likewise كمكام *hamkām*). The uncleanness of leprosy. (pl. اضري *azrī* and ضراء *zirāʼ*) A hunting-dog. *Zarw* or *zurūw*, (v. n. of ضرا for ضرو) Streaming (blood from a vein or wound).

A ضروب *zarūb*, A striker, beater. *Zurūb*, (pl. of ضرب *zarb*) Modes, forms of speech, idioms, phrases.

A ضروح *zarūh*, Kicking (horse). Far-shooting (bow). *Zurūh*, (v. n. of ضرح) Being dull, a market (where no goods are sold).

A ضرور *zarūr*, Necessary, expedient, unavoidable, indispensable. Essential.

A ضرورة *zarūrat*, Violence, compulsion, constraint. Necessity, need. بالضرورة *bi'z zarūrat*, By compulsion. Of necessity. ضرورات بشريّه *zarūrāti bashariya*, The necessities of men.

A ضروريّ *zarūrīy*, Necessary. Happening of necessity. Forced, compelled, constrained. ضروريّات معاشي *zarūrīyāti maʻāshī*, The necessaries of life.

A ضروس *zarūs*, A vicious camel that bites her milker. A biting she-camel that has recently brought forth. *Zurūs*, (pl. of ضرس *zirs*) Stones by which a well is built up. Grinders. Rough hills. Gentle rains. ذو ضروس *zū zurūs*, Name of a famous sword.

A ضروط *zarūt* or *zirrawt*, A great farter.

A ضرّوط *zarrūt*, Thick, bulky.

A ضروع *zarūʻ*, Humble, suppliant. *Zurūʻ*, (v. n. of ضرع) Approaching his prey (a wild beast). Being near upon setting (the sun). A kind of grape. (pl. of ضرع *zarʻ*) Teats, dugs, nipples, paps. (pl. of ضرع *zirʻ*) Similitude: like, equals. Rope-threads.

A ضري *zary*, (v. n. of ضري) Flowing. *Zaraʼ*, (v. n. of ضري) Being turned to hunt (a dog). A hunting-dog. *Zaraʼ* or *zary*, (v. n. of ضري) Being greedy, addicted to.

A ضريّ *zarīy*, Profusely-bleeding (vein). A species of date-wine.

A ضريب *zarīb*, The third gaming arrow. A part, portion, lot, destiny. A small tribe, an offset from a larger one. A striker, beater. Beaten, struck. (pl. ضرباء *zurabāʼ*) One who presides, shakes, or throws the arrows at games of hazard. Thick oxygal of a bad quality, or a morsel broken off. Milk drawn from several camels into one pail. Snow, frost, ice. The belly of a man. Like. Kind, species. ضريب الشول *zarību'sh shawl*, The milk of several camels milked into one dish.

A ضريبة *zarībat*, (pl. ضرائب *zarāʼib*) Nature, disposition. Whatever is received in tribute. Wages. Cotton or woollen threads rolled into a clew or hank. Struck with a sword. Any thing on which a sword is tried. Slain with the sword. A sword. Edge of a sword. A bit of cotton. Name of a river. كريم الضريبة *karīmu'z zarībat*, Of a generous nature. لئيم الضريبة *laʼīmu'z zarībat*, Of a base disposition.

A ضريّة *zarīyat*, Name of a village on the road from Basra to Mecca.

A ضريج *zarīj*, Rapid, swift (course).

A ضريجيّ *zarījīy*, Clipt money.

A ضريح *zarīh*, Far distant. A sepulchre, tomb, grave dug in the middle of a burying-place (if dug in the side it is called لحد *lahd*).

A ضرير *zarīr*, (pl. اضرّاء *azirrāʼ*) Blind, made blind (not born so). Sick, emaciated. Afflicted with pain, loss, or hardship. Patience, constancy. Loss, damage. Remains of the body. Side of a river. Soul, mind. Jealousy. A quiet quadruped. A polygamist, a husband of two or more wives. ما اشدّ ضريره عليها *mā ashadda zarīrahu ʻaloyhā*, How jealous he is over her! ذات ضرير *zāti zarīr*, (A camel) enduring much labour, not easily fatigued. ذو ضرير علي شيء *zū zarīr ʻala' shayʼ*, Constant in any thing.

A ضريرة *zarīrat*, A woman, sick, lean, and blind.

A ضريس *zarīs*, (pl. ضراسي *zarāsa'*) (A well) lined all the way up with stones. The vertebræ or joints of the back. Very hungry. A cant name for dates and biscuit (such as grub or tuck).

A ضريط *zarīt*, (v. n. of ضرط) Breaking wind. A fart.

A ضرّيطة *zurraytat*, A large, bulky ewe.

A ضرّيطي *zurrayta'*, (*zirrīta'*, ضريط *zurayt*, or ضريطا *zurayta'*) (See سرّيطي *surrayta'*).

P ضريع *zarīʻ*, Name of a plant growing on the sea-shore.

A ضريع *zarīʻ*, Large-breasted (woman); large-uddered (sheep). The periosteum. Prickles on palm-trees. A species of thorn, particularly when dry. A certain plant called شبرق *shibrik* when green, and ضريع *zarīʻ*, when dry. A kind of bramble. A certain plant growing in stagnant water. Something in hell more bitter than the aloe, more fetid than carrion, and hotter than fire. A certain offensive vegetable cast up by the sea. Wine (especially weak).

A ضريعة *zarīʻat*, Large-breasted (woman); large-uddered (ewe).

A ضريفطيّة *zurayfiṭīyat*, A kind of game.

A ضريك *zarīk*, (pl. ضرائك *zarāʼik* and ضركاء *zurakāʼ*) Poor, unfortunate, tried, afflicted. Blind. Paralytic. Foolish. An eagle. A male vulture.

A ضريم *zarīm*, Burnt. A conflagration. *Ziryam*, The gum of a certain tree.

A ضزّاز *zuzzāz*, (pl. of اضزّ *azazz*) Ill-natured, passionate, surly. Unable to speak clearly from a bad formation in the jaws or adhesion of the teeth.

A ضزز *zazaz*, A being so as described above.

A ضزن *zazn*, (v. n. of ضزن) Snatching out of another's hand, taking from him by force.

A ضطط *zatat*, (and ضطيط *zatīt*) Strong (mud). *Zutut*, Evils, calamities.

A ضع *zaʻ*, (for موضوع *mawzūʻ*) Placed, put.

A ضعّ *zaʻʻ*, The exercising or training of camels, or the word used in so doing: as, ضعّ ضعّ *zaʻʻ zaʻʻ*.

A ضعاضع *zuʻāziʻ*, A little pit, into which water runs from a mountain.

A ضعاف *ziʻāf*, (pl. of ضعيف *zaʻīf*) Weak.

A ضعافة *zaʻāfat*, (or ضعافية *zuʻāfiyat*) (v. n. of ضعف) Being weak, infirm.

A ضعافي *zaʻāfa'*, (pl. of ضعيف *zaʻīf*) Weak.

A ضعة *zaʻat*, (v. n. of وضع) Humbling one's self. Cutting off the head. Taking away, removing (sin). Situation, position, posture. Name of a salt and bitter shrub, the food of camels; or a plant resembling the ثمام *sumām*. *Zaʻat* or *ziʻat*, (v. n. of وضع) Losing in trade. Being lowered, let down. A sinking or lowering in rank or character. Meanness. *Ziʻat*, Situation, posture, position.

A ضعز *zaʻz*, (v. n. of ضعز) Treading violently.

A ضعضع *zaʻzaʻ*, (and ضعضاع *zaʻzāʻ*) Weak in body or mind; silly, simple, trifling.

A ضعضعة *zaʻzaʻat*, (v. n. of ضعضع Q) Demolishing, levelling with the ground. (Fortune) humbling, depressing (any one).

A ضعط *zaʻt*, A slaying, a slaughtering.

A ضعف *zaʻf*, Weakness of intellect. Semen genitale. *Zaʻf* or *zuʻf*, (v. n. of ضعف) Being weak. Being twice as much. Being superior to, exceeding in number or in fortune. Augmenting. *Zaʻf*, *zuʻf*, or *zaʻaf*, Infirmity, weakness, imbecility of disposition. ضعف معده *zaʻfi miʻda*, Weakness of stomach. *Ziʻf*, (pl. اضعاف *azʻāf*) Equal, alike, so much again, double. A pair. Capital punishment. *Zuʻf*, Weakness of body. *Zaʻaf*, Doubled or lined garments.

A ضعفاء *zuʻafāʼ*, (pl. of ضعيف *zaʻīf*) Weak.

A ضعفان *zaʻfān*, Weak. *Ziʻfāni*, (dual of ضعف *ziʻf*) The double, twice as much (which being added to the thing doubled, trebles it).

A ضعفة *zaʻafat*, (or ضعفي *zaʻfa'*) (pl. of ضعيف *zaʻīf*) Weak.

A ضعل *zaʻal*, Thinness of body, puniness (from

intermarriages with one's own relations).

A ضعو *zaʿw*, (v. n. of ضعا for ضعو) Lying hid, concealing one's self.

A ضعوف *zaʿūf*, Weak (male or female).

A ضعويّ *zaʿawiy*, Of the tree ضعة *zaʿat*.

A ضعيف *zaʿīf*, (pl. ضعاف *ziʿāf*, ضعفاء *zuʿafā*, ضعفة *zaʿafat*, ضعفى *zaʿfa'*, and ضعافى *zaʿāfa'*) Weak, feeble, infirm, impotent, attenuated, emaciated, enfeebled, powerless, frail, fearful, timid. A fool. Blind. Of little weight or authority (a word, or form of spelling a word).

A ضعيفان *zaʿīfāni*, A woman and a slave (the two weak ones).

P ضعيف بينا *zaʿīf-bīnā*, Weak-sighted.

A ضعيفة *zaʿīfat*, A weak female.

Á ضعيفي *zaʿīfī*, Weakness, imbecility.

A ضغاء *zughāʿ*, (v. n. of ضغا for ضغو) Cheating (at play). Crying out (as a fox, cat, or one in distress).

A ضغاب *zughāb*, Cry of a hare or wolf. Noise of a horse's yard within the sheath.

A ضغابيس *zaghābīs*, (pl. of ضغبوس *zughbūs*) Small cucumbers. Branches of the ثمام *sumām*. An esculent thorny shrub. A kind of vegetable resembling asparagus.

A ضغادر *zaghādir*, (pl. of ضغدرة) Hens.

A ضغامة *zughāmat*, Any thing seized or bitten by the teeth. Whatever is ejected from the mouth.

A ضغائن *zaghāʾin*, (pl. of ضغينة) Hatreds.

A ضغب *zaghb*, (v. n. of ضغب) Crying (as a hare or wolf). Terrifying by imitating the cry of a wild beast. Lying with. One fond of a species of small cucumber or asparagus, called ضغبوس.

A ضغبوس *zughbūs*, (pl. ضغابيس *zaghābīs*) A small cucumber. A camel neither aged nor fat. A weak man. A young fox.

A ضغت *zaght*, (v. n. of ضغت) Masticating with the canine and wisdom-teeth.

A ضغث *zaghs*, (v. n. of ضغث) Pronouncing words confusedly and inarticulately. Leaving (clothes) still dirty after washing. Feeling if a camel's bunch be fat. Crying out (the lizard called ورل *waral*). *Zighs* or *zaghs*, (pl. اضغاث *azghās*) A handful of herbs, partly green and partly dry. A handful of saplings from one root. ضغث الحديث *zighsu'l hadīs*, A confused, intricate story.

A ضغد *zaghd*, A strangling, throttling.

A ضغدرة *zughdarat*, (pl. ضغادر *zaghādir*) A hen.

A ضغرس *zaghras*, A greedy man.

A ضغز *zighz*, A lion. A malignant wild beast.

A ضغضغة *zaghzaghat*, (v. n. of ضغضغ Q) Muttering. Chewing, mumbling (a toothless person). Making a noise (as a wolf) when devouring food. Talkativeness.

A ضغط *zaght*, (v. n. of ضغط) Pressing, squeezing, forcing, driving up against (a wall).

A ضغطة *zaghtat*, Narrowness (of the tomb). *Zughtat*, Difficulty, straits, narrowness. Pressure. Anguish. A dilatoriness on the part of a debtor to pay a debt, so that the creditor, being disgusted, consents to accept of a part instead of the whole. اخذه ضغطة *akhazahu zughtatan*, He seized it by force against the owner's will.

A ضغطى *zaghta'*, (pl. of ضغيط) Weak in mind.

A ضغم *zaghm*, (v. n. of ضغم) Biting, seizing with the teeth. Filling the mouth with any thing one is fond of.

A ضغن *zighn*, Hatred, malevolence. Affection, inclination, attachment. A side, quarter. The armpit of a camel. *Zaghan*, (v. n. of ضغن) Hating. Liking, having an inclination for. Resting, reposing. *Zaghin*, Crooked (spear).

A ضغو *zaghw*, (v. n. of ضغا for ضغو) Using perfidy, cheating (at game). Crying (as a fox, a cat, or one in distress). Being wearied, weak, beaten, and knocked up.

A ضغوث *zaghūs*, (A camel) felt to know if fat.

A ضغيب *zaghīb*, The cry of a wolf or a hare. The noise made by a horse's sheath.

A ضغيط *zaghīt*, A well adjoining to another filled up, and overflowed by its stagnated water. (pl. ضغطى *zaghta'*) Weak in mind.

A ضغيطة *zaghītat*, Weak, feeble (plant).

A ضغيغ *zaghīgh*, Plenty of provision or produce. ضغيغ دهره *zughīghu dahrihi*, The whole of his time.

A ضغيغة *zaghīghat*, A delightsome, flourishing garden. Thin dough; rice cake made of the same. A confused multitude. An easy, comfortable life.

A ضغيفة *zaghīfat*, A garden green with herbs. Freshness, greenness, verdure.

A ضغيل *zaghīl*, The sound made by the surgeon's mouth when sucking the air from a cupping-glass applied to the body.

A ضغينة *zaghīnat*, (pl. ضغائن *zaghāʾin*) Hatred, enmity. Inclination, attachment.

A ضغينيّ *zaghīnīy*, A lion.

A ضفّ *zaff*, (v. n. of ضفّ) Collecting. Contracting the fingers and rubbing the hands when warming them at the fire. Milking (a camel) with the whole hand. One in a tender, distempered state. One who has a numerous family and little means. *Zuff*, (pl. ضففة *zifafat*) An insect resembling the tike, whose bite raises pustules on the skin.

A ضفا *zafa'*, (dual ضفوان *zafwānī*) A side.

A ضفّات *zaffāt*, (pl. of ضفّة *zaffat*) Banks of rivers. Sea-shores. Bodies of men.

A ضفادع *zafādiʿ*, (or ضفادي *zafādī*) (pl. of ضفدع *zafdaʿ*) Frogs. ضفادع مشويّة *zafādiʿi mashwiya*, Roasted frogs. نقّت ضفادع بطنه *nakkat zafādiʿu batnihi*, The frogs in his belly croaked, *i.e.* he had a roaring (or ravenous) appetite.

A ضفار *zafār*, Any thing twisted, wherewith they bind camels or pack-saddles.

A ضفاريط *zafārīt*, (pl. of ضفروط *zufrūt*) Wrinkles in the face between the cheek and the nose, near either corner of the eye.

A ضفّاز *zaffāz*, A calumniator, whisperer.

A ضفّاط *zaffāt*, A hirer of camels. A camel-owner or driver. One who goes from place to place (with slaves or cattle). Fat and flabby. Heavy, sluggish, not going forth with the people. Troubled with diarrhœa. *Zuffāt*, The scum of the people.

A ضفاطة *zafātat*, (v. n. of ضفط) Being foolish, stupid. Being large-bellied. An Arabian drum; also be who beats it.

A ضفّاطة *zaffātat*, A large body travelling together. A burden-bearing camel.

A ضفافة *zafāfat*, Weak in mind.

A ضفائر *zafāʾir*, (pl. of ضفيرة *zafīrat*) Braided locks. ضفائر الجنّ *zafāʾiru'l jinn*, (Elf-locks) The plant maidens'-hair.

A ضفائز *zafāʾiz*, (pl. of ضفيزة) Large mouthsful.

A ضفّة *zaffat*, One violent rush of a crowd towards water. The first gush of water, a freshet. A river's bank; the sea-shore. A body of men. ضفّة الشخب *zaffatu'sh shukhb*, (A sheep) that gives milk in wide streams. *Ziffat*, A river's bank: brink of a well. (pl. of ضفّ *zuff*) Ash-coloured insects.

A ضفّتان *zaff* or *ziffatāni*, Both sides (of a river).

A ضفد *zafd*, (v. n. of ضفد) Striking with the palm of the hand, giving a slap or box.

A ضفدع *zufdaʿ*, *zifdiʿ*, *zufdaʿ*, or *zifdaʿ*, (pl. ضفادع *zafādiʿ* or ضفادي *zafādī*) A frog. ضفدع ببطنه *zafdaʿ bi batnihi*, He hungered. *Zifdiʿ*, A bone in the cavity of a horse's hoof called the frog.

A ضفدعة *zafdaʿat*, (v. n. of ضفدع Q) Containing frogs (water). *Zifdiʿat*, (fem. of ضفدع *zifdiʿ*) A female frog.

A ضفر *zafr*, (v. n. of ضفر) Plaiting, braiding (the hair of the head). Drawing together (the hair). Twisting (a rope). Jumping, running. Throwing provender into a horse's mouth. (pl. ضفور *zufūr* and ضفر *zufur*) Any thing twisted or plaited, with which they bind camels or pack-saddles. A large pile or hill of sand. A lock of braided hair. Any structure of stone without clay or mortar. Putting food into a horse's mouth. *Zufur*, (pl. of ضفار *zafār*) Ropes with which camels are bound.

A ضفران *zafrāni*, (dual) Two locks of hair.

A ضفرة *zafirat*, (pl. ضفر *zafir*) A heap or hillock of sand. A quiver filled with arrows. An insect which torments camels.

A ضفرط *zifrit*, Large-bodied (camel).

A ضفرطة *zafratat*, Largeness of belly.

A ضفروط *zufrūt*, (pl. ضفاريط *zafārīt*) A wrinkle in the face between the nose and the cheek, and round the exterior or internal angle of the eye.

A ضفز *zafz*, (v. n. of ضفز) Forcing any thing into the mouth. Swallowing a mouthful against his will (a camel). Putting a bit into the mouth of a horse. Impulse. Coition. A running, a leaping. A blow given by the hand or foot. *Zafaz*,

Bruised barley given to camels. A coarse grinding of barley for that purpose.

A ضفس zafs, A making up mouthsful of hard and dry thistles, and feeding a camel with them.

A ضفضفة zafzafat, A crowd of people.

A ضفط zaft, (v. n. of ضفط) Tying. Riding upon and not quitting. Purging.

A ضفّط zifitt, Heavy, sluggish, not going forth with the people. Full of flesh.

A ضفطار ziftār, An old, ugly Lybian lizard.

A ضفطة zaftat, (pl. ضفطات zafatāt) Folly, absurdity, whim. Weakness.

A ضفطى zafta', (pl. of ضفيط) Stupid, silly.

A ضفع zafع, (v. n. of ضفع) Voiding excrement. Breaking wind. Elephant's dung.

A ضفعانة zafعānat, Fruit of the سعدان saعdān.

A ضفف zafaf, A multitude of people eating together, where there are more mouths than meat. The rush of a crowd running to water together. An insufficiency to fill a measure. Any thing less than full. A number of domestics, a numerous household. Necessity. Weakness. Adversity, anguish, straits. Haste.

A ضففة zifafat, (pl. of ضفّ zuff) Certain insects which blister the skin.

A ضفق zafk, (v. n. of ضفق) Voiding at once what is in the belly.

A ضفن zafn, (v. n. of ضفن) Dashing (the foot against a stone). Striking with the foot (a camel). Kicking on the backside. Throwing a person with violence on the ground. Accomplishing (one's business). Dunging (a camel). Exciting the male camel against the female. Loading (a camel). Grasping a camel's teat to milk. Voiding excrement. Lying with. Approaching (to sit down near one).

A ضفنّ zifann or zifinn, Foolish. Thick and short.

A ضفنّد zafannad, Soft, loose, and gorbellied.

A ضفندد zafandad, Foolish. Short and thick.

A ضفنّس zafannas, Soft. Numerous. Flabby.

A ضفنط zafant, Fat and flabby.

A ضفو zafw, (v. n. of ضفا for ضفو) Abounding. Redundancy, overflow, profusion, redundance. The side of any thing.

A ضفوة zafwat, Affluence, happiness.

A ضفور zufūr, (pl. of ضفار zafār) Camels' halters. (pl. of ضفرة zafirat) Large heaps or hillocks of sand.

A ضفوف zafūf, (A camel) full of milk.

A ضفير zafīr, A braided or plaited lock of hair. The sea-shore.

A ضفيرة zafīrat, (pl. ضفائر zafāسir) A braided lock; hair twisted or plaited. A heap or hill of sand. Name of a certain ground in the valley of عقيق عahīk.

A ضفيز zafīz, Thick. Coarsely-ground barley.

A ضفيزة zafīzat, (pl. ضفائز) A large mouthful.

A ضفيط zafīt, (pl. ضفطى zafta') Stupid, ignorant. Liberal, generous. Vicious (camel). Fat and flabby. Gentle (camel). See عذيوط عizyawt.

A ضفيف zafīf, One admitted to the society of persons at the time when he is ruining their affairs.

A ضفيفة zafīfat, A garden green with herbs.

A ضق zakk, (v. n. of ضقّ) Imitating the noise of one stone falling or impinging on another.

A ضكّ zakk, (v. n. of ضكّ) Squeezing, pressing. Being oppressive and irksome.

A ضكاضك zukāzik, (and ضكضاك zakzāk, fem. ضكضاكة zakzākat) Firm-fleshed, compact, short of stature.

A ضكز zakz, Slander, calumny. A hard squeeze.

A ضكضكة zakzakat, (v. n. of ضكضك Q) Squeezing, pressing. Quick pace.

A ضكل zakl, A little water.

A ضلّ zalla, (fut. يضلّ yazillu) He erred.

A ضلّ zall or zull, (v. n. of ضلّ) Erring, straying, losing one's way. Being lost. Error. ضلّ اضلال zillu azlāl or zullu azlāl, Extremely subtle and worthless. Zull, Miss, loss, destruction, or deviation from the way. ضلّ بن ضلّ zillu'bnu zillin or zullu'bnu zullin, Error, the son of error, one who persists in error, i.e. a worthless fellow, who is not known by his own or his father's merit.

A ضلاضل zalāzil, Remains (of water). Zulāzil, A skilful guide. Rugged ground.

A ضلاعة zalāعat, (v. n. of ضلع) Being strong, iron-sided. Strength.

A ضلال zalāl, (v. n. of ضلّ) Erring. Losing one's way, being unable to find (one's horse or home). Being lost or overcome (any thing). Being absent. Disappearing. Turning to earth and bones. Lying hid. Going away from. Dying. Perishing. Forgetting. Error. Ruin. ضلال محض zalāli mahz, Mere heresy, an error in faith. هو ضلال ابن التلال huwa zalāl ibnu't talāl, He and his father are unknown.

A ضلّال zullāl, Wanderers, strayers.

A ضلالة zalālat, Aberration, deviation, error.

A ضلّة zallat, The uncertainty of the mind when surprised with any thing uncommon, good or bad; ecstacy. Error, deviation from the way. A word concerning the absent (good or bad). Zillat, Error, mistake, blunder. تبع ضلّة talعu zillatin, Extremely subtle and worthless. هو ابنه لضلّة huwa ibnuhu li zillatin, He is his illegitimate son. Zillatan, With impunity. Zullat, Skill in shewing the way.

A ضلضل zalzal, zulazil, or zulzul, Rugged ground. Zalazil, Rugged, hilly ground, where travellers easily lose themselves.

A ضلضلة zalzalat, Error. Zalzalat or zulazilat, Rugged ground. Zalazilat or zulazilat, Rugged, hilly ground, where travellers easily lose themselves. Zulazilat, A stone which one can barely lift. A skilful guide.

A ضلع zalع, (v. n. of ضلع) Inclining, stooping. Deviating from the right way. Limping. Stuffing one's self with food. Striking on the rib. Crookedness by nature. Inclination; sympathy. Zilع, (pl. اضلع azluع, ضلوع zulūع, and اضلاع azlāع) A rib. A side. (in geometry) A square number. Zulع, (pl. of اضلع azlaع) Strong and thick (men or horses). Those whose teeth bend inwards, resembling the curvature of ribs. (pl. of ضليع zalīع) Compact (horses). Zalaع, (v. n. of ضلع) Being curved (a sword). Limping naturally (a camel). Leaning towards, and having a liking or sympathy. Being strong, robust (in bearing loads). Disputing, litigating. Patience (under any thing burdensome). Strength. A load of debt. Crookedness by nature. Zaliع, Crooked, lame by nature, leaning to a side. Zilaع, (pl. اضلع azluع, ضلوع zulūع, and اضلاع azlāع) A rib. A side, part. A district, quarter of land. A column (in the page of a book). A mountain; a small mountain standing alone; a low mountain easy to cross. A lute. Any thing broad and curved like a rib; a piece of wood of that shape. An oblong slice of a melon. ضلع الخلف zilaعu'l khalf, A brand behind the ribs towards the back. ضلع عوجاء zilaعun عawjāس, Woman (a crooked rib). هم عليّ ضلع جائرة hum عalayya' zilaع jāسirat, They are unjust towards me.

A ضلعة zilaعat, A little green short-boned fish.

P ضلع دار zilaع-dār, One who presides over the collections of a zilla or district (in India).

A ضلفع zalfaع, (or ضلفعة) Mulier amplâ rimâ.

A ضلفعة zalfaعat, A shaving (of the head).

A ضلل zalal, An error. Running water (especially among trees or under rocks, to which the sun does not penetrate).

A ضلمة zulmat, A sea-port in Hijāz.

A ضلوع zulūع, (pl. of ضلع zilع or zilaع) Ribs. Grounds rising in a curve. Roads through stony places.

A ضلوعة zalūعat, A bow in whose wood is curvature and straightness, whilst the whole resembles that part which is called كبد kabid.

A ضلول zalūl, Straying, stray; a wanderer.

A ضلي zaly, (v. n. of ضلي) Perishing.

A ضليع zalīع, (pl. ضلع zulع and اضلاع azlāع) Strong-sided. Firm, muscular, compact-bodied (horse). Wide-mouthed, with closely-set teeth.

A ضليل zalīl, One who errs greatly. A name of Amru'l kays.

A ضلّيل zillīl, Greatly erring, very erroneous.

A ضمّ zamm, (v. n. of ضمّ) Drawing to one's self. Hugging, clasping to one's bosom. Adding, joining, incorporating, inserting. Closing. Marking a consonant with the vowel ـُ zammah (u). The vowel itself. Zimm, Great calamity.

A ضماد zamād, A poultice. Zimād, An embrocation. A narrow bandage or fillet for binding the head or a wound. A plaster.

A ضمادة zimādat, A bandage for the head or a wound. A plaster.

A ضمار zimār, Any thing uncertain (as debt, for

the payment of which there is no fixed term; a mercantile adventure, the returns for which are doubtful; a suspended punishment, or any other probable but undetermined event). Property, the return of which is not looked for. Name of an idol.

A ضمارز *zumāriz*, Thick (stallion). Old, milkless (camel).

A ضماريط *zamārīt*, (pl. of ضمروط *zumrūt*) Wrinkles between the cheeks and nose.

A ضمازر *zumāzir*, Strong (camel).

A ضماضم *zumāzim*, (A lion) stirred up, seizing all before him. Angry (man).

A ضماطير *zamātīr*, Places were streams end.

A ضمام *zimām* or *zumām*, That by which one thing is collected or drawn to another.

A ضمامة *zimāmat*, A load, bundle. (du. ضمامتان *zimāmatāni*) The boards of a book.

A ضمّامة *zammāmat*, Any thing for binding or holding together books or papers.

A ضمان *zamān*, (v. n. of ضمن) Answering, being surety for another. A chronical distemper, paralysis. *Zimān*, Recompense. ضمان تملك *zimāni tamalluk*, Recompense for the assumption of property. ضمان فساد *zimāni fasād*, Indemnification for damage.

A ضمانة *zamānat*, Ailment. Paralysis. Love.

A ضمائر *zamāʼir*, (pl. of ضمير *zamīr*) Secrets. Ideas, minds, thoughts. Affixed pronouns.

A ضمائم *zamāʼim*, (pl. of ضميمة) Additions.

A ضمائن *zumāʼin*, Properties implanted by God.

A ضمّة *zammat*, Horses running for a wager.

A ضمج *zamj*, (v. n. of ضمج) Anointing (the body) profusely, so that the unguent drops off. A stinking, biting animalcule. *Zamaj*, (v. n. of ضمج) Having his passions excited (a catamite). Cleaving to the ground. A misfortune, calamity.

A ضمخ *zamkh*, An anointing (the body) profusely.

A ضمخة *zimkhat*, A fat woman or she-camel. Ripe dates dropping juice.

A ضمّخر *zummakhr*, Proud. Large and fat.

A ضمخز *zimakhz* or *zumakhz*, Large (man or camel). Bulky (stallion).

A ضمد *zamd*, (v. n. of ضمد) Striking on the head with a stick. Binding up (a wound). Laying on a plaster. Joining, yoking together. Dissembling, acting the hypocrite. Moist; dry (herbage). Fat. Lean. The best; or the worst of a flock. A woman having two sweethearts. *Zimd*, A friend. *Zamad*, (v. n. of ضمد) Being dry, withered. Hating. Being angry. Hatred. Remainder of a debt.

A ضمر *zamr*, Slender in the body, thin in the belly. Narrow, strait. (A horse) with thin eyebrows. Concealment. *Zumr* or *zumur*, Leanness. Slenderness. Lightness of flesh. Collapse of belly.

A ضمّر *zummar*, (pl. of ضامر *zāmir*) Lank, slender.

A ضمران *zamrān*, A species of plant. *Zumrān*, Name of a certain bitch.

A ضمرة *zamrat*, (fem. of ضمر *zamr*) Slender-bodied. *Zumrat*, (v. n. of ضمر) Being slender, thin, and lank-bellied.

A ضمرز *zamraz*, A lion. *Zamruz*, Hard ground. *Zimriz*, Old and milkless (camel).

A ضمرزة *zamrazat*, (v. n. of ضمرز Q) Being rough and hard (a country or the grave). Rough stony ground which cannot be travelled by night. Thick (woman). Rugged-tempered (woman).

A ضمروط *zumrūt*, A place of concealment. A hidden and narrow place. (pl. ضماريط *zamārīt*) A wrinkle between the cheek and the nose.

A ضمز *zamz*, (v. n. of ضمز) Holding one's peace. Keeping food in the mouth, whether ruminated or not, without chewing the cud (a camel). Sticking closely to, keeping fast. Making up and swallowing mouthfuls. A rugged place. A low hill or solitary mountain with red stones without clay.

A ضمزر *zamzar*, Hard ground. Thick woman. A lion. *Zimzir*, Strong (she-camel).

A ضمزرة *zamzarat*, Roughness (of a country).

A ضمس *zams*, (v. n. of ضمس) Chewing gently. Hard, difficult.

A ضمضام *zamzām*, One who comprehends, contains, grasps, or holds every thing.

A ضمضم *zamzam*, Corpulent. *Zamzam* or *zumazim*, (A lion) excited, and seizing every thing that comes in his way. Angry (man). Bold.

A ضمضمة *zamzamat*, (v. n. of ضمضم Q) Taking courage. Seizing the whole (property). Roaring.

A ضمعج *zamʻaj*, Thick, squat, corpulent (woman).

A ضمن *zamn*, (v. n. of ضمن) Answering or being surety for. Redeeming, ransoming. *Zimn*, Cover, fold, or envelope, of a letter. Endorsement of a grant. Contents, any thing comprehended, contained, or inserted. Idea, conception. Obligation, suretyship. Aid, assistance. *Zaman*, (v. n. of ضمن) Being impaired in constitution from disease. Indisposition, ailment. *Zamin*, Impaired in constitution from disease. An invalid. Smitten with love.

A ضمناً *zimnan*, Comprehensively, intimately. By way of surety or assistance.

A ضمنة *zumnat*, Distemper: disease, bodily injury, ailment. Inability to move from bodily ailment.

P ضمندار *zamn* or *zimn-dār*, A sponsor. An ally.

A ضمنى *zamnaʼ*, (pl. of ضمن) Ailing. Invalids.

A ضمور *zumūr*, A being slender, thin, lank.

A ضموز *zamūz*, Silent. A lion. A low hill or solitary mountain with red stones without clay.

A ضموم *zamūm*, Any stream flowing between two long hills.

A ضمي *zamy*, (v. n. of ضمي) Being dark. Injuring, oppressing.

A ضمير *zamīr*, (pl. ضمائر *zamāʼir*) Mind, heart; thought, reflection, sense, conscience, conception, comprehension, idea. A secret. A pronoun. Dried, shrivelled, withered grapes. ضمير منفصل *zamīri munfasil*, A detached pronoun. ضمير متصل *zamīri muttasil*, An affixed pronoun.

A ضمّير *zimmīr*, A secret.

P ضميران *zamīrān*, Sweet basil.

A ضميل *zamīl*, Dry.

A ضميلة *zamīlat*, Limping (woman); also one decaying or withering from age.

A ضميم *zamīm*, Joined.

A ضميمة *zamīmat*, Addition, increment.

A ضمين *zamīn*, A sponsor, surety: undertaker.

A ضنّ *zinn*, (v. n. of ضنّ) Being avaricious, parsimonious, tenacious. Peculiar, special.

A ضنأ *zanʼ*, (v. n. of ضنأ) Going off. Having many children (a woman). Being abundant (wealth). Lurking under ground. *Zanʼ* or *zinʼ*, (pl. ضنوء *zunūʼ*) Numerous offspring, progeny. *Zinʼ*, Origin. A mineral.

A ضناء *zanāʼ*, (v. n. of ضني) Having many children (a woman). Being increased, abounding.

A ضناءة *zunāʼat*, Grief, anguish. Necessity.

A ضنأة *zanʼat*, (v. n. of ضنأ) Being prolific (a woman). Being numerous (camels). *Zunʼat*, Necessity. Grief, anguish, vexation.

A ضناط *zināt*, A crowd flocking to a well.

A ضناك *zanāk* or *zināk*, Firm in flesh. Swelling-hipped (woman). *Zināk*, A large tree. *Zunāk*, Rheum, defluxion.

A ضنأك *zunʼak*, Large (she-camel). *Zunʼak* or *zanʼak*, Firm-fleshed.

A ضناكة *zanākat*, (v. n. of ضنك) Being narrow, straitened. Being weak in mind or body. Being low-spirited. *Zunākat*, Firm-fleshed (woman).

A ضنأكة *zunʼakat*, Large (she-camel).

A ضنان *zinān*, (or ضنانة *zanānat*) The being avaricious, parsimonious, tenacious.

A ضنائن *zanāʼin*, The choicest or most peculiar of the creation of God.

A ضنب *zamb*, (v. n. of ضنب) Dashing (on the ground), daubing (with mud). Seizing, grasping.

A ضنبس *zimbis*, Enervated, sluggish, slothful. Easily broken.

A ضنّة *zannat*, Parsimony. *Zinnat*, Name of five tribes.

A ضندل *zandal*, Big-headed.

A ضنط *zant*, Narrowness, straits. A woman who has two lovers. *Zanat*, (v. n. of ضنط) Being compact and full of flesh. Boasting. Being disliked by her husband (a woman). Alacrity. Scarce year. Fat.

A ضنفس *zinfis*, Enervated, soft.

A ضنك *zank*, (v. n. of ضنك) Being narrow. Narrow. Straitness of circumstances, wretchedness.

A ضنكة *zunkat*, Rheum, defluxion.

A ضنن *zanan*, Strong, brave. Versed in business.

A ضنو *zanw* or *zinw*, Offspring.

A ضنوء *zunūʼ*, (v. n. of ضنأ) Being fruitful, having many children (a woman). Being abundant (wealth). Offspring. (pl. of ضنء *zanʼ* or *zinʼ*)

Numerous progenies.

A ضنوط *zanūt*, (A woman) who has two lovers.

A ضنوكة *zunūkat*, A being narrow. Straits.

A ضنئ *zana'*, (v. n. of ضني) Increasing. Having many children (a woman). Abounding. Being sick of a secret, latent, and tedious disease. A disease. *Zana'* or *zanī*, Sick.

A ضنيك *zanīk*, Weak in mind or body. Low-spirited. An indigent state. A follower, domestic who serves for his maintenance. Cut, amputated.

A ضنين *zanīn*, Avaricious, close-fisted.

A ضوء *zaw'* or *zū'*, (v. n. of ضاء) Shining, sparkling. Light, splendour. الضوء الازرق *az'zaw'u'l azrak*, Morning-twilight. الضوء الاسود *az'zaw'u'l aswad*, Evening-twilight. في ضوء القمر *fī zaw'i'l kamar*, By moonlight, in the light of the moon.

A ضواء *ziwā'*, Light, splendour, brilliancy, resplendence. *Zuwā'*, (v. n. of ضاء) Shining, sparkling.

A ضوابح *zawābih*, (pl. of ضابح *zābih*) Horses which breathe with noise; roarers.

A ضوابط *zawābit*, (pl. of ضابطة *zābitat*) Regulations, rules, precepts. Lists.

A ضواة *zawāt*, A wen, swelling, gland. A substance resembling a bladder coming out of the uterus of a camel before bringing forth. Hubbub, noise.

A ضواجع *zawāji'*, A crowd, company. (pl. of ضاجع *zāji'*) Setting stars. Windings of a river. Low hills.

A ضواحك *zawāhik*, (pl. of ضاحكة *zāhikat*) The laughing teeth, those seen when laughing.

A ضواحي *zawāhī*, (pl. of ضاحية *zāhiyat*) Outer sides of any thing exposed to the sun. Tracts of the heaven. Projecting parts (as the shoulders). Sides of a cistern. Exposed parts of Roumelia.

A ضؤاد *zu'ād*, (v. n. of ضئد) Having a rheum.

A ضوادي *zawādī*, Shameful, exasperating words. Lies, amusing, cajoling words.

A ضوارب *zawārib*, (pl. of ضارب *zārib*) Valleys planted with trees. Camels which kick their milkers. Swimmers. Dark nights. Strips of rough ground. طير الضوارب *tayru'zzawārib*, Birds which seek their own food.

A ضواريب *zawārīb*, Mutual beatings.

A ضوازة *zuwāzat*, A stick used as a dentifrice.

A ضواضي *zuwāzī*, Thick.

A ضواضية *zuwāziyat*, A misfortune.

A ضواطر *zawātir*, (pl. of ضوطر *zawtar* or ضوطري *zawtara'*) Corpulent.

A ضواع *zuwā'*, The hoot of an owl.

A ضوّاع *zawwā'*, A fox.

A ضواكة *zawākat*, A crowd, body, troop.

A ضوالّ *zawāll*, (pl. of ضالّ) Strayers, wanderers.

A ضوامر *zawāmir*, (pl. of ضامر) Slender camels.

A ضوامن *zawāmin*, (pl. of ضامن) Pregnant camels.

A ضوائع *zawā'i'*, Slender camels, thin of flesh.

A ضوائن *zawā'in*, (pl. of ضائنة *zā'inat*) Ewes.

A ضوب *zawb*, (or ضؤوب *zu'ub*) (v. n. of ضاب for ضوب) Lying in wait, circumventing (an enemy).

A ضوبان *zawbān* also *zūbān*, A strong, robust camel. *Zūbān*, The withers of a camel.

A ضؤبان *zu'bān*, A strong, robust camel.

A ضوّة *zawwat*, Noise, hum of men.

A ضوتع *zawta'*, Name of a volatile. A fool.

A ضوج *zawj*, (v. n. of ضاج for ضوج) Inclining, leaning. Turning aside, swerving. Being wide, diffuse, spacious. (pl. اضواج *azwāj*) The winding or bend of a river.

A ضوجان *zawjān*, (or ضوجانة *zawjānat*) Hard, dry (man, horse, or palm-tree).

A ضؤدة *zu'dat* or *zu'udat*, Rheum, defluxion.

A ضور *zawr*, Extreme hunger. Hurt, injury. يحيى بن ضور *yahya' bin zawr*, Name of a renowned hunter. *Zūr*, A black cloud.

A ضورة *zūrat*, Vile, abject. Poor.

A ضوز *zawz*, (v. n. of ضاز for ضوز) Diminishing. Defrauding one (of his right). Oppressing. Chewing (dates or a dentifrice). A bit of a dentifrice.

A ضؤزي *zu'za'*, A part. Deficient (portion). Unjust (woman).

A ضوس *zaws*, The eating of meat.

A ضوضا *zawza'*, Vociferation, noise of men.

A ضوضؤ *zu'zu'*, Origin, root, or family. A mine. A numerous offspring. A black and white bird.

A ضوضوء *zu'zū'*, Hubbub. A numerous offspring.

A ضوط *zawat*, A distortion of the jaw.

A ضوطار *zawtār*, One who goes to market without money, and gains somewhat by his wits or labour.

A ضوطر *zawtar*, A corpulent, large-hipped man. A mean, worthless fellow.

A بنو ضوطري *banū zawtara'*, Hunger. Name of a tribe.

A ضوع *zaw'*, (v. n. of ضاع for ضوع) Moving, shaking, agitating. Splitting, dividing. Striking with terror. Emaciating a horse (fatigue). Diffusing an odour (musk when shaken). Bending a tree (wind). Feeding her young (a bird). Extirpating. Writhing or throwing himself about (as a boy crying). *Ziwa'* or *zuwa'*, (pl. اضواع *azwā'*) and ضيعان *zī'ān*) An owl. A species of crow.

A ضوقى *zūka'*, (fem. of اضيق *azyak*) Narrow.

A ضوك *zawk*, (v. n. of ضاك for ضوك) Leaping on the mare (a horse).

A ضوكع *zawka'*, Corpulent, heavy, stupid.

A ضوكعة *zawka'at*, (v. n. of ضوكع Q) Being tired (in walking). A man, corpulent, heavy, torpid, and of weak intellect. A woman who walks slowly and languidly.

A ضؤلاء *zu'alā'*, (pl. of ضئيل *za'īl*) Small, slender, contemptible.

A ضؤلان *zu'lān*, (or ضولان *zawalān*) A heavy burden, trouble.

A ضؤلة *zu'alat*, Thin, slender, weak (man).

A ضولج *zawlaj*, Refined silver.

A ضولع *zawla'*, Very desirous, much inclined.

A ضوم *zawm*, A defrauding, injuring.

P ضومر *zawmar*, Cocks'-comb (an herb).

A ضومران *zawmarān*, Sweet basil.

A ضون *zawn*, A yellow putredinous ferment in the stomach of a camel or kid, used in curdling milk.

A ضونة *zawnat*, A little doe. A numerous offspring.

A ضوئ *zawa'*, (v. n. of ضوي) Being thin, meagre, slender by nature, or attenuated by distemper. Leanness. Slenderness of bone or smallness of body.

A ضويّ *zawiy*, Bright, light. *Zuwiy*, (v. n. of ضوي) Repairing to, taking refuge. Coming in the night. Inquiring about news. Becoming lean.

A ضويضية *zuwayziyat*, A misfortune. A raging stallion.

A ضويطة *zuwaytat*, Clay or mud at the bottom of a cistern or pond. Butter melted, mixed with fat, and laid up in a skin. Soft dough.

A ضويكة *zawīkat*, A crowd, body, troop.

A ضهّ *zahh*, (v. n. of ضهّ) Resembling.

A ضهاء *zihā'*, (v. n. 3 of ضهي not in use) Resembling, matching.

A ضهب *zahb*, (v. n. of ضهب) Altering (by fire). Mixed (multitude).

A ضهباء *zahbā'*, A bow made straight by the heat of the fire.

A ضهت *zaht*, A treading violently.

A ضهد *zahd*, A subduing, a forcing.

A ضهدة *zuhdat*, One who submits to every body. هو ضهدة لكلّ احد *huwa zuhdatun li kulli ahadin*, He gives way to every one.

A ضهر *zahr*, A mountain-top. A tortoise. A rock on a mountain of a different colour from the rest.

A ضهز *zahz*, (v. n. of ضهز) Trampling upon. Lying with. Beating hard. Biting with the fore-part of the mouth.

A ضهزم *zihzim*, Worthless, mean (man).

A ضهس *zahs*, A biting with the front teeth.

A ضهضبة *zahzabat*, (v. n. of ضهضب Q) Raking together a fire.

A ضهل *zahl*, (v. n. of ضهل) Returning to its origin. Bringing (intelligence). Giving little (to one). Defrauding. Having little milk (a sheep or camel). Being small and little. Milk. Any thing made up of different parts; a collection. A little water. *Zuhul*, (pl. of ضهول *zahūl*) (Sheep) which yield little milk.

A ضهلة *zahlat*, A small quantity (of money). Little (present).

A ضهواء *zahwā'*, Ground without herbage. (A woman) whose breasts do not swell.

A ضهوب *zuhūb*, (v. n. of ضهب) Failing in promise or duty. Being weak and unlike other people.

A ضهوة *zahwat*, (pl. اضهاء) A pond, reservoir.

A ضهول *zahūl*, (pl. ضهل *zuhul*) (A sheep) having little milk, or (a well) water. (An ostrich) laying many eggs. A white ostrich. *Zuhūl*, (v. n. of ضهل) Being collected together in parts, or by little and little. Having little milk (a sheep). Being thin and little (drink). Returning. Defrauding (of his right).

A ضهى *zaha'*, (v. n. of ضهي) Not conceiving nor being menstruous (a woman). Producing nothing (ground).

A ضهيّ *zahīy*, Resembling, answering to another.

A ضهيا *zahyaʼ*, (ضهياء *zahyāʼ*, ضهيا *zahya'*, or ضهيأة *zahyaʼat*) A woman wanting breasts and not conceiving. A woman not menstruous. A kind of shrub resembling a thistle.

A ضهيأة *zahyaʼat*, A desert place with no water. A slight putting together or construction.

A ضهيد *zahyad*, Hard, strong, firm.

A ضيّ *zayy*, (v. n. of ضوي) Repairing to, or taking refuge with. Coming in the night. Being drawn together. Inquiring (about news).

A ضياء *ziyāʼ*, Light, splendour, brilliancy.

A ضياب *zayʼab*, (more correctly ضيأن *zayʼan*) One who plunges into business, or interferes inconsiderately in any thing.

P ضيا پاش *ziyā-pāsh*, Light-diffusing.

P ضيا پذير *ziyā-pazīr*, Admitting light, enlightened, illumined.

A ضياح *zayāh*, Thin, watery milk.

A ضياريب *zayārīb*, Mutual beatings.

A ضيّاط *zayyāt*, A corpulent man shaking his body as he walks.

A ضياطر *zayātir*, (and ضياطرة *zayātirat*) (pl. of ضيطر *zaytar* and ضيطار *zaytār*) Corpulent, heavy-hipped (men). Low, mean fellows.

A ضياع *zayāʻ*, (v. n. of ضاع for ضيع) Perishing. Being ruined, lost. Domestics. A wife and children. Any poor dependants. A kind of medicinal herb. Ruin, destruction. مات ضياعا *māta zayāʻan*, He died, and nobody cared about him. *Ziyāʻ*, (pl. of ضائع *zāʼiʻ*) Wanderers; perishing, lost. (pl. of ضيعة *zayʻat*) Fields, villas, estates, farms.

A ضيافة *ziyāfat*, (v. n. of ضاف for ضيف) Being a guest. A feast, banquet, convivial entertainment. Hospitality. Invitation. دار الضيافة *dāru'z ziyāfat*, A banqueting-hall.

P A ضيافت خانه *ziyāfat-khāna*, Banqueting-house.

A ضياق *ziyāk*, (v. n. of ضاق for ضيق) Squeezing, oppressing, being hard upon. Aspasia, a kind of astringent or contracting lotion used by women.

A ضياكل *zayākil*, (or ضياكلة *zayākilat*) (pl. of ضيكل *zaykal*) Thick, corpulent. Naked. Poor.

P ضيا گستر *ziyā-gustar*, Light-diffusing.

A ضئال *ziʼāl*, (pl. of ضئيل) Slender, small, mean.

A ضياون *zayāwin*, (pl. of ضيون) Ram-cats.

A ضيائيّ *ziyāʼīy*, Luminous, bright, brilliant.

A ضئب *ziʼb* (or ضيب *zayb*) A pearl. Any marine production.

A ضئبل *ziʼbil* or *ziʼbul*, A misfortune.

A ضيثم *zaysam*, A lion.

A ضيج *zayj*, (or ضيجان *zayajān*) (v. n. of ضاج for ضيج) Inclining, leaning.

A ضيح *zayh*, (v. n. of ضاح for ضيح) Mixing milk with water. Being void and waste (a country). Thin milk mingled with water. Honey. Wild dates (called مقل *mukl* when ripe). *Zīh*, The sun. Any thing exposed to the sun.

A ضير *zayr*, (v. n. of ضار for ضير) Hurting, injuring. Harm. Want, need, necessity, helplessness.

A ضيراب *zīrāb*, (pl. ضواريب *zawārīb* and ضياريب *zayārīb*) A mutual beating.

A ضيراك *zīrāk*, A sort of fish.

A ضيرم *zayram*, Burned.

A ضيز *zayz*, (v. n. of ضاز for ضيز) Injuring, hurting. Defrauding. Acting unjustly, oppressing.

A ضيزان *zayzān*, A horse that has never covered.

A ضيزن *zayzan*, A rival to his father in a woman's love. One who contends with another who shall first draw water for their cattle. One that hoards commodities to enhance the price, a regrater. Offspring, children, domestics, family. A troublesome foe. A smart, active water-carrier or cupbearer. A punctual observer of agreements. Trusty. A brass ring within the axle-hole of a pulley. Name of an idol. Associates, partners.

A ضيزى *ziza'*, (or ضئزى *ziʼza'*) Deficient, short. Not properly distributed (portion).

A ضيس *zays*, (v. n. of ضاس for ضيس) Beginning to wither (a plant). *Zays*, (or ضيّس *zayyis*) An herb shrinking and beginning to dry or wither.

A ضئضئ *ziʼziʼ*, (or ضئضيّ *ziʼzīy*) Origin, root. Family. A numerous offspring. A mine.

A ضيط *zayt*, (or ضيطان *zayatān*) (v. n. of ضاط for ضيط) Shaking the shoulders or body when walking from fat or flabbiness.

A ضئط *zaʼit*, One who shakes his arms and shoulders in walking.

A ضيطار *zaytār*, (pl. ضياطرة *zayātirat*, ضياطر *zayātir*, and ضياطرون *zayātirūn*) A large-hipped man. A mean, worthless fellow. A merchant who does not quit his place.

A ضيطان *zaytān*, One who moves his shoulders in walking from abundance of flesh. *Zayatān*, (v. n. of ضيطن Q) Shaking the shoulders and body in walking.

A ضيطر *zaytar*, (pl. ضياطرة *zayātirat*) A large-hipped man. A mean fellow.

A ضيطرى *zaytara'*, One who goes to market without money, and earns by his wits or labour.

A ضيطن *zaytan*, One who moves his shoulders in walking from abundance of flesh.

A ضيطنة *zaytanat*, (v. n. of ضيطن Q) Shaking the shoulders or body in walking.

A ضيع *zayʻ* or *ziʻ*, (v. n. of ضاع for ضيع) Perishing, being lost. Becoming obsolete. مات ضيعا *māta ziʻan* (*ziyaʻan*, or ضيعة *ziʻatan*), He died, and none inquired after him. *Ziyaʻ*, (pl. of ضيعة *zayʻat*) Farms, estates, villas.

A ضيّع *zuyyaʻ*, (pl. of ضائع) Perishing, lost.

A ضيعان *ziʻān*, (pl. of ضوع *ziwaʻ* and *zuwaʻ*) Owls. Birds resembling crows.

A ضيعة *zayʻat*, (v. n. of ضاع for ضيع) Perishing, being lost. Becoming obsolete. Want. (pl. ضيع *ziyaʻ*, ضياع *ziyāʻ*, and ضيعات *zayʻāt*) An estate, productive farm, villa; any immoveable possession. Land and water. Trade, craft, profession.

A ضيغم *zaygham*, A biter. A lion.

A ضيغميّ *zayghamīy*, A lion.

A ضيف *zayf*, (v. n. of ضاف for ضيف) Becoming a guest. Being menstruous. Seizing one (melancholy). Flying wide of the mark (an arrow). Inclining. Being nigh to setting (the sun). (pl. اضياف *azyāf*, ضيوف *zuyūf*, and ضيفان *zīfān*) A stranger, foreigner, guest. *Zīf*, A side. The arm. ضيفا الوادي *zīfā'l wādī*, The two sides of a river.

A ضيفان *zīfān*, (pl. of ضيف *zayf*) Guests.

A ضيفة *zayfat*, A female guest. Menstruous.

A ضيفن *zayfan*, The friend of a guest, who, though uninvited, accompanies him to a feast.

A ضيق *zayk* or *zīk*, (v. n. of ضاق for ضيق) Being narrow, strait, or tight. Being close, covetous. Being unable to hold. Anguish, vexation, grief, sadness, melancholy, affliction, anxiety, doubt, oppression of spirits, or any thing which tortures the mind: straits. (pl. of ضيقة *zīkat*) Afflicted circumstances. ضيق النفس *zīku'n nafas*, Asthma.

A ضيّق *zayyik*, Strait, narrow. Narrow, tight, narrow-hearted (miser).

A ضيقة *zaykat*, The mansion of the moon between النجم *an'najm* and الدبران *ad'dabarān*. *Zaykat* or *zīkat*, (pl. ضيق *zīk*) A melancholy situation, narrow circumstances, poverty, straits.

A ضيق نفس *zīk-nafas*, Asthmatic.

A ضيقى *zīka'*, (fem.) Narrower, straiter.

A ضيك *zayk*, (v. n. of ضاك for ضيك) Straddling (from heat), and being unable to bring her thighs close to her udder. Swelling with anger.

A ضيّك *zuyyak*, (pl. of ضائك *zāʼik*) Straddling (camels).

A ضيكان *zaykān*, The straddling pace of a fat man.

A ضيكل *zaykal*, (pl. ضياكل *zayākil* and ضياكلة *zayākilat*) Thick, fleshy. Poor, naked from poverty.

A ضيم *zaym*, (v. n. of ضام for ضيم) Diminishing, defrauding. (pl. ضيوم *zuyūm*) Injustice, oppression. *Zīm*, The flank of mountain.

A ضيمران *zaymurān*, A species of odoriferous herb.

A ضئنيّ *ziʼnīy*, A large bottle of a single skin in which they churn milk.

A ضيوج *zuyūj*, (v. n. of ضاج for ضيج) Inclining.

A ضيور *zayūr*, Want, need, necessity.

A ضيوف *zuyūf*, (pl. of ضيف *zayf*) Guests.

A ضئولة *zuʼūlat*, Slenderness of body.

A ضيوم *zuyūm*, (pl. of ضيم *zaym*) Oppressions.

A ضيون *zaywan*, (pl. ضياون *zayāwin*) A ram-cat.

A ضيهب *zayhab*, A spit or instrument for roasting meat. Any place heated by the sun, wherein meat may be cooked.

A ضييعة zuyayʻat, (dim. of ضيعة) A small estate.

A ضُئَيل zaʼīl, (pl. ضُوَلاء zuʼalāʼ and ضئال ziʼāl) Slender, small, contemptible.

A ضُئَيلة zaʼīlat, A slender serpent. The uvula.

A ضَئين zaʼīn, (pl. of ضأن or ضائن) Wethers.

A ضيين zuyayn, zuyayyin or ضييون zuyaywin, (dim. of ضيون zaywan) A male kitten, a little tom-cat.

ط

ط tā or to, (called طاى حطّي tāʼi huttī, طائُ غير منقوطة tāʼi ghayr manḳūta, or طاىُ مهمله tāʼi muhmala, Undotted tā) Is the sixteenth letter of the Arabic alphabet, and the nineteenth of the Persian; expressing 9 in arithmetic, Capricorn in the zodiac, and the moon's descendant. The just pronunciation of this letter can only be learned from the mouth of a native of Arabia. The Persians give to it the same power as that of our t, and in spelling English words in Persian characters they generally use ط for t. It is interchangeable with ص, ض, ظ, and ك.

P طاء tāʼ, A man who frequents the society of women very much.

A طاءة tāʼat, A going far off in pasturing. Thin clay or mud.

A طاب tāb, (v. n. of طاب for طيب) Being sweet, fragrant, agreeable, good, lawful. Rendering so. Abounding in pasturage (land). Odour, perfume. An excellent flavour. رطب بن طاب rutbu'bnu tāb, A sort of date. عذق بن طاب ʻizh bin tāb, A kind of Madīna date. (in prayer) طاب سرّه tāba sirruhu, May his grave be fragrant! may he rest in peace!

A طاباق tābāḳ, A large brick.

A طابة tābat, Wine. The town of Madīna.

A طابخ tābikh, (pl. طبّخ tubbakh) A cook. An angel who torments the damned. A burning fever.

A طابخة tābikhat, Mid-day heat, grilling heat.

A طابع tābaʻ or tābiʻ, (pl. طوابع tawābiʻ) A seal-ring, or any other instrument by which an impression is made, or with which tithe-cattle are branded. Stamp, mark, impression. Tābiʻ, A printer. A stamper, sealer. A fixed or settled habit of body.

A طابق tābaḳ or tābiḳ, (from P تابه tāba) (pl. طوابق tawābiḳ and طوابيق tawābīḳ) A frying-pan. A large brick. A cellar. A trap-door. A joint, a limb. The hand. Half of a sheep; as much as will satisfy two or three persons.

A طابقيّ tābiḳiy, A mode of wrapping a turban round the head without passing it under the chin.

A طابن tābin, Very skilful or cunning.

T طابوت tābūt, (for A تابوت tābūt) A bier.

A طابون tābūn, A pit, or other place where they cover up fire.

P طابه tāba, A frying-pan, a skillet.

A طأة taʼat, (v. n. of وطئ) Being even, level, soft (ground or bed). A treading, trampling. على طأة ʻala' taʼatin, Commodiously.

P طات tāt, Persians; so called by a tribe who inhabit between Hamadān and Kurdistān.

A طاجن tājan or tājin, A frying-pan.

A طاحل tāhil, Turbid. Spleen-coloured.

A طاحن tāhin, A grinder. An ox placed in the middle of a thrashing-floor, round which the other oxen move when treading out the grain.

A طاحنة tāhinat, (pl. طواحن) A back-tooth.

A طاحونة tāhūnat, (pl. طواحين) A water-mill.

A طاحي tāhī, Extending a great way (a multitude). Large, spacious (arbour or shade). Drawn out a great way. Whatever fills up. Exalted, high.

A طاخر tākhir, A black cloud covering the sky.

P طاخك tākhak, A sort of tree in Tabaristān.

A طاخي tākhī, Thick (darkness).

A طاخية tākhiyat, Name of an ant said to have held a discourse with Solomon.

A طاد tād, Heavy. Furious (he-camel).

A طادي tādī, (fem. طادية tādiyat) Old, long-established (custom).

A طارّ tārr, A youth whose mustachios are beginning to appear.

A طارد tārid, Persecutor, pursuer. Hard driver.

A طارط tārit, One who has thin eyebrows.

P طارطقه tāratha, A cherry.

P طارف tāraf, Newly-acquired wealth.

A طارف tārif, Newly-acquired or discovered.

A طارفة tārifat, Plenty (of money).

P طارق tārik, A door.

A طارق tārik, (fem. طارقة tārikat) (pl. طرّاق turrāk) A nocturnal traveller. A prophet; a diviner by throwing stones, magician. The morning-star.

A طارقة tārikat, (pl. طوارق tawārik) A family, kindred, tribe. A small throne, sofa, or couch. An event, accident. A prophetess.

A طارقيّة tārikiyat, A sort of collar or necklace.

P طارم tāram, A wooden building of a circular form with an arched roof. A dome. A roof. A palisade to exclude people from a garden. طارم اخضر tārami akhzar (فيروزه fīroza, or نيلگون nīlgūn), Sky. طارم چارم tārami chārum, The fourth heaven, the firmament, solar sphere or orbit.

A طارمة tārimat, An arch-roofed wooden house.

A طارونيّ tārūniy, Raw silk or stuff made of it.

A طاري tārī, (pl. طرّاء turrāʼ or طرّآء turraʼāʼ) Who or what comes suddenly and unexpectedly.

A طارئة tāriʼat, Calamity, heavy misfortune.

P طاريقه tārīka, A purgative seed.

A طازج tāzaj, (from P تازه tāza, a mute ه becomes ج) Fresh. Sound, good, pure (tradition).

P طازي tāzī, An Arab; Arabia. A greyhound.

P A طاس tās, A cup, goblet. A dish. The vessel in which water is cooled. Brocade. P طاس آبگون tāsi āb-gūn (also نگون nigūn), Heaven.

A طاس افلاك tāsi aflāk, The vault of heaven.

P طاس زر tāsi zar, The sun (the golden dish).

A طاسّات tāssāt, Cups.

P طاس‌باز tās-bāz, A juggler or conjurer.

A طاسّة tāssat, Deeply-penetrating (stab).

P طاسچه tāscha, A little cup.

A طاسل tāsil, Flying (dust).

P طاسه tāsa, A kind of drum.

P طاسه نواز tāsa-nawāz, A player on the طاسه.

A طاسئ tāsiʼ, Oppressed, sick from eating fat.

A طاط tāt, Long, tall. Strong. Courageous. Quarrelsome. A libidinous and noisy stallion.

A طأطاء taʼtāʼ, A camel with a short, thick neck. Low ground, a hollow where one can lie hid.

A طأطأة taʼtaʼat, (v. n. of طأطأ Q) Lowering (the head). Giving (a horse) the rein, or jogging (him) with the thigh that (he) may mend his pace or caper. Being lavish in spending money.

A طاطة tātat, (pl. of طائط) Raging stallions.

A طاع tāʻ, Obedient.

A طاعة tāʻat, (v. n. of طاع for طوع) Obeying, submitting to. Obedience, obsequiousness. The service or worship of God. A proper name of a woman.

P طاعتگاه tāʻat-gāh, A mosque, temple, church.

A طاعل tāʻil, A straight, firm arrow.

A طاعم tāʻim, A taster of food. A man who feeds delicately. Independent (of a person's food).

A طاعن tāʻin, Reproaching, blaming: stabbing. A piercer, spearer. An asperser, slanderer. طاعن في السنّ tāʻin fi's sinn, Stricken in years.

A طاعون tāʻūn, (pl. طواعين) Plague, pestilence.

P طاعون زده tāʻūn-zada, Smitten with pestilence.

A طاعية tāʻiyat, A woman diseased in the liver.

A طاغوت tāghūt, (pl. طواغيت tawāghīt and طواغي tawāghī) An idol, a demon, or any object worshipped (excepting Omnipotence), particularly an ancient idol at Mecca. Satan. A diviner, soothsayer, augur. Juggling, magic. An heresiarch.

A طاغي tāghī, A rebel, leader of faction or insurrection; a refractory, disobedient, insolent man. A tyrant (applied by the Muhammadans to the Greek emperors of Byzantium or Constantinople).

A طاغية tāghiyat, (pl. طواغي tawāghī) A tyrant. A ringleader of rebellion. A Greek emperor. A proud, insolent fool. A thunderbolt, lightning. An idol. A loud shriek under the infliction of castigation or torment. Crimes, sins, trespasses.

A طاف tāf, (A man) who goes much round. Wool of the neck, the nape of the neck.

A طافّة tāffat, Any thing dividing a plain from a mountain. A hedge, border, or whatever surrounds a garden.

A طافح tāfih, Overflowing (pond). Full of drink.

A طافلة tāfilat, Good. Utility, profit.

A طافي tāfī, Extinguished. Overspreading.

A P طاق tāk, (pl. طاقات tākāt and طيقان tī-

kān) An arch. An arched building, cupola, or any species of vaulted work. The space between any two planks of a ship. A window, balcony. A kind of tree. A kind of garment, cloak, cloth, or green scarf. Open. A peculiar noise or echo. The prominent part of a mountain. A projecting part of a well. Odd. Unique, singular, one part or fold of any thing doubled (as a single or double sole). A fold, plait, or ply. P دو طاق *du tāk*, Double, two-fold. سه طاق *sih tāk*, Three-fold. طاق ابرو *tāki abrū*, The eyebrow (of a mistress). A طاق ازرق *tāki azrak*, The azure vault, *i.e.* heaven, sky. (Synonymous to which are the following, in composition with طاق *tāk*: P بازيچه رنگ *bāzīcha-rang*, خضرا *khazrā*, طارم *tāram*, فيروزة *fīroza*, كحلي *kuhlī*, لاجوردي *lājawardī*, نيلوفري *nilūfarī*, نيم خانه *nīm-khāna*, or نيم خايه *nīm-khāya*). P طاق بر نهادن *tāk bar nihādan*, To forget, leave, omit. طاق جفت *tāk-juft*, (or طاق يا جفت *tāk yā juft*) Odd or even. طاق شكر بورة *tāki shakar-būra*, A kind of sweet triangular pasty. A طاق مقرنس *tāki mukarnas*, The throne of Solomon. P طاق و ترنب *tāk u turumb*, (or طاق و طرم *tāk u turum*) Pomp, pride. A في الطاق *fi't tāk*, In the window. قصر زمرد طاق *kasri zumurrud-tāk*, The palace of the azure vault, *i.e.* heaven, sky. P نه طاق *nuh tāk*, The nine vaults or heavens. طاق شدن *tāk shudan*, To be folded or doubled up.

A طاقة *tākat*, Power, force, strength. Ability. Patience. Rest, repose. Order, series. One heap, bundle, or handful. A single plat of a rope.

P طاقچه *tākcha*, A little window.

P طاقدانه *tākdāna*, The cornel-tree.

P طاقديس *tākdes*, Archwise. A portico, verandah. A royal pavilion. The throne of Khusraw; likewise that of king Solomon.

P طاقه *tāka*, A single twist of a rope. One sprig of a flower. A single silken garment. Power, strength. Patience, endurance.

P طاقي *tākī*, A kind of high-crowned hat or mitre. The froth of urine in a chamber-pot. Sediment in the urine of a sick person. A cloud. Wall-eyed (horse).

P A طاقيه *tākiya* or *tākīya*, A fillet, especially one worn under the head-dress. A balcony, penthouse. A cornice. طاقيه دوز *tākiya-doz*, A head-dress maker. A deceiver.

A طال *tāla*, (in prayer) May it be long! طال بقاه *tāla bakāhu*, May his existence be prolonged!

A طالب *tālib*, (pl. طلاب *tullāb*, طلب *tullab*, طلبة *talabat*, and طلب *talab*) One who asks, inquires, demands, interrogates, or requests: craving, importunate. A beggar. An inquisitor, inquirer. A pursuer. Studious, desirous of knowledge, curious. طالب علم *tālibi ɛilm*, A student. P طالبان فضيلت گستر *tālibāni fazīlat-gustar*, Learned and excellent men. ابو طالب *abū tālib*, The name by which عبد مناف *ɛabd manāf*, the paternal uncle of Muhammad and father of Alīy, is usually designated.

A طالة *tālat*, A she-ass.

A طالح *tālih*, (pl. طلح *tullah*) Wicked, villainous. Wearied (she-camel). P اگر صالح و اگر طالح *agar sālih u agar tālih*, Whether good or bad. A لولا الصالحون لهلك الطالحون *law lā as sālihūna, la halaka't tālihūna*, Were it not for the righteous, verily the wicked would be cut off.

A طالع *tāliɛ*, Who or what arises, appears, breaks forth, is born or produced. The false dawn, twilight. The horoscope or predominant star at a person's nativity. Fortune (good or bad), fate, destiny, chance. An arrow which flies beyond the mark. The new moon. طالع مسعود المطالع *tāliɛi masɛūdu'l matāliɛ*, A constellation of a happy ascendant; good fortune.

P طالع آزمائي *tāliɛ-āzmāɛī*, Trial of one's fortune.

P طالعمند *tāliɛmand*, Fortunate, prosperous.

P طالعور *tāliɛwar*, Fortunate. Wealthy.

A طالق *tālik*, (pl. طلق *tullak*) Divorced, repudiated (woman). (A camel) without a halter, or one going to water. (A camel) left a day and a night without being milked.

A طالقة *tālikat*, (pl. طوالق *tawālik*) Divorced (woman). Temperate (night). (A camel) allowed to pasture where she likes without being milked.

P طالقون *tālkūn*, (or طاليقون *tālīkūn*) A species of poisonous brass or mixed metal, composed of iron, antimony, lead, gold, tin, copper, and silver, of which tweezers are made for pulling out hairs, which never grow afterwards, or at least but slowly.

A طالم *tālim*, (pl. طلمة *talamat*) A baker.

A طالما *tāla mā*, It is a long time that.

A طالوط *tālūt*, (or طالوت *tālūt*) Saul (the king).

A طالي *tālī*, Covered with green scum (a horse-pond). Dark (night).

T طاليان *tālyān*, (Italiano) An Italian.

P طاليسفر *tālīsfar*, The bark of an Indian olive; applied to the mouth it is a cure for certain diseases.

A طامّ *tāmm*, Conquering, victorious (army).

P طامات *tāmāt*, Doubtful words, without certainty, raving nonsense. Barbarously pronounced.

A طامّة *tāmmat*, Adversity. A calamity which overtops all others. The resurrection.

A طامث *tāmis*, A menstruous woman.

A طامح *tāmih*, High, elevated. (A woman) who flies from her husband to her friends. Looking upwards. Covetous, eager. High, lofty. طامح الطرف *tāmihu't tarf*, A quick-sighted horse.

A طامر *tāmir*, A flea. طامر بن طامر *tāmiru'bnu tāmirin*, Unknown, either himself or his father.

A طامس *tāmis*, (pl. طوامس *tawāmis*) Far distant or separate, invisible. Hollow in heart (a man); without a soul. A concealer.

A طامع *tāmiɛ*, (pl. طمعاء *tumaɛāɛ*, طماعى *tamāɛa'*, and اطماع *atmāɛ*) Covetous, greedy, desirous, hopeful. Appetitive.

A طامعة *tāmiɛat*, Appetite.

A طامل *tāmil*, Wicked, scurrilous, shameless.

A طامور *tāmūr*, (pl. طوامير *tawāmīr*) A book, volume, roll, scroll.

A طامي *tāmī*, Swelling, raging (deep).

A طان *tān*, Full of clay, clayey. The body.

A طانز *tāniz*, Sarcastic, satirical, derisive.

A طاني *tānī*, (pl. طناة *tunāt*) A whoremonger.

A طاوس *tāɛus*, (pl. اطواس *atwās* and طواويس *tawāwīs*) A peacock. A handsome man, a beau. Ground verdant with herbage, or covered with herbage of various kinds. Silver. P طاوس آتش پر *tāwusi ātish-par*, (The peacock with wings of fire) The sun. طاوس پران اخضر *tāwus-parāni akhzar*, Angels. Stars. طاوس خلد *tāwusi khuld*, Virgins of Paradise. طاوس مشرق خرام *tāwusi mashrik khirām*, The sun. Heaven.

P طاوس مادة *tāɛus-māda*, A peahen.

A طاوي *tāwī*, (fem. طاوية *tāwiyat*) Starved, hungry, eating nothing.

A طاويّ *tāwīy*, Any one.

A طاهر *tāhir*, (pl. اطهار *athār* and طهاري *tahāra'*) Clear, pure, unsullied, chaste, clean, holy. A clean woman. طاهر الثياب *tāhiru's siyāb*, (and طاهر الذيل *tāhiru'z zayl*) Immaculate, of unsullied life. قلب طاهر *kalbi tāhir*, A pure heart.

A طاهرة *tāhirat*, (A woman) clear of all impurity.

A طاهل *tāhil*, Fetid (water).

A طاهي *tāhī*, (pl. طهاة *tuhāt* and طهي *tuha'*) Cooking. A cook. A roaster. A baker.

A طائب *tāɛib*) Good, pleasant, lawful.

A طائبين *tāɛibīn*, (obliq. pl. of طائب *tāɛib*) The good, the lawful.

A طاية *tāyat*, A flat roof, terrace, or surface. A place where they dry dates. A large stone in sandy ground. Soil in which are no stones.

A طائر *tāɛir*, Flying. A flier. (pl. طير *tayr*) A bird. Work, act. An omen (especially a bad one); and also the thing from which the omen is taken. Anger, rage. The brain. Any thing which is put upon a man to execute. Dignity, happiness. Whatever is necessary for the support of life, daily bread. طائر سدرة *tāɛiri sidra*, The bird of Sidra (a species of paradisaical tree), the angel Gabriel. طائر قدسي *tāɛiri kudsī*, An angel. ساكن الطائر *sākinu't tāɛir*, Grave, modest. طار طائره *tāra tāɛiruhu*, He flew in a passion.

A طائش *tāɛish*, Volatile, light, flighty; pettish.

A طائط *tāɛit*, (pl. طاطة *tātat* and اطواط *atwāt*) A raging and noisy stallion. A litigious and quarrelsome man. Long, tall.

A طائع *tāɛiɛ*, (pl. طوع *tuwaɛ*) Obedient, cheerful, willing. طائعا بلا اكراه *tāɛiɛan bilā ikrāhin*, Consenting without compulsion.

A طائف *tāɛif*, Who, what goes round. A night-watch or patrole. A wall surrounding any place. The ox which is stationed at the outer edge of the threshing-floor. A rock projecting from a mountain. A domestic who serves gently and carefully. Name of a town and of a district in Arabia. The middle of the bow, between ابهر abhar and سئة siʼat, upon which the arrow rests. A spectre, phantom, vision. Temptation of the devil, a vile thought.

A طائفة tāʼifat, (pl. طوائف tawāʼif) A people, nation, tribe, family; a troop, band, body, company, clique, suite, train, equipage, attendants. A person, individual. A portion. Part (of any thing, especially of the night).

A طائفتان tāʼifatāni, Two companies, *i. e.* Jews and Christians.

A طائق tāʼik, Prominent part of (a mountain or well). Space between any two planks of a ship.

A طائل tāʼil, Long. Power. Profit, advantage. The comforts of life, riches. Excellence. لا طائل lā tāʼil, (There is) no profit. غير طائل ghayr tāʼil, Dull, blunt (sword). ما هو بطائل mā huwa bi tāʼilin, He is low, useless, good for nothing. لم يحل منه بطائل lam yahla minhu bi tāʼilin, No good came of him (or it).

A طائلة tāʼilat, Excellence. Power, riches. The comforts of life. Enmity, hatred.

A طائيّ tāʼiy, Of the tribe of طيّ tayy.

A طبّ tabb, (v. n. of طبّ) Strengthening (a leathern bottle) by covering the seams with a strap. Skilful, an adept, able practitioner; expert (stallion). (A camel) placing his hind-feet in the prints left by his fore-feet). *Tibb, tabb,* or *tubb,* (v. n. of طبّ) Executing any work leisurely and commodiously. Making up medicine. Being an adept in any science. Medicine for body or mind. Magic, witchcraft, necromancy, fascination. Benevolence, courtesy. Assistance. علم طب ʻilmi tibb, Science of medicine. *Tibb,* Will, desire, inclination. Nature, habit, custom. State, condition. ما ذاك بطبّي mā zāka bi tibbī, That is not my custom.

A طباب tabāb, A long, streaky cloud. *Tibāb,* (pl. of طبّة tibbat, طبابة tibābat, and طبيبة tabībat) Oblong tracts of land or clouds. Leathern straps of a finger's breath for covering the seams of a leathern bottle.

A طبابة tabābat, A long, streaky cloud. *Tibābat,* The medical art. A strip of leather for covering the seams of the bottom of a water-bottle.

P طبابه tabāba, Meat dressed soft.

A طباءة tabāʼat, Nature, disposition (good or bad).

A طباخ tabākh or tubākh, Strength, stability. Plumpness, fatness.

A طبّاخ tabbākh, A cook.

A طباخة tibākhat, The art of cookery. *Tubākhat,* The scum of a pot boiling over, slush.

A طباخية ta or tubākhiyat, A beautiful and sensible young woman, also one firm and well-made.

A بنات طبار banātu tabār, Heavy calamities.

A طبّار tubbār, A tree resembling the fig.

P طباز tibāz, A kind of large red fig.

A طباشير tabāshīr, A substance of a silicious nature produced in the bamboo, used in medicine; also the ashes of the roots and joints. In a high wind these bamboos rub against each other and emit fire. طباشير الخيّاط tabāshīru'l khayyāt, Chalk, lime, plaster. طباشير صبح tabāshīri subh, The light of dawn.

A طباطبا tabātabā, Name of the great-great-grandson of Alīy.

A طباع tibāʻ, Nature, temperament, complexion, disposition, nature's stamp; understanding, genius, intellect, judgment. دار الطباع dāru't tibāʻ, A printing-office. (pl. of طبع tabʻ) Natures, forms.

A طبّاع tabbāʻ, A sword-cutler: potter: sealer.

A طباعة tibāʻat, The art of forging swords or moulding earthen pots.

A طباق tibāk, (v. n. 3 of طبق) Agreeing, suiting, fitting, matching. Higher part or surface (of ground). Antithesis. (pl. of طبق tabak) Things similar to one another (plates, dishes, orbs, cupolas, the stories of a house, the orders of the heaven).

A طبّاق tubbāk, A certain tree found on the mountains near Mecca, a specific against poisons, scab, or fever, or inveterate obstructions in the liver.

A طباقاء tabākāʼ, Impotent (stallion camel). Weak, helpless, impotent (man). Heavy and fat (man). A stammerer.

A طبّال tabbāl, A drummer.

A طبالة tibālat, The art of drum-beating.

A طبّالة tabbālat, A female drummer.

A طبانة tabānat, (or طبانية tabāniyat) (v. n. of طبن) Being sensible, intelligent, knowing, expert. Quickness, sagacity.

P طبانچه tabāncha, A box, blow, slap.

A طباهج tabāhij, Meat fried in butter.

A طباهجة tabāhijat, A dish composed of slices of meat, onions, eggs, and water.

P طباهجه tabāhja, (or طباهيج tabāhīj) An omelet. Soft meat.

A طبائخ tabāʼikh, Hot pestilential winds.

A طبائع tabāʼiʻ, (pl. of طبيعة) Natures, tempers.

A طبائعيّ tabāʼiʻiy, Natural, physical.

A طبب tibab, (pl. of طبّة tibbat, طبابة tibābat, طبيبة tabībat) Sorts, kinds. Oblong tracts of ground or clouds. Segments of cloth or leather. طبب شعاع شمس tibabi shiʻāʻi shams, The rising sun's rays darting through the air.

A طبّة tibbat, (pl. طبب tibab) An oblong tract of grassy ground or clouds; also a long segment of cloth, or a leathern strap about the breadth of the finger. A house. A garment open in front, and long-skirted. A sun-beam. Goats' leather, used by shoemakers. *Tubbat,* A strip of leather for covering the seams of the bottom of a water-bottle.

A طبج tabj, (v. n. of طبج) Striking any thing hollow (as the head). Confirmed stupidity. *Tabaj,* (v. n. of طبج) Being foolish, insane.

A طبخ tabkh, A cooking; cookery. جيّد الطبخ jayyidu't tabkh, Well-baked (loaf). Well-burnt (brick.)

A طبّخ tubbakh, (pl. of طابخ tābikh) Cooks. Angels who torment the damned.

A طبخة tabkhat, Quite foolish or stupid.

P طبخ خانه tabkh-khāna, A cook's shop.

A طبر tabr, (v. n. of طبر) Leaping, skipping. Concealing one's self. Covering (as a stallion). *Tibr,* The angle; also the side curtain or buttress of a castle. (for تبر tibr) Native gold. *Tabar,* (from P تبر tabar) An axe. A mattock.

P طبر tabar, Name of a district in Persia.

A طبرانيّ tabarāniy, Belonging to Tiberias.

A طبرج tabraj, An emmet, a pismire.

P طبرخون tabarkhūn, The red Hyrcanian or Tabristān willow. The jujube. A red colour.

P طبرزد tabarzad, (طبرزذ tabarzaz, طبرزن tabarzan, or طبرزل tabarzal) Sugar-candy. Conserve of roses.

A طبرس tabras or tibris, An arrant liar.

P طبرستان tabaristān, The ancient Hyrcania.

P طبري tabarī, A native of Tabaristān.

A طبريّ tabariy, Native of Tabariyat in Wāsit. The third part of a درهم dirham in Syria.

A طبريّة tabariyat, Tiberias. Name of a village in Wāsit. بحيرت طبريّه buhayrati tabariya, The lake of Tiberias.

A طبز tabz, (v. n. of طبز) Filling. Lying with. *Tibz,* The angle of a mountain. A boulder-stone. (A camel) with a double bunch.

A طبس tabs, Black. *Tibs,* A wolf.

P طبسه tabsa, Tapestry, a carpet.

A طبش tabsh, Men: a body, troop. ايّ الطبش هو ayyu't tabsh huwa, Who he is (I know not).

A طبطاب tubtāb, A bird with large ears.

A طبطابة tabtābat, The club, bat, or racket, with which they strike the ball at the game of tennis.

A طبطبة tabtabat, (v. n. of طبطب Q) Making noise. The sound made by the dashing of torrents or water-falls, or in walking, or in whipping.

A طبطبيّة tabtabiyat, A twisted garland, with which they strike one another when dancing.

P طبطو tabtū, A kind of water-bird.

A طبع tabʻ, (v. n. of طبع) Forging (a sword). Coining (money). Moulding (a pitcher). Printing, stamping. Signing, sealing, making an impression with a seal. Presenting a fair mark for a blow (the nape of the neck). Striking the back of the head with the hand. Casting a veil over the heart (God). Filling (a bucket or measure). An impression made with a seal. Nature, genius, complexion, temperament, quality, intellect, judgment. Mould, make. Form, shape, air. Likeness, resemblance. طبع الهي tabʻi ilāhī, Divine nature. طبع كافوري tabʻi kāfūrī, A cold and dry temperament. A dull, stupid, reserved, frigid fellow. Death. الطبع املك من الادب at'tabʻ amlak mini'l adab, Nature is more powerful than education. بالطبع *bi't tabƹ*, Naturally. P تيزطبع *tez-tabƹ*, Ready-witted, ingenious; capricious, whimsical, fantastic. A حاتم طبع *hātim-tabƹ*, Of the nature of Hātim (a generous Arabian), *i.e.* incomparably munificent. P خوش طبع *khwush-tabƹ*, Good-natured, benevolent. A مدنيّ بالطبع *muduniy bi't tabƹ*, Of an urbane disposition. *Tibƹ*, A channel, stream, rivulet. (pl. اطباع *atbāƹ*) A place of little water. A measure full. A leathern bottle for churning. Rust, soil, dirt. *Tabaƹ*, (v. n. of طبع) Becoming rusty (a sword). Being mean, sordid, abject. Being idle, slothful, sunk in low and vicious habits (as a sword is covered with rust). Excessive rust, dirt, and nastiness. Disgrace, vice, infamy. *Tabiƹ*, Sordid, mean, abject; unblushing, not ashamed of his sordid manners or filthiness. Rusty (sword).

P طبع آزما *tabƹ-āzmā*, Trying the disposition.

A طبعان *tubƹān*, Sealing-wax or clay.

P طبعخانه *tubƹ-khāna*, A printing-office.

P طبع زاد *tabƹ-zād*, Invention.

A طبعيّ *tabƹiy*, Natural, physical.

A طبق *tabk*, (v. n. of طبق) Cleaving to the side (the hand). Being near (doing any thing). *Tibk*, Any thing corresponding with, or joined to, another. A multitude (of men or locusts). The fruit of a certain tree. An hour of the day. A long time. Bird-lime. (pl. of طبقة *tibkat*) Gins, springes, snares. *Tubk*, (pl. of طبيق *tabīk*) Hours of the night. *Tabak*, (from طبق) Cleaving to. Being contracted, shut, or clapt to the side (the hand). Setting about a thing which one intends to finish. A dish, plate, tray. (pl. اطباق *atbāk* and اطبقة *atbikat*) A lid, cover. An orb, disk. A thin bone between the joints of the backbone. The story of a house. Vault of heaven. Universal (rain) covering the surface of the globe. Surface of the earth. A leaf. Gold-leaf, tinfoil. One thing following another. Whatever matches, tallies with, or fits (another thing). An age. A period of twenty years. The greater part (of night or day). A flight of locusts. A company of people. State, condition. The exterior of the vulva. طبق زنبور *tabaki zambūr*, A bee-hive. طبق طبق *tabak tabak*, One above another (as plate upon plate, story over story). طبقا عن طبق *tabakan ƹan tabakin*, Consecutively, following in order. بنات طبق *banātu tabakin*, Misfortunes. Tortoises. Serpents. احدي بنات طبق *ihda' banāt tabak*, Misfortune, sorrow (literally, the mother, or one of the daughters of the tortoise, the old Arabians believing, that of 79 eggs, the usual number laid by her, one of them produced a black serpent). بنت طبق *bintu tabakin*, A tortoise which lays 99 eggs, each of which produces a tortoise, and lays one egg which produces a serpent. *Tibak*, (pl. of طبقة *tibkat*) Gins, nooses, snares.

A طبقا *tibkan*, For a long time (we abode with him). *Tabakan*, One after another, successively.

A طبقات *tabakāt*, (pl. of طبقة) Kinds (of men).

A طبقة *tibkat*, An hour of the day. (pl. طبق *tibak* or *tibk*) A gin, noose, snare. *Tabakat*, One thing following another. A degree, stage, story, floor, stratum. Race, generation. A class or order of men. P طبقهٔ بالا *tabakaʼi bālā*, An upper story. طبقهٔ پائين *tabakaʼi pāʼīn*, A lower story. A *Tabikat*, Contracted or shut (hand). A hand which cleaves to the side.

P طبقچه *tabakcha*, A small plate, saucer.

P طبقچي *tabakchī*, One who has charge of dishes or plate, clerk of the scullery.

P طبقري *tabkarī*, A small plate. Side, border.

A طبل *tabl*, (v. n. of طبل) Drumming. (pl. اطبال *atbāl* and طبول *tubūl*) A drum, single or double. A tambourine. Garments on which are figures of drums. The pool in which gamesters deposit the stakes. A money-till, a save-all. People. Tribute.

P طبل آسايش *tabli āsāyish*, Sounding a retreat. طبل خوردن *tabl khwurdan*, To be afraid, to fly in terror. طبل در زير گليم زدن *tabl dar zīri gilīm zadan*, To strive to conceal what is notorious. طبل در زير گليم ماندن *tabl dar zīri gilīm māndan*, To be obscure, little known. طبل زدن *tabl zadan*, To beat a drum. طبل واپس *tabli wāpas*, (or طبل ماتم *tabli mātam*) A drum which they beat on the day عاشورا *ƹāshūrā*. A ما ادري ايّ الطبل هو *mā adrī ayyu't tabli huwa*, I know not what man he is.

P طبل باز *tabl-bāz*, A drum hung at the saddle. A drummer.

A طبلة *tablat*, A tray in the shape of a sieve.

P طبلخانه *tabl-khāna*, Warlike music; a concert of drums. A band of music.

P طبل زن *tabl-zan*, A drummer.

A طبلق *tablak*, A bundle of papers.

P طبلك *tablak*, A little drum; also a drum made of two kettles, joined bottom to bottom, and covered with a skin. A mitre, cap, tiara. A fillet.

P طبل نواز *tabl-nawāz*, A drummer.

P طبل نوازي *tabl-nawāzī*, Drum-beating

P طبله *tabla*, A large wooden dish in which fruits are exposed to sale. A small tambourine. A round butt or mark for archers. A sandal or slipper. Any thing thrown or shot at birds, sprung by a pointer, which brings them down. طبلهٔ عطّار *tablaʼi ƹattār*, A perfumer's tray.

P طبله خوار *tabla-khwār*, Eating gratis; a parasite.

P طبله نواز *tabla-nawāz*, A drummer.

A طبليّة *tabliyat*, Tributary money.

A طبن *tabn* or *taban*, (v. n. of طبن) Covering up (a fire) to prevent (its) dying away. Person, people. A great concourse of people. ايّ الطبن هو *ayyu't tabni huwa*, What countryman is he? *Tubn*, A lute, a guitar. *Taban*, (v. n. of طبن) Knowing, perceiving, understanding well. Quickness, sagacity. *Taban, tabn, tibn, tubn*, or *tuban*, A kind of game with lines scored on the ground. A carcase laid to entice vultures. *Tabin*, Sensible, intelligent, knowing, sagacious. *Tiban*, (pl. of طبنة *tibnat*) Intellectual powers, subtilties. *Tuban*, (pl. of طبنة *tubnat*) Games of nine-pins.

A طبنة *tibnat*, (pl. طبن *tiban*) Understanding, quickness of apprehension. *Tubnat*, The sound of a lute or guitar. (pl. طبن *tuban*) A kind of game with three or nine stones or pieces.

A طبندر *tabandar*, Mischief, malice, evil.

P طبنگ *tabang*, A green-grocer's tray.

A طبو *tabw*, A calling to.

A طبواء *tabwāʼ*, (A she-camel) with a pendulous udder. A serious and important affair.

P قريهٔ طبور *karyaʼi tabūr*, The city of Tiberias.

P جبل طبور *jabali tabūr*, Mount Tabor.

A طبوع *tubūƹ*, (pl. of طبع *tibƹ*) Rivulets.

A طبّوع *tabbūƹ*, An insect of the tike-species, whose bite is extremely painful, a crab-louse.

A طبول *tubūl*, (pl. of طبل *tabl*) Drums.

A طبونة *tabūnat*, (v. n. of طبن) Perceiving, knowing, understanding well. Quickness, sagacity. Covering up (a fire) to prevent (its) dying away.

P طبه *taba*, An European carpet with a short pile.

A طبي *taby*, (v. n. of طبي) Inviting, calling to. Guiding, leading. Turning from. Having a loose, pendulous udder (a camel). *Tiby* or *tuby*, (pl. اطباء *atbāʼ*) A nipple, a dug.

A طبيّ *tabiy*, Consenting, accepting. An udder easily milked.

A طبّيّ *tibbiy*, Medicinal, medical.

A طبيب *tabīb*, (pl. اطبّة *atibbat* and اطبّاء *atibbāʼ*) A physician, doctor: a skilful practitioner in general. A mistress.

A طبيبة *tabībat*, (pl. طباب *tibāb*) An oblong tract of ground or clouds. A segment of cloth, or a leathern strap of a finger's breadth.

A طبيبي *tabībī*, Profession of a physician.

A طبيّة *tabiyat*, (A camel) with a long, swaggy udder. A grave, important affair.

A طبّيجة *tibbījat*, Podex.

P طبيخ *tabīkh*, A melon.

A طبيخ *tabīkh*, Cooked. Any thing dressed, especially half-roasted or parboiled. A decoction, apozem. A spirituous liquor obtained from dates. A brick, tile. Plaster, mortar. A violent burning or fever.

A طبّيخ *tibbīkh*, A melon.

P طبيدن *tabīdan*, To palpitate, throb, beat.

A طبيس *tabīs*, Abounding, overflowing (sea).

A طبّيع *tibbīƹ*, The centre or heart of the early blossom of the date.

A طبيعة *tabīƹat*, (pl. طبيعات *tabīƹāt* and طبائع *tabāʼiƹ*) Nature, essence, quality, property, genius, complexion, temperament, constitution, humour, instinct, temper, disposition. لطيف الطبيعة *latīfu't tabīƹat*, Gracious, mild, gentle by nature. P تيز طبيعت *tez-tabīƹat*, Constitutionally sharp, impatient, irascible.

P طبيعت شناس *tabīʿat-shinās*, A physician.

A طبيعي *tabīʿīy*, Natural, intrinsic, physical, حرارت طبيعيه *harārati tabīʿīya*, Natural heat.

A طبيق *tabīk*, (pl. طبق *tubk*) An hour of the night. A long time. Any thing agreeing with, or equal to, another.

A طبيقا *tabīkan*, For a long while.

A طبيقة *tabīkat*, What is suitable, agreeable.

P طپان *tapān*, Restless, agitated, distracted.

P طپانچه *tapāncha*, A blow, box, slap. A pistol. طپانچه خوردن *tapāncha khwurdan*, To be slapped, cuffed, buffeted.

P طپانيدن *tapānīdan*, To cram, stuff.

P طپش *tapish*, Palpitation. طپش دل *tapishi dil*, A palpitation of the heart.

P طپيدگي *tapīdagī*, Palpitation.

P طپيدن *tapīdan*, To palpitate (as the heart), to throb, beat. To wallow. To totter, fall.

A طتو *tutūw*, The act of going away.

A طتيليق *tutaylīk*, (dim. of اطلاق *ittilāk*) A moderate degree of expansion.

A طث *tass*, A boy's game, throwing a ball.

A طثا *tass*, (v. n. of طثا) Casting forth the contents of the belly. Playing at hockey.

A طثر *tasr*, (v. n. of طثر) Being thick (milk), covered with cream.

A طثرة *tasrat*, Thick milk covered with cream. Thick water full of weeds or sediment. Thickness of milk. Water-moss. Stinking black mud. Wool; the grease and sweat on sheeps' shoulders. Affluence, happiness.

A طثرج *tasraj*, A small yellow ant, a pismire.

A طثن *tasn*, *tisn*, or *tusn*, Affluence, ease, enjoyment. Mirth, jollity.

A طثو *tusūw*, (v. n. of طثا for طثو) Playing with the قلة *kulat*. Voiding excrement.

A طثور *tusūr*, (v. n. of طثر) Being thick and covered with cream (milk).

A طثي *tasaʾ*, Small pieces of wood.

A طثيار *tasyār*, A lion. A gnat. A brave man.

A طجن *tajn*, (v. n. of طجن) Frying in a pan.

A طح *tahh*, (v. n. of طح) Expanding, stretching. Scratching, rubbing, bruising with the heel.

A طحا *tahaʾ*, Expanded, wide, level ground.

A طحار *tuhār*, (v. n. of طحر) Sighing. A deep-fetched sigh. Painful gripes.

A طحاف *tahāf*, High, elevated (cloud).

A طحال *tihāl*, (pl. طحل *tuhul*) The milt, spleen.

A طحامر *tuhāmir*, Large, gorbellied.

A طحان *tahhān*, (fem. طحانة *tahhānat*) A miller.

A طحانة *tihānat*, Grinding, trade of a miller.

A طحانة *tahhānat*, Many camels.

A مدوّنة الطحاوي *mudawwinatu't tahāwī*, (Vultures) hovering round their prey.

A طحث *tahs*, (v. n. of طحث) Pushing, thrusting, driving away (with the hand).

A طحح *tuhuh*, Scraped. A scraper, that wherewith any thing is scraped.

A طحر *tahr*, (v. n. of طحر) Throwing out a mote (the eye). Casting away a green film (a fountain). Driving away. Extirpating the foreskin (a circumciser). Lying with. *Tahr*, (*tahar*, طحرة *taharat*, طحرور *tuhrūr*, طحرورة *tuhrūrat*, or طحرية *tihriyat*) A bit of a thin cloud.

A طحرب *tihrib*, Leaves of trees, pieces of wood, or rubbish carried down by a stream.

A طحربة *tahrabat*, (v. n. of طحرب Q) Filling (a water-bottle). Rubbing (a substance) to make (it) soft and supple. Becoming open. Saturating. Shaking (a vessel) that (it) may be thoroughly filled. Breaking wind. Running away and breaking wind. *Tahrabat*, *tihribat*, or *tuhrubat*, (He has not) a rag of clothes. A small cloud, a bit of a cloud.

A طحرة *taharat* or *tahrat*, Hair. Wool. Any thing covering another.

A طحرف *tihrif*, (and طحرفة *tihrifat*) Thin (broth, cream, or cloud).

A طحرمة *tahramat*, (v. n. of طحرم Q) Filling (a leathern bottle). Stringing and drawing (a bow). *Tihrimat*, A rag, bit of cloth.

A طحز *tahz*, Coition.

A طحس *tahs*, (v. n. of طحس) Lying with.

A طحطاح *tahtāh*, A lion. *Tihtāh*, (v. n. of طحطح Q) Separating, scattering. Destroying. Breaking. Smiling, shewing the teeth.

A طحطحة *tahtahat*, (v. n. of طحطح Q) Separating, scattering, destroying. Breaking. Smiling. *Tihtihat*, (There is not upon him) a rag, a hair, or any thing.

A طحك *tuhhak*, (A camel) that has not yet learned to kneel down.

A طحل *tahl*, (v. n. of طحل) Filling (a vessel). *Tahl* or *tahal*, (v. n. of طحل) Hurting in the spleen. Bringing on a complaint in the spleen. *Tahal*, (v. n. of طحل) Having a complaint in the spleen. Having a large spleen. Becoming corrupt, stinking from mud (water). Being dust-coloured, or the colour of the spleen (a wolf or a sheep). *Tahil*, Splenetic, irascible. Black. Full. (Water) filled with moss. One whose spleen is enlarged and painful. (Wine) neither turbid nor bright. (A crow) neither of a dark nor of a light colour. *Tuhul*, (pl. of طحال *tihāl*) Spleens.

A طحلاء *tahlāʾ*, (fem. of اطحل) Dust-coloured. (Wine) neither of a turbid nor of a bright colour.

A طحلب *tihlib*, *tuhlab*, or *tuhlub*, Water-moss.

A طحلبة *tahlabat*, (v. n. of طحلب Q) Being covered with a green mantle, film, or water-weeds (stagnant water). Being overspread with verdure (ground). Shearing (a camel); killing (him). *Tihlibat*, (There is not upon him) one hair, one rag.

A طحلة *tuhlat*, A whitish ash-colour, the colour of the milt or spleen.

A طحلمة *tihlimat*, The smallest cloud.

A طحماء *tahmāʾ*, A plant called نجيل *najīl*.

A طحمة *tahmat*, A mass, the major part. A sort of plant. A kind of saltish plant. طحمة الفتنة *tahmatu'l fitnat*, The crowded state of a throng in a mutiny. طحمة ابليس *tahmatu iblīs*, Satanic agency or mischief. *Tahmat*, *tihmat*, and *tuhmat*, Impulse. A setting in (of the night). A crowd, multitude. *Tuhamat*, Intrepid in battle. Many camels.

A طحمرة *tahmarat*, (v. n. of طحمر Q) Filling (a bottle) with water. Stringing a bow. Jumping, leaping. *Tihmirat*, A small thin cloud. A single hair.

A طحمريرة *tahmarīrat*, A small cloud: any thing.

A طحمير *tihmīr*, A small or thin cloud.

A طحن *tahn*, (v. n. of طحن) Grinding (a mill). Fatiguing, harassing, crushing, routing (a host). Coiling up (as a serpent). *Tihn*, Meal, flour. *Tuhan*, A dwarf. A species of animalcule. A lion. The animal called ليث عفرين *lays ʿifrīna*.

A طحو *tahw*, (v. n. of طحا for طحو) Throwing (a man) on his face. Travelling, going (across the country). Being spread. Expanding, spreading abroad. Being sad and melancholy. Being absent. Perishing. Drawing out lengthwise. Inclining, carrying one strongly to. Lying on the left side.

A طحور *tahūr*, Swift, rapid. A strong bow shooting with velocity. *Tahūr*, (or طحورة *tahūrat*) (An eye) throwing out motes, or (a fountain) green film.

A طحوم *tahūm*, A propeller. *Tuhūm*, Once.

A طحون *tahūn*, A multitude, phalanx bearing down all before them. A fierce battle. Many camels (about 300).

A طحي *tahy*, (v. n. of طحي) Lying down. Spreading abroad. Being spread out. Travelling (across a country). Entering cordially with one into any thing.

A طحية *tahyat*, Part of a cloud, little cloud.

A طحير *tahīr*, (v. n. of طحر) Sighing. A deep-fetched sigh. Gripes which force out deep sighs.

A طحين *tahīn*, Flour, meal.

A طخ *takhkh*, Projection: removal: coition.

A طخاء *takhāʾ*, A high cloud. Sorrow, or what clouds the mind.

A طخارم *tukhārim*, Enraged, passionate.

A طخارية *takhāriyat*, An active, sprightly she-ass.

A طخارير *takhārīr*, A mixed multitude. A scattered multitude. (pl. of طخرور *tukhrūr*) Thin clouds.

A طخاطخ *tukhātikh*, Darkness.

A طخاف *takhāf*, A thin, high cloud. *Tikhāf* or *takhāf*, A thin cloud through which the sky is seen. (pl. of طخفة *takhfat*) Thin, transparent clouds.

A طخامة *takhāmat*, (v. n. of طخم) Being proud.

A طخر *takhr*, A thin cloud veiling the sky.

A طخربة *takhrabat*, A rag of clothes.

A طخربية *tukhrubīyat*, A rag of clothes.

A طخرور *tukhrūr*, (pl. طخارير *takhārīr*) A thin

cloud. A slender, relaxed man. A man neither brisk nor languid. A stranger.

A طخز *tihhz*, A lie, a falsehood.

A طخس *tikhs*, Root, origin, base, cause, author.

A طخش *takhsh* or *takhash*, (v. n. of طخش) Being dark, dim-sighted (the eye).

A طخطاخ *takhtākh*, Malignant, evil-minded. Clouds closely packed. The rattling of a necklace.

A طخ طخ *tikh tikh*, Laughing, ha! ha! ha!

A طخطخة *takhtakhat*, (v. n. of طخطخ Q) Equalling, making even, equal, or level, joining one thing to another. The noise made in laughing.

A طخف *takhf*, Grief which clouds the mind. Sour milk. A thin, high cloud.

A طخفاء *takhfā*, Black-muzzled (she-ass).

A طخفة *takhfat*, (pl. طخاف *tikhāf*) A thin cloud.

A طخم *takhm*, (v. n. of طخم) Being proud, haughty, overbearing.

A طخمة *takhmat*, A herd of goats. *Tukhmat*, Blackness on the tip of the nose.

A طخمورث *takhmūras*, Name of a Persian monarch (dynasty?), said to have reigned 700 years.

A طخميل *tikhmīl*, A roost-cock.

A طخوة *takhwat*, A thin cloud.

A طخوخ *tukhūkh*, Depravity, malignity.

A طخوم *tukhūm*, Limits, bounds, boundaries.

A طخيّ *tukhayy*, A cock.

A طخياء *takhyā*, A dark night. An unintelligible discourse.

A طخية *takhyat*, A piece of a cloud. (pl. طخيون *takhyūn*) Foolish, stupid. *Takh, tikh*, or *tukhyat*, Darkness. *Tukhyat*, A cloud (is not in the sky).

A طخيفة *takhīfat*, Gravy-soup; broth with meat.

A طخيم *takhīm*, Flesh dry and black.

A طدة *tidat*, (v. n. of وطد) Establishing, confirming. Rendering heavy. Ramming hard, making (ground) solid. Being firm, solid, perpetual. Travelling, marching, going. Treading upon, trampling under foot.

A طرّ *tarr*, (v. n. of طرّ) Compelling; driving (cattle) together from different quarters, and ranging (them) up to the right and left. Seizing, carrying off. Splitting, cleaving, cutting (purses). Sharpening (a sword or knife). Shining, glittering (stars). Carrying (a building) up a good height. Patching or covering (a cistern) with clay. Giving a slap or a blow. Falling. Sprouting (as herbage, or mustachios). Dismembering, cutting off. New hair appearing on an ass which has cast his coat. *Turr*, The generality. طرًّا *turran*, All of them (came).

A طرأ *tar*, (v. n. of طرأ) Coming by surprise, arriving suddenly.

A طرا *tara'*, Innumerable kinds of creatures.

A طراء *tarā*, (or طراءة *tarāat*) (v. n. of طرؤ) Being fresh, moist, succulent (a vegetable).

A طرّاء *turrā*, (and طرآء *tura-ā*) (pl. of طاري *tārī*) Comers by surprise.

A طرابلوس شام *tarābulūsi shām*, Tripoli in Syria. طرابلوس غرب *tarābulūsi gharb*, Tripoli in Barbary.

A طرابوزن *tirābūzan*, Trebisond.

A طرابيل *tarābīl*, (pl. of طربال *tirbāl*) Lofty towers. Syrian churches or cloisters.

A طرأة *tur-at*, Force or impetuosity (of a torrent).

P طرائيث *tarāsis*, A fruit called بل *bil*.

A طراح *tarāh*, A distant place.

A طرّاح *tarrāh*, An architect.

A طرّاحة *tarrāhat*, The covering of a sofa.

A طراحيّ *turāhiy*, Far distant (journey).

A طراخنة *tarākhinat*, (pl. of طرخان *tarkhān*) Princes, dukes (in Khurāsān).

A طراد *tirād*, (v. n. 3 of طرد) Making a headlong attack in battle. A hunting-spear, javelin. Stratagem in hunting.

A طرّاد *tarrād*, A long day. A small swift ship. A spacious place. An open and flat roof. One who wearies the patience of his hearers by a tedious delivery.

A طرار *tirār*, (pl. of طرّة *turrat*) q. v.

A طرّار *tarrār*, A cut-purse, pickpocket.

P طرّارة زبان *tarrāra-zabān*, Chattering, clack.

P طرّاري *tarrārī*, Quickness, fluency. Impudence.

P طراريدن *turārīdan*, To inquire, search.

P طراز *tarāz*, A royal robe, or rich dress so ornamented; also the places in Persia where they are generally made. A place where water is distributed in small canals from a river or fountain. The decoration of a city upon any public solemnity. An ornament. Painting, embroidery. Sugar-cane. A sugar-refinery in the province of Khuzistān. A work-shop, factory. A manufactory of brocade. Way, form, manner, rule. A company of people. Wild, desert, scenite. Name of a district in Badakhshān. Name of a city on the confines of China, celebrated for the comeliness of its inhabitants and the excellence of its musk. (in comp.) Ornamenting, adorning, embroidering. Singing, trilling. اثر طراز *asar* (or آثار *āsār*) *tarāz*, A historiographer. ديباجه طراز *dībāja-tarāz*, A composer of prefaces or exordiums (as being written in a highly-ornamented style).

A طراز *tirāz* or *tarāz*, Border, fringe, edge. Mode, manner. عبقري طراز *ʿabkarī-tarāz*, Having edgings or fringes of various colours or figures. ليس هذا من طرازك *laysa hāzā min tirāzika*, This is not after your nature or fashion.

A طرّاز *tarrāz*, An embroiderer.

A طرازدان *tirāzdān*, (from P ترازودان *tarāzūdān*) A case in which scales are kept.

P طرازگر *tarāzgar*, An embroiderer.

P طرازنده *tarāzanda*, A decorator, embroiderer.

P طرازيدن *tarāzīdan*, To embroider. To sing.

G طراغيس *tarāghīs*, (or طراقيس) Pearl-barley.

P طراغيون *tarāghayūn*, Name of a gum-tree.

A طراف *tirāf*, (pl. طرف *turf*) A tent made of tanned leather. Whatever is taken from the sides of a sown field. توارثوا المجد طرافًا *tawārasu'l majda tirāfan*, They succeeded to greatness by inheritance.

A طرافة *tarāfat*, (v. n. of طرف) Being new, coming out (something original and elegant). Being distinguished by a long line of ancestry.

A طرافش *turāfish*, Depraved, ill-tempered.

P طراق *tarāk*, The rattling noise made by any thing tumbling down, or in breaking a bone.

A طراق *tirāk*, (v. n. 3 of طرق) Putting on two garments. Sewing together (two soles). Lining, especially thin leather with which they line boots or shoes. The curvature of a crest on a helmet. A piece of leather cut in the form of a shield, and stuck thereupon. Any piece of workmanship that fits another. (pl. طرق *turk*) A mark set on the middle of a goat's ear. Feathers lying one over the other.

A طرّاق *tirrāk*, Treacle (an antidote). *Turrāk*, (pl. of طارق *tārik*) Necromancers, diviners.

P طراك *tarāk*, Noise, din, clatter.

A طرامة *turāmat*, A greenish tartar on the teeth. Shreds of meat sticking between the teeth.

A طرآن *tur-ān*, A mountain abounding with doves. Unpleasant and bad (road or business).

A طرآني *tur-āniy*, A dove arriving, or an affair happening from some unknown quarter.

A طراوة *tarāwat*, A being fresh. Freshness.

P طراوت ناك *tarāwatnāk*, Fresh, moist, juicy.

P طراوه *tarāwa*, A pennant, a vane.

A طرائد *tarā-id*, (pl. of طريدة *tarīdat*) Things driven, as game into nets. Schooners.

A طرائز *tarā-iz*, Fringes.

A طرائف *tarā-if*, Name of a country. Rare and choice vessels or pieces of furniture: rarities.

A طرائق *tarā-ik*, (pl. of طريقة *tarīkat*) Ways, tracts. Lines or grooves (on a sword-blade). Troops, bodies, sects, assemblies (especially of the superior orders of men). ثوب طرائق *sawb tarā-ik*, A torn or worn garment.

A طرب *tarab*, (v. n. of طرب) Skipping, leaping, dancing for joy. Cheerfulness, mirth, hilarity, joy, gladness, rejoicing, jubilee. Desire, inclination. Motion. Emotion (joyous or sad). Grief, sadness. حسن طرب *husni tarab*, Joyous emotion. *Tarib*, Name of a horse which belonged to Muhammad.

A طربا *taraban*, Joyfully. With emotion.

A طربال *tirbāl*, (pl. طرابيل *tarābīl*) A high tower built on the top of a hill. A Christian church in Syria, with lofty steeples or a belfry. A part of a wall or mountain towering above the rest. A large stone projecting from a mountain. Any building large and lofty. طربال مائل *tirbāli māil*, A leaning tower or wall.

P طرب انگيز *tarab-angez*, Mirth-exciting.

A طربلة *tarbalat*, A making water in the air.

A طربيل *tirbīl*, A flail, a thrashel.

A طرّة *tarrat*, The waist. Impregnation effected by a single covering. *Turrat*, (pl. طرر *turar* and

طرار tirār) The bank (of a river). A coast, shore, tract of country (especially bordering upon another). The edge of a garment, plain or sewed, but not fringed, the selvage. The side, border, or extreme verge. The border of a garment, especially when embroidered of different colours. Long, thin (cloud). Forelocks, ringlets. A particular fashion of dressing the forelocks of a girl. A wallet.

A طرّتان turratāni, (dual of طرّة turrat) Two black streaks on the shoulders of an ass.

A طرثمة tartamat, (v. n. of طرثم Q) Being corrupt and covered by a green film (water). Overspreading. Suiting, agreeing with.

A طرث tars, Any building fresh and new. Tirs, The extremity of the clitoris.

A طرثخة tarsakhat, Lightness, levity, volatility.

A طرثمة tarsamat, A fixing the eyes on the ground in pride or anger.

G طرثوث tarsūs, A fruit, called in Persian بل bil.

A طرثوث tursūs, (pl. طرائيث tarāsīs) A species of fungus, of the form of parsnips, growing under trees, penetrating deep into the ground (one kind is red and sweet, the other white and bitter). Glans penis.

A طرجهارة tarja, (tirjihārat, طرجهالة tarji, or tirjahālat) A drinking vessel. A small cup or bowl.

A طرح tarh, (v. n. of طرح) Throwing, casting, flinging. Making a move at chess, or a throw at backgammon. Driving to a distance. Fixing, laying, placing. Position, establishment, disposition, location. Manner, mode. Foundation of an edifice. P طرح اساس كردن tarhi asās kardan, To lay the foundations. طرح افگندن tarh afgandan, To practise. طرح كردن tarh kardan, To throw away. بطرح دادن ba tarh dādan, To give gratis or for nothing. A Tirh, A distant place. Thrown away, driven forward. Tarah, (v. n. of طرح) Being evil and odious (the disposition). Being blessed with an abundance of the conveniences of life. Distant (place), remote (design). The barberry.

A طرّح turrah, A distant place. Thrown away.

A طرحان tarhān, Prostrate, enfeebled (by disease).

A طرحة tarhat, A kind of cloak of camels' hair hanging from the shoulders.

P طرحدار tarh-dār, Beautiful, well-shaped.

P طرحداري tarh-dārī, Beauty, elegance.

A طرحوم turhūm, Tall. Corrupted, changed in colour and taste (water).

A طرحى tarha', (pl. of طريح) Prostrate. Abject.

A طرخان tarkhān, (pl. طراخنة tarākhinat) A prince (in Khurāsān). One who says whatever he pleases. A kind of vegetable.

P طرخانه tarkhāna, Wheat coarsely ground, boiled to a consistency, and after milk has been poured upon it, is made up into balls, dried, and laid up for future use.

A طرخة tarkhat, A large reservoir at the mouth of a water-pipe.

A طرخثة tarkhasat, Agility, lightness.

P طرخشقون tarkhashkūn, Wild endive.

A طرخف tirkhif, (or طرخفة tirkhifat) Thin butter in a fluid state. The very worst kind of butter.

A P طرخون tarkhūn, Tarragon, a herb.

A طرد tard or tarad, (v. n. of طرد) Banishing, chasing, driving away: persecuting. Putting to flight. Hunting. Seizing or watching for prey, applying one's self to the chace. Driving (camels) from different quarters into one body. Coming to, overtaking, and passing by. Banishment, persecution, propulsion, expulsion. طردا للباب tardan li'l bāb, By driving at the door; done at once. Tarid, Water befouled by the dung of cattle.

A طردة tirdat, One attack or charge of cavalry.

A طردسة tardasat, A tying, binding, fastening.

A طردين turdīn, A kind of food of the Kurds.

G طرذيلون tarzīlūn, Assafœtida.

A طرر turar, (pl. of طرّة turrat) Banks (of rivers). Edges of garments, plain or sewed, but not fringed.

A طرز tarz, Form, manner, habit, fashion. Rule, law. طرز كلام tarzi kalām, Idiom. Taraz, (v. n. of طرز) From being thick and rough, becoming elegant; from being bad, becoming good. Being well-dressed, being nice and neat in regard to dress.

P طرز tirz, Decoration. An embroiderer.

P طرزدان tarz-dān, Acquainted with forms.

P طرزيدن tirzīdan, To embroider, work with the needle.

A طرس tars, (v. n. of طرس) Erasing (writing), cancelling. Tirs, (pl. اطراس atrās and طروس turūs) A leaf of paper, a book; a page (especially erased and re-written).

P طرستوج tarastūj, A kind of sea-fish.

A طرسعة tarsaʻat, (v. n. of طرسع Q) Scampering away with fright.

A طرسمة tarsamat, (v. n. of طرسم Q) Keeping silence, fixing the eyes upon the ground. Retiring, retreating (from battle).

A طرسوس tarsūs or tursūs, Tarsus in Cilicia.

P طرسيقوس tursīkūs, Name of a Christian monk or learned man.

A طرش tursh, Deaf (persons). Tarash, (v. n. of طرش) Being deafish, heavy of hearing. Deafness.

A طرشة turshat, A slight deafness.

A طرشحة tarshahat, (v. n. of طرشح Q) Rendering soft (by beating). Softness, flaccidity.

A طرشمة tarshamat, (v. n. of طرشم Q) Being dark.

P طرشيدن tirshīdan, To engage in any work heedlessly. To be anxious, sad, grieved.

A طرط tarat, (v. n. of طرط) Having thin eyebrows or eyelashes. Folly, stupidity. Tarit, Foolish. طرط الحاجبين taritu'l hājibayn, Thin-eyebrowed.

A طرطاء tartāʼ, (fem. of اطرط) Thin of eyelash.

A طرطب turtub or turtubb, Large, flagging breasts. دهدرّين و طرطبّين duhdurrayn wa turtubbayn, A term applied to any one in ridicule.

A طرطبة tartabat, (v. n. of طرطب Q) Calling (sheep or goats) to milk. Running away, fleeing. The whistling sound made by the lips to goats whilst milking them. The agitation of water in the belly. Turtubat, Long-dugged.

A طرطبّة turtubbat, (and طرطبانيّة turtubānīyat) (A she-goat) which has long dugs.

A طرطبّى turtubba', A large, flabby dug. Penis. Large and flabby-breasted (woman).

A طرطبيس tartabīs, Plenty of water. A languid old woman. A she-camel full of milk, and quiet whilst milking.

A طرطر turtur, (imper.) Maintain a frequent and intimate acquaintance with the house of God.

A طرطرة tartarat, (v. n. of طرطر Q) Boasting, vaunting, saying and not doing. Calling (a sheep) by name. Whisking or cocking the tail. The cry of the kata bird.

A طرطور turtūr, Long and slim. Weak and worthless. A high-peaked turban worn by the Arabians.

A طرطوس tartūs, Name of a champion.

A طرطوشة turtūshat, Tortosa in Spain.

A طرعب tarʻab, Disproportionably tall.

A طرغشة targhashat, A walking, stirring about.

P طرف tarf, A side, corner. An angle of the eye. A girdle. An iron hoop round a chest. Taraf, Part, portion.

A طرف tarf, (v. n. of طرف) Averting, turning away, repelling. Giving one a blow on the eye and making the tears to flow. Looking at, beholding. Winking. Closing the eyelid. Giving a slap. (pl. اطراف atrāf, disallowed by some) The eye. The ninth mansion of the moon (two small stars being so named, likewise called عينا الاسد ʻaynā'l asad, The eyes of the lion). A blow, box, slap. A noble, liberal man. Extremity (of a thing). طرف الايوان tarfu'l aywān, The extremity of the piazza, i. e. the upshot of any business. P طرف بربستن tarf bar bastan, To derive advantage. A طرف ثاني tarfi sānī, A defendant. An enemy. A wife. ارتداد الطرف irtidādu't tarf, The twinkling of an eye. Tirf, (pl. اطراف atrāf) (A man) noble, well descended, having a long series of illustrious ancestors. (pl. طروف turūf) High-bred (horse). A liberal, generous man. Grass just sprouted. Newly-acquired (wealth). One who is soon tired and weary of another's society. A camel wandering from pasture to pasture. One recently ennobled. Pleased with, and anxious to possess all he sees. طرف الحديث tirfu'l hadīs, (A woman) pleasant at telling a story. Turf, (pl. of طراف tirāf) Tents of tanned leather. (pl. of طريف tarīf) Fresh, newly-acquired (riches). Taraf, (v. n. of طرف) Cropping the top of herbage and not mingling with the others (a camel). (pl. اطراف atrāf) Side, quarter. End, extremity. Coast, shore, extreme part. A portion. A noble, generous man. طرف البدن *tarafu'l badan*, Hands, feet, and head; also the fingers and those parts subject to ablution. طرف من الارض *taraf mini'l arz*, The nobles or learned of the earth. The distant parts of the earth. طرف من الرجل *taraf mini'r rajul*, A father, brother, paternal uncle, or near relation. طرف بطرف *taraf bi taraf*, (or طرف طرف *taraf taraf*) From side to side, from different quarters. P بر طرف *bar taraf*, Apart, aside, separated. لطيفه بر طرف *latifa bar taraf*, Raillery apart. طرف گرفتن *taraf giriftan*, To protect. To retire into a corner. A اقطع طرفاً *aktaꜥu tarafan*, Sharper-tongued. *Tarif*, (A man) not adhering to one woman or companion. One whose nobility is not of modern date. Nobly-descended on both sides (man).

A طرفاء *tarfāꜥ*, The tamarisk-tree (which is of four kinds.).

A طرفاة *tarfāt*, A single tamarisk-tree.

A طرفاس *tirfās*, A heap of sand round a tree.

A طرفان *tarafāni*, (oblique طرفين *tarafayn*) (dual of طرف *taraf*) Both ends. Tongue and penis. Mouth and anus. Kill or cure.

A طرفة *tarfat*, One wink or twinkle with the eye. A red blood-spot on the eye from a blow or other accident. A scar. Name of a star. One tamarisk-tree. A slap, blow. في طرفة العين *fī tarfati'l ꜥayn*, In the twinkling of an eye. *Turfat*, A watery running from the eyes. A wound from a malignant eye. Any thing new, agreeable, rare, or wonderful, and never possessed before. Newly-acquired property. *Tarafat*, A single tamarisk-tree. *Tarifat*, A she-camel roaming from pasture to pasture. A she-camel, the tip of whose muzzle is peeled with age.

P طرفدار *taraf-dār*, A partisan, follower, or sectary. An assistant. Partial. A prince, magistrate. An officer employed to collect the revenue of particular parts. طرفدار انجم *taraf-dāri anjum*, The sun. طرفدار پنجم *taraf-dāri panjum*, The planet Mars. The monarch of Turkistān. The fifth climate. The Greeks.

P طرفداري *taraf-dārī*, Partiality. Sectarism.

A طرفساء *tirfisāꜥ*, A dark night. Darkness.

A طرفسان *tirfisān*, Darkness. A heap of sand (especially collected about a tree).

A طرفسة *tarfasat*, (v. n. of طرفس Q) Sharpening (sight). Looking through half-shut eyes. Putting on many clothes. Being dark (night), muddy (water). Being much frequented (cistern).

A طرفشة *tarfashat*, (v. n. of طرفش Q) Being weak and dim (eye). Looking through half-shut eyes. Going, stirring one's self, rising.

P طرفگي *turfagī*, Wonderfulness: a rarity.

P طرفگير *taraf-gīr*, A partisan. Partial.

P طرفگيري *taraf-gīrī*, Partiality, partisanship.

P طرفه *turfa*, Any thing new and agreeable. Surprise. طرفهٔ شش طاق *turfaꜥi shash tāk*, The world.

A طرفيل *tirfīl*, Trefoil, clover.

A طرفين *tarafayn*, (oblique of طرفان *tarafāni*, du.) Both sides. ذو الطرفين *zū't tarafayn*, A kind of serpent that has a sting at either extremity, without being deadly. كريم الطرفين *karīmu't tarafayn*, Noble by father and mother.

A طرق *tark*, (v. n. of طرق) Arriving in the night. Knocking at a door. Covering the female (a camel). Striking violently or with a smith's hammer. Beating with a rod (cotton), in order to separate and to rarefy it. Mixing wool and cotton when practising divination. Throwing pebble-stones and gravel, in order to prognosticate future events (a diviner). Defiling water by their dung (cattle). Drinking muddy water. Touching a harp, lute, or similar instrument. Water defiled by the dung of cattle. Weakness of intellect. A palm-tree. A stallion that covers. Once. Sperma genitale. الوضوء بالطرق احبّ اليّ من التيمّم *al wazūꜥ bi't tark ahabbu ilayya' mini't tayammum*, Ablution with water defiled by the dung and urine of cattle is more pleasing to me than that with sand. طرقا او طرقين *tarkan aw tarkayn*, Once or twice. *Tirk*, Fat, tallow, grease. Fatness. Craft, trade, calling. Strength, courage: as, ما به طرق *mā bihi tirk*, He has no strength. *Turk*, (v. n. of طرق) Arriving at night. Leaping on the female (a stallion). (pl. of طريق *tarīk*) Roads. (pl. of طراق *tirāk*) Marks on (goats') ears. *Tarak*, (v. n. of طرق) Limping; being bow-legged and weak in the knees. Lying one over another (bird's feathers). A place where water collects. (pl. اطراق *atrāk*) A ply, fold, wrinkle (of the belly or of a leathern bottle almost empty). The turning down the top of a leathern bottle in order to drink. (pl. of طرقة *tarakat*) Orders, lines, rows. Places where waters stagnate. The prints of camels' feet following each other. Gins, snares. *Turak*, (pl. of طرقة *turkat*) Grooves in bows. *Turuk*, (pl. of طريق *tarīk*) Ways, roads.

A طرقاء *tarkāꜥ*, (A she-camel) crook-legged; weak in the knees.

A طرقات *turukāt*, (pl. of طرق *turuk*, pl. of طريق *tarīk*) Ways, paths, roads. Many ways.

A طرقة *tarkat*, A work, art, craft. A fowler's net, gin, snare. Once. طرقة او طرقتين *tarkat aw tarkatayn*, Once or twice. *Tirkat*, A gin, snare. One thing laid on another. *Turkat*, (pl. طرق *turak*) The guiding line on the handle of a bow. A road, way. Custom, habit. Darkness. A heap of stones. Fold upon fold. Any one thing laid upon another. Foolish, silly; a fool. Handiwork. Concupiscence. *Tarakat*, (pl. طرق *tarak*) One line (of camels). A fowler's snare. The print of a camel's foot. *Turakat*, One who travels much by night (to join his friends).

A طرّكونة *tarrakūnat*, Tarragon in Spain.

A طرم *tarm* or *tirm*, Butter. Honey. A full honeycomb. *Turm*, A chafing-dish. A kind of tree. *Taram*, (v. n. of طرم) Being covered with tartar (the teeth). Dropping from a full comb (honey). The flowing of honey from the comb.

P طرم *turum*, The noise of a drum.

A طرمّاح *tirimmāh*, High and celebrated. Aspiring, ambitious. Provident, foreseeing.

A طرماذ *tirmāz*, Vain-glorious. A boaster.

A طرمة *tarmat*, The liver. *Tarmat*, *tirmat*, or *turmat*, A pimple on the middle of the upper lip. *Turmat*, A chafing-dish.

A طرمح *tarmah*, One who takes long strides.

A طرمحانيّة *tarmahāniyat*, Pride, haughtiness.

A طرمحة *tarmahat*, The carrying out an edifice to a considerable length.

A طرمذار *tarmazār*, A boaster.

A طرمذان *tirmizān*, Vain-glorious: a boaster.

A طرمذة *tarmazat*, (v. n. of طرمذ Q) Boasting, vaunting. Promising but not performing. *Tirmizat*, One who makes false promises. One who does not act in a straightforward manner.

A طرمساء *tirmisāꜥ*, Thick darkness. A thin cloud. Dust.

A طرمسة *tarmasat*, (v. n. of طرمس Q) Being drawn in, contracted. Departing, desisting through fear. Erasing writing. Knitting the eyebrows. Contraction. Austerity, sternness. Retreat, flight.

A طرمشة *tarmashat*, Darkness (of the night).

A طرموث *turmūs*, Weak. Bread baked under the ashes.

A طرموح *turmūh*, Long, tall.

A طرموس *turmūs*, Bread baked in the ashes.

A طرموق *turmūk*, A bat or rere-mouse.

P طرموي *tarmoy*, A kind of hawk.

A طرن *turn*, Raw silk. Stuff of the same.

G طرنجومانس *taranjūmānis*, Maidens'-hair.

A طروّ *turūw*, An arriving from afar.

A طروء *turūꜥ*, A coming unexpectedly.

A طروب *tarūb*, One who moves with alacrity from joy or sorrow.

A طروح *tarūh*, A distant place. Strong and far-shooting (bow). Long-branched (palm-tree). A man who lies with a woman and begets a child.

A طروحة *turūhat*, Tribute.

A طرور *turūr*, (v. n. of طرّ) Driving cattle together from different parts. Splitting, cleaving. Patching or plastering (a cistern) with clay. Elevating (a building). Falling by a blow of a sword (the hand). Shining (the stars). Sharpening (a knife or spear). Sprouting (herbage or whiskers). A certain mode of dressing the forelocks of a girl.

A طرورة *turūrat*, The sprouting (of grass).

A طروس *turūs*, (pl. of طرس *tirs*) Erased, cancelled sheets of paper.

A طروف *turūf*, (pl. of طرف *tirf*) Excellent, high-bred (horses).

A طروق *turūk*, (v. n. of طرق) Arriving at night. Covering the female (a camel).

A طروقة *tarūkat*, A marriageable girl. Any young female ready for the male.

G طروقوقون *tarūkūkūn*, A medlar.

G طروقون *turūkūn*, Cock's-comb (an herb).

P طرّة *turra*, A waving ringlet, dangling forelock, tuft of frizzled, braided, or curled hair. The end of a turban hanging loose. A nosegay. Twisted leathern thongs, with which they beat the small brazen drums hung at their saddle-bows. The black stripe on either shoulder of an ass. طرّهٔ عنبرين *turrasi ɛambarīn*, (or طرّهٔ مشكين *turrasi mushkīn*) Tresses of ambergris or musk (from their colour). از طرّهٔ مشك شام تا غرّهٔ بيضائ بام *az turrasi mushki shām tā ghurrasi bayzāsi bām*, From the musk-like (or sable) locks of the evening to the white star on the forehead of Aurora, *i. e.* from night till morning.

A طرهدة *tarhadat*, A vain boast.

A طرّي *tara'*, (v. n. of طري) Approaching, advancing. Passing by.

A طرّيٰ *turra'*, A she-ass pursued to a distance.

A طريّ *tariy*, (or طرىٔ *tariء*) Fresh, green, moist, humid, new. P گياه سرسبز طري *giyāhi sar-sabzi tari*, Herbs green and fresh.

A طرياق *tiryāk*, Treacle, theriaca. Opium.

P طرياقي *tiryākī*, A chewer of opium.

A طرّيان *tirriyān*, Tables with meat laid thereon.

P طريبله *tirībula*, The lote-tree.

A طريح *tarīh*, Thrown prostrate. Abject.

P طريخ *tarīkh*, A small kind of fish.

A طرّيخ *tirrīkh*, Small fish pickled: a sardine.

A طريد *tarīd*, Banished. Driven, propelled. The trunk of a tree, crooked and destitute of leaves and branches. A bunch of dates. Long (day). (A brother) born immediately after another.

A طريدان *tarīdāni*, (du. of طريد) Night and day.

A طريدة *tarīdat*, Any thing forced or driven (as prey into a net). Stolen or driven away by stealth (herd of camels). A narrow strip of ground or pasturage. A long strip of silk. A sort of game, commonly called مسّة *massat* or ضبطة *zabtat*. A dampcloth, with which an oven is cleaned. A notched reed, used for smoothing a spindle or an arrow.

P طريده *tarīda*, A swift arrow. A robber.

A طرير *tarīr*, Sharpened (spear-head). A youth whose mustachios begin to grow. Sharp-sighted.

P طريغان *tarīghān*, A kind of endive.

A طريف *tarīf*, (pl. طرف *turf*) New, fresh, newly acquired. One who traces his descent through a long line of ancestors. Foreign, strange, rare.

A طريفة *tarīfat*, The plant نصيّ *nasīy*, when compact and full-grown.

P طريفلن *tarīfalan*, The lote-tree.

P طريفه ناك *tarīfanāk*, Abundant in the plant نصيّ *nasīy*, when compact and full-grown.

A طريق *tarīk*, (pl. اطرق *atruk*, طرق *turuk*, *turk*, اطرقاء *atrikāء*, اطرقة *atrikat*, and طرقات *turukāt*) A way, road, path. Manner, mode. (pl. of طريقة *tarīkat*) Tall palm-trees. طريق اوسط *tarīki awsat*, The middle road. طريق عام *tarīki ɛām*, A public road. طريق ما *tarīki mā*, A water-course. *Turayk*, A palm-tree.

A طرّيق *tirrīk*, Taciturn. A male bustard or crane. امّ طرّيق *ummu turrayk*, The hyena.

A طريقة *tarīkat*, A road, way, path. A furrow. A line. State, condition. Manner, way, fashion. Religion, sect. (pl. طريق *tarīk*) A tall palm-tree. Palm-trees growing in a row. A strip of cloth of woollen or camels' hair about a cubit in breadth, connecting the opening parts of a tent. A head man, or (plurally) the chiefs or better sort of people. The stick of a parasol. A musical air. A Christian burial-ground. P پير طريقت *pīri tarīkat*, A prior or head man of a sect.

A طرّيقة *tirrīkat*, Gentleness, softness. Obedience. Soft, even ground.

A طريم *tarīm*, Anger. طار طريمه *tāra tarīmuhu*, He waxed wroth. *Tiryam*, A thick cloud, mass lying upon mass. Honey. Tall of stature (man).

A طرين *tiryan*, Thin clay. اتىٰ بالطرين والغرين *ata' bi't tiryan wa'l ghiryan*, He was enraged.

A طرينة *taryanat*, (v. n. of طرين Q) Being muddled with intoxication (a drinking-party).

A طزر *tazr*, A shoving away with a blow or a kick. *Tazar*, (from P تزر *tazar*) A summer-dwelling. A plant growing in the summer.

A طزع *tazɛ*, (v. n. of طزع) Sitting still, not attacking the enemy. Lying with. *Tazaɛ*, (v. n. of طزع) Being free from jealousy. Being destitute of meat or money. Being greedy and needy. Being impudent. *Taziɛ*, Free from jealousy or punctilio. In want of meat and money.

A طزيع *tazīɛ*, Indigent, destitute of meat or money. Free from jealousy, unsuspecting. Greedy.

A طسّ *tass*, (v. n. of طسّ) Overcoming, silencing (an opponent). Putting or plunging under water. Going away. *Tass*, (طسّة *tassat*, or *tissat*) (pl. طسوس *tusūs*, طساس *tisās*, طسيس *tasīs*, and طسّات *tassāt*) A cup, a bason, tassie.

A طسأ *tasء*, (or طساء *tasāء*) (v. n. of طسأ) Having the stomach oppressed with any thing fat. Being ashamed, blushing.

A طسا *tasa'*, (v. n. of طسي) Having the stomach overloaded with any thing fat. Oppressing, causing indigestion.

A طسّات *tassāt*, (pl. of طسّ *tass*) Cups, basons.

A طساس *tisās*, (pl. of طسّ *tass*, طسّة *tassat*, *tissat*, and طست *tast*) Bowls, basons, cups.

A طسّاس *tassās*, A cup or bason-maker.

A طساسة *tisāsat*, The art of bason-making.

A طساسيج *tasāsīj*, (pl. of طسّوج *tassūj*) Parts, tracts. Quarters of a دانق *dānik*, or twenty-fourth parts of drams.

A طسام *tasām*, (*tusām*, *tassām*, and طسّان *tassān*) Dust when raised and driven about by the wind.

A طست *tast*, (طسّة *tass*, or *tissat*) A cup, bason.

A طستخان *tastikhān* or *tistikhān*, (from P تست *tast*, Bowl, cup, and خوان *khwān*, A table) A large flat plate of silver or other metals, upon which other cups or dishes are placed, and used as a table by those who eat sitting on the ground.

A طسع *tasɛ*, (v. n. of طسع) Traversing (a country). Lying with. *Tasaɛ*, (v. n. of طسع) Being impudent, wanton-eyed, and free from due respect towards women. Being desirous, covetous, greedy. *Tasiɛ*, Impudent, wanton-eyed. Desirous, greedy.

A طسق *task* or *tisk*, A tax upon lands. Tribute exacted. A sort of measure.

A طسك *task*, A kind of measure. Land-tax.

A طسل *tasl*, Water flowing on the surface of the ground. The glittering of the water-like vapour سراب *sarāb*.

A طسم *tasm*, (v. n. of طسم) Being obliterated (a path). An extinct branch of the tribe of عاد *ɛād*. (Tasm was son of لاوي *lāwa'*, son of Shem, son of Noah). ذوات طسم *zawāt tasm*, Name of certain chapters of the Kur'ān. *Tasam*, (v. n. of طسم) Being oppressed with indigestion, and swollen. Darkness, beginning of night. A dusty colour.

A طسن *tāsan*, (pl. ذوات طسن *zawāt tāsan*) Name of a certain chapter of the Kur'ān.

A طسّوج *tassūj*, (pl. طساسيج *tasāsīj*) A weight of two grains of barley; the twenty-fourth part of a dram. A coast, shore, tract of land.

A طسوس *tusūs*, (pl. of طسّ *tass*, طسّة *tassat*, and *tissat*) Cups, bowls, basons.

A طسوم *tusūm*, (v. n. of طسم) Erasing, obliterating. Becoming defaced, cancelled, obliterated.

A طسيء *tasīء*, Oppressed, incommoded by indigestion or fat meat.

A طسيت *tusayt*, (dim. of طست *tast*) A small cup or bason.

A طسيس *tasīs*, (pl. of طسّ *tass*, طسّة *tassat*, and *tissat*) Bowls, cups, basons. *Tusays*, (dim. of طسّ *tass*) A little bason. A small cup.

A طسيع *tasīɛ*, Impudent. Desirous, greedy.

A مياه طسيم *miyāh tusaym*, Error, delusion.

A طشّ *tashsh*, A raining gently. Thin rain.

A طشاءة *tashāsat*, (v. n. of طشأ) Lying with.

A طشأة *tush* or *tushasat*, Rheum. A stammerer.

A طشاش *tashāsh*, A sprinkling (with water, tears, or blood). *Tushāsh*, Rheum, defluxion.

A طشّة *tishshat*, An infant. *Tushshat*, Rheum.

P طشت *tasht*, A large bason, ewer, cup, bowl. طشت زر *tashti zar*, A golden dish. The sun. طشت زرّين *tashti zarrīn*, A golden bowl, goblet. طشت نگون *tashti nigūn*, (Inverted bowl) Sky.

P طشت دار *tasht-dār*, (Ewer-holder) The servant who pours water on the hands when washing.

طشت دار خانه *tasht-dār khāna*, A butler's pantry.

P طشتگر *tashtgar*, A maker of basons. Name of a musician.

P A طشت و خايه *tasht u khāya*, (Bason and egg) The filling of an eggshell with a fluid (in Persian شبنم *shab-nam*, Dew), and placing it in a bason exposed to the sun; when the bason becomes heated, the eggshell ascends and flies in the air like a balloon (a kind of philosophical toy). Heaven and earth. Astronomy. Magic.

A طشط *tasht*, (pl. طشوط *tushūt*) A bason.

A طشيش *tashīsh*, Gentle rain.

A طع *tagg*, (v. n. of طع) Licking (a dish).

A طعام *taʻām*, (v. n. of طعم) Eating, tasting. (pl. اطعمة *atʻimat*) A meal. Wheat. Meat, viands, victuals, food, refreshment. Water; or the water of the well Zamzam. طعام عروسي *taʻāmi ʻarūsī*, A wedding-feast. طعام ماتم *taʻāmi mātam*, A funeral-banquet. بعد الطعام الكلام *baʻdu't taʻām al kalām*, After meat, conversation (a saying).

P طعام بخش *taʻām-bakhsh*, A ladle.

P طعام تلاش *taʻām-talāsh*, A sponger.

A طعاميّه *taʻāmiya*, Expenses for provisions.

A طعان *taʻān*, (v. n. of طعن) Spearing in battle.

A طعّان *taʻʻān*, A spearer. A slanderer.

A طعب *taʻb*, Pleasure, delight, enjoyment.

A طعثنة *taʻsanat*, Bad-tempered (woman). Numerous (flock of sheep).

A طعر *taʻr*, (v. n. of طعر) Marrying. Bringing to justice by compulsion.

A طعز *taʻz*, (v. n. of طعز) Repelling. Copulating.

A طعزبة *taʻzabat*, Ridicule, irony.

A طعس *taʻs*, (v. n. of طعس) Lying with.

A طعسبة *taʻsabat*, Extreme iniquity, oppression.

A طعسفة *taʻsafat*, (v. n. of طعسف Q) Stamping on the ground. Walking unevenly.

A طعطع *tuʻtuʻ*, Plain, level ground.

A طعطعة *taʻtaʻat*, The sound made when licking or sucking any thing nice and savoury.

A طعل *taʻl*, (v. n. of طعل) Piercing, stabbing. Cursing or reviling.

A طعم *taʻima*, (fut. يطعم *yatʻamu*) He ate.

A طعم *taʻm*, (v. n. of طعم) Eating, tasting. (v. n. of طعم) Being grafted upon. Being satiated. *Taʻm* or *tuʻm*, Intellect. Power, strength. (pl. طعوم *tuʻūm*) The finest flavour of victuals. Taste, flavour. Any thing that excites the appetite. *Tuʻm*, (v. n. of طعم) Tasting. Sipping to try the taste or flavour of any thing. Being able. Being full of marrow (a bone). Food, eatables. Meat which satiates. Taste, flavour, relish. *Taʻim*, A man who eats elegantly, or hunts after delicacies. *Tuʻam*, (pl. of طعمة *tuʻmat*) Eatables, viands. Dinners.

A طعمة *tiʻmat*, A manner in eating or tasting. *Tuʻmat*, (pl. طعم *tuʻam*) Meat, food, fodder, forage. Birds' food. A bait, lure. An invitation to an entertainment. Dinner. A meal. A dining-room, or any place where people eat. Gain, profit, any mode of acquisition. Wages, salary. The woof.

P طعمت دادن *tuʻmat dādan*, To bait, set a bait.

A طعن *taʻn*, (v. n. of طعن) Piercing with a spear. Chiding, reviling, reproaching, cursing. Departing (for the desert), penetrating (into it). Travelling all night. Giving a full and loose rein (to a horse). Blame, disapprobation. Accusation. طعن في السنّ *taʻuna fi's sinn*, He is stricken in years. طعن و لعن *taʻn u laʻn*, Reproaching and cursing. *Tuʻn*, (pl. of طعين *taʻīn*) Speared.

P طعن آميز *taʻn-āmez*, Mixed with reproach.

A طعنان *taʻnān*, (v. n. of طعن) Cursing, reproaching, reviling. Spearing one another in battle.

A طعنة *taʻnat*, One blow (with spear or tongue). Contumely, taunt, reproach, sarcasm, gibe, ignominy, disgrace (as conveyed by reproachful words).

P خامهٔ سيه زبان و نامهٔ طعنه زنان *khāmaʼi siyah-zabān u nāmaʼi taʻna-zanān*, Pens having sable tongues, and letters which strike with reproach.

P طعنه زن *taʻna-zan*, Reproaching, vilifying.

A طعوم *taʻūm*, (or طعيم *taʻīm*) A camel in good case, neither too fat nor lean. *Tuʻūm*, (pl. of طعم *taʻm*) Fine flavours in viands. Tastes, flavours.

A طعومة *taʻūmat*, Home-fed (sheep) for killing.

A طعين *taʻīn*, (pl. طعن *tuʻn*) Pierced with a spear. Afflicted with pestilence (طاعون *tāʻūn*).

A طغ *taghgh*, A bull.

A طغا *tagha'*, A sound, voice.

A طغاة *tughāt*, (pl. of طاغي) Rebels, insurgents.

A طغام *taghām*, Of a mean inferior order (a man or men); the worst species of birds. A fool.

A طغامة *taghāmat*, A mean kind of bird or man. A fool.

A طغر *taghr*, (v. n. of طغر) Rushing, coming down upon. Thrusting, pushing away. *Tughar*, (pl. طغران *tighrān*) Name of a bird.

P طغرا *tughrā*, The imperial signature. The royal titles prefixed to letters, diplomas, or other public deeds, which are generally written in a fine ornamented hand.

A طغران *tighrān*, (pl. of طغر) Kinds of birds.

P طغرائي *tughrāʼī*, Expert in writing the Toghra character. Name of the author of an admired Arabic poem, which has been translated into Latin by Pocock under the title of Carmen Tograi, and into English verse by Carlyle.

P طغرل *tughril*, Name of a king of the Seljukian dynasty. *Tughrul*, A kind of falcon.

P طغري *tughrī*, A sort of falcon for hunting.

P طغك *taghak*, A tree like a cypress or pine.

A طغم *tagham*, The sea. Much water.

A طغمشة *taghmashat*, Weakness of sight.

A طغموس *tughmūs*, Wicked, malignant (demon).

A طغوان *tughwān*, An exceeding of bounds in wickedness, a being insolent. Insolence, rebellion.

A طغوة *taghwat*, A high place. A little, small quantity (of any thing). The summit of a mountain.

A طغومة *tughūmat*, (or طغوميّة *tughūmiyat*) Folly, stupidity, ignorance. Baseness, meanness.

A طغوي *taghwa'*, Rebellion, disobedience. Insolence. معين تقوي و مانع طغوي *muʻīni takwa' u māniʻi taghwa'*, The assister of piety, and repeller of wickedness. *Tughwa'*, An exceeding of bounds in wickedness, a being insolent. Insolence.

A طغي *taghy*, (v. n. of طغي) Being rebellious, insolent, impious, unjust, exceeding bounds in wickedness. Breaking forth, overflowing (water). Dashing (billows). Boiling (blood). Lowing (the wild cow). *Tagha'*, Sound, noise, voice.

A طغيا *ta* or *tughya'*, A small wild cow. A bull.

A طغيان *tughyān* or *tighyān*, (v. n. of طغى) Being very rebellious, exceeding bounds in wickedness. Overflowing (a torrent). Raging (the sea). Boiling (blood). Lowing (the wild cow). Rebellion, sedition, disobedience, perverseness, insolence. اهل طغيان *ahli tughyān*, Rebellious. Rebels. P بازمرهٔ طغيان *bāzumraʼi tughyān*, With a body of insurgents.

A طغية *taghyat*, The loftiest and most difficult ridge of a mountain. A tract, a coast. A smooth stone. A small portion, particle.

A طفّ *taff*, (v. n. of طفّ) Filling (a measure or a vessel) to the brim. Happening, offering itself, being possible. Being near. Lifting with the hand or foot. Tying (a camel) by the feet. The upper part of a measure not filled. That which is heaped above the measure; also what remains in it after that surplus is smoothed off. Fulness to the brim. A side, shore, coast, bank (especially high). The higher part of Mesopotamia, bordering on Arabia and Chaldea. Sprightly, swift (horse). طفّ الصاع *taffu's sāʻ*, Short of filling the measure.

A طفاح *tifāh*, Plentitude, fulness.

A طفاحة *tufāhat*, What runs over a boiling pot, the froth or scum.

A طفّاحة *taffāhat*, Swift, nimble (she-camel).

A طفاسة *tafāsat*, (v. n. of طفس) Being dirty, filthy (a man or a garment). Filth, nastiness.

A طفاشاء *tafāshāʼ*, Emaciated, lean (woman).

A طفاطف *tafātif*, (pl. of طفطفة *taftafat*) Hypochondria, those parts lying under the spurious ribs. Soft parts of the belly.

A طفاف *tafāf*, Darkness of the night. The brim. *Tafāf* or *tifāf*, Fulness to the brim. That which is heaped above the measure; also what remains in it after that surplus is smoothed off. *Tifāf*, Darkness of the night. *Tufāf*, That which is heaped above the measure.

A طفّاف *taffāf*, Sprightly, swift (horse).

A طفافة *tufāfat*, The compliment; also the redundancy of a measure. The upper part of a measure not filled.

A طفال *tafāl* or *tufāl*, Dry clay. *Tifāl*, (pl. of طفل *tafl*) Young and tender (boys or girls).

A طفالة *tafālat*, (v. n. of طفل) Being young and tender. Tender age, infancy.

A طفّان *taffān*, Filled to the brim.

A طفانية *tafāniyat*, A contumelious reproach.

A طفانين *tafānīn*, A lie; idle, trifling, discourse. A prison. A lingering behind.

A طفاوة *tufāwat*, Part (of spring). Halo round the sun or moon. Overflowings of a boiling pot.

A طفح *tafh*, (v. n. of طفح) Being full, running over (a vessel). Filling (a thing) till it overflows. Departing, going away. (Wind) carrying off (cotton). Bringing forth (a fœtus) fully formed.

A طفحان *tafhān*, (fem. طفحي *tafha'*) Overflowing (dish).

A طفذ *tafz*, (v. n. of طفذ) Burying, laying in the grave. *Tafz* or *tafaz*, (pl. اطفاذ *atfāz*) A tomb.

A طفر *tafr*, A crupper.

A طفرة *tafrat*, A leap, upward spring. Cream.

A طفرس *tifris*, Soft, easy, smooth.

A طفس *tafs*, (v. n. of طفس) Lying with. *Tafas*, (v. n. of طفس) Being dirty, filthy (garment or man). Filth, nastiness. *Tafis*, Dirty, filthy.

A طفش *tafsh*, Concubitus. Filth.

G طفشيقون *tafshīkūn*, Toxicum, with which they poison arrows.

A طفشيل *tifshīl*, (P طفشيله) Boiled lentils.

A طفطاف *taftāf*, A coast, shore. The sides (of a tree).

A طفطفة *taftafat*, (v. n. of طفطف Q) Becoming weak and submissive in the hand of an adversary. (pl. طفاطف *tafātif*) The hypochondria; also all tremulous loose flesh, or soft part of the belly.

A طفف *tafaf*, A heaped-up measure. Fulness to the brim; also what remains after the surplus has been smoothed off.

A طففة *tafafat*, Redundancy of any measure: also the surplus which falls off.

A طفق *tafk*, (v. n. of طفق) Being fixed to, or busy in any place. Realizing one's wish. Setting about any thing which one means to finish.

A طفل *tafl*, (v. n. of طفل) Beginning to turn dark, near sunset. Rising (the sun). Reddening towards setting (the sun). Bringing up well her young (a she-camel). Entering upon darkness. (pl. طفال *tifāl* or طفول *tufūl*) Young and tender (boy or girl). *Tifl*, (pl. اطفال *atfāl*) An infant, a little boy. The young of wild beasts. Necessity. Night. Sunset. Part of any thing, especially a spark of fire from a tinder-box. P طفل چهل روزه *tifli chihal roza*, A child of forty days, *i. e.* Adam. طفل خوني *tifli khūnī*, The sun. طفل زبان دان *tifli zabān-dān*, A child who understands and remembers what his teacher has once told him. طفل غازيان *tifli ghāziyān*, Beardless youths. Wandering monks. طفل مشيمهٔ رزان *tifli mashīmaʼi razān*, Red wine. طفل هندو *tifli hindū*, The pupil of the eye. طفلان آتش *tiflāni ātish*, Sparks of fire. A *Tafal*, (v. n. of طفل) Being soiled with dirt (grass). Going uninvited to a feast. Tender age, infancy. The time from عصر *ʻasr* (which is the middle point between the meridian and sunset) till sun-down. The close of the evening. The dawn. Darkness. Rain.

P طفلانه *tiflāna*, Infantine. Childishly.

A طفلة *taflat*, Young and tender (female).

P طفلگان *tiflagān*, Children.

P طفله *tafla*, Cumine-seed. *Tifla*, A child.

A طفلي *tiflī*, Infancy. Childishness.

A طفليّة *tifliyat*, Childhood, infancy.

A طفليل *tiflīl*, Who comes uninvited to a feast.

A طفن *tafn*, Death. A prison. Durance.

A طفنّش *tafannash*, One whose feet are broad at the root of the toes.

A طفنشأ *tafanshaʼ*, (or طفنشاء *tafanshāʼ*) Weak-sighted. Weak, enervated. Timid.

A طفنشل *tafanshal*, Weak, feeble (man).

A طفو *tafw*, (or طفوّ *tufūw*) (v. n. of طفا for طفو) Swimming, floating. Appearing (as a bull upon a hill). Springing (leaves). Bounding, leaping (a doe). Dying (a man). Plunging into business.

A طفوء *tufūʼ*, (v. n. of طفئ) Being extinguished, going out (fire). Being darkened, blinded (eye).

A طفوة *tafwat*, A slender plant.

A طفوح *tufūh*, (v. n. of طفح) Being full, running over (a vessel).

A طفور *tufūr*, (v. n. of طفر) Leaping, rearing.

A طفوس *tufūs*, (v. n. of طفس) Dying (a horse).

A طفوق *tufūk*, (v. n. of طفق) Realising one's wish. Being fixed to, or busy in, a place. Setting about any thing which one intends to finish.

A طفول *tufūl*, (pl. of طفل *tafl*) Young and tender.

A طفولة *tufūlat*, (v. n. of طفل) Being young and tender. *Tufūlat*, (or طفوليّة *tufūliyat*) Infancy, childhood, boyhood. P در اعوام طفوليّت *dar aʻwāmi tufūliyat*, In the years of childhood.

A طفي *tufy*, A leaf of the dwarf palm-tree.

A طفية *tufyat*, (pl. طفيً *tufa'*) A leaf of the dwarf palm-tree; also (in the dual) two lines resembling it on the back of a serpent. A malignant serpent, marked on the back with two such black lines.

A طفيشل *tafayshal*, A kind of broth.

A طفيف *tafīf*, Little, deficient, incomplete.

A طفيل *tafīl*, Muddy water remaining in a cistern or a pond. *Tifyal*, An infant. The young of man or beast. *Tufayl*, (dim. of طفل *tifl*) A little child. *Tufayl*, (and طفيليّ *tufayliy*) A companion, especially an humble one. A parasite, feast-hunter, trencher-fly. Cause, means.

A طق *tak*, The sound made by the collision or rattling of stones. *Tik*, That of a frog jumping out of or into the water.

A طقس *taks*, (pl. طقوس *tukūs*) Order, ceremony, ecclesiastical constitution.

P طقطق *taktak*, A noise in general. The noise made by the teeth in masticating.

A طقطقة *taktakat*, (v. n. of طقطق Q) Making a clatter when gallopping over stones (a horse). The noise thus made.

A طلو *tahw*, Quickness of step.

P طل *tul*, A widow.

A طلّ *tall*, (v. n. of طلّ) (Dew) slightly moistening (the ground). Shedding blood with impunity. Being bedewed (the ground). Keeping back, restraining. Being spilt unrevenged (blood). Driving (camels) violently. Defrauding, cheating. Making void. Plating, washing over. Delaying payment of a debt. (pl. طلال *tilāl* and طلل *tilal*) A gentle rain, dew. Beautiful, charming (hair, water, or night). Milk. Scarcity of camels' milk. A serpent. A very old man. *Till*, A serpent. *Tull*, (v. n. of طلّ) Being shed with impunity (blood). Milk. Blood. Fat. A scarcity of camels' milk. The neck. A draught of milk.

A طلا *tala'*, (pl. اطلاء *atlāʼ*, طلاء *tilāʼ*, طليان *tulyān*, or *tilyān*) A fawn just dropt. The young, especially of any animal which parts the hoof. A person, body. Sick, diseased. Desire, will, wish. Spittle drying in the mouth. Anointed with saffron or pitch. جميل الطلا *jamīlu't tala'*, Handsome, beautiful. *Tila'*, Pleasure, delight, enjoyment.

P طلا *tilā*, Gold. Gold fringe or wire. طلا و سيم *tilāʼu sīm*, Gold and silver.

A طلاء *tilāʼ*, Any thing used in anointing, especially pitch. Ointment, liniment, embrocation. Must boiled down to one half. Delicious wine. A rope by which a calf or lamb is tied to a stake. Contumely, contempt, outrage. (pl. of طلا *tala'*) Fawns just dropt. Young animals. *Tulāʼ*, A pellicle, thin skin or film upon blood.

A طلّاء *tallāʼ*, Blood shed with impunity. Blood. *Tullāʼ*, A pellicle upon blood. A scratch which fetches blood. Blood.

A طلاب *tilāb*, (v. n. 3 of طلب) Inquiring, searching, asking. Exhorting, encouraging.

A طلّاب *tallāb*, (pl. طلّابون *tallābūn*) One who asks, seeks, or inquires. *Tullāb*, (pl. of طالب *tālib*) Students, curious inquirers.

P طلابه *talāba*, A scout, spy. Watch and ward.

A طلاة *tulāt*, The neck. A scabby she-camel. A bit of rag with which a she-camel is anointed.

A طلاح *talāh*, A bad state (the reverse of صلاح *salāh*). *Tilāh*, The acacia.

A طلاحة *talāhat*, (v. n. of طلح) Being fatigued (a camel). Tiring (a camel).

A طلاحيٌ *talāha'*, (Camels) griped from eating of the acacia.

A طلاحيّ *tilāhiy* or *tulāhiy*, (A camel) feeding on the acacia. Belonging to that tree.

P طلادوز *tilā-doz*, An embroiderer with gold.

A طلّاسة *tallāsat*, A cloth with which they wipe tablets, effacing what is written: a wiper.

A طلاسم *talāsim*, (pl. of طلسم) Talismans.

A طلاطل *tulātil*, Death. A calamity. *Tulā* or *talātil*, An incurable distemper corroding the back.

A طلاطلة *tulātilat*, A misfortune. Death. A disease affecting the loins of an ass. A swelling of the throat, or the falling of the uvula.

A طلاع *tilāʻ*, (v. n. 3 of طلع) Considering. Being attentive to, looking at, reading. Proposing. Exhibiting for inspection or to be read. (pl. طلع *tulʻ*) Fulness, plenty of earth or soil. Whatever the sun shines upon. رجل طلاع الثنايا و الانجد *rajulun tallāʻu's sanāyā' wa'l anjudi*, A man who meditates and masters high things.

A طلافح *talāfih*, Things wide and broad. A broad mark upon the thigh. *Tulāfih*, Thin marrow.

A طلاق *talāk*, (v. n. of طلق) Being divorced (a wife). Divorce, repudiation. طلاق بدعت *talāki bidʻat*, Irregular divorce. طلاق حسن *talāki hasan*, Laudable divorce. كتاب الطلاق *kitābu't talāk*, A bill of divorcement.

A طلاقة *talākat*, (v. n. of طلق) Being temperate (the day or night). Being of an open countenance. Eloquence, glibness of tongue. Openness, freshness, joyousness of countenance.

P طلاق نامه *talāk-nāma*, A bill of divorce.

P طلاكاري *tilā-kārī*, Gilding.

A طلال *tilāl*, (pl. of طلّ *tall*) Gentle rains.

A طلالة *talālat*, (v. n. of طل) Being pleasant, agreeable. Being amazed, astonished, delighted. Joy, gladness. A beautiful, handsome state, quality, form, or appearance. A body, figure. Any thing extant, as traces of a house.

A طلّام *tullām*, Hemp-seed.

A طلاوة *talāwat*, Delay, expectation, a waiting for, looking for. *Ta*, *ti*, or *tulāwat*, Beauty, grace, loveliness, elegance. Joyousness. Attractiveness. A pellicle on the surface of blood or milk. Remains of meat in the mouth after eating. Saliva drying up in the mouth from indisposition. Magic.

A طلائح *talāʼih*, (pl. of طليح *talīh*) (Camels) jaded and attenuated with travelling.

A طلائع *talāʼiʻ*, (pl. of طليعة) Advanced guards.

A P طلايه *talāya*, Advanced guard, reconnoitering party. *Tilāya*, Nightwatch, rounds.

P طلائي *tilāʼī*, Golden.

A طلب *talb*, (in Morocco) Learned, of general information. A priest. *Tilb*, (pl. اطلاب *atlāb* and طلبة *tilabat*) A lover, a suitor. A woman sought after. طلب علم *tilbi ʻilm*, A student. *Talab*, (v. n. of طلب) Petitioning, begging, requesting, seeking desiring. Being absent, afar off. Petition, request, demand, application, summons, call. Desire, wish. Inquiry, search, quest, summons, sending for. Pay, wages, salary. طلب خزانه *talabi khizāna*, Demand of rent or of revenue. طلب داخله *talabi dākhila*, Demand of rent brought to account.

P طلب كردن *talab kardan*, To ask, petition, request, demand, exact, solicit, pursue with ambition. معاونت طلب كردن *muʻāwanat talab kardan*, To ask help. A *Talab*, (or طلّب *tullab*) (pl. of طالب *tālib*) Inquirers, seekers. *Tulub*, (pl. of طلوب *talūb*) Inquisitors, inquirers.

P طلب *tulb*, A company of persons assembled.

A طلباء *tulabāʼ*, (pl. of طليب *talīb*) Inquisitors.

P طلبانه *talbāna*, Daily pay to constables, paid by those whom they guard.

A طلبة *tilbat*, (v. n. of طلب) Inquiring, searching. Any thing sought after. A woman sought after. A mistress. امّ طلبة *umm tilbata*, An eagle. *Tulbat*, A long journey. Angels who register the acts of the servants of God. *Talabat*, A proper name, Thalaba. (pl. of طالب *tālib*) Seekers, inquirers. Students. *Talibat*, Any thing sought after. *Tilabat*, (pl. of طلب *tilb*) Lovers.

P طلبدار *talab-dār*, One who asks or inquires. Desirous. One who receives pay.

P طلبگار *talabgār*, Requiring, demanding.

P طلبگاري *talabgārī*, A desiring, wishing.

P طلب نامه *talab-nāma*, Summons, citation.

A طلبي *talabī*, Requisite, demandable.

P طلبيدن *talbīdan*, To inquire, search, call. To call for, summon into one's presence.

A طلّة *tallat*, A wife. Delicious wine. Exquisite odours. A garden wet with dew. Affluence; plenty of food and raiment. Immodest (woman). An old woman. *Tillat*, (pl. of طليل *talīl*) Mats. *Tullat*, (pl. طلل *tulal*) The neck. A draught of milk.

A طلثة *tulsat*, Weak in mind or body.

A طلح *talh*, (v. n. of طلح) Being fatigued. Tiring (a camel). Palm-flowers. Empty-bellied. Jaded (camel). A large thorny tree: acacia. The banana or plantain-fruit. The muddy water at the bottom of a cistern. *Tilh*, (pl. اطلاح *atlāh*) Fatigued (camel). Attenuated. A fatigued shepherd. The insect called the tike. One who manages flocks or any kind of estate. A follower of women. *Talah*, (v. n. of طلح) Being empty-bellied. Grace, favour. Joy, delight.

A طلّح *tullah*, (pl. of طليح) Attenuated (camels).

A طلحافاً *tilhāfan*, By a violent blow.

A طلحان *talihāni*, (du.) A camel and his rider.

A طلحة *talhat*, A single tree of the kind طلح *talh*. *Talihat*, (A she-camel) griped from feeding on the acacia. (Land) abounding in acacia trees.

A طلحثة *talhasat*, (v. n. of طلحث Q) Bedaubing, defiling with a dirty, disagreeable business.

P طلحستان *talhistān*, A grove of acacias.

A طلحف *tilahf* or *tilhaff*, Excessive (hunger).

A طلحفاً *talahfan*, *tilhaffan*, (*tilahfan*, or طلحفي *tilahfaʼ*) By a violent blow.

P طلحند *talhand*, A king of Hindūstān.

A طلحوم *tulhūm*, Stinking water, unfit to drink.

A طلحيّة *talhiyat*, A sheet of paper.

A طلحيف *talhīf*, Excessive (hunger). *Tilhīf*, Violent (shock or blow).

A طلخ *talkh*, (v. n. of طلخ) Blotting out writing. Dirtying, staining. Dirty, fetid water, full of black mud and tadpoles. Defilement, filth.

A طلخاء *talkhāʼ*, (for لطخاء) Foolish (woman).

A طلخام *tilkhām*, A she-elephant.

A طلخثة *talkhasat*, (v. n. of طلخث Q) Bedaubing, dirtying one's self.

A طلخف *tilakhf*, A violent blow.

A طلخوم *tulkhūm*, Corrupted, stinking water.

A طلخيف *tilkhīf*, Violent (blow).

A طلس *tals*, (v. n. of طلس) Erasing, defacing. Throwing (any thing) down on (its) face. Becoming lost (the sight). Breaking wind. Being cast into prison. A black hood. طلس به في السجن *tulisa bihi fī's sijn*, He was cast into prison. P طلس كردن *tals kardan*, To cancel, expunge. A *Tils*, (pl. اطلاس *atlās*) A book, page. Smooth, bald. A bald wolf. The skin of a camel's thigh bare. Any thing erased. Old, ancient. Dirty (raiment).

A طلسة *tulsat*, An ash-coloured satin.

A طلسم *tilsam*, (pl. طلاسم *talāsim*) A talisman, or magical image, upon which, under a certain horoscope, are engraved mystical characters, as charms against enchantment or fascination. They use talismans as preservatives in various ways, particularly in burying them with treasure, to prevent it from being discovered.

A طلسمة *talsamat*, (v. n. of طلسم Q) Keeping silence, looking on the ground. Arming, defending, preserving, securing by talismanic charms.

A طلش *talsh*, (for شلط *shalt*) A knife.

A طلطل *taltal*, A misfortune. *Tultul*, A chronic disease.

A طلطلة *taltalat*, (v. n. of طلطل Q) Moving, puting in motion. A misfortune.

A طلطين *tulatīn*, A very cunning fellow.

A طلع *talʻ*, The spathe of a palm-tree, in which the fruit is enclosed; also the buds, flowers, and incipient fruit. Quantity, number, measure. الجيش طلع الف *al jayshu talʻu alfin*, The corps amounts to a thousand. *Talʻ* or *tilʻ*, A high place whence any thing is viewed. A tract of country. *Tilʻ*, Level ground. Full of hills. A long serpent. Inspection of any business. Sight, view. Arcana of any business. طلع العدوّ *tilʻa'l ʻadūw*, In sight, in view of the enemy. *Tulʻ*, (pl. of طلاع *tilāʻ*) Fulnesses (of earth or soil). *Talaʻ*, (v. n. of طلع) Ascending (a mountain).

A طلعاء *tulaʻāʼ*, A vomit.

A طلعة *talʻat*, Aspect, face, countenance. Appearance. طلعة ذكر *talʻatu zakarin*, The foreskin. حيّا الله طلعتك *hayyā'llāh talʻataka*, May God give your face life! (a form of benediction). *Tulaʻat*, A mind that considers any thing attentively. Inclined to love. طلعة خباة *tulaʻat khubaʼat*, (A woman) who now peeps out, and anon withdraws.

A طلغان *talaghān*, Fatigued, tired, wearied.

A طلف *talaf*, A gift, present. Any thing easy, agreeable, or excellent. Much, excess.

A طلفا *talf* or *talafan*, Gratis, with impunity.

A طلفان *talafān*, Fatigued, tired, weary.

A طلفحة *talfahat*, (v. n. of طلفح Q) Rendering thin, making broad and thin.

A طلق *talk*, (v. n. of طلق) Travelling night and day to water. Opening (the hand), *i.e.* giving any thing. Being distant. Feeling the pangs of childbirth. A heat at a race. Open (in countenance). Free from fetters. Liberal, open-handed. Eloquent. Temperate, agreeable, wholesome (day or night). (pl. اطلاق *atlāk*) A fawn. A hunting-dog. Free, unfettered (camel). طلق اليد اليمنى *talku'l yadi'l yumna'*, A horse on whose off fore-leg there is not any white (contrary to محجل *muhajjal*). P طلق روان *talki rawān*, Wine. A *Talk* or *tilk*, Talc, a translucent mineral, consisting of broad, flat, smooth laminæ or plates, and used in the skylights of baths, &c. *Tilk*, Free, clear, quit. Eloquent. Open (in countenance). The purest and best. Allowed, permitted, lawful. هولك طلقا *huwa laha tilkan*, It is lawful or allowed to thee. *Tulk*, Open (in countenance). Free from fetters. *Talak*, (v. n. of طلق) Going to a distance. An intestine. The sheath of a horse. A nocturnal journey to a watering-place two nights' distance. The first night of that journey. Free from fetters, unchained (captive). A leathern fetter or foot-band (for a camel). A kind of liniment good for burns. One heat at a horse-race. Tythimallus, or a plant used in dyeing. A part, portion. *Talik*, Open in countenance, smiling. Eloquent. *Tulak*, Eloquent. Unfettered (captive or camel). *Tuluk*, Free, unchained (captive or camel). Liberal, open-handed. Eloquent. Having three feet white and one of another colour (a horse).

A طلّق *tullak*, (pl. of طالق *tālik*) Divorced (women). Camels pasturing freely.

A طلقاء *tulakās*, (pl. of طليق) Liberated (captives).

A طلقة *talkat*, Temperate (night). *Tulakat*, One who frequently divorces his wives.

A طلل *talal*, (pl. اطلال *atlāl* and طلول *tulūl*) A body, figure, substance. Projecting remains or ruins of a house. Any thing moist, fresh, and green. The sail of a ship. A bench upon which they sit (in an office or house). Surface (of water). حيّا الله طللك *hayyā'llāhu talalaka*, May God preserve thy body! (a form of benediction). *Tilal*, (pl. of طلّ *tall*) Gentle rains. *Tulal*, (pl. of طلّة *tullat*) Necks. Draughts of milk. *Tulul*, (pl. of طليل *talīl*) Mats.

A طلم *talm*, (v. n. of طلم) Working a mass of dough, making it ready for baking. *Tulm*, A table or dresser on which bread is kneaded or spread out. *Talam*, Foulness of the mouth from neglect in cleaning the teeth.

A طلمة *tulmat*, Coarse bread baked under the ashes. *Talamat*, (pl. of طالم *tālim*) Bakers.

A طلمساء *tilmisās*, A tract of land without turret or land-mark. Darkness.

A طلمسانة *tilimsānat*, Dark, hazy (night). (Land) without water.

A طلمسة *talmasat*, A knitting (of the brows).

A طلنفأ *talanfas*, (or طلنفاء *talanfās*) Verbose, loquacious, talkative.

A طلنفح *talanfah*, Empty, hungry. Fatigued.

A طلنفى *talanfa'*, Verbose, talkative.

A طلو *talw*, (v. n. of طلا for طلو) Tying a lamb to the stake (for slaughter). A fawn just dropped. The young of any animal which parts the hoof. *Tilw*, Contracted, slender in the body. A wolf.

A طلواء *tulawās*, Delay, expectation.

A طلوان *tulwān* or *talawān*, Saliva drying up in the mouth. Delay, expectation.

A طلوب *talūb*, Inquiring; diligent, inquisitive.

A طلوة *tilwat*, The young of any wild beast. *Tulwat*, Whiteness, clearness of the dawn. The neck.

A طلوث *tulūs*, The flowing (of water).

A طلوع *tulūʿ*, (v. n. of طلع) Rising (as the sun or star), ascending. Ascending (a mountain). Appearing, growing (teeth). Budding, beginning to shoot out branches or flowers (palm-trees). Arriving, happening, approaching. Seeking, asking, searching, making for. Being absent, going away, becoming hid. Knowing, viewing, considering. The rising (of the sun or of a star). طلوع كوكب سلطان محمّد *tulūʿi kawkabi sultān muhammad*, The ascendant of the star of Sultān Muhammad.

A طلوق *tulūk*, (v. n. of طلق) Going freely to water through a day's journey (camels).

A طلوقة *tulūkat*, (v. n. of طلق) Being temperate (day or night).

A طلول *tulūl*, (v. n. of طلّ) Shedding blood with impunity. (pl. of طلل *talal*) Vestiges, traces.

A طله *talh*, (v. n. of طله) Traversing (a country). Creeping. *Tulh*, (pl. of اطله *atlah*) Smooth, bare. *Tulah*, A small or thin cloud.

A طلهة *tulhat*, A remnant of wealth or of camels.

A طلهس *tilhis*, A large army.

A طلهيس *talahyas*, The darkness of the night. *Talahyas* or *tilhis*, A large army.

A طلي *taly*, (v. n. of طلي) Anointing, besmearing. Detaining, imprisoning. Tying a lamb to a stake by the foot. *Tala'*, (v. n. of طلي) Having yellow teeth (a mouth). Yellowness of teeth. (pl. اطلاء *atlās*) A body, person. Anointed with pitch. Very sick. Desire, wish, will. *Tila'*, Pleasure, delight. *Tula'*, One draught of milk. (pl. of طلية *tulyat*) Necks.

A طلّى *tulla'*, A draught of milk.

A طلّي *taliy*, (v. n. of طلي) Having yellow teeth (a mouth). Yellowness of teeth. Bound, fettered. Anointed, besmeared. (pl. طليان *tulyān*) A lamb.

A طلياء *talyās*, Anointed, besmeared (she-camel). Scabby (she-camel). A menstruous cloth. The scab. Ringworm, dry scab.

A طليان *tilyān*, A yellowness of the teeth. *Tulyān*, (pl. of طلّي *taliy*) Lambs. *Tulyān* or *tilyān*, (pl. of طلا *tala'* and طلو *talw*) Young fawns recently born. The young of any animals.

A طليب *talib*, (pl. طلباء *tulabās*) Inquiring. An inquirer. Studious.

A طلية *tulyat*, (pl. طلي *tula'*) The neck. The base of the neck.

A طليح *talih*, (fem. طليحة *talihat*) Fatigued, attenuated with travelling (camel). The sheep-tike.

A طليس *tillis*, Blind.

P طليسا *talisā*, A kind of oyster.

A طليعة *taliʿat*, (pl. طلائع *talāiʿ*) The vanguard, picket, advanced post: a spy, scout.

A طليف *talif*, Received, accepted. Given gratis. False.

A طليق *talik*, Liberated (captive). Open (in countenance). Eloquent. طليق ذليق *talik zalik*, Eloquent. طليق الاله *taliku'l ilāh*, The wind.

A طلّيق *tillik*, (A man) frequent in divorcing.

A طليل *talil*, Sweet. (Blood) shed with impunity. (pl. اطلّة *atillat*, طلّة *tillat*, and طلل *tulul*) A mat made of palm-leaves or of the bark of the palm.

A طمّ *tamm*, (v. n. of طمّ) Abounding. Overflowing. Prevailing. Running rapidly, going easily. Perching on a tree (a bird). Biting. Cutting (the hair). Filling (a vessel). Filling up, making level (a well). *Timm*, A male ostrich. A large penis. A generous steed. Water; also whatever rubbish is carried by it along the ground. The sea. A vast number. Much wealth. Ingenious, shrewd. Admiration. A marvellous thing. طمّ و رمّ *timm u rimm*, Much wealth.

A طماح *timāh*, Stubbornness, viciousness in a horse. Refractoriness, disobedience in a wife.

A طمّاح *tammāh*, Covetous, wishful.

A طماحر *tumāhir*, Large-bellied.

A طماخر *tumākhir*, A male camel.

A طمار *tamār*, (v. n. of طمر) Leaping (a horse), hopping (a crow). An elevated spot. بنات طمار *banātu tamāri*, Misfortune.

A طماسة *tamāsat*, (v. n. of طمس) Guessing. Observing, watching. Conjecture.

A طماسلة *tamāsilat*, (pl. of طمسل) Robbers.

A طماع *tamāʿ*, (v. n. of طمع) Wishing greedily, hankering after.

A طمّاع *tammāʿ*, Wishful, covetous, greedy.

A طماعة *tamāʿat*, A wishing greedily.

A طماعى *tamāʿa'*, (pl. of طمع *tamiʿ* and طامع *tāmiʿ*) Greedy.

A طماعية *tamāʿiyat*, A coveting, hankering after.

A طماليخ *tamālikh*, White clouds, thin, dispersed.

A طمأنة *tamsanat*, (v. n. of طمأن Q) Stooping till the back is level and flat. Resting from labour.

P طمانچه *tamāncha*, A pistol. A slap, blow.

A طمأنينة *tumaʼnīnat*, Rest, repose, tranquillity, quiet, serenity of mind. Evenness, equality.

A طمّة *tummat*, Human excrement. A bit of dry herbage.

A طمث *tams* or *tims*, (v. n. of طمث) Deflowering (a woman). Being menstruous. Being nasty and dirty. Touching. The courses. Dirt, filth.

A طمح *tamh*, (v. n. of طمح) Raising (the countenance towards an object). Running away from her husband (a woman). Going a long way in search. Looking after other men besides her husband (a woman). Coveting. *Timah*, A kind of tree.

A طمحات *tamh or tamhāt*, Bad, adverse (fortune).

A طمحرير *tamharīr*, Large-bellied.

A طمخ *tamkh*, (v. n. of طمخ) Being proud, tossing the nose.

A طمخرير *tamkharīr*, Large-bellied.

A طمر *tamr*, (v. n. of طمر) Springing, leaping (a horse), hopping (a crow), jumping up and down. Hiding, concealing, burying under ground. Filling (a subterraneous store-house). Swelling (a wound). طمر في ضرسه *tumira fī zirsihi*, His tooth ached. *Timr*, (pl. اطمار *atmār*) A tattered garment. A worn-out cloak (not of wool). Poor, penniless. A green magpie. High-blooded, swift, spirited (horse), or long-legged and prepared to run. ذو طمر *zū timr*, Clad in rags. *Tamar*, (v. n. of طمر) Swelling (the hand).

A طمّر *tummar*, Root, origin, cause. Youthful inexperience and ignorance.

A طمّر *timirr*, A steed, high-bred and swift. A horse compactly built.

P طمرا *tamrā*, The plant called Palma Christi.

A طمّرة *tummarat*, The earliest part of youth.

A طمّرة *timirrat*, A horse compactly built.

A طمرر *timrir*, High-blooded, spirited, and compactly-built (horse).

A طمرس *timris*, A low, base, lying fellow.

A طمرساء *timrisāʼ*, Dust, fine dust.

A طمرسة *tamrasat*, Contraction. Departure, desistence from fear.

A طمرور *tumrūr*, Old, worn-out clothes, not woollen. Poor, penniless. A kind of speckled bird. A generous horse. A long-bodied, sprightly horse. A horse ready to run or leap.

A طمروس *tumrūs*, Bread baked under the ashes. A lamb. A horse-colt six months' old. A liar. A low, base, worthless, lying fellow.

A طمرير *timrīr*, High-blooded, spirited (horse).

A طمس *tams*, (v. n. of طمس) Erasing, defacing, obliterating, destroying, extirpating, eradicating. Looking to a great distance. Withdrawing to a distance.

A طمسل *tumsul*, (pl. طماسلة *tamāsilat*) A thief.

A طمسلة *tamsalat*, (v. n. of طمسل Q) Being impotent, deficient in virility.

A طمسلي *tamsalaʼ*, Misfortune, calamity. على الطمسلى *ʻala't tamsalaʼ*, Stealing or creeping softly (as a thief).

A طمش *tamsh*, (pl. طموش) A man, person.

A طمطام *tamtām*, The middle of the sea.

P طمطراق *tumturāk*, Magnificence, pomp, great attendance, grandeur.

A طمطم *timtim*, (طمطمي *timtimīy*, or طمطماني *tumtumānīy*) Stuttering in speech, unintelligible.

A طمطمانية *tumtumāniyat*, Vulgar, disallowed phraseology, a coarse provincialism.

A طمطمة *tamtamat*, (v. n. of طمطم Q) Swimming in the midst of the sea. Talking barbarously and unintelligibly.

A طمع *tamaʻ*, (v. n. of طمع) Coveting, desiring, hankering. Being filled with concupiscence. Desire, concupiscence. Greediness. (pl. اطماع *atmāʻ*) A soldier's pay; also the time when paid. P طمع ازجان بريدن *tamaʻ az jān burīdan*, To give up hope of life. طمع خام *tamaʻi khām*, Vain-expectation. طمع دادن *tamaʻ dādan*, To seduce by promises, to bring over to one's own party. A *Tamiʻ* or *tamuʻ*, (pl. طمعون *tamiʻūn*, طمعاء *tumaʻāʼ*, طماعي *tamāʻaʼ*, and اطماع *atmāʻ*) Greedy, eager.

A طمعاء *tumaʻāʼ*, (pl. of طمع or طامع) Covetous.

P طمعكار *tamaʻ-kār*, Greedy, covetous. Gluttonous. Avaricious. Interested, ambitious.

A طمغ *tamagh*, A copious running (of the eye).

P طمغا *tamghā*, (and طمغه *tamgha*) A mark impressed by burning on the king's horses; also on false witnesses. The standard mark of gold or silver. A royal edict. A diploma. Toll for transit of goods. A grant of land in perpetuity. (This is properly a Turkish word, and the correct orthography is التمغا *altamghā*, which means, The red seal).

P طمغاج *tamghāj*, A country in Turkistan.

P طمغاج خانه *tamghāj-khāna*, Name of the king of Samarkand; according to others of the king of Tibet and Yaghmā.

A طمل *taml*, (v. n. of طمل) Rolling out a mass of leaven. Making (a thing) broad and even. Driving hard. Weaving (a mat) of a flimsy texture, putting (threads) into it. Dyeing deep (a garment). Smearing an arrow (blood). Falling into any mess, getting into any shameful business. People, mortals, creatures. Creation. *Timl*, A garment dyed of a full deep colour. Black. A black habit. A green robe. Ignoble, mean, worthless. Muddy water. A robber. (pl. طمول *tumūl*) Foul-mouthed, scurrilous. A villain, daring wretch, scoundrel. A blockhead. Disobedient, rebellious. Foolish, stupid. Poor. Ill-tempered. Naked. Sordid. A bald wolf slily stealing along. A necklace or collar. A threadbare garment. *Tamal*, (v. n. of طمل) Being smeared (with blood, pitch, or grease).

A طمّل *timill*, A dark-coloured wolf creeping along stealthily.

A طملال *timlāl*, Poor. Of a bad disposition, malignant. A sorry condition; bad food and clothing. Scantily clad, naked. A dark-coloured wolf creeping stealthily along.

A طملة *tam*, *tum*, or *tamalat*, Mud, clay, slime (at the bottom of a cistern). A remainder of muddy water in a vessel. صار الماء طملة واحدة *sāraʼlmāʼu tamlatan wāhidatan*, The water became downright mud. *Timlat*, A weak woman. Mud. *Tumlat*, A shameful, dirty, or disagreeable business.

A طملس *tamallas*, Dry (bread), a dry crust.

A طملسة *tamlasat*, Toilsome effort, painful exertion. Blandishment, favour, obligingness. A lying hid, concealment. Hatred, malevolence.

A طملول *tumlūl*, Coarse fare and raiment. Wicked, profligate. Poor and coarsely fed. Naked.

A طمليل *timlīl*, A robber, scoundrel. Poor and coarsely fed. Coarse fare and raiment.

A طمن *tamn*, (pl. طمون *tumūn*) Quiet, quiescent.

A طموّ *tumūw*, (v. n. of طما for طمو) Raising one's self. Being high-minded. Being filled (a channel), swelling (the sea or a river). Becoming tall (a plant).

A طموح *tumūh*, (v. n. of طمح) Lifting up the eyes towards any object.

A طمور *tumūr*, (v. n. of طمر) Springing, leaping (a horse); hopping (a magpie). Travelling by land, passing by.

A طمّور *timmawr*, Root, origin, stock.

A طموس *tumūs*, A being obliterated, defaced.

A طموش *tumūsh*, (pl. of طمش *tamsh*) Crowds of people. Men, persons.

A طمول *tamūl*, (pl. طمول *tumūl*) Wicked, scurrilous, shameless. *Tumūl*, (pl. of طمل *timl*) Foul-mouthed, impudent, scurrilous.

A طمولة *tumūlat*, Impudence, profligacy, shamelessness, scurrilousness.

A طموم *tumūm*, (v. n. of طمّ) Plaiting (the hair). Filling (a vessel). Abounding, overflowing (water).

A طمون *tumūn*, (pl. of طمن *tamn*) Quiescent.

P طمه *tama*, Account of revenues estimated by measurement of the lands and a regular rent-roll.

A طمي *tamy*, (v. n. of طمي) Passing rapidly by (as a horse). Being high (water, mind, or design). Being full (the sea). Growing long (a plant).

A طمّي *tumīy*, (v. n. of طمي) Being filled (the channel of a river). Getting the upper hand of her husband (a woman).

A طميس *tamīs*, Blind, blinded. Going blind.

A طميل *tamīl*, Bloody (arrow). Hidden, concealed. A kid. Water of mud. The prickle of a palm-tree. A mat. Rolled out (dough). A broad point (of a spear). A necklace.

A طميلة *tamīlat*, A kid.

A طميم *tamīm*, (v. n. of طمّ) Running with rapidity. Going softly. A swift and generous steed.

A طميئن *tumayʼin*, (dim. of مطمئن) Quietish.

A طميئنة *tumayʼinat*, (dim. of طمأنينة *tuma-*

nīnat) Little rest, somewhat of quiescence.

A طنّ *tann*, (v. n. of طنّ) Making (a bason) ring. Making a noise, ringing (a bason). *Tinn*, A sweet and fresh date. *Tunn*, (pl. اطنان *atnān* and طنان *tinān*) The human body. A truss, or what a horse carries on the top between two loads. A bundle of reeds.

A طنأ *tanɛ*, (v. n. of طنأ) Being ashamed, blushing. *Tanaɛ*, (v. n. of طنئ) Having a disease (a camel) in which the spleen sticks to the side. Having something in the mind which one is ashamed of revealing.

A طنء *tinɛ*, The last breath. Remains of water in a cistern. Extinguished ashes. Sickness, disease. Wickedness, lewdness. A pit dug for a lion, especially on high ground. High ground to which water does not reach. White ground. A garden. Love, affection, inclination. A serious design or proposal. A mansion, inn, halting-place. A bed, carpet, or cushion. A stone enclosure for cattle.

A طنا *tana'*, The mortal bite of a serpent.

A طناب *tanāb* or *tināb*, A tent-rope. A scaling-ladder. A springe. P طناب اندر طناب *tanāb andar tanāb*, Close together, as close as possible.

A طنابير *tanābīr*, (pl. of طنبور *tumbūr*) Lutes.

A طناة *tanaɛat*, Whoremongers, adulterers.

A طناة *tunāt*, (pl. of طاني) Whoremongers.

A طنّاز *tannāz*, Facetious, ludicrous, sportive, jocund, mirthful. Sarcastic, satirical, derisive.

A طنافة *tanāfat*, (v. n. of طنف) Being suspicious. Being internally evil, intrinsically bad.

A طنافس *tanāfis*, (pl. of طنفسة *tanfa, tanfi, tinfa, tinfi*, and *tunfusat*) Carpets.

A طنان *tinān*, (pl. of طنّ *tunn*) Bodies.

A طنب *tanab*, A bend in a spear. Length of leg with looseness. Length of back (a blemish). *Tunub*, (pl. اطناب *atnāb* and طنبة *tinabat*) A thong which connects a bowstring to the horns of a bow. A tent-rope. Root of a tree. A tendon, especially in the neck. طنب الاطناب *tunubu'l itnāb*, Sublime style, hyperbole, bombast.

A طنباء *tambāɛ*, (fem. of اطنب *atnab*) Long-legged but lax. Long-backed.

A طنبار *timbār*, A lute or guitar.

A طنبة *tinabat*, (pl. of طنب *tunub*) Tent-ropes.

A طنبزيز *tambazīz*, Vulva.

P طنبسه *tambasa*, (for طنفسة) A carpet.

P طنبك *tumbak*, A bagpipe. A trumpet, clarion.

P طنبل *tambal*, A small drum.

A طنبلة *tambalat*, (v. n. of طنبل Q) Feigning to be a fool, or shewing signs of folly after having made pretensions to wisdom.

A طنبور *tumbūr*, (from P دنبهٔ برّه *dumba-barra*) A kind of lute or guitar with a long neck.

A طنبوراني *tumbūrāniy*, A guitar-player.

A طنبورة *tambūra*, A kind of mandolin.

P طنبي *tambī*, An open-fronted summer-room.

A طنّة *tannat*, A tinkling noise. *Tunnat*, One reed drawn from a bundle.

A طنثرة *tansarat*, (v. n. of طنثر Q) Eating fat, indigestible things.

P طنجة *tanjat*, Tangiers in Africa.

A طنجير *tinjīr*, A cauldron, a kettle, or a copper saucepan for cooking sweetmeats in.

A طنح *tanh*, (v. n. of طنح) Labouring under indigestion. Becoming fat (camels).

A طنخ *tinhh*, A part of the night. *Tanahh*, (v. n. of طنخ) Nauseating, having an indigestion (from fulness). Growing fat.

A طنخة *tanahhat*, Foolish, ignorant.

A طنز *tanz*, (v. n. of طنز) Holding up to ridicule, bantering. Irony, ridicule, jest, banter, derision. insult, sarcasm. A kind of fish. P طنز كردن *tanz kardan*, To calumniate, banter, ridicule.

A طنس *tanas*, Great darkness.

A (ذو) طنطان (*zū*) *tantān*, Noisy, clamorous.

A طنطنة *tantanat*, Sound, resounding, re-echoing of musical instruments. The murmuring of water. Noise. Pomp.

A طنف *tanaf*, (v. n. of طنف) Being suspicious. Being internally evil, intrinsically bad. *Tanf, tanaf, tunf*, or *tunuf*, (pl. اطناف *atnāf* and طنوف *tunūf*) The projection of a mountain, a promontory, peak. The coping of a wall, a projection, slab, or pent over a door. *Tanaf*, Thongs of red leather over boxes. Suspicion. *Tanif*, Suspected. A little eater. Inwardly bad, depraved, of evil intentions.

A طنفس *tinfis*, Deformed, hideous, ugly, bad.

A طنفسة *tanfasat*, (v. n. of طنفس Q) Becoming vicious, corrupt, and wicked, after having been good. Putting on many clothes. *Tanfa, tanfi, tanfu, tinfa, tinfi*, or *tunfusat*, (pl. طنافس *tanāfis*) A carpet or rug with a shaggy pile. Mats made with palm-leaves, about a cubit in breadth. Garments.

A طنفش *tanfash*, (or طنفشيّ) Weak, enervated.

A طنفشاء *tinfishāɛ*, Weak and cowardly.

A طنفشة *tanfashat*, (v. n. of طنفش Q) Contracting the eyes to look with greater steadiness.

A طنو *tanw*, A bed, carpet, or cushion. *Tunw*, Debauchery and wickedness.

A طنوج *tunūj*, The different parts of a book. Different sorts or forms. Volumes, papers.

A طنوف *tunūf*, (pl. of طنف *tanf, tanaf, tunf*, and *tunuf*) Promontories, mountain-tops.

A طنوفة *tunūfat*, (v. n. of طنف) Being internally bad, intrinsically evil. Suspecting.

A طني *tany*, Suspicion, *Extinct (ashes). Disease, sickness. Water-moss. The purchase of a tree. The sale of a palm-tree. *Tiny*, Debauchery, wickedness. *Tana'* or *tanī*, One whose spleen adheres to the left side. *Tina'*, (v. n. of طني) Launching out into wickedness and debauchery. Having the spleen and lungs adhering to the left side. Recovering from the effects of the sting of a scorpion.

A طنّي *tunnīy*, A stout, corpulent man.

P طنيدن *tanīdan*, To tingle (the ear).

A طنين *tanīn*, (v. n. of طنّ) Tingling (in the ear). Humming (flies). Quacking (a duck). Dying. (pl. اطنّاء *atinnāɛ*) A tinkling noise. The ringing of a bason. طنين ذباب *tanīni zubāb*, The buzzing of a fly.

A طوء *tawɛ*, (v. n. of طاء) Travelling. Going far.

A طوّاب *tawwāb*, A maker of brick (طوب *tūb*).

A طوابع *tawābiɛ*, (pl. of طابع) Seal-rings.

A طوابق *tawābik*, (or طوابيق *tawābīk*) (pl. of طابق *tābak* and *tābik*) Frying-pans.

A طواجن *tawājin*, (pl. of طاجن) Frying-pans.

A طواحن *tawāhin*, (pl. of طاحنة *tāhinat*) Back teeth, grinders, molars.

A طواحي *tawāhī*, Vultures hovering o'er a corse.

A طواحين *tawāhīn*, (pl. of طاحونة) Water-mills.

A طوار *tawār*, Any thing situated on a border or opposite another. *Tawār* or *tiwār*, The area of a house or ground which it covers, including the court. The length and breadth of a house. *Tuwār*, Edge, limit, border. Quantity.

A طوارف *tawārif*, Eyes. Such wild beasts as hunt their prey. Those parts of a tent which are lifted up in order to look out.

A طوارق *tawārik*, (pl. of طارقة *tārikat*) Female augurs, diviners, soothsayers, necromancers. Calamities. Dangers, accidents (of the night).

A طوارقات *tawārikāt*, Female diviners.

P طوارة *tawāra*, Name of a poisonous herb.

A طوّاز *tawwāz*, Soft, smooth. Old, aged.

A طواس *tawās*, One of the three last nights of a lunar month. A drinking-vessel.

A طواسيم *tawāsīm*, (more correctly ذوات طسم *zawāt tāsam*) Certain sūras in the Kur'ān.

A طواشي *tawāshī*, Eunuchs.

A طوّاشي *tawwāshī*, A eunuch.

A طواط *tuwāt*, Strenuous, intrepid.

A طواعية *tawāɛiyat*, Obedience. Service.

A طواعين *tawāɛīn*, (pl. of طاعون *tāɛūn*) Pestilential diseases, plagues.

A طواغيت *tawāghīt*, (or طواغي *tawāghī*) (pl. of طاغوت *tāghūt*) Idols. Augurs.

A طواف *tawāf*, (v. n. of طاف for طوف) Going round, making a procession, circumambulating (especially the tomb of a pious person). Going to the necessary. طواف بيت الله الحرام *tawāfi baytu'llāhi'l harām*, The procession round the Kaaba or temple of Mecca, which the pilgrims are enjoined by the Kur'ān to do seven times, the three first in a quick, the four last in a grave, ordinary pace.

A طوّاف *tawwāf*, One who goes round and round, and gads about. One who serves or waits on another with affectionate solicitude. One who joins in the sacred procession at Mecca or in other places. A deluge. P طوّاف سركش *tawwāfi sarkash*, One who carries fruit about to sell. The night-patrol. A thief, robber.

A طوال *tawāl*, The term of life. Absence. طوال الدهر *tawāla'd dahri*, At no time, never. *Tiwāl*, (pl. of طويل *tawīl* and طوال *tuwāl*) Long. *Tuwāl*, Very long.

A طوّال *tuwwāl*, Very long.

A طوالع *tawāliꜥ*, (pl. of طالع *tāliꜥ*) Horoscopes.

A طوالق *tawālik*, Temperate (night). Camels sent to a distant watering-place at the end of the first day's journey. (pl. of طالقة) Divorced (women).

A طوامس *tawāmis*, (pl. of طامس *tāmis*) Far distant, separate, out of sight.

A طوامير *tawāmīr*, (pl. of طامور or طومار) Volumes.

A طواويس *tawāwīs*, (pl. of طاوس) Peacocks.

A طوائح *tawāïh*, Adverse, harassing accidents.

A طوائف *tawāïf*, (pl. of طائفة *tāïfat*) Peoples, tribes, nations. Troops, bands. Sorts. طوائف تجّار *tawāïfi tujjār*, Merchants, traders. طوائف نسا *tawāïfi nisā*, Different kinds of women. ملوك الطوائف *mulūku't tawāïf*, The kings of those provinces into which the empire of the Arabs in Spain was broken up; but not those kings exclusively.

A طوائق *tawāïk*, Collars, necklaces.

A طوب *tūb*, A brick, a tile (in Egypt).

A طوبا *tūbā'*, (in regim. for طوبيٰ *tūba'*) Good, excellent (woman). طوباك *tūbāka*, Happy art thou.

A طوباز *tūbāz*, A topaz.

A طوبالة *tūbālat*, (pl. طوبالات) A ewe.

A طوبيٰ *tūba'*, Good, excellent. Agreeable, or sweet. (fem. of اطيب *atyab*) Better, best, sweetest. (pl. of طيّبة *tayyibat*) Things lawful or excellent. Hail! bravo! excellent! Name of a tree in Paradise, the fruit of which is supposed to be most delicious. طوباك *tūbāka*, How happy thou art! Bravo! Well done!

A طوبيّ *tūbīy*, Any one.

T طوپ *top*, A cannon, piece of ordnance.

T طوپچي *topchī*, A cannonier, artillery-man.

T طوپخانه *top-khāna*, An arsenal. Artillery.

A طوح *tawh*, (v. n. of طاح for طوح) Perishing, or being in imminent danger. Falling. Going. Wandering about as a vagabond. *Tawah*, A distant aim, remote design.

A طوحة *tawahat*, A remote design.

A طوخ *tawkh*, (v. n. of طاخ for طوخ) Harassing (one) with opprobrious words or injurious acts. Suspecting. *Tūkh*, Name of several places in Egypt.

A طود *tawd*, (v. n. of طاد for طود) Being firm, immoveable. (pl. اطواد *atwād* and طودة *tiwadat*) A large mountain. A high sandhill. ابن الطود *ibnu't tawd*, (Son of the large mountain) A huge rock which tumbles from it, a boulder-stone.

A طودة *tiwadat*, (pl. of طود *tūd*) Huge mountains.

A طور *tawr*, (v. n. of طار for طور) Going round, wheeling about, skimming in circles. Mode, manner, condition, state, action. Quantity, measure. Limit, boundary, whatever separates two objects; a partition. Equal, parallel. (pl. اطوار *atwār*) A time, turn. طور و حركت *tawr u harakat*, Action and motion. *Tawr* or *tūr*, Any thing situated on a border, or facing and opposite to. *Tūr*, A limit, boundary. End, extremity. A mountain, especially Mount Sinai. A court-yard. The precincts of a palace. جبل طور *jabali tūr*, (طور سينا *tūri sīnā*, or طور موسيٰ *tūri mūsa'*) Mount Sinai, or the mountain of Moses. طور زيبا *tūri zībā*, Name of a mountain near Jerusalem. طور هارون *tūri hārūn*, Mount Hor, the place of Aaron's death.

P طور *tor*, Wild, terrified.

A طورًا *tawran*, Now this, now that.

A طوران *tawarān*, (v. n. of طار for طور) Going round, wheeling about, circumgyrating.

A طورانيّ *tūrānīy*, Wild or mountain (pigeon). A man, any body (is not therein).

A طورة *tiwarat* or *tūrat*, A bad omen.

P طوردان *tūrdān*, A strong horse, mule, or camel.

P طورسيقوس *tūrsīkūs*, Name of a certain individual, a Christian monk or doctor.

P طورك *tūrak*, Name of a general of Zahhāk.

P طوري *torī*, Fear, dread, terror, horror.

A طوريّ *tuïrīy*, Any one, any body.

A طوريّ *tūrīy*, Wild, mountain (man or pigeon). Any one, any body (is not therein).

A طوس *taws*, (v. n. of طاس for طوس) Being of a fair countenance. Trampling. The moon. Freshness and clearness of the face after sickness. *Tūs*, Continuation, perpetuity. A medicine which assists the memory. Name of a city in Khurāsān.

P طوسك *tūsak*, A kind of thorn.

A طوسيّ *tūsīy*, A colour so called. A kind of purple. Native of the city of Tūs.

A طوش *tawsh*, Levity of mind.

A طوط *tūt*, (v. n. of طاط for طوط) Being libidinous and noisy (a stallion). Long, tall. Quarrelsome. Cotton. A sparrow-hawk. A bat. Small. A serpent. Strong, courageous. (pl. اطواط *atwāt*) A libidinous stallion. The funnel or chimney of a bath.

A طوطرة *tawtarat*, A prostrating time after time.

P طوطك *tūtak*, A little parrot. A paroquet.

P طوطي *tūtī*, A parrot. طوطيء صحرا *tūtīï sahrā*, Verdure (literally, parrot) of the plain.

P طوطي نامه *tūtī-nāma*, Parrot-tales (a book).

P طوطي نواي *tūtī-nawāy*, Parrot-voiced. Eloquent.

P طوطي وار *tūtīwār*, Parrot-like. Eloquent.

P طوطي واري *tūtīwārī*, Parrotry. Habits of parrots; imitation of parrots.

A طوع *tawꜥ*, (v. n. of طاع for طوع) Obeying, complying with, humouring. Lying open, affording plenty of pasture (a field). Easy, gentle, obedient to the rein (horse). Obedience, voluntary submission. Obedient.

A طوّع *tuwwaꜥ*, (pl. of طائع *tāïꜥ*) Obedient.

A طوعًا *tawꜥan*, Obsequiously, willingly. طوعًا وكرهًا *tawꜥan wa karhan*, Willingly and unwillingly, whether he will or not, nolens volens.

A طوعة *tawꜥat*, A proper name of a woman. *Tuwaꜥat*, Obedient to every body, compliant.

P طوغان *tūghān*, A royal falcon.

A طوف *tawf*, (v. n. of طاف for طوف) Going round, circumambulating. Going all about or everywhere. Going to the privy. Visiting (one's wives) in succession. Appearing (a spectre). Inflated leathern bottles which they use to float rafts or assist swimmers. A wall. Human excrement. *Tūf*, Wool of the neck. The nape of the neck.

P طوف *tūf*, A decrepit, doting old woman.

A P T طوفان *tūfān*, A flood, a universal deluge. Violent rain. Storm, tempest, hurricane, tornado. Any thing that completely envelopes. A general mortality. Sudden death, a killing at once. A quarrelsome person. Night. A very dark night. Torment, punishment. A *Tawafān*, (v. n. of طاف for طوف) Going round, circumambulating.

A طوفانة *tūfānat*, One deluge, flood, inundation.

A طوفاني *tūfānī*, Stormy. Quarrelsome.

A طوق *tawk*, (v. n. of طاق for طوق) Being able, equal to, a match for, or having the power. Power, ability, capacity. (pl. اطواق *atwāk*) A necklace, chain, collar. A bird's ruff. A circle, ring. A rope for climbing a palm-tree. An opening. The pillory. P طوق بهار *tawki bahār*, The rainbow. طوق زنجير *tawki zanjīr*, Irons, manacles. A طوق طاقت *tawk tākat*, A valuable chain, such as the servants of great men wear round the neck. طوق عنبر *tawki ꜥambar*, The sprouting of a beard. P طوق ماه *tawki māh*, A halo round the moon. A هو في طوقي *huwa fī tawkī*, He is in my power.

A طوقة *tawkat*, Plain ground surrounded by rocky districts (forming a ring or collar).

P طوقدار *tawk-dār*, Collared. Pilloried; prisoner. A youth whose beard begins to appear. Lunar.

A طول *tawl*, (v. n. of طال for طول) Conferring favours, benefiting. Excelling in goodness and liberality. Excelling in length. Duration of life, age. Absence. Excellence. Power. Riches, the conveniences of life. اولو الطول *ulū't tawl*, The wealthy. ذو الطول *zū't tawl*, Long-suffering (God). *Tūl*, (v. n. of طال for طول) Being long, tall, extensive, lasting long, of a long duration. Exceeding in length. Length of life. Absence. (pl. اطوال *atwāl*) Longitude. طول الدهر *tūla'd dahri*, At no time, never. طول زمان *tūli zamān*, Length of time. *Tawal*, Length of the upper lip hanging over the under one (especially in camels). *Tiwal*, Duration of life, age. Absence, distance, remoteness. A long rope with which pasturing cattle are tethered. ارخ للفرس من طوله *arkhi li'l faras min tiwalihi*, Give the horse a little more tether. *Tuwal*, Duration of life, age. Absence. (pl. of طوليٰ *tūla'*) Longer, taller. High stations. السبع الطول *as sabꜥu't tu-*

wal, The seven long chapters or sūras of the Kur'ān, viz. from the second to the eighth inclusive.

A طوّل *tūwal*, A certain long-legged water-fowl.

A طوّل *tiwall*, A tethering-rope.

A طولاً *tūlan*, In length, lengthwise.

A طولاني *tūlānī*, Long. Lofty. Loud.

A طولع *tawlaʿ*, A vomit.

A طولمبة *tūlumba*, A hydraulic musical instrument. A trumpet. A pump, a syphon.

P طوله *tawla*, A stable or stall for horses. A set of horses, of six or eight, exactly matched. A long rope or tether. A kind of trick-track or draughts.

A طولى *tūla'*, (fem. of اطول *atwal*) (pl. طول *tuwal*) Longer. A high situation, post, rank. يد طولى *yad tūla'*, Pre-eminence.

G طوليدون *tūlīdūn*, Fox-grapes, nightshade.

A طومار *tūmār*, (pl. طوامير *tawāmīr*) A book, volume, long roll. A kind of writing. Household-accounts. طومار جمع *tūmāri jamʿ*, A rent-roll.

P طومار نويس *tūmār-navīs*, An accountant.

A طومة *tūmat*, Death. Calamity, misfortune. A female tortoise.

G طونسلس *tūnuslus*, The bog-rush.

A طوّوي *tuʾwīy*, (طوويّ *tūwīy*, also *tuwawīy*) Any body (is not within).

A طوي *toy*, A feast, festival.

A طوى *tawa'*, (v. n. of طوي) Suffering hunger, fasting involuntarily; hunger. A leathern bottle. *Tawī*, Thin, pliable (about the belly). One who abstains from food.

A طويّ *tawīy*, Built, constructed with stones (a well). A bale or bundle as big as one can carry. A bale, roll, or web of linen or muslin. An hour of the night.

A طويّة *tawīyat*, Purpose, design, intention, mind, heart, thought. A secret. A well built of stones.

A طوير *tuwayr*, A little bird. A flying insect.

A طويس *tuways*, (dim. of طاوس *tāʾus*) A small peacock. Name of a certain catamite and singer, who used to say of himself, "My mother was in the habit of circulating slanders amongst the wives of the Ansārs, and brought me forth the night the prophet died; and weaned me the day Abū bakr died. I attained the age of puberty on the day Omar died, and I married on the day Othmān was murdered; and on the day of Aliy's death a child was born to me:" hence the saying, اشأم من طويس *ashʾam min tuways*, More ill-fated than Tuways.

P طويل *tawīl*, Name of one of the seven games at نرد *nard*.

A طويل *tawīl*, (pl. طوال *tiwāl* and طيال *tiyāl*) Long, tall. Prolix. A species of long verse, فعولن مفاعيلن *faʿūlun mufāʿīlun*, repeated. طويل الذيل *tawīlu'z zayl*, A robe with a long train, a garment with long skirts. Any thing protracted to a great length. عمر طويل *ʿumri tawīl*, A long life. مدّت طويل *muddati tawīl*, (or زمان طويل *zamāni tawīl*), A long space of time. كلّ طويل احمق *kull tawīl ahmak*, Every tall fellow is a blockhead (a ridiculous proverb).

A طويلة *tawīlat*, (fem. of طويل *tawīl*) Long. A tether, foot-band, fetter. A stable, stall. A string of pearls. قصيرة عن طويلة *kasīratun ʿan tawīlat*, Compendiousness in speaking.

A طوئيّ *tuʾīy*, Any body.

A طويئر *tuwayʾir*, (dim. of طائر *tāʾir*) A little bird. A flying insect.

P طه *tah*, Tea (little used).

A طه *tah*, An interjection commanding silence; (hence) a pause in the Kur'ān. O man!

A طهاء *tahāʾ*, A high cloud.

A طهاة *tuhāt*, (pl. of طاهي *tāhī*) Cooks. Bakers.

A طهّار *tahhār*, A cleaner, cleanser, purifier.

A طهارة *tahārat*, (v. n. of طهر) Being pure, clean, holy. Purity, cleanness, ablution. Sanctity.

P طهارت خانه *tahārat-khāna*, A privy.

P طهارت نامه *tahārat-nāma*, A treatise on cleanliness, or corporeal and mental purity.

A طهاري *tahāra'*, (pl. of طاهر) Clean, pure, holy.

A طهاطه *tahātih*, Neighings (of horses).

A طهاف *tahāf*, A high cloud.

A طهافة *tuhāfat*, (or طهاوة *tuhāwat*) The pellicle on the top of milk or coagulated blood.

A طهامل *tahāmil*, (pl. of طهمل) Deformed.

A طهاية *tahāyat*, A dressing, cooking, roasting.

A طهب *tahab*, Name of a dwarf-tree.

A طهبلة *tahbalat*, Peregrination through cities.

A طهثة *tuhsat*, Corpulent. Weak in mind.

A طهر *tahr*, (v. n. of طهر) Placing at a distance. *Tuhr*, (v. n. of طهر) Being clean. (pl. اطهار *athār*) Cleanliness, purity. *Tahir*, Clean, pure.

A طهران *tuhrān*, Clean, pure.

A طهرة *tuhrat*, Purity, cleanness, cleanliness.

A طهس *tahs*, (v. n. of طهس) Entering into the interior of a country, thither to remain, or to pass on. Going (nobody knows where). طهس به *tuhisa bihi*, He was carried off.

A طهش *tahsh*, Confusion. The spoiling of any thing commenced by one's self or by any one else.

A طهطاه *tahtāh*, A young, well-made, lively horse.

A طهف *tahf*, Bread made from millet. *Tahf* or *tahaf*, A kind of grass, slender and weak, bearing a grain which is eaten in seasons of scarcity.

A طهفة *tahfat*, Soft butter. The upper parts of a fresh scallion. The plant صليان *silliyān* when tall. *Tihfat*, A part or segment of any thing.

A طهفلة *tahfalat*, (v. n. of طهفل Q) Eating continually bread made from millet.

A طهق *tahk*, A going fast. Quickness of step.

A طهل *tahl*, Fetid (water). *Tahal*, (v. n. of طهل) Stinking, being spoiled (water).

A طهلبة *tahlabat*, The traversing of a country.

A طهلة *tuhlat*, A certain tender pot-herb. A little forage.

A طهلس *tihlis*, A large army.

A طهلئة *tihliʾat*, A small cloud (is not in the sky). A fool. New plaster dropping off into a cistern. Darkness.

P طهليزج *tihlīzaj*, Bitter herbs which the Jews used to eat at the passover.

A طهم *tahm* or *tuhm*, A word expressive of disgust. ما ادري ايّ الطهم هو *mā adrī ayyu't tahm huwa*, I know not who he is.

P طهماسب *tahmāsb*, Name of a king of Persia.

A طهمة *tuhmat*, Blackness inclining to yellow. Red inclining to white. *Tahimat*, (fem.) Thin-faced.

A طهمل *tahmal*, Any thing which, when felt, has no thickness about it. Slender (woman). (pl. طهامل *tahāmil*) Corpulent and ugly-shaped.

A طهمليّ *tahmalīy*, Black and dwarfish.

P طهمورث *tahmūras*, The third of the Persian kings of the Peshdādian dynasty, and the supposed founder of Babylon, Niniveh, and Isfahān. He reigned about 830 years before the Christian æra, though some carry him beyond that period.

A طهنبى *tahamba'*, Strong (camel).

A طهو *tahw*, (or طهوّ *tuhūw*) (v. n. of طها for طهو) Dressing, roasting (meat). Performing, executing. Travelling. Work, action, labour.

A طهور *tahūr*, (v. n. of طهر) Purifying, cleaning. Purification, ablution. A purifier. That by which any thing is purified or cleaned.

A طهي *tahy*, (v. n. of طهي) Dressing, roasting meat. Performing, executing. Travelling. *Taha'*, Small bits of straw. *Tuha'*, Cooked. A decoction. A wolf. (pl. of طاهي *tāhī*) Cooks. Bakers.

A طهيّ *tuhīy*, (v. n. of طهي) Cooking, roasting. Executing. Travelling.

A طهياء *tahyāʾ*, A person, individual.

A طهيان *tahayān*, The summit of a mountain. Filings, scrapings, chips.

A طهياية *tahyāyat*, A dressing or roasting meat.

A طهيّة *tuhayyat*, Name of a tribe.

A طهير *tahīr*, Clean, pure.

A طهيلة *tahyalat*, (v. n. of طهيل Q) Eating the herb طهلة *tuhlat*. *Tahīlat*, (or طهلئة *tihʾilat*) New plaster dropping off into a cistern. Foolish; a fool.

A طيّ *tayy*, (v. n. of طوي) Folding up. Abridging, making a compendium. Constructing with stones (a well). Concealing, suppressing, keeping secret. Travelling. Declining, turning from. Passing by, through, or beyond. Ending, finishing. Drawing near, in order to sit down or reside. Bringing near, causing to approach. Fasting voluntarily. Dropping the fourth quiescent letter of مستفعلن *mustafʿilun* and مفعولات *mafʿūlāt*. The cover or envelope of a letter. A fold. Name of an Arabian tribe. P طي كردن *tay kardan*, To cross.

A طيا *taya'*, Fasting (woman).

A طيّاء *tayyāʾ*, (A woman) who fasts on purpose.

A طياب *tiyāb*, A kind of Basra palm-tree.

A طيّاب *tuyyāb*, Good, excellent, sweet, clean, pure. Odour, perfume.

A طيار *tiyār*, (v. n. 3 of طار for طير) Making fly, putting in rapid motion.

A طيّار *tayyār*, Flying. Fleet (horse). Quicksilver. A winged animal.

A طيّارة *tayyārat*, A kind of fast-sailing vessel.

A طيّاش *tayyāsh*, Inconstant, light, vain, fickle, incapable of steady application to one pursuit.

P طياف *tiyāf*, The nightmare.

A طيال *tiyāl*, Duration of life, age. Absence. (pl. of طويل *tawīl*) Long, tall.

A طيالس *tayālis*, (pl. of طيلسان *taylasān*) Hoods, coifs, turban-sashes. Cloaks, scarfs, mantles hanging down from the shoulders.

A طيالسة *tayālisat*, (pl. of طيلسان *taylasān*, *taylisān*, or *taylusān*) Ends of turban-sashes hanging down behind. Mantles, scarfs hanging from the shoulders as badges of literary distinction.

A طيالسيّ *tayālisiy*, A maker of the cloak, hood, scarf, or sash طيلسان *taylasān*.

P طيان *tayān*, Wild jasmine.

A طيّان *tayyān*, A starved person, one who eats nothing. One who prepares or mixes up plaster, mortar, or clay (طين *tīn*). A plasterer.

A طيانة *tiyānat*, The art of preparing or working in clay.

A طياهيج *tayāhīj*, (pl. of طيهوج *tayhūj*) Small species of partridges.

A طيب *tīb*, (v. n. of طاب for طيب) Being good and lawful. Being sweet and delicate. Being favourable (wind). Abounding in pasturage (land). Deliciousness. (pl. اطياب *atyāb*) Odour, perfume; an aromatic unguent, essence. Any thing lawful. The best part of any thing. بطيب نفسى *bi tībi nafsī*, With a willing mind (I did it). اظفار الطيب *azfāru't tīb*, Perfumed nails.

A طيّب *tayyib*, Good, excellent. Sweet, agreeable. Legal. Name of a son of Muhammad. طيّب الرائحة *tayyibu'r rāʼihat*, Fragrant, odoriferous.

A طيّبات *tayyibāt*, (pl. of طيّبة *tayyibat*) Good, excellent works, pious foundations. Delights.

A طيبة *taybat*, Madīna. ابو طيبة *abū taybat*, Name of Muhammad's barber or surgeon. *Tībat*, (v. n. of طاب for طيب) Being good, lawful. Being sweet, delicious. Abounding in pasturage (land). A lawful thing. The purest wine. The well Zamzam. بطيبة نفسى *bi tībati nafsī*, With a willing mind (I did it). *Tiyabat*, Fair, not treacherous (captivity).

A طيّبة *tayyibat*, (fem. of طيّب *tayyib*) Good. A name of the city Madīna.

A طيبي *tība'*, Paradise.

A طئة *tiʼat*, (v. n. of وطئ) Being smooth, level (bed or place). Convenience. A treading, a trampling. Softness. على طئة *ʻala' tiʼatin*, Conveniently.

A طيّة *tayyat*, Intent, design. *Tiyat*, A mode of folding or wrapping up (of any thing). A long fold. Intention, purpose, mind, heart, thought. Any distant shelter or rest whither one is travelling.

A طيثار *taysār*, A lion. A gnat. Fearless (man).

A طيجن *tayjan*, A frying-pan.

A طيح *tayh*, (v. n. of طاح for طيح) Perishing, being in imminent danger. Falling. Wandering about in astonishment. The plough-tail.

A طيحة *tayhat*, Any cause of discord.

A طيخ *taykh*, (v. n. of طاخ for طيخ) Contaminating. Being defiled by any thing nefarious. Growing proud, strutting, behaving loftily. *Tīkh*, Pride. *Tīkhi tīkhi*, The noise made in laughing.

A طيخة *taykhat*, A fool, a worthless person. Insurrection, seduction.

P طير *tayr*, Sal ammoniac.

A طير *tayr*, (v. n. of طار for طير) Flying. Being carried rapidly along. Being long or tall. Flight. (pl. طيور *tuyūr* and اطيار *atyār*) A bird. An omen from the flight of birds (especially a bad one). Lightness. (pl. of طائر *tāʼir*) Birds. على رأسه الطير *ʻala' raʼsihi't tayru*, The birds are on his head, *i.e.* he remains immoveable, tranquil, grave (as a camel, on whose head crows alight to pick out the tikes). طير الليل *tayru'l layl*, The bird of night, the owl.

P طيران *tayrān*, (pl. of Arab. طير *tayr*) Birds.

A طيران *tayarān*, (v. n. of طار for طير) Flying. Flight. P طيران كردن *tayarān kardan*, To fly.

P طيراني *tayrānī*, Belonging to birds, volatile.

A طيرانيّ *tīrāniy*, Native of طيري *tīra'*.

A طيرة *tayrat*, Agility, lightness, levity of mind. *Tīrat* or *tiyarat*, A bad omen.

A طيرورة *tayrūrat*, (v. n. of طار for طير) Flying with velocity. Levity.

P طيرة *tīra*, Grief, pain, uneasiness. Shame, modesty. Bashful.

A طيري *tīra'*, A village near Ispahān.

A طيس *tays*, (v. n. of طاس for طيس) Being many, numerous, copious. *Tays*, (or طيسل *taysal*) A great number, multitude, plenty (of water or sand). Living things which multiply exceedingly (as flies or ants). Dust on the surface of the ground.

A طيسر *taysar*, Abundance, plenty (of water).

A طيسع *taysaʻ*, A large, roomy place. Covetous.

P طيسفون *taysakūn*, Name of a city in Irān, formerly a royal residence.

A طيسل *taysal*, A dark night. A violent wind. Dust. A bowl-dish. Much of any thing. The semblance of water on a plain.

A طيسلة *taysalat*, (v. n. of طيسل Q) Taking a short journey. Being wealthy, having many camels.

P طيسه *taysa*, A bed, couch, pillow, bolster.

A طيش *taysh*, (v. n. of طاش for طيش) Being light, inconstant. Being foolish, losing one's wits. Passing beyond the mark (an arrow). Levity, inconstancy, folly, irresolution. Anger.

A طيط *tīt*, Foolish, ignorant. Long, tall. A libidinous stallion.

A طيطان *tītān*, A wild leek or scallion.

P طيطو *tītū*, A kind of water-fowl.

A طيطوي *tītawa'*, A species of the قطا *katā*.

A طيع *tayʻ*, The act of obeying.

A طيّع *tayyiʻ*, Obsequious, obedient; willing.

A طيّعاً *tayyiʻan*, Voluntarily, of one's own accord.

A طيف *tayf*, (v. n. of طاف for طيف) Appearing (as a ghost). A phantom, spectre, apparition. Rage, anger. Madness. طيف من الشيطان *tayfun mini'sh shaytān*, A spectre raised by the devil: a suggestion or persuasion of the devil.

A طيّف *tayyif*, Imagination, fancy, idea. A suggestion of the devil.

P طيفسون *tayfasūn*, Ctesiphon: Madain: Bagdad.

P طيفور *tayfūr*, A bird or winged insect.

A طيفور *tayfūr*, Name of a little bird.

A طيقان *tīkān*, (pl. of طاق *tāk*) Arches.

P طيقي *tīkī*, A kind of red grain.

A طيل *tīl* or *tiyal*, Duration of life, age. Absence. *Tiyal*, (or طيّل *tiyall*) A tethering rope.

P طيلافيون *taylāfiyūn*, Houseleek. The anemone.

A طيلة *tīlat*, Life, age. Absence. Delay.

A طيّلة *tayyilat*, One wind blowing in an opposite direction to another.

A طيلسان *taylasān*, *taylisān*, or *taylusān*, (also طيلس *taylas*, *taylis*, or *taylus*) (pl. طيالس *tayālis* or طيالسة *tayālisat*) (from P تالشان *tālishān*) The end of the turban-sash hanging down behind like a tail or lappet. A hood. A mantle, scarf, or tippet hanging from the shoulders. A pall (worn as a badge by literary men). طيلسان مزعفر *taylasāni muzaʻfar*, The rays of the sun. طيلسان مطرّا *taylasāni mutarrā*, Night. ابن طيلسان *ibni taylasān*, A Persian, a barbarian. يا ابن طيلسان *yā ibni taylasān*, O son of a barbarian!

A طلئلهة *tislihat*, A fool. New plaster dropping off into a cistern.

A طيم *taym*, (v. n. of طام for طيم) (God) forming (any one for good). Being good (any body's work). Doing a good work.

A طين *tayn*, (v. n. of طان for طين) Sealing (a letter) with clay. Working up clay well. Plastering (a roof) with clay. (God) forming any one for a good end, creating him with a good disposition. *Tīn*, Clay, loam. طين اصفر *tīni asfar*, Yellow earth or chalk. طين مختوم *tīni makhtūm*, Sealing-clay or wax; earth of Lemnos, ruddle. طين ارمني *tīni armanī*, Armenian bole.

A طينة *tīnat*, A bit of clay. Nature, complexion, temperament, disposition, genius.

P طينوث *taynūs*, A species of the cantharides.

A طينيّ *tīniy*, Earthy, clayey. Natural, innate.

A طيور *tuyūr*, (pl. of طير *tayr*) Birds. Winged animals, volatiles. طيور سدرة *tuyūri sidra*, Angels.

P طيّور فيّور *tayyūr fayyūr*, Quick, sharp, active.

A طيوريّ *tuyūriy*, A dealer in birds.

A طيوط *tuyūt*, (v. n. of طاط for طيط) Being

milk to drink before the butter is formed. *Zulm*, (v. n. of ظلم) Digging (ground) in a place not to be dug. Slaughtering (a camel) without disease. Rising higher than ever known before (a river). Drinking milk out of the churning-bottle before the butter is formed. Covering the female when pregnant (an ass). Putting a thing not in its place. Tyranny, oppression, injustice, injury, cruelty, outrage, ferocity, barbarity. Idolatry. Obscurity, darkness.

P ظلم كردن *zulm kardan*, (or ظلم و تعدّي كردن *zulm u taʿaddī kardan*) To oppress. A *Zalam*, A body. (pl. ظلوم *zulūm*) A figure appearing black at a distance. A mountain. ادنى ظلم *adnaʼ zalamin*, Near, neighbouring. First of all, before all. *Zilam*, A certain plant having long tendrils. *Zulam*, (pl. of ظلمة *zulmat*) Obscurities, darknesses. (pl. of ظلماء *zalmāʼ*) Three dark nights in the month immediately following درع *duraʻ*. *Zulum*, Obscurity, darkness. (pl. of ظلم *zulm*) Oppressions.

A ظلماً *zulman*, Oppressively, tyrannically.

A ظلماء *zalmāʼ*, Obscurity, darkness. Dark (night).

A ظلمات *zulmāt*, *zulamāt*, and *zulumāt*, (pl. of ظلمة *zulmat* and *zulumat*) Darknesses.

A ظلمان *zilorzulmān*, (pl. of ظليم) Male ostriches.

A ظلماني *zulmānīy*, Dark, obscure.

A ظلمانيان *zulmāniyān*, (Pers. pl.) Those who are dark, or sitting in darkness.

A ظلمانيّة *zulmānīyat*, Darkness, obscurity.

P ظلم پيشه *zulm-pesha*, A tyrant, oppressor.

A ظلمة *zilmat* or *zulmat*, Name of a certain woman proverbially lewd. *Zulmat*, (pl. ظلم *zulam*) Darkness, obscurity. Severity. Torment. A dark place at the extremity of the world, where the fountain of life is supposed to be placed; also the fountain itself. *Zalamat*, (pl. of ظالم *zālim*) Oppressors, tyrants. *Zalimat*, Dark (night). *Zulumat*, Darkness. Near, the first thing which meets the eye.

P ظلمتيان *zulmatiyān*, Heathens, idolaters.

P ظلم كاه *zulm-kāh*, A diminisher of injustice.

P ظلمه كده *zulma-kada*, The mansion of darkness, this present world.

P ظلم كيش *zulm-kesh*, Oppressive, tyrannical.

P ظلم گاه *zulm-gāh*, A dark place. A place where iniquity or oppression abounds.

A ظلميّة *zulmīyat*, Iniquity, oppression.

A ظلوف *zulūf*, (pl. of ظلف *zilf*) Hoofs, cloven feet. ظلوف ظلف *zulūf zullaf*, Hard cloven feet.

A ظلول *zulūl*, (v. n. of ظلّ) Executing any work by day, not by night. Becoming, happening. (pl. of ظلّ *zill*) Shadows.

A ظلوم *zalūm*, One who puts a thing not in its proper place. Most cruel, unjust, tyrannical. *Zulūm*, (pl. of ظلم *zalm*) Fresh, natural colours of teeth. (pl. of ظلم) Figures appearing black. Mountains.

A ظلّيّة *zillīyat*, Shadiness, umbrageousness.

A ظليف *zalīf*, (pl. ظلف *zulf* and *zuluf*) Of a bad natural disposition, mean, abject, criminal (man). In an evil plight. Rough, rocky (ground); painful (business). Gratuitous. The whole, the entire. Adversity, difficulty. The root of the neck. ظليف النفس *zalīfu'n nafs*, Pure, ingenuous.

A ظليفاً *zalīfan*, Gratis, without price.

A ظليفة *zalīfat*, The whole (of any thing). اخذ الشيء بظليفته *akhaza'sh shayʼ bi zalīfatihi* (or بظليفه *bi zalīfihi*) He took the whole thing.

A ظليل *zalīl*, Shady (place). A cool place. Perpetual (shade). ظلّ ظليل *zilli zalīl*, A perpetual shade.

A ظليلة *zalīlat*, (pl. ظلائل *zalāʼil*) A hole in the bed of a river where water stagnates. A place full of thickets.

A ظليم *zalīm*, Milk not quite turned. Name of two stars. Earth thrown from a new well: virgin soil. (pl. ظلمان *zilmān* or *zulmān*) A male ostrich.

A ظلّيم *zillīm*, Very unjust, most oppressive.

A ظليمة *zalīmat*, Injustice, oppression. Loss, damage. Requisition of justice. Milk not fully concreted or coagulated.

A ظمء *zimʼ*, (pl. اظماء *azmāʼ*) Thirst. The space of time between one drinking and another: hence, ظمء الحيٰوة *zimʼu'l hayāt*, The interval between birth and death. قدر ظمء الحمار *hadr zimʼi'l himār*, As long as an ass can be kept from water, *i.e.* a very little time (this animal, of all others, being least able to endure thirst).

A ظماء *zamaʼ*, (v. n. of ظمئ) Being very thirsty. Burning with desire.

A ظماء *zamāʼ*, (or ظماءة *zamāʼat*) (v. n. of ظمئ) Being very thirsty. *Zimāʼ*, rarely *zumāʼ*, (pl. of ظمئ *zamiʼ* or ظمآن *zamʼān*) Thirsty.

A ظماءة *zamāʼat*, An evil disposition, bad temper; unfairness. *Zimāʼat*, (v. n. of ظمئ) Being thirsty. Burning with desire.

A ظمآن *zamʼān*, (fem. ظمآنة *zamʼānat*) (pl. ظماء *zimāʼ* or *zumāʼ*) Thirsty.

A ظمأي *zamʼaʼ*, Hot, dry (wind).

A ظمخ *zimakh*, A fig. A kind of plantain.

A ظمخة *zimakhat* or *zimkhat*, A single fig-tree. A plane-tree.

A ظمى *zamaʼ*, (v. n. of ظمي) Being livid (the lip). A scarcity of blood at the roots of the teeth.

A ظمئ *zamiʼ*, (pl. ظماء *zimāʼ*) Thirsty.

A ظمياء *zamyāʼ*, Livid and withered (lip). Bloodless (gum). Fleshless (limb). Thin of eyelashes (eye). A woman whose gums are bloodless, whose eye is destitute of eyelashes, and whose limbs are slender and spindling. Black (she-camel).

A ظنّ *zanna*, (fut. يظنّ *yazunnu*) He thought.

A ظنّ *zann*, (v. n. of ظنّ) Thinking, suspecting. Knowing for certain, being sure. (pl. ظنون *zunūn* and اظانين *azānīn*) Opinion, thought, belief, persuasion. Knowledge. Doubt, wavering. سوء ظنّ *sūʼi zann*, Bad thought, rash judgment.

A ظنابيب *zanābīb*, (pl. of ظنبوب *zumbūb*) Shank-bones. Nails or studs in the side of spear-blades. قرع الظنابيب *karʻu'z zanābīb*, Any thing vile; whatever makes one contemptible. قرع ظنابيب الامر *karaʻa zanābība'l amr*, He gained the mastery, he subdued. He rendered contemptible. He prepared for war. He engaged in arduous matters.

A ظنب *zimb*, Trunk of a tree. A root.

A ظنبة *zumbat*, A macerated nerve from a camel's neck, which fastens the feathers to an arrow.

A ظنبوب *zumbūb*, (pl. ظنابيب *zanābīb*) A shank-bone. A stud in the side of a spear-head. قرع ظنبوبه *karaʻa zumbūbahu*, He exerted himself, he stirred his stumps.

A ظنّة *zinnat*, (pl. ظنن *zinan*) Suspicion.

A ظنمة *zanamat*, A draught of milk ere the butter has been extracted.

A ظنون *zanūn*, A suspicious man. Any subject which engages the mind, especially if doubtful; whether (a debt) be discharged or not; or if (a well) contain either little or much water. A well of little water. Weak in mind, barren in mental resources. A noble lady, matron, or wife. *Zunūn*, (v. n. of ظنّ) Thinking, supposing, deeming. (pl. of ظنّ *zann*) Opinions, doubts, surmises.

A ظنّي *zannī*, Supposed, surmised.

A ظنين *zanīn*, (pl. اظنّة *azinnat*) Suspected.

A ظوءة *zawʼat*, Foolish, insane.

A ظؤار *zuʼār*, Trevets. (pl. of ظئر) Foster-mothers.

A ظواهر *zawāhir*, Pot-herbs. High lands. Nobles. Arabs of Kuraysh, who pitched their tents outside of Mecca.

A ظؤرة *zuʼrat*, (pl. of ظئر) Foster-mothers, nurses.

A ظؤري *zuʼraʼ*, A cow in want of the bull.

A ظوف *zūf*, Hairs of the neck. بظوفه *bi zūfihi*, (He left him) alone. اخذه بظوف رقبته *akhazahu bi zūfi rakabatihi*, He took it all.

A ظؤوب *zuʼūb*, (pl. of ظأب *zaʼb*) Husbands of wives' sisters. Noises, clamours. Marriages. Oppressions. Cries of he-goats.

A ظؤور *zuʼūr*, (pl. of ظئر) Nurses, foster-mothers.

A ظؤورة *zaʼūrat*, (A camel) fond of another's colt. *Zuʼūrat*, (pl. of ظئر *ziʼr*) Nurses, foster-mothers.

A ظهار *zahār*, The surface of stony ground. *Zihār*, (v. n. 3 of ظهر) Pronouncing the words انت عليّ كظهر امّي *anti ʻalayya ka zahri ummī*, "Thou art unto me as my mother's back," a formula of repudiation by which a man is divorced from his wife. *Zuhār*, A crowd, multitude. (pl. ظهران *zuhrān*) The narrowest side of the feather of a bird's wing.

A ظهارة *zahārat*, (v. n. of ظهر) Being strong in the back. Being effaced, obliterated (a blemish or defect). Having (a camel) ready prepared for any occasion. *Zihārat*, The outside (of a garment, opposed to بطانة *bitānat*, The inside or lining).

A ظهاري *zahārīy*, (pl. of ظهري *zihrīy*) (Camels) trained and ready for use on any occasion.

A ظهاريّة *zuhārīyat*, A mode of tripping in wrestling, or throwing the adversary on his back. Modus coeundi. اوثقه الظهارية *awsakahu'z zuhāriyat* (or *zuhāriyat*), He held him fast by the shoulder-blade, or he pinioned him.

A ظهائر *zahāʼir*, (pl. of ظهيرة *zahīrat*) She-camels strong in the back.

A ظهر *zahr*, (v. n. of ظهر) Striking on the back. Training, breaking in for any kind of use (a camel). Boasting, glorying in. (pl. اظهر *azhur*, ظهور *zuhūr*, and ظهران *zuhrān*) The back. The superficies, especially the harder and more hilly part (of ground). A camel for the saddle. A road through the desert. The external or exoteric part of the Kur'ān, *i. e.* the text (بطن *batn* implying the esoteric part, or interpretation). Much wealth. An old kettle. A thing absent, concealed, hidden. The narrowest side of a bird's feather. Story, news, history, tradition. ظهر الكفّ *zahru'l kaff*, The back of the hand. على ظهر *ءala' zahrin*, Ready for a journey. على ظهر لسانه *ءala' zahri lisānihi*, (He read) by heart. قرأت على ظهر لساني *karaʼtu ءala' zahri lisānī*, I read off by heart. هو يأكل علي ظهر يدي *huwa yaʼkulu ءala' zahri yadī*, He eats at my charges. من ظهر القلب *min zahri'l kalb*, From memory, by heart. اعطاه عن ظهر يدن *aءtāhu ءan zahri yadin*, He gave to him without any recompense. جعل الحاجة بظهره *jaءala'l hājata bi zahrihi*, He placed the affair behind him, *i.e.* he forgot or neglected it. خفيف الظهر *khafīfu'z zahr*, (and ثقيل الظهر *sakīlu'z zahr*) Possessor of few (and many) domestics. قرين الظهر *karīnu'z zahr*, One who stands at another's back, or follows behind him in battle. اقران الظهر *akrānu'z zahr*, They who fight in the rear. لصّ عادي ظهر *lassun ءādī zahrin*, A thief who skulks in the rear and steals. اصبت منك مطر ظهر *asabtu minka matara zahrin*, I have received from thee much good. ولد الظهر *waladu'z zahr*, A boy neglected or turned adrift by his parents. سال واديهم ظهرا *sāla wādihim zahran*, Their valley streamed from rain fallen on their own land (درء *darʼan* signifying their neighbours' land). *Zuhr*, Mid-day, or a little time after the sun has passed the meridian, when it is most sultry. صلوة الظهر *salātu'z zuhr*, Afternoon-prayer. *Zahar*, (v. n. of ظهر) Complaining of or having a pain in the back. A pain in the back. Household utensils. *Zahir*, Pained in the back. Lumbaginous. Painful to the back.

A ظهران *zuhrān*, (pl. of ظهر *zahr*) Backs. (pl. of ظهار *zuhār*) The narrowest sides of birds' feathers.

A في الظهرانين *fi'z zahrānayni*, In two or three days. بين ظهرانينهم *bayn zahrānaynihim*, Between them, among them.

A ظهرة *zihrat*, An assistant. Assistance, help. *Zihrat*, *zuhrat*, or *zaharat*, Families, relations, allies. *Zuhrat*, A tortoise. An assistant.

A ظهريّ *zihrīy*, Thrown behind the back, forgotten, neglected. (pl. ظهاريّ *zahāriy*) Ready for use on every occasion (a camel).

A في الظهرين *fi'z zahrayni*, In two or in three days. بين ظهريهم *bayn zahrayhim*, Amongst them.

A ظهور *zahūr*, High, raised, prominent. *Zuhūr*, (v. n. of ظهر) Appearing, being conspicuous, happening. Flowing or proceeding from, emerging, being born, starting into being, springing up. Throwing behind one's back, forgetting, neglecting, despising, slighting. Appearance, birth. Reign, dominion, fame. ظهور اقبال *zuhūri ikbāl*, Reign of prosperity, happy progress, fortunate coincidence. صاحب ظهور *sāhib zuhūr*, Famous, glorious. (pl. of ظهر *zahr*) Backs.

A ظهير *zahīr*, Troubled with a pain in the back, afflicted with lumbago. Strong in the back. An assistant, supporter, protector, patron, associate, second, backer. A poetical name of a Persian poet.

A ظهيرة *zahīrat*, Mid-day, during the hot season. (pl. ظهائر *zahāʼir*) (A she-camel) strong in the back. قائم الظهيرة *kāʼimu'z zahīrat*, (or حدّ الظهيرة *haddu'z zahīrat*) The meridian, the highest altitude of the sun.

A ظيّ *zayy*, Honey.

A ظياة *zayʼat*, Foolish; a fool.

A ظئار *ziʼār*, (v. n. of ظأر) Hiring a nurse. Giving suck to the young of another: taking a liking to. Tying a bag over a camel's nose to induce her to suckle another's colt. الطعن ظئار قوم *at' taءn ziʼār kawmin*, Spearing inclines people to seek reconciliation.

A ظيّان *zayyān*, Wild jessamine; also another plant, with which they tan leather. Honey.

A ظيّة *zayyat*, A dead carcase ere it has burst.

A ظئر *ziʼr*, (pl. اظؤر *azʼur*, اظآر *azʼār*, ظؤور *zuʼūr*, ظؤورة *zuʼūrat*, ظؤار *zuʼār*, and ظؤرة *zuʼrat*) A nurse, foster-mother. Kind, benevolent. A pillar, prop, buttress of a citadel or for shoring up a wall.

ع

ع *ءayn*, (called عين غير منقوطه *ءayni ghayr mankūta* or عين مهمله *ءayni muhmala*, Undotted *ءayn*) The eighteenth letter of the Arabic alphabet, and used as the twenty-first of the Persian; expressing 70 in arithmetic. The power of this letter is that of ا *alif*, pronounced with greater exertion of the throat, not easy to be explained. As the Roman alphabet does not furnish any character of similar power, in imitation of Meninski, we have, in this edition, used the original letter itself in spelling the words with the European alphabet.

A عاب *ءāb*, (v. n. of عاب for عيب) Being damaged (merchandize). Injuring, spoiling. Accusing, reproaching, treating opprobriously. A defect, blemish. Disgrace, infamy.

A عابث *ءābis*, A player, a dallier.

A عابد *ءābid*, An adorer, or servant of God. A votary. Enraged, indignant. Loathing, refusing. Disgusted. Denying: a denier, disowner.

P عابدانه *ءābidāna*, Devoutly, as servant of God.

A عابديّة *ءābidiyat*, Name of a sect.

A عابر *ءābar*, Heber, son of Arphaxad, son of Shem. *ءābir*, Weeping (man or woman). A passenger. An interpreter, commentator, expounder. عابر السبيل *ءābiru's sabīl*, A passenger, traveller.

A عابرة *ءābirat*, Whatever passes current, or may be admitted (as a word or idiomatic phrase).

A عابس *ءābis*, (pl. عوابس *ءawābis*) Austere, stern, sour, crabbed, grim. A lion.

A عابية *ءābiyat*, Beautiful (woman).

A عاتر *ءātir*, (pl. عتر *ءutur*) Inflamed with lust.

A عاتق *ءātik*, (pl. عتق *ءutk*) Free, manumitted. Ancient, old, antique (coin). Wine long kept. (pl. عواتق *ءawātik*) (A girl) in the bloom of youth, kept confined at home, and not yet seen by her future husband. A girl somewhat past the bloom. A large leathern wine-bottle. An old bow red with age. (A young bird) ready for flight. That part of the back next the neck, the shoulders, withers. اميل العاتق *amyalu'l ءātik*, Distorted in that part, high-shouldered. حبل العاتق *hablu'l ءātik*, The nerve or tendon between the neck and back.

A عاتقة *ءātikat*, An old bow red with age.

A عاتك *ءātik*, Noble, generous. Excellent. Pure (wine), bright (colour). An old bow red with age. Changeable, inconstant; quarrelsome.

A عاتكة *ءātikat*, An old bow become red with age. A palm-tree which has not been fructified. (A woman) imbued with perfume. A woman's name.

A عاتم *ءātim*, Late (in the evening), tardy.

A عاتمات *ءātimāt*, Darkened by dust (stars).

A عاتن *ءātin*, (pl. عتن *ءutun*) Strong, intense.

A عاته *ءātih*, (pl. عتهاء *ءutahāʼ*) One who takes a pleasure in molesting or mimicking.

A عاتي *ءātī*, (pl. عتاة *ءutāt*) Proud, overbearing, exorbitant. Violent.

A عاثر *ءāsir*, A stumbler: in danger of falling.

A عاثور *ءāsūr*, A pit dug for catching lions or other wild beasts. Adversity, evil, an unlucky affair. A dangerous place.

A عاثي *ءāsī*, (pl. عثاة *ءusāt* and عثيّ *ءusiy*) Mischievous, destructive.

A عاج *ءāj*, Ivory. The bone of an elephant. Tortoiseshell. Gentle (she-camel). تخت عاج *takhti ءāj*, An ivory throne.

A عاجّ *ءājj*, Full of travellers (road).

A عاجب *ءājib*, Wonderful.

A عاجز *ءājiz*, (pl. عواجز *ءawājiz* and عجزة *ءajazat*) Weak, imbecile, impotent, exhausted, defective, hopeless, powerless, dejected. عاجز الرأي *ءājizu'r raʼy*, Weak in counsel. P عاجز كردن *ءājiz kardan*, To baffle, defeat, confound, perplex.

P عاجزانه *ءājizāna*, Weakly, hopelessly. Weak.

A عاجزي *ʿājizi*, Weakness.

A عاجل *ʿājil*, Hastening. Swift, expeditious. Agile. Transitory, frail, fading, fleeting (opposed to آجل *ājil*). حيات عاجله *hayāti ʿājila*, (This) transitory life (in opposition to حيات آجله *hayāti ājila* and حيات باقيه *hayāti bākiya*, Life eternal).

A عاجلاً *ʿājilan*, (P عاجلانه *ʿājilāna*) In haste. Hastily. In regard to the present life.

A عاجلة *ʿājilat*, The present fleeting life.

A عاجمة *ʿājimat*, That which bites: a tooth.

A عاجن *ʿājin*, (A camel) whose fœtus does not remain quiet in the womb.

A عاجنة *ʿājinat*, The middle (of a place).

A عاجيّ *ʿājiy*, Made or consisting of ivory.

A عاد *ʿād*, Name of an ancient Arabian tribe. (pl. of عادة *ʿādat*) Customs, usages.

A عادّ *ʿādd*, (in arithmetic) Any number which will divide two commensurable numbers without a remainder (as 6 and 3 which can measure 12 and 18).

A عادة *ʿādat*, (pl. عادات *ʿādāt*, عاد *ʿād*, and عيد *ʿīd*) Custom, mode, manner, habit, usage, rite, observation. امر عادت *amri ʿādat*, Ordinary business, any thing common or indifferent. علي عادته *ʿala' ʿādatihi*, According to his custom.

A عادةً *ʿādatan*, Habitually, customarily.

A عادتي *ʿādati*, Customary, habitual. A catamite.

A عادر *ʿādir*, A liar.

A عادق *ʿādik*, Uncertain, irresolute (in opinion).

A عادل *ʿādil*, One who deviates: devious. Equal, resembling. (pl. عدول *ʿudūl* and عدل *ʿadl*) Just, equitable: one who administers justice. A judge. One who gives associates to God; a polytheist.

P عادلانه *ʿādilāna*, Justly, equitably.

A عادن *ʿādin*, (A she-camel) continuing at one pasture. A camel feeding continually on a kind of salsuginous herbage (called حمض *hamz*).

A عادّون *ʿāddūn*, (pl. of عادّ *ʿādd*) Numberers. Angels who number the days of men.

A عادي *ʿādi*, (pl. عدي *ʿida'* or *ʿuda'*) A passer by, runner on foot. A transgressor, wicked, rapacious, fierce. A thief. A lion. Side of a plank. (pl. عداة *ʿudāt*) An enemy. ما ادري اي عاد هو *mā adrī ayyu ʿādin huwa*, I know not who he is. (irreg. from عادت *ʿādat*, but much used in Hindūstān) Accustomed, addicted.

A عاديّ *ʿādiy*, Belonging to the ancient tribe of عاد *ʿād*. Ancient, old (thing).

A سموءل بن عادياء *samawʾal bin ʿādiyāʾ*, Name of a man proverbial for keeping his promise.

A عاديات *ʿādiyāt*, (pl. of عادية *ʿādiyat*) Swift (horses). Hard running camels.

A عادية *ʿādiyat*, Injustice, iniquity. Hostility. Infantry (and sometimes cavalry) rushing before the rest to battle. Swift horses. (pl. عوادي *ʿawādi*) Camels pasturing upon حمض *hamz*. Distance. Business which diverts the attention. Camels not inclined for salsuginous pasture. Hard-running.

A عاذب *ʿāzib*, One abstaining from eating on account of excessive thirst. (Beasts of burden) standing without meat or drink. Under the open sky.

A عاذر *ʿāzir*, A circumciser. One who makes excuses, an apologist. The scar of a wound. Dung, excrement. A menstruous vein.

A عاذرة *ʿāzirat*, Ordure, excrement.

A عاذف *ʿāzif*, One eating nothing: fasting.

A عاذل *ʿāzil*, (pl. عذلة *ʿazalat*, عذّال *ʿuzzāl*, and عذّل *ʿuzzal*) One who reproves and blames, a railer. (pl. عواذل *ʿawāzil*) A certain vein from which menstruation flows. The old name of the Arabian month Shaabān or Shawwāl.

A عاذور *ʿāzūr*, (pl. عواذير *ʿawāzīr*) Adversity, evil. A long mark made on cattle.

A عاذوراء *ʿāzūrāʾ*, An inflammation in the throat.

A عاذي *ʿāzī*, (A place) far from water.

A عاذية *ʿāziyat*, (Camels) staying in a place without the salsuginous plant حمض *hamz*.

A عار *ʿār*, Reproach, scorn. Disgrace, ignominy, dishonour, shame. Bashfulness, modesty.

P عارداشتن *ʿār dāshtan*, To be ashamed, to blush. To cause to blush, to put to the blush.

A عارّ *ʿārr*, Scabby (camel).

A عارب *ʿārib*, Deep (river); plenteous in water (well). Pure, genuine (Arab).

A عارة *ʿārat*, Any thing lent or borrowed.

A عارج *ʿārij*, Absent. Concealed, hidden.

A عارد *ʿārid*, One who retires to one side.

A عارض *ʿāriz*, Happening, occurrent, accidental. Accident, event. Contingence. A misfortune, evil, disease. Diseased, broken down with age (she-camel). Reviewer of an army. Muster-master. General of an army. Side of the face, cheek. A large, heavy cloud; a low-hanging cloud bounding the horizon, resembling a mountain; also such a mountain. Any thing that meets the eye (as a curtain, and the like). A gift, present. The grinding teeth; or any except those in front. P عارض گرديدن *ʿāriz gardīdan* or شدن *shudan*, To happen, occur. عارض لشكر *ʿārizi lashkar*, A field-deputy. A عارض ممالك *ʿārizi mamālik*, Paymaster of the empire.

A عارضاً *ʿārizan*, Accidentally.

A عارضان *ʿārizāni*, (oblique عارضين *ʿārizayni*) (dual of عارض *ʿāriz*) Both sides of the face, the cheeks. خفيف العارضين *khafīfu'l ʿārizayn*, Thin of hairs on the sides of the face.

A عارضة *ʿārizat*, (pl. عوارض *ʿawāriz*) Any thing necessary to be done. A note or memorial. Accident, event. The side of the face. A transverse or horizontal piece of wood over a doorway or on a roof. A side-tooth. The side of the face, beard, or cheek. Eloquence. Strength, hardiness, courage. Skill, ability. A camel killed when labouring under any infirmity (عبيط *ʿabīt* implying one slaughtered without a blemish). A flush, heat, or scurf on the face.

A عارضةً *ʿārizatan*, Obliquely, askance.

P عارض نامه *ʿāriz-nāma*, Particulars of receipts of revenue.

A عارضيّ *ʿāriziy*, Accidental. صفت عارضيّه *sifati ʿāriziya*, An accidental quality.

A عارف *ʿārif*, Knowing, perceiving; scientific; wise, skilful, intelligent, sagacious. Well-known, notorious. Patient. A holy man. Head man, chief.

A عارفانه *ʿārifāna*, Wisely, acutely. Piously. A symbol. A reckoning, proportion of any payment.

A عارفة *ʿārifat*, (fem.) (pl. عوارف *ʿawārif*) Ingenious. Known. Patient. Benefit, favour, gift. حبست نفسا عارفة *habasat nafsan ʿārifatan*, She preserved a patient mind, she kept her temper.

A عارك *ʿārik*, (pl. عوارك *ʿawārik*) A menstruous woman. A camel whose elbow cuts his side.

A عارم *ʿārim*, Intense, violent. Impudent. Of a bad disposition. Dirty, obscene. Cold (day). سجن عارم *sijnu ʿārimin*, Name of a prison in Kūfa.

A عارن *ʿārin*, Distant (place). A lion.

A عارورة *ʿārūrat*, Sordid, hateful, wicked (man). Unlucky. Bunchless (camel).

A عاري *ʿāri*, Whatever surprises or comes unlooked for. (pl. عراة *ʿurāt*) Naked, denuded, bare. Destitute of hair. Exempt from, pure. Simple (prose), without rhyme or measure. Ignorant.

A عارية *ʿāriyat*, (pl. عواري *ʿawāri*) Any thing borrowed or lent. P عاريت دادن *ʿāriyat dādan*, To lend. عاريت گرفتن *ʿāriyat giriftan*, To borrow.

A عاريّة *ʿāriyat*, (pl. عواريّ *ʿawāriy*) Any thing borrowed or lent.

P عاريت سرا *ʿāriyat-sarā*, The present world.

A عاريتي *ʿāriyati*, Borrowed. False (hair). Common, of every day's wear. Transient, fading.

A عازّ *ʿāzz*, A long mountain.

A عازب *ʿāzib*, Unmarried. Distant pasture. A sheep feeding in a distant pasture. (pl. عزيب *ʿazīb*) A camel which feeds abroad all night.

A عازبة *ʿāzibat*, A wife. A camel.

A عازر *ʿāzar*, Lazarus.

A عازف *ʿāzif*, A singer or player of music.

A عازم *ʿāzim*, One who applies his mind. One undertaking (a journey). An enterprizer. عازم الزيارة *ʿāzimu'z ziyārat*, One who designs a visit.

P عازم شدن *ʿāzim shudan*, To set out on a journey.

A عاسّ *ʿāss*, (pl. عسس *ʿasas* and عسيس *ʿasīs*) Nightwatch, patrole.

A عاسف *ʿāsif*, Dying (camel). (A camel) afflicted with pestilence. One which has a trembling or falling of the larynx.

A عاسل *ʿāsil*, One who takes the honey from the hives. Tremulous (spear). (pl. عسل *ʿusul*) A good man. One whose deeds are praiseworthy, and whose fame is as sweet as honey. (pl. عسّل *ʿussal* and عواسل *ʿawāsil*) A wolf.

A عاسلة *ʿāsilat*, (A hive) full of honey.

A عاسم *ʿāsim*, (pl. عسم *ʿusum*) Who earns his

bread by labour. One who brings trouble and vexation upon his household. Covetous, greedy.

A عاسن *ʻāsin*, Narrow, confined (place).

A عاسي *ʻāsī*, A palm-tree. A branch and bunch of dates. Hard and dry (branch).

A عاشب *ʻāshib*, (A camel) pasturing on fresh grass (عشب *ʻushb*). (A field) abundant in herbage.

A عاشر *ʻāshir*, A tenth. A tithe-collector. A publican, revenue-collector.

A عاشرة *ʻāshirat*, (pl. عاشرات *ʻāshirāt*) A female hyena. The circle in which the عواشر *ʻawāshir* (10th verses) of the Kur'ān is contained. (pl. عواشر *ʻawāshir*) Every tenth verse of the Kur'ān. (pl. اعشار *aʻshār*) A prize at a game of hazard. A portion of a slaughtered camel. The outer feather of a bird's wing.

A عاشق *ʻāshik*, A lover, inamorato, sweetheart, mistress. Amorous. Transported with divine love.

P عاشق بيچاره *ʻāshiki bichāra*, A species of ivy. عاشق خشك *ʻāshiki khushk*, A faithless lover. عاشق سگ جان *ʻāshiki sag-jān*, A worldling. عاشق شدن *ʻāshik shudan*, To fall in love. عاشق مفتون *ʻāshiki maftūn*, (عاشق ديوانه *ʻāshiki dīwāna*, or عاشق مجنون *ʻāshiki majnūn*) Frantic, mad, dying with love. A عاشق و معشوق *ʻāshik u maʻshūk*, Lover and beloved.

P عاشقانه *ʻāshikāna*, Amorously. A lover.

P عاشق با *ʻāshik-bā*, (or عاشق وا *ʻāshik-wā*) A dish made of fruits, as dried peaches, prunes, grapes, walnuts, or almonds boiled with the acid of sumach and pomegranates.

A عاشقة *ʻāshikat*, A mistress.

A عاشقي *ʻāshikī*, Love. The condition of a lover.

P عاشقي نمودن *ʻāshikī namūdan*, To fall in love.

A عاشقية *ʻāshikīyat*, A being enamoured.

A عاشم *ʻāshim*, A sort of tree. A sand-hill.

A عاشوراء *ʻāshūrā*, (or عاشورا *ʻāshūra'*) (pl. عواشير *ʻawāshīr*) (or يوم عاشورا *yawmi ʻāshūra'*) The tenth or ninth of the first month, محرّم *muharram*.

A عاشي *ʻāshī*, One who eats or prepares (for a journey) in the evening. A traveller. One who approaches or makes up to.

A عاشية *ʻāshiyat*, A camel grazing in the evening.

A عاص *ʻās*, (v. n. of عاص for عوص) Confounding (an adversary), reducing (him) to a nonplus.

A عاصب *ʻāsib*, One intensely hungry, who ties a stone round his waist. Red and dusky (horizon).

A عاصد *ʻāsid*, A dying camel turning his head over his shoulders.

A عاصر *ʻāsir*, A presser, squeezer.

A عاصف *ʻāsif*, Strong, violent (wind). Stormy, blowing (day). Declining, deviating (an arrow from the mark). Whatever inclines or is bent.

A عاصفة *ʻāsifat*, A strong, violent wind.

A عاصل *ʻāsil*, Firm, strong (arrow).

A عاصم *ʻāsim*, A defender. Safe, protected. Chaste, virtuous. A man's name. ابو عاصم *abū ʻāsim*, Father of safety, *i.e.* Barley-broth.

A عاصمة *ʻāsimat*, (The protected) Madina.

A عاصي *ʻāsī*, (pl. عصاة *ʻusāt*) Disobedient, rebellious, seditious, refractory, stubborn. A sinner, rebel. A camel's colt independent of his dam. A vein, the blood of which cannot be stanched. The Orontes.

P عاصي شدن *ʻāsī shudan*, To rebel, mutiny.

A عاصية *ʻāsiyat*, Inaccessible, impregnable.

A عاضّ *ʻāzz*, A biter. (A camel) feeding on the plant عضّ *ʻizz*.

A عاضّة *ʻāzzat*, (pl. عواضّ *ʻawāzz*) A camel feeding on the thorny plant عضّ *ʻizz*.

A عاضد *ʻāzid*, An ass which hugs the sides of the female when covering. One who walks by the side of his beast. A male camel, which biting the arm (عضد *ʻazud*) of the female, forces her to crouch.

A عاضر *ʻāzir*, Who or what hinders: an obstacle.

A عاضه *ʻāzih*, (pl. عواضه *ʻawāzih*) Pasturing on the thorny shrub عضاه *ʻizāh* (a camel). A magician, sorcerer. حيّة عاضه *hayyatun ʻāzihun* (or عاضهة), A serpent stinging to death on the spot.

A عاضهة *ʻāzihat*, A she-camel pasturing on the thorny shrub عضاه *ʻizāh*.

A عاضي *ʻāzī*, Well clothed and delicately fed.

A عاطر *ʻātir*, (pl. عطر *ʻutur*) Fond of odours. Odoriferous. Benevolent, generous, noble. Gracious.

A عاطس *ʻātis*, Sneezing. Dawn. (A deer) advancing towards or meeting a person (a good omen).

A عاطش *ʻātish*, Thirsty.

A عاطف *ʻātif*, (pl. عطف *ʻutf*) Inclined to. Benevolent, gracious. A sheet or mantle. A fawn whose neck is bent when couchant. The horse which comes in sixth in a race. واو عاطفه *wāwi ʻātifa*, The conjunction و, And, connecting two synonymes, or two opposites, which is then pronounced *u*: as, درون و بيرون *darūn u bīrūn*, Interior and exterior. When joining different sentences it is pronounced *wa*.

A عاطفة *ʻātifat*, (pl. عواطف *ʻawātif*) Affection benevolence. Kin, relationship. Grace, favour.

A عاطل *ʻātil*, Idle, vacant, wanting. Vain, useless. (pl. عواطل *ʻawātil* and عطّل *ʻuttal*) (A woman) whose neck is destitute of ornaments.

A عاطم *ʻātim*, (pl. عطم *ʻutum*) Perishing.

A عاطن *ʻātin*, (A camel) lying down near the cistern after he has quenched his thirst.

A عاطنة *ʻātinat*, (pl. عواطن *ʻawātin* and عطون *ʻutūn*) (A camel) lying down near the cistern after he has quenched his thirst. A sea-port in Yaman.

A عاطوس *ʻātūs*, Any thing exciting sneezing, a sternutatory. A certain animal of bad omen.

A عاطوف *ʻātūf*, A trap or gin formed of a bent stick; a springe.

A عاطي *ʻātī*, A taker, receiver.

A عاظب *ʻāzib*, One who alights in a sandy country.

A عاظل *ʻāzil*, (pl. عظّلی *ʻazla'*) (Locusts) sticking close together.

A عاف *ʻāf*, A level country with soft soil.

A عافط *ʻāfit*, Breaking wind. Bleating. Sneezing.

A عافطة *ʻāfitat*, A shepherdess. A ewe.

A عافق *ʻāfik*, A man going constantly to and fro.

A عافل *ʻāfil*, One who wears short garments over long ones.

A عافور *ʻāfūr*, Misfortune: as, وقع في عافور شرّ *wakaʻa fī ʻāfūri sharrin*, He fell into trouble.

A عافي *ʻāfī*, (pl. عفاة *ʻufāt*) Who asks or receives a favour or food. Plentiful, abundant, numerous, long, luxuriant. Forgiving. Arriving. A guest. Long-haired. Meat left in a kettle in return for the loan of it. (pl. عفيّ *ʻufīy*) Obliterated, effaced. One who obliterates, effaces, or destroys.

A عافية *ʻāfiyat*, A preserving in, or a restoring to, health. A defending from harm. Health, safety. (pl. عوافي *ʻawāfī*) Searching for food (man, beast, or bird). (A crowd) approaching to water. Those who ask favours. عافية اللحم *ʻāfiyatu'l lahm*, Fleshy (she-camel). كثير العافية *kasīru'l ʻāfiyat*, One who entertains many guests.

A عاق *ʻāk*, (or عاق باق *ʻāk bāk*) A raven's caw.

A عاقّ *ʻākk*, (pl. عققة *ʻakakat*) Disobedient, undutiful, rebellious, disloyal.

A عاقب *ʻākib*, A successor or deputy, one who comes last (hence an epithet of Muhammad, as being styled the last of the prophets). (pl. عواقب *ʻawākib*) A she-camel that eats up the remains of the provender; also one that, after drinking a little, goes to her lair, and presently returns to the water.

A عاقبة *ʻākibat*, (v. n. of عقب) Coming after, succeeding. Considering the end of any thing. (pl. عواقب *ʻawākib*) End, conclusion, success, accomplishment, issue. Recompense, reward. A son, offspring. Finally, at length, in the end. عاقبة الامر *ʻākibatu'l amr*, Termination of any business. The long and short of the matter. Finally.

P عاقبت انديش *ʻākibat-andesh*, Provident.

P عاقبت بيني *ʻākibat-bīnī*, Foresight.

A عاقد *ʻākid*, One binding, fastening, tying in a knot. A binder. A she-camel when she has conceived (as she then twists her tail in a knot). A doe which turns her head back, placing it on her rump. The environs of a well.

A عاقر *ʻākir*, (pl. عقّر *ʻukhar*) Barren (woman). Addle, not procreating (man). One who hamstrings. (Large tracts of) unfertile sands. A high sand-hill. An incomparable woman.

A عاقر قرحا *ʻāhir karhā*, Dracunculus.

A عاقف *ʻākif*, Crooked-legged (sheep).

A عاقل *ʻākil*, (pl. عقلاء *ʻukalā* and عقّال *ʻukkāl*) Prudent, judicious, intelligent, sensible, wise, sagacious. A mountain-goat securely perched on a high rock. A deer. The relations of a man who may inherit his property, as a father, grandfather, or son's son.

P عاقلانه *ʻākilāna*, Prudently, wisely. Prudent.

A عاقلة *ǥākilat*, A sensible woman. A bride-dresser, tire-woman. Paternal relations who pay the expiatory mulct for manslaughter. Magistrates.

A عاقلي *ǥākilī*, Wisdom, sense, intellect.

A عاقور *ǥākūr*, (A saddle) galling a (horse's) back. Biting (ass).

A عاقول *ǥākūl*, (pl. عواقيل *ǥawākīl*) The winding of a river. A country in which there is no open road. An intricate affair. A whirlpool, gulf. A kind of caper. A river. A heap of sand. A wave. The teak-tree.

A عاقولى *ǥākūla'*, A name of the city of Kūfa.

A عاكب *ǥākib*, (pl. عكوب) A great multitude.

A عاكف *ǥākif*, (pl. عكوف *ǥukūf*) Assiduous, diligent. One who remains behind. Constantly employed in devotion. P عاكفان قدس *ǥākifāni kuds*, Those who reside constantly at Jerusalem from motives of piety.

A عاكل *ǥākil*, (pl. عكل *ǥukul*) A dwarf. A miser, a niggard. Inauspicious.

A عاكوب *ǥākūb*, Dust.

A عاكي *ǥākī*, Dead. Dying. One who sells عكي *ǥuka'*, or who is given to drink the milk or beverage called عكيّ *ǥakiy*.

A ما له عال و لا مال *mā lahu ǥālun wa lā mālun*, He has nothing.

A عالّ *ǥāll*, Whose camels have drunk twice.

A عالة *ǥālat*, A parapluie, or any thing that shelters from rain. A she-ostrich. Poverty. (pl. of عائل *ǥāʼil*) Poor. (pl. of عيّل *ǥayyil*) Domestics, persons who are maintained in a family.

A عالّة *ǥāllat*, (Camels) which have drunk twice.

A عالج *ǥālij*, (pl. عوالج *ǥawālij*) (A camel) feeding on the herb علجان *ǥalajān*. Sand lying layer upon layer.

A عالط *ǥālit*, A poet.

A عالق *ǥālik*, (pl. عوالق *ǥawālik*) (A camel) feeding on the plant علقى *ǥalka'*. A camel browsing on the higher parts of thorny shrubs (as if suspended from them).

A عالك *ǥālik*, Hard, tough (meat).

A عالك عاليا *ǥālaka ǥāliyan*, An exclamation made to any one when about to stumble.

A عالم *ǥālam*, (pl. عالمون *ǥālamūn* and عوالم *ǥawālim*) The world. The universe. Time, age. Condition, state. Men, creatures, every thing which the world contains. P عالم آب *ǥālami āb*, A great drinker. A drinking-bout. A عالم ارواح *ǥālami arwāh*, The world of spirits. عالم اسباب *ǥālami asbāb*, The world, this life. عالم باقي *ǥālami bāķī*, Future state. P عالم بالا *ǥālami bālā*, The world above, heaven. عالم تر *ǥālami tar*, The world of pagan ignorance. A عالم تربيت *ǥālami tarbiyat*, World of discipline. P عالم جان *ǥālami jān*, World of spirits. This world. The elements. A عالم جبروت *ǥālami jabarūt*, (or عالم ملكوت *ǥālami malakūt*) World of the angels, or the heaven above the starry firmament, where the angels, according to the Muhammadan system, are supposed to dwell; and immediately under عالم عظمت *ǥālami ǥazamat*, The high empyrean heaven, the residence of Omnipotence. P عالم خاك *ǥālami khāk*, The earth. The human body. عالم دورنگ *ǥālami du rang*, The earth as subject to the vicissitudes of day and night. A hypocrite. عالم ديگر *ǥālami dīgar*, The other world. A عالم ذوق *ǥālami zawk*, The world of delight. عالم سفلي *ǥālami siflī*, The earth. عالم شهادت *ǥālami shahādat*, The visible world. عالم صباوت *ǥālami sabāwat*, (and عالم طفوليّت *ǥālami tufūliyat*) The age of youth, childhood, infancy. عالم صغير *ǥālami saghīr*, The world; men; kings. عالم صوري *ǥālami sūrī*, The visible world. عالم عالم *ǥālam ǥālam*, The greatest, highest, most. عالم علوي *ǥālami ǥalwī*, The upper world. عالم غيب *ǥālami ghayb*, The world of absence, *i.e.* a future state. عالم كبير *ǥālam kabīr*, Nature, condition. عالم كون *ǥālami kawn*, The visible world. عالم لاهوت *ǥālami lāhūt*, Court of heaven. P درعالم مثال *dar ǥālami masāl*, In the world of fancy, in a dream, in ecstasy. A عالم معقول *ǥālami maǥkūl*, The rational world. عالم معنى *ǥālami maǥna'*, The invisible world. عالم ناسوت *ǥālami nāsūt*, The world of mortals. عالم نباتات *ǥālami nabātāt*, Botany. مشهور عالم *mashhūri ǥālam*, Known to all the world. *ǥālim*, (pl. علّام *ǥullām*) Learned, intelligent, wise. Theoretic (in contradistinction to عامل *ǥāmil*, Practical). One who makes a fissure in the upper lip. عالم الغيب والشهادة *ǥālimu'l ghayb wa'sh shahādat*, (God) who knows the past and the present, the invisible and the visible, omniscient. P عالم تر *ǥālimi tar*, (A wet or green doctor) A hypocrite or ignorant pretender.

P عالم آرا *ǥālam-ārā* or آراي, World-adorning.

P عالم افروز *ǥālam-afroz*, World-illuminating.

P عالمانه *ǥālimāna*, Wisely, learnedly.

P عالمپناه *ǥālam-panāh*, Asylum of the world.

P عالمتاب *ǥālam-tāb*, World-inflaming.

P عالمسوز *ǥālam-soz*, World-inflaming. برق عالمسوز *barki ǥālam-soz*, World-inflaming lightning.

P عالم گرد *ǥālam-gard*, A great traveller.

P عالم گير *ǥālam-gīr*, Conquering the universe. One of Awrang-zeb's titles.

P عالم نورد *ǥālam-naward*, A great traveller.

A عالمون *ǥālamūn*, (pl. of عالم *ǥālam*) Worlds. ربّ العالمين *rabbu'l ǥālamīn*, Lord of hosts or worlds.

P عالمي *ǥālamī*, Worldly, existing in the world.

P عالميان *ǥālamiyān*, Men, mankind.

A عاله *ǥālih*, Inconstant, light, vain, fickle (woman). A (female) ostrich.

A عالي *ǥālī*, High, sublime, eminent, excellent, grand. *ǥālī*, (with tanwīn عال *ǥālin*) The upper part. Above. من عال *min ǥālin*, From the upper part, from above. عالي حضرت *ǥālī-hazrat*, عالي شان *ǥālī-shān*, عالي جناب *ǥālī-janāb*, عالي جاه *ǥālī-jāh*, عالي قدر *ǥālī-kadar*, عالي مقام *ǥālī-makām*, عالي مقدار *ǥālī-mikdār*, عالي منقبت *ǥālī-mankibat*, عالي مكان *ǥālī-makān* (with other similar phrases, which are often joined in one word, as عالیحضرت *ǥālī-hazrat*), are titles of dignity and address, occurring frequently in letters to and from men of high rank; implying, majesty, excellence, of exalted dignity, powerful. عالي الكعب *ǥālī'l kaǥb*, Noble. عالي و دون *ǥālī u dūn*, High and low.

A عاليّ *ǥāliy*, Native of, belonging to, Hijāz.

A عالية *ǥāliyat*, (fem.) (pl. عوالي *ǥawālī*) High, exalted. Sublimity. Any thing high or tall. The upper half of a spear. The upper part. The higher part of Arabia, from above Najd to Tihāmat, behind Mecca; the province of Hijāz or Arabia Petræa.

P عالي سراي *ǥālī sarāy*, The high seraglio, a monarch's court.

P عاليشان *ǥālī-shān*, Of high degree. Imperial, royal, most noble, excellent, dignified. نشان عاليشان *nishāni ǥālī-shān*, The imperial signet.

P عالي گهر *ǥālī-guhar*, Valuable pearl or gem.

A عالي همّت *ǥālī-himmat*, High-minded, noble, gracious, generous.

P عالي همّتي *ǥālī-himmatī*, Elevation of mind.

A عام *ǥām*, (pl. اعوام *aǥwām*) A year. A day. العام *al ǥām*, This year. عام اوّل *ǥāmi awwal*, Last year. P عام ديگر *ǥāmi dīgar*, Next year. عام سنة *ǥāmu sanatin*, A year of dearth. A عام عام اوّل *ǥāmu ǥāmi awwal*, The year before last. عام الفيل *ǥāmu'l fīl*, A feast in commemoration of the defeat of a king of Egypt who besieged Mecca before the time of Muhammad. (pl. of عامة *ǥāmat*) Many handsful (of corn).

A عامّ *ǥāmm*, Complete, perfect. A year. *ǥāmm* or *ǥām*, Common, universal, public, popular, vulgar. The vulgar, common people, commons, commonalty. حاسّة عامّة *hāssaǥi ǥāmma*, Common sense. خاصّ و عامّ *khāss u ǥāmm*, Noble and plebeian, gentle and simple.

A عامة *ǥāmat*, (pl. عام *ǥām*) A handful, or number of handsful (of corn). The wreath, sash, or turban rolled round the head. The head of a horseman, as appearing above the crowd. Inflated leathern bottles, used as rafts in crossing streams.

A عامّة *ǥāmmat*, (fem.) Common, universal, vulgar. (pl. عمم *ǥamam*) The vulgar, commons, plebeians. The general resurrection. A community, society. All, every body. A raft. عامّة افاضل *ǥāmmaǥi afāzil*, All the doctors or learned men. عامّة برايا *ǥāmmaǥi barāya'*, All the nobility and vassals. عامّة رعيّت *ǥāmmaǥi raǥiyat*, The lower order of men, the common people, peasantry. عامّة عباد الله *ǥāmmaǥi ǥibādu'llāh*, All the servants of God. All the subjects. عامّة ناس *ǥāmmaǥi nās*, All mankind. عامّة كافّة *ǥāmmatan kāffatan*, Generally, universally, commonly.

A عامد *ǥāmid*, One who proposes, purposes,

designs, pursues, or makes for.

A عامدا ʿāmidan, Purposely, designedly.

A عامر ʿāmir (pl. عمّار ʿummār) Cultivated, inhabited, flourishing. Rich, abundant. A visitant. Frequented, standing, in preservation (building). An inhabitant. A family, part of a tribe. Rustic. Royal, imperial. A hyena's cub. A serpent. A proper name. امّ عامر ummu ʿāmir, A hyena.

A عامرة ʿāmirat, (fem.) Long-lived. Cultivated (country). Well-replenished (treasury). (pl. عوامر ʿawāmir) A serpent. خزينهٔ عامره khazīnaʾi ʿāmira, The royal treasury.

A عامس ʿāmis, A kind of dish. (See آمس āmis).

A عامق ʿāmiḳ, (A camel) feeding on the plant عمقى ʿimḳaʾ.

A عامل ʿāmil, A maker, performer. (pl. عملة ʿamalat and عمّال ʿummāl) An operator, workman. An intendant of finance, collector of revenue (inferior to an امين amīn and a زميندار zamīn-dār). An officer, functionary. Practical (opposed to عالم ʿālim, Theoretical). (pl. عوامل ʿawāmil) (in grammar) Governing. That part of the spear-staff nearest to the iron head. P عاملان درياوكان ʿāmilāni daryāwakān, The planets Saturn, Jupiter, Mars, the Sun, Venus, Mercury, and the Moon. A عامل طبع ʿāmili tabʿ, The animal spirit. P عامل جان ʿāmili jān, Creator of the soul, i.e. God. Elements.

A عاملة ʿāmilat, (pl. عوامل ʿawāmil) One word governing another: a governing power (as a preposition or particle). That part of the spear-staff nearest to the iron head.

P عامل نامه ʿāmil-nāma, A government warrant or order empowering one to take possession.

A عام منفعت ʿām-manfaʿat, Universally useful.

A عامود ʿāmūd, (pl. عواميد ʿawāmīd) A column.

A عاموص ʿāmūṣ, Emmaus.

A عامه ʿāmih, (pl. عمّه ʿummah) Astonished, confounded, puzzled, perplexed, nonplused.

A عامّى ʿāmmī, The common people. Ignorant.

A عامىّ ʿāmīy, General, common, universal. Plebeian. Dry herbage a year old.

A عامّىّ ʿāmmīy, Annual, or a year old (plant). Common, plebeian. Popular, vulgar.

A عامية ʿāmiyat, Weeping, wailing (woman).

A عانّ ʿānn, A long rope.

A عانب ʿānib, Possessor of grapes (عنب ʿinab).

A عانة ʿānat, (pl. عون ʿūn) A herd of wild asses, or of asses' colts. A she-ass. Hair about the privy parts. Certain white stars below those called سعود suʿūd. A town in Mesopotamia, or Diyār-bakar, on the banks of the Euphrates, famous for its asses.

A عانّة ʿānnat, A cloud.

A عانت ʿānit. See عانس ʿānis.

A عاند ʿānid, (pl. عنّد ʿunnad) A strayer from the road. Obstinate, refractory, wilful, perverse, contumacious. Flowing (sweat), which will not stop.

A عانذة ʿānizat, The root of the chin and of the ear.

A عانس ʿānis, (pl. عوانس ʿawānis, عنس ʿuns, عنّس ʿunnas, and عنوس ʿunūs) (A girl) remaining long in her parents' house after the marriageable age; an old maid. An old bachelor. Handsome, fat, and full-grown.

A عانسة ʿānisat, (fem.) Fat and full-grown.

A عانقاء ʿāniḳāʾ, The hole of a field-mouse.

A عانك ʿānik, Sands heaped together, high, pathless, and difficult of passage. Necessary. A hanger-on. A fat woman. Red (blood). Menstruous.

A عاني ʿānī, (pl. عناة ʿunāt) Captive. Flowing, fluid (blood). Fatiguing, toilsome, distressing.

A عانىّ ʿānīy, (An ass) from the town عانة ʿānat.

A عاوز ʿāwiz, Poor.

A عاهة ʿāhat, Murrain. Blight.

A عاهر ʿāhir, A whoremonger. A whore.

A عاهرة ʿāhirat, A female thief. A witch, hag. A whore.

A عاهل ʿāhil, A mighty king. A woman in want of a husband.

A عاهن ʿāhin, (pl. عواهن ʿawāhin) A palm-branch lying close to the heart of the tree. A member of the human body. A vein in the uterus of a camel, or in the human members. Hereditary (wealth). (A camel) bred by its owner. Present. Fixed, established (in a place). Poor, indigent. Lazy, slothful, relaxed, enervated.

A عائب ʿāʾib, Thick milk.

A عائث ʿāʾis, A lion.

A عائج ʿāʾij, Standing.

A عائد ʿāʾid, Who or what returns, refers to, turns towards, appertaineth to, belongs, relates, or is connected. (pl. عود ʿawd, عوّاد ʿūwād, and عوّد ʿūwad) A visitor of the sick. A payer, restorer.

A عائدة ʿāʾidat, (pl. عوائد ʿawāʾid) Return, produce, profit. Custom. Merit, reward. Favour. Benefit, utility. Kindness. A present. Pity.

P عايده ʿāyida, A trowel.

A عائذ ʿāʾiz, (pl. عوذ ʿūz and عوذان ʿūzān) (A mare, camel, or doe) the tenth or fifteenth day after colting, from that time called مطفل mutfil.

A عائر ʿāʾir, Striking out, piercing, or blinding the eye (an arrow or stone, especially thrown by an unseen hand). Any hair, straw, or mote paining the eye. A sty on the lower eyelid. Wateryness, bloodshot. عائرة عينين ʿāʾiratu ʿaynayni, Abundance, as much as can satisfy both eyes.

A عائس ʿāʾis, An able manager of stock.

A عائش ʿāʾish, Living comfortably (man).

A عائشة ʿāʾishat, The daughter of Abū bakr, and the favourite wife of Muhammad. She was distinguished by the title of Mother of the faithful. A name common to men and women.

P عايشه ʿāyisha, A wagtail. عايشهٔ لب جوى ʿāyishaʾi labi joy, Name of a small bird called in Arabic صعوه saʿwa.

A عائص ʿāʾis, (pl. عوص ʿūs) A sheep not conceiving for some years.

A عائض ʿāʾiz, Given in exchange for another.

A عائضين ʿāʾizīn, At any time, ever. عوض العائضين ʿawza'l ʿāʾizīna, Ever, at any time.

A عائط ʿāʾit, (pl. عوط ʿūt, عيط ʿīt, عيّط ʿuyyat, عوطط ʿūtat, ʿawtat, or ʿawtut) Not conceiving for some years, yet not barren (woman, camel). A camel not conceiving when covered the first time.

A عائف ʿāʾif, Averse, loathing: one who nauseates (meat or drink). A soothsayer, augur, prophet. Blushing, ashamed, disdainful. (A bird) hovering over a corse or water, with intent to alight.

A عائفة ʿāʾifat, A female soothsayer.

A عائق ʿāʾiḳ, (pl. عوّق ʿūwaḳ) Who or what prevents, hinders, diverts, frustrates, detains. Slack in paying. An accident; hindrance.

A عائل ʿāʾil, Inclining to one side (judge), weighing down (scale). One who undertakes to support, mind, or look after. Conquering, prevailing. Preponderating. (pl. عالة ʿālat, عيّل ʿuyyal, and عيلى ʿaylaʾ) Poor, indigent. Embarrassed, at a loss where to search for a thing that is missing.

A عائلة ʿāʾilat, A painful motion or gait.

A عائم ʿāʾim, A swimmer. Name of an idol.

A عائن ʿāʾin, Flowing (water). One who looks with a fixed and malignant eye. A spectator, beholder, looker on, seer, eyer. Some, any one.

A عائنة ʿāʾinat, Any thing apparent. Cattle and shepherds. اوّل عائنة awwala ʿāʾinatin, (or ادنى عائنة adnaʾ ʿāʾinatin) The first thing (I stumbled upon him).

A عائهة ʿāʾihat, Clamour, exclamation.

A عب ʿab, The light of the sun.

A عبّ ʿabb, (v. n. of عبّ) Drinking (like a horse, or) without suction (as a dove). Drinking with the mouth (without using a vessel or the hands). Falling to the water with noise (a bucket). Being long (a plant). The light of the sun. Hail. ʿubb, A gusset, or the arm-hole of a sleeve.

A عبء ʿabʾ, (v. n. of عبا) Mixing (perfumes). Dressing or doing up properly (merchandise). Being anxious (about any thing). Drawing up an army in battle-array. Sunshine. ما اعبا به mā aʿbaʾu bihi, What shall I do with him? I care not about him. ʿibʾ or ʿabʾ, (pl. اعباء aʿbāʾ) A bale of merchandise. A burden, load, weight. Any thing equivalent or equiponderant. Like.

A عباء ʿabāʾ, (pl. اعبئة aʿbiʾat) A coarse cloth of which they make surtout coats. A cloak forming the outer garment over all others, worn open in front, and much resembling an English boat-cloak. A black striped cloak or habit worn by dervishes. Heavy, unwholesome. A foolish fellow. P عباپوش ʿabā-posh, Clothed in the garment abā.

A عباءة ʿabāʾat, A sort of garment of goats' hair.

A عباب ʿibāb, (v. n. 3 of عبّ) Contending about glory or augmentation. ʿubāb, A wave, surge, billow; a great body of water. A palm-leaf. An inundation, overflow of water. First or uppermost part. لا عباب *lā ʿabāba*, He does not drink.

A عبّاب *ʿabbāb*, One who fills himself with drink.

A عبابيد *ʿabābīd*, Men or horses going different ways. Distant roads. Hillocks.

A عباة *ʿabāt*, A black striped cloth of goats' hair.

A عباد *ʿibād*, A servant. (pl. of عبد *ʿabd*) Servants. Men, mankind. A society, fellowship. عباد الله *ʿibādu'llāh*, The servants of God. *ʿibād* or *ʿabād*, Certain dispersed Arabian tribes who, in Hīra in Mesopotamia, embraced Christianity.

A عبّاد *ʿubbād*, (pl. of عابد *ʿābid*) Monks or others dedicated to the service of God.

A عبادة *ʿibādat*, Divine worship, adoration. Obedience. Service, servitude. Pious works.

P عبادتخانه *ʿibādat-khāna*, A house of worship.

P عبادتكار *ʿibādat-kār*, Religious, devout.

P عبادتگاه *ʿibādat-gāh*, A place of worship; a church, chapel, mosque, temple, synagogue.

A عبادلة *ʿabādilat*, Name of certain companions of Muhammad, in number two hundred and twenty, of whom four were his most intimate friends.

A عباديّ *ʿibādīy*, A Christian of Diyār-bakar.

A عباديد *ʿabādīd*, Men or horses going different roads. مرّ راكبا عباديده *marra rākiban ʿabādīdahu*, He went his own way.

A عباديديّ *ʿabādīdīy*, Resembling bodies of men running to and fro; erratic, discursive, desultory.

A عبّار *ʿabbār*, Robust, always travelling.

A عبارة *ʿibārat*, (v. n. of عبر) Interpreting (a dream). Explaining. (pl. عبارات *ʿibārāt*) Explanation, interpretation, commentary. Trope, figure, metaphor, metaphorical allusion; a mode of expressing: synonym. Sense, meaning, intent. Style (in writing), speech, phrase: word, dialect, idiom.

P عبارت سنج *ʿibārat-sanj*, Attentive to style.

A عبارد *ʿubārid*, Tender, delicate beautiful girl. Soft, limber (branch).

A عبارى *ʿabāra'*, (pl. of عبرى *ʿabra'*) Weeping (women). (pl. of عبران) Weeping (men or eyes).

A عبّاس *ʿabbās*, A lion. The son of عبد المطلب *ʿabdu'l mutlab*, Muhammad's uncle, and ancestor of the Abbāssi caliphs, who reigned from A. D. 749 till the extinction of the califat in 1258. Name of a plant, marvel of Peru.

A عبّاسيّ *ʿabbāsīy*, Belonging unto the house of Abbās; also a species of coin named from those caliphs. Red colour. صوت عبّاسي *sawti ʿabbāsī*, A stentorian voice. P لشكر عبّاسي *lashkari ʿabbāsī*, The Arabian or Abbāssi army, and afterwards used to signify the Turkish troops.

A عبّاسى صوت *ʿabbāsī-sawt*, One with a sonorous voice, like that of Abbās. A stentor.

A عباط *ʿibāt*, (pl. of عبيط *ʿabīt*) Fat, unblemished (camels) slaughtered.

A عباقاء *ʿabāqāʾ*, A man who sticks close to one.

A عباقة *ʿabākat*, (v. n. of عبق) Adhering to a thing (perfume). Dwelling in a place.

A عباقريّ *ʿabāqarīy*, A kind of carpet.

A عباقية *ʿabākiyat*, (v. n. of عبق) Adhering to any thing (perfume). Abiding in a place. A shrewd, cunning rogue. A certain thorny tree. A robber. The scar of a wound on the principal part of the face.

A عباقيس *ʿabākīs*, The remainder of the remains of any thing, a remnant of a remnant.

A عباقيل *ʿabākīl*, Remains of disease or love.

A عبال *ʿabāl*, A thick mountain rose-tree, whence they cut rods; of such tree they say was Moses' rod. *ʿibāl*, (pl. of عبلاء *ʿablāʾ*) Whitish stones. (pl. of عبلة *ʿablat*) Perfectly-formed and elegantly-shaped (women).

A عبالة *ʿabālat*, (v. n. of عبل) Being thick, stout, lusty. Being symmetrically formed. Being white.

A عبالّة *ʿabāllat*, (or عبالة *ʿubālat*) Weight.

A عبام *ʿabām*, A stuttering man. Distressed, helpless. *ʿubām*, Much (water).

A عباماء *ʿabāmāʾ*, Foolish; a fool.

A عبامة *ʿabāmat*, A being foolish. Folly.

A عباهر *ʿabāhir*, Fleshy, delicate, beautiful, large, and tall.

A عباهل *ʿabāhil*, Free, without keeper (camels).

A عباهلة *ʿabāhilat*, Kings of Arabia Felix.

A عباية *ʿabāyat*, A black garment of goats' hair. Cruel, injurious. Heavy, dull.

A عبائر *ʿabāʾir*, (pl. of عبور) Yearling (sheep).

P عبائي *ʿabāʾī*, A saddle-cloth.

A عبب *ʿubab*, (pl. of عبّة *ʿubbat*) Berries of nightshade. The shrub Palma Christi. A tree of the sort called اعلاث *aʿlās*. *ʿubub*, Waters swelling and diffusing themselves.

A عبّة *ʿubbat*, (pl. عبب *ʿubab*) A berry of the nightshade. The shrub Palmi Christi.

A عبث *ʿabs*, (v. n. of عبث) Mixing up, preparing the curd called اقط *akit*. Preparing the dish called عبيثة *ʿabīsat*. *ʿabas*, (v. n. of عبث) Being vain, idle. Trifling, playing. Vanity, folly.

A عبثا *ʿabasan*, In vain.

A عبجة *ʿabajat*, Odious and worthless. Careless and reckless in speech.

A عبد *ʿabd*, (pl. عبدون *ʿabdūn*, عبيد *ʿabīd*, اعبد *aʿbud*, عباد *ʿibād*, عبدان *ʿubdān*, *ʿibdān*, عبدّان *ʿibiddān*, معبدة *maʿbadat*, معابد *maʿābid*, عبدّاء *ʿibiddāʾ*, عبدّي *ʿibidda'*, عبد *ʿubud*, *ʿabud*, معبوداء *maʿbūdāʾ*, and اعابد *aʿābid*) A servant, slave. A man (bond or free). A sort of fragrant herb. A spear-head short and broad. Quicksilver. عبد الله *ʿabdu'llāh*, A proper name, implying servant of God (this epithet the Muhammadans gave particularly to the apostate Christians who embraced the Mussulmān religion). عبد البطن *ʿabdu'l batn*, A slave to his belly, a glutton. عبد قنّ *ʿabdu kinnin*, A servant whose parents are slaves. عبد مملوك *ʿabdi mamlūk*, A purchased slave. عبد مملكة *ʿabdu mamlukatin*, A servant whose parents are free-born. *ʿabad*, (v. n. of عبد) Being penitent. Penitence, self-displacency. A bad scab or itch. Reprobation, denial, refusal. Avidity. Rage. *ʿabid*, Ashamed, disgusted, loathing, disdainful. *ʿabud*, A servant. (pl. of عبد *ʿabd*) Servants, slaves. *ʿubud*, (pl. of عبد *ʿabd*) Servants, slaves.

A عبدّاء *ʿibiddāʾ*, (pl. of عبد *ʿabd*) Slaves.

A عبدان *ʿibdān*, (*ʿubdān*, or عبدّان *ʿibiddān*) (pl. of عبد *ʿabd*) Servants. Slaves.

A عبدة *ʿabadat*, A loathing, disdaining; indignation. Permanence, durability. Corpulence, fatness. Firmness, strength, thickness of cloth. Power. Life. A stone for grinding perfumes upon. One against whom anger is kindled.

A عبدريّ *ʿabdarīy*, Related to the tribe of بني عبد الدار *banī ʿabdi'd dār*.

A عبدل *ʿabdal*, A servant, a slave. A man's name. The province of Hazramawt.

A عبدون *ʿabdūn*, (pl. of عبد) Servants, slaves.

A عبدّي *ʿibidda'*, (pl. of عبد) Servants, slaves.

A عبديّة *ʿabdīyat*, Servitude, slavery. Submission, obedience. دراهم عبديّه *darāhimi ʿabdīya*, Name of an excellent coinage.

A عبر *ʿabr*, (v. n. of عبر) Crossing (a river). Passing, travelling, walking. Dying, becoming extinct. Reading (a letter or a book) in silence. Explaining, interpreting (a dream). Leaving (a ram) a year unshorn. Examining (money or merchandise with regard to weight or quality). Chiding, driving off, scaring (birds). Weeping, being sad. The bank of a river. عبر الاسفار *ʿabru*, *ʿibru*, or *ʿubru 'l asfār*, Continually travelling (a man or she-camel). *ʿibr*, The country which lies between the western bank of the Euphrates and the Arabian desert. بنات عبر *banātu ʿibrin*, A lie, falsehood. Any thing vain, false, or absurd. *ʿibr* or *ʿabr*, Fully-attended (meeting or session). مجلس عبر *majlisu ʿibr*, A numerous assembly. *ʿubr*, Many, copious. Bereaved (woman). Clouds travelling rapidly. A shore. Weakness and heat of the eye fetching tears. Rams left a year unshorn. An eagle (especially black). Name of a tribe. *ʿabar*, Weakness or heat of the eyes from crying. Respect, reverence. ابو العبر *abū'l ʿabar*, A nonsensical fellow. *ʿabir*, Weeping (man). *ʿibar*, (pl. of عبرة *ʿabrat*) Tears. (pl. of عبرة *ʿibrat*) Examples. Admonitions. Miracles, wonders. P چشم عبربين *chashmi ʿibar-bīn*, An eye beholding wonders.

A *ʿubur*, (pl. of عبور *ʿabūr*) Uncircumcised.

A عبرات *ʿabarāt*, (pl. of عبرة *ʿabrat*) Tears.

A عبران *ʿabrān*, Weeping (man).

A عبرانيّ *ʿibrānīy*, Hebraic, the Hebrew language. ناموس عبراني *nāmūsi ʿibrānī*, The Jewish law.

A عبرانيّة *ʿibrāniyat*, The Hebrew language.

A عبرب *ʿabrab*, The eatable herb sumach.

A عبربيّة *ʿabrabīyat*, Dressed with sumach.

A عبرة *ʻabrat,* (v. n. of عبر) Weeping. Being sad and melancholy. Explanation. (pl. عبرات *ʻabarāt* and عبار *ʻibār*) A tear just starting. Silent grief, without crying. Suppressed sobs in the chest. *ʻabrat* or *ʻubrat,* The bank of a river. *ʻibrat,* (pl. عبر *ʻibar*) A miracle, prodigy, mystery, any thing wonderful. Example, warning. P عبرت شش روزه *ʻibrati shash roza,* (A six-days' wonder) Heaven and earth. The face of the earth. A strange event. عبرت پذيرفتن *ʻibrat pazīruftan,* To take warning. عبرت شدن *ʻibrat shudan,* To be an example. A ابو عبرة *abū ʻabarat,* A nonsensical, idly-talking fellow. A *ʻubrat,* Much, many: large quantity. A crowd. A kind of bead or shell. *ʻubrat* or *ʻabarat,* Inflammation of the eyes by hot tears (from sorrowful weeping). *ʻabirat,* Weeping (woman).

P عبرت آميز *ʻibrat-āmez,* Mysterious: wondrous.

P عبرت بخش *ʻibrat-bakhsh,* Exemplary.

P عبرت نما *ʻibrat-namā,* Exemplary. Mysterious. A prototype, exemplar.

P عبرت نمون *ʻibrat-namūn,* Mystical. Wonderful. مضمون عبرت نمون *mazmūni ʻibrat-namūn,* The wonderful or mysterious contents.

A عبرد *ʻubrud,* Slender, flagging (herb). *ʻubrud,* (*ʻubarid,* or عبردة *ʻubaridat*) Tender, delicate, beautiful (girl).

A عبرود *ʻubrūd,* Soft, limber (branch). Trembling, flabby (fat).

A عبري *ʻabra',* (pl. عباري *ʻabāra'*) Weeping (female). عين عبري *ʻaynun ʻabra',* A tearful eye.

A عبريّ *ʻibrīy,* Hebrew, Hebraic. *ʻubrīy,* The lote growing on a river's bank.

A عبريّة *ʻibrīyat,* The Hebrew language.

A عبس *ʻabs,* (v. n. of عبس) Being austere, crabbed; frowning, contracting the countenance. Mother of thyme. *ʻabas,* (v. n. of عبس) Having a dry hand and dirt sticking to it. A dry filthy substance adhering to a camel's tail.

A عبسور *ʻubsūr,* (or عبسر *ʻabsur*) Swift (camel).

A عبش *ʻabsh,* Any thing proper, decent, suitable, becoming. *ʻabsh,* (*ʻabash,* عبشة *ʻabshat,* or *ʻabashat*) Carelessness, negligence. Folly, stupidity.

A عبشميّ *ʻabshamīy,* Related to the tribe of عبد شمس *ʻabd shams.* The title of Abd Shams, or servant of the sun, was first given to the elder سبا *saba',* son of يشجب *yashjab,* son of يعرب *yaʻrab,* son of قحطان *kahtān,* son of هود *hūd,* because he introduced the worship of that luminary.

A عبط *ʻabt,* (v. n. of عبط) Splitting, tearing (a new garment). Slaughtering (a camel) without a blemish. Peeling the surface of the ground (wind). Distressing (unmerited misfortune). Going cheerfully to battle. Newly digging (earth or a well). Absconding, lying concealed. Inventing (a lie). Spurring (a horse) to the gallop, causing him to perspire. Raising the dust. Making (an udder) bleed. Being split, torn, full of fissures. (Dying) in full health and vigour. *ʻubut,* (pl. of عبيط *ʻabīt*) Rent (garments). Unblemished cattle slaughtered.

A عبطة *ʻabtatan,* In full vigour (he died).

A عبعاب *ʻabʻāb,* A tall man, corpulent and handsome. Of ample throat and capacious paunch.

A عبعب *ʻabʻab,* The softness and gracefulness of youth. A healthy, plump young man. A large garment. A soft garment made of camels' hair. A tall man. An idol-temple. Name of an idol and of a man. Colour. A mountain-goat.

A عبعبة *ʻabʻabat,* (v. n. of عبعب Q) Being put to flight (the enemy). A quantity of red wool.

A عبق *ʻabak,* (v. n. of عبق) Adhering to any thing (perfume). Dwelling in a place, being fixed. Being greedy. Adversity. *ʻabik,* Slightly scented.

A عبقان *ʻabkān,* (fem. عبقانة) Naturally bad.

A عبقة *ʻabakat,* Butter sticking to a churn.

A عبقر *ʻabkar,* Name of a solitary place where demons dwell. Name of a town noted for cloth.

A عبقرّ *ʻabakurr,* Hail. ابرد من عبقرّ *abrad min ʻabakurr,* Colder than hail.

A عبقرة *ʻabkarat,* (v. n. of عبقر Q) Glittering (the vapour سراب *sarāb*). Fat, sleek, smooth-skinned (woman).

A عبقريّ *ʻabkarīy,* Perfect in every respect, excelled by none. Intense, excessive, severe. A lord, chief. A kind of carpet or tapestry. A sheer lie.

A عبقس *ʻabkas,* (عبقص *ʻabkas,* عبقوس *ʻubkūs,* or عبقوص *ʻubkūs*) A sort of animalcule.

A عبقسيّ *ʻabkasīy,* Related to, or descended from, the tribe of عبد القيس *ʻabdu'l kays.*

A عبطة *ʻubtat,* Freshness.

A عبك *ʻabk,* A mixing of things together.

A عبكة *ʻabakat,* A vine-root. Barley-meal. Somewhat, a little. A bit of bread or of butter sticking to the churn. Any thing light and weak. Distressed, helpless, and disliked.

A عبل *ʻabl,* (v. n. of عبل) Twisting (a rope). Putting a long, broad point on an arrow. Stripping (a tree) of leaves. Driving or casting back. Detaining, imprisoning. Cutting. Taking away. Throwing one's weight upon. Shedding its leaves (a tree). Putting forth leaves (a tree). Thick-armed (man). Thick-legged (horse). *ʻabal,* (v. n. of عبل) Being thick. Being white. (pl. اعبال *aʻbāl*) A curled and jagged leaf of a tree. A leaf fallen from a tree. A new leaf. *ʻabil,* Thick. White.

A عبلاء *ʻablāʼ,* (fem. of اعبل *aʻbal*) Whitish (stone). Rugged (hillock). White and thick (tree). Name of a copper-mine.

A عبلة *ʻablat,* (pl. عبال *ʻibāl*) Perfectly-formed, elegantly-shaped (woman). Thick. Name of a woman and mother of a tribe.

A عبليّ *ʻablīy,* Of the tribe عبلة *ʻablat.*

A عبمّ *ʻibamm,* Large and long-bodied.

A عبن *ʻabn,* Thickness and roughness of body. *ʻubun,* Jolly, handsome (men).

A عبنّ *ʻabann,* (fem. عبنّة *ʻabbanat*) Large. Corpulent (camel or vulture).

A عبنّاة *ʻabannāt,* (pl. عبنّيات *ʻabannayāt*) Large and fat (she-camel).

A عبنبل *ʻabambal,* Large and strong.

A عبنة *ʻubnat,* Strength (in a camel).

A عبنجر *ʻabanjar,* Large and thick.

A عبنقاء *ʻabankāʼ,* (or عبنقاة *ʻabankāt*) Rapacious, sharp-clawed (eagle).

A عبنقس *ʻabankas,* Of a bad disposition. Tall, soft (man). One whose paternal and maternal grandmothers were foreigners.

A عبنقساء *ʻabankasāʼ,* Brisk, cheerful.

A عبنّك *ʻabannak,* Hard, firm, strong (man).

A عبنّى *ʻabanna',* Corpulent (camel or vulture).

A عبو *ʻabw,* (v. n. of عبا for عبو) Having a shining face. Arranging (household furniture).

A عبوثران *ʻabawsarān* or *ʻabawsurān,* Name of a fine-scented herb.

A عبود *ʻubūd,* (pl. of عبد *ʻabd*) Servants, slaves.

A عبّود *ʻabbūd,* Name of a man who is said to have slept seven years.

A عبودة *ʻubūdat,* Service, servitude.

A عبوديّة *ʻubūdīyat,* Servitude, slavery. Submission, subjection. خلوص و عبوديت *khulūs u ʻubūdīyat,* Profound devotion or reverence.

A عبور *ʻabūr,* (pl. عبائر *ʻabāʼir*) A young lamb. (pl. عبر *ʻubur*) Uncircumcised. شعري العبور *shiʻra'l ʻabūr,* The great dog-star, Syrius. *ʻubūr,* (v. n. of عبر) Crossing (a river), passing, travelling, walking. Dying, becoming extinct. Transition, transit, passage. P عبور نمودن *ʻubūr namūdan,* To cross over. باج عبور *bāji ʻubūr,* Toll for a passage.

A عبوس *ʻabwas,* A vast number. *ʻabūs,* Austere, morose, stern, grim. Adverse, unfortunate (day). A lion. P عبوس روي *ʻabūs-rūy,* Of a sour, disagreeable, sullen countenance. A *ʻubūs,* (v. n. of عبس) Being austere, crabbed, stern.

A عبوسة *ʻubūsat,* Austerity, moroseness.

A عبوسيّة *ʻabūsīyat,* Moroseness, crabbedness.

A عبول *ʻabūl,* Death.

A عبهال *ʻibhāl,* A being angry: expostulation.

A عبهر *ʻabhar,* The narcissus; jessamine; anemone. Fleshy, delicate, beautiful, large, and tall (male or female). P عبهر جانان *ʻabhari jānān,* The eye of a mistress. عبهر لرزان *ʻabhari larzān,* A ringlet of the prophet.

A عبهرة *ʻabharat,* Full of flesh, delicate, beautiful and fair-complexioned (woman).

A عبهلة *ʻabhalat,* (v. n. of عبهل Q) Turning (camels) loose without a keeper. Manifesting signs of anger. Expostulation, accusation, recrimination.

A عبّى *ʻubba',* A woman whose children all die.

A عبيّ *ʻabīy,* A portion of a slaughtered camel. Furnished, equipped.

A عبيبة *ʻabībat,* Something resembling tears distilling from the plant عرفط *ʻurfut;* meat or drink impregnated with this herb. A camel's pasturage of bitter herbage in a salt-marsh. The plant رمث *rims.*

A عبّيّة *ɛibbiyat* or *ɛubbiyat*, Haughtiness, vain boasting. عبّيّة الجاهليّة *ɛubbiyatu'l jāhiliyat*, The vain-glorious boasting of the Arabs in paganism.

A عبيث *ɛabīs*, An aromatic herb.

A عبّيث *ɛibbīs*, Much addicted to play or sport.

A عبيثة *ɛabīsat*, A mixture (especially of various flocks; of wheat and barley; of flour, dates, and butter; or of different tribes). (A man) of a mixed race. A kind of dried sour milk preserved with herbs, sour milk, and cheese. A dish in which locusts are used in place of meat.

A عبيثران *ɛabaysarān* or *ɛabaysurān*, Name of a fragrant herb. A thing difficult or disagreeable. *ɛabaysurān*, A certain thorny tree.

A عبيد *ɛabīd*, (pl. of عبد *ɛabd*) Servants, slaves. *ɛubayd*, (dim. of عبد *ɛabd*) A little servant. امّ عبيد *umm ɛubayd*, An uninhabited desert. بنو عبيد *banū ɛubayd*, Name of a tribe.

A عبيدة *ɛubaydat*, Belly, paunch, rough tripe.

A عبير *ɛabīr*, Ambergris or any other grateful perfume. A perfume composed of musk, sandal-wood, and rose-water. Saffron; also a composition in which it is an ingredient. Full-feathered (arrow). Numerous (concourse). P پر عبير *pur ɛabīr*, Full of ambergris: fragrant, odoriferous.

A عبيراء *ɛubayrā*, Name of a plant.

A عبير تأثير *ɛabīr-tasīr*, Having the effect of ambergris. Fragrant as ambergris.

A عبير تعطير *ɛabīr-taɛṭīr*, Fragrant as ambergris.

A عبيط *ɛabīṭ*, Pure (blood). Fresh (blood, meat, or saffron). (pl. عبط *ɛubuṭ* and عباط *ɛibāṭ*) An unblemished (camel or ox) killed. The flesh of such an animal. Rent, though new (garment).

A عبيلة *ɛabīlat*, (fem.) Thick, stout, lusty.

A عتّ *ɛatt*, (v. n. of عتّ) Repeating over and over, being troublesome, importunate. Reproaching with bitterness. Biting any one (a serpent).

A عتّا *ɛatta'*, (equiv. to حتّي *hatta'*) To, until.

A عتاب *ɛitāb*, (v. n. of عتب) Chiding. (v. n. 3 of عتب) Reproving (lovers or friends). Expostulating. Reprehension, reproach, rebuke. Anger. P عتاب كردن *ɛitāb kardan*, To chide, to reproach, reprove, rebuke, rail at.

A امّ عتّاب *umm ɛattāb*, A hyena.

P عتّاب *ɛuttāb*, The inventor of waved silk.

P عتابي *ɛutābī*, A porter. A kind of rich undulated silk, named after the inventor.

A عتاة *ɛutāt*, (pl. of عاتي *ɛātī*) Proud. Violent.

A عتات *ɛitāt*, The carrying on an altercation.

A عتاد *ɛatād*, (v. n. of عتد) Being ready, prepared. (pl. اعتد *aɛtud*) Preparation or necessary apparatus (for a journey or war). A large cup.

A عتادة *ɛatādat*, A being ready, prepared.

A عتار *ɛatār*, Penis.

A عتّار *ɛattār*, A strong horse. A rugged and desolate place. A bold man.

A عتاق *ɛatāk*, (v. n. of عتق) Being set free (a male or female slave). Becoming noble or honourable. Liberty. *ɛitāk*, (pl. of عتيق *ɛatīk*) Nobles. Animals of the nobler kind (as high-blooded horses, camels, or falcons). *ɛutāk*, Wine long kept.

A عتاقة *ɛatākat*, (v. n. of عتق) Getting the start, taking the lead (a horse). Being set free. Becoming noble and honourable. Being clear and tender-skinned on recovery from sickness. Being bound on any one (an oath). Being old and good (wine). Being in excellent condition (flocks). Manumission, liberty. مولى عتاقة *mawla' ɛatākat*, A freedman.

A عتّال *ɛattāl*, A digger of turf (عتلة *ɛatalat*).

A عتان *ɛitān*, Dung and salt for tanning hides.

A عتاه *ɛutāh*, (v. n. of عته) Being distracted in mind, stupid. Being intelligent, studious, desirous to learn. Loving to annoy or to mimic another's talk.

A عتاهة *ɛatāhat*, Wanderers. Delirium, stupidity. Mimicry.

A عتاهية *ɛatāhiyat*, Wanderers. Insane. Foolish. ابو العتاهية *abū'l ɛatāhiyat*, Name of a man.

A عتائق *ɛatāɛik*, (pl. of عتيقة *ɛatīkat*) Manumitted, emancipated, liberated (female slaves).

A عتب *ɛatb*, (v. n. of عتب) Being enraged, chiding, reviling. Limping, halting on three legs (a quadruped), or on one foot (a man). Treading a threshold. *ɛitb*, One who reproves and chides much. *ɛatab*, The space between the fore and middle-finger, or the middle and ring-finger. Perplexity, distress. A bridge upon a stringed musical instrument. Rough ground. Corruption. (pl. of عتبة *ɛatabat*) Thresholds. Steps. Pavements.

A عتبات *ɛatabāt*, (pl. of عتبة *ɛatabat*) Steps.

A عتبان *ɛatbān*, (v. n. of عتب) Reproaching. *ɛatbān* or *ɛatabān*, (v. n. of عتب) Hopping on one foot (a man); halting on three (a camel). امّ عتبان *umm ɛitbān*, A hyena.

A عتبة *ɛatabat*, (pl. عتب *ɛatab*) A gate, a port; the lower and also the upper threshold. A pavement. The round of a ladder, a step. Any thing adverse and disagreeable. A royal court. A wife.

A عتبي *ɛutba'*, Contentment, satisfaction.

A عتت *ɛatat*, Roughness, coarseness, of speech.

A عتد *ɛatad* or *ɛatid*, Ready for the course (a horse). Strong, bulky, perfectly-formed (horse).

A عتدان *ɛitdān*, (pl. of عتود) Yearling kids.

A عتدة *ɛutdat*, Instruments, equipage, apparatus for a journey.

A عتر *ɛatr*, (v. n. of عتر) Being strong, trembling, vibrating (as a spear). Producing an erection. Sacrificing the victim called عتيرة *ɛatīrat*. *ɛatr* or *ɛitr*, Penis. *ɛitr*, Root, origin. An idol. A dwarfish, thorny shrub. Whatever was sacrificed (as a sheep, &c., see عتيرة *ɛatīrat*). Name of a tribe. The handle of a spade, rake, or hoe; also that part upon which the delver sets his foot when digging. Deliriousness, raving, doting. *ɛatar*, Strength, power. *ɛutur*, (pl. of عاتر *ɛātir* and عتور *ɛatūr*) Open and ruttish (vulvæ).

A عتران *ɛatarān*, (v. n. of عتر) Trembling (a spear). Being strong (a spear).

A عترب *ɛutrub*, Sumach, an esculent vegetable.

A عترة *ɛitrat*, Little balls formed of musk or other aromatics, and worn as a necklace. A progeny, family, near relations. Beauty, also sharpness, of teeth. Fresh and sweet saliva. Sweet marjoram. A bit of pure musk. That part of a spade upon which the delver puts his foot when digging. The caper-cucumber. عترة الطاهرين *ɛitratu't tāhirīn*, The family of Muhammad. عترة عينين *ɛitrat ɛaynayn*, Plenty, what will satisfy the eyes.

A عترس *ɛatras*, (also عترّس *ɛatarras*) Firm, compact-bodied, strong-jointed (man). Large round the girth (beast). A lion. A cock.

A عترسان *ɛutrusān*, A lion. A cock.

A عترسة *ɛatrasat*, (v. n. of عترس Q) Seizing with rudeness and violence.

A عترفان *ɛutrufān*, A dunghill-cock. A certain broad plant growing in the summer.

A عترفة *ɛatrafat*, Vehemence, severity, intensity.

A عتروف *ɛutrūf*, (or عتريف *ɛitrīf*) A villain, scoundrel. A daring fellow careless of reputation. Strong (camel). Iniquitous, oppressive.

A عتريس *ɛitrīs*, A powerful, angry tyrant. A male sylvan demon. A calamity, misfortune.

A عتريفة *ɛitrīfat*, (A camel) which gives little milk, is high spirited, and indifferent to threats.

A عتش *ɛatsh*, (v. n. of عتش) Bending. Inclining, being favourable.

A عتص *ɛats*, An obsolete verb, supposed to be synonymous with اعتياص *iɛtiyāṣ*, A being difficult.

A عتعت *ɛutɛut* or *ɛatɛat*, A kid. Strong, able. A tall, full-grown man. Tall and staggering.

A عتعتة *ɛatɛatat*, (v. n. of عتعت Q) Calling to a kid *ɛatɛat*. Madness, phrenzy.

A عتف *ɛatf*, (v. n. of عتف) Plucking up (hairs, wool, or feathers). *ɛitf*, A part of the night.

A عتق *ɛatk*, (v. n. of عتق) Seizing with the teeth. Being liberated, manumitted (a male or a female slave). Becoming noble or honourable. Being old and good (wine). Managing (flocks) well. Being well managed (flocks). Taking the lead (a horse). Freedom, manumission. (Wine) long kept. *ɛitk*, (v. n. of عتق) Making haste, preceding, getting the start (a horse). Being free or manumitted (a male or female slave). Becoming noble or honourable. Being clear, but tender-skinned (on recovering from an indisposition). Being bound upon one (an oath). Being in good condition (cattle, an estate). A tree from which bows are made. Generosity, excellence. Nobility. Liberty. Freedom. *ɛitk* or *ɛutk*, Age (applicable to inanimate objects, as wine or dates). *ɛutk*, Freedom. (pl. of

عاتق ʿātik) Liberated, manumitted. ʿutuk, A tree from which bows are made.

A عتقاء ʿutakāʾ, (pl. of عتيق) Free. Old, antique.

A عتك ʿatk, (v. n. of عتك) Adhering to the body (unguents). Drying on (a camel's) gaskoin (dung and urine). Attacking, striking without let or hindrance. Running at, intending to bite (a horse). Inclining to. Governing, protecting. Rallying, repeating an attack in battle. ʿatak, (v. n. of عتك) Becoming red with age (a bow). Time.

A عتكيّ ʿatakīy, Of the family of عتيك ʿatīk.

A عتل ʿatl, (v. n. of عتل) Dragging or using with violence (a man). Leading (a camel). Pulling away (the clitoris). ʿatal, (v. n. of عتل) Making haste, running headlong (to any thing bad). (pl. of عتلة ʿatalat) Strong Persian bows. ʿatil, One who hastens to any thing bad.

A عتلّ ʿutull, A savage, malignant man. A glutton. A thick spear. عتلّ و زنيم ʿutull u zanīm, A worthless fellow.

A عتلاء ʿutalāʾ, (pl. of عتيل) Hirelings, servants.

A عتلة ʿatalat, A large turf or clod torn from the ground. A wimble, gimblet. An instrument with which they pull up the roots or lop off the suckers of palm-trees. An iron instrument for undermining walls. A piece of iron like the head of an axe. A thick cudgel or walking-staff. A she-camel refusing the male. (pl. عتل ʿatal) A Persian bow.

A عتم ʿatm, (v. n. of عتم) Being milked at even (camels). Becoming dark at the crepuscle (a night). Abstaining from that to which one has been addicted. Being slow, late, lazy. Retiring, desisting through timidity. Having a portion of itself past (the night). Pulling out the hairs. ʿutm or ʿutum, A wild olive.

A عتمة ʿatamat, A third division of the night, beginning at the evening-twilight; the time of the last evening-prayer. Return of cattle from pasture. Darkness of night. Milk remaining in the udders at that time.

A عتن ʿatn, (v. n. of عتن) Dragging, hauling to prison. ʿutun, (pl. of عاتن ʿātin and عتون ʿatūn) Strong, vehement.

A عتوّ ʿutūw, (v. n. of عتا for عتو) Exceeding all bounds in wickedness, insolence, or pride. عتوّ و بغضا ʿutūw u baghzā, Haughtiness and extreme hatred.

A عتوادة ʿitwādat, A short, dwarfish man.

A عتوارة ʿitwārat, A particle of musk. A short, dwarfish man. ʿit or ʿutwārat, Name of a tribe.

A عتوب ʿatūb, One railed at or chidden in vain.

A عتود ʿatūd, (pl. اعتدة aʿtidat or عدّان ʿiddān) A kid one year old. The lote-tree. The acacia-tree.

A عتور ʿatūr, (pl. عتر ʿutur) Ruttish and open (vulva). ʿutūr, (v. n. of عتر) Producing an erection.

A عتوك ʿutūk, (v. n. of عتك) Departing alone, travelling, rambling. Doubling the hand back to the breast. Inclining to. Being disobedient, untractable (wife). Meeting, encountering (for good or evil). Becoming red with age (a bow). Being very sour (milk or wine). Drying and sticking to the buttocks of a camel (urine). Establishing, incontrovertibly maintaining (an argument or position). Being noble, illustrious (a woman). Governing, guarding. Swearing falsely.

A عتول ʿitwal, One who cannot possibly dispense with women. A deer.

A عتوم ʿatūm, Giving milk only in the evening (a she-camel).

A عتون ʿatūn, (pl. عتن ʿutun) Strong, powerful.

A عتوه ʿatūh, Delirious, insane.

A عته ʿath or ʿuth, (v. n. of عته) Being distracted in mind, stupid. Delighting to molest or to mimic another's talk. Being intelligent, studious, desirous to learn.

A عتهاء ʿutahāʾ, (pl. of عاته ʿātih) Molesters, annoyers. Mimics.

A عتي ʿaty, (v. n. of عتي) Being proud, exorbitant, and overbearing.

A عتّي ʿatta', (equiv. to حتّي hatta') Until.

A عتيّ ʿatīy, (pl. ʿutīy) Proud, overbearing. (pl. اعتاء aʿtāʾ) Low, mean. A destroyer. ʿitīy or ʿutīy, (v. n. of عتا for عتو) Being proud, haughty. ʿutīy or ʿatīy, (v. n. of عتا for عتو) Beginning to break (an old man).

A عتيب ʿatīb, Name of a tribe.

A عتيبة ʿatībat, (A city) neither remarkable or praiseworthy.

A عتّيبي ʿittība', A reproaching, a chiding.

A عتيد ʿatīd, Ready, prepared, present.

A عتيدة ʿatīdat, A dish in which are placed the perfumes for the bridegroom or bride.

A عتيرة ʿatīrat, Whatever was sacrificed (as a sheep) in the month رجب rajab by the old Arabians to their gods.

A عتيق ʿatīk, (pl. عتق ʿuth and عتقاء ʿutakāʾ) Liberated, manumitted, discharged, free. Old, ancient, antique, the past. Chronic (disease). Thin and clear-skinned. (pl. عتاق ʿitāk) Noble, generous, choice, excellent (in any kind or degree). A palm-tree whose fructifying pollen does not become exhausted. A liniment, embrocation. Name of Abū bakr. Wine boiled down to a third. Water. Milk. Wine. A date. A man whose cheek is fresh and clear, after having been coarse and rough. البيت العتيق al baytu'l ʿatīk, The old house; i.e. the كعبه kaʿba or temple at Mecca. مولي عتيق mawla' ʿatīk, A freedman.

A عتيقة ʿatīkat, (pl. عتائق ʿatāʾik) Manumitted, freed (female slave). مولاة عتيقة mawlāt ʿatīkat, A freed-woman.

A عتيك ʿatīk, Sultry (day). Name of a family.

A عتيل ʿatīl, (pl. عتلاء ʿutalāʾ) A hireling, a servant. Severe (ailment).

A عثّ ʿass, (v. n. of عثّ) Gnawing, fretting (as a moth). Importunity. The bite of a serpent. ʿuss, (pl. of عثّة ʿussat) Moths. عثّ مال ʿussu mālin, An unskilful, wasteful manager of property.

A عثاء ʿasāʾ, A serpent.

A عثاة ʿusāt, (pl. of عاثي) Mischievous, destructive.

A عثاث ʿisās, A modulation of the voice, trill, quaver. Serpents devouring each other in scarcity.

A عثاجل ʿusājil, Large-bellied.

A عثار ʿasār, Evil, adversity, an unlucky affair. ʿisār, (v. n. of عثر) Stumbling, striking the foot against any thing, falling.

A عثاعث ʿasāʿis, Adversities, tribulations.

A عثاكيل ʿasākīl, (pl. of عثكال ʿiskāl, عثكول ʿuskūl, and عثكولة ʿuskūlat) Palm-branches laden with clusters of dates.

A عثالط ʿusālit, Thick, (sour milk).

A عثان ʿusān, (v. n. of عثن) Smoking (fire). Ascending (a mountain). (pl. عواثن ʿawāsin) Smoke. Dust.

A عثانين ʿasānīn, (pl. of عثنون ʿusnūn) Long hairs under a camel's chin. Rain whilst falling from the clouds to the earth.

A عثّة ʿussat, (pl. عثّ ʿuss) A moth, book-worm. A serpent that eats another serpent through hunger in a barren year. An old woman; also one silly and shameless.

A عثج ʿasj, (v. n. of عثج) Drinking by little and little, sipping. ʿasj or ʿasaj, A body of men travelling together. Part (of the night).

A عثجة ʿusjat, A crowd, company of men.

A عثجج ʿasjaj, A numerous collection.

A عثجل ʿasjal, Large-bellied. Wide (wallet or water-bottle).

A عثجلة ʿasjalat, (v. n. of عثجل Q) Rising with difficulty through age or infirmity.

A عثر ʿasara, (fut. يعثر yaʿsuru) He stumbled. He lied. (The artery) beat.

A عثر ʿasr, (v. n. of عثر) Stumbling, or falling. Knowing, perceiving, stumbling upon, discovering. Watered only by rain (a sown field). ʿusr, An eagle. A lie. ʿasar, A lie. A field watered only by rain.

A عثّر ʿassar, Name of a place abounding in lions.

A عثرات ʿasarāt, Slips, lapses, falls. Sins.

A عثرب ʿusrub, A kind of pomegranate.

A عثرة ʿasrat, A slip, stumble. Offence, sin, crime.

A عثريّ ʿasarīy, (A sown field) watered only by rain. ʿasarīy, (and sometimes عثّريّ ʿassarīy) Unconcerned about this world or the next.

A عثعث ʿasʿas, (pl. عثاعث ʿasāʿis) A hill of sand producing nothing. Corruption, depravity. The soft part of the thigh. Soft earth.

A عثعثة ʿasʿasat, (v. n. of عثعث Q) Putting in motion. Stopping, staying. Having in one's power, possessing authority. Being firm. Soft earth.

A عثق ʿasak, A highway. A certain tree.

A عثقة ʿasakat, Fertile (ground). A fruitful, plenteous year.

A عثك *ʻasak, ʻasik, ʻusak*, or *ʻusuk*, Roots of the palm-tree.

A عثكال *ʻiskāl*, (عثكول *ʻuskūl*, or عثكولة *ʻuskūlat*) (pl. عثاكيل *ʻasākīl*) A branch of the palm-tree laden with many clusters.

A عثكة *ʻasakat*, Mud, clay mixed with water.

A عثكلة *ʻaskalat*, (v. n. of عثكل Q) Decorating a camel-litter with hanging ornaments. A heavy mode of running.

A عثكولة *ʻuskūlat*, Any hanging ornament, as of various-coloured wools.

A عثل *ʻisl*, A steward, guardian. One who is entrusted with the management of live stock. *ʻasal*, (v. n. of عثل) Being large and thick. The caul of a sheep's intestines. *ʻasal* or *ʻasil*, Large, thick, much. Very fleshy. *ʻusul*, (pl. of عثول *ʻasūl*) Fools.

A عثلبة *ʻaslabat*, (v. n. of عثلب Q) Taking a bit of wood called زند *zand* from the tree without knowing whether it will emit sparks of fire or not. Spoiling (any business). Burying (meat) under the ashes, or grinding (wheat), that it may not be lost. Gulping water. Investigating, examining, searching diligently.

A عثلط *ʻusalit*, Thick (sour milk).

A عثلول *ʻuslūl*, The nerve of the neck of a horse, whence the mane grows.

A عثم *ʻasm*, (v. n. of عثم) Setting crookedly a broken (bone). Being thus set. Becoming hard and dry (unhealed wound). Sewing slightly (a wallet).

A عثمان *ʻusmān*, The ancestor of the Grand Seignor. A young bustard or dragon. A serpent or its young. عثمان بن عفان *ʻusmānu'bn ʻaffān*, Osmān, the third caliph.

A عثمانيّ *ʻusmānīy*, Ottoman, Ottomite, Turkish.

P عثمانيان *ʻusmāniyān*, Turks, Ottomites.

A عثمثم *ʻasamsam*, A tall, strong camel. A lion.

A عثمرة *ʻusmurat*, A sucked grape.

A عثن *ʻasn*, (v. n. of عثن) Smoking (as a fire). Ascending (a mountain). *ʻisn*, Wool. A kind of palm-leaf eaten green by cattle. A manager of an estate or property. *ʻasan*, (v. n. of عثن) Adhering (as perfume to clothes). Smoke. (pl. اعثان *aʻsān*) A little idol. *ʻasin*, Smoked, unfit to be eaten (food).

A عثنج *ʻasanjaj*, A camel, swift, thick, bulky.

A عثنون *ʻusnūn*, (pl. عثانين *ʻasānīn*) The peaked point of the beard. Long hairs under a camel's throat. The beginning of wind or rain. Rain. Rain whilst in the act of falling between heaven and earth.

A عثو *ʻasw*, (v. n. of عثا for عثو) Committing depredations, damaging, doing mischief.

A عثواء *ʻaswāʼ*, A female hyena. A decrepit old woman.

A عثوة *ʻaswat*, (pl. عثّي) A long lock of hair.

A عثوثج *ʻasawsaj*, (or عثوجج *ʻasawjaj*) A camel, swift, thick, and corpulent.

A عثور *ʻasūr*, Failing, fading (world). Apt to trip. *ʻusūr*, (v. n. of عثر) Comprehending, perceiving, discovering, stumbling upon.

A عثول *ʻasūl*, (pl. عثل *ʻusul*) A fool. Thick and rough (palm-tree).

A عثولّ *ʻiswall*, Very hairy in head and body. *ʻiswall*, (or عثوثل *ʻasawsal*) A stutterer, stammerer. Weak, relaxed.

A عثوليّ *ʻaswalīy*, Thick and entangled (beard).

A عثون *ʻusūn*, (v. n. of عثن) Smoking. Ascending (a mountain).

A عثّي *ʻussaʼ*, (pl. of عثوة) Long locks of hair.

A عثيّ *ʻusīy*, (pl. of عاثي *ʻāsī*) Mischievous, destructive. *ʻusīy* or *ʻisīy*, (v. n. of عثي) Committing depredations, damaging, doing mischief.

A عثيان *ʻisyān*, A hyena. *ʻasayān*, (v. n. of عثي) Doing mischief.

A عثيثة *ʻusaysat*, (dim. of عثّة) A little moth.

A عثير *ʻasīr*, (v. n. of عثر) Stumbling, falling. *ʻisyar*, Dust. Dirt, clay, mud, or sludge thrown up by the feet. A slight mark or impression.

A عثيل *ʻisyal*, A male hyena. One who neither decorates or anoints his person. امّ عثيل *umm ʻisyal*, A female hyena.

A عجّ *ʻajj*, (v. n. of عجّ) Scattering dust (wind). Being clamorous, noisy, vociferous. Pealing (thunder). Driving a camel by calling out to him عاج *ʻāji* عاج *ʻāji*. Being very expert in different modes of riding.

A عجاب *ʻujāb*, A wonderful thing, wonder.

A عجّاب *ʻujjāb*, A very wonderful thing.

A عجاج *ʻajāj*, Dust. Smoke. Foolish. Base, upstart young fellows.

A عجّاج *ʻajjāj*, Hard-blowing, dusty (day). Braying in the throat (libidinous camel). Roaring lustily.

A عجاجة *ʻajājat*, A whirlwind. A large herd of camels. Clamour. لبّد عجاجته *labbada ʻajājatahu*, He desisted from what he was engaged in. لفّ عجاجته عليه *laffa ʻajājatahu ʻalayhi*, He rushed upon him to snatch it.

A عجاجير *ʻajājīr*, Balls of dough; also he who eats them.

A عجاجيل *ʻajājīl*, (pl. of عجّول *ʻijjawl*) Calves. Certain preparations of the new cheese called اقط *akit*, about the bigness of the hand.

A عجّار *ʻajjār*, One who eats balls of dough. A wrestler whom no one can throw down on his side. A wrestler who entwines his leg between those of his adversary and throws him down.

A عجارة *ʻijārat*, A veil, a covering.

A عجارد *ʻujārid*, Penis.

A عجاردة *ʻajāridat*, Name of a schismatical sect.

A عجارف *ʻajārif*, The accidents (of fortune). Violence (of rain).

A عجارم *ʻujārim*, Strong (man). Penis.

A عجاريّ *ʻajārīy*, (or عجاري *ʻajārī*) Heavy calamities. Heads, knobs, or processes of bones.

A عجارير *ʻajārīr*, Streaks in the sand.

A عجاريز *ʻajārīz*, (pl. of عجروز) Streaks in sand.

A عجاريف *ʻajārīf*, The accidents (of fortune). Violent rain.

A عجاز *ʻijāz*, A macerated sinew whipped about the haft of a sword.

A عجازة *ʻijāzat*, A little cushion worn by women to give a false prominency to the hips. The spur of a bird.

A عجاساء *ʻajāsāʼ*, Darkness. A large troop of camels. A part of the night. Impediments, obstacles, hindrances.

A عجاسى *ʻajāsaʼ*, A large troop of camels.

A عجاف *ʻijāf*, Misfortune. Time. Fortune. The colocynth, the wild gourd. (pl. of اعجف *aʻjaf*) Lean, emaciated. Thin (spear-heads). *ʻujāf*, A kind of date.

A عجافة *ʻajāfat*, (v. n. of عجف) Being lean.

A عجال *ʻajāl* or *ʻijāl*, (pl. of عجلة *ʻijlat*) Bottles of oil. Water-wheels. Wallets. She-calves. *ʻijāl*, (pl. of عجيل *ʻajīl* and عجلان *ʻajlān*) Hasteners. (pl. of عجلة *ʻajalat*) Carts. Wheels.

A عجّال *ʻujjāl*, A quantity of dates, with milk, butter, and flour taken in haste. Whatever one is in haste to eat. A handful of dates.

A عجالة *ʻijālat*, A kind of plant. *ʻijālat* or *ʻujālat*, Any thing that is ready and at hand. Any thing hastily procured and set before a guest. New milk which the milkers send home to their friends. First-fruits or new corn toasted slightly, and rubbed between the hands. التمر عجالة الراكب *at' tamru ʻujālatu'r rākib*, Dates are a ready and convenient thing for one who is riding a journey. P عجالت الوقت بي انسجام *ʻijālatu'l wakt bī insijām*, Early fruit not watered (implying any thing done or written hastily, without being well digested).

A عجالةً *ʻijālatan*, Instantly, without delay.

A عجالد *ʻujālid*, Thick milk, coagulated, and turned to cheese.

A عجالز *ʻujāliz*, Thick milk.

A عجالط *ʻujālit*, Thick (sour milk).

A عجالم *ʻajālim*, Name of a people in Yaman.

A عجالى *ʻajālaʼ*, (pl. of عجلى *ʻajlaʼ*) Quick, hasty (women). *ʻajālaʼ* or *ʻujālaʼ*, (pl. of عجلان *ʻajlān*) Quick, speedy, nimble, active, expeditious.

A عجام *ʻujām*, A fruit-stone.

A عجّام *ʻajjām*, A large bat. A swallow.

A عجان *ʻijān*, (pl. اعجنة *aʻjinat* and عجن *ʻujun*) The ligament or seam between the scrotum and anus, the perinæum. The part of the penis extending from the testicle to the anus. The neck. The fundament. The part below the chin.

A عجّان *ʻajjān*, An idiot. Silly.

A عجانس *ʻajānis*, Beetles, may-bugs.

A عجاوة *ʻajāwat*, A date close and fleshy. A Madīna date. *ʻujāwat* or *ʻijāwat*, Milk with which they feed a child that has lost its mother. *ʻujāwat*, (or عجاية *ʻujāyat*) (pl. عجى *ʻujaʼ*, عجيّ *ʻujīy*, and عجايا *ʻajāyaʼ*) A tendon from the knee to the hoof.

A عجاهن *ɛujāhin*, A hedgehog. The friend of the bridegroom until he has taken home his wife. A match-maker. A cook, domestic, sewer, table-decker. A man of mean or doubtful birth.

A عجاهنة *ɛajāhinat*, Servants. Cooks. Sewers, table-deckers. *ɛujāhinat*, A bride-maid, or dresser.

A عجايا *ɛajāya'*, (pl. of عجاية *ɛujāyat*) Tendons running from the knee to the hoof. (pl. of عجيّ *ɛujīy* or عجيّة *ɛujīyat*) Children not suckled till after the stated time.

A عجائب *ɛajāɛib*, (pl. of عجيب *ɛajīb*) Wonders, miracles. Prodigies, portents, things wonderful and stupendous. عجائب الدنيا *ɛajāɛibu'd dunya'*, The wonders of the world. عجائب وغرائب *ɛajāɛib u gharāɛib*, Wonderful and strange things.

P عجايبي *ɛajāyabī*, A sort of tent.

A عجاية *ɛajāyat*, A close, fleshy date. A Madina date. *ɛujāyat*, A protuberance on the hinder part of a horse's foot.

A عجائز *ɛajāɛiz*, (pl. of عجوز *ɛajūz*) Old women.

A عجائل *ɛajāɛil*, (pl. of عجول *ɛajūl*) Bereaved (mothers) agonized at the loss of their young.

A عجب *ɛajb*, (pl. عجوب *ɛujūb*) Termination of sandy tracts. Root of a horse's tail. Rump-bone (of a man or woman). The hinder part of any thing. *ɛujb*, Pride, presumption, haughtiness, self-admiration, conceit. P فخر و عجب كردن *fakhr u ɛujb kardan*, To think highly of one's self. A *ɛajb*, *ɛijb*, or *ɛujb*, A man fond of the society of women, or in whose society women find pleasure. Ignorance of that which may befal one. *ɛajab*, (v. n. of عجب) Being astonished, remaining thunder-struck, being lost in admiration. Strange, marvellous, wonderful. A marvellous thing. Admiration, wonder, astonishment. Ignorance of what may happen. The grace, favour, and good pleasure of God. عجب عاجب *ɛajab ɛājib*, A strange thing. عجب العجائب *ɛajabu'l ɛajāɛib*, A wonder of wonders, strange portents, monstrous appearances. ابو العجب *abū'l ɛajab*, Fate. العجب *al ɛajab*, (or يا للعجب *yā li'l ɛajab*) Strange! P عجب داشتن *ɛajab dāshtan*, To wonder, to be surprised.

A عجبا *ɛajaban*, (P عجبا *ɛajabā*) Astonishing! strange! Is it possible? Wonderfully, strangely.

A عجباء *ɛajbāɛ*, (fem.) A miracle of beauty. A prodigy of deformity. Slender and prominent about the buttocks (she-camel): also rough, coarse.

P عجب رود *ɛajab-rūd*, A psaltery. The sound of a musical pipe.

P عجبناك *ɛajabnāk*, Astonished, amazed.

A عجّة *ɛujjat*, An egg-fritter, omelet; to which they add sometimes a little meat, onions, and pepper.

A عجد *ɛajd* or *ɛujd*, Grape-stones. Bad raisins. *ɛujd*, Dried grapes. *ɛajad*, (pl. of عجدة) Crows.

A عجدة *ɛajadat*, (pl. عجد *ɛajad*) A crow.

A عجر *ɛajr*, (v. n. of عجر) Rushing (upon one with a sword). Scampering swiftly by (as a horse when frightened). Importuning, soliciting, urging. Prohibiting, preventing, keeping back. *ɛajar*, (v. n. of عجر) Being thick, coarse, fat, and large-bellied. Being hard and firm (a horse). Protuberance. *ɛajir* or *ɛajur*, Thick (leg, especially above the ancle). *ɛujar*, (pl. of عجرة *ɛujrat*) Knots in wood or in the veins of the body. عجره و بجره *ɛujaruhu wa bujaruhu*, His blemishes and his difficulties. The things he does openly and those he does secretly.

A عجراء *ɛajrāɛ*, A knotty cudgel.

A عجران *ɛajarān*, (v. n. of عجر) Running away and bending the neck in fear. Scampering by (horse).

A عجرة *ɛijrat*, The mode of tying the turban. *ɛujrat*, (pl. عجر *ɛujar*) A knot in wood or in the veins of the body. A thick and knotty place in any thing. A blemish, defect. A difficult and intricate affair. Any thing which one conceals or exposes to public view.

A عجرد *ɛajrad*, Light and nimble. Strong and corpulent. Penis.

A عجرّد *ɛajarrad*, Bold, brave. Stript, denuded.

A عجرفة *ɛajrafat*, Harsh speech, injurious language. *ɛajrafat*, (or عجرفيّة *ɛajrafīyat*) Celerity; precipitation, unskilfulness, inconsiderateness, temerity, rashness, heedlessness, fearlessness.

A عجرقب *ɛajarkab*, Impure, scandalously bad.

A عجرم *ɛajram*, The part where the muscles unite inside the thigh of a horse; the root of his pizzle. *ɛajram* or *ɛujrum*, Strong (man). *ɛujrum*, Hard, strong (camel). *ɛijrim*, A certain hard insect found in trees. *ɛijrim* or *ɛajram*, Short, fat, compact.

A عجرمة *ɛajramat*, (v. n. of عجرم Q) Going quick. *ɛajramat*, *ɛujrumat*, and *ɛijrimat*, One hundred, two hundred, or from fifty to a hundred (camels). *ɛujrumat* and *ɛijrimat*, (pl. عجرم *ɛujrum* and *ɛijrim*) A kind of tree.

A عجرور *ɛujrūr*, (pl. عجارير *ɛajārīr*) A groove made in sand by the wind.

A عجروز *ɛujrūz*, (pl. عجاريز) A streak in sand.

A عجروف *ɛujrūf*, A long-legged ant. Light and nimble (she-camel). A sort of insect. An old woman.

A عجروفة *ɛujrūfat*, An old woman.

A عجريّ *ɛujrīy*, A lie. A misfortune.

A عجز *ɛajz*, (v. n. of عجز) Being infirm, weak. Leaving undone what ought to be done. Weakness, infirmity, impotence. The hilt of a sword. A disease in the buttocks of a quadruped. بنات العجز *banātu'l ɛajz*, Arrows. A kind of bird. ردّ العجز علي الصدر *raddu'l ɛajzi ɛala's sadr*, A species of poetry, where a verse concludes with the same word with which it began. *ɛijz*, That part of a bow which is grasped by the hand. *ɛujz*, (pl. of اعجز *aɛjaz* and عجزاء *ɛajzā*) Large-buttocked. *ɛujz*, *ɛajz*, or *ɛijz*, Buttocks, bottom, bum. *ɛajaz* or *ɛujz*, (v. n. of عجز) Being large (buttocks). *ɛajuz*, *ɛajaz*, and *ɛajiz*, (pl. اعجاز *aɛjāz* and اعجز *aɛjuz*) The hinder or last part of the back, buttocks, hips. A penultimate letter. *ɛujuz*, (pl. of عجوز *ɛajūz*) Old women.

A عجزاء *ɛajzāɛ*, Large-buttocked (woman). Short-tailed (eagle), or one having a white feather in her tail. A high hill of sand. A woman, the palm of whose hand is rough.

A عجزان *ɛajazān*, (v. n. of عجز) Being weak and impotent. Leaving undone what ought to be done. Being negligent. Weakness, impotence.

A عجزة *ɛijzat* or *ɛujzat*, The youngest of a man's offspring, whether male or female. *ɛajazat*, (pl. of عاجز *ɛājiz*) Weak, helpless. P عجزۀ بي تاب و توان *ɛajazaɛi bī tāb u tuwān*, Feeble persons without strength or vigour.

A عجس *ɛajs*, (v. n. of عجس) Retaining, detaining, hindering, throwing obstacles in the way, creating delays. Apprehending, grasping, taking by the hand. Running off the road with her rider from skittishness (a camel). *ɛajs*, *ɛijs*, or *ɛujs*, The middle or handle of a bow. The latter part of the night. *ɛajus*, (pl. اعجاس *aɛjās*) The hinder part, buttocks.

A عجسة *ɛujsat*, An hour of the night. The dawn.

A عجسمة *ɛajsamat*, Quickness, activity, haste.

A عجعاج *ɛajɛāj*, One who vociferates greatly. A noble and aged camel.

A عجعجة *ɛajɛajat*, (v. n. of عجعج Q) Crying out from being beaten, or from being loaded with a heavy burden (a camel). Being incessantly clamorous and noisy. Driving a she-camel by crying عاج عاج *ɛāj ɛāj*. Substituting a ج *jīm* for ي *yā*.

A عجف *ɛajf*, (v. n. of عجف) Abstaining from eating, although hungry, that another may have enough. Making lean. Bearing with and not reproving. Subduing one's own spirit. Being separated, remaining at a distance. Accommodating one's self to the wants and humours of a sick person by care and attention. *ɛajaf*, (v. n. of عجف) Being lean, losing fat (cattle). Leanness, loss of fat.

A عجفاء *ɛajfāɛ*, (fem. of اعجف *aɛjaf*) Lean, thin. Good-for-nothing (country or soil).

A عجفاوان *ɛajfāwāni*, (dual) Two thin (lips).

A عجفة *ɛajifat*, Lean (woman).

A عجفي *ɛajfa'*, (pl. of عجيف) Thin, lean.

A عجل *ɛijl*, (pl. عجول *ɛujūl*) A calf. (For the first year he is called عجل *ɛijl*, then تبيع *tabīɛ*, then جذع *jazaɛ*, then ثنيّ *sanīy*, then رباع *rabāɛ*, then سديس *sadīs*, and then سالغ *sāligh*). *ɛujl*, Whatever is ready at hand. New milk which a milker sends home to his friends. *ɛajal*, (v. n. of عجل) Making haste. Haste, expedition, despatch. Clay, mud black and fetid. (pl. of عجلة *ɛajalat*) Carriages. Wheels. *ɛajil* or *ɛajul*, One who makes haste. Quick, speedy, nimble. *ɛijal*, (pl. of عجلة *ɛijlat*) Bottles of oil. Water-wheels. Wallets. Female calves, heifers. *ɛujul*, (pl. of عجول *ɛajūl*) Bereaved (mothers) distracted by the loss of their young.

A عجلان *ɛajlān*, (pl. عجالي *ɛajāla'* and *ɛujāla'*) One who makes great haste. The month Shaabān.

عجلان ام *umm ʿajlān*, Name of a bird.

A عجلة *ʿajalat*, Haste, velocity, expedition, precipitation. (pl. عجل *ʿajal*, اعجال *aʿjāl*, and عجال *ʿijāl*) A carriage, vehicle, chariot, cart, waggon. A water-wheel. A large pulley for drawing water. A piece of wood on which loads are carried. Mud, clay. A ladder for ascending a palm-tree (which is made by notching the tree in steps). على العجلة *ʿala'l ʿajala*, In haste, readily, expeditiously. *ʿijlat*, A cow-calf, heifer. (pl. عجل *ʿijal*, عجال *ʿijāl* and *ʿajāl*) A bottle. A water-wheel. A certain herb. *ʿujlat*, New milk which a milker sends home to his friends. Whatever is ready at hand.

A عجلد *ʿujalid*, Thick milk coagulated and turned into cheese.

A عجلز *ʿajlaz*, Strong, robust (male camel).

A عجلزة *ʿajlazat* or *ʿijlizat*, Strong, robust (she-camel). *ʿijlazat*, Strong, robust (mare).

A عجلط *ʿujalit*, Thick (sour milk).

A عجلمي *ʿajlamīy*, Belonging to the عجالم *ʿajālim* (a people in Yaman).

A عجلى *ʿajla'*, (fem. of عجلان *ʿajlān*) (pl. عجالى *ʿajāla'*) Quick, hasty, expeditious. (A bow) shooting with velocity.

A عجم *ʿajm*, (v. n. of عجم) Seizing or biting with the teeth to try whether a substance is hard or soft. Assaying, proving, examining. Understanding, perceiving, beholding, distinguishing, discovering, exploring. Marking with points. Pointing a consonant. Hating. (pl. عجوم *ʿujūm*) Little or young camels. The root of (a horse's) tail. Intelligent, discerning, discreet. *ʿujm*, Root of the tail. A grape-stone. Barbarians, persons other than Arabians. *ʿajam*, (pl. اعجام *aʿjām*) A barbarian. Barbarians (not born Arabians). A Persian. Stones, grains or kernels of fruit. Little or young camels. ولايت عجم *wilāyati ʿajam*, Persia. نفط عجم *nafti ʿajam*, Oil extracted from fruit-stones.

A عجّم *ʿujumm*, Camels feeding on thorny plants.

A عجماء *ʿajmāʾ*, (fem. of اعجم *aʿjam*) Persian. Barbarian (woman). A brute (as being dumb). Silent, mental (prayer). A sandy tract without trees.

A عجمات *ʿajamāt*, Hard stones or kernels.

A عجمة *ʿijmat* or *ʿujmat*, Part of a sandy tract. *ʿujmat*, Heaped-up sand. Barbarism, foreignness. An impediment of the tongue. *ʿajamat*, One stone or kernel. *ʿaja* or *ʿajmat*, (pl. عجمات *ʿajamāt*) A palm-tree sprung from a stone. A hard rock.

A عجمجمة *ʿajamjamat*, Strong (she-camel).

P عجمستان *ʿajamistān*, Persia.

A عجمضى *ʿajamzaʾ*, A small kind of date.

A عجمي *ʿajamīy*, (pl. عجم *ʿajam*) Barbarian, foreign, although a correct speaker of Arabic. A Persian, a native of Persia (عجم *ʿajam*).

A عجمية *ʿajamīyat*, Barbarism, foreignness.

A عجن *ʿajn*, (v.n. of عجن) Making up a mass of paste, kneading. Rising or leaning upon the hands (a feeble man). Striking the ground with the feet (a camel). Striking on the perinæum. *ʿajan*, (v. n. of عجن) Being fat (camel). Being affected with a tumour which prevents conception (a camel). *ʿajin*, Fat and firm of body. *ʿujun*, (pl. of عجين *ʿajīn*) Effeminate. (pl. of عجان *ʿijān*) Seams between the scrotum and anus, perinæa.

A عجناء *ʿajnāʾ*, Fat and giving little milk (she-camel). Afflicted with the tumour عجن *ʿajan*. A camel, the glandular flesh of whose udder hangs level with her dugs.

A عجنة *ʿajinat*, A she-camel which has a swelling in the matrix.

A عجنجرة *ʿajanjarat*, Short, fat, and of lively spirits (a woman). Fat and fleshy (she-camel).

A عجنّس *ʿajannas*, A large, hard, strong camel.

A عجو *ʿajw*, (v. n. of عجا for عجو) Suckling (an infant). Afflicting. Turning away (the face). Being malicious and bad-tempered (a camel). Braying (a camel). Opening (the mouth).

A عجوب *ʿujūb*, (pl. of عجب) Ends of sandy tracts.

A عجوبه *ʿujūba*, Wonderful.

P عجوبها *ʿujūbahā*, (pl. of A عجوبه) Wonders.

A عجوة *ʿajwat*, A fine Madina date. A date very fleshy and compact. Date-paste. A delaying to suckle an infant beyond the proper time. *ʿujwat*, Milk with which an orphan child is fed.

A عجوجر *ʿajawjar*, Large-boned (man).

A عجوز *ʿajūz*, (pl. عجائز *ʿajāʾiz* and عجز *ʿujuz*) An old woman. (To this, the regular meaning, are to be added the following, much of which is mere slang:) A young woman of a delicate constitution. An old man. A traveller. A king. A champion. A kingdom. An army; battalion. A thousand. A year. Government of a province or city. Vice-gerency. A companion, familiar. A merchant. Heaven. The world. Earth. A continent, dry land. The sun. A parhelion, halo, or circle surrounding the sun. Road, way, path. The temple of Mecca. Mecca. The Kibla, towards which they turn the face in prayer. A Christian church or monastery. The sea. A ship. A well. A hot pestilential wind. Fire. Hell. Calamity, misfortune. Contrariety. Repentance. Abstinence from sin. Vanity. Hunger. Hungry. Fever. Health. Weak. The right hand. Plaster. War. A tent. A shield. A kind of dart. The point of a sword. A stud or nail in a sword-hilt. A needle. A sting. A scorpion. A bow. A quiver. A standard, ensign, colours. A drum. A feather. A dish. A kettle, pot. A leathern bottle. A trevet, grate, any thing supporting a pot or holding fire. A page. A leaf, sheet of paper. A woman's shift or under-garment. A dish made of a sea-herb. Butter. Wine. A kind of perfume. A pelican. Musk. Silver. Price, value. Delay. A lion. A horse. A bull. A cow. A he or she-wolf. A she-camel, a large she-camel. A hare. A hyena. A dog. Poison. Tremor, palsy. Uterus, pubes feræ. A balance, scales. A palm-tree. A certain tree. Name of a certain sandy tract. ايّام العجوز *ayyāmu'l ʿajūz*, Five (or according to some) seven days at the winter-solstice. They are as follow: صنّ *sinn*, صنّبر *sinnabr*, وبر *wabr*, الآمر *al āmir*, المؤتمر *al muʾtamir*, المعلّل *al muʿallil*, and مطفئ الجمر *mutfiʾu'l jamr*, (or مكفئ الظعن *mukfiʾu'z zaʿn*). P عجوز بدنما *ʿajūzi bad-namā*, An ill-looking old woman. عجوز خشك پستان *ʿajūzi khushk-pistān*, A dry-breasted old woman, *i.e.* who has never borne children. The disappointing world. A *ʿujūz*, (v. n. of عجز) Leaving undone what ought to be done. Weakness, impotence. Waxing old (a woman).

A عجوزة *ʿajūzat*, An old woman. عجوزهٔ فرتوت *ʿajūzaʾi fartūt*, The world full of troubles.

A عجوس *ʿajūs*, Pouring down copiously (rain). A heavy cloud. *ʿujūs*, The march of a large herd of camels.

A عجّوس *ʿijjaws*, Very swift. A calf. A handful of dates. Dates eaten with milk and flour.

A عجوف *ʿujūf*, (v. n. of عجف) Abstaining from eating, though hungry, that another may have enough. Accommodating one's self to the wants and humours of a sick person by care and attention.

A عجول *ʿajūl*, Fast-going. Death. Breakfast, a whet. (pl. عجل *ʿujul* and عجائل *ʿajāʾil*) Bereaved (woman). Distracted for the loss of her colt (a she-camel). *ʿujūl*, (pl. of عجل *ʿijl*) Calves.

A عجّول *ʿijjawl*, (pl. عجاجيل *ʿajājīl*) A calf. A handful of dates. A quantity of dates eaten in haste with milk and flour.

A عجوم *ʿujūm*, (v. n. of عجم) Seizing or biting with the teeth to try whether (a thing) is hard or soft. Understanding, perceiving. Proving, assaying. Exploring, examining. (pl. of عجم *ʿajm*) Little or young camels.

A عجومة *ʿajūmat*, Strong, able (she-camel).

A عجهرة *ʿajharat*, Inhumanity, coarseness.

A عجهوم *ʿujhūm*, Name of a certain waterfowl.

A عجى *ʿujaʾ*, Dried skins, which when cooked are eaten. *ʿujaʾ*, (or عجىّ *ʿujīy*) (pl. of عجاية *ʿujāyat*) Tendons running from the knee to the hoof, leaders.

A عجيّ *ʿajīy*, A child or young camel, whose mother being dead is suckled by another. *ʿajīy*, (fem. عجيّة *ʿajīyat*) (pl. عجايا *ʿajāyaʾ*) A child not suckled until after the proper time.

A عجيب *ʿajīb*, (pl. عجائب *ʿajāʾib*) Wonderful, strange, surprising, astonishing.

A عجيبة *ʿajībat*, A thing wonderful or worthy of admiration. A marvel, a wonder.

A عجيبي *ʿajībī*, A sort of tent.

A عجية *ʿujyat*, (pl. عجى *ʿujaʾ*) A dried skin which they boil and eat.

A عجيّة *ʿujayyat*, A small or thin sinew.

A عجيج *ʿajīj*, (v. n. of عجّ) Being clamorous,

noisy. Scattering dust (the wind).

A عجير *ʿajir*, (عجز *ʿajiz*, or عجيس *ʿajis*) Impotent (man or stallion).

A عجيز *ʿajīz*, The buttocks.

A عجيز *ʿujjayiz*, (dim. of عجوز) A little old woman.

A عجيزة *ʿajīzat*, (A woman's) hips.

A عجيس *ʿajīs*, A palm-tree which does not take the fecundating pollen of the male. A stallion unable to cover.

A عجيساء *ʿajīsāʾ*, A stallion unable to cover. *ʿujīsāʾ*, (or عجيسي *ʿajīsaʾ*) A slow step.

A عجّيسى *ʿijjīsaʾ*, A slow step.

A عجيف *ʿajīf*, (pl. عجفي *ʿajfaʾ*) Thin. Lean.

A عجيل *ʿajīl*, Making haste. (pl. عجال *ʿijāl* and عجالي *ʿujālaʾ*) Quick, speedy, nimble. *ʿujayl*, A whet before dinner. Any thing prepared in haste.

A عجيلة *ʿujaylat*, Quick march, rapid journey.

A عجيلى *ʿujaylaʾ*, A rapid journey.

A عجين *ʿajīn*, (v. n. of عجن) Kneading. (pl. عجن *ʿujun*) Kneaded. Effeminate. Flour and water, paste, dough. An electuary.

A عجينة *ʿajīnat*, A troop, multitude. Silly, foolish. Effeminate. ام عجينة *umm ʿajīnat*, A pelican.

A عدّ *ʿadd*, (v. n. of عدّ) Numbering, counting, computing, reckoning, estimating. Numeration, number. *ʿidd*, (pl. اعداد *aʿdād*) A perennial fountain. A multitude. An old well. The right number (when one guesses any thing exactly, as age). A fellow, a companion. Alike, equal. ذو عدّ *zū ʿidd*, Numerous. *ʿudd*, A pimple breaking out on the face of the beautiful.

A عدا *ʿadaʾ*, (v. n. of عدا for عدو) Rushing (as bandits upon merchandise). Beside, except.

A عداء *ʿadāʾ*, (v. n. of عدا for عدو) Transgressing (the law). Acting unjustly towards another. Averting, diverting from. Transgression of the law or any other iniquity. Any employment which diverts the mind from another pursuit. Length and breadth. Distance. *ʿidāʾ*, (v. n. 3 of عدا for عدو) Passing through one to another (as piercing two animals with one shot). Detesting, being inimical and hostile. Seeking immediately one after another. (pl. of عدو *ʿidw*) Thin flat stones with which things are covered. (pl. of عدوة *ʿidwat* and *ʿudwat*) High places. (pl. of عدوة *ʿidwat*) Banks of rivers. *ʿidāʾ* or *ʿadāʾ*, One heat at a race. Length, breadth, limit, or extent.

A عدّاء *ʿaddāʾ*, (pl. عدّاءون *ʿaddāʾūn*) Swift of foot; an excellent runner. Fleet (courser).

A عداب *ʿadāb*, A place thin of sand.

A عدابة *ʿadābat*, Uterus: pecten et pubes (feminæ).

A عدابس *ʿadābis*, Strong (camels).

A عداة *ʿudāt*, (pl. of عادي *ʿādī*) Enemies.

A عداد *ʿidād*, Number, enumeration. A rising up against an enemy. A preparing for a fight. The pain from the bite of a scorpion or other animal, which grows raw and rankles on the anniversary. The time when the moon, after her monthly course, returns to the Pleiades. Equal, alike. A gift, present. A companion, fellow. A fit of madness. The hour of death. لقيته عداد الثريا *lakītuhu ʿidāda's surayyaʾ*, I met him once a month. عداد القوس *ʿidādu'l kaws*, The twang of a bow-string. عداده في بني فلان *ʿidāduhu fī banī fulān*, He is thought to be of the family of such-a-one. هو في عداد اهل الخير *huwa fī ʿidādi ahli'l khayr*, He is numbered amongst the good, *i. e.* he is dead, gone to heaven. يوم عداد *yawmu ʿidād*, Either of the days of جمعة *jumuʿat*, فطر *fitr*, or اضحى *azhaʾ*. يوم العداد *yawmu'l ʿidād*, A day dedicated to presents. P عداد كردن *ʿidād kardan*, To prepare. To number.

A عدار *ʿudār*, A certain beast said to exist in Yaman, which generates with human beings, and whose sperm consists of worms. A proper name.

A عدّار *ʿaddār*, A sailor.

A عداري *ʿadārī*, A kind of grape (in Morocco).

A عداس *ʿidās*, A departing, travelling.

A عداف *ʿudāf*, Any thing (eatable).

A عدال *ʿidāl*, (v. n. 3 of عدل) Being crooked. Hesitating, remaining in doubt with regard to two matters before one.

A عدالة *ʿadālat*, (v. n. of عدل) Being just, right, equitable, lawful, legitimate. Justice, equity, law. A court of justice (for the trial of causes respecting property). P عدالت ديواني *ʿadālati dīwānī*, A civil court. عدالت فوجداري *ʿadālati fawjdārī*, A criminal court. A عدالت قاسمة *ʿadālati kāsima*, Distributive justice. P عدالت كردن *ʿadālat kardan*, To administer justice, to proceed with equity.

P عدالت پيشه *ʿadālat-pesha*, Practiser of justice.

A عدالت قرين *ʿadālat-karīn*, Connected with justice.

A عدالي *ʿadālī*, (pl. of عدولي) Old, large trees.

A عدامة *ʿadāmat*, A being foolish. Idiocy.

A عدامس *ʿudāmis*, (or كلأ عدامس *kalaʾun ʿudāmis*) A heap of dry herbage. Thick, old (tree or Lybian lizard).

A عدامل *ʿudāmil*, (or عداملىّ *ʿudāmiliy*) Old.

A عدان *ʿadān*, Shore (of the sea); bank (of a river). Space of seven years.

A عدّان *ʿaddān*, The first or best part of any thing. *ʿaddān* or *ʿiddān*, The time in which any thing is done: as, كان ذالك علي عدّانه *kāna zālika ʿala' ʿaddānihi*, That was in his time. هو في عدّان شبابه *huwa fī ʿaddāni shabābihi*, He is in the prime of youth. *ʿiddān*, (for عتدان *ʿitdān*) Yearling kids.

A عدانة *ʿadānat*, A body, troop, crowd of men. A patch on the bottom of a leathern bucket.

A عداوة *ʿadāwat*, Enmity, hatred, hostility.

P عداوت گزين *ʿadāwat-guzīn*, Inimical.

A عداول *ʿadāwil*, (pl. of عدولي) Old, high trees.

A عدائم *ʿadāʾim*, A kind of Madīna date.

A عدائن *ʿadāʾin*, (pl. of عدينة) Leathern patches.

A عدبّس *ʿadabbas*, (pl. عدابس *ʿadābis*) Strong, firm-bodied (camel). Bad-tempered, malignant. Coarse, thick, corpulent.

A عدبيّ *ʿadabiy*, Excellent, unblemished.

A عدة *ʿidat*, (v. n. of وعد) Predicting any thing good to another, promising. Threatening. A promise. A term.

A عدّة *ʿiddat*, Number, multitude (of children); many. A certain (also a computed) number or body (of men or cattle). The state of a woman when it is unlawful to have intercourse with her (as when divorced, when mourning the death of her husband, or when menstruous). The time of probation which a divorced woman is to wait before she can engage in a second marriage, in order to determine whether or not she be pregnant by the former. *ʿuddat*, Disposition, preparation, readiness. A provision made for any necessary occasion (as scarcity). A pimple or eruption on a comely face. كونوا على عدّة *kūnū ʿala' ʿuddatin*, Be ye in readiness. هو من عدّة مال *huwa min ʿuddatin mālun*, His wealth is laid up against a time of want.

A عدث *ʿads*, Softness of disposition.

A عدد *ʿadad*, Number. Numbered. The computed years of a person's life. عدد اوّل *ʿadadi awwal*, A prime number. عدد تامّ *ʿadadi tāmm*, A perfect number, *i.e.* one whose aliquot or even parts joined together will exactly make that whole number: as 6, which is equal to 1+2+3. عدد صحيح *ʿadadi sahīh*, A whole number, a unit. عدد كثير *ʿadadi kasīr*, A great multitude. العدد المعدود *al ʿadadu'l maʿdūd*, The age of any person. عدد مركب *ʿadadi murakkab*, A compound number. *ʿidad*, A return of the pain from the bite of a scorpion at the end of a year. *ʿudad*, (pl. of عدّة *ʿuddat*) Preparations against a time of scarcity.

A عدديّ *ʿadadiy*, Numeral, numerical.

A عدر *ʿadr*, Excessive rain. Boldness. *ʿudr*, Much and heavy rain. *ʿadar*, (v. n. of عدر) Abounding in water (a place).

A عدرّج *ʿadarraj*, Light, nimble. ابن عدرّج *ibn ʿadarraj*, Any one, such a one (is not at home).

P عدرنا *ʿadarnā*, Glasswort. Pearl-ashes, lye.

A عدس *ʿads*, (v. n. of عدس) Wandering. Labouring. Conjecturing. Trampling hard. Pasturing, tending (cattle). Calling out to a mule. Serving (as a domestic). Carrying any one off (death). *ʿadas*, A mule; also a word used in calling to him. A lentil. Name of a harsh muleteer who lived in the time of Solomon.

A عدسان *ʿadasān*, (v. n. of عدس) Travelling.

A عدسة *ʿadasat*, One lentil. A species of pustules on the body, which are often mortal.

A عدسيّة *ʿadasiyat*, A dish of lentils.

A عدعد *ʿadʿad*, Used in speaking to a mule.

A عدعدة *ʿadʿadat*, Haste, expedition in walking. The cry of the bird called kata.

A عدف *ʻadf*, (v. n. of عدف) Eating. Any thing eatable. A little fodder. A small present. *ʻidf*, Part (of the night). A company of men, from 10 to 50. Root, origin. *ʻudf*, (pl. of عدوف *ʻadūf*) Eatables. *ʻadaf*, Chips, straws, motes. Any thing eatable. *ʻidaf*, A company of men, 10 to 50.

A عدفة *ʻadfat*, Root, origin. *ʻidfat*, The upper part of the breast, the thorax. Part (of a flock, or of the night). A small body of men, from 10 to 50. An assembly, a company. The border of a garment, whether plain or ornamented. A short shift or inner garment. *ʻidfat* or *ʻadafat*, (pl. عدف *ʻidaf* and *ʻadaf*) The root of a tree under ground.

A عدق *ʻadk*, (v. n. of عدق) Collecting, gathering. Being irresolute, uncertain what to do, ask, or take. Moving the hand about in any place full of water (as if in search of any thing), groping. *ʻadak*, (v. n. of عدق) Doing (any thing) of one's own will without certain knowledge. Moving the hand about in any place full of water (as if searching).

A عدقة *ʻadakat*, (pl. عدق *ʻadak*) A hooked instrument with which they pull buckets out of wells.

A عدك *ʻadk*, A beating wool with a mallet.

A عدل *ʻadl*, (v. n. of عدل) Appointing what is just, administering justice. Equaling, equalising. Making of the same weight. Inclining, turning away from. Being crooked (a road). Being like, equal to. Desisting from covering (a stallion). Driving off a stallion. Riding in company, occupying the opposite panier or hawda. Composing differences. Giving companions or equals to God, being an idolater. Being irresolute, wavering in one's choice betwixt two things. Returning. Name of an executioner. Equity, justice, correctness, rectitude, probity, integrity. Measure. Just, equitable, equal (man or woman). Legal, unobjectionable, competent (witness). Any thing alike, equal, equivalent in value. An ordinance of God. Recompense, redemption, ransom; any thing which redeems another. Irregularity, anomaly. Deviation from the right way. (pl. of عادل *ʻādil*) Just, equitable. ذو عدل *zū ʻadlin*, Competent (witness). الشاهد العدل *ash shāhidu'l ʻadl*, A just, unexceptionable witness, who avoids sins great and small, even to eating or making water on the high-road. *ʻidl*, (pl. اعدال *aʻdāl* and عدول *ʻudūl*) Any thing equal or equiponderant to another (as load to load; what a beast of burden carries on one side); whatever resembles another, animate or inanimate. *ʻadal*, The equalizing of two packages on one horse.

A عدلاء *ʻudalāʼ*, (pl. of عديل *ʻadīl*) Pairs, equals.

A عدلة *ʻadlat*, Just (woman). *ʻadalat*, Persons competent and worthy to give evidence. *ʻudalat*, One competent and worthy to give evidence.

P عدلي *ʻadalī*, A sort of good money.

A عدلية *ʻadlīyat*, Justice. Followers of Aliy.

A عدم *ʻudm*, (v. n. of عدم) Becoming poor. Being a fool. Leaving, abandoning, and going away (any business). *ʻudm* or *ʻadam*, (v. n. of عدم) Losing, being deprived of. Being destitute of, wanting. *ʻudm*, *ʻadam*, or *ʻudum*, Want, privation, defect, inexistence, nothing, nonentity. Annihilation. Poverty. عدم مقاومت *ʻadami mukāwamat*, Inability of resistance, weakness. P عدم كردن *ʻadam kardan*, To annihilate, reduce to want, make defective. A *ʻadim*, Poor, indigent.

A عدماء *ʻadmāʼ*, White (earth). Desolate (country). White on the head (a sheep). *ʻudamāʼ*, (pl. of عدم *ʻadim*) Poor, needy, indigent.

A عدمل *ʻudmul*, (or عدملي *ʻudmulīy*) Old, aged. Thick, old (tree or Lybian lizard). *ʻudmul*, The male bird رخم *rakham*.

A عدمول *ʻudmūl*, Old, aged. A frog.

A عدمي *ʻadamīy*, Privative. Inexistent.

A عدمية *ʻadamīyat*, Annihilation, non-existence.

A عدن *ʻadn*, (v. n. of عدن) Settling in any country; remaining in one place (as cattle at pasture). Dunging (land). Pruning or defacing with a hatchet (a tree). Waxing tall (a palm-tree). Pulling up (a stone). جنات عدن *jannātu ʻadnin*, Gardens of permanent occupation. *ʻadan*, A permanent dwelling. Eden. The town now called Aden.

A عدنان *ʻadnān*, Name of the father of Maadd.

P عدنگ *ʻadang*, Foolish, stupid.

A عدني *ʻadanīy*, A native of Aden.

A عدو *ʻadw*, (v. n. of عدا for عدو) Averting, diverting from. Passing by or over, leaving. Rushing upon. Running (a horse). Being iniquitous, unjust. *ʻidw*, (pl. عداء *ʻidāʼ*) The length, breadth, extent, or limit of a thing. A limit, extremity. A thin stone with which any thing may be covered.

A عدو *ʻadūw*, (pl. اعداء *aʻdāʼ*, اعادي *aʻādī*, and عدي *ʻuda'*) An enemy. عدو عاقل خير من صديق جاهل *ʻadūwun ʻāhilun khayrun min sadīkin jāhilin*, Better a prudent enemy than a foolish friend (a proverb). *ʻudūw*, (v. n. of عدا for عدو) Running, passing by. Being iniquitous, unjust.

A عدواء *ʻudawāʼ*, (A vehicle) unequal, inconvenient for sitting on. Ground hard and dry. A distant house or home. Impediments, obstacles (to any work). Any occupation which diverts from other pursuits.

A عدوان *ʻidwān*, (v. n. of عدا for عدو) Being iniquitous. Hating. *ʻudwān*, (v. n. of عدا for عدو) Being iniquitous, unjust. Averting from. Passing by or over, leaving. Rushing upon (as bandits upon merchandise). Flagrant injustice. Evil, iniquity. Hostility, hatred, oppression. اهل عدوان *ahli ʻudwān*, Resentful, rancorous, inimical. بغض و عدوان *bughz u ʻudwān*, Hatred and enmity. غيظ و عدوان *ghayz u ʻudwān*, Indignation and hatred. *ʻadawān*, (v. n. of عدا for عدو) Rushing (as bandits upon merchandise). Running. Who runs fast. ذو عدوان *zū ʻadawān*, Very rapacious, cruel, fierce.

A عدوب *ʻadūb*, Many sands, abundant sand.

P عدوبند *ʻadū-band*, Subduer of enemies.

A عدوة *ʻadwat*, *ʻidwat*, or *ʻudwat*, (pl. عداء *ʻidāʼ*) The side of a river. *ʻidwat* or *ʻudwat*, Length, breadth, extent. Limit, extremity. A thin stone or slab for covering. (pl. عداء *ʻidāʼ* and عديات *ʻudyāt*) A high place. *ʻudwat*, A distant place. High ground.

A عدوة *ʻadūwat*, (fem. of عدو) A female foe.

A عدودني *ʻadawdanīy*, Swift, strong (camel).

A عدوس *ʻadūs*, Bold, brave (woman). عدوس السري *ʻadūsu'ssura'*, One who travels by night, bold. A hyena. *ʻudūs*, (v. n. of عدس) Departing.

A عدوف *ʻadūf*, Any thing eatable: provender.

A عدوفة *ʻadūfat*, Any thing eatable.

A عدوقة *ʻadwakat*, (pl. عدق *ʻuduk*) Hooked instruments with which they pull buckets out of wells.

A عدول *ʻadawl*, Name of a renowned shipbuilder. *ʻudūl*, (v. n. of عدل) Returning. Deviating, swerving, wandering, receding, deserting. Declining, inclining. Refusing. Composing differences. Driving off (a stallion). Reversion. Defection, deviation. (pl. of عدل *ʻidl*) Things equal or equiponderant. Things resembling each other (animate or inanimate). (pl. of عادل *ʻādil*) Just, equitable. P عدول نمودن *ʻudūl namūdan*, To turn away from.

A عدولة *ʻudūlat*, (v. n. of عدل) Administering justice. Justice, equity.

A عدولي *ʻadawla'*, (pl. عدالي *ʻadālī* and عداول *ʻadāwil*) An old and tall tree. A maritime town in Bahrayn, on the east coast of Arabia.

A عدولي *ʻadawlīy*, A sailor.

A عدولية *ʻadawlīyat*, A kind of ship (named from عدولي *ʻadawla'*).

A عدوم *ʻadūm*, Poor, needy, destitute.

P عدو مال *ʻadū-māl*, Crushing foes.

A عدون *ʻudūn*, (v. n. of عدن) Settling in a country; remaining in one place (cattle at pasture).

A عدوي *ʻadwa'*, Assistance, aid, protection. An action brought before a judge for revenge of an injury. Any contagious disease. Contagion. *ʻudwa'*, (v. n. of عدا for عدو) Transgressing, being iniquitous, unjust. Hostility, hatred. Evil, injustice.

A عدوي *ʻadawīy*, Inimical. Of the family of عدي *ʻadīy*. *ʻidawīy*, Promissory.

A عدوية *ʻadawīyat*, Plants or shrubs on which cattle pasture at the end of spring. Small sheep.

P عدّه دار بكر *ʻidda-dār bikr*, Wine not yet tasted. An unbroached cask of wine.

A عدي *ʻada'*, (v. n. of عدا for عدو) Running. Wishing to run. *ʻuda'*, (v. n. of عدا for عدو) Rushing (as bandits upon merchandise). *ʻida'*, or *ʻada'*, (pl. اعداء *aʻdāʼ*) A side, quarter. A river's brink. A beam between two others. A thin, flat stone for covering any thing. *ʻida'* or *ʻuda'*, Enemies, strangers. Travellers. Absent (persons). قوم عدي *kawmi ɛida'*, Hostile people, enemies.

A عديّ *ɛadīy*, Name of a family of the tribe of Kuraysh. (pl. of عادي *ɛādī*) Runners, especially on their toes. *ɛidīy*, Promissory.

A عديات *ɛudyāt*, (pl. of عدوة *ɛidwat* or *ɛudwat*) High places.

A عديد *ɛadīd*, Numerous. A number. Enumerated. A companion, fellow, match. Equal, alike. A widow's weeds. هم عديد الحصا *hum ɛadīdu'l hasa'*, They are as numerous as the pebbles. عديد القوم *ɛadīdu'l kawm*, One of the people.

A عديدة *ɛadīdat*, A lot, part, portion.

A عديل *ɛadīl*, (pl. عدلاء *ɛudalā*) In quantity or weight equal to a load on one side of a horse or camel. Any one riding in an opposite litter on the other side of a camel. Equal. Alike. Just, equitable. A rival.

A عديم *ɛadīm*, Destitute. Poor, indigent. Not be found, non-existent. Senseless: crazed: a fool. عديم المثال *ɛadīmu'l misāl*, Incomparable; a nonpareil. عديم النظير *ɛadīmu'n nazīr*, Matchless, peerless. عديم الوفا *ɛadīmu'l wafā*, Faithless, dishonest.

A عدينة *ɛadīnat*, (pl. عدائن *ɛadāɛin*) A patch on the bottom of a leathern bucket. Name of a place wherein are the graves of sundry pious men, and the tomb of ذو اشرف *zū ashraf*. *ɛudaynat*, Name of Taizz, in Yaman; also of a woman.

A عديّي *ɛadayīy*, Of the family of عديّ *ɛadīy*.

A عذاءة *ɛazāɛat*, Healthiness, salubrity of air.

A عذاب *ɛazāb*, (pl. اعذبة *aɛzibat*) Pain, punishment. Torment, torture, martyrdom; a whipping. عذاب اليم *ɛazābi alīm*, Severe punishment. عذاب الحريق *ɛazābu'l harīk*, The punishment of hell-flames. عذاب عذبين *ɛazābu ɛuzabīn*, Incessant torture: torment from which there is no escape.

A عذابة *ɛazābat*, Uterus. Pecten et pubes feminæ.

A عذاة *ɛazāt*, (pl. عذوات *ɛazawāt*) Level, excellent, healthy soil.

A عذار *ɛizār*, The cheek. That part of the jaws over which the bridle passes to the head. The side of the beard. (pl. عذر *ɛuzr*) That part of the bridle which presses upon the jaws. A mark or scar upon the cheek. The side of a spear-head. A road. An entertainment made on any novel occasion (as finishing a house, or circumcising a child). Shame. An extensive hill of sand. Rough ground reaching to a great distance. خلع العذار *khalaɛa'l ɛizār*, He went on fearlessly, shamelessly. P عرض عذار كردن *ɛarzi ɛizār kardan*, To uncover the face, to appear or shew one's self.

A عذاري *ɛazāra'* or *ɛazārī*, (pl. of عذراء) Virgins.

A عذاف *ɛazāf*, Any thing eatable. *ɛuzāf*, Deadly (poison).

A عذافر *ɛuzāfir*, A lion. A large, strong camel.

A عذّال *ɛazzāl*, A railer, accuser. *ɛuzzāl*, Railers.

A عذّالة *ɛazzālat*, The fundament.

A عذّام *ɛazzām*, (pl. عذم *ɛuzum*) A flea. *ɛuzzām*, A kind of salt bitter plant.

A عذانة *ɛazānat*, The podex.

A عذاوات *ɛazāwāt*, (pl. of عذاة) Level grounds.

A عذاويط *ɛazāwīt*, (or عذاييط *ɛazāyīt*) (pl. of عذيوط *ɛizyawt*, *ɛuzyawt*, or *ɛuzyūt*, q. v.).

A عذائم *ɛazāɛim*, (pl. of عذيمة *ɛazīmat*) Reprehensions, reproofs, rebukes.

A عذب *ɛazb*, (v. n. of عذب) Hindering. Prohibiting. Abandoning. Abstaining from, or loathing meat from excessive thirst. Sweet water. A kind of tree. Meat and drink which glides easily down the throat. لسان عذب البيان *lisāni ɛazbu'l bayān*, A flowing or eloquent tongue. *ɛazub*, That which accompanies the birth. A kind of tree. A strip of cloth worn round the waist by mourning women. The string by which they lift a balance or scales. The extremity or edge of any thing. The tip of a camel's pizzle. A strap hanging from the hinder part of a camel's saddle. (pl. of عذبة *ɛazabat*) Sticks and straws. ذو عذب *zū ɛazub*, (Water) covered with rubbish. *ɛazib*, (Water) covered with fenny weeds.

A عذبة *ɛazbat*, A kind of tree fatal to camels. Name of a certain medicine. A fenny weed floating on water. *ɛazbat*, *ɛazabat*, or *ɛazibat*, Water-lentils, fen-weeds. *ɛazabat*, The tip of the tongue. The extremity of the turban or sash hanging behind. A strap hanging from the hinder part of a camel's saddle. The string by which they lift a balance or scales. A branch. Rubbish; a bit of stick. *ɛazibat*, Chaff. Scum. The lash of a scourge.

P عذبه *ɛazba*, The fruit of the tamarisk.

A عذبيّ *ɛazabīy*, Generous, noble-minded.

A عذج *ɛazj*, (v. n. of عذج) Drinking. A drink. عذج عاذج *ɛazji ɛāzij*, A great draught.

A عذره *ɛazara*, (fut. يعذر *yaɛziru*) He excused.

A عذر *ɛazr*, (v. n. of عذر) Circumcising. Bridling (a horse), or rather putting on him the headstall (called عذار *ɛizār*). *ɛazr* or *ɛazar*, (v. n. of عذر) Being prolific in vices, sins, mischief. *ɛuzr*, (v. n. of عذر) Excusing. (pl. اعذار *aɛzār*) Excuse, apology, pretext, objection. Virginity. (pl. of عذار *ɛizār*) Those parts of bridles which press upon the jaws. Good success, fortunate issue. Victory, conquest. ابو عذر *abū ɛuzr*, A first husband. ذو عذر *zū ɛuzr*, Excusable. ما انت بذي عذر هذا الكلام *mā anta bizī ɛuzri hāza'l kalām*, Thou art not the author of this discourse. عذر قدم *ɛuzri kadam*, Welcome (a form of salutation). Humility. P عذر آوردن *ɛuzr āwardan*, To apologize. عذر خواستن *ɛuzr khwāstan*, To ask pardon. عذر لنگ *ɛuzri lang*, A lame excuse. A عذر ما فات *ɛuzri mā fāt*, An excuse for past faults. P عذر كردن *ɛuzr kardan*, To make an excuse or apology. A *ɛuzur*, (v. n. of عذر) Excusing. (pl. of عذير *ɛazīr*) Apologists. Situations urged in extenuation of a fault.

P عذرا *ɛazrā*, A virgin. A mistress. The sign Virgo. Plainly, openly. A word used at the game of نرد *nard*. Name of the mistress of وامق *wāmik*.

A عذراء *ɛazrāɛ*, (pl. عذاري *ɛazāra'*, *ɛazārī*, and عذراوات *ɛazrāwāt*) A virgin, a maiden. The sign Virgo. An iron instrument of torture, to extort confession. &c. Sand yet untrodden. A pearl not yet bored. Gemini. Madīna. A place near Damascus. رسالت عذرا *risālati ɛazrā*, A maiden letter.

P عذر آور *ɛuzr-āwar*, One who offers an excuse; an apologist, apologizer.

P عذر پذير *ɛuzr-pazīr*, Excuse-accepting.

A عذرة *ɛizrat*, A mode of excuse. *ɛuzrat*, Virginity. The taking of a maidenhead. A lad's foreskin. Circumcision. The uvula and jaws, or any pain in them from inflammation. A mark or scar on the cheek. The mane of a horse's withers. A handful of hair, a ringlet growing from the crown of the head. A disease in the throat producing pain and inflammation. The clitoris. A mark, sign. Five stars in the extremity of the milky way. A certain star which, when it has risen, the heat increases. ابو عذرة *abū ɛuzrat*, (Father of a maidenhead) A first husband. *ɛazirat*, Dung, human excrement, ordure. A court-yard or place where rubbish or ordure is thrown. Light wheat, tail-end, and rubbish. An assembly, convivial meeting.

P عذرخواه *ɛuzr-khwāh*, Seeking an excuse, asking pardon. An apologist; apologizer.

P عذر خواهانه *ɛuzr-khwāhāna*, As an excuse.

P عذر خواهي *ɛuzr-khwāhī*, Excuse; an apology. عذر خواهي نمودن *ɛuzr-khwāhī namūdan*, To beg pardon. To offer an excuse: to apologize.

P عذرة ناك *ɛaziranāk*, Full of rubbish and filth.

A عذريّ *ɛuzra'*, (v. n. of عذر) Excusing.

A عذط *ɛazt*, A stooling in coitu.

A عذف *ɛazf*, (v. n. of عذف) Eating. Any thing eatable.

A عذفوط *ɛuzfūt*, An animalcule, white and soft, resembling a girl's finger.

A عذق *ɛazk*, (v. n. of عذق) Upbraiding one with any thing infamous. Tracing, charging, imputing. Distinguishing any thing by its own peculiar mark (as a sheep or camel, by tying round them a lock of different-coloured wool). Driving away (a stallion camel from the females). Collecting, bringing (them) together. Letting the two ends of the turban-sash or head-dress flow behind. Dunging (a camel). Lopping the branches of a palm-tree. Producing an ear (the sweet rush). (pl. اعذق *aɛzuk* and عذق *ɛizk*) A palm-tree with its produce. A sort of date. *ɛizk*, (pl. اعذاق *aɛzāk* and عذوق *ɛuzūk*) A bunch of dates or grapes. A bunch of which the grapes have been eaten. Any branch bearing twigs. Glory, dignity. *ɛazik*, Cunning, artful, clever. Fragrant (perfume). Glib-tongued.

A عذقانة *ɛazkānat*, A clamorous, brawling woman.

A عذقة *ʻazhat* or *ʻizkat*, A mark of different-coloured wool tied round a sheep's neck.

A عذل *ʻazl*, (v. n. of عذل) Reproving, chiding. *ʻazl* or *ʻazal*, Reprehension. *ʻuzul*, Sultry (days).

A عذّل *ʻuzzal*, Railers, reproachers.

A عذلاج *ʻizlāj*, Agreeable, easy (life).

A عذلة *ʻazalat*, (pl. of عاذل *ʻāzil*) Railers, reproachers. *ʻuzalat*, A continual railer.

A عذلجة *ʻazlajat*, (v. n. of عذلج Q) Feeding (an infant) well. Filling (a leathern bottle).

A عذلط *ʻuzalit*, Thick (milk).

A عذلوج *ʻuzlūj*, Beautiful, healthy, well-fed (boy).

A عذلوق *ʻuzlūk*, A light, active lad.

A عذم *ʻazm*, (v. n. of عذم) Biting (as a horse). Eating voraciously. Reproaching, blaming (her husband) for making unnatural proposals to her (a wife). عذمه عن نفسه *ʻazamahu ʻan nafsihi*, He drove him from him. *ʻazam*, A kind of plant. *ʻazim*, (A horse) apt to bite. *ʻuzum*, (pl. of عذام *ʻazzām*) Fleas.

A عذمذم *ʻazamzam*, Measure by guess. Death of great numbers.

A عذمهر *ʻazamhar*, Spacious, extensive (city).

A عذو *ʻazw*, (v. n. of عذا for عذو) Having a pleasant, wholesome air (a town).

A عذوب *ʻazūb*, (A horse) abstaining from eating on account of excessive thirst. A beast of burden standing without meat or drink. Employed in the open air.

A عذوبة *ʻuzūbat*, (v. n. of عذب) Being pure (water). Purity or sweetness of water.

A عذوّر *ʻazawwar*, Of a bad disposition, hard hearted. Large-bellied (ass). A mighty king.

A عذوط *ʻizwat*, (or عذووط *ʻizwawt*) One who stools in coitu. See عذيوط *ʻizyawt*.

A عذوف *ʻazūf*, Whatever is eaten. One who eats much, or who takes a taste. علىٰ غير عذوف *ʻala' ghayr ʻazūf*, Without any thing to eat.

A عذوفر *ʻazawfar*, Large and strong (camel).

A عذوق *ʻuzūk*, (pl. of عذق) Clusters of dates.

A عذويّة *ʻazawiyat*, Camels feeding in a sweet pasture where the plant حمض *hamz* does not grow.

A عذي *ʻazy* or *ʻizy*, A field watered only by rain. A country in which the salsuginous plant حمض *hamz* does not grow. *ʻaza'*, (v. n. of عذي) Having a pleasant air. Being far situated from water.

A عذية *ʻaziyat*, (pl. عذوات *ʻazawāt*) A level, healthy country. Sticks or straws floating on water.

A عذير *ʻazīr*, (pl. عذر *ʻuzur*) One who excuses, an apologist. An assistant, defender. A situation, especially that which a man pleads in excuse for a fault. A convivial meeting. A feast on the occasion of building a house or circumcising a child.

A عذيرة *ʻazīrat*, A circumcision-feast.

A عذيطة *ʻazyatat*, (v. n. of عذيط Q) Stooling in coitu. Experiencing an effusion antecedent to coition.

A عذيق *ʻuzayk*, (dim. of عذق *ʻazk*) A small loaded palm-tree.

A عذيمة *ʻazīmat*, (pl. عذائم *ʻazāʼim*) Reprehension, reproof, blame. A biting or chewing. A stoneless date.

A عذيوط *ʻizyawt* or *ʻuzyūt*, (pl. عذاييط *ʻazāyīt* or عذاويط *ʻazāwīt*) Qui se concacat in coitu. One who experiences an effusion before coition.

A عرّ *ʻarr*, (v. n. of عرّ) Injuring, vexing, rendering sad (any one). Defaming, accusing. Pulling (hair) up by the roots. Being necessitous. Bringing one's necessities before any one. Giving without being asked. Being ulcerated, scabby (camels). The scab. A child who is weaned early. *ʻirr*, Noise which a horse makes less than neighing. *ʻurr*, (v. n. of عرّ) Becoming pregnant (camels). An ulcer in the neck of a young camel. A disease which causes a camel's coat to fall off. The scab. A boy, a slave. Dung of birds.

A عرا *ʻara'*, A court-yard, area, piazza.

A عراء *ʻarāʼ*, (pl. اعرية *aʻriyat* and اعراء *aʻrāʼ*) An open place, area; spacious place in the open air. An empty place. Surface of the ground. *ʻirāʼ*, (v. n. 3 of عري) Riding (horses) without saddles.

P عراء *ʻirā*, The square lying between the king and the tower at chess.

A عرّاء *ʻarrāʼ*, A girl, a virgin. Scabby (she-camel). Bunchless or small-bunched (she-camel).

A عراب *ʻarāb*, Fruit of a tree, from whose bark ropes are made. *ʻirāb*, Fine Arab horses or camels.

A عرّاب *ʻarrāb*, A maker of the bag عرابة.

A عرابة *ʻarābat*, (pl. عرابات *ʻarābāt*) A bag put over the dugs of sheep to prevent them being sucked. *ʻirābat*, Coarse, indecent, obscene language.

A عرابض *ʻurābiz*, Thick and strong.

P عرابه *ʻarāba*, A curricle. A two-wheel cart.

A عراة *ʻarāt*, A court-yard, area. A vestibule. A shore. Intense cold. *ʻurāt*, (pl. of عاري *ʻārī*) Naked. Unarmed.

A عرّات *ʻarrat*, Hard (spear).

A عراج *ʻurāj*, Hyenas.

A عراجين *ʻarājīn*, (pl. of عرجون *ʻurjūn*) Bunches of dates (dry), stalks of bunches.

A عراد *ʻarād*, A thick, hard plant. A kind of plant.

A عرادة *ʻarādat*, A state, quality, condition. A female locust.

A عرّادة *ʻarrādat*, A kind of small balista or engine for hurling missiles.

A عراديس *ʻarādīs*, A joint of the fingers. Articulation or joining-place of bones (in man or beast).

A عرار *ʻarār*, A fragrant forest-herb resembling camomile. Women bringing forth only male children. A child weaned early. Retaliation, lex talionis. A being equal to, or match for. Adversity. Elevation, sublimity. Principality, dominion. Depravity. Name of a cow, which fought with another called كحل *kahl* till they were both killed: hence, when two things are equal they say, باءت عرار بكحل *bāʼat ʻarār bi kahl*. *ʻirār*, (v. n. of عرّ) Being scabby (a camel). (v. n. 3 of عرّ) Being dilatory. *ʻirār* or *ʻurār*, (v. n. of عرّ) Making a noise (as an ostrich).

A عرارة *ʻarārat*, Depravity, badness of temper. A female child soon weaned. Principality, chiefship. Adversity.

A عراز *ʻirāz*, A corrupting, vitiating, spoiling.

A عرّاز *ʻurrāz*, Slanderers of the absent.

A عرازم *ʻarāzim*, A lion.

A عرازيل *ʻarāzīl*, Gangs of thieves.

A عراس *ʻirās*, A rope for binding a camel.

A عرّاس *ʻarrās*, A seller of the young camel عرس *ʻars*.

A عراص *ʻirās*, (pl. of عرصة *ʻarsat*) Court-yards, areas, open spaces without buildings.

A عرّاص *ʻarrās*, A thundering, flashing cloud. Incessantly flashing (lightning). Tremulous, limber (spear or sword).

A عراصم *ʻurāsim*, A lion.

A عراصيف *ʻarāsīf*, (pl. of عرصوف *ʻursūf*) Four pieces of wood used in making a camel's saddle. Projecting parts of the vertebræ of a camel's back. Bones of a proboscis bending inwards to the nose.

A عراض *ʻirāz*, (v. n. 3 of عرض) Going side by side, and step for step. Doing equal with another. Collating (books). Retiring to a side, giving place, going away, shunning, avoiding. Taking (a thorny plant) obliquely in his mouth (a camel). Bringing forth a son illegitimately (a woman). Covering the female when brought to him (a camel). A side, tract, quarter. A half or side. Primary (argument). The greater part. A broad mark on the thigh or buttocks of any animal. An iron with which the hoofs of a camel are marked, in order that he may be tracked through the sand. (pl. of عريض *ʻarīz*) Broad, wide. *ʻurāz*, Broad, wide.

A عراضة *ʻarāzat*, (v. n. of عرض) Having breadth. *ʻurāzat*, A present (especially in provisions). Provisions carried from place to place. قوس عراضة *kaws ʻurāzat*, A broad bow.

A عراعر *ʻarāʻir*, Sides or extremities of a camel's bunch. (pl. of عراعر *ʻurāʻir*) Nobles, chiefs. *ʻurāʻir*, Fat (camel). (pl. عراعر *ʻarāʻir*) A noble. The chief of a family. Name of a place whence salt is brought.

A عرّاف *ʻarrāf*, A priest, augur. A physician.

A عرافة *ʻarāfat*, (v. n. of عرف) Becoming an عريف *ʻarīf*, *i. e.* one next in rank to a chief, a lieutenant, or deputy. *ʻirāfat*, (v. n. of عرف) Exercising the office of deputy. The rank next to a commander or chief judge, lieutenant, deputy.

A عرافج *ʻarāfij*, Pathless, trackless deserts.

A عرافيص *ʻarāfīs*, (pl. of عرفاص *ʻirfās*) Scourges for whipping criminals. Ropes made of sinews for fastening the heads of the timbers of camels' saddles.

A عراق *ʻirāk*, The part of the belly above the navel, the diaphragm. What surrounds the nails.

The external part of the ear. The court of a house. The stitched border of a circular leathern tablecloth. The side of a mountain. (pl. اعرقة aɛrikat and عرق ɛuruk) A double stitch in the bottom of a bottle or provision-bag. A piece of leather with which stitches are covered. Remains of salt and bitter plants. The inside of a quill. Babylonia, Chaldea. (Irāk extends in length from عبّادان ɛabbādān to Mawsil, and in breadth from Kādisīya to Hulwān). (pl. عرق ɛuruk) The sea-shore. The bank of a river during the whole of its course. (pl. of عرق ɛirk) Veins, arteries. Roots. عراق عجم ɛirāki ɛajam, Persian Irāk or Media. عراق عرب ɛirāki ɛarab, Arabian Irāk, Babylonia, Chaldea. ɛirāk or ɛurāk, (pl. of عرق ɛark) Bones without flesh. ɛurāk, Herbage, the immediate produce of a shower. Clear water. Copious rain. A fleshless bone.

A عراقان ɛirākāni, The cities of Basra and Kūfa.

A عراقة ɛurākat, Clear water. Copious rain.

A عراقي ɛarākī, (pl. of عرقوة ɛarkuwat) Cross-bars on buckets. ذات العراقي zātu'l ɛarākī, A calamity, misfortune, distress, adversity.

A عراقيّ ɛirākīy, Produced in, or belonging to, Irāk (especially applied to a breed of horses from that country). A Parthian.

A عراقيب ɛarākīb, (pl. of عرقوب ɛurkūb) Large tendons in the leg reaching to the heel, leaders. Projecting parts of mountains. Narrow mountain-passes. عراقيب الامور ɛarākību'l umūr, Important and difficult affairs. طير العراقيب tayru'l ɛarākīb, The bird شقرّاق shikirrāk (a species of pie).

A عراقيل ɛarākīl, Misfortunes, difficulties.

A عراك ɛarāk, (v. n. of عرك) Having her courses (a woman). ɛirāk, (v. n. 3 of عرك) Fighting hand to hand, jostling one another in battle. A watering (of camels) in a body.

A عراكة ɛurākat, Whatever is milked before the first فيقة fīkat, or interval between two milkings.

A عرام ɛurām, (v. n. of عرم) Being malignant, of corrupted morals, impudent, saucy (boy). Without flesh (bones). Unbarked (trees). What has fallen from the bark of a bramble-bush. Malignity, sauciness. The impetuosity, brunt, or multitudinousness of a large army.

A عرامة ɛarāmat, (v. n. of عرم) Being malignant and impudent. Malignity, impudence.

A عرامين ɛarāmīn, (pl. of عرمان ɛurmān) Piebald. Flocks of sheep and goats. Uncircumcised. Wells or places where water collects.

A عران ɛirān, (v. n. of عرن) Being distant (a house). Being hard and rough. Whipping a bruised sinew round the head of an arrow. Killing; fighting. Being soft and smooth. The block of a pulley. A disease in the heel of a beast of burden causing the hair to fall off, and the foot to crack. A callosity in the pastern of a horse. The stud or nail fastening the hilt of a sword. A bit of wood thrust between a camel's nostrils (to make way for the rein-ring). Battle, conflict. A hyena's den. A horn. Far-distant (places). Distance from home.

A عرانية ɛurāniyat, The main ocean, the middle or deepest part of the sea. A rising tide.

A عرانين ɛarānīn, (pl. of عرنين) Leaders of people.

A عراهل ɛurāhil, Finely-shaped (horse).

A عراهم ɛurāhim, A lion. Tender, soft, fresh. ɛurāhim, (or عراهمة) Large-bodied (she-camel).

A عراهن ɛurāhin, Corpulent (he-camel).

A عراهيل ɛarāhīl, A multitude ranging at liberty with nothing to do.

A عراهين ɛarāhīn, (pl. of عرهون ɛurhūn) Mushrooms. Funguses, puffs.

A عرايا ɛarāya', Naked (objects). (pl. of عريّة ɛarīyat) Palm-trees of which the owner allows others to partake. The sale of dates upon the tree.

A عرائس ɛarāɛis, (pl. of عروس ɛarūs) Brides. ابيات عرائس abyāti ɛarāɛis, Verses, the letters of which are marked with diacritical points.

A عرائك ɛarāɛik, (pl. of عريكة) Dispositions.

A عرب ɛarb, (v. n. of عرب) Eating. ɛarb or ɛarab, Alacrity, briskness. ɛirb, The plant بهمى buhma' when dry. ɛurb, An Arabian who inhabits a city. ɛarab, (v. n. of عرب) Being brisk. Having much water (a well or a river). Swelling, suppurating (a wound), and leaving a scar. Being turned, becoming squeamish (the stomach). Being deep (a river). Arabia. An Arabian (applied to those who inhabit cities, اعراب aɛrāb denoting the roving and plundering Arabs). Much pure water. عرب عاربة ɛarab ɛāribat, (or عرب عرباء ɛarab ɛarbāɛ, or عرب عربة ɛarab ɛaribat or عربات ɛaribāt) The true genuine Arabians, of unmixed blood; عرب مستعربة ɛarab mustaɛribat, (or عرب متعرّبة ɛarab mutaɛarribat) (commonly called Mosarabians) implying Arabians descended from intermarriages with other nations. ɛarib, Squeamish (stomach). Much pure water. ɛurub, (pl. of عروب ɛarūb) Women who love their husbands.

A عربات ɛarabāt, Vessels moored in the Tigris, to serve the purpose of a bridge.

A عرباض ɛirbāz, Strong and large (man, lion, or camel). The lock of a door.

A عربان ɛurbān, Earnest-money.

A عربانة ɛurbānat, A sort of lizard.

P عربانه ɛarabāna, A drum. A tambourine.

A عربب ɛurbub, Water plentiful and pure. A scar left by a wound.

A عربة ɛarabat, A rapid river. Soul, mind, self. A wheel. A place near Madīna. ɛaribat, Pure, genuine Arab. A woman fond of her husband. Refractory, disobedient, and laughing (wife). Abundant in water (a well).

A عربج ɛurbuj, A stout, fat dog.

A عربد ɛirbid, A serpent. Rough ground.

A عربدّ ɛirbadd or ɛirbidd, Strong, firm. Custom, manner, habit. A male viper. A hissing but harmless snake. A red malignant serpent. ركبت عربدّي rakibtu ɛirbaddī, I passed on, but inclined not to any thing.

A عربدة ɛarbadat, Malignity of disposition, quarrelsomeness. Conflict, dispute, battle, riot, uproar.

P عربده جوي ɛarbada-joy or jūy, Quarrelsome, uproarious. A flatterer. A juggler.

P عربده كار ɛarbada-kār, One who assaults his pot-companions and friends.

A عربرب ɛarabrab, The esculent herb sumach.

A عربربيّة ɛarabrabīyat, (Meat) dressed with sumach; a pot seasoned with sumach.

A عربس ɛirbis, Level land prepared for planting. An elevated hillock, smooth and suitable for alighting upon at the end of night.

P عربستان ɛarabistān, The land of Arabia.

A عربسيس ɛarbasīs, Level ground ready for planting. An elevated hillock, level and well adapted for pitching upon at the end of night.

A عربض ɛirbaz or ɛirabz, Strong, bulky (camel or lion). ɛirabz, Broad.

A عربنة ɛarbanat, A giving earnest-money.

A عربون ɛurbūn or ɛarabūn, Earnest-money. ɛarabūn, The contents of the belly.

P عربه ɛaraba, Any wheeled carriage; a chariot, coach, curricle, chaise, waggon, cart, &c.

A عربيّ ɛarabīy, (fem. عربيّة ɛarabīyat) A civilized Arabian. Arabic, Arabian. The Arabic language: hence, عربيّات ɛarabīyāt, Arabic books or phrases; Arabicisims. White barley: or an ear of it.

A عربيد ɛirbīd, A noisy, drunken, riotous fellow, who injures his pot-companions.

A عرّة ɛarrat, (v. n. of عرّ) Annoying, vexing. Strength, fortitude, military courage. Fierceness of battle. A bad temper. A female child weaned early. ɛurrat, The dung (of a man or bird). The infliction of what is distasteful and unpleasant. The fat of a camel's bunch. Injury, crime. The scab. A young girl. Sordid, wicked, hateful (man), the disgrace of his tribe.

A عرت ɛart, (v. n. of عرت) Trembling, vacillating. Flashing, shining. Rubbing (the nose). Being hard (a spear).

A عرتبة ɛartabat, (or عرتمة ɛartamat) The nose, tip of the nose, or the soft part of it. The groove in the middle of the upper lip. على عرتمته ɛala' ɛartamatihi, Against his will.

A عرتن ɛartan, ɛartun, or ɛaratan, A species of tanning shrub.

A عرتنة ɛartanat, A tanning with the plant عرتن.

A عرتون ɛaratūn, A certain shrub used in tanning.

A عرث ɛars, (v. n. of عرث) Being uprooted. Rubbing hard. Tearing up forcibly.

A عرثمة ɛarsamat, The tip of the nose.

A عرج ɛarj or ɛirj, (pl. اعراج aɛrāj and عروج ɛurūj) A troop of camels, from 80 to 90, or 150, or a little more, or from 500 to 1000. *ʻurj*, (pl. of اعرج *aʻraj*) Lame. Hyenas. *ʻaraj*, (v. n. of عرج) Limping naturally. Lameness from birth. Setting (the sun), or inclining westward. ما اشدّ عرجه *mā ashadda ʻarajuhu*, How lame he is! *ʻarij*, A camel that suffers from incontinence of urine, or that squirts it out awry.

A عرجاء *ʻarjāʼ*, (fem.) Naturally lame. A hyena.

A عرجان *ʻurjān*, (pl. of عارج *ʻārij*) Lame from birth. *ʻarajān*, Lameness, limping mode of walking.

A عرجة *ʻurjat*, Lameness. Delay, pause.

A عرجد *ʻurjad*, (or عرجدّ *ʻurjudd*) The stalk from which dates hang.

A عرجلة *ʻarjalat*, A herd of horses. A flock of sheep or goats. A multitude of men on foot.

A عرجنة *ʻarjanat*, (v. n. of عرجن Q) Striking (any one) with the stalk of the palm-tree. Marking (a garment) with the figure of date-stalks. Besmearing with blood or saffron. Dyeing, tinging.

A عرجود *ʻurjūd*, A date-stalk. A vine-bud.

A عرجوف *ʻurjūf*, A strong she-camel.

A عرجول *ʻirjawl*, A troop, body, herd.

A عرجوم *ʻurjūm*, A strong she-camel.

A عرجون *ʻurjūn*, (pl. عراجين *ʻarājīn*) A bunch of dates (dry). A kind of mushroom. A tree become crooked, and having its branches lopped; an old pollard.

A عرد *ʻard*, (v. n. of عرد) Fleeing, running away. Hard, strong. Erect. Stiff, inflated (yard). An ass. The root or base of the neck. *ʻarid*, (or عردّ *ʻurudd*) Hard.

A عرداد *ʻirdād*, An elephant. Brave, intrepid, hardy. Robust. A piece of wood with which they fasten horses and camels.

A عردام *ʻirdām*, A branch on which are clusters of dates. A large branch, from which smaller branches issue.

A عردة *ʻuradat*, A mountain with water at its base.

A عردسة *ʻardasat*, A throwing prostrate.

A عردل *ʻurdal*, Hard and strong. Tall.

A عردلة *ʻardalat*, Laxity of gait.

A عردم *ʻardam*, Thick, coarse, gross. Of little flesh. Strong and hard. The neck.

A عردمان *ʻurdumān*, Obstinate, stiff-necked, stubborn. Strong.

A عردمة *ʻurdamat*, Hardness.

A عرر *ʻarar*, (v. n. of عرّ) Being bunchless (a camel). Smallness of bunch. Scab, itch, mange.

A عرز *ʻarz*, (v. n. of عرز) Being contracted, drawn together, and wrinkled. Pulling, drawing violently. Blaming, reproving, chiding. Being strong and thick. Holding (a thing) in the clenched fist, and allowing a part (of it) to be seen. Being contrary. *ʻaraz*, (v. n. of عرز) Being hard and strong.

A عرزال *ʻirzāl*, A place on the summit of a tree where those sit who watch fields (for fear of wild beasts). A piece of meat roasted, which hunters use in catching wild beasts. A lion's den or nest for his whelps. Remains of flesh-meat. A kind of large sack. A portable, moveable house built for the use of a king when on a military expedition. A hut for a gatherer of mushrooms. A serpent's hole. A little furniture. The branch of a tree. A tavern. A sect, troop, band. Heavy. Abject, mean, contemptible. The mouth of a large water-bottle. Any thing whereby a man is preferred or distinguished.

A عرزام *ʻirzām*, A lion.

A عرزب *ʻarzab* or *ʻirzabb*, Hard, firm, strong.

A عرزم *ʻarzam*, Compact, solid. A lion. *ʻirzim*, An old serpent.

A عرزمّ *ʻirzamm*, A lion.

A عرس *ʻars*, (v. n. of عرس) Tying a camel neck and fore-leg. Turning away from. Continuing in a state of joy. A rope. The middle pole of a tent. A wall (between two other walls it does not touch), upon which the roof rests in a peculiar manner, which conduces to warmth. A fair held at the tomb of a saint in honour of him. *ʻars* or *ʻurs*, (pl. اعراس *aʻrās*) A young camel weaned from the dam. *ʻirs*, (pl. اعراس *aʻrās*) A spouse, husband, or wife. A lioness. ابن عرس *ibn ʻirs*, (pl. بنات عرس *banāt ʻirs*) A species of weasel, small-eared, and with eyelids turned up. A pole-cat. *ʻurs* or *ʻurus*, Matrimony, nuptials. (pl. اعراس *aʻrās* and عرسات *ʻurusāt*) A marriage-feast. *ʻaras*, (v. n. of عرس) Refusing, denying, withholding. Being confounded, astonished, losing one's wits. Being proud and insolent. Being necessary. Being assiduous, fixed to. *ʻaris*, Struck with astonishment. Timid, afraid. Assiduous, fixed to. A lion. *ʻurus*, (pl. of عروس *ʻarūs*) Bridegrooms.

A عرسات *ʻurusāt* or *ʻurasāt*, (pl. of عرس *ʻurs*) Marriage-feasts.

A عرسان *ʻirsāni*, (dual) A lion and lioness.

A عرسيّ *ʻirsiy*, Of a weasel or tawny colour.

A عرش *ʻarsh*, (v. n. of عرش) Propping up (a vine), training (it) over a trellis. Making a trellis for a vine, or a cover for a well. Building (a wooden house). Pitching (a tent). Abiding in one place. Striking (any one) on the side of the neck. Sticking close (to a debtor). Being thunderstruck, lost in amazement. Being struck with fear, and not approaching the game (a dog). Being difficult to obtain. Constructing the lower part of a well for six feet of stone and the remainder of wood. Keeping fast hold of what is in one's possession. Retiring, turning away. (pl. عروش *ʻurūsh*, عرش *ʻurush*, اعراش *aʻrāsh*, and عرشة *ʻirashat*) A throne, chair of state. A palace, citadel. The throne of God. Roof of a house. A wooden cover to a well. The convex part of the foot. The buttocks of a lion. A bier. An awning, shade, arbour, alcove. A tent. A nest. A prop, buttress, stay, support. A leader or chief of the people. A piece of wood whereon a drawer of water stands. Mecca and its old wooden houses. Glory. عرش اكبر *ʻarshi akbar*, The human heart. عرش اعلا *ʻarshi aʻla'*, (عرش رحمن *ʻarshi rahmān*, and عرش شريف *ʻarshi sharīf*) The throne of God. عرش سبائي *ʻarshi sabāī*, The throne of Bilkīs, the queen of Sheba. عرش السماك *ʻarshu's simāk*, Four small stars below the constellation عوّاء *ʻawwāʼ*. عرش و فرش *ʻarsh u farsh*, Heaven and earth. ذو العرش *zū'l ʻarsh*, Lord of the throne, *i. e.* God. *ʻursh*, The side of the neck. The root of the neck, or the part to which the cupping-glass is applied. A bone near the throat which forms a fulcrum for the tongue. The hair under a horse's mane. The ear. Thick, large (she-camel). *ʻursh* or *ʻarsh*, (pl. عرشة *ʻirashat* and اعراش *aʻrāsh*) What lies between the instep and the toes. *ʻarash*, (v. n. of عرش) Being thunderstruck, lost in amazement. *ʻurush*, (pl. of عرش *ʻarsh*) Thrones. (pl. of عريش *ʻarīsh*) Shades, arbours, bowers, alcoves.

P عرش آشياني *ʻarsh-āshyānī*, A name given to the Emperor Akbar after his decease.

A عرشة *ʻirashat*, (pl. of عرش *ʻarsh*) Thrones. (pl. of عرش *ʻursh* or *ʻarsh*) Convex parts of feet.

P عرش منزل *ʻarsh-manzil*, A title given to Alam-gīr the Second.

P عرش وران *ʻarshwarān*, Prophets, saints.

P عرشيان *ʻarshiyān*, Angels who carry the throne of God, bearers of the celestial throne.

A عرص *ʻars*, (v. n. of عرص) Having lightning incessantly flashing (the sky). Going with a tottering gait (a camel). Tying a camel by the fore-leg. A rafter. *ʻaras*, (v. n. of عرص) Flashing incessantly (lightning). Being cheerful, brisk. Smelling badly, a house or plant (especially from dampness). *ʻaris* or *ʻars*, Incessantly flashing (lightning).

A عرصات *ʻarasāt*, (pl. of عرصة) Courts, areas.

A عرصاف *ʻirsāf*, (pl. عراصيف *ʻarāsīf*) Pack-saddles. A scourge of sinews or twisted thongs. A long sinew. Various pieces of wood used in constructing a camel's saddle. A nail in a camel's saddle. Points, processes of the vertebræ of a camel's back. The bones of the nose bent inwards.

A عرصام *ʻirsām*, A lion.

A عرصة *ʻarsat*, (pl. عراص *ʻirās*, عرصات *ʻarasāt*, and اعراص *aʻrās*) A court, square, quadrangle, area, open space free from buildings. A plain. A field of battle. A chess-board or table for playing at dice. عرصة الجمع *ʻarsatu'l jamʻ*, Day of the resurrection. P عرصهٔ زمين *ʻarsaʼi zamīn*, Surface of the earth.

A عرصتان *ʻarsatāni*, (dual) Two open places in the عقيق *ʻakīk* of Madīna.

A عرصف *ʻarsaf*, Ground-pine.

A عرصفة *ʻarsafat*, (v. n. of عرصف Q) Drawing. Cleaving down lengthwise.

A عرصم *ʻarsam*, A glutton. Active, cheerful.

ɛirsim, The wild egg-plant or brinjāl.

A عرصم ɛirsamm, Thin. Strong. A lion.

A عرصوف ɛursūf, (pl. عراصيف ɛarāsīf) A piece of wood used in a camel's saddle.

A عرصوفان ɛursūfāni, Two pieces of wood at the plough-tail.

A عرصوم ɛursūm, A miser.

A عرض ɛarz, (v. n. of عرض) Presenting itself, appearing. Happening, occurring, befalling. Meeting, confronting. Exhibiting, offering for sale. Bartering, exchanging. Giving (cloth in payment of a debt). Rendering manifest. Presenting or representing (to a superior). Perusing (a book). Reviewing an army. Running with extended neck; also going on one side (a horse). Putting aloe-wood into a censer. Clapping (a sword) across (the thigh). Being cheated (in buying or selling). Marking (a camel) crosswise. Having an inclination or desire. Smiting with sword or stick. Cropping the extremities of a tree. Striking the side of any thing. Filling (a tank or leathern bottle). Dying, not from disease. Arriving in the country of Mecca and Madīna. An offering. Exposition, proposition. Petition, request. A valley. Breadth, amplitude, width. The measurement of a heap of grain from the bottom to the top, as opposed to طول tūl, Length (an Indian term of revenue). A mountain, or the foot of one, or side of one, or the place whence a mountain rises. A large army. The mass of men. A cloud obscuring the horizon. Many locusts. An hour. An hour of the night. Madness. Merchandise, household furniture, or other effects (money excepted, which is expressed by عين ɛayn). (pl. اعراض aɛrāz) A village of Hijāz. العرض al ɛarz, Day of review, *i.e.* the last judgment. عرض حال ɛarzi hāl (or only عرض ɛarz), Explanation of the state of a case, memorial, petition. عرض عين ɛarza ɛaynin, Before one's eyes. P عرض ديدار كردن ɛarzi dīdār kardan, To shew the face, to discover one's self. عرض لشكر كردن ɛarzi lashkar kardan, To muster (review) an army. عرض كردن ɛarz kardan, To speak, say, represent humbly, put, place, state, beg, request. عرض مراد كردن ɛarzi murād kardan, To explain one's intentions. A اشتريت المتاع بعرض ishtaraytu'l matāɛ bi ɛarzin, I bought the goods with other goods. جراد عرض jarādun ɛarzun, Many locusts. طول و عرض tūl u ɛarz, Length and breadth. في عرض الناس fī ɛarzi'n nās, (I saw him) near certain people. يوم العرض yawmu'l ɛarz, The day of the resurrection. P زعرض دور كردن zi ɛarz dūr kardan, To mortify. To kill. A ɛirz, Reputation, honour, fame, estimation. The soul. The body. Effluvia of the body (good or bad). A pore of the body. A valley having villages, water, and trees. Skin, leather. An army. Ancestral dignity. A praiseworthy disposition. A side of the neck. A salt, bitter plant. The thorny tree اراك arāk. The side of a valley. A city, town, or district. A large cloud. Many locusts. One who imposes on others with follies and lies. عرض و ناموس ɛirz u nāmūs, A good name. ɛurz, The foot of a mountain. The middle (of a river or of the sea). Primary (argument). The mass (of mankind). The broad part of a sword. A pace approved in a horse, but disapproved of in a camel. The side (of any thing). Care, anxiety. (pl. of عارض ɛāriz) The back-teeth, grinders. The jaws. عرض الحائط ɛurzu'l hāʼit, The side of the wall. عرض السفر ɛurzu's safar, (A she-camel) travelling well. بعرض وجهه bi ɛurzi wajhihi, (Looking) at him obliquely. في عرض الناس fī ɛurzi'n nās, Amongst the people. من عرض الناس min ɛurzi'n nās, From among the vulgar. ɛaraz, (v. n. of عرض) Bursting from eating too much herbage (a sheep). An accident, any thing that befals a person. Disease, sickness. A philosophical accident. Any thing which has no duration. Worldly goods, which being transient and fleeting, are bestowed alike on the evil and the good. Any kind of wealth (except gold and silver). Prey, spoil, plunder. An army. Desire, concupiscence. سهم عرض sahmu ɛarazin, (or حجر عرض hajaru ɛarazin, An arrow or a stone with which any one is struck accidentally or by mistake. ɛiraz, (v. n. of عرض) Possessing breadth. ɛuruz, A side, tract, confine, border, extremity. Corner of the eye.

A عرضا ɛarzan, In breadth. ɛurzan, (or عن عرض ɛan ɛurzin) At the side, sideways; as it may happen, without choice. Indiscriminately, without inquiry. ɛarazan, Accidentally.

A عرضان ɛirzān or ɛurzān, (pl. of عريض ɛarīz) Rampant he-goats. Yearling kids.

T عرض بيگی ɛarz-begī, The person who presents all petitions, either written or by word of mouth.

A عرضة ɛarzat, An offering, exposition, exhibition. A review. ɛurzat, Impediment, obstacle. An object exposed to loss or depredation. One who is evil spoken of. Inclination, favour, affection. Intention, thought, care. A manœuvre employed in wrestling. Adapted (as a man for business, or any one thing to another); agreeing together (as man and wife). An equal, peer, match. Any thing constantly occuring (as an oath on every slight occasion). Accustomed to affect grief.

P عرضدار ɛarz-dār, Broad. A military muster. An accident, any thing befalling: disease, sickness.

P عرض داشت ɛarz-dāsht, A memorial or address from an inferior to a superior. Breadth.

P عرضگاه ɛarz-gāh, (or عرضه گاه ɛarza-gāh) A rendezvous for an enemy.

A عرضنة ɛiraznat, A she-camel leaning to one side from sprightliness. ɛiraznatan, (Looking at one) obliquely, with half-shut eyes.

A عرضني ɛirazna', (also العرضني al ɛirazna') Obliquely from sprightliness.

P عرضه داشت ɛarza-dāsht, A petition.

A عرضي ɛarza', A kind of cloth. Certain conveniences in a house (as sinks or drains).

P عرضي ɛarzī, A petition, memorial, or humble representation.

A عرضي ɛirizza', Alacrity, cheerfulness.

A عرضي ɛurzīy, Leaning to one side, sprightly (camel), because badly broke in. Disobedient, untractable. Not firmly seated in the saddle. ɛarazīy, Accidental.

A عرضية ɛurzīyat, Intractable (she-camel). Fearlessness, stubbornness, intractableness.

A عرط ɛart, (v. n. of عرط) Slandering and traducing the absent. Losing his teeth by feeding on certain trees (a camel). ɛurut, (pl. of عروط ɛarūt).

A عرطب ɛartab, (عرطبة ɛartabat, or ɛurtabat) A lute, harp; a small drum. A drum used by the natives of Abyssinia.

A عرطزة ɛartazat, (v. n. of عرطز Q) Being far from one's friends. Falling out, contending. See عرطسة ɛartasat.

A عرطسة ɛartasat, (v. n. of عرطس Q) Retiring to a distance from mankind, and quietly declining to oppose or withstand them.

A عرطل ɛartal, (and عرطليل ɛartalīl) Thick. Deformed from disproportioned length.

A عرطنيثا ɛartanīsā, A root yellow without and white within, good for cleaning woollens: sowbread.

A عرطوج ɛurtūj, Name of a king.

A عرطويل ɛartawīl, Young, well-proportioned.

A عرعار ɛarɛār, A boy's game.

A عرعر ɛarɛar, The juniper. حبّ العرعر habbu'l ɛarɛar, Juniper-berries. ɛurɛur, The septum of the nostrils. Lower part of the belly. ركب عرعره rakiba ɛurɛurahu, He behaved perversely.

A عرعرة ɛarɛarat, (v. n. of عرعر Q) Pulling out (an eye). Uncorking a bottle. Putting in motion, shaking. Name of a boy's game. Skin of the head. ɛarɛarat or ɛurɛurat, A cork, stopple. ɛurɛurat, Summit (of a mountain). The upper and the best part of a camel's bunch. The head or chief part of any thing. The gristle partition of the nose. The lower part of the belly. The nose. Depravity.

A عرف ɛarafa, (fut. يعرف yaɛrifu) He knew.

A عرف ɛarf, (v. n. of عرف) Polling, clipping a horse's mane. Perfuming very much. Confessing a sin, acknowledging a fault, or confessing one part and suppressing the remainder. Being patient. Compensating, requiting. Being ulcerated in the palm of the hand. A certain plant, the ثمام sumām; or a plant neither of the kind حمض hamz nor عضاه ɛizāh. Smell (good or bad, though generally the former). ɛirf, (v. n. of عرف) Knowing, discerning. Knowledge. Being patient. Patience. Tardiness, lateness in attaining the knowledge of a thing. ɛurf, Known, public, notorious. A just, lawful, proper, agreeable thing. Corresponding to, equal. A benefit, favour, largess, present, gift, liberality. Confession, acknowledgment, avowal of a deed. Knowledge. The mane (of a horse); comb (of a cock), crest. A wave of the sea. The boundary between heaven and hell. A high place. Heaped up sands. The name by which a person or thing is generally called (or known), commonly called; alias. Common parlance. A kind of palm-tree; one that has not yet borne dates. A sort of date-tree called برشوم *burshūm*, growing in Bahrayn. An orange-tree. (pl. of عروف *ɛarūf*) Patient. (pl. of اعرف *aɛraf*) Thick-maned (horses). Crested (serpents). (pl. of عرفاء *ɛarfāɛ*) Hyenas. Long-maned (mares or she-camels). عرف انام *ɛurfi anām*, A multitude, all mankind. الف عرفا *alf ɛurfan*, A thousand certain or confessedly. اهل عرف *ahli ɛurf*, Officers of justice, attendants upon a judge or tribunal. في عرف *fī ɛurf*, Notorious, well known. مرسلات عرفا *mursalāti ɛurfan*, Angels or horses following in a line as the hairs in a horse's mane. *ɛuraf*, (pl. of عرفة *ɛurfat*) High hills of sand. Boundaries, partitions. *ɛuruf*, Heaped up sands. A high place. A horse's mane.

A عرفاء *ɛarfāɛ*, (fem. of اعرف *aɛraf*) Long-maned (mare). A hyena (because of the thickness of its mane). *ɛurafāɛ*, (pl. of عريف *ɛarīf*) Acquaintances. Intelligent, ingenious. Judges.

A عرفات *ɛarafāt*, A mountain twelve miles from Mecca, from which, among other ceremonies, the pilgrims make a procession to the Holy Monument situated on another mountain at a little distance. It was on Mount Arafāt where the Muhammadans imagine Adam, conducted by the angel Gabriel, met Eve after a separation of 200 years, in consequence of their disobedience and banishment from Paradise, whence he carried her afterwards to Ceylon. Eastern writers make Adam of a prodigious size, the most moderate giving him the height of a tall palm-tree, whilst others say that his foot was seventy cubits long, and the rest of his body in proportion.

A عرفاس *ɛirfās*, (pl. عرافيس *ɛarāfīs*) A camel bearing great fatigue. A lion.

A عرفاص *ɛirfās*, A scourge for whipping criminals. A rope made of sinews for fastening the timbers of a camel-litter.

A عرفان *ɛirfān*, Name of a celebrated female singer. *ɛirfān*, (or عرفان *ɛiriffān*) (v. n. of عرف) Knowing, discerning. Confessing, owning, acknowledging, admitting. Knowledge, learning, science. اهل عرفان *ahli ɛirfān*, Learned.

A عرفان *ɛuruffān* or *ɛiriffān*, A large kind of locust. Another kind of insect.

P عرفان مآب *ɛirfān-maɛāb*, Learned.

A عرفة *ɛarfat*, Wind. An ulcer on the palm of the hand. Diligent inquiry. *ɛirfat*, (v. n. of عرف) Knowing. Diligent inquiry. Knowledge, acquaintance. *ɛurfat*, A college. A corporation, company, or body of artisans; also the master of such company or guild. A large fertile district. (pl. عرف *ɛuraf* and اعراف *aɛrāf*) A high sand-hill producing long grass. (pl. عرف *ɛuraf*) Boundary or partition, party-wall. A high place. *ɛarafat*, A vigil, wake. يوم عرفة *yawmi ɛarafat*, The ninth day of the month ذي الحجة *zi'l hijjat*.

A عرفج *ɛarfaj*, A species of thorny plants growing in plains. A man.

A عرفجة *ɛarfajat*, A single specimen of the plant *ɛarfaj*. لي العرفجة *layyu'l ɛarfajat*, Modus coeundi.

A عرفسيس *ɛarfasīs*, Large (camel or woman).

A عرفط *ɛurfut*, A species of the plant عضاه.

A عرفيّ *ɛurfiy*, (fem. عرفيّة *ɛurfiyat*) Accumulated, accessory, aggravated. Notorious, known, public. تكاليف عرفيه *takālīfi ɛurfiya*, Public impositions, extraordinary taxation. حقيقت عرفيه *hakīkati ɛurfiya*, A self-evident or well-known truth. *ɛarafiy*, A resident at عرفات *ɛarafāt*.

A عرق *ɛark*, (v. n. of عرق) Gnawing a bone, and stripping it of the flesh. Having little flesh on the bones. Travelling. Putting an عراق *ɛirāk* to a leathern bottle. Any thing wrought of palm-leaves; a basket. (pl. عراق *ɛirāk* and *ɛurāk*) A bare bone; a bone with a little flesh; likewise one with a great deal. A path beaten and made bare. *ɛirk*, (pl. عروق *ɛurūk*, اعراق *aɛrāk*, and عراق *ɛirāk*) A vein, an artery. Root of a tree. Spur of a mountain. Origin, stock: kind, species. Milk. The body. A small dash of water in wine. Remains of salt and bitter plants. A long sand-hillock. A high place. Salt and barren ground. A rugged, steep, and inaccessible mountain. A small mountain. Prolific breed. Saltish ground producing the tamarisk. عرق الرية *ɛirku'r riya*, The windpipe. عرق من الماء *ɛirk mini'l māɛ*, A little dash of water (amongst wine). عرق النسا *ɛirku'n nisa'*, Sciatica, hip-gout. العرق الظالم *al ɛirku'z zālim*, When one man sows in a field which another has ploughed, in order to claim the land. فيه عرق من العبودية *fīhi ɛirk mini'l ɛubūdiyat*, There is in him a dash of vassalage. *ɛarah*, (v. n. of عرق) Being torpid and sluggish. Gaining, making a profit. Acquiring or becoming possessed of camels' colts. Sweat. A heat. Juice, spirit, sap. Honey flowing from dates. Spirituous liquor, rack. Milk. Currants. A string or row (of horses, birds, or stones). A course of bricks in a wall. Tracks of camels following one another. Any thing wrought of palm-leaves; a basket. Exudation from a wall. Earth, dust, or a little of it. Roads through a mountain. The breed of cattle. عرق الخلال *ɛaraku'l khilāl*, A friendly present. عرق القربة *ɛaraku'l kirbat*, Adversity, labour, toil. جري عرقا او عرقين *jara' ɛarakan aw ɛarakayni*, (The horse) ran again and again, a heat or two. P عرق استخوان *ɛaraki ustukhwān*, Any thing chewed. A عرق انفعال *ɛaraki infiɛāl*, Blush, funk. P عرق بهار *ɛaraki buhār*, The aroma of orange-flowers. عرق كردن *ɛarak kardan*, To give something. To blush, funk. A *ɛarik*, Sour milk impregnated with a sweaty smell of a camel on which it has been carried. Even, level (place). *ɛurak*, A man who sweats much. *ɛuruk*, (pl. of عراق *ɛirāk*) Double stitches in the bottoms of bottles or provision-bags. Pieces of leather with which stitches are covered. Remains of salt and bitter plants. Insides of quills. Sea-shores. Banks of rivers during the whole of their course.

A عرقاة *ɛarkāt*, (v. n. of عرقي Q) Fixing two cross bars (called عرقوتان *ɛarkuwatāni*) on the top of a bucket. Clear water. *ɛarkāt* or *ɛirkāt*, A root. Capital, stock. The butt end of a tree, from which the roots strike out. *ɛarakāt*, A cross bar on the top of a bucket.

A عرقال *ɛirkāl*, Who swerves from the right way.

A عرقان *ɛarkān*, Sweating, in a sweat.

A عرقبة *ɛarkabat*, (v. n. of عرقب Q) Houghing (a quadruped). Lifting one up by the hams in order that he may stand upright. Laying snares, dealing deceitfully.

A عرقة *ɛarkat*, Roads through a mountain. *ɛirkat*, A root. Capital, stock. The butt end of a tree from which the roots strike out. *ɛarakat*, (pl. عرق *ɛarak* and عرقات *ɛarakāt*) A cross beam between two buttresses of a wall. A bull's pizzle or other scourge. A leathern thong for binding a captive. Flaps fastened to the side of a tent. A string of birds. A course of bricks in a wall. *ɛurakat*, (A man) sweating much, very sudatory.

A عرقچين *ɛarak-chīn*, A handkerchief, napkin, sudary. A little cap.

A عرقدة *ɛarkadat*, A twisting very hard.

A عرقصاء *ɛurkusāɛ*, (or عرقصان *ɛarakusān*) A herb like fennel, very efficacious in medicine.

A عرقصة *ɛarkasat*, A leaping or dancing. The motion of a serpent.

P عرق كرده *ɛarak-karda*, A horse that can run much without being distressed or sweating.

P عرق گير *ɛarak-gīr*, A handkerchief, napkin, sudary. Ashamed: sweating, funking.

A عرقلة *ɛarkalat*, (v. n. of عرقل Q) Swerving from the right way. Distorting, wresting (a meaning). Speaking to, and acting tortuously towards any one. Circulating a falsehood respecting one.

A عرقلي *ɛarkala'*, A stately, swaggering walk.

P عرقناك *ɛaraknāk*, Sweating to excess.

A عرقوب *ɛurkūb*, The tendon Achilles. The hough of a quadruped. A winding track through a valley. A narrow pass over a mountain. Fraud, stratagem. The leg of the bird قطا *katā*. The knowledge of an argument. A man notorious for breach of promise: hence, مواعيد عرقوب mawāʻidi ʻurkūb, Promises of ʻurkūb (never meant to be performed).

A عرقوة ʻarkuwat, (pl. عراقي ʻarāki) The cross-bar on a bucket. A cross-timber in a camel's saddle. A hillock in the form of a hog's back.

A عرقيّ ʻarkīy, Related to, connected with, belonging to the cross-bar عرقوة ʻarkuwat.

P عرقيّه ʻarakīya, A silken pocket-handkerchief, a sudary.

A عرقيل ʻirkīl, The yolk of an egg.

A عرك ʻark, (v. n. of عرك) Rubbing (the ear or side). Feeling (a camel's bunch) if fat. Devouring plants (cattle). Falling heavily upon one (misfortunes and evils). Trying any one (fortune). Cutting his side with his elbow until the flesh appears (a camel). Turning (camels) into a pasture of salt and bitter plants that they may take their fill. Being menstruous (a woman). Dung of wild beasts. ʻarak, (v. n. of عرك) Locking hands with another in fight, wrestling, bruising. Fishermen. Sound. Salt and bitter pasturage for camels. Seamen. ʻarik, Sound, Tried, proved: powerful in battle. The middle of the sea, the main ocean. Athletic, overthrowing (men). Intermixed (sands). ʻuruk, (pl. of عروك ʻarūk) (She-camels) whose fat cannot be ascertained except by feeling.

A عركات ʻarakāt, (pl. of عركة ʻarkat) Times. ʻarakātin, Often, oftentimes.

A عركانيّة ʻarakānīyat, An adultress. A coarse, thick woman.

A عركة ʻarkat, One time or turn. ʻurakat, One who puts up with inconvenience and trouble. A dirty, nasty fellow.

A عركرك ʻarakrak, A strong, thick camel. A camel whose elbow cuts his side. Powerful, athletic. Patient.

A عركركة ʻarakrakat, A corpulent woman. A meagre-hipped, ill-looking woman.

A عركسة ʻarkasat, A collecting, accumulating.

A عركل ʻarkal, A drum.

A عركون ʻarikūn, (pl. of عرك) Wrestlers, strong.

A عركي ʻarakīy, A fisherman. A mariner.

A عركيّة ʻarakīyat, An adultress. A coarse, thick woman.

A ذو العركين zū'l ʻarkayn, Name of a plant.

A عرم ʻarm, (v. n. of عرم) Baring (a bone) of flesh, or (a tree) of its bark. Eating a little meat. Using blandishments and playfulness. Being headstrong, malignant, and saucy. Sucking the mother (a child). Browsing a tree (a camel). Assaulting with malice and impudence. A well; a ditch. Fat. Remains in a pot. ʻurm, An egg or eggs, especially of the قطا katā. (pl. of اعرم aʻram) Spotted with black and white. ʻaram, (v. n. of عرم) Being weak and languid. White upon the lips of a sheep. A variegated colour (especially black and white). The egg of the katā. (pl. of عرمة ʻaramat) Heaps of grain upon the floor. ʻarim, Ungrateful, petulant, malignant, corrupted. Of a black and white colour. (pl. of عرمة ʻarimat) Mounds, banks, or dykes, for confining water. Great rains. سيل العرم saylu'l ʻarim, A great flood which destroyed an embankment constructed by the Sabeans.

P عرم ʻarim, A kind of fish, a sardine.

A عرماء ʻarmāʼ, (fem. of اعرم aʻram) White-lipped (ewe). A flock of different coloured sheep and goats. Speckled (snake).

A عرماض ʻirmāz, (v. n. of عرمض Q) Being covered with a green film (water). A green film which floats on water.

A عرمان ʻurmān, (pl. of اعرم aʻram) Pie-bald, dappled. Flocks of sheep and goats. Uncircumcised. Wells, ditches.

A عرما والله ʻarmā wa'llāh, Verily, truly, by God!

A عرمة ʻarmat, A place where sands are heaped up. عرمة الرجل ʻarmatu'r rajul, The tribe or people of a man. ʻurmat, A mixture of black and white. White upon the lips of a sheep. The egg of the kata. ʻaramat, A heap of grain in a barn trodden out or threshed, but not winnowed. Accumulated sand. The smell of cooked meat. ʻarimat, A vineyard. A male field-mouse. Great rain. A dam for impounding water.

A عرمرم ʻaramram, A numerous army. Strong, vehement. عرمرم كثير الزحام ʻaramrami kasīru'z zihām, Troops in prodigious, overwhelming masses.

A عرمس ʻirmis, A rock. A hardy she-camel.

A عرمّس ʻarammus, Sharp, penetrating. Ingenious, clever, witty.

A عرمسة ʻarmasat, (v. n. of عرمس Q) Becoming firm after having been soft and relaxed (the body).

A عرمض ʻarmaz, A dwarfish tree of the lote, or the اراك arāk-kind. A green film or moss which floats on the surface of stagnant water. ʻarmaz or ʻirmiz, A species of the tree called عضاه ʻizāh.

A عرمضة ʻarmazat, (v. n. of عرمض Q) Being covered with a green film called duck-weed (water).

P عرن ʻarn, A horny excrescence in the inside of a horse's leg, inside the knee and hough.

A عرن ʻarn, (v. n. of عرن) Passing a piece of wood through (a camel's) nose, and inserting a ring, or fastening the reins to it. Anointing the worn part of a camel's hoof. Whipping a bruised sinew round the head of an arrow. ʻirn, The smell of cooking. ʻaran, (v. n. of عرن) Being hard about the pastern (the foot of a beast). Cracks in the feet of beasts of burden above the ankle (from dryness). A sore in a camel's neck. A hardness in a horse's pastern. Deep. The main sea. Smoke. The smell of cooking. Cooked meat. A tree used in tanning. ʻarin, One who sticks close to the distributor of the joints of a slaughtered camel, that he may come in for a share. ʻurun, (pl. of عرين ʻarīn and عرينة ʻarīnat) Haunts of lions, hyenas, wolves and snakes.

A عرناس ʻirnās, A bird like a pigeon, which you hardly perceive till it rises from under your feet. A projecting part of a mountain, a nose or ness. A place for receiving the refuse of the cotton which drops whilst carding.

A عرنة ʻirnat, Fallen through weakness. An unconquered wrestler. Veins in the nose. Wood of the tree ظمخ zimakh. The root of a tree with which they tan. Impure. Name of a shrub for tanning hides. ʻurnat, A disease in the heel of a beast of burden, causing the hair to fall and the foot to crack. Roots of the shrub عرنتن ʻarantan. ʻarinat, Hard about the pastern (a horse).

A عرنتن ʻarantan, tin, or tun, A kind of shrub.

A عرند ʻurund, Thick (nerve). Hard.

A عرندد ʻarandad, Hard.

A عرندس ʻarandas, Strong (camel). A great torrent, a heavy flood. A lion.

A عرندل ʻarandal, Long. Hard and strong.

A عرنقصان ʻurankusān, Name of a certain efficacious medicinal plant.

A عرنيّة ʻuranīyat, An adultress. A coarse, thick woman.

A عرنين ʻirnīn, (pl. عرانين ʻarānīn) The anterior, beginning, or best of any thing. The nose. The bony part of the nose. A prince, lord.

A عرو ʻarw, (v. n. of عرا for عرو) Covering (any thing) by surrounding (it). Descending, alighting. Visiting, alighting, coming upon one (as a guest to a host). Approaching (especially to ask a favour). ʻirw, (pl. اعراء aʻrāʼ) A side, part. Negligent, lazy. Free. عرو من الذنوب ʻirw mini'z zunūb, Free from crimes.

A عرواء ʻurawāʼ, Tremor, ague; paroxysm (of a fever). The low growl of a lion. The pale hue of the sun toward night, the wind blowing cold.

A عروان ʻurwān, A sort of evergreen.

A عروب ʻarūb, (or عروبة ʻarūbat) (pl. عرب ʻurub) A woman who loves her husband, and discovers her affection. Refractory (wife); also a laughing and mocking one.

A عروباء ʻarūbāʼ, Name of the seventh heaven.

A عروبة ʻurūbat, (v. n. of عرب) Speaking Arabic well. An Arabism. يوم العروبة yawmu'l ʻarūbat, Friday (in old Arabic).

A عروبيّة ʻurūbīyat, An Arabicism, an Arabism. The Arab race pure and unmixed.

A عروة ʻurwat, (pl. عري ʻura') The handle (of a jug or flagon). A loop or hole for a button. A fleshy excrescence. An evergreen. Any thing precious which one possesses (as a horse). A multitude. A lion. Whatever lies round a city. A large quantity of the عضاه ʻizāh and حمض hamz eaten in a time of scarcity. ابو عروة abū ʻurwat, Name of a man whose shout would frighten a lion to death. عروة الوثقي ʻurwatu'l wuska', The firmest, strongest handle, (metaphorically) Genuine religion.

A عروج ʻurūj, (v. n. of عرج) Climbing up (a ladder). Ascending, becoming high. Limping from an accident. (pl. of عرج ʻarj and ʻirj, q.v.) P حصار گردون عروج hiṣāri gardūn-ʻurūj, A fort as high (or as hard to climb) as heaven.

A عرود ʻurūd, (v. n. of عرد) Arising, springing up, growing (plants or teeth). Being hard. Throwing (a stone) far.

A عرور ʻurūr, (v. n. of عرّ) Being itchy, mangy, or scabby. Itch, scab, mange.

P عروس ʻarūs, Name of the first treasure of Khusraw. A treasure of Kay Kāwus. Sulphur.

A عروس ʻarūs, (pl. عرس ʻurus) A bridegroom. (pl. عرائس ʻarāʼis) A bride when carried home to her husband's house. A spouse (in general). P عروس ارغنون زن ʻarūsi arghanūn-zan, The planet Venus. عروس پرده ʻarūsi parda, A species of ruby-coloured rose; any thing of that hue. عروس جهان ʻarūsi jahān, The world. The planet Venus. عروس چهارم فلك ʻarūsi chahārum falak, (عروس چرخ ʻarūsi charkh, عروس خاوري ʻarūsi khāwarī, عروس روز ʻarūsi roz, or عروس فلك ʻarūsi falak) The sun. عروس خشك پستان ʻarūsi khushk-pistān, A barren woman. The disappointing world. عروس در پرده ʻarūsi dar parda, A species of nightshade. A عروس الشام ʻarūsu'sh shām, (Bride of Syria) The town Askelon. عروس عدن ʻarūsi ʻadn, The moon. The stars. A servant, handmaid. عروس عرب ʻarūsi ʻarab, The temple of Mecca. P عروس كج ʻarūsi kaj, A figure dressed up to terrify children. عروس نه فلك ʻarūsi nuh falak, The sun. The nine firmaments. عروسان باغ ʻarūsāni bāgh, (or عروسان چمن ʻarūsāni chaman) Flowers, fruits; shoots, suckers. عروسان بيابان ʻarūsāni biyābān, Camels of burden. Camels employed on a pilgrimage. عروسان خلد ʻarūsāni khuld, The virgins of Paradise. عروسان درخت ʻarūsāni dirakht, Young shoots.

P عروسانه ʻarūsāna, Like a bride, bridelike.

P عروس بر ʻarūs-bar, (Leading the bride, *i. e.*) A brideman.

P عروسك ʻarūsak, A little spouse. A doll, a girl's puppet. A small machine for throwing stones and other missile weapons. A flying insect of the cantharides genus. A cricket. A glowworm. A ruby colour. A female owl. عروسك در پرده ʻarūsak dar parda, The herb nightshade.

P عروسه ʻarūsa, A bride.

P عروسي ʻarūsī, Nuptials. A marriage-feast. شمع عروسي shamʻi ʻarūsī, The nuptial torch.

A عروسيّ ʻarūsiy, Nuptial.

A عروش ʻurūsh, (v. n. of عرش) Training, propping (a vine). Making a trellis. (pl. of عرش ʻarsh) Thrones. Houses of Mecca. Vaulted roofs. خاوية علىٰ عروشها khāwiyat ʻala' ʻurūshihā, (A city) entirely overthrown.

A عروشة ʻarwashat, (v. n. of عروش Q) Being mounted, riding on a beast of burden.

A عروص ʻarūṣ, (A she-camel) smelling sweetly when she sweats.

A عروض ʻarūz, (pl. اعارض aʻāriz or اعاريض aʻārīz) Poetry, poesy, verse, measure, prosody. The last foot of the first hemistich of a couplet. Mecca and Madina, with their territories. Want, necessity. Whatever occurs as necessary to be done. Any person or thing blocking up the road and impeding a passenger. A way through a mountain. An unbroken, stubborn she-camel. (A camel) devouring thorns. Victuals. Many, much. A cloudy sky. Argument or scope (of a speech). Way, track. Border, confine, limit. ʻurūz, (v. n. of عرض) Making one's appearance, arising to view (any thing), coming in sight. Bursting from eating too much herbage (a sheep). Cropping the highest parts of trees. Giving (a kind of cloth in payment of a debt). Arriving in the territory of Mecca and Madina. (pl. of عرض ʻarz) Furniture, clothes, or any kind of effects (which are not sold by weight or measure, also exclusive of money and any thing that has life). عروض الجسد ʻurūzu'l jasad, Accidents of the body, whatever affects it (as disease).

A عروط ʻarūṭ, (pl. عرط ʻuruṭ) (A camel) losing the teeth by devouring trees.

A عروف ʻarūf, Clear-sighted. Knowing, intelligent. (pl. عرف ʻurf) Patient.

A عروفة ʻarūfat, Very wise or clever.

A عروق ʻurūḳ, (v. n. of عرق) Departing, travelling, wandering. A plant which dyes yellow. Capital, said to be of four kinds, two outward, viz. plantations and buildings; and two inward, namely, wells and mines. (pl. of عرق ʻirḳ) Veins. Roots, origins. العروق الحمر al ʻurūḳu'l humr, Madder. العروق البيض al ʻurūḳu'l bīz, A certain fattening plant. عروق الشجر ʻurūḳu'sh shajar, Pine-gum. عروق الصفر ʻurūḳu's ṣufr, (or الصبّاغين as ṣabbāghīn) Turmeric. Saffron. عروق الكافور ʻurūḳu'l kāfūr, Zedoary. عروق نابضة ʻurūḳi nābiza, The pulse, beating arteries.

A عروك ʻarūk, (pl. عرك ʻuruk) A camel whose fat cannot be ascertained except by feeling. ʻurūk, (v. n. of عرك) Being menstruous (a woman). Fishermen. Sailors.

A عرون ʻarūn, Hard about the pastern (horse); or one that has lost the hair about his feet.

A عرويٰ ʻarwa', A hillock.

A عرهلّ ʻirhall, A strong camel.

A عرهم ʻarham, (or عرهمّ ʻirhamm) A lion.

A عرهوم ʻurhūm, Withered (tamarisk-tree). A vine. Tender, soft, fresh. A drop. Rain.

A عرهون ʻurhūn, (pl. عراهين ʻarāhīn) A fungus, puff, or kind of mushroom.

A عري ʻariya, (fut. يعريٰ yaʻra') He was naked.

A عري ʻary, (v. n. of عري) Making a handle for a wallet. Covering any thing. Approaching, coming upon. ʻury, (v. n. of عري) Being naked. Nudity. (pl. اعراء aʻrāʼ) A horse without a saddle. ʻura', Nudity. (pl. of عروة ʻurwat) Handles. ʻura' or ʻira', A handle. A loop or button-hole.

A عريّ ʻariy, A cold wind.

A عريان ʻuryān, (fem. عريانة ʻuryānat) (pl. عريانون ʻuryānūn) Naked, stripped. Name of a fortress in Madina. A heap of sand without a tree. Long-legged (horse). نذير عريان nazīr ʻuryān, A faithful monitor. عريان النجيّ ʻuryānu'n najiy, A woman or a man unable to keep a secret.

A عرياني ʻuryānī, Nakedness, nudity.

A عريب ʻarīb, No one (at home).

A عرية ʻiryat or ʻuryat, Nakedness. Those parts of a woman which are seen, as the face, hands, and feet. ʻuryat, (v. n. of عري) Being naked.

A عريّة ʻariyat, (pl. عرايا ʻarāya') Any thing of which the proprietor allows others to partake (as a grazing-field or palm-tree). Sold without any bidding being permitted (the produce of a palm-tree). A palm-tree without fruit, or whose fruit has been eaten. A cold wind.

A عريج ʻarīj, Lame, trifling (business).

A عريجاء ʻurayjāʼ, A watering of camels one day in the morning, the other at mid-day. A taking of food once a day. Mid-day heat.

A عريد ʻarīd, Distant. Disposition. Custom, mode, habit, usage.

A عرير ʻarīr, A stranger. A traveller.

A عريس ʻarīs, A bridegroom, spouse.

A عرّيس ʻirrīs, (or عرّيسة) A lion's den.

A عريش ʻarīsh, (pl. عرش ʻurush) A shade from the sun, an arbour, bower. A vine-prop. Mecca. A wooden machine in which women are carried on the backs of camels. Four or five palm-trees from one root. ابو عريش abū ʻarīsh, Name of a town.

A عريض ʻarīz, (pl. عراض ʻirāz) Broad, large. Wide. Expanded. (pl. عرضان ʻirzān or ʻurzān) A kid one year old. A rampant he-goat. A wether. عريض البطان ʻarīzu'l biṭān, Rich, wealthy. P اين عرصة عريضة īn ʻarsaʼi ʻarīza, This extensive plain. A دعاء عريض duʻāʼ ʻarīz, Much prayer. ʻurayz, Name of a valley near Madina.

A عرّيض ʻirrīz, One who calls bad names, abusive. One who lays stumbling-blocks in the way of others. Busy in useless and trifling pursuits.

A عريضة ʻarīzat, A petition.

A عريضن ʻurayzin, An oblique sprightly gait.

A عريضي ʻarīzī, Latitude, breadth, width.

A عريط ʻiryaṭ (امّ ummu ʻiryaṭin), A scorpion.

A عريف ʻarīf, One who knows. (pl. عرفاء ʻurafāʼ) An acquaintance. The next man to a chief or general: a lieutenant. An usher at a school.

A عريفي ʻarīfī, The office of lieutenant.

A عريق ʻarīḳ, Of noble blood (man or horse). Rooted in noble or base qualities. Homogeneous.

A عريقصاء *ɛurayḳisā*, (or عريقصانة *ɛurayḳisānat*) Name of a certain plant useful in medicine.

A عريقطة *ɛuraykitat*, (or عريقطان *ɛuraykitān*) A species of animalcule somewhat like a beetle.

A عريك *ɛarīk*, Compactly-built (man).

A عريكة *ɛarīkat*, (pl. عرائك *ɛarāɛik*) Nature, disposition. Soul, spirit, self. The bunch of a camel, or the remainder of one. لين العريكة *layyinu'l ɛarīkat*, Modest, gentle.

A عريم *ɛarīm*, A calamity, misfortune.

A عرين *ɛarīn*, (or عرينة *ɛarīnat*) (pl. عرن *ɛurun*) The haunt of a lion, hyena, wolf, or serpent. The hole of the Lybian lizard. A lion's prey. Game, or game the neck of which has been broken. Dry, withered (shrub عضاه *ɛizāh*). The area of a house. A city, a town. A thorn. Glory, greatness, might. *ɛarin*, The murmur of a dove. Flesh. A forest, a thicket.

A عرينة *ɛuraynat*, Name of a sect that apostatized in the time of Muhammad.

A عز *ɛazz*, (v. n. of عز) Disputing. Conquering, overcoming. *ɛizz*, (v. n. of عز) Being rare, scarce, excellent, precious, incomparable, honourable, glorious. Waxing great and powerful after having been poor and mean. Flowing (water). Running, discharging (a sore). Being vehement, heavy, hard, painful, adverse. Being necessary, becoming, befitting. Glory, dignity, grandeur, magnificence. Pride, rebellion. Heavy, copious (rain). Rare. عز و شان *ɛizz u shān*, Dignity and rank. *ɛazza*, (3d pers. pret. used optatively) May he be glorified! عز و جل *ɛazza wa jalla*, May he be honoured and glorified! *i.e.* The glorious God. عزاسمه *ɛazza ismuhu*, His name be glorified!

A عزاء *ɛazāɛ*, (v. n. of عزا for عزو) Ascribing, relating, attributing, referring. Professing to belong. Claiming or asserting, either for one's self or for another, a relationship to such a person or thing. Pretension, claim. Evincing patience. (v. n. of عزي) Being patient. Referring, tracing (one to his father). Consolation, condolence. Lamenting. A benefit. Lineage, stock, race. Patience. ايام عزا *ayyāmi ɛazā*, Days of mourning or condolence.

A عزاء *ɛazzāɛ*, Severe (year).

A عزاب *ɛuzzāb*, Those who go far with camels to pasture. (pl. of عزب *ɛazab* and عزبة *ɛazabat*) Bachelors. Maidens.

A عزا بزا *ɛazzanbazzān*, Inevitably: without doubt.

P عزا پرستي *ɛazā-parastī*, Mourning, grief.

A عزاز *ɛazāz*, Hard ground. *ɛizāz*, (v. n. of عز) Having the orifice of the teat narrow (a ewe or a camel). (v. n. 3 of عز) Overpowering by words. (pl. of عزيز *ɛazīz*) Powerful, eminent. Rare, scarce.

A عزازة *ɛazāzat*, (v. n. of عز) Being rare, valuable. Being great, powerful, honourable. *ɛizāzat*, (pl. of عزيز *ɛazīz*) Glorious. Rare, excellent.

A عزازيل *ɛazāzīl*, An evil spirit. A small bird so called.

A عزاف *ɛazzāf*, A cloud noisy with thunder. Name of a sandy tract.

A عزاقة *ɛazzākat*, The fundament. The ring of the fundament.

A عزال *ɛizāl*, Weak.

A عزالان *ɛazālāni*, (dual) Two large feathers at the end of an eagle's tail.

A عزالي *ɛazāla'* or *ɛazālī*, (pl. of عزلاء *ɛazlāɛ*) The lower mouths of travellers' wallets.

A عزام *ɛazzām*, The lion.

A عزاهل *ɛuzāhil*, Finely-shaped (horse).

A عزاهي *ɛizāhī*, (pl. of عزه *ɛizh*, *ɛazih*, عزهى *ɛizha'*, عزهات *ɛizhāt*, and عزهاة *ɛizhāɛat*) Those who abstain from women and all amusements.

A عزاهيل *ɛazāhīl*, Camels feeding at large.

A عزائر *ɛazāɛir*, Price of fodder cut down.

A عزائم *ɛazāɛim*, (pl. of عزيمة *ɛazīmat*) Incantations. Verses of the Kur'ān used as spells. Necessary laws prescribed in that book. عزائم الله *ɛazāɛimu'llāh*, Divine decrees regarded as obligatory. عزائم المغفرة *ɛazāɛimu'l maghfirat*, Acts or dispositions insuring forgiveness. سلطان مسعود العزائم *sultāni masɛūdu'l ɛazāɛim*, A prince of happy auspices or undertakings.

P عزائم خوان *ɛazāɛim-khwān*, Conjuror, exorcist.

A عزب *ɛazb*, (v. n. of عزب) Leading a single life. Being empty and deserted (a country). عزب طهر المرأة *ɛazaba tuhru'l marɛat*, The season of the woman's cleanness was passed in celibacy (*i.e.* her husband was then absent). *ɛazab*, (pl. اعزاب *aɛzāb* and عزاب *ɛuzzāb*) An unmarried person. A bachelor. A maid.

A عزباء *ɛazbāɛ*, An unmarried woman, a maid.

A عزبة *ɛuzbat*, A single life, celibacy. *ɛuzabat*, A maiden, an unmarried woman.

A عزة *ɛizat*, (pl. عزون *ɛizūn* and عزي *ɛiza'*) A multitude, crowd. A sect.

A عزة *ɛazzat*, A young doe. A young woman. Name of a woman. *ɛizzat*, (v. n. of عز) Being rare, valuable. Agreeing with, suiting. Being great, powerful. Conquering. Victory. Grandeur, glory. Power, might. Honour, esteem. Rareness, infrequency. Scarcity.

A عزت آثار *ɛizzat-āsār*, Bearing the emblem of honour.

P عزتخواه *ɛizzat-khwāh*, A friend, follower, attached to the glory of another.

A عزت قرار *ɛizzat-kirār*, Seat of magnificence, *i.e.* Illustrious, glorious (a royal title).

A عزتموفور *ɛizzat-mawfūr*, Glorious, honourable.

A عزج *ɛazj*, (v. n. of عزج) Beating off, driving back. Lying with. Turning over (earth) with a spade.

A عزد *ɛazd*, (v. n. of عزد) Lying with.

A عزر *ɛazr*, (v. n. of عزر) Censuring. Compelling, forcing against one's will. Forbidding, repelling. Expounding, explaining matters relating to religion. Assisting. Matrimony. The price of cut down forage.

A عزرائل *ɛizrāɛil*, Name of the angel of death.

A عزز *ɛuzuz*, (pl. of عزوز *ɛazūz*) (She-camels) the orifices of whose teats are narrow.

A عزط *ɛazt*, (v. n. of عزط) Marrying (a girl).

A عزعز *ɛazɛaz*, A word used in calling to a goat.

A عزعزة *ɛazɛazat*, (v. n. of عزعز Q) Calling out (to a goat). Conquering, overpowering by words.

A عزف *ɛazf*, (v. n. of عزف) Remaining a long time eating and drinking. Throbbing at the time of death (a camel's gullet). The sound of winds. The imaginary nocturnal sounds of demons in the desert. (pl. معازف *maɛāzif*) A stringed instrument. *ɛuzf*, A queest.

A عزق *ɛazk*, (v. n. of عزق) Cleaving, digging (the ground). Inflicting (a blow). Running swiftly. Retaining, witholding. Adhering, sticking close. *ɛazak*, (v. n. of عزق) Adhering. *ɛazik*, Unkind, severe. Low, worthless. *ɛuzuk*, Malicious, bad-tempered. A winnower of wheat.

A عزل *ɛazl*, (v. n. of عزل) Removing from office, deposing. Keeping back, withholding. Resigning abdicating. Living apart from (one's wife). Removal from office. Whatever is paid beforehand into the exchequer without being weighed or counted prior to the time fixed for the regular payments. *ɛuzl*, Weak. An unarmed state. Want of employ. *ɛuzl* or *ɛuzzal*, (pl. of اعزل *aɛzal*) Unarmed. *ɛazal*, The hinder parts of (an ass). An unarmed state. Want of employ. *ɛuzul*, (pl. *ɛuzl* and اعزال *aɛzāl*) Unarmed.

A عزلاء *ɛazlāɛ*, (pl. عزالي *ɛazālī* or *ɛazāla'*), The mouth of a traveller's bag. The fundament. The place in a cistern through which water runs in or out.

A عزلان *ɛuzlān*, (pl. of اعزل *aɛzal*) Unarmed.

A عزلبة *ɛazlabat*, (v. n. of عزلب Q) Marrying or lying with (a girl).

A عزلة *ɛuzlat*, Retirement from office, resignation. A retired, sequestered life. *ɛazalat*, The top or projecting bone of the hip (which comes in contact with the ground).

P عزلي *ɛazlī*, Abdication, resignation.

A عزم *ɛazm*, (v. n. of عزم) Running hard. Rendering necessary. A design, undertaking, purpose, resolution. (pl. عزم *ɛuzum*) Dregs of raisins subsiding or expressed. عزم الامور *ɛazmu'l umūr*, The divine purpose concerning human affairs. P عزم بزم رفتن *ɛazmi bazm raftan*, To go to an entertainment. عزم راه كردن *ɛazmi rāh kardan*, To set out on a journey. عزم سفر گرفتن *ɛazmi safar giriftan*, To undertake an expedition, to go to war. A اولو العزم *ulū'l ɛazm*, Those endued with a resolution to obey the commands of God, as Noah, Abraham, Moses, and Muhammad. Those endued with constancy and patience; as Noah, Abraham, Isaac, Jacob, Joseph, Job, Moses, David, and Jesus. *ɛazm* or ʻuzm, (v. n. of عزم) Applying the mind to, undertaking. Determining to accomplish, being resolved on an affair. Adjuring. Inviting. Reading charms or verses from the Kur'ān to avert evil. Being undertaken. ʻazam, Constant, trusty, sincere friends. ام العزم ummu'l ʻizm, (and امّ العزمة ummu'l ʻizmat) Podex. ʻuzam, (pl. of عزمة ʻuzmat) Paternal relations. Tribes.

A عزمان ʻuzmān, (v. n. of عزم) Purposing stedfastly to accomplish. Applying the mind, undertaking.

A عزمة ʻazmat, Design. Necessary, obligatory. Firm, fixed, stable. A claim, right, due. The decree of God. ʻuzmat, (pl. عزم ʻuzam) Paternal kindred. A tribe. ʻazamat, Persons sincere in their affection.

A عزمىّ ʻazmīy, A vender of the expressed dregs of raisins. A man who fulfils an engagement.

A عزو ʻazw, (v. n. of عزا for عزو) Referring, tracing (one to his father), naming (him from him). Being related to, descended from.

A بنو عزوان banū ʻazwān, A race of جنّ jinn.

A عزوب ʻuzūb, (v. n. of عزب) Being far off (meekness, patience, or wits). Going far away. Wandering to a distance (camels at pasture) and not returning in the evening. Being separated (husband and wife). Lying hid, being concealed and out of sight. Being uncultivated, uninhabited, widowed (a country). Absence, distance.

A عزوبة ʻazūbat, A country where the pasturage is a great distance off. ʻuzūbat, A single life, celibacy.

A عزوة ʻizwat, Relationship, race, stock. Claim, pretension.

A عزور ʻazwar, Wicked, malignant. A cuckold.

A عزورة ʻazwarat, A hill, hillock, heap of stones.

A عزوز ʻazūz, (pl. عزز ʻuzuz) (A camel) the orifices of whose teats are very narrow. ʻuzūz, (v. n. of عزّ) Having the holes of the teats narrow (a camel or a sheep). Becoming strong.

A عزوف ʻazūf, One who abstains from: averse, loathful; a loather. ʻuzūf, (v. n. of عزف) Abstaining, being averse from, loathing.

A عزوق ʻazwak, Untimely, unformed (pistachio-nuts), unfit to be eaten, and used in tanning. Bad-flavoured, disagreeable (fruit).

A عزوم ʻazūm, An old woman. An aged she-camel with some remains of strength. Resolved.

A عزومة ʻazūmat, A pic-nic party held in a garden, fête-champêtre. ʻuzūmat, An entertainment.

A عزون ʻizūn, (pl. of عزة ʻizat) Sects, companies.

A عزوي ʻazwa', A word expressive of a desire to conciliate affection.

A عزه ʻizh, (ʻazih, عزهي ʻizha', عزهىّ ʻizhīy, عزهاة ʻizhāt, عزهاءة ʻizhāʼat, عزهوة ʻizhuwat, and عزهانى ʻuzhānīy) One who abstains from women and every amusement; a worthless, stupid fellow. One who hates a partner or associate.

A عزهاة ʻizhāt, A woman advanced in years, but still indulging juvenile propensities.

A عزهل ʻizhil, A male pigeon. Swift, outstripping the others. ʻizhil or ʻazhal, Tottering (man). Irresolute. A male pigeon. A young pigeon.

A عزهلّ ʻizhall, A strong camel. Free, empty.

A عزهول ʻuzhūl, Light, swift, outstripping others. Merry, jovial, facetious. (pl. عزاهيل ʻazāhīl) A camel feeding at large without a keeper.

A عزهون ʻizhūna, also ʻuzhūna, Those who abstain from women and every kind of amusement.

A عزي ʻazī, Patient. ʻiza', (pl. of عزة ʻizat) Multitudes, crowds, sects.

A عزّي ʻuzza', Excellent, rare, precious (thing). Name of an ancient idol. (fem. of اعزّ aʻazz) Better, more excellent, more or most glorious. Rare, excellent (woman). Beloved (woman).

A عزيب ʻazīb, Camels which feed separate from the flock. A man who lives far from his property and home. A bachelor. (pl. of عازب ʻāzib) Camels which feed abroad all night.

A عزية ʻizyat, Race, stock. Claim, pretension.

A عزير ʻazīr, Price of forage. ʻuzayr, Esdras.

A عزيز ʻazīz, (pl. عزاز ʻizāz, عزازة ʻizāzat, اعزّة aʻizzat, and اعزّاء aʻizzāʼ) Excellent. Precious, dear, valuable. Rare, choice. Magnificent, incomparable, glorious. Powerful. Venerable, pious, holy. Centaury. A well-known collyrium for the eyes. A king (especially of Egypt). Difficult. عزيز الانتقام ʻazīzu'l intiķām, God the avenger. عزيز مقتدر ʻazīzi muķtadir, God Almighty. عزيز الوجود ʻazīzu'l wujūd, Hard to find. P پدر عزيزم pidari ʻazīzam, My revered father.

A عزيزاء ʻuzayzāʼ, A horse's buttocks.

A عزيزة ʻazīzat, An eagle.

A عزيزي ʻazīzī, Greatness, valuableness.

A عزيزي ʻuzayza', A horse's buttocks.

A عزيف ʻazīf, The imaginary nocturnal sound of demons in the desert. The noise of thunder, or of moving sands.

A عزيق ʻazīķ, Level, flat, low ground.

A عزيم ʻazīm, (v. n. of عزم) Applying the mind to, undertaking. Determining to accomplish. A powerful enemy. (pl. of عزيمة ʻazīmat, q. v.).

A عزيمة ʻazīmat, (v. n. of عزم), Undertaking. (pl. عزائم ʻazāʼim), An incantation, spell, amulet (against fascination, serpents, disease, or any other evil); verses of the Kur'ān employed for that purpose. Resolution, determination; an undertaking. Departure. عنان عزيمت ʻināni ʻazīmat, The reins of departure. ماضي العزيمة māzī'l ʻazīmat, Successful in (his) plans. P عزيمت كردن ʻazīmat kardan, To intend, purpose, design. To travel. To charm, exorcise. To use enchantments.

P عژك ʻajak, A certain musical instrument bearing a resemblance to a Turkish guitar.

A عسّ ʻass (v. n. of عسّ), Going the rounds, patroling at night. Arriving late (intelligence). Giving little meat. Pasturing alone (a she-camel). Refusing to let her milk flow before any person. ʻuss, (pl. عساس ʻisās) A large cup. Penis.

A عسا ʻasa', (v. n. of عسا for عسو) Drying, or waxing firm and hard; coming to maturity (a plant). Growing dark (the night).

A عساء ʻasāʼ, (v. n. of عسا for عسو) Growing old, withering, drying; becoming firm and hard; also thick and strong (a plant). A large cup.

A عساجر ʻasājir, (pl. of عيسجور) Hardy camels.

P عسار ʻusār, Poverty. A religious life.

A عسارة ʻasārat, (v. n. of عسر) Being difficult. Having a hard time in labour (a woman). Being hard (the times). Refusing to come forth (the contents of the belly). Opposing, resisting, thwarting.

A عساري ʻusāra', (or عساريات ʻusārayāt) One after another. Scattered, dispersed.

A عساريات ʻusārayāt, Scattered on all sides.

A عساس ʻisās, (pl. of عسّ ʻuss) Large cups. درّت عساسا darrat ʻisāsan, She (i.e. the camel) gave her milk unwillingly, only by compulsion.

A عسّاس ʻassās, A wolf (as a prowler at night).

A عساعس ʻasāʻis, Hedgehogs (because they go to and fro in the night).

A عساف ʻusāf, (v. n. of عسف) Being near death (a camel). A trembling or a falling of the larynx. The agony, or last breath. A camel afflicted with pestilence.

A عساقب ʻasāķib, (pl. of عسقبة ʻiskibat) Small bunches of grapes at the bottom of a large cluster.

A عساقل ʻasāķil, (pl. of عسقل ʻaskal) Large mushrooms. Detached pieces of a cloud.

A عساقيل ʻasāķīl, Appearance of water. (pl. of عسقول ʻuskūl) Large white mushrooms.

A عساكر ʻasākir, (pl. of عسكر ʻaskar) Armies. عساكر منصورة ʻasākiri manṣūra, (or عساكر نصرت ماثر ʻasākiri nuṣrat-maʼāṣir) Victorious troops.

A عسّال ʻassāl, Mellifluent. A vender of honey. A taker of honey from hives. A trembling spear. A wolf. A small black and white fig, very sweet.

A عسّالة ʻassālat, The honey-making bees. A hive. A bee's nest.

A عسالج ʻasālij, (pl. of عسلج) Tendrils, shoots.

A عسالق ʻasālik, (pl. of عسلق ʻaslak and ʻislik) Bad-tempered. Deformed. Light, nimble. Long-necked. Lions. Beasts of prey. Ostriches. Foxes. Wolves. Vapours. ʻusālik, see عسلق ʻaslak or ʻislik.

P عسالنج ʻasālinj, (probably an error for عسالج ʻasālij) A vine-leaf.

A عساود ʻasāwid, (pl. of عسودّة ʻiswaddat) White animalcules resembling maidens' fingers.

A عسب ʻasb, (v. n. of عسب) Hiring, letting out a (stallion). Covering (the female). The price paid; and the colt brought forth. Sperma. ʻusb, Straight palm-branches without leaves. ʻasib, (Hair) long uncombed.

A عسبار *ɛisbār*, (or عسبارة *ɛisbārat*) A whelp between a wolf and hyena. A young wolf.

A عسبان *ɛusbān*, (pl. of عسيب *ɛasīb*) Straight, leafless palm-branches.

A عسبة *ɛusbat*, A cleft in a mountain.

A عسبر *ɛusbur*, (fem. عسبرة) A leopard.

A عسبرة *ɛusburat*, A swift, excellent she-camel.

A عسبق *ɛisbik*, A bitter plant good for dressing wounds.

A عسلبة *ɛasbalat*, A going to and fro, a popular commotion.

A عسبور *ɛusbūr*, (or عسبورة *ɛusbūrat*) The offspring of a dog and a she-wolf.

A عسبورة *ɛusbūrat*, A swift, excellent she-camel.

A عسج *ɛasj*, (v. n. of عسج) Stretching out the neck in travelling (a camel or horse). *ɛasaj*, (v. n. of عسج) Being distempered by feeding on the bramble عوسج *ɛawsaj*, (flocks or herds.)

A عسجد *ɛasjad*, Gold. Any sort of jewel, as a pearl or ruby. A large camel.

A عسجديّة *ɛasjadiyat*, Camels upon which kings ride, or such as are employed in the transport of gold. Large camels' colts. Horses of the breed of Dīnārīy.

A عسجر *ɛasjar*, Salt.

A عسجرة *ɛasjarat*, (v. n. of عسجر Q) Looking intently. Being wicked, malignant, impure. Being constantly on the march (camels). Salting (meat).

A عسجمة *ɛasjamat*, Agility, quickness, lightness.

A عسد *ɛasd*, (v. n. of عسد) Travelling. Twisting (a rope) tightly. Lying with.

A عسر *ɛasr*, (v. n. of عسر) Pressing a debtor for payment. Coming from the left. Tossing the tail in running (a camel). Having a hard time in labour (a woman). Taking away (property) per force. *ɛisr* or *ɛasr*, Name of a tribe of demons; also of the place they inhabit. *ɛusr*, (v. n. of عسر) Being difficult. Difficulty. عسر البول *ɛusru'l bawl*, Strangury. عسر النفس *ɛusru'n nafas*, Asthma. *ɛusr* or *ɛusur*, (v. n. of عسر) Having a hard time (a woman in labour). Being difficult. Being hard and pinching (the times). Refusing to come forth (the contents of the belly). Opposing, resisting, thwarting. *ɛasar*, (v. n. of عسر) Being difficult and perplexing. Being equally expert (both hands). Being left-handed. Difficulty. A hard and griping disposition. *ɛasir*, Difficult, intricate, perplexed. Hard, ill-tempered. Disastrous, unfortunate. Pressing (necessity). An unbroken camel whereon a person rides. A she-camel which cocks her tail when running. *ɛusur*, Difficulty.

A عسراء *ɛasrāʼ*, (fem. of اعسر *aɛsar*) Left-handed. (An eagle) having more feathers on the left than the right wing; also one having white quill-feathers. A white quill-feather.

A عسران *ɛasarān*, (v. n. of عسر) Tossing her tail (a camel) in running. Coming from the left hand.

A عسرب *ɛasrab*, The lion.

A عسرة *ɛusrat*, A difficult or indigent condition. Difficulty. جيش العسرة *jayshu'l ɛusrat*, The army of Tabūk (because sent against that place during the hottest season). *ɛasarat*, A white quill-feather.

A عسري *ɛasra'*, also *ɛusra'*, A certain pot-herb. *ɛusra'*, Difficulty. Distress. Torment. A difficult, perplexing affair.

A عسس *ɛasas*, (v. n. of عسّ) Going the rounds at night. (pl. of عاسّ *ɛāss*) Patrols, nightly watches.

A عسطس *ɛistis*, Marsh-mallows.

A عسطلة *ɛastalat*, An incoherent speech.

A عسطوس *ɛasatūs*, (or عسّطوس *ɛassatūs*) Name of a tree, a cane, or rattan. The head of the Christians in Greek.

A عسطوسة *ɛasatūsat*, (or عسّطوسة *ɛassatūsat*) Cold fresh water. Snow.

A عسعاس *ɛasɛās*, The vapour سراب. A wolf.

A عسعس *ɛasɛas*, (pl. عساعس *ɛasāɛis*) A wolf. A hedgehog. Name of a place; also of a man. *ɛusɛus*, A varicious and greedy merchants. A large vase.

A عسعسة *ɛasɛasat*, (v. n. of عسعس Q) Prowling at night (as a wolf). Beginning to close in (night). Approaching the earth (clouds). Being ended (night). Setting in motion, shaking. Covering, concealing, making perplexed, intricate.

A عسف *ɛasf*, (v. n. of عسف) Oppressing. Extorting with violence, seizing unjustly. Patroling by night in search of. Straying, deviating from the right way, or travelling without direction. Employing, taking into one's service. Managing an estate for any one. Working for another, and giving satisfaction. Being near death from a glandular swelling (a camel). The agony of death. The last breath. A capacious cup.

A عسفاء *ɛusafāʼ*, (pl. of عسيف) Working-classes.

A عسفات *ɛasafāt*, A trembling or a falling of the larynx. The agony of death.

A عسفان *ɛusfān*, Name of a place.

A عسق *ɛasak*, (v. n. of عسق) Keeping close to the male (a she-camel). Being assiduous, sticking close, importuning. A twisting, contortion. Illnature, malice. Sadness, anguish. Darkness, dimness. A cluster of bad dates. *ɛasik*, Bad-tempered. *ɛusuk*, Severe to debtors. They who cause (palmtrees or camels) to be fecundated and impregnated.

A عسقبة *ɛaskabat*, A dryness and stiffness in the eyes from weeping. *ɛiskibat*, (pl. عسقب *ɛiskib* and عساقب *ɛasākib*) A small bunch of grapes attached to the bottom of the cluster.

A عسقد *ɛuskud*, Long, tall. Foolish. Coarse and full of flesh.

A عسقفة *ɛaskafat*, (v. n. of عسقف Q) Wishing to weep without being able; growing stiff on that account (eyes). Proposing, intending to do (any thing good) without having the power.

A عسقل *ɛaskal* (pl. عساقل *ɛasākil*), (and عسقول *ɛuskūl*) (pl. عساقيل *ɛasākīl*) A large white mushroom.

A عسقلان *ɛaskalān*, Askelon in Palestine. The top of the head.

A عسقلة *ɛaskalat*, (v. n. of عسقل Q) Moving to and fro (the vapour called سراب *sarāb*). A detached piece of a cloud. A hard place full of white stones.

A عسك *ɛasak*, (v. n. of عسك) Being necessary. Adhering.

A عسكبة *ɛiskibat*, A bunch with about ten grapes.

A عسكر *ɛaskar*, (from P لشكر *lashkar*) An army, forces, troops. A collection. Any thing numerous. Darkness of night. عسكر اسلام *ɛaskari islām*, The army of the faithful, *i. e.* the Ottoman troops. P عسكر ظفر رهبر *ɛaskari zafar-rahbar*, Troops leading to victory.

A عسكران *ɛaskarāni*, (du.) Arafat and Mina.

A عسكرة *ɛaskarat*, (v. n. of عسكر Q) Encamping. Assembling, coming together. Drawing up, preparing an army. Being thick (darkness of night). Falling into difficulties. Vehemence. Difficulty, adversity. A barren year. Enlisting as a soldier.

P عسكرگاه *ɛaskar-gāh*, A camp.

P عسكري *ɛaskare*, A soldier. *ɛaskarī*, Military, belonging to the army.

A عسل *ɛasl*, (v. n. of عسل) Dressing (meat) with honey. Giving, providing with honey. Commending, praising. Lying with (a woman). Tottering when running (a wolf or horse). Trembling much (a limber spear). Being ruffled by the wind (water). *ɛisl*, A steward, bailiff, manager, controller. A tribe of جنّ *jinn*. *ɛusl*, (pl. of عسل *ɛasal*) Honeys. Bubbles. *ɛasal*, (v. n. of عسل) Tasting (of any meat). Making (one) universally beloved (God). Making haste, running, skipping, hopping. Hasting across a desert (a guide). Being agitated by the wind (water). (pl. اعسال *aɛsāl*, عسل *ɛusul*, *ɛusl*, عسول *ɛusūl*, and عسلان *ɛuslān*) Honey (of bees or of dates). A honied dew gathered from flowers. Gum of the plant عرفط *ɛurfut*. A bubble on running water. Praise, fame. Ruin, perdition. Swift she-camel. عسل داؤد *ɛasali dāwud*, (David's honey) The oily exudation of a certain tree. عسل الرمث *ɛasalu'r rims*, A pearly whiteness. عسل طبرزد *ɛasali tabarzad*, Treacle. عسل لبن *ɛasali laban*, Liquid storax. عسل اللبني *ɛasalu'l lubna'*, Liquid gum storax. عسل مصفّا *ɛasali musaffa'*, Clarified honey. احلي من العسل *ahla' mini'l ɛasal*, Sweeter than honey. شمع عسل *shamɛi ɛasal*, Bees' wax. عليك العسل *ɛalayka'l ɛasal*, Make haste, walk fast. *ɛasil*, Nimble-handed (thief). Striking rapidly and with vehemence. *ɛusul*, (pl. of عسل *ɛasal*) Bubbles. Honeys. (pl. of عاسل *ɛāsil*) Good, honest men. (pl. of عسول *ɛasūl*) Tremulous spears. (pl. of عسيل *ɛasīl*) Pizzles of elephants or camels.

A عسّل *ɛussal*, (pl. of عاسل *ɛāsil*) Wolves.

A عسلاً *ɛasalan*, Perdition (seize thee).

A عسلان *ʻuslān*, (pl. of عسل *ʻasal*) Honeys. Bubbles. *ʻasalān*, (v. n. of عسل) Being ruffled by the wind (water). Hastening across the desert (a guide). Trembling (as a limber spear). Tottering (a wolf or horse).

A عسلبة *ʻaslabat*, Discord, division: irresolution.

A عسلة *ʻasalat*, A little honey. Root, basis. مضرب عسلة *mazribu ʻasalatin*, Any thing noble (is not in him). ابو عسلة *abū ʻislatin*, A wolf.

A عسلج *ʻusluj*, A tendril, young shoot. قوام عسلج *kawāmun ʻuslujun*, A delicate form, graceful shape.

A عسلّج *ʻasallaj*, Soft, delicate (meat).

A عسلجة *ʻaslajat*, (v. n. of عسلج Q) Producing shoots and verdure (a tree).

A عسلطة *ʻaslatat*, An incoherent speech.

A عسلق *ʻaslak*, (*ʻislik*, or عسلّق *ʻasallak*) (pl. عسالق *ʻasālik*) Vapour. A wolf. A lion. A beast of prey. A male ostrich. A fox. Light. Long-necked. Bad-tempered.

A عسلقة *ʻas* or *ʻislakat*, (fem.) Of a bad disposition. Light, nimble. Long-necked. A bitch-fox.

A عسلوج *ʻuslūj*, A tendril, shoot, vine-branch.

A عسلوجة *ʻuslūjat*, A tendril, a delicate young shoot. Soft, delicate (girl).

P عسلي *ʻasalī*, A bit of yellow cloth which the Jews are compelled to wear on the shoulder by way of distinction. A garment worn by the fire-worshippers. A particular colour with which the fakirs of India dye their garments.

A عسلّي *ʻasalīy*, The most learned man amongst the Jews. A mark or sign of the Jews.

P عسلي رنگ *ʻasalī-rang*, A dervish's garment.

A عسم *ʻasm*, (v. n. of عسم) Coveting. Striving. Endeavouring to procure subsistence, or to acquire any thing. Precipitating one's self (into any danger); rushing into a crowd. Shedding tears (the eye). Winking (the eye), being closed (the eyelids). *ʻasam*, (v. n. of عسم) Being stiff and distorted (hand or foot). *ʻusum*, (pl. of عاسم *ʻāsim* or عسوم *ʻasūm*) Those who toil for their bread.

A عسماء *ʻasmāʼ*, (fem.) Crooked-handed or footed.

A عسمان *ʻasamān*, An ambling pace.

A عسمة *ʻasmat*, One meal. A bit of dry bread. *ʻasamat*, Fragments of dry bread.

A عسمطة *ʻasmatat*, (v. n. of عسمط Q) Mixing.

A عسمّي *ʻasmīy*, One who manages well his affairs. One whose business is all awry. A deceiver.

A عسن *ʻasn*, Tallness with beauty of hair and fairness of complexion. *ʻasn*, *ʻisn*, or *ʻusn*, (pl. اعسان *aʻsān*) Fat, grease, lard. *ʻisn*, Like, equal, resembling. *ʻusn* or *ʻusun*, Fatness. *ʻusun* or *ʻasan*, The beneficial effect of fodder upon cattle. *ʻasin*, (A horse) satisfied with a little corn. Fat, in good condition (beast). *ʻusun*, Old fat.

A عسنّج *ʻasannaj*, Injured, unjustly dealt with. An ostrich.

A عسنق *ʻusnuk*, Beautiful: finely proportioned.

A عسو *ʻasw*, Wax. A wax-candle. *ʻasw*, (or عسوّ *ʻusūw*) (v. n. of عسا for عسو) Becoming hard or thick with labour (a hand). Growing old, become feeble (from age).

A عسوّ *ʻusūw*, (v. n. of عسا for عسو) Withering, drying; becoming firm and hard (a plant). Growing dark (night).

A عسوب *ʻasūb*, A prince, chief. The king bee.

A عسودّ *ʻiswadd*, A male animal bigger than a lizard, on which demons are supposed to ride. A serpent. Strong, vigorous.

A عسودّة *ʻiswaddat*, (pl. عسودّات *ʻiswaddāt* (or عساود *ʻasāwid*) A kind of white animalcule, which resembles maidens' fingers.

A عسوس *ʻasūs*, One in search of prey or game. A woman not shy of approaching men. (A she-camel) pasturing alone, and giving little or no milk unless at a distance from men. A she-camel examined if she have milk or not. A camel which looks out for bones and breaks them. A she-camel bad tempered at milking-time. A good-for-nothing fellow. A wolf.

A عسوف *ʻasūf*, Violent, unjust. An oppressor, extortioner. One who loses his way.

A عسوفة *ʻusūfat*, (v. n. of عسف) Being near death from a glandular swelling and pestilence (a camel); experiencing a trembling or falling of the larynx. Fetching a short and cold breath.

A عسول *ʻasūl*, (pl. عسل *ʻusul*) A good man. Tremulous (spear). *ʻusūl*, (v. n. of عسل) Trembling (a limber spear). (pl. of عسل *ʻasal*) Honeys. Bubbles.

A عسوم *ʻasūm*, A camel with many foals. (pl. عسم *ʻusum*) One who earns his bread by labour. One who brings much trouble and plague upon his household. *ʻusūm*, (v. n. of عسم) Gaining, earning. Rushing into a crowd. Winking (the eye), being closed (eyelids). Striving. Shedding tears. Paucity, penury. Fragments of dry bread.

A عسى *ʻasaʼ*, (v. n. of عسا for عسو) Waxing old. It wanted but little that. It may be, perhaps. He became. A palm-branch. بعسى و لعلّ *bi ʻasaʼ wa laʻall*, By perhaps and may be. *ʻasī*, Apt, fit, proper, suitable.

A عسيّ *ʻasīy*, Apt, fit, proper, suitable. *ʻusīy*, (v. n. of عسا for عسو) Growing old.

A عسيب *ʻasīb*, The exterior part of the foot, the instep. The longest feather of the wing. The outer side of a feather. (pl. عسبان *ʻusbān*) A straight palm-branch without leaves. A cleft in a mountain. *ʻasīb*, (and عسيبة *ʻasībat*) The bone of the tail, and the skin whence the hairs grow.

A عسير *ʻasīr*, Difficult. Pressing (necessity). Disastrous, unfortunate. Unbroken (she-camel), on which a person rides. Covered (camel), but not conceiving. (A she-camel) tossing her tail when running. عسير الاستخراج *ʻasīru'l istikhrāj*, Difficult to extract. شرائط عسير الرعاية *sharāʼiti ʻasīru'r riʻāya*, Conditions difficult to be observed. يوم عسير *yawmi ʻasīr*, The day of judgment. مرض عسير العلاج *marazi ʻasīru'l ʻilāj*, A disease difficult of cure. P دربند عسير المرور *dar-bandi ʻasīru'l murūr*, A pass difficult to penetrate.

A عسيس *ʻasīs*, (pl. of عاسّ *ʻāss*) Night-patroles.

A عسيف *ʻasīf*, (pl. عسفاء *ʻusafāʼ*) A mercenary, labourer, assistant, servant. A decrepit old man.

A عسيقة *ʻasīkat*, Vapid, watery wine.

A عسيل *ʻasīl*, (pl. عسل *ʻusul*) The pizzle of an elephant or camel. A man who strikes a heavy blow and brings his hand quickly back again. Feathers, or any thing similar, with which a perfumer brushes together drugs or civet brayed on a stone.

A عسيلة *ʻusaylat*, Sensual pleasures as sweet as honey. Sperma virile. A term of endearment.

A عشّ *ʻashsh*, (v. n. of عشّ) Disturbing, frightening (a deer) from (its) place. Turning (one) away from (his) purpose. Alighting upon a spot, molesting the occupants and forcing them to quit. Beating. Having a slender trunk and few branches (a palm-tree). Giving sparingly. Being attentive to gain, industrious; gathering, collecting. Nestling (a bird). Mending, patching a shirt. Lean, spare, dry man. A scanty gift. A stallion camel conscious of the wish of the female, and yet leaving her unmolested. *ʻushsh* or *ʻashsh*, (pl. اعشاش *aʻshāsh*, عشاش *ʻishāsh*, or عششة *ʻishashat*) The nest of a bird building on trees (that of such as nestle on rocks or in houses being called وكر *wakr* (or وكن *wakn*), and that of such as burrow in the ground is named ادحيّ *udhīy* and افحوص *ufhūs*). ليس بعشّك فادرجي *laysa bi ʻushshiki, fadruji*, (O woman!) you have no right in it; go your way.

A عشا *ʻashaʼ*, (v. n. of عشي) Being purblind. Purblindness, nocturnal blindness.

A عشاء *ʻashāʼ*, (pl. اعشية *aʻshiyat*) A supper. Purblindness. عشاءِ ربّاني *ʻashāʼi rabbānī*, The Lord's Supper, the Eucharist. *ʻishāʼ*, The first watch of the night, or, according to some, from the time when the sun begins to go down till twilight, or from sunset until dawn.

A عشاءان *ʻishāʼāni*, (dual of عشاء *ʻishāʼ*) The first and second watch of the night.

A عشابة *ʻashābat*, Plenty of herbage, grassiness.

A عشار *ʻishār*, (v. n. 3 of عشر) Living upon terms of familiarity. Forming an alliance with. (pl. of عشراء *ʻusharāʼ*) She-camels ten months gone with young. A word applied to camels until some have brought forth, and of others whose parturition is expected. *ʻushār*, In tens. جاء القوم عشار عشار *jāʼa'l kawm ʻushāra ʻushāra*, The people came ten and ten, in companies of ten.

A عشّار *ʻashshār*, A tithe-collector, tithe-proctor.

A عشارب *ʻushārib*, A lion.

A عشارة *ʻushārat*, A piece, or a tenth, broken off

a pot or any thing else.

A عشارم *ɛashārim*, A lion.

A عشاري *ɛushāriy*, Ten cubits long (garment). A kind of barge used upon the Nile. ذهبوا عشاريات *zahabū ɛushārayātin*, They went off dispersed.

A عشازن *ɛashāzin*, (pl. of عشوزن *ɛashawzan*) Difficult, intricate. Strong, thick.

A عشاش *ɛishāsh*, (pl. of عش *ɛushsh*) Birds' nests built in trees or hedges.

A عشاشة *ɛashāshat*, (v. n. of عش) Being lean, slender (body). Having few branches and a slender stem (a palm-tree).

P عشاق *ɛushāk*, Name of a musical tone.

A عشاق *ɛushāk*, A dear little boy, a bantling.

A عشاق *ɛushshāk*, (pl. of عاشق *ɛāshik*) Lovers.

P عشاق سگ جان *ɛushshāki sag-jān*, Covetous, worldly-minded, dog-souled people. A جزيرة العشاق *jazīratu'l ɛushshāk*, The lover's isle, *i.e.* Sinope.

A عشان *ɛushshān*, The root of a palm-branch.

A عشانة *ɛushānat*, The root of a palm-branch. Dates picked off the ground. The trunk of a tree. ابو عشانة *abū ɛushānat*, A cant name for a man.

A عشانط *ɛashānit*, (pl. of عشنط *ɛashannat*) Tall and handsome.

A عشانق *ɛushānik*, Tall and moderately stout.

A عشانقة *ɛashānikat*, (pl. of عشنق *ɛashannah*) Tall and moderately thick.

A عشاوة *ɛashāwat*, Nocturnal blindness.

A عشاوز *ɛashāwiz*, (pl. of عشوزن *ɛashawzan*) Difficult, intricate.

A عشايا *ɛashāya'*, (pl. of عشية *ɛashīyat*) Evenings. Clouds.

A عشائر *ɛashāɛir*, (pl. of عشيرة *ɛashīrat*) Kindreds, tribes. The nearest relations on the father's side.

A عشب *ɛushb*, Green fodder, grass. *ɛashab*, (v. n. of عشب) Being hard and dry. Grown up, adult (family). *ɛashib*, Grassy (field).

A عشبة *ɛushbat*, Sarsaparilla. عشبة مقدسة *ɛushbat muhaddisat*, Name of a plant. *ɛashabat*, A dwarf (male or female). A large tooth. Old or decrepit (man or woman). An ugly woman. An aged sheep or camel. An army.

A عشة *ɛashshat*, (A tree) which has slender branches and grows badly. (A woman) lean, tall, and slender in the bones of the hand and foot. Ground dry and rugged. (A palm-tree) having few branches and a slender stem.

A عشج *ɛashij*, (for عشي *ɛashīy*) Evening.

A عشجب *ɛashjab*, A languid, relaxed man.

A عشجذة *ɛashjazat*, A raining feebly.

A عشد *ɛashd*, A collecting, gathering.

P عشر *ɛashr*, Every milky plant. Name of a poisonous milky tree in India. Saffron. An artichoke. Senna of Mecca.

A عشر *ɛashr*, (v. n. of عشر) Being ten months gone with young (a camel). Taking one from ten, decimating. Adding one to nine, making ten, making the tenth. Making twenty. The ten fingers. Ten (females). *ɛishr*, A watering of camels on the tenth or ninth day (from their last drinking). A piece or tenth part broken off a cauldron, or any thing else. *ɛushr*, (v. n. of عشر) Decimating, receiving (as tithes from the people) the tenth of their flocks. (pl. عشور *ɛushūr* and اعشار *aɛshār*) A tenth part, tithe. A decade of verses in the Kur'ān (of which there are 621). Camels which emit small quantities of milk in streams without collecting any amount. عشر شرعي *ɛushri sharɛī*, The tenths prescribed by law. *ɛashara*, Ten (females). عشر كلمات *ɛashara kalimāt*, The ten words, *i.e.* the decalogue or ten commandments. احد عشر *ahad ɛashara*, Eleven. *ɛushar*, A certain tree containing inflammatory matter; emitting better fire than any other kind. It is used in making bolsters; and from its blossoms and branches a certain kind of sugar is made. There is a bitterness also about it.

A عشراء *ɛusharāɛ*, (pl. عشراوات *ɛusharāwāt* and عشار *ɛishār*) A camel gone with young ten months or eight months. A woman in labour, or who has borne a child within forty days. The summit of a mountain. (pl. of عشير *ɛashīr*) Companions (especially husband and wife). Familiars, intimate friends.

A عشرب *ɛashrab*, (or عشرب *ɛasharrab*) An arrow flying. A lion. One who runs violently.

A عشرة *ɛashrat* or *ɛasharat*, Ten (males). *ɛishrat*, Conversation, society, agreeable familiarity. Pleasure, delight, enjoyment; sociableness, the pleasures of the table. *ɛusharat*, A certain tree or gum.

P عشرتخانه *ɛishrat-khāna* (or عشرت گاه *ɛishrat-gāh*), A house of pleasure, a place of entertainment.

P عشر خوان *ɛashar-khwān*, A reader of the Kur'ān. Deposed from office.

P عشرستان *ɛusharistān*, A grove of *ɛushar*-trees.

A عشرق *ɛishrik*, Name of a plant good for the piles, producing milk and dyeing the hair black.

P عشرق *ɛushrik*, A medicinal seed called تخم مرو *tukhmi marv*.

A عشرقة *ɛashrakat*, (v. n. of عشرق Q) Flourishing (a plant). Being verdant (ground).

A عشرم *ɛashram*, Strong and rough.

A عشرم *ɛasharram*, Bold, active. A lion. An arrow flying.

A عشرون *ɛishrūna*, (obl. عشرين *ɛishrīna*) Twenty. عشري *ɛishrīya'*, My twenty. عشروك *ɛishrūka*, Thy twenty.

A عشرة *ɛashara*, First ten days of Muharram.

A عشري *ɛushariy*, Subject to tithe, tithable.

A عشرين *ɛishrayni*, (obl. dual of عشر *ɛishr*) Two waterings of camels, *i. e.* a space of eighteen days.

A عشرينات *ɛishrīnāt*, Companies of twenty.

A عشرينية *ɛishrīnīya*, A monthly pension, payable upon the twentieth day.

A عشز *ɛashz*, Thickness of body. Thick-bodied and full of flesh.

A عشزان *ɛashazān*, (v. n. of عشز) Walking like one that has lost his leg. Leaning on a stick.

A عشزب *ɛashzab*, (also عشزب *ɛashazzab*) A lion, strong and fierce.

A عشزن *ɛashazzan*, Naturally hard.

A عشزنة *ɛashzanat*, Opposition, contradiction.

A عششة *ɛishashat*, (pl. of عش) Birds' nests.

A عشط *ɛasht*, A drawing greedily to one's self.

A عشعش *ɛashɛash* or *ɛushɛush*, Birds' nests built one under the other.

A عشق *ɛishk*, Love. Intensity of the passion and a blindness to the failings of the object loved. *ɛishk* or *ɛashak*, (v. n. of عشق) Being sick or dying for love. Love. عشق الهي *ɛishki ilāhī*, Divine love. *ɛashak*, (v. n. of عشق) Sticking, cleaving to. (pl. of عشقة *ɛashakat*) Ivies. *ɛushuk*, Those who have the charge of planting, trimming, and keeping in order odoriferous herbs.

P عشق *ɛashak*, A species of ivy.

P عشقباز *ɛishk-bāz*, A man of gallantry. A tumbler-pigeon.

P عشق بازي *ɛishk-bāzī*, Gallantry, amorous talk.

P عشق پيچا *ɛishk-pechā*, American jasmine.

P عشق پيچان *ɛishk-pechān*, Ivy.

A عشقة *ɛashakat*, (pl. عشق) Ivy, convolvulus.

P عشقه *ɛashiha*, A kind of ivy.

A عشم *ɛasham*, (v. n. of عشم) Coveting, desiring greatly. Becoming dry. Beginning to fatten. Desire, concupiscence. Dry bread (without meat). Mouldy, dry, spoilt bread. *ɛashim*, A sort of tree. *ɛushum*, (pl. of عاشم *ɛāshim*) Trees of a certain kind.

A عشماء *ɛashmāɛ*, (Trees) dried to a powder. Ground, where trees wither. Dusty (ground).

A عشمة *ɛashamat*, A piece of dry bread. Decrepitude, dotage. An old man or woman bent double. Withered, dry from leanness. Desire, concupiscence.

A عشن *ɛashn*, A conjecturing, guessing.

A عشنج *ɛashannaj*, Wrinkled and ugly-faced. Sour-faced and bad-tempered.

A عشنزر *ɛashanzar*, Large and robustly framed.

A عشنط *ɛashannat*, (pl. عشانط *ɛashānit*) Tall and handsome. Full of flesh and delicately formed. Ingenious, intelligent.

A عشنق *ɛashannah*, (pl. عشانقة *ɛashānikat*) Tall and moderately thick. Light and thin of flesh.

A عشو *ɛashw*, (or عشو *ɛushūw*) (v. n. of عشا for عشو) Eating supper. Giving meat to men, or forage to cattle in the evening. Travelling in the night-time. Seeing a fire at night from a distance and making for it. Drawing near a fire or light in order to see better. Receding, turning away from, shifting. *ɛishw*, A cup of milk drank after the flocks return from pasture in the evening.

A عشواء *ɛashwāɛ*, (fem. of اعشى *aɛsha'*) Purblind. A she-camel that cannot see before her and paws the ground. A sort of date. خبط عشواء *khabta ɛashwāɛ*, With great confusion. ركب العشواء *ra-*

hiba'l ʿashwāʾ, He rode the purblind camel, *i. e.* He made a jumble of the concern, or he went to work in the dark.

A عشوان *ʿushwān*, A sort of date.

A عشوة *ʿashwat*, The thick darkness following the crepuscle. *ʿashwat, ʿishwat*, or *ʿushwat*, An attempting or engaging in a gloomy, dark affair, stupendous and dangerous. *ʿishwat*, Amorous playfulness, blandishment, caresses, coquetting, ogling, gallantry. *ʿushwat* or *ʿishwat*, A lighted fire.

A عشور *ʿushūr*, (v. n. of عشر) Decimating, tithing. (pl. of عشر *ʿushr*) Tithes, legal tenths. (pl. of عشير *ʿashīr*) Tenths.

A عشوراء *ʿashūrāʾ*, (or عشورا *ʿashūra'*) The tenth or the ninth of the month محرّم *muharram*.

A عشوز *ʿashwaz*, (or عشوّز *ʿashawwaz*) Hard ground: rough (road): strong (camel): much (flesh).

A عشوزن *ʿashawzan*, (pl. عشازن *ʿashāzin* and عشاوز *ʿashāwiz*) Difficult, intricate. Hard. Strong, thick (camel). Roughly-built (man).

A عشوشة *ʿushūshat*, (v. n. of عش) Being thin and lean (the body).

A عشوف *ʿushūf*, A dry tree.

A عشوم *ʿushūm*, (v. n. of عشم) Coveting. Becoming dry.

P عشوه زن *ʿishwa-zan*, One playing the gallant or coquette.

P عشوه ساز *ʿishwa-sāz*, Gallant: coquettish.

P عشوه سازي *ʿishwa-sāzī*, Gallantry: coquetry.

A عشويّ *ʿashawīy*, Belonging to the evening.

A عشويّة *ʿashwīyat*, A dark place.

A عشي *ʿashy*, (v. n. of عشي) Acting like a purblind man. Providing meat or forage in the evening. Supping. *ʿushy*, (pl. of اعشى *aʿsha'*) Purblind. *ʿasha'*, (v. n. of عشي) Being purblind. Pasturing at night (a camel). Injuring, oppressing. Shortness of sight at night. *ʿashī*, Purblind. Blind at night. *ʿisha'*, (pl. اعشية *aʿshiyat*) Supper, also the evening food of cattle.

A عشيّ *ʿashīy*, The evening; the time from sunset to the first watch; also the first watch. A camel long in eating his evening meal. A cloud. عشيّ امس *ʿashīya amsin*, Yester eve. صلوتا العشي *salātā'l ʿashīy*, Afternoon and evening-prayers.

A عشيان *ʿashyān*, Supping, who takes supper.

A عشيّان *ʿushayyān*, (dim. of عشيّ *ʿashīy*) A short evening.

A عشيب *ʿashīb*, Grassy (field). A dwarf. *ʿushayb*, A dwarf.

A عشيّة *ʿashīyat*, (pl. عشايا *ʿashāya'*) The evening. A cloud.

A عشير *ʿashīr*, (pl. اعشراء *aʿshirāʾ*, عشور *ʿushūr*, and اعشار *aʿshār*) A tenth. The tenth part of a قفيز *kafīz* (a measure of land). The cry of the hyena. (pl. عشراء *ʿusharāʾ*) A friend, intimate companion (especially husband or wife).

A عشيرة *ʿashīrat*, (pl. عشائر *ʿashāʾir*) Parentage, kindred, brethren by whole blood, a family, tribe, house. Fellowship. P عشيرت و خويشان *ʿashīrat u khweshān*, Kindred and domestic relations.

A عشيش *ʿashīsh*, (v. n. of عش) Being thin and slender (the body).

A عشيشات *ʿushayshāt*, Short evenings.

A عشيشان *ʿushayshān*, (or عشيشيان *ʿushayshiyān*) (dim. of عشيّ *ʿashīy*) A short evening.

A عشيشيانات *ʿushayshiyānāt*, Short evenings.

A عشيشية *ʿushayshiyat*, (dim. of عشيّ *ʿashīy*) A short evening.

A عشيق *ʿashīḳ*, (fem. عشيقة *ʿashīkat*) A lover.

A عشيق *ʿishshīḳ*, Desperately in love.

A عصّ *ʿaṣṣ*, (v. n. of عصّ) Being strong, hard, firm. Being severe, hard on a debtor. Root, origin.

A عصا *ʿaṣa'*, (v. n. of عصا for عصو) Bastinadoing, striking with a stick or sword. Making a cudgel. Using a sword like a cudgel. (pl. اعصي *aʿṣī*, اعصاء *aʿṣāʾ*, عصيّ *ʿuṣīy* or *ʿiṣīy*) A stick, a staff, cudgel, baton, bludgeon. An instrument used in taking altitudes. A woman's veil or head-dress. The tongue. The leg-bone. Chastisement, discipline. A society (of Muslims). عصا الراعي *ʿaṣa'r rāʿī*, Shepherds'-staff, a pot-herb of a red colour. عصاي متره پوليت *ʿaṣayi matrapolīt*, A bishop's crosier. عصاي موسيٰ *ʿaṣayi mūsa'*, Moses' rod. القي عصاه *alka' ʿaṣa'hu*, He threw away his staff, *i.e.* he stopt, he gave up proceeding on a journey, he desisted from any design. He arrived at his journey's end; he halted; or he pitched his tent. انشقاق العصا *inshiḳāḳu'l ʿaṣa'*, Discord. شقّ العصا *shakku'l ʿaṣa'*, A breaking of the stick, *i. e.* a sowing of discord. ضعيف العصا *zaʿīfu'l ʿaṣa'*, One who pastures (camels) properly, and beats them but little. ليّن العصا *layyinu'l ʿaṣa'*, Of a mild disposition. One who administers justice well. عبيد العصا *ʿabīdu'l ʿaṣa'*, Servants of the stick, *i. e.* those who are liable to be beaten.

A عصاب *ʿiṣāb*, A rope tied round a she-camel's thigh to make her give milk plentifully. Whatever any part of the body except the head is tied with. A grasp or seizure of any thing. *ʿuṣāb*, Fumitory.

A عصّاب *ʿaṣṣāb*, A vender of thread. A spinner.

A عصابة *ʿiṣābat*, (pl. عصائب *ʿaṣāʾib*) A bandage (for a wound); a fillet, wreath, tiara, turban, or any thing which they bind round, or wear upon, the head. A body (of men or horses); a flock (of birds). A red cloud. Difficulty, trouble.

A عصاة *ʿaṣāt*, A stick. عصاة الجنّ *ʿaṣātu'l jinn*, Name of a Syrian plant. *ʿuṣāt*, (pl. of عاصي *ʿāṣī* and of عصيّ *ʿaṣīy*) Rebels, obstinate sinners.

A عصاثج *ʿuṣāʾij*, Hard, strong, thick, and fat.

A عصار *ʿiṣār*, Great dust. Wind gently expelled from the belly. جاء علي عصارمن الدهر *jāʾ ʿala' ʿiṣārin mini'd dahri*, He came at a fixed, or at the appointed time. *ʿuṣār*, Expressed juice.

A عصّار *ʿaṣṣār*, An oil-maker or presser. A presser of grapes.

A عصارة *ʿuṣārat*, Expressed juice. عصارهٔ افسنتين *ʿuṣāraʾi afsintīn*, Wormwood-water. عصارهٔ مهك *ʿuṣārai mahk*, Liquorice-juice. كريم العصارة *karīmu'l ʿuṣārat*, Liberal, when appealed to.

A عصافة *ʿuṣāfat*, Chaff, beards, leaves of corn.

A عصافير *ʿaṣāfīr*, (pl. of عصفور *ʿuṣfūr*) Sparrows. A certain kind of tree. عصافير القتب *ʿaṣāfīru'l ḳutub*, Four pegs for keeping together a camel's saddle. عصافير المنذر *ʿaṣāfīru'l munzir*, An excellent kind of camels used by princes. نقّت عصافير بطنه *naḳḳat ʿaṣāfīru baṭnihi*, He hungered.

A عصافيريّ *ʿaṣāfīrīy*, A sort of olive.

A عصاقياء *ʿaṣāḳiyāʾ*, (or عصاقية) Uproar.

A عصاقيل *ʿaṣāḳīl*, Whirlwinds.

A عصال *ʿiṣāl*, Crooked. A crooked arrow. (pl. of اعصل *aʿṣal*) Crooked with hardness.

A عصّال *ʿaṣṣāl*, One who twists very much.

A عصام *ʿaṣām*, (pl. اعصام *aʿṣām*) A dog's collar. *ʿiṣām*, Name of a man who acquired celebrity by his own merits, not from his ancestry. نفس عصاميّة *nafsi ʿiṣāmīya*, One who does not glory in his father's virtues, but in his own. (pl. اعصمة *aʿṣimat*, عصم *ʿuṣum*, and عصام *ʿiṣām*) A collyrium with which they anoint or paint the eyebrows. The small part of the tail. The rope or other fastening of a leathern bottle, bucket, and the like. A rope by which the camel-litter is fastened to the breast-harness or girth of a camel to prevent it from slipping back. The handle of any vessel.

A عصامير *ʿaṣāmīr*, Water-wheels.

P عصاول *ʿaṣāwal*, A state-messenger.

A عصاويد *ʿaṣāwīd*, Perplexed, obscure words. Thick, accumulated clouds. Thirsty persons. Camels tumbling one over another. Warriors standing by their comrades in battle. *ʿaṣāwīda*, One after another.

A عصائب *ʿaṣāʾib*, (pl. of عصابة) Bodies, herds.

A عصائر *ʿaṣāʾir*, (pl. of عصيرة *ʿaṣīrat*) Juices.

A P عصايم *ʿaṣāyam*, My stick, my staff.

A عصب *ʿaṣb*, (v. n. of عصب) Surrounding, encircling, enclosing. Drying round the mouth (spittle). Twisting hard. Spinning. Assembling, flocking. Being necessary. Putting on a turban or tiara; binding a fillet round the head. Tying a rope round a camel's thigh to make her give milk plentifully. Tying tight the testicles of a ram or goat that they may perish without being extracted. Grasping, griping. Laying fast hold. Taking separate things in hand, and holding them together (as branches of trees to prune or strip off the leaves). Acquiring power over. Changing the cesura مفاعلتن *mufāʿalatun*, in the metre وافر *wāfir* (exuberant) to مفاعيلن *mafāʿīlun*. Reddening (as the horizon). A kind of striped Arabian cloth. Cotton-thread. Dirt upon the teeth. A cloud, especially a little red cloud appearing in very dry seasons. A grasp, a tight fold or twist. The superior rank of men. حسنة العصب *hasanatu'l ɛasb*, (A damsel) of an elegant shape. *ɛasb, ɛusb*, or *ɛasab*, Ivy. *ɛasab*, (v. n. of عصب) Having large tendons (flesh). Assembling round a cistern (camels). A tendon, nerve, ligament. Chiefs, upper ranks. (pl. of عصبة *ɛasabat*) Nerves, tendons, ligaments. Children and near relations. *ɛusab*, (pl. of عصبة *ɛusbat*) Crowds. *ɛusub*, (pl. of عصيب *ɛasib*) Hearts, lights, and livers dressed with other intestines.

P عصب *ɛusab*, Gum-tragacanth.

A عصبة *ɛisbat*, A mode or fashion of binding on the turban. *ɛusbat*, A body of men, horses, or birds (from ten to forty). A substance which cleaves to trees and thorns, and which cannot be detached without difficulty. *ɛasabat*, (pl. عصب *ɛasab*) A nerve, tendon, ligament. (pl. عصبات *ɛasabāt*) Kindred, distant relations. Sons. Male relations on the father's side.

A عصبصب *ɛasabsab*, Intense, oppressive (day with heat). Disastrous (day).

P عصبه *ɛasba*, Name of a fragrant creeper.

A عصبيّة *ɛasabīyat*, Zeal. Bigotry, prejudice, party-spirit, tenacity. Love of kindred or country. Help, assistance.

A عصد *ɛasd*, (v. n. of عصد) Bending (the neck). Lying with. Forcing unwillingly. Semen genitale.

A عصر *ɛasr*, (v. n. of عصر) Squeezing, pressing (grapes). Imprisoning, detaining, hindering, preventing. Giving (a gift). Taking refuge, escaping. Milking. *ɛasr* or *ɛasar*, Afternoon. Day. Night. Morning. A number of men (without women) under ten. Kindred, family, tribe. Rain. A prison. A gift. صلوة العصر *salātu'l ɛasr*, Afternoon-prayer. كريم العصر *karīmu'l ɛasr*, Of a noble race. *ɛasr, ɛisr, ɛusr*, or *ɛusur*, (pl. اعصار *aɛsār*, عصور *ɛusūr*, اعصر *aɛsur*, and عصر *ɛusur*) Time, an age. Evening-prayer. جاء لكن لم يجئ لعصر *jāɛ lākin lam yajiɛ li ɛusrin*, He came, but not at the right time. *ɛusr*, A refuge, asylum. Escape, deliverance. *ɛasar*, A refuge, asylum. Dust. بنو عصر *banū ɛasar*, Name of a tribe. *ɛusur*, (pl. of عصر *ɛasar*) Times, ages.

A عصراً *ɛusran*, (adverb) Late.

A عصران *ɛasrāni*, Morning and evening; day and night. Morning and evening-prayer.

A عصرة *ɛasrat*, A kind of large tree. *ɛusrat*, Refuge, a place of escape. Obedience. One who is of an inferior order. *ɛasarat*, A whirlwind, raising the dust in the form of columns, driving about the clouds fraught with lightning. Much dust.

A عصرة *ɛusratan*, (adverb) Below the rest.

A عصريّ *ɛasarīy*, Of the tribe of بنو عصر.

A عصص *ɛusas* or *ɛusus*, Root of a (horse's) tail.

A عصعص *ɛusɛus*, Bad-tempered. A worthless fellow. Firm and compact in body. *ɛusɛus, ɛusaɛis*, or *ɛasɛas*, The rump-bone, root of the tail.

A عصعصة *ɛasɛasat*, A pain in the rump-bone, at the root of the tail.

A عصعوص *ɛusɛūs*, The root of a horse's tail.

A عصف *ɛasf*, (v. n. of عصف) Cutting unripe (corn). Blowing with violence (wind). Being carried with velocity. Labouring to gain a livelihood for one's family. Inclining, being bent. Carrying off, destroying (war). A blade of corn, or corn in the blade. Straw after the grain has been thrashed out. A storm, hurricane.

A عصفة *ɛasfat*, The scent of wine.

A عصفر *ɛusfur*, Saffron in the flower. A red colour.

A عصفرة *ɛasfarat*, A dyeing with saffron.

A عصفور *ɛusfūr*, (fem. عصفورة *ɛusfūrat*) (pl. عصافير *ɛasāfīr*) A sparrow. The place where the forelocks grow. Protuberant bones on each side of a horse's forehead; also a white spot on his forehead. The half of the brain. A male locust. A book. A nail in a ship. A king, lord. Various pieces of wood used in putting together a camel's saddle or litter. عصفور التين *ɛusfūru't tīn*, The fig-pecker. عصفور الشوك *ɛusfūru'sh shawk*, A wagtail.

A عصفوريّ *ɛusfūrīy*, A two-bunched camel.

A عصقول *ɛuskūl*, A male locust.

A عصل *ɛasl*, (v. n. of عصل) Inclining. Bending, making crooked (a stick). *ɛusl*, (pl. of اعصل *aɛsal*) Crooked (arrows). Bandy-legged (men). Those who apply closely to any thing. Bent, inclined. *ɛasal*, (v. n. of عصل) Being naturally crooked and distorted. A crookedness in a horse's tail. A crookedness with hardness. A crookedness in the teeth and leg. (pl. اعصال *aɛsāl*) A small gut. A certain tree which purges camels. Rhododaphne or laurel-rose. *ɛasil*, (pl. عصال *ɛisāl*) Crooked (tree). Crooked and hard. Crooked-tailed. *ɛisal*, A small gut.

A عصلاء *ɛaslāɛ*, Lean, fleshless (woman).

A عصلب *ɛuslab*, Large, robust, strong, firm. *ɛuslub*, Long-bodied and tottering.

A عصلبة *ɛaslabat*, Excess of rage.

A عصلبيّ *ɛuslubīy*, Hard and strong (man).

A عصلّج *ɛasallaj*, Bow-legged, crooked.

A عصلد *ɛaslad*, (or عصلود *ɛuslūd*) Hard, strong.

A عصلوب *ɛuslūb*, Strong, firm, large-bodied.

A عصم *ɛasm*, (v. n. of عصم) Gaining, acquiring. Defending, protecting, preserving. Fastening a belt or guard called عصام *ɛisām* to a leathern bottle. *ɛusm*, (pl. اعصام *aɛsām*) Whiteness on the arm of a deer, and the like. *ɛusm* or *ɛusum*, Marks left (of pitch, or of privet on the hands or soles of the feet. *ɛasam*, (v. n. of عصم) Having white on the fore-feet, the rest of the body being red or black (a doe). *ɛisam*, (pl. of عصمة *ɛismat*) Collars, necklaces. Protections, safeguards. *ɛusum*, Remains, vestiges. (pl. of عصام *ɛisām*) Belts, guards.

A عصماء *ɛasmāɛ*, White on the fore-legs (she-goat).

A عصمة *ɛismat*, (v. n. of عصم) Guarding, defending. Keeping back (from sin or danger). Sticking the claws into. Preserving from famishing (food). (pl. عصم *ɛisam*) A defence, a guard, protection. Continence, chastity. Integrity. Honour. A necklace, collar, or belt. *ɛusmat*, Whiteness on the leg of a doe. A collar. (pl. اعصام *aɛsām*) A dog's collar. A guard. *ɛasamat*, (pl. of عصم *ɛisam*) (pl. of عصمة *ɛismat*) Collars. Defences, guards.

P عصمتيان *ɛismatiyān*, Prophets. Holy and self-denying men. Chaste and holy women. Mary the mother of Jesus Christ.

A عصمور *ɛusmūr*, A water-wheel, or the bucket attached to it.

A عصنصى *ɛasansaʼ*, Weak.

A عصو *ɛasw*, (v. n. of عصا for عصو) Cudgelling. Beating at cudgel-playing. Collecting, drawing together. Binding up a wound.

A عصواد *ɛiswād* or *ɛuswād*, Malignant, boisterous, surly-tempered (man or woman). A difficult and important affair. A watering-place difficult of access.

A عصوب *ɛasūb*, (A camel) giving no milk unless her thigh is bound with a cord. Dirt on the teeth. Meagre-hipped (woman).

A عصود *ɛusūd*, (v. n. of عصد) Dying.

A عصوّد *ɛasawwad*, Long (day).

A عصوّد *ɛiswadd*, Slim, slender (woman).

A عصودة *ɛaswadat*, A shouting and fighting.

A عصور *ɛusūr*, (pl. of عصر *ɛasr, ɛisr, ɛusr*, or *ɛusur*) Ages, times.

A عصوف *ɛasūf*, Violent (wind), storm, hurricane. (A camel or an ostrich) borne rapidly along. Opaqueness, dimness, dulness. Wine. *ɛusūf*, (v. n. of عصف) Blowing violently (wind).

A عصوم *ɛasūm*, A glutton, devourer, great eater.

A عصويّ *ɛasawīy*, Belonging to a staff.

A عصى *ɛasy*, (v. n. of عصى) Being disobedient, rebellious, revolting. Disobedience, rebellion, revolt. *ɛasaʼ*, (v. n. of عصى) Striking with a stick.

A عصىّ *ɛasīy*, Rebellious, stubborn, disobedient. *ɛisīy*, The bones of a bird's wing. *ɛisīy* or *ɛusīy*, (pl. of عصا *ɛasaʼ*) Sticks, staffs, cudgels, batons.

A عصيان *ɛisyān*, (v. n. of عصى) Being disobedient, rebellious. Rebellion, disobedience, opposition to lawful authority. Sin, transgression.

P عصيان گر *ɛisyāngar*, Rebellious, sinful.

A عصيب *ɛasīb*, Intense, vehement, oppressive (as a day with heat). Calamitous (day). (pl. اعصبة *aɛsibat* and عصب *ɛusub*) The heart, lungs, or liver dressed with other intestines.

A عصيّة *ɛusayyat*, (dim. of عصا *ɛasaʼ*) A little staff, stick, wand, rod, or switch. Name of an offset of a tribe.

A عصيد *ɛisyad*, Infamous, suspected, abhorred.

A عصيدة *ɛasīdat*, Broth, so thick that it can scarcely be stirred with a ladle. A kind of sweetcake, generally given to friends on the birth of a child.

A عصير *ʻaṣīr*, Squeezed. Expressed juice. Juice pressed from grapes. عصير معدني *ʻaṣīri maʻdanī*, Mineral juices or essences.

A عصيرة *ʻaṣīrat*, Expressed juice.

A عصيفة *ʻaṣīfat*, The blade or broad leaf when containing the ear of corn.

A عصيفر *ʻuṣayfir*, (dim. of عصفور) A little sparrow.

A عصيفرة *ʻuṣayfirat*, The yellow violet.

A عصيفير *ʻuṣayfīr*, (dim. of عصفور *ʻuṣfūr*) A little sparrow.

A عصيم *ʻaṣīm*, Remains, vestiges. Marks of pitch, remains of privet or tincture on the hands or feet. Black hair growing under a camel's coat. Sweat, urine, and filth adhering to a camel's thighs.

A عضّ *ʻazz*, (v. n. of عضّ) Seizing between the teeth, or holding by the tongue. Being shrewd and clever. Severity (of the times or of war). *ʻizz*, (pl. عضوض *ʻuzūz*) Cunning, clever, shrewd (man). Provident, attentive (to matters of property). Eloquent. Strong, able to travel. عضّ سفر *ʻizzu safarin*, Able to travel. عضّ مال *ʻizzu mālin*, An able manager of live stock. Bad-tempered. A rival. A miser. (A lock) difficult to be opened. *ʻizz* or *ʻuzz*, (pl. اعضاض *aʻzāz*) A dwarf thorny shrub eaten by camels. *ʻuzz*, Food which in towns they give to camels (as sesame-grains after the oil is expressed, or the broken macerated stones of dates). Dough with which they feed camels. Clover. Barley. Wheat. A date-stone. A rough, rugged tree remaining in the ground. Firewood. Dry grass.

A عضاب *ʻizāb*, (v. n. 3 of عضب) Repelling.

A عضّاب *ʻazzāb*, An abuser, reviler, railer.

A عضات *ʻazāt*, Any thorny tree.

A عضاد *ʻazād*, Short, compact, powerfully-built (youth). Thick and unsightly about the upper part of the arm (a woman). Short, squab (man or woman). *ʻizād*, (v. n. 3 of عضد) Helping each other. An ornament for the arm, an armlet. A hook or bill with which a herdsman pulls down branches to feed camels. A mark branded on the arm of a camel. *ʻuzād*, Short, square-built (youth). (A woman) whose upper arm is thick and ugly.

A عضادة *ʻizādat*, Side-post of a gate or door. عضادتا الباب *ʻizādatā'l bāb*, The two jambs of a door. *ʻuzādat*, Ugly and thick-armed (woman).

A عضاديّ *ʻaz, ʻiz,* or *ʻuzādiy*, One who has big arms (عضد *ʻazud*) from the shoulder to the elbow.

A عضارس *ʻazāris*, (pl. of عضرس *ʻazras* and عضارس *ʻuzāris*) Hails. *ʻuzāris*, Hail. Snow. Cold water. A wild ass. Cold. See عضرس *ʻazras*.

A عضارط *ʻazārit*, (pl. of عضرط *ʻuzrut*) Hired labourers. *ʻuzārit*, A hired labourer.

A عضارطة *ʻazāritat*, Hired labourers.

A عضارطيّ *ʻuzāritiy*, Flabby female parts. Podex.

A عضارف *ʻazārif*, (pl. of عضرفوط *ʻazrafūt*) Male animals on which the demons are said to ride.

A عضاريط *ʻazārīt*, Veins in the arm-pits. (pl. of عضروط *ʻuzrūt*) Hired labourers.

A عضاض *ʻazāz*, Thick (tree). Whatever may be taken in the teeth and eaten. ما ذقت عضاضا *mā zuktu ʻazāzan*, I have not tasted aught. *ʻizāz*, (v. n. 3 of عضّ) Biting one another. A habit of biting in a horse. Living, life. Scarcity. (pl. of عضوض *ʻazūz*) Deep wells. عضاض عيش *ʻizāzu ʻayshin*, Patient under misfortune. *ʻuzāz*, (or عضّاض *ʻuzzāz*) The root of the nose, the part next the eyebrow.

A عضاضيّ *ʻuzāziy*, Fatted, saginated (camel). Soft, tender, delicate (man).

A عضافج *ʻuzāfij*, Hard, strong, thick, and fat.

A عضال *ʻuzāl*, Troublesome, serious, or important (business). Strong (ring). Difficult to be cured (disease).

A عضام *ʻizām*, The rump-bone (of a horse or camel). (pl. of عضم *ʻazm*) Handles or middles of bows.

A عضامين *ʻazāmīn*, Old camels.

A عضّان *ʻizzāni*, Name of two individuals proverbial in their day for their sound knowledge.

A عضاهة *ʻizāhat*, (pl. عضاه *ʻizāh*, عضون *ʻizūn*, عضوات) A thorny shrub on which camels feed.

A عضاهيّ *ʻizāhiy*, A camel feeding on this plant.

P عضايت *ʻazāyat*, A kind of green lizard.

A عضب *ʻazb*, (v. n. of عضب) Reproaching, reviling. Striking. Piercing. Cutting off. Weakening. Returning. Taking, receiving. Slitting (a camel's ear). Having one horn broken, or having a slit ear (a sheep). Breaking the horn (of a sheep). Virulent-tongued (man). Smooth-tongued (man). A sharp sword. A light-headed, volatile youth. A calf beginning to have horns.

A عضباء *ʻazbā*, (fem. of اعضب *aʻzab*) Broken-horned (sheep). Slit-eared (camel or sheep). (A mare) having above a fourth part cut off the ears. Short-handed (woman). Name of a camel which belonged to Muhammad.

A عضبار *ʻizbār*, A small millstone. A stone whereon a fuller cleans clothes.

A عضبرة *ʻazburat*, (v. n. of عضبر Q) Being bold as a lion (a dog).

A عضبل *ʻazbal*, Hard.

A عضة *ʻizat*, (pl. عضون *ʻizūn* or عضوات *ʻizawāt*) A multitude. A section. A lie. Thorny shrubs.

A عضّة *ʻazzat*, A bite.

A عضد *ʻazd*, (v. n. of عضد) Helping, aiding. Binding a thing on one's upper arm. Being strong in the upper arm. Seizing (a she-camel) by the upper arm, and forcing (her) to lie down (a male camel). Striking, wounding, or taking in the arm. Wounding (a camel's) arm (the saddle قتب *katab*). Cutting or felling (a tree) with the instrument called معضد *miʻzad*. Approaching the arms of camels and tying them one to another. A tall palm-tree. A side, quarter, tract, coast. *ʻazd, ʻuzd, ʻizd, ʻazid, ʻazud,* or *ʻuzud*, An arm (from the shoulder to the elbow; or the corresponding part in a quadruped). فتّ في عضده *fatta fī ʻazudihi*, He frustrated the plans of his allies and scattered them. *ʻazd* or *ʻazud*, (pl. اعضاد *aʻzād*) A companion, an assistant. *ʻazad*, (v. n. of عضد) Being diseased in the upper arm (a camel). A beating pain or disease in the upper arm; or in the corresponding part of the fore-leg of a beast. Cut (tree). *ʻazid*, One who approaches the side-post of a well. One who complains of a pain in the arm. An ass that hugs the sides of the female when covering. Short-armed.

A عضدان *ʻizdān*, (pl. of عضيد) Tall palm-trees.

A عضدة *ʻazidat*, A hand, *i.e.* the whole arm whose عضد *ʻazud* (or upper arm) is short.

A عضر *ʻazr*, (v. n. of عضر) Speaking, uttering (not a word). Name of a tribe in Yaman.

A عضرة *ʻazrat*, News, intelligence, information.

A عضرس *ʻazras*, (pl. عضارس *ʻazāris*) Hail. Cold. Snow. Cold and sweet water. A wild ass, an onager. A leaf wet with morning-dew, or adhering to a stone soaking in water. Grass of a bright green colour bearing much dew. *ʻizris*, Wild mallows.

A عضرط *ʻazrat* or *ʻizrit*, The podex. *ʻizrit*, The rump-bone. The perinæum, or seam which connects the anus and scrotum. *ʻuzrut*, A mercenary, hired labourer, one who works for his victuals. (pl. عضارط *ʻazārit*) Mean, base, worthless.

A عضرفوط *ʻazrafūt*, (pl. عضارف *ʻazārif*) A male animal larger than a lizard, on which they believe the demons ride. A white worm, to which a maiden's fingers are compared.

A عضروط *ʻuzrūt*, (pl. عضاريط *ʻazārīt* also عضارطة *ʻazāritat*) A hired servant. Mean, base, worthless. The gullet, or the head of it.

A عضز *ʻazz*, (v. n. of عضز) Hindering, preventing. Chewing. (The school of Basra refuses to acknowledge this root).

A عضض *ʻuzaz*, (pl. of عضوض) Deep (wells).

A عضط *ʻazt*, (v. n. of عضط) Stooling in coitu.

A عضعضة *ʻazʻazat*, (v. n. of عضعض Q) Biting.

A عضفوط *ʻuzfūt*, Name of an animal whereon demons are said to ride.

A عضل *ʻazl*, (v. n. of عضل) Hemming in, reducing to straits. Being troublesome and difficult (business). *ʻazl* or *ʻizl*, (v. n. of عضل) Preventing (a kinswoman, a widow) from marrying. *ʻizl*, A deep, designing, malicious fellow. *ʻuzl*, (pl. of عضلة *ʻuzlat*) Misfortunes. *ʻazal*, (v. n. of عضل) Being muscular (a man). (pl. عضلات *ʻazalāt* and عضلان *ʻizlān* or *ʻuzlān*) A field-mouse. (pl. of عضلة *ʻazalat*) Muscles. *ʻazil* or *ʻazul*, Muscular (arm). *ʻuzal*, A field-mouse. (pl. of عضلة *ʻuzlat*) Misfortunes. انّه لعضلة من العضل *innahu la ʻuzlat mini'l ʻuzal*, It is a misfortune of misfortunes.

A عضلان *ʻizlān*, (v. n. of عضل) Tyrannically preventing (a woman) from marrying. *ʻuzlān* or ƹizlān, (pl. of عضل ƹazal) Field-mice.

A عضلة ƹuzlat, (pl. عضل ƹuzal and ƹuzl) Misfortune. ƹazalat, A muscle.

P عضله ناك ƹazalanāk, Muscular.

A عضم ƹazm, The plough-tail. The shelve board of a plough, at the end of which the share is fixed. (pl. اعضمة aƹzimat and عضم ƹuzm) A pronged implement for winnowing corn. A mountain-goat. A streak in a mountain of a different colour from the rest. Rump-bone, root of the tail of horse or camel. (pl. عضام ƹizām) Handle or middle part of a bow.

A عضمجة ƹazmajat, A bitch-fox, a vixen.

A عضمّر ƹazammar, Avaricious, narrow-minded, bad-tempered.

A عضمّز ƹazammaz, (fem. عضمّزة ƹazammazat) A lion. Strong. Covetous.

A عضمّزة ƹazammazat, An old woman with large teeth and a hideous appearance; also short, deformed, and sly. A woman, the corners of whose mouth are thick.

A عضمور ƹuzmūr, A water-wheel. A wheel at a well. A bucket.

A عضنّك ƹazannak, Thick. Strong. ƹazannak, (or عضنّكة ƹazannakat) Large and fleshy (female parts). Plump-thighed (woman).

A عضنّكة ƹazannakat, Fleshy, flabby (woman).

A عضو ƹazw, (v. n. of عضا for عضو) Cutting in pieces, dissecting, dismembering. ƹizw or ƹuzw, (pl. اعضاء aƹzāʼ) A member, limb, joint.

A عضوّ ƹuzūw, A being well-clad, in good circumstances, and passing the time agreeably.

A عضوات ƹizwāt, Certain thorny trees.

A عضوبة ƹuzūbat, (v. n. of عضب) Being sharp and reproachful (tongue). Having a smooth, flattering tongue. Being sharp (a sword).

A عضوبر ƹazawbar, Thick, gross, large, corpulent. A huge stone for breaking rocks. A he-wolf.

A عضوبرة ƹazawbarat, A she-wolf.

A عضوض ƹazūz, (pl. عضض ƹuzaz and عضاض ƹizāz) Whatever may be taken in the teeth and eaten. Biting (horse). Adverse (fortune). Deep and abundant in water. A string sticking close to the belly of a bow. Narrow (woman). A kingdom wherein oppression is rife. ƹuzūz, (pl. of عضّ ƹuzz) Shrewd, cunning. Strong, able.

A عضوم ƹazūm, A hardy she-camel.

A عضون ƹizūn, (pl. of عضة ƹizat) Crowds. Sects. Sections. Lies. Thorny trees.

A عضه ƹazh or ƹazah, (v. n. of عضه) Cutting the tree عضاه ƹizāh. Feeding on it (a camel). Lying, deceiving. Accusing falsely. Enchanting. Suspecting. ƹazah, (v. n. of عضه) Being indisposed from feeding on the thorny tree عضاه ƹizāh (a camel). ƹazih, A camel feeding on the thorny plant عضاه ƹizāh. ƹizah, A lie, false pretence, groundless accusation. Magic, sorcery. ƹizah, (or عضهة ƹizahat) A thorny kind of tree.

A عضهة ƹizhat, (v. n. of عضه) Lying. False accusation. Sorcery. ƹazihat, A she-camel feeding on the thorny plant عضاه ƹizāh. (A country) abounding in such plants.

A عضهلة ƹazhalat, (v. n. of عضهل Q) Stopping (the mouth of a flask).

A عضويّ ƹazawīy, (or عضهيّ ƹizahīy) A camel feeding on the plant عضاه ƹizāh. ƹazawīy, Pertaining to the members. Membered.

A عضيد ƹazīd, (pl. عضدان ƹizdān) A tall palm-tree. A palm-tree within arm's reach.

A عضيرف ƹuzayrif, (and عضيريف ƹuzayrīf) (dim. of عضرفوط ƹazrafūt) A small animal on which they believe a demon rides.

A عضيض ƹazīz, (v. n. of عضّ) Taking in the teeth, or holding by the tongue. Sticking close (to a friend). Biting hard. Affliction, calamity. A hard bite. A cotemporary, compeer; same-aged, of the same age.

A عضيلّ ƹizyall, Mean, sordid, avaricious.

A عضيلة ƹazīlat, A muscle.

A عضين ƹizīn, Magic, enchantment.

A عضيوط ƹizyawt. (See عذيوط ƹizyawt).

A عضيهة ƹazīhat, (v. n. of عضه) Lying. Cutting the thorny tree عضاه ƹizāh. A lie, false accusation. Sorcery. A country abounding in the thorny plant عضاه ƹizāh.

A عطّ ƹatt, (v. n. of عطّ) Tearing (a garment). Tearing (a shirt) lengthwise without separating. Throwing down. Overcoming, conquering.

A عطا ƹataʼ, (or عطاء ƹatāʼ) (v. n. of عطا for عطو) Giving. (pl. اعطية aƹtiyat) A present, gift, donation, favour. عطاي كبري ƹatāyi kubraʼ, The great gift, *i. e.* The age of 120 years. P عطا كردن ƹatā kardan, To give, confer a benefit, present.

A عطاء ƹitāʼ, (v. n. 3 of عطا for عطو) Labouring for, serving. Submitting. Giving.

P عطا بخش ƹatā-bakhsh, Giving presents, liberal, munificent. عطا بخش و كرم گستر ƹatā-bakhsh u karam-gustar, Bestowing benefits, and diffusing liberality.

A عطابل ƹatābil, (or عطابيل ƹatābīl) (pl. of عطبول ƹutbūl) Beautiful (women).

A عطّار ƹattār, (fem. عطّارة ƹattārat) A dealer in perfumes, drugs, spices, or groceries.

A عطارة ƹitārat, The profession of a perfumer, druggist, or grocer. Perfumery.

A عطّارة ƹattārat, Excellent (she-camel) and vendible in the market.

A عطارد ƹutārid, The planet Mercury (whose orbit is in the second heaven). Quicksilver.

P عطارد نصاب ƹutārid-nisāb, In rank, Mercury.

A عطّاري ƹattārī, The business of a perfumer.

A عطاس ƹutās, (v. n. of عطس) Breaking forth (the dawn). Dying. Sneezing. Aurora, dawn.

A عطّاس ƹattās, A sneezer.

A عطاش ƹitāsh, (pl. of عطشان ƹatshān and of عطشى ƹatshaʼ) Thirsty. ƹutāsh, A disease in which the thirst cannot be quenched. Intensity of thirst.

A عطاشى ƹatāshaʼ, (pl. of عطشان) Thirsty.

A عطاط ƹatāt, A bold or strong man. A lion. Corpulent.

A عطاف ƹitāf, (v. n. 3 of عطف) Shewing kindness. (pl. عطف ƹutf) A loose upper garment wrapped round the body. A sword.

A عطّاف ƹattāf, Much bent. One who makes repeated attacks and charges. A trap or gin made of a bent stick, a springe. A successful arrow. An arrow which neither brings profit or loss.

A عطامس ƹatāmis, (or عطاميس ƹatāmīs) (pl. of عيطموس ƹaytamūs) Beautiful, elegant, completely-formed (women).

A عطان ƹitān, Dung or salt rubbed on a hide to season it, and preserve it from rotting and stinking.

A عطّان ƹuttān, Persons who halt near a watering-place.

A عطايا ƹatāyaʼ, (pl. of عطيّة ƹatiyat) Gifts.

A عطب ƹatb, (v. n. of عطب) Being soft (cotton). Softness of cotton. ƹutb or ƹutub, Cotton. ƹatab, (v. n. of عطب) Perishing. Breaking down (a camel or horse). Destruction.

A عطبة ƹutbat, A bit of cotton or burnt cloth.

A عطبل ƹutbul, Beautiful, well-formed, full of flesh, and long-necked (girl).

A عطبول ƹutbūl, (or عطبولة ƹutbūlat, (pl. عطابل ƹatābil, or عطابيل ƹatābīl) Beautiful, well-formed.

A عطر ƹitr, (pl. عطور ƹutūr) Odour, perfume, fragrance, otto, attar, ottar (of roses). عطر مثلّث ƹitri musallasi, A composition of musk, ambergris, camphor, and oil of ban-nuts. ƹatir, Smelling well, fragrant, aromatic. Perfumed, scented (man). ƹutur, (pl. of عاطر ƹātir) Persons fond of perfumes.

A عطرة ƹatirat, (fem. of عطر ƹatir) Perfumed (woman). Excellent and vendible (she-camel).

A عطرّد ƹatarrad, Long (day or rope). Noble, generous (man). Open (road). Sharp (spear). Entire (year). A quick step. Difficult, troublesome (affair).

P عطردان ƹitrdān, A scent-box.

A عطردة ƹatradat, (v. n. of عطرد Q) Preserving, keeping. Making preparation, providing necessary apparatus.

P عطرسا ƹitrsā, Fragrant, odoriferous.

A عطرم ƹitrim, Lions' dung.

A عطرود ƹutrūd, Arms, apparatus, equipment.

A عطريّ ƹitrīy, Perfumed, scented.

A عطريّات ƹitrīyāt, Perfumes, scents.

A عطس ƹats, (v. n. of عطس) Sneezing. Breaking forth (as the dawn). Dying. عطست به اللجم ƹatasat bihiʼl lujamu, He died.

A عطسة ƹatsat, A sneeze. Similar to another in form or temper. فلان عطسة فلان fulān ƹatsatu fulānin, So-and-so (is) the very image of so-and-so. P عطسهٔ چاه ƹatsaʼi chāh, Echo from a well. عطسه زدن *ʿatsa zadan* (or دادن *dādan*), To sneeze. عطسهٔ شب *ʿatsaʾi shab*, Break of day. A عطسهٔ صبح *ʿatsaʾi subh*, The sun. P عطسهٔ عنبرین *ʿatsaʾi ʿambarīn*, A fragrant scent.

A عطش *ʿatsh*, (v. n. of عطش) Exceeding, beating in thirst. *ʿatash*, (v. n. of عطش) Thirsting. Thirst. *ʿatish*, Thirsty, parched (place). *ʿatish* or *ʿatush*, Thirsty.

A عطشان *ʿatshān*, (pl. عطشی *ʿatsha'*, عطاشیٰ *ʿatāsha'*, and عطاش *ʿitāsh*) Thirsty, parched with drought. Consumed with desire. عطشان نطشان *ʿatshān natshān*, Thirsty to excess.

P عطشان *ʿatashān*, Name of a thorny tree.

A عطشانة *ʿatshānat*, (pl. عطشانات *ʿatshānāt*) Thirsty (woman).

A عطشة *ʿatishat*, Thirsty (woman).

A عطشی *ʿatsha'*, (fem. of عطشان *ʿatshān*) Very thirsty (woman). (pl. of عطشان *ʿatshān*) Thirsty.

A عطط *ʿutut*, Sheets cut ready for sewing.

A عطعط *ʿutʿut*, A yearling lamb: a kid: an ass colt.

A عطعطة *ʿatʿatat*, (v. n. of عطعط Q) Making a confused noise, as in battle or in a tumult, or in beating and winning, calling out عیط عیط *ʿīt ʿīt*.

A عطف *ʿatf*, (v. n. of عطف) Inclining. Being propitious, favourably disposed towards. Turning. Bending (a stick). Folding, doubling (a pillow). Connecting by a copulative conjunction, as و or ف. Rushing upon. Inclination. Conversion. Favour, affection. Departure. A copulative conjunction. A present, bounty. The horn of a bow, or the notch into which the string goes. عطف بیان *ʿatfi bayān*, A copulative conjunction. عطف تفسیر *ʿatfi tafsīr*, An explicative conjunction (connecting several synonymous or explanatory words). P عطف داشتن *ʿatf dāshtan*, To have an affection, to be propitious or favourable. عطف عنان کردن *ʿatfi ʿinān kardan*, (or عطف زمام کردن *ʿatfi zimām kardan*) To turn the reins towards. عطف گردن *ʿatfi gardan*, A turning of the head either in coquetry or in anger. A حرف عطف *harfi ʿatf*, A copulative conjunction. *ʿitf*, Side. Arm-pit. ثنّی عطفه عنه *sanna' ʿitfahu ʿanhu*, He turned from him. ینظر فی عطفیه *yanzuru fī ʿitfayhi*, He admires himself. جاء ثانی عطفه *jāʾa sānī ʿitfihi*, He came free and cheerful. He came bending the neck, proud, and disdainful. *ʿitf* or *ʿatf*, The highest part of a road. *ʿutf*, (pl. of عاطف *ʿātif* and عطوف *ʿatūf*) Favourably inclined. (pl. of عطاف *ʿitāf*) Loose upper garments thrown over the body. *ʿataf*, Length of eyelids.

A عطفة *ʿatfat* or *ʿitfat*, Small beads or shells hung by women round their necks as a charm to gain the affections of their lovers. An alley. A tree to which a vine-tendril hangs. *ʿitfat*, Goats'-vine. Pendulous extremities of a vine. Ivy. *ʿatafat*, A kind of plant, without leaf or branch, encircling trees.

P عطفل *ʿatfal*, A kind of willow.

A عطل *ʿutl*, Stringless (bow). *ʿutl* or *ʿutul*, Poor, indigent (man). Ill-mannered. *ʿutul*, (pl. عطّل *ʿuttal* and اعطال *aʿtāl*) Unornamented, without bracelets (a woman). *ʿatal*, (v. n. of عطل) Being without a necklace or other ornaments (a woman). Being empty and vacant. Being in need (of wealth). Having a big belly, being fat. Wanting manners. (pl. اعطال *aʿtāl*) Any thing standing up erect. Stature, figure, body. The neck. A cluster of dates. *ʿutul*, (pl. اعطال *aʿtāl*) (A camel or horse) without any thing round their neck, or any distinguishing mark. Unarmed (man). Stringless (bow).

A عطلة *ʿutlat*, Idleness, absence of employment, omission, or slackness of business. The absence of female ornaments. *ʿatilat*, Beautifully-shaped, and choice (she-camel). Rich in milk (a camel or sheep). (A bucket) whose rope or handle is broken (and therefore useless). سین عطلة *sīn ʿatilat*, س *sīn* without diacritical points.

A عطلس *ʿatallas*, Long, tall.

A عطم *ʿutm*, Plucked wool. Coloured wool. *ʿutum*, (pl. of عاطم *ʿātim* and عطیم) Perishing.

A عطموس *ʿutmūs*, Beautiful, young, and barren (female).

A عطن *ʿatn*, (v. n. of عطن) Macerating (hides) with dung, salt, and the plant علقیٰ *ʿalka'*, or burying (them) to soften and take off the hair. *ʿatan*, (v. n. of عطن) Stinking (skins). Being thrown into a pit, or after having been wet being buried, to fetch off the hair (a hide). (pl. اعطان *aʿtān*) A place near a well where camels recline after drinking. A sheep-cote near water. One's native soil. رحب العطن *rahbuʾl ʿatan*, Wealthy. Liberal. Powerful. ضربوا بعطن *zarabū bi ʿatanin*, They drank their fill, and then remained near the cistern. ضربت الابل بعطن *zarabatiʾl ibl bi ʿatanin*, The camels reclined upon bended knees. واسع العطن و البلد *wāsiʿuʾl ʿatan waʾl balad*, Liberal, munificent.

A عطنة *ʿatanat*, The lying down of camels; also people who halt near a watering-place.

A عطو *ʿatw*, (v. n. of عطا for عطو) Receiving in the hand; raising the head or hands when taking any thing. Overcoming, conquering in giving. *ʿatw*, *ʿitw*, *ʿutw*, عطوّ *ʿatūw*, (A wild buck) that stretches out his neck to reach something from a tree.

A عطوب *ʿutūb*, Softness of cotton.

A عطوّد *ʿatawwad*, A quick step. Wide, open (road). Noble, generous (man). Difficult, troublesome, perplexing. Long (day or rope). Sharp (spear). Entire (year). یوما عطوّدا *yawman ʿatawwadan*, The whole day: an entire day.

A عطور *ʿutūr*, (pl. of عطر *ʿitr*) Odours, perfumes, ottars, ottos, attars.

A لجم العطوس *lujamuʾl ʿatūs*, Death.

P عطوسی *ʿatūsī*, Snuff.

A عطوف *ʿatūf*, (pl. عطف *ʿutf*) Favourable, well-affected. A she-camel which is induced to take a liking to a بوّ *bavv* (q. v.), and to part with her milk freely. A trap or gin formed of a bent stick, a springe. A successful gaming arrow. An arrow which brings no luck, good or bad. An arrow which is shot time after time. A sheet, mantle.

A عطوفة *ʿatufat* or *ʿutūfat*, Inclination. Affection, favour. P عطوفت پدریه *ʿutūfati pidariya*, Fatherly affection.

A عطول *ʿutūl*, (v. n. of عطل) Being without a necklace or other ornaments (a woman).

A عطون *ʿatūn*, A camel, male or female lying down after having drunk their fill. *ʿutūn*, (v. n. of عطن) Lying down after drinking to their fill (camels). Camels thus laid down. People who halt near a watering-place.

A عطوی *ʿatwa'*, (A bow) which discharges arrows easily; easy, flexible (bow).

A عطیّ *ʿutayy*, (dim. of عطاء) A small gift.

A عطیّة *ʿatiyat*, (pl. عطایا *ʿatāya'*) A gift.

A عطیّد *ʿatayyad*, A quick step. Wide, open (road). Noble, generous (man). Difficult, troublesome, perplexing. Long (day or rope). Sharp (spear). Entire (year).

A عطیف *ʿatīf*, Gentle, mild, docile (woman).

A عطیل *ʿatīl*, A long branch of a palm-tree.

A عطیم *ʿatīm*, (pl. عطم *ʿutum*) Perishing.

A عطین *ʿatīn*, Macerated with dung and salt to strip off the hair (a hide). Stinking (man or hide).

A عطینة *ʿatīnat*, Stinking (man).

A عظّ *ʿazz*, (v. n. of عظّ) Distressing one (war). Throwing down, causing to cleave to the ground.

A عظا *ʿaza'*, (v. n. of عظی) Having a swollen belly from eating the herb عنظوان *ʿunzuwān*.

A عظاء *ʿizāʾ*, (pl. of عظایة *ʿizāyat*) Certain reptiles larger than lizards.

A عظاءة *ʿazāʾat*, (pl. عظاء *ʿazāʾ* or *ʿizāʾ*) An animal larger than a lizard.

A عظارة *ʿizārat*, Repletion with wine, fulness of drink.

A عظاری *ʿazāra'*, Male locusts.

A عظاظ *ʿizāz*, (v. n. 3 of عظّ) Biting one another. Calling one another bad names. Vehemence, intrepidity in battle. Difficulty, trouble.

A عظال *ʿizāl*, (v. n. 3 of عظل) Sticking together (dogs or locusts). Inserting the verses of another amongst one's own. Repetition, reiteration.

A عظام *ʿizām*, (pl. of عظم *ʿazm*) Bones. عظام رمیم *ʿizāmi ramīm*, Dry, carious bones. (pl. of عظیم *ʿazīm*) Great. *ʿuzām*, (or عظّام *ʿuzzām*) Great.

A عظامة *ʿazāmat*, (v. n. of عظم) Being great. *ʿizāmat*, (pl. of عظم *ʿazm*) Bones. A cushion, or any thing similar, with which women shew a false prominence about the hips.

A عظّامة *ʿuzzāmat*, A cushion with which women give a false prominency to the hips. Pomp, pride, grandeur.

A عظاية ɛizāyat or ɛazāyat, (pl. عظاء ɛizāɛ or ɛazāɛ) An animal larger than a lizard.

A عظائم ɛazāɛim, Great, mighty things.

A عظب ɛazb, (v. n. of عظب) Adhering to one with patience and perseverance. Wagging the tail briskly (a bird). Managing properly (cattle or any other estate). ɛazab, (v. n. of عضب) Being fat, corpulent. Adhering with patience and perseverance. Growing hard from labour (the hands). ɛazib, One who alights in a dry and sandy place.

A عظة ɛizat, (v. n. of وعظ) Admonishing, exhorting. Admonition, exhortation, preaching.

A عظّة ɛazzat, Vehemence, intrepidity in battle.

A عظر ɛazar, (v. n. of عظر) Loathing, abhorring. Filling (a leathern bottle). Pregnancy. A fœtus. عرق العظر ɛirku'l ɛazar, A certain vein which prevents a she-camel from bearing. ɛuzur, (pl. of عظور ɛazūr) Filled with wine.

A عظرب ɛizrib, A small viper.

A عظرة ɛazirat, (A camel) taking the male and conceiving. A camel which does not conceive.

A عظرم ɛizrim, The dung of a lion.

A عظعاظ ɛizɛāz, (and عظعظة ɛazɛazat) (v. n. of عظعظ Q) Wavering, going with a zig-zag motion, or turning in the flight (an arrow). Retiring from battle, swerving through cowardice. Going up (a hill). Wagging the tail and travelling uneasily.

A عظل ɛazl, (v. n. of عظل) Sticking fast together (dogs or locusts). ɛuzul, A pathic. Persons suspected of vicious and unnatural propensities.

A عظلام ɛizlām, Dark-coloured dust.

A عظلم ɛizlim, The juice of woad or the indigo-plant. A dark night.

A عظلمة ɛazlamat, Darkness.

A عظلى ɛazla', (pl. of عاظل ɛāzil) (Locusts) sticking together, riding one another.

A عظم ɛazm, (v. n. of عظم) Giving (a dog) a bone. Striking the bone (of a man). A plough-tail. The naked timbers of a camel's saddle. (pl. اعظم aɛzum, عظام ɛizām, and عظامة ɛizāmat) A bone. عظم وضّاح ɛazmu wazzāhin, A kind of game. ɛuzm, Magnitude, greatness. Pride. A vast crowd, numerous assemblage. ɛuzm or ɛazm, The principal or major part of any thing. عظم البطن بطنك ɛuzma'l batnu batnuka, Ha! your belly is very prominent! ɛazam, The middle of the road: an open, spacious road. ɛizam, (v. n. of عظم) Being great. Being grievous, pressing sorely. Magnificence. Bigness, magnitude.

A عظماء ɛuzamāɛ, (pl. of عظيم ɛazīm) Grandees.

A عظمات ɛazamāt, Princes, lords, leaders.

A عظمة ɛazmat, (v. n. of عظم) Thrashing, belabouring the bones. ɛuzmat, A cushion, or any thing similar, with which women shew a false prominence round the hips. ɛazamat, (or عظموت ɛazamūt) Magnitude, magnificence, pride, pomp, grandeur. The largest elbow-bone, the muscular part of the arm nearest the elbow. Thickness of tongue, or the thick of the arm. ɛazimat, A female that longs for a large penis.

A عظمى ɛazma', A sort of pigeon inclining to white. ɛuzma', (fem. of اعظم aɛzam) Greatest, most supreme. وزارت عظمى wizārati ɛuzma', The grand-vazirship, the dignity of prime-minister.

A عظو ɛazw, (v. n. of عظا for عظو) Grieving, saddening. Doing evil. Assaulting, attacking suddenly, overcoming and destroying. Poisoning. Diverting, turning one away (from good). Traducing, slandering, inveighing against the absent.

A عظوب ɛuzūb, (v. n. of عظب) Adhering with patience and perseverance. Wagging the tail briskly (a bird). Managing properly (cattle or any other estate). Becoming dry (the skin). Growing hard from labour (the hands). Becoming fat.

A عظور ɛuzūr, Filled (with wine or drink).

A عظي ɛazi, (or عظيان ɛazyān) Swollen from eating the plant عنظوان ɛunzuwān (a camel).

A عظيبّ ɛizyabb, Large, robust, or big-bodied. Of a bad disposition.

A عظير ɛizyar, (or عظيرّ ɛizyarr) Short, thick, strong. Bad-tempered. Ugly.

A عظيم ɛazīm, (pl. عظام ɛizām and عظماء ɛuzamāɛ) Great, large, much. Grand, magnificent, glorious. High in quality or dignity, much esteemed. Grave, serious. Fat. Severe (punishment). An epithet of God. عظيم القدر ɛazīmu'l kadar, High in rank. ɛuzaym, (dim. of عظم ɛazm) A small bone. عظيم وضّاح ɛuzaymu wazzāhin, A kind of game.

P عظيم آباد ɛazīm-ābād, Patna, capital of Bahār.

A عظيمة ɛazīmat, (pl. عظائم ɛazāɛim) A sore calamity. An important affair, extraordinary event.

A عظيوط ɛizyawt. (See عذيوط ɛizyawt.)

A عظيوطة ɛizyawtat, The female jerboa.

A عفّ ɛaff, (v. n. of عفّ) Abstaining from what is unlawful. Remaining in the udder (milk). Abstinence, chastity. Chaste, abstaining from what is forbidden.

A عفا ɛafa', An ass's colt. Untrodden ground, uninhabited, and without the trace of a building. ɛifa', An ass's colt.

A عفاء ɛafāɛ, (v. n. of عفا for عفو) Perishing (a vestige). Obliterating, effacing (vestiges). Being clear and undisturbed (water). Surpassing, getting beyond (in learning). Covering the ground (plants). Shearing (wool). Obliteration. Decay, ruin. Dust, earth. Any thing white on the pupil of the eye. An ass's colt. Rain. ɛifāɛ, An ass's colt. A multitude, luxuriancy of ostrich-feathers, abundance of camels' hair. (pl. of عفو ɛifw) Asses' colts. ابو العفاء abū'l ɛifāɛ, An ass.

A عفاة ɛufāt, (pl. of عافي ɛāfī) Askers of favours. Guests. كثير العفاة kasīru'l ɛufāt, One who entertains many guests.

A عفار ɛafār, A species of tree, which easily kindles, used for striking a fire. The fecundation of the female palm-tree by sprinkling over it the male flowers. Meal of wheat or barley without any admixture of sweets. Dry bread, *i. e.* without meat. ɛifār, (pl. of عفر ɛufr) Strong, robust, valiant.

A عفّار ɛaffār, One who fecundates a palm-tree.

A عفارة ɛafārat, Detestable, malicious cunning. Impurity.

A عفاري ɛafāra', (pl. of عفرية) Cocks' feathers.

A عفاريّ ɛufāriy, Excellent (spear-head).

A عفاريات ɛufāriyāt, Certain dams or weirs in the valley of عقيق ɛakīk.

A عفارية ɛufāriyat, A sly, wicked, and dangerous man. Strong (lion).

A عفاريت ɛafārīt, (pl. of عفريت ɛifrīt) Horrible demons or giants. عفاريت الجنّ واقاعي مسموم السنّ ɛafārītu'l jinn, wa afāɛīɛi masmūmu's sinn, Dreadful demons and vipers with envenomed teeth.

P عفاريت آثار ɛafārīt-āsār, Diabolical in acts.

A عفاز ɛafāz, A walnut.

A عفازة ɛafāzat, A hill, heap, tumulus. ɛufāzat, The fruit of the cotton-plant.

A عفاس ɛifās, Corruption, wickedness, villainy.

A عفاش ɛufāsh, Thick-bearded (man).

A عفاشة ɛufāshat, A mob, crowd. Good-for-nothing people.

A عفاص ɛifās, A little purse of leather or cloth for holding petty cash. A small strap of leather, with which they fasten the mouth of a bottle. The cover of a flask.

A عفاضج ɛufāzij, Thick, corpulent, soft.

A عفّاط ɛaffāt, (or عفاطيّ ɛifātiy) A stutterer.

A عفّاطة ɛuffātat, A shepherdess.

A عفاف ɛafāf, (or عفافة ɛafāfat) (v. n. of عفّ) Abstaining (from what is forbidden). Chastity, continence. عفاف الحبّ ɛafāfu'l hubb, Chaste love. ɛifāf, Medicine, remedy.

A عفافة ɛufāfat, Milk left in the udder.

A عفاق ɛifāk, (v. n. 3 of عفق) Coaxing, deceiving, circumventing. Applying remedies. Ravaging a flock (a wolf). Frequency in milking. Rapidity in travelling.

A عفّاقة ɛaffākat, Podex. كذبت عفّاقته kazabat ɛaffākatuhu, He broke wind.

A عفال ɛafāli, A term of reproach to a woman.

A عفّان ɛaffān, Name of the father of the caliph عثمان ɛusmān. ɛiffān, Time, season. على عفّانه ɛala' ɛiffānihi, In good time; seasonably.

A عفانش ɛufānish, Thick-bearded (man).

A عفاوة ɛa, ɛi, or ɛufāwat, The fat of broth. ɛufāwat, Broth which remains in the kettle, as the hire paid to the person from whom it is borrowed. Food which children send as a present.

A عفاهم ɛufāhim, Strong and active (she-camel). Affluence, enjoyment of life. Hard running.

A عفاهن ɛufāhin, Strong and active (she-camel).

A عفاهية ɛufāhiyat, Thick, large, bulky

A عفائف ʿafāʾif, (pl. of عفيفة) Chaste matrons.

A عفّة ʿaffat, A modest woman. ʿiffat, (v. n. of عفّ) Abstaining (from what is unlawful). Chastity, continence, purity, abstinence, modesty, virtue. اهل عفّت ahli ʿiffat, Chaste. ʿuffat, Milk remaining in the udder. An old woman. A certain small, smooth white fish.

A عفت ʿaft, (v. n. of عفت) Twisting (the hand), so that it becomes broken. Twisting. Breaking, but without effecting a separation of the parts. Committing blunders in speaking.

A عفتّان ʿifittān, Large-bodied. Smooth, succulent, full of flesh, and compact. Cruel, oppressive.

A عفج ʿafj, (v. n. of عفج) Striking (with a stick). Lying with. Beating clothes with the mallet when washing معفاج mifʿāj. Committing sodomy. ʿifj, ʿafaj, or ʿafij, (pl. اعفاج aʿfāj) The small guts. ʿafaj, (v. n. of عفج) Being large (the intestines).

A عفجة ʿafijat, Ditches, receptacles for water near a tank. The small guts.

A عفد ʿafd, A pigeon, or a bird resembling it. ʿafd, (عفدان ʿafdān, or ʿafadān) (v. n. of عفد) Leaping with the feet close.

A عفر ʿafr, (v. n. of عفر) Rolling in the dust, throwing (any one) on the ground. Burying under ground, concealing. Dust. ʿifr, Swine: a young pig. A hog, boar. A dangerous, wicked, shrewd, cunning man. Strong (lion). ʿufr, (pl. اعفار aʿfār and عفار ʿifār) Strong, robust, valiant. Sharp, shrewd, arch. Dull (market). The 7th, 8th, and 9th night of the moon. A boar. (pl. of اعفر aʿfar and عفراء ʿafrāʾ) Short-necked and reddish white (hinds). عن عفر ʿan ʿufrin, About a month or fortnight ago. ʿafar, (v. n. of عفر) Being of a whitish red (a deer). (pl. اعفار aʿfār) Earth, dust. The first watering of sown fields. Difficulty, ambiguity. The arrow called مخاط الشيطان mukhāṭu'sh shayṭān. كلام لا عفر فيه kalām lā ʿafara fīhi, A discourse in which is nothing hard to be understood. ʿufur, Time, season. A month.

A عفرّ ʿifirr, A dangerous, wicked, impure, and cunning man.

P عفرا ʿafrā, Name of the mistress of عروة.

A عفرا ʿafraʾ, Feathers on a cock's neck.

A عفراء ʿafrāʾ, (fem. of اعفر aʿfar) Whitish red (deer). White (woman). Trackless (waste). White (mortar or bread-crumbs). Red sand. Bright night.

A عفرات ʿifrāt, Hairs growing in the middle of the head. A sly, dangerous, inhuman person.

A عفراس ʿifrās, A powerful and cruel lion.

A عفرة ʿifrat, A filthy woman. ʿifrat or ʿufrat, The mane, hair, or feathers on the neck of a lion or cock, which bristle up when they are angry. ʿufrat, The beginning (of cold). Redness of a deer's back inclining to white. ʿufrat or ʿafrat, Whiteness, but not clear.

A عفرّة ʿufurrat, The beginning (of cold). The intenseness of summer-heat. Mixed crowds of men.

A عفرتى ʿafartaʾ, Strong (lion).

A عفرجع ʿafarjaʿ, Of a bad disposition.

A عفرزان ʿafarrazān, Name of a Basra catamite.

A عفرس ʿifris, A strong, fierce, ravenous lion.

A عفرسة ʿafrasat, (v. n. of عفرس Q) Prostrating. Overcoming. Rending, tearing (as a lion).

A عفرفرة ʿafarfarat, Impure, wicked, base, malignant. A lion.

A عفرن ʿifarn, A lion.

A عفرناة ʿafarnāt, Strong (lioness or she-camel). The sylvan demon called غول ghūl.

A عفرنس ʿafarnas, A thick-necked camel. A ferocious lion.

A عفرنى ʿafarnaʾ, Ravenous (lion or lioness).

A عفرنية ʿufarniyat, Hairs growing on the middle of the head. A dangerous, wicked, cunning man.

A عفروس ʿufrūs, A strong, ravenous lion.

A عفرى ʿafraʾ, The feathers on a cock's neck. The hair on the nape of a man's neck. The forelocks of a horse. Hairs on the middle of the head.

A عفريّ ʿifriy, Dangerous, wicked, cunning man.

A عفرية ʿifriyat, (pl. عفارى ʿafāraʾ) The hackles on a cock's neck. Hairs on the nape of a man's neck. The forelock of a horse. Hairs growing on the middle of the head. The mane, hair, or feathers on the neck of a lion or cock, which bristle up when they are angry or pugnacious. Contentious, quarrelsome. Tyrannical, oppressive. A strong lion. A dangerous, wicked, cunning man.

A عفريت ʿifrīt, (pl. عفاريت ʿafārīt) A giant, demon, any fancied spectre of a horrible appearance, a fright. Powerful, independent, master of one's own possessions. One who does a thing in a careful, artistical, and masterly way. Strong (lion). ʿifrīt or ʿafrīt, A sly, dangerous, inhuman man.

A عفرّيت ʿifirrīt, Powerful, independent, master of one's own possessions. One who does any thing with care, art, and in a masterly manner.

A عفريتة ʿifrītat, (A woman) powerful and shrewd in managing (her) affairs.

P عفريت ديدار ʿifrīt-dīdār, Of diabolical aspect.

A عفريس ʿifrīs, A fierce, ravenous lion.

A عفرين ʿifrīn, Powerful, independent, master of one's possessions. One who does a thing attentively and well.

A عفرّين ʿifirrīn, Name of a place frequented by lions. Powerful, independent, master of one's possessions. A large, powerful lioness. One who does any thing attentively, artfully, masterly. ليث عفرّين lays ʿifirrīn, A lion. A certain insect that lives in soft ground at the foot of a wall. A reptile resembling a chameleon, troublesome to a rider, and striking with his tail. A full-grown, strong, and powerful man. A clever man, one who brings every thing to perfection.

A عفز ʿafz, (v. n. of عفز) Ordering (a camel) to lie down. Toying with one's wife. A walnut.

A عفزر ʿafzar, One who runs before. A fellow noisy in any frivolous and trifling matter.

A عفس ʿafs, (v. n. of عفس) Restraining, retaining, imprisoning. Making vile and despicable. Driving with violence. Dragging on the ground. Rubbing, currying (a skin). Using (a garment) every day. Kicking the posteriors.

A عفش ʿafsh, A collecting, bringing together.

A عفشال ʿifshāl, Of little fortitude (man). Impudent, undaunted.

A عفشج ʿafshaj, Long, tall: corpulent.

A عفشل ʿafshal, Heavy, and troubled with indigestion (man).

A عفشليل ʿafshalīl, Inhuman, stern, severe, heavy (man). Very hairy (garment). A hyena. Flabby (old woman).

A عفص ʿafs, (v. n. of عفص) Closing the mouth of a flask or glass bottle with leather. Treading under foot. Squeezing hard, enfeebling (in wrestling), twisting the hand. Lying with (a damsel). Bending, doubling. Pulling up, tearing out. A gall (both tree and nut). ʿafas, An obliquity in the nose. ʿafis, Styptic, astringent (food).

A عفضج ʿafzaj, Hard. ʿafzaj, (and عفضاج ʿifzāj) Thick, corpulent, soft.

A عفضجة ʿafzajat, A waxing fat.

A عفط ʿaft, (v. n. of عفط) Sneezing, breaking wind (sheep or goats). Driving sheep so that they sneeze. Calling to sheep. Making a noise with the lips. Stammering, stuttering. A fart. Mucus from the nose of a sheep. ʿafit, A farter.

A عفطان ʿafatān, (v. n. of عفط) Farting (a sheep or a goat).

A عفطلة ʿaftalat, A mixing, mingling.

A عفطىّ ʿiftiy, A stutterer, a stammerer.

A عفعف ʿafʿaf, The fruit of the طلح talh.

A عفعفة ʿafʿafat, (v. n. of عفعف Q) Eating the fruit of the طلح talh.

A عففة ʿafafat, (pl. of عفّ ʿaff) Pure, chaste.

A عفق ʿafk, (v. n. of عفق) Going at discretion, at full liberty, disappearing, and afterwards returning. Coming, going, or repeating any thing often; visiting frequently. Milking very often. Covering frequently (an ass). Whipping severely. Travelling fast. Waking, sleeping little. Doing any thing slightly. Collecting. Retaining, restraining, hindering. Retiring, concealing one's self; lying hid. Shaking any thing (wind). Breaking wind. ʿafak, A going to and fro of camels to the cistern. ʿufuk, A fly.

A عفقة ʿafkat, Absence: concealment. A kind of game with earth.

A ما عفقسه mā ʿafkasahu, How bad-tempered he is become after having been good-tempered!

A عفقسة ʿafkasat, A spoiling, making bad.

A عفقل ʿafkal, Large-faced (man).

A عفك *ɛafk*, (v. n. of عفك) Being very stupid. Not connecting well (one's discourse). Restraining. Deferring, postponing. *ɛafak*, (v. n. of عفك) Being very stupid. *ɛafik*, Foolish, stupid.

A عفكاء *ɛafkāʼ*, Stubborn, intractable (she-camel).

A عفكل *ɛafkal*, Foolish, stupid, insane.

A عفل *ɛafl*, (v. n. of عفل) Feeling cattle about the thighs if fat. *ɛafal*, (v. n. of عفل) Having a rupture (a female); a female rupture. The perinæum. Fat of a ram's testicles, or parts adjacent which are felt. Fat between the buttocks of cattle.

A عفلاء *ɛaflāʼ*, Ruptured (woman or she-camel).

A عفلاة *ɛaflāt*, A lip which becomes turned out in laughing.

A عفلة *ɛafalat*, The female rupture.

A عفلط *ɛiflit*, (or عفلّط *ɛafallat*) Foolish, awkward, dull.

A عفلطة *ɛaflatat*, A mingling, mixing.

A عفلق *ɛaflak*, (and عفلّق *ɛafallak*) A lazy, unskilful woman; an ill-spoken one. Wide and flabby (vulva). Soft and fleshy (thing).

A عفلّقة *ɛafallakat*, A lazy woman; a foul-tongued one.

A عفلوق *ɛufluk*, Silly, foolish.

P عفله زده *ɛafala-zada*, Ruptured (female).

A عفليط *ɛiflīt*, A fool.

A عفن *ɛafn*, (v. n. of عفن) Ascending (a hill). Corrupting, causing to stink (meat). *ɛafan*, (v. n. of عفن) Rotting, falling in pieces when touched (a rope). *ɛafin*, Rotten, putrid, falling in pieces.

A عفنجج *ɛafanjaj*, Foolish, dull, thick. A swift she-camel.

A عفنجش *ɛafanjash*, Injurious, cruel, unfeeling.

A عفنجل *ɛafanjal*, Heavy and disagreeable (person). Very talkative.

A عفنّش *ɛafannash*, A very aged man. Thick-bearded. One who has bushy eyebrows.

A عفنشة *ɛafnashat*, Thickness (of the beard).

A عفنشل *ɛafanshal*, Heavy (man), and troubled with indigestion.

A عفنّط *ɛafannat*, Vile, contemptible. Bad-tempered. The creature called دابّة الارض *dābbatu'l arz*.

A عفنقس *ɛafankas*, Mean, base. Morose, touchy (temper); a man of such a disposition.

A عفو *ɛafw*, (v. n. of عفا for عفو) Erasing, cancelling, obliterating. Effacing (the vestiges of a house) the wind, covering them with dust. Being effaced. Being long, luxuriant (hair or herbage). Allowing to grow long. Being pure (water). Giving the best part of broth. Leaving in the pot the best part of the broth, in return for the loan of the kettle. Cropping the herbage near to the roots (a camel). Being fat, and in easy circumstances, and good case. Going to beg a favour. Forgiving, remitting, passing by a transgression. Good pasture. The largest, best, or choicest part of any thing. Pardon, forgiveness, absolution. A benefit, favour, gift. The balance of one's estate after all necessary disbursements are deducted. Water left after people have drunk. Untrodden ground, uninhabited, and without the trace of a building. Easy. P عفو كردن *ɛafw kardan*, To forgive, excuse, spare. A *ɛafw*, *ɛifw*, or *ɛufw*, (pl. عفوة *ɛafwat* and عفاء *ɛifāʼ*) A wild ass's colt.

A عفوّ *ɛafūw*, One who forgives much. عفوّ و غفّار *ɛafūw wa ghaffār*, (God) granting pardon to sinners. *ɛufūw*, (v. n. of عفا for عفو) Being obliterated. Obliteration.

A عفوا *ɛafwan*, Gratuitously, without asking for. Without trouble or difficulty.

P عفو پيشه *ɛafw-pesha*, Forgiving, merciful.

A عفوة *ɛafwat*, An expiatory mulct for murder, the price of blood. (pl. of عفو *ɛifw*) Asses' colts. *ɛafwat*, *ɛifwat*, or *ɛufwat*, The fat of broth. *ɛifwat*, The purer, better, or choicest part (of any thing). A she-colt of an ass. Excellent pasture.

A عفوصة *ɛufūsat*, Astringency, stypticity. Bitterness.

A عفوق *ɛufūk*, (v. n. of عفق) Ranging at liberty, pasturing where they please (camels).

A عفونة *ɛufūnat*, (v. n. of عفن) Rotting, falling in pieces when laid hold of (a rope). Corruption, infection, stink, funk, miasm, rottenness.

A عفوه *ɛufūh*, (v. n. of عفه) Overspreading. Covering with a lid.

P عفّه *ɛuffa*, A lamb's skin covered with soft wool.

A عفيّ *ɛufīy*, (pl. of عافي *ɛāfī*) Obliterated, effaced. Those who ask or receive benefits.

A عفيتة *ɛafītat*, A kind of sweet cake (called also عصيدة *ɛasīdat*).

P عفيدن *ɛafīdan*, To bark.

A عفير *ɛafīr*, (Flesh) laid on sand to be dried by the sun. Dry bread without meat or condiment. A kind of wheat boiled without sweets. Meal of wheat or barley without any admixture of sweets. (A woman) giving nothing to her female slave. *ɛufayr*, Name of an ass whereon Muhammad rode.

A عفيرة *ɛafīrat*, A woman who makes not a present to any body. Dung rolled into an orbicular form by a beetle. *ɛufayrat*, Name of a woman ranked amongst the sages of pagan antiquity.

A عفيط *ɛafīt*, (v. n. of عفط) Sneezing (as a sheep). Breaking wind (a goat). Mucus from a sheep's nose.

A عفيف *ɛafīf*, (pl. اعفّاء *aɛiffāʼ*) Chaste, abstaining (from any thing forbidden).

A عفيفة *ɛafīfat*, (pl. عفيفات *ɛafīfāt* and عفائف *ɛafāʼif*) A chaste, modest woman.

A عفيقان *ɛafīkān*, A species of thorn.

A عفيك *ɛafīk*, Foolish, stupid. Unsteady.

A عقّ *ɛakk*, (v. n. of عقّ) Splitting. Shooting (an arrow) towards the sky. Slaughtering (a sheep) and giving it in alms on the birth of a child, or when its head is first shaved, which is upon the seventh day. Undutiful, disobedient (son). A deep furrow or trench in the ground. Bitter and thick (water). *ɛikk*, A deep trench. *ɛukk*, Bitter (water).

A عقاء *ɛikāʼ*, (pl. of عقاة *ɛakāt* and عقوة *ɛakwat*) Areas, courts.

A عقاب *ɛikāb*, (v. n. 3 of عقب) Coming behind, following at the heels of. Punishing, chastising. Changing turns (with another), doing duty alternately. Making gain or plunder. Punishment, chastisement, torment. (pl. of عقبة *ɛakabat*) Declivities or difficult passes of mountains. P خوف عقاب شاه *khawfi ɛikābi shāh*, Dread of royal resentment or punishment. A *ɛukāb*, (pl. اعقب *aɛkub* and عقبان *ɛukbān* or *ɛikbān*) An eagle (especially black). Name of a constellation. A standard belonging to Muhammad. A projecting stone in a mountain, or in a well under water, on which pitchers are broken. A stone whereon a water-drawer stands. A rivulet, or any place whence water flows into a cistern or reservoir. High ground; any high place. An excrescence, in shape like an almond, on the leg of a horse. A small thread in the hole of an ear-ring. Name of a woman; also of a bitch. P عقاب آهنين منقار *ɛukābi āhanīn-minkār*, An iron-beaked eagle. عقاب شدن *ɛukāb shudan*, To hanker after.

A عقابيس *ɛakābīs*, Evils, misfortunes.

A عقابيل *ɛakābīl*, (pl. of عقبولة *ɛukbūlat*) Remains of a disease, enmity, or friendship. Pustules breaking out on the lips after a fever. Adversities, tribulations. ذو عقابيل *zū ɛakābīl*, Wicked, evil.

A عقاة *ɛakāt*, (pl. عقاء *ɛikāʼ*) A mansion; the court or ground surrounding it.

A عقادة *ɛikādat*, A knotting, platting.

A عقار *ɛakār*, (v. n. of عقر) Being barren (a woman). An immoveable estate in land, water, or palm-trees. A palm-tree. Any thing dry. A red dye. The choicest fodder. A mansion, palace, or citadel. Household furniture. A kind of grass which wounds cattle. ما له دار ولا عقار *mā lahu dār wa lā ɛakār*, He has neither house or land. *ɛakār* or *ɛukār*, Choice furniture, used only on high days and holidays. *ɛikār*, (v. n. 3 of عقر) Boasting against another in regard to hamstringing (camels). *ɛukār*, Wine. A kind of coloured cloth. عقار آدم *ɛukāri ādam*, Name of a medicinal plant. P عقار كوهان *ɛukāri kohān*, Dracunculus.

A عقّار *ɛakkār*, A medicinal plant or root. A tree. Name of a dog. (pl. عقاقير *ɛakākīr*) An aromatic root.

A عقارات *ɛakārāt*, (pl. of عقار *ɛakār*) Immoveable estates in land, water, or palm-trees.

A عقارب *ɛakārib*, Whisperings, slanders. Adversities. The depth of winter. (pl. of عقرب *ɛakrab*) Scorpions.

A عقارة *ɛukārat* or *ɛakārat*, (v. n. of عقر) Being barren (a woman).

A عقاري *ɛakāraʼ*, Hamstrung (horses).

A عقاص *ɛikās*, A fillet for the hair. (pl. of عقصة *ɛiksat* and *ɛakisat*) (Women's) plaited or braided locks. *ʻukās*, A disease incident to sheep.

A عقاف *ʻukāf*, A distemper making the feet of sheep crooked.

A عقافة *ʻukkāfat*, A stick curved at the end, by which one can draw any thing.

A عقاق *ʻakāk*, (v. n. of عقّ) Being with young (a mare). Undutifulness. *ʻakāk* or *ʻikāk*, Fruit borne in the womb. *ʻikāk*, (pl. of عقوق *ʻakūk*) Pregnant (mares). (pl. of عقق *ʻukuk*) Pregnant animals of single hoof. *ʻukāk*, Bitter (water).

A عقاقل *ʻakākil*, (pl. of عقنقل *ʻakankal*) Large hills in sandy grounds. Ventricles of crocodiles.

A عقاقير *ʻakākīr*, (pl. of عقّار *ʻakkār*) Aromatic roots. جيّد العقاقير *jayyidu'l ʻakākīr*, (Iron) of an excellent quality.

A عقال *ʻikāl*, Whatever is given in one year by way of tithes. A young she-camel. (pl. عقل *ʻukul*) A rope which binds together the feet and neck of a camel (to make him obedient when otherwise untractable). A fetter. عقال المئين *ʻikālu'l miʼīn*, A prince, whose ransom is hundreds of camels.

A عقّال *ʻukkāl*, A disease in a horse's foot causing him to limp. The limping of cattle. (pl. of عاقل *ʻākil*) Prudent, intelligent, wary. ذو العقّال *zū'l ʻukkāl*, Name of a very celebrated stallion.

A عقالان *ʻikālāni*, (du.) Alms paid for two years.

A عقام *ʻakām*, (pl. عقماء *ʻukamāʼ*) Barren, childless (man or woman). A strong she-camel in her ninth year. A kind of sea-serpent. *ʻikām*, (pl. of عقيم *ʻakīm*) Childless (men). *ʻukām*, Disastrous (day). *ʻukām* or *ʻakām*, A man of a bad disposition. Raging (war). An incurable distemper.

A عقّان *ʻikkān*, An excrescence at the roots of palms and vines, which, if not pruned, destroys them.

A عقائد *ʻakāʼid*, (pl. of عقيدة *ʻakīdat*) Confections of sugar. Fundamental articles of faith.

A عقائص *ʻakāʼis*, (pl. of عقصة *ʻiksat* and عقيصة *ʻakīsat*) Locks of women's hair brought together on the top of the head.

A عقائق *ʻakāʼik*, (pl. of عقيق *ʻakīk*) Cornelians.

A عقائل *ʻakāʼil*, (pl. of عقيلة) Things excellent in their kind. Camels of the finest description.

A عقائم *ʻakāʼim*, (pl. of عقيم) Barren (women).

A عقب *ʻakb*, (v. n. of عقب) Striking upon the heel. Coming behind or after, succeeding, filling (a father's place). Assailing, assaulting maliciously. Putting forth green leaves after the former had withered (a tree). Running (a horse) again and again. Taking a second wife after the death or divorce of the first. Winding (a bow or an arrow) about with a bruised gut. A son. A son's son. Posterity, grand-children. A second heat or course. The heel. A side, quarter. من اين عقبك *min ayn ʻakbuka*, From whence comest thou? *ʻikb*, The latter part of the month. *ʻukb*, The end or final issue of any thing. في عقب الشهر *fī ʻukbi'sh shahri*, (He came) about the close of the month. *ʻakab*, The heel. (pl. of عقبة *ʻakabat*) Nerves, macerated tendons. P عقب لشكر *ʻakabi lashkar*, Rear of an army. A بعقب *bi ʻakabi*, At the heels of, after. P در عقب *dar ʻakab*, In the rear, after, behind. A *ʻakib*, (pl. اعقاب *aʻkāb*) The heel. Offspring, children, grand-children, successors, posterity. End of a month. عقب الشيطان *ʻakibu'sh shaytān*, A mode of sitting like a dog. *ʻukab*, (pl. of عقبة *ʻukbat*) Times, turns. Remains, things left behind. *ʻukub*, End or issue of a thing.

A عقّب *ʻikkab*, Signs or traces of any thing good.

A عقبا *ʻukbaʼ*, The future world. End. Reward, or punishment.

A عقبات *ʻakabāt*, Summits of mountains.

A عقبان *ʻikbān* or *ʻukbān*, (pl. of عقاب *ʻukāb*) Eagles. *ʻukbān*, End of the month (the whole being elapsed).

A عقبة *ʻakbat*, Green leaves coming out to succeed those that have withered. *ʻakbat* or *ʻikbat*, A kind of painted litter-cloth. *ʻukbat*, Posterity. A time, turn. The turning or sweep of a bird from the beginning to the end of his career. Day and night. Any thing received for another commodity, hire (especially part of the broth made in a pot given to the owner for the loan of it). Exchange, substitute. عقبة الجمال *ʻukbatu'l jamāl*, Remains of beauty. عقبة الشيطان *ʻukbatu'sh shaytān*, A mode of sitting like a dog. *ʻukbat* or *ʻikbat*, Outward form. Remains, vestige. عقبة القمر *ʻikbatu'l kamar*, Once a month. *ʻakabat*, (pl. عقب *ʻakab*) A nerve, tendon (particularly the nerve of a camel's neck, used when macerated to bind the heads of arrows). The summit of Mina, where Muhammad was first publicly acknowledged by twelve persons, and in the year following by seventy. (pl. عقاب *ʻikāb*) Summit of a mountain, steep declivity.

A عقبلة *ʻukabilat*,, A follower.

A عقبولة *ʻukbūlat*, (or عقبول *ʻukbūl*) (pl. عقابيل *ʻakābīl*) Dregs of a disease; remains of enmity or friendship. Pustules breaking out on the lips after a fever. Hardness, severity.

A عقبي *ʻukbaʼ*, End, accomplishment, issue, success. A return, requital, reward, or punishment: hence, the life to come.

A عقّة *ʻakkat*, A long streak of lightning in the sky. A deep trench. *ʻikkat*, (pl. عقق *ʻikak*) A deep trench. The hair of young animals, with which they are born. *ʻukkat*, A child's plaything.

A عقد *ʻakd*, (v. n. of عقد) Binding, fastening, tying in a knot. Twisting (the beard). Knotting her tail (a camel that has conceived). Making an oath without any exception or reserve. Building. Confirming an agreement. Marrying. Entering into partnership, or forming any commercial contract. Establishing a confederacy, concluding an alliance. Counting. Counting on the ten fingers. Becoming thick and concrete (conserves). Forming a stone (a peach, date, &c.). Being ready for mischief. A knot, compact, league, confederacy, alliance; a chain, connection (in matrimony or trade), bargain, agreement. Opinion, belief, judgment, thought. Tongue-tied. An arch. The key-stone of an arch. A decimal. P عقد بستن *ʻakd bastan*, To tie a knot. To betroth, engage to marry. عقد مجلس داشتن *ʻakdi majlis dāshtan*, To meet, or to hold a conference. عقد نكاح كردن *ʻakdi nikāh kardan*, To make a marriage-contract. A اهل الحلّ و العقد *ahlu'l hall wa'l ʻakd*, Authorised to loose and to bind. *ʻikd*, (pl. عقود *ʻukūd*) A collar. A necklace. A guard. عقد الجمان *ʻikdu'l jumān*, A string of pearls. A *ʻakad*, (v. n. of عقد) Being tied, fettered (the tongue). Sticking fast (a dog and a bitch). P عقد شب افروز *ʻakadi shabafroz*, Stars and planets. عقد شب و روز *ʻakadi shab u roz*, Night and day. Time, fortune. The world. A *ʻakid*, Dwarfish but hardy, patient of labour (camel). A sort of tree whose leaf has the property of healing wounds. (pl. of عقدة *ʻakidat*) Tracts of accumulated sands. عقد اللسان *ʻakidu'l lisān*, Tongue-tied. Having an impediment in speech. *ʻukad*, (pl. of عقدة *ʻukdat*) Knots. Angers, indignations. Prefectures, commands. Perplexed affairs, confused words. تحلّلت عقده *tahallalat ʻukaduhu*, His anger subsided.

A عقداء *ʻakdāʼ*, Knotty-tailed. A sheep with such a tail. (A woman) who has an impediment of speech. A maid-servant.

A عقدان *ʻukdān*, Name of Farazdak (from his dwarfish stature). *ʻakadān*, A sort of date.

P عقدانه *ʻakdāna*, Marriage-fees, formerly paid to the Kāzī or Musulmān priest in India.

A عقدة *ʻukdat*, (pl. عقد *ʻukad*) An excrescence (especially at the joints, or where bones have been broken). A crookedness in the setting of a broken hand. A knot. An impediment in speech. A bundle. A bargain, covenant, compact. An estate, manor, villa in fee-simple. Prefecture, government, presidency, command. A place thick planted with trees; abounding with pasture; or provision for men. A dog's pizzle. An arch. A corner of a pasture. Cattle forced or driven up to trees. Name of a country near Yazd. آلف من غراب عقدة *ālaf min ghurābi ʻukdat*, More tame than a crow of Ukdat (which flies to a very short distance, so numerous are the trees). عقدة اعراس *ʻukdaʼi iʻrās*, The marriage-knot. *ʻakadat*, Root of the tongue. *ʻakadat* or *ʻakidat*, A tract of accumulated sand.

A عقدتان *ʻukdatāni*, (obliq. عقدتين *ʻukdatayn*) (du. of عقدة *ʻukdat*) Head and tail of the dragon.

P عقدت كشا *ʻukdat-kushā*, Resolver of difficulties.

A عقر *ʻakr*, (v. n. of عقر) Wounding (a horse) in the feet (or a camel). Hamstringing. Cutting off the head of a palm-tree and killing it. Lopping, felling, destroying. Galling, wounding the back. Falling in with game. Eating up forage. Detaining long, keeping bound. Preventing from going. Being barren (a woman). Killing (a camel) over the grave of his master. A palace, mansion, or citadel; or one falling to ruin. A lofty edifice. Space between two objects (as the legs of a table). A white cloud. A mist rising before the eye and concealing the sun and what is about it; or grows up in the expanse of the sky and passes away unseen, only its thunder is heard from a distance. Any thing white. A mark like a crack in the foot of a horse or camel. *ɛakr* or *ɛukr*, The foundation, also the area or court of a house. A place where people alight. *ɛukr*, (v. n. of عقر) Being barren (a woman). Not yielding any result (an affair). Stripping off the bark of a palm-tree and taking away the medullary substance. Abstaining from intercourse with a wife to ascertain whether she be a virgin or not. Barrenness (of a woman or camel). The centre of a fire. The examination of a girl to discover if she be a virgin or not. A woman's marriage portion; also the fine paid for vitiated virginity. *ɛukr*, Food, fodder, forage. The finest verses in a poem or elegy. A palace, a citadel. بيضة العقر *bayzatu'l ɛukr*, The egg of a cock (being supposed to lay one every year). A gift which arrives unexpectedly from a quarter unlooked for. The first or last egg which a hen lays. An egg by which trial of a woman's virginity is made. A childless man. The place behind the reservoir where the camels stand when watering. لقحت الناقة عن عقر *lakihati'n nākat ɛan ɛukrin*, The camel conceived after having been barren. *ɛakar*, (v. n. of عقر) Being seized with sudden fright, and unable to advance or recede. Misfortune. *ɛakir*, (A bird) whose feathers having received injury do not grow again. *ɛukar*, (A saddle) galling (a horse's) back. A man who by over-work galls the back of his beast. *ɛukur*, Centre, heart of a fire. (pl. of عقور *ɛakūr*) Biting (dogs).

A عقّر *ɛukkar*, (pl. of عاقر *ɛāķir*) Barren (women).

A عقراء *ɛakrāɛ*, Lofty (sand-hill). *ɛukarāɛ*, (pl. of عقور *ɛakūr*) Wounding (animals), biting (dogs).

A عقرب *ɛakrab*, (pl. عقارب *ɛakārib*) A scorpion. The sign Scorpio. The wheel of an arquebuse. The pin of a dial, hand of a watch. A needle. A halter. A shoe-latchet. A crupper-strap. A quarrelsome fellow. P عقرب پريشان *ɛakrabi pareshān*, A lady's veil. عقرب نيلوفري *ɛakrabi nīlūfarī*, The sign Scorpio.

A عقرباء *ɛakrabāɛ*, A female scorpion.

A عقربان *ɛakrubān*, Name of a plant. *ɛukrubān*, (or عقرّبان *ɛukrubbān*) A male scorpion. Any other animal with a tail and long feet. An earwig.

A عقربانة *ɛukrubānat*, Firmness, invincibleness.

A عقربة *ɛakrabat*, A (female) scorpion. A hook fastened to a saddle. A shoe-latchet: bucket-strap. An intelligent handmaid, clever at serving.

P عقربخانه *ɛakrab-khāna*, A needle-case.

A عقرة *ɛakrat* or *ɛukrat*, Barrenness (of women). *ɛakirat*, (A she-camel) which drinks not except in fear. *ɛukarat*, (A woman) diseased in the womb. A little spherical amulet or charm which some women wear about their haunches to prevent them from becoming pregnant. A man who galls the backs of his beasts by over-work. (A saddle) galling a horse's back. Any thing which bites or stings (not having life). عقرة العلم النسيان *ɛukaratu'l ɛilm an nisyān*, Forgetfulness is the sterilizer of (or that which renders barren) learning.

A عقرطل *ɛakurtal* or *ɛikirtil*, A she-elephant.

A عقري *ɛakraʼ*, Menstruous (woman). (pl. of عقير *ɛakīr*) Cut, wounded. عقري حلقي *ɛakraʼ halkaʼ*, May God wound in the feet and throat! *ɛukraʼ*, An estate, farm, or immoveable property.

A عقز *ɛakz*, (v. n. of عقز) Creeping close to each other (ants).

A عقش *ɛaksh*, (v. n. of عقش) Bending (a stick). Collecting, accumulating (wealth). *ɛaksh* or *ɛakash*, A kind of pot-herb. Extremities of vine-branches. Fruit of the tree اراك *arāk*.

A عقص *ɛaks*, (v. n. of عقص) Plaiting or twisting the hair. *ɛakas*, (v. n. of عقص) Being avaricious and bad-tempered. In the measure of verse called وافر *wāfir* (Exuberant), a dropping of the م *mīm* of مفاعلتن *mufāɛalatun* after it had been previously changed into مفاعيلن *mafāɛīlun*. *ɛakis*, Covetous and froward. Sand unequally heaped and difficult to cross. *ɛikas*, (pl. of عقصة *ɛiksat*) Spiral ringlets. *ɛukus*, A miser. The tripe.

A عقصاء *ɛaksāɛ*, (A woman) whose fingers and teeth are distorted, and cross each other.

A عقصة *ɛiksat*, (pl. عقص *ɛikas*) (A woman's) braided hair. *ɛuksat*, An excrescence on a horn.

A عقط *ɛakt*, (for قعط *kaɛt*) The tying on a turban.

A عقعق *ɛakɛak*, A magpie.

A عقعقة *ɛakɛakat*, The chattering (of a magpie).

A عقف *ɛakf*, (v. n. of عقف) Bending. A fox.

A عقفاء *ɛakfāɛ*, (fem. of اعقف *aɛkaf*) Crooked, curved. An iron with a crooked point. A certain herb resembling rue, which kills sheep but not camels.

A عقفان *ɛukfān*, The grandsire of the red ants.

A عقفرة *ɛakfarat*, (v. n. of عقفر Q) Ruining, destroying. Throwing on the ground.

A عقفسة *ɛakfasat*, A spoiling, a deteriorating.

A عقق *ɛakak*, (v. n. of عقّ) Being in foal (a mare). Being cleft, divided, branching out. Undutiful. *ɛikak*, (pl. of عقّة *ɛikkat*) Hairs upon young animals. *ɛukak*, Lightning piercing the clouds like a flaming sword. Undutiful to parents, froward, audacious. *ɛukuk*, (pl. عقاق *ɛikāk*) Any pregnant animal dividing the hoof. (pl. of عقوق *ɛakūk*) Mares in foal.

A عققة *ɛakakat*, (pl. of عاقّ *ɛākk*) Undutiful.

A عقل *ɛakl*, (v. n. of عقل) Confining, tying up (a camel's) foot. Constipating the belly (astringent medicine). Understanding, perceiving, finding out. Fleeing for refuge. Standing erect on a high rock (a goat). Eating the plant عاقول *ɛākūl* (a camel). Excelling in genius or wisdom, being intellectual. Undertaking to pay a mulct or fine in case of dishonesty in the offending party, and afterwards paying it. Paying every one his quota of a fine for manslaughter. Paying a mulct for manslaughter, and pacifying those who threaten revenge. Combing (her) hair (a woman). Being vertical and perpendicular (the sun at mid-day). Not retaliating, having received an amercement. Tripping up the heels in wrestling. Dropping the letter ي *ye* in مُفاعيلن *mufāɛīlun*. (pl. عقول *ɛukūl*) Intellect, knowledge, reason, prudence, judgment, sense, wisdom, mind. The faculty of discrimination. The heart. An asylum. A fortification, citadel. A fine, mulct. A red cloth with which a camel-litter is covered. A sort of embroidery. عقل اوّل *ɛakli awwal*, (or عقل كلّ *ɛakli kull*) Natural genius or instinct. The throne of God. The Holy Spirit. Muhammad. Gabriel. عقل بالغ *ɛakli bāligh*, Maturity of mind, when the judgment is formed (about eighteen years of age). عقل فعّال *ɛakli faɛɛāl*, Superior wisdom. عقل معاد *ɛakli maɛād*, Meditation on a future state. عقل اليقين *ɛaklu'l yakīn*, Believing without suspicion. عقل معاش *ɛakli maɛāsh*, Economy, industry, prudence. خلاف عقل *khilāfi ɛakl*, Unreasonable, inconsistent. *ɛakal*, A distortion in the feet of camels. A knocking together of the knees. *ɛukul*, (pl. of عقال *ɛikāl*) Ropes with which the fore-feet of camels are tied up to the shoulder.

A عقلاء *ɛaklāɛ*, (fem. of اعقل *aɛkal*) Bow-legged (she-camel). *ɛukalāɛ*, (pl. of عاقل *ɛāķil*) Prudent, intelligent, wise, sensible, judicious.

P عقلانه *ɛaklāna*, Prudently, wisely, reasonably.

A عقلة *ɛuklat*, A tripping or twisting of the feet of an adversary in wrestling. Magic charms. The character ÷ in geomancy.

P عقل رفتگي *ɛakl-raftagī*, Loss of reason.

P عقل رفته *ɛakl-rafta*, Bereft of reason.

P عقلمند *ɛaklmand*, Sensible, judicious.

A عقليّ *ɛakliy*, Reasonable. Intellectual. Theoretical. Judicious. افعال عقليّه *afɛāli ɛakliya*, Prudent, judicious actions.

A عقم *ɛakm*, Any thing intervenient or intervening. *ɛakm*, *ɛakam*, or *ɛukm*, (v. n. of عقم) Being barren (the womb). Withering, drying (the joints of the hand or feet). A garment of a reddish colour. *ɛakm* or *ɛikm*, A reddish sort of garment. Colour, paint. *ɛikm*, (v. n. of عقم) Keeping silence. *ɛukm* or *ɛakm*, A hurt or mal-conformation of the womb, whereby it is sterilized. *ɛukm* or *ɛukum*, (pl. of عقيم *ɛakīm*) (Women) who conceive not.

A عقماء ɛukamāɛ, (pl. of عقيم) Childless (men).

A عقمة ɛakmat or ɛikmat, A reddish sort of garment. Colour, paint. ɛakamat, A lunar revolution.

A عقمى ɛakma', (pl. of عقيم) Childless (men).

A عقم عقي ɛak, ɛik, or ɛukmiy, Obsolete, uncommon, or unintelligible (speech). ɛukmiy, A man of hereditary nobility or virtue. Liberal, generous.

A عقنباة ɛakambāt, Sharp-taloned (bird).

A عقنبس ɛakambas, Bad, vicious.

A عقنفس ɛakanfas, Bad-tempered. A bad temper.

A عقنقسة ɛakankasat or ɛukankisat, A certain animalcule.

A عقنقل ɛakankal, (pl. عقاقل ɛakākil) A large open valley. A hill in sandy grounds. Intestine of the Lybian lizard. A cup, goblet. A sword.

A عقو ɛakw, (v. n. of عقا for عقو) Being high, lifted up (a banner). Digging in the sides of a well to get more water. Abhorring, loathing, disliking.

A عقوب ɛakūb, A successor (in any good work). ɛukūb, (v. n. of عقب) Coming behind or after, succeeding, filling (a father's) place.

A عقوبة ɛukūbat, Punishment, chastisement, torment, torture.

A عقوة ɛakwat, (pl. عقاء ɛikāɛ) A mansion, or the court surrounding it. A sort of tree.

A عقود ɛukūd, (pl. of عقد ɛakd) Knots, ties. Those parts of a building which serve to hold and connect the whole together (as doors, &c.). Agreements, obligations. Decimals, numbers above units. (pl. of عقد ɛikd) Necklaces.

A عقودات ɛukūdāt, (pl. of عقود ɛukūd) Knots. Those parts of an edifice which connect the whole together, ties. Doors. Arches.

A عقور ɛakūr, (pl. عقر ɛukur) Biting (dog).

A عقوف ɛakūf, The teat of a cow whose milk when drawn does not come out straight.

A عقوق ɛakūk, (pl. عقق ɛukuk and عقاق ɛikāk) Pregnant (mare); also one not in foal. ɛukūk, (v. n. of عقّ) Being disobedient, undutiful. Being pregnant (a mare). Disobedience, rebellion. Soft date-stones (with which young camels are fed).

A عقول ɛakūl, Wise, sagacious, intelligent. An astringent medicine. ɛukūl, (v. n. of عقل) Standing erect on a high rock (a goat). Being vertical, perpendicular (as the sun at noon). Fleeing for refuge. (pl. of عقل ɛakl) Wisdoms, sciences. Intellects, reasons, judgments. ارباب عقول سديدة arbābi ɛukūli sadīda, Persons of sound judgment.

A عقي ɛaky, (v. n. of عقى) Hindering, detaining, preventing. Coming from any place. Disliking, disapproving. Giving a new-born babe something to make it void its first excrement. Voiding excrement for the first time (a new-born babe). ɛiky, (pl. اعقاء aɛkāɛ) Excrement of a new-born infant. احرص من كلب على عقي صبي ahras min kalbin ɛala' ɛikyi sabīyin, Greedier than is a dog of a child's excrement.

A عقيان ɛikyān, Purest gold produced from plants, or growing like vegetables, but not dug from mines. See عقيون ɛikyawn.

A عقيب ɛakīb, A follower. The after part. Behind, after, following, at the heels of.

A عقّيب ɛukkayb, A kind of bird.

A عقيّب ɛukayyib, (dim. of عقاب) An eaglet.

A عقيد ɛakīd, Thick, concrete, coagulated. Confederate. عقيد الكرم ɛakīdu'l karam, Very liberal. عقيد اللؤم ɛakīdu'l luɛm, Extremely covetous.

A عقيدة ɛakīdat, (pl. عقائد ɛakāɛid) A fundamental article of religion. Faith. Conserve of roses, dry sweetmeats.

P عقيدت منش ɛakīdat-manish, Faithful.

A عقير ɛakīr, (pl. عقرى ɛakra') Cut, wounded. Lamed, hamstrung. Seized with sudden fear, thunderstruck. Childless (man). ɛukayr, A bitter date.

A عقّير ɛikkīr, (pl. عقاقير ɛakākīr) A tree.

A عقيرب ɛukayrib, (dim. of عقرب ɛakrab) A small scorpion.

A عقيرة ɛakīrat, A wild beast, whose legs are cut by the noose with which he is caught. A cut leg. A noble person who is killed. The cries of wounded men; also the noise made in singing, weeping, or reading. Truncated (palm-tree).

A عقّيص ɛikkīs, A miser. The tripe.

A عقيصاء ɛukaysāɛ, A small stomach united to the larger one.

A عقيصة ɛakīsat, (pl. عقاص ɛikās and عقائص ɛakāɛis) (A woman's) braided or plaited hair.

A عقيصير ɛukaysīr, A certain animal found in the desert.

A عقيفاء ɛukayfāɛ, A herb resembling rue, fatal to sheep, but not to camels.

A عقيفان ɛukayfān, A long-legged ant, found in baths and ruinous places.

A عقيق ɛakīk, (pl. عقائق ɛakāɛik) A cornelian, agate, red gem. (pl. اعقّة aɛikkat) Any place excavated by a torrent; a channel filled by a stream. Hair upon new-born infants or animals. Name of a valley near Madīna. P عقيق ناب ɛakīki nāb, The lip of a mistress. Tears of blood. Red wine.

A عقيقة ɛakīkat, A thunderbolt piercing the clouds like a flaming sword. A wallet. A river. A bandage or fillet torn from a garment. The foreskin of a child. An arrow shot towards the clouds. A sheep slaughtered on the birth of a child. A christening or name-day. Hair upon new-born infants or animals. Hair on a kid. Soft date-stones with which young camels are fed.

A عقيل بن ابي طالب ɛakīl bin abī tālib, Name of the brother of the caliph Alīy, and the most skilful genealogist of the tribe of Kuraysh.

A عقيلة ɛakīlat, Any thing excellent in its kind; (as a prince or chief; a chaste and noble lady; the best camel). عقيلة البحر ɛakīlatu'l bahr, Pearls (as being the most precious product of the sea).

A عقّيلى ɛukkayla', Sour fruit. Unripe dates.

A عقيم ɛakīm, (pl. عقائم ɛakāɛim, عقم ɛukum and ɛukm) Barren (woman). (pl. عقماء ɛukamāɛ, عقام ɛikām, and عقمى ɛakma') Childless (man). Vain, futile, trifling, worthless. Barren (womb). Useless, unprofitable (intellect). The present world. A gentle wind moving neither clouds nor trees. Vehement, raging (war). Unhappy (day), especially the last judgment. P رنج عقيم ranji ɛakīm, Useless toil, labour in vain.

A عقيمة ɛakīmat, Barren (woman).

A عقيون ɛikyawn, A sea of air under the throne of God, in which, the Muhammadans say, angels stand armed with spears of the winds, their faces turned towards the throne, and repeating the praises of Omnipotence.

A عكّ ɛakk, (v. n. of عكّ) Restraining, diverting (from any purpose). Delaying, putting off (payment of debt). Repeating often (orders, words, injuries). Attacking charging. Explaining (a speech). Turning, inclining. Overcoming (by solid argument). Striking, scourging, chastising. Requesting one to speak a second time or explain. Putting on a cloak (a woman), so that the ends hang loose. Being intensely hot (the day). Continuing incessantly hot (a fever). Relating, reiterating even to satiety. Sultry (day) without a breath of air. Hardy, strong (man).

A عكّا ɛakka', Acre, Ptolemais.

A عكاء ɛikāɛ, (pl. of عكوة) Roots of tails.

A عكاب ɛikāb, (pl. of عنكبوت ɛankabūt) Spiders. ɛukāb, Smoke. Dust.

A عكابة ɛukābat, Name of the father of a tribe.

A عكابر ɛakābir, Male jerboas.

A عكابس ɛukābis, Numerous (camels) approaching to a thousand.

A عكّار ɛakkār, One who makes repeated charges and attacks.

A عكّاز ɛukkāz, A staff with a ferrule, crutch.

A عكّازة ɛukkāzat, (pl. عكاكيز ɛakākīz) A ferruled walking-staff. A crutch. A shepherd's crook. A bishop's crosier.

A عكازيل ɛakāzīl, A lion's whelp. The soft parts under the claws of a lion.

A عكاس ɛikās, A rope (especially tying the neck of a camel to his fore-feet in order to make him quiet). عكاس مكاس ɛikās mikās, A seizing one another by the forelocks.

A عكّاش ɛukkāsh, A spider: male spider: spider's web. A banner wound about a tree and unfurled.

A عكّاشة ɛukkāshat, A spider; a cobweb.

A عكاظ ɛukāz, The celebrated fair formerly held nigh to Mecca, which lasted three weeks.

A عكاظى ɛukāzīy, (Leather) bought or sold at the annual fair of عكاظ ɛukāz.

A عكاك ɛikāk, Intenseness of heat without a breath of wind. (pl. of عكّة ɛukkat) Bottles in which butter is preserved.

A عكاكيز *ʻakākīz*, (pl. of عكّازة *ʻukkāzat*) Ferruled walking-sticks; crutches.

A عكال *ʻikāl*, A rope with which a camel's fore-foot is tied up.

A عكالد *ʻukālid*, Thick (milk).

A عكام *ʻikām*, (pl. عكم *ʻukum*) A rope, or any thing similar, for tying up bales.

A عكام *ʻakkām*, One who loads camels with trusses, bales, &c.

A عكامس *ʻukāmis*, Very dark (night). Many camels, about a thousand in number.

A عكان *ʻikān*, The neck.

A عكب *ʻakb*, (v. n. of عكب) Travelling hard. Light, nimble, brisk. Strength in travelling. Dust. *ʻakab*, (v. n. of عكب) Being thick (smoke). Thickness of lip, chin, or teeth. Closeness of toes. *ʻukub*, (pl. of عنكبوت *ʻankabūt*) Spiders.

A عكبّ *ʻikabb*, A corpulent dwarf. Proud, disobedient (man or devil). One whose mother has a husband. Name of the jailer of Nomān bin Munzir.

A عكباء *ʻakbās*, Malignant (woman). Thick, stout (woman), with thick lips and large teeth.

A عكباش *ʻikbāsh*, A budding-horned fawn.

A عكبر *ʻikbir*, Whatever a bee carries on his legs to the hive.

A عكبرة *ʻukburat*, A rude, inhuman woman; a coarse woman.

A عكبز *ʻukbuz*, Glans penis virilis.

A عكبس *ʻukabis*, Numerous (camels), near 1000.

A عكبشة *ʻakbashat*, A tight fastening.

A عكّة *ʻakkat*, (pl. عكاك *ʻikāk*) Intense heat without a breath of wind. Scorching sands from the reflection of the sun. Hot (night) without a breath of wind. Ascalon, called likewise Acca, Ptolemais, or St. Jean d'Acre. طوبيٰ من رأى عكة *ṭūba' man rasa' ʻakkat*, Fortunate is he who hath seen Acre. *ʻikkat* or *ʻukkat*, Intensity of heat without a breath of air. *ʻukkat*, A paroxysm of a fever. The change of colour in a she-camel after conception. Sands heated by the reflection of the sun. (pl. عكك *ʻukak* and عكاك *ʻikāk*) A leathern bottle in which butter is preserved.

A عكث *ʻaks*, Union, agreement, coalition.

A عكد *ʻakada*, (fut. يعكد *yaʻkidu*) (The thing) was possible (to me). He took refuge.

A عكد *ʻukd*, The middle (of any thing). *ʻakad*, (v. n. of عكد) Becoming fat (a camel or lizard). Adhering, coalescing. *ʻakid*, Fat (camel or lizard). Dry (trees) one upon another.

A عكدة *ʻukdat*, The rump-bone. Strength, power. The den of the Lybian lizard. *ʻakadat*, The root of the tongue or heart. A feather with which a cake is dotted. *ʻakidat*, Fat (camel or lizard).

A عكر *ʻakr*, (v. n. of عكر) Rushing upon, assaulting. Returning to a charge, renewing a fight. Inclining to, departing for. Running home to his own people in spite of his rider (an ass). *ʻikr*, Root, origin, principle, foundation. رجع الي عكره *rajaʻa ila' ʻikrihi*, It returned to its beginning or origin. *ʻakar*, (v. n. of عكر) Being or becoming turbid, muddy, feculent. Dregs or sediment, mother of oil, lees of wine. Rust. (pl. of عكرة *ʻakarat*) Herds of camels. Roots of tongues. *ʻakar* or *ʻakr*, A number of camels, exceeding 500. Sixty camels. Any number of them, between 50 and 100. *ʻakir*, Muddy, feculent, dreggy, unracked (wine).

A عكرة *ʻakrat*, One assault or attack. *ʻakarat*, (pl. عكر *ʻakar*) A large herd of camels, from 50 to 100. The root of the tongue.

A عكرد *ʻakrad*, *ʻukrud*, or *ʻukarid*, Near to puberty and fat (boy).

A عكردة *ʻakradat*, (v. n. of عكرد Q) Becoming fat and strong. Running back to her former owners against the will of the rider (a she-camel).

A عكرش *ʻikrish*, A sort of plant growing at the root of a palm-tree and destroying it. A he-goat.

A عكرشة *ʻikrishat*, A fat female hare. An old woman who pretends to the character of a female شيخ *shaykh*, or one who assumes an aged and venerable appearance.

A عكركر *ʻakarkar*, Thick milk.

A عكرم *ʻikrim*, Darkness of the night.

A عكرمة *ʻikrimat*, A female dove.

A عكرود *ʻukrūd*, (A boy) approaching puberty.

A عكز *ʻakz*, (v. n. of عكز) Seizing, grasping, griping. Leaning on a crutch. Driving (a spear) into the ground. Strengthening (the end of a spear) with a ferrule of iron. Finding one's way to any thing, knowing it. Wrinkling, shrivelling, puckering. *ʻikz*, Wicked, ill-disposed. Covetous.

A عكس *ʻaks*, (v. n. of عكس) Turning upside down, inverting, placing the last first, transposing. Checking, keeping back, pulling in the reins. Tying the rein of a camel to his fore-leg in order to make him quiet. Pouring milk upon any kind of food. Tying (a camel) with the rope called عكاس *ʻikās*. Mixing up milk with fat. Reflection, inversion. Reverberation, recoil, repercussion. Refraction. The contrary, opposite. عكس نور *ʻaksi nūr*, Reflection of light. P عكس انداز كردن *ʻaks-andāz kardan*, To represent by reflection (as in a mirror). برعكس *bar ʻaks*, On the contrary.

A عكش *ʻaksh*, (v. n. of عكش) Collecting, bringing together. Rushing (upon any one). Surrounding a bull (dogs). Tying tight. Spinning her web (a spider). *ʻakash*, (v. n. of عكش) Being curly and heaped together (hair). Growing luxuriantly and becoming entangled (grass or plants). *ʻakish*, A collection. Curled (hair). One who collects or brings together. A man shewing himself good for nothing.

A عكشة *ʻakishat*, (A tree) whose branches are numerous and entangled.

A عكص *ʻaks*, (v. n. of عكص) Repelling, driving back. Closeness, compactness. Malignity, badness of temper. *ʻakis*, Bad-tempered. (Sand) difficult to walk through. *ʻakas*, (v. n. of عكص) Being stubborn, refusing to proceed (a horse).

A عكض *ʻakz*, (v. n. of عكض) Compelling, subduing. Separating. Silencing, taking down (a boaster). Confining, detaining. Deposing.

P عكعك *ʻakʻak*, A magpie.

A عكف *ʻakf*, (v. n. of عكف) Confining in chains or in prison. Keeping back, hindering, preventing. Hovering (a bird round a carcase). Staying. Being assiduous. Being threaded (pearls). *ʻakif*, Curled hair.

P عكك *ʻakak*, A magpie.

A عكك *ʻakak*, Intense heat without a breath of air. *ʻukak*, (pl. of عكّة *ʻukkat*) Leathern bottles in which butter is kept.

A عكل *ʻakl*, (v. n. of عكل) Being obscure, doubtful. Throwing in prison, keeping in chains. Binding (a camel) with the ropes عكال *ʻikāl*. Bringing back. Piling (furniture, as carpets) one upon the other. Throwing headlong on the ground. Driving (camels) hard. Collecting, assembling. Labouring diligently, striving. Conjecturing, giving as one's opinion. Dying. *ʻikl* or *ʻukl*, (pl. اعكال *aʻkāl*) Inglorious, mean, avaricious. *ʻukl*, Name of the father of a tribe noted for stupidity. *ʻakal*, (v. n. of عكل) Being sullied by the oil (a lamp). *ʻukul*, (pl. of عاكل *ʻākil*) Dwarfs. Misers, niggards.

A عكلد *ʻukalid*, (or عكلط *ʻukalit*) Thick (milk).

P A عكله *ʻakla*, A kind of ivy.

A عكم *ʻakm*, (v. n. of عكم) Tying (effects or furniture) with a garment. Loading (a camel) with two trusses; assisting another in binding burdens. Desisting. Attacking, rushing upon, turning back upon. Expecting, waiting for. Delaying, deferring. Travelling, making for. The interior of the side. *ʻikm*, A casket for jewels. A portmanteau. (pl. اعكام *aʻkām*) A rope, or any thing similar, for tying up bales. The pulley of a well. Half a horse or camel-load, as much as is carried on one side. (pl. عكوم *ʻukūm*) A bundle of clothes. *ʻukum*, (pl. of عكام *ʻikām*) Ropes for tying up bales.

A عكمة *ʻakmat*, A corner of the belly.

A عكمز *ʻukmuz*, Glans penis.

A عكمزة *ʻukmuzat*, A woman firm and full of flesh. Talis penis.

A عكمس *ʻukamis*, Many camels (about 1000).

A عكمسة *ʻakmasat*, A being dark.

A عكمص *ʻukamis*, Misfortune. Cautious, wary, on one's guard, timid. ابو العكمص *abū'l ʻukamis*, Name of an individual.

A عكموز *ʻukmūz*, Glans penis.

A عكموزة *ʻukmūzat*, A woman firm and full of flesh. Talis penis.

A عكموس *ʻukmūs*, An ass.

A عکن *ʻukan*, (pl. of عکنة *ʻuknat*) Wrinkles on the belly from fatness.

A عکناء *ʻaknāʼ*, (A girl) whose belly is wrinkled from corpulence. Thick about the teats (camel).

A عکنان *ʻaknān* or *ʻakanān*, Many, plentiful (camels or ostriches).

A عکنباة *ʻakambāt*, A spider.

A عکنة *ʻuknat*, (pl. عکن *ʻukan* and اعکان *aʻkān*) A wrinkle on the belly from fatness.

A عکنکع *ʻakankaʻ*, The male sylvan demon called Ghūl.

P عکنه *ʻakna*, Hermodactyls.

A عکو *ʻakw*, (v. n. of عکا for عکو) Tying in a knot (the tail of a horse). Binding up her hair (a woman). Partly coming out and partly remaining (dung in the fundament). Making a spiral protuberance with the garment round the middle. Ascending (as smoke). Covering and impregnating the female (a camel). Throwing into irons. Being propitious, affectionate. Being fat, plump (camels).

A عکواء *ʻakwāʼ*, (A ewe) white on the tail and black in every other part.

P عکوب *ʻakūb*, A kind of artichoke.

A عکوب *ʻakūb*, Dust. *ʻukūb*, (v. n. of عکب) Boiling. Pressing upon one another (camels when watering). Standing. Crying aloud. (pl. of عاکب *ʻākib*) Great multitudes.

A عکوب *ʻakkūb*, Dust. A dense multitude.

A عکوة *ʻukwat*, The farina of the wild date. *ʻukwat* or *ʻakwat*, (pl. عکی *ʻuka'* or عکاء *ʻikāʼ*) The thicker or greater part of any thing. A nerve split and twisted. A thick waistband of the breeches. (pl. عکی *ʻuka'*) The root of (a horse's) tail. A period, time, turn. Middle, centre. Root of the tongue.

A عکور *ʻukūr*, (v. n. of عکر) Returning. Rushing upon, assaulting. Renewing a charge.

A عکوز *ʻakwaz*, A walking-stick with an iron ferrule: a crutch. An iron case for the stump of one who has lost his foot.

A عکوف *ʻukūf*, (v. n. of عکف) Remaining constantly in the mosque. Remaining behind. Being assiduous, sticking close to. Hovering round a carcase (a bird). Being threaded, turning round on the string, or strung (pearls or gems). Paying attention, shewing kindness. Approaching, advancing towards. Surrounding, encircling. (pl. of عاکف *ʻākif*) Those who remain behind; who remain constantly at a place from motives of piety. و الناس عکوف *wa'n nās ʻukūf*, And the people waiting (outside for his coming forth).

A عکوك *ʻakawwak*, Plump, short, firm-bodied. A hard place. A plain, level country.

A عکوکع *ʻakawkaʻ*, Short, dwarfish.

A عکول *ʻakawwal*, Short of stature and fat.

A عکوم *ʻakūm*, One who recedes or departs. The place of receding or departing. A woman accustomed to bring forth a boy and girl alternately. *ʻukūm*, (pl. of عکم *ʻikm*) Bundles of clothes.

P عکه *ʻakka*, A magpie.

A عکی *ʻaky*, (v. n. of عکی) Dying. Tying the waistband of one's dress with a hard knot. Being bunchy round the girdle; that part of the Asiatic dress which is wrapped about the middle. *ʻuka'*, (pl. of عکوة *ʻukwat*) Roots of horses' tails.

A عکی *ʻakka'*, (Wearing an upper garment) with the train hanging loose. *ʻukka'*, The farina of the wild date.

A عکیّ *ʻakīy*, The stale milk of sheep, upon which they milk fresh to make it coagulate. Milk unmixed with water. A leathern bottle in which they put it. A drink made from the fruit of the wild date.

A عکیث *ʻakīs*, The urine of an elephant.

A عکیس *ʻakīs*, A shoot of a vine laid under the ground, the other extremity re-appearing above ground at a little distance. Sour milk (especially poured upon broth); also new milk upon which fat is poured. A dish made of flour and milk, stir-about.

A عکیسة *ʻakīsat*, Dark (night). A great number of camels.

A عکیظ *ʻakīz*, Short of body.

A عکیك *ʻakīk*, (pl. عکاك *ʻikāk*) Intense heat without a breath of wind. A paroxysm. Hot (day).

A عل *ʻal*, The upper part of a house. *ʻalu*, Above. من عل *min ʻalu* or *ʻali*, (or من علا *min ʻala'*) From above, from the upper or highest part.

A علّ *ʻall*, (v. n. of علّ) Striking one with repeated blows. Drinking, or causing another to drink a second time. Becoming sick. A second draught. An attenuated tike (sheep-louse), or a man like it, emaciated with sickness or age. A plump tike. One who visits and converses with women much. One whose skin is shrivelled much from disease. A large, bulky he-goat. *ʻalla*, Perhaps. علّي *ʻallī* or علّني *ʻallanī*, Perhaps I (may do). علّك *ʻallaka*, Peradventure thou (mayest see him).

A علا *ʻala'*, High. من علا *min ʻala'*, From above. (pl. of علاة) Anvils. حق جلّ وعلا *hakk jalla wa ʻala'*, God, be He glorified and exalted!

A علاء *ʻalāʼ*, (v. n. of علی) Being superior to, above, on the upper part. Being high in rank and dignity. Glory, sublimity, height, exaltation, eminence, dignity, superiority. علاء الدين *ʻalāʼu'd dīn*, (Glory of religion) A proper name (Aladdin). *ʻilāʼ*, (v. n. 3 of علا for علو) Exalting, elevating.

A علاب *ʻilāb*, An oblong mark impressed on the neck. (pl. of علبة *ʻulbat*) Milk-pails of wood or camels' leather.

A علابط *ʻulābit*, (pl. علابط *ʻalābit* or علابيط *ʻalābīt*) Thick milk. Any thing thick. One's own weight or person. A flock of sheep. Corpulent.

A علابيّ *ʻalābiy*, Lead, tin. (pl. of علباء *ʻilbāʼ* or *ʻalbāʼ*) Strong nerves on each side of a camel's neck.

A علاة *ʻalāt*, (pl. علا *ʻala'*) An anvil. A kind of stone on which they place اقط *akit* in the form of a milk-pail, surrounded with dung, and then milk upon it. A tall she-camel.

A علّات *ʻillāt*, (pl. of علّة *ʻillat*) Accidents. Causes. Diseases. علی کلّ علّاته *ʻala' kulli ʻillātihi*, In all respects. ابناء علّات *abnāʼi ʻallāt*, (or بنو العلّات *banū'l ʻallāt*) Sons of one father by different mothers.

A علاثة *ʻulāsat*, Mixture of two things; as اقط *akit* with butter. One who collects here and there.

A علاج *ʻilāj*, (v. n. 3 of علج) Applying (a remedy). Adjusting, managing (affairs). A medicine. Remedy, cure, treatment, management. P بي علاج *bī ʻilāj*, Without remedy, incurable.

P علاج پذير *ʻilāj-pazīr*, Curable.

A علاجيم *ʻalājīm*, Strong, robust camels.

A علادي *ʻulāda'*, Strong (camel).

A علاس *ʻulās*, A thing, somewhat (eatable).

A علاص *ʻilās*, An advance of money made to one on condition of sharing the profits.

A علاط *ʻilāt*, A rope round a camel's neck. (pl. اعلطة *aʻlitat*) A transverse mark made by burning. Gossamer floating in the rays of the sun. The side of a camel's neck. A black ring round a dove's neck. Thread (of a needle). Mischief, dispute, strife.

A علاف *ʻilāf*, (pl. of علف *ʻalaf*) Provenders.

A علّاف *ʻallāf*, A vender of forage or fodder, a purveyor of provender. A corn-chandler.

A علافيّات *ʻilāfīyāt*, Strong pack-saddles, large in the middle and behind, made by علاف *ʻilāf*.

A علاق *ʻalāk*, Food, fodder sufficient for cattle. A road. The beam which supports the pulley of a well. The pulley itself; also the rope. A large bucket. Wish, desire. Friendship. A piece of meat. A glance. *ʻalāki*, Hang on, strike your claws in.

A علّاق *ʻullāk*, A kind of plant.

A علاقة *ʻalākat*, (v. n. of علق) Falling in love, being attached. A strong inclination towards. (pl. علائق *ʻalāʼik*) Relation, parentage, connection, dependency, attachment, interest. An art or a trade upon which one is dependent for a subsistence. A sufficiency for the support of life. Food sufficient for the day. Friendship. Enmity, altercation. Death. A road. A camel employed in bringing provisions. The beam from which the pulley of a well is suspended. The pulley itself; also the rope. A large bucket. Wish, desire. A woman's portion, which the husband is bound to pay in case he sues for a divorce. علاقهٔ قرابت *ʻalākaʼi karābat*, Connection of kindred. *ʻilākat*, A rope or strap by which any thing is fastened (as a shield, bow, whip, &c.). (pl. علائق *ʻalāʼik*) Fixed love. علاقة الصيد *ʻilākatu's sayd*, Game suspended by the legs.

A علّاقة *ʻallākat*, Death. Calamity, adversity.

P علاقه بند *ʻilāka-band*, A tape-maker.

A علاقي *ʻalāka'*, (pl. of علقی *ʻalka'*) Kinds of

brooms. ʻulāka', (pl. of علاقية ʻalākiyat) Titles, surnames. Attachments, fixed affections. Game suspended by cords fastened to the legs.

A علاقية ʻalākiyat, (A man) devoted wholly to any thing. (pl. علاقى ʻulāka') A title, surname.

A علاك ʻalāk or ʻulāk, Any thing eatable. A certain tree in Hijāz.

A علاك ʻallāk, A vender of the gum علك ʻilk.

A علاكد ʻulākid, Thick milk.

A علاكم ʻulākim, (pl. ʻalākim) Strong (camel).

A علال ʻilāl, A being milked at mid-day.

P علالا ʻalālā, An acclamation of reproof.

A علالة ʻulālat, Whatever diverts one from any pursuit. Remains of any thing. Strokings (in milking). The mid-day-milking of cattle.

A علالى ʻalāliy, (pl. of عليّة ʻilliyat) Supper-rooms, upper rooms, parlours.

A علام ʻilām, (pl. of علامة ʻalāmat) Signs, marks. (pl. of علم ʻalam) Milestones. Landmarks. Mountains. ʻulām, A sparrow-hawk. ʻalāma, (for على ما ʻala' mā) Upon what?

A علام ʻallām, Omniscient, God (as knowing every thing). A very learned man. One skilled in genealogies. علام الغيوب ʻallāmu'l ghuyūb, Acquainted with things future and invisible (an epithet of God). بحمد الله الملك العلام bi hamdi 'llāhi'l malihi'l ʻallām, With praise to God, the king of knowledge, or the Omniscient. ʻillām, (v. n. 2 of علم) Teaching, instructing. Wearing any mark or badge of recognition (as soldiers do in battle). ʻullām, A sparrow-hawk. Privet. A very learned man. Skilled in genealogies. (pl. of عالم ʻālim) Learned men.

A علامة ʻalāmat, (pl. علام ʻalām) A sign, signal, mark; any distinguishing characteristic or impression. Diagnosis (of a disease). A pedigree, coat of arms, armorial bearing, cognizance. A miracle, prodigy. A standard, banner, ensign. A road-post, milestone, or any thing similar for shewing the way or the boundaries of lands.

A علامة ʻallāmat, A very learned man. Skilled in genealogies. علامهٔ عصر ʻallāmaʼi ʻasr, The most learned man of the age. علامة الوري ʻallāmatu'l wara', The most learned of men. ʻullāmat, That whereby a thing is proved or demonstrated.

A علامض ʻulāmiz, Slow, heavy, oppressed at the stomach. One whose company is disagreeable.

A علامه ʻalāmah, (for على ما ʻala' mā) Upon what.

A علامي ʻallāmī, My very wise man, the familiar title which Akbar, Emperor of Hindūstān, gave to his minister Abū'l Fazl.

A علامي ʻulāmiy, Light, active. Acute, intelligent.

A علامي ʻallāmiy, Most exceedingly wise.

A علاميد ʻalāmīd, (or علامدة ʻalāmidat) (pl. of علماد ʻilmād or علمادة ʻilmādat) Things round which threads are wound.

A علان ʻilān, An acting openly with.

A علان ʻallān, Ignorant (man).

A علانة ʻallānat, Ignorant (woman).

A علاند ʻalānid, (pl. of علندي ʻalanda') Thick, gross, fat. Certain thorny trees.

A علاني ʻalāniy, (pl. علانيين ʻalāniyīn) Public, open, manifest, notorious.

A علانية ʻalāniyat, (v. n. of علن) Becoming manifest, public, open, notorious. Publication, divulgation, notoriety, publicity. (pl. علانين ʻalānīn) Public, open, notorious. External (behaviour or conduct). ʻalāniyatan, Publicly. سرا و علانية sirran wa ʻalāniyatan, Privately and publicly.

A علانين ʻalānīn, (pl. of علانية ʻalāniyat) Open, public, notorious.

A علاوة ʻalāwat, Redundancy, superabundance, excess. Height. ʻalāwat or ʻulāwat, The upper or better part. ʻilāwat, (pl. علاوي ʻalāwa') The upper part, any thing placed above another; the head (as above the neck), a small package laid on the top of a horse or camel-load. ʻulāwat, The upper part. علاوة الريح ʻulāwatu'r rīh, An upper current of air.

A P علاوه ʻalāwa, Moreover, beside, o'er and above.

A علاوي ʻalāwa', (pl. of علاوة ʻilāwat) Bundles placed on loads of horses and camels.

A علاه ʻilāh, (and علاهى ʻalāha') (pl. of علهان ʻalhān) Hungry. Sprightly (horses).

A علاهم ʻulāhim, Large and fat camel.

A علاية ʻalāyat, A high place.

A علائق ʻalāʼik, (pl. of علاقة ʻalākat or ʻilākat) Affections, studies, attachments. (pl. of عليقة ʻalīkat) Marriage-portions. She-camels employed in bringing provisions.

A علائم ʻalāʼim, Signs, indications.

A علب ʻalb, (v. n. of علب) Making an impression, marking. Cutting. Scraping. Fastening tight the handle of a sword, or the like, with the sinew of a camel's neck. Aiming at the nerve of a camel's neck with the sharp part of a sword. (pl. علوب ʻulūb) A mark, vestige, impression. A rough, rocky, unfruitful place. A hard substance. ʻilb, (pl. علوب ʻulūb) A worthless fellow from whom no good is to be expected. A place which no rain can render fruitful. A rough, rugged place. Ground where lote-trees grow. ʻilb or ʻulb, Old (lizard or goat). ʻalab, (v. n. of علب) Being firm, solid (flesh). Beginning to corrupt (meat). Being broken in the edge (a sword). A disease in the neck or in the two nerves of the neck (of a camel). ʻalib, A hard substance. Old and tough (goat or lizard). ʻulab, (pl. of علبة ʻulbat) Milk-pails of wood or leather.

A علباء ʻilbā, (v. n. of علبي Q) Piercing or cutting the علباء ʻilbāʼ of a slave. Becoming very prominent from age (the علباء ʻilbāʼ of a man). ʻilbāʼ or ʻalbā, (pl. علابي ʻalābiy) A strong nerve on each side of a camel's neck, between which the mane grows.

A علبة ʻilbat, A piece of hard wood whereof they make stocks or fetters, also censers. ʻulbat or ʻilbat, (pl. علاب ʻilāb and علب ʻulab) A milk-pail of wood or camel's leather. A case, coffer. A pill-box. A tall palm-tree.

A علبط ʻulabit, A corpulent man. A flock of sheep. Thick milk. Any thing thick. One's own weight or person.

A علبطة ʻulabitat, A flock of sheep.

A علبوبة ʻulbūbat, The better sort of people.

A علبية ʻilbiyat, A nasty, dirty she-camel.

A علّة ʻallat, Harm, hurt. Need, want, indigence. ʻillat, An accident, misfortune, infirmity, casualty, calamity, disease, suffering, ailing, ailment. Dirt. A pretence, excuse. A cause, reason. Any thing which diverts one from his object. A corrupt bias, perversion. علت پشت ʻillati pusht, An unnatural propensity. علت زيارت ʻillati ziyārat, Under pretence of a visit. علت صوري ʻillati sūrī, Formal cause, i. e. that form in which its essence consists. علت غائي ʻillati ghāʼī, Final cause or purpose for which it was made. علت فاعلي ʻillati fāʻilī, Efficient cause, (as the maker, if the work of man). علت مادّي ʻillati māddī, Material cause, or the matter of which the thing is made. علت قمّي ʻillati kummī, A plague or endemial disease peculiar to the city of Kumm. (metaph.) Obscurities, difficulties in a book. بعلة bi ʻillatin, On pretence, on pretended ground. حرف علة harfu ʻillatin, A letter of infirmity. حروف العلة hurūfu'l ʻillat, The infirm letters ا, و, and ي. P بعلت ba ʻillat, For the sake of. By reason of, on account. بي علت bī ʻillat, Without cause. Independent.

P علت دانه ʻillat-dāna, Small-pox.

A علث ʻals, (v. n. of علث) Mixing (wheat with barley). Collecting. Tanning a leathern bottle with the plant ارطى arta'. Failing to strike fire (a flint). ʻalas, Intrepidity in battle, fierceness of combat. ʻalis, An adopted son, the putative son of a man not his father. Attached, sticking close to in order to secure his rights.

P علث ʻils, A kind of wild endive.

A علثة ʻulsat, Any thing within the reach of cattle. Food sufficient for the day. Somewhat.

A علج ʻalj, (v. n. of علج) Conquering, overcoming, excelling in adjusting or healing. ʻilj, (pl. علوج ʻulūj, اعلاج aʻlāj, معلوجاء maʻlūjāʼ, معلوجي maʻlūja', علجة ʻilajat or ʻalajat) A proselyte (either in a religious or a political light). An infidel, one of no religion. An ass, the onager (especially fat and strong). Rough, fierce. A cake with a thick edge. علج مال ʻilju mālin, A steward, skilful manager of camels. ʻalaj, A dwarf-species of palm-tree. ʻalij, ʻulaj, or علّج ʻullaj, Solid, grave, firm (man). An able, skilful, vigorous manager.

A علجان ʻuljān, A quantity of thorny shrubs

called عضاه *ʻizāh*. *ʻalajān*, The waving pace of a she-camel. Name of a plant, from the stem of which toothpicks are made.

P علجان *ʻalajān*, Name of a plant used in washing the hands.

A علجانة *ʻalajānat*, Dust collected by the wind round the roots of trees.

A علجة *ʻil* or *ʻalajat*, (pl. of علج) Proselytes.

A علجم *ʻaljam*, Long, tall.

A علجن *ʻaljan*, A woman careless of what she says or does. A stout she-camel.

A علجوم *ʻuljūm*, (pl. علاجيم *ʻalājīm*) A robust, choice camel. A male frog. An old bull. A drake. A male ostrich. A ram. A mountain-goat. A wild buck of a brown colour. A certain white bird. A tike. A wave of the sea. A garden thickly set with palms. Very deep water. Darkness of night.

A علجون *ʻuljūn*, Strong (she-camel).

A علحدّة *ʻalahidda*, Separate, apart, distinct.

A علد *ʻald*, (v. n. of علد) Being hard and strong. Hard, strong. A nerve in the neck. Hardness.

A علدمي *ʻaldamiy*, Greedy, eating all he can get.

A علز *ʻalaz*, (v. n. of علز) Being covetous. Fretting, chafing, crying out, being impatient under mental or bodily distress or bondage. *ʻaliz*, Avaricious. Fretful, restless, unable to sleep.

A علس *ʻals*, (v. n. of علس) Drinking, eating, tasting. Meat, drink. *ʻalas*, Thick (tike). A tike. A lentil. A sort of ant. A species of wheat grown in Arabia, having two grains in each husk.

A علسيّ *ʻalasiy*, A robust, undaunted man. A plant whose flower resembles the lily.

A علش *ʻalsh*, Greediness.

A علشط *ʻalashshat*, Of a bad disposition.

A علصة *ʻulsat*, A small quantity.

A علض *ʻalz*, (v. n. of علض) Wagging (a stake) from side to side to pull (it out of the ground).

A علط *ʻalt*, (v. n. of علط) Marking (a camel) on the neck with a transverse mark. Aiming at or hitting (with an arrow). Speaking ill of any one. A black mole or ornamental patch on the face. *ʻulat*, A male camel without a bridle. *ʻulut*, (pl. اعلاط *aʻlāt*) A she-camel without a burnt mark or a bridle. Short (asses). Long (she-camels). (pl. of اعليط *iʻlīt*) Transverse marks on a camel's neck.

A علطبيس *ʻaltabīs*, Resplendent, bright, glittering, smooth.

A علطة *ʻultat*, A necklace, chain, or any similar ornament. A black mole, or any black ornamental patch on a woman's face.

A علطسة *ʻaltasat*, A running in a wrong road.

A علطميس *ʻaltamīs*, Plump, healthy, delicate (girl). A large head bald. A glutton. Tall and strong (she-camel).

A علطوس *ʻiltaws*, Active, excellent (she-camel). Tall (man).

A علع *ʻalaʻ*, (and علعل *ʻalʻala*) Words used in calling out to sheep or camels.

A علعال *ʻalʻāl*, A male lark.

A علعل *ʻalʻal* or *ʻulʻul*, The breast-bone situated above the belly and in shape like a tongue. Membrum virile. The male lark. *ʻalʻalla*, Haply.

A علعلان *ʻalʻalān*, A certain large tree.

A علعول *ʻulʻūl*, Continued evil. Wavering, uncertain, irresolute. A battle, conflict, strife.

A علف *ʻalf*, (v. n. of علف) Feeding cattle, giving them plenty of meat and drink. Much drink. *ʻilf*, Who devours much. *ʻilf* or *ʻulf*, A certain tree growing in Yaman, the leaf of which resembles that of the vine, and is used as a substitute for vinegar in cookery. *ʻulf* or *ʻuluf*, (pl. of علوفة *ʻalūfat*) Stipends, salaries. *ʻalaf*, (pl. علوف *ʻulūf*, اعلاف *aʻlāf*, and علاف *ʻilāf*) Grass, forage, fodder, hay, straw, provender. P علف شيرين *ʻalafi shīrīn*, (or علف خورش *ʻalafi khwurish*) The medlar. *ʻuluf*, (pl. of علوفة *ʻalūfat*) Provisions for horses.

A علّف *ʻullaf*, The fruit of the acacia, resembling beans (with which they feed camels).

A علفتاني *ʻalfatāniy*, Foolish: chattering fellow.

P علفخانه *ʻalaf-khāna*, The world.

P علفخوار *ʻalaf-khwār*, Pasture. علفخوارهاي خرّم *ʻalaf-khwārahāyi khurram*, Charming pastures.

P علفخور *ʻaluf-khwur*, Any beast fed in the stall (as a horse, ass, or mule), stall-fed. A glutton.

P علفدان *ʻalafdān*, A hay or corn-bin. The crop of a bird. The maw or paunch of a beast.

P علفزار *ʻalafzār*, Pasturage, a meadow.

A علفصة *ʻalfasat*, Force, compulsion, harshness, severity. A tripping or twisting in wrestling of an adversary, though stronger than one's self.

A علفطة *ʻalfatat*, (v. n. of علفط Q) Mixing.

P علف ناك *ʻalafnāk*, Abundant in pasturage.

A علفوت *ʻilfawt* or *ʻulfūt*, Ignorant, careless of what one says.

A علفوف *ʻulfūf*, An ill-tempered old fellow; also one fleshy and hairy. A coarsely-made man. An old woman. A thick, bulky stallion. A she-camel with a compact bunch.

A علق *ʻalh*, (v. n. of علق) Browsing the summit of a tree (a camel). Tormenting with opprobrious language. Part of a garment torn by adhering to any thing. Any thing very precious (especially old wine or costly raiment). A certain tree used in tanning. An earthern vessel; a bag or sack. *ʻilk*, (v. n. of علق) Falling in love, being attached. A shield. A sword. (pl. اعلاق *aʻlāk* and علوق *ʻulūk*) Any thing most excellent or precious (especially wine of the best kind, or costly garments). A leathern bag or sack. An interest. A sword or shield. علق علم *ʻilku ʻilmin*, Devoted to learning. علق شرّ *ʻilku sharrin*, Addicted to wickedness. *ʻalak*, (v. n. of علق) Browsing on the topmost leaves of a tree (a camel), as if suspended from it. Being suspended, hanging (a deer in a noose). Having a horse-leech fastening upon his chin whilst drinking (a camel). Falling in love, being deeply affected with that passion (a girl). Conceiving, being pregnant (a woman). Quarrelling, litigating. Setting about, commencing. Knowing, understanding. Lasting love, affection, attachment. Suspension. Any thing suspended or hoisted up by a pulley. A rogue who deserves the halter. Any thing tenaciously adhering (as viscous clay). Lasting litigation, quarrelling, or any thing bad to which one is remarkably addicted. Thick, clotted blood. The middle or main part of a road. A rent in a garment from something sticking to it. A sufficiency of fodder for daily consumption. The tender leaves of trees which cattle cannot reach and crop. A pulley with all its tackling, including the rope and bucket. (pl. of علقة *ʻalakat*) Leeches. علق القربة *ʻalaku'l kirbat*, Water dripping from a leathern bottle. Shame. Labour, exertion. *ʻulak*, A large body, troop, herd. Deaths. Employments, occupations. A great calamity, prodigy, portent.

A علقة *ʻalkat*, A drawing, a dragging or trailing (of a garment). *ʻilkat*, The first garment worn by a boy. A sleeveless shirt. A girl's frock open at the sides as far as the waist. A rich garment. A certain tree used in tanning. *ʻulkat*, A part or one of any thing, somewhat. Any thing necessary for the support of life. An interest. Suspension. Whatever cattle can reach on a tree. A tree upon which camels browse all winter until spring. A glance. A bit of meat. Any thing precious. *ʻalakat*, Suspension. A quantity of coagulated blood. One drop of thick clotted blood. A horse-leech.

A علقم *ʻalkam*, The wild gourd. The bitter lote-fruit. Any thing bitter. Bitter water.

A علقمة *ʻalkamat*, Bitterness. A putting of any thing bitter amongst victuals. Name of two poets.

A علقى *ʻalka'*, (pl. علاقى) A kind of broom.

A علك *ʻalk*, (v. n. of علك) Chewing. Chewing (gum). Grating the teeth. Champing the bit (a horse). *ʻilk*, (pl. علوك *ʻulūk*) The gum of pine, juniper, or turpentine, which may be chewed. *ʻalak*, A certain tree found in Hijāz. *ʻalik*, Adhesive, viscous. Tough (meat).

A علكات *ʻalikāt*, Strong canine teeth.

A علكة *ʻalakat*, A fine fat she-camel. *ʻalikat*, Ground having water near it. A substance like lights, protruding from the mouth of a camel in rut.

A علكد *ʻalkad*, *ʻilkid*, *ʻulkud*, or *ʻulakid*, Thick. *ʻilkid*, A monstrous-looking and shrewd old hag. A woman of a short and mean appearance. *ʻulakid*, Thick milk.

A علكدّ *ʻilkadd*, Fat, grease.

A علكز *ʻalkaz* or *ʻilkiz*, A strong big man, and full of flesh.

A علكم *ʻalkam*, (or علكوم) A strong camel.

A علكمة ɛalkamat, Bigness of a camel's bunch.

A علل ɛalal, (v. n. of علّ) Drinking or causing another to drink a second time. A second draught. ɛilal, (pl. of علّة ɛillat) Pretences. Causes. Defects, infirmities. علل اربعه ɛilali arbaɛa, Four causes. P علل دریاوکان ɛilali daryāwakān, The sun.

A علم ɛalm, (v. n. of علم) Signing, marking. Excelling in science, being learned. Making a fissure in the upper lip. The world. Men, creatures, every thing that the world contains. ɛilm, (v. n. of علم) Knowing, understanding, being learned. Doing any thing firmly and well. (pl. علوم ɛulūm) Knowledge, science, doctrine. Known. Art, profession. Theory. (in the language of Sūfis or mystics) The great veil which conceals the Almighty. علم الادب ɛilmu'l adab, (or علم الاخلاق ɛilmu'l akhlāḳ) Ethics, morals. علم استخراج ɛilmi istikhrāj, Astrology. علم اسما ɛilmi asmā, The knowledge of the names, i.e. of the attributes of God. علم الاكتاف ɛilmu'l aktāf, The science of divining by the shoulder-blades of sheep. P علم اندازه ɛilmi andāza, Geometry. A علم انشا ɛilmi inshā, Letter-writing. علم باطن ɛilmi bātin, Speculative science. علم بیان ɛilmi bayān, (علم بلاغت ɛilmi balāghat, علم خطابت ɛilmi khitābat, علم كلام ɛilmi kalām, or علم معاني ɛilmi maɛānī) The explanatory science, i.e. rhetoric, oratory, eloquence. علم تشريح ɛilmi tashrīh, Anatomy. علم تصريف ɛilmi tasrīf, (or علم الصرف ɛilmu's sarf) Grammar. علم تصوّف ɛilmi tasawwuf, The mystic or the contemplative science. علم تنظر ɛilmi tanazzur, Optics. علم تواريخ ɛilmi tawārīkh, Chronology; history. علم الجبر ɛilmu'l jabar, Algebra. P علم چل صباح ɛilmi chil sabāh, The leavening of the clay of which Adam was formed. A علم حديث ɛilmi hadīs, Knowledge of Muhammadan tradition. علم حساب ɛilmi hisāb, (علم غبار ɛilmi ghubār, علم رقم ɛilmi raḳam, or علم عدد ɛilmi ɛadad) Arithmetic, science of numbers. علم حكمت ɛilmi hikmat, Philosophy, physics. علم الحوادث ɛilmu'l hawādis, Astrology. P علم خدا ɛilmi khudā, (or علم الهى ɛilmi ilāhī) Theology. A علم رمل ɛilmi raml, Geomancy. علم رياضت ɛilmi riyāzat (or رياضي riyāzī) Mathematics. P علم زمين ɛilmi zamīn, Geology, geography. علم ستاره ɛilmi sitāra, Astronomy. A علم سحر ɛilmi sihr, Magic. علم سيميا ɛilmi sīmiyā, Alchymy. Chiromancy, palmistry. علم شريف ɛilmi sharīf, The noble science, that of the stars. علم شعر ɛilmi shiɛr, Poetry. علم الطبّ ɛilmu't tibb, (or علم ادويه ɛilmi adwiya) The medical art. علم طبيعي ɛilmi tabīɛī, Natural philosophy. علم العبارة ɛilmu'l ɛibārat, The science of interpreting dreams. علم عروض ɛilmi ɛarūz, Poetry, versification. Scansion. علم عقل ɛilmi ɛaḳl, Natural knowledge. علم الفقه ɛilmu'l fiḳh, Jurisprudence. علم القوافي ɛilmu'l ḳawāfī, Art of rhyming. علم الكف ɛilmu'l kaff, (or علم اليد ɛilmu'l yad) Palmistry. علم الكلام و العقائد ɛilmu'l kalām wa'l ɛaḳāid, Scholastic theology. Metaphysics. علم كيميا ɛilmi kīmiyā, Alchymy. علم لغت ɛilmi lughat, Lexicography. علم مثلّث ɛilmi musallas, (or علم رصد ɛilmi rasad) Gnomics, trigonometry. علم مرايه ɛilmi marāya, Study of perspective. علم المساحة ɛilmu'l masāhat, Geometry. Mensuration. علم ملاحة ɛilmi mallāhat, Nautical art. علم المنطق ɛilmu'l mantiḳ, Logic. علم الموسقى ɛilmu'l mūsīḳī, (or علم تأليف اللحون ɛilmi taɛlīfi'l luhūn) Art of music. علم نباتات ɛilmi nabātāt, Botany. علم نجوم ɛilmi nujūm, Astronomy; astrology. علم نحو ɛilmi nahv, Grammar, syntax. علم نقل ɛilmi naḳl, Borrowed or revealed science. علم الوجوه ɛilmu'l wujūh, Physiognomy. علم الهندسة ɛilmu'l handasat, Geometry. علم الهئة ɛilmu'l hiɛat, Astronomy. علم هئة دنيا ɛilmi hiɛati dunya', Cosmography. علم اليقين ɛilmu'l yaḳīn, Certain knowledge, demonstration. A religious life. العلم عند الله al ɛilm ɛinda'llāh, The knowledge is with God, God knows. اهل علم ahli ɛilm, Learned; a learned person. طالب علم tālibi ɛilm, Studious, searching for knowledge. A student. ɛalam, (v. n. of علم) Having a fissure on the upper lip, or at the corner of the mouth. A standard, ensign, colours, flag, banner, cornette, guidon. (pl. علام ɛilām and اعلام aɛlām) A sign, mark, boundary-stone; a road, direction-post, milestone. The border of a garment, especially when embroidered of different colours. An epaulette. A fissure in the upper lip, or at the corners of the mouth. A long mountain. A prince, lord. (in grammar) A proper name. P علم انداختن ɛalam andākhtan, To strike or throw away one's colours. To forget, neglect. علم برداشتن ɛalam bar dāshtan, To set up the standard, take the field. علم روز ɛalami roz, Break of day. The sun. علم صبح ɛalami subh, False or true dawn. علم كشيدن ɛalam kashīdan, To draw, unsheath. A علم كائنات ɛalami kāɛināt, The sky. P علم ماتم ɛalami mātam, A flag borne in a funeral procession. A علم معكوس ɛalami maɛkūs, With the colours reversed. P علم نمودن ɛalam namūdan, To prepare, unfurl. علم همايون ɛalami humāyūn, The imperial standard. علمهاي روز ɛalamhāyi roz, The true dawn. The false dawn. The morning-star. The sun. مير علم mīr ɛalam, The prefect of the standard, i.e. the governor of a small territory. علم الله لافعلنّ كذا ɛalima'llāh la afɛalanna kazā, By the all-wise God, or God knows, I will surely do so.

A علماء ɛalmāɛ, (fem. of اعلم aɛlam) One with a fissure in the lip. Slit (lip). Armour, mail. A woman's shift. (for علي الماء ɛala'l māɛ) On the water. ɛulamāɛ, (pl. of عليم ɛalīm) Doctors, theologians. The learned. علماى محقق ɛulamāɛi muhaḳḳiḳ, Men of undoubted learning.

A علماد ɛilmād, (and علمادة ɛilmādat) (pl. علامدة ɛalāmidat and علاميد ɛalāmīd) Any thing upon which threads are wound into clews; a ball of thread.

P علم بخش ɛalam-bakhsh, Prize-money given to soldiers who have fought under the same colours.

A علمة ɛulmat or ɛalamat, A fissure in the upper lip, or at the corners of the mouth.

P علمخوان ɛilm-khwān, Studious.

P علمدار ɛalam-dār, A standard-bearer.

P علمدان ɛilm-dān, Learned, wise.

A علمص ɛulamis, A wonderful thing.

A علمى ɛilmīy, Scientific, theoretic: doctrinal.

A علمية ɛalamīyat, Quality of proper name.

A علميس ɛilmīs, A fatiguing nocturnal journey (in search of water).

A علن ɛalan, (v. n. of علن) Becoming published, divulged. Publishing, divulging.

A علنة ɛulanat, Who conceals nothing, a blab.

A علنداة ɛalandāt, A thorny tree.

A علندس ɛalandas, Strong, robust. A lion.

A علندي ɛalanda' or ɛulanda', (pl. علاند ɛalānid) Corpulent, large, bulky. A kind of thorn.

A علنكد ɛalankad, Hard and strong.

A علنكز ɛalankaz, A thick, gross, fat, big man.

A علو ɛalw, ɛulw, or ɛilw, Upper or better part (of any thing). Height, eminence. علو الدار ɛulwu'd or ɛilwu'd dār, The upper stories of a house.

A علوا ɛalwan, By force, forcibly. من علو min ɛalwin, From on high.

A علوّ ɛulūw, (v. n. of علا for علو) Being high, lofty, sublime, lifted up. Being high in rank. Penetrating, being thoroughly up to, knowing. Behaving proudly. Ascending, mounting. Conquering, overcoming. Striking (with a sword). Eminence, height, sublimity. علوّ شان و سطوع ɛulūwi shān u sutūɛ, Height of dignity and exaltation.

A علواء ɛalwāɛ, A lofty business, a high matter.

A علوان ɛulwān, (v. n. of علون Q) Prefacing or writing a title-page to a book. Title-page, preface.

A علوب ɛulūb, (pl. of علب ɛalb) Vestiges, tracks, traces. (pl. of علب ɛilb) Good-for-nothing men.

A علوج ɛalūj, An embassy, message. An ambassador. علوج صدق ɛalūju sidḳin, A faithful ambassador. ɛulūj, (pl. of علج ɛilj) Asses. Proselytes. Barbarians.

A علوّد ɛalwadd, Great. Long. A man of rank and gravity. علوّد العنق ɛilwaddu'l ɛunuḳ, Long-necked (man).

A علودة ɛalwadat, (v. n. of علود Q) Adhering firmly, remaining immoveable.

A علوّدة ɛilwaddat, (Horses) unmanageable unless goaded from behind. Old, decrepit (camels).

A علو رتبت ɛulū-rutbat, High dignity.

A علوز ɛillawz, Cholic. Fury, madness. Sudden death. A thick clitoris.

A علوس ɛalūs, Any thing (especially eatable). ما علسنا علوساً mā ɛalasnā ɛalūsan, We have not tasted any thing.

A علّوس *ʿallūs*, A certain fort belonging to the Kurds. *ʿillaws*, The cholic.

A علّوش *ʿillawsh*, A jackal. A wolf. A certain small animal. A species of beast of prey. Light, not heavy. Greedy, covetous.

A علّوص *ʿillaws*, Indigestion. Cholic.

A علّوض *ʿillawz*, A jackal.

A علوف *ʿulūf*, (pl. of علف *ʿalaf*) Provisions.

A علّوف *ʿillawf*, An old man.

A علوفة *ʿalūfat*, (A camel or sheep) fed at home on the fruit of the acacia, called علّف *ʿullaf*. (pl. علف *ʿuluf* or *ʿulf*) Provender for a horse. Stipend, salary, pension, soldier's pay, subsistence-money.

P علوفجي *ʿalūfjī*, A stipendiary.

A علوق *ʿalūk*, Death. A demon of the woods. A draught of milk. Any thing hanging about a man. What a camel eats, especially cropping the tender foliage and branches of trees. Semen genitale viri. A tree eaten by she-camels ten months gone with young. A she-camel giving suck to another's colt, thinking it her own (if she discovers the mistake by smell, she gives none; they therefore stop her nose). A woman liking none but her own husband. A she-camel not liking the male, or not keeping close to her colt. A woman who suckles another's child, a wet-nurse. One who talks but does not perform. A calamity, misfortune. *ʿulūk*, (v. n. of علق) Loving, being inclined. An interest. (pl. of علق *ʿilk*) Most precious of wines or clothes.

A علوك *ʿulūk*, (pl. of علك) Resins, pine-gums.

A علوم *ʿulūm*, (pl. of علم *ʿilm*) Sciences. علوم عقليّه و نقليّه و رياضيّه *ʿulūmi ʿakliya u nakliya u riyāziya*, Speculative, practical, and mathematical sciences. علوم المتعارفة *ʿulūmu'l mutaʿārifat*, Axioms, common sayings. جوامع العلوم *jawāmiʿu'l ʿulūm*, An encyclopedia.

A علون *ʿulūn*, A becoming public, notorious.

A علونة *ʿalwanat*, (v. n. of علون Q) Prefacing or writing a title-page to a book.

A علويّ *ʿulwīy*, Native of the upper parts of Arabia called عالية *ʿāliyat*. High, sublime. جواهر علويّه *jawāhiri ʿulwiya*, The gems above, *i. e.* the stars. *ʿalawīy*, A descendant of عليّ *ʿalīy*, Alīy.

P علويان *ʿulwiyān*, Angels. Planets. *ʿalawiyān*, Princes, lords (descendants of عليّ *ʿalīy*, Alīy.

A علويّة *ʿulwiyat*, Sublimity.

A عله *ʿalah*, (v. n. of عله) Being astonished, amazed; running to and fro in terror. Falling under a reproof. Being of a malignant mind, quarrelling. Being hungry, starving. Being sprightly (horse), obeying cheerfully the reins. Applying diligently. Experiencing a slight crop-sickness. Sharpness, ardour. Foulness, impurity. *ʿalih*, Astonished, confounded.

A علهاء *ʿalhāʾ*, A vest doubled and lined with camels' hair, worn under armour.

A علهاص *ʿilhās*, The stopple of a bottle.

A علهان *ʿalhān*, (pl. علاه *ʿilāh* and علاهى *ʿalāhā'*) Hungry. A male ostrich. Sprightly (horse).

A علهب *ʿalhab*, (fem. علهبة *ʿalhabat*) Tall (man). Long-horned (goat). A mountain-ox.

A علهج *ʿalhaj*, A sort of tree.

A علهجة *ʿalhajat*, (v. n. of علهج Q) Softening a skin at the fire, preparing it for eating.

A علهدة *ʿalhadat*, A feeding (a child) well.

A علهز *ʿilhiz*, A kind of food which the Arabians prepare, of blood and camels' hair; these are eaten in great scarcity. An aged she-camel with some remains of strength. A sort of plant. A large tike.

A علهسة *ʿalhasat*, A handling rudely.

A علهصة *ʿalhasat*, (v. n. of علهص Q) (or علهضة *ʿalhazat*) (v. n. of علهض Q) Handling a bottle to draw the stopple. Wishing to pull out an eye. Incommoding. Dealing roughly with, compelling, forcing. Taking forcibly, obtaining. Importuning.

A علّهم *ʿillahm*, Large and fat (camel).

A علهمّ *ʿilhamm*, Large and fat (camel).

A علهى *ʿalha'*, (fem.) Hungry. Sprightly (mare).

A علي *ʿaly*, A high place. *ʿaly* also *ʿily*, (v. n. of علي) Ascending (a flat roof or terrace). *ʿily*, Chiefs, nobles. *ʿala'* Above, upon, over. On, upon. In addition to. Before. Towards. Against, opposite. Alongside. To. According to. Of. For, on account of, in consideration of. Although. Notwithstanding. In. From. By. عليّ زيدا *ʿalayya' zaydan*, Shew me, tell me, Zayd. عليك زيدا *ʿalayka zaydan*, Take Zayd, bring him here. عليه *ʿalayhi*, He owes. It behoveth him. علي الاتّصال *ʿala'l ittisāl*, Connectedly, continually, without interruption. علي اثر *ʿala' asar*, Instantly. علي الاستمرار *ʿala'l istimrār*, Continually, incessantly. Perseveringly. علي اسعد الحال و ايمن الفال *ʿala' asʿada'l hāl wa aymana'l fāl*, In the happiest situation, and with the most aupicious omen. علي الاطلاق *ʿala'l itlāk*, Absolutely, universally. علي ان *ʿala' an*, On condition that. Seeing that. Although, notwithstanding. علي الانفراد *ʿala'l infirād*, Separately. علي اي حال *ʿala' ayyi hālin*, In every manner, howsoever that may be. علي باب الله *ʿala' bāb allāh*, Carelessly, slightly. علي التحقيق *ʿala't tahkīk*, Certainly, surely, in truth. علي التعجيل *ʿala't taʿjīl*, Hastily. علي التفصيل *ʿala't tafsīl*, (or علي وجه التفصيل *ʿala' wajhi't tafsīl*) Prolixly, diffusedly, at full length, in detail. علي تقدير الضرر *ʿala' takdīri'z zarar*, In case of loss. علي تقدير الوقوع *ʿala' takdīri'l wukūʿ*, In case it happens. علي تلك النعم *ʿala' tilki'n niʿam*, For these favours. علي التوالي *ʿala't tawālī*, Successively, in a continued series. علي حسب ترتيب *ʿala' hasbi tartīb*, In order, regularly. علي حسب مراتبهم و ترتيب مناصبهم *ʿala' hasbi marātibihim wa tartībi manāsibihim*, According to their rank and dignity. علي الخصوص *ʿala'l khusūs*, Especially, particularly. Precisely. علي الدوام *ʿala'd dawām*, Continually, perpetually, always. علي الرأس و العين *ʿala'r raʾs wa'l ʿayn*, On the head and eye, *i. e.* willingly, cheerfully. علي الرغم *ʿala'r rughm*, Against one's will. علي رؤس الاقران *ʿala' ruʾusi'l akrān*, Above the heads of his equals. علي السحر *ʿala's sahar*, About dawn, towards daybreak. علي السويّة *ʿala's sawīya*, (or علي سواء *ʿala' sawāʾ*) Equally, in a similar manner. علي الصباح *ʿala's sabāh*, In the morning. علي طريق عكس القضيّة *ʿala' tarīki ʿaksi'l kazīyat*, On the contrary. علي العادة *ʿala'l ʿādat*, According to custom. علي العمياء *ʿala'l ʿamyāʾ*, Blindly, like a blind man. علي عهده *ʿala' ʿahdihi*, (It happened) in his time. علي الغفلة *ʿala'l ghafla*, Rashly, imprudently, inconsiderately. علي الفور *ʿala'l fawr*, Suddenly, immediately. علي فوق *ʿala' fawk*, Upwards. علي قدر الطاقة *ʿala' kadari't tākat*, According to his strength or powers. علي كلّ شيء قدير *ʿala' kulli shayʾin kadīrun*, Omnipotent. علي ما *ʿala' mā*, Wherefore? علي ما نطق به الكتاب المستطاب *ʿala' mā nataka bihi'l kitābu'l mustatāb*, As the sacred book declares. علي مرور الشهور و الاعوام *ʿala' murūri'sh shuhūr wa'l aʿwām*, In the course of months and years. علي المصنّف *ʿala'l musannif*, (It lies) upon the author (to prove). علي ملأ الناس *ʿala' malaʾi'n nās*, Before the world, publicly. علي ميلين من *ʿala' mīlayn min*, At two miles distance from. علي وجه العموم *ʿala' wajhi'l ʿumūm*, All, universally. علي وفق المراد *ʿala' wafki'l murād*, At pleasure, ad libitum. علي ولا *ʿala' wilā*, Consequently. علي هذا التقدير *ʿala' hāza't takdīr*, In this case. علي يد *ʿala' yad*, By the hand of. لي عليك *lī ʿalayka*, To me against thee, *i.e.* thou owest me. من علي *min ʿala'*, From above. *ʿula'*, Elevation, height, dignity, nobility.

A عليّ *ʿalīy*, Strong, powerful. Ascended high. Name of a man, the son-in-law and fourth caliph, or successor, to Muhammad. (pl. علية *ʿilyat*) High, eminent, noble. عليّ القدر و جليّ الصدر *ʿalīyu'l kadr wa jalīyu's sadr*, Eminent in power, and exalted in dignity. *ʿilīy*, Height, eminence.

A علّيّ *ʿillīy*, (pl. علّيّون *ʿilliyūn*) High, sublime.

A عليا *ʿulya'*, (fem. of اعلي *aʿla'*) More or most high, eminent. Upper.

A علياء *ʿalyāʾ*, Heaven. The summit of a mountain. A high place. Any thing elevated. A momentous affair.

A عليان *ʿalyān*, Disproportionately tall (man or woman). *ʿilyān*, Tall, big, and corpulent. High (she-camel). Male (hyena). Loud (voice). *ʿulyān*, The title-page of a book.

A علّيان *ʿilliyān*, High (she-camel). Loud (voice). A male hyena.

A علية *ʿilyat*, (علّية *ʿillayat*, *ʿiliyat*, علّيّة *ʿillīyat*, and *ʿulīyat*) Chiefs, nobles. هو من علية الناس *huwa min ʿilyati'n nās*, He is one of the upper classes.

A عليّة *ɛaliyat*, (fem. of عليّ *ɛaliy*) High, exalted, sublime. The posterity of Aliy, son-in-law of Muhammad.

A عليّة *ɛilliyat* or *ɛulliyat*, (pl. علالىّ *ɛalāliy*). A parlour. An upper room. A handful of water.

A عليث *ɛalis*, Wheat mixed with barley.

A علىحدة *ɛala'hidda*, Separately, distinct, apart.

A عليس *ɛalis*, Any thing roasted in the skin.

A عليص *ɛullays*, Name of a plant which furnishes a condiment for broth.

A عليط *ɛilyat*, Name of a tree.

A عليف *ɛalīf*, Pastured, fed, fatted.

A عليفة *ɛalīfat*, (A sheep or camel) fed at home on the fruit of the acacia.

A عليفىّ *ɛulayfiy*, A small pack-saddle made by علاف *ɛilāf*, a celebrated maker.

A عليق *ɛalik*, Parchment. Suspended. A nose-bag. Barley or clover given to a horse. Weak, soft. ثمر العليق *samaru'l ɛalik*, The blackberry.

P عليق *ɛulayk*, Name of a certain tree, from the leaves of which a composition is prepared for tinging the nails or hair.

A عليق *ɛullayk*, Dodder. عليق الخيل *ɛullayku'l khayl* (or حبل *habl*), Name of a plant. عليق الكلب *ɛullayku'l kalb*, Name of a plant.

A عليقة *ɛalīkat*, (pl. علائق *ɛalāɛik*) Affection, attachment, intercourse, commerce, conversation. A marriage-portion. A she-camel employed in bringing provisions.

A عليقى *ɛullayka'*, Dodder.

A عليك *ɛalayka*, Above, on, or to thee. عليكم *ɛalaykum*, Above you. Take. عليك زيدا *ɛalayka zadan*, Take Zayd.

A عليل *ɛalīl*, (pl. اعلاء *aɛillāɛ*) Weak, sick, indisposed, ailing, infirm. A valetudinarian.

A عليلة *ɛalīlat*, A woman who perfumes herself often.

A عليم *ɛalīm*, (pl. علماء *ɛulamāɛ*) Wise, learned. Conversant with every subject. A name of God. *ɛala'ma*, Wherefore? why?

A عليين *ɛillīna*, or *ɛullīna*, Nobles, grandees.

A عليّون *ɛilliyūn*, (pl. of علّى *ɛilliy*) High, sublime. A place in the seventh heaven, where the records of men's actions are laid up; the books themselves. The seventh heaven, whereunto the souls of believers ascend.

A عليه *ɛalayhi*, Upon, against, with him (or it). عليه السلام *ɛalayhi's salām*, Peace be with him, which is often abbreviated thus عم *ɛam*, when following the name of any prophet; after that of Muhammad they frequently add عليه افضل الصلوة و اكمل التحية *ɛalayhi afzalu's salāt wa akmalu't tahiya*, On whom be the highest blessing and the most perfect health; or صلوات الله عليه و سلامه *salawātu'llāh ɛalayhi wa salāmuhu*, With whom be the blessing and peace of God; or صلى الله تعالي عليه و سلم *salla' allāh taɛāla' ɛalayhi wa sallam*, May heaven bless him and place him in safety; and others similar. After the names of Aliy and others famed for sanctity, they write رضوان الله عليه *rizwān allāh ɛalayhi*, God's good-will be upon him! رحمة الله عليه *ɛalayhi'r rahmat*, (or عليه الرحمة *rahmatu'llāh ɛalayhi*) On him be the mercy of God.

A الثنيّتان العليان *as saniyatāni'l ɛulyayāni*, The two upper front teeth.

A عليّين *ɛaliyīna*, High, sublime. The starry sky.

A علّيّين *ɛilliyīn*, (obliq. of عليّون *ɛilliyūn*, High, sublime. في العليّين *fi'l ɛilliyīn*, In excelsis.

A عم *ɛam*, (for عليه السلام *ɛalayhi's salām*) On him be peace!

A عمّ *ɛamm*, (pl. اعمام *aɛmām*, عمومة *ɛumūmat*, اعمّة *aɛimmat*, اعمّ *aɛumm*, and اعمون *aɛmumūn*) A paternal uncle, father's brother. Tall. A crowd of men. Grass. *ɛamm* or *ɛumm*, (pl. of عميمة *ɛamīmat*, Tall palm-trees. Excellent-shaped (women). *ɛamma*, Of what? concerning what? For what reason? From that which.

A عما *ɛamā*, Verily, truly.

A عمّا *ɛammā*, (for عن ما *ɛan mā*) For what reason? From that which, concerning what. عمّا قريب *ɛammā karīb*, In a little time.

A عماء *ɛamāɛ*, Deviation, aberration, loss of the way. Blindness. Contention, litigation. A cloud on a mountain's top. A cloud, high, dense, rainy, or transparent; or black or white; or which has shed rain. عماي جبلى *ɛamāyi jibillī*, Natural blindness.

A عمّاء *ɛammāɛ*, Tall (girl or palm-tree).

A عماد *ɛimād*, A house. Lofty buildings. A column, pillar, pilaster, tent-pole. Confidence, trust, faith, reliance, support. The confidential bearer of a message to an army. A pronoun of the nominative case interposed between the subject of a proposition and the predicate; as, زيد هو المنطلق *zayd huwa'l muntalik*, Zayd, he is the jolly (fellow). One on whose behalf, or along with whom, men engage to fight. عماد الدين *ɛimādu'd dīn*, The pillar of religion, *i. e.* The Kur'ān. ارم ذات العماد *iram zātu'l ɛimād*, Iram with her columns pointing to the skies. اهل العماد *ahlu'l ɛimād*, People who dwell in tents (particularly in lofty ones). رفيع العماد *rafīɛu'l ɛimād*, Tall, lofty. طويل العماد *tawīlu'l ɛimād*, The owner of lofty buildings, bearing signals for visitors. A house (celebrated or visited) from afar.

A عمادة *ɛimādat*, One column or lofty building.

P عمادية *ɛamādiya*, A kind of silken stuff.

P عمار *ɛamār*, A myrtle: a laurel. Name of the inventor of the litter عماري *ɛimārī*; the litter itself.

A عمار *ɛamār*, A salutation, compliment, congratulation. A complimentary gift. Nosegays which decorate a banqueting-room.

A عمّار *ɛammār*, Frequent in prayer and fasting. Strong in faith. One whose whole life is regulated by the precepts of Muhammad, and who keeps his household and dependants in the same path. Agreeable, sweet (in praise and in perfumes). Benevolent, favourably inclined towards the ruling power, and attached to the people. Mild, grave in word and deed. Firm, steady in business. *ɛummār*, The inhabitants of a house. Visitors.

A عمارة *ɛamārat*, (v. n. of عمر) Enduring. Living long. Any covering for the head, as a crown, turban, cap. (pl. عمائر *ɛamāɛir*) A tribe, society (smaller than قبيلة *kabīlat*); a large حيّ *hayy*, or part of a tribe. An ornamental patch sewed on a parasol. Salutation, compliment, congratulation. A gift, offering. *ɛimārat*, (v. n. of عمر) Cultivating, rendering habitable. Cleaving, sticking close to one's house or property. Worshipping, praying. Fasting. Being cultivated, inhabited. An edifice, pious foundation, sacred fabric, temple, church, mosque, seminary, college, academy. Any inhabited place; habitation. Culture, cultivation. The means whereby a place is rendered habitable. A tribe, society, multitude. The fourth degree of consanguinity. P عمارت كردن *ɛimārat kardan*, To repair, refit. عمارتهاي عالى *ɛimārathāyi ɛālī*, Lofty buildings. A *ɛumārat*, The cost of rendering a place habitable.

P عمارت گر *ɛimāratgar*, A builder.

P عمارت گري *ɛimāratgarī*, Edification, building.

A عمارس *ɛamāris*, (pl. of عمروس) Lambs.

A عمارطة *ɛamāritat*, (pl. of عمروط) Robbers.

P عماري *ɛimārī*, An elephant-litter.

A عماريس *ɛamārīs*, (pl. of عمروس) Lambs.

A عماريط *ɛamārīt*, (pl. of عمروط) Robbers.

A عماس *ɛamās*, A furious battle. A misfortune. (pl. عمس *ɛumus* and *ɛums*) Dull, dark (day or night). A fierce lion. Perplexed (business).

A عماسة *ɛamāsat*, (v. n. of عمس) Being dark and heavy (the day).

A عماص *ɛamās*, Obscure, gloomy (day).

A عماضج *ɛumāzij*, Strong, stout (horse, camel).

A عماعم *ɛamāɛim*, Dispersed (crowds).

A عماق *ɛimāk*, (pl. of عميق) Deep (wells).

A عماقة *ɛamākat*, (v. n. of عمق) Being deep. Depth, deepness, profundity.

A عمّال *ɛummāl*, (pl. of عامل *ɛāmil*) Artificers, artisans, workmen. Agents. Tax-gatherers.

A عمالة *ɛamālat*, Sprightliness, activity. *ɛamā*, *ɛimā*, or *ɛumālat*, Workmen's wages. Perquisites.

A عماليق *ɛamālīk*, (or عمالقة) Amalekites.

A عمام *ɛimām*, (pl. of عمامة *ɛimāmat*) Turbans.

A عمامة *ɛimāmat*, (pl. عمائم *ɛamāɛim* and عمام *ɛimām*) A turban. A head-dress worn by judges, or doctors. A helmet, or a cap worn under it. A raft. The snake of a hooka.

A عمان *ɛumān*, The southern coast of Arabia, extending from Maskat to Aden, *i. e.* from the entrance into the Persian Gulf to the Straits of Babelmandel. Name of a town in Yaman. بحرعمان *bahri ɛumān*, That part of the ocean comprised betwixt Ethiopia and India."

A عمان ʻammān, Name of a town in Syria.

A عمانية ʻumāniyat, A kind of palm-tree in Basrah, always in flower and bearing fruit.

A عماه ʻamāh, (v. n. of عمه) Being astonished, distracted, wandering. Being bewildered in argument or losing one's road.

A عماهج ʻumāhij, Thick milk. Self-important, proud, haughty. Tall. Swift. Fleshy and fat.

A عماهيج ʻamāhīj, (pl. عمهوج ʻumhūj) Plants green and entangled.

A عماية ʻamāyat, Deviation, aberration, loss of the way. Contention, litigation. Remains of the darkness of night.

A عمائر ʻamāʼir, (pl. of عمارة ʻamārat) Tribes, or part of tribes. (pl. of ʻimārat) Public buildings.

A عمائق ʻamāʼik, (pl. of عميق) Deep (places).

A عمائم ʻamāʼim, (pl. of عمامة ʻimāmat) Turbans. Helmets, or caps worn under. Scattered bodies or herds. ارباب عمائم arbābi ʻamāʼim, Judges, ecclesiastics (as wearing large turbans).

A عمّة ʻammat, A paternal aunt, a father's sister. ʻimmat, A mode of wrapping the turban round the head.

A عمت ʻamt, (v. n. of عمت) Clewing wool, or winding it in skeins round the hand preparatory to spinning. Beating, bastinadoing. Overcoming by force, warding of. ʻumut, (pl. of عميتة ʻamītat) Clews of wool.

A عمج ʻamj, (v. n. of عمج) Making haste, travelling fast. Swimming. Flying aside (an arrow). Twisting, coiling, crawling (a serpent). ʻamaj or ʻumaj, A serpent, snake.

A عمد ʻamd, (v. n. of عمد), Intending, proposing. Looking out for. Making for. Setting seriously and deliberately about any thing. Supporting, propping (by pillars), establishing. Breaking the constitution (distemper, love, or any oppression of body or mind). Grieving, making sad. Having a spite against. Striking with a column (a mace?) Striking the back. Weighing (a man) down (debt). Resolution, resolve, purpose, design, intention. بلا عمد bilā ʻamdin, Unintentionally, unwittingly. عمد على عين ʻamda ʻala' ʻaynin, Diligently, attentively, purposely. In fact. ʻamad, (v. n. of عمد) Being wet with rain (ground), so that the dust conglomerates. Being weakly and ailing. Being angry. Cleaving, sticking close to. Being surprised, astonished. Being swelled from riding (the buttocks). Having the inside of the bunch crushed and injured from riding (a camel). Wetting the dust, and causing it to stick (rain). A raft. Any bodily swelling, wound, or sickness. (pl. of عمود ʻamūd) Columns. ʻamid, (A camel) hurt inside the hump. Moist earth. عمد الثري ʻamidu's sara', Extremely beneficent. ʻumud, (pl. of عمود ʻamūd) Columns, pillars.

A عمدّ ʻumudd, A youth full of youthfulness.

A عمدا ʻamdan, Deliberately: with malice prepense.

A عمدان ʻumdān, The bearer of a message to an army.

A عمّدان ʻummadān, Long, tall.

A عمدّاني ʻumuddāniy, Full of youthfulness.

A عمدة ʻumdat, A support, pillar, prop. Whatever is trusted or confided in. The bearer of a message to an army. Great, rich, consequential. A minister, vazīr. عمدة الخواص ʻumdatu'l khawāss, A prime-minister. عمدة الملك ʻumdatu'l mulk, Pillar of the state (a title conferred upon the great officers of state).

A عمر ʻamara, (fut. يعمر yaʻmuru) He built.

A عمر ʻamr, (v. n. of عمر) Preserving. Living long. Visiting. Bringing. Life, age. Faith, religion. (pl. عمور ʻumūr) The gums. A ring for the nose or the top of the ear. Any thing long between two cloves of garlic. A tall tree. The sugar palm-tree, which bears a superior kind of date. عمر الله ʻamra'llāh, (or لعمر الله la ʻamru'llāh) By the life of God! عمرك الله ʻamraka'llāhu, May God keep you! ʻamraka'llāha, By thy acknowledgment of the life of God! (a form of adjuration). لعمري la ʻamrī or la ʻamarī, By my life! ʻumr, (pl. اعمار aʻmār) (Long) life, age, lifetime. A mosque or church. The gums. The sugar date-tree. عمرابد ʻumri abad, Eternal life, immortality. P عمردراز ʻumri darāz, A long life. A عمر عزيز ʻumri ʻazīz, (or P عمر گرامي ʻumri girāmī) Precious life. P عمر فرسا ʻumri farsā, Perishable life. A ʻamar, A kerchief with which a free-born or noble woman covers her head. She who, in the absence of a veil, thrusts her head into her sleeve. ʻumar, Omar (a man's name). ʻumur, Life, age.

A عمرا ʻumran, In his life, never.

A عمران ʻimrān, Name of the father of Moses. ʻumrān, Cultivated, inhabited. ʻamrāni, (dual) عمرو بن جابر ʻamr bin jābir, and بدر بن عمر badr bin ʻamr. Two bits of flesh suspended over the uvula. ʻamrāni or ʻamarāni, The two ends of the sleeves. ʻumarāni, (dual) The two Omars, *i.e.* Abū bakr and Omar, the two first caliphs; or Omar and عمر بن عبد العزيز ʻumar bin ʻabdi'l ʻazīz.

A عمرة ʻamrat, Any covering for the head, as a crown, tiara, turban, or cap. A small pearl or bead by which a string of pearls is divided at intervals. A woman. ابو عمرة abū ʻamrat, Penury and hunger. Name of a man who carried misfortune and war wherever he went. ʻumrat, (pl. عمر ʻumar) The sacred visitation or pilgrimage to Mecca. One of the essential elements of pilgrimage. The visiting or cohabiting with a woman in the house of her parents or kindred.

A عمّرتان ʻammaratāni, Two small bones at the root of the tongue.

P عمرد ʻamrud, Parsley.

A عمرّد ʻamarrad, Of a bad disposition. Strong. Exceedingly cunning and mischievous. Noble (camel), an excellent roadster. A fierce wolf. Long (horse or road).

A عمرّس ʻamarras, Robust, strong (man). Accelerated, vehement (approach). Malignant. Severe, disastrous (day).

A عمرط ʻimrit or ʻumrut, Long.

A عمرّط ʻamarrat, Light, nimble. Bold, strong. A misfortune.

P عمركاه ʻumr-kāh, Life-consuming.

A عمرو ʻamrū, (pronounced ʻamr, the و being employed solely to distinguish this word from عمر ʻumar, Omar) (pl. اعمر aʻmur and عمور ʻumūr) A proper name. Name of Farazdak. امّ عمرو umm ʻamr, A hyena.

A عمرود ʻumrūd, Long (horse or road).

P عمرورشدن ʻumrwar shudan, To grow old. To draw towards a close (life).

A عمروس ʻumrūs, (pl. عماريس ʻamārīs and عمارس ʻamāris) A sucking lamb. A fat camel's colt. Plump, firm (youth).

A عمروط ʻumrūt, (pl. عمارطة ʻamāritat and عماريط ʻamārīt) A robber. A poor wretch. Wicked, malignant, stubborn, insolent.

A عمره الله ʻamaruhu allāh, God grant him a long life!

A عمريّ ʻumra', A life-grant, a life-interest.

A عمري ʻumre, An age, long space of time.

A عمريّ ʻamrīy, A sort of date. ʻumrīy, Ancient (tree). The lote-tree growing on a river's bank.

P عم زاده ʻam-zāda, An uncle's son.

A عمس ʻams, (v. n. of عمس) Being erased (any writing). Concealing, hiding. Being dull, cloudy (day). Feigning dulness or ignorance. A cruel war. Perplexed (business). ʻums or ʻumus, Dark nights. ʻamas, (v. n. of عمس) Being dull, cloudy (day).

A عمش ʻamsh, An undesigned blow. A convenient, proper, becoming thing. ʻamash, (v. n. of عمش) (An exhortation) suiting (one) well, making a suitable impression. Recovering from sickness (the body). Being weak-sighted. Weakness of sight, and a defluxion in the eyes.

A عمشاء ʻamshāʼ, Weak-sighted (woman).

A عمشوش ʻumshūsh, A branch of a vine, from which the grapes have been partially eaten.

A عمص ʻums, A kind of food. ʻamis, Addicted, given to eat acids.

A عم صباحا ʻim sabāhan, Good morrow to you.

A عمضج ʻamzaj, Strong (horse or camel).

A عمط ʻamt, (v. n. of عمط) Disgracing or disparaging. ʻamt or ʻamat, (v. n. of عمط) Not gratefully acknowledging the mercies of God.

A عمعمة ʻamʻamat, (v. n. of عمعم Q) Having a numerous army, after having had a small one.

A عمق ʻamk or ʻumk, (pl. اعماق aʻmāk) A widely-extended desert. Unripe dates laid in the sun to dry. *ɛamk, ɛumk*, or *ɛumuk*, Depth or bottom (of a well). *ɛumk*, (v. n. of عمق) Being deep. *ɛamak*, A right, due, or claim. *ɛumuk* or *ɛimak*, Deep (wells).

A عمقة *ɛamakat*, Grease of butter sticking to a leathern churn.

A عمقى *ɛimka'*, Name of a tree or plant.

A عمقيّت *ɛumkīyat*, Depth.

A عمكوس *ɛumkūs*, An ass.

A عمل *ɛamal*, (v. n. of عمل) Working. Doing, making, acting, effectuating, operating, executing, labouring, putting in practice. Being active and sprightly (a camel). Continuing, lasting (lightning). Governing, exercising a syntactical government. (pl. اعمال *aɛmāl*) Action, operation. Work, labour. Servile work. Practice (as opposed to علم *ɛilm*, Theory). Effect. Rule, power, dominion. A border, a country. The collection of the revenue. Seizure, confiscation, or any thing liable to confiscation. Trouble, vexation. عمل صالح *ɛamali sālih*, A good action. عمل معمول *ɛamali maɛmūl*, Ancient usage. بنو العمل *banū'l ɛamal*, Pedestrians, footmen. ذو عمل *zū ɛamalin*, A workman. دستور العمل *dastūru'l ɛamal*, A manual of practice. *ɛamil*, Fit for work, business, or action. Long-continued (lightning). He who executes an office; a revenue-officer. عمل به العملين *ɛamila bihi'l ɛimillīn* (عملين *ɛimlīn* or *ɛumalīn*), He gave him hard usage, he sedulously strove to annoy him.

A عملاً *ɛamalan*, In very deed, truly, in earnest.

A عملاق *ɛimlāk*, One who deceives by his elegance and address.

A عملة *ɛamlat*, Theft. Deceit, perfidy. *ɛimlat*, Work. What is made or done. Wages, hire. The mode or style of doing any thing. Wickedness, depravity of the heart. *ɛumlat*, Wages, workmen's wages. *ɛamalat*, (pl. of عامل *ɛāmil*) Labourers. Officers. *ɛamilat*, Active, brisk, sprightly (she-camel). What is made or done. Work.

P عملج *ɛamlaj*, A kind of winter-melon.

P عملدار *ɛamal-dār*, One in command. A tax-gatherer. (in India) A native collector of revenue.

A عمّلس *ɛamallas*, Indefatigable and swift (camel). A fierce wolf. A hunting-dog. Name of a dutiful son, who bore his mother on his back a pilgrim to Mecca; hence, ابرّ من عمّلس *abarr min ɛamallas*, More pious than Amallas.

A عملسة *ɛamlasat*, Speed, velocity.

A عمّلط *ɛummalit*, Robust, strong, hardy to travel.

A عملّط *ɛamallat*, Robust, strong, hardy to travel.

A عملقة *ɛamlakat*, (v. n. of عملق Q) Making water. Voiding excrement. Speaking profoundly. Urine. Excrement.

P عمل نامه *ɛamal-nāma*, A lease, title-deed. A warrant, a power of attorney.

A عملوسة *ɛumlūsat*, A strong bow which discharges an arrow swiftly.

A عمليّ *ɛamalīy*, Practical (in opposition to theoretical). Laboured, artificial, wrought. Forged. حكمت عملي *hikmati ɛamalī*, Practical philosophy.

A عمليّة *ɛamalīyat*, Practice.

A عمليص *ɛimlīs*, A fatiguing nocturnal journey in search of water.

A عمليق *ɛimlīk*, Amalek.

A عمم *ɛamam*, Complete, perfect (body). Universal (in beneficence). Bigness, size. Universality, generality. (pl. of عامّة *ɛāmmat*) The commons, plebeians. *ɛumum*, A perfect stature of body. The entire (of the body, wealth, or youth). (pl. of عميم *ɛamīm*) Complete, common, general (things).

A عمن *ɛamn*, (v. n. of عمن) Staying (in one place). *ɛumun*, Tarriers, abiders.

A عمّن *ɛamman*, (for عن من *ɛan man*) From that which.

A عمو *ɛamw*, (v. n. of عما for عمو) Being humble and submissive. Being tame and quiet. Inclining, leaning to. (pl. اعماء *aɛmāɛ*) Error, aberration. Humility, submissiveness.

A عمّو *ɛammū*, A paternal uncle.

A عمواس *ɛamwās*, Emmaus, in Palestine. *ɛamwās* or *ɛimwās*, A pestilence which raged in Syria during the early days of Muhammadism.

A عموج *ɛamūj*, (An arrow) flying aside.

A عمود *ɛamūd*, (pl. اعمدة *aɛmidat*, عمد *ɛamad*, and *ɛumud*) A column, pillar, post, prop. A mace, bludgeon. The support of a family. A chief, great man. A line on the back of a sword. One who conveys a message to an army. One along with whom one agrees to fight. A vein extending from the breast-bone to a little below the navel. A vein which conveys moisture to the liver. The larger or more important part of the ear. Gloomy, sad. The legs of an ostrich. The posts of the pulley of a well. That part of a spear which lies between the two shanks of the iron head. عمود البطن *ɛamūdu'l batn*, The back. P عمود رخش *ɛamūdi rakhsh*, The yard of a horse. A عمود السحر *ɛamūdu's suhr*, The heart-string. عمود الصبح *ɛamūdu's subh*, The spreading light of the dawn. A morning beam. خط عمود *khati ɛamūd*, A perpendicular line. على عمود رأيهم *ɛala' ɛamūdi raɛyihim*, Upon their fixed principle.

A عموداً *ɛamūdan*, Perpendicularly.

A عمور *ɛumūr*, (v. n. of عمر) Cleaving, sticking close to house or property. Worshipping. Praying. Fasting. (pl. of عمر *ɛamr*) Gums. (pl. of عمرو *ɛamr*) Amrs, names of men.

A عمورة *ɛamūrah*, The city of Gomorrah.

A عموس *ɛamūs*, Obscure, perplexed (business). One who goes in darkness or uncertainty. A fierce lion. *ɛumūs*, (v. n. of عمس) Being heavy, dark (day).

A عموق *ɛumūk*, Depth.

A عمول *ɛamūl*, Fit for work, business, or action. Workmen's wages.

A عموم *ɛumūm*, (v. n. of عمّ) Being common, universal, embracing all. Doing, giving, or lending in common. Community, universality.

A عموماً *ɛumūman*, Commonly, vulgarly.

A عمومة *ɛumūmat*, (v. n. of عمّ) Being a paternal uncle. Relationship of paternal uncle. (pl. of عمّ *ɛamm*) Paternal uncles.

A عموميّ *ɛumūmīy*, Common, universal.

A عموميّة *ɛumūmīyat*, Generality, universality.

A عمون *ɛamūn*, (pl. of عمي *ɛamī*) Blind.

A عموه *ɛumūh*, (or عموهة *ɛumūhat*) (v. n. of عمه) Wandering here and there. Being bewildered in argument or on the road.

A عمويّ *ɛamawīy*, Belonging to a blind, foolish, silly person. Belonging to a paternal uncle.

A عمه *ɛamh*, (v. n. of عمه) Being astonished, distracted, wandering. Being bewildered in argument or on the road. *ɛamah*, (v. n. of عمه) Being without land-marks or direction-posts (a country). Astonishment, bewilderment. Irresolution, uncertainty. Aberration, perplexity, puzzle, nonplus. *ɛamih*, (pl. عمهون *ɛamihūna*) Astonied, perplexed.

A عمّه *ɛummah*, (pl. of عامه) Astonished, puzzled.

A عمهاء *ɛamhāɛ*, (A country) without sign-posts.

A عمهان *ɛamahān*, (v. n. of عمه) Being astonished, distracted, wandering. Being bewildered in argument or on the road.

A عمهج *ɛamhaj*, Thick milk. Self-important, proud, haughty. Tall. Swift. Fleshy and fat.

A عمهوج *ɛamhūj*, (pl. عماهيج *ɛamāhīj*) Herbage, green and luxuriantly entangled.

A عمّهى *ɛummaha'*, Wandering, straying.

A عمى *ɛamy*, (v. n. of عمى) Casting up rubbish (water). Throwing his foam about (a camel). Running, flowing. *ɛumy*, (pl. of اعمى *aɛma'* or عمياء *ɛamyāɛ*) Blind. *ɛama'*, (v. n. of عمى) Being blind or ignorant. Being dark, obscure (business). Blindness (physical or mental). Stature. Length. Dust. صكّة عمى *sakkat ɛama'* (or عمىّ *ɛumayy*), Midday heat. *ɛamī*, (pl. عمون *ɛamūn*) Blind. Ignorant. عمي القلب *ɛamī'l kalb*, Blind-hearted.

A عمّي *ɛammī*, My uncle, or (simply) a paternal uncle. *ɛumma'*, (pl.) On the brink of death.

A عمّيّ *ɛummīy*, Common, plebeian (man).

A قتيل عمّيّا *katīlu ɛimmīya'*, Killed, but nobody knows by whom.

A عمياء *ɛamyāɛ*, (fem. of اعمى *aɛma'*) Blind.

A عميان *ɛumyān*, (pl. of اعمى *aɛma'*) Blind.

A عميانس *ɛumyānis*, Name of an idol formerly worshipped by the tribe of خولان *khawlān*.

A عمية *ɛamyat*, An object of choice. Choice, election. *ɛamiyat*, Blind or ignorant (woman).

A عميّة *ɛamiyat*, Blind (woman). *ɛamiyat* or *ɛumīyat*, Deviation, aberration, loss of the way. Ignorance. Contention, litigation.

A عمّيّة *ɛummīyat* or *ɛimmīyat*, Pride. Ignorance. Blind bigotry, ignorant pertinacity.

A عميت *ʻamit*, (pl. of عميتة) Clews of wool.

A عمّيت *ʻimmīt*, A vigilant watchman. Drunk. Imprudent, rash. A simpleton, idiot.

A عميتة *ʻamītat*, (pl. اعمتة *aʻmitat*, عمت *ʻumut*, and عميت *ʻamīt*) A clew, hank, or skein of wool or camels' hair (سليلة *salīlat* signifying a clew of other hair, and سبيجة *sabījat* one of cotton).

A عميثل *ʻamaysal*, One who drags or trails (as a man or woman their garments, or beasts their tails). A lion. Slow, dilatory from bulk and flabbiness. Long-tailed (mountain-goat). Long (garment). Short and loose (garment). Thick, strong, broad. Quick, active, brisk. A noble personage, a prince.

A عميثلة *ʻamaysalat*, Corpulent, fat (she-camel). Quick, active (woman).

A عميثليّة *ʻumaysiliyat*, A sluggish, trailing pace.

P عميد *ʻamīd*, A house in which one is forced to take refuge.

A عميد *ʻamīd*, A chief, a great man. Indisposed. Sick with love.

A عيدر *ʻamaydar*, A delicate youth. Opulent.

A عمير *ʻamīr*, Cultivated, inhabited. Coarse, thick (cloth). كثير بجير عمير *kasīr bajīr ʻamīr*, Very numerous. ابو عمير *abū ʻumayr*, Penis.

A عميرة *ʻamīrat*, A bee-hive. جلد عميرة *jaldu ʻumayrat*, Mastupration, onanism, self-abuse.

A عميرتان *ʻumayratāni*, Two bones at the root of the tongue.

P عمي زاده *ʻamī-zāda*, A cousin, uncle's son.

A عميس *ʻamīs*, Obscure, intricate (business). One who pretends to be ignorant of what he well knows. عميس الحمائم *ʻamīsu'l hamāʼim*, Name of one of Muhammad's halting-places to Badr.

A على العميسة *ʻala'l ʻamīsat*, (or العميسيّة *al ʻumaysiyat*) Rashly, falsely-taken (oath).

A عميق *ʻamīk*, (pl. عمق *ʻumuk*, *ʻimak*, عمائق *ʻamāʼik*, and عماق *ʻimāk*) Deep, profound (well). Distant, deep, and long (valley). Widely extensive. A gulf.

A عميل *ʻamīl*, Operator. Revenue-collector.

A عميم *ʻamīm*, Full, complete, perfect. The superior rank, better sort of men. (pl. عمم *ʻumum*) Common to all or to many, universal, general. Dry plants called بهمي *buhma'*. Dry provender. عميم الاحسان *ʻamīmu'l ihsān*, Benevolent or beneficent unto all. عميم البركات *ʻamīmu'l barakāt*, Enriching universally. عميم النفع *ʻamīmu'n nafʻ*, Advantageous to all, of universal benefit.

A عميمة *ʻamīmat*, (pl. عمّ *ʻumm*) Of a perfect shape and good figure (a woman). Tall (palm-tree).

A عميمرتان *ʻumaymiratāni*, Two bones at the root of the tongue.

A عمينة *ʻamīnat*, A plain, level ground.

A عمّيهى *ʻummayha'*, Wandering one knows not where.

A عن *ʻan*, Off. From. From off. After. Out of. Without. Through. By. With. Concerning, because, on account of, for. Above, on. Before. Instead of, in exchange of. According to, on the authority of. عن بيّنة *ʻan bayyinatin*, After a clear demonstration. عن دبر *ʻan duburin*, After one's decease. عن صميم القلب *ʻan samīmi'l kalb*, From the bottom of the heart. عن قريب الزمان *ʻan karībi'z zamān*, (or عن قريب *ʻan karīb*) In a little time, soon, immediately, shortly. عن قصد *ʻan kasd*, Designedly. عن قولك *ʻan kawlika*, On your word. عن لاشي *ʻan lā shay*, In vain. عن يسار مكّة *ʻan yasāri makkat*, To the left of Mecca. عن نفسه *ʻan nafsihi*, Against his will. ما عن في السماء نجم *mā ʻan fi's samāʼ najm*, As long as a star is in the sky. مات عن ولد *māta ʻan waladin*, He died, leaving a child. وجد عن طلب *wajada ʻan talabin*, He found without seeking. عن *ʻan* is used by the tribe of Tamīm for ان *an*; as, اعجبني عن تفعل *aʻjabanī ʻan tafʻala*.

A عنّ *ʻann*, (v. n. of عنّ) Pulling in a horse (with the reins). Putting reins to a bridle. Putting a title or inscription to a book, or a direction to a letter. Appearing before the eyes, presenting itself. Reproaching, reviling. *ʻanna*, Perhaps.

A عنا *ʻana'*, A side.

A عنّا *ʻannā*, (for عن نا *ʻan nā*) From us.

A عناء *ʻanāʼ*, (v. n. of عنو or عني) Being detained (a captive). Being fatigued. Being humble and suppliant. Affliction, labour, lassitude, adversity, distress. P رنج و عنا *ranj u ʻanā*, Labour and affliction. A مقرّ عنا *makarri ʻanā*, The house of sorrow. *ʻināʼ*, (v. n. 3 of عني) Opposing strenuously. Becoming callous to evil, enduring it with all its consequences. Taking care (of property).

A عناب *ʻunāb*, Large-nosed. A female hernia, or imperviousness. An excrescence which they who practise female circumcision cut off. A small black mountain. A long round mountain.

A عنّاب *ʻannāb*, A vender of grapes. *ʻunnāb*, A jujube-tree and fruit. The fruit of the اراك *arāk* tree. The lip of a mistress. P عنّاب تر *ʻunnābi tar*, The finger of a mistress.

A عنابج *ʻunābij*, Cruel, severe, morose, unjust.

A عنابس *ʻanābis*, Six men of the tribe of Kuraysh. *ʻunābis*, A lion.

A عنابل *ʻunābil*, A thick bow-string. Thick. (A man) of a full, perfect stature.

A عنّابي *ʻunnābiy*, Of a carnation-colour.

A عناة *ʻunāt*, (pl. of عاني *ʻānī*) Captives.

A عناتل *ʻanātil*, Hyenas that rend their prey. A deer cut in pieces and laid to entice beasts of prey.

A عناج *ʻunāsij*, Powerful, fat, and thick (mountain-goat).

A عناثي *ʻanāsī*, (pl. of عنثوة *ʻansuwat* and *ʻunsuwat*) Grasses, hard, dry, and beginning to wither.

A عناج *ʻināj*, A rope passed round the bottom of a large bucket, and fastened to the cross bars at the top. An affair, business; or that by which it is held together. A pain in the loins. قول لا عناج له *kawlun lā ʻināja lahu*, A speech without consistency, or uttered without deliberation.

A عناجيج *ʻanājīj*, (pl. of عنجوج) Swift (horses).

A عناد *ʻinād*, (v. n. 3 of عند) Declining, receding, departing. Being contumacious: obstinacy, stubbornness, perverseness, resistance, repugnance.

A عناداً *ʻinādan*, Obstinately, perversely.

A عنادل *ʻanādil*, (pl. of عندليب) Nightingales.

A عنادلان *ʻanā* or *ʻunādilāni*, The testicles.

A عناديّ *ʻinādiy*, Opposing, incompatible.

A عناز *ʻināz*, (pl. of عنز *ʻanz*) She-goats.

A عناس *ʻinās*, (v. n. of عنس) Remaining long unmarried in her parent's house (a nubile virgin). A mirror, looking-glass.

A عناش *ʻināsh*, (v. n. 3 of عنش) Hugging one another in battle.

A عنّاش *ʻannāsh*, Who fights with an adversary.

A عناصر *ʻanāsir*, (pl. of عنصر) The elements.

A عناصل *ʻanāsil*, (pl. of عنصل) Squills.

A عناصي *ʻanāsī*, (pl. of عنصوة *ʻunsuwat*) Small parts (of cattle or hair).

A عناظب *ʻanāzib*, Yellow male locusts.

A عنافة *ʻanāfat*, (v. n. of عنف) Incommoding, being troublesome. Inconvenience.

A عنافش *ʻunāfish*, Long and thick-bearded.

A عنافط *ʻanāfit*, (pl. of عنفط *ʻunfut*) Bad-tempered. Low, mean.

A عناق *ʻanāk*, (pl. اعنق *aʻnuk* and عنوق *ʻunūk*) A female kid. A calamity. A troublesome business. Disappointment, failure. The middle star in the Great Bear. Two years' tithes. عناق الارض *ʻanāku'l arz*, The animal called سياه گوش *siyāh-gosh*. *ʻināk*, (v. n. 3 of عنق) Catching in the arms, hugging (either in love or wrath).

A عناقة *ʻanākat*, Disappointment, failure.

A عناقيد *ʻanākīd*, (pl. of عنقود) Clusters of grapes.

A عناك *ʻanāk*, A sand-hill.

A عناكب *ʻanākib*, (pl. of عنكبوت) Spiders.

A عنان *ʻanān*, (pl. of عنانة *ʻanānat*) Clouds. *ʻinān*, (v. n. 3 of عنّ) Opposing, resisting. (pl. اعنّة *aʻinnat* and عنن *ʻunun*) A rein, a bridle. Any object present to the eye. A conspicuous part of the heavens. An artery in the back. Opposition or resistance to the purchaser of a chattel on the ground of a personal interest in the thing. Equality in partnership in one particular part of the property to the exclusion of the rest. The environs (of a house). (pl. of عنّة *ʻunnat*) Enclosures for camels. P عنان أمل سبك شدن *ʻinānī amal sabuk shudan*, To despond, despair. عنان بر عنان *ʻinān bar ʻinān*, Equality. عنان تافتن *ʻinān tāftan*, To be weak. To turn away the face. عنان دزديدن *ʻinān duzdīdan*, To remain behind, become dispirited. عنان ريز كردن *ʻinān-rez kardan*, To relax the reins, ride full gallop. عنان زنان رفتن *ʻinān-zanān raftan*, To go at full speed. عنان سبك

كردن *ʻinān sabuh kardan*, To proceed gently. To take time to consider. عنان سبك شدن *ʻinān sabuk shudan*, To travel. عنان فرو گرفتن *ʻinān faro giriftan*, To set about any thing leisurely. باد عنان *bād-ʻinān*, Swift as the wind. A شركة عنان *shirkat ʻinān*, Partnership in trade solely in regard to one particular object. طرق العنان *tarku'l ʻinān*, Active, nimble. عنانك ان تفعل كذا *ʻunānāka an tafʻala hazā*, The whole for you to do (is) this.

A عنان *ʻannān*, Slow, dilatory.

A عنانا المتن *ʻinānā'lmatn*, Two veins in the back.

A عنانك *ʻunānāka*, Your object or effort.

P عنان پيچيدة *ʻinān-pechīda*, Contumacious, disobedient, headstrong.

A عنانة *ʻananat*, Disinclination to women, arising from impotency or fascination. (pl. عنان *ʻanān*) A cloud. A cloud containing water.

P عنان كش *ʻinān-kash*, Pulling the reins.

A عناهج *ʻunāhij*, Long, tall.

A عناية *ʻanāyat* or *ʻināyat*, (v. n. of عني) Meaning, signifying, intending (somewhat by one's words). Rendering anxious, engaging one's careful attention. Belonging to, concerning. Bestowing pains upon. Happening, occurring. Agreeing with one (food). Producing herbage (ground). Guarding, preserving. Assistance, aid, favour. A gift, present. Solicitude, anxiety, care. Cloth half silk. P عنايت كردن *ʻināyat kardan*, To aid, succour, favour. عنايت الهى *ʻināyati ilāhī*, Divine favour.

P عنايت نامة *ʻināyat-nāma*, A certificate or a grant in writing. A deed of exemption.

A عنب *ʻinab*, (and عنباء *ʻinabāʼ*) The grape, grapes. Wine. عنب الثعلب *ʻinabu's saʻlab*, Fox grapes, nightshade.

A عنبان *ʻanabān*, Light, active. Heavy, dull, aged (hart).

A عنبب *ʻumbab*, Plenty of water. The fore part of a torrent. Name of a river and of a plant.

A عنبة *ʻinabat*, (pl. عنبات *ʻinabāt*, عنوب *ʻunūb*, عنب *ʻinab*, عنباء *ʻinabāʼ*, and اعناب *aʻnāb*) One grape. A tubercle, pustule, pimple, button.

A عنبج *ʻumbuj*, Languid, slow, dull, foolish.

A عنبر *ʻambar*, Ambergris, a rich perfume, said to be the excrement of a marine animal. A certain sea-fish. Something that rises in the bottom of the sea, consumes marine animals, and dies; and is mostly found in the belly of a fish. A kind of wax, which in process of time dissolves and falls into the sea, and by the waves is cast on shore. The skin of a sea-fish; also a shield made of it. Saffron. P عنبر ارزان *ʻambari arzān*, (or عنبر لرزان *ʻambari larzān*) The musky ringlets of the prophet. عنبر تر *ʻambari tar*, The ringlets of a mistress; also a mole on the face. Night.

P عنبر آگين *ʻambar-āgīn*, Full of amber.

P عنبر بار *ʻambar-bār*, Odoriferous, fragrant.

P عنبر بارس *ʻambar-bāris*, Barberis.

P عنبر بوي *ʻambar-boy*, Smelling of ambergris.

A عنبرة *ʻambarat*, Severity of winter. Onions cooked in a pot. A pure, unmixed genealogy.

P عنبرچة *ʻambarcha*, An ornament for the neck full of amber.

A عنبريّ البلد *ʻambarīyu'l balad*, A name for guidance or direction.

P عنبرين *ʻambarīn*, Of ambergris. عنبرين سنبل *ʻambarīn-sumbul*, The locks of a mistress.

P عنبرينة *ʻambarīna*, A perfume compounded of ambergris, musk, and wood of aloes. A woman's ornament for the neck full of amber.

A عنبس *ʻambas*, A lion.

A عنبط *ʻumbut*, (or عنبطة *ʻumbutat*) Short, compact in body, and full of flesh.

A عنبل *ʻumbul*, (or عنبلة *ʻumbulat*) The clitoris.

A عنبلة *ʻumbulat*, (A woman) with a clitoris.

A عنبليّ *ʻumbulīy*, Thick. An Ethiopian.

A عنبوج *ʻumbūj*, Languid, slow, dull, foolish.

A عنة *ʻunnat*, (pl. عنن *ʻunan* and عنان *ʻinān*) A wooden pen for camels. An aversion to women. A fire-place, a stove. A rope. Impotency produced by witchcraft. A judicial declaration of impotency. عين عنّة *ʻayna ʻunnatin*, (I gave him) something more than the rest. Unexpectedly, with the glance of the eye (I saw him).

A عنت *ʻanat*, (v. n. of عنت) Being liable to offend. Being vicious and corrupt. Falling into misfortune or difficulty, from which a man cannot extricate himself. Disobeying. Being broken again, (a bone) scarcely consolidated. Being weak and despondent. A fault, crime. Corruption, depravity. Ruin, destruction. Difficulty and trouble coming upon a man. Fornication, adultery. A rent, split. *ʻanit*, (A bone) re-broken, the former fracture not having been consolidated.

A عنتتة *ʻantatat*, (v. n. of عنتت Q) Turning away from. Being high and erect (the horn of a yearling kid).

A عنتر *ʻantar* or *ʻuntar*, A gad-fly, horse-fly.

A عنترة *ʻantarat*, (v. n. of عنتر Q) Making a buzzing noise (flies). Encountering with intrepidity the dangers of war. Piercing with a spear. Name of one of the seven Arabian poets, whose poems were hung up on the temple of Mecca, and were called معلّقات *muʻallakāt*, *i.e.* Suspended.

A عنتريس *ʻantarīs*, A camel whose flesh is compact. A calamity, misfortune.

A عنتل *ʻuntul* or *ʻuntal*, Hard. The clitoris.

A عنتلة *ʻantalat*, A tearing in pieces.

A عنتوت *ʻuntūt*, Grass, hard, dry, and beginning to wither. A small mountain in a desert. The beginning of any thing. A hill difficult of ascent.

A عنته *ʻuntuh*, (or عنتهيّ *ʻuntuhīy*) One who exerts himself and strains every nerve.

A عنثة *ʻansat*, Grass, hard, dry, and withering.

A عنثج *ʻansaj*, Languid, corpulent, thick. Powerful, thick, and fat (mountain-goat).

A عنثل *ʻansal*, (or امّ عنثل) A hyena.

A عنثوة *ʻansuwat* or *ʻunsuwat*, (pl. عناثي *ʻanāsī*) Grass, hard, dry, and beginning to wither. *ʻunsuwat*, The hair of the chin.

A عنج *ʻanj*, (v. n. of عنج) Training, exercising (a camel), by bringing the halter back to his fore-legs. Passing a rope round the bottom of a large bucket, and fastening it to the handle or cross-bar. *ʻanaj*, The training of a camel. An old man.

A عنجة *ʻanajat*, The jamb or side-post of the door of the hawda or camel-litter.

A عنجج *ʻanjaj*, Great, large. *ʻunjuj*, A sort of fragrant herb.

A عنجد *ʻanjad*, *ʻunjad*, or *ʻunjud*, A bad sort of dried grape.

A عنجدة *ʻanjadat*, (v. n. of عنجد Q) Being black and bad (a grape).

A عنجرة *ʻanjarat*, (v. n. of عنجر Q) Making mouths, pouting the lips in contempt. A bold woman.

A عنجرد *ʻanjarid*, An impudent, brawling woman.

A عنجش *ʻunjush*, A decrepit, withered, contracted, wrinkled old man.

A عنجف *ʻunjuf*, A lean, withered dwarf, shrivelled in body.

A عنجل *ʻunjal*, A badger. *ʻunjul*, An old man thin of flesh and raw-boned.

A عنجوج *ʻunjūj*, (pl. عناجيج *ʻanājīj*) An excellent horse. A swift camel. Early youth.

A عنجورة *ʻunjūrat*, The cover of a flask.

A عنجوف *ʻunjūf*, A lean and withered dwarf. Contracted, shrivelled in body. An old woman.

A عنجول *ʻunjūl*, A certain little beast.

P عنجه *ʻunja*, A collection. Mixing, kneading.

A عنجهانية *ʻunjahānīyat* or *ʻunjuhānīyat*, Pomp, pride. Ignorance.

A عنجهيّ *ʻunjuhīy*, Proud. Foolish, mad, crazy.

A عنجهيّة *ʻunjuhīyat*, Ignorance, stupidity. Pride.

A عند *ʻanada*, (fut. يعند *yaʻnudu*) He deviated.

A عند *ʻand*, *ʻind*, or *ʻund*, A side, part, quarter. *ʻanda*, *ʻinda*, or *ʻunda*, (An adverb of time and place) Near, nigh, with, before, about, in, according to. عند الله *ʻinda'llāh*, With or before God. عند البعض *ʻinda'l baʻz*, According to some. عند التحقيق *ʻinda't tahkīk*, Of a truth, certainly. عند الخلائق *ʻinda'l khalāʼik*, In the estimation of men. عند ذلك *ʻinda zālika*, Then, at the same moment. عند العاقبة *ʻinda'l ʻākibat*, At length, finally. عند الوصول *ʻinda'l wusūl*, On the arrival, when it happens, in such an event. عند الوقت *ʻinda'l wakt*, In time, at the critical juncture. عندك زيدًا *ʻindaka zaydan*, Take thou (this) Zayd. عندمّ زيد *ʻindimmu zayd*, (for عندي امّ زيد *ʻindī ummu zayd*) Zayd's mother is with me. عنده *ʻindahu*, With him, in his possession. عندما *ʻindamā*, In the meanwhile. من عندك *min ʻindika*, On thy part. عندي *ʻindī*, According to my notion, in my opinion. من عندي *min ɛindī*, By my authority. *ɛind*, Heart, mind, intelligence. *ɛanad*, Side, part.

A عنّد *ɛunnad*, (pl. of عاند *ɛānid*) Obstinate, wilful. Bleeding veins which cannot be stanched.

A عندأ *ɛindaɂ*, Bold, brave.

A عندأوة *ɛindaɂwat*, Bold. Difficulty, intricacy. Trouble. Wrong, injury. A heavy misfortune. Fraud, stratagem, deceit, guile.

A عنديل *ɛandabīl*, A nightingale.

A عندد *ɛundad*, Art, cunning, fraud, stratagem. Old, ancient. *ɛundad* or *ɛundud*, Flight, escape.

A عندرة *ɛandarat*, (v. n. of عندر Q) Being heavy (rain).

A عندقة *ɛundukat*, The lower part of the belly below the navel, the abdomen.

A عندل *ɛandal*, A long or tall camel. Large-headed (camel).

A عندلة *ɛandalat*, (v. n. of عندل Q) Being strong and sinewy (a camel). Warbling (a nightingale). Long (she-camel). Large-breasted woman.

A عندليب *ɛandalīb*, (pl. عنادل) A nightingale.

A عنديل *ɛandalīl*, A sort of sparrow.

A عندم *ɛandam*, Dragons' blood. Brazil-wood.

A عنذاء *ɛinzāɂ*, An instigating, an exciting.

A عنذيان *ɛinziyān*, A shrew.

A عنز *ɛanz*, (v. n. of عنز) Declining, turning away the face from. Skirmishing or piercing (with a small spear). (pl. اعنز *aɛnuz*, عنوز *ɛunūz*, and عناز *ɛināz*) A she-goat, doe, fawn, gazel. A female eagle, vulture, or bustard. Little, black, and bare (hill). Name of a certain water-fowl. A stone in water. Name of a horse, woman, and sword. Name of a large fish (which a mule can scarcely carry). كركبتي العنز *ka rukbatayi'l ɛanz*, Like the two knees of a goat, *i.e.* equal (in honour and rank). لقي يوم العنز *lakiya yawma'l ɛanz*, He met his destruction.

A عنزب *ɛunzub*, The edible herb sumach.

A عنزة *ɛanazat*, A short spear with an iron ferrule at bottom. Edge of a hatchet. A kind of animal resembling a weasel, which is said to crawl into the vulva of a camel when asleep.

A عنزروت *ɛanzarūt*, A Persian gum or balsam. Flesh-glue.

A عنزهاني *ɛunzuhānīy*, (عنزهو *ɛinzahw*, or عنزهوة *ɛinzahwat*) One who abstains from all amusements. One who dislikes partners or associates.

A عنزهوة *ɛinzahwat*, Pride.

A عنس *ɛans*, (v. n. of عنس) Bending (a stick). A strong she-camel with a long tail. An eagle. Crookedness of wood. *ɛuns*, (or عنّس *ɛunnas*) (pl. of عانس *ɛānis*) (Girls) who remain long in their parents' house after the marriageable age. *ɛanas*, A frequent glance at a mirror.

A عنسل *ɛansal*, A swift she-camel.

A عنش *ɛansh*, (v. n. of عنش) Bending. Disturbing, frightening, driving away. Uprooting, displacing, separating.

A عنشط *ɛanshat*, (or عنشّط *ɛanashshat*) Of a bad disposition. Long, tall (man or woman).

A عنشطة *ɛanshatat*, (v. n. of عنشط Q) Being angry. Tall (woman).

A عنشنش *ɛanashnash*, Long, light, swift (man or horse).

A عنشوش *ɛunshūsh*, A remnant, somewhat.

A عنصاة *ɛinsāt*, (عنصوة *ɛansuwat*, *ɛinsuwat*, *ɛunsuwat*, or عنصية *ɛinsiyat*) (pl. عناصي *ɛanāsī*) Scattered herbage; dispersed cattle; remains of any estate (in money or flocks), from a third to a half.

A عنصر *ɛunsur*, also *ɛunsar*, (pl. عناصر *ɛanāsir*) An element. A foundation. Temperament, constitution, complexion. Root, origin, principle. Reputation, estimation. Misfortune, calamity. Care, study: aim, design. Necessity, need, want. Grief.

A عنصرة *ɛansarat*, The Jewish Pentecost.

A عنصريّ *ɛunsurīy*, Elementary, elemental.

A عنصل *ɛunsal* or *ɛunsul*, (عنصلاء *ɛunsalāɂ* or *ɛunsula'*) (pl. عناصل *ɛanāsil*) A sea-leek. A wild onion. A squill. طريق العنصلين *tarīku'l ɛunsalayn*, Any road where one is lost.

A عنصنص *ɛanasnas*, A fatiguing nocturnal journey in search of water.

A عنصوة *ɛunsuwat* or *ɛunsawat*, (pl. عناصي *ɛanāsī*) A handful of hair.

A عنصية *ɛinsiyat*, A lock of hair.

A عنط *ɛanat*, Length (of a beautiful neck).

A عنطبول *ɛantabūl*, Tall (woman).

A عنطنط *ɛanatnat*, Long, tall. A jug, water-pot.

A عنطيان *ɛintiyān*, The beginning of youth.

A عنظاب *ɛinzāb*, (*ɛunzāb*, عنظب *ɛunzab*, or *ɛunzub*) A thick, fat locust. A yellow male locust.

A عنظباء *ɛunzubāɂ*, (or عنظبان *ɛunzubān*) A yellow male locust.

A عنظل *ɛanzal*, A spider's web.

A عنظلة *ɛanzalat*, (v. n. of عنظل Q) Running.

A عنظوان *ɛunzuwān*, A wicked, foul-mouthed, obscene, worthless man. A hypocrite. A boaster. A sorcerer, magician. One who forces another to go to war. A kind of salt and bitter plant which gripes camels. The best of the herb alkali.

A عنظوانة *ɛunzuwānat*, A female locust.

A عنظوب *ɛunzūb*, A thick, fat locust. A yellow male locust.

A عنظوبة *ɛunzūbat*, A she-locust.

A عنظيان *ɛinziyān*, A very wicked man. Flagitious, obscene, foul-mouthed. A sorcerer, an enchanter. Rude, unfeeling. The beginning of youth.

A عنظية *ɛanzayat*, A telling obscene stories.

A عنعنة *ɛanɛanat*, Change of ء *hamza* into ع *ɛayn*.

A عنف *ɛanf*, (v. n. of عنف) Incommoding, being troublesome to. Inconvenience. Hindrance. Beginning, commencement, first. *ɛinf*, Inconvenience. *ɛunf*, Inconveniency; severity, rigour, violence, fury, force, oppression. P عنف عتاب آميز *ɛunfi ɛitāb-āmez*, Mixed with severity and reproach.

A عنف *ɛunuf*, (pl. of عنيف *ɛanīf*) Imperious, tyrannical, violent, cruel.

A عنفا *ɛunfan*, In the first place.

A عنفة *ɛunfat*, Beginning, commencement. *ɛunfat* or *ɛunufat*, Aversion, detestation, disgust. *ɛanafat*, Any thing forced by water, which turns a mill. The space between two rows of corn, a furrow.

A عنفجيج *ɛanfajīj*, A straddling she-camel; also sharp and cunning; old and fat.

A عنفس *ɛinfis*, Vile, abject, mean. Short, dwarfish.

A عنفش *ɛanfash*, (and عنفشيش *ɛanfashīsh*) One who has a long, thick beard.

A عنفشة *ɛanfashat*, (v. n. of عنفش Q) Being thick and bushy (the beard).

A عنفص *ɛinfis*, An impudent, unchaste, or depraved woman. A short, small-bodied woman. A malicious or proud and arrogant woman. A woman who moves much. Malignant, bad-tempered (man). A fox's cub.

A عنفصة *ɛinfisat*, (fem.) Loquacious. Stinking.

A عنفط *ɛunfut*, (pl. عنافط *ɛanāfit*) Bad-tempered. The space between the mustachios on the upper lip. The animal called سياه گوش *siyāh-gosh*.

A عنفق *ɛanfak*, Lightness (of any thing).

A عنفقة *ɛanfakat*, Lightness. The hair between the under lip and the chin.

A عنفك *ɛanfak*, Foolish. Heavy, unwholesome.

A عنفو *ɛunfūw*, First, beginning. Beauty.

A عنفوان *ɛunfuwān*, (and عنفوة *ɛunfūwat*) Vigour, freshness, beauty. Flower of youth. Beginning, first or early stage (of any thing).

A عنفيّ *ɛunfīy*, Rigorous, severe, violent, lordly, tyrannical. تكاليف عنفيّة *takālīfi ɛunfīya*, Exactions, oppressive extortions.

A عنق *ɛunk*, A company. Nobles, princes. The lower orifice of the stomach, the pylorus. A crust of bread. *ɛunk*, *ɛunuk*, or *ɛunak*, (pl. اعناق *aɛnāk* and اعنق *aɛnuk*) The neck. هم عنق اليك *hum ɛunuhun ilayka*, They incline to thee, are anxiously looking for thee. كان ذلك علي عنق الدهر *kāna zālika ɛala' ɛunuki'd dahr*, That is of high antiquity. *ɛanak*, Length of neck. The straddling pace of a tired horse with out-stretched neck.

P عنقا *ɛankā*, Name of a note in music.

A عنقاء *ɛankāɂ*, (fem. of اعنق *aɛnak*) Long-necked. A hillock on the top of a mountain. Calamity, misfortune. A fabulous bird which makes a distinguished figure in Eastern romance, and is described by naturalists as معلوم الاسم مجهول الجسم *maɛlūmu'l ism, majhūlu'l jism*, (A creature) known as to name, unknown as to body. العنقاء المغرب *al ɛankāɂu'l mughribu*, (or عنقاء مغرب *ɛankāɂ mughribun*, مغربة *mughribatun*, or مغرب *mughribin*) A name for any bird of mighty wing. An unmeaning speech. Calamity, adversity. A woman who sets out on a journey, and is heard of no more.

A عنقاد *ɛinkād*, A bunch of grapes. A bunch

from the fruit اراك *arāk* or بطم *butm*.

A عنقاش *ɛinkāsh*, Vile, abject, base, ignoble. A lad who serves for his victuals. A higgler, a retailer in villages.

A عنقر *ɛankar* or *ɛankur*, Root of the reed, or the first sprouting of the papyrus whilst yet white. Pith of a palm-tree. The stock or origin of man. The children of villagers (on account of their fresh and florid complexion). *ɛunkur*, Name of a camel, the dam of a noble race.

A عنقرة *ɛunkurat*, The female of a hawk.

A عنقريب *ɛan karīb*, Soon, near to, about, presently, shortly.

A عنقز *ɛankaz*, Sweet marjoram. An ass's pizzle.

A عنقزة *ɛankazat*, A flag. Poison. Misfortune.

A عنقس *ɛankas*, Sly, cunning, and malignant.

A عنقش *ɛankash*, Lean, spare, thin.

A عنقشة *ɛankashat*, (v. n. of عنقش Q) Hanging upon, being dependent.

A عنقفير *ɛankafīr*, Misfortune, calamity. A scorpion. An impudent, noisy woman. An aged camel, the back of whose head well nigh touches her shoulder.

A عنقل *ɛankal*, The intestine of the Lybian lizard.

A عنقود *ɛunkūd*, (pl. عناقيد *ɛanākīd*) A bunch of grapes. A bunch of the fruit of the اراك *arāk* or بطم *butm*. A name for a bull.

P عنك *ɛank*, An ass which goes before the herd. *ɛink*, An oil-mill. Pillar of a house or oil-mill.

A عنك *ɛank*, (v. n. of عنك) Becoming thick (milk). Being heaped up (sands in the deserts, leaving no trace of a road, dangerous and difficult to travel over); getting slowly through such sands (a camel). Travelling through a country. Attacking or returning to a charge. Disobeying her husband (a woman). Being very red (blood or sand). Shutting, bolting (a door). *ɛank*, *ɛink*, or *ɛunk*, The greater part of any thing. The greater part of the night elapsed, a third left. *ɛink*, Root, origin. A door. *ɛunk*, (pl. of عنيك *ɛanīk*) Sands heaped up. *ɛanak*, Root, origin. *ɛanka*, From or by thee.

A عنكب *ɛankab*, (fem. عنكبة *ɛankabat*) A spider.

A عنكباء *ɛankabāɛ*, A spider.

A عنكبوت *ɛankabūt*, (and عنكباة *ɛankabāt*) (fem. عنكبوتة *ɛankabūtat*) (pl. عناكب *ɛanākib*) A spider. P مگس وار در پردهٔ عنكبوت افتاده *magaswār dar pardaɛi ɛankabūt uftāda*, Like a fly fallen into the web of a spider.

A عنكث *ɛankas*, Name of a plant. Impacted wool.

A عنكد *ɛankad*, Hard. Foolish, stupid.

A عنكرة *ɛankarat*, (v. n. of عنكر Q) Becoming fat (a camel's bunch). Large (she-camel).

A عنكش *ɛankash*, Negligent, slovenly, dirty, filthy in one's person.

A عنكشة *ɛankashat*, (v. n. of عنكش Q) Beginning to wither and turn yellow (grass). Becoming mouldy (bread).

A عنكل *ɛankal*, Hard, firm. The back-bone from the shoulders to the buttocks.

A عنكم *ɛankum*, From you.

P عنگ *ɛang*, Braying of an ass. A jackass.

P عنم *ɛanm*, Pomegranate-flowers.

A عنم *ɛanam*, A species of Arabian tree bearing red fruit, to which a finger tinged with henna is compared; also the extremities of the Syrian carob-tree. The tendrils of a vine twining round an arbour. A kind of lizard. The thorn of the acacia.

A عنمة *ɛanamat*, A fissure on the lip.

A عنمّي *ɛanamīy*, A beautiful, ruddy, rosy face.

A عنن *ɛanan*, (v. n. of عنّ) Happening, occurring. Presenting itself before one's face. A side, quarter. False, vain, wrong. An object present to the eye. *ɛunan*, (pl. of عنّة *ɛunnat*) Wooden camel-pens. *ɛunun*, (pl. of عنان *ɛinān*) Reins of a bridle.

A عنو *ɛanw* (v. n. of عنا for عنو) Bringing out. Producing (grass). Approaching a thing and smelling it (a dog). *ɛinw*, (pl. اعناء *aɛnāɛ*) A tract, district, expanse. A crowd or body of men of different ranks or families.

A عنوّ *ɛunūw*, (v. n. of عنا for عنو) Being humble, suppliant. Being detained (captive). Happening to, coming down upon. Producing grass (the earth). Going up to any thing and smelling it (a dog). Being full of water and unable to retain it (a leathern bottle). Being difficult and perplexing (business).

A عنواش *ɛinwāsh*, Tall, long-legged she-camel.

A عنوان *ɛunwān* or *ɛinwān*, Title-page, frontispiece, or lettering of a book (generally gilded and highly ornamented). Beginning of any thing. Most conspicuous and decorated front of a palace. Royal signature on the top of a letter. Pretext, appearance. That whereby any thing is known. Mode, manner. صاحب عنوان *sāhib ɛunwān*, Sovereign, supreme, distinguished. سعادت عنوان *saɛādat-ɛunwān*, Happy, glorious, august.

A عنوب *ɛunūb*, (pl. of عنبة *ɛinabat*) Grapes.

A عنوة *ɛanwat*, Any thing produced, published, brought forth. Production. Force, compulsion. Love, affection. *ɛanwatan*, By force.

A عنوت *ɛanūt*, (A hill) difficult of ascent.

A عنود *ɛanūd*, Contumacious, refractory, wayward. A cloud big with rain. An arrow coming out victorious in a mode different from the rest. *ɛunūd*, (v. n. of عند) Deviating (from the right way). Acting unjustly, being contumacious, rejecting what one knows to be right and proper, and obstinately sticking for what is false. Emitting blood which cannot be stanched (a vein). Flowing without drying up (sweat). Pasturing alone (a she-camel).

A عنوز *ɛunūz*, (pl. of عنز *ɛanz*) She-goats.

A عنوس *ɛunūs*, (v. n. of عنس) Remaining long unmarried in her parents' house (a girl). Producing an alteration in a man's countenance (old age). (pl. of عانس *ɛānis*) Girls who remain long in their parents' house after the marriageable age.

A عنوق *ɛunūk*, (pl. of عناق *ɛanāk*) Female kids. العنوق بعد النوق *al ɛunūk baɛda'n nūk*, She-kids after she-camels, *i. e.* poverty after opulence.

A عنوك *ɛunūk*, (v. n. of عنك) Becoming thick (milk). Getting slowly through sands (a camel). Travelling through a country. Disobeying her husband (a woman). Being very red (sand or blood). Shutting (a door). Attacking, returning to a charge. Being heaped up and drifted (sands in a desert, leaving no trace of a road).

A عنون *ɛunūn*, (A camel) outstripping others in travelling. *ɛunūn*, (v. n. of عنّ) Appearing, offering (itself) to one's view.

A عنونة *ɛanwanat*, (v. n. of عنون Q) Putting the title-page or frontispiece to a book, or the heading to a letter.

A عنه *ɛanhu*, From him (or it). (See عن *ɛan*.)

A عنيٰ *ɛana'*, (fut. يعني *yaɛnī*) He meant.

A عنيٰ *ɛana'*, (v. n. of عني) Being held a captive. *ɛanī*, Solicitous, anxious, careful: afflicted.

A عنيان *ɛinyān* or *ɛunyān*, Title of a book.

A عنية *ɛanyat*, Labour, affliction, distress.

A عنيّة *ɛanīyat*, Camels' urine and dung dried in the sun, used as a liniment for scab or mange.

A عنيد *ɛanīd*, (pl. عند *ɛunud*) Obstinate, stubborn, refractory. One who strays from the right way purposely and intentionally.

A عنيدل *ɛunaydil*, (dim. of عندليب *ɛandalīb*) A little nightingale.

A عنيز *ɛanīz*, Unfortunate, distressed.

A عنيزة *ɛunayzat*, A girl's name.

A عنيف *ɛanīf*, (pl. عنف *ɛunuf*) One riding with pain. Violent (speech or act). Hard (pace). Imperious, tyrannical, rigorous, cruel, severe in reproach. Troublesome, inconvenient.

A عنيق *ɛanīk*, The neck. One who embraces or who seizes by the neck.

A عنيقيد *ɛunaykīd*, (dim. of عنقود *ɛunkūd*) A small bunch of grapes.

A عنيك *ɛanīk*, (pl. عنك *ɛunk*) Sand heaped up.

A عنيكب *ɛunaykib*, (dim. of عنكبوت *ɛankabūt*) A small spider.

A عنين *ɛanīn*, Unable to retain wind in his belly.

A عنّين *ɛinnīn*, Impotent, averse from women (through dislike, natural deficiency, or fascination).

A عنينة *ɛinīnat* or *ɛinnīnat*, Impotency, aversion to women. *ɛinnīnat*, A woman averse from men.

P عو *ɛav*, Clamour, noise. A cry for help.

A عواء *ɛuwāɛ*, (v. n. of عوي) Making an indistinct noise. Barking, howling. Attaining the age of thirty (a man). Bending, folding, twisting.

A عوّاء *ɛawwāɛ*, (or عوّا *ɛawwa'*) A dog (especially barking much). The fundament. The thirteenth mansion of the moon, or four or five stars of the shape of an ا *alif* in Virgo. An aged she-camel.

A عوابس *ʻawābis*, pl. of عابس *ʻābis*, Grim (lions).

A عواتق *ʻawātiḳ*, (pl. of عاتق *ʻātiḳ*) Blooming girls. Shoulders. Large bottles. Old bows red with age. Birds ready for flight.

A عواتك *ʻawātik*, (pl. of عاتكة *ʻātikat*) Names of women.

A عواثن *ʻawāsin*, (pl. of عثان *ʻusān*) Smokes. *ʻuwāsin*, Hairy (lion).

A عوّاج *ʻawwāj*, Dealer in ivory or tortoiseshell.

A عواجز *ʻawājiz*, (pl. of عاجز) Weak, impotent.

A عواجم *ʻawājim*, (pl. of عاجمة *ʻājimat*) Teeth.

A عواد *ʻawād*, *ʻiwād*, or *ʻuwād*, Any agreeable object to which one always returns with pleasure. *ʻawādi*, Return, descend, or alight thou. *ʻiwād*, (v. n. 3 of عاد for عود) Making a habit or custom.

A عوّاد *ʻawwād*, A performer on the lute or harp (عود *ʻūd*). A visitor of the sick. *ʻuwād*, (pl. of عائد *ʻāʼid*) Visitors of the sick.

A عوادة *ʻuwādat*, A visit to the sick. A return. Victuals served up a second time (particularly to any one after the others have finished).

A عوّادة *ʻawwādat*, A female player on the lute.

A عوادي *ʻawādī*, Enemies. Detainers. (pl. of عادية *ʻādiyat*) Camels feeding continually on the plant حمض *hamz*. Vines planted at the roots of large trees.

A عواذ *ʻawāz*, A disliking, a disapproving.

A عواذا *ʻawāzan*, Unwillingly.

A عواذل *ʻawāzil*, (pl. of عاذل *ʻāzil*) Certain veins from which the remains of menstruous blood trickle. Blamers.

A عواذي *ʻawāzī*, Camels pasturing in a field where the salsuginous plant حمض *hamz* grows not.

A عواذير *ʻawāzīr*, (pl. of عاذور) Adversities.

A عوار *ʻawār*, (*ʻiwār*, *ʻuwār*, also عوّار *ʻūwār*) A mote paining the eye. A rent in a garment. Blemish, fault, defect. ذات عوار *zāti ʻawār*, Torn or spoilt (merchandise).

A عوّار *ʻūwār*, (pl. عواوير *ʻawāwīr*) Pusillanimous, timid, weak. A swallow. Dust, motes, or any thing similar in the eye. A bit of flesh extracted from the eye after having injected a medical powder. One unable to see his way. Those whose حاجات *hājāt* are in their ادبار *adbār*.

A عوارد *ʻawārid*, Things thrown aside.

A عوارض *ʻawāriz*, (pl. of عارضة *ʻārizat*) Camels killed when labouring under any disease. Side-teeth. Cross timbers in the roof of a house. Things necessary to be done. Accidents, incidental distempers. Taxes, extraordinary contributions. عوارض جسمانيه *ʻawārizi jismāniya*, Bodily infirmities. *ʻuwāriz*, Name of a mountain whereon is the burial place of the celebrated حاتم طائي *hātim tāʼiy*.

A عوارف *ʻawārif*, (pl. of عارفة *ʻārifat*) Known, public, notorious (things). Kindnesses.

A عوارق *ʻawāriḳ*, Teeth, grinders. Years.

A عواري *ʻawārī*, (and عواريّ *ʻawāriy*) (pl. of عارية *ʻāriyat* or عاريّة *ʻāriyyat*) Loans.

A عوّاري *ʻūwāraʼ*, A tree from which they make collars at Mecca.

A عوازب الاطهار *ʻawāzibu'l athār*, Wives.

A عوّاس *ʻawwās*, A night-patrol.

A عواساء *ʻawāsāʼ*, A beetle carrying dung-balls.

A عواسة *ʻuwāsat*, One draught of milk.

A عواسل *ʻawāsil*, (pl. of عاسل *ʻāsil*) Wolves.

A عواشر *ʻawāshir*, Camels used to drink once only in ten or nine days. عواشر القرآن *ʻawāshiru'l kurʼān*, The tenth verses of the Kur'ān, those verses which complete the decades into which the entire volume is divided.

A عواشي *ʻawāshī*, Camels and sheep grazing by night.

A عواشير *ʻawāshīr*, (pl. of عاشوراء *ʻāshūrāʼ*) Tenth days of the month محرّم *muharram*.

A عواص *ʻawāṣ*, The track by which a fox goes to and fro.

A عواصر *ʻawāṣir*, Three stones with which they press grapes.

A عواصف *ʻawāṣif*, (pl. of عاصف *ʻāṣif* or عاصفة *ʻāṣifat*) High winds, hurricanes, violent gales.

A عواصم *ʻawāṣim*, Those countries of which Antioch is the capital city.

A عواصي *ʻawāṣī*, (pl. of عاصية *ʻāṣiyat*) Inaccessible mountains.

A عواضّ *ʻawāzz*, (pl. of عاضّة *ʻāzzat*) (Camels) feeding on the thorny plants عضّ *ʻizz*.

A عواضة *ʻawāzih*, (pl. of عضه *ʻazih* and عاضه *ʻāzih*) (Camels) feeding on the plants عضاه *ʻizāh*.

A عواطف *ʻawāṭif*, (pl. of عاطفة *ʻāṭifat*) Affections, favours. Benevolent inclinations.

A عواطل *ʻawāṭil*, (pl. of عاطل *ʻāṭil*) (Women) unadorned with necklaces. Letters without diacritical points (as س *sīn*, ص *ṣād*, &c.)

A عواطن *ʻawāṭin*, (pl. of عاطنة *ʻāṭinat*) (Camels) lying down about the cistern after watering.

A عواف *ʻuwāf*, (or عوافة *ʻuwāfat*) Whatever a lion prowls after by night and devours. Any thing won.

A عوافي *ʻawāfī*, (pl. of عافية *ʻāfiyat*) Healths, safeties. (Birds or beasts) in quest of food.

A عواق *ʻuwāḳ*, The rumbling noise in the belly of a trotting horse.

A عواقّ *ʻawāḳḳ*, Shoots, sprouts growing out of a palm-tree.

A عواقب *ʻawāḳib*, Camels which drink alternately and return to their places. (pl. of عاقبة *ʻāḳibat*) Ends, conclusions, issues, consequences.

P عواقب بين *ʻawāḳib-bīn*, Foresightful.

A عواقر *ʻawāḳir*, (pl. of عاقر) Barren (women).

A عواقيل *ʻawāḳīl*, (pl. of عاقول *ʻāḳūl*) Windings of rivers. عواقيل الامور *ʻawāḳīlu'l umūr*, Intricate affairs, or the intricacies of things.

A عوالج *ʻawālij*, (pl. of عالج *ʻālij*) Camels feeding on the plant علجان *ʻalajān*. Sands heaped up layer upon layer, drifted high.

A عوالق *ʻawāliḳ*, (pl. of عالق *ʻāliḳ*) (Camels or goats) which browse the tops of plants. Name of a tribe in Yaman.

A عوالك *ʻawālik*, (pl. of عولك) Uterine veins.

A عوالم *ʻawālim*, (pl. of عالم) Worlds. Ages.

A عوالي *ʻawālī*, (pl. of عالية) Straight, tall spears.

P عوالي پناه *ʻawālī-panāh*, Illustrious.

A عوّام *ʻawwām*, A swimmer. Swimming (horse). Swift-going (horse). One going on or attacking with intrepidity. A raft, or any thing similar, on which people pass rivers.

A عوامّ *ʻawāmm*, (pl. of عامّة *ʻāmmat*) The common people, public, vulgar. عوامّ الناس *ʻawāmmu'n nās*, The populace. عوامّ و خواصّ *ʻawāmm u khawāṣṣ*, Plebeians and nobles, every body.

A عوامر *ʻawāmir*, (pl. of عامرة *ʻāmirat*) Serpents.

A عوامل *ʻawāmil*, (pl. of عاملة *ʻāmilat*) Words, particles, or prepositions, which govern other words. Oxen which plough or tread out corn. Feet.

A عواميد *ʻawāmīd*, (pl. of عامود) Columns.

P عوان *ʻawān*, A seizer, holder, griper.

A عوان *ʻawān*, (pl. عون *ʻūn*) A middle-aged woman (especially married), a lady, mistress of a family. A middle-aged mare or cow. War determined by one battle. Land wet with rain. *ʻiwān*, (v. n. 3 of عان for عون) Assisting, bringing help.

P عوانان *ʻawānān*, (pl. of عوان *ʻawān*) Gripers, oppressors. عوانان فلك *ʻawānāni falak*, The planets Saturn, Jupiter, Mars, the sun, Venus, Mercury, and the moon.

A عوانة *ʻawānat*, Ground overflowed with rain. A tall palm-tree. A sand-worm. An animal smaller than a hedgehog.

A عوانس *ʻawānis*, (pl. of عانس *ʻānis*) (Girls) remaining at home long unmarried.

A عواني *ʻawānī*, (pl. of عانية *ʻāniyat*) Female captives. Women.

A عواور *ʻawāwir*, (and عواوير *ʻawāwīr*) (pl. of عوّار *ʻūwār*) Swallows.

A عواوير *ʻawāwīr*, (pl. of عوّار) Weak, cowardly.

A عواهج *ʻawāhij*, Name of an Arabian tribe.

A عواهق *ʻawāhiḳ*, (pl. of عوهق *ʻawhaḳ*) Mountain swallows.

A عواهن *ʻawāhin*, (pl. of عاهن *ʻāhin*) Palm-branches which communicate with the heart of the tree. Veins in the uterus of a camel, or in the members of the human body. رمي بالكلام على عواهنه *ramaʼ bi'l kalām ʻalaʼ ʻawāhinihi*, He cared not whether he spoke right or wrong.

A عوائد *ʻawāʼid*, (pl. of عائدة *ʻāʼidat*) Favours, kindnesses. Returns, profits, gains.

A عوائذ *ʻawāʼiz*, Name of four stars forming an irregular square, in the centre of which are the stars called ربع *rubaʻ*.

A عوائر *ʻawāʼir*, Swarms (of locusts).

A عوائق *ʻawāʼiḳ*, (pl. of عائق *ʻāʼiḳ*) Hinderers.

Accidents, calamities, misfortunes. Affairs which occupy greatly.

A عوبث ɛawbas, A road over a mountain.

A عوبر ɛawbar, The whelp of the cheeta.

A عوبطة ɛawbatat, Misfortune, calamity. The depth of the sea.

A عوّة ɛawwat, (v. n. of عوي) Howling, barking. Curling or plaiting (hair); bending (a bow). Attaining the age of thirty (a man). Noise, clamour. Noise of combatants. ɛawwat or ɛūwat, The backside.

A عوث ɛaws, (v. n. of عاث for عوث) Restraining, hindering even to bewilderment.

A عوج ɛawj, (v. n. of عاج for عوج) Stopping (in any place). Standing. Continuing, allowing to remain. Receding, retiring. Bending with the reins (the head of a camel or horse). Drawing in (reins). ɛūj, Og, king of Bashan. (pl. of اعوج aɛwaj) Crooked. ɛawaj, (v. n. of عوج) Being crooked, distorted. Curvature. A distorted form (of erect bodies). ɛiwaj, Curvature, crookedness. Obliquity (whether physical or moral).

A عوجاء ɛawjāʼ, (fem. of اعوج aɛwaj) Crooked. Perverse. A bow. Slender, attenuated camels.

A عود ɛawd, (v. n. of عاد for عود) Returning. Turning. Becoming (learned). Restoring, bringing back. Visiting (the sick). Coming step by step. A coming back. Return. Relapse. Habit, custom. Repetition. (pl. عودة ɛiwadat and عيدة ɛiyadat) Aged (camel or sheep). The second in rank. A man of ability, experience, or prudence. An old road. Ancient dominion. (pl. of عائد ɛāʼid) Visitors of the sick. عود سودد ɛawdi sawdad, An old beaten path. رجع عودا على بدء rajaɛa ɛawdan ɛala' badʼin, (or عوده على بدئه ɛawdahu ɛala' badʼihi) He did not break off his journey till he returned, he kept moving on till he had got back. ɛūd, (pl. عيدان ɛīdān and اعواد aɛwād) Wood, timber, the trunk or branch of a tree, a staff, stick. Wood of aloes. Marine costus. A lute, harp, lyre. The bone at the root of the tongue. P عود زدن ɛūd zadan, To strike the lyre. A عود الدرقة ɛūdu'd darka, Root of the assafœtida-plant. P عود سيمين ɛūdi sīmīn, The dawn. A عود الصليب ɛūdu's salīb, Name of a wood called فاوانيا fāwāniyā. A kind of wood on which fire makes no impression. A sort of wood which breaks in squares. A triangular bit of wood, used as an amulet to keep off frightful dreams. Streaks of the dawn. عود العطاس ɛūdu'l ɛutās, Sneezewort. عود قماري ɛūdi kamārī, A species of aloe-wood brought from Kamār. عود كلاني ɛūdi kalānī, Whiteness and blackness. P عود و گلاب ɛūd u gulāb, Whiteness and blackness. عود هندي ɛūd hindī, Lignum aloes. A ام العود ummu'l ɛūd, The rough tripe.

A عوّد ɛūwad, (pl. of عائد) Visitors of the sick.

A عودان ɛūdān, Muhammad's pulpit or staff.

A عودة ɛawdat, A return, coming back. ɛiwadat, (pl. of عود ɛawd) Aged (camels or sheep).

P عودسوز ɛūd-soz, A censer, in which they burn aloe-wood.

A عودق ɛawdak, (or عودقة ɛawdakat) A hooked instrument for pulling buckets out of wells.

A عودقة ɛawdakat, (v. n. of عودق Q) Moving the hand in a place full of water as if in search of something. Doing (any thing) in doubt and uncertainty. Pulling a bucket out of a well with a hooked instrument. A hook baited with flesh, with which they catch wolves and other wild beasts.

P عودي تخت ɛūdi-takht, Heaven, sky.

A عوذ ɛawz, (v. n. of عاذ for عوذ) Fleeing for refuge. Flying to God from any thing bad. عوذ بالله منك ɛawzun bi'llāhi minka, God defend me from thee. ɛūz, (pl. of عائذ ɛāʼiz) (Mares, camels, or does) the 10th or 15th day after colting. ɛawaz, A disliking, a disapproving. Refuge, asylum. Falling (leaf). Low, base, mean. افلت منه عوذا aflata minhu ɛawazan, He frightened, but struck not. عوذا منه ɛawazan minhu, (I did it) unwillingly. ɛuwaz, (pl. of عوذة ɛūzat) Amulets.

A عوّذ ɛūwaz, That part of the flesh next to the bone. Herbage growing at the roots of thorns, or in rough places where cattle cannot crop it. A bird which takes refuge in a mountain. اطيب اللحم عوّذه atyabu'l lahm ɛūwazuhu. The nicest meat is that nearest the bone.

A عوذا ɛawazan, (Escaping) hardly, with danger.

A عوذان ɛūzān, (pl. of عائذ ɛāʼiz) Mares, camels, or does, the 10th or 15th day after bringing forth.

A عوذة ɛūzat, An amulet, a thing repelling evil.

A عور ɛawr, (v. n. of عار for عور) Depriving of one eye, blinding. Taking away, carrying off. Destroying. Obliterating. ɛūr, (pl. of اعور aɛwar) One-eyed. ɛawar, (v. n. of عور) Being blind of an eye. ɛawir, Inwardly bad, secretly wicked.

A عوراء ɛawrāʼ, (fem. of اعور aɛwar) One-eyed; also one who sees double. Without water (desert). Obscene (discourse), disgraceful (action).

A عورات ɛawrāt, (and ɛawarāt when applied to females) (pl. of عورة ɛawrat) Parts of the body which it is indecent to expose. Fissures in mountains.

A عوران ɛūrān, A ruined well or wells. (pl. of اعور aɛwar) One-eyed.

A عورة ɛawrat, (pl. عورات ɛawrāt) Any part of the body which it is indecent to expose (particularly from the navel to the knee). Any place exposed to hostile incursions, the frontier nearest an enemy. Any weak part in a regiment or fortress. The state of having only one eye, monoculousness. P عورت زن ɛawrati zan, Pudenda mulieris. عورت مرد ɛawrati mard, Pudenda viri. A ɛawirat, Possessed of weak parts, flaws, or chinks.

P عورت ɛawrat, A woman. A wife.

P عورت پوش ɛawrat-posh, Breeches.

P عوري ɛūrī, Nakedness.

A عوز ɛawz, A grape-stone. ɛawaz, (v. n. of عوز) Being strong, hard, and severe. Being difficult. Wanting, not being found. Being poor. Poverty. Need, necessity.

A عوزب ɛawzab, An old woman.

A عوزة ɛawzat, A single grape-stone.

A عوزر ɛawzar, The mountain-plant نصيّ nasīy.

A عوزلوز ɛawiz lawiz, Poor and needy.

A عوزم ɛawzam, An old woman or she-camel with some remains of strength. A dwarfish woman.

A عوس ɛaws, (v. n. of عاس for عوس) Ranging in the night; catching (as a wolf) any thing to devour. Governing, managing judiciously (one's property). Labouring industriously for the support of one's family. ɛūs, A species of sheep. ɛawas, A going inwards of the corners of the mouth when laughing.

A عوساء ɛawsāʼ, (fem. of اعوس aɛwas) (A woman) who draws in the corners of her mouth when laughing.

A عوسان ɛawasān, A going about at night.

A عوسج ɛawsaj, (or عوسجة) A kind of bramble.

A عوسجة ɛawsajat, Name of a certain silver-mine.

A عوسرانة ɛawsarānat, An unbroken she-camel ridden upon.

A عوسرانيّة ɛawsarānīyat, A she-camel accustomed to carry her tail high in running. A she-camel ridden before she is fairly broke in.

A عوسن ɛawsan, Tall and slightly hump-backed.

A عوسيّ ɛūsīy, A species of ram.

A عوص ɛaws, A mark, a sign. ɛūs, Uz, the son of Iram, the son of Shem, and the father of عاد ɛād. (pl. of عائص ɛāʼis) (Sheep) which have not conceived for several years. ɛawas, (v. n. of عوص) Being unintelligible (affair or speech). Being hard and difficult. Confounding (an antagonist), reducing him to a nonplus.

A عوصاء ɛawsāʼ, Foreign (word). Intricate (business). Difficulty.

A عوض ɛawz, (v. n. of عاض for عوض) Doing or giving an equivalent. Compensation. Time, an age. Name of an old Arabian idol. At no time, never, usually in a future sense, from henceforth (قط katt implying never before). عوض العائضين ɛawzu'l ɛāʼizīna, Never. من ذي عوض min zi ɛawzin, Anew, afresh from the beginning. ɛiwaz, (v. n. of عاض for عوض) Giving or doing an equivalent, or one thing for another. (pl. اعواض aɛwāz) Reward, recompense, compensation, premium, price, exchange, any thing substituted for another. عوضه ɛiwazahu, (or عوضا عنه ɛiwazan ɛanhu) In his room, instead of it. P عوض كردن ɛiwaz kardan, To barter, exchange. A بلا عوض bilā ɛiwazin, Gratuitously, without reward, return, or equivalent.

A عوضي ɛiwazī, Equivalent, in compensation.

A عوط ɛūt, (pl. of عائط ɛāʼit) Camels not conceiving for several years, though not barren.

A عوطب *ʿawṭab*, An accident, calamity, misfortune. The midst of the sea, abyss, gulf. The smooth space between two waves. A kind of tree.

A عوطط *ʿawṭaṭ*, *ʿūṭaṭ*, or *ʿawṭuṭ*, (pl. of عائط *ʿāʾiṭ*) (Camels or women) not conceiving for several years, though not barren.

A عوعاء *ʿawʿāʾ*, Noise, cry, tumult, clamour.

A عوعاة *ʿawʿāt*, Driving (sheep) by calling عا *ʿā*.

A عوف *ʿawf*, (v. n. of عاف for عوف) Flying round any thing (as birds round a watering-place or a carcase). Sticking, adhering to. State, condition. Good fortune, happiness. A guest. Penis. Work, business. A grandfather. Name of a bird. A dunghill-cock. Name of an idol; also of a mountain. A lion. A wolf. Good pasturage. A certain fragrant plant. One who looks well after his camels. One who labours for his family. ابو عوف *abū ʿawf*, A male locust. امّ عوف *umm ʿawf*, A female locust.

A عوفيّ *ʿawfiy*, Addicted, given to.

A عوق *ʿawḳ*, (v. n. of عاق for عوق) Hindering, detaining, preventing. Changing, turning. Engaging the heart of her husband (a wife). Delay, procrastination. One who diverts another from any thing good. Time. The bending of a valley. آخر عوق *āḵhir ʿawḳin*, The end of time. *ʿawḳ* or *ʿūḳ*, (pl. اعواق *aʿwāḳ*) Worthless, good for nothing. *ʿawḳ*, *ʿūḳ*, or *ʿawiḳ*, An accident (hindered me). *ʿūḳ*, One who diverts from any thing good. Name of the father of عوج *ʿūj*, Og. *ʿawaḳ*, Hunger. *ʿawiḳ*, *ʿuwaḳ*, or *ʿiwaḳ*, A hinderer, a preventer. عوق لوق *ʿawiḳ lawiḳ*, Foolish, sheepish, bashful. *ʿuwaḳ*, A hinderer. A coward. One who meets with continual interruptions and hindrances. One who having set his mind on any thing performs it.

A عوّق *ʿūwaḳ*, One who meets with continual interruptions and hindrances. One who having set his mind on a thing accomplishes it. One who diverts people from their business. A coward. (pl. of عائق *ʿāʾiḳ*) Hinderers, preventers.

A عوقة *ʿawḳat*, One who diverts from any thing good. *ʿuwaḳat*, A hinderer, preventer. Dilatory.

A عوك *ʿawk*, (v. n. of عاك for عوك) Being supported (by hope). Returning to (her) house and eating what is there (a woman). Turning to, inclining, advancing towards. Fleeing unto, taking refuge. Returning. Rushing upon, charging. Gaining (a livelihood). Motion. A thing. اوّل عوك و بوك *awwalu ʿawkin wa bawkin*, The first thing. عوكي على بيتك اذا اعياك بيت جارتك *ʿūkī ʿala' baytiki izā aʿyāki baytu jāratiki*, Return home (O woman!) when thy neighbour's house becomes irksome to thee.

A عوكشة *ʿawkashat*, A fan, winnowing machine.

A عوكل *ʿawkal*, Foolish (woman). Biting (hare). A dwarfish, bandy-legged man. Sands heaped up. A kind of seasoning. A particular kind of broth. قلائد عوكل *ḳalāʾid ʿawkal*, Disgraceful deeds.

A العوكلان *al ʿawkalāni*, Name of two stars.

A عوكلي *ʿawkaliy*, Food prepared with عوكل.

A عول *ʿawl*, (v. n. of عال for عول) Deviating, swerving, straying. Leaning to one side (a scale). Being partial (a judge). Exceeding bounds, being high, heavy, and exorbitant. Exacting or levying more than what is due. Being troublesome, oppressive, and vexatious (affair). Being crooked. Exhausting the patience of. Overcoming, getting the better of, excelling. Becoming exhausted and worn out (patience). Supporting (a family). Having a large family to maintain. Asking aid. Provision for a family. Lamentation, howl, wail. Any thing in which one reposes trust or relies for help. عول زيد *ʿawla* or *ʿawlu zaydin*, Fie on thee, Zayd! *ʿiwal*, Confidence, reliance. Aid implored.

A عولة *ʿawlat*, (v. n. of عول) Being bereaved (a mother). Wailing, lamentation.

A عولق *ʿawlaḳ*, A demon inhabiting the woods. An appendix or the tail of a discourse. (A bitch) which wants the male. A wolf. Hunger.

A عولك *ʿawlak*, (pl. عوالك *ʿawālik*) A rolling of the tongue in speaking. A vein in the uterus of mares, asses, and sheep.

A عوم *ʿawm*, (v. n. of عام for عوم) Swimming (a man). Floating, sailing (a ship). Travelling (a camel). *ʿuwam*, (pl. of عومة *ʿūmat*) Black animalcules swimming on water.

A عوّم *ʿūwam*, (pl. of عام *ʿām* or عائم *ʿāʾim*) Years. سنون عوّم *sinūna ʿūwamun*, Many years.

A عومة *ʿūmat*, (pl. عوم *ʿuwam*) A black animalcule swimming on water. A kind of fish.

A عومج *ʿawmaj*, A serpent.

A عومرة *ʿawmarat*, The collecting or detaining of a number of men in one place. The noise of a mixed multitude.

A عون *ʿawn*, (v. n. of عان for عون) Being middle-aged (a woman). Aid, assistance, succour, help. (pl. اعوان *aʿwān*) A defender, helper, patron, ally. A servant. عون الهي *ʿawni ilāhī*, Divine aid. *ʿūn*, (pl. of عانة *ʿānat*) Herds of wild asses. (pl. of عوان *ʿawān*) Middle-aged women. Matrons. ابو عون *abū ʿūn*, Dates. Salt.

A عووص *ʿawūṣ*, A sheep giving milk sparingly.

A عوول *ʿuwūl*, (v. n. of عال for عول) Maintaining a family (عيال *ʿiyāl*).

A عوهبة *ʿawhabat*, (v. n. of عوهب Q) Accusing of error, charging (one) with seducing or leading astray.

A عوهج *ʿawhaj*, Long-necked or long-legged (ostrich, camel, or roe). A serpent. A young she-camel. (A roe) marked on the flank with two stripes.

A عوهق *ʿawhaḳ*, Long, tall. Name of a remarkable camel, to which all camels of a superior quality are traced. A black crow. A black camel. The best kind of the tree نبع *nabʿ*. Lapis lazuli, or its blue tincture. A bull inclining to black. A mountain-swallow. A tall dust-coloured ostrich.

A عوهقان *ʿawhaḳāni*, Two stars at the side of the فرقدان *farḳadāni* in a line towards the polar star.

A عوهقة *ʿawhaḳat*, A seducing, leading into error.

A عوهكة *ʿawhakat*, (v. n. of عوهك Q) Fighting. Struggling. Wrestling. Vociferating.

A عوية *ʿawiyat*, (v. n. of عوي) Making an inarticulate noise. Barking, howling. (A camel) bending (his nose-ring). Attaining the age of thirty. Bending (a bow, or a camel's head with the rein).

A عويد *ʿuwayd*, (dim. of عود) A little stick.

A عوير *ʿuwayr*, (dim. of اعور *aʿwar*) A crow. An odious disposition. كسير عوير *kusayr ʿuwayr*, Corrupted, depraved.

A عويشراء *ʿuwayshirāʾ*, Summit of a mountain.

A عويص *ʿawīṣ*, Difficult to be understood (verse); foreign, obsolete (word). Severe (misfortune). Difficult, distressing (affair). Hard (ground), rugged, gravelly (place). Soul, self, spirit. Strength, power. Force, vehemence, severity. Motion. The tracks by which a fox goes to and fro.

A عويكة *ʿawīkat*, A battle, a combat.

A عويل *ʿawīl*, A groan, wail, lamentation. P پر عويل *pur ʿawīl*, Full of groans.

A ذات العويم *zāta'l ʿuwaym*, In a certain year.

A عوين *ʿawīn*, All, every. Helpers.

A عهّ *ʿahh*, Impudent. Proud. Quarrelsome.

A عهاد *ʿihād*, Showers in spring following one another close. (pl. of عهد *ʿahd*) Early vernal showers.

A عهار *ʿihār*, (v. n. 3 of عهر) Visiting a woman either by night or day and committing fornication.

A عهارة *ʿahārat*, (v. n. of عهر) Fornicating, whoring. Being addicted to lewdness and thieving.

A عهان *ʿihān*, Root of a cluster of dates.

A عهب *ʿahb*, A being ignorant of, not knowing.

A عهبّاء *ʿihibbāʾ*, (or عهبّى *ʿihibba'*) The beginning (of youth). Feebleness of dominion. عهبّى الملك *ʿihibba'l malik*, Time or reign of the king.

A عهخع *ʿuhkhuʿ*, Name of a tree, the leaves of which are used in medicine.

A عهد *ʿahd*, (v. n. of عهد) Commanding; recommending: enjoining. Making a will or testament. Stipulating. Fulfilling a promise, treaty, covenant, or engagement. Becoming surety for another. Meeting with. Being civil and polite, dissimulating. Observing; taking care of, keeping, preserving. Being moistened with rain (ground). Knowing. Knowledge, acquaintance. A promise, agreement, compact, contract, engagement, obligation, treaty, peace, truce. An oath; faith, security. Protection. A mandate, precept, commission, or patent for any office or dignity. A place which one frequents, in which one does a thing oft. Testament, last will. A religious vow. Time, season. A profession in or belief of the unity of God. Honour, reverence, respect, esteem. Precedency. Modesty. Successive rains. Early spring-rains. Age, time, reign: as, علىٰ عهد رسول الله *عala' عahdi rasūli'llāh*, In the time of the prophet. P عهد بستن *عahd bastan*, To strike a bargain. A علىّٰ عهد الله لافعله *عalayya' عahdu'llāh la afعaluhu*, By God I will do it! P عهد و پيمان جانبين *عahd u paymāni jānibayn*, The conditions on both sides. A عهد الله *عahdu'llāh*, The command of God. وليّ عهده *walīy عahdihi*, His heir apparent, his successor. *عahid*, A manager of the affairs of a kingdom.

A عهدان *عihdān*, A pledging of faith, suretiship.

A عهدة *عahdat* or *عihdat*, Early spring-rains. *عuhdat*, An obligation, debt; an obliging one's self to pay, a becoming surety for another. A written agreement or treaty. A bargain, contract. A mulct, a fine. Office, trust, post, business, employment, situation. A returning of goods (when damaged). A return. Deficiency, weakness (in understanding or business). العهدة علىٰ الراوي *al عuhdatu عala'r rāwī*, It rests with the author to prove. لا عهدة *lā عuhdata*, There is no returning or taking back (an article sold). P از عهدهٔ عهد بيرون آمدن *az عuhdasi عahd bīrūn āmadan*, To pay a vow, to fulfil, or get quit of, an obligation.

P عهد شكن *عahd-shikan*, A promise-breaker.

P عهد شكني *عahd-shikanī*, Breach of promise.

P عهد نامه *عahd-nāma*, Letters of agreement, articles of peace or capitulation. A diploma.

P عهده برائي *عuhda-barāئī*, Performance of an agreement, ability to perform; means; performance.

P عهده بندي *عuhda-bandī*, Stated periods for the discharge of a debt or payment of money.

P عهده دار *عuhda-dār*, Entrusted with a business, employed, holding a commission; an officer. A contractor, collector: security for rents.

A عهر *عahr*, (v.n. of عهر) Being addicted to whoredom or theft. *عahr*, *عihr*, or *عahar*, (v. n. of عهر) Whoring, fornicating. *عihr*, Adultery, whoredom.

A عهعخ *عuhعuhk*, Name of a tree whose leaves and stem are useful in medicine.

A عهن *عahn*, (v. n. of عهن) Withering (as the branch of a tree). Being fixed, established, remaining (in a place). Going out, and travelling. Making a treaty. Being present. Taking pains with any business. Hastening to accomplish the wishes of another. *عihn*, An able manager of an estate, one thoroughly conversant with the management of camels. (pl. عهون *عuhūn*) Dyed wool.

A عهنة *عihnat*, A tree bearing a red flower. A part of a lock of wool, especially when dyed. Hatred. Rage. *عuhnat*, The fracture of a bough or twig without a separation of the parts.

A عهو *عihw*, A colt. A camel, fine-shouldered, slender in the back, and strong withal.

A عهود *عuhūd*, (pl. of عهد *عahd*) Conditions, capitulations, promises, agreements. Successive rains.

A عهور *عuhūr*, (v. n. of عهر) Visiting a whore by night or day. Being given to whoring and thieving.

A عهون *عuhūn*, (pl. of عهن *عihn*) Various coloured wools.

A عهيد *عahīd*, United in a bond, confederate. Cotemporary. Tributary. Old, ancient.

A عهيديٰ *عuhhayda'*, Suretyship.

A عيّ *عayy*, (v. n. of عوي) Plaiting (hair), twisting (a rope). (A camel) bending (his nose-ring). Folding, doubling. Exciting to sedition and discord. Bending. Distorting (the head of a camel by pulling tight the reins). Treating as a liar. Driving or casting back. Making an indistinct noise. Barking, howling. Attaining the age of thirty, having a strong gripe, and twisting the hand of another. (pl. اعياء *aعyā*) Unable to accomplish a work, embarrassed. *عiy*, (v. n. of عوي) Stammering. Being ignorant of. (v. n. of عيّ) Being embarrassed, unequal to any business or enterprise. Stammering, stuttering.

A عياء *عayāء*, (pl. اعياء *aعyāء*) Difficult, incurable (disease). Impotent, unable to generate.

A عياب *عiyāb*, (pl. of عيبة *عaybat*) Portmanteaus. Breasts and hearts as the repositories of secrets. An instrument which separates or cards cotton.

A عيّاب *عayyāb*, (or عيّابة *عayyābat*) Slanderous, loquacious: a reviler.

A عيّاث *عayyās*, A lion.

A عياد *عiyād*, (v. n. of عاد for عود) Visiting (the sick). Occupant of the second post or rank.

A عيادة *عiyādat*, (v. n. of عاد for عود) Visiting (the sick). A visitation. P عيادت خستگان *عiyādati khastagān*, Visitation of the sick.

A عياذ *عiyāz*, (v. n. of عاذ for عوذ) Flying from evil to good, taking refuge. Having recently brought forth (young camels, mares, or deer). Sticking, cleaving, adhering. Refuge, asylum. A bird which takes refuge in a mountain. The first birth, also a recent birth. هي في عياذها *hiya fī عiyāzihā*, She is within ten days or a fortnight after colting. عياذاً بالله *عiyāzan bi'llāh*, By flying for refuge to God; synonymous to, God avert! Heaven forefend!

A عيار *عiyār*, (v. n. 3 of عار for عور) Marking (weights and measures) with a just standard, assaying. Dividing, apportioning. Seeing, examining. A standard of weight, measure, or firmness. Mark, proof, touchstone, assay. The pace of a horse or dog running away when escaping or set at liberty. (pl. of عير *عayr*) Asses, wild or tame. P عيار دانش *عiyāri dānish*, Criterion of knowledge (title of a book). A تمام عيار *tamām-عiyār*, (P درست عيار *durust-عiyār*, or A مستقيم العيار *mustakīmu'l عiyār*) Of full or standard-measure. Legal-marked (weight). دار العيار *dāru'l عiyār*, The assay-office. P درست عياران *durust-عiyārān*, (or راست عياران *rāst-عiyārān*) The just, those who weigh exactly. عيار گير *عiyār-gīr*, (or A صاحب عيار *sāhib عiyār*) An assayer, the officer of the mint who tries and marks gold or silver; also a skilful jeweller.

A عيّار *عayyār*, A cheat, knave, impostor, charlatan, conjuror, juggler. A horse curveting or prancing from sprightliness. One who travels much, who goes and comes a great deal; who goes round and round much. A lion.

A عيارات *عiyārāt*, (pl. of عيار *عiyār* which is pl. of عير *عayr*) Many wild or tame asses.

P عيّار پيشه *عayyār-pesha*, A knave in conduct.

A عيارة *عiyārat*, Publicity, notoriety.

A P عيّارة *عayyāra*, A sly, cunning, woman.

A عيّاري *عayyārī*, Deceit, imposture, knavery.

A عيازر *عayāzir*, A certain herb smaller than عضاه *عizāh* and larger than دق *dikh*. Small branches or loppings.

A عياسة *عiyāsat*, (v. n. of عاس for عوس) Managing (property) carefully and judiciously.

A عيّاش *عayyāsh*, A jovial fellow, jolly toper, boon companion; one fond of good cheer.

A عياص *عayās*, (v. n. of عاص for عوص) Confounding (an adversary) reducing (him) to a nonplus. *عiyās*, (v. n. of عوص) Being unintelligible (speech), difficult (an affair). (v. n. 3 of عوص) Wrestling, struggling.

A عياض *عiyāz*, Retribution, compensation.

A عياط *عiyāt*, (v. n. of عاط for عوط) Not conceiving for some years though not barren (a woman or camel). Noise, clamour, wail.

A عياف *عayāf*, A kind of game. *عiyāf*, (v. n. of عاف for عيف) Nauseating, loathing (food).

A عيافة *عiyāfat*, (v. n. of عاف for عوف) Having an aversion to, loathing meat or drink. Divining, auguring from the flight of birds. Divination. Disgust, loathing, aversion. اهل العيافة *ahlu'l عiyāfat*, A diviner by birds: an augur.

A عيال *عiyāl*, (pl. of عيّل *عayyil*) Family, children, domestics. A wife.

A عيّال *عayyāl*, Proudly-moving (man or horse).

A عيالة *عiyālat*, (v. n. of عال for عول) Maintaining a family. Having a numerous household to maintain. Forage, provender.

A عيّالة *عayyālat*, A woman who walks with a haughty carriage, or with a delicate, mincing air.

P عيال دار *عiyāl-dār*, Maintainer of a family.

P عيال داري *عiyāl-dārī*, Maintenance of a family.

P عيال مند *عiyālmand*, Possessed of a family.

A عيام *عayām*, A day.

A عيان *عiyān*, (v. n. 3 of عان for عين) Seeing. Observing, contemplating, beholding face to face. Ocular demonstration. (pl. اعينة *aعyinat* and عين *عuyun*) A ploughshare. ابنا عيان *ibnā عiyān*, Two birds or two lines traced on the ground, from which they divine; whence, when any one wins at chance-games they say جري ابنا عيان *jara' ibnā عiyān*.

A عيّان *عayyān*, Tired, embarrassed, unequal to.

A عياناً *عiyānan*, Publicly, clearly, plainly, visibly.

A عيانة *ɛiyānat*, (v. n. of عان for عين) Being a spy on another's acts, eyeing.

A عياني *ɛiyānī*, A spy.

A عياهمة *ɛuyāhimat*, Swift, strong (she-camel).

A عياهير *ɛayāhīr*, (pl. of عيهران) Male ghūls.

A عياياء *ɛayāyāɛ*, Deficient (in action), embarrassed, unequal to: one with an impediment (in speech). Impotent, unable to generate (camel).

A عيائل *ɛayāɛil*, (pl. of عيال *ɛiyāl*, which is pl. of عيّل *ɛayyil*) Household servants. Persons maintained in a family.

A عيب *ɛayb*, (v. n. of عاب for عيب) Accusing, reproaching, treating opprobriously. Spoiling, damaging. Being damaged (wares). Making (milk) thick (a churn). (pl. عيوب *ɛuyūb*) Vice, fault, defect, blemish, stain, disgrace, affront, crime, infamy, dishonour. *ɛiyab*, (pl. of عيبة *ɛaybat*) Portmanteaus, bags for keeping clothes in.

A عيبة *ɛaybat*, Fault, disgrace, vice, defect, or blemish. (pl. عيب *ɛiyab*, عياب *ɛiyāb*, and عيبات *ɛaybāt*) A portmanteau, or any thing similar in which they put clothes. A repository of secrets. *ɛuyabat*, Slanderous, loquacious, reviling; a great fault-finder.

P عيب جوي *ɛayb-joy*, Fault-seeking.

P عيب چيني *ɛayb-chīnī*, Criticism.

P عيب گوي *ɛayb-goy* or *gūy*, A slanderer.

P عيبناك *ɛaybnāk*, Disgraceful, vicious, faulty, blemished. Damaged, spoiled (goods).

P عيب ناكي *ɛaybnākī*, Blemish, vice, faultiness.

A عيتوم *ɛaytūm*, A big man. A slow camel.

A عيث *ɛays*, (v. n. of عاث for عيث) Destroying, wasting (as a wolf the flock). ذو العيث *zū'l ɛays*, Mischievous, destructive.

A عيثام *ɛaysām*, The plane-tree. Food in which are dressed locusts.

A عيثة *ɛaysat*, Soft and level ground.

A عيثر *ɛaysar*, A slight trace, vestige. Essence, individual, the thing itself. Thin clay.

A عيثرة *ɛaysarat*, (v. n. of عيثر Q) Seeing (a bird) running and frightening (it) away.

A عيثمي *ɛaysamīy*, The wild ass.

A عيثوم *ɛaysūm*, Large-bodied (camel). An elephant (male or female). A hyena.

A عيثي *ɛaysa'*, Wonder, amazement, surprise. Astonishing! strange! is it possible? عيثي جعار *ɛīsi jaɛāri*, A particle of contempt, used when any thing is rejected as false or trifling.

A عيج *ɛayj*, (v. n. of عاج for عيج) Fearing, minding, caring for. Taking in good part, being pleased and satisfied. Quenching one's thirst. Being any better (for medicines).

A عيجلوف *ɛayjalūf*, Name of the ant of which mention is made in the Kur'ān.

A عيد *ɛīd*, Any thing which returns (of care, grief, or sickness). (pl. اعياد *aɛyād*) A solemnity, feast, festival, holiday. Name of an excellent camel, the sire of a noble race. A sort of mountain-tree. (pl. of عادة *ɛādat*) Manners, customs, habits. عيد شريف *ɛīdi sharīf*, The grand festival, *i.e.* Easter, the passover. عيد فقر *ɛīdi fakr*, (Poverty's feast) A ceasing from man, and the union of the soul with the Supreme Spirit. عيد اضحي *ɛīdi azha'*, The festival of sacrifices at Mecca. عيد مسيح *ɛīdi masīh*, The day upon which a table descended from heaven at the prayer of Jesus Christ.

A عيدان *ɛaydān*, (pl. of عيدانة *ɛaydānat*) Tall palm-trees. *ɛīdan*, (pl. of عود *ɛūd*) Timbers; trunks or branches of trees, sticks.

A عيدانة *ɛaydānat*, (pl. عيدان) A tall palm-tree.

A عيداء *ɛaydāh*, Bad-tempered (man, camel).

A عيدة *ɛiyadat*, (pl. of عود) Old (camels, sheep).

A عيدشوق *ɛaydashūk*, A certain kind of insect.

A عيدشون *ɛaydashūn*, A certain kind of insect.

A عيدف *ɛaydaf*, A part, portion.

P عيد گاه *ɛīd-gāh*, A place where solemn feasts and festivals are held.

A عيدة *ɛaydah*, Proud, unfeeling. Ill-tempered (man). Stubborn (camel). Badness of disposition.

A عيدهة *ɛaydahat*, (also عيدهيّة *ɛaydahīyat*) Badness of disposition.

A عيدهور *ɛayhahūr*, Swift (she-camel).

A عيدي *ɛīdiy*, Belonging to Easter, or to any solemn feast. Paschal.

A عيديّة *ɛīdiyat*, An Easter-offering. ناقة عيديّة *nākat ɛīdiyat*, An excellent she-camel of the breed of عيد *ɛīd*.

A عيذان *ɛayzān*, Malignant, spiteful.

A عير *ɛayr*, (v. n. of عار for عير) Travelling, roaming. Coming and going. Escaping, running away as if set at liberty (a horse or a dog). Taking (any thing), going off with (it), or destroying (it). Leaving one female and going to another (a male camel). Travelling, circulating (a poem). Going about in every direction when grazing (a horse). An eyelid. The inner corner of the eye. The pupil of the eye. A glance of the eye. A prince, chief. The middle or thickest part of a spear. The middle fibre of a leaf. A bone with a lump in the middle. A bump or prominence in any even substance or just below the instep; also in the ear, or in the artery of the back. A peg, nail. A mountain. The point of the shoulder. A piece of wood in the fore-part of a camel-litter. Excessive heat. A drum. One side of the back. Name of a place once rich and fruitful, but now sterile and desert. An increase of salary of ten dirhams made by each succeeding caliph of the house of Umayya. Name of a mountain near Madīna. (pl. اعيار *aɛyār*, عيار *ɛiyār*, عيور *ɛuyūr*, عيورة *ɛuyūrat*, معيوراء *maɛyūrāɛ*, and عيارات *ɛiyārāt*) An ass (particularly the wild ass). عير السراة *ɛayru's sarāt*, A bird resembling a pigeon. جوف العير *jawfu'l ɛayr*, The belly of an ass (*i.e.* any being, place, or thing in which nothing good is to be found). قبل عير *kabla ɛayrin*, At the first glance of the eye, in less than a twinkle. ما ادري اي من ضرب العير هو *mā adrī ayyu man zaraba'l ɛayra huwa*, I know not what man he is. *ɛīr*, A caravan. (pl. عيرات *ɛiyarāt* and عيرة *ɛīrat*) A great number of beasts of burden travelling together, especially with provisions.

A عيران *ɛayrān*, Scattered swarms of locusts. *ɛayrāni*, (dual of عير *ɛayr*) Both sides of the back or loins. *ɛīrān*, (pl. of اعور *aɛwar*) One-eyed.

A عيرانة *ɛayrānat*, A she-camel running away swift as a wild ass.

A عيزار *ɛayzār*, Firm, hard, solid. Brisk, lively (youth). A sort of drinking-glass. A kind of tree. ابو العيزار *abū'l ɛayzār*, An aquatic bird with a long neck, a crane. Satan.

A عيزاريّة *ɛayzāriyat*, A kind of glass cup.

P عيزران *ɛīzrān*, A medlar.

A عيز عيز *ɛayza ɛayza*, Used in calling to sheep.

A عيس *ɛays*, (v. n. of عاس for عيس) Impregnating the female (a camel). Semen admissarii. *ɛīs*, (pl. of اعيس *aɛyas*) (Camels) of a whitish yellow colour. *ɛayas*, Whitish yellow (in a camel).

A عيساء *ɛaysāɛ*, (fem. of اعيس *aɛyas*) (A female camel) of a yellowish white colour. A (female) locust. A woman's name.

A عيسان *ɛaysān*, Men, people.

A عيسجور *ɛaysajūr*, (pl. عساجر *ɛasājir*) A hard and swift she-camel. A horrid dragon.

A عيسران *ɛaysarān*, (or عيسرانيّ *ɛaysurānīy*) An unbroke camel on which a person rides. *ɛaysurān*, A sort of a plant.

P عيسوب *ɛaysūb*, Sweet marjoram.

A عيسويّ *ɛīsawīy*, Of the religion of Jesus. A Christian. A Jesuit. ملّت عيسويّه *millati ɛīsawīya*, The Christian religion or people.

A عيسي *ɛīsa'*, (pl. عيسون *ɛīsawna*, *ɛīsūna*, عيسين *ɛīsayna*, or *ɛīsīna*) Jesus. *ɛīsa'* is a name occasionally met with amongst Muhammadans, but not amongst Christians. مولود عيسي *mawlūdi ɛīsa'*, The nativity of (the Lord) Jesus.

A عيسيّ *ɛīsīy*, Belonging to Jesus, Christian.

P عيسي خورد *ɛīsa' khwurd*, A bunch of grapes.

P عيسي دهقان *ɛīsa' dihkān*, Grape-wine.

P عيسي ره نشين *ɛīsa' rah-nishīn*, The sun. A sun-beam. A skilful physician.

P عيسي ششماهه *ɛīsa' shash māha*, Fruits which come to maturity in six months.

P عيسي كده *ɛīsa'-kada*, The mansion of Jesus; the fourth heaven. A Christian church.

P عيسي نه ماهه *ɛīsa' nuh māha*, A bunch of grapes. Grape-wine.

P عيسي هردرد *ɛīsa' har dard*, Wine.

A عيش *ɛaysh*, (v. n. of عاش for عيش) Living. Food, bread. Life. Pleasure, delight, luxury. P عيش ده روزه *ɛayshi dah roza*, A short life. A short life and a merry one.

A عيشا *ʿīsha'*, The womb.

A عيشة *ʿīshat*, (or عيشوشة *ʿayshūshat*) (v. n. of عاش for عيش) Living, leading an agreeable life. عيشة راضية *ʿīshat rāẓiyat*, An agreeable life.

P عيش سازي *ʿaysh-sāzī*, Pleasure, enjoyment.

A عيشم *ʿaysham*, Dry, mouldy (bread).

A عيش محل *ʿaysh-mahal*, Place of joy. One of the apartments in a palace.

A عيشوم *ʿayshūm*, (pl. of عيشومة *ʿayshūmat*) Withering plants. Name of a tree.

P عيشه *ʿīsha*, A plant resembling a reed.

A عيص *ʿays*, (v. n. of عوص) Being unintelligible (a speech), intricate (an affair). Esau. *ʿīs*, (pl. اعياص *aʿyās*) A thick grove of the سدر *sidr*; entangled trees. A place where choice trees grow. Root, origin. Name of a planted valley at Madīna.

A عيصان *ʿīsān*, Certain mines in Arabia.

A عيصو *ʿīsū*, Esau (the brother of Jacob).

A عيصوم *ʿaysūm*, A glutton, gormandizer.

A عيضفوط *ʿayzafūt*, An animal whereon demons ride.

A عيضموز *ʿayzamūz*, An old woman. Large, bulky (she-camel), unable to conceive for fatness. (A she-camel) long, large, thick, strong, and compactly built, and apparently full of wrath. A rock long and large.

A عيضمون *ʿayzamūn*, (pl. عضامين) An old camel.

A عيضوم *ʿayzūm*, A glutton. A biter.

A عيط *ʿayt*, (v. n. of عيط) Having a long neck. Not conceiving for several years (a woman or a camel, although not barren). *ʿīt*, Excellent young camels. The shouts of a drunken or riotous fellow; or of young chaps when winning a game. (pl. of اعيط *aʿyat*) Long-necked. *ʿīt*, (or عيّط *ʿuyyat*, (pl. of عائط *ʿāʾit*) (Women or camels) not conceiving for several years though not barren. *ʿayat*, Length of neck.

A عيطاء *ʿaytāʾ*, (fem. of اعيط *aʿyat*) Long-necked. High, lofty. Proud, refractory.

A عيطبول *ʿaytabūl*, Beautiful, well-formed (girl).

A عيطل *ʿaytal*, Long-necked and handsome-bodied (woman, camel, or mare). Any thing long. A long neck. A long branch of a male palm-tree.

A عيطموز *ʿaytamūz*, Long and large (she-camels or rocks).

A عيطموس *ʿaytamūs*, (pl. عطامس *ʿatāmis* or عطاميس *ʿatāmīs*) Completely-formed (woman or camel). Beautiful, tall, smooth, and succulent (woman), but barren withal. A decrepit camel.

A عيعاة *ʿayʿāt*, (or عيعاء *ʿīʿāʾ*) (v. n. of عيعي Q) Calling out to sheep.

A عيف *ʿayf*, (v. n. of عاف for عيف) (A bird) planing, hovering, being suspended in the air (over water or a carcase) intending to alight. Loathing.

A عيفان *ʿayafān*, (v. n. of عاف for عيف) Loathing, nauseating (meat or drink).

A عيّفان *ʿayyifān*, Naturally averse from any thing. Querulous, disposed to complain.

A عيفة *ʿayfat*, An obstruction of milk in the breasts of a child-bearing woman. A woman who sucks the milk of one who has an obstruction in her breast. A bird's flying round and round, or balancing itself in the air. *ʿīfat*, Choice camels. The best part of cattle or other wealth.

A عيفس *ʿiyafs*, Short of stature.

A عيق *ʿayk*, A worthless, good-for-nothing fellow. A hinderer, preventer. An allowance of water. Hindrance. Dilatory, delaying. *ʿīk*, A word used in checking or driving cattle.

A عيّق *ʿayyik*, A hinderer, a preventer. Dilatory, delaying.

A عيقة *ʿaykat* or *ʿīkat*, The sea-shore. A corner or part of a house. A part, an allowance of water.

A عيقص *ʿaykas*, A miser. Stomach, rough tripe.

A عيكان *ʿayakān*, (v. n. of عاك for عيك) Shaking the shoulders in going.

A عيكة *ʿaykat*, A grove, thicket. A lote-grove.

A عيل *ʿayl*, (v. n. of عال for عيل) Walking pompously, moving with a noble carriage (a man or horse). Hunting (a leopard). Travelling, wandering, rambling, making a tour. Wishing or searching for without finding. Tiring, exhausting. Being poor, indigent, destitute. Impoverishing, disappointing, rendering necessitous. *ʿayal*, A telling of a story to a deaf person, or to one who will not hear.

A عيّل *ʿayyil*, (pl. اعيلة *aʿyilat*, اعولة *aʿwilat*, عالة *ʿālat*, عيال *ʿiyāl*, and عيائل *ʿayāʾil*) A wife, children, domestic, or any person maintained in a family. *ʿuyyal*, (pl. of عائل *ʿāʾil*) Poor.

A عيلام *ʿaylām*, A male hyena.

A عيلان *ʿaylān*, A male hyena. *ʿayalān*, (v. n. of عال for عيل) Being unable to find a thing lost.

A عيلة *ʿaylat*, (v. n. of عال for عيل) Becoming poor. Poverty, want, indigence. (pl. of عائل *ʿāʾil*) Poor, needy.

A عيلم *ʿaylam*, A male hyena. A well full of water. Brackish water. The sea. Water under the earth. A frog. A soft, delicate youth.

P عيلم *ʿelim*, (from Arab. عالم *ʿālim*) Learned.

A عيلى *ʿayla'*, (pl. of عائل *ʿāʾil*) Poor, needy.

A عيم *ʿaym*, A thirsting (especially after milk).

A عيمان *ʿaymān*, (fem. عيمى *ʿayma'*) One who thirsts for milk. Thirsty. One who loses his wife or his camels. عيمان ايمان *ʿaymān aymān*, (A man) whose wife and camels are dead and gone.

A عيمة *ʿaymat*, (v. n. of عام for عيم) Thirsting (for milk). An intense longing for milk. Thirst. *ʿīmat*, The best of one's estate. Choice camels.

A عين *ʿayn*, (v. n. of عان for عين) Flowing (water). Following or wounding with a malignant eye, eyeing. Reaching a spring or fountain. Injuring (the eye). Inclining to one side (the tongue of a balance). Acting as watch, keeping a look out. (pl. اعيان *aʿyān*, اعين *aʿyun*, عيون *ʿuyūn*, *ʿiyūn*, and اعينات *aʿyunāt*) The eye. Sight, aspect, vision. The sense of seeing. A look, a glance. (pl. اعين *aʿyun* and عيون *ʿuyūn*) A fountain, spring, source, conduit; flowing water. The letter ع (the head of which resembles the eye). A spy, scout, watchman. The eye in which the tongue of the scales plays. A small chink or eye-hole. The leather or sling of a balista, in which they place the ball or stone to be thrown. The ring of a coat of mail. The cavity of the knee, the knee-pan. A cloud proceeding from Irāk. A rain with little interruption for several days. Profit on goods, usury. The best kind or part of any thing. (pl. اعيان *aʿyān*) A distinguished or dignified man; a lord. A man, person; any one. Appearance. Any thing present. Essence, reality, individual, thing itself. Ready (camels or grapes). Fine circles on the skin. The true point of the قبله *kibla*. The people of a house, a family. The brother of a father or mother. Inclination, inequality, bias (in scales). The half of a دانق *dānak*, or seven dinars. A crowd, multitude. A brother-germain. A kind of bird. Citizens. A tract of country. The body of the sun; also his rays. Money, coin, gold, or silver specie. Very, exact; intrinsic, real. Just. The eastern part of Irāk. عين الانسان *ʿaynu'l insān*, The eye of men, *i.e.* the first or most distinguished. عين سخين *ʿayni sakhīn*, A hot eye, *i.e.* anguish, distress. P عين تباهي و محض گمراهي *ʿayni tabāhī u mahzi gumrāhī*, Complete destruction and absolute ruin. A عين الثور *ʿaynu's sawr*, The bull's eye (name of a star). عين الحيوة *ʿaynu'l hayāt*, Fountain of life or immortality. Quicksilver. عين الحيوان *ʿaynu'l haywān*, Quicksilver. عين سلوان *ʿayni salwān*, The river Jordan. A fountain. عين الشمس *ʿaynu'sh shams*, The sun's eye (a flower). عين صلاح *ʿayni salāh*, Sincere advice. عين الصواب *ʿaynu's sawāb*, A right road. The thing itself. Right reason. عين عبرت *ʿayni ʿibrat*, An example-giving countenance. عين عنايت *ʿayni ʿināyat*, A look of favour. عين القطر *ʿaynu'l katr*, Brimstone. عين كمال *ʿayni kamāl*, The height of perfection; also the eyes of some Arabians (called كمال *kamāl*), which were supposed piercing enough to kill people. عين ميزان *ʿayni mīzān*, The eye of a balance, (*i.e.* wherein the tongue moves). عين اليقين *ʿaynu'l yakīn*, Experimental knowledge, certainty. بعينه *bi ʿaynihi*, The self-same. هو بعينه *huwa bi ʿaynihi*, He himself, propriâ personâ. انت على عيني *anta ʿala' ʿaynī*, You are in my regard, you possess my esteem. انسان العين *insānu'l ʿayn*, The image or pupil of the eye. لقيته اوّل عين *lakītuhu awwala ʿaynin*, I met him the first thing. عبد عين *ʿabdi ʿayn*, (or صديق عين *sadīki ʿayn*) An eye-server, friend to the eye, *i.e.* a false friend, a hypocrite, cheat, dissembler. عرض عين *ʿarzu ʿaynin*, Near. عمداً على عين *ʿamdan ʿala' ʿay-*

nin, (or عمد عين ʻamda ʻaynin) Certainly, attentively, uninterruptedly (I did it). قرير العين karīru'l ʻayn, Cold-eyed, i.e. cheerful, happy. لا عين و لا اثر lā ʻayn wa lā asar, Neither shadow nor trace. عين عنة ʻaynu ʻunnatin, Near, hard by. ʻīn, Wild cattle. (pl. of عيون ʻayūn) Stedfast lookers with malignant eyes. (pl. of اعين aʻyan) Large-eyed (oxen). (pl. of عيناء ʻaynā) Black-eyed (virgins). ʻayan, (v. n. of عين) Having large black eyes. Width and blackness of the eyes. Domestics, a household. Citizens. A crowd, company. ʻuyun, (pl. of عيان ʻiyān) Ploughshares. (pl. of عيون ʻayūn) Those who look with evil eyes.

A عيّن ʻayyin or ʻayyan, (A leathern bottle) full of holes and leaky. New (leathern bottle).

A عينا ʻaynan, (بعين bi ʻaynin and بعينه bi ʻaynihi) Exactly, justly, clearly, truly, effectually, precisely, to the point.

A عيناء ʻaynās, (fem. of اعين aʻyan) (pl. عين ʻīn) Large-eyed (cow). Black-eyed (virgin). Green. Ready to burst (bottle). Widely circulating (verse).

A عينان ʻayanān, (v. n. of عان for عين) Flowing (water from a fountain, tears from the eye).

A عينة ʻīnat, (v. n. of عين) Having large and handsome black eyes. The choicest part of cattle or other wealth. Money lent or paid in advance. The part round the eye of a sheep or a wild cow. Handsome to the eye, having a handsome external surface (a garment). The subject of a war. A loan without interest.

A عينتاب ʻayn-tāb, Name of a city in Syria.

A عينك ʻaynak, Spectacles, eye-glasses.

P عينك دان ʻaynakdān, A spectacle-case.

A عينوم ʻaynūm, A male frog.

A عينيّ ʻaynīy, Genuine, essential, real.

A عيوب ʻayūb, Dishonest, shameful. Faulty, vicious. ʻuyūb, (pl. of عيب ʻayb) Vices, defects, faults, blemishes, bad points or qualities.

A عيوث ʻayūs, A lion.

A عيور ʻuyūr, (pl. of عير ʻayr) Asses.

A عيورة ʻuyūrat, (pl. of عير ʻayr) Asses.

A عيوف ʻayūf, (A camel) smelling the water without drinking, although thirsty. A woman whose milk will not flow after childbirth. Nice, dainty with respect to food. Unwilling. One who divines by the flight of birds: an augur.

A عيّوق ʻayyūk, A certain bright red star which follows the Pleiades.

A عيول ʻuyūl or ʻayūl, (v. n. of عال for عيل) Wandering, travelling. Being poor. Poverty.

A عيون ʻayūn, (pl. عين ʻīn and ʻuyun) One who looks stedfastly with a malignant eye. ʻuyūn, (pl. of عين ʻayn) Eyes. Fountains. Buds of trees. عيون البقر ʻuyūnu'l bakar, A grape called the ox-eye. A damson.

A عيه ʻayh, (v. n. of عاه for عيه) Being attacked by murrain called عاهة ʻāhat (cattle).

A عيهاب ʻīhāb, Accused, charged with error.

A عيهاق ʻayhāk, Error, aberration.

A عيهال ʻayhāl, A swift she-camel.

A عيهامة ʻayhāmat, Swift (she-camel).

A عيهب ʻayhab, Corpulent. Indisposed, digesting badly. Thick, woolly (cloth). Weak, timid, fearful of purpose, incapable of retaliation.

A عيهبة ʻayhabat, (v. n. of عيهب Q) Seducing.

A عيهران ʻayharān, (pl. of عياهير ʻayāhīr) A male غول ghūl. A strong camel.

A عيهرة ʻayharat, (v. n. of عيهر Q) Behaving with levity. Playing the whore. A woman light and sprightly, but withal unchaste. The animal called غول ghūl. A strong camel.

A عيهق ʻayhak, Alacrity, joy, glee.

A عيهقة ʻayhakat, A kind of bird.

A عيهكة ʻayhakat, (v. n. of عيهك Q) Fighting. Throwing down. Wrestling. Vociferating.

A عيهل ʻayhal, Swift (she-camel). Powerful, strong (she-camel). A he-camel. Restless (man). A strong wind. A tall woman.

A عيهلّ ʻayhall, Swift (she-camel). Violent (wind). Restless (woman).

A عيهلة ʻayhalat, A swift she-camel. Restless (woman). An old woman.

A عيهم ʻayham, Swift (she-camel). Strong. A male elephant.

A عيهمان ʻayhamān, Unable to prosecute one's journey at the beginning of night, and on that account sleeping on the road.

A عيهمة ʻayhamat, Swiftness.

A عيهميّ ʻayhamīy, Thick, bulky, and tall.

A عيهول ʻayhūl, A swift she-camel.

A عيهوم ʻayhūm, The root of a certain tree.

A عيهون ʻayhūn, Name of a delicious vegetable or fragrant plant.

A عيّ ʻayīy, (pl. اعياء aʻyiyā and اعيية aʻyiyat) A stammerer. Let, hindered, embarrassed, puzzled, perplexed, unequal to a work.

A عيير ʻuyayr, (dim. of عير ʻayr) A little ass. عيير وحده ʻuyayru wahdihi, A man wedded to his own opinion. One who takes his meals alone.

A عيينة ʻuyaynat, (dim. of عين ʻayn) A little eye. ذو عيينتين zū ʻuyaynatayn, A spy.

غ

غ ghayn, (called غين منقوطه ghayni mankūta or غين معجمه ghayni muʻjama, Dotted ghayn) The nineteenth letter of the Arabic alphabet, and the twenty-second of the Persian. In arithmetic it expresses 1000, and denotes quadrature in the aspects of the stars. This letter is articulated in the throat with a vibration producing a sound like that given to r by the Northumbrians, or the noise made in gargling. It is occasionally changed to ق k or گ g, and is sometimes redundant. It seems to bear the same relation to خ kh as ب b does to پ p, د d to ت t, ز z to س s, and گ g to ك k. Poets sometimes use this letter to imply the nightingale, one of whose epithets is the bird of a thousand notes, غ being the character for a thousand.

P A غاب ghāb, A forest, wood, thicket, grove, brake. The haunt or den of a wild beast.

P غاب ghāb, Foolish, unmeaning gabble. Fallen back, remaining afar off. Spoiled, destroyed; useless. Powerless, paralyzed. Leavings, orts.

A غابّ ghābb, (pl. غوابّ ghawābb) (A camel) watered every second day. Corrupted, stinking, tainted (meat), stale (bread).

P غابانك ghābānk, A kind of herb.

A غابة ghābat, (pl. غاب ghāb) A forest, a dense thicket; a wild beast's haunt. (Ground) lying low, flat land, out of sight. A gulf, pit. A multitude of men. A long limber spear waving in the air. ليث غابة laysu ghābatin, A lion of the forest.

A غابر ghābir, (pl. غبّر ghubbar) Remaining. Solid, lasting. Past, passing by. The future tense.

A غابرة ghābirat, Remaining. A remainder.

P غابش ghābish, Name of a mountain-tree.

A غابش ghābish, False, insincere, deceitful, traitorous. Weak-sighted.

A غابط ghābit, (pl. غبط ghubut) Anxious one's self to possess something equal to what another enjoys (it implies emulation without envy).

A غابن ghābin, Languid, remiss. An impostor.

P غابندن ghābandan, To slip, slide, stumble.

P غابوق ghābūk, Wine drunk at night.

P غابوك ghābūk, Ball for cannon or cross-bow.

A غابي ghābī, Careless, heedless, stupid.

P غاتفر ghātfar, Name of a city in Turkistān; also of a quarter in Samarkand. Name of a wrestler.

A غاتية ghātiyat, Simple, silly, weak (woman).

A غاثر ghāsar, Ghāsar, son of Iram, son of Shem, and father of ثمود samūd.

A غادّ ghādd, (pl. of غداد ghidād) Infected with the plague (a camel).

A غادة ghādat, Fat, fresh, tender, fine-necked (woman). Tender, delicate, limber (shrub).

A غادر ghādir, Deceitful. A swindler.

A غادف ghādif, A seaman. A rower.

A غادوف ghādūf, An oar.

A غادي ghādī, A goer out at morn. A lion.

A غادية ghādiyat, Morning-rain or clouds.

A غاذّ ghāzz, A lachrymal duct which ceases not to run. Sense, feeling.

A غاذّة ghāzzat, Two bones in the upper part of the head (which are tender and moist in infants).

A غاذي ghāzī, Digestive, peptic. One who looks after cattle or manages property well.

A غاذية ghāziyat, The faculty of digestion. A certain vein or artery. Two bones in the upper part of the head (which are tender and moist in infants).

P غار *ghār*, The laurel.

A غار *ghār*, (v. n. of غار for غير) Being jealous. (pl. اغوار *aghwār* and غيران *ghīrān*) A cavern, cave, pit, or niche in a mountain. The den of a wild beast. Low land. The cavity or socket of the eye. The interior part of the mouth. An army. A large oil-yielding tree. A large congregation. A vine-leaf. A large measure in use amongst the people of نسف *nasaf*, containing a hundred قفيز *kafīz*. Corn carried from place to place. Envy, jealousy. Dust. Name of a cave near Mecca. غارغم *ghāri gham*, A prison. The grave of the wicked. P يار غار *yāri ghār*, A companion in a cave or prison, *i.e.* an intimate friend. A الغار الاعلي *al ghāru'l a'la'*, The roof of the mouth (hollow like a cavern).

A غارّ *ghārr*, Imprudent, heedless, thoughtless. A well-digger. (pl. غرور *ghurūr*) A vain hope, trifle.

A الغاران *al ghārāni*, The two cavities (venter et pudenda). The sockets of the eyes.

A غارب *ghārib*, One who comes from afar. The summit of a wave. (pl. غوارب *ghawārib*) The upper part of a camel's bunch; also the space between that and the neck. حبلك علي غاربك *habluka 'ala' ghāribiha*, Your halter is on your withers, *i.e.* you may go where you please.

A غارة *ghārat*, (v. n. of غار for غور) Making a hostile incursion into an enemy's country. Twisting a rope firmly. (pl. غارات *ghārāt*) A hostile incursion into an enemy's country to carry off spoil or captives. The navel. A predatory troop of horse. Rapine, plunder. شديد الغارة *shadīdu'l ghārat*, Firmly-twisted (rope). P غارت و خسارت كردن *ghārat u khasārat kardan*, To plunder and lay waste.

A غارّة *ghārrat*, A certain long fish.

P غارت غول *ghārat-ghol*, Sudden loss or destruction. Suddenly or unexpectedly lost.

P غارت گر *ghāratgar*, Marauder, robber, assassin.

P غارت گري *ghāratgarī*, Spoliation, pillage.

P غارتنگ *ghārtang*, The bar of a door.

P غارتيدن *ghāratīdan*, To ravage, plunder, pillage, rifle. To be plundered. To roll over.

P غارج *gharaj*, (*ghārij*, also غارچ *ghārich*) A morning draught of wine. Wine.

P غارجي *ghāriji*, A morning draught of wine. A cup-bearer. One who drinks in the morning.

A غارز *ghāriz*, (A camel) having little milk. هو غارز رأسه في سنته *huwa ghārizun ra'suhu fī sinatihi*, He is ignorant and stupid. *Ghāriz*, (or غارزة *ghārizat*) (A locust) fixing her tail in the ground to lay.

A غارس *ghāris*, A planter.

P غارستان *ghāristān*, A place full of caverns.

A غارض *ghāriz*, One who leads out animals to water early in the morning. Who does any thing betimes. Long (nose).

A غارضا *ghārizan*, Betimes, early in the morning.

A غارفة *ghārifat*, (pl. غوارف *ghawārif*) (A woman) shorn in front. Swift (she-camel).

A غارق *ghārik*, Submerged, drowned.

A غارم *ghārim*, A debtor.

P غارنگ *ghārang*, An idiot, a fool.

P غار و غور *ghār u ghūr*, Chaos, confusion.

A غاروق *ghārūk*, The mosque of Kūfa.

P غارة *ghāra*, Plunder. Plunderers. A morning draught of wine. A twist, plat. A cavern.

P غاري *ghārī*, A bushel. A sponge.

A غاريقون *ghārīkūn*, Agaricum.

P غاز *ghāz*, A patch on a garment. Split, opened. A rent, slit, crack. Want, scarcity, dearness. Eating with a relish. A certain water-bird. Beating cotton. غاز كردن *ghāz kardan*, To tease cotton. To take to pieces the worn cloth of a garment or tent (called shoddy) to be woven again.

P غازغاز *ghāz ghāz*, Cleft asunder.

P غازغان *ghāzghān*, A cauldron, a kettle.

A غازلة *ghāzilat*, (fem. غزّل *ghuzzal* or غوازل *ghawāzil*) A female spinner.

P غازة *ghāza*, Rouge for the face. Noise, cry. Root of the tail. A peg for fastening planks.

P غازي *ghāzī*, A courtesan. A rope-dancer. Sheep's chitterlings stuffed with spiceries.

A غازي *ghāzī*, (pl. غزّي *ghuzza'*, غزيّ *ghuzīy*, غزّاء *ghuzzā'*, and غزاة *ghuzāt*) A conqueror, hero, gallant soldier (especially combating infidels). A general, leader of an expedition. غازي الدين *ghāzī'd dīn*, Champion of the faith (a proper name). P پادشاه غازي *pādshāhi ghāzī*, Victorious king.

P غازيانه *ghāziyāna*, Bravely.

P غازي مرد *ghāzī-mard*, A hero. A horse.

P غازي ميان *ghāzī-miyān*, Name of the nephew of Sultān Mahmūd Ghaznawī. (A festival is held in commemoration of him at the beginning of May).

P غاژ *ghāj*, A wide-mouthed man. A thorn.

P غاژ كردن *ghāj kardan*, To separate the seed from the cotton. To beat wool and prepare it for spinning. To take to pieces the worn cloth of a garment or tent called shoddy, to be woven again.

A غاسق *ghāsik*, That part of the night immediately succeeding the crepuscle. The moon.

A غاسل *ghāsil*, A washer. A washerman.

A غاسلة *ghāsilat*, A woman whose business is to wash female corpses. A washerwoman.

A غاسول *ghāsūl*, A herb whence potash is made.

A غاسي *ghāsī*, Frail, feeble (old man).

P غاش *ghāsh*, A sincere man. An ardent and sincere lover. Petulant, perverse. Stupid, dull. Tumult. A cluster of unripe grapes. A cucumber kept for seed. Partial. A dissembler, hypocrite.

A غاشّ *ghāshsh*, False, insincere, deceitful. Malicious, filled with hatred.

A غاشم *ghāshim*, Iniquitous, injurious.

A غاشية *ghāshiyat*, (pl. غواشي *ghawāshī*) A covering. A leather covering for a saddle or for the hilt of a sword. The pericardium. A piece of iron in the hinder part of a camel's saddle. The resurrection. The day of judgment. Hell fire. An internal complaint, cholic, gripes. Friends. Visitors. Beggars. A porter's burden.

P غاشيه بر دوش *ghāshiya bar dosh*, Obedient.

P غاشيه دار *ghāshiya-dār*, One who has the care of saddles. The angel Gabriel. A porter.

A غاصّ *ghāss*, Troubled with something in the throat. (A habitation) crammed full of people.

A غاصب *ghāsib*, A usurper, a forcible seizer.

A غاضّ *ghāzz*, An anklet which fits the leg tight.

A غاضب *ghāzib*, Angry, wrathful.

A غاضر *ghāzir*, A hide good for tanning. Active, bustling, stirring in one's affairs.

A غاضف *ghāzif*, Delicate (life). One in agreeable and comfortable circumstances. (A dog) whose ears hang forward. Loose. Soft, worn.

A غاضي *ghāzī*, Dark (night). Bright (night or fire). Great (luminary). Plentiful, accumulated, heaped up. Excellent. Well fed and well clothed. A camel eating the tree غضاة *ghazāt*.

A غاضية *ghāziyat*, (pl. غواضي *ghawāzī*) A she-camel feeding on the tree غضاة *ghazāt*.

A غاط *ghāt*, A multitude, assembly, congregation. Low-lying ground.

A غاطس *ghātis*, (pl. غواطس *ghawātis*) Immersed. Covered with a coat of mail.

A غاطية *ghātiyat*, A vine (as covering all).

A غاغ *ghāgh*, Pennyroyal.

A غاغاء *gha'ghā'*, The twittering of the mountain-swallow. The caw of the black mountain-crow.

P غاغاطي *ghāghātī*, A bituminous stone brought from Syria.

A غاغة *ghāghat*, A confused medley of people. A certain plant. A gnat. Locusts unable to fly.

P غاغه *ghāgha*, Mint.

A غاف *ghāf*, Name of a tree bearing sweet fruit.

P A غافت *ghāfat*, (or غافث *ghāfis*) Swallow-wort. Agrimony.

A غافر *ghāfir*, Forgiving. Clement, merciful.

A غافصة *ghāfisat*, Difficulty, pressure of times.

A غافل *ghāfil*, Imprudent, inconsiderate, careless, incautious, off one's guard, negligent, indolent, incurious, inattentive, thoughtless. P شهزادۀ غافل نظر *shah-zāda'i ghāfil-nazar*, An inconsiderate and improvident prince.

A غافلا *ghāfilan*, (P غافلانه) Imprudently.

P غافل گير *ghāfil-gīr*, Attacking unawares.

A غافلي *ghāfilī*, Negligence, inattention.

A غاق *ghāk*, A crow. Name of an aquatic bird. *Ghāki*, The croaking of a raven.

A غاقة *ghākat*, A certain aquatic bird.

P غاك *ghāk*, Noise, disturbance, riot, tumult, sedition. The croaking of a raven. Fraud, deceit.

P غال *ghāl*, Rolling, wallowing. A cavern in which they keep cattle. A burrow, fox's hole. A bee-hive. Going round.

A غالّ *ghāll*, (pl. غلّان *ghullān*) Thirsty. Level or low ground producing wild trees or thorns, or the tree سلم *salam*. Name of a plant. Productive (estate). The hole of the Lybian lizard.

P غالالوط *ghālālūt*, The Egyptian bean.

A غالب *ghālib*, Overcoming, overpowering, prevailing, predominant. Triumphant, victorious. A conqueror. Chief. The greater part.

A غالبا *ghāliban*, (or في الغالب *fi'l ghālib*) Chiefly, principally; finally, upon the whole; apparently, probably; necessary, without fail, beyond a doubt. For the most part.

P غالبانه *ghālibāna*, Triumphantly.

A غالبيّة *ghālibīyat*, Victory, prevalence.

P غالج *ghālij*, A morning-draught of wine.

P غالد *ghālad*, Who moves from side to side.

P غالوك *ghāluk*, A play-ball; a cannon-ball.

P غاله *ghāla*, A kid.

P غالي *ghālī*, A carpet, tapestry.

A غالي *ghālī*, (pl. غلاة *ghulāt*) Dear, costly, high-priced, precious, valuable. Fat meat. One who exceeds bounds. A zealot. One who shoots an arrow with his whole might.

P غاليا بار *ghāliyā-bār*, Fragrant, odoriferous.

A غالية *ghāliyat*, A kind of perfume; civet.

P غاليچه *ghālīcha*, A carpet.

P غاليدن *ghālīdan*, To tumble, roll, wallow. To surround, wheel round either in defending a friend or assailing an enemy. To instigate, animate. To start up suddenly.

P غالينوس *ghālīnūs*, Galen the physician.

A غاليون *ghāliyūn*, Name of an herb which causes milk to coagulate instantly.

P غاليه *ghāliya*, Civet. A composition of musk, ambergris, camphor, and oil of ban-nuts.

P غاليه بار *ghāliya-bār*, Fragrant, odoriferous.

P غاليه ساي *ghāliya-sāy*, Fragrant. A perfumer.

A غامّ *ghāmm*, Intensely hot (day). Gloomy, dull (day). Melancholy, sad, glum (day).

A غامد *ghāmid*, Filled, freighted (ship).

A غامدة *ghāmidat*, Filled up, fallen in (well). Full, filled, loaded, freighted (ship).

A غامر *ghāmir*, Uninhabited, uncultivated, waste, abandoned (the opposite of عامر *ʿāmir*). Overflowed (country).

A غامرة *ghāmirat*, A palm-tree which requires not to be watered.

A غامز *ghāmiz*, Expressed by amorous winks.

A غامس *ghāmis*, Plunging, sinking.

A غامش *ghāmish*, Weak-sighted.

A غامض *ghāmiz*, (pl. غوامض *ghawāmiz*) Low-lying (place). Obscure, unintelligible (speech). Mean, obscure, base, contemptible. Depressed, sunk, subsiding, or falling to the bottom, precipitating. Doubtful (pedigree). Weak, languid in making a charge or attack. (An anklet) that sits tight upon the leg. Large and fat (leg or ankle).

A غامضة *ghāmizat*, A house situated at a distance from the high road.

P غامي *ghāmī*, Poor. Weak, feeble. Lean.

A غامياء *ghāmiyāʼ*, The dens or holes of beasts or reptiles. The burrow of the field-mouse.

A غانة *ghānat*, Loop at the end of a bow-string.

P غانج *ghānj*, (or غانغا *ghāngkā*) The Ganges.

A غانذ *ghāniz*, The windpipe, throat.

A غانم *ghānim*, Laden with spoil. Impotence, effeminacy, want of spirit or manliness.

P غانه *ghāna*, Name of a place in Arabia where they find gold.

A غاني *ghānī*, Rich: able to do without.

A غانية *ghāniyat*, (pl. غواني *ghawānī*) A woman despising ornaments, satisfied with the native beauty of her person. A girl much courted, yet remaining contentedly unmarried in her parents' house; also a chaste woman in general, whether married or unmarried. A singing girl. A harlot.

P غاو *ghāw*, An ox. A hole in the ground made for the security of sheep and other animals.

P غاوش *ghāwash* or *ghāwush*, A cucumber kept for seed. A bunch of ripe grapes.

P غاوشنگ *ghāw-shang*, An ox-goad.

P غاوشو *ghāwshū*, An ardent and sincere lover. A cucumber for seed. An unripe bunch of grapes.

A غاووش *ghāwūsh*, A cucumber kept for seed.

P غاوون *ghāwūn*, (pl. of غاوي *ghāwī*) Those who are in error. Devils. Those who countenance scurrilous or flattering poets.

P غاوه *ghāwa*, Name of a mountain.

A غاوي *ghāwī*, (pl. غاوون *ghāwūn*) Wandering, erring, straying, seduced. Hopeless. Small (head). A locust. A demon.

A غاوية *ghāwiyat*, A leathern bag wherein is water. A traveller's leathern provision-bag.

A غاي *ghāy*, (pl. of غاية *ghāyat*) Ends, extremities. Goals. Standards.

A غائب *ghāʼib*, (pl. غيّب *ghuyyab*, غيّاب *ghuyyāb*, غوائب *ghawāʼib*, and غيب *ghayab*) Absent, latent, concealed, invisible. Vanished. (in gram.) The third person. P غائب شدن *ghāʼib shudan*, To be absent, disappear, vanish.

P غائبانه *ghāʼibāna*, In absence, invisibly.

P غائب باز *ghāʼib-bāz*, A conjuror.

A غاية *ghāyat*, (pl. غاي *ghāy*) End, extremity, termination, final point. The goal. The starting post, or the winning post. A ne plus ultra. A sovereign remedy. A standard, flag. A vintner's shop. Chiefly, greatly, extremely. غاية الاصابع *ghāyatu'l asābiʿ*, The little finger. غاية الغاية *ghāyatu'l ghāya*, For the most part, very much. الغاية القصوىٰ *al ghāyatu'l kuswaʼ*, The utmost extremity.

A غائر *ghāʼir*, (Water) flowing down upon low grounds. One whose eyes are sunk in the sockets.

A غائرة *ghāʼirat*, Meridian, mid-day, noon.

A غائص *ghāʼis*, A diver. One who is carried on with great zeal and earnestness in any affair. One who comes down upon, or arrives suddenly.

A غائصة *ghāʼisat*, A woman who, from greedy desire of venery, fails to apprise her husband that she is menstruous.

A غائض *ghāʼiz*, Falling, decreasing, subsiding, sinking (water).

A غائط *ghāʼit*, (pl. غوط *ghūt*, اغواط *aghwāt*, غياط *ghiyāt*, and غيطان *ghītān*) Low, level ground widely spread. A hollow, a lurking-place. Dung, ordure, human excrement.

A غائكة *ghāʼikat*, Foolish, silly (woman).

A غائلة *ghāʼilat*, (pl. غوائل *ghawāʼil*) A misfortune. A secret grudge, malignity. An unfair attack. A crack, a flaw. غائلة الحوض *ghāʼilatu'l hawz*, A rent in a cistern. غائلة الصداع *ghāʼilatu's sudāʿ*, An excruciating headache.

A غبّ *ghabb* or *ghibb*, (v. n. of غبّ) Drinking every second day (camels). *Ghibb*, (v. n. of غبّ) Visiting every alternate day. Attacking thus (as a tertian ague). Passing the night with. Succeeding, coming to an issue, drawing to a close. Success, issue, termination. An unfrequent or weekly visit. Becoming stale, stinking (meat). *Ghibba*, After. غبّ ذا *ghibba zā*, After that. غبّ ما *ghibba mā*, After which. غبّ الدعا *ghibba'd duʿā*, After salutations. *Ghubb*, One who travels far inland from the sea. (pl. اغباب *aghbāb* and غبوب *ghubūb*) Low ground, whereon water lies.

A غبا *ghabaʼ*, (v. n. of غبي) Not considering, or adverting to, from weakness of mind. Being hidden, not apprehended, from stupidity. Dust raised.

A غبأ *ghabaʼa*, (fut. يغبأ *yaghbaʼu*) He went in search of, he made for.

A غبّا *ghibban*, Seldom, rarely.

A غباء *ghabāʼ*, Rugged ground.

P غباد *ghubād*, The invention or production of something new. A man resolutely bent on doing what is right.

A غبار *ghubār*, Dust. (metaphorically) Vexation, affliction, plague, perplexity. غبار خاطر *ghubāri khātir*, Affliction or disturbance in mind. P غبار رنجش و آزار *ghubāri ranjish u āzār*, The dust of vexation and disgust.

P غبار آلوده *ghubār-ālūda*, Covered, soiled, or defiled with dust.

P غبار گونه *ghubār-gūna*, Dust-coloured. Dust.

P غباره *ghibāra*, An ox-goad. *Ghubāra*, A bomb.

A غبارين *ghabārīn*, (pl. of غبران *ghubrān*) Double dates growing from one stalk.

P غباريه *ghubārīh*, Name of a mountain-tree.

P غباز *ghabāz*, A dervish's staff.

P غبازه *ghabāza*, A dervish's staff.

A غباشير *ghabāshīr*, The twilight.

A غبانة *ghabānat*, (v. n. of غبن) Being weak in mind, liable to deception. Weakness, deficiency.

A غباوة *ghabāwat*, (v. n. of غبي) Not considering, or adverting to, from weakness of mind. Being hidden and not apprehended through stupidity. Stupidity. Want of feeling or pity.

P A غبب *ghabab*, The dewlap of an ox. The wattles of a cock. The loose flesh beneath the chin.

A غبّة *ghubbat*, An eaglet. Food sufficient for one day.

A غبث *ghabs*, A mixing new cheese with butter.

A غبج *ghabj*, A drinking, gulping (of water).

A غبجة *ghubjat*, A sip, a draught.

A غبر *ghabr*, (v. n. of غبر) Passing, going by. Being of a dusty colour. *Ghibr*, Hatred, secret grudge. *Ghubr*, (pl. اغبار *aghbār*) A remainder, remnant (particularly of milk in the udder). *Ghubar*, (v. n. of غبر) Swelling with matter (a wound). A great misfortune, the like of which it is difficult to find. Dust, earth. One who becomes friendly and obedient after having been hostile and refractory. A sore in a camel's hoof. The breaking out again of a sore apparently healed. The corruption or matter of a wound. صمّاء الغبر *sammāʼu'l ghabar*, A heavy misfortune, sore calamity. One who becomes friendly and obedient after having been hostile and refractory. داهية الغبر *dāhiyatu'l ghabar*, A grievous calamity. *Ghabir*, Corrupt, stinking (wound). A vein that had been tied up breaking out again. *Ghubar*, A sort of fish. Name of a certain low, swampy country. A large stream amongst rocks uniting with other gravelly streams. Name of a boy born of an elderly woman.

A غبّر *ghubbar*, (pl. of غابر *ghābir*) Remaining. Passed by. A remainder, remnant (of catamenia).

A غبراء *ghabrāʼ*, (fem. of اغبر *aghbar*) Of the colour of dust. Defaced, obliterated (path). Barren (year). A female partridge. Earth, land. Name of a country abounding in trees. A plant growing in soft ground. According to some, غبراء *ghabrāʼ* is the fruit and غبيراء *ghubayrāʼ* is the tree, or vice versâ. وطأة غبراء *watʼatun ghabrāʼ*, A footmark, new or old. An obliterated footmark. بنو الغبراء *banū'l ghabrāʼ*, Children of the dust, *i.e.* the poor; also strangers, travellers, or pilgrims met together to drink. سجّادۂ غبرا *sajjādaʼi ghabrā*, A carpet: any covering for the ground.

A غبران *ghubrān*, (pl. غبارين *ghabārīn*) A double date growing from one stalk.

A غبرة *ghubrat*, A dusty colour. Dust. A residue, remainder. *Ghabarat*, Dust.

A غبرقة *ghubrukat*, Large black-eyed (woman).

A غبرور *ghubrūr*, A small kind of sparrow.

A غبرون *ghubrūn*, A sort of bird. A small sparrow.

A غبس *ghabas*, (and غبسة *ghubsat*) Obscurity, darkness. A dark, dull, ashy colour. *Ghubs*, (pl. of اغبس *aghbas*) Dun-coloured (wolves).

A غبش *ghabash*, (v. n. of غبش) Being dark (the latter part of the night). *Ghabash*, (or غبشة *ghubshat*) (pl. اغباش *aghbāsh*) The latter part of the night. *Ghabish*, Dark (night).

A ابو غبشان *abū ghabshān* or *ghubshān*, Name of a man who had charge of the keys of the Kaaba, which privilege, (Esau-like) he was persuaded in a drunken fit to sell for a bottle of wine; an act of which he afterwards fruitlessly repented.

A غبشة *ghubshat*, Dust-colour mixed with red.

A غبص *ghabas*, (v. n. of غبص) Being full of white sordes (the eyes). Being deeply sunk in the socket (the eye). A flux from the eyes.

A غبط *ghabt*, (v. n. of غبط) Wishing to be like or equal to another without envy. Feeling the buttocks of cattle to ascertain their fatness. Envy, emulation. اللّهمّ غبطاً لا هبطاً *allāhumma ghabtan la habtan*, O God, may this happy state continue! *Ghabt* or *ghibt*, (pl. غبوط *ghubūt*) A handful of corn when reaping. *Ghubut*, (pl. of غابط *ghābit*) Those who wish to possess something equal to what another enjoys without envy. (pl. of غبيط *ghabīt*) Dorsers on which camel-litters are fixed.

A غبطة *ghibtat*, (v. n. of غبط) Wishing to be like unto another without envy. Emulation without envy. Envy. A happy condition. Joy, gladness. *Ghubtat*, The string of a leathern wallet.

A غبطى *ghabtaʼ*, Raining incessantly (sky).

A غبغب *ghabghab*, A dewlap. The wattles of a cock. A double chin. Name of an idol. Name of a hill at Mina where sacrifices are offered. P چاه غبغب *chāhi ghabghab*, The pit in the chin.

A غبق *ghabk*, (v. n. of غبق) Giving wine to drink, or drinking it in the evening.

A غبقان *ghabkān*, (fem. غبقاء *ghabkāʼ*) One who drinks wine in the evening.

A غبقة *ghabakat*, A cord fastened on the head of the yoke of an ox employed in drawing water or in ploughing.

A غبن *ghabn*, (v. n. of غبن) Laying up in a secret store (grain or provisions) against a scarcity. Cheating, gulling (in a sale), imposing upon one. Doubling up and sewing part of a garment to render it shorter. Forgetting. Passing over. Mistaking. Being negligent, forgetful. Being ignorant. Deceit, fraud. P غبن كردن *ghabn kardan*, To deceive. A *Ghaban*, (v. n. of غبن) Being weak in mind, liable to deception. Being negligent, forgetting. Mistaking, erring. Imposing upon, cheating, deceiving. Weakness. Forgetfulness. Weakness of mind, defect of judgment.

A غبوب *ghubūb*, (v. n. of غبّ) Being watered, drinking on every other day (camels). (pl. of غبّ *ghubb*) Low-lying grounds.

A غبوة *ghabwat*, (or غبوّة *ghubūwat*) Negligence, inadvertency, forgetfulness, thoughtlessness.

A غبور *ghubūr*, (v. n. of غبر) Remaining, being left. Departing, passing by.

A غبوط *ghabūt*, (A camel) whose fatness cannot be ascertained except by feeling. *Ghubūt*, (pl. of غبط *ghibt*) Handsful of reaped corn.

A غبوق *ghabūk*, Wine drank at night. *Ghubūk*, (v. n. of غبق) Drinking, or giving to drink, wine in the evening.

A غبيّ *ghabīy*, A dolt, blockhead, fool. Weak in mind, forgetful. *Ghubīy*, Negligence, inadvertency, forgetfulness.

A غبياء *ghabyāʼ*, Thick, entangled (trees).

A غبيبة *ghabībat*, Ewes' milk, milked in the morning, upon which in the evening they milk a little fresh to make it thicken, in order to churn it into butter the day after.

A غبية *ghabyat*, A slight rain, just sufficient to wet the surface of the ground; also one heavy plump of rain or torrent of water. Dust raised. A lash, a scourge. Setting of the sun. A quick pace, full gallop.

A غبيثة *ghabīsat*, A mixture of new cheese and butter. See عبيثة *ʻabīsat*.

A غبير *ghabīr*, A kind of date.

A غبيراء *ghubayrāʼ*, An intoxicating drink made from millet. Name of a plant. A kind of fruit. تركه على غبيراء الظهر *tarakahu ʻalaʼ ghubayrāʼi'z zahr*, (or غبراء الظهر *ghabrāʼi'z zahr*, He returned disappointed.

A غبيس *ghubays*, (dim. of اغبس *aghbas*) A tawnyish wolf. ما غبا غبيس *mā ghaba' ghubays*, As long as the wolf will seize the sheep, *i.e.* for ever.

A غبيط *ghabīt*, (pl. غبط *ghubut*) Dorsers on which they fix the camel-litters in which women travel. A stream flowing from high ground. Low, level ground widely extended and high at the extremities. Quicksilver. Name of a valley and desert.

A غبين *ghabīn*, Weak in mind. A fool, a gull. Deceived, gulled, cheated.

A غبينة *ghabīnat*, Deceit, fraud, cheating. Deficiency, defect. Weakness of mind, dulness, liability to be imposed upon, cheated, and gulled.

P غپك *ghapak*, A grass of which mats are made.

P غت *ghut* or *ghat*, An idiot, fool.

A غتّ *ghatt*, (v. n. of غتّ) Plunging (any one) into water head foremost. Employing. Afflicting, vexing. Making sad. Concealing, smothering (laughter, laughing in one's sleeve). Subjoining, or causing one (thing) to follow another. Following or prosecuting. Strangling. Fatiguing, tiring. Chiding, reproaching, railing, sneering at. Sipping, drinking often without removing the cup from the lips.

A غترفة *ghatrafat*, (v. n. of غترف Q) Being proud and consequential. Pride. Petulance.

P غتفر *ghutfar*, Foolish, stupid.

P غتفره *ghutfara*, Ignorant, inexperienced, foolish, stupid. A whoremonger.

A غتل *ghatal*, (v. n. of غتل) Being thickly set with trees (a place). *Ghatil*, (A place) thickly set with trees. Crowded (grove of palm-trees).

A غتم *ghatm*, A suffocating heat. The oppressive sensation of suffocating heat. *Ghutm*, (pl. of غتم *aghtam*) Indistinct speakers.

A غتمة *ghutmat*, Barbarism in speech.

A غتمي *ghutmīy*, A person who speaks unintelligibly. (Milk) noiseless when poured out.

A غتيم *ghutaym*, in composition with حياض *hiyāz*, as حياض غتيم *hiyāz ghutaym*, Death.

A غث *ghass*, (v. n. of غث) Calling (any thing) bad and leaving (it). Failing to ask every person. Being full of pus, suppurating (a wound). Brisk. Corrupt (discourse). Lean (meat). غث و ثمين *ghass u samīn*, Little and much. Good and bad. Strong and weak. Rich and poor.

A غثاء *ghusā* or *ghussā*, (pl. اغثاء *aghsā*) Foam, decayed leaves of trees, bits of wood, or any rubbish dirtied by foam carried down by the stream.

A غثاثة *ghasāsat*, (v. n. of غث) Being lean (sheep or meat). Being smutty (speech or story).

A غثار *ghusār*, A hyena.

A غثاغث *ghusāghis*, A lion.

A غثة *ghassat*, Lean (sheep). *Ghussat*, A sufficient part. Food sufficient to sustain life.

A غثث *ghasis*, A lion.

A غثر *ghasr*, (v. n. of غثر) Waving with grass, being verdant (the earth). *Ghusr*, (pl. of اغثر *aghsar*) Of a dusty red colour. The rabble, the canaille. *Ghasar*, Nap, pile. Fringe.

A غثراء *ghasrā*, (fem. of اغثر *aghsar*) Ignorant. Low, vile. Dust-coloured. A mixed multitude, rabble, mob. A certain long-necked water-fowl. A film floating on stagnant water. (Cloth) of thick woollen. A hyena.

A غثرة *ghasrat*, Plenty of provisions, cheapness, abundance, ease, convenience. *Ghusrat*, A black colour mixed with red. Dust-colour inclined to green. A crowd. *Ghasarat*, Dregs of the people.

A غثري *ghasariy*, A sown field watered by rain.

A غثغثة *ghasghasat*, (v. n. of غثغث Q) Making a feeble fight without weapons. Abiding in a place. Folding up (a garment) at the sides. Washing.

A غثم *ghasm*, (v. n. of غثم) Giving the best part of one's property at once. *Ghusm*, A crumb.

A غثمة *ghusmat*, Black inclining to dust-colour. Colour of hair more inclined to white than black. *Ghasimat*, The belly or paunch; tripe.

A غثمرة *ghasmarat*, (v. n. of غثمر Q) Destroying, wasting (one's substance).

A غثو *ghasw*, (v. n. of غثا for غثو) Carrying down sticks and leaves (a river). Spoiling the sweetness of water (sticks and leaves).

A غثوثة *ghusūsat*, (v. n. of غث) Being lean. Being corrupt and smutty (conversation or story).

A غثوثر *ghasawsar*, A lion.

A غثي *ghasy*, (v. n. of غثي) Carrying down sticks and leaves (a river). Sweeping away fodder into heaps, and destroying the flavour of it (a flood). Mixing, jumbling together (words). Striking. *Ghasy*, (or غثيان *ghasayān*) (v. n. of غثي) Being disturbed and fainting (the mind and spirits). Being overcast (sky). Being luxuriant in herbage.

A غثيث *ghasīs*, (v. n. of غث) Discharging matter (a wound). Lean. Pus, matter.

A غثيثة *ghasīsat*, Corrupted flesh (of a wound). Degeneracy, corruption, failure of intellect. A fool: worthless. (A palm-tree) bearing black sour dates.

A غثيمة *ghasīmat*, A dish prepared with locusts. Conflict, disturbance, confusion.

A غجوم *ghujūm*, (for غموج *ghumūj*) Camels' colts.

P غجك *ghichak*, A kind of lute, guitar, or violin.

P غجكي *ghichakī*, A player on the غجك *ghichak*.

P غجموك *ghachmūk*, A frog.

A غد *ghad*, Morrow. غدا *ghadan*, To-morrow. بعد غد *baʿda ghadin*, The day after to-morrow.

A غد *ghadd*, (v. n. of غد) Being afflicted with pestilence (a camel).

A غداء *ghadā*, (pl. اغدية *aghdiyat*) Meat, victuals, provisions. Breakfast. غداء روحاني *ghadāi rūhānī*, Food for the soul, spiritual food. غداء جسماني *ghadāi jismānī*, Nourishment for the body. *Ghidā*, A coming early.

A غداة *ghadāt*, Morning: the interval between dawn and sunrise.

A غداد *ghidād*, (pl. of غدة *ghuddat*) Portions, parts. Glands. Wens. (pl. of غاد *ghādd*) Camels infected with the plague.

A غدار *ghidār*, (v. n. 3 of غدر) Leaving, relinquishing. Remaining.

A غدار *ghaddār*, Fraudulent, perfidious (man or woman). A traitor. P آن غدار بدكردار *ān ghaddāri bad-kirdār*, That perfidious traitor. اين غدار خونريز *īn ghaddāri khūn-rez*, This treacherous blood-shedder. A يا غدار *yā ghadāri*, O perfidious (woman)!

A غدارة *ghudārat*, A thing left behind.

A غدارة *ghaddārat*, False, deceitful (woman).

P غداره *ghadāra*, The broad point of a spear. A copper vessel. An hour-glass.

A غداري *ghaddārī*, Perfidy, fraud, deception.

A غداف *ghudāf*, (pl. غدفان *ghidfān*) A black crow. Long black hair. A vulture with many feathers. A black wing.

A غدافل *ghadāfil*, (pl. of غدفل *ghidafl*) Old clothes. *Ghudāfil*, Bushy-tailed (camel or ram).

A غدافي *ghudāfiy*, Dark (night).

A غدان *ghidān*, A cane or any pole on which they hang clothes, a clothes-horse.

A غداني *ghudānīy*, Delicate, full of juice (youth).

A غدايا *ghadāya'*, (pl. of غدية) Mornings.

A غدائد *ghadāid*, (pl. of غدة *ghuddat*) Portions, parts. Glands, wens.

A غدائر *ghadāir*, (pl. of غديرة) Women's curls.

A غدب *ghudubb*, Short, thick, muscular.

A غدبة *ghudbat*, Thick flesh, or the bump under the soft part of the ear.

A غدة *ghuddat*, (pl. غداد *ghidād* and غدائد *ghadāid*) The pestilence in camels. A wart or wen which gives no pain. What lies between the fat and the bunch of a camel. A part, a portion of wealth. A herd of camels. *Ghuddat*, (or غددة *ghudadat*) (pl. غدد *ghudad*) A hard lump formed in the flesh, a glandular swelling, a kernel. Extravasated blood between the skin and flesh.

A غدد *ghadad*, The pestilence in camels. *Ghudad*, The intestines which are the receptacle of excrement. *Ghudud*, A hard lump formed in the flesh, a glandular swelling.

A غدر *ghadr*, (v. n. of غدر) Acting perfidiously, breaking a treaty or agreement; persecuting. Drinking pond-water. Perfidy, fraud, treachery, deceit, malevolence, malignity, hostility, injury. Villainy, ingratitude. Noise, bustle. اهل غدر *ahli ghadr*, Perfidious, cruel, malignant. *Ghadar*, (v. n. of غدر) Drinking rain-water. Remaining behind the flock (a she-camel or sheep). Being satiated with pasture when beginning to grow (sheep). Being hard and difficult for a horse to cross (ground). Being dark (night). Hard, stony, gravelly ground; a pond, ditch, furrow, or rut in such ground. Ground full of holes, along which a beast can scarcely travel. Any thing left. A great stone. Boldness in speech, in battle, or in any thing that one undertakes. ثبت الغدر *sabtu'l ghadar*, Firm, not swerving (in battle, or in any thing one takes in hand). *Ghudar*, A sink, drain, sewer. Water left by a flood. Treacherous. يا غدر *yā ghudara*, O traitor! (pl. of غدير *ghadīr*) Ponds, ditches, stagnant waters. *Ghudur*, Knaves, rogues.

P غدر *ghadar*, Breast of a garment. A breast-plate.

A غدراء *ghadrā*, Darkness.

A غدران *ghudrān*, (pl. of غدير *ghadīr*) Ponds, ditches, stagnant waters. (pl. of غديرة *ghadīrat*) Slips of plants. *Ghadarān*, (v. n. of غدر) Acting perfidiously, violating a treaty or agreement.

A غدرة *ghudrat*, also *ghidrat*, (pl. غدرات *ghudrāt*) Any thing left. Any thing left behind. *Ghadirat*, Dark (night).

P غدرك *ghadrak*, A breast-plate. A warlike instrument.

P غدغن *ghadaghan*, Speed; hurry. Confusion.

A غدف *ghadf*, (v. n. of غدف) Giving liberally. *Ghadaf*, Plenty, abundance. Cheapness.

A غدف *ghidaff*, A lion.

A غدفان *ghidfān*, (pl. of غداف *ghudāf*) Black crows. Vultures with many feathers.

P غدفره *ghudfara*, A stupid fellow.

A غدفل *ghidafl*, (pl. غدافل *ghadāfil*) A worn garment. Comfortable (life). Tall (man). Large-bodied (camel). Wide, ample (mercy or outer covering).

A غدفلة *ghadfalat*, (v. n. of غدفل Q) Enjoying the conveniences of life.

A غدفن *ghidafn*, Complete, ample, full, profuse. Full-bodied.

A غدق *ghadak*, (v. n. of غدق) Flowing plentifully (water). Plenty of water. بئر غدق *bi*,*r ghadakin*, Name of a well at Madīna.

A غدن *ghadan*, (v. n. of غدن) Being soft and smooth. Being loose, hanging down. Sleeping. Any thing within one's power. A flat and drowsy interval between two prophets. Softness, gentleness, smoothness. Languor, relaxation. Somnolency.

A غدنة *ghudnat*, Softness, smoothness. Looseness, flabbiness.

A غدنّة *ghudunnat*, Softness, smoothness. Flabbiness. A lump of flesh behind the ears.

P غدنگ *ghadang*, Disproportioned, ill-shaped. Rude, unpolished. Restless. Stupid.

A غدو *ghadw*, (v. n. of غدا for غدو) Coming in the morning. The morrow.

A غدوّ *ghudūw*, The morning. بالغدوّ و الآصال *bi'l ghudūw wa'l āsāl*, Morning and evening.

A غدوة *ghudwat*, (v. n. of غدا for غدو) Coming in the morning. (pl. غدوات *ghadawāt*) The morning. The interval between dawn and sunrise.

A غدودنيّ *ghadawdaniy*, Swift.

A غدور *ghadūr*, Fraudulent, most perfidious (man or woman).

A غدورة *ghadūrat*, (A she-camel) lagging behind the herd.

A غدويّ *ghadawiy*, Of to-morrow. The fœtus in the womb (especially of a sheep).

A غديّ *ghadīy*, Of to-morrow.

A غديان *ghadyān*, (fem. غدياء *ghadyā*,) Breakfasting; at breakfast.

A غدية *ghadyat*, (pl. غدايا *ghadāya'* or غديات *ghadayāt*) Morning. The interval between dawn and sunrise.

A غدير *ghadīr*, (pl. غدر *ghudar* and غدران *ghudrān*) A ditch, pool, stagnant water. Water left by a flood. A sword.

A غدّير *ghiddīr*, Very perfidious.

A غديرة *ghadīrat*, (pl. غدائر *ghadā*,*ir*) A curling lock of a woman's hair. Left behind the flock (a camel or sheep). A kind of hasty pudding. (pl. غدران *ghudrān*) A slip, graft. A bit of grass.

A غديا *ghadya'*, Breakfasting (woman).

A غذّ *ghazz*, (v. n. of غذّ) Swelling, suppurating (a wound). Diminishing.

A غذاء *ghizā*,, Meat or drink, diet, provision, food, victuals. Aliment, nutriment. (pl. of غذىّ *ghazīy*) Fœtuses of sheep.

A غذارم *ghuzārim*, Indefinite, conjectural (measurement). Abundant (water).

A غذامة *ghuzāmat*, Great plenty of milk.

A غذّامة *ghuzzāmat*, A sort of plant salt and bitter.

A غذامر *ghuzāmir*, Much (water).

A غذامس *ghuzāmis*, Name of a city in Africa whence they bring skins, called الجلود الغذامسيّة *al julūdu'l ghuzāmisiyat*.

A غذامير *ghazāmīr*, (pl. of غذمرة) Noises.

A غذائم *ghazā*,*im*, Things piled one upon another.

A غذرمة *ghazramat*, (v. n. of غذرم Q) Buying and selling (any thing) in the lump by conjecture. Mixture, confusion of words.

A غذغذة *ghazghazat*, The act of diminishing.

A غذم *ghazm*, (v. n. of غذم) Giving away the best part of one's property. Eating voraciously. Eating with difficulty. *Ghazam*, A kind of herb. *Ghuzam*, A sort of sour plant.

A غذمة *ghazmat*, Trouble, inconvenience. One word (was not heard). غذمة منكرة *ghazmatun munkaratun*, An inconvenient place. *Ghuzmat*, A dusky colour. A portion of wealth, a part of one's camels. (pl. غذم *ghuzam*) A large quantity of milk. *Ghazamat*, A large quantity of milk.

A غذمرة *ghazmarat*, (v. n. of غذمر Q) Suppressing one's words through pride, menace, or anger. Being angry. Selling in the lump by conjecture. Bringing out bit by bit. Crying out, making a great clamour. Separating. Mixing. Seizing by violence from one and giving to another. (pl. غذامير *ghazāmīr*) Clamour, brawl, quarrel. *Ghuzāmirat*, Mixed grass.

A غذو *ghazw*, (v. n. of غذا for غذو) Feeding, maintaining. Affording nutriment. Being suppressed (urine). Stopping, suppressing (urine). Flowing (water). Making haste. Running, flowing (blood from a vein).

A غذوّ *ghuzūw*, (v. n. of غذو) Flowing (water). Emitting blood (a vein). Cutting. Being cut.

A غذوان *ghazawān*, Brisk, swift (horse). Sharp-tongued. Flagitious, refractory, disobedient.

A غذوانة *ghazawānat*, A sharp tongue. Impudent, obscene (woman).

A غذويّ *ghazawiy*, (or غذيّ *ghazīy*) (pl. غذاء *ghizā*,) New-born (lamb or kid). The fœtus in the belly of a goat or sheep. Cattle sold with young.

A غذي *ghazy*, (v. n. of غذي) Feeding, nourishing. *Ghaza'*, Camels' urine.

A غذيّ المال *ghaziyu'l māl*, Young camels.

A غذيذة *ghazīzat*, Pus, matter, blood, or proud flesh (of a wound).

A غذيرة *ghazīrat*, Milk-pottage warmed by a hot stone.

A غذيم *ghazīm*, Wide (well).

A غذيمة *ghazīmat*, Trouble, inconvenience. (A country) yielding plentifully the plant غذم *ghazam*. A wide well. غذيمة منكرة *ghazīmatun munkaratun*, Inconvenient place.

P غر *ghar*, A whore. A coward. *Ghur*, Ruptured. Filling the mouth with wind, and striking it so that the wind escapes with noise. Swelling in the neck, a wen. Rupture. A Turkish nation.

A غرّ *gharr*, (v. n. of غرّ) Deceiving, flattering, feeding with vain hopes, cajoling, coaxing. Misleading. A bird feeding its young, putting bill into bill. Tending, feeding (camels). Sinking into the ground (water). Taking a gargle. (pl. غرور *ghurūr*) A wrinkle in the skin, or fold in a garment. طويته علي غرّه *tawaytuhu ʻala' gharrihi*, I folded (it) up in the old fold, *i. e.* I left it as it was. *Ghirr*, (pl. اغرار *aghrār*) Unskilled, inexperienced, raw, easily duped (youth or girl). A dupe. *Ghurr*, That wherewith a bird feeds her young. A fissure in the ground. A rivulet, a slender water-course. A wrinkle in the skin, a crease in a garment. The edge of a sword. A certain water-fowl. (pl. of اغرّ *agharr*) Most illustrious or noble.

A غرا *ghara'*, (v. n. of غري) Being attached, wholly dedicated (to any thing). Being cold (the water of a spring). Beauty. Glue, isinglass. (pl. اغراء *aghrā*,) Lean, attenuated. The young of a cow.

P غرا *ghurā*, White, bright. The sun.

A غراء *gharā*,, (v. n. of غري) Being devoted, wholly given up to. Being extremely irascible, indulging anger to excess. Greediness. *Ghirā*,, (v. n. of غري) Being attached, wholly given to. Being cold (the water of a spring). (v. n. 3 of غرا for غرو) Joining, subjoining. (A man) destitute of a horse. Glue, isinglass.

A غرّاء *gharrā*,, (fem. of اغرّ *agharr*) White, bright, splendid, illustrious, noble. Distinguished by a white star on the forehead (a mare). Intense (noon-day heat). The city of Madīna. A certain aromatic plant. Name of a certain white-headed bird. ليلة الغرّاء *laylatu'l gharrā*,, Thursday-night.

A غراءي *ghurā*,*a'*, (pl. غراءي *gharā*,*a'*) Froth of milk. A large stone or rock.

A غراب *ghurāb*, The curved part of the edge of a sword or of an axe (with which the blow is struck). (pl. اغرب *aghrub*, اغربة *aghribat*, غربان *ghirbān*, and غرب *ghurb*) A crow, raven, rook, jackdaw. A kind of ship (commonly called a grab). The prominent part of the hips of horses or camels, immediately above the leg. Name of a constellation. Hail. Snow. The back part of the head behind the ears. A cluster of the fruit of the tree اراك *arāk*. غراب البين *ghurābu'l bayn*, A certain bird with red legs and beak. P غراب زمين *ghurābi zamīn*, A dark night. A رجل الغراب *rijlu'l ghurāb*, Crows'-foot (an herb). A very secure kind of fastening with which they tie the dugs of camels to prevent the young from sucking.

A غرابة *gharābat*, (pl. غرابات *gharābāt*) Any thing admirable, strange, foreign. Strangeness, singularity. *Ghurābat*, The first or beginning of any thing. Edge, sharpness.

A غرابليّ *gharābiliy*, A sieve-maker.

A غرابيّ *ghurābiy*, A kind of date.

A غرابيب *gharābīb*, (pl. of غربيب) Very black.

A غرابيل *gharābīl*, (pl. of غربال) Large sieves.

A غرابيليّ *gharābīliy*, Maker or vender of sieves.

A غرابين *gharābīn*, (pl. of غربان *ghirbān*, which is pl. of غراب *ghurāb*) Crows: many crows.

A غراة gharāt, Lean. Instigation.

A غراث ghirās, (pl. of غرثان gharsān) Hungry (men). (pl. of غرثي gharsa') Hungry (women).

A غراثي gharāsa', (pl. of غرثان gharsān) Hungry.

P غراچه gharācha, Infamous, unmanly. A contented cuckold, a pimp to his own wife, a wittol. Ignorant, foolish. Name of a country.

A غراد gharād, (pl. ghirād) A kind of fungus.

A غرادة gharādat, A kind of mushroom.

A غرار ghirār, (v. n. of غرّ) Feeding its young (a bird), putting bill into bill. (v. n. 3 of غرّ) Giving little milk (a camel). Returning improperly a salutation: as, سلام عليك salām ɛalayka, when the first saluter had said سلام عليكم salām ɛalaykum. Being cold, dull (market). A deficiency or short-coming in the performance of the ablutions, prostrations, and ceremonies at prayer. Slumber. Edge of a sword, point of a spear. Haste, speed. Space (of a month). A little sleep. A way, mode of doing any thing. A model, figure, form, mould. A mould in which they cast arrow-heads. علي غرار ɛala' ghirārin, In a hurry. One after another.

A غرارة gharārat, (v. n. of غرّ) Being white (the face). Having a white spot (on the forehead). Being seduced and beguiled after having had experience. Being inexperienced, unacquainted with the use of things. Inexperience, youth. كان ذالك في غرارتي kāna zālika fi gharārati, That happened in the season of my inexperience or nonage. Ghirārat, (pl. غرائر gharāɛir) A large sack.

P غراره gharāra, Washing, rinsing the mouth. Ghirāra, A helmet. A gardener's sack with meshes.

A غراز gharāz, Hard ground. Ghirāz, (v. n. of غرز) Having little milk (a camel).

P غراس gharās, Sadness, sorrow.

A غراس gharās, Whatever is voided by one who has taken a cathartic draught. Ghirās, The season proper for planting. A sapling, a young plant. (pl. of غرس ghars) Saplings.

A غرّاس gharrās, A planter. Learned.

P غراش gharāsh, A fracture, rent, scratch, wound. Rage. Force, violence. Grief.

P غراشيدن gharāshīdan, To chide. To scratch.

P غراشيده gharāshīda, Angry. Scratched.

A غراضيف gharāzīf, (pl. of غرضوف ghurzūf) Gristles, cartilages.

A غراف ghirāf, A large measure for dry goods. (pl. of غرفة ghurfat) Draughts of water.

A غرّاف gharrāf, Capacious. (A river) abundant in water. Wide-stepping (horse).

A غرافة ghurāfat, A draught (of water) taken with the hand.

A غرام gharām, Desire, cupidity, greediness. A fine, mulct. A debt which must be paid. Torture, torment. A tedious calamity, destruction. شوق و غرام shawk u gharām, Desire and alacrity.

A غرامة gharāmat, A debt which must be paid. A fine. P غرامت زده gharāmat-zada, Mulcted.

P غران gharān or gharrān, Rapacious, fierce. Iron.

A غرّان ghurrān, (pl. of اغرّ agharr) White. Illustrious. (pl. of غرير gharīr) Excellent dispositions. Sureties. Lives free from care. Bubbles on water.

A غرانق gharānik, The root of the bramble. (pl. of غرنوق ghurnūk) Braided locks of hair. Gharānik, (or غرانقيّ gharānikīy) Delicate (lock of hair flowing behind the ear). Ghurānik, (pl. غرانق gharānik, غرانيق gharānīk, and غرانقة gharānikat) A delicate, beautiful youth. Young, fleshy (woman).

A غرانقة ghurānikat, Young (woman) full of flesh.

A غرانيق gharānīk, (pl. of غرنوق ghurnūk) Roots of brambles.

P غراورنگ gharāwrang, Large. Ghirāwrang, A great throne.

A غرائب gharāɛib, (pl. of غريبة gharībat) Strange, extraordinary things. Foreign, outlandish (women).

A غرائر gharāɛir, (pl. of غرارة ghirārat) Sacks.

A غرائس gharāɛis, (pl. of غريسة gharīsat) Young palm-trees just appearing.

A غرب gharb, (v. n. of غرب) Being hid. Being absent. Going to a great distance, or to one side. Going. Rejoicing. Delaying, procrastinating. Being shed (tears). Sunset. The west. Africa. The flowing of tears. The overflowing of wine or tears. A lachrymal vein or duct. Beginning or first. The sharpest parts of the teeth; also their brightness. A sturdy kind of tree common in Hijāz. The most prominent part of any thing, as the curvature of a sword. Removal, departure. A day of watering. A leathern water-bag. Quickness or vehemence of speech. Distance, longinquity. A large bucket. A beast employed in drawing water. The first course, race, or starting of a horse. Cheerfulness, briskness. (A horse) running much. A distemper or swelling in the inner corners of the eye, a pimple in the eye. The outer or inner corner of the eye. Protraction. Spawl, sputter. A traveller's leathern provision-bag. The stone of a grape. سهم غرب sahm gharb, An arrow from an unknown hand. Ghurb, Distance from home. (pl. of غراب ghurāb) Crows, ravens. Gharab, (v. n. of غرب) Being very black. Being obscure, unintelligible. Lying hid. Being afflicted with a disease in the eye (sheep). Silver. Gold. Plate. Wine. The white poplar. Water dripping from the bucket whilst drawing up from the well. A distemper incident to sheep, making the hairs to drop from their eyelids. Blueness in the eye of a horse. A goblet, a bowl. The odour of water or mud. A willow. سهم غرب sahmi gharab (or gharb), An arrow of which one loses sight, and knows not where it has struck. Ghurub, A foreigner. Rare, strange.

A غرباء ghurabāɛ, (pl. of غريب gharīb) Strangers, foreigners, aliens. Poor people. Travellers.

A غربال ghirbāl, (pl. غرابيل gharābīl) A large sieve, riddle, screen. A drum. A slanderer, whisperer.

P غربال آبگون ghirbāli āb-gūn, The sky, firmament.

P غربال بند ghirbāl-band, A sieve-maker.

A غربان ghirbān, (pl. of غراب ghurāb) Crows.

A غربة gharbat, Distant. Distance, longinquity. غربة نويّ nawan gharbatun, A great distance. غربة النويّ gharbatu'n nawa', The distance of any place to which one goes. Ghurbat, (v. n. of غرب) Travelling, going away, departing, retiring. Being far distant from country and friends. Being thin and fine. Being concealed. Distance from home. Condition of a stranger. Exile. Wretchedness.

P غربتان gharbatān, A roller for smoothing the flat roofs of houses. A cuckold, pimp to his own wife.

P غربد gharbad, A blemished bride.

A غربلة gharbalat, (v. n. of غربل Q) Sifting, searcing; riddling. Cutting. Grinding. Killing.

P غربه ghurba, Hiding tears, weeping privately.

A غربيّ gharbīy, West, western, westerly. Exposed to the setting sun. Smitten by the heat of the setting sun. A sort of date. A red dye. Wine prepared from unripe grapes without fermentation.

P غربيب gharbīb, A kind of black grape.

A غربيب ghirbīb, (pl. غرابيب gharābīb) Very black. The best kind of grape. An old man who dyes his grey hairs with privet.

P غربير gharbīr, (or غربيل gharbīl) A sieve.

P غربيله gharbīla, Alternate motion and rest.

A غرة ghirat, A promise.

A غرّة ghirrat, (v. n. of غرّ) Deceiving or flattering. Feeding with vain hopes. Inexperienced (girl). Inexperience. Carelessness, inattention, thoughtlessness. علي غرّة ɛala' ghirratin, Unawares, without notice, off one's guard. عن غرّة ɛan ghirratin, Through negligence or inattention.

P غرّه شدن ghirra shudan, To be deceived, cheated.

A Ghurrat, (v. n. of غرّ) Being white (the face), having a white spot (the forehead). (pl. غرر ghurar) Whiteness, brightness, an ornament, a blaze on the forehead of a horse (larger than درهم dirham). The dawn. The human face (implying also a shining brightness). The heart. Noble, illustrious. A lord, chief of a people. The most excellent of any thing (especially the richest furniture). The first appearance of any thing (particularly of teeth, denoting likewise their whiteness). The new moon. The first night of the moon. The splendour of the moon (especially the first three days). Rapidity of growth in a vine. A servant, male or female; a slave, captive, boy or girl. A fine of 500 dirhams, derived from the appellation generally given in Arabic to an infant male or female slave of that value. Quickness of growth in grapes. P غرّهٔ اين دولت روز افزون ghurraɛi īn dawlati roz-afzūn, The founder of this daily-increasing empire. غرّهٔ ماه محرّم ghurraɛi māhi muharram, The beginning of the month Muharram. A غرّهٔ ناصيهٔ سلطنت واقبال ghurraɛi *nāsiyaẖi sultanat u ikbāl,* The star and ornament on the forehead of the state (a title).

A غرث *gharas,* A being hungry, hungering.

A غرثان *gharsān,* (pl. غرثى *gharsa',* غراثى *gharāsa',* and غراث *ghirās*) Hungry.

A غرثى *gharsa',* (pl. of غرثان *gharsān*) Hungry (men). (fem. of غرثان *gharsān*) (pl. غراث *ghirās*) Hungry (woman). غرثي الوشاح *gharsa'l wishāh,* Slender-waisted (woman).

P غرچه *gharcha,* Ignorant, stupid. Infamous. A catamite. A contented cuckold. Georgia.

P غرد *ghard,* A habitation for the summer.

A غرد *ghard,* A house of reeds. A house roofed with planks. A certain building appropriated to the use of the governors of سرّ من راي *surr man rāy.* *Ghard, ghird,* or *gharad,* (pl. غردة *ghiradat*) A species of mushroom or puff. *Gharad,* (v. n. of غرد) Singing, warbling. The motion of the body whilst singing. *Gharid* or *ghird,* Singing (bird). *Ghirad,* Warbling, melodious (voice).

A غردة *ghirdat,* A kind of mushroom. *Ghiradat,* (pl. of غرد *ghard* and *ghird*) Mushrooms.

A غردقة *ghardakat,* Dust, or the darkness of the night obscuring every object. The dropping of a curtain, or the hiding with a veil.

P غردل *ghar-dil,* Timid, cowardly-hearted.

P غرده *gharda,* A wheel. *Ghurda,* A tumour, wen.

A غرر *gharar,* (v. n. of غرّ) Having a white spot (the forehead). Being white (the face). Any thing subject to the caprice of fortune or of uncertain events. Engaging for what is not in one's power, (as selling a bird in the bush). Personal risk, exposure of one's self to danger. *Ghurar,* (pl. of غرّة *ghurrat*) The three first nights of the month. Ornaments. (pl. of اغر *agharr*) White. Illustrious.

A غرز *gharz,* (v. n. of غرز) Piercing, pricking, poking (with a sword, needle, or sting). Fixing (a stake) in the ground, or an ornament on the person. Yielding obedience to a prince after having been rebellious. Having little milk, or not yielding it (a camel). Putting (the foot in a stirrup) when going to mount. Commands and prohibitions, edicts and interdicts. A leathern stirrup (one of iron or wood being called ركاب *rikāb*). (pl. غروض *ghurūz*) A sucker ingrafted into the trunk of a vine. *Gharaz,* Very bad herbage or bog-rush.

P غرز *gharaz,* Sort of the herb shepherds'-staff.

P غرزاد *ghar-zād,* A son of a whore.

A غرزحلة *ghirzahlat,* A staff, a stick.

P غرزن *ghar-zan,* A strumpet.

P غرس *ghars* or *ghirs,* Rage, passion, excitement. Soon angry. Wearied. *Ghirs,* A scratch.

A غرس *ghars,* (v. n. of غرس) Planting, setting (trees). (pl. اغراس *aghrās* and غراس *ghirās*) A plant, a sapling. *Ghirs,* A black crow. (pl. اغراس *aghrās*) A membrane covering the head of a new-born camel; the caul; also a mucous substance which comes along with the fœtus.

P غرسا *gharsā,* The herb elecampane.

P غرش *gharsh,* Force. A scratch. Anger.

A غرش *gharsh,* The fruit of a certain tree.

P غرّش *ghurrish,* Force. Anger.

P غرّشت *ghurrisht,* The roaring of a lion. The braying of an ass. The neighing of a horse.

P غرشنه *ghurshna,* Name of an herb for washing the hands.

P غرشيدن *gharshīdan,* To be angry.

P غرشيده *gharshīda,* Angry.

A غرض *gharz,* (v. n. of غرض) Girthing (a camel). Filling (a vessel); not filling (it) quite full. Withholding, keeping back. Shaking (a bottle) in order to make butter. Giving whey or buttermilk to drink. Taking, receiving, cutting, or gathering (any thing) whilst fresh or new. Being doubled, folded. Weaning (a kid) before the proper time. Hurrying, expediting, doing (any thing) before the time. Being wrinkled (the body), as the effect of leanness after having been fat. The space of any place or vessel which is not completely filled (as from the surface of the water to the parapet of a well). The breast-strap of a camel. A vessel which is left without any thing being put into it. A bend, a fold. After having been fat, a becoming thin, and having lines or corrugations remaining on the belly. The palm of the hand. The hastening of any thing before the time. (pl. غروض *ghurūz* and اغراض *aghrāz*) The girth of a camel's saddle. (pl. غرضان *ghurzān* and *ghirzān*) An incomplete rivulet, or a large branch from a river. *Ghurz* or *ghuruz,* (pl. of غرضة *ghurzat*) Girths of camels' saddles. *Gharaz,* (v. n. of غرض) Being tired of (any place). Having a strong inclination for (it). Longing, desiring greatly. Fearing. Wish, design, aim, motive, end, view, meaning, intention. Desire, longing. Ennui, langour. Vexation. Want. Machination, interestedness, selfishness. Hatred, rancour, malignity, rage, spite. (pl. اغراض *aghrāz*) A butt or mark for archers. غرض خفي *gharazi khafī,* Concealed malevolence. P غرض كردن *gharaz kardan,* To persecute, conspire against, entertain a secret but mortal grudge. To lay a train for the ruin of another. To intend. A الغرض *al gharaz,* Upon the whole, to sum up all, in short, in fine. لغرضه *ligharazihi,* For his own sake. P با غرض *bā gharaz,* Deliberately, on purpose. بي غرض *bī gharaz,* Without intention, interest, design, or selfish motive. A *Ghiraz,* (v. n. of غرض) Being fresh (meat).

P غرض آشنا *gharaz-āshnā,* Interested.

P غرض آلودگي *gharaz-ālūdagī,* Defilement by selfishness. غرض آلوده *gharaz-ālūda,* Defiled, tainted, or stained by selfishness.

P غرض آميز *gharaz-āmez,* Malicious.

A غرضان *ghurzān* or *ghirzān,* (pl. of غرض *gharz*) Large branches from deep rivers. Deep valleys.

P غرضانه *gharazāna,* Malevolently. محبّت بي غرضانه *mahabbati bī gharazāna,* Disinterested love.

A غرضة *ghirzat* or *ghurzat,* (pl. غرض *ghuruz* and *ghurz*) The girth of a camel's saddle.

P غرضمند *gharazmand,* Self-interested.

P غرضمندي *gharazmandī,* Selfishness.

A غرضوف *ghurzūf,* (pl. غراضيف *gharāzīf*) Gristle, cartilage. غرضوفان *ghurzūfāni,* Two pieces of wood tied right and left between the middle and the back of a camel's saddle.

A غرطمانيّ *ghurtumānīy,* Comely (youth).

P غرغاب *ghargkāb,* Noise, clamour. A whirlpool.

P غرغان *gharghān,* A loud voice.

P غرغر *gharghar,* Axis, axle, cylinder, or barrel around which the rope is coiled in drawing water. *Ghurghur,* Ruptured. A man muttering with rage.

A غرغر *ghirghir,* The Guinea-hen or jungle-fowl. A kind of herb.

A غرغرة *ghargharat,* (v. n. of غرغر Q) Gargling. Piercing the throat with a spear, or cutting it with a knife. The sound of boiling water or of meat when roasting. Overflowing. Being near death. A sound made in the throat when dying or gargling. The guttural noise made by a shepherd. A fracture in the gristle of the nose. The top of a jug or bottle. The maw of a bird. A gargarism, gargle. *Ghurghurat,* A noble, illustrious man. A white star on the forehead of a horse. The maw, crop.

P غرغره *ghargkara,* The cylinder or axis about which the rope is entwined in drawing water. *Ghurghura,* Rupture. Murmuring, muttering.

A غرغريّات *ghurghurīyat,* Excellent camels.

P غرغشه *gharghasha,* Dispute, causeless quarrel.

P غرغن *gharghan* or *gharghin,* A kind of leather of which shoes are made.

P غرغنجه *gharghanja,* A lewd woman.

P غرغند *gharghand,* A kind of leather.

P غرغنده *gharghanda,* Cordovan. Angry.

A غرف *gharf,* (v. n. of غرف) Taking up (water in the hand). Cutting, lopping. Cutting (the forelocks). Clipping, polling, shearing. Tanning with the plant غرف *gharf.* *Gharf* or *gharaf,* A tree used in tanning. *Gharaf,* (v. n. of غرف) Being griped from feeding on the plant غرف *gharf* (a camel). The plant ثمام *sumām,* or only as long as it is green. Any evergreen. Any one of the trees شث *shass,* طبّاق *tubbāh,* بشم *basham,* غفار *ghafār,* غنم *ghunm,* صوم *sawm,* حج *habaj,* شدن *shadn,* حيّهل *hayyahal,* هيشر *hayshar,* and ضرم *zirm.* The leaf of a tree. *Ghiraf,* (pl. of غرفة *ghirfat*) Slippers. *Ghuraf,* (pl. of غرفة *ghurfat*) Parlours, supper-rooms.

A غرفة *gharfat,* One draught out of the hand. A single cutting, clipping, or shearing. A single taking up of water in the hands. *Ghirfat,* (pl. غرف *ghiraf*) A sandal or slipper. A mode of drinking with the hands. *Ghurfat*, (pl. غرفات *ghur, ghura*, or *ghurufāt*) A parlour, upper room, or other apartment for supping. Paradise, the seventh heaven. (pl. غراف *ghirāf*) A draught of water taken up with the hand, as much as one drinks at once. A ringlet of hair. A knotted cord or fringe round a camel's neck by way of ornament.

P غرفج *ghurfuj*, Wormwood. Touchwood.

A غرفش *ghurfish*, Reproof, intimidation, bullying (that of a coward that affects bravery).

P غرفنج *ghurfanj*, Ruptured.

A غرفي *gharfiy*, (A leathern bottle) tanned with the plant غرف *gharf*.

A غرق *gharak*, (generally pronounced *ghark*) (v. n. of غرق) Sinking, being submerged or drowned. Being contented, independent, in want of nothing. Taking a pailful of milk by guess. Drinking a draught to satiety. Submersion. A drowning. P غرق چشمهٔ سيماب *gharki chashmasi simāb*, Fascinated by worldly objects. غرق چشمهٔ قير *gharki chashmasi kīr*, Diving. Grovelling in the world. Sunset. غرق شدن *ghark shudan*, To be drowned. To sink. غرق كردن *ghark kardan*, To drown. To dive to the bottom, to plunge. A *Gharik*, Drowned. Immersed. غرق الصوت *ghariku's sawt*, One whose voice is drowned, and unable to speak from terror. *Ghurak*, (pl. of غرقة *ghurkat*) Draughts (of milk).

P غرقاب *gharkāb*, Deep water. A whirlpool. A shipwreck. غرقاب شدن *gharkāb shudan*, To sink, be drowned. خطر غرقاب *khatari gharkāb*, Danger of shipwreck.

A غرقأة *gharkasat*, (v. n. of غرقأ Q) Coming forth with the pellicle on (an egg). Laying an egg before the outer shell is formed (a hen).

A غرقة *ghurkat*, (pl. غرق *ghurak*) One draught (of milk). *Gharikat*, Very humid, saturated with moisture (land).

A غرقد *gharkad*, A species of large trees, or of the thorn عوسج *pawsaj*. The white of an egg. بقيع الغرقد *bakīpu'l gharkad*, The cemetery of Madina (because formerly thickly set with these trees).

P غرق شده *ghark-shuda*, Drowned.

A غرقلة *gharkalat*, (v. n. of غرقل Q) Becoming addle (an egg). Rotting (a melon, squash, gourd). Pouring out (water) on the head.

A غرقم *gharkam*, Glans penis.

A غرقه *gharka*, Drowned. P غرقه شدن *gharka shudan*, To be drowned.

A غرقى *gharka'*, (pl. of غرق *gharik*, غارق *ghārik*, or غريق *gharīk*) Drowned. A *Gharkī*, Injury to standing crops from a flood.

A غرقئ *ghirkis*, The white of an egg. The pellicle which encloses the white of an egg.

A غرل *gharil*, A man of a loosely-built frame. A long spear.

A غرلة *ghurlat*, The foreskin, prepuce.

P غرم *gharm* or *gharam*, Anger. *Ghurm*, A mountain-sheep. A horned fighting ram.

A غرم *gharm*, (v. n. of غرم) Paying or owing a fine. *Ghurm*, A fine. Bad fortune. A debt which must be paid.

A غرماء *ghuramās*, (pl. of غريم *gharīm*) Debtors. Creditors.

P غرماسنگ *gharmāsang* or *gharamāsang*, A cake fried in butter.

P غرمان *gharmān*, Angry, passionate, choleric.

P غرمانوش *gharmānūsh*, Dragon-wort.

P غرمج *gharmij*, Carraways.

P غرمچ *gharmich*, Coriander-seed.

P غرمنده *gharmanda*, Passionate.

A غرمول *ghurmūl*, A thick, dangling, and uncircumcised penis. A horse's pizzle.

A غرمى *gharma'*, Heavy (woman). Yes, verily.

P غرميدن *gharmīdan*, To fly in a passion. To chide, reproach. To thunder. To murmur, mutter. To roar, bray. To rock a child in the cradle.

P غرميده *gharmīda*, Enraged, indignant.

P غرن *gharan*, Loud weeping and sobbing.

A غرن *gharan*, (v. n. of غرن) Drying on a fur garment (dough). (pl. أغران *aghrān*) An eagle, or a bird resembling an eagle. A crab. *Gharin*, Weak.

A غرناطة *gharnātat*, Grenada in Spain.

A غرناق *ghirnāk*, A comely, tender youth.

P غرنبش *ghurumbish*, A loud and a dreadful noise made by a man or beast. Thunder.

P غرنبه *ghurumba*, Exclamation, clamour. A tumult. A walking-stick.

P غرنبيدن *ghurumbīdan*, To thunder: bray, roar.

P غرّنده *ghurranda*, Roaring, fierce (lion).

A غرنف *ghirnif*, Jessamine. Papyrus.

A غرنقة *gharnakat*, The resemblance of a thread in the eyes.

P غرنگ *gharang* also *ghirang*, A noise in the throat when sobbing or being strangled. *Gharang* or *ghurang*, Weeping, lamentation, groaning.

A غرنوق *ghirnawk*, A crane, or any aquatic bird with a long neck. *Ghurnūk*, (pl. غرانق *gharānik*) A braided lock of hair. (pl. غرانيق *gharānīk*) Roots of brambles. *Ghurnūk* or *ghirnawk*, A certain black (according to some, white) water-fowl. A tender, comely youth. *Ghurnūk*, A crane or long-necked water-bird. Delicate (plant) lying concealed.

P غرنيچى *gharnīchī*, Intense cold.

A غرنيق *ghurnayk* or *ghirnīk*, A tender, comely youth. *Ghurnayk*, A certain water-fowl. A crane or long-necked aquatic bird.

P غرو *gharw*, A reed, an uncut reed or pen. A musical pipe made of a reed.

A غرو *gharw*, (v. n. of غرا for غرو) Glueing. Adhering (as fat to the heart), covering it. Being filled with wonder, surprised. Being carried far in rage. Wonder. لا غرو *lā gharwa*, No wonder.

P غرواش *gharwāsh*, A plant resembling a brush used by weavers. The herb elecampane. *Gharawāsh*, Anger, indignation. Sadness, sorrow. A scratch with the nails.

P غرواشه *gharwāsha*, A herb with which weavers sprinkle their cloth, or curriers anoint leather. Anger.

A غروب *ghurūb*, (v. n. of غرب) Setting (as the sun or moon). The west. (pl. of غرب *gharb*) The angles of the eyes.

P غروبه *ghurūba*, Exclamation, cry, clamour.

A غرود *gharūd*, A bride whom her husband finds not a virgin.

A غرور *gharūr*, A deceiver. The world. Satan. A gargle. *Ghurūr*, (v. n. of غرّ) Deceiving, flattering, feeding with false hopes. Pride, presumption, vain-glory, vanity. Folly. (pl. of غرّ *gharr*) Folds in garments. (pl. of غارّ *ghārr*) Trifles, things with which one is amused or deceived. P غرور خريدن *ghurūr kharīdan*, To behave proudly.

A غروز *ghurūz*, (pl. of غرز *gharz*) Suckers ingrafted into a vine.

A غروض *ghurūz*, A wrinkle or corrugation in the belly, arising from leanness after having been fat. (pl. of غرض *gharz*) Girths of camels' saddles.

A غروف *gharūf*, Water (in a well) which may be reached with the hand. A large bucket holding much water.

P غرونبه *ghurūmba*, Noise, clamour, outcry.

A غروى *gharwa'*, Any thing on which the attention is wholly fixed. Wonder. Instigation. لا غروى *lā gharwa'*, No wonder.

P غرويدن *ghurwīdan*, To make a noise: thunder.

P غرويزن *gharwīzan*, A sieve.

P A غرّه *gharra*, Haughty, proud. Deceived. Cross. Pride. غرّه شدن *gharra shudan*, To be deceived.

A غرى *ghara'*, Beauty. *Gharī*, (or غريّ *gharīy*) Handsome (man or edifice).

A غرّى *ghurra'*, A lady, princess in her own tribe.

P غرياسنگ *gharyāsang*, A kind of pancake fried in butter.

A غرياق *ghiryāk*, Name of a bird.

A غريب *gharīb*, (pl. غرباء *ghurabās*) Uncommon, strange, outlandish, foreign. Extraordinary. Exotic. A foreigner, stranger. Gentle, humble, meek, docile. Poor, needy. الغريب كالاعمى *al gharīb ka'l aqma'*, (proverb) A stranger is like one blind. P مرد غريب *mardi gharīb*, A foreign man.

P غريبانه *gharībāna*, Fit for the poor.

P غريب پرور *gharīb-parwar*, Cherisher of the poor. غريب پرورى *gharīb-parwarī*, Kindness to the poor.

A غريبة *gharībat*, (pl. غرائب *gharāsib*) Any thing rare, strange, or elegant. A hand-mill.

P غريب نواز *gharīb-nawāz*, Kind to strangers.

A غريبى *gharībī*, Foreignness, strangeness. Indigence. Humility. P غريبى كردن *gharībī kardan*, To travel, become a stranger.

P غريچى *gharīchī*, Intense cold. Winter.

P غريد *gharīd*, A bride falsely given as a virgin.

A غرّيد *ghirrīd*, Singing; a warbler, singer.

P غريدن *ghurīdan*, To thunder; to cry with a loud voice; to roar, bray. To yawn, stretch.

P غرّيدن *ghurrīdan*, To roar (as a wild beast).

A غرير *gharīr*, (pl. اغرّاء *aghirrā*, and اغرّة *aghirrat*) Simple, deceived, inexperienced. Buoyed up with false hopes. A raw youth, easily imposed upon. (pl. غرّان *ghurrān*) A noble disposition. An agreeable temper. Beauty. Cheerfulness, a life free from care. A surety, caution. One who cautions, bids beware. انا غريرك منه *ana gharīruka minhu*, I advise you to be diffident of him.

A غريراء *ghurayrā*, Name of an aromatic plant.

A غريرة *gharīrat*, (fem. of غرير *gharīr*) Inexperienced (girl).

P غريرن *ghareran*, Black mud lying at the bottom of a pond.

P غريز *gharīz*, Meekness, gentleness, forbearance.

P غريزان *gharezān*, A sieve.

A غريزة *gharīzat*, Nature. (A camel) abounding in milk.

P غريزن *gharīzan*, Mud at the bottom of a pond. A sieve.

A غريزيّ *gharīzīy*, Innate, natural. حرارت غريزيّه *harārati gharīzīya*, Natural heat.

P غريژنگ *gharījang*, Black mud at the bottom of a pond.

A غريس *gharīs*, A sheep. A word used in calling them to be milked.

A غريسة *gharīsat*, (pl. غرائس *gharāïs*) A young palm-tree just appearing, any sapling just planted till it has rooted. A name common to handmaids.

A غريض *gharīz*, Flowers of the palm-tree. Fresh (meat). Any thing fresh, bright, and shining. Rain-water. An excellent singer.

A غريف *gharīf*, A reed-bed, a papyrus-bed. The haunt or den of a lion. Water in a reed-bed; a marsh, swamp. A thick forest; or a forest of the reeds papyrus and حلفاء *halfā*. A bed of the ضال *zāl* and سلم *salam*. Capacious (bucket). *Ghiryaf*, A soft and limber kind of plant; the papyrus.

A غريفة *gharīfat*, A wood, dense thicket. A shoe. A slipper (especially an old one). A piece of ornamental leather of a span long which hangs from the hilt of a sword.

P غريفج *gharefaj*, (or غريفژ *gharefaj*) Mud, clay. High ground from which boys slide down.

A غريق *gharīk*, (pl. غرقى *gharka'*) Immersed, sunk, drowned, shipwrecked. A drowned or drowning person. Cased (in armour). غريق امواج بحار *gharīki amwāji bihār*, Swallowed by the waves of the sea. غريق رحمت *gharīki rahmat*, Overwhelmed with mercy, drowned in the mercy of God.

P غريق آب *gharīk-āb*, Deep, out of one's depth.

A غريل *ghiryal*, A remainder of water in the bottom of a cistern, unfit for drinking, in which only tadpoles live. Sediment in a jug. Thin clay left by water on the surface of the ground. Dirty foam left on the ground by a torrent. Dust. The mucus of any solid-hoofed animal.

A غريم *gharīm*, A debtor. A creditor.

A غرين *gharīn* or *ghiryan*, Folly. Thin clay. Clay left by a flux of water, whether moist or dry. Dirty water at the bottom of a pond. Fresh butter.

P غريو *ghirev*, Clamour, exclamation, lamentation, complaint, groaning, crying, howling, shrieking. Uproar, tumult, mob.

P غريوان *ghirevān*, One who laments or exclaims.

P غريويدن *ghirevīdan*, To exclaim, lament, make a clamour.

P غز *ghuz*, Name of a Turkish nation.

A غزّ *ghazz*, (v. n. of غزّ) Choosing, selecting from amongst others. Putting various-coloured things round children's necks to defend them from malignant eyes. *Ghuzz*, The corners of the mouth inside. Name of a Turkish nation.

A غزّاء *ghuzzā*, (pl. of غازي) Soldiers: generals.

A غزاة *ghazāt*, A warlike expedition against infidels. Battle. *Ghuzāt*, (pl. of غازي *ghāzī*) Warriors, soldiers, heroes, champions.

A غزار *ghizār*, (v. n. 3 of غزر) Giving somewhat to receive more. (pl. of غزيرة *ghazīrat*) (Camels) which abound in milk, (or fountains) with water.

A غزارة *ghazārat*, (v. n. of غزر) Being plentiful (milk). Abounding in milk (cattle). Being plenteous (water in a fountain, or tears in the eyes). Plenty, abundance.

P غزاره *ghazāra*, Plenty, abundance.

A غزاز *ghizāz*, An outstripping, getting before.

A غزّاز *ghuzzāz*, (pl.) Beneficent to children, relations, or neighbours.

A غزال *ghazāl*, (pl. غزلة *ghizlat* and غزلان *ghizlān*) A fawn just able to walk, or till it can run at full speed. A delicate young person. غزال شعبان *ghazālu shaʻbān*, Name of an insect. دم الغزال *damu'l ghazāl*, Name of a biting herb. Tarragon.

A غزّال *ghazzāl*, A vender of cotton-thread.

P غزالان *ghazālān*, Singers, musicians.

A غزالة *ghazālat*, A young deer, fawn, roe, gazelle. The sun, light, rays; especially the sun's meridian lustre. A certain sweet esculent herb. Name of a woman. غزالة الضحي *ghazālatu'z zuha'*, Breakfast, luncheon. *Ghazālatu'z zuha'*, (or غزلات الضحي *ghazalātu'z zuha'*) Beginning of the part of the day called ضحي *zuha'*, or from the hour the sun is fairly up until a fifth of the day is gone. غزالهٔ فلك *ghazāla-i falak*, The sun. Aries.

A غزاوة *ghazāwat*, (v. n. of غزا for غزو) Making war, fighting. Advancing against an enemy.

A غزّة *ghazzat*, Gaza in Palestine, (the birthplace of the Imām Shāfiī).

A غزر *ghazr*, (pl. غزر *ghuzr*) Plenty, abundance. A basket made of reeds or palm-leaves. *Ghazr* or *ghuzr*, (v. n. of غزر) Being plentiful (milk in cattle, water in a fountain, or tears in the eyes). Abounding in milk (cattle).

A غزران *ghuzrān*, (Camels) yielding an abundance of milk.

A غزز *ghazaz*, (v. n. of غزّ) Having the sole property (in any person or thing). Choosing, selecting from among others.

A غزغز *ghuzghuz*, The corners of the mouth inside.

P غزغن *ghazghan*, A kind of leather. A cauldron.

P غزغند *ghazghand*, Kind of leather. Cauldron.

A غزل *ghazala*, (fut. يغزل *yaghzilu*) He spun.

A غزل *ghazl*, (v. n. of غزل) Spinning. Spun. (Cotton) thread, twist. *Ghazal*, (v. n. of غزل) Speaking in the language of love or in verse. Spinning. Stopping short, astonished at the voice of a fawn of which he was in pursuit (a dog). An ode. *Ghazil*, A poet, writer of erotic poetry. One who talks or amuses himself with the ladies. Weak, flexible.

A غزّل *ghuzzal*, (pl. of غازلة) Female spinners.

A غزلان *ghizlān*, (and غزلة *ghizlat*) (pl. of غزال *ghazāl*) Fawns, gazelles, antelopes.

P غزل خوان *ghazal-khwān*, A repeater of odes.

P غزلدان *ghazldān*, A basket in which a woman lays up her thread when sewing.

P غزلولاور *ghuzlūlāwar*, A copper vessel.

A غزليات *ghazliyāt*, Odes.

P غزم *ghuzm*, Fear. Anger, passion. Hatred.

P غزنك *ghuznak*, A herb used in washing clothes.

P غزنو *ghaznū*, (غزني *ghaznī*, or غزنين) Ghaznin.

P غزنه *ghazna*, Ghizneh.

A غزو *ghazw*, (v. n. of غزا for غزو) Making war, going against an enemy. Intending, undertaking, purposing, willing, wishing. Aim, intent, purpose.

A غزوات *ghazawāt*, (pl. of غزاة *ghazāt*) Battles, wars with infidels. Victories, heroic achievements.

A غزوان *ghazawān*, (v. n. of غزا for غزو) Going against (an enemy), waging war with (infidels).

A غزوة *ghazwat*, A military engagement.

A غزويّ *ghazwīy*, Warlike, heroic, military.

P غزه *ghaza*, Noise, sound, clamour. The root of the tail. Rouge for the face. A wooden peg for uniting boards.

A غزيّ *ghuzza'*, (pl. of غازي) Warriors, generals.

A غزيّ *ghazīy*, Warriors. *Ghuzīy*, (pl. of غازي *ghāzī*) Warriors. Generals.

A غزيد *ghizyad*, Loud, sonorous. Tender, delicate (plant).

A غزير *ghazīr*, Copious, plentiful, ample; abounding in milk (cattle), water (a fountain), tears (eyes).

A غزيرة *ghazīrat*, (pl. غزار *ghizār*) (A camel) giving plenty of milk.

P غزيور *ghuzyūr*, A copper pan.

P غژ *ghaj*, Crawling on his posteriors (like a child).

P غژب *ghujb*, A grape-berry separated from the stalk. A grape-stone; also the skin of a grape. Anger. A cluster of dates. A cow's teat.

A غژغا *ghajghā*, (غژغاو *ghajghāw*, غژگا *ghajgā*,

or غژگاو *ghajgāw*) A sea-horse or cow, of the hair of whose tails they make little tufts to hang round the necks of horses, as well for ornament as to defend them from fascinating eyes. A sort of ox found on the mountains of Tibet.

P غژك *ghijak*, A lute, harp, kind of violin.

P غژم *ghujm*, A grape-stone or seed. Anger, rage. Hatred. Vindictiveness. A wart.

P غژوليدن *ghujūlīdan*, To be diligent, attentive, to make haste. To make one industrious. To break wind.

P غژيدن *ghajīdan*, To accumulate, pile up, story upon story. To be heaped one upon another. To pick, gather. To be demolished. To hitch forward or backward on the buttocks (as children or cripples).

P غژيده *ghajīda*, Stuck together.

A غسّ *ghass*, (v. n. of غسّ) Entering into and travelling over (a country). Eating, being fed. Accusing, reproaching. Driving away a cat by saying غسّ غسّ *ghass ghass*. Plunging (into water). *Ghuss*, A worthless man or men; weak, languid.

P غسا *ghasā*, An unripe date.

A غساة *ghasāt*, (pl. غسيٌ *ghasa'* or غسيات *ghasayāt*) An unripe date.

A غساس *ghusās*, A disease incident to camels.

A غساق *ghasāk*, (also غسّاق *ghassāk*) A cold, clammy, fetid humour, such as they suppose flows from the damned. Any thing cold and stinking.

P غساك *ghasāk*, Ivy.

A غسّال *ghassāl*, A washer. One whose business is to wash the bodies of the dead.

A غسالة *ghusālat*, Water with which any thing has been washed, dirty water. Water which has dropped, trickled, or oozed out. Filth which is washed out or from off any thing. Bathing. Washed (garment).

P غسّال خانه *ghassāl-khāna*, The house in which the bodies of the dead are washed. A wash-house.

A غسالي *ghasālā'*, (pl. of غسيلة) Washed.

A غسان *ghisān*, A leathern dress worn by boys. *Ghusān*, The deepest recesses of the heart.

A غسّان *ghassān*, The impetuosity of youth. Sort, kind. Men, people. Name of a tribe from which sprang kings in Yaman.

A غسّاني *ghassāniy*, Very beautiful, handsome.

A غسر *ghasr*, (v. n. of غسر) Covering the female when she was not in heat (a camel). A dunning, harassing of a debtor. *Ghasar*, Whatever is blown into a pond. *Ghasir*, Dark, intricate (business).

A غسغسة *ghasghasat*, (v. n. of غسغس Q) Driving away (a cat) by saying غسّ غسّ *ghass ghass*.

A غسف *ghasaf*, Darkness.

A غسق *ghash*, (v. n. of غسق) Being dark (night). Dropping rain (the sky). Flowing from the udder (milk). *Ghasak*, (v. n. of غسق) Becoming dark (the night). Darkness, especially at the beginning of the night, just after twilight. Tares, darnel.

A غسقان *ghasakān*, (v. n. of غسق) Becoming dark (the night). Emitting a yellow matter (a wound). Being dim and watery (the eye). Dropping down rain (the sky). Flowing from the udder (milk). The flowing of water and the like.

P غسك *ghasak*, A bug.

A غسك *ghasak*, Darkness at night-fall.

P غسل *ghasl*, Marshmallows.

A غسل *ghasl*, (v. n. of غسل) Washing, performing ablutions. Enfeebling with pains or stripes. Pouring down sweat (a horse). Cohabiting much (a man), or covering frequently (a stallion), in vain. *Ghisl* or *ghusal*, Whatever is used for washing the head, as water, in which is infused marshmallows or myrtle-leaves. (A man or horse) making frequent but ineffectual efforts to impregnate. *Ghusl* or *ghusul*, A washing, an ablution (especially of the whole body after connubial intercourse or any ceremonial uncleanness). غسل صحّت *ghusuli sihhat*, The first bathing after sickness. P غسل دادن *ghusl dādan*, To wash. غسل كردن *ghusul kardan*, To bathe.

A غسلاء *ghusalā*, (pl. of غسيل *ghasīl*) Washed.

A غسلبة *ghaslabat*, The removing, drawing, or tearing of a thing from any one.

A غسلة *ghislat*, Whatever is employed for washing the head, as water, in which is infused marshmallows or leaves of myrtle. Perfumes with which a woman sprinkles her hair whilst combing. ابو غسلة *abū ghislat*, The wolf. *Ghusalat*, A stallion which covers, or a man who cohabits much, in vain.

P غسلج *ghaslaj*, Pearl-ashes, lye.

A غسلج *ghaslaj*, The plant بنج *banj* (the black kind). One affair intervening between two. *Ghaslaj*, (or غسلّج *ghasallaj*) Insipid (meat or drink).

P غسل خانه *ghusul-khāna*, A bath, bagnio.

A غسلي *ghasla'*, (pl. of غسيل *ghasīl*) Washed. (fem. of غسيل *ghasīl*) (pl. غسالي *ghusāla'*) Washed.

A غسلين *ghislīn*, Washed (garment). Water, blood, and matter, supposed by the Muhammadans to run from the skin and flesh of the damned. Intense heat. Name of an infernal tree. Very hot.

A غسم *ghasam*, (v. n. of غسم) Being dark, obscure (the night). Dust. Darkness. Confusion in a speech. *Ghusam*, Bits of clouds.

A غسن *ghasn*, Mastication. *Ghusn*, Weak, soft, or flaccid. *Ghusan*, (pl. of غسنة *ghusnat* and غسناة *ghusnāt*) Ringlets, locks (hanging over the forehead or from the mane).

A غسنبة *ghasnabat*, A putting (water) in motion.

A غسنة *ghusnat*, (and غسناة *ghusnāt*) (pl. غسن *ghusan*) A ringlet, a lock hanging over the forehead or from the mane.

A غسوّ *ghusūw*, (v. n. of غسا for غسو) Becoming dark (night). Being frail, decrepit (an old man).

A غسوة *ghaswat*, The fruit of the lote-tree.

A غسوس *ghasūs*, Food of any kind. غسوس صدق *ghasūsu sidkin*, Real, substantial food.

A غسوق *ghusūk*, (v. n. of غسق) Being dark (night). Being dim and shedding tears (the eye).

A غسول *ghasūl*, (or غسّول *ghassūl*) Any thing for washing the hands (as water, soap, mallows, &c.).

A غسولة *ghaswalat*, A stirring up (of water).

A غسويل *ghaswīl*, A plant found in salt land.

A غسي *ghasy*, (v. n. of غسي) Being dark. *Ghasa'*, (and غسيات *ghasayāt*) (pl. of غساة *ghasāt*) Unripe dates.

A غسيس *ghasīs*, New-gathered but spoilt dates.

A غسيل *ghasīl*, (pl. غسلي *ghasla'* and غسلاء *ghusalā*) Washed. Purified. *Ghasīl*, (or غسّيل *ghissīl*) A stallion which covers often, but in vain.

A غسيلة *ghasīlat*, (pl. غسالي) Washed (woman).

P غش *ghash*, Longing (as a pregnant woman). A slight repose, slumber. Astonished. Stupor, fainting. Wheeling round (as a horse).

A غشّ *ghashsh*, (v. n. of غشّ) Dissembling, deceiving by false pretences, beguiling by pretended friendship, giving treacherous advice. Adulterating. Overlaying with a thin coat of base metal. (A man) with a large navel. *Ghishsh*, Fraud, vice, treachery, dissimulation; hatred. *Ghushsh*, (pl. غشّون) A deceiver, traitor. Weak. An adulterer.

A غشاء *ghishā*, The pericardium. The covering of a sword or saddle. The membrane of the brain. A pericarp.

A غشارب *ghushārib*, Bold, brisk, alert.

A غشاش *ghishāsh*, Beginning and end of darkness. (Drink) small in quantity, doing little good.

A غشاشا *ghashāshan* or *ghishāshan*, About sunset, or at night. Suddenly, unexpectedly.

P غشاك *ghashāk*, Fetid breath. The mouth.

A غشامر *ghashāmir*, (pl. of غشمرة *ghashmarat*) Oppressions. Voices, noises.

A غشانة *ghushānat*, A tree shot up again after having been cut to the root. Single dates gathered from the branches after the clusters are cut off.

A غشاوة *gha, ghi*, or *ghushāwat*, A veil, covering. A dimness in the eye-sight, purblindness.

A غشاية *ghi* or *ghushāyat*, A veil, covering.

A غشب *ghashb*, Iniquity, injury.

P غشتة *ghashta* or *ghishta*, Mixed. Moistened. Smeared, soiled. Brackish, sterile ground.

A غشرّب *ghasharrab*, A lion.

A غشش *ghashash*, Not clear, turbid, mixed.

A غشفل *ghashfal*, A fox.

A غشق *ghashk*, The striking of any thing soft (as flesh).

A غشم *ghashm*, Iniquity, injury. *Ghasham*, (v. n. of غشم) Leaving no place unanointed with pitch, whether sound or unsound. Cutting wood hastily (especially at night, without considering quantity or quality, whether dry or green).

A غشمرة *ghashmarat*, (v. n. of غشمر Q) Coming down, advancing (as a torrent or night). Injuring, defrauding. An accident, an event unexpected, or without stability and permanency. (pl. غشامر *ghashāmir*) Injustice, violence. A voice, cry.

(A man's) running heedlessly and at random into a business without caring if it be right or wrong.

A غشمريّة *ghashmariyat*, Injustice, oppression.

A غشمشم *ghashamsham*, Intrepid, steady. Persevering, constant: obstinate, headstrong, self-opiniated.

A غشمشمة *ghashamshamat*, (or غشمشميّة *ghashamshamiyat*) Boldness, daring. Talent, ability.

A غشمير *ghishmir*, Violence; force, strength.

A غشن *ghashn*, A striking (with a sword or stick).

A غشو *ghashw*, (v. n. of غشا for غشو) Approaching, drawing near. The fruit of the lote-tree.

A غشواء *ghashwā*, (fem. of اغشي *aghsha'*) White-headed (mare or goat). Name of a mare.

A غشوة *gha, ghi,* or *ghushwat*, A veil.

A غشوم *ghashūm*, Iniquitous (man). War. سلطان غشوم خير من فتنة تدوم *sultān ghashūm khayr min fitnat tadūm*, An oppressive ruler is preferable to perpetual anarchy.

A غشّون *ghushshūn*, (pl. of غشّ *ghushsh*) Weak. Worthless. Deceitful, treacherous.

P غشه *ghishih*, Leaves of reeds.

A غشي *ghashy*, (v. n. of غشي) Being stupefied, fainting. Surprising, coming unawares, rushing upon. Lying with. Striking with a scourge.

A غشيان *ghishyān*, (v. n. of غشي) Coming unawares, rushing on. Striking. Lying with. *Ghashayān*, (v. n. of غشي) Fainting, losing one's senses.

A غشية *ghashyat*, A fainting fit, swoon. *Ghushyat*, A veil.

A غشيم *ghashīm*, Simple, easily imposed upon.

A غصّان *ghassān*, Choked (with meat or drink), or any thing sticking in the throat.

A غصب *ghasb*, (v. n. of غصب) Seizing violently, ravishing, sacking, plundering; compelling one to do any thing. Pulling the hair or wool from a hide without tanning. Any thing taken by force. (in law) The taking the property of another which is valuable and sacred, without the consent of the proprietor, in such a manner as to destroy the proprietor's possession of it.

A غصّة *ghussat*, (pl. غصص *ghusas*) Strangulation, suffocation. A choking affliction, grief, anguish, passion, sorrow, or sadness. Any thing sticking crosswise in the throat. ذو الغصّة *zū'l ghussat*, Name of Husayn Ibn Yazid (so called from an obstruction in his throat which prevented him from speaking clearly).

A غصص *ghasas*, (v. n. of غصّ) Having food sticking in the throat. Sticking in the throat (meat). *Ghusas*, (pl. of غصّة *ghussat*) Griefs, sorrows.

A غصغص *ghasghas*, Name of a plant.

A غصلب *ghuslub*, A tall, slim, loosely-built, shambling fellow.

A غصلجة *ghaslajat*, (v. n. of غصلج Q) Dressing meat insufficiently, and without salt or pot-herbs.

A غصلقة *ghaslakat*, A not seasoning, salting, or dressing properly (meat).

A غصن *ghasn*, (v. n. of غصن) Taking and cutting off. Repelling, restraining, averting. Having many berries (a cluster of grapes). Pulling (a branch) towards one's self. *Ghusn*, (pl. غصون *ghusūn*, غصنة *ghisnat*, and اغصان *aghsān*) A branch, especially one branch growing out of another.

A غصنة *ghisnat*, (pl. of غصن *ghusn*) Branches. *Ghusnat*, A twig, wand.

A غصون *ghusūn*, (pl. of غصن *ghusn*) Branches.

P غصّه دار *ghussa-dār*, Angry, choking with rage.

P غصّه ناك *ghussanāk*, Afflicted. Passionate.

A غضّ *ghazz*, (v. n. of غضّ) Casting down (the eyes), lowering (the voice). Being broken without separation (a branch). Enduring any thing disagreeable. Lessening, taking away a part. Breaking partially (a branch). Fresh, new, tender, smiling; full of vigour (youth). The tender buds of palm-trees. (pl. غضاض *ghizāz*) The young offspring of kine. غضّ الطرف *ghazzu't tarf*, Patience under any thing odious and disagreeable.

A غضا *ghaza'*, (v. n. of غضي) Being griped through eating of the tree غضاة *ghazāt* (camels). Name of a country. A forest. A kind of tree. اهل الغضا *ahlu'l ghaza'*, The inhabitants of Najd.

A غضاب *ghizāb*, (v. n. of غضب) Being afflicted with small-pox. Any mote in the eye. The small-pox. (pl. of غضبان *ghazbān*) Angry, passionate.

A غضابر *ghuzābir*, Hard, thick.

A غضابي *ghazāba'* or *ghuzāba'*, (pl. of غضبان *ghazbān*) Enraged, wrathful, passionate, choleric.

A غضابيّ *ghuzābiy*, Gloomy, saturnine, unsocial.

A غضاة *ghazāt*, (pl. غضا *ghaza'*) A kind of tree.

A غضار *ghazār*, Pure, adhesive, and greenish clay. A bit of earthenware carried about one to ward off the influence of evil eyes.

A غضارب *ghuzārib*, Full of herbage and water.

A غضارة *ghazārat*, Affluence, abundance, comfort, happiness. Pure, adhesive, and greenish clay. The female of the bird قطا *katā*.

A غضاريف *ghazārif*, (pl. of غضروف) Gristles.

A غضاض *ghazāz* and *ghuzāz*, The space between the eyebrows. The nose. The part of the face which joins the nose. The part between the nose and the root of the forelocks. *Ghazāz*, (*ghizāz*, and غضاضة *ghazāzat*) (v. n. of غضّ) Enduring any thing disagreeable. Breaking partially (a branch). Casting down (the eye). Lessening, taking away a part. *Ghizāz*, (pl. of غضّ *ghazz*) The young of cows.

A غضاضة *ghazāzat*, (v. n. of غضّ) Being fresh, vigorous (youth). Harm, injury, loss, detriment. Defect, deficiency. A mean, base condition, baseness.

A غضافر *ghuzāfir*, A lion.

P غضان *gha* or *ghuzān*, Orts, broken victuals.

A غضان *ghizān*, Abortion, miscarriage of a camel.

A غضايا *ghazāya'*, (pl. of غضية *ghaziyat*) (She-camels) griped from browsing too freely on the غضاة.

A غضاية *ghazāyat*, A herd of choice camels.

A غضب *ghazb*, Extremely red. A bull. A lion. Stoniness. *Ghazab*, (v. n. of غضب) Being angry or in a rage. Rage, anger, ire, wrath. غضب الله *ghazabu'llāh*, The wrath of God. *Ghazib*, Angry, wrathful, irate, passionate. Oppressive.

A غضبّ *ghuzubb*, Very angry, irate, choleric.

A غضبا *ghazaban*, In a rage.

P غضبان *ghazbān*, A stone hurled by a battering-ram. A balista. غضبان فلك *ghazbāni falak*, The sun. Mars.

A غضبان *ghazbān*, (fem. غضبانة) (pl. غضاب *ghizāb*, غضابي *ghazāba'*, or *ghuzāba'*) Enraged.

A غضبانة *ghazbānat*, Angry (woman).

A غضبة *ghazbat*, The skin of an old mountain-goat; a shield made of it. Hard, rocky, stony. The skin of the head or of a fish; also that between the horns of a bull. A pimple on the upper eye-lid (from the birth). One scurf or incrustation (as of small-pox on the skin).

A غضبّة *ghazubbat, ghuzubbat,* and *ghazabbat*, Prone to anger, passionate (man).

A غضبر *ghuzabir*, Hard and thick.

P غضبناك *ghazabnāk*, Enraged, angry.

A غضبي *ghazba'*, A herd of one hundred camels. (fem. of غضبان *ghazbān*) Angry (woman). (pl. of غضبان *ghazbān*) Angry (men).

A غضّة *ghuzzat*, Detriment. Diminution. A mean condition.

A غضر *ghazr*, (v. n. of غضر) Assigning to another part of one's estate. Bestowing plenty (God). Inclining to. Cutting, dividing. Declining, receding. Imprisoning, detaining, probibiting, preventing. *Ghazar*, (v. n. of غضر) Abounding in produce after having been in straits. غضر مضر *ghazir mazir*, Comfortable, easy (life). غضر الناصية *ghaziru'n nāsiyat*, Fortunate, favoured by fortune.

A غضراء *ghazrā*, Conveniency, happiness, comforts of life. Land wherein the palm-tree will not grow until it has been trenched. Good earth lying near water. Viscous and greenish earth. Ground possessing pure clay.

A غضرب *ghazrab*, Full of herbage and water.

A غضرة *ghazrat*, A sort of plant.

A غضرم *ghazram* or *ghizrim*, A place abounding in good soil. Red clay dry and cracked. Soft, adhesive (soil). Soft, mortary (place). Coarse, thick.

A غضروف *ghuzrūf*, Gristle, cartilage.

A غضريف *ghizrīf*, Jasmine.

A غضس *ghazas*, (in Yaman) Caraway-seed.

A غضغضة *ghazghazat*, (v. n. of غضغض Q) Lessening in quantity (water). Being lessened and diminished. Decrease, diminution.

A غضف *ghazf*, (v. n. of غضف) Breaking (wood). Letting (his) ears drop (a dog). Setting off to run (a she-ass). Farting (a she-ass). *Ghuzf*, A black kind of the bird قطا *katā*. (pl. of اغضف *agh-*

zaf) Bangle-eared (dogs). *Ghazaf*, (v.n. of غضف) Having pendulous, flagging ears, or letting his ears hang down (a dog). Being dark, dusky (night). An Indian palm-tree. Flabbiness (of the ear).

A غضفة *ghazafat*, (pl. غضف *ghuzf*) The bird قطا *katā*; also another bird. A hill, hillock, tumulus.

A غضفر *ghazfar*, Rough, cruel, coarse, unfeeling.

A غضفرة *ghazfarat*, The being heavy.

A غضن *ghazn*, (v. n. of غضن) Detaining, retaining, keeping back (a man). Bringing forth an abortion (a camel). غضن العين *ghaznu'l ʻayn*, The skin outside of the eye. *Ghazn* or *ghazan*, (pl. غضون *ghuzūn*) A wrinkle, plait, fold. Lassitude.

A غضنة *ghaznat*, One scurf or incrustation (as of small-pox).

A غضنفر *ghazanfar*, A lion. Coarse, strong-bodied. Injurious, cruel, unfeeling.

A غضوّ *ghuzūw*, (v. n. of غضا for غضو) Being silent. Being dark (night). Plenty, abundance.

A غضوب *ghazūb*, Enraged, choleric (man or woman). Wayward, dogged (woman or camel). A malignant serpent. A lion. A bull.

A غضور *ghazwar*, Viscous, adhesive clay. A kind of tree. Name of a well in the tribe of Tayy.

A غضوّر *ghazawwar*, A lion.

A غضورة *ghazwarat*, A being angry.

A غضوضة *ghuzūzat*, (v. n. of غض) Being fresh, vigorous (youth).

A غضون *ghuzūn*, (pl. of غضن *ghazan*) Wrinkles. Roots of the ears. في غضون ذلك *fi ghuzūni zālika*, In the meantime, then.

A غضويّ *ghazawiy*, Belonging to the herb غضاة.

A غضي *ghazy*, (v. n. of غضي) Being well-off, and able to maintain a family. *Ghaza'*, (v. n. of غضي) Being griped with eating of the tree غضا *ghaza'* (a camel). A forest. Name of a country. اهل الغضيٰ *ahlu'l ghaza'*, The inhabitants of نجد *najd*. ذباب الغضيٰ *zubābu'l ghaza'*, Sons of Kaab. *Ghazī*, (A camel) griped from eating غضاة *ghazāt*.

A غضياء *ghazyā*, (or غضيا *ghazya'*) (A country) abounding in the trees غضاة *ghazāt*.

A غضيانة *ghazyānat*, A troop of choice camels.

A غضية *ghaziyat*, (pl. غضايا *ghazāya'*) (A she-camel) griped with eating غضاة *ghazāt*.

A غضير *ghazīr*, Green, flourishing. Soft, tender, delicate.

A غضيرة *ghazīrat*, Soil containing pure mould.

A غضيض *ghazīz*, (pl. اغضة *aghizzat*) Deficient, diminished. Languid, weak, dim-sighted (eye). Mean, abject, submissive. Fresh, green. Tender buds of palm-trees. Deficiency, loss.

A غضيضة *ghazīzat*, Harm, hurt, injury. A mean condition. Defect, deficiency.

A غضيٰ *ghazya'*, A herd of a hundred camels.

A غطّ *ghatt*, (v. n. of غطّ) Plunging, ducking (any one) into water. Braying (a camel).

A غطاء *ghitā*, A covering, a veil.

A غطارس *ghatāris*, (pl. of غطرس *ghitris*) Proud, unjust, oppressive, tyrannical.

A غطارفة *ghatārifat*, (pl. of غطراف *ghitrāf* and غطريف *ghitrīf*) Illustrious princes, lords, chiefs.

A غطاريس *ghatārīs*, (pl. of غطريس *ghitrīs*) Proud, unjust, oppressive, tyrannical.

A غطاس *ghatiās*, A diver.

A غطاط *ghatāt*, A species of the bird قطا *katā*. *Ghatāt* or *ghutāt*, First dawn. *Ghitāt*, (v. n. 3 of غطّ) Ducking one another.

A غطاغط *ghatāghit*, (pl. of غطغط *ghutghut*) Ewe-lambs just dropt.

A غطامط *ghutāmit*, A heavy, rolling sea. The noise of boiling water or of the sea.

A غطاية *ghitāyat*, A kind of quilted stuff worn under a coat of mail; also by women to give them a protuberance round the hips.

A غطر *ghatr*, (v. n. of غطر) Swinging the arms. One who walks with a swinging or graceful air.

A غطراف *ghitrāf*, A great prince, lord, chief.

A غطرب *ghitrab*, A serpent.

A غطرس *ghitris*, (pl. غطارس *ghatāris*) Proud, unjust, oppressive, tyrannical.

A غطرسة *ghatrasat*, (v. n. of غطرس Q) Provoking to anger. Indulging in self-admiration. Being overbearing and insolent toward equals.

A غطرشة *ghatrashat*, (v. n. of غطرش Q) (The night) beclouding (the sight). Being dim (the eye-sight). Being proud and haughty.

A غطرفة *ghatrafat*, A being proud. Pride.

A غطروف *ghitrawf*, A clever, intelligent youth. *Ghitrawf* or *ghutrūf*, A handsome youth.

A غطريس *ghitrīs*, (pl. غطاريس *ghatārīs*) Proud, unjust, oppressive, tyrannical.

A غطريف *ghitrīf*, (pl. غطارفة *ghatārifat*) A great prince, young, liberal, and generous. A young hawk. A fly. Beautiful.

A غطس *ghats*, (v. n. of غطس) Plunging or throwing (into water). Immersing one's person. Drinking with the mouth (without using a vessel). غطس به اللجم *ghatasa bihi'l lujamu*, Death carried him off.

A غطش *ghatsh*, (v. n. of غطش) Walking slowly from disease or age. *Ghatash*, Weakness of sight attended with an incessant flux from the eye.

A غطشاء *ghatshā*, Weak-sighted (woman). *Ghatshā*, (or غطشيٰ *ghatsha'*) (A desert) without road or direction-post, blind (so to speak).

A غطشان *ghatashān*, (v. n. of غطش) Walking slowly from disease or age.

A غطغط *ghutghut*, (pl. غطاغط *ghatāghit*) A ewe-lamb just dropt. *Ghut*, A word used to excite a mob in an uproar.

A غطغطة *ghatghatat*, (v. n. of غطغط Q) Foaming (the sea). Boiling violently (a pot). Overcoming (as sleep). A cry like that of the قطا.

A غطف *ghataf*, Comforts (of life). Length and folding over of the eyelid. Hairiness of eyebrows.

A غطفان *ghatafān*, Name of a tribe.

A غطل *ghatl*, (v. n. of غطل) Being overcast with clouds, layer upon layer (the sky). *Ghatal*, (v. n. of غطل) Being intensely dark (the night).

A غطلّس *ghatallas*, (and ابو الغطلّس *abū'l ghatallas*) A wolf.

A غطمّ *ghitamm*, The great ocean. Vast, deep (sea). A large assembly or congregation. Liberal, munificent (man), of an open, generous disposition.

A غطماط *ghitmāt*, Dashing, rolling waves.

A غطمّش *ghatammash*, Dull-sighted. Unjust, violent, cruel, oppressive. The lion.

A غطمشة *ghatmashat*, A seizing by force.

A غطمطة *ghatmatat*, The dashing and agitation of the waves of the sea. The boiling of a pot. The noise of a torrent.

A غطمطم *ghatamtam*, Surgy (sea), vasty (deep).

A غطمطيط *ghatmatīt*, The noise of the sea, roar of the deep. A heavy, rolling sea.

A غطو *ghatw* or *ghutūw*, (v. n. of غطا for غطو) Being dark (the night). Rising, swelling (water). Hiding, covering, enveloping.

A غطوان *ghatawān*, Dignity. Abundance, wealth.

A غطوس *ghatūs*, Undaunted in battle or danger.

A غطومط *ghatawmat*, A heavy, rolling sea.

A غطي *ghaty* or *ghuty*, (v. n. of غطي) Being full of vigour (a youth). Being long and spreading on the ground (the branches of a tree). Hiding, covering. Enveloping in its darkness (the night). Existing or remaining (above any thing). Travelling well (a she-camel).

A غطيّر *ghit* or *ghutyarr*, A corpulent dwarf.

A غطيط *ghatīt*, (v. n. of غطّ) Braying (a camel). Snoring. The noise made in the throat when choking.

A غطيلة *ghatyalat*, (v. n. of غطيل Q) Being rich, keeping up a large establishment. Investing one's money in cattle. Being diffusive in conversation and raising the voice.

A غطيم *ghatīm*, The vast ocean, mighty deep.

P غف *ghaf*, A curling lock.

A غفّ *ghaff*, Dry leaves. *Ghuff*, Food sufficient for a day.

A غفاة *ghufāt*, Any white or pearly substance on the pupil of the eye.

A غفار *ghifār*, A helmet fitting the head. Name of the father of a tribe. *Ghufār*, Hairs on the legs, forehead, cheek, jaws, neck, or back of the neck.

A غفّار *ghaffār*, One who pardons greatly. غفّار الذنوب *ghaffāru'z zunūb*, The forgiver of sins (God). حضرت ملك الغفار *hazrati maliku'l ghaffār*, The most merciful God.

A غفارة *ghifārat*, A cloth worn under the veil or head-dress to keep them from being soiled by the perfumed unguent with which women anoint their hair. Mail, net steel-work worn under the cap to protect the head. A patch of cloth round the horns of a bow. One cloud overtopping another. The summit of a mountain.

A غفّان *ghiffān*, Time, convenient time, a proper season.

A غفّة *ghuffat*, A sufficiency to sustain life. A mouse. A hasty mouthful snatched by a camel.

P غفج *ghufj*, (or غفچ *ghufch*) A sword having an undulating surface. An anvil. A place full of caverns or of hollows, especially where water stagnates. Any thing long, straight, and thick.

P غفچي *ghafchī*, A low place where water collects. A shining sword.

A غفر *ghafr*, (v. n. of غفر) Covering. Laying up, enclosing in a case or in a repository. Tinging, dyeing (grey hairs). Pardoning (crimes). Relapsing (a sick person). Relapsing into melancholy (a lover). Rankling, growing raw (a wound). Rendering the market cheap (the arrival of grain). Little hairs on the forehead or the thigh. Nap, shagginess of cloth. (pl. اغفار *aghfār*, غفرة *ghifarat*, and غفور *ghufūr*) The young of a mountain-goat. The belly. A bag, a sack, or any thing resembling it. A mansion of the moon, consisting of three small stars in Libra. *Ghifr*, A calf. A certain insect. *Ghufr*, A covering. (pl. اغفار *aghfār*, غفرة *ghifarat*, and غفور *ghufūr*) The young of a mountain-goat. (pl. of غفور *ghafūr*) Forgivers, merciful. *Ghafar*, (v. n. of غفر) Relapsing (a sick person). Growing raw (a wound). Being hairy and shaggy (cloth). Hair on the lower jaw, on the back of the neck, and about the thighs of a woman. Shagginess of a garment, nap of cloth. The fifteenth mansion of the moon. Small, young grass. *Ghafir*, Hairy (nape of neck).

A غفران *ghufrān*, (v. n. of غفر) Covering over. Forgiving (sin). Pardon, remission, absolution. غفران كامل *ghufrān kāmil*, A plenary absolution. عليه الرحمة والغفران والرضوان *ʻalayhi'r rahmat wa'l ghufrān wa'r rizwān*, On him be (divine) mercy, and pardon, and complacency. P غفران پناه *ghufrān-panāh*, Asylum of pardon. Dead, defunct.

A غفرة *ghifrat*, (v. n. of غفر) Forgiving. Pardon, a formula of remission or absolution. A covering. Any thing worthy, suitable, and seemly for adorning or perfecting any business. *Ghafirat*, Hairy-faced, hairy-necked (woman). *Ghifarat*, (pl. of غفر *ghafr* or *ghufr*) Young mountain-goats.

A غفش *ghafash*, A winking, twinkling of the eyes. Dirt in the eye.

A غفق *ghafk*, (v. n. of غفق) Coming every hour to water (camels). Striking often (with a scourge). Approaching (the female) frequently (an ass). Emitting an odour. A gentle rain. An assault, a sudden attack. A sudden return from an absence.

A غفقة *ghafkat*, One sleep, a slumber.

A غفل *ghufl*, (pl. اغفال *aghfāl*) A desert without roads or direction-posts; a place naked, without the vestige of habitations or people. One from whom no good is expected or evil feared. An ignorant, inexperienced (man). A man without rank or character. Anonymous (poet). (Verses) of an unknown author. A blank (in a lottery). A camel without milk. Unmarked (cattle or arrow). Camels' hair. *Ghafal*, Carelessness, negligence, inadvertency. Comfort, abundance. High. Much.

A غفلان *ghaflān*, Inconsiderate, incautious. *Ghuflān*, Negligence, carelessness, inadvertency.

A غفلة *ghaflat*, (v. n. of غفل) Doing (any thing) inconsiderately. Forgetting. Neglecting, overslipping. Leaving (a beast) unbranded. Imprudence, carelessness, negligence, indolence, forgetfulness, inadvertency. *Ghaflatan*, Imprudently, inconsiderately. Unexpectedly, unawares.

P غفلت ورز *ghaflat-warz*, Negligent, careless. Uninformed. غفلت ورزي *ghaflat-warzī*, Negligence, carelessness, imprudence.

A غفلّقة *ghafallakat*, A lazy woman speaking ill.

A غفو *ghafw*, High ground where water does not reach. A pit dug for a lion. *Ghafw*, (or غفوّ *ghufūw*) (v. n. of غفا for غفو) Sleeping, slumbering. Floating or swimming (upon water).

A غفوة *ghafwat*, High ground where water does not reach. A pit dug for a lion.

P غفوده *ghufūda*, A week, se'nnight, hebdomad.

A غفور *ghafūr*, (pl. غفر *ghufr*) Forgiving, merciful, clement. A name of God. ربّ غفور *rabb ghafūr*, Most merciful God. *Ghufūr*, (v. n. of غفر) Forgiving, pardoning, condoning, absolving. (pl. of غفر *ghafr*) The young of mountain-goats.

A غفول *ghafūl*, A she-camel which shies not at any thing. *Ghufūl*, (v. n. of غفل) Neglecting, forgetting, leaving. Imprudence, heedlessness.

P غفه *ghufa* or *ghuffa*, A lamb's skin; a curled sheep-skin.

A غفى *ghafa'*, (v. n. of غفي) Cleaning (grain) from tares, darnel, or chaff. Chaff, tares, and refuse of corn when winnowed. Rubbish carried down by a stream. Refuse of camels. A kind of disease or blight incident to palm-trees, which prevents the dates from ripening. Grains of corn which drop from the ear, sheddings of grain.

A غفية *ghafyat*, (v. n. of غفي) Sleeping, slumbering. High ground where water does not reach. A pit dug for a lion.

A غفير *ghafīr*, (v. n. of غفر) Pardoning. All, many. Hairs on the jaws and back of the neck. الجمّاء الغفير *al jammāʼu'l ghafīr*, A helmet which completely encloses the head. جاؤا جمّا غفيرا *jāʼū jamman ghafīran*, جمّاء غفيرا *jammāʼa ghafīran*, جمّ الغفير *jamma'l ghafīri*, جمّاء الغفير *jammāʼa'l ghafīri*, الجمّاء الغفير *al jammāʼa'l ghafīra*, جمّاء الغفيري *jammāʼa'l ghafīra'*, جمّ الغفيرة *jamma'l ghafīrati*, جمّاء الغفيرة *jammāʼa'l ghafīrati*, الجمّاء الغفيرة *al jammāʼa'l ghafīrata*, جمّاء غفيرة *jammāʼ ghafīratan*, الجمّ الغفير *al jamma'l ghafīra*, بجمّا الغفير *bi jammā'l ghafīri*, or غفيرة *ghafīratin*, All came, none excepted, noble and plebeian.

A غفيرة *ghafīrat*, (v. n. of غفر) Pardoning. Any thing worthy, suitable, and seemly for adorning or perfecting. A covering of faults, forgiveness.

A غفيفة *ghafīfat*, A garden green with herbs.

A غقّ *ghakk*, The hoarse croak of a raven. *Ghakk*, (and غقيق *ghakīk*) (v. n. of غقّ) Screaming (a hawk). Boiling and making a noise (pitch). The noise made by water when passing from a wide into a narrow place.

A غق غق *ghik ghik*, Noise (of water) boiling.

A غقغقة *ghakghakat*, Chattering of a hawk.

A غققة *ghakakat*, Mountain-swallows.

P غك *ghak*, Fat and dwarfish; ludicrous.

P غكه *ghuka*, A hiccough.

P غل *ghul*, A saw. A yoke. A mountain-demon. (for غلغل *ghulghul*) Tumult. غل غدر *ghul ghadar*, Noise and tumult.

A غلّ *ghall*, (v. n. of غلّ) Suffering extremely from thirst. Mixing bruised date-stones with clover as food for camels. Being introduced, entering. Greasing the roots of the hair. Turning away from looking straight (the eye). Flowing amongst trees (water). Hurting in the viscera. Putting on an under-waistcoat. Yielding a revenue (an estate). Handcuffing, manacling, or fettering. Putting a chain round the neck. *Ghill*, (v. n. of غل) Fostering enmity, cherishing malevolence in the heart, being faithless, perfidious. Hatred, malice, envy, malevolence, perfidy, fraud, treachery. غلّ وغشّ *ghill u ghishsh*, Oppression. Objection, hesitation. P بي غل *bī ghill*, Without guile. A *Ghull*, Extreme thirst, the burning heat of thirst. (pl. اغلال *aghlāl*) A yoke (for oxen); the pillory (for men); a collar or any thing put round the neck (of iron, wood, or undressed leather). A fetter, chain. غلّ قمل *ghull kamil*, Handcuffs and lice, (a proverb denoting) an ill-tempered woman. ما له غلّ و ال *mā lahu ghullun wa ullun*, May he possess nothing at all! (an imprecation).

A غلاء *ghalāʼ*, (v. n. of غلي) Being dear or high-priced. Scarcity, dearness. (A man) who shoots an arrow with force. (pl. اغلية *aghliyat*) Name of a short-bodied fish. بالغلاء *bi'l ghalāʼ*, Dearly (I sold it). *Ghilāʼ*, (v. n. 3 of غلي) Bidding against, raising the price upon another. Shooting (an arrow) with all one's might. (pl. of غلوة *ghalwat*) Arrow-shots discharged as far as possible.

A غلاب *ghilāb*, (v. n. 3 of غلب) Contending mutually for victory or superiority. Prevailing against, overpowering.

A غلّاب *ghallāb*, One who conquers often.

A غلابية *ghalābiyat*, Power which subjugates.

A غلاة *ghulāt*, (pl. of غالي *ghālī*) Those who exceed all reasonable bounds, zealots.

A غلّات *ghallāt*, (pl. of غلّة) All sorts of grain.

A غلاصيم *ghalāṣīm*, The parts about the throat.

A غلاط *ghilāt*, (v. n. 3 of غلط) Throwing into confusion. Leading each other into error.

A غلاظ *ghilāz*, (pl. of غليظ *ghalīz*) Coarse, thick, gross. *Ghulāz*, Thick, rough, rude.

A غلاظة *ghilāzat*, Thickness, spissitude, grossness. Hardness, roughness. Rudeness. Valour.

A غلاف *ghilāf*, (pl. غلف *ghulf*, *ghuluf*, and غلّف *ghullaf*) The sheath of a sword or knife. A slip, a cover. The cover of a flask. The foreskin. P غلاف دل *ghilāfi dil*, (A غلاف القلب *ghilāfu'l kalb*) The pericardium.

A غلافيّ *ghilāfiy*, Testaceous (fish).

A غلال *ghulāl*, (pl. of غليل *ghalīl*) Thirsty. Low or level grounds producing the trees غلّان *ghullān*.

A غلالة *ghalālat*, A certain disease incident to sheep. *Ghilālat*, An under-waistcoat. A cushion, or any thing similar, with which women shew a false prominency about the hips. A pin or stud for uniting the rings of a coat of mail.

P غلاله *ghilāla*, Grease at the roots of the hair. Running water at the roots of trees. Error, deviation from the right road. *Ghulāla*, Curls, ringlets.

A غلام *ghulām*, (pl. اغلمة *aghlimat*, غلمة *ghilmat*, and غلمان *ghilmān*) A boy, lad, youth, one whose mustachios begin to grow: adolescent, pubescent. A servant, slave. Of full age. P غلام فلکم *ghulāmi falakam*, The termination of any affair in a manner contrary to one's wishes.

P غلام بارگي *ghulām-bāragī*, Pederasty.

P غلام باره *ghulām-bāra*, A sodomite.

A غلامة *ghulāmat*, A servant-girl, female slave.

P غلام گردش *ghulām-gardish*, A sitting-room for servants, a servants' hall.

P غلامي *ghulāmī*, Belonging to a servant. Servitude, slavery. A sodomite.

A غلاميّ *ghulāmīy*, Youth-like.

A غلاميّة *ghulāmīyat*, Youth, boyhood. Adolescence, pubescence.

A غلّان *ghallān*, Thirsty (camel). *Ghullān*, (pl. of غالّ *ghāll*) Certain plants. Low or level grounds producing these plants.

A غلانية *ghalāniyat*, An exceeding of bounds in any thing. Dearness. Ebullition.

A غلائل *ghalā,il*, (pl. of غليل *ghalīl*) Low, level grounds producing the trees *ghullān*. (pl. of غليلة *ghalīlat*) Coats of mail. Studs by which the rings are fastened. Quiltings under coats of mail.

A غلب *ghalb* or *ghalab*, (v. n. of غلب) Conquering, excelling. Prevailing. Victory, dominion, power. *Ghulb*, (pl. of اغلب *aghlab*) Thickly-planted (orchards). *Ghalab*, (v. n. of غلب) Being thick-necked.

A غلباء *ghalbā,*, (fem. of اغلب *aghlab*) Thick-necked. Noble and powerful (tribe). High (dignity). Lofty, high (hill). Thickly-set (orchard).

A غلبة *ghalabat*, Victory, conquest, superiority, assault, strength, power, dominion, prevalence, predominance. A multitude. Copiousness, abundance.

A غلبّة *ghalabbat* or *ghulubbat*, Victory. *Ghulubbat*, Easily provoked, soon in a passion.

P غلبکن *ghalbakan*, (or غلبکين *ghalbakīn*) A latticed door. A garden-door behind which they sit.

P غلبگي *ghalabagī*, Victory.

P غلبه *ghulba*, (or غلپه *ghulpa*) A magpie.

A غلبّى *ghulubba'* or *ghilibba'*, Victory, conquest.

P غلبيز *ghalbīz*, A sieve.

A غلّة *ghallat*, (pl. غلّات *ghallāt*) Corn, grain, fruits, harvest, produce. The return of an estate, rent, income. Wages. *Ghullat*, Excessive thirst: also its burning heat. An under-waistcoat.

P غلت *ghalt*, A rolling, tossing, wallowing.

A غلت *ghult*, (v. n. of غلت) Breaking a bargain, declining to buy. *Ghalat*, Error (in calculation).

P غلتان *ghaltān*, Any thing round. A pearl.

P غلتانيدن *ghaltānīdan*, To cause to roll.

P غلتبان *ghaltbān* or *ghaltabān*, A roller for smoothing the flat roofs of houses. A man who keeps a mistress or connives at the infidelity of his wife.

A غلتة *ghaltat*, Beginning of night. *Ghultat*, An error in calculation.

P غلتک *ghaltak*, (or غلتنک *ghaltanak*) A carriage-wheel. The pulley of a well.

P غلته *ghalta* or *ghulta*, A rolling-pin.

P غلتيدن *ghaltīdan*, To tumble, wallow, roll.

A غلث *ghals*, (v. n. of غلث) Mixing wheat with barley; eating them, or bread made of that composition. Not striking fire (the stick زند *zand*). Tanning (a leathern bottle) with the plant ارطى *arta'*. *Ghalas*, (v. n. of غلث) Fighting hand to hand. Sticking close to the enemy. Failing to emit fire (the stick زند *zand*). Thick of the fight, brunt of the battle. *Ghalis*, Fighting fiercely, hand to hand. One who exhales a smell of meat or of drink. Staggering, waving from side to side from drowsiness. Insane.

A غلثى *ghalsa'*, A certain bitter tree.

A غلج *ghalj*, (v. n. of غلج) Running well (as a horse), with an even pace. *Ghuluj*, Beautiful youth.

P غلج *ghilj* or *ghilaj*, (غلچ *ghilch* or *ghilach*) A knot which cannot be unloosed.

P غلچه *ghalcha*, A villager. A vagabond, strolling fellow. A rustic, peasant. A wandering soldier.

A غلس *ghalas*, (pl. اغلاس *aghlās*) The darkness before the dawn, cock-crowing. بغلس *bi ghalasin*, Before day-break.

A غلص *ghals*, A cutting or seizing by the throat.

A غلصمة *ghalsamat*, The top of the windpipe, root of the tongue; the fleshy part between the head and neck. A cutting or seizing by the throat. Princes. An assembly, multitude, crowd. Number or nobility.

A غلط *ghalat*, (v. n. of غلط) Blundering in speaking. Making an error in an account. Error, blunder, solecism, barbarism (in speech). غلط العامّ *ghalatu'l ꜥāmm*, A popular mistake, a vulgar error. غلط مشهور *ghalati mashhūr*, A received abuse, an idiomatical expression, or mode of speech currently used, though erroneous.

P غلطان *ghaltān*, Rolling, wallowing. Any thing round. A pearl. غلطان پيچان *ghaltan-pechān*, Wallowing, rolling, foundering.

P غلطک *ghaltak*, A wheel. A roller. A pulley.

P غلط گو *ghulat-go* or *ghalat-gū*, A false relater.

P غلط گوئي *ghalat-go,ī*, Relation of falsehoods.

P غلط نويس *ghalat-navīs*, An erroneous writer.

A غلطي *ghalatī*, A mistake, error.

P غلطيدن *ghaltīdan*, To roll, wallow.

A غلظ *ghalz*, Rough, rocky ground. *Ghilaz*, (v. n. of غلظ) Being thick (the body or a humour), coarse (cloth or fare), rocky (the ground). Swelling with grains (an ear of corn). Thickness, coarseness.

A غلظة *ghal, ghil*, or *ghulzat*, Thickness, grossness, rudeness, asperity. *Ghilzat*, Enmity, hostility.

P غلغج *ghilghij*, A yellowish bee. A tickling.

P غلغل *ghulghul*, Tumult, confusion, contest. Vociferation, clamour. The chirping of birds. The noise made by liquor when decanting out of a narrow-necked vessel. غلغل تهليل وتکبير *ghulghuli tahlīl u takbīr*, The resounding noise made by the Muhammadan armies when pronouncing aloud, before an engagement, الله الله *allāh allāh*, or الله اکبر *allāh akbar*, Great God!

P غلغلاج *ghulghalāj*, Throwing any thing violently into the air.

A غلغلة *ghalghalat*, (v. n. of غلغل Q) Being introduced. Haste. A quick pace. A bringing in.

P غلغله *ghulghula*, Riot, uproar. A kind of dish. غلغلهٔ غمزه *ghulghula,i ghamza*, A wink of the eye.

P غلغليچ *ghalghalīch*, (*ghilghilīch*, or غلغليچه *ghalghalīcha*) Tickling, titillation.

P غلغونه *ghulghūna*, Paint for the face.

A غلف *ghalf*, (v. n. of غلف) Putting up (a glass or flask) into (its) case. Perfuming (the hair or beard) with civet. Name of a tree with which they tan or dress hides. *Ghulf*, (pl. of اغلف *aghlaf*) Uncircumcised. قلوب غلف *kulūbun ghulfun*, Hearts uncircumcised. *Ghulf* and *ghuluf*, (pl. of غلاف *ghilāf*) Sheaths. *Ghalaf*, Uncircumcision.

A غلّف *ghullaf*, (pl. of غلاف *ghilāf*) Sheaths.

A غلفاء *ghalfā,*, (fem. of اغلف *aghlaf*) Uncircumcised. Cased, sheathed (bow). Fruitful (year). Uncropped, ungrazed (field).

A غلفاق *ghilfāk*, (A woman) who walks fast. Tall (woman).

A غلفة *ghulfat*, The prepuce, foreskin.

P غلفچ *ghalafch*, (*ghalfach*, or غلفج *ghalafj*) A hornet, wasp. A bee. A leech.

A غلفق *ghalfak*, Water-moss; a broad-leafed water-herb. Delicate, agreeable, easy (life). Relaxed, unstrung (bow). The fibrous wood of a palm-tree. Unskilful, foolish (woman) in conversation or at work. The leaf of a vine whilst on the tree.

A غلفقة *ghalfakat*, (v. n. of غلفق Q) Becoming poor and straitened. Talking badly.

A غلق *ghalk*, (v. n. of غلق) Shutting, closing, bolting, or locking (a door). Travelling far into a country. Large, lean, and red (man or camel). A bolt, bar, lock, chain, or any fastening of a door. *Ghalak*, (v. n. of غلق) Being dangerously galled on the back from overloading. Belonging of right to the pawnee if not redeemed within a given time (a pledge). Being full of worms, and consequently unfruitful (a palm-tree). Sticking fast. Perishing. A bolt, bar, or lock. *Ghalik*, Difficult to be comprehended (speech). *Ghuluk*, Shut, fastened (door).

P غلقا *ghalkā*, A plant resembling capers, but which contains a milky poisonous juice.

A غلقة *ghalkat*, (*ghilkat* or غلقى *ghalka'*) A bitter Arabian shrub used in tanning; one with which the Ethiopians poison their arrows.

P غلّك *ghullak*, A jar used as a till or save-all.

A غلل *ghalal*, (v. n. of غلّ) Being thirsty. Drinking, but not sufficiently (camels). (pl. اغلال *aghlāl*) Water flowing amongst trees. Water not flowing, but one while visible, at other times hid from view. A colander. The burning heat of excessive thirst. Excessive thirst. A disease incident to sheep.

A غلم *ghalm*, (v. n. of غلم) Being lustful; lust. *Ghalim*, Lustful, libidinous, salacious.

A غلمان *ghilmān*, (pl. of غلام *ghulām*) Boys, youths, lads. Servants. غلمان و جواري *ghilmān u jawārī*, Boys and girls, lads and lasses.

A غلمة *ghilmat*, (pl. of غلام *ghulām*) Boys. *Ghulmat*, (v. n. of غلم) Being libidinous. Lust. *Ghalimat*, Lascivious, lustful (woman).

P غلمچ *ghalmach*, (or غلمليچ *ghalmalīch*) A tickling under the arm-pits. غلمچ دادن *ghalmach dādan*, (or غلمليچ دادن *ghalmalīch dādan*) To tickle under the arms.

P غلمشك *ghalmashak*, A harsh, rough, or perverse fellow.

A غلن *ghaln*, (v. n. of غلن) Outstepping bounds (youth). Being quick and hasty.

P غل نهاده *ghul-nihāda*, Pilloried; in the stocks.

A غلو *ghalw*, (v. n. of غلا for غلو) Flying high and overshooting the mark (an arrow). Shooting an arrow with the greatest force. Becoming long and entangled (herbage).

A غلوّ *ghulūw*, (v. n. of غلا for غلو) Shooting (an arrow) with the greatest force. Flying high and overshooting the mark (an arrow). Becoming long, tangly (grass). Exceeding bounds. Excess.

A غلواء *ghulwā* or *ghulawā*, (v. n. of غلا for غلو) Exceeding bounds. Passing away (youth). The briskness, vivacity, or insolence of youth.

A غلوان *ghulwān*, Youthful vivacity. Early youth.

A غلوة *ghalwat*, (pl. غلوات *ghalwāt* and غلاء *ghilā*) The shooting of an arrow as far as possible. Bow-shot distance. The utmost stretch of a horse, when at full gallop. A butt for archers. مائة غلوة *miat ghalwat*, A hundred lengths (of a horse).

A غلوطة *ghalūtat*, Any question liable to error, reprehension, or criticism.

A غلول *ghalūl*, Food which one puts into one's belly. Soft food, such as is eaten by old men. A traitor, deceiver. *Ghulūl*, (v. n. of غلّ) Defrauding, cheating, purloining a part (of any plunder). (Water) flowing (amongst trees)

P غلول *ghulūl*, Meat sticking in the throat.

P غلوله *ghalūla*, A ball.

A غلومة *ghulūmat*, (and غلوميّة *ghulūmīyat*) Youth, boyhood, adolescence, pubescence.

A غلوي *ghalwa'*, A kind of black perfume: civet.

P غله *ghala*, Unsteadiness, anxiety.

P غلّه *ghalla*, Corn, produce of the earth. *Ghulla*, A till: a save-all. A narrow-necked gugglet.

P غله دان *ghuladān*, A money-box or till.

P غلّه دان *ghalladān*, A granary. غلّه دان عدم *ghalladāni ʿadam*, The earth. *Ghulladān*, A money-box or till: a save-all.

P غلّه زار *ghallazār*, A place abounding in grain.

P غلّه فروش *ghalla-farosh*, A corn-factor.

A غلي *ghaly*, (v. n. of غلي) Boiling (a pot).

A غليّ *ghalīy*, Dear, high-priced. بالغليّ *bi'l ghalīy*, Dearly (sold).

P غليان *ghilyān*, A kind of pipe for smoking tobacco through water.

A غليان *ghalayān*, (v. n. of غلي) Boiling. Working (as liquors in a state of fermentation).

A غلية *ghalyat*, One boiling or ebullition.

P غليته *ghalīta*, A grass for making baskets.

P غليث *ghalīs*, Adulterated (as wheat with barley). A poisoned bait laid for a vulture.

P غليجن *ghulījan*, Mint.

P غليدن *ghalīdan*, To wallow in the clay from excessive thirst (cattle). To flow (as water). To dive. To faint, swoon.

A غليز *ghalīz*, Gross, thick, rough, coarse.

P غليژن *ghalījan*, (or غليزن *ghalīzan*) Clay or blackish mud at the bottom of ditches or ponds.

A غليس *ghalīs*, Asses.

A غليظ *ghalīz*, Coarse, thick. Gross, rude, rugged, rough. Rustic. Avaricious. Dirty, foul, filthy. Severe in punishing. Sore punishment. غليظ القلب *ghalīzu'l kalb*, Hard-hearted: gross, unfeeling.

A غليظة *ghalīzat*, Uncultivated and hard (land). Rough, rugged, craggy, uneven ground.

A غليظى *ghalīzī*, Coarseness, thickness.

P غليغر *ghileghar*, (or غليگر *ghilegar*) A master-builder or worker in clay.

A غليل *ghalīl*, (pl. غلائل *ghalāʾil*) Thirst. The pangs of thirst. Malevolence, hatred, enmity, envy. Warmth of love or hatred. A mixture of trefoil and crushed date-stones, with which camels are fed. Low or level ground producing the species of trees called غلان *ghullān*. Thirsty, parched with thirst.

P غليل *ghulel*, A pellet-bow.

P غليل باز *ghulel-bāz*, A pelleter with a bow.

P غليل بازي *ghulel-bāzī*, Pelleting.

A غليلة *ghalīlat*, (pl. غلائل *ghalāʾil*) A coat of mail. A stud by which the rings are fastened. A quilting worn under a coat of mail.

A غلّيم *ghillīm*, Libidinous.

A غليّم *ghulayyim*, (dim. of غلام) A little boy.

A غلّيمة *ghillīmat*, Libidinous (female).

P غليو *ghalev*, Astonished. Folly, wild fancy.

P غليواج *ghalewāj*, (غليواژ *ghalewāj*, *ghalīwāj*, or غليواژه *ghalīwāja*) A kite (bird).

P غليون *ghalīwan*, Black mud at a pond's bottom.

sp. غليون *ghilyūn*, A galleon, a sort of ship.

A غمّ *ghamm*, (v. n. of غمّ) Being cloudy (day). Being intensely hot and suffocating (the day). Making sad. Covering. Stopping the mouth or nostrils, muzzling. Gloomy (day). Intensely hot, suffocating (day or night). (pl. غموم *ghumūm*) Grief, sadness, anxiety, trouble care. A source of regret. Remorse. Loss, harm. P غم خوردن *gham khwurdan*, To commiserate, sympathize, care. دفع غم كردن *dafʿi gham kardan*, To dispel, drive off care.

A غماء *ghamā*, Grief, sadness. Any thing laid upon a horse to throw him into a sweat. *Ghimā*, The roof of a house, especially the upper part covered with reeds or sand; also these materials.

A غمّاء *ghammā*, Dark, cloudy (night). Calamity, misfortune. (fem. of اغمّ *aghamm*) One who has many locks of hair hanging before or behind.

A غمار *ghamār*, *ghimār*, or *ghumār*, A great crowd. *Ghimār*, (pl. of غمر *ghamr*) Whirlpools. Beneficent. Deep seas. (pl. of غمرة *ghamrat*) Intensities, severities. Crowds, throngs.

A غمارة *ghamārat*, (v. n. of غمر) Being inexperienced, rude, ignorant, and silly. Being plenteous and abundant (water). Want of experience.

A غماريد *ghamārīd*, Sorts of mushrooms.

A غمّاز *ghammāz*, An informer, accuser, detractor, sycophant, tale-bearer. The eyes of a mistress.

A غمّازة *ghammāzat*, A girl of comely countenance and limbs when beckoning and making signs.

P غمّازك *ghammāzak*, A bit of wood, cork, or quill, by which the angler discovers the bite of a fish, a float.

A غمّازي *ghammāzī*, Slander, detraction.

A غمّاسة *ghammāsat*, (pl. غمّاس *ghummās*) The diver (a bird).

A غماض *ghamāz* or *ghimāz*, (v. n. of غمض) Winking. A wink of sleep. ما اكتحلت غماضا *mā iktahaltu ghimāzan*, I did not sleep a wink.

A غماضة *ghamāzat*, (v. n. of غمض) Being low and level (ground).

P غم آلوده *gham-āluda*, Drenched in sorrow, sad.

P غمام *ghamām*, A sponge.

A غمام *ghumām*, Rheum, defluxion, cold.

A غمامة *ghamāmat*, (pl. غمائم *ghamāsim*) A cloud overspreading the sky. A white cloud. *Ghimāmat*, (pl. غمائم *ghamāsim*) Hoodwinks. A bag used as a muzzle. A bridle, halter. *Ghimāmat* or *ghumāmat*, The foreskin of a boy.

A غماهج *ghumāhij*, Thick and fat.

A غمائم *ghamāsim*, (pl. of غمامة *ghamāmat*) Clouds. (pl. of غمامة *ghimāmat*) Halters, bridles. Muzzles. Hoodwinks. Blinkers.

P غم بادة *gham-bāda*, Sickness caused by sorrow.

A غمّة *ghammat*, Cloudy (night). Intensely hot (night). *Ghummat*, Grief, anguish. Obscurity, darkness. The bottom of a churning-bottle. The bottom of the sea. Difficult, intricate, unknown (thing), being a source of grief.

A غمت *ghamt*, (v. n. of غمت) Oppressing the stomach (meat), making the head to ache. Covering. Lifting the head to breathe (when drinking). Plunging (into water). *Ghamat*, (v. n. of غمت) Being indisposed or stupefied from eating meat which disagrees with one.

A غمج *ghamj*, (v. n. of غمج) Drinking, gulping (water). *Ghamij*, Sucking (colt). Not sweet (water).

A غمجار *ghimjār*, A glue with which they varnish bows to prevent them from cracking.

A غمجة *gham* or *ghumjat*, One sip or draught.

A غمجرة *ghamjarat*, (v. n. of غمجر Q) Varnishing (a bow) with glue. Watering (a garden) thoroughly (rain). Swallowing (water) gulp after gulp.

P غمخانه *gham-khāna*, House of mourning.

P غمخوار *gham-khwār*, Devouring sorrow, *i. e.* afflicted, vexed, sad. Condoling, pitying. An intimate friend (as partaking in another's feelings).

P غمخوارگي *gham-khwāragī*, Sympathy.

P غمخواري *gham-khwārī*, Sympathy.

P غم خورك *gham-khwurak*, A heron.

A غمد *ghamd* or *ghimd*, (v. n. of غمد) Sheathing (a sword). *Ghimd*, (pl. اغماد *aghmād* and غمود *ghumūd*) A sheath, scabbard. A pod, husk, shell. *Ghamad*, (v. n. of غمد) Being abundant, also scanty (water in a well).

P غمدان *ghamdān*, Name of a certain edifice. The world (as being the abode of sorrow).

A غمدان *ghumdān*, Name of a magnificent palace in Sanaa, the capital of Yaman.

A غمدّان *ghumuddān*, A sheath, scabbard.

P غمديدة *gham-dīda*, Having seen sorrow, inured to misfortune, afflicted, distressed.

A غمذرة *ghamzarat*, (v. n. of غمذر Q) Measuring and giving more than full measure.

A غمر *ghamr*, (v. n. of غمر) Covering, overflowing (water). Appearing above, being higher, taller (men). (pl. غمار *ghimār* and غمور *ghumūr*) Plenty of water, sufficient to cover any thing; a whirlpool, gulf, abyss. Full, spacious (garment). A crowd, mob, mixed multitude. Deep, the main (sea). Excellent, swift (horse). Liberal, generous. غمر الخلق *ghamru'l khuluk*, (and غمر الرداء *ghamru'r ridā*) Liberal, beneficent. *Ghamr*, *ghimr*, *ghumr*, and *ghamar*, Inexperienced in business, raw. *Ghimr*, Thirst. Malevolence, hatred. *Ghumr*, Saffron. *Ghumr* or *ghumur*, (pl. اغمار *aghmār*) An inexperienced, rude, unlearned, boorish fellow. *Ghamar*, (v. n. of غمر) Hating, detesting. Stinking from meat (the hands). The smell of any thing on the hands; as meat, fish, or rust. A mob, crowd. (pl. غمور *ghumūr*) Hatred, ill-will. منديل الغمر *mindīlu'l ghamar*, A napkin, towel. *Ghamir*, What stinks of fish or any other disagreeable thing. *Ghumar*, A small dish, cup, or vessel (the smallest used by the Arabians). (pl. of غمرة *ghamrat*) Adversities, misfortunes.

A غمرات *ghamarāt*, (pl. of غمرة *ghamrat*) Intensities, severities. Crowds, throngs.

A غمرة *ghamrat*, (pl. غمرات *ghamarāt* or غمار *ghimār*) Intensity, severity. (pl. غمرات *ghamarāt*, غمار *ghimār*, and غمر *ghumar*) A mob, crowd, mixed multitude. Adversity, misfortune, danger. Agony of death. An abyss, a whirlpool. *Ghumrat*, A kind of liniment (of the ورس *wars*-genus), used by women to impart a lustre to their complexions. An inexperienced and foolish woman. Saffron. *Ghamirat*, (A hand) stinking of meat or of fish. A black garment worn by slaves and handmaids.

A غمز *ghamz*, (v. n. of غمز) Accusing, impeaching, defaming. Beckoning, making a signal (with head, hand, or eye). Limping, leaning to a side. Being evident, apparent (a disease or a blemish). Feeling cattle (if fat). Pressing, squeezing, pushing. Poking or sticking in the ground. غمز عين *ghamzi ʿayn*, A winking with the eye; dissimulation: connivance. *Ghamaz*, The worst of one's property. Weak (man). Lean beasts.

A غمزة *ghamzat*, One wink.

P غمزدا *gham-zidā*, (or غمزداي *gham-zidāy*) Who or what drives away, or wipes off, care: cheerful, exhilarating.

P غمزداي *gham-zidāy*, The 8th day of the month.

P غمزدگي *gham-zadagī*, Affliction, grief.

P غمزدة *gham-zada*, Sorrow-stricken, afflicted.

P A غمزه *ghamza*, A wink or a signal with the eye. An amorous glance, coquetry, ogling. The eyelid. P غمزهٔ اختر *ghamzaʾi akhtar*, The twinkling of a star. Starlight at break of day. غمزهٔ سرتيز *ghamzaʾi sar-tez*, Joy, gladness. غمزهٔ گل *ghamzaʾi gul*, The opening of a flower. غمزهٔ لاجوردي *ghamzaʾi lājwardī*, Glances, winks not repeated.

A غمس *ghams*, (v. n. of غمس) Immersing, ducking into water, dipping, steeping. Tinging (her) hand (a woman). Setting (as a star).

A غمش *ghamash*, (v. n. of غمش) Being dim (the eyesight) from hunger or thirst.

A غمص *ghams*, (v. n. of غمص) Despising. Disparaging. Slighting, neglecting. Being ungrateful. Lying. Reviling, accusing. *Ghamas*, A flux from the eyes.

A غمض *ghamz*, (v. n. of غمض) Being easy, conniving, indulgent. Travelling, posting across a country. Penetrating deep into the flesh (a sword). (pl. غموض *ghumūz* and اغماض *aghmāz*) Low and level (ground). Connivance. *Ghumz*, (v. n. of غمض) Winking. A wink of sleep.

A غمط *ghamt*, (v. n. of غمط) Despising, holding cheap. Being ungrateful for health. Living inconsiderately, returning no thanks for prosperity. Swaggering. Absorbing greatly, drinking much water. Slaughtering (a victim). Low ground.

A غمطى *ghamataʾ*, (A sky) raining incessantly.

A غمغمة *ghamghamat*, The lowing of an affrighted bull. Noise of warriors in battle. An obscure, unintelligible speech.

P غم فرسودگي *gham-farsūdagī*, Care-crazedness.

P غم فرسودة *gham-farsūda*, Care-worn.

A غمق *ghamak*, (v. n. of غمق) Being moist with dew (ground). Lying on the earth (dew). *Ghamik*, Rank from too much moisture (a herb). Soaked with dew, heavy with moisture, or near to water (ground or night).

A غمقة *ghamakat*, A disease in the loins. *Ghamikat*, A watered field.

P غمكدة *gham-kada*, The mansion of sorrow.

P غمكسار *gham-kusār*, (or غمكسار وفادار *gham-kusāri wafā-dār*) A friend, an intimate companion, confidant. بادهٔ غمكسار *bādaʾi gham-kusār*, Wine, the dispeller of care.

P غمكساري *gham-kusārī*, The driving away of melancholy. Friendship, society, companionship.

P غمگسار *gham-gusār*, Whatever drives away sorrow; a dear friend. The 8th day of the month.

P غمگين *gham-gīn*, Sorrowful, full of grief.

P غمگيني *gham-gīnī*, Grief, sadness.

A غمل *ghaml*, (v. n. of غمل) Putting under ground (a skin) with the hair upon it, till it smells, becomes soft, and loses the hair; also letting it remain too long till it rots. Putting green (fruits) under straw to ripen. Covering (a person) with bed-clothes to produce perspiration. Amending, correcting, adjusting. Riding (one plant upon another). *Ghamal*, (v. n. of غمل) Growing sore, angry from bandaging (a wound). Heaping up (grapes).

A غملاس *ghimlās*, Large and thick (substance called ششقة *shikshikat*).

A غملج *ghamlaj*, (غملّج *ghamallaj*, غملاج *ghimlāj*, غملوج *ghumlūj*, غمليج *ghimlīj*, or غمالج *ghumālij*; fem. غملج *ghamlaj*, غملّج *ghamallaj*, غملوجة *ghumlūjat*, غمليجة *ghimlījat*) Inconstant, variable, fickle.

A غملّس *ghamallas*, Wicked, bold. A wolf.

A غملّط *ghamallat*, Long-necked.

A غملول *ghumlūl*, A species of pot-herb eaten boiled. A field or a valley abounding with trees and plants. A shady grove. A certain esculent vegetable. High ground. Dark, cloudy. A cloud. Obscurity, darkness. A valley, long, narrow, and full of thickly-entangled plants.

A غمم *ghamam*, Length and thickness of hair on the head.

A غمن *ghamn*, (v. n. of غمن) Putting green fruit under ground to ripen and mellow. Putting under ground a skin with the hair upon it in order to soften and become smooth. Throwing clothes on (any one) to make (him) sweat.

P غمناك *ghamnāk*, Disconsolate, melancholy.

A غمنة *ghumnat*, Ceruse, a paint used by women. A wash or cosmetic lotion for the face. Civet.

P غمنده *ghamanda*, Sorrowful. Enraged.

A غمو *ghamw*, (v. n. of غما for غمو) Covering (a house) with clay and wood.

A غمود *ghumūd*, (v. n. of غمد) Becoming covered with leaves (the plant عرفط *'urfut*). Drying up (water in a well). (pl. of غمد *ghimd*) Sheaths, scabbards, cases.

A غمور *ghumūr*, (pl. of غمر *ghamr*) Whirlpools. Great waters. Beneficent, liberal persons. (pl. of غمر *ghamar*) Hatreds, ill-wills.

A غمورة *ghumūrat*, (v. n. of غمر) Being plenteous and abundant (water). Depth. Liberality, munificence. Plenty of water.

A غموز *ghamūz*, (A she-camel) of whose fatness one cannot be certain except by feeling.

A غموس *ghamūs*, Deep (stab). Difficult, mysterious (affair). False (oath), gross (perjury). (A she-camel) having no appearance of pregnancy. A she-camel, concerning the marrow of whose bones doubts are entertained whether it be stinking and melted, or sweet and firm. A she-camel pregnant without raising her tail.

A غموص *ghamūs*, False (oath), perjury. غموص حنجرته *ghamūsu hanjaratihi*, A lying fellow. الغموص *al ghamūs*, The lesser dog-star.

A غموض *ghumūz*, (v. n. of غمض) Being low and level (ground). Being unintelligible (speech), having an occult and latent meaning. Being easy, conniving in buying and selling. (pl. of غمض *ghamz*) Low, level (grounds).

A غموضة *ghumūzat*, (v. n. of غمض) Being low and level (ground). Being unintelligible (speech), having an occult meaning.

A غموم *ghumūm*, (pl. of غمّ *ghamm*) Cares, griefs. Small, invisible stars.

A غمي *ghamy*, (v. n. of غمى) Fainting, swooning (a sick person). Recovering from a fainting fit. Covering the roof of a house with earth or reeds. *Ghamy* or *ghama'*, Cloudiness, absence of the moon. *Ghama'*, (pl. اغماء *aghmā's*) Fainting, swooned. (pl. اغمية *aghmiyat* and اغماء *aghmā's*) The roof of a house or soil laid upon it. غمىً والله *ghama' wa'llāh*, Verily, as God is true.

P غمي *ghamī*, Unhappy, sad, sorrowful.

A غمّىٰ *ghamma'*, Moonless and cloudy (night). Intensely hot (night), also a melancholy one. A calamity, misfortune, a serious affair. Dust. Darkness. Severity, intensity. صام الغمّىٰ *sāma'l ghamma'* (or *ghumma'*), He fasted late in the evening, the new moon being concealed. *Ghumma'*, Calamity, misfortune. A serious affair.

A غميا *ghamyā*, The fifth door of hell.

P غميار *gham-yār*, Yawning, gaping. Sad.

A غميذر *ghamayzar*, Confused in speech or action. One who perceives or understands nothing. Fat, in good case; full of youthful, animal spirits.

A غمير *ghamīr*, (pl. اغمراء *aghmirā's*) Green grass which is over-topped and sheltered from the sun by the taller and drier herbage. Seed of the plant بهمىٰ *buhma'*. A sort of plant. Green stuff vegetating at the root of hay or grass. Plenty of water, an abyss.

A غميزة *ghamīzat*, A place exposed to piercing and reproach. A place or object of desire. Defect, blemish. Weakness of intellect.

A غميس *ghamīs*, Dark (night). Unknown (thing). Darkness, obscurity, invisibility. Green grass growing amidst higher and drier herbage. A reed-bed or jungle, wherein one may conceal one's self. A small water-course flowing among plants or pot-herbs. قصيدة غميس *kasīdatun ghamīsun*, A poem hitherto unrivalled.

A غميصاء *ghumaysā's*, Name of a place. الغميصاء *al ghumaysā's*, The lesser dog-star.

A غميضة *ghamīzat*, Any thing censurable. Defect, blemish. Meanness, obscurity.

A غميل *ghamīl*, (A skin) buried under ground in order to become soft and lose the hair. (Unripe fruits) buried in order to mellow. Rank from moisture, or from being heaped together (herbs). Thick and rank (herb نصيّ *nasiy*).

A غميم *ghamīm*, Milk thickened by boiling. Sour, coagulated milk. Green herbage growing at the roots of the dry.

P غمين *ghamīn*, Sad, sorrowful.

A غمين *ghamīn*, (Skins or unripe dates) buried in the earth, in order that the hair of those may come off, and that these may ripen.

P غن *ghan*, A heavy stone suspended for pressing oil or cheese. A stone or wooden mortar.

A غنّ *ghanna*, Perhaps.

A غناء *ghanā's*, (v. n. of غني) Abiding (anywhere). Giving in marriage. Living. Supplying the place of another. Becoming. Meeting, encountering. Riches. Profit, advantage. Power, ability. Usefulness. لا غناء عنده *lā ghanā's 'indahu*, He has not enough. *Ghinā's*, A song, vocal music.

A غنّاء *ghannā's*, (fem. of اغنّ *aghann*) One who speaks through the nose. Abounding with trees or herbage (a valley), through whose trees the wind passes with a whistling sound. (A town) full of buildings, and resonant with the busy hum of men.

A غناة *ghunāt*, (pl. of غاني *ghānī*) Rich.

A غنّاث *ghunnās*, Well-bred people at a convivial party.

A غناج *ghināj*, Smoke of a furnace. *Ghunāj* or *ghināj*, Amorous gesture.

A غناجل *ghanājil*, (pl. of غنجل) Badgers.

A غنادب *ghanādib*, (pl. of غندبة *ghundubat* or غندوب *ghundūb*) Hard glands or swellings about the throat.

P غناده *ghunāda*, Name of an instrument; also of a game.

A غناظيك *ghanāzayka* or *ghināzayka*, In order to give you increased trouble and embarrassment (he acted in such a manner).

A غنافر *ghunāfir*, A shaggy male hyena. Dull-witted, stupid.

A غناما *ghunāmā*, A great endeavour. هذا غناماك *hāzā ghunāmāka*, This is your concern, or should be your chief aim.

A غنان *ghunān*, The buzzing of flies.

A غنائم *ghanā'im*, (pl. of غنم *ghanam*) Sheep. (pl. of غنيمة *ghanīmat*) Spoils, preys, booties. Enemies.

A غنب *ghamb*, Much plunder. *Ghunab*, (pl. of غنبة *ghumbat*) Dimples round the mouth.

A غنبة *ghumbat*, A dimple about the mouth.

A غنبول *ghumbūl*, A sort of bird.

P غنبه *ghumba*, Clamour. Reproach, defamation.

A غنّة *ghunnat*, (v. n. of غنّ) Talking through the nose. Being full of trees (a valley). Coming to maturity (the fruit of a palm-tree). A sound emitted through the nose: a nasal twang, nasality. The clatter of the collision of stones.

A غنتل *ghantal*, Low, obscure. ام غنتل *umm ghantal*, A hyena.

A غنث *ghanas*, (v. n. of غنث) Breathing after drinking. Being disturbed (the mind). Being ill-disposed, bad-tempered.

A غنثر *ghansar*, *ghunsar*, or *ghunsur*, Foolish, infatuated. One whose company is shunned as disagreeable. يا غنثر *yā ghunsaru*, O foolish! abject! doltish! heavy! base!

A غنثرة *ghansarat*, (v. n. of غنثر Q) Drinking without being thirsty. Brightness of head, with abundance of hair. A blue fly.

P غنج *ghanj*, A paint for the face. A large sack. An amorous gesture, a leer. When affixed to nouns it denotes affection: as, بيمارغنج *bīmār-ghanj*, Sick, in pain. *Ghanj* or *ghinj*, Buttocks.

A غنج *ghunj*, Black smoke. *Ghunj* or *ghunuj*, Amorous gestures. *Ghanaj*, (v. n. of غنج) Darting amorous glances, or walking gracefully; alluring, playing the coquette (a lovely woman). An old man. غنج القوم *ghanaju'l kaum*, The head of the tribe.

P غنجار *ghanjār*, (or غنجاره *ghanjāra*) A red paint for the face. Amorous playfulness, blandishment.

P غنجال *ghanjāl*, Green sour fruit.

A غنجة *ghanijat*, Attractive, lovely, fascinating (woman), a coquette.

P غنجر *ghanjar*, (or غنجرة) Paint for the face.

P غنجرش *ghanjrash* or *ghanjrish*, A frog.

A غنجل *ghunjul*, (pl. غناجل *ghanājil*) A badger, brock. The animal called سياه گوش *siyāh-gosh*.

P غنج مرش *ghanjmarish*, (or غنجموش) A frog.

A غنجول *ghunjūl*, Name of a certain animal, particulars of which are unknown.

P غنجه *ghunja*, A rose-bud; the plush of a rose. غنجه كردن *ghanja* or *ghunja kardan*, To bake; to knead. To collect.

P غنجيدن *ghunjīdan*, To speak obscenely. To jest, play, toy.

P غنچه *ghuncha*, A rose-bud. غنچهٔ آب *ghuncha-i āb*, A bubble of water. غنچهٔ ارغوان *ghuncha-i arghawān*, A spark of fire; a live coal. غنچه شدن *ghuncha shudan*, To assemble, be collected together. غنچهٔ كبگ دري *ghuncha-i kabgi darī*, Name of the seventh note of the barbut. غنچه دهن *ghuncha-dahan*, With a mouth like a rose-bud; a mistress.

P غند *ghund*, Collected, assembled. A crowd.

A غندار *ghandār*, One who thinks evil. One who guesses right.

A غندبة *ghundubat*, (pl. غنادب *ghanādib*) A hard gland or swelling about the throat.

A غندبتان *ghundubatāni*, Two lumps at the root of the tongue. Two pieces of flesh encircling the palate. Two pieces of flesh resembling a gland covering the prominent bones under the ears.

A غندر *ghundar* or *ghundur*, Fat, thick. Soft, delicate (youth). يا غندر *yā ghundar*, O importunate (teaser or questioner)! O you bore!

A غندرة *ghandarat*, Evil, wickedness.

P غند رود *ghund-rūd*, A small brazen trumpet for collecting people together.

P غندش *ghundish*, Cotton beaten out of the pod.

A غندلاني *ghundulāniy*, Large-headed.

P غندماش *ghundmāsh*, A kind of pulse, a sort of French bean.

A غندوب *ghundūb*, A hard gland or swelling about the throat.

P غنده *ghunda*, Collected, accumulated. A ball of dough. Cotton made up into rolls for spinning. A small brazen trumpet. A kind of spider or tarantula. Stink. A sour cake. A bubble.

P غنده بر *ghunda-bur*, A knife, scissors.

P غنده رود *ghunda-rūd*, A small trumpet for collecting people together.

A غنذاء *ghinzāʼ*, (or غنذاة *ghanzāt*) (v. n. of غنذي Q) Instigating, exciting.

A غنذمة *ghanzamat*, (v. n. of غنذم Q) Draining the dam's udder (a camel's colt).

A غنشوش *ghunshūsh*, Somewhat. Remains (of possessions, or of an army).

A غنص *ghanas*, (v. n. of غنص) Having a pain or tightness in the breast. A tightness in the chest.

A غنظ *ghanz*, (v. n. of غنظ) Weighing heavily upon, breaking the spirits. *Ghanz* or *ghanaz*, Excessive grief. Grief or melancholy that brings one nigh unto the grave, but from which one afterwards recovers.

A غنظاءة *ghanzāʼat*, (v. n. of غنظى Q) Reviling, reproaching. Talking obscenely.

A غنظيان *ghinziyān*, Obscene, impudent, ribald.

G غنقيلي *ghunkīlī*, A turnip.

P غنگ *ghang*, A strong piece of hard wood, from which they suspend the stone غن *ghan*. A loud noise. An ass. A wooden or stone mortar.

A غنم *ghanm*, *ghunm*, or *ghanam*, (v. n. of غنم) Carrying off as plunder, getting booty. Acquiring luckily. *Ghunm*, Plunder, spoil. A fortunate hit. *Ghanam*, (pl. اغنام *aghnām*, غنوم *ghunūm*, and اغانم *aghānim*) Sheep or goats; cattle; a flock.

A غنمان *ghunmān*, (v. n. of غنم) Carrying off booty, robbing. *Ghanamānī*, Two flocks of sheep.

P غنو *ghunav*, Sleep. *Ghunū* or *ghunav*, Sleeping.

A غنوة *ghunwat*, Independence, ability to do without. Affluence.

P غنودگاه *ghunūd-gāh*, A bed-chamber.

P غنودگي *ghunūdagī*, Drowsiness, slumber.

P غنودن *ghunūdan*, To slumber, sleep, doze, rest, repose. To roll. To faint.

P غنوده *ghunūda*, Sleepy, dozing, drowsy.

A غنوم *ghunūm*, (pl. of غنم) Sheep. Flocks.

P غنوند *ghunwand*, Condition, pact, covenant.

A غنوي *ghanawiy*, Pertaining to a rich man.

P غنويدن *ghunawīdan*, To doze, slumber.

A غنيٰ *ghanaʼ*, (v. n. of غني) Being independent of ornament (a woman). Abiding in a place, settling. Living. Seeing. Remaining. Being. Ability to do without. Worthy. Remedy, help. Escape. ما له غنيً عنه *mā lahu ghanan ʻanhu*, He cannot do without it, or avoid it. *Ghinaʼ*, (v. n. of غني) Being rich. Giving in marriage. Joining, associating. Riches, affluence.

A غنيّ *ghaniy*, Rich, wealthy. Independent, able to dispense with. غني و محتاج *ghanī u muhtāj*, Rich and poor.

A غنيان *ghunyān*, (v. n. of غني) Being contented with (any thing), considering it as sufficient. Ability to do without. Affluence, independence.

A غنية *ghunyat*, (v. n. of غني) Being able to do without, being independent. Ability to do without. Remedy, help. *Ghunyat* or *ghinyat*, Affluence.

A غنيظ *ghanīz*, Unripe dates cut off in clusters, and hung up.

A غنيم *ghanīm*, Plunder, spoil. The acquisition of a thing without labour and trouble.

A غنيمة *ghanīmat*, (v. n. of غنم) Carrying off booty. Making a fortunate hit. (pl. غنائم *ghanāʼim*) Plunder, booty, spoil, prey (taken especially in a war with infidels). Abundance, wealth, plenty, affluence, good fortune. P غنيمه شمردن *ghanīma shumurdan*, To account as gain. To have his life as a prey. A *Ghunaymat*, (dim. of غنم *ghanam*) A little sheep.

P غنينه *ghanīna*, A bees' nest. A swarm.

P غو *ghaw*, Thunder. Tumult, noise. A voice. Shouts of soldiers or clang of warlike instruments.

A غو *ghaw*, Free, at liberty.

A غوابّ *ghawābb*, (fem. of غابّ *ghābb*) (Camels) watered every second day. Stale (meats).

A غواث *ghuwās*, (rarely *ghawās*) A cry for help. An assistant, a defender.

A غوار *ghiwār*, A making a hostile excursion.

A غوارب *ghawārib*, (pl. of غارب *ghārib*) Summits of waves. Upper parts of camels' bunches.

A غوارف *ghawārif*, (pl. of غارفة *ghārifat*) Swift (she-camels).

A غوازل *ghawāzil*, (pl. of غازلة) Female spinners.

A غواس *ghawās*, (A day) of rout, flight, plunder, robbery, or bloodshed.

A غواشي *ghawāshī*, (pl. of غاشية *ghāshiyat*) Coverings for saddles. Gloomy thoughts overspreading the mind. Faintings, swoonings.

A غوّاص *ghawwās*, A diver (for pearls). Subtile, penetrating. Name of a bird.

A غوّاصي *ghawwāsī*, Diving; a plunge into water. P غوّاصي كردن *ghawwāsī kardan*, To dive.

A غواضي *ghawāzī*, (pl. of غاضية *ghāziyat*) (Camels) eating the tree غضاة *ghazāt*.

A غواطس *ghawātis*, (pl. of غاطس *ghātis*) Immersed, covered.

A غوامض *ghawāmiz*, (pl. of غامض *ghāmiz*) Low-lying places. Intricate questions.

A غواني *ghawānī*, (pl. of غانية *ghāniyat*) Songs. Singing-women. Women despising ornaments, satisfied with their own natural beauty. Girls much courted, yet remaining contentedly unmarried in their parents' houses. Chaste women in general.

A غوائب *ghawāʼib*, (pl. of غائب *ghāʼib*) Absent.

A غواية *ghawāyat*, (v. n. of غوي) Being deceived, erring. Desperation.

A غوايت *ghawāyat*, Extremities.

A غوائل *ghawāʼil*, (pl. of غائلة) Misfortunes.

A غوبر *ghawbar*, A kind of fish.

P غوبنك *ghūbinak*, An herb used in washing.

P غوت *ghot*, A sling. A plunge into water. A certain downy plant. Cheerful, ready.

P غوته *ghaw* or *ghūta*, A plunge under water.

A غوث *ghaws*, A cry for assistance, generally with the word وا غوثاه *wā ghawsāh*, *i.e.* Help! help! An assistant, defender; one who redresses complaints. A title of Muhammadan saints, whose ardour of devotion, according to vulgar tradition, is such, that in the act of worship their head and limbs fall asunder.

A غوج *ghawj*, (v. n. of غاج for غوج) Being doubled, bent, folded. غوج اللبان *ghawju'l labān*, (A horse) with a wide brisket-skin.

P غوج *ghūch*, A horned ram used to fight.

P غوچي *ghawchī*, A deep well.

P غور *ghor*, A pathick. *Ghūr*, A sort of measure weighing twelve سخ *sukhkh*. Name of a country contiguous to Kandahār.

A غور *ghawr*, (v. n. of غار for غور) Setting (the sun). Waxing hot (the day). Arriving in any low-lying country. Entering into any thing. Flowing down upon low grounds (water). Gulping water. Being deeply sunk in the socket (an eye). Benefiting, doing good. Giving rain and a plentiful crop (God). Expiating murder by a mulct. Water which flows down upon low grounds. The bottom (of any thing). A cave, cavern. Depth, profundity. Whatever lies between ذات عرق *zāt ɛirk* and the sea. Sloping ground west of Tihāma. A low-lying district betwixt Jerusalem and Hawrān, three days' journey in length and two leagues in width. Low ground. Reflection, consideration, deliberation, meditation, attention, observation, circumspection. بعيد الغور هو *baɛīdu'l ghawr huwa*, He is of a deep or close disposition. *Ghiwar*, The price of blood.

A غُؤُر *ghuɛur*, The setting (of the sun).

P غور پرداخت *ghawr-pardākht*, Attendance on.

A غورة *ghawrat*, The sun. Noon.

P غوررسي *ghawr-rasī*, Deep research.

A غور كار *ghawr-kār*, Bottom of any thing.

A غور كلّي *ghawr kullīy*, Attentive investigation.

P غورمكس *ghor-magas*, A fly of reddish green.

P غورواشه *ghūrwāsha*, A kind of herb with which weavers smear their cloth and curriers their hides.

P غوره *ghūra*, Unripe grapes or dates. A colour in pigeons. غوره افشردن *ghūra afshurdan*, To cause to weep. To envy. To rejoice at another's distress. To overcome.

P غوره با *ghūra-bā*, Meat dressed with the juice of unripe dates.

A غوريٰ *ghawra'*, The bottom. Depth.

P غوري *ghorī*, A sort of porcelain which breaks the moment poison is put into it.

P غوريدن *ghūrīdan*, To encourage to fight. To put to flight. To be satiated, satisfied.

A غوز *ghawz*, (v. n. of غاز for غوز) Intending, purposing, aiming at.

P غوزه *ghoza*, A cotton-pod. A string of silver beads, rosary. غوزهٔ آب *ghozaʼi āb*, Bubble of water.

P غوژه *ghūja*, A cotton-pod or nut. The bud of a flower.

P غوش *ghosh*, A very hard wood, of which they make arrows, darts, and saddle-timbers. The ear. Dung of animals. A led horse. A look, a looking about, amusement. Stark-naked. The birch-tree.

P غوشا *ghoshā*, Dung of animals. A bunch of dates or grapes. An ear of corn. A fold for cattle.

P غوشاد *ghoshād* or *ghawshād*, A circular area. A halo. A nocturnal fold for cattle. A halting-place for caravans. A resorting-place of demons. An inn. A tall tree. Dung of animals.

P غوشاك *ghoshāk*, Dung of animals. A fold for cattle.

P غوشاي *ghoshāy*, An ear of corn, especially those left by the reapers for the poor to glean. Dried cows' dung, used as firing. A nocturnal fold for cattle.

P غوشت *ghosht*, Stark-naked.

P غوشنه *ghoshna*, An alkaline herb, used to wash the hands. A species of mushroom.

P غوشه *ghosha*, A herb, eaten when fresh, and used when dry for washing clothes. A kind of food. The birch-tree. An ear of corn. A cluster.

A غوص *ghaws*, (v. n. of غاص for غوص) Diving, plunging under water to bring any thing up. Floundering, sinking. Studying any subject to the bottom, knowing. Coming down upon suddenly.

A غوط *ghawt*, (v. n. of غوط) Being dipped or plunged into; sinking (as the feet amongst sand). Entering (one thing into another). Digging downwards. Bread crumbled in pieces. Low-lying ground. *Ghūt*, (pl. of غائط *ghāɛit*) Low grounds.

A غوطة *ghawtat*, A valley, a hollow, low, level ground. The city or country round Damascus.

A P غوطم غاته *ghotam-ghāta*, A game in which swimmers dip one another under water.

A غوطه *ghota*, Dipping, diving. A dip, a dive.

P غوطه خوردن *ghota khwurdan*, To dive, plunge. غوطه دادن *ghota dādan*, To give a ducking.

P غوطه باز *ghota-bāz*, A diver.

P غوطه خور *ghota-khwur*, A diver. Whatever dips or is dipped.

P غوطه خوري *ghota-khwurī*, The being dipt.

P غوغا *ghawghā*, A noise, cry, tumult, uproar, clamour, disturbance, contest, squabble, quarrel, debate. A company, assembly. غوغاي هراسندگان *ghawghāyi hirāsandagān*, Cry of penitents for mercy.

A غوغاء *ghawghāɛ*, Locusts of a reddish colour, scarcely able to fly. A certain harmless insect resembling a gnat. A confused multitude of people, a mob. A mixing pell-mell in battle.

P غوغائي *ghawghāɛī*, Noisy, riotous. Uproar.

P غوغو *ghūghū*, A pigeon, a dove.

A غوفر *ghawfar*, A kind of melon or cucurbitaceous plant growing in the autumn.

P غوق *ghok*, (for غوك *ghok*) A frog.

P غوك *ghok*, A frog. A butt for archers.

P غوكان *ghokān*, A frog. Frogs.

P غوك چوب *ghok-chob*, A stick for playing at hockey or tip-cat. Faithless, fickle.

A غول *ghawl*, (v. n. of غال for غول) Assaulting suddenly and unexpectedly, overcoming and destroying. Carrying off unawares. An oppression of the mind, a loss of the senses (from drunkenness). Drunkenness. A headache. A grove of the thorny trees called طلح *talh*. Low-lying, sloping ground. Much earth. Distance of a desert, stretch, extension. *Ghūl*, (pl. اغوال *aghwāl* and غيلان *ghīlān*) Destruction, ruin. An accident, misfortune. A serpent, a dragon. A sorceress of the jinns. Death, fate. A man-devouring demon, a demon of the woods. A certain beast which appeared in Arabia, and was slain by Ta'abbat Sharran. One who assumes various forms by magic. غول الحلم *ghūlu'l hilm*, The demon that destroys mildness, *i. e.* anger. *Ghūl* or *ghawl*, Whatever robs a man of his senses.

P غول *ghol*, An imaginary sylvan demon, of different shapes and colours, supposed to devour men and animals (from which our European loup-garou, or man-wolf, seems to be borrowed). Caverns made for the protection of cattle by night. Twin children. The seed of a plant called horses'-ear. A rogue, rascal, whoreson. The ear. غول بيابان *gholi biyābān*, The dragon of the desert. غول سياه *gholi siyāh*, A dark night. غولان روزگار *gholāni rozgār*, Worldly-minded, unprincipled people.

A غوّل *ghuwwal*, Easy, comfortable (life).

A غولان *ghawlān*, A species of salsuginous plant.

P غولانيدن *gholānīdan*, To cause to put to flight.

P غولتاش *ghūltāsh*, A helmet.

P غولك *gholak*, A money-till, save-all. The pool in which gamesters put the stakes.

P غوله *ghawla*, Silly, out of one's mind. *Ghola*, A granary. A money-till, save-all. The pool.

P غوليدن *gholīdan*, To put to flight. To instigate to battle. To chide, revile. To quench (thirst).

P غولين *gholīn*, A wide-mouthed cup, ewer, or jar.

A غؤور *ghuɛūr*, (v. n. of غار for غور) Arriving in a low-lying country. Setting (the sun). Entering into any thing.

A غوهق *ghawhak*, Cheerfulness, sprightliness. Madness. A crow.

A غويٰ *ghawa'*, (v. n. of غوي) Suffering from indigestion, or by being kept from milk, pining away (a lamb or a camel's colt). Empty-bellied, unsatiated. *Ghawī*, Erring, straying, wandering at large. Sickly, pining (colt). Hopeless.

A غويّ *ghawīy*, Seduced, led astray. At liberty.

A غويث *ghawīs*, Full speed. Any thing affording aid (whether food or courageous interposition).

A غوير *ghuwayr*, (dim. of غار) A little cavern.

P غويشه *ghawīsha*, A kind of mushroom.

P غويه *ghūyah*, A churn-staff. A churn. A crane. غويه زدن *ghūya zadan*, To churn.

A غهب *ghahab*, (v. n. of غهب) Doing any thing carelessly or thoughtlessly. Forgetting.

A غهبا *ghahaban*, By chance, unawares.

A غهبيٰ *ghihibba'*, (or غهباء *ghihibbā*) The flower of youth.

A غهق *ghahik*, Long-bodied (camel).

A غيّ *ghayy*, (v. n. of غويٰ) Erring, straying or being deceived. Deceiving, leading astray. (v. n. of غيّ) Planting a standard. Error, sin. Deviation. Disappointment, despair. Name of a river or valley in hell.

A غياب *ghayāb*, (v. n. of غاب for غيب) Being absent. Lying hid. *Ghiyāb*, (v. n. of غاب for غيب) Lying hid, being invisible. Setting (the sun). Being doubtful, occult, mysterious. (pl. of غيب *ghayb*) Doubts.

A غيّاب *ghuyyāb*, pl. of غائب, Absent, concealed.

A غيابة *ghayābat*, Bottom (of a well or valley). Any place which conceals. *Ghiyābat*, (v. n. of غاب for غيب) Lying hid, being invisible. Entering, being enclosed (one thing within another).

A غياث *ghiyās*, Assistance, redress, succour. Cry for help, clamour for justice. A redresser.

A غياثة *ghiyāsat*, Aid, help, succour, redress.

A غياديق *ghayādīk*, Serpents.

A غياذير *ghayāzīr*, (pl. of غيذار *ghayzār*) Asses.

P غيار *ghiyār*, A strip of yellow cloth worn by Jews in Persia.

A غيار *ghiyār*, (v. n. of غار for غور) Giving rain and a plentiful crop. Entering into. Setting (the sun). Alighting or reposing at noon-day. (v. n. of غار for غير) Providing for one's dependants, being useful, doing good. Sending rain or any thing good (God). Being jealous. Bartering (goods). Any piece of dress or uniform which distinguishes soldiers or sects of people (as the girdles which are worn by fire-worshippers).

A غياري *ghayārā'*, (pl. of غيري *ghayra'*) Jealous (women). *Ghayārā* or *ghuyārā'*, (pl. of غيران *ghayrān*) Jealous.

P غيازه *ghayāza*, A goad.

A غياص *ghiyās*, (v. n. of غاص for غوص) Diving. Studying deeply.

A غياصة *ghiyāsat*, (v. n. of غاص for غوص) Diving. Studying to the bottom. Pearl-fishing. A place where a diver goes down. The upper part of the thigh.

A غياض *ghiyāz*, (pl. of غيضة *ghayzat*) Forests, places abounding in trees, but having little water.

A غياط *ghiyāt*, (pl. of غائط *ghā,it*) Low lands.

A غياطل *ghayātil*, (pl. of غيطلة *ghaytalat*) Milch-kine or does.

A غياظك *ghiyāzaka*, (or غياظيك *ghiyāzayka*) (He did so) to increase your embarrassment.

A غيّاف *ghayyāf*, Long and large-bearded.

A غيّال *ghayyāl*, A lion.

A غيان *ghayān*, Quicksilver.

A غيّان *ghayyān*, Erring: deceived, seduced.

A غياهب *ghayāhib*, (pl. of غيهب) Darknesses.

A غياية *ghayāyat*, The splendour of the shining sun. The bottom of a well. Darkness. Any thing casting a shade (as clouds or dust).

A غيب *ghayb*, (v. n. of غاب for غيب) Being absent, hidden; lying hid. Being invisible. Setting (the sun). Being doubtful, or concealed. (pl. غياب *ghiyāb* and غيوب *ghuyūb*) Absence, invisibility, concealment, mystery, doubt. Any thing in the womb of futurity. A low-lying place. Low-lying ground. Fat. Latent, concealed, absent, invisible, mysterious. عالم غيب *ālami ghayb*, The invisible world, future state. جنود و رجال الغيب *junūd u rijālu'l ghayb*, An army of invisible spirits. *Ghayab*, (or غيّب *ghuyyab*) (pl. of غائب *ghā,ib*) Absent. Concealed, invisible.

A غيبان *ghay* or *ghayyibān*, Roots (of trees).

A غيبة *ghaybat*, (v. n. of غاب for غيب) Being absent, invisible. Concealment, Low ground. (pl. غيبات *ghaybāt*) Things concealed or mysterious. *Ghaybat* or *ghībat*, (v. n. of غاب for غيب) Lying hid, being concealed. Being invisible. *Ghībat*, Slander, detraction, calumny; any thing secretly whispered of an absent person (implying truth, however, as بهتان *buhtān* expresses a false accusation).

P غيبت گر *ghībatgar*, A slanderer.

P غيب دان *ghayb-dān*, Skilful in discovering mysteries. A prophet, diviner. Omniscient.

A غيبوبة *ghaybūbat*, (v. n. of غاب for غيب) Being absent. Absence. Concealment, invisibility.

P غيبه *ghayba*, Bits of iron from which coats of mail and armour are wrought. A quiver. Rings in a shield of wood or twisted silk. Carded cotton.

A غيبيّ *ghaybīy*, Absent. Concealed: invisible. Future. Fatal. Heavenly, divine.

A غيّة *ghayyat*, Rashness, carelessness. هو لغيّة *huwa li ghayyatin*, He acts rashly. ولد غيّة *waladu ghayyatin* or *ghiyatin*, A bastard.

A غيث *ghays*, (v. n. of غاث for غيث) (Rain) watering the earth. Being rained upon. Giving rain, causing it to fall (God). Shining, giving light. Rain widely spread. Plants, especially such as grow with rain. ذات غيّث *zātu ghayyisin*, At full gallop (a horse). (A well of) running water, perennial (spring).

A غيثرة *ghaysarat*, Dregs of the people. A mixed multitude, rabble. A scuffle in which people trample on one another. Threat, denunciation.

A غيثمة *ghaysamat*, A quarrelling, fight, scuffle.

A غيد *ghīd*, (pl. of غيداء *ghaydā,*) Soft, delicate women. *Ghīd* or *ghīda*, Make haste, go quickly. *Ghayad*, (v. n. of غيد) Having a tender, flexible (neck). Being fresh, soft, tender, flexible. Softness.

A غيداء *ghaydā,*, (fem. of اغيد *aghyad*) Soft, flexible, or mild.

A ابو غيداس *abū ghaydās*, Penis.

P غيداق *ghaydāk*, A place in the desert of Kipjāk.

A غيداق *ghaydāk*, Delicate, and of a fair countenance (youth). A noble, generous man. A young Lybian lizard or crocodile. Long (horse). The prime of youth.

P غيداقي *ghaydākī*, Proceeding or coming from Ghaydāk. تير غيداقي *tīri ghaydākī*, An arrow of a very hard wood manufactured there.

A غيدان *ghaydān*, Tender age of youth.

A غيدق *ghaydak*, Soft and delicate (youthfulness or young man).

A غيدقان *ghaydakān*, Youthful prime. Of a delicate and noble disposition. Delicate, handsome, and good-tempered (youth).

A غيدقة *ghaydakat*, (v. n. of غيدق Q) Being plentiful (spittle). Being full of saliva.

A غيدل *ghaydal*, Easy, comfortable (life).

A غيذار *ghayzār*, (pl. غياذير *ghayāzīr*) An ass.

A غيذان *ghayzān*, One who conjectures or guesses accurately.

A غيذر *ghayzar*, Flour upon which they pour new milk, and warm with a hot stone.

A غيذرة *ghayzarat*, Evil. Abundance of talk, and confusion in the same.

A غير *ghayr*, (v. n. of غار for غير) Being jealous. Watering the earth (rain). Sending rain or any thing good (God). Being useful, doing good. Destroying, causing to perish. Expiating murder by paying a fine. Change, alteration. Other, different. No, not, un; except, beside, unless. P غير آن *ghayri ān*, Besides that. A من غير ان *min ghayr an*, Although, notwithstanding. غير ان *ghayr an*, Except that. غير بعيد *ghayri ba‛īd*, Not far distant. غير جازم *ghayr jāzim*, Inconclusive. P غير جاوداني *ghayr* (or *ghayri*) *jāwidānī*, Not eternal, frail. A غير جائز *ghayr jā,iz*, Illegal. غير جنس *ghayr jins*, A different species. غير حاضر *ghayr hāzir*, Absent. غير حاضري *ghayr hāzirī*, Absence. غير خالص *ghayr khālis*, Insincere, impure. غير زيد *ghayr zaydin*, (It was) not Zayd. غير شي *ghayr shay*, Nothing. عمل غير صائب *‛amali ghayri sā,ib*, An unworthy action. غير كامل *ghayr kāmil*, Imperfect. غير كرّه *ghayr karra*, Another time. غير مترقب *ghayr mutarakhib*, Unexpected, unlooked-for. غير متساوي *ghayr mutasāwī*, Unequal. غير متناهي *ghayr mutanāhī*, Unlimited, boundless. غير مثمر *ghayr musmir*, Unfruitful, barren. غير مشكوك *ghayr mashkūk*, Doubtless, undoubted. غير معهود *ghayr ma‛hūd*, Unusual, extraordinary. غير معيّن *ghayr mu‛ayyan*, Undetermined. غير مغلوب *ghayr maghlūb*, Unconquered. غير مفيد *ghayr mufīd*, Unprofitable. غير مقدور *ghayr mahdūr*, Impossible. غير مقرّر *ghayr mukarrar*, Indefinite. غير مقشّر *ghayr mukashshar*, Unpeeled, in the bark. غير واقع *ghayr wāki‛*, Unfounded, untrue. بنات غير *banātu ghayrin*, A lie. بغير *bi ghayr*, Otherwise. Without. ليس غير *laysa ghayrin* or *ghayran*, Not otherwise. و غير ذالك *wa ghayru zālika*, Besides, et cætera. الي غير ذلك *ila' ghayri zālika*, And so of the rest. *Ghīr*, (pl. اغيار *aghyār*) The atonement or mulct for murder. An altered state. *Ghiyar*, (or غير الدهر *ghiyaru'd dahr*) Vicissitudes of fortune. (pl. of غيرة *ghīrat*) Provisions. *Ghuyur*, (pl. of غيور *ghayūr*) Jealous.

P غير *ghīr*, A florid ulceration of the skin.

A غيران *ghayrān*, (pl. غياري *ghayārā'* and *ghuyārā'*) Jealous. *Ghīrān*, (pl. of غار *ghār*) Caverns.

A غيرة *ghayrat*, (v. n. of غار for غير) Being jealous. Jealousy. Zeal. A nice sense of honour. غيرت الهيّه *ghayrati ilāhīya*, A holy zeal. P غيرت خوردن *ghayrat khwurdan* (or داشتن *dāshtan*), To be jealous. A *Ghīrat*, (pl. غير *ghiyar*) Provision, especially brought from abroad. Rain. A plenteous crop. The atonement or mulct for murder. Perdition, destruction.

P غيرت مند *ghayratmand*, Jealous.

A غيرها *ghayruhā*, (غيرهم *ghayruhum*, or غيرهما *ghayruhumā*) (comp. of غير *ghayr* and the affixed pronouns, and sometimes preceded by و *wa*: as, وغيرها *wa ghayruhā*) And the others, the rest, the above-mentioned.

A غيرى *ghayra'*, (pl. غيارى) Jealous (woman).

A غيرية *ghayrīyat*, Change, alteration. Unreality.

P غيژيدن *ghejīdan*, To move along or hitch forwards on the hips. To walk upon all fours; to crawl upon hands and knees. To crawl as a serpent.

A لمم غيس *limamun ghīsun*, Locks flowing behind the ears full and luxuriant.

A غيسات *ghaysāt*, Bloom or flower of youth.

A غيسان *ghaysān*, Youth. The impetuosity of youth. Flower of youth. Sort, kind. Men, people.

A غيسانة *ghaysānat*, The flower of youth. Delicate (woman), well-fed, and in good health.

A غيسانيّ *ghaysānīy*, Beautiful and graceful.

P غيش *ghīsh*, Sorrow, sadness. Afflicted circumstances. A thick wood.

P غيشه *ghīsha*, A forest. A reed-bed. A reed of which they make sacks for carrying earth; such a sack. غيشهٔ مشك *ghīshaï mushk*, Name of a drug often mixed with musk.

A غيض *ghayz*, (v. n. of غاض for غيض) Decreasing, sinking into the ground (water); falling (as the price of commodities). Coming short of the proper time for delivery (a woman or animal). Causing to subside (water), or become cheap (goods). Immature fruit of the womb. غيض من فيض *ghayzun min fayzin*, Any little out of a large quantity. *Ghīz*, The pod, sheath, or spathe which contains the buds, flowers, and fruit of the palm-tree.

A غيضة *ghayzat*, (pl. غياض *ghiyāz* and اغياض *aghyāz*) A forest; a place abounding in trees, but having a little water. A swamp, a low-lying place. A haunt, a den.

A غيط *ghayt*, (v. n. of غاط for غيط) Entering (one thing into another). Lying hid.

A غيطان *ghītān*, Low-lying grounds.

A غيطل *ghaytal*, A cat. The same distance of the sun from the meridian in the forenoon at which he is in the afternoon at the hour called ظهر *zuhr*, the hottest time of the day. Thickets, groves.

A غيطلة *ghaytalat*, (v. n. of غيطل Q) Eating, drinking, and enjoying one's self without fear. Sleeping securely. One thicket. A crowd (of tamarisk-trees or men). Meat and drink. Pleasure with safety. Worldly blessings. Prosperity which renders insolent. An overpowering propensity to sleep. The sound of men's voices. The intense darkness of the night. (pl. غياطل *ghayātil*) A milch cow or doe.

A غيطمّ *ghaytamm*, Thick milk.

A غيطول *ghaytūl*, Thick darkness. Darkness. Mixed voices, noise, hubbub.

A غيظ *ghayz*, (v. n. of غاظ for غيظ) Rendering extremely angry, putting in a passion. Rage, fury, wrath, anger, passion, indignation, impetuosity. Anger suppressed through weakness. نائرهٔ غيظ تيمور *nāïraï ghayzi tīmūr*, The fire of Tīmūr's wrath.

A غيف *ghayf*, A flock of birds.

A غيفان *ghayfān*, (or غيّفان *ghayyafān*) The trees مرخ *markh*, غاف *ghāf*, or ينبوت *yambūt*. *Ghayafān*, (v. n. of غاف for غيف) Waving (as a tree from side to side).

A غيفة *ghayfat*, The haunt of a lion.

A غيل *ghayl*, (v. n. of غال for غيل) Suckling a child or cohabiting with a man when pregnant (which is prohibited by the Muhammadan law). The milk of a pregnant woman, or of one cohabiting with a man. Thickly-entangled trees. A valley of fountains and springs. Water overflowing the surface of ground in tillage. Whatever appears near although a great way off. A line drawn upon any thing. A variegated purple border or list of cloth. A wide garment. A strong, nervous, brawny arm. A corpulent, fat lad. *Ghīl*, (pl. اغيال *aghyāl* and غيول *ghuyūl*) A forest, wood, thicket, grove. A bed of canes or water-plants. A valley full of trees and water. A lion's den. *Ghiyal*, (pl. of غيلة *ghīlat*) Unexpected and treacherous attacks. *Ghuyul*, Many and fat (camels or beeves).

A غيلان *ghaylān*, Name of a man. امّ غيلان *umm ghaylān*, Egyptian-thorn, acacia. *Ghīlān*, (pl. of غول *ghūl*) Sylvan demons. Destructions. Accidents, misfortunes. غيلان الوغي *ghīlānu'l waghy*, Valiant soldiers.

A غيلة *ghaylat*, A fat woman. *Ghīlat*, (v. n. of غال for غيل) Suckling a child or cohabiting with a man when pregnant. An unexpected and treacherous attack. The substance شقشقة *shikshikat*. قتله غيلة *katalahu ghīlatan*, He slew him treacherously.

A غيلم *ghaylam*, A male tortoise. A pretty and lascivious girl. Broad-crowned and abounding in hair (boy). A well-spring. A frog. Any body.

A غيلميّ *ghaylamīy*, (A lad) the crown of whose head is large and thick of hair.

P غيم *ghaym*, A sponge.

A غيم *ghaym*, (v. n. of غام for غيم) Thirsting, being hot within. Being overspread with clouds (the sky). A cloud. Thirst, internal heat. A camel's distemper. Anger, rage. Secret anger.

A غيمان *ghaymān*, (fem. غيماء *ghaymā* or غيمي *ghayma'*) Thirsty, hot within.

A غين *ghayn*, (v. n. of غان for غين) Thirsting. Covering. Being altered, stupefied, and fainting (the mind). Pressing (any one) on all sides (debts). Darkness. Being diseased (camels). A cloud covering the sky. Thirst. Name of the letter غ. *Ghīn*, Name of a place where fever is prevalent.

A غيناء *ghaynā*, (fem. of اغين *aghyan*) (A tree) having many green leaves and thick branches.

A غينة *ghaynat*, A place full of trees without water. *Ghīnat*, The matter exuding from a corpse.

A غينف *ghaynaf*, An abyss, whence issue rivers and fountains. ذو غينف *zū ghaynaf*, Of immense depth (the sea).

P غيو *ghev*, Clamour, noise great and loud.

A غيوب *ghuyūb*, (v. n. of غاب for غيب) Lying hid. Being invisible. (pl. of غيب *ghayb*) Doubts.

A غيوبة *ghuyūbat*, (v. n. of غاب for غيب) Lying hid, being concealed. Doubt. A secret, mystery.

A غيوث *ghuyūs*, (pl. of غيث *ghays*) Rains.

A غيور *ghayūr*, (pl. غير *ghuyur*) Jealous in point of love or honour. An epithet of God. P آتش غيور سوز *ātishi ghayūr-soz*, Jealousy's consuming fire.

P غيوران *ghayūrān*, Holy men. غيوران شب *ghayūrāni shab*, Those who keep watch by night.

A غيول *ghuyūl*, (pl. of غيل *ghīl*) Woods. Reed-beds. Valleys full of water.

A غيوم *ghuyūm*, (pl. of غيم *ghaym*) Clouds.

P غيه *ghiya*, A cry for help.

A غيهب *ghayhab*, (pl. غياهب *ghayāhib*) Darkness. Extremely black (horse); pitchy-coloured (night). An indolent, careless, foolish man. Very woolly (garment). Heavy, troubled with indigestion. Disagreeable (companion).

A غيهبان *ghayhabān*, Darkness. The belly.

A غيهبة *ghayhabat*, Sounds, noises in battles.

A غيهق *ghayhak*, Long-bodied (camel). Cheerfulness, sprightliness. Madness.

A غيهقة *ghayhakat*, (v. n. of غيهق Q) Weakening the sight (darkness).

A غيهم *ghayham*, Darkness.

ف

ف *fā*, (called فاءِ سعفص *fā'i sa'fas*) The twentieth letter of the Arabic alphabet, and the twenty-third of the Persian, expressing 80 in arithmetic, and, in almanacks, the moon in her altitude. It is in Persian frequently interchangeable with ب *be*, پ *pe*, or و *vāv*, (as فيل *fīl* for پيل *pīl*, فام *fām* for وام *vām* or *wām*). In Arabic it is a prefixed particle of inference and sequence, signifying, "and, then, for, therefore, so that, in order that, in that case, in consequence, afterwards, at least, lest, for fear that, truly." Its power is that of *f*. ضربت زيدا فعمرا *zarabtu zaydan fa 'amran*, I struck Zayd, and then Amr.

P فا *fā*, A beloved object. Bashful. (for با *bā*)

With: as, فا او گفت *fā u guft*, He spoke with him; فا او رفت *fā u raft*, He went with him. (for وا *wā*) Again, once more. Against, opposite to, from the other side. فا داشتن *fā dāshtan*, To meet, confront. To oppose.

A فا *fā*, (accus. of فم *fam* or فوه *fūh*) The mouth. فا كرشن *fā kirshin*, The nearest road.

P فاء *fās*, Froth of the sea.

G فابش *fābish*, A bean.

P فات *fāt*, Fate. Death. فات يافتن *fāt yāftan*, To die.

A فات *fāta*, (fut. يفوت *yafūtu*) He died.

A فاتح *fātih*, (pl. فتحة *fatahat*) Who or what opens. A conqueror: a taker (of a city).

A فاتحة *fātihat*, (fem.) Who or what opens. (pl. فواتح *fawātih*) A beginning, exordium, commencement. الفاتحة *al fātihat*, (or سورة فاتحه *sūrasi fātiha*) The first chapter of the Kur'ān, (which the Muhammadans frequently repeat in their prayers).

P فاتحهٔ بزرگان *fātihasi buzurgān*, Prayers for the dead. فاتحه خواند *fātiha khwānd*, He recited the first chapter of the Kur'ān. He cursed. A فاتحهٔ فكرت *fātihasi fikrat*, The first word of a sentence.

A فاتر *fātir*, Weak, languid. Remiss. Dim-sighted (eye). Lukewarm, tepid (water). P خاطر فاطرش *khātiri fātirash*, His languid soul, dull wit.

P فاترسين *fātarsīn*, Wild rue. Seed of nasturtium.

P فاتر شدن *fātar shudan*, To ascend, be on high.

A فاتق *fātik*, One who cleaves open.

A فاتك *fātik*, (pl. فتّاك *futtāk*) Intrepid, strong. A robber.

A فاتن *fātin*, Tempter, trier, prover. One who leads astray; a seducer. The devil. Tempted, tried. Seduced, fascinated.

A فاتور *fātūr*, Tepid, lukewarm (water).

P فاتوريدن *fātūridan*, (or فاتوليدن *fātūlīdan*) To be farther off. To keep on one side, to shun, to avoid. To be afraid. To put away. To straighten.

P فاتوسين *fātūsīn*, Wild rue. Seed of nasturtium.

A فاتون *fātūn*, Pharaoh's baker slain by Moses.

A فاثج *fāsij*, A young (camel) in foal; also one fat, and not conceiving the first year. Large-bunched and fat (she-camel).

A فاثور *fāsūr*, A slab of marble, gold, or silver. A large brazen salver or plate, upon which other cups or dishes are placed. A large cup, goblet, or vessel from which smaller ones are filled. An earthen or other vessel in which wine is kept. A large dish or saucer. The sun's disk. A spy. A troop of soldiers stationed on the confines of an enemy's country, for the purpose of making inroads upon his territory. A post of honour, dignity, station. Cheerfulness, gladness. The breast.

P فاج *fāj*, (or فاخ *fākh*) A branch.

P فاجام *fājām*, Straggling fruits remaining on trees after the general gathering. Above.

A فاجر *fājir*, (fem. فاجرة *fājirat*) (pl. فجّار *fujjār* and فجرة *fajarat*) A sinner, liar; an adulterer, fornicator. A corrupter. Disobedient, rebellious. Rich. An enchanter, magician. False (oath).

P فاجره بچه *fājira-bacha*, A son of a whore.

P فاجشه *fājisha*, The testicles of a beaver.

A فاجع *fājiꜥ*, Disastrous, calamitous (death). (A woman) sorely afflicted. A sort of black bird having the beak and legs red.

A فاجعة *fājiꜥat*, Adversity, choaking grief.

A فاجل *fājil*, A gamester. A winner at gaming.

A فاجور *fājūr*, Wicked, adulterous, debauched.

A فاحش *fāhish*, Shameful, dishonest, indecent, obscene, impudent, flagitious. Enormous, exceeding bounds (in any thing bad), glaring, outrageous. Avaricious. Ugly, mis-shapen. Disproportionate. فاحش الطول *fāhishu't tūl*, Disproportionately long.

A فاحشا *fāhishan*, Exceedingly, outrageously.

A فاحشة *fāhishat*, A whore. Any thing extremely bad, an abominable crime. Whoredom, adultery. Whatever God has forbidden.

P فاحشگی *fāhishagī*, Whoredom, prostitution.

P فاحشه دوست *fāhisha-dost*, A whoremonger.

P فاحشه دوستي *fāhisha-dostī*, Whoremongery.

A فاحص *fāhis*, An examiner, searcher.

A فاحم *fāhim*, Hoarse-voiced (ram). Very black, coal-black (hair). Water stagnating, not flowing.

A فاختة *fākhitat*, (pl. فواخت *fawākhit*) A ring-dove. A woman's name.

P فاختك *fākhtak*, A little ring-dove.

P فاخته *fākhta*, A ring-dove. فاخته گون *fākhta-gūn*, Dove-coloured, or of a quince-flower.

A فاختيّ *fākhitīy*, Dove-coloured.

P فاختئی *fākhtasī*, Dove-colour.

A فاخر *fākhir*, A boaster. Precious, valuable, sumptuous, splendid, brave. Excellent, honourable, distinguished. A large sort of date without stone. حبق الفاخر *habaku'l fākhir*, Large-leaved basil.

A فاخرة *fākhirat*, (fem. of فاخر) Excellent. Name of a city in Turkistān. خلعت فاخره *khilꜥati fākhira*, A rich dress presented by Eastern princes to those whom they mean to honour.

P فاخره *fākhara*, Name of a medicinal grain.

A فاخز *fākhiz*, A kind of stoneless date.

A فاخور *fākhūr*, A species of sweet-smelling herb. A woman walking flauntingly.

P فاخيدن *fā khīdan*, To pluck, pull. To beat or card cotton. To throw a javelin. To take, receive. To assemble, collect.

P فاخيز آمدن *fākhez āmadan*, To crawl. To go staggering or tottering along (as a drunken man or child).

A فأد *fasd*, (v. n. of فأد) Hitting, wounding in the heart. Making a coward. Making a place under the ashes for baking bread. Roasting (meat). Baking (bread) under the ashes. *Fasad*, (v. n. of فئد and فؤد) Labouring under, or complaining of, a disease of the heart (فؤاد *fusād*).

P فاداشتن *fādāshtan*, To retain. To keep before or opposite, to front. To oppose, to meet face to face.

P فادج *fādaj*, Name of a stone from China. The bezoar-stone.

A فادح *fādih*, Important, difficult. Oppressive.

A فادحة *fādihat*, A misfortune.

A فادر *fādir*, (pl. فدر *fudr*) Weak, knocked up (stallion). (pl. فوادر *fawādir*) Aged or large (mountain-goat). A she-camel separating from the herd.

A فادرة *fādirat*, A large, solid rock on the summit of a mountain.

P فادزهر *fādzahar*, The bezoar-stone.

A فاذا *fa izā*, Then, in that case, therefore, after that. When, lo!

A فار *fār*, A human muscle.

A فأر *fasr*, (v. n. of فأر) Digging, burying, hiding. (pl. فئران *fisrān*, فئرة *fisarat*, and فؤر *fusar*) A mouse. Musk.

A فارّ *fārr*, (pl. فرّ *farr*) Flying. A deserter.

P فاراب *fārāb*, Name of a province in Turkistān. Name of a city in the same province, called by the Turks سيرام *sīrām*. Land watered by irrigation.

A فأرة *fasrat*, A mouse (male or female). Wind which collects round the pastern of camels, which dissipates on being rubbed, and collects again when let alone, wind-gall. Name of a tree. A bag of musk. فأرة الابل *fasratu'l ibl*, A fragrant smell from the wind of a camel after eating odoriferous herbs. فارة الابل *fāratu'l ibil*, The smell of camels' hides when they become moist after watering. فارة المسك *fāratu'l mish*, A bag, or the strong smell of musk.

A فارج *fārij*, A dispeller of grief. A bow bellying out from the string. A she-camel which has long ceased to breed, and therefore spurns the male.

A فارح *fārih*, (fem. فارحة *fārihat*) Glad, happy.

P فارد *fārd* or *fārid*, Name of the first round at the game of نرد *nard* (of which there are seven).

A فارد *fārid*, Alone. Solitary. (A tree) standing alone. (A doe) separated from the herd. The best and whitest sugar. A wild ox.

A فاردة *fāridat*, (A tree) growing by itself. (A she-camel) pasturing alone.

A فارز *fāriz*, Clear, distinct (speech). Plain (tongue). The grandsire of the black ants.

A فارزة *fārizat*, A road through soft sands.

P فارس *fārs*, Persia, Parthia.

A فارس *fāris*, Mounted upon any solid-hoofed animal except a horse (as a mule or an ass). (pl. فوارس *fawāris* and فرسان *fursān*) A horseman, a cavalier. A lion. The Persians. Persia.

G فارسطاريون *fāristāriyūn*, Valerian.

P فارسی *fārsī*, Persian, Persic. زبان فارسی *zabāni fārsī*, The Persian language.

A فارسيّ *fārisīy*, Persic, Persian. A Persian.

P فارسيان *fārsiyān*, The Persians. Pārs is the proper and original name of this country, Fārs being a corruption of the Arabians, who have not the letter پ pe in their language.

A فارسيّة fārisīyat, A Persian word or phrase.

A فارض fāriz, Aged (cow). (pl. فرّض furraz) Large, bulky, corpulent. Thick (beard). Old, ancient. One who knows or understands الفرائض al farāïz, i.e. the statutes and commandments of God.

A فارط fārit, (pl. فرّاط furrāt) A leader; one who goes on before a herd, a troop, or a caravan to prepare water for them; also the first in a flight of the birds called قطا katā.

A الفارطان al fāritāni, Two stars before the Bear.

A فارع fāriʻ, A high mountain overhanging another. One who ascends. One who descends. Handsome, good-looking. (pl. فرعة faraʻat) An ally, auxiliary (of a king).

A فارعة fāriʻat, The upper part (of a mountain). The surface of a valley. Name of a woman.

P فارغ fārigh, Leisure. Joy. A summer-breeze.

A فارغ fārigh, (pl. فرّغ furragh) Free; ceasing from labour, having just finished any work. At leisure; discharged, ceased, stopped. Free from care. Empty, hollow. فارغ البال fārighu'l bāl, (or فارغ الحال fārighu'l hāl) Independent. Contented.

A فارغبالي fārigh-bālī, Joy, gladness.

T فارغخطّي fārigh-khattī, A written release.

P فارفتن fā raftan, To be before or greater than others, to excel. Fā ruftan, To sweep out.

A فارق fārik, Who or what decides or distinguishes. A separator, divider. A discerner. (pl. فوارق fawārik, فرّق furrak, and فرق furuk) (A camel or ass) near delivery and withdrawing from the herd. A cloud (especially separated from others).

A فارقات fārikāt, Angels who are sent down to separate truth from falsehood.

G فارقليط fāraklīt, The Comforter.

A فارقيّ fārikīy, Of ميّافارقين mayyāfārikīn.

A فارك fārik, (A woman) hating her husband.

A فارنة fārinat, A female baker, a fornarina.

P فارنديدن fā randīdan, To shovel away.

A فاروق fārūk, Timid to an extreme. Name of the caliph Omar (as able to discriminate truth from falsehood, or to make orthodoxy triumphant over infidelity). Fārūk, (or ترياق فاروق tiryāki fārūk) The best sort of treacle, or theriaca.

A فاروقة fārūkat, Very timid (man or woman).

A فاره fārih, (pl. فرّه furrah, فرهة furrahat, فرهة furhat, فره furuh, and furh) Ingenious, clever. Active, brisk, sprightly (horse or mule).

A فارهة fārihat, A beautiful girl, extremely voracious. A singing girl.

P فارياب fāryāb, (or فاريّاو fāryāv) Ground watered by irrigation. Name of a country and city in Turkistān.

A فازة fāzat, An awning supported by two poles. A triumphal arch.

A فازر fāzir, An open road. A reddish black ant.

A فازرة fāzirat, A way leading through sand-hills.

A فازع fāziʻ, Afraid, frightened.

P فاژ fāj, Yawning.

P فاژده fājada, Yawning. A canopy, shade.

P فاژیدن fājīdan, To yawn, gape, stretch.

A فاس fa‹s, (v. n. of فأس) Cleaving. Striking with a hatchet. Touching or hurting on the hind-head. Eating (food). (pl. افؤس af‹us and فؤس fu‹us) A hatchet, an axe. The bit of the bridle, or rather a piece of iron suspended to the bit. The hind-head protuberant.

A فاس fās, Fez in Africa.

P فاسترك fāstarak, A little behind. A swallow.

A فاسج fāsij, (A she-camel) covered when too young. A she-camel young and swift.

A فاسخ fāsikh, A violator, dissolver, breaker.

A فاسد fāsid, (pl. فسدى fasdā') Vicious, corrupt, perverse, depraved, naught. Invalid, null and void. فاسد المزاج fāsidu'l mizāj, Of a bad disposition. فكر فاسد المال fikri fāsidu'l ma‹al, Bad counsel.

A فاسق fāsik, (pl. فسقة fasakat) A worthless, impudent fellow, scoundrel, prevaricator. A sinner, fornicator, adulterer. A sodomite. (in law) One who neglects decorum in his dress and behaviour, and whose evidence is therefore not held admissible. (A ripe date) that quits the husk.

A فاسقة fāsikat, A whorish, lewd woman.

A فاسقيّة fāsikīyat, A mode of wrapping the turban round the head.

A فاسياء fāsiyā‹, (and فاسية fāsiyat) A beetle.

P فاش fāsh, Manifest, clear, public, divulged, spread abroad. Scattered. فاش كردن fāsh kardan, To reveal, divulge, publish, blazon abroad.

A فاشّة fāshshat, Disobedient, stubborn (woman).

P فاشرا fāshrā, A species of ivy, producing clustering fruit. Bryony.

P فاش رستني fāsh rastanī, Seed of nose-smart.

SY فاشرستين fāshiristīn, A kind of wild vine: the black vine.

P فاشرسين fāsharsīn, Mustard-seed. Wild rue.

A فاشريّ fāshirīy, A certain medicine useful against the bite of a snake.

A فاشغة fāshighat, Scattered, flying (forelocks).

A فاشي fāshī, Divulged, diffused, made known. Propagated, multiplied. موت فاشي mawt fāshī, Wide-spreading death; plague, pestilence. P ناشي و فاشي شدن nāshī u fāshī shudan, To be brought to light and published.

A فاشية fāshiyat, Cattle multiplying or breeding. Property in general. Desultory (foray).

A فاصخة fāsikhat, (pl. فواصخ fawāsikh) Unfortunate, disappointed in one's views. A man to whom an acute intellect has been denied.

A فاصل fāsil, A separator. Decisive (sentence).

A فاصلة fāsilat, Space, intermediate space, distance. Any thing separating one from another, distinguishing between the true and false religion. Intervening (letter). A bead which separates other beads upon a string. (pl. فواصل fawāsil) The end of a verse or period in the Kur'ān; also of a poetic distich. A species of metrical foot. الفاصلة الصغرى al fāsilatu's sughra', (in poetry) Three inflected letters before a quiescent one: as, ضربت zarabat. الفاصلة الكبرى al fāsilatu'l kubra', Four inflected letters before a quiescent one: as, ضربتا zarabatā.

A فاضّة fāzzat, (pl. فواضّ fawāzz) Misfortune.

A فاضح fāzih, Gross, shameful (blunder).

A فاضل fāzil, Abounding, excelling, exceeding. Overflowing, redundant. Excellent, virtuous. Learned. Bountiful. Large (bucket). Much (wealth). Preponderating (scale). Whatever is realized over and above the estimated produce. A remainder. فاضل الدهر fāzilu'd dahr, The best of his age.

A فاضلة fāzilat, Beneficence. A valuable present. Distinguished virtue. Prerogative, privilege. الفاضلة al fāzilat, A metrical foot, called likewise الفاصلة الكبرى al fāsilatu'l kubra'.

P فاضلتر fāziltar, Better, more excellent.

P فاط fāt, Zedoary. Nux vomica. Poison.

A فاطر fātir, The Creator. (A camel) breeding new teeth. فاطر السموات و الارض fātiru's samāwāt wa'l arz, Creator of the heavens and earth.

A فاطم fātim, A colt ready to wean. A camel whose colt is a year old.

A فاطمة fātimat, (pl. فواطم fawātim) Name of Muhammad's daughter, called also فاطمة الزهراء سيّدة النساء fātimatu'z zahrā‹ sayyidatu'n nisā‹.

P مرغ فاطمه murghi fātima, A wagtail.

A فاطميّة fātimīyat, The Fātimites; a dynasty which reigned in Egypt from the year 908 to 1171.

A فاطن fātin, Intelligent, penetrating.

A فاعل fāʻil, One who makes or performs; a maker, doer, performer; an agent, actor. Governing (as one word another). The participle active, or noun of agency. The nominative case. A pederast (the pathic, or person abused, being called مفعول mafʻūl, Patient). فاعل حقيقي fāʻili hakīkī, The true agent (God). فاعل مختار fāʻili mukhtār, Master of one's own actions. تقدير فاعل مختار takdīri fāʻili mukhtār, Divine predestination. اسم فاعل ismi fāʻil, (in gram.) A noun denoting the agent.

A فاعليّ fāʻilīy, Effective, efficient. علت فاعليه ʻillati fāʻilīya, An efficient cause.

A فاعليّة fāʻilīyat, The quality or the nature of agent or noun of agency: agency.

A فاعوس fāʻūs, A sluggish old beast. A stammerer. A serpent. A mountain-goat. A misfortune. A narrow-necked traveller's water-bottle. Glans penis. A kind of Arabian game.

A فاعوسة fāʻūsat, The privities of a woman.

A فاعي fāʻī, Enraged, foaming.

A فاعية fāʻiyat, The plant called ثمامة sumāmat. Privet-flowers. Whispering, tell-tale (woman).

P فاعيه fāʻiya, Root of the water-lily.

P فاغر *fāghir*, A fragrant flower in India.

A فاغر *fāghir*, A species of animalcule.

A فاغرة *fāghirat*, A certain medicinal root. Roots of the water-lily. Cubebs, an aromatic.

P فاغره *fāghara*, A spice of the size of a vetch.

P فاغوش *fāghūsh*, An acrid Indian medicine.

A فاغية *fāghiyat*, Flowers of the privet.

P فاغيه *fāghiya*, A certain fragrant yellow Indian flower. Privet-flowers. Any fragrant blossom.

P فافا *fāfā*, Choice, excellent, rare, astonishing.

A فأفأ *fa,fa,* (or فأفاء *fa,fā,*) A stutterer, stammerer. One who pronounces badly, or very frequently, the letter ف *fā* or *fe*.

A فأفأة *fa,fa,at*, A vicious pronunciation, or reiteration, of the letter ف *fā*.

A فاق *fāk*, (v. n. of فوق, passively) Being broken in the notch (an arrow). A large dish full of meat. Cooked olive-oil. A desert. Tall, shambling, and loosely-framed (man). Name of a long-necked water-bird.

A فاقة *fākat*, Poverty, necessity, want. A day's fast. فقر و فاقه *fakr u fāka*, Poverty and want.

A فاقد *fākid*, (A woman) lamenting the loss of husband and children; or who marries after the decease of her husband. (A doe) missing her young, which has been carried off by a wild beast. فاقد البصر *fākidu'l basar*, Wanting the sight.

A فاقرة *fākirat*, A misfortune. A bridle, halter running through a ring inserted in a camel's nose.

A فاقع *fākiɛ*, Intense (yellow or red). Pure, unmixed, bright (colour).

A فاقعة *fākiɛat*, (pl. فواقع *fawākiɛ*) A misfortune.

P فاقه كش *fāka-kash*, A faster. Famished.

P فاقه كشي *fāka-kashī*, Fasting, hunger.

P فاقه مست *fāka-mast*, One who is starving, but conceals his distress.

A فاقياء *fākiyā,*, A membrane enclosing the head of a fœtus. A child's caul.

A فاك *fākk*, (pl. فككة *fakakat* and فكاك *fikāk*) Silly. Decrepit (old man). Wide-mouthed (old camel). فاك فاك *fākk fākk*, Very stupid.

A فاكه *fākih*, Soft, delicately brought up. Merry, blithe, joyous, jocose. A possessor of fruit.

A فاكهاني *fākihāniy*, A fruit-seller, fruiterer.

A فاكهة *fākihat*, (pl. فواكه *fawākih*) Fruit. Sweetmeats. A beautiful palm-tree. Jovial, gay, lively, merry, entertaining. فاكهة الشتاء *fākihatu'sh shitā,*, (Winter-fruits) Fire, firing.

P فاگرفتن *fā giriftan*, To meet: interrupt, intercept.

A فأل *fa,l*, (pl. فؤول *fu,ul* and افؤل *af,ul*) (vulg. *fāl*) An omen, augury, presage. علم الفال *ɛilmu'l fāl*, Sortilege, augury. لا فأل عليك *lā fa,la ɛalayka*, Nothing can harm thee: no spell against thee.

A فال *fāl*, (pl. افيال *afyāl*) Weak (in mind), imprudent. The flesh on one side of the hips. A certain vein in the gaskoin of a horse. Name of a place in Persia.

P فالج *fālij*, Assisted, defended. Victorious.

A فالج *fālij*, The palsy, or rather a paralytic affection of one side of the body, hemiplegia. A measure for dry goods. Name of a wind. A large camel with two bunches. An arrow reaching the mark. Name of a person, the son of Khalāwat; whence the adage, انا من ذلك الامر فالج بن خلاوة *ana min zāliha'l amr fālij bin khalāwat*, I am as clear of that matter as Fālij, the son Khalāwat.

P فالج زده *fālij-zada*, Paralytic.

A فالح *fālih*, Prosperous, successful.

G فالرغس *fālirghus*, (or فالرغوس) A stork.

P فالزن *fāl-zan*, A soothsayer, diviner.

P فال سنگك *fāl-sangak*, Pebbles for divining.

A فالعة *fāliɛat*, (pl. فوالع) A misfortune.

A فالق *fālik*, He who creates, brings forth, or splits open. A palm-tree whose blossoms have burst forth from the pod. A cleft in a mountain. Low ground between two heights. فالق الاصباح *fāliku'l asbāh*, Creator of the morning.

A فالقة *fālikat*, Low ground between two heights.

A فالك *fālik*, A girl whose breasts begin to shew.

P فالكباز *fālak-bāz*, A conjurer, fortune-teller.

P فال گرفتن *fāl giriftan*, To foretell, divine.

P فالگو *fāl-go* or *gū*, (فال گوي *fāl-goy* or *gūy*) A fortune-teller. A soothsayer.

P فال گوئي *fāl-go,ī* or *gū,ī*, Fortune-telling, soothsaying, divination, augury.

A فالود *fālūd*, (from P پالود *pālūd*) Strained.

A فالودج *fālūdaj*, (فالودق *fālūdak*, فالوذ *fālūz*, or فالوذق *fālūzak*, P فالوده *fālūda*) A dish made of starch, honey, and water: sweet flummery.

A فالوذ *fālūz*, Steel. A kind of sweetmeat.

A فالي *fa,līy*, (or *fālī*) A soothsayer, enchanter.

A فالية الافاعي *fāliyatu'l afāɛī*, The beginnings of evil. A kind of speckled beetle.

P فاليز *fālez*, A field of melons.

P فالينوس *fālīnūs*, Fumitory.

P فام *fām*, Form, appearance. Like, resembling. Name of a town in Khurāsān. (Joined to nouns of colour, implies a tendency to such colours: as) زمرد فام *zumurrud-fām*, Of an emerald-colour; سيه فام *siyah-fām*, Somewhat black; كبود فام *habūd-fām*, Of a cerulean or turquoise-colour; كحل فام *kuhl-fahm*, Blackish. (Equiv. to وام *wām*) Debt.

A فأم *fa,m*, (v. n. of فأم) Having the mouth full of grass (a camel). Drinking to satiety. *Fa,am*, (v. n. of فئم) Being full of fat (the withers of a camel).

A فأمّا *fa'ammā*, But, surely, if.

P فام ترش *fām-tursh*, Morose, disagreeable.

P فامر *fāmir*, (or فامره) A city in Turkistān.

A فامي *fāmiy*, Vender of wheat. Seller of garlic.

A فامية *fāmiyat*, Name of a city in Syria.

A فانّ *fa inna*, And. Indeed. But.

P فاناك *fānāk*, One who strongly articulates the letter ف *fā* in talking.

P فاناكي *fānākī*, The fault of pronouncing the letter ف *fā* much when speaking.

A فانق *fānik*, Soft, easy, delicate.

P A فانوس *fānūs*, A pharos, a light-house. A lantern. A whisperer, a tale-bearer, a pick-thank.

A فانوس خيال *fānūsi khiyāl*, A magic lantern (or P فانوس گردان *fānūsi gardān*, A revolving lantern), A lantern which revolves by the smoke of the candle within, and has on the sides of it figures of various animals. The heavens.

P فانه *fāna*, A wedge. A wooden peg, which, dropping into a lock, prevents it being opened till that is drawn up. A small cistern. (for زفانه *zafāna*) Flame. The tongue of a balance.

A فاني *fānī*, Frail, transitory, perishable, inconstant; tottering (old man). P اين جهان فاني *īn jahāni fānī*, This transitory world.

A فانيذ *fānīz*, (from P پانيد *pānīd*) Sugar-candy. A kind of sweetmeat.

A فأو *fa,w*, (v. n. of فأو) Striking, splitting (the head with a sword). A fissure between two mountains. An extensive, pleasant tract of country surrounded by hills. Low and trodden ground between rocky or rough grounds. A narrow pass through a valley, leading into an open country. A round heap of sand. A smooth, bare place. Night. The west.

P فاوا *fāwā*, Shamed, dishonoured. Dishonour, disgrace. فاوا بودن *fāwā būdan*, To be exposed.

A فاوانيا *fāwāniya*, Name of a wood, called also عود الصليب *ɛūdu's salīb*, (Wood of the cross).

A فأوي *fa,wa'*, Glans penis.

A فاه *fāh*, (pl. افواه *afwāh*) The mouth.

A فاهقة *fāhikat*, A stab with a spear fetching blood or hurting the first joint of the neck. A brand on the first joint of the neck.

P فاهم *fāham*, Together. فاهم آمدن *fāham āmadan*, To suit. To be drawn together.

A فاهم *fāhim*, Understanding; intelligent.

A فأي *fa,y*, A striking, splitting (of the head).

A فائت *fā,it*, A passer by: dead: escaped, lost.

A فائجة *fā,ijat*, A crowd, body. A large valley between two mountains or sand-hills.

A فائح *fā,ih*, Diffusing odour.

A فائحة *fā,ihat*, Fragrance, perfume.

P فايد *fāyad*, Until.

A فائدة *fā,idat*, (pl. فوائد *fawā,id*) Profit, gain (of learning or wealth); utility, advantage, emolument. The application or point of a moral or tale. A note, notice, advertisement. A sign, mark, or asterisk. Observation. Explanation. P پر فائده تر *pur-fā,idatar*, More replete with advantage, more beneficial.

P فائده مند *fā,idamand*, Profitable, useful.

A فائر *fā,ir*, Boiling. (A horse) whose sinews are inflated. (pl. فور *fūr*) A doe, a deer. Hatred. فار فائره *fāra fā,iruhu*, His anger raged, his passion was strong.

A فائز *fā,iz*, An overcomer. A flier. Overtaking, reaching, obtaining.

A فائض *fāʼiz*, Abundant, overflowing, affluent, exuberant. Excellent. فائض السرور *fāʼizu's surūr*, Diffusing joy. فائض النور *fāʼizu'n nūr*, Luminous.

A فائغة *fāʼighat*, Acrid, pungent, overpowering, intoxicating (smell).

A فائق *fāʼik*, Superior, super-excellent, superfine, transcendental, overtopping. The joining of the head with the neck. دواء فائق *dawāʼun fāʼikun*, A sovereign remedy.

A فائل *fāʼil*, The flesh of the side or the hollow part of the hip. Weak in mind, silly.

A فائلتان *fāʼilatāni*, Two veins in the thighs.

A فائية *fāʼiyat*, A large district, an extensive tract, partly hilly, partly level.

A فبأة *fabʼat*, A smart shower but short.

P فبال *fabāl*, A beginning, commencement.

A فبها *fabihā*, Well and good! Then, be it so!

P فپوس *fapūs* or *fupūs*, Ridicule, derision, laughter, mockery, sarcasm. Cream.

A فتّ *fatt*, (v. n. of فتّ) Breaking with the fingers. Crumbling. A crack in a stone. فتّ في ساعده *fatta fī sāʻidihi*, He weakened him, he crippled his arm. *Futt*, *fitt*, or *futt*, (The members of a family) scattered here and there.

A فتأ *fatʼ*, (v. n. of فتأ) Ceasing, desisting, abstaining. Breaking. Extinguishing. ما افتأت اذكره *mā aftaʼtu azkuruhu*, I have not ceased to remember him. *Fataʼ*, (v. n. of فتئ) Forgetting. Desisting.

A فتاء *fatāʼ*, (v. n. of فتي) Being young, and begetting offspring then. Being generous. Youth, juvenile age. *Fitāʼ*, (pl. of فتيّ *fatīy*) Young (animals).

A فتاة *fatāt*, (pl. فتيات *fatayāt*) A young girl.

A فتات *futāt*, A crumb. A fragment.

A فتاتيح *fatātīh*, (pl. of فتّاح) Kinds of birds.

A فتّاح *fattāh*, An opener. A conqueror. A judge. An arbiter. (pl. فتاتيح *fatātīh*) A sort of bird.

A فتاحة *fatāhat*, Aid, assistance. Victory, conquest. *Futāhat* or *fitāhat*, Judgment, award, decision; judicature.

A فتاحية *futāhiyat*, A kind of bird.

P فتادن *futādan*, To fall.

P فتاده *futāda*, Fallen. A fall, slip, tumble.

A فتار *fitār*, (v. n. of فتر) Being weak, languishing; slackening, flagging. Being lukewarm (water). Measuring with the فتر *fitr*, *i.e.* the tip of the thumb and fore-finger extended. *Futār*, The beginning of ebriety.

P فتاريدن *fitārīdan*, To dig up. To scatter. To tear. To cleave, to sunder.

A فتّاش *fattāsh*, An exact inquirer, inquisitor.

A فتافت *fatāfit*, Secrets mysteriously whispered.

A فتاق *fitāk*, A lump of leaven. The white root of the fibrous bark of the palm-tree. A bunch of dry dates. The upper limb of the sun's disk. The sun itself. The disappearance of a mist from the face of the sun. Mixtures of medicines.

P فتاك *fatāk*, Particular, special. Intense.

A فتّاك *fattāk*, A daring robber. *Futtāk*, (pl. of فاتك *fātik*) Intrepid, strong. Robbers.

P فتال *fatāl*, A twisting, coiling. A tearing up. Dispersion, diffusion. A newly-planted tree. *Fitāl*, Tearing. A cutting or breaking.

A فتّال *fattāl*, A rope-maker. A nightingale.

P فتاليدن *fatālīdan* or *fitālīdan*, To tear up, pull away. To draw off, by twisting, any thing which adheres tenaciously. To split, to tear. To shed, spill. To disperse. To dig up.

A فتان *fitān*, A leathern saddle-cover.

P فتان *futān*, Falling.

A فتّان *fattān*, An assayer (of gold). A tempter. Malicious, villainous, factious, seditious. Bewitching, seductive. Satan. A robber, thief. An inquisitor (such as the angels منكر *munkar* and نكير *nakīr*).

A فتّانان *fattānāni*, (dual) Gold and silver coin. Two angels named نكير و منكر *nakīr u munkar*, who are supposed to subject men to an initiatory examination in the grave.

P فتانيدن *futānīdan*, To cause to fall.

A فتاوي *fatāwa'*, (pl. of فتوي *fatwa'*) Legal decrees, judicial sentences given by the mufti.

A فتائل *fatāʼil*, (pl. of فتيلة *fatīlat*) Wicks.

A فتة *fitat*, (pl. فتون *fitūn*) A water-pot.

A فتّة *fattat* or *futtat*, Any thing crumbled; as fuel mixed with camels' dung. A portion of dates. A bit of dry dung placed as tinder under a fire-steel.

A فتح *fataha*, (fut. يفتح *yaftahu*) He opened.

A فتح *fath*, (v. n. of فتح) Opening (a door). Taking (a city). Having the orifices of the teats wide (a camel). Beginning, undertaking. Deciding, giving judgment in a law-suit. Assisting. Marking (a letter) with the vowel فتحه *fat'ha* ـَ. Opening, aperture. Victory, conquest; the taking of a city. Water overflowing a tract of land. Judgment, award, decision. The vowel *fat'ha* ـَ. Fruit of the tree نبع *nabʻ*, resembling a green berry. Aid. The commencement of the spring-rains. مجري فتح السنخ من القدح *majra's sinkhi mini'l kidhi*. فتح باب *fathi bāb*, The setting in of the rainy season. Rain. Opposition of two planets. P فتح باب كردن *fathi bāb kardan*, To open a door. To commence a business. فتح كلام دادن *fathi kalām dādan*, To begin a speech. A *Futuh*, Wide. Open (gate). Wide-mouthed (bottle) and without a stopple.

P فتح پيچ *fath-pech*, A mode of tying a turban.

A فتحة *fathat*, The vowel *fat'ha* ـَ, which, in Arabia, Persia, and Turkey, with a sound like "a" in "bat," or even approaching the "e" in "bet," is pronounced in India more like "u" in "but." *Futhat*, An ostentatious display of wealth or learning. An opening, an expanding. *Fatahat*, (pl. of فاتح *fātih*) Conquerors. Takers of cities.

P فتح مند *fathmand*, Victorious.

P فتح نامه *fath-nāma*, Despatches announcing victory.

P فتح نشان *fath-nishān*, A victorious banner.

A فتح نصيب *fath-nasīb*, Of victorious fortune.

A فتحي *fatha'*, The wind.

P فتح ياب *fath-yāb*, Obtaining victory.

A فتخ *fathh*, (v. n. of فتخ) Contracting and expanding the fingers or toes. *Fatakh*, Softness and flexibility of the joints. Breadth and length of the palm of the hand or sole of the foot. The appearance of fat in a camel. A little bell which emits no sound. (pl. of فتخة *fathkat*) Rings of silver on the hands or feet.

A فتخاء *fathkhāʼ*, (fem. of افتخ *aftakh*) Soft and limber about the palms of the hand, soles of the feet, or finger-joints. (A camel or woman) whose teats are large round the base. (In the former it is regarded as a blemish; in the latter, a beauty). Soft-jointed (hand). A frame whereon a bee-hive is placed. Soft-winged (eagle).

A فتخة *fatkhat* or *fatakhat*, (pl. فتخ *fatakh*, فتوخ *futūkh*, and فتخات *fatakhāt*) A ring upon the hands or feet, especially of silver, and without a bezel (with a bezel it is called خاتم *khātam*).

A فتر *fatr*, A woman's name. *Fitr*, The distance between the stretched-out tips of the thumb and the fore-finger. (From the index to the long finger the space is called رتب *ratab*; from this to the ring-finger, عتب *ʻatab*; and from this to the little finger, بصم *busm*). *Futr*, A mat of palm-leaves, on which they sift meal. *Fatar*, Languor, relaxation. Weakness. Intermission of the pulse. A muscle. A certain fixed quantity of meat or grain.

A فتّر *fittar*, The torpedo, (a fish).

P فتراك *fitrāk*, Saddle-straps. Cords fixed to the saddle for hanging game to.

A فترة *fatrat*, Languor, debility, relaxation, remission, intermission. An interregnum. An interval of time between two apostles or prophets. The torpedo (a fish). علي فترة *ʻala' fatratin*, After an interval. P بي فترت *bī fatrat*, Without intermission, incessantly.

P فترد *fatard*, Old, worn, rent. A tearer.

P فتردن *futardan*, To scatter. To destroy, tear. To pull to pieces. To cleave asunder.

A فترصة *fatrasat*, A cutting, an amputating.

P فتريد *fatrīd*, Any thing old, worn, torn.

P فتريدن *fitrīdan* or *fatrīdan*, To tear, break in pieces, tear asunder. To scatter.

A فتش *fatsh*, (v. n. of فتش) Examining, searching, making strict inquiry.

A فتغ *fatgh*, (v. n. of فتغ) Treading on (a thing) until (it) splits open.

A فتفتة *fatfatat*, A drinking short of repletion.

A فتق *fatk*, (v. n. of فتق) Breaking, splitting. Leavening (dough). Rendering (musk) more fragrant by an admixture of other odours. Breach of friendship or peace, quarrel, law-suit, feud, division. A rupture, hernia. A disease in the scrotum. Dawn. Ground without rain, between neighbouring fields which have it. An opening. An open country. فتق مائي *fatk māʼiy*, Watery hernia, hydrocele. فتق معوي *fatk maʻwiy*, Intestinal hernia. فتق ريحي *fatk rīhiy*, Windy hernia. فتق ثربي *fatk sarbiy*, Hernia of the omentum. *Fatak*, (v. n. of فتق) Being plentiful (season). Being open, large, patent. Plenty, luxuriance. The dawn. *Futuk*, Talkative, fluent (woman).

A فتقاء *fatkāʼ*, Ravished. Wide (woman).

P فتك *fatk*, A badger, a brock.

A فتك *fatk*, *fitk*, or *futk*, (v. n. of فتك) Daring to perpetrate whatever one meditates; attacking unawares, and treacherously destroying another. Being impudent (a wench). Importuning, urging, dunning, harassing.

A فتكر *fitakr*, (*fitkir*, فتكرين *fitakrīn*, *fatakrīn*, *futakrīn*, and *fitkarīn*) A great and wonderful thing. Misfortune.

A فتكلين *futaklīn*, An accident, misfortune.

A فتل *fatl*, (v. n. of فتل) Twisting (a rope). Converting, diverting (from any plan). Averting (the face). Following in the track of deceit and cunning. Removing the forelocks from before the eyes. Singing, warbling (as the nightingale). A plant which does not spread but twists up. A pod which stands in place of a leaf. *Fatal*, A lump or callosity on a camel's elbow. Wideness between a camel's elbow and side.

A فتلاء *fatlāʼ*, (A she-camel) whose legs are bent.

A فتلة *fatlat*, The pod which contains the berries of the سلم *salam* and سمر *samur* trees. A certain part of a camel's ear. *Fatlat* or *fatalat*, The fruit of the shrub عرفط *ʻurfut*.

P فتليدن *fitlīdan*, To tear. To scatter. To pluck up.

A فتن *fatn*, (v. n. of فتن) Proving, trying. Assaying (metals). Tempting. Seducing. Making mad (as a woman her lover). Filling with wonder and astonishment. Burning, scorching. Tormenting. Meeting with trials. State, condition, situation. Mode, manner. *Fitan*, (pl. of فتنة *fitnat*) Temptations. Seditions, wickednesses. *Futun*, (pl. of فتين *fatīn*) Black stony grounds.

P فتن *fatan*, Figure, form, shape. Endowments. Name of a province in India.

A فتنان *fatnāni*, Two kinds. العيش فتنان *al ʻaysh fatnāni*, Life is checkered with pain and pleasure. *Futnāni*, (dual) Morning and evening.

A فتنة *fitnat*, (v. n. of فتن) Proving (men) by temptations, or (gold) by fire. Seducing (from loyalty), leading into sedition and rebellion. Being tried by evils. The smelting of gold or silver. Sedition, insurrection, tumult, mutiny, discord, disturbance, riot, rebellion. War. Calamity, distress. Toil, pain, torment. Malignity, impiety, iniquity, infamy. Crime, sin, wickedness. Ingratitude. Temptation, seduction: any thing diverting a man from his duty. Discordance in opinion. Anarchy. Error. Madness, delirium. Wealth. Children. فتنهٔ آخر زمان *fitnaʼi ākhir zamān*, The wickedness of the last times. P فتنه را كمر كشادن *fitna rā kamar gushādan*, To quell a mutiny. فتنه شدن *fitna shudan*, To revolt, mutiny.

P فتنه *fitna*, Wickedness. Fraud. The eyes, hair, or figure of a woman (as that whereby a man is bewitched). Name of a female slave of Bahrām Gūr.

P فتنه انگيز *fitna-angez*, Rebellious, seditious.

P فتنه جوي *fitna-joy* or *jūy*, Fond of tumults, seeking disturbance, quarrelsome, seditious.

A فتو *fatw*, An excelling in liberality.

P فتو *fataw*, Proud: quarrelsome. Deceived.

A فتوّ *futūw*, (pl. of فتىً *fata'*) Young men. Liberal-minded.

A فتوا *fatwa'*, (for فتوي *fatwa'*) A judicial decree pronounced by a مفتي *muftī*; judgment, sentence.

A فتوان *fatawāni*, du. of فتىً *fata'*, Two young men.

A فتوة *fitwat*, (pl. of فتىً *fata'*) Young men. Liberal.

A فتوّة *futūwat*, Liberality. Childhood, boyhood. The rank of mufti, chancellor, or patriarch.

A فتوت *fatūt*, Crumbled: ground coarsely.

A فتوح *fatūh*, The commencement of vernal rains. (A camel) having the orifices of the teats wide. *Futūh*, (pl. of فتح *fath*) Victories, conquests, the taking of towns. Plenty, easy circumstances, income received gratuitously.

A فتوحات *futūhāt*, (pl. of فتوح *futūh*, pl. of فتح *fath*) Numerous victories, conquest of many towns.

A فتوحي *futūhī*, A jacket without sleeves.

A فتوخ *futūkh*, (pl. of فتخة *fatkhat*) Rings upon the fingers or toes without a bezel. The joints of a lion's claws.

P فتودن *futūdan*, To speak with premeditation.

P فتوده *futūda*, Deceived. Deceitful (world).

A فتور *futūr*, (v. n. of فتر) Slackening. Languishing, flagging. Being weak, languid, relaxed (the joints). Being tepid (water). Measuring with the extended tip of the thumb and index. Weakness, languor, infirmity. Coolness, want of affection. P فتور پذير شدن *fūtur-pazīr shudan*, To become languid.

P فتورة *futūrat*, Lukewarmness. A temperate atmosphere.

A فتوريا *fatūriyā*, Dispersed, ruined, undone. Exciting quarrels.

A فتوق *futūk*, Calamities. Wants. Diseases. Debt. ذو فتوق *zū futūk*, (A year) of little rain.

A فتوك *futūk*, (v. n. of فتك) Daring to perpetrate whatever one meditates. Importuning, urging, dunning, harassing. Being impudent (a wench). Exceeding bounds in wickedness. Attacking unawares, and treacherously destroying another.

A فتون *fitūn*, (pl. of فتة *fitat*) Water-pots. *Futūn*, (v. n. of فتن) Proving, trying. Throwing into trouble or temptation. Filling with wonder and astonishment. Falling into trouble or temptation. Desiring to commit fornication.

A فتوي *fatwa'* or *futwa'*, (pl. فتاوي *fatāwa'*) A judicial or religious sentence pronounced by a mufti.

A فتويّ *fatawiy*, Fragmentary.

A فتىً *fata'*, (pl. فتيان *fityān*, فتوة *fitwat*, فتية *fityat*, فتوّ *futūw*, and فتيّ *futiy*) A youth, boy. A man-servant. Liberal, generous, munificent.

A فتيّ *fatiy*, (pl. فتاء *fitāʼ* and افتاء *aftāʼ*) Young in years (any animal). New. *Futayy*, The cup or bowl of daring, impudent fellows. *Futiy*, (pl. of فتىً *fata'*) Young men. Liberal, munificent.

A فتيا *futya'* or *fatya'*, A judicial or religious decree pronounced by a mufti or expounder of the law.

A فتيات *fatayāt*, (pl. of فتاة) Young (girls).

A فتيان *fityān*, (pl. of فتىً *fata'*) Youths. Liberal. *Fatayāni*, Two young men. Night and day.

A فتية *fityat*, (pl. of فتىً *fata'*) Young men.

A فتيّة *fatiyat*, (fem. of فتيّ *fatiy*) Young.

A فتيت *fatīt*, Crumbled (bread), crumbs.

A فتيق *fatīk*, Shining (dawn). Eloquent. Bursting with fat (a camel). Double-pointed (spear).

A فتيل *fatīl*, Twisted (rope). A rope made of the fibres of the palm-tree. A match for a cannon or lamp, a linstock, candle-wick. A tent for wounds. A thin membrane in the groove of a date-stone. Aught, any thing. Little rolls of skin which are peeled off the body by friction in the baths.

A فتيلة *fatīlat*, (pl. فتائل *fatāʼil*) Particles of skin rubbed off the body in the bath. A wick. A match. A clyster. Aught, any thing. فتيلت طويلة *fatīlati tawīla*, A long wick, (metaph.) A man who supports the honour of his family. حجر فتيلة *hajari fatīla*, A stone which burns like a match.

P فتيله دهنج *fatīla-dahanj*, Small forceps for plucking up hairs. Snuffers.

P فتيله سوز *fatīla-soz*, A candlestick.

P فتيله مو *fatīl-mo*, Silly, stupid, mad, crazy.

A فتين *fatīn*, Burnt (silver). (pl. فتن *futun*) Stony, burnt ground.

A فثّ *fass*, (v. n. of فثّ) Dispersing, scattering. A certain herb, of which they make a kind of coarse bread in scarce seasons. The colocynth. Scattered (dates).

A فثأ *fasʼ*, (v. n. of فثأ) Pacifying anger. Stilling (a boiling pot) by pouring in cold water. Averting, turning off. Casting up froth (boiling milk). Taking the chill off any thing.

A فثائد *fasāʼid*, (or فثافيد *fasāfīd*) White clouds, one piled upon another. Lining of garments.

A فثج *fasj*, (v. n. of فثج) Diminishing, decreasing. Cooling (boiling water) by the pouring in of cold. Bearing heavily.

A فثح *fasih*, (pl. افثاح *afsāh*) The belly, paunch. A large serpent which resembles a wallet or purse.

A فثغ *fasgh*, A breaking (of the head).

A فثوء *fusūs*, (v. n. of فثأ) Stilling (a boiling pot) by pouring in cold water. Taking the chill off any thing. Averting (evil). Casting up froth (boiling milk) and then ceasing.

P فج *fuj* or *fij*, A camel or other animal whose lip hangs loose.

A فجّ *fajj*, (v. n. of فجّ) Being very wide between the feet, straddling. Pulling and rendering distant from the string (the middle of a bow). (pl. فجاج *fijāj*) A broad way, especially between two mountains. من كل فجّ فجاج *min kull fajj fijāj*, (or من كل فجّ عميق *min kull fajj ʻamīk*) From every wide or deep valley, from every quarter. *Fijj*, Raw, unripe (fruit). The Syrian melon.

A فجأ *fajs*, (v. n. of فجأ) Lying with, knowing carnally. *Fajas*, (v. n. of فجئ) Being large-bodied (a camel). (pl. of فجوة *fajwat*) Court-yards.

A فجا *faja'*, (v. n. of فجي) Being wide between the feet, straddling. Being distant from the string (the middle of a bow). Bigness of belly in a she-camel. Width between the thighs, knees, and legs.

P فجا *fajā* or *fijā*, Gleanings of grapes or dates.

A فجاء *fijās*, (v. n. 3 of فجأ) Taking by surprise, rushing upon unawares. (pl. of فجوة *fajwat*) The courts or squares of a house.

A فجّاء *fajjās*, (fem. of افجّ *afajj*) (A bow) whose string is distant from the handle. Wide between the legs.

A فجاءة *fujāsat*, (v. n. of فجأ) Rushing upon and destroying unawares. Taking by surprise. An unforeseen accident. موت الفجاءة *mawtu'l fujāsat*, Sudden death. فجاءةً *fujāsatan*, Suddenly.

A فجأة *fajsat*, (v. n. of فجأ) Happening unexpectedly, taking by surprise. Rushing upon and destroying unawares. فجأةً *fujsatan*, Suddenly, unexpectedly, unawares.

A فجاج *fijāj*, (pl. of فجّ *fajj*) Broad roads between mountains. *Fujāj*, A wide road between mountains.

A فجاجة *fajājat*, Crudity, rawness. Raw fruit.

A فجار *fajār*, Wickedness. Adultery, fornication, harlotry. يا فجار *yā fajāri*, O adultress! *Fijār*, Roads, ways. (pl. افجرة *afjirat*) Name of an unjust war (of which there were four) waged between the Arabian tribes Kuraysh and Kays.

A فجّار *fujjār*, (pl. of فاجر *fājir*) Wicked; sinners, fornicators.

A فجائع *fajāsiʻ*, (pl. of فجيعة) Afflictions, pains.

A فجائي *fujāsiy*, Unforeseen, casual.

A فجّة *fujjat*, Interstice, space, gap.

A فجج *fujaj*, A wide divarication of the feet, the heels being close, and the toes turned out (considered more ungraceful than فحج *fahaj*). *Fujuj*, Heavy, disagreeable persons.

A فجر *fajr*, (v. n. of فجر) Setting a-flowing (water). Deviating from one's duty, swerving from truth. Launching out into wickedness and debauchery. Recovering from sickness. Crepuscle, dawn, morning, early. صلوة الفجر *salātu'l fajr*, Morning-prayer. كوكب الفجر *kawkabu'l fajr*, The morning-star. وقت فجر *wakti fajr*, Day-break. *Fajar*, Munificence, beneficence, liberality. Opulence. *Fujur*, (pl. of فجور *fajūr*) Very wicked. Adulterers, debauchees.

A فجرة *fajrat*, (v. n. of فجر) Launching out into debauchery and wickedness. The widest part of a valley, towards which the waters flow. *Fujrat*, A channel or valley down which a torrent runs. *Fajarat*, (pl. of فاجر *fājir*) Impious, infidel, wicked, unchaste. ركب فجرة *rakiba fajarata*, He lied.

A فجز *fajz*, (for فجس *fajs*) Pride, haughtiness.

A فجس *fajs*, (v. n. of فجس) Being haughty. Originating a shameful or odious act. Pride, haughtiness. A malicious action. Violence, oppression.

A فجش *fajsh*, (v. n. of فجش) Breaking a hollow substance (as head or cup). Widening, stretching.

A فجع *fajʻ*, (v. n. of فجع) Vexing, causing grief (the loss of a thing on which one has prided himself).

A فجفاج *fajfāj*, (فجفج *fajfaj*, or *fujfuj*) Loquacious, talkative, crammed with other people's ideas.

A فجل *fajl* or *fajal*, (v. n. of فجل) Being thick. Being loose or soft. *Fujl* or *fujul*, A radish. حبّ الفجل *habbu'l fujl*, A kind of medicine.

A فجو *fajw*, (v. n. of فجا for فجو) Opening (a door). Drawing a bowstring wide from the handle.

A فجواء *fajwās*, (A bow) whose string is distant from the handle. (Cattle) wide or straddling between the thighs, knees, or legs (from fatness). An extensive tract of land.

A فجوة *fajwat*, (pl. فجوات *fajawāt*, فجاء *fijās*, or *fajās*) An interval, intervening space. A cleft between two mountains. The space between the right and the left side of a hoof. A court-yard. A wide tract of land.

A فجور *fajūr*, (pl. فجر *fujur*) Very wicked; adulterous; a debauchee. *Fujūr*, (v. n. of فجر) Deviating from the right way, launching out into wickedness and debauchery. Lying. Charging with falsehood, giving the lie. Rebelling against, resisting, opposing divine authority. Leaning from the saddle (a horseman). Being spoiled (business). Becoming dim (the sight). Recovering (from indisposition). Wickedness, adultery, lust, luxury, lying, villainy, impiety. فجور القرابة *fujūru'l karābat*, Incest. فسق و فجور *fisk u fujūr*, Iniquity and debauchery.

A فجوع *fajūʻ*, Calamitous (death).

A فجوي *fajwa'*, (fem. of افجي *afja'*) (Cattle) wide or straddling between the thighs from fatness.

A فجيعة *fajiʻat*, (pl. فجائع *fajāsiʻ*) Adversity, poignant grief.

P فچفچه *fuchfucha*, Whispering.

A فحّ *fahh*, (v. n. of فحّ) Hissing (a serpent). Being hoarse; making a hoarse, snoring noise in sleep.

A فحا *faha'* or *fiha'*, (pl. افحاء *afhās*) An onion or other herb used in seasoning meat when dressing.

A فحاحيل *fahāhīl*, (pl. of فحّال) Male palm-trees.

A فحّاش *fahhāsh*, Wicked, obscene, indecent.

A فحاشة *fahāshat*, Salaciousness, obscenity.

A فحال *fihāl*, (pl. of فحل *fahl*) Males, stallions.

A فحّال *fuhhāl*, (pl. فحاحيل *fahāhīl*) The male palm-tree bearing no fruit.

A فحالة *fihālat*, (v. n. of فحل) Gendering (a stallion). Male energy. (pl. of فحل *fahl*) Males.

A فحام *fihām*, (pl. of فحم *fahm*) Coals. *Fuhām*, (v. n. of فحم) Sobbing, being unable to breathe any more (a lad). Bleating hoarsely (a ram).

A فحّام *fahhām*, A charcoal-burner.

A فحاوي *fahāwī*, (pl. of فحوي) Significations.

A فحّة *fuhhat*, Heat (of pepper).

A فحث *fahs*, (v. n. of فحث) Examining, investigating, inquiring. *Fahis*, Belly, paunch; tripe.

A فحج *fahj*, (v. n. of فحج) Being proud. Pointing the toes inward in walking. *Fahaj*, A mode of walking, with the toes turned in and heels out.

A فحجاء *fahjās*, (fem. of افحج *afhaj*) (A woman or mare) going with the toes turned in and the heels out: pigeon-toed.

A فحح *fuhuh*, Vipers in motion or irritated.

A فحس *fahs*, (v. n. of فحس) Taking any thing with the tongue or mouth from the hand (as water). Rubbing barley in the hand until the piles drop off.

A فحش *fuhsh*, (v. n. of فحش) Being shameful, infamous. Talking obscenely. Being stingy. Exceeding bounds. Answering outrageously. Ribaldry, shameful discourse or action.

A فحشاء *fahshās*, Stinginess in giving (especially that which is ordained by the Muhammadan law for pious uses). Whoredom, adultery.

P فحش گو *fuhsh-go* or *gū*, Obscene in conversation.

A فحشيات *fahshiyāt*, Obscenities.

A فحص *fahs*, (v. n. of فحص) Examining, investigating, inquiring into. Choosing a certain place for her nest, called افحوص *ufhūs* (the bird قطا *katā*). Being loose, moving (the front teeth). Turning the soil over (rain). Making haste. Shaving the middle of the head, so as to resemble a bird's nest on the ground. A place fully inhabited. A dimple.

P فحص مراد كردن *fahsi murād kardan*, To examine into a design.

A فحصة *fahsat*, A dimple on the chin.

A فحض *fahz*, (v. n. of فحض) Breaking or squashing any thing soft (as a cucumber or melon).

A فحفاح *fahfāh*, Hoarse. A river in Paradise.

A فحفحة *fahfahat*, (v. n. of فحفح Q) Being sincere (in love or friendship). Being hoarse. Whistling in one's sleep.

A فحل *fahl*, (v. n. of فحل) Allowing a stallion camel free access to the females. Choosing an excellent stallion camel. (pl. فحول *fuhūl*, افحل *afhul*, فحال *fihāl*, فحالة *fihālat*, and فحولة *fuhūlat*) A male animal, stallion. Fruitless (tree). The male palm-tree; also a mat made of its filaments. One who looks after horses. (pl. فحول *fuhūl*) A historian, narrator. A repeater of poetry. Wise, learned. The star Canopus. Name of a poet, called also علقمة *ʿalkamat*; one who excels his rivals, especially in poetry. فحل آفاق *fahli āfāk*, The world.

A فحلة *fahlat*, The business and duty of a stallion. Audacious, impudent, masculine (woman). *Fihlat*, (v. n. of فحل) Gendering (a stallion). Male energy.

A فحم *fahm*, (v. n. of فحم) Sobbing, being unable to breathe, speak, or cry aloud. Bleating (a ram). Drinking after twilight. Sound, sensible, eloquent (speech). *Fahm* or *faham*, (pl. فحام *fihām* or فحوم *fuhūm*) Charcoal. *Fahim*, Hoarse (ram).

A فحمة *fahmat*, One coal. The hour of twilight or dawn. فحمة العشاء *fahmatu'l ʿishāʾ*, The beginning; also darkest part of the night (after twilight. فحمة بن جمير *fahmatu'bn jumayr*, Midnight.

A فحواء *fahwāʾ*, Seed, pot-herb seed. *Fahwāʾ*, (*fuhawāʾ*, or فحواى كلام *fahwāʾi kalām*) Signification, sense, meaning, argument, scope, spirit, style, contents. فحواى مسرّت احتوا *fahwāʾi masarrat-ihtiwā*, The joyful sense.

A فحوة *fahwat*, The choicest honey.

A فحول *fuhūl*, A male palm-tree. (pl. of فحل *fahl*) Males. Those who excel others. Historians, chroniclers. Mats made of palm-leaves. فحول الشعراء *fuhūlu'sh shuʿarāʾ*, Masculine, vigorous poets. Caustic satirists.

A فحولة *fuhūlat*, (v. n. of فحل) Gendering (a stallion). The virtue or energy of the male. (pl. of فحل *fahl*) The males of any sort of animal.

A فحوم *fuhūm*, (v. n. of فحم) Being hoarse-voiced. Sobbing; being unable to speak, reply, breathe, or cry aloud. Being black. Stagnating, not flowing (a well). (pl. of فحم *fahm* or *faham*) Coals.

A فحومة *fuhūmat*, (v. n. of فحم) Being of a coal black; dark, or jetty. Blackness.

A فحوى *fahwa'*, Meaning, sense, scope. لفظ فلا فحوى *lafz fa lā fahwa'*, A word without meaning.

A فحية *fihyat* or *fahiyat*, A sip, a small draught.

A فحيح *fahīh*, (v. n. of فح) Hissing (a serpent).

A فحيص *fahīs*, A prier into secrets or failings.

A فحيل *fahīl*, Potent (man or stallion). Clever, distinguished (man). Excellent (ram).

A فحيم *fahīm*, Very black. A coal: charcoal.

P فخ *fahh*, A gin, noose, snare. The chase. A hunting-place. A nose-bag for a horse.

A فخ *fakhkh*, (v. n. of فخ) Snoring; sleeping on the back. Being diffused (perfume). (pl. فخاخ *fikhākh* and فخوخ *fukhūkh*) A gin, snare. Weakness in the feet.

A فخاخ *fikhākh*, (pl. of فخ *fakhkh*) Snares, gins.

A فخار *fakhār*, Glory, boast. *Fikhār*, (v. n. 3 of فخر) Boasting against, or contending for glory.

A فخّار *fakhkhār*, One who glories, boasts, vaunts greatly: boastful, vauntful. A potter. Potters' clay. (pl. of فخّارة *fakhkhārat*) Earthenwares.

A فخارة *fakhārat*, Glory, boast, vaunt.

A فخّارة *fakhkhārat*, Earthenware, crockery.

A فخّاري *fakhkhāriy*, A seller of earthenware.

A فخام *fikhām*, (pl. of فخيم) Great, illustrious.

A فخامة *fakhāmat*, A being thick and corpulent.

A فخّة *fakhkhat*, Sleeping, snoring. A morning slumber (especially on the back, or after coition). A corpulent, greasy woman. A flexible, slender bow. Weakness in the foot.

P فخت *fakht*, Trodden. Wide, expanded. Gain.

A فخت *fakht*, (v. n. of فخت) Cutting. Uncovering (a vessel). Striking (the head) with a sword. Cooing (a ring-dove). (A cook) taking meat out of a cauldron, piece after piece. Light or splendour of the moon. Round holes in the roof. A noose, snare, gin.

A فخج *fakhj*, (v. n. of فخج) Being proud. A mode of turning in the toes (worse than فحج *fahaj*).

A فخخ *fakhakh*, Weakness in the foot.

A فخذ *fakhz*, (v. n. of فخذ) Smiting, hurting in, or breaking the thigh. *Fakhiz*, *fakhz*, or *fikhz*, (pl. افخاذ *afkhāz*) The thigh. *Fakhiz*, Part of a tribe. Relations, brethren.

A فخذاء *fakhzāʾ*, (A woman) embracing, clasping, and holding fast by a femoral hug.

A فخر *fakhr*, (v. n. of فخر) Excelling in glory. Preferring, exalting, regarding as more eminent in glory. *Fakhr* or *fakhar*, (v. n. of فخر) Excelling in glory. Boasting, glorying. Glory, ornament, grace. Egotism, vaunt, boast. فخر الاقران *fakhru'l akrān*, The glory of his cotemporaries. فخر الاماجد و الاعيان *fakru'l amājid wa'l aʿyān*, The most illustrious amongst the nobles. فخر الامراء الملة المسيحية *fakhru'l umarāʾi'l millati'l masīhiya*, The ornament of the Christian princes. فخر انبيا و رسل *fakhri ambiyā u rusul*, The glory of prophets and apostles (Muhammad). P اظهار فخر و غرور كردن *izhāri fakhr u ghurūr kardan*, To make a vainglorious display, to boast, to vaunt.

A فخرانيّة *fakhrāniyat*, Glory. Beatitude, felicity.

P فخرز *fakhriz*, Fat. Strong, lusty.

A فخري *fakhrī*, A kind of grape so called.

A فخرية *fakhrīya*, Boasting, vain-glorious.

A فخز *fakhz*, (v. n. of فخز) Excelling, exceeding. Being proud, haughty, arrogant. Causing an excess, making a surplus, leaving a remainder. Boasting. Triumphing in a contest for vain-glory. Doing good. A residue, remainder.

A فخش *fakhsh*, (v. n. of فخش) Losing, wasting. Neglecting, not minding, leaving unattended to.

A فخفخة *fakhfakhat*, A boasting vainly.

P فخفره *fakhfara*, Bran. Mouldy. Stale.

P فخفور *fakhfūr*, Title of the Emperor of China.

P فخلمه *fakhlama*, A wooden instrument with which they strike the bow when preparing cotton for spinning.

A فخم *fakhm*, Noble, illustrious, honourable. A grandee, magnificent man. (A discourse) delivered with a full voice.

P فخم *fakham*, A sheet stretched on poles for catching money thrown about at festivals; also one placed under a tree to receive the fruit as it drops.

P فخمده *fakhamda*, Carded cotton.

P فخمنده *fakhminda*, (Cotton) separated from the seed.

P فخميدن *fakhmīdan*, To separate cotton from the seeds. To pluck hairs from the body.

P فخن *fakhn* or *fakhan*, The interior or centre of a garden. *Fakhn*, A fathom.

A فخوخ *fukhūkh*, (pl. of فخ *fakhkh*) Snares.

A فخور *fakhūr*, One who glories, a boaster. (A camel) with a large udder and little orifice. Thick-trunked and branched (palm-tree). Large-pizzled (horse). Large (udder) with a small orifice and little milk. *Fukhūr*, Glory, boast, vaunt.

A فخوز *fakhūz*, Thick (teat) with a small orifice.

A فخيخ *fakhīkh*, (v. n. of فخ) Snoring. The hiss of a serpent. A snore.

A فخير *fakhīr*, One who glories (against another), boastful, vauntful. Excelled in glory.

A فخّير *fikhkhīr*, Very proud, vain-glorious.

A فخّيري *fikhkhīra'*, (or فخّيراء) Glory, boast.

P فخيز *fakhīz*, A spur.

A فخيم *fakhīm*, Great in rank and honour.

A فخيمة *fukhaymat*, Elevation, grandeur.

P فدا *fadā*, Root, origin. A model, design, precept, canon, rule.

A فداء *fadāʾ*, A heap, pile (of grain). A granary. A store-room for dates. A swelling. *Fidāʾ*, (v. n. of فدي) Ransoming. Paying a ransom. Devoting one's self for another. A redemption, ransom. Sacrifice, offering. فداءٍ لك ابي *fidāʾin laka abī*, May my father be a ransom for thee!

A فدّاد *faddād*, (pl. فدّادون *faddādūn*) Loud-voiced. Possessing from 200 to 1000 camels. Proud, arrogant, lofty. One whose tread is firm and strong.

A فدادة *fadādat* or *faddādat*, A frog. Timid. *Fudādat*, A sort of bird.

A فدّادون *faddādūna*, (pl. of فدّاد *faddād*) Loud-voiced, noisy (fellows). People calling out with a strong, rough voice (especially they who drive oxen at plough, shepherds or camel-drivers). Possessing from 200 to 1000 camels.

A فدادين *fadādīn*, (pl. of فدان *fadān* and *faddān*) Yokes of oxen. Ploughs.

A فداكل *fadākil*, Important affairs.

A فدام *fidām*, (*fadām* or *faddām*) A covering or a veil for the mouth, worn by the Parsis when they drink or say certain prayers. A strainer. The stopple of a bottle or other vessel. *Fidām*, A muzzle for an ox when treading out the corn. A turban or other head-dress. (pl. of فدم *fadm*) Stammerers. Fools.

A فدامة *fadāmat*, (v. n. of فدم) Having an impediment in speech. Being weak in intellect, dull, heavy. Being cross and moody.

A فدان *fadān*, (also فدّان *faddān*) (pl. فدادين *fadādīn*) An ox: yoke of oxen. A plough: plough-gear.

A فداويّ *fidāwīy*, (P فداوي *fidāvī*) Self-sacrificing, devoted. A volunteer.

P فدائي *fidāʼī*, (pl. فدائيان *fidāʼiyān*) One who volunteers or risks his life in any perilous service: devoted. A lover. A robber, murderer.

A فدح *fadh*, (v. n. of فدح) Pressing heavily, weighing down (as debt or shocks of fortune).

A فدخ *fadkh*, (v. n. of فدخ) Breaking, cleaving open (the head with a stone).

A فدر *fadr*, (v. n. of فدر) Being languid, impotent from too much work (a stallion). Becoming cold after having been cooked (meat). *Fudr*, (pl. of فادر *fādir*) Weak, knocked up (stallions). *Fadar*, (pl. فدور *fudūr*, مفدرة *mafdarat*, or *mafdurat*) An aged or full-grown mountain-goat. *Fadir*, Foolish, silly. Easily broken (wood). *Fudur*, (pl. of فدور *fadūr*) Mountain-goats.

A فدرّ *fudurr*, Silver. A plump boy arrived at the age of puberty.

A فدرة *fidrat*, Piece of meat. Part (of night or a mountain). *Fudarat*, (A man) who travels alone.

P فدرنجك *fadranjak*, Nightmare. The lips, mouth, or parts about the mouth.

P فدرنك *fadrang*, The bar of a door. A piece of wood used in wringing clothes. A calender, mangle. A cuckold. Food carried in a napkin. Leave, permission.

P فدرونك *fadrūnak*, Loopholes, embrasures in the walls of a citadel, through which stones are hurled. The stones thus thrown.

P فدره *fadra*, A mat of palm-leaves laid on the roof of a house and incrusted with clay.

A فدس *fuds*, (pl. فدسة *fidasat*) A spider.

A فدسيّ *fadasīy*, One whose family and tribe are unknown.

A فدش *fadsh*, (v. n. of فدش) Breaking (the head). فدش مدش *fadish madish*, Dull, unskilful.

A فدع *fadaع*, (v. n. of فدع) Having the hands or feet distorted and turning inwards. A distortion of the wrist or ankle. A mode of walking on the outer edge of the foot. An elevation of the fore and hinder part of the sole of the foot, so that a sparrow might lie underneath uncrushed. A crookedness between the groin and hoof of a beast. A prominence in the front of a camel's hoof. A crookedness in the joints.

A فدعاء *fadعāʼ*, (fem. of افدع *afdaع*) (A woman or she-camel) whose wrist-joints or fetlocks bend inwards (as is always the case in ostriches).

A فدعة *fadaعat*, A joint bent inwardly. The place of distortion in the hand or foot.

A فدغ *fadgh*, (v. n. of فدغ) Breaking (any thing) hollow. Moistening (meat) with fat. *Fadagh*, Crookedness, obliquity in the soles of the feet.

A فدغم *fadgham*, Corpulent, handsome (man). Full of flesh (cheek). Succulent (pot-herb).

A فدغمة *fadghamat*, A being chubby-cheeked.

A فدفد *fadfad*, Level ground. An extensive desert. A hard, hilly, rocky district. *Fudfud* or *fudafid*, Loud-voiced. *Fudafid*, Very thick milk.

A فدفدة *fadfadat*, (v. n. of فدفد Q) Fleeing away from the face of a wild beast or an enemy. A noise resembling that of a snake casting his slough.

A فدك *fadak*, Name of a town near خيبر *khaybar*. Name of a son of Ham.

A فدم *fadm*, (v. n. of فدم) Covering up (the mouth of a vessel). Muzzling (an ox). (pl. فدام *fidām*) A stammerer, stutterer, one who has a hesitation or obscurity of speech. Weak in mind, dull, stupid. Deep red.

A فدن *fadan*, Red tincture. (pl. افدان *afdān*) A strong castle covered with plaster. A palace.

A فدور *fadūr*, (pl. فدر *fudur*) An old mountain-goat; also one young and full grown. *Fudūr*, (v. n. of فدر) Being weak, languid from too much covering (a stallion). (pl. of فدر *fadar*) Aged or full-grown mountain-goats.

A فدوكس *fadawkas*, A lion. A strong man. A large and strong camel. Name of a man.

A فدّوم *faddūm*, A covering or veil for the mouth worn by the Parsīs or fire-worshippers. A strainer.

A فدومة *fudūmat*, (v. n. of فدم) Being weak, dull, and heavy in intellect. Having an impediment in speech. Being cross and moody.

P فدوند *fadwand*, The bar of a door.

P فدوي *fidvī*, *fidavī*, *fidwī*, or *fidawī*, Your devoted servant. It is much used by inferiors instead of the pronoun من *man*, I.

P فدويانه *fidwiyāna*, Like your devoted servant.

A فدويّة *fidawīyat*, Devotedness, devotion.

A فدى *fidaʼ* or *fadaʼ*, (v. n. of فدي) Paying a ransom, ransoming. A ransom, sum paid. فديً لك ابي *fidan laka abī*, May my father be a ransom for thee!

A فدية *fidyat*, A ransom. فدية الفطر *fidyatu'l fitr*, Half a صاع *sāع* of wheat, and a صاع *sāع* of all other kinds of grain. خذ علىٰ هديتك و فديتك *khuz عala' hidyatika wa fidyatika*, Take the way you were going.

A فديد *fadīd*, (v. n. of فدّ) Running. Promising. Threatening. Crying aloud. The noise made by sheep running. A loud noise. A noise, as that of a snake casting his slough. فديد من الابل *fadīd mini'l ibl*, Many camels.

A فديكات *fudaykāt*, A sect of schismatics.

A فذّ *fazz*, (v. n. of فذّ) Driving on with violence. Putting to a distance. (pl. افذاذ *afzāz* and فذوذ *fuzūz*) Alone, singular, unique. Scattered (dates). The first arrow used in casting lots or gaming, the names of which follow: 1. فذّ *fazz*, 2. توام *tawʼam*, 3. رقيب *rakīb*, 4. حلس *hils*, 5. نافس *nāfis*, 6. مسبل *musbil*, 7. معلّى *muعalla'*, 8. سفيح *safīh*, 9. منيح *manīh*, 10. وغد *waghd*. When drawn they all have different values, the three last excepted, which are blanks. فذّ بذّ *fazz bazz*, Single, odd.

A فذاذى *fazāza'*, (*fuzāza'*, فذاذا *fuzāzan*, or فذّاذا *fuzzāzan*) Separately, distinctly.

A فذاك *fa zāka*, Very well, well and good.

A فذفذة *fazfazat*, (v. n. of فذفذ Q) Drawing one's self together in order to spring upon (any one) by surprise. Walking stately.

A فذلك *fazālik*, In the same manner.

A فذلكة *fazlakat*, (v. n. of فذلك Q) Bringing (an account) to a close. Ascertaining, taking, or concluding (so much) to be the sum. (This root is coined from the words فذلك كذا و كذا *fa zālika kazā wa kazā*) It was then so and so.

A فذوذ *fuzūz*, (pl. of فذّ *fazz*) Sole, singular. Separate, scattered (dates).

P فر *far*, Beauty, comeliness, ornament, elegance, decoration. Light, splendour, brilliancy, lustre. Voice, sound. A feather. A torrent of water. Justice. Government. Infliction of punishment. Above, upper part. Magnificence, glory, power, dignity, dominion, pomp, state. شاه فريدون فر *shāhi farīdūn-far*, A king equal in power to Farīdūn. *Fur*, A Jewish library or bookseller's shop.

A فرّ *farra*, (fut. يفرّ *yafirru*) He fled away.

A فرّ *farr*, (v. n. of فرّ) Fleeing away. Examining, clearing up by investigation. Looking into (a horse's) mouth to discover (his) age. Fleeing, fugitive (man or men, woman or women). (pl. of فارّ *fārr*) Flying, fugitive. كرّ و فرّ *karr u farr*, Attack and retreat. *Furr*, Better, more respectable.

P فرا *farā*, Back. Behind. Again. Open. Over. Before. Foremost. Opposite, facing, over against. Towards. Onwards, along. Above, up, on, upon. Higher. Height. All. Side, quarter, nook, corner. Far. Near. Middle, midst. Increase, much, more. A taking, seizing. A particle of applause. (It is often prefixed or added to words to prevent a cacophony; and is frequently redundant).

A فرأ *faraʼ*, (and فراء *farāʼ*) (pl. فراء *firāʼ*, افراء *afrāʼ*, and افرء *afruʼ*) A wild ass, or its young. كلّ الصيد في جوف الفرا *kullu's sayd fī jawfi'l faraʼ*, (not فرأ *faraʼi*; because in proverbs a final inflected letter is made quiescent, as in Italian, amore is often written amor) All game is in the belly of the onager, *i.e.* the onager is the most valuable of all game.

A فراء *firāʼ*, (pl. of فرو *farw*) Fur-garments, furs.

A فرّاء *farrāʼ*, A skinner, furrier, vender of furs. White, splendid. Beautiful (woman). (A woman) who acts well. الفرّاء *alfarrāʼ*, Name of a grammarian.

P فرا آر *farā ār*, Stop thou up.

P فرا بافتن دروغ *farā bāftani durogh*, The making a lie, inventing, feigning.

P فرابرز *farāburz*, Name of a mighty champion and minister of Irān.

P فرا پوش *farā posh*, Stupidity, folly, madness.

P فرا پوشانيدن *farā poshānidan*, To cover.

P فرا پيش *farā pesh*, Before, in the presence of. Leading the van in battle, the forlorn hope. فرا پيش كشيدن *farā pesh kashīdan*, To draw towards one. To attract.

A فرات *furāt*, (pl. فرتان *fartān*) Very fine, sweet water or waters. The river Euphrates. The sea.

A فراتان *furātāni*, The Euphrates and Tigris.

P فراتر *farātar*, More behind. Higher. Name of an ancient king. فراتر شدن *farātar shudan*, To be in a higher situation. To tend upwards.

P فراته *furāta*, New wine boiled to a consistence with fine flour, nuts, and almonds, then cooled and made up in the form of sausages.

P فراتين *farātīn*, Heavenly (speech).

A فراثة *furāsat*, That which is contained in the ventricle, or in the liver of a beast.

A فرّاج *farrāj*, A dispeller (of grief).

P فراچنگ آوردن *farāchang āwardan*, To clutch.

A فراح *farāh*, Gladness, joyousness, cheerfulness. Skittishness, wantonness.

A فراحى *farāha'*, (pl. of فارح *fārih*) Joyful, glad.

P فراخ *farākh*, Open. Wide, spacious. Large, broad. Much, plentiful, abundant. Cheap. سال فراخ *sāli farākh*, A plenteous year.

A فراخ *firākh*, (pl. of فرخ *farkh*) The young of birds or beasts. Chickens. Young plants. (Plants) beginning to branch out. Vile, abject, (men).

P فراخا *farākhā*, Width, breadth, openness, spaciousness. A spacious place.

P فراخ آستين *farākh-āstīn*, Wide-sleeved, *i. e.* Liberal, munificent. High-minded.

P فراخ بال *farākh-bāl*, In affluent circumstances.

P فراختن *farākhtan*, To exalt, extol.

P فراخ حوصلگي *farākh-hawsalagī*, Nobleness.

P فراخ دست *farākh-dast*, Open-handed.

P فراخ دستي *farākh-dastī*, Open-handedness, liberality. Wealth. Power.

P فراخ دهانه *farākh-dahāna*, Wide-mouthed (vessel or river).

P فراخ دهن *farākh-dahan*, Open-mouthed: blab.

P فراخ رو *farākh-rav*, Wide-stepping. Swift, quick. Extravagant, lavish, profuse. *Farākh-rū*, Of an open countenance, good-natured, merry.

P فراخ روزي *farākh-rozī*, Abundance of the comforts and conveniences of life.

P فراخ روي *farākh-ravī*, Extravagance, profusion. *Farākh-rūy*, A pleasant countenance.

P فراخ سال *farākh-sāl*, A plentiful year. فراخ سالي يافتن *farākh-sāli yāftan*, To enjoy abundance.

P فراخ كام *farākh-kām*, Rich, happy. Swift.

P فراخ گام *farākh-gām*, Wide-stepping (horse).

P فراخنا *farākhnā*, Width, spaciousness. Interval, interstice. An open, spacious place.

P فراخور *farākhwur*, Worthy, fit, proper, suitable, suited. Corresponding, proportioned. فراخور آمدن *farākhwur āmadan*, To be equal. To correspond, to agree, to quadrate, to suit, to fit.

P فراخه *farākha*, Tremor, trembling, horror.

P فراخه گرفته *farākha-girifta*, Seized with a fit of trembling, trepidation, or horror; horrified.

P فراخي *farākhī*, Wideness, width, openness; largeness. Abundance, plenty. Cheapness (of provisions). A girth. فراخيء رزق *farākhīi rizk*, Abundance of wealth, plenty of provisions.

P فراخيدن *farākhīdan*, To separate, put asunder. To stand on end (the hair of the head). To be broad, large, abundant. To be dissolved. To belch.

P فراخيز *farākhez*, The tottering pace of infants or drunkards. فراخيز آمدن *farākhez āmadan*, To begin to creep. To walk staggeringly, to toddle.

A فراد *firād*, (pl. of فرد *fard*) Parts tallying with other parts. *Furāda*, (*farāda*, فرادا *furādan*, *firādan*, and فرادي *furāda'*) Separately. One after another. Sheet by sheet.

A فرّاد *farrād*, A maker or a vender of gems or gold beads called فريد *farīd*.

P فرا دار *farā dār*, Lift up.

P فرادر *farādar*, The bar of a door.

A فرادس *furādis*, Large-boned (man).

P فرادون *farādūn*, (also فرادين *farādīn*) Any thing minute. Certain small stars.

A فرادي *furāda'*, (pl. of فرد *fard*) Unique, incomparable. One by one.

A فراديس *farādīs*, (pl. of فردوس) Paradises.

A فرار *farār*, *firār*, or *furār*, (v. n. of فرّ) Looking into a (horse's) mouth to discover (his) age. Clearing up by investigation. عينه فراره *ʿaynuhu farāruhu* (*firāruhu*, or *furāruhu*), His eye for his tooth, *i. e.* From his exterior you may judge of his interior. *Firār*, (v. n. of فرّ) Running away. Flight, escape. Quicksilver. الفرار عن الزحف *al firār ʿani'z zahf*, Flying from an attacking enemy. P فرار نمودن *firār namūdan*, To flee, shew flight. A *Furār*, The young of the wild cow, sheep, or goat. Lambs, kids, or wild calves.

A فرّار *farrār*, Fleeing, fugitive, runaway.

P فرا راه افتادن *farā rāh uftādan*, To be taught, instructed, trained. فرا راه افكندن *farā rāh afkandan*, To instruct, educate, train.

A فرارة *farārat*, Flight, running off, absconding.

P فرا رسيدن *farā rasīdan*, To arrive.

P فرا رسيده *farā rasīda*, Surrounding, comprehending. Arrived.

P فرا رفتن *farā raftan*, To go on, proceed.

P فرارون *farārūn*, Untoward, unlucky, retrograde.

A فراري *farārī*, A runaway, deserter. Absconded.

A فراريج *farārīj*, (pl. of فرّوج *farrūj*) Chickens.

P فراز *farāz*, Above, up, upon, on, upwards, aloft, on the top. Above and below, up and down. Back, behind. After, hereafter. Again, on the contrary. Opposite. Before, in presence. In the way, hindering. Near. Almost. Together. Since. Open. Opening. Trodden, flattened. Broad, wide. Shut. Shutting. The ascent, declivity, or summit of a mountain. Height, altitude. Concealment. Kindling, illuminating. Exalted. Stubborn, obstinate, headstrong. A light or smooth thing. An assembly, congregation. Entrance, ingress; interior. Union. Increase. Additional, redundant. Progress. Blood. Membrum virile. A particle of praise, approbation, or redundant pleonasm, often prefixed to verbs without altering the sense: as, فراز اندوختن *farāz andokhtan*, (the same as اندوختن *andokhtan*) To gain. فراز آر *farāz ār*, Carry or bring up. فراز آوردن *farāz āwardan*, To obtain. فراز ده *farāz dih*, Give back, give again. فراز رساندن *farāz rasāndan*, To cause to arrive. فراز رسيدن *farāz rasīdan*, To arrive, occur, happen. فراز كردن *farāz kardan*, To open (a door). To shut, cover, hide. To build. فراز گرفتن *farāz giriftan*, To encompass, surround, light upon, overtake. فراز و نشيب *farāz u nishīb*, Ascent and declivity. از صباح فراز *az sabāh farāz*, From, since morning. از ديروز فراز *az dīroz farāz*, From, since yesterday. *Farāz* or *firāz*, High. Height. Exalting; who raises or elevates.

A فرازد *farāzid*, (pl. of فرزدق) Crumbs of bread.

P فرازدن *farā zadan*, To open, discover, unveil. To release.

A فرازع *farāziʿ*, (pl. of فرزعة *furzuʿat*) Handfuls of fodder.

A فرازق *farāzik*, (pl. of فرزدق *farazdak*) Crumbs of bread. Masses of paste.

P فرازمان *farāzmān*, An order, command.

P فرازنده *farāzanda*, A raiser. A planter.

P فرازنو *firāzinav*, A butterfly. A moth.

P فرازه *farāza*, A high place.

P فرازي *farāzī*, Highness, exaltation.

P فرازيد *farāzīd*, (pl. of فرزدق *farazdah*) Cakes.

P فرازيدن *farāzīdan*, To erect. To open. To shut. To unite, join.

A فرازين *farāzīn*, (pl. of فرزان) Queens at chess.

A فراس *farās*, A kind of date, black, though not the شهريز *shihrīz*. ابو فراس *abū firās*, Name of Farazdak the poet. A lion.

A فرّاس *farrās*, The lion (as tearer or render).

A فراسة *farāsat*, (v. n. of فرس) Being skilful in horsemanship, and in whatever appertains to horses. *Firāsat*, Physiognomy, a judging of the mind of another from external appearances; sagacity, discernment, shrewdness, penetration, judgment, understanding, ingenuity, address, dexterity. علم فراست *ʿilmi firāsat*, The science of physiognomy. P فراست كردن *firāsat kardan*, To conjecture, divine, judge. فراست نامه *firāsat-nāma*, A book which treats of physiognomy.

P فراستو *farāstū*, (or فراستوك) A swallow.

P فراسته *farāsta*, A little backwards.

A فراسخ *farāsikh*, (pl. of فرسخ) Parasangs.

A فراسن *furāsin*, A lion.

P فراسوده *farā sūda*, Old, worn out, tattered.

P فراسياب *farās-yāb*, A bubble. Name of a king of Tūrān, Turkistān, or Transoxiana.

P فراسين *farāsīn*, Wild leek.

A P فراسيون *farāsiyūn* or *furāsuyūn*, Wild leek.

P فراش *farāsh*, A bird whose wings are well fledged. The teeth of a mill, the cogs or paddles of a wheel. The radii or arms of a reel, or any thing similar. A runner. *Firāsh*, Numbness of limbs.

A فراش *farāsh*, A moth flying round a lighted candle. Mud dried on the surface of the ground. Bubbles on wine. Drops of sweat. Two greenish veins under the tongue. The two pieces of a bit pressing on the jaws, to which the reins are fastened. فراش الرأس *farāshu'r rass*, The thin scaly bones of the skull reaching to the neck. *Firāsh*, (v. n. of فرش) Spreading (any thing, as a carpet); strewing with stones, paving. Propagating. Expanding, smoothing the way, clearing business of any difficulty. (pl. فرش *furush*) A bed, couch, quilt, or any thing upon which one reclines. A bird's nest. The place where the tongue lies in the hollow of the mouth. (metaphor.) A wife, woman. صاحب فراش *sāhib-firāsh*, Confined to (one's) bed, bed-ridden. خستهٔ وُ صاحب فراش *khasta u sāhib firāsh*, Sick and confined to bed.

A فرّاش *farrāsh*, One who spreads the carpets or cushions, *i.e.* the chamberlain in the palaces of kings and great men; an officer who superintends the pitching of tents. فرّاش غضب *farrāshi ghazab*, Executioners who wait in the royal antichamber.

P فراشا *farāshā*, Horripilation. Horror, the tremor of a fever.

A فراشة *farāshat*, One moth. The tongue or bolt (of a lock). A small, thin bone. A little water. A light man.

P فراشترو *farāshtarū*, (or فراشتروك) A swallow.

P فراشتك *farāshtuk*, A swallow.

P فراشتن *farāshtan*, To lift up, raise.

P فراشخانه *farāsh-khāna*, The room where carpets are spread.

A فرّاشى *farrāshī*, Spreading carpets; the business of a farrāsh.

P فراشيدن *farāshīdan*, To tremble with horror. To shake (with cold). To stand on end (as the hair of a man in terror, the pile of a cat on the appearance of a dog, the plumage of a bird).

P فراشيون *farāshīwan*, Wild leek.

A فراص *firāṣ*, (v. n. 3 of فرص) Observing rotation, doing any thing alternately with another. A garment, clothing. Strong, thick. Red. (pl. of فرصة *firṣat*) Menstruous cloths.

A فراض *firāz*, The mouth of a river. A garment. Ways, roads. (pl. of فرض *farz*) Notches in the horns of a bow.

A فراضة *farāzat*, (v. n. of فرض) Being conversant with the commandments and ordinances of God (called فريضة *farīzat*). Being old (a cow).

A فراط *firāt*, (v. n. 3 of فرط) Endeavouring to get before another. (Water) which is yielded to the first comer, though other families have a right to it. تكلّم فراطاً *takallama firātan*, He spoke precipitately, his tongue outstripped his judgment.

A فرّاط *furrāt*, (pl. of فارط *fārit*) Leaders, those who go before to get water ready for the caravan. فرّاط القطا *furrātu'l kata*, Kata birds which take the lead in quest of water.

A فراطة *farātat*, (v. n. of فرط) Preceding (especially any one sent before a caravan to prepare the buckets and other conveniences for drawing water for the camels on their arrival at the end of the stage. *Furātat*, (Water) which is yielded to the first comer.

A فراطيس *furātīs*, Large, thick (glandes penum).

A فراع *firāɛ*, (pl. of فرع *farɛ*) Channels, gutters. (pl. of فرعة *farɛat*) Mountain-tops.

A فراعة *farāɛat*, A rag used as a pen-wiper.

A فراعل *farāɛil*, (and فراعلة *farāɛilat*) (pl. of فرعل *furɛul*) Hyenas' whelps.

A فراعنة *farāɛinat*, (pl. of فرعون *firɛawn*) Pharaohs. Tyrants, haughty oppressors.

A فراغ *farāgh*, (v. n. of فرغ) Finishing, bringing to a close. Making for. Being poured forth (water.) Termination, close. *Firāgh*, (pl. افرغة *afrighat*) Cessation from labour: rest, repose, leisure, retirement, retreat. Happiness, competency. (A camel) having a capacious and distended udder. A large leathern water-vessel. A horse going with wide steps. Half a horse-load, a pack. The broad head of a javelin. A large cup which one can scarcely carry. A bow which shoots to a great distance and inflicts a deep wound. A place between the handles of a bucket, over which they pour the water. للفراغ *li'l firāgh*, In vain, uselessly. فراغ بال *firāghi bāl*, Repose of mind, contentment.

P فراغ *firāgh*, Opportunity. A cool summer-wind. Joy. *Furāgh*, Splendour, coruscation.

A فرّاغ *furrāgh*, Idle, unemployed (men.)

A فراغة *farāghat*, (v. n. of فرغ) Being wide and broad (a wound.) Leisure. Cessation, quiet, freedom from business and care. Forgetfulness. Impatience, restlessness. اوقات فراغت *awkāti farāghat*, Hours of leisure. P فراغت شدن *farāghat shudan*, To be at leisure, to desist, have a relaxation from toil after having finished any thing. To abandon any pursuit, to leave a thing untouched. A *Furāghat*, Genitura viri quæ effunditur.

T فراغ خطّى *firāgh-khattī*, Discharge, release.

P فراغة *furāgha*, A piece of thin black silk for wiping pens.

A فرافب *farāfib*, A certain kind of tree, of which they make camels' saddles.

A فرافر *furāfir*, Who breaks every thing. The young of a sheep, a goat, or a wild cow. A boy or young slave. An idle or unskilful fellow. A horse which champs the bit. A camel eating and chewing the cud. The blast of a trumpet. A lion which shakes and breaks his fellow. A ptisan made of the fruit of the tree ينبوت *yambūt*. The clash of swords. Name of a horse. Name of a sword.

A فرافرة *furāfirat*, A lion that shakes and breaks to pieces his fellow.

A فرافص *furāfis*, A strong, thick lion. A stout, savage beast. A powerful, vigorous man.

A فرافصة *furāfisat*, A strong, thick lion.

A فرافل *furāfil*, Ptisan of pulse of Oman.

A فراق *farāk* or *firāk*, Departure. Separation. Distance. Grief, regret on account of absence. *Firāk*, (v. n. 3 of فرق) Parting (from a friend.)

P فراق زده *firāk-zada*, Absent, separated.

A فراقيّة *firākīyat*, A poem made on the absence of a mistress.

P فراك *furāk*, The back. A catamite. Impure. Vile, bad.

P فراكن *farā-kan*, The channel of a river newly dug. A deep ravine excavated by a torrent. High.

P فرا گرفتن *farā giriftan*, To take, assume, resume. To fill. To hold, seize. To be costive. To have a dysentery. To adopt (as a habit or temper).

P فرا گوش داشتن *farā gosh dāshtan*, To listen.

A فرام *firām*, A constrictive medicine, wash, or lotion used by women. A menstruous cloth.

A فرامة *firāmat*, A menstruous cloth.

P فرامرز *farāmarz*, Name of the son of Rustam.

P فرامش *farāmush*, Forgotten. Forgetfulness. فرامش كردن *farāmush kardan*, To forget.

P فرامشت *farāmusht*, Forgetfulness. Grasped, clutched in the fist.

P فرامشكار *farāmush-kār*, Unmindful.

P فرامشي *farāmushī*, Forgetfulness, oblivion.

P فراموش *farāmosh*, Forgotten. Forgetfulness. فراموش كردن *farāmosh kardan*, To forget. فراموش گرديدن *farāmosh gardīdan*, To be forgotten.

P فراموش شده *farāmosh shuda*, Forgotten.

P فراموشگار *farāmoshgār*, Forgetful.

P فراموشي *farāmoshī*, Forgetfulness.

P فراموشيدن *farāmoshīdan*, To forget.

A فرامين *farāmīn*, (pl. of P فرمان *farmān*) Orders, mandates. Passports.

P فرانج *faranaj*, The nightmare.

T فرانچه *frāncha*, (or فرانسه *frānsa*) France.

A فرانِد *farānid*, (pl. of فرند) Herbs, seasonings. (pl. of فرند *firind*) Glittering surfaces of swords.

A فرانس *furānis*, A lion.

A فرانسة *farānisat*, (pl. of فرناس *firnās*) Chief men of villages.

A فرانق *furānik*, (from P پروانك *parwānak*) An animal which, they say, precedes the lion, and points him out his prey. A guide (especially to an army). A courier. A lion.

P فرانك *farānak*, Name of Farīdūn's mother.

P فرا نمودن *farā namūdan*, To shew, exhibit.

A فراني *farānī*, Large round cakes.

P فراوار *farāwār*, (or فروار *farwār*) A balcony.

P فراوان *farāwān*, Much. Abundant, copious. Sufficient. Opulent. Wide, spacious. Deep. Abundantly. نعمت فراوان *niʻmati farāwān*, Plenty of victuals, an abundance of good things.

P فراواني *farāwānī*, Abundance. Depth.

P فراور *farāwar*, Name of a fountain in Turkistān which removes a quartan fever.

P فرآوريدن *far āwarīdan*, To bring down, or cause to descend. To swallow, or make swallow.

P فراوند *farāwand*, The bar of a door.

P فراويز *farāwez*, Lace, fringe, edging, any ornament round a garment. Any thing spread as carpets.

A فراهة *farāhat*, (or فراهية *farāhiyat*) (v. n. of فره) Being ingenious, clever, and sprightly (a man). Being sprightly (an ass). Sprightliness.

P فراهت *farāhat*, Elegance, beauty, pomp, state.

P فراهختن *farāhikhtan*, To suspend. To instruct, educate. To draw (a sword).

P فراهم *farāham*, Collected, gathered. Collection, conjunction, contraction. A collective particle preceding verbs (similar to *con* or *ad* in Latin). Together: as, فراهم آمدن *farāham āmadan*, To come together. فراهم آوردن *farāham āwardan*, To bring together. To adjust. To collect, accumulate. To clench (the fist). فراهم كردن *farāham kardan*, To assemble. فراهم كشيدن *farāham kashīdan*, To draw together. To contract, wrinkle. فراهم گرفتن خودرا *farāham giriftan khwudrā*, The drawing of one's self into a heap, a shrinking into one's self.

P فراهم آمدگي *farāham-āmadagī*, A collection.

P فراهيختن *farāhekhtan*, To educate. To draw (a sword).

A فراهيد *farāhīd*, Lambs.

A فراهيذ *farāhīz*, (pl. of فرهود *furhūz*) Compact, firm of body, corpulent. Small sheep.

A فرائد *farāʼid*, (pl. of فريد *farīd*) Precious gems. Ones. Beads separating pearls from gold in a necklace or a bracelet. فرائد الدرّ *farāʼidu'd durr*, Large pearls. Unios.

A فرائس *farāʼis*, (pl. of فريسة) Preys of lions.

P فرايسته *farāyista*, More, greater. Increase.

A فرائش *farāʼish*, (pl. of فريش *farīsh*) Solid-hoofed animals which have brought forth their young seven days. Concubines.

A فرائص *farāʼis*, (pl. of فريصة *farīsat*) Nerves and muscles, between the inner parts of the shoulder by the sides, which quiver in horses. Veins in a horse's neck where he is let blood.

A فرائض *farāʼiz*, (pl. of فريضة *farīzat*) The divine precepts, statutes, laws. The legal knowledge of dividing inheritances.

A فرائضيّ *farāʼiziy*, Skilled in the Muhammadan law of inheritance.

P فرايوش *farāyūsh*, Silly, beside one's self.

P فرب *farb*, Name of a large river.

P فربارة *farbāra*, Pomp, state, dignity.

P فربال *farbāl*, (or فرباله *farbāla*) A summer-apartment, a latticed balcony.

G فربانيون *farbāniyūn*, Camomile.

P فربود *furbūd*, Straight, right, orthodox.

P فربود كيش *farbūd-kesh* (or فربود دين *farbūd-dīn* or فربودي *farbūdī*) Sound in the faith, orthodox.

P فربه *farbih*, Fat. Gross. Corpulent. Much, abundant. Immense (mountain). Heavy (stone). Deep (gash). Flourishing (kingdom).

P فربهن *farbhan* or *farbhin*, Purslain.

P فربهي *farbihī*, Fatness. Corpulence.

P فربي *farbī*, Fat.

P فربيدن *firbīdan*, To deceive.

P فربيون *furbiyūn*, Euphorbium.

P فرپرك *far parak*, A bat.

A فرة *firat*, (v.n. of وفر) Becoming full, complete, entire, numerous, copious, exuberant, abundant, rife. Filling, completing, making plentiful. Abundance.

P فرّة *furrat*, Flight. *Furrat*, Severity, hardness. Mixture. Intensity of heat. Beginning of heat. Better, more respectable.

P فرت *fart*, The warp of a web in the loom. *Furt*, Name of a medical plant. Devotional exercises, holy obedience.

A فرت *fart*, (v.n. of فرت) Being wicked. *Firt*, The distance between the stretched-out tips of the thumb and fore-finger. *Farat*, (v. n. of فرت) Becoming weak after having been endued with a sound understanding.

P فرتاب *fartāb*, Revelation.

A فرتاج *firtāj*, A mark burnt on a camel.

P فرتاش *fartāsh*, Existence.

A فرتان *fartān*, (pl. of فرات) Sweet waters.

A فرتخة *fartakhat*, (v. n. of فرتخ Q), Becoming easy from being difficult, or tame from being wild.

A فرتك *fartak*, (or رأس الفرتك *raʼsu'l fartak*) Name of a promontory on the Indian Ocean.

A فرتكة *fartakat*, (v. n. of فرتك Q) Cutting to atoms. Marring. Walking with short, close steps.

P فرتك زدن *furtak zadan*, To snap the fingers.

A فرتنة *fartanat*, (v. n. of فرتن Q) Speaking in a muttering, unintelligible tone of voice. Going with short steps.

A فرتنى *fartana'*, A hand-maid. A lewd woman. A hyena's whelp. Name of a woman.

P فرتوت *fartūt*, A decrepit, doting old man.

P فرتوت شدگي *fartūt-shudagī*, Decrepitude.

P فرتوتي *fartūtī*, Decrepitude. Dotage.

P فرتود *fartod*, A decrepit old dotard.

P فرتور *fartawr* or *fartor*, Reflexion, inversion.

P فرتوك *fartūk*, A swallow.

A فرث *fars*, (v. n. of فرث) Splitting, loosing; opening a basket, hamper, paunch, letting out and scattering its contents. Pouring out any thing which has been cut up. Sticking and cutting in pieces the heart of a man still alive. (pl. فروث *furūs*) The fæces in the paunch of an animal. A small ship. A small bottle or water-pot. A fainting to which pregnant women are subject. *Faras*, (v. n. of فرث) Being satiated. Being separated, scattered (people). *Faris*, A place neither sandy nor mountainous.

A فرثدة *farsadat*, A being fleshy in the face.

A فرثطة *farsatat*, A hanging towards the ground.

A فرج *faraja*, (fut. يفرج *yafriju*) He cleft.

P فرج *farj*, Price, worth, value. Esteem, honour. Dignity, rank.

A فرج *farj* (v. n. of فرج) Splitting. Separating. Opening (a gate). Dispelling (grief). Privities of man or woman. The space between the two hind-feet of a horse. Confines of a hostile country; a dangerous or an infested place. *Furj* or *firj*, Unable to keep a secret. *Faraj*, (v. n. of فرج) Having the haunches wide apart and the privities exposed (through fatness). Joy, comfort, pleasure, cheerfulness, delight. An exposure of the privities. *Farij*, Habitually cheerful. *Furuj*, Unable to keep a secret; leaky, not close. A bow wide apart from the string. (A woman) dressed in a single robe.

P فرجا *farjā*, Here, behold!

A فرجاء *farjāʼ*, (A woman) whose hips stand wide apart; one who, from negligence, has her privities (فرج *farj*) exposed.

P فرجاد *farjād*, Excellent, eminent in learning.

A فرجار *firjār*, (or فرجارز *farjāraz*) (from P پركار *parkār*) A pair of compasses.

A فرجاريّ *firjāriy*, Drawn with compasses.

P فرجام *farjām*, End, conclusion, issue. Utility, profit. Happiness. Convenient, agreeable. Custom. The newest; that which is last poured from a flagon into a cup. اسب نا فرجام *asbi nā farjām*, An unbroke horse. سخن نا فرجام *sukhuni nā farjām*, An useless, impertinent, foolish speech. مضمون خجسته فرجام *mazmūni khujasta-farjām*, The august contents (of a royal letter).

P فرجامگاه *farjām-gāh*, The final home, the grave.

A فرجان *farjāni*, (or الفرجان *al farjāni*) Khurāsān, and Sigistān or Sinde.

A فرجة *farjat*, *firjat*, or *furjat*, The cheerfulness of a mind freed from sorrow, straits, and difficulties. *Furjat*, Interstice (or space between two fingers). A crevice (in a wall), gap, chink, breach.

P فرجد *farjad*, A great-grandfather.

A فرجلة *farjalat*, (v. n. of فرجل Q) Running with the fore-feet close, the hind-feet wide (a horse).

P فرجمند *farjmand*, Adorned. High in rank.

A فرجنة *farjanat*, A currying, cleaning (a horse).

P فرجود *farjūd*, A miracle.

A فرجول *firjawl*, (or فرجون) A curry-comb.

A فرجيّ *farjīy*, A kind of garment.

A فرح *fariha*, (fut. يفرح *yafrahu*) He was glad.

A فرح *farah*, (v. n. of فرح) Being joyful, glad, fain. Being saucy, wanton. Gladness, cheerfulness, joyousness, glee, briskness, wantonness. *Farih*, Free from care, gay, happy, joyful, cheerful, joyous, blithe, satisfied. Saucy, skittish, pert.

A فرحًا *farahan*, Gladly, cheerfully.

P فرح افزا *farah-afzā*, Mirth-increasing.

A فرحان *farhān*, (fem. فرحانة *farhānat*) (pl. فرحى *farha'* and فراحي *farāha'*) Joyful, joyous, glad, happy. Saucy.

A فرحانة *farhānat*, A white mushroom.

A فرحة *farhat* or *furhat*, Delight, pleasure, cheerfulness, joy, amusement. Sauciness, insolence. A gift for any thing which has been a source of joy. *Farihat*, Cheerful (woman).

A فرحت آثار *farhat-āsār*, Pleasant, happy.

P فرحت افزاي *farhat-afzāy*, Increasing delight.

A فرحت اللقا *farhatu'l likā*, Pleasant to look at. Name of a kite. The Pondicherry eagle.

A فرحجة *farhajat*, (v. n. of فرحج Q) Walking with the toes turned inwards.

A فرحجي *farhaja'*, A straddling gait.

P فرحناك *farahnāk*, Joyful, delighted.

A فرحى *farha'*, Cheerful (woman). (pl. of فرحان *farhān*) Joyful, glad.

A فرخ *farkh*, (pl. افرخ *afrukh*, افراخ *afrākh*, فراخ *firākh*, فروخ *furūkh*, افرخة *afrikhat*, and فرخان *firkhān*) The young of any bird or beast. Young herbage or plants. Vile, base, abject, mean. The fore part of the brain. (A plant) beginning to spread into branches. Corn ready to burst into ear. *Farakh*, (v. n. of فرخ) Being secure, exempt from fear or danger. Cleaving to the ground.

P فرّخ *farrukh*, Happy, fortunate. Beautiful-faced. Name of the second of the five supplemental days added to the Persian year.

P فرخا *farkhā*, Breadth. Affliction, grief, pain.

P فرخاد *farkhād*, Victorious.

P فرخار *farkhār*, Ornament, decoration. Name of a city remarkable for the beauty of the inhabitants and a number of idols.

P فرخاش *farkhāsh*, War, battle. Dispute, strife.

P فرخاك *farkhāk*, (or فرخال *farkhāl*) A lock of hair hanging down neither plaited or curled.

P فرخاگ *farkhāg*, A dish of meat and eggs.

A فرخان *firkhān*, (pl. of فرخ *farkh*) Young birds or beasts.

A فرخة *farkhat*, A broad spear-head.

P فرختار *firukhtār*, A seller.

P فرختن *firukhtan*, To sell. To kindle, inflame.

P فرخجسته *farkhujasta*, Prosperous. Happy. A musician. Name of a certain flower.

P فرخجه *farkhaja*, Deformed, sordid, filthy.

P فرخجي *farakhji*, Shamefulness. Impurity. Vileness, wickedness.

A فرخجيّ *farkhajīy*, One who straddles in walking.

P فرخچ *farakhch*, Rump or buttocks of a quadruped. Ugly, ill-shaped. Unclean. A bribe.

P فرّخ روز *farrukh-roz*, Name of a note in music.

P فرّخ زاد *farrukh-zād*, Happy. Prosperous. Name of an angel stationed on the earth.

P فرخسته *farkhasta*, Lying on, or dragged along, the ground.

P فرّخ سير *farrukh-siyar*, A happy disposition.

P فرخش *farakhsh*, The rump or buttocks of a quadruped. A crupper.

P فرخشته *farkhashta*, A sort of cake made with leaven, in which they put almonds and the like. Dragged along the ground.

P فرخشور *farakhshūr*, A messenger from heaven, a prophet.

P فرخشه *farkhasha*, Almond-cake.

P فرخميدن *farkhamīdan*, To beat. To clean cotton from the seed. To pull, pluck, gather.

P فرخنج *farkhanj*, Vain, foolish, useless. Disagreeable (voice). Joy, pleasure, merriment, sport, dalliance. Interest, profit, share, lot, fortune.

P فرخندگي *farkhundagi*, Happiness.

P فرخنده *farkhunda*, Happy. Fortunate, prosperous. سال فرخنده فال *sāli farkhunda-fāl*, A year of prosperity. وزرائ فرخنده راي *wuzarā-i farkhunda-rāy*, Sage ministers. فرخنده پاي *farkhunda-pāy*, Of auspicious footstep.

P فرخنده طالع *farkhunda-tāliʿ*, Fortunate.

P فرخنده مال *farkhunda-maāl*, Happy issue.

P فرخو *farkhav*, The lopping of a vine, pruning. Clearing a garden or field from weeds. The Lybian lizard.

P فرخواگ *farkhwāg*, A dish of meat and eggs.

P فرخور *farkhwar* or *farkhūr*, A water-course. The young of the bird تيهو *tīhū*.

P فرخوي *farkhuy*, Nature, disposition.

P فرخويدن *farkhawīdan*, To prune, lop (a tree).

P فرّخي *farrukhī*, Prosperity.

A فرد *fard*, (v. n. of فرد) Being alone. Entering upon (any business) alone, achieving (it) by one's self. (pl. فراد *firād*) One thing, one out of two, a half. One person, an individual. An odd number. A single sheet or strip of paper; a list, roll. A verse, piece. The singular number. Alone. (pl. افراد *afrād* and فرادي *furāda'*) Incomparable, sole, single, only, unique. God. One cheek or jaw. Single-soled (shoe). P هرفرد *har fard*, Every one. A *Fard, farad, farid, farud*, and *furud*, A glittering sword. *Farad, farid, farud*, and *furud*, Alone, sole, unique, incomparable. *Farad* or *farid*, One.

P فردا *fardā*, To-morrow. فرداي قيامت *fardāyi kiyāmat*, The resurrection-morn.

P فرداب *fardāb*, Manifestation, revelation.

A فردات *furdāt*, Hillocks.

P فردا شب *fardā-shab*, To-morrow-night.

A فرداً فرداً *fardan fardan*, One by one.

A فردان *fardān*, One. Alone, solitary.

A فردانيّة *fardānīyat*, Unity, singularity.

P فردادوم *fardāwum*, (or فردايينه *fardāyina*) Relating to to-morrow, of to-morrow, crastine.

A فردة *furadat*, One who travels alone.

P فردجان *fardajān*, The month of October.

A فرد حقيقت *fard-hakīkat*, A memorial.

P فردخانه *fard-khāna*, A house where strangers put up on the road. A private apartment. A cell in a monastery.

A فردد *fardad*, An excellent sword.

P فردر *fardar*, (or فردره *fardara*) A large wooden bar to fasten a door.

A فردسة *fardasat*, (v. n. of فردس Q) Throwing prostrate. Stuffing (a basket of dates) quite full. Ease, facility, amplitude.

A فرد سوال *fard suwāl*, Petition, application.

P فردفر *fardfar*, (God) the supporter of men.

A فردود *furdūd*, Certain stars ranged in a line behind the Pleiades.

A فردوس *firdaws*, (pl. فراديس *farādīs*) A garden, vineyard, paradise. A fertile vale. Name of several delightful places. *Furdūs*, Provisions set before a guest.

A فردوس مكاني *firdaws-makānī*, A title of a deceased emperor (located in Paradise).

P فردوسي *firdawsī*, A famous Persian poet, the author of the great epic poem شاهنامه *shāh-nāma*.

A فرده *farda*, A poll-tax.

A فردي *farda'*, Singly, one by one.

A فردي *fardī*, A roll, catalogue.

A فرديات *fardiyāt*, A topical remedy.

A فرديّة *fardīyat*, Unity, singleness.

A فردين *fardayn*, (oblique dual of فرد *fard*) Without a third person, tête-a-tête.

P فردين *fardīn*, The first month of the Persian year, when the sun is in Aries.

A فررة *furarat*, Fleeing, fugitive (man).

P فرز *farz*, Great. Learned. *Firz*, The queen at chess. *Firz* or *furz*, Grass, verdure. *Furz*, Excess. Victory, conquest. A bank of a large river where boats may harbour.

A فرز *farz*, (v. n. of فرز) Separating, parting, or distinguishing. A plain not having a mountain. *Firz*, A road through hilly ground.

A فرّز *furuzz*, One quite free, or a mere slave, sleek and full of flesh.

P فرزاده *farzāda*, A large mass of leaven.

P فرزام *farzām*, Worthy, suiting, befitting.

P فرزان *farzān*, Science, learning. Strength, constancy. Wise, learned. *Firzān*, The queen at chess.

A فرزان *firzān*, (pl. فرازين) The queen at chess.

P فرزانگان *farzānagān*, (pl. of فرزانه *farzāna*) Learned men. Privy counsellors. Excellent.

P فرزانگي *farzānagi*, Learning, science. Wisdom. Excellence.

P فرزانه *farzāna*, A learned man, wise, excellent, intelligent. Noble, honourable. Happy, blest.

P فرز بود *farz būd*, Wisdom, understanding.

A فرزة *firzat*, Part, a thing separated. *Furzat*, Occasion, time, turn. A road through hilly ground.

P فرزجه *farzaja*, A suppository, clyster.

P فرزد *furuzd*, A green weed covering stagnant water. Verdure, bright, moist, and succulent.

A فرزدق *farazdak*, (pl. فرازد *farāzid*, فرازق *farāzik*, and فرازيد *farāzīd*) A cake baked in the oven. A crumb of bread. A name given to همام بن غالب بن صعصعة *humām bin ghālib bin saʿsaʿa*, A poet, celebrated alike for his extravagance of praise and bitterness of censure; hence, he is not unfrequently designated شيطان فرزدق *shaytān farazdak*, Devil Farazdak.

A فرزدقة *farazdakat*, (pl. فرازق *farāzik*) A lump of dough, a mass of paste or leaven.

A فرزع *furzuʿ*, The seed of cotton.

A فرزعة *furzuʿat*, (pl. فرازع *farāziʿ*) A handful of fodder. Name of one of Lokman's vultures.

A فرزل *firzil*, Fetters. Smiths' shears. *Furzul*, Thick, lusty.

A فرزلة *farzalat*, A chaining, a fettering.

P فرزند *farzand*, A son. A child. Offspring. فرزند آب *farzandi āb*, Aquatic animals. Bubbles. فرزند ارجمندش *farzandi arjmandash*, His illustrious son. فرزند آفتاب *farzandi āftāb*, A ruby. فرزند بكر *farzandi bikr*, Eldest son. An evergreen. فرزند خاور *farzandi khāwar*, The sun. فرزند رشيد *farzandi rashīd*, A good child. فرزند زنا *farzandi zinā*, A bastard. فرزند شاد *farzandi shād*, Meditation. فرزند نيك نهاد عالي نژاد *farzandi nek-nihādi ʿāli-nijād*, A son of high quality and noble race.

P فرزندك *farzandak*, A little child, a bantling.

P فرزند مرده *farzand-murda*, Bereaved (parent).

P فرزو *farzū*, Wisdom, intelligence.

A فرزوم *furzūm*, A shoe or bootmaker's board on which he cuts his leather. A cobbler's last.

P فرزة *farza*, A green herb: a place full of grass. *Furza*, The bank of a river where ships are moored.

P فرزي *farzī*, The queen at chess.

P فرزي بند *farzī-band*, A term used at chess.

P فرزين *farzīn*, The queen at chess. Learned.

P فرژ *furj* or *farj*, Root of galangale. Rhubarb.

A فرس *fars*, (v. n. of فرس) Catching, tearing (prey). Breaking the neck, killing. Eating habitually the black date فراس *farās*. Pasturing, tending (horses). Slaughter. *Firs*, Name of an herb, either the قضقاض *kizhāz*, asphodel, or rhododaphne. *Faras*, (pl. افراس *afrās* and فروس *furūs*) A horse or mare. The knight at chess. P فرس نهادن *faras nihādan*, To be weak and vanquished.

A فرس *furs*, Persia. The Persians.

P فرسا *farsā*, (and فرساي *farsāy*) (in compos.) Destroying, wearing. Old, worn out. Rubbing against, reaching (the sky). جان فرسا *jān-farsā*, Distracting the mind, unhappy, melancholy, fatal.

A فرساح *firsāh*, A widely-extended country.

P فرساد *farsād*, Wise, learned. A mulberry.

P فرسان *farsān*, Any animal of whose skin they make fur-garments.

A فرسان *fursān*, (pl. of فارس *fāris*) Horsemen.

P فرسانيدن *farsānīdan*, To cause to rub or wear.

P فرسايندة *farsāyinda*, Waxing old, impaired.

P فرسب *farsub*, (or فرسپ *farasp*) The main beam which enters the walls. Tapestry with which they adorn the walls on feast-days.

A فرسة *farsat*, Wind which settles in the back; also a painful swelling on the neck. *Farasat*, A mare.

P فرست *farast*, Magic, incantation. *First*, Send. A letter. Any thing sent as a present. A mission.

P فرستادن *firistādan*, To send.

P فرستادة *firistāda*, (pl. فرستادگان *firistādagān*) Sent. An ambassador, envoy, apostle, legate.

P فرستگان *firistagān*, Ambassadors, apostles.

P فرستگاني *firistagānī*, Apostolical.

P فرستو *farastū*, *firistū*, (فرستوك *farastūk*, or *firistūk*) A swallow.

P فرستوة *furistūh*, A certain king of China.

P فرستة *firista*, Sent. An ambassador, apostle. A present.

A فرسخ *farsakh*, (pl. فراسخ *farāsikh*) A parasang, a league, about 18,000 feet in length. An interval. A chink, cleft. Without interval, intermission, chink, or cleft. Rest, quiet, repose. An hour. A long time; perpetual; much. فرسخ فرسخ *farsakh farsakh*, From one distant place to another.

A فرسخة *farsakhat*, The dispelling of grief; curing of a fever; expulsion of the cold.

P فرسد *farsad*, It decays, wears away.

P فرسدن *farsudan*, To be worn, to wax old.

G فرسطاريون *firistāriyūn*, A species of pulse.

G فرسطون *farastūn*, A public standard of weights or measures.

A فرسق *firsik*, (and فرسك *firsik*) The finest red peach, or one which separates from the stone.

P فرسك *firisk*, A peach.

P فرسلوس *farslūs*, A fabulous stone obtained by Alexander the Great, which, when placed on mercury, was changed to silver.

P فرسلون *farsulūn*, Talc, mica.

A فرسن *firsin* or *san*, Hoof of a camel or sheep.

P فرسناف *firisnāf*, (or فرسنافه) New-year's night.

P فرسنداج *farsandāj*, A messenger, prophet.

P فرسنگ *farsang*, A parasang, league. A distance of twelve thousand cubits.

P فرسنگسار *farsangsār*, A league-stone.

P فرسودگي *farsūdagī*, Obliteration. Wear, waste.

P فرسودن *farsūdan*, To rub, scrub, wear, tear, consume, diminish. To be torn, worn, old, inveterate. To rot. To kick, strike, shake. To torment, persecute. To press, urge, compel, importune. To expose one's self to danger. To hitch along sitting on the backside; or to be dragged by any thing when lying. To be fatigued, languid, spiritless. To detest, loathe. To anoint. To be anointed. To repent. To congeal.

P فرسودة *farsūda*, Torn, worn, old, decayed.

A فرسيٰ *farsaʾ*, (pl. of فريس *farīs*) Killed.

A فرسيّ *fursiy*, Persian, Persic.

A فرسيّات *fursiyāt*, Persian affairs or phrases.

A فرش *farsh*, (v. n. of فرش) Spreading (a carpet or the like). Furnishing (a house). Paving, laying flag-stones. Lying. Dispersing, scattering. Being broad, spreading out (a camel's hoof). Enlarging, rendering easy. A bed, couch, cushion, mat, carpet, bed-clothes, or any similar household furniture. A large court or quadrangle. Blades of corn just sprouting above ground. Small, slender trees or sticks. Small camels unfit for burdens. Animals reared for slaughter. A lie, a falsehood. State, condition. Grief, sorrow. A place where many shrubs grow (particularly the plant عرفط *ʿurfut*). The middle-sized and best-shaped camels' feet. P فرش باستان *farshi bāsitān*, (or فرش خاك *farshi khāk*) The earth. فرش دو رنگ *farshi du rang*, The world. The earth. Night and day. A فرش عاج *farshi ʿāj*, (A carpet of ivory) Snow. *Furush*, (pl. of فراش *firāsh*) Beds, mattrasses.

P فرش *fursh*, Biestings. *Farish*, Tired of.

A فرشاح *firshāh*, A widely-extended country. A solid, broad, and flat hoof. Clouds without rain. Large, hideous, stinking (woman or camel).

A فرشة *firshat*, A mode of spreading a carpet. Face, aspect, external form.

P فرشتگان *firishtagān*, (pl. of فرشته) Angels.

P فرشتگاني *firishtagānī*, Angelical.

P فرشتو *farashtū*, (or فرشتوك) A swallow.

P فرشته *firishta*, An angel. فرشتهٔ سحاب *firishtaʾi sahāb*, The angel Michael, the angel of the clouds. فرشتهٔ صوري *firishtaʾi sūrī*, Israel.

P فرشته تنان *firishta-tanān*, Angelic beings.

P فرشته سيرت *firishta-sīrat*, Angel-tempered.

A فرشحة *farshahat*, (v. n. of فرشح Q) Striding, either when sitting or standing at prayer. Straddling (cattle when milking). Sitting down with the hams closely touching the ground.

A فرشحيٰ *farshahaʾ*, (v. n. of فرشح Q) Sitting down with the thighs close to the ground. Straddling (cattle when being milked).

A فرشخ *farshakh*, Rest, quiet, cessation.

A فرشخة *farshakhat*, (v. n. of فرشخ Q) Being wide, easy, in one's power. Amplitude, capacity.

A فرشدة *farshadat*, (v. n. of فرشد Q) Sitting or standing in a straddling posture.

A فرشط *firshit*, (or فرشاط *firshāt*) Seated with the legs apart.

A فرشطة *farshatat*, (v. n. of فرشط Q) Sitting with the legs wide apart, and the hams touching the ground. Riding with both legs dangling on one side. Lying down in a loose and languid manner (a camel). Cutting (meat) in pieces. Stretching (a thing). Straddling to be milked (a she-camel), or to stale (a he-camel).

P فرشك *farishk*, A small bunch joining a larger.

P فرشه *fursha* or *firsha*, New milk, biestings.

A فرشي *farshī*, A kind of hookah.

A فرشيح *firshīh*, The male organ of generation.

P فرشيد *farshed*, The brother of Pīrān Vīsa.

P فرشيم *farshīm*, A share, division: a section.

A فرص *fars*, (v. n. of فرص) Cutting, cleaving, tearing, slitting. Hurting in the فريصة *farīsat*. Stone of the wild date مقل *mukl*. *Furas*, (pl. of فرصة *fursat*) Occasions, opportunities.

A فرصاء *farsāʾ*, A camel standing aside waiting her turn to drink.

P فرصاد *firsād*, The white mulberry, the leaves of which being boiled with those of the black fig and of the vine in rain-water, produce a liquor which will stain hair black.

A فرصاد *firsād*, A grape-stone. A white mulberry. A red dye.

A فرصة *farsat*, Wind in a tumour, especially on the back. *Firsat*, (pl. فراص *firās*) A menstruous cloth. *Fursat*, Occasion, opportunity, fit time, convenience. Coincidence. Advantage. A time, turn, (drinking in) rotation. P فرصت يافتن *fursat yāftan*, To find an opportunity. فوت فرصت كردن *fawti fursat kardan*, To neglect, lose, or miss one.

P فرصت جو *fursat-jo*, Seeking an occasion.

A فرصمة *fursamat*, A breaking; a cutting.

A فرصيد *firsīd*, (or فرصد) A grape-stone.

A فرض *farz*, (v. n. of فرض) Cutting, notching, nicking. Ordering (any thing) to be observed (as an article of religion). Rendering necessary and obligatory. Paying what is enjoined by law, discharging a debt. Appointing a time for any thing. Giving, allowing a stipend. An indispensable duty, divine command; a necessary observation of certain precepts of the Muhammadan religion (the omission of which is considered as a mortal sin); a definition or injunction (of any kind). The reading of the Kur'ān. The Sunna, or traditions of Muhammad. An incision, notch, indent, cutting, splitting. Any thing given away from a sense of duty, without expectation of reward. Troops in the receipt of regular pay. A garment. (pl. فراض *firāz*) The notch at the horn of a bow. An unfeathered arrow. A sort of date. One of the timbers in a house. A widow's jointure, a fourth of her husband's property if she have borne children, and an eighth if she have not. The mouth of a river. A shield. That part of the steel or wood which strikes fire. على فرض المحال *ʿala' farzi'l muhāl*, Granting an impossibility. *Firz*, The fruit of the dwarf palm-tree whilst yet green. *Furaz*, (pl. of فرضة *furzat*) Notches in the horns of a bow. Indents in the bank of a river, bights.

A فرّض *furraz*, (pl. of فارض *fāriz*) Large, bulky (men or uvulas).

A فرضا *farzan*, (or بالفرض *bi'l farz*) Supposing the case, for example. Clearly, distinctly, altogether, entirely, principally, above all; so that, surely.

A فرضاخ *firzākh*, Thick, broad, tall (man).

A فرضاخة *firzākhat*, (and فرضاخية *firzākhiyat*) Full-breasted (woman).

A فرضة *furzat*, (pl. فرض *furaz*) The notch in the horn of a bow, or in the top of a yarn-spindle into which the thread goes. An indent of a river where they draw water. A bight where ships ride at anchor; a harbour, dock, or station for shipping. The mouth of a river. The interior part of an ink-holder. The hinge of a door; also the socket in which a turnstile or any thing similar turns.

A فرضخ *firzikh*, A scorpion.

A فرضم *firzim*, A large, broken-horned, and old sheep. Toothless.

A فرضميّ *firzimīy*, (A camel) large, strong, and which treads firmly.

A فرضول *farzūl*, The hammer of a musket.

A فرضيّ *farazīy*, Skilled in the law, ordinances, and commandments of God.

A فرضيّة *farzīyat*, An indispensable precept.

A فرط *fart*, (v. n. of فرط) Getting before, outstripping. Passing beyond. Preceding (especially one sent before a caravan to prepare the buckets and other conveniences for drawing water for the camels immediately on their arrival at the end of the stage). Sending (an ambassador). Being rashly and injuriously reproachful. Being careless, deficient in duty, or inattentive. Losing any thing, or delaying till it escapes. Being sprinkled late with the male flowers, when the pods are ready to burst (the female palm). Losing (a son) by an untimely death. (pl. افرط *afrut* and افراط *afrāt*) Excess. Too much. Victory, superiority, prevalency. Time recently passed (especially from three to about fifteen days). The summit of a hill. A small hill. A post or stone placed for directing the way. فرط محبّت *farti mahabbat*, Excess of fondness. وفور صداقت و فرط مودّت *wufūri sadākat u farti mawaddat*, The greatest sincerity and affection. *Farat*, A person or persons who goes, or who go before to prepare buckets, ropes, and whatever is requisite for drawing water. Water taking the precedency of other waters. Good works, reward, or recompense, sent before. A son dying under the age of puberty. اللّهمّ اجعله لنا فرطا *allāhumma ijʿalhu lanā furatan*, O God! place him amongst the good works we have sent before (a form of condolence when any person has lost a son). *Furut*, A swift horse (outstripping all the rest). Left or neglected (business). Any thing done beyond bounds. Iniquity, injustice, oppression. (pl. افراط *afrāt*) A high hill.

A فرطاح *firtāh*, Broad (head).

A فرطاس *firtās*, Broad, wide.

A فرطة *fartat*, One procession or departure (noun of unity). *Furtat*, Precedence. A going forth.

A فرطحة *fartahat*, A making broad, widening.

A فرطسة *fartasat*, A putting forth the snout.

A فرطمة *fartamat*, A mending the toe (of a boot).

P فرطوس *fartūs*, Name of a wrestler.

A فرطوسة *furtūsat*, Snout or pizzle of a hog.

A فرطوم *furtūm*, A boot, or the toe of it.

A فرطي *fara* or *furatīy*, Difficult to manage.

A فرطيسة *firtīsat*, A hog's snout and pizzle. Tip of the nose. منيع الفرطيسة *maniʿu'l firtīsat* is equivalent to منيع الحورة *maniʿu'l hawrat*.

A فرع *farʿ*, (v. n. of فرع) Excelling others (in birth or in beauty). Deflowering (a virgin). Climbing (a mountain). Descending. Amending, correcting, adjusting. Reconciling, making peace. Holding a stick over (the crown of the head) in a threatening manner. Prohibiting, preventing. Checking (a horse), pulling the bridle. Interposing. Top, head. Chief of a people or family. An excellent bow. The top of the ear. Effect, produce, descent, offspring. Ready and available property. A bow made of the extremity of a branch. A bow made of a single piece. The branch of a tree (especially the top). (pl. فروع *furūʿ*) A woman's head of hair. A full head of hair. (pl. فراع *firāʿ*) A channel, a gutter. *Farʿ* or *faraʿ*, (pl. of فرعة *farʿat* or *faraʿat*) Large lice. P فرع خواران خاك *farʿ khwārāni khāk*, Men. A قوس فرع *kawsun farʿun* or *farʿatun*, A bow made of a single branch or piece. *Furʿ*, (pl. of افرع *afraʿ*) Well-haired (persons). *Faraʿ*, (v. n. of فرع) Having a large head of hair. (pl. فرع *furuʿ*) Firstlings of camels or sheep, which the pagan Arabians offered in sacrifice to their gods. A part, portion, division. A piece let into a leathern bottle. (pl. of فرعة *faraʿat*) Large lice.

A فرعاء *farʿāʾ*, (fem. of افرع *afraʿ*) (A woman) with a fine head of hair.

A فرعان *furʿān*, (pl. of افرع *afraʿ*) Men who have much hair on their heads. A man's name.

A فرعة *farʿat*, (pl. فراع *firāʿ*) The top or declivity of a mountain. (pl. فرع *farʿ*) A louse. A bow of the best kind. (pl. of فارع *fāriʿ*) Royal allies, helpers, or defenders. *Faraʿat*, (pl. فرع *faraʿ*) One large louse.

A فرعل *furʿul*, (fem. فرعلة *furʿulat*) (pl. فراعل *farāʿil* and فراعلة *farāʿilat*) A young hyena.

A فرعلان *furʿulān*, A male cub of a hyena.

A فرعنة *farʿanat*, (v. n. of فرعن Q) Being crafty, sly, subtle. Craftiness, sagaciousness, slyness.

A فرعون *firʿawn*, A crocodile. *Firʿawn*, *furʿūn*, or *furʿawn*, (pl. فراعنة *farāʿinat*) Pharaoh; and in general, any cruel tyrant. Proud. The name of the Pharaoh of the Old Testament is said to have been وليد بن مصعب *walīd bin musʿab*.

A فرعوني *firʼawnī*, Haughtiness. Pharaonic.

A فرعي *farʼiy*, Derivative, descending.

P فرغ *fargh*, A chicken.

A فرغ *fargh*, The place between the handles of a bucket, over which they pour the water. A vessel wherein is date-honey. فرغ الدلو *farghu'd dalw*, Name of two lunar mansions: one called المقدم *al mukaddam*, The foremost; the other, المؤخر *al muaḳhkhir*, The hindmost. They form the 26th and 27th of the lunar mansions. *Firgh*, (v. n. of فرغ) Being shed with impunity (blood). Leisure, disengagement. *Faragh*, (v. n. of فرغ) Being poured out (water). *Farigh*, Free, ceased from labour, just finished a work, disengaged.

A فرّغ *furragh*, (pl. of فارغ *fārigh*) Empty.

A فرغا *farghan* or *firghan*, With impunity.

A فرغاء *farghāʼ*, Deep, wide (wound).

P فرغار *farghār*, Moistened, wetted. Kneaded. Mixed. Broken, bruised. Name of a scout belonging to Afrāsyāb.

P فرغاريدن *farghāridan*, To moisten well: to mix (leaven) with any liquid. To scratch (the head).

A فرغان *farghāni*, Two stars, lunar mansions.

P فرغانج *farghānj*, (or فرغانچ *farghānch*) A plump fat cow or mule full of flesh. A vineyard.

P فرغانه *farghāna*, Name of a country in Turkistān. Name of a note in music. Name of a mountain where mandrakes are found in abundance.

P فرغر *farghar*, The bed of a river when almost dry; also the small quantity of water remaining in such a river. A minor stream derived from a more considerable one. A ditch, pool.

P فرغرده *fargharda*, Mixed, kneaded.

P فرغن *farghan*, A channel newly made through which they cause water to flow.

P فرغند *farghand*, (or فرغنده *farghanda*) Any thing stinking. Ivy.

P فرغور *farghūr*, A bird resembling a partridge, but smaller. A lark. A frog.

P فرغوك *farghok*, Silent, taciturn, modest. Delay, slowness.

P فرغول *farghol*, Procrastination. Negligence.

P فرغوي *firghūy*, A sparrow-hawk, merlin.

P فرغيش *farghīsh*, Old, worn out. A fur-garment, the hair of which is dropping off. Negligence.

A فرفار *farfār*, Loquacious. Full of levity, light, fickle. One who breaks every thing. A species of vehicle for the women. Name of a tree black and hard as ebony, of which they make dishes. *Farfār* or *firfār*, A lion which shakes and breaks in pieces his fellow.

A فرفارة *farfārat*, Talkative (woman).

P فرفت *farfat*, Fumitory.

P فرفتن *firiftan*, To deceive, cozen, cheat.

A فرفح *farfah*, Soft ground.

P فرفخ *farfakh*, (or فرفخيز *farfakhez*) Purslain. Joints in stalks of corn.

P فرفر *farfar*, Reading or writing expeditiously. A word spoken in haste. Quickness, hurry, expedition. A boy's top. فرفر نوشتن *farfar navishtan*, To write in haste.

A فرفر *firfir* or *furfur*, Name of a bird. A sparrow. *Furfur*, The young of a wild cow, goat, or sheep. A lion which shakes and breaks his fellow.

A فرفرة *farfarat*, (v. n. of فرفر Q) Calling out to. Talking much and confusedly. Breaking. Cutting. Putting in motion. Shaking. Defaming. Shaking himself (a camel), and running fast with short steps. Being light in mind and swift of foot. Champing the bit and shaking his head (a horse). Making the vehicle called فرفار *farfār*. Tearing (a leathern bottle). Lighting a fire from the tree called فرفار *farfār*. Being joyous and cheerful.

P فرفروزان *farfurūzān*, The Creator.

P فرفروك *farfarūk*, A child's peck-top.

P فرفره *farfara*, Hurry in speaking, writing, or working. A child's plaything, formed of a piece of leather cut round; and which, by means of a double string, is made to whirl about, making a humming noise. A paper-toy like the sweeps of a windmill applied on a pin to the end of a stick.

P فرفور *farfūr*, A kind of bird smaller than a partridge; a quail. A fat sheep. *Furfūr*, Sour milk, dried and become black.

A فرفور *furfūr*, A boy, servant. A fat camel; a camel eating or chewing the cud. A ptisan made of the fruit of the tree ينبوت *yambūt*. A sparrow.

P فرفوز *farfūz*, A bird smaller than a partridge.

P فرفوس *farfūs*, A kind of pumice-stone applied to wounds.

P فرفه *farfa*, Purslain.

P فرفهن *farfahan* or *farfahn*, Purslain.

P فرفير *farfīr*, A small kind of partridge; a quail. A fat sheep.

A فرفير *firfīr*, Purple. A violet.

P فرفين *farfayn*, (or فرفينه *farfīna*) Purslain.

A فرفيون *farfayūn* or *furfiyūn*, Euphorbium.

A فرق *farḳ*, (v. n. of فرق) Separating, dividing. Deciding judicially. Giving to a woman in child-bed the preparation called فريقة *farīkat*. Voiding dung. Possessing fruit-stones. Separation, distinction, division, difference, discrimination. The head, summit, or top of any thing. The division of the hair along the top of the head. (pl. فرقان *furkān*) A certain measure at Madīna. Flax. A kind of bird. Away! Aside! P فرق فرقد ساي *farki farkad-sāy*, (His) head reaching the stars. A بلا فرق *bilā farḳ*, Indiscriminately, without distinction, indifferently. *Firk*, A part separated from the whole. A piece split off any thing. A mountain inaccessible and separate from others. A large flock of sheep. A herd of cattle or deer. A flock of stray sheep under a hundred. Date-stones, the food of camels. A troop of children. A wave.

Furk, Whatever distinguishes truth from falsehood. The Kur'ān. *Farak*, (v. n. of فرق) Trembling, being frightened. Diving, plunging into. Drinking from the measure فرق *farak*. (pl. فرقان *furkān*) A certain measure at Madīna. Dispersion (as of darkness by the dawn). Dawn. (pl. افراق *afrāk*) An interval or space (between the teeth, cloven hoofs of cattle, beard of an old man, or comb of a cock). An interval in the growth of plants, *i.e.* when they are not close, or in continuous rows. Fright, fear. The dawn. An inequality in the hips of a horse, one being higher than another. ابين من الفرق *abyan mini'l farak*, Clearer than the dawn. *Farik*, Small (plant) not covering the ground. Timid, frightened. *Faruk*, Naturally timid. *Firak*, (pl. of فرقة *firkat*) Crowds, bodies, sects. *Furuk*, (pl. of افرق *afrak*) White cocks. Rams whose testicles are wide apart. (pl. of فريق *farīk*) Troops, bodies. *Furuk* or *furrak*, (pl. of فارق *fārik*) (Camels or asses) bringing forth.

A فرقاء *farkāʼ*, Wide between the points of the teats (ewe).

A فرقاع *firkāʼ*, A fart.

A فرقان *furkān*, (v. n. of فرق) Separating, dividing, discriminating, distinguishing. The Kur'ān. The Pentateuch. Any sacred book (as distinguishing right from wrong, truth from falsehood). Assistance. Victory. Demonstration, proof. The dividing of the Red Sea. The dawn. Boys, children. يوم الفرقان *yawmu'l furkān*, The day of the battle of Badr. (pl. of فرق *fark* and *farak*) Measures of Madīna.

A فرقاني *furkāniy*, Kuranic.

A فرقب *furkub*, Name of a place in Egypt.

A فرقبية *furkubīyat*, A kind of Egyptian linen.

A فرقة *firkat*, (pl. فرق *firak*, افارقة *afārikat*, افراق *afrāk*, and افاريق *afārīk*) A body, sect, clan, troop, band. A leathern bottle, so full that it cannot be churned until it be partially emptied. فرقة نصارا *firkaï nasāra'*, The Christian people. *Furkat*, Separation, distinction. Distance. *Farikat*, (A country) whose plants grow up at intervals.

A فرقد *farkad*, A calf, or a wild one. A bright star near the north pole.

A فرقدان *farkadān* or *farkadāni*, Two stars near the pole of the Lesser Bear.

A فرقعة *farkaʼat*, (v. n. of فرقع Q) Running violently. Twisting the neck. Pulling the fingers till the joints crack. Farting. *Furkuʼat*, Podex.

A فرقم *farkam*, Glans penis.

A فرقود *furkūd*, A calf. A bright star near the north pole.

P فرقور *farkūr*, A bird resembling a partridge.

A فرك *fark*, (v. n. of فرك) Rubbing (an ear of corn or cloth) with the hands; cracking (a louse). Conjugal hatred. *Firk*, Hatred (between husband and wife). *Farak*, Limberness in the root of the ear. *Farik*, Whose bark or skin is rubbed or peeled off.

A فركاء *farkā*, Limber, loose, flagging at the root (soft ear).

A فركاح *firkāh*, One whose buttocks stand prominently out.

P فركامخ *farkāmukh*, A young lion. Milk poured over meat.

A فركان *furukhān*, A hating. Conjugal hatred.

A فركة *farikat*, Limber, loose, flagging (ear).

A فركحة *farkahat*, Width betwixt the buttocks.

P فركن *farkan*, A canal newly dug from a large river. Rotten, falling to pieces from age. An excavation formed by a torrent, with water lodging here and there.

P فركند *farkand*, An excavation formed by a torrent. An artificial canal newly dug. A ditch. A stream above ground flowing from one spot to another. A subterraneous canal which works its way from one well to another. Any thing falling to pieces from age.

P فركندن *farkandan*, To dig a canal, and to bring water into fields and gardens. To do one an unpremeditated or accidental injury, to lead one into danger without design. To destroy, tear, when pulling up (herbs, hair, and the like).

P فركنده *farkanda*, Old, worn, decayed, falling to pieces, torn, destroyed. Dug.

P فركنديدن *farkandīdan*, To cause to be dug.

P فرگاه *fargāh*, Presence. Worship. Majesty.

P فرگفت *farguft*, Order, command, decree.

P فرگوهر *far gohar*, Essence.

P فرگويا *far goyā*, Speaking. Rational (animal).

A فرم *farm*, A constrictive lotion used by women.

P فرم *faram*, Grief, anguish. Baseness.

P فرما *farmā*, (and فرماي *farmāy*) Commanding. فرمان فرما *farmān-farmā*, An issuer of orders.

A فرماء *farmāʼ*, Narrowed (woman) by the use of a constrictive lotion or medicament.

P فرمان *farmān*, A mandate, command, order, or royal patent. فرمان عاليشان *farmāni ʻālī-shān*, The exalted or the imperial mandate. This is synonymously expressed in a variety of different ways: as, فرمان واجب الاذعان *farmāni wājibu'l izʻān*, Orders proper to be submitted to. فرمان واجب الامتثال *farmāni wājibu'l imtisāl*, Ordinances necessary to be obeyed. فرمان جليل عنوان *farmāni jalīl-ʻunwān*, Diplomas with the illustrious imperial signature. فرمان جليل القدر *farmāni jalīlu'l kadar*, Precepts of high authority. فرمان جهان مطاع *farmāni jahān-mutāʻ*, Injunctions obeyed by all the world. فرمان قدر توان *farmāni kadar-tuwān*, Decrees of powerful efficacy. فرمان قضا جريان *farmāni kazā-jarayān*, Commands flowing like, or irresistible as, destiny. فرمان بردار *farmān-bardār*, Obeying commands, *i.e.* A subject. Obedient.

P فرمان بر *farmān-bar*, Order-bearing; a servant.

P فرمانبرداري *farmān-bardārī*, Obedience, subjection. فرمان برداري كردن *farmān-bardārī kardan*, To obey, to yield obedience to commands.

P فرمان پذير *farmān-pazīr*, Submissive.

P فرمان ده *farmān-dih*, (فرمان روا *farmān-rawā*, or فرمان گذار *farmān-guzār*) Issuing mandates, *i.e.* A monarch, emperor, king, reigning prince.

P فرمانده‌ي *farmān-dihī*, (فرماني *farmān-farmāʼī*, or فرمان گذاري *farmān-guzārī*) Empire, sovereignty. فرمان دهيء قاضي *farmān-dihīʼi kāzī*, A written order or sentence of a judge.

P فرمان روايان *farmān-rawāyān*, Monarchs.

P فرمايش *farmāyish*, Order, will, commands.

P فرمايشي *farmāyishī*, Ordered. Excellent.

P فرماينده *farmāʼinda*, Ordering: a commander.

A فرمة *farmat*, A constrictive medicament or lotion used by women.

P فرمد *farmad*, Name of a village near Tūs.

P فرمرست *farmarust*, Weak from want of food.

P فرمس *farmus*, The old name of Dāmaghān.

P فرمش *faramush*, Forgetfulness.

P فرمگن *faram-gin*, (or فرمگين *faram-gīn*) Afflicted, melancholy, grieved, full of anguish.

P فرمگيني *faramgīnī*, Sadness, grief, anguish.

P فرمند *farmand*, Wise, enlightened. Pure.

P فرمودن *farmūdan*, To command, order. To deign, to favour. To come. To sit down.

P فرموده *farmūda*, Ordered, commanded. A mandate, order, command, injunction, prescription. Fat. فرمودهٔ خدا *farmūdaʼi khudā*, The commandments of God.

P فرموش *farmosh*, Forgetfulness.

P فرموك *farmūk*, A ball of thread upon its spindle. A boy's top set in motion by a string.

P فرموهد *farmūhad*, A village near Tūs.

P فرمه *farma*, A violet.

A فرن *furn*, An oven. An earthen pan in which bread is baked. A furnace.

A فرناة *farnāt*, A breaking of the neck, a killing. A cutting to pieces.

P فرناخيدن *farnākhīdan*, To blush. To become gentle, well-mannered. To hang the ears. To become sly. To card cotton.

P فرناد *farnād*, Power, strength. Bottom of water. A fish-pond. End, extremity.

P فرناس *farnās*, Careless. Indolent, yawning, slumbering, drowsy, oppressed with sleep. Ignorant, untaught. Ignorance, carelessness.

A فرناس *firnās*, A thick-necked lion. Strong and courageous. (pl. فرانسة *farānisat* and فرانيس *farānīs*) The head man of a Persian village.

P فرناك *farnāk*, A privy.

A فرنب *firnib*, A mouse. A young jerboa.

A فرنتي *faranta'*, Name of a woman, of a female servant, and of a castle.

P فرنج *furunj*, *faranj*, or *firunj*, The environs of the mouth. A large branch lopped off, in order that smaller ones may shoot forth.

P فرنجك *faranjak* or *firinjak*, Nightmare.

A فرنجمسك *faranjmisk*, Sweet basil.

P فرنجمشك *faranjmushk*, A sweet basil.

P فرنجه *faranja* or *firanja*, France.

A فرنخة *farnakhat*, Softness after hardness. Rest after flight. Repose after rude alarm.

P فرند *fa* or *firand*, A sword's glittering surface.

A فرند *firind*, (pl. فراند *farānid*) A sword, or its glittering surface. A red rose. A sheet. The seed of the pomegranate. A sort of garment. The plant حوجم *hawjam*. *Firnid*, (pl. فراند *farānid*) Pot-herbs, seasoning for meat.

A فرنداة *firindāt*, The bird قطا *katā*.

A فرنداد *firindād*, A sort of tree.

A فرنسة *farnasat*, Skilfulness in domestic management, good housewifery.

A فرنع *firniʻ* or *furnuʻ*, A middle-sized louse.

A فرنق *furnuk*, Bad, worthless, useless.

P فرنگ *farang* or *firing*, A Frank, an Italian, European. A Christian. All nations which wear short garments. A galley. *Firnag*, A boy's plaything.

P فرنگستان *frangistān* or *firingistān*, Italy, France, or the country of the Franks. Europe.

P فرنگي *frangī* or *firingī*, French. Italian. An European Christian. A matchlock.

P فرنگيس *farangīs*, The daughter of Afrāsyāb.

P فرنود *farnūd*, Demonstration, proof.

P فرنودسار *farnūdsār*, Name of an encyclopædia.

P فرنه *farna*, Malediction, execration.

A فرنيّ *furnīy*, Cooked in an oven: also bread baked in the oven, *i.e.* round and thick. Stiff, sturdy (fellow). Bulky (dog).

A فرو *farw*, (pl. فراء *firāʼ*) A garment of fur.

P فرو *farū*, A species of fine fox-fur. *Firū*, *faro*, *firo*, or *furo*, Down, downward. Below. Under, beneath. Low. فرو آمدن *furo āmadan*, To come down. To descend. To go down (as the sun). To plunge into water. فرو بردن *furo burdan*, To carry down. To swallow. To duck, to plunge. فرورفتن *furo raftan*, To go down, descend, be swallowed, absorbed. سر فرو كردن *sar furo kardan*, To bow the head, to bend; to subject. فرو گفت *furo guft*, He spoke low, he whispered. فرو نشاندن *furo nishāndan*, To put down, quell, stifle.

P فروار *farwār*, A house for the summer. A winter-habitation.

P فرواره *farwāra*, A summer-house. Treasury.

P فرواز *farwāz*, A summer-parlour. A short piece of wood or lath connecting the rafters, and supporting the roof, which is mostly of clay.

P فروال *farwāl*, (or فرواله *farwāla*) A summer-habitation. An upper-room, open on all sides.

P فروانچه *farwāncha*, A moth. A little moth.

P فرو بردگي *furo burdagī*, Deglutition.

P فروبستن *faro bastan*, To fasten, to close.

P فرو پريدن *faro parīdan*, To fly low.

P فرو پوشيدن *faro poshīdan*, To hide, conceal

A فروة *farwat*, The skin of the head. A fur-pelisse. Peltry. A purse in which a mendicant puts his alms. A heap of dried provender. Ground without herbage. A crown, diadem. A woman's veil or head-dress. A tunic having tucked-up sleeves. Half a cloak made of camels' hair. ذوالفروة *zū'l farwat*, A mendicant. (for ثروة *sarwat*) Riches, plenty.

P فروت *fa* or *furawt*, Much, many, abundant.

A فروت *furūt*, (v. n. of فرت) Being corrupt and wicked. Fornicating.

A فروتة *furūtat*, Sweetness (of water).

P فروتر *farotar*, Lower, inferior.

P فروترين *farotarīn*, Lowest.

P فروتن *faro-tan*, *firo-tan*, or *firū-tan*, Lowly. Humble, depressed. Submissive.

P فروتنده *furotanda*, Hard. Pressed, compressed.

P فروتني *faro-tanī*, Submission. Humility, lowliness. فروتني كردن *firū-tanī kardan*, To humble one's self, to submit.

A فروث *furūs*, (pl. of فرث *fars*) Fæces in the belly of an animal.

A فروج *farūj*, A bow bellying out distant from the string. *Furūj*, (pl. of فرج *farj*) Privities.

A فرّوج *farrūj*, A small shirt; a boy's garment, having an opening behind. *Farrūj* or *furrūj*, (pl. فراريج *farārīj*) A chicken.

A فرّوجة *furrūjat*, A hen-chicken.

P فرو چكيدن *faro chakīdan*, To distil, drop.

P فروچيدن *faro chīdan*, To pick up, gather.

A فروح *farūḥ*, Glad, happy, joyous.

A فروخ *furūkh*, (pl. of فرخ *farkh*) Young birds or beasts.

A فرّوخ *farrūkh*, Name of the brother of Ishmael and Isaac.

P فروخت *firūkht*, *farokht*, or *furokht*) He sold. Sale, selling. فروخت كردن *farokht kardan*, To sell. خريد و فروخت *kharīd u farokht*, Buying and selling, purchase and sale.

P فروختار *firūkh*, *farokh*, or *furokhtār*, A seller.

P فروختگي *farokhtagī*, Sale, vendition, vend.

P فروختن *firūkhtan*, *farokhtan*, or *furokhtan*, To sell. To inflame, kindle, set on fire.

P فروختني *firūkh* or *farokhtanī*, Venal, saleable.

P فروخته *firūkhta*, Sold. Shining, radiant.

P فروخفتن *faro khuftan*, To become thick (as milk), to concrete (as honey).

P فروخفته *faro khufta*, Concreted. A low hill.

P فروخواندن *faro khwāndan*, To call. To read.

P فروخوردن *faro khwurdan*, To eat, swallow. To suppress anger, to swallow one's rage.

P فرود *farwad*, The bar of a door. *Firod* or *farod*, Below, under, down. Descent. Lower part, bottom. A door-sill. A cheat, rogue, deceiver. Vile, bad, unlucky, wicked. Proud, arrogant. Deceived. Name of the son of Siyāwush. فرود آمدن *firod āmadan*, To alight. فرود آوردن *farod āwardan*, To cause to alight. *Furod*, Fried or baked (meats).

A فرود *farwad*, Incomparable, glittering (sword).

Farūd, Single, alone. (A camel) grazing alone. *Furūd*, Appearing distinct and bright (rising stars).

P فروداشت *firo-dāsht*, End, term, extremity. The dying away of sound. The lower or latter part of any thing.

P فروداشتن *faro dāshtan*, To keep down. To preserve.

P فرود آمدن گاه *firod āmadan-gāh*, A halting-place.

P فرودست *faro-dast*, Inferior, powerless. *Firo-dast*, Speaking, singing, reciting together. A chorus, concert. The province of Bengal is also so called by the people of the upper provinces, and its inhabitants فرودستي *firo-dastī*.

P فرود گاه *farod-gāh*, Halting-place, camp.

P فروده *farwada*, The bar of a door. *Furūda*, Meanness, vileness. Mean, avaricious. *Furoda* or *firoda*, Fried in a pan, baked in the oven.

P فرودين *farwadīn*, Name of a month. Name of an angel. The nineteenth day of every month. *Furodīn*, Lowest. A threshold. The west wind.

P فرور *farwar*, Separation. Genius.

A فرور *farūr*, Fleeing (man). Flying from man or fairy (woman). *Farūr*, (or فرّور *furrūr*) The young of a goat, sheep, or wild cow.

A فرورة *farūrat*, Fleeing, fugitive (man).

P فروردگان *farwardgān*, or فروردیان *farwardyān*) Five supplementary days added to the Persian year.

P فروردن *farwardan*, To nourish, foster, educate.

P فروردين *farwardīn*, The nineteenth day of the month. The first month of the Persian year, corresponding with March; also the name of an angel supposed to preside over it.

P فرو رها كردن *furo rahā kardan*, To drop, to let fall (a veil or curtain).

P فرو ريختن *faro rekhtan*, To pour out, to spill. To fall off, or in pieces. To be shed.

P فروز *furoz*, Splendour, light, brilliancy, heat. Quality, property. (in comp.) Inflaming; illuminating, kindling. دل فروز *dil-furoz*, Inflaming the heart (with love). فروزان شدن *furozān shudan*, To kindle, inflame, burn. To be in flames.

P فروزان *furozān*, Luminous, resplendent, radiant.

P فروزان فر *furozān-far*, The Creator.

A فروزة *farwazat*, (v. n. of فروز Q) Dying. Perishing.

P فروزد *furozad*, The planet Jupiter. A fresh, juicy pot-herb.

P فروزگان *furozgān*, Qualities, properties.

P فروزندگي *furozandagī*, Light, lustre.

P فروزنده *furozanda*, Kindler, shiner, illuminator; polisher. فروزنده خاور *furozanda-khāwar*, The world-illuminating sun.

P فروزها *furozhā*, Lights, splendours. Qualities.

P فروزيده *furozīda*, Illuminated. Qualified, described.

P فروزينه *furozīna*, Chips: tinder-box. Quality.

A فروس *farūs*, A lion. *Furūs*, (pl. of فرس *fars*) Horsemen, cavaliers. (pl. of فرس *faras*) Horses.

A فروسة *furūsat*, (or فروسيّة *furūsiyat*) The art of horsemanship. Skill in whatever relates to horses; manege. Sharpness, quickness of intellect.

P فروش *farosh*, Selling. A seller. حلوافروش *halwā-farosh*, A seller of sweetmeats. خود فروشان *khwud-faroshān*, Venders of themselves, *i.e.* boasters.

A فروش *furūsh*, (pl. of فرش *farsh*) Carpets.

P فروشا *faroshā*, Selling; a seller.

P فروشاندن *furoshāndan*, To put or throw away, to put aside.

P فروشتن *faroshtan*, To let or send down.

P فروشدن *faro shudan*, To sink, to be drowned. To descend. To dive. To set (as the sun).

P فروشك *faroshak*, A dish of bruised wheat.

P فروشنده *faroshanda*, A vender. فروشندگان متاع *faroshandagāni matāʿ*, Sellers of wares.

P فروشه *farosha*, Any species of pastry made with almonds. *Furosha*, Bruised wheat.

P فروشيدن *faroshīdan*, To sell.

A فروض *furūz*, The growing old (of a cow).

A فروط *furūt*, A preceding, an outstripping.

A فروع *furūʿ*, (v. n. of فرع) Excelling in birth or beauty. (pl. of فرع *farʿ*) Heads, tops, summits. Heads of hair. Branches. Chiefs of a people or a family. فروع الجوزاء *furūʿu'ljawzāʾ*, (or نجم الفروع *najmu'l furūʿ*) The greatest intenseness of heat.

A فروعات *furūʿāt*, (pl. of فروع *furūʿ*) Summits. Branches. Ramifications.

A فروغ *farūgh*, A star, the sign Gemini. *Furūgh*, (v. n. of فرغ) Finishing, bringing to a conclusion. Dying. Being at leisure. Making for.

P فروغ *furogh*, Splendour, light, brightness, flame.

P فروغاني *furoghānī*, Luminous, resplendent.

P فروغته *firoghta*, (or فروغده *firoghda*) Sold. Lighted up, flashing, radiant.

A فروق *farūḳ*, Timid. A name of Constantinople. *Furūḳ*, (v. n. of فرق) Arriving where two roads meet. Retiring from a herd (a camel or ass) when near delivery. Possessing date-stones, the food of camels. (pl. of فريق *farīḳ*) Troops, bodies.

A فرّوق *farrūḳ*, Timid.

A فروقة *farūḳat*, An armful (of wood or corn). Fat of the reins or kidneys. *Farūḳat*, (or فرّوقة *farrūḳat*) Pusillanimous, timid, cowardly (man or woman). ربّ فروقة يدعى ليثا *rubba farūḳatin yudʿaʾ laysan*, Many a craven is called a lion.

P فروك *farūk*, A young bird that has not yet laid.

A فروك *farūk*, (A woman) who hates her husband. *Furūk*, Conjugal hatred.

P فروكاس *farokās*, Mean, vile, contemptible.

P فرو كش كردن *firo kash kardan*, To squabble, to call one by a bad name. To stay in one place.

P فرو كشيدن *faro kashīdan*, To pull down. To drag along the ground.

P فرو كوفتن *faro koftan*, To knock down, bruise.

P فرو گذاشت *furo guzāsht*, Negligence, remissness, carelessness. Shortness.

P فرو گذاشتن *faro guzāshtan*, To dismiss, discharge, quit, leave, omit, neglect, let alone. To dissipate, destroy. To let down.

P فرو گرفتن *faro giriftan*, To seize. To strike a hard blow.

P فرو گشتن *firo gashtan*, To disappear.

P فرو ماليدن *firo mālidan*, To pluck, collect, gather. To twist. To press, squeeze, strain.

P فرو ماندگي *firo māndagī*, Helplessness, indigence, poverty. Distress, despondency.

P فرو ماندن *firo māndan*, To expect, wait for. To adhere. To be astonished, weak, helpless.

P فرو مانده *faro mānda*, Broken, weak, fatigued, tired, dejected, depressed, oppressed. Helpless, without relief. Defective. عاجز و فرومانده شدن *ǎjiz u faromānda shudan*, To be powerless, oppressed, fatigued.

P فرو مايگان *faro-māyagān*, Base people.

P فرو مايگی *faro-māyagī*, Baseness, meanness, despicableness.

P فرو مايه *faro* or *firo-māya*, Ignoble, mean, abject, petty, base, worthless, sordid. Humble, low. Ignorant, unskilful. Poor. A miser. A spendthrift.

P فرومد *farūmad*, Name of a village near Tūs.

P فرو ميرانيدن *faro mīrānīdan*, To extinguish.

P فرونجك *furūnjak*, The parts about the mouth externally. The nightmare.

P فروند *farwand*, (or فرونده) A bar for a door.

P فرو نشاندن *faro nishāndan*, To extinguish.

P فرو نشانيدن *faro nishānīdan*, To put down, quell, lessen, check, quench, extinguish.

P فرو نشستن *faro nishastan*, To be quenched.

P فرو نهادن *faro nihādan*, To put down. To leave, dismiss.

A فروهة *furūhat*, Cleverness, sprightliness.

P فروهخته *farohikhta*, Making an agreement. Arriving.

P فروهر *furūhar*, Matter, essence (distinguished from accident).

P فرو هشتگی *faro hishtagī*, Pendulousness.

P فرو هشتن *faro hishtan*, To hang down.

P فروهشته *farohishta*, Loose, pendulous.

P فرو هليدن *furo hilīdan*, To quit, leave, loose, let go, throw away.

P فروهنده *furohinda*, An angel. Beautiful. Good-tempered.

P فرو هيختن *faro hīkhtan*, To teach. To draw (a sword).

P فروهيدن *farohīdan*, To abandon, throw away.

P فروهيده *farohīda*, Ingenious, wise. *Firohīda*, Manifest, plain. Pompous, stately.

P فرويز *farwez*, Lace, fringe, edging.

P فرويش *farwesh*, Error, fault. Omission, negligence, forgetfulness. Leisure. Want of employ, idleness. Roughness.

A فره *furh, furuh,* or *furrah*, (pl. of فاره *fārih*) Ingenious, clever. Brisk (mules). *Farah*, (v. n. of فره) Being active, nimble, saucy, petulant. *Farih*, Brisk, active. Saucy, petulant.

P فره *fira*, Much. More. Increase. Precedency, priority. Good-tempered, cheerful. Thoughtful, attentive. High-minded.

P فرّه *farra*, State, dignity, pomp, grandeur, magnificence, power.

A فرّه *firruh*, (in the dialect of Morocco) Iron. *Furrah*, Lively (colts).

P فرهاد *farhād*, A cutter of stones, a digger of mines; so named from a celebrated Persian statuary, who, it is said, to please his mistress Shīrīn, dug through an immense mountain.

P فرهانج *farhānj*, The circumference of the mouth. The nightmare. A gore, gusset. A large branch lopped, that others may grow. The bough of one tree tied to the bough of another. A vine-branch bent under ground, so that the other extremity shoots up and flourishes at a distance from the mother trunk.

A فرهة *furhat*, (pl. of فاره) Brisk (mules).

A فرّهة *furrahat*, (or فرهة *furhat*) (pl. of فاره *fārih*) Ingenious, clever.

P فرهت *farhat*, Decency, propriety, gravity. Grandeur, pomp, state.

P فرهخت *farhakht*, Propriety, decency, decorum.

P فرهختن *farhakhtan* or *farhikhtan*, To teach, instruct, educate. To draw a sword. To hang.

P فرهخته *farhakhta*, Instructed, well educated.

A فرهد *farhad* or *furhud*, A fresh, handsome youth. A lion's cub. *Furhud*, Compact, square-built, firm of body, corpulent. Soft and succulent. Rough and hasty.

A فرهذ *furhuz*, Compact, firm of body, corpulent.

P فرهست *farhast*, Fascination, magic, conjuring.

P فرهمند *farhmand* or *farhamand*, Intelligent, wise. Near.

P فرهنج *farhanj*, Science, skill, knowledge, learning. Politeness, good manners. Understanding, intellect. A Persian lexicon. A vine-branch bent under ground, so that the extremity shoots up at a distance from the parent trunk. Name of the mother of Kay Kāwus.

P فرهنجه *farhanja*, One of polite and of elegant manners, of good temper and handsome person.

P فرهنجيدن *farhanjīdan*, To be polite, mannerly. To teach.

P فرهنجيده *farhanjīda*, Instructed, well-mannered.

P فرهنگ *farhang*, Good-breeding. Greatness. Excellence. Gravity. Wisdom, science. Jurisprudence. A dictionary, lexicon, vocabulary, glossary. A vine-branch bent under ground, so that the other extremity shoots up at a distance from the mother trunk. A subterraneous canal. Name of the mother of Kay Kāwus.

P فرهنگاه *farhangāh*, Inside, middle.

P فرهنگدار *farhang-dār*, A magistrate, judge.

P فرهنگسار *farhangsār*, Obliteration, erasement. Transformation, change of shape, transmigration.

P فرهنگي *farhangī*, A preceptor, tutor, teacher, instructor. A man learned in the law.

P فرهنگيان *farhangiyān*, Preceptors, teachers.

A فرهود *furhūd*, A young mountain-goat. Compact, square, firm of body, corpulent, soft, succulent.

P فرهودي *farhūdī*, One stedfast in religion.

A فرهوذ *furhūz*, (pl. فراهيذ *farāhīz*) Compact, firm of body, corpulent.

P فرهومند *farhomand*, Virtuous and enlightened.

P فرّهی *farrihī*, Possession of honour and glory.

P فرهيختن *farhekhtan*, To teach politeness and good manners. To hang. To draw a sword.

A فري *fary*, (v. n. of فري) Cleaving, splitting, cutting (either to mend or to mar). Measuring accurately, cutting out and making (a wallet). Feigning, inventing a lie. Travelling. *Fara'*, (v. n. of فري) Being astonished, stupefied. Being astonished at, or admiring, one's own performance.

A فريٌ *faris*, Great, wonderful (thing).

A فرّي *furra'*, (A legion) put to flight.

A فريّ *fariy*, Great, wonderful, astonishing, surprising (thing). Large (bucket). Fresh, new (milk just from the cow or the camel). Important (business). Made, formed, prepared. Artificial. False, lying.

P فرياد *faryād* or *firyād*, An exclamation, cry for help or redress: clamour. Lamentation, complaint. فرياد بر آوردن *firyād bar āwardan*, To cry out. فرياد رسيدن *faryād* (or بفرياد *ba faryād*) *rasīdan*, To assist, succour. فرياد و فغان كردن *firyād u fighān kardan*, To cry out, to lament, complain. داد و فرياد كردن *dād u firyād kardan*, To call aloud for justice.

P فرياد خوان *firyād-khwān*, (or فرياد خواه *firyād-khwāh*) Calling for redress; a plaintiff.

P فرياد رس *firyād-ras*, An assistant, defender. Redressing complaints.

P فرياد رسي *firyād-rasī*, Assistance, redress.

P فريادناك *far* or *firyādnāk*, Noisy, clamorous.

P فريادي *firyādī*, A complainant, plaintiff.

A فرياض *firyāz*, Wide.

P فريب *firīb, fireb, fareb,* or *farīb*) Deception, fraud, duplicity, trick, deceit, treachery, imposture, fallacy. Any thing by which one is beguiled. A talisman. Amorous playfulness, blandishment. (in comp.) Deceiving: as, مردم فريب *mardum-firīb*, Betraying men. ناظر فريب *nāzir-firīb*, Deceiving beholders. فريب خوردن *fareb khwurdan*, To be cheated, gulled. فريب دادن *fareb dādan*, To deceive, cheat, gull.

P فريبا *firībā*, A deceiver. Deceived.

P فريب آميز *fareb-āmez*, Mixed with deceit.

P فريب اندازي *fareb-andāzī*, Imposture.

P فريب انگيز *fareb-angez*, Cheating; a cheat.

P فري برز *fariburz*, Name of the son of Kay Kāwus. Name of a certain woman.

P فريب خور *firib-khwur*, A gull, geck, dupe.

P فريب خوري *firib-khwurī*, A being cheated.

P فريب ساز *fareb-sāz*, An impostor, cheat.

P فريبگاه *firib-gāh*, (or فريبگه *firib-gah*) A talisman. Any thing to which a talisman is tied.

P فريبندگي *firibandagī*, Deceit, subtlety, fraud.

P فريبنده *firibanda*, Fallacious. A deceiver.

P فريبي *farebī*, A cheat, impostor.

P فريبيدن *firībidan*, To deceive, or be deceived.

A فرية *faryat*, A heat. A single milking. *Firyat*, A lie, a fiction.

A فريّة *fariyat*, Wide (bucket).

P فريج *farij*, Galangale.

A فريج *farij*, A long bow bellying from the string. (A camel) delivered of her first colt. Cold.

P فريجاب *farijāb*, Small rain; dew.

A فريخ *furaykh*, Illustrious descendants (of Kuraysh). (dim. of فرخ *farkh*) A chickling.

P فريد *farid*, The middle bead of a necklace. *Furid*, A hunter. Congealed.

A فريد *farid*, (pl. فرائد *farāʼid*) A precious gem, pearl, especially one of a larger size, or a bead of gold placed alternately between smaller ones in a necklace or bracelet. The back-bone between the vertebræ of the neck and the vertebræ above the hip-bone. One, unique, incomparable. Singular, only. Bright, glittering (sword). فريد الدهر *farīdu'd dahr*, The phœnix of the age.

A فريدة *faridat*, A precious stone, a pearl.

P فريدون *farīdūn* or *firidun*, Name of an ancient and celebrated king of Persia, the commencement of whose reign is placed about 750 years before the Christian æra. The zodiac.

P فريده *farīda*, Proud, conceited.

P فريدي *farīdī*, Sudden, unpremeditated.

P فريديس *farīdis*, A shrimp.

P فرير *farir*, The herb borage.

A فرير *farir*, (pl. فرار *furār*) A wild calf. The young of a sheep or goat. The mouth, or that part of it where the teeth are examined (in a horse). The part of the mane which a rider lays hold of when going to mount. Name of the father of قيس *kays*.

P فريرون *farīrūn*, Unlucky, unsuccessful.

P فريز *farez* or *firez*, A fattening kind of grass. *Firez*, The edging of a garment. Meat dried and hardened. Shaving, shearing, peeling. A kind of scented grass. فريز كردن *firez kardan*, To shear, clip.

P فريز كردني *firez kardanī*, Fit for shearing.

P فريز كرده شده *firez karda shuda*, Shorn, sheared. فريز ناكرده *firez nākarda*, Unshorn.

P فريس *faris*, Name of a sweet-scented herb. Meat dried and hardened.

A فريس *faris*, (pl. فرسي *farsa'*) Killed, slain. A wooden ring or hoop. *Furays*, (dim. of فرس *faras*) A little horse, a tit, a pony.

A فريسة *farisat*, (v. n. of فرس) Catching and breaking the bones of game or prey. A lion's prey.

G فريسموس *farismūs*, A priapism.

A فريسي *farisīy*, A Pharisee.

P فريش *faresh*, Rapine, spoil, plunder. Roasted meat. Bravo! well done! The parts round about the mouth. *Firaysh*, Scattered, dispersed.

A فريش *farīsh*, (pl. فرائش *farāʼish*) Any solid-hoofed animal immediately, or for seven days, after being delivered of young. A concubine.

P فريشته *firishta*, An angel.

A فريص *fariṣ*, One who drinks or does any thing alternately with another. (pl. of فريصة *fariṣat*, q.v.)

A فريصة *fariṣat*, (pl. فريص *fariṣ* and فرائص *farāʼiṣ*) The vein in a horse's neck where he is let blood; also a nerve, and a muscle between the interior part of the shoulder and the side (which is observed to quiver).

A فريض *fariz*, Properly notched (bow or arrow). Old, ancient. Conversant with the ordinances and commandments of God.

A فريضة *farīzat*, (pl. فرائض *farāʼiz*) An ordinance of God, an indispensable religious or legal duty. Tithes or other proportion of cattle due for pious uses. A part or portion cut off. A knowledge of the law of inheritance. A decrepit old woman, a crone. الفريضتان *al farīzatāni*, Two-year-old sheep and four-year-old camels (they pay no tithes before that time).

A فريع *furayʻ*, A little Pharaoh; petty tyrant.

A فريعة *furayʻat*, (dim. of فرعة *faraʻat*) A small louse. A woman's name.

A فريغ *farīgh*, Wide, stretched out, large, broad, ample. Flat, level (spot). Long-stepping (horse).

A فريغة *farīghat*, A large bottle. Wide (wound).

P فريفتار *firīftār* or *fireftār*, A deceiver, cheat.

P فريفتن *firif* or *fareftan*, To deceive, seduce.

P فريفته *firef* or *firīfta*, Deceived, seduced. Enamoured. فريفته شدن *firīfta shudan*, To be beguiled, deceived, cheated, gulled.

A فريق *farīk*, (pl. افرقاء *afrikāʼ*, افرقة *afrikat*, فرق *furuk*, and فروق *furūk*) A troop or squadron. A sect. Strayed sheep. فريق ثاني *farīki sānī*, The defendant party in a law-suit, if consisting of several individuals.

A فريقة *farīkat*, (A few sheep) separated from the flock, and not returning at night. A preparation of dates and fenugreek given to women in childbed. الفريقتين *al farīkatayn*, (or الفريقتان *al farīkatāni*) Two kinds of creatures (as men and demons).

A فريقين *farīkayn*, (oblique of فريقان *farīkāni*) Both parties.

A فريك *farīk*, Ripe, dry, or rubbed (ear of corn).

A فريكتان *farīkatāni*, (dual) Two bones at the root of the tongue.

P فرين *farīn*, An oven.

P فرين پخت *farīn-pukht*, Baked in the oven.

P فريور *farewar* or *firewar*, Straight. Just, right, true. Orthodox. Name of a fragrant herb.

P فريوردن *farewardan*, To be just and true.

P فريوركيش *farewar-kesh*, Orthodox in religion.

P فريوري *farewarī*, Justness, rectitude. Truth. Steadiness in religious matters.

P فريوريدن *farewarīdan*, To be a true and orthodox believer in religion.

P فريوك *furīwak*, A melon.

P فريه *farya*, A curse. *Firya*, An imprecation, curse. Detestation, abhorrence. Imposture, lie.

P فز *faz*, The male organ of generation.

A فزّ *fazz*, (v. n. of فزّ) Retiring, turning away. Separating one's self. Springing up (as a surprised deer), trembling. Removing, tearing from a place. Disturbing, making restless. (pl. افزاز *afzāz*) A light, active man. The calf of a wild cow.

P فزا *fizā* or *fazā*, More. Increase. Increasing. Grown, augmented. Yawning. هجنت فزا *hujnat-fizā*, Increasing in wickedness or infamy.

P فزار *fazār*, A tool. Spiceries, seasonings.

A فزارة *fazārat*, A she-leopard. Name of the founder of a tribe. Name of a woman.

A فزازة *fazāzat*, A being stirred up, inflamed.

A فزّاعة *fazzāʻat*, A very dreadful man, one who inspires great terror.

P فزاك *fazāk*, The crown of the head. Impure, defiled, polluted. Carrion. Uncleanness, ordure.

P فزّان *fazzān*, Name of a son of Ham. Fezzan in Western Africa.

P فزاي *fizāy*, Augmenting, increasing (used in composition). More, greater.

P فزايسته *fazāyista*, More, greater. Increase.

P فزايش *fazāyish*, Increase, augmentation.

P فزاينده *fazāyanda*, Augmenting.

A فزد *fuzd*, Camels' blood.

A فزر *fazr*, (v. n. of فزر) Rending (a garment). Striking the back (with a stick). Having a large excrescence on the back or breast. *Fizr*, A flock of sheep, from 10 to 40, or from 3 to 10; also two or more sheep. A kid. Root, origin. A tumour growing near the pubes (of a man or sheep). فزر معزي *fizrun miʻzan*, A flock of goats (used proverbially for any thing improbable, as those animals do not herd together). *Fazar*, (v. n. of فزر) Having a large excrescence on the back or breast. *Fizar*, Fissures, clefts.

A فزراء *fazrāʼ*, Full of flesh and fat, and near the age of puberty (a girl).

A فزرة *fuzrat*, A wide road. A wen.

A فزع *fazʻ*, *fizʻ*, or *fazaʻ*, (v. n. of فزع) Fearing, flying in terror. Calling for help. Taking refuge. Assisting, succouring. Waking from sleep. *Fuzʻ*, Any thing dreadful, whatever frightens people. *Fazaʻ*, (pl. افزاع *afzāʻ*) Terror. Cry, lamentation. جزع و فزع *jazaʻ u fazaʻ*, Complaint and lamentation. يوم الفزع الاكبر *yawmu'l fazaʻi'l akbar*, The day of great lamentation, *i.e.* The last judgment. *Fazi'*, Terrified, frightened, afraid.

A فزعة *fuz'at*, One of whom all are afraid. *Fuza'at*, One who implores relief; much frightened.

A فزفزة *fazfazat*, A banishing, a driving away.

P فزودن *fuzūdan*, To increase, multiply.

P فزورة *fazwara*, A bar for fastening a door.

A فزوزة *fuzūzat*, A being stirred up, inflamed.

P فزون *fuzūn*, More, greater. Increase. Multitude. Size.

P فزونا *fuzūnā*, Greatly, very much.

P فزوني *fuzūnī*, Augmentation.

P فزة *fizih*, Ugly, nasty, filthy. Conquering.

P فزيدون *fazīdūn*, More, greater.

A فزيز *fazīz*, (v. n. of فزّ) Flowing, running (blood from a wound).

P فژ *faj*, Dirt, nastiness. A lie. A nasty, sordid fellow. Flame. *Fuj*, The mane of a horse.

P فژاك *fajāk*, (فژاكن *fajākin*, or فژاگين *fajāgīn*) Dirty, nasty. Squalid, loathsome.

P فژدرة *fajdara*, A bar for fastening a door.

P فژژ *fajaj*, Galangale or sweet cane (good for stomach-complaints).

P فژغردة *fajgharda*, Moistened, wet, softened.

P فژغند *fajghand*, An herb winding round plants like ivy, and drying them up. Filthy, nasty, dirty.

P فژغندة *fajghanda*, (فژگن *fajgan*, فژگند *fajgand*, or فژگندة *fajganda*) Impure, nasty, filthy. Ugly.

P فژم *fajm*, Affliction, distress, indigence.

P فژوليدن *fijūlīdan*, To wither, or to cause to wither. To be scattered. *Fujūlīdan*, To provoke, stimulate, or urge (to battle). To importune, dun. To drive away. To shake dirt and dust from the skirts of one's garment.

P فژة *faja*, A squalid, filthy, disgusting fellow. Wards of a key. *Fijih*, Dirty, nasty. Rugged, rough.

P فژيژ *fajīj*, Galangale.

P فژيغون *fajeghūn*, Name of a Persian physician.

A فسء *fas'*, (v. n. of فسأ) Tearing (a garment). Striking on the back with a stick. Preventing, warding off. *Fasa'*, (v. n. of فسيء) Being hollow-backed, and having a protuberant breast. Suffering a pain in the backside, loins, or thighs when walking. Being unable to rise without difficulty.

P فسا *fasā*, Name of a city in Persia, whence stuffs are brought.

A فساء *fusā'*, A breaking wind without noise. A slight wind (from the belly).

A فسّاء *fassā'*, One who often breaks wind gently, who frequently lets a quiet فسوة *faswat*.

A فساح *fusāh*, Spacious, roomy (apartment).

A فساحة *fasahāt*, (v. n. of فسح) Being large, wide, ample, roomy, spacious, commodious.

A فساد *fasād*, (v. n. of فسد) Being corrupted, spoiled. Corruption, depravity, mischief, malignity, perverseness, iniquity, villainy, wickedness, violence, war, horror. Mutiny, sedition, rebellion. Unjust seizure of property. Barrenness, scarcity. A diseased state, unsoundness, affection (in surgery). اهل فساد *ahli fasād*, A villain, criminal. باعث فتنه و فساد *bā'isi fitna u fasād*, The author (or exciter) of sedition and mischief.

A فسادات *fasādāt*, (pl. of فساد *fasād*) Evils. Wars. Villainies. Diseased conditions.

P فساد آيين *fasād-āyīn*, Of bad principles.

P فسادكار *fasād-kār*, A mischief-maker.

A فسادي *fasādī*, Quarrelsome, mutinous.

P فسار *fasār*, A headstall. Yawning, gaping.

A فسّاط *fussāt* or *fissāt*, A tent of goats' hair. The first Cairo, metropolis of Egypt. Any large city.

A فساطيط *fasātīt*, (pl. of فسطاط *fustāt*) Tents made of goats' hair.

A فسافس *fasāfis*, Wall or paper-lice. Bugs.

A يا فساق *yā fasāki*, O lewd wench! slut!

A فسّاق *fussāk*, (pl. of فاسق *fāsik* and فسق *fasik*) Scoundrels. Highway-robbers.

A فساقيّ *fasākīy*, (pl. of فسقيّة) Fountains.

A فسال *fisāl*, (pl. of فسل) Worthless fellows.

A فسالة *fasālat*, (v. n. of فسل) Being of the worst and meanest rank (men). *Fusālat*, Whatever flies or falls from iron or other metals when hammering or forging.

P فسان *fasān*, History, story, fable. A whetstone.

P فسانه *fasāna*, A story, fable. Celebrated.

P فسانيدن *fasānīdan*, To rub, make true or even. To tame, charm, fascinate, enchant. To romance. To observe.

P فسانيدة *fasānīda*, Rubbed, made even. Tamed, charmed, fascinated. An enchanter, magician.

P فساي *fasāy*, (in compos.) Fascinating. A charmer, fascinator. A grape-stone.

A فسائل *fasā'il*, (pl. of فسيلة *fasīlat*) Shoots or suckers of palm-trees.

P فسايندة *fasāyanda*, A fascinator, charmer.

P فساييدن *fasāyīdan*, To fascinate, charm.

A فستات *fustāt*, (*fistāt*, فسقاط *fustāt*, or *fistāt*) A tent made of goats' hair. Cairo, the metropolis of Egypt.

P فستان *fistān*, A loose gown, petticoat.

A فستق *fustuk* or *fustak*, A pistachio. Pine.

P فستقى *fustukī*, Of a pistachio or sea-green.

A فسح *fas-h*, (v. n. of فسح) Making more room for one in an assembly. Being spacious and roomy. Granting a firmān or passport. A passport. Width of step. Easter. *Fus-h*, Large-breasted (man). *Fasah*, Width of step. *Fusuh*, Spacious, capacious (sitting-room).

A فسحة *fus-hat*, Largeness, width, amplitude, room, space. Liberty.

P فسحت سراي *fus-hat-sarāy*, A spacious palace.

A فسحم *fus-hum*, A man having a large breast. Spacious, roomy (apartment). Glans penis.

A فسخ *faskh*, (v. n. of فسخ) Violating, dissolving (a marriage), breaking (an agreement or bargain). Dislocating (the hand). Spoiling, corrupting, vitiating. Throwing aside (one's clothes). Separating, scattering. Laying waste, desolating. Being corrupted. Becoming weak. Being old and tattered (a garment). Being dislocated, bruised (the hand). Being ignorant. Ignorance; weakness of mind and body. Weak in mind and body, and unable to manage one's own affairs. P فسخ كردن *faskh kardan*, To break. A *Fasakh*, (v. n. of فسخ) Being spoiled.

A فسخة *faskhat*, Unable to manage his affairs.

A فسدى *fasda'*, (pl. of فسيد *fasīd*) Corrupted, spoiled, vitiated.

A فسر *fasr*, (v. n. of فسر) Explaining, interpreting, or declaring, making clear. The inspection of urine, and the discovery thereby of a disease.

P فسرانيدن *fusurānīdan*, To allow to become thick and congealed.

P فسرد *fusard*, Jelly.

P فسردگى *fusurdagī*, Congelation.

P فسردن *fis* or *fusurdan*, To congeal, concrete.

P فسردة *fisurda* or *fusurda*, Congealed, frozen. Cold-hearted. The chace.

P فسردة بيان *fusurda-bayān*, Any one whose conversation is destitute of force or meaning, cold, and uninteresting. An unimpressive orator.

P فسردة پستان *fusurda-pistān*, A barren or an old woman past bearing or giving suck.

P فسردة دل *fusurda-dil*, Cold, hard-hearted.

P فسرة *fisara*, Tremor from cold or fear.

A فسس *fusus*, (pl. of فسيس *fasīs*) Weak in mind and body.

A فسطاط *fustāt*, (pl. فساطيط *fasātīt*) A tent made of goats' hair. The metropolis of Egypt, ancient Cairo, built by عمرو بن عاص *'amr bin 'ās*, Any large collection of houses and inhabitants, a city.

P فسطفى *fastafī*, Name of a musical instrument.

A فسفس *fusfas*, Extremely foolish. Blunt (sword). A certain nasty-smelling herb.

P فسفس *fisfis*, A whispering, a humming. A bug. A wall-louse.

A فسفسة *fisfisat*, A sort of clover-grass.

P فسفسة *fasfasa*, Trefoil, clover, Burgundian hay.

A فسفسى *fasfasa'*, A kind of game.

A فسفيس *fasfīs*, A wren.

A فسق *fisk*, (v. n. of فسق) Slipping out of its husk (a ripe date). Deviating, swerving from the way of truth and righteousness. Slighting the commands of God. Disobedience, rebellion. Iniquity, villainy, sin, impiety, falsehood, prevarication. Impudence, obscenity, adultery. *Fasik*, A scoundrel, transgressor, law-breaker. *Fusak*, Very wicked; ever bent on villainy. يا فسق *yā fusak*, O scoundrel!

A فسقة *fasakat*, (pl. of فاسق) Wicked; adulterous.

A فسقية *fiskīyat* or *faskīyat*, (pl. فساقيّ *fasākīy*) A cistern. A place for washing the hands and face. An ornamented, artificial fountain.

A فسكل *fiskil*, (A man) of the worst kind: lazy,

worthless. *Fiskil* or *fuskul*, The last horse in a race.

A فسكلة *faskalat*, (v.n. of فسكل Q) Coming in last. Following. Delaying, tarrying, lingering behind. Becoming a follower. Making (any one) a follower.

A فسكول *fuskūl* or *fiskawl*, The last horse in a race. One who remains behind, comes in the rear.

A فسل *fasl*, (v. n. of فسل) Weaning (a child). (pl. افسل *afsul*, فسول *fusūl*, فسال *fisāl*, فسل *fusl*, فسولة *fusulat*, and فسلاء *fusalāʼ*) A worthless man. A vine-tendril or slip fit for planting. *Fisl*, A fool.

A فسلاء *fusalāʼ*, (pl. of فسل *fasl*) Base fellows.

A فسلان *fuslān*, (pl. of فسيلة *fasīlat*) Palm-shoots.

A فسلة *faslat*, The sucker of a palm-tree.

P فسله *fusla*, A herd of horses. *Fisla*, A narrative, history. A similitude.

G فسليون *fasliyūn*, The herb flea-bane.

P فسن *fasan*, A whetstone.

A فسو *fasw*, A breaking wind without noise.

A فسوّ *fasūw*, One who oft breaks wind gently.

A فسوات الضباع *fasawātu'z zibāʻ*, A kind of fungus (what we call the devil's snuff-box?)

A فسوة *faswat*, Wind without noise. فسوة الضبع *faswatu'z zabuʻ*, A kind of fungus or mushroom.

P فسوجن *fusūjan*, A food eaten in Gīlān.

A فسود *fusūd*, (v. n. of فسد) Being corrupted, spoiled, marred.

G فسوس *fasūs*, Ephesus.

P فسوس *fisos*, Seduction or straying from the way of safety. Reproach, blame, sarcasm, gibe, joke, jest, raillery, ridicule. Play, sport, wit, humour. Vexation, sorrow, regret, grief. Ah! alas! فسوس كردن *fisos kardan*, To rail at, ridicule, banter.

P فسوسكاري *fisos-kārī*, Chequered, inlaid work.

P فسوسيدن *fisosīdan*, To sigh after, grieve for. To joke, jeer. To seduce, lead, or go astray.

A فسوق *fusūk*, (v. n. of فسق) Going out. Deviating, swerving from the commands of God. Being wicked, adulterous.

A فسول *fusūl*, (pl. of فسل *fasl*) Men of the worst kind. Vine-tendrils.

A فسولة *fusūlat*, (v. n. of فسل) Being worthless, of a vile stock (a man). (pl. of فسل *fasl*) Worthless fellows.

P فسون *fusūn*, Incantation, fascination. Fraud, deceit. فسانه و فسون *fasāna u fusūn*, Fables and enchantments.

P فسونا *fusūnā*, An enchanter, fascinator.

P فسونگري *fusūngarī*, Fascination.

A فسيح *fasīh*, Ample, large, capacious, spacious, roomy. حيات فسيحة الحسنات *hayāti fasīhatu'l hasanāt*, A life employed in pious actions.

A فسيخ *fasīkh*, Weak in mind and in body. Unable to manage his own affairs.

A فسيد *fasīd*, (pl. فسدي) Corrupted, vicious.

A فسيس *fasīs*, (pl. فسس *fusus*) Weak in mind and body.

A فسيط *fasīt*, A nail-paring. A date-stalk.

A فسيفساء *fusayfisāʼ*, A sort of pearl or bead fixed on the inner walls of houses.

A فسّيق *fissīk*, Intent on villainy. An adulterer.

A فسيل *fasīl*, (pl. of فسيلة *fasīlat*) Palm-shoots.

A فسيلة *fasīlat*, (pl. فسائل *fasāʼil*, فسيل *fasīl*, and فسلان *fuslān*) A palm-shoot or sucker.

P فسيله *fasīla*, A herd, flock, bevy. A branch.

P فش *fash*, Scattered. The noise made in untying garments. The parts about the mouth (especially of a horse). The end of a turban-sash, to the length of a few inches, hanging down the back or side. A horse's forelocks. (Sometimes used for وش *wash*) A particle of similitude: as, ماه فش *māh-fash*, Like the moon. *Fush*, Mane or tail of a horse. End or tail of any thing.

A فشّ *fashsh*, (v. n. of فشّ) Squeezing (the air) out of a bag or bladder. Belching. Milking expeditiously (a camel). A kind of thorny tree. The fruit of an African carob or bean. Foolish. Detraction. The pursuit of insignificant thieves. Places wherein water collects or settles. A coarse cloak of open, flimsy texture.

A فشء *fashʼ*, (v. n. of فشأ) Being proud, arrogant, playing the great man. Pride, pomp, boasting.

A فشاء *fashāʼ*, Breed or increase of cattle.

A فشاح *fashāh*, A hyena.

P فشار *fashār* or *fishār*, A scattering. Diffusion. Compression, constriction, squeezing. The piercing of one thing with another.

A فشار *fushār*, A word used by the vulgar in the sense of هذيان *hazayān*, Vain, idle talk or gibberish. (It is not an Arabic word).

P فشاردن *fishārdan*, To press, squeeze, wring. To pierce or thrust one thing into another.

P فشارش *fishārish*, A squeezing, pressure.

A فشاشي *fashāshi*, Disobedient, shrewish.

P فشاع *fishāʻ*, The white or black vine.

A فشاغ *fishāgh*, Laziness, slowness. (See also شغار *shighār*). *Fushāgh*, A patch on a leathern bottle. *Fushāgh* or *fushshāgh*, A species of herb, which, like ivy, twines about trees and destroys them.

P فشافاش *fashāfāsh*, The whizzing of arrows.

P فشافش *fashāfash*, The whizzing of arrows.

P فشان *fashān*, A mace of iron, silver, or gold. *Fishān*, (in compos.) Scattering, strewing, shedding. A strewer. خون فشان *khūn-fishān*, Blood-shedding. زرفشان *zar-fishān*, Strewing gold. چشمش سيّاله فشان *chashmash sayyāla-fishān*, Her (or his) eyes shedding a torrent of tears.

P فشاندن *fishāndan*, To scatter. To ventilate.

A فشج *fashj*, (v. n. of فشج) Straddling in running or when about to stale (a horse).

A فشح *fashh*, (v. n. of فشح) Spreading open the legs. Turning away from.

A فشخ *fashkh*, (v. n. of فشخ) Striking the head or back of the neck with the hand. Injuring. Telling lies at play.

P فشردن *fashurdan*, To squeeze, press, wring. To plant the foot firmly.

P فشرده قدم *fashurda-kadam*, Steady. Resolute.

A فشع *fashʻ*, (v. n. of فشع) Drying at the tops, withering (ears of millet).

A فشغ *fashgh*, (v.n. of فشغ) Rising above, overtopping, and covering. Striking (with a whip), bringing (one) under the whip.

A فشغاء *fashghāʼ*, Diffused, dishevelled (forelocks), overhanging the eyebrows.

A فشغة *fashghat*, Ivy, bind-weed, pellitory. A cottony substance found within a reed. Whatever flies from within the plant صوصلاة *sawsalāt*.

A فشفاش *fashfāsh*, A coarse and flimsy cloak.

A فشفش *fishfish*, Vapid wine.

A فشفشة *fashfashat*, (v. n. of فشفش Q) Being weak in intellect. Lying grossly. Scattering urine.

A فشق *fashk*, (v. n. of فشق) Giving themselves up to play and pastime by reason of the abundance of worldly possessions (people). A breaking. A violent mode of eating. *Fashak*, Cheerfulness, sprightliness. Greediness. Speed, flight. Width between the horns, or between the fore and hind part of a camel's dug.

P فشك *fishak*, A parasol.

A فشل *fashl*, (pl. افشال *afshāl*) Weak. Slow. Cowardly. *Fishl*, (pl. فشول *fushūl*) The hood of a camel-litter, or that whereon a woman sits. *Fashal*, (v. n. of فشل) Being cowardly, timid, languid, dull, slow. *Fashil*, (pl. فشل *fushl*) Cowardly, languid, torpid, lazy, dull, slow.

A فشو *fashw*, (and فشوّ *fushūw*) (v. n. of فشا for فشو) Being divulged, published (news).

A فشوش *fashūsh*, (A camel) scattering, spilling milk whilst milking. A vain, boasting fellow. A rough, coarse cloak of open texture. The bean-pod or carob. A leathern milk-pail. A deceitful, lying woman; one whose parts make a noise in coitu.

A فشول *fushūl*, (pl. of فشل *fishl*) Covers of camel-litters. Cushions to sit upon in camel-litters.

A فشيّ *fushīy*, (v. n. of فشا for فشو) Being divulged, published (news or fame).

A فشيان *fashyān*, Sorrow, heaviness of heart.

A فصّ *fass*, (v. n. of فصّ) Separating, pulling (one thing from another). Making a whizzing noise (a locust). Weeping slightly (a boy). Eloquence. ما فصّ في يدي شيء *mā fassa fī yadī shayʼun*, Nothing remains in my hand. *Fass*, *fiss*, or *fuss*, (pl. فصوص *fusūs*) The bezel, or rather the precious stone of a ring. Pupil of the eye. Juncture or joint of bones, articulation. A clove of garlic. An article or distinct part of a writing or business.

A فصا *fasaʼ*, (or فصاة *fasāt*) A grape-stone.

A فصاح *fisāh*, (pl. of فصح *fas-h* or فصيح *fasīh*) Eloquent, rhetorical (men). (pl. of فصيحة *fasīhat*) Eloquent (women).

A فصاحة *fasāhat*, (v. n. of فصح) Employing

elegant, perspicuous language. Eloquence.

P فصاحت پرداز fasāhat-pardāz, Eloquent.

A فصاد fisād, (v. n. of فصد) Breathing a vein, bleeding. Assigning, fixing for any one a certain sum. Venesection, phlebotomy.

A فصّاد fassād, A bleeder, phlebotomist, surgeon.

A فصادة fisādat, Bleeding, venesection.

A فصّادي fassādī, Surgery, phlebotomy.

A فصّاص fassās, A maker of ring-bezels. One who cuts or sets the precious stone in the collet.

A فصاعدًا fa sāʿidan, And more, and upwards.

A فصافص fasāfis, (pl. of فصفصة fisfisat) Fresh clover-grasses. Fusāfis, Quick, active, brisk.

A فصافصة fusāfisat, A lion.

A فصال fisāl, (v. n. of فصل) Weaning (a colt). (v. n. 3 of فصل) Breaking off and settling accounts (with one's partner), dissolving partnership. (pl. of فصيل fasīl) Young camels weaned. Low breast-works on the outside of fortified towns.

A فصّال fassāl, One who praises people to gain their favour. An accuser.

A فصائح fasāʾih, (pl. of فصيحة) Eloquent (women).

A فصّة fassat, Medica, a sort of trefoil.

A فصح fas-h, (v. n. of فصح) Bursting forth and overcoming one (the light of the morning). Employing elegant, perspicuous language. Being eloquent. (pl. فصحاء fusahā, فصاح fisāh, and فصح fusuh) Eloquent, clear (man or speech). Fis-h, A day without cloud or cold. Easter, the Christian passover. Fusuh, (pl. of فصح fas-h and فصيح fasīh) Orators, eloquent, rhetorical men.

A فصحاء fusahā, (pl. of فصح fas-h and فصيح fasīh) Eloquent men.

A فصحىٰ fusha', (fem. of افصح afsah) More or most eloquent. Clearer, clearest.

A فصخ faskh, (v. n. of فصخ) Neglecting, taking no heed. Dislocating (a hand). Cheating (in a sale).

A فصد fasd, (v. n. of فصد) Bleeding, opening a vein. Assigning, fixing upon a thing as a present. Phlebotomy, venesection, blood-letting, surgery.

A فصدة fusdat, Dates mixed with blood (which they dress in this manner with meat).

A فصع fasʿ, (v. n. of فصع) Pressing (a fresh date, so that it slips out of the skin). Rubbing (an almond) to take off the bark, blanching (it). Giving away part of one's property. Taking off (the turban). Drawing back the foreskin over the gland (an uncircumcised lad). Opening and shutting the pudendum alternately (a mare).

A فصعاء fasʿā, A female mouse.

A فصعان fasʿān, Constantly bare-headed on account of heat.

A فصعة fusʿat, The foreskin drawn back. A wide foreskin which will allow the nut to come out.

A فصعل fisʿil and fusʿul, A scorpion, or its fœtus. A worthless fellow, a miser.

A فصفصة fasfasat, (v. n. of فصفص Q) Bringing true information. Being hasty, rapid (in utterance). Fisfisat, (pl. فصافص fasāfis) A species of clover-grass when green (if dry it is called قتّ katt).

A فصل fasl, (v. n. of فصل) Cutting, dissecting, disjoining, separating, dividing, interrupting, interposing, intervening. Weaning. Cutting off one or more letters at the end of a verse. Stringing a bead between every two pearls. Distinguishing, discerning. Deciding, determining, defining. Being divided. A section, article, chapter, or other division of a book. Difference, distinction, decision (between right and wrong). A right and true saying or speech. Decision of a cause. A division between two provinces. Any thing intervenient, interposing, or uniting. The juncture or joint of bones. A pronoun in the nominative case placed between the subject of a proposition and the predicate: as, زيد هو المنطلق zaydun huwa'l muntalik, Zayd, he is the jolly fellow. Time, season, juncture. Any one of the four seasons. Harvest. A crop. فصل الخطاب faslu'l khitāb, The phrase امّا بعد ammā baʿd. A verdict against the defendant. A verdict decisive between right and wrong. P فصل خصومت كردن fasli khusūmat kardan, To decide law-suits. فصل بهار fasli bahār, The spring season. The vernal equinox. A فصل خريف fasli kharīf, The latter end of the year. فصل ربيع fasli rabīʿ, The first harvest of the year. P فصل مهرجان fasli mihrjān, Autumnal equinox. چهار فصل chahār fasl, The four seasons. A يوم الفصل yawmu'l fasl, The day of decision, last day, day of judgment.

A فصلان fislān or fuslān, (pl. of فصيل fasīl) Weaned camels' colts.

P فصلانه faslāna, A fee received by the kāzī on the harvest.

A فصلة faslat, One segment. A transplanted palm-tree. A single section or chapter.

A فصلي faslī, A fasly, time, season. A term designating the official revenue-year of the Muhammadans (in which no months are reckoned), commencing on the 12th of July. (The year A. D. 1840 corresponds with 1249-1250, Fasly).

A فصم fasm, (v. n. of فصم) Breaking, bruising (without separation). Being demolished (a house).

A فصوص fusūs, (pl. of فصّ fass) Stones set in rings. Bezels of rings. Fish-scales.

A فصول fusūl, (v. n. of فصل) Departing, going out. Coming out small (the stone of the grape). (pl. of فصل fasl) Sections. Seasons of the year.

A فصي fasy, (v. n. of فصي) Separating, dividing. Releasing, giving deliverance. Fasa', A grape-stone.

A فصية fasyat, (v. n. of فصي) Separating, dividing. Releasing, giving deliverance. Temperature, neither extreme heat nor cold. Fasyat, (or فصيّة fasiyat) Liberty, freedom from ill, deliverance.

A فصيح fasīh, (pl. فصحاء fusahā, فصاح fisāh, and فصح fusuh) Eloquent, rhetorical (man or discourse). Correct, accurate (expression). Frothless or skimmed (milk).

A فصيحة fasīhat, (pl. فصاح fisāh and فصائح fasāʾih) Eloquent (woman).

A فصيخ fasīkh, (or فصيخة fasīkhat) Unfortunate, disappointed in one's views. A man to whom an acute intellect has been denied.

A فصيد fasīd, Bled in a vein. Blood drawn from a vein (especially that of a camel, which is eaten fried, and even set before a guest in scarce seasons).

A فصيدة fasīdat, Dates mixed with blood (which they dress in this manner with meat).

A فصيص fasīs, (v. n. of فصّ) Being purulent, running (a wound). Oily (date-stone or kernel).

A فصيط fasīt, A nail-paring. Stalk of a date.

P فصيل fasīl, A kind of French bean.

A فصيل fasīl, (pl. فصلان fuslān, fislān, and فصال fisāl) A child or young camel weaned from the mother. A breast-work inside a fortification.

A فصيلات fusaylāt, Commas.

A فصيلة fasīlat, A young she-camel. A family; kindred, the nearest relations. A slice of flesh from the thigh, or a piece from any member. جاؤا بفصيلتهم jāʾu bi fasīlatihim, They came all together.

A فصيم fasīm, Large (battle-axe or halbert).

A فضّ fazz, (v. n. of فضّ) Breaking (the seal of a letter). Tearing asunder, breaking so as to separate. Dispersing, separating (people). A scattered multitude.

A فضا faza', A grape-stone. Any thing mixed. امرهم فضا بينهم amruhum fazan baynahum, They have no chief over them. سهم فضا sahmun fazan, A single arrow. بقيت فضا bakītu fazan, I remained alone.

A فضاء fazāʾ, (v. n. of فضا for فضو) Being roomy and spacious (a place). Not putting (one's money) into the purse. A plain, field, or open place. A court, area. فضاءُ واسع fazāʾi wāsiʿ, A wide field. P در فضاءُ خاطر dar fazāʾi khātir, In (his) enlarged mind. A Fizāʾ, Water overflowing ground.

A فضاح fizāh, (or فضاحة fazāhat) Disgrace, ignominy, infamy.

A فضّاح fazzāh, A detector, exposer. المدام فضّاح al mudām fazzāh, Wine exposes. In vino veritas.

A فضاض fizāz, Scattered fragments of rock torn from a mountain, lying one upon another. Fizāz or fuzāz, A fragment flying off from any thing broken or beat.

A فضال fizāl, (v. n. 3 of فضل) Contending about excellence. An every-day garment. Every-day garments. Wine. Wines.

A فضّال fazzāl, An excellent, deserving man.

A فضالة fuzālat, (pl. فضالات fuzālāt) A remainder, redundancy, exuberance. A proper name.

P فضالهٔ خوان fuzālaʾi khwān, Remains of an entertainment, scraps after a meal.

A فضالى fuzāla', Those who try to excel their peers.

A فضائح *fazāsih*, (pl. of فضيحة) Disgraceful acts.

A فضائل *fazāsil*, (pl. of فضيلة *fazīlat*) Virtues, excellencies. Sciences. Literary attainments. Excesses. فضائل شعار حقائق دثار *fazāsil-shiʻāri haķāsik-disār*, Clothed, enriched, or conspicuous for learning (a title bestowed upon judges).

A فضة *fazzat* or *fizzat*, (pl. فضض *fizaz*) Gravelly ground high and burnt. *Fizzat*, Silver.

A فضح *fazh*, (v. n. of فضح) Detecting villainies and exposing them to infamy. Blushing (as the dawn). Breaking out, overpowering one (the light of the morning). *Fazah*, (v. n. of فضح) Being of a whitish colour. Ruddy (dawn).

A فضحة *fuzhat*, A pale white.

A فضخ *fazkh*, (v. n. of فضخ) Breaking, bruising (the head, or any thing hollow). Tearing out (an eye). Pouring out (water) at one plump, or dash.

A فضض *fazaz*, Water scattered about during the performance of ablutions. *Fazaz* or *fuzuz*, A part separated, torn, or scattered. *Fizaz*, (pl. of فضة *fazzat* and *fizzat*) Gravelly lands high and burnt.

A فضع *fazʻ*, (v. n. of فضع) Breaking wind. Voiding excrement.

A فضغ *fazgh*, (v. n. of فضغ) Breaking (a stick).

A فضفاض *fazfāz*, Large (coat of mail). Convenient, easy (life).

A فضفاضة *fazfāzat*, Large (coat of mail). A girl tall and full of flesh.

A فضفضة *fazfazat*, Conveniency, comfort of life. Largeness of a coat of mail or garment.

A فضل *fazl*, (v. n. of فضل) Remaining over and above, exceeding, being redundant. Excelling. (pl. فضول *fuzūl*) Redundancy, excess. A remnant, remainder. Science, wisdom, learning, knowledge, sense. Sediment. A gift, present, recommendation, reward, favour, benefit, grace, bounty. Name of a mountain; also of several compilers of traditions. اهل فضل و معرفت *ahli fazl u maʻrifat*, Endowed with wisdom and learning. *Fuzul*, Clad in the same garment every day (man or woman). A garment worn every day (by working people).

A فضلاً *fazlan*, The more, much less. فضلاً عن *fazlan ʻan*, Much less. فضلاً عن ان *fazlan ʻan an*, Not but that, much less.

A فضلاء *fuzalās*, (pl. of فاضل *fāzil*) Learned men.

A فضلات *fazalāt*, (pl. of فضلة) Leavings, orts.

A فضلة *fazlat*, (pl. فضلات *fazalāt* and فضال *fizāl*) A remainder, abundance, redundancy; leaving, refuse, orts. Excrement. An every-day or a sleeping-garment. Wine. *Fizlat*, The habit or mode of wearing an every-day garment.

A فضلي *fazlī*, Learning, science.

A فضوّ *fuzūw*, (v. n. of فضا for فضو) Being spacious (place). Not putting (money) in one's purse.

A فضوح *fazūh*, as يا فضوح *yā fazūh*, O thou exposed to disgrace! *Fuzūh*, Disgrace, ignominy.

A فضوحة *fuzūhat*, Disgrace, ignominy.

A فضوخ *fuzūkh*, Strong, intoxicating wine.

A فضول *fazūl* or *fuzūl*, Exuberant, excessive, redundant, disproportioned (about the head). Any kind of plunder which cannot be divided (as one horse). *Fuzūl*, Violence. Excess. Flabbiness of skin. A busy, meddling spirit; folly; impertinent interference. (pl. of فضل *fazl*) Augmentations, redundancies, excesses. حلف الفضول *hilfu'l fuzūl*, Name of a (chivalrous?) treaty entered into by certain tribes to vindicate the rights of the oppressed.

P فضول خرچ *fazūl-kharch*, Lavish, profuse.

P فضول گو *fazūl-go* or *gū*, A great talker. A boaster, egotist.

A فضولي *fazūlī*, Redundance, extravagance. Independence.

A فضوليّ *fuzūlīy*, Proud, haughty, presuming. An idle talker. One who busies himself in things not belonging to him, or acts without authority. A busy-body, meddler, impertinent fellow. A tailor.

A فضولي بيع *fuzūlī-bayʻ*, The sale of another's property without his consent.

A فضّيّ *fizzīy*, Made of silver, silver, silvery.

A فضيج *fazīj*, Sweat.

A فضيح *fazīh*, A bad manager (of an estate); one who improperly employs (wealth). Ignominious, infamous, disgraceful. افعال فضيحه *afʻāli fazīha*, Dishonest, dishonourable actions.

A فضيحة *fazīhat*, Disgrace, ignominy.

A فضيحتي *fazīhatī*, Disgraceful, infamous.

A فضيخ *fazīkh*, The expressed juice of grapes. Wine made from unripe dates without fermentation. Watery (milk).

A فضيض *fazīz*, Fresh or flowing water. Water scattered about in performing one's ablutions. Bud of a palm-tree yet unexpanded. Any thing scattered.

A فضيل *fazīl*, Excellent, eminent, admirable. *Fuzayl*, Name of a celebrated saint.

A فضيلة *fazīlat*, (pl. فضائل *fazāsil*) Excess. Excellence, eminence, virtue, perfection, greatness. Science, art, ingenuity, learning, knowledge, doctrine. Superior excellence; qualification which one has in a higher degree than others. Reward, benefit.

P فضيلت انتساب *fazīlat-intisāb*, Allied to excellence: excellent, highly distinguished.

A فطأ *fatas*, (v. n. of فطئ) Being pigeon-breasted, *i. e.* having a depression of the back with a projection of the breast. A flatness of the nose.

A فطاء *fatsās*, Pigeon-breasted (woman).

A فطأة *futsat*, (v. n. of فطأ) Smiting. Striking one (on the back with the open hand). Throwing prostrate. Lying with. Voiding dung. Breaking (any thing hollow, as the head or a cup). Breaking wind. Loading (a camel) so heavily as to produce a depression in his back. Turning (any one) away from his design. Casting up scum (a boiling pot). Imposing on people that which is disagreeable to them. *Futsat*, A depression of the back with a projection of the breast.

A فطار *futār*, Notched, blunt (sword).

A فطاريّ *futārīy*, A man without a good or bad quality.

A فطاطيس *fatātīs*, (pl. of فطّيس *fittīs*) Smiths' hammers.

A فطافط *fatāfit*, Noises made in checking animals, or in coition.

A فطام *fitām*, Weaning, ablactation.

A فطانة *fatānat*, (or فطانية *fatāniyat*) (v. n. of فطن) Understanding, perceiving. Being quick, shrewd, intelligent, sagacious.

A فطح *fath*, (v. n. of فطح) Widening, making broad. Striking with a bludgeon. Hewing, chipping, smoothing (wood). Casting (a fœtus). Impregnating (a palm-tree). *Fatah*, (v. n. of فطح) Being impregnated with the pollen of the male (a female palm). Breadth or largeness of head or tail; also of the tip of the nose.

A فطحل *fitahl*, The time before the creation of man, or when stones were supposed to be fluid. The age of Noah. A great inundation. Large-bodied (camels). Fat, sleek, and large.

A فطذ *fatz*, A chiding, checking, driving away.

A فطر *fatr*, (v. n. of فطر) Commencing, broaching, beginning. Creating, producing, stamping an impress. Breaking a fast. Causing one to breakfast. Not saturating (a hide) with the tanning material. Baking unleavened bread. Splitting, cleaving. Coming forth (teeth). Milking with the thumb and fore-finger, or with the tips of the fingers. A seminal effusion. (pl. فطور *futūr*) A fissure. *Fitr*, He or those who breakfast. Breakfast. عيد الفطر *ʻīdu'l fitr*, The festival of breaking the fast, which immediately follows the Muhammadan Lent. *Fitr* or *futr*, A grape when the heads appear. *Futr*, The kneading of flour. *Futr* or *futur*, Unfermented. A sort of fungus, puff, or mushroom which is deadly. The froth of new milk.

G فطراساليون *futrāsāliyūn*, Rock-parsley.

A فطرة *fitrat*, Nature, creation, form (which an embryo takes in the womb). Religion. The power of the Creator. Alms given upon the عيد الفطر *ʻīdu'l fitr*, above-mentioned. The Catholic mass, or wafer. Wisdom, sagacity. Deceit, trick.

A فطرتي *fitratī*, Sagacious, cunning.

A فطرس *futrus*, Peter.

A فطريء *fatra'*, Unleavened (bread).

A فطريّ *fitrīy*, Natural, constitutional.

A فطز *fatz*, (v. n. of فطز) Dying.

A فطس *fats*, (v. n. of فطس) Flattening, making wide (iron). Speaking to one's face. Myrtle-berries. *Fatas*, (v. n. of فطس) Being flat-nosed, having the nose broad, flattened, and depressed.

A فطساء *fatsās*, (fem. of افطس) Flat-nosed.

A فطسة *fatsat*, A glass bead, or any such thing, by which men or animals are said to be charmed.

A single myrtle-berry. The skin of an animal which has died a natural death. *Fatasat*, Flatness or depression of nose, a camous state.

A فطفطة *fatfatat*, (v. n. of فطفط Q) Voiding dung. Speaking unintelligibly.

A فطم *fatm*, (v. n. of فطم) Weaning. Cutting. Restraining. *Futum*, (pl. of فطيم *fatīm*) Weaned.

A فطن *fatn, fitn, futn, fatan*, or *futun*, (v. n. of فطن) Understanding, perceiving, comprehending. *Fatin, fatun*, or *fatn*, (pl. فطن *futn*) Wise, intelligent, sagacious.

A فطنة *fitnat*, (v. n. of فطن) Perceiving, knowing. Understanding, intelligence, shrewdness. اهل فطنت *ahli fitnat*, Intelligent. *Fatinat*, (v. n. of فطن) Knowing, understanding: being quick, shrewd, intelligent. Intelligent, clear-sighted (woman).

A فطو *fatw*, A driving violently.

A فطوح *fatūh*, Large-bellied (she-camel).

A فطور *fatūr*, (or فطوريّ *fatūrīy*) Any thing on which one breakfasts. Breakfast. *Futūr*, (v. n. of فطر) Splitting (the gum), appearing (teeth). (pl. of فطر *fatr*) Fissures.

A فطورة *fatūrat*, A sheep sacrificed on the عيد الفطر *ɛīdu'l fitr*.

A فطوس *futūs*, (v. n. of فطس) Dying.

A فطوطیٰ *fatawta'*, Very crooked in the back.

A فطون *fatūn*, Clear-sighted, intelligent.

A فطونة *futūnat*, (v. n. of فطن) Understanding.

A فطه *fatah*, Width of back.

A فطير *fatīr*, An unleavened mass of paste. Any thing precipitately done, or meat hastily dressed. Fresh (dates, butter, and milk).

A فطيرة *fatīrat*, A sheep sacrificed on the feast called عيد الفطر *ɛīdu'l fitr*.

A فطيس *fittīs*, (pl. فطاطيس *fatātīs*) A large smiths' hammer. Very large.

A فطّيسة *fittīsat*, The snout, or any adjacent part of a hog. The lip of a man, or of any hoofed animal. The proboscis of wild beasts.

A فطيم *fatīm*, (pl. فطم *futum*) Weaned.

A فطيمة *fatīmat*, A species of sea-bird. A weaned camel's colt.

A فطين *fatīn*, Intelligent, quick, clear-sighted.

A فظّ *fazz*, (v. n. of فظّ) Forcing water out of the stomach of a camel and drinking it. Inhuman, rough, morose, unamiable, hard, speaking harshly. Water in the ventricle of an animal.

A فظا *faza'*, The womb.

A فظاظ *fizāz*, Roughness, inhumanity, harshness of speech. (pl. of فظيظ *fazīz*) Inhuman, cruel.

A فظاظة *fazāzat*, (v. n. of فظّ) Being inhuman, villainous. Roughness, inhumanity, harshness of speech. *Fuzāzat*, A portion of any thing; or of that which is in the loins of a man.

A فظاعة *fazāɛat*, (v. n. of فظع) Being disagreeable, shameful, exceeding bounds in turpitude.

A فظظ *fazaz*, Roughness, inhumanity, harshness of speech.

A فظع *fazaɛ*, (v. n. of فظع) Considering (a thing) to be arduous, troublesome, and beyond one's power. Being filled (a vessel). Being unequal (to a task).

A فظیٰ *faza'*, The womb.

A فظيظ *fazīz*, Inhuman, villainous. Sperm (of a stallion or woman).

A فظيع *fazīɛ*, Base, shameful (affair). Important. Difficult, troublesome. Sweet, fresh, cold, and limpid water.

A فعارير *faɛārīr*, The young of the herbs called ذآنين *zaɛānīn*.

A فعافع *fuɛāfiɛ*, A light, active fellow. A shepherd. A butcher.

A فعال *faɛāl*, (v. n. of فعل) Acting, doing. Making. Nobility. Generosity. A good deed. A scandalous deed (restricted to one agent). (pl. فعل *fuɛul*) The handle of an axe. *Fiɛāl*, (pl. فعول *fuɛūl*) A handle (of an axe). Acts, deeds (good or bad performed by two agents). (pl. of فعل *fiɛl*) Actions, operations, works. سوء فعال *sūɛi fiɛāl*, Bad works. *Faɛāli*, Do thou.

A فعّال *faɛɛāl*, A doer.

A فعالة *faɛālat*, Name of خزاعة *khuzāɛat*.

A فعامة *faɛāmat*, (v. n. of فعم) Being brawny, nervous (arm). Being well made and stout-legged (a woman). Being filled (a vessel).

A فعر *faɛr*, (v. n. of فعر) Eating the small herbs called ذآنين *zaɛnīn*.. Those herbs themselves.

A فعفاع *faɛfāɛ*, A coward.

A فعفع *faɛfaɛ*, A kid. A light, active fellow. Swift. A word used in calling to cattle.

A فعفعان *faɛfaɛān*, A shepherd. A butcher.

A فعفعانيّ *faɛfaɛānīy*, A coward. A shepherd. A butcher.

A فعفعة *faɛfaɛat*, (v. n. of فعفع Q) Driving and calling out to flocks, using the word فعفع *faɛfaɛ*.

A فعفعيّ *faɛfuɛiy*, A coward. A shepherd. A butcher.

A فعل *faɛl*, (v. n. of فعل) Acting. Doing, making, performing. *Fiɛl*, (pl. فعال *fiɛāl*) An action, work, deed, operation. The matrix of an animal. (in gram.) A verb. فعل اصمّ *fiɛli asamm*, A surd verb (called also مضاعف *muzāɛaf*, Reduplicated). فعل ثلاثي *fiɛli sulāsī*, A triliteral verb. فعل ثلاثي مزيد فيه *fiɛli sulāsī mazīdun fīhi*, An increased triliteral verb. فعل رباعي *fiɛli rubāɛī*, A quadriliteral verb. فعل خماسي *fiɛli khumāsī*, A quinqueliteral verb. فعل رباعي مزيد فيه *fiɛli rubāɛī mazīd fīhi*, An increased quadriliteral verb. فعل سالم *fiɛli sālim*, (or صحيح *sahīh*) A sound verb. فعل غير سالم *fiɛli ghayr sālim*, An infirm or defective verb, *i.e.* which contains an ا *alif*, و *wāw*, or ي *yā*. فعل غير قياسي *fiɛli ghayr kiyāsī*, An irregular verb. فعل قياسي *fiɛli kiyāsī*, A regular verb. فعل ماضي *fiɛli māzī*, A verb in the preterite. فعل متعدّي *fiɛli mutaɛaddī* (or واقع *wākiɛ*), A transitive verb. فعل غير متعدّي *fiɛli ghayr mutaɛaddī* (or لازم *lāzim*), An intransitive or a neuter verb. فعل مجرّد *fiɛli mujarrad*, A simple or primitive verb. فعل مزيد فيه *fiɛli mazīd fīhi*, An increased or derivative verb. فعل مضارع *fiɛli muzāriɛ*, A verb in the aorist. فعل معروف *fiɛli maɛrūf* (or معلوم *maɛlūm*), An active verb. فعل مجهول *fiɛli majhūl*, A passive verb. فعل معيل *fiɛli muɛtall*, An infirm verb. فعل معتلّ الفا *fiɛli muɛtallu'l fā*, A verb infirm in its first radical (called also مثال *misāl*, Assimilated). فعل معتلّ العين *fiɛli muɛtallu'l ɛayn*, A verb infirm in the medial radical (called also اجوف *ajwaf*, Concave). فعل معتلّ اللام *fiɛli muɛtallu'l lām*, A verb infirm in its final radical (called also ناقص *nākis*, Defective). فعل معتلّ اللام الاولیٰ *fiɛli muɛtallu'l lāmu'l ūla'*, A verb infirm in its third radical. فعل معتلّ اللام الثاني *fiɛli muɛtallu'l lāmu's sānī*, A verb infirm in its fourth radical. فعل معتل الفا و اللام *fiɛli muɛtallu'l fā wa'l lām*, A verb infirm in the first and third radical, called also لفيف المفروق *lafīfu'l mafrūk*, Twined together, but with an interval (as, وقیٰ *waka'*). فعل معتلّ العين و اللام *fiɛli muɛtallu'l ɛayn wa'l lām*, A verb infirm in its second and third radical, called also لفيف المقرون *lafīfu'l makrūn*, Twined together without an interval (as, شوي *shawa'*). فعل ممات *fiɛli mumāt*, An obsolete verb. فعل مهموز *fiɛli mahmūz*, A verb, having a أ *hamza* for one of its radicals. فعل مهموز الفا *fiɛli mahmūzu'l fā*, A verb hamzated in its first radical. فعل مهموز العين *fiɛli mahmūzu'l ɛayn*, A verb hamzated in its second radical. فعل مهموز اللام *fiɛli mahmūzu'l lām*, A verb hamzated in its third radical. فعل عبث *fiɛli ɛabas*, Lost labour, an absurd undertaking. P فعل كردن *fiɛl kardan*, To perform an action, to labour. فعل نا سزا *fiɛli nā sazā*, An unworthy deed. A بالفعل *bi'l fiɛl*, In fact, actually. Immediately. بالفعل و القوّة *bi'l fiɛl wa'l kūwat*, Actually and powerfully. قول و فعل *kawl u fiɛl*, Word and deed. *Fuɛul*, (pl. of فعال *faɛāl*) Handles (of axes).

A فعلاً و قولاً *fiɛlan wa kawlan*, In deed and word.

A فعلة *fiɛlat*, An act, work, deed. *Faɛalat*, A work, action. A shameful deed. (pl. of فاعل *fāɛil*) Agents, labourers. Workers in clay, excavators. *Faɛilat*, Custom, habit.

A فعليّ *fiɛlīy*, Derived from a verb, verbal. Actual. Effectual, efficient, operative.

A فعم *faɛm*, (v. n. of فعم) Filling (a vessel). Filling with perfume (the olfactory nerves). Enraging. A sort of tree. A rose. *Faɛm*, (and فعمل *faɛmal*) Brawny. Plump (arm).

A فعمة *faɛmat*, Symmetrical and stout-legged (woman).

A فعول *faɛūl*, Effecting, doing; a doer.

A فعومة *fuɛūmat*, (v. n. of فعم) Being full and

brawny (the arm). Being well made and stout legged (a woman). Being filled (a vessel).

P فغ *fagh* or *fugh*, A lover, a mistress. A handsome man or woman. An idol. Drunk.

A فغّ *faghgh*, (v. n. of فغّ) Perfuming, impregnating, blowing upon one (sweet scents).

A فغا *fagha'*, Rotten unripe dates. A milk-pail. A large dish. An obliquity in the mouth. Chaff, tares, and refuse of corn when winnowed. Rubbish carried down by a stream. Refuse of camels. A species of malady incident to palm-trees which prevents the dates from ripening. Grains of corn which drop from the ear.

A فغار *faghāri*, Penetrating (stab). *Fughār*, A man's name.

A فغّار *faghghār*, A man's name.

A فغافرة *faghāfirat*, (pl. of فغفور *faghfūr*) Chinese emperors.

P فغاك *fughāk*, Foolish, stupid. A bastard. A pimp to his own wife; a voluntary cuckold.

P فغان *fighān*, Complaint, lamentation, clamour. Oh! alas! فرياد و فغان كردن *firyād u fighān kardan*, To cry aloud and to lament. *Fughān*, (pl. of فغ *fugh*) Idols. Lovers, mistresses. Drunkards.

A فغّة *faghghat*, Diffusion or breathing of odours.

A فغر *faghr*, (v. n. of فغر) Opening (the mouth). Unclosing itself (the mouth). Expanding (as a flower). A full-blown rose or flower. واسع فغر الفم *wāsiꜥ faghri'l fam*, Wide-mouthed. *Fughar*, (pl. of فغرة *fughrat*) Mouths of rivers.

A فغرة *faghrat*, (or الفغرة *al faghrat*) The rising of the Pleiades. *Fughrat*, (pl. فغر *fughar*) The mouth of a river.

P فغستان *fughistān*, An idol-temple. The haram of a prince. Handsome persons of either sex. *Fughsutān*, The favourite mistress of a king.

A فغفور *faghfūr*, The general name of the emperors of China. The porcelain of China. P فغفور چيني *faghfūri chīnī*, An emperor of China. A porcelain vessel.

P فغفوري *faghfūrī*, Royal, imperial, belonging to the emperors of China. China-ware.

A فغم *faghm*, (v. n. of فغم) Filling, stopping the nose (perfume); also loosing, unstopping, de-obstructing. Sucking (the dam). Kissing. Blooming, blossoming. Whatever is brought away by the tongue from between the teeth. *Fughm* or *fughum*, The mouth. The chin with the beard. اخذه بفغمه *akhazahu bi fughmihi*, He threw him into trouble and difficulty. *Fagham*, (v. n. of فغم) Being desirous and greedy of. Sticking closely to, abiding in. *Faghim*, Greedy, wishful (dog).

A فغمة *faghmat*, A sweet breath; odour, scent.

P فغند *faghand*, *fighand*, or *fughand*, A leap, dance. Bounding like a deer.

P فغنشور *faghanshor* or *fughanshor*, Name of a city in China.

A فغو *faghw*, (v. n. of فغا for فغو) Being diffused. Withering (corn). Flowers of privet.

P فغوارة *fughwāra*, (Like a statue) Unable to speak from bashfulness, anguish, or excessive pride.

A فغوم *fughūm*, (v. n. of فغم) Filling, stopping the nose (perfume); also loosing, unstopping, and de-obstructing. Kissing. Sucking (the dam).

P فغياز *faghyāz*, An extra gratuity given over and above the wages due. A present. Good news, glad tidings.

P فغيازي *faghyāzī*, A present made to a bringer of good news. Alms.

P فف زدن *fuf zadan*, To breathe or blow upon.

A فقّ *fakk*, (v. n. of فقّ) Opening.

A فقء *fakꜥ*, (v. n. of فقأ) Tearing out (the eye, or otherwise depriving it of sight). Bursting (a boil). Appeasing the anger of any one. The caul enveloping the head of a new-born infant. A hollow in a stone in which water stagnates.

A فقاءة *fukaꜥat*, A membrane enveloping the head of a fœtus.

A فقاح *fikāh*, (pl. of فقحة) Annuli podicum.

A فقّاح *fukkāh*, Any species of flowers producing hairs or fibres. Handsome women.

A فقاحة *fakāhat*, The palm of the hand.

A فقاحيّ *fukāhiy*, (A garment) of a rose-colour.

A فقاخ *fikākh*, (v. n. 3 of فقخ) Striking one (upon the head).

A فقار *fakār*, (pl. of فقارة *fakārat*) Vertebræ or joints of the back. A thing without head or tail. ذو الفقار *zu'l fakār*, Name of the celebrated sword of العاص بن منبّه *al ꜥās bin munabbih*, an unbeliever who was slain at Badar. It became the property of Muhammad, and afterwards fell into the possession of his son-in-law Aliy.

A فقارة *fakārat*, (pl. فقار *fakār*) A joint of the back, vertebræ.

A فقاريّ *fakāriy*, Vertebral.

A فقاس *fukās*, A disease in the joints.

A فقاع *fukāꜥ* or *fakāꜥ*, Ruddy (man).

A فقّاع *fukkāꜥ*, Dirty, wicked, mischievous. *Fukkāꜥ*, A kind of drink made of water and barley, or dried grapes; beer, ale. Name of a plant, which, when withered, is hard, and of a horny appearance.

A فقّاعة *fakkāꜥat*, A bubble on water.

P فقاع گشودن *fukāꜥ gushūdan*, To belch. To boast, brag.

A فقاعيّ *fukāꜥiy*, Intense (yellow or red).

A فقّاعيّ *fukkāꜥiy*, A seller of beer called فقّاع *fukkāꜥ*: also of snow and syrup of grapes or dates.

A فقاق *fakāk*, (or فقاقة) Foolish, silly (man).

A فقاقة *fakākat*, (pl. فقاق) A kind of bird.

A فقاقيع *fakākīꜥ*, (pl. of فقاعة) Bubbles.

A فقام *fikām*, (v. n. 3 of فقم) Lying with.

A فقامة *fakāmat*, (v. n. of فقم) Being grave, serious, important, and difficult (business).

A فقاه *fikāh*, (v. n. 3 of فقه) Disputing with on a point of law.

A فقاهة *fakāhat*, (v. n. of فقه) Being intelligent. Being learned in the law. Legal knowledge.

A فقائر *fakāꜥir*, (pl. of فقيرة) Poor (women).

A فقائه *fakāꜥih*, (pl. of فقيهة *fakīhat*) Female doctors of law and divinity.

A فقح *fak-h*, (v. n. of فقح) First opening (his) eyes (a whelp). Smiting in the anus. Taking (medicine) dry and unmixed. Flourishing and blossoming (a plant). The anus.

A فقحة *fak-hat*, (pl. فقاح *fikāh*) The arse-hole (especially when wide). The palm of the hand. The garment worn by the pilgrims at Mecca during the month محرّم *muharram*. (Ears of corn or flowers) shooting out into hairs, fibres, or beards.

A فقحل *fuk-hul*, Soon angry, easily irritated.

A فقحلة *fak-halat*, (v. n. of فقحل Q) Growing soon angry unseasonably.

A فقخ *fakhkh*, The act of striking on the head.

P فقد *fakd*, Cinquefoil. Seed of cinquefoil.

A فقد *fakd*, (v. n. of فقد) Being deprived of, losing, missing. Loss, deprivation. Name of a plant. A kind of drink made of grapes, honey, or dodder. *Fakad*, Certainly. Only.

A فقدان *fikdān*, (v. n. of فقد) Losing, missing, being deprived of. Deprivation, loss, miss, want.

A فقدد *fukdud*, A drink made of grapes, honey, or dodder.

A فقر *fakr*, (v. n. of فقر) Piercing, perforating, boring (beads for threading). Making an incision in a camel's nose, and inserting a ring, to which the reins are made fast. Digging, excavating. Breaking the vertebræ of the back. Being poor. Poverty; just a competency for the support of life, and no more. Asceticism, ascetic mortification. (pl. فقور *fukūr*) Anxiety, care, grief. الفقر فخري *al fakr fakhrī*, Poverty (is) my glory (a saying of Muhammad). فقر و فاقه *fakr u fāka*, Poverty and hunger. سدّ الله وجوه فقره *sadda'llāh wujūha fakrihi*, May God put a stop to his poverty! *Fukr*, Poverty. (pl. فقر *fuhar*) A side. *Fakir*, One who has the vertebræ of the back broken. *Fikar*, (pl. of فقرة *fikrat*) Vertebræ of the back. *Fukar*, (pl. of فقر *fuhr*) Sides. *Fukur*, (pl. of فقير *fakīr*) Ditches for planting palms: palm-trees so planted.

A فقراء *fukarāꜥ*, (pl. of فقير *fakīr*) The poor, the common people. Fakīrs, religious mendicants.

A فقرة *fikrat* or *fakrat*, (pl. فقر *fikar*, فقرات *fikrāt*, *fakarāt*, *fikarāt*, *fikirāt*, فقران *fikrān*, and *fikirān*) Vertebræ of the back. A necklace jointed like vertebræ. The finest verse in a poem; the greatest beauty of a speech; the similar terminations in the members of an Arabian oration, having a kind of rythmical cadence. A sown field destitute of trees and buildings. *Fakrat*, (pl. فقر *fakr*) A species of plant. *Fikrat*, A mark, a sign (such as a mountain or target). The best of land in tillage. *Fukrat*, Propinquity. A pit, ditch. The breast or part of a shirt thro' which the head goes. هو منّي فقرة *huwa minnī fukratan*, He is near me.

P فقره بندي *fikra-bandī*, Arrangement, order.

A فقري *fukra'*, The loan of a camel.

A فقز *fahz*, (v. n. of فقز) Dying.

A فقس *fahs*, The breaking (of an egg).

A فقش *fahsh*, The breaking (of an egg).

A فقص *fahs*, (v. n. of فقص) Breaking (an egg). Broken (egg). Cloven (skull).

A فقط *fahat*, Only, solely, merely, simply.

A فقع *fahʿ*, (v. n. of فقع) Expiring from heat. Overwhelming any one (misfortunes). Stealing. Farting. Being very yellow. Moving, growing (a lad). *Fahʿ* or *fikʿ*, (pl. فقعة *fihaʿat*) A white soft mushroom. اذل من فقع بقرقرة *azallu min fahʿin bi karkaratin*, More contemptible (or helpless) than a mushroom on a plain (easily trodden upon, or culled without difficulty). *Fuhʿ*, (pl. of افقع *afhaʿ*) Intensely white. *Fahaʿ*, (v. n. of فقع) Being red.

P فقع *fahaʿ*, A fungus. *Fuhaʿ*, Beer, ale. فقع گشودن *fuhaʿ gushūdan*, To boast, brag. To belch.

A فقعة *fihaʿat*, (pl. of فقع *fahʿ* or *fikʿ*) White mushrooms.

P فقعگان *fukaʿgān*, Pride, boasting, vain-glory.

A فقفاق *fahfāk*, One who talks nonsense. A blunder in speaking.

A فقفاقة *fahfākat*, One who talks nonsense.

A فقفقة *fahfakat*, (v. n. of فقفق Q) Barking, howling (a frightened dog). Being reduced to the depth of poverty. Mouthing much in speaking. The noise made by the running or dropping of water.

A فقفوق *fahfūk*, Intelligence, genius.

A فققة *fahakat*, Fools.

A فقل *fahl*, Ventilation, fanning, or winnowing. Richness, productiveness (of land). ارض كثيرة الفقل *arz kasīratu'l fahl*, Land rich in produce. *Fuhl*, Name of a small poisonous fish.

A فقم *fahm*, (v. n. of فقم) Having the upper front teeth overhanging the lower. Exulting, being insolent with joy. Being exhausted (wealth). Being abundant. Lying with. Taking by the jaw or by the tip of the nose. *Fahm* or *fuhm*, The jaw. The tip of a dog's nose. ما بين الفقمين *mā bayna'l fahmayn*, The tongue. *Fahm* or *faham*, (v. n. of فقم) Being weighty and not going on smoothly (business). *Faham*, (v. n. of فقم) Being filled up. Having the front upper teeth overhanging the lower ones, or the contrary. Suffering from indigestion. Exulting, being insolent with joy. Being exhausted (wealth). Being abundant. Fulness, abundance. Inequality of the front teeth, either overhanging or underhanging. *Fahim*, Intelligent, and more than a match for one's adversaries. *Fuhum*, The mouth.

A فقو *fahw*, A tracking, a following the steps.

A فقوء *fuhūʾ*, (v. n. of فقأ) Bespattering the plant بهمى *buhma'* with soil, so that cattle refuse to eat it (a shower or a torrent).

A فقوة *fukwat*, (pl. فقى *fuhaʾ*) Notch of an arrow.

A فقود *fukūd*, The act of losing or missing.

A فقور *fuhūr*, (pl. of فقر *fahr*) Cares, anxieties.

A فقوس *fukūs*, (v. n. of فقس) Dying. Killing (an animal). Breaking or spoiling her eggs (a bird). Preventing, restraining. Dragging down by the hair.

A فقّوس *fakkūs*, A Syrian melon.

A فقّوص *fakkūs*, A small unripe Egyptian melon.

A فقوع *fukūʿ*, (v. n. of فقع) Being very yellow. Moving, growing (a lad). Overwhelming any one (misfortune). Dying from heat. White soft funguses.

A فقوم *fuhūm*, (v. n. of فقم) Being weighty, serious (an affair).

A فقه *fah-h*, (v. n. of فقه) Conquering, beating in a contest respecting law and divinity. *Fik-h*, (v. n. of فقه) Knowing, understanding (law and divinity). Understanding, comprehending. Knowledge, especially of religion and jurisprudence. فقه السياسة *fik-hu's siyāsat*, Political knowledge. *Fakuh*, Deeply versed in theology and jurisprudence.

A فقهاء *fuhahāʾ*, (pl. of فقيه *fakīh*) Doctors of law and divinity. Jurisconsults. Theologians.

A فقهة *fukihat*, (A woman) skilled in law.

A فقهيّ *fik-hīy*, Relating to law and jurisprudence. Theological. Juridical.

A فقى *fuha'*, (pl. of فقوة) Notches of arrows.

A فقىء *fakīʾ*, Griped (camel). A disease producing in a camel costiveness and strangury. A hollow in a stone wherein water lodges.

A فقيد *fahīd*, Destitute, deprived of. Missed, regretted, or lamented.

A فقير *fakīr*, (pl. فقراء *fukarāʾ*) Poor, indigent. A poor man. A pauper. A poor mechanic. A religious order of mendicants. Broken in the back. Pierced in the nose (a camel). The channel through which the water flows from the well into the canal or cistern at which the cattle drink. Contiguous wells communicating with one another; any plain in which they are dug. The mouth of a subterraneous canal. Ditches prepared for planting palm-trees. P فقير كردن *fakīr kardan*, To impoverish.

A P فقيران *fakīrān*, Land bestowed upon Muhammadan fakirs or mendicants as a provision.

P فقيرانه *fakīrāna*, Poorly, in the manner of a poor man, after the fashion of pauper or mendicant.

A فقيرة *fakīrat*, (pl. فقائر *fakāʾir*) A poor woman.

A فقيري *fakīrī*, Poverty.

A فقيص *fakīs*, Broken (egg). A kind of farming implement.

A فقيع *fakīʿ*, Red, ruddy. Dirty. Wicked.

A فقّيع *fikkīʿ*, Intense (white). A white pigeon.

A فقيه *fakīh*, (pl. فقهاء *fukahāʾ*) A Muhammadan lawyer, theologian (in Spanish, with the article *alfaqui*). A preceptor, pedagogue, or schoolmaster. Expert (stallion).

A فقيهة *fakīhat*, (pl. فقائه *fakāʾih*) (A woman) skilled in law and divinity.

A فكّ *fakk*, (v. n. of فكّ) Unloosing, disjoining. Liberating, manumitting (a servant). Releasing a prisoner. Releasing (a pawn or pledge). Opening the hand and shewing what is in it. Putting (medicine) into a child's mouth. Being aged, decrepit. The upper and under jaw. A luxation of the hand. فكّ اسفل *fakki asfal*, The lower jaw. فكّ اعلى *fakki aʿla'*, The upper jaw. P فك رهن كردن *faki rahn kardan*, To release a pledge.

A فكاك *fakāk* or *fikāk*, (v. n. of فكّ) Manumitting (a slave or servant). Releasing a prisoner. Opening the hand and shewing what is in it. The ransom or release of a pledge or a pawn. *Fikāk*, (pl. of فاكّ *fākk*) Fools. Decrepit (men or camels).

A فكاه *fikāh*, (v. n. 3 of فكه) Jesting (with another), being merry, jocose, festive, and joyous.

A فكاهة *fakāhat*, (v. n. of فكه) Being cheerful, joyous, jocose, festive, sociable, sprightly. Admiring, being filled with astonishment. *Fukāhat*, A jest. Joyousness, cheerfulness.

A فكّة *fakkat*, (v. n. of فكّ) Being relaxed or disjointed. Being slip-shouldered (man). Being foolish and weak. Folly, stupidity. Languor. الفكّة *al fakkat*, A star behind Pisces and Sagittarius (vulgarly called قصعة المساكين *kasʿatu'l masākin*, The beggar's dish).

A فكر *fikr* or *fakr*, (v. n. of فكر) Thinking. (pl. افكار *afkār*) Thought, reflection, consideration, opinion, deliberation, counsel, advice, sentiment. Care, solicitude, anxiety. *Fikr*, Need, necessity. P فكر فرمودن *fikr farmūdan*, To consider. To spy, ken, or perceive. بي فكر *bī fikr*, Inconsiderate, thoughtless.

A فكرة *fikrat*, (or فكري *fikra'*) Thought.

P فكرمند *fikrmand*, Thoughtful. Sorrowful.

P فكز *fakz* or *fakaz*, A hole to let out smoke, a louvre-window, a chimney.

A فكع *fukʿ*, (v. n. of فكع) Looking to the ground from grief or rage. Going no one knows where.

A فكك *fakak*, (v. n. of فكّ) Being disjointed, dislocated, relaxed. Being slip-shouldered (man). Being broken (the jaw).

A فككة *fakakat*, (pl. of فاكّ *fākk*) Fools. Decrepit (men or camels).

A فكن *fakn*, (v. n. of فكن) Persevering, persisting (in a lie).

P فكن *fikan*, One who throws away.

A فكنة *fuknat*, Repentance, regret for the past.

P فكندن *fikandan*, To throw, cast, spread.

P فكندني *fikandanī*, A carpet, or any similar thing that may be spread.

P فكنده سر *fikanda-sar*, (Hanging the head) Contemplative. Ashamed, confounded, abashed.

P فكنده سرين *fikanda-surīn*, Sitting four-square.

A فكور *fakūr*, One who recollects much, or considers attentively: extremely thoughtful.

A فكوع *fukūʻ*, (v. n. of فكع) Looking down from grief or rage. Going no one knows where.

A فكوك *fukūk*, (v. n. of فك) Releasing (a pawn or pledge). Being aged and decrepit.

A فكه *fakah*, (v. n. of فكه) Being cheerful, joyous, blithe, merry, jocose, festive, social, entertaining. Being surprised, astonished. *Fakih*, Jovial, gay, blithe, lively, merry, entertaining, boisterous. One who takes pleasure in speaking ill of the absent. An eater of fruit (فاكهة *fākihat*).

A فكهاني *fak-hānīy*, A fruiterer.

A فكير *fikkīr*, Very thoughtful.

A فكيف *fakayf*, Why then? How much more! So much the more (or less); the stronger the argument is.

A فكيهة *fakīhat*, A jest. Jocularity, pleasantry, blithsomeness.

P فگار *figār*, (or فگال *figāl*) Soreness of back of a beast of burden. Lame, crippled, wounded, galled. Afflicted, confused, distracted. دل فگار *dil-figār*, Heart-afflicting.

P فگانه *fagāna*, (*figāna*, or فگامه *fagāma*) An abortion, a castling.

P فگندن *figandan*, To throw away or lay aside.

P فل *ful*, A species of water-lily; also its root. The wood of the quince-tree.

A يا فل *yā fulu*, O! such a one.

A فلّ *fall*, (v. n. of فل) Breaking, notching (a sword). Routing (an army). Leaving one and afterwards returning (one's intellect). (pl. فلول *fulūl*) A crack or notch on a sword-blade. A crowd, troop, body. (pl. فلول *fulūl* and افلال *aflāl*) (An army, cohort, or single man) put to flight. *Fill*, Bare, barren ground. Thin hair. Freshness, moisture. *Full*, Ground wet with rain, and yet producing nothing. Land not rained upon for several years. Ground not wet with rain lying between grounds that have so been. Any thing that flies off from any substance (as filings or sparks). *Full* or *fill*, (pl. افلال *aflāl*) Ground without rain and without produce, a desert.

A فلا *fala'*, (pl. of فلاة *falāt*) Deserts.

A فلاء *falā*, (v. n. of فلا for فلو) Weaning. Drawing out, striking (with a sword on the head). Undertaking a journey. Recovering one's senses, becoming wise again. (pl. of فلاة *falāt*) Deserts.

A فلاة *falāt*, (pl. فلا *fala'*, فلوات *falawāt*, فلوّ *fulūw*, فليّ *fulīy*, *filīy*, and افلاء *aflāʼ*) An extensive desert without water or herbage.

P فلات *falāt*, The warp of a web.

A فلات *filāt*, (v. n. 3 of فلت) Coming upon unawares. A sudden and unexpected seizure. يا فلات *yā fulāt*, O ye Mesdames So-and-so!

P فلاته *filāta* or *fulāta*, A species of sweet cake made with sheep's milk.

A فلاح *falāḥ*, Prosperity, happiness. Escape, deliverance. Safety; asylum, refuge. Permanency, continuance in good. Breakfast. حي على الفلاح *hay ʻala'l falāḥ*, Come unto the asylum, or to safety.

A فلّاح *fallāḥ*, A farmer, villager, peasant, boor. A hirer out of camels or horses. A seaman.

A فلاحة *falāḥat*, Agriculture. Fraud, cheating in selling. P فلاحت نامه *falāḥat-nāma*, A treatise on agriculture (a book so called).

P فلاخان *falākhān*, (or فلاخن) A sling.

P فلاد *falād*, (فلاده *falāda*, *filāda*, or *fulāda*) A trifle, useless thing. Vain, unprofitable.

A فلّاس *fallās*, A boss-seller (for swords).

A فلاسفة *falāsifat*, (pl. of فيلسوف) Philosophers.

P فلاسنگ *falāsang*, A sling.

A فلاط *filāt*, Any thing sudden and unexpected.

P فلاطن *falātun*, (or فلاطون *falātūn*) Plato.

P فلاطوس *falātūs*, The preceptor of عذرا *ʻazrā*.

A فلاق *filāḳ*, The separation of milk into particles from sourness. (pl. of فلاقة *fulāḳat*) Brickbats. Bits of an egg broken in pieces. *Filāḳ* or *fulāḳ*, Distinct, separate particles. *Fulāḳ*, Curdled (milk). A sheer lie. An egg broken to pieces.

A فلاقة *fulāḳat*, (pl. فلاق *filāḳ*) A brickbat.

A فلاك *filāk*, (pl. of فلك *falak*) Circular hills or tumuli of sand rising in the midst of a plain.

A فلاكة *falākat*, Evil, misfortune, adversity, misery. فلاكت فلك *falākati falak*, Fortune's frowns.

A فلاكتي *falākatī*, Unfortunate.

A فلال *filāl*, (pl. of فل *fall*) Routed hosts.

A فلّال *fullāl*, Routed (squadron).

A فلالّي *falālīy*, (pl. of فليّة *filliyat*) Lands not having a year's rain.

A فلاليج *falālīj*, (pl. of فلّوجة *fallūjat*) Lands ready for sowing.

A فلان *fulān*, (or فلانة *fulānat*) The name of any unknown or undefined person, He, that man. Such a one, such, a certain. الفلان *al fulān*, Such, so-and-so (applicable to all except men). في سنة فلان *fī sanati fulān*, In such a year. P در فلان تاريخ *dar fulān tārīkh*, At such a date, on such a day.

A يا فلان *yā fulān*, Ho! you there! يا فلان *yā fulāni*, (dual of فل *fulu*) O ye two men!

P فلان از فلان *fulān az fulān*, Boasting, bragging.

P فلانستان *fulānistān*, Such a place, the residence of any one.

A فلانه *falāna*, Penis. *Fulāna*, Such a one.

A فلانيّ *fulānīy*, Of so-and-so; of such a place.

A فلاورة *falāwirat*, (equiv. to صيادلة *sayādilat*).

P فلاوه *falāwa*, Distracted, giddy.

A فلاوي *falāwa'*, (pl. of فلوّ) Full-grown colts.

A فلاية *filāyat*, A hunting for lice, a lousing.

A يا فلة *yā fulata*, O Madam So-and-so!

A فلت *falat*, Escape, liberation, deliverance. *Fulat*, (or فلّت *fullat*) Quick, swift, sudden.

A فلتات *falatāt*, Errors, blunders, slips, mistakes.

A فلتان *filtān* or *falatān*, Brisk, spirited, and fleet (horse). *Falatān*, Hard, strong. Bold, brave. A certain bird with which they hunt monkeys. يا فلتان *yā fulatāni*, O ye two Mesdames So-and-so!

A فلتة *faltat*, The last night of every month. The last day before any sacred month, when fighting was prohibited.

A فلتة *faltatan*, Suddenly, unexpectedly, without previous thought or consideration.

P فلج *falj*, (also فلجم *faljam*) A bolt, bar, lock, chain, or fastening for a door.

A فلج *falj*, (v. n. of فلج) Dividing into two parts, separating, making a partition. Ploughing (the ground). Laying a tax, imposing tribute. Being prosperous. Conquering, escaping. Loss, injury, damage. Victory, triumph. (pl. فلوج *fulūj*) A half. Palsy, hemiplegia. *Filj*, (pl. فلوج *fulūj*) A part, half. A kind of measure for dry goods. *Fulj*, Victory, safety, escape. *Falaj*, (pl. افلاج *aflāj*) Brooks. Width, space (between the teeth or feet).

A فلجاء *faljāʼ*, (fem. of افلج *aflaj*) One with wide-set teeth. (A woman) whose hands are far apart from one another.

A فلجان *faljāni*, (dual) Two halves. *Falajān*, The space between the legs or teeth.

A فلجة *fuljat*, Victory, safety, escape.

A فلح *falḥ*, (v. n. of فلح) Ploughing, tilling the ground. Cutting, cleaving, splitting. Cheating, defrauding in a sale. Traducing, speaking ill of. *Falah*, Prosperity, happiness. Safety, refuge. A fissure in the nether lip.

A فلحاس *filḥās*, Ugly, stinking, and ill-tempered.

A فلحة *falahat*, A sown field destitute of trees or buildings.

A فلحس *fulhas*, Greedy, avaricious. One who waits for the time for people to be at meals. A dog. An old bear. Name of a man proverbial for begging.

A فلحسة *fulhasat*, Lank-hipped, ugly (woman).

P فلخ *falkh*, Taking the seed out of cotton. *Falakh*, The beginning of any work.

A فلخ *falkh*, (v. n. of فلخ) Breaking, fracturing. Cleaving. Making clear, rendering manifest.

P فلخم *falakhm*, A sling. *Falkham*, A wooden instrument wherewith they strike the string of a bow, with which they separate cotton. A burial-place of the fire-worshippers.

P فلخمان *falakhmān*, A sling.

P فلخمه *falkhama*, A lock. An instrument used by cotton-dressers. A burial-place of the fire-worshippers. *Falakhma*, A sling.

P فلخميدن *falkhamīdan* or *falakhmīdan*, To beat and separate cotton.

P فلخود *falkhūd*, (or فلخيد *falkhīd*) A seed sticking in cotton. A separator of cotton from the seed.

P فلخودن *falkhūdan*, (or فلخيدن *falkhīdan*) To dress cotton and clear it from the seeds.

P فلخوده *falkhūda*, Cleaned cotton. Pure, mere.

P فلخيده *falkhīda*, Cotton cleaned of its seed. Any thing pure, freed from admixture.

A فلذ *falz,* (v. n. of فلذ) Cutting. Cutting off a slice for any one. Giving liberally, at once, without delay or promise. *Filz,* (pl. افلاذ *aflāz*) A camel's liver. *Filaz,* (pl. of فلذة *filzat*) Pieces, slices of livers, meat, or ears.

A فلذة *filzat,* (pl. فلذ *filaz* and افلاذ *aflāz*) A part, slice, segment, bit (of an ear, meat, or camel's liver: also of gold or silver).

A فلذلك *fa lizālika,* And on that account.

P فلرز *falarz,* (or فلرزنگ *falarzang*) Victuals carried home by the guests from an entertainment.

A فلز *filizz, filazz,* or *fuluzz,* Ore, metal in general. A kind of white brass. Stone. Dross, scoria. A thick, robust man. Any thing on which swords are tried. Avaricious.

A فلزات *filizzāt,* (pl. of فلز *filizz*) Ores, metals.

A فلزي *filizziy,* Metallic, mineral, fossil.

A فلس *fals,* (generally pronounced *fils*) (pl. افلس *aflus* and فلوس *fulūs*) A small coin, an obolus, or any thing of similar shape; as the scale of a fish, the boss on a bridle or a book. The part of the throat called خاتم الجزية *khātimu'l jizyat.* *Fils,* Name of an idol. Indigence, insolvency, bankruptcy.

A فلسطون *filastūn* or *falastūn,* Palestine.

A فلسطي *filastiy,* A Philistine. Belonging to Palestine.

A فلسطين *falastīn* or *filastīn,* Palestine.

G فلسفة *falsafat,* Philosophy.

A فلشك *filishk,* A gugglet painted for children.

A فلط *falt,* (v. n. of فلط) Being astonished, confounded. *Falat,* Any thing unexpected.

A فلطا *falatan,* Unexpectedly.

A فلطاح *filtāh,* Broad, large (head).

A فلطاس *filtās,* (فلطوس *filtaws,* or فلطيس *filtīs*) Large and broad (glans penis).

A فلطحة *faltahat,* A spreading, expanding dough.

A فلطيسة *filtīsat,* A hog's snout.

A فلع *falع,* (v. n. of فلع) Cutting, splitting, cracking. *Falع* or *filع,* (pl. فلوع *fulūع*) A crack in the foot. *Fulع,* (pl. of فلوع *falūع*) Sharp swords.

A فلعة *filعat,* A slice from a camel's bunch. A cleft, chink, cranny. لعن الله فلعتها *laعana'llāh filعatahā,* An untranslatable phrase of detestation.

A فلغ *falgh,* (v. n. of فلغ) Breaking (the head).

P فلغند *falghand* or *fulghund,* Thorns or spikes put upon a wall to prevent men or animals from getting over it. A dangerous place in the sea.

P فلغود *falghūd,* A seed sticking in cotton.

A فلفل *filfil* or *fulful,* Pepper. Long pepper. فلفل ابيض *filfili abyaz,* White pepper. فلفل بري *filfili barrī,* Seed of agnus castus. P فلفل دراز *filfili darāz,* Long pepper. فلفل در آتش افكندن *filfil dar ātish afkandan,* To render uneasy. A فلفل سرخ *filfili surkh,* Red pepper, capsicum. دار فلفل *dār filfil,* Long pepper. *Fulful,* A clever servant. The fibre of the palm-tree.

A فلفلة *falfalat,* (v. n. of فلفل Q) Walking with a starched air. Cleaning the teeth with a stick.

P فلفل مون *filfil mūn,* Wild mint.

P فلفل مويه *filfil-mūya,* Root of long pepper.

A فلق *falk,* (v. n. of فلق) Splitting. Pulling the wool off a rotten skin. Breaking forth (the dawn). The opening or middle of the mouth. A misfortune. فلق المفرق *falku'l mafrik,* The middle of the crown of the head. *Filk,* A branch split into two parts, of which they make a bow, each half being called *filk*; also a bow made of half a branch. A misfortune. Any thing wonderful and portentous. The opening or middle of the mouth. *Falak,* (pl. فلوق *fulūk*) A fissure, crevice. The stocks, in which offenders are placed. The dawn or its spreading light. All men or creatures. (pl. فلقان *fulkān*) A low place or valley between higher grounds. Hell; or a pit therein. An open space between two heaps of sand. Milk separating into particles from acidity. Milk remaining at the bottom of a cup. يا ابن شارب الفلق *yā ibna shāribi'l falak,* (a term of reproach). علق فلق *عulak fulak,* Wonderful and uncommon calamities.

A فلقاء *falkā,* Wide in the teat (ewe).

A فلقان *fulkān,* A sheer, palpable, manifest lie. (pl. of فلق *falak*) Low places between hills.

A فلقة *falkat,* A certain mark under a camel's ear in the shape of a boy's kite. *Filkat,* A fragment. A half. A wonder. Calamity, adversity.

A فلقحة *falkahat,* (v. n. of فلقح Q) Eating or drinking up whatever is in the dish or goblet.

A فلقحي *falkahiy,* A laugher in people's faces.

A فلقس *falkas,* Base, vile. A miser.

A فلقطة *falkatat,* A talking or walking fast.

A فلقم *falkam,* Large, ample.

A فلقي *falka',* A prodigy, portent, calamity.

P فلك *filk,* A fire-worshipper.

A فلك *fulk,* A ship. Ships. *Falak,* (v. n. of فلك) Having round breasts (a maiden). Becoming round (the breasts of a maiden). (pl. افلاك *aflāk* or فلك *fuluk*) Heaven, sky, firmament. Time, an age. Fortune, fate. The orbit wherein the heavenly bodies revolve. A stick to which a thong is fastened for punishing naughty boys. The round or swelling part of any thing. Water set in motion by the wind. A wave. (pl. فلاك *filāk*) A hill or tumulus of sand on a plain. فلك اطلس *falaki atlas,* (P فلك پرده دار *falaki parda-dār* or فلك ساده *falaki sāda*) The crystalline sphere. فلك افلاك *falaki aflāk,* The primum mobile, empyrean heaven. P فلك اندازه كردن *falak andāza kardan,* To obtain promotion. A فلك القمر *falaku'l kamar,* The moon's orbit. فلك مكوكب *falaki mukawkab,* The starry firmament. *Falik,* One whose bones are out of joint, or whose joints are thick and hard. Pained in the knee-pan. One whose buttocks are round like the whirl of a spindle (as the Ethiopians). *Fuluk,* (pl. of فلك *falak*) Celestial orbits.

A فلكة *falkat,* (pl. فلك *falak* and فلاك *filāk*) A round tract or hillock of sand in the midst of a flat desert. The joint between each vertebra of a camel's back. A bit of flesh on the head of the root of the tongue and extremity of the breast-bones. Any thing of that kind which is round. A circular hillock consisting of a single stone. Any thing circular of bones. The knee-pan. A round substance made of bristles, with which the tongue of a weanel is scratched to prevent him from sucking. That part of a camel between the gaskoin and the root of the tail. *Falkat* or *filkat,* The whirl of a woman's spindle, *i.e.* a globular bit of wood or leather upon which the thread is wound in a ball. *Falakat,* A boy's top, which he either throws from his hand or whips on the ground.

P فلك دبدبه *falak-dabdaba,* Pompous as the spheres, stately as the firmament.

P فلك زده *falak-zada,* Oppressed by fortune.

A فلك سير *falak-sayr,* Extremely swift.

P فلك نواز *falak-nawāz,* An ignorant upstart.

A فلكي *falkī,* A tasteless sort of pear.

A فلكي *falakiy,* Heavenly. Astronomical.

A فلكية *falakīyat,* Astrologers. Astronomers.

A فلل *falal,* Broken edge, notch (of a sword).

P فلماخن *falmākhun,* A sling.

P فلنجمشك *falanjmishk,* A sort of sweet basil.

P فلنجه *falanja,* A red seed used as a perfume.

P فلنجيدن *falanjīdan,* To assemble, collect, gain.

A فلندح *falandah,* Thick, gross. A man's name.

A فلنص *falans,* The citrul.

A فلنقس *falankas,* Born of a slave father, but of a free mother. Born of slave parents. One whose parents were free, but both grandmothers slaves; or whose mother, though not his father, was free. Bad, vile. A miser.

A فلو *falw,* (v. n. of فلا for فلو) Weaning (a colt or a child). Undertaking a journey. Growing wise after having been foolish. Fostering, bringing up. Striking with a sword. *Filw,* (pl. افلاء *aflāء*) A horse-colt (especially when weaned).

A فلو *falūw* or *fulūw,* (pl. فلاوي *falāwa'*) A horse-colt (especially when weaned). *Fulūw,* (pl. of فلاة *falāt*) Deserts, wastes, wildernesses.

A فلوات *falawāt,* (pl. of فلاة) Deserts, solitudes.

A فلوة *filwat,* A filly weaned or one year old.

A فلوت *falūt,* Small, narrow (garment).

A فلوج *fulūj,* (pl. of فلج *falj* or *filj*) Parts, pieces cut off. Halves.

A فلوج *fallūj,* A writer, a scribe.

A فلوجة *fallūjat,* (pl. فلاليج *falālīj*) Ground ready for sowing. A village in Arabian Irāk.

A فلوح *fulūh,* Fissures, cracks (in the feet).

P فلوزة *fulūza,* (also فلورة *fulūra*) The timber which supports the roof of a building.

A فلوس *fulūs,* (pl. of فلس *fals*) Small coins of uncertain value. Scales of fish. Bosses of bridles.

P فلوس ماهی *fulūsi māhī*, Dogs'-bane, a plant.

P فلوس دار *fulūs-dār*, Scaly (fish). Bossy.

A فلوع *falūʻ*, (pl. فلع *fulʻ*) Sharp (sword). *Fulūʻ*, (pl. of فلع *falʻ* or *filʻ*) Fissures in the feet.

A فلوق *falūk*, Curdled (milk). *Fulūk*, (pl. of فلق *falk*) Fissures, cracks.

A فلول *fulūl*, (pl. of فل) Notches. Routed hosts.

A یا فلون *yā fulūna*, (pl. of فل *fulu*) O ye men, Messieurs So-and-so!

P فله *fala* or *falla*, Biestings. Sour, curdled milk.

A فلهد *falhad*, (*fulhud*, or فلهود *fulhūd*) A stout and fat youth who has arrived at puberty.

A فلهذا *falihāzā*, And because, therefore.

A فلهم *falham*, A large, wide well. A weaver's shuttle. Pudendum muliebre.

A فلي *faly*, (v. n. of فلي) Striking (the head) with a sword. Hunting for lice, lousing. Searching carefully into the meaning of a poem. Assaying, testing the intellect of any one. *Falaʼ*, (v. n. of فلي) Being cut off, broken, detached.

A فلي *fullaʼ*, Routed (squadron).

A فلي *fulīy* or *filīy*, (pl. of فلاة *falāt*) Deserts, wastes.

A فلية *filliyat*, (pl. فلالي *falālīy*) Land which is without a year's rain.

P فليته *falīta*, (for فتيله *fatīla*) A gun-match. A torch. A wick. A wick composed of paper inscribed with mystic words, by inhaling the smoke of which demons are said to be expelled from those possessed. A cord of twisted thread sewed between the two folds of the hem of a garment to strengthen it. فليته دار *falīta-dār*, A match-lock. Any thing that has a match or wick. Cloth hemmed with a cord.

A فليج *falīj*, One whose teeth stand apart.

A فليجة *falījat*, Part of a tent. A single breadth of the skirts of a tent. One board or plank in a house.

A فليحة *falīhat*, The split leaf of the مرخ *markh* tree.

P فليدن *falīdan*, To be a coward. To seize with violence. *Falīdan* or *filīdan*, To thrust with violence so as to leave a wound.

P فليفس *filīfus*, Philip.

P فليفله *fulayfala*, Fruit of the aloe-tree.

P فليق *falīk*, The silkworm's cocoon.

A فليق *falīk*, Any thing wonderful. A misfortune. A vein in the neck or in the upper part of the arm. The lower and flat side in the upper part of a camel's throat.

A فليق *fullayk*, A peach which separates from the stone.

A فليقة *falīkat*, An evil, a misfortune. Thin-haired (woman). A portent, prodigy. يا للفليقة *yā liʼl falīkat*, O monstrous!

A فليل *falīl*, Broken, notched (sword). A crowd, body, troop. Fibres, filaments (of palm-trees). The projecting tooth (of a camel) broken into small parts or holes. *Falīl*, (or فليلة *falīlat*) Hair tied up in a large bunch.

P فليو *falīv*, (or فليوه *falīwa*) Useless, fruitless, vain, foolish.

P فم *fam*, A sheet stretched on poles in which people collect the money scattered on occasions of public rejoicings.

A فم *fam*, A single tanning. *Fam*, *fim*, *fum*, فمّ *famm*, *fimm*, *fumm*, (in the oblique case فم *famin*, فما *fuman*, فمّ *fammin*, and *fummin*; in the genit. في *fī*; accus. فا *fā*; dual فمان *famāni* and فموان *famawāni*, and فميان *famayāni*; pl. افمام *afmām* and افواه *afwāh*, which last is most commonly used, فم *fam* being supposed to be corrupted from فوه *fūh*) The mouth. فم المعدة *famuʼl miʻda*, The orifice of the stomach. P نهنگ فم *nahang-fam*, Having the (voracious) mouth of a crocodile.

A فمّ *fumma*, Then, after which.

A فمويّ *famawīy*, (or فميّ *famīy*) Oral, belonging to the mouth.

A فنّ *fann*, (v.n. of فنّ) Driving (camels). Adorning, garnishing. Forgetting. Being cheated, gulled, or imposed upon. Delaying, putting off (a debt). Fraud, deceit. A song. A musical voice. Delay. Riches. (pl. افنان *afnān* and فنون *funūn*) A species, form, mode, manner, ratio. A state. فنّ اخلاق *fanni akhlāk*, The science of morality, ethics. P فن فريب *fan fareb*, Art and cunning. فن فريبي *fun-farebī*, Artful, cunning. A *Finn*, One who gives close application and attends sedulously (to erudition).

A فنء *fanʼ*, A crowd, multitude. جاء فنء منهم *jāʼa fanʼun minhum*, A crowd of them came.

A فنا *fanaʼ*, Solanum hortense, or a tree with red berries, which, when dry, they hang round the neck.

A فناء *fanaʼ*, Excess, redundancy, much.

A فناء *fanāʼ*, (v. n. of فني) Vanishing, passing away, being ended and finished. Being old, frail, and decrepit. Mortality, frailty. Corruption. (in the language of Soofism) Annihilation or loss of all consciousness or perception of this world or the next, whilst the soul is absorbed in the contemplation of the divine glory. دار فنا *dāri fanā*, (P كشور فنا *kishwari fanā*) The frail house, this kingdom of corruption, *i.e.* the present world. P فنا شدن *fanā shudan*, To die. فنا كردن *fanā kardan*, To annihilate, reduce to nothing. A *Fināʼ*, (pl. افنية *afniyat* and فنيّ *funīy*) A court before a house.

A فنّاء *funnāʼ*, Very branchy (tree).

P فنا پذير *fanā-pazīr*, Transitory, frail.

A فناة *fanāt*, (pl. فنوات *fanawāt*) A wild cow. (pl. فنا *fanaʼ*) Fox-grapes, nightshade.

A فناخر *funākhir*, Large-bodied. One who has inflated nostrils.

A فناديد *fanādīd*, (pl. of فنداية *findaʼyat*) Axes.

A فنادير *fanādīr*, (pl. of فندير *findīr*) Large stones fallen from mountains, boulders.

P فنار *fanār*, A lighthouse.

A فناطيس *fanātīs*, (pl. of فنطيس *fintīs*) Abject, base-born. Broad-nosed. Flat noses with wide nostrils. Penes.

A فنّان *fannān*, A wild ass with various paces.

P فنانيدن *funānīdan*, To make a pause between speaking and doing something. To do deliberately and prudently.

A فنائق *fanāʼik*, (pl. of فنيقة) Large sacks.

A فنة *fannat*, An hour, a small portion of a day. Space. A part, the end of an age. *Funnat*, Plenty of forage.

G فنتق *funtuk*, An inn, caravansera.

P فنج *fanj*, Ruptured. Ugly. Hernia or rupture. فنج مادة *fanji māda*, A female hernia. *Funj*, Ruptured. Rupture. Name of a town in Zanguebar. *Fanaj*, A harmless kind of snake.

A فنج *funuj*, Persons heavy and disagreeable.

P فنجا *fanjā*, Yawning. Snow. The first symptom of an approaching fever; a shivering-fit. فنجا كردن *fanjā kardan*, To yawn. *Finjā*, Wind and snow.

P فنجان *finjān*, Porcelain dish, tea, or coffee-cup.

P فنجر *fanjar*, (or فنجره *fanjara*) A man with a large organ of generation.

A فنجش *fanjash*, Wide, spacious, ample.

A فنجل *fanjal*, One who has straddling legs or feet, who walks with his toes turned in and his heels out. *Funjul*, A badger. The animal called سياه گوش *siyāh-gosh*.

A فنجلة *fanjalat*, (and فنجلی *fanjalaʼ*) A languid, slow, straddling pace (especially of an old man).

A فنجليس *fanjalīs*, Large (glans penis).

P فنج مادة *funj-māda*, A swelling of the clitoris.

P فنجنگشت *fanjangusht*, Cinquefoil.

P فنجنوش *fanjnosh*, An electuary composed of iron filings, wine, and oil of almonds.

P فنجيدن *fanjīdan*, To yawn from crop-sickness. To yawn and stretch as on the approach of a fever.

A فنح *fanh*, (v. n. of فنح) Drinking (a horse) but not to the full.

A فنخلس *fanhalas*, Glans penis crassior.

A فنخ *fankh*, (v. n. of فنخ) Conquering, overcoming, subduing, humbling. Breaking small (a bone) without cracking or spilling blood.

A فنخر *finkhir*, Hard and unmoved when butted against. *Funkhur*, Large-bodied.

A فنخرة *fankharat*, (v. n. of فنخر Q) Swelling (the nostrils) with wind. Boasting vainly.

A فنخيرة *finkhīrat*, Vain-glorious, boastful. A substance resembling stone, but softer, detached from the summit of a mountain.

P فند *fand*, Trifles, vain words. A lie. Fraud, treachery, deceit. A point, dot, mole, or freckle. *Find*, Name of a poet.

A فند *find*, Ground without rain, parched. A branch, twig. A species. People assembled. Name of a servant of Aāyishah, who, being sent by his mistress in quest of fire, fell in with a party going to Egypt, which he joined, and did not return with the fire till a year after; hence the proverb ابطأ من

ابطا من فند *abtaʼ min find*, More dilatory than Find. *Find* or *fand*, A large mountain, or a long portion of it. *Fanad*, (v. n. of فند) Being impaired by age (the intellect). Blundering (in speaking), making mistakes. Telling a lie. Dotage, impairment of intellect (from indisposition or from age). A lie. Ingratitude. Weakness.

A فنداق *fundāḳ*, A cash-book, account-book.

A فنداوة *findaʼwat*, (or فنداوة) A sharp hatchet.

A فندأية *findaʼyat*, (pl. فناديد *fanādīd*) An axe.

P فندرسگ *fandarsag*, A town near Astarābād.

A فندسة *fandasat*, (v. n. of فندس Q) Passing by or through. Running.

A فندش *fandash*, Robust and clever (youth).

A فندشة *fandashat*, The act of conquering.

P A فندق *funduḳ*, A filbert-nut. A nut good against the sting of a scorpion. A ball for cannon, musketry, or cross-bow. The lip of one's beloved. P فندق زدن *funduḳ zadan*, To make a particular noise by striking the fore-finger of the right hand against the fore and middle fingers of the left. فندق سنجاب رنگ *funduḳi sinjāb-rang*, The earth. فندق سیم *funduḳi sīm*, The stars. فندق شکستن *funduḳ shikastan*, (To crack a nut) To kiss.

G فندق *funduḳ*, An inn, house for travellers.

A فندلة *fandalat*, Name of the father of the vazīr and scribe Abū Bakr ibn abi Muhammad.

A فندير *findīr*, (and فنديرة *findīrat*) (pl. فنادير *fanādīr*) A large stone projecting from a mountain. A large lump of dates.

P فنديره *findīra*, A large boulder-stone rolled from the summit of a mountain.

A فنزج *fanzaj*, (from P پنجه *panja*) A dance with joined hands.

A فنزر *fanzar*, A box built for sentinels raised on pillars about sixty cubits high.

A فنس *fanas*, Depressing poverty.

A فنشخة *fanshakhat*, (v. n. of فنشخ Q) Being tired, and shrinking from any work. Straddling when making water. Growing old.

A فنطاس *fintās*, The hold of a ship, in which bilge-water lodges. A tank in a ship for holding fresh water. A bowl in which fresh water is dealt out.

G فنطافلون *fantāfilūn*, Cinquefoil.

A فنطليس *fantalīs*, Glans penis magna.

A فنطيس *fintīs*, (pl. فناطيس *fanātīs*) Abject, worthless. Base-born. Broad-nosed. Penis. A flat nose with wide nostrils.

A فنطيسة *fintīsat*, A hog's snout. A wolf. منيع الفنطيسة *manīʻuʼl fintīsat*, Firm-minded, prudent. Jealous of one's honour, zealous in its defence.

A فنع *fanaʻ*, (v. n. of فنع) Abounding (in wealth). Increasing, growing. Plenty, riches. Excellence, reputation, fame. Fragrance. Generosity, liberality. ذو فنع *zū fanaʻ*, Fragrant (musk). *Faniʻ*, Increased, opulent, wealthy.

A فنفنة *fanfanat*, (v. n. of فنفن Q) Allowing one's camels to stray all about from laziness.

A فنق *funuḳ*, Delicately-brought up (girl). A fat young she-camel. (pl. of فنيق *fanīḳ*) Stallions held in high estimation.

A فنقع *fanḳaʻ*, Death. *Funḳuʻ*, A mouse.

A فنقعة *funḳuʻat* or *fanḳaʻat*, Podex.

A فنقور *funḳūr*, (or فنقورة) The arse-hole.

A فنك *fank*, (v. n. of فنك) Eating up entirely without shame or cessation. Entering upon. Being surprised. Oppressing, behaving tyrannically or unjustly. Triumphing, conquering. Lying. Victory, superiority. Contention, striving. A lie. Transgression. A door. The root of the tail. *Fank* or *fanak*, Any thing wonderful. *Fink*, A door. *Fink* also *funk*, An hour of the night. *Fanak*, (v. n. of فنك) Being surprised. A P A hay-weasel; a marten; a castor or beaver.

P فنك *fanak*, A kind of fur-pelisse. A leech. A sort of dark lantern used by robbers and by travellers by night.

P فنگ *fang*, Distress, misfortune. A colocynth.

A فنن *fanan*, (pl. افنان and افانين) A branch.

P فنو *fanav*, Fallacy, deception. Deceived, flattering one's self. Quiet. Agreeing.

A فنواء *fanwāʼ*, Branchy and shady (tree). Thick-haired (woman).

P فنود *fanūd* or *funūd*, Slow in speaking or walking. Weeping, cry, lamentation.

P فنودن *funūdan*, To deceive. To be deceived. To make a long pause between speaking or doing any thing. To desist, cease, finish. To be negligent, sluggish.

P فنوده *funūda*, Deceived. Resting, halting.

P فنور *funūr*, Separation.

A فنوك *funūk*, (v. n. of فنك) Being pertinacious, persevering. Adhering. Entering into an affair. Lying. Being impudent (a wench). Abiding, staying, stopping. Remaining. Eating the whole up without stopping or being ashamed.

A فنون *funūn*, (pl. of فنّ *fann*) Sciences, arts. Modes, ways. Tricks.

A فنيّ *funīy*, (pl. of فناء *fināʼ*) Court-yards.

A فنيخ *fanīkh*, Weak, soft, and flabby.

A فنيع *fanīʻ*, Rich, increased in goods.

A فنيق *fanīḳ*, (pl. فنق *funuḳ* and افناق *afnāḳ*) A camel or a horse-stallion of a noble breed, and never ridden or worked.

A فنيقة *fanīḳat*, (pl. فنائق *fanāʼiḳ*) A large sack for removing earth.

A فنيك *fanīk*, The joint of the chin-jaw. Root of the tail of a bird.

A فنثل *finsil*, Short woman. An elephant's neck.

A فنين *fanīn*, A painful swelling in the arm-pit. (A camel) troubled with that swelling.

A فو *fū*, The mouth. Phu, valerian.

A فوات *fawāt*, (v. n. of فات for فوت) Passing by. Slipping by, escaping (an opportunity). Dying. موت الفوات *mawtuʼl fawāt*, Sudden death.

A فواتح *fawātiḥ*, (pl. of فاتحة *fātiḥat*) Openings. Beginnings. Commencements of the chapters of the Kur'ān. Introductions, prefaces.

A فواتر *fawātir*, (pl. of فاتر) Languid (eyelids).

A فواجر *fawājir*, Wicked, loose, lewd persons.

A فواحش *fawāḥish*, (pl. of فاحشة *fāḥishat*) Shameful things, lewd practices: ribaldries.

A فواخت *fawākhit*, (pl. of فاختة) Ring-doves.

A فواخر *fawākhir*, (pl. of فاخرة) Precious (things).

A فؤاد *fuʼād*, (generally pronounced فواد *fuwād* or *fawād*) (pl. افئدة *afʼidat*) The heart, liver, or lungs. Mind, soul.

A فوادح *fawādiḥ*, Calamities, shocks of fortune.

A فوادر *fawādir*, (pl. of فادر) Old (mountain-goats).

P فواده *fawāda*, Dough mixed up with a kind of gruel or drink called آبکامه *āb-kāma*.

A فوار *fuwār*, (v. n. of فار for فور) Diffusing its perfume (musk). Froth, scum of a boiling cauldron.

A فؤارة *fuʼārat*, Fenugreek and dates given to women in child-bed.

A فوارة *fuwārat*, Heat (of a boiling cauldron).

A فوّارة *fawwārat*, A hollow in the hip not concealed or enclosed by any bone. A jet d'eau, fountain, spring. Any thing round and immoveable. *Fūwārat*, Any thing round and moveable.

A فوّارتان *fawwāratāni*, (dual) Two lines between the buttocks and the bone which encircles the anus to the edge of the buttocks.

A فوارد *fawārid*, Excellent, incomparable camel-stallions. Excellent she-camels, with which the stallions cannot remain.

A فوارس *fawāris*, (pl. of فارس *fāris*) Horsemen.

A فوارض *fawāriz*, Those whose bones are sound; also those whose bones are unsound.

A فوارع *fawāriʻ*, (pl. of فارعة *fāriʻat*) Upper parts of mountains. تلاع الفوارع *tilāʻuʼl fawāriʻ*, The higher parts of streams.

A فوارغ *fawārigh*, (pl. of فارغ *fārigh* or فارغة *fārighat*) Empty. Remnants of a meal. مراکب فوارغ *marākibi fawārigh*, Ships in ballast.

A فوارق *fawāriḳ*, (pl. of فارق *fāriḳ*) Brood-camels or asses.

A فواشی *fawāshī*, Flocks feeding freely.

A فواصح *fawāsiḥ*, (pl. of فاصحة *fāsiḥat*) Unfortunate, disappointed in expectation.

A فواصل *fawāsil*, (pl. of فاصلة *fāsilat*) Ends of verses, periods of the Kur'ān or of poetic distichs: pauses, cesuras.

A فواضّ *fawāzz*, (pl. of فاضّة *fāzzat*) Misfortunes.

A فواضل *fawāzil*, (pl. of فاضلة *fāzilat*) Benefits. فواضل المال *fawāziluʼl māl*, The benefits and advantages derived from cattle, such as hiring out, &c. (which are small when camels are pasturing far from home).

A فواطم *fawātim*, (pl. of فاطمة *fātimat*) Fātimas.

A فواظ *fuwāz*, (v. n. of فاظ for فوظ) Dying.

A فواق *fawāḳ*, (v. n. of فاق for فوق) Being superior to, excelling (one's companions). *Fawāḳ* or *fuwāḳ*, The re-collection of milk in the udder after milking. Delay, waiting. Rest. (pl. افوقة *afwiḳat* and آفقة *āfiḳat*) The interval between two milkings; also the time between opening the hand and closing it again on the teat. P فواق شيشه *fawāḳi shīsha*, Pouring out wine into a glass with noise. *Fuwāḳ*, (v. n. of فاق for فوق) Sobbing, hiccupping. Breaking the notch of an arrow. Giving up, or being about to give up, the last breath. A sob. Hiccup. The last breathings of a dying person. Tall, but loosely knit together.

A فؤاق *fuʼāḳ*, Belching. A belch. Hiccup. Pain.

A فواقا فواقا *fuwāḳan fuwāḳan*, At intervals.

A فواقع *fawāḳiʻ*, (pl. of فاقعة) Misfortunes.

A فواكه *fawākih*, (pl. of فاكهة *fākihat*) Fruits.

A فوّال *fawwāl*, A dealer in beans (فول *fūl*).

A فوالج *fawālij*, Large double-bunched camels.

A فوالع *fawāliʻ*, (pl. of فالعة) Misfortunes, evils.

A فوائد *fawāʼid*, (pl. of فائدة *fāʼidat*) Gains, profits, advantages, benefits. Notices, signs, observations. فوائد عميمه *fawāʼidi ʻamīma*, Common benefits. P فوائد بسيار داشتن *fawāʼidi bisyār dāshtan*, To possess many advantages.

A فوائه *fawāʼih*, (pl. of فوّهة *fūwahat*) Mouths of streets or rivers, embouchures. Beginnings.

P فوب *fūb*, Wind from the mouth blown by those who fascinate; also in lighting a fire, or in blowing out any thing lodged in the eye.

A فوّة *fūwat*, Madder, a red dye.

A فوت *fawt*, (v. n. of فات for فوت) Passing away. Escaping. Slipping (as an occasion). Escape loss. Death. (pl. افوات *afwāt*) The space between two fingers. فوت فم *fawta famin*, (فوت يد *fawta yadin*, or فوت رمح *fawta rumḥin*) Any thing near to the mouth, to the hand, or to a spear, but which, however, cannot be reached. جعل الله رزقه فوت فمه *jaʻala'llāh rizḳahu fawta famihi*, May God tantalize him! P فوت شدن *fawt shudan*, To die. To be lost, escape. فوت كردن *fawt kardan*, To die. فوت گرفتن *fawt giriftin*, To brave or seek death.

P فوت شده *fawt-shuda*, Dead or perishing. Ruined. Passed away. Neglected. Lost.

A فوتنج *fūtanaj*, (from P پودنه *pūdina*) Pennyroyal. Mint.

P فوته *fūta*, A cloth which they wrap round the middle when going to bathe.

A فوتي *fawtī*, Dead. (Property) of any person who dies intestate and without legal heirs; which escheats to the sovereign. فوتي فراري *fawtī-firārī*, Killed and missing. (Property) of persons dying intestate or absconding.

P فوتي نامه *fawtī-nāma*, A list of killed.

A فوج *fawj*, (v. n. of فاج for فوج) Diffusing odour (musk). Being cold (the day). (pl. فووج *fuwūj*, افواج *afwāj*, افاوج *afāwij*, and افاويج *afāwīj*) A body of men, company, troop, squadron, army. فوج فوج *fawj fawj*, In troops.

P فوجدار *fawj-dār*, An officer of the police in Hindūstān, and chief magistrate of a chaklah, who takes cognizance of all criminal matters.

P فوجداري *fawj-dārī*, The office or jurisdiction of a fawjdār.

A فوح *fawḥ*, (or فوحان *fawaḥān*) (v. n. of فاح for فوح) Diffusing odour (musk). Bleeding (a wound). Being widely-spread (a marauding party). Boiling. (pl. افواح *afwāḥ*) Fragrance, perfume.

A فوحات *fawḥāt*, (pl. of فوح *fawḥ*) Odours, fragrant substances.

A فوخ *fawkh*, (or فوخان *fawakhān*) (v. n. of فاخ for فوخ) Diffusing (an odour). Coming forth with or without noise from man or beast (wind). Making a hissing noise (as in making water). Breaking wind. كلّ بائلة تفوخ *kull bāʼilat tafūkh*, Every female whilst making water farts.

A فود *fawd*, (v. n. of فاد for فود) Dying. Circulating, or being fixed, but profitable (property). A troop. Confusion, mixture. The side of the head. A mass of hair about the ear. A side. Any thing equal or equiponderant, one side of saddle-bags.

P فود *fūd*, (equiv. to پود *pūd*) Cloth in the loom.

A فودج *fawdaj*, The camel-litter in which Arabian ladies travel. A vehicle in which a bride is carried. A camel's groin. Wide-groined (she-camel).

P فوده *fūda*, Dry fermented dough, from which the drink آبكامه *āb-kāma* is prepared.

A فوذنج *fūẕanaj*, Pennyroyal.

A فور *fawr*, (v. n. of فار for فور) Boiling (as a pot), bubbling (as a fountain). Causing to boil. Making فيارين *fiyārayn* for a pair of scales. Heat. Celerity, haste, expedition. Way, mode, manner. على الفور *ʻala'l fawr*, (or في الفور *fi'l fawr*) Quickly, instantly, in haste. من فورهم *min fawrihim*, Immediately on their arrival, before they had rested. *Fūr*, (pl. of فائر *fāʼir*) Does, deer.

P فور *fūr*, Palish red, russet. Name of a Rāja of Kanūj slain by Alexander (Porus?).

A فؤر *fuʼar*, A he-mouse.

A فورا *fawran*, Immediately, quickly, directly.

P فوران *fūrān*, The city of Kanūj in India.

A فوران *fawarān*, (v. n. of فار for فور) Boiling (as a pot), bubbling (as a fountain). Beating, throbbing, bursting forth (a vein or artery). Diffusing perfume (musk).

P فورانيان *fūrāniyān*, The citizens of Kanūj.

A فورة *fawrat*, Intenseness (of heat). The table-land of a mountain. فورة الجبل *fawratu'l jabal*, The summit of a mountain. The back of a mountain. فورة العشاء *fawratu'l ʻishāʼ*, A part of the evening, after sunset. *Fūrat*, Fawns.

A فؤرة *fuʼarat*, (or فورة *fūrat*) Wind which collects round the pastern of camels, which dissipates on being rubbed, and re-collects when left alone.

P فوردگان *fūrdagān*, (فوردجان *fūrdajān*, or فورديان *fūrdiyān*) Five days added to the end of the Persian year.

P فوردين *fūrdīn*, Fur, made of fur. *Fawardīn*, The first month of the solar year.

P فورك *fūrak*, Daughter of the king of Kanūj.

P فور موي *fūr-moy* or *mūy*, One whose hair is dark-coloured inclining to red: russet-haired.

P فوريان *fūriyān*, Descendants of Rājā Fūr.

A فوز *fawz*, (v. n. of فاز for فوز) Possessing, getting, gaining. Taking, carrying off. Escaping, getting clear of. Perishing. Dying. Victory, superiority. Escape, refuge, freedom, safety, salvation. Death, destruction.

P فوز *fūz*, Onset, attack: impetuosity. Belching. *Fūz*, (or فوزه *fūza*) The borders or parts about the mouth externally.

A فوزي *fawzī*, Triumphal, triumphant.

P فوژان *fūzhān*, A dreadful voice or sound.

P فوشنج *fūshanj*, A village near Harāt.

P فوشنه *fūshina*, A kind of fungus.

A فوضوضاء *fawzūzāʼ*, (or فوضوضى *fawzūzaʼ*) A partnership concern.

A فوضى *fawzaʼ*, Equals without a chief. Scattered (people). Mixed (cattle). Intermingled (ostriches). Confused (business). Equally shared by all (cattle).

A فوط *fuwat*, (pl. of فوطة *fūtat*) Striped cloths brought from Sinde.

A P فوطة *fūtat*, (pl. فوط *fuwat*) A kind of striped Indian cloth, of which trousers are made. A sash, bandage. A wrapper for the body, worn by Turkish women in the bathing-room. Treasure, revenue. A purse. A testicle.

P فوطه دار *fūta-dār*, A treasurer, banker.

A فوظ *fawẓ*, (v. n. of فاظ for فوظ) Dying, giving up the ghost. Death.

A فوعة *fawʻat*, Fragrance (of aromatics). The strength or virulence of poison. The beginning of night and day.

A فوغ *fawgh*, (v. n. of فاغ for فوغ) Diffusing odour (musk). *Fawagh*, (v. n. of فاغ for فوغ) Diffusing itself (perfume). Thickness of mouth.

A فوغة *fawghat*, Fragrance, perfume.

A فوف *fawf*, (v. n. of فاف for فوف) Asking for any thing (joining the nails of the fore-finger and thumb together). White specks on the nails. An ox's bladder. *Fūf*, White specks on the nails. A white kernel in the interior part of a date, whence the palm-tree germinates. The red skin of a date-stone. A thing, somewhat, a small matter. A kind of striped stuff of Yaman. Bits of cloth.

A فوفل *fawfal* or *fūfal*, Betel-nut.

A فوق *fawḳ*, (v. n. of فاق for فوق) Being above, superior to (one's fellows). Superiority, excellence. The top, upper part. *Fūḳ*, (v. n. of فاق for فوق) Breaking (an arrow) in the notch. (pl. فوق *fuwaḳ* and افواق *afwāk*) The notch of an arrow, into which the string goes. Tall, but loosely knit together. The upper part of the penis. The first road. A sort of bird. A mode of speech. Vulva. The tip of the tongue. The aperture of the mouth. Name of a monarch, Phocas. ما ارتدّ علىٰ فوقه *mā irtadda ʿala' fūkihi*, He went and returned not. رمينا فوقاً *ramaynā fūkan*, We discharged a rapid arrow. *Fawka*, Above, more than, beyond. Besides, except. الي فوق *ila' fawk*, Upwards. من فوق *min fawk*, From above, downwards. فوق التراب *fawka't turāb*, Above ground. فوق الحدّ *fawka'l hadd*, Above measure, excessively. فوق العادة *fawka'l ʿādat*, Unusual, out of the common rule. فوق المأمول *fawka'l maʾmūl*, Beyond expectation. *Fawak*, A bend or crack in the notch of an arrow.

A فوقاء *fawkāʾ*, (A pulley) notched twice in every tooth. Sharp at the point (glans penis).

A فوقان *fūkāni*, (dual.) The two sides of the notch of an arrow. *Fawakān*, (v. n. of فاق for فوق) Being superior (to one's associates).

A فوقانيّ *fawkāniy*, Superior, upper. Dotted above as some letters (such as ت *tā* or ن *nūn*).

A فوقة *fūkat*, Tall, but loosely knit together. The notch of an arrow. *Fawakat*, Polite, learned men: eloquent preachers.

A فوقيّ *fawkiy*, Dotted above (as ت *tā* or ن *nūn*).

A فوقيّة *fawkiyat*, Supremacy, superiority. Preference. *Fūkiyat*, (Coin) of the emperor Phocas.

P فوك *fūk*, A vetch, a bean. Tares.

P فوكان *fūgān*, A kind of drink, beer, ale.

A فول *fūl*, A kind of bean (when dry): a vetch.

A فؤول *fuʾul*, (pl. of فأل *faʾl*) Omens (especially such as are favourable).

P فولاد *fūlād*, (equiv. to پولاد *pūlād*) Steel.

P فولادي *fūlādī*, Made of steel. A pike-staff.

A فولاذ *fūlāz*, (from P پولاد) The best kind of steel.

A فولف *fawlaf*, A large vessel, basket, or pannier made of palm-leaves. Any covering (especially for clothes).

P فوليون *fūliyūn*, A medicine brought from Syria.

A فوم *fūm*, Wheat, vetches, pulse, grain of any kind. Bread. Garlic. A head of onion, clove of garlic. A large mouthful.

A فؤوم *fuʾum*, (pl. of فئام *fiʾām*) Coverings or cushions of camel-litters. فؤوما *fuʾaman*, (or فوما *fuwaman*) (He cut) into small pieces.

A فومة *fūmat*, An ear of corn. Any thing carried between two fingers.

A فووج *fuwūj*, (pl. of فوج *fawj*) Bodies of men, troops, squadrons.

A فووح *fuwūh*, (v. n. of فاح for فوح) Diffusing a smell (musk). Bleeding (a wound). Boiling (as a (kettle).

A فؤور *fuʾūr*, (v. n. of فار for فور) Boiling (as a pot), bubbling (as a fountain).

A فؤوس *fuʾūs*, (pl. of فأس) Axes, hatchets.

A فؤوق *fuʾūk*, (v. n. of فأق) Dying, expiring, giving up, or being about to give up, the ghost.

A فوه *fawh*, (v. n. of فاه for فوه) Pronouncing, speaking, uttering a word. *Fūh*, (pl. افواه *afwāh* or افهاه *afhāh*) Any thing fragrant, with which they make up ointments or perfumes. Pot-herbs, spices. The colour of a flower or blossom. Sort, species, kind. The teeth. *Fūh*, (for which فم *fam* and فو *fū* are generally used in construction, or with the affixed pronouns) (pl. افواه *afwāh*) The mouth. فوه *fūhu*, His mouth. *Fawah*, Width of mouth. Length, projection of the fore-teeth in the upper jaw.

P فوه *fawa* or *fūwa*, Madder.

A فوّه *fūwah*, Certain long slender red roots used in dyeing. Madder.

A فوهاء *fawhāʾ*, Large-mouthed (woman, well, wound, or pulley). A clothes-horse or line.

A فوهة *fawhat*, The mouth. A word. *Fūhat*, The mouth or entrance of a river, road, street, or lane. Noise, uproar, disturbance.

A فوّهة *fūwahat*, (pl. فوائه *fawāʾih*) The mouth. The entrance or mouth of a street or river. A word, saying. Slander, detraction behind the back. A commencement. Sweetish milk. Noise, uproar.

A فوهد *fawhad*, Fat (boy) and near puberty.

P فوهل *fūhil*, Saltpetre.

A فوهيّ *fūhiy*, Oral.

A فويت *fuwayt*, A man or woman singular in their opinion.

A فويق *fuwayk*, (dim. of فوق) A little above.

A فويسقة *fuwaysikat*, A mouse issuing from his hole.

A فويطة *fuwayta*, A little strip of cloth.

A فويه *fuwayh*, (dim. of فوه) A little mouth.

P فه *fah*, An oar. A paddle. *Fih*, An oar. A rake or shovel. An agricultural implement for levelling the ground.

A فهّ *fahh*, A stutterer. Weak.

A فهّاد *fahhād*, The man who trains the panther, hunting-leopard, or cheeta, and teaches it to hunt.

P فهار *fahār*, A precious stone from the East.

A فهارس *fahāris*, (pl. of فهرس *fihris*) Indexes.

A فهّام *fahhām*, Very intelligent, learned.

A فهامة *fuhāmat*, (*fihāmat*, or فهامية *fahāmiyat*) (v. n. of فهم) Understanding, comprehending, perceiving.

A فهّامة *fahhāmat*, A very intelligent man.

P فهانه *fahāna*, A wedge.

A فهاهة *fahāhat*, (v. n. of فهّ) Stammering, pronouncing improperly. Forgetting. Being weak, impotent. Hesitation in speech.

A فهّة *fahhat*, A stammering or hesitation in speech. A slip, fall. Ignorance.

A فهد *fahd*, (v. n. of فهد) Attending well to any one's interests during his absence. (pl. فهود *fuhūd* and افهد *afhud*) The cheeta or hunting-panther; the ounce. A nail or peg in the middle of a camel's saddle. The constellation Fera, *Fahad*, (v. n. of فهد) Sleeping. Neglecting one's duty. Resembling the cheeta in sloth. *Fahid* or *fihid*, Torpid, sleepy.

A فهدة *fahdat*, The fundament.

A فهدتان *fahdatāni*, Two prominences on the breast of a horse. Two bones growing behind a camel's ears.

A فهدر *fuhdur*, Compact, firm-bodied, corpulent. Flesh full of juices (a young man).

A فهر *fahr* or *fahar*, (v. n. of فهر) Lying with a woman, and withdrawing from her embrace before consummation, in order to lie with another (a practice forbidden by the سنّة *sunna* or Muhammadan law). *Fihr*, (pl. افهار *afhār* and فهور *fuhūr*) A stone filling the hand, wherewith they bray drugs or crack nuts. *Fuhr*, A Jewish university or college. The festival of Purim, which the Jews celebrate with much feasting.

A فهرس *fihris*, (or P فهرست *fihrist*) An index, summary, syllabus, table of contents; catalogue, inventory, list. A canon, rule. Preface or beginning of a book. فهرست اجناس *fihristi ajnās*, An invoice. P بعد از فهرست كتاب *baʿda az fihristi kitāb*, After the preface or beginning of the book.

A فهرسة *fahrasat*, (v. n. of فهرس Q) Making an index or catalogue, cataloguing.

A فهض *fahz*, (v. n. of فهض) Breaking.

A فهفاه *fahfāh*, One who manages (property) well.

A فهفه *fahfah*, A stammerer.

A فهفهة *fahfahat*, (v. n. of فهفه Q) Stammering, hesitating; hesitation in speech.

A فهق *fahk* or *fahak*, (v. n. of فهق) Being full (vessel); running over with liquor. Hurting the first joint of the neck.

A فهقة *fahkat*, The first vertebra of the neck.

P فهل *fahal*, Wide, open.

A فهلل *fahlala*, (or ابن فهلل) Vain, futile.

A فهلمّ *fahalumma*, Come along then, do so.

A فهم *fahm* or *faham*, (v. n. of فهم) Understanding. Intellect, knowledge, comprehension. P تيزفهم *tez-fahm*, Of a quick capacity. سخن فهم *sukhan-fahm*, Understanding words. A معقول فهم *maʿkūl-fahm*, Rational, comprehending the meaning (of any thing). *Fahim*, Intelligent.

P فهمانيدن *fahmānīdan*, To give to understand.

P فهميد *fahmīd*, Understanding, perception.

P فهميدگي *fahmīdagī*, Comprehension.

P فهميدن *fahmīdan*, To understand, perceive.

P فهميده *fahmīda*, Understood, comprehended.

A فهو *fahw*, (v. n. of فها for فهو) Forgetting. Slighting, neglecting. *Fahwa*, And, indeed, but it is. فهو المأمول *fahwa'l maʾmūl*, And that is the intention, that is what is wished, asked, or hoped for.

A فهود *fuhūd*, (pl. of فهد *fahd*) Cheetas, hunting-panthers, ounces.

A فهور *fuhūr*, (pl. of فهر *fihr*) Stones filling the

hand, with which they crack nuts.

P فهوله *fahūla*, A bundle.

A فهوم *fuhūm*, (pl. of فهم *fahm*) Intellects, understandings. اصحاب فهوم *as-hābi fuhūm*, Intelligent, learned men.

A فهه *fahah*, (v. n. of فهه) Stuttering, stammering. Forgetting. *Fahih*, A stammerer.

P فهه *fiha*, An oar.

A فهيرة *fahīrat*, Milk mixed with flour, and boiled by throwing into it a hot stone.

A فهيم *fahīm*, Learned, intelligent.

A فهيه *fahīh*, Weak. A stutterer. Ignorant.

A في *fī*, In, into, among. Above, on, upon. Of. To, with, for, by, against. Concerning. For the sake of. Notwithstanding. According to. In comparison of, each (or for each), per: as, في من *fī man*, Per maund. ثلاثون ذراعا في عشرين *salāsūna zirāɛan fī ɛishrīna*, Thirty cubits by twenty. في الامس *fī'l ams*, Yesterday. في اناء الليل واطراف النهار *fī anāɛi'l layl wa atrāfi 'n nahār*, By night and by day. في اوّل الدهر *fī awwali'd dahr*, A while ago. في البديهة *fī'l badīhat*, Readily, quickly, extempore. في الجملة *fī'l jumla*, Wholly, totally, entirely, universally, in all things, upon the whole, to sum up all. في الحال *fī'l hāl*, Now, immediately, suddenly, directly, instantly. في الحقيقة *fī'l hakīka*, Really, truly, in effect, in fact. في داخل *fī dākhil*, Within. في غضون ذلك *fī ghuzūni zāliha*, In the mean time, after which, then. في الفور *fī'l fawr*, Now, in short, immediately, directly. في كل مكان *fī kull makān*, Everywhere. في المثل *fī'l masal*, As, for example. Allegorically. في النار و السقر *fī'n nār wa's sakar*, In hell-flames. في نفس الامر *fī nafsi'l amr*, To the bottom of the affair. في نفسه *fī nafsihi*, In his own person, personally. في الواقع *fī'l wākiɛ*, Really, effectively. في يوم *fī yawm*, One day, in the day-time. اقبل في الف فارس *akbala fī alf fārisin*, He approached with a thousand horse. *Fī* is the oblique of فو *fū*, (for فم *fam*) The mouth. مات لفيه *māta li fīhi*, He died for his sake.

A فيّ *fīya*, My mouth.

A فيء *fayɛ*, (v. n. of فاء for فيأ) Returning. Paying a fine and taking one's wife back again. Receiving plunder and booty. (pl. افياء *afyāɛ* and فيوء *fuyūɛ*) A shadow (applied particularly to an alteration in position, pointing to the west before mid-day, then shortening, disappearing, and afterwards taking an opposite direction). Shade caused by the departure or shifting of the sun (that which is perpetual being called ظلّ *zill*). A flight of birds. Return. Spoil, prey. Tribute. سريع الفيء من غضبه *sarīɛu'l fayɛ min ghazabihi*, One who soon recovers from passion. يا فيء *yā fayaɛ*, Strange! alas!

A فيأة *fayɛat*, A return, bringing back. A kind of bird. Time, season.

A فئات *fiɛāt*, (pl. of فئة *fiɛat*) Troops, bodies.

A فياح *fayāh*, A word used when making an onset for plunder. *Fayāhi*, Make room, O woman!

A فيّاح *fayyāh*, fem. فيّاحة *fayyāhat*, Wide (sea).

A فيّاحة *fayyāhat*, Full-uddered (camel).

A فياخر *fayākhir*, Long-pizzled (horses).

A فيّاد *fayyād* A man who walks haughtily. A male owl. One who seizes and eats all he can get at.

A فيّادة *fayyādat*, (A beast) seizing whatever he can catch in order to devour it. Walking proudly.

P فيار *fayār*, Employ, work, business, art.

A فياران *fiyārāni*, (dual.) The two upright bars between which the tongue of a balance vibrates.

A فياش *fiyāsh*, Boast. A vain, empty threat.

A فيّاش *fayyāsh*, A vain-boaster. A noble lord, chief of a family. One who excels in beneficence.

A فياشل *fayāshil*, A sort of tree. (pl. of فيشلة *fayshalat*) Glandes penis.

A فيّاض *fayyāz*, Overflowing (river). Liberal, generous, charitable, profuse, bountiful. فيّاض مطلق *fayyāzi mutlak*, God the bounteous bestower of benefits. P ابر فيّاض *abri fayyāz*, A cloud full of rain.

A فيّاضي *fayyāzī*, Liberality, bountifulness.

A فياف *fiyāf*, (pl. of فيف *fayf*) Plains. Deserts without water.

A فيافي *fayāfī*, (pl. of فيفاء) Soft deserts.

A فياق *fuyāk*, Tall, but loosely knit together.

P فيال *fiyāl*, First, beginning. Land cultivated after first rain. Two-barbed arrow.

A فيال *fiyāl*, (*fayāl*, also فئال *fiɛāl*) A game among the Arabians (something is hid in a heap of earth, which, being then divided into several smaller heaps, he who discovers that which contains it gains).

A فيّال *fayyāl*, The keeper or driver of an elephant.

A فيالة *fiyālat*, (v. n. of فال for فيل) Being weak in mind. Erring in opinion or conjecture. Imbecility, folly, mental weakness.

A فيالق *fayālik*, (pl. of فيلق) Armies, legions.

A فئام *fiɛām*, (pl. فؤم *fuɛum*) The covering or cushion of a camel-litter or similar vehicle. A multitude, body of men.

P فياوار *fayāwār*, (or فياور *fayāwar*) Art, trade, profession. A mechanic. Skilful at work.

A فئة *fiɛat*, (pl. فئون *fiɛūn* and فئات *fiɛāt*) An army, body of men. تلاقيء فئتين *talākiɛi fiɛatayn*, The meeting of two armies.

A فيتق *faytak*, A carpenter. A blacksmith. A porter at a gate. A king.

A فيتن *faytan*, A carpenter.

A فيج *fayj*, A valley, low ground. (from P پيك *payk*) A messenger; attendant. A crowd, company.

A P فيجن *fayjan*, Rue.

A فيح *fayh*, Fruitfulness of herbage in an extensive tract. *Fayh*, (or فيحان *fayahān*) (v. n. of فاح for فيح) Being diffused (odour). Boiling. Flowing with blood (a wound). *Fayah*, Amplitude.

A فيحاء *fayhāɛ*, (fem. of افيح *afyah*) Large (house). Open, spacious, vast (country). الفيحاء *al fayhāɛ*, A kind of spoon-meat made of herbs.

A فيحق *fayhak*, Extensive (country).

A فيحقة *fayhakat*, (v. n. of فيحق Q) Straddling. Extensive (country).

A فيحي *fīhī*, Make way, O woman!

A فيخ *faykh*, (v. n. of فاخ for فيخ) Being diffused, scattered (an odour). Making a noise, whistling (the wind). Dispersion.

A فيخة *faykhat*, A platter, a dish. Amplitude, width in the urinary passage. Excessive heat. Abundance and luxuriancy of plants.

A فيخر *faykhar*, An earthen vessel. (pl. فياخر *fayākhir*) Large and long-pizzled (horse).

A فيخز *faykhaz*, The yard of any solid-hoofed animal. (A horse or man) which has a large yard.

A فيخمان *faykhamān*, Self-willed, determined to have one's own way. A great man. An umpire, judge, referee.

A فيد *fayd*, (v. n. of فاد for فيد) Dying. Walking pompously. Accruing to any one (advantage). Moistening, macerating, diluting saffron and other aromatics. Circulating freely, or remaining fixed (property). Turning aside from, avoiding. Clearing away the ashes from baked bread. Emolument, advantage. Saffron macerated. Hairs upon the lips of a horse.

P فيدار *faydār*, Trade, profession, art, craft.

P فيداقه *faydāka*, Name of a woman who reigned over the country of بردع *bardaɛ*.

A فيدس *faydas*, A large water-pot, such as persons carry with them on a sea-voyage.

P فيدوم *faydūm*, A kind of white manna.

A فئر *fuɛir*, (A place) full of mice. (Milk) rendered impure by a mouse fallen into it. *Fuɛar*, (pl. of فأر *faɛr*) Mice.

P فير *fīr*, Laughter, laughing-stock. Vexation.

A فئران *fiɛrān*, (pl. of فأر *faɛr*) Mice.

A فئرة *fiɛrat*, (*fiɛarat*, *faɛirat*, or فيرة *fīrat*) Fenugreek and dates administered to women in child-bed. *Fiɛarat*, (pl. of فأر *faɛr*) Mice.

P فيرندگي *ferandagī*, A triumphant, insolent boast.

P فيرنده *feranda*, Proud, boastful.

P فيروز *fīroz* or *feroz*, Victorious, triumphant, prosperous, successful. Victory. Prosperity. The third of the five supplemental days added to the Persian year. لشكر فيروز *lashkari fīroz*, The conquering army.

P فيروزاباد *fīrozābād*, Mansion of prosperity; a city in Persia near Shīrāz; also name of several other towns.

P فيروزاثر *fīroz-asar*, Victorious, conquering.

P فيروز بخت *fīroz-bakht*, Victorious.

A فيروزج *fīrūzaj*, (P فيروزه) A turquoise-stone.

P فيروزگرد *fīrozgard*, The city of Ardabīl.

P فيروزمند *fīrozmand*, A conqueror.

P فيروزمندي *fīrozmandī*, Victory, prosperity.

P فيروزنين *fīrozanīn*, A good work or act.

P فيروزة *fīroza,* A turkois, or turquoise.

P فيروزة تاج *fīroza-tāj,* (Blue diadem) The crown of Kay Khusraw. Holy men, dervishes.

P فيروزة تخت *fīroza-taht,* (or فيروزة سقف *fīroza-sakf*) Heaven (the azure vault).

P فيروزة دريا *fīroza-daryā,* (or فيروزة دريا گون *fīroza daryā gūn*) The azure sea. The sky.

P فيروزة طشت *fīroza-tasht,* The throne of Khusraw. The sky. The seven stars of the Great Bear disposed in the form of a چوگان *chawgān, i.e.* bandy or shinty, and called بنات النعش *banātu'n naꜥsh.*

P فيروزة كاخ *fīroza-kākh,* (or فيروزة مرقد *fīroza-markad*) The world.

P فيروزي *fīrozī,* Victorious, happy, glorious.

P فيريدگي *ferīdagī,* Sauciness, insolence, excessive joy. Pride of purse.

P فيريدن *ferīdan,* To swagger, walk pompously. To be very benevolent. To vex, deride.

A فيز *fiyazz,* A strong nervous arm. One whose flesh and sinews are hard and firm.

A فيزلة *fayzalat,* Lands soon flooded.

P فيزوم *fīzūm,* The river Ganges.

P فيسا *fīsā,* A peacock.

A فيسحي *faysaha',* Width of step.

A فيش *faysh,* (v. n. of فاش for فيش) Mounting (an ass the female). Boasting, swaggering, entertaining a wrong opinion of one's self. Glans penis.

A فيشة *fayshat,* Glans penis.

A فيشلة *fayshalat,* (pl. فياشل *fayāshil*) Glans penis (particularly of a stout one).

A فيشوشة *fayshūshat,* Weakness, languor.

A فيشون *fayshūn,* Name of a river, Pison.

A فيص *fays,* (v. n. of فاص for فيص) Flying, escaping, eluding one's pursuit (a lizard). Going, departing, budging from a place, travelling. Declaring, uttering.

A فيصل *faysal,* A decision, decree, determination of a law-suit, a definitive sentence from which there lies no appeal. Separation, division, rupture, disjunction. A stab piercing between two joints. A judge, arbitrator. P فيصل كردن *faysal kardan,* To settle a law-suit or dispute.

P فيصل نامه *faysal-nāma,* Decree, award; an instrument denoting that a cause has been settled.

A فيصله *faysala,* Decree, settlement, adjustment.

A فيصلي *faysalīy,* A judge, arbitrator.

P فيصور *faysūr,* Name of a city whence they bring camphire.

A فيصور *faysūr,* A sprightly ass.

A فيض *fayz,* (v. n. of فاض for فيض) Being plentiful, copious (water, tears). Being bank-full (a river). Overflowing (a river). Being very numerous, swarming (wicked men). Appearing, peeping out. Being published, spreading (news). Revealing, divulging, disclosing, allowing (a secret) to escape. Dying, expiring, giving up the ghost. Quitting the body (the vital spirit). Plenty, abundance. Grace, favour. Bounty, liberality. Death. The river Nile. The river of Basra. Swift (horse): an excellent runner. فيض اقدس *fayzi akdas,* Communications of divine grace made to angels, prophets, and other superior intelligences, without the intervention of the Holy Spirit. فيض حق *fayzi hak,* (or فيض ربّاني *fayzi rabbānī*) The grace of the Lord. فيض عام *fayzi ꜥām,* Creating general abundance, liberal, profuse. فيض كرم *fayzi karam,* Divine bounty. فيض مقدّس *fayzi mukaddas,* Communications of divine grace bestowed by means of the Holy Spirit. اعطاه غيضاً من فيض *aꜥtāhu ghayzan min fayzin,* He gave him little out of much.

A فيضان *fayazān,* (v. n. of فاض for فيض) Overflowing. Redundancy.

P فيض بخش *fayz-bakhsh,* (or فيض رسان *fayz-rasān*) Bestowing favours.

A فيضة *fayzat,* Effusion, a pouring forth.

A فيضوضاء *fayzūzā',* (or فيضوضي *fayzūza'*) Equally shared by all (cattle or goods); a partnership concern.

A فيضوضة *fayzūzat,* (v. n. of فاض for فيض) Overflowing. Divulging.

A فيضيضاء *fayzīzā',* (or فيضيضي *fayzīza'*) (Goods) shared in common, a partnership concern.

A فيظ *fayz,* Death. *Fayz,* (or فيظان *fayazān*) (v. n. of فاظ for فيظ) Expiring, giving up the ghost.

P فيظل *fayzal,* Wild anise.

A فيع *fayꜥ,* (or فيعة) Beginning of business.

A فيف *fayf,* (pl. افياف *afyāf,* فيوف *fuyūf,* and فياف *fiyāf*) A level place. Solitude, plain, desert without water. A country where the winds are variable.

A فيفاء *fayfā',* (فيفا *fayfā,* or فيفاة *fayfāt*) (pl. فيافي *fayāfī*) A level place. A solitude. A place or desert without water.

A فيفرع *fayfaraꜥ,* A kind of tree.

A فيفعي *fayfaꜥīy,* A shepherd. A butcher.

A فيق *fayk,* (v. n. of فاق for فيق) Giving up the ghost. The cackling of a hen. *Fīk,* The mountain which surrounds the world. Tall (man), but loosely knit together.

A فيقة *fīkat,* (pl. فيق *fīk, fiyak,* فيقات *fīkāt,* افواق *afwāk,* and افاويق *afāwīk*) Milk collected in the udders between two milkings. The half-way hour between sunrise and mid-day.

A فيقر *faykar,* A calamity, misfortune.

P فيك *fayk,* A footman, courier, messenger.

A فيكر *faykar,* Very thoughtful.

A فيّل *fayil,* Corpulent and full of flesh (man).

A فيل *fīl,* (pl. افيال *afyāl,* فيول *fuyūl,* and فيلة *fiyalat*) An elephant. Heavy. Base, ignoble, paltry. *Fīl* or *fayl,* Weak in judgment, silly. ذات الفيل *zātu'l fīl,* Elephantiasis. ناب الفيل *nābu'l fīl,* Ivory, the tusk of an elephant.

A فيّل *fayyil,* Weak in mind, silly. فيّل اللحم *fayyilu'l lahm,* Very fleshy.

G فيلا *fīlā,* A lover.

G فيلاسوف *filāsūf,* A philosopher.

P فيلاق *faylāk,* A legion.

P فيلبان *fīlbān,* An elephant-keeper or driver.

P فيلپا *fīl-pā,* Swollen-legged. Elephantiasis.

P فيلپايه *fīl-pāya,* A pillar.

A فيلة *faylat,* (v. n. of فال for فيل) Being weak (the mind). Being weak-minded. Making a mistake in playing at the game of فيال *fiyāl. Fīlat,* A female elephant. *Fiyalat,* (pl. of فيل *fīl*) Elephants.

P فيلجه *faylaja,* Power, strength.

A فيلخ *faylakh,* A mill. The nether mill-stone.

P فيلخانه *fīl-khāna,* An elephant-stable.

P فيلدندان *fīl-dandān,* Ivory.

P فيل زهره *fīl-zahra,* The box-thorn.

P فيلسته *fīlasta,* A cheek. An arm. A finger.

A فيلسوف *faylasūf,* A philosopher. Intelligent, knowing. Cunning, artful.

P فيلسوفگي *faylasūfagī,* Philosophy.

A فيلق *faylak,* (pl. فيالق *fayālik*) An army, legion. A misfortune. A great man.

P فيلقوس *faylakūs,* Philip of Macedon.

P فيلك *faylak,* A double-headed arrow. The planet Mercury.

A فيلكون *faylakūn,* The plant papyrus. A reed. Pitch. Barley-meal.

P فيلگوش *fīl-gosh,* Flowers of different colours with jagged leaves. The iris or elephants'-ears. Name of a sweetmeat.

A فيلم *faylam,* One who has a large forehead and a large head of hair. Wide, deep (well). A comb. A sheet of dressed leather used as a table-cloth. Numerous (host). *Faylam,* (or فيلماني *faylamānīy*) A big man. A coward.

P فيلمرغ *fīl-murgh,* (Elephant-bird) A turkey.

P فيلنشين *fīl-nishīn,* Seated on an elephant.

A فيلولة *faylūlat,* (v. n. of فال for فيل) Being weak (the judgment). Being weak-minded (a man). Making a mistake in playing at the game فيال *fiyāl.*

P فيلي *fīlī,* Of an elephant, elephantine.

A فيم *fīma,* Because that, inasmuch as.

A فيّم *fayyim,* (pl. فيوم *fuyūm*) A strong man.

A فيما *fīmā,* In that which, from that which; so that, on which, whence; why; whilst, in the mean time. According to. في ما بعد or فيما بعد *fī mā baꜥd,* After this, henceforward. فيما بين *fīmā bayn,* Between. Reciprocal, mutual. يا فيما *yā fīmā,* A cry of astonishment.

A فيمان *faymān,* (P پيمان) Compact, agreement.

P فيمان *fīmān,* Aiming at moral perfection.

P فيمون *faymūn,* A name given to عذرا *ꜥazrā.*

A فين *fayn,* The act of coming.

P فين *fīn,* A place of recreation in Kāshān.

A فينان *faynān,* Hair long and handsome. One who has such hair.

A فينانة *faynānat,* (A woman) with fine long hair.

A فينة *faynat,* An hour, time, a small space of

time. لقيته الفينة بعد الفينة *lakītuhu'l faynata baʿda'l faynati,* (or *faynatan baʿd faynatin*) I met him again and again.

P فينك *fīnak,* Froth of the sea, meerschum.

A فيوء *fuyūʾ,* (pl. of فيء *fayʾ*) Shadows.

A فيوج *fuyūj,* (pl. of فيج *fayj*) Messengers, attendants. Keepers of a prison.

A فيّور *fayyūr,* Acute, quick, intelligent.

A فيوض *fiyūz,* (v. n. of فاض for فيض) Overflowing (water). *Fuyūz,* (v. n. of فاض for فيض) Overflowing (water). Dying. (pl. of فيض *fayz*) Overflowings of water.

A فيوضات *fuyūzāt,* (pl. of فيوض) Inundations.

A فيوضى *fuyūzaʾ,* Intricate, confused (business).

A فيوظ *fuyūz,* (or فيوظة *fuyūzat*) (v. n. of فاظ for فيظ) Giving up the ghost.

A فيوف *fuyūf,* (pl. of فيف *fayf*) Level grounds. Deserts destitute of water.

A فيول *fuyūl,* (pl. of فيل *fīl*) Elephants.

A فيولة *fuyūlat,* (v. n. of فال for فيل) Being weak in mind. Erring in opinion or conjecture. Imbecility, folly.

A فيوم *fuyūm,* (pl. of فيّم *fayyim*) Strong men.

A فيّوم *fayyūm,* A city and district in Egypt.

A فئون *fiʾūn,* (pl. of فئة *fiʾat*) Bodies, troops.

A فيوي *fiyawiy,* Relating to في *fī,* In.

A فيه *fīh,* The mouth. *Fīhi,* In him, in it.

A فيّه *fayyih,* (fem. فيّهة *fayyihat*) Eloquent, loquacious, talkative. Voracious.

A فيهج *fayhaj,* A cup filled with wine. Wine. A wine-measure. A strainer.

A فيهر *fayhar,* Large, robust (she-camel).

A فيهرة *fayharat,* (v. n. of فيهر Q) Being tired, breathing hard (a horse). Large, robust (she-camel).

A فيهق *fayhak,* Large, wide. (A camel) plentiful in milk.

A فيهك *fayhak,* Silly, foolish (woman).

A فيئة *fayʾat* or *fiʾat,* A large bird, a species of eagle. Time, age. *Fiʾat,* A return, bringing back.

A فئيد *faʾīd,* Heartless, spiritless, cowardly. Fire. Roasted (meat).

P فييدن *fayīdan,* To be displeased at, timid, afraid.

ق

ق *kāf,* The twenty-first letter of the Arabic, and twenty-fourth of the Persian alphabets, expressing 100 in arithmetic. The Persians, it may be observed, however, do not acknowledge this letter as originally belonging to their alphabet. Its sound is harder than that of ك *kāf,* being formed deep in the throat, by the pressure of the root of the tongue against it; and has been compared to the cawing of a raven. ق *kāf* is sometimes used for ك *kāf* and غ *ghayn.* *Ki,* (imper. of وقى *waka'*) Preserve, take care. ق على ظلعك *ki ʿala' zalʿika,* Mind your own business.

P قاآن *kāʾān,* Title of the Emperor of China.

A قآب *kaʾāb,* A being filled with wine.

A قأب *kaʾb,* (v. n. of قأب) Devouring (meat). Drinking (water or wine). *Kaʾab,* (v. n. of قئب) Drinking much, being filled with drink. Being full (of wine).

P قاب *kāb,* A vessel or a case: as, قاب عينك *kābi ʿaynak,* A spectacle-case; قاب قلم *kābi kalam,* A pen-case; قاب آينه *kābi āyina,* A case for a looking-glass.

A قاب *kāb,* Quantity, space, interval. (du. قابان *kābāni*) The distance between the extremities and middle of a bow. قاب قوسين *kāb kawsayn,* Two bows' (or according to others) two cubits' length.

A قابّ *kābb,* The year after next.

A قابة *kābat,* An egg. A chicken.

A قابّة *kābbat,* Thunder. Drops of rain.

A قابض *kābiz,* A taker, seizer, griper, grasper, clutcher. A receiver. A possessor. Swift, expeditious. One who drives fast. An astringent, constipator. قابض الارواح *kābizu'l arwāh,* The seizer of souls, *i.e.* The angel of death. قابض جريمه *kābizi jarīma,* A receiver of fines.

A قابضات *kābizāt,* Astringents.

A قابع *kābiʿ,* Short-winded, breathing hard.

A يا ابن قابعاء *yā ibna kābiʿāʾ,* O thou fool!

A قابل *kābil,* Approaching, ensuing, that which is next or approaches, following (year). A recipient. Capable, able, skilful, clever. Worthy, sufficient. He who receives the bucket from the drawer of water. Cain. قابل امانت *kābili amānat,* A human being. قابل تحمّل *kābili tahammul,* Tolerable, supportable. قابل التوب *kābilu't tawb,* (God) the accepter of repentance. قابل دعويء شرعى *kābili daʿwaʾi sharʿī,* Authorised by law. P قابل شدن *kābil shudan,* To be able, qualified, capable. To be possible. A قابل الغلط *kābilu'l ghalat,* Fallible. قابل و هابل *kābil u hābil,* Cain and Abel.

P نا قابل *nā kābil,* Incapable, unskilful.

P قابلة *kābilat,* A midwife. Next night.

A قابليّة *kābiliyat,* Aptitude to receive, fitness, capacity, skill. Possibility. Ability. Sufficiency. Desire, appetite.

P قابو *kābū,* Ability, power, opportunity. قابو يافتن *kābū yāftan,* To find an opportunity. To be revenged of. قابو پرست *kābū-parast,* Tyrannical.

P قابو پرستي *kābū-parastī,* Tyranny.

P قابوس *kābūs,* Name of a king of Astarābād.

A قابوس *kābūs,* A man with a handsome face and a fine complexion. (for P كاووس *kāvūs*) Name of an ancient king of Persia. ابو قابوس *abū kābūs,* Name of Nuʿmān, son of Munzir, king of Arabia.

P قابول *kābūl,* (قابوك *kābūk,* or قاپول *kāpūl*) A pent, eaves. A trough for water under the eaves.

P قابون *kābūn,* (equiv. to برون داشت).

A قابياء *kābiyāʾ,* Worthless. بنو قابياء *banū kābiyāʾ,* (Sons of infamy) Wine-drinkers at taverns.

A قابية *kābiyat,* A woman culling saffron-flowers.

A قابيل *kābīl,* Cain.

A قاتر *kātir,* Elegant, well-proportioned (saddle) that sits well. Parsimonious, stingy in housekeeping. Of a just proportion (shield). (A rider) careful not to hurt a camel's back.

A قاتل *kātil,* (pl. قتلة *katalat*) A killer, murderer, slayer. Deadly, mortal. قاتل الذئب *kātilu'z ziʾb,* Wolfs'-bane. قاتل الكلب *kātilu'l kalb,* Dogs'-bane. P زهر قاتل *zahri kātil,* Deadly poison.

A قاتم *kātim,* (or قاتن *kātin*) Dusty. Blackish.

A قاثم *kāsim,* Liberal, most munificent.

A قاح *kāha,* (fut. يقوح *yakūhu*) (The wound) became purulent. He swept (the house).

A قاحب *kāhib,* Violent (cough).

A قاحة *kāhat,* The middle court of a house.

A قاحد *kāhid,* Single, solitary.

A قاحزات *kāhizāt,* Adversities, tribulations.

A قاحط *kāhit,* (pl. قواحط) Severe (season).

A قاحف *kāhif,* Rain coming suddenly and sweeping away all before it. An emptier of a cup.

A قاحل *kāhil,* Withered, dry.

A قاحم *kāhim kāhim,* Jet black.

A قاخ *kākh,* Dark, black (night).

A قاد *kāda,* (fut. يقود *yakūdu*) He led.

A قاد *kād,* Quantity. قاد رمح *kādu rumhin,* A spear's length.

A قادة *kādat,* (pl. of قائد) Leaders, captains.

A قادح *kādih,* A black corrosion of the teeth; also of a tree. A crack in wood. A blamer, accuser.

A قادحة *kādihat,* A worm in a tooth or tree.

P قادر *kādir,* An arrow.

A قادر *kādir,* Potent, powerful, able, capable, skilful. The powerful, an attribute of God. Cooked in a pot (قدر *kidr*). P قادر بي ريب و خلاف *kādiri bī rayb u khilāf,* Potent without doubt or opposition, *i.e.* Omnipotent. قادر شدن *kādir shudan,* To be able, sufficient, powerful.

P قادر انداز *kādir-andāz,* An expert archer.

A قادرة *kādirat,* (fem.) Powerful. ليلة قادرة *laylatun kādiratun,* An easy night's journey.

A قادس *kādis,* Cadiz (in Spain). A large ship.

A قادسيّه *kādisīya,* Name of a city in Chaldea, famous for the battle which subjected Persia to the Arabian califat.

A قادم *kādim,* Arriving; a comer. (pl. قدم *kudum* and قدّام *kuddām*) One who arrives off a journey. (pl. قوادم *kawādim*) A (man's) head. The fore part of a camel's saddle. A camel's front teat.

A قادمان *kādimāni,* Fore-dugs (of sheep or camel).

A قادمة *kādimat,* The advanced guard or van of an army. The fore part of a camel's saddle. (pl. قوادم *kawādim* and قدامى *kudāma'*) The first or longest feather of the wing.

A قادمتان *kādimatāni,* The fore-dugs (of a ewe or camel). The two fore timbers of a camel's saddle.

A قاديـة *kādiyat*, A small body of men.

A ما يدع شاذة و لا فاذة *mā yadaɛu shāzzatan wa lā fāzzatan*, He is a brave fellow, slaying all.

A قاذف *kāzif*, One who pelts with stones. One who accuses: or who convicts. Going swiftly and running before the males (she-camel).

A قاذور *kāzūr*, (or ذو قاذورة *zū kāzūratin*) A misanthrope. قاذورات *kāzūrāt*, Dirt, impurities.

A قاذية *kāziyat*, A small body of men.

P قار *kār*, Any thing very white or very black, as snow or pitch. قارخشك *kāri khushk*, Thick, hard pitch. قارسيّال *kāri sayyāl*, Liquid pitch.

A قار *kār*, Pitch. A large herd of camels. Name of a bitter tree. (pl. of قارة *kārat*) Small hills separate from others. Large stones.

A قارّ *kārr*, Cold (day). Cheerful (eye).

A قاراة *kārāt*, A town, *i.e.* a fixed residence.

G قاراسيا *kārāsiyā*, Cherries.

A قارب *kārib*, (pl. قوارب *kawārib*) A boat belonging to a large ship. A camel employed to make nocturnal journeys in quest of water. The owner of such a camel. (pl. قاربون *kāribūn*) One who goes to water in the night-time.

T قارپوز *kārpūz*, A water-melon.

A قارة *kārat*, (pl. قور *kūr* and قيران *kīrān*) A small hill detached from the others. A large stone. Ground abounding in black stones. A black stone. A she-bear. Name of a tribe expert in throwing the javelin.

A قارّة *kārrat*, Cold, cheerful (eye).

A قارت *kārit*, One who seizes every thing for himself. The best and driest (musk).

A قارح *kārih*, A veteran. A lion. Pregnant, and visibly so (camel). A bow distant from the string. (fem. قارحة *kārihat*) (pl. قراح *kirāh*, قوارح *kawārih*, قرّح *kurrah*, and مقاريح *makārīh*) A tooth that has reached its full size. Five-year-old, or a full-aged (horse), having then shed all (his) teeth.

A قارس *kāris*, Cold. Intense (cold). Old, ancient.

A قارشة *kārishat*, A bleeding wound in the head.

A قارص *kāris*, Acid, acrid, sour (milk upon which they pour fresh milk till its acidity be gone). A bug.

A قارصة *kārisat*, (pl. قوارص *kawāris*) Biting word.

A قارض *kāriz*, Corroding, corrosive.

A قارظ *kāriz*, One who collects the leaves of the tree سلم *salam*.

A قارع *kāriɛ*, A gainer at drawing lots. A striker.

A قارعة *kāriɛat*, (pl. قوارع *kawāriɛ*) Adversity, evil. A curse. A court-yard. The highest part of a road. القارعة *al kāriɛat*, The day of judgment.

P قارن *kāran*, Name of a wrestler.

A قارن *kārin*, An assistant, companion. Possessor of a sword and an arrow.

A قارورة *kārūrat*, (pl. قوارير *kawārīr*) A flask containing wine or any thing similar. A glass bottle, decanter. A urinal. An alabaster-vase (for ointment). The pupil or black of the eye.

P قارورة *kārūra*, A glass urinal, in which the urine of a sick person is shewn to the physician; hence, a name for urine.

A قارون *kārūn*, Supposed to be the same person called Korah, and proverbial for his wealth and avarice. Galangale.

P قاره *kāra*, A plant resembling a leek.

A قارئ *kāri*, The appointed time (of any thing, especially of a periodical wind to blow).. (pl. قرأة *karaɛat*, قرّاء *kurrāɛ*, and قارئون *kāriɛūn*) A reader, especially of the Kur'ān. Devout, worshipping (man). Pure, holy.

A قاري *kārī*, Inhabitant of a town (بادي *bādī* implying one who lives in the country or desert).

A قارية *kāriyat*, (pl. قواري *kawārī*) A species of bird with a long beak (a great favourite with the Arabians, being considered as a bird whose appearance is hailed as a presage of rain, and frequently denoting a liberal man). A witness, testimony, evidence. A spy upon the actions of another. The head or sharp point (also the lower part) of a spear. Edge of a sword. A town, fixed abode.

A قاريط *kārit*, Seed of the tamarind.

A قارئون *kāriɛūn*, (pl. of قاريٌ *kāriɛ*) Readers of the Kur'ān.

T قاز *kāz*, A goose.

A قازّ *kāzz*, Satan.

A قازب *kāzib*, A merchant voyaging by sea or travelling by land athirst for gain.

A قازح *kāzih*, Penis durus. High (price or tax). Coarse (garment).

T قازقان *kāzkān*, A large cauldron.

A قازوزة *kāzūzat*, A cup, jug, drinking-vessel.

A قاس *kāsa*, (fut. يقيس *yakīsu*) He measured.

P قاس *kās*, A frog. An eyebrow.

A قاس *kās*, Quantity, measure.

A قاسان *kāsān*, A city beyond the Oxus.

A قاسب *kāsib*, Weak, flaccid (yard).

A قاسط *kāsit*, One who deviates from the truth. Unjust, tyrannical, oppressive.

A قاسم *kāsim*, A divider, a distributor. Distributive. قاسم الارزاق *kāsimu'l arzāk*, The distributor of daily bread, *i.e.* God. عدالت قاسمه *ɛadālati kāsima*, Distributive justice.

A قاسي *kāsī*, Hard, unfeeling (heart).

A قاش *kaɛsh*, A cable, hawser.

P قاش *kāsh*, A slice (a of melon). Alike.

T قاش *kāsh*, A bit, piece. The eyebrow.

A قاشان *kāshān*, Name of a city.

A قاشب *kāshib*, A tailor. Weak-minded.

A قاشح *kāshih*, Thick (cloth).

A قاشر *kāshir*, Skin-grazing (blow). Ground-brushing (rain). The last horse in a race. Name of a certain horse: hence, اشأم من قاشر *ashɛam min kāshir*, More unlucky than Kāshir.

A قاشرة *kāshirat*, A slight wound grazing the skin. A woman rubbing her face to make it shine.

T قاشق *kāshik*, A wooden spoon.

P قاش قاش *kāsh kāsh*, Scattered, dispersed.

P قاشق تراش *kāshik-tarāsh*, A spoon-maker.

A قاش ماش *kāsh māsh*, Utensils. Furniture. Stuff, merchandize.

A قاشور *kāshūr*, Unlucky. The last horse in a race. Excoriating every thing, *i.e.* a barren season.

A قاشورة *kāshūrat*, A scarce year.

A قاشي *kāshī*, A bad obolus.

A قاصّ *kāss*, An historian, story-teller.

A قاصب *kāsib*, One who blows the flute, a piper. A butcher. Loud thunder. A male or female camel leaving off drinking before quenching thirst.

A قاصد *kāsid*, Travelling, going. One who aims at or who makes for. Near. A traveller. (pl. قصّاد *kussād*) A messenger, courier, express, postman, cossid. P قاصد چرخ *kāsidi charkh*, The moon. The sun. A ليلة قاصدة *laylatun kāsidatun*, An easy night's journey.

A قاصر *kāsir*, Defective, insufficient, unequal, impotent, falling short of. Cold (water). (Water) far distant from pasture. Water around which cattle feed. One who hangs down the head. قاصر البيان *kāsiru'l bayān*, Failing in relation, whose meaning is defective; inexplicable. قاصر اليد *kāsiru'l yad*, Short-handed, weak, puny. قاصرة الطرف *kāsiratu't tarf*, A woman looking down, turning her eyes to none but her husband.

A قاصعاء *kāsiɛāɛ*, (pl. قواصع *kawāsiɛ*) The hole of the jerboa or field-mouse.

A قاصف *kāsif*, Who or what breaks, shakes, or drives. Vehement, violent (wind). Loud (thunder). One who presses at a door for admittance.

A قاصل *kāsil*, Sharp (sword or tongue).

A قاصم *kāsim*, A breaker in pieces.

A قاصي *kāsī*, (fem. قاصية *kāsiyat*) (pl. اقصاء *aksāɛ*) Remote, far distant.

A قاصيّة *kāsiyat*, A country, territory, district. Decrepit (sheep or wild cow).

A قاضب *kāzib*, (pl. قواضب *kawāzib* and قضب *kuzb*) Sharp (sword).

A قاضويّ *kāzawiy*, Judicial.

A قاضي *kāzī*, (pl. قضاة *kuzāt*) A cādi or cāzi, a judge, civil, criminal, and ecclesiastic. Deadly (poison). P قاضيء چرخ *kāziɛi charkh*, (or قاضيء فلك *kāziɛi falak*) The planet Jupiter. A قاضي الحاجات *kāzi'l hājāt*, (God) the judge of the necessities (of mankind). P قاضيء شهر *kāziɛi shahr*, Judge or mayor of a city. A قاضيء عسكر *kāziɛi ɛaskar*, An army-judge; also sometimes the chief judge of the empire. قاضي القضاة *kāzi'l kuzāt*, Judge of judges, *i.e.* chief judge, lord chief-justice.

A قاضيّ *kāziy*, Judicial, juridical.

A قاضية *kāziyat*, Death, fate. A certain number of camels by which manslaughter is expiated. Fixed alms. قاضية الموت *kāziyatu'l mawt*, A sentence of death.

A قاطّ *kātt*, Dear (provisions), high (assize).

A قاطب *kātib*, Who knits his brows. A lion.

A قاطبة *kātibat*, All (mankind), every one.

A قاطبة *kātibatan*, Generally, universally.

T قاطر *kātir*, A mule.

A قاطر *kātir*, Gum-distilling (tree, especially the one called dragon's blood). Dropping urine incessantly (a camel). The tears or gum of a tree.

A قاطط *kātit*, High, dear (assize or tariff).

A قاطع *kātiʿ*, Who or what cuts. Keen, sharp. Any cutting instrument; shears, scissors. One who forsakes, forsaker. Decisive, peremptory, explicit, categorical. Acid (milk). قاطع الرحم *kātiʿu'r rahim*, One who abandons his parents or kindred. قاطع الطريق *kātiʿu't tarīk*, A cutpurse, highwayman, assassin.

A قاطن *kātin*, (pl. قطّان *kuttān*) An inhabitant, a settled resident. A servant. قاطن الدنيا *kātinu'd dunya'*, An inhabitant of the world, *i.e.* man.

A قاطنة *kātinat*, Inhabitants. Servants, domestics.

A قاطول *kātūl*, Name of a place on the Tigris.

T قاطون *kātūn*, Sal-ammoniac.

A قاع *kāʿ*, (pl. قيع *kiʿ*, قيعة *kiʿat*, قيعان *kiʿān*, اقواع *akwāʿ*, and اقوع *akwuʿ*) A plain, level ground. A flat, level country. A fortress in Madina.

A قاعب *kāʿib*, A howling wolf.

A قاعة *kāʿat*, A court-yard. A saloon.

A قاعد *kāʿid*, (pl. قعود *kuʿūd*) Sitting, sedentary. Full of corn (sack). (pl. قواعد *kawāʿid*) A dwarf palm-tree which the hand can reach. (A woman) remaining at home, and separated from her husband (in child-bed, or during her courses). A discharged soldier whose name is not inscribed in the muster-book. A sect or people who go not to war. Nastiness, ordure. Weakness in the pastern joint of a quadruped. (pl. قعد *kaʿad*) A schismatic.

A قاعدة *kāʿidat*, (pl. قواعد *kawāʿid*) Base, basis, foundation, ground-work. A pedestal. A metropolis, capital, seat of government. Rule, custom, institution, mode, manner, style, regulation. A rule of grammar. قاعدۀ عمود *kāʿidaʾi ʿamūd*, The base of a column.

A قاعف *kāʿif*, Rain, a torrent, deluge.

A قاعلة *kāʿilat*, (pl. قواعل *kawāʿil*) A high, extensive mountain.

A قاف *kāf*, A fabulous mountain, anciently imagined by the Asiatics to surround the world, and to bind the horizon on all sides. Mount Caucasus. P از قاف تا قاف *az kāf tā kāf*, From Kāf to Kāf, *i.e.* the whole world. A Independent, able to do without. The letter ق *kāf*. The Kur'ān. The upper part or tip of the ear. قاف ودال *kāf u dāl*, Vain, foolish. Foolish prating, idle talking. A discourse, argument. Magnificence, great attendance, grandeur. اخذه بقاف رقبته *akhazahu bi kāfi rakabatihi*, He took him by the nape of the neck.

A قافة *kāfat*, (pl. of قائف *kāʾif*) Tracers, those who can track footsteps.

A قافز *kāfiz*, (pl. قوافز) Prancing (horse).

A قافل *kāfil*, Dry (skin). Dry-skinned. Dry-handed. (pl. قفّال *kuffāl*) Returning from a journey.

A قافلة *kāfilat*, (pl. قوافل *kawāfil*) A caravan, body of travellers, a coffle. A travelling party returned from a journey. P قافله شد *kāfila shud*, The caravan is departed (metaph.), The prophet (Muhammad) is dead.

P قافله سالار *kāfila-sālār*, Chief of a caravan.

A قافور *kāfūr*, The envelope of palm-flowers.

A قافي *kāfī*, A follower, attendant.

A قافية *kāfiyat*, (pl. قوافي *kawāfī*) A poem, rhyme, cadence, metre. The last consonant in a verse, to which all the other distichs rhyme. The neck behind. على قافيته *ʿala' kāfiyatihi*, Close behind him, at his heels. P قافيه تنگ شدن *kāfiya tang shudan*, To be feeble in speaking or acting. A ذو قافيتين *zū kāfiyatayn*, Double-rhymed (verse).

P قافيه سنجان *kāfiya-sanjān*, Poets.

P قافيه سنجي *kāfiya-sanjī*, Versification.

P قاق *kāk*, Flesh or fish smoked or dried. Tall, lank.

A قاق *kāk*, Very tall. Silly, light, flighty.

A قاقاء *kaʾkāʾ*, The cawing of the ravens of Irāk.

A قاقزة *kākuzzat* or *kākizzat*, A drinking-vessel, cup, or goblet.

A P قاقلّة *kākullat*, (or قاقلة *kākulat*) Cardamoms.

A قاقلّي *kākulla'*, A species of salt herb.

P قاقم *kākum*, The ermine. An emblem of day.

P قاقم نماي *kākum-namāy*, Appearing white.

A قاقوزة *kākūzat*, A drinking-vessel, cup, goblet.

P قاقيا *kākiyā*, All juices expressed from any thing of a styptic quality; but especially the juice-pods of an Egyptian thorn.

A قال *kāl*, A word, a saying. Loquaciousness. A beginning, commencement. (pl. قيلان *kīlān*) A stick striking another, called قلة *kulat*, in the boy's game of hockey. A speaker. قال الحق *kālu'l hakk*, Jesus Christ, the Word of God. قيل و قال *kīl u kāl*, Much conversation.

P قالب *kālab*, A form, model, mould; any thing in which, or from which, another is made. The body, bust, shape, figure. قالب بي جان *kālabi bī jān*, A body without a soul; a trunkless head.

A قالب *kālib*, Who or what turns or changes. Unripe dates reddening. Of a different colour from the mother (a sheep). (pl. قوالب *kawālib*) A form, mould, model: a last on which shoes are made.

A قالبي *kālibiy*, Cast in a mould, moulded.

A قالة *kālat*, A saying, speech, talk (generally in a bad light, قول *kawl* implying a good sense). Fluency of speech. (pl. of قائل *kāʾil*) Speakers.

A قالس *kālis*, Vomiting. Throwing away.

P قالش *kālish*, A friend, fellow-student.

A قالص *kālis*, Increasing (water in a well). Contracted (shadow), shrivelled (lip).

A قالع *kāliʿ*, One who plucks up, a puller or a stripper off. A patch of white hairs under the saddle (considered a blemish in a horse).

A قالم *kālim*, (pl. قلمة *kalamat*) Unmarried man.

A قال مقال *kāl makāl*, Altercation, wrangling.

P قالنجه *kālinja*, A magpie.

P قالوس *kālūs*, Name of a note in music.

P قالون *kālūn*, Good. Beautiful. Name of a fabulous island, of which marvellous things are related.

P قالي *kālī*, A costly kind of carpet.

A قالي *kālī*, A cook. One who hates, a hater.

P قاليچه *kālīcha*, A small carpet.

T قاليون *kālyūn*, A kind of pipe for smoking through water.

A قامة *kāmat*, (v. n. of قام for قوم) Standing, stopping. Being tired (a horse). Beginning. Rising. Being set over any business, attending to it. Being moderate, middling. Being thronged, brisk (a market). Giving pain. Freezing (water). Being worth (ten dīnars). (pl. قامات *kāmāt*) Stature, shape, form, figure, body. A measure of six feet, a fathom. (pl. قيم *kiyam*) A pulley, with its apparatus, for drawing water.

A قامح *kāmih*, (pl. قمّح *kummah*) Raising the head, refusing to drink (a camel). Languid from intense thirst (a camel).

A قامر *kāmir*, A gamester.

A قامع *kāmiʿ*, Large-kneed or large-houghed (horse). A subduer, conqueror. One who tears up.

A قاموس *kāmūs*, The main ocean, the middle or deepest part of the sea. Name of an Arabic lexicon, compiled by Fīrozabādī, who lived in the fourteenth century, cotemporary with Tamerlane; who made him a present of 5000 ducats, as a reward for his industry and learning. This dictionary was translated into Latin by Giggeus, and published at Milan, A.D. 1632.

A قامه *kāmih*, (pl. قمّه *kummah*) (A he-camel) which raises the head. Travelling well (a camel).

P قان *kān*, A title of the emperor of China.

A قان *kān*, A tree from which bows are made.

A قانب *kānib*, A howling wolf. Quick, rapid (diffusion of odour or flow of blood).

A قانت *kānit*, Godly, devout, prayerful.

A قانز *kāniz*, A hunter.

A قانسة *kānisat*, The gizzard or entrails of a bird.

A قانص *kānis*, A hunter.

A قانصة *kānisat*, (pl. قوانص *kawānis*) The crop of a bird. The intestine of a bird.

A قانط *kānit*, Desperate, despairing.

A قانع *kāniʿ*, Contented, satisfied with one's lot. One who makes humble request, an abject suppliant. One who moves from place to place.

A قانم *kānim*, Rotten (walnut).

A P قانون *kānūn*, (pl. قوانين *kawānīn*) A species of dulcimer, harp, or sackbut; the strings of which, from fifty to sixty in number, rest upon two bridges, and are touched with both hands, without making use of any kind of plectrum or bow. A psaltery with catgut strings. A canon, rule, regulation, form, mode, manner, law, usage, custom, constitution, statute, ordinance. A قانون شفا *kānūni shifā*, Rules for health (the title of a book).

P قانون كردن *kānūn kardan*, To make a law, to lay down a rule, to introduce a custom.

P قانونچه *kānūncha*, Name of a treatise on medicine. A certain musical instrument.

P قانون‌دان *kānūn-dān*, Conversant with business.

P قانون گو *kānūn-gū* or *go*, An officer whose duty is to register and expound the laws of the empire. An officer in each district acquainted with the customs, the nature of the tenures of the land.

P قانونگوئی *kānūn-goʼī* or *gūʼī*, Office of kānūn-go.

P قانون نامه *kānūn-nāma*, Book of canons or laws.

P قانون نويس *kānūn-navis*, Writer of institutes.

A قانوني *kānūniy*, Regular, canonical.

A قاني *kānī*, (or قانئ *kāniʼ*) Very rosy. Of a beautiful full red or scarlet colour. احمر قانئ *ahmar kāniʼ*, Intense red.

P قاورد *kāward*, A sort of sweetmeat.

P قاوند *kāwand*, A kind of congealed fat.

A قاوي *kāwī*, Taking; a taker.

A قاوية *kāwiyat*, An egg. Name of a flower or kitchen-garden. (A year) of little rain.

P قاويل *kāwīl*, Name of a northern nation.

A قاه *kāh*, Obedience. Dignity. Power. Quickness in despatching victuals set before one. Easy and comfortable (life).

A قاهر *kāhir*, Who or what subdues or triumphs. A conqueror. Violent, forcible, oppressive. P قاهر الزهر *kāhiru'r zahr*, An antidote to poison.

A قاهرة *kāhirat*, A conqueress, victrix, Augusta. The fleshy part between the neck and shoulder. The breast, bosom. Haste, expedition. Beginning of any thing. القاهرة *al kāhira*, (The victorious) Al Cairo, or Grand Cairo, the metropolis of Egypt. دولت قاهره *dawlati kāhira*, The conquering dynasty, *i.e.* the Arabian califat; also the Turkish power.

P قاه قاه *kāh kāh*, A horse-laugh.

A قاهي *kāhī*, A man in easy and prosperous circumstances. Quick, sharp, intelligent.

A قاهيّ *kāhiy*, Affluent.

P قاي *kāy*, Name of a place.

A قأي *kaʼy*, (v. n. of قأي) Confessing, acknowledging, telling the truth.

A قائب *kāʼib*, Absent.

A قائبة *kāʼibat*, An egg. A cock. A chicken.

A قائت *kāʼit*, Subsistence, competency. A lion.

A قائد *kāʼid*, (pl. قوّد *kūwad*, قوّاد *kūwād*, and قادة *kādat*) A leader, general, governor, president. A leader of horses. The greatest of the فلجان *fuljān* of the ploughman. A prominent part of a mountain. A long tract of country, or a depressed mountain. القائد *al kāʼid*, The last star in the tail of the Lesser Bear. قائد الجيش *kāʼidu'l jaysh*, The general of an army.

A قائدة *kāʼidat*, A hillock or bank reaching far.

A قائف *kāʼif*, (pl. قافة *kāfat*) Skilful in tracking, knowing footsteps.

A قائل *kāʼil*, (pl. قوّل *kūwal*, قيّل *kuyyal*, قالة *kālat*, and قوول *kuwūl*) A speaker, spokesman. One who asserts or professes a belief, or stoutly maintains an opinion. The author of a verse. (pl. قيل *kayl*, قيّل *kuyyal*, and قيّال *kuyyāl*) One who sleeps at mid-day.

A قائلاً *kāʼilan*, Saying.

A قائلة *kāʼilat*, (v. n. of قال for قيل) Sleeping at noon. Noon. A nap at noon.

A قائم *kāʼim*, (pl. قوم *kūwam*, قيّم *kuyyam*, قوّام *kūwām*, and قيّام *kuyyām*) Standing. Erect, perpendicular. Firm, fixed, durable, perpetual, constant, stedfast. Vigilant, attentive. Stopped, drawn (game). The hilt of a sword. Name of a building in Surr man ray. P قائم پنجم آسمان *kāʼimi panjum āsmān*, The planet Mars. قائم ريختن *kāʼim rekhtan*, To be feeble, to decline a contest. A قائم الصبح *kāʼimu's subh*, Early in the morning. قائم مقام *kāʼim makām*, A lieutenant, vicegerent, the Kaimacām, or governor of Constantinople. A vicar, administrator, overseer. قائم النار *kāʼimu'n nār*, Standing the fire, uninjured by fire.

P قائم انداز *kāʼim-andāz*, An expert player at chess. Weak, feeble.

A قائمة *kāʼimat*, Erect, perpendicular. A perpendicular line. A right angle. Sightless (eye), but whose pupil appears perfect and unblemished. (pl. قوائم *kawāʼim*) Foot of a quadruped. Hilt of a sword. An hour. Leaf of a book.

A قائم مزاج *kāʼim mizāj*, Of a settled temper, fixed. Resolute, persevering.

A قائم مزاجي *kāʼim-mizājī*, Fixedness, firmness. Resolution.

A قائن *kāʼin*, Cain.

A قب *kab*, The sound of a sword falling upon any object.

A قبّ *kabb*, (v. n. of قبّ) Cutting off (the hand). Withering (a plant). Being heard (the grinding of the teeth of a lion or stallion). A king, general, chief, lieutenant. The axle, also the axle-hole of a pulley. The interstice between the hips. A man of a noble race. The cross-beam of a pulley. A gore, side, breast, or collar of a shirt, or other garment. A stallion of a good breed, and skilful at covering. A strong, hard bridle. *Kibb*, The rump-bone. A governor, chief, leader. *Kubb*, (pl. of اقبّ *akabb*) Gaunt-bellied (horses).

A قبء *kabʼ*, (v. n. of قبأ) Eating. Being filled with drink.

P قبا *kabā*, A garment; a short tunic open before. A close long gown worn by men. قبا تنگ شدن *kabā tang shudan*, To be weak, feeble, or poorly off. قبا كردن *kabā kardan*, To tear up a shirt. قباي آهنين *kabāyi āhanīn*, A coat of mail.

قباي زربفت *kabāyi zar-baft*, The sky on a dark night without a cloud. قباي كحلي *kabāyi kuhlī*, Sky. قباي معلم *kabāyi muʼlam*, The lunar sphere.

A قبا *kuba'*, A sort of plant. A demolishing.

A قباء *kabāʼ*, (pl. اقبية *akbiyat*) A vesture, garment. قباء قوسين *kibāʼu kawsayni*, Two bows' length. Two cubits' length.

A قبّاء *kabbāʼ*, (pl. قبّ *kubb*) (A woman) slender round the middle.

A قباب *kibāb*, A sort of fish. (pl. of قبّة *kubbat*) Towers, vaults, cupolas. *Kubāb*, Sharp (sword). Large (nose). Name of a fortress in Madīna.

A قبّاب *kabbāb*, A lion.

A قباءة *kabaʼat*, (or قباءة) Grass, pasturage.

A قباتر *kubātir*, Short, dwarfish: a dwarf.

A قباثر *kubāsir*, Vile, mean, base, abject. Obscure, unknown.

P قباچاي *kabāchāy*, (or قباچه) A little tunic.

A قباح *kabāh*, The joint of the knee and thigh. *Kibāh*, (pl. of قبيح *kabīh*) Hideous, shameful, ugly. *Kubāh*, (v. n. of قبح) Being ugly, foul, offensive.

A قبّاح *kubbāh*, A bear.

A قباحة *kabāhat*, (v. n. of قبح) Being base, ugly, shameful. Ugliness. Villainy, baseness, dishonesty. Evil, ill. Inconvenience. Crime, fault, rascality.

A قباحى *kabāha'*, (pl. of قبيح) Shameful, ugly.

P قباد *kubād*, Name of a king of Persia and father of Noshīrawān. A kind of thorny shrub of which camels are fond.

A قباذ *kubāz*, The father of كسري *kisra'*.

A قباذية *kubāziyat*, Old, spoilt, damaged (wheat).

A قبّار *kubbār*, Name of a place in Mecca. A company collected together to draw the game from out of the nets. A hunter's lantern.

P قباس *kubās*, The sun.

A قباسة *kabāsat*, (v. n. of قبس) Covering quickly, impregnating at once (a camel).

A قبّاض *kabbāz*, A fast driver. A taker, seizer.

A قباضة *kabāzat*, Quickness, expedition, swiftness.

A قبّاضة *kabbāzat*, One who drives fast.

A قبّاط *kubbāt*, White sweetmeats.

A قباطيّ *kabātiy*, (or قباطي *kabātī*) (pl. of قبطيّ *kibtiy*) Copts, Egyptians.

A قباع *kibāʼ*, (v. n. of قبع) Grunting (as swine). A large measure. *Kubāʼ*, A foolish man. A hedgehog. A large corn-measure used at Basra. The rough tripe. An ample woman. A wide mirror. Name of حارث *hāris*, governor of Basra.

A قبّاع *kabbāʼ*, A timorous, cowardly pig.

A قباعث *kabāʼis*, (pl. of قبعثري *kabaʼsara'*) Large and strong.

A قباعيّ *kubāʼiy*, Large-headed (man).

A قباقب *kubākib*, The third year from the present, exclusive. A cruel, savage, unfeeling man. A great talker, a doter. انّك لن تفلح العام ولا قابل ولا قابّ ولا قباقب ولا مقبقب *innaka lantuflihaʼl ʼāma, wa lā kābila, wa lā kābba, wa lā kubākiba, wa lā mukabkiba*, Verily thou wilt not succeed this year, nor the next, nor the ensuing, nor the one after it, nor the next to that.

A قبال *kibāl*, A strap which passes between the toes and fastens the sandal to the foot. قصيري قبال *husayra' kibālin*, A deadly sort of viper.

A قبالة *kabālat*, (v. n. of قبل) Being surety for another. Management of an affair. Deputyship. Suretiship. *Kibālat*, (v. n. of قبل) Bringing a woman to bed, acting as midwife. Midwifery. Being surety for another. Deputyship. *Kubālata*, Opposite, over against. جلست قبالته *jalastu kubālatahu*, I sat opposite to him.

P قباله *kabāla* or *kubāla*, Any contract, especially of bargain and sale, signed by a judge. A grant. A deed, writing, written agreement. Bail, bond. Title-deeds.

P قباله نويس *kabāla-navis*, A conveyancer.

A قبان *kabān*, Scales or steelyard.

A قبّان *kabbān*, A pair of scales. Faithful, trusty. حمار قبّان *himār kabbān*, (or عير قبّان *ʿayr kabbān*) An oval insect of the locust kind, with six feet and a target-back, bred in moist places: a scarabæus.

P قبا نمد *kabā-namad*, A coarse, rain-tight cloak.

P قباه *kabāh*, A garment.

A قباية *kabāyat*, An even plain, a desert.

A قبائح *kabāʾih*, (pl. of قبيحة *kabihat*) Crimes, shameful thoughts, words, or deeds, turpitudes.

A قبائر *kabāʾir*, (pl. of قبراء *kubrāʾ*) Larks.

A قبائل *kabāʾil*, (pl. of قبيلة *kabilat*) Tribes.

A قبب *kabab*, Slenderness, slimness of waist. *Kubab*, (pl. of قبّة *kubbat*) Cupolas, domes, arches.

A قبة *kibat*, The rough tripe of a sheep.

A قبّة *kibbat*, Rough tripe of sheep. *Kubbat*, (pl. قباب *kibāb* and قبب *kubab*) A cupola, vault, dome, arch, alcove. A turret. A cathedral church, duomo. A tent, tabernacle. A parasol. قبّة الاسلام *kubbatu'l islām*, Basra. قبّة الزمان *kubbatu'z zamān*, The tabernacle of the covenant.

A قبتر *kubtur*, Short, dwarfish: a dwarf.

A قبتور *kubtūr*, Name of an island in the West.

A قبث *kabs*, (v. n. of قبث) Taking, seizing, grasping, clutching.

A قبثر *kabsar*, Vile, mean, base: obscure, unknown.

A قبج *kabj*, (or قبجة *kabjat*, P كبك) A partridge.

P قبچاق *kibchāk*, Name of a desert in Tartary.

A قبح *kubh* or *kabh*, (v. n. of قبح) Being shameful or ugly. Ugliness, foulness, shamefulness. قبحاً له *kubhan lahu*, May God keep him from all good!

A قبحى *kabha'*, (pl. of قبيح *kabīh*) Ugly, hideous.

A قبر *kabr*, (v. n. of قبر) Burying. (pl. قبور *kubūr*) A grave, sepulchre, tomb, monument. P قبر كوهانى *kabri kohānī*, A grave raised in the middle like a camel's back. A *Kibr*, A worm-eaten place in aloe-wood. *Kubar*, A delicious sort of grape long and white. *Kubar* or *kubbar*, A lark.

A قبراء *kubrāʾ*, (pl. قبائر *kabāʾir*) A lark.

A قبراة *kibirrāt*, Glans penis.

A قبّرة *kubbarat*, A single lark.

A قبرشع *kabarsaʿ*, A skilful manager of camels.

A قبرس *kubrus*, Cyprus. The finest Cyprus brass.

P قبرستان *kabristān*, A cemetery, graveyard.

A قبرسلامى *kabr-salāmī*, A consideration or dues paid to the zamīndār by the Muhammadans for his allowing them to dig a grave for their deceased relations (an Indian phrase).

A قبرسىّ *kubrusiy*, A Cypriot.

P قبركن *kabr-kan*, A grave-digger.

P قبرگاه *kabr-gāh*, A burying-ground.

A قبرّى *kibirra'*, A nose. Large-nosed.

A قبز *kibz*, Short. Avaricious.

A قبس *kabs*, (v. n. of قبس) Lighting or obtaining (fire) from another. Acquiring learning. Deriving knowledge. *Kibs*, Root, origin. *Kubas*, (v. n. of قبس) Being quick, expeditious (a stallion camel). A portion of fire, firebrand for kindling a fire. *Kabis*, A quick and sure foal-getter.

A قبشور *kubshūr*, Not menstruous (woman).

A قبص *kabs*, (v. n. of قبص) Taking up (any thing) with the tips of the fingers. Making (any one) break off drinking before his thirst is quenched. Mounting the female (a stallion). Running a string into one's trousers and drawing it. Being brisk, spirited, and striking the ground with the fore-edge of his feet (a horse). *Kibs*, A great multitude of men. Root, origin. *Kibs* or *kabs*, A great heap of sand. *Kabas*, (v. n. of قبص) Being brisk, spirited (horse). Being closed up (the womb of a camel). Alighting on a tree in a swarm (locusts). Being long and large (the head, or the crown of the head). Being joyful. Having a pain in the liver (caused by eating dates fasting). The pain itself. Lightness, briskness. A projection or excrescence on the crown of the head. *Kabis*, Brisk, sprightly. Slack (rope).

A قبصاء *kabsāʾ*, Thick and lofty (mountain-top). هامة قبصاء *hāmat kabsāʾ*, A head thick and high.

A قبصة *kabsat*, A locust. *Kabsat* or *kubsat*, Whatever can be taken with the tip of the fingers. As much wheat as can be taken in the two hands.

A قبصّى *kibissa'*, Hard running.

A قبض *kabaza*, (fut. يقبض *yakbizu*) He clutched.

A قبض *kabz*, (v. n. of قبض) Taking, seizing, arresting, grasping, griping, clutching. Refraining, withholding one's hand from taking hold of. Flying or walking swiftly. Contracting, drawing in. Driving (camels) fast. Dying. Capture, sequestration, confiscation. Possession. Constipation, astringency. Contraction (of the wings). Swiftness. Agitation. Compulsion. Power. A receipt, voucher. قبض خاطر *kabzi khātir*, Contraction of mind. قبض الوصول *kabzu'l wusūl*, A receipt, discharge, acknowledgment. *Kabaz*, Grasped, clutched. Tribute, tax, whatsoever is exacted from the people.

A قبّض *kubbaz*, An animal resembling a tortoise.

A قبضة *kabzat*, Power. Grasp. The gripe of a sword; a hilt, handle. Seized, grasped, clutched. *Kabzat* or *kubzat*, A handful. A grasp, gripe. *Kubazat*, A shepherd who skilfully manages his flock. *Kubazat*, (or قبضة رفضة *kubazatun rufazatun*) (A man) suddenly snatching and immediately dropping any thing, playing fast and loose.

A قبضّى *kibizza'*, A mode of running or leaping.

A قبضية *kabziyat*, Seizure. Costiveness.

A قبط *kabt*, (v. n. of قبط) Gathering together, and holding with the hand. *Kibt*, Egypt. Copts.

A القبطريّة *al kubturiyat*, White linen cloth.

A قبطىّ *kibtiy*, (pl. قباطىّ *kabātiy* or قباطى *kabāti*) Egyptian. *Kubtiy* or *kibtiy*, Fine linen of Egypt. Coptic.

A قبطيّة *kibtiyat*, Egyptian (woman). مارية القبطيّة *māriyatu'l kibtiyat*, Mary the Copt.

A قبع *kabʿ*, (v. n. of قبع) Lowering the head in worship. Turning inwards the mouth of a leather bottle, or putting the corner to one's mouth and drinking. Grunting (a hog). Breathing hard, puffing and blowing. Sound, noise; the cry of an elephant. *Kubaʿ*, A brazen trumpet. *Kubaʿ*, A hedgehog. A certain marine animal.

A قبعة *kubaʿat*, A woman now peeping out and then withdrawing herself. القبعة *al kubaʿat*, A bird smaller than a sparrow, which shrinks its head into its neck when frightened. يا ابن قبعة *yā ibna kubaʿat*, O thou stupid fellow!

A قبّعة *kubbaʿat*, A garment like the برنس *burnus*.

A قبعثاة *kabaʿsāt*, A female rupture.

A قبعثر *kabaʿsar*, Great in size, large, bulky (man).

A قبعثرى *kabaʿsura'*, (pl. قباعث *kabāʿis*) Great, large, strong. A large camel. An emaciated weanel. A certain marine animal.

A قبعثى *kabaʿsa'*, (fem. قبعثاة *kabaʿsāt*) Large-footed (man or camel).

A قبعرور *kabaʿrūr*, A kind of a bad date.

A قبعلة *kubʿalat*, The projection of one foot beyond another. Distance of heels. A weak step, such as ploughs up the dust.

A قبقاب *kabkāb*, Loud-roaring (lion). Murmuring or braying (camel). The grinding of the teeth of a stallion camel. Vulva. A lake or cistern full of water. A wooden shoe, clog, patten. A great liar. A shell, or any thing similar, with which they glaze cloth. A great talker, raver, doter.

A قبقب *kabkab*, The belly. *Kibkib*, A species of sea-shell.

A قبقبة *kabkabat*, (v. n. of قبقب Q) Making a rumbling noise in the belly (a horse). Gnashing with the teeth. Roaring (a lion). Being insane.

P قبك كتك وقبك گرگ قبك كتك وقبك گرگ *kabk kath, u kabk gurg, kabk kath, u kabkgurg*, Behold, a stranger comes!

P قبك آب *kubki āb*, Duck-weed.

A قبل *kabl*, (v. n. of قبل) Putting the thongs

قبال *kibāl* to a sandal. Tying this thong. Blowing from the east (wind). Looking to the tip of one's nose. The fore part, front, face. A siege, blockade. Before. P قبل كردن *kabl kardan*, To besiege. A قبل الامس *kabla'l ams*, The day before yesterday. قبل ان *kabla an*, Before that. قبل الدخول *kabla'd dukhūl*, Before entering or arriving. قبل الزمان *kabla'z zamān*, Before the time. قبل الصبح *kabla's subh*, Before dawn. قبل وصول المجاهدين *kabla wusūli'l mujāhidīn*, Before the arrival of the soldiers of the faith, *i.e.* Muhammadans. قبله *kablahu*, Before that. قبل هذا *kabla hāzā*, A little before, not long since. قبل *kablu*, قبلا *kablan*, and من قبل *min kabli*, Formerly, before all, in the fore part. Heretofore. *Kubl*, Aim, design, intent, purpose. (pl. of اقبل *akbal* and قبلاء *kablās*) Those who have the pupil of the eye directed to the tip of the nose. *Kubl* or *kubul*, The fore part. Pudenda(viri vel fœminæ). Commencement(of time). The foot (of a mountain). بقبل الهدف *bi kubli'l hadaf*, Forward, before the mark. في قبل *fī kubli*, In the beginning (of winter). من قبل *min kubuli*, In front (Joseph's shirt was torn). *Kabal*, (v. n. of قبل) Looking to the tip of one's nose. Having the toes turned inward; or the horns of a sheep bent over the face. Coming on (night). Drinking water (camels), which is suddenly thrown over their heads. Speaking extempore. Having a first sight of the new moon. A squinting inwards. Gentleness and lightness of manipulation of a midwife in extracting a child. An open highway. Any thing seen for the first time. A shell or bead used for incantation. A piece of polished ivory hung to the neck of a woman or horse. The top of a hill or sand tumulus; also that part of any rising ground which is opposite to us. (pl. of قبلة *kabalat*) Whirls upon spindles. *Kibal*, Power. Plenty. A part, side. Presence. With, in (my) possession. P در قبل عزت دوستم محمد *dar kibali ɛizzati dostam muhammad*, To the presence of my glorious friend Muhammad (a mode of addressing letters). A من قبل *min kibali*, In respect of, aside, apart. من قبل انفه *min kibali anfihi*, (He speaks) through his nose. *Kubul*, (pl. of قبيل *kabīl*) Tribes.

A قبلاً *kabalan*, Extempore, unpremeditated. Never before seen. *Kabalan, kubulan, kubalan*, or *kibalan*, For the first time. Before, in my presence or sight. *Kubulan*, By troops of different nations. Before the eyes.

A قبلاء *kablās*, (fem. of اقبل *akbal*) (A woman) whose eye looks to the tip of her nose, squinting inwardly. (A sheep) whose horn is bent over the face.

A قبلة *kablat*, A small shell or bead used for purposes of fascination, or to avert the influence of malignant eyes. *Kiblat*, Any thing opposite. That part to which people direct their faces in prayer; (especially Mecca, towards the Kaaba, or temple, of which city the Muhammadans, in whatever quarter of the world they are, turn themselves when going to pray). The tomb of Muhammad at Madīna. An altar, temple. Worship. Side, part. Mode, manner. A father. P قبلهٔ جمشيد *kiblasi jamshed*, The cup or mirror of Jam; which, according to the Eastern fabulists, represented the whole world. Fire. The sun. Red wine. قبلهٔ دهقان *kiblasi dihkān*, (or قبلهٔ زردشتيان *kiblasi zardushtiyān*) Fire. A قبلهٔ عالم *kiblasi ɛālam*, (Kibla of the world) A title which some Eastern princes have given themselves. قبلهٔ كونين *kiblasi kawnayn*, The kibla of both worlds, applied to a father. *Kublat*, A kiss. A philtre, by which witches pretended to reconcile enemies. A mark on a sheep's ear. Bail, surety. The thread which is drawn forward whilst sewing. P قبله دادن *kubla dādan*, To kiss. A *Kabalat*, (pl. قبل *kabal*) A spindle; likewise the whirl used in spinning with a distaff. A small shell or bead, with which enchanters pretend to fascinate people, whilst they pronounce the words يا قبلة اقبليه *yā kabalatu akbilīhi*, O shell go to him (these shells they also hang round the necks of cattle to defend them from fascination). The cabalistic art, dealing in any thing mysterious or supernatural. A cough, hoarseness. A heap of sand.

A قبلتين *kiblatayn*, (oblique dual of قبلة *kiblat*) The two Kiblas, *i.e.* Mecca and Jerusalem (the latter having not only been the Christian Kibla, but also originally that of the Muhammadans; till their prophet, to conciliate the good-will of his fellow-citizens, changed it to Mecca in the second year of the Hijra).

A قبلش *kaballash*, Glans penis.

P قبله گاه *kibla-gāh*, Any place towards which one looks during prayer (Daniel vi. 10). قبله گاه مجوس *kibla-gāhi majūs*, Fire.

P قبله نامه *kibla-nāma*, A mariner's compass; also قبله نما *kibla-namā*, (Showing a place) a machine, directing the Muhammadans, at a distance from Mecca, to that point where the Kibla stands.

A قبليّ *kibliy*, Southern.

A قبليًّا *kabiliyan*, Before, in my presence or sight.

A قبنة *kubnat*, Expedition in necessary affairs.

A قبنجر *kabanjar*, Large-bellied.

A قبو *kabw*, (v. n. of قبا for قبو) Collecting in the fingers. Raising (an edifice). Gathering (saffron).

A قبوب *kubūb*, (v. n. of قبّ) Drying up or losing its moisture (meat, a skin, a wound, or a date). Brawling, squabbling aloud (people).

A قبوة *kabwat*, A contracting of the lips.

A قبوح *kubūh*, (and قبوحة *kubūhat*) (v. n. of قبح) Being deformed, ugly, foul. Ugliness.

A قبور *kabūr*, Low and soft (ground). A palm-tree which bears quickly: or one whose fruit is on the branch. *Kubūr*, (pl. of قبر *kabr*) Tombs, graves. اصحاب قبور *as-hābi kubūr*, The dead, the buried.

A قبوص *kabūs*, Firm, strong, swift, or mettlesome (horse). A horse that strikes the ground with only the fore-edge of his hoofs.

A قبوع *kubūɛ*, (v. n. of قبع) Hanging or hiding his head in his garment (a man); rolling itself up (a hedgehog). Travelling. Grunting (swine). Breathing hard. Remaining behind one's companions.

A قبول *kabūl*, (v. n. of قبل) Receiving favourably, taking well, consenting, granting. Blowing from the east (wind). Submitting to. Coming, approaching. Receiving the bucket from the water-drawer. Sticking, cleaving to. Beginning. Wind blowing from the east. A midwife. Beauty. Ornament. Garb, dress. Consent, compliance, a favourable reception, concession, approbation, assent. Approved, consented. Tolerated. P قبول افتادن *kabūl uftādan*, To prove acceptable. قبول كردن *kabūl kardan*, To agree, consent, accept, approve, submit to. A ذو قبول *zū kabūl*, Capable of receiving. قرين قبول *karīni kabūl*, Acceptable, agreeable. عليك قبول *ɛalayka kabūl*, Is it agreeable to you? *Kubūl*, (v. n. of قبل) Approaching, coming. Blowing from the east (wind). Taking, receiving, accepting. Receiving a bucket from the water-drawer. Beauty. Ornament. Garb, dress.

A قبولي *kabūlī*, Acceptable. A kind of food, rice and pulse boiled together.

A قبوليّ *kabūliy*, Belonging to, fanned by, or exposed to the morning breeze (قبول *kabūl*).

A قبوليّة *kabūliyat*, A receipt, acceptance. An agreement in writing. A counter agreement.

A قبون *kubūn*, (v. n. of قبن) Travelling.

P قبّه *kubba*, A vault, arch. A dome, cupola. A cupping-horn. قبّهٔ آب *kubbasi āb*, A bubble of water. قبّهٔ زبرجدي *kubbasi zabarjadī* (or مينا *mīnā*), The azure vault. قبّهٔ زربفت *kubbasi zarbaft*, A starlight night. قبّهٔ زرين *kubbasi zarīn*, The sun. The dawn. قبّهٔ عليا *kubbasi ɛulyā*, (or قبّهٔ گردنده *kubbasi gardanda*) The firmament. قبّهٔ فلك *kubbasi falak*, The ninth heaven.

P قبّه دار *kubba-dār*, (or قبّه وار *kubbawār*) Convex.

A قبّي *kubbiy*, One who fasts till his flanks shrink.

A قبيب *kabīb*, (v. n. of قبّ) Being heard (the grinding of the teeth of a horse or a lion). Making a grating noise (teeth). The preparation of milk called اقط *akit* mixed in its moist and dry state.

A قبيح *kabīh*, (pl. قباح *kibāh*, قباحى *kabāhā'*, قبحى *kabhā'*) Deformed, ugly. Shameful, vile, detestable, bad. قبيح المنظر *kabīhu'l manzar*, Of a hideous appearance. القبيح *al kabīh*, Tip of the elbow. Joint of the knee or thigh.

A قبيحة *kabīhat*, (pl. قبائح *kabāɛih* or قباح *kibāh*) A foul, shameful, unworthy act. قبيحة الشخب *kabīhatu'sh shukhb*, A camel with wide teat-holes.

A قبيرة *kubayrat*, (dim. of قبّراة *kibirrāt*) Small glands or nuts of yards.

A قبيس *kabīs*, (A camel) soon impregnating.

Kubays, in composition with ابو *abū*: as, ابو قبيس *abū kubays*, Name of a mountain near Mecca.

A قبيصة *kabīsat*, Any thing taken up with the tips of the fingers. Earth heaped up. Gravel, pebbles, small stones. Name of an Arab who refused to surrender to the mighty hunter Bahrām Gūr a gazel which had sought refuge in his tent; whence he was styled مجير الغزلان *mujīru'l ghizlān*.

A قبيض *kabīz*, Rapid, hasty, expeditious. Skilful in one's profession. قبيض الشد *kabīzu'sh shadd*, Moving the feet nimbly.

A قبيط *kubbayt*, (قبيطي *kubbayta'*, or قبيطاء *kubaytā͗*) A white sweetmeat.

A قبيعة *kabīʿat*, The pommel of a sword, of silver or of iron. The nostril of a pig.

A قبيعة *kibbīʿat*, The nostril of a hog.

A قبي قوسين *kabyu kawsayn*, Two bows' length: two cubits' length.

A قبيل *kabīl*, A midwife. Capable. A thread drawn forward in spinning. A surety, bail. A second in command. Obedience (opposed to دبير *dabīr*, which implies disobedience). A winning arrow at games of hazard. The lobe of the ear. Cotton. (pl. قبل *kubul*) A crowd of different nations; also of one tribe, or any miscellaneous multitude. A spouse, a husband or wife. A proper name.

A قبيلاً *kabīlan*, Before, in my presence or sight. *Kubaylan*, A little before.

A قبيلة *kabīlat*, (pl. قبائل *kabā͗il*) Tribe, family, house, kindred, parentage, race, line, stock, generation, progeny. The various parts of the skull united together. The thong of a bridle. A stone on the mouth or front of a well. عن قبيلة *ʿan kabīlatin*, By their tribes.

A قبين *kabīn*, Swift, active in business.

T قپان *kuppān*, A large pair of scales; or rather, a scale at one end and a heavy stone at the other.

P قپچاق *kipchāk*, (or دشت قپچاق *dashti kipchāk*) The Precop or Kipjāk Tartars. Many Persian words have been borrowed from the language of those people.

P قت *kut*, Trefoil, clover, hay.

A قتّ *katt*, (v. n. of قتّ) Slandering, whispering, calumniating. Cutting into strips or thongs. Diminishing, lessening. Following another clandestinely. Following footsteps. Collecting by little and little. Directing properly. Preparing, fitting, adjusting, amending. Smelling the urine of a diseased camel (a keeper). Perfuming (oil) by putting (it) amongst flowers. Detraction, slander, lying. Clover, Burgundian hay.

A قتا *kata'*, *kita'*, or *kuta'*, (v. n. of قتا for قتو) Serving well (a domestic). Serving a king.

A قتات *kattāt*, A spy, scout. A listener, eavesdropper, tale-bearer. A slanderer, sycophant.

A قتاد *katād*, (pl. اقتاد *aktād*, اقتد *aktud*, and قتود *kutūd*) A thorny tree, called the tragacanth; hence, خرط القتاد *khartu'l katād*, The stripping of this tree with the hand is an expression employed to denote a thorny, troublesome business.

A قتادي *katāda'*, Griped from eating this tree.

A قتادية *katādiyat*, (Camels) feeding on the tree قتاد *katād*.

A قتار *kutār*, The smell of meat roasting, of a boiling cauldron, or of a burning bone. Perfume, odour (of wood of aloes, &c.). Soot of a kettle.

A قتال *katāl*, The soul. Remains of life. Strength. The body. ذات قتال *zāti katāl*, Compact (she-camel). *Kitāl*, (v. n. 3 of قتل) Fighting for. Opposing, fighting. Battle, conflict, combat, engagement. Slaughter, carnage. قتال البحر *kitālu'l bahr*, A sea-fight, a naval engagement.

A قتّال *kattāl*, A killer, slayer, murderer. Deadly (poison). *Kuttāl*, (pl. of قاتل *kātil*) Murderers.

A قتّالة *kattālat*, Very destructive and deadly.

A قتام *katām*, Black dust.

A قتان *katān* or *kutān*, Dust.

A قتانة *katānat*, (v. n. of قتن) Having little meat. Being a little eater.

A قتائد *kutā͗id*, The declivity of a mountain.

A قتب *katb*, (v. n. of قتب) Feeding with roasted intestines. Putting the saddle-cloth or saddle قتب *kitb* upon a beast. *Kitb*, The bowels. A saddle-cloth (to imbibe the sweat) laid under a pack-saddle. A small saddle-cloth of the size of a camel's bunch. All the furniture of a she-camel employed in carrying water for purposes of irrigation. A roundness of belly. *Katab*, (pl. اقتاب *aktāb*) A small saddle for a camel's bunch. A pack-saddle, particularly a small one. *Katib*, Peevish, touchy.

A قتبة *kitbat*, One intestine, a bowel.

A قتبي *kutabīy*, Of the tribe of قتيبة *kutaybat*.

A قتد *katad*, (v. n. of قتد) Eating of the thorny tree قتاد *katād*, and being griped (a camel). (pl. اقتاد *aktād* or قتود) The timber of a camel's saddle.

A قتدة *katidat*, Camels griped with قتاد *katād*.

A قتر *katr*, (v. n. of قتر) Sending forth a scent (a boiling pot, meat roasting, or a burning bone). Being parsimonious (in housekeeping); half-starving (one's domestics). Joining one thing to another. Driving the nails قتير *katīr* into a coat of mail. Sticking close to a thing. Short commons, a bare sustenance. *Katr* or *katar* (equiv. to قدر *kadr*). *Kitr*, The small head of a kind of arrow (or the reed itself), used in shooting at marks. *Kutr* or *kutur*, (pl. اقتار *aktār*) A tract, side, or quarter (especially of the heavens). *Katar*, Dust. *Katir*, Proud, haughty, arrogant, lofty. *Kutar*, (pl. of قترة *kutrat*) Hunters' lurking-places.

P قتر *katir*, A mule.

A قترة *kitrat*, or ابو قترة *abū kitrat*, The devil. ابن قترة *ibn kitrat*, A small virulent serpent. *Kutrat*, A hunter's lurking-place. A heap of globular dung or gravel. *Katrat* or *katarat*, Dust.

A قتع *kitʿ*, A bee-hive in a cavern, but not deep. *Kataʿ*, A wood-louse or worm.

A قتعة *kataʿat*, Submissive, mean, abject, vile. A single wood-louse.

P قتق *katik*, Butter-milk or any thing acid put into broth.

A قتقتة *kathatat*, Detraction, whispering.

A قتل *katl*, (v. n. of قتل) Killing, slaying, slaughtering, murdering. Striking on the body. Diluting (wine) with water. Knowing for sure. Cursing. Slaughter, murder, death. قتل بالسبب *katl bi's sabab*, Homicide by an intermediate cause. قتل عام *katli ʿām*, A general massacre. قتل عمد *katl ʿamd*, Homicide by misadventure. قتل قائم مقام بخطا *katl kā͗im makām bi khutā*, Homicide of the same nature as that by misadventure. *Kitl*, (pl. اقتال *aktāl*) An enemy, adversary. A companion, equal, peer, associate, friend, cousin, kinsman. A strong intrepid man. A vital part, which being hurt death ensues. A horn. قتل شرّ *kitlu sharr*, One up to mischief. *Kutl* or *kutul*, (pl. of قتول *katūl*) Sanguinary, murderous.

A قتلان *kitlāni*, (dual of قتل *kitl*) A pair.

A قتلة *kitlat*, (v. n. of قتل) Killing. A mode of killing. قتلة سوء *kitlatu saw͗in*, An infamous murder, parricide. شرّ قتلة *sharr kitlat*, A cruel death. *Katalat*, (pl. of قاتل *kātil*) Slayers, murderers.

P قتلگاه *katl-gāh*, A place of execution. The seat of carnage.

A قتلى *katla'*, (pl. of قتيل *katīl* or قتيلة) Slain.

A قتلي *katlīy*, A murderer. Meriting death.

A قتمة *kutmat*, A dusty colour. A certain disgusting plant. *Katamat*, An offensive smell.

A قتن *katan*, A certain fish of a hand's breadth.

A قتو *katw*, (v. n. of قتا for قتو) Serving well (a domestic). Serving a king.

A قتوبة *katūbat*, Saddled with the small saddle قتب *katab* (she-camel).

A قتوة *katwat*, Detraction, slander, whispering.

A قتوت *katūt*, A spy, scout, listener, an eavesdropper, sycophant.

A قتود *kutūd*, (pl. of قتد *katad*) Timbers of camels' saddles. (pl. of قتاد *katād*) Tragacanth-trees.

A قتور *katūr*, Avaricious, parsimonious, stingy (to one's household). *Kutūr*, (v. n. of قتر) Being parsimonious in housekeeping. Emitting a flavour or effluvia (roast meat or a boiling pot), stinking (a burning bone).

A قتوع *kutūʿ*, A being mean, base, abject.

A قتول *katūl*, (pl. قتل *kutl* and *kutul*) Sanguinary, murderous.

A قتول *kitwall*, A stammerer, a stutterer. Relaxed, enervated.

A قتوم *kutūm*, (v. n. of قتم) Being raised (dust).

A قتون *kutūn*, (v. n. of قتن) Becoming dry (a fish).

A قتيبة *kutaybat*, (dim. of قتبة *kitbat*) A small intestine. Name of a tribe.

A قتّيتي *kittīta'*, Detraction; whispering. A spy, eaves-dropper, tale-bearer.

A قتير *katīr*, The heads of the nails used in fastening coats of mail. Hoariness; or the beginning of it.

A قتيرة *kutayrat*, Name of the father of a tribe.

A قتيل *katīl*, (pl. قتلى *katla'*) Killed, murdered (man or woman). قتيل الرعد *katīlu'r raȝd*, (Killed by thunder) a quail.

A قتيلة *katīlat*, (A woman) killed or beheaded.

A حياض قتيم *hiyāzu kutaymin*, Death: ruin.

A قتين *katīn*, (A man) who has little meat. The tike (an insect infesting sheep or camels). A man or woman (implying elegance; and baseness, or deformity). White dressed silk. A spear, or the point of it. A spear-head thin and old. A man who is a little eater.

A قثّ *kass*, (v. n. of قثّ) Driving into one body (cattle). Pulling up, tearing out. Drawing, dragging. A kind of plant.

A قثا *kasa'*, Eating a crisp thing (as cucumbers).

A قثاء *kisāȝ* or *kusāȝ*, A cucumber.

A قثّاء *kassāȝ*, A possessor of cucumbers. *Kissāȝ*, A cucumber. قثّاء الاصف *kissāȝu'l asaf*, Caper-cucumber. قثّاء الحمار *kissāȝu'lhimār*, Wild cucumber.

A قثاث *kusās*, Household furniture.

A قثّاث *kassās*, A spy, whisperer, sycophant.

A قثاثة *kasāsat*, A herd, flock, troop, body.

A قثارد *kasārid*, The tails or skirts of a shirt or garment. *Kusārid*, Household furniture. Rich in sheep or furniture.

A قثام *kasām*, The female hyena. Much spoil. A maid-servant; whence يا قثام *yā kasām*, (reproachfully) O sluttish!

A قثامة *kasāmat*, (v. n. of قثم) Being dusty.

A قثد *kasd*, (v. n. of قثد) Eating of the plant قثد *kasad*, which resembles a cucumber.

A قثرة *kasarat*, Household furniture.

A قثرد *kasrad*, Furniture which is not carried on a journey. Clippings of wool. *Kasrad*, *kisrid*, or *kusrud*, Household furniture. *Kasrad* or *kusarid*, Rich in furniture and sheep. *Kisrid*, Dry twigs and rubbish at the root of a vine. A multitude of men.

A قثع *kusȝ*, A cornet, trumpet.

A قثقثة *kashasat*, Fulness of measure. The shaking of a peg in order to draw it out.

A قثم *kasm*, (v. n. of قثم) Giving away a considerable part (of one's property). Collecting. Being dusty. A defiling with dung. *Kasam*, (v. n. of قثم) Being dirtied with dung. *Kusam*, Beneficent, liberal, generous, munificent. Assembling, collecting a great number or quantity (good or bad). A male hyena. Great spoil. One who has a large family. Name of a man.

A قثمة *kusmat*, (v. n. of قثم) Being defiled with dung. Dust. Ash-colour. Defilement with dung.

A قثو *kasw*, (v. n. of قثا for قثو) Collecting (wealth). Chewing (a cucumber). An assemblage of sheep or other wealth. Coriander.

A قثول *kiswall*, A stammerer. Flaccid, withered. A big bunch of dates. A big piece of meat and bones.

A قثوم *kasūm*, One who collects much good. One with a large family. Very liberal.

A قثوي *kaswa'*, A concourse, collection.

A قثي *kasy*, (v. n. of قثي) Collecting. Eating cucumbers. An assemblage of sheep or other wealth.

A قثيثة *kasīsat*, A herd, flock, troop, body.

A قثيثي *kissīsa'*, A collection, amount of property.

A قثيرة *kusayrat*, (dim. of قثرة) Little furniture.

A قجقجة *kajkajat*, A kind of game.

P قچ *kuch*, A fighting horned ram.

P قچقار *kuchkār*, A ram.

P قچك *kachak* or *kichuk*, A kind of musical instrument.

P قچل *kachal*, A magpie.

A قحّ *kuhh*, True, real, genuine, unsophisticated, unblemished (used in a good or in an ironical sense). Brutal (man). Unripe and full of pulp (pumpkin). اعرابيّ قحّ *aȝrābiyun kuhhun*, A genuine Arab.

A قحاب *kihāb*, (pl. of قحبة *kahbat*) Whores. *Kuhāb*, (v. n. of قحب) Coughing. The dry cough (of horses, camels, and also of men).

A قحاح *kuhāh*, The best part. The purest. Simple, guileless.

A قحاحة *kahāhat*, (v. n. of قحّ) Being pure and unmixed. Being unripe (a pumpkin). Being fat and full of marrow.

A قحاد *kihād*, (pl. of قحدة *kahadat*) Roots of camels' bunches.

A قحّاد *kahhād*, Alone, having no son or brother.

A قحارة *kahārat*, Old age (in a camel) with yet some remains of strength.

A قحارية *kuhāriyat*, Aged (camel) with some remains of strength. A man, large-bodied, irascible, a great drinker, and short of stature.

A قحاز *kuhāz*, A disease incident to sheep. A cough among camels.

A قحّازة *kuhhāzat*, A snare for catching birds.

A قحازن *kahāzin*, pl. of قحزنة, Staves, bludgeons.

A قحاف *kihāf*, (v. n. of قحف) Drinking much; drinking out of wooden bowls. Wine. اليوم قحاف وغدا نقاف *al yawm kihāf wa ghada' nihāf*, Drinking to-day, and breaking of pates to-morrow. *Kuhāf*, Rapid, irresistible (torrent).

A قحافة *kuhāfat*, Whatever any one carries off.

A قحال *kuhāl*, The drying of a sheep's gums.

A قحامة *kahāmat*, Great age; decrepitude.

A قحب *kahb*, (v. n. of قحب) Coughing. Speaking, talking to. Aged. Taken with a fit of coughing.

A قحبة *kahbat*, A cough. An old woman. A whore (because she is said to invite attention by a cough or hem). A woman who has an offensive stomach arising from disease.

P قحبگان *kahbagān*, (pl. of قحبه) Prostitutes.

P قحبگی *kahbagi*, Whoredom, prostitution.

P قحبه *kahba*, A whore, courtesan, prostitute.

P قحبه خانه *kahba-khāna*, A brothel.

A قحة *kahat* or *kihat*, (v. n. of وقح) Being hard (a hoof). Being impudent, bare-faced.

A قحث *kahs*, (v. n. of قحث) Taking the whole of any thing. Commencing at the end.

A قحثرة *kahsarat*, A scattering, throwing away.

A قحد *kahd*, (v. n. of قحد) Having a large, high bunch (a camel).

A قحدة *kahdat*, A she-camel with a large bunch. *Kahadat*, (pl. قحاد *kihād* and اقحد *ak-hud*) A camel's bunch, or the root of it.

A قحر *kahr*, (pl. اقحر *ak-hur* and قحور *kuhūr*) Decrepit (old man). Aged (camel) with some remains of strength. (The female is not called قحرة *kahrat*, but ناب *nāb*).

A قحز *kahz*, (v. n. of قحز) Leaping, springing. Wavering, tottering. Striking (with a stick). Throwing prostrate. Falling at the archer's foot (an arrow). Squirting urine (a dog).

A قحزان *kahazān*, (v. n. of قحز) Squirting urine.

A قحزة *kahzat*, A striking of one dry substance against other.

A قحزلة *kahzalat*, (v. n. of قحزل Q) Causing to fall. Striking. A staff.

A قحزمة *kahzamat*, A changing, turning.

A قحزنة *kahzanat*, (v. n. of قحزن Q) Throwing prostrate. (pl. قحازن *kahāzin*) A club, a bludgeon.

A قحزي *kahaza'*, A springy, elastic bow.

A قحص *kahs*, (v. n. of قحص) Passing by swiftly, running. Sweeping (a house). Striking with the feet, kicking.

A قحط *kaht*, (v. n. of قحط) Being withheld, failing (rain). Suffering from drought. Scarcity, barrenness, sterility. Dearness. Penury, hunger, want, famine. A hard blow. قحط رجال *kahti rijāl*, A scarcity of men. قحط و طاعون *kaht u tāȝūn*, Famine and pestilence. *Kuht*, A kind of plant. *Kahat*, (v. n. of قحط) Being withheld, failing (rain). Experiencing drought. *Kahit*, Severe (blow, year).

A قحطان *kahtān*, Son of عامر *ȝāmir* son of سالح *sālih*, father of a tribe. Name of a man called the father of Yaman (1 Chron. i. 17—20).

A قحطاني *kahtāniy*, Of the tribe of Kahtān.

A قحطبة *kahtabat*, (v. n. of قحطب Q) Throwing prostrate on the ground. Standing over one with a drawn sword. Striking.

A قحطرة *kahtarat*, (v. n. of قحطر Q) Stringing a bow. Lying with (a woman).

P قحط رسيده *kaht-rasīda*, Visited by dearth.

P قحط سال *kaht-sāl*, A year of dearth.

P قحطناك *kahtnāk*, Barren, unproductive.

A قحطي *kahtiy*, A glutton (causer of scarcity).

A قحف *kahf*, (v. n. of قحف) Wounding, cutting, or breaking (the skull). Draining the contents of a vessel. Drawing out of a vessel or a pudding. Drinking all up (especially emptying a wooden bowl). Winnowing (wheat). *Kihf*, (pl. اقحاف *ah-hāf*, قحوف *kuhūf*, and قحفة *kihfat*) The skull. A wooden cup resembling it in shape. A potsherd. Hard drinking. ما له قدّ ولا قحف *mā lahu kiddun wa lā kihfun*, He has nothing (قدّ *kidd* implying the same form of cup in leather). افلس من ضارب قحف استه *aflasu min zāribi kihfi istihi*, Poorer than he who strikes the sides of his buttocks, very poor. *Kuhf*, (pl. of قاحف *kāhif*) Emptiers of vessels.

A قحفاء *kahfāʼ*, A sweeping whirlwind.

A قحفة *kihfat*, (pl. of قحف *kihf*) Skulls.

A قحفزة *kahfazat*, (v. n. of قحفز Q) Employing harsh and severe language. Walking fast. Stuffing softly (a cloak-bag).

A قحفليز *kahfalīz*, Vulva.

A قحقاح *kahkāh*, A hard nocturnal journey in quest of water.

A قحقح *kuhkuh*, The bone round the anus, above what is called قبّ *kibb*.

A قحقحة *kahkahat*, (v. n. of قحقح Q) Laughing loudly. The laugh, chatter, or grin of an ape.

A قحل *kahl* or *kahal*, (v. n. of قحل) Being shrivelled (the skin). *Kahl* or *kahil*, Dry-skinned and worn with age (old man). *Kahal*, (v. n. of قحل) Being dry-skinned (an old man).

A قحلزة *kahlazat*, (v. n. of قحلز Q) Going the pace of a dwarf. Using harsh and gross language.

A قحم *kahm*, (v. n. of قحم) Crossing (deserts). Approaching. Decrepit, shrivelled (old man). *Kuham*, Difficulties (of the way). The three last days of a month. Law-suits.

A قحمة *kahmat*, Decrepit, and old (she-camel). *Kuhmat*, (v. n. of قحم) Attacking rashly, rushing upon suddenly and with precipitation. Peril, danger, difficulty. A law-suit. The hardship of a dry barren season, which forces people to emigrate.

A قحو *kahw*, A taking, a seizing.

A قحوان *kuhwān*, Anthemis, camomile.

A قحوحة *kuhūhat*, (v. n. of قح) Being pure, unmixed. Being unripe (a melon). Being fat and full of marrow.

A قحور *kuhūr*, (pl. of قحر *kahr*) Decrepit (old men). Aged (camels).

A قحورة *kuhūrat*, Old age (in camels) with some remains of strength.

A قحوز *kuhūz*, (v. n. of قحز) Falling down as dead. Squirting his urine (as a dog).

A قحوط *kuhūt*, (v. n. of قحط) Being withheld, failing (rain). Suffering from drought.

A قحوف *kuhūf*, (pl. of قحف *kihf*) Skulls. Ladles.

A قحول *kuhūl*, (v. n. of قحل) Becoming dry, withered (skin upon the bone).

A قحوم *kahūm*, Decrepit (old man). (A pulley) having a rapid fall. *Kuhūm*, (v. n. of قحم) Attacking rashly, entering upon with precipitation.

A قحومة *kuhūmat*, Infirmities of old age.

A قحيح *kahīh*, A gulping down of liquor.

A قحيط *kahīt*, Severe (blow). Scarce (year).

A قخر *kahhr*, (v. n. of قخر) Knocking against one another (especially dry substances).

A قخزة *kahhzat*, (v. n. of قخز) Knocking against one another (especially dry substances).

P قد *kad*, Stature, figure. An oblong rent in a sleeve. A cutting out of cloth to make a garment. Excoriation. قد الف چو میم کردن *kadi alif chu mīm kardan*, To hang the head in a contemplative posture. قد لاجوردي *kadi lājawardī*, The sky. قد مریم *kadi maryam*, A kind of houseleek.

A قد *kad*, (A particle preceding verbs, signifying in the preterite) Certainly, doubtless, already, meanwhile, some time since, long ago, formerly, just now, sometimes, never, when (he did it); (before verbs in the present or future) sometimes, now and then (he will come); in which sense لقد *la kad* is also used; though both, as well as many other Arabic and Persian particles, are often mere expletives, which give a nervousness or elegance to the style, whilst the sense would be complete without them. A sufficiency. Sufficiently. قد زیداً درهم *kad zaydan dirhamun*, (or قد زید درهم *kad* (also *kadu*) *zaydin dirhamun*) A dirhem is enough for Zayd. قدني درهم *kadnī dirhamun*, A dirhem is sufficient for me. قد مات زید *kad māta zaydun*, Zayd is just dead. قد کنت في خیر *kad kuntu fī khayr*, Never was I well off. قد یقدم الغائب *kad yakdumu'l ghāʼib*, Without doubt the absent (man) will arrive. قد یصدق الکذوب *kad yasduku'l kazūb*, Sometimes a liar speaks the truth. قد اترك القرن مصفرًّا انامله *kad atruku'l kirna musfarran anāmiluhu*, Often do I leave my opponent with the tips of his fingers yellow. قد افلح من زکّیها *kad aflaha man zakkahā*, Surely he who pays tithes for it (or them) will prosper.

A قدّ *kadd*, (v. n. of قدّ) Tearing (a garment) lengthwise. Cutting up by the roots. Traversing (a desert). Interrupting, breaking short (a discourse). A lash, a scourge. The cesura in verse; the dividing any thing with propriety. A quantity, part. A fissure, split, crack, crevice. (pl. اقدّ *akudd*, قداد *kidād*, اقدّة *akiddat*, and قدود *kudūd*) A kid's or lamb's skin. Stature of the body. Length. *Kidd*, (pl. اقدّ *akudd*) A leather strap or thong cut from an untanned hide. A vessel made of leather. A lash, a scourge. *Kudd*, A kind of sea-fish.

A قداة *kadāt*, Good flavour of meat in the pot.

A قداح *kidāh*, (pl. of قدح *kidh*) Arrows ere they have received heads or wings.

A قدّاح *kaddāh*, A fire-steel, or fire-striking wood. A potter, a maker of glass-ware. The extremities of young, tender plants. The flexible buds of clover-grass. A flint.

A قداحة *kidāhat*, Potter or glass-blower's trade.

A قدّاحة *kaddāhat*, A flint, or fire-striking wood.

A قداحس *kudāhis*, A strong, intrepid man. Of a bad disposition. A lion.

A قداد *kadād*, A hedgehog, an urchin. A field-mouse. *Kidād*, (pl. of قدّ *kadd*) Kid-skins. Human statures. *Kudād*, The belly-ache, gripes.

A قدار *kidār*, (v. n. 3 of قدر) Doing exactly as another does. Instituting a comparison between two things. Agreeing with, or answering to another in measure or comparison. *Kidār* or *kadār*, (v. n. of قدر) Being able, powerful, obtaining the superiority. Power, strength, ability. *Kudār*, A camel-butcher. A cook. One who cooks in a pot (قدر *kidr*). A table-decker. A large serpent or dragon. A middling-sized man.

A قدارة *kadārat*, (v. n. of قدر) Directing properly, amending. Appointing a time for any thing. Power, strength.

P قدّارة *kaddāra*, A two-edged sword.

A قداس *kudās*, A string of silver beads, a rosary. صاحب القداس *sāhibu'l kudās*, A presbyter. A stone placed at the spot where water is poured into a cistern. A stone placed in a cistern for measuring out water equally amongst camels. High, inaccessible dignity.

A قدّاس *kaddās*, A stone placed at the spot where water is poured into a cistern. *Kuddās*, The catholic mass. The consecrated wafer, the host.

A قداف *kudāf*, A dish, earthen water-pot.

A قدام *kudām*, Old, ancient.

A قدّام *kaddām*, A king, prince, leader. *Kuddām*, Anterior, prior. The front, projecting part. A king, prince, leader. A butcher, slaughterer of camels. Before. (pl. of قادم *kādim*) Comers from a journey. قدّام الباب *kuddāmu'l bāb*, A portico. قدّام البعض *kuddāma'l baʻz*, Before some. قدّام عسکر *kuddāmi ʻaskar*, The front or first line of an army. قدّام و خلف *kuddām u khalaf*, First and last. الی قدّامك *ila' kuddāmika*, (Wind blowing) from the opposite quarter in your face. من قدّامك *min kuddāmika*, In your presence.

A قدامة *kadāmat*, (v. n. of قدم) Preceding in point of time, being prior, ancient, eternal.

A قدامی *kudāmaʼ*, The advanced guard of an army. (pl. of قدیم *kadīm*) Ancient. (pl. of قادمة *kādimat*) Quill-feathers.

A قدامیس *kadāmīs*, (pl. of قدموس) Large camels.

A قداوة *kadāwat*, (v. n. of قدي) Being well-flavoured (meat).

P قد آور *kad-āwar*, Tall of stature.

A قدائم *kadāʼim*, (pl. of قدوم *kadūm*) Hatchets. (pl. of قدیمة *kadīmat*) Ancient (things).

A قدة *kadat*, (pl. قدات *kadāt*) A kind of serpent. *Kidat*, (v. n. of وقد) Being kindled, blazing (a fire). An excellent man, a model, exemplar.

A قدّة *kiddat*, (pl. قدد *kidad*) A thong. Rule, regulation, institution. A scattered multitude going different ways, each following a plan of his own.

A قدح *kadh*, (v. n. of قدح) Reviling, reproaching, cursing, anathematizing. Striking fire from a flint and steel. Striking fire. Taking (broth) out of a pot with a ladle. Sinking in the socket (an eye). Cracking (the bottom of a spear-head). Reproach, cursing, malediction, satire, lampoon. قدح و مذمت *kadh u mazammat*, Reproach and detraction. *Kidh*, (pl. قداح *kidāh*, اقدح *akduh*, and اقاديح *akādīh*) An arrow ere it has received head or wing. An arrow employed in drawing lots. *Kadah*, (pl. اقداح *akdāh*) A cup, goblet, glass, bowl; any drinking-vessel (especially of the larger size, sufficient for two persons). A black corrosion of the teeth; also of a tree. A crack in wood. P زرّين قدح *zarrīn kadah*, The narcissus.

A قدحة *kadhat*, One stroke of the fire-steel. *Kidhat*, A striking of fire. The management of an affair. *Kudhat*, A sup of broth.

A ذهبوا بقدّحرة *zahabū bi kiddahrat*, They went where none could get at them.

P قدحكار *kadah-kār*, A cup-bearer.

A قدد *kidad*, (pl. of قدّة *kiddat*) Slips or strips of leather, thongs. Different ways.

P قد دار *kad-dār*, Of a fine stature.

A قدر *kadr*, (v. n. of قدر) Making great, magnifying, honouring. Measuring, determining. Disposing, arranging, adapting, regulating. Cutting out or making (a garment) exactly. Confining, reducing to difficulties. Looking to the end. Appointing, predestinating. Cooking in a pot. Measuring, comparing one thing with another. Whatever is fixed or ordained of God. Fate. Divine Providence. Quantity. Worth, value, price. Power, strength. Size, dimensions, measure. Affluence, opulence. The head of the shoulder. The centre of a saddle. ذو القدر *zū'l kadr*, Possessed of power, high in station. P شب قدر *shabi kadr*, (or A ليلة القدر *laylatu'l kadr*) The night of power; the night the Kur'ān was sent down. A عظيم القدر *ʿazīmu'l kadr*, Of exalted rank. ما قدروا الله حقّ قدره *mā kadarū'llāha hakka kadrihi*, They honoured not God as he deserved to be honoured. *Kidr*, (pl. قدور *kudūr*, قدرات *kidarāt*, *kidirāt*, and اقدر *akdur*) A cauldron, pot, kettle. Certain stars disposed in a circle. *Kudr*, Quantity, price, worth. *Kadar*, (v. n. of قدر) Measuring. Pre-ordaining, rendering necessary. Being short-necked. A decree, mandate, judgment. Whatever is fixed, decreed, and commanded of God. (pl. اقدار *akdār*) Power. The power of directing one's own actions without restraint, necessity, or irresistible fate (in opposition to جبر *jabr*). Quantity, price, worth, value. Shortness of neck. P اين قدر *īn kadar*, So much, this quantity. چه قدر *chi kadar*, How much? what quantity? A قضا و قدر *kazā u kadar*, Fate and the divine decree.

A قدراء *kadrāʾ*, A well-proportioned ear, neither too large nor too small. بنو قدراء *banū kadrāʾ*, Easy matters.

A قدران *kidrān*, (v. n. of قدر) Being able. Power, ability.

P قدر انداز *kadr-andāz*, An excellent archer.

P قدر بخش *kadr-bakhsh*, Conferring dignity. The source of dignity, fountain of honour.

A قدرة *kudrat*, (v. n. of قدر) Being able. Power, ability, potency, vigour, force, prowess, authority, virtue. Courage, audacity. One of the attributes of God: omnipotence, providence, prescience, destiny. So much. قدرت حلوا *kudrat-halwā*, The sweet cake of God, *i. e.* the manna of the Israelites. ذو قدرة *zū kudrat*, Potent, powerful. *Kadurat*, A small flask, decanter, or bottle. The distance at which palm-trees are planted apart.

A قدرتيّ *kudratīy*, Not produced by man.

P قدرت ياب *kudrat-yāb*, Who finds the power.

P قدرتي رنگ *kudratī-rang*, White; natural colour (not dyed).

P قدر خان *kadar-khān*, Title of the emperor of China and of the king of Samarkand.

P قدردان *kadr-dān*, A just appreciator, one who knows the worth (of men or things).

P قدرشناس *kadar-shinās*, Acquainted with the value or quality (of persons or things).

P قدرف *kadraf*, Name of a city.

P قدرفي *kadrafī*, Name of a gold coin.

P قدر قدرت *kadar-kudrat*, Powerful as fate.

P قدر مايه *kadar-māya*, A little.

A قدري *kadrī*, A certain order of dervishes. Whatever is predestined. Name of a celebrated author. *Kadare*, A little, small quantity; somewhat.

A قدريّ *kadarīy*, One who maintains the doctrine of free-will (opposed to جبريّ *jabarīy*).

A قدريّة *kadarīyat*, Name of a Muhammadan sect which holds the doctrine of free-will (the opposite of جبريّة *jabarīyat*, which denies the freedom of the human will).

A قدس *kuds*, (v. n. of قدس) Being holy, pure. *Kuds* or *kudus*, Sanctity, holiness. Paradise. The angel Gabriel. Jerusalem (which is likewise called قدس مبارك *kudsi mubārak*, قدس شريف *kudsi sharīf*, and كعبۀ قدس *kaʿbaʾi kuds*, The holy city). حظيرة القدس *hazīratu'l kuds*, The holy fold, *i. e.* Paradise. روح القدس *rūhu'l kudus*, The Holy Spirit. The angel Gabriel. *Kadas*, A two-handed vessel, from which they pour water on bathers. *Kudas* or *kudus*, A cup about as big as غمر *ghumar*.

A قدّس *kaddasa*, (passively *kuddisa*) (3d pers. sing. pret. of the second conj. used optatively) May he be blessed! قدّس سرّه *kuddisa sirruhu*, May his tomb be purified! (speaking of a departed king or great man). قدّس الله تعالي سرّه و افاض علينا برّه *kaddasa'llāhu taʿāla' sirrahu, wa afāza ʿalaynā birrahu*, May the most high God hallow his grave, and shed on us his virtues!

A قدسيّ *kudsīy*, Holy, divine. Celestial. Belonging to Paradise or Jerusalem. The angel Gabriel.

P قدسيان *kudsiyān*, Angels, holy intelligences.

A قدع *kadʿ*, (v. n. of قدع) Prohibiting, hindering, diverting (one) from any thing. Checking, reining in (a horse). Striking on the nose with a spear or a staff (a stallion, a horse, or camel when good for nothing). Causing to pass, transmitting, despatching. Sipping, drinking by little and little. *Kadaʿ*, (v. n. of قدع) Being weak (the eyes). Approaching or being near, pressing upon. Being bashful and of few words (a woman). Being weak-sighted and shying (a horse). *Kadiʿ*, Timid, frightened (horse), that sees badly and shies. (A man) that cries and wails piteously. (Water) brackish, undrinkable.

A قدعة *kidʿat*, A short tunic. *Kadiʿat*, (A woman) bashful and sparing of speech.

P قدغ *kadgh*, A drinking-vessel made of horn.

P قدغن *kadaghan*, Corroboration, stress. Seeking, inquiring, solicitude, care.

A قدف *kadf*, A lading out with the hand, or a pouring out of the water (of a well). The stump of the larger palm-branches after the lighter branches have been cut away.

A قدقد *kidkid*, Name of a mountain, out of which stone cauldrons are hewn.

A قدم *kadm*, (v. n. of قدم) Preceding, going before. Being prior in point of time, place, or degree. Being bold and intrepid. A red garment. *Kidm*, Antiquity, a former age, ancient times. *Kudm*, (v. n. of قدم) Preceding, going before, being prior to. Bold, audacious. *Kadam*, (pl. اقدام *akdām* and اقدم *akdum*) A foot. The toe of the foot. A footstep, track, trace. A foot's length. A step, pace. A going before. Merit, especially any qualification which one has in a superior degree to others. Bold, heroic (man, woman, men or women). Very meritorious (man, men, woman, women). P قدم ازجان بر آوردن *kadam az jān bar āwardan*, To bid adieu to life. قدم از سر ساختن *kadam az sar sākhtan*, To proceed, set out, or go away. قدم افشردن *kadam afshurdan*, To keep a firm footing. قدم بقدم *kadam ba kadam*, Step by step, gently. قدم خاك *kadami khāk*, The ground. قدم رنجه نمودن *kadam ranja namūdan*, To take the trouble to come. To go, march, step. A قدم شريف *kadami sharīf*, A relic. قدم مبارك *kadami mubārak*, A stone on which the foot of Muhammad is said to be impressed, and therefore greatly venerated. ثابت قدم *sābit-kadam*, Constant, firm, solid, immoveable. له قدم صدق عنده *lahu kadamu sidkin ʿindahu*, He was held in great esteem by him on account of his superior merit. P وضع قدم كردن *wazʿi kadam kardan*, To enter, step in. A *Kadim*, Bold, courageous, taking the lead in battle. Rough, stony (ground). *Kidam*, (v. n. of قدم) Preceding in point of time, being ancient, eternal. A going before. Age. Antiquity, olden time. *Kudam*, Name of a place in Yaman, where cloths are made. *Kudum*, Precedence. An intrepid man, excelling in courage. The fore part, before. (pl. of قادم *kādim*) Comers off a journey. (pl. of قدوم *kadūm*) Hatchets. مضى قدما *maza' kuduman*, He preceded, led the van.

P قدم *kudum*, Effect or consequence of an act.

A قدما *kidman*, Formerly, of old. It is long that.

A قدماء *kudamā*, (pl. of قديم *kadīm*) The ancients. Excellent (men).

A قدمان *kidmān*, A coming (off a journey).

P قدم باز *kadam-bāz*, Fleet, nimble-footed.

P قدمبوسى *kadam-bosī*, Foot-kissing: obeisance.

A قدمة *kudmat*, (v. n. of قدم) Walking pompously, stately, or gracefully. A pompous, graceful, or stately carriage. A going before, a taking the lead. Intrepidity. A footstep, track, trace. *Kadamat*, Meritorious (woman). *Kadimat*, Rugged, stony ground.

P قدم جا *kadam-jā*, A privy.

P قدمگاه *kadam-gāh*, Place of arrival. A privy.

A قدموس *kudmūs*, (pl. قداميس *kadāmīs*) Ancient, antique. A large camel. A great king.

A قدموسة *kadmūsat*, Big (woman); large (stone).

P قدميا *kadamiyā*, Litharge of gold or silver.

A قدمية *kadamīyat*, A kind of goats' leather. *Kadumīyat*, A haughty air in walking. *Kudumīyat*, Precedence. مشى القدمية *masha'l kudumīyat*, He was superior in birth and bravery.

P قدمى چند *kadame chand*, A few paces.

A قدن *kadn*, A sufficiency. A sufficing.

A قدو *kadw*, (v. n. of قدا for قدو) Being finely flavoured (meat). Arriving off a journey. Propinquity. *Kidw*, A trunk whence branches germinate.

A قدوة *kadwat*, *kidwat*, or *kudwat*, An example, exemplar, pattern, model; any person or thing imitated; a man of renown. A trodden road. قدوة الابرار *kidwatu'l abrār*, An example of justice, a model of equity. قدوة الاقران *kidwatu'l akrān*, (or قدوة الاصحاب *kudwatu'l as-hāb*) An honour or pattern to (his) peers or companions.

A قدوح *kaduh*, A fly. (A well) from which water may be drawn by the hand.

A قدود *kudūd*, (pl. of قد *kadd*) Goat-skins. Statures of human bodies.

A قدور *kudūr*, Power, strength. (pl. of قدر *kidr*) Pots, cauldrons.

A قدورة *kudūrat*, Power, strength.

A قدوس *kadūs*, Bold, intrepid, dauntless.

A قدّوس *kuddūs* or *kaddūs*, Pure, holy, blessed: hence a name of God.

A قدّوسيّة *kuddūsiyat*, Extreme purity or sanctity.

A قدوع *kadūʿ*, (A horse) which stands in need of being checked when at full gallop, and made obedient to the word of command. Abject, submissive, easily kept in check. One who prevents from calling out. Poured out.

A قدوم *kadūm*, Bold, magnanimous, taking the lead. (pl. قدائم *kadāʾim* and قدم *kudum*) A hatchet, axe. *Kudūm*, (v. n. of قدم) Arriving, coming near. Preceding. Coming off a journey. Accession, approach, advent.

P قدومه *kudūma*, Mallows.

A قدومية *kudūmīyat*, A present from a prince to any person that approaches him. مشى القدومية *masha'l kudūmīyat*, He walked before.

A قدوي *kadwa'*, Rectitude. Stability.

A قدي *kady*, (v. n. of قدي) Coming from the desert (famine-stricken people). Being well-flavoured (meat). *Kada'*, (v. n. of قدي) Being well-flavoured (meat). Arriving (off a journey). A spear's length. *Kadī*, Of an excellent flavour (meat in the pot). *Kida'*, Quantity. Length (of a spear).

A قديّ *kadiy*, Well-flavoured (meat in a pot).

A قديان *kadayān*, (v. n. of قدي) Running fast.

A قدية *kidyat*, Custom or situation in which one finds himself.

A قديّة *kadīyat*, A present, an offering.

A قديح *kadīh*, Broth, especially the remains at the bottom of the pot, which requires trouble to obtain.

A قديد *kadīd*, Flesh smoked or dried by the wind and cut into long strips, jerked. A thread-bare garment. *Kudayd*, A small striped dervish's habit.

A قديديم *kudaydīm*, (قديديمة *kudaydīmat*, or قديدمة *kudaydimat*) (dim. of قدّام *kuddām*) (Any thing) a very little anterior or prior.

A قديديّون *kadīdīyūn*, The followers of an army, camp-followers (such as tailors, farriers, tinkers, and the like).

A قدير *kadīr*, Powerful. An epithet of God. Cooked in a pot (قدر *kidr*). بعون الملك القدير *bi ʿawni'l maliki'l kadīr*, By the aid of the all-powerful King. تقدير قدير *takdīri kadīr*, Divine predestination. *Kudayr*, (dim. of قدر *kidr*) A little pot, cauldron, kettle, or pipkin.

A قديس *kadīs*, Fresh milk. Milk.

A قديم *kadīm*, (pl. قدماء *kudamā*, قدامى *kudāma'*, and قدائم *kadāʾim*) Ancient, olden. Former. Without beginning or end. القديم *al kadīm*, God. قديم لايام *kadīmu'l ayyām*, Ancient of days.

A قديما *kadīman*, (من قديم *min kadīm*, P ازقديم *az kadīm*) Anciently, in former times, from of old.

A قدّيم *kiddīm*, A king. A prince, leader.

A قديميّ *kadīmiy*, Ancient, olden.

A قذّ *kazz*, (v. n. of قذّ) Cutting, clipping, and fitting feathers to an arrow. Throwing a stone or any thick substance. Striking on the back of the head or behind the ears.

A قذا *kaza'*, Chips, straws, motes.

A قذاء *kizā*, A recompensing, a repaying.

A قذاذات *kuzāzāt*, Small particles which fall when cutting (feathers for an arrow).

A قذاذة *kuzāzat*, A filing (of gold, silver, &c.).

A قذارة *kazārat*, (v. n. of قذر) Being unclean, impure, nasty, dirty.

A قذاريف *kazārīf*, (pl. of قذروف *kuzrūf*) Vices, blemishes.

A قذاف *kizāf*, The velocity of a galloping horse. Any thing grasped in and filling the hand, either to carry or to throw. A she-camel running before the males. (pl. of قذف *kuzf*) Sides, parts, tracts. (pl. of قذفة *kuzfat*) Battlements, pinnacles, turrets.

A قذّاف *kazzāf*, A pair of scales. A balista, catapulta, cross-bow, or any engine for throwing stones or darts. Rapid (nocturnal journey in quest of water). A horse, camel, or carriage of any kind.

A قذّافة *kazzāfat*, A sling or single balista.

A قذال *kazāl*, (pl. قذل *kuzul* and اقذلة *akzilat*) The back part of a horse's head behind the ears, over which the headstall passes.

A قذامل *kuzāmil*, Wide, broad, large.

A قذّان *kizzān*, (pl. of قذّة *kuzzat*) Fleas. *Kuzzān*, Hoariness in the temple-locks. White on the wing of a bird.

A قذّان قذّان *kuzzāna kuzzāna*, A sort of game.

A قذائف *kazāʾif*, (pl. of قذيفة *kazīfat*) Things thrown away.

A قذّة *kuzzat*, (pl. قذذ *kuzaz*) A feather. The wing of an arrow. Ala vulvæ. The ear (of a man or horse). (pl. قذّان *kizzān*) A flea.

A قذّة قذّة *kuzzata kuzzata*, A sort of game.

A قذحمة *kizhamat*, Illustration, elucidation. *Kizahmat*, Concealment. A veil.

A قذذ *kuzaz*, The hinder part of the head betwixt the ears. A flea. (pl. of قذّة *kuzzat*) Wings of an arrow.

A قذر *kazr*, (v. n. of قذر) Abhorring, abominating as being filthy. *Kazar*, (v. n. of قذر) Being unclean, impure, dirty. Abhorring, abominating (as being filthy). Dirt, filth. *Kazar*, *kazr*, *kazir*, or *kazur*, Filthy. افكار قذر *afkāri kazir*, Unclean thoughts.

A قذرة *kuzarat*, Pure, unsullied, free from censure (man).

A قذروف *kuzrūf*, (pl. قذاريف *kazārīf*) Vice, fault, defect, blemish.

A قذع *kazʿ*, (v. n. of قذع) Reproaching, reviling, traducing, cursing. Striking with a stick. *Kazaʿ*, Obscenity, ribaldry, turpitude, impurity, filthiness.

A قذعل *kizaʿl* or *kuzʿul*, Worthless. Paltry, stingy.

A قذعمل *kuzaʿmal*, Corpulent (camel).

A قذعملة *kuzaʿmalat*, Short of body; deformed, vile, base (woman). Corpulent (she-camel). Somewhat, any thing. Weakness.

A قذعيل *kuzaʿmil*, A decrepit old man.

A قذف *kazf*, (v. n. of قذف) Accusing, criminating, convicting, impeaching, reproaching, censuring. Accusing (a virtuous woman) of incontinence. Pelting with stones. Rowing (a boat). Throwing (stones). Vomiting. *Kazf* or *kazaf*, The side (of a valley or river). *Kuzf*, (pl. قذاف *kizāf*)

A side, part, place, tract. *Kazaf* or *kuzuf*, Remote (habitation). Distant (purpose). Weary (waste). A slippery place. A side. *Kuzaf* or *kuzuf*, (pl. of قذفة *kuzfat*) Battlements.

A قذفة *kuzfat*, (pl. قذاف *kizāf*, قذف *kuzaf*, *kuzuf*, قذفات *kuzafāt*, or *kuzufāt*) A battlement, turret. A prominence on the top (of a hill). A side.

A قذل *kazl*, (v. n. of قذل) Striking on the back part of the head called قذال *kazāl*. Inclining. Accusing, reproaching. Striving, straining every nerve. Deviation. Injustice. *Kazal*, A vice, fault, defect, blemish. *Kuzul*, (pl. of قذال *kazāl*) Hind-heads.

A قذم *kazm*, (v. n. of قذم) Being liberal, munificent. Munificence; a present. Giving away much at once. *Kuzam*, A magnificent, generous prince who gives away much at one time. *Kuzum*, Wells dug in rocks which spring continually.

A قذمّ *kizamm*, Strong, vehement. Swift. Very liberal, munificent.

A قذمة *kuzmat*, The drinking of a draught.

A قذمور *kuzmūr*, A silver table or tray.

A قذور *kazūr*, (A woman) abhorring all impurity, and keeping at a distance from men. (A she-camel) avoiding the males. A misanthrope, one who shuns society.

A قذوف *kazūf*, Far-distant (dwelling). Weary (waste), wide (desert).

A قذي *kazy*, (v. n. of قذي) Coming, arriving Casting forth a mote (the eye). Throwing out a whitish substance from the uterus (a sheep in want of the ram). *Kaza'*, (v. n. of قذي) Being annoyed by a mote fallen into it (the eye). Casting forth a mote (the eye). A chip, straw, or mote swimming on water or paining the eye. Water or blood discharged by a camel or sheep before or after the birth. هو يغضي على القذي *huwa yughzī ɛala'l kaza'*, He closes his eye on a mote, *i.e.* he is silent under contempt and affront. *Kazi*, Troubled with a mote in the eye. *Kiza'*, (pl. اقذاء *akzas* and قذيّ *kuzīy*) Pounded, pulverized earth.

A قذيّ *kazīy*, Troubled with a mote in the eye. *Kuzīy*, (v. n. of قذي) Casting forth a mote (the eye). (pl. of قذي *kiza'*) Pounded, pulverized earths.

A قذيان *kazayān*, (v. n. of قذي) Having a mote fallen into it (the eye). Casting forth a mote (the eye).

A قذية *kaziyat*, (or قذيّة *kazīyat*) (An eye) troubled with a mote in it.

A قذيعم *kuzayɛim*, (dim. of قذعملة *kuzaɛmilat*) Any thing very small.

A قذيف *kazīf*, Very remote (halting-place or habitation). A cloud rising up before the eye.

A قذيفة *kazīfat*, Any thing thrown or darted. Any thing that brings suspicion or reproach.

A قذّيفي *kizzīfa'*, A mutual reviling; also a flinging of stones at one another.

P قر *kir*, An ape, monkey, baboon.

A قرّ *karr*, (v. n. of قرّ) Drinking for the first time, but not to repletion (a camel). Remaining firm, resting, dwelling (in any place). Being affected by cold. Ceasing to cackle (a hen). Pouring in water to still a boiling pot or to prevent the pot from being burned. Throwing water over one's head or another's. Pouring words into another's ear, *i.e.* whispering or communicating a secret. A kind of saddle. The camel-litter called هودة *hawda*. A chicken. Cold (day). قرّ الثوب *karru's sawb*, A crease or fold in a garment. قرّ عين *karri ɛayn*, Coldness (or liveliness) of eye. يوم القرّ *yawmu'l karr*, The eleventh of ذو الحجة *zū'l hija*, the day after a great solemnity at Mecca, because people then repose either in the valley of Mina or at home after the performance of the sacrifices and other ceremonies. *Kurr*, Cold; coldness. A place of rest, mansion of repose.

A قرء *kars*, (v. n. of قرأ) Reading. Communicating tidings relative to health. Being pregnant (a camel). *Kars* or *kurs*, (pl. اقراء *akrās*, قروء *kurūs*, and اقرؤ *akrus*) Catamenia. Purifications, or the period when they are over. Time, season. A similar ending of verses in a poem.

A قرا *kara'*, The back. A kind of esculent gourd.

P قرا *kirā*, A machine for hurling stones or dirt.

A قرأ *karasa*, (fut. يقرأ *yakrasu* or *rusu*) He read.

A قرأء *hurras*, (pl. of قارئ) Readers of the Kur'ān.

A قراء *karās*, (v. n. of قرأ) Being kind, receiving (a friend) hospitably. Gathering together, collecting and conveying (water). Being pregnant (a camel). Bringing forth. (v. n. of قري) Receiving (a guest) hospitably. Swelling from a pain in the teeth (a camel's chops). Pursuing, travelling from place to place. Reading a book. *Kirās*, (v. n. 3 of قرأ) Teaching to read, practising.

A قرّاء *karrās*, (pl. قرّاؤن *karrāsun*) One who reads well. *Kurrās*, (pl. قرّاؤن *kurrāsun* and قراريّ *karāris*) A devout and holy man, given to sacred reading. (pl. of قاريّ *hāris*) Readers of the Kur'ān.

A قراءة *kirāsat*, (v. n. of قرأ) Reading the Kur'ān. A proper manner of reading the Kur'ān: a correct pronunciation. علم قراءت *ɛilmi kirāsat*, Skill in reading (particularly the Kur'ān with a solemn tone). P قراءت كردن *kirāsat kardan*, To read.

A قراب *karāb*, Near. بقراب *bi karābin*, Shortly. *Kirāb*, (v. n. 3 of قرب) Drawing near, approaching. Taking short steps. Lifting the leg. Speaking gently or soothingly. Letting alone excess and aiming at what is right and just. A sword-sheath; also a case in which it is laid up with all its appurtenances. (pl. of قربان *harbān*) (Vessels) nearly full. *Kirāb* or *kurāb*, Any thing almost full, or any business nearly accomplished. *Kurāb*, Sagacity, penetration, judgment.

A قرابات *karābāt*, Kinsmen, relations. هم قراباتي *hum karābātī*, They are my relations (an inaccurate mode of speaking).

A قراباذين *karābāzīn*, pl. قراباذيناب, An antidote.

A قرابة *karābat*, (v. n. of قرب) Becoming near. (pl. قرابات *karābāt*) Propinquity, nearness, affinity, connexion, relationship, kindred, consanguinity, kin, parentage, alliance. قرابت قريبه *karābati kariba*, A near relationship. هو قرابتي *huwa karābatī*, He is my kinsman (an inaccurate phrase). هو ذو قرابتي *huwa zū karābatī*, He is related to me. *Kirābat*, (v. n. of قرب) Going to water, distant a night's journey. An approach to fulness. *Kurābat*, One who comes near. Any thing almost full, or any business nearly accomplished. Nigh, near. Sagacity, penetration. Like, resembling. A relation. لا بقرابة منك *lā bi kurābatin minka*, Not nigh thee.

P قرابه *karāba*, A large flagon or vessel having two handles and a spout (made of glass, in which they allow wine to stand forty days in order to refine). قرابهٔ زرين *karābasi zarīn*, The sun.

A قرابي *kurāba*, Near to each other.

A قرابيس *karābīs*, (pl. of قربوس) Saddle-bows.

F قرابين *karābīn*, A carbine.

A قرابين *karābīn*, (pl. of قربان *kurbān*) Sacrifices, victims. Intimate associates of a king.

A قرأة *kirsat*, Plague, pestilence. *Karusat*, (pl. of قارئ *hāris*) Readers, particularly of the Kur'ān.

P قرات *kurāt*, A strip of cloth.

A قراثاء *karāsās*, An excellent sort of date.

P قراچور *karāchūr*, A long sword: a swordsman.

P قراچوري *karāchūrī*, A swordsman: a sword.

A قراح *karāh*, (pl. اقرحة *akrihat*) A sown field destitute of trees and of buildings. Land especially appropriated to sowing and planting. (Water) cold, sweet, pure, limpid, unmixed with any thing. *Kirāh*, (v. n. 3 of قرح) Meeting face to face. (pl. of قارح *kārih*) Mature, full-aged (horses). *Kurāh*, The coast of the sea of قطيف *katif*.

A قراحيّ *kurāhīy*, One who recedes or gives up any business. One who abides in a town and never goes into the country. One who has never been seen in a battle-field.

A قراحيّتان *kurāhīyatāni*, du., The hypochondria.

P قراخان *karākhān*, Name of a king of India cotemporary with Alexander. Name of one of Afrāsyāb's champions.

A قراد *kurād*, (pl. قردان *kirdān*) The tike or tick, a parasitical insect infesting dogs, camels, or cattle. A nipple or dug. The point of a nipple or of the orifice of a horse's pizzle.

A قرّاد *karrād*, A keeper or trainer of apes.

A قرادد *karādid*, (and قراديد *karādīd*) (pl. of قردد *kardad* and قردودة *kurdūdat*) High, rugged grounds.

A قرار *karār*, (v. n. of قرّ) Dwelling, fixing one's abode in any place. Resting. Constancy, firmness, stability. A safe, undisturbed habitation. Rest, tranquillity, peace, quietness, repose. Conclusion, determination, ratification, agreement, engagement. Certainty, truth, reality. Waiting, patience. Short-legged and ill-looking sheep. Ground low and level. P قرار داشتن *karār dāshtan*, To acquire stability. To be confirmed, settled, ratified. قرار كردن *karār kardan*, To conclude, confirm, ratify. To resolve. قرار گرفتن *karār giriftan*, To be still and quiet. To be firm or steady. A قرار واقع *karāri wāķiģ*, Completely, entirely. قرار و مدار *karār u madār*, Promise and agreement. P بر قرار *bar karār*, Firm, established. بر قرار شدن *bar karār shudan*, To be or remain firm, unshaken. بر قرار كردن *bar karār kardan*, To confirm, strengthen. بي قرار *bī karār*, Without firmness; inconstant, fickle, variable. بي قراري *bī karārī*, Inconstancy. دوزخ قرار *dozakh-karār*, A hell-hound, firebrand, infernal villain. كفّار دوزخ قرار *kuffāri dozakh-karār*, Accursed infidels. A معدلت قرار *maģdilat-karār*, Equitable, just, of unshaken integrity. *Kirār*, A name.

A قرارة *ka, ki*, or *kurārat*, Cold water poured into a pot to prevent it from being burned. *Karārat*, Short-legged, ill-looking sheep. Dwarfish. Level and roundish ground. Rest, tranquillity, quietness, repose. A small pond. *Kurārat*, (Meat, broth, or seasoning) sticking to the bottom of a pot.

P قرار داد *karār-dād*, Possessed of firmness, *i.e.* established, confirmed, ratified. An engagement, contract, agreement. A prescription. صلح قرار داد *sulhi karār-dād*, A peace concluded and ratified.

P قرار داده *karār-dāda*, Confirmed, established.

P قرار كمي *karār-kamī*, Decrease in rent of land.

P قرارگاه *karār-gāh*, A mansion, quiet place of residence. قرار گاه نطفه *karār-gāhi nutfa*, The womb. Fundus uteri.

P قرار گيري *karār-girī*, Quiet, peace, security.

P قرار نامه *karār-nāma*, A written agreement.

A قراريء *karāriء*, (pl. of قرّاء *kurrāء*) Persons devoted to sacred reading, especially the Kur'ān.

A قراريّ *karāriy*, Firm, stable, ratified, agreed to. A citizen who does not leave home. A tailor. A butcher. Any tradesman or mechanic. A flute-player, a piper.

A قراريط *karārīt*, Seed of tamarind. (pl. of قيراط *kīrāt*) Half-dāngs (the name of a coin).

A قراس *karās*, Name of a mountain in Yaman. آل قراس *āl karās*, Name of certain cold mountains near السراة *as'sarāt*.

P قراسنقر *karāsunkur*, Name of a bird of prey of a black colour. Night. Name of a king.

T قراسو *karāsū*, A river near Khwārazm.

P قراسيا *karāsiyā*, (or قراسيه *karāsiya*) A cherry.

A قراسية *kurāsiyat*, Robust (camel or camels).

P قراش *kurāsh*, (or قراشه *kurāsha*) A fever in which the hair stands on end.

A قراشب *karāshib*, (pl. of قرشبّ *kirshabb*) Aged, old. Ill-tempered. Badly circumstanced. Thick. Tall. Gluttonous. Lions.

A قراشم *karāshim*, A large tike or tick.

A قراشماء *kurāshimāء*, A sort of plant.

A قراشمة *kurāshimat*, (pl. قراشيم *karāshīm*) A white animalcule, which afterwards turns to a tike, and is bred in the plant رمث *rims*.

A قرّاص *kurrās*, Anthemis, camomile, especially the dry flowers. Spring-grass. The plant ورس *wars*. احمر قرّاص *ahmar kurrās*, Intense red.

A قرّاصة *karrāsat*, A reviler.

A قراصيا *karāsiyā*, A cherry. قراصياءِ حلو *karāsiyāءi hulv*, The sweet cherry. قراصياءِ حامض *karāsiyāءi hāmiz*, The morel-cherry.

A قراض *kirāz*, (v. n. 3 of قرض) Repaying, requiting (good or bad). Going partnership, and trading with another's capital. Challenging one to dispute, especially in verse. Debt.

A قراضب *kurāzib*, A hungry fellow, who devours whatever is placed before him.

A قراضبة *karāzibat*, (pl. of قرضاب *kirzāb*) Sharp swords. (pl. of قرضوب *kurzūb*) Poor, starving men. Thieves.

A قراضة *kurāzat*, What falls off in filing; filings. A fragment, small particle (of gold or silver).

A قراط *kirāt*, A light, lamp, or the flame thereof. Snuff of a candle or lamp-match. A funeral-prayer or oration. (pl. of قرط *kurt*) Ear-rings.

A قرّاط *kirrāt*, A carat, the 24th part of an ounce.

A قراطب *kurātib*, Sharp, cutting.

A قراطط *karātit*, (pl. of (قرطان) Saddle-cloths.

A قراطف *karātif*, Shaggy carpets.

A قراطيس *karātīs*, (pl. of قرطاس *kirtās*) Papers.

A قرّاظ *karrāz*, A vender of سلم *salam*-leaves.

A قراع *kirāģ*, (v. n. of قرع) Bulling. Covering.

A قرّاع *karrāģ*, (pl. قرّاعات *karrāģāt*) Hard, firm. A bird that digs with his bill a nest in solid wood.

A قرّاعة *karrāģat*, Scarcity of pasture. Podex.

A قراف *kirāf*, (v. n. 3 of قرف) Having to do (with one's wife). Drawing near, approaching.

A قرافة *kurāfat*, The bark of a tree.

A قرافص *kurāfis*, Hard, strong, large, and thick. Quick, brisk, active.

A قرافصة *karāfisat*, Thieves, robbers.

P قرافه *karāfa*, Name of a city.

A قرافيص *karāfīs*, (pl. of قرفصاء *kurfusāء*, q.v.).

A قراقر *karāhar*, Grumbling of the guts (borborygmi). Noise, outcry, hubbub. *Kurāhir*, (and قراقريّ *hurākiriy*) Melodious, tunable (applied particularly to camel-drivers, who sing as they travel).

A قراقرة *kurākirat*, Talkative (woman). A substance resembling lights, which protrudes from the mouth of a male camel when in heat.

A قراقف *kurākif*, Sonorous (crowing cock).

A قراقل *karākil*, (pl. of قرقل) Women's shifts.

T قرال *krāl* or *kirāl*, (Sclav.) A king. A chief.

A قرام *kirām*, A painted or embroidered veil or curtain; a garment of coloured or figured stuff. A place where the skin is cut, by way of mark, in a camel's nose.

A قرامة *kurāmat*, Part of the skin cut, by way of mark, from a camel's nose. Part of the crust of bread sticking to the oven. A mark, spot, stain, blemish. An orbicular callosity on a camel's breast.

A قرامص *kurāmis*, Sour (milk).

A قرامطة *karāmitat*, (pl. of قرمطيّ *karmatiy*) Certain sects of people.

A قرامل *karāmil*, Camels with two bunches.

A قراميد *karāmīd*, (pl. of قرمود *hurmūd*) Young of wild goats. (pl. of قرميد *hirmīd*) Bricks. Tiles.

A قراميص *karāmīs*, (pl. of قرماص *hirmās* and قرموص *hurmūs*) Holes dug in plains, into which shepherds retire to shelter themselves in winter.

A قرآن *kurءān*, (v. n. of قرأ) Gathering together, collecting. Conveying, carrying. Reading. Teaching. Invoking. Bringing forth. The Kur'ān. قرآن شريف *kurءāni sharīf*, (or قرآن عظيم *kurءāni ءazīm*) The great, the noble book.

A قران *kirān*, (v. n. of قرن) Being in a transition state from green to moist (a date). (v. n. 3 of قرن) Living together, being intimate. Being in conjunction (two stars). Eating two dates at once. Conjunction of planets. A performing together of the sacred visitations called حجّ *hajj* and عمرة *ءumrat*. A pair of arrows matched. A rope joining camels, or oxen to a plough. An arrow finished by one man. (pl. of قرن *karn*) Small hills. Tops of mountains. قران اعظم *kirāni aءzam*, The greatest conjunction (in astrology). قران سعدين *kirāni saءdayn*, Conjunction of the two beneficent planets (Jupiter and Venus). قران نحسين *kirāni nahsayn*, Conjunction of the two malignant planets (Saturn and Mars). صاحب قران *sāhib-kirān*, Lord of felicity, august hero (a royal title).

A قرّان *karrān*, A flask or decanter.

P قرآن خوان *kurءān-khwān*, A reader of the Kur'ān. Cashiered, dismissed from a post or office.

A قراني *kurāna'*, Associated, nearly allied.

A قرآنيّ *kurءāniy*, Coranic.

A قرانيا *karāniya'*, Cornel-tree. Sorb-apple.

A قرانيس *karānis*, An inundation, or its beginning, with leaves and rubbish borne on its surface.

A قرانيص *karānīs*, (pl. of قرنوص *hurnūs*) Seams on the tops of boots. Fore parts or toes of boots.

P قراول *karāwul*, A sentinel, watchman, spy, guard. The vanguard. قراول كردن *karāwul kardan*, To mount guard.

P قراولي *karāwulī*, A skirmish, running fight.

A قرّاؤن *karrāءun*, (pl. of قرّاء *karrāء*) Readers of the Kur'ān. *Kurrāءun*, (pl. of قرّاء *kurrāء*) Addicted to sacred reading.

A قرّاويّ *kurrāwiy*, Belonging to a reader.

A قراويح *karāwīh*, (pl. of قرواح *kirwāh*) Long-legged (she-camels). Tall and smooth (palm-trees). Countries exposed to the sun.

A قراهيد *karāhīd*, Young sheep, lambkins.

A قرائث *karāءis*, (pl. of قريثاء *karīsāء*) Excellent sorts of dates.

A قراي صاحب طيلسان *harāyi sāhib taylasān*, The planet Jupiter. The planet Saturn. (or قراي طيلساني *harāyi taylasānī*) The planet Saturn.

A قرائن *karāɛin*, Houses opposite each other. ذوات القرائن *zawātu'l karāɛin*, (pl. of ذو القرينتين *zū'l harīnatayn*) Nerves inside the thigh. دور قرائن *dūrun harāɛin*, Houses facing each other.

A قرائيّ *kurrāɛiy*, Belonging to a reader.

A قرب *harb*, (v. n. of قرب) Putting up a sword into a case, wherein the scabbard and appendages are kept. Making a sheath for holding a sword with its scabbard. Feasting a guest on the parts betwixt the haunches and the soft parts of the belly. *Kurb*, (v. n. of قرب) Drawing near, approaching. Neighbourhood, nearness, vicinity, approach. *Kurb* or *kurub*, (pl. اقراب *akrāb*) The hypochondria, or space between the haunches and short ribs. قربا و بعدا *kurban wa buɛdan*, Near and far. بقرب *bi kurbin*, (عن قرب *ɛan kurbin*, or من قرب *min kurbin*) Immediately. هو بالقرب منّي *huwa bi'l kurbi minnī*, He is my relation. *Karab*, (v. n. of قرب) Complaining of pain in the hypochondria. A nocturnal journey (especially towards water in the deserts). Relationship. A well whose water is near the top. ليلة القرب *laylatu'l karab*, A night on which water is sought at a little distance. *Kirab*, (pl. of قربة *kirbat*) Large leathern milk-bags or water-bottles.

A قرباء *kurabāɛ*, (pl. of قريب *karīb*) Relations.

A قربات *kirbāt*, *kirabāt*, and *kiribāt*, (pl. of قربة *kirbat*) Leathern water-bottles, or milk-bottles.

A قربان *karbān*, (pl. قراب *kirāb*) A vessel nearly full. *Kirbān*, Coition. *Kirbān* or *kurbān*, (v. n. of قرب) Approaching, being, or standing near to another. *Kurbān* or *karbān*, (pl. قرابين *karābīn*) That whereby one draws nigh to God. A sacrifice, victim, oblation. The Christian communion; or rather, the sacrifice of the mass. One who has access to the king, a royal favourite.

P قربان *kurbān*, A case for a bow.

P قربانگاه *kurbān-gāh*, Place of sacrifice, altar.

A قرباني *kurbānī*, Devoted. Sacrificed. P قرباني كردن *kurbānī kardan*, To sacrifice.

G قربانيون *karbāniyūn*, Ox-eye (a plant).

A قربة *kirbat*, (pl. قربات *kirbāt*, *kirabāt*, *kiribāt*, or قرب *kirab*) A large leathern milk-bottle or water-bag, particularly stitched on one side. عرق القربة *ɛaraku'l kirbat*, Adversity. *Kurbat* or *kurubat*, Kindred: affinity, vicinity, proximity, intimacy, familiarity. *Karabat*, An approach to fulness.

A قربج *kurbaj*, A tavern, a wine-shop.

A قربز *hurbuz*, (from P گربز *gurbuz*) A cheat.

A قربشوش *karbashūsh*, Household furniture.

A قربق *kurbak*, A green-stall or shop. A vintner's shop. Basra.

A قربوت *karabūt*, Saddle-bow or pommel.

A قربوس *karabūs*, (dual قربوسان *karabūsāni*) (pl. قرابيس *karābīs*) The bow or pommel of a saddle.

P قربولة *karbūla*, A kind of ivy.

A قربيٰ *karba'*, (fem. of قربان *karbān*) Nearly full (vessel). *Kurba'*, Affinity, relationship. ذو القربيٰ *zū'l kurba'*, A relation, relative, kinsman.

P قربوس *karpūs*, The bow of a saddle.

A قرة *kirat*, (v. n. of وقر) Being quiet, modest, grave, sedate. Loading a beast of burden. A flock with the shepherd, his dog, and his ass. Family, children, domestics. A burden, load, weight. A very aged man. A time of sickness. Pestilence. A sheep. Property, substance. Patience, quietness, gravity.

A قرّة *harrat*, (v. n. of قرّ) Being cold and cheerful (the eye). (fem. of قرّ *harr*) Cold (night). *Kirrat*, The cold; the cold fit of an ague. *Kurrat*, (v. n. of قرّ) Being cold and cheerful (the eye). Being charmed by the sight of a beloved object (the eye). Remains of meat or of jelly sticking to the bottom of a pot. Joy, gladness. A gush or a rush (of water). قرّة العين *kurratu'l ɛayn*, A coldness (*i. e.* a lustre or cheerfulness) of the eye. A beloved object. A kind of water-cress. ابو قرّة *abū hurrat*, A chameleon. *Kurrat*, *karrat*, or *kirrat*, A frog.

P قرت *hart*, (or قرته) A contented cuckold.

A قرت *karat*, (v. n. of قرت) Changing colour, becoming pale (from pain or anger). Ice. Snow. Jelly.

A قرّتان *harratāni*, Evening and morning.

P قرتبان *hartabān*, A contented cuckold.

P قرتبوس *hartabūs*, A contented cuckold.

A قرث *hars*, (v. n. of قرث) Labouring, toiling. Gaining. Giving much trouble (any business). A small leathern bottle.

A قرثع *karsaɛ*, Foolish, simple, silly (woman), painting one eye and not the other, or dressing preposterously. Immodest, shameless (woman). A male ostrich. A lion. A little kind of shell-fish. Mean, paltry. Small hairs or down upon a beast.

A قرثعة *karsaɛat*, Small hairs or down upon an animal. *Kirsiɛat*, An excellent shepherd, under whose care a flock thrives.

A قرثل *karsal*, A man of a middling size; dwarfish. A small leathern bottle.

A قرح *harh*, (v. n. of قرح) Wounding, ulcerating. Digging a well where there is no water. A wound, scar, painful ulcer. A pustule tending to corruption. A sore ulcer destructive to young camels. *Kurh*, A painful wound, or the pain of a wound. The beginning of any thing. The three first nights of the month. Water gushing from a well. قرح الربيع *hurhu'r rabīɛ*, Beginning of spring *Karah*, (v. n. of قرح) Finishing the teething when full five years old (solid-hoofed animals). Being ulcerous. *Karih*, Scabby, pimply, pustulous, ulcerous.

A قرّح *kurrah*, (pl. of قارح) Five-year-old (horses).

A قرحاء *karhāɛ*, White with flowers (garden).

A قرحان *karhān*, A lion. *Kurhān*, One who recedes, or gives up, or is free and clear of business. A species of mushroom or fungus. One who has never been present in a battle. (A camel) having never had the scab or any small pustules. (A boy) who has not had the small-pox. (A man) never having been ill. Ulcerous, scabby. One who has had the small-pox. (pl. of اقرح *akrah*) Mushrooms.

A قرحانة *kurhānat*, A single mushroom.

A قرحانون *kurhānūn*, (pl. of قرحان) Ulcerated.

A قرحاني *kurhāniy*, One who recedes or gives up any work.

A قرحة *karhat*, One wound with a sword. One ulcer, sore, pimple, or pustule. Ulceration. *Kurhat*, A small star on the forehead of a horse. Commencement of spring or winter.

A قرحيٰ *karha'*, (pl. of قريح *karīh*) Ulcerated.

A قرحياء *kirhiyāɛ*, A sown field destitute of trees and of buildings, appropriated exclusively to planting and sowing.

P قرخواك *karkhwāk*, Broth of meat cut small.

A قرد *hard*, (v. n. of قرد) Gaining. Collecting (as butter in a churn). Short, dwarfish. The neck. *Kird*, (pl. اقراد *akrād*, قرود *kurūd*, قرد *karid*, قردة *kiradat*, and *karidat*) A male ape, monkey, baboon. *Kurd*, A tike, tick, louse infesting sheep, camels, or horses. *Karad*, (v. n. of قرد) Being corroded, worm-eaten (leather). Being silent (especially from an impediment in speech). Being small (teeth). Being crisp and curly (hair). Being matted together and impacted (wool). Being spoiled in flavour (resin). The worst or coarsest parts of wool. Small particles beneath a cloud which do not amalgamate. Palm-branches stripped of their leaves. A kind of down adhering to the طرثوث *tursūs*. A repeating of words, tautology. *Karid*, Heaped up, cumulated. (A camel) swarming with tikes. (pl. of قرد *kird*) Apes. قرد الخصيل *karidu'l khasīl*, Firmly-knit, not flabby (horse).

G قردامن *hardāman*, Seed of wild rue.

G قردامومن *hardāmūman*, Cresses.

G قردامينى *hardāmīnī*, The herb lady's-smock. Water-mint.

A قردان *kirdān*, (pl. of قراد *kurād*) Tikes, ticks. امّ القردان *ummu'l kirdān*, A place between the hinder part of a horse's hoof, over which the hairs hang.

A قردة *kirdat*, A she-ape. *Karadat*, A flock of coarse wool. *Kiradat* or *karidat*, (pl. of قرد *kird*) Male apes.

A قردح *kardah* or *kurduh*, A striped cloth. *Kurduh*, A large ape.

A قردحة *hardahat*, (v. n. of قردح Q) Acknowledging, owning any thing about which one is asked. Submitting, humbling one's self. *Kurduhat*, A swelling in the throat, Adam's apple.

A القردحمة *alkirdahmata*, *al kardahmata*, (or بقردحمة *bi kirdahmata*, Every where, here and there, on all sides. بقردحمة *bi kardahmatin* or *kirdah-*

matin, Plainly, distinctly.

A قردد *kardad*, (pl. قرادد *karādid* and قراديد *karādid*) High, rugged ground. The upper part of the back. Hardness. Severity of cold. The face. Name of a mountain.

A قردسة *kardasat*, (v. n. of قردس Q) Tying, binding, fastening tight. Calling (a whelp). Firmness, hardness.

A قردع *kirdaع* or *kirdiع*, A camel-louse, or a hen-louse. A fowl, a hen.

A قردعة *kardaعat*, Baseness, meanness. *Kirdiعat*, The neck.

A قردم *kardam*, A stammerer.

G قردمانا *kardamānā*, Cardmine. *Kurdumānā*, Wild caraway.

A قردماني *kurdamāna'*, Caraway.

A قردماني *kurdumāniy*, A coat of mail, cuirass, either of rings of iron or quilted cloth. A helmet, or a cap worn under the helmet.

A قردوح *kurdūh*, A large ape.

A قردوحة *kurdūhat*, A lump or swelling in the throat, Adam's apple.

A قردود *kurdūd*, High and rugged ground.

A قردودة *kurdūdat*, High and rugged ground. The most prominent part of the back, the shoulders. Severity (of winter).

A قردوس *kurdūs*, Name of the founder of a tribe.

A قردوع *kurdūع*, A small ant.

A قردوعة *kurdūعat*, A nook in a mountain-cleft.

A قرديدة *kirdīdat*, Rude language. A stripe along the back. The head of a man. The summit of a mountain. See كرديدة.

A بقرذحمة *biki* or *karzahmatin*, Plainly, clearly.

A قرذع *karzaع*, A foolish, silly woman.

A قرر *kurar*, Soup, broth, pottage.

A قررة *kararat*, Cold water poured into a pot that it may not be burned. *Kurarat* or *kururat*, Meat or jelly which adheres to the bottom of a pot.

A قرز *karz*, (v. n. of قرز) Taking up earth with the tips of the fingers. Making up little balls between the fingers. A hillock. Rugged (ground). *Kurz*, An ointment-box: a cupper's ointment-glass.

A قرزام *kirzām*, A mean poet, poetaster.

A قرزة *kurzat*, A handful.

A قرزح *kurzuh*, A female vest. Name of a tree and a horse.

A قرزحة *kurzuhat*, A short, mean woman. A kind of pot-herb. A kind of small tree.

A قرزحلة *kirzahlat*, An amulet hung round a child's neck. A bludgeon, a stick. A dwarfish woman. Necessary things.

A قرزل *kurzul*, Vile, abject, mean. The hair worn in a certain fashion by women round the head. A fetter. Hard, scirrhous. Elegant, graceful. Compactly built. Name of a horse.

A قرزلة *karzalat*, (v. n. of قرزل Q) Collecting her hair, and winding it in a certain fashion round her head (a woman).

P قرزم *hurzum*, The Red Sea.

A قرزمة *karzamat*, (v. n. of قرزم Q) Composing or bringing out doggrel verse.

A قرزوم *kurzūm*, A shoemaker's block or table on which he cuts out.

A قرس *kars*, Severe cold, hoar-frost. Cold. ليلة ذات قرس *laylat zāt karsin*, A chilly, frosty night. *Kars* or *karas*, (v. n. of قرس) Being very cold, freezing. *Kirs*, A small gnat. *Karas*, Congealed, stiff.

P قرسنه *kirisna*, A scab.

A قرش *karsh*, (v. n. of قرش) Collecting from all quarters. Mixing. Attacking each other with spears. Adding one to another. Cutting, splitting. A kind of marine animal or fish that preys upon fish.

A قرشام *kirshām*, (pl. قراشم) A large tike.

A قرشامة *kirshāmat*, A sparrow-hawk. A kind of animalcule.

A قرشبّ *kirshabb*, (pl. قراشب *karāshib*) Old, aged. Thick. Tall. Of an evil disposition. In evil case. A lion. A glutton. Badly circumcised. Fat.

A قرشحة *karshahat*, A leaping with short steps.

A قرشع *kirshiع*, A heat in the breast or the throat, heartburn. A white eruption like salt on the body.

A قرشمّ *kirshamm*, Hard and strong. An old Lybian lizard.

A قرشوم *kurshūm*, A kind of tree to which tikes resort. A large tike or tick.

A قرشيّ *kurashiy*, Of the tribe of قريش *kuraysh*.

A قرص *kars*, (v. n. of قرص) Taking with the finger and thumb. Pinching, nipping. Making up balls of leaven between the fingers. Biting (a flea). Squeezing with the points of the fingers in washing. Spreading out dough. Cutting. A flea-bite. *Kurs*, (pl. اقراص *akrās* and قرصة *kirasat*) A round loaf or cake. A pastil. A lozenge. The sun's orb or disk. P قرص خورشيد *kursi khwurshed*, The orb or disk of the sun. قرص زر *kursi zar*, (قرص زر مغربي *kursi zar maghribi*, or قرص هفت درة *kursi haft dara*) The sun. قرص سيمين *kursi simin*, (or قرص مه *kursi mah*) The moon. قرص گرم و سرد *kursi garm u sard*, Sun and moon. قرص نان *kursi nān*, A cake or loaf of bread. A *Karas*, (v. n. of قرص) Persevering in a contest for honour or glory, or in slander and detraction. *Kuras*, (pl. of قرصة *kursat*) Round loaves or cakes. Pastiles.

A قرصافة *kirsāfat*, (A woman or a camel) that rolls, as if she were a ball. See خذروف *khuzrūf*. قاصة قرصافة *hāssat kirsāfat*, A kind of game.

A قرصبة *karsabat*, An amputating, a cutting.

A قرصة *kursat*, (pl. قرص *kuras*) A round loaf. A pastil. The holy wafer, the host. P قرصۀ زر *kursa-i zar*, The sun (the loaf of gold). A *Kirasat*, (pl. of قرص *kurs*) Crusts of bread.

A قرصد *karsad*, What remains on a threshing-floor after threshing.

A قرصع *karsaع*, Veretrum breve. Name of a base and sordid fellow in Yaman; hence the proverb, الأم من قرصع *alام min karsaع*, (or من ابن القرصع *min ibni'l karsaع*) More sordid than Karsaa.

A قرصعة *karsaعat*, (v. n. of قرصع Q) Writing in close lines. Walking awkwardly (a woman). Contracting one's self. Seeking to hide one's self. Eating sparingly, or eating alone. Sitting at home.

A قرصعنة *karsaعnat*, Sea-holm, sea-holly.

P قرصك *kursak*, A small sweet cake.

A قرصمة *karsamat*, A breaking. A cutting.

A قرصنّة *kursunnat*, (A woman) who takes not up with the finger and thumb what she supposes.

A قرصوف *kursūf*, Keen, sharp.

A قرض *karz*, (v. n. of قرض) Cutting (a rope). Gnawing (as a rat). Rehearsing or composing (verse). Repaying, requiting. Leaning to the right or left in travelling. Declining, moving from one thing to another. Going out of the right road. Turning aside from a place. Passing by a place, leaving it on one side. Dying. Threatening death. *Karz* or *kirz*, Debt, a loan; money borrowed or lent on interest (especially without any fixed term of payment, that being expressed by دين *dayn*). Retribution, retaliation (good or bad). Good or evil sent on before, and for which a future recompense will be awarded. قرض حسن *karzi hasan*, Money advanced without interest, and repaid at the pleasure of the borrower; literally, a good loan. P قرض دادن *karz dādan*, To lend. قرض كردن *karz kardan* (or داشتن *dāshtan*), To borrow.

A قرضاب *kirzāb*, (pl. قراضبة *karāzibat*) A lion. A robber. A thief. A needy thief. A sharp sword. One who eats any thing dry. A poor, starving man, who eats whatever is set before him. A small matter.

A قرضابة *kirzābat*, A starving fellow, who eats up whatever is placed before him.

A قرضب *kirzib*, Chaff thrown out of a sieve.

A قرضبة *karzabat*, (v. n. of قرضب Q) Collecting meat in a cauldron. Dividing. Scattering. Eating dry things. Eating the whole of any thing. Cutting. Running.

P قرض خواه *karz-khwāh*, A creditor. A dun.

P قرض دار *karz-dār*, A borrower, debtor.

P قرضداري *karz-dārī*, The being in debt.

A قرضمة *karzamat*, (v. n. of قرضم Q) Cutting, amputating. Taking every thing.

A قرضوب *kurzūb*, (pl. قراضبة *karāzibat*) A robber. A needy thief. A sharp sword. A poor or a starving man, one who eats all placed before him.

A قرضوف *kurzūf*, A shepherd's staff. A great eater.

A قرضيُ *kirzis*, Name of a yellow flowering shrub.

A قرضيّ *karziy*, Borrowed.

A قرضيّة *karzīya*, A loan.

P قرط *kart*, The fruit of a certain thorny shrub. *Kurt*, A kind of trefoil. The noise made in swallowing water. Patience.

A قرط *kart*, (v. n. of قرط) Slicing in pieces (a

leek). *Kirt*, A leek. *Kurt*, (pl. اقرطة *akritat*, اقراط *akrāt*, قراط *hirāt*, قروط *kurūt*, and قرطة *kiratat*) An ear-ring. Clover. A little boy's cock. A dug, an udder. Fire, flame. قرطي مارية *kurtay māriyat*, The ear-rings of Mary, (proverbially) any thing extremely valuable. *Karat*, (v. n. of قرط) Having the lobes of the ears hanging down (a goat).

A قرطاجنة *kurtājannat*, Carthage. Carthagena.

A قرطاس *kartās*, *kirtās*, or *kurtās*, (pl. قراطيس *karātīs*) Paper. *Kirtās*, A beautiful, fine-made, fair-complexioned girl. A leaf, a page. A target, a butt for archers. A brown dusky colour. A young she-camel. An Egyptian striped stuff.

A قرطاسيّ *kirtāsiy*, (A horse) of a pure, unmixed white (as white as paper).

A قرطاط *kurtāt* or *kirtāt*, A soft cloth laid under a saddle to imbibe the sweat. Evil, misfortune.

A قرطال *kirtāl*, (pl. of قرطالة *kirtālat* or قرطلّة *kirtallat*) Fruit-baskets. Panniers; as much as an ass carries on one side.

A قرطالة *kirtālat*, An ass-load. A fruit-basket.

A قرطان *kurtān*, Misfortune, evil. (pl. قراطط) A soft cloth laid under a saddle to imbibe the sweat.

A قرطبان *kartabān*, A pimp to his own wife; a voluntary cuckold, a wittol.

A قرطبة *kartabat*, (v. n. of قرطب Q) Throwing on the back. Cutting up a slaughtered camel. Being angry. Running fast. Fleeing away. *Kurtubat*, Cordova in Spain.

A قرطبي *kurtuba'*, (or القرطبي) A sword.

A قرطبّي *kirtibba'*, Name of a game. A mode of wrestling.

A قرطة *kiratat*, (pl. of قرط *kurt*) Ear-rings. *Kuratat* or *kiratat*, When a goat has the lobes of the ears hanging down.

A قرطس *kartas* or *kirtas*, Paper.

A قرطسة *kartasat*, (v. n. of قرطس Q) Hitting the mark, the blank or the white (an arrow).

A قرطع *kirtaɛ* or *kirtiɛ*, A camel or hen-louse.

A قرطعب *kirtaɛb*, A cloud. Name of an animal.

A قرطعبة *kirtaɛbat*, *kuratɛabat*, or *kurutɛubat*, Any thing little or much. A rag, bit of cloth.

A قرطعن *kirtaɛn*, Foolish.

A قرطعنة *kirtaɛnat*, A little. A rag, bit of cloth.

A قرطف *kartaf*, Velvet, satin. A certain pot-herb, or the fruit of the رمث *rims*.

A قرطق *kurtak*, (P كرته) A kind of garment.

A قرطقة *kartakat*, (v. n. of قرطق Q) Putting the garment قرطق *kurtak* on (any person).

A قرطلّة *kirtallat*, A pannier, that which an ass carries on one side.

A قرطم *kirtim* or *kurtum*, Seed of safflower.

P قرطمان *kurtumān*, Oats.

A قرطمانا *kartamānā*, Wild caraway-seeds.

A قرطمة *kartamat*, (v. n. of قرطم Q) Cutting. *Kirtimat*, (or dual قرطمتان *kirtimatāni*) Two dots on the root of a (pigeon's) beak.

A قرطور *kartūr*, A fortress in Azarbayjān.

P قرطه *karta*, Sewing, the stitches of which appear distinctly. A kind of short garment. قرطهٔ فستقي *kartaɪ fistikī*, A reddish-green kind of garment.

A قرطيّة *kar* or *kurtiyat*, A species of camel.

A قرطيط *kirtīt*, Misfortune, evil. Somewhat.

A قرطيطة *kirtītat*, A little, somewhat.

A قرظ *karaz*, (v. n. of قرظ) Becoming great and honourable, from being contemptible. The fruit of the acacia. Leaves of the tree سلم *salam*, with which they tan leather. بلاد القرظ *bilādu'l karaz*, Arabia Felix (from the number of those trees which grow there). مروان القرظ *marwānu'l karaz*, Name of the fourth caliph of the house of Umayya.

A قرظيّ *ka* or *kuraziy*, Native of Arabia Felix.

A قرع *karɛ*, (v. n. of قرع) Knocking (at a door or gate). Beating, striking (the head with a stick). Winning, beating at drawing lots. Covering (a camel), bulling (a bull). Grinding the teeth (from remorse or vexation). Befalling any one (calamity). Knocking one's forehead with an empty cup (a drinker, *i.e.* draining the cup dry). Being empty, or not crowded. Emptiness of court. A kind of gourd. *Kurɛ*, (pl. of اقرع *akraɛ* and قرعاء *karɛās*) Bald (men or women). Hard (places or shields). Fields without herbage. Name of certain valleys in Syria. *Karaɛ*, (v. n. of قرع) Being overcome in archery. Throwing the javelin for a wager. Taking advice, acquiescing in it. Departing from any advice given and acquiesced in. Being bald through disease. Being empty (a fold). Being thinly attended (a court or religious festival). An empty camel-fold. A leathern buckler. A fluid resembling froth floating on the surface of camels' milk. A small corn-sack with a wide bottom. White pustules on the feet of young camels. A wager at a horse-race. An instrument for cauterizing. Precedency. Money paid in advance. Any thing for which money has been paid in advance. *Kariɛ*, Unable to sleep. Rotten (nail or hoof). One who takes advice, but neglects to follow it. قرع جبهته بالاناء *karaɛa jabhatahu bi'l inās*, He struck his forehead against the cup, *i.e.* he drank the whole up. من قرع بابا ولجّ ولج *man karaɛa bāban wa lajja, waluja*, Whoever knocks at a door and perseveres, gains admittance.

A قرّع *hurraɛ*, (pl. of اقرع *akraɛ*) Hard (places or shields).

A قرعاء *karɛās*, (fem. of اقرع *akraɛ*) Bald (woman). A field eaten bare. Adversity, distress. A court, a quadrangle. The highest part of a road. Decayed (finger).

A قرعامة *kirɛāmat*, Of full growth (a palm).

A قرعان *kurɛān*, (pl. of اقرع *akraɛ* and قرعاء *karɛās*) Bald (people, men and women).

A قرعبل *karaɛbal*, (or قرعبلانة *karaɛbalānat*) A species of marine animal, broad, short, and thick.

A قرعة *karɛat*, One gourd. A mark branded on the hardest and least fleshy part of the leg of a camel. *Kurɛat*, A wager, bet, wagering, drawing lots. The seeking of one's fortune by opening of a book; bibliomancy. A lot (such as the Arabians draw with arrows). The best part of cattle. A mark branded (especially on the middle of a camel's nose). كانت له القرعة *kānat lahu'l kurɛat*, The lot fell upon him. *Karaɛat*, Baldness. A bald place on the head.

A قرعث *karɛas*, A congregation, collection.

A قرعوس *kirɛaws* (*kurɛūs*, قرعوش *kirɛawsh* or *kurɛūsh*) Double-bunched (camel).

A قرعوش *kurɛūsh*, A lion's whelp.

A قرعون *karɛūn*, Name of a village between Balbeck and Damascus.

A قرعي *karɛa'*, (pl. of قريع *kariɛ*) Young camels.

P قرغوي *kir ghūy*, A sparrow-hawk, merlin.

A قرف *karf*, (v. n. of قرف) Unbarking, skinning, laying bare (a sore). Peeling, barking (a clove when dry). Accusing, criminating. Gaining a livelihood (for one's family). Overbearing, tyrannizing. Mixing. Lying. Suspecting. A bag of camels' or cows' leather, tanned with pomegranate-rinds, in which they carry pickled meats. A certain tree used in tanning. Forage, provender. Proper, fit, worthy, suitable. Very red. *Kirf*, The bark of certain trees (as the pomegranate). Earth which comes away sticking to vegetables or roots. Crust of bread adhering to the oven. Dry mucus of the nose. *Kurf*, (pl. of قروف *karūf*) Extremely insolent and pugnacious. *Karaf*, (v. n. of قرف) Being near happening. A certain disease fatal to camels. A relapse. The spread (of plague or contagion). Infected with an epidemic disease (a country). Proper, fit, worthy, suitable. Mixture, commerce. *Karif*, Worthy, suitable.

A قرفاص *kirfās*, A stallion that satisfies.

A قرفة *kirfat*, A kind of cinnamon. Suspicion. Suspected. Dry mucus of the nose. Turpitude, baseness, vileness. Gain. Bark (as of a pomegranate). هو قرفتي *huwa kirfatī*, He it is whom I suspect. بنو فلان قرفتي *banū fulān kirfatī*, The sons of So-and-so are those in whose possession I expect to find the object of my search. سل بني فلان عن ناقتك فانّهم قرفة *sal banī fulān ɛan nāhatika fa innahum kirfat*, Enquire of the sons of So-and-so respecting thy camel: they can tell thee about her. امّ قرفة *ummu kirfat*, Name of a woman who had so many male relations that their swords, to the number of fifty, were suspended in her tent.

A قرفصاء *kurfusās* or *kurufsās*, (قرفصي *karfasa'*, *kirfisa'*, or *kurfusa'*) An Arabian mode of sitting on the hips, with the knees close to the belly, and the hands folded under the arm-pits, or embracing the legs.

A قرفصة *karfusat*, (v. n. of قرفص Q) Tying together the hands and feet. Modus coeundi.

A قرفطة *harfatat*, A mode of walking with short steps. Modus coeundi.

P قرفه *kirfa*, A sort of cinnamon.

A قرفيّ *karfiy*, Ruddy (man).

A قرق *kark*, Any sound uttered by a fowl. *Kirk*, A bad origin. Custom, habit. Small people. A kind of game called سدّر *suddar*. *Kurk*, Embargo, confiscation, seizure. Enclosure, hindrance, prevention of success. *Karak*, (v. n. of قرق) Travelling over level ground. *Karak* or *karik*, Plain ground. Level.

P قرقار *karkār*, A pigeon of Baghdād.

A قرقار *karkār*, The braying in a clear voice (of a camel). The cooing of a dove. A kind of vase or vessel. *Karkāri*, Remain, be quiet (O woman)!

A قرقارة *karkārat*, A substance resembling lights, protruding from the mouth of a male camel in rut.

A قرقب *karkab*, *hurkub*, or *kurkubb*, The belly. *Kurkub*, Name of a little bird.

A قرقبة *kurkubbat*, A piece of flesh or bait for catching game.

A قرقر *karkar*, The suburbs of a town. A woman's garment. Level, smooth, and slippery ground. The back. اذلّ من فقع بقرقر *azallu min fakʻin bi karkarin*, More worthless (more easy to be taken) than a fungus on soft ground.

A قرقرا *karkarā*, Name of a bird (Ardea Virgo).

A قرقرة *karkarat*, (v. n. of قرقر Q) Cooing (as a dove). Braying (a camel). Laughing until the tears run and a rattling noise in the throat is heard. Pouring cold water into a pot that it may not be burned. Level, soft ground. That part of the face which is uncovered. A mode of laughing, giggling.

P قرقرون *kurkurūn*, Galangale.

P قرقري *karkarī*, A mode of tying on a turban.

A قرقرّي *kirkirrīy*, (or قرقريّ *kirkiriy*) The back.

A قرقرير *karkarīr*, The cooing of a dove.

A قرقس *kirkis*, A species of small gnat.

A قرقسة *karkasat*, A calling (of a dog).

P قرقسيا *karkasyā*, Cubeb (a drug).

P قرقشه كردن *karkasha kardan*, To contend.

A قرقصة *karkasat*, A calling (of a whelp).

P قرقف *kurkuf*, Name of a book of the Magi.

A قرقف *karkaf*, Wine which, when drunk, causes a trembling. *Kurkuf*, A kind of small bird.

A قرقفة *karkafat*, (v. n. of قرقف Q) Causing to tremble. Cooing (a dove). Braying (a camel). Having one's teeth chattering with cold. Thundering. Trembling. Laughing loudly. Tremor.

A قرقفنّة *karkafannat*, Glans penis. A certain bird that spreads his wing over the eye of a shameless, contented cuckold, to increase his shamelessness and want of spirit.

A قرقل *karkal*, (or قرقلّ *karkall*) (pl. قراقل *karākil*) A woman's shift.

A قرقم *kirkim*, Glans penis.

P قرقمان *karkamān*, Wood found in the middle of the tree مقل *mukl*, and used as a dentifrice.

A قرقمة *karkamat*, (v. n. of قرقم Q) Being badly fed (a child).

P قرقوبي *kar* or *kurkūbī*, A garment made in Irāk.

A قرقور *kurkūr*, A long and large ship.

A قرقوس *kurkūs*, A word used in calling a dog or kid. A wide desert. *Karakūs*, Hard, level soil, rugged and bare, raised or depressed, without herbage, and abounding in hot springs.

A قرقوص *kurkūs*, A whelp.

A قرقوف *kurkūf*, Wine which, when it hath been drunk, causes a trembling. A silver coin.

P قرقومي *karkūmī*, A sort of garment.

A قرقي *kurkī*, Confiscated. P قرقي پروانه *kurkī-parwāna*, A warrant issued to sequester a property.

P قركن *karkan*, The bed of a river fresh dug. A channel excavated by a torrent.

A قرلّى *kirillaʼ*, Name of a very wary bird.

A قرم *karm*, (v. n. of قرم) Marking (a camel) by cutting part of the skin of the nose and leaving it dangling. Unbarking, peeling. Eating (meat). Eating gently (as an infant); nibbling the herbage (a camel). Reviling. Detaining, imprisoning, keeping back. (pl. قروم *kurūm*) An excellent camel stallion kept for covering, or fed for slaughter. A lord, a prince. A notch upon a gaming arrow. *Kurm*, A kind of marine plant. *Karam*, (v. n. of قرم) Having an insatiable craving for flesh meat. Having a longing desire for a mistress or a friend. *Karim*, Carnivorous. *Kirim*, A term of reproach. The Crimea. T قرم خاني *kirim-khānī*, The khan of the Crim Tartars. A بحر القرم *bahru'l kirim*, The sea of Azof. The Euxine Sea.

A قرماء *karmāʼ*, (A she-camel) the skin of whose nose is cut and left dangling as a mark.

A قرماز *kirmāz*, A loaf round and flat.

A قرماص *kirmās*, (pl. قراميص *karāmīs*) Shortness of the cheeks. (See قرمص *kirmis*).

A قرمان *karmān* or *haramān*, Caramania (Cilicia). *Karamān*, (v. n. of قرم) Eating languidly.

A قرمة *karmat*, A notch upon a game-arrow. A cloth with which they clean beds or carpets. *Karmat* or *kurmat*, Part of the skin cut, and left dangling by way of mark, from a camel's nose. *Kurmat*, The part of a camel's nose where the skin is cut, and left dangling as a mark.

A قرمد *karmad*, Plaster, parget. A stone that softens by fire, of which they make plaster. Saffron. A brick or tile.

A قرمدة *karmadat*, (v. n. of قرمد Q) Building (a house) with burnt bricks or tiles. Writing closely or finely. Going with short steps.

A قرمز *kirmiz*, Kermes, an insect produced upon the kermes-oak, and used in dyeing red; hence, Crimson. Cochineal. A grain resembling a vetch.

A قرمزيّ *kirmiziy*, Crimson, scarlet. P قرمزي روز *kirmizī roz*, A ruddiness in the sky before sunrise.

U قرمساق *kurram sāk*, A pimp, cuckold.

A قرمش *karmash* or *kirmish*, A mixed crowd.

A قرمّش *karammash*, One who eats any thing. Rogues, scoundrels.

A قرمشة *karmashat*, (v. n. of قرمش Q) Spoiling. Damaging. Collecting.

A قرمص *kirmis*, A kind of ditch dug in plains, narrow at top and wide at bottom, into which shepherds retire to shelter themselves from cold in winter. A dove's nest. The place where they bake bread under ashes. Smallness of the cheeks.

A قرمصة *karmasat*, (v. n. of قرمص Q) Entering the shelter قرمص *kirmis*.

A قرمطة *karmatat*, (v. n. of قرمط Q) Writing in close lines. Going with short steps. *Kirmitat*, The nostril of a winged animal.

A قرمطيّ *karmatiy*, (pl. قرامطة) Name of a people.

A قرمطيط *karmatīt*, One who writes small and close. Close writing. One who takes short steps.

A قرمل *karmal*, A kind of weak tree without thorns. *Kirmil*, (pl. قرامل *karāmil*) A species of camel with two bunches; called also بختيّ *bukhtīy*. Whatever fastens a woman's hair. A very hairy young camel.

A قرمليّة *kirmilīyat*, Small and hairy camels.

A قرمود *kurmūd*, (pl. قراميد *karāmīd*) A mountain-goat. Fruit of the tree غضاة *ghazāt*.

A قرموص *kurmūs* (pl. قراميص *karāmīs*). (See قرمص *kirmis*).

A قرموط *kurmūt*, A globule of dung formed by a beetle. The red fruit of the tree غضا *ghazaʼ*.

A قرمول *kurmūl*, The fruit of the tree غضا *ghazaʼ*.

A قرميّة *kirmīyat*, A knot at the root of the hair nose-ring of a camel. *Kuramīyat*, (fem.) Original. حجّة قرميّة *hujjat kuramīyat*, An original decree.

A قرميد *kirmīd*, A roof or gutter-tile. A drain made of earthen pipes (اردبّة *irdabbat*). A female mountain-goat (ارويّة *urwīyat*). Some think this last is an error, the words being much alike.

A قرميز *kirmīz*, Weak.

A قرميش *kirmīsh*, A miscellaneous crowd.

A قرن *karn*, (v. n. of قرن) Joining one thing to another. Yoking (two camels). Falling into the mark of the fore-foot (the hind-foot of a horse). (pl. قرون *kurūn*) A horn. قرن البحر *karnu'l bahr*, Amber. A smooth clean stone. The side of the head (whence the horns grow). A lock of hair, either hanging down straight or curled. A lock of wool. A rope made of the fibres or bark of a tree. The anterior part or entrance into the desert. One time, once. First and the last (of forage). (pl. قران *kirān*) Top of a mountain. (pl. قرون *kurūn* and قران *kirān*) A little hill or part of a mountain rising above the rest. The bottom of a sand-hill. A small tumour like the hernia (anteriore vulvæ parte enascens). Two stars near Capricorn. The covering of a camel-litter or هودة *hawda*. The upper limb of the sun's disk (which appears above the horizon); the rays of the sun. A plump of rain. A prince, a lord. A stone pillar erected at each side of a well, over which is thrown a cross-beam, to which the bucket-pulley is suspended. An instrument for anointing or painting the eyes. Point or the edge of a sword. A certain station for the pilgrims of Najd. A generation, a period of forty years. Many years (from 10 to 80); a decade or space of ten years; also a century, an age, a space of 120 years. Age: as, هو علي قرني *huwa ʿala' karnī*, He is about my age. Coeval, cotemporary. A race, or heat, course. قرن الشيطان *karnu'sh shaytān*, (or قرنا الشيطان *karnā'sh shaytān*) The adherents of Satan. The dominion of the devil. عصر الفرس قرنا او قرنين *ʿasara'l farasa karnan aw karnayn*, He urged his horse to one and another heat, *i.e.* he made him go at full speed. *Kirn*, Equal to, or a match for, another in bravery, wrestling, battle, or art. *Karan*, (v. n. of قرن) Having joined eyebrows. Any animal joined with another (as a yoke of oxen). A rope with which two camels are tied, or two oxen are fastened to the yoke. A leathern quiver. An arrow and a sword. Name of a station for pilgrims.

A قرناء *karnās*, Horned (ewe). Any verse of the Kur'ān that is read at every inclination of the head or genuflexion called ركعة *rakʿat*. *Kuranās*, (pl. of قرين *karīn*) Companions, peers.

A قرناس *kirnās* or *kurnās*, A part of a mountain projecting like a nose. Having projecting sides (a she-camel). The place for receiving picked, teazed, or carded cotton.

P قرناس *kurnās*, A knave, villain, scoundrel, cheat, a man of the worst description. A pimp to his own wife, a cuckold.

A قرنان *karnān*, A cuckold, cornuto; one who allows another to share in his wife's favours.

P قرناي *kar-nāy*, A flute, trumpet.

A قرنب *karnab*, A mouse, either of the domestic or field-species. *Kurnub*, The flank where the small guts are.

P قرنباد *kurumbād*, Wild caraway-seeds.

A قرنباع *kirimbāʿ*, Contracted. Avaricious.

A قرنبضة *kurambazat*, A dwarfish woman.

A قرنبي *karambaʾ*, A kind of large beetle.

A قرنة *kurnat*, The extremity, projecting part, or horn of a thing (as of a spear or mountain). The point of a spear. The edge of a sword. The neck of the womb; or rather, os tincæ. A corner, angle.

P قرنجك *karanjak*, The nightmare.

A قرنس *kirnis*, Prominent-sided (she-camel).

A قرنسة *karnasat*, (v. n. of قرنس Q) Changing plumage; moulting (as birds). Flying when beat (a cock). Being hooded (a falcon recently taken).

A قرنصة *karnasat*, (v. n. of قرنص Q) Running away beaten (a cock). Hunting (a falcon). Sitting on his perch (a falcon). Keeping (a falcon) on his perch. Training or keeping (a falcon) for hunting.

A قرنفش *karanfash*, Thick, large.

A قرنفل *karanful*, A clove. A gilly-flower. P قرنفل بستاني *karanfuli bustānī*, A kind of sweet basil.

A قرنفول *karanfūl*, A clove.

A قرنوة *karnuwat*, An herb growing in the clefts of sand-hills useful in tanning. A horned serpent.

A قرنوص *kurnūs*, (pl. قرانيص *karānīs*) A seam on the top of a boot. The toe of a boot.

A قرنوي *karnawīy*, Tanned with the herb قرنوة *karnuwat* (a leathern bottle). Horned (serpent).

A قرني *karanīy*, One whose eyebrows join.

A ذو القرنين *zū'l karnayn*, Two-horned: a name of Alexander the Great. Name of a certain Arab.

A قرو *karw*, (v. n. of قرا for قرو) Intending. Piercing with a spear. Reproaching. Pursuing. Travelling from place to place. Mode, manner, rule, regulation, institution. A cup or small vessel. A wine-press, or that part through which the juice flows. (pl. قرو *kurūw*) A long cistern for watering camels. A country one can scarcely cross. The lower part of the palm-tree, which, when hollowed out, serves as a trough or wash-tub. A tumour in the scrotum, either from wind, water, or a descent of the bowels. على قرو واحد *ʿala' karwin wāhidin*, In one and the same manner. قروا واحدا *karwan wāhidan*, The same. (Ground covered) equally by one shower. *Karw*, *kirw*, or *kurw*, (pl. اقراء *akrās*, اقري *akrī*, اقروة *akriwat*, and قري *kurīy*) A vessel from which a dog laps his food.

A قروء *kurūs*, (pl. of قرء *kars*) Catamenia. Purifications. Times, seasons. The last consonants in verses to which all the others rhyme.

A قرواء *karwās*, Long-bunched and strong-backed (she-camel). The back, or back-side. Custom, manner, usage.

A قرواح *kirwāh*, A camel refusing to drink with the larger ones, but drinking with the smaller ones. Gone out and exposed to the open air. A sown field destitute of trees and buildings. A wide, extensive tract of country exposed to the sun. (pl. قراويح *karāwīh*) Long-legged (she-camel). Tall and smooth (palm-tree).

A قرواش *kirwāsh*, A parasite. Big-headed.

A قروان *karwān* or *karawān*, The back.

A قرواني *karwānīy*, Troubled with a swelled testicle or hydrocele.

A قروة *karwat*, The side of the head. A tumour in the scrotum from wind, rupture, or hydrocele.

P قروت *kurūt*, Dried curds.

A قروت *kurūt*, (v. n. of قرت) Coagulating or drying (as blood). Assuming a livid appearance (the skin from a blow). قروتي شدن معامله *kurūti shudani muʿāmala*, Confusion, jumble of business.

A قروح *kurūh*, (v. n. of قرح) Having the teeth completely grown (solid-hoofed animals). Being pregnant, and visibly so (a camel). (pl. of قرح *karh*) Ulcers, sores. ذو القروح *zū'l kurūh*, The surname of Amru'l kays, an Arabian prince and famous poet, cotemporary with Muhammad, whom he opposed and satirized. He was the author of one of the seven celebrated Arabian poems called معلقات *muʿallakāt* (*i.e.* suspended), from being hung up in the temple of Mecca on account of their superior excellence, written on silk in letters of gold. He took refuge from his revolted subjects at Ancyra in Galatia, where he died a violent death; in consequence of wearing (according to some Muhammadan writers) a poisoned shirt, sent to him as a present by Heraclius, emperor of Greece, who had taken offence at his lampoons.

A قرود *karūd*, A camel which does not run away from having the tikes picked off him. *Kurūd*, (pl. of قرد *kird*) Apes.

A قرور *karūr*, (A woman) who stands still without offering resistance to a man who kisses (her). Cold water with which any one washes himself. *Kurūr*, (v. n. of قر) Being cold, brisk, and ceasing from tears (an eye). Stopping, resting, standing firm. Being charmed by the sight of a beloved object (the eye).

A قرورة *karūrat*, Base, contemptible. *Kurūrat*, Meat or seasoning sticking to the bottom of a pot. Cold water poured in to still a boiling pot.

A قروري *karūrīy*, Long-bodied, long-legged horse.

A قروش *karwash*, A collection from all quarters.

A قروض *kurūz*, (pl. of قرض *karz*) Debts.

A قروط *kurūt*, (pl. of قرط *kurt*) Ear-rings.

A قروع *karūʿ*, A well dug from the summit to the bottom of a mountain. A well of little water.

A قروف *karūf*, (pl. قرف *kurf*) Exceedingly insolent and pugnacious.

P قرول *kurūl*, Coral.

P قرولي *karūlī*, A duty on game, fish, &c.

P قروم *kurūm*, A stone of seven colours.

A قروم *kurūm*, (v. n. of قرم) Eating languidly or gently (a child or a young camel). (pl. of قرم *karm*) Excellent stallion camels. Princes.

A قرون *karūn*, Who eats two dates or two mouthsful at once. (A camel) having the two fore and the two hinder dugs close together; also kneeling on both knees at once. A camel that collects milk in the udder between two milkings. (A horse) placing the hind-feet in the footsteps of the fore. (A beast) soon sweating. Soul, body, self. *Kurūn*, (pl. of قرن *karn*) Horns. Ages. Small hills. قرون السنبل *kurūnu's sumbul*, A poisonous plant, the filaments of which are sometimes found amongst Indian spikenard.

A قرونة *karūnat*, The soul.

P قروهه *kuroha*, A ball, a globular substance.

A قروي *karawīy*, A citizen, townsman, villager.

A قره karah, (v. n. of قره) Having a dirty, squalid skin. Blackness, dirtiness of teeth; squalidness or blackness of skin; the black and blue marks of stripes: seams left by the scab.

A قرهاء karhās, (fem. of اقره) Squalid (woman).

A قرهب karhab, An old bull; or one big, bulky. Hairy goats. An aged goat. A prince, a leader.

A قرهد hurhud, Soft, delicate, tender, or luxuriously brought up.

A قره سنقر karah sanhar, Black. Blackness. Name of a bird of prey.

A قري kary, (v. n. of قري) Following, pursuing. Reading. Kary or kara', (v. n. of قري) Drawing (water into a reservoir). Laying up (provender) in one side of the mouth (a camel or ruminating animal). Kara', The back. A pumpkin. Kira', (v. n. of قري) Receiving hospitably. Hospitality. Water collected in a reservoir. Kura', (pl. of قرية karyat) Villages, towns. اهل قري ahli kura', Villagers, peasants. Townsmen.

A قرّئ kurra', Evil, misfortune befalling after due precautions had been taken. Water in a desert.

A قرّي kariy, (pl. اقرية akriyat, اقراء akrās, and قريان karyān) A canal, aqueduct. A stream let into a sown field. Thick milk not yet churned. Kuriy, (pl. of قرو karw) Cups, small vessels. Vessels from which dogs eat their food. Lower parts of palm-trees.

A قرياح kiryāh, A sown field destitute of trees and buildings.

A قريان karyān, (pl. of قرّي) Canals, aqueducts.

A قريب karib, (sing. and plur.) Near, in point of time, place, or connexion. (pl. اقرباء akribās) A relation, kinsman. Neighbouring (place); near (the time); connected (by relationship). Nearly, hard by, with, in his possession. Salted fish still retaining its freshness. About. عن قريب ɛan karib, In a short time, shortly.

A قريبة karibat, A female relation.

A قرية karyat or kiryat, (pl. قري hura') A village; town, city. A nest of ants. قرية الانصار karyatu'l ansār, Madīna, the town of Muhammad's allies.

A قريّة kariyat, A notched piece of wood, into which slides the head of the pole which supports the tent. The yard of a sail. The cross stick in the upper part of a camel-litter. A stick. An ant-hill.

A قرّيّة kirriyat, The crop of a bird.

A قريت karit, Jelly (of fish). Congealed water.

A القريتان al haryatāni, Mecca and Tāyf.

A قرّيث kirrīs, A kind of sea-fish.

A قريثاء karisās, (pl. قرائث karāsis) An excellent sort of date.

A قريثي karisa', An excellent sort of date.

A قريح karih, (pl. قرحي karha') Wounded, covered with ulcers. Water from the clouds. Clear, limpid water. Pure, uncorrupt, unmixed. A cloud beginning to appear.

A قرّيح hirrīh, Ulcerated.

A قريحاء kurayhās, A wen on a horse's belly the bigness of a man's head. A camel that makes the pebbles fly about in going.

A قريحة karīhat, Nature, genius. Any thing to which the mind has a peculiar bias. The first or beginning of any thing. Water gushing from a well.

A قريد hurayd, (dim. of قرد hird) A little ape.

A قرير karīr, (v. n. of قرّ) Ceasing to cackle (a hen). Hissing (a serpent). Cold, cool. قرير العين karīru'l ɛayn, Happy, cheerful, whose eye is cold.

A قريرة karīrat, Cold, cheerful (eye).

A قريس karīs, Cold. Intense (cold). Frozen (water). Jelly of fish. Old, ancient.

A قريش karīsh, Strong (camel). Kuraysh, A tribe in Arabia, of which Muhammad's grandfather, عبد المطّلب ɛabdu'l muttalib, was prince. A shark.

A قريشيّ kurayshiy, Of the tribe of Kuraysh.

A قريص karīs, Meat or fish eaten with bread.

A قرّيص kurrays, A nettle. A ship's anchor.

A قريض karīz, Verse, poetry. That which a beast brings up when chewing the cud. A nettle.

A قريظة kurayzat, A Jewish tribe at Khaybar.

A قريع karīɛ, Choice, excellent. A prince, a leader. A messmate. An antagonist at play. A camel stallion. (pl. قرعي karɛa') A camel's colt affected with the pustules called قرع karaɛ. قريع الدهر karīɛu'd dahr, The hero of the age. قريعك karīɛuha, Thine adversary.

A قرّيع kirrīɛ, A prince, leader of the people.

A قريعبة kurayɛibat, (dim. of قرعبلانة karaɛbalānat) A small marine animal, broad, thick, and short.

A قريعة karīɛat, The choice part of one's estate. The roof, also the bettermost part of a house, the coolest in summer and the warmest in winter. Slow of conception (a she-camel).

A قريم huraym, A term of reproach.

A قرين karīn, (pl. قرناء huranās) Connected, joined, next, contiguous, adjoining; related, allied; adhering. Tied with the same rope. A friend, companion, cotemporary, coeval, of the same age; an associate. A demon indissolubly connected with a man. One who unites the حجّ hajj and the عمرة ɛumrat. The soul. The body. Self. P قرين قبول شدن karīni habūl shudan, To take well, to approve. A قرين القبول karīnu'l habūl, Acceptable, agreeable. عزت قرين ɛizzat-karīn, Honourable, magnificent, illustrious.

A قريناء kuraynās, A kind of pulse or bean.

A قرينان karīnāni, Abū bakr and Talhat (because tied together by one rope).

A قرينة karīnat, (pl. قرائن karāsin) A female friend, a wife. Context. Cause. Conjecture. Adversity. The soul. An accompaniment. ذو القرينتين zū'l karīnatayn, (pl. ذوات القرائن zawātu'l harāsin) A sinew inside the thigh.

A قرييّ karayiy, A villager. A townsman.

P قز kaz, Raw silk.

A قزّ kazz, (v. n. of قزّ) Refusing, disliking. Leaping, springing, drawing one's self together, preparing to leap. Raw silk. A silken garment. Kazz, kizz, or kuzz, (pl. اقزّاء akizzās) One who abstains from every thing impure or base. Kuzz, Aversion to every thing impure; cleanliness.

A قزاح kuzāh, A disease incident to sheep.

A قزّاح kazzāh, A dealer in onions or seasoning-herbs (قزح kizh or kazh).

A قـزاز kazāz, A large dragon. Short serpents.

A قزّاز kazzāz, A silk-merchant, spinner, or weaver. A maker of loops or flexible handles. Kuzzāz, Free from impurity. One who shuns vices.

A قزاع kizāɛ, A bit of cloth. ما عليه قزاع mā ɛalayhi kizāɛ, He has not a rag on him.

A قزّاق kazzāk, A partisan. A light-armed soldier. A highway-robber. A cossack.

A قزاقز kazākiz, Parts, portions, particles.

P قزّاقي kazzāki, A military incursion. Guerilla warfare.

P قزاگند kazāgand, (قز آگنگ haz-āgang, also قزاغند kazāghand) A garment quilted with silk or cotton, and either worn in battle by itself or under the armour. A quilt. Bedding. Night-garments.

A قزام kizām, Vile, base persons. Kuzām, Dextrous; one whom none can excel. Sudden death.

A قزامي kazāma', Mean, worthless (men).

P قزاوه kazāwa, A camel-litter for long journeys.

A قزب kazb, Much coition. Kizb, A title, style. Kazab, Hardness. Strength. Severity.

A قزبر kuzbur, (or قزبريّ kuzburīy) Penis longus crassusque.

A قزبرة kazbarat, (v. n. of قزبر Q) Lying with.

P قزبين kazbīn, A city in Persian Irāk.

P قزبيني kazbīnī, A copper coin worth five oboli.

A قزّة kuzat, A kind of serpent with a short train. A sort of game.

A قزّة kazzat, kizzat, or kuzzat, A woman who abstains from every thing impure and base.

A قزح kazh, (v. n. of قزح) Seasoning (a pot) with herbs and the like. Making water squirtingly (as a dog). Casting urine on the root of a tree. Dropping its liquor (a pot). Being high. Elevation, height. A dog's urine. Kizh, The dung of a serpent. Kizh or kazh, Onions or other roots for seasoning victuals; also their seeds. Kuzah, Satan. An angel supposed to preside over the clouds. قوس قزح kaws kuzah, The rainbow.

A قزحان kazahān, (v. n. of قزح) Dropping its liquor (a pot).

A قزحة kuzhat, A blending of the colours yellow, red, and green.

A قزحلة kazhalat, A bow.

A قزد kazd, (v. n. of قزد) Purposing, intending. Design, purpose, intention. (See قصد kasd).

P قزدار kazdār, Name of a city in Hindūstān.

A قزدير *kazdīr*, Tin, pewter.

A قزز *hazaz*, Elegant, polite, clever, witty. Free from impurity: one who shuns vice.

A قزع *kazaȝ*, Bits of clouds. Small camels. Tufts or patches of hair left untouched when shaving a boy's head. Locks of wool that fall or are plucked off in the spring. Leaves, sticks, rubbish borne by a stream. Foam on the tip of (a camel's) nose.

A قزعة *hazaȝat*, One bit of a cloud. A bit of cloth, rag, or piece of a garment. A bastard. ما عنده قزعة *mā ȝinduhu kazaȝat*, Not a rag on him.

A قزعة *kuzzaȝat*, A side lock. A tuft left on a boy's head.

P قزغند *kuzghund*, Seed of the pine used in dressing leather.

P قزقان *hazkān*, A cauldron.

A قزل *kazal*, (v. n. of قزل) Limping ungracefully, staggering. Having thin, attenuated legs. Walking as if with an amputated foot. A pompous and stately gait.

A قزلان *kazalān*, (v. n. of قزل) Leaping, springing up. Halting.

T قزل باشي *kazal-bāshī*, (comp. of T قزل *kizil*, Red, and باش *bāsh*, The head) A kind of Mogul soldier. The kazal-bāshīs are considered to be the descendants of the captives given to Shaykh Haydar by Tamerlane. They wore the red caps assumed by those captives as a mark of distinction, and are considered as the best troops of the Persian armies.

A قزم *hazm*, (v. n. of قزم) Accusing, reproaching. *Kazam*, (v. n. of قزم) Having a small body. Smallness of body (in cattle), meanness of disposition (in man). Baseness, meanness, worthlessness. (Any thing) of a bad sort. *Kazim*, *huzum*, or *hazam*, (pl. قزم *huzum* and اقزام *ahzām*) Small, mean, worthless, useless (man). Cattle of the worst kind. *Kuzum*, Mean, worthless (men).

A قزمة *hazamat*, Vile, ignoble (woman). Short (man or woman).

A قزمل *kazmal*, Abject. A dwarf.

A قزميلة *kazmīlat*, Penis.

A قزو *hazw*, (v.n. of قزا for قزو) Playing at the game of قزة *kuzat*. Striking the ground with the point of a stick, and leaving a mark. Hating and shunning all kinds of impurity and sin.

A قزوح *kuzūh*, (v. n. of قزح) Making water squirtingly (a dog).

A قزوع *kuzūȝ*, (v. n. of قزع) Being quick, nimble; flying swiftly (a deer). Being slow, going gently.

P قزوين *hazwīn*, A city in Persian Irāk.

P قزويني *hazwīnī*, Stupid, silly. A fool.

A قزي *kizy*, A surname, style, or title.

A قزّي *hazzīy*, Made of the silk قزّ *hazz*.

A قزيح *hazīh* is often put after مليح *malīh*; as, مليح قزيح *malīh kazīh*, Handsome, agreeable.

A قزيعة *hazīȝat*, A side lock. A tuft of hair left untouched when shaving a boy's head.

P قزين *hazīn*, Any thing made of silk, silken.

P قژاوة *kajāwa*, A camel-litter for long journeys.

P قژه *hijih*, Any thing impure, filthy, nasty.

A قسّ *hass*, (v. n. of قسّ) Slandering, detracting, hurting with foul language. Eating, devouring the flesh from the bone. Extracting marrow. Driving or pasturing well (camels). Feeding by herself (a she-camel). Seeking, desiring, pursuing, prosecuting. A camel-keeper who never quits his herd. Hoar-frost, rime. A bishop. (pl. قسوس *kusūs*) A presbyter. *Kiss* and *kuss*, (v. n. of قسّ) Seeking, desiring, pursuing. Slander, detraction. *Kuss*, Name of a very eloquent man in Arabia, cotemporary with Muhammad. و قسّ على هذا *wa kuss ȝala' hāzā*, And so with regard to the rest, &c.

P قسا *kasā*, Cassia of Arabia.

A قساء *kasāʼ*, (v. n. of قسا for قسو) Being hard, unfeeling (the heart). Being coined of hard and bad silver, or clipt (money). *Kisāʼ*, (v. n. 3 of قسا for قسو) Becoming callous with regard to any evil, and enduring it with all its inconveniences. *Kusāʼ*, Name of a mountain.

A قسابة *kusābat*, A worthless date.

A قسابريّ *kusābirīy*, Penis longus.

A قساة *kusāt*, (pl. of قاسي *hāsī*) Hard.

A قساح *kusāh*, Dry and hard.

A قساحة *kasāhat*, (v. n. of قسح) Being hard. Twisting a rope. Having a tremendous priapism.

A قساس *kusās*, Name of a mountain in Yaman where the cornelian is found. القساس *al kusās*, Iron mines in Armenia.

A قساسيّ *kusāsīy*, Made of the iron of Al kusās.

A قساط *kisāt*, (pl. of قسطاء *hastāʼ*) Stiff necks.

A قساطرة *kasātirat*, (pl. of قسطريّ *kastarīy*) Expert money-changers.

A قساقس *kusāhis*, A lion.

P قسالاون *husālāwan*, Oil of pitch.

A قسام *kasām*, Beauty. Intenseness of heat. Sultry afternoon-heat. The hour of sunrise. *Kisām*, (v. n. 3 of قسم) Dividing with another. Swearing, declaring on oath.

A قسّام *kassām*, A distributor, divider, partitioner.

A قسامة *kasāmat*, (v. n. of قسم) Being handsome. Beauty. The administration of an oath. Truce, peace between the enemy and Musulmāns. A party swearing or testifying. *Kusāmat*, Alms. That which a distributor appropriates to himself.

A قساملة *kasāmilat*, (and قساميل *kasāmīl*) Arabian tribes.

A قساميّ *hasāmīy*, One who laps or folds cloth. A horse اقرح *ahrah* on one side, and رباع *rabāȝ* on the other. One thing situate between two others.

A قسانينة *husānīnat*, Hardness, thickness of the hand from labour. Feebleness from age. Darkness.

A قساوة *kasāwat*, (v. n. of قسا for قسو) Being hard (the heart). Being coined of bad silver or clipt (money). Hardness of heart. Hard fortune. Grief, melancholy, sadness, affliction, anguish, anxiety, care, pain, chagrin. Stinginess.

A قساوسة *kasāwisat*, (pl. of قسّيس) Presbyters.

A قسب *hasaba*, (fut. يقسب *yaksibu*) (The water) ran. (The sun) began to decline.

A قسب *hasb*, Hard and ugly. A dry date which crumbles in the mouth.

A قسبار *kisbār*, (or قسبريّ *kusburīy*) Longus penis.

A قسبرة *kasbarat*, (v. n. of قسبر Q) Lying with.

A قسبند *kusband*, (from P گوسپند) A sheep.

A قسّة *kassat*, A small town or village.

A قسح *kasah*, Dryness. A continuous priapism.

A قسحبّ *kus-hubb*, Corpulent, large, thick.

A قسر *kasr*, (v. n. of قسر) Compelling. Compulsion. Violence.

A قسري *kasrī*, Forcible, violent, compulsive.

A قسس *kusus*, Intelligent (persons). Expert camel-drivers.

A قسط *hasata*, (fut. يقسط *yaksitu*) He was unjust.

A قسط *hast*, (v. n. of قسط) Being unjust. Distributing, dividing, scattering. *Kist*, (v. n. of قسط) Appointing what is just. Administering justice. Justice, equity. A stipend, salary, pension. A portion, one's share of any thing distributed. A pair of scales, a balance. A jug, decanter. A stipulated rate and time of paying the public revenue or a private debt; an instalment, dividend. A tax paid by whores every three months. A dry-measure, half a صاع *sāȝ*, or one sixth of a فرق *fark*. قسط اوفى *kisti anfa'*, A full share. قسط مبادله *kisti mubādala*, Commutative justice. *Kust*, The costus, a shrub, the root of which, of a spicy flavour, is used medicinally. The leg, shank. (pl. of اقسط *aksat*) Straight-legged (horses). Stiff (knees). *Kasat*, Stiffness in the neck. A perpendicular formation of the hinder-legs of a horse (which is reckoned a blemish, a degree of curvature being esteemed). *Kusut*, Straight-footed (man).

P قسطا *kistā* or *kustā*, Name of a celebrated physician. Name of the son of Luke, who, father and son, were eminent physicians.

A قسطاء *kastāʼ*, (fem. of اقسط *aksat*) Perpendicular-legged (mare). Crooked (leg). Stiff (knee). (pl. قساط *kisāt*) Stiff (neck). (A she-camel) dry and stiff in the nerves of the legs.

A قسطار *kistār*, A banker, money-changer. Clever, clear-sighted.

A قسطاس *kistās* or *kustās*, A balance, a pair of scales. A just balance.

A قسطال *kastāl*, Dust. *Kistāl*, Purling (stream).

A قسطان *kustān*, Dust. *Kustān*, قسطاني *kustānīy*, or قسطانيّة *kustānīyat*) The rainbow.

P قسط بندي *kist-bandī*, An obligation for the discharge of a debt by instalments.

A قسطبيلة *kustabīlat*, Penis. Glans penis.

A قسطبينة *kastabīnat*, Penis. Glans penis.

A قسطة *kustat*, The leg, the shank.

A قسطر *kastar*, A banker, money-changer.

A قسطرة *kastarat*, (v.n. of قسطر Q) Separating good from bad coin. Money-changing.

A قسطري *kastariy*, Gross, corpulent. (pl. قساطرة *kasātirat*) Acute, intelligent. Able to distinguish good money from bad.

A قسطل *kastal*, Dust. امّ قسطل *ummu kastal*, Calamity, misfortune. *Kustul*, A chesnut.

A قسطلان *kastalān*, Dust.

A قسطلانيّة *kastalāniyat*, The rainbow. Ruddiness of the crepuscle. Name of a red stuff.

A قسطلة *kastalat*, The bray of a camel. The noise of a running stream. Castile in Spain.

A قسطناس *kustanās*, A stone for grinding perfumes. Name of a tree.

A قسطنطنيّة *kustantiniya*, (or قسطنطينه *kustantina*) Constantinople.

A قسطنطين *kustantīn*, Constantine.

G قسطوريون *kastūriyūn*, (or قسطورة) Castor.

A قسطول *kustūl*, Dust.

A قسطه *kista*, Stated payment, instalment of rent.

G قسطير *kistīr*, Lead.

A قسطيليّة *kastīliyat*, Castile in Spain.

A قسقاس *kaskās*, A journey in quest of water prosecuted with despatch. A guide who points out the right way. Intense cold. Keen hunger. Blunt (sword). Dark (night). Nimble, swift. A lion. A good rope. A plant resembling parsley.

A قسقاسة *kaskāsat*, A rod, a staff. The moving of a stick.

A قسقبّ *kuskubb*, Thick, large.

A قسقس *kaskas*, A lion.

A قسقسة *kaskasat*, (v. n. of قسقس Q) Moving, shaking (a staff). Using expedition (in travelling). Calling to a dog, and using the words قوس قوس *kūs kūs*. Rapid travelling, especially in the night-time. Travelling all night. Acquiring a habit of travelling at night. Devouring the meat which cleaves to the bone.

A قسقيس *kiskīs*, Expeditious (journey).

A قسم *kasm*, (v. n. of قسم) Dividing. Observing the turn or time. Scattering, dispersing. Measuring, disposing, arranging. A gift, a present. Division. Judgment, opinion. Doubt. Irresolution. Rain widely spread. Water. Power. An opinion which gains strength in the mind, and ripens into a conviction. حصاة القسم *hasātu'l kasm*, The pebble of division, *i.e.* a stone put into a jar when water is scarce on a journey, so as to make an equitable distribution. P قسم كردن *kasm kardan*, To divide, to make a partition amongst others. To make a measure agreeable to its just standard. To expend, dispose of. To begin (a business). A *Kasm* or *kism*, Nature, quality, habit, custom. *Kism*, (pl. قسيم *kasīm*, اقسام *aksām*, اقسماء *aksimāʼ*, and اقاسيم *akāsīm*) Part, portion, division. Kind, sort, species. قسم وافي *kismi wāfī*, Complete manner, perfection. P دو قسم *du kism*, Two-fold. Two sorts. A *Kusm*, (pl. of قسيم *kasīm*) Handsome, beautiful. *Kasam*, An oath. Beauty. P قسم خوردن *kasam khwurdan*, To swear. قسم بالله كردن *kasam bi'llāh kardan*, To take God to witness, to swear by God.

A قسماء *kusamāʼ*, (pl. of قسيم *kasīm*) Coparceners.

A قسمة *kismat*, Division, distribution; partition of inheritance. Any thing to be divided; portion, lot, share. Fate, fortune; decree of God. Destiny. A perfume-phial. A druggist's tray. P قسمت كردن *kismat kardan*, To distribute. To discern, foresee. A *Kasamat* or *kasimat*, The face (especially between the cheeks and nose). Beauty. A druggist's phial or perfume-box. A market.

A قسمل *kismil*, A lion's whelp. Name of a branch of the tribe of Azd.

A قسنطينيّة *kusantīniyat*, Constantine in Africa.

A قسني *kasnī*, Galbanum.

A قسو *kasw*, (v. n. of قسا for قسو) Becoming hard (the heart). Being coined of bad silver, or being clipt (money).

A قسوب *kasūb*, A boot. *Kusūb*, (v.n. of قسب) Being hard.

A قسوبّ *kaswubb*, (or قسّوب *kassūb*) Boots.

A قسوبة *kusūbat*, (v. n. of قسب) Being hard.

A قسوة *kaswat*, (v. n. of قسا for قسو) Being hard (the heart). Being bad or clipt (money).

A قسوحة *kusūhat*, (v. n. of قسح) Being hard. Twisting a rope. Having a priapism.

A قسودّ *kiswadd*, Thick-necked and strong.

A قسور *kaswar*, A lion. A species of sea-herb. A hunter hurling a spear.

A قسورة *kaswarat*, (v. n. of قسور Q) Growing luxuriantly (plants). Being old (a man). A lion. Hunters darting spears. The beginning, middle, or better part of the night. A certain plant which grows in a plain. Glorious, powerful. A buzz or low noise of men. Youthful and strong (man).

A قسوس *kasūs*, A she-camel pasturing alone. A vicious camel. A camel whose milk begins to diminish. *Kusūs*, Ivy. (pl. of قسّ *kass*) Presbyters.

A قسّوسة *kussūsat*, The sacerdotal office.

A قسوط *kusūt*, (v. n. of قسط) Being unjust. Being formed perpendicularly (the hind-legs of a horse). Distributing.

A قسويّ *kusawiy*, Belonging to a bow.

A قسيّ *kasiy*, Hard. (pl. قسيان *kisyān*) Of bad silver (coin). Hard, severe (cold, barrenness, drought, fortune). Name of a man called ثقيف *sakīf*. *Kisīy* and *kusīy*, (pl. of قوس *kaws*) Bows.

A قسّيّ *kassiy*, (Coin) of bad silver. *Kassīy* or *kissīy*, A species of Egyptian cloth mixed with silk.

A قسيان *kisyān*, (pl. of قسيّ) Spurious (coins).

A قسيب *kasīb*, Sound (of running water).

A قسيبّ *kisyabb*, Strong, long, and hard.

A قسّيس *kissīs*, (pl. قسّيسون *kissīsūn* and قساوسة *kasāwisat*) A bishop, presbyter, priest. A learned man.

A قسّيسة *kissīsat*, The sacerdotal office.

A قسّيسيّة *kissīsiyat*, The rank of presbyter.

A قسيط *kasīt*, Straight-footed (man).

A قسيم *kasīm*, (pl. قسم *kusm*) Beautiful, handsome. A side or a half. (pl. اقسماء *aksimāʼ* and قسماء *kusamāʼ*) A coparcener. (pl. of قسم *kism*) Portions. قسيم الوجه *kasīmu'l wajh*, Comely-faced.

A قسيمة *kasīmat*, A perfume-box. A druggist's or perfumer's tray. An oath.

P قش *kash*, Alike, resembling. A friend.

A قشّ *kashsh*, (v.n. of قشّ) Becoming fat after having been lean. A bad species of palm-tree. A large bucket.

A قشا *kasha'*, Spittle.

A قشاء *kishāʼ*, (pl. of قشوة *kashwat*) Baskets of palm-leaves, wherein women put perfumes or cotton.

A قشابة *kashābat*, Whiteness, brightness, purity.

A قشابر *kushābir*, Spreading (scab or mange).

قشابر اللحية *kushābiru'l lihyat*, Long-bearded (man).

A قشاح *kashāh*, A hyena. *Kushāh*, Dry.

A قشادة *kushādat*, Sediment of melted butter cooked with barley-meal and dates.

A قشارة *kushārat*, Peelings, shavings, scrapings.

A قشاسار *kushāsār*, The name of a place. ملح قشاساريّ *milh kushāsāriy*, Salt from Kushāsār.

A قشاش *kushāsh*, A thing picked up; fragments.

A قشّاش *kashshāsh*, A mendicant, one who collects and eats scraps.

A قشاط *kishāt*, The removal of a veil, curtain, or covering. Denudation. (See كشاط *kishāt*).

A قشاع *kishāʻ*, A bit of cloth. (pl. of قشعة *kashʻat*) Dry skins. *Kushāʻ*, Cry of the female hyena.

A قشاعة *kushāʻat*, Phlegm, spittle.

A قشاعر *kashāʻir*, (pl. of مقشعرّ *mukshaʻirr*) Trembling with horror. (Men) whose hair stands on end. *Kushāʻir*, Old and rough-skinned.

A قشاعم *kashāʻim*, (pl. of قشعم *kashʻam*) Lions. Old. Thick.

A قشّاف *kushshāf*, A thin stone.

A قشافة *kashāfat*, (v. n. of قشف) Being of a scorbutic, squalid habit. Being sun-burnt, tanned; or having the face discoloured or affected by distemper, disease, or poverty of living.

A قشاق *kashāk*, Palma Christi, castor.

A قشام *kashām*, A woollen-garment. *Kushām*, (pl. قشومة *kushūmat*) Crumbs, fragments left at table. Any thing affecting palm-trees, which makes the fruit drop off before being ripe.

A قشامة *kushāmat*, Crumbs, orts left at table.

A قشاوة *kushāwat*, A long bank, mound, or dike.

A قشب *kashb*, (v. n. of قشب) Mixing. Infecting, contaminating, corrupting, hurting, being offensive. Reproaching, defaming, calumniating. Shaming, putting to the blush. Giving poison. Acquiring praise or censure. Rendering insane or stupid. Polishing (a sword). *Kashb*, *kishb*, or *ka-*

shab, (pl. اقشاب *akshāb*) Poison, venom. *Kishb*, Soul, spirit. A kind of plant. Rust. قشب خشب *kishbun khishbun*, Sluggish, worthless (man).

A قشبار *kishbār*, Rough (stick). قشبار اللحية *kishbār* or *kushbāru'l lihyat*, Long-bearded (man).

A قشبانية *kushbāniyat*, An old worn-out garment.

A قشبة *kishbat*, A mean man. A young ape.

A قشبر *kishbir*, The refuse of wool.

A قشبر *kishbarr*, Thick.

A قشة *kishshat*, A young and little girl, a child. A female ape with her young she-cub. Wool used in anointing scabby camels with pitch. An insect like a beetle.

A قشد *kashd*, (v. n. of قشد) Moving from (its) place, taking off (a cover). Making bare, denuding. Flaying (a camel).

A قشدة *kishdat*, Sediment of butter dressed with meal and dates. An old milch camel. A thin skin upon milk.

A قشذة *kishzat*, Sediment of butter.

A قشر *kashr*, (v. n. of قشر) Being unfortunate. Bringing bad luck. Unbarking, peeling. *Kishr*, (pl. قشور *kushūr*) Bark, skin, crust, husk, peel, or shell. A garment. قشر البيضة *kishru'l bayzat*, An egg-shell. *Kushr* or *kishr*, A certain fish a span long. *Kashir*, (A date) enveloped in several husks.

A قشراء *kashrā*, (fem. of اقشر *akshar*) Stripped of the outward bark, peeled, excoriated. A snake that has cast his slough.

A قشران *kushrān*, The wings of a locust.

A قشرة *kishrat*, Any covering, natural or accidental; a shell, husk, scale, skin, bark, cuticle, crust. (pronounced *keshre*) A decoction made from the skin of the coffee-bean. A small sheep, round as a ball. *Kushrat* or *kusharat*, Rain which abrades the surface of the ground. *Kusharat*, Unlucky.

A قشط *kasht*, (v. n. of قشط) Uncovering, denuding. Skinning (a camel). Bastinadoing.

A قشع *kashع*, (v. n. of قشع) Milking (a camel). Uncovering. Shaking off, dispelling, scattering, dispersing. A scattered cloud. Sweepings or rubbish of baths. Crust on dry clay. A thin coat of ice. Loose earth scraped off the ground with the hand and thrown about. A chameleon. A worn-out fur-garment. A leathern table-cloth, or a piece of one. A basket. A male hyena. Phlegm (spit out). Ostrich-feathers. A man losing his flesh from age. Insane, foolish. (pl. قشع *kishaع*) A dry bottle or skin. (pl. قشوع *kushūع*) A tent made of skins. *Kishع* or *kushع*, Rubbish of baths. A vanishing cloud. *Kashaع*, (v. n. of قشع) Being light. *Kashiع*, Inconstant, fickle. Dry. *Kishaع*, (pl. of قشع *kashع* or قشعة *kishعat*) Dry skins.

A قشعام *kishعām*, A large male vulture.

A قشعامة *kishعāmat*, A gin, snare.

A قشعة *kashعat*, (pl. قشاع *kishāع*) A worn-out bit of a skin-garment: a crust of clay. A withered old woman. Dodder. *Kashعat* or *kishعat*, A part of a cloud. A dry skin. *Kishعat*, Phlegm spit out. *Kashiعat*, Lean (sheep).

A قشعر *kushعur*, A cucumber.

A قشعريرة *kushaعrīrat*, Horror making the hair stand erect. The trembling of a fever or ague.

A قشعم *kashعam*, Aged (man or vulture). Thick. A lion. ام قشعم *umm kashعam*, Death. Misfortune. War. A hyena. A spider. An ant's nest.

A قشعمان *kashعamān* or *kushعumān*, A large male vulture.

A قشعوم *kushعūm*, A dwarf. The like insect.

A قشف *kashf*, (v. n. of قشف) Being scorbutic and squalid in spite of washing. *Kashf* or *kashaf*, Squalid and scorbutic. *Kashaf*, (v. n. of قشف) Being of a scorbutic, squalid habit of body. Being sun-burnt, or having the face discoloured or affected by distemper or penury. Squalidness, unsightliness. Scurf. A wretched condition, penury. *Kashif*, Sun-burnt. Squalid. Poverty-stricken.

P قشقه *kashka*, A sectarial mark, such as the Hindūs make on their forehead. قشقه كشيدن *kashka kashīdan*, To mark the face (as the Hindūs), a ceremony used by the Marhattas at the installation of their chief.

A قشلب *kushlub* or *kishlib*, A kind of plant.

A قشم *kashm*, (v. n. of قشم) Eating the best and leaving the worst of any thing. Picking, choosing. Sifting, winnowing. Splitting palm-leaves for weaving. Eating much. Dying. The channel through which water passes into a cistern or reservoir. *Kishm*, Nature. (pl. قشوم *kushūm*) A narrow channel in a valley. Any channel of water. Fat. A root. The body, habit of body. Meat nearly dressed. Red meat. *Kushm*, (pl. of قشيم *kashīm*) Withered fruits of dwarf palm-trees. *Kasham* or *kashm*, Dates beginning to ripen, being then white and sweet.

A قشمذين *kashmazīn*, (in Yaman) Heaven.

P قشمش *kishmish*, Dried grapes or currants.

A قشنيزة *kishnīzat*, Name of an esculent plant.

A قشو *kashw*, (v. n. of قشا for قشو) Stripping off (the skin). Peeling (a stick). Shaving (wood). Stripping the leaves off a bough. Rubbing (the face). Wiping.

A قشوان *kash* or *kushwān*, Slender, thin of flesh.

A قشوة *kashwat*, (pl. قشوات *kashawāt* and قشاء *kishā*) A wicker-basket, in which women put perfumes or cotton.

A قشور *kashwar*, A woman not subject to menstruation. *Kashūr*, A medicine that excoriates the face that the skin may become clear. *Kushūr*, (pl. of قشر *kishr*) Barks, skins. Garments. قشور شجرة الحيّة *kushūri shajaratu'l hayya*, Gentian bark.

A قشورة *kashwarat*, A thumping (with a stick).

A قشوش *kushūsh*, (v. n. of قش) Recovering flesh. Walking in a debilitated manner. Rubbing any thing with the hand to make it fit properly. Milking (a camel) quickly. Collecting. Eating whatever one can obtain, clearing the table of what one can lay one's hand upon. Eating whatever is thrown on the dunghill, or orts given in charity. Withering (a plant). Departing, going away.

A قشوع *kushūع*, (pl. of قشع) Tents made of skin.

A قشوم *kushūm*, (pl. of قشم *kishm*) Channels through which water passes into a reservoir.

A قشومة *kushūmat*, Fragments left on a table.

P قشون *kushūn*, A body, company, troop.

A قشونيّة *kushūniyat*, Thin-skinned and small-mouthed camels.

A قشيّ *kashīy*, (Money) made of bad silver.

A قشيب *kashīb*, A new garment. Sharp. Old, worn out. White, bright, clean, newly-polished (sword). (A vulture) killed for his feathers and skin (by throwing him a piece of poisoned meat). Rusty (sword).

A قشيش *kashīsh*, Any thing picked up here and there. Scrapings. The sound of a serpent's skin in motion.

A قشيع *kashīع*, Scattered (forage).

A قشيف *kashīf*, Scantily, coarsely fed or clad.

A قشيم *kashīm*, (pl. قشم *kushm*) Withered fruit of the dwarf palm-tree.

A قص *kass*, (v. n. of قص) Following (the footsteps of another). Bringing one to death's door. Being near (death). Shaving. Shearing. Paring (the nails). Cutting (hair). Appearing to be pregnant by refusing the male (mares or sheep). Explaining, narrating. (pl. قصاص *kisās*) The breast, especially the top or middle of it. Shorn wool.

A قصا *kasa'*, (v. n. of قصي) Going to a distance. Retiring to one side. A court in front of a house. Remote (ancestry). A region, country. A slight incision in a camel's or sheep's ear.

A قصاء *kasā*, (v. n. of قصا for قصو) Being far distant. A court before a house. Remote (ancestry). The excision of a camel's ear. Distance. A region, country.

A قصاب *kisāb*, (pl. of قصبة *kasabat*) Mounds erected to save a wall or house from being undermined by torrents.

A قصّاب *kassāb*, A blower of a flute or a pipe. A butcher. One who cuts up joints, puddings, and entrails. *Kussāb*, (pl. of قصّابة *kussābat*) Flutes, pipes.

A قصابة *kisābat*, The art of playing the flute.

A قصّابة *kassābat*, The part between the joints or knots of a cane or hollow stalk. A pipe. Slanderous, malevolent. *Kussābat*, A lock of hair twisted but not plaited. (pl. قصّاب *kussāb*) A tube, spout, syphon. A flute, pipe, psaltery. Cane-root.

P قصّاب خانه *kassāb-khāna*, A butcher's shop.

P قصابك *kasābak*, Name of a bird generally found on the banks of rivers.

A قصابه *kasāba*, A handkerchief tied round the

head (worn by women principally).

A قصّابيّة *kassābīyat*, A duty payable on hides.

A قصّاد *kussād*, (pl. of قاصد *kāsid*) Messengers, couriers, postmen, cossids.

A قصادة *kasādat*, (v. n. of قصد) Becoming fat.

A قصار *kasār*, Slothfulness, worthlessness. *Kasār* or *kusār*, End, termination. Ultimate aim or object. *Kisār*, A mark impressed on the necks of cattle. A clipping, or a shortness of the hair. Bleaching. (pl. of قصير *kasīr* and قصيرة *kasīrat*) Short.

A قصّار *kassār*, A fuller, a cleaner of clothes.

A قصارا *kusāra'*, End, termination, limit. قصاراك ان تفعل كذا *kusārāka an tafzala kazā*, Your great point should be to do so (or thus).

A قصارة *kasārat*, (v. n. of قصر) Being short. Shortness. *Kisārat*, The fuller's art. (pl. of قصيرة *kasīrat*) Short (women). Closely-confined (women). (for قصيرة *kasīrat*) Short (woman). *Kusārat*, A cabinet or closet for privacy or retirement. Corn after winnowing or sifting. Grains remaining in the ear after threshing. What comes out of clover at the first threshing. The outer skin of a serpent. قصارة الارض *kusāratu'l arz*, A small quantity of ground, 50 cubits or upwards, of the fattest and most productive soil.

A قصاري *kusāra'*, End, extremity. The last or utmost effort, final aim. Strong desire.

A قصاص *kasās*, A certain tree from which bees extract a particular kind of honey. *Kasās*, *kisās*, or *kusās*, The part before or behind where the growth of the hair finishes. The meeting-place of the haunches. *Kisās*, Law of retaliation. Revenge, retribution. Reproof, correction. (pl. of قص *kass*) Breasts. (pl. of قصّة *kassat*) Particles of plaster. (pl. of قصّة *kussat*) Forelocks. *Kusās*, The termination of the back of the head.

A قصاصاء *ka* or *kisāsāɛ*, Law of retaliation.

A قصاصة *kusāsat*, Nail-parings. Hair-cuttings. A trifle of money.

A قصاع *kisāɛ*, (pl. of قصعة) Dishes, plates.

A قصاعة *kasāɛat*, (v. n. of قصع) Growing slowly (a boy). *Kusāɛat*, Hole of the jerboa or field-mouse.

A قصاعيّ *kisāɛīy*, A maker or vender of dishes.

A قصاف *kisāf*, Large, bulky (woman).

A قصاقص *kusākis*, (pl. قصاقص *kasākis* and قصاقصات *kusākisāt*) Thick and short (man). Malignant (serpent). Big, bulky (camel). Strong (lion).

A قصّال *kassāl*, Sharp (sword). A lion.

A قصالة *kusālat*, Chaff, winnowings. Light, shrivelled corn, tail-end cast off in winnowing.

A قصاه *kasāhu*, Towards him.

A قصايا *kasāya'*, (pl. of قصيّة *kasīyat*) She-camels kept apart and exempted from labour, and not milked. Camels of the worst kind.

A قصائب *kasāɛib*, (pl. of قصيبة) Curled locks.

A قصائد *kasāɛid*, (pl. of قصيدة) Poems, elegies.

A قصائم *kasāɛim*, (pl. of قصيمة *kasīmat*) Sandy places producing the plant غضا *ghaza'*.

A قصب *kasb*, (v. n. of قصب) Cutting. Cutting up a sheep into joints (a butcher). Interrupting (a camel) when drinking. Leaving off drinking before his thirst is quenched (a camel); refusing to drink (not having eaten enough). Accusing, blaming, censuring, reproaching. *Kusb*, (pl. اقصاب *aksāb*) An intestine. A fiddle-string made of gut. The back. The hypochondria. *Kasab*, A reed, pen, or any thing similarly hollow (as a bone, tube of silver, or other metal). The windpipe. A brilliant pearl. A brilliant emerald set about with rubies. The bones of the fingers. Lachrymal ducts. Tubes, water-pipes, canals. A fine linen cloth made in Egypt. A citadel. قصب البطحاء *kasabu'l batḥāɛ*, Waters flowing to the fountains of wells. قصب بوا *kasab bawā*, Calamus aromaticus. قصب الحائك *kasabu'l hāɛik*, A weaver's reed. قصب الحبيب *kasabu'l habīb*, Friendly pen. Sugar-cane. قصب الذريرة *kasabu'z zarīrat*, Worm-seed plant. قصب السكر *kasabu's sukkar*, A sugar-cane. P قصب سه دامني *kasabi sih dāmani*, A torn garment. The sea. A قصب مصري *kasabi misrī*, Fine linen of Egypt. Rays of the sun. Lightning.

A قصباء *kasbāɛ*, A reed. A reed-bed.

A قصباة *kasabāt*, A single reed.

A قصبة *kasabat*, A town, or the middle of it. A citadel, or its interior. A large village. The head station in a district. A marrow-bone. The bone or bridge of the nose. The greater part of a town. A lock of hair twisted but not plaited. A single reed. A well newly dug. (pl. قصاب *kisāb*) A dam erected to prevent the foundations of a wall or a house from being washed away by a torrent. *Kasibat*, Ground where reeds or canes grow.

P قصبك *kasbak*, A snail.

A قصبلة *kasbalat*, An eating all (the food).

A قصبور *kasbūr*, Coriander.

A قصبيّ *kasabīy*, One piece of قصب *kasab* cloth.

A قصّة *kassat* or *kissat*, (pl. قصاص *kisās*) Plaster. *Kissat*, (pl. قصص *kisas*) A thing, affair, business, condition, accident. Case, suit-at-law. History. A tale, fable, apologue, or theme. *Kussat*, (pl. قصص *kusas* and قصاص *kisās*) Forelocks.

A قصد *kasd*, (v. n. of قصد) Intending, proposing to one's self. Breaking, splitting (wood). Giving one's attention to making verses. Sparing expense. Being in a middle state, neither corpulent nor slender, neither prodigal nor sparing, neither swift nor slow. Keeping the right middle path. Acting justly. Making distinct and clear. Aiming at one with intent to hurt or kill. Intention, design, resolution, resolve, determination, scope, view, preparation, project, purpose, deliberation, pretension, attempt, endeavour. Desire, wish, will. A part, side. A road. Neither corpulent nor slender. قصد مصمّم *kasdi musammam*, A fixed resolution, firm intention. P قصد كردن *kasd kardan*, To aim at, pursue, make for. A *Kasad*, A species of thorn, of which they said the rod of Moses was made. A soft twig of the same. Hunger. A leaf of the tree عضاه *ɛizāh* in the autumn. *Kasid*, Broken (spear). *Kisad*, (pl. of قصدة *kisdat*) Fragments.

A قصداً *kasdan*, (عن قصد *ɛan kasdin*, or بقصد *bi kasdin*) Deliberately, expressly, intentionally, on purpose. علي قصد *ɛala' kasdin*, On the right road.

A قصدة *kisdat*, (pl. قصد *kisad*) A fragment. *Kasadat*, The first appearance of buds on a thorny tree.

A قصدير *kasdīr*, Tin.

A قصر *kasr*, (v. n. of قصر) Approaching, beginning, drawing in (evening), growing dark. Diminishing, shortening, abbreviating, abridging, contracting. Cutting the hair, cropping it so that it cannot hang down, shaving. Driving back, causing to turn back. Restraining any thing within certain bounds. Beating, washing clothes (as fullers or bleachers). Confining, imprisoning. Casting down her eyes (a woman), looking only at her husband. Dropping or drawing aside (her) veil. Shortening the ceremony of prayer by performing only two instead of four inclinations. Main object, ultimate design. Shortness, lowness of stature. Brevity. Firewood. Evening, twilight. (pl. قصور *kusūr*) A citadel. A palace, mansion, or any house of stone. A name peculiar to fifty-seven places, either town, village, hall, or fortress, the most remarkable of which was the palace of Bahram Gūr, of one stone, near Hamadān. P قصر دوازده دري *kasri duwāzdah dari*, The eighth heaven, *i.e.* of the zodiac. A قصر رفيع سلطنت *kasri rafīɛi saltanat*, The sublime palace, the principality, or kingdom. P قصر شاهي *kasri shāhī*, A royal palace. A قصر قيصر *kasri kaysar*, The palace of Cæsar. قصر وجود *kasri wujūd*, Palace of existence, *i.e.* the world. قصرك ان تفعل ذاك *kasruka an tafɛala zāka*, Your great point is to do that. *Kasar*, (v. n. of قصر) Suffering from a crick in the neck. Roots of palm-trees, or trees in general; or remains of roots. A disease which makes the neck stiff or crooked. Whatever remains of corn in the sieve after sifting or winnowing, or what comes out of clover after the first treading. The outer skin of a serpent. Weakness, negligence. Necks or roots of them. *Kasir*, Troubled with a stiff neck. *Kisar*, Brevity, shortness. Lowness of stature.

A قصراً *kasran*, In the evening.

A قصراء *kasrāɛ*, (fem. of اقصر *aksar*) Pained in the neck. *Kusarāɛ*, (pl. of قصير *kasīr*) Short.

A قصرة *kasrat*, The back of the neck. *Kusrat*, Shortness, brevity. *Kasarat*, A bride's bed-chamber. (pl. اقصار *aksār*) The neck, or root of it (in man or beast). Rumps of birds. What remains of corn after winnowing or sifting, or what comes out of clover after the first treading. The outer skin of a serpent. A bit or splinter of iron or of wood. A smith's hammer; also his anvil. Slothfulness, torpor. *Kasratan* or *kusratan*, In the nearest degree of consanguinity.

A قصري *kisra'* or *kusra'*, What remains of corn after winnowing or sifting, or what comes out of clover after the first treading. The outer skin of a serpent. *Kusra'*, A short rib. A kind of dragon. سورة النساء القصري *sūratu'n nisā'i'l kusra'*, The chapter of the Kur'ān called طلاق *talāk*. *Kasara'* or *kusra'*, A kind of viper.

A قصريّ *kasrīy*, Noble, patrician. *Kisrīy*, Grains remaining in the ear after threshing.

A قصريان *kusrayāni*, (du.) The two shortest ribs.

A قصص *kasas*, (v. n. of قصّ) Following, tracking footsteps. Explaining, narrating. History. Speech. Relation, exposition. Shorn wool. The lower part of the breast in cattle. *Kisas*, (pl. of قصّة *kissat*) Histories, narrations, fables. P قصص پر حصص *kisasi pur hisas*, Instructive histories. A *Kusas*, (pl. of قصّة *kussat*) Forelocks.

A قصطاس *kustās* or *kistās*, A balance, scales.

A قصطبير *kastabīr*, Penis.

A قصطل *kastal*, A castle, a fort. Dust.

A قصع *kasaꜥ*, (v. n. of قصع) Chewing the cud. Biting, pressing, or masticating hard. Killing (a louse) between the nails. Shining, flashing, appearing. Suppressing, stunting growth. Striking on the crown of the head with the palm of the hand. Despising, disparaging, treating with contempt. Quenching the thirst (water). Gulping draughts of water. Keeping close at home. Being full of blood (a wound). *Kasaꜥ*, (v. n. of قصع) Not growing in proportion to age (a boy). *Kasiꜥ*, (A boy) stunted in his growth. *Kisaꜥ*, (pl. of قصعة *kasꜥat*) Dishes, plates, saucers.

A قصعاء *kasaꜥāꜥ*, The hole of the jerboa.

A قصعة *kasꜥat*, (pl. قصعات *kasaꜥāt*, قصع *kisaꜥ*, and قصاع *kisāꜥ*) A dish, plate, saucer. The bason or scale of a balance. A box or casket. *Kusꜥat*, (pl. قصع *kusaꜥ*) The foreskin drawn back. *Kusaꜥat* or *kusꜥat*, The hole of the jerboa or field-mouse.

A قصعل *kusꜥul*, Worthless, contemptible, avaricious. *Kusꜥul* or *kisꜥil*, A scorpion or its young. A young wolf.

A قصف *kasf*, (v. n. of قصف) (A gale of wind) breaking, dashing to pieces (a ship). Thundering. Playing. Any thing ludicrous; play, game. (pl. of قصفة *kasfat*) Heaps of sand broken off from the mass. *Kasaf*, (v. n. of قصف) Being broken in the midst (a tooth). Being crooked from its disproportioned length (a tree or pole). Becoming rotten and fragile (a stick). Being broken, though not separated (a cane). Being split lengthwise (a spear). The braying of a camel. *Kasif*, Weak, infirm (man). Broken in two halves. Speedily broken down by misfortune (man). Limber (stick).

A قصفان *kusfān*, (pl. of قصفة *kasfat*) Sand-hills.

A قصفة *kasfat*, Impulse, pressure, thronging of a multitude. (pl. قصف *kasf* or قصفان *kusfān*) A hill or tumulus of sand broken off from the mass. The step of a stair or ladder. Slenderness of the tree ارطى *arta'*. *Kasafat*, The braying of camels. The worst camels.

A قصفلة *kasfalat*, An eating (of all the) meat.

A قصقاص *kaskās*, Thick and short. Malignant, dangerous (serpent). Roaring (lion).

A قصقص *kaskas*, The place in the breast where hairs grow. Sound, voice. *Kuskus*, Thick and short.

A قصقصة *kaskasat*, (v. n. of قصقص Q) Calling to (a whelp). *Kuskusat*, Short-bodied, yet thick and strong. A lion.

A قصل *kasala*, (fut. يقصل *yaksilu*) He cut.

A قصل *kasl*, (v. n. of قصل) Cutting. Beheading. Treading out wheat. Cutting green corn as food for horses. Blossom of the سلم *salam*. *Kasl*, *kisl*, or *kasal*, Chaff. *Kisl*, A herd of camels, from 10 to 40. Ignoble, worthless. A fool. Weak.

A قصلة *kaslat*, A shock of cut corn. A weak tree. *Kaslat* or *kislat*, A herd of 30 or 40 camels. A flock of quadrupeds. *Kislat*, A foolish woman.

A قصم *kasm*, (v. n. of قصم) Breaking so that the parts separate. Returning unto a place from whence one came. *Kasm*, *kism*, or *kusm*, A fragment. *Kism* or *kasm*, (pl. اقصام *aksām*) The root of pasture-ground. *Kusm*, (pl. of قصماء *kasmā'*) Broken-horned (she-goats). *Kasam*, A fracture, with separation of parts. A fracture in the front teeth. Locusts' eggs. *Kasim*, Fragile, easily broken. One who is soon broken by age or grief. *Kusam*, One who breaks whatever he meets. *Kusum*, (pl. of قصيمة *kasīmat*) Places producing the plant غضا *ghazā*.

A قصماء *kasmā'*, (pl. قصم *kusm*) (A she-goat) whose anterior horn is broken.

A قصمة *kasmat*, The step of a stair or of a ladder. A splinter of the wood مسواك *miswāk* with which they rub the teeth. *Kas*, *kis*, or *kusmat*, A fragment.

A قصمل *kismil*, A lion. *Kusmul*, A fatal disease in the joints. A disease fatal to young camels. *Kusamil*, *kasmal*, or *kismil*, A hard or violent man.

A قصملة *kasmalat*, (v. n. of قصمل Q) Breaking, cutting. Taking short steps. Throwing prostrate. Eating up every thing. Being afflicted with a fatal disease in the joints. A hard bite or graunch. A little worm that corrodes the teeth. Remains of water in a vessel.

A قصملى *kasmala'*, Violently (he swallowed).

A قصنصع *kasansaꜥ*, Short, dwarfish.

A قصو *kasw*, (v. n. of قصا for قصو) Being far distant (place). Retiring a great way from one's friends. Conquering, overcoming, excelling in travelling to a great distance. Cropping (a camel's) ears.

A قصوّ *kusūw*, (v. n. of قصا for قصو) Being very distant (a place).

A قصواء *kaswā'*, (A sheep or she-camel) the tips of whose ears are cropt.

A قصوب *kasūb*, Sheep that are sheared. *Kusūb*, (v. n. of قصب) Leaving off drinking before his thirst is quenched (a camel).

A قصوة *kaswat*, A mark at the extremity of the ear.

A قصود *kasūd*, Marrow.

A قصور *kusūr*, (v. n. of قصر) Beginning the evening; doing any thing then. Falling in price (goods, provisions). Becoming dear. Being unequal to, and therefore desisting. Not reaching the mark, falling short (an arrow). Subsiding (as anger or pain). Defect, default, decrease, failure, want, deficiency, impotence, remainder; error, sin, fault, omission. (pl. of قصر *kasr*) Palaces, villas, castles. P قصور كردن *kusūr kardan*, To fail, neglect, omit.

A قصورة *kasūrat*, A closet. A bride's bed-chamber. (A woman) closely confined.

A قصوف *kusūf*, Earnestness, perseverance in eating and drinking.

A قصوي *kuswa'*, (fem. of اقصى *aksa'*) Farthest distant, remotest. A remote extremity. The side of a valley.

A قصّة *kissa*, (properly قصّة *kissat*) A thing, affair, business, negociation. History, tale, romance, fable, apologue, narration. Pudenda. القصّة *al kissa*, On the whole, to sum up all. P قصّه كوتاه *kissa kotāh*, (or كوته *kotah*) To make short of the story.

P قصّه خوان *kissa-khwān*, قصّه گذار *kissa-guzār*, or قصّه گوي *kissa-goy*, A teller of stories, a narrator.

A قصى *kasa'*, (v. n. of قصي) Retiring far from one's friends. Distance. A country. Side, direction.

A قصيّ *kasīy*, (pl. اقصاء *aksā'*) Remote, distant (place). *Kusayy*, Name of a man.

A قصيا *kusya'*, (fem. of اقصى *aksa'*) Distant, remote. A remote extremity. The side of a valley.

A قصيب *kasīb*, (A male or female camel) that leaves off drinking before the thirst is quenched.

A قصيبة *kasībat*, (pl. قصائب *kasā'ib*) A lock of hair twisted but not plaited. A tube, spout, syphon. The part between two knots or joints of a cane.

A قصيّة *kasīyat*, (pl. قصايا *kasāya'*) A she-camel of value kept apart by herself and exempted from labour. One of the worst kind. Distant.

A قصيد *kasīd*, Broken (spear). Fat (camel's bunch). Marrow. A marrow-bone. A fat she-camel with marrow in her bones. Dried meat. A staff, a rod. (pl. قصائد *kasā'id*) A poem, of which half the stanzas must rhyme, but the other half need not. According to some authorities, it cannot be less than three verses; according to others, not less than sixteen. Elegantly-written (poem).

A قصيدة *kasīdat*, (pl. قصائد *kasā'id*) A poem, kasīda, or elegy being a kind of longer ghazal or ode (which last seldom exceeds thirteen, but never eighteen distichs). A staff, rod. A fat she-camel.

A قصير *kasīr*, (pl. قصراء *kusarāʼ* and قصار *kisār*) Short. (A horse) kept in the stable. A current of water which flows not in a channel that bears a name. قصيرالنسب *kasīru'n nasab*, One whose pedigree is known on mentioning his father without the need of mentioning his grandfather. *Kusayr*, Cosseir, a town on the western shore of the Red Sea. Name of a small island.

A قصيراك ان تفعل كذا *kusayrāka an tafʻala kazā*, Your great point is to do that.

A قصيرة *kasīrat*, Closely-confined (woman). (pl. قصار *kisār*) Short (woman). قصيرة من طويلة *kasīratun min tawīlatin*, A date from a palm-tree. A compendious discourse made from a long one.

A قصيرة *kasīratan*, In the nearest degree of kin.

A قصيري *kusayra'*, The lowest rib of the side. The lower part of the neck. The rib nearest the hypochondria, and the one nearest the collar-bone. القصيري *al kusayra'*, A species of viper.

A قصيريان *kusayrayāni*, The two shortest ribs.

A قصيص *kasīs*, The place in the breast where the hairs grow. Sound, voice. (pl. of قصيصة *kasīsat*) Certain plants.

A قصيصة *kasīsat*, A species of plant. A camel following a troop of camels. A camel employed in the transport of provisions or of household furniture. A weak camel carrying a small burden. A crowd, mob. A history, fable, tale, story.

A قصيع *kasīʻ*, A dwarfish lad. A mill.

A قصيعاء *kusayʻāʼ*, The hole of the jerboa.

A قصيعة *kusayʻat*, (dim. of قصعة *kasʻat*) A small dish, plate, or saucer.

A قصيف *kasīf*, (v. n. of قصف) Being violent (thunder or any thing else). Thundering. Impatient of hunger, soon sinking if food be withheld. The grating of a stallion camel's teeth. Broken in two halves. A broken branch.

A قصيل *kasīl*, Green corn cut for horses. A crowd.

A قصيلة *kisyallat*, Short and broad (camel or man). Big-bellied and thick-set (man).

A قصيم *kasīm*, An old cotton-tree.

A قصيمة *kasīmat*, (pl. قصيم *kasīm*, قصم *kusum*, and قصائم *kasāʼim*) A sandy place producing the plant الغضا *al ghazaʼ*, or a crowd of these plants.

A قض *kazz*, (v. n. of قض) Boring (pearls). Deflowering (a maid). Detaching (horsemen against an enemy). Throwing sugar or candy into a ptisan. Hurting the teeth by champing gravel amongst one's victuals. Having gravel mixed with it (meat). Bruising, pounding small. Cutting a stake. Small gravel. A place rough with pebbles or gravel, and inconvenient to recline upon. قضيض *kazīz* signifying large pebbles, they say قضهم بقضيضهم *kazzahum bi kazīzihim*, All, great and small (came).

A P قض *kazs*, (v. n. of قضي) Eating up, consuming. Being rotten and stinking from damp, and falling to pieces. Being red, becoming flaccid and dim (the eye). Being tarnished (reputation).

A قضا *kazaʼ*, A decree, mandate, judgment.

A قضاء *kazāʼ*, (v. n. of قضي) Decreeing, appointing. Pre-ordaining, pre-judging. Condemning, sending destruction (amongst any people). Commanding, enjoining. Concluding, finishing, consummating, Causing to arrive. Going to the necessary. Performing, creating, making. Paying (a debt). Reaching. Dying. Killing. Relating (any thing to another), giving complete information (on any point). Office or sentence of a judge. Jurisdiction, diocese. (pl. اقضية *akziyat*) Decree, mandate, judgment, order, charge, edict. An act, deed. Fate, destiny, predestination, fatality. Death. Accident, chance. Arrival, approach. Departure. Prayer repeated at the appointed time. By accident. P قضائ حاجت كردن *kazāʼi hājat kardan*, To go to the privy. قضائ شهوت كردن *kazāʼi shahwat kardan*, To indulge one's lusts. قضائ عمري *kazāʼi ʻumrī*, Repeating the prayers to make up for having omitted prayers in the former part of one's life. قضا كردن *kazā kardan*, To judge, determine. To make up for any former omission (as fasting afterwards, on account of a non-observance of Ramazān when sick or on a journey. A قضائ مبرم *kazāʼi mubram*, (or قضائ وطر *kazāʼi watr*) Inevitable fate or misfortune. P قضا ممكنست *kazā mumkinast*, The remedy is possible, it may yet do. قضائ ناگهاني *kazāʼi nāgahānī*, Sudden death, a fatal accident. A قضا و قدر *kazā u kadar*, The decree existing in the Divine mind from all eternity, and the execution and declaration of the decree at the appointed time. ديون واجب القضا *duyūni wājibu'l kazā*, Debts necessary to be discharged.

A قضّاء *kazzāʼ*, Rough to the touch, not yet rendered smooth by wearing (a coat of mail). Fastened with nails (a coat of mail). Camels, from 30 to 40. An aged man. *Kizzāʼ*, (v. n. 2 of قضي) Performing, finishing, consummating.

A قضاءة *kazāʼat*, (v. n. of قضئ) Being sullied (reputation).

A قضّاب *kazzāb*, Sharp (sword).

A قضابة *kuzābat*, Loppings, cuttings of a tree.

A قضّابة *kazzābat*, Active in the management of business. Sharp (sword).

A قضأة *kazʼat* or *kuzʼat*, Corruption, sully, tarnish, stain, defect, blemish.

A قضاة *kuzāt*, The membrane which envelopes the head of a new-born babe, the caul. (pl. of قاضي *kāzī*) Judges. اعظم قضات زمان *aʻzami kuzāti zamān*, The greatest of the judges of the age.

P قضارا *kazārā*, By chance, providentially.

A قضاض *kizāz*, (pl. of قضّة *kizzat*) Stones piled one upon another.

A قضاع *kuzāʻ*, The gripes. A pain inside the teeth. *Kuzāʻ*, (or قضاعة *kuzāʻat*) Small dust. Fine soil at the base of a wall.

A قضاعة *kuzāʻat*, A beaver. The cheeta or hunting-leopard. Name of the founder of a tribe.

A قضاف *kizāf*, (pl. of قضيف *kazīf*) Slender.

A قضافة *kazāfat*, (v. n. of قضف) Being slender-bodied. Leanness.

A قضاقض *kuzākiz*, Prey-rending (lion).

U قضّاك *kazzāk*, A robber, cossack.

A قضام *kazām*, A thing eaten (with the fore-teeth).

A قضّام *kuzzām*, (pl. قضاضيم *kazāzīm*) A kind of salt and bitter plant. A palm-tree becoming so tall that its fruit shrivels.

A قضايا *kazāyaʼ*, (pl. of قضيّة *kazīyat*) Commands. Things done. Philosophical propositions.

A قضب *kazb*, (v. n. of قضب) Cutting, lopping, pruning. Striking (with a switch). Mounting a young unbroke (camel). Any wide-spreading tree. Branches lopped off to be converted into bows and arrows. A tree from which bows are made. *Kazb*, (or قضبة *kazbat*) Green clover-grass (especially when mowed). *Kuzb*, Young branches. (pl. of قاضب *kāzib*) Sharp swords. *Kuzub*, (pl. of قضيب *kazīb*) Twigs.

A قضبان *kuzbān* or *kizbān*, (pl. of قضيب *kazīb*) Long and slender branches. Yards (of men or asses). Unbroke camels.

A قضبة *kazbat*, (pl. قضبات *kazabāt*) A long slender branch. An arrow made from the tree نبع *nabʻ*. *Kizbat*, Light, slender (man or camel). A herd (of camels), a flock (of sheep).

A قضة *kizat*, (pl. قضي *kizaʼ* and قضات *kizāt*) A sort of herb. *Kuzat*, Vice, defect, blemish.

A قضّة *kazzat*, Bits of gravel. Remains of any thing. A small clew or ball of thread. A hillock. *Kizzat* or *kazzat*, Small gravel. Virginity. A gravelly place. A low or sandy place alongside high ground. Genus, kind, sort. The deflowering of a virgin. *Kuzzat*, Vice, defect, blemish.

A قضض *kazaz*, (v. n. of قض) Being rough with gravel and inconvenient to lie upon. Being gritty with gravel (a piece of meat). Gravel, or bits of stone, making any place inconvenient for reclining upon. Food mixed with gravel. *Kaziz*, Wheat mixed with gravel. A place rough with gravel and incommodious to lie upon.

A قضع *kazʻ*, (v. n. of قضع) Subduing, taming, conquering, overcoming. Belly-ache, gripes, cholic.

A قضعة *kuzʻat*, Corruption, vice, disgrace, stain.

A قضعم *kazʻam*, An old, decrepit man. *Kizʻim*, An old, debilitated she-camel.

A قضف *kazaf*, Small stones. *Kazaf* or *kizaf*, Slenderness, leanness.

A قضفان *kizfān* or *huzfān*, (pl. of قضفة *kazafat*) Rough grounds. *Kuzfān*, (pl. of قضيف *kazīf*) Slender, slim.

A قضفة *kazafat*, A kind of bird, the kata. (pl. قضف *kazaf*, قضاف *kizāf*, قضفان *kizfān*, and *kuzfān*) Rocky ground raised in the middle. A hillock, as if consisting of a single stone. Small hills between which water runs in low ground. Elevated spots of stones and mud. *Kizafat,* A tract of moving sands.

A قضقاض *kazkāz,* The herb alkali, or a certain salt and bitter plant. *Kazkāz* or *kizkāz,* Level ground. *Kazkāz* or *kuzkāz,* Prey-tearing (lion).

A قضقضة *kazkazat,* Noise of breaking a bone.

A قضلام *kizlām,* Biting (stallion).

A قضم *kazm,* (v. n. of قضم) Eating with the fore-teeth, or any thing dry. An action performed gradually, and with ease. *Kazam,* (v. n. of قضم) Breaking, cutting. Being notched and broken at the edges and black (teeth). A sword. (pl. of قضيم *kazīm*) Membranes, parchments whereon they write. *Kazim,* Old and notched (sword).

P قضم *kuzm,* Cotton.

A قضماء *kuzmāʼ,* Notched and blackish-toothed (woman).

A قضمة *kuzmat,* Aught eaten with the fore-teeth.

A قضون *kizūn,* (pl. of قضة *kizat*) Plants growing in soft ground.

A قضي *kazy,* (v. n. of قضى) Determining, predestinating, decreeing. Judging, passing sentence. *Kazaʼ,* A bad sort of dried grape. *Kizaʼ,* (pl. of قضة *kizat*) Certain kinds of herbs.

A قضئ *kaziʼ,* (fem. قضئة *kaziʼat*) Rotten from damp (cloth or leathern bottle).

A قضيّ *kaziy,* Death. One who quickly decides, ready at returning a verdict. One who readily pays.

A قضيب *kazīb,* (pl. قضبان *kuzbān* and *kizbān*) Sharp (sword). A long slender branch or rod, a switch. A bow made of the branch of a tree. An elastic sword. A yard (of man or ass). A soldier. An unbroke camel. Name of a date-dealer in Bahrayn, who, having purchased a hamper of dates wherein lay hid a purse of 10,000 dirhems, was persuaded by the seller to restore his purchase. On discovering what a treasure he had missed, he stabbed himself through vexation with the knife which the seller had brought to kill himself withal, in case of his not being able to recover his property: hence, الهف من قضيب *alhaf min kazīb,* More vexed at a loss than Kazīb.

A قضيّة *kaziyat,* (v. n. of قضى) Decreeing. Predestinating. A thing, substance, action, fact. (pl. قضايا *kazāyaʼ*) A declaration, proposition, decision, or determination. A syllogism. History, narrative. Quarrel, dispute, contention. A case, legal question, suit, cause. A command, order. Death. Vulva. P قضيّهٔ مشهورست *kaziyaʼi mashhūrast,* It is a celebrated story. قضيّهٔ نا مرضيّه *kaziyaʼi nā marziya,* An unworthy, displeasing action.

A قضيض *kazīz,* (v. n. of قضّ) Cracking as if bursting (girth, belt). The noise itself. Large gravel. جاؤا بقضيضهم *jāʼū bi kazīzihim,* They all came.

A قضيف *kazīf,* (pl. قضفان *kuzfān* and قضاف *kizāf*) Slender, slim.

A قضيم *kazīm,* (pl. قضم *kazam*) A white skin or membrane on which they write. Barley given to horses. Any thing eaten with the front teeth. A leathern table-cloth. A mat woven of leathern thongs. A defect, blemish. Silver. One whose teeth are notched and blackish. An old broken-edged sword.

A قضيمة *kazīmat,* Barley given to a horse. A leathern table-cloth.

A قضيّه دلّال *kaziya-dallāl,* Exciter of a quarrel.

A قط *kat* or *katt,* Enough. قطك *katka,* Let it suffice thee. قطى *katī,* (قطني *katnī,* also قطّني *kattanī*) It is enough for me. قط عبد الله درهم *kattu ʻabdaʼllāh dirhamun,* (or قطن عبد الله درهم *katnu ʻabdiʼllāh dirhamun*) (or قط عبد الله درهم *kat ʻabdaʼllāh dirhamun*) A dirhem is enough for Abdallah. *Kat, kut, katt,* or *kutt,* Ever, never. ما رأيته قط *mā raʼaytuhu katt,* I never saw him.

A قطّ *katt,* (v. n. of قطّ) Cutting (a thing) transversely, side-ways, across; cutting or making (a pen). Cutting out any thing hard (as a box or casket). Calling the kata bird. Becoming dear, increasing beyond the common price (provisions). Short, curly hair. (pl. اقطاط *aktāt* and قطاط *kitāt*) One whose hair is much curled. Dear (provisions). *Kitt,* (pl. قطاط *kitāt* and قططة *kitatat*) A he-cat. (pl. قطوط *kutūt*) A written decree of a judge. An hour of the night. A gift of conveyance. A part, portion, share. An account-book.

A قطا *kataʼ,* A bird of the tetraonidæ or grouse family, flying in large flocks, and knowing where water is to be found at a great distance. It makes a noise resembling *katā katā*; whence it receives the name. There are two kinds; one is called كدري *kudrī,* the other جوني *jūnī*; the first of a brown colour, the back and belly variegated with black and white, the neck yellow, and the tail short; the other much larger, the interior part of the wings and the tail black, the back tawny, with a mixture of yellow; whence the proverb ليس القطا كالقطيّ *laysaʼl kataʼ kaʼl kutayy,* The *kata* is not like the *kutayy, i.e.* The small are not like the great. A bustard. A bittern. A disease incident to sheep.

A قطاب *kitāb,* (v. n. of قطب) Mixing wine. A mixture. The meeting of the breast of a garment.

A قطابة *kutābat,* A slice, a bit of meat.

P قطابي *kutābī,* A kind of triangular pasty.

A قطاة *katāt,* One bird of the قطا *kataʼ* species. The buttocks, the place on which a person sits who rides behind another on a camel or horse.

A قطاج *katāj* or *kitāj,* The hawser of a ship.

A قطار *kitār,* (v. n. 3 of قطر) Coming and going. (pl. قطر *kutur* and قطرات *kuturāt*) A string of camels following one another. A rank, order, series, row. (pl. of قطر *katr*) Showers, drops. *Kutār,* (A cloud) having large drops.

A قطارب *katārib,* (pl. of قطرب *kutrub*) Sylvan demons.

A قطارة *kutārat,* Whatever drops from any thing, droppings, dribblings of a barrel. A little water.

A قطاريّ *kutāriy,* (fem. قطاريّة *kutāriyat*) Black (serpent); or which lodges in the trunk of a palm-tree; or one from which poison drops through the abundance of the same.

P قطاس *kutās,* A fringed knot made of the mane or tail of a sea-horse, set often in gold, and hung round the necks of horses, by way of ornament, or as a defence against fascination.

A قطاط *kitāt,* Curly-haired (men). (pl. اقطّة *akittat*) A model or pattern on which any thing is cut. The circumference of the hoof of a quadruped. Extreme curliness or crispness of the hair. The upper part of the side of a cavern. The edge of a mountain or of a cliff. (pl. of قطّ *kitt*) Cats. *Katāti,* It suffices to me.

A قطّاط *kattāt,* Turner, maker of boxes or caskets.

A قطاطة *katātat,* Extreme curliness (of the hair).

A قطاع *katāʻ,* (v. n. of قطع) Flying from a cold to a hot climate, or vice versa. Migrating (as birds). Failing (as water in a well). Cutting clusters of dates. *Kitāʻ,* (v. n. of قطع) Migrating from a cold to a warm climate. Cutting clusters of dates. Any cutting instrument (as a knife or shears). (pl. of قطع *kitʻ*) The points of spears, small but broad. (pl. of قطيع *katīʻ*) Loppings of trees. Herds, flocks. Monies, coins.

A قطّاع *kattāʻ,* Keen, sharp, tranchant. *Kuttāʻ,* (pl. of قاطع *kātiʻ*) Robbers, assassins. قطّاع الطريق *kuttāʻuʼt tarīk,* Highway-robbers.

A قطاعة *katāʻat,* (v. n. of قطع) Being unable to speak, abashed, or interrupted in the middle of a speech. *Kutāʻat,* A part. A mouthful. Loppings, chippings. Any fragment which drops in cutting, such as a nail-paring, or a bit of leather.

A قطاف *katāf* or *kitāf,* The vintage, the season for cutting grapes. *Katāfi,* A handmaid. *Kitāf,* (v. n. of قطف) Taking slow and short steps (a horse). The slow short step of a horse.

A قطّاف *kattāf,* A vintager. A vine-dresser.

A قطافة *kutāfat,* Whatever drops in gathering grapes: gleanings of the vintage.

P قطال *katāl,* A soldier.

A قطام *katām,* Flesh.

P قطامه *katāma,* A lascivious woman.

A قطاميّ *katāmiy* or *kutāmiy,* A kind of hawk (especially when darting his eye upon his prey). Flesh of a hawk. Strong wine from dates or grapes.

A قطان *kitān,* (pl. قطن *kutun*) The frame of a camel-litter. The bar of a door.

A قطّان *kattān,* A cleaner or spinner of cotton. *Kuttān,* (pl. of قاطن *kātin*) Inhabitants. Servants. قطّان ارضين وسماوات *kuttāni arzīn u samāwāt,* The inhabitants of earth and heaven.

A قطانة *katānat,* A kettle, pot. Catania in Sicily.

P قطاني *katānī*, A sort of meat-pasty.

A قطانيّ *katāniy*, (pl. of قطنيّة) Vegetables.

A قطايات *katāyāt*, (pl. of قطاة *katāt*) Kata-birds.

A قطائط *katāʼit*, Detached companies.

P قطائف *katāʼif*, A cake of fine flour, honey, and sesame-oil and almonds.

A قطائف *katāʼif*, A red date. (pl. of قطيفة *katīfat*) Velvets, satins.

A قطب *katb*, (v. n. of قطب) Frowning, knitting the brows, looking stern. A buying by sample, a conjecturing of the weight or value of the whole by the examination of a small quantity. *Katb*, *kitb*, *kutb*, or *kutub*, The iron axle around which a wheel turns. *Kutb*, (v. n. of قطب) Cutting. Collecting. Mingling (wines). Putting in a passion. Filling (a vessel). Drawing together the two ears of a sack, and fastening it. Assembling, flocking together. (pl. اقطاب *aktāb*, قطوب *kutūb*, and قطبة *kitabat*) The polar star, north pole. A centre round which any thing revolves; an axis, a pivot. A prince, lord, chief. A general, a commander-in-chief. قطب جنوبي *kutbi janūbī*, The south pole. قطب الدين *kutbu'd dīn*, The axis of religion. قطب سما *kutbi samā*, The axis of heaven, *i.e.* the pole. قطب شمالي *kutbi shimālī*, The north pole. قطب العارفين *kutbu'l ʻārifīn*, Chief of the wise men, *i.e.* Plato. قطب فلك رسالت *kutbi falaki risālat*, The celestial pole of prophecy, *i.e.* Muhammad. قطب الملك *kutbu'l mulk*, The pole-star of the empire. *Kutab*, (pl. of قطبة *kutbat*) Points of spears on which they fix targets to shoot at.

A قطبان *kutbān*, A kind of plant.

A قطبة *kutbat*, The iron axle round which a wheel turns. (pl. قطب *kutab*) The point of a spear at which they shoot. Name of a plant. *Kitabat*, (pl. of قطب *kutb*) Polar stars. Centres about which objects revolve. Princes, chiefs.

P قطب نما *kutb-namā*, A compass.

A قطبّى *kitibbaʼ*, Name of a plant from which the strongest ropes are made.

A قطّة *kattat*, The nib of a pen. *Kittat*, A queen-cat.

A قطج *katj*, (v. n. of قطج) Twisting (a hawser) firmly. Drawing water from a well with such a rope.

A قطر *katr*, (v. n. of قطر) Dropping (as water or tears). Letting (water) fall in drops. Tying (camels) so that they follow each other in a line. Seizing, holding, detaining. قطرت استه *katarat istuhu*, His stool fell in liquid drops. (pl. قطار *kitār*) Rain. (pl. of قطرة *katrat*) Drops. *Kitr*, Fusile brass, or a kind of it. A species of striped cloth. Property, paternal inheritance. *Kutr*, (pl. اقطار *aktār*) The side of the body. A tract, quarter. A diameter-line. Wood of aloes. *Katar*, (v. n. of قطر) Tying (camels) in a string. A buying by sample, guessing the weight or value of the whole by the examination of a small quantity. Name of a place. *Kutur*, Wood of aloes. (pl. of قطار *kitār*) Strings of camels following one another.

A قطرات *katarāt*, (pl. of قطرة *katrat*) Drops.

P قطرات شبنم *katarāti shabnam*, Drops of dew.

A *Kuturāt*, (pl. of قطار *kitār*) Strings of camels following one another.

A قطران *katrān*, *kitrān*, or *katirān*, Liquid pitch, tar, the juice of the pine. زفت و قطران *zift u katirān*, Tar and pitch. *Katarān*, (v. n. of قطر) Distilling, falling in drops (water or tears). The dropping of water from the eaves of houses. *Katirān*, Name of a poet.

P قطران ماليدگي *katirān-mālīdagī*, An anointing or daubing with pitch. قطران ماليده *katirān-mālīda*, Besmeared with pitch.

P قطراني *katrānī*, A sort of money.

A قطرب *kutrub*, A species of sylvan demon, the male غول *ghūl*. A little demon, goblin, fairy, elf. A whelp. A little animal perpetually in motion on the surface of the water. A kind of bird. A mouse. A robber. A bald wolf; hence, a species of deep melancholy, which makes men fancy themselves wolves, and run howling to the woods. An oaf. A coward. Ignorant. Mean, vile. Thrown prostrate. Epileptic.

A قطربة *katrabat*, (v. n. of قطرب Q) Making haste. Throwing prostrate.

A القطربلية *al kutrubbuliyat*, (also قطربليّة *kutrubullīyat*) Name of a wine grown in Irāk.

A قطربوس *katrabūs* or *kitrabūs*, A severe-stinging scorpion. A swift and strong she-camel.

A قطرة *katrat*, (pl. قطر *katr*) One drop. قطرة قطرة *katra katra*, Drop by drop. P قطرهٔ آب *katraʼi āb*, A drop of water. A sword. A spear's point. قطرهٔ دزد *katraʼi duzd*, A cloud. قطره زدن *katra zadan*, To run to and fro, to make haste. قطرهٔ زرد *katraʼi zard*, The sun. A *Kutrat*, Small, few, mean. A trifling thing.

A قطروب *kutrūb*, A sylvan demon, a غول *ghūl*.

P قطره زن *katra-zan*, A fast runner.

A قطرى *kitrīy*, Cloth or stuff made at قطر *katar*.

A قطريات *katarīyāt*, Excellent camels of *katar*.

A قطرية *kitrīyat*, A kind of striped cloth.

P قطزن *kat-zan*, A piece of bone on which they nib their writing-reeds or pens.

A قطط *katat*, (v. n. of قط) Curling much (hair). Very curly (hair). (pl. قطاط *kitāt*) One whose hair is very curly. *Kitat*, (pl. of قطّة *kittat*) Cats.

A قططة *kitatat*, (pl. of قط *kitt*) Tom-cats.

A قطع *katāʻa*, (fut. يقطع *yaktaʻu*) He cut.

A قطع *katʻ*, (v. n. of قطع) Cutting off, amputating. Splitting, cracking. Dividing. Stanching (blood). Breaking off. Giving up (hope). Rejecting, discarding (a name or a title). Retiring, withdrawing (from one's kindred). Terminating, concluding, finishing, stopping short. Filling (a cistern) half-full and then cutting off the water. Fixing the price of a ransom. Defining or ordaining any thing necessary to be observed. Passing (a river or bridge). Traversing, crossing. Convincing by clear proofs. Silencing, stopping the mouth of an adversary by good offices. Strangling. Being sufficient for one's stature (stuff for a garment). Striking with a scourge. Migrating (a bird of passage). Infesting (a road). A section, segment, cutting. A shape, form, cut. A separation from kindred. Cut out (garment). قطع كامل *katʻi kāmil*, Folio-size. قطع جواب *katʻi jawāb*, A definitive answer. P قطع جواب دادن *katʻi jawāb dādan*, To give a categorical answer. قطع رحم كردن *katʻi rahim kardan*, To break off all connexion with relations. قطع طريق كردن *katʻi tarīk kardan*, To infest the roads, rob, assassinate. قطع علاقه كردن *katʻi ʻalāka kardan*, To renounce all right to. To manumit a slave. قطع مسافه كردن *katʻi masāfa kardan*, To travel, make a journey. قطع نزاع كردن *katʻi nizāʻ kardan*, To decide a law-suit. قطع نظر دادن *katʻi nazar dādan*, To turn away the eyes. To abandon or think no more of. A *Kitʻ*, Whatever is cut from a tree. A bad arrow. A failure of water in a well. A shortness of breath from over-exercise; asthma. The darkness at the extremes of the night; the first watch. (pl. اقطع *aktuʻ*, اقطاع *aktāʻ*, and قطاع *kitāʻ*) A small broad head to an arrow. (pl. قطوع *kutūʻ* and اقطاع *aktāʻ*) A shaggy cloth spread under a man when riding a camel. *Kutʻ*, (v. n. of قطع) Being amputated (the hand). A failure of water in a well in the intense heat of summer. Shortness of breath. Highway-robbers. (pl. of اقطع *aktaʻ*) Those whose hands are amputated. (pl. of قطيع *katīʻ*) Branches from which they make arrows. *Kataʻ*, (v. n. of قطع) Losing (the hand), having it cut off on account of a distemper. Being cut off (the hand). (pl. of قطعة *kataʻat*) The stumps remaining after the hands are cut off. *Katiʻ*, Dumb. *Kitaʻ*, The darkness of the latter part of the night; the space between the first and second watch. (pl. of قطعة *kitʻat*) Segments, cuts, slices. *Kutaʻ*, One who forsakes his relations. (pl. of قطعة *kutʻat*) Portions cut off. *Kutuʻ*, (pl. of قطيع *katīʻ*) Loppings, or any thing cut from trees.

A قطعا *katʻan*, In no shape, not at all, never.

A قطعاء *katʻāʼ*, (Commerce) with relations cut off. *Kutaʻāʼ*, (pl. of قطيع *katīʻ*) Scourges cut off at the end. Like, resembling, equal to.

A قطعات *kutaʻāt*, *kataʻāt*, or *kutuʻāt*, Points of knots of a tree which project when they are cut.

A قطعان *kutʻān*, (pl. of قطيع *katīʻ*) Herds of oxen. Branches from which they make arrows. (pl. of اقطع *aktaʻ*) Amputated in the hands. Deaf.

A قطعة *katʻat*, (v. n. of قطع) Being amputated on account of disease (the hand). *Kitʻat*, A segment, section, portion, part, division, piece, cut, morsel. A strophe. Distichs corresponding in measure and rhyme but without a مطلع *matlaʿ*. A name of the female kata. قطعه قطعه *kitʿa kitʿa*, In pieces. *Kutʿat*, The failure of water in a well. The place at which any thing is cut off or fails. (pl. قطع *kataʿ*) The stump of an amputated arm. (pl. قطع *kutaʿ*) A part or portion cut off. A piece of land given in feudal tenure. A vicious pronunciation peculiar to the tribe of طيّ *tayy*; as instead of saying يا ابا الحكم *yā abā'l hakam*, they say ياابا الحكا *yā abā'l hakā*. The bran of fine flour. *Kataʿat*, (pl. قطع *kataʿ*) The place where cut; the stump of an arm or branch. *Kutaʿat*, One who does not associate with his kindred (who cuts them). A place where any thing is cut off or finishes.

P قطعه بند *kitʿa-band*, A kind of verse in which the meaning of the first verse of each stanza is completed in the last.

A قطعي *katʿī*, Verily. A tailor's measure.

A قطعيّ *katʿiy*, Disjunctive. P حكم قطعي دادن *hukmi katʿī dādan*, To insist. A *Kutʿiy*, Related to the tribe of بني قطعة *banī kutʿat*.

A قطف *katf*, (v. n. of قطف) Gathering in the vintage, cutting the clusters. Scratching with the finger-nails. Going slowly (a horse). A kind of broad-leafed herb. Orage. (pl. قطوف *kutūf*) A scratch. *Kitf*, (pl. قطوف *kutūf*) Grapes, a cluster. Gathered fruit. Orach. *Kataf*, A vestige, mark, trace. Orage. A certain hard mountain-tree, of which rings are made. *Kutuf*, (pl. of قطيفة *katīfat*) Velvets.

A قطفة *kitfat*, A certain herb, long and prickly, red within, and with leaves of dust colour. *Katafat*, A mark, trace, vestige.

A قطقاط *katkāt*, A hasty journey performed during the first watch of the night.

A قطقط *kitkit*, Hail; small hailstones. Very small rain, or successively falling in large drops.

A قطقطة *katkatat*, (v. n. of قطقط Q) Raining. Crying in solitude (the bittern).

A قطل *katl*, (v. n. of قطل) Cutting, amputating. Beheading. *Kutul*, (The trunk of a palm-tree) cut off and thrown away.

A قطلب *katlab*, A wild strawberry or cherry.

A قطم *katm*, (v. n. of قطم) Biting, seizing with the teeth. Cutting. Tasting. *Katam*, (v. n. of قطم) Having a strong desire for eating flesh or for coition (man or beast). A strong desire for any thing. *Katim*, Eager for food or venery.

A قطمور *kutmūr*, The dog of the seven sleepers.

A قطمير *kitmīr*, (or قطمار *kitmār*) The thin pellicle on a date-stone. A white speck on the back of a date-stone. Name of the seven sleepers' dog. نقير و قطمير *nakīr u kitmīr*, Minute, particular.

A قطن *kutn*, (*kutun*, قطّن *kuttan*, or قطنّ *kutunn*) Cotton. *Katan*, The rump. The part between the hip-bone and the root of the tail in a bird. Curvature. *Kutun*, (pl. of قطان *kitān*) Frames of camel-litters. (pl. of قطين *katīn*) Servants.

A قطنة *kitnat* or *katinat*, Part of the stomach; the many folds. A pomegranate. A quantity of twisted cotton.

A قطنيّ *kutnīy*, Made of cotton. A garment of silk and cotton.

A قطنيّة *kutnīyat* or *kitnīyat*, (pl. قطانيّ *katānīy*) Millet, pulse, or grain in general (excepting wheat, barley, currants, and dates). Garments.

A قطو *katw*, (v. n. of قطا for قطو) Going with a short, sprightly step. Having a heavy step. Crying *kata kata* (the kata bird, a kind of grouse).

A قطوات *katawāt*, (pl. of قطا *kata'*) Kata birds.

A قطوان *katwān* or *katawān*, One who moves with a short step. Long-legged. *Katawān*, Name of a place in the district of Kūfa.

A قطوانيّ *katawānīy*, A kind of Kūfic garment.

A قطوب *katūb*, One who knits his brows, stern, austere, crabbed. A lion. *Kutūb*, (v. n. of قطب) Knitting the brows, frowning, looking stern. (pl. of قطب *kutb*) Polar stars. Centres around which things revolve. Princes, chiefs.

A قطور *katūr*, (A cloud) that drops much water. *Kutūr*, (v. n. of قطر) Falling in drops (water, tears, or liquid gum). Travelling, going. Making haste. Throwing (one) prostrate with violence. Sewing (a garment).

A قطوراء *kutūrā*, Name of a plant.

A قطوط *kutūt*, (v. n. of قطّ) Becoming dear (provisions). (pl. of قطّ *kitt*) Portions, shares. Written sentences of a judge. Account-books.

A قطوّط *katawwat*, Light and swift.

A قطوطى *katawta'*, One who moves with a short, sprightly step.

A قطوع *katūʿ*, (A camel) soon ceasing to give milk. *Kutūʿ*, (v. n. of قطع) Passing (a river or a bridge). Convincing by clear proofs. Silencing, stopping the mouth of an adversary by good offices. Splitting, cracking. Striking with a scourge. Strangling. Flying from a cold to a warm climate, or vice versâ. Failing, drying up (water in a well). (pl. of قطع *kitʿ*) Rough camel saddle-cloths.

A قطوف *katūf*, Slow-paced, short-stepping (horse). *Kutūf*, (v. n. of قطف) Taking slow short steps (a horse). (pl. of قطف *katf*) Scars, scratches. (pl. of قطف *kitf*) Grapes. Clusters of grapes.

T قطولكي *katolikī*, (from the Greek) Catholic.

A قطون *kutūn*, (v. n. of قطن) Dwelling in (a place), making it one's home. Serving, waiting on.

A قطونا *kitūnā*, Flea-wort.

A قطى *katy*, A disease in the buttocks. *Katī*, Troubled with the disease قطا *kata'* (a sheep).

A قطيّا *kutayya'*, A rope made of cocoa-nut fibre.

A قطيب *katīb*, Mixed (wine).

A قطيبة *katībat*, A mixture of camels' with sheep or goat-milk. A crowd, multitude.

A قطيرة *kutayrat*, (dim. of قطرة *katrat*, A drop) A little drop, a droplet. A particle. A trifle.

A قطيس *kitīs*, Cytisus (an herb).

A قطيطة *katītat*, Upper part of a mountain-cave.

A قطيع *katīʿ*, (pl. قطعان *kutʿān*, اقطعة *aktiʿat*, قطاع *kitāʿ*, اقطع *aktuʿ*, اقاطع *akātiʿ*, قطع *kutuʿ* and *kutʿ*) A branch from which they make arrows. (pl. اقطاع *aktāʿ*, قطعان *kutʿān*, قطاع *kitāʿ*, and اقاطيع *akātīʿ*) A herd (of oxen). A flock (of sheep). (pl. قطعاء *kutaʿā*) A scourge cut off at the end. Alike, resembling, equal (in figure or stature). Any thing lopped from a tree and soon taking fire. قطيع القيام *katīʿu'l kiyām*, Unable to rise, worn out, weak; lazy; corpulent. قطيع الكلام *katīʿu'l kalām*, (A woman) keeping silence, but not dumb.

A قطيعاء *kutayʿā*, Alienation or dislike among relations. Dissensions. A kind of date.

A قطيعة *katīʿat*, (v. n. of قطع) Retiring, withdrawing from one's kindred. Separation from kindred. A portion of land (especially in feudal tenure). Tribute, toll, impost.

A قطيفة *katīfat*, (pl. قطائف *katāʾif* and قطف *kutuf*) Velvet, satin. Any inner garment with a long pile. A mantle or sheet folded up.

A قطيل *katīl*, Cut. Cut up by the root (a palm-tree). Name of a man.

A قطيلة *katīlat*, A clout for imbibing water.

A قطيّم *kityamm*, A rampant stallion.

A قطيمة *katīmat*, Milk which has lost its flavour. A fragment. A large dish of meat.

A قطين *katīn*, Inhabitants. Handmaids. Servants, domestics, followers, attendants.

A قطينة *katīnat*, Pulse. The inmates of a house.

A قعّ *kaʿʿ*, (v. n. of قعّ) Using bold and confident language. *Kuʿʿ*, Exceedingly bitter (water).

A قعا *kaʿā'*, (v. n. of قعي) Turning up, so as almost to touch the bridge (the tip of the nose).

A قعاب *kiʿāb*, (pl. of قعب) Wooden bowls.

A قعاث *kuʿās*, A disease on the nose of a sheep.

A قعاد *kuʿād*, A distemper affecting the haunches of camels. Lameness from that disease. A lameness disabling any one from moving.

A قعادة *kuʿādat*, A wife.

A قعارة *kaʿārat*, (v. n. of قعر) Being deep.

A قعاس *kuʿās*, A disease incident to sheep from too much food.

A قعاسب *kuʿāsib*, Long.

A قعاص *kuʿāṣ*, A distemper which carries off sheep immediately when attacked, the neck appearing broken.

A قعّاص *kaʿʿāṣ*, A lion that kills instantly.

A قعاط *ka* or *kiʿāt*, A violent driver of cattle.

A قعاع *kuʿāʿ*, Exceedingly bitter (water).

A قعاف *kuʿāf*, All-sweeping (torrent).

A قعاقع *kaʿākiʿ*, Incessant claps of thunder. Noise of cuirasses in battle.

A قعال *kuʿāl*, Flowers of vines full blown and beginning to fall. Camels' hair dropping off.

A قعان *kaʿān*, Shortness of the nose with a cocking up of the point.

A قعانب *kuʿānib*, Strong and hard. A lion.

A قعائد *kaʿāʾid*, (pl. of قعدة *kuʿdat* or قعود *kaʿūd*) Able to travel (young camels). (pl. of قعيدة *kaʿidat*) Sacks. Husbands.

A قعب *kaʿb*, (pl. اقعب *akʿub*, قعاب *kiʿāb*, and قعبة *kiʿabat*) A cup. A large wooden bowl, holding as much as a man may drink at a single draught. The hidden meaning (of a speech). *Kuʿb*, A deep furrow or cavern in a mountain.

A قعبة *kaʿbat*, A little box or casket. *Kuʿbat*, A hopper in which seed is put for sowing. *Kiʿabat*, (pl. of قعب *kaʿb*) Cups, wooden bowls.

A قعبريّ *kaʿbariy*, Hard, unkind towards one's family and friends. Avaricious. Bad-tempered.

A قعبل *kaʿbal* also *kiʿbil*, Rough-mannered. Rooted up. Hard, rugged. Mushrooms, funguses. A milk-dish. A side, edge, margin. A kind of white plant.

A قعبلة *kaʿbalat*, (v. n. of قعبل Q) Turning in the toes. Distance of heel. A weak, shuffling step.

A قعبول *kuʿbūl*, A kind of white plant, or sort of mushroom. A milk-dish.

A قعترة *kaʿtarat*, Extirpation, eradication.

A قعثب *kaʿsab*, Many.

A قعثبان *kaʿsabān*, Many. *Kuʿsubān*, An insect resembling a beetle.

A قعثة *kaʿsat*, A giving sparingly.

A قعثرة *kaʿsarat*, A tearing up by the roots.

A قعثلة *kaʿsalat*, A turning of the toes in and of the heels out. A weak, straddling pace.

A قعد *kaʿada*, (fut. يقعد *yakʿudu*) He sat.

A قعد *kiʿd*, A companion. قعدك الله *kaʿdaka* or *kiʿdaka'llāh*, May God preserve you! I beseech you for God's sake! *Kaʿad*, Human excrement. Weakness in a camel's pastern. Schismatics. Disbanded soldiers who are not inscribed in the muster-book. *Kuʿud*, (pl. of قعود *kaʿūd*) (Young camels) fit for riding.

A قعدان *kiʿdān*, (pl. of قعود *kaʿūd*) (Young camels) fit for the saddle. *Kuʿdān*, (pl. of قعدة *kuʿdat*) Asses.

A قعدة *kaʿdat*, One sitting, or a single session. *Kaʿdat* or *kiʿdat*, The space which one person occupies when sitting. ذو القعدة *zū'l kaʿdat* or *kiʿdat*, (pl. ذوات القعدة *zawātu'l kaʿdat*) The eleventh month of the Arabian year. *Kiʿdat*, A mode of sitting. The youngest child (male or female). *Kuʿdat*, (pl. قعدان *kuʿdān*) An ass. A camel which the keeper rides on all occasions. A camel's saddle. A saddle. *Kaʿadat*, A carriage or beast employed in carrying women. A shaggy camel saddle-cloth. *Kuʿadat*, Sedentary.

A قعدد *kuʿdad*, (*kuʿdud*, or قعدود *kuʿdūd*) One who is nearly related to the head of his family or tribe. *Kuʿdud*, One very remotely so allied. Ignoble, mean, worthless, pusillanimous.

A قعديّ *kiʿdiy* or *kuʿdiy*, Weak. *Kuʿdiy* or *kiʿdiy*, (قعديّة *kuʿdiyat* or *kiʿdiyat*) One who sits much, or sleeps much. *Kaʿadiy*, A schismatic.

A قعر *kaʿr*, (v. n. of قعر) Going to the bottom. Making (a well) deep. Eating to the bottom of the dish, devouring all up. Drinking up the contents of a vessel. Bringing forth an abortion (a sheep). Eradicating, unrooting (a tree) so that it falls. Throwing down, levelling with the ground. (pl. قعور *kuʿūr*) The bottom or depth (of a well). A ditch, hollow, or low ground. A large dish, wooden saucer. A town. P قعر دريا *kaʿri daryā*, Bottom of the sea. A *Kaʿar*, Intellect, knowledge.

A قعران *kaʿrān*, A deep dish, one especially containing remains of food.

A قعرة *kaʿrat* or *kuʿrat*, Any thing remaining in, and just covering, the bottom of a dish. A ditch, hollow, low ground, or declivity. *Kaʿirat*, A vessel whose bottom is just covered with the contents. Libidinous (woman), whose passion is deep seated.

A قعرطة *kuʿratat*, Demolition of a structure.

A قعريٰ *kaʿraʾ*, (A vessel) the bottom of which is just covered.

A قعز *kaʿz*, (v. n. of قعز) Filling (a vessel). Drinking up (the contents of a vessel).

A قعس *kaʿs*, Fetid earth. *Kaʿas*, Protuberance of breast and concavity of back. A hollow in the middle of the back, with high shoulders and crupper. *Kaʿis*, One who has such breast and back, cradle-backed, sway-backed.

A قعساء *kaʿsāʾ*, (fem. of اقعس *akʿas*) Hollow-backed, with a protuberance on the breast. A grave, steady woman. Firm, solid (glory). (An ant) with an erected tail and breast.

A قعسبة *kaʿsabat*, A swift running through fear.

A قعسر *kaʿsar*, Ancient. A small pumpkin. *Kaʿsar*, (or قعسريّ *kaʿsariy*) Thick and strong.

A قعسرة *kaʿsarat*, (v. n. of قعسر Q) Being powerful, strong, bearing up against. Firmness, hardness.

A قعسريّ *kaʿsariy*, A small mill's wooden axle.

A قعسوس *kuʿsūs*, A word applied to a mean, deformed woman.

A قعش *kaʿsh*, A collection. Destruction, demolition (of a house). The turning or bending of a piece of wood. (pl. قعوش *kuʿūsh*) A camel-litter in which women travel.

A قعص *kaʿs*, (v. n. of قعص) Killing on the spot. A sudden death without moving or stirring. *Kaʿas*, (v. n. of قعص) Acquiring a habit of striking the milker and withholding her milk (a ewe). Being struck with the distemper قعاص *kuʿās*.

A قعض *kaʿz*, (v. n. of قعض) Bending. Bent.

A قعضب *kaʿzab*, (or قعضبيّ *kaʿzabiy*) Strong, thick. Expeditious. Bold, brave. Name of a certain maker of spear-heads.

A قعضبة *kaʿzabat*, (v. n. of قعضب Q) Extirpating, eradicating. Hardness, vehemence.

A قعضم *kaʿzam* or *kiʿzim*, Decrepit, toothless.

A قعط *kaʿt*, (v. n. of قعط) Binding hard. Straitening, crowding, confining, distressing (a debtor). Being abject, contemptible. The binding on of a turban. Rage, anger. Cowardice, pusillanimity. Great noise, clamour. Driving, forcing. A discovery, an uncovering. Drought, dryness. Numerous sheep. *Kaʿat*, (v. n. of قعط) Being humble, supplicating.

A قعطبة *kaʿtabat*, A cutting, an amputating.

A قعطبيّ *kaʿtabiy*, Quick (journey). Strong.

A قعطرة *kaʿtarat*, (v. n. of قعطر Q) Throwing prostrate. Tying, binding (any one). Filling.

A قعطلة *kaʿtalat*, (v. n. of قعطل Q) Talking much. Pressing hard, distressing (a debtor). Throwing prostrate.

A قعف *kaʿf*, (v. n. of قعف) Rooting out (palm-trees). Exhausting, eating, or drinking up (whatever is in a vessel). (Rain) going rapidly, (or any person) brushing (the ground) with the feet, sweeping off (pebbles). *Kaʿaf*, The falling of a wall. Little hills rising one above another.

A قعفزة *kaʿfazat*, (v. n. of قعفز Q) Walking with short steps. Sitting with the knees and thighs joined in a contemplative mood. قعفز له الكلام *kaʿfaza lahu'l kalāma*, He wished by words to drive him off. جلس القعفزيٰ *julasa'l kaʿfazaʾ*, He rested on the tips of the toes as ready to rise.

A قعفوز *kuʿfūz*, A kind of plant.

A قعقاع *kaʿkāʿ*, A clashing of arms or any thing similar. A trembling fever; ague. One who makes a noise with the joints of the feet when walking. Dry, hard (dates). Difficult, troublesome, and painful to walk in (road). Painful, laborious (nocturnal journey in quest of water). Name of Ibn Shawr, a man proverbial for his conversational powers. *Kiʿkāʿ*, (v. n. of قعقع Q) Making a crashing noise (as thunder, arms, or the teeth when eating any thing crisp or dry). Shaking and rattling any thing hard and dry. Driving a bull and crying قع قع *kaʿ kaʿ*. Travelling, making a tour or circuit.

A قعقبة *kaʿkabat*, A wound.

A قعقع *kuʿkuʿ*, A magpie; also another forest-bird, large, black, and white, with a long beak, tail, and feet.

A قعقعانيّ *kaʿkaʿāniy*, One who makes a noise with the joints of his feet when walking. *Kuʿkuʿāniy*, Loud-braying (ass).

A قعقعة *kaʿkaʿat*, (v. n. of قعقع Q) Making a crashing noise (as thunder, arms, or the teeth when eating any thing crisp or dry). Shaking and rattling any thing hard and dry (especially an old and shrivelled leathern-bottle, which being struck with a stick is used to frighten camels and make them mend their pace). Shaking the gaming-arrows preparatory to drawing. Driving a bull and calling out قع قع *kaع kaع*. The noise itself. Travelling, making a tour or circuit. The crash of thunder. قعقعت عمدهم *kaعkaعat عumuduhum*, Their tent-poles have rattled, *i.e.* they have migrated. ما يقعقع له بالشنان *mā yukaعkaع lahu bi'sh shinān*, He is not to be intimidated by empty noise.

A قعل *kaعl*, A stick serving to prop young vine-branches. Short in body. A miser. Base, unlucky.

A قعم *kaعm*, The mewing of a cat. *Kaعam*, (v. n. of قعم) Being attacked by disease. Distortion of the nose. An inclination or height of the buttocks.

A قعمة *kuعmat*, The choice part of one's estate.

A قعمصة *kaعmasat*, A voiding excrement.

A قعموص *kuعmūs*, Whatever is contained in the belly: excrement. Funguses, mushrooms.

A قعموط *kuعmūt*, Infants' swaddling bands.

A قعموطة *kuعmūtat*, Dung rolled up by a beetle.

A قعن *kaعn*, A large dish in which they knead paste. *Kaعan*, A deformed shortness of nose. A prominency of nose, and turned up at the point. Wideness between the feet.

A قعنب *kaعnab*, Strong; hard. A lion. A male fox. Name of a man. *Kuعnub*, A hooked nose.

A قعنباة *kaعambāt*, Hooked-taloned (eagle).

A قعنبة *kaعnabat*, Curvature or crookedness of nose. Short (woman).

A قعو *kaعw*, (pl. قعيّ *kuعiy*) The wooden cheek of a pulley which supports the axle; also the pulley itself and the iron axle. Lanky, firm, prominent-hipped (man). *Kaعw* or قعوّ *kuعūw*, (v. n. of قعا for قعو) Mounting, leaping on the female. Treading (as a bird).

A قعواء *kaعwās*, (fem. of اقعي *akعa'*) Pug-nosed; also, slender-thighed, or slender-legged (woman).

A قعوان *kaعwāni*, The two cheeks of a pulley.

A قعود *kaعūd*, (A young camel) ready for the saddle. (pl. اقعدة *akعidat*, قعد *kuعud*, قعدان *kiعdān*, and قعائد *kaعāsid*) A camel on which the keeper claps the saddle on every occasion. *Kuعūd*, (v. n. of قعد) Sitting. Remaining at home and separated from her husband (in child-bed, or during courses). Rising up. Reclining on the breast (a pelican). Bearing one year and not another (a palm-tree). Being a match for a rival. Preparing, accoutring (one's fellow) for conflict. Getting a stem (a young palm-tree). Becoming. Widowhood. (pl. of قاعد *kāعid*) Sitters.

A قعودة *kaعūdat*, A camel which the keeper rides on any occasion whatever; a hack-camel.

A قعور *kaعūr*, Deep. *Kuعūr*, (pl. of قعر) Bottoms.

A قعّور *kaععūr*, A deep well.

A قعوس *kaعwas*, A very old man.

A قعوش *kaعwash*, Light. A corpulent camel. *Kuعūsh*, (pl. of قعش *kaعsh*) Camel-litters for women.

A قعوشة *kaعwashat*, The act of prostrating.

A قعوص *kaعūs*, Striking the milker, and holding her milk (a ewe).

A قعوطة *kaعwatat*, Demolition of a structure.

A قعولة *kaعwalat*, (v. n. of قعول Q) Walking in a shuffling manner and kicking up the gravel before him. Sitting on the top of a hill.

A قعيّ *kuعiy*, (pl. of قعو *kaعw*) The wooden cheeks of a pulley which support the axle.

A قعيب *kaعib*, A great number.

A قعيث *kaعis*, Easy, light, small. A large present. Much rain, a great torrent.

A قعيد *kaعid*, He who sits with another; *i.e.* a colleague, confederate. Coeval. Coming behind, following. Game coming behind one. One whose father or ancestors are nearly related to the prince or chief of a tribe. A guardian. A father. A locust whose wings have not yet grown. قعيدك *kaعidaka*, By thy father! قعيدك الله *kaعiduka'llāh*, May God preserve you! I beseech you for God's sake!

A قعيدات *kaعidāt*, Saddles. Pack-saddles.

A قعيدان *kaعidāni*, (dual of قعيد *kaعid*) Guardian angels, especially two whom they suppose constantly to attend on the right and left of man.

A قعيدة *kaعidat*, A sack. A wife. A heap of sand.

A قعير *kaعir*, Profound, deep.

A قعيرة *kaعirat*, Libidinous (woman), whose passion lies deeply seated.

A قعيس *kuعays*, (dim. of مقعنسس *mukعansis*) Moderately strong (ن, م, and س, being rejected).

A قعيل *kaعil*, A male hare.

A قف *kif*, (imp. of وقف *wakafa*) Stop, halt.

A قفّ *kaff*, (v. n. of قف) Being collected, heaped together so as to resemble a gourd. A dry herb, chiefly such as they eat raw. *Kuff*, (pl. قفاف *kifāf* and اقفاف *akfāf*) A rugged hill, or any piece of rough ground. Clouds piling one over another, representing the appearance of mountains. The back of any thing. The hole in a hatchet, in which the handle is fixed; any thing resembling an axe. A mob, a mixed crowd. Short. Stones piled one upon another without admixture of loose earth. A hill whereon huge stones lie about as big as recumbent camels.

A قفء *kafs*, (v. n. of قفئ) Being rained upon (land), and rendered unfit for grazing by dirt and grit brought by a flood.

A قفا *kafa'*, (fut. يقفو *yakfū*) He followed (him).

A قفا *kafa'*, (or قفاء *kafās*) (pl. اقفى *akfī*, اقفية *akfiyat*, اقفاء *akfās*, قفيّ *kufiy*, *kifiy*, and قفين *kifin*) The hind-head, back part or nape of the neck, nuke. Following, pursuit. قفا الدهر *kafa'd dahr*, At no time, never. قفاء فلك *kafāsi falak*, Accidents which occur by the influence of the heavenly bodies. على قفاه *عala' kafāhi*, After him, at his back, close at his heels. ردّ قفا *rudda kafan*, (or على قفاه *عala' kafāhi*) He became decrepit.

A قفاخ *kifākh*, (v. n. 3 of قفخ) Striking on the head, or on any thing hollow. *Kufākh*, A woman of an elegant shape, and well-proportioned.

A قفاخر *kufākhir*, Thick-bodied.

A قفاخرة *kufākhirat*, Handsome (woman).

A قفاخرىّ *kufākhiriy*, Thick-bodied. The best of its sort. Delicately formed and fleshy.

A قفاخريّة *kufākhiriyat*, Large, fine (woman).

P قفادار *kafā-dār*, Assistant, helper, comrade.

A قفار *kafār*, Bread without meat. Meal of wheat or barley not moistened. Name of خالد بن عامر *khālid bin عāmir*, who served up an entertainment with bread and milk without meat. اكل خبزه قفارا *akala khubzahu kafāran*, He ate his bread without meat. *Kifār*, (pl. of قفر *kafr*) Deserts without grass or water.

A قفاز *kafāz*, (v. n. of قفز) Leaping, jumping, bounding. Dying.

A قفّاز *kuffāz*, A glove lined with cotton. A muff. Ornaments for the hands or feet. A kind of iron lattice on which a falcon perches. White hairs round the hoof of a horse. P قفّازپوشيدن *kuffāz poshīdan*, To put on gloves: to wear a muff.

A قفاس *kafās*, Vile, abject, base (woman).

A قفاص *kufās*, The mountain-goat. A certain disease incident to quadrupeds, shrivelling their legs.

A قفّاص *kaffās*, A maker of bird-cages.

A قفاع *kifāع*, (pl. of قفعة *kafعat*) Baskets without handles made of palm-leaves. *Kufāع*, A distemper which crooks the legs of sheep.

A قفّاع *kaffāع*, Parsimonious, thrifty. *Kuffāع*, A kind of shrub, which, when hard and dry, has the appearance of horns; whence it is called كفّ الكلب *kaffu'l kalb*.

A قفّاعة *kuffāعat*, (or قفاعة *kufāعat*) A net for catching birds, made of the fibres of the palm-tree.

A قفاعيّ *kufāعiy*, Red. One whose nose is intensely red and excoriated. احمر قفاعيّ *ahmar kufāعiy*, Intense red.

A قفاف *kifāf*, (pl. of قفّ *kuff*) Hills. Clouds piled up.

A قفّاف *kaffāf*, One who steals money between his fingers.

P قفاگيران *kafā-girān*, The oppressed.

A قفّال *kaffāl*, A locksmith. *Kuffāl*, (pl. of قافل *kāfil*) Comers off a journey.

A قفّان *kaffān*, The hind-head. End, conclusion, result. A troop, herd, body, collection of any kind. Time, season, opportunity. Trusty. Attention, study, diligence in getting the knowledge of a thing. A large pair of scales. على قفّانه *عala' kaffānihi*, Close on his steps.

A قفاند *kafānid*, (pl. of قفندد *kafandad*) Broad-shouldered (men).

A قفاوة *kafāwat*, Any thing by which a guest is honoured. Joy, exultation. Kindness, favour.

P قفاهير *kafāhīr*, A handsome face.

A قفّة *kaffat*, A little, weak man. *Kaffat*, *kiffat*, or *kuffat*, The trembling of an ague, paroxysm of fever. *Kiffat*, The first excrement of a new-born

A قفقفة *kafkafat*, (v. n. of قفقف Q) Trembling with cold. Chattering (as the teeth). Making a noise (the jaws when eating). Withering (as a plant).

A قفل *kafl*, (v. n. of قفل) Preserving. Withering (a tree). Laying up (corn) against a season of scarcity. Measuring. Estimating, guessing at the amount of any thing. Withered (tree), dry (wood). *Kufl*, (pl. اقفال *akfāl*, اقفل *akful*, and قفول *kufūl*) A lock, bolt, bar. A standard, ensign, banner. A sort of tree found in Hijāz. A proper name. P قفل آسمان *kufli āsmān*, (or قفل فلك *kufli falak*) Impiety, heresy, infidelity. قفل رومي *kufli rūmī*, A padlock. Name of the fifteenth musical note of the bārbud. قفل سست كردن *kufl sust kardan*, To open the door. A قفل وسواس *kufli waswās*, An intricate kind of lock. *Kafal*, A multitude returned from a journey.

A قفلة *kaflat*, The hind-head. Giving a present once. (Money) of just weight. *Kaflat* or *kafalat*, A dry tree. *Kufalat*, One who remembers all he hears.

A قفلطة *kaflatat*, (v. n. of قفلط Q) Snatching.

P قفلگر *kuflgar*, A locksmith.

P قفلوط *kuflūt*, A kind of leek.

A قفن *kafn*, (v. n. of قفن) Striking. Beating, lashing. Smiting on the back of the head. Fighting. Slaughtering (especially on the back of the head or neck). Lapping with his tongue (a dog). Drinking water out of an earthen vessel. A whip, lash, scourge. *Kafan*, The hind-head.

A قفنّ *kafann*, The hind-head. *Kifann*, Severe, hard, unjust. Foul-mouthed. A fool.

A قفنّد *kafannad*, One with a large hard head.

A قفندد *kafandad*, (pl. قفانِد *kafānid* and قفنددون *kafandadūn*) Broad-shouldered (man).

A قفندر *kafandar*, Hideous, ugly. Who has a strong, hard, and small head. One who has a little thick foot. Short and compact-bodied. White.

A قفنزعة *kafanzaʻat*, A very dwarfish woman.

A قفو *kafw*, (and قفوّ *kufūw*) (v. n. of قفا for قفو) Following another, tracking closely his steps. Striking the nape of the neck. Preferring, esteeming rather. Choosing, selecting for any particular business. Involving in any unpleasant affair. Accusing publicly of any shameful action, especially of adultery. Suspecting. Calling bad names. Setting food before a guest. Obliterating, effacing. *Kafw*, Heat at a time of rain.

A قفوة *kifwat*, Any thing agreeable which one prefers. An unpleasant thing. Any shameful act with which one is charged. A crime, sin, fault. An accusation (true or false). Suspicion. Greatness, honour, glory. Calumny, falsehood, detraction. Disgrace.

A قفور *kufūr*, (pl. of قفر *kafr*) Deserts.

A قفّور *kaffūr*, The branch of a palm-tree; also the envelope of the flower. Name of an herb.

P قفورا *kafūrā*, Name of a medicinal plant.

A قفوز *kafūz*, Jumping, limping (deer). *Kufūz*,

P قفس *kafas*, A bird's cage: a lattice, grate, window-bars. قفس مركب *kafasi markab*, The netting of a ship, especially on the tops.

A قفساء *kafsās*, The belly. The stomach. Vile, base, abject (woman).

A قفش *kafsh*, Agility, cheerfulness. A taking, a collecting. A striking with a stick or sword. Voracity in eating. A short boot. Milking hastily. Multus coitus. *Kafash*, Terror-inspiring robbers.

A قفشليل *kafshalīl*, (P قفشيل *kafshīl*) A ladle.

A قفص *kafs*, (v. n. of قفص) Tying (a deer) by the feet. Confining (a queen-bee) in the hive, or (a bird) in the cage. Putting (its) parts very near each other. Giving pain. Ascending, being high. (pl. اقفاص *akfās*) A bird's cage. *Kufs* or *kafas*, Net-work. *Kafas*, A bird-cage. A wicker-basket. An agricultural machine in which the wheat is carried to the stack. Lightness, briskness, joy. A shrivelling up from cold. A burning heat in the throat. Acidity on the stomach, heart-burn from drinking water after eating dates. *Kafis*, Contracted, drawn together (horse). (A locust) whose wings are stiff with cold.

P قفص گر *kafasgar*, A maker of cages.

A قفصل *kufsul*, A lion.

A قفط *kaft*, (v. n. of قفط) Treading (as a bird), gendering (any cloven-footed animal). Collecting. Recompensing, requiting. *Kift*, Copt, a city in Upper Egypt, settled on the descendants of Aliy.

A قفطلة *kaftalat*, (v. n. of قفطل Q) Snatching from another's hand.

A قفطى *kafata'*, (A man) addicted to venery.

A قفع *kafʻ*, (v. n. of قفع) Striking on the fingers (with a ferrule). Refusing, denying. Prohibiting, driving back, withholding, hindering. Being contracted, shrivelled, shrunk. Being shrivelled or scorched from top to bottom (an ear). A pent-house, or any thing similar, under which soldiers made formerly their approaches to the walls of a besieged town. *Kufʻ*, Those whose fingers are bent inwards. *Kafaʻ*, Straits, anguish. Labour, toil.

A قفعاء *kafʻāʼ*, A female whose fingers bend downwards, or whose toes turn in towards the sole. Singed, scorched (ear). A pent-house. A limber or slender stick. A kind of tree bearing green rings, which fall off when dry. (A foot) whose toes are turned downwards towards the sole.

A قفعة *kafʻat*, (pl. قفاع *kifāʻ*) A basket without a handle made of palm-leaves. A date-hamper. A sack of hair-cloth, in which they put the grain sesame in order to be pressed for oil. A circular vessel in which they gather fresh dates.

A قفعدد *kafaʻdad*, A dwarf.

A قفف *kufaf*, (pl. of قفّة *kuffat*) Hatchets.

A قفقف *kafkaf*, (dual قفقفان *kafkafāni*) The jaw or beard of a camel. Wing of an ostrich.

animal. *Kuffat*, A hare. A mouse. (pl. قفف *kufaf*) Any thing like a hatchet. A tree withered and dead. A decrepit, spent old man. Any thing gourd-shaped made of palm-leaves. A case, casket, box, basket (especially of palm-leaves, or a dry, empty gourd or calabash in which women keep their sewing-cotton). High ground.

T قفتان *kaftān*, A robe of honour which Eastern princes present to ambassadors and other persons of distinction.

A قفثلة *kafsalat*, (v. n. of قفثل Q) Sweeping off with haste. Uprooting.

A قفح *kafh*, (v. n. of قفح) Abhorring, disliking, disapproving. Nauseating food. Taking medicine in powders.

A قفحاء *kafhāʼ*, (Smoke or dust) which appears to branch out.

A قفخ *kafkh*, (v. n. of قفخ) Striking (especially on the head, or on any hollow substance).

A قفخة *kafkhat*, A cow in want of the bull.

A قفد *kafd*, (v. n. of قفد) Striking one slightly on the back of the head (with the palm of the hand). Finishing any work. Having a thick, flabby neck, short hands, feet, fingers, or toes. Turning inward the point of the hoof (a camel). Folding the turban-sash round the head, so that no part hangs down. A perpendicular straightness of the pastern. An oblique position of the human foot, the toes being seen from behind.

A قفداء *kafdāʼ*, A folding of the turban-sash round the head, so that no part hangs down.

A قفدانة *kafadānat*, (or قفدان *kafadān*) A casket, case, or sheath in which the collyrium-pot is kept. A leathern box in which druggists put up aromatics.

A قفدر *kafdar*, Ugly, of a hideous aspect.

P قفر *kafr*, Dodder.

A قفر *kafr*, (v. n. of قفر) Following (another's steps). Having little (money). Being without meat (bread). (pl. قفار *kifār* and قفور *kufūr*) A desert without herbage. Bread without meat. Bitumen. Hair. A steer taken from the mother in order to be yoked to the plough. قفر اليهود *kafru'l yahūd*, Jew's pitch. بات القفر *bāta'l kafra*, He slept in the open air (finding no shelter). *Kafir*, Thin of hairs. A wolf.

A قفرة *kafrat*, A desert, a solitude.

A قفز *kafz*, (v. n. of قفز) Skipping. Dying.

A قفزان *kufzān*, (pl. of قفيز *kafīz*) Measures containing about eight مكاكيل *makākīl*. *Kafazān*, (v. n. of قفز) Leaping, skipping. Dying.

A قفزي *kafaza'*, A spring, a leap. A particular pace of horses and camels.

A قفس *kafs*, (v. n. of قفس) Dying. Tying by the feet (a deer). Seizing by the hair. Seizing in an angry mood. *Kufs*, Name of a people in Karamania resembling the Kurds. *Kafas*, (v. n. of قفس) Having the tip of the nose large.

(v. n. of قفز) Leaping, jumping, skipping. Dying.

A قفوس *kufūs*, (v. n. of قفس) Dying. Tying (a deer) by the feet. Seizing by the hair. Seizing any thing in an angry mood.

A قفوس *kafūs* also *kufūs*, Name of a country whence a fragrant fumigating herb is procured.

A قفوف *kufūf*, (v. n. of قف) Withering (as a plant). (Any thing) becoming wrinkled, shrivelled. Drying after being washed (clothes). Filching, stealing. Standing on end from fear (hair).

A قفول *kufūl*, (v. n. of قفل) Returning from a journey. Becoming dry (skin). Measuring. Estimating, guessing at the amount of a thing. Hoarding up (grain) against scarcity. Being very impatient and excited (a stallion). (pl. of قفل *kufl*) Locks.

P قفوله *kufūla*, A clew, a ball.

A قفون *kufūn*, (v. n. of قفن) Lapping (as a dog). Striking on the back of the head. Slaughtering (a sheep) on the back part of the head or neck. Dying.

A قفي *kafy*, (v. n. of قفي) Striking on the hind-head. Slaying a sheep on the back of the head.

A قفيّ *kafīy*, Killed by an incision or blow on the back of the head or neck. An honoured guest. Food set before a guest. One who inquires minutely into people's affairs. Benevolent. A follower, one who marks the motions of another. A lieutenant, locum-tenens, vicegerent. Any shameful act with which one is charged. Any person preferred before or esteemed above another. Accused, suspected. Learned, knowing. Suspicion. Ill-name, abuse, reproach. *Kufīy* or *kifīy*, (pl. of قفا *kafa'*) Hind-heads.

A قفية *kufyat*, A pit dug for a lion.

A قفيّة *kafīyat*, A successor, a follower. A vicegerent, lieutenant. Excellence, superiority. Any thing by which a guest is honoured. A sheep slaughtered behind the head.

A قفيحة *kafīhat*, Cream, upon which milk is poured drawn fresh from the ewe.

A قفيخة *kafīkhat*, Food prepared with dates dressed with fat. A fleshy limb.

A قفير *kafīr*, Dry bread. A basket. A large date-basket made of palm-leaves. Dry dung.

A قفيرة *kufayrat*, The mother of Farazdak.

A قفيز *kafīz*, (pl. اقفزة *akfizat* and قفزان *kufzān*) A measure containing about eight مكاكيل *makākīl*. A space of ground containing about 144 cubits square, equal to a fourth of a جريب *jarīb*. *Kufayz*, Name of a servant of Muhammad.

A قفيزي *kuffayza'*, A boy's game.

A قفيص *kafīs*, A ploughshare; also the ring of it.

A قفيط *kafīt*, A man much given to venery.

A قفيف *kafīf*, (v. n. of قف) Shrivelling, drying, withering. Dry, withered herbage. Vegetables which are eaten raw.

A قفيل *kafīl*, Dry (skin or wood). A scourge. A narrow pass through a mountain. A turn-again lane. Name of an herb. Rose-water.

A قفين *kafīn*, Slaughtered by a cut on the back of the head. *Kifīn*, (pl. of قفا *kafa'*) Hind-heads.

A قِقة *kikat*, The scream of a child. A noise by which they frighten or deter children.

A قَقّة *kakkat* or *kikkat*, The excrement of a child. Bad counsel.

P ققدان *kakadān*, A perfumer's bag.

A ققق *kakak*, The excrement (of a child).

A قققة *kakakat*, Tame crows taught to speak. The excrement of a child.

P ققنس *kaknus*, ققنوس *kak* or *kuknūs*, Phœnix.

A قل *kall*, A low wall. *Kill*, (pl. قلل *kilal*) A tremor which seizes a man. A date-stone that germinates alone weakly. *Kill* or *kull*, (v. n. of قل) Being rare, not happening. Lifting, raising up. *Kull*, A little, small quantity, paucity. Solitary (man). The least thing. قل بن قل *kullu bin kullin*, An unknown man.

P قلا *kalā*, A sling. Lixivium, potash.

A قلا *kilā'*, (v. n. of قلا for قلو) Hating, detesting.

A قلاء *kalā'*, (v. n. of قلا for قلو) Hating, detesting. Leaving. Hatred.

A قلّاء *kallā'*, One that fries. A frying-pan maker. A burner of potash (قلي *kily* or *kila'*).

A قلاءة *kalā'at*, A manufactory of frying-pans.

A قلاب *kilāb*, A wolf. *Kulāb*, A disease of the heart. A disease of which a camel instantly dies.

P قلاب *kulāb*, A fish-hook.

A قلّاب *kallāb*, A counterfeiter of coin.

A قلات *kilāt*, (pl. of قلة *kulat*) Small pieces of wood, struck forward by a larger, in boys' games.

A قلّات *kullāt*, (pl. of قلة *kullat*) Mountain-tops.

P قلات گازران *kalāti gāzurān*, Name of the burial place of the Shaykh Sādī in Shīrāz.

P قلاتين *kalātīn*, A tub, a cistern.

P قلاچو *kalāchū*, A dervish's leathern drinking-cup. A channel from which cattle drink in winter.

P قلاچوري *kalāchūri*, A glittering sword.

A قلاح *kulāh*, Yellowness, dirt of the teeth.

A قلاد *kilād*, A copper-thread running through the nose-ring of a camel or round an ear-ring.

A قلادة *kilādat*, (pl. قلائد *kalā'id*) A collar, necklace, chain, or any ornament for the neck. A leash, by which a courser holds his dog. A term applied to elephants (as سير *sar* is to horses).

A قلار *killār*, (or قلاريّ *killārīy*) The white fig.

P قلارون *kalārūn*, Generals, military tribunes.

P قلاري *kulārī*, A kind of white fig.

P قلازارة *kalāzāra*, (or قلازاره) A magpie.

A قلّاس *kallās*, Foaming (sea). A seller of the high caps or mitres called قلنسوة *kalansuwat*.

P قلاسنگ *kalāsang*, A sling. A ball, sling-stone.

A قلاسي *kalāsiy*, (or قلاسي *kalāsī*) (pl. of قلنسوة *kalansuwat* and قلنسية *kulansiyat*) Mitres, high caps.

A قلاش *kalāsh*, A shrivelled pistachio.

P قلّاش *kallāsh*, Cunning, crafty. A drunkard, a haunter of taverns. A needy, worthless fellow.

A قلاشة *kalāshat*, Smallness, shortness.

P قلاشي *kallāshī*, Revelry, drunkenness.

P قلاشيرة *kalāshīra*, Ashes of which soap is made.

A قلاص *kilās*, (pl. of قلوص) Young she-camels.

A قلّاص *kallās*, Increasing (water in a well).

A قلاط *kulāt*, Extremely dwarfish (man, cat, or dog). The brood of demons.

A قلاع *kilā'*, (pl. of قلع *kal'*) Scrips, shepherds' bags. (pl. of قلع *kil'*) Sails. (pl. of قلعة *kal'at*) Castles; forts, citadels. (pl. of قلعة *kala'at*) Large and high stones or pieces of rock detached from a mountain. P قلاع سپهر ارتفاع *kilā'i sipihr-irtifā'*, Castles high as heaven. A *Kulā'*, St. Anthony's fire, or any similar disease, corroding the flesh to the bone. Pustules in the mouth. Clay which dries and cracks when the water covering it evaporates or runs off. A fragment or crust of earth, underneath which mushrooms are found. Sudden death overtaking a healthy camel.

A قلّاع *kallā'*, A beadle or officer attending a magistrate or collector of revenue. One who rakes up the ashes of the dead. Unsteady, not firm on his feet, or tottering in his saddle. A pimp. Stupid. A sycophant, whisperer, tale-bearer, slanderer, or liar. *Kullā'*, Clay which dries and cracks when the water covering it evaporates or runs off. A fragment or crust of earth, beneath which mushrooms lie. A plant eaten by camels, dry or fresh.

A قلاعة *kilā'at*, The sail of a ship. *Kulā'at*, A bit of clay. A stone or a ball thrown by a sling. A large stone standing perpendicular in a plain. A stone or a piece of earth torn from the ground to throw at any thing.

A قلافة *kilāfat*, The art of caulking a ship. *Kulāfat*, Skin, husk, bark.

P قلاقل *kilākal*, The wild pomegranate.

A قلاقل *kulākil*, An active ally. A sort of plant.

A قلال *kalāl* or *kulāl*, Little, small (thing). *Kilāl*, (v. n. 3 of قل) Giving little. A vine-prop. (pl. of قلة *kullat*) Buckets. Mountain-tops.

A قلّال *kullāl*, Few (persons).

A قلام *kilām*, (pl. of قلم *kalam*) Pens, reeds.

A قلّام *kullām*, A plant of the حمض *hamz* sort.

A قلامة *kulāmat*, A nail-paring.

P قلان *kalān*, A tax in Shīrwān. A catamite.

A قلانس *kalānis*, (or قلانيس *kalānīs*) (pl. of قلنسوة *kalansuwat*) Mitres, high caps.

P قلاوز *kalāwuz*, A road-guide. Horsemen who guard the flank of an army. Spies, scouts.

P قلاوزي *kalāwuzī*, Guidance.

P قلاوژون *kalāwajūn*, A magpie.

P قلاووز *kalāwūz*, A road-guide.

A قلايا *kalāya'*, (pl. of قلية *kalīyat*) Fried victuals.

A قلائد *kalā'id*, Necklaces. Poems which remain from age to age.

A قلائص *kalā'is*, (pl. of قلوص *kalūs*) Young she-camels.

A قلائل *kalāʼil*, (pl. of قليل *kalīl*) Few (men).

P قلب *kalb*, Bad money. Left (not right).

A قلب *kalb*, (v. n. of قلب) Converting, inverting, turning, turning inside out, changing, permuting, transmuting, commuting. (God) receiving to himself. Striking, hurting (especially in the heart). Beginning to redden (unripe dates). Robbing (a palm-tree) of (its) pith. Heart, mind, soul, understanding, intellect. Kernel, marrow. Middle. Centre (of an army). Permutation of one letter with another, inversion. Pure, genuine, unmixed (Arabian). Inverted. Adulterated. Counterfeit coin. Rugged, difficult ground. القلب *al kalb*, The heart is the name of the eighteenth lunar mansion. قلب الاسد *kalbu'l asad*, Name of a star in Leo. قلب طاهر *kalbi tāhir*, A pure heart. قلب العقرب *kalbu'l ʻakrab*, The heart of the scorpion, *i.e.* A bright star in Scorpio, the twenty-eighth mansion of the moon. استكبار القلب *istikbāru'l kalb*, Loftiness of soul, pride, arrogance. قلب اقبال *kalbi ikbāl*, The inversion of اقبال *ikbāl*, Prosperity, *i.e.* لا بقا *lā bakā*, No permanency. P قلب ريش *kalbi rish*, The inversion of ريش *rish*, *i.e.* شير *shir*, Milk. *Kalb, hilb*, or *kulb*, (pl. اقلاب *aklāb*, قلوب *kulūb*, and قلبة *kilabat*) The pith of a palm-tree, or the best leaves thereof. *Kulb*, A bracelet. A whitish serpent. A very hard species of grain. Pure, genuine (in descent). *Kulb* or *kulub*, (pl. of قليب *kalīb*) Ancient wells. *Kalab*, Inversion of the lip.

A قلب *kullab*, Skilful in managing affairs. An artful fellow, a cheat. Changeable.

A قلبا *kalban*, Cordially, heartily.

A قلباء *kalbāʼ*, (fem. of اقلب *aklab*) Inverted-lipped (woman). Inverted (lip).

A قلبة *kalbat*, True (Arabian woman). *Kulbat*, Redness (of unripe dates). Purity (of descent). *Kalabat*, Pain, disease, grief (either from love or vexation). Fatigue, lassitude. *Kilabat*, (pl. of قلب *kalb* or *kilb*) Hearts. Kernels. Marrows.

P قلبخانه *kalb-khāna*, The barbican of the fortress of Herat.

P قلبزن *kalb-zan*, (or قلب ساز *kalb-sāz*) A coiner of false money.

P قلبگاه *kalb-gāh*, Middle; centre of an army.

P قلبنگ *kalabang*, A sort of odoriferous wood.

T قلبور *kalbūr*, A sieve.

P قلبه *kulba*, A plough.

P قلبه ران *kulba-rān*, Ploughing. A ploughman. گاو قلبه ران *gāvi kulba-rān*, A ploughing-ox. قلبه راني كردن *kulba-rānī kardan*, To drive plough. To plough.

A قلبي *kalbiy*, Cordial, hearty. Adulterated.

A قلبي *kullabiy*, Skilful in managing business. Artful, cunning. Changeable, changeful, versatile.

A قلة *kulat*, (pl. قلات *kilāt*, قلون *kilūn*, and *kulūn*) A small piece of wood struck forward by a larger in the game of hockey.

A قلة *kallat*, A rising up from sickness or poverty. *Killat*, (v. n. of قل) Being little, few; diminishing. Paucity, littleness, fewness, scarcity. Tremor, palpitation. قلت فهم *killati fahm*, Poverty of understanding. *Kullat*, (pl. قلل *kulal* and قلال *kilāl*) Summit of a mountain, top or head of any thing: head of a man: pommel of a sword. A crowd. A large jar or water-pot. A small jug.

P قلت *kalt*, A pimp. *Kilt*, Kind of vetch.

A قلت *kalt*, (pl. قلات *kilāt*) A hollow in a mountain, or tarn where water collects. قلت الابهام *kaltu'l ibhām*, A hollow under the thumb. *Kalt* or *kalit*, One who has little flesh on the bones. *Kult*, Saxifrage. *Kalat*, (v. n. of قلت) Perishing. Death, destruction.

P قلتاق *kaltāk* A saddle-tree. A housing.

P قلتبان *kaltabān* or *kaltbān*, A contented cuckold, wittol, pimp. A roller for levelling clay roofs.

P قلتباني *kaltabānī*, Panderism. قلتباني كردن *kaltabānī kardan*, To pimp or pander.

P قلتبوس *kaltbos*, A contented cuckold. Faithless, irreligious.

A قلتة *kalitat*, (A sheep) whose milk is not sweet.

P قلته *kalta*, A cuckold, wittol. A pimp.

A قلتين *kullatayn*, A warm-bath. A cup which is in common use by many.

P قلج *kulj*, A four-footed animal, whose feet stand wide apart, and whose knees are close together.

A قلح *kalh*, An old ass. *Kilh*, A dirty garment. *Kalah*, (v. n. of قلح) Having dirty, yellow teeth. Foulness or yellowness of teeth. *Kalih*, Dirty.

A قلحاس *kilhās*, Ugly, ill-looking, deformed.

A قلحامة *kilhāmat*, Decrepit (old man).

A قلحز *kilhazz*, Fat. A vain boaster.

A قلحزة *kalhazat*, A dwarf's pace.

A قلحم *kilhamm*, Of a noble or elevated mind. Aged, old, worn. Proud, haughty, stately.

A قلحمة *kalhamat*, A being decrepit.

A قلحوم *kulhūm*, Large-bodied.

A قلخ *kalkh*, (v. n. of قلخ) Braying in the throat (a stallion camel). Striking one dry substance against another. Eradicating (trees). An aged ass. A hollow reed. An impatient stallion.

A قلخم *kilkhamm*, A large thick camel.

A قلد *kald*, (v. n. of قلد) Collecting (water in a cistern, milk in a pail, or drink in the belly). Attacking any body (a fever, especially a quotidian ague). Watering (sown fields). Making thin (a piece of iron) and folding it over any thing. Folding (one thing over another). Twisting (a rope). Bracelets of twisted silver. *Kild*, The periodical return of an ague fit. A quartan fever. Weekly rain. The caravans passing between Mecca and Judda (because they only drink once in the four days' journey). A kind of bowl. Water given away. A multitude. A horse's yard. اعطيته قلد امري *aʻtaytuhu kilda amrī*, I committed my business into his hand.

A قلداء *kaldāʼ*, A she-camel having a long copper-string put through the nose-ring. Long-necked (she-camel).

A قلدة *kildat*, Sediment of melted butter: dregs.

A قلذ *kalaz*, A tike, tick, or sheep-louse.

A قلذة *kalizat*, Flocks infested with the tike.

A قلذم *kalzom*, Wide and watery (pudendum).

A قلز *kalz*, (v. n. of قلز) Drinking the beverage called قلز *kalz*. Causing (one) to drink. Pricking the ground with the point of a stick and leaving a mark. Laying eggs (a locust). Striking, beating, shooting, darting. Being nimble. Leaping, rushing upon, or assaulting. Limping. A kind of drink. A light and weakly man. Briskness, cheerfulness.

A قلز *kuluzz* also *kilizz*, A hardy, strong man. Hard copper on which iron makes no impression.

A قلزم *kilzim*, Base, avaricious. *Kulzum*, Clysma, a town in Egypt near Mount Sinai. بحر قلزم *bahr kulzum*, The Red Sea. P قلزم پنج شاخ *kulzumi panj shākh*, The palm of the hand. The hand of the liberal. قلزم نگون *kulzumi nigūn*, The sky.

A قلزمة *kalzamat*, (v. n. of قلزم Q) Swallowing. Reprehension. Noise, clamour.

A قلس *kals*, (v. n. of قلس) Vomiting at one time a small quantity. Spilling (wine) from an overflowing cup. Dashing its water over the bank (an overflowing stream). Dancing to vocal music. Good singing. Drinking largely of date or raisin-wine. Being disturbed (the mind). (pl. قلوس *kulūs*) A thick rope or halser made of the fibres of the palm-tree or cocoa-nut. A cable. Any acid humour which the stomach throws up into the mouth, vomiting once in a slight degree (when repeated again and again it is called قيء *kayʼ*, or the true vomit).

A قلساة *kalsāt*, (v. n. of قلسي Q) Putting a hat or the high cap قلنسوة *kalansuwat* on a person.

A قلص *kalas*, (v. n. of قلص) Being disturbed (the mind). *Kulus*, (pl. of قلوص) Young she-camels.

A قلصة *kalasat*, Well-water flowing, increasing.

A قلط *kalt*, Ugliness of face. *Kalat*, The offspring of demons.

A قلطبان *kaltabān*, A pimp, voluntary cuckold.

A قلطفة *kaltafat*, Lightness, smallness of body.

A قلطي *kalatiy*, Extremely dwarfish (man, cat, or dog). Impure, wicked, obstinate.

A قلع *kalʻ*, (v. n. of قلع) Drawing out, tearing off, extirpating, eradicating, extracting, pulling down, subverting, overturning, ruining, removing from (his) place. Cashiering. A removal from office. A builder's hatchet. (pl. قلوع *kuluʻ*, اقلع *akluʻ*, قلاع *kilāʻ*, and قلعة *kilaʻat*) A scrip, a shepherd's bag. Any thing paid into the exchequer by anticipation. *Kalʻ, kilʻ*, or *kalaʻ*, Intermission (of a fever); the period of such intermission. Mines from which they dig the best lead (or tin) called

قلع *kalʻ. Kilʻ,* (pl. قلاع *kilāʻ* and قلوع *kulūʻ*) The sail of a ship. Standing infirmly on the feet, or tottering in the saddle. Stupid. Any clothing for a man's breast. *Kulʻ,* A stout walker. (pl. of قلوع *kalūʻ*) Large-bodied (she-camels). Bows which, when drawn, fly back. *Kulʻ* or *kalaʻ,* A lifting up of the feet high in walking. *Kalaʻ,* (v. n. of قلع) Being moveable, unfixed, ready to fall. Being stupid and unable to comprehend. Blood. Scurf or scab. Thick, clotted blood. A stone under a rock. (pl. of قلعة *kalaʻat*) Parts of a large cloud. *Kaliʻ,* Slipping the foot (in wrestling). Sitting totteringly on horseback; unsteady. Stupid. Lifting the feet high in travelling. (pl. قلعة *kilaʻat*) A shepherd's wallet. *Kilaʻ,* (pl. of قلعة *kalaʻat*) Stones high and large, detached from a mountain. (pl. of قلعة *kilʻat*) Halves of things split lengthwise.

A قلعة *kalʻat,* (in India *kilʻa*) (pl. قلاع *kilāʻ* and قلوع *kulūʻ*) A castle, fort (especially on the top of a mountain). Name of a place in India where the best lead is found and the best swords are made. P قلعهٔ بندر *kalʻaʼi bandar,* Name of a fortress in Shīrāz. قلعهٔ کهرباگون *kalʻaʼi kah-rubāgūn* (or پیکر *paykar*), The world. A *Kalʻat,* A sucker torn from the root of a palm-tree. A palm-tree torn up by the root. Part of a camel's bunch. A scrip, a shepherd's bag. *Kilʻat,* (pl. قلع *kilaʻ*) The half (especially of any thing split the wrong way). *Kulʻat,* A moving from place to place (the having no fixed habitation, or when sitting, compelled frequently to rise up). A removal from office. Any sum paid into the exchequer unweighed. Borrowed money. Fleeting treasures. Any thing not permanent. Weak, unable to maintain one's ground in wrestling, or one's seat in the saddle. Any thing borrowed or lent. A mouthful pulled off a tree. دار قلعة *dāru kulʻatin,* The present world. علیٰ قلعة *ʻala' kulʻatin,* On a journey. *Kulʻat, kulaʻat,* or *kuluʻat,* Slipping the foot. Unsettledness, absence of stability and permanence. Unsteady. Stupid. *Kalaʻat,* (v. n. of قلع) Being unsteady, tottering, ready to fall from a saddle. Being stupid and unable to comprehend. A citadel. A purse, scrip, or shepherd's bag. مرج القلعة *marju'l kalaʻat,* Name of a place where swords are made. (pl. قلاع *kilāʻ* and قلع *kilaʻ*) A huge piece of rock uprooted from a mountain, and difficult to pass by. A great stone, a boulder. (pl. قلع *kalaʻ*) A piece of a large cloud. A cloud veiling one side of the sky. A big she-camel. *Kilaʻat,* (pl. of قلع *kalʻ*) Shepherds' bags, scrips.

A P قلعجات *kilʻajāt,* (pl. of قلعه) Fortresses.

A P قلعچه *kilʻacha,* A redoubt.

A قلعطة *kalʻatat,* Exceeding crispness or curliness of the hair.

P قلعگیان *kilʻagiyān,* Garrison-soldiers.

A قلعم *kalʻam,* An old woman.

A قلعمّ *kilʻamm,* A decrepit old man.

P قلعه دار *kilʻa-dār,* The commandant of a garrison, governor of a fort. قلعه دار سپهر *kilʻa-dāri sipihr,* The sun.

P قلعه نشین *kalʻa-nishīn,* Besieged. A besieger.

A قلعيّ *kalʻiy,* Tin (from the mine قلع *kalʻ,* where it is found). P قلعي کردن *kalʻī kardan,* To tin (pots and kettles). A *Kalaʻiy,* (A sword) of the make of مرج القلعة *marju'l kalaʻat.* Part of a large cloud.

P قلعیگر *kalʻīgar,* A tinman.

P قلغنج *kalghanj,* A lock. The ring of a gate.

P قلغند *kalghand,* Driving a nail into a horse's hoof and clenching it. An enclosure of wicker-work.

P قلغه *kalgha,* A flower. An insignia of rank worn in the turban.

P قلغه سلطان *kalgha-sultān,* The lieutenant or next brother to the khan of Crim Tartary.

A قلف *kalf,* (v. n. of قلف) Stripping off the bark of a tree, tearing off a nail. Circumcising, cutting the foreskin clean off. Opening up, giving free vent, by carrying off any obstruction. Unbunging (a wine-cask). Caulking, pitching, filling up seams of a ship with the fibres of palm-leaves or moss. Turning, inverting. Foaming, frothing. *Kilf,* A basket made of palm-trees, which is drawn together at the top. Skin, husk, bark. Bark of the mastich-tree, or of the pomegranate. A rough place. *Kulf,* (pl. of اقلف *aklaf*) Uncircumcised. *Kalaf,* (v. n. of قلف) Being uncircumcised. Cutting the foreskin clean off. Uncircumcision. *Kuluf,* (pl. of قليفة *kalīfat*) Baskets for holding dates.

A قلف *killaf,* Thin clay left by the water and become dry.

A قلفاء *kalfāʼ,* (fem. of اقلف) Plenteous (year).

A قلفان *kalafāni,* (or قلفتان *kulfatāni,* du.) The edges of the whiskers.

A قلفة *kalfat,* (v. n. of قلف) Unbunging (a wine-cask). Turning, inverting. Caulking (a ship). Foaming, frothing. (pl. قلف *half*) A hamper full of dates (in Bahrayn). *Kilfat,* A certain plant. Covetous, greedy. Torn off (nail). *Kulfat* or *kalafat,* The prepuce, foreskin.

A قلفحة *kalfahat,* An eating up of the whole.

A قلفع *kilfaʻ* or *kilfiʻ,* Cracked crust of clay. A splint flying off from iron when hammering.

A قلفعة *kilfiʻat,* A crust of earth covering a mushroom. A kind of crust upon a scabby camel.

G قلفونيا *kulfūniyā,* A kind of pine-tree gum.

P قلفه *kalfa,* A sub-preceptor.

A قلفي *kulfī,* A small hukka-snake. A cup with a cover in which ice is moulded.

A قلق *kalak,* Fretfulness, restlessness, disquietude, agitation, commotion. *Kalik,* Unquiet, restless, fretful. قلق الوشاح *kaliku'l wishāh,* A woman whose necklace hangs loose.

A قلقاس *kulkās,* The root of a plant which is edible when cooked. (It is stimulating and fattening, but when eaten for long, breeds melancholy).

A قلقال *kalkāl,* Violent motion. *Kilkāl,* (v. n. of قلقل Q) Moving, disturbing. Travelling through a country. The lip of a camel.

G قلقديس *kulkadīs,* Shoemakers' black, vitriol.

A قلقطار *kulkatār,* (or قلقنطار) Yellow vitriol.

A قلقل *kilkal,* A pomegranate growing in a place without water. *Kilkil,* A species of plant producing a grain, hard, black, and odoriferous. *Kulkul,* The noise made by water in the neck of a bottle when pouring out, guggling. A light, brisk, active man. Swift (horse). An expeditious helper.

P قلقلان *kulkulān,* Name of a plant.

A قلقلانيّ *kulkulāniy,* A species of pigeon.

A قلقلة *kalkalat,* (v. n. of قلقل Q) Moving, disturbing. Travelling through a country. Crying. حروف القلقلة *hurūfu'l kalkalat,* The letters قد طبج.

A قلقله *kulkula,* A hookah.

G قلقنت *kalkant,* (or قلقند *kalkand*) Copperas.

G قلقنه *kulkuna,* A sore in a horse's foot.

A قلقئ *kalka',* A sort of necklace.

A قلل *kilal,* (pl. of قلّ *kill*) Tremors, agitations. *Kulal,* Scattered people assembled together. (pl. of قلّة *kullat*) Tops of mountains. Jars. *Kulul,* (pl. of قلال *halāl, kulāl,* and قليل *halīl*) Few. Small. Thin. Scattered men of different tribes.

A قللون *kululūn,* Few or thin (persons).

A قلم *kalm,* (v. n. of قلم) Paring (the nails). *Kalam,* (pl. قلام *kilām* and اقلام *aklām*) A pen, reed. A pen-knife. An engraving-tool. Sheep-shears. A character, mode of writing. An arrow without wings for gaming. A weaver's reed. The state of a woman remaining long unmarried. Cuttings of trees for planting. A kind of fire-work. P قلم انداختن *kalam andākhtan,* To throw away the pen, *i. e.* to neglect writing. قلم آوردن *kalam āwardan,* To write. قلم بر آفتاب راندن *kalam bar āftāb rāndan,* To draw a pen across the sun, (met.) To have a beard just appearing. قلم جعد کردن *kalam jaʻd kardan,* To write. قلم در سیاهی نهادن *kalam dar siyāhī nihādan,* To draw the pen over any one's words. قلم در کشیدن *kalam dar kashidan,* To obliterate. قلم زدن *kalam zadan,* To write. To erase. قلم سرب *kalami surb,* A lead-pencil. قلم شدن *kalam shudan,* To be written. قلم کردن *kalam kardan,* To cut, lop, prune. To cut in two at a single blow. قلم کندگري *kalami kandagari,* A chisel. قلم موي *kalami mūy* or *moy,* A hair-pencil. قلم نیست *kalam nīst,* He has no account, he is clear. اهل قلم *ahli kalam,* Men of the pen, viziers, scribes, &c. دوات و قلم *dawāt u kalam,* Pen and ink.

P قلما *kulmā,* A sling.

A قلّما *kallāmā,* It is very rare that, it is seldom that.

P قلماسنگ *kalmā-sang,* A sling. A round stone for a sling.

P قلماش *kalmāsh,* Vain, futile, frivolous, absurd, nonsensical. *Kulmāsh,* A worthless, despicable man. A liar. Taken, received, occupied.

P قلماق *kalmāk*, A Calmuck Tartar.

P قلم بندي *kalam-bandī*, Signature, signing. An agreement.

A قلمة *kalamat*, (pl. of قالم) Unmarried persons.

P قلمتراش *kalam-tarāsh*, A pen-knife.

P قلمدان *kalamdān*, A pen-case. A standish. The ensign of the vazīrship.

P قلمدر *kalamdar*, A young tree or shoot.

A قلم رسّام *kalam-rassām*, An engraver on brass.

P قلمرو *kalam-rav*, (or قلمروي *kalam-ravī*) Empire, dominion, sovereignty, jurisdiction, district.

A قلمّزة *kalammazat*, A female dwarf.

P قلم زده *kalam-zada*, Committed to writing.

P قلم زن *kalam-zan*, A scribe (quill-driver).

A قلمّس *kalammas*, Overflowing (sea or well). An intelligent, generous, honourable man; a great lord. A deep, cunning fellow.

A قلمعة *kalmaʻat*, (v. n. of قلمع Q) Beheading, knocking on the head, or (according to others) shaving (the head). The dregs of the people.

P قلمكار *kalam-kār*, An engraver on brass, silver, or gold.

P قلمكاري *kalam-kārī*, The engraving art.

P قلم كشي *kalam-kashī*, Writing, caligraphy.

P قلمون *kalamūn*, (بو *bū*, or ابو قلمون *abū kalamūn*) A chameleon. A changing-coloured cloth.

P قلمونيا *kalmūniyā*, Resin of the pine-tree.

P قلمه *kulma*, A sausage, or any food stuffed into the intestines of animals, haggis, black pudding.

A قلمي *kalamī*, Crystallized (saltpetre, &c.).

P قلمي *kalumī*, A kind of quilted garment. قلمي فرمودن *kalamī farmūdan*, To write.

P قلنبك *kalambak*, A fragrant kind of wood.

A قلنّة *kalannat*, Corunna in Spain.

P قلندر *kalandar*, A kind of wandering Muhammadan monk, with shaven head and beard; who abandons every thing, wife, friends, possessions, and retires from the world. Name of the founder of this religious order. The fly of a tent.

A قلندرا *kalandarā*, A kind of silk cloth. The fly of a tent.

P قلندري *kalandarī*, A fly for a tent.

A قلندريّة *kalandariyat*, Kalandars, a Mussulman sect of Sufis, indifferent to the externals of religion, unobservant of the common rules of good breeding, and seeking only internal tranquillity.

G قلنديس *kalandīs*, Shoemakers' black, vitriol.

A قلنسة *kalnasat*, (v. n. of قلنس Q) Putting a hat or high cap (قلنسوة *kalansuwat*) on any one.

A قلنسوة *kalansuwat*, (pl. قلانس *kalānis*, قلانيس *kalānīs*, قلنسي *kalansī*, قلاسي *kalāsī*, or قلاسيّ *kalāsiy*) A high cap, tall hat, or mitre.

A قلنسي *kalansī*, (pl. of قلنسوة) High caps.

A قلنسيّة *kulansiyat*, A high-crowned cap.

A قلو *kalw*, (v. n. of قلا for قلو) Frying (meat) in a pan. Running away furiously (as a camel with a rider). Driving the female before him (an ass). Driving fast (a herd of camels). Striking with a large club (the smaller piece of wood called قلة *kulat* in the game of hockey). *Kilw*, Light, nimble (animal). Potash, barilla. A young ass.

A قلوب *kalūb*, Very versatile. A wolf. *Kulūb*, (pl. of قلب *kalb*) Hearts, kernels, piths, marrows.

P قلوب آدميان *kulūbi ādamiyān*, The hearts of men.

A قلوب *kallūb* or *killawb*, A wolf.

A قلوبع *kalawbaʻ*, A sort of game.

A قلوة *kilwat*, A horse running off with his rider.

P قلوز *kalawuz*, A highway-robber. Horsemen who lead the van of an army.

A قلوس *kulūs*, (pl. of قلس *kals*) Thick ropes made of the fibres of palm-trees. قلوس السفائن *kulūsu's safāʼin*, Ships' cables, or hawsers.

A قلوص *kalūs*, (pl. قلائص *kalāʼis*, قلص *kulus*, and قلاص *kilās*) A young she-camel; or one which keeps on travelling; or when ready for the saddle, and before she has changed her first teeth (when she is called ناقة *nākat*). A she-ostrich, and her female young one. A young bustard. A proper name for a young girl. *Kulūs*, (v. n. of قلص) Rising, increasing (as water in a well). Packing up one's things and setting off. Diminishing, decreasing; contracting (as a shadow); shrinking (a garment with washing); shrivelling (the lips). Leaping, springing upon. Being disturbed (the mind).

A قلّوط *killawt*, The offspring of demons.

A قلوع *kalūʻ*, A large she-camel. (pl. قلع *kulʻ*) A bow which, when drawn, flies back. *Kulūʻ*, (pl. of قلع *kalʻ*) Wallets, shepherds' scrips. (pl. of قلع *kilʻ*) Sails of ships. (pl. of قلعة *kalʻat*) Citadels.

A قلولي *kalawlā*, A bird soaring in flight.

G قلومس *kulūmus*, Bears'-ears (a plant).

G قلومن *kulūman*, Froth of the sea.

A قلون *kilūn* or *kulūn*, (pl. of قلة *kulat*) Small pieces of wood struck forward by a larger one or bat in the boy's game of tip-cat, hockey, or shinty.

A قلة *kalah*, (v. n. of قله) Being dirty (the body), being covered with spots (the skin) from scab. Being black (skin). Being peeled (skin). Dirtiness.

P قله *kula*, A sort of grape. Dun-coloured (horse).

P قلّه *kulla*, The top of a mountain. A large ewer.

A قلهب *kalhab*, Corpulent, gross. Aged.

A قلهبان *kalhabān*, Long.

A قلهبة *kalhabat*, A white cloud.

A قلهبس *kalahbas*, Aged (wild ass). Glans penis. Circular (crown of the head).

A قلهدم *kalahdam*, Light, active. The great sea.

A قلهزم *kalahzam*, Light, active. The great sea. A square-shaped, large-headed man. A short dwarf. A high-bred horse. A little bump under the lobe of the ear.

A قلهمة *kalhamat*, Swiftness, velocity.

A قلهمس *kalahmas*, Short, but closely and compactly built.

A قلهنف *kalahnaf*, Tall in stature.

A قلي *kaly*, (v. n. of قلي) Cooking in a frying-pan. Striking on the head. Playing the game of hockey. *Kily* or *kilā'*, Potash, barilla. *Kilā'*, (v. n. of قلي) Abhorring, detesting. Hatred. A small piece of wood struck forward by a larger one in the game of tip-cat, hockey, or shinty. *Kulā'*, Mountain-tops. Crowns of heads.

P قلي *kilī*, Potash.

A قلّي *kullā'*, A dwarfish girl.

P قليا *kalyā* or *kilyā*, Potash. Black vitriol.

P قليان *kalyān*, A pipe for smoking through water.

A قليب *kalīb*, (pl. اقلبة *aklibat*, قلب *kulb*, and *kulub*) An old well. A wolf. *Kulayb*, (dim. of قلب *kalb*) A little heart. An amulet. قليبي *kulaybī*, My little heart (an endearing expression).

A قلّيب *killīb*, A wolf.

A قلّيسة *killīyat*, A cell, a Christian cloister.

A قليّة *kaliyat*, (pl. قلايا *kalāyā'*) Any thing fried.

A قليّة *kallīyat*, A crowd. The whole or best part. *Killīyat*, All, the whole: bones and all.

A قليخ *kalīkh*, (v. n. of قلخ) Braying inwardly.

A قليد *kalīd*, Twisted (rope). A palm-leaf rope.

A قلّيد *killīd*, A treasury, a magazine.

G قليدس *kulīdus*, Euclid.

A قليذم *kalayzam*, An overflowing well.

A قليس *kalīs*, A miser.

A قلّيس *kullays*, Name of a church in Sanaa built by Abraha.

A قليسيّة *kulaysīyat*, (or قليسية) A little cap.

A قليص *kalīs*, Rising, increasing (water in a well).

A قليط *kalīt*, Ruptured, having a swelled testicle.

A قلّيط *killīt*, Rupture, hydrocele.

A قليف *kalīf*, Unbunged (barrel). A date-basket. (pl. of قليفة *kalīfat*) Date-baskets. *Kilyaf*, A strong, thick she-camel.

A قليفة *kalīfat*, (pl. قليف *kalīf* and قلف *kuluf*) A pannier, hamper, or basket for holding dates.

A قليل *kalīl*, (pl. قلل *kulul* and اقلّاء *akillāʼ*) Little, small, moderate. Few, rare. Lean. Short. قليل الاعتبار *kalīlu'l iʻtibār*, Of small estimation. قليل البضاعة *kalīlu'l bizāʻat*, Poor, indigent. A merchant with a small capital. قليل الحرمة *kalīlu'l hurmat*, Profane, unworthy of veneration. P لشكر قليل العدد *lashkari kalīlu'l ʻadad*, A small army, a handful of troops. A قليل المفاد *kalīlu'l mafād*, Of little advantage. Teaching little. قليل و كثير *kalīl u kasīr*, Small and great. خرج قليل *kharji kalīl*, Small expense, parsimony. شيء قليل *shayʼun kalīl*, A small thing, a trifle, a bagatelle.

A قليلاً *kalīlan*, Little; a little. قليلاً قليلاً *kalīlan kalīlan*, By degrees, sparingly, by little and little.

A قلّيلة *killīlat*, The whole.

A قليلون *kalīlūna*, (pl. of قليل) Few (men).

A قلّيلي *killīlā*, The whole.

A قليميا *kilimiyā*, Litharge of gold and silver. Dross of metals. Gold or silver filings. Name of Adam's daughter.

A قلينسة *kulaynisat*, (or قلنيسة) A small hat.

P قليون *kalyūn*, A sort of pipe for smoking through water. A galley, a pinnace.

P قليه *kalya*, Fried. Ashes of which they make soap. A species of pumice-stone. A kind of earth or composition from herbs put amongst colours. Flesh-meat dressed with any thing. قليهٔ سغدي *kalyaʼi sughdī*, A dish made of meat, suet, and eggs.

P قليه خوار *kalya-khwār*, A pimp, cuckold.

P قليه مشك *kalya mishk*, Civet.

P قم *kum*, Name of a city in Persian Irāk, situated between Kazwīn and Ispahān.

A قمّ *kamm*, (v. n. of قمّ) Impregnating the female (a camel). Sweeping (a house). Eating any thing picked off the ground (a sheep). Eating every thing that is on the table. Drying. Collecting.

A قمأ *kamʼ*, (v. n. of قمأ) Growing fat (a sheep). Abiding in rich pasture and growing fat. Rooting up. Being small and mean (a man). Digging up. *Kumʼ* or *kimʼ*, (v. n. of قمأ) Being little and mean.

A قماء *kamāʼ*, (v. n. of قمأ) Growing fat (a sheep). Abiding in rich pasture and growing fat. *Ki* or *kumāʼ*, (pl. of قمئ *kamiʼ*) Short and contemptible.

A قماءة *kamāʼat*, (v. n. of قمأ) Being small and mean. Becoming fat (a sheep). Abiding in luxuriant pasturage and becoming fat.

A قمأة *kamʼat*, (v. n. of قمأ) Being little, mean, and contemptible. A place sheltered from the sun. *Kamʼat* or *kumʼat*, Much fodder, plenty. Ease.

A شهرا قماح *shahrā kumāh* or *kimāh*, The two coldest months.

A قمّاحة *kummāhat*, Saffron: also another plant dyeing yellow. The dregs; also the musty flavour of wine.

A قماحد *kamāhid*, (pl. of قمحدوة) Hind-heads.

A قماد *kumād*, (or قمادي) Large, strong, bulky.

P قمار *kamār*, Name of a place. *Kumār*, Name of a city in India.

A قمار *kimār*, (v. n. 3 of قمر) Playing at dice. Dice or any game of hazard. P قمار باختن *kimār bākhtan*, To game.

P قمارباز *kimār-bāz*, A gamester.

P قمارخانه *kimār-khāna*, A gaming-house.

A قمارص *kumāris*, Acid, acrid, sour (milk).

T قمار كاغذي *kumār-kāghizī*, Playing-cards.

A قماريّ *kamāriy*, (pl. of قمريّة *kumriyat*) Female turtle-doves. A kind of wood so called from قمار *kamār*. الورق القماريّ *al waraku'l kumāriy*, A certain leaf of a pungent scent and pleasant taste brought from قمر *kumr*, a country beyond Ethiopia.

A قماس *kimās*, (v. n. 3 of قمس) Contending (with another) in diving. A dip, a plunge. Abundance of water in a well.

A قمّاس *kammās*, A diver.

A قماش *kimāsh*, Name of a suit at cards. *Kumāsh*, (pl. اقمشة *akmishat*) Silken cloth, fine linen. Merchandize, goods, stuff. Any thing picked up here and there. Trifles, things of no value. Household furniture. The meanest of mankind, the rabble. ما اعطاني الّا قماشا *mā aʿtānī illā kumāshan*, He gave me but the worst he could find.

A قماشير *kamāshīr*, Gum of the wild parsley.

A قماص *kimās*, A contraction in the sinews of a horse. *Kimās* or *kumās*, (v. n. of قمص) Dashing (waves), driving, tossing, heaving (a ship). Galloping, cantering (a horse). Motion, leaping, dancing. Restlessness, unsteadiness. ما بالعير من قماص *mā bi'l ʿayri min kimāsin*, A proverbial expression, used in reference to any one who, after having been powerful, has become weak and contemptible.

A قماط *kimāt*, A swaddling or cradle-band. A rope for tying a sheep for slaughter, or the hands or feet of a captive. وقعت علي قماطه *wakaʿtu ʿala' kimātihi*, I am up to his tricks.

A قماطر *kumātir*, Calamitous (day). Injury done to milk by rennet.

A قماعيل *kamāʿīl*, (pl. of قمعولة *kumʿūlat*) Flower-cups, buds. Knots in the veins.

A قماقم *kamākim*, Small tikes or sheep-lice. A kind of louse. (pl. of قمقمة *kumkumat*) Jugs, tankards. *Kumākim*, A liberal-minded nobleman. A large number.

A قمال *kamāl*, A louse.

A قمام *kumām*, (pl. of قمامة) Sweepings.

A قمامة *kumāmat*, Sweepings, rubbish. A crowd, body of men. كنيسة القمامة *kanīsatu'l kumāma*, The church of the holy sepulchre at Jerusalem.

A قمامسة *kamāmisat*, Commanders of 10,000.

A قماميس *kamāmīs*, (pl. of قمّيس *kimmīs*) Seas.

A قمائع *kamāʼiʿ*, (pl. of قميعة *kamīʿat*) Protuberances behind horses' ears. Tips of stumps of horses' tails.

A قمّة *kimmat*, The body. Stature, figure. Fat, grease. Crown of the head, top of any thing. A crowd, a body of men. القي عليه قمّته *alkaʼ ʿalayhi kimmatahu*, He threw his body upon him. حسن القمّة *hasanu'l kimmat*, Handsome, of a fine person. *Kummat*, Whatever a lion takes in his mouth. A crowd.

A قمح *kamh*, (v. n. of قمح) Taking up any thing with the hand. Putting somewhat dry (as a medicine) into the mouth. Wheat.

A قمّح *kummah*, (pl. of قامح *kāmih*) (Camels) which raise their heads and refuse to drink.

A قمّحان *kummuhān* or *kummahān*, A plant dyeing yellow, found in Arabia Felix. A pellicle floating on the surface of wine. Saffron.

A قمحانة *kimhānat*, The part betwixt the hind-head and the hollow of the neck.

A قمحة *kumhat*, A mouthful. Saffron. A yellow-dyeing plant. A pellicle on the surface of wine.

A قمحدوة *kamahduwat*, (pl. قماحد *kamāhid*) The hind-head. A projection, little bump behind the ears.

P قمحه *kamha*, Name of a medicinal plant.

A قمحى *kimhaʼ*, (or قمحاة *kimhāt*) Glans penis.

A قمد *kamd*, (v. n. of قمد) Refusing, rejecting, hanging back. Persevering in any thing (good or bad). *Kamad*, Length and thickness of neck. *Kumud*, Strong, hard, of a large body or weight.

A قمدّ *kumudd*, Long-necked. Hard, strong, robust. Very stiff (penis).

A قمداء *kamdāʼ*, (fem. of اقمد *akmad*) Thick-necked (woman).

A قمدّان *kumuddān*, Hard, strong, and bulky.

A قمدّانيّ *kumuddāniy*, Hard, strong, and bulky.

A قمدّانيّة *kumuddāniyat*, (fem.) Long-necked.

A قمدّة *kumuddat*, Long-necked (woman).

A قمدر *kamdar*, Long.

A قمدود *kumdūd*, Hard, strong, and bulky.

A قمر *kamr*, (v. n. of قمر) Gaming and gaining at dice. Marrying a wife. *Kumr*, (pl. of قمريّة *kumriyat*) Female turtle-doves. Name of a country beyond Ethiopia, from whence they bring a certain leaf called الورق القماريّ *al waraku'l kumāriy*. *Kamar*, The moon (especially from the third day to the end). قمر المقنع *kamaru'l mukannaʿ*, The moon of Mukanna. (See نخشب *nakhshab*). (v. n. of قمر) Having the eyes blinded or contracted from the reflection of snow or any bright colour. Satisfying thirst (camels). Being abundant (forage, water, &c.). Being spoilt, as a leathern bottle, the water entering between the outward and interior skin. Watching, lying awake in moonlight. *Kamir*, Much, abundant (water).

A قمراء *kamrāʼ*, (fem. of اقمر *akmar*) Of a whitish colour, with a mixture of brown or green; a she-ass of this colour. The splendour of the moon. A bright moonlight night. A kind of bird.

A قمران *kamarāni*, (dual) The sun and moon.

A قمرة *kumrat*, A dusky white colour, with a mixture of green. *Kamirat*, A bright moonlight night.

A قمّرز *kummariz*, (or قمرز *kumariz*) Dwarfish and small-eared.

A قمرصة *kamrasat*, The eating (of almonds).

P قمرگاه *kamar-gāh*, The hunting-ring formed to enclose the game in the grand royal chase.

P قمرون *kamrūn*, A shrimp.

P قمري *kumrī*, A turtle-dove, ring-dove.

A قمريّ *kamariy*, Lunar. Lunatic.

A قمريّة *kumriyat*, (pl. قماريّ *kamāriy* and قمر *kumr*) A female turtle-dove (the male being called ساق حرّ *sāku hurrin*).

A قمرين *kamarayn*, (obliq. du.) Sun and moon.

A قمز *kamz*, (v. n. of قمز) Scraping together, or taking up with the points of the fingers. *Kamz kamz*, Separate, sparse, here and there. *Kamaz*, The worst part of any thing. Low, worthless, good for nothing.

A قمزة *kumzat*, A handful of dates. The follicle, containing the seed of a plant. Compact flesh.

A قمس *kams*, (v. n. of قمس) Plunging (one's

self or another into water). Stirring (as a fœtus in the womb).

A قمّس *kummas*, A nobleman.

A قمش *kamsh*, (v. n. of قمش) Collecting, gleaning from every quarter.

A قمص *kams*, (v. n. of قمص) Cantering, galloping (a horse). Dashing (waves), tossing, heaving, driving (a ship). A contraction of the sinew in a horse. *Kamas*, Little flies swimming on water. Locusts just hatched. *Kumus*, (pl. of قميص *kamīs*) Shirts, shifts.

A قمصان *kumsān*, (pl. of قميص) Shirts, shifts.

A قمصّى *kimissa'*, Hard running, hard shaking.

A قمط *kamt*, (v. n. of قمط) Binding (a captive or sheep for slaughter). Swaddling (an infant). Treading (as a bird). Failing, falling short. Taking. Pleasure, voluptuousness. *Kimt*, A rope with which a reed cottage is girded, or a sheep for slaughter is fast bound.

A قمطر *kimatr*, A library, a book-case. A large strong camel. A short man. That which is placed on the legs of men: gyves. A pot for holding plants or sugar. قمطر الرجل *kimatru'r rijl*, (A dog) whose legs being crooked are supported by a stick.

A قمطرة *kamtarat*, (v. n. of قمطر Q) Tying close (a leathern bottle). Lying with. Drawing (itself) together. *Kimatrat*, A library, book-case.

A قمطري *kimatra'*, A short man. A mode of walking with short steps.

A قمطرير *kamtarīr*, Calamitous (day).

A قمع *kamʻ*, (v. n. of قمع) Striking on the head with a mace. Smiting an (elephant) with the hook wherewith (he) is driven. Humbling, suppressing, putting down. Diverting one from his purpose. Destroying, breaking. Subduing, bringing into subjection. Drinking the entire contents of a leathern bottle. Entering. Nipping plants (cold). Running down the throat without being gulped (liquor). Listening, paying attention to. Adjusting (a leathern bag) for the reception of liquor, either by introducing a funnel or bending outwards the orifice. Large-kneed, or large-houghed (horse). P قمع فتنهٔ اشرار کردن *kamʻi fitnaʻi ashrār kardan*, To quell sedition, to quiet the public discontent. A *Kamʻ*, *kimʻ*, or *kimaʻ*, A funnel. The stalk of a date, or the hollow place of the fruit to which it joins. *Kumʻ*, (pl. of قمعة *kumʻat*) Best parts of any thing. (pl. of اقمع *akmaʻ*) (Men) troubled with the fistula lachrymalis. *Kamaʻ*, (v. n. of قمع) Suffering from a fistula lachrymalis. Having a mote fallen into the eye, and trying to extract it with a ring. Taking medicine simple and unmixed. Getting a bunch (a camel's colt). A kind of smoke or dust rising in the air. The head or lid of the windpipe. Flies tormenting the heads of cattle in hot weather. A small projecting bone in the windpipe. A pimple on the edge of the lip. A diseased state of the inner corner of the eye, a redness and inflammation of that part. The incessant watering of the eye, and weakness of sight. A largeness in the knee or hough of a horse. (pl. of قمعة *kamaʻat*) Tops of camels' bunches. Heads. *Kamiʻ*, Large-bunched (camel). Large (bunch). Pimpled (eye). Timid (horse). *Kumaʻ*, Indigestion.

A قمعاء *kamʻāʼ*, (fem. of اقمع) Troubled with fistula lachrymalis. Large-kneed or boughed (mare).

A قمعال *kimʻāl*, Chief of a tribe. Head shepherd.

A قمعالة *kimʻālat*, A large glans penis.

A قمعان *kamʻāni*, Handles of a date-hamper.

A قمعة *kumʻat*, A plug, stopple, or fastening for the mouth of a wallet. *Kum*, *kam*, or *kamaʻat*, (pl. قمع *kumʻ*) The best part (of a thing), the best (of camels). *Kamaʻat*, (pl. قمع *kamaʻ*) The head. The top of a camel's bunch. (pl. مقامع *makāmiʻ*) A blue fly infesting camels in hot seasons.

A قمعل *kumʻal* or *kumʻul*, Nympha, clitoris. *Kumʻul*, A large goblet. A small cauldron or copper having a narrow neck. A little bird with a short neck and beak. A small bowl.

A قمعلة *kamʻalat*, (v. n. of قمعل Q) Being the head of his family, the chief of his tribe.

A قمعوث *kumʻūs*, A pimp to his own wife.

A قمعول *kumʻūl*, A large goblet.

A قمعولة *kumʻūlat*, (pl. قماعيل *kamāʻīl*) Cup of a flower, bud. A knot in a vein.

A قمقام *kamkām* or *kumkām*, The deep sea. An important affair, deep business. A great number. Larger or better part. A prince, lord. Small tikes.

A قمقامة *kamkāmat*, One tike or sheep-louse.

A قمقم *kimkim*, A withered, unripe date. *Kumkum*, A decanter. A water-pot. A cucumber-shaped vessel, used for warming water. News, intelligence. The throat or gullet.

A قمقمان *kumkumān*, A great number. The larger or better part.

A قمقمة *kamkamat*, (v. n. of قمقم Q) Assembling. Surrounding, encircling. Taking, seizing. Sending lice (God). *Kumkumat*, (pl. قماقم *kamākim*) A bowl, jug, or tankard.

A قمل *kaml*, A louse. قمل قريش *kamlu kuraysh*, Seed of fir. *Kamal*, (v. n. of قمل) Being lousy (the head). Being large (the belly). Being black, as covered with insects (a thistle). Becoming fat after leanness. Being very numerous (a tribe). *Kumal*, The tike or louse (which infests sheep or camels). غلّ قمل *ghull kamil*, Handcuffs and lice, an expression employed to denote any troublesome affair. (The Arabians used to handcuff their prisoners, who frequently had lousy heads, which required scratching).

A قمّل *kummal*, An insect less than the tike, found on lean camels. A small ant. A locust without wings.

A قملة *kamlat*, One louse. قملة النسر *kamlatu'n nasr*, A kind of insect. *Kamilat*, Very short (woman).

A قمّلة *kummalat*, Very short (woman). A weevil, which destroys corn. قمّلة الاذن *kummalatu'l uzn*, The beetle. The earwig. The centiped.

A قملى *kamala'*, Short, little. Mean-looking, base, contemptible (man). An inhabitant of the desert who has chosen a town-residence.

A قملية *kamalīyat*, A short, little woman.

A قمم *kimam*, (pl. of قمّة) Tops, summits.

A قمن *kamn*, Near. A neighbour. A mode, manner. *Kaman*, A mode, form. *Kaman* or *kamin*, Fit, proper, worthy, well adapted.

A قمنانة *kamnānat*, A tike in its smallest form.

A قمنة *kaminat*, Filthy (smell).

A قموء *kumūʼ*, (or قموءة *kumūʼat*) (v. n. of قمأ) Becoming fat (a sheep).

A قموح *kumūh*, (v. n. of قمح) Raising (his) head and refusing to drink (a camel).

A قموس *kamūs*, So abundant in water that the bucket disappears (a well).

A قموص *kamūs*, Gallopping (horse) that shakes his rider. A lion. Restless.

A قموع *kamūʻ*, Troubled with a fistula lachrymalis.

A قمه *kamah*, A little appetite for meat.

A قمّه *kummah*, (pl. of قامه *kāmih*) Travelling well (camels), carrying their heads high.

A قمهد *kamhad*, Sordid, base, ugly. *Kumhad*, Stationary, that stirs not from his place.

A قمهزية *kumahziyat*, Very dwarfish (woman).

A قمى *kamiʼ*, Small and contemptible.

A قميذل *kamaysal*, (A man) who walks awry.

A قميحة *kamīhat*, As much of medicine as one puts into the mouth at once. Any thing taken to aid digestion.

A قمير *kamīr*, (pl. اقمار *akmār*) An antagonist at play. *Kumayr*, (dim. of قمر *kamar*) A little moon.

P قمير *kumīr*, Name of a city in Hindūstān.

A قمّيس *kimmīs*, (pl. قماميس *kamāmīs*) The sea.

A قميشة *kamīshat*, A dish composed of milk and the seeds of the colocynth.

A قميص *kamīs*, (pl. قمص *kumus*, اقمصة *akmisat*, and قمصان *kumsān*) A shirt, shift, or any kind of inner garment of linen; also a tunic, a surplice (of cotton, but not of wool). The membrane which inwraps the fœtus in the womb, and comes along with the birth. Purse of the heart, pericardium. A gallopping horse that shakes his rider.

A قميط *kamīt*, Entire, whole, full (year).

A قميع *kamīʻ*, The top of a camel's bunch. An exostosis on the spinal vertebræ.

A قميعة *kamīʻat*, (pl. قمائع *kamāʼiʻ*) The protuberance behind the ears in horses. The tip of the stump of a horse's tail.

A قميم *kamīm*, A dry, withered pot-herb.

A قمين *kamīn*, The chimney of a bath. Fit, proper. Swift.

A قميئة *kamīʼat*, Name of an Arabian poet.

A قنّ *kann*, (v. n. of قنّ) Examining (a messenger), inquiring after news. Scrutinizing. Striking with a stick. *Kinn*, (pl. اقنان *aknān* and اقنّة *akinnat*) A slave, especially one born in the family, whose father and mother are slaves. One whose father is free, but whose mother is a slave. *Kunn*, Sleeve (of a shirt). A small mountain.

A قنء *kans*, (v. n. of قنئ) Dying. Being spoiled (tanned leather).

A قنا *kana'*, A Roman or hawk-nose. (pl. of قناة *kanāt*) Canes. Spears. قنا الانف *kana'l anf*, A hookedness and height of nose, with length and narrowness of nostril (similar to the nostril of a bird). *Kana'* or *hina'*, A bunch of dates.

A قناء *kanās*, Water. The shady side of a wall. *Kinās*, (pl. of قناة *kanāt*) Spears. Canes.

A قنّاء *kannās*, A spearman, or a spear-maker. Skilful in discovering water. قنّاء الارض *hannāsu'l arz*, The hoopoo (as skilful in discovering water).

A قناب *kināb*, A bow-string. The claw of a lion. *Kināb* or *kunāb*, The appearance of the leaves of corn when the grain begins to form.

A قنابة *kunābat*, Name of a fort at Madīna.

A قنّابة *kunnābat*, The leaf or husk enveloping the grain. Name of a fort at Madīna.

A قنابر *kanābir*, (pl. of قنبراء *kumburās*) Larks.

A قنابري *kunābira'*, A kind of wild pot-herb.

A قنابع *kanābiȥ*, (pl. of قنبعة) Boys' tunics.

A قنابل *kanābil*, (pl. of قنبلة *hambalat*) Troops of horses or horsemen, from 30 to 40. *Kunābil*, A kind of ass. Gross, rude (man).

A قناة *kanāt*, (pl. قنوات *kanawāt*, قنى *kana'*, قنيّ *huniy*, and قنيات *kanayāt*) A cane, spear, javelin (the Arabians in general making use of cane-spears). The back-bone, the vertebræ of the back. (pl. قنيّ *kunīy*) A subterraneous canal. A syphon.

A قنات *kanāt*, The walls of a tent or canvas-enclosure, with which a sort of court-yard is formed in a camp. A screen.

A قناتة *kanātat*, Abstinence, abstemiousness.

A قنّاحة *kunnāhat*, A long crooked key.

A قناخر *kunākhir*, Corpulent.

A قنّاد *kannād*, A maker of sugar-candy.

A قنادل *kunādil*, Large-headed (camel). Long.

A جاء الامر علي قناديده *jāsa'l amr ȥala' kanādidihi*, The business came in its regular course.

A قناديل *hanādīl*, (pl. of قنديل *kindīl*) Candles. Lamps. P قناديل چرخ *hanādīli charkh*, (Candles of the sky) The stars.

A قنانع *kanāziȥ*, Obscene talk, ribaldry. Misfortune. (pl. of قنذعة *hunzuȥat*) Long hairs left on the crown of the head.

A قنّارة *hann* or *kinnārat*, A slaughter-house.

P قنّاره *hannāra*, Shambles.

A قنّاز *kannāz*, A huntsman.

A قنازع *kanāziȥ*, (pl. of قنزعة *kanzaȥat*) Long hairs about the head. Heavy calamities. Remains of the plant نصيّ *nasiy* and of camels' bunches.

A قناسر *kunāsir*, Hard, vehement.

A قنّاص *kannās*, A hunter.

A قناصر *kunāsir*, Strong, vehement.

A قناصرين *kunāsirīn*, Name of a place in Syria.

A قناطة *kanātat*, (v. n. of قنط) Despairing.

A قناطر *kanātir*, (pl. of قنطرة) Bridges. Arches.

A قناطير *kanātīr*, (pl. of قنطار *kintār*) Weights of 100 lbs. قناطير مقنطرة *kanātīri mukantara*, Talents heaped together.

A قناع *kanāȥ*, A name for a sheep. *Kināȥ*, (pl. قنع *kunuȥ*) A sort of plate or dish made of palm-wood. A large kerchief or hood. The pericardium. Arms, armour.

A قناعة *kanāȥat*, Content, contentment, tranquillity, resignation. Ability to do without.

A قناعس *kunāȥis*, (pl. *kanāȥis*) Large-bodied.

A قناعيس *kanāȥīs*, (pl. of قنعاس *kinȥās*) Large camels. Men, stout, strong, and inaccessible.

A قناف *kināf* or *kunāf*, One who has a large nose or a long and thick beard. Glans penis grandior.

A قنافذ *kanāfiz*, (pl. of قنفذ *kunfaz*) Hedgehogs. Hillocks, sand-hills.

A قنافر *kunāfir*, Short-bodied. A dwarf.

A قنافش *kunāfish*, One who has an excoriated nose or a neglected beard.

A قنافي *kunāfī*, Crassior glans penis.

A قناقن *kunākin*, (pl. قناقن *kanākin*) Skilful in discovering water.

A قنان *kinān*, (pl. of قنّة *kunnat*) Mountain-tops. *Kunān*, Sleeve (of a shirt). Stench of arm-pits.

A قنانة *kinānat* or *kunānat*, Servitude.

A قناني *kanānī*, (pl. of قنّينة) Glass wine-bottles.

A قناوة *kināwat*, Desert, merit.

A قنب *kumb*, A large sail. A bow-string. Clitoris. The claw of a lion. The sheath of a horse or other solid-hoofed animal.

A قنّب *kinnab* or *kunnab*, Hemp. A hempen rope.

A قنبراء *kumburās*, (pl. قنابر *kanābir*) A lark.

A قنبرانيّة *kumburānīyat*, A sort of crested hen.

A قنبرة *kumburat*, A lark. A bird's crest.

A قنبريّ *kumburiy*, Crested (cock).

A قنبس *kambas*, A woman.

A قنبض *kumbuz*, A serpent. Short-bodied and well-fed (man).

A قنبضة *kumbuzat*, Short and ugly (woman).

A قنبع *kumbuȥ*, A place where they lay up wheat. Short, dwarfish.

A قنبعة *hambaȥat*, (v. n. of قنبع Q) Concealing one's self in one's own house, or itself in its cup (a flower). Swelling with rage. *Kumbuȥat*, A kind of tunic worn by boys. A kind of veil or head-dress worn by women. Short (woman). The pod in which the flower is concealed.

A قنبل *kambal*, A body or troop of men or horse (from 30 to 40). *Kumbul*, A sharp, lively boy. A kind of tree. Gross, rude (man).

A قنبلاني *kumbulānīy*, A cauldron sufficient for a whole tribe.

A قنبلة *kambalat*, (v. n. of قنبل Q) Joining one's self to a troop after having been alone. Firing the tree قنبل *kumbul*. (pl. قنابل *kanābil*) A troop of horsemen, herd of horses. A band, small body of men. *Kumbulat*, A sparrow-hawk net.

A قنبير *kimbīr*, A kind of plant.

A قنبيط *kimbīt* or *kunnabīt*, A cauliflower.

A قنبيعة *kimbīȥat*, The nostril of a pig.

P قنبيل *kambīl*, An earth which, when baked, becomes yellow and is good for worms in the bowels.

A قنبيل *kimbīl*, A small grain like manna falling in Yaman fatal to earth-worms and good against the mange.

P قنبيله *kambīla*, Name of a medicinal herb.

A قنّة *kinnat*, (pl. قنن *kinan*) A single thread of a rope made of palm-tree fibres called ليف *līf*. Galbanum. *Kunnat*, (pl. قنن *kunan*, قنان *kinān*, and قنون *kunūn*) A mountain-top. A little mountain. A mountain separated from the others and reaching far, or stretching up into the sky.

A قنتة *kantat*, A decanter, flagon.

A قنتر *kantar*, (or قنثر *kansar*) Short-bodied.

A قنثلة *kansalat*, (v. n. of قنثل Q) Raising the dust (as a horse when travelling).

P قنج *kanj*, Pressure, compression. Dissimulation. Amorous playfulness. *Kunj*, Idle, vain, futile. An ass with his tail docked.

A قنجل *kunjul*, A slave (of the worst kind).

A قنجور *kunjūr*, Small-headed. Weak-minded.

P قنجه *kanja*, Amorous, languishing. The cup of a flower.

A قنح *kanh*, (v. n. of قنح) Bending, curving. Quenching the thirst and raising the head. Setting up (a door) of planed wood. Refusing to drink.

A قنحل *kunhul*, A slave (of the worst kind).

A قنخر *kinnakhr*, One with a large mouth and nostrils, strong voice, or hard head. Large-bodied. A substance like stone, but softer, torn from the top of a mountain.

A قنخورة *kunkhūrat*, (or قنخيرة) A large stone.

P A قند *kand*, Sugar, sugar-candy. P قند خام *handi khām*, Sugar. A قند مكرّر *kandi mukarrar*, The lips of a mistress.

A قند *kund*, (from P كند *kund*) The testicles. ابو القندين *abū'l kundayn*, Name of a certain man.

P قند آب *kand-āb*, Wine.

A قنداو *kindasw*, Light, active, nimble. *Kindasw*, (or قنداوة *hindaswat*) A foul feeder, or one poorly fed. Bad-tempered. Rough. Short, dwarfish. Large-headed. Small-bodied. Lean. Bold, intrepid. Short-necked, strong-headed. Agile, nimble (epithets chiefly applicable to a camel). The loins.

A قنداوة *kindāwat*, Active. Swift (she-camel). Sharp (axe).

A قندة *kandat*, Sugar-candy. قندة الرقاع *kan-*

datu'r rikāɛ, A sort of date.

A قندهر *kindahr*, An opponent, hinderer.

A ذهبوا بقندحرة *zahabū bi kindahrata*, They went where none could find them.

A قندد *kindid*, Condition of man (good or bad).

P قندز *kunduz*, The beaver. Sable. An emblem of night. A dark night. Wine. Name of a country on the confines of the region of darkness. قندز آمدن *kunduz āmadan*, To become night.

P قندز قوري *kunduz-kūrī*, Testicles of the beaver.

P قندس *kundus*, Alkali. A kind of animal.

A قندسة *handasat*, (v. n. of قندس Q) Repenting, turning away from sin. Wandering, travelling through the earth.

A قندع *kunduɛ*, A contented cuckold.

A قندعل *kindaɛl*, (or قنذعل) Foolish; a fool.

A قندفير *kandafīr*, (from P كنده پير *handa-pīr*) An old woman.

A قندفيل *kandafīl*, Bulky, big-headed (camel).

A قندل *kandal* or *kunadil*, Large-headed (horse or camel). Long.

A قندلة *kandalat*, (v. n. of قندل Q) Having a large head. Going with a slow, languid pace.

A قندلّي *kandalīy*, A sort of tree.

A قندول *kandūl*, A certain tree found in Syria, whose flower yields a costly oil. *Kindūl*, An aromatic bark of a prickly tree.

A قنديل *kandawīl*, Large-headed (horse or camel). Long.

P قندهار *kandahār*, Name of a city, Candahār.

A قنديّ *kandiy*, Sugared, made of sugar.

A قنديد *kindīd*, Wine. Saffron. Expressed juice rendered more fragrant by an admixture of aromatic herbs. Ambergris. Camphor. Musk. A perfume compounded with saffron. The state of man (good or bad). Candied sugar.

A قنديل *kindīl*, (pl. قناديل *kanādīl*) A candle; a lamp, lantern, chandelier, branched candlestick. P قنديل ترسا *kindīli tarsā*, A lamp kept perpetually burning in a church. قنديل چرخ *kindīli charkh*, The sun and moon. قنديل دو سر *kindīli du sar*, The sky. قنديل شب *kindīli shab*, The darkness of the night. A قنديل عيسيٰ *kindīli ɛīsa'*, The sun (situated in the fourth heaven, which is said to be the abode of Jesus Christ).

T قنديلچي *kindīlchi*, A lamp-lighter in a mosque.

T قنديه *kandiya*, The isle of Candia or Crete.

A قنذع *hunzuɛ*, A contented cuckold.

A قنذعة *kunzuɛat*, Long hair about the head.

A قنذعل *hinzaɛl*, A fool.

A قنز *kinz*, A small flagon or wine-vessel. *Kinz* or *kunz*, (A man) hating uncleanness. *Kanaz*, Any kind of earthenware. Prey, game.

A قنزعة *kanzaɛat*, (v. n. of قنزع Q) Running away from the fight (a cock), shewing a white feather. *Kunzuɛat*, *hanzaɛat*, or *hinziɛat*, (pl. قنازع *kanāziɛ* and قنزعات *kunzuɛāt*) Hair round about the head. A tuft of hair left on the head of children. Long hairs. A patch of ground without vegetation. A few remaining feathers. The root of the tail. The feathers on a cock's neck, his hackles. A stone bigger than a nut. A knot of hair of the size of a pomegranate on a woman's head.

A قنس *kans* or *kins*, A root. The root or foundation of greatness. *Kins*, (pl. قنوس *kunūs*) Crown of the head. *Kanas*, Elecampane. A slight vomit.

A قنسر *kansar*, (قنسّر *kinsarr*, or قنّسر *kinnasr*) Old, aged, worn out, decrepit.

A قنسرة *kansarat*, (v. n. of قنسر Q) Rendering hoary (age or care).

A قنسريّ *kansarīy*, Old, aged, decrepit.

A قنّسريّ *kinnasrīy*, A native of Kinnasrīn.

A قنّسرين *kinnasrīn*, (*kinnisrīn*, or قنّسرون *kinnasrūn* or *kinnisrūn*) Name of a town in Syria.

A قنّسرينيّ *kinnasrīnīy*, Native of Kinnasrīn.

A قنسطيط *kunsatīt*, A sort of tree.

A قنشورة *kanshūrat*, A woman free from menses.

A قنص *kans*, (v. n. of قنص) Taking by hunting. *Kins*, Root, origin. *Kanas*, Prey, game.

A قنصعر *kinsaɛr*, Short in the neck. Contracted in the back. Compact-bodied.

A قنصف *kinsif*, Cotton of the papyrus.

A قنصل *kunsul*, Short.

A قنط *kant*, Hindrance, prohibition. Penis pueri. *Kanat*, (v. n. of قنط) Despairing. *Kanit*, Overwhelmed with despair.

G قنطا *kintā*, Dragons'-blood.

A قنطار *hintār*, (pl. قناطير *kanātīr*) A weight of 40 اوقية *ūkiyat* (ounces) of gold; or of 1200 dīnārs; or of 1200 اوقية *ūkiyat*, *i.e.* a talent of 120 lbs.; or of 70,000 dīnārs, or 80,000 dirhams, or 100 رطل *ratl* of gold or silver, or of 1000 dīnārs. An ox's skin full of gold or silver. The freshness of fragrant aloe-wood.

A قنطثة *kantasat*, Flight from terror.

A قنطر *kintir*, Misfortune. A black bird with a tuneful note. A wood-pigeon, a queest.

A قنطرة *kantarat*, (v. n. of قنطر Q) Dwelling in cities or villages. Abandoning the desert. Possessing wealth by the قنطار *kintār*. Marrying a girl. Abiding, lengthening out a stay. (pl. قناطر *kanātir*) A bridge. An arch. Any lofty building.

A قنطريس *kantarīs*, A mouse. A large and strong she-camel.

P قنطس *kantus*, The myrtle-tree.

A قنطعر *kintaɛr*, Centaury, a medicine.

A قنطوراء *kantūrāɛ*, Keturah, Abraham's concubine, from whom the Turks are descended. بنو قنطوراء *banū kantūrāɛ*, Turks and Negroes.

G قنطوريون *kantūriyūn*, Centaury.

A قنطير *kintīr*, A misfortune.

A قنع *kanɛ*, (v. n. of قنع) Turning downwards (the mouth of a ewer). Being high, with no disposition to come down (a sheep's udder). *Kinɛ* or *kunɛ*, A kind of plate or dish made of the wood of a palm-tree. *Kinɛ*, Root, origin. (pl. اقناع *aknāɛ*) Arms. (pl. of قنعة *kinɛat*) Level grounds between two hills. *Kunɛ*, A brazen trumpet. *Kanaɛ*, (v. n. of قنع) Being contented. Longing for the meadow (camels). Contentment. Fine sands. A level spot at the foot of a sand-hill. من قنع شبع و من شبع ذاك *man haniɛa shabiɛa, wa man shabiɛa zāka*, He that is contented is full, and he that is full has enough. *Kaniɛ*, Taking well, satisfied with what one receives, contented. *Kunuɛ*, (pl. of قناع *kinūɛ*) Plates or dishes made of palm wood. Large kerchiefs or hoods. Pericardia. Arms.

A قنعات *kinɛāt*, Hairy-faced.

A قنعاث *kinɛās*, Very hairy-faced and bodied.

A قنعار *kinɛār*, A large, fat, wild goat.

A قنعاس *kinɛās*, (pl. قناعيس *kanāɛis*) A large camel. A man strong and unassailable.

A قنعان *kinɛān*, (pl. of قنعة *kinɛat*) Level grounds between two hills. (pl. of اقناع *aknāɛ*, pl. of قنع *kinɛ*) Arms. *Kunɛān*, (v. n. of قنع) Being content with one's lot. Sufficient, satisfactory, valid (witness, witnesses, or evidence).

A قنعب *kinaɛb*, Gluttonous, greedy.

A قنعة *kanɛat*, A camel's desire for the fold, or a longing for sweet herbage. *Kinɛat*, (pl. قنع *kinɛ* and قنعان *kinɛān*) A level place between two hills, a valley. *Kunɛat*, A petition, request, begging. *Kanaɛat*, The top of a mountain or camel's bunch.

A قنعدل *kanaɛdal*, Short. A fool.

A قنعسة *kanɛasat*, Shortness and strength of neck.

A قنعل *kunɛul*, A dwarf, dandiprat.

A قنغر *kanghar*, A tree like the caper (but firmer in the wood), of which camels are fond.

A قنف *kanaf*, (v. n. of قنف) Cracking (dry mud left on the surface of the ground). Thickness of nose. Smallness and thickness of the ear and closeness to the head. White upon the pizzle of an ass.

A قنّف *kinnaf*, Clay or mud which a flood leaves behind, and which cracks.

A قنفاء *kanfā*, (fem. of اقنف *aknaf*) Small and thick-eared (woman). (A mare) whitish on the back of the neck. Thick and flat (goat's ear). A large glans penis. Straight (human ear).

A قنفج *kinfij*, A corpulent she-ass.

A قنفخ *kanfahh* also *kinfikh*, A severe misfortune. A kind of plant.

A قنفخر *kinfakhr*, Bulky. Root of the papyrus.

A قنفد *kunfud*, A hedgehog.

A قنفذ *kunfuz* also *kunfaz*, (pl. قنافذ *kanāfiz*) A porcupine. A hedgehog. A protuberance behind a camel's ear. A high sand-hill. A mouse. A tree growing in the midst of sands. A place producing luxuriant plants. قنفذ ليل *kunfuzu laylin*, A whisperer, slanderer, defamer.

A قنفذة *kunfa* or *kunfuzat*, A she-porcupine.

A قنفر *kanfar*, Penis.

A قنفرش *kanfarish*, A decrepit woman. Crassum penis caput.

A قنفشة *kanfashat*, (v. n. of قنفش Q) Being collected, contracted, wrinkled. Collecting (any thing) quickly. Being costive. Containing, restraining one's self. *Kinfishat*, A species of reptile with a shrivelled skin.

A قنفل *kunful*, A bulky she-goat. A proper name.

A قنفلة *kanfalat*, A sluggish gait.

A قنفور *kunfūr*, Anus, podicis foramen.

A قنفير *kinfīr*, A dwarf; short-bodied.

A قنقاب *kankāb*, A shell for glazing clothes.

A قنقع *kinkiʻ* or *kunkuʻ*, A mouse. *Kunkuʻ*, Short, low, ignoble, trifling, paltry.

A قنقعة *kunkuʻat*, Podex. A she-urchin.

A قنقل *kankal*, A large measure for dry goods. The crown of Khusraw, king of Persia. Heavy-stepping (man).

A قنقن *kinkin* or *kankan*, A skilful guide. Ingenious in discovering water in a desert. A field-mouse. A kind of sea-shell.

A قنقهر *kankahir*, Name of a certain gum.

A قنم *kanam*, (v. n. of قنم) Smelling strong of oil (the hand). Stinking (a leathern bottle). Being rotten (a walnut). Being wet with dew and then made dirty by the dust. *Kanim*, (A hand) which stinks (of oil).

A قنمة *kanamat*, (v. n. of قنم) Smelling strong (a leathern bottle). Being rotten (a nut). The strong smell of oil or any thing fat.

A قنن *kanan*, Rule, mode, manner. *Kinan*, (pl. of قنة *kinnat*) Threads of ropes made of palm-tree fibres. *Kunan*, (pl. of قنة *kunnat*) Mountain-tops.

A قنو *kanw*, (v. n. of قنا for قنو) Blushing continually. Creating. Gaining, acquiring. Keeping goats for milking. *Kinw* or *kunw*, (pl. اقناء *aknāʼ*, قنيان *kun, kan, kinyān*, قنوان *kun, kan*, or *kinwān*) A cluster of dates.

A قنوء *kunūʼ*, (v. n. of قنأ) Being very red (as a woman with paint, or fingers after pressing fruits). Mixing milk with water. Killing. Urging any one to kill. Being put into a tan-pit (a hide). Dyeing (the beard) black.

A قنوّ *kunūw*, (v. n. of قنا for قنو) Gaining, acquiring. Keeping goats for milking. Blackness.

A قنواء *kanwāʼ*, (fem. of اقنى *akna'*) Hook-nosed.

A قنوات *kanawāt*, (pl. of قناة) Canes. Spears.

A قنوان *kinwān, kanwān*, or *kunwān*, (pl. of قنو *kinw*) Clusters of dates. *Kunwān*, The sleeve of a shirt. *Kanawān*, (v. n. of قنا for قنو) Gaining, acquiring. Keeping goats for milking.

A قنوب *kunūb*, (v. n. of قنب) Setting (sun). Entering. Pruning (a vine). Sprouting from the envelope (a flower). Buds, cups of flowers.

A قنوة *kin* or *kunwat*, (v. n. of قنا for قنو) Acquiring (sheep). Gain: mode of acquisition. A flock wholly and entirely one's own. A cluster of dates.

A قنوت *kunūt*, (v. n. of قنت) Standing long in prayer. Refraining from speaking. Being silent. Obedience. Supplication.

P قنّوج *kinnawj*, Name of a city of India.

P قنود *kunūd*, Animated, or presuming, in saying or doing any thing.

A قنّور *kannūr*, Name of a salt-pit whence the finest salt is brought. *Kinnawr*, A slave, servant. Tall, handsome. Long. Long-headed.

A قنوّر *kanawwar*, Having a large head. Hard and rough. Bad-tempered. Untractable (camel).

A قنوس *kunūs*, (pl. of قنس *kins*) Tops of heads.

A قنوط *kunūt*, (v. n. of قنط) Despairing: despair.

A قنوع *kanūʻ*, Contented. A humble suppliant. Steep, sloping (ascent or descent). *Kunūʻ*, (v. n. of قنع) Humbly begging. Being content with what is given. Longing for sweet pasture or for the fold (a camel). Being high and not coming down (a sheep's udder). Ascending. A petition, asking. Contentment. خير الغنى القنوع و شرّ الفقر الخضوع *khayru'lghina'lkunūʻ, washarru'l fakri'l khuzūʻ*, The best riches is contentment, and the worst poverty is humble entreaty.

A قنون *kunūn*, (pl. of قنّة *kunnat*) Mountain-tops.

A قنونية *kunūnat*, Servitude.

A قنّه *kinna*, Galbanum.

A قنهور *kanahwar*, Tall. Flaccid, weak.

A قنى *kany*, (v. n. of قني) Gaining, acquiring. *Kana'*, A hookedness of the nose. (pl. of قناة *kanāt*) Canes. Spears. *Kanī*, Badly-smelling (leathern bottle). *Kina'*, (v. n. of قني) Being contented. Being independent, needing nothing. Any thing which satisfies a person. Contentment, satisfaction. (pl. of قنية *kinyat* or *kunyat*) Gains.

A قنيّ *kaniy*, A part of a flock kept for store or milking. *Kuniy*, (pl. of قناة *kanāt*) Spears. Subterraneous aqueducts.

A قنيات *kanayāt*, (pl. of قناة *kanāt*) Spears.

A قنيان *kinyān* or *kunyān*, (v. n. of قني) Gaining, acquiring. Acquired wealth (in flocks). *Kin, kan*, or *kunyān*, (pl. of قنو *kinw*) Clusters of dates. *Kunyān*, (v. n. of قني) Preserving inviolate (chastity). Blushing continually.

A قنيب *kanīb*, Crowds of men. Clouds.

A قنيبر *kunaybir*, A sort of plant.

A قنية *kinyat*, (v. n. of قني) Keeping (a girl) at home, not permitting (her) to play with the boys. *Kinyat* or *kunyat*, (v. n. of قني) Acquiring (sheep). (pl. قنيً *kina'*) Gain, acquisition. A store.

A قنيت *kanīt*, Eating little (a woman). Holding water badly (a bottle).

A قنيص *kanīs*, A huntsman. Game.

A قنيع *kanīʻ*, Contented. An abject beggar.

A قنيف *kanīf*, Crowds of men. A cloud fraught with rain. Part (of the night). Eating little (a man). Thin of hairs.

A قنئل *kinʼil*, An elephant's neck. A short woman.

A قنّين *kinnīn*, The Grecian lyre. A kind of game.

A قنّينة *kinnīnat*, (pl. قناني) A glass bottle.

A قوا *kuwa'*, (for قوى *kuwa'*) Powers, forces.

A قواء *kawāʼ*, A mansion without inhabitants. بات القواء *bāta'l kawāʼ*, He remained in the open air, without shelter; starving, wanting every necessary. *Kawāʼ* or *kiwāʼ*, A desert, uncultivated ground.

A قوأب *kawʼab*, (or قوأبي *kawʼabiy*) Capable of holding much (a vessel).

A قوابع *kawābiʻ*, Horses outstripped and left behind in a race.

A قوابل *kawābil*, (pl. of قابلة *kābilat*) Midwives. Beginnings (of affairs).

A قوات *kuwāt*, Aliment, nourishment.

A قوّات *kūwāt*, (pl. of قوّة *kūwat*) Powers, virtues.

A قواتل *kawātil*, (pl. of قاتلة) Deadly (things).

A قواحط *kawāhit*, (pl. of قاحط) Severe, hard times.

A قوّاد *kawwād*, A pimp. (in Himyaritic) The nose. *Kūwād*, (pl. of قائد *kāʼid*) Leaders, governors.

A قوّادة *kawwādat*, A bawd, procuress.

A قوادح *kawādih*, Curses, censures.

P قوادگي *kawādagī*, Pimping, panderism.

A قوادم *kawādim*, (pl. of قادم *kādim*) Heads. (pl. of قادمة *kādimat*) The first or the longest feathers in a bird's wing.

P قواده *kawāda*, A procuress.

A قوادي *kawādī*, (pl. of قادية *kādiyat*) Small bodies of men.

A قواذف *kawāzif*, Missiles, things with which any one is pelted.

A قوارب *kawārib*, Camels hastening to water by night. Camels on the second night of a journey to a watering-place. (pl. of قارب *kārib*) Ships' boats.

A قوارة *kuwārat*, A round piece cut (out of cloth, or more especially of leather). A slice from the side of any thing. Any thing from the side of which a slice has been cut.

A قوارح *kawārih*, Five-year-old horses.

A قوارش *kawārish*, Spears intermixed in battle.

A قوارص *kawāris*, Harsh, biting words.

A قوارع *kawāriʻ*, (pl. of قارعة *kāriʻat*) Adversities, evils. Harsh, biting words. Verses of the Kur'an, which the Muhammadans repeat incessantly when in apprehension of danger from men or demons.

P قواره *kawāra*, A remnant, piece, bit, fragment, scrap, shred. A finger.

A قواري *kawārī*, (pl. of قارية *kāriyat*) Witnesses. Points or lower ends of spears. Edges of swords.

A قوارير *kawārīr*, (pl. of قارورة *kārūrat*) Flasks, decanters. Broken bottles. قوارير من فضة *kawārīr min fizzatin*, Decanters brilliant as silver.

A قوّاز *kawwāz*, Soft, smooth. Old, aged.

A قوازح *kawāzih*, Bubbles (of water).

A قوازع *kawāziʻ*, (pl. of قوزع *kawzaʻ*) Chains round the neck, from which men will never be free.

A قوّاس *kawwās*, A bow-maker. An archer.

A قواشة *kawāshat*, The stump of a lopped vine.

A قواصر *kawāsir*, (pl. of قوصرة *kawsarat*) Baskets or hampers for dates.

A قواصع *kawāsiʿ*, (pl. of قاصعاء *kāsiʿāʾ*) Holes of field-mice.

A قواصف *kawāsif*, (pl. of قاصفة) Violent winds.

A قواصل *kawāsil*, (pl. of قاصل) Sharp swords.

A قواضب *kawāzib*, (pl. of قاضب) Sharp swords.

A قوّاط *kawwāt*, A shepherd.

A قواطع *kawātiʿ*, Birds of passage. Incisors.

A قواع *kuwāʿ*, A hare.

A قوّاع *kawwāʿ*, A howling wolf.

A قواعد *kawāʿid*, (pl. of قاعد *kāʿid*) Dwarf palm-trees. Women remaining at home, and not visited by their husbands (on account of child-birth or menses). Women who have no hope of being married. Four pieces of wood whereon the litter of a cripple is laid. (pl. of قاعدة *kāʿidat*) Bases, foundations, pillars, props. Rules, canons. Military exercises. قواعد دين *kawāʿidi dīn*, Articles of religion.

A قواعل *kawāʿil*, (pl. of قاعلة *kāʿilat*) Long, extensive mountains.

A قوافز *kawāfiz*, (pl. of قافز *kāfiz*) Leaping (horses). Frogs.

A قوافص *kawāfis*, High grounds.

A قوافل *kawāfil*, (pl. of قافلة *kāfilat*) Caravans, bodies of travellers. Animals lean and weak.

A قوافي *kawāfī*, (pl. of قافية) The last consonants or syllables in verses with which all the others rhyme.

A قواقلة *kawākilat*, Descendants of قوقل *kawkal*.

A قواقي *kawākī*, (pl. of قيقاءة) Rugged grounds.

A قوّال *kawwāl*, (or قوّالة *kawwālat*) Loquacious. One who speaks fluently, eloquent. A professional story-teller. ابن قوّال *ibn kawwāl*, Eloquent. حمام قوّال *hamām kawwāl*, (Talking pigeon) The cuckoo.

A قوالب *kawālib*, (pl. of قالب) Moulds, forms.

A قوام *kawām*, Straightness. Justice, equity. Truth, consistency. A well-proportioned shape. The stature of a man. That on which any thing rests, or in which it consists; essence; substance, competency; syrup. *Kiwām*, The chief or support of a family. The joining together, connexion, direction, or constitution of any thing. That whereon a thing rests, or in which it consists. (pl. of قويم *kawīm*) Of a fine stature. *Kuwām*, A disease incident to the feet of sheep.

A قوّام *kawwām*, Standing. Superior to. Erect, upright. Of a fine stature. *Kuwwām*, (pl. of قائم *kāʾim*) Standers.

A قوامس *kawāmis*, Heavy calamities.

A قوانص *kawānis*, A small column for the support of a roof or any thing similar. (pl. of قانصة *kānisat*) Birds' intestines.

A قوانين *kawānīn*, (pl. of قانون *kānūn*) Canons, regulations, rules, statutes. Harps.

A قوأي *kūʾaʾ*, (fem. of اقوي *akwaʾ*) Stronger.

A قواية *kawāyat*, A field not watered by rain, between two others which are. Strength. A desert country.

A قوائم *kawāʾim*, (pl. of قائمة) Quadrupeds' legs.

A قوب *kawb*, (v. n. of قاب for قوب) Digging. Breaking. Crushing (as her bird her egg). Fleeing. Approaching. *Kūb*, (pl. اقواب *akwāb*) A chick. امّ القوب *ummu'l kūb*, Misfortune. *Kuwab*, An egg-shell.

A قوّب *kaʾub*, A great drinker.

A قوب *kūwab*, (pl. of قوباء *kūbāʾ*) Ring-worms.

A قوباء *kūbāʾ* or *kuwabāʾ*, (A woman) losing the hair by an old scab. Ring-worm, dry scab.

A قوبة *kūbat* or *kuwabat*, A woman made bald by an old scab. *Kuwabat*, One who keeps at home.

A قوبع *kawbaʿ*, The pommel of a sword. A certain red-legged bird.

A قوبعة *kawbaʿat*, A certain insect.

A قوبيّ *kūbiy*, Fond of eating young birds.

A قوّة *kūwat*, (v. n. of قوي) Being strong, powerful. Excelling in strength. (pl. قوي *kuwaʾ* and *kiwaʾ*) Power, force, vigour, strength, firmness; virtue, authority, faculty. A stedfast determination to observe a law. A single thread of a rope. قوّت آخذه *kūwati ākhiza*, Strength of mind. قوّت باصره *kūwati bāsira*, Visible faculties, sight. قوّت باه *kūwati bāh*, Lust. قوّت جاذبه *kūwati jāziba*, Power of attraction; allurement. قوّت حفظ *kūwati hifz*, (حافظه *hāfiza*, or محافظه *muhāfiza*) The conservative power, *i.e.* memory. قوّت حيوانيّه *kūwati haywānīya*, Animal, vital power. قوّت دافعه *kūwati dāfiʿa*, Expulsive, repelling power. قوّت دل *kūwati dil*, Strength of mind. قوّت ذاتيّه *kūwati zātīya*, Natural virtue or powers. قوّت ذائقه *kūwati zāʾika*, Tasting. قوّت سامعه *kūwati sāmiʿa*, Hearing. قوّت شامّه *kūwati shāmma*, Smelling. قوّت شهوانيّه *kūwati shahwānīya*, Concupiscent power. قوّت غضبيّه *kūwati ghazabīya*, Irascible power (also rage, anger). قوّت لامسه *kūwati lāmisa*, Touching. قوّت ماسكه *kūwati māsika*, Retentive power. قوّت متخيّله *kūwati mutakhayyila*, (or خيال *khayāl*) The power of fancy. قوّت متصرّفه *kūwati mutasarrifa*, Volition. قوّت محركه *kūwati muhrika*, Moving power. قوّت مدركه *kūwati mudrika*, Apprehending, comprehending. قوّت معده *kūwati miʿda*, Strength of stomach. قوّت مميّزه *kūwati mumayyiza*, Power of discrimination, discernment. قوّت واهمه *kūwati wāhima*, (واهميّه *wāhimīya*, and وهم *wahm*) Faculty of imagination. قوّت هاضمه *kūwati hāzima*, Digestion.

A قوت *kawt* or *kūt*, (v. n. of قات for قوت) Maintaining (one's family). *Kūt*, Nourishing, aliment, food, victuals, livelihood, sustenance. قوت روح *kūti rūh*, Food for the soul. قوت لا يموت *kūti lā yamūt*, Food sufficient to keep body and soul together. قوت ليلة *kūtu laylatin*, A night's provision. قوت مسيح *kūti masīh*, One night's wine.

P قوت مسيح يكشبه *kūti masīhi yakshaba*, A date.

P قوّت پذير *kūwat-pazīr*, Acquiring strength.

A قوتة *kūtat*, A day's provision.

P قوت خواه *kūt-khwāh*, Food-seeking.

P قوتي *kūtī*, A box, generally of wood, though sometimes of silver, in which precious stones or electuaries are preserved.

P قوتيل *kūtīl*, A weight of three drams.

P قوثر *kūsir*, Sweet cane, galangale.

P قوچ *koch*, A horned fighting ram.

A قوح *kawh*, (v. n. of قاح for قوح) Being full of matter (a wound). Sweeping (a house). *Kūh*, (pl. of قاحة *kāhat*) Courts.

A قوخ *kawkh*, (v. n. of قاخ for قوخ) Becoming corrupted from disease (the stomach or belly).

A قود *kawd*, (v. n. of قاد for قود) Leading (opposed to سوق *sawk*, which means driving). A led horse or mule (not mounted). A troop of horse. *Kūd*, (pl. of اقود *akwad*) Long-necked or long-backed (camels or horses). *Kawad*, Retaliation, lex talionis. Length of neck or back.

A قوّد *kūwad*, (pl. of قائد *kāʾid*) Governors.

A قوداء *kawdāʾ*, (fem. of اقود *akwad*) Long-backed or long-necked (camel or mare). High, lofty (road over a mountain).

A قور *kawr*, (v. n. of قار for قور) Walking on tiptoe, so as not to be heard. Attacking suddenly from an ambush. Circumventing (game). Making a circular incision in the middle of any thing. Circumcising (a woman). A new rope of fine cotton. Fresh cotton. Riband, tape. A cotton-plant of the present year's sowing. *Kūr*, (pl. of قارة *kārat*) Hills. Black stones. *Kawar*, (v. n. of قور) Being blind of an eye. Purblindness, dimness of sight. The state of having only one eye, monoculousness.

P قور *kūr*, The top of a gourd, or any ball placed on an eminence, at which they shoot with arrows. Cotton. A testicle. A knot, wen. Armour.

A قوراء *kawrāʾ*, Large, roomy (house).

A قورب *kawrab*, A large mass of water.

P T قوربيگي *kūr-begī*, Keeper of the arsenal.

P قورچي *kūrchī*, The keeper of the armoury. A horseguard, a cuirassier.

P قورخانه *kūr-khāna*, An arsenal, armoury.

G قورسا *kūrsā*, The balsam-tree.

P قورلتان *kūrlatān*, (in Khwārazm) A consultation.

P قوريون *kūriyūn*, Coriander.

A قوز *kawz*, (pl. اقواز *akwāz*, قيزان *kīzān*, اقاويز *akāwīz*, and اقاوز *akāwiz*) A round heap, hill, or high tract of sand.

P قوز *kūz*, Curved, crooked. A sheep.

P قوز پشت *kūz-pusht*, Crook-backed.

A قوزع *kawzaʿ*, (pl. قوازع *kawāziʿ*) A chain round the neck, from which one will never be freed.

A قوزعة *kawzaʿat*, (v. n. of قوزع Q) Running away beaten (a cock).

A قوس *kaws*, (v. n. of قاس for قوس) Measuring, comparing. Preceding, outstripping, surpassing. Drawing up (race-horses) in a row preparatory to starting. A cubit. (pl. قسيّ *kisīy, kusīy,* اقواس *akwās,* and قياس *kiyās*) A bow. Sagittarius the zodiacal sign. The lesser segment of a circle. A few dates lying at the bottom of the bin. قوس الله *kawsu'llāh,* God's bow, the rainbow. قوس قزح *kaws kuzah,* The rainbow. *Kūs,* A cloister, hermit's cell. The lurking-place of a hunter. A word used in scaring away dogs. *Kawas,* (v. n. of قوس) Being crook-backed. Curvature in the back. *Kawis,* Difficult (times).

P قوس *kūs,* The cell of a monk.

A قوساء *kawsā,* (fem. of اقوس *akwas*) Crook-backed (woman).

A قوسرّة *kawsarrat,* (or قوسرة *kawsarat*) A basket or hamper made of reeds or osier-twigs.

P قوسه *kawsa,* The rainbow.

A قوسيّ *kawsīy,* Of the form or colour of the rainbow (قوس *kaws*). *Kūsīy,* Troublesome (times).

SY قوسيا *kūsiyā,* The costus (a shrub).

A قوش *kūsh,* (from P كوچك *kūchak*) Small-bodied (man). A word used in scaring dogs.

P قوشباز *kūshbāz,* A fowler. A seller of birds.

P قوشون *kūshūn,* A house. A hospital.

P قوشي *kūshī,* A scarecrow.

A قوص *kūs,* Name of a place in Egypt.

A قوصرة *kawsarat,* (or قوصرّة *kawsarrat*) (pl. قواصر *kawāsir*) A basket or hamper of reeds or osier-twigs for holding grain or dates. A woman.

A قوصف *kawsaf,* A carpet with a long pile, striped and four-square.

A قوض *kawz,* (v. n. of قاض for قوض) Destroying, demolishing (a building). قوضا بقوض *kawzan bi kawzin,* Instead of.

A قوط *kawt,* (pl. اقواط *akwāt*) A flock of sheep, or a hundred of them.

A قوطة *kawtat,* A large date-basket.

A قوظ *kawz,* Midsummer-heat.

A قوع *kawꜥ,* (v. n. of قاع for قوع) Covering (as a camel). Retiring, receding, retreating, desisting. (pl. اقواع *akwāꜥ*) A piece of plain ground, on which dates or corn are gathered.

A قوعان *kawaꜥān,* (v. n. of قاع for قوع) Mounting, covering (a camel), lining (a dog). Limping.

A قوعس *kawꜥas,* Thick-necked; strong-backed.

A قوعلة *kawꜥalat,* (v. n. of قوعل Q) Sitting on a hillock. An eagle that soars round high mountains called قواعل *kawāꜥil.* A little hill, hillock.

P قوغا *kawghā,* (for غوغا *ghawghā*) Tumult.

A قوف *kawf,* (v. n. of قاف for قوف) Following (the footsteps), coming behind, tracking. *Kūf,* The upper part or opening of the ear. Margin, extremity. The hinder part of the back. بقوف رقبته *bi kūfi rakabatihi,* (or بقوفة رقبته *bi kūfati rakabatihi,* (He took) by the nape of his (or its) neck.

P قوفا *kūfā,* Turpentine of fir.

A قوفل *kūful,* Betel-nut.

A قوق *kawk,* (v. n. of قاق for قوق) Clucking (as a hen). *Kūk,* An aquatic bird with a long neck. Rima mulieris. Disproportionably tall. Name of one of the Greek emperors.

A قوقأة *kawkaꜥat,* (v. n. of قوقأ Q) Clucking.

A قوقاة *kawkāt,* (v. n. of قوقي Q) Screaming.

P قوقبا *kūkabā,* An opening medicine. Name of an herb.

A قوقة *kūkat,* A bald place on the head.

A قوقل *kawkal,* The male partridge. The bird kata. Name of the father of a tribe.

A قوقلة *kawkalat,* (v. n. of قوقل Q) Ascending a hillock. Name of the father of a tribe.

P قوقنس *kūknus,* (or قوقنوس *kūknūs*) A phœnix.

P قوقو *kūkū,* (or قوقه *kūka*) A top-knot on a turban, a button on a garment.

P قوقي *kūkī,* A kind of beaver.

A قوقية *kūkīyat,* Coins bearing the image and superscription of the Greek emperor قوق *kūk.*

A قول *kawl,* (v. n. of قال for قول) Speaking, saying, pronouncing, or giving an opinion upon (any thing). Thinking. Killing. Striking. Dying. Leaning. Reposing. Advancing. Preparing for any thing. Overcoming, conquering. (pl. اقوال *akwāl* and اقاويل *akāwīl*) A word, saying. Promise, agreement, compact, consent, acquiescence. Contract, bargain. (in India) A lease or agreement in writing given to the ryots, to shew the principles and rules by which the demands of government on the land in their occupation are to be regulated. Kind of song. P قول كاسه گر *kawli kāsagar,* A term of music. A قول و فعل *kawl u fiꜥl,* Word and deed. قول و قرار *kawl u karār,* An agreement.

A قُوُل *kuwul,* (pl. of قؤول *kaꜥūl*) Talkative.

A قوّل *kuwwal,* (pl. of قائل *kāꜥil*) Speakers.

P قولاج *kūlāj,* A fathom. قولاج كردن *kūlāj kardan,* To measure with a fathom, to fathom.

A قولة *kawlat,* (v. n. of قال for قول) Speaking. A speech. *Kuwalat,* Talkative. Eloquent.

P قولنامه *kawl-nāma,* Treaty, written agreement.

A قولنج *kawlanj, kawlinj,* or *kūlinj,* Cholic.

A قوليّ *kawlīy,* Verbal.

A قولية *kawlīyat,* Noise, tumult. A mob.

A قوم *kawm,* (v. n. of قام for قوم) Being brisk (the market). Freezing (water). Being dull, at a stand (the market). Rising up. Rebelling against. Being middling, moderate. Beginning. Paining. Fetching (its) value (a thing). Overseeing, minding, tending. Standing. Being set over (any business), attending to, executing. Stopping (as a fatigued horse). Being straightforward (business). (pl. اقوام *akwām,* اقاوم *akāwim,* اقاويم *akāwīm,* and اقائم *akāꜥim*) People. A nation; a tribe, family, kindred. A sect, caste. Some, somewhat, a certain person. A company of men (exclusive of women). قوم لوط *kawmi lūt,* The people of Lot, *i.e.* inhabitants of Sodom. قوم موسيٰ *kawmi mūsaꜥ,* The people of Moses, the Israelites. قوم يونس *kawmi yūnas,* The people of Jonah, *i.e.* the Ninevites. P قوم و خويش *kawm u khwesh,* People and kin, friends and relations.

A قوّام *kuwwām,* (pl. of قائم *kāꜥim*) Standers.

A قومة *kawmat,* (v. n. of قام for قوم) Being brisk, bustling (the market). Freezing (water). Rising up. Standing. Beginning. Being middling, moderate. Paining. Being appointed to any charge, giving attention to any trust. Being tired (a horse). Standing. One standing erect between two prostrations. One rising up. Stature. *Kawamat,* (pl. of قائم *kāꜥim*) Administrators, prefects.

A قومس *kawmas,* A prince, commander. The main ocean, middle of the sea. *Kūmas,* Name of a tract of country between Khurāsān and Irāk. Name of a province in Spain.

P قوميني *kūminī,* An intoxicating liquor made from barley and other species of grain.

A ابنة قومي *ibnatu kūmī,* A maid-servant.

A قومية *kawmīyat,* Connexion, the being of the same tribe: clanship. Stature, figure. That by which any thing subsists or is supported; stay, support.

A قونة *kūnat,* A thin plate of copper or of iron, with which they repair vessels.

P قونج *kūnj,* A kind of beech-mast employed in tanning leather. The oxyacanth; the wild plum.

P قوندروج *kondurūj,* Frankincense.

A قونس *kawnas,* Crest of a helmet. Crown of the head. A prominent bone between the ears of a horse. The beaten part of a road.

A قونوس *kawnūs,* The crest of a helmet.

A قونية *kūniyat,* (or قونيه *kūniya*) Iconium.

A قؤود *kaꜥūd,* Manageable, well-trained (horse).

A قؤول *kaꜥūl,* (pl. قُوُل *kuwul*) Loquacious, talkative. Eloquent.

A قوول *kuwūl,* (pl. of قائل *kāꜥil*) Speakers.

A قوهة *kūhat,* Milk beginning to spoil.

A قوهستان *kūhistān,* Name of a place famous for the manufacture of cloths.

A قوهيّ *kūhīy,* A kind of white cloth.

A قوي *kawaꜥ,* (v. n. of قوي) Being empty and deserted (a house). Being famished. Being withheld (rain). Hungry. A desert. بات القوي *bāta'l kawaꜥ,* He passed the night famishing. *Kawī,* A rope made of threads of unequal thickness. *Kuwaꜥ,* Intellect, sense, mind. (pl. of قوّة *kuwwat*) The different threads of a rope. *Kuwaꜥ* or *kiwaꜥ,* (pl. of قوّة *kuwwat*) Powers, virtues, energies.

A قويّ *kawīy,* (pl. اقوياء *akwiyāꜥ*) Robust, firm, strong, solid, powerful, vigorous. P دلاوران قوي دل *dilāwarāni kawī-dil,* Warlike and courageous soldiers. A سلطان قويّ الجنان *sultāni kawiyu'l janān,* A prince of a great soul. *Kuwayy,* The young of any bird or beast.

P قوي بازو *kawī-bāzū,* (or بال *bāl*) Strong-armed.

P قوي بخت *kawī-bakht,* Fortunate, prosperous.

P قوي پي *kawī-pay,* Sinewy, muscular.

A قوي جثّه *kawī-jussa*, Strong-bodied.

A قويس *kuways*, (and قويسة *kuwaysat*) (dim. of قوس *kaws*) A little bow.

A قوي طبع *kawī-tabʻ*, Of strong natural parts.

A قويّ الفؤاد *kawiyu'l fuʼād*, (and قويّ الاقتدار *kawiyu'l iktidār*, Firm-hearted; most potent.

A قويل *kuwayl*, (dim. of قول *kawl*) An unusual, inaccurate, cant, trivial, trite, or familiar word.

A قويم *kawīm*, (pl. قوام *kiwām*) Right, straight. Of a fine stature. *Kuwaym*, (and قويمة *kuwaymat*) (dim. of قوم *kawm*) A little people.

A قويمة *kuwaymat*, (dim. of قامة *kāmat*) An hour, a little while.

A قوي هيكل *kawī-haykal*, Robust.

A قه *kih*, (imper. of وقى) Preserve thou.

A قه *kahh*, Loud laughter.

A قهاب *kuhāb*, (and قهابيّ *kuhābiy*) White.

A قهابي *kahābī*, (or قهاوب *kahāwib*) (pl. of قهوباة *kahawbāt*) Triple-pointed arrows.

A قهاد *kihād*, (pl. of قهد) Small-eared sheep.

A قهّار *kahhār*, Powerful. A conqueror, subduer. An avenger. An oppressor. القهّار *al kahhār*, The omnipotent or avenging (God).

A قهّاري *kahhārī*, Vindictive: the avenger. Divine. غضب قهّاري *ghazabi kahhārī*, Divine wrath.

A قهاقر *kuhākir*, That by which any thing is rubbed or pulverized.

A قهب *kahb*, Of a brown, also of a dark colour, between black and white. A large mountain. An aged camel. *Kahab*, (v. n. of قهب) Being of a black and white colour.

A قهباء *kahbāʼ*, (fem. of اقهب *ak-hab*) Brown.

A قهبة *kuhbat*, A dark colour, between black and white. *Kahibat*, (fem.) Of such a colour.

A قهبسة *kahbasat*, A thick, fat she-ass.

A قهبل *kahbal*, The face.

A قهبلة *kahbalat*, (v. n. of قهبل Q) Saying حيّا الله قهبلك *hayya'llāhu kahbalaka*, May God preserve your charming face! A stout wild she-ass. A mode of walking.

A قهبلس *kahbalis*, A large and thick penis. A dull white. A small louse. A large, stout woman.

A قهبيّ *kahbīy*, A male partridge.

A قهة *kihat*, Pure milk.

A قهد *kahd*, (v. n. of قهد) Going with short steps. (pl. قهاد *kihād*) A species of red sheep with very small ears, and reddish, and whose mouth is something like a dog. Small black sheep without tail or ears. A small ox. An unblown narcissus. Brown, dark. Clear-coloured. White. A hart. A wild ox.

A قهر *kahr*, (v. n. of قهر) Conquering, overcoming, subduing. Force, violence. Power. Oppression, subjection. Lordship or rule. Vengeance, severity. Torment, punishment, chastisement. Judgment. Rage, indignation. P قهر كردن *kahr kardan*, To conquer, oppress, tame. قهر گرفتن *kahr giriftan*, To take fire, to fly in a passion. A *Kahir*, Lean, scraggy (thigh).

A قهرا *kahran*, (P قهرانه *kahrāna*) By force, compulsively, by authority.

A قهرة *kuhrat*, Force. *Kuharat*, Wicked, malignant (woman). A large needle.

A قهرة *kuhratan*, Forcibly.

P قهرمان *kahramān*, A valiant warrior, an invincible hero. Name of a celebrated fabulous hero of Persia. Power, authority.

P قهرناك *kahrnāk*, Disturbed, indignant.

A قهريّ *kahriy*, Vested with the power to punish (as a magistrate), avenging, vindicating.

A قهز *kahz*, (v.n. of قهز) Leaping, springing. *Kahz* or *kihz*, Cloth made of red wool mixed with silk.

A قهزب *kahzab*, A dwarf. Short.

A قهزيّ *kihziy*, Cloth made of red wool and silk.

P قهستان *kuhistān*, The country of Kohistān.

A قهطم *kihtim*, Base, sordid, and clamorous.

A قهقار *kahkār*, A hard stone.

A قهقاع *kihkāʻ*, (v. n. of قهقع Q) Gnashing the teeth, grinning, raging (as a bear).

A قهقاة *kahkāh*, A short night-journey for water.

A قهقب *kahkab*, Tall, handsome, and jolly. The brinjal or egg-plant. *Kahkab*, (or قهقبّ *kahkabb*) Thick, corpulent, and aged.

A قهقر *kahkar*, Much wheat stored up in vessels. That with which any thing is rubbed or reduced to a powder. A very black crow.

A قهقرّ *kahkarr*, A hard stone. A he-goat. Aged, old. *Kuhkurr*, A red cuticle over the pith of a palm-tree. Gum.

A قهقرة *kahkarat*, (v. n. of قهقر Q) Retiring, retreating back. Green wheat turning black.

A قهقري *kahkara'*, Much wheat stored up in vessels. (dual قهقران *kahkarāni*) A retreat, a retrograde motion. رجوع قهقري *rujūʻ kahkara'*, A shameful retreat.

A قهقز *kahkaz*, Black.

A قهقزة *kahkazat*, High-blooded (camel).

A قهقزيّة *kahkaziyat*, Dwarfish (female).

A قهقمّ *kihkamm*, Voracious, gluttonous.

A قهقور *kuhkūr*, A long structure of pebbles, such as children build.

P قهقه *kahka*, A horse-laugh. Name of a place.

A قهقهة *kahkahat*, (v. n. of قهقه Q) Laughing loudly or indecently. Walking hastily. A loud laugh, horse-laugh.

A قهل *kahl*, (v. n. of قهل) Praising immoderately. Being ungrateful for benefits, inhuman; using one shamefully and ungratefully in word or action. Shrivelling (the skin). Unaccustoming the body to the use of water, keeping the person dirty. Esteeming little (a gift).

A قهم *kaham*, (v. n. of قهم) Having little appetite for food.

A قهمد *kahmad*, Of base origin, low. Ugly-faced.

A قهمزة *kahmazat*, A spring, leap. Short-bodied (man or woman). Bulky, slow-paced (she-camel).

A قهميزي *kahmaza'*, Celerity, alacrity.

A قهنّب *kahannab*, Tall and hump-backed. Long.

A قهنبان *kahnabān*, Long.

A قهوان *kahwān*, Stout-horned, aged (he-goat).

A قهوبة *kahūbat*, (or قهوباة *hahawbāt*) (pl. قهابي *kahābī* or قهاوب *kahāwib*) A tri-forked spear-head. A small arrow hitting the mark.

A قهوة *kahwat*, Wine. Coffee, or a decoction of berries called بنّ *bunn*, which gives an appetite. Breakfast, a collation. A coffee-house. A plentiful, satisfying meal. Pure milk. Odour, smell.

A قهوس *kahwas*, Tall. A he-goat with large horns browsing on sandy grounds.

A قهوسة *kahwasat*, Celerity, swiftness.

A قهول *kuhūl*, (v.n. of قهل) Shrivelling (the skin).

T قهوه جي *kahwajī*, A coffee-house keeper.

P قهوه خانه *kahwa-khāna*, A coffee-house.

P قهوه دان *kahwadān*, A coffee-pot.

P قهوه رنگي *kahwa-rangī*, Coffee-coloured.

A قهي *kahy*, (v. n. of قهي) Having no desire for food, loathing, detesting.

A قهيبة *kahībat*, A sort of bird.

A قهيرة *kahīrat*, The fleshy part between the neck and shoulder. The breast, bosom. القهيرة *al kahīrat*, Cairo, the metropolis of Egypt.

A قهيز *kahīz*, A coarse silk.

A قهيقران *kuhaykirān*, A sort of insect.

A قي *kiy*, A desert.

A قيأ *kays*, (v. n. of قاأ for قيأ) Vomiting. Drinking in the dye (cloth), being thoroughly saturated.

A قياء *kuyāʼ*, Frequent vomiting. An emetic.

A قياتة *kiyātat*, The act of nourishing.

A قياد *kiyād*, Reins, a bridle. A halter for leading. عسر القياد *ʻasiru'l kiyād*, Difficult to guide.

A قيادة *kiyādat*, (v. n. of قاد for قود) Leading (a horse). Conduct, guidance. Panderism, pimping.

A قياديد *kayādīd*, (pl. of قيدود *kaydūd*) Long-bodied (she-asses).

A قيّار *kayyār*, Possessed of, or vender of pitch.

P قي آرنده *kay-āranda*, An emetic, vomitive.

A قياس *kiyās*, (v. n. 3 of قاس for قيس) Agreeing, answering to in measure or comparison. Measuring, comparing. Regular form, analogy. The regular measure (of a noun, verb, &c.). Reasoning, logic; syllogism. Opinion, judgment, argument, thought, design, conjecture, imagination, supposition, guess. قياس استثنائي *kiyāsi istisnāʼī*, Conditional syllogism. قياس استقراني *kiyāsi istikrānī*, Absolute syllogism. P بي قياس *bī kiyās*, Immense, above measure. A خلاف القياس *khilāfu'l kiyās*, Anomalous. علی القياس *ʻala'l kiyās*, According to analogy, regularly. علی غير القياس *ʻala' ghayri'l kiyās*, Without rule, irregular, anomalous. P قياس كردن *kiyās kardan*, To estimate, judge, or imagine. A (pl. of قوس *kaws*) Bows.

A قيّاس *kayyās*, One who starts horses at a race.

A قياسر *kayāsir*, (and قياسرة *kayāsirat*) (pl. of قيسريّ *kaysarīy*) Large camels.

A قياسيّ *kiyāsīy*, Analogical, analogous, regular. Conjectural. Probable. غير قياسيّ *ghayru kiyāsīyin*, Irregular, anomalous.

A قيّاصة *kayyāsat*, (A well) whose parapet has fallen to ruin.

A قياصرة *kayāsirat*, (pl. of قيصر *kaysar*) Cæsars.

A قياض *kiyāz*, Equal.

A قياظ *kiyāz*, (v. n. 3 of قاظ for قيظ) Agreeing with any one for the summer-season (called قيظ *kayz*). Summer-heat.

A قياع *kiyāʿ*, (v. n. of قاع for قوع) Mounting, covering (a camel).

A قيافة *kiyāfat*, Appearance, semblance, likeness, resemblance, imitation, representation, port, air, manner, mode, habit.

A قياق *kiyāk* or *kuyāk*, Long.

A قياقي *kayākī*, (pl. of قيقاءة) Rugged grounds.

A قيّال *kuyyāl*, (pl. of قائل *kāʾil*) Those who sleep (taking their siesta), or who drink at mid-day.

A قيالة *kiyālat*, Noon-day. Siesta.

A قيام *kiyām*, (v. n. of قام for قوم) Standing upright, rising up. Making an insurrection. Giving pain. Beginning. Being appointed (to any charge), watching over, preserving (it); giving attention to any trust, overseeing, managing, tending. Being worth, fetching the value. Being middling, moderate. Being brisk (as a market where much business is done). Being congealed (water). Being fatigued (a horse). Resurrection. Insurrection. Assistance. Application, attention. Station, dignity. The woof in weaving. Residence, settlement. That by which any thing subsists or is supported. Alvi dejectio et fluxus. قيام و قعود و ركوع و سجود *kiyām u kuʿūd, u rukūʿ u sujūd*, Standing, sitting, stooping, and prostration (Muhammadan postures in worship). P قيام كردن *kiyām kardan*, (or قيام نمودن *kiyām namūdan*) To observe, fulfil. To set about, attend to. A (pl. of قائم *kāʾim*) Standers.

A قيّام *kayyām*, Subsisting, eternal; hence, God. *Kuyyām*, (pl. of قائم *kāʾim*) Standers.

A قيامة *kiyāmat*, The resurrection, last day. Confusion, tumult. Calamity. Excessively great. P قيامت كردن *kiyāmat kardan*, To achieve wonders. A صحراىٔ قيامت *sahrāʾi kiyāmat*, The plain or valley of the last judgment, on which they suppose the souls of mankind will be assembled. يوم القيامة *yawmu'l kiyāmat*, (often written القيمة) The day of the resurrection.

A قيامي *kiyāmī*, Stability, steadiness. Stagnant.

A قيان *kiyān*, (pl. of قين *kayn*) Servants, slaves. (pl. of قينة *kaynat*) Girls, maidens. Singing women.

P قياوار *kayāwār*, Work, employ, business, trade. A badger. A jackal. A workman. Interrupted in work.

A قيب *kīb*, Quantity, longitude, space, interval. The part of a bow between the handle and extremity.

A قيت *kīt*, Food, victual, provision (for a day).

A قيتار *kītār*, A guitar, harp, lyre.

A قيتال *kītāl*, (v. n. 3 of قتل, irregularly formed) Fighting, resisting, opposing, striving to kill.

A قيتة *kītat*, A day's provisions. Fuel. اقتت لنارك قيتة *iktat li nāriha kītatan*, Put fuel on your fire.

P قيجك *kījak*, A violin.

T قيجي *kaychī*, Scissors.

A قيح *kayh*, (v. n. of قاح for قيح) Being purulent (a wound). Matter unmixed with blood.

A قيخم *kaykham*, Eminent, high.

A قيخمان *kaykhamān*, A chief or leader who acts agreeably to his own will.

A قيد *kayd*, (pl. اقياد *akyād* and قيود *kuyūd*) Confinement, restraint, imprisonment, restriction, obstacle. A fetter, pinion, manacle. The thong with which the two timbers of a camel's saddle are held together. The straps which connect the rings of a sword-sheath with the belt. Tractable, manageable (horse). A paction, bond, compact, treaty, bargain, rule, regulation, article of agreement, obligation, restriction, modification. Length and quantity. Measurement. The enrolling of any thing in a public register. The quiescent letter (excepting ا, و, or ي of prolongation), which immediately precedes the رويّ *rawīy*, or final consonant of the rhyme (as the ر *ra* in مرد *mard*). القيد و الرتعة *al kayd wa'r ratʿat*, Captivity, and plenty to eat and drink. قيد الاسنان *kaydu'l asnān*, The gums. قيد الاوابد *kaydu'l awābid*, A generous horse outstripping the wild beasts. قيد عياني *kayd ʿayānī*, Before my eyes. قيد الفرس *kaydu'l faras*, A mark burnt on the neck of a camel. P قيد فرنگ *kaydi farang*, A kind of fetter used by the Europeans. A قيد النكاح *kaydu'n nikāh*, The bonds of matrimony. P قيد كردن *kayd kardan*, To confine. بي قيد *bī kayd*, Free, unfettered. A *Kīd*, Quantity. Worth, value. قيد رمح *kīdu rumhin*, A spear's length.

A قيّد *kayyid*, Ductile, tractable (horse).

A قيدار *kaydār*, A proper name.

P قيدافه *kaydāfa*, Name of a queen of بردع *bardaʿ*.

A قيدام *kaydām*, (or قيدوم *kaydūm*) The projecting part or ness (of a mountain). A prow. Before.

P قيد بند *kayd-band*, A fortress.

A قيدحور *kaydahūr*, Of a bad disposition.

P قيد خانه *kayd-khāna*, A prison.

P قيد كرده *kayd-karda*, Fettered, imprisoned.

P قيدو *kaydū*, Name of a Mogul emperor.

A قيدود *kaydūd*, (pl. قياديد *kayādīd*) Long-bodied and long-necked (she-camel). Long.

A قيدودة *kaydūdat*, (v. n. of قاد for قود) Leading (a horse): conduct, guidance.

A قيدون *kaydūn*, The third or heaven of rubies.

A قيدي *kaydī*, Imprisoned. A prisoner, captive.

A قيذار *kayzār*, Kedar, son of Ishmael, and progenitor of the Arabians.

A قيذحور *kayzahūr*, Of a bad disposition.

A قير *kīr*, A kind of pitch, used in smearing ships or camels. Black.

A قيّر *kayyir*, A skilful darter of javelins.

A قيراط *kīrāt*, (pl. قراريط *karārīt*) A weight of four grains. Half a dang.

A قيران *kīrān*, (pl. of قارة *kārat*) Little mountains. Black stones.

P قير اندود *kīr-andūd*, Besmeared with pitch, pitched, tarred. قير اندودكي كردن *kīr-andūdagī kardan*, To tar, pitch.

P قيردار *kīr-dār*, (or زده) Besmeared with pitch.

P قيرگون *kīr-gūn*, Of the colour of pitch.

P قيروان *kīrwān*, The environs of a cultivated place. Going through, viewing cities. The horizon, east and west. A caravan.

A قيروان *kayrawān* or *kayruwān*, (Arabicised) A caravan, a body of travellers. A battalion. A lock, bar, bolt. Cyrene in Africa.

G قيروطي *kayrūtī*, A cerecloth.

A قيروطيّ *kayrūtīy*, A kind of plaster cerecloth.

P قيري *kīrī*, Of a pitchy blackness.

P قيز *kīz*, A wife of the infidels.

A قيزان *kīzān*, (pl. of قوز *kawz*) Round sand-hills.

A قيس *kays*, (v. n. of قاس for قيس) Measuring one thing by another, comparing, estimating. A pompous mode of walking. Hunger. Vehemence. Penis. Name of the founder of a tribe. The tribe itself. امرؤ القيس *amrusu'l kays*, A name common to several men. قيس مجنون *kaysi majnūn*, Name of a lover famous in the east. *Kīs*, Quantity, measure. قيس رمح *kīsu rumhin*, A spear's length.

G قيسارية *kaysāriyat*, Cæsarea in Palestine.

A قيسب *kaysab*, A kind of salt bitter plant.

A قيسبان *kaysabān*, Thick, strong (penis).

A قيسبة *kaysabat*, A man's name.

P قيست *kīst*, A small apricot.

A قيسريّ *kaysarīy*, (pl. قياسر *kayāsir* and قياسرة *kayāsirat*) A large camel. Great, large. Aged. An old man. A kind of beetle.

P قيسوس *kīsūs*, A kind of ivy.

A قيسيّ *kaysīy*, Of the tribe of قيس *kays*.

P قيشور *kayshūr*, A sort of stone found in the sea.

A قيص *kays*, The dropping out of a tooth. A commotion in the belly. (pl. اقياص *akyās* and قيوص *kuyūs*) Braying (camel).

A قيصاريه *kaysāriya*, Cæsarea.

A قيصانة *kaysānat*, Name of a round yellow fish.

A قيصر *kaysar*, (pl. قياصرة *kayāsirat*) Cæsar, an emperor. قيصر روم *kaysari rūm*, The Roman or the Grecian emperor. قيصر الروميّ *kaysaru'r rūmīy*, The Roman Cæsar, *i.e.* Julius Cæsar.

P قيصران *kaysarān*, Name of a note in music.

A قيصريّ *kaysarīy*, Imperial. Cæsarean.

A قيصرية *kaysariyat*, Imperial dignity. Cæsarea.

P قيصور *kaysūr*, Name of a city whence the

finest musk is brought. Name of a mountain.

A قيصوم *kaysūm*, Southernwood (a plant).

A قيض *kayz*, (v. n. of قاض for قيض) Breaking, cracking (an egg). Changing, exchanging. Doing exactly like another. Drawing, pourtraying a countenance. Being divided, split, cleft. Being full of water (a well). An egg-shell, or a fragment of it. A chick, or the water which comes out of an egg. A fissure in a well (through which the water runs off). Equal. Recompense, compensation. Comparison. Similitude. *Kiz*, (pl. of قيضة *kizat*) Small bits of bones.

A قيّض *kayyiz*, A hot stone with which they cauterize cattle. One who offers goods in exchange.

A قيّضان *kayyizāni*, (dual) Buyer and seller.

A قيضة *kizat*, (pl. قيض) A small bit of a bone.

A قيّضة *kayyizat*, A hot stone with which they cauterize cattle.

G قيطس *kaytis*, A myrtle. *Kitas*, The constellation called the whale.

A قيطون *kaytūn*, A magazine, store-room. A small house within a larger.

P قيطون *kītūn*, A border, edging of silk.

A قيظ *kayz*, (v. n. of قاظ for قيظ) Being extremely hot (midsummer). Passing the summer, summering. (pl. اقياظ *akyāz* and قيوظ *kuyūz*) Midsummer, the two hottest summer-months.

A قيظيّ *kayziy*, Produced in summer's height.

A قيع *kayʿ*, (v. n. of قاع for قيع) Grunting (a hog). *Kiʿ*, (pl. of قاع *kāʿ*) Level grounds, plains.

A قيعار *kayʿār*, (or قيعر *kayʿar*) One who moves his mouth much in speaking.

A قيعان *kiʿān*, (pl. of قاع) Level grounds, plains.

A قيعة *kiʿat*, Level ground, field, plain. (pl. of قاع *kāʿ*) Level grounds without mountains.

A قيعلة *kayʿalat*, An eagle that soars round lofty mountains. A large masculine woman.

A قيعم *kayʿam*, A cat. Old, thick (camel).

A قيعون *kayʿūn*, Name of an herb.

A قيف *kīf*, A funnel.

G قيفال *kīfāl*, (or قيفل) The cephalic vein.

A قيفط *kayfat*, A man greatly addicted to venery.

A قيق *kayk*, (v. n. of قاق for قيق) Clucking as a hen. *Kīk*, Disproportionately long. Foolish, giddy. A mountain surrounding the world. *Kiyak*, (pl. of قيقاءة *kīkāʾat*) Rugged grounds.

A قيقاء *kaykāʾ*, (v. n. of قوقى Q) Screaming, clucking, cackling. *Kaykāʾ* or *kīkāʾ*, Rugged, rocky ground. A flagon with a spout. The white of an egg, or the pellicle surrounding it; also the envelope of a palm-flower.

A قيقاءة *kīkāʾat*, (pl. قواقي *kawākī*, قياقي *kayākī*, and قيق *kiyak*) Rugged ground. *Kīkāʾat*, (or قيقاة *kīkāt*) A kind of drinking-vessel.

A قيقاب *kaykāb*, A shell for glazing stuffs.

A قيقب *kaykab*, A saddle. A kind of wood whereof saddles are made. Leather with which saddle-bows are covered. The bit of a bridle.

A قيقبان *kaykabān*, A saddle. A kind of wood of which saddles are made.

A قيقة *kīkat*, The interior skin of an egg.

A قيقم *kaykam*, Wide-throated (man).

P قيقهن *kaykahin*, Name of a certain gum.

A قيقئ *kiʾkiʾ*, (or قيقئ *kīkiʾ*) The white of an egg, or the membrane in which it is enclosed.

A قيل *kayl*, (v. n. of قال for قيل) Sleeping at mid-day; also drinking then. Breaking off a bargain, putting an abrupt end to any negociation. A camel milked at noon. One who sleeps at noon. Milk drank at mid-day. (pl. اقوال *akwāl* and اقيال *akyāl*) A king of the Himyarit Arabs. (pl. of قائل *kāʾil*) Sleepers at noon-day. شراب للقيل *sharābun li'l kayl*, One whose constitution requires him to drink at mid-day. *Kayl* or *kīl*, A rupture; swelled testicle. *Kīl*, (v. n. of قال for قول) Speaking, saying, pronouncing. A word, speech, saying (especially in answer, قال *kāl* being used in the commencement of a discourse or by way of a question). قيل و قال *kīl u kāl*, Proposition and answer; conversation, dialogue, chitchat.

P قيل *kīl*, Pitch. Name of a vast desert.

A قيّل *kuyyal*, (pl. of قائل *kāʾil*) Those who sleep or take their siesta at noon. Speakers.

A قيلان *kīlān*, (pl. of قال *kāl*) Sticks, bandies, or clubs for striking in the game of قلة *kulat*.

A قيلة *kaylat*, A camel milked at noon.

A قيلع *kaylaʿ*, A woman who has large feet and a large stature.

P قيلقي *kaylakī*, Pearl-ashes, lye.

P قيلموس *kaylamūs*, Prudence, wisdom, caution.

P قيلوط *kaylūt*, A kind of leek.

A قيلولة *kaylūlat*, An afternoon's nap, siesta.

A قيم *kiyam*, (pl. of قامة *kāmat*) Pullies, blocks. (pl. of قيمة *kīmat*) Prices, values. Statures. Fathoms.

A قيّم *kayyim*, True. One who has charge of, who looks after; a guardian. A prince, chief. *Kuyyam*, (pl. of قائم *kāʾim*) Standers.

T قيماق *kaymāk*, (or قيماغ *kaymāgh*) Cream.

A قيمة *kīmat*, (pl. قيم *kiyam*) Price, value, worth. Estimation. Measure or stature (of a man). Steadiness, fixedness. *Kiyamat*, Resurrection.

A قيّمة *kayyimat*, (fem. of قيّم *kayyim*) Straight. القيّمة *al kayyimat*, The true religion, orthodoxy.

A قيمتي *kīmatī*, Valuable, high-priced, costly.

A قيموليا *kaymūliyā*, Slabs of white polished marble, on which fire makes no impression.

P قيمه *kīma*, Hashed meat.

P قيمه پلاو *kīma-pilāw*, A dish of meat and rice.

P قيمه شوربا *kīma-shorbā*, A sort of soup.

A قين *kayn*, (v. n. of قان for قين) Hammering (iron). Collecting together, adjusting. Repairing, composing, mending (broken pots or pans). Forming, framing, creating, adapting. Smithcraft. (pl. اقيان *akyān* and قيون *kuyūn*) A blacksmith. (pl. قيان *kiyān*) A slave, captive, servant. بنو القين *banū'l kayn*, (contracted to بلقين *balkayn*) Name of an Arabian tribe. سعد القين *saʿdu'l kayn*, A lie.

P قينا *kīnā*, A kind of purslain.

A قيناب *kaynāb*, A rapid effusion of blood.

A قينان *kaynān*, The parts of the feet of cattle to which the tether is fastened. Cainan, son of Enos, son of Seth.

A قينة *kaynat*, (pl. قيان *kiyān*) A maid-servant, female slave, singer, or musician. A tire-woman. Middle of the back between the haunches. Podex.

H قينچي *kaynchī*, Scissors. St. Andrew's cross.

A قينس *kaynas*, A bull.

A بنو قينقاع *banū kaynukāʿ*, (*kaynakāʿ*, or *kaynikāʿ*) A society of Jews that lived at Madīna.

A قينيّ *kayniy*, Of the tribe of Banū'l kayn.

A قيوء *kayūʾ*, (or قيوّ *kayūw*) One who vomits much. An emetic.

A قيود *kuyūd*, (pl. of قيد *kayd*) Chains, fetters, pinions. Obligations; laws. شروط و قيود صلح *shurūt u kuyūdi sulh*, Articles and conditions of peace.

A قيّور *kayyūr*, Of a mean origin, unknown as to pedigree.

A قيوس *kuyūs*, (pl. of قيص) Braying camels.

A قيوظ *kuyūz*, (v. n. 3 of قاظ for قيظ, irreg.) Bargaining with (any one) for the summer. (pl. of قيظ *kayz*) Midsummers, hottest months.

A قيول *kayūl*, Milk drank at mid-day.

A قيولة *kayūlat*, A camel which the owner keeps tied up for the purpose of drinking her milk at mid-day, or for the mid-day draught (قيل *kayl*).

A قيّوم *kayyūm*, Permanent, lasting. Stable, fixed, steady. Peerless, matchless. The eternal God. An appraiser, valuer.

A قيّوميّة *kayyūmīyat*, Permanency, stability.

A قيون *kuyūn*, (pl. of قين *kayn*) Blacksmiths.

P قيوند *kīwand*, A concreted oil drawn from the pistachio-nut.

A قيه *kīh*, (for وقيّة *wakīya*) An ounce.

A قيهل *kayhal*, (or قيهلة *kayhalat*) Countenance, face, aspect.

A قيّ *kaʾiy*, Who vomits much. An emetic.

ك

ك *kāf*, (called كاف تازي *kāfi tāzī* or كاف عربي *kāfi ʿarabī*) The twenty-second letter of the Arabic alphabet, and the twenty-fifth of the Persian. In arithmetic it expresses 20. In Persian writing it is frequently confounded with گاف *gāf*; but in some books, in order to mark this sound, it is written with three points, or a line over it thus, ڭ or ګ. This letter is interchangeable with ج *jīm*, خ *khā*, غ *ghayn*, ق *kāf*, and ه *he*.

P ك *ak*, (*i.e.* ك preceded by َ *fatha*) added to Persian nouns, forms diminutives, or denotes contempt: as, پسرك *pisarak*, A little boy, from پسر *pisar*, A boy. مردك *mardak*, A little man, or one of no value, from مرد *mard*, A man. It is also an expression of endearment: as, مامك *mā-mak*, Dear little mother. It is also employed pleonastically: as, شانه سرك *shāna-sarak*, (for شانه سر *shāna-sar*) The hoopoo, or crest-head.

A ك *ka* is an inseparable adverb of similitude prefixed to Arabic nouns or particles (never to pronouns), signifying, "As, like, so. As soon as. Because of, for." كالاوّل *ka'l awwal*, As at the first, like the first, as before. كأن *kaan*, As if. كذا *kazā*, So, thus: as, كرجل *ka rajulin*, Like a man; and others, which will be found in their alphabetical places. *Ka* (masc.), *ki* (fem.), is the affixed pronoun of the second person singular, having, with verbs or prepositions, a relative or personal signification, and a possessive or relative with nouns: as, ضربك *zarabaka*, He beat thee. كتابك *kitābuka*, Thy book.

A كاء *kās*, (v. n. of كأ for كوأ) Being weak and cowardly. *Kās*, (or كاءة *kāsat*) Weak, cowardly.

A كآبة *kaābat*, (v. n. of كئب) Being sad.

A كأب *kasb*, (v. n. of كئب) Desponding. Despondency, depression, grief.

A كاب *kāba*, (fut. يكوب *yakūbu*) He drank from a vessel having neither handle or spout.

A كأباء *kasbās*, Grief, sadness.

A كأبة *kasābat*, (v. n. of كئب) Being sad.

A كأبة *kasbat*, (v. n. of كئب) Being disconsolate, sad, melancholy. Grief, sadness.

P كابتره *kābtara*, Foolish discourse.

A كابح *kābih*, (pl. كوابح *kawābih*) A bird or other object of ill omen.

P كابخ *kābahh*, A condiment eaten with bread.

A كابد *kābid*, Any evil or inconvenience which a person endures, and against which he bears up.

A كابر *kābir*, Great, grand. توارثوا المجد كابرا عن كابر *tawārasū'l majda kābiran ʿan kābirin*, They inherited glory in an uninterrupted succession.

A كابس *kābis*, Prominent (tip of the nose), advancing towards the upper lip. (So-and-so came) running. Alone, separate from the rest.

P كابك *kābuk*, A bird's nest. A pigeon-house. A basket hung up in a house, in which domestic pigeons lay their eggs and rear their young. Old clouts sewed together, whereon bread is laid and baked in the oven.

P كابل *kābil*, Short. *Kābul*, Name of a country and of a city. Name of a musical instrument.

P كابلج *kāblij*, The little finger; the smallest toe.

P كابلي *kābilī*, Myrobalan. *Kābulī*, Kind of pea.

A كابليّ *kābuliy*, Short, dwarfish.

P كابليج *kāblīj*, The little finger. The smallest toe. A basket hung up in a court-yard for pigeons.

P كابن *kabin*, A marriage-portion.

P كابنه *kābina*, The eye.

A كابوس *kābūs*, Nightmare. Modus coeundi.

P كابوك *kābūk*, A bird's nest. A hen's nest. A pigeon-house. A kind of basket in which a pigeon lays her eggs. Old clouts sewed together, whereon bread is laid to be baked in the oven.

A كابول *kābūl*, A hunter's net.

A كابي *kābī*, Falling prostrate, prone. Elevated, exalted, high. Great. كابي الرماد *kābi'r ramād*, Very hospitable, one whose ashes form a high heap.

P كابيدن *kābīdan*, To dig. To excavate, hollow out. To scratch. To cleave asunder.

P كابيشه *kābīsha*, Saffron in the flower.

P كابيله *kābīla*, A mortar.

P كابين *kābīn*, Matrimony, or rather the ratification of it before the judge. A marriage-portion or settlement which a husband is obliged to pay to his wife if he divorces her without sufficient cause.

P كابيني *kābīnī*, A marriage-portion. كابيني زن كردن *kābīnīʾi zan kardan*, To assign or promise a portion or settlement to a woman before marriage.

P كات *kāt*, A kind of rice which, with one sowing, will yield crops for seven years. A drop. Name of a drug. Name of a city in Khurāsān, or, according to others, in Turkistān.

A كاتب *kātib*, (pl. كتبة *katabat* or كتاتيب *katātīb*) A writer, scribe. An amanuensis, copier, clerk, notary. One who stitches (leathern bottles). Learned. The planet Mercury. كاتب ازلي *kātibi azalī*, The eternal writer (*i. e.* God, whom they suppose to have written from all eternity every thing that was to happen till the end of time). P كاتب جان *kātibi jān*, An epithet of the Almighty. A كاتب الحروف *kātibu'l hurūf*, The writer of these lines. كاتب سر *kātibi sir*, (كاتب السرّ *kātibu's sirr*, or T سركاتبي *sir-kātibī*) A secretary. كاتب وحي *kātibi wahy*, Name of the caliph Othmān. كلّ كاتب جاهل *kull kātib jāhil*, Every scribe is a blockhead (implying that he who writes a fine hand is generally ignorant of every thing else).

P كاتبي *kātibī*, A kind of short-sleeved vest.

A كاتف *kātif*, Abhorring: one who abhors. A locust beginning to fly.

A كاتم *kātim*, Concealed, secret. A concealer. Absconding. A stitcher of leathern bottles. Noiseless (bow).

A كاتمة *kātimat*, Noiseless (bow).

P كاتوره *kātūra*, The headache. Astonished, stupefied, amazed. Astonishment, amazement. One who announces news.

P كاتوزي *kātūzī*, Religious, devoted to the service of God. The sacerdotal class, or the first of the four orders or castes into which Jamshed, an ancient king of Persia, divided his subjects.

A كاثّ *kāss*, That which sprouts up from the scattered grains left by the reapers. Self-sown grain.

A كاثبة *kāsibat*, (pl. اكثاب *aksāb*) The lower part of the withers of a horse.

A كاثر *kāsir*, Much, many.

A كاثعة *kāsiʿat*, Thick (lip). Turgid (gum).

A كاثم *kāsim*, Thick (mushroom).

A كاج *kasj*, (v. n. of كأج) Being very foolish.

P كاج *kāj*, A blow, box, slap. A wild pine-tree. Squint-eyed. Would to heaven! Name of a caravansera between Kum and Ray.

P كاجكي *kājakī*, Would to heaven that!

P كاجيره *kājīra*, A seed whence oil is extracted.

P كاچ *kāch*, A blow, cuff, slap on the nape of the neck. A varnish with which earthen vessels are glazed. Crown of the head. Would to heaven! كاچ خوردن *kāch khwurdan*, To receive a blow on the nape of the neck. To turn tail, to run away.

P كاچار *kāchār*, Household furniture.

P كاچال *kāchāl*, Household furniture.

P كاچره *kāchra*, Seed of bastard saffron.

P كاچغر *kāchghar*, Name of a city in Turkistān.

P كاچك *kāchak*, The crown of the head.

P كاچوره *kāchūra*, Seed of bastard-saffron.

P كاچول *kāchūl*, Wagging the hips in dancing or buffoonery.

P كاچه *kācha*, The chin. Joy, gladness.

P كاچي *kāchī*, Milk-pottage. A kind of sweetmeat. A sort of varnish with which earthen vessels are glazed over.

P كاچيره *kāchīra*, Seed of bastard-saffron.

P كاچيك *kāchīk*, An electuary or hard balls prepared from honey; syrup of raisins, or dry grapes.

P كاچينه *kāchīna*, Seed of bastard-saffron.

A كاح *kāh*, (pl. اكياح *akyāh* and كيوح *kuyūh*) The side of a mountain; also the hinder part, croup, or breadth of it.

A كاحبة *kāhibat*, Much. A multitude. Fire blazing into flame.

A كاحص *kāhis*, One who strikes with the feet. (pl. كواحص *kawāhis*) Obliterated (vestige).

A كاحط *kāhit*, Scarce, barren, without rain.

P كاخ *kākh*, A palace, villa, summer-dwelling; an apartment at the top of the house open to the front. An upper story. A tower, gallery, balcony, battlements, or any similar erection for the benefit of air or a prospect. Rain. Name of a town in Khurāsān. كاخ ماه *kākhi māh*, The sign Scorpio, and the first heaven or region of the moon. كاخ مشتري *kākhi mushtarī*, Mansion of Jupiter, *i.e.* the signs Sagittarius and Pisces. The sixth heaven.

A كاخ *kākh*, A hut or house without windows. (pl. كوخة *kiwakhat*) An upper apartment.

P كاخج *kākhij*, Rust, spot, stain, dirt.

P كاخر *kākhar*, Jaundice. Blight. Rain.

A كاخرة *kākhirat*, The lower part of the ring of the fundament.

P كاخوسته *kākhwusta*, Seed of bastard saffron.

P كاخول *kākhūl*, A variegated starling; the locust-destroyer.

P كاخه *kākha*, Rain. Jaundice. Winter.

A كاد *kad*, (v. n. of كاد) Being sad, disconsolate, and broken-hearted.

P كاد *kād*, Avidity, greediness.

A كاد *kād*, is often pleonastic: as, ما كاد يفهمه *mā kāda yafhamuhu*, He understood it not.

A كادّ *kādd*, One who labours, studies to gain.

A كأداء *ka,dā*, (A mountain) difficult of ascent. A dark night. Severity, adversity. Tyranny, cruelty. Grief. Prudence, fear, caution.

A كادح *kādih*, Studious, attentive, laborious.

A كادس *kādis*, (pl. كوادس *kawādis*) Any thing from which one takes an omen (as sneezing); especially a bad omen (as a deer appearing at your back).

A كادئ *kādi,*, Of slow growth, dwarfish.

A كادئة *kādi,at*, (Ground) slow in producing.

A كادية *kādiyat*, Hard earth in which vegetation is slow. Misfortune, adversity.

A كاذان *kāzān*, Large, fat, corpulent.

A كاذب *kāzib*, (pl. كذّب *kuzzab* and كواذب *kawāzib*) A liar. False. (A camel) failing to conceive. False (lightning not followed by rain). صبح كاذب *subhi kāzib*, The false dawn. قياس كاذب *kiyāsi kāzib*, A false syllogism. ناقل كاذب *nākili kāzib*, A false reporter.

A كاذبة *kāzibat*, (v. n. of كذب) Lying. A lie.

A كاذة *kāzat*, The groin. The flesh on the back of the thighs.

P كاذي *kāzī*, Name of a fragrant flower.

A كاذي *kāzī*, A sort of unguent. A certain fragrant plant. Red.

A كاذيّ *kāziy*, A certain tree whose flowers are used to give a perfume to ointment.

P كار *kār*, An action, work, thing, affair; business, occupation, labour, art, profession, trade, commerce. Effect, impression. Exigency, need. Tillage, agriculture. Strife. Contention, battle. A word. (participle of كاريدن *kāridan* or of كاشتن *kāshtan*) Labouring, acting. Sowing (land). An agent, operator. A sower. This word is much used in composition (but should not be confounded with گار *gār*). كار آب *kāri āb*, Excessive drinking. كار بستن *kār bastan*, To set to work, put in practice. To use, exert, apply. To obey, yield obedience. كار چراغ خلوتيان *kāri charāgh khalwatiyān*, Continually burning. The lighting up of a dark place. The manufacture of lamp-black. كار فرمودن *kār farmūdan*, To enjoin, order, give directions, oversee any work. To employ, make use of, adopt, put in practice. كار كردن *kār kardan*, To work, toil, labour, trade. To give effect, penetrate, pervade. كار گيا *kāri giyā*, A king. A prime-minister. Any one who commands, or is skilful in, business. Each of the four elements. كار و بار *kār u bār*, Negociation, transaction. Occupation. كار و كسب *kār u kasb*, (or جهد و كار *jahd u kār*) Labour and industry, any thing by which one gains daily bread. بكار آمدن *ba kār āmadan*, To be fit, proper, useful. بكار آوردن *ba kār āwardan*, To perform, execute, cause to take place. To bring to use. در كار بود *dar kār būd*, He was at work. در كارند *dar kārand*, They are useful. از كار رفته *az kār rafta*, Useless, powerless (limb). بد كار *badkar*, A bad action, an infamous business. حيله كار *hīla-kār*, A layer of snares, deceiver.

A كار *kār*, Wheat-laden vessels foundering at sea.

P كار آزمودة *kār-āzmūda*, (or كار آموز *kār-āmoz*) Skilful, expert, intelligent, practised.

P كاراسته *kārāsta*, Planks, building-materials.

P كاراسي *kārāsī*, Name of a whining little animal; also of a plaintive singing bird.

P كارافژول *kār-afjūl*, An overseer. A workman.

P كار آگاه *kār-āgāh*, Acquainted with the truth of any affair. Sagacious, penetrating, intelligent. One who brings news; a spy, informer. An astrologer. An historian. كار آگاهان *kār-āgāhān*, Clever people. Overseers.

P كار آگاهي *kār-āgāhī*, Knowledge of the matter.

P كار آمدني *kār-āmadanī*, Useful, serviceable.

P كارانيدن *kārānīdan*, To cause to labour or till.

P كاراوژول *kār-arjūl*, An overseer. A hireling.

P كاربا *kā-rubā*, (for كاه ربا *kāh-rubā*) Amber.

P كاربار *kār-bār*, Work, labour, or business.

P كارباري *kār-bārī*, A trader. A transacter of business, a manager, officer.

P كاربان *kārbān*, A string of camels, horses, or mules. A caravan, body of travellers. كاربانرا بست كردن *kārbānrā bast kardan*, To intercept a caravan.

P كاربرداري *kār-bardārī*, Undertaking a work.

P كاربند *kār-band*, Any one giving attention to any work or regulating himself properly. كاربند شدن *kār-band shudan*, To obey.

P كارپرداز *kār-pardāz*, Transacter of business.

P كارپردازي *kār-pardāzī*, Completion, management of work.

P كارپرورد *kār-parward*, One who thinks, works, or expends with propriety.

P كارپيچ *kār-pech*, A truss, pack, bundle. A wrapper in which an embroiderer folds up his work when he leaves off. One who makes up goods into bales.

A كارة *kārat*, A bundle of clothes. Any large quantity of corn.

P كارتن *kārtan*, A spider.

P كارتنه *kārtana*, A spider. *Kāratna*, Fenugreek.

A كارث *kāris*, Troublesome (business).

P كارچان *kārchān*, Thigh or rump of a bird.

P كارچوب *kār-chob*, The instrument by which the web is stretched when working. A weaver's loom. Embroidery. An embroiderer.

P كارچوبي *kār-chobī*, Embroidered.

A كارح *kārih*, (or كارحة) Windpipe of a man.

A كارخ *kārikh*, A conductor of water.

P كارخانجات *kār-khānajāt*, (Arabic pl. of كارخانه *kār-khāna*) Workshops.

P كارخانه *kār-khāna*, A shop, workshop, manufactory. A laboratory. An arsenal, dock-yard, or any place where public works are carried on. A great work. كارخانهٔ فلك *kār-khānaï falak*, The world. The sky.

P كارخانه دار *kār-khāna-dār*, Steward, butler.

P كارد *kārd*, A knife.

P كاردار *kār-dār*, Busy, occupied. A money-maker. One in office, a prime-minister. كارداران فلك *kār-dārāni falak*, The planets.

P كاردان *kār-dān*, Intelligent, skilful, expert, versed. A prime-minister. كاردان فلك *kār-dāni falak*, The planet Mercury. كاردانان فلك *kārdānāni falak*, The (seven) planets.

P كاردانك *kārdānak*, A bustard, crane.

P كارداني *kār-dānī*, Skill, experience, sagacity.

P كارد رسيدة *kārd-rasīda*, (A hide) touched, injured by the knife.

P كاردگر *kārdgar*, A cutler, knife-maker.

P كاردو *kārdū*, The flower of the palm-tree. A fragment, broken meat served up the second day. A pair of large shears (for clipping wool); sheep-shearing; a lock of wool.

P كارديدة *kār-dīda*, Experienced. A veteran.

P كارران *kār-rān*, (Business-driving) Skilful in business. A factor, agent, broker.

P كاررَوا *kār-rawā*, Useful, fit for use.

P كارروائي *kār-rawā,ī*, Usefulness. The carrying on a business; occupation, management, conduct.

A كارز *kāriz*, A preacher; a public crier.

P كارزار *kārzār*, A battle; engagement, conflict, combat. A field of battle.

P كارزارجاي *kārzār-jāy*, A battle-field.

P كارزارگاه *kār-zār-gāh*, The field of battle.

P كارزاري *kārzārī*, Warlike.

P كارژول *kārjūl*, An inspector of workmen.

P كارساز *kār-sāz*, Dexterous, skilful, clever. Consenting, agreeing, adapting. The Deity.

P كارسازي *kār-sāzī*, Dexterity. Preparation. Intrigue, under-hand practice, setting up false pretences for not settling an account, and the like.

P كارسان *kārsān*, A wooden chest or an earthen vessel, in which bread and sweetmeats are kept.

P كارسپردگي *kār-sipurdagī*, An intrusting of an affair; a commission.

P كارستان *kāristān*, The seat of action.

P كارشناس *kār-shināş*, Skilful in business.

P كارشناسان *kār-shināsān*, Wise, learned, intelligent, experienced men. Astronomers, astrologers.

P كارشناسي *kār-shināsī*, Knowledge of business.

P كارطلب *kār-talab*, Seeking action or work.

A كارع *kāriʿ*, Any one who goes into the water, whether he drinks or not.

A الكارعة *al kāriʿat*, A palm-tree near water.

P كارفرما *kār-farmā*, An emperor. A minister, commander, superintendant, any one vested with power. كارفرمايان دولت *kār-farmāyāni dawlat*, The ministers or grandees of the kingdom.

P کارکن *kār-kun,* Labouring. Impressive, effective. A director, manager. An operator. The registrar of the collections under a Zamindār.

P کارکني *kār-kunī,* Office of a کارکن *kār-kun.*

P کارگاه *kār-gāh,* A shop, workshop. A weaver's instrument supporting the web. The world. کارگاه فلك *kār-gāhi falak,* The world. The sky. کارگاه پرِ وسواس *kār-gāhi pur waswās,* The world. کارگاه کن فکان *kār-gāhi kun fakān,* The world and all that it contains. The laboratory of (Him who said), Be, and it was.

P کارگذار *kār-guzār,* A curator. Skilful.

P کارگذاري *kār-guzārī,* Discharge of duty. کارگذاري کردن *kār-guzārī kardan,* To achieve, perform.

P کارگر *kārgar,* One who labours in adjusting affairs; a skilful negociator, an intelligent man of business, one who penetrates to the foundation, and brings matters to bear with address. Any thing that takes effect (as a moving oration, medicine, penetrating sword). A workman. Effective. Quality, attribute. Description.

P کارگه *kār-gah,* A workshop.

P کارگیا *kār-giyā,* An emperor. An element.

P کارگیر *kār-gīr,* A man who superintends, undertakes, or bears the weight of any business. A cavern, cellar, vault. A kind of coarse cloth. A solid structure of stone, supporting or strengthening a house. کارگیر بنا *kār-gīr binā,* A stone building.

P کارمند *kārmand,* Performing work.

P کارنا آزمودگي *kār nā āzmūdagī,* Inexperience.

P کارنا آزموده *kār-nā āzmūda,* Inexperienced.

P کارنامه *kār-nāma,* A model, design, specimen, example, plan, draught. Any difficult or delicate handicraft which few can attain unto. A record of battles. A commentary, memoirs. A register, chronicle, date. کارنامه کردن *kār-nāma kardan,* To oblige, caress. To glorify, praise.

P کارنجك *kāranjak,* A large fresh cucumber.

P کارنده *kārinda,* Laborious, working. A manager, agent.

P کارنگ *kārang,* Joyful, glad. Eloquent.

P کاروان *kārwān,* A caravan, a large company of travellers or merchants. کاروان سراي *kārwān-sarāy,* A caravansera, a public building for the reception of caravans.

P کاروانك *kārwānak,* A crane, a heron.

P کارواني *kārwānī,* (pl. کاروانیان *karwāniyān*) One who forms part of a caravan.

P کاروژول *kār-wujūl,* A head man, superintendant, inspector, overseer. A workman.

P کارو کرد *kār u kard,* Business, trade, profession.

P کارو گر *kār u gar,* Prop, refuge. Design.

P کاره *kāra,* As much as a man can carry on his back (of faggots, straw, and the like).

A کاره *kārih,* One who abhors, detests, loathes, or abominates. Loath, averse, unwilling.

P کارها *kārhā,* (pl. of کار *kār*) Difficulties.

P کاري *kārī,* Sharp, acid. Vehement, impetuous. Effectual. An able wrestler. A champion. A warrior. کاري زخم *kārī zakhm,* (or زخم کاري *zakhmi kārī*) A deep wound. A mortal wound.

P کاریدن *kāridan,* To sow. To work. To saw.

P کاریز *kārez,* A subterraneous canal, a sewer; a ditch dug round a field to convey water.

P کاریگر *kārīgar,* An artisan, clever workman.

P کاریگري *kārīgarī,* Good work, workmanship.

P کارین *kārīn,* Far off, distant.

P کاز *kāz,* Shears, scissors, forceps, or any thing similar, or two-pronged. A pruning-hook. A branch. Branches on which old rags are hung to frighten wild beasts into the hunter's toils. A swing. The den of a wild beast. A hut built of wood, canes, or straw on the border of a sown field or melon-ground. A hermitage on a hill. Caverns in which, in some places, men or sheep are lodged in winter-time. A pine-tree. A slap, box, or cuff on the neck.

P کازرون *kāzarūn,* A city and country in Persia.

P کازره *kāzura,* Seed of bastard saffron.

P کازود *kāzūd,* Shears, scissors.

P کازه *kāza,* A house. A hut erected in the corner of a field or melon-ground. A bed-chamber built of wood and supported by columns. A hermitage on a hill. A malkin to terrify game into a net. A hunter's hiding-place. A canopy. A shady place.

P کازیره *kāzīra,* A small cauldron.

P کاژ *kāj,* (or کاژو) Squint-eyed. A pine-tree.

P کاژرون *kājarūn,* Name of a city in Persia.

P کاژغر *kājghar,* Name of a city in Turkistān.

P کاژه *kāja,* A residence. A hunter's lurking-place.

P کاژیره *kājira,* Wild saffron.

P کاس *kās,* A cup, goblet, bowl (especially when filled with wine). A hog. A large drum.

A کاس *kaʼs,* (pl. اکوس *akʼus,* کوس *kuʼus,* کاسات *kāsāt,* and کیاس *kiyās*) A cup filled with wine. A drinking-cup. Wine.

A کاسات *kāsāt,* (pl. of کاس *kaʼs*) Drinking-cups. Cups filled with wine.

P کاسان *kāsān,* A village near Samarkand.

P کاسانه *kāsāna,* A kind of bird of a reddish green colour found in Khūzistān.

A کاسب *kāsib,* A gainer, acquirer: one who toils for his bread. An artist, tradesman. An inquisitor. A receiver of fines. ابو کاسب *abū kāsib,* A wolf.

P کاست *kāst,* He diminished. Diminution. Loss, damage. A lie.

P کاست کار *kāst-kār,* A liar.

P کاستن *kāstan,* To lessen, diminish, damage, destroy. To finish.

P کاسته *kāsta,* Diminished, lessened.

P کاستي *kāstī,* Decrease, diminution.

P کاسج *kāsuj,* (or کاسجوك *kāsjūk*) A porcupine.

A کاسد *kāsid,* Worthless, deficient in quantity or quality, not selling or passing current, despicable, in no esteem. Dull of sale, unsaleable (goods). Dull, flat (market). Destitute, in debt. حیوان کاسد الاذعان *haywāni kāsidu'l izʻān,* An irrational animal.

A کاسر *kāsir,* (pl. کسّر *kussar*) A breaker. An eagle closing his wings when about to pounce. کاسر الحجر *kāsiru'l hajar,* (Stone-breaker) Saxifrage.

A کاسرة *kāsirat,* (fem. of کاسر *kāsir*) (pl. کواسر *kawāsir* and کسّر *kussar*) Breakers.

A کاسع *kāsiʻ,* (An animal) clapping the tail between the legs.

A کاسف *kāsif,* In a bad situation. Austere, frowning. Unfortunate, disastrous (day).

A کاسفة *kāsifat,* Eclipsed (sun).

P کاسك *kāsak,* A small goblet.

P کاسکینه *kāskīna,* Name of certain birds: as, a kind of swallow, the bee-eater, a green magpie.

A کاسل *kāsil,* Slow.

P کاسمو *kās-mū* or *mo,* (or کاسموي *kās-mūy* or *moy*) Hogs' bristles. The whiskers of the wolf or fox. Hair about the pubes. Inexperienced, ignorant. Improper, unsuitable, useless, trifling.

P کاسن *kāsan,* A village near Samarkand.

P کاسني *kāsnī,* Endive, white succory. The sunflower. *Kāsanī,* An inhabitant of کاسن *kāsan.*

P کاسو *kāsū,* (or کاسوره *kāsūra*) A cloth at the end of a pole with which bakers damp their ovens.

A کاسور *kāsūr,* A village green-grocer.

A P کاسه *kāsa,* A cup, goblet. A plate, saucer, large or small, of brass, wood, or clay. Porcelain. The body of a violin or guitar. A large drum. The firmament. The sun. The earth, world. کاسهٔ آتشین *kāsaʼi ātishīn,* The sun. کاسهٔ بلوط *kāsaʼi ballūt,* The cup of an acorn. کاسهٔ پنیر *kāsaʼi panīr,* (or کاسهٔ جغرات *kāsaʼi jughrāt*) The full moon. کاسهٔ درویشان *kāsaʼi darweshān,* (or کاسهٔ یتیمان *kāsaʼi yatīmān*) (Beggar's or orphan's dish) A kind of drinking-cup, in the form of a ship on one side, with a groove or a spout on the other. A certain star, Corona Borea, or Ariadne. کاسهٔ رود *kāsaʼi rūd,* Name of a certain river. کاسهٔ سر *kāsaʼi sar,* The skull. کاسهٔ سرنگون *kāsaʼi sar-nigūn,* (The inverted bowl) The heavens. کاسهٔ سفالین *kāsaʼi sifālīn,* An earthen jug or bason. کاسه شدن *kāsa shudan,* To labour, strive. To search, inquire. To be curved, bent. کاسهٔ گردان *kāsaʼi gardān,* The heavens. کاسهٔ گردون *kāsaʼi gardūn,* The sun. کاسهٔ مینا *kāsaʼi mīnā,* (or کاسهٔ نگون *kāsaʼi nigūn*) The sky. کاسهٔ همسایه *kāsaʼi hamsāya,* A portion of meat sent to one's friends. سیه کاسه *siyah-kāsa,* Mean, sordid, avaricious.

P کاسه بند *kāsa-band,* Mender of cups or dishes.

P کاسه پشت *kāsa-pusht,* A tortoise. The sky.

P کاسه تن *kāsa-tan,* Hump-backed. Destitute of all capacity or ability. A corpse.

P کاسه دوز *kāsa-doz,* A mender of pots and pans.

P کاسه سرنگون *kāsa-sar-nigūn,* (One whose cup is inverted) Liberal, hospitable.

P کاسه سیاه *kāsa-siyāh*, A miser.

P کاسه شکنك *kāsa-shikanak*, A green magpie.

P کاسه کباب *kāsa-kabab*, Meat drest in a pot.

P کاسه کجا برم *kāsa kujā baram*, A parasite, who, by means of a common friend, obtains an introduction to a person's table.

P کاسه گاه *kāsa-gāh*, A band of music. The place at the porch of a palace where the drums are beaten at stated intervals.

P کاسه گر *kāsagar*, A maker of plates and dishes. A drummer. Name of a note in music; also of the inventor of it. The sixth line on the cup of Jam.

P کاسه گردان *kāsa-gardān*, A beggar. A cup-bearer. Pass the bowl. Again, anew, afresh.

P کاسه گردون *kāsa-gardūn*, A cup-bearer.

P کاسه گري *kāsagarī*, The manufacture of cups, plates, dishes, or porcelain.

P کاسه ليس *kāsa-lis*, (Plate-licker) A parasite, feast-hunter. A flatterer. A beggar. A miser. A mean, low fellow.

P کاسه نواز *kāsa-nawāz*, A drummer.

A کاسي *kāsī*, Clothed, clad, dressed.

P کاش *kāsh*, Would to God! I wish to heaven! The city of Kāshān.

A کاش *kaₑsh*, (v. n. of کأش) Eating.

P کاشان *kāshān*, A winter-habitation. Name of a city in Irāk.

P کاشانه *kāshāna*, A small house. A hall, dining-room, or parlour. A gallery, balcony, portico, lodge. A stove. A winter-dwelling. A bird's-nest.

P کاشتن *kāshtan*, To turn up or cultivate the earth, to labour, plough, sow. To disappoint, render hopeless. To turn away, avert.

P کاشته *kāshta*, Sown, laboured. Seed.

A کاشح *kāshih*, Secret enemy; dissembling foe.

A کاشد *kāshid*, (pl. کشد *kushud*) A man who labours to support his family. One who is kind to, and mingles much with, his relations.

A کاشر *kāshir*, Modus coeundi. A grinner.

P کاشغر *kāshghar*, A city in Turkistān.

A کاشف *kāshif*, A discoverer, revealer.

A کاشفة *kāshifat*, (pl. کواشف *kawāshif*) Manifestation, disclosure, apocalypse.

P کاشك *kāshk*, Would to heaven! کاشکي *kāshake*, May it happen! God send; would to heaven!

P کاشکي دانستمي *kāshake dānistame*, O would that I knew!

A کاشم *kāshim*, The assafœtida-plant.

P کاشمر *kāshmar*, Name of a city in Turkistān. Name of a village in Khurāsān, where there formerly stood a cypress of great size said to have been planted by Zoroaster. It was cut down and conveyed to Baghdad by order of the caliph Mutawakkil.

P کاشني *kāshnī*, Succory, endive.

P کاشو *kāshū*, The crupper of a horse.

P کاشه *kāsha*, Wild saffron. Ice. A straw hut erected in the corner of a sown field.

P کاشي *kāshe*, Would to heaven *Kāshī*, Painted and glazed tiles, with which they cover the insides of baths or houses. Of the city of Kāshān.

P کاشي پز *kāshī-paz*, A potter.

A کاص *kaₑs*, (v. n. of کأص) Overpowering, subjugating, mastering. Eating. Eating or drinking much. Extremely patient in regard to eating and drinking, one who fares hardly.

A کاص *kās*, Extreme avarice. A quick pace.

A کاظم *kāzim*, (pl. کظم *kuzzam*) (A camel) that ruminates not. Silent. *Kāzim*, (or کاظم الغيظ *kāzimu'l ghayz*) One who restrains his anger.

A کاظمة *kāzimat*, Name of a place.

A کاظي *kāzī*, Dry (ground).

A کاع *kāₑ*, The wrist-bone (especially the outer side, *i.e.* the side next the little finger). Fearful.

A کاعب *kāₑib*, (pl. کواعب *kawāₑib*) (A girl) with swelling breasts. A swelling breast.

A کاعي *kāₑī*, One who takes to flight.

P کاغ *kāgh*, Fire. That which ruminant animals bring up to be masticated, the cud. The rattling noise of beads shaken in a goblet. Complaint, lamentation. A moor-hen, coot. Croak of a raven.

P کاغاله *kāghāla*, A seed whence oil is extracted.

A P کاغذ *kāghiz* or *kāghaz*, (کاغد *kāghid* or *kāghad*) Paper. A letter. A charter or patent, presented by the kings of Persia to those whom they mean to honour; by virtue of which, the governors of every district through which a کاغذ دار *kāghiz-dār* travels must supply him, the moment he presents it, with carriages and every necessary to which his rank is entitled. P کاغذ چسپانيده *kāghizi chaspānīda*, (or کاغذ وصلي *kāghizi waslī*) Pasteboard. کاغذ دفتر *kāghizi daftar*, A sheet upon which the revenue-accounts are drawn out. کاغذ زر *kāghizi zar*, Gilt paper. Gold leaf. Any paper in which gold-beaters envelope gold and silver leaf. A roll of gold coin. A draft. A کاغذ نشاف *kāghizi nashshāf*, Blotting-paper.

P کاغذ باد *kāghaz-bād*, A paper-kite.

P کاغذ خانه *kāghiz-khāna*, A paper-mill.

P کاغذگر *kāghizgar*, A paper-maker or dealer.

P کاغذي *kāghizī*, A paper-maker or vender. A stationer. A paper-case. Any thing covered with a thin skin, as nuts or almonds. Delicate, thin, soft. A kind of lime. A writer.

P کاغذين جامه *kāghizīn-jāma*, Weakness, destitution. Cries of the oppressed, lamentation.

P کاغك *kāghak*, Happiness, joy, content.

P کاغ کاغ *kāgh kāgh*, Caw or croak of a raven.

P کاغله *kāghla*, A seed whence oil is extracted.

P کاغنه *kāghuna*, (or کاغنو *kāghnū*) A venomous worm of a reddish-black colour. A certain bird which flies in the night. Cantharides.

G کاغولتا *kāghūltā*, Golgotha.

P کاغه *kāgha*, An idiot, a simpleton.

A کاغي *kāghī*, One who takes to flight, routed.

P کاف *kāf*, A fissure, breach, crack. The science of alchymy. One who manages well his affairs. Cleave thou. (in compos.) Cleaving, splitting.

A P کاف *kāf*, The letter ك *k*. A کاف لو لاك *kāfi law lāka*, An epithet of Muhammad. کاف و لام *kāf u lām*, A man bald from disease. Vanity; an idle saying or empty boasting. A lie. Play, amusement. کاف و نون *kāf u nūn*, Two chapters of the Kur'ān so called. بقلم الكاف و النون *bi kalami'l kāf wa'n nūn*, With the pen of omnipotence. (The letters ك *kāf* and ن *nūn* being abbreviations of كن فيكون *kun fa yakūnu*, Be, and it is).

A کاف *kāff*, A preventer, a hinderer. Preventive. One who refrains or abstains.

A کافة *kāffat*, All, universal, whole, total. کافهٔ انام *kāffaₑi anām*, (or بريّت *barīyat*) All mankind. (or کافهٔ معشر بشر *kāffaₑi maₑshari bashar*) The whole human race. کافهٔ رعايا *kāffaₑi raₑāyā'*, All the subjects. کافهٔ علوم *kāffaₑi ₑulūm*, All the sciences.

A کافة *kāffatan*, All of them (came).

A کافت *kāfit*, A certain cavern wherein thieves lay up their spoils.

P کافتن *kāftan*, To split, cleave. To dig, bore. To examine, investigate.

P کافته *kāfta*, Cleft, riven. Searched, examined.

P کافتيده *kāftīda*, Cleft.

A کافر *kāfir*, (pl. کفّار *kuffār*, کفرة *kafarat*, and کفار *kifār*) One denying God. Ungrateful, unthankful for divine favours. An infidel, pagan, impious wretch. A Caffre. A mistress. Armour, a coat of mail. Dark (cloud). Darkness (night). A farmer, a sower. The envelope of the flowers of the palm-tree. The sea. A mighty river. Low or level ground trodden. A plant. A large valley. Land far from habitations. One who wears a garment over his coat of mail. کافر ماجرا *kāfiri mā jarā'*, A denier of facts, quarrelsome fellow. کافر النعمة *kāfiru'n niₑma*, Ungrateful, unthankful for benefits.

P کافرانه *kāfirāna*, Infidel-like, impiously.

A کافرة *kāfirat*, (pl. کوافر *kawāfir*) Unbelieving, impious, unthankful, ungrateful (woman).

A کافرتان *kāfiratāni*, (dual) Buttocks. Groins.

P کافرکيش *kāfir-kesh*, Infected with infidelity.

A کافرنعمت *kāfir-niₑmat*, Ungrateful, thankless.

A کافرنعمتي *kāfir-niₑmatī*, Ingratitude.

A کافل *kāfil*, (pl. کفّل *kuffal*) One who fasts often, and imposes silence upon himself whilst fasting. One who maintains, or manages, the affairs of another, an administrator. One who undertakes to support, attend to, or look after. A sponsor, surety.

P کافور *kāfūr*, Flowers of the palm-tree or vine; also their envelope. Camphor. A fountain in Paradise. Any thing white. Name of a tyrannical king put to death by Rustam. کافور باريدن *kāfūr bāridan*, To snow. کافور جودانه *kāfūri jawdāna*, A very fragrant sort of camphor. کافور خوردن *kāfūr khwurdan*, Eating camphor (an expression used to imply deficiency of virility).

A کافور *kāfūr*, (pl. کوافیر *kawāfīr* and کوافر *kawāfir*) The flowers, buds, spathe, or envelope of the flowers of the palm-tree. Name of a plant bearing a fragrant blossom like the camomile. Camphor, the produce of a tree growing in the island of Formosa. (The camphor-tree is large enough to overshadow a hundred horsemen). The bud of the vine.

P کافور بار *kāfūr-bār*, (Raining camphor) Any thing cold or fragrant. Snowing.

P کافوري *kāfūrī*, Pure, an emblem of whiteness. Camomile-flowers. Title of an eunuch. شمع کافوري *shamʻi kāfūrī*, A wax-candle, camphorated wax.

A کافه *kāfih*, The commander of an army.

A کافي *kāfī*, Sufficient, enough. Efficacious. Entire, perfect. کافیك *kāfīka*, Let it suffice thee.

P کافیدن *kāfīdan*, To dig. To split. To seek.

P کافیشه *kāfīsha*, Saffron in the flower.

P کافیلو *kāfīlū*, A kind of slender-stemmed Arabian thorn, to which slim persons are compared.

P کاك *kāk*, Biscuit. Dry bread. Bread indifferently baked. Any thing dried (especially meat). A thin man or beast. The moon on the fourteenth night. The pupil of the eye. A man. A boy, infant. A master, preceptor. Small, minute. Empty. Name of a fortress in Azarbayjān.

P کاکا *kākā*, An old slave. An elder brother. Dry fruit. A paternal uncle. A schoolboy's satchell.

A کاکاء *kaʻkāʻ*, Pusillanimous. Very impatient and greedy. The running of a thief.

A کاکاة *kaʻkaʻat*, (v. n. of کاکا Q) Being weak, cowardly. Retiring from fear. Congregating, being collected together.

P کاکاو *kākāw*, A boy's game.

P کاکبان *kākbān*, Saffron in the flower.

P کاکره *kākira* or *kākara*, Pellitory.

P کاکریز *kākrez*, Name of a purplish colour.

P کاکریزي *kākrezī*, Purple-coloured.

P کاکل *kākil*, Flowers growing in water. *Kākul*, (or کاکول *kākūl*) Origany, marjoram. The herb alkali. A salt, bitter plant. A kind of wheat. A lock of hair, of boys, men, or horses; a forelock.

P کاکله *kākula*, Name of a champion of Irān.

P کاکنج *kāknaj*, Winter-cherry. Nightshade.

A کاکنج *kākanaj*, A gum produced by a tree in the mountains of Herat.

P کاکو *kākū*, Mother's brother. Name of a man.

P کاکوتي *kākūtī*, A kind of origany, marjoram.

P کاکوش *kākosh*, The violet.

P کاکول *kākūl*, A ringlet, a forelock.

P کاکولي *kākūlī*, Origany. Penny-royal.

P کاکویه *kākūya*, A mother's brother.

P کاکي *kākī*, Name of ماکان *mākān's* father.

P کاکي *kākī*, An aunt.

P کاکیا *kākiyā*, A spider's web.

P کاکیان *kākiyān*, Seed of wild saffron.

P کاگره *kāgara*, Name of a medicine.

P کاگل *kāgal*, A pen, a hollow reed.

P کال *kāl*, Unripe fruit. A gourd. A leek. A kind of rose. Breaking the line of battle and flying, put to flight. Confused, mixed. Rout, dispersion, flight; a clandestine flight. Cracked ground. A ditch. Bent, crooked. A place.

A کال *kaʻl*, (or کالة *kaʻlat*) (v. n. of کال) Transferring, buying or selling a debt.

A کال *kāll*, Dull, thick, blunt: hebetated.

P کالا *kālā*, Silk cloths, and in general any kind of household furniture. (zand and Pāz.) Cry, wail.

P کالار *kālār*, A torrent, very deep, and so wide that a man or horse cannot leap over. Slabs or flag-stones, with which they cover sewers or subterraneous water-courses.

P کالاشکن *kālāshkan*, A kind of sweetmeat.

A کالاوّل *ka'l awwal*, As before, like the first.

P کالب *kālab*, A mould. Confection of fruits.

A کالب *kālib*, A pack of dogs. Keeper of dogs.

P کالبد *kālbud* or *kālbad*, The body of a man or animal. The heart. A model, figure, form, mould. Unripe, sour fruit. A finger-joint. کالبد تن *kālbudi tan*, Stature, size, bulk, mould of the body. کالبد یارانه *kālbudi yārāna*, Any thing preserved in vinegar, syrup, or honey.

P کالبدگر *kālbudgar*, A sculptor. A founder.

P کالبوت *kālbūt*, A bird fastened to a net to decoy others, a lure.

P کالبوي *kālboy*, (or کالبو *kālbo*) Astonished, surprised. Ignorant, foolish.

P کالجار *kāljār*, War, battle. Rice-grounds.

P کالجوش *kāljosh*, Spoon-meat, food of dervishes.

A کالح *kālih*, Adverse (fortune). White. Cold (winter). Frowning, crabbed, austere (man). One who grins and shews his teeth.

A کالد *kālid*, Old (cluster of dates).

P کالفته *kālufta*, (or کالفه) Smitten with love.

P کالك *kālak*, An unripe melon. A cupping-glass. A kind of sandal. Hideous.

P کالم *kālum*, A woman whose husband is dead, or who has been divorced.

P کالنج *kālanj*, A medlar.

P کالنجر *kālanjar*, Name of a fort in Hindūstān from whence they bring indigo.

P کالنجه *kālinja*, A ring-dove: quest: magpie.

P کالو *kālū*, (or کالوب *kālūb*) The body. A model, mould, figure.

P کالوج *kālūj*, (or کالوچ *kālūch*) The little finger. A pigeon.

A کالوخ *kālūkh*, Name of a stinking plant: leek.

A کالوز *kālūz*, (pl. کوالیز *kawālīz*) One who goes to water armed (in case of attack).

P کالوس *kālūs*, Foolish, stupid.

P کالوسك *kālūsak*, A bean.

P کالوشه *kālūsha*, A cauldron. A dish peculiar to the people of Delam, made of rice, vetches, beet, and vinegar, over which they pour coriander-seed and mint pounded and fried in butter.

P کالوني *kālūnī*, Origany.

P کاله *kāla*, Household furniture or utensils. Worldly goods or gain. A yarn-reel. A large hank, clew, or heap of cotton, of which they make sewing-thread. An unripe melon or cucumber. A dry hollow gourd full of wine. Ground prepared for sowing. کاله بر خرش بنه *kāla bar kharash bi nih*, Place the goods upon his ass, *i.e.* Let him know who he is.

P کاله دان *kāladān*, A basket in which women keep thread. A wardrobe. A casket.

P کالي *kālī*, A guard, keeper.

A کالئ *kāliʻ*, Purchased on credit. Earnest.

P کالیا *kālyā*, An unripe melon.

P کالیار *kālyār*, A sandal, slipper. Spittle. Galls, oak-apples.

P کالیدن *kālīdan*, To be routed, put to flight. To rout, defeat. To dissolve, scatter, cut in pieces. To be confounded, disturbed. To have the hair stand on end (from terror). To grow grey (the hairs). To have scales or scurf on the head. To have dishevelled or neglected hair.

P کالیده *kālīda*, One whose hair is dishevelled, or stands up when terrified. Mixed. Any thing covered with dust or earth.

P کالیو *kālīv*, (or کالیوه *kālīva*) Foolish, mad, insane, crazy. Astonished, bewildered. Ignorant. Deaf. Beautiful. Intrepid. Liberal-minded. Unsuitable, inconvenient. Ostentation, boasting. Accident, event. A narrative. Dispersion. Quiet, rest. Headache.

P کالیوس *kālyūs*, Crumbled bread, with buttermilk, walnuts, and spices (on which dervishes live).

P کام *kām*, Desire, wish. Design, intention, pursuit. The palate. The uvula. The mouth. Chewing well, digesting well. Masticated food. Any thing which assists digestion. A bar, fastening of a door. کام خاریدن *kām khārīdan*, To long for, hanker after. کام فرو آمده *kām faro āmada*, Disappointed in one's wishes. بکام رسیدن *ba kām rasīdan*, To arrive at perfection. To attain one's object.

P کام بخش *kām-bakhsh*, Giving the enjoyment of one's desires. Name of Awrangzīb's youngest son.

P کامبخشي *kām-bakhshī*, Fulfilment of one's wishes. Liberality. Power.

P کامبین *kām-bīn*, Fortunate, happy, rich, content, successful in every undertaking or wish, gratified. Absolute, powerful.

P کامته *kāmata*, A town in Kutch (India).

P کام جو *kām-jo* or *jū*, Seeking enjoyment.

A کامخ *kāmakh*, (from P کامه *kāma*) A sourish kind of stomach-water for creating an appetite and promoting digestion. Sauce, condiment. Ordure.

A کامد *kāmid*, Sad, sorrowful. One who conceals or smothers his grief.

P کامران *kām-rān*, Successful in every undertaking, fortunate, happy, blest. Voluptuous.

P كامراني *kām-rānī*, Happiness, felicity, pleasure, delight. August, royal. Absolute, despotic. Fortune, prosperity, success. كامراني كردن *kām-rānī kardan*, To live in the gratification of one's desires.

P كامرو *kāmrū*, The city of Kāmrūp, situated between Bengal and Khotā, famed for its magicians.

P كامروا *kām-rawā*, Enjoying; gratified.

P كامروائي *kām-rawāī*, Fruition, enjoyment.

P كامزن *kām-zan*, Having an intention or desire (especially to go any where). Striking the palate.

P كام طبع *kām-tabʻ*, Greedy, covetous.

P كام فيروز *kām fīroz*, Name of a city in Persia.

P كامگار *kāmgār*, One who accomplishes whatever he wishes. Powerful. An absolute monarch. Fortunate, happy. A hunting-bird which infallibly secures its prey.

P كامگاري *kāmgārī*, Power. Happiness.

P كامگذار *kām-guzār*, One who has the means of gratifying all his desires.

A كامل *kāmil*, (pl. كملة *kamalat*) Perfect, complete, full, plenary, entire. Folio-sized (paper). Learned. A kind of verse containing the measure متفاعلن *mutafāʻilun* six times repeated. A name common to several celebrated horses. كامل الوزن *kāmilu'l wazn*, Of full weight. كامل العيار *kāmilu'l ʻiyār*, Of perfect standard.

P كام لگام *kām-ligām*, That part of a bridle which touches the palate, the bit.

A كاملية *kāmiliyat*, The worst sect of the روافض *rawāfiz*, (called from their leader ابوكامل *abū kāmil*).

A كامن *kāmin*, Concealed, hidden, latent.

P كام نا كام *kām nā kām*, Willing or unwilling. Necessarily.

P كامو *kāmū*, A particular kind of skin.

P كامود *kāmūd*, Simple (opposed to compound).

P كامور *kāmwar*, Successful according to his wishes. (Any thing) worthy of one's choice.

P كامورة شده *kāmwara shuda*, Renowned. Successful.

P كام وريژ *kāmwarij*, Wish, purpose, intention.

P كاموس *kāmos*, Name of an ally of Afrāsyāb.

P كامون *kāmūn*, Cummin-herb or seed.

P كامه *kāma*, Acid bread soured with vinegar or meat dressed with it. A sourish kind of stomach-water for creating an appetite and promoting digestion. Milk or butter-milk boiled together. A confection, electuary; preserved fruits; pickles. Desire, wish, will, intent, object, scope, aim. A bridle. Coral. Name of a township or district in Kābul, containing one hundred villages or hamlets.

A كامه *kāmih*, A blundering man, going he knows not where.

A كامي *kāmī*, Armed: cased in armour. Warlike, brave.

P كامياب *kām-yāb*, One who obtains what he desires. Prosperous.

P كاميابي *kām-yābī*, Fruition, prosperity.

P كاميدن *kāmīdan*, To desire, wish.

P كامين *kāmīn*, The root of galangale.

A كأن *kaʼn*, A being firm and strong.

P كان *kān*, A sheath. A mine or quarry. Digging, excavating. The backside. (for كه آن *ki ān*) Because that, since he.

A كان *kāna*, It was, existed, became, happened. كان له *kāna lahu*, He possessed. It became him, it was lawful or expedient for him. كان لي *kāna lī*, It was in my power. I had. كان للشيء *kāna li'l shayʼ*, He was equal to the thing. كان علی امر *kāna ʻala' amrin*, He was engaged about a business. كان علی التأبي *kāna ʻala't taʼabbī*, He refused. كان علی شفا حفرة *kāna ʻala' shafa' hufratin*, He was on the edge of a gulf of fire.

A كأنّ *kaʼanna*, As if, as though. Verily.

P كانا *kānā*, Foolish, stupid, senseless. The stem of a bunch of grapes or dates. A part of a bunch of grapes.

P كاناز *kānāz*, That part of the stem of a bunch of grapes or dates which joined the main branch or tree. A bunch of dates.

A كانب *kānib*, Full from repletion.

P كانجي محال *kānjī-mahāl*, Licensed stews.

P كاند *kānd*, Sugar, sugar-candy.

P كاندر *k'andar*, (for كه اندر *ki andar*) For within.

A كانس *kānis*, (A deer) hiding under a cover.

A كانسه *kānsa*, (prop. كاسه *kāsa*) A cup, bowl, glass, goblet.

P كانسه گر *kānsagar*, A cup or bowl-maker.

A كانع *kāniʻ*, (A nose) beaten flat on the face. (A prisoner) confined tight with thongs.

A كانعة *kāniʻat*, (pl. of كوانع *kawāniʻ*) A nose beaten flat on the face.

A كانفة *kānifat*, A fortification, bulwark, obstruction, a means of protection.

P كان كن *kān-kan*, A miner. Name of Farhād.

A كانم *kānim*, A certain race of negroes, of whom there was a celebrated poet called الكانميّ *al kānimiy*.

P كانور *kānūr*, A fruit-basket.

A كانون *kānūn*, (pl. كوانين *kawānīn*) A fire-grate, a chafing-dish, or place for holding fire. Any man to whom others look up, or whose words are generally attended to. Heavy, dull, phlegmatic, whose society is shunned. Form, manner, habit, fashion, rule, law. Name of two Syrian winter months. كانون الاوّل *kānūnu'l awwal*, December, and كانون الآخر *kānūnu'l ākhir* (or كانون الثاني *kānūnu's sānī*) January.

A كانونة *kānūnat*, A chafing-dish, any place for holding fire. Grave, heavy, dull (woman).

P كانه *kāna*, Price of provisions. Dissimulation, hypocrisy. A place for sitting down.

A كأنّه *kaʼannahu*, As if he (or it), as if indeed.

P كاني *kānī*, Mineral.

A كاني *kānī*, (pl. كانون *kānūn*) One who calls any thing by a figurative or metonymical name.

P كانيرو *kānerū*, Mezereon.

P كان يسار *kān yasār*, Opulent, wealthy.

P كاو *kāw*, Excavation, hollowing out, digging. Examination, investigation, disputing about the truth of any thing. (in compos.) Digging, excavating. A digger, excavator. Bold, intrepid, warlike.

A كأو *kaʼw*, Fearing, a being cowardly.

P كاواك *kāwāk*, Hollow. ميان كاواك *miyān kāwāk*, Hollow in the middle.

P كاواكي *kāwākī*, Hollowness. Presumption.

A كاوان *kāwān*, Name of an island.

P كاواني درفش *kāwānī-dirafsh*, Kāwa's standard.

P كاوانيدن *kāwānīdan*, To cause to dig.

P كاورك *kāwark*, A bird's nest. *Kāwarak*, Name of a plant resembling a cucumber.

P كاوش *kāwish*, Digging. Investigation, inquiry, meditation.

P كاوك *kāwak*, Empty, hollow.

P كاوكاو *kāwkāw*, A tap with a pick or sharp-pointed tool. Speed, diligence, haste. Investigation, inquiry, search. Perturbation. In small pieces.

P كاوكلور *kāw kalūr*, A man's yard.

P كاول *kāwul*, A table-decker, sewer. Wild-leek. Kābul.

P كاونجك *kāwanjak*, A fresh cucumber.

P كاونده *kāwinda*, An examiner, investigator.

P كاونه *kāwuna*, A Spanish fly. A fire-fly.

P كاووس *kāwūs*, (or, according to the modern orthography, كأوس *kāʼus*) Name of an ancient king of Persia. Pure. Elegant, graceful. Radical. Firm, constant. Generous, noble. Strengthened by divine aid. A subduer, conqueror. A spark. Light, splendour, corruscation. Swiftness, impetuosity.

P كاووك *kāwūk*, A bird's nest.

P كاوول *kāwūl*, A taster, table-decker.

P كاوه *kāwa*, The famous smith of Ispahān who defeated the usurper Zahhāk. A bag of musk.

A كاوي *kāwī*, Caustic.

A كاوياء *kāwiyāʼ*, The cautery, a hot instrument applied to the skin, leaving an impression or scar.

P كاوياني درفش *kāwiyānī-dirafsh*, Kāwa's banner.

P كاويدن *kāwīdan*, To examine, to investigate, search. To dig, excavate, hollow out. To plough. To dispute, contend, struggle, wrestle, strain every nerve. To mix, disturb, trouble. To fight, make war.

P كاويش *kāwīsh*, A milk-pail.

P كاوين *kāwīn*, A dower.

P كاوينك *kāwīnak*, A year.

P كاه *kāh*, Straw. Hay. كاه مكي *kāhi makkī*, Camels'-hay, bog-rush. (in comp., from the verb كاستن *kāstan*) Diminishing: as, لذّت كاه *lazzat-kāh*, Weakening or destroying pleasure.

A كاهب *kāhib*, Dark red or brown (camel).

P كاهبان *kāhbān*, A keeper of a straw-bin.

P كاهبن *kāh-bun*, Stubble. A stubble-field.

P كاه خانه *kāh-khāna*, A straw-bin, hay-loft.

P كاهدان *kāhdān*, A hay or straw-loft.

P كاهربا *kāh-rubā*, (or كاهرباي *kāh-rubāy*) Yellow amber (from its attracting straws). Gum of the walnut-tree; also of a tree resembling the pistachio.

P كاهريز *kāh-rez*, (or كاهريزه *kāh-reza*) Straws or dust blown into the eyes. Chaff.

P كاهسته *kāhista*, Diminished.

P كاهش *kāhish*, Diminution. Consumption.

P كاه فروش *kāh-farosh*, A seller of straw.

P كاه فروشي *kāh-faroshī*, A dealing in straw. كاه فروشي كردن *kāh-faroshī kardan*, To deal in straw.

P كاهكشان *kāh-kashān*, The milky-way.

P كاهگل *kāh-gil*, Clay and straw for plastering.

P كاهگير *kāh-gīr*, Stubborn mule; unbroke beast.

P كاهگيري *kāh-gīrī*, Restiveness, stubbornness.

A كاهل *kāhil*, Slow, tardy, languid; indolent, idle, lazy, negligent. Sick. One to whom people look, and on whom they depend. Middle-aged. (pl. كواهل *kawāhil*) The space between the shoulders, withers. ذو كاهل *zū kāhil*, Boiling with rage. شديد الكاهل *shadīdu'l kāhil*, Difficult of access.

A كاهلا *kāhilā*, Ailing, sick, indisposed.

P كاهلانه *kāhilāna*, Slowly.

A كاهل مزاج *kāhil-mizāj*, Indolent.

A كاهلي *kāhilī*, Sloth, inactivity. Slowness, tardiness, languor, indolence, cowardice. Sickness.

A كاهن *kāhin*, (pl. كهنة *kahanat* and كهّان *kuhhān*) A soothsayer, augur, prophet, priest. An administrator, agent, factor.

P كاهنگان *kāhangān* The milky-way.

P كاهو *kāhū*, Lettuce. A bier (of the Pārsīs).

P كاهوكب *kāhūkub*, A bier, a coffin.

P كاهي *kāhī*, Greenness. Name of a dish.

P كاهيدن *kāhīdan*, To be diminished. To languish, pine. To diminish.

A كاي *kāsy*, A paining by words.

A كأيّ *ka'ayy*, How many?

A كائد *kāsid*, Fraudulent, deceitful. A deceiver.

A كائع *kāsiʿ*, (pl. كاعة *kāʿat*) Timid, fearful.

A كائن *kāsin*, Being, existent. A creature. كائناً من كان *kāsinan man kān*, Be he who he may, whoever he was, whatever it was.

A كأيّن *ka'ayyin*, (or كائن *ka-a-in*) How many?

A كائنات *kāsināt*, (pl. of كائنة *kāsinat*) Beings, creatures, existences. The universe. زبدهٔ كائنات *zubdaṣi kāsināt*, The cream or most excellent of creatures (title of Muhammad).

A كائنة *kāsinat*, Existing. A creature. A novelty, event, accident. Any thing new or original, that never existed before.

P كاينه *kāyina*, (or كابينه *kāyīna*) Turn not away your eyes from me.

P كب *kab*, The inside of the cheek.

A كبّ *kabb*, (v.n. of كبّ) Inverting, overthrowing, tumbling on the ground, throwing one upon his face. Winding thread into clews. Being heavy. Kindling a fire with the herb كبّ *kubb*. *Kubb*, A kind of bitter and salt herb.

A كباء *kiba'*, (pl. أكباء *akbās*) Dung, filth, rubbish, sweepings; a dunghill.

A كباء *kabās*, A spring of water. Scattered rays of the moon. *Kibās*, (pl. كبي *kuba'*) Wood of aloes. *Kubās*, Elevated, exalted, high.

A كباب *kabāb*, Meat cut in small pieces and roasted with onions and eggs stuck on skewers. Meat. Roast meat. P كباب ترازران آهو *kabābi tar az rānī āhū*, Flakes of snow. كباب كردن *kabāb kardan*, To roast. A *Kubāb*, Waving hills of sand. A herd of camels. A flock of sheep. Mud, clay. Earth, moist and dewy.

A كبابة *kabābat*, (P كبابه *kabāba*) Cubebs.

P كباب چيني *kabāb chīnī*, Cubebs.

P كبابخانه *kabāb-khāna*, A kitchen, cook's shop.

A كبابي *kabābī*, Fit to be roasted. Roasting. One who roasts, a roaster. A maker of kabobs.

A كباث *kabās*, Ripe fruit of the tree اراك.

A كباخ *kubākh*, Greatness, pomp, haughtiness.

A كباد *kibād*, (v. n. 3 of كبد) Waxing callous to evil, enduring it with all its inconveniences. *Kubād*, Disease of liver, liver-complaint.

P كباده *kabāda*, A weak bow for practising.

P كبار *kabār*, A man who brings wood from the forest for sale.

A كبار *kibār*, (pl. of كبر *kabar*) Capers. (pl. of كبير *kabīr*) Great. Grandees, nobles: men renowned for wealth and knowledge. *Kubār*, Great, huge.

A كبّار *kibbār*, (v.n. 2 of كبر) Making or esteeming great. Magnifying God by saying الله اكبر *allāh akbar*, God is great! *Kubbār*, Great, huge, very large. (vulgarly for كبر *kabar*) Capers.

A كبارة *kabarat*, The being large and bulky.

P كباره *kabāra*, A kind of basket. A bee-hive. A sort of earthenware-cup.

A كبّاريّة *kubbārīyat*, Greatness.

A كباس *kubās*, Great and large-headed (penis). One who wraps his head in his garments and sleeps.

A كباسة *kibāsat*, A bunch of dates.

A كباش *kibāsh*, (pl. of كبش *kabsh*) Rams, tups.

A كباص *kubās*, (or كباصة *kubāsat*) (Camels or asses) strong to labour.

P كباك *kabāk*, (also كبال *kabāl*) A rope made of the fibres of the palm-tree.

A كباكب *kabākib*, (pl. of كبكب *kubkub*) Compact, closely built. *Kubākib*, Compact, closely built.

A كبان *kubān*, A camel's disease. (in the dialect of Yaman) Millet.

A كبائر *kabāsir*, (pl. of كبيرة *kabīrat*) Great, large, enormous things. Mortal sins.

A كبائس *kabāsis*, Clusters, bunches.

A كبب *kubab*, (pl. of كبّة) Balls of thread.

A كبة *kubat*, (pl. كبون *kubūn*) Sweepings.

A كبّة *kabbat*, A blow, collision. A crowd. One heat at a race. One attack or charge in battle. Severity (of winter). A shot discharged into the air. *Kubbat*, (pl. كبب *kubab*) A herd of horses. A troop, body of men. A large and valuable camel. A clew or hank of thread.

P كبت *kabt* or *kibt*, A bee.

A كبت *kabt*, (v. n. of كبت) Throwing prostrate with the face downwards. Bringing under, subjugating, humbling, disgracing. Driving back, repelling with wrath and severity. Turning, averting. Grieving.

P كبتا *kabitā*, A kind of sweetmeat.

P كبتر *kabtar*, A pigeon.

A كبث *kabs*, (v. n. of كبث). Being tainted, stinking (meat). Rendering sad and melancholy. *Kabis*, Corrupted.

P كبج *kabj*, Self-praise. Conveniency, utility. Part, portion. A stick for stirring beer. A hook with which they remove ice. A little garden. *Kabj*, (or كبجه *kabja*) A docked ass. A beast of burden having the lower part of the throat swelled.

P كبچ *kabch*, A beast, the lower part of whose mouth is swelled.

P كبچه *kabcha*, A ladle, skimmer: spatula, trowel.

A كبح *kabh*, (v. n. of كبح) Reining in (a horse). Keeping back, hindering from business. Striking with a sword. *Kubh*, A kind of dark-coloured whey.

P كبد *kabd*, (or كبدا) Solder, glue. Haste. Fat.

A كبد *kabd*, (v. n. of كبد) Striking in, or aiming at, the liver. The liver. The middle of the vault of heaven. Cutting, distressing (cold). *Kibd* or *kabid*, (pl. كبود *kubūd* and اكباد *akbād*) The liver. كبد السماء *kabidu's samās*, The midst of heaven. *Kabad*, (v. n. of كبد) Being in pain, suffering from a diseased liver. Air, atmosphere. The midst of heaven. The centre of a sand-hill. Adversity. Severity (of winter). Bigness of the belly. *Kabid*, The belly. The interior cavity of a thing. The bulging part of a bow, or a cubit's length from the part which the archer grasps. A side.

A كبداء *kabdās*, (fem. of اكبد *akbad*) (A woman) corpulent, especially about the middle. Slow-paced. Thick-handled (bow). (A sand-hill) large in the middle. A hand-mill. The middle of the celestial vault.

A كبدة *kabdat*, A spell or philtre to conciliate love.

A كبر *kabara*, (fut. يكبر *yakburu*) He was old. He exceeded in age by a year.

P كبر *kabr*, (in Pehlevi) A corslet of iron. *Kabar*, Capers.

A كبر *kibr*, An enormous crime. Pomp, pride, haughtiness. Magnitude, magnificence. Power. *Kibr* or *kubr*, Nobility, eminence. The greater or better part. *Kubr*, (v. n. of كبر) Being large and bulky. Great, greater, greatest. *Kubr* or *kuburr*, The chief of a family, the first degree of kindred, the nearest of kin of the head of a family. *Kabar*, (pl. كبار *kibār* and اكبار *akbār*) Capers. A drum. *Kibar*, (v. n. of كبر) Reaching to an advanced age, being full of years. Being large and bulky. Full age. A great age. *Kubar*, (pl. of كبري *kubra'*) Great. Majors, (in syllogisms).

A كبراء *kubarā*ء, (pl. of كبير *kabīr*) Great.

P كبربا *kabar-bā*, Broth seasoned with capers.

A كبرة *kabrat* or *kaburat*, A great age. *Kibrat*, The last born son or daughter. A great crime. Greatness. Pride. The head (of a family). *Kabarat*, One caper (pickle).

A كبّرة *kuburrat*, The head of a family. The nearest kin to the head of a family.

A كبرتة *kabratat*, (v. n. of كبرت Q) Anointing with sulphur or brimstone (كبريت *kibrīt*).

A كبرثل *kabarsal*, A male beetle. A beetle. A young beetle.

P كبرك *kabarak*, Name of a thorny plant.

P كبروا *kabar-wā*, Meat dressed with capers.

P كبره *kabra*, A coat of mail.

A كبري *kubra'*, (fem. of اكبر *akbar*) (pl. كبر *kubar*) Greater. Great (city). The major proposition of a syllogism.

A كبرياء *kibriyā*ء, Grandeur, magnificence, power, excellence. Pride, haughtiness. A name or an attribute of God.

A كبريائي *kibriyāī*, Almightiness.

A كبريّة *kabariyat*, Food dressed with capers.

A كبريت *kibrīt*, Fine (gold or silver). Sulphur, brimstone. A match dipped in sulphur. A ruby. كبريت احمر *kibrīti aḥmar*, The philosopher's stone.

P كبريتي *kibrītī*, Of the colour of sulphur.

A كبس *kabs*, (v. n. of كبس) Filling up (a well or river). Lying once with. Wrapping up one's head in a garment. Alighting at the foot of a mountain. Coming under a mountain. Assaulting suddenly and surrounding (a house). *Kibs*, Earth filling up a well or river. A large head. A house of mud. Root, origin. هو في كبس غنيً *huwa fī kibsi ghinan*, He is in the source of wealth.

A كبّس *kubbas*, Hard, granitic (mountains).

P كبست *kabast*, The dog or ass-cucumber.

P كبستو *kabastū*, (or كبسته) The bitter gourd.

A كبش *kabsh*, (pl. اكبش *akbush*, كباش *kibāsh*, and اكباش *akbāsh*) A ram. A battering ram. A prince, chief, leader.

A كبع *kabع*, (v. n. of كبع) Prohibiting, restraining. Cutting off. Counting out money, separating the good from the bad. *Kubaع*, A sea-camel; hence يا وجه الكبع *yā wajha'l kubaع*, O face of a sea-camel (applied to an ill-favoured woman).

A كبعثاة *kabaعsāt*, A sort of female hernia.

P كبك *kabk*, The hand; palm of the hand. كبك شكستن *kabk shikastan*, To lose a track.

A كبكاب *kabkāb*, A coarse and fat date.

A كبكابة *kabkābat*, Fat and jolly (woman).

A كبكب *kibkib* or *kabkab*, A sort of game. *Kibkib* or *kubkub*, A troop. A ball of thread. A large camel. Weight, heaviness. *Kubkub*, (pl. كباكب *kabākib*) Compactly-built (man).

A كبكبة *kabkabat*, (v. n. of كبكب Q) Overturning, throwing (one) prostrate on the ground. *Kabkabat* or *kubkubat*, Any thing thrown or shot to a height. *Kibkibat*, *kubkubat*, or *kabkabat*, A troop. A ball of thread. A large camel. Weight, heaviness. *Kubkubat*, A troop closely wedged together.

P كبكبه *kabkaba*, The noise made by the feet of camels, horses, or men.

P كبكنجير *kabkanjīr*, A sling. A woodcock.

A كبكوب *kubkūb*, (or كبكوبة *kubkūbat*) A troop. A crowd pressed closely together.

P كبگ *kabg*, A partridge. كبگ دري *kabgi darī*, A beautiful kind of partridge. كبگ رقّاص *kabgi raḳḳāṣ*, A prancing horse. كبگ كر *kabgi kar*, A woodcock. كبگان بزم *kabgāni bazm*, Cup-bearers.

A كبل *kabl*, (v. n. of كبل) Fettering (a prisoner). Keeping fast bound in jail. Deferring payment of a debt. Granting (a debtor) a respite or time for paying a debt. (pl. كبول *kubūl*) A large chain or fetter. Very furry (garment). The edge or lip of a leathern bottle folded down. *Kibl*, (pl. كبول *kubūl*) A large and heavy fetter. *Kabal*, (A skin) with short hair or wool.

P كبل *kabal*, A garment made of sheep-skin.

A كبن *kabn*, (or كبون *kubūn*) (v. n. of كبن) Sewing (cloth or a leathern bottle) which has been turned in. Keeping back, withholding. Deviating from. Cleaving to the ground, being low-bodied (a deer). Causing to disappear, be invisible, or not to be found. Turning away (a benefit from any body). Turning in the lip of a bucket. Running gently, coming short, breaking down (a horse). Having the upper part of the front teeth inclining inwards. Becoming fat. Being cowardly, retreating, turning back. The edge of a leathern bottle turned in and sewed. *Kaban*, (v. n. of كبن) Being thick and fat (the finger).

A كبنّ *kubunn*, A miser. (See كبنّة *kubunnat*.)

A كبنة *kubnat*, A sort of game.

A كبنّة *kubunnat*, Covetous, avaricious; contracting the body, shrugging the shoulders, looking down (as a miser when applied to). Dry bread.

A كبو *kabw*, (or كبوّ *kubūw*) (v. n. of كبا for كبو) Falling on the face. Rising (as dust). Failing (as a flint to strike fire). Refraining from, breathing hard (a horse). Being high, piled up (live coals). Running without sweating (a horse). Collecting (rubbish) by sweeping. Withering (a plant). Emptying (a flagon).

A كبوة *kabwat*, (v. n. of كبا for كبو) Keeping back, standing off, on account of something shameful or dirty. Being high (ashes). Being covered with ashes (fire). Dust. A dusty colour. A falling flat on the face. A flint which fails to strike fire. *Kubwat*, A chafing-dish. A censer.

P كبوتر *kabūtar*, A pigeon, dove. كبوتر تيز پر *kabūtari tez-par*, A swift-flying pigeon. كبوتر حرم *kabūtari ḥaram*, Mecca pigeons which are not allowed to be killed. A lady of high birth whose hand it is difficult to obtain. كبوتر شلواري *kabūtari shalwārī*, A sort of pigeon plumaged about the feet. كبوتر نامه بر *kabūtari nāma-bar*, A carrier-pigeon. كبوتر نياز *kabūtari niyāz*, A sort of pigeon.

P كبوتر باز *kabūtar-bāz*, Playing or gaming with pigeons, laying bets on their flight.

P كبوتر بان *kabūtarbān*, A breeder, feeder, or trainer of pigeons: a pigeon-fancier.

P كبوتر بچه *kabūtar-bacha*, A young pigeon. An unripe poppy-head, wrapped in pease-meal, and fried in butter or oil.

P كبوتر خانه *kabūtar-khāna*, A pigeon-house.

P كبوتر دم *kabūtar-dam*, Kissing and billing (as lovers). *Kabūtar-dum*, (Pigeon's tail) The end of a turban-sash or waistband standing straight out.

P كبوتروار آب *kabūtarwār āb*, Fordable place.

A كبوثل *kabawsal*, A kind of locust.

P كبود *kabūd*, Blue. Name of a mountain.

A كبود *kubūd*, (pl. of كبد *kibd* or *kabid*) Livers.

P كبودان *kubodān*, Coriander-seed. Name of a village in the dependencies of Nishābūr.

P كبود پشت *kabūd-pusht*, (كبود حصار *kabūd-ḥiṣār*, or كبود طشت *kabūd-tasht*) The sky.

P كبود چشم *kabūd-chashm*, Blue or grey-eyed.

P كبودر *kabūdar*, An animalcule living in water, which the small fry devour. A heron.

P كبودوش *kabūdwash*, A blue colour.

P كبوده *kabūda*, The gnat-tree. A kind of tough willow growing spontaneously.

P كبودي *kabūdī*, A turban with a blue sheep-skin border. كبودي كبود *kabūdī kabūd*, Of a deep blue.

P كبودي رنگ *kabūdī-rang*, Blue, azure.

P كبوس *kabos*, Crooked, bent.

A كبوع *kubūع*, Submission, obsequiousness.

P كبوك *kabūk*, A female bird (there being, it is said, no male of the species) which flocks and pairs with birds of different kinds. A certain water-fowl.

A كبّوك *kabbūk*, A lark.

A كبول *kubūl*, (pl. of كبل *kabl* or *kibl*) Fetters.

A كبولاء *kabūlā*ء, A kind of thick broth.

A كبون *kubūn*, (v. n. of كبن) Running gently; failing or breaking down in running (a horse). Stillness, quiet. (pl. of كبة *kubat*) Sweepings.

P كبه *kaba*, *kuba*, or *kubba*, A cupping-glass. A rising, a swelling.

P كبي *kabī*, An ape, a baboon.

A كبيٰ *kuba'*, (pl. of كباء *kibā*ء) Aloe-woods.

P كبيتا *kubaytā*, A sweetmeat made of almonds, pistachios, walnuts, and oil of sesame. A cake made of sesame and sugar. *Kubītā*, A cake made of fine flour, honey, and sesame-oil.

P كبيتك *kubaytak*, A tool for notching millstones.

P كبيته *kubīta*, A sort of sweetmeat.

A كبيث *kabīs*, Stinking, tainted (meat).

P كبيچه *kabīcha*, An animal whose lower jaw is swollen. An instrument for scratching the back, a curry-comb.

P كبيد *kabīd*, Solder. Glue.

A كبيداء *kubaydās*, (or كبيداة *kubaydāt*) The higher parts of the sky, the zenith.

P كبيدن *kabīdan*, To put out of its place.

P كبيده *kabīda*, Meal baked in the oven. A dish made of barley, rice, and butter. Coarsely-ground (wheat or barley).

A كبير *kabīr*, (pl. كبار *kibār*, مكبوراء *makbūrās*, and كبراء *kubarās*) Great. Large in body. Great in power and wealth. Heavy, serious. One arrived at full age, completely grown, elder. P كبير شدن *kabīr shudan*, To grow up (to man's estate), to become strong or great. A فساد كبير *fasādi kabīr*, An enormous sin, capital crime. وادي الكبير *wādī'l kabīr*, (The Great River) The Guadalquiver.

A كبيس *kabīs*, A kind of date. A little hollow ornament filled with scent, and hung on the neck.

A كبيسة *kabīsat*, Intercalary, embolismal. P سال كبيسه *sāli kabīsa*, Leap year.

P كبيكج *kabīkaj*, A kind of wild-parsley, and a deadly poison.

P كبين *kabīn*, A dower, marriage-portion.

P كپ *kup*, The mouth.

P كپاك *kapāk*, A wagtail.

P كپان *kapān*, A balance with a scale at one end and a stone weight at the other. A steelyard.

P كپچه *kapcha*, A ladle, skimmer.

P كپراس *kaprās*, Joke, jest, wit, humour.

P كپوك *kapūk*, A female bird (there being, it is said, no male of the species) which pairs with birds of different kinds.

P كپّه *kappa* or *kuppa*, A cupping-glass.

P كپي *kapī* or *kappī*, An ape.

P كپيدن *kapīdan*, To rob, seize, ravish.

P كت *kat*, A subterraneous canal, common sewer. A royal throne. The throne of the kings of India. *Kit*, (for كه تو *ki tu*) Who thou, that thou. (for كه ترا *ki turā*) What to thee? Who to thee?

A كتّ *katt*, (v. n. of كتّ) Whispering in the ear. Injuring, compelling. Making sad, depressing, humbling. Numbering, counting, computing; comprehending in a number. Boiling (as a pot). Lean (man or woman). Braying softly (a camel).

P كتا *katā*, (in zand and Pāz.) A writing, mandate.

A كتاب *kitāb*, (v. n. of كتب) Writing. Describing. (pl. كتب *kutub* or *kutb*) A book, volume; writing. A letter, missive, despatch. A commission, command. Law, a statute. Release, discharge. Fate. An inkstand. الكتاب *al kitāb*, The book. The Bible. The Kur'ān. الكتاب المستطاب *al kitābu'l mustatāb*, (or كتاب الله *kitābu'llāh*) The holy or the divine book, the book of God (used by Christians to denote the Scriptures, and by Muhammadans the Kur'ān). اهل الكتاب *ahlu'l kitāb*, Instructed in the sacred writings, *i.e.* A Christian or a Jew. امّ الكتاب *ummu'l kitāb*, The first chapter of the Kur'ān. غير كتابي *ghayr kitābī*, Without a book, *i.e.* a heathen, as having no scripture.

A كتّاب *kuttāb*, (pl. كتاتيب *katātīb*) A small arrow with which boys learn to shoot. A writing-school. (pl. of كاتب *kātib*) Writers, secretaries, scribes. Learned men.

A كتابة *kitābat*, (v. n. of كتب) Writing, describing, inscribing. An inscription, motto, title of a book. A painting (on the walls of houses). An epitaph. A tax. The ransom of a slave.

P كتاب خانه *kitāb-khāna*, A library. A study. A bookseller's shop.

P كتابدان *kitābdān*, A book-case.

P كتاب فروش *kitāb-farosh*, A bookseller.

P كتابون *katābūn*, Name of a man and woman. The daughter of Cæsar and wife of Gushtāsb.

A كتابيّ *kitābiy*, Belonging to a book. A Jew.

A كتأة *katsat*, The herb rocket.

A كتاتب *katātib*, (pl. of كتّاب *kuttāb*) Writing-schools. Small arrows with which boys learn to shoot. (pl. of كاتب *kātib*) Scribes.

H كتاره *katāra*, A spear, javelin. A short sword.

A كتاع *kitāʿ*, (v. n. 3 of كتع) Fighting, assaying to kill. (pl. of كتعة *katʿat*) Pieces, bits. *Kutāʿ*, Any body (is not here).

A كتاف *kitāf*, (pl. كتف *kutf*) A chain, fetter, tether. A cord for tying the hands behind the back. *Kutāf*, A pain in the shoulder-blades.

A كتّاف *kattāf*, Shaky in the shoulder-blades.

A كتال *katāl*, Thickness of the body. Flesh. The soul. Any thing needful, as food and raiment. Bad diet. *Kitāl*, (v. n. 3 of كتل) Fighting. *Kutāl*, A mountain or hill-pass, a ghaut.

P كتاله *katāla*, A short spear.

P كتام *katām*, A place raised on pillars six or seven yards high, where they sleep on account of the dampness of the ground.

P كتّان *kattān*, Linen, flax. رنگ كتّان *rangi kattān*, Of the colour of linen, grey (as in French gris-de-lin). *Kattān* or *katān*, A kind of garment made of straw. *Kattān* or *kitān*, A grain from which they extract oil: linseed.

A كتّان *kattān*, Water-moss. Foam or rubbish floating on water. Flax. Linen. *Kuttān*, A red biting insect.

A كتائب *katāsib*, (pl. of كتيبة *katībat*) Armies, battalions, troops, cohorts, squadrons.

A كتب *katb*, (v. n. of كتب) Writing, describing. Ordering, enjoining. Knowing. Joining, binding firmly. Closing the mouth of a leathern bottle with a stopple. Sewing a leather bottle or bag with two thongs. Stitching up behind (a camel) so as not to afford access to the male. Putting an iron ring through the nostrils of a camel in order that she may not scent the young of another, but may be induced to suckle it as her own. *Kutub* or *kutb*, (pl. of كتاب *kitāb*) Books. Letters. كتب سلطانيه *kutubi sultānīya*, The royal books, divine books, word of the Lord. كتب سماوي *kutubi samāwī*, The holy Scriptures. كتب موسيٰ *kutubi mūsa'*, The books of Moses. دار كتب *dāri kutub*, A library.

A كتبة *kitbat*, The requesting of another to write a letter that one is dictating. Description, inscription, the writing of a book. *Kutbat*, A stitch, a suture. A leathern thong with which they stitch up any thing. *Katabat*, (pl. of كاتب *kātib*) Writers.

P كتب خانه *kutub-khāna*, A library.

P كتبستان *kutubistān*, A library, a museum.

A كتبيّ *kutubiy*, A bookseller, bibliopolist.

A كتبيّة *kutubīyat*, A library.

A كتة *kattat*, Verdure. *Kuttat*, The worst kind of property or camels. Goats of the worst sort.

A كتح *kath*, (v. n. of كتح) Eating to the full. Throwing any thing so that it penetrates. Striking the skin and making an impression. Devouring the grass (locusts). Driving dust and scattering it over a person (wind). Any thing thrown and hurting the body. A slight scratch from grit or gravel.

P كتخ *katakh*, Butter-milk. Milk, butter-milk, and salt. *Katikh*, A mixture of sweet and sour.

P كتخدا *kat-khudā*, (for كدخدا *kad-khudā*, Master of the house) A lord-lieutenant, a viceroy, vicegerent, vicar, locum tenens, deputy. A rich or great man, the chief inhabitant of a place. (astrologically) The lord of the ascendant, the predominant star at a person's birth.

P كتخدا پسند *kat-khudā-pasand*, Common, low.

P كتخدائي *katkhudāsī*, The office of overseer. State of a householder, house-keeping. Marriage.

P كتخ شير *katakh-shīr*, Butter-milk mixed with milk and butter.

A كتد *katad*, Name of a star. *Katad* or *katid*, (pl. اكتاد *aktād* or كتود *kutūd*) The place of union of the shoulders, or part between the shoulders and the back. The withers of a horse.

A كتر *katr*, A small camel-litter in which the ladies travel. Quantity, quality. Dignity, estimation. Numbered. The middle of any thing. A wall enclosing a place where dates are dried, or where corn is stacked. A staggering pace like that of a drunken man. *Ka, ki*, or *katar*, A camel's bunch. *Kitr*, A cupola or arched building resembling it. A tomb of the old tribe of عاد *ʿād*.

P كتران *katrān*, Liquid pitch.

A كترة *katrat*, A camel's bunch.

P كترونتن *katrūnitan*, (in zand) To remain still.

P كتس *katas*, (in zand and Pāzand) Small.

A كتع *kutʿ*, (v. n. of كتع) Going off with. Being active, alert, quick in the despatch of business. Being contracted, drawn together. Fleeing, running away. Swearing. Running. *Kataʿ*, (v. n. of كتع) Being active, stirring in business. Drawing one's self together, restraining one's self. *Kitaʿ*, (pl. كتع *kutaʿ*) A small piece. *Kutaʿ*, (pl. كتعان *kitʿān*) A fox's cub (especially the worst). A wolf. Mean, abject, sordid, despicable. A light, active, nimble man. Clever, expert, intelligent. Contracted within (himself). (pl. of كتعاء *katʿāʾ*) All. (pl. of كتعة *kutʿat*) The ends of glass phials. Small buckets.

A كتعاء *katʿāʾ*, A female slave, maid-servant. *Katʿāʾ*, (or جمعاء كتعاء *jamʿāʾ katʿāʾ*) All, the whole.

A كتعان *kitʿān*, (pl. of كتع *kutaʿ*) Fox-cubs. Wolves. Mean.

A كتعة *katʿat*, (pl. كتاع *kitāʿ*) A bit, piece. *Kutʿat*, (pl. كتع *kutaʿ*) A small bucket. End of a glass phial.

P كتغ *katagh*, Sour milk dried.

A كتف *katf*, (v. n. of كتف) Striking on the shoulders. Galling the shoulders of a horse (a saddle). Tying one's hands behind his back. Drawing tight the curved timbers of a camel's saddle one upon the other. Hooping a barrel or other vessel. Being high in the withers (a horse). Walking softly, moving the shoulders in walking. Being kind and easy; favouring. Loathing, detesting, nauseating. *Kitf*, (v. n. of كتف) Flying and compressing his wings towards his hinder parts (a bird). *Kitf, katif*, or *kataf*, (pl. كتفة *kitafat* and اكتاف *aktāf*) The shoulder, or the shoulder-blade. لوح كتف *lawhi kitf* (or *katif*), The shoulder-blade, omoplate. P كتف برزدن *kitf bar zadan*, To shrug the shoulders, to rejoice. A *Kutf*, (pl. of اكتف *aktaf*) Wide-shouldered. Lame in the shoulder. *Kataf*, (v. n. of كتف) Being broad-shouldered. Being broad in the withers (a horse). Walking softly. Breadth of shoulder. A halting from dislocation or pain of the shoulders.

A كتفاء *katfāʾ*, (fem. of اكتف *aktaf*) Slip-shouldered (mare).

A كتفان *kitfān*, (v. n. of كتف) Flying and compressing his wings towards his hinder parts (a bird). *Kitfān* or *kutfān*, A locust beginning to fly. *Katafān*, A quick step.

A كتفة *kitafat*, (pl. of كتف *katif*) Shoulders. Shoulder-blades.

P كتف سارة *kitf-sāra*, The withers of a horse. The shoulder-blade.

P كتك *kuth*, A stick. *Katak*, A species of ugly short-legged sheep (peculiar to Bahrayn).

H كتك *katak*, Cuttak. The crab-apple.

A كتكات *kathāt*, A blabber, a prater.

P كتكار *katkār*, (or كتكر *katkar*) A carpenter.

A كتكت *kathat*, The note of a bustard. *Kutkut*, A sort of game.

A كتكتة *kathatat*, (v. n. of كتكت Q) Laughing low. Taking short and quick steps.

P كتكتو *kuthutū*, A kind of origany.

A كتكتى *kuthuta'*, A sort of game.

P كتكن *kat-han*, A well-digger.

P كتكنه *kathina*, Portion of a farm re-let. كتكنه كردن *kathina kardan*, To re-farm, or re-let.

P كتكنه دار *kathina-dār*, An under tenant.

P كتگر *katgar*, (or كتگار *katgār*) A carpenter.

A كتل *katl*, (v. n. of كتل) Binding, imprisoning. *Katal*, (v. n. of كتل) Being viscous, adhering. Grossness of body.

P كتل *kutal*, A led horse for parade. A high hill. The skirts of a hill. شتر كتل *shuturi kutal*, A led camel.

A كتلة *kutlat*, (pl. كتل *kutal*) A mass of clay. A quantity of dates in a lump. A little ball of gum. *Kutlat* or *katlat*, A piece of meat.

P كتلجيان *kutaljiyān*, (or كتلچيان *kutalchiyān*) The king's domestics, those who have the care of pitching the royal tent.

P كتم *katm* or *katam*, Leaves of woad or indigo.

A كتم *katm*, (v. n. of كتم) Hiding, lurking, absconding; covering, veiling, concealing. Suppressing (anger). P كتم سر كردن *katmi sir kardan*, To keep a secret. كتم شهادت كردن *katmi shahādat kardan*, To refuse to give testimony. *Kutm*, Indigo-leaf. *Katam*, A species of herb which, mixed with privet, makes a tincture for the hair. *Kutum*, (pl. of كتوم *katūm*) Camels which conceal their pregnancy by not cocking their tails.

A كتمان *kitmān*, (v. n. of كتم) Concealing, keeping in. Retaining liquor (a leathern bottle). كتمان اسرار *kitmāni asrār*, The keeping of secrets. *Kutmān*, A species of herb which, combined with hinna, makes a dye for the hair.

A كتمة *katmat*, A word in reply. *Kitmat*, Secrecy, concealment. *Kutamat*, (A man) who conceals his thoughts.

A كتن *katan*, (v. n. of كتن) Being dirty, nasty (as a house with smoke, hands with blackness, the lips of cattle with eating viscous herbage). Nastiness, filth. Viscosity. Soil at the root of a palm-tree. *Katin*, Dirty, grimy (leathern bottle). *Katin* or *kitn*, A large platter or dish.

P كتنبر *katambar*, (or كتنبل) Slow. A glutton.

A كتنة *kitnat*, A certain fragrant tree.

A كتو *katw*, A going with short steps.

P كتو *katū*, Name of a bird which devours gravel. *Kutū*, A cotton-pod.

A كتوال *kutwāl*, The porter of a castle. A kind of officer of police or magistrate, who apprehends rogues, inspects taverns and houses of promiscuous entertainment, and determines disputes of inferior moment.

P كتوالي *kutwālī*, The office of kutwāl.

A كتود *kutūd*, (pl. of كتد *katad*) Interscapulæ.

A كتوع *kutūʿ*, (v. n. of كتع) Travelling far off.

A كتول *katūl*, High (ground).

A كتوم *katūm*, Close, who conceals (his) thoughts. Notchless (bow). (A bow) emitting no sound. (A camel) silent when mounted upon. (pl. كتم *kutum*) A camel that does not cock her tail though pregnant. *Kutūm*, (v. n. of كتم) Concealing her pregnancy by not cocking her tail (a camel). Emitting no sound (a bow). Retaining liquor (leathern bottle).

P كت و مت *kut u mut*, Really, truly, exactly.

A كتيب *katīb*, Sewed. Fastened, closed (bottle).

P كتيب *kitīb*, A chain, fetter; manacle, shackles. (from A كتاب *kitāb*) A book.

A كتيبة *katībat*, (pl. كتائب *katāʾib*) An army; a troop, squadron, battalion of men from 100 to 1000.

A كتيت *katīt*, (v. n. of كت) Walking gently, or taking quick, short steps. A miser. Any gentle noise, as the cry of a young camel when beginning to bray, or in the chest of a very angry man. The noise of a boiling pot, or of fermenting liquor.

A كتيتة *katītat*, Broth so thick as scarcely to be stirred with a ladle.

P كتير *katīr* or *kutīr*, The appearance of water in the desert. Marshy, unfertile ground. A kind of stuff.

P كتيران *katīrān*, Pitch.

P كتيرة *katīra*, Gum-tragacanth.

A كتيع *katīʿ*, Any body, any thing (is not there). Entire, full, whole (year). Worthless, vile, sordid.

A كتيف *katīf*, (pl. كتف *kutf*) Broad (sword). A barrel-hoop. Broad plates for casing doors.

A كتيفة *katīfat*, A large iron plate for strengthening, and occasionally enough for covering, a door. Malevolence. A crowd, troop. Blacksmith's pincers.

A كتيلة *katīlat*, A palm-tree beyond hand-reach.

P كتيم *katīm*, A leathern bag or bottle from which the water has not entirely run out. Brackish, unfruitful soil.

A كتيم *katīm*, Well-sewed (bottle). (A stitch) which does not leak. Silent (camel). Twangless (bow). A bow made of a piece of unsplit wood. A bow in which there is no notch for the arrow.

A كث *kass*, (v. n. of كث) Voiding excrement. (pl. كثاث *kisās*) Thick-bearded (man). *Kuss*, Thick-bearded (persons). Thickly-congregated (people).

A كثأ *kasʾ*, (v. n. of كثأ) Floating on the surface of the whey (milk). Throwing up scum (a pot). Taking off the cream or scum. Growing long, thick, and entangled (herbage, the beard, or camels' hair).

A كثا *kasa'*, (pl. كثى *kasa'*) The herb ايهقان.

A كثاء *kassāʾ*, Thick (beard).

A كثاب *kisāb*, Any thing which strikes one (as an arrow or stone). *Kusāb*, Many, much.

A كثاب *kassāb* or *kussāb*, An arrow without point or wings.

A كثأة *kasʾat* or *kusʾat*, Cream. Scum. *Kasʾat*, (or كثاة *kasāt*) A species of the herb rocket.

A كثاة *kasāt*, (pl. كثى *kasa'*) The herb ايهقان.

A كثاث *kisās*, (pl. of كث) Thick-bearded men.

A كثاثاء *kasāsāʾ*, (Land) of strong deep soil.

A كثاثة *kasāsat*, (v. n. of كث) Being thick and dense. Being bushy, curling, and short (beard).

A كثار *kasār* or *kisār*, Troops, herds. *Kusār*,

Much. A great multitude.

A كثافة *kasāfat*, (v. n. of كثف) Being thick, dense; much; numerous. Density, thickness. Luxuriance. Multitude, number, abundance.

A كثب *kasb*, (v. n. of كثب) Collecting together, heaping up. Pouring in or out. Entering, being introduced. Making an assault, charging upon. Inverting (a quiver). Decreasing (the milk of a camel). *Kasab*, Nearness, neighbourhood. من كثب *min kasab*, Near at hand, from hard-by. *Kusub*, (pl. of كثيب *kasīb*) Sands blown in a heap.

A كثباء *kasbā*, Earth.

A كثبان *kusbān*, (pl. of كثيب *kasīb*) Sand-hills.

A كثبة *kusbat*, (pl. كثب *kusab*) A pail of milk, as much as is milked at once. A little milk or water. As much remaining in a vessel as is sufficient for a draught. Meat, drink, and in general any thing collected or composed from smaller quantities. A valley between two mountains. A heap.

A كثة *kassat*, Thick (beard).

A كثث *kasas*, (v. n. of كث) Being thick, bushy, and short (the beard).

A كثج *kasj*, (v. n. of كثج) Eating food and laying up an abundant store.

A كثح *kas-h*, (v. n. of كثح) Taking or collecting. Separating, scattering. Driving about the dust (wind). Baring (the buttocks).

A كثحة *kas-hat*, A small crowd.

A كثحم *kus-hum*, (A man) having a short, thick, bushy beard.

A كثحمة *kus-hamat*, Small bits of wood, broken branches, dry leaves, or other rubbish. *Kus-humat*, A short, thick, curly beard.

A كثر *kasr*, Much. Surplus. *Kasr* or *kasar*, The marrow or pith of a palm-tree; also a branch and the envelope of the flower. *Kusr*, (v. n. of كثر) Excelling in multitude. Being numerous. Abundance, riches. The greater part of a thing.

A كثرة *kasrat*, (v. n. of كثر) Becoming numerous. *Kasrat* or *kisrat*, Multitude, plenty, abundance, superfluity, excess. The best or greatest part. كثرت خلائق *kasrati khalāʼik*, (also كثرت خلق *kasrati khalk*) Many people. كثرة السهر *kasratu's suhr*, Too much watching. كثرت غذا *kasrati ghidā*, A superfluity of victuals. كثرت كلام *kasrati kalām*, Loquacity, tautology.

A كثري *kasra'*, Name of an idol of the Arabian tribes جديس *jadīs* and طسم *tasm*, destroyed by نهشل *nahshal*, who embraced Islām under Muhammad. *Kusra'*, The habit of drinking much wine.

A كثع *kasʻ*, (v. n. of كثع) Having cream swimming on the surface (milk). *Kasʻ* or *kasaʻ*, (v. n. of كثع) Being red, turgid with blood (the lip).

A كثعب *kasʻab*, A woman whose privities are large. Large and thick (female privities).

A كثعة *kasʻat* or *kusʻat*, Scum of a pot, fat of broth. Cream of milk. *Kusʻat*, The groove in the upper lip. *Kasaʻat*, Clay, mud.

A كثعم *kasʻam*, A panther. A cross breed between a wolf and hind. (See also كثعب *kasʻab*).

A كثف *kasf*, A crowd, a multitude.

A كثكث *kaskas* or *kiskis*, Small fragments of stone. Earth.

A كثكثة *kaskasat*, (v. n. of كثكث Q) Having a thick and bushy beard.

A كثكثي *kuskusa'* or *kaskasa'*, A certain game played with sand or earth.

A كثل *kasl*, A crowd. A heap of corn.

A كثم *kasm*, (v. n. of كثم) Collecting, assembling. Filling. Eating a cucumber, or any thing green and crisp. Following (the traces or footsteps). Turning (a quiver) upside down. Diverting from (any purpose). Approaching. Delaying, being slow. عن كثم *ʻan kasamin*, In the neighbourhood, near at hand. From near, from hard-by. *Kasim*, Thick.

A كثمة *kasamat*, Drunk, or full of drink (woman). *Kasimat*, Hard and thick (mushroom).

A كثنب *kasnab*, Strong, hard, robust.

A كثنة *kusnat*, Any thing made of myrtle, osier, or palm-leaves (as wicker-work or matting), on which they lay fragrant herbs or flowers.

A كثو *kusw*, Heaped-up earth. A little milk. The bird قطا *kata'*.

A كثوثة *kusūsat*, (v. n. of كثّ) Being thick. Being short, curling, and bushy (beard).

A كثوع *kusūʻ*, (v. n. of كثع) Having diarrhœa or liquid stools. Throwing up scum (a pot). Producing cream (milk). Being red, turgid (the lip).

A كثي *kasa'*, (pl. of كثا *kasa'* or كثاة *kasāt*) Plants called ايهقان *ayhukān*.

A كثيب *kasīb*, (pl. أكثبة *aksibat*, كثب *kusub*, or كثبان *kusbān*) Sand-hill, sand blown in a heap.

A كثيبي *kasībiy*, Hillocky, prominent (buttocks).

A كثيث *kasīs*, Thick, dense. كثيث اللحية *kasīsu'l lihyat*, Thick-bearded, bushy-bearded.

A كثير *kasīr*, Many, much, copious, abundant, plentiful, numerous. Superfluous. Fruitful. كثير الاحسان *kasīru'l ihsān*, Most beneficent. كثير الجهاد *kasīru'l jihād*, Warlike, heroic. كثير الضرر *kasīru'z zarar*, Most noxious or hurtful. كثير اللون *kasīru'l lawn*, Many-coloured. P دشمن كثير التحكم *dushmani kasīru't tahakkum*, A powerful enemy. شاه كثير النوال *shāhi kasīru'n nawāl*, A most beneficent prince. A الكثير ضرّ و القليل نفع *al kasīru zarra, wa'l kalīlu nafaʻa*, Superfluity is hurtful, whilst a little does good. زمان كثير *zamāni kasīr*, A long time. قليل و كثير *kalīl u kasīr*, Little and much.

A كثيرا *kasīran*, Many times, often.

A كثيراء *kasīrā*, Gum-tragacanth.

A كثيرة *kasīrat*, (fem. of كثير *kasīr*) Much. Many. رجال كثيرة *rijāli kasīra*, Many men. مرّات كثيرة *marrāti kasīra*, (or دفعات كثيرة *dufaʻāti kasīra*) Many times, often.

A كثيرةً *kasīratan*, Oftentimes.

A كثيف *kasīf*, Thick, dense. Opaque. Many, much, numerous, abundant.

P كج *kaj*, Crooked, curved, wry, distorted, bent, dislocated. A kind of silk of little value. A hook. A grappling-iron. *Kuj*, A sort of herb used in setting broken bones. A species of the shell called concha veneris.

A كج *kajj*, (v. n. of كج) Playing at the game كجة *kujjat*, or racket, bandy, shinty, or hockey.

P كجا *kujā*, Where? Whither? After what manner? how? Who? what? Everywhere, wherever. When? A place. كجا ميروي *kujā mī ravī*, Whither goest thou? تا كجا *tā kujā*, How long? تا كجا *tā kujā*, (or تا بكجا *tā ba kujā*) Whither? to what place? از كجا *az kujā*, Whence? by which way? هر كجا *har kujā*, Everywhere. Wheresoever. خيال زهد كجا نشاي شراب كجا *khayāli zuhd kujā, nashāyi sharāb kujā*, How (can any one reconcile) the idea of piety and the fumes of wine?

P كج ابرو *kaj-abrū*, Finely-arch-browed.

P كج ابروئي *kaj-abrūʼī*, The possession of finely-arched eyebrows, graceful curvature of eyebrow.

P كجابه *kajāba*, A camel-litter for women.

P كجاز *kajāz*, A hatchet, axe, pick, mattock.

P كج آغند *kaj-āghand*, (or كج آكند *kaj-āgand*) A cuirass quilted with silk.

P كجاوه *kajāwa*, A camel-litter for females.

P كجاوه نشين *kajāwa-nishīn*, Seated in a litter.

P كجائي *kujāʼī*, Where thou art. Where art thou? Whence art thou? A dweller, inhabitant.

P كج باز *kaj-bāz*, An unfair player. Fraudulent.

P كج بحث *kaj-bahs*, An absurd reasoner.

P كج بحثي *kaj-bahsī*, Absurd, tortuous reasoning.

P كج بسته *kaj-basta*, Ill-set (broken bone).

P كجبه *kajaba*, A camel-litter for women.

P كج بين *kaj-bīn*, Squint-eyed, looking awry.

A كجّة *kujjat*, A boy's game, the game of racket.

P كج چشم *kaj-chashm*, Squint-eyed.

P كج چشمي *kaj-chashmī*, Strabism, squint.

P كج خلق *kaj-khulk*, Ill-tempered, cross.

P كج خواه *kaj-khwāh*, Deceitful.

P كج خواهي *kaj-khwāhī*, Deceitfulness.

P كجدار مريز *kaj-dār marez*, Evasion, subterfuge, putting off.

P كج را *kaj-rā*, Of crooked policy.

P كجرو *kaj-rav*, Going awry. Unprincipled.

P كج روي *kaj-ravī*, A walking obliquely or awry. The want of principle: perverseness.

P كج طبع *kaj-tabʻ*, Cross-tempered.

P كج فهم *kaj-fahm*, Misunderstanding, perverting a meaning.

P كجك *kajak*, A hook used in driving elephants. An iron curved at one end. A rod having one end bent, from which is suspended balls of gold and silver for shooting at. A drum-stick. A black feather in a duck's tail, which couriers wear on their head and women in their hair. A jar for keeping rose-water and dates in. A kind of shell from which a medicament for the eye is prepared. A snail.

A کجکجة *kajhajat*, Name of a game called است الکلبة *istu'l kalbat*.

P کج کلاه *kaj-kulāh*, A beau, (lit.) wearing the cap awry. A beloved object.

P کجله *kajala*, A magpie.

P کج مزاج *kaj-mizāj*, Cross, peevish. Stupid.

P کج نال *kajnāl*, A small cannon carried on an elephant.

P کج نظر *kaj-nazar*, Envious, malignant looks.

P کج نهاد *kaj-nihād*, Crooked-minded.

P کجواج *kajwāj*, Crooked, bent, wry.

H کجور *kajūr*, Zedoary, a Chinese root.

P کجوك *kujūk*, Sciatica or hip-gout.

P کجومن *kajūman*, A kind of nightshade.

P کجوه *kajawa*, A camel-litter for women.

P کجه *kaja*, A thing crooked at the extremity. A hook on which they hang meat.

P کجي *kaji*, Raw-silk from the cones. Crookedness, wryness, distortion. Crossness.

P کجیرده *kujīrda* or *kujayrda*, A leader, head of a party, chief of a religious sect.

P کجیم *kajīm*, Armour for man or horse. صهیل اسب کجیم پوشیده *sahīli asbi kajīm-poshīda*, The neighing of a barbed warhorse.

P کجین *kajīn*, Made of raw-silk. Armour quilted with silk. *Kijīn*, Flour and oil.

P کچ *kuch*, The scale of a fish.

P کچري *kichrī*, A kind of food made of rice, pulse, and butter (eaten in Hindūstān).

P کچك *kachak*, Name of an animalcule which frets a leathern water-bottle.

P کچکول *kachkūl*, A beggar, mendicant.

P کچل *kachal*, One who has no hair, and is marked with wounds or scars. Crooked, bandy-legged. *Kachal* or *kuchal*, An animalcule which eats holes in a leathern water-bottle.

P کچله *kuchula*, Dogsbane. Wolfsbane.

P کچلي *kachalī*, A disease incident to the heads of children and causing the hair to fall off. Name of a valley near Ispahān.

P کچول *kachol*, Motion of the hips in dancing.

P کچه *kacha*, A ring without a bezel. The chin. A ladle. A hook on which they hang meat.

P کچه بازي *kacha-bāzī*, Tricks done with a ring.

P کچه گل کردن *kacha gul kardan*, To become manifest (any thing concealed).

P کچیر *kachīr*, (کچیرده *kachīrda*, or *kuchayrda*) A leader, head, chief of a party.

A کح *kuhh*, (fem. کحة) True, aboriginal (Arabian).

A کحال *kihāl*, A species of antimony. A collyrium. Small beads, or any thing similar, used as amulets against the fascination of malignant eyes.

A کحال *kahhāl*, An oculist. کحال شریعت *kahhāli sharīʻat*, An epithet of Muhammad.

A کحائل *kahāʼil*, (pl. of کحیل *kahil*) Anointed with antimony (eyes).

A کحب *kahb*, (v. n. of کحب) Striking on the backside. Sour grapes. The backside.

A کحبة *kahbat*, A single sour grape.

A کحث *kahs*, (v. n. of کحث) Drawing (part of any thing) towards one with the hand.

A کحثلة *kahsalat*, Protuberance of belly.

A کحح *kuhuh*, Old decrepit women.

A کحص *kahs*, (v. n. of کحص) Obliterating, defacing. Being obliterated. Running round, going over. Going off, and being lost sight of (an ostrich). Searching, groping with the foot. A kind of plant the seed of which resembles locusts' eyes.

A کحط *kaht*, (v. n. of کحط) Giving over, ceasing (rain). Sterility, barrenness.

A کحف *kahf*, (pl. کحوف *kuhūf*) A limb, member.

A کحکح *kihkih* or *kuhkuh*, A decrepit old woman; aged camel.

A کحل *kahl*, (v. n. of کحل) Being barren (the year). Afflicting and distressing people (a barren year). Anointing the eyes with antimony. Being covered with green herbage for the first time (ground). A barren year. Dearth, scarcity. Heaven, sky. Name of a cow. صرحت کحل *sarrahat kahlun*, The sky was serene and cloudless. *Kuhl*, (pl. اکحال *ak-hāl*) A collyrium, or antimony reduced to a fine powder, used for the eyes. Accumulated wealth. (pl. اکاحل *akāhil*) A sort of pot-herb. P کحل خولان *kuhli khawlān*, Juice of boxthorn. A کحل السودان *kuhlu's sūdān*, A tree bearing black berries, which are excellent for the eyes. P کحل فارس *kuhli fārs*, Sarcocolla, a Persian gum or balsam, used in dressing wounds. کحلي پرند *kuhlī parand*, (کحلي روز *kuhlī roz*, or کحلي شب *kuhlī shab*) Darkness of the night. کحلي چرخ *kuhlī charkh*, The lower heaven. Darkness of the night. A *Kahal*, (v. n. of کحل) Having black at the roots of the eyelashes (naturally, without the aid of paint). *Kahil*, (pl. کحلي *kahla'* and کحائل *kahāʼil*) Anointed with antimony (eye).

P کحلا *kuhlā*, Ox-tongue (an herb). Melilot. Chickweed. Wild mustard.

A کحلاء *kahlāʼ*, (fem. of اکحل *ak-hal*) One who has naturally black eyes and eyelashes without the assistance of art. (A woman) whose eyes are anointed with collyrium. Black-eyed and white-bodied (sheep). A kind of bird. A certain plant on which bees feed. The herb bugloss.

A کحلة *kahlat*, Small beads used as amulets against the fascination of malignant eyes. The sky.

A کحلي *kahla'*, (pl. of کحیل *kahil*) (Eyes) anointed with antimony.

A کحمة *kahmat*, The eye.

A کحوص *kuhūs*, (v. n. of کحص) Departing, vanishing, disappearing, being obliterated, and effaced.

A کحوف *kuhūf*, (pl. of کحف) Members, limbs.

A کحي *kahy*, A spoiling, damaging, injuring.

A کحیل *kahīl*, (pl. کحائل *kahāʼil* and کحلي *kahla'*) An eye anointed with collyrium or antimony. An eye of the colour of antimony. *Kuhayl*, Pitch or naphtha (with which they anoint camels).

A کحیلاء *kuhaylāʼ*, Ox-tongue (an herb).

P کخ *kakh*, Name of a city. *Kakh, kikh*, or *kukh*, A mask, a deformed appearance, any thing similar with which they frighten boys. *Kikh*, Tasteless, insipid. *Kukh*, A reed of which mats are made. A worm.

A کخ *kikh, kakhkh*, or *kikhkh*, A word used in deterring children from doing any thing, or in detestation of any thing dirty.

P کخته *kukhta*, A flame of fire.

P کخج *kukhj*, (or کخچ *kukhch*) Birch, broom.

P کخ جنده *kakh janda*, An evil spirit, a demon.

P کخکخ *kikhkikh*, A word used in deterring children from doing any thing. Laughter. *Kukhkukh*, Coughing. Heat, warmth.

A کخکخة *kakhkhakhat*, (v. n. of کخکخ Q) Crying out to a child کخ کخ *kikh kikh*.

A کخم *kakhm*, A pushing, thrusting away.

A کخیخ *kakhīkh*, (v. n. of کخ) Snoring in sleep.

P کد *kad*, A house. Beginning, first. (in zand and Pāzand) A person, somebody.

A کدّ *kadda*, (fut. یکدّ *yakuddu*) He laboured.

A کدّ *kadd*, (v. n. of کدّ) Importuning, urging a request. Combing the head. Making a signal with the finger. Plaguing, tormenting, desiring one to take any trouble. Taking away (any thing, fluid or solid) with the hand. Trouble, labour, fatigue, diligence, endeavour. A mortar (in which any thing is pounded). Examination, search, inquiry. کدّ فرج *haddi farj*, Meretricious work. P کدّ وکاوش *kadd u kāwish*, Search, inquiry, examination, application.

A کدأ *kadʼ*, (v. n. of کدأ) Being nipped by cold, or knocked down by hail (a plant); also growing slowly for want of rain. Pinching a plant (cold). *Kadaʼ*, (v. n. of کدئ) Appearing to vomit when croaking (a raven). Being stunted (plants).

A کداء *kadāʼ*, A name of عرفات *ʻarafāt*. *Kidāʼ*, Hindrance, prohibition. A cutting.

A کداة *kadāt*, A collection of meat and drink.

A کداد *kudād*, Name of a celebrated stallion-ass. The refuse of the herb صلیان *silliyān*.

A کدادة *kudādat*, Remains of meat at the bottom of a pot. Sediment of butter dressed with pounded grain (سویق *sawīk*) and dates.

A کدادیس *kadādīs*, (pl. of کدّاس) Shocks of corn.

A کدارة *kadārat*, (v. n. of کدر) Being muddy and opaque. *Kudārat*, Broth remaining at the bottom of the kettle. Sediment of butter.

A کداري *kudāriy*, A transparent cloud.

A کداس *kidās*, (v. n. of کدس) Sneezing (an animal). *Kudās*, A heap of snow. The sneezing of an animal.

A کدّاس *kuddās*, A shock of unthreshed corn.

A کداسة *kudāsat*, Any thing collected from different quarters.

A كدّاش kaddāsh, One who pinches or nips.

P كدام kudām, Which? whosoever. Who? what?

A كدام kudām, An old man. The root of grass trodden and invisible till the rain brings it to light.

A كدامة kudāmat, Remainder of any victuals.

P كدامي kidāmī, A light rough stone of a dark green colour, found on the sea-shore, used by tinmen. Kudāmī, Who? what? which?

P كدامين kudāmīn, Which of them? در كدامين dar kudāmīn, Where? in what place? In whom? بكدامين ba kudāmīn, What? whither?

A كدان kidān, A piece of untwisted, unravelled rope sticking in a knot.

A كدانة kadānat, Turpitude, baseness.

A كداية kudāyat, A collection of meat and drink.

A كدب kadb, kadib, kadab, or kudb, A white speck on the nail. Kadib, Whitish, thin, watery (blood).

P كدبا kadbā, (in zand and Pāzand) A lie.

P كدبانو kad-bānū, A married woman, mistress of a family, lady, matron. The body. An iron instrument, used by engravers, seal-cutters, and painters.

A كدّة kiddat, Rough, rugged (ground).

A كدج kadaj, (v. n. of كدج) Drinking wine at pleasure to one's fill.

A كدح kadh, (v.n. of كدح) Scratching (the face with the nails). Combing (hair). Studying, giving attention, labouring (especially in providing for a family). (pl. كدوح kudūh) A scratch, a scar.

P كدخدا kad-khudā, God. Master of a family. A magistrate. Any one looked up to with reverence and respect. A bridegroom; married man. The soul. A king.

P كدخدائي kad-khudāʼī, A family-establishment, housekeeping. Marriage.

A كددة ka or kudadat, Broth left in a pot.

A كدر kadr, (v. n. of كدر) Pouring out (water). Kadr or kadir, Muddy, obscure. Kadar, (v. n. of كدر) Being turbid, dirty, muddy (water). Being distracted, perplexed with misfortunes (life). Trouble, affliction, agitation, vexation, sorrow, sadness, grief, anguish, solicitude, anxiety, perturbation, melancholy. Darkness, dimness, impurity (of colour, of the eye or water). (pl. of كدرة kadarat) Handsful of corn cut down. Cisterns. Kudur, A stout, thick ass.

P كدر kadar, Name of a fragrant plant.

A كدرّ kudurr, A well-made young man, strong-built, and fat.

A كدراء kadrāʼ, (fem. of أكدر akdar) Dark; brown, tawny. Name of a place in Yaman famous for goats' leather.

P كدرپذير kadar-pazīr, Disturbed, afflicted.

A كدرة kudrat, (v. n. of كدر) Being muddy, opaque (as colour), perplexed (life). Darkness, dimness of colour. Kadarat, The mud at the bottom or the green-weed swimming at the top of a cistern. A thin cloud. A large lump of clay scraped together. A huge clod. (pl. كدر kadar) A handful or a shock of cut-down corn.

P كدرم kudram, A vegetable like millet.

A كدريّ kudrīy, A thin cloud. A species of the bird قطا katā, of a brown colour, neck yellow, back and belly powdered with black and white spots.

A كدس kads, (v. n. of كدس) Sneezing (beasts). Going fast, though heavy laden (a camel). Throwing or spreading on the ground. Accumulating, heaping up. Kuds, (pl. أكداس akdās) A stack of unthreshed corn. A heap of snow.

A كدسان kadasān, (v. n. of كدس) Sneezing.

A كدسة kadsat, Sneezing (as brutes, though sometimes applied to men; this, however, is generally expressed by عطسة ʻatsat).

P كدست kudist, A span.

A كدش kadsh, (v.n. of كدش) Scratching with the nails. Cutting. Striking with a sword or spear. Driving, urging onward. Communicating a portion of intelligence. Endeavouring to provide for a family. Acquiring, obtaining. Receiving (a present). Pushing, thrusting violently.

A كدع kadʻ, (v. n. of كدع) Driving away, beating off, averting.

A كدعة kudʻat, Vile, base, mean, abject.

A كدف kadaf, The noise of feet or of any thing unseen, or of feet falling on a hard place.

P كدفت kaduft, The skull.

A كدكاد kidkād, Immoderate laughter.

A كدكدة kadkadat, (v. n. of كدكد Q) Driving, thrusting, pushing with violence. Running gently. A heavy, slow pace. Immoderate laughter. A blow of the furbishing instrument on a sword when being polished. The noise of the hammer descending on the anvil.

P كدكده kadkada, The noise made by a hammer when striking a red-hot iron.

A كدم kadm, (v. n. of كدم) Biting or seizing with the fore-teeth; taking any thing with the lips (in the manner of an ass). Marking with an iron instrument, making an impression. Pursuing, hunting. Searching, looking for. Kudam, A black locust with a green head.

A كدمة kadmat, An impression, mark, or scar. Kadamat, Motion. Kadimat, A fat sheep.

A كدمّة kudummat, A strong, brawny man.

A كدمّل kudummul, An island in the sea of Yaman.

A كدن kadn, (v. n. of كدن) Girding (one's vest) with a girdle. Kadn or kidn, (pl. كدون kudūn) An upper garment put on to keep the clothes clean. A cloth in which women wrap their feet when travelling in the hawda or camel-litter; also that vehicle. A camel-saddle. The skin of an animal's leg tanned, which they use as a mortar for braying drugs. Kadan, (v. n. of كدن) Being black from eating viscous plants (a camel's lip). Having its tops cropped and the roots remaining (the herb صلّيان silliyān). Muddy, obscure. Kadin, Corpulent.

P كدن kidin, A village in which near ten thousand people assemble on the day called عاشورا ʻāshūrā. A pathic.

A كدنة kidnat, Flesh. Fat. The bunch of a camel. People.

P كدنگ kudang, (or كدنگه) A fuller's beetle.

A كدو kudw, (or كدوّ kudūw) (v. n. of كدا for كدو) Producing plants slowly (ground). Growing unkindly (corn).

P كدو kadū, A gourd. A cupping-glass.

A كدوء kudūʼ, (v. n. of كدأ) Being nipped by cold, or lodged by hail (a plant). Nipping and laying plants (cold).

P كدواده kad-wāda, Foundation of a house.

P كدوبا kadū-bā, Pumpkin-soup.

A كدوح kudūh, (pl. of كدح kadh) Scratches with the nails.

P كدوخ kadokh, A bath. A cup.

A كدود kadūd, A well, the water of which is difficult to draw.

P كدودانه kadū-dāna, Intestinal worms. A fatal disease, breaking out internally like seeds of gourds.

A كدور kudūr, (v. n. of كدر) Being turbid, muddy.

A كدورة kudūrat, (v. n. of كدر) Being turbid, muddy, opaque. (pl. كدورات kudūrāt) Foulness, impurity in water. Dimness of the eye. Anguish, perturbation, oppression of spirits. Resentment.

P كدوكش kadū-kash, An instrument for cutting pumpkins.

A كدون kudūn, (pl. of كدن kadn or kidn) Upper garments for keeping the clothes clean. Wrappers for the feet when travelling.

P كدونيمه kadū-nīma, A half-gourd; a decanter.

P كدوه kudūh, A tearing, wounding. Seizure.

A كدوه kudūh, (v. n. of كده) Scratching (the face) with the nails. Striking, wounding, and leaving a mark (a stone). Parting (hair). (pl. of كده kadh) Hard blows (with a stone).

A كده kadh, (v. n. of كده) Scratching, wounding. Breaking. Parting (hair with a comb). Victory. (pl. كدوه kudūh) A hard knock (with a stone) leaving a mark. Kadh or kudh, A word used in frightening wild beasts.

P كده kada, A habitation. A tavern. A vault, cavern, or cellar. A village. (added to any word is a noun of place: as) آتش كده ātish-kada, (Place of fire) A temple of the Magi. مى كده may-kada, A wine-cellar; a tavern, an inn. Kuda, A scratch. The uvula. The wards of a key. The bolt or lock of a door. The wooden bar of a gate.

A كدي kady, (v. n. of كدي) Being good for nothing, giving little. Retaining, detaining, imprisoning. Occupying, keeping employed. Scratching (the face). Perishing (sown corn). Kadā, (v. n. of كدي) Biting. Drinking milk, and having the belly-ache in consequence (a young camel). Being choked by a bone in the throat. Vomiting, coughing (a whelp). Being worn (finger-nails) by digging earth. Milk and bruised dates, which girls eat to gain flesh. A disease to which whelps are subject. *Kadī*, Inodorous (musk). *Kuda'*, (pl. of كدية *kudyat*) Hard soils.

A كديّ *kadīy*, Inodorous (musk).

A كديباء *kudaybā'*, A white speck on the nail.

A كدية *kudyat*, (pl. كدي *kuda'*) Hard ground or clay. Misfortune. A store of meat and drink. A large and hard rock.

A كديد *kadīd*, An extensive tract of country. Large-grained salt; and the sound made in pouring it out. Rough, rocky ground.

A كدير *kadīr*, Muddy, turbid, obscure.

A كديراء *kudayrā'*, Milk and bruised dates, which women eat to recover flesh.

P A كدي زاد *kadī-zād*, House-born (man or beast). The son of a man of distinction by a female slave.

A كدين *kadīn*, A girdle.

P كدين *kudīn*, (or كدينه *kudīna*) A large beetle or wooden mallet used by bleachers.

P كديور *kadewar*, A landlord, master of a family. The head man of a village. A farmer, sower. A gardener. Time. Fortune. The world.

P كديوري *kadewarī*, Agriculture. Horticulture.

A كديون *kidyawn*, Fine sand and dung mixed with dregs of oil, with which they scour armour.

A كذّ *kazz*, (v. n. of كذّ) Being rough.

A كذا *kazā*, (comp. of ك *ka* and ذا *zā*) This, that. Thus, such. Some, such and such. ليلة كذا *laylatu kazā*, This or that night. هكذا *hākazā*, Thus. كذا و كذا *kazā wa kazā*, So-and-so, consequently, consecutively, et cætera.

A كذّاب *kazzāb*, A liar. An impostor. *Kizzāb*, (v. n. of كذب) Lying. Denying stoutly. Being necessary to be done. (v. n. 2 of كذب) Calling one a liar. *Kuzzāb*, A lie.

A كذّابان *kazzābāni*, The two liars, viz. مسيلمة الحنفي *musaylimat al hanafiy*, and اسود العنسيّ *aswad al ɛansiy*.

A كذّان *kazzān*, Soft stones resembling clay.

A كذب *kazaba*, (fut. يكذب *yakzibu*) He lied.

A كذب *kizb* or *kazib*, (v. n. of كذب) Lying. Taking the male and not conceiving. Being necessary to be done or observed (as pilgrimage, the sacred visit called عمرة *ɛumrat*, or war with infidels). *Kizb*, A lie. P كذب وانكار كردن *kizb u inkār kardan*, To deny with a lie, to speak falsely. A *Kuzb*, A white speck on the nail. *Kazib*, (v. n. of كذب) Delaying. False. A lie. *Kuzub*, (pl. of كذوب *kazūb*), and كذّب *kuzzab* (pl. of كاذب *kāzib*) (Men) of lying tongues, liars.

A كذبان *kazbān*, A liar. *Kuzbān*, A lie.

A كذبة *kazbat* or *kizbat*, (v. n. of كذب) Lying. Being necessary to be done. *Kuzabat*, A liar.

A كذبذب *kuzubzub* or *kuzzubzub*, A liar.

A كذبذبان *kuzubzubān* A liar.

A كذبي *kuzba'*, A lie.

A كذج *kazaj*, (from P كده *kada*) A habitation.

A كذع *kazh*, (v. n. of كذع) Driving gravel against one (wind).

P كذر *hazar*, A silly, stupid man.

A كذكذة *kazkazat*, Intense redness.

A كذلك *kazālik*, So, thus, in the like manner (compounded of ك *ka*, Like, and ذلك *zālik*, That).

A كذوب *kazūb*, (pl. كذب *kuzub*) A liar. Soul.

A كذوبة *kazūbat*, A liar. The soul.

P كر *kar*, Deaf. Strength, power. Intention, design, will, desire. Felicity. كر و فر *kar u far*, Pomp and pride. كر كردن *kar kardan*, To deafen, to stun. *Kur*, Rice. Name of two rivers.

A كرّ *karra*, (fut. يكرّ *yakarru*) He returned.

A كرّ *karr*, (v. n. of كرّ) Repeating, reiterating. Returning, retiring, retreating. Inclining to. Shewing kindness. Making an attack, rushing upon. A chain, fetter, tether made of palm-leaves or fibres. A thick rope, hawser, cable. A rope in general. That whereby the two sides of a camel's saddle are united. A rope for climbing palm-trees. (pl. اكرار *akrār*) A napkin for kneeling on at prayers. A well. (pl. كرار *kirār* and كرور *kurūr*) A low place where water collects and filters itself clear (as in sandy grounds). *Kurr*, (pl. اكرار *akrār*) A dry Babylonish measure of six ass-loads, or sixty قفيز *kafīz*, or forty اردبّ *irdabb*. A garment, apparel. A well. An upper garment, a short cloak.

A كرا *kara'*, A mode of walking with the toes turned in and the heels turned out. Slenderness of leg. Lustiness of arm.

P كرا *kirā*, To whomsoever. To whom? Whom?

A كراء *kirā'*, (v. n. 3 of كري) Hiring, renting. Letting on hire. Hire, rent. P كرا كردن *kirā kardan*, To farm, rent, give or take upon hire.

A كراب *kirāb*, (v. n. of كرب) Ploughing and sowing land. Water-courses through valleys.

A كرّاب *karrāb*, Somebody, any one.

A كرابة *karābat* or *kurābat*, (pl. اكربة *akribat*) Dates which are gathered from the roots of the branches after the clusters are cut off.

A كرابيس *karābīs*, (pl. of كرباس) Fine linens.

A كرابيسيّ *karābīsiy*, Made of fine white muslin. One who deals in fine linen.

A كرات *kurāt*, (pl. of كرة *kurat*) Globes.

A كرّات *karrāt*, (pl. of كرّة *karrat*) Times, many times. كرّات مرّات *karrāt marrāt*, Repeatedly.

A كراث *karās*, A kind of large tree found growing in the mountains of طائف *tāif*.

A كرّاث *kurrās* or *karrās*, A leek, purret.

A كراثاء *karāsā'*, A good unripe date.

A كرّاثي *kurrāsiy*, Leek (seed).

T كراجي *kirājī*, A hirer. A renter. A hireling.

P كراجيدن *karājīdan*, (or كراچيدن *karāchīdan*) To cluck (as a hen when she has laid an egg).

P كراخ *karākh*, (or كراج *karāj*) The clucking of a hen after laying.

P كراخان *karākhān*, The eldest son of Afrāsyāb.

A كراخة *karākhat*, A mat.

A كراد *kirād*, (pl. of كرديدة *kirdīdat*) Hampers of dates. Dates left in the bin.

P كراده *kurād*, كراده *ka* or *kurāda*, An old garment.

A كرادح *kurādih*, Short, dwarfish.

A كراديد *karādīd*, (pl. of كرديدة *kirdīdat*) Dates remaining at the bottom of a bin or hamper.

A كراديس *karādīs*, Herds of horses. Members.

A كرار *karār*, A little bead, shell, or other charm used by the Arabian women, saying, يا كرار كرّيه و يا همرة اهمريه ان اقبل فسرّيه و ان ادبر فضرّيه *yā karāri kurrīhi, wa yā hamratu ahmarīhi: in akbala fa surrīhi, wa in adbara fa zurrīhi*. *Kirār*, (pl. of كرّ *karr*) Low places in sandy grounds where water collects.

P كرار *kurār*, (or كرارا *kurārā*) The threshold of a door. A plot of ground with a raised border prepared for sowing.

A كرّار *karrār*, Impetuous: an attacker, an assailant. An epithet of Aliy. Kind, friendly.

A كرارجة *karārijat*, A kind of short, green fish.

A كرارزة *karārizat*, (pl. of كرّز *kurraz*) Falcons. Birds a year old.

P كرارة *karāra*, An old ragged garment.

A كراريس *karārīs*, (pl. of كرّاسة *kurrāsat*) Sheets, writings. التاجر مجده في كيسه والعالم مجده في كراريسه *at'tājir majduhu fī kīsihi, wa'l ɛālim majduhu fī karrārīsihi*, The glory of a merchant is in his purse; the glory of a learned man in his writings.

P كراز *karāz*, The fever and heat which women in labour suffer. *Kirāz*, A wanton or proud air in walking. A harrow which they draw over a field to make it even. *Kurāz*, A phial. A bottle with a close mouth. The crop, gizzard.

A كراز *kurāz*, (pl. كرزان *kirzān*) A jug, narrow-necked gugglet. An earthen vessel without handle.

A كرّاز *karrāz*, The ram on which the shepherd lays his wallet. *Kurrāz*, An earthen vessel without a handle. A jug, a gugglet with a narrow neck.

P كرازان *kirāzān*, One who walks pompously.

P كرازيدن *kirāzīdan*, To walk haughtily; to affect such a gait, or to wave from side to side with a coquettish air (a woman).

A كرازين *karāzīn*, (pl. of كرزين) Woodmen's axes.

P كراس *kurās*, A wagtail.

A كرّاسة *kurrāsat*, (pl. كرّاس *kurrās* and كراريس *karārīs*) A sheet of paper folded so as to form a tract or pamphlet consisting of several leaves.

P كراسه *kurāsa*, The Kur'ān.

A كراسيّ *karāsiy*, (pl. of كرسيّ *kursiy*) Chairs.

P كراش *karāsh*, Distraction, perplexity. Name of a reddish green bird.

A كرّاش *kurrāsh*, Name of an animalcule.

P کراشه *karāsha*, Form, habit, quality, colour.

P کراشیدن *karāshidan*, To be disturbed in mind. To be spoiled. To be dispersed.

P کراشیده *karāshīda*, Distracted, insane. Destroyed. Dispersed.

A کراض *kirāz*, (v. n. of کرض) Bringing forth before the time (a camel). Casting forth seed from the womb (a she-camel). Preparing the food called کریض *karīz*. An imperfect work. A stallion, or his seed, which the female casts out. The corrugations of the womb. The notch in the extremity of a bow into which the string goes.

A کراع *kurāع*, (pl. اکرع *akruع* and اکارع *akāriع*) The smaller part of a sheep's or cow's leg, the shin. Camp-followers. (pl. کرعان *kirعān*) The rocky projection of a mountain. A troop of horses. The extremity of any thing; the part below the knee in a man.

A کرّاع *karrāع*, The friend or companion of worthless men. One who gives a flock rain-water.

A کراعيّ *kurāعiy*, A dresser and vender of the shins of cattle.

P کراغ *kurāgh*, Name of an herb used in setting dislocated joints.

A کرّاف *karrāf*, A follower of women.

P کراك *karāk*, A wagtail. A quail. *Karāk* or *kurāk*, A magpie.

P کراکا *karākā*, A wagtail.

P کراکر *karākar* or *kurākar*, A crow, rook.

A کراکيّ *karākiy*, (pl. of کرکيّ *kurkiy*) Cranes.

A کرام *kirām*, (pl. of کريم *karīm*) Generous, noble. Mild, benign, eminent. *Kurām*, (pl. کرامون *kurāmūn*) Generous, kind, noble.

A کرّام *kurrām*, (pl. کرّامون *kurrāmūn*) Extremely generous, very beneficent.

A کرامة *karāmat*, (v. n. of کرم) Being venerable, liberal, beneficent, precious, valuable, worthy, dignified. Being fertile (land). Pouring forth rain (a cloud). Generosity, munificence, dignity, nobleness, excellence, reverence. A miracle. The cover of a wine-jar. ذو کرامات *zū karāmāt*, Endued with miraculous powers. صاحب الکرامات *sāhibu'l karāmāt*, A worker of miracles. ارباب الکرامات *arbābu'l karāmāt*, Workers of miracles.

P کرامت فرمودن *karāmat farmūdan*, To grant.

A کرامة لك *karāmatan laka*, In honour of thee.

P کرامي *kirāmī*, Most noble, honourable, revered. Precious. کرامي کردن *kirāmī kardan*, To honour.

A کراميّة *karāmiyat*, Name of a sect which ascribes materialism to the Great Supreme.

P کراميدن *kirāmīdan*, To honour, venerate.

P کران *karān*, A shore, coast, margin, bank, side, boundary. An end. Retiring into solitude, courting privacy. بي کران *bī karān*, Immense, boundless. *Kurān*, A dun-coloured horse.

A کران *kirān*, A lute, harp. A fiddle. Cymbals. (pl. of کرينة *karīnat*) Female musicians.

P کرّان *karrān*, Name of a quarter in Ispahān; of a country near Tibet; and of a fort in the west.

P کرانه *karāna*, A margin, side, quarter, corner. A tip. A black bird slow of flight.

A کرانيف *karānīf*, (pl. of کرناف *kir* or *kurnāf*) Trunks of palm-trees after the branches are cut off.

P کراوش *kirosh*, An oil-press.

P کراويا *karāwiyā*, Caraway-seeds.

A کراوين *karāwīn*, (pl. of کروان *karawān*) Red-legged partridges.

P کراه *karāh*, A side. An end. *Kurāh*, Alike, resembling. A wagtail.

A کراهة *karāhat*, (v. n. of کره) Abhorring, loathing. Becoming abominable. Aversion, horror, detestation, disgust, dislike. Hard, rough, uneven ground. P کراهت داشتن *karāhat dāshtan*, To abhor, abominate, nauseate, hold in detestation.

A کراهة *karāhatan*, Unwillingly.

A کراهية *karāhiyat*, (v. n. of کره) Abhorring, detesting, disliking, disapproving. Disgust, aversion.

A کراهين *karāhīn*, Loathing, abhorrence.

A کرائب *karāـib*, (pl. of کريبة) Misfortunes.

A کرائم *karāـim*, (pl. of کريمة) Generous, noble.

P کرايه *karāya*, A certain black bird slow of flight. *Kirāya*, Hire, price paid for labour, fare, rent. بکرايه دادن *ba kirāya dādan*, To hire out, to let or farm to another. بکرايه ستاندن *ba kirāya satāndan*, To take on hire.

P کرايه دار *kirāya-dār*, A tenant, renter.

P کرايه دهنده *kirāya-dihinda*, Who lets on hire.

P کرايه دهي *kirāya-dihī*, Hire, rent.

P کرايه کش *kirāya-kash*, One who draws rent.

A کرايیس *karāyis*, (pl. of کرياس *kiryās*) Privies on the roofs of houses.

A کرب *karb*, (v. n. of کرب) Pressing heavily, weighing down the spirits (grief). Drawing tight (a fetter). Taking the root of a palm-branch. Sowing an open field. Ploughing (land). Twisting. Tying (a bucket) with a double or treble rope to the cross bar called عرقوة *عarkuwat*, lest the long rope should rot in the well. (pl. کروب *kurūb*) Anguish, vexation. *Kurb*, Nigh, thereabout. *Karab*, (v. n. of کرب) Being broken (the rope of a bucket). The root of a palm-branch broad and thick. A rope tied to the handle of a water-bucket that the main rope may not become wet and rotten.

P کرباس *karbās*, A white cotton garment, muslin.

A کرباس *kirbās*, (pl. کرابيس *karābīs*) Fine linen, carbasus. A garment of white muslin. قطعة کرباس *kitعaـi kirbās*, A web or piece of cloth.

P کرباسه *kirbāsa*, Fine linen or cotton. A web. Lint. A lizard.

A کرباسيّ *kirbāsiy*, Belonging to cotton, cottony: muslin. A vender of linen, a linen-draper.

A کربال *kirbāl*, A bow for separating cotton.

P کربال *kurbāl*, Name of a rice-district in Persia.

P کربايس *karbāyis*, (or کربايش *karbāyish*) A venomous kind of lizard.

A کربة *kurbat*, Affliction, mental anguish, distress. *Karabat*, (pl. کراب *kirāb*) A water-course through a valley. A socket of wood, into which they fix the head of the principal pole that supports a tent.

A کربج *kurbaj*, A warehouse, a shop. A greengrocer's stock.

A کربحة *karbahat*, (v. n. of کربح Q) Throwing prostrate. A severe attack. A kind of ambling pace.

A کربدة *karbadat*, (v. n. of کربد Q) Exerting one's self in running.

A P کربز *kirbiz* or *kurbuz*, A large cucumber.

P کربس *karbas*, A large venomous lizard.

A کربسة *karbasat*, The pace of a man fettered.

P کربسو *karbasū* or کربسه, A poisonous lizard.

P کربش *karbash*, A large and poisonous lizard.

P کربش پايه *karbash-pāya*, Name of a plant found on the sea-shore.

A کربشة *karbashat*, (v. n. of کربش Q) Taking and binding. Going with the feet bound. Joining the feet in order to jump.

P کربشو *karbashū*, A large and poisonous lizard.

P کربشه *karbasha*, A lizard.

A کربعة *karbaعat*, (v. n. of کربع Q) Prostrating. Cutting off (with a sword). Separating (the feet).

A کربل *karbal*, Name of a scarlet flowering plant.

A کربلاء *karbalāـ*, Name of a place in Irāk, noted for the murder of Husayn, son of Aliy.

A کربلة *karbalat*, (v. n. of کربل Q) Sifting, winnowing (wheat). Mixing. Relaxation or languor in the limbs. Going through clay or water. A weakness in the foot.

P کربه *karba*, Name of a bird (coracias). A large kind of venomous lizard. *Kurba*, A shop. Name of an esculent plant.

P کرپا *kurpā*, Trefoil.

P کرپاس *kirpās*, Fine linen.

P کرپاسو *karpāsū*, (کرپاسه *karpāsa*, کرپاشو *karpāshū*, or کرپاشه *karpāsha*) A sort of poisonous lizard.

P کرپاوان *karpāwān*, A kind of trefoil.

A کرة *kurat*, (pl. کرين *kurīn*, *kirīn*, کريّ *kuriy*, کريء *kuraـ*, and کرات *kurāt*) A globe, a sphere, ball. P کرهٔ آب *kuraـi āb*, The water which surrounds the earth. A کرهٔ ارض *kuraـi arz*, (P کرهٔ خاك *kuraـi khāk*) The terrestrial globe. کرهٔ لاجورد *kuraـi lājaward*, (or کرهٔ وهم سوز *kuraـi wahm-soz*) The sky. تخم کره *tukhmi kura*, Tares, darnel.

A کرّة *karrat*, (pl. کرّات *karrāt*) Once, one time or turn. One assault or attack. A retreat. The whole, sum total. Morning. Evening. P يك کرّه *yak karra*, (or يك کرّت *yak karrat*) Once. دو کرّه *du karra*, (or دو کرّت *du karrat*) Twice. صد کرّه *sad karra*, (or صد کرّت *sad karrat*) A hundred times. بعضي کرّه *baعze karra*, (or بعضي کرّت *baعze karrat*) Sundry times. هر کرّه *har karra*, (or هر کرّت *har karrat*) Every time, as often as. A *Kurrat*, Putrid pill-like dung of cattle, with which they scour coats of mail.

A کرّةً *karratan*, Sometimes.

P کرت *kart*, The fruit of a certain thorn.

P کرتاخ *kartākh*, An important affair pending.

A کرّتانِ *karratāni*, Morning and evening.

A کرتحة *kartahat*, (v. n. of کرتح Q) Going like a dwarf, waddling. Throwing prostrate.

A کرتع *kartaع*, Short, dwarfish.

A کرتعة *kartaعat*, (v. n. of کرتع Q) Meddling in any affair which does not concern one.

P کرتك *kartak*, A wooden mallet. *Kurtak*, A short tunic close to the body like a cuirass, with sleeves reaching to the elbows. Feathers (of ostriches, cranes, or herons) which they wear in the head-dress. A species of sewing or embroidery. A thorny shrub.

P کرتله *kartala*, A beardless and perverse youth.

A کرتم *kirtim*, An axe.

A کرتوم *kurtūm*, Large smooth stones. High, elevated ground.

P کرتوما *kartūmā*, Name of a Persian sage.

P کرته *karta*, A piece of ground in tilth. *Kirta*, A camel-thistle or thorn. A kind of shrub of which brooms are made. کرتهٔ دشتي *kirtaِi dashtī*, The bog-rush. *Kurta*, A tunic, waistcoat, jacket. A long loose-skirted under-gown or shirt. A shirt.

P کرتي *kurtī*, A waistcoat for women, a short bodice reaching to the hips, with very short, if any sleeves, open under the throat. A soldier's jacket.

A کرتيم *kirtīm*, A hatchet, axe for felling trees.

P کرتينه *kartīna*, A spider's web.

A کرث *kars*, (v. n. of کرث) Oppressing, grieving, afflicting.

A کرثأة *karsaٔat*, Great thickness (of hair).

A کرثئ *kirsiٔ*, A towering-cloud. An egg-shell.

A کرثئة *kar* or *kirsiٔat*, Thick, entangled grass.

P کرج *karj*, A collar-button. A slit in a garment. *Kirj* or *kirij*, A slice of a melon. *Kirij*, A piece cut out of the collar of a garment.

A کرج *karaj*, (v. n. of کرج) Becoming stale and mouldy (bread).

A کرّج *kurraj*, (P کرّه *kurra*) A foal, horse-colt.

P کرجفو *karjafū*, A quail.

P کرجن *kurjan*, Gristle.

A کرّجيّ *kurrajiy*, A sodomite.

P کرچ *kurch* or *karach*, A segment, cut, slice.

P کرچه *kircha*, Cotton, raw-silk put into an ink-holder. *Kurcha*, A hut of boughs or reeds, whence husbandmen watch their fields or melon-grounds.

A کرح *kirh*, (pl. أكراح *akrāh*) A monk's cell.

P کرخ *karkh*, A mansion, habitation, turreted building. Name of a place in Baghdād. *Karakh*, Destitute of feeling, bereft of consciousness, insensible, paralyzed, benumbed. A place in Turkistān.

P کرخت *karakht*, Insensible, deprived of feeling.

P کرختگي *karakhtagī*, Dryness, austerity.

P کرخ زراه *karkh zarāh*, A pedestrian.

P کرد *kard*, He made. Work, labour, employment. An action, good or bad. *Kard* or *kird*, The loppings of trees. *Kurd*, A sown field having a raised bank, border, or balk about it. Land in tillage. A rice-ground. Low land where water stagnates; a small lake, a ditch. A shepherd.

A کرد *kard*, (v. n. of کرد) Driving, repelling, pursuing (a foe). Cutting, shaving. The neck, or the root of it. *Kurd*, (pl. أكراد *akrād*) The Curds, a nation in Armenia near the Gordian mountains. Part of a field; a furrow.

P کردا *kardā*, Yesterday.

A کرداح *kirdāh*, A swift runner.

P کرداد *kardād*, (or کردادة *kardāda*) The erection of a wall.

P کردار *kirdār*, Work, business, continued labour. Employment in which a man is constantly engaged; profession, trade, art, occupation. Effect. Manner, conduct. Action (good or bad). بد کردار *bad-kirdār*, Malignant, trained to villainy.

A کردار *kirdār*, An edifice. Trees. A place filled with earth.

P کردانيدن *kardānīdan*, To cause to do. To effect, render. To change from one state to another.

A کردبية *kurdabiyat*, A half-sleeved tunic, reaching to mid-thigh.

A کردة *kurdat*, Part of a sown field.

A کردحة *kardahat*, (v. n. of کردح Q) Running (an ass). Throwing on the ground. Running fast.

A کردح *kirdih*, An old woman. A hard, strong man.

A کردحاء *kardahāٔ*, A mode of walking.

P کردر *kardar*, Hillocky ground. Hard ground. A plain, valley, or pass between mountains.

A کردسة *kardasat*, (v. n. of کردس Q) Dividing (horses) into troops. Going with a short step, as if the feet were tied. Driving violently. A rope, ligature, or other fastening.

P کردستان *kurdistān*, Kurdistān.

P کردك *kirdak*, An enigma in prose or verse.

P کردگار *kirdigār*, God the omnipotent. Knowingly, wittingly, on purpose, expressly.

P کردگاز *kirdigāz*, God the omnipotent. Knowingly, designedly.

A کردم *kardam*, Short and thick. A dwarf. An intrepid man.

A کردمة *kardamat*, (v. n. of کردم Q) Leaning to one side, walking or running. Running dwarfishly. Assembling, collecting, and drawing up (an army).

P کردمند *hardmand*, Very quick, swift, expeditious, brisk, hasty.

P کردن *kardan*, To do, make, perform. آهنگ گريز کردن *āhangi gurez kardan*, To make preparation for flight. تمام کردن *tamām kardan*, To complete. در آفتاب کردن *dar āftāb kardan*, To expose to the sun. در زندان کردن *dar zindān kardan*, To imprison. دروغ کردن *durogh kardan*, To lie, feign. دو تا کردن *du tā kardan*, To double. دور کردن *dūr kardan*, (also جدا کردن *judā kardan*) To remove, alienate, separate. زن کردن *zan kardan*, To take a wife, to marry. شمار کردن *shumār kardan*, To number, reckon. فريب کردن *fareb kardan*, To deceive. فساد کردن *fasād kardan*, To act like a villain. To commit adultery. کارزار کردن *kārzār kardan*, To make war. گوش کردن *gosh kardan*, To lend an ear, to listen.

P کردنگ *kardang*, (or کردنگل *kardangal*) A cuckold. A silly fellow. Deformed.

P کردني *kardanī*, Fit to be done, practicable.

P کردو *kardū*, A branch lopped from a tree.

A کردوسة *kurdūsat*, A troop of horsemen. A number of horses. A member, a limb. A bone having another adapted to it, or one joint corresponding to another, as the knee, hip, or shoulder-joints. Any bone thickly clothed with flesh.

A کردوم *kurdūm*, Short. A dwarf.

P کرده *karda*, Made. Done, performed, executed, effected. What is done. Who has done. A short spear. کرده آمدن *karda āmadan*, To become. خوي کرده *khway-karda*, Sweating.

P کرده شده *karda shuda* added to substantives or adjectives forms a passive participle: as, سکه کرده شده *sikka karda shuda*, Coined. محاصره کرده شده *muhāsara karda shuda*, Besieged. گرم کرده شده *garm karda shuda*, Heated, made hot.

P کرده‌کار *karda-kār*, Experienced in business.

P کردي *kurdī*, A native of Kurdistān.

A کرديّة *kurdīyat*, Dates remaining in the corners of a hamper.

A کرديدة *kirdīdat*, (pl. کراديد *karādīd* and کراد *kirād*) A hamper of dates. Dates left in the bin.

P کرديلن *kardaylin*, A kind of pellitory, which is said to make cattle very prolific.

A کرز *karz*, (v. n. of کرز) Persevering in eating the preparation of acid milk called اقط *akit*. Preaching (the gospel). *Kurz*, (pl. کرزة *kirazat*) A wallet, sack, bag, purse.

P کرز *kurz*, A field prepared for sowing, having a raised border, bank, or balk round it.

A کرّز *kurraz*, (pl. کرارزة *karārizat*) A worthless fellow. Dishonest, villainous, filthy. Masterly, ingenious. A stammerer. A hawk. A falcon. A bird one year old.

A کرزان *kirzān*, (pl. of کراز) Narrow-necked phials.

A کرزة *kirazat*, (pl. of کرز) Sacks, wallets, purses.

A کرزم *karzam*, An axe. Short-nosed. *Kurzum*, Voracious, devouring.

P کرزمان *karzamān*, Heaven. *Karzamān* or *karazmān*, The throne of God. Religious people.

A کرزمة *karzamat*, An eating at mid-day.

P کرزن *karzan*, A crown richly adorned with gold and jewels. An embroidered coronet. A basket.

A کرزن *karzan* or *kirzin*, A large hatchet.

P کرزه *karza*, An infant born without the organ of generation. *Kurza*, A field prepared for sowing, having a raised border, bank, or balk round it.

P کرزه ماه *kurza māh*, A species of sweet-scented grass and herb.

A کرزي *kurraziy*, Worthless, covetous. Dishonest, villainous, filthy.

A كرزم *kirzim*, A hatchet. A misfortune.

A كرزين *kirzin*, (pl. كرازين *karāzīn*) A woodman's axe.

A كرس *kirs*, A heap of dung and of urine, consisting of different layers. (pl. اكراس *akrās*, اكاريس *akāris*, and اكارس *akāris*) An adjoining house. A crowd of men. A string of pearls or other beads. A building erected for young goats. A pigeon-house. (more correctly كلس *kils*) Chalk, lime.

P كرس *kurs*, also *kuras*, A lock of hair. A curl or ringlet of hair. *Kuras*, Dirt on the body. *Kurus*, Scurf, foulness of the skin, dirt on the body.

A كرسافة *kirsāfat*, Dimness of the eye.

P كرسان *karsān*, An earthen or wooden vessel in which they keep sweetmeats and the like. *Kirsān*, An agriculturist.

P كرسب *karasb*, Parsley. Celery.

P كرستون *karastūn*, (or كرستوان *karastwān*) A large public weighing-engine.

P كرس طوس *karastūs*, (in the language of the Gospel) Christ. *Kiristūs*, A name of God.

A كرسعة *karsaʿat*, (v. n. of كرسع Q) Running. Smiting the wrist-bone with a sword. *Kursaʿat*, A multitude, a crowd.

P كرسف *karasf*, Parsley.

A كرسف *kursuf*, Cotton, or similar thing, put in an inkholder. A menstruous cloth. A pessary.

A كرسفة *karsafat*, (v. n. of كرسف Q) Hamstringing. Tethering (a camel) very tight.

A كرسفي *kursufiy*, A whitish kind of honey.

A كرسمة *karsamat*, (v. n. of كرسم Q) Keeping silence. Closing the eye. Hanging the head.

A كرسنة *karsanat*, A sort of tree bearing a medicinal fruit. A vetch.

P كرسنج *karsanj*, Cowardice, want of resolution.

P كرسنه *karsana*, A kind of pulse. A bread-basket. *Kirisna*, A scab.

A كرسوع *kursūʿ*, The wrist-bone, particularly the prominent bone near the little finger.

A كرسوعة *kursūʿat*, A multitude, crowd.

A كرسوف *kursūf*, Cotton put into an inkstand.

P كرسه *kurasa*, Curly hair. Filth, impurity.

A كرسيّ *kursiy*, (pl. كراسيّ *karāsiy*) A throne, chair, seat, stool, bench (of a judge). A pulpit. The crystalline or the empyrean heaven (as being the supposed throne of God). A falcon's nest. The stone or seal-part of a ring. Learning, knowledge. A learned man. A king. The power, sovereignty, or providence of God. Name of a place within about 14 miles of Lucknow, the inhabitants of which are said to be foolish or mad. P كرسي خاك *kursī khāk*, The earth. كرسي دار مجلس طور *kursī-dāri majlisi tūr*, The prophet Moses. كرسي زر *kursī zar*, (Golden-throne) The sun. Day. White hips. كرسي شرف *kursī sharaf*, Aries. كرسي شش گوشه *kursī shash gosha*, The world. A كرسيّ الملك *kursiyu'l mulk*, The metropolis of the empire.

P كرسي خاك *kurusī khāk*, A hen that has done laying.

P كرسيدن *karsīdan*, To deceive, to act meanly. To endeavour, strive, strain every nerve. To dispute, controvert. To shrivel, wrinkle, contract.

A كرسين *karsīn*, The barbel (a sort of fish).

P كرسي نامه *kursī-nāma*, A genealogical tree.

P كرسي نشين *kursī-nishīn*, Enthroned.

P كرش *karsh*, Scurf, dirt of the body. *Karsh* or *karash*, Deceit, meanness, baseness. *Kirsh*, Snoring. *Kurush*, A hair-line, cord.

A كرش *karsh*, (v. n. of كرش) Putting into the stomach or paunch. *Kirsh* or *karish*, (pl. كروش *kurūsh*) The rough tripe or stomach of a beast chewing the cud. A body, crowd of people. Children or domestics whom one maintains. A kind of pasturage. A piece of high ground. كرش منشورة *karishi manshūra*, Infants. *Karash*, (v. n. of كرش) Shrivelling (the skin). Becoming possessed of a legion after having been alone.

A كرشاء *karshāʾ*, Big-bellied (woman). A deep womb. Swelling, but hollow in the belly (a she-ass). Thick, fleshy, flat in the soul (foot), with short toes.

A كرشافة *kirshāfat*, Hard, rough (ground).

A كرشاني *karshāni*, The tribes of ازد *azd* and عبد القيس *ʿabdu'l kays*.

A كرشبّ *kirshabb*. (See قرشبّ *kirshabb*.)

P كرشته *kirishta*, Rubbish, chips.

P كرشف *karshaf*, Cotton.

A كرشفة *karshafat* or *kirshafat*, Rough, hard, uncultivated (ground).

A كرشمة *karshamat*, The face. The cheek.

P كرشمه *kirishma*, A wink, nod, glance, looking languishingly through half-shut eyes, an amorous gesture or blandishment, coquetry; consenting, agreeing with a look of love or benignity; also refusing with an oblique or side glance.

P كرشنه *kirshana*, A species of pulse.

A كرشوم *kurshūm*, Deformed in face, ugly.

P كرشوني *karshūnī*, The Arabic language written in Syriac characters; any Syriac writing.

P كرشه *karsha*, Deceit, flattery, pretended submission. *Kurusha*, A hair-line.

P كرشيدن *kar* or *karashīdan*, To deceive, defraud, act meanly. *Kirshīdan*, To go on badly.

A كرشيّون *kirshiyūn*, Inhabitants of Wāsit.

A كرص *kars*, (v. n. of كرص) Beating, pounding. Mixing milk with dates.

A كرضمة *karzamat*, (v. n. of كرضم Q) Giving battle, attacking a foe.

A كرظ *karz*, (v. n. of كرظ) Slandering, defaming. *Kirz*, A slanderer, detractor.

A كرظة *kurzat*, A notch in the end of an arrow or horn of a bow. A bit of wood at the end of a bow. A sinew within the notch of an arrow.

A كرع *karaʿ*, (v. n. of كرع) Drinking with the mouth (without using a vessel or hands). Hitting on the shank. Courageously eating up shank-bones. Having a pain in the small of the leg. Being slender (the shank). Being of the most infamous class (a man). Raining. Arriving at a stony and burnt-up spot. Perfuming one's self. Longing for a man (a woman). *Karaʿ*, (v. n. of كرع) Courageously eating up shins and shank-bones. Longing for a man, being lustful (a woman). A base, abject wretch. Slenderness of shin. The leg of a quadruped. Rain-water collected in a cistern. A place.

A كرعان *kirʿān*, (pl. of كراع *kurāʿ*) Promontories.

A كرعة *kariʿat*, Libidinous (girl).

P كرغ *kuragh*, A plant used to bind up a dislocated shoulder.

P كرغست *harghast*, A plant bearing a yellow flower with which they feed cattle. A kind of potherb eaten boiled.

P كرف *karf*, Liquid pitch. A black stuff used by goldsmiths. *Kurf*, Pitch.

A كرف *karf*, (v. n. of كرف) Smelling to. Smelling the urine of the female (a male-ass), and then raising the head and inverting the lips.

A كرفأة *karfaʾat*, (v. n. of كرفأ Q) Foaming (a boiling pot). Being mingled together (men). Being very thick (hair). Compact, unblown (flower).

P كرفت *kirift*, Dirt, soil, foulness. A man who does not purify himself after any uncleanly act, or take care to avoid pollution.

P كرفج *karfaj*, A species of grass, broom, or heather, with which they light fires.

P كرفس *karafs*, A plant of which they make a salad, the seeds of which are said to promote venery.

A كرفس *karafs*, Parsley. كرفس صحرائي *karafsi sahrāʾī*, Wild parsley. كرفس كوهي *karafsi kohī*, Rock or mountain-parsley. *Kurfus*, Cotton.

A كرفسة *karfasat*, (v. n. of كرفس Q) Being close fettered (a camel). Going as if the feet were bound.

P كرفش *karfash*, A species of poisonous lizard infesting houses. (Whoever destroys one of these reptiles is considered entitled to a reward of seven maunds (من *man*) of wheat).

P كرفه *kirfa*, Virtue, merit.

A كرفئ *kirfiʾ*, A high-towering cloud.

A كرفئة *kirfiʾat*, A part of a high cloud. The outward shell of an egg. The caper-tree.

P كرك *kark*, A domestic fowl. A partridge. A crab. The pupil of the eye. The limb of a tree. *Karak*, A kind of quail. The roof of a house. Name of a town near Jerusalem.

A كرك *kark* or *karak*, Name of a place on the confines of Arabia Petrea. *Karik*, Red.

A كرّك *kurrak*, A kind of game.

P كركاس *karkās*, A plant that grows among

corn; tares, darnel.

P کرکام *karkām*, Strength, ability. Desire, will.

A کرکب *kurkub*, Name of a fragrant plant.

A کرکدن *karkaddan*, (often pronounced as if written کرکدنّ *karkadann*) A rhinoceros.

P کرکر *karkar*, God. A powerful prince. A fir, pine-tree. *Kirkir*, A kind of bean or pea.

A کرکر *karkar*, The sheath of a camel, goat, or bull. Name of a town near بیلقان *baylakān*, built by Noshiravān.

P کرکرانك *karkarānak*, Gristle or soft bone.

A کرکرة *karkarat*, (v. n. of کرکر Q) Turning (a mill). Grinding coarsely. Driving, agitating (as wind the clouds). Thrusting away, repelling. Collecting, gathering together. Retaining, detaining. Calling (to a fowl). Being routed, put to flight. Laughing immoderately. (v. n. 2 of کرّ) Causing to return time after time. *Kirkirat*, The callous part of the breast, on which a camel or other soft-footed animals recline. A crowd, assembly of people. ابن کرکرة *ibn kirkirat*, Name of a lexicographer.

P کرکرك *karkarak*, A wagtail. A magpie. A quail.

P کرکروهن *karkarūhan*, A tonic electuary, composed of split cubebs, mace, sandal, spikenard, oak-apples, honey, and the seed called فلنجه *falanja*.

A کرکرة *karkara*, Immoderate laughter.

P کرکرهن *karkarhin*, Pellitory.

P کرکري *karkarī* or *kurkurī*, Gristle, soft bone.

P کرکز *karkuz*, A directing-post: road-guide.

A کرکسة *karkasat*, (v. n. of کرکس Q) Driving about, tossing to and fro. Making prisoner.

P کرکفیز *karkafīz*, A skimmer.

A کرکم *karkam* or *kurkum*, Saffron; a yellow root which dies of a saffron colour; dioscorides; name of a medicine. The gum of pine or juniper. The rainbow.

P کرکما *karkamā*, A wagtail.

P کرکمان *kurkumān*, The lot-tree.

A کرکمان *kurkumān*, Sufficiency to support life.

P کرکمیسه *karkamīsa*, Name of a fine, sweet-smelling flower, chiefly found on the mountain Alwand.

P کرکن *karkan*, *karkin*, or *karkun*, Wheat, barley, vetches, or beans, cooked when half ripe.

P کرکوز *karkūz*, A direction-post: road-guide.

A کرکیٰ *karka'*, One who suffers himself to be abused contrary to nature; a catamite.

P کرکی *kurkī*, A sort of crane, whose brains, if applied to the eyes, are said to cure blindness.

A کرکیّ *kurkiy*, (pl. کراکي *karākiy*) A sort of crane, whose brain and gall are supposed to possess marvellous medicinal virtues.

A کرکیدة *kirkidat*, A hamper of dates. Dates left in a bin.

P کرگ *karg*, A rhinoceros. *Kurg*, A hen which has done laying, and is inclined for the cock. A kind of down or fine wool combed from the roots of the long hair of a goat, of which shawls are manufactured. *Kurag*, A head rendered bald from a scald; the disease called the scald head.

P کرگدن *kargadan*, The rhinoceros. A huge kind of bird which pursues an elephant ten years old.

P کرگس *kargas*, A vulture. A sort of arrow. کرگس ترکش *kargasi tarkash*, Arrows left in the quiver. کرگس فلك *kargasi falak*, The dog-star. کرگسان فلك *kargasāni falak*, The constellations called نسر طائر *nasri tāïr*, The Eagle; and نسر واقع *nasri wākiꜥ*, The falling vulture, *i. e.* the Lyre.

P کرگسار *karagsār*, Name of a place and hero.

P کرگسي *kargasī*, The nature of a vulture. کرگسي کردن *kargasī kardan*, To imitate a vulture.

P کرم *karm*, Any species of plant growing by the water-side. *Kirm*, A worm. کرم ایوب *kirmi ayyūb*, The worm of Job, the silkworm. کرم بادامه *kirmi bādāma*, The silkworm. کرم شبتاب *kirmi shab-tāb*, The glowworm. کرم گرفتن *kirm giriftan*, To breed worms. *Kurm*, Grief, sorrow, affliction, wound, hurt. *Karam*, A cauliflower, cabbage.

A کرم *karm*, (v. n. of کرم) Excelling in honour, nobility, generosity, munificence. Land from out of which the stones have been picked. A mode of founding, casting, or moulding. A kind of ornament worn in the days of paganism. (pl. کروم *kurūm*) A grape-vine. A necklace, ornament for the neck. A true believer, religious man. P کرم دشتي *karmi dashtī*, Bryony. A *Kurm*, Generosity, nobility. *Karam*, (v. n. of کرم) Being generous, liberal, honourable. Noble, generous. Good, generous (land). Generosity, liberality, nobleness, grandeur, magnificence, beneficence, grace, favour, clemency, courtesy, graciousness, goodness, kindness, benignity. High breed. *Kuram*, Good, generous (lands).

A کرماً *karman*, For the sake of honouring.

A کرماء *kuramā*, (pl. of کریم) Noble, generous.

P کرمان *karmān* or *kirmān*, Carmania, famous for steel. The capital of Caramania. *Kirmān*, A castle; an emporium.

A کرمان *kurmān*, Generosity, liberality. کرماناً له *kurmānan lahu*, In honour of him.

P کرمانشاه *karmān-shāh*, Name of a province in Persian Irāk.

P کرمان شهان *kirmān-shahān*, Name of a city.

P کرماني *kirmānī*, Belonging to Karmān. Carmanian, also Damascus steel.

P کرمائیل *karmāïl*, One of Zahhāk's cooks.

P کرم پیشه *karam-pesha*, Munificent, liberal.

P کرمپیله *kirm-pīla*, A silkworm.

A کرمة *karmat*, One vine. The top of the thigh-bone. *Kirmat*, Noble, generous (woman). *Kurmat*, Liberality, magnificence. Benignity. *Karamat*, (v. n. of کرم) Being generous, liberal, honourable.

A کرمة *kurmatan*, (or کرمة عین *kurmata ꜥayn*) In honour of.

A کرمحة *karmahat*, (v. n. of کرمح Q) Waddling like a dwarf. Throwing on the ground.

P کرم خورده *kirm-khwurda*, Worm-eaten.

P کرمدانه *kirm-dāna*, A species of mezereon. Myrtle-seed.

A کرمدة *karmadat*, A running in the track of.

P کرمك *karmak*, A food prepared from pulse. *Kirmak*, A small worm. A fire-fly. An herb with which they wash. An enigma.

P کرمکار *karam-kār*, Generous, gracious. Merciful. Benevolent.

P کرم کن *karam kun*, Do (me) the favour.

P کرمگستر *karam-gustar*, Gracious, diffusive.

A کرمل *kirmil*, Carmel, in Palestine.

P کرمند *karmand*, Quick, speedy, hasty, expeditious. Haste, expedition.

P کرموش *kar-mosh*, A deaf mouse. A mole.

A کرميٰ *kurma'*, Generosity, liberality.

P کرمیخ *kur-mekh*, A nail having a large broad head. A large-headed peg, pin, or stake.

P کرن *kuran*, A dun-coloured horse.

P کرنا *karnā*, The ass-mushroom or fungus. The red gooseberry. A trumpet.

P کرناتك *karnātak*, The Carnatic.

A کرناس *kirnās*, A cotton or muslin garment.

A کرناف *kirnāf* or *kurnāf*, (pl. کرانیف *karānīf*) The palm-tree's trunk after the branches are cut off.

P کرنامه *kar-nāma*, Example, model, exemplar.

P کرّناي *karranāy*, A kind of trumpet.

P کرنب *karamb*, Cabbage, cauliflower. کرنب رومي *karambi rūmī*, A cauliflower. *Karnab*, A species of poison for dogs.

A کرنب *kurnub* or *karamb*, Beet; a kind of beet.

P کرنبا *karambā*, A dish prepared from cabbage. A carpet. *Kurimbā*, Name of a carpenter's tool.

A کرنبة *karnabat*, Gift of milk and dates to a guest.

A کرنبیّة *karnabīyat*, A dish made of cabbage.

P کرنج *kiranj* or *karanj*, A sort of date. Poison. *Karinj*, *kiranj*, or *kurinj*, Coriander-seed. *Kurinj*, Rice. Black pepper. Silver. A falcon, a hawk. کرنج خانه *kurinj-khāna*, A falconry, a house for hawks.

P کرنجو *karanjū*, The nightmare.

P کرند *kurand*, (کرنده *karinda*, or *kuranda*) A course for racing. A concourse or circle of men. A grey colour in a horse. A large circle formed by huntsmen. A dyer's vat. Name of a river in Loristān. *Kurund*, (کرنده *karinda*, or *kuranda*) A sort of brush, used by weavers and the like in putting their size or glue on their yarn.

A کرنفة *karnafat*, (v. n. of کرنف Q) Cutting with a sword. Striking with a stick. Cutting the trunks of palm-trees (called کرانیف *karānīf*). *Kurnafat*, Slender-bodied (man or camel).

P کرنگ *kurang*, A bay-horse. A place for exercising troops. A ring made by hunters or troops. Name of a river in Loristān.

P کرنگاني *karangānī*, A species of grapes.

P کرنگه *kurangah*, A race-ground. A place for reviewing troops. A bay colour. A dyer's vat. Name of a river in Loristān. *Kurungah*, A weaver's brush.

P کرنه *karna*, Name of a village in Badakhshān famous for its pears. *Kirna*, A kind of thorn eaten by camels. A sort of snake. A tike, sheep-louse.

A کرنیب *karnib* or *kirnib*, Milk and dates.

A کرنیفة *kirnīfat*, A thick nose.

A کرو *karw*, (v. n. of کرا for کرو) Walking pompously or gracefully (a woman). Digging. Building up (a well with wood). Playing or striking with a ball. Going fast (a horse). Repeating, reiterating, doing over again. *Kirw* or *kurw*, Price, hire.

P کرو *karū*, That part of a spider's web in which it lays its eggs. *Karv* or *kirav*, A hollow tooth. Broken, rugged. Bitter lettuce, endive. *Kirav*, A small ship, boat. *Kurū*, Name of Afrāsyāb's kinsman.

P کروا *karwā*, A joining, uniting.

A کرواء *karwā*, Slender-legged and thick-armed (woman).

P کروان *karwān*, Name of a plant of an exhilarating property. Name of a bird.

A کروان *karawān*, (pl. کروان *kirwān* and کراوین *karāwīn*) A red-legged partridge. A bustard. A woodpecker. Name of a village in Tūs.

P کروانك *karwānak*, A bustard, crane.

A کروب *kurūb*, (v. n. of کرب) Approaching. Being near setting (sun), near expiring (life or fire); being near doing any thing. Lading a beast of burden. Eating the dates کرابة *kurābat*. Making (the rolling-pin) clatter. (pl. of کرب *karb*) Griefs, cares.

P کرّوبیان *karrūbiyān*, Angelic ranks, cherubim.

A کروبین *karūbīn*, Cherubim. ملائکهٔ کروبین *malāʼikaʼi karūbīn*, The cherub angels.

A کروبیّون *karūbiyūn*, (pl. of کروبيّ) Cherubim.

A کروة *kirwat* or *kurwat*, Price, hire.

P کروت *kurūt*, Fat.

P کروتنه *karawtana*, A spider.

P کروخ *kurūkh*, Name of a village in Khurāsān.

P کروخان *kurūkhān*, The brother of Pīrānwīsah.

P کرود *karūd* or *kurūd*, A well so deep that it is with difficulty water can be drawn from it.

A کرور *kurūr*, (v. n. of کرّ) Rushing upon, attacking. Returning, receding. Shewing kindness, inclining to. (pl. of کرّ *karr*) Napkins for kneeling on at prayers.

P کروز *kurūz*, (or کروژ *kurūj*) Cheerfulness; song, dance. Sorrow, distress of mind.

A کروز *kurūz*, (v. n. of کرز) Entering. Absconding, lurking, taking refuge. Inclining. Smelling urine (a stallion).

P کروس *kirwas*, An enigma.

A کروّس *karawwas* or *karawwus*, Large-headed. Black. (A camel) with large hoofs and legs.

A کروش *kurūsh*, (pl. of کرش *kirsh* and *karish*) Paunches, maws of ruminants.

A کروع *kurūʻ*, (v. n. of کرع) Drinking with the mouth (without using a vessel or hands).

P کروکر *karūkar*, A name of God. A workman

A کروم *kurūm*, (pl. of کرم *karm*) Vines.

P کرون *kurwan*, A dun-coloured horse.

P کرونیس *karūnīs*, Name of an island in which وامق *wāmik* the lover of عذرا *ʻazrā* lived.

P کروه *karwa*, A hollow or a rotten tooth. *Kuroh*, A road-measure of about two miles. The nest or roost of birds. *Karawa*, An animal whose bite is said to be worse than that of a serpent.

A کرويّ *kurawiy*, Spherical, globular.

A کرویا *karawya'*, Caraways.

A کروياء *karwiyā* or *karawyā*, Caraway-seeds or plant.

P کرویز *karwīz* or *karawīz*, Speech, reason.

P کرویه *karwiya*, Caraway.

A کره *kariha*, (fut. یکره *yakrahu*) He detested.

A کره *karh*, Whatever one is compelled by another to do reluctantly. A strong-headed camel. *Karh* or *kurh*, (v. n. of کره) Hating, abhorring, objecting to, disliking, disapproving. Aversion, abomination, detestation, abhorrence. Trouble, molestation. *Karh* or *karih*, Detestable, abominable. *Kurh*, What one forces one's self to do reluctantly.

P کره *kara*, Filth, dirt, nastiness. Fresh butter. The skin of the hands or feet become hard and stiff from labour. A chamber in a place of repose for travellers, or a school. Staleness, mustiness. Mouldiness of bread or fruit. A bracelet of gold or silver. A clasp. A spider's web where she lays her eggs. A kind of thorn. Name of a city. کره بستن *kara bastan*, (or بر آوردن *bar āwardan*) To contract mould, become mouldy, stale, or musty. *Kura*, A cannon-ball. A globe. A thing spherical. A lock. A ward of a lock. A smith's forge. A colt. An element. کرهٔ آب *kuraʼi āb*, The water which surrounds the globe. کرهٔ ارض *kuraʼi arz*, (or کرهٔ خاك *kuraʼi khāk*) The terrestrial globe. کرهٔ لاجورد *kuraʼi lājuward*, (or کرهٔ وهم‌سوز *kuraʼi wahm-soz*) The sky.

P کرّه *kurra*, The colt of a horse, camel, or ass (one or two years old). A girth, surcingle, belt. کرّهٔ آب *kurraʼi āb*, A wave.

A کرهاً *karhan*, (or علیٰ کره *ʻala' karhin*) With difficulty, inconveniently. *Kurhan*, Unwillingly.

P کره بسته *kara-basta*, Mouldy, musty.

P کره‌تن *kara-tan*, A spider.

P کره‌دان *karadān*, A place for rubbish.

P کرّه گري *kurragari*, A strapping, a flogging.

A کرهيْ *kar* or *kurha'*, The upper part of the cavity of the hind-head. The face with the head.

A کري *kary*, (v. n. of کري) Digging. Playing with a ball. *Kara'*, (v. n. of کري) Inclining to sleeping, dozing. Being slender-limbed. Throwing her legs about when running (a she-camel). Running fast, or leaping. An inclination to sleep. Digging (a well). A bustard. A male red-legged partridge. A male woodpecker. Sleep. *Karī*, Sleepy; slumbering. A runner. *Kura'*, (pl. of کرة *kurat*) Balls, globes, spheres.

P کري *karī*, Deafness. That part of the spider's web where she lays her eggs.

A کرّيْ *kurra'*, Once, one time. One attack.

A کريّ *kariy*, Sleepy; slumbering. A runner. A hirer out of mules, asses, or horses, a muleteer. A taker on hire. Much of any thing. A kind of plant. A tree growing in sand. (pl. of کرة *kurat*) Balls, globes, spheres. *Kuriy*, Spherical, globular.

P کریاس *kiryās*, Court or levee of a prince.

A کریاس *kiryās*, (pl. کرابیس *karāyis*) A privy on the roof of a house, having a communication with a subterraneous passage.

A کریان *karyān*, Somnolent, sleepy. A runner.

P کریان *kiryān* or *kuryān*, Sacrifice, ransom.

A کریب *karīb*, Ploughed land or a sown field destitute of trees and buildings. Sad, mournful. The knot of a reed. A baker's rolling-pin.

A کریبة *karībat*, (pl. کرائب *karāʼib*) Misfortune.

A کریّة *kariyat*, A tree growing in sand. A plant.

A کریت *karīt*, Entire, complete (year).

P کریتونتن *karītūnitan*, (in zand & Pāz.) To read.

A کریث *karīs*, Troublesome (business). A coward, one who shrinks from any disagreeable business. کریث الامر *karīsu'l amr*, Bothered, nonplused by any affair.

A کریثاء *karīsā*, A good unripe date.

P کریچ *kārij*, (or کریچ *kurīch*) A roof for protecting unthreshed corn from the rain. The moulting of birds' feathers. *Karīj*, (کریجه *kurīja*, or کریچه *kurīcha*) A small house. A hut or cottage formed of wood, reeds, and straw on the side of a cornfield or melon-ground.

A کریر *karīr*, (v. n. of کرّ) Returning, receding. Rushing upon, attacking. Shewing kindness, inclining to. Making a rattling noise in the throat (a strangling man). A sound in the breast resembling that of a person strangling or dying. Hoarseness from dust. Name of a river.

P کریر *kurīr*, An overseer, superintendant.

A کریرج *kurayraj*, A kind of short green fish.

P کریز *karīz* or *kurīz*, The moulting of birds. A hut built of reeds. A corner. *Kurīz*, A falconry.

A کریز *karīz*, Soft cheese called اقط *akit*.

P کریزه *kurīza*, A hut, hovel, shed. Moulting.

P کریزی *kurīzī*, An old man bent with age and infirmities, and in a state of dotage. A falcon moulting in the desert. Any thing given to birds to make them shed their feathers.

P کریس *kirīs*, Fraud, deceit. Flattery.

P کریسه *kirīsa*, Fraud, deceit.

P کریسیدن *kirīsīdan*, To deceive, defraud, cheat.

P کریشك *kireshak*, A warrior. A deep hollow place, a cavern. A chick, chicken.

P کریشنگ *kurīshang*, A mountain. A cavern.

A کریص *karīs*, (v. n. of کرص) Mixing soft cheese with dates. The soft, acid cheese called اقط *akit* mixed with طراثيث *tarāsis* or حماصيص *ḥamāṣiṣ*. A treasure, hoard. A cooking of wild-sorrel and milk, and a drying and eating of it in the summer. The place where the cheese اقط *akiṭ* is made.

A کريض *karīẓ*, A sort of cheese.

A کريع *karīʻ*, One who drinks water from a river with the hands (having no vessel).

P کريغ *kurīgh*, Flight. Moulting of birds.

P کريفتن *kurēftan*, To flee, escape, retreat.

P کريم *karīm*, Name of an ancestor of Rustam-Zāl. Name of a city in Karmania.

A کريم *karīm*, (pl. اکرماء *akrimāʼ*, کرماء *kuramāʼ*, and کرام *kirām*) Generous, munificent, liberal, magnificent, splendid, grand. Benign, benevolent, beneficent, kind, courteous, gracious, merciful, forgiving, venerable, reverend: respectable, high-bred. One of the attributes of God. A religious man, fearing God. Easy, kind, conciliatory (language). Abundant and good (food). کريم الشان *karīmu'sh shān*, (or کريم الاخلاق *karīmu'l akhlāḳ*) Most noble, generous. کريم النفس *karīmu'n nafs*, Of a noble, generous soul. الله کريم *allāh karīm*, God is merciful.

P کريما *karīmā*, O merciful (God)!

P کريمان *karīmān*, The great-great-grandfather of Rustam-Zāl. A city in Karmania.

A کريماني *karīmāni*, du., Pilgrimage and holy war.

P کريمانه *karīmāna*, Generous. Generously.

A کريمة *karīmat*, (fem. of کريم *karīm*) (pl. کرائم *karāʼim*) Noble, generous. A princess, lady. The nose. The ear. The hand. A verse of the Kur'ān: as, کريمهٔ انا فتحنا لک فتحا مبينا *karīmaʼi* (for آيت کريمهٔ *āyati karīmaʼi*) *innā fataḥnā laka fatḥan mubīnan*, That sacred verse of the Kur'ān, "We have granted to thee a decisive victory" (a mode of expression used by the Muhammadan writers when they quote the standard of their religion).

A الکريمتان *al karīmatāni*, The two eyes (as the noblest or most precious parts of the body).

A کريمية *karīmīyat*, Bountifulness.

A کرين *kirīn* or *kurīn*, (pl. of کرة *kurat*) Globes, spheres. Cannon-balls.

A کرينة *karīnat*, (pl. کران) A female musician.

P کرينونتن *karīnūnitan*, (zand and Pāz.) To read.

P کريودوم *karayūdūm*, Perfidy, breach of faith.

P کريون *karyūn*, Centaury.

A کريه *karīh*, Detestable, abominable, dirty, filthy, offensive. A lion. کريه الصوت *karīhu's sawt*, Harsh, unpleasing-voiced. کريه المنظر *karīhu'l manẓar*, Ugly in countenance. الکريه *al karīh*, The lion.

A کريهة *karīhat*, (fem. of کريه *karīh*) Detestable. War, and the calamitous circumstances attending it. A disaster. Impetuosity, vehemence. ذو الکريهة *ẕū'l karīhat*, A sharp sword penetrating at one blow.

P کز *kaz*, Raw silk. *K'az*, (for که از *ki az*) From which, by what, whence. That from. *Kaz* or *kaza*, Name of a country in India.

A کز *kazz*, (v. n. of کز) Contracting (one's steps). Being seized with ague or a shivering fit. (pl. کز *kuzz*) Dry, contracted, shrivelled. Avaricious. Ugly (in face). Hard, rigid, stiff.

P کزابه *kazāba*, A camel-litter for women.

P کزاد *ka* or *kizād*, An old, worn-out garment.

P کزار *kuzār*, A lancet.

A کزاز *kuzāz*, (or کزاز *kuzzāz*) A disease from cold; trembling, ague.

A کزازة *kazāzat*, (v. n. of کز) Being dry, drawn together. Being of an acrid and astringent taste. Being stingy and good for nothing.

P کزاغ *kuzāgh*, An herb used in bandaging dislocated joints.

P کزاوه *kazāwa*, A camel-litter for women.

P کزايش *kizāyish* or *kuzāyish*, Fit, proper, suitable. A stick for driving cattle.

A کزب *kuzb*, The sediment of fruits or sesame remaining in the hair-cloth after the juice or oil is expressed. (It is given to the poor or to cattle). A kind of hard tree. *Kazab*, A smallness and narrowness of the instep (regarded as a blemish).

P کزبا *kazbā*, A gooseberry or bastard corinth.

A کزبرة *kuzburat*, Coriander.

P کزبود *kazbūd*, A chief, master of a family.

P کزبه *kazba*, Dregs of oil and the like.

A کزة *kazzat*, Shrivelled (woman). Close, creaking (pulley). Dry, rigid, stiff (bow), difficult to bend.

P کزد *kazd*, The loppings of a tree.

P کزديدن *kazdīdan*, To lop, clip, trim, polish.

P کزردن *kuzardan*, To seek for help or aid.

P کزره *kuzra*, Name of a sweet-scented grass. A watered field. Irrigation.

A کزز *kazaz*, Avarice.

P کزطرخون *kaztarkhūn*, Pellitory. Dracunculus.

P کزغ *kuzgh* or *kuzagh*, An herb which they fasten round dislocated bones. *Kazagh*, A kind of medicine.

P کزف *kuzf*, Black stuff used by goldsmiths. *Kuzf*, *kazaf*, or *kazif*, Pitch. Silver burnt black.

P کزلک *kizlik*, A knife, penknife, scraper, clasp-knife, razor. The curved point of a sword or dagger.

P کزم *kazm*, An herb growing on banks of rivers.

A کزم *kazm*, (v. n. of کزم) Breaking with the front-teeth, and extracting the contents to eat them. *Kazam*, Shortness and thickness of lips in quadrupeds. Shortness of nose or of fingers. Avarice. Voraciousness. *Kazim*, A poltroon, coward. *Kuzam*, A nightingale. A young sparrow. A bird resembling a sparrow.

A کزماء *kazmāʼ*, Short-lipped (mare). Short in the nose or arms (woman). Short (nose or hand). Short-fingered (hand).

A کزمازج *kizmāzaj*, (or کزمازک *kazmāzak*) The berries of the tamarisk. The tamarisk.

A کزمة *kazmat*, Compact, close (fat).

P کزن *kazan*, A catamite. A village where many people meet on the day called عاشورا *ʻāshūrā*.

P کزنده *kazinda*, A teasel. A meshy sack.

P کزنه *kaz* or *kizna*, A rock-swallow. Nettle-seed.

P کزني *kaznay*, Wet, withered (plant in winter).

P کزو *kazu*, (for که ازاو *ki azu*) Who or which, from that or him.

P کزوا *kazwā*, A gooseberry or bastard currant.

P کزوان *kizwān*, Mountain-balm.

A کزوزة *kuzūzat*, (v. n. of کز) Being dry, shrivelled. Being of an acrid and astringent taste. Being stingy and good for nothing.

P کزوغ *kazūgh*, The vertebræ in man or beast.

A کزوم *kazūm*, An old toothless camel.

A کزي *kazy*, (v. n. of کزي) Conferring favours on an emancipated slave.

P کزين *kazīn*, (Made) of raw silk.

P کزين فروش *kazīn-farosh*, A vender of raw silk.

P کژ *kaj*, Crooked, curved, distorted. Coarse silk of little value. کژ کردن *kaj kardan*, To crook, bend, twist. *Kuj*, The root of a tree.

P کژابه *kajāba*, A camel-litter in which Persian ladies travel; it may be covered or opened at pleasure. The arched covering of cradles.

P کژاته *kajāta*, Cod of the silkworm, cocoon.

P کژار *kajār*, A strip or piece of any thing torn off. *Kujār*, The crop of a bird.

P کژاريدن *kajārīdan*, To tear, tear in pieces.

P کژآغند *kaj-āghand*, (کژآغندش *kaj-āghandish*, کژآگند *kaj-āgand*, or کژآگندش *kaj-āgandish*) A kind of jerkin, of thick quilted cotton or silk, worn in battle instead of armour.

P کژاوه *kajāwa*, A litter on a camel's back.

P کژبين *kaj-bīn*, Squinting. Malignant.

P کژپا *kaj-pā*, Wry-footed, whose foot is distorted.

P کژترخون *kajtarkhūn*, Pellitory. Dracunculus.

P کژچشم *kaj-chashm*, Squint-eyed.

P کژچشمي *kaj-chashmī*, Strabism, squint.

P کژخاطران *kaj-khātirān*, (pl.) Cross-grained.

P کژدست *kaj-dast*, One with a distorted hand.

P کژدم *kaj-dum*, A scorpion (crook-tail). The sign Scorpio. کژدم بحري *kajdumi baḥrī*, Name of a dark-coloured fish of the sword-fish kind. کژدم گردون *kajdumi gardūn*, (کژدم طاس آبگون *kajdumi tāsi āb-gūn*, کژدم فلک *kajdumi falak*, or کژدم نيلوفري *kajdumi nīlūfarī*) The sign Scorpio.

P کژدم خواره *kajdum-khwāra*, Name of a poisonous reptile.

P کژدمناک *kajdumnāk*, Abounding in scorpions.

P کژدمه *kajduma*, A whitlow.

P کژرف *kajraf*, Name of a stinking herb.

P کژرفتار *kaj-raftār*, Walking shamblingly, going awry, crooked, in-kneed.

P کژرنگ *kaj-rang*, Whitish-coloured.

P کژطرخون *kaj-tarkhūn*, Pellitory. Dracunculus.

P کژغا *kajghā*, (or کژغاو *kajghāw*) The mountain-ox of Tibet with a bushy tail. The sea-ox.

P کژغان *kajghān*, A cauldron, pot.

P کژف *kujf*, Burnt silver. Pitch.

P کژک *kajak*, The iron hook with which they goad and regulate the motions of the elephant. A crooked stick attached to a tall post, to which they fasten balls of gold and silver as marks and prizes to archers. A crooked stick with which they strike their large kettle-drums. Any kind of hook or crook. The wards of a lock. The feathers of a duck's tail with which women adorn their heads. An earthen jar in which rose-water and dates are kept.

P کژگا *hajgā*, (or کژگاو *hajgāw*) The bushy-tailed cow of Tibet. The sea-ox; also his tail.

P کژمازون *kajmāzūn*, Name of a medicine.

P کژمژ *kajmaj*, Crooked, distorted.

P کژمژزبان *kajmaj-zabān*, A child that cannot yet speak plain.

P کژمیان *kaj-miyān*, Crooked about the loins.

P کژنظر *kaj-nazar*, Squint-eyed.

P کژنه *kajna*, A patch.

P کژور *kajūr*, Zedoary, a Chinese root.

P کژوند *kajwand*, The wards of a lock.

P کژه *kaja*, A hook or crook. An iron hook with which they drive and guide elephants. A curved stick with which they beat a drum. Shambles. The uvula. The wards of a lock. A piece of wood so placed as to prevent a lock from being opened.

P کژي *kajī*, Crookedness, curvature, obliquity.

P کژيغ *kajīgh*, Flight, departure.

P کژيم *kajīm*, (or کژين *kajīn*) A quilted jacket worn in battle. Horse-armour.

P کس *kas*, A man, person. One, any one, some one. Intelligent, learned (persons). کس وناکس *kas u nākas*, Every body, noble and plebeian. همه کس *hama kas*, (or هرکس *har kas*) Every body, all the world. *Kus*, Pudendum muliebre. کس و کن *kus u kun*, Vulva et podex.

A كسّ *kass*, (v. n. of كسّ) Pounding small. *Kuss*, (pl. اكساس *aksās*) Vulva.

A كسء *kas*, (v. n. of كسأ) Following, pursuing, driving (one beast) after another. Striking (with a sword). Overcoming (at law). (pl. كسوء *kusūs*) Part of the night. *Kus*, (pl. اكساء *aksās*) The latter part (of any thing). ركب كساه *rakiba kussahu*, He fell on his back.

P كسا *kasā*, A sort of coarse woollen cloth.

A كساء *kasās*, Glory, nobility, eminence. *Kisās*, (v. n. 3 of كسا for كسو) Contending about glory. (pl. اكسية *aksiyat*) A garment, an upper short cloak. Milk covered with cream. (pl. of كسوة *kuswat* or *kiswat*) Vestments, clothes, garments.

A كساب *kasābi*, A wolf.

A كسّاب *kassāb*, (A man) who gains much.

A كسابر *kasābir*, (pl. of كسبر) Ivory bracelets.

A كساح *kusāh*, A disease incident to camels.

A كساحة *kusāhat*, Impotency in the hands or feet, lameness. Sweepings, rubbish. Swept snow.

A كساد *kasād*, (v. n. of كسد) Not meeting with customers. Difficulty in despatching of any thing, badness of markets, cheapness of merchandise, decline of trade, unsaleableness, flatness, dulness.

P كسار *kusār*, (in comp.) Drinking. Suffering, undergoing: as, ميكسار *may-kusār*, Drinking wine. غمكسار *gham-kusār*, Experiencing sorrow.

A كسار *kusār*, Chips, fragments.

A كسّار *kassār*, A breaker in pieces.

A كسارة *kusārat*, A fragment. A fraction.

P كساردن *kusārdan*, To endure. To drink.

P كسارنده *kusāranda*, A drinker. Suffering.

A كساري *kasāra'*, (pl. of كسير *kasīr*) Broken.

A كساسرة *kasāsirat*, (pl. of كسري *kisra'*) Chosroes, kings of Persia.

A كسافة *kasūfat*, Eclipse: obscuration. Sediment.

A كسالة *kasālat*, Heaviness, slowness, gravity. Sickness, grief, affliction, distress. Embarrassment.

A كسالى *kasāla'*, *kisāla'*, *kusāla'*, and *kasālī*, (pl. of كسلان *kaslān*) Lazy, slothful, slow, heavy.

P كسان *kasān*, (pl. of كس *kas*) Men, persons.

P كسانه *kasāna*, Human, like a man; humanity.

A كساوي *kasāwī*, Garments, vestments.

A كسائي *kisāīy*, Name of an Arabian grammarian.

A كسب *kasb*, (v. n. of كسب) Gaining, acquiring, earning. Seeking one's daily bread. Causing to get or gain. Gain; acquisition (by labour), industry. Art, trade, profession, employment, handicraft. P كسب فضائل كردن *kasbi fazāil kardan*, To acquire science. A *Kisb*, Gain, acquisition. *Kush*, Sediment after the oil is extracted.

A كسبة *kasbat*, A bitch's name. *Kisbat*, Gain, or a mode of acquisition.

P كسبت *kisbat*, The case (or the bag) in which barbers or surgeons keep their instruments. A bit of leather worn by a waterman on his left hip, on which he rests the bag containing water.

P كسبت نامه *kisbat-nāma*, A book containing the histories of barbers or surgeons, with directions for their practice. The bhishtis (water-carriers in India) have also such a book.

A كسبج *kusbuj*, Sediment, dregs.

A كسبر *kusbar*, (pl. كسابر) An ivory bracelet.

A كسبرة *kusburat* or *kusbarat*, Coriander.

P كسبند *kus-band*, A belt, a girth.

P كسبه *kusba*, Sesame-grains remaining in the hair-cloth after the oil has been expressed, which they give to the poor, or as food to buffaloes.

A كسبي *kasbī*, An artisan. A prostitute.

P كسپرج *hasparaj*, A pearl.

P كست *kast*, Shameful, dirty, base. A blueish gem with a tincture of red. *Kist*, (for كه است *ki ast*) Who is he? *Kust*, Cauliflower, cabbage.

A كست *kust*, The costus, a kind of shrub.

A كستج *kustaj*, An armful (of palm-tree fibres).

P كستر *kastar*, A black thorn.

P كستل *kastal*, A beetle, tumble-dung.

P كستن *kustan*, To pound. To seize. To put on a girdle.

P كسته *kusta*, Pounded; rice that has been separated from the husk by pounding, but not cleared from the chaff. Shepherd's-staff (an herb).

P كستي *kustī*, Wrestling. A girdle worn by the Parsis and Brahmins; also by the wrestlers of Khurāsān.

A كستيج *kustīj*, (from P كستي *kustī*) A girdle.

P كستيمه *kustīma*, A thorny plant of which camels are fond.

A كسح *kas-h*, (v. n. of كسح) Sweeping (a house with a broom). Brushing the earth (wind). Weakness, impotency. *Kasah*, (v. n. of كسح) Having a weakness in the hands or feet. *Kāsih*, One who does not give assistance when called to.

A كسحان *kas-hān*, Weak in the hands or feet. *Kus-hān*, (pl. of اكسح *aksah*) Lame, unable to move.

A كسحبة *has-habat*, The motion of any one who is frightened, and who strives to conceal himself.

A كسد *husd*, The costus, a kind of shrub.

A كسر *kasara*, (fut. يكسر *yaksiru*) He brake.

A كسر *kasr*, (v. n. of كسر) Breaking. Destroying. Routing, putting to flight. Marking with the vowel point kasra. Closing the wings (as a bird descending). Bringing forth merchandise by degrees (as one piece when another is sold). Casting down the eyes. Taking little trouble in looking after one's camels. Doubling a cushion and lying down upon it. A rupture, breach, rout. A fraction in arithmetic. Affliction, contrition. An allowance upon the exchange of rupees. The vowel point kasr or kasra ـِـ, or short *i*. A small, trifling, or insipid affair. P كسرنفس كردن *kasri nafs kardan*, To mortify the flesh, to humble one's self. A *Kasr* or *kisr*, (pl. اكسار *aksār* and كسور *kusūr*) The lower part of a tent, or the flap nearest the ground, in which are openings for the convenience of going in and out. The side of a house. A portion of the body or members. A complete member. Half a bone with flesh upon it. A bone with a little flesh on it. كسرقبيح *kisru kabīhin*, The bone of the fore-arm, half-way of the elbow. كسر الصحراء *kasru's sahrās*, Both sides to a desert. *Kasar* or *kasir*, Trouble which one is unable to bear. *Kisar*, (pl. of كسرة *kisrat*) Fragments, broken pieces. *Kusar*, High and low lands.

A كسّر *kussar*, (pl. of كاسر and كاسرة) Breakers.

A كسرات *kasarāt*, (or ذو كسرات *zū kasarāt*) One who is cozened in buying or selling.

A كسرة *kasrat*, The vowel ـِـ *i*. One fracture. Affliction. Flight, rout (of an enemy). *Kisrat*, (pl. كسر *kisar*) A fragment, broken piece.

A كسرويّ *kisrawīy*, (or كسريّ *kisrīy*) Royal.

A كسري *kasra'*, (pl. of كسير *kasīr*) Broken. *Kisra'* or *kasra'*, (from P خسرو *khus-rav*, Of wide dominion) (pl. كساسرة *kasāsirat*, اكاسرة *akāsirat*, اكاسر *akāsir*, and كسور *kusūr*) Chosroes, Cyrus, an emperor, the surname of several kings of Persia (like Ptolemy among the Egyptians, or Cæsar with the Romans).

P كسري *kisrī*, Name of Noshīrwān the Just, or of any of the kings of Persia.

A كسس *kasas*, Shortness and smallness of teeth, or firm adhesion by their roots.

A كسط *kust*, Costus (a shrub). Justice.

A كسطال *kastāl*, (or كسطل *kastal*) Dust.

A كسطان *kastān*, Dust.

A كسع *kasɛ*, (v. n. of كسع) Striking one upon the buttocks with foot or hand. Clapping the tail between the legs (a camel or a doe). Leaving a little milk in a camel's udder in order to increase the quantity. Throwing cold water upon (a camel's) udder to make her retain or increase her milk. *Kasaɛ*, Whiteness about the fetlocks of horses. *Kusaɛ*, Name of a tribe in Yaman. Crumbs of bread. (pl. of كسعة *kusɛat*) White spots on beasts' foreheads. White feathers under birds' tails.

A كسعة *kusɛat*, (pl. كسع *kusaɛ*) A white spot upon a beast's forehead. White feathers under a bird's tail. A she-camel lent in order to be milked. Name of an idol. An ass. An ox of burden. A slave.

A كسعوم *kusɛūm*, (in the Himyarit) An ass.

A كسعي *kusaɛiy*, Of the tribe of كسع *kusaɛ*.

A كسف *kasf*, (v. n. of كسف) Cutting into pieces (cloth). Houghing (a camel). Being crabbed (the countenance). Causing (an eclipse). Casting down (the eye). Being sorry (the condition of a man). An eclipse. In poetry, the substitution of a quiescent for an inflected letter at the cæsura: as when مفعولات *mafɛūlātu* becomes مفعولن *mafɛūlun*. *Kisf*, (pl. of كسفة *kisfat*) Parts, segments. *Kisaf*, (pl. of كسفة *kisfat*) Segments, sections, parts.

A كسفة *kisfat*, (pl. كسف *kisf*, *kisaf*, اكساف *aksāf*, and كسوف *kusūf*) A part, section, segment.

P كسك *kasak*, A fricassee of meat. A magpie. A fragment of brick, or of a broken wall.

A كسكاس *kaskās*, Thick, short; a dwarf.

A كسكر *kaskar*, A tract of country whose capital was واسط *wāsit*, and whose revenue was twelve millions of مثقال *miskāl*, similar to Ispahān.

A كسكس *kuskus*, A farinaceous dish, prepared in the way of millet, common in Morocco.

A كسكسة *kaskasat*, (v. n. of كسكس Q) Beating, pounding small. Adding the letter س *s* to the ك *k* of the second person singular feminine: as, اكرمتكس *akramtukis* for اكرمتك *akramtuki*, بكس *bi kis* for بك *bi ki* (a practice peculiar to the tribe of بني تميم *banī tamīm*).

P كس كش *kus-kash*, A pimp: contented cuckold.

AP كسگر *kasgar*, A plasterer. A potter.

A كسل *kisl*, A string hanging from a bow for beating cotton. *Kasal*, (v. n. of كسل) Being torpid, sluggish. Not emitting (in coitu), being unsolicitous for offspring. Laziness. Laxness, slowness, indolence; cowardice. Sickness. *Kasil*, Cowardly, slothful, lazy, indolent.

A كسلان *kaslān*, (pl. كسالى *kasālā'*, *kisālā'*, *kusālā'*, *kasālī*, and كسلى *kaslā'*) Lazy, cowardly.

P كسلمند *kasalmand*, Languid, sick, relaxed.

P كسلناك *kasalnāk*, Cowardly, lazy, sluggish.

A كسلي *kaslā'*, (pl. of كسلان *kaslān*) Slothful.

A كسم *kasm*, (v. n. of كسم) Breaking or crumbling (any thing) with the hand. Labouring, studying, endeavouring, working to maintain a household. Kindling the flame (of war). Much herbage.

A كسملة *kasmalat*, A going with short steps.

P كسمه *kasma*, A ringlet of hair parted to hang over the cheek. An artificial or false lock of hair. A sort of cake.

P كسناج *kasnāj*, Endive, succory.

P كسنذر *kasan* or *kusundar*, Mean, worthless.

P كسنك *kisnak*, A grain used to fatten cattle.

P كسني *kasnī* or *kisnī*, Succory. كسنيء تلخ *kasnīi talkh*, Wild succory. *Kisnī*, Assafœtida.

A كسو *kasw*, (v. n. of كسا for كسو) Clothing.

A كسؤ *kusɛ*, (pl. اكساء *aksāɛ*) The hinder part.

A كسوء *kusūɛ*, (pl. of كسء *kasɛ*) Parts of the night.

A كسوب *kasūb*, A great gainer. Any thing.

A كسّوب *kassūb*, Name of a plant.

A كسوة *kiswat* or *kuswat*, (pl. كسي *kusā'* or كساء *kisāɛ*) A robe, habit, dress, apparel. A mode of dressing. P كسوت جان كردن *kiswati jān kardan*, To impart life. To invest with a property. كسوت كافوري *kiswati kāfūrī*, (Dress of camphor) Snow covering the face of the ground.

P كسود *kiswad*, Harshness, unkind behaviour.

A كسود *kusūd*, (v. n. of كسد) Not going off (goods). Flatness, dulness of markets.

A كسور *kasūr*, Large-bunched (camel); or one which draws his tail down after cocking it. *Kusūr*, (v. n. of كسر) Clapping close the wings when descending or pouncing (a bird). Inequalities, high and low places. The bendings or reaches of valleys or rivers. (pl. of كسر *kasr* or *kisr*) Bones having little meat upon them. Lower parts of tents. Portions of the body, or the members. Sides of houses. (pl. of كسرة *kasrat*) Fractures, chinks, breaches. Fractional parts (in arithmetic). (pl. of كسري *kisrā'*) Cæsars, emperors. كسور الاودية *kusūru'l awdiyat*, Bendings, windings of valleys.

P كسور *kusūr*, Gaining, preserving, keeping.

A كسوف *kusūf*, (v. n. of كسف) Being sad (circumstances of a man). Being obscured, eclipsed (the sun). Frowning. An eclipse. (pl. of كسفة *kisfat*) Parts, sections, segments of any thing.

A كسول *kasūl*, Slow, dull, lazy, tardy. (A damsel) delicately educated, who scarcely moves from her seat (this being considered as an accomplishment).

A كسوم *kasūm*, Expeditious, sharp.

P كسون *kasūn*, Name of a Magian philosopher.

P كسه *kasa*, Facility, ease.

P كسي *kase*, One, some one, any one, a certain person. كسي چند *kase chand*, Some persons.

A كسي *kusy*, (pl. اكساء *aksāɛ*) The hinder part, extremity of the rump. *Kasā'*, A putting on of clothes. *Kusā'*, (pl. of كسوة *kuswat* or *kiswat*) Vestures, clothes, garments.

A كسيب *kusayb*, Name of a dog. ابن الكسيب *ibnu'l kusayb*, A bastard.

A كسيح *kasīh* or *kusayh*, Infirm in hands or feet, lame, unable to move from place to place. Impotent.

A كسيد *kasīd*, Not selling or passing current; a drug in the market. Base, mean, despicable.

P كسيدا *kasīdā*, Cassia of Arabia.

A كسير *kasīr*, (pl. كسري *kasrā'* and كساري *kasārā'*) Broken. Routed. Poor. Dried pitch. *Kusayr*, Name of a mountain overhanging the furthest point of the sea of Omān.

P كسيس *kasīs*, A kind of drug which gives a lustre to steel. Wine. Wine from dates or millet.

A كسيس *kasīs*, Date-wine. Meat dried upon heated stones, reduced to powder, and carried as travelling provision; pemmican. Broken bread.

A كسيف *kasīf*, Thick, gross, impure.

A كسيفه *kasīfa*, Dregs, dross, scoria.

P كسيقون *kasīkūn*, A kind of wild lily.

P كسيل *kusel*, A betrothing. The prosecution of a journey. A driving away.

P كسيلا *kasīlā*, Cassia of Arabia.

P كسيله *kasayla*, A sort of cassia.

A كسّيلي *kissīlā'*, A certain medicinal bark.

P كش *kash*, The arm-pit, or that part of the side under it (as servants carry their master's clothes under the arm). The groin. A corner, angle. The breast. The planet Saturn. A running sore in the foot of a camel, for which they cauterize the feet of healthy camels to prevent the contagion from spreading. A mode of putting the hands to the sides as a mark of respect. Empty. Good. Beautiful. Name of a city in Turkistān. كش ران *kashi rān*, The groin. (imperat. of كشيدن *kashīdan*) Draw thou; and in composition it is used for the part. كشنده *kashanda*, Drawing, pulling, carrying, bearing: who draws; a drawer, drainer. آب كش *āb-kash*, A drawer of water. باركش *bār-kash*, A porter or a bearer of burdens. پياله كش *piyāla-kash*, A wine-drinker. دست خنجركش *dasti khanjar-kash*, The dagger-drawing hand. درد كش *durd-kash*, A drainer of the dregs. دل كش *dil-kash*, Heart-attracting. سركش *sar-kash*, Drawing in the head, *i.e.* refractory, stubborn, disobedient. كينه كش *kīna-kash*, Bearing malice. ملهم كش *malham-kash*, A spatula for spreading plasters. هيزم كش *hezam-kash*, Carrying wood. سركشي *sar-kashī*, Disobedience (in which manner, by adding ي, abstract nouns may be formed from the whole). *Kish*, A line drawn through a word to erase it. It is also often for كه اورا *ki urā*: as, كش گفت *kish guft*, *i.e.* كه اورا گفت *ki urā guft*, Who said to him. *Kish* or *kish kish*, A word announcing the approach of a king or great man, that the by-standers may keep silence and behave with propriety (similar to, Have a care! stand by!); it is used likewise at chess when the king receives a check; or in driving fowls. *Kush*, A male. (imp. of كشتن *kushtan*, in composition used for كشنده *kushanda*) A killer; who kills, slays, murders, oppresses. اژدها كش *ajdahā-kush*, A dragon-killer. زبون كش *zabūn-kush*, The oppressor of the distressed or weak. صفرا كش *safrā-kush*, The bile-killer, *i.e.* breakfast. عالم كش *ʿālam-kush*, Destroying the world, killing whom he will. خشم عالمكش *khishmi ʿālam-kush*, Fury, universally destructive.

A كش *kish*, occasionally *kash*, by a particular idiom, is sometimes employed in place of the affixed pronoun ك *ki*, in the second person fem.: as, عليكش *ʿalaykish*, Above thee, for عليكِ *ʿalayki*.

A كش *kashsh*, (v. n. of كش) Lowing (a cow). *Kushsh*, The male palm-tree's fructifying flowers.

A كشء *kashʾ*, (v. n. of كشأ) Being filled (with). Being transparent (the under skin of a leathern bottle appearing through that which is above). Striking with a sword, cutting. Lying with. Being chapt (the hand). Roasting (meat) until it becomes quite dry. Eating (cucumbers). Peeling, unbarking.

P كشا *kashā*, (from كشيدن *kashīdan*) Drawing. *Kushā*, (from كشادن *kushādan*, used in composition for كشاينده *kushāyanda*) An opener: one who opens, solves, loses, reveals, displays. Who makes cheerful. Who besieges, who conquers. دل كشا *dil-kushā*, Heart-expanding, exhilarating. كشور كشا *kishwar-kushā*, Conquering provinces.

A كشاء *kashāʾ*, (v. n. of كشي) Being filled (with food). Being transparent (the under skin of a leathern bottle appearing through that which is above). Being chapt, rough, or shrivelled (the hand).

A كشأة *kushʾat*, Vice, defect, fault, blemish.

A كشاح *kishāh*, (v. n. 3 of كشح) Harbouring a secret grudge (against another). A mark burnt on the sides of animals.

P كشاخل *kushākhal*, A grain for making bread.

P كشاد *kushād*, He opened, displayed, uncovered. He exhilarated. He seized. An opening, uncovering; cheerfulness. Expansion. A seige. The shooting of an arrow. A move at chess. Open, wide. كشاد نامه *kushād-nāma*, A royal diploma, privilege, or license. A bill of divorce. خاطر كشاد *khātir-kushād*, Cheerfulness of mind, lightness of heart.

P كشادگي *kushādagī*, An opening, an aperture. Openness, expansion. Joy, cheerfulness, openness of heart. Siege or taking of a town. An area, court. An interstice, interval, space between two things. در كشادگي *dar kushādagī*, Openly, in face of day.

P كشادن *kushādan*, To open, disclose, detect, discover, explain, expose (merchandise to sale). To take (a town), to subdue. To laugh. To polish. To shoot an arrow. To move at chess.

P كشاده *kushāda*, Opened, discovered, uncovered, expanded, detected, revealed, explained, displayed (goods for sale), diffused, stretched. Wide, ample, extensive. Taken (castle), subjected. Glad, cheerful, rejoiced, jovial, happy, frank. Serene, clear. Who opens. كشاده وُباز *kushāda u bāz*, Open and back (as a door), displayed. بازار كشاده *bāzāri kushāda*, An open market. رنگ كشاده *rangi kushāda*, An open, clear colour.

P كشاده ابرو *kushāda-abrū*, With wide eyebrows, not joined at the nose. Of an open countenance.

P كشاده پيشاني *kushāda-peshānī*, Of an open countenance, having a broad forehead.

P كشاده دست *kushāda-dast*, Open-handed. Liberal, generous.

P كشاده دهان *kushāda-dahān*, Open-mouthed.

P كشاده رو *kushāda-rav*, Straddling (horse).

P كشاده روي *kushāda-rūy*, Of an open, serene countenance.

P كشاده سخن *kushāda-sukhan*, Plain-spoken. Distinct, perspicuous, clear.

P كشاده مشرب *kushāda-mashrab*, Open by nature, candid, sincere. Jovial.

A كشاط *kishāt*, Nudity, nakedness. A covering of skin. The taking off of a covering, skinning. A skin taken off.

A كشاف *kishāf*, (v. n. of كشف) Taking the male (a camel) followed by her foal, and thus breeding two years consecutively. Taking the male (although in foal).

A كشّاف *kashshāf*, A detector, discoverer, looser, solver, explainer. كشّاف مشكلات *kashshāfi mushkilāt*, A resolver of doubts, a solver of difficulties. شرح كشّاف *sharhi kashshāf*, A clear explanation.

P كشاك *kashāk*, Mind, thought, reflection.

P كشاكش *kash-ā-kash*, Attraction, allurement. Taking, fetching. Distraction. Orders issued in continued succession. Commands and prohibitions. Contention, tumult. War, battle. Deep sorrow, intense sadness. Pleasant and unpleasant.

A كشامر *kushāmir*, Deformed, ugly (man).

A كشامرة *kashāmirat*, (pl. of كشميري *kishmīrīy*) Natives of Kashmir, or Cashmere.

P كشان *kashān*, (part.) Drawing, attracting. Drawn, carried. A single-posted tent. Name of a country. كشان كشان *kashān kashān*, (or كشان بر كشان *kashān bar kashān*) Drawing, attracting, alluring, ravishing. (pl. of كش *kash*) Drawing: as, دردي كشان *durdī-kashān*, (Dreg-drawers) Wine-drinkers, or such as drain the bowl.

P كشانيدن *kashānīdan*, To cause to draw.

P كشاورز *kashāwarz*, A husbandman, cultivator. A cultivated field. A sowing; seed-time.

P كشاورزي *kashāwarzī*, Cultivation, ploughing, farming. كشاورزي نمودن *kashāwarzī namūdan*, To follow agriculture, to cultivate.

P كشايانيدن *kushāyānīdan*, To cause to open.

P كشايش *kushāyish*, Aperture, opening, unloosing. Clearness, serenity. كشايش روزه *kushāyishi roza*, The breaking of a fast, breakfast.

P كشاينده *kushāyanda*, An opener.

A كشب *kashb*, A greedy devouring (of flesh).

A كشّة *kushshat*, The forelocks, or any spiral or twisted ringlets.

P كشت *kasht*, An herb, red, and resembling a thread, which creeps twiningly along the ground. Very dry and friable. Salt, salsuginous. Ugly, deformed. *Kisht*, Seed; a sown field. Tillage. The hypochondria, the body between the haunches and short ribs. Check at chess. خداوند كشت *khudāwandi kisht*, A husbandman. كشت كاريده *kishti kārīda*, A sown field. *Kusht*, He killed. Killing. The back, belly, waist, side.

P كشت آب *kisht-āb*, Seed sown during the rains.

P كشتار *kushtār*, Slain in sacrifice. Slaughtered. A sacrifice. كشتار كردن *kushtār kardan*, To slay.

P كشتاو *kashtāw*, Compassion, condolence.

P كشتاور *kishtāwar*, A husbandman.

P كشت زار *kisht-zār*, A field sown and beginning to look green. Ripe corn. A seminary. كشت زار ديو *kisht-zāri dev*, The devil's corn-field, *i. e.* the world.

P كشتك *kushtak*, A beetle.

P كشتكار *kisht-kār*, A sower, husbandman, agriculturist. A sown field.

P كشتكاري *kisht-kārī*, Tillage, husbandry.

P كشتگان *kushtagān*, (pl. of كشته *kushta*) The slain. كشتگان زنده *kushtagāni zinda*, Martyrs.

P كشتگي *kushtagī*, Murder, slaughter. كشتگي در راه خدا *kushtagī dar rāhi khudā*, Martyrdom.

P كشتگير *kusht-gīr*, A wrestler.

P كشتمند *kishtmand*, A cultivated field.

P كشتن *kishtan*, To till, sow. To reap, mow. *Kushtan*, To kill, murder. To slay, sacrifice. To beat, bruise. To extinguish (a fire or candle).

P كشتن گاه *kushtan-gāh*, The time or place of slaughter.

P كشتني *kushtanī*, Fit to be killed, destined for slaughter. كشتني شدن *kushtanī shudan*, To be fit for the butcher.

P كشتو *kashtū*, Half-ripe grapes.

P كشتوك *kashtūk*, A tortoise.

P كشته *kashta*, Squint-eyed. *Kishta*, Tilled, sown. Seed. Seed-time. An apple-pippin. Dried fruit. *Kushta*, Killed, murdered, sacrificed. Extinguished. Killing; a killer. كشته شدن *kushta shudan*, To be killed.

P كشتي *kashtī*, (in India *kishtī*) A boat, ship, vessel, bark. A tray. A beggar's plate. A drinking-vessel in the form of a ship. كشتيِ روندهٔ صبح *kishtī rawandaʾi subh*, A camel. كشتيِ زر *kishtīʾi zar*, The golden skiff, *i.e.* The new moon. The sun. A drinking-vessel in the form of a ship. كشتي سوار شدن *kishtī-suwār shudan*, To go on board ship or boat, to embark. كشتي شدن *kishtī shudan*, To swim. كشتيِ غم *kishtīʾi gham*, The vessel of sorrow, *i. e.* The world. كشتيِ گذاره *kishtīʾi gu-*

zāra, A ferry-boat. كشتيء نوح *kishtī-i nūh*, Noah's ark. دود كشتي *dūd-kishti*, (Smoke-boat) A steamer, steam-boat. *Kushtī*, Fighting. Wrestling. A belt, a girdle. كشتي كردن *kushtī kardan*, To wrestle, fight, struggle, contend.

P كشتيبان *kishtībān*, The captain or commander of a ship. A pilot. A sailor.

P كشتي باني *kishtībānī*, Seamanship.

P كشتي جاي *kushtī-jāy*, An arena for wrestlers.

P كشتي ساز *kishtī-sāz*, A ship-builder, shipwright.

P كشتي سازي *kishtī-sāzī*, Ship-building.

P كشتي سوار *kishtī-suwār*, Embarked in a vessel.

P كشتي كش *kishtī-kash*, A pilot. A wine-bibber.

P كشتي گاه *kishtī-gāh*, An arsenal; sea-port. An anchorage. *Kushtī-gāh*, A place where wrestlers exercise their strength, a gymnasium.

P كشتي گر *kishtīgar*, A ship-builder.

P كشتي گير *kushtī-gīr*, A wrestler.

P كشتي گيري *kushtī-gīrī*, Wrestling.

P كشتي مال *kishtī-māl*, A tax levied on boats.

P كشتي نشين *kishtī-nishīn*, Seamen: on shipboard.

A كشح *kash-h*, (v. n. of كشح) Burning or cauterizing under the short ribs. Clapping the tail between the legs. Having a private hatred (to any person). Sweeping (a house). Becoming dispersed. Separating, scattering, dispersing. (pl. كشوح *kushūh*) The side, the short ribs, hypochondria, waist. A kind of shell. كشح مخصر *kash-hun mukhassarun*, A slender waist. طوي كشحه على الامر *tawa' kashhahu ʿala'l amr*, He kept the matter secret. *Kashah*, Pleurisy. A disease of the side requiring the cautery.

P كشخ *kashakh*, A line on which they hang grapes to dry.

A كشخان *kashkhān* or *kishkhān*, A pimp to his own wife; one who winks at his own cuckoldom.

P كشخر *kushkhar*, A climate.

P كشخرما *kush-khurmā*, A male palm-tree.

A كشخنة *kashkhanat*, (v. n. of كشخن Q) Calling one a كشخان *kishkhān*, *i.e.* cuckold, or wittol.

A كشد *kashd*, (v. n. of كشد) Cutting with the teeth (as in biting a carrot). Milking (a camel) with three fingers. A species of edible grain. *Kashad*, One who labours hard for the support of his family. *Kushud*, (pl. of كاشد *kāshid*) Those who labour hard for the support of a family, and endeavour to keep relations united. (pl. of كشود *kashūd*) Camels milked with three fingers. Camels whose teats are short and orifices narrow.

A كشر *kashr*, (v. n. of كشر) Displaying the teeth in laughter or otherwise. A smile. Certus quidam coeundi modus. *Kashar*, (v. n. of كشر) Fleeing, running away. Dry bread. A bunch or cluster whose grapes have been eaten off.

A كشرة *kishrat*, A discovery of the teeth in laughter or otherwise.

P كش رفتار *kash-raftār*, An elegant walker.

P كشسه *kushsa*, A written document, particularly in Arabic, Persian, or Hindī.

P كشش *kashish*, A drawing. Attraction, allurement. Blandishments, coquetry, amorous playfulness; a wink, nod, glance. A walking with a graceful air. Travelling night and day. *Kushish*, Killing, slaughter. Sacrifice. كشش كردن *kushish kardan*, To fight, to try to kill. To slaughter.

A كشط *kasht*, (v. n. of كشط) Removing from its place, taking off (a cover or horse-cloth). Denuding, stripping. Flaying (a camel).

A كشطة *kashatat*, Sharers or proprietors of a slaughtered camel.

A كشع *kashʿ*, (v. n. of كشع) Retiring, departing from one killed. *Kashaʿ*, Anxiety, difficulty, sorrow, anguish, grief.

A كشعج *kashaʿsaj*, (or كشعطج *kashaʿtaj*) A bundle of fibres off the palm-tree. A thick cord or girdle worn by tributaries.

A كشف *kashf*, (v. n. of كشف) Opening, manifesting, revealing, declaring, solving, explaining. Exposing to shame. Averting evil. Manifestation, disclosure, apocalypse, revelation. P كشف راز كردن *kashfi rāz kardan*, To disclose a secret. A *Kashaf*, (v. n. of كشف) Being put to flight, routed. The curling of the hair on the forehead (when sprouting after being shaved). The twisting of a horse's tail; the bending of the bone.

P كشف *kushf*, Burnt silver. Pitch. A black substance used by goldsmiths. *Kashaf*, A tortoise. The sign Cancer. A large vessel for cooling liquors.

A كشفاء *kashfā*, Bare (forehead) whose locks turn backwards.

A كشفة *kashafat*, Part of the forehead marked by كشف *kashaf*. *Kushufat*, The hair of the forehead grown again, and the curling thereof.

P كشفت *kushuft* or *kashaft*, He dissolved, scattered. Separated. Scattered. *Kushift*, A Jew's synagogue.

P كشفتن *kashaftan* or *kushuftan*, To open. To cleave. To dissolve, scatter, disperse, separate. To wither, decay, perish.

P كشفته *kashafta* or *kushufta*, Dispersed, dissipated, scattered, dissolved. Annihilated, consumed.

P كشف رود *kashaf-rūd*, Name of a certain river.

P كشك *kashk*, Sour milk dried. A sort of condiment made of butter-milk. A kind of thick pottage made of wheaten flour or barley-meal with sheep's milk, to which they add flesh or wheat. *Kushk*, An upper chamber, gallery, or balcony on the top of a house; a hall, parlour. *Kashak*, A magpie. A line, stripe. كشكهاي پرتو *kashakhāyi partav*, The sun's rays.

A كشك *kashk*, Barley-broth. Barley.

P كشكاب *kashkāb*, Barley-water. A ptisan.

P كشكاو *kashkāv*, Food. Barley-broth.

P كشكبا *kashk-bā*, A kind of milk-diet dressed in the Muharram.

P كشك خانه *kushk-khāna*, A granary.

P كشكدار *kushk-dār*, A guard, sentinel.

P كشكرك *kashkrak*, (in Kazwīn) A magpie.

P كشكشان *kashkashān*, Travelling gently.

A كشكشة *kashkashat*, (v. n. of كشكش Q) Lowing (a cow). Substituting كش *kish* for ك *ki*, the affix pronoun of the second person singular feminine: as, عليش *ʿalayshi*, (or عليكش *ʿalaykish* for عليك *ʿalayki*). Exhausting by drawing water. The noise of a serpent's skin when crawling. Flight.

P كشكك *kashkak*, Barley or wheat (especially boiled whole with meat till it has become soft).

P كشكله *kashkala*, A covering for the feet, as worn by running footmen. A buskin.

P كشكنجير *kashkanjīr*, A column with a pulley on the summit, over which they pass a rope, at the end of which is fastened a bag of sand. (It is chiefly used by archers as a trial of strength). A sling. *Kushkanjīr*, A cannon. A cannon-ball. A stone slung from a balista.

P كشكنه *kashkina*, Barley-bread. Bread made of wheat, barley, beans, and vetches. Fried wheat, which, with onions, beet, and purslain-seed, is steeped in fish-jelly and dried in the sun.

P كشكو *kashkū*, Barley-broth. A magpie.

P كشكول *kashkūl*, A beggar. A goblet. A beggar's cup, generally made in the form of a boat.

P كشكين *kashkīn*, Bread made of barley, millet, beans, and lentils. Wheat soaked in sour milk and dried in the sun.

P كشكينه *kashkīna*, Barley-bread. Wheat softened by boiling.

P كش گفتار *kash-guftār*, An elegant speaker.

A كشم *kashm*, An amputation of the nose. The hunting-leopard. *Kasham*, A defect in the formation of the body, or a flaw in one's pedigree.

P كشمان *kishmān*, A field ploughed and sown.

A كشمخة *kushmakhat*, Sea-purslain, an herb.

P كشمر *kishmar*, Name of a village in Khurāsān, where one of Zoroaster's two cypresses formerly grew. Name of a village in Turkistān.

A كشمرة *kashmarat*, (v. n. of كشمر Q) Breaking (the nose). Being about to weep.

A كشمش *kishmish*, Dried grapes, corinths, or currants, a species of small grape without stones. Raisins. The Armenian apricot with a bitter kernel.

P كشمكش *kash-ma-kash*, Pulling different ways. Orders issued successively. Sorrow, distress. Commands and prohibitions. Pleasing and displeasing. Want, distress. *Kush-ma-kush*, Fear, terror. The noise of combatants (crying Kill! do not kill! &c.).

A كشملخ *kushmalakh*, Sea-purslain, an herb.

P كشمور *kashmūr*, Name of a desert. Name of a place in the desert of مور *mūr*.

P كشميده *kashmīda*, A line drawn over writing to erase it. A line. Written.

P کشمیر *kashmīr*, Cashmere.

A کشمیرِيّ *kishmīriy*, (pl. کشامرة *kashāmirat*) A Cashmerian, a native of Cashmere.

P کشن *kashan*, *kashn*, or *kashin*, Large, copious, ample, much, numerous.

P کشنج *kashnaj*, A species of fungus.

P کشندگي *kushandagī*, Slaughter.

P کشندة *kashanda*, A drawer, attracter. *Kushinda* or *kushanda*, A killer. Fatal, mortal.

P کشنك *kishnak*, A kind of black-coloured vetch of a fattening quality, which, when deprived of its husk, is given to cattle.

P کشنگ *kashang*, A large melon or gourd flat like a plate. A rope made of palm-tree fibres, used by weavers.

P کشنه *kashna*, A fungus resembling an egg. A plant resembling a fungus. A sort of medicinal plant. Coriander. Thirsty. Facility. *Kashna*, *kushna*, *kashana*, or *kushana*, Pease, pulse, a vetch.

P کشني *kashnī* or *kishnī*, A thick forest, a wood, wilderness. *Kishnī*, A vetch, pea. *Kushnī*, A goat.

A کشنیٰ *kushna'*, A vetch.

P کشنیج *kishnīj*, Coriander. Name of a blue flower. کشنیج دشتي *kishnīji dashtī*, Mountain-balm.

P کشنیز *kishnīz*, Coriander.

A کشو *kashw*, (v. n. of کشا for کشو) Biting and extracting with the teeth.

P کشو *kashav*, A tortoise. The sign Cancer. Name of a plant from which ropes are made.

P کشواد *kishwād*, Name of a strong man.

P کشوبا *kashūbā*, (in zand and Pāz.) A bow.

A کشوث *kashūs*, (*kushūs*, کشوثیٰ *kashūsa'*, or کشوثاء *kashūsā'*) Dodder. کشوث رومی *kushūsi rūmī*, Grecian wormwood, species of southernwood.

A کشوح *kashūḥ*, One of the seven swords brought by Bilkīs to Solomon. *Kushūḥ*, (pl. of کشح *kashḥ*) Hypochondria. Waists.

P کشود *kashwad*, The basest profligacy. *Kushūd*, Dodder.

A کشود *kashūd*, (pl. کشد *kushud*) A man who labours to support his family. One who is kind to his relations. A camel milked with three fingers; also one short in the teat and narrow in the orifice.

P کشودن *kushūdan*, To open.

P کشودة *kushūda*, Opened. Open. کشودة شدن *kushūda shudan*, To be opened.

P کشودة شکم *kushūda-shikam*, Loose in the belly.

P کشور *kishwar*, A climate, country, quarter, or region of the world, as divided into seven climates, each of which is supposed to be more immediately dependent on one of the planets; thus, the first climate, *i.e.* Hindūstān, is assigned to the planet Saturn; the second, *i.e.* China and Khotā, to Jupiter; the third, *i.e.* Turkistān, to Mars; the fourth, *i.e.* Irāk and Khurāsān, to the sun; the fifth, *i.e.* Transoxania, to Venus; the sixth, *i.e.* Greece, or the Turkish empire (Rūm), to Mercury; and the seventh, *i.e.*, the hyperborean regions, to the moon.

P کشور خدا *kishwar-khudā*, (کشور خداي *kishwar-khudāy*, also کشور خدیو *kishwar-khidīv*) A king, paramount sovereign.

P کشور خدائي *kishwar-khudā,ī*, Sovereignty.

P کشور داري *kishwar-dārī*, Sovereignty.

P کشورز *kishwarz*, Great. A great man.

P کشورزیان *kishwarziyān*, Grandees, nobles.

P کشورستان *kishwar-satān*, (کشور کشا *kishwar-kushā*, کشور کشاي *kishwar-gushāy*, or کشور گیر *kishwar-gīr*) A conqueror of kingdoms or countries.

P کشور کشائي *kishwar-kushā,ī*, (or کشور گیري *kishwar-gīrī*) Conquest of provinces.

A کشوف *kashūf*, A camel having colts two following years. A camel covered although in foal.

P کشوف *kushūf*, A scattering, dispersion.

P کشوفتن *kushūftan*, To open. To cleave, to be burst open. To scatter, to dissolve. To wither, to dry. To vanish, disappear.

P کشونا *kashūnā*, (in ancient Persian) A bow.

P کشه *kasha*, A mendicant, poor man. A girth, surcingle, or other fastening for saddles or loads. Ease. *Kisha*, French lavender. A line drawn to erase writing. *Kisha* or *kusha*, A line in general, whether drawn on paper, on a wall, or on the ground. کشه کردن *kisha kardan*, To erase.

P کشه *kashsha*, A beast which has thrown his pack-saddle.

P کشي *kashī*, Health, happiness, goodness.

A کشيء *kashī'*, (or کشيء *kashī'*) Full, overloaded (with food).

A کشیٰ *kusha'*, Fat parts of the Lybian lizard.

A کشیة *kushyat*, (pl. کشیٰ *kusha'*) The fat of a crocodile or Lybian lizard; also the root of its tail.

P کشیخان *kashīkhān*, A cuckold, a wittol.

P کشیخاني *kashīkhānī*, Cuckoldom.

P کشیدگي *kashīdagī*, Stretch. Displeasure.

P کشیدن *kashīdan*, To draw, extract, attract, protract, extend, prolong. To draw lines, delineate. To exhaust, draw out. To bring, bear, carry. To bring before, present. To withdraw, remove. To conquer. To support, suffer, endure, put up with. To experience. To lead, induce. To bind. To see. آواز کشیدن *āwāz kashīdan*, To extend the voice. آه کشیدن *āh kashīdan*, To fetch a sigh. بر دار کشیدن *bar dār kashīdan*, To hang on a gibbet. خط کشیدن *khat kashīdan*, To draw a line. درهم کشیدن *darham kashīdan*, To contract, draw together, wrinkle, shrivel. روي کشیدن *rūy kashīdan*, To knit the brows, disdain, turn away the face. گرسنگي کشیدن *gursnagī kashīdan*, To suffer hunger.

P کشیدة *kashīda*, Drawn. Extended, lengthened. Long. Shrivelled, wrinkled (face). Disturbed in mind, stupefied, thunder-struck. Weighed. One who has suffered or felt. Sullen, supercilious. A kind of needle-work. A clenched fist ready to strike a blow. High, tall. کشیدة شدن *kashīda shudan*, To be drawn, extended. الم کشیدة *alam-kashīda*, Afflicted, pained, distressed.

P کشیدة ابرو *kashīda-abrū*, (or ابرو کشیدة *abrū-kashīda*) One who has distant or long eyebrows.

P کشیدة بالا *kashīda-bālā*, Tall of stature.

P کشیدة خاطر *kashīda-khātir*, Displeased.

P کشیدة دوزي *kashīda-dozī*, A kind of embroidery.

P کشیدة رو *kashīda-rū*, Long or wrinkled-faced.

P کشیدة ریش *kashīda-rīsh*, Long-bearded.

P کشیدة عقل *kashīda-ʻakl*, A fool.

P کشیدة گر *kashīdagar*, An embroiderer.

P کشیش *kashīsh*, A priest, presbyter.

A کشیش *kashīsh*, (v. n. of کش) Making a noise (a serpent's skin in motion). Braying for the first time (a young camel). The sound of a serpent's skin in motion. The noise made by the collision of the steel and flint. First brayings of a young camel. Noise made by wine in fermentation.

P کشیشي *kashīshī*, A monastic life, priesthood.

A کشيء *kashī'*, Roast meat.

A کصّ *kass*, (v. n. of کصّ) Speaking in a thin, piping voice. A shrill, small voice. A congregation, meeting, assembly.

G کصنیثون *kasnīsūn*, The wild egg-plant.

A کصوم *kusūm*, (v. n. of کصم) Retiring, returning, turning one's back. Failing to attain the whole of one's wishes. Driving, repelling with vehemence.

A کصي *kasy*, (v. n. of کصي) From being exalted, becoming debased.

A کصیر *kasīr*, Short, dwarfish.

A کصیص *kasīs*, (v. n. of کصّ) Having a shrill, small voice. Being moved, agitated, trembling. (Water) being frequented (by people). Twisting, writhing, contracting one's self, shrinking with fatigue. The chirping of a locust. A shrill, small voice. Thunder. Commotion, tremor. Terror.

A کصیصة *kasīsat*, Crowd. Net for taking deer.

A کضکضة *kazkazat*, The act of going fast.

A کضل *kazl*, A repulse.

A کظّ *kazz*, (v. n. of کظّ) Oppressing, indisposing (too much meat). Perplexing, overwhelming one (business). Overwhelmed with business. کظّ لظّ *kazzun lazzun*, Ill-tempered.

A کظاظ *kazāz*, (and کظاظة *kazāzat*) (v. n. of کظّ) Burdening, oppressing, vexing, harassing. *Kizāz*, (v. n. 3 of کظّ) Doing business with difficulty, going heavily or reluctantly to work. Involving one's self in the thick of the battle. Difficulty, trouble, labour. Enmity, hatred.

A کظام *kizām*, Whatever obstructs or fills up; stop-gap. Firmness, solidity. (pl. of کظم) Mouths.

A کظامة *kizāmat*, That part of an arrow where they place the feathers; also the sinew with which they are bound. The string run through a camel's nose. The mouth of a valley. The place whence urine issues forth (in a woman). One at the extremity of a bow. The ring where the ropes or chains meet which suspend the scale of a balance. A well dug near another (especially such as are supplied under ground by the same spring).

A كظّة *kizzat*, Repletion. Indigestion. Nausea from over-eating, squeamishness.

A كظر *kazr*, (v. n. of كظر) Notching the horn of a bow to receive the string. Notching (a fire-steel). *Kizr*, A bruised nerve whipt about the notch of an arrow. *Kuzr*, Fat of the reins or between the two clavicles of the breast. The notch in the horn of a bow into which the string goes. The edge of the pudendum. *Kuzr*, (or كظرة *kuzrat*) A bit of wood at the corner of a bow. The middle of the collar-bone.

A كظكظة *kazkazat*, (v. n. of كظكظ Q) Being (equally) distended every way (a bag with water, or the belly with victuals).

A كظم *kazm*, (v. n. of كظم) Restraining (anger). Shutting (a door), stopping or damming up (a water-course). *Kazam*, The mouth. The throat.

A كظّم *kuzzam*, (pl. of كاظم *kāzim*) Silent people.

A كظو *kazw*, (v. n. of كظا for كظو) Waxing firm, compact, and hard (the flesh on the body).

A كظوب *kuzūb*, The being full of fat.

A كظوم *kazūm*, An animal that does not chew the cud. *Kuzūm*, (v. n. of كظم) Abstaining from chewing the cud (camels). Keeping silence.

A كظيظ *kazīz*, Over-fatigued, overwhelmed.

A كظيم *kazīm*, Who checks his rage, restrains his passion. Afflicted, sorrowful. A lock, bolt, bar.

A كظيمة *kazīmat*, A well dug near another (especially such as are supplied under ground from one spring). A large water-bottle of a double skin.

A كعّ *kaǥǥ*, Timid, cowardly. Thin-faced.

A كعاب *kaǥāb*, (A girl) with swelling breasts. *Kiǥāb*, (pl. of كعب *kaǥb*) Ankle-bones. Dice.

A كعابة *kiǥābat*, (v. n. of كعب) Having swelling breasts (a young girl).

A كعابر *kaǥābir*, (pl. of كعبرة *kuǥbarat*) Joints in stalks of corn.

A كعابير *kaǥābīr*, Sheaths, pods, capsules.

A كعاس *kiǥās*, (pl. of كعس *kaǥs*) The joint-bones in the hands or feet of men or cattle.

A كعاسم *kaǥāsim*, (pl. of كعسم) Wild asses.

A كعاسيم *kaǥāsīm*, (pl. of كعسوم) Domestic asses.

A كعام *kiǥām*, (v. n. 3 of كعم) Muzzling (a camel). Kissing. A camel's halter or muzzle. (pl. of كعم *kiǥm*) Sheaths, repositories for arms.

A ذو كعان *zū kiǥān*, Name of a certain king of Yaman, whose height was ten cubits.

A كعانب *kaǥānib*, Swellings or bumps (on the head). *Kuǥānib*, Short. A lion.

A كعب *kaǥb*, (v. n. of كعب) Filling (a vessel). Being round and plump (a girl's breast). (pl. اكعب *akǥub*, كعوب *kuǥūb*, and كعاب *kiǥāb*) The protuberant joint-bone of the foot and leg, the ankle: any joint resembling it. The top of the foot, the instep. Dice, tables, or the bones with which they play at those or similar games. A geometrical cube. The projecting part in the joint of a cane or reed. Any quantity of milk poured out at once. A roundish piece of butter. Nobility, grandeur, ancestral glory. كعب الحبر *kaǥbu'l habr* (or *hibr*), Name of a certain Jewish doctor, who embraced the religion of Muhammad. كعب الغزال *kaǥbu'l ghazāl*, (كعب غزال *kaǥbi ghazāl*, or كعب الغزا *kaǥbu'l ghazā*) A kind of sweetmeat. A lump of sugar. Wine. *Kuǥb*, The breast. (pl. of كعب *kaǥb*) Dice.

A كعبات *kaǥbāt*, (pl. of كعبة *kaǥbat*) Dice.

A كعبة *kaǥbat*, A die or play-bone. A parlour. A kind of comb. Hair plaited in four divisions. Any kind of square building; hence, the square temple at Mecca. P كعبۀ جان *kaǥbaʼi jān*, Aim or object of one's life. كعبۀ جهان گرد *kaǥbaʼi jahān-gard*, (كعبۀ رهرو *kaǥbaʼi rah-rav*, or كعبۀ محرم نشان *kaǥbaʼi muhrim-nishān*) The sun. A *Kuǥbat*, Virginity.

A كعبتين *kaǥbatayn*, (obliq. ca. du. of كعبة *kaǥbat*) Two dice. The two temples, Mecca and Jerusalem.

P كعبده *kaǥbada*, The site of the temple of Mecca. A theatre, or any place for public spectacles.

A كعبرة *kaǥbarat*, (v. n. of كعبر Q) Cutting off (with a sword). A woman of foreign origin, coarsely made and bad-tempered. *Kuǥburat*, A large protuberant bone. A piece of flesh. Protuberance of the wrist-bone next the thumb. The root of the head. Any thing drawn together or compact. A lusty hip. Dry dung about the tails of camels. *Kuǥburat*, (or كعبرّة *kuǥburrat*) (pl. كعابر *kaǥābir*) A joint-knob on a stalk of corn; also the refuse in winnowing.

A كعبشة *kaǥbashat*, (v. n. of كعبش Q) Seizing and binding. Going as if fettered. Joining the feet to leap.

A كعبورة *kaǥbūrat*, Any thing drawn together.

P كعبه رو *kaǥba-rav*, A visitor to the Kaaba.

A كعت *kaǥt*, Short-bodied (man).

A كعتان *kiǥtān*, (pl. of كعيت) Nightingales.

A كعتة *kaǥtat*, Short-bodied (woman). *Kuǥtat*, The stopple, cover, or casing of a glass bottle.

A كعتر *kuǥtur*, A bird resembling a sparrow.

A كعترة *kaǥtarat*, (v. n. of كعتر Q) Reeling like a drunkard. Running with speed. Walking fast.

A كعثب *kaǥsab*, Magna et ampla (pubes); rima mulieris; magnâ pube prædita mulier.

A كعد *kaǥd*, A sack, a bag.

A كعدب *kaǥdab*, (or كعدبة) Slothful, cowardly.

A كعدبة *kuǥdubat*, A bubble of water.

A كعدة *kaǥdat*, The stopple of a glass bottle.

A كعر *kaǥr*, (v. n. of كعر) Being big-bellied from over-eating (a boy). *Kuǥr*, Name of a smooth-leaved, thorny plant. *Kaǥar*, (v. n. of كعر) Having a large belly from much food, waxing fat (a boy). Beginning to grow fat in the bunch (a young camel). *Kaǥir*, Fat, full-bellied (boy).

A كعرة *kaǥrat*, A glandulous tumour.

A كعز *kaǥz*, A scraping together with the fingers.

A كعس *kaǥs*, (pl. كعاس *kiǥās*) The joint-bones in the hands or feet (of men or cattle).

A كعسبة *kaǥsabat*, (v. n. of كعسب Q) Running, going fast. Fleeing. Proceeding leisurely. Staggering (like a drunken man).

A كعسم *kaǥsam*, The onager or wild ass.

A كعسمة *kaǥsamat*, A turning the back, fleeing.

A كعسوم *kuǥsūm*, (pl. كعاسيم) A domestic ass.

A كعص *kaǥs*, (v. n. of كعص) Eating.

A كعطل *kaǥtal*, Stretching the body, or expanding the nails. A lion.

A كعطلة *kaǥtalat*, (v. n. of كعطل Q) Running, passing quickly, or slowly. Outstretching (the hand).

A كعظل *kaǥzal*, Stretching the body, or expanding the nails. A lion.

A كعك *kaǥk*, Biscuit. Cake without milk or butter in it.

A كعكبّة *kuǥkubbat*, Four braids of hair plaited together in one. A sort of comb.

A كعكبيّة *kuǥkubīyat*, A sort of comb.

A كعكع *kuǥkuǥ*, Timid, cowardly.

A كعكعة *kaǥkaǥat*, An imprisoning, detaining.

A كعل *kaǥl*, Fresh dung (of any animal). Sweat of sheep's wool. Filth adhering to the testicles of a goat. A careless shepherd. A rich miser. Dates adhering closely together. A mountain. *Kaǥl* or *kuǥal*, A black dwarfish man.

A كعم *kaǥm*, (v. n. of كعم) Muzzling (a camel). Closing, stopping (the mouth of a vessel). Kissing. *Kiǥm*, (pl. كعام *kiǥām*) A sheath, scabbard, or repository for arms.

A كعنب *kaǥnab*, Short. A lion. One who has bumps or swellings on the head.

A كعنكع *kaǥankaǥ*, A male sylvan demon, a Ghūl.

A كعو *kaǥw*, The being cowardly.

A كعوب *kuǥūb*, (v. n. of كعب) Having swelling breasts (a girl). Filling (a vessel) so that the contents make a convex swelling above the brim. (pl. of كعب *kaǥb*) Ankle-bones. Cubes. كعوب الرمح *kuǥūbu'r rumh*, Knots or joints of a cane-spear.

A كعوبة *kuǥūbat*, (v. n. of كعب) Having swelling breasts (a girl).

A كعورة *kaǥwarat*, Large, thick-nosed.

A كعوع *kuǥūǥ*, (v. n. of كعّ) Being timid, pusillanimous, weak.

A كعوم *kuǥūm*, (v. n. of كعم) Kissing. Mouths, open ends, embouchures (of roads).

A كعيت *kuǥayt*, (pl. كعتان) The nightingale.

A كعيص *kaǥīs*, The piping of chick or mouse.

A كعيظ *kaǥīz*, A dwarf, a short man.

A كعيم *kaǥīm*, Muzzled (camel).

P كغالة *kaghāla*, A seed whence oil is drawn.

P كف *kaf*, Froth, foam, scum, soap-suds, spittle. A black tincture with which the eyebrows of a bride are dyed. Purslain. Cleave thou. (from

A كفّ *kaff*) The palm of the hand. The sole of the foot. كف آبگينه *kafi ābgīna*, The scum or dross which floats on the surface of glass when in fusion. كف بيضا *kafi bayzā*, A white hand. (It generally denotes the miracle wrought by Moses, as recorded in Exod. iv. 6). كف پا *kafi pā*, Sole of the foot. كف دريا *kafi daryā*, Froth of the sea. Scuttle-bone. دريا كف *daryā-kaf*, Bountiful as the ocean. كف دست *kafi dast*, Palm of the hand. A level, bare, desert plain. كف زدن *kaf zadan*, To foam, to froth. كف سفيد *kafi safed*, Snow. كف غنچه كردن *kaf ghuncha kardan*, To clench the fist. كف مس *kafi mis*, A scoria produced by pouring water on brass when in a state of fusion. علم كف *ɛilmi kaf*, Chiromancy, fortune-telling by the lines on the palm. بكف آوردن *ba kaf āvardan*, To seize, to grasp, to clutch.

A كفّ *kaff*, (v. n. of كفّ) Prohibiting, restraining, averting. Abstaining, refraining, containing one's self. Turning in and hemming a garment. Shutting (a purse), drawing together the strings. Wrapping (the feet) in swathes. Being holden (the eye so that it cannot see). Filling a vessel till it overflows. (pl. اكفّ *akuff*, كفوف *kufūf*, and كفّ *kuff*) The hand. The palm of the hand. A handful. The foot of a quadruped having toes. Purslain. Plenty, comfort, abundance (of good things). When, in verse, the seventh quiescent consonant drops: as, ن *nūn* from the end of فاعلاتن *fāɛilātun* or مفاعيلن *mafāɛīlun* becoming فاعلاتُ *fāɛilātu* and مفاعيلُ *mafāɛīlu*. كف الكلب *kaffu'l kalb*, كف السبع *kaffu's sabuɛ*, (or ضبع *zabuɛ*), كفّ القرد *kaffu'l kird*, كف الاسد *kaffu'l asad*, كف الذئب *kaffu'z ziɛb*, كف الاجذم *kaffu'l ajzam*, (or الجذماء *al jazmāɛ*), كفّ آدم *kaffu ādam*, كف عايشه *kaffi ɛāyisha*, كفّ مريم *kaffu miryam*, Names of plants. *Kuff*, (pl. of كفّ *kaff*) Hands. Palms of hands.

A كفأ *kafɛ*, (v. n. of كفأ) Turning back (any thing). Turning off, diverting from one thing to another. Inverting (a vessel). Following. Entering on a path between mountains (sheep). Driving. Departing, being put to flight. Missing a mark. Like, equal. *Kifɛ*, The bed of a river.

P كفا *kafā*, Adversity, straits, difficulty; affliction, sickness, disease. Strangulation.

A كفاء *kafāɛ*, Recompense, requital. Resemblance. *Kifāɛ*, (v. n. 3 of كفأ) Being equal, alike, resembling, corresponding. Repelling, warding off. Spearing alternately (two horsemen). Observing, watching. Rewarding, requiting, recompensing. A kind of skirt fastened to the lower part of a tent. Power. (pl. اكفاء *akfāɛ*) Like, equal. (pl. of كفيء *kafīɛ*) Equals. لا كفاء له *lā kifāɛ lahu*, None like him.

A كفاءة *kafāɛat*, Resemblance.

A كفاة *kafɛat* or *kufɛat*, The produce of camels for one year, viz. colts, milk, and hair. A year's produce of a palm-tree, or crop of the fruits of the earth.

A كفاة *kufāt*, (pl. of كافي *kāfī*) Sufficient, enough. Entire, perfect. Efficacious. Those who perform their duties efficiently.

A كفات *kifāt*, (v. n. of كفت) Going fast. Drawing one's self together. (v. n. 3 of كفت) Getting the start in a race, surpassing, excelling, straining every nerve against another. A place where any thing is collected and contained. مات كفاتا *māta kifātan*, He died suddenly.

A كفّات *kaffāt*, A lion.

A كفاح *kifāh*, (v. n. 3 of كفح) Looking in the face and speaking to. Kissing with unveiled lips. Fighting. War, battle. An abundance of the goods of this world and the next. نائرة كفاح *nāɛiraɛi kifāh*, The heat of battle.

A كفار *kifār*, (pl. of كافر *kāfir*) Unbelievers.

A كفّار *kaffār*, Ungrateful. A farmer. *Kuffār*, (pl. of كافر *kāfir*) Infidels, unbelievers, pagans, idolaters. P كفار تيره روزگار *kuffāri tīra-rozgār*, Wicked infidels. كفار خاكسار *kuffāri khāksār*, Grovelling pagans. كفّار دوزخ قرار *kuffāri dozakh-karār*, Infernal unbelievers.

A كفّارة *kaffārat*, Penitence, penance, atonement (by alms, fasting, &c.). كفّارت ذنوب *kaffārati zunūb*, Expiation of sins.

A كفاريّ *kufāriy*, Large-eared.

A كفاس *kifās*, Swaddling-bands, swathes for the hands and feet. An upper garment.

A كفاف *kafāf*, Sufficiency, competency, enough (to keep one from begging). Pittance, daily bread. Alike, resembling, equal to. Measure. كفاف نفس *kafāfi nafs*, Sufficient for the sustenance of life. وجه كفاف *wajhi kafāf*, A sufficient quantity. دعني كفافِ *daɛnī kafāfi*, Let me alone, and I will not trouble you. *Kifāf*, The external part of the ear. Edge, hem. Edge of a sword. (pl. of كفّة *kiffat*) Scales of a balance. (pl. of كفّة *kuffat*) Hems, borders.

A كفالة *kafālat*, (v. n. of كفل) Becoming surety, giving bail. Security, caution, responsibility, bail. A pledge, pawn. كفالة بالدرك *kafālat bi'd dark*, Bail for whatever may happen. كفالة بالنفس *kafālat bi'n nafs*, Personal security.

P كفانه *kafāna*, An abortion, castling.

P كفانيدن *kafānīdan*, To cleave lengthwise. To cut or split open.

A كفاية *kifāyat*, (v. n. of كفي) Being sufficient, sufficing. A sufficiency, a supply adequate to wants. Ability, adequacy, adequate means, enough, abundance, plenty. A surplus. Prudence, good sense. Economy, thrift. Profit, advantage. بيع الكفاية *bayɛu'l kifāyat*, Purchasing on condition of transferring to the seller the debt of a third person. كفايت كردن *kifāyat kardan*, To suffice, serve, do. To save, spare. كفايت شدن *kifāyat shudan*, To be saved, spared. To be sufficient.

A كفايتي *kifāyatī*, Abundance, plenty, sufficiency, adequacy. Thrifty. Cheap, purchased for less than its value.

A كفّة *kiffat* or *kaffat*, (pl. كفف *kifaf* and كفاف *kifāf*) The bason or scale of a balance. كفّة كفّة *kaffata kaffata*, (كفّة لكفّة *kaffatan likaffatin*, or كفّة عن كفّة *kaffatan ɛan kaffatin*) Openly and fairly, face to face, hand to hand. *Kiffat*, Any thing circular or spherical. The wooden rim (of a drum). A wet ditch, or any piece of stagnating water. A (fowler's) net. The lower part (of the gum). *Kiffat* or *kuffat*, A flaccid gum. *Kuffat*, (pl. كفف *kufaf* and كفاف *kifāf*) Hem (of a garment); border or list (of cloth); extremity (of a sandy desert). The net of a hunter or fowler. A crowd (of people), those nearest to you. Any part of the world where night and day meet. The part where a tree has been cut off. The edge of a cloud. The bottom of a coat of mail. An oblong tract of sand. A stone round which they place ox-dung and mud, and then cook thereon the cheese اقط *akit*.

P كفت *kaft*, He burst, he split. He dug. Split, cleft. A bursting, splitting, rupture. *Kift*, The shoulder. *Kuft*, A rupture. A fissure. A breaking, pounding in pieces. A sprain.

A كفت *kaft*, (v. n. of كفت) Receiving, collecting together. Diverting (one from any design). Grasping. Flying fast (a bird). Getting up to, overtaking. Shrinking, drawing one's self together. Being turned upon the back. Killing, destroying. (Bread) without meat. Death. Swift, active, nimble. *Kaft* also *kift*, A small pot. *Kift*, A sack which lets not any thing drop out. *Kufat*, (or كفتة *kufatat*) A horse drawing himself together when taking a leap.

P كفتا *kaftā*, Broken, burst.

P كفتار *kaftār*, A hyena.

A كفتان *kafatān*, (v. n. of كفت) Flying or running fast. Drawing one's self together.

A كفتة *kaftat*, The cemetery of Madina.

P كفتر *kaftar*, A pigeon.

P كفتري *kaftarī*, A weaver's comb.

P كفتگي *kaftagī*, A split, crack, rent. *Kuftagī*, A sprain. A bruise.

P كفتن *kaftan*, To split. To be divided or split. *Kuftan*, To beat, bruise, smite. To pound. To sprain.

P كفتور *kaftūr*, Perseverance in any undertaking, patience in affliction.

P كفته *kafta*, Split, burst, cracked. Divided. Bipartite. *Kufta*, Sprained. Bruised.

P كفته سم *kafta-sum*, Cloven-hoofed. نا كفته سم *nā kafta-sum*, Solid-hoofed.

P كفجول *kafjūl*, A chopping-block.

P كفچ *kafch*, A skimmer. Froth, scum. Soap-suds. Spittle. A curl. The hood of a snake.

P كفچك *kafchak*, A skimmer. Saddle-flaps.

P كفچل *kafchal*, Crupper, haunches of a horse.

P كفچل پوش *kafchal-posh*, A horse-cloth.

P كفچليز *kafchalez,* A ladle full of holes for taking rice out of a pot: a skimmer. The dog-fish. A tadpole.

P كفچليزك *kafchalezak,* A little skimmer. A tadpole. A small crocodile. A red-tailed lizard.

P كفچليزه *kafchaleza,* A small skimmer. A tadpole.

P كفچه *kafcha,* A ladle, spatula, spoon. A skimmer. A curl, a ringlet. A kind of serpent. The hood of a snake. An open jacket.

P كفچه نول *kafcha-nol,* Spoonbill (a bird).

A كفح *kafh,* (v. n. of كفح) Revealing, uncovering. Looking at, or speaking to, face to face. Kissing with naked lips. Drawing in the bridle, checking (a horse). Striking with a stick. *Kafah,* (v. n. of كفح) Being timid, pusillanimous, cowardly.

A كفخ *kafkh,* (v. n. of كفخ) Giving one a blow on the head (with fist, stick, or spear).

A كفخة *kafkhat,* White fresh butter.

P كفداري *kaf-dārī,* Play, trick, sport.

P كف دست برهم سودن *kaf-dast bar ham sūdan,* To wring the hands. To rub the palms.

A كفر *kafr,* (v. n. of كفر) Covering, hiding, concealing, enveloping. Relapsing into infidelity. A Persian's magnifying or honouring his king. Unbelief, impiety. The grave. Earth, dust. A piece of wood. A short and thick piece of wood. A short staff or cudgel. A village. Obscurity, the darkness of the night. Any place remote from habitations. *Kifr,* Darkness of the night. *Kufr,* (v. n. of كفر) Being unbelieving, impious, ungrateful. Blasphemy, incredulity, impiety. Unbelief. Ingratitude. Pitch. كفر نفسه *kufri nafsihi,* Denying himself. P كفر گرفتن *kufr giriftan,* To blaspheme. A *Kafar,* An eagle. The envelope of the flowers of the palm-tree. A high mountain. A *Kafir,* A large mountain, or a declivity of it. *Kufur,* (pl. of كفور *kafūr*) Infidels. Ungrateful.

P كفرا *kufrā,* Blossoms of the date-tree. *Kufrā,* (or كفراه *kufrāh*) The envelope of the flowers of the female palm-tree.

A كفرًا كفرًا *kafran kafran,* From village to village, from street to street.

A كفران *kufrān,* (v. n. of كفر) Being ungrateful to one's Divine Benefactor. Ingratitude. Unbelief. كفران نعمت *kufrāni niʻmat,* Unthankfulness for benefits.

A كفرة *kafrat,* Darkness. *Kafarat,* (pl. of كافر *kāfir*) Infidels, pagans, unbelievers.

P كفرگوي *kufr-goy* or *gūy,* A blasphemer.

A كفرني *kafarnaʼ,* Mean, obscure, ignorant fellow.

A كفرّي *kufurraʼ, kufarraʼ,* or *kufirraʼ,* The envelope of the flowers of a palm-tree.

A كفرّين *kifirrin,* Sly, cunning, astute.

A كفس *kafas,* A turning in of the toes, so that the person walks limpingly on the outer edges of the feet. A curvature of the breast.

A كفساء *kafsāʼ,* (fem. of اكفس *akfas*) Bow-legged (woman), who walks limpingly on the outer edges of her feet.

P كف سفيد *kaf-safed,* (White hand) Liberal.

P كف سنگ *kaf-sang,* A hand-stone; a stone held in the hand with which any thing is brayed upon a slab; a muller. A stone for cracking nuts.

P كفش *kafsh,* A shoe, sandal, slipper, high-heeled and shod with iron. كفش خواستن *kafsh khwāstan,* (To ask for one's shoes) To set out on a journey. كفش نهادن *kafsh nihādan,* (To lay by one's shoes) To remain at home, not to travel.

P كفش دوز *kafsh-doz,* A shoemaker.

P كفشگر *kafshgar,* Dealer in shoes. A shoemaker.

P كفشير *kafshīr,* Solder. Borax. Lead, tin, pewter. كفشير كردن *kafshīr kardan,* To solder. كفشير گرفتن *kafshīr giriftan,* (or پذيرفتن *pazīruftan*) To be soldered, closed up, united. To heal.

P كفش كن *kafsh-kan,* A place where the slippers are pulled off.

P كفشن *kafshan,* A desert; also ground which has formerly been cultivated.

A كفاف *kafaf,* A sufficiency, competency, enough to keep one from begging. A request made with outstretched hand. *Kifaf,* (pl. of كفّة *kiffat*) Scales of a balance. *Kifaf* or *kafaf,* Lines of a circular form stained upon the hands. *Kifaf,* Holes from whence springs of water arise. *Kufaf,* (pl. of كفّة *kuffat*) Hems of garments.

A كففة *kifafat,* (pl. of كافّ *kāff*) Hinderers.

P كفك *kafk,* Froth, scum. Soap-suds. Spittle. كفك بر آوردن *kafk bar āwardan,* To cast up scum. To froth, foam.

A كفكفة *kafkafat,* (v. n. of كفكف Q) Repelling, averting, preventing, stopping.

P كفك گير *kafk-gīr,* A spoon, ladle, skimmer.

P كفگير *kaf-gīr,* A skimmer, spoon, ladle, generally perforated like a colander.

A كفل *kafl,* (v. n. of كفل) Fasting continually. Maintaining or educating. Being security for another. *Kifl,* Alike, equal. A part, portion. (pl. اكفال *akfāl*) The cloth covering a camel's bunch, on which the rider sits. Hair growing after hair has fallen off. One who throws himself upon people. A piece of cloth under the yoke of an ox. One who sits badly on horseback. Flight. Any thing on which one is carried. One who keeps in the rear of an army that he may easily escape. *Kafal,* (pl. اكفال *akfāl*) The buttocks, the rump.

P كفل *kafal,* The buttocks, haunches; crupper (of a horse). A kind of cloth used instead of a saddle.

A كفّل *kuffal,* (pl. of كافل *kāfil* and كفيل *kafīl*) Sureties, bondsmen. Persons who fast continually.

A كفلاء *kufalāʼ,* (pl. of كفيل *kafīl*) Securities, sureties, bondsmen, pledges, bail.

P كفل پوش *kafal-posh,* A horse-cloth.

P كفلگاه *kafal-gāh,* The hips, buttocks.

P كفليز *kaflez,* (or كفليزه *kafleza*) A ladle, skimmer. A colander, strainer.

A كفن *kafn,* (v. n. of كفن) Spinning. Burying bread in the ashes (to bake). Wrapping (a body) in a winding-sheet. *Kafan,* (pl. اكفان *akfān*) Grave-clothes, a winding-sheet, a shroud. Meat without salt. P كفن بر گردن *kafan bar gardan,* With a winding-sheet round one's neck.

P كفن آهنج *kafan-āhanj,* (also كفن دزد *kafan-duzd*) A stripper or plunderer of the dead.

P كفن آهنجي *kafan-āhanjī,* A stripping of the dead. كفن آهنجي كردن *kafan-āhanjī kardan,* To plunder or strip the dead of their grave-clothes.

A كفنة *kafnat,* Name of a tree. *Kufnat,* Good ground producing all kinds of vegetables.

P كفنج *kafanj,* A fish which stimulates to venery.

A كفني *kafnī,* A dress worn by fakīrs.

A كفو *kufw,* Like, equal.

A كفوء *kafuʼ* (pl. كفاء *kifāʼ*), or *kufuʼ* (pl. اكفاء *akfāʼ*) Like, equal.

A كفور *kafūr,* (pl. كفر *kufur*) Unthankful. An infidel. *Kufūr,* (v. n. of كفر) Being impious, ungrateful to one's Divine Benefactor. Infidelity.

A كفوف *kafūf,* (A camel) whose teeth are worn to the stump with age. *Kufūf,* (v. n. of كفّ) Having teeth worn down with age (a camel). (pl. of كفّ *kaff*) Palms of the hands. Hands.

A كفول *kufūl,* (v. n. of كفل) Being security for.

P كفه *kafa,* A heap of corn in a barn winnowed. Ears of wheat or barley not threshed or trodden out. A tambour de basque.

P كفّه *kaffa,* Name of a city.

A كفي *kafy, kify,* or *kufy,* Sufficient. *Kufaʼ,* Like, equal. (pl. of كفية *kufyat*) Sufficiencies. Victuals, livelihoods.

A كفيّ *kafiy,* Sufficient. Rain.

P كفيار *kafyār,* Laborious, pains-taking in praiseworthy deeds.

A كفية *kufyat,* A sufficiency. (pl. كفي *kufaʼ*) Food, sustenance.

A كفيت *kafīt,* (v. n. of كفت) Running or flying fast. Drawing one's self together. A sufficiency, a competency. Swift, active, nimble. A sack which lets not any thing drop out of it.

A كفيح *kafīh,* Alike, equal, resembling. A husband, a bedfellow. An unexpected guest.

P كفيدن *kafīdan,* To burst, crack, break. To foam.

P كفيده *kafīda,* Burst, broken, cracked, split.

P كفيز *kafīz,* A measure containing about 64 lbs. weight.

A كفيل *kafīl,* (pl. كفلاء *kufalāʼ*) A security, surety, cautioner, bail. Like, equal. Sureties.

A كفيء *kafīʼ,* (pl. كفاء *kifāʼ*) Like, resembling, equal. Changed (colour). The bed of a river.

A كفيئة *kafīʼat,* Like, resembling, equal.

P كك *kak,* Dry biscuit. Name of a sour herb. *Kuk,* A hen that has left off laying and wants the cock.

A كك *kak,* (for كذلك *ka zālika*) Like that.

P ککا *kakā*, (in zand and Pāzand) The teeth.

P ککچه *kakcha*, Cotton-seed.

P ککري *kakrī*, Name of a city in India.

P ککژ *kakij*, The herb rocket.

P ککش *kakish*, A pungent plant like nosesmart.

P ککمک *kakmak*, A mole or freckle.

P ککه *kaka*, (or ککي *kakī*) Human excrement.

P کل *kal*, A man who has wounds and scars on his head and has lost his hair; bald. The male of any animal. A male buffalo. *Kul*, Crooked-backed. Bent, curved. A village, hamlet. Short, defective.

A کلّ *kalla*, (fut. يـكلّ *yakillu*) He was wearied.

A کلّ *kall*, (v. n. of کلّ) Being blunt (a sword); dull, dim (sight); slow, stammering (tongue). Being tired. Having neither parent nor child. (pl. کلول *kulūl*) A heavy burden. Trouble. Injustice, oppression. Domestics, or those whom a person maintains. An orphan. Blunt (sword); dim (sight). One who has neither parents nor children. Heavy. Worthless. An agent, a commissioner. The back of a knife or sword. خفيف الکلّ *khafīfu'l kall*, One who has a small family. *Kull*, All, universal, the whole. Each. کلّ حضر *kullun hazara*, (or کلّ حضروا *kullun hazarū*) All were present. کلّ رجل *kullu rajulin*, Every man. کلّ امرأة *kullu imraʼatin*, Every woman. کلّ اناس *kullu anās*, All men. کلّ کاس *kullu kās*, The whole cup. بالکلّ *bi'l kull*, In toto. هو العالم کلّ العالم *huwa'l ʻālim kullu'l ʻālim*, He is a learned man every inch of him. بيده کلّها *bi yadihi kullihā*, With his whole hand. کلّ احد *kullu ahadin*, Every one. کلّما *kullamā*, As often as. من کلّ جانب *min kulli jānibin*, From every side, from all quarters.

A کلء *kalʼ*, (v. n. of کلأ) Guarding (as God does man). Flogging, lashing. Being deferred (a debt). Abounding in forage (land). Turning (the eye) again and again. Devouring forage (a camel).

A کلأ *kalaʼ*, (v. n. of کلئ) Abounding in green herbage (ground). Devouring forage (a camel). Forage, fodder, herbage.

P کلا *kalā*, A frog. Potash.

A کلا *kilā*, (dual of کلّ *kull*) Both.

P کلّا *kallā*, A cabbage. The head.

A کلّا *kallā*, Not at all, not in the least. By no means. Certainly, by all means, yes. Verily, truly.

A کلاء *kilāʼ*, (v. n. of کلأ) Guarding. Flogging. Being deferred (a debt). Abounding in forage (land). Directing (the eye) again and again. Drawing to a close (life).

A کلّاء *kallāʼ*, The station or mooring of a ship, a dock. A river's bank. Name of an anchoring-place at Basrah. A place little exposed to the wind.

A کلاءة *kilāʼat*, (v. n. of کلأ) Guarding. Flogging. Being deferred (debt). Abounding in forage (land). Turning (the eye) again and again. Drawing to a close (life). اذهب في کلاءة الله *izhab fī kilāʼat allāh*, Go under the protection of God.

P کلاو *kalāū* or *kulāū*, A frog.

A کلاب *kalāb*, Madness, loss of reason. Hydrophobia. *Kilāb*, (v. n. 3 of کلب) Feeding on thorns (a camel). Being malignant, snarling. Being pinched with want. (pl. of کلب *kalb*) Dogs.

A کلّاب *kallāb*, A keeper of dogs. A hook whereby a traveller suspends his provision-bag from the saddle. *Kullāb*, (pl. کلاليب *kalālīb*) A pot-hook; or for drawing bread from ovens. A saw. A spur.

P کلابتون *kalābatūn*, A kind of needle-work or embroidery. Gold-thread.

A کلابث *kulābis*, Avaricious, stingy.

P کلابه *kalāba*, A raw thread as it is wound from the spindle, yarn. A ball of thread, a clew, hank, skein. A reel, wheel for winding thread on.

P کلابه سنگ *kalāba-sang*, A stone for a sling.

P کلابيه *kulābiya*, A wafer: marchpane.

P کلّا پايچه *kallā pāycha*, Name of a dish, the head and trotters.

P کلاپشت *kulā-pusht*, (or کلاپشته *kulā-pushta*) A kind of goats'-hair cloth black and green.

P کلاپيسه *kalāpesa*, A rolling and shewing the whites of the eyes from anger, debility, or voluptuousness.

A کلاءة *kulʼat*, A debt to be paid hereafter. Earnest-money. Any thing purchased on credit.

P کلات *kalāt*, A castle on the top of a mountain or other high ground (either inhabited or deserted and in ruins). A market-town. Name of a city in Turkistān; also of a fortress in Kandahār. کلات ديوان *kalāti devān*, Devil's castle, *i. e.* A sort of mushroom or fungus growing among ruins.

P کلاته *kalāta*, A market-town. A palace or superb building surrounded by other houses. A castle on a hill. A small level sown field.

A کلاثب *kulāsib*, Close-fisted, stingy, crabbed.

P کلاج *kulāj*, A wafer: marchpane.

P کلاجک *kalājak*, A small white species of the concha venerea, with which they ornament the collars of dogs. The shell of the murex or purple fish, out of which they drink wine.

P کلاجو *kalājū*, A cup, for wine or coffee.

P کلاجود *kalājūd*, A small dish, plate, or saucer, whether of gold, of silver, or of earthenware, on which another dish or cup is placed. A full cup or bumper drank to another's health.

P کلاچه *kalācha*, Marrow. A magpie.

P کلاچه گاو *kalācha-gāv*, A party-coloured ox.

A کلاح *kilāh*, *kalāh*, or *kulāh*, A barren year. *Kulāh*, (v. n. of کلح) Putting on a sour, stern, grinning countenance.

P کلاخ *kalākh*, A fillet, a head-band.

P کلّا خشک *kallā khwushk*, Lantern-jawed. Treacherous, cunning, malicious. Noise, tumult.

P کلاذه *kalāza*, Squint-eyed.

P کلار *kalār*, A frog.

P کلاري *kalārī*, A salt-pan, or salt-work.

P کلاژ *kalāj*, Squint-eyed. A magpie. Mouldiness.

P کلاژاره *kalājāra*, A magpie.

P کلاژکه *kalājaka*, A grappling-hook or iron, particularly that used to recover things from a well.

P کلاژه *kalāja*, Squint-eyed. A magpie. A green magpie.

A کلّاس *kallās*, Extremely sharp.

P کلاسنگ *kalā-sang*, A sling.

P کلاسه *kalāsa*, Wells where travellers drink (especially pilgrims going to or from Mecca).

P کلاش *kalāsh*, A spider.

P کلاش جامه *kalāsh-jāma*, The film in which the spider deposits her eggs. A cobweb.

P کلاشخانه *kalāsh-khāna*, A spider's web, cobweb.

P کلاشک *kalāshak*, A sling.

P کلاشکن *kalāshkan*, A kind of sweetmeat.

P کلاشکه *kalāshaka*, A hook for recovering things from a well.

A کلاع *kulāʻ*, (v. n. of کلع) Having cracks in the feet. Patience, fortitude in battle or conflict.

A کلاعيّ *kulāʻiy*, Strong, bold, strenuous.

P کلاغ *kalāgh*, An enclosure of wood or stone erected about the tombs of the great. *Kalāgh* or *kulāgh*, A crow, rook, raven. کلاغ گرفتن *kalāgh giriftan*, To laugh at, hold in derision.

P کلاغ پيشه *kalāgh-pesha*, A jackdaw.

P کلاغچه *kalāghcha*, A magpie. A little rook.

P کلافه *kalāfa*, A raw thread as it is wound from the spindle. A reel.

A کلافيّ *kulāfiy*, (A grape) grown at Kulāf.

P کلاک *kalāk*, A mere desert. The upper part of the forehead. *Kilāk*, A crook stick for gathering fruit. *Kulāk*, Empty, void. A large wave.

P کلّا کار *kallā-kār*, Noisy, tumultuous.

A کلاکل *kalākil*, Crowds, bodies. *Kulākil*, Short, thick, and strong (man).

P کلاکموش *kalāk-mush*, The jerboa. A mole.

P کلاگر *kalāgar*, A kind of food. Whatever deepens colour (as vinegar), or gives a flavour to victuals (as spices or honey).

P کلال *kalāl*, The crown of the head. Top of a mountain. Weakness. A natural defect. An orphan. A childless man. *Kulāl*, A potter.

A کلال *kalāl*, (v. n. of کلّ) Being tired (a man or camel). Weakness, languor, fatigue, lassitude, impotency. Dimness. *Kilāl*, (pl. of کلّة *killat*) Bits of red wool on the top of a hawda for ornament.

A کلالة *kalālat*, (v. n. of کلّ) Being fatigued. Being blunt (sword). Being dim-sighted. Stammering, being slow in speech. Being crowned. Ceasing (as wind). One who has neither parents nor offspring. Remote relationship.

P کلال خانه *kalāl-khāna*, A place where arrack is sold. An arrack-farm (an Indian term).

P کلاله *kulāla*, Hair, locks, ringlets dangling from the forehead. A handful of flowers, a nosegay.

A کلاليب *kalālīb*, (pl. of کلّاب *kullāb* and کلّوب

kallūb) Pot-hooks. Spurs. Saws. The talons of a hawk. The thorns of trees.

P کلالیوه *kalālīwa*, Astonied, amazed, confounded.

A کلام *kalām*, A word, speech, oration, harangue; discourse, talk, conversation. A sentence or proposition complete in itself. Disputation. Scholastic theology. Combat. A salutation, compliments. کلام الله *kalāmu'llāh*, The word of God. کلام شریف *kalāmi sharīf*, (or کلام عزّت *kalāmi ʻizzat*) The holy writings, *i.e.* the Kur'ān. P کلام کردن *kalām kardan*, To speak. To reason. To relate. A بطئ الکلام *batīu'l kalām*, Slow of speech. P ردّ کلام کردن *raddi kalām kardan*, To refute, to contradict, to oppose. A علم کلام *ʻilmi kalām*, Metaphysics. Scholastic theology. Rhetoric. فصیح الکلام *fasīhu'l kalām*, (میر کلام *mīri kalām*, or ملیح الکلام *malīhu'l kalām*) Eloquent. خلاصهٔ کلام *khulāsaʻi kalām*, (محصّل کلام *muhassali kalām*, حاصل کلام *hāsili kalām*, also الحاصل *al hāsil*) The substance of the discourse is, *i.e.* in a word, to sum up all, upon the whole. *Kilām*, (pl. of کلم *kalm*) Wounds. *Kulām*, Coarse, thick, and hard earth.

A کلّام *killām*, (v. n. 2 of کلم irregular) Speaking.

P کلان *kalān*, Large, great, big, stout, grand, bulky. Elder. High. More. A great bulk, mass. Crown of the head. A large public standard for weights and measures. کلان روضه *kalāni rawza*, An epithet of Muhammad. روز کلان *rozi kalān*, A great day: a festival. Christmas. *Kilān*, A fastening for an out-house.

P کلان بینی *kalān-bīnī*, Large-nosed.

P کلان پیشه *kalān-pesha*, Amplification, dimness in the eyesight, confusion of vision.

P کلانتر *kalāntar*, Bigger, greater, larger. The chief man (especially for life) in a town, in whose name every thing is done.

P کلان سال *kalān-sāl*, Aged, old, grandevous.

P کلان سالی *kalān-sālī*, Old age, grandevity.

P کلان شکم *kalān-shikam*, Big-bellied.

P کلان گوش *kalān-gosh*, Large-eared.

P کلانی *kalānī*, Greatness, size, bigness.

P کلاو *kalāv*, A frog. A clew. A reel.

P کلاور *kalāwar*, A frog.

P کلاوو *kalāwū*, A species of field-mouse.

P کلاوه *kalāwa*, A hank, a skein. A reel. A frog. Astonished, confounded, amazed. کلاوهٔ چرخ *kalāwaʻi charkh*, The Zodiac. The revolution of the heavens.

P کلاه *kulāh*, A cap, cowl, night-cap, especially one worn by the Muhammadan monks or dervīshes; also in general any similar head-dress. A mitre, tiara, turban, a Tartar cap, hat, fillet, or wreath. A crown. کلاه انداختن *kulāh andākhtan*, (or بر انداختن *bar andākhtan*) To fling away one's hat; (met.) To rejoice greatly, to exult extravagantly. کلاه برسر نهادن *kulāh bar sar nihādan*, To put on one's hat; (met.) To shew respect, to honour. کلاه چرخ *kulāhi charkh*, The sky. The sun. کلاه زر *kulāh-zar*, (or زرّین کلاه *zarrīn-kulāh*) A golden fillet or head-dress worn by the Persian ladies. کلاه زنگله *kulāhi zangula*, A ridiculously-shaped cap, from which are suspended many little bells and foxes' tails, and in which any person detected in selling short weight is exposed to public view. کلاه زمین *kulāhi zamīn*, The sky. The sun. The moon. A fungus, toadstool. کلاه شکستن *kulāh shikastan*, To turn down the corner of one's cap or turban. To wear one's hat awry. کلاه قاضی *kulāhi kāzī*, A kind of cap worn by the cāzis or judges. A fungus, a toadstool. کلاه ملك *kulāhi mulk*, A king. کلاه مولوی *kulāhi mawlavī*, The dervīsh's cap, called in general mawlavī. کلاه نهادن *kulāh nihādan*, To salute respectfully, to make humble reverence. زره کلاه *zirih-kulāh*, A helmet, casque.

P کلاه داری *kulāh-dārī*, Sovereignty, royalty.

P کلاهو *kalāhū*, A sort of deer without horns.

P کلاهور *kalāhūr*, Name of a champion.

P کلاهون *kalāhūn*, Name of a renowned warrior.

A کلب *kalb*, (v. n. of کلب) Imitating the barking of dogs to induce them to respond. Acquiring the habit of eating men (a dog). Being seized with a fever. Cutting leather. Spurring. (pl. اکلب *aklub*, اکالب *akālib*, کلاب *kilāb*, کلابات *kilābāt*, and کلیب *kalīb*) A dog. Any biting animal. The dog-star. A lion. A sort of fish. Side of a hill. The first gush or flush of a torrent. The pivot of a mill-wheel. A leathern thong cut from an untanned hide. A stripe along the middle of a horse's back. An offshoot of the tribe of قضاعة *kuzāʻat*. A thong with which a bag is sewed. A beam which props or supports a wall. A round knob on the hilt of a sword; also any thing fixed there by which it is hung to the belt. A hook by which a traveller suspends his provision-bag to the saddle. کلب البحر *kalbu'l bahr*, (Sea-dog, or river-dog) A beaver. لسان الکلب *lisānu'l kalb*, (Dog's-tongue) Name of a plant. Name of a certain famous sword. امّ الکلب *ummu'l kalb*, Name of a thorny little tree. کفّ الکلب *kaffu'l kalb*, (Dog's-paw) A spreading kind of grass. *Kalab*, (v. n. of کلب) Being severe (winter). Being hard (the times). Being enraged or rabid. Being seized with hydrophobia. Slipping between the cheek of the pulley and the wheel (a rope). Producing hard leaves (a tree for want of watering). Being foolish, losing one's senses. Eating much without being satisfied. Acting meanly and basely. Extreme cold. Canine madness (whether affecting men, dogs, or other animals). A canine appetite. Thirst. Procurement, panderism. The yelp of one bitten by a mad dog. Avidity. Vehemence. Severity. *Kalib*, Mad, rabid (dog or camel). Hard, pinching (times).

P کلب *kalab*, The circumference of the mouth. The beak of a bird.

P کلبا *kalbā*, (in zand and Pāzand) A dog.

P کلباد *kalbād*, A mighty man of Tūrān, killed by Fariburz in the combat of the twelve champions.

P کلباسو *kalbāsū*, A noxious kind of lizard.

A کلبة *kalbat*, A bitch. A thorny tree. A thorny shrub destitute of branches. An opprobrious epithet given to a woman. کلبة الماء *kalbatu'l māʼ*, A beaver. امّ کلبة *ummu kalbat*, A fever. *Kulbat*, A thong or the fibres of bark used in stitching. A closet, cell. Severity (of cold). A tavern or wine-cellar. Straits. Sterility of a season. Whiskers of a dog or cat. *Kalibat*, Mad (bitch). A thorny tree.

A کلبتان *kalbatāni*, A blacksmith's or farrier's forceps, with which they take hold of hot iron or pull out nails.

P کلبتان *kalbitān*, A smith's forceps or pincers.

A کلبث *kalbas*, *kulbus*, or *kulabis*, Avaricious.

P کلبد *kulbad*, A closet, a cell.

P کلبسو *kalbasū*, A large lizard.

P کلبك *kulbak*, A covering for a stack of grain. A hut built for those who keep watch over sown fields or melon-grounds.

P کلبه *kulba*, A closet, a cell. A cot. A shop, warehouse. A corner. کلبهٔ احزان *kulbaʻi ihzān*, (Cell of sorrow) An afflicted, distressed family.

A کلبيّ *kalbiy*, Canine. Of the tribe کلب *kalb*.

P کلپتره *kalpatra*, Foolish sayings.

A کلّة *kallat*, A large blunt knife. *Killat*, (v. n. of کلّ) Being blunt (sword); dull, dim (sighted). Being slow, stammering (tongue). (pl. کلال *kilāl*) State, condition. A woman's veil. A bit of red wool on the top of a hawda for ornament. A canopy; an awning for keeping off gnats, a mosquito-curtain. *Kullat*, (fem. of کلّ *kull*) All, every (woman). Delay.

A کلت *kalt*, (v. n. of کلت) Collecting, drawing together. Pouring (into a vessel). Spurring, galloping (a horse). Flinging (a thing). فلت کلت *fullat kullat* or *fulat kulat*, A swift horse.

A کلتا *kiltā*, (in regimen) Both females.

P کلتان *kaltān*, Jambs, side-posts of a door.

A کلتان *kiltāni*, (dual fem. of کلّ *kull*) Both.

P کلتب *kaltab* or *kultub*, Hypocrisy, deceit.

A کلتب *kaltab* or *kultub*, Weakness, inability, want of efficiency.

P کلتبان *kaltabān*, A pimp to his own wife.

A کلتة *kultat*, A portion of meat or corn. A little, somewhat. فلتة کلتة *fulatat kulatat*, A horse drawing himself together when preparing to leap.

A کلتحة *kaltahat*, A mode of walking.

A کلتويّ *kiltawiy*, Relating to both females.

P کلته *kalta*, Dock-tailed. A short stick which fills the hand. Short, defective, little, mean, contemptible. Any thing old of its kind; past his labour, or any animal that can no longer hunt from age. One who has an impediment in his speech.

P کلته چوب *kalta-chob*, A dervīsh's short staff.

A کلثب *kalsab*, Stingy. Crabbed, contracted.

A كلثمة *kalsamat*, (v. n. of كلثم Q) Being full-faced, plump-cheeked, chubby (yet handsome).

A كلثوم *kulsūm*, Full of flesh about the face and cheeks. An elephant. The silk flag at the top of a standard. امّ كلثوم *ummu kulsūm*, The mother of plumpness, (by the figure metonymy) the name of a woman, as of Fātima the daughter of Muhammad.

P كلج *kilj*, Baskets in which they carry coals or dried dung for heating baths. A fold, wrinkle. Proud, arrogant, conceited.

A كلج *kalaj*, Generous. Bold, brave. *Kuluj*, Strenuous, strong, robust, bold men.

P كلجان *kaljān*, A dunghill or receptacle for dirt and sweepings.

P كلچ *kalch*, Dirt, filth. A wrinkle. Pride, arrogance, self-conceit. A dung-basket. *Kulch*, A sort of cloth brought from Cashmere. Crumbs of bread.

P كلچنگ *kulachang*, A crab.

P كلچيچه *kal* or *kilchīcha*, Tickling, titillation.

P كلح *kilh*, A gum, benzoin or benjamin.

A كلحبة *kalhabat*, (v. n. of كلحب Q) Striking with a sword. The crackling sound of fire.

A كلحة *kalahat*, The mouth; the environs of the mouth, especially when stretched to a grin.

A كلحم *kilhim*, Earth, dust.

P كلخ *kulkh*, A kind of herb.

P كلخچ *kalakhch*, Filth of the body. كلخچ بستن *kalakhch bastan*, To become nasty, contract dirt.

A كلد *kald*, (v. n. of كلد) Heaping, accumulating. *Kalad*, Hard, rough, soil, without gravel. A hill. A leopard. A weasel.

A كلدة *kaldat*, A tract of hard ground. ابو كلدة *abū kaldat*, A hyena.

A كلدح *kaldah*, Hard, rough. An old woman.

A كلدحة *kaldahat*, A certain manner of walking.

A كلدم *kaldam*, Hard, thick.

A كلدوم *kuldūm*, Short. A dwarf.

P كلده *kalda*, Dry, barren ground. A name.

A كلز *kalz*, (v. n. of كلز) Collecting.

P كليز *kilz*, Root of the wild pomegranate.

A كلزّ *kilazz*, Strong-muscled, compactly built.

A P كلس *kils*, Quick-lime.

P كلس *kuls*, Carded cotton.

A كلسة *kulsat*, A blackish ash-colour.

P كلسرا *kalsirā*, Depraved, vicious. An enemy.

A كلسمة *kalsamat*, (v. n. of كلسم Q) Being slothful, negligent in doing any thing. Going quickly. Directing one's steps towards.

G كلسيا *kalisiyā*, A church.

A كلشمة *kalshamat*, An old woman.

A كلصمة *kalsamat*, (v. n. of كلصم Q) Passing by (a fugitive).

A كلط *kulut*, Saucy, petulant people.

A كلطة *kaltat*, (*kalatat*, كلظة *kalazat*, or *kalzat*) A limping, halting gait.

A كلع *kalaʻ*, (v. n. of كلع) Drying on the head (dirt). Being dirty and chapt (the foot). Being cracked in the feet (a camel). *Kilaʻ*, (pl. كلعة *kilaʻat*) Rough, of a repulsive aspect. Vile, abject, sordid. كلع مال *kilaʻu mālin*, The steward or manager of an estate; an able manager of camels. *Kalaʻ*, (v. n. of كلع) Being dirty (the foot, a vessel, or the head). Being cracked, chapt (the foot). Filth adhering to the feet, to a vessel, or bottle. Fissures in the feet. The sorest of the fight, the brunt of the battle. *Kaliʻ*, Dirty (leathern bottle). (A camel) afflicted with the disease called شقاق *shukāk*.

A كلعة *kulʻat*, A distemper in the hips of a camel. *Kalaʻat*, A part of a flock. *Kilaʻat*, (pl. of كلع *kilaʻ*) Rough, repulsive. Vile, sordid.

P كلعند *kulʻund*, Uncouth, froward, perverse. A strong beardless youth. A foolish talker.

P كلغر *kalghar*, A species of very fine soft wool. A sort of wood used for fuel.

A كلف *kilf*, A man in love. *Kulf*, (pl. of اكلف *aklaf*) Of a blackish red colour. *Kalaf*, (v. n. of كلف) Attending carefully to any thing, being engrossed by any object; being in love. Inclining to a dirty black (red). A blackish yellow. Any pimple or spot in the face of a reddish black. A freckle.

P كلف *kalaf*, A freckle.

A كلف *kalaf*, (from قفل *kufl*) A padlock.

A كلفاء *kalfāʼ*, (fem. of اكلف *aklaf*) Of a blackish red colour. Wine.

A كلفة *kulfat*, A blackish red colour. Trouble, vexation, distress, inconvenience.

P كلفت *kalaft*, The beak of a bird. *Kuluft*, Rough, uncouth.

P كلفخشنگ *kalfakhshang*, (or كلفهشنگ *kalfahshang*) An icicle.

P كلك *kalk* or *kulk*, The side under the arm-pit. *Kilk*, A hollow reed, a kex; a pen. An arrow. The canine teeth. A brasier. Flesh-glue. كلك خوش رفتار *kilki khwush-raftār*, An easy-going pen. كلك عنبربار *kilki ʻambar-bār*, An odoriferous reed. *Kulk*, The fine wool of which shawls are made, which they comb from the root of the hair of a species of goat. *Kalak*, A lancet. An earthen fire-stove. A concourse of people. Headache. A kind of float for passing rivers, constructed of bundles of reeds and the like, and a number of inflated skins. Ill-omened, unlucky. An owl. A pod of cotton not yet ripe. A young he-buffalo. Name of a place nigh unto Dāmaghān remarkable for its excellent wheat. كلك خسپ *kalak khasp*, A crowd of people huddled together round a fire in winter. Poor, indigent. *Kalik*, An owl. *Kilik*, Squint-eyed. The little finger. *Kuluk*, Squint-eyed. Gripes.

A كلكال *kalkāl*, Breast. Girth-place of a horse.

P كلكته *kalkatta*, Calcutta, capital of Bengal.

P كل كل *kal kal*, Vain words, nonsensical talk. Search, inquiry. *Kal kal*, *kil kil*, or *kul kul*, Bdellium.

A كلكل *kalkal*, The breast. The girth-place of a horse. *Kulkul*, Short but robust (man).

A كلكلان *kulkullān*, (from كلّ *kull*) One entrusted with the whole economy of a house; a factotum, or major domo.

P كلكله *kulkula*, A small kind of hooka.

P كلكم *kalkam*, A cleaving, splitting. The rainbow. *Kalkam* or *kulkum*, A balista, catapulta.

P كلكنك *kilkank* or *kilkanak*, Purslain.

P كلكي *kalakī*, A plume worn on the head by the youths of Persia in battle and on great occasions.

P كلكينه *kulkīna*, Soft, shaggy silk or velvet.

P كلل *kalal*, A plume worn on the head by the Persian youths in battle or on festivals.

A كلل *kalal*, State, condition.

A كلم *kalm*, (v. n. of كلم) Wounding. (pl. كلوم *kulūm* and كلام *kilām*) A wound. *Kalim* and *kilam*, (pl. of كلمة *kalimat* and *kilamat*) Words.

P كلم *kalam*, A cabbage, cauliflower.

P كلما *kalmā*, (in zand and Pāzand) A vine.

A كلما *kullamā*, Whatever. *Kullamā*, As often as, every time.

A كلمات *kalimāt*, (pl. of كلمة *kalimat*) Words, vocables, discourses, speeches.

P كلماسنگ *kalmāsang*, A sling.

A كلماني *kalmāniy* or *kalamāniy*, Eloquent.

A كلّماني *killimāniy*, Loquacious, chatty. Eloquent.

A كلّماني *kilimmāniy*, Eloquent.

A كلمة *kalmat* or *kilmat*, (pl. كلمات *kalmāt*) A word. *Kalimat*, (pl. كلم *kalim* and كلمات *kalimāt*) A word, saying, discourse, vocable, part of speech. A poem, complete or incomplete. كلمة الله *kalimatu'llāh*, The word of God. Jesus Christ. الكلمة الباقية *al kalimatu'l bāḳiyat*, (The enduring word) A profession of the unity of God. كلمةٌ طيبه *kalimaṭi tayyiba*, Good words. P كلمه به كلمه *kalima ba kalima*, Word for word. A ذو كلمة نافذة *zū kalimatin nāfizatin*, (or نافذ الكلمتين *nāfizu'l kalimatayn*) Possessed of a penetrating, or of two penetrating words, *i. e.* such as produce conviction or enforce obedience; one from whose "Yes" and "No" there is no appeal: of absolute authority. عشر كلمات *ʻashara kalimāt*, The decalogue. *Kilamat*, (pl. كلم *kilam*) A word.

A كلمتان *kalimatāni*, (dual, oblique case كلمتين *kalimatayni*) Two voices, two words, or two divisions of a discourse: as, كلمتي الشهادة *kalimatayi'sh shahādat*, The two members of the Muhammadan confession of faith, *i. e.* لا اله الّا الله *lā ilāha illa'llāh*, There is no god but God, و محمّد رسول الله *wa muhammad rasūlu'llāh*, And Muhammad is the apostle of God.

A كلمح *kilmih*, Earth, dust.

P كلمرغ *kalmurgh*, A species of vulture.

A كلمسة *kalmasat*, (v. n. of كلمس Q) Going.

P كلموژ *kalmūzh*, A lizard with a head like a serpent.

P كلن *kulan*, A swelling in the body. A wen. Elephantiasis. Carded cotton.

P كلنبه *kulumba*, Almond-cake. A ball.

P کلنج *kilanj*, Dirt, filth. Vain-glory. The little finger.

P کلنجار *kilinjār*, A crab, a crayfish.

P کلنجر *kilanjar*, A place and fort in Hindūstān.

P کلنجري *kalinjarī*, A kind of black grape. *Kilanjarī*, A native of Kilanjar.

P کلنجك *kilanjak*, The little finger. *Kulanjak* or *kilinjak*, A crab.

P کلند *kaland* or *kuland*, A mattock, a pick-axe, shovel. A vine-dresser's pruning-hook. *Kuland*, A lock, key. Rough, unshaved, unsmoothed. A log fastened to a dog's neck.

P کلند بردار *kuland-bardār*, A pioneer.

P کلندر *kalandar*, The stocks. Bar of a door. A rough, untrimmed stick. A rough, uncouth man.

P کلندره *kalandara* also *kulandara*, A rough, unshaved stick. A man uncouth in his manners.

P کلندن *kulandan*, To shake a garment or carpet.

P کلنده *kalanda*, The hopper of a mill.

A کلندي *kalunda'*, A hillock, a bank.

P کلندي *kalandī*, Hard and rough ground.

P کلنديدن *kalandīdan*, To dig, to excavate.

A کلنز *kalnaz*, Of a squat shape, with a plump jolly countenance.

P کلنك *kalink*, Squint-eyed. *Kilnak*, Purslain. *Kilnak* or *kilank*, A key-hole. *Kulank*, A crane, heron. A large cock. *Kulunk*, A pick-axe.

P کلنکك *kilnakak*, Purslain.

P کلنکی *kulunkī*, Greedy, overreaching. A sort of cock. One who uses a mattock or pick-axe.

P کلنګ *kilang*, A key-hole. *Kulung*, A pick-axe.

P کلنه *kulna*, A bird's beak.

P کلو *kulo*, The head man of a ward. The judge of a market. A large buttered cake.

A کلوء *kalū'*, Able to do with very little sleep.

P کلوا *kalwā*, A joining of two things. A frog.

A کلواذ *kilwāz*, The ark of the Mosaical law. ام کلواذ *umm kilwāz*, Misfortune.

P کلوب *kulūb*, A form, model, mould.

A کلوب *kallūb*, (pl. کلاليب *kalālīb*) Forceps, pincers. A spur. A saw.

P کلوبنده *kulūbanda*, A head servant.

A کلوة *kulwat*, (pl. کلی *kula'*) Reins, kidneys.

P کلوتك *kulotak* or *kalotak*, An implement of wood used by fullers and washers of linen.

P کلوته *kulota*, A kind of veil of net-work worn by the Persian ladies, through which may be seen the ornaments or gems of their head-dress without distinguishing the features. A sort of angular cap wadded with cotton worn by children.

P کلوج *kaluj*, Bread which has fallen from the wall of the oven into the ashes and become baked there. A hand or foot which has lost its fingers or toes by frost. *Kulūj*, A large round cake. Crumbs.

P کلوچ *kaloch*, Exchange, return, requital. Chewing any thing which makes a noise: scranching.

P کلوچيدن *kalochīdan*, To scranch, to bite or chew things which make a noise in masticating, such as biscuits and the like.

A کلوح *kulūh*, (v. n. of کلح) Putting on a sour, stern, grinning countenance. Drawing the lips so that the teeth appear.

P کلوخ *kalūkh*, An unburnt brick. *Kulūkh*, A clod of earth. Dried clay. Fragments of an old wall, brickbats. Dull, stupid, mean-spirited. کلوخ بر لب ماليدن *kulūkh bar lab mālīdan*, (زدن *zadan*, or نهادن *nihādan*) To conceal any thing.

P کلوخ امرود *kulūkh-amrūd*, A hard, insipid pear.

P کلوخ انداز *kulūkh-andāz*, Apertures in a fortified wall, through which they may throw down stones and combustibles. A grandchild. A sling. *Kulūkh-andāz*, (or کلوخ اندازان *kulūkh-andāzān*) A festival celebrated at the close of the month Shaabān.

P کلوخ کوب *kulūkh-kob*, A clod-crusher.

P کلور *kalūr*, Gleanings of corn.

P کلوز *kulūz*, (or کلوزه *kulūza*) A cotton-pod.

P کلوس *kulūs*, A horse white about the face, eyes, and muzzle.

A کلوف *kalūf*, Difficult, troublesome (affair).

P کلوك *kaloh*, A smooth-faced boy. A grain somewhat resembling a French-bean. *Kuloh*, Ill-bred, impudent, shameless.

A کلول *kulūl*, (v. n. of کلّ) Being dim (the sight); blunt (a sword). Stammering (the tongue). (pl. of کلّ *kall*) Heavy burdens.

A کلولة *kulūlat*, (v. n. of کلّ) Being dim (the sight); blunt (a sword). Stammering (the tongue).

A کلوم *kulūm*, (pl. of کلم *kalm*) Wounds.

P کلوند *kalwand*, A kind of cucumber. Figs, walnuts, or dates strung on a string. Name of a mountain.

P کلونده *kalwanda*, A cucumber. A small and slender cucumber. A large cucumber kept for seed. An unripe melon.

A کلويّ *kilwiy*, Relating to both.

P کله *kala*, The face or cheek; the risings about the mouth in laughing. The inside of the lips. A bow. A stitch in sewing; the act of stitching. The motion in venery. A trevet. An iron mace. A city in an island. کلهٔ سائلي *kalaᵢ sāᵢilī*, Misfortune, ill-luck. A name given to the infidels of Hindūstān. Crows gathered about a carcase. *Kila*, Stitching or quilting. Name of a city. *Kula*, Short, defective. A short man. *Kulah*, A cap, tiara, mitre, or fillet. A wriggling motion. کله انداختن *kulah andākhtan*, (or کله بر انداختن *kulah bar andākhtan*) To be in high spirits, to shout with joy on obtaining the object of one's wishes. زرّين کلهان *zarrīn-kulahān*, (Golden-caps) Certain officers about the king of Persia's household that wear golden tiaras.

P کلّه *kalla*, The head. The crown or hinder part of the head. Top, summit. Faithless, insincere, dishonest. Everywhere. *Killa*, The roof of a house, or any thing which answers the purpose of a roof. A screen. A curtain formed into a kind of dressing-room for the ladies. کلّهٔ خضرا *killaᵢ khazrā*, The sky. کلّهٔ دخاني *killaᵢ dukhānī*, The sky. A black cloud. A dark night. کلّهٔ نيلوفري *killaᵢ nīlūfarī*, The sky. *Kullah*, The hair of the head, a lock of hair tied in a knot. The heel, the protuberant joint-bone of the foot and leg. کله مشکين *kullahi mushkīn*, Curls, ringlets.

P کله پز *kalla-paz*, (or فروش *farosh*) One who dresses and sells the heads, feet, and tripe of cattle.

P کله پوش *kālla-posh*, A tiara, mitre, or cap, a square bonnet worn by young girls.

P کله خشك *kulla-khushk*, Mad, crazy; sad. An opium-eater. A hen's egg which has been placed with the head downwards and left to dry.

P کله دار *kalla-dār*, A conqueror. An absolute sovereign. Proud, haughty, arrogant. Stubborn.

P کله داري *kalla-dārī*, Sovereignty. Obstinacy.

P کلهري *kalahrī*, A squirrel.

P کلّه زده *killa-zada*, A throne with a canopy.

P کله زن *kalla-zan*, A boaster, swaggerer.

P کله زني *kalla-zanī*, Boasting, swaggering.

A کلهسة *kalhasat*, (v. n. of کلهس Q) Walking with the breast projecting, the head low, and the shoulders contracted. Fearing, dreading. Attending diligently to. Attacking manfully (the enemy).

A کله شجرا *kulah-shajarā*, Succession and property of a saint, fakīr, &c.

P کلهګوشه *kulah-gosha*, The corner of a cap. کله ګوشه بر آسمان *kulah-gosha bar āsman*, High rank, exaltation, dignity. کله ګوشهٔ ملك *kulah-goshaᵢ mulk*, A king's son, prince.

A کلّهم *kulluhum*, All of them, the whole.

P کله مشکين *kullah-mushkīn*, A lock, a ringlet.

A کلی *kaly*, (v. n. of کلي) Striking the reins or kidneys. *Kila'*, (v. n. of کلی) Being hurt in the kidneys. *Kula'*, (pl. of کلية *kulyat*) Reins, kidneys. Sides of a river. Lower parts of clouds. حمراء الکلی *hamrāᵤu'l kula'*, Lean, emaciated (sheep). لقيته بشحم کلاه *lakītuhu bi shahmi kulahu*, I met him in his early youth and lively spirits.

P کلي *kalī*, An eruption on the head which children are subject to. *Kulī*, A tambourine. A large cake. A small kind of fish which stimulates to venery. Any thing which eats or corrodes (as rust, the moth, leprosy, or gangrene). Rustic, rural. One village. A country life.

A کلّيّ *kulliy*, Universal, total, all, every.

P کليا *kilyā*, A plant used by soap-boilers, pot-ash. (in zand and Pāzand) A sheep.

A کليات *kulyāt*, (pl. of کلية) Reins, kidneys.

A کلّيّات *kulliyāt*, (pl. of کلّيّة *kulliyat*) All, every one, every thing, the whole work of an author: as, کلّيّات نظامی *kulliyāt nazāmī*, Nazāmī's works.

P کلياس *kilyās*, The door or entrance to a house. A privy on the roof of a house.

P کلياني *kilyānī*, Gum-ammoniac, galbanum, assafœtida.

P كلياوه *kalyāwa*, Deaf.

A كليب *kalīb*, A pack of dogs.

A كلئة *kaliʼat*, Land fruitful in herbage.

A كلية *kulyat*, (pl. كليات *kulyāt*, *kulayāt*, and كلي *kulaʼ*) A kidney. A piece of leather of a kidney-form sewed about the handle of any thing in order to strengthen it. The curved part of a bow between the handle and the extremes, about three spans from the middle. Feathers of a bird next those called اباهر *abāhir*. The lower part of a cloud.

A كلّيّة *kulliyat*, (fem. of كلّيّ *kulliy*) All. Universality, the total, whole. بالكلّية *biʼl kulliya*, Universally, totally, in toto, on the whole.

A كليت *kalīt*, (or كلّيت *killīt*) An oblong stone with which they block up the hole of the hyena.

A كليتان *kulyatāni*, (dual) The reins or kidneys. The two sides of a spear-head.

P كليج *kalīj*, Vain, proud. Dirt, filth. *Kilej*, A horse whose hind-legs are crooked. *Kulīj*, Bread which, having fallen from the side of the oven (the ovens in Asia are often mere holes in the ground), has been baked in the ashes. A large cake.

A كليجن *kulījan*, Galangale.

P كليچ *kalīch*, Pus. Dirt, filth.

P كليچه *kalīcha*, A wooden bolt or key. *Kulīcha*, The disk or body of the sun or moon. A small buttered loaf. A splendid garment closely sewed. Stitched, quilted. كليچۀسيم *kulīchaʼisīm*, Full moon.

P كليد *kilīd*, A key. A ploughshare. كليد ايمان *kilīdi īmān*, (or كليد بهشت *kilīdi bihisht*) A testimony, attestation, confession of faith. كليد گنج حكيم *kilīdi ganji hakīm*, The sentence بسم الله الرحمن الرحيم *biʼsmiʼ llāhiʼr rahmāniʼr rahīmi*, In the name of the most merciful God.

P كليدان *kalīdān*, A lock, stocks, or any thing similar by which a number of people are confined by the feet. *Kilīdān*, A lock, bolt, bar.

P كليدانه *kilīdāna*, A lock, bolt, bar.

P كليز *kalīz*, A bee.

P كليزدان *kalīzdān*, A bee-hive.

P كليزه *kalīza*, A cup for water, a ewer.

P كليسا *kalīsā*, (or كليسه *kilesa*) A church, synagogue. ارباب كليسا *arbābi kalīsā*, Christians, the patrons of churches, churchmen.

P كليك *kalīk*, An owl. Seed of roses. *Kalīk* or *kilīk*, Squint-eyed. The little finger.

P كليكان *kalīkān*, Name of a very stinking plant. *Kilīkān*, Dragon-wort.

P كليكي *kalīkī*, Squint-eyed. Strabism.

A كليل *kalīl*, Dim-sighted. Stammering. Blunt (sword); dim (eye); stammering (tongue). كليل الظفر *kalīluʼz zufr*, Short-nailed: despicable, abject.

P كليله و دمنه *kalīla u dimna*, Name of two jackals (who make a conspicuous figure in a book called انوار سهيلي *anwāri suhaylī*, همايون نامه *humāyūn-nāma*, or Pilpay's fables).

A كليم *kalīm*, Wounded. One who speaks to another, a familiar. كليم الله *kalīmuʼllāh*, One who speaks to God, *i.e.* Moses.

P كليم دست *kalīm-dast*, Dexterous, successful (as though having the hand of Moses).

P كليواج *kalewāj*, (or كليواژ *kalewāj*) A kite.

P كليون *kulyūn*, A kind of cloth of seven colours.

P كم *kam*, Few, little. Deficient, defective, mutilated, wanting, diminished, scarce, less. Worse. Poor, wretched. Base. Abandonment. Deficiency, destitution. Excellent, precious, glorious, honoured. The waist, side. كم زار خوردن *kam zār khwurdan*, To eat little. كم زار خورش شدن *kam zār khwurish shudan*, To be diminished or scarce of provisions. كم شدن *kam shudan*, (بودن *būdan*, or آمدن *āmadan*) To fail, become deficient, be lessened. كم عدد *kam-ʻadad*, Deficient in number, small in quantity. كم عقل *kam-ʻakl*, Distressed in mind. Stupid, ignorant. كم كاشتي *kam-kāshti*, Shameful. Disgrace. كم كردن *kam kardan*, To diminish. To withhold, defraud. كم گوشت *kam-gosht*, Lean. كم گرفتن *kam giriftan*, To abandon, give up, consider as lost. كم و كاست *kam u kāst*, Loss, deficiency; defect and diminution. كم ياب *kam-yāb*, Rare, scarce. *Kum*, A thorn which bears the gum tragacanth. Name of a city in Irāk.

A كم *kam*, How much? How many? How long? Many, much. A multitude, a quantity. كم كرّة *kam karra*, How often? كم من آية *kam min āyat*, How many a sign? كم من القرون *kam miniʼl kurūn*, How many ages?

A كمّ *kamm*, (v. n. of كمّ) Covering, concealing. Stopping up, corking. Muzzling. Producing date-pods (a palm-tree). Covering a young transplanted palm-tree in order to protect it. Assembling together (men). A quantity. كمّ متّصل *kammi muttasil*, A continued quantity. كمّ منفصل *kammi munfasil*, A separate quantity. *Kimm*, (pl. اكمّة *akimmat* and اكمام *akmām*) A rose-bud; the follicle or outward leaf of an unblown palm or other flower. An envelope or cover. *Kumm*, (pl. اكمام *akmām* and كممة *kimamat*) A sleeve.

A كمء *kamʼ*, (pl. اكمؤ *akmuʼ* and كمأة *kamʼat*) A mushroom. A substance resembling manna.

A كمأ *kamaʼ*, (v. n. of كمئ) Being worn in the feet (a man) although shod. Being cracked and chapt (the feet). Being ignorant of. Being a fool.

P كما *kamā*, A sleeve. Old cloth sewed together, whereon they lay bread to be baked in the oven. *Kamā*, *kimā*, or *kumā*, The envelope of nutmegs, mace. *Kumā*, A certain stinking plant.

A كما *kamā*, (comp. of ك *ka* and ما *mā*) Like, as. Because, on account of. كما ذكر *kamā zukira*, As it is asserted, as above related. كما في الاوّل *kamā fiʼl awwal*, (or كما اوّل *kamā awwal*) As before, as in the beginning. كما قال تعالى *kamā kāla taʻālaʼ*, As God spake. كما قيل *kamā kīla*, As it is said, as hath been said. كما كان *kamā kāna*, As it was, in the same manner and situation, equally, alike. كما مرّ تفصيله *kamā marra tafsīluhu*, As before fully enlarged upon. كما ورد في الحديث *kamā warada fiʼl hadīs*, As it is related in the sayings (of Muhammad). كما هو حقّه *kamā huwa hakkuhu*, As it ought; agreeable to justice. كما هو الواجب *kamā huwaʼl wājib*, As it may suit or be agreeable. كما هي *kamā hiya*, As things are, as the affair stands. كما ينبغي *kamā yambaghī*, As it is proper, perfectly. كما تدين تدان *kamā tadīn tudān*, As you judge, you will be judged.

A كمّاء *kammāʼ*, A seller or gatherer of mushrooms.

P كمابيش *kam-ā-besh*, Less or more.

A كمأة *kamʼat*, (pl. of كمء *kamʼ*) Mushrooms. A single mushroom.

A كماة *kumāt*, (pl. of كميّ *kamīy*) Heroes, champions, warriors, armed men. فوارس كماة *fawārisu kumāt*, Cavaliers armed at all points, from top to toe.

A كماتة *kumātat*, (v. n. of كمت) Being bay-coloured (a horse).

A كماتر *kumātir*, Short and thick-bodied.

A كماتل *kumātil*, Strong, hard, firm.

A كماتيّ *kamātīy*, Bay horses.

A كماثر *kumāsir*, Short-bodied.

P كماج *kumāj*, (or كماچ *kumāch*) Unleavened bread; bread baked in the ashes. A round bit of wood, perforated in the middle for receiving the top of a tent-pole.

A كماد *kimād*, A beating of cloths. *Kimād*, (or كمادة *kimādat*) Hot cloth, or any fomentation applied to an afflicted part. The gripes. الكماد احبّ اليّ من الكيّ *al kimād ahabb ilayyaʼ miniʼl kayy*, Fomentation is more agreeable to me than cautery.

G كمادريوس *kamādaryūs*, The herb germander.

P كمار *kamār*, Land cultivated by contract.

P كماره *kamāra*, A mortar or howitzer.

P كماريدن *kamārīdan*, To smile.

P كم آزار *kam-āzār*, Uninjurious, not cruel.

P كم آزاري *kam-āzārī*, Mildness, humanity.

P كماس *kamās*, Little, few. *Kamās*, (كمّاس *kummās*, or كماش *kamāsh*) A kind of short-necked earthen or wooden vessel, flat on one side (carried under the arm, in which they smuggle home wine). A beggar's wooden dish.

P كماسه *kamāsa*, A wooden bowl. A short, narrow-necked vessel. *Kumāsa*, A well-digger, canal-cutter. A mistress, courtezan. A hermaphrodite. Name of a mountain in Khurāsān.

P كماسي *kamāsī*, Littleness, deficiency.

A كماشة *kamāshat*, (v. n. of كمش) Being quick, brisk, active. Being consumed (provisions). Being sufficient, sufficiency.

P كماشير *kamāshīr*, A gum like opoponax.

P كم اصل *kam-asl*, Of mean origin.

A كماع *kimāʻ*, (v. n. 3 of كمع) Lying within one garment with another. Drawing to one's self.

G كمافيطس *kamāfītus*, The herb ground-pine,

a strong diuretic, which opens obstructions, and powerfully promotes the menstrual discharge.

A كمال *kamāl*, (v. n. of كمل) Being complete, entire, perfect. Perfection, excellence, integrity. Completion, conclusion. Punctuality. كمال مرتبه *kamāl martaba*, Perfectly, entirely, punctually, exactly. علي وجه الكمال *ʿala' wajhi'l kamāl*, In a perfect way, in perfection.

A كمّال *kummāl*, (pl. of كامل *kāmil*) Perfect.

A كمالات *kamālāt*, (pl. of كمال) Perfections. ذات جامع الكمالات *zāti jāmiʿi'l kamālāt*, Endued with every perfection.

P كمالكي *kamāl-kamī*, A gift from the tenants to their landlord.

P كماله *kumāla*, Coarse, low-priced silk.

A كمالية *kamāliyat*, Perfection.

P كماليون *kamāliyūn*, A kind of mezereon.

P كمام *kimām*, Frankincense.

A كمام *kimām*, A halter or muzzle (for a biting camel). (pl. of كمامة *kimāmat*) Rose-buds, follicles, outward leaves.

A كمامة *kimāmat*, (pl. كمام *kimām*) The follicle or outward leaf of an unblown flower. A muzzle for a camel. The nose-bag for a horse.

P كمان *kamān*, A bow. The sign Sagittarius. (pl. of كم *kam*) Few, small. Deficient. كمان آسمان *kamāni āsmān*, (كمان بهمن *kamāni bahman*, كمان رستم *kamāni rustam*, كمان سام *kamāni sām*, or كمان شيطان *kamāni shaytān*) The rainbow. كمان حكمت *kamāni hikmat*, A species of balista for throwing arrows. كمان زنبوري *kamāni zambūrī*, A musket, firelock. كمان ساده *kamāni sāda*, The sun. Moonlight. Sunshine. كمان فلك *kamāni falak*, The sign Sagittarius. كمان گردون *kamāni gardūn*, The rainbow. The sign Sagittarius. كمان قروهه *kamāni kuroha*, (كمان گروهه *kamāni guroha*, or كمان مهرة *kamāni muhra*) A cross-bow.

P كمان ابرو *kamān-abrū*, One who has arched eyebrows. A mistress.

P كمان جوله *kamān-jola*, A bow and arrow-case.

P كمانچه *kamāncha*, A little bow. A bow with which women strike cotton. The bow of a violin. A lute, harp, species of violin. A figure in the shape of a bow at the head of a royal patent instead of the طغرا *tughrā*. A cup.

P كماندار *kamān-dār*, An archer, a bowman.

P كمانداري *kamān-dārī*, Bow-holding, archery.

P كماندان *kamāndān*, A bow-case.

P كمانساز *kamān-sāz*, A bow-maker. An archer.

P كمانكش *kamān-kash*, An archer. ابروي كمانكش *abrūyi kamān-kash*, Eyebrows like bows (letting fly the arrows of love).

P كمانگر *kamāngar*, One who makes bows.

P كمان گردن *kamān-gardan*, (Bow-necked) A large, strong, hairy camel with two bunches. Any thing thin, lean, and weak.

P كمان گير *kamān-gīr*, An expert bowman. Name of the archer آرش *ārash*, who shot an arrow from آمل *āmul* to مرو *marw*, a journey of forty-days.

P كمانه *kamāna*, A plectrum or bow of an instrument. A bow. The bow for a drill. A cup. A harp. A digger of graves, wells, or ditches; a miner. A hole dug in the ground in order to try the quality of the water.

P كماني *kamānī*, Bowed, bent.

P كمأة *kamʾah*, A white mushroom like an egg; a toadstool, puff, devil's snuff-box. A truffle.

P كماهه *kumāha*, An amulet, any thing worn on the arm as a preservative from fascination.

P كما هي *kamā hiya*, As it is; true state.

P كماي *kumāy*, Name of a very stinking herb. Name of a champion of Irān.

P كمايش *kamāyish*, Affairs, business. The management of affairs.

P كمايوك *kumāyūk*, Old clothes sewed together, on which they lay bread to be baked in the oven.

P كمبار *kambār*, A rope made of the fibres of the palm or cocoa-nut tree.

P كم بخت *kam-bakht*, An unlucky wight.

P كم بختي *kam-bakhtī*, Adversity, misfortune.

P كم بر *kam-bar*, A division of the suit at cards.

P كم بضاعت *kam-bazāʿat* or *bizāʿat*, Poor, possessed of little capital.

P كمبها *kam-bahā*, Low-priced, worthless.

P كم بيش *kam besh*, Less or more.

P كمپاي *kam-pāy*, Remissness, backwardness.

P كمپايه *kam-pāya*, Mean, of low degree.

P كمپير *kam-pīr*, A feeble old man, a dotard.

A كمّة *kummat*, A round cap.

A كمت *kamt*, (v. n. of كمت) Restraining anger. Being bay-coloured. *Kumt*, (pl. of كميت *kumayt*) Bay-coloured (horses).

A كمتة *kamtat*, (v. n. of كمت) Being bay-coloured. *Kumtat*, A dark red or bay colour.

P كمتر *kamtar*, Less, least. Smaller. Meaner, baser, viler, more contemptible. Lower, inferior. كمتر يافتن *kamtar yāftan*, Not to find. من فقير كمتر *man fakīri kamtar*, I, a poor, low man.

A كمتر *kumtur*, Short, thick, and strong-bodied.

P كمترآشنا *kamtar-āshnā*, Little versed, unskilled.

A كمترة *kamtarat*, (v. n. of كمتر Q) Fastening the mouth of, or tying tight (a bottle). Filling. Taking short steps. *Kimtirat*, The walk of a broad, thick-set man.

P كمترغبار *kamtar-ghubār*, The least dust.

P كمترين *kamtarīn*, (or كمترينه *kamtarīna*) Least, most vile, despicable, infamous, defective, or insignificant. The rabble.

A كمتل *kamtal*, Strong, hard, firm.

A كمّثراة *kummasrāt*, One pear.

A كمثرة *kamsarat*, Compression, compactness.

A كمّثري *kummasra'*, A pear; pears.

A كمثل *ka misli*, Like, as, according to.

A كمج *kamaj*, The hip-joint, the point of the huckle-bone. The groin.

P كم جرأت *kam-jurʾat*, Cowardly.

P كمچه *kamcha*, (in zand and Pāz.) A locust.

A كمح *kamh*, (v. n. of كمح) Checking (a horse).

P كم حركت *kam-harakat*, Indolent, lazy.

P كم حرمتي نمودن *kam-hurmatī namūdan*, To disparage, to shew little respect or reverence.

P كم حوصله *kam-hawsala*, Unaspiring, unambitious. Poor-spirited, not high-stomached.

A كمخ *kamkh*, (v. n. of كمخ) Pulling the bridle and checking (a horse). Drawing up the nose, *i.e.* being proud, behaving contemptuously. Going to the necessary, voiding excrement.

P كمخا *kamkhā*, Damask silk of one colour. *Kimkhā*, Damask silk of different colours.

P كمخاب *kamkhāb*, An embroidered garment of one colour. *Kimkhāb*, An embroidered cloth of divers colours.

P كمخاباف *kimkhā-bāf*, A satin-weaver.

P كمخابافي *kimkhā-bāfī*, Satin-weaving.

P كمخت *kumakht*, (in zand and Pāz.) Mixed.

P كم خرچ *kam-kharch*, Parsimonious. كم خرچ بالا نشين *kam-kharch bālā-nishīn*, Applied to any thing of good quality purchased cheaply.

P كم خرچي *kam-kharchī*, Parsimony.

P كم خرد *kam-khirad*, Unwise, ignorant.

P كم خواب *kam-khwāb*, One who sleeps little.

P كم خوار *kam-khwār*, A little eater.

P كم خوارگي *kam-khwāragī*, Abstemiousness.

P كم خور *kam-khwur*, Abstemious, eating little.

P كم خوراك *kam-khwurāk*, A little eater.

P كمخوري *kam-khwurī*, Abstemiousness.

P كم خير *kam-khayr*, Good for little or nothing.

A كمد *kamd*, (v. n. of كمد) Beating (a garment). *Kamd* or *kamad*, Change of colour. Excessive grief, inward pain. *Kamad*, (v. n. of كمد) Being afflicted, vexed, anxious. *Kamid*, Sad, sorrowful. Concealing one's grief.

A كمدة *kumdat*, Change of colour. Inward pain.

A كمدّة *kumuddat*, Penis, veretrum.

P كم ذات *kam-zāt*, Low-bred, of low caste.

P كم ذهن *kam-zihn*, Forgetful. Without abilities.

A كمر *kamr*, (v. n. of كمر) Excelling any one in the size of the glans penis. *Kimr*, A date which has fallen to the ground and is very soft. *Kamar*, (pl. of كمرة *kamarat*) Glandes penum. الكمر اشباه الكمر *al kamaru ashābu'l kamar*, Glands are like glands (said of things which resemble; as like as two peas).

P كمر *kamar*, The waist, loins. A girdle, zone, belt. The middle of a mountain. The flank of an army. An arch, cupola, dome, arched bridge. Rocks tumbled from a mountain, especially when presenting an arched appearance. Height. An apartment open in front. A fold: enclosure for cattle. كمر آفتاب *kamari āftāb*, A line passing the sun's centre. A mountain; also the hollows or caverns in it. كمر بر كمر *kamar bar kamar*, Height above height.

کمر بستن *kamar bastan*, To prepare for action, to engage heart and soul in business. To choose. To be opposite, over against (an enemy). کمر بستن آب *kamar bastani āb*, The freezing of water. کمر رستم *kamari rustam*, The rainbow. کمر کوه *kamari koh*, The middle of a mountain. The world-illuminating sun. The fourth heaven. Jesus Christ. The heavenly temple, *i.e.* Mecca, being built in imitation of the vault of heaven. کمر کشادن *kamar kushādan*, (or گشودن *gushūdan*) To abandon, resign, give up, desist. To wait. To turn away the eyes. کمر هلال پیکر *kamari hilāl-paykar*, A waist like the face of the new moon, *i.e.* extremely slender.

A کمرّ *kumurr*, Penis. Magnum habens penem.

P کمرا *kamrā*, A sheepfold. A tower or lofty archway. A high wall. The string worn by the followers of Zoroaster.

P کمراه *kam-rāh*, (A horse) slow, without bottom.

P کمر بسته *kamar-basta*, Ready, prepared. A servant. کمر بستهٔ عبودیت *kamar-bastaʼi ʻubūdiyat*, Attentive in serving.

P کمربند *kamar-band*, A waistband, sash, belt, girdle, zone. Alert, ready for battle, prepared, armed. A servant.

P کمربندگي *kamar-bandagī*, A girding of the waist, a readiness for service.

P کمربندي *kamar-bandī*, Armament, preparation for battle. Readiness for service.

A کمرة *kamarat*, (pl. کمر *kamar*) Glans penis.

A کمرّة *kumurrat*, Penis.

P کمردار *kamar-dār*, A servant, serving-man.

P کمردوال *kamar-duwāl*, A leathern belt.

P کمردون *kamardūn*, The rainbow.

P کمررخت *kamar-rakht*, An ornamented bridle.

P کمرساز *kamar-sāz*, A horse-belt or girth. A maker of girdles. A clasp, buckle.

P کمرکش *kamar-kash*, A hero, a brave man.

P کمرکشائي *kamar-kushāʼī*, Ungirding the loins. An exaction made by peons placed in restraint over any one for permission to pull off his clothes and perform the ordinary functions of life.

P کم رنگ *kam-rang*, Pale, faint-coloured.

P کم رو *kam-rav*, Slow-paced (horse).

P کمري *kamrī*, (A horse) weak in the loins.

A کمرّيٌ *kimirra'*, Short-bodied. Qui grandi est penis glande.

P کمريا *kamriyā*, (in zand) Moonlight.

A کمز *kamz*, (v. n. of کمز) Rolling any thing into a globular form. *Kumaz*, (pl. of کمزة *kumzat*) Lumps of dates. Heaps of earth or sand.

A کمزة *kumzat*, (pl. کمز *kumaz*) A heap of earth or sand. A mass of dates.

P کمزدن *kam zadan*, To diminish.

P کمزده *kam-zada*, One who always throws low at dice. A hypocrite. An infidel. Perverse, untoward, miserable. کم زدهٔ چند *kam-zadaʼi chand*, Unbelievers, hypocrites.

P کم زن *kam-zan*, A low thrower at dice. Unfortunate. One who does not entertain too high notions of his own excellence. A prudent manager.

P کم زور *kam-zor*, Weak, powerless, feeble.

P کم زوري *kam-zorī*, Weakness, feebleness.

P کم سال *kam-sāl*, Young, juvenile.

P کمست *kamast*, It is little. A kind of stone of little value. A low, ignorant fellow. A kind of cup.

P کم سخن *kam-sukhan*, Taciturn, of few words.

P کم سفره *kam-sufra*, One who keeps a poor table.

P کمسك *kamask*, Milk and butter-milk mixed together, called by the Arabs شيراز *shīrāz*.

A کمش *kamsh*, (v. n. of کمش) Lopping (the extremities). Being spent (provisions). Swift, quick, penetrating (man). Small-pizzled (horse). (A mare) with small dugs. A string with which they tie the dugs of camels to prevent the young from sucking.

P کم شان *kam-shān*, Humble, unassuming.

A کمشة *kamishat*, (A camel) having short teats or a small udder.

P کم شده *kam-shuda*, Lost.

P کم شر *kam-shar*, Well-disposed, good-natured.

P کم شرح *kam-sharh*, Low wages.

P کم شرم *kam-sharm*, Shameless, immodest.

P کم شوق *kam-shawk*, Indifferent.

P کم شير *kam-shīr*, Giving little milk.

A P کم صلا *kam-salā*, A method of transmuting words, so as to form, in writing, a cypher, and in speech, a gibberish or cant language, unintelligible to all who do not possess the key. The rule is contained in the following couplet:

کم صلا او حطله درسع
ham salā aw hatun lahu dar saʻ;
حرف منقوطش را بجايش دع
harfi mankūtishrā bajāyish daʻ.

That is, the letters composing the following pairs are mutually interchanged for one another, and all those which have diacritical points remain unaltered: عس, رد, ه‌ل, طح, وا, لاص, مك. The word سلامت, written according to this rule, becomes عصكت.

P کم طاعت *kam-tāʻat*, Disobedient.

P کم ظرف *kam-zarf*, Shallow. Stupid, silly, witless. Ignoble, vile.

A کمع *kamʻ*, (v. n. of کمع) Cutting off (the feet). Going into (water). Plunging the head (into a vessel). Going slowly (a horse). *Kimʻ*, A tunic, garment. A tract of low ground rising at the extremities. The brink (of a river). A bed-fellow. A house, mansion, home. *Kamaʻ*, The joint of the thigh. *Kamiʻ*, Weak, at everybody's beck and call.

A کمعرة *kamʻarat*, (v. n. of کمعر Q) Being fat (a camel's bunch).

P کم عرض *kam-ʻarz*, Narrow.

P کم عيار *kam-ʻiyār*, Below standard, alloyed.

P کم فروش *kam-furosh*, A seller of short weight.

P کم فهم *kam-fahm*, Stupid.

P کم قدر *kam-kadar*, Worthless.

P کم قدم *kam-kadam*, Slow-paced.

P کم قوت *kam-kūwat*, Feeble, powerless.

P کم قيمت *kam-kīmat*, Low-priced.

P کمك *kumak*, A corps of auxiliaries.

P کم کار *kam-kār*, Inexperienced in business.

P کم کاسه *kam-kāsa*, (pl. کم کاسگان *kam-kāsagān*) Niggardly, sordid. Mean-spirited.

A کمکام *kamkām*, Compressed, squat. Tears or gum of a tree found in the hilly parts of Yaman.

P کمکم *kumkum*, A tankard. A quicksand. Saffron. *Kumkum*, (or کم کم آفتاب *kumkumi āftāb*) The noise made in counting out gold. *Kumkum*, (or کم کم نقاب *kumkumi nikāb*) The noise made in digging a well or mine.

P کمکي *kumakī*, Auxiliary.

P کم گفتار *kam-guftār*, Of few words, taciturn.

P کم گو *kam-go* or *gū*, Taciturn, speaking little.

A کمل *kamal*, The whole.

A کملاً *kamalan*, Altogether, wholly, entirely.

A کمّل *kummal*, (pl. of کامل) Perfect. Learned.

A کملة *kamalat*, (pl. of کامل *kāmil*) Perfect.

P کملکان *kamalkān*, A streamlet.

A کملول *kumlūl*, A kind of wild pot-herb. A desert.

P کمله *kamla*, A kind of blanketing. *Kumla*, Foolish, ignorant, stupid.

P کملي *kamlī*, A very coarse woollen dress worn by the poor.

P کم مايگي *kam-māyagī*, Smallness of capital.

P کم مايه *kam-māya*, Ill-provided or stocked.

A کممة *kimamat*, (pl. کمّ *kumm*) Sleeves.

P کمنام *kam-nām*, Unknown. Anonymous. Of little repute.

P کم نامي *kam-nāmī*, Obscure reputation.

A کمنة *kamnat*, Men lying in ambush. *Kumnat*, A dulness in the eyesight; also an itching or a gummy redness round the eyes.

A کمنجه *kamanja*, A sort of violin.

P کمند *kamand*, A halter, noose, snare, lasso. A scaling-ladder. A lock of hair. کمند انداختن *kamand andākhtan*, To throw a noose, to catch any fugitive man or animal. کمند کردن *kamand kardan*, To scale a wall. درکمند کردن *dar kamand kardan*, To catch in a noose or toil.

P کم نظر *kam-nazar*, Dim or weak-sighted.

A کمنون *kimnūn*, (for کمّون *kammūn*) Cumine.

P کم نيت *kamnayt*, An archer.

P کم نيتي *kamnaytī*, Archery.

A کمودة *kumūdat*, Change of colour, lividness.

A کموس *kumūs*, Moroseness, austerity, sternness.

A کموش *kamūsh*, (A sheep) having short dugs or a small udder.

A کمول *kumūl*, (v. n. of کمل) Being perfect, entire, complete.

A کمون *kamūn*, A camel which does not whisk her tail when covered or in foal. *Kumūn*, (v. n.

of (كمن) Lurking, lying hid, lying in ambush. Being dim-sighted, and having a gummy redness about the eyes. An ambuscade.

A كمّون *kammūn*, Cummin-seed. الكمّون الارمنيّ *al kammūnu'l armaniy*, Caraways. الكمّون الحبشيّ *al kammūnu'l habashiy*, A sort of coriander. الكمّون الحلو *al kammūnu'l hulw*, Aniseed.

A كموني *kamūnī*, A medicine in which cummin-seed is mixed.

A كمّونيّ *kammūniy*, Dressed with cumine.

A كمويّ *kamwa'*, A moonlight night.

A كمه *kumh*, Name of a fish. *Kamah*, (v. n. of كمه) Being blind from one's birth; having a dimness of sight. Being dark (day). Changing colour. Being ignorant of. Losing one's reason.

A كمهد *kumhud*, Having a large glans penis. A large glans penis.

A كمهدة *kumhudat*, (or كمهدر) Glans penis.

A كمهلة *kamhalat*, (v. n. of كمهل Q) Tucking up the garments, girding up the loins, preparing to set out on a journey. Gathering together (cattle). Concealing, mystifying (any thing). Denying a debt, or defrauding any one of his due.

P كم همّت *kam-himmat*, Unambitious. Mean-spirited.

A كمي *kamy*, (v. n. of كمي) Concealing, suppressing (evidence). Covering one's self with a coat of mail or a helmet.

P كمي *kamī*, Smallness, deficiency, paucity, loss; abatement. Lurking-place, ambush. A horoscope. كمي كردن *kamī kardan*, To be scanty or deficient.

A كميّ *kamiy*, (pl. كماة *kumāt* and اكماء *akmā'*) Armed. Bold, brave.

A كمّيّ *kammiy*, How much?

P كمياب *kam-yāb*, Rare, difficult to be found.

P كميابي *kam-yābī*, Rarity.

P كمي بيشي *kamī-beshī*, An abstract account of the increase and decrease of the rental of each individual in a village (a revenue-term in India).

A كمّيّة *kammiyat*, Quantity: form: number: value.

A كميت *kumayt*, (pl. كمت *kumt*) A bay horse with a black tail and mane. Wine of a deep red colour. كميت احمّ *kumayt ahamm*, Dark chesnut or bay. كميت مدمّى *kumayt mudamma'*, Bright chesnut. Name of a poet. كميت نشاط *kumayti nishāt*, Red wine.

A كميتة *kamītat*, (or بكميتتة) Wholly, altogether.

A كميثرة *kumaysirat*, A small pear.

A كميثل *kamaysal*, Short, dwarfish.

P كميچه *kamecha*, A small bow. A harp, lute. A fire-fly.

P كميخت *kumīkht*, (in zand) Mixed together.

A كميد *kamīd*, Sad, sorrowful, one who smothers his grief.

P كميدن *kamīdan*, To grow less, be diminished. To rise in the scale. To suck.

P كميز *kimīz* or *kumīz*, Urine. Dung, ordure. كميز بشتاب *kumīz ba shitāb*, Diabetes. كميز كردن *kumīz kardan*, (or انداختن *andākhtan*) To urine, stale. كميز منجمد *kumīzi munjamid*, Gravel or stone in the bladder.

P كميزدان *kumīzdān*, The bladder. A chamber-pot.

P كميز گرفتگي *kumīz-giriftagī*, Strangury.

P كميز گرفته *kumīz-girifta*, Strangurious.

P كميزيدن *kumīzīdan*, To make water, urine, stale.

A كميش *kamīsh*, Swift, quick, penetrating (man). (A mare) having small dugs. كميش الازار *kamīshu'l azār*, One whose breeches or apron are tucked up.

A كميع *kamīg*, A bed-fellow.

A كميل *kamīl*, Entire, perfect.

A كميم *kamīm*, Wrapped in, folded in.

A كميثرة *kumaymisrat*, (كميثريّة *kumaymisriyat*, or كميثراة *kumaymisrāt*) A small pear.

P كمين *kamīn*, Deficient, defective. Meaner, baser. The little finger. An ambush.

A كمين *kamīn*, An ambush, lurking-place where any one can make observation without being seen. Liers in wait. An entering into an affair which one does not understand. P كمين ساختن *kamīn sākhtan*, To lie in wait, to form an ambuscade.

P كمينساز *kamīn-sāz*, (or دار *dār*) A lier in wait.

P كمين سازي *kamīn-sāzī*, A laying of snares.

P كمينگاه *kamīn-gāh*, An ambush.

P كمينه *kamīna*, Defective. Base, abject, in a mean condition. Humble, servile.

A كمّيهى *kummayha'*, Going none knows where.

P كن *kan*, A tree. A place full of trees. A fish-spear, trident. (from كندن *kandan* in comp.) Dig, tear out, eradicate; and in composition a digger: as, خاراكن *khārā-kan*, Breaking stones. قلعه كن *kalʿa-kan*, Demolisher of castles. كوه كن *koh-kan*, An underminer of mountains. فرهاد كوه كن و سنگ افكن *farhādi koh-kan u sang-afkan*, Farhād, the underminer of mountains, and the piercer of stones. (This is a celebrated Persian lover, who is said to have dug quite through a large mountain on account of his mistress Shīrīn). عدوي بيخ كن *ʿadūyi bekh-kan*, An enemy who extirpates by the roots, and gives a total overthrow. *Kin*, Close stitching. *Kun*, The podex. (imperative of كردن *kardan*). It is used in a compound form from كننده *kunanda*, A maker or doer, who makes or does: as, درميان كن *dar miyān kun*, Producing in the middle.

A كن *kun*, (imp. of كان *kāna*) Be, let it be: as, كن فيكون *kun fa yakūn*, (God says) Be, and it is. مالك كن فكان *māliku kun fa kāna*, An epithet of Omnipotence.

A كنّ *kann*, (v. n. of كنّ) Covering, preserving, protecting. Shading from the sun. Concealing, keeping secret. Laying up in the mind (knowledge). *Kinn*, (pl. اكنان *aknān*) A veil, or any covering by which, or under which, persons or things are protected. A cocoon. A shade, umbrella. An asylum, refuge. The court or middle of a house.

P كنا *kanā* or *kunā*, Ground. A field prepared with a raised border for sowing. *Kinā*, (in zand and Pāzand) A fish. *Kunā*, Doing, making.

A كناب *kināb*, A branch or cluster of dates.

A كنابث *kunābis*, Hard, contracted. A miser.

P كنابد *kanābad*, Name of the place where the twelve champions of Irān and Tūrān fought.

A كنابد *kunābid*, Deformed, hideous, ugly (face).

A كنابذ *kunābiz*, One who has a large, crabbed, and hideous face.

A كنابل *kunābil*, Hard and robust.

A كناة *kunāt*, (pl. of كاني *kānī*) Those who employ figurative or metonymical names, called كناية *kināya*.

A كنّات *kunnāt*, (pl. كنّة *kunnat*) Shades or pents, eaves or cornices over doorways.

A كناتب *kunātib*, A dwarf.

A كناثب *kunāsib*, Strong, hard, robust.

A كناثر *kunāsir*, Compressed, contracted. Glans.

P كناد *kanād*, A turtle-dove. *Kunād*, (God) grant!

A كنّاد *kannād*, An ungrateful man.

P كنّادار *kannādār*, A kind of shoe or slipper.

A كنادر *kunādir*, A short, thick man. A dwarf. A short, thick ass.

P كنار *kanār*, A side, brink, coast, shore, extremity, limit, boundary, edge; hem (of a garment); margin (of a book). The stalk whence bunches of grapes or dates hang. Banana or plantain-fruit. كنار بحر *kanāri bahr*, The sea-shore. كنار گرفتن *kanār giriftan*, To fly, retire. *Kinār*, The lap. The bosom. An embrace. Dalliance. Separation, disunion. كنار كردن *kinār kardan*, To embrace. To approximate, draw to one. *Kunār*, (or كنّار *kunnār*) The lote-fruit.

A كنار *kunār*, The lote-fruit.

A كنّارة *kannārat* or *kinnārat*, (pl. كنّارات *kannārāt*, *kinnārāt*, and كنانير *kanānīr*) A harp, lute. A drum, tabor.

P كنارگير *kanār-gīr*, A circle, hoop, ring.

P كنارنگ *kanā* or *kunā-rang*, Governor of a province; a grandee. A lord-marcher, margrave, landgrave. A petty dynasty. Weeping in secret. Whispering, speaking privately. A tax-gatherer, revenue-collector. A night-watch.

P كناره *kanāra*, A side, shore, coast, verge. A hem, border. A hook, especially that whereon a butcher hangs his meat, shambles. كناره گرفتن *kanāra giriftan*, To retire, withdraw.

P كناره گيران *kanāra-girān*, Coasters. Withdrawers from a crowd, from business, from the world.

H كناري *kinārī*, (Gold or silver) lace.

P كناري فروش *kinārī-farosh*, A laceman.

P كنارين *kanārīn*, An extremity. Extreme.

P كناز *kanāz*, The stalk whence bunches of grapes or dates hang.

A كناز *kanāz* or *kināz*, (v. n. of كنز) Laying up dates in store. Dates heaped up, in order to be packed up for preservation. زمن الكناز *zamanu'l kanāz*, The season of packing up dates for store. *Kināz*, (pl. كنز *kunuz* and كناز *kināz*) (A she-camel or girl) firm in flesh.

A كناس *kinās*, (v. n. of كنس) Fleeing to cover, hiding amongst the bushes (a deer). (pl. كنس *kunus* or كنّس *kunnas*) The place where a deer lies.

A كنّاس *kannās*, A sweeper. An avaricious man.

A كناسة *kunāsat*, Sweepings, rubbish, dust.

A كنّاسي *kannāsī*, The office of a sweeper.

A كنّاشات *kunnāshāt*, Roots, principles. This word is sometimes inscribed on books, implying treatises, digests, and the like.

A كناص *kunāṣ*, Strong to labour (camel or ass).

A كناعر *kanāʼir*, (pl. of كنعرة) Large she-camels.

P كناغ *kunāgh*, Silk, a thread of silk. A silkworm's cocoon. A spider's web. A side, border, margin.

A كناف *kināf*, A helping, bringing assistance.

A كنافث *kunāfis*, Short.

A كنافج *kunāfij*, Many, copious, numerous. Full of flesh, firm. Compact (ear of corn).

P كناك *kanāk*, Belly-ache, gripes.

P كنام *kunām*, (or كنّام *kunnām*) A house, dwelling. The den or retreat of a wild beast. A bed, resting-place. A bird's nest. Pasture.

A كنان *kinān*, (pl. اكنّة *akinnat*) A veil, covering. (pl. of كنّة *kunnat*) Shades over doorways, eaves.

P كنان *kunān*, (part. pres. of كردن *kardan*) Making, doing. تفرّج كنان *tafarruj-kunān*, Taking recreation, walking. جلوه كنان *jilwa-kunān*, Shining, resplendent. جنگ كنان *jang-kunān*, Making war, fighting. سير كنان *sayr-kunān*, Travelling, going, walking. غارت كنان *ghārat-kunān*, Making depredations. ناله كنان *nāla-kunān*, Groaning.

A كنانة *kinānat*, A quiver of leather without any wood, or vice versâ. Name of the father of a tribe.

P كنانه *kanāna*, Old, not new. Worn out.

P كنانيدن *kunānīdan*, To cause to do or make.

A كنانير *kanānīr*, (pl. of كنّارة *kannārat*) Harps, lutes. Drums, tabors.

A كناية *kināyat*, (v. n. of كني) Calling (any thing) by a significant name. A metaphor, metonymy, nickname. (Under the words ابو *abū*, امّ *umm*, ابن *ibn*, or بنت *bint*, many examples may be seen).

A كنائس *kanāʼis*, (pl. of كنيسة *kanīsat*) Churches.

A كنائن *kanāʼin*, (pl. of كنّة *kannat*) Sons' or brothers' wives.

A كنب *kamb*, (v. n. of كنب) Collecting (in a bag). *Kanab*, Callousness of the feet, or of the hands, from labour. *Kanib*, Hemp.

P كنب *kumb*, Cassia fistularis. The city of Kum. *Kanab*, Hemp. A hempen rope. The inebriating hemp-seed.

A كنبار *kimbār*, A rope made of cocoa-nut fibres.

P كنبانيدن *kambānīdan*, To incline.

P كنبت *kanabt* or *kinibt*, A bee.

A كنبث *kumbus*, Hard, strong. Contracted, shrivelled. Miserly.

A كنبثة *kambasat*, (v. n. of كنبث Q) Being shrivelled, wrinkled (the skin). Being costive.

P كنبدانه *kanab-dāna*, Hemp-seed.

A كنبرة *kimbarat*, A thick tip or ridge of the nose.

A كنبل *kumbul*, Hard. Robust.

A كنبوث *kumbūs*, Hard and contracted. A miser.

P كنبور *kambūr*, Fraud, deceit.

P كنبوره *kambūra*, Fraud, deceit. Usury.

P كنبوريدن *kambūrīdan*, To defraud, deceive.

P كنبه *kanaba*, Raw thread.

P كنبهن *kimbahn*, Seed of turpentine. Juniper-berries.

P كنبيدن *kambīdan*, To draw (a thing) from a place and take it away. *Kumbīdan*, To rise up, to ascend. To leap.

P كنبيزه *kumbīza*, A species of cucumber. An unripe melon.

A كنّة *kannat*, (pl. كنائن *kanāʼin*) The wife of a son or of a brother. *Kinnat*, A veil, any covering by which, or under which, persons or things are preserved. A shade, umbrella. Whiteness. *Kunnat*, (pl. كنان *kinān*) A pent over a doorway or projecting from a wall. A cupboard or safe. An arch with a wall.

A كنت *kant*, (v. n. of كنت) Being strong and powerful. *Kanat*, (v. n. of كنت) Being rough.

A كنتأة *kintaʼat*, A plant resembling rocket.

A كنتأل *kuntaʼl*, A dwarf.

A كنتأو *kintaʼw*, A strong rope. A man with a large, handsome, bushy beard.

A كنتب *kuntub*, A dwarf.

A كنتح *kantah*, Foolish.

A كنتع *kuntuʼ*, Short. A dwarf.

A كنتلّ *kintall*, Short.

A كنتني *kuntuniy*, Large and strong. Of great age. An egotist.

P كنتو *kinatū*, Seed of the Palma Christi.

A كنتيّ *kuntiy*, Strong. Large. Old, decrepit (from كنت *kunta*, Thou hast been). An egotist.

A كنثاب *kinsāb*, Sand poured out.

A كنثأة *kansaʼat*, (v. n. of كنثأ Q) Being large and bushy (a beard).

A كنثأو *kinsaʼw*, A strong rope. A man with a large bushy beard.

A كنثب *kunsab* or *kunsub*, Strong, robust.

A كنثة *kunsat*, A myrtle or a willow-basket, in which they keep aromatic herbs.

A كنثح *kansah*, Foolish.

A كنثر *kunsur*, Compressed, contracted. Glans.

A كنثرة *kansarat*, The nostril of an ass.

P كنج *kanj*, The uvula. A vain, foolish fellow. Saying, telling. Coagulated milk. Drawn out. Chosen. The little toe. *Kinj*, A huge, powerful, formidable elephant. *Kunj*, A corner. A narrow street, confined place. A subterraneous excavation. Wrinkle, plait. Bent double, crooked, hump-backed. كنج چشم *kunji chashm*, The inner corner of the eye.

P كنجار *kunjār*, (كنجاره *kunjāra*, كنجال *kunjāl*, or كنجاله *kunjāla*) Sediment, dregs, caput mortuum, remains of any thing squeezed.

P كنجد *kunjud*, The grain sesame. Rape-seed.

P كنجدك *kunjudak*, (كنجده *kunjada*, *kunjida*, or *kunjuda*) A kind of gum, sarcocolla, flesh-glue. Bezoar-stone. A freckle, a mole.

P كنجده *kunjada*, Sediment, dregs, remains of any thing squeezed, caput mortuum.

P كنجر *kinjar*, A large, stout, wild elephant.

P كنجر و پنجر *kinjar u pinjar*, Pinching.

P كنجشنج *kunj shunj*, A subterraneous passage, a mine. The undermining of a wall. A covered way. A ditch.

P كنجك *kanjak*, A tree called پشّه غال *pashshaghāl*, having a thick, smooth stem, and dense foliage. *Kunjak*, A curiosity of any kind, whatever is new and excites admiration.

P كنج كنج *kinj kinj*, (or كنچ كنچ *kinch kinch*) Little, small. By little and little.

P كنجل *kunjul*, Any thing contracted, shrunk up, or wrinkled; the hand or foot with the fingers or toes contracted. Bread which, by accident, has fallen into the embers of the oven.

P كنجلك *kunj* or *kunjulak*, Wrinkle, fold, plait.

P كنج لنج *kunj lunj*, Full of folds and wrinkles.

P كنجور *kunjūr*, Treasure. *Kanjwar*, Treasurer.

P كنجه *kunja*, An ass whose lower jaw is swollen. An ass that has lost his tail.

P كنجيد *kunjīd*, Sesame-seed.

P كنجيده *kunjīda*, Oil-cake, the husks of seeds, after the oil has been expressed.

A كنحب *kanhab*, Name of a plant.

P كنخ *kanakh*, Sour milk thickened by straining off the whey.

A كنخبة *kankhabat*, A confused, blundering speech.

P كنخت *kanakht*, The water of a sword-blade.

P كند *kand*, Hemp. Sugar. A wound. A pick-axe. Flight. A village. Name of a village in Turkistān whence they bring the best almonds. *Kund*, Dull, blunt. A stupid man, blockhead, dolt. A blunt sword or knife. Any thing unsaleable, not fetching its value. Bold, brave, strong. Wise, learned, sage; a philosopher. A fetter, clog; stocks. Penis. The testicles. كند نمودن *kund namūdan*, To set (the teeth) on edge, to dull, benumb.

A كند *kand*, (v. n. of كند) Cutting.

P كندا *kundā* or *kandā*, Learned, wise. A philosopher, prophet, soothsayer. Bold, warlike. *Kundā*, Name of a painter.

A كندارة *kindārat*, A sort of high-backed fish.

P كنداگر *kandāgar*, A carver, engraver. *Kundāgar*, Learned, wise. Brave, bold.

P كنداگري *kandāgarī*, Carving, engraving.

P كنداموية *kundāmoya*, The hair a child is born with. The small yellow plumage on young birds.

P كنداواله *kundāwāla*, Tall, corpulent, robust.

A fat, ugly, ill-formed, beardless youth.

A كنداو *kindaw*, A strong camel.

P كنداور *kundāwar*, Brave, bold, valiant, courageous, warlike. A hero, champion. Wise, learned.

A كندة *kindat*, A part, segment (of a mountain). Name of an Arabian tribe.

A كندث *kundus*, Hard.

A كندجة *kandajat*, (P كنده *kanda*) Excavation.

P كند خانه *kand-khāna*, Depressed, humble. A small basket. A bed, or sleeping-place.

P كندر *kandar*, A town, city. Name of a city in Khurāsān. (for كه اندر *ki andar*) Who or which (is) in. *Kandur*, An earthen vessel in which they put wheat and bread. *Kundur*, Mastich. كندر رومي *kunduri rūmī*, Mastich.

A كندر *kandar*, A species of astrological calculation, borrowed from the Greek. *Kundur*, A dwarf, a thick, short man. Frankincense. A kind of juniper-gum, which, when chewed, is good for the bile. A stout ass.

A كندرة *kandarat*, High rough ground. A hawk's perch or nest.

P كندرك *kundurak* or كندرو *kundrū*, Mastich.

P كندرو *kundrū*, Name of the vazir of Zahhāk.

P كندروش *kandarūsh*, Hillocky, hilly ground.

P كندرة *kandara*, Name of a small water-bird.

P كندز *kun-diz*, An old fortress. An old palace or upper room. Name of a city built by Farīdūn in Tūrān. *Kunduz*, Name of a city built by Jamshed.

P كند زبان *kund-zabān*, A stammerer.

P كند زباني *kund-zabānī*, An impediment or hesitation in speaking, stammering.

A كندس *kundus*, A certain root, black without, yellow within, and a sternutatory in medicine.

P كندسه *kundusa*, Glasswort.

P كندش *kandush* or *kundish*, A lump of cotton prepared for spinning. A stick for winding cotton upon. Glasswort.

A كندش *kundush*, A magpie. Name of a sternutative medicine.

P كند فهم *kund-fahm*, Dull of intellect.

P كند فهمي *kund-fahmī*, Dulness of intellect.

P كندك *kundak*, Bread broken in pieces.

P كندگوش *kund-gosh*, Hard of hearing, deafish.

P كندگي *kandagī*, Sculpture, engraving. A ditch.

P كندلان *kandulān* or *kundalān*, A sort of tent.

P كندله *kundula*, Any thing surrounded and brought together.

A كندلى *kandala'*, (or كندلاء *kandalā*) Name of a marine plant whose bark is used in tanning.

P كندمند *kandmand*, A house in ruins.

P كندن *kandan*, To dig. To pluck, extract, tear up, root out, extirpate; to raze (the foundations of a house). To skin, peel, unbark. To carve, engrave. To separate. To gather. To flee. To be entangled, embroiled.

P كندو *kandū* or *kundū*, A vessel made of clay, in which they keep grain. A demon of the woods. A bee-hive.

P كندوالة *kundwāla*, Firm, robust, and tall (man). An ugly, ill-made, beardless youth.

A كندوج *kandūj*, (from P كندو *kandū*) A clay vessel in which they keep grain.

P كندو خانه *kandū-khāna*, A vessel in which the butter is separated from the churned milk. A small basket. A bee-hive.

P كندورة *kandūra*, A large table. A linen or leathern cover for a table, a table-cloth.

P كندوري *kandūrī*, A leathern cover for a table. A napkin. A feast held in honour of Fātima, of which only women (and those the most virtuous) can partake. No male is ever permitted to see the food dressed on this occasion and set apart for an offering to the prophet's daughter. Name of a gourd.

P كندوز *kundoz*, A large needle.

P كندوش *kandosh*, A stony, rough, difficult road. The wages of a day's labour, daily pay. Mastich, white resin. *Kundosh*, A poisonous weed.

P كندوك *kundūk*, A shop. A capacious jar made of clay, in which they lay up grain for future use.

P كندوكوب *kand u kob*, Disquiet, unsteadiness.

P كندوله *kundūla*, A basket, a jar for holding grain. Broken pottery.

P كندويدستر *kundwidastar*, Testicles of beaver.

P كنده *kanda*, Digged, excavated. Engraved, carved. A ditch round fortified towns, gardens, or fields; a fosse, moat. A mound, dike. Any hollow place made as a shelter for travellers. A fold for cattle cut out at the foot of a mountain. An old man or woman. Misfortune. Inconvenient. Of a bad disposition. كندهٔ چهاربند *kandaِi chahār band*, The world. كندهٔ هيزم *kandaِi hezam*, An engraver in wood. *Kunda*, The stocks for offenders, a kind of clog or wooden fetters for captives. Stump of a tree. A butcher's chopping-block, a shoemaker's cutting-board. Stock of a gun. A fool, blockhead, man of dull understanding. A robust, beardless youth. A demon of the woods. Any thing brayed in a mortar. The silken bands with which a falcon's wings are confined when travelling; his collar and fastenings of bells to his legs. A falconer's cage. A potter's wheel. A stable.

P كنده پير *kanda-pīr*, An old woman.

P كنده خايه *kanda-khāya*, Ruptured. Castrated.

P كنده روي *kanda-rūy*, A table-cloth or towel.

P كنده كار *kanda-kār*, An engraver. Engraved, carved (as seal-rings or sword-hilts).

P كنده گر *kandagar*, A carver, engraver.

P كنده گري *kandagarī*, Engraving. كنده گري كردن *kandagarī kardan*, To grave, to carve.

P كنده موي *kanda-moy*, The down upon a new-hatched bird.

P كنده وش *kanda-wash*, A stony road.

P كنده هيزم *kanda-hezam*, Wood felled upon the mountains. The stocks.

P كندي *kandī*, Name of a flower (Pandanus odoratissimus). *Kundī*, Dulness, hebetude, stupidity. كنديء بينائي *kundīِi bīnāī*, Dimness of sight. كنديء دندان *kundīِi dandān*, The stupor of the teeth from eating any thing acid.

P كنديدن *kandīdan*, To dig, or cause to dig.

A كندير *kindīr*, A thick ass.

A كنديرة *kindīrat* or *kandīrat*, Largeness, magnitude, bulk, thickness.

P كنر *kanar*, (or كنره *kanara*) Canara in India.

A كنز *kanz*, (v. n. of كنز) Treasuring, storing, hoarding, laying up; putting any thing into a case or repository. Fixing (a spear) in the ground. Forcibly thrusting one thing into another or into the ground. Treasure (especially buried gold or silver). *Kunuz*, (pl. of كناز *kināz*) Firm-fleshed (she-camels or girls).

P كنز *kanaz*, That part of the stem of a bunch of dates which joins the tree.

P كنزا *kanzā*, Wise, learned, philosophic. An herb or flower which grows spontaneously.

A كنس *kans*, (v. n. of كنس) Sweeping, cleaning. *Kunus*, (pl. of كناس *kinās*) Coverts of deer.

A كنّس *kunnas*, (pl. of كانس *kānis*) Stars. Angels. Wild cows or their young. (pl. of كناس *kinās*) The coverts of deer.

P كنست *kanast* or *kunist*, A fire-temple.

P كنستو *kanastū*, An alkaline herb for washing.

A كنسح *kinsih*, (or كنسح) Root, origin; race.

A كنش *kansh*, A plaiting or flouncing of the fringe of a garment. A softening of the rough dentifrice called مسواك *miswāk*.

P كنش *kanish*, A digging, plucking up. جان كنش *jān-kanish*, Agony of death. *Kunish*, Action, operation, business. Custom, habit, manner, disposition. A criminal. A Christian church. A Jewish synagogue. A fire-temple.

A كنشاء *kinshāِ*, Curly-haired (man). Ugly-faced.

P كنشت *kunisht*, A fire-temple. A Jew's synagogue. A pigsty. Profession, occupation. بدكنشت *bad-kunisht*, Malignant, villainous.

P كنشتو *kanashtū*, An alkaline herb with which they wash clothes. Unripe grapes. Rubbish.

P كنشتوك *kanashtūk*, An alkaline herb for washing clothes.

P كنشك *kinishk*, A throbbing pain.

P كنشن *kunishn*, An act, work. A fire-temple. A Jews' synagogue. A pigsty.

P كنشو *kanshū*, Unripe grapes.

A كنظ *kanz*, (v. n. of كنظ) Afflicting, grieving, annoying, oppressing. Filling.

A كنظة *kunzat*, Anguish, distress: squeeze, pressure.

A كنع *kinaʿ*, The greater part of the night elapsed, a third remaining. Root, origin. A gate. *Kunaʿ*, (pl. of اكنع *aknaʿ*) Disabled in the arms, by fracture or dislocation. Unequal to any business. *Ka-*

naʻ, (v.n. of كنع) Being drawn together and wrinkled (the fingers). Being assiduous, sticking to. Being thrown flat on the chin. *Kaniʻ*, Broken with age, wrinkled (old man).

P كنعال *kanʻāl*, A falcon raising his head and body when he eyes his prey. A dangler after women. Greedy of prey.

A كنعان *kanʻān*, Canaan.

A كنعانيون *kanʻāniyūn*, Canaanites.

A كنعت *kanʻat*, A kind of fish.

A كنعد *kanʻad*, A kind of sea-fish.

A كنعرة *kanʻarat*, (pl. كناعر) A large she-camel.

P كنغ *kingh*, The matter which hardens in the corner of the eye.

P كنغال *kinghāl*, A wencher. *Kunghāl*, An interview in private between friends.

P كنغاله *kanghāla*, Whoredom. A matrimonial suit. A whore. A request, wish. A miser. A whoremonger. Avarice. A hero. Name of a mountain in Khurāsān.

A كنف *kanf*, (v. n. of كنف) Guarding, preserving, protecting, aiding, assisting. Enclosing. Driving (cattle) into a fold or enclosure. Preparing a covering or the shelter called كنيف *kanīf*. Placing both hands on the head of a measure, and holding grain in them. Constructing a privy or place to throw filth into. Turning from, retiring. *Kinf*, A shepherd's scrip. A kind of bag in which a trader puts up the meaner sort of commodities. *Kunf*, (pl. of كنوف *kanūf*) (She-camels) lying down among the males. (pl. of كنيف *kanīf*) Privies, necessaries. *Kanaf*, Side, edge, margin, coast, shore. Wing (of a bird). Protection, guardianship. Shade, shadow.

P كنف *kanaf*, A cord made of flax.

A كنفاء *kanfāʼ*, A sheep whose rump-bone is conspicuous from leanness.

A كنفة *kanafat*, A tract of country where camels feed. A side, margin, coast.

A كنفث *kunfus*, Short.

A كنفرة *kinfirat*, The tip, also the side of the nose.

A كنفكان *kun fa kān*, Let it be, and it was; (or, مالك كن فكان *māliki kun fa kān*, Lord of Let it be, and it was), An epithet of the Almighty.

P كنفليل *kanfalīl*, A large beard.

A كنفليل *kanfalīl*, Large-bearded (man).

A كنفليلة *kanfalīlat*, A large beard.

P كنك *kank*, Hump-backed. A cat. A cock. A dwelling for the spring-season. A temple: an Indian pagoda. *Kink*, A mandate. A young man whose beard begins to grow. *Kunk*, Earthen water-pipes or conduits. *Kanak*, *kinik*, or *kinak*, A kind of grass of which they make cord. A walnut, the kernel of which it is difficult to pull out. Parsimonious, stingy.

A كنكنة *kankanat*, (v. n. of كنكن Q) Fleeing away. Being lazy and inactive. Sitting in the house.

P كنكوس *kankūs*, A demon.

P كنگ *kang*, Wing of a bird. Arm of a man from the tips of the fingers to the shoulder. Limb or branch of a tree. *King*, A youth of a clumsy, ill-shaped body. A vulgar, impudent, talkative fellow. *Kung*, A man of a gross, stout habit. A beardless and impudent youth. Name of a certain sea-port. The end of the stalk of a bunch of dates next the tree.

P كنگاب *kangāb*, Syrup, jalap, ptisan.

P كنگاج *kankāj*, A crab. *Kangāj* or *kingāj*, Counsel, consultation, deliberation.

P كنگار *kangār* or *kungār*, A snake which has recently cast his slough.

P كنگاس *kin* or *kangās*, Counsel. A crab.

P كنگاش *kingāsh*, Counsel, deliberation. كنگاش خواستن *kingāsh khwāstan*, To ask counsel. كنگاش نمودن *kingāsh namūdan*, To consult, deliberate.

P كنگاله *kangāla*, A dangling after women. A matrimonial suit. A courtesan. A miser. Name of a mountain in Khurāsān.

P كنگر *kangar*, A kind of artichoke. Obstinacy, contentiousness. كنگر كندن *kangar kandan*, To toil in vain. *Kingir*, Name of a musical instrument used in India. *Kungur*, A large owl. A beam projecting from a wall. A player on the kettle-drum. A young branch. Shameless. A kind of beggar (see شاخشانه *shākh-shāna*). A battlement, pinnacle. كنگر كبريا *kunguri kibriyā*, Pinnacle of greatness.

P كنگران *kangarān*, An owl. Rye.

P كنگرزد *kangar-zad*, Artichoke-gum.

P كنگره *kingira*, A musical instrument having only two wires. *Kungura*, A niched battlement, notched parapet, pinnacle, turret. An acroterium. Plumes upon helmets, ornaments upon crowns.

P كنگره دار *kungura-dār*, Embattled, crested.

P كنگري *kangarī*, Artichoke-gum. *Kingirī*, Name of a musical instrument made of two gourds, used in Hindūstān; a kind of lute.

A كنمة *kanmat*, A wound.

P كن مكن *kun makun*, Do and do not; irresolute, hesitating in giving orders. A sovereign, a commander. Commands and prohibitions.

P كنند *kanand*, A hoe, spade, or instrument for turning up ground which cannot be ploughed.

P كننده *kananda*, A digger, one who tears any thing up. *Kunanda*, A maker. A factor, agent, doer.

P كنو *kanav* or *kanū*, Hemp.

A كنوب *kunūb*, (v. n. of كنب) Being thick, coarse, and rough. Being contented, independent, able to dispense with, and to do without.

A كنوة *kinwat* or *kunwat*, A patronymic.

A كنود *kanūd*, Ungrateful, unthankful, rebellious against God or man; avaricious. One who does no good, beats his servants, and eats by himself. A woman untrue in her love, unfaithful in her attachment. Barren (ground). *Kunūd*, (v. n. of كند) Being ungrateful. Ingratitude.

P كنودان *kanawdān*, (*kanūdān*, كنودانه *kanawdāna*, or *kanūdāna*) Hemp-seed (eat roasted to procure an appetite or get fat).

P كنور *kanūr*, A basket or wooden vessel for holding bread or corn. A large jar of unbaked clay, in which grain is preserved from fire. *Kanūr* or *kinūr*, Fraud, deceit. *Kunūr* or *kanūr*, Thunder.

P كنوره *ka* or *kinūra*, A cheat, deceiver, trifler.

P كنوريدن *ka* or *kinūridan*, To cheat, deceive.

A كنوز *kunūz*, (pl. of كنز *kanz*) Treasures.

P كنوزه *ka*, *ku*, or *kinūza*, Dressed cotton-wool.

A كنوع *kunūʻ*, (v. n. of كنع) Drawing one's self together; contracting or clapping close the wings when flying downward (an eagle). Running away from, being cowardly. Approaching, being near. Setting (as a star). Being submissive, gentle, humble. Adhering to the garments (musk or other perfume). Striking the fingers so that they become dry. Swearing by God. Striking. Contracting or withering (fingers). Desiring, being greedy of (any thing).

A كنوف *kanūf*, (pl. كنف *kunf*) (A she-camel) lying down among the males. Retiring from the herd or flock (a she-camel or a sheep). A sheep blissomed although pregnant.

P كنون *knūn*, (used for اكنون *aknūn*) Now. God willing. *Kanūn*, A large jar of unbaked clay to preserve corn.

A كنون *kunūn*, (v. n. of كن) Covering, veiling, protecting, preserving. Shading from the sun.

A كنه *kunh*, Substance. Quantity, species, mode. Time. Face, aspect. Sum, extreme, or height (of any thing). يعرفه كنه معرفته *yaʻrifuhu kunha maʻrifatihi*, He knows it thoroughly.

P كنه *kanah*, (pl. كنهها *kanahhā*) A tike.

P كنه *kunna*, Shady.

A كنهان *kanhān*, A plant like the juniper.

A كنهبل *kanahbal* or *kanahbul*, A kind of large tree. Barley with large ears.

A كنهدر *kanahdar*, An instrument upon which they carry grapes, unburnt bricks, or milk, &c.

A كنهدل *kanahdal*, Large, thick, strong.

P كن هزه *kan haza*, A yawning-fit before a fever.

A كنهفة *kanhafat*, (v. n. of كنهف Q) Going away, making haste in walking or running.

A كنهور *kanahwar*, Clouds like mountains. A large man.

A كنهورة *kanahwarat*, A large old she-camel.

A كنى *kunaʼ*, (pl. of كنية *kunyat*) Metonymics.

A كني *kaniy*, One who jokes with another's name. One who has a patronymic similar to that of another person; cognominal.

P كنيا *kanyā*, (in zand and Pāz.) Hollow within.

A كنيب *kanīb*, A tree, dry, withering, or having the thorns broken.

A كنية *kinyat* or *kunyat*, (v. n. of كني) Calling or naming (any one) by a word which has another meaning, dubbing: as, ابو حذر *abū hazar*, Father

Timidity, a name for the chameleon. (pl. كنى *kuna'*) A patronymic, or a filionymic: any name beginning with اب *ab*, Father; امّ *umm*, Mother; ابن *ibn*, Son; بنت *bint*, Daughter; اخ *akh*, Brother; or اخت *ukht*, Sister.

A كنيت *kanīt*, (A bottle) that holds water well.

P كنيت *kunet*, (for كنيد *kuned*) Do you.

A كيدر *kanaydar* or *kunaydir*, Thick, gross.

P كنير *kanīr*, A glutton. A lazy fellow.

P كنيز *kanīz*, A female slave, maid-servant. A maid, virgin, girl. *Kanīz* or *kunīz*, The stalk where bunches of grapes or dates hang. كنيز سزا *kanīzi sazā*, A retributive particle. كنيز وازده *kanīzi wāzada*, A conditional particle.

A كنيز *kanīz*, Dates packed in hampers and laid up in store for winter-use.

P كنيزك *kanīzak*, A girl. كنيزك فراشي *kanīzaki firāshī*, A kept mistress.

P كنيزكي *kanīzagī*, The condition or duty of a female servant, or girl.

P كنيزي *kanīzī*, Maidenhood, girlhood.

A كنيسة *kanīsat*, (pl. كنائس *kanāʼis*) A Christian church. A Jew's synagogue; a pagan temple. A beautiful woman.

A كنيّسة *kunayyisat*, (dim. of كنيسة *kanīsat*) A small church, a chapel.

P كنيش *kunīsh*, An action, good or bad.

A كنيع *kanīʻ*, Broken-armed or broken-handed. One who strays from the right path, or wandering from one road to another. Extreme (hunger).

A كنيف *kanīf*, (pl. كنف *kunf*) A privy, necessary. A place where rubbish or excrement is thrown. A place for washing the face and hands. A veil, covering. A shield. An enclosure for cattle made of rushes. A palm-tree sprouting after being cut down to the height of a cubit. *Kunayf*, (dim. of كنف *kinf*) A small shepherd's wallet.

A كنين *kanīn*, Hidden, concealed.

P كو *kaw*, Clever, ingenious. Power. Stature. *Ku*, (for كه او *ki u*) That he. Who, which, what. *Kū*, Where? Where is he gone? A broad street, square, market-place. A narrow street, an alley.

A كوّ *kaww*, A window.

A كوء *kawʼ*, (v. n. of كوأ) Being pusillanimous, infirm, weak.

A كواء *kiwāʼ*, (v. n. 3 of كوي) Reviling one another. (pl. of كوّة *kawwat* or *kūwat*) Windows.

A كوّاء *kawwāʼ*, Foul-mouthed, abusive; reviler. ابو الكوّاء *abū'l kawwāʼ*, An Arabian nickname.

A كوابح *kawābiḥ*, (pl. of كابح) Objects of omen.

A كواتل *kawātil*, Name of a halting-place on the road to Rakkah.

A كواثر *kawāsir*, (pl. of كوثر) Fountains in Paradise.

A كواثل *kawāsil*, Name of a country.

A كواح *kiwāḥ*, A good manager (of cattle).

A كواحص *kawāḥis*, Obliterated (vestiges). اطلال كواحص *atlāl kawāḥis*, Effaced marks of a house.

A كوادس *kawādis*, (pl. of كادس *kādis*) Omens taken from sneezing.

P كوادة *kiwāda*, The wooden sill of a door. The piece of wood in which the lower pivot turns.

A كواذب *kawāzib*, (pl. of كاذب) False. Liars.

P كوار *kawār*, A leek. A thick mist which appears in summer-nights. *Kawār* or *kuwār*, A basket for carrying about fruit on the back. *Kuwār*, Name of a town near Shīrāz.

P كوارا *ka* or *kuwārā*, The wooden sill of a door.

A كوارات *kuwārāt*, Domestic hives.

A كوارة *kiwārat*, A sort of wine. *Kiwārat*, *kuwārat*, or *kūwārat*, (pl. كوّارات *kūwārāt* or كواثر *kawāʼir*) A hive, or place where bees make honey.

A كوارث *kawāris*, Troublesome (affairs).

P كوارون *kuwārūn*, Disease of skin, prickly heat.

P كوارة *kawāra*, A basket or pannier for carrying fruit about upon the back. A thick mist which appears during the night in the summer-months. A bee-hive. *Kuwāra*, An earthen vessel.

P كوارة دان *kawāra-dān*, A shepherd, herdsman.

P كواز *kawāz*, A kind of bottle carried by travellers. A stick for driving cattle.

P كوازة *kawāza*, A close-mouthed travellers' bottle. *Kiwāza*, An ox-goad. *Kuwāza*, A poached egg.

P كواژ *kawāj*, Reproach, reprehension, taunt.

P كواژة *kawāja*, Jesting, bantering, jeering, ridiculing. A jester. Bread half baked. A poached egg.

P كواس *kuwās*, Quality, property; way, manner.

A كواسب *kawāsib*, (or الكواسب *al kawāsib*) Wild beasts. Extremities of the body, hands, feet.

A كواسر *kawāsir*, (pl. of كاسرة *kāsirat*) Breakers. Eagles. Camels which break the branches.

P كواسمه *kuwāsama*, Easy, not difficult.

P كواسة *kuwāsa*, Quality, property, way, manner.

P كواسيه *kuwāsima*, Easy. Easiness, facility.

P كواش *kuwāsh*, Mode: quality, property.

A كواشة *kuwāshat*, A large glans penis.

A كواشف *kawāshif*, (pl. of كاشفة *kāshifat*) Disclosures, discoveries, revelations.

P كواشمه *kuwāshama*, Easy, not difficult. Ease.

P كواشه *kuwāsha*, Quality, way, manner.

P كواشير *kawāshīr*, (or گواشير *gawāshīr*) Name of a place whence they bring turquoise-stones of a light colour and little value.

P كواشيه *kuwāshima*, Easy. Easiness, facility.

A كواعب *kawāʻib*, (pl. of كاعب *kāʻib*) Swelling-breasted girls.

A كواغذ *kawāghiz*, (pl. of P كاغذ *kāghiz*) Papers.

A كوافر *kawāfir*, Wine-jars. (pl. of كافرة *kāfirat*) Infidels, unbelieving (women). (pl. of كافور *kāfūr*) Flowers of the palm-tree. (See كافور *kāfūr*).

A كوافير *kawāfīr*, (pl. of كافور) Flowers of the palm.

A كواكب *kawākib*, (pl. of كوكب *kawkab*) Stars, constellations. ذو كواكب *zū kawākib*, Sorrowful, mournful (day). *Kuwākib*, Name of a mountain whence they cut mill-stones.

P كواكب شناس *kawākib-shinās*, An astronomer. An astrologer.

A كوأكل *kawaʼkal*, (كوألل *kawaʼlal*, and كوالل *kawālil*) Short-bodied. One who turns his toes in and his heels out.

A كواكية *kuwākiyat*, A dwarf.

P كوال *ka* or *kuwāl*, Gain, growth, increase.

P كوالغنجه *kuwālghuncha*, Red paint for the face.

P كوالف *kawālif*, A kind of white thorn or thistle of which camels are fond.

P كواليدن *ka* or *kuwālīdan*, To gain, acquire, heap up. To grow, increase, abound; to flourish, ripen.

P كواليده *kawālīda* also *kuwālīda*, Gained, acquired. Grown, increased.

A كواليز *kawālīz*, (pl. of كالوز *kālūz*) Those who go armed to water.

A كوانع *kawāniʻ*, (pl. of كانعة *kāniʻat*) Noses beaten flat on their faces.

A كوانين *kawānīn*, (pl. of كانون) Chafing-dishes.

P كواوم *kūūm*, The bog-rush.

A كواهل *kawāhil*, (pl. of كاهل *kāhil*) The cavities between the scapula and the vertebræ. من كواهل الصواهل *min kawāhili's sawāhil*, From the backs of neighing steeds.

A كوائر *kawāʼir*, Domestic hives.

A كوائف *kawāʼif*, Particulars, contents.

P كوايم *kūīm*, Name of an herb.

A كوب *kawb*, (v. n. of كاب for كوب) Drinking water out of a vessel without handle or spout. *Kūb*, (pl. أكواب *akwāb*) A cup, or any such vessel without spout or handle, a ewer. *Kawab*, Largeness of head, with a slenderness of neck.

P كوب *kob*, (in compos. from كوفتن *koftan* or كوبيدن *kobīdan*) Beating, striking, smiting; or who beats or strikes. (پاي كوب *pāy-kob*, A dancer. دشمن كوب *dushman-kob*, Routing enemies. طوپ قلعه كوب *topi kalʻa-kob*, Cannon battering a fort. زركوب *zar-kob*, A goldsmith.) A stroke, bang, whack, knock, blow, thump. A touch. An elephant-goad. A mat made of very coarse reeds.

P كوبانيدن *kobānīdan*, To cause to beat, bruise, bang, whack, or thump.

A كوبة *kawbat*, A sigh for any thing lost or irretrieveable. *Kūbat*, The game of chess; tables. A small drum. A kind of lute. A stone filling the hand, with which they bray drugs or crack nuts.

A كوءبة *kuʼabat*, Shame.

P كوبخي *kūbakhī*, A great, distinguished man.

P كوب كاري *kob-kārī*, Chastisement.

P كوبكو *kū ba kū*, From street to street, from place to place.

P كوبل *kūbal*, Camomile.

P كوبله *kūbala* or *kawbala*, The hair on the top of the head.

P كوبن *koban*, A sledge-hammer.

P كوبه *koba*, An instrument with which any thing is brayed. A mallet, beetle. A whip, scourge.

A drum formed of two kettles, joined on their convex sides, and covered with a skin, played upon like a bagpipe. A wave of the sea. A vessel in which butter is separated from the milk. Name of an edible plant.

P كوبه كاري *koba-kārī*, A thumping.

P كوبيازه *kobyāza*, A sledge-hammer, hammer.

P كوبيدن *kobīdan*, To beat, strike, bruise, pound. پاي كوبيدن *pāy kobīdan*, To dance, strike the feet.

P كوبين *kobīn*, A hammer, mallet. A bleacher's beetle. A strainer of reeds used by those who sell oil; a sack made of reeds, in which they put seeds to be squeezed for the oil. The press of an oil-mill.

P كوپ *kūp*, A hill or mountain. A large water-jar. A mat.

P كوپاره *kūpāra*, A herd.

P كوپال *kūpāl*, A ponderous club, a mace. A thick neck. Name of a wrestler.

P كوپل *kūpal*, A young shoot, sprout, or bud.

P كوپله *kūpala* or *kawpala*, The bud or young shoot of a tree. A cupola, an arch decorated with festoons of flowers. A lock for a chest. Bubbles on wine or water. The hair on the top of the head.

P كوپه *kūpa*, A surgeon's cupping-glass.

A كوّة *kawwat* or *kūwat*, (pl. كواء *kiwās*, كوي *kawa'*, or *kuwa'*) A window.

P كوت *kawt* or *kot*, The buttocks. *Kut*, (for كه او ترا *ki u turā*) Who to thee.

H كوت *kot*, A fort.

P كوتار *kotār*, A covered market-house.

P كوتاه *kotāh*, Short, small, little. Mean. A dwarf. كوتاه شدن *kotāh shudan*, To be shortened. كوتاه كردن *kotāh kardan*, To abridge.

P كوتاه انديش *kotāh-andesh*, Short-sighted.

P كوتاهانه *kotāhāna*, Like a dwarf, dwarfishly.

P كوتاه بالا *kotāh-bālā*, Short of stature.

P كوتاه بين *kotāh-bīn*, Short, or dim-sighted.

P كوتاه پا *kotāh-pā*, (كوتاه پاي *kotāh-pāy*, also كوتاه پاچه *kotāh-pācha*) Name of a quadruped with a spotted back and horns like a deer. A hare.

P كوتاه پاچه *kotāh-pācha*, A very short man.

P كوتاه زندگاني *kotāh-zindagānī*, Short-lived.

P كوتاه قد *kotāh-kad*, Short of stature.

P كوتاه گردن *kotāh-gardan*, Short-necked.

P كوتاه نظر *kotāh-nazar*, Short-sighted: careless, negligent, improvident. Stingy, avaricious.

P كوتاهي *kotāhī*, Shortness, brevity. Littleness, deficiency.

P كوتر *kawtar* or *kūtar*, (for كبوتر) A pigeon.

A كوتعة *kawtaʻat*, The nut of an ass's yard.

P كوتنگ *kotang*, A washer's beetle.

P H كوتوال *kotwāl*, The porter of a castle. A magistrate.

P كوته *kotah*, (for كوتاه *kotāh*) Short, contracted.

P كوته امل *kotah-amal*, Moderate in one's hopes.

P كوته انديش *kotah-andesh*, Short-sighted, imprudent, rash, improvident, wanting foresight.

P كوته بال *kotah-bāl*, Of short stature.

P كوته پا *kotah-pā*, (or كوته پاچه *kotah-pācha*) An animal resembling a deer. A hare.

P كوته قد *kotah-kad*, Of a short stature.

P كوته گردن *kotah-gardan*, Short-necked. Wicked, deceitful.

A كوتئ *kawta'*, Short. Dwarf. Corn sprouting up after rain.

A كوتيّ *kūtiy*, Short. A dwarf. A man's name.

P كوتينا *kotīnā*, (in zand and Pāzand) A mule.

A كوث *kaws*, (pl. اكواث) A shoe, a short boot.

A كوثة *kawsat*, Plenty, fruitfulness.

A كوثر *kawsar*, (pl. كواثر *kawāsir*) A river in Paradise whence all the other rivers derive their source. A river. Name of a village in Taif. The Muhammadan religion. Prophecy. A liberal, munificient man. A prince or chief. Much. Much (dust) piled up.

A كوثل *kawsal*, Stern or poop of a ship; helm.

P كوج *kūj*, Squint-eyed. *Kawaj*, A quilted jacket worn in battle. Gum exuding from a tree.

P كوچ *koch*, A robber, footpad, assassin. A wandering tribe. Migration, decamping. Marching, setting off. Squint-eyed. A kingdom. A man's family, wife, children. An owl. Assistance, service. Name of a country lying between Bengal and Khutā. كوچ كردن *koch kardan*, To decamp, move to another place. To set off on a march. To run away. To set. كوچ دادن *koch dādan*, To serve. كوچ و بلوچ *koch u buloch*, A wandering tribe settled on the mountains bordering on كرمان *karmān*.

P كوچانيدن *kochānīdan*, To cause to march on.

P كوچ بكوچ *koch ba koch*, Travelling one after another. A highwayman's horse.

P كوچك *kūchak*, Small, little. A musical mode or style. ايلچيء كوچك *īlchīi kūchak*, A little ambassador, internuncio, envoy, resident.

P كوچك بالا *kūchak-bālā*, Small in stature.

P كوچكتر *kūchaktar*, Less, smaller.

P كوچكي *kūchakī*, Smallness. Purple.

P كوچكين *kūchakīn*, (or كوچكترين *kūchaktarīn*) Smallest, least.

P كوچه *kūcha*, (dim. of كو *kū*) A narrow street. A lane, slum, row, passage. A street, square, market-place. A thread. Migration. كوچهٔ باستان *kūchai bāsitān*, (or كوچهٔ خطر *kūchai khatar*) The world. كوچهٔ سربسته *kūchai sar-basta*, A blind alley, cul-de-sac. كوچه فتادن *kūcha fitādan*, To be a stranger, far from country and friends.

P كوچه گرد *kūcha-gard*, A vagrant. A street-walker, perambulator of the streets.

P كوچه گردي *kūcha-gardī*, Vagrancy. Street-walking. Perambulation of the streets.

A كوح *kawh*, (v. n. of كاح for كوح) Conquering in war. Immersing in water, or burying in the earth.

P كوخ *kokh*, A small hut of reeds. A house without a window. A species of grass of which they make mats. The matter which hardens in the corner of the eye. A worm.

A كوخ *kūkh*, (pl. اكواخ *akwākh*, كوخان *kūkhān*, كيخان *kīkhān*, and كوخة *kiwakhat*) A small hut or house of reeds without a window.

A كوخان *kūkhān*, (or كوخة *kiwakhat*) (pl. of كوخ *kūkh*) Small huts of reeds without windows.

A كوخة *kuwakhat*, (pl. of كاخ) Upper rooms.

P كوخك *kūkhak* or *kawakhk*, A bunch of grapes. A branch after the grapes have been pulled off.

A كود *kawd*, (v. n. of كاد for كود) Being just on the point; every thing but; hardly being able (to accomplish). Preventing, hindering. Wishing, desiring. Being liberal. This verb is sometimes pleonastic: as, لم يكد يراها *lam yakad yarāhā*, which is equivalent to لم يراها *lam yarāhā*, He saw her not. و لا كودا *wa lā kawdan*, In no shape, by no means.

P كود *kod*, A stack or heap of corn. Collected, the reverse of scattered. Manure. *Kawud*, Blue.

A كوداء *kusadās*, Deep, long-fetched breath, sigh.

P كوداب *kodāb*, Food dressed with grape-juice.

A كوداة *kawdasat*, (v. n. of كودا Q) Running.

P كودال *kodāl*, A ditch. A well. A hoe.

P كودبان *kūdbān* or *kūdabān*, A kind of camel's saddle. The timber of a camel's saddle.

A كودة *kawdat*, (pl. اكواد) A heap of earth.

A كودر *kawdar*, Name of a king; also of a certain general or lieutenant.

P كودر *kūdar*, The skirt of a mountain. Thin leather for lining boots and shoes.

P كودره *kawdara*, A water-fowl. A cormorant. A sort of duck.

P كودك *kūduk*, A boy, lad, youth, child, infant. A slave-boy.

P كودكانه *kūdakāna*, Childish, childishly.

P كودكه *kūdaka*, A little infant.

P كودكي *kūdakī*, Puerile, infantine. Childhood. Childishness, puerility.

P كودگر *kodgar*, A digger, an excavator.

P كودن *kawdan*, Weak in mind, dull, stupid, thick-headed. An old beast of burden. A bustard.

A كودن *kawdan*, Lazy, slow, and stupid. *Kawdan*, (or كودني *kawdaniy*) A mean or sorry horse. A pack-horse. An elephant. A mule.

P كودني *kawdanī*, Stupidity.

P كوده *kūda*, The bow of a saddle. A key with the head or extremity bent. Teeth or work of a key. كودهٔ پستان *kūdai pistān*, The nipples of animals.

P كودينه *kūdīna*, A large hammer or mallet. A bleacher's beetle.

A كوذان *kawzān*, Large and fat.

P كوذر *kūzar*, A calf-skin; leather boot-lining.

P كور *kawr*, Ground full of hollows and unfit for cultivation. The semblance of water floating over the plain. *Kūr*, Blind. كور شدن *kūr shudan*, To be or become blind. كور كردن *kūr kardan*, To make blind. *Kawar*, Capers.

A كور *kawr*, (v. n. of كار for كور) Wrapping (the turban-sash) round the head in a spiral form. Digging, excavating in the ground. Carrying a bundle of clothes. Killing. Haste, expedition, acceleration. Nature. Plenty, increase, abundance. (pl. اكوار *akwār*) A herd of camels, from 150 to 200 or upwards. A herd of oxen. نعوذ بالله من الحور بعد الكور *naʻūzu bi'llāh mini'l hawr baʻda'l kawr*, God defend us from want after plenty! *Kūr*, (pl. اكيار *akyār*, اكور *akwur*, and كيران *kīrān*) A camel's saddle with the furniture. A smith's forge made of clay. A bee-hive. A hornet's nest. *Kuwar*, (pl. of كورة *kūrat*) Cities, towns. Regions.

P كوراب *kūrāb*, A false appearance of water on a sandy plain. One very thirsty, but drinking little.

P كورابين *kūrābīn*, A sack made of palm-leaves or reeds, wherein seeds are put to be squeezed for oil.

P كوران *kūrān*, (pl. of كور *kūr*) Blind.

P كوربا *kawar-bā*, Food dressed with capers.

P كوربخت *kūr-bakht*, Blind-fortune, *i. e.* unfortunate, wretched. A whisperer, tale-bearer, spy.

A كورة *kūrat*, (pl. كور *kuwar*) A city. A town. A tract of country, region. A term of contempt addressed to a female.

P كورت *kūrt*, A long narrow-necked jug.

P كورچشم *kūr-chasm*, A kind of garment.

P كورد *kūrd*, A Curd.

P كوردستان *kūrdistān*, Country of the Curds.

P كوردل *kūr-dil*, Blind-hearted, mad, foolish, dull.

P كوردي *kūrdī*, A woollen garment.

P كوردين *kūrdīn*, A woollen garment. A blanket. A sock.

P كورز *kawarz*, (or كورزة *kawarza*) Capers.

P كورس *kawars*, A curl. *Koras* or *kururs*, A lock of hair, a curl. Dirt, pus, matter.

P كورسي *kūrsī*, A seat, chair.

P كورش *kūrash*, Cyrus, king of Persia.

P كورشبك *kūrshabak*, The mole (an animal).

P كورشت *kūrisht*, Two sticks, the one long, the other short, with which they play the game of hockey.

P كورك *kawark*, Capers. Name of a place near Ormuz. Name of an infidel sect.

P كور كور *kor kor*, A kite.

P كورگاني *kūrgānī*, A sort of Morocco leather.

P كورگيا *kawargiyā* or *korgiyā*, Capers. Carobs.

P كورموش *kūr mūsh*, A species of mouse or rat very offensive.

P كورميخ *kūr mekh*, A large wooden pin or peg.

P كورنش *kornish*, Obeisance, salutation. Prostration. Adoration.

P كورنمايش *kūr-namāyish*, Dark, obscure.

P كورنمك *kūr-namak*, An ungrateful fellow.

P كورنه *kūrana*, An onion.

P كورنين *kawarnīn*, Household furniture. Immoveable effects. A ditch, a furrow.

P كوروا *kawar-wā*, A dish dressed with capers.

P كورة *kawra*, A channel hollowed out by a torrent. A torrent. A river-shell or worm. Name of a people in India. *Kūra*, A large village or market-town. A number of contiguous villages. Hard ground excavated by a torrent. A wild ass, the onager. A fire-place. A smith's forge. A furnace. A brick-kiln. A lime-kiln. Little, most minute. An earthen vessel which has not been used. كورة يابان كيمياي سپهر *kūra-yābāni kimiyāyi sipihr*, Astronomers. Astrologers, almanack-makers. *Kora*, A fifth part, one of the five ancient divisions of Persia called Ardshīr, Istikhar, Dārāb, Shāhpūr, and Kobād. Unbleached cloth.

P كورة خر *kūra-khar*, An elk.

P كورة راه *kūra-rāh*, An indirect road, which winds like a labyrinth, and leads one astray.

P كورة مز *kūra-maz*, A dish of milk and curds.

P كوري *kawrī*, A large leathern dish in which drugs are offered for sale. *Kūrī*, Blindness. A sort of wild grain. A lively, dancing pace. An easy, agreeable life; jovialness, cheerfulness.

A كوز *kawz*, (v. n. of كاز for كوز) Collecting, assembling. Drinking out of a cup. *Kūz*, (pl. كيزان *kīzān*, اكواز *akwāz*, and كوزة *kiwazat*) A jug, decanter, drinking-cup.

P كوز *kūz*, A hump, crooked back. The sky.

P كوزاورة *kūzāwara*, A glass bottle.

P كوزاويز *kūz-āwez*, Any thing by which a pitcher is suspended.

A كوزب *kawzab*, Close, stingy, avaricious.

P كوزپشت *kūz-pusht*, Hump-backed.

A كوزة *kiwazat*, (pl. of كوز *kūz*) Jugs, gugglets.

P كوزدار *kūz-dār*, Crooked, hump-backed.

P كوزر *kūzar*, Grain left in the ear after threshing. A sieve or screen for lime or gravel.

P كوزرة *kūzara*, Name of a blue water-bird.

P كوزشب *kūzashb*, Name of a certain king.

P كوزگاني *kūzyānī*, A kind of Morocco leather.

P كوزن *kūzan*, A wooden mallet.

P كوزورة *kūzwara*, A glass bottle.

P كوزة *kūza*, An earthen bottle with a long narrow neck for water. A gugglet. A kind of rose. Sugar which has been crystallized in an earthen pan.

P كوزة آويز *kūza-āwez*, That whereby a gugglet is suspended.

P كوزة پشت *kūza-pusht*, Hump-backed. The firmament.

P كوزة پنبه *kūza-pamba*, A cotton-pod.

P كوزة گر *kūzagar*, A potter.

P كوزة گردانك *kūza-gardānak*, Name of a game.

P كوزي *kūzī*, A reservoir, small lake, pond.

P كوژ *kūj* or *kuwij*, A species of medlar. *Kūj*, Crooked, curved, bent in two.

P كوژانك *kūjānuk*, The wards of a lock.

P كوژبرتا *koj bartā*, (in zand and Pāz.) Coriander.

P كوژپشت *kūj-pusht*, Hump backed, having a gibbous excrescence upon it; ill-made, deformed.

P كوژد *kojad*, (or كوژدة *kojada*) Flesh-glue.

P كوژگرة *kūj-girih*, A button, a button-hole.

P كوژنوك *kūjnūk*, The wards of a lock.

P كوژة *kūja*, A whitish ass.

A كوس *kaws*, (v. n. of كاس for كوس) Walking gently. Limping upon three feet (cattle). Coiling up (as a serpent). Throwing (any one) down. Pushing, shoving (in sexual intercourse). Beating down a price (when buying). The north-west wind. An exclamation uttered when in fear of drowning.

P كوس *kos*, A tymbal, large brass drum, which is beat in the palaces or camps of eastern princes. A road-measure of about two miles. A row, rank, line. Two persons who knock their sides or shoulders together. Collision, shock. A game in which the men are drawn up in rows like chess. The longest corner of a garment or a mantle. A nod, a wink, signal, or intimation. Name of a town in Māzanderān. كوس رحلت *kosi rihlat*, (or كوس رحيل *kosi rahīl*) Beating the retreat; a signal for departure. كوس فرو كوفتن *kos faro koftan*, To decamp, to set off to another place. كوس كردن *kos kardan*, To fight; to assault; to pierce or strike one upon the side when fighting. *Kūs*, A drum. A triangular instrument or rule used by carpenters in squaring their wood.

A كوس *kūs*, Accumulated sand-hills.

A كوس *kusus*, (pl. of كاس *kās*) Drinking-cups. Cups filled with wine.

A كوساء *kawsās*, (pl. كوس *kūs*) A thick, entangled plant, beginning to wither and turn white.

A كوسالة *kūsālat*, Glans penis.

P كوسان *kosān*, Name of a famous flute-blower to one of the ancient kings of Persia. A mode of singing. A town in Māzandarān.

P كوست *kost*, Concussion, shock, collision. A blow. Affliction. A drum. *Kawast*, A colocynth.

P كوستن *kostan*, To beat, strike, hurt, injure.

A كوسج *kawsaj* or *kūsaj*, A thin-bearded man. The sword-fish. Toothless. Slow (pack-horse).

A كوسجة *kawsajat*, (v. n. of كوسج Q) Becoming كوسج *kawsaj*, *i.e.* thin-bearded.

P كوس رحيل *kos-rahīl*, Beating a retreat.

P كوسك *kawisk*, A bean.

A كوسلة *kūsalat*, Glans penis.

P كوسه *kosa*, (A man) with little or no beard. One who has eight and twenty teeth. The fifth figure in geomancy. كوسه برنشين *kosa bar nishīn*, Name of a festival held at the beginning of the month آذر *āzur* by the ancient Persians.

A كوسيٓ *kūsa'*, Ingenious, sensible (woman).

A كوسي *kūsy*, Short in the fore-leg (horse).

P كوسياد *kūsyād*, A hard and black stone, which if thrown into the water attracts the fish, and if reduced by fire unites with iron and fixes mercury.

P كوش *kawsh*, A shoe, a slipper. *Kosh*, Exertion, effort, pains. The fourth day of every month. (from كوشيدن *koshīdan*, used in forming compounds) Striving, labouring. Industrious, doing one's endeavour, attentive. سلطان عطا كوش و خطاپوش *sultāni ʿatā-kosh u khatā-posh*, A monarch attentive (to confer) benefits and hide offences, *i.e.* beneficent and merciful.

A كوش *kawsh*, (v. n. of كاش for كوش) Being frightened, calling for help. Lying with. *Kūsh*, A large glans penis.

P كوشا *koshā*, One who displays a great energy in war. Labouring, striving.

P كوشاب *koshāb*, Syrup of grapes, new wine boiled with herbs. Barley-water, ptisane; the juice or broth of meat. Pollution.

P كوشاد *kūshād*, Gentian.

P كوشادن *kūshādan*, To open.

P كوشاسب *kūshāsb*, Sleep: a dream. Nightmare. Pollution. A youth whose beard begins to grow.

A كوشالة *kawshālat*, Glans penis magna.

P كوشالنگ *kūshālang*, A spade. A wooden bolt. A log fastened to a dog's neck. A stupid man. A crane. A large cock.

A كوشان *kawshān*, A dish made of rice and fish.

P كوشان *koshān*, Endeavouring; pains-taking.

P كوشش *koshish*, Study, endeavour, striving, effort, exertion, attention, application, labour, work. Search. War, battle, strife. A mustachio. كوشش بيهوده *koshishi bihoda*, A vain attempt. كوشش كردن *koshish kardan*, (or نمودن *namūdan*) To labour, exert one's self, be deeply engaged. To try, endeavour, strive.

P كوشك *kūshk*, A palace, villa. A castle, citadel. *Kūshak*, Small, little; a dwarf.

P كوشكنجير *kūshkanjīr*, A stone or iron ball projected from a catapulta or cannon.

A كوشلة *kawshalat*, A large glans penis.

P كوشه *kosha*, Sought, hunted after: object of endeavour, search. Any thing acquired by labour.

P كوشيار *koshyār*, Name of a physician under whom the celebrated Avicenna studied medicine.

P كوشيدن *koshīdan*, To labour, struggle, strive, endeavour, try, exert one's powers. To force, compel, beat. To dispute, wrangle, debate. To wander, stray. To search.

A كُوصة *kuṣat*, Extremely patient in regard to eating and drinking: accustomed to hard fare.

A كوع *kawʿ*, (v. n. of كاع for كوع) Going obliquely on one side of the feet (as a dog) on hot sand. Having a large wrist-bone, or a distorted wrist. *Kūʿ*, (pl. اكواع *akwāʿ*) The protuberance of the wrist-bone. The wrist-bone (especially on the thumb-side). *Kawaʿ*, A pain in the wrist-bone next the thumb.

A كوعاء *kawʿāʾ*, Distorted-wristed (woman).

A كوعرة *kawʿarat*, (v. n. of كوعر Q) Becoming fat (a camel's bunch).

P كوغ *kogh*, A going within, concealment.

A كوف *kawf*, (v. n. of كاف for كوف) Doubling down and sewing the edges of leather.

P كوف *kūf*, A large owl. A weaver's sley.

A كوفان *kawfān*, (v. n. of كوف) Being of a circular form. *Kawfān*, (*kūfān*, كُوَفان *kūwafān*, or *kawwafān*) The city of Kūfa in Arabian Irāk (or Chaldea). Any thing round (especially a heap of sand). A circle, circuit, compass. Estimation, esteem, honour. Dignity, glory, grandeur. A garrison. Difficulty, trouble. A whirlwind, hurricane. Mixture. Confusion. Hateful, disagreeable. A forest, grove, or thicket of reeds.

A كوفة *kūfat*, A round tumulus of sand (especially red and mixed with gravel). The city of Kūfa. A blemish. ليست به توفة و لا كوفة *laysat bihi tūfatun wa lā kūfatun*, There is no vice in him.

P كوفت *koft*, Interwoven. A blow, bruise. Grief, sadness. Anguish, vexation.

P كوفتر *koftar*, A sauce made of plums and grapes.

P كوفت كوب *koft-kob*, Beating.

P كوفت گر *koftgar*, A gilder; a gold-beater.

P كوفتگي *koftagi*, A bruise. A treading, trampling.

P كوفتن *koftan*, To break, bruise, knock, strike, smite, beat, thrash, shake, trample under foot, tread upon. To precipitate, to throw down. To bleach. كوفتن دل *koftani dil*, A palpitation of the heart. در كوفتن *dar koftan*, To knock at a gate or door.

P كوفته *kofta*, Thrashed. Trampled upon. Distressed, vexed, grieved. Wearied, knocked up. Inlaid. Hashed meat. Balls of pounded meat cooked in soup. An ignorant, weak, silly fellow. كوفته كردن *kofta kardan*, To inlay.

P كوفته بريان *kofta-biryān*, Meat pounded and spiced, fried in butter, and poured upon boiled rice.

P كوفج *kofaj*, (or كوفجان *kofjān*) Name of a tribe of Karmanian mountaineers.

P كوفجان *kofjān*, A cage.

P كوفشانه *kofshāna*, A weaver.

A كوفيّ *kūfiy*, (pl. كوفيّون *kūfiyūn*) Native of Kūfa in Chaldea.

A كوفيّة *kūfiyat*, A kind of female garment.

P كوك *kok*, Lettuce, a soporiferous lettuce. A cough. Long stitches in sewing, called basting. Tuning an instrument. A dome, cupola. كوك كردن *kok kardan*, To tune, accord, make even, harmonize. *Kūk*, A bow. A very loud noise.

P كوكا *kawkā*, Tumult, loud noise. The moon.

A كوكاة *kawkāt*, A dwarf.

P كوكان *kokān*, Apparatus of fuller or bleacher.

A كوكب *kawkab*, (pl. كواكب *kawākib*) A star. A little star formed by nails on the sole of a shoe. Any thing shining of a round figure. The white of the eye. The pupil of the eye. A flower. A tall plant. The lustre (of a sword). A mountain. A woman's name. A fountain, jet-d'eau. Water. A mushroom, fungus, puff. Nocturnal dew. The greater part of any thing. A prince, chief, general. A cavalier. An armed man. A youth at the age of puberty. Talc. Intenseness of heat. A sword. A nail, pin. A prison. A strip of land whose colour differs from the other part. كوكب شاموس *kawkabi shāmūs*, Samian earth. ذهبوا تحت كل كوكب *zahabū tahta kulli kawkabin*, They were dispersed everywhere, under every star.

P كوكبا *kawkabā*, (in zand and Pāzand) A star.

A كوكبة *kawkabat*, (v. n. of كوكب Q) Shining (star); glittering (steel). A star. Crowd, company.

P كوكبوس *kawkbūs* or *kawakbūs*, Crooked, bent.

P كوكبه *kawkaba*, A polished steel ball suspended to a long pole and carried as an ensign before the king. A concourse of people. A royal train, retinue, cavalcade. Splendour.

P كوكلك *koklak*, The pod which contains the cotton before it is ripe.

P كوكله *kokila* or *kawkala*, A kind of hoopoo.

P كوكما *kokmā*, (in zand in Pāzand) The sun.

P كوكن *kokan*, An owl. Unripe parched grain.

P كوكنار *koknār*, Poppy (after the opium has flowed from it they bruise and boil the heads, the oil of which, called koknār, has a strong inebriating quality).

P كوكنك *kokanak*, A small owl.

P كوكو *kūkū*, A fried egg, fritter. The cooing of a dove.

A كوكوة *kawkawat*, (v. n. of كوكو Q) Walking like a dwarf. Hastening, making haste.

P كوكوز *kūkūz*, A kind of embroidered silk.

P كوكوه *kawkawa*, An owl.

P كوكه *koka*, An owl. A little round cake.

P كول *kol*, A pond or reservoir. An owl. *Kūl*, The shoulder. The back. The back of a hill or mountain. A carp. A salmon-trout. A ford, shallow water, ditch, or place where water stagnates. Inexperienced, rude. *Kawal*, A baggage-horse, clumsy and slow. Leather of a large coarse sheep-skin. A coarse kind of woollen stuff. Name of a town in Persia.

P كولاب *kolāb*, A pond, reservoir. A large wave. Name of a district in Badakhshān; also of a town.

P كولاج *kūlāj*, A certain kind of sweetmeat.

P كولاك *kolāk*, A large wave.

A كولان *kawlān* or *kūlān*, The plant papyrus.

P كولان *kawalān*, Name of a mountain. Name of an aquatic plant from which mats are made.

P كولانج *kūlānj*, A kind of sweetmeat. Cholic.

P كولاويان *kūlāwiyān*, Able wrestlers.

P كولپر *kūlipar*, Name of an herb.

A كُولة *kuwulat*, (v. n. of كال) Transferring, buying, or selling a debt.

A كولح *kawlah*, Ugly, hideous.

P كولخ *kolakh*, Name of a champion. *Kūlakh*, A chafing-dish.

A كولع *kawlaʿ*, Filth, nastiness, dirt.

P كولغنچه *kūlghuncha*, Red paint for the face.

P كولك *kolak*, A hollow gourd or calabash in which women put their cotton for spinning.

P کولم *kawlam*, Black pepper.

P کولنج *kūlanj*, Cholic. Lumbago. A fire-hearth. A chafing-dish. Name of a note in music.

P کولنگ *kolang*, A sodomite.

P کوله *kola*, A place where hunters lie to surprise their game. Foolish, stupid, dull, ignorant. Short, dwarfish. A bastard. A porcupine, hedgehog.

P کولیدن *kolīdan*, To dig, excavate, hollow out. To eradicate, tear out, pluck up.

A کوم *kawm*, (v. n. of کام for کوم) Leaping (as a horse upon the mare). Lying with. Pudenda. *Kūm*, A herd of camels. *Kawam*, (v. n. of کوم) Having a large bunch (a camel).

P کوم *kūm*, Hay. Dry herbage growing in ploughed ground. The bog-rush.

A کوماء *kawmāʼ*, Large-bunched (she-camel).

P کوماج *kūmāj*, (or کوماچ) Unleavened bread.

A کومة *kawmat*, (v. n. of کام for کوم) Lying with. *Kūmat*, (pl. کیمان *kīmān*) A high heap of earth.

A کومح *kawmah*, Large-hipped. One whose teeth so fill his mouth as to prevent him from articulating distinctly.

P کومر *kūmar*, (in zand and Pāzand) A pear.

P کومش *kūmish*, A well-digger.

A کومل *kawmal*, Name of a fort in Yaman.

P کومه *koma*, A straw-hut or shed for sheltering those who watch the fields. *Kūma*, A coat of mail.

A کون *kawn*, (v. n. of کان for کون) Being, becoming, happening. Continuing at. Being permanent and firm. Becoming surety for another. Staying, stopping. Thinking, supposing, fancying. (pl. اکوان *akwān*) Essence, existence, entity. Nature, the universe. Any thing novel or original. Motion. Rest, quiescence. کون و مکان *kawn u makān*, The universe, world, every created being. لکونه *likawnihi*, Because of its being or its existence.

P کون *kūn*, The backside. کون خاریدن *kūn khārīdan*, To scratch the backside, (met.) To be ashamed, to be sorry. کون خر *kūni khar*, The fundament of an ass, (met.) A great fool. Mischievous, depraved. سوراخ کون *sūrākhi kūn*, The arse-hole. *Kawan* or *kuwan*, A sodomite. *Kuwin* or *kawan*, A concourse of people assembled on the tenth of the first month. *Kuwan*, A kind of willow.

P کونج *kawinj*, A falcon. Coriander.

P کون خري *kūn-kharī*, Evil, wickedness. Folly.

P کونده *kawanda*, A net made of straw or long grass in which they carry about dry cow-dung for sale. An unripe melon. A corn-sack.

P کونسته *kūnasta*, Buttocks of man or horse.

P کونه *kūna*, Buttocks of man or horse.

P کوني *kūnī*, A catamite.

A کوني *kawnīy*, Existent. *Kūnīy*, Very aged.

P کونیان *kūnyān*, Sleep.

P کونیز *kawnīz*, A basket of oats. A measure (especially one of 24 lbs.).

A کونین *kawnayn*, (dual. of کون *kawn*) Both worlds; both kinds of beings, corporeal and spiritual, men and angels.

A کوود *kaʼūd*, (A mountain) of difficult ascent.

P کوود *kavūd*, (for کبود *kabūd*) Blue.

A کوولة *kuʼūlat*, (v. n. of کال) Transferring, buying, or selling a debt.

A کوه *kawh*, (v. n. of کاه for کوه) Bidding a person breathe in one's face (to discover if he be drunk). *Kawah*, (v. n. of کوه) Being astonished, confounded.

P کوه *koh* or *kūh*, A mountain, hill. کوه ابراهیم *kohi ibrāhīm*, Name of a mountain in Karmania. کوه اخضر *kohi akhzar*, The green mountain, *i.e.* The mountain Kāf. کوه اسد *kohi asad*, A burning mountain, volcano. کوه بکوه *koh ba koh*, From mountain to mountain. کوه تیغ *kohitegh*, A mountain of light, a blaze of light. کوه جلیل *kohi jalīl*, Name of a mountain in which Noah dwelt, and from which the first waters of the flood gushed out. کوه رحمت *kohi rahmat*, Name of a mountain near Mecca. کوه رونده *kohi rawanda*, A moving mountain, (met.) A horse. کوه محروق *kohi mahrūk*, Name of a black mountain on the confines of ارمن *arman*. کوه نور *kohi nūr*, The mountain of light, a name given to a large and celebrated diamond. قلهٔ کوه *kullaʼi koh*, The peak of a mountain. آفتاب بکوه رفتن *āftāb ba koh raftan*, To die. *Kuwa*, The pod which contains the cotton; the seed-vessel of any plant. A silkworm's pod.

P کوهامون *ko-hāmūn*, A table-mountain.

P کوهان *kohān*, A saddle for a horse. A camel's bunch. The hump of a camel or of the Indian ox. کوهان ثور *kohāni sawr*, The hump on an ox's back. (metaphorically) The Pleiades.

P کوه بر کوه *koh bar koh*, A kind of amber.

P کوه بودنده *koh-būdanda*, A mountaineer. An anchoret.

P کوه پاره *koh-pāra*, A piece of a mountain. A horse (this meaning is metaphorical).

P کوه پایه *koh-pāya*, The base or foot of a mountain. A mountainous tract.

P کوه پشت *koh-pusht*, Curved, hump-backed.

P کوه پیکر *koh-paykar*, In form, a mountain.

P کوهج *kūhij*, The oxyacanth-fruit. A bramble.

P کوه جگر *koh-jigar*, Valiant, courageous.

P کوهچه *kohcha*, A hillock, small mountain.

P کوه خر *koh-khar*, The onager, mountain-ass.

A کوهد *kawhad*, Tremulous from age.

P کوهري *kūharī*, Exchange, equal return.

P کوهریدن *kūharīdan*, To exchange; to substitute one thing in the place of another.

P کوهسار *kohsār*, Mountainous; hilly country.

P کوهستان *kohistān*, A forest, a place surrounded with mountains or forests, and almost impassible. Persian Irāk (ancient Parthia). Samarkand.

P کوه فحم *koh-fahm*, Name of a black mountain, whose stones are burnt to make soap. Mountain-coal.

P کوهکن *koh-kan*, One who cuts through mountains. Name of Farhād, lover of Shīrīn. A horse.

P کوه کوب *koh-kob*, A horse. A camel. Name of فرهاد *farhād*, the lover of شیرین *shīrīn*.

P کوه گین *koh-gin*, A lord, master, great man.

P کوهم *kohim*, (pronounced *koim*) Name of an herb which grows amongst corn.

P کوه مزوه *koh-mazwa*, A disease in the eye.

P کوهنگ *kohang*, Jumping up, rising.

P کوه نورد *koh-naward*, Traversing mountains.

P کوهه *koha*, The hunch of a camel or ox. The prominent parts of a saddle before and behind. A saddle. Height; any thing high and elevated. A hillock, knoll. A wave. Fear, terror. An attack, a charge. A fairy. کوههٔ آب *kohaʼi āb*, A large wave, billow. کوههٔ آسمان *kohaʼi āsmān*, The height of heaven. کوهه بر آوردن *koha bar āwardan*, To toss its waves (as the sea). زین کوهه *zin-koha*, The stuffing of a saddle, cushion, saddle-cloth.

P کوهها موي *kohhā-mūy*, A boy's game, in which hair is hidden in a heap of wet earth.

P کوهه گرفته *koha-girifta*, Bewitched.

P کوهي *kohī*, Mountainous. A mountaineer. The medlar.

P کوهیج *kūhīj*, A medlar. Burnt lime.

P کوهین *kohīn*, An herb growing amongst corn.

P کوي *kūy*, A town, village. A side, quarter, district. A turn-again lane, a street without a thoroughfare. کوي هفتاد راه *kūyi haftād rāh*, The world.

A کوئ *kawaʼ*, (pl. of کوّة *kawwat*) Windows. *Kuwaʼ*, (pl. of کوّة *kūwat*) Windows, small apertures for the admission of light.

A کويّ *kuwayy*, Name of a star.

A کوّي *kūwīy*, Belonging to a window.

P کو یافت *kū-yāft*, A foundling, bastard.

P کویچه *kūycha*, A narrow street. A small village. A cell.

P کوي داش *kūy-dāsh*, A fellow-townsman.

P کویر *kiver*, Salt and sour ground, where nothing grows. The vapour called سراب *sarāb*. Wet ground made uneven by the trampling of men or beasts, and afterwards become hard. A fierce lion.

P کویز *kawez*, A hollow place. A corner of a house.

P کویژ *kawīj*, A measure, bushel. A medlar.

P کویست *kuwīst*, A blow. Hurt, injury.

P کویستن *kuwīstan*, *kiwīstan*, or *kawīstan*, To beat, pound, thresh. To shake.

P کویسته *kawīsta*, Beaten, pounded, threshed.

P کویستیدن *kuwīstīdan*, *kiwīstīdan*, or *kawīstīdan*, To beat, pound, thresh.

P کویش *kawish*, (or کویشه) A vessel in which they separate the butter from the churned milk.

P کویل *kawel*, Camomile-flowers.

P کویله *kawela* or *kūyala*, A lock of hair on the crown of the head.

P کوین *kuwīn*, A basket made from palm-leaves, used by oil-pressers.

P کویه *kūya*, A sweet esculent herb.

P كوي يافت *kūy-yāft*, A foundling.

P كه *kah*, Straw. Grass. *Ki*, Who? what? which? Whom. That. While, whereas. Lest. When. Lo! behold! Whether. For, because. And. Than. Nay, no. *Ki* is much used as an explanatory particle at the beginning of a sentence, in passing from narrative to the very words used by the speaker: as, ملك عابدي را پرسيد كه اوقات عزيزت چه گونه مي گذرد *malik ʻābiderā pursīd, ki awkāti ʻazīzat chi gūna mī guzarad*, A king asked a certain holy man what? "How are thy precious hours spent?" It may be therefore rendered by, "saying, namely, videlicet." حيران ماندند كه ايا چه چيز است *hayrān māndand, ki ayā chi chīz ast*, They stood astonished, saying, "Oh! what is the matter?" *Kih*, Little. Small, slender. *Kuh*, A hill or mountain. *Kuha*, (for كوهه *koha*) Prominent parts of a saddle before and behind. Bunch of a camel, hump of an Indian ox. A wave.

A كهّ *kahh*, (v. n. of كهّ) Belching in another's face (a drunken man).

P كها *kahā*, Modest, ashamed, bashful.

A كهاء *kihāʼ*, A contending for glory.

P كهاب *kahāb*, A fomentation of hot herbs and drugs for a bruise or wound.

A كهاة *kahāt*, An old fat she-camel. A camel, the skin of whose teats is loose.

A كهال *kihāl*, (pl. of كهل *kahl*) Men of full age, *i.e.* from thirty to fifty. Men beginning to turn grey. *Kuhāl*, Name of a pagan soothsayer.

A كهام *kahām*, Blunt (sword). Slow (tongue). Sluggish (horse). Old and worn-out (man or men).

A كهامة *kahāmat*, (v. n. of كهم) Waxing old.

P كهان *kahān*, The world, the universe. *Kihān*, (pl. of كه *kih*) Little, small.

A كهّان *kuhhān*, (pl. of كاهن *kāhin*) Priests. Prophets, soothsayers.

A كهانة *kahānat*, (v. n. of كهن) Turning prophet, priest, or soothsayer. Soothsaying, auguring. *Kihānat*, Divination, soothsaying. The priesthood.

A كهب *kahb*, An old camel (or, an old buffalo).

P كهب *kuhib* or *kihib*, Disgrace, infamy.

A كهبة *kuhbat*, A ruddy brown (in camels).

P كهبد *kahbad, kahbud, kihbud*, or *kuhbud*, A broker (that examines goods, and buys and sells for others). A king's tax-gatherer. A treasurer. A banker, money-changer. *Kuhbud*, A hermit, recluse. A villager.

P كهبر *kahbar*, Name of a country in India.

A كهبل *kahbal*, A kind of large tree. Barley with large ears. A dwarf.

P كهبل *kuhbal*, (*kahbul*, كهبله *kahbala*, or *kuhbala*) An idiot.

P كهپرك *kahparak*, The brinjal or egg-plant.

P كه پيكر *kuh-paykar*, A huge elephant. A powerful horse (in size a mountain).

A كهّة *kahhat*, A large aged she-camel (whether fat or lean). An old woman.

P كهتاب *kahtāb*, Hot herbs laid on a swelling.

P كهتر *kihtar*, Less, junior, very small, low.

P كهتري *kihtarī*, Littleness, smallness: minority.

P كهترين *kihtarīn*, The least, the smallest.

P كهج *kahj*, The common or wild strawberry. A cherry. *Kuhj*, A large strawberry.

A كهد *kahd*, (v. n. of كهد) Making haste. Causing or ordering to make haste. Being fatigued. Importuning. Labour, endeavour, exertion.

A كهداء *kahdāʼ*, A maid-servant.

A كهدان *kahadān*, (v. n. of كهد) Being swift, running fast (an ass). Being fatigued. Importuning. Causing or ordering one to make haste.

A كهدب *kahdab*, Heavy. Ill with indigestion.

A كهدل *kahdal*, A plump girl; one in the bloom of youth, kept at home from the sight of men. An old woman. A spider. Name of a poet.

A كهر *kahr*, (v. n. of كهر) Advancing (as the day), being hot or bright. Assuming a severe, indignant look, giving a contemptuous reception. Oppressing, subjugating. Shouting. Laughing. Playing, amusing one's self. Forming a matrimonial alliance, marrying into a family.

P كهر *kuhar*, A chesnut or bay colour (particularly in a horse or mule).

P كهرام *kuhrām*, Name of a fort in Hindūstān.

P كهربا *kah-rubā*, Attracting straws, *i.e.* Amber.

P كهربا خاصيّت *kah-rubā-khāṣiyat*, Having an attractive virtue, or the properties of amber.

P كهربا رنگ *kah-rubā-rang*, Amber-coloured, yellow. Possessed of the virtues of amber. Quick, light-fingered. A robber.

P كهرم *kuhram*, Name of a champion of Tūrān.

A كهرور *kuhrūr*, (or كهرورة *kuhrūrat*) A scowl, grim look. A scolder, chider, rebuker, or railer.

P كهره *kahra*, A kid six months old.

P كهزك *kahzak*, Mustard-seed: nosesmart: rocket.

P كهزل *kahzal*, The herb nosesmart. Rocket.

P كهسار *kuhsār*, Mountainous. A mountain-peak.

P كهست *kihist*, A stone.

P كهستان *kuhistān*, Persian Irāk (Parthia).

P كهسته *kuhasta*, (or كهشته *kuhashta*) A cup full of water. An idiot, simpleton.

P كهسله *kahsala*, A fool.

A كهف *kahf*, (pl. كهوف *kuhūf*) A cave. A large cavern, grotto. An asylum, especially a cave dug by men, or formed by nature, in a mountain. A place of refuge. Speed in running or walking. كهف الراجين *kahfu'r rājīn*, The asylum of supplicants. كهف القوم *kahfu'l kawm*, A chief or leader of the people. اصحاب كهف *as-hābi kahf*, The companions of the cave, *i.e.* the seven sleepers. This is founded on a legend of seven young Christians of Ephesus, who fled, they say, from the persecution of the Emperor Decius, and slept in a cave, accompanied only by their dog, for 309 years. Muhammad has adopted this story in the 18th chapter of the Kur'ān.

A كهكامة *kahkāmat*, A timid, terrified man.

P كهكان *kuh-kān*, One who breaks rocks in pieces, or who digs through mountains. Name of Farhād.

A كهكاهة *kahkāhat*, Fearful, afraid. A fat girl.

P كهكاهي *kahkāhī*, A kind of dervish's cap.

A كهكب *kahkab*, The brinjal or egg-plant.

P كهكشان *kahkashān*, The milky-way, galaxy.

A كهكم *kahkam*, Timid. Aged. The egg-plant.

P كه كوب *kuh-kob*, A horse. A camel. Farhād.

A كهكهة *kahkahat*, The roaring of a lion. The braying of a camel. A warming of the hands with the breath. Heat, warmth.

P كهگل *kah-gil*, Plaster of mud and straw.

A كهل *kahl*, (pl. كهول *kuhūl*, كهلون *kahlūn*, كهلان *kuhlān*, كهال *kihāl*, and كهّل *kuhhal*) Of full age, *i.e.* from 30 to 50. A full-grown, flourishing plant. A man beginning to grow grey and venerable. طارله طائر كهل *tāra lahu tāʼirun kahlun*, He has worldly happiness and good fortune.

A كهلان *kahlān*, Name of a man; also of a tribe. *Kuhlān*, (pl. of كهل *kahl*) Men beginning to turn grey.

A كهلة *kahlat*, (pl. كهلات *kahlāt* or *kahalāt*) A middle-aged woman.

P كهلم *kahlam*, The brinjal or egg-plant.

A كهلول *kuhlūl*, A great laugher. Noble, generous.

A كهلون *kahlūn*, (pl. of كهل *kahl*) Full-grown men.

P كهله *kahla*, Current silver: bits of gold or silver.

A كهم *kahm*, (v. n. of كهم) Depressing, dispiriting, dejecting one (misfortune).

A كهمس *kahmas*, Short of stature. A lion. Ugly-faced. (A she-camel) with a large bunch.

A كهمسة *kahmasat*, (v. n. of كهمس Q) Being close together, and kicking up the dirt (the feet).

A كهمل *kahmal*, A dwarf. Heavy, unwholesome. A heavy, disagreeable man, whose society is avoided.

P كهن *kuhan*, Old, ancient. Worn. امرائ كهن سال *umarāʼi kuhan-sāl*, Ancient chiefs. يار كهن *yāri kuhan*, An old friend.

P كهنبار *kahambār*, A stack of straw. *Kuhambār*, A house, habitation. A court. (See كاهبارها).

P كهن پير *kuhan-pīr*, A very old man.

A كهنة *kahanat*, (pl. of كاهن *kāhin*) Priests. Prophets, soothsayers.

P كهنج *kuhunj*, The oxyacanth fruit.

P كهن خرابات *kuhan-kharābāt*, The present transitory world.

P كهن دز *kuhan-diz*, An old fort in Badakhshān.

P كهن دير *kuhan-dayr*, The world. Heaven.

P كهنزه *kahanza*, Yawning, stretching.

P كهن فرش *kuhan-farsh*, The earth.

P كهن گرگ *kuhan-gurg*, (Old wolf) The world.

P كهنگي *kuhnagī*, Old age or clothes. Oldness.

P كهنه *kuhna*, Old, ancient. Inveterate, chronic. Beardless; a youth. كهنه شدن *kuhna shudan*, To become old or inveterate. جامۀ كهنه *jāmaʼi kuhna*, An old or tattered garment.

P کهني *kihnī*, A winter-house. A bear.

P کهود اليدين *kahūdu'l yadayn*, Swift (she-ass).

A کهوف *kuhūf*, (pl. of کهف) Caves, caverns.

A کهول *kahwal* or *kahūl*, A spider. *Kuhūl*, (pl. of کهل *kahl*) Full-grown men, *i. e.* from 30 to 50.

A کهولة *kuhūlat*, Cowardice, laziness.

A کهوه *kuhūh*, (v. n. of کهّ) Being decrepit. Breathing in another's face, making the sound که *kah*.

P کهوين *kuhwīn*, Old.

P کهي *kihe*, Name of a fortress in Sīstān.

A کهي *kuha'*, A being weak or cowardly.

P کهيانا *kahyānā*, The herb piony.

P کهيچ *kahech*, Name of a fortress in Sīstān.

P کهير *kaher*, A wild apple, medlar.

P کهيلا *kahīlā*, Name of a champion of Irān.

P کهيله *kahīla*, Name of a medicinal bark.

P کهيم *kahīm*, Old, decrepit.

P کهين *kihīn*, (or کهينه *kihīna*) Least, less, younger. The little finger. A medlar.

P کي *kay*, When? A great king. A strong giant, genie. Any one of the four elements. Clear, pure, innocent, elegant, graceful. Noble, excellent. Just. کي قباد *kay kubād*, Cyaxares. کي کاوس *kay kāwus*, Darius the Mede. کي خسرو *kay khusraw*, Cyrus or Chosroes; the three first kings of the Kayānian or second Persian Dynasty. *Kī*, Who? which? what?

A کي *kay*, That, in order to, in order that. How?

A کيّ *kayy*, (v. n. of کوي) Marking with a brand. Cauterizing the skin. Stinging (as a scorpion). Looking intently at. A mark burnt upon the skin. A cautery.

A کيء *kay*, (v. n. of کاْ for کيأ) Fearing. Weak, pusillanimous (man).

P کيا *kiyā*, A king, protector, defender. A hero, champion. A lord, master. A lord marcher, landgrave, margrave. A peasant. Powerful. Work, labour. The four elements. Pure, clear, innocent. Heat, cold, dryness, or moisture. The mouth. Mastich.

P کياباد *kayābād*, Power, dominion.

A کياْة *kay,at*, (v. n. of کاْ for کيأ) Dreading, fearing. Weak, pusillanimous, timid.

A کئاج *ki,āj*, Folly, stupidity, with badness of disposition, and an impediment in the speech.

P کياجور *kayājūr*, Wise, learned.

P کيا خره *kiyā-khura*, (or کيا خوره *kiyā-khwura*) Divine light imparted to enable kings to govern.

P کياخن *kayākhan*, Working slowly, doing any thing imperceptibly, by degrees. Soothing expressions, flattery, with an intention to deceive.

P کياده *kiyāda*, Dishonourable, infamous. Disgrace, infamy.

P کيار *kiyār* or *kuyār*, Slowness, laziness. Name of a plant. بي کيار *bī kiyār*, Brisk, cheerfully.

P کيارا *kayārā*, Grief, trouble. A longing for any thing (particularly in women). Blackness of face from having any thing tight about the neck.

P کيارش *kayārash*, A son of Kay Kubād.

P کي ارمين *kay armīn*, A son of Kay Kubād.

P کيارنگ *kiyārang*, Pure, fair, white, clear.

P کيازند *kiyāzand*, A great king.

A کئاس *ki,ās*, (pl. of کاس *ka,s*) Cups filled with wine. Drinking-cups.

A کياسة *kayāsat* or *kiyāsat*, (v. n. of کاس for کيس) Being quick, ingenious. Sagacity, ingenuity, quickness of parts, vivacity; cunning. صاحب کياست *sāhib kiyāsat*, Ingenious, sagacious.

A کياسم *kayāsim*, Persons of the tribe of Kaysam (now extinct).

A کيّاص *kayyās*, Languid. One who walks with his thighs wide apart.

P کياغ *kiyāgh*, Grass.

A کياکي *kayākī*, (pl. of کيکاة *kaykāt*) Eggs.

P کياگن *kayāgin*, Repugnant, contrary, absurd, improper. Rugged, uneven.

A کيّال *kayyāl*, A measurer of grain, weighman. A title given to a certain silly man who was perpetually weighing dust.

A کيالج *kayālij*, (and کياجلة *kayālijat*) (pl. of کيلجة *kaylajat*) Measures of wheat.

A کيّالي *kayyālī*, Fees for weighing.

P کيان *kayān*, A star. The point made by the compasses at the centre of a circle. (pl. of کي *kay*) Great kings. The surname of the second dynasty of the Persian kings. *Kiyān*, Who? what persons? کيانند *kiyānand*, Who are they? سمع الکيان *sam-ߢu'l kiyān*, Name of a Persian book. *Kuyān* or *kiyān*, A round tent propped by one column.

A کيان *kiyān*, (v. n. of کان for کون) Becoming surety for another. Being, existing. Existence, state, mode of being.

P کيانا *kayānā*, The elements. Heat, cold, dryness, and moisture. Root, foundation. A landgrave.

A کيانة *kiyānat*, (v. n. of کان for کون) Becoming surety for. Suretiship.

P کيان خره *kiyān-khura*, (or کيان خوره *kiyān-khwura*) Divine light, whereby kings reign well, or people are instructed.

P کيانند *kiyānand*, Who are?

P کياني *kayānī*, Royal. کمر کياني *kamari kayānī*, A royal girdle, a precious belt or cincture.

A کيانيات *kiyāniyāt*, Medicine, physic.

P کيانيان *kayāniyān*, The second Persic dynasty.

P کيب *kīb*, Twisting, bending. Confused.

A کئب *ka,ib*, Afflicted, distressed, melancholy.

P کيبو *kībū*, Name of a large bird called دينار *dīnār*. Name of a small motley-coloured bird which builds a hang-nest in trees.

P کيبيدن *kebīdan*, To twist, turn, turn on one side, deviate, to go from place to place.

P کيپا *kaypā*, (in zand and Pāzand) Silver.

P کيپا *kīpā*, A sheep or goat's ventricle stuffed with minced meat and rice. A pudding.

P کيپانيدن *kaypānīdan*, To light a candle. *Kīpānīdan*, To incline. To administer justice.

P کي پشين *kay-pushīn*, A son of Kay Kubād.

P کيپو *kīpū*, Lettuce. Ignorant. The chaffinch. A butterfly.

A کيّة *kayyat*, A place where the skin is cauterized or branded.

P کيت *kīt*, A bee. Astonished. How much, how great. Of what kind or quality.

A کيت *kayta* or *kayti*, Only. Thus. کيت و کيت *kayta wa kayta*, In this or that way.

A کيّت *kayyit*, (or کيت *kayt*) (pl. اکيات *akyāt*) Ingenious, shrewd, clever.

P کيتو *kītū*, Name of a bird said to feed on gravel and sand instead of grain.

A کيثر *kaysar*, Much, many. Liberal, munificent.

P کيثه *kīsa*, Dross of silver.

P کيج *kīj*, An ass which has lost his tail. A quadruped, the lower part of whose mouth is swollen.

P کيچ *kīch*, Distracted, scattered. A species of silken cloth. Small, little. Slow. Name of a country near Sīstān. کيچ کيچ *kīch kīch*, By little and little, slowly.

P کيچه *kīcha*, A lane or narrow road or street.

A کيح *kayh*, (v. n. of کاح for کيح) Making an impression (a sword). *Kayh* or *kīh*, Thick (teeth). *Kayh*, (also کيح اکيح *kayhun akyahu*) A rough, hairy, gross man. *Kīh*, (pl. اکياح *akyāh* and کيوح *kuyūh*) The side of a mountain. *Kayah*, Roughness. Thickness.

P کيخ *kīkh*, Matter which collects in the corner of the eye; dirt which settles on the hands and feet.

A کيخان *kīkhān*, (pl. of کوخ *kūkh*) Huts of reed.

P کيخرس *kaykhurs*, A species of vetch.

P کيخسرو *kay khusraw*, Cyrus. A great monarch.

P کيخسروي *kaykhusrawī*, Name of a note in music.

A کيخم *kaykham*, Great king (a royal title).

P کي خور *kay-khwur*, Treasure.

P کيد *kayd*, A king of Kanūj, whose daughter is said to have been married to Alexander. Solder.

A کيد *kayd*, (v. n. of کاد for کيد) Deceiving, laying snares, entrapping, plotting mischief. Adapting, adjusting, addressing, applying a remedy. Exerting one's self liberally. Being near. Dying. Vomiting, casting forth. Being menstruous (a woman). Using harshness and severity. War. Striking fire (a steel). The loud croak of a raven. Deceit, fraud, stratagem. Malignity, malice. کيد الله *kaydu'llāh*, The recompense of God in kind to those who act deceitfully. لا کيد و لا همّا *lā kayda wa lā hamman*, Neither stratagem or serious design (is purposed by me).

P کيدپا *kaydapā*, Name of a queen of *Bardaঃ*.

A کيذبان *kayzabān* or *kayzubān*, A liar.

P کير *kīr*, Penis. کير و خايه, Penis et testes.

A کير *kīr*, (pl. اکيار *akyār*, کيرة *kiyarat*, and کيران *kīrān*) A smith's bellows.

A کیّر *kayyir*, A horse cock-tailed when running.

A کیران *kīrān*, (pl. of کور *kūr*) Camels' saddles. (pl. of کیر *kīr*) Smiths' bellows.

P کیرآور *kīr-āwar*, (or کیرآورد) Large-yarded.

A کیرة *kiyarat*, (pl. of کیر *kīr*) A smith's bellows.

P کیرخ *kīrakh*, A desk or support for a book.

P کیردارو *kīr-dārū*, Fern, brake.

P کیرکاشي *kīr-kāshī*, (or کیرمان) A dildo.

P کیرو *kīrū*, Custody, care, retention. Memory. Getting the knowledge of a secret.

P کیریان *kīriyān*, An offering by way of expiation or protection from misfortune.

P کیز *kīz*, Felt-cloth.

A کیزان *kīzān*, (pl. of کوز *kūz*) Cups, goblets.

A کیس *kays*, (v. n. of کاس for کیس) Being clever, shrewd (a boy). Excelling in genius. Sagacity, ingenuity, intellect, reason. Coition (especially with moderation and circumspection, without overstraining the natural powers, or touching uncleanness). Medicine. Goodness, beneficence. *Kīs*, (pl. اکیاس *akyās* and کیسة *kiyasat*) A purse. The membrane which envelopes the fœtus in the womb. The scrotum. کیس تفریك *kīsi tafrīk*. A red camelot bag for rubbing the body in a bath.

P کیس *kīs*, A wrinkle, fold.

A کیّس *kayyis*, (pl. کیسیٰ *kīsa'* and اکیاس *akyās*) Ingenious, sagacious, prudent; cunning, shrewd, sly, crafty.

A کیسان *kaysān*, Imposture, perfidy, treachery. امّ کیسان *umm kaysān*, The knee. A kick on the backside. Measure, quantity.

A کیسانیّة *kaysāniyat*, Name of a sect of schismatics called روافض *rawāfiz*. A sect of those who hold the two principles, who maintain that all things were created from water, fire, and earth.

A کیسبة *kaysabat*, A wolf.

A کیسة *kiyasat*, (pl. of کیس *kīs*) Purses.

P کیست *kīst*, Who or what is he?

P کیستار *kīstār*, Torment, torture. A screw.

P کیستان *kīstān*, An oil or wine-press. A churn.

P کیستو *kīstū*, The colocynth or wild gourd.

P کیسر *kesar*, Saffron.

P کیسرگونه *kaysar-gūna*, The herb poley.

A کیسم *kaysam*, The father of a tribe extinct.

P کیسنه *kīsana*, A rope. A clew of thread from the distaff.

P کیسو *kaysū*, The herb poley.

A P کیسوم *kaysūm*, (pl. اکاسم *akāsim*) (A garden) full of herbs, moist and verdant. Dry herbage in large quantities.

P کیسه *kīsa*, A purse either for money or for enclosing letters (when sent to persons of distinction they are generally made of rich silk and muslin). A kind of small sack made of goats' hair, which they put upon their hands, and use in the manner of a flesh-brush; a purse of money containing about 500 dollars. A complete horse-load. کیسه بصابون زدن *kīsa ba sābūn zadan*, To expend. کیسه دوختن *kīsa dokhtan*, To wait for, to expect. کیسهٔ صورت کشادن *kīsaï sūrat kushādan*, To be metamorphosed, to undergo a transformation.

P کیسه بر *kīsa-bur*, A cutpurse.

P کیسه دار *kīsa-dār*, A purse-bearer. A letter-carrier. A forestaller, regrater.

A کیسیٰ *kīsa'*, Ingenious, clever (woman). (pl. of کیّس *kayyis*) Clever, shrewd, sly.

P کیش *kaysh*, Matrimony. A dowry. Muslin, fine cotton cloth. Filth. *Kesh*, Faith, religion, sect. A quiver, case for bows and arrows. A feather, particularly of an arrow. A kind of animal of whose skin they make fur-garments. The box-tree. A kind of linen-garment. A word used to drive away birds; also at chess, as when the king is in check. Name of a city in the isle of Ormūz. (in composition it denotes) Practising: as, ظلم کیش *zulm-kesh*, Oppressive. کافرکیش *kāfir-kesh*, Prone to infidelity. A mistress, a sweetheart.

P کیشمند *kayshmand*, (in zand and Pāzand) Strong, powerful.

A کیص *kays*, Extreme avarice. A swift pace. *Kays*, (and کیصان *kayasān*) (v. n. of کاص for کیص) Abstaining, being cautious from fear. Eating (especially alone or much). Feasting (with any one). Making haste. *Kīs*, Narrow-minded, very covetous. Short and fleshy. *Kiyas*, Very muscular.

A کیّص *kayyis*, Narrow-minded, very covetous. Short and full of flesh.

A کیّص *kiyass*, Very muscular.

A کیصیٰ *kaysa'* or *kīsa'*, One who lives alone, and eats alone, caring only for himself.

A کیع *kayᶜ*, (or کیعوعة *kayᶜūᶜat*) (v. n. of کاع for کیع) Declining, forbearing, abstaining from timidity.

A کیعر *kayᶜar*, Fat (whelp).

P کیغ *kīgh*, Matter in the corners of the eyes.

P کیغا *kayghā*, Distress, affliction. Pain.

P کیغباد *kay-ghubād*, Just, equitable, stedfast in the truth. Name of the greatest of the ancient kings of Persia. (It is now written کیقباد *kay-kubād*).

A کیف *kayf*, (v. n. of کاف for کیف) Cutting. Hilarity, good humour, high spirits produced by drinking or chewing bang. *Kayfa*, How? How! How, in what manner. کیف شاء *kayf shāᵃ*, At his pleasure. فکیف *fa kayfa*, How then! How much the more.

P کیفال *kīfāl*, A scoundrel: a loose, dissolute fellow. A frequenter of stews. Fond of wine and women.

P کیفانیدن *kīfānīdan*, To incline. To administer justice.

A کیفة *kīfat*, A section, segment. A patch in the front skirt of a shirt.

P کیفتن *kīftan*, To do justice. To incline.

P کیفر *kayfar*, A return for good or evil, repayment, reward, exchange. Thirst for revenge. Repentance. A river. A vessel of a peculiar form, in which sour coagulated milk is prepared. Calamity, affliction, injury, oppression. Name of a certain impregnable fort. *Kayfar* or *kīfar*, A stone placed on the battlements of a fortress, ready to be rolled on any assailant.

P کیفسام *kayfasām*, The keeping of a secret.

A کیفما *kayfamā*, In whatever manner, in whatsoever way.

P کیفوس *kayfūs*, Connivance, lenity.

P کیفه *kayfa*, The palm of the hand.

A کیفي *kayfī*, Intoxicated. Any thing of an intoxicating nature.

A کیفیّة *kayfiyat*, Quality, mode, story, statement, account, relation, state, detailed circumstances, particulars, news. Hilarity, mirth caused by drinking. کیفیّت تسخیر *kayfiyati tashkhīr*, The manner of attack. کیفیّت راسخه *kayfiyati rāsikha*, A fixed, permanent quality. کیفیّت عارضیّة *kayfiyati ᶜārizīya*, A moveable or accidental quality.

P کیقباد *kaykubād*, A great king. Name of a king of Irān.

P کیك *kayk*, A flea. کیك درپاچه افکندن *kayk dar pācha*, (پازه *pāza*, or شلوار *shalwār*) *afkandan*, To throw a flea into (another's) trowsers, (met.) To disturb, disquiet, render fidgetty. *Kīk*, A man. The pupil of the eye. *Kiyak*, A kind of fruit. A cat. An ash-coloured horse.

A کیکاء *kaykāᵃ*, Worthless, good for nothing.

P کیکاوس *kay-kāwus*, Just, noble. Name of a king of Persia.

A کیکة *kaykat*, (or کیکیّة *kaykīyat*) (pl. کیاکي *kayākī*) An egg.

P کیکن *kīkin* or *kīkan*, Darkness. Solder.

P کیکیر *kaykīr*, (کیکیز *kīkīz*, کیکیش *kaykīsh*, or *kīkīsh*) The herb rocket.

A کیل *kayl*, (v. n. of کال for کیل) Measuring (grain). Measuring out to any one. Weighing (money). Satisfying (as regards measure). Computing or measuring (one thing by another). Failing (as a flint and steel to strike fire). A measure of grain; also of other dry goods and liquids. Heat, also cold, with certain modifications of both. Sparks struck with flint and steel.

P کیل *kīl*, Crooked. Anxious, longing. Dressed in a warm blanket. *Kiyal*, Name of a fruit. A medlar.

A کیّل *kayyil*, Refuse, chaff. The best and choicest of any thing.

A کیلا *kay lā*, Lest, that not.

A کیلة *kaylat*, Measure. *Kīlat*, Any thing measured. The mode of measuring.

A کیلجة *kaylajat*, (pl. کیالجة *kayālijat* and کیالج *kayālij*) A corn-measure of 3 lbs. 3 qrs., or 1 and $\frac{7}{8}$ths of a منا *mana'*.

P کیلدار *kayl-dār*, One who over-sees the measurement of grain, or an officer employed to attend the measurement of grain.

P کیلك *kiyalak*, A medlar.

P كيلكان *kīlakān*, A certain black medicinal wood from the shores of the Caspian. A sort of leek.

P كيلو *kīlū*, A pond, ditch. A place on the bank of a river or other piece of water where the Muhammadans ease and purify themselves before performing their religious ablutions. *Kiyalū*, A medlar.

P كيلواس *kīlwās*, Name of a city, the birth-place of the Hindū saint شاكموني *shākmūnī*.

G كيلوس *kaylūs*, Chyle.

P كيله *kīla*, A measure of corn.

A كيم *kīm*, (in Himyaritic) A master, an owner.

A كيما *kaymā*, Why? In order to.

P كيماك *kī* or *kaymāk*, A sort of surcingle with which they secure the loads of asses and camels. Name of a city in Tartary, and of a river. Cream.

P كيمال *kīmāl*, A weasel. A certain furred animal.

A كيمان *kīmān*, (pl. of كومة *kūmat*) Hillocks, heaps.

A كيماوي *kīmāwiy*, An alchymist. A deceiver.

P كيمخاب *kīmkhāb*, Brocaded silk.

P كيمخت *kīmukht*, The back-leather of a horse or ass, shagreen. A wrinkled skin. كيمخت ماه *kīmukhti māh*, The sky.

P كيمختي *kīmukhtī*, Made of kīmukt.

P كيمخواب *kīmkhwāb*, Brocade.

A كيمر *kaymar*, Name of غالب *ghālib*, grandfather of the satirical poet فرزدق *farazdak*.

A كيموح *kaymūḥ*, Imminent, impending. Earth.

G كيموس *kaymūs*, Humour. Chyme.

P كيمونستن *kīmūnistan*, (in zand and Pāzand) To request, beg, ask.

P A كيمياء *kīmiyā*, Fraud, deceit, art. Chemistry, alchymy; the philosopher's stone. Lead. Love. The sagacity of an instructor, or guide. Elixir. The basis of gold and silver. كيمياء اكبر *kīmiyāʼi akbar*, The grand alchymy, the philosopher's stone or tincture, of which they say مشهور الاسم و معدوم الجسم *mashhūru'l ism wa maʻdūmu'l jism*, A name celebrated, but the existence unknown. P كيمياي جان *kīmiyāyi jān*, Wine. A كيمياء معاني *kīmiyāʼi maʻānī*, The chemistry of meanings, *i.e.* the study of truth. اهل كيميا *ahli kīmiyā*, An alchymist. A deceiver, cheat.

A كيميا اثر *kīmiyā-asar*, Effective as chemistry.

P كيمياگر *kīmiyāgar*, An alchymist. A deceiver. A lover.

P كيمياگري *kīmiyāgarī*, Love. Alchymy.

A كين *kayn*, (v. n. of كان for كين) Being humble and submissive. (pl. كيون *kuyūn*) A caruncle, gland within the matrix.

P كين *kīn*, Hatred, enmity, rancour, malice. Revenge. كين ايرج *kīni īraj*, (or كينهٔ ايرج *kīnaʼi īraj*) Name of the nineteenth note of the bārbud. كين سياوش *kīni siyāwush*, (or كينهٔ سياوش *kīnaʼi siyāwush*) Name of the twentieth note of the bārbud. كين گرفتن *kīn giriftan*, To conceive resentment. *Kʼīn*, (for كه اين *ki īn*, written also كاين) Which, for, because, that this.

A كينا كينا *kīnā kīnā*, Chinchina, a medicinal bark.

P كينال *kīnāl*, A sot, drunkard.

A كينة *kaynat*, The lote-tree. Security, caution, bail. *Kīnat*, Bad situation, plight, ill-luck.

P كين توز *kīn-toz*, One who foments dissensions and law-suits; malevolent-minded.

P كين گذار *kīn-guzār*, A revenger of injuries; full of fury, athirst for vengeance.

P كينور *kīnwar*, Malevolent, inimical.

A كينونة *kaynūnat*, (v. n. of كان for كون) Being, existing. Happening, coming to pass.

P كينه *kīna*, Hatred, rancour, malevolence. كينه داشتن *kīna dāshtan*, To hate. كينه كشيدن *kīna kashīdan*, To take vengeance. باكس كينه گرفتن *bā kas kīna giriftan*, To conceive hatred against any one. دشمن كينه خواه *dushmani kīna-khwāh*, A mortal foe. سينهٔ پر كينه *sīnaʼi pur kīna*, A breast full of enmity or revenge.

P كينه خواه *kīna-khwāh*, Malevolent, vindictive.

P كينه خواهي *kīna-khwāhī*, Malevolence, vindictiveness, thirst for vengeance.

P كينه كش *kīna-kash*, Revengeful. Name of the twelfth day of the month.

P كينه كشي *kīna-kashī*, Vindictiveness, revenge.

P كينه گاه *kīna-gāh*, A field of battle. Any place of quarrel.

P كينه ور *kīnawar*, Hostile, malicious, spiteful, revengeful, rancorous.

P كيو *kayū*, Lettuce. A bier. Cause, motive.

P كيوان *kaywān*, The planet Saturn; likewise his orbit. A bow. The seventh heaven.

A كيوح *kuyūḥ*, (pl. of كيح or كاح) Mountain-sides.

P كيود *kayūd*, (or كيوده) Cause, motive, matter.

P كيوس *kayūs*, Name of an island where they sold عذرا *ʻazrā*, mistress of وامق *wāmik*. Name of the brother of Anoshīrwān. *Kiyos*, Curved, crooked.

P كيوغ *kayūgh*, Clay unmixed with straw.

A كيول *kayyūl*, The rear of an army, the rear-rank. Timid, pusillanimous. High or projecting ground. Gold-filings. Refuse, chaff. The best and choicest of any thing.

P كيومرث *kayūmars*, (also كيومرت *kayūmart*) Name of the first of Adam's offspring who ever exercised regal authority. He is generally considered as the first king of the Peshdādian dynasty, and is sometimes confounded with Adam and Noah.

A كيون *kuyūn*, (pl. of كين *kayn*) Caruncles.

P كيوه *kaywa*, Lettuce. Name of a plant that bears a fragrant fruit. *Kīwa*, A kind of cotton-shoe used chiefly in Persia by prize-runners.

A كيوي *kayawiy*, Belonging to the particle كي *kay*; That, in order that.

A كيه *kayh*, (v. n. of كاه for كيه) Desiring a person to breathe in one's face (to discover if he be drunk).

P كيه *kiya*, Mastich.

A كيّه *kayyih*, A man odious and shunned on account of his deceitfulness.

A كيهاء *kayhāʼ*, An old fat she-camel.

P كيهان *kīhān* or *kayhān*, The world.

P كيهان خديو *kīhān-khidīv*, Lord of the world. The universal monarch, *i.e.* God.

P كيه كيه *kayha kayha*, (or كيهه *kayha*) So-and-so.

P كيهونستن *kīhūnistan*, (in zand and Pāzand) To spring up, to grow, to be fresh and green.

P كيهوئيدن *kīhūʼīdan*, (in zand and Pāzand) To come up, to grow.

P كيهه *kīha*, The bramble. A kind of ivy.

A كيّ *kayy*, Fearful.

P كيِي *kiʼī*, Who art thou?

A كئيب *kaʼīb*, Afflicted, distressed, melancholy.

A كيئة *kayʼat*, (v. n. of كاءَ for كيأ) Fearing. Weak, pusillanimous (man).

P كيش *kaorkiyish*, Conqueror, tyrant, oppressor.

A كييكة *kuyaykat*, (and كييكية *kuyaykiyat*) (dim. of كيكة *kaykat*) A little egg.

A كيئن *kayʼin*, How many?

گ

گ *gāf*, (called كاف فارسي *kāfi fārsī* or كاف عجمي *kāfi ʻajamī*) The twenty-sixth letter of the Persian alphabet, the power of which is precisely that of *g* before *a, e, o, u*. In manuscripts it is often confounded with ك *kāf*, as well in sound as shape; and some words will be found indifferently spelled with either. It is interchangeable with غ *ghayn*.

P گابارة *gābāra*, A cavern or a cleft in a rock. A herd of cows.

P گاخوارة *gākhwāra*, A cradle.

P گادن *gādan*, To embrace, lie with.

P گادة *gāda*, Lain with, depucelated.

P گار *gār*, A particle which, subjoined to a word, denotes agency or possession: as, آمرزگار *āmurzgār*, سازگار *sāzgār*, ستمگار *sitamgār*, خدمتگار *khidmatgār*.

P گاري *gārī*, Frail, unsteady, inconstant (thing).

P گاز *gāz*, Shears, scissors. Pincers, tweezers, snuffers. The teeth; biting the lips or any other part with the teeth; biting, chewing. Seizing, taking away. Pasturage. A cavern in a rock. A hole or trench dug in the ground as a shelter for men and cattle. A hermitage on the top of a hill.

P گازر *gāzur*, A bleacher, fuller. A wagtail.

P گازرك *gāzurak*, A wagtail.

P گازرگاه *gāzur-gāh*, (The bleaching-ground) Name of a place at Shīrāz where the Shaykh Sādī lies interred; also of a place in Harāt, containing the remains of Khʼājah Abdu'llāh Ansārī.

P گازري *gāzurī*, Bleaching. گازري كردن *gāzurī kardan*, To wash, bleach, or full.

P گازه *gāza*, A small gardener's hut covered with a coarse cloth (to which the world is sometimes compared). A swing. A cradle. A hermitage on a hill. The lurking-place of a hunter.

P گازي *gāzi*, Name of a sweet-smelling flower.

P گاژ *gāj*, A place, situation. A stage.

P گاشاك *gāshāk*, A sausage made of the small guts stuffed with meat and condiments.

P گاشتن *gāshtan*, To turn, cause to revolve.

P گاف *gāf*, Name of the letter گ. Boasting. A crack, fissure. Exceeding bounds.

P گاگا *gāgā*, Any thing given at entertainments with wine, as fruits or sweetmeats.

P گال *gāl*, Far, distant. The pod in which the cotton is produced. A sort of millet. A jackal. A cock. Rolling, tumbling. Deceit, fraud, imposture. A species of spider. Dung hanging to the wool of a sheep's tail.

P گالبنگ *gāl-bang*, Name of an intoxicating herb growing amongst wheat.

P گاله *gāla*, Far, distant. A ball of carded cotton. A bag made of wool and hair.

P گاليچه *gālicha*, A magpie.

P گام *gām*, A step, pace. The distance between the feet in walking. A foot's length. A cubit. The jaw. The palate. The uvula. A bridle. A village. گام زدن *gām zadan*, To step. گام نهادن *gām nihādan*, To go, to travel.

P گاموس *gāmūs*, A buffalo.

P گاميدن *gāmīdan*, To go, walk, step, travel.

P گاميش *gāmesh*, A buffalo.

P گان *gān*, Coition. A whore. Worthy, fit, proper. A tyrannical king. Joining, uniting. گان دادن *gān dādan*, To play the whore. *Gān* at the end of a word terminating in silent ه *he* forms the plural number when the ه *he* is dropped; as from ايستاده *īstāda*, Standing, is formed ايستادگان *īstādagān*, Those who are standing.

P گانداده *gān-dāda*, An infamous boy. A whore.

P گانگاه *gān-gāh*, The nuptial-bed.

P گانور *gānūr*, A fruit-basket.

P گانه *gāna*, A redundant particle used after numerals: as, هفت گانه *haft gāna*, Seven.

P گاني *gānī*, A whore. An infamous boy.

P گاو *gāu*, *gāo*, *gāw*, or *gāv*, A bull. A bullock. A cow. A drinking-vessel made in the shape of an ox. Bold, intrepid. A land-measure of about six miles. گاو دياس *gāvi diyās*, A threshing-ox. گاو زادن *gāv zādan*, To inherit. To derive advantage from. گاوزر *gāvi zar*, (or گاو زرّين *gāvi zarrīn*) A golden cup made in the form of an ox. Name of the golden calf made by سامري *sāmirī*, a relation of Moses. گاو زرّين *gāvi zarrīn*, Name of a green-coloured animal of the beetle-kind. گاو زمين *gāvi zamīn*, The energy implanted by the Creator in the heart of the earth. گاو سفالين *gāvi sifālīn*, An earthen vessel made in the shape of an ox. گاو سيمين *gāvi sīmīn*, A silver cup made in the form of an ox. گاو كار *gāvi kār*, (or گاو ورزه *gāvi warza*) A working-ox. گاو فلك *gāvi falak*, The sign Taurus. گاو قلبه ران *gāvi kulba-rān*, A ploughing-ox. گاو كوهي *gāvi kohī*, The mountain-cow. گاو گردون *gāvi gardūn*, The sign Taurus. A draught-ox. گاو گلين *gāvi gilīn*, An earthen vessel made in the form of an ox. گاو نه ليسيده *gāvi na līsīda*, Proud, vain; untaught, ignorant of the world (an unlicked cub).

P گاوآب *gāv-āb*, Green scum collected on the surface of stagnant pools, duck-weed.

P گاواره *gāvāra*, A cradle. A herd of oxen.

P گاوآهن *gāv-āhan*, A ploughshare.

P گاوبان *gāwbān*, A herdsman. A bullock-driver. A blacksmith.

P گاو بنده *gāw-banda*, A neatherd.

P گاو بيشه *gāw-besha*, The world.

P گاو پشت *gāw-pusht*, The sky.

P گاو پلنگ *gāw-palang*, A cameleopard.

P گاوپيكر *gāw-paykar*, (or گاو چهر *gāw-chihr*) The mace of Farīdūn, having a head like that of an ox.

P گاو تازي *gāw-tāzī*, Threat, intimidation.

P گاوچشم *gāw-chashm*, or گاوچشمه *gāw-chashma*, Ox-eye (a plant). A fragrant forest-herb resembling camomile. A kind of wild grape. Large-eyed.

P گاود *gāwid*, (in zand and Pāz.) The wild ox.

P گاودشتي *gāw-dashtī*, A wild bull or cow. Adeer.

P گاودل *gāw-dil*, Ignorant, foolish.

P گاودم *gāw-dum*, A cow-tail. A trumpet, tube. Any thing thick at one end and thin at the other. Acclivity, descent.

P گاودنبال *gāw-dumbāl*, A cow-tail. Any thing broad at one end and narrow at the other.

P گاودوش *gāw-dosh*, (گاو دوشنه *gāw-doshna*, or گاودوشه *gāw-doshna*) A vessel for milking, having a broad mouth and narrow bottom. A milking-pail. A churn.

P گاودي *gāwdī*, Ignorant, foolish.

P گاوديده *gāw-dīda*, A kind of bread.

P گاور *gāwr*, An infidel. *Gāwar*, The opoponax.

P گاورزه *gāwarza*, An ox yoked to the plough.

P گاورس *gāwars*, Millet. A kind of vetch. گاورس سيم *gāwarsi sīm*, (A silver vetch) A star. گاورسهٔ نقره گون *gāwarsasi nukra-gūn*, The lustre of a sword. The milky-way.

P گاورشير *gāwar-shīr*, Gum of the opoponax.

P گاورنگ *gāw-rang*, King Farīdūn's mace.

P گاوريش *gāw-rīsh*, (Cow-beard) A fool.

P گاوزاد *gāw-zād*, Unexpected good fortune, an inheritance.

P گاوزبان *gāw-zabān*, Bugloss, ox-tongue (an herb). A plaster. A kind of bread.

P گاوزر *gāw-zar*, A cup made of gold.

P گاوزنه *gāw-zana*, An ox-goad.

P گاوزور *gāw-zor*, Rude, brutal, an able wrestler.

P گاوزوري *gāw-zorī*, Violence.

P گاوزهره *gāw-zahra*, A stone found in the gall-bladder of an ox, considered as an antidote against poison. A coward.

P گاوسار *gāw-sār*, Like an ox. Ox-headed. Name of Farīdūn's mace.

P گاوسر *gāw-sar*, (or گاو سره) Farīdūn's mace.

P گاوسنگ *gāw-sang*, A stone found in the gall-bladder of an ox. An ox-goad.

P گاوش نليسيده *gāwash na līsīda*, Proud, vain. Ignorant of the world.

P گاوشنگ *gāw-shang*, An ox-goad. A sort of pot-herb.

P گاوشيد *gāwshed*, Name of a dreadful dragon, said to have long infested Persia, but killed at length by Cyrus; in commemoration of which event, they add, he built a splendid آتشگاه *ātish-gāh*, or temple to the sun or fire.

P گاوشير *gāw-shīr*, Gum of the opoponax-tree.

P گاوعنبر *gāw-ʿambar*, Ambergris; the Persians believe it to be the excrement of the sea-cow, thrown on shore by the waves, and there concreted by the sun. Sādī calls a stupid man گاوعنبر *gāw-ʿambar*, The ambergris-bullock.

P گاوك *gāwak*, A little ox. A tike or a louse infesting cattle. A kind of mule.

P گاو كار *gāw-kār*, A sown field.

P گاو كون كردن *gāw kūn kardan*, To purify. To ease nature.

P گاوكي *gāwakī*, A kind of mule.

P گاو گون *gāw-gūn*, (Ox-like) Stupid, dull.

P گاو ماده *gāw-māda*, A cow.

P گاو مشنگ *gāu mashang*, Grain like a vetch.

P گاوميش *gāu-mesh*, A buffalo.

P گاو نر *gāw-nar*, A bull.

P گاوو *gāwū*, A mountain-ox.

P گاوه *gāwa*, A wooden wedge. A chief magistrate. The master of a family.

P گاوهيدن *gāwahīdan*, To agitate, shake.

P گاوي *gāwe*, One bull or cow.

P گاويزن *gāwīzan*, A beautiful yellow pigment made from the gall of an ox. The gall of an ox.

P گاويش *gāwīsh*, A vessel for holding milk.

P گاه *gāh*, Time. Place (always in composition). A throne. A golden seat. A noun of time and place. A crucible (for melting gold). The dawn. A bed. A large cushion. The sign Capricorn. An alligator. Office, dignity, public employment. A ditch dug for planting or preserving vines. A dimple in the chin. A bridegroom, wooer, suitor. Sometimes, now and then. آن گاه *ān gāh*, In that time. تختگاه *takht-gāh*, A throne. Residence of a prince. تهي گاه *tihī-gāh*, The waist. دستگاه *dast-gāh*, A workhouse, shop. شكارگاه *shikār-gāh*, A place proper for hunting, a chace. عبادتگاه *ʿibādat-gāh*, A place of worship. منزل گاه *manzil-gāh*, A caravansera, inn, lodging, or halting-place. گاه بگاه *gāh ba gāh*, (or گاه گاه *gāh gāh*) Sometimes, at times, from time to time, now and then. گاه وبي گاه *gāh u bī gāh*, Well-timed or ill-timed, at every turn, at all times. In season and out of season.

P گاهبارها *gāh-bārhā*, (or گاهنبارها *gāhambārhā*) The six days or periods in which (according to the cosmogony of the ancient Persians) God created the world. The first period, called in the language of the Zand ميديوزرم *midyūzaram*, embraces an interval of forty days (forty-five days, HYDE), in which God is said to have created the heavens. The second period is called ميديوسمه *midyūsama*, and is made to comprise a space of sixty days, in which God created the waters. The third period, called پيتي سهيم *piti sahīm*, includes an interval of seventy-five days, in which the earth was created. In the fourth period, called ايا تهريم *ayyā tahrīm*, the duration of which is limited to thirty days, the trees and grass were created. The fifth period, called ميدياريم *maydiyārīm*, consists of eighty days, in which the animal tribes were created. In the sixth period, called همشپتمهديم *hamshpatamahdīm*, which lasted for seventy-five days, man was created.

P گاه گاهي *gāh gāhe*, Sometime or other.

P گاهنگان *gāhangān*, The milky-way.

P گاهواره *gāhwāra*, A cradle.

P گاهي *gāhe*, Sometimes. گاهي كه *gāheki* Whenever.

P گاهيدن *gāhidan*, To embrace, to copulate.

P گاهين *gāhīn*, Root of sweet cane.

P گايان *gāyān*, A buffalo. Coition.

P گايه *gāya*, Coition.

P گائيدن *gāīdan*, To embrace, copulate.

P گائيده *gāīda*, A woman depucelated.

P گب *gab*, Large and thick.

P گباره *gubāra*, A herd of oxen.

P گبيبمن *gabibmin*, (in zand and Pāzand) Low (پست *past*). (according to another reading) The back (پشت *pusht*).

P گبر *gabr*, A guebre, ancient Persian, one of the Magi of the sect of Zoroaster, a priest of the worshippers of fire. A pagan, infidel. A plant resembling ginger. A vest. A stone. *Gabr* or *gabar*, A corslet or coat of mail. A helmet. *Gabar*, A kind of transparent stone, whence cups and the like are made. A tent supported by a column. Name of a city.

P گبرآباد *gabr-ābād*, (Habitation of fire-worshippers) The suburbs of Ispahān.

P گبركي *gabrakī*, A vessel for holding wine.

P گبرونت *gabrūnat*, Raining.

P گبري *gabrī*, The Magian religion. Paganism.

P گبز *gabz*, Any thing thick, gross, dense.

P گبست *gabast*, Poison of a serpent. A kind of bitter herb. A kind of wild gourd.

P گبنا *gabnā*, (in zand and Pāzand) A man.

P گبه *gabba*, A cupping-glass.

P گبها *gubhā*, Grass, herbage.

P گپ *gap*, Idle report, gossip, chit-chat, news, false rumour. Word, saying. Thick, gross, dense; large.

P گپتن *guptan*, (for گفتن *guftan*) To say, speak.

P گت *gut*, Great, large, grand.

P گترم *gutrum*, Vain, idle conversation.

P گته *guta*, Great, large, grand.

P گج *gaj*, A species of white earth used in building; also of which they make lime. Advantage, conveniency. Self-admiration, folly. A fool. Spurning, kicking.

P گجرات *gujrāt* or *gujarūt*, Guzerat.

P گجيل *gajīl*, Name of a certain quarter in Tabrīz; also of a burial-ground.

P گچ *gach*, A kind of white earth of which they make lime. Plaster.

P گچ بر *gach-bar*, A plasterer. A hodman.

P گچ پز *gach-paz*, A lime-burner.

P گچري *gachrī*, A dish of rice and beans.

P گچك *gichak*, Name of a musical instrument.

P گچكاري *gach-kārī*, Whitewash.

P گچ گر *gachgar*, A plasterer.

P گچگري *gachgarī*, Plastering, working in plaster.

P گچن *gachan*, Passed, elapsed.

P گچه *gacha* or *gachcha*, A stammerer.

P گد *gad*, A beggar. Begging, mendicity.

P گدا *gadā*, Poor, indigent, beggarly. گدا كردن *gadā kardan*, To beggar, impoverish, ruin.

P گداختن *gudākhtan*, To melt, liquify; clean, purify, clarify. To be melted.

P گداخته *gudākhta*, Melted. Purified, clarified.

P گداد *gudād*, A worn or patched habit. A wide garment.

P گداره *gudāra*, A lofty summer-house. A balcony. Planks on which is laid the terrace of a house.

P گداز *gudāz*, Liquefaction. Melted. Mild, gentle, affable. Anguish. (in comp.) Melting, consuming. جگر گداز *jigar-gudāz*, Melting the liver. سوز و گداز *soz u gudāz*, Burning and consuming.

P گدازان *gudāzān*, Melters, refiners (of gold).

P گدازانيدن *gudāzānīdan*, To cause to melt.

P گدازش *gudāzish*, Liquefaction. Consumption.

P گدازنده *gudāzanda*, A melter, dissolver. A solvent, dissolvent. گدازندهٔ ظلم و فسق و بدع *gudāzandaï zulm u fisk u badaɛ*, The destroyer of injustice, iniquity, and impiety (innovation, heresy).

P گدازيدن *gudāzīdan*, To melt. To be melted.

P گداش *gadāsh*, A horn. An antler.

P گدا طبع *gadā-tabɛ*, Beggarly-natured; greedy.

P گدا غازي *gadā-ghāzī*, A rope-dancer.

P گداي *gadāy*, Poor, a mendicant.

P گدايه *gadāya*, Beggary, mendicity.

P گدائي *gadāī*, Beggary, mendicity.

P گدر *gadr*, A warlike instrument.

P گدرك *gadrak*, An instrument of war.

P گدست *gidast*, A span.

P گدك *gadak*, Little. The ventricle of a sheep or kid (stuffed with meat and dressed), a haggess.

P گد گدي *gud gudī*, Tickling. A call to goats.

P گدمن *gadmin*, (in zand) Light, illumination.

P گده *gada*, The wards of a key.

P گديور *gadīvar*, A beggar.

P گديه *gidya*, Begging, mendicity. A beggar.

P گذار *guzār*, A passage, transit, passing. A ferry. Haste, expedition. Payment. Desertion. A broker, factor. A beam, joist. Pasturage. A lancet. (in comp.) Passing. Passing by, remitting. Paying, performing, satisfying. خراج گذار *kharāj-guzār*, Who pays tribute, tributary. خنجر سينه گذار *khanjari sīna-guzār*, A dagger piercing the breast. شكر گذار *shukr-guzār*, Giving, or a giver of thanks. قصه گذار *kissa-guzār*, A moralist. مال گذار *māl-guzār*, A farmer, renter. مال گذاري *māl-guzārī*, Rent, revenue. مصلحت گذار *maslahat-guzār*, (or مصالح گذار *masālih-guzār*) Expert in business.

P گذارا *guzārā*, A ferry, ferry-boat.

P گذارانيدن *guzārānīdan*, To cause to pass.

P گذاردن *guzārdan*, To pass. To cause to pass. To pay, perform, satisfy. To clean, purge. To discern, distinguish.

P گذارش *guzārish*, A quitting, leaving, passing. Payment. Tribute. Representation, explanation. Petition. گذارش كردن *guzārish kardan*, To suggest.

P گذارنده *guzāranda*, A passer, transmitter. A messenger, bearer. Who causes to pass.

P گذاره *guzāra*, Passing, penetrating.

P گذاري *guzārī*, (in compos.) Performance. شكر گذاري *shukr-guzārī*, Thanksgiving.

P گذاريدن *guzārīdan*, To pass by. To cause to pass. To transact. To pay.

P گذاشتن *guzāshtan*, To quit, leave, relinquish, forsake, dismiss, discharge, leave off, cease, put away, place. To perform. To allow, let, suffer, permit. To pay.

P گذاشتني *guzāshtanī*, Proper to be relinquished.

P گذاشته *guzāshta*, Passed by. Left off.

P گذاف *guzāf*, A vain, rash, inconsiderate word, falsehood, lie. Useless act. بگذاف *ba guzāf*, With impunity. لاف و گذاف *lāf u guzāf*, Boasting.

P گذر *guzar*, Pass thou. Passing by. A passage, ferry, ford. A pass, passage, way. گذر كردن *guzar kardan*, To pass. *Guzir*, A carrot.

P گذرا *guzarā*, Passing. Livelihood, maintenance, employment.

P گذرآب *guzar-āb*, A canal, aqueduct. A ford.

P گذران *guzarān*, Passing by. Exceeding.

P گذرانيدن *guzrānīdan*, To cause to pass, to present. To raise (a disturbance). To live, to get along. پيغام گذرانيدن *payghām guzrānīdan*, To deliver a message.

P گذربان *guzarbān*, A ferryman. An officer who collects the customs at the ferries. A guardian at a pass, a road-watch.

P گذرش *guzarish*, Sigh, complaint; accusation.

P گذرگاه *guzar-gāh*, A ferry, ford, passage.

P گذرنامه *guzar-nāma*, A passport, safe-conduct.

P گذريدن *guzarīdan*, To pass by. To omit, to leave undone.

P گذشت *guzasht*, A road, a pass. After. Other, beside. Fetching the last breath. از گذشت آن *az guzashti ān*, After that.

P گذشتگان *guzashtagān*, The ancients.

P گذشتن *guzashtan*, To pass, pass by, outstrip, precede, proceed, go on, advance, ascend, surpass. To cross over, to abandon. To pass by a fault. To die.

P گذشته *guzashta*, Past, elapsed. ايّام گذشته *ayyāmi guzashta*, Time past, past days.

P گر *gar*, If. Scab, mange. Purpose, design, intent. Power, strength. Felicity. A performer, workman, maker (when added to nouns, as "er" in plasterer): as, آهنگر *āhangar*, A blacksmith. كفشگر *kafshgar*, A shoemaker. گر خشك *gari khushk*, Dry scab. *Gir*, A smith's bellows. Take. *Gur*, Ruptured. Name of a river.

P گرّا *garrā*, Confined, not free. A slave. A barber. A term of abuse. A sort of harrow.

P گراد *girād*, An old garment.

P گرارون *garārūn*, Ring-worm, dry scab.

P گراز *gurāz*, A hog, a boar. A rake, a harrow. A shovel, spade. A large iron mace. A shepherd or buffalo-driver's staff. A heat, to which women in labour are subject. A phial, or traveller's bottle. A chink, crevice. Growth, increase. A haughty air in walking. A cushion or pillow. A brave man.

P گرازان *gurāzān*, A polisher. One who walks pompously. A pompous air. (pl. of گراز *gurāz*) Boars. Hogs. Sturdy wrestlers.

P گرازنده *gurāzanda*, A proud, stately walker.

P گرازه *gurāza*, A boar. Name of a champion of Irān.

P گرازيدن *gurāzīdan*, To march, walk pompously.

P گراس *garās*, A mouthful.

P گراسيدن *girāsīdan*, To be necessary. To cheat.

P گراش *garāsh*, A scratch. Distracted, disturbed.

P گراشيدن *garāshīdan*, To scratch. To disturb, confuse. To be disturbed, confused.

P گرامي *garāmī* or *girāmī*, Precious, excellent. Dear, beloved. Revered.

P گراميدن *girāmīdan*, To honour, respect.

P گران *girān*, Heavy, weighty, ponderous. Slow. Great, important. Difficult. Precious, dear, valuable. Gain, profit. Penury. بي گران *bī girān*, (or بي گرانه *bī girāna*) Immense, infinite. گران بها *girān-bahā*, Of high price, of immense value, sumptuous. *Gurān*, A handful of corn as cut by the reaper.

P گران بار *girān-bār*, Heavy-laden. Fruit-bearing (tree). Pregnant (woman or animal). Wealthy.

P گران پاي *girān-pāy*, Slow-footed.

P گران پشت *girān-pusht*, Strong, sturdy. A porter. Arrogant, proud, silly.

P گرانجان *girān-jān*, Oppressed in mind, unhappy, unfortunate. Wearied with life. Poor, sick. Slow, sluggish, tremulous with age. Lazy. Proud. A sweet beverage made of water, flour, and honey.

P گرانجاني *girān-jānī*, Affliction. Misfortune. Laziness. Pride.

P گران خاطر *girān-khātir*, Afflicted at heart.

P گران خواب *girān-khwāb*, One who goes to sleep late and rises late, a heavy sleeper.

P گرانخوار *girān-khwār*, A great eater, a glutton.

P گران دست *girān-dast*, Heavy-handed, slow.

P گراندن *girāndan*, To look, behold.

P گران دو *girān-dav*, Slow-running (horse).

P گران دود *girān-dūd*, Dark cloud, fog, mist.

P گران ركاب *girān-rikāb*, A bold rider. (A horse or a man) going slowly and heavily. One who does not flinch from the impetuous assault of his enemy. Grave, sedate. گران ركاب شدن *girān-rikāb shudan*, To attack impetuously. To die.

P گران سال *girān-sāl*, Old, aged, great in years.

P گران سالي *girān-sālī*, Old age.

P گران سايه *girān-sāya*, Of exalted dignity.

P گران سر *girān-sar*, Proud. The commander of an army. Heavy (dragoons). A numerous army.

P گران سرشت *girān-sirisht*, Proud. Grave, sedate, dignified. Slow, tardy, languid.

P گران سنگ *girān-sang*, Heavy, weighty. Grave, dignified. Precious, valuable. Low-spirited. Patient, contented.

P گران سير *girān-sayr*, Slow-going, heavy-moving. كشتيء گران سير *kashtīi girān-sayr*, A slow-sailing ship.

P گران عنان *girān-ʻinān*, Slow (man or horse).

P گران گوش *girān-gosh*, Heavy of hearing, deaf.

P گران گوشي *girān-goshī*, Heaviness of ear.

P گرانمايگي *girān-māyagī*, Preciousness. Excellence of birth. Weightiness.

P گران مايه *girān-māya*, Precious. Of noble birth. Weighty, ponderous.

P گراني *girānī*, Heaviness, weight, gravity. Importance. Scarceness, dearth, dearness. گرانيء گوش *girānīi gosh*, Heaviness of hearing, deafness.

P گرانيدن *girānīdan*, To be heavy, grave, ponderous. To weigh, or guess the weight of, any thing in the hand. To make heavy. To augment the price of. To esteem, to think highly of, extol. *Gurānīdan*, To make one take or hold any thing.

P گرانيده *girānīda*, Poor. Oppressed.

P گراووس *garāvūs*, (or گراوس) An oil-mill.

P گراه *girāh*, Inclination, will. Inclined. Like.

P گراي *garāy*, Mentioned, recorded. A title of the princes of Tartary. *Girāy*, Inclination, wish, desire; intention, preparation. Diminution. Merchandize. Heavy. Seizing by the hand, the feet, the waist, or the hem of the garment. Attacking, pretending to strike or throw stones; threatening. Inclining, propense. Examining, investigating.

P گرّاي *garrāy*, A barber. A slave.

P گرايستن *girāyistan* or *garāyistan*, To incline towards, to love. To intend, prepare, or make for. To explore, examine. To happen. To behold. To rebel. *Girāyistan*, To move any thing up and down whilst weighing it. To scatter, disperse. To macerate or soften hides.

P گرايش *girāyish* or *garāyish*, Inclination, desire, will, wish. Disobedience, rebellion.

P گراييدن *girāyīdan* or *garāyīdan*, To have an inclination or affection, to love. To examine, prove, try. To weigh in the hand; to lay out of the hand. To intend. To contend, endeavour. To attack. To compose, accord, tune (the string of an instrument). To lessen, diminish. To estimate, esteem, think. To involve, to wrap round, to cover. To disobey, rebel.

P گرباك *gurbāk*, A wide dish.

P گربال *girbāl* or *garbāl*, A sieve.

P گربز *gurbuz*, (or گربژ *gurbij*) A deceiver, seducer, flatterer, cheat. Artful. Ingenious, skilful, intelligent. Strong, invincible.

P گربزي *gurbuzī*, Fraudulence, seduction, deception. Intelligence, wisdom. Greatness, valour.

P گربگو *gurbagū*, Name of a fragrant shrub.

P گربه *gurba*, A cat. Wild thyme. Name of an odoriferous tree called بيد مشك *bīdi mushk*. گربهٔ آبي *gurbai ābī*, An otter. گربه از بغل افكندن *gurba az baghal afgandan*, Throwing the cat from under the arm; letting the cat out of the bag, discovering the secret. Leaving off deceitful ways. گربه در انبان داشتن *gurba dar ambān dāshtan*, To practise deceit. گربه در زندان كردن *gurba dar zindān kardan*, To be extremely avaricious. گربهٔ دشتي *gurbai dashtī*, A kind of panther or wild cat. Bog-rush. گربهٔ مسكين *gurbai miskīn*, A wicked rogue.

P گربه بيد *gurba-bīd*, A species of willow.

P گربه چشم *gurba-chashm*, Grey-eyed.

P گربه چشمي *gurba-chashmī*, Grey-eyedness.

P گربه دله *gurba-dala*, A ferret, marten, weasel.

P گربه سان *gurbasān*, (or گربه گون *gurba-gūn*) Cat-like, wily, cunning, deceitful.

P گرپا *gurpā*, Trefoil.

P گرت بايد *garat bāyad*, (for گرترا بايد *gar turā bāyad*) If thou meanest (if it must be to thee).

P گرج *gurj*, Georgia. Native of Georgia.

P گرجستان *gurjistān*, Georgia.

P گرجي *gurjī*, A Georgian. A servant boy. A hut. A kind of dog.

P گرچ *girach*, Mortar, plaster.

P گرچند *garchand*, How much soever.

P گرچه *garcha*, Although, though, notwithstanding. Certainly, indeed. *Gurcha*, A cottage. A dungeon. A subterraneous excavation.

P گرختن *gurikhtan*, To fly, escape, flee for refuge.

P گرد *gard*, Turning round. Revolving. The celestial globe. Fortune. The sun. Dust, earth. Flying dust. Advantage, profit, emolument. Reflexion, inversion, repercussion, refraction. Lightning. Joy, mirth. Sadness, sorrow. A kind of silk. A fragrant smell. گرد آفتاب *gardi āftāb*, Atoms which appear playing in the sun-beams. گرد بر آوردن *gard bar āwardan*, To trample under foot. To annihilate. گرد زمرّد *gardi zumurrud*, A sprouting beard. *Gird*, Round. A circle, orbit, circumference, circuit, rotundo. Environs, parts adjacent. A collection, assembly. A city. A tent, pavilion. گرد آمدن *gird āmadan*, To convene, meet together.

To accumulate, collect, mount up. گرد آوردن *gird āwardan*, To accumulate. گرد راه *girdi rāh*, The circuit of a road. گرد رو *girdi rū*, The contour of the face. A woman's ornament worn about the face set with jewels. گرد شهر *girdi shahr*, Suburbs. گرد کار گشتن *girdi kār gashtan*, To engage in, to attempt or commit any thing. گرد کردن *gird kardan*, To collect, assemble, bring together. To make round, to encompass, environ. To wrinkle, shrivel, contract. To wager, especially at a horse-race. To put in. گرد گشتن *gird gashtan*, To go round. داراب گرد *dārāb-gird*, The city of Dārāb. *Gurd*, Strong, brave, valiant; a hero. گرد زابل *gurdi zābul*, The hero of Zābul, *i.e.* Rustam. *Girad*, (for گیرد *gīrad*) He may take. *Girid*, Crete or Candy.

P گردا *gardā*, Returning, wheeling, encircling. A boy's top. *Girdā*, Pretence, pretext, excuse.

P گرداب *gird-āb*, A whirlpool, abyss, gulf, vortex. *Gurd-āb*, A wave.

P گرداباد *girdābād*, The city of Madāin, founded by Tahmūras and finished by Jamshed.

P گردار *gar-dār*, Scabby, mangy.

P گرداس *gurdās*, An oppressor, tyrant.

P گرداش *gurdāsh*, An oppressor, tyrant.

P گرداگرد *gard-ā-gard*, Step by step. Continually revolving. *Gird-ā-gird*, Round about, round and round. The winding of a river, road, or mountain. Parts, sides, boundaries.

P گرد آلوده *gard-ālūda*, Soiled with dust. Encumbered with riches or worldly cares.

P گردان *gardān*, Turning, winding, changing, inverting, converting. One who turns or goes round. Conjugation, inflexion. Meat parboiled and roasted with spices. گردان شدن *gardān shudan*, To revolve, turn round. گردون گردان *gardūni gardān*, The spheres, the heavenly heavens. قبهٔ گردون گردان *kubba-i gardūni gardān*, The vault of heaven (perpetually) revolving.

P گرداناد *gardānād*, May (God) effect it!

P گرد اندام *gird-andām*, Of a middling stature, square, compactly built.

P گرداندن *gardāndan*, To turn round.

P گردانك *gardānak*, The pointers (two stars in the Bear).

P گردانه *gardāna*, An iron ring (to which any thing is suspended). *Girdāna*, A child's go-cart, leaning against which it learns to walk.

P گردانیدگی *gardānīdagī*, A rolling about.

P گردانیدن *gardānīdan*, (transitive of گردیدن *gardīdan*) To change, alter, avert, convert, divert, drive round, surround. To cause to become. To represent as becoming, to regard as. آواز گردانیدن *āwāz gardānīdan*, To make inflections of the voice, *i.e.* to sing, modulate, shake, quaver, or trill. بر گردانیدن *bar gardānīdan*, To invert, transpose. بچرا گردانیدن *ba charā gardānīdan*, To lead to pasture.

P گردانیده *gardānīda*, Turned round. Meat parboiled and roasted.

P گردانیه *gardāniya*, Name of a note in music.

P گرداوا *girdāwā*, A patrol.

P گرد آور *gird-āwar*, All round, round.

P گردآوردن *gird āwardan*, To assemble, collect.

P گرد آوري *gird-āwarī*, A drawing together.

P گرداوژند *gurdāwjand*, Name of a champion.

P گردباد *gird-bād*, (or گردباده) A whirlwind. A demon. گردبادآسا *gird-bādāsā*, Like a whirlwind.

P گردبالش *gird-bālish*, (or بالین) A small pillow laid under the cheek. A large cylindrical pillow.

P گردبان *gardbān*, A leader, commander-in-chief. The tree of paradise. An artificer's wooden block fixed in the ground for polishing his work. A shirt-collar; neck and breast of a shirt.

P گردبر *girdbur*, A wimble, gimlet.

P گردبر آوردن *gard bar āwardan*, To raise a dust. To trample down, destroy.

P گرد بر آورده *gird bar āwarda*, Vaulted, domed.

P گرد بگرد *gird ba gird*, All round.

P گرد بندن *gard-bandan*, Collar, neck-ornament.

P گردپاي *gird-pāy*, The space about the foot of a throne or other seat. گردپاي حوض گردیدن *gird-pāyi hawz gardīdan*, To wander about any place incognito in search of any thing. گرد پاي نشستن *gird pāy nishastan*, To sit in a square posture.

P گردپستان *gird-pistān*, Round-breasted maiden.

P گرد پوش *gird-posh*, Bed-clothes.

P گرد پیش *gird-pesh*, All round.

P گرد خوان *gird-khwān*, A circular table.

P گردر *gardar*, Hard ground at the foot of a mountain. Hilly ground. A city.

P گردران *gird-rān*, A fleshy thigh. An easy life. Root of the thigh, groin.

P گردش *gardish*, Revolution, turning round, reversion, conversion, motion. Turn, change. A bend. گردش آسمان *gardishi āsmān*, Revolution of the heavens.

P گردشب *gard-shab*, Darkness of the night.

P گردشنده *girdshanda*, Reptiles.

P گردك *girdak*, (dim. of گرد *gird*) A small royal tent. A large round tent. A bride's chamber. An enigma. A rich cake. A sum, total, whole, collection.

P گردكنا *gird-kunā*, A collector. Surrounding.

P گردگان *girdgān*, A walnut. The ball of a pellet-bow. Any thing round.

P گردگاه *gird-gāh*, The navel.

P گردگریبان *gird-girībān*, A shirt, a shift.

P گرد گشتگي *gird-gashtagī*, A going round.

P گردگي *girdagī*, Roundness, rotundity.

P گردگیر *gurd-gīr*, A conqueror of heroes. The title of the son of Afrāsyāb.

P گردمانه *girdmāna*, Seed of mezereon.

P گردن *gardan*, The neck. A pole. Strong, robust, firm, powerful. A brave, stout man; a hero. Strength, power. گردن خاریدن *gardan khārīdan*, To scratch the neck; (met.) To seek an excuse. گردن زدن *gardan zadan*, To decapitate. گردن شتر *gardani shutur*, A camel's neck; (met.) A purse full of gold. گردن نهادن *gardan nihādan*, To place the neck, *i.e.* to submit, obey. با خون لشكر در گردن او *bā khūni lashkar dar gardani u*, With the blood of the (whole) army on his neck, *i.e.* he was the cause of their destruction. با شمشیر و كفن بر گردن *bā shamshīr u kafan bar gardan*, With a scimeter and a winding-sheet about (his) neck.

P گردنا *gardanā*, A spit. A go-cart, in which a child learns to walk. A boy's top. Meat parboiled and then roasted with spices. The peg of a musical instrument. گردناي چرخ *gardanāyi charkh*, The sky. *Girdanā*, A spit. The kneepan. A red rose. A deep dish.

P گردناج *gardanāj*, Meat parboiled and roasted.

P گردناك *gardnāk*, Full of dust, dusty.

P گردنامه *gird-nāma*, An incantation written upon a bit of paper, accompanied by the name of a slave who may have run away from his master, which, being hidden under a stone or in the ground, is supposed to have the power of preventing his escape and obliging him to return. A die for coining, the impression on money.

P گردنان *gardanān*, (pl. of گردن *gardan*) Strong, powerful, illustrious. گردنان بنظم *gardanān ba nazm*, Illustrious poets.

P گردناي *gardnāy*, A boy's top. *Girdnāy* or *gardnāy*, A red rose. A child's go-cart.

P گردن بسته *gardan-basta*, Chained or fastened by the neck. گردن بسته و دل شكسته *gardan-basta u dil-shikasta*, With the neck in chains and a broken heart.

P گردن بند *gardan-band*, A chain, collar, necklace, ornament for the neck.

P گردن فراز *gardan-firāz*, Stretching the neck. Long-necked.

P گردنكش *gardan-kash*, Exalting the neck, *i.e.* proud, haughty, refractory, disobedient, stubborn, obstinate. گردن كشان نظم *gardan-kushāni nazm*, Poets of distinguished merit.

P گردنكشي *gardan-kashī*, Pride, arrogance, presumption, stubbornness. گردنكشي كردن *gardan-kashī kardan*, To rebel.

P گردنگ *gardung*, A fool, idiot. A cuckold.

P گردنگل *gardangal*, A fool. *Gardangul*, A rolling-pin.

P گرد نواحي *gird-nawāhī*, Environs.

P گردنه *gardana*, A rolling-pin. A saw worked by two men. A musical instrument. Name of an herb.

P گردنها *gardanhā*, (pl. of گردن *gardan*) Necks.

P گردني *gardanī*, A horse-cloth. A blow on the nape of the neck. گردني كردن *gardanī kardan*, To disobey, to rebel.

P گردو *girdū*, A nut, a walnut.

P گردون *gardūn*, A wheel. Heaven, the celestial globe or sphere. Chance, fortune, and her revolving wheel. A chariot, calash, chaise. A child's go-cart, by which he learns to walk. A gun-carriage. A cobweb. گردون دون نواز و چرخ کینه ساز *garduni dūn-nawāz, wa charkhi kīna-sāz*, Fortune smiling on the base, and preparing adversity (for the deserving). گردون مینا *garduni mīnā*, The azure sky.

P گردون اقتدار *gardūn-iktidār*, Powerful as heaven.

P گردونچه *gardūncha*, (or گردونچهٔ کودك *gardūnchaꜜi kūdak*) A child's go-cart, by which it learns to walk.

P گردون سرشت *gardūn-sirisht*, Proud, conceited, pompous, dignified. Slow, negligent. Absurd.

P گردونه *gardūna*, A chariot, calash, gig.

P گرده *garda*, Powder used by painters, which, tied in a cloth, they rub over the outlines of their designs pricked on paper, and which passing through the holes transfers a dotted outline of the subject to another piece of paper; also the pricked paper. A shield. *Girda*, A kind of round cake, but not thin. Any thing round. A round pillow. A round yellow patch sewed upon a garment to distinguish a Jew. All, the whole. Watch, guard. گردهٔ چرخ *girdaꜜi charkh*, (or گردهٔ گردون *girdaꜜi gardūn*) The sun and moon. *Gurda*, A kidney. The reins. Courage.

P گرده آلو *gurda-ālū*, A fruit like an apricot.

P گرده بالش *girda-bālish*, A round pillow.

P گرده بان *girdabān*, One who claps his hands upon meat on a table, to prevent it from being carried off. A watchman.

P گرده بر *girda-bur*, A wimble, augur, gimlet.

P گرده پیچ *girda-pech*, A circuit, surrounding, investing, besieging. Herb-seeds dressed with meat.

P گردیدن *gardīdan*, To turn, become, return, change. To be inverted, converted. To go round, walk about, saunter. To be surrounded, embraced, comprehended. To embrace. To stretch one's self (especially when waking from sleep). از حال گردیدن *az hāl gardīdan*, To change one's state or condition. باز گردیدن *bāz gardīdan*, To turn back, to retire.

P گردیده *gardīda*, Become, changed. Surrounded. Tumbled down, revolved.

P گرز *gurz*, A mace of gold, silver, or iron. A club, battle-axe. A pestle. Penis.

P گرز بردار *gurz-bardār*, A mace-bearer.

P گرزدمن *garazdamin*, (zand & Pāz.) An enemy.

P گرزدن *gurazdan*, To help, aid; tend the sick.

P گرزده *gar-zada*, Smitten with scab, scabby.

P گرزش *garzish*, A cry against injustice, remonstrance, supplication, the groans of the oppressed.

P گرزم *gurazm*, Name of a brother of Isfandiyār.

P گرزمان *garazmān* or *garzmān*, The highest heaven. Heaven.

P گرزن *garzan*, Crown of the old Persian kings.

P گرزه *garza*, A very venomous kind of serpent. *Gurza*, A large wooden club. A mace. A large-headed serpent. Ravenous, fierce. Membrum virile. گرزهٔ گاو پیکر *gurzaꜜi gāu-paykar*, (گرزهٔ گاو چهر *gurzaꜜi gāu-chihr*, گرزهٔ گاو سار *gurzaꜜi gāu-sār*, گرزهٔ گاو سر *gurzaꜜi gāu-sar*, or گرزهٔ گاومیش *gurzaꜜi gāu-mesh*) The mace of king Farīdūn, which had the figure of an ox's head on the top of it.

P گرزیدن *gurazīdan*, To help, assist. To cure.

P گرزین *girzīn*, A rich crown worn by the ancient kings of Persia. A basket. A pointed arrow.

P گرس *gurs*, Hunger. Dirt upon the body or linen. Curled hair; a ringlet.

P گرست *garast*, Full of drink, intoxicated.

P گرستن *giristan*, To weep, to cry.

P گرستودن *garastūdan*, A steelyard for weighing large weights.

P گرستون *garastūn*, A large public standard or weighing engine.

P گرسنگي *gursnagī*, Hunger.

P گرسنه *gursna* or *gurusna*, Hungry, famished.

P گرسنه چشم *gursna-chashm*, Hungry-eyed. Envious. Niggardly. Poor; a beggar. One who has just escaped from a famine. گرسنه چشمان کنعان *gursna-chashmāni kanꜥān*, An epithet of the brethren of Joseph.

P گرسیان *garsiyān*, Name of a certain stone.

P گرسیوز *garsewaz*, Name of Afrāsyāb's brother.

P گرش *girish*, An amorous glance or gesture.

P گرشاسب *garshāsb*, (گرشاسف *garshāsf*, or گرشسب *garshasb*) Name of an ancestor of Rustam. Name of the son of Tahmāsb.

P گرشال *gurshāl* or *girshāl*, An animal between a wolf and a jackal, or between a bear and a jackal.

P گرغست *gar ghast*, Name of a plant resembling spinage.

P گرفت *girift*, He took or seized. Capture, seizure, detention, sequestration, fine, mulct. A handle, catch, clutch. A fault, sin, crime (for which one is reviled). Blame, reproach, taunt. Objection, criticism. Observation, watch. An eclipse of the sun or moon. A thrust with a spear. Friction. Shaking with the fingers, or pressing upon the finger-board of a musical instrument, so as to produce a tremulous sound. A small shrill trumpet. گرفت کردن *girift kardan*, To shake upon a musical instrument. To turn away from.

P گرفتار *giriftār*, A captive, prisoner, slave; involved (in trouble). A commencement. گرفتار کردن *giriftār kardan*, To take prisoner, carry off captive.

P گرفتاري *giriftārī*, Captivity, bondage, imprisonment, embarrassment.

P گرفتگاه *girift-gāh*, The handle, hilt, or grasping-place (of a sword, knife, and the like).

P گرفتگي *giriftagī*, Capture, seizure, detention, imprisonment. The setting of a broken bone. A contraction. An impediment. گرفتگيِ آواز *giriftagīꜜi āwāz*, Hoarseness. گرفتگيِ شکم *giriftagīꜜi shikam*, Costiveness, constipation.

P گرفتم *giriftam*, I admit, take it (for granted).

P گرفتن *giriftan*, To take, seize, catch, snatch. To make prisoner. To intercept. To rebuke. To begin. To set a broken bone. To close up. To undergo an eclipse. To make (a dwelling). بازگرفتن *bāz giriftan*, To keep back, retain. بر گرفتن *bar giriftan*, To take up, to pick up. گرفتن ماه *giriftani māh*, A lunar eclipse. بر خود گرفتن *bar khwud giriftan*, To take upon one's self. To assume airs, presume, arrogate. پیش گرفتن *pesh giriftan*, To anticipate. To undertake. در دل گرفتن *dar dil giriftan*, To conceive (fear) in the mind. درمیان خود گرفتن *dar miyāni khwud giriftan*, To contain or restrain one's self. زیر پاي گرفتن *zīri pāy giriftan*, To trample under foot. فال بد گرفتن *fāli bad giriftan*, To take a bad presage. قوّت گرفتن *kūwat giriftan*, To gain strength; to prevail. ناخن گرفتن *nākhun giriftan*, To pare the nails.

P گرفتي *giriftanī*, Criticism.

P گرفته *girifta*, Taken, received, seized, captured. Adopted, assumptive. Blamed, reproached. Obstructed, shut, closed. Eclipsed. A prisoner, captive. Blame, reproach, contumely. A crime, sin. A mulct, fine. A boasting, bragging; a foolish saying or action. A thrust, stab. Wages, price of labour. Avaricious, stingy, sordid; a niggard. گرفته زدن *girifta zadan*, To reproach. To pierce. To boast. گرفته شدن *girifta shudan*, To be eclipsed. ادب گرفته *adab-girifta*, Polite, well-bred. پاي گرفته *pāy-girifta*, Fled, escaped. Baked, kneaded. پسر گرفته *pisari girifta*, An adopted son. پند گرفته *pand-girifta*, Admonished; taking advice. درهم گرفته *darham girifta*, Contracted, drawn together.

P گرفته خاطر *girifta-khātir*, Afflicted at heart.

P گرفته دم *girifta-dam*, Asthma. Asthmatic.

P گرفته زبان *girifta-zabān*, Stammering, having an impediment in speech.

P گرفته لب *girifta-lab*, Tongue-tied, dumb. Silent. Silence.

P گرگ *garg*, Scabby, mangy. *Gurg*, A wolf. گرگِ سیمین سم *gurgi sīmīn-sum*, A strong, able-bodied man. گرگِ فسونگر *gurgi fusūngar*, The world. The sky.

P گرگابي *gurgābī*, A kind of sandal or shoe.

P گرگ آشتي *gurg-āshtī*, An insincere peace.

P گرگ آشنائي *gurg-āshnāꜜī*, Hollow friendship.

P گرگان *gurgān*, A desert. Name of a city.

P گرگانج *gurgānj*, The metropolis of Khwārazm.

P گرگاو *gurgāv*, A kind of shoe or sandal.

P گرگ بند *gurg-band*, Conquered, made captive: a prisoner. Light (not heavy). گرگ بند کردن *gurg-band kardan*, To take prisoner. To oppress. To render light.

P گرگج *gargaj*, A redoubt in front of a fort.

P گرگ دو *gurg-dav*, A trot like that of a wolf.

P گرگ دیزه *gurg-deza*, A dun colour. Satin.

P گرگر *gargar*, One of the names of God. A throne. Name of a town in the province of Azarbayjān. *Girgir*, A species of bean or pea. *Gur-*

gur, A whisper, what is said aside.

P گرگ مست *gurg-mast*, A beloved object, cruel and fickle.

P گرگن *gargan*, The scab. *Gargin*, One who has a cutaneous eruption. Scabby. *Gurgun*, Unripe corn gathered for food.

P گرگنج *garganj*, The capital of Khwārazm.

P گرگوز *gur* or *gargūz*, Governor of a province.

P گرگوي *gargoy*, Name of a champion and ally of Afrasyāb.

P گرگي *gurgī*, Wolfishness.

P گرگيج *girgīj*, Name of a certain city.

P گرگين *gargīn*, Scabby, mangy. *Gurgīn*, Name of a champion.

P گرگينه *gurgīna*, A fur-garment.

P گرم *garm*, Warm, hot. Choleric, fiery. Ardent, active, zealous. Thronged, busy (market). Anguish, vexation. Haste, despatch. گرم شدن *garm shudan*, To grow warm. To fly in a passion. گرم كردن *garm kardan*, To make hot. To excite, inflame, put in a rage. گرم و سرد *garm u sard*, Hot and cold, ups and downs, prosperity and adversity. گرم و سرد چرخ *garm u sardi charkh*, The sun and moon. Accidents of fortune. *Gurm* or *garm*, Grief, sorrow, affliction, distress of mind. Taking little when much is required. *Gurm*, The rainbow.

P گرما *garmā*, Heat, warmth, sultriness.

P گرمابان *garmābān*, A hot-bath. A bath-keeper.

P گرمابدار *garmāb-dār*, A bagnio-keeper.

P گرمابه *garmāba*, A hot bath.

P گرمابه بان *garmābabān*, Keeper of a hot-bath.

P گرمابي *garmābī*, Warmth, heat.

P گرما زده *garmā-zada*, Smitten with heat.

P گرمافزاي *garmā-fizāy*, Increasing heat. Name of the third month in the era of Yazdagird, corresponding to May.

P گرماله *garmāla*, Name of a certain medicine.

P گرماوه *garmāwa*, A hot bath.

P گرماوه بان *garmāwabān*, Keeper of a hot bath.

P گرماهي *gar-māhī*, (Scab-fish) A shad.

P گرمائيل *girmā-il*, Name of one of the princes who were compelled to perform the office of cook to the tyrant Zahhāk.

P گرم جوشي *garm-joshī*, Warmth of affection.

P گرمخانه *garm-khāna*, A hot-house, subterraneous dwelling for warmth.

P گرم خون *garm-khūn*, Of a hot blood; lively. An ardent lover. Wine containing much alcohol.

P گرمخيز *garm-khez*, An early riser. Quick, active. One who passes part of the night in prayer.

P گرمدان *garmdān*, A kind of fruit.

P گرم دلان *garm-dilān*, Ardent lovers.

P گرمران *garm-rān*, A furious driver.

P گرم روان *garm-rawān*, Quick travellers. Impatient lovers.

P گرمسير *garm-ser*, A warm climate. A winter-habitation in low grounds. Waiting impatiently.

P گرمش *garmish*, Heat. A fever.

P گرمك *garmak*, Boiled beans. An early melon. (dim. of گرم *garm*) Somewhat hot, warmish.

P گرمگاه *garm-gāh*, A warm place. Mid-day.

P گرمه *garma*, Fruits which ripen early (especially melons); first-fruits. Hot or white bread.

P گرمه بيز *garma-bez*, (or *wez*) A fine sieve.

P گرمي *garmī*, Heat, warmth. Briskness of market. The venereal disease.

P گرميت *garmiyat*, Heat, warmth, ardour.

P گرميخ *gur-mekh*, A large pin or stake to which they fasten the heel-ropes of horses.

P گرمي خونابه *garmī-khūnāba*, Excessive weeping.

P گرميدانه *garmī-dāna*, A rash, prickly heat.

P گرميدن *garmīdan*, To be hot, wax warm.

P گرنج *gurinj*, A wrinkle. The corner of a house. *Gurinj* or *guranj*, Rice.

P گرنجار *gurinjār*, A rice-ground.

P گرنج بشير *gurinj ba shīr*, Rice with milk.

P گرنده *gurinda*, A sort of brush used by weavers to apply paste or size to their warp.

P گرنگ *garang*, The rendezvous of an army; a field of battle. *Giring*, Broken to pieces.

P گرنه *garna*, (or گرني *garnī*) Unless. *Gurna*, Name of an herb.

P گرو *giraw* or *girav*, A wager, stake, bet. A pledge, pawn, earnest. A contract. گرو بردن *giraw burdan*, To win the game, carry off the stakes. گرو بستن *giraw bastan*, (گرو دادن *giraw dādan*, گرو كردن *giraw kardan*, گرو كشيدن *giraw kashīdan*, or گرو نهادن *giraw nihādan*) To wager, bet.

P گروانيدن *girwānīdan*, To cause to bet. To make believe.

P گروچه *gurūcha*, Gristle, a tendon.

P گرودار *giraw-dār*, A layer of bets. A holder of stakes.

P گرور *girwar*, Fit, proper, necessary, expedient.

P گرور فرتاش *girwar-fartāsh*, Whose existence is necessary.

P گروزه *gurūza*, An assembly, concourse.

P گروس *gurūs*, A ringlet or braid of hair. Dirt on the body or clothes. Hunger.

P گروغ *gurogh*, A lie.

P گروگان *girawgān*, A wager, stake. A slave. *Gurūgān*, The male organ of generation.

P گروگر *garūgar*, An attribute of God, signifying, "Who grants our desires."

P گروند *girwand*, Pustules on the lips (which are said to rise in consequence of horrible dreams). The ringworm or tetter excoriating the skin and becoming white.

P گروه *guroh*, A troop, squadron, company, band, levy of people, crew. A body of travellers. گروه كبت انگبين *gurohi kabti angubīn*, Swarm of bees. گروه سگان *gurohi sagān*, Pack of hounds. گروه گروه *guroh guroh*, In troops, company by company.

P گروه شدگي *guroh-shudagī*, Association, a uniting in a body, confederation.

P گروهه *giroha*, The clew of thread as formed upon the spindle. *Guroha*, A ball, bowl, globe, or any spherical figure. A ball of thread, ball for a cannon, balista, or cross-bow. The head, crown of the head. A kind of sweetmeat. An assembly, concourse, multitude of people.

P گروي *girawī*, Pledged, pawned. *Gurwī*, Name of a kinsman of Afrāsyāb.

P گرويدگي *girawīdagī*, Admiration, adoration, adherence, attachment.

P گرويدن *girawīdan*, To follow, admire, obey, adore. To believe, confide in. To form a sincere alliance with any one. To be attached. To pledge.

P گرويده *girawīda*, Attracted, attached to, admiring, captivated. A believer. Confiding.

P گره *gara*, A cup or ewer. Mouldiness. *Girih*, A knot, a knur (as in a thread or on wood), a knob, a joint. A button or any thing for fastening garments. An abscess. A knuckle. Articulation. Three finger-breadths. A difficulty. The seed of a thorny tree used for tanning. The heart. گره بر گره *girih bar girih*, Knot upon knot, difficulty upon difficulty. گره بر گوش زدن *girih bar gosh zadan*, To be deaf or hard of hearing. گره بستن *girih bastan*, To knot, to concrete (as honey). گره زبان *girihi zabān*, Impediment in the speech. گره زدن *girih zadan*, To lay up a treasure, to amass wealth. To knot the hair. گره گرفتن *girih giriftan*, To be tied (as the tongue), and unable to articulate. گره گوشت *girihi gosht*, A gland in the body, kernel in the flesh.

P گره بر *girih-bur*, A cutpurse.

P گره بر باد *girih bar bād*, (Difficulties to the wind) Indifference to worldly concerns.

P گره بند *girih-band*, A coat-button. The waistband of drawers. One who ties a knot.

P گرهچه *girihcha*, (or گرهك *girihak*) A little knot.

P گرهكشا *girih-kushā*, A looser of knots. A solver of difficulties.

P گره گردان *girih-gardān*, Name of a game.

P گرهه *giriha* or *girihha*, A little knot. A joint in an herb. *Guruha*, A ball. A company of people.

P گري *garī*, Any standard of measure, whether for land, cloth, grain, liquids, or time. A measure of time, twenty-two minutes and thirty seconds. The itch, scab. *Gire*, (for گره *girih*) A knot. The neck. *Girī*, Weep thou; weeping. The neck. A mountain. (for گيري *gīrī*) Thou mayest take.

P گريا *giryā*, Weeping: one who weeps.

P H گريال *garyāl*, A round flat plate of bell-metal, used in the east as a bell to strike the hours upon.

P گريا لقا *giryā-likā*, A monstrous appearance, a hideous figure.

P گريان *giryān*, Weeping, crying excessively. Causing to weep. A weeper. گريان شدن *giryān shudan*, To weep, bewail. *Guryān*, The fire-place or furnace of a hot-bath. A sacrifice or offering made for deliverance from calamity.

P گريانيدن *giryānidan*, To cause to weep.

P گريبان *girībān*, A collar, the opening or breast of a garment. A pocket. گريبان دامن كردن *girībān dāman kardan*, To meditate, to be wrapt in ecstacy.

P گريبان گير *girībān-gīr*, An accuser, a plaintiff. An apologist.

P گريباني *girībānī*, A kind of loose vest. A leathern binding sewed to the collar of a coat.

P گريچ *gurīch*, (or گريچه *gurīcha*) A hut, hovel, cottage, cell. A small building set upon posts.

P گريچه *gurīcha*, A sort of sweetmeat.

P گريختن *gurekhtan*, To fly, flee, run away. To escape. To take refuge, retire, retreat.

P گريخته *gurekhta*, A fugitive.

P گريد *girīd*, The island of Crete or Candy.

P گريز *gurez*, Flying, a fugitive. Flight. Deviation, regression, abhorrence, aversion, abstinence, fasting. The general or leader of an army. An eloquent man. A part of a beam projecting beyond a wall. گريز داشتن *gurez dāshtan*, To dispense with. مارا از شما گريز نيست *mārā az shumā gurez nist*, You are indispensable to us, we cannot do without you.

P گريزان *gurezān*, Taking flight. گريزان شدن *gurezān shudan*, To fly.

P گريزاندن *gurezāndan*, To put to flight. To cause to escape. در گريزاندن *dar gurezāndan*, To cause to take refuge.

P گريزانيدن *gurezānīdan*, To put to flight.

P گريزگاه *gurez-gāh*, Time or place of fleeing. A place of escape. An asylum, place of refuge, retreat.

P گريزنده *gurezanda*, A fugitive. Quicksilver.

P گريزي *gurezī*, Flight.

P گريزيدن *gurezīdan*, To fly, to flee.

P گريس *girīs*, Deceit, fraud, artifice.

P گريستن *girīstan*, To weep, cry, bewail. گريستن هوا *girīstāni hawā*, Weeping of the atmosphere, *i.e.* raining.

P گريسنگ *garīsang*, A ditch, a hollow place in the ground. *Gurīsang*, The note of the nightingale. The shout made by a party of religious mendicants.

P گريسه *girīsa*, Fraud, deceit.

P گريسيدن *girīsīdan*, To deceive, defraud, cheat.

P گريش *garesh*, Name of a little, long-legged, and swift animal.

P گريغ *gurīgh*, Flying: a fugitive. Flight.

P گريفتن *gureftan*, To flee, to run away.

P گريگاه *girī-gāh*, That part of the pilaw which touches a neck of mutton when stewing in a pot.

P گرينده *giryanda*, A weeper, a wailer.

P گريو *girīv*, A stake, pledge, hostage.

P گريواره *girīwāra*, A necklace.

P گريوازه *girewāza*, A string of beads.

P گريوان *girīwān*, A collar.

P گريودوم *garayūdūm*, Perfidy, treachery.

P گريون *garīwan*, Scab, ringworm.

P گريوه *garīwa* or *girīwa*, A low hill. A high bank, high ground, a mound of earth which has been worn into gullies by the rain.

P گريه *girya*, A plaint, lamentation. Crying, weeping, tears. گريه كردن *girya kardan*, To weep, to cry. گريه كنان و سينه زنان *girya-kunān u sīna-zanān*, Bewailing and beating the breast. گريه و زاري *girya u zārī*, Weeping and wailing.

P گز *gaz*, The tamarisk-tree. A yard for measuring cloth. A cubit, a length of 24 finger-breadths, or six hands. A ramrod. A sort of arrow or dart without wing or point, the two ends being small and the middle thick. گزشايگان *gazi shāygān*, (or گز ملك *gazi mulk*) A measure equal to half the height of a man of ordinary stature (used chiefly in Khurāsān). (in comp.) Biting, pungent. زبان گز *zabān-gaz*, Biting the tongue, acrid. *Giz*, A tooth.

P گزا *gazā*, Biting. Hurtful. Harm, loss.

P گزار *guzār*, A pass, passage. A surgeon's lancet or cupping-instrument. The outline of a drawing. Payment of debt. Performance of prayer. Sleep, dream. (imper. of گزاشتن *guzāshtan*) Leave thou. (in composition) Who leaves, quits, or pays.

P گزارا *guzārā*, Paying. An utterer of words.

P گزاردن *guzārdan*, To quit, leave. To pay, discharge. To draw the outline of a picture.

P گزارده *guzārda*, Discharged, paid (debt).

P گزارش *guzārish*, The interpretation of a dream; explanation. Utterance. A quitting, a leaving. A discharging, paying.

P گزارش گر *guzārishgar*, An interpreter of dreams. One who transmits, brings, conveys, carries. One who agrees or consents.

P گزارشن *guzārishn*, Interpretation of a dream; explanation. Utterance. A quitting, discharging.

P گزارش نامه *guzārish-nāma*, (گزارشي نامه *guzārishī-nāma* or گزارنامه *guzār-nāma*) A book on the interpretation of dreams. A commentary.

P گزارنده *guzāranda*, Who leaves or quits. Who causes to pass. A payer. A speaker. A drawer of pictures.

P گزاره *gazāra*, A thing, substance, fact, history. *Guzāra*, The interpretation of dreams. Explanation. Excess, much.

P گزاره نامه *guzāra-nāma*, A book containing the interpretation of dreams. A commentary.

P گزاريدن *guzārīdan*, To pay, perform, or satisfy. To speak. To sketch, draw an outline, mark, or trace. نقطه گزاريدن *nukta guzārīdan*, To put a dot.

P گزاز *guzāz*, The uneasiness which men suffer from heat, passion, and the like.

P گزاستن *guzāstan*, To curry hides, dress skins. To lay stones.

P گزاشتن *guzāshtan*, To pass by. To quit, leave. To pay a debt or fine, make a present on the renewal of a lease and the like. To transmit, remit an offence. To make a sketch of a drawing, to mark or trace.

P گزاف *gizāf* or *guzāf*, Foolish, vain, idle, extravagant. Very much, innumerable, extreme. بگزاف *ba guzāf*, At random, by guess. بگزاف ستاندن *ba guzāf satāndan*, To take, to buy any indefinite quantity, without weight, measure, or number. بگزاف فروختن *ba guzāf farokhtan*, To sell in the gross.

P گزافرنگان *gazāf-rangān*, Quickness, activity.

P گزافه *gizāfa*, Innumerable, much. Boundless. Vanity, an idle, foolish saying or action.

P گزان *gazān*, Biting, pungent. *Guzān*, Choosing.

P گزانگبين *gaz-angubīn*, Basrah honey, manna; bitter honey.

P گزانيدن *gazānīdan*, To cause to bite. To injure.

P گزاو رنگان *gazāv-rangān*, Quickness, haste.

P گزاونگان *gazāwangān*, Haste, speed, activity.

P گزاوه *gazāwa*, A litter for camel or elephant.

P گزاي *gazāy*, Who wounds or injures.

P گزايان *gazāyān*, Injurious, hurtful, detrimental.

P گزايستن *guzāyistan*, To pass, pervade.

P گزايش *gazāyish* or *gizāyish*, A stick for driving cattle. A twisting, contortion. *Guzāyish* or *gazāyish*, Fit, proper.

P گزر *gazar*, A carrot. *Guzar*, A passage, transit. A scrip. A dream. *Guzir* or *guzar*, Remedy, help.

P گزرد *guzard*, A remedy, help, or cure. لا گزرد *lā guzard*, Remediless.

P گزردن *guzardan*, To apply a remedy.

P گزرنامه *guzar-nāma*, A book on the interpretation of dreams.

P گزره *gazura*, An herb called سرزيره *sarzīra*.

P گزف *gazf* or *guzf*, Pitch or tar. Silver burnt black. Goldsmiths' black (a kind of composition).

P گزك *gazak*, A relish (eaten with wine), a devil. Nipped with cold.

P گزلك *gizlik*, A small long-handled knife. A sort of penknife with a crooked point, and narrow at the other end, chiefly brought from Egypt.

P گزم *gazm*, The tamarisk-tree.

P گزما *gazmā*, A kind of sorrel.

P گزمازك *gazmāzak*, (or گزمازو *gazmāzū*) The fruit of the tamarisk-tree.

P گزند *gazand*, Loss, injury, damage, mishap, misfortune, ruin, calamity. A fatal accident in consequence of witchcraft.

P گزند رسان *gazand-rasān*, Injurious, hurtful.

P گزند رساني *gazand-rasānī*, Injuriousness.

P گزندگي *gazandagī*, Mordacity, bite, sting.

P گزنگبين *gazangubīn*, Manna.

P گزنند *gaznand*, A sack filled with straw.

P گزنه *gazna*, A nettle.

P گزني *gaznay*, Wet and withered (winter-plant).

P گزيت *gazīt* or *gizyat*, An annual tax exacted by government. Capitation-tax paid by Jews and Christians. *Guzīt*, Chosen, approved.

P گزيد *gazīd*, A gift, present, douceur, bribe. A tribute imposed by conquerors. *Guzīd*, Selected, chosen, distinguished. A game like leap-frog.

P گزيدگر gazīdgar, Tributary, subject.

P گزيدگي gazīdagī, A bite, a sting.

P گزيدن gazīdan, To bite. To sting, prick with a needle. To wound with weapon or tongue. To cut off. To fear. To imagine. Guzīdan, To choose, select, prefer. To assist.

P گزيده gazīda, Bitten. Alarmed, afraid. Vexed, indignant. Imagined. Guzīda, Chosen, excellent. Peculiar, private. A selection. Assistance. Name of a boy's game. گزيدهٔ اخيار guzīda-i akhyār, Chosen above all people, the most excellent of the just. گزيدهٔ شهان guzīda-i shahān, The best of kings. اي شاه عالم و گزيدهٔ بني آدم ay shāhi ʿālam u guzīda-i banī ādam, O king of the world, and chosen of the sons of Adam!

P گزير gazīr or gizīr, A vazīr. The superintendant or collector of the revenue. A hero, champion. Guzīr, Aid, help, remedy. Escape. گزير كردن guzīr kardan, To help. نا گزير nā guzīr, Remediless, helpless.

P گزيره guzīra, A remedy, help, cure.

P گزين gazīn, Biting. A nettle. Guzīn, Electing, choosing. Chosen. خلوت گزين khalwat-guzīn, Fond of solitude, solitary, retiring from the world.

P گزينش guzīnish, Approbation. Property, peculiarity. Chosen.

P گزيننده guzīnanda, A chooser.

P گزينه gazīna, An iron or wooden mallet. A coppersmith's hammer. A storehouse, treasury. A thick (or close) and rather coarse kind of cotton cloth for making tents or for clothing for the poor. Guzīna, Choice, excellent, chosen, approved. Property, innate quality.

P گزيني guzīnī, Property, quality, disposition.

P گزيه gizya, A poll-tax, capitation-tax.

P گژاژ gujāj, The crop or gizzard of a bird.

P گژدهم gajdaham, Name of a champion of Persia.

P گژف gajf, Pitch. Silver burnt black.

P گژم gujm, Sorrow, distress of mind. A large-stemmed and leafy tree, called the gnat-tree.

P گسار gusār, Carrying away, removing. غم گسار gham-gusār, Removing grief, i.e. A friend. ميگسار may-gusār, Who drinks wine. غم گسار gham-gusār, Who experiences sorrow.

P گساردن gusārdan, To quit, leave. To drink (wine). To experience (sorrow).

P گسارده gusārda, Left, quitted.

P گست gast, Ugly, shameful, base, displeasing.

P گستاخ gustākh, Arrogant, presumptuous, bold, rash, audacious, uncivil, rude, impudent, cruel.

P گستاخانه gustākhāna, Impudently. Rashly.

P گستاخ دست gustākh-dast, Quick, dexterous.

P گستاخي gustākhī, Arrogance, want of urbanity or politeness, rudeness, freedom, familiarity.

P گستر gustar, A bed. A bolster, a pillow. The black or white thorn. (in comp.) Spreading, strewing, scattering, diffusing. A spreader, strewer, scatterer. ضيا گستر ziyā-gustar, Light-diffusing. وفا گستر wafā-gustar, A propagator of religion, one of the true believers. خان مكرمت گستر khāni makramat-gustar, A most merciful prince.

P گستراندن gustarāndan, (and گسترانيدن gustarānīdan) To spread, strew. To cause to spread.

P گسترانيده gustarānīda, Strewn, spread.

P گستردن gustardan, To expand, diffuse; to make (a bed). To spread. To arrange.

P گستردني gustardanī, A bed, cushion, carpet, &c.

P گسترده gustarda, Spread (bed). A foundation.

P گسترش gustarish, Any thing that may be spread; a carpet.

P گستريدن gustarīdan, To spread. To arrange.

P گستوان gustuwān, Horse-armour.

P گسته gasta, The dung of horses and the like. Gusta, Starving, hungry.

P گستهم gustaham, Name of the grandson of Minūchihr; also of a certain champion of Irān.

P گستي gastī, Ugliness, deformity.

P گسختن gusikhtan, To break, tear, pull, or twist off. To burst, be broken.

P گسستگي gusistagī, Breach, interruption.

P گسستن gusistan or gusustan, To break off. To be broken or twisted off.

P گسسته gusis or gususta, Broken, broken off.

P گسسته روده gusista-rūda, Griped in the bowels.

P گسسته مهار gusista-mahār, Ungovernable.

P گسسته نور gusista-nūr, The new moon. A drinking-vessel in the form of a ship.

P گسل gusil, A breaking. Breaking, tearing. جان گسل jān-gusil, Heart-breaking. غم گسل gham-gusil, Destroying care.

P گسله gusila, A bit broken off, a fragment.

P گسليدن gusilīdan, To break.

P گسن gusn, Hunger.

P گسنامار gus-nāmār, Extreme hunger.

P گسنده gusanda, Desire, appetite. Pith of a tree.

P گسنگي gusnagī, Hunger.

P گسنه gusna, Hungry.

P گسي gusī, Dismission, discarding, a sending away. A bidding farewell. Sloth, heaviness, torpor.

P گسيختن gusīkhtan, To snap asunder, separate.

P گسيخته gusīkhta, Broken off.

P گسيل gusīl, Dismission. Farewell. A breaking, tearing. گسيل كردن gusīl kardan, To send away.

P گسيلا gusīlā, Bending, doubling. Nux vomica.

P گش gash, Delicate, handsome, genteel. The blandishments and coquetry of girls; the elegant air of a pretty woman. Joy, gladness. A boat. Interruption, hindrance, impediment. Gish, The heart. Gush, Humour or temperament of the body, of which there are four: as, گش زرد gushi zard, (Yellow humour) Bile; گش سفيد gushi safed, (White humour) Phlegm; گش سرخ gushi surkh, (Red humour) Blood; گش سياه gushi siyāh, (Black humour) Bile, gall.

P گشاد gushād, He opened. Wide. Victory, conquest. Happy, well. Happiness. Discharging an arrow. گشاد كار gushādi kār, The opening or accomplishing of an affair.

P گشادگي gushādagī, Width, space, openness.

P گشادن gushādan, To open.

P گشاد نامه gushād-nāma, A royal mandate, diploma, patent, or privilege. Lettering or title-page.

P گشاده gushāda, Opened. Open.

P گشاده دل gushāda-dil, Open-hearted, liberal.

P گشاده زبان gushāda-zabān, Eloquent.

P گشاد هنگامان gushād-hangāmān, Four seasons.

P گشاسب gushāsb, Name of an ancient king of Persia (the same as گشتاسب gushtāsb).

P گشاك gushāk, An arm long from the shoulder to the elbow.

P گشب gushb, Leaping. A leaper, jumper.

P گشت gasht, It came to pass. Walking, strutting, looking about, surrounding, going round (especially guards patrolling), perambulation, recreation, amusement, diversion. Erasure, obliteration. State, condition, posture of affairs. A pumpkin. The bitter purging apple. گشت كوه ودشت gashti kohu dasht, A tour through hills and deserts. گشت وگذار كردن gasht u guzār kardan, To take a walk. To wander, stray, stroll, saunter.

P گشتا gushtā, Heaven.

P گشتاسپ gushtāsp, Name of a king of Persia (Darius Hystaspes). A channel by which communications of divine grace are made from the Creator to the creature.

P گشت بر گشت gasht bar gasht, Fold upon fold. A certain creeping plant.

P گشتسب gushtasb, An ancient king of Persia.

T گشت سلامي gasht-salāmī, A tax exacted by the kāzīs when on a circuit.

P گشتك gashtak, A beetle.

P گشتگي gashtagī, Perversion, perverseness.

P گشتن gashtan, To turn, return, change, alter, repeat, renew. To become, to be changed, converted, perverted. To twist. To go away, depart. گشتن روي gashtani rūy, A distemper attended with convulsions. A squint of the eye, twist of the nose or mouth to one side. A wrinkle. بازگشتن bāz gashtan, To return, come back. Gishtan, To bend, incline.

P گشته gashta, Returned, converted, perverted. Inverted, reversed. Become, formed. Firm. Changed. Squint-eyed. Gushta, Hungry.

P گشتي gashtī, Watch, sentinel, patrol. Gladness, happiness, health. A merry, sportive air.

P گشسب gashasb, Splendour, lustre. (in comp.) A worshipper. Leaping, jumping. Name of a king.

P گشف gashf, Pitch. Silver burnt black. Goldsmiths' black.

P گشن gashn, gashan, or gushn, Much, abundant, numerous. Gushn, The male of any animal.

A male palm-tree. A desire for the male. Pregnancy, gestation. Fruitfulness of a palm-tree. به گشن آمدن *ba gushn āmadan*, To be in heat (a bitch). گشن دادن *gushn dādan*, To give the male (to any animal). To sprinkle the female palm-tree with the male flowers. گشن گرفتن *gushn giriftan*, To take the male. To be impregnated.

P گشنبز *gushn-buz*, A he-goat.

P گشن خواه *gushn-khwāh*, In want of the male. گشن خواه شدن *gushn-khwāh shudan*, To be in heat.

P گش نشین *gash nishīn*, The fourth of the month.

P گشن ناك *gushnnāk*, Pregnant.

P گشنه *gushna*, Hungry.

P گشني *gushnī*, The act of generation. Application of the male flowers of the palm to the female. گشني كردن *gushnī kardan*, To engender, to cover.

P گشن يافته *gushn-yāfta*, Taken the male, covered, lined, impregnated (female).

P گشني داده *gushnī-dāda*, Fructified, impregnated (female palm-tree).

P گشنيز *gashnīz*, A mirthful, sportful, joyous air. Joy, mirth. Joyful. *Gishnīz*, Coriander-seed.

P گشنيز حصرم *gishnīz-hisrim*, Grape-wine.

P گشودن *gushūdan*, To open.

P گشي *gashī* or *gashshī*, Health, happiness. *Gashshī*, A graceful air in walking.

P گطا *gatā*, A trap-ball stick.

P گفت *guft*, He said, he spoke. A word, saying, speech, discourse. Any thing thick and dense. A garment of a close texture. گفت و گوي *guft u gūy* or *goy*, (گفت و گو *guft u gū*, or گفت گو *guft-gū*) Conversation, common talk, discourse, rumours, reports, news; disputes, jarring pretensions, lawsuits, squabbles; superfluity of words; also eloquence. گفت و شنيد *guft u shunīd*, Speaking and hearing, question and answer, dialogue, conversation, conference, debate, controversy.

P گفتا *guftā*, He said.

P گفتار *guftār*, Speech, conversation; a saying. A chapter. شكر گفتار *shakar-guftār*, Speaking sweetly, eloquent.

P گفتاريدن *guftārīdan*, To speak.

P گفتان *guftān*, A locust, or a bird like it. A green fish.

P گفتگو *guftgū*, Parley.

P گفتن *guftan*, To say, speak, call, relate, rehearse, repeat. To tell. To compose (a poem). To open, cleave. باز گفتن *bāz guftan*, To state fully, openly.

P گفتني *guftanī*, Fit to be said or spoken.

P گفته *gufta*, Said, related, spoken. A speech. گفته شدن *gufta shudan*, To be related or published.

P گفتي *guftī*, Speech.

P گل *gil*, Clay, mud. گل ارمني *gili armanī*, (or گل سرخ *gili surkh*) Bole armoniac. گل اقريطس *gili ikrītus*, Cretan earth. گل پارسي *gili pārsī*, A kind of clay with which women wash their heads. گل پرورده *gili parwarda*, The human body. گل حكمت *gili hikmat*, Lute, cement. گل خراساني *gili khurāsānī*, A kind of chalk which they eat. گل زرد *gili zard*, A kind of yellow clay brought from the neighbourhood of Constantinople. گل سرشوي *gili sar-shūy*, Persian earth used for cleansing the head. گل سفيد *gili safed*, Chalk. گل شاموسي *gili shāmūsī*, Samian earth. گل قبرسي *gili kubrusī*, Cyprus clay. گل مختوم *gili makhtūm*, (or گل نبشته *gili nibishta*) Sealing-clay or wax, the earth of Lemnos, ruddle. گل مصري *gili misrī*, Egyptian clay. *Gul*, A rose. A flower. Embers. A red colour. Snuff of a lamp or a candle. Albugo. A seton, an issue. A mark made by burning. Balls of charcoal used for burning the tobacco in a hooka. The caput mortuum of tobacco left on the tile of a hooka after smoking. Good fortune. گل اربه *guli urba*, Name of a medicinal plant. گل آسمان *guli āsmān*, The sun. گل اشرفي *guli ashrafī*, Calendula. گل آگين كردن *gul-āgīn kardan*, To fill to the brim. گل اورنگ *guli awrang*, Name of a flower. گل با فرمان *gul bā farmān*, A violet. گل بي فرمان *gul bī farmān*, A reddish rose growing in the meadows. The anemone. گل پارسي *guli pārsī*, A very red and fragrant rose. گل پياده *guli piyāda*, Any flower that grows on a small plant. Wild flowers. گل تر *guli tar*, A fresh rose. The cheek or hand of the fair sex. گل جعفري *guli jaʻfarī*, Tagetes patula. گل حجر *guli hajar*, Fire. گل خيرا *guli khayrā*, (or گل خيرو *guli khayrū*) Chinese and Persian hollyhock. گل دو رنگ *guli du rang*, The rose of two colours (pale yellow and red). گل رعنا *guli raʻnā*, A sort of rose, yellow within and red without. گل زرد فلك *guli zardi falak*, The sun. گل سرخ *guli surkh*, A red rose. گل سنگ *guli sang*, Lichen. گل سورنجان *guli sūranjān*, Flower of the hermodactyl-plant. گل سوري *guli sūrī*, A remarkably beautiful and odoriferous Persian rose. گل سوسن *guli sūsan*, A lily. گل شدن *gul shudan*, To become manifest. To arrive at the summit of greatness. گل صد برگ *guli sad barg*, The hundred-leaved rose. گل صد برگ آسمان *guli sad bargi āsmān*, The world-illuminating sun. گل طرّه *guli turra*, Poinciana pulcherrima. گل عبّاس *guli ʻabbās*, Name of a plant, marvel of Peru. گل عجائب *guli ʻajāʼib*, Name of a flower (Hibiscus mutabilis). گل فرنگ *guli farang*, Name of a flower (Vinca Rosea). گل قبرسي *guli kubrusī*, A Cyprus rose. گل قحبه *guli kahba*, A red and yellow rose. گل كاچيره *guli kāchīra*, (or گل كاجيله *guli kājīla*) A kind of saffron-flower used for dyeing. گل كردن *gul kardan*, To extinguish, to snuff (a candle). To become apparent, manifest. گل كوزه *guli kūza*, A wild rose. گل گرفتن *gul giriftan*, To snuff a candle. گل گيتي *guli gītī*, A particular species of rose. گل مخمل *guli makhmal*, Globe amaranth. گل مشكين *guli mishkīn*, Narcissus. گل مكرّر *guli mukarrar*, Syrup of roses. گل نشاط *guli nishāt*, Grape-wine. گل يوسف *guli yūsuf*, The anemone.

P گلاب *gilāb*, Clay and water. *Gulāb*, Rose-water. Julap.

P گلاب پاش *gulāb-pāsh*, A bottle for sprinkling rose-water. A rose-water bottle, generally of silver or gold.

P گلابدان *gulābdān*, A vessel for rose-water.

P گلابي *gulābī*, Rose-colour. A flagon. A kind of sweetmeat.

P گلاج *gulāj*, A Persian cake of flour, honey, and sesame-oil. A delicate confectionary made of starch and eggs.

P گلاگونه *gulāgūna*, A red paint for the face.

P گل آلوده *gil-ālūda*, Bedaubed with clay.

P گلاله *gulāla*, A shirt. A long lock of hair hanging loose. A bunch of flowers. A nosegay.

P گلان *gulān*, A kind of cake fried in butter and eaten with syrup. Shaking a carpet or skin of a garment. (pl. of گل *gul*) Roses.

P گل اندازي *gil-andāzī*, An embankment of earth with a ditch, for confining water on the lands, and to serve as a reservoir.

P گل اندام *gul-andām*, Slender, graceful, delicate.

P گلاندن *gulāndan*, To strew, to scatter.

P گلانيدن *gulānīdan*, To shake (a carpet, or the skirts of one's garment). To scatter.

P گلاه *galāh*, Black.

P گلبار *gulbār*, Name of a city.

P گل باغ *gul-bāgh*, Paradise.

P گلبام *gulbām*, A loud shout or noise made by a concourse of mendicants or travellers. The noise of a kettle-drum.

P گلبانگ *gulbāng*, A loud shout. The war-cry of "Allah! Allah!" The note of the nightingale.

P گلبت *galbat*, A large boat or ship.

P گلبدن *gul-badan*, With a body like a rose (epithet of a mistress). A kind of silken cloth.

P گلبرگ *gul-barg*, A rose-leaf. A mistress.

P گلبرگه *gulbargah*, A place in the Deccan.

P گلبشكر *gul ba shakar*, Conserve of roses.

P گلبن *gul-bun*, A rose-bush. The foot of a tree. The root of a rose-tree.

P گلبنگ *gulbang*, The noise of a drum.

P گل به شكر *gul ba shakar*, Conserve of roses.

P گلبيز *gul-bez*, Scattered rose-leaves.

P گلپايگان *gulpāyagān*, Name of a city in Irāk.

P گل پياده *gul-piyāda*, A kind of inodorous rose.

P گلتراش *gul-tarāsh*, Snuffers.

P گلتنگ *gil-tang*, Viscous clay.

P گل چشم *gul-chashm*, Troubled with albugo.

P گل چگان *gul-chagān*, A kind of fire-work. *Gul-chigān*, Name of tree.

P گلچه *galcha*, A magpie. *Gilcha*, A quail. *Gulcha*, A small rose or flower, a floweret, floret.

P گل چهره *gul-chihra*, Name of the mistress of a man called اورنگ *awrang*.

P گل چين *gul-chīn*, Gathering roses or flowers.

A gardener. Name of a certain woman.

P گلخ *galkh*, A wrinkle.

P گل خال *gul-khāl*, Spotted. Flowered.

P گل خنج *gul khaj*, A round lump of dough.

P گلخن *gul-khan*, The fire-place in a bath; stove.

P گلخن تاب *gulkhan-tāb*, One who lights the furnaces of baths.

P گلخوچه *gulkhocha*, Tickling.

P گل خور *gul-khwur*, A horse's halter.

P گل خوردني *gil khwurdanī*, Chalk.

P گلدار *gil-dār*, Full of clay. *Gul-dār*, Possessing roses. A rose-garden. Spotted. Flowered.

P گلدان *guldān*, A flower-pot.

P گلدرخت *gul-dirakht*, A rose-bush. Barberry.

P گلدسته *gul-dasta*, A handful of roses; a nosegay. A minaret whence people are called to prayer.

P گلرخ *gul-rukh* (or رخسار *rukhsār*) Rosy-cheeked.

P گلرعنا *gul-raʻnā*, A beautiful, delicate-scented rose. Rouge with which ladies paint their cheeks. A bed of roses in full blow.

P گل رنگ *gul-rang*, Rose-coloured, roseate.

P گل رو *gul-rū*, Rosy-faced, red-faced, ruddy.

P گلروي *gul-rūy*, Rosy-faced, ruddy, having a blooming complexion. A mistress, sweetheart.

P گل روئي *gul-rūʼī*, Rosy-facedness.

P گلريز *gul-rez*, A kind of silken stuff.

P گلزار *gilzār*, Clay, mud. A miry place. *Gulzār*, A garden of roses. Name of a note in music.

P گل زريون *gul zaryūn*, Name of a city and river in Turkistān.

P گل ساز *gil-sāz*, A worker in clay.

P گلست *galast*, Dead-drunk.

P گلستان *gulistān*, A rose-garden. A flower-garden. A celebrated Persian book in prose and verse, by Shaykh Saadī Muslihu'd dīn ash' Shīrāzī. Sādī was born at Shīrāz, the capital of Persia Proper, A. D. 1175, and spent most of his life in travelling as a dervish. He died A. D. 1291, aged 116. رشك گلستان ارم *rashki gulistāni iram*, The envy of the gardens of Iram.

P گلستو *gulistū*, A flower-garden.

P گلسرخ *gul-surkh*, A red flower. The world-illuminating sun.

P گلسون *gulsūn*, A net in which women confine their hair. A row of pearls.

P گلشاه *gil-shāh*, King of the earth. Name of the first monarch of the Peshdādian dynasty, called also كيومرث *kayūmars*. Adam. *Gulshāh*, Name of the mistress of ورقه *warka*.

P گلشكر *gul-shakar*, (گل با شكر *gul bā shakar*, or بشكر *ba shakar*) Conserve of roses.

P گلشن *gulshan*, A rose or flower-garden. A delightful spot; a place where a person enjoys himself. Florid, cheerful, agreeable. گلشن قدس *gulshani huds*, The highest heaven. گلشن كردن *gulshan kardan*, To recreate or amuse one's self. To sing, dance, and be happy.

P گلشن سراي *gulshan-sarāy*, A garden-palace.

P گلشو *gil-shū*, A depilatory used in baths.

P گلشه *gil-shah*, The king Kayūmars. Adam. *Gulshah*, Name of the mistress of ورقه *warka*.

P گلشهر *gulshahr*, Name of the wife of پيران ويسه *pīrān wīsa*, commander of the forces of Afrāsyāb.

P گلعذار *gul-ʻizār*, Rosy-cheeked.

P گلغر *gilghar*, An architect. *Gulghar*, A fine down or wool, combed from the roots of a species of goat bred in Tibet, of which shawls are made.

P گلغنچه *gul-ghincha*, Tickling. *Gul-ghuncha*, A rose-bud. A red paint for the face, rouge, fard.

P گلغنده *gulghanda*, Cotton ready for spinning.

P گلغونده *gulghūnda*, A ball of cotton ready for spinning. A fat, lazy, sluggish fellow.

P گلغونه *gulghūna*, Paint for the face, fard.

P گلغيچه *gulghīcha*, Tickling.

P گلفام *gul-fām*, Of a rose colour. A mistress.

P گلفشان *gul-fishān*, Scattering roses. Agreeable, pleasant.

P گلفهشنگ *gulfahshang*, Water which petrifies in the form of icicles.

P گلقند *gul-hand*, Candied conserve of roses. گل قند عسلي *gul-handi ʻasalī*, Conserve of roses made with honey.

P گلك *gulak*, (dim. of گل *gul*) A little rose. A floweret. A satire, lampoon, abuse. A reddish sort of gum. گلك انار *gulaki anār*, A pomegranate-flower.

P گلكار *gil-kār*, A worker in clay. A potter.

P گلكاري *gil-kārī*, A working in clay. گلكاري كردن *gil-kārī kardan*, To work in clay. *Gul-kārī*, Flowering. Flower-painting.

P گلكج *gulkaj*, A lump of dough.

P گلكنده *gulkunda*, Golconda (in India).

P گلكوي *gil-kūy*, Mud in the street.

P گلكيش *gul-kesh*, The cock's-comb flower.

P گلكچه *gul-gaja*, Certain ceremonies ordained to be performed upon infants.

P گلگشت *gul-gasht*, A pleasant place for walking or recreation, especially blooming with roses and other flowers. An evening walk. Name of a charming place near Shīrāz in Persia.

P گل گل *gal gal*, A very acid kind of citron. *Gulgul*, Name of an Arabian gum, bdellium.

P گل گندم *gil-gandum*, Name of a medicinal root.

P گل گنده *gul ganda*, Name of a very stinking plant, which women render sweet, and eat in order to become fat.

P گلگورستان *gul-goristān*, A fungus.

P گل گولي *gul gūlī*, A walk in a garden in spring.

P گلگون *gul-gūn*, Of a vermilion colour. Paint for the face. A goblet of wine. A bright bay horse, especially one belonging to Shīrīn, the mistress of Farhād. گلگون چرخ *gulgūni charkh*, The sky. شير گلگون *sheri gul-gūn*, A tawny lion.

P گلگونه *gul-gūna*, Cosmetic. Rosy-cheeked. Rose-coloured. گلگونهٔ اديم آدم *gul-gūnaʼi adīmi ādam*, An epithet of Muhammad. گلگونهٔ چرخ *gul-gūnaʼi charkh*, A ruddiness in the sky after sunset.

P گلگير *gul-gīr*, Snuffers.

P گل لاله *gul lāla*, The anemone.

P گل لحنه *gul lahana*, Cauliflower.

P گلمج *galmij*, The fin of a fish.

P گلمر *gulmar*, Name of a fragrant flower. A kind of arrow-head.

P گلموژ *galmūj*, A species of lizard.

P گلموش *gulamūsh*, A species of the willow.

P گل مهره *gil-muhra*, A ball of clay for a cross-bow. The terrestrial globe. Man.

P گلميخ *gul-mekh*, A large-headed, rose-shaped nail fixed in gates. A spike-nail, tent-pin. A stud, tack.

P گلنار *gulnār*, Sour cherry. Pomegranate-flowers.

P گلناري *gulnārī*, Of the colour of the pomegranate-flower. گلناري رنگ *gulnārī-rang*, Carnation-coloured.

P گل نا فرمان *gul nā farmān*, A violet.

P گلناك *gilnāk*, Muddy, miry, clayey (place). *Gilnāk* or *gulnāk*, A fortification, a castle or fortress. *Gulnāk*, A rose-garden; a flower-bed.

P گلنده *gulanda*, A woman of bad character.

P گلنسرين *gul-nasrīn*, Camomile-flowers.

P گل نفسي *gul-nafsī*, A sweet smell. Pleasant conversation.

P گلنگبين *gulangubīn*, A conserve of roses made with honey.

P گلو *gulū*, The neck, gullet, throat. گلوي آسيا *gulūyi āsyā*, The hopper of a mill. گلوي سرخ *gulūyi surkh*, The gullet. گلو روشن كردن *gulū roshan kardan*, To hem, to clear the throat. گلو فرو آمدگي *gulū furo āmadagī*, A catarrh in the throat. گلو گرفتن *gulū giriftan*, To strangle. بگلو فرو بردن *ba gulū furo burdan*, (or در گلو بردن *dar gulū burdan*) To swallow. Deglutition.

P گلو بند *gulū-band*, A neckcloth. A necklace. A cloth worn by women on their head, and fastened under the chin, to keep their head-dress from being stained by the unguent or pomatum of the hair.

P گلو بنده *gulū-banda*, A grown lad. A glutton.

P گلوته *gulū-tah*, A kind of cornered cap for children, lined with cotton, and tied under the chin.

P گلوچ *gulūch*, A wink with the eye.

P گلودن *gulūdan*, To fill.

P گلوز *galūz*, A filbert. A pistachio-nut. A mountain-almond.

P گلو گرفتگي *gulū-giriftagī*, Hoarseness.

P گلو گرفته *gulū-girifta*, Throttled. Hoarse, gruff.

P گلو گرفته آواز *gulū-girifta-āwāz*, Hoarse-voiced.

P گلوگير *gulū-gīr*, Suffocating, throttling. Sour or unsavoury food, which sticks in the throat and is digested with difficulty. A wild or choke-pear. An accuser.

P گلوله *gulūla*, A reel. A ball of thread. A stone for a cross-bow or balista, a bullet.

P گلوند *galwand*, Any thing sent as a present,

especially a composition of nuts and figs.

P گلوه *gulwa*, The mouth of an oven.

P گله *gala*, (or گلّه *galla*) A flock, herd, bevy. A crowd, heap. *Gila*, A complaint, lamentation, reproach, blame. A pass between two hills. A single grape. گله کردن *gila kardan*, To complain. *Gula*, A cannon, musket, or cross-bow ball. A cotton reel. A cotton-pod. A ringlet, a curl.

P گلّه *gulla*, A swallow, a martinet. An arbour, bower, projecting roof. Hair collected together. گلّهٔ مرغان *gulla-i murghān*, Tapestry embroidered with every kind of bird. A shadow cast by an immense flight of birds.

P گله بان *galabān*, A pastor, shepherd, keeper.

P گله باني *galabānī*, Pastoral care.

P گله دوست *gala-dost*, A cough, a sore throat.

P گله کرده شده *gila-karda-shuda*, Complained of, complained against.

P گله گاه *gala-gāh*, A lodging-room in an inn.

P گله مند *gilamand*, Complaining: a complainer.

P گله مندي *gilamandī*, Murmur, complaint.

P گله موش *gula-mūsh*, A kind of willow.

P گلي *gilī*, Earthen, made of clay.

P گليچه *gulīcha*, A sob. The hiccough. The sun or moon's disk. A small round cake.

P گليز *gīz* or *galīz*, Spittle, saliva, slaver, drivel.

P گليگان *guligān*, Name of a stinking plant.

P گليگر *giligar*, Maker of mortar, worker in clay.

P گليم *gilīm*, A garment made of goats' hair or wool. A carpet or rug to lie down upon.

P گليم پوش *gilīm-posh*, Clad in a گليم *gilīm*.

P گليم شوي *gilīm-shūy*, A scourer of cloths. Pearl-ash, lye; root چوبك اشنان *chūbak ushnān*.

P گليم گوشان *gilīm-goshān*, (pl.) A race of men whose ears are so large that the one serves them for a mattress, and the other as a counterpane.

P گلين *gilīn*, Made of clay or mud, clayey.

P گلين گوي *gilīn gūy*, The terrestrial globe.

P گليون *galyūn*, A kind of stuff of seven colours.

P گم *gum*, Lost, wanting, missing. Absent, invisible. Wandering, distracted, confounded. گم شدن *gum shudan*, To be lost. To lose one's self. گم كردن *gum kardan*, To lose. گم كردن نعمت كسي را *gum kardani niʻmati kase rā*, To lose the remembrance of any one's services; to be ungrateful. گم گشتهٔ دار و ديار *gum-gashta-i dār u diyār*, Losing house and home, driven from country and friends.

P گمار *gumār*, A large ladle. The noise made by the feet in walking. (Imp. of, and contracted from, گماشتن *gumāshtan* and گماريدن *gumāridan*).

P گمارا *gumārā*, Committing. A fold for cattle.

P گماريدن *gumāridan*, To gnash the teeth in indignation. To force, compel. To sew, so that the threads and stitches are seen. وا گماريدن *wā gumāridan*, To shew the teeth in laughing; smile, grin.

P گماشتگي *gumāshtagī*, Lieutenancy, commission, delegation, charge, appointment.

P گماشتن *gumāshtan*, To dismiss, set at liberty, to let alone. To set over, to place at the head. To commit, deliver over, recommend, consign, assign, entrust to another (any business); to commission, furnish with plenipotentiary powers. To send upon any special business. To prefix. To view the actions of another (in a bad light). To compel one to speak. To pursue or prosecute one by the power and authority of a prince or judge. To extort.

P گماشته *gumāshta*, Appointed, set over. A minister, vazīr, superintendant, commissary, agent, factor, head clerk, accountant, or servant. One whose sayings and doings are noticed.

P گماشه *gumāsha*, Silver.

P گمان *gumān*, Doubt, suspicion, surmise. Opinion, fancy, supposition, imagination. (in comp.) Thinking, suspecting. بد گمان *bad-gumān*, Suspicious, jealous, malignant. گمان بردن *gumān burdan*, (گمان كردن *gumān kardan*, گمان داشتن *gumān dāshtan*, or در گمان بودن *dar gumān būdan*) To think, imagine, suppose, believe, conjecture, fancy, doubt, suspect. در گمان شدن *dar gumān shudan*, To be doubtful, suspicious.

P گمانه *gumāna*, Doubt, suspicion. A shaft sunk in order to ascertain the depth of the water when making a subterraneous canal. A well-digger.

P گمانيدن *gumānīdan*, To think, imagine, suppose. To doubt.

P گمراه *gum-rāh*, Losing the way, wandering, stray, deviating, seduced. Abandoned, depraved. Intrepid, bold, rash, perverse, fearing neither God nor man. گمراه شدن *gum-rāh shudan*, To be seduced, to deviate. گمراه كردن *gum-rāh kardan*, To seduce, to lead astray.

P گمراهي *gum-rāhī*, A missing or losing of one's way. Deviation, seduction.

P گمره *gum-rah*, Erring, lost.

P گمست *gamast*, An inferior precious stone.

P گم شدگي *gum-shudagī*, A lost condition.

P گم شده *gum-shuda*, Lost. گم شدهٔ لب دريا *gum-shuda-i labi daryā*, Lost on the sea-shore.

P گم كرده پي *gum-karda-pay*, One of whom all traces are lost. Unrivalled, beyond another's reach.

P گمنام *gum-nām*, Whose name is lost, extinct.

P گمه *gima*, Name of an herb resembling fennel. *Guma*, A kind of fish.

P گميز *gimīz*, Urine.

P گميزيدن *gimīzīdan*, To make water.

P گميژه *gimīja*, Mixed together.

P گن *gin*, A particle put after substantives to form attributives: as, شرمگن *sharmgin*, Ashamed. *Gun*, A testicle. گن ابليس *guni iblīs*, (Devil's testicle) Name of a certain hard black grain about the size of a nutmeg.

P گناه *gunāh*, Sin, crime, error, vice, fault, iniquity.

P گناهان *gunāhān*, (pl. of گناه *gunāh*) Crimes.

P گناهگار *gunāhgār*, A sinner, culprit, criminal.

P گناهگاري *gunāhgārī*, A state of sin, a habit of vice, criminality, sinfulness. A fine for an offence.

P گناه نكرد *gunāh na kard*, Faultless.

P گنبد *gumbad*, An arch, vault, cupola, dome, tower. An arched gateway. Bud of a flower. A cup. A leap, tumble heels over head, summersault. گنبد آب *gumbadi āb*, A bubble. گنبد ازرق *gumbadi azrak*, The azure vault, *i.e.* the vault of heaven. (Synonymous to which are the following: گنبد آفت پذير *gumbadi āfat-pazīr*, گنبد تيزرو *gumbadi tezrav*, گنبد چار بند *gumbadi chār band*, گنبد جان ستان *gumbadi jān-satān*, گنبد حرّاقه رنگ *gumbadi harrāka-rang*, گنبد خضرا *gumbadi khazrā*, گنبد دود گشت *gumbadi dūd-gasht*, گنبد دور گشت *gumbadi dūr-gasht*, گنبد دولاب رنگ *gumbadi dolāb-rang*, گنبد دولابي *gumbadi dolābī*, گنبد شگرف *gumbadi shigarf*, گنبد صوفي لباس *gumbadi sūfī-libās*, گنبد طاقديس *gumbadi tākdes*, گنبد فيروزه خشت *gumbadi fīroza-khisht*, گنبد گيتي نورد *gumbadi gītī-naward*, گنبد مقرنس *gumbadi mukarnas*, گنبد نارنج *gumbadi nāranj*, گنبد نارنگ *gumbadi nārang*, and گنبد نيلوفري *gumbadi nīlūfarī*). گنبد اعظم *gumbadi aʻzam*, The great vault, *i.e.* the highest heaven. گنبد دماغ *gumbadi dimāgh*, The palate, roof of the mouth. گنبد گل *gumbadi gul*, A rose-bud. A golden goblet. گنبد مايل *gumbadi māyil*, The fourth heaven. گنبد معنبر *gumbadi muʻambar*, The hair of a mistress (her head being uncovered).

P گنبده *gumbada*, An arch, vault. A tumble head over heels. Bud of a flower. A cup.

P گنبدي *gumbadī*, A dome, vault, arch. A summersault. A tent supported by one column.

P گنج *ganj*, A store, hoard, hidden treasure. A magazine, granary, grain-market, storehouse. A mart. A case. گنج افراسياب *ganji afrāsyāb*, Name of the fourth of Khusraw's treasures. گنج الهي *ganji ilāhī*, The divine treasure, *i.e.* The word of God. Contentment. گنج باد *ganji bād*, (گنج بادآورد *ganji bād-āward*, or گنج باد آور *ganji bād-āwar*) Hidden treasure, any thing which one gets without any trouble. A windfall. Name of the second of Khusraw's treasures. Name of a note of the barbud. گنج بار *ganji bār*, Name of the eighth of Khusraw's treasures (called likewise گنج گاو *ganji gāu* and گنج شاد آورد *ganji shād-āward*). گنج حكيم *ganji hakīm*, The sage's treasure, *i.e.* The first chapter of the Kur'ān. گنج خاكي *ganji khākī*, Adam or his posterity. گنج خضرا *ganji khazrā*, The sixth of Khusraw's treasures. گنج دار *ganji dār*, Name of a note in music. گنج ديبه *ganji dība*, Name of the third treasure of Khusraw. گنج روان *ganji rawān*, Name of Korah's treasure. گنج سوخته *ganji sokhta*, Name of the fifth of Khusraw's treasures; also name of a note in music. گنج شاد آورد *ganji shād āward*, Name of one of Khusraw's treasures. گنج شايگان *ganji shāygān*, Name of another of Khusraw's treasures. گنج عروس *ganji ɛarūs*, Name of the first of Khusraw's treasures; also of a musical note. گنج فریدون *ganji farīdūn*, Name of a note in music. گنج کاوس *ganji kāwus*, Name of a musical note. گنج گاو *ganji gāv*, (گنج گاوان *ganji gāvān*, and گنج گاومیش *ganji gāwmesh*) Name of one of Jamshed's treasures, dug up in the reign of Bahram, and distributed amongst the poor. Name of a note in music. *Ginj*, A proud, conceited man. Astonished, surprised, bewildered. *Gunj*, Space, room, capacity. A proportion, or ration, observed where large numbers are to be served with provisions, so that they may all share alike.

P گنجا *gunjā*, Capability of being contained.

P گنجار *ganjār*, Rouge for the face.

P گنجاره *ganjāra*, Rouge for the face. Sesame.

P گنجانیدن *gunjānīdan*, To cause to be held.

P گنجایش *gunjāyish*, Capacity, holding, containing. Profit. Room to contain, stowage. گنجایش پذیر شدن *gunjāyish-pazīr shudan*, To be contained. گنجایش داشتن *gunjāyish dāshtan*, To have room or stowage, to be able to contain.

P گنجائی *gunjāī*, The power of containing.

P گنجبار *ganj-bār*, One of Khusraw's treasures.

P گنج بخش *ganj-bakhsh*, Liberal, lavish.

P گنجدار *ganj-dār*, A treasurer. Name of a note in music.

P گنجر *ganjar*, Rouge, fard for the face.

P گنجره *ganjara*, Red paint for the face.

P گنج ریزی *ganj-rezī*, A scattering of treasure.

P گنجشك *gunjishk*, A sparrow. A chick. Any small bird.

P گنجگاه *ganj-gāh*, A high note in music.

P گنجلنج *gunjulunj*, Any thing small.

P گنجور *ganjūr*, A treasurer. A rich man. Treasure. A treasury.

P گنجوبر *ganjwer*, (in zand and Pāz.) A treasurer.

P گنجه *ganja*, Name of the city where شیخ نظامی *shaykh nazāmī* was born. An ass without a tail; docked. Saddle-bags.

P گنجیدن *gunjīdan*, To be contained or held. To hold exactly, to be filled. To be gathered in (corn).

P گنجیده *gunjīda*, Contained, held, stowed.

P گنجیفه *ganjīfa*, Pack of cards. Game of cards.

P گنجینه *gunjīna*, A treasury, magazine, granary, barn. Any place for holding provisions. A pantry. Revenue. A pocket-book.

P گنجینه دار *gunjīna-dār*, A treasurer.

P گنجینه داری *gunjīna-dārī*, Treasurership.

P گنجینه نه *gunjīna-nih*, A treasurer.

P گنجینه نهی *gunjīna-nihī*, Treasurership.

P گند *gand*, Any thing fetid, bad smell, stink, funk. گند بغل *gandi baghal*, Stench of the arm-pits. *Gund*, A testicle. گند بیدستر *gundi bīdastar*, Testicles of the beaver. گند سگ *gundi sag*, Orchis.

P گندا *gandā*, Any thing putrid, stinking, fetid.

P گنداب *gandāb*, Fetid, stagnate water: a ditch.

P گندآور *gund-āwar*, A brave man, commander.

P گندای *ganday*, Stinking. *Gunday*, A diviner.

P گند بیدستر *gund bīdastar*, Castor.

P گندژ *gandij*, Name of a fortress built in Babylon by Zahhāk.

P گندش *gandish*, Sulphur, brimstone.

P گندك *gandak*, Brimstone. Gunpowder.

P گندگی *gandagī*, Filth, stink, stench. Putrefaction. *Gundagī*, Coarseness, thickness.

P گندگیاه *gand-giyāh*, Name of an herb of which bears are fond.

P گندلاش *gandalāsh*, A stinking kind of herb. A rotten egg.

P گندم *gandum*, Wheat. گندم دیوانه *gandumi dīwāna*, Tares, darnel. گندم کرمانی *gandumi kirmānī*, Vermicelli.

P گندم با *gandum-bā*, (Wheat-food) A dish called حلیم *halīm*, made of wheat.

P گندملك *gandumak*, Lingula vulvæ.

P گندم گون *gandum-gūn*, Wheat-colour, *i.e.* brown.

P گندم گونی *gandum-gūnī*, Tawniness, brownness.

P گندم گونی وام *gandum-gūnī vām*, Brown-coloured, of the colour of wheat, tawny.

P گندم مایهٔ خشك *gandum māyaɪ khushk*, Wheat coarsely ground.

P گندمه *gandama*, A wart. A freckle. *Ganduma*, A kind of grain deprived of the husk.

P گندن *gandan*, To rot, stink. To wax hot.

P گندنا *gandanā*, A leek. Chives.

P گندنازار *gandanāzār*, A bed of leeks.

P گندنا گون *gandanā-gūn*, Of a bright green.

P گندنا گوهر *gandanā-gawhar*, A colocynth.

P گنده *ganda*, Fetid, stinking, rotten. Ruptured. Castrated. An old man or woman. گنده شدن *ganda shudan*, To stink. *Gunda*, Coarse, thick. A wart. Hashed meat. A lump of dough. Marrow. A shoemaker's board. A pit in which hunters conceal themselves from the sight of wild beasts. گندهٔ پشم *gundaɪ pashm*, A clew or ball of wool. گندهٔ خمیر *gundaɪ khamīr*, A lump of dough. گنده کردن *gunda kardan*, To paint, figure with needle-work. To cut, clip, pare.

P گنده بغل *ganda-baghal*, One whose arm-pits emit a stench.

P گنده بوی *ganda-boy*, Smelling bad, stinking.

P گنده بهار *ganda-bahār*, Rain in cold weather.

P گنده پیچ *gunda-pech*, A spinning-wheel; a reel; a piece of wood or hand-reel for winding cotton. A potter's wheel (turned by the hand).

P گنده پیر *ganda-pīr*, A decrepit old woman. گنده پیر کابلی *ganda-pīri kābulī*, Name of a celebrated enchantress who lived in Kābul.

P گنده خایه *ganda-khāya*, A stale egg.

P گنده دهن *ganda-dahan*, Stinking-breathed.

P گنده فیروزه *ganda-fīroza*, Olibanum.

P گنده مغزی *ganda-maghzī*, Pride, insolence, boast, bluster. Foolish, absurd talk. Harshness, severity. Any one in whom these qualities appear.

P گندیدگی *gandīdagī*, Putrefaction.

P گندیدن *gandīdan*, To stink, to putrefy.

P گندیده *gandīda*, Putrid, fetid, stinking.

P گنر *ganar*, Name of a place where a battle was fought by Mahmūd Ghaznavi.

P گنگ *gang*, The Ganges. Name of a temple in China, and of another in Turkistān. Any thing bent or distorted; one born crooked. Wind in the body brought on by melancholy. Handsome, fine. Name of several cities; and of a certain mountain and island. *Gung*, Dumb. One who converses by signs. Stupid. An earthen pipe for conveying water under ground. گنگ ده زبان *gungi dah zabān*, (or صد زبان *sad-zabān*) A red rose.

P گنگار *gungār*, A serpent that has just changed his skin, that has recently cast his slough.

P گنگ بهشت *gang bihisht*, A fort in Babylon.

P گنگ دژ *gang-dij*, Name of a fortress in Babylon. Name of a place in the East.

P گنگ دژهخت *gangi dijhukht*, (دژهرج *dijhirj*, *dijhurj*, *dijhirj*, *dijharaj*, or دژهوخت *dijhūkht*) Jerusalem. An idol-temple.

P گنگل *gangal*, Play, joke, jest.

P گنگلاج *gungalāj* or *gunglāj*, A stammerer.

P گنگلاجی *gunglājī*, Stammering, stuttering.

P گنگی *gungī*, Dumbness.

P گنوار *ganwār*, A thief, robber, plunderer.

P گنور *ganūr*, Name of a fort in Hindūstān.

P گنوره *gunūra*, A workman, a mechanic.

P گنه *gunah*, (for گناه *gunāh*) A sin, crime. نیم گنه *nīm gunah*, Half a crime, a peccadillo.

P گنهگار *gunahgār*, A sinner. A criminal. نهایت گنهگار *nihāyat gunahgār*, An arrant villain.

P گنهگاری *gunahgārī*, A fine for crimes and misdemeanours.

P گنیز *gunīz*, A glutton.

P گو *gaw*, A ditch, or any low or hollow place. The sun. Venerable, respected. A hero; bold, warlike, powerful; a chieftain. *Go*, A cow. *Gū*, A ball. A button. Dung. Little, small. *Gū*, (though by some *go*) (verbal noun, and imp. of گفتن *guftān*) Saying. Say thou. Suppose. Although. A word, speech. دروغ گو *durogh-go*, A liar. معجز گو *muɛjiz-go*, Speaking miracles, expressing himself admirably. گفت و گو *guft u gū*, Conversation.

P گوا *guwā*, A witness.

P گواب *gawāb*, A ditch. The socket of the eye.

P گواچو *guwāchū*, (or گواچه *guwācha*) A swing.

P گوار *gawār*, A race of gipsies in India. *Guwār*, A thing easy of digestion. Digesting. خوش گوار *khwush-guwār*, Sweet, agreeable, easy of digestion. Wholesome, salubrious.

P گوارا *guwārā*, Digestible. Agreeable, pleasant. Digesting. Approval, consent. Bearing, enduring, submitting to. گوارا کردن *guwārā kardan*, To consent, approve. زود گوارا *zūd-guwārā*, Quick of digestion. دیر گوارا *dīr-guwārā*, Slow of digestion.

P گواران *guwārān*, Agreeable, easy of digestion.

P گوارانیدن *guwārānīdan*, To help digestion. To cook. فرو گوارانیدن *furo guwārānīdan*, To digest.

P گوارائي *guwārāī*, Wholesomeness, digestibility.

P گوارش *guwārish*, (or گوارشت *guwārisht*) Any electuary for assisting digestion.

P گوارندگي *guwārandagī*, Wholesomeness.

P گوارنده *guwāranda*, Wholesome, easy of digestion. That which digests. طعام نا گوارنده *taām-i nā guwāranda*, Meat overloading the stomach; difficult to be digested. هوايش گوارنده *hawāyash guwāranda*, Its salubrious air.

P گوارون *guwārūn*, A disease of the skin, scab.

P گواره *gawāra*, A bee-hive. A herd of oxen or buffaloes. (for گهواره *gahwāra*) A cradle. *Guwāra*, Digesting. Meat light and easy of digestion.

P گواريدن *guwārīdan*, To digest, to be digested.

P گواز *gawāz*, (or گوازه *gawāza*) A large wooden mortar in which they beat off the husk of rice. *Gawāz*, (*guwāz*, or گوازه *gawāza*) An ox-goad.

P گواژه *gawāja*, A jest, joke, fun, merriment. Jovial, jolly, jocose. A woman's coif.

P گواش *gu* or *gawāsh*, Quality, species, colour.

P گواشتن *guwāshtan*, To digest.

P گواشمه *gawāshma*, A large veil of fine linen.

P گواشير *gawāshīr*, Name of a country in which are produced white turquoise-stones of little value. Gum of the opoponax-tree.

P گواك *guwāk*, A wagtail.

P گوال *guwāl*, A closet. A carp. *Guwāl* or *gawāl*, Increase, augmentation, growth. Gain, acquisition. A sack. A rubbing, polishing, furbishing. A herdsman.

P گوالنده *guwālanda*, A crawling infant.

P گواليار *guwāliyār*, Gualior, in India.

P گواليدگي *guwālīdagī*, Increase, growth.

P گواليدن *guwālīdan*, To creep, as an infant upon hands and knees. To wave from side to side in walking. *Guwālīdan* or *gawālīdan*, To grow up, to come to maturity.

P گوان *gawān*, (pl. of گو *gaw*) Valiant warriors.

P گوانجي *gawānjī*, A hero, a captain or commander of an army.

P گوانگله *gū-angula*, A button and loop. A kind of knot. The sun.

P گواه *guwāh*, An evidence, witness, testimony. گواه آوردن *guwāh āwardan*, (or گرفتن *giriftan*) To take to witness; to bring evidence, to invoke. گواه دروغ *guwāhi durogh*, A false witness.

P گواهي *guwāhī*, Testimony, evidence. گواهي دادن *guwāhī dādan*, To give evidence, to attest.

P گوائي *guwāī*, Testimony, evidence.

P گوباره *go-bāra*, A herd of oxen. A cow-stall.

P گوبان *gobān*, A herdsman.

P گوبشا *gobashā*, (in zand and Pāz.) Honey.

P گوبيا *gobiyā*, (in zand and Pāz.) The tongue.

P گوپال *gūpāl*, An iron mace. A throne of iron or wood. Name of a Scythian warrior.

P گوپان *gopān*, A herdsman.

P گوپيازه *gūpiyāza*, A kind of food in Balkh.

P گوت *gawt*, The hips or buttock.

P گوچ *gawach*, Gum.

P گوچاه *gaw-chāh*, A shallow ditch or trench.

P گوچه *gawcha*, Threads on the edge of a garment.

P گوچي *gawchī*, A deep trench.

P گود *gawd*, Deep; a ditch; low-lying ground. *Guwad*, (a contraction of گويد *gūyad*) He says.

P گوداب *gūdāb*, (or گوزاب *gūzāb*) Syrup of dates boiled down. A dish of meat, rice, vetches, and walnuts, on which a condiment of vinegar and syrup is poured. Food dressed under roast meat.

P گودر *gawdar*, (or گودره *gawdara*) The young of the wild cow. A calf. A calf-skin. *Gawdar*, A fawn. A species of goose. A plant growing amongst wheat and barley. Name of a son of Shāpur; also of a wrestler.

P گودرز *gūdarz*, Name of a bird which frequents the banks of rivers. Name of two kings of the Ashkānian dynasty. Any two bodies which never separate, and yet are never found close together (a term chiefly applied to the heavenly bodies).

P گوده *gūda*, Reins, kidneys. Marrow, kernel. گوده بحرام *gūda ba harām*, Lazy, sluggish, do-nothing.

P گور *gawr*, A pagan, infidel, guebre, or worshipper of fire. Name of a city in Bengal, now in ruins. *Gor*, A wild ass, the onager. A tomb, grave, sepulchre, monument. A desert, a plain without water. Wine, mirth, hilarity, the pleasures of the table. A miser. Name of a Persian king of the Sassanian dynasty (called Bahrām gor). گور با مدفون *gori bā madfūn*, (or گور نا مدفون *gori nā madfūn*) (Tomb of the unburied one) The fish which swallowed Jonah. گور غريبان *gori gharībān*, A burying-place for strangers. گور نفس *gori nafs*, (Grave of the soul) The human body. در گور کردن *dar gor kardan*, To bury, inter, entomb.

P گوراب *gorāb*, A horse-course. A cupola raised over a tomb. Short socks worn under stockings in the winter-season. A false appearance of water on a sandy plain common in hot countries, mirage. Name of a city.

P گورابه *gorāba*, A cupola raised over a tomb. Name of a place where Rustam's father is interred.

P گورا گور *gor-ā-gor*, Very swift, active, quick.

P گوران *gawrān*, (pl. of گور *gawr*) Pagans, infidels. *Gūrān*, The rendezvous of an army. An assembly-room. Rice browned in the oven.

P گورب *gorab*, Short socks.

P گوربان *gorbān*, Keeper of a burial-ground.

P گورب بافك *gorab-bāfak*, Name of a bird which builds a stocking-form hanging-nest in trees.

P گورجا *gor-jā*, A burial-ground, cemetery.

P گورجستان *gūrjistān*, Georgia, a province lying between the Euxine and Caspian Seas.

P گورجي *gūrjī*, A Georgian.

P گورچشم *gor-chashm*, A kind of silken stuff in which are woven spots like the eyes of the wild ass.

P گورخان *gor-khān*, Name of an Emperor of China.

P گورخانه *gor-khāna*, A sepulchre, a tomb. A cavern. An empty room without a window; a cell.

P گور خر *gor-khar*, The onager or wild ass.

P گورد *gawrd*, A beetle.

P گوردين *gordīn*, A rough carpet. A dress worn by dervishes.

P گورس *gūrs*, Hunger.

P گورستان *goristān*, A burying-ground. A hermit's cell.

P گورشكاونه *gor-shikāwana*, One who digs up dead bodies and carries off the grave-clothes.

P گورك *gūrk*, Beauty. *Gūrak*, A stone on which washers beat their linen.

P گوركن *gor-kan*, A grave-digger. A digger up of graves in order to strip dead bodies.

P گورگاني *gūrgānī*, Goats' leather.

P گور گندم *gor gandum*, A kind of wheat.

P گورگور *gorgor*, Very swift, active, quick, nimble. Name of a certain bird.

P گورگيا *gor-giyā*, (or گور گياه *gor-giyāh*) Camels' hay, bog-rush.

P گور ماست *gor-māst*, New cheese prepared from wild asses' milk.

P گورنين *gawarnīn*, Household furniture. Immoveable effects. A ditch, a furrow.

P گوره *gawra*, Name of a tribe in Hindūstān.

P گوري *gorī*, Avarice. A lively, dancing pace, like that of the wild ass. An easy, agreeable life. Jovial cheerful in company.

P گوز *gawz*, A walnut. گوز كنا *gawzi kunā*, The thorn-apple. *Gūz*, A walnut. A fart. Bad. Bdellium. گوز ارغ *gūzi urugh*, A rotten nut. گوز از كن خر *gūz az kuni khar*, Wind from the anus of an ass (a proverb applied when nothing is expected). گوز بلغار *gūzi balghār*, A filbert. گوز دادن *gūz dādan*, (or زدن *zadan*) To fart. *Gawaz*, A fallow deer. The mountain-ox.

P گوز آب *gawz-āb*, A dish of walnuts, vetches, and rice.

P گوزاز *gūzāz*, A bird like the nightingale.

P گوز آگند *gawz-āgand*, A dried apricot stuffed with walnut-kernels.

P گوزبان *gozbān*, The crupper of a saddle.

P گوز بن *gawz-bun* or *gūz-bun*, A walnut-tree.

P گوزد *gawzad*, A beetle.

P گوزده *gūzada*, A red kind of gum.

P گوززن *gūz-zan*, One who breaks wind.

P گوزستان *gawzistān*, A place full of nut-bushes.

P گوز شكسته *gawz-shikasta*, The sky.

P گوزغه *gawzagha*, A cotton-pod.

P گوزك *gūzak*, The heel.

P گوزگاني *gūzgānī*, (or گوزگاني) Goats' leather.

P گوزگره *ganz-girih*, A sort of ornamental button.
P گوز گند *gūz-gand*, Vain-boasting, idle talk, lie.
P گوز گندم *ganz gandum*, Name of a plant.
P گوزن *gawazn*, A kind of mountain-ox. A deer, doe, elk.
P گوزنخ *gaw-zanakh*, A dimple in the chin.
P گوزه *goza*, A cotton-pod. The silkworm's cone. The head of a poppy.
P گوزهر *gawizahr*, The dragon's head or tail. The sphere of the moon.
P گوزمخ *goza-mukh*, The spathe of the date-flower.
P گوزي *gūzī*, Badness.
P گوزيدن *gūzīdan*, To break wind.
P گوزينه *gawzīna*, A sweetmeat made of walnuts.
P گوژاب *gojāb*, Syrup of grapes or dates.
P گوژده *gūjada*, A kind of red gum.
P گوساله *go-sāla*, A calf. A young camel or elephant. Young in years. A dolt, a blockhead. گوسالهٔ فلك *gosālaᵢi falak*, The sign Taurus.
P گوساله پرست *gosāla-parast*, A calf-worshipper.
P گوسپند *gospand*, A sheep, a ram. A goat.
P گوسپند چران *gospand-charān*, A shepherd.
P گوسپند کشان *gospand-kushān*, (Sheep-slaying) Name of a certain Muhammadan festival called عيد قربان *īdi kurbān*.
P گوست *gost*, A breach, break. A large drum.
P گوسفند *gosfand*, A sheep. A ram. A goat.
P گوش *gosh*, The ear. (from گوشيدن *goshīdan*) Hearing. A hearer, listener. A spy, emissary, informer. A corner. Look, sight. Desire, expectation. Custody, preservation. Name of an angel. Name of the fourteenth day of the month. گوش افتادن *gosh uftādan*, To be deaf. گوش بشنفتن چيزي کردن *gosh ba shiniftani chīze kardan*, To give ear to any thing. گوش بر داشتن *gosh bar dāshtan*, To expect, to wait for. To give up hope, to despair. گوش بر در داشتن *gosh bar dar dāshtan*, To expect, to wait for. گوش خاريدن *gosh khārīdan*, To scratch the ear, (met.) To wait, tarry. To think, meditate. گوش دادن *gosh dādan*, To give or lend an ear. گوش داشتن *gosh dāshtan*, To give ear. گوش زدن *gosh zadan*, To prick up the ears, to listen attentively. گوش شدن *gosh shudan*, To listen, pay profound attention. گوش کردن *gosh kardan*, To hear, listen. گوش نهادن *gosh nihādan*, To listen, attend to. To leave, abandon. گوش موش *goshi mūsh*, Mouse's-ear (a plant). گوش هوش *goshi hosh*, The ears of the understanding. *Gūsh*, A mustachio, whisker.
P گوشاسب *gūshāsb*, Sleep. A dream. Pollution. The nightmare. A youth whose beard has scarcely begun to appear.
P گوشان *goshān*, Juice pressed from grapes.
P گوشانه *goshāna*, An ambush, lurking-place.
P گوش آوائی *gosh-āwāᵢi*, One who understands and remembers all he hears.
P گوش بدر *gosh bi dar*, Expecting impatiently.

P گوش بريدگي *gosh-burīdagī*, A cutting off of the ear.
P گوش بريده *gosh-burīda*, Crop-eared.
P گوش بستر *gosh-bistar*, A race whose ears were so large as to serve for a mattress and a counterpane.
P گوش پيچ *gosh-pech*, Twisting the ears. Punishment. A cap covering the ears against cold. An ornament worn in the turban.
P گوش پيچيده *gosh-pechīda*, One who has had his ears pulled or twisted. A scholar, pupil, schoolboy.
P گوشت *gosht*, Flesh, meat. Pulp of fruit. گوشت گرفتن *gosht giriftan*, To gather flesh, to wax fat. گوشت مرده *goshti murda*, Proud flesh. *Gawasht*, Name of a note in music.
P گوشتاب *goshtāb*, (Meat-water) Gravy.
P گوشتاب *gosh-tāb*, A twisting of the ears as a punishment. Castigation. Any thing worn round the head to keep the ears warm.
P گوشتابه *goshtāba*, Minced-meat soup.
P گوشتاسپ *gūshtāsp*, Pollution; the nightmare. A bird's beak.
P گوشت آگنده *gosht-āganda*, Meat-pie, sausage.
P گوشت آوه *gosht-āwa*, Gravy, soup.
P گوشت آويز *gosht-āwez*, A flesh-market.
P گوشت آهنج *gosht-āhanj*, (or آهنگ *āhang*) A flesh-hook. A trident, eel-spear. A little spit. A kite.
P گوشت پاره *gosht-pāra*, Bit of meat; a kernel.
P گوشت خوره *gosht-khwura*, Carnivorous.
P گوشت دار *gosht-dār*, Full of flesh, corpulent.
P گوشت ربا *gosht-rubā*, (or گوشت رباي *gosht-rubāy*) A kite, crow. A flesh-hook.
P گوش تر شدن *gosh tar shudan*, To listen.
P گوشت رفته *gosht-rafta*, Lean, emaciated.
P گوشت فروش *gosht-farosh*, A seller of meat.
P گوشتکوب *gosht-kob*, A butcher's cleaver.
P گوشتمند *goshtmand*, Fleshy, made of flesh.
P گوشت ناك *goshtnāk*, Fleshy. Pulpy.
P گوشت ناکي *goshtnākī*, Fleshiness.
P گوشتين *goshtīn*, Fleshy, fat. Meat-dishes.
P گوشچي *goshchī*, A listener, hearer. A spy, watchman, sentinel, emissary, informer.
P گوش خارك *gosh-khārak*, (or خرك *kharak*) Any thing which scratches the ear. An earwig.
P گوش خبه *gosh-khaba*, (or گوش خيه *gosh-khaya*) An ear-pick. An earwig.
P گوش خزم *gosh-khaz*, (or گوش خزك *gosh-khazak*) Scolopendra, millipede. An earwig.
P گوش خورده *gosh-khwurda*, Boxed on the ears.
P گوشدار *gosh-dār*, Guardian, keeper, preserver.
P گوش زد *gosh-zad*, What strikes the ear: hearsay.
P گوش سراي *gosh-sarāy*, One who remembers or thoroughly understands all he hears.
P گوش سوراخ *gosh-sūrākh*, One whose ears are bored.
P گوشك *goshak*, (dim.) A little ear. The uvula.
P گوش گذار *gosh-guzār*, A hearer. Heard.
P گوش لب *gosh-lab*, One whose beard has not yet sprouted.
P گوشمال *gosh-māl*, Chastisement, especially that of schoolmasters upon boys by rubbing their ears.
P گوشماهي *gosh-māhī*, A small Indian shell with which they ornament bridles. Tortoiseshell. A cup made of mother-o'-pearl.
P گوشوار *goshwār*, An ear-ring (befitting the ear).
P گوش واره *gosh-wāra*, An ear-ring. A large pearl (the only one in the shell). An embroidered cloth worn as an ornament over the sides of a turban. Total, aggregate amount. Abstract of an account. Boring the ears of female children. گوشوارهٔ فلك *gosh-wāraᵢi falak*, The ear-ring of the sky, *i.e.* the new moon.
P گوشه *gosha*, An angle, corner, nook, closet. Retirement, privacy, side. The handle of a vessel. A button-hole, loop, or noose. A species of wicker travelling-basket. A notch (at the end of a bow, into which the string goes). The womb. گوشهٔ جام شکسته *goshaᵢi jāmi shikasta*, The new moon. گوشهٔ جگر *goshaᵢi jigar*, The lobe of the liver. گوشهٔ چشم *goshaᵢi chashm*, The corner of the eye. گوشهٔ چيزي *goshaᵢi chīze*, Extremity or point of a thing. گوشهٔ دهن *goshaᵢi dahan*, Corner of the mouth. گوشهٔ زمين *goshaᵢi zamīn*, Corner of the earth, tract of land. گوشهٔ کمان *goshaᵢi kamān*, The notch for the string at the end of a bow. گوشه گرفتن *gosha giriftan*, (or گوشهٔ باغي گرفتن *goshaᵢi bāghe giriftan*) To seek retirement, court privacy. To retire, withdraw. گوشه گوشه *gosha gosha*, (They searched for it) from corner to corner. سه گوشه *sih gosha*, A triangle.
P گوشه گير *gosha-gīr* (Possessing a corner), or گوشه نشين *gosha-nishīn* (Sitting in a corner), Solitary. A hermit.
P گوشيار *goshyār*, Name of a learned man under whom the celebrated ابن سينا *ibn sīnā* (Avicenna) studied medicine.
P گوشيدن *goshīdan*, To listen, hear, hearken.
P گو كه *gū* or *go ki*, Although.
P گوگ *gog*, A button. A wart. A calf.
P گوگار *gūgār*, (or گوگال *gūgāl*) A beetle.
P گوگال ناك *gūgālnāk*, Full of beetles.
P گوگرد *gūgird*, Sulphur, brimstone.
P گو گردانك *gū-gardānak*, A tumble-dung.
P گوگه *goga*, A coat-button. A calf. A wart.
P گول *gawl*, A dervish's coarse woollen garment. *Gol*, A fool. Stupid, rude, unlearned, ignorant. An owl. Fraud, deceit. A pond containing little water. A ball. گول زدن *gol zādan*, To play the fool, to play tricks.
P گولاج *golāj*, A kind of sweetmeat.
P گولاد *gūlād*, Name of a champion of Irān.
P گولاك *gūlāk*, A fuller's beetle.
P گولان *gawlān*, A medicine made from the root of boxthorn.
P گولانج *gūlānj*, A kind of sweetmeat. A very thin sort of cake eaten in soup.

P گولبند *gol-band*, (in Gīlān) Swaddling-bands.

P گوحاج *gol-haj*, (Foolish pilgrim) A pilgrim travelling on foot to Mecca; also a pilgrim ignorant of the rites to be performed there.

P گولخ *golakh*, (or گولخن) Stove of a bath.

P گولغنچه *gūlghuncha*, Red paint for the face.

P گولك *golak*, The kotwāl's treasure-pot. A till, a drawer. *Gūlak*, Root of assafœtida.

P گولنداز *golandāz*, A cannonier, bombardier.

P گولندازي *golandāzī*, Gunnery.

H گوله *gola*, A store-house for keeping grain, salt, and the like.

P گوله *gola*, A ball in general. A cannon-ball. A cotton-pod. The silkworm's cocoon. A poppy-head. A hedgehog. A porcupine. An earthen pitcher for water.

P گوله انداز *gola-andāz*, A cannonier, gunner.

P گولي *golī*, Folly, thoughtlessness. *Golī* also *gūlī*, A ball, bullet, bowl, orb, pill.

P گوليدن *gūlīdan*, To bark (as a dog).

P گوم *gom*, The bog-rush.

P گوما *gūmā*, Name of a plant used as a topic, and cure for ear-ache, ague, &c. (Pharnaceum Mollugo).

P گومباش *gū ma bāsh*, Say, let it not be. Leave done, if it cannot happen it won't happen.

H گومتي *gūmtī*, Name of a river in India.

P گومست *gawmist*, Name of a book that descended to a Magian priest named جومست *jawmist*.

P گومشون *gūmashūn*, (in zand) Them, these.

P گومن *gūman*, (in zand and Pāzand) This.

P گومه *goma*, A hovel made of reeds or straw.

P گون *gūn*, Colour. Species. Form, kind, mode, manner, fashion, law, rule, regulation. Like, resembling. (When added to nouns it implies a similitude of colour): as, گل گون *gul-gūn*, Rose-coloured. لاله گون *lāla-gūn*, Of the colour of, or like, the tulip. ديگرگون كردن *dīgar-gūn kardan*, To make of another colour. *Guwin*, Name of a city in Persia.

P گونا *gūnā*, Colour. Paint for the face. Form, figure, habit, mode, manner, rule, law, regulation. (in zand and Pāzand) A lamb.

P گوناب *gūnāb*, Paint or wash for the face.

P گونا گون *gūn-ā-gūn*, Of different kinds, species, sorts, or colours. كتب گونا گون *kutubi gūn-ā-gūn*, Various authors, all sorts of books, a miscellany.

P گوناگوني *gūnāgūnī*, Variety.

P گونجي *guwinjī*, Noble, excellent, brave, courageous. Dear, precious.

P گون ژده *gūn jada*, A cricket.

P گونسته *gūnasta*, Buttocks of man or horse.

P گونند *gūnand*, A packing-needle. A sack-maker.

P گونه *gūna*, Colour. Species. Form, figure, external appearance, mode, manner, kind. The cheek. The buttocks. Various, diversified. Red paint for the face. گونه گونه *gūna gūna*, (or گونه گون *gūna gūn*) Of different kinds, of various sorts. گونه گونه شدن *gūna gūna shudan*, To be distinguished by genus or species, to be of different sorts. باز گونه *bāz gūna* (or واز گونه *wāz gūna*) كردن *kardan*, To overset, turn topsy-turvy. To reserve. دو گونه *du gūna*, Double, of two kinds. يك گونه *yak gūna*, Simple, in one manner.

P گونه گون *gūna gūn*, Of various kinds or colours.

P گونيا *gūnyā*, A perpendicular, a mason's or carpenter's rule. An architect's line.

P گو واره *gaw-wāra*, A herd of oxen. A cradle.

P گوه *gūh*, Human dung. *Guwah*, A witness.

P گوه بين *gūh-bīn*, Inspector, or cleaner of privies.

P گوهدان *gūhdān*, A necessary, jakes, privy.

P گوهر *gohar* or *gawhar*, A gem, jewel, pearl, precious stone. Lustre of a gem or sword. Root, origin. Of a noble family. Essence, substance, form. Offspring. Any hidden virtue. Intellect, wisdom. A substitute. عالي گوهر *ǣālī-gohar* was the title of the late Great Mogul, Shāh Aālam, before he ascended the throne. گوهر آدم *gawhari ādam*, The origin and substance of man. Earth, dust. The offspring of Adam. گوهر آسمان *gawhari āsmān*, The origin and matter of the firmament. The stars. گوهر تر *gawhari tar*, A liquid pearl, (met.) A tear. گوهر خانهٔ خيز *gawhar-khānaʼi khez*, (or گوهر خاي *gawhar-khāy*) An epithet of Muhammad. گوهر سفتن *gawhar suftan*, To begin a discourse, to tell a story. گوهر شكستن *gawhar shikastan*, To befriend (as fortune). To laugh. گوهر مريخ صفت *gawhari mirrīkh-sifat*, A live coal. گوهر مطهر *gawhari mutahhar*, Any thing pure and excellent. گوهر ملك *gawhari mulk*, A prince. A king. گوهر نيم سفت *gawhari nīm-suft*, A half-bored pearl, (met.) A discourse, imperfect, or but partially understood.

P گوهر آگين *gawhar-āgīn*, Set with pearls, filled with jewels. Brave, mettlesome.

P گوهران *gawharān*, (pl. of گوهر) The elements.

P گوهر اندوز *gawhar-andoz*, Collecting jewels.

P گوهرتاب *gawhar-tāb*, A transparent summer-garment, worn by ladies. A wreath, fillet. A veil adorned with gold.

P گوهردار *gawhar-dār*, Bright, glittering (sword).

P گوهرزاي *gawhar-zāy*, Nobly-born. Good, benevolent, virtuous. Just. Prudent. Skilful. Generous, bold. Eloquent.

P گوهر كش *gawhar-kash*, A female ornament for the wrists or arms, of gems, gold, or silver.

P گوهرگر *gawhargar*, A jeweller.

P گوهر گش *gawhar-gish*, Bold, courageous.

P گوهر نثار *gawhar-nisār*, (or گوهر ريز *gawhar-rez*) Scattering gems.

P گوهري *gawharī*, Generous, noble. High-bred (horse). Innate, essential. Adorned with gems. A dealer in precious stones, connoisseur in gems, jeweller. اسب گوهري *asbi gawharī*, A generous horse.

P گوهريدن *gawharīdan*, To exchange, barter.

P گوه غلطان *gūh-ghaltān*, (Tumble-dung) A beetle.

P گوه گردان *gūh gardān*, Name of a game.

P گوهين *gūhīn*, A ditch, a channel.

P گوي *gūy*, A ball, golf-ball, globe, sphere, button; any thing globular. Dung. *Gūy* or *goy*, Saying. A speech, word. گوي بردن *gūy burdan*, To bear away the ball, to excel. گوي انگله *gūyi angula*, A button with the loop. A button-hole. A particular kind of coat-button. The sun. گوي زر *gūyi zar*, The sun. گوي ساكن *gūyi sākin*, The terrestrial globe. A dot, a diacritical point. گوي سيم *gūyi sīm*, The moon. گوي شدن *gūy shudan*, To place the head on the knee, to watch narrowly. بيهوده گوي *bīhoda-goy*, (or ياوه گوي *yāfa-goy*) A trifling babbler, idle talker. مذمت گوي *mazammat-goy*, (or عيب گوي *ǣayb-goy*) Satirical, censorious. A facetious man, a jester, an agreeable story-teller.

P گويا *goyā* or *gūyā*, Saying, speaking. A speaker, singer. Loquacious, talkative. The tongue. A singing-bird. Well-tuned (instrument). Thus, in this manner, as you would say, as it were. Chiefly, principally, apparently, probably. خوش گويا *khwush-goyā*, Speaking elegantly (as a man), distinctly (as a parrot); singing melodiously (as a bird). عندليب گويا *ǣandalībi goyā*, The sweet-singing nightingale. گويا شدن *goyā shudan*, To speak. گوياي گهواره *goyāyi gahwāra*, (or گوياي مهد *goyāyi mahd*) Jesus Christ (speaking in the cradle).

P گوياك *goyāk*, Talkative, loquacious.

P گويائي *goyāʼī*, Conversation, talk.

P گوي باز *gūy-bāz*, A player at trap-ball or at shinty. One who throws several balls in the air successively and catches them. Name of the nineteenth day of the month.

P گوير *gawer*, A desert. A vapour which appears like water in a desert. The prefect of a city.

P گويس *gawīs*, A churn or the staff.

P گويست *gawest* or *guwīst*, A blow, kick.

P گويسته *gawista*, Beaten, pounded.

P گويسه *gawīsa*, A milk-churn or the stick.

P گويش *gawīsh*, (or گويشه *gawīsha*) A churn. A churn-stick. *Gūyish*, A word, a speech, discourse.

P گويك *gūyak*, A button. A little ball.

P گوي گردان *gūy-gardān*, (or گوي گردانك *gūy-gardānak*) A beetle, a tumble-dung.

P گويند *gūyand* or *goyand*, They say.

P گويندگي *gūyandagī*, A dialect. A mode of speech.

P گوينده *gūyanda*, An orator, speaker; a singer. The tongue. An instrument well tuned.

P گويه *gūya*, A cavern, place of shelter.

P گويي *gūyī*, (or گوئي *gūʼī*) Thou shouldst say.

P گوييدن *gūyīdan* or *goyīdan*, To speak.

P گه *gah*, Time. Place. A throne. A crucible. Quickly. خوابگه *khwāb-gah*, A sleeping-place. گه گه *gah gah*, Sometimes. *Guh*, Dung, excrement.

P گهان *gihān*, The world.

P گهبار *gahbār*, (or گهبارها *gahbārhā*) The six days or periods of the creation.

P گهر *guhar*, Race, stock, family. Offspring. Essence, quality. Wisdom, intelligence. Substitute, exchange, recompense. Root, origin, form, substance. A gem, jewel. گهر عقد فلك *guhari ɛikdi falak*, The stars. گهر بار *guhar-bār*, Raining or scattering gems.

P گهر پاره *guhar-pāra*, A piece of a gem. A precious pearl.

P گهر پاش *guhar-pāsh*, Strewing jewels.

P گهر پرور *guhar-parvar*, Nourishing pearls, *i.e.* the shell in which they grow. مادر گهر پرور *mādari guhar-parvar*, Mother of an incomparable daughter.

P گهر خانۀ اصلي *guhar-khānaɛi aslī*, A phrase denoting nearness to the Deity.

P گهر ريز *guhar-rez*, Sprinkling, scattering gems.

P گهر گستر *guhar-gustar*, A faithful adviser.

P گهري *guharī*, Adorned with gems. A dealer in precious stones. High-bred (horse). Recompense.

P گهزن *gahzan*, A shoemaker's tool.

P گهله *gahla*, Uncoined gold or silver.

P گهن *guhn*, A worm bred in trees, wood-louse.

P گهنبار *gahambār*, (or گهنبارها *gahambārhā*) The six days of the creation. (See گاهبارها *gāh-bārhā*).

P گهوارگي *gahwāragī*, Cradled (infant).

P گهواره *gahwāra*, A cradle. گهوارۀ فنا *gahwāraɛi fanā*, The cradle of mortality, *i.e.* the present transitory world.

P گهولي *gahūlī*, Exchange, barter.

P گهوليدن *gahūlīdan*, To barter, exchange.

P گي *gay*, Name of a speckled bird whose wings are used in feathering arrows. *Gī*, taking the place of mute ه *he*, is an affix employed to form the abstract noun: as, بخشندگي *bakhshandagī*, Liberality, from بخشنده *bakhshanda*, Liberal; خوانندگي *khwānandagī*, Perusal, from خواننده *khwānanda*, A reader; مردانگي *mardānagī*, Manliness, from مردانه *mardāna*, Manly; همسايگي *ham-sāyagī*, Vicinity, from همسايه *ham-sāya*, A neighbour.

P گيا *giyā*, Dry herbage. Enclosure of a village.

P گياخن *gayākhun*, A doing slowly, deliberately.

P گيارنگ *giyārang*, A general or commander.

P گيازار *giyāzār*, A meadow, place full of grass.

P گيا شير *giyā-shīr*, The milk of any plant.

P گياغ *giyāgh*, Grass, herbage.

P گياه *giyāh*, Green herbage, grass; also dry hay. گياه آبگينه *giyāhi ābgīna*, A plant used in giving a lustre to glass. گياه اخضر *giyāhi akhzar*, Green herbage. گياه شتر *giyāhi shutur*, Tragacanth, which camels like. گياه قيصر *giyāhi kaysar*, The herb melilot. گياه نمناك *giyāhi namnāk*, Purslain.

P گياهان *giyāhān*, (pl. of گياه *giyāh*) Grasses.

P گياه ناك *giyāhnāk*, Grassy, full of grass.

P گياه ناكي *giyāhnākī*, Grassiness.

P گيبر *gaybur*, A kind of spear-head.

P گيپا *gīpā*, A sheep or goat's ventricle stuffed with minced meat and rice; a sausage, pudding.

P گيپائي *gīpāɛī*, A seller of sausages.

P گيتي *gītī*, The world. Time, fortune.

P گيتي آراي *gītī-ārāy*, World-adorning: the ornament of mankind. A beautiful Basrah rose, which preserves its leaves a long time (when withered they put these roses amongst clothes and linens, which give them a perfume resembling a mixture of musk and ambergris).

P گيتي بان *gītībān*, Protector of the world, king.

P گيتي پژوه *gītī-pijūh*, Worldly. A king.

P گيتي ستان *gītī-satān*, Conqueror of the world.

P گيتي ستاني *gītī-satānī*, Conquest of the world.

P گيتي فروز *gītī-faroz*, World-illuminating.

P گيتي نما *gītī-namā*, Shewing the world; implying a mirror supposed to be in possession of Alexander the Great, which represented every transaction on the face of the earth.

P گيتي نورد *gītī-naward*, Who has travelled the world over. The sun. Alexander. A horse.

P گيج *gīj*, (گيجه *gīja*, or گيچ *gīch*) A fool pleased with, or praising himself. Light or giddy-headed, one that has the vertigo. Distracted.

P گيجيده *gījida*, Astonished, confounded, amazed.

P گيد *gīd*, A kite. Spiritless, dastardly.

P گيدي *gīdī*, Stupid, a blockhead.

P گير *gīr*, (imper. of گرفتن *giriftan*) Take, seize, hold. Rebuke, chiding. A bitter taste (in an almond or walnut). (in compos.) Seizing, taking. Keeping, holding. A captor, taker, seizer. شيرگير *shergīr*, A conqueror of lions. غافل گير *ghāfil-gīr*, One who surprises the unwary. شمشير عالم گير *shamshīri ɛālam-gīr*, A world-subduing scimeter.

P گيرا *gīrā*, One who holds or is held firmly. Prehensile. A captive. Detention, captivity. Treating, handling. A cough. ميراث گيرا *mīrās-gīrā*, Who takes an inheritance, *i.e.* an heir.

P گيرا گير *gīr-ā-gīr*, Take, seize, hold fast.

P گيرانيدن *gīrānīdan*, To cause to take. To hold together.

P گيرائي *gīrāɛī*, Grasp, seizure. The power of taking or laying hold; prehension, prehensility.

P گيرخ *gīrakh*, A desk or support for a book.

P گيردار *gīr-dār*, Take and hold. The confused clamour of combatants; battle.

P گيرفتن *gīriftan*, To take.

P گيرم *gīram*, I take, take for granted, allow, admit.

P گيرنده *gīranda*, A taker.

P گيرنگ *gīrang*, Name of a place in Khurāsān.

P گيروج *gīrūj*, The herb restharrow.

P گير و دار *gīr u dār*, Take and hold. The confused noise of combatants; battle, combat. Absolute authority, dominion.

P گيروي *gīrūy*, Name of a champion of Irān.

P گيره *gīra*, A basket.

P گيري *gīrī*, A taking, a handling.

P گيريان *gīryān*, Sacrifice, ransom. Weeping.

P گيز *gīz*, The pine-tree.

P گيسو *gīsū*, (or گيس *gīs*) A ringlet of hair, a forelock, a side-lock, curl. گيسوي عنبر آميز *gīsūyi ɛambar-āmez*, Locks fragrant as amber.

P گيسوبند *gīsū-band*, A hair-fillet. A purse.

P گيسودار *gīsū-dār*, An old man of authority. An aged prince.

P گيسينه *gīsīna*, Belonging to the hair.

P گيل *gīl* or *gel*, The country called Gīlān. (in the dialect of Gīlān) A subject, peasant, plebeian.

P گيلان *gīlān*, Name of a country and city between the Caspian and Euxine; also of a warlike tribe, and of a mountain.

P گيلاني *gīlānī*, A native of Gīlān.

P گيلدارو *gīl-dārū*, Name of a certain medicinal wood, black without and green within, found on the shores of the Caspian Sea.

P گيلك *gelak*, (in the dialect of Gīlān) A subject, plebeian, villager, peasant.

P گيلو *gīlū*, Name of a mountain.

P گيله *gīla*, Name of a place.

P گيلي *gelī*, Native of Gīlān. Name of a tribe.

P گيميا *gīmyā*, A kind of garment of fine texture.

P گين *gīn*, (a contraction of آگين *āgīn*, Filled) A particle added to substantives, forms adjectives of possessions: as, from غم *gham*, Sorrow; غمگين *ghamgīn*, Sorrowful, filled with sorrow.

P گينه *gīna*, (for آبگينه) A glass. A mirror.

P گيو *gev*, Warlike, brave. Name of the son of گودرز *gūdarz*. *Gayū*, A speaker. The tongue. Chiefly, principally, apparently, probably.

P گيور *gīwar*, An historian. Common sense.

P گيوگان *gevgān*, Name of a champion of Irān.

P گيومرث *gayūmars*, Name of the first monarch.

P گيوه *gewa*, A kind of cotton-shoe used chiefly in Persia by prize-runners. *Gīwa*, Name of an ancient king.

P گيه *giyah*, Fresh grass.

P گيها *giyahā*, (in zand and Pāzand) Grass.

P گيهان *gayhān*, The world. Time. Fortune.

P گيهه *gīha*, The bramble (red or black).

ل

ل *lām*, The twenty-third letter of the Arabic alphabet, and the twenty-seventh of the Persian. In arithmetic it denotes 30; and in the ephemerides it expresses night, the planet Saturn, and the opposite aspect in astrology; and is also an abbreviation of شوّال *shawwāl*, the tenth Arabian month. It is interchangeable with ب, ث, ج, ر, ز, ع, ف, ن, م, and ه; and in poetry it is the emblem of a ringlet of hair.

A ل *la*, (a particle of asseveration) Surely, verily, certainly. It is also employed in swearing: as, لعمرك *la ɛumrika*, By thy life! It marks the dative when followed by the affixed pronouns: as, لك *laka*, To thee; له *lahu*, To him; لنا *lanā*, To us; لكم *lakum*, To you. It may sometimes be rendered by "from:" as, سمعت له صراخاً *samiztu lahu surākhan*, I heard from him a cry. (*La* becomes *li* before the pronoun of the first person singular: as, لي *li*, To me). It serves also to express wonder and admiration, as يا لها *yā lahā*: and is occasionally employed with the vocative case; as, يا لزيد *yā la zaydin*, O Zayd (help)! *Li*, (an inseparable particle, denoting the genitive as well as the dative case) That, to, unto, for. By, because of, against, on account of, belonging to. Therefore, in order to. On, upon. After. In favour of (opposed to علي *zala'*, Against). للربّ *li'r rabbi*, Of, or to, the Lord; and also, because of the Lord. للتأديب *li't tasdib*, For instruction or correction. لنفسه *li nafsihi*, For himself. لله *li'llāh*, By God; for God. لله و لرسوله *li'llāhi wa li rasūlihi*, For the love of God and his apostle. كتبته لخمس خلون *katabtuhu li khamsin khalawna*, I wrote him, five (nights) being passed, *i.e.* on the fifth of the month. (This particle is often prefixed likewise by way of pleonasm or expletive, without having any precise meaning).

P لا *lā*, A particle expressive of multiplication: as, دولا *dulā*, Double. Boasting, bragging, vain-glory.

A لا *lā*, No, not, not at all. (for ليس *laysa*) It is not. لا اله الا الله *lā ilāha illa'llāh*, There is no god but God. لاشي *lā shay*, Nothing. بلا *bilā*, Without. و لا *wa lā*, Neither. *Lā* is the correct name for ا *alif*.

A لاء *lāsi*, (with the article اللاء *allāsi*) (pl. of التي *allatī*) (The women) who.

A لأّء *lassās*, A dealer in pearls.

A لا ابال *lā ubāl*, I don't care, I fear not.

A لا ابالي *lā ubālī*, I fear not. Fearing nothing, insolent, licentious, petulant. Fearless.

A لأاة *lasāt*, (fem. of لأي *lasa'*) The wild cow. A shield.

A لأامة *lasāmat*, (v.n. of لؤم) Being inglorious, ignoble, sordid. Meanness, sordidness.

P لاب *lāb*, The sun. Request, supplication.

A لاب *lāb*, (pl. of لابة *lābat*) Black stony places.

A لاباس *lā bāsa*, It is not bad; there's no harm.

A لا با له *lā bā lahu*, (for لا ابا له *lā abā lahu*) He has no father.

A لابة *lābat*, (pl. لاب *lāb*) A place full of stones (especially black). Black she-camels congregated.

A لابث *lābis*, A delayer, dilatory.

A لابد *lābid*, Much wealth. اللابد *al lābid*, The lion. *Lābud*, A key for tuning an instrument.

A لابدّ *lā budda*, No flight or escape. Necessarily, infallibly. Entirely. It cannot be but.

P لا برلا *lā bar lā*, Fold upon fold. Manifold, multiplied. A kind of confection of almonds, nuts, and a little fine flour.

A لابس *lābis*, Clothed: one who puts on clothes.

P لا بلا *lā ba lā*, Manifold, multiplied.

A لابد لك *lāba laka*, By all means, of necessity.

A لابن *lābin*, Who abounds in or gives milk.

A لابنة *lābinat*, (pl. لوابن) The breast or udder.

P لابه *lāba*, A supplication, prayer, request, desire. A word. Submission. Confession of weakness. A demonstration of sincere friendship. Ridicule, irony, jest, joke, any thing facetious. Adulation, flattery, coaxing. A root. Any thing entwined about another from head to foot. لابه كردن *lāba kardan*, To ask, pray, petition. To jest, ridicule.

P لابيدن *lābīdan*, To boast, brag. To ask, pray.

A لآة *lasāt*, The wild cow. A shield.

A لات *lāt*, Name of an idol worshipped of old by the pagan Arabians. *Lāta*, (for لا *lā*) (or لات حين *lāta hīna*) It is not time.

A لاتب *lātib*, Firm, sticking. Necessary.

A لاتح *lātih*, Ingenious, intelligent, skilful.

A لا ترما *lā tara mā*, Especially.

P لاتو *lātū*, A boy's top. A trap, snare. A paddle. Steps; a ladder.

A لاتي *lātī*, (with the article اللاتي *al lātī*) (fem. of التي *allatī*) (The women) who.

A لاث *lās*, (fem. لاثة) Entangled herbage.

A لاثاني *lā sānī*, Incomparable, without a second.

A لاثم *lāsim*, (pl. لثم *lusm*) A breaker, hurter.

P لاج *lāj*, A bribe. Naked. A bitch.

A لاجرم *lā jaram*, Undoubtedly. Necessarily, of necessity, indispensibly, by all means. Consequently, of course.

A لاجل *li ajli*, Because of. لاجل ماله و جماله و فضله و كماله *li ajli mālihi wa jamālihi wa fazlihi wa kamālihi*, On account of his wealth and his beauty, and his learning and his perfection. لاجل اسلامه *li ajli islāmihi*, Because of his orthodoxy. لاجلي *li ajlī*, On my account. لاجل ذلك *li ajli zālika*, On that account, on account of that.

A لاجواب *lājawāb*, Incapable of answering, silenced, speechless, disconcerted.

P لاجورد *lājaward*, Lapis lazuli.

P لاجورد خم *lājaward-khum*, Azure vault.

P لاجوردي *lājawardī*, Azure, cerulean.

P لاجوردي سقف *lājawardī sakf*, The sky.

P لاجوردي نقاب *lājawardī-nikāb*, Mourning.

P لاجوردينه خم *lājawardīna-khum*, The sky.

A لاجئ *lājis*, A refugee.

P لاچ *lāch*, A deception, a trick; a jest.

P لاچار *lā chār*, Helpless, destitute, poor.

P لاچارگي *lā chāragī*, Forlornness, helplessness, destitution. Poverty.

P لاچي *lāchī*, Common cardamoms.

P لاچين *lāchīn*, A servant, slave.

A لاح *lāhh*, Narrow (place).

A لاحاصل *lā hāsil*, Unproductive, profitless.

A لاحب *lāhib*, An open, beaten road.

A لاحج *lāhij*, Sticking, remaining fast.

A لاحد *lāhid*, (A grave) dug in upon one side, or which has a niche cut in one side.

A لاحسة *lāhisat*, Calamitous (year).

A لاحظة *lāhizat*, (pl. لواحظ) Glancing (eye).

A لاحق *lāhik*, Who or what touches or reaches unto. Adhered, conjoined, adjoining, affixed. An appendage. A name of several horses. ابو لاحق *abū lāhik*, (Father reacher or overtaker) A falcon.

A لاحلّ *lā hall*, Difficult, not to be solved, abstruse.

A لاحم *lāhim*, (pl. لواحم *lawāhim*) (A hawk) which eats flesh. Who feeds with meat. One who gives or possesses meat (لحم *lahm* or *laham*).

A لاحن *lāhin*, One who pronounces vowels improperly. Who perceives the true meaning of a speech.

A لاحوس *lāhūs*, Unfortunate, unhappy.

A لاحول ولا قوّة الا بالله *lā hawla wa lā kūwata illā bi'llāh*, There is no power nor strength except in God, *i.e.* there is no striving against fate. (It is uttered also to drive away evil spirits).

A لاحي *lāhī*, A rebuker, reprover, chider.

P لاخ *lākh*, Cotton or silk put into an ink-holder. Hard. A rock, a stone. Much, copious, numerous. (in composition it signifies "place") سنگلاخ *sanglākh*, A stony place.

A لاخ *lākh*, Wry-mouthed.

A لاخ *lākhkh*, Narrow, choked up (valley).

A لاخراج *lā kharāj*, Rent-free, allodial.

P لاخشه *lākhisha*, (or لاخشته *lākhishta*) Vermicelli, or long slices of paste put into broth.

A لا خطر علي قلب الناس *lā khatara zala' kalbi'n nās*, It never entered into the heart of men; it is incomprehensible.

P لاخه *lākha*, A piece, a patch.

P لاخه دوز *lākha-doz*, A mender of old clothes.

P لاخيز *lākhez*, A flood; a torrent.

P لاد *lād*, An incrustation, plastering of a wall. Earth, dust. A wall. Rows of bricks or turfs in a wall. A foundation. Root. Reason, cause, motive. The gum-herb ladon. A flower; a rose. Soft, thin silk. The cultivation or improvement of a place. A fortress. The city of Lār.

A لادّ *lādd*, An adversary, an antagonist.

P لادرز *lād-raz*, A partition made of wattles.

P لادرزة *lād-raza*, A wall.

A لا دعوي *lā dazwa'*, A release, acquittance.

A لادم *lādim*, A mender, a patcher.

P لادن *lādan*, The gum-herb lada.

P لادنه *lādina*, A kind of grass from the outer coat of whose stalk they make ropes.

A لا دوا *lā dawā*, Incurable, irremediable.

P لاده *lāda*, Idiot, fool, blockhead. A bitch.

A لاذة *lāzat*, (pl. لاذ) A dress of red China silk.

A لاذقية *lāzikīyat*, Laodicea, or Lattakia, a seaport on the coast of Syria.

A لاذن *lāzan*, Moisture adhering to the hair and beards of goats whilst feeding on a certain herb called قلسوس *kalsūs* or قستوس *kastūs*.

P لار *lār*, Name of a country in Persia. Name of a city in the same province, four days' journey from Bandar Abbās.

P لارجان *larjān*, Name of a mountain in Tabaristān, in which there is a petrifying well.

P لاردة *lārda*, A quail.

P لارنگ *lārang*, A kneading-trough.

P لارو *lārū*, Southernwood.

P لارودة *lārūda*, (or لارورة *lārūra*) A quail.

P لاري *lārī*, Name of a Persian silver coin.

A لاريب *lā rayb*, No doubt. Undoubted. Infallible. Unquestionably, infallibly, certainly.

A لاريبي *lā raybī*, Indubitable.

A لاز *lāz*, (or لازوري *lāzūrī*) Lazarus.

A لا زال *lā zāla*, (in prayer) May it never fail! may it last for ever! Not deficient.

A لازب *lāzib*, Firm, solid. Firmly adhering. طين لازب *ṭīni lāzib*, Adhesive mud. صار الشيء ضربة لازب *ṣāra'sh shayʼu ẓarbata lāzibin*, The thing was done necessarily.

A لازق *lāzik*, Adhering, coalescing, adhesive.

A لازم *lāzim*, Necessary, urgent, indispensable, obligatory, important. Proper, suitable. Inseparable, inherent, adhering. An attendant, hanger-on. Necessarily, in consequence. (in gram.) Intransitive or neuter. لازم الادا *lāzimu'l adā*, Necessary to be done. لازم الانقياد *lāzimu'l inkiyād*, Necessary to be obeyed. لازم البناء *lāzimu'l bināʼ*, Indeclinable (word). لازم التقديم *lāzimu't taḳdīm*, Proper to be prefixed or placed over. لازم التكريم *lāzimu't takrīm*, (or لازم الرعاية *lāzimu'r riʻāya*) Honourable, worthy of reverence. P لازم شدن *lāzim shudan*, To be necessary. مهم و لازم شدن *muhimm u lāzim shudan*, To be urgent; to be of great consequence. لازم گرفتن *lāzim giriftan*, To adhere, stick close. A لازم الوقا *lāzimu'l wakā*, Necessary to be preserved, carefully to be watched or kept. لازم متعدي *lāzim mutaʻaddī*, Neuter and active, intransitive and transitive (verb). فعل لازم *fiʻli lāzim*, A neuter or intransitive verb.

A لازمة *lāzimat*, (pl. لوازم *lawāzim*) Necessary (thing). Contumelious (word). Necessity, exigence. Obligation, debt.

P لازم گير *lāzim-gīr*, One who abides in, and who keeps close to.

P لازم گيرنده *lāzim-gīranda*, One who regards as obligatory and indispensable.

A لازم ملزوم *lāzim malzūm*, Intimate friendship.

A لازمي *lāzimī*, Any thing that is necessary.

A لا زوال *lā zawāl*, Imperishable, eternal.

P لازوردي *lāzuwardī*, (A لازوردي *lāzawardīy*) Of a blue colour, of the colour of lapis lazuli.

A لازوق *lāzūḳ*, A plaster left on a wound till it be healed.

P لاژ *lāj*, Name of a village in Khurāsān.

P لاژورد *lājuward*, Lapis lazuli.

P لاس *lās*, Refuse of silk or lint. Coarse silk. The female of any animal. A bitch.

P لا سخن *lā sukhan*, Silent, taciturn. Abuse, improper talk.

A لاسع *lāsiʻ*, Who or what stings.

P لا سكوي *lā sakwī*, Name of a melodious bird.

A لاسيّما *lā siyamā*, Especially.

P لاش *lāsh*, A dead body, carcase. A kind of bread. Devastation, plunder, laying waste a country. Spoil, plunder, booty. A mean fellow unworthy of credit. Ruined, undone. Small, little, mean, base, ignoble. Nothing. الرأي اللاش *ar'raʼyu'l lāsh*, A vain, foolish notion.

A لاشبيه *lā shabīh*, Incomparable, unequalled.

A لاشك *lā shakk*, Without doubt. Indubitable.

P لاشه *lāsha*, A carcase. One reduced to skin and bones. Rude, rough. Slow, negligent. A shoulder.

A لاشيء *lā shayʼ*, Nothing, a trifle, of no value.

P لاشيدن *lāshīdan*, To strew, to scatter.

A لاصف *lāṣif*, A stone whence comes antimony.

A لاصق *lāṣiḳ*, Adhering, joined, adhesive. Low (building), as if cleaving to the ground.

A لأط *laʼṭ*, (v. n. of لأط) Commanding. Urging, importuning. Wounding with an arrow. Striking with a stick. Dunning, exacting. Looking after one, following him with one's eyes till he disappears. Fleeing, passing rapidly by without casting a look behind. Being severe upon.

A لاط *lāṭ*, The act of persevering in.

A لاطّ *lāṭṭ*, Impure, dirty. لاطّ ملطّ *lāṭṭ mulaṭṭ*, One filthy himself, and whose associates are filthy.

A لاطائل *lā ṭāʼil*, Useless, unprofitable.

A لاطة *lāṭat*, Sodomites, people of Lot.

A لاطع *lāṭiʻ*, One who licks, a licker.

A لاطم *lāṭim*, A striker, boxer.

A لاطئ *lāṭiʼ*, A refugee. Cleaving to the ground.

A لاطئة *lāṭiʼat*, An incurable wound in the pericranium, or from the bite of an insect.

A لأظ *laʼẓ*, A driving away any one who is near. A dunning, exacting rigorously. Gloom, sadness.

A لاع *lāʻ*, (pl. لاعون *lāʻūna*, لاعة *lāʻat*, and الواع *alwāʻ*) Fearful, timid. Distempered, impatient, from love or disease. هاع لاع *hāʻun lāʻun*, Trembling, cowardly. Impatient. Greedy. Bad, wicked.

A لاعاقل *lā ʻāḳil*, Foolish, stupid.

A لاعب *lāʻib*, A player, gamester.

A لاعبة *lāʻibat*, Name of a certain milky plant.

A لاعة *lāʻat*, A prudent, discreet woman. One who inflames a lover with words, but permits no liberties. An ass, astonished, stupefied, and fearfully agitated by maternal affection. (pl. of لاع *lāʻ*) Fearful, timid. Distempered.

A لاعج *lāʻij*, Ardent, passionate (love).

A لاعط *lāʻiṭ*: as, مرّ لاعطاً *marra lāʻiṭan*, He passed by the wall (of a house), or the side (of a hill).

A لاعلاج *lā ʻilāj*, Incurable, remediless, hopeless.

A لاعن *lāʻin*, One who drives away. One who curses and pours forth imprecations.

A لاعي *lāʻī*, Terrified by the slightest trifle. One who licks with the tongue. ما بالدار لاعي قرو *mā bi'd dār lāʻī karwin*, There is no plate-licker (*i. e.* nobody) in the house.

A لاعية *lāʻiyat*, A shrub of a yellow colour which kills fish. It is a strong purgative and vomitive.

P لاغ *lāgh*, A jest, burlesque. Deception, deceit, fraud, imposition. Cowardice, heartlessness.

A لاغب *lāghib*, Weak and foolish (man).

P لاغر *lāghar*, Lean, meagre, gaunt, slender, poor. لاغر شدن *lāghar shudan*, To be or grow lean. لاغر كردن *lāghar kardan*, To make lean.

P لاغر ميان *lāghar-miyān*, Slender-waisted.

P لاغري *lāgharī*, Leanness.

P لاغريدن *lāgharīdan*, To grow thin, poor, lean.

G لاغون *lāghūn*, A hare.

A لاغية *lāghiyat*, (v. n. of لغي) Blundering, erring (in speech). Talking triflingly and nonsensically. Obscene (discourse). A base, shameful, rash, obscene, or foolish saying.

P لاغيدن *lāghīdan*, To trifle, to jest.

P لاغينه *lāghīna*, Tithymal, sea-lettuce.

P لاغيه *lāghiya*, A plant bearing a flower like the aniseed flower (Tithymal).

P لاف *lāf*, Praise. Boasting, self-praise, bragging. لاف زدن *lāf zadan*, To praise, vaunt, boast, commend one's self. To traduce.

A لأف *laʼf*, (v. n. of لأف) Eating gracefully.

A لافح *lāfiḥ*, (pl. لوافح) Scorching (wind).

P لافزن *lāf-zan*, A boaster, a braggart.

P لاف زني *lāf-zanī*, Boasting. لاف زني نمودن *lāf-zanī namūdan*, To boast, brag, bluster, swagger.

A لافظة *lāfiẓat*, The sea (as that which throws up amber, &c.). A mill. A millstone. The world. (A bird) feeding young ones. A dunghill-cock. A sheep which runs readily to be milked when called.

P لافي *lāfī*, Boastful, braggart.

P لافيدن *lāfīdan*, To boast, to vaunt. To talk nonsense. To fail in keeping one's promise.

P لافيس *lāfīs*, (or لاقيس *lāḳīs*) Name of a demon which, during the hour of prayer, suggests wicked thoughts to the mind.

A لاقح *lāḳiḥ*, Distressing, cruel (war). (pl. لواقح *lawāḳiḥ*) A camel which has been covered and holds.

A لاقس *lāḳis*, A railer. Itch, mange.

A لاقط *lāḳiṭ*, One who picks up; a gatherer. An emancipated slave. A mender of clothes; a darner.

A لاقطة *lāḳiṭat*, (fem. of لاقط *lāḳiṭ*) Low, despicable (man or woman). لاقطة الحصى *lāḳiṭatu'l ḥaṣa'*, The crop of a bird (as enclosing gravel). لكل ساقطة لاقطة *li kulli sāḳiṭat lāḳiṭat*, For every thing that drops there is a picker up.

P لاك *lāk*, Lac, a kind of lake produced from lac, used for dyeing red. A parget-trough, or any place in which they make plaster or mortar; also a kneading-trough. A tortoise. A wooden cup. Spoiled, ruined. Bad, useless, good for nothing.

P لاك پشت *lāk-pusht*, A tortoise. لاك پشت دريائي *lāk-pushti daryāʼī*, The sea-turtle. لاك پشت صحرائي *lāk-pushti ṣaḥrāʼī*, The land-tortoise.

P لاكچه *lākcha*, Vermicelli, macaroni, or long

slices of paste put into broth.

A لاكز *lākiz*, A striker.

A لاكلام *lā kalām*, Without a word; indisputably, no question: let it pass, agreed, no more to be said.

A لا كلام باقي *lā kalām bākī*, Undisputed balance.

P لاكن *lākan*, Name of a mountain on the confines of Russia.

A لاكن *lākin*, But.

A لاكي *lākī*, A seeker of faults; critical, malevolent.

A لآل *laءāl*, (for لآلي *laءāliء*) Pearls, gems.

A لأّل *laءءāl*, A seller of pearls.

P لال *lāl*, A ruby. Red. Inflamed. Darling, dear. An infant boy. To-morrow. Dumb. Name of a bird (the male of Fringilla Amandava).

P لالا *lālā*, Incomparable. The anemone. The water-lily. The chief servant, intrusted with the education of his master's sons: a major-domo. A slave. Babbling, prating. A grain resembling sesame. A certain plant brought from the neighbourhood of Mecca. Shining, resplendent.

A لا لا *lā lā*, No, no, not at all.

A لألاء *laءlāء*, A dealer in pearls. Excessive joy.

A لالأء *lālaءءaء*, A pearl-merchant.

A لألأة *laءlaءat*, (v. n. of لألأ Q) Glancing her eye (a woman). Blazing (flame). Wagging the tail (a deer). Pouring out, shedding (tears). Desiring the male (a she-goat). ما افعله ما لألأت الفور *mā afءaluhu mā laءlaءati'l fūr*, I'll not do it as long as the deer continues to whisk her tail, *i. e.* ever.

P لالا سرا *lālā-sarā*, A eunuch who has the chief superintendence of the women.

P لالأل *lālaءءāl*, A pearl-merchant.

P لالان *lālān*, (pl. of لال *lāl*) Dumb (people).

A لآلة *liءālat*, Pearl-dealing. The wild cow.

P لالس *lālas*, A kind of red silken stuff of a delicate texture. The face. Love, friendship.

P لال ساگ *lāl sāg*, Name of a vegetable (Amaranthus gangeticus).

P لالك *lālak*, A cock's comb. A crest. A crown. A shoe or slipper. A fritter.

P لالكا *lālakā*, A slipper, sandal. A cock's comb. A crown.

P لالنگ *lālang*, Broken victuals which poor people carry away from an entertainment.

P لاله *lāla*, A tulip. Any wild flower. A passionate lover. The lip of a mistress. لالهٔ دختري *lālaءi duhhtarī*, The anemone.

P لاله رخ *lāla-rukh*, Tulip, vermilion-cheeked.

P لاله زار *lālazār*, A bed or garden of tulips.

P لاله سار *lāla-sār*, Name of melodious bird.

P لاله سان *lālasān*, Tulip-like.

P لاله سرا *lāla-sarā*, A eunuch.

P لاله گون *lāla-gūn*, Of a tulip-colour.

P لاله وش *lālawash*, Like a tulip.

A لآلي *laءāliء*, (pl. of لؤلؤ *luءluء*) Pearls.

P لالي *lālī*, Redness, rubicundity.

A لأم *laءm*, (v. n. of لأم) Consolidating, healing (a wound), cementing, mending, soldering (a broken vessel), repairing (any thing). Receiving into favour. Putting good feathers or wings to an arrow. Charging with meanness and avarice. An arrow furnished with the wing called لؤام *luءām*. A person, a figure. (pl. of لأمة *laءmat*) Coats of mail closely woven.

P لام *lām*, The ragged garments of a dervish. Ornament, decoration, dress. A tree green and hanging down. Boasting. A composition of drugs against fascination and evil eyes. A sash or belt.

A لام *lām*, The letter ل *lām*; (and hence, from the similitude) Crooked, curved, twisted, bent (especially in body, ا *alif* implying a straight erect shape). The article ال *al*, The. A ringlet. A wing. Culpable, criminal, obnoxious to punishment or censure; doing any thing which deserves it. Strong, vehement, violent. The person or stature of man. Fear, dread. Nearness.

A لام الف *lām alif*, This compound character لا *lā* some Arabian grammarians consider as the 29th letter of the alphabet; and support it by saying, that Muhammad denounced eternal damnation to all who refused to adopt it as such.

P لامان *lāmān*, Bragging, boasting. Active, ready, nimble. Adulation, flattery. A musical mode of reciting verses. (in zand and Pāzand) Bread.

A لأمان *laءmān*, Ignoble, knavish, avaricious.

P لاماني *lāmānī*, Flattery, adulation. A lie. Vain boasting. A request, prayer, petition. Singing verses. A flatterer. Any thing fastening a fillet or head-dress. One who accompanies verses with song. The being clad in a coat of mail.

A لآمة *laءāmat*, (v. n. of لؤم) Being inglorious, ignoble, or sordid. Baseness, sordidness, avarice.

A لأمة *laءmat*, A coat of mail closely woven.

A لامة *lāmat*, Any thing deserving of reproof. Fear, dread. A coat of mail.

A لامّة *lāmmat*, Malignant (eye). Dreaded thing.

A لامج *lāmij*, One who eats much, and indulges much in venery.

P لامچه *lāmcha*, A charm against evil eyes.

A لامح *lāmih*, Who looks slily, but attentively. Shining, glancing, glittering.

A لامحاله *lā mahāla*, Inevitable. Inevitably, assuredly, undoubtedly.

P لامخ *lāmihh*, The father of نوح *nūh*, Noah.

A لامس *lāmis*, Touching, feeling. A feeler, a groper. One who strokes with the hand. امرأة لا تمنع يد لامس *imraءatun lā tamnaءu yada lāmisin*, An immodest woman, an adultress. رجل لا يمنع يد لامس *rajulun la yamnaءu yada lāmisin*, A spiritless, powerless man, making no resistance.

A لامسة *lāmisat*, Touch, sense of feeling. قوّت لامسه *kūwati lāmisa*, The sense of touch.

P لامشگر *lāmishgar*, A tree having a large smooth stem and thick foliage, called the gnat-tree.

A لامطمع *lā matmaء*, Hopeless, desperate.

A لامع *lāmiء*, Who or what shines. Bright, flashing, splendid. لامع الانوار *lāmiءu'l anwār*, The vibrating rays of light, luminous, resplendent. آثار لامعة الانوار *āsār lāmiءatu'l anwār*, Most clear or striking signs and miracles.

A لامعة *lāmiءat*, The bregma of a new-born child.

A لامق *lāmik*, One who gives a slap on the eye.

P لامك *lāmak*, A piece of cloth worn over the turban. Lamech, the father of Noah.

P لامكان *lā makān*, Inexistent, with no abode.

P لامه *lāma*, A piece of cloth worn over the turban. Whatever fastens the head-dress. An ornament. A thing entwined about another from head to foot. A corslet of iron. Spiritless.

A لاميّ *lāmīy*, Belonging to the letter ل *lām*, or to the end of a word; as, اضافت لاميه *izāfati lāmiya*, The regimen of two nouns: in which the first is pronounced with كسر *kasr* or short *i*; as, شب تاريك *shabi tārīk*, A dark night. A العظم اللاميّ *al ءazmu'l lāmīy*, A forked bone at the root of the tongue called hyoides os.

P لان *lān*, A wall round a house. An area. A fold or enclosure for cattle. A ditch, furrow, pit. Ingratitude, insincerity. A tremor from excess of pain. Affixed to nouns, it denotes abundance or place; as, نمك لان *namaklān*, A salt-warehouse.

A لان *lān*, Name of a country and people adjacent to Armenia. *Lāna*, (for الآن *alءān*) Now.

A لأنّ *laءanna*, Perhaps. *Liءanna*, Because, since, in order to.

P لاندن *lāndan*, To move, shake, agitate. To totter, stagger. To tumble. To bark.

A لا نسلّم *lā nusallim*, We do not grant or admit.

A لانظير *lā nazīr*, Incomparable, unequalled.

A لانم *lā nam*, (a contraction of لا نسلّم *lā nusallim*) We do not grant or yield.

P لانه *lāna*, A nest. A bee-hive. A hen-coop. Vain, empty. Idle, lazy, negligent. Spiritless. Singing. A shout, noise, cry. Torn to pieces, broken to pieces. Driven away. A guide.

A لأنّي *la annī*, (or لا انّي *lā annanī*) Haply I.

P لانيدن *lānīdan*, To move, agitate, shake.

P لاو *lāu*, Plaster, whitewash. Submission. Flattery. Supplication, request. A jest, joke. A small piece called the cat, which is struck in the game of tipcat or hockey.

A لأواء *laءwāء*, Distress, trouble. A wild cow.

A لا وارث *lā wāris*, Heirless, leaving no heir.

A لا وارث محال *lā wāris-mahāl*, Revenue arising fom persons dying without heirs.

A لا و الله *lā wa'llāh*, No, by God

A لاوذ *lāwaz*, Name of a son of Shem.

P لاورشير *lāwarshīr*, Gum of the opoponax-tree. Food given to boys.

P لاوشير *lāwashīr*, Gum of the opoponax-tree.

P لاوك *lāwuk*, A kneading-trough. A wash-tub.

A thin round cake.

A لا ولد *lā walad*, Without offspring, childless.

A لا و نعم *lā wa naʻam*, No and yes.

A لاؤون *lāʼūna*, (or with the article اللاؤون *al lāʼūna* and اللاوو *allāwū*) (pl. of الذي *allazī*) (The men) who.

P لاوه *lāwa*, Supplication, request. Trick, fraud. Adulation, flattery. A jest, joke. A kite. The game of tipcat. لاوه كردن *lāwa kardan*, To supplicate.

A لاوِيّ *lāwiy*, A Levite. Levitical.

A لاوياء *lāwiyāʼ*, A kind of plant. A mark set on cattle, a brand.

P لاويدن *lāwīdan*, To ask. To boast, vaunt.

P لاه *lāh*, A kind of red silken stuff.

A لاه *lāh*, God.

A لاهة *lāhat*, A serpent.

A لاهز *lāhiz*, A mountain or rising ground making a road narrow. *Lāhiz*, (or دائرة اللاهز *dāʼiratu'l lāhiz*) A spot upon a horse's jaw below the ear.

A لاهزان *lāhizāni*, (du. of لاهز *lāhiz*) Two mountains almost meeting, leaving only a narrow pass.

A لاهف *lāhif*, Injured, afflicted, sad, sighing (man or woman). لاهف القلب *lāhifu'l kalb*, Pained at heart.

A لاهمّ *lāhumma*, (for اللّهمّ *allāhumma*) O God!

P لاه نور *lāhnor*, Lahore in the Panjāb.

A لاهوت *lāhūt*, Divinity.

P لاهوتي *lāhūtī*, Divine.

P لاهور *lāhor*, Lahore in the Panjāb.

P لاهوره *lāhūra*, Cucumber or melon-parings.

A لاهون *lāhūna*, (pl. of لاهي *lāhī*) Men or boys lazy, lounging, trifling away time. Those who, if they do wrong, do it thoughtlessly, not designedly.

A لأي *laʼaʼ*, (fut. يلأي *yalʼaʼ*) He was slow.

A لأي *laʼy*, (v. n. of لأي) Being slow, tardy; retained, contained. Hanging back. Adverse fortune, indigence. Delay, slowness. *Laʼaʼ*, (pl. الآء *alāʼ*) A bull, a wild ox. Adverse fortune.

P لاي *lāy*, A speaker. A complainer, lamenter. A kind of silken stuff brought from India and China. Black, viscous mud. Sediment, lees. One-half of a horse-load. A valley between mountains. A fold, ply. دو لاي *du lāy*, Double, twofold.

A لائب *lāʼib*, (pl. لؤوب and لوائب) Thirsty.

A لايتبدل *lā yutabaddal*, Incommutable.

A لايتحمّل *lā yutahammal*, Intolerable.

A لايتغيّر *lā yataghayyar*, Unalterable.

A لا يتناهي *lā yatanāhaʼ*, Boundless.

A لائث *lāʼis*, Entangled (herbage). A lion.

A لايجوز *lā yajūz*, Prohibited, illicit, unlawful.

A لائح *lāʼih*, Evident, clear, appearing. Bright, splendid (star). Flashing (lightning).

A لائحة *lāʼihat*, Any thing evident. Clearness, splendour. Proof.

A لايحصي *lā yuhsaʼ*, Innumerable.

A لايحلّ *lā yuhall*, Unlawful, illegitimate.

A لايدرك *lā yudrak*, Incomprehensible.

A لا يذاب *lā yuzāb*, Indissoluble.

A لا يزال *lā yazāl*, Eternal, durable, unfading.

A لائس *lāʼis*, A glutton, an epicure.

P لايستان *lāyistān*, A miry place.

A لايصبر *lā yusbar* or لايطاق *lā yutāk*, Intolerable.

A لائط *lāʼit*, A Sodomite, one of Lot's people.

A هائع لائع *hāʼiʻ lāʼiʻ*, Trembling, cowardly. Bad, wicked. Impatient, greedy.

A لائعة *lāʼiʻat*, (An ass) whose affection for her foal is mingled with stupefaction and fear.

A لا يعدّ *lā yuʻadd*, Innumerable. مفاسد لا يعدّ *mafāsidi lā yuʻadd*, Innumerable evils.

A لا يعقل *lā yaʻkil*, Insane. Mad, drunk.

A لا يعلم *lā yaʻlam*, It means nothing.

A لا يعني *lā yaʻnī*, Unmeaning, absurd. Obscene.

A سائغ لائغ *sāʼigh lāʼigh*, (Food or wine) which flows gently down the throat.

A لا يغلب *lā yughlab*, Invincible, unconquered.

A لا يفوت *lā yafūt*, Immortal.

A لا يفهم *lā yufham*, Unintelligible.

A لائق *lāʼik*, Worthy, proper, suitable, capable, adapted, consistent, convenient, congruent, congruous, decent, due, fit for, able, qualified.

P لائقانه *lāʼikāna*, Worthy, proper. Suitably.

A لائك *lāʼik*, A seeker of faults, critical; cynic.

A لائل *lāʼil*, in comp., as, ليل لائل *laylun lāʼilun*, A night long and dark. Misfortune.

A لائم *lāʼim*, (pl. لوّم *luwwam*, لوّام *luwwām*, and ليّم *luyyam*) A blamer, censurer, reprover. An accuser of any thing mean or criminal. ربّ لائم مليم *rubbu lāʼimin mulīm*, Many (or ofttimes) a censurer is himself deserving of censure.

A لائمة *lāʼimat*, Reproof, accusation, censure.

A لايموت *lā yamūt*, Immortal.

P لاين *lāyin*, A short, narrow-sleeved shirt.

P لاي ناك *lāynāk*, Filled with black mud.

A لا ينبغي *lā yambaghī*, Indecent, impertinent.

P لاينده *lāyanda*, A complainer. A vain talker.

A لاينفكّ *lā yunfakk*, Indissoluble, inseparable.

A لاينكسر *lā yankasir*, Infrangible.

P لايني *lāyinī*, A short shirt with narrow sleeves worn at work. A short vest worn by dervishes.

P لايه *lāya*, A kind of silk stuff brought from India and China. Speech. Black, adhesive mud. Sediment at the bottom of a cistern. Half a horse-load. A valley between two mountains.

A لائيّ *lāʼiy*, Of, belonging, or relating to the particle of negation لا *lā*, Negative, negatory.

P لاييدن *lāyidan*, To talk idly. To complain.

P لب *lab*, The lip. Edge, margin. Shore, bank, coast. A blow on the nape of the neck with the open hand edgewise. لب آتش فشان *labi ātishfishān*, Lips scattering fire. The lips of one who pours forth sighs and groans; also curses and imprecations. The lip of a mistress. لب آفتاب *labi āftāb*, Sunshine intercepted by a shadow. لب برلب *lab bar lab*, Full, stuffed. Brimful. لب را چشمهٔ خضر ساختن *lab rā chashmaʼi khizr sākhtan*, To drink incessantly. لب خضرا *labi khuzrā*, The horizon, welkin's bound. لب در *labi dar*, The lips of a door, *i.e.* a bolt, bar, or any thing which keeps a door shut. The post or cheek of a gate. لب دريا *labi daryā*, Sea-shore. A mighty river or sea. لب سفيد كردن *lab safed kardan*, To smile. لب شمشير *labi shamsher*, Edge of a sword. لب كشتيگاه *labi kashtigah*, A pass, ferry, ford. لب لپان *labi lapān*, The shining brightness of a sword. لب و لهجه *lab u lahja*, Conversation.

A لب *lab*, A lioness.

A لبّ *labb*, (v. n. of لبّ) Standing, stopping, remaining in a place. Putting on the poitrel or breast-harness. Steadiness, assiduity. Facing another (a house). Striking (any one) on the throat. One who stands still. One who sticks close. لبّ طبّ *labb tabb*, Assiduous, attentive, industrious. *Lubb*, (pl. الباب *albāb*, البّ *alubb*, and البب *albub*) The heart, soul, mind. (pl. لبوب *lubūb*) Marrow, kernel of an almond or walnut: pith of a tree. The best part of any thing. Understanding, genius, judgment. Poison. لبّ جوز *lubbi jawz*, Kernel of a nut.

A لبء *labʼ*, (v. n. of لبأ) Milking the biestings from a sheep. Giving biestings to drink. Boiling biestings. The first milk after delivery, biestings. The first watering of a sown field. The first draught.

A لبأ *libaʼ*, Biestings, first milk after delivery.

A لباب *labāb*, A little green fodder. A small quantity, less than a mouthful. *Libāb*, (pl. of لبيب *labīb*) Prudent, intelligent. *Lubāb*, Pure, unsullied, untarnished, unmixed (nobility, reputation). لباب القمح *lubābu'l kamh*, Starch. *Labābi*, There is no harm.

A لبابة *labābat* or *lubābat*, (v. n. of لبّ) Being intelligent, ingenious. Intelligence, judgment.

A لبأة *labʼat*, *lubaʼat*, (لباة *labāt*, or لباءة *labāʼat*) (pl. لبآت *labʼāt*) A lioness.

A لبآت *labʼāt*, (pl. of لبأة *labʼat*) Lionesses.

A لبّات *labbāt*, (pl. of لبّة *labbat*) The throats of animals where they are stuck. Excellent women who love their husbands.

A لباث *labās*, (v. n. of لبث) Delaying, tarrying. Slow-paced (horse). Delay.

A لباثة *labāsat*, (v. n. of لبث) Delaying. Delay.

A لباج *libāj*, Foolish. Weak.

P لباچه *labācha*, A mantle. An outer garment. A judge's robe.

A لباخ *libākh*, A striking, buffeting. Wrestling.

A لباخيّة *lubākhiyat*, (A woman) full of flesh, unblemished in body, tall, and handsome.

P لباد *labād*, Any garment worn over all in wet weather. *Lubād*, A yoke for oxen.

A لبّاد *labbād*, A felt-manufacturer or vender.

A لبّادة *lubbādat*, A short, thick woollen coat worn in rainy weather. A wrapper.

P لبادة labāda, A cloak for rain. *Lubāda*, A yoke.

A لبادي labāda', (Camels) suffering from a disease in the throat. *Lubāda'*, (or لبّادي lubbāda') A kind of bird which is taken when lying on the ground. An assembled throng.

A لباس libās, (pl. البسة albisat) A garment, vesture, robe, apparel. Drawers. A spouse, husband, or wife. An assembling, flocking together. Mixture, confusion. لباس البأس libāsu'l baʼs, Deep distress. لباس التقوي libāsu't takwa', The robe of piety. A thick, rough garment. Bashfulness, shame, modesty. A covering for the nakedness. Religion, faith. لباس الجوع libāsu'ljūʻ, Extreme hunger. لباس راهب libāsirāhib, (P لباس عنبرسا libāsi ʻambarsā) Black clothing. لباس الرجل libāsu'r rajul, A wife. لباس المرأة libāsu'l marʼat, A husband. اخلاص لباس ikhlās-libās, Clothed with sincerity and candour. P زن بد لباس zani bad-libās, A slatternly, untidily-dressed woman.

A لبّاس labbās, Possessed of a great deal of clothing. A mixer. A thorough dissembler.

P لباسي labāsī, Forgery.

P لباشن labāshan, (or لباشه labāsha) An instrument for holding a horse's lip or nose while shoeing, a farrier's twitch.

A لباقة labākat, (v. n. of لبق) Being intelligent, clever, skilful: mental abilities. Fitting well (a garment).

A لباكة lubākat, A body, heap, multitude. Sheep mixed with other sheep.

P لبالب lab-ā-lab, Lip to lip. Brimful.

A لبالب labālib, The bleating of sheep.

P لبان labān, A kind of gum. A partner in labour. (A slave or beast of burden) that has toiled long in service. (pl. of لب lab) Lips.

A لبان lubān, Breast, bosom: brisket or chest of any cloven-hoofed animal. *Libān*, (v. n. of لبن) Sucking. (pl. of لبون labūn) Milch (camels or ewes). *Lubān*, Frankincense. Benzoin. Any cone-bearing tree. Juniper-gum. Work undertaken from generous motives, not from necessity.

A لبّان labbān, A brick-maker. A milk-seller.

A لبانة lubānat, (pl. لبان lubān) An affair undertaken gratuitously. Want, necessity in any high and arduous affair.

A لباية lubāyat, A sort of the tree امطيّ umṭīy.

A لبائن labāʼin, (pl. of لبون labūn) Milch (camels or ewes).

A لبب labab, (pl. الباب albāb) The throat, that part in particular about which they hang ornaments, or where they slaughter animals. Poitrel, breast-harness of a horse. A small heap (of sand).

P لب بسته lab-basta, With closed lips.

A لبة labat, A lioness.

A لبّة labbat, The throat, especially the sticking-place in animals. Excellent (woman), loving her husband; lovely, elegant.

A لبت labt, (v. n. of لبت) Twisting (the hand). Striking on the breast, belly, or ribs with a stick.

A لبث labs, (v. n. of لبث) Delaying, tarrying. Delay. *Labis*, A delayer; tedious, dilatory.

A لبثة lubsat, A delay, stay, stop, halt.

A لبج labj, (v. n. of لبج) Throwing on the ground, strewing. Striking with a stick. *Labaj* or *lubaj*, (pl. of لبجة lubjat, labajat, or lubujat) Traps for wolves.

A لبجة lubjat, labajat, or lubujat, A forked trap made of iron for catching wolves.

P لب چرا lab-charā, Fruits and sweetmeats handed about at an entertainment, and which people eat slowly when chatting together. Food in general for man or beast.

A لبح labh, (v. n. of لبح) Growing old (a man). *Labah*, Fortitude, strength, bravery. An old man.

A لبخ labkh, (v. n. of لبخ) Laying snares. Taking. Beating. Killing. Using ill in word or deed.

P لب خا lab-khā, One who bites his lip: fastidious, fretful. A prig.

A لبخة labakhat, A large tree which bears fruit resembling dates, sweet, but disagreeable.

P لبخند lab-khand, (or خنده khanda) Smiling agreeably: of a gracious, cheerful countenance.

A لبد labd, (v. n. of لبد) Carding or teazing (wool), moistening it and stuffing it into the head of the sheath to save the sword-belt. *Libd*, (pl. الباد albād and لبود lubūd) Felt-cloth; any kind of carpeting or saddle-cloths made of it. Business. *Labad*, (v. n. of لبد) Having a violent pain and tightness in the throat from eating too freely of the plant صلّيان silliyān (a camel). Stopping, remaining. Sticking, cleaving to. Wool. ما له لبد ولا سبد mā lahu labad wa la sabad, He has neither woollen-cloth nor hair-cloth, *i.e.* he has nothing. *Lubad* and *libad*, One who keeps close at home; sluggish in seeking a livelihood. *Lubad*, Much wealth. Name of the last vulture of Locman. (This Locman was sent on an apostolic mission by the tribe of عاد ʻād, and is said to be a different person from Locman the sage and fabulist). ابو اللبد abū'l lubad or libad, The lion.

A لبدًا labadan, Closely (like felt), pell-mell.

A لبّد lubbad, Much wealth.

A لبدة libdat, A piece of woollen-cloth united together without weaving. Felt. A lion's mane. The inside of the thigh. A patch on the breast of a shirt. A string or line round the collar of a shirt. A locust. A number of men in one place. A shoot of the tree صلّيان silliyān. ذو لبدة zū libdat, A lion. امنع من لبدة الاسد amnaʻ min libdati'l asad, More unapproachable than the lion's mane. *Lubdat*, A crowd, mass of people packed together. Felt.

A لبدي lubada' or lubbada', A kind of bird.

A لبّدي lubbada', Assembled (people).

P لبريز lab-rez, Brimful, running over. سر نثار و لبريز شدن sar-nisār u lab-rez shudan, To be too full and overflowing.

A لبز labz, (v. n. of لبز) Eating fast and greedily. Striking violently; hitting on the back with the hand. Driving. Calling bad names. Putting on a veil worn across the nose by the Arabian women. Going a gentle pace, the whole foot touching the ground (a camel). *Libz*, (v. n. of لبز) Anointing a sore with an embrocation.

A لبس labs, (v. n. of لبس) Proposing to one any thing obscure or confused, mystifying. Mixture, confusion, ambiguity. *Libs*, A covering, especially that of the kaabah, or square temple of Mecca. The covering of a camel-palankin. A kind of dress. The membrane of the brain. *Lubs*, (v. n. of لبس) Putting on a garment. Enjoying long the company (of a wife), or the society (of a friend). لبس المسوح lubsu'l musūh, The wearing of sackcloth.

A لبساء (داهية) dāhiyat labsāʼ, A great misfortune.

P لبسان labsān, Like a lip. Name of an herb eaten with sour milk. Wild mustard.

A لبسة libsat, A mode of dressing, costume. A kind of dress. *Lubsat*, Obscurity, mystification, doubt. *Labasat*, A kind of pot-herb.

A لبط labt, (v. n. of لبط) Falling flat. Being seized with epilepsy. Throwing (on the ground). Striking the ground with the fore-feet (a camel).

A لبطة lubtat, A rheum in the head. *Labatat*, The gait of one who limps or is spindle-shanked. The pace of any quadruped where the fore-feet move at once.

A لبعًا labʻan, (or ضبعًا لبعًا zabʻan labʻan) With impunity, unrevenged (blood was spilt).

A لبق labk, (v. n. of لبق) Softening (as cake amongst broth, or a leathern bottle). Being intelligent, skilful, ingenious, worthy, proper, fit. Fitting well (a garment). Ingenuity, quickness. *Labik*, Intelligent, clever, skilled, glib-tongued. Finely clad. A garment which fits well.

A لبقة lubkat, Ingenuity, quickness. *Labikat*, (A woman) well versed in the lore of looks.

A لبك labk, (v. n. of لبك) Mixing (flour with honey). Taking (pudding) with the fingers. Mixing, confounding. A mixture. *Labik*, Any thing mixed or confused.

A لبكة labkat, A mixture. *Labakat*, A bit or mouthful (of steeped bread or of dates, butter, and coagulated milk).

P لبلاب lablāb, A conjurer. *Liblāb*, Ivy.

A لبلاب lablāb, Ivy, bind-weed, pellitory.

A لبلب lablab, Bleating (ram). *Lablab* or *lublub*, Benevolent, kind to domestics or neighbours.

A لبلبة lablabat, (v. n. of لبلب Q) (A sheep) licking tenderly her new-dropt lamb. Being scattered. Being tender-hearted and affectionate. The rattling of a goat at rutting-time. Separation, discrimination. Parental affection.

P لبلبو lablabū, Beet boiled and eaten with whey and garlic.

P لب لعل *lab-laʿl*, Lip-ruby, or ruby-lipped.

A لبم *labam*, Inequality in the shoulders.

A لبن *labn*, (v. n. of لبن) Giving milk to drink. Striking; bruising the breast (with a stick or a brick). Making brick. Eating voraciously. *Libn*, *labin*, or *libin*, A brick or tile. *Libn* or *lubn*, (pl. of لبون *labūn*) (Ewes or camels) having plenty of milk in the udder. *Laban*, (v. n. of لبن) Having plenty of milk in the udder (a ewe). Being seized with a pain in the neck from the pillow. (pl. البان *albān*) Milk. Coagulated sour milk. Gum, or any juice exuding from a tree. Quicksilver. بنات لبن *banāti laban*, Lacteal glands. *Labin*, Fond of, or drinking milk. A gore in the side of a shift. The breast of a shirt. (pl. of لبنة *labinat*) Bricks.

A لبنان *lubnān*, Mount Libanus.

A لبنانية *lubnāniyat*, Great, important (affair).

A لبنة *libnat* or *labinat*, Breast of a shirt. A brick or tile. A mural quadrant. *Lubnat*, A large mouthful or morsel. *Labinat*, (A sheep) abounding in milk. A gusset in a shirt. (pl. لبن *labin*) A square brick.

P لبنج *labanj*, A kind of plane-tree.

P لبنگ *labang*, A timber or ship-worm.

P لبنه *labna*, An insect which injures grain. *Lubna*, Part of an astrolabe.

A لبنى *lubnaʼ*, A tree which emits a gum from which a fumigating perfume is made. عسل اللبنى *ʿasalu ʼl lubnaʼ*, Liquid gum-storax.

P لبنى *labanī*, Storax. Any thing made of milk and curd.

A لبنيات *labaniyāt*, Aliments made of milk.

A لبؤ *lubaʼ*, (*lubuʼ*, or لبوء *lubūʼ*) (pl. of لبوة *lubuʼat*) Lionesses.

A لبوات *labuwāt*, (pl. of لبوة) Lionesses.

A لبوب *lubūb*, (pl. of لبّ) Kernels. Piths.

A لبوة *labuʼat*, (لبوة *labwat*, *libwat*, or *labuwat*) A lioness.

A لبوخ *lubūkh*, Fulness of flesh.

A لبود *labūd*, A tike or sheep-louse. *Lubūd*, (v. n. of لبد) Stopping, remaining. Adhering, cleaving (to the earth); sticking. Lighting (a bird on the ground). (pl. of لبد *libd* or لبدة) Felt-cloths.

A لبوديّ *lubūdiy*, A dealer in felt, a felt-maker.

A لبوس *labūs*, Coat of mail. Clothing, raiment.

A لبون *labūn*, (or لبونة *labūnat*) (pl. لبان *libān*, لبن *libn*, *lubn*, and لبائن *labāʼin*) (Cattle) with milk in the udder, milch. ابن اللبون *ibnu ʼl labūn*, (fem. ابنة اللبون *ibnatu ʼl labūn*) A young camel two years old. بنات لبون *banātu labūn*, Young dwarfish thorny plants called عرفط *ʿurfuṭ*.

P لبوه *labwa*, Rennet for curdling milk.

A لبي *laby*, (v. n. of لبي) Consuming much meat.

P لبي *labī*, A slice of bread or melon. *Labe*, Yes, sir; hey.

P لبياب *labyāb*, A great river.

A لبيب *labīb*, (pl. الباء *alibbāʼ*) Prudent, intelligent, wise, sagacious, acute. Industrious, attentive, assiduous, who sticks to his work. Dressed in a cloak.

A لبيبة *labībat*, A kind of cloak. A sleeveless vest, tunic, or shirt.

A لبيث *labīs*, (as خبيث لبيث *khabīs labīs*) Wicked, malignant.

A لبيثة *labīsat*, (v. n. of لبث) Delaying. A multitude out of different tribes and nations.

A لبيج *labīj*, A herd of camels about a tent.

A لبيخ *labīkh*, Fleshy.

A لبيخة *labīkhat*, A bag of musk.

P لبيد *labīd*, Boast, brag. A historian. A poet.

A لبيد *lubīd*, A small woollen sack (which, filled with food, they hang round the neck of a horse). Name of a poet. *Labīd* or *lubayd*, Name of a bird.

P لبيدن *labīdan*, To boast, to brag.

P لبيدي *labīdī*, Poetry; story-telling.

A لبيرة *labīrat*, Name of a province in Spain.

A لبيس *labīs*, Often worn, threadbare (dress). Clothed, clad. Like, resembling. Name of a fish.

P لبيش *labīsh*, (لبيشه *labīsha*, or لبيشن *labīshan*) Barnacles for holding a horse's nose when shoeing, a farrier's twitch.

A لبيق *labīk*, Intelligent, clever, skilled. Glib-tongued. Fitting well (garment).

A لبيقة *labīkat*, (A woman) well versed in the lore of looks: coquettish.

A لبّيك *labbayk*, What dost thou want with me? What wouldst thou have? Here I am: I wait your commands.

A لبيكة *labīkat*, A multitude. A mixture of sheep. A dish of meat, flour, sliced sour curd or oxygal, dates, and butter. (See بكيلة *bakīlat*).

A لبين *labīn*, (A horse) fed with milk. ابو لبين *abū lubayn*, Membrum virile.

P لبينا *labīnā*, A certain musical mode.

A لبينة *labīnat*, (Cattle) having plenty of milk in the udder. The breast of a shirt.

A لبيني *lubaynaʼ*, The devil's daughter; a woman's name. ابو لبيني *abū lubaynaʼ*, A name of the devil.

P لپ *lap*, A large mouthful.

P لپاچه *lapācha*, An outer garment. Breaking.

P لپان *lipān*, Splendid, shining, glittering.

P لپچور *lapchūr*, Large-lipped.

P لپ لپ *lap lap*, The noise made in taking soup or lapping.

A لت *lat*, A hammer. A mace, battle-axe. A stick. A knock, blow, thump, flagellation. A part, fragment. A piece, as a piece of cloth and the like. One half of a folding-door. Linen. The belly. Name of a river.

A لتّ *latt*, (v. n. of لتّ) Breaking. Bruising, pounding, braying small. Moistening, rendering fluid a ptisan, and mixing it up with fat. Collecting, drawing close, tying tight, causing to adhere closely together. Making firm. Being united in friendship. A blow, stroke, bastinado. Punishment. (pl. لتوت *lutūt*) A long-necked glass drinking-vessel.

A لتأ *latʼ*, (v. n. of لتأ) Beating on the breast. Striking (with a stone). Going. Being deficient. Lying with. Fixing the eyes upon (any thing). Bringing forth. Voiding dung. Breaking wind.

A لتات *lutāt*, Bark of trees pounded small. Any thing triturated, broken, pounded, or mixed.

A لتاح *lutāḥ*, Intelligent, clever.

P لتالت *lat-ā-lat*, In pieces. Fragile.

P لتانبان *lat-ambān*, A glutton. A term of abuse.

A لتب *latb*, (v. n. of لتب) Adhering, sticking. Being firm, fixed. Spearing. Tying tight. Putting on clothes. Girding a housing on a horse.

A لتح *latḥ*, (v. n. of لتح) Striking the face or body of any one with gravel, so as to leave marks. Tearing out (an eye). Casting a look. Lying with. Spoiling of every thing. Striking with the hand. Clever, intelligent. *Lataḥ*, (v. n. of لتح) Being hungry. Hunger. *Latiḥ*, Ingenious, intelligent, skilful.

A لتحان *laṭḥān*, Hungry, starved. Intelligent.

A لتحة *lutaḥat*, Ingenious, intelligent.

A لتحى *lathaʼ*, Hungry, starved (woman).

A لتخ *latkh*, (v. n. of لتخ) Staining, contaminating. Splitting, cleaving. Cutting (with a scourge). Peeling, skinning.

A لتخان *latkhān*, Hungry, famished.

A لتخة *latikhat*, Ingenious, skilful (man).

A لتد *latd*, (v. n. of لتد) Striking (with fist).

P لتر *latar*, A certain weight, half a من *man* of Tabrīz. A vessel for holding wine.

P لتره *latra*, A part, fragment. A man rendered indolent by fat. Rent, torn in pieces. Old. Low, base, vile. *Lutra*, By-words used by two persons and not understood by others. One who tells whatever he hears. Expelled, ejected, driven off.

P لتره لتره *latra latra*, In pieces, piecemeal.

A لتز *latz*, (v. n. of لتز) Striking on the breast or jaws with the fist in fighting. Pushing, thrusting, beating off.

A لتغ *latgh*, (v. n. of لتغ) Striking (with the fist). Biting (as a serpent).

P لتك *latak*, Name of a game.

P لت لت *lat lat*, In pieces, piecemeal.

A لتلتة *latlatat*, Perjury.

A لتم *latm*, (v. n. of لتم) Piercing in the nostril with a spear. Throwing, darting. Striking, beating. *Latam*, A wound.

A لتن *latin*, Sweet.

P لتنبار *latambār*, (لتنبان *latambān*, or لتنبر *latambar*) Lazy; slothful. A glutton. Ignorant.

A لتنة *latnat*, Any thing necessary to be done.

A لتنة *lutunnat*, A hedgehog.

A لتوب *lutūb*, (v. n. of لتب) Being firm, fixed. Sticking close to. Piercing with a spear. Tying tight. Putting on raiment.

A لتوت *lutūt*, (pl. of لتّ *latt*) Long-necked drinking-decanters made of glass.

P لتّه latta, Linen-rags.

P لته لته lata lata, Piecemeal. Broken in bits.

A لتيّا latayya' or lutayya', (dim. of اللتي allatī) The little she who. Misfortune.

A لتيم latīm, A proper name.

L لتين latīn, Latin.

A لتيّ latīs, One who moves not from his place.

A لث lass, (v. n. of لثّ) Being importunate. Remaining (in a place). Hitting, reaching, getting to. (Raining) for several days. Dew.

A لثأ lass, (v. n. of لثأ) Thrusting his muzzle into a pot (a dog) and lapping the contents.

A لثا lasa', (v. n. of لثي) Being very wet (dress).

A لثاة lasāt, The uvula. A sort of tree.

A لثات lisāt, (pl. of لثة lisat) Gums.

A لثام lisām, A veil or a fillet bound over the mouth to disguise the face or to keep out the dust.

A لثة lisat, (pl. لثات lisāt and لثي lisa') The gum. A kind of tree.

A لثد lasd, (v. n. of لثد) Filling a dish with grated bread levelled ready for the reception of milk or broth. Laying (furniture or wares) side by side.

A لثدة lisdat, A crowd, stationary multitude.

A لثط last, (v. n. of لثط) Throwing lightly or gently. Abusing, reviling in an under tone. A throw. A slight blow (especially slap on the back). A slow and gradual voiding of excrement.

A لثعة lasẓat, That part of the lip which adheres to the roots of the teeth.

A لثغ lasgh, (v. n. of لثغ) Making (any one) stammer, or looking on (him) as a stutterer. Lasagh, (v. n. of لثغ) Stammering, stuttering, being large-tongued, pronouncing غ ghayn, ي yā, or ل lām, instead of ر rā; or ث thā instead of س sā.

A لثغاء lasghās, (fem. of الثغ alsagh) A woman who has the defect above-mentioned.

A لثغة lusghat, The defect in the pronunciation of the letters mentioned above. Lasaghat, The mouth.

A لثق lasak, (v. n. of لثق) Being moist. Being calm, with much dew (a day). Moisture. Lasik, (A bird) wet with dew or water.

A لثلاث laslās, (and لثلاثة laslāsat) Slow, tardy; one who recedes from what he was expected to do.

A لثلثة laslasat, (v. n. of لثلث Q) Wavering, being inconstant in any business. Giving a little rest. Working, making (a camel) toil. Detaining, hindering. Tumbling (in the sand). Being obscure in speech. Importunity. Sojourn. Weakness. Several days' rain.

A لثم lasm, (v. n. of لثم) Kissing. Veiling the mouth. Breaking stones with the foot (a camel). Giving a blow (on the nose) with the fist. Bruising, wounding (as stones do a camel's foot). Lusm, (pl. of لاثم lāsim) Camels breaking stones with their feet.

A لثمة lismat, A manner of veiling the mouth.

A لثوي lisawiy, Pertaining to the gum, gingival.

A لثي lasy, (v. n. of لثي) Drinking (water) sparingly. Licking (a pot) violently. Dirtying, soiling (a garment). Lasa', (v. n. of لثي) Being moist and dewy. Distilling gum or juice (a tree). Thin gum or exudation which distils from a tree. Moisture, dew. The tread of a boot in water or blood. Adhesive, viscous (grease of milk). Dirt. Lasī, Moist (garment). (A tree) which distils gum or juice. Lisa', (pl. of لثة lisat) The gums.

A لثي lasiy, Greedily fond of the gum lasa.

A لثياء lasyās, (A woman) who sweats in front or all over her body.

A لثية lasyat, (A woman) who sweats about the privities, or over the whole body. Lasiyat, A tree, or gum which distils from a tree.

A لثيمية lusaymīyat, A costly kind of habit.

P لج laj, A kick. Dispute, quarrel. A cross rent. A wound from a blow with the foot.

A لجّ lajja, (fut. يلجّ yalajju) He was litigious.

A لجّ lujj, A great crowd. The rugged part of a mountain. Plenty, especially a great body of water. A sword. Side of a channel or valley. ادهم لجّ adhamu lujjun, Intensely dusky-coloured (camel).

A لجأ lajas, (v. n. of لجأ) Taking refuge. An asylum, place of refuge. A frog.

A لجاب lijāb, (pl. of لجبة laj, lij, or lujbat) Ewes whose milk fails four months after yeaning.

A لجابة lajābat, (v. n. of لجب) Beginning to fail four months after delivery (a sheep's milk).

A لجأة lajasat, A female frog.

P لجاج lajāj, Quicksilver.

A لجاج lajāj, (v. n. of لجّ) Quarrelling, wrangling. Contest, litigation, quarrel, squabble. في لجاج fī lajāj, (or على لجاج ẓala' lajāj) Importunely. Lijāj, Hard riding.

A لجّاج lajjāj, A brawler; litigious fellow.

A لجاجة lajājat, (v. n. of لجّ) Disputing, quarrelling. Contention, litigation. Importunity. Adulation. Palpitation of the heart from hunger.

A لجاذ lijāz, (v. n. of لجذ) Doing any thing successively and by degrees. Disputing, contending, wrangling. Glue, isinglass.

A لجاف lijāf, The threshold of a door. A stone projecting from a mountain (over a cave's mouth).

A لجام lijām, (from P لگام ligām) (pl. لجم lujum and الجمة aljimat) A bridle, reins. A mark resembling a bridle made upon cattle by burning. A menstruous cloth. Name of a famous horse. لفظ لجامه lafaza lijāmahu, He desisted from what he was doing (from fatigue). Lujām, Any thing from which one takes a bad omen. Inclination, affection.

A لجان lajān, (v. n. of لجن) Being stubborn and lazy. Being slow, sluggish (a camel). Lijān, Stubbornness, refractoriness (in a camel).

A لجب lajab, (v. n. of لجب) Making a noise, shouting. Roaring agitation (of the sea); voices of men. Lajib, (or ذو لجب zū lajab) Noisy (cloud). (A host) numerous, tumultuous, and uproarious.

A لجبة laj, lij, luj, laja, laji, or lijabat, (pl. لجاب lijāb) (A ewe) with much, or little milk. A ewe four months after yeaning, and whose milk has dried up.

A لجة lijat, (v. n. of ولج) Creeping into (a hole).

A لجّة lajjat, Noise, vociferation, clamour. Lujjat, A large body, multitude. Plenty (of water), the great deep, middle of the sea; an abyss. Silver. A looking-glass, mirror.

A لجج lujaj, (pl. of لجّة lujjat) Large bodies, multitudes. Bodies of water, mighty deeps. Silvers.

A لججة lujajat, Quarrelsome, contentious.

A لجح lujh, A hole in the bottom of a well or channel of a river. Lajah, A pimple in the inner corner of the eye. A flux from the eye.

A لجذ lajz, (v. n. of لجذ) Eating, pasturing (as cattle). Cropping the pasture with the tip of the tongue. Taking or receiving little. Asking again and again after having received a present. Rousing, stirring up. Licking a pot (a dog).

A لجز lajiz, Extensively drawn out, or ductile. Tenacious, adhesive, viscous, clammy, ropy.

A لجف lajf, A blow, stroke. A digging at the foot of the hiding-place of a deer. Lajaf, (pl. الجاف aljāf) A well or trench in a stable. A cut in the side of a well, through which some part of the water runs off. Any part round the bottom of a well eaten away by the water. A well narrow at top and wide at bottom. A dam, mound, weir. The channel of a torrent. A trench cut at the side of a deer's covert.

P لجلاج lujlāj, One who gives instruction in games of hazard. Name of the author of the game of chess. Irresolute, perplexed, hesitating. Tongue-tied; a stammerer. Silver. Quicksilver.

A لجلج lajlaj, Any thing embarrassing, or in which one errs; obscure, doubtful, shifting, uncertain. الحق ابلج والباطل لجلج al hakk ablaj, wa'l bātil lajlaj.

A لجلجة lajlajat, (v. n. of لجلج Q) Repeating words, being tautological.

P لجلجه lajlaja, An aromatic electuary.

P لجم lajm, Black mud at the bottom of a pond.

A لجم lajm, (v. n. of لجم) Sewing (a garment). Unripe grapes. Lujm, A frog. Air, atmosphere. Lajam, Any thing from which one takes a bad omen. That part of a horse's cheek which is covered by the headstall. A frog. Lujam, A large and venomous kind of lizard. A frog. Lujum, (pl. of لجام lijām) Reins, bridles.

A لجمة lujmat, An extensive and flat mountain. The side of a valley. Lajamat, That part of a horse's cheek which is pressed by the headstall.

A لجن lajn, (v. n. of لجن) Licking. Mixing leaves of trees with meal or barley as food for cattle. Lajan, (v. n. of لجن) Sticking, hanging by. Leaves shaken from trees for fodder. Lajin, Filth.

P لجن lajan or lajin, Black mud or clay in the bottom of a pond. Any thing mixed up with clay.

A لجنة *lajnat*, Many men consenting to, and approving any thing.

A لجوج *lajūj*, (or لجوجة) Litigious, quarrelsome.

A لجون *lajūn*, Stubborn and lazy (camel). *Lujūn*, (v. n. of لجن) Being stubborn and lazy. Being heavy and sluggish (a camel).

A لجي *lu* or *lijjiy*, Deep (sea), fathomless (ocean).

A لجيف *lajīf*, Broad-headed arrow. Door-post.

A لجيفة *lajīfat*, (du. لجيفتان) A door-post.

A لجين *lajīn*, Leaves shaken from trees for feeding camels. Foam of a camel. *Lujayn*, Silver.

P لچ *lach*, Face, cheek, complexion. *Luch*, Naked.

P لچك *lachak*, A square mantle which women wear doubled into a triangular form.

A لح *lahh*, (v. n. of لح) Being very close and intimate (relationship). A near relation. ابن عمي لحا *ibnu ʻammī lahhan*, (or ابن عم لح *ibnu ʻammin lahhin*) A very near relation.

A لحاء *lihāʼ*, (v. n. 3 of لحي) Opposing, contending with. The bark of a tree or of a stick.

A لحادة *lahādat*, A piece of meat. A mistake in reading or inflecting a noun or verb.

A لحاس *lahhās*, A greedy licker.

A لحاسة *lahhāsat*, A lioness.

A لحاسم *lahāsim*, (pl. of لحسم *luhsum*) Narrow water-courses.

A لحاص *lahāsi*, An affair of great importance. Misfortune, calamity. Mixture, confusion.

A لحاظ *lahāz*, The outer corner of the eye. *Lihāz*, (v. n. 3 of لحظ) Observing attentively, looking through half-shut eyes. Look, glance, view, observation. Sense, respect. A mark burnt under the eyes of sheep. A feather plucked from the wing. The feathered part of an arrow.

A لحاف *lihāf*, (pl. لحف *luhuf*) An upper garment. A blanket, coverlet, quilted counterpane. A wife. P لحاف چشم *lihāfi chashm*, The upper eyelid.

A لحاق *lahāk*, (v. n. of لحق) Overtaking, reaching to, touching. A collapse. *Lihāk*, A bow-case.

A لحام *lihām*, Metallic cement, solder. (pl. of لحم *lahm*) Meats, bits of meat.

A لحام *lahhām*, A meat-seller, vender of flesh.

A لحان *lahhān*, One who pronounces very badly.

A لحانة *lahānat*, Error in pronouncing words.

A لحانة *lahhānat*, One who pronounces badly.

A لحانية *lahāniyat*, An inaccurate mode of reading.

A لحب *lahb*, (v. n. of لحب) Beating, wearing (a road). Proceeding straight; passing briskly on, going forward. Throwing on the ground. Lying with (a woman). Drawing the bark off a tree, or the flesh from a bone. Being sleek and plump (a horse's back). Cutting (meat) the long way. Striking (with a sword). Making an impression, marking the way. Making (a road) clear. A wide and clear road. *Lahab*, (v. n. of لحب) Being emaciated with age. *Lahib*, Beaten (path), broad (road).

P لحبتان *luhbatān*, A doll, a puppet.

A لحت *laht*, (v. n. of لحت) Striking (with a staff). Taking the bark off a branch. بحت لحت *bahtun lahtun*, True, sincere. Excessive, intense, clear, and stunning (cold).

A لحج *lahaja*, (fut. يلحج *yalhaju*) He struck.

A لحج *lahj*, (v. n. of لحج) Sticking in the scabbard (a sword). Striking. Hurting (the eye). Wounding with an evil eye. Fleeing for refuge. *Luhj*, Corner of a house. Corner of the eye. *Luhj* or *lahj*, (pl. الحاج *alhāj*) The socket of the eye. A hollow, a cavity. *Lahij*, Narrow (place).

A لحح *luhah*, (v. n. of لح) Having the eyelids glued together by viscous matter. *Lahih*, Narrow (place).

A لحد *lahd*, (v. n. of لحد) Burying or preparing a place in the side of a tomb for depositing the dead. Burying (the dead). Inclining towards. Deviating from; becoming an infidel. *Lahd* or *luhd*, (pl. الحاد *alhād* and لحود *luhūd*) A place dug in the side of a grave, a sepulchral niche, a catacomb.

A لحز *lahz*, (v. n. of لحز) Being importunate. Striking on the breast with the fist. *Lahaz*, (v. n. of لحز) Being avaricious. Being of a sour, crabbed temper. *Lahiz* or *lihz*, Avaricious, narrow-minded.

A لحس *lahs*, (v. n. of لحس) Licking (a dish). Eating, corroding (as a moth or locust). اسرع من لحس الكلب انفه *asraʻ min lahsi'l kalb anfahu*, Quicker than a dog can lick his nose.

A لحسة *lah* or *luhsat*, (v. n. of لحس) Licking.

A لحسم *luhsum*, A narrow water-course.

A لحص *lahs*, (v. n. of لحص) Engaging in, sticking (to business). Hunting after or publishing news by little and little. *Lahas*, A shrinking of the upper eyelid.

A لحصان *lahasān*, Velocity. A running, leaping.

A لحط *laht*, (v. n. of لحط) Sprinkling, pouring (water). Thrusting, poking, driving.

A لحظ *lahz*, (v. n. of لحظ) Looking through half-shut eyes, or through the outer corner of the eye.

A لحظان *lahazān*, (v. n. of لحظ) Looking through half-shut eyes, or through the outer corner of the eye.

A لحظة *lahzat*, One look, glance. A moment. The twinkling of an eye. Name of a part of Tihāma abounding in lions. و لو لحظة *wa law lahzatan*, But for a moment, if only for an instant, though but a glance.

A لحظي *lahze*, One moment. Straightways.

A لحف *lahf*, (v. n. of لحف) Covering with a cloak or coverlet. Licking (with the tongue). *Lihf*, Foot of a mountain. Cleft of the buttocks. *Luhuf*, (pl. of لحاف *lihāf*) Upper garments. Bow-cases.

A لحفة *lahfat*, (v. n. of لحف) Losing part of one's flock. *Lihfat*, A mode of putting on a cloak.

A لحق *lahk*, (v. n. of لحق) Joining, adhering. Reaching, overtaking, attaining to. *Lahak*, Any thing following and joining another. (pl. الحاق *alhāk*) Part of a valley or bank of a river which is sown after the overflowing waters subside. Dates or figs produced under others.

A لحك *lahk*, (v. n. of لحك) Putting one thing into another, and making them to adhere closely. Putting medicine into another's mouth. Drenching Licking (honey). *Lahik*, Qui lente sperma fundit.

A لحكاء *luhakāʼ*, (or لحكة *luhakat*) An animal like a lizard, livid, shining, swift, and short-tailed.

A لحلح *lahlah*, Narrow (place).

A لحلحة *lahlahat*, (v. n. of لحلح Q) Remaining fixed, without moving from the spot. Dry bread, crust.

A لحم *lahm*, (v. n. of لحم) Feeding (one) with meat. Gnawing or picking (a bone). Fixing, establishing, doing firmly and well. Soldering (gold or silver). (pl. الحم *alhum*, لحوم *luhūm*, لحام *lihām*, and لحمان *luhmān*) Flesh, meat. Pulp, heart, core. *Lihm*, (v. n. of لحم) Abiding in a place. *Laham*, (v. n. of لحم) Longing for meat. Coming into a place. Hanging by, sticking to. Being fleshy about the body. Flesh. *Lahim*, Carnivorous. A lion. A house where people meet for slanderous gossip.

A لحمان *luhmān*, Slices of meat.

A لحمة *lahmat*, A piece of meat. A bruising match, fisticuffs. *Lahmat* or *luhmat*, Woof of a web. That part of prey which is given to a hawk, his reward. *Luhmat*, Propinquity, relationship. The fleshy skin of the head.

A لحن *lahn*, (v. n. of لحن) Speaking or reading in a tuneful pronunciation or recitative, chanting. Inclining to one. Deviating, pronouncing the vowels erroneously. Saying any thing to one which he understands, but is unintelligible to every other person. Understanding, perceiving a thing said by another. (pl. الحان *alhān* and لحون *luhūn*) A sound, note, tone. Melody, modulation. An error in pronouncing the vowels, cacophony. The signification of a word. P سي لحن *sī lahn*, The thirty notes in music as arranged by the celebrated musician Bārbud. (See سي لحن). A *Lahan*, (v. n. of لحن) Being intelligent, sagacious, understanding what is said. Reading incorrectly, pronouncing badly.

A لحنة *luhnat*, One who pronounces badly. *Lahanat*, One who pronounces very incorrectly. *Luhanat*, One who charges others with inaccuracy in pronunciation.

A لحو *lahw*, (v. n. of لحا for لحو) Stripping the bark off a branch. Reviling, reproaching.

A لحوب *luhūb*, (v. n. of لحب) Being open (way).

A لحوجة *lahwajat*, (v. n. of لحوج Q) Confusing, puzzling, mystifying.

A لحوح *luhūh*, A kind of Arabian cake.

A لحود *lahūd*, Deep down (water of a well). *Luhūd*, (pl. of لحد *lahd*) Niches dug in the side of tombs.

A لحوس *lahwas*, Desirous, wishful, greedy. *Lahūs* (A person or fly) fond of any thing sweet.

A لحوق *luhūk*, (v. n. of لحق) Following, reaching. Being thin, slender, and lank. Arrival. Conjunction, touch, adhesion.

A لحوم *luhūm*, (pl. of لحم *lahm* or لحمة) Meats.

A لحون *luhūn*, An error or inaccurate mode of pronouncing the vowels. (pl. of لحن *lahn*) Sounds, notes, keys, tunes, modulations, melodies.

A لحويّ *lihawīy*, Belonging to beard or jaw.

A لحي *lahy*, (v. n. of لحي) Peeling (a tree). Reprehending, reproaching. Confounding, cursing. Speaking evil of, traducing. (pl. الحي *alhī* and لحيّ *luhīy*) The chin. Bark. *Laha'*, (pl. الحي *alhī* and لحيّ *luhīy*) The part where the beard grows; jaw, chin. *Liha'* or *luha'*, (pl. of لحية *lihyat*) Beards.

A لحيّ *lihīy* or *luhīy*, (pl. of لحية *lihyat*) Beards. *Luhīy*, (pl. of لحي *laha'*) Chins. Jaws.

A لحيان *lihyān*, Drops of water. A furrow made by a torrent, a ditch, gutter, gully.

A لحيانيّ *lihyānīy*, Large or long-bearded.

A لحيب *lahīb*, Thin of flesh on the back.

A لحية *lihyat*, (pl. لحي *liha'* and *luha'*) Beard, mustachio, or whisker. لحية التيس *lihyatu't tays*, Goats'-beard (a shrub). لحية الحمار *lihyatu'l himār*, (Ass's-beard) The plant maidens'-hair.

A لحيج *lahīj*, Fraud, guile, deceit. ما فيه لحيجاء *mā fīhi lahījāʼ*, There is no deceit in him (or it).

A لحيجاء *luhayjāʼ*, Revocation, repeal, reversal.

A لحيزاء *luhayzāʼ*, A treasure.

A لحيص *lahīs*, Narrow, strait. Calamitous.

A لحيظ *lahīz*, Alike, resembling, equal to.

A لحيف *lahīf*, An outer garment. *Lahīf* or *luhayf*, Name of a horse belonging to Muhammad.

A لحيم *lahīm*, Fleshy. One who has meat in the house. Killed, slain. Like, resembling. Suitable, befitting.

P لخ *lukh*, A bulrush.

A لخّ *lakhkh*, (v. n. of لخّ) Being tearful (an eye). Being obscure, confused, barbarous, and unintelligible. Pursuing upon the mountains. Inclining in excavating. Anointing with perfume. Giving a blow. Inquiring (news).

P لخا *lakhā*, A shoe, slipper, sandal.

A لخاء *lakhāʼ*, A gallipot for holding medicines. An instrument, or the skin of a fish, by means of which a sternutatory is injected into the nostrils. Moist (female pudendum). *Likhāʼ*, (v. n. 3 of لخي) Cultivating mutual friendship. Endeavouring to conciliate, soothing by presents. Opposing, contradicting, dissenting from. Instigating, setting by the ears. Lying, colouring with falsehoods. Soaked bread, or the soaking of bread. Pap for children.

A لخاص *likhās*, (pl. of لخصة *lakhasat*) Pimples in the inner part of the eye.

A لخاف *likhāf*, (pl. of لخفة) Thin whitish stones.

A لخاقيق *lakhākīk*, (pl. of لخقوق *lukhkhūk*) Cracks in the ground.

A لخام *lakhām*, Bones.

A لخامة *lakhāmat*, (v. n. of لخم) Being very fleshy (the face). Being thick and hard.

A لخب *lakhb*, (v. n. of لخب) Marrying. Smiting upon the cheek, slapping, boxing. *Lakhab*, A kind of tree.

A لخّة *lakhkhat*, A dirty, stinking woman.

P لخت *lakht*, An iron mace. An iron hook used in driving or managing an elephant. A stick, a scourge. Flagellation. Somewhat, some, a little. A piece, bit, part, portion. A shoe, slipper, sandal. Hose worn over boots to keep them clean. Leather for making soles. Strife, contention. Breaking in pieces. A butcher's knife. An iron helmet. A horse's mane. A gad-fly. لخت جگر *lakhti jigar*, A piece of one's liver (applied generally to a beloved child). سنگ لخت *sang-lakht*, Solid rock.

A لخت *lakht*, Great, large, corpulent. A woman abused so that both passages have become one. سخت لخت *sakhtun lakhtun*, Excessive (heat).

P لختان *lakhtān*, (pl. of لخت) Parts, portions.

P لخت دوز *lakht-doz*, Mender of old clothes.

P لختة *lakhta*, A piece, part, portion.

P لختينه *lakhtīna*, A place raised upon wooden pillars seven or eight yards high, where they sleep on account of the dampness of the ground.

P لختيها *lakhtīhā*, Parts, portions. Trifles.

P لخج *lakhaj*, A white humour congealed about the eyes.

A لخجة *lakhijat*, Blear, dirty (eye).

A لخجم *lakhjam*, An open road. A large-bellied camel. Frigidioris vulvæ mulier.

P لخچ *lakhch* or *lakhach*, Vitriol, copperas. Potash.

P لخچه *lakhcha*, Flame, live coals.

A لخز *lakhz*, A sharp knife.

P لخشان *lakhshān*, Slipping, sliding. Clear. Plain, level.

P لخشش *lakhshish*, A slip, slide.

P لخشك *lakhshak*, A kind of frumenty. A certain sweetmeat. A stone on which a man sits and slides to the bottom of a mountain. Level ground frozen over, on which boys slide.

P لخشه *lakhsha*, A live coal. A spark of fire. A kind of frumenty. Fallen down in a slippery place.

P لخشيدن *lakhshīdan*, To slide.

A لخص *lakhs*, (v. n. of لخص) Examining the eye of a camel to see if she be fat or not. *Lakhas*, (v. n. of لخص) Having a hard fleshiness of the upper eyelid. Becoming swollen round about (the eye). A hard fleshiness of the upper eyelid. *Lakhis*, Very fleshy (udder), with difficulty milked.

A لخصاء *lakhsāʼ*, (An eye) swollen round about.

A لخع *lakhaʻ*, Languor, relaxed habit of body.

A لخف *lakhf*, (v. n. of لخف) Branding with a broad mark. Thin foam or froth. Thin fresh butter. A hard blow.

A لخفة *lakhfat*, (pl. لخاف *likhāf*) A thin whitish stone. A brand on cattle. Posteriors, backside.

A لخقوق *lukhkhūk*, (pl. لخاقيق *lakhākīk*) A gap or crack in the earth, like the hole of a field-mouse.

P لخلخ *lakhlakh*, Weak, feeble, languid, lean.

A لخلخانيّ *lakhlakhānīy*, One who speaks badly.

A لخلخانية *lakhlakhānīyat*, Rudeness of speech.

A لخلخة *lakhlakhat*, A kind of aromatic unguent.

P لخلخه *lakhlakha*, A cephalic medicine. *Lakhlakha*, (or لخلخهاي عنبري *lakhlakhāyi ʻambarī*) A ball composed of aloe-wood, musk, and camphor. The hours of the night.

A لخم *lakhm*, A cutting, amputation. A box, a blow. *Lukhm*, A kind of fish.

A لخمة *lakhmat*, Languor, heaviness. *Lakhamat*, A back-sinew. A difficult pass over rough ground. *Lakhamat* or *lukhamat*, Heavy, dull.

A لخن *lakhn*, White matter which collects within the foreskin of an uncircumcised lad, or in the sheath of an ass. *Lukhn*, (pl. of الخن *alkhan* and لخناء *lakhnāʼ*) Stinking, uncircumcised. *Lakhan*, (v. n. of لخن) Being stinking, rank, rancid, or rotten. Rank smell of female pudendum: of arm-pit or groin.

A لخناء *lakhnāʼ*, Rank, uncircumcised (girl).

A لخنة *likhnat*, The fleshy part below the shoulder-blades.

A لخو *lakhw*, (v. n. of لخا for لخو) Injecting medicine or snuff into the nostrils of any one.

A لخواء *lakhwāʼ*, A prating woman, gossip. (An eagle) which has the upper beak longer than the under one. (A she-camel) having one knee larger than the other. Wide (woman).

A لخوخ *lakhūkh*, Vicious, blemished (root, stock).

A لخي *lakhy*, (v. n. of لخي) Giving one's property. Making one sneeze, putting medicine into his nose or mouth. Much nonsensical talk. *Lakha'*, An instrument, or the skin of a fish, by means of which a sternutatory is introduced into the nostrils. Flabby and moist (pudendum). *Lakhi*, (A camel) having one knee larger than another.

A لخيفة *lakhīfat*, The noise of running water, the sound of wind or of an eagle flying, or of one being strangled.

A لد *ladu*, *lad*, or *lud*, To, with, nigh, at.

A لدّ *ladd*, (v. n. of لدّ) Contending with animosity. Disputing at law; gaining a suit at law or victory in the field; being a formidable or severe enemy. Confining, imprisoning. Pouring medicine into the corner of the mouth of a sick man: giving a drench. Taking in medicine at one corner of the mouth. A sack, bag. *Ludd*, Lydda in Palestine. (pl. of الدّ *aladd*) Bold (antagonists).

A لدا *ladā*, To, with, nigh, at.

A لدات *lidāt*, (pl. of لدة *lidat*) Contemporaries.

A لداد *lidād*, Bold, unfair antagonists.

A لدّاغ *luddāgh*, A sharp thorn, a sting.

A لدّاغة *luddāghat*, A curse, cutting speech. A troublesome, disagreeable fellow.

A لدام *lidām*, (v. n. of لدم) Patching a garment or shoe. A patch (on a boot or garment).

A لدان *lidān*, (pl. of لدن) Limber (spears).

A لدانة *ladānat*, Limberness (of a spear).

A لدة *lidat*, (v. n. of ولد) Bringing forth (as a woman). A birth-day. (pl. لدون *lidūn* and لدات *lidāt*) Coeval, contemporary, born at the same time.

A لدح *ladh*, (v. n. of لدح) Striking or slapping with the hand on the back.

A لدد *ladad*, Litigation.

P لدروه *ladrūh*, Name of a fort in India.

A لدس *lads*, A throw. A blow with the hand. Gentle lowing or bleating. A licking, lapping.

A لدغ *ladgh*, (v. n. of لدغ) Stinging (a scorpion). Biting (a serpent). Using a cutting expression.

A لدغاء *ludaghā*, Detractors, slanderers.

A لدغة *ladghat*, A sting or venomous bite.

A لدغي *ladgha'*, Detractors, slanderers. (pl. of لديغ *ladīgh*) Bitten by a serpent.

A لدك *ladk* or *ladak*, A sticking close, adhering.

A لدم *ladm*, (v. n. of لدم) Beating. Giving a box or a blow. Striking with any thing hard. Striking the bosom or face (as a woman in grief). Making dough flat by striking it. Mending, patching (a garment). The sound of a stone falling to the ground. Weak in mind, dull. *Ladam*, The honouring or acknowledging as a relation; whence this formula in confirming any alliance, اللدم اللدم *al ladama'l ladama*, Your honour will be our honour. (pl. of لادم *lādim*) Strikers. Menders.

A لدمة *ladmat*, A part, portion.

A لدن *ladn*, (pl. لدن *ludn* and لدان *lidān*) Flexible, limber (spear). *Ladun*, Soft, ill-dressed (meat). *Ladun, ladan, ludun, ludn, ladin*, or *ladni*, To, with. Nigh, near. At.

A لدنّة *lu* or *ladunnat*, A thing needful to be done.

P لدني *ladunī*, Inspired, infused (knowledge).

A لدود *ladūd*, An adversary, opponent. (pl. الدّة *aliddat*) A medicine poured through a tube into the corner of the mouth of a sick person: a drench. A pain in the mouth or throat. *Ludūd*, (v. n. of لدّ) Pouring medicine into the corner of the mouth of a sick person. Giving a drench. Taking in medicine at one corner of the mouth.

A لدون *lidūn*, (pl. of لدة) Born at the same time.

A لدونة *ludūnat*, (v. n. of لدن) Being supple, flexible, and limber.

A لدويّ *ladawiy*, Pertaining to the particle لدي.

A لدي *lada'*, To, with, nigh, near, after, at. Whither? لديك *ladayka*, Near or with thee.

A لديد *ladīd*, (pl. الدّة *aliddat*) Medicine poured into the corner of the mouth. A drench.

A لديدان *ladīdāni*, The two sides of the neck below the ear. Banks of a river. Sides of a valley.

A لديدة *ladīdat*, A gay, flourishing garden.

A لديس *ladīs*, (pl. الداس *aldās*) Fat, firm in flesh.

A لديغ *ladīgh*, (pl. لدغي *ladgha'*) Bitten by a serpent. Stung by a scorpion.

A لديم *ladīm*, A worn or tattered garment; also one mended.

A لذّ *lazz*, Sweet, agreeable (water). اللذّ *al lazz*, Sleep. *Luzz*, (pl. of لذيذ *lazīz*) Sweet, pleasant, delectable. Wines.

A لذّات *lazzāt*, (pl. of لذّة *lazzat*) Delights. لذّات حسّيّة *lazzāti hissīya*, Pleasures of sense.

A لذاذ *lazāz*, (or لذاذة *lazāzat*) (v. n. of لذّ) Taking delight in, finding (a thing) agreeable. Being sweet and delicious. هادم اللذاذ *hādimu'l lazāz*, The destroyer of pleasure, *i. e.* death. *Lizāz*, (pl. of لذيذ *lazīz*) Sweet, delicious, delightful. Wines.

A لذّاع *lazzā*, A liar, promise-breaker.

A لذّة *lazzat*, (pl. لذّات *lazzāt*) Pleasure, delight, enjoyment, content, sweetness, deliciousness; taste, flavour, relish, savour. اللذّة *al lazzat*, Wine.

A لذج *lazj*, A sipping. A being importunate.

A لذع *laz*, (v. n. of لذع) Burning, scorching, singeing. Paining the heart (love). Making a mark by burning. Reproaching with words.

A لذعة *lazat*, One mark made by the cautery, a dot with the end of the branding-iron; one reproach.

A لذلاذ *lazlāz*, Quick, expeditious at work. اللذلاذ *al lazlāz*, The wolf.

A لذلذة *lazlazat*, A being quick at work.

A لذالك *lizālika*, Because, on account of.

A لذم *lazm*, (v. n. of لذم) Affording pleasure, causing surprise. Dwelling, being fixed (to a spot). Breaking stones with his feet (a camel). Kissing.

A لذمة *luzamat*, One who keeps always at home.

A لذوب *luzūb*, A remaining, a stopping.

A لذي *laza'*, (v. n. of لذي) Being assiduous, adhering to, cleaving unto. *Lazī*, Who.

A لذيذ *lazīz*, (pl. لذّ *luzz* and لذاذ *lizāz*) Sweet, full of juice, delicious, savoury, tasteful, pleasant, delightful. اللذيذ *al lazīz*, Wine.

P لر *lar*, A water-course. Arm-pit. Poor, thin, meagre. *Lur*, Name of a people of large stature dwelling in the open fields. The men of Kohistān. Ability, wish, will, object. A lamb. Name of a city.

P لرد *lard*, A race-course, public place.

P لرز *larz*, Tremor, fear, terror.

P لرزان *larzān*, Trembling, tremulous.

P لرزانا *larzānā*, (or لرزانان) Terrifying.

P لرزانيدن *larzānīdan*, To make tremble, frighten.

P لرزش *larzish*, Shivering, quaking, trembling.

P لرز ماهي *larz-māhī*, The torpedo.

P لرزة *larza*, A shaking, shivering, trembling, quaking. Tremor. The paroxysm or cold fit of an ague. An earthquake. لرزة گرفتن *larza giriftan*, To shiver. لرزة زدة شدة *larza-zada shuda*, Struck with a tremor, seized with a shivering fit.

P لرزي *larzī*, Ague, cold fit of an ague.

P لرزيدن *larzīdan*, To tremble, shiver, quake.

P لرس *lars*, A blow, cuff, kick. *Lurs*, Pity, commiseration. Playing (on an instrument) with a plectrum or bow.

P لرستان *luristān*, A country in Persia.

P لرك *lurk*, Sour milk thickened by boiling. *Lurah*, A bow for cleaning and separating cotton.

P لرلر *larlar*, A name of Omnipotence.

A لزّ *lazz*, (v. n. of لزّ) Fastening, joining, glueing together. Adhering. Tying, binding. Piercing with a spear. The ring of a door. كزّ لزّ *kazzun lazzun*, Dry, shrivelled (man). A miser. لزّ شرّ *lizzu sharrin*, Addicted to evil.

A لزء *laz*, (v. n. of لزأ) Giving. Filling. Feeding (camels) well. Bringing forth.

A لزاب *lizāb*, (pl. of لزب *lazib*) Few, small.

A لزاز *lizāz*, The bar of a door. One inveterate in his hatred against his enemy.

A لزاق *lizāk*, Glue. Coition. لزاق الذهب *lizāku'z zahab*, Gum-ammoniac. A certain medicine made from the urine of children; also of one leek-coloured, brought from Armenia. لزاق الحجر *lizāku'l hajar*, (or لزاق الرخام *lizāku'r rukhām*) A medicine extracted from a certain stone.

A لزام *lazām*, (or لزامة *lazāmat*) (v. n. of لزم) Being necessary, ensuing of necessity. Remaining constantly firm. Being assiduous, inseparable, adhering steadily. سبّة لزام *subbat lazām*, An eternal reproach. *Lazāmi*, Contumelious (expression). *Lizām*, (v. n. 3 of لزم) Being conjoined, individual, adhering. Death. Number, reckoning. Assiduous, attentive. An equitable judge. A judge who makes a just decision between what is right and wrong.

A لزائز *lazāiz*, Breast-bones.

A لزب *lazb*, (v. n. of لزب) Adhering, having his several parts united. Becoming hard (clay). (pl. of لزبة *lazbat*) Straits, difficulties. *Lizb*, A narrow path. *Lazib*, (pl. لزاب *lizāb*) Few, small.

A لزبات *lazbāt*, (pl. of لزبة) Straits, difficulties.

A لزبة *lazbat*, Difficulty, penury, want, scarcity.

A لزج *lazaj*, (v. n. of لزج) Being drawn out (any thing viscous). Being joined, glued together; adhering. Being greedy. *Lazij*, Tenacious, adhesive, viscous, ropy, stringy, ductile.

A لزجة *laz* or *lazijat*, A man who keeps at home.

A لزز *lazaz*, (v. n. of لزّ) Fastening, joining, glueing together. Tying, binding. The bar of a bar.

A لزق *lazika*, (fut. يلزق *yalzaku*) (It) adhered.

A لزق *lizk*, Contiguous, adjoining, close to the side. لزقي *lizkī*, My companion (as being close to my side). *Lazak*, Whatever grows up on a rainy morning and adheres to the lower parts of stones.

A لزك *lazk*, Coalescence (of the lips of a wound).

A لزم *lazm*, (v. n. of لزم) Being necessary, necessarily following. Being assiduous, adhering steadily, or inseparably. Keeping, observing strictly. Sticking close to. لزمه *lazimahu*, It stuck to him. *Lazam*, A distinction (between what is right and wrong). *Lazim*, A judge who makes a decision between right and wrong.

A لزمان *luzmān*, (or لزمة *luzmat*) (v. n. of لزم) Being necessary, following as a thing of course. Remaining steady. Being assiduous, inseparable, adhering.

A لزمة *luzamat*, Always fixed on one object.

A لزن *lazn*, Narrowness of circumstances, bad fortune, an indigent situation. (pl. of لزنة *laznat* and *liznat*) Straits, difficulties, distresses. *Lazn* or *lazan*, (v. n. of لزن) Pressing upon one another (people in a narrow spot, or round a watering-place). *Lazn* or *lazin*, (A well or drinking-place) beset by a throng of people.

A لزنة *laznat* or *liznat*, (pl. لزن *lazn*) Indigence, scarcity, a life of distress. ليلة لزنة *laylatun laznatun* or *liznatun*, A night of intense cold or great scarcity.

A لزوب *luzūb*, (v. n. of لزب) Adhering tenaciously. Being firm, settled. Stinging (as a scorpion). Dearth, scarcity.

A لزوجة *luzūjat*, Adhesiveness, viscosity.

A لزوز (عجوز *ɛajūzun*) *lazūzun*, An old woman.

A لزوق *lazūk*, A plaster, sarcocolla (a Persian medicine for wounds). *Luzūk* (v. n. of لزق) Adhering, sticking.

P لزوم *luzūm*, A weak bow for practising with.

A لزوم *luzūm*, (v. n. of لزم) Necessarily following, behoving. Being inseparable adhering steadily, keeping close. Necessity, compulsion, obligation. Necessary connection. Expediency, behoof. Imposition of a task upon one's self. Debt. قدوم بهجت لزوم *kudūmi bahjat-luzūm*, (His) fortunate or auspicious arrival.

A لزيجة *lazījat*, One who keeps much at home.

P لزيچه *lazīcha*, A clew of thread.

P لزير *lazīr*, Clever, expert, wary.

A لزيز *lazīz*, (pl. لزائز *lazāʼiz*) The breast-bone, where the flesh is thickest. لزيز شرّ *lazīzu sharrin*, Addicted to evil.

A لزيق *lazīk*, An inseparable companion.

A لزيقاء *luzaykāʼ*, Whatever grows up in a rainy morning and adheres to the lower parts of stones.

A لزّيقى *luzzayka'*, Any thing agreeable (in speech), (which adheres or is remembered).

P لژم *lajum*, Black mud at a pond's bottom.

P لژن *lajan*, Mud at the bottom of a pond.

A لسّ *lass*, (v. n. of لسّ) Cropping herbage. Eating. Licking.

A لساس *lusās*, Early grass which cattle can just crop with their lips. A kind of forage.

A لسّاس *lussās*, A kind of forage.

A لسّاع *lassāɛ*, Stinging; a stinger.

A لسام *lisām*, (v. n. of لسم) Tasting (any thing). ما لسم لساماً *mā lasama lisāman*, He tasted nothing.

A لسان *lisān*, (pl. السن *alsun*, السنة *alsinat*, and لسن *lusn*) The tongue. Language, dialect, idiom, diction, speech, brogue, jargon. Tongue of a balance, or of a buckle. Flame of fire. A mission; an epistle. Style of a book. An interpreter. A ready spokesman (for the people). The hilly ground of Kūfa. لسان الله *lisān allāh*, The word of God. لسان الابل *lisānu'l ibl*, A kind of medicinal plant. لسان البحر *lisānu'l bahr*, Sebestens. لسان الثور *lisānu's sawr*, Ox-tongue. A sole. لسان الحمل *lisānu'l hamal*, Plantain. لسان السبع *lisānu's sabuɛ*, Name of a plant. لسان الصدق *lisānu's sidk*, A high encomium. Suitable praise. لسان العصافير *lisānu'l ɛaṣāfīr*, Seed of the ash. لسان الفرس *lisānu'l faras*, Horse-tongue (an herb). لسان القلزم *lisānu'l kulzum*, Tongue or bay of the Egyptian Sea. The Red Sea. لسان الكلب *lisānu'l kalb*, The herb dogs'-tongue. لسان المزمار *lisānu'l mizmār*, Head of the windpipe, larynx. لسان النار *lisānu'n nār*, Tongue of fire, *i.e.* lambent flame without smoke. بلسان حال *ba lisāni hāl*, In language (expressive) of (one's) state or condition (as a haggard countenance, or tattered garments, in contradistinction to language uttered by the lips, and which is called لسان قال *lisāni kāl*). ذو لسانين *zū lisānayn*, Two-tongued, bilingual. Deceitful.

A لساناً *lisānan*, Verbally, orally.

A لسّان *lassān*, Eloquent. *Lussān*, An herb.

P لسان آشنا *lisān-āshnā*, A philologist, linguist.

P لسان آشنائي *lisān-āshnāʼī*, Philology.

A لسّانية *lassāniyat*, Eloquence.

A لسب *lasb*, (v. n. of لسب) Stinging (as a scorpion). Striking (with a scourge). Licking (honey). Adhering, persisting in.

A لسبة *lasbat*, Bite of serpent, sting of scorpion. المرأة عقرب حلوة اللسبة *al marʼat ɛakrab hulwatu'l lasbat*, Woman is a scorpion with a sweet sting.

P لست *last*, Firm, strong. Good, handsome.

A لست *lastu*, (from the negat. verb ليس *laysa*) I am not. الست بربكم *a lastu bi rabbikim*, Am I not your Lord? (spoken by the Almighty when He entered into covenant with Adam and his seed, Kur'ān, ch. vii. See Maracci or Sale in loc. Allusion to this transaction is not unfrequent among the mystic poets of Persia, in such expressions as روز الست *rozi a last*, عهد الست *ɛahdi a last*, &c.)

A لسد *lasd* or *lasad*, (v. n. of لسد) Sucking (as a kid). Licking (a plate).

A لسس *lusus*, Expert managers of camels.

A لسع *lasɛ*, (v. n. of لسع) Stinging (as a serpent or scorpion). Reproaching. Travelling.

A لسعة *lasɛat*, A scorpion's sting. *Lusaɛat*, One who has a reproachful tongue.

A لسق *lisk*, Close, contiguous, near, adjoining. هو لسقي *huwa liskī*, He is my companion (close to my side). *Lasak*, (v. n. of لسق) Having the lights adhering to the side from excessive thirst (a camel).

A لسلاس *lislās*, A camel's bunch cut.

A لسلسة *lislisat*, A camel's bunch cut.

A لسم *lasam*, (v. n. of لسم) Being dumb, silent from stammering in speech and from ignorance. Keeping (the road). Tasting.

A لسن *lasn*, (v. n. of لسن) Taking hold of another's tongue. Sucking (a damsel's) tongue. Making (a shoe) tapering to a point. Overcoming in argument. Stinging (as a scorpion). *Lisn*, Idiom, tongue, language. *Lusn*, (pl. of لسن *lasin* and of السن *alsan*) Eloquent. (pl. of لسان *lisān*) Tongues. *Lasan*, (v. n. of لسن) Being eloquent. Eloquence. *Lasin*, Eloquent. Sharp-pointed like a tongue.

A لسناء *lasnāʼ*, Talkative, tongued (woman).

A لسو *lasw*, The act of eating voraciously.

A لسوب *lasūb*, (or لسّوب *lassūb*) Whatever is or may be licked; hence, any thing, somewhat.

A لسوع *lasūɛ*, A woman who hates her husband. *Lusūɛ*, Fissures, gaps.

A لسوق *lusūk*, (v. n. of لسق) Adhering, sticking.

A لسيع *lasīɛ*, Stung (by a serpent or scorpion).

A لسيعة *lasīɛat*, A kind of herb.

A لسيق *lasīk*, An inseparable companion.

P لش *lush*, Mud at the bottom of a pond.

A لشّ *lashsh*, (v. n. of لشّ) Driving, compelling. Sumach. A kind of pease.

P لشتن *lashtan*, To sport, play, amuse. *Lishtan*, To lick.

P لشك *lushk*, A bit or piece. *Lashk* or *lishk*, Dew, hoar frost.

P لشكر *lashkar*, An army. لشكر كشيدن *lashkar kashīdan*, To muster or lead an army. لشكر مور شمار *lashkari mūr-shumār*, An army numerous as ants. پيش لشكر *pesh lashkar*, Advanced guard, van, forlorn hope. پس لشكر *pas lashkar*, The rear.

P لشكرپژوه *lashkar-pijūh*, A spy, a scout.

P لشكرخلاص *lashkar-khalās*, A trull, strumpet.

P لشكرشكن *lashkar-shikan*, (or لشكرشكوف *lashkar-shikūf*) A conqueror of armies.

P لشكركش *lashkar-kash*, A commander, general.

P لشكر كشي *lashkar-kashī*, Generalship.

P لشكرگاه *lashkar-gāh*, A camp, parade, or any place where an army is quartered or manœuvres.

P لشكرنشين *lashkar-nishīn*, A military station.

P لشكرنويس *lashkar-navīs*, Paymaster-general.

P لشكري *lashkarī*, A soldier. Any thing belonging to an army: military. An officer.

P لشك صفت *lashk-sifat*, Like hoar frost.

P لشك لشك *lashk lashk*, In pieces.

P لشكه *lashka*, A bit, a piece. Dew.

P لشكه لشكه *lashka lashka*, In pieces.

A لشلاش *lashlāsh*, Disturbed in the bowels. Timid (man).

A لشلشة *lashlashat*, Commotion in the bowels. Disquietude. A going to and fro in fear and alarm.

A لشن *lashn*, *lashan*, or *lashin*, Soft, nice, delicate. Plain, smooth, even. *Lashan*, A prop, support.

A لشو *lashw*, (v. n. of لشا for لشو) Becoming wretched after having been in a high station.

A لشيّ *lashīy*, Abounding in new milk.

A لصّ *lass*, (v. n. of لصّ) Shutting a door. Doing any thing slily. *Liss*, *lass*, or *luss*, (pl. لصوص *lusūs* and الصاص *alsās*) A robber.

A لصّاء *lassāʼ*, (fem. of الصّ *alass*) (A sheep) whose one horn projects forwards, the other backwards. Close-thighed (woman). Narrow (forehead).

A لصاب *lisāb*, Narrow passes between hills.

A لصّات *lassāt*, (pl. of لصّة) Female thieves.

A لصاص *lasās*, The act of robbing: robbery.

A لصائص *lasāʼis*, (pl. of لصّة) Female thieves.

A لصب *lisb*, (pl. لصاب *lisāb* and لصوب *lusūb*) A fissure in a mountain, or narrow pass or valley between hills (greater than شعب *shiʻb* and less than لهب *lihb*). *Lasab*, (v. n. of لصب) Sticking fast (a sword in the scabbard). Adhering (skin to the flesh from leanness). Being tight upon the finger (a ring). *Lasib*, A kind of barley. Avaricious.

A لصّة *lassat*, (fem. of لصّ *lass*) (pl. لصّات *lassāt* and لصائص *lasāʼis*) A female robber.

A لصت *last*, *list*, or *lust*, (pl. لصوت) A robber.

A لصص *lasas*, (v. n. of لصّ) Robbing. Robbery. Closeness of shoulder-blades, teeth, or thighs.

A لصف *lasf*, (v. n. of لصف) Shining, lightening. Joining together (stones in pavements), laying (stones upon each other in a building). Whipping an arrow-head about with a bruised sinew. Agreeing, being suitable. *Lasaf*, The caper-tree. A substance resembling a cucumber springing from the root of the capers. A sort of date. Hares'-ears (an herb). Dryness and adhesiveness of skin.

A لصق *lish*, The side. لصقي *liskī*, (or بلصقي *bi liskī*) A companion (as close to one's side). *Lasak*, (v. n. of لصق) Having the lights adhering to the side from excessive thirst (a camel).

A لصلصة *laslasat*, A setting in motion. Motion.

A لصو *lasw*, (v. n. of لصا for لصو) Joining one's self to another to avoid suspicion. Accusing, convicting.

A لصوب *lusūb*, (pl. of لصب *lisb*) Narrow paths between mountains.

A لصوت *lusūt*, (pl. of لصت *last*) Robbers.

A لصوز *lusūz*, Robbers.

A لصوص *lusūs*, (v. n. of لصّ) Robbing. (pl. of لصّ *liss* and *luss*) Robbers.

A لصوصة *lusūsat*, The being a robber: robbery.

A لصوصيّة *lusūsiyat*, (v. n. of لصّ) Robbing. Robbery, the profession of a robber.

A لصوغ *lusūgh*, (v. n. of لصغ) Cleaving to the bones from leanness (the skin).

A لصوق *lusūk*, (v. n. of لصق) Adhering, being joined to. Conjunction, adhesion.

A لصيف *lasīf*, Lightning. Effulgence.

A لصيق *lasīk*, An inseparable companion.

A لضّ *lazz*, A man who drives away, or who commands to drive away.

A لضلاض *lazlāz*, Intelligent (guide).

A لضلضة *lazlazat*, A looking to right or left.

A لضم *lazm*, A being inconvenient, troublesome.

A لضو *lazw*, (v. n. of لضا for لضو) Being clever, intelligent (as a guide through sandy deserts).

A لضي *lazy*, (v. n. of لضي) Being added, joined, attached.

A خضيّ بضيّ لضيّ *khaziy baziy laziy*, Impotent.

A لطّ *latt*, (v. n. of لطّ) Being assiduous, adhering steadily to, sticking close. Joining, fastening to. Clapping the tail between the legs (as a camel when going to run). Denying (a debt). Loosing, letting drop (a veil). Covering, veiling. Closing, bolting (a door). Concealing, suppressing (news). (pl. لطاط *litāt*), Any thing hung round the neck (especially a necklace of dyed colocynth-berries).

A لطأ *lats*, (v. n. of لطأ) Adhering to, or being near the ground. Striking (with a stick). Beating, thumping (the back).

A لطاة *latāt*, A place, ground. Robbers near at hand. The forehead, or the middle of it. A weight, load. دائرة اللطاة *dāʼiratu'l latāt*, A star on the forehead of a horse.

A لطاخة *lutākhat*, Whatever falls from the hands or mouth in eating.

A لطاط *latāt*, A year of scarcity, when gifts and presents are forgotten to be made. *Litāt*, A salient point from the side or summit of a mountain. (pl. of لطّ *latt*) Necklaces made of dyed colocynth-berries.

A لطّاع *lattāʻ*, A licker of his fingers in eating.

A لطافة *latāfat*, (v. n. of لطف) Being small, slender, yet handsome. Slimness, slenderness. Grace, elegance, beauty. Pleasantness, facetiousness, wit.

A لطام *litām*, (v. n. 3 of لطم) Buffeting each other. Giving a blow, box, slap, or cuff.

A لطائف *latāʼif*, (pl. of لطيفة *latīfat*, Jests, jokes. لطائف الحيل *latāʼifu'l hiyal*, Arts of finesse.

A لطائم *latāʼim*, (pl. of لطيمة) Perfume-boxes.

A لطب *latab*, (v. n. of لطب) Adhering (as skin to the flesh from leanness).

A لطّة *lattat*, Vermicelli.

A لطث *lats*, (v. n. of لطث) Striking (with the palm of the hand, a broad stick, or a stone). Assembling, collecting. Being severe, distressing (affair). Being overloaded (a camel). Mischief.

A لطح *lath*, (v. n. of لطح) Striking (gently on the back) with the palm of the hand. Throwing (a man) on the ground. (Any thing) becoming dry, or worn down (no vestige remaining).

A لطخ *latkh*, (v. n. of لطخ) Staining, defiling, contaminating. Defaming, accusing. Striking with the hand. A small part (of a cloud). *Latikh*, Uncleanly in diet. Badly fed.

A لطخة *lutakhat*, (pl. لطخات *lutakhāt*) A fool.

A لطس *lats* and *latas*, (v. n. of لطس) Striking, dashing (as stone against stone). Striking with any thing broad. Pelting (with stones). Bruising. Kicking. Boxing.

A لطط *latat*, (v. n. of لطّ) Denying (a debt). Dropping out (teeth) being worn to the stumps.

A لطع *latʻ*, (v. n. of لطع) Licking. Kicking (the backside). Giving one a blow (upon the eye). Striking with a stick. Hitting (the mark). Establishing, confirming. Erasing (a name). Having no water (a well). لطع اصبعه *lataʻa isbaʻahu*, He died. (pl. الطاع *altāʻ*) The jaw. *Lataʻ*, Whiteness in the interior part of an Ethiopian's lips. Thinness of lips. A wearing away of the teeth to the roots. A lack of flesh about the female privities.

A لطعاء *latʻāʼ*, Toothless (old woman). (A woman) small, lean, or skinny about the privities.

A لطف *latf*, (v. n. of لطف) Being small, slender, yet elegant. *Lutf*, (v. n. of لطف), Approaching, drawing near. Being propitious, favourable (God). Being small, slender (but elegant). The grace or protection of God. Gentleness, humanity, graciousness, goodness, favour, courtesy, kindness, benignity, bounty, generosity, benevolence. P لطف كردن *lutf kardan*, To do a favour, confer an obligation. A لطفا و كرما *lutfan wa karaman*, Graciously, generously. *Lataf*, A benefit, favour, kindness. A small quantity (of food).

A لطفان *latfān*, Kind, gentle, courteous.

A لطفة *latafat*, A present, an offering.

A لطفي *lutfī*, Adopted, brought up in the family.

A لطلط *litlit*, Toothless, decrepit (she-camel or old woman). One who has large thick teeth.

A لطم *latm*, (v. n. of لطم) Slapping (the face) buffeting. Joining, glueing together. A blow, box, slap on the face. لو ذات السوار لطمتني *law zātu's siwār latamatnī*, Had one wearing a bracelet slapped me . . . . (indignantly said by a lady who had received a slap from a menial).

A لطمة *latmat*, A blow.

A لطميّ *latamīy*, Aromatic.

A لطو *latw*, A fleeing to a rock or cave.

A لطوّ *lutuw*, A cleaving (to the earth).

A لطوخ *latūkh*, Filth, defilement, stain.

A لطي *laty*, (v. n. of لطي) Cleaving to the ground. Supposing (any thing to be in another's possession). Being oppressive, distressing.

A لطّيخ *littīkh*, A fool; foolish.

A لطيف *latīf*, Elegant, graceful. Beautiful, agreeable, lovely, genteel, gallant, pleasant. Gentle, benign, benevolent, affable, kind, courteous. Thin, delicate, slender with elegance. (A speech) having an occult or mysterious meaning, a quaint saying. Acute, quick-sighted, penetrating, knowing occult subjects. اللطيف *al latīf*, God.

A لطيفة *latīfat*, (fem. of لطيف *latīf*) Elegant, fine. Delicate, delicious. (pl. لطائف *latāʼif*) A jest, joke, pleasantry, jeu d'esprit. P لطيفه بر طرف *latīfa bar taraf*, Jesting apart. لطيفه كردن *latīfa kardan*, To laugh at, jest.

A لطيف طبع *latīf-tabʻ*, Of gentle disposition.

A لطيف مشرب *latīf-mashrab*, Facetious.

P لطيفه گوي *latīfa-gūy*, Facetious, witty.

A لطيم *latīm*, (pl. لطم *lutum*) Cut with blows. اللطيم *al latīm*, A camel's colt. (The Arabian shepherd has a peculiar ceremony in weaning the young camel. When the proper time arrives, he turns the colt towards the rising star Canopus, and saying, "Seest thou Canopus? from this moment you taste not, by Allah, one other drop of milk;" gives it a slap on the cheek, drives it from the mother, and sends it to feed on herbage with the rest of the herd). A horse distinguished by a white mark on the cheek. An orphan (deprived of both parents, or of the father; a motherless child being called عجيّ *ɛajīy*). The ninth horse in a race (when ten is the number started). Musk, or any odour with which they perfume the temples. A stallion-camel. لطيم لطيم *latim latim*, Used in calling sheep to be milked.

A لطيمة *latimat*, A perfume-box. Musk. A market where perfumes are sold. A troop of camels carrying perfumes and fine cloths.

A لظّ *lazz*, (v. n. of لظّ) Importuning, urging, harassing. Being assiduous, persevering. Repelling, driving away. A bad-tempered, grasping fellow. لظّ كظّ *lazzun kazzun*, An ill-tempered man.

A لظا *laza*, A small thing, a trifle.

A لظلاظ *lazlāz*, Warm (day). Ill-tempered (man).

A لظلظة *lazlazat*, (v. n. of لظلظ Q) Coiling, writhing, or twisting (as a serpent). Tossing and turning the head with indignation.

A لظه *lazh*, A slap with the palm of the hand.

A لظى *laza'*, (v. n. of لظي) Blazing, sending forth a flame (fire). Hell, or hell-fire. Fire, flame.

A لظيظ *laziz*, (v. n. of لظّ) Being assiduous, persevering. Urging, importuning.

A لعاً لك *laɛan laka*, May you rise from your fall (a formula of benediction when any one stumbles)!

A لعّ *laɛɛ*, (v. n. of لعّ) Shining (as the vapour سراب *sarāb*). Greedy. Hot, lascivious.

A لعاء *liɛāɛ*, (pl. of لعو *laɛw*) Bad-tempered and low-bred. Gluttons.

A لعاب *liɛāb*, (v. n. 3 of لعب) Playing, joking, toying. *Luɛāb*, Spittle. Slaver running from the mouth (of an infant). Snot, mucus, sliminess, viscosity. لعاب الشمس *luɛābu'sh shams*, (Saliva of the sun) Floating substances in the air during warm weather, resembling spider's webs, gossamer. لعاب عنكبوت *luɛābi ɛankabūt*, A spider's web. Drawing, painting. P لعاب گاو *luɛābi gāv*, (or لعاب گوزن *luɛābi gawazn*) Brightness of the sun or of lightning. Morning-light. Snow. Dew. لعاب لعل *luɛābi laɛl*, The sun. لعاب لعل سان *luɛābi laɛl-sān*, Red wine. لعاب مگس *luɛābi magas*, Honey. Wine. A لعاب النحل *luɛābu'n nahl*, Honey.

A لعّاب *laɛɛāb*, A player. An instructor in any game or exercise.

P لعاب ناك *luɛābnāk*, A slaverer, slabberer.

A لعابي *luɛābīy*, Slimy, snotty, ropy, stringy.

A لعاة *laɛāt*, A bitch.

A لعاع *luɛāɛ*, Herbage when just sprouting.

A لعاعة *luɛāɛat*, Endive. Young grass, excellent pasture quickly eaten up. Fruitfulness of a year (in grass). The world. A draught of wine.

A لعّاعة *laɛɛāɛat*, One who makes an ineffectual effort to sing.

A لعاق *luɛāk*, The lickings of the lips or teeth.

A لعامظة *laɛāmizat*, (or لعاميظ *laɛāmīz*) (pl. of لعموظ *luɛmūz*) Greedy, gluttonous people.

A لعان *liɛān*, (v. n. 3 of لعن) Execrating, cursing (one another). Pronouncing judgment, sentencing (as a judge). A malediction, curse. Exclusion from society. (pl. of لعنة *laɛnat*) Curses.

A لعانية *laɛāniyat*, A malediction, curse. Exclusion from society.

A لعب *laɛb*, Play, sport. *Laɛb*, *liɛb*, and *laɛib*, (v. n. of لعب) Playing. *Liɛb* and *laɛib*, Addicted to play. *Laɛab*, (v. n. of لعب) Slavering, drivelling (as an infant). *Laɛib*, Play, sport, game. *Luɛab*, (pl. of لعبة *luɛbat*) Games, sports.

A لعباء *laɛbāɛ*, Name of a place, whence are brought the dogs called لعبانيّة *laɛbāniyat*.

A لعبان *laɛbān*, Given to play, playful.

A لعبة *laɛbat*, One game. Any sort of game. لعبت بربري *laɛbati barbarī*, Hermodactyls. P لعبت زرنيخ *laɛbati zarnīkh*, The world-illuminating sun. A لعبت مطلّقة *laɛbati mutallaka*, (or لعبت معلّقة *laɛbati muɛallaka*) The mandrake. *Liɛbat*, A mode of play. *Luɛbat*, Play of any kind (as chess or cards): a game. Any thing with which one plays (as dice). A ludicrous man, of whom they make game. A puppet, doll, or plaything. *Luɛabat*, Addicted to play.

A لعبتان *luɛbatān*, (Pers. pl. of A لعبة *luɛbat*) Dolls, puppets. P لعبتان ديده *luɛbatāni dīda*, The pupils of the eyes.

P لعبتباز *luɛbat-bāz*, A player, comedian, buffoon, punch, punchinello. A player of puppets. A fascinator, conjurer. لعبتباز شطرنج *luɛbat-bāzi shatranj*, A player at chess.

P لعبتبازي *luɛbat-bāzī*, Play, amusement; comedy, theatrical representation: ombres chinoises.

A لعبيّ *luɛbīy*, Ludicrous, belonging to play.

A لعّة *laɛɛat*, Beautiful, chaste (woman).

A لعث *laɛs*, A being slow and heavy.

A لعثمة *laɛsamat*, (v. n. of لعثم Q) Delaying, hesitating. Considering attentively, descrying, perceiving. Not daring, being deficient, coming short.

A لعج *laɛj*, (v. n. of لعج) Entering, occurring, forcing a way into the mind. Giving pain (a blow), making the skin smart. Inflaming, paining (love).

A لعدن *laɛdan*, The gum-herb lada.

A لعذمة *laɛzamat*, (v. n. of لعذم Q) Delaying. Considering attentively. Not daring, coming short.

A لعذميّ *laɛzamīy*, Greedy, covetous.

A لعز *laɛz*, (v. n. of لعز) Lying with. Licking (her) colt (a camel). Striking on the breast with the fist.

A لعس *laɛs*, (v. n. of لعس) Biting. *Luɛs*, (pl. of العس *alɛas* and of لعساء *laɛsāɛ*) Blackish-lipped. *Laɛas*, (v. n. of لعس) Being ruddy, with a mixture of black. Blackness of the lips, natural or artificial (sometimes esteemed a beauty in Arabia).

A لعساء *laɛsāɛ*, (fem. of العس *alɛas*) A girl of a dark complexion, with a mixture of red; also one blackish-lipped. Blackish (lip).

A لعص *laɛas*, Difficulty, hardness, severity. Gluttony, guzzling, swilling.

A لعض *laɛz*, A taking (with the tongue).

A لعط *laɛt*, (v. n. of لعط) Burning, cauterizing, branding in the neck. Wounding (with an arrow or a malignant eye). Feeding, grazing (camels). Making haste. Asking for, and taking care of, the whole of one's due. (pl. العاط *alɛāt*) A line on the face, such as the Ethiopians disfigure themselves with. *Luɛt*, The side of a wall or mountain parallel to which they travel.

A لعطاء *laɛtāɛ*, (A sheep) marked with a black line in the neck.

A لعطة *luɛtat*, A malignant eye; fascination. Blackness mixed with red on a falcon's head. Blackness across a sheep's neck. Black or yellow lines, with which a woman paints her cheeks. A black mole or ornamental patch on the face. Archery.

A لعظمة *laɛzamat*, A devouring (of flesh).

A لعق *laɛika*, (fut. يلعق *yalɛaku*) He licked.

A لعق *laɛk*, (v. n. of لعق) Scraping a dish with the fingers; licking a plate or the fingers. Dying. لعق فلان اصبعه *laɛika fulānun isbaɛahu*, So-and-so licked his finger (a phrase denoting, He died). وعق لعق *waɛikun laɛikun*, Greedy, gluttonous.

A لعقة *laɛkat*, One lick or one scrape. A little, lick (of spring-grass). *Laɛkat* or *luɛkat*, (v. n. of لعق) Scraping with the finger, licking. *Luɛkat*, Any thing licked. A ladleful.

A لعقط *liɛkit*, Foul-mouthed, scurrilous (woman).

P لعل *laɛl*, A gem, a ruby of the most brilliant lustre. A species of red rose. The vermilion lips of a lovely woman. Red wine; called also لعل مذاب *laɛli muzāb* or *mazāb*, (لعل روان *laɛli ravān*, or لعل سفته *laɛli sufta*) Liquid ruby. Blood. لعل آبدار *laɛli āb-dār*, (or لعل خوشاب *laɛli khwush-āb*) A most brilliant ruby. The lip of a mistress. لعل از سنگ دادن *laɛl az sang dādan*, (or زادن *zādan*) To acquire any thing with great difficulty. لعل با طبرزد جفت كردن *laɛl bā tabarzad juft kardan*, To speak agreeably. لعل پيازي *laɛli piyāzī*, A kind of ruby red and white. لعل پيكاني *laɛli paykānī*, A ruby of the size of an arrow-head worn in the ear. لعل شكر بار *laɛli shakar-bār*, Lip of a mistress. لعل فلك *laɛli falak*, The world-illuminating sun. لعل قبائي *laɛli kabāɛī*, Drunkenness. لعل كهربا *laɛli kah-rubā*, Lip of a mistress. لعل نا سفته *laɛli nā sufta*, (An unbored ruby) Original airs or compositions. An agreeable discourse on a new topic.

A لعلّ *laɛalla* or *laɛal*, Perhaps, haply, would that. لعلّي *laɛallī*, (and لعلّني *laɛallanī*) Perhaps I. لعلّك *laɛallaka*, Perhaps thou.

A لعلاع *laɛlāɛ*, Pusillanimous, timid. A coward.

P لعل طراز *laɛl-tarāz*, He who creates rubies and imparts to them their lustre.

A لعلع *laɛlaɛ*, A wolf. The semblance of water

appearing over a plain. Name of an Arabian tree and of a mountain. (See لعا *laʻā*).

A لعلعة *laʻlaʻat*, (v. n. of لعلع Q) Shining (the vapour سراب *sarab*). Being restless (from hunger or any other cause). Moving, shaking. Breaking (bones). Grief, affliction. Anguish through hunger.

P لعل قبا *laʻl-kabā*, The thread of a crimson robe. Blood. The liver. Red wine.

P لعل گون *laʻl-gūn*, (or لعل رنگين *laʻl-rangīn*) Ruby-coloured, ruddy, rosy. A species of red rose.

P لعل ماهي *laʻl-māhī*, A kind of red-boned fish.

P لعله *laʻla*, A tulip.

P لعلين *laʻlīn*, Ruby, ruby-coloured. Set with rubies. Name of a red and white flower.

A لعم *laʻam*, Saliva.

A لعماظ *liʻmāz*, A taking of a bone in the mouth. A stripping of the flesh from a bone with the teeth. A vain boaster.

A لعمظ *laʻmaz*, Greedy. A gluttonous man.

A لعمظة *laʻmazat*, Gluttony. The taking of a bone in the mouth. A stripping of the flesh from the bone with the teeth.

A لعموظ *luʻmūz*, A humble companion, parasite, feast-hunter. *Luʻmūz*, (or لعموظة *luʻmūzat*) (pl. لعامظة *laʻāmizat* and لعاميظ *laʻāmīz*) A glutton.

A لعن *laʻana*, (fut. يلعن *yalʻanu*) He cursed.

A لعن *laʻn*, (v. n. of لعن) Cursing, imprecating. Driving away (from any thing good). Pulsion. ابيت اللعن *abayta'l laʻna*, A formula of congratulation or compliment, implying, you have done nothing, or will do nothing deserving of censure. P لعن كردن *laʻn kardan*, To curse. A *Luʻan*, (pl. of لعنة *luʻanat*) Those who execrate or speak ill of.

A لعنّ *laʻanna*, Perhaps. لعنّي *laʻannī*, (or لعنّني *laʻannanī*, Perhaps I.

A لعنة *laʻnat*, (pl. لعان *liʻān* and لعنات *laʻanāt*) Imprecation, curse, anathema. لعنة الله عليه *laʻnatu'llāh ʻalayhi*, (لعنة عليه *laʻnatun ʻalayhi*, or عليه اللعنة *ʻalayhi'l laʻna*) May the curse of God be upon him (an imprecation generally added to the name of the devil, or any worthless wretch). شيطان لعنت مآب *shaytāni laʻnat-maʼāb*, The accursed devil. P لعنت به هيچ *laʻnat ba hech*, So so, better than bad. لعنت كردن *laʻnat kardan*, To curse. To excommunicate. A *Luʻnat*, Execrable, accursed. *Luʻanat*, (pl. لعن *luʻan*) One who execrates, curses, or speaks ill of others.

A لعنتي *laʻnatī*, Cursed.

A لعو *laʻw*, (pl. لعاء *liʻāʼ*) Bad-tempered and low-bred. A glutton. Greedy. Lecherous.

A لعوب *laʻūb*, Playful (woman). Beautiful (girl).

A لعوة *laʻwat*, A bitch. Greedy (she-wolf or bitch). *Laʻwat* or *luʻwat*, Excess (of hunger). A blackness round the nipple.

A لعوس *laʻūs*, Something, any thing. *Laʻwas*, A wolf. A man suddenly devouring any thing; greedy.

A لعوض *laʻwaz*, A jackal.

A لعوق *laʻwak*, Ignorant. *Laʻūk*, Licked. An electuary, or any medicine which may be licked or sucked, a linctus, a lambative.

A لعوقة *luʻūkat*, Activity, expedition at work.

A لعيّ *laʻaʼ*, Of a bad disposition or stock. A glutton. Greedy. Lecherous.

A لعيعة *laʻiʻat*, Bread baked of millet.

A لعين *laʻīn*, Detested, execrable, abominable, accursed, anathematized, excommunicated. Driven out of society. (A woman) who curses others. A wolf. A scarecrow. Deformed, transformed into any vile shape. Destroyed, ruined, covered with shame and ignominy. اللعين *al laʻīn*, (Satan), the accursed. رجل لعين *rajulun laʻīnun*, A scarecrow.

P لغ *lagh*, Bald, having no hair. A desert without vegetation. An addle egg.

A لغا *lagha'*, (v. n. of لغي) Blundering, making mistakes (in speech or in pronunciation). Talking triflingly and nonsensically. Being addicted to any thing (as drinking); drinking much (without satisfying thirst). Making a noise.

A لغاب *lughāb*, The worst feather of an arrow. An arrow badly trimmed.

A لغابة *laghābat* or *lughābat*, Folly, weakness.

A لغات *lughāt*, (pl. of لغة *lughat*) Tongues, languages, brogues, dialects, idioms. Forms, modes of writing and pronouncing words.

A لغاثين *laghāsīn*, (pl. of لغثون *lughsūn*) The insides and roots of noses.

A لغاديد *laghādīd*, (pl. of لغدود *lughdūd*) The parts of the mouth about the throat and jaws.

A لغّاز *laghghāz*, A slanderer.

A لغاط *lighāt*, (v. n. of لغط) Making a confused, unintelligible noise (people).

A لغّاف *laghghāf*, A hectorer, blusterer, bully.

P لغام *lughām*, A bridle, a bit.

A لغام *lughām*, The foam of a camel's mouth.

A لغانين *laghānīn*, (pl. of لغنون *lughnūn*) The fleshy parts between the palate and throat.

A لغب *laghb*, (v. n. of لغب) Becoming fatigued, tired, weary. Corrupting, injuring, causing mischief. Relating any thing wide of the truth. Thrusting his muzzle into a pot (a dog). The weakest of a bird's quills near the belly. A bad arrow, roughly polished. A vicious pronunciation. Weak, foolish (man). Flesh between the fore-teeth. *Laghab*, The hair of the neck. اخذ بلغب رقبته *akhaza bi laghabi rakabatihi*, He apprehended or understood it.

A لغة *lughat*, (pl. لغات *lughāt*, لغون *lughūn*, and لغي *lugha'*) Tongue, idiom, speech, language, dialect; word, vocable. A dictionary, lexicon, vocabulary. An error in pronunciation. لغة في *lughatun fī*, Another or a less accurate mode of writing: as, سدغ *sudgh* for صدغ *sudgh*, زدق *zidk* for صدق *sidk*, &c. اهل لغت *ahli lughat*, The writer of a dictionary, a lexicographer. علم لغت *ʻilmi lughat*, Lexicography. كتاب لغت *kitābi lughat*, A dictionary, vocabulary (literally a book of words).

A لغثون *lughsūn*, (pl. لغاثين *laghāsīn*) The inside and root of the nose.

A لغد *laghd*, (v. n. of لغد) Driving (camels) into the right road. Keeping in order. Restraining (from any thing). Pricking the ears. *Lughd*, (لغدود *lughdūd*, and لغديد *lighdīd*) (pl. الغاد *alghād* and لغاديد *laghādīd*) The flesh about the throat and jaws; also the lobe and the interior part of the ear.

A لغدة *lughdat*, Name of a grammarian of Isfahān.

A لغذميّ *laghzamīy*, A violent eater, glutton.

P لغز *laghz*, A slip, stumble, fall.

A لغز *laghz*, (v. n. of لغز) Changing, inverting, distorting. *Lughz*, *laghaz*, *lughaz*, or *lughuz*, (pl. الغاز *alghāz*) An enigma, riddle; any thing occult, ambiguous, or mysterious, difficult to be understood; any speech liable to misinterpretation, or to give offence. *Lughz*, *laghz*, or *laghaz*, (pl. الغاز *alghāz*) The hole of a lizard, rabbit, field-mouse, or mole (as formed in an intricate manner). A labyrinth, maze, crooked path, meander.

P لغزان *laghzān*, Slipping down. Slippery.

P لغزاني *laghzānī*, Slipperiness.

P لغزانيدن *laghzānīdan*, To make any thing slip, slide, or fall. To lubricate.

P لغزش *laghzish*, A slip, slide. Offence. Anger.

P لغزناك *laghznāk*, A slippery place.

P لغزيدن *laghzīdan*, To slipe, slide, fall. To drink. To milk.

P لغسر *lagh-sar*, Bald-headed. Scald.

A لغط *laght*, A court in front of a house. *Laght* or *laghat*, (v. n. of لغط) Making a loud noise, uttering a cry. Cooing (a turtle-dove, or the bird katā). (pl. الغاط *alghāt*, A confused noise, indistinct voices.

A لغف *laghaf*, (v. n. of لغف) Making up (meat) into balls and eating (it).

A لغفاء *lughafāʼ*, (pl. of لغيف *laghīf*) Companions of thieves.

A لغفة *lughfat*, A morsel, a mouthful.

A لغلغ *laghlagh*, A stork or similar bird.

A لغلغة *laghlaghat*, (v. n. of لغلغ Q) Stuttering, being barbarous in speech. Tautology. Moistening (a bread-pudding) in soup.

A لغم *laghm*, (v. n. of لغم) Foaming (camel), throwing saliva out of his mouth. Relating uncertain news. *Lagham*, A little perfume or unguent. The veins or nerves of the tongue. Extreme heat, restlessness, or disturbance.

P لغم *lagham*, Reins, a bridle.

A لغماء *laghmāʼ*, White-faced (sheep).

A لغن *laghn*, Juvenile warmth and sprightliness. *Lughn*, The flesh between the palate and the throat. The flesh about the ear and neck. The gristly part of the ear. A lie. جئت بلغن غيرك *jiʼta bi lughni ghayrika*, (Spoken to one when you understand not what he says).

A لغنّ *laghanna*, Perhaps.

A لغنون *lughnūn*, (pl. لغانين *laghānīn*) A nerve within the ear. The flesh between the palate and throat. The inside of the nose. Root of the nose.

A لغنّي *laghannī*, (or لغنّني *laghannanī*) Perhaps I.

A لغو *laghw*, (v. n. of لغا for لغو) Talking triflingly and nonsensically. Barking (a dog). Swearing rashly. Moistening (a cake) in soup. Being disappointed, cut off from hope, despairing. The barking of a dog. The cry of the bird katā. Thoughtless and improper conversation. A blunder, mistake. Battology in prayer. Any thing contemptible, low-priced, of small value. A camel's colt or sheep, small and of little or no value.

A لغوب *laghūb*, Foolish, weak. *Lughūb* also *laghūb* (v. n. of لغب) Being exceedingly tired, greatly fatigued. Fatigue.

A لغوبة *lughūbat*, Folly, weakness.

A لغوس *laghwas*, A wolf, a greedy eater, gobbler. A robber, villain. A kind of fattening herb. A delicate, slender plant, which trembles from its delicacy and flexibility.

A لغوسة *laghwasat*, Any uncertain news or information, of which nothing sure is known.

A لغون *lughūn*, (pl. of لغة *lughat*) Tongues, idioms.

P لغونه *laghūna*, Decoration, ornament, dress.

A لغوي *laghwa'*, Foolish, trifling talk. The cry of the bird katā.

A لغويّ *lughawīy*, (pl. لغويّون *lughawīyūn*) Belonging to language. A lexicographer. The literal meaning (of a word). معناي لغوي *maʻnāyi lughawī*, The literal sense (of a passage).

A لغي *laghy*, (v. n. of لغى) Barking (a dog). *Lagha'*, Talk of which no account is made. A blunder, mistake. Any thing mean, little, contemptible; spoken rashly. *Lugha'*, (pl. of لغة *lughat*) Words, vocables. Idioms, phrases.

A لغيب *laghīb*, Bad or spoilt (feather).

A لغيّة *lughayyat*, (dim. of لغة *lughat*) A little error, a trifling inaccuracy. A trivial word.

A لغيث *laghīs*, Mixed, adulterated; a mixture. Wheat and barley mixed. A poisoned bait set for a vulture.

A لغيزاء *lughayzā*, or لغّيزي *lughghayza'*, Enigma.

A لغيط *laghīt*, (v. n. of لغط) Making a confused noise, uttering unintelligible sounds (people). Cooing (a turtle-dove).

A لغيف *laghīf*, (pl. لغفاء *lughafā*) A friend, an intimate companion. An abettor of thieves; one who takes care of their concerns, without accompanying them in their robberies; a receiver of stolen goods.

A لغيفة *laghīfat*, Gruel or porridge so thick that it can scarcely be stirred with a ladle.

A لفّ *laff*, (v. n. of لفّ) Involving, wrapping, folding. Joining, adding one thing to another. Assembling, collecting. Mixing in battle (two hosts). Refusing to give another his due. Being thick and entangled (trees). Eating many kinds of food, mixing them together in a disgusting manner. Being reckoned amongst, belonging to. A crowd of different sorts of people. جاؤا بلفّهم *jāʼu bi laffihim* or *bi liffihim*, They came with their mixed multitude. *Liff*, (pl. لفوف *lufūf*, A crowd, multitude, troop, legion, body of men. A sort or kind of men. A body of false witnesses packed together from various places. كنّا لفّا *kunnā liffan*, We were congregated in one spot. جاؤا و من لفّ لفّهم *jāʼu wa man laffa liffahum*, They came with all that were reckoned to belong to them. *Liff* or *laff*, A garden thickly planted with trees. (pl. الفاف *alfāf*) Thick, entangled trees. *Luff*, (pl. of الفّ *alaff*, and لفّاء *laffā*) Thick, fleshy-thighed. Tall, plump girls.

A لفء *lafʼ*, (v. n. of لفأ) Peeling off the bark of trees. Denuding. Diverting (one from any pursuit). Striking (with a stick). Railing at, traducing (the absent). Paying the whole that one owes; or something short. Remaining over.

A لفاء *lafāʼ*, (v. n. of لفأ) Peeling off the bark. Denuding. A thing of little moment, a trifle. Something short of one's due. Rubbish or furniture on the ground. Ground, earth.

A لفّاء *laffāʼ*, (fem. of الفّ *alaff*) Plump-thighed (woman). Plump thigh. Thick, entangled (foliage).

A لفات *lafāt*, Ill-tempered, foolish.

A لفّاح *luffāh*, A well-known plant resembling the brinjal or egg-plant. Fruit of the يبروح *yabrūh*.

A لفاظ *lifāz* or *lufāz*, A pot-herb.

A لفّاظ *laffāz*, Eloquent.

A لفاظة *lufāzat*, Any thing thrown out, especially from the mouth. A thing uttered. A word dropped from the mouth. Remains (of any thing).

A لفّاظي *laffāzī*, Eloquence.

A لفاع *lifāʻ*, A cloak or upper garment of a man or woman. A covering, carpet, quilt. A table-cloth. The front teat of a quadruped.

A لفاعة *lifāʻat*, A patch upon a garment.

A لفافة *lifāfat*, (pl. لفائف *lafāʼif*) Any kind of bandages, swathes, or rollers wrapped round the feet of a corpse, mummy, &c. A wrapper. Outside cover of a letter, an envelope.

A لفاق *lifāk*, Two cloths sewed together.

A لفام *lifām*, A fillet or veil which covers the tip of the nose or only the mouth.

A لفائف *lafāʼif*, (pl. of لفافة *lifāfat*) Swathes for the feet, rollers. Wrappers, covers, envelopes.

A لفّة *laffat* or *liffat*, A garden studded with trees. *Liffat*, A light, sprightly, and pretty woman.

A لفت *laft*, (v. n. of لفت) Twisting, bending, rolling. Peeling, barking. Turning away the face from (any body). Leading away, diverting, preventing from following (his plan). Putting (feathers) askew (upon an arrow). Striking (cattle) cruelly and indiscriminately. *Lift*, A rape, turnip. One half of any thing. Side, edge, margin. A cow. The genitals of a lioness. Foolish (woman). Inclination, proneness. A friend.

A لفتاء *laftāʼ*, (fem. of الفت *alfat*) Crooked-horned (she-goat). Squinting (woman).

A لفتة *lufatat*, One who strikes cattle cruelly and indiscriminately.

P لفترة *laftara*, Vile, mean, ignoble.

A لفتيّة *liftiyat*, A dish of turnips.

P لفج *lafj*, (لفچ *lafch*, لفچن *lafchan*, or *lafchin*) A thick lip like the lip of a camel, dirty, or hanging down when angry. A piece of meat without bone. A woman of loose character.

A لفج *lafj*, Affliction, wretchedness.

P لفجان *lafjān*, One who hangs his lip from extreme anger.

P لفچن *lafchan*, Thick-lipped.

A لفح *lafh*, (and لفحان *lafahān*) (v. n. of لفح) Burning (fire). Striking slightly, but briskly (with a sword). Being full of virulence (poison).

A لفخ *lafkh*, A giving a blow on the head.

A لفظ *lafz*, (v. n. of لفظ) Ejecting, throwing out (of the mouth). Pronouncing, articulating (words). Dying. A word, vocable. Pronunciation. لفظ و معنى *lafz u maʻna'*, Pronunciation and signification. مثله لفظا و معنى *misluhu lafzan wa maʻnan*, (A word) resembling another in sound and sense.

A لفظا *lafzan*, Explicitly, distinctly pronounced.

A لفظة *lafzat*, (pl. الفاظ) Word, speech, saying.

A لفظيّ *lafzīy*, Enunciative. Verbal.

A لفع *lafʻ*, (v. n. of لفع) Covering the head (grey hairs).

A لفف *lafaf*, A stuttering, stammering. The distortion of a vein in the fore-arm which disables a man from working.

A لفق *lafk*, (v. n. of لفق) Sewing two things together. Being unable to find what one seeks. Setting about any thing which one intends to finish. Finding and taking. Catching nothing (a hawk let loose). *Lifk*, One part, side, or edge of two pieces sewed together.

P لفگر *lafgar*, Smoke, soot.

A لفلاف *laflāf*, Weak, infirm.

A لفلف *laflaf*, Infirm, weak.

A لفلفة *laflafat*, (v. n. of لفلف Q) Eating voraciously. Tottering from a distortion of the sinews (a camel's leg).

A لفم *lafm*, (v. n. of لفم) Binding a fillet over the nose or mouth. Binding, fastening.

A لفوت *lafūt*, (A woman) staring, looking about. Perverse, ill-tempered, and foolish. (A she-camel) braying when milking, and giving it with reluctance. (A married woman) who has children by another husband.

A لفوح *lafūh*, Scorching wind.

A لفوف *lufūf*, (pl. of لفّ) Assembled crowds.

A لفيتة *lafītat*, A kind of thick soup.

A لفيظ *lafīz*, Thrown out. Spoken, pronounced.

A لفيعة *lafiʿat*, Patch, addition to a garment.

A لفيف *lafif*, Wrapped, folded, involute. Complex. A crowd, mixed multitude, or congregation out of every tribe. Mixed grain. The doubly imperfect Arabic verb; where infirm letters are separated it is then called لفيف مفروق *lafifi mafrūk*, (Complex separated) as in وقي *waka'*, He preserved; and when united it is called لفيف مقرون *lafifi makrūn*, (Complex joined) as in شوي *shawa'*, He roasted.

A لفيفا *lafifan*, Assembled from every tribe.

A لفيفة *lafifat*, Flesh on a camel's rump.

A لفيك *lafik*, Ill-tempered. Foolish.

A لفيئة *lafiʾat*, A piece of meat without bone.

P لق *lak*, Destitute of hair, bald. An addle egg. لق و تق *lak u tak*, A desert, a wild uncultivated country. *Lak* or *luk*, Cheating, deceiving.

A لق *lakk*, (v. n. of لق) Striking with the hand. Striking on the eye. A crack in the ground. P دق و لق كردن *dakk u lakk kardan*, To clap the hands, to applaud; to make a noise.

A P لقا *likā*, Face, form, visage, countenance. P حور لقا *hūr-likā*, With a face like an angel, *i.e.* beautiful. خورشيد لقا *khwurshed-likā*, With a face like the sun.

A لقاء *likāʾ*, (v. n. of لقي) Meeting, encountering, being opposite; lighting or hitting upon. Thrown into. (pl. of لقوة *lakwat* or *likwat*) Soon conceiving (as women or she-camels). Female eagles. لقاء الله *likāʾu'llāh*, The meeting of God: day of judgment.

A لقاءة *likāʾat*, (v. n. of لقي) Meeting. One meeting or encounter. (An inaccurate word).

A لقاة *lakāt*, A meeting. The middle of the road.

A لقاح *lakāh*, (v. n. of لقح) Taking the male and conceiving (a she-camel). Being impregnated with the flowers of the male and bearing fruit (a female palm-tree). The male palm-flowers. A masculine or noble tribe (such in Pagan times being so distinguished, who had never known captivity, nor a dependence upon kings). *Likāh*, Sperma admissarii. A milch-camel. A she-camel that has a colt two or even three months' old. (pl. of لقحة *lik-hat*) Souls. Minds. (pl. of لقوح *lakūh*) Male camels. (pl. of لقحة *lik-hat* and *luk-hat*) Milch-camels.

A لقّاح *lakkāh*, One who causes the fructifying energy to be imparted to a she-camel or palm-tree.

A لقاس *likās*, A railing, a calling names.

A لقاط *lakāt*, Stalks of corn left uncut by the reapers, being missed by the sickle. *Likāt*, (v. n. 3 of لقط) Meeting from opposite quarters. Being left in the field by the reapers (stalks of corn). بلقاطه *bilikātihi*, Over against, opposite him. *Lukāt*, Ears of corn picked up. لقاط السنبل *lukātu's sumbul*, Gleanings of corn.

A لقاطة *lukātat*, Any thing gathered from off the ground. Gleanings, pickings. Sweepings, rubbish.

A لقاع *likāʿ*, A coarse garment or covering.

A لقّاع *lakkāʿ*, A fly.

A لقّاعات *lukkāʿāt*, Sounds from the bottom of the throat.

A لقّاعة *lukkāʿat*, Ready and prompt at giving an answer. A fool. A railer, slanderer, giver of ill names, or nicknames.

A لقالق *lakālik*, (pl. of لقلاق *laklāk*) Storks.

A لقانة *lakānat*, (and لقانية *lakāniyat*) Quickness of apprehension.

A لقاية *likāyat*, (v. n. of لقي) Meeting.

A لقب *lakab*, (pl. القاب *alkāb*) A title of honour, style, surname, addition; a nickname.

A لقث *laks*, (v. n. of لقث) Mixing. Taking (any thing) quickly and entirely.

A لقح *lak-h* or *lakah*, (v. n. of لقح) Taking the male and conceiving (a she-camel). *Lakah*, A mountain. The fructifying sperm taken from the male to be put into any thing else. That by which a palm-tree is fructified. *Likah* (pl. of لقحة *lik-hat*), and لقح *lukkah*, (pl. of لقوح *lakūh*) Milch (camels).

A لقحة *lik-hat*, An eagle. A crow. A woman giving suck. (pl. لقاح *likāh*) Soul. *Lik-hat* or *lak-hat*, (pl. لقح *likah* and لقاح *likāh*) Milch (camel).

A لقز *lakz*, (v. n. of لقز) Striking on the breast or neck in fighting.

A لقس *laks*, (v. n. of لقس) Accusing, reproaching, treating opprobriously. Inclining, drawing (one) towards. اللقس *al laks*, Itch, scab. *Lakas*, (v. n. of لقس) Being ill inclined toward any thing, being disturbed, perplexed. Being spoiled and depraved. *Lakis*, A slanderer, reviler; ridiculer; fomenter of discord. One who calls men by nicknames. Intelligent. A man who is never in one stay.

A لقش *lakish*, Old, dried-up (leathern bottle).

A لقص *laks*, (v. n. of لقص) Burning, scorching (the skin). *Lakas*, (v. n. of لقص) Being narrow and tight. Being disturbed (the mind). Being impure (the soul). *Lakis*, Narrow. Loquacious, verbose. Prone to evil.

A لقط *lakt*, (v. n. of لقط) Gathering, picking from the ground. Mending or darning (a garment). *Likt*, (v. n. of لقط) Escaping the reaper's sickle (stalks of corn). *Lakat*, Any thing picked up or gleaned from the ground. A little, somewhat. A species of odoriferous pot-herb. لقط السنبل *lakatu's sumbul*, Gleaning of corn. لقط المعدن *lakatu'l maʿdan*, Particles or small pieces of gold in the mine, or mixed with ore.

A لقطاء *lukatāʾ*, (pl. of لقيط) Foundling-boys.

A لقطة *luktat* or *lukatat*, Any thing gathered from off the ground. Property which a person finds on the ground and takes away to preserve it in the manner of a trust; stray, trove. A foundling.

A لقع *lakʿ*, (v. n. of لقع) Throwing away. Hitting (with a pebble). Flinging (camel's dung at any one). Hurting, wounding with a malignant eye. Biting (a serpent). Overcoming in talk or disputation. Taking up with its proboscis (a fly).

A لقعان *lakaʿān*, (v. n. of لقع) Passing quickly.

A لقعة *lukaʿat*, One who speaks foolishly. One who terrifies by opprobrious and abusive words.

A لقف *lakf*, (v. n. of لقف) Seizing, snatching eagerly (like a hungry man). لقف ثقف *lakfun sakfun*, Of a quick genius. *Lakaf*, (v. n. of لقف) Falling, ruinous (wall or cistern), bursting at the lower part. (pl. القاف *alkāf*) Side of a well or cistern. *Lakif*, (A well) tumbled down or sunk at the bottom. A weak structure of bad bricks. A well constructed of weak and bad materials. A well full of water, which flows as soon as dug. Quick, intelligent (man).

A لقفان *lakafān*, A snatching, taking eagerly.

A لققة *lakakat*, Wells narrow at top. Those who strike with the palm of the hand (on the eyes).

A لقلاق *laklāk*, (pl. لقالق *lakālik*) A stork. Sound, voice. لقلاق بقباق *laklāk bakbāk*, Talkative.

A لقلق *laklak*, A stork. The tongue.

A لقلقة *laklakat*, (v. n. of لقلق Q) Crying tremulously. Moving, shaking, agitating. Chattering (a stork). The voice of a stork. A continued sound or motion of the jaws; or thrusting out the tongue (of a serpent). Eloquence, pronunciation.

A لقم *lakm*, (v. n. of لقم) Blocking (up the road). Eating fast, gobbling. Eating or swallowing leisurely (any thing). *Lakam* or *lukam*, The middle or main part of the road. *Lukam*, (pl. of لقمة *lukmat*) Morsels, gobbets, mouthsful.

A لقمان بن باعورا *lukmān bin bāʿūrā*, Name of a certain wise man, by some said to have been a son of Job's sister or aunt: by others, to have been a disciple of David: by others, a judge in Israel: while others declare him to have been an emancipated Ethiopian slave. He is the author of some Arabian fables, and is supposed by many to be the same as Æsop.

P لقماني *lukmānī*, Locmanic; wise, sage.

A لقمة *lukmat* or *lakmat*, A mouthful, morsel. A kind of globular fritter made of flour, dried grapes, and oil; also mixed with new wine, and fried with sesame-oil. P لقمهٔ آهن كشيدن *lukmaʾi āhan kashīdan*, (To get a taste of iron) To receive a sabre-wound. To be fettered. A لقمهٔ خليفه *lukmaʾi khalīfa*, (Caliph's bonne bouche) Name of a sweetmeat.

P لقمه شمار *lukma-shumār*, One who attends feasts uninvited, and counts the number of mouthsful.

P لقمه لقمه *lukma lukma*, In mouthsful.

A لقن *lakn*, (v. n. of لقن) Perceiving, understanding. Quickness of apprehension. *Likn*, A side, edge, border, margin, coast. A pillar, prop, buttress. Sharp, quick, intelligent (lad). *Lakan*, (v. n. of لقن) Having a quickness of apprehension. *Lakin*, Who soon comprehends or easily retains.

A لقنة *laknat*, Quickness of apprehension.

A لقو *lakw*, (v. n. of لقا for لقو) Bringing on the

disease لقوة *lakwat.*

A لقوة *lakwat,* A disease or distortion of the mouth. ذو اللقوة *zū'l lakwat,* Name of a certain eagle. A black eagle. *Lakwat* or *likwat,* (pl. لقاء *likāz* or القاء *alkāz*) A female eagle. A light, nimble, active woman. Soon conceiving (woman or camel).

A لقوح *lakūh,* (pl. لقاح *likāh*) A he-camel. (pl. لقح *lukkah*) A she-camel that has taken the male. A she-camel that is milked. (This word is used for two or three months after foaling).

P لقوم *lukūm,* A kind of fritter made of flour, butter, and honey.

G لقوماش *lakūmāsh,* (or لقومه *lakūma*) Nicomachus, the father of Aristotle.

A لقي *luky, liky,* or *luka',* (v. n. of لقي) Meeting. *Laka',* (pl. القاء *alkāz*) Any thing thrown away as worthless.

A لقيّ *lakīy,* Any person or thing one meets. Thrown into, hitting, or lighting on. شقيّ لقيّ *shakīyun lakīyun,* Miserable, abject. *Lukīy,* (v. n. of لقي) Meeting.

A لقيان *lik* or *lukyān,* (v. n. of لقي) Meeting.

A لقيّان *lakīyāni,* Two persons meeting together.

A لقيانة *likyānat* or *lukyānat,* (v. n. of لقي) Meeting, encountering. *Lukyānat,* One meeting.

A لقية *lukyat,* (v. n. of لقي) Meeting. A meeting, an encounter.

A شقيح لقيح *shakīh lakīh,* Deformed.

A لقيط *lakīt,* Picked up. A child exposed to chance, a foundling-boy. An old well upon which one alights unawares.

A لقيطة *lakītat,* A contemptible man or woman; one of the meanest rank. بنو اللقيطة *banū'l lakītat,* Name of a tribe.

A لقيطي *lukhayta',* A tell-tale, whisperer, spy.

A لقيف *lakīf,* Quick, intelligent (man). (A well) fallen in at the bottom. Badly-constructed (cistern). A well full of water, which flows as soon as it is dug.

A لقيم *lakīm,* A globular morsel or any thing similar swallowed.

A لقيميّة *lukaymīyat,* A large sort of wheat.

P لك *lak,* A hundred thousand. Weak of mind, foolish; idle, foolish words. An old garment in holes. The dress worn by country people. A spot, stain. Bald. Name of a tribe of gipsies. لك روپيه *laki rūpiya,* A lack of rupees. *Lik,* Name of a well-flavoured bird. *Luk,* The substance commonly called gum-lac, being the nidus of an insect found deposited on the twigs of certain trees in India, and from which a beautiful red lake is extracted, used in dyeing. A red colouring substance produced from gum-lac. A knot, bump, or swelling. Any thing not pared or trimmed. A wound in the belly, an imposthume. A ball. The ankle-bone.

A لك *laka,* To thee.

A لك *lakk,* (v. n. of لك) Striking one, especially on the nape of the neck with the clenched fist. Knocking and beating off. Tearing the flesh from a bone. Mixture. Flesh. A plant used in dyeing. *Lukk,* The expressed juice or residuum of the plant لك *lakk,* used as a dye. Firm in flesh. *Lukk* or *lakk,* The scrapings of skins dyed with the juice lukk, used in fastening knife-handles.

A لكء *laks,* (v. n. of لكأ) Striking. Paying the whole of what is due. Throwing prostrate.

A لكأ *lakas,* A stopping, staying, abiding.

P لكا *lakā,* (A baker's) kneading-trough. A stain upon cloths. A soft kind of skin. Goats' leather. A red flower. A shoe or slipper. Undressed leather. *Lakā* or *lukā,* Sediment of lac, used in fastening knife-handles. *Lukā,* A red colouring substance produced from gum-lac. An inhabited country, region, district. A window.

A لكا *laka',* A being greatly addicted, cleaving to.

A لكاء *lakkās,* Leather coloured with lukk.

P لكات *lakāt,* A thing spoilt, good for nothing.

A لكاث *lakās,* A sparkling stone amidst plaster. Pustules in the mouth of a camel.

A لكاث *lukkhās,* Pargeters, workers in plaster.

A لكاثي *lukāsīy,* White, very bright.

A لكاز *likāz,* A piece of brass or cloth put into the axle-hole of a pulley when grown too wide in order to tighten it (technically, a bush or box).

A لكاع *lakāʿi,* Dirty, slatternly (woman).

A لكاعة *lukāʿat,* A being mean, sordid, dirty.

A لكاف *likāf,* A thick coarse cloth placed under an ass's pack-saddle.

A لكاك *likāk,* (pl. لكك *lukak*) Compression, squeezing, crowding. Fleshy or fat (she-camel). Fleshy (camels). (pl. of لكيك *lakīk*) Closely arrayed, compact (squadrons). Firm in flesh.

A لكالك *lukālik,* Thick, firm-fleshed (camel).

P لكام *lukām,* Shameless, impudent, bold, saucy. Name of a mountain.

A لكّام *lakkām,* Hard (hoof) breaking stones.

P لكامه *lakāma,* (or لكانه *lakāna*) A sheep's pudding, chitterling, sausage. Penis.

P لكائي *lakāʾī,* Red colour, red.

A لكث *laks,* (v. n. of لكث) Striking. Overloading, oppressing. *Lakas,* (v. n. of لكث) Adhering to any one (dirt). Having pustules in the mouth (a camel). The pustules themselves.

A لكثة *lakisat,* Fat (she-camel).

A لكح *lak-h,* A striking with the fist on the chin.

A لكد *lakd,* (v. n. of لكد) Striking with hand or foot. Driving away. *Lakad,* (v. n. of لكد) Adhering (dirt). *Lakid,* Avaricious, narrow-minded.

P لكد *lakad,* A kick, cuff, blow. لكد زدن *lakad zadan,* To strike, kick, cuff. To tread, trample.

P لكد زده *lakad-zada,* Kicked, cuffed. Trod.

P لكد زن *lakad-zan,* Striking. A kicker.

P لكد كوب *lakad-kob,* Kicking. Kicked, trodden.

A لكز *lakz,* (v. n. of لكز) Striking with the fist on the breast or jaws in fighting. *Lakiz,* Avaricious.

A لكس *lakis,* Stubborn, obstinate, untractable.

A لكض *lakz,* A blow with the clenched fist.

A لكع *lakʿ,* (v. n. of لكع) Stinging (as a serpent or scorpion). Striking the udder with his head (a sucking lamb). Eating, drinking. Bite, puncture. *Likʿ,* A dwarf. *Lakaʿ,* (v. n. of لكع) Being mean, sordid, dirty. Adhering (especially mud or dung, and hardening). *Lukaʿ,* Worthless, criminal, sordid, avaricious, abject, slavish, servile, base, mean, despicable. Lascivious. Careless, heedless, inattentive. Filth, dirt. A slave. An infant. A fool. A horse. The young of any quadruped. A colt. The two sons of Alīy, Hasan and Husayn. يا لكع *yā lukaʿ,* O wretched, sordid, abject!

A لكعاء *lakʿāz,* Mean, servile (woman).

A لكعة *lukaʿat,* A mare.

A لكفو *lakfū,* A tribe of Ethiopians.

P لكك *likak,* A sour plum.

A لكك *lukak,* (pl. of لكاك) Firm-fleshed (camels).

P لكل *likal,* A pear.

P لكلك *laklak,* Idle talk. *Liklik,* A mill-hopper.

A لكلك *laklak* or *lukluk,* Thick and short (camel).

P لكلكه *lukluka,* Vain, idle talk. *Liklika,* A mill-hopper.

A لكم *lakm,* (v. n. of لكم) Driving, knocking off. Striking with clenched fist. *Lakum,* To you, your.

A لكمة *lakmat,* A blow with the fist.

P لكن *lakan,* Any bason or vessel in which the hands, feet, or body are washed. A candlestick. A censer. A chafing-dish. A cotton-cover or screen for a candle. A fire-steel. A large grate.

A لكن *lakan,* (v. n. of لكن) Speaking barbarously (especially bad Arabic). A bason, a bowl.

A لكن *lākin,* (or لكنّ *lākinna*) But, still, notwithstanding, nevertheless.

A لكنة *luknat,* (v. n. of لكن) Stammering, stuttering. Pronouncing (Arabic) barbarously. Impediment in speech.

A لكنونة *luknūnat,* A stammering, a stuttering.

P لكوپك *lak u pak,* Running up and down. An old carpet; household furniture, especially when worse for the wear. Rude, unskilful, inexpert. *Luk u puk,* Coarse, thick, rough, untrimmed.

P لك و پكي *luku puki,* Thickness, coarseness.

A لكوع *lakūʿ,* Abject, wretched, mean, servile.

A لكونة *lukūnat,* (v. n. of لكن) Pronouncing (Arabic) barbarously.

P لكه *laka,* Spot, stain. Red dye, lac. Timid.

P لكهن *lak-han,* Hunger. A fast-day.

A لكي *laka',* (v. n. of لكي) Being greedy. Sticking close to. *Likay,* That, so that, in order to.

A لكيّ *lakīy,* Addicted to.

A لكيع *lakīʿ,* Abject, wretched, mean, servile.

A لكيعة *lakīʿat,* Mean, servile (wench).

A لكيك *lakīk,* (pl. لكاك *likāk*) Closely arrayed, compact (army). Flesh. Firm in flesh. Liquid pitch.

Name of a certain slender tree.

A لكيكة *lukaykat*, Fleshy, firm (she-camel).

A لكيلا *likaylā*, So as not.

A لكيما *likaymā*, That, so that. So as not.

P لكين *lukīn*, A coarse woollen cloth.

P لگ *lag*, Pain, trouble, sorrow, affliction, suffering. Imprisonment: a prison. A stick. Flagellation.

P لگام *ligām* or *lugām*, A bridle; the bit. لگام خائيدن *lugām khāīdan*, To champ the bit. To be refractory. لگام دادن *lugām dādan*, To attack.

P لگام ريز *lugām-rez*, Slack-rein, full-speed.

P لگلگ *laglag*, A stork.

P لگله *lagala*, A kick, blow with the foot.

P لگن *lagan*, A brazen or copper pan in which the hands are washed; also in which they bake.

P لگور *lagūr*, A tribe of gipsies living in the vicinity of Harāt.

A للوقت *li'l wakt*, Suddenly, extempore.

A لله *li'llāh*, (for لالله *li'llāh*) For God. لله العظيم *li'llāhi'l ʻazim*, By the great God, for the love of God. لله الحمد و المنة *li'llāhi'l hamd wa'l minnat*, To God be the praise and glory (or thanks).

P لم *lam*, Mercy, forgiveness. Rest; tranquillity.

A لم *lam*, Not. When prefixed to the aorist it gives it the preterite signification: as, لم ينصر *lam yansur*, He did not assist. لم يخلق مثلها في البلاد *lam yukhlak misluhā fī'l bilād*, The like hath not been created on earth. لم يزلي *lam yazalī*, (fem. لم يزلية *lam yazalīya*) Eternal. *Lam* is sometimes pleonastic. *Lima*, Wherefore? For that which.

A لم *lamm*, (v. n. of لمّ) Assembling, collecting what had been dispersed. Repairing, mending, restoring. Eating one's own substance, and that of one's friends. Descending, alighting at.

A لمأ *lamʼ*, (v. n. of لمأ) Stealing, taking the whole. Striking the hand on. Looking askance, glancing at.

P لما *lamā*, Nightshade, foxgrapes.

A لما *lamā*, Surely not. *Limā*, (from ل *li* and ما *mā*) For that which, whereas. Why? Wherefore?

A لمّا *lammā*, Not yet, never. Why? If not. When. لمّا يضرب *lammā yazrib*, He has not yet struck.

A لمات *lumāt*, (pl. of لمة *lumat*) Bodies of men, from three to ten. Peers, equals, cotemporaries.

A لمّات *lammāt*, pl. of لمّة, Fortunes. Misfortunes.

A لماج *lamāj*, A small bit, morsel, taste, sip.

A لمّاح *lammāh*, One who looks slily but attentively. Shining, glancing. *Lummāh*, Intelligent birds of prey.

A لماخ *limākh*, A striking, a giving of blows.

A لماذا *limāzā*, (comp. of ل *li*, ما *mā*, and ذا *zā*) For what reason? why? wherefore?

A لماز *lamāz*, A defamer (of one present).

A كواه لماس *kawāhu lamāsi*, He cauterized his diseased part.

A لماسة *lumāsat*, Necessity, but not extreme.

A لماظ *lamāz*, Something. Any thing. Whatever is tasted with the tip of the tongue.

A لماظة *lumāzat*, Shreds of meat about the teeth; remains in the corners of the mouth after eating.

A لماع *limāʻ*, (pl. of لمعة *lumʻat*) Parts of a plant beginning to wither and turn white.

A لمّاع *lammāʻ*, Bright, glittering (sword).

A لمّاعة *lammāʻat*, A desert where the vapour سراب *sarāb* glitters. The middle of an infant's head, as long as it remains soft. An eagle.

A لماق *lamāk*, Aught (I have not tasted).

A لماك *lamāk*, A small bit, morsel, taste. *Lumāk* or *limāk*, A collyrium used for clearing or brightening the eyes.

A لمال *la* or *lumāl*, Collyrium for the eyes.

P لمالم *lam-ā-lam*, Up to the brim.

A لمام *limām*, (pl. of لمّة *limmat*) Locks of hair flowing below the ears. لماما *limāman*, (He) seldom (visited) us. Sometimes, from time to time.

A لمة *lumat*, A peer, equal, cotemporary. A chief, leader, exemplar. A body of men, from three to ten.

A لمّة *lammat*, Fortune; misfortune. Vehemence, intensity. A little. A slight touch (of insanity). *Limmat*, (pl. لمم *limam* and لمام *limām*) A head of hair, locks flowing below the ears (that which flows to the shoulders is called جمّة *jummat*). The ragged appearance of the head of a stake which has been much thumped by a mallet. *Lummat*, A companion, partner, fellow-traveller. Companions, friends. A company, from three to ten. Of the same age. Like, resembling; a match. A leader.

P لمتر *lamtur*, Uneven, rough. Strong-bodied. Coarse, thick. Fat. Idle, tardy, languid.

A لم تر ما *lam tara mā*, Especially.

A لمج *lamj*, (v. n. of لمج) Eating with the fore-teeth, or with the corners of the mouth. Lying with. سمج لمج *samjun lamjun* or *samijun lamijun*, Deformed, base.

A لمجة *lumjat*, A whet before dinner.

A لمح *lamh*, (v. n. of لمح) Looking at slily, glancing the eyes at any object. Shining, twinkling (star), flashing (lightning). A glance, twinkling of an eye, instant. لمح البصر *lamhu'l basr*, The twinkling of an eye. لمح باصر *lamhun bāsirun*, Any thing clear.

A لمحان *lamahān*, (v. n. of لمح) Shining, twinkling (a star), flashing (lightning).

A لمحة *lamhat*, A glance with the eye; a wink. Lightning. (pl. ملامح *malāmih*) Similitude, resemblance. *Lumhat*, (pl. لمح *lumah*) A shining spot.

A لمحه لمحه *lamha lamha*, Every moment.

A لمد *lamd*, (v. n. of لمد) Beating, lashing, boxing, slapping. Humility, submission.

A لمدان *lamdān*, Humble, submissive.

A لمذ *lamz*, The stealing of a glance.

A لمز *lamz*, (v. n. of لمز) Defaming, accusing, reproaching. Winking, making a signal with the eye. Striking, pushing, thrusting, beating off, bruising. Trampling upon. Appearing (as grey hairs).

A لمزة *lamzat*, A wink. *Lumazat*, A slanderer (of the absent).

P لمزدن *lamzadan*, To sleep soundly. To stretch out.

P لمس *lams*, Soft, tender, delicate.

A لمس *lams*, (v. n. of لمس) Touching, handling, feeling. Lying with. Prying into the mysteries of heaven, and longing to overhear. The sense of feeling or touch. *Lumus*, (pl. of لموس *lamūs*) Camels which must be felt before it is ascertained if they be fat or not. Spurious.

A لمش *lamsh*, Play. Folly, trifle.

P لمشك *limishk*, A sort of curd eaten with fresh milk and salt.

A لمص *lams*, A dish resembling فالوذ *fālūz*, without sweetness, which children eat with date-honey. (v. n. of لمص) Eating of, partaking of, the aforesaid dish. Taking up (honey) on the point of the finger and eating it. Pinching.

A لمط *lamt*, Agitation, commotion. A spearing.

A لمطة *lamtat*, Name of a country famous for shields of solid leather soaked in milk for a year.

A لمظ *lamz*, (v. n. of لمظ) Rolling the tongue about the mouth to pick the teeth. Licking the lips. Tasting. Giving one his due. *Lamaz*, Whiteness on the under lip of a horse.

A لمظة *lumzat*, Whiteness on the nether lip of a horse. A little white on the fore or hind-foot of a horse. Any white spot. The heart's core. A bit of meat. A particle of butter taken on the finger.

A لمع *lamʻ*, (or لمعان *lamaʻān*) (v. n. of لمع) Shining, glittering, glancing, twinkling, flashing, glaring. Going off with. Pointing at. Moving his wings in flight (a bird). Going out of the door. Convulsions (of death).

A لمعات *lamaʻāt*, Splendours, effulgencies.

A لمعة *lamʻat*, One flash. Splendour, brilliancy. The glare of the sun. *Lumʻat*, (pl. لماع *limāʻ*) Part of a plant beginning to wither. Part of a limb remaining dry during the performance of ablutions. Any part untouched by water when making ablution. A glossiness on the human body. A competency, a sufficiency to support life. A crowd, a congregation.

A لمعظة *lamʻazat*, Greedy (man). A licker.

P لمغان *lamghān*, Name of a quarter of the city of Ghaznīn; or of a city near Ghaznīn.

A لمق *lamk*, (v. n. of لمق) Striking (especially with the palm upon the eye). Writing. Obliterating. Looking steadily at. *Lamak*, The greater part or the middle of a road. *Lumuk*, (pl. of لامق *lāmik*) Those who strike upon the eye with the open hand.

A لمك *lamk*, (v. n. of لمك) Kneading leaven. A collyrium for clearing or brightening the eyes.

P لمك *lamak*, Lamech, the father of Noah.

A لملم *lamlam*, Numerous (tribe or host).

A لملمة *lamlamat*, (v. n. of لملم Q) Wishing, desiring. Turning round, causing to revolve.

A لملوم *lamlūm*, A crowd, a company.

A لمم *lamam*, (v. n. of لمّ) Being on the verge

of sin, without positively committing it. A slight touch of madness. Venial sins. *Limam*, (pl. of لمة *limmat*) Locks flowing below the ears.

A لمن *liman*, (from ل *li* and من *man*) To him or to them who. To whom? whose?

A لمو *lamw*, An eating of the whole.

A لموح *lamūh*, One who looks slily but attentively. Glittering, bright, shining.

A لموس *lamūs*, (pl. لمس *lumus*) (A camel) which must be felt before it can be known if she is fat. Spurious, one whose gentility is doubtful.

A لموسة *lamūsat*, A road through which one must grope or feel one's way.

A لموص *lamūs*, A liar. An impostor. A defamer. One who winks or makes signs with the eye.

A لمؤلفه (بيت *bayt*) *limu,allifihi*, A verse of the author (*i.e.* such as the reader can perceive is not borrowed, but the composition of the author).

A لموم *lamūm*, (or لمومة *lamūmat*) (A house) which holds many people and supports them.

A لمه *limah*, Wherefore?

A لمهج *lamhaj*, Rich and sweet (milk).

A لمى *lama'*, (v. n. of لمي) Having brown or blackish lips. *Lama'*, *limā'*, or *luma'*, A brown or blackish colour of the lips (in some instances esteemed beautiful in Arabia).

A لمّي *limmīy*, Pertaining to لم *lima*, Why?

A لمياء *lamyā,*, Black or brown-lipped (female).

A لمّية *limmīyat*, State of why or wherefore.

A لميج *lamīj*, A great eater. One who indulges much in venery. سميج لميج *samīj lamīj*, Deformed.

A لم يزل *lam yazal*, (or لم يزلي *lam yazalī*) Unchangeable.

A لميس *lamīs*, (A woman) soft to the touch. A woman's name. *Lumays*, Name of a man.

A لميك *lamīk*, One whose eyes are anointed with collyrium.

A لن *lan*, Not, it shall not be that, certainly never (from لا *lā*, Not, and ان *an*, That). لن تراني *lan tarānī*, (Thou shalt never see me) Boasting, bragging. (Why it means this is not very obvious).

P لنبان *lambān*, A used-up strumpet who acts as a procuress. *Lumbān*, Name of a village near Ispahān.

P لنبر *lambar* or *lumbur*, Strong, fat. Buttocks.

P لنبك *lambak*, Name of a cup-bearer. *Lumbak*, Fat and unwieldy.

P لنبوس *lumbos*, The inside lining of the cheek.

P لنبه *lamba*, Any thing round like an orange or an apple. *Lumba*, Fat. Large.

P لنبه سر *lamba-sar*, (Round-head) Name of a mountain in Māzandarān.

P لنج *lanj*, A proud or graceful air in walking. Pulling up and carrying from place to place. Tearing any thing from the ground, eradicating. Hanging, suspending. *Lunj*, The cheek, the inside (according to some, the exterior part) of the cheek. The lower parts of the face, the mouth and chin. A lip. A cripple, without the use of hands or feet.

P لنجا *lanjā*, A pulling out, a tearing up.

P لنجا *lunjā*, A cripple, without hands or feet.

P لنجان *linjān*, Name of a district in Ispahān, abounding in rice-grounds and gnats.

P لنجه *lanja*, A proud air in walking, a waving from side to side. Pulling up and carrying away. *Lunja*, Lip. Environs of the mouth. A cripple.

P لنجيدن *lanjīdan*, To pull up by the roots, to eradicate. To chide, reproach; to mock, ridicule, or point at with the fingers. To wave from side to side in walking, with a swagger. To diffuse odour.

P لند *land*, Membrum virile. A boy, youth, son. *Lund*, Vain boasting. A grumbling from anger.

P لندا *lundā*, Murmuring.

P لندش *lundish*, Murmur.

P لندهور *land-hor*, (Offspring of the sun) Name of a great king in Hindūstān.

P لنديدن *lundīdan*, To boast. To murmur, mutter.

P لنطي *lantī*, Name of the son of Yūnān.

A لنفسه *li nafsihi*, For his (or its) own sake.

P لنگ *lang*, Lame. Maimed. The halting of a caravan for a day or two. Penis. *Ling*, The leg, from the groin to the tip of the toe. The ankle. *Lung*, A cloth worn round the loins and passed between the legs.

P لنگاك *langāk*, An opprobrious, reproachful, contemptuous, or disagreeable word.

P لنگان *langān*, Halting, limping. Sneezing.

P لنگان رفتگي *langān-raftagī*, Lameness in walking, a limping, halting mode of going.

P لنگر *langar*, An anchor. A stay or rope for supporting a tent. The house or monastery of the Calendars or Muhammadan monks. A wall of stone, brick, wood, or clay round the tomb of a distinguished person. An alms-house. Worthless, mean, fraudulent, deceitful, disliked by every body. Strong. Majesty, authority. لنگر انداختن *langar andākhtan*, (نهادن *nihādan*, or زدن *zadan*) To cast anchor. لنگر برآوردن *langar bar āwardan*, (or برداشتن *bar dāshtan*) To weigh anchor.

P لنگر خانه *langar-khāna*, An hospital or bede-house for the entertainment of the poor and indigent. A house or arsenal where anchors are stored.

P لنگرگاه *langar-gāh*, An anchorage, sea-port.

P لنگري *langarī*, Provisions distributed to the poor. A kind of drinking-glass.

P لنگ زن *lang-zan*, Bow-legged.

P لنگن *langan*, Hunger. A fast kept by Hindūs.

P H لنگوته *lungota*, A narrow strip of cloth which poor people wear about their waists. لنگوته بستن *lungota bastan*, To tie on the lungotah; to renounce the world.

P لنگی *langī*, Lameness. *Lungī*, A cloth worn round the loins and passed between the legs.

P لنگيدن *langīdan*, To halt, lame, limp. To roll, wallow (as a horse or dog).

P لو *lav*, The lip. An eminence. Bile. A kind of sweetmeat. Name of a town in Māzandarān. *Lū*, A repository, any vessel containing somewhat. *Lū* or *lo*, A ply, fold. دو لو *du lū*, Two-fold, double. سه لو *sih lū*, Threefold, triple. كفش يك لو *kafshi yak lū*, A single-soled or unlined shoe.

A لو *law*, If, but if, did but, had but. That. لو كان *law kāna*, Had (he or it) been. لو لا *law lā*, If not, unless, but for. لو لم *law lam*, If not, unless. ولو *wa law*, Although, notwithstanding, even then. و لو سلم *wa law sallam*, Although he surrendered or submitted. When used as a noun, لو *law* takes tashdīd: as, اكثرت من اللوّ *aksarta mini'l laww*, You multiply or deal too plentifully in ifs.

A لواء *liwā,*, The twisting or coiling of a serpent. The winding (of a river, of a valley, or channel). (pl. الوية *alwiyat*) Standard, flag, ensign, banner, colours. A government (of a small district, town, or castle). لواي نصرت التوا *liwāyi nusrat-iltiwā*, The victorious banner. ميرلوا *mīrilivā*, The governor of a small province or of a city. بعثوا بالسواء واللواء *ba,asū bi's siwā, wa'l liwā,*, They sent to implore help.

A لوّاء *lawwā,*, A kind of bird.

A لؤاب *lu,āb*, Thirst.

A لواب *luwāb*, (v. n. of لاب for لوب) Thirsting. Thirst. Saliva, spittle.

A لوابن *lawābin*, (pl. of لابنة) Breasts. Udders.

A لواة *law,at*, The privities of man or woman. Any thing shameful and bad.

A اللواتي *allawātī*, (pl. of التي *allatī*) (The women) who.

A لواث *luwās*, Flour sprinkled on the table under the dough.

A لواثة *luwāsat*, A crowd, company. Flour sprinkled on the table under dough. One who mixes in every thing.

A لواح *luwāh*, A thirsting. Thirst.

A لواحظ *lawāhiz*, (pl. of لاحظة) Glancing (eyes).

A لواحق *lawāhik*, (pl. of لاحق *lāhik*, or of fem. لاحقة *lāhikat*) Dependencies, appurtenances. Followers, clients, domestics. Consequent upon.

A لواحم *lawāhim*, (pl. of لاحم *lāhim*) Hawks fond of flesh (لحم *lahm* or *laham*).

A لواخة *liwākhat*, Butter melted amongst milk.

A لواذ *liwāz*, (v. n. 3 of لاذ for لوذ) Fleeing for refuge to one another. Wrestling against, opposing, contradicting. Using art or fraud. *Lawāz*, *liwāz*, or *luwāz*, (v. n. of لاذ for لوذ) Taking for one's defence or safeguard.

A لواذع *lawāzi,*, Bitter, poignant words.

P لوارة *lawāra*, Name of a town in Hindūstān.

A لوّاز *lawwāz*, A seller of almonds (لوز *lawz*).

A لوازم *lawāzim*, Necessary things, requisites, accompaniments, consequences, inevitable results. Baggage. A fee, perquisite.

A لوازمات *lawāzimāt*, Necessaries, requisites.

A لواس *lawās*, A taste, any thing to be tasted.

A لوّاس *lawwās*, A glutton, an epicure, one who hunts after delicacies.

A لواسة *luwāsat*, A small mouthful or morsel.

P لواش *lawāsh*, A thin cake or biscuit.

P لواشه *lawāsha*, Barnacles for restive horses, a farrier's twitch.

A لواص *lawāṣ*, Pure honey. A kind of sweetmeat made of flour, water, and honey.

A لواصب *lawāṣib*, Narrow and deep wells.

A لواط *liwāṭ*, The commission of sodomy.

A لوّاط *lawwāṭ*, A sodomite (people of Lot).

A لواطة *liwāṭat*, Sodomy, pederasty. P لواطت كردن *liwāṭat kardan*, To commit sodomy, to bugger.

P لواطت كن *liwāṭat-kun*, A sodomite, buggerer.

A لواطف *lawāṭif*, The short ribs next the chest.

A لوّاف *lawwāf*, A maker of carpets. A spinner, particularly of materials for tent-making.

A لوافح *lawāfiḥ*, (pl. of لافح) Scorching blasts.

A لواق *lawāḳ*, Something, any thing. لا ذاق لواقا *lā ẕāḳa lawāḳan*, He tasted nothing.

A لواقح *lawāḳiḥ*, (pl. of لاقح *lāḳiḥ*) (Camels) which have taken the male. (Winds) which drive about rainy clouds, and which shake the trees.

A لواقن *lawāḳin*, The lower part of the belly.

A لواك *lawāk*, What is eaten or chewed. ما ذاق لواكا *mā ẕāḳa lawākan*, He tasted nothing.

A لوالب *lawālib*, (pl. of لولب *lawlab*) Staples, holes into which a bolt shoots. Screws, vices.

P لوالو *lav-ā-lav*, Light, trifling, undignified.

P لوا لوا *lawā lawā*, Light, fickle, inconstant.

A لؤام *luʼām*, The wing or feather of an arrow, especially the best kind. Feathers skilfully set on an arrow. Necessity, need, lack. Unavoidable business. A call of nature.

A لوّام *lawwām*, An accuser, censurer, blamer. *Luwwām*, Accusers, blamers.

A لوامع *lawāmiʻ*, (pl. of لامعة) Lights, rays.

A لو انّ *law anna*, Perhaps, haply. لو انّي *law annī*, (or لو انّني *law annanī*) Perhaps I.

A لواهس *lawāhis*, Light, active, swift (persons).

A لواي *liwāy*, A standard, banner.

A لوايا *lawāyā'*, (pl. of لويّة *lawīyat*) Portions or messes of meat which one lays by for another.

A لوائب *lawāʼib*, Thirsty camels going round a well without being able to get to it for the crowd.

A لواية *liwāyat*, The spear-staff of a banner.

A لوائح *lawāʼiḥ*, (pl. of لائح *lāʼiḥ* or لائحة *lāʼiḥat*) Lights, splendours, luminous appearances.

A لوائم *lawāʼim*, (pl. of لائمة *lāʼimat*) Accusations, reproaches. Slanders. Faults.

A لوب *lawb*, (v. n. of لاب for لوب) Going round a well without being able to get to it on account of the crowd (thirsty camels). *Lawb* or *lūb*, (v. n. of لاب for لوب) Thirsting. Thirst. *Lūb*, A piece of meat turning and rolling about in a pot. A bee. (Palm-trees or camels) thirsty, remote from water.

A لؤوب *luʼūb*, Thirst.

A لوباء *lūbāʼ*, A kind of pulse.

A لوبان *lūbān*, A thirsting.

A لوبان *lobān*, Male frankincense reddish, incense, benzoin.

A لوبة *lūbat*, A place full of stones (especially black). Negroes. Ethiopians. People living amongst others without consulting them. Lybia.

P لوبره *lobara*, A wild ram. A wild buffalo.

P لوبشه *lūbasha*, Thrashed grain still in the chaff.

A لوبيّ *lūbīy*, An Ethiopian, Lybian.

P لوبيا *lūbiyā*, (لوبيه *lūbiya*, and لوبا *lūbā*) A kind of pulse, a species of French bean.

A لوّة *lawwat*, Ugliness of face. *Luwat*, A fragrant kind of wood.

A لوت *lawt*, (v. n. of لات for لوت) Relating, declaring, telling news without being asked. Suppressing, concealing (intelligence).

P لوت *lot*, Delicious viands. A sort of pastry. A large mouthful. A harsh, disagreeable youth. *Lūt*, Naked, bare.

P لوتر *lotar*, (لوترا *lotarā*, also لوتره *lotara*) A secret mode of conversation. An enigma.

P لوت وپوت *lot u pot*, Sorts of meat and drink.

A لوث *laws*, (v. n. of لاث for لوث) Being powerful, strong. Rolling a mouthful or globular fritter in fat. Wrapping (a turban, sash, or fillet round the head). Remaining close at home. Taking refuge, flying to. Rolling any thing in the mouth to masticate it. Macerating, dissolving in water. The semblance of an argument or demonstration. Slowness, tediousness. Wounds. Wickedness. Queries. Hatreds, rancours. Power, strength. Contamination, defilement, impurity.

A لوثاء *lawsāʼ*, (fem. of الوث *alwas*) Languid, feeble. Gentle (rain) causing grass to be entangled. Slow of speech or gait.

A لوثة *lūsat*, Impetuosity. Languor, weakness, slowness. Relaxedness. Folly, insanity. Abundance of fat or flesh. A ball of cloth used in a game. ذات لوثة *zātu lūsatin*, Fat, fleshy (she-camel).

A لوج *lawj*, (v. n. of لاج for لوج) Rolling (any thing) about in the mouth.

P لوج *loj*, A country in Irān. *Lūj*, Naked.

A لوجاء *lawjāʼ*, Necessity, a necessary thing. Doubt, scruple. A reply (good or bad).

P لوچ *loch*, Squint-eyed.

A لوح *lawḥ*, (v. n. of لاح for لوح) Rising, appearing, or shining (as the sun, or a star). Flashing (lightning). Turning the colour, tanning (as by travelling, the sun, or thirst). Being manifest. Looking at. (pl. الواح *alwāḥ*) A table, plank, or any thing flat, of wood or bone, especially on which any thing is inscribed. A black board used as a slate to write on. The pannel of a door. The shoulder-blade. The air, atmosphere. The brilliant appearance (of a star). P لوح پا *lawḥi pā*, The foot-board or treadle of a weaver's loom. لوح خاموشي *lawḥi khāmoshī*, Silence. لوح دو رنگ *lawḥi du rang*, The world. Time. Fortune. A لوح محفوظ *lawḥi maḥfūẓ*, (or اللوح المحفوظ *lawḥu'l maḥfūẓ*) The indelible tables (on which, according to Muhammadan belief, the transactions of mankind have been written by God from all eternity). *Lūḥ*, (v. n. of لاح for لوح) Thirsting. Thirst. A glance.

A لؤوح *luʼūḥ*, Thirst.

A لوحان *lawaḥān*, A thirsting. Thirst.

A لوحة *lawḥat*, One table, plank, or board.

A لوحش *lawḥash*, (or لوحش الله *lawḥash allāh* for لا اوحش الله *lā lawḥash allāh*) God forbid! may God remove all sorrow from him! Bravo! well done!

A لوحي *lawḥaʼ*, Thirsty (camels).

A لوخ *lawkh*, The act of mixing.

P لوخ *lūkh*, A reed. Hump-backed.

P لوخن *lokhan*, The moon.

A لود *lawad*, (v. n. of لاد for لود) Being perverse, obstinate, refractory.

P لوده *lawda*, A pannier.

A لوذ *lawẕ*, (v. n. of لاذ for لوذ) Fleeing unto, taking refuge. Taking for a protection or fortress. Surrounding, embracing, comprehending. The side or circuit of a mountain. Name of the son of Shem. (pl. الواذ *alwāẕ*) The winding of a vale or a river. A mountain, asylum.

A لوذان *lawẕān*, A side, border, quarter.

A لوذانيّة *lawẕānīyat*, A taking refuge with one another. The use of art and fraud. A wrestling or striving with.

A لوذع *lawẕaʻ*, (or لوذعيّ *lawẕaʻīy*) Eloquent, ingenious. Nimble, dexterous. Smart, witty, capable of saying piquant things.

P لور *lor*, The channel of a torrent, a torrent. A dish made of new milk or sour whey boiled and thickened. The bow of a cotton-dresser. Impudent, shameless. A sort of cheese. Name of a bird. Name of a country, and of a people in India.

P لورا *lorā*, Cream-cheese. A quicksand.

P لورانك *lorānak*, (or لورادر *lorādar*) An oil-bottle made of skins. A copper vessel for making butter.

P لورستان *loristān*, A country in Persia.

P لورك *lorak*, A cotton-dresser's bow.

P لوركند *lor-kand*, A gulley made by a torrent.

P لوره *lora*, A torrent, water-course.

P لوري *lorī*, Bold, impudent, shameless. A singer, street-beggar. Nice, delicate. Name of a bird. Name of a people in Persia. *Lūrī*, Leprosy.

A لوز *lawz*, (v. n. of لاز for لوز) Fleeing unto, taking refuge. Eating. Saving one's self, escaping, being delivered. An almond. A kind of sweetmeat. لوز الهند *lawzu'l hind*, The quince. *Lawiz*, (or عوز لوز *ʻawiz lawiz*) Indigent, needy.

A لوزة *lawzat*, One almond. Preserved fruit.

P لوزتان *lawzatān*, The uvula.

P لوزه *loza* or *lawza*, Any thing sweet, nice, and delicate, whether to the palate or ear. Deceit.

A لوزيّات *lawzīyāt*, Sweetmeats in which almonds are used, almond-confections.

A لوزينج *lawzīnaj*, A confection of almonds.

P لوزينه *lawzīna*, Any food in which almonds form a part. در لوزينه سير خوردن *dar lawzīna sīr khwurdan*, (or دادن *dādan*) To eat (or put) garlic with almonds, (met.) To experience an alloy to one's pleasures. To be cheated or gulled. To render another's existence miserable.

A لوس *laws*, (v. n. of لاس for لوس) Tasting, hunting after delicacies. Rolling any thing round the mouth. Taste. *Lūs*, Meat, food.

P لوس *los*, Flattery, seduction, deceit. Pretended humility. Adulteration, debasement. Wry-mouthed. A wry mouth. Adhesive mud.

P لوسانه *losāna*, Flattery.

P لوسيدن *losīdan*, To cheat, act dishonestly.

P لوش *lawsh*, A withered melon. *Losh*, The Grecian painter Zeuxis. *Lūsh*, Leprous. Torn in pieces. Ignorant, stupid. Black thin clay; mud adhering to cattle. Wry-mouthed.

P لوشا *loshā*, Name of the painter Zeuxis.

P لوشابه *loshāba*, Sweet, agreeable to the palate or the ear.

P لوشاره *loshāra*, Ground worn into gullies.

P لوشانه *loshāna*, Sweet, agreeable to the palate or ear. Flattery, adulation. Pretended humility.

A لوشب *lawshab*, A wolf.

P لوشن *loshan*, Black mud at a pond's bottom.

P لوشناك *loshnāk*, Full of mud. Muddy water.

A لوص *laws*, (v. n. of لاص for لوص) Prying, peeping through the chinks of a door. Swerving, turning aside from. A pain in the ear or throat.

A لوصة *lawsat*, A pain in the back, lumbago.

A لوط *lawt*, (v. n. of لاط for لوط) Possessing one's affections, being dear to one. Joining, uniting, bringing together (friends). Aiming at or wounding (with an arrow or malignant eye). Bedaubing with mud, plastering (a cistern) with mud. Hiding. Committing sodomy. A cloak. A man expert and expeditious in business. Profit, usury. Any thing which sticks and adheres. *Lūt*, Lot.

A لوطيّ *lūtīy*, The people of Lot or Sodom; a sodomite. An impudent, forward fellow; a bravo, bully.

A لوظ *lawz*, (v. n. of لاظ for لوظ) Driving away one who is near. Dunning, exacting rigorously.

A لوع *lawʻ*, (v. n. of لاع for لوع) Being avaricious, villainous, and cowardly. Tanning, freckling, turning the colour of the skin (the sun).

A لوعة *lawʻat*, (v. n. of لاع for لوع) Afflicting, distempering any one (love). Being indisposed either from disease or fear. A blackness round the nipples. Heat, pain, indisposition arising from love, care, or sickness.

A لوغ *lawgh*, (v. n. of لاغ for لوغ) Rolling (any thing) in the mouth, and then casting (it) out. Sticking close to.

P لوغ *lūgh*, Drinking. A milking. A drinker. A milker. A roller.

P لوغانيدن *lūghānīdan*, To cause to milk.

P لوغيدن *lūghīdan*, To drink. To milk. To spill.

A لوف *lawf*, (v. n. of لاف for لوف) Eating, chewing. Eating dry fodder (cattle). Meat or fodder which is not agreeable. *Lūf*, A certain bulbous plant called صرّاحة *sarrāhhat*.

P لوف *lūf*, Dragon-wort. The plant elephants'-ear.

P لوفا *lūfā*, A species of the herb sempervivus. Centaury.

A لوفى *lūfaʼ*, Name of a certain plant.

A لوق *lawk*, (v. n. of لاق for لوق) Softening with butter. Remaining firm and quiet in a place. Striking (on the eye). Putting silk or cotton into an ink-holder. *Lawak*, (v. n. of لوق) Being a fool. Folly.

P لوقا *lūkā*, The evangelist Luke.

SY لوقابين *lūkābīn*, Seed of wild rue.

A لوقة *lawkat*, An hour. *Lūkat*, Butter. A dish of fresh dates and butter.

SY لوقيون *lūkiyūn*, The box-thorn.

A لوك *lawk*, (v. n. of لاك for لوك) Rolling any thing in the mouth to masticate it. Chewing any thing hard (as a horse champing the bit). Injuring one's reputation.

P لوك *lok*, A sort of burden-bearing camel having very little hair. Weak, silly, mean, contemptible. Ivy. Milk boiled to a consistency. One who crawls on hands and knees.

P لوكر *lūkar*, Name of a city in Hindūstān.

SAN. لوكشور *lokishwar*, A being who translates perfect souls from the fetters of the brute form into the human form (a notion of the followers of Sākyamuni, who are believers in metempsychosis).

P لوكه *lūka*, Cotton separated from the seed. Any kind of flour. The cry of dog or cat. Toasted meal.

P لوكيدن *lūkīdan*, To crawl on hands and knees like an infant. To stagger or walk uneven.

P لول *lol*, Shameless, bold, impudent.

A لولا *lawlā*, Unless, save, except, but for. Come on! لولاك *law lāka*, But for thee (the world would not have been called out of non-existence).

A لولاء *lawlāʼ*, Adversity, affliction. Loss.

A لولاة *lawlāt*, (v. n. of لولي Q) Turning the back in flight.

P لولانج *lūlānch*, A kind of sweetmeat.

P لولانك *lūlānak*, (or لولاور *lūlāwar*) A sort of bottle for keeping oil and the like.

A لولب *lawlab*, The staple or place into which a bolt goes. A spring. A screw, a vice. Much water flowing through a narrow tube, and spouting out with a noise. An alembick-spout. Any tube or canal through which water flows.

A لولبيّ *lawlabīy*, Belonging to, or resembling a screw or vice.

A لولع *lawlaʻ*, Blackness round the nipples.

P لولو *law law*, A light, frivolous, undignified man. *Lū lū*, A figure dressed up to frighten children.

A لؤلؤ *luʼluʼ*, (pl. لآلي *laʼālī*) A pearl, gem, jewel. The wild cow. لؤلؤ مكنون *luʼluʼ maknūn*, A pearl concealed in the shell, (metaph.) An unblemished maid. لؤلؤ منضّد *luʼluʼ munazzad*, Pearls neatly and regularly strung, (metaphorically) Well-set teeth.

A لؤلؤان *luʼluʼān*, Pearl-coloured.

P لؤلؤ بار *luʼluʼ-bār*, Raining, scattering gems.

P لؤلؤ پاش *luʼluʼ-pāsh*, Scattering gems. لؤلؤ پاش دموع شدن *luʼluʼ-pāshi dumūʻ shudan*, To shed pearly tears.

A لؤلؤة *luʼluʼat*, A single pearl. ابو لؤلؤة *abū luʼluʼat*, The slave who assassinated the caliph Omar.

A لؤلؤيّ *luʼluʼiy*, Pearl-coloured, pearly. A pearl-merchant, a dealer in pearls.

P لوله *lola*, Flour toasted. A handful of flour kneaded into dough. *Lūla*, A canal, tube, syphon, the pipe or spout of a ewer or alembick. A tobacco-pipe. A reed used by weavers to wind thread upon. با لوله كوزه *bā lūla kūza*, A flagon with a spout.

P لولي *lolī*, Nice, delicate. Merry, glad. Intelligent, clever. A public singer. A strumpet. Name of a handsome people called Karaji.

P لوليخانه *lolī-khāna*, A bawdy-house, brothel.

P لولين *lūlīn*, A jug, flagon, or any similar vessel with a spout.

A لؤلؤيّ *luʼluʼīy*, A pearl-merchant.

A لوم *lawm*, (v. n. of لام for لوم) Blaming, reprehending, accusing. Reproof. Fear, dread. Fault, error, sin, crime. P لوم و توبيخ كردن *lawm u tawbīkh kardan*, (or لوم كردن *lawm kardan*) To accuse. A *Lawam*, A perpetual finding of fault.

A لؤم *luʼm*, (v. n. of لأم) Being ignoble, inglorious, mean, sordid, avaricious. Covetousness, villainy, vice. *Luʼam*, (pl. of لأمة *laʼmat*) Coats of mail.

A لوّم *luwwam*, (pl. of لائم *lāʼim*) Blamers, censurers, accusers.

A لوما *law mā*, If not, unless.

A لوماء *lawmāʼ*, Reproof.

A لؤماء *luʼamāʼ*, (pl. of لئيم *laʼīm*) Mean, sordid.

A لؤمان *luʼmān*, Deserving of, obnoxious to, reproof. (pl. of لئيم *laʼīm*) Mean, sordid, base, grovelling, avaricious.

A لومة *lawmat*, (v. n. of لام for لوم) Reproving, blaming. A severe reproof. Any thing deserving of reproof. The choicest honey. *Lūmat*, (A man) accused. Expectation. Delay. *Luwamat*, (A man) who blames others.

A لؤمة *luʼamat*, One who relates or imitates the actions of another. Plough-gear. A choice piece of household furniture, which one is very reluctant to lend or part with.

A لومى *lawmaʼ*, Reproach, accusation.

A لون *lawn*, (pl. الوان *alwān*) Colour. Complexion. External form. A species, genus. A kind of palm-tree. Any thing intervening, interposing, or uniting. كثير اللون *kasīru'llawn*, Many-coloured, variegated; deeply tinged. قليل اللون *kalīlu'l lawn*, Discoloured, of a bad or weak colour.

A لونة *lūnat*, A species of palm-tree.

P لوند *lawand*, Free, independent. A soldier, volunteer, adventurer. Without a fixed residence. A libertine who fears not God nor regards man. Ignorant. Slothful, sluggish, lazy. A frequenter of taverns and stews. A whore. A man who is fond of his wife; gallant. A servant or labourer. A naughty boy. Good news.

T لوندره *londra*, (ITAL. Londra) London.

P لوندزن *lawand-zan*, A whore. Married to a harlot, wedded to a whore.

P لونه *lawna*, Paint for the ladies.

A لؤوس *la,ūs*, An epicure, one who hunts after delicacies. Any thing tasted.

A لووع *luwū,*, (v. n. of لاع for لوع) Being greedy and ill-tempered, and cowardly.

A لووهة *luwūhat*, Shining of the سراب *sarāb*.

P لوويا *lūviyā*, (or لويا *luviyā*) A French bean.

A لوة *lawh*, (or لوهان *lawahān*) (v. n. of لاة for لوة) Shining as the vapour سراب *sarāb*. Creating; creation. *Lawh*, The vapour سراب *sarāb*.

P لوه *lawa*, A kite. A bird like a partridge.

P لوهاور *lawhāwar* or *lohāwar*, Lahore.

P لوهر *lawhur*, (or لوهور *lawhūr*) Lahore.

P لوهنين *lohanīn*, An instrument for separating cotton from its seed.

A لوي *lawa'*, (fut. يلوي *yalwī*) He bent.

A لوي *lawa'*, (v. n. of لوي) Having the cholic. Being crooked (an arrow). Winding (a valley). Withering (herbage). A pain or contortion in the stomach. (for لائي *lāī*) (pl. of التي *allatī*) Those females who. *Lawī*, Griped in the belly. Crooked, sinuous (arrow or tract of sand). *Liwa'*, (pl. الوية *alwiyat*) The extremes of sandy deserts bordering upon more solid ground. (pl. الواء *alwā,* and الوية *alwiyat*) A distorted hill of sand. The termination of a sand-hill. *Luwa'*, Vain things.

A لوّي *lawiy*, Withering, dry (herbage). *Luwayy*, A kind of tree. *Luwīy*, (v. n. of لوي) Bending, twisting (a rope).

A لوّي *lawwīy*, Pertaining to لو *law*, If.

A لوية *lawiyat*, (pl. لوايا *lawāya'*) A part of meat which one lays aside for another.

A لويثة *lawīsat*, A mixed multitude.

A لويجاء *luwayjā,*, Hope, desire, wish, expectation.

A لويحق *luwayhik*, A partridge-hawk.

P لويد *lawīd*, (*liwīd*, or لوير *lawīr*) A large cauldron or kettle, especially of brass.

P لويزه *lawīza*, Name of Abel's twin-sister.

P لويش *lawesh*, (لويشن *lawīshan*, or لويشه *lawīsha*) A blacksmith's twitch for holding the nose of a horse whilst shoeing.

A لويطة *luwaytat*, A dish of different meats; a hodge-podge.

P له *lah*, Scent, smell. Wine made from grapes. *La*, The pine-tree. Name of a town in Turkistān. *Lih*, Any thing old and ready to fall in pieces. *Luh*, A black eagle.

A له *lahu*, His, to (from, or of) him.

A لهّ *lahh*, (v. n. of لهّ) Making (the hair) appear delicate, beautifying (it).

A لها *lahā*, To her. *Laha'*, (pl. of لهاة) Uvulas.

A لهاء *lihā,*, (pl. of لهاة *lahāt*) Uvulas. *Luhā,*, A quantity, sum. لهاء مائة *luhā,u mi,atin*, The number of a hundred (men).

A لهاب *lihāb*, (pl. of لهب *lihb*) Spaces between mountains. Fissures. (pl. of لهبان *lahbān*) Thirsty people. *Luhāb*, (v. n. of لهب) Burning, flaming (fire). Being inflamed. Heat of the fire. Flame without smoke. Thirst.

A لهابة *lihābat*, (pl. of لهب *lihb*) Spaces between mountains. Fissures, narrow passes. *Luhābat*, Flame.

A لهاة *lahāt*, pl. لهوات *lahawāt*, لهيات *lahayāt*, لهيّ *luhīy*, *lihīy*, لها *laha'*, and لهاء *lihā,*, The uvula.

A لهاث *lahās*, (v. n. of لهث) Thirsting. Thirst. *Luhās*, (v. n. of لهث) Lolling out the tongue (as a dog, either from thirst or fatigue). Burning thirst. Pangs of death. Red points on palm-leaves.

A لهّاث *luhhās*, Those who weave palm-leaves into baskets.

A لهاثيّ *luhāsiy*, A person having many red moles on the face.

A لهاد *luhād*, A sigh, a sob. Hiccup.

A لهاذم *lahāzim*, (pl. of لهذم *lahzam*) Sharp points of spears. Robbers.

P لهار *luhār*, Name of a city.

A لهاز *lihāz*, A bit of wood driven into an axle-hole, or into the head of a hatchet, to tighten it.

A لهازم *lahāzim*, (pl. of لهزمة *lihzimat*) Jaw-bones projecting under the ear.

A لهاس *luhās*, (and لهاسة) A little food.

A لهاسم *lahāsim*, (pl. of لهسم *luhsum*) Narrow parts of streams.

P لهاشم *lahāshum*, An ugly, disagreeable thing.

A لهاعة *lahā,at*, Sluggishness, languor; carelessness (in purchase), a liability to be cheated.

A لهاف *lihāf*, (and لهافي *lahāfa'*) (pl. of لهفى *lahfa'*) Afflicted, oppressed, suffering (women).

A لهاق *lahāk*, A white bull. White. *Lihāk*, (pl. of لهق) Brown, tawny (camels). Very white. ابيض لهاق *abyazu la* or *lihākin*, Intense white.

P لهاك *luhāk*, Cause, motive, reason, argument.

A لهّاك *lahhāk*, Name of the brother of Pīrān Wīsah, Afrāsyāb's general.

A لهاله *lahālih*, (pl. of لهلهة *luhluhat*) Widely-extended plains, over which the vapour سراب *sarāb* is seen to float.

A لهام *luhām*, A numerous army (as devouring or destroying all opposition).

A لهاميم *lahāmīm*, (pl. of لهموم) Generous.

P لهانور *la* or *luhānūr*, The city of Lahore.

P لهاور *lahāwar*, The city of Lahore.

A لهب *lahb*, Flame, blaze. *Lahb* or *lahab*, (v. n. of لهب) Blazing, flaming without emitting smoke (fire). *Lihb*, (pl. الهاب *alhāb*, لهوب *luhūb*, لهاب *lihāb*, and لهابة *lihābat*) The space between two mountains. A fissure or narrow pass. A steep or perpendicular precipice, which it is impossible to climb. *Lahab*, Flame (especially without smoke). Redness. Flying (dust). ابو لهب *abū lahab* or *lahb*, Name of one of Muhammad's uncles, of whom mention is made in the Kur'ān.

A لهبان *lahbān*, (pl. لهاب *lihāb*) Thirsty. *Lahabān*, (v. n. of لهب) Blazing, flaming without emitting smoke (fire). Excessive heat. Flame without smoke. A hot day. Thirst.

A لهبة *luhbat*, Thirst. A burning or shining brightness.

A لهبرة *lahbarat*, Short, mean-looking (woman); or one whose speech or clamour is unintelligible; or one who walks slow and heavily.

P لهبله *lahbala*, Foolish, stupid; unlearned, ignorant, unskilful.

A لهبي *lahba'*, (fem. of لهبان) Thirsty (woman).

A لهث *lahs*, (v. n. of لهث) Lolling the tongue (a dog, from thirst or fatigue). *Lahas*, Thirst.

A لهثان *lahsān*, Thirsty. *Lahasān*, Thirst.

A لهثة *luhsat*, Lassitude; Thirst. A red point on a palm-leaf.

A لهثى *lahsa'*, (fem. of لهثان) Thirsty (woman).

A لهج *lahaj*, (v. n. of لهج) Being greedy, devoted, or habitually addicted to. *Lahij*, Greedy, one who hankers after.

A لهجة *lahjat* or *lahajat*, The tongue. Voice, sound, tone. فصيح اللهجة *fasīhu'l lahjat*, Eloquent. *Luhjat*, Breakfast; a whet before dinner.

A لهجم *lahjam*, A cup, goblet. A highway, open road, beaten path.

A لهد *lahd*, (v. n. of لهد) Oppressing, overwhelming, beating down (a load). Wearing out (cattle) by overworking. Beating, thrusting, pushing; striking on the back or breast in contempt. Accusing, impeaching. Eating or licking with the tongue. Any kind of fissure in the feet or thighs of men or animals. A fissure in the breast of a camel from a blow. A tumour under the shoulder-blades of beasts of burden A grave, also an indolent, or sedentary man. Ignoble, sordid.

A لهذا *lihāzā*, (from ل *li* and هذا *hāzā*) Because of, therefore, consequently, for this reason.

A لهذب *lahzab*, A close joining.

A لهذم *lahzam*, (pl. لهاذم *lahāzim*) Sharp, penetrating (spear). Wide pudendum.

A لهذمة *lahzamat*, A cutting, amputating.

P لهر *lahar*, A tavern, public house, where they sell wine and strong liquors. A brothel.

P لهراسپ *luhrāsp*, A king of Persia, father of Gushtasb. Justice.

A لهز *lahz*, (v. n. of لهز) Beginning to come upon

one (grey hairs). Striking on the breast, or on the lump under the ear, with the fist. Piercing the breast (with a spear). (Any young animal) striking the udder of the mother with its head when sucking. Mixing in any society.

A لهزة *lahazat*, That part of the jaw under the ear. *Lahizat*, A woman having plump cheeks, or the corners of whose mouth are protuberant.

A لهزمة *lahzamat*, (v. n. of لهزم Q) Cutting away the jaw-bone projecting under the ear. Beginning to appear on the cheeks (grey hairs). *Lihzimat*, (pl. لهازم *lahāzim*) The jaw-bone under the ear.

A لهس *lahs*, (v. n. of لهس) Licking (a dish). (A child) pulling or licking the teat without sucking. Running hungrily and eagerly to victuals.

A لهسة *luhsat*, A little, somewhat.

A لهسم *luhsum*, (pl. لهاسم *lahāsim*) A narrow part of a stream.

A لهط *laht*, (v. n. of لهط) Striking with the open hand. Aiming at (with an arrow). Sewing (a garment). Throwing or dashing one upon the ground. Bringing forth. Dashing water on the privities.

A لهطة *lahtat*, Doubtful, uncertain news.

A لهع *lahaȝ*, (v. n. of لهع) Accommodating one's self to the temper of another; being sociable, free and easy. Twisting the mouth to a side when speaking. *Lahiȝ*, Accommodating, obliging, affable.

A لهف *lahf*, Ah! alas! (a particle of regret). *Lahaf*, (v. n. of لهف) Lamenting (especially for any thing neglected and gone).

A لهفان *lahfān*, Injured, oppressed; afflicted, sad, sighing.

P لهفت *luhfat* or *lihufat*, A doll, puppet.

P لهفتان *luhfatān*, (pl. of لهفت *luhfat*) Dolls.

A يا لهفه *yā lahfahu*, (يا لهفي عليه *yā lahafa' ȝalayhi*, يا لهفة *yā lahfatu*, يا لهفي عليه *yā lahfī ȝalayhi*, يا لهف *yā lahfi*, يا لهفا *yā lahfā*, يا لهف *yā lahfa*, يا لهفاه *yā lahfāhu*, يا لهفتاه *yā lahfatāhu*, or يا لهفتياه *yā lahfatayāhu*) Alas!

A لهفى *lahfa'*, (pl. لهافي *lahāfa'* and لهاف *lihāf*) Afflicted, oppressed, suffering (woman).

A لهق *lahh* or *lahak*, (v. n. of لهق) Being intensely white (but not glossy or shining). *Lahih*, White but not glossy (bull, garment, or hoariness). *Lahik* or *lahak*, (pl. لهاق *lihāk*) A white bull. Whitish. Brown, tawny (camel). ابيض لهق *abyazu lahak*, (or *lahik*) Intense white.

A لهله *lahlah*, Cloth of a fine thread and open texture. Flimsy verse, or other composition. *Luhluh*, (pl. لهاله *lahālih*) A plain over which the vapour سراب *sarāb* is seen to move to and fro.

P لهلهان *lahlahān*, A species of sweet basil.

A لهلهة *lahlahat*, (v. n. of لهله Q) Weaving (cloth) slightly. *Luhluhat*, (pl. لهاله *lahālih*) A wide country, over which the vapour سراب *sarāb* floats.

A لهم *lahm*, (v. n. of لهم) Swallowing. Liberal, munificent. *Lahm* or *laham*, (v. n. of لهم) Swallowing quickly and at once. *Lihm*, (pl. لهوم *luhūm*) Aged (bull). *Lahim*, Voracious, gluttonous. *Luham*, A glutton.

A لهمّ *lihamm*, Outstripping in the race (a horse). The ocean. Wise, prudent. Liberal, munificent.

A لهمة *luhmat*, A handful of barley-meal.

A لهمم *lihmim*, (*luhmum*, or لهميم *lihmīm*) Excellent, fleet (horse). Liberal, munificent (man).

A لهموم *luhmūm*, (A camel) giving much milk. Liberal (man). A large number. A vast army. A deep or large wound. Clouds full of rain. Vulva. Female dress or appurtenances.

A لهنة *luhnat*, A breakfast; whet or collation before dinner. Any present brought by a traveller.

P لهنج *lahanj*, A stone upon which washers beat their linen. A whetstone. Concord, harmony.

A لهنّك *lahinnaka*, Because thou. Certainly.

P لهنه *lahna*, A fool, idiot. A stone. لهنهٔ جانگزا *lahna-i jān-gazā*, A stone which causes any one who looks on it to burst out into a violent fit of laughter.

A لهو *lahw*, (v. n. of لها for لهو) Playing, amusing one's self, passing the time agreeably, unbending. Dismissing, letting alone. Lying with. Play, any thing ludicrous or jocular; whatever diverts the thoughts from any thing serious (especially women or children). لهو و لعب *lahw u laȝb*, Playing and toying. Sport, amusement, game, fun. *Lahw*, (or لهوّ *luhūw*) (v. n. of لها for لهو) Listening to a story and being amused by it.

A لهوّ *lahūw*, One who dismisses any thing, or turns away from it; negligent, careless.

A لهوات *lahawāt*, (pl. of لهوة *lahwat*) Uvulas.

A لهوب *luhūb*, (pl. of لهب *lihb*) Spaces between two mountains. Clefts between mountains.

A لهوة *lahwat*, A woman with whom one plays or toys. *Lahwat* or *luhwat*, (pl. لهى *luha'*) What the miller throws with his hand into the hopper. As much gold as the two hands can hold; a thousand pieces of gold or silver. A valuable present.

A لهوجة *lahwajat*, (v. n. of لهوج Q) Not dressing (meat) enough, leaving (it) half-cooked. Doing (any business) wretchedly.

A لهوق *lahwak*, A vain boaster; who speaks or acts carelessly, or who says but does not. Unpractised, inexperienced.

A لهوقة *lahwakat*, (v. n. of لهوق Q) Making a vain boast, putting forth false pretensions. Saying or doing any thing carelessly.

A لهوم *lahūm*, A glutton. Milch (camel). Liberal (man). Excellent (horse). *Luhūm*, (pl. of لهم *lihm*) Aged (bulls).

A لهويّ *lahwīy*, Pronounced from the uvula, as ق *kāf* (by some spelt *qāf*) and ك *kāf*.

A لهى *laha'*, (and لهيان *luhyān*) (v. n. of لهي) Loving, delighting in, solacing one's self, diverting by one thing the thoughts of another. Dismissing from one's thoughts, forgetting. Dismissing, abandoning. *Luha'*, (pl. of لهوة *luhwat*) Valuable gifts. معطاء اللهى *miȝtāu'l luha'*, Munificent, liberal.

P لهي *lihī*, Leave, dismissal, discharge, liberty.

A لهيّ *luhīy*, (v. n. of لهي) Loving, delighting in, solacing one's self, diverting one's self. Dismissing from one's thoughts, forgetting. Abandoning. *Luhīy* or *lihīy*, (pl. of لهاة *lahāt*) Uvulas.

A لهيات *lahayāt*, (pl. of لهاة *lahāt*) Uvulas.

A لهيب *lahīb*, (v. n. of لهب) Burning, blazing without smoke (fire). Ardour, inflammation, heat. The passion of love. Heart-burn.

A لهية *luhyat*, A costly present.

A لهيد *lahīd*, Tired, jaded (beast).

A لهيدة *lahīdat*, Pulse, pottage, panado, neither thick nor thin.

A لهيعة *lahīȝat*, Sluggishness, languor. Carelessness in making purchases: a liability to be imposed upon. Name of a man.

A لهيف *lahīf*, Injured, afflicted. Oppressed, ruined. Sighing. Tall, coarse, and thick. لهيف القلب *lahīfu'l kalb*, Pained at heart.

A لهيفة *lahīfat*, (pl. لهاف *lihāf*) Sighing, afflicted, injured (woman).

A لهيم *lahīm*, Death, fate. *Luhaym*, A large kettle or pot. امّ اللهيم *ummu'l luhaym*, Misfortune; fever; fate; death.

A لهّيم *lihhīm*, A horse outstripping in a race.

P لي *lay*, A vessel, casket. Clay.

A لي *lī*, To me.

A لي *layy*, (v. n. of لوي) Bending, crooking, turning, twisting (a rope). Inclining (the head). Denying what he ought to say. Concealing, suppressing. Attaining his twentieth year (a youth). Moving, wagging (the tail). Desisting from any thing through indolence. Preferring one to another. Inclining to. Expecting. *Layy* or *liy*, (v. n. of لوي) Delaying, deferring, putting off payment of a debt. *Luyy*, (pl. of الوى *alwa'*) Crooked (horns).

A لياء *liyāʼ*, A kind of white vetch. A fair woman. A sort of fish which supplies good materials for making shields. Land far distant from water.

A ليّاء *layyāʼ*, (fem. of الوى *alwa'*) Crooked, distorted. Disputatious. Lone, solitary. A place distant from water.

A لياح *lay* or *liyāh*, White. A white wild bull. Morning. ابيض لياح *abyazu liyāhun*, Pure white.

A لياخة *liyākhat*, Butter melted amongst milk.

A لياد *layād*, A thing, any thing.

A لياذ *liyāz*, (v. n. 3 of لاذ for لوذ) Taking refuge. Taking for a protection or fortress.

A لياذة *liyāzat*, A taking refuge.

A لياس *liyās*, A wittol, a cuckold. One who never moves abroad.

A لياط *liyāt*, Profit, usury. Plaster, lime, mortar. Dung. (pl. of ليطة *lītat*) Barks of canes or reeds.

A لياط *layyāt*, An active man.

A لياع *liyāȝ*, Violent, strong (wind).

A لياغة liyāghat, Foolish, frantic.

A لياق layāḳ, Perseverance in any business, permanence in. A wide, open, grassy field. Liyāḳ, Flame, heat.

A لياقة liyāḳat, Propriety, fitness, suitableness. Congruence, congruity. Dignity, worth, merit. Skill, ability. Prudence, judgment.

A ليالى layālī, (pl. of ليل layl) Nights. (pl. of ليلي layla') Scents of black wines. Laylas.

A لئام liʼām, (pl. of لئيم laʼīm) Mean, sordid, avaricious. Like, equal. خيارو لئام khiyāru liʼām, The good and the bad, the precious and the vile.

P ليان layān or liyān, Splendour, brightness (of a sword). Lightning. Flashing, glittering.

A ليان layān, (v. n. of لان for لين) Being smooth and soft: softness, gentleness: lenity, smoothness. Conveniency, ease, comfort. Liyān, (v. n. 3 of لان for لين) Behaving placidly, compassionately, humanely. Being soft and smooth. (v. n. of لوي) Delaying, putting off payment of a debt. (pl. of لين līn) Certain kinds of palm-trees.

A لیّان layyān, (v. n. of لوي) Delaying, deferring, putting off payment of a debt. Concealing, suppressing. Inclining to. Expecting. Inclining (the head). Wagging (the tail). Preferring.

A ليايل layāyil, (pl. of ليل layl) Nights.

P ليپا līpā, (or ليپان līpān) Sheep's tripe stuffed with minced meat and rice.

A ليّة layyat, One ply, fold. (pl. لوي liwa') A woman. Union of relations. اللّيّة al līyat, Aloe-wood.

A ليت layt, (v. n. of لات for ليت) Hindering, preventing, diverting one (from a pursuit). Defrauding; diminishing. ليت و لعلّ layt u laʻall, Evasion, prevarication, subterfuge, procrastination. Līt, Side of the neck. Layta, (or ياليت yā layta) Would to God! I wish. Oh! if. ليتي laytī, (or ليتني laytanī) Would to heaven that I! ليتك laytaka, I wish that thou. Sometimes it is used in the sense of وجدت wajattu, I found.

P ليتك letak, Poor, indigent, distressed. A slave boy. A girl agreeably plump. One of mean origin. Remainder of any thing, dregs and the like. Confounded, bewildered.

A ليث lays, A lion. A spider that jumps upon flies. Eloquent. ليث عفرّين laysu ʻifirrīn, A strong lion. A forest for lions. A kind of animal that lurks in the ground at the foot of a wall. A well-made, strong, powerfully-built man. Clever, expert at business. An animal resembling a chameleon. Līs, A species of plant. Thick herbage. (pl. of اليث alyas) Brave, strong.

A ليّث layyis, Entangled herbage. Strong (camel). A beard black and grey.

A ليثة laysat, A strong, stout camel.

P ليچار lechār, (or ليچال lechāl) A confection, electuary, preserved fruits, pickles.

P لير ler, Slaver running from the lips and corners of the mouth.

P ليرت lerat or lert, A helmet. A kind of armour.

P ليرد lerd, A kind of armour.

A ليز layz, A fleeing unto, a seeking refuge.

P ليز līz, Soft and slippery ground. Any thing smooth and soft. Drawing a manual instrument across any thing. Mixed. Any thing rare, choice, delicate, good.

P ليزم lezam, A kind of bow with an iron chain instead of a string, with which the natives of the East exercise their bodies.

P ليزه līza, Mixed. Drawing a manual instrument across any thing.

P ليزيدن līzīdan, To mix. To slip, slide.

P ليس līs, (in comp.) Licking (with the tongue). كاسه ليس kāsa-līs, A plate-licker, glutton.

A ليس līs, (pl. of اليس alyas) Bold, strong. Layas, Fortitude, boldness. Imprudence, carelessness, negligence. Laysa, Not; is not. Except. ليس في الدار غيرنا ديّار laysa fi'd dār ghayrunā dayyār, There is nobody at home but us. ليس كارادتي laysa ka irādatī, It is not according to my wish.

P ليسپنه lespana, (or ليسنه lesana) A weaver's reed on which he winds his thread.

P ليسش līsish, (from ليسيدن līsīdan) Licking.

P ليسيدن līsīdan, (and ليسيستن) To lick.

P ليسيدني līsīdanī, Capable of being licked. An electuary. داروي ليسيدني dārūyi līsīdanī, A linctus, a lambative medicine.

A ليص lays, (v. n. of لاص for ليص) Being crooked and wry. Bending or shaking (any thing) in order to extract (it).

A ليط layt, (v. n. of لاط for ليط) Being dear to, intwining (itself) round the heart. Wounding with an arrow or malignant eye. Cursing. Being worthy, deserving. Concealing. Attaching, causing to unite. Layt or līt, Colour. Līt, Skin, bark. Disposition, temper, nature, habit, constitution. (pl. of ليطة līṭat) Barks of canes. Bows. Canes.

A ليطان laytān, (or شيطان ليطان) Satan.

A ليطة līṭat, (pl. ليط līt, لياط liyāt, and الياط alyāt) Bark of a cane or reed. A bow. A cane. A spear. Disposition, temper, nature, habit, constitution.

A ليع layʻ, A being timid, cowardly.

A ليعان layaʻān, A being vexed, melancholy.

A ليعة layʻat, Pangs of hunger, starvation.

A ليغ laygh, (v. n. of لاغ for ليغ) Asking, desiring. Layagh, Downright folly.

A سيّغ ليّغ sayyigh layyigh, (Wine or food) which glides gently down the throat.

A ليف layf, (v. n. of لاف for ليف) Eating food. Līf, Fibres, filaments, especially of palm-trees.

P ليف līf, A brush made of palm-tree fibres.

A ليفانيّ līfānīy, One with a very large beard.

A ليفس liyafs, Bold, brave, courageous.

P ليفه دان līfadān, An inkholder. A shell for holding vermilion.

A ليق layḳ, (v. n. of لاق for ليق) Putting silk or cotton into an inkholder. Adhering. Having the ink adhering to the cotton (an inkstand). Preserving, reserving, keeping. Flying to, taking refuge. Being proper (as an action), fitting well (as a garment). Līḳ, A black substance which they mix with collyriums. Liyaḳ, Thin clouds, or the openings in them.

A ليقة layḳat, (v. n. of لاق for ليق) Putting silk or cotton into an inkholder. Līḳat, Raw silk or cotton put into an inkholder. Clay, or any thing similar, with which they plaster walls.

P ليك lek, But, notwithstanding, nevertheless. A bustard. A measure for corn or dates.

P ليكك līkak, A bustard.

P ليكن lekin, (or ليكه leka) But.

A ليل layl, (pl. ليالي layālī and ليايل layāyil) Night. A female, also a young bustard. ليل لائل layli lāʼil, (or ليل اليل laylu alyalu) A long and dark night; that which precedes the new moon. Misfortune. ليل و نهار layl u nahār, Night and day. اجبن من ليل ajban min laylin, More timorous than a young bustard.

A ليلاً laylan, In the night-time.

A لئلّا liʼallā, (comp. of ل li, ان an, and لا lā) Lest, that not, in order that not.

A ليلاء laylāʼ, (or ليلا layla') (as ليلة ليلاء laylatu laylāʼ or ليلا layla') A long and dark night; that which precedes the new moon.

A ليلاة laylāt, Night.

A ليلة laylat, One night. ليلة القدر laylatu'l ḳadr, The night of power (the 27th of Ramazān). ليلهٔ زفاف laylaʼi zifāf, The wedding-night.

P ليلج līlaj, (ليلنج, or ليلنگ) Indigo-plant.

P ليلو līlū, A pond, a ditch.

P ليلوپر līlūpar, (or ليلوپل) The water-lily.

A ليلى layla', (pl. ليالي layālī) The odour of black wine, or the commencement of its intoxicating influence. Name of a lady frequently alluded to in the East. The loves of مجنون majnūn and ليلى layla' are celebrated in a fine Persian poem by نظامي nazāmī. امّ ليلي umm layla', Black wine.

A ليليّ laylīy, Nocturnal. One who does any thing by night.

P ليليا layliyā, (in zand and Pāzand) Night.

A لئم liʼm, Consent, concord. Peace. Honey.

A ليم līm, Peace, concord. Equal, resembling in form, stature, and disposition.

A لیّم luyyam, Accusers, blamers, censurers.

P ليمو līmū, (ليمون līmūn, or ليمونا līmūnā) A lemon, citron.

P ليمودارو līmū-dārū, Name of a plant or herb which grows in rocky places, and has the odour of a lemon: verbena.

A ليمون laymūn, (or ليمو laymū) A lemon.

P ليمونا līmūnā, Lemon-juice. A lemon, citron.

P ليمون كاغذي līmūn-kāghzī, A lime.

P لیمونی *līmūnī*, Made or imbued with lemon.

A لین *layn*, (v. n. of لان for لین) Being smooth. Being gentle, mild, placid, humane. Soft, smooth, mild, placid. هین لین *haynun laynun*, Easy, convenient. *Līn*, Softness, smoothness. (pl. لیان *liyān*) A kind of palm. حرف اللین *harfu'l līn*, A letter of softness, *i. e.* the diphthong او *aw*, *au*, or اي *ay*, *ai*, in such words as یوم *yawm* or بیت *bayt*.

A لئن *laɹin*, Certainly if.

A لیّن *layyin*, (pl. لیّنون *layyinūn* and الیناء *al-yināɹ*) Soft, smooth (thing). لیّن الجانب *layyinu'l jānib*, Of gentle manners.

A لینة *laynat*, A leathern cushion. *Līnat*, (v. n. of لین) Being smooth. (pl. لین *līn*) A kind of palm.

P لینج *līnaj*, A litharge produced in Cyprus.

A لینيّ *līniy*, Soft, as applicable to ا, و, or ي.

P لیو *lev*, The sun.

P لیوان *līwān*, (pl. لواوین) An ante-chamber.

A لیوث *luyūs*, (pl. of لیث *lays*) Lions. Spiders.

P لیوك *līvak*, A stout, uncouth young man.

P لیولنك *levlank*, Butter-milk dried in the sun. *Levlank* or *layūlank*, Snow.

P لیوه *līwa*, A deceiver, flatterer. Jocular.

A لیه *layh*, (v. n. of لاه for لیه) Being covered, veiled, concealed. Being high, eminent, exalted.

A لییل *luyayl*, (dim. of لیل *layl*) A short night.

A لییلیة *luyayliyat*, (dim. of لیلاة *laylāt*) A short night.

A لئیم *laɹīm*, (pl. لئام *liɹām*, لؤماء *luɹamāɹ*, and لؤمان *luɹmān*) Vile, abject, mean, base, worthless, inglorious, ignoble, sordid, avaricious, cowardly. A miser. (pl. الآم *alɹām* and لئام *liɹām*) Like, equal.

P لئیمان *laɹīmān*, (pl. of A لئیم *laɹīm*) Base.

P لییدن *layedan*, To chew.

م

م *mīm*, The twenty-fourth letter of the Arabic alphabet, and the twenty-eighth of the Persian. In arithmetic it denotes 40, and in almanacs is the character for Sunday. It is also a contraction of the month محرّم *muharram*, and the word منطق *mantik*, Logic; and when preceded by the letter ع is an abbreviation of علیه السلام *ɛalayhi's salām*. It is interchangeable with ب, ت, ل, ن, and و. *Ma*, (for ما *mā*), as الام *ilāma*, To what?

P م *mīm* preceded by *fathah* ـَ added to a noun forms a possessive pronoun: as, پدرم *pidaram*, My father. کتابم *kitābam*, My book. It stands also for مرا *marā*: as, دیدنش بردم از هوش *dīdanash burdam az hosh* for مرا از هوش برد *marā az hosh burd*, The sight of her robbed me of my understanding. زرم داد *zaram dād*, He gave me gold. نیستم پروای کسی *nīstam parwāyi kase*, I care for nobody. It occasionally stands also for من *man*, as in the first person singular of the tenses of verbs. It is also prefixed to the second person singular and plural imperative mood to imply "forbidding or dissuading:" as, مخور *makhwur*, Don't eat. مگو *ma gū*, Do not speak. مروید *ma ravīd*, Go not ye. م *m*, preceded by *zamm*, is added to cardinal numbers to form ordinals: as, یکم *yakum*, First; دوم *duwum* or دویم *duyum*, Second; سیوم *sīwum*, Third.

P ما *mā*, We. Us, our. از ما *az mā*, From us. پدر ما *pidari mā*, Our father.

A ما *mā*, Which, what, that which, whatsoever. Somewhat, something. Why, wherefore. Whilst, during, as long as. As much as, as far as. No, not, nothing. How! What! What? Who, he who. Beside, except. لتکن دائرة ما *litakun dāɹiratu mā*, Let there be some (or a given) circle. انّ زیدا ممّا ان یکتب *inna zaydan mimmā an yaktub*, Indeed Zayd is an excellent writer, or of those who write well. علی ما کان *ɛala' mā kāna*, According as it was. ما لك *mā laka*, What's the matter? what ails thee? ما من احد *mā min ahadin*, There is not one. ما احسن عمر *mā ahsan ɛumar*, How excellent is Omar! ما ارشق *mā arshak*, How rapid! With what velocity it vibrates! ما ازهاه *mā azhāhu*, Most superb; how glorious! ما اشبه *mā ashbaha*, How like! ما اموت قلبه *mā amwata kalbuhu*, How dead-hearted he is! ما اوسم *mā awsam*, How barren of herbage! ما استطیع *mā astatiɛu*, As far as I can. ما دمت حیّا *mā dumtu hayyan*, As long as I live. ما بقي *mā baka'*, The rest, remainder, arrears, balance. ما به الاحتیاج *mā bihi'l ihtiyāj*, Whatever is (or may be) necessary. ما الحاضر *mā al hāzir*, Whatever comes first to hand. ما نحن فیه *mā nahnu fīhi*, The subject which we are about. This particle is frequently added to others, without making any sensible difference of sense: as, امّا *ammā*, If, but if. انّما *innamā*, (for انّ *inna*) Because, certainly; although. اذاما *izāmā*, (for اذا *izā*) When. اینما *aynamā*, Wheresoever. کلّما *kullamā*, As often as. Whatsoever. کما *kamā*, As, as if, like, according to. کیفما *kayfamā*, How? In any manner. کیما *kaymā*, That, in order to. لکیما *likaymā*, In order to. مهما *mahmā*, As often as. Wherefore.

A ماء *māɹ*, (originally ماه *māh*) (pl. امواه *amwāh* and میاه *miyāh*) Water. Juice, sap, humour, liquor. Semen, sperm. Splendour, lustre, temper (as of a sword). Clearness (of the face). ماء اجوج *māɹi ajūj*, Brackish water. ماء جاري *māɹi jārī*, Flowing or running water. ماء جامد *māɹi jāmid*, Stagnant water. Ice. Jelly. ماء جبن *māɹi jubn*, Serum or whey which drops from new-made cheese. ماء الحیوة *māɹu'l hayāt*, Water of life or immortality. ماء ذکر *māɹi zakar*, Sperma. ماء الزجاج *māɹu'z zujāj*, Scum or dross which floats on the surface of glass when in fusion. ماء زلال *māɹi zulāl*, (ماء قراح *māɹi karāh*, or ماء صافی *māɹi sāfī*) Pure water. ماء الشعیر *māɹu'sh shaɛīr*, Barley-water. ماء الظهر *māɹu'z zahr*, Sperma. ماء العسل *māɹu'l ɛasal*, Water and honey, metheglin. ماء القرع *māɹu'l karɛ*, Juice of the pumpkin. ماء اللحم *māɹu'l lahm*, Distilled water from (kid's) flesh with spices. ماء المرآة *māɹu'l mirɹāt*, Lustre of a mirror. ماء مطر *māɹi matar*, Rain-water. ماء مقطر *māɹi muktar*, Distilled water. ماء نبع *māɹi nabɛ*, A fountain, spring, source. ماء ورد *māɹi ward*, (or ماء الورد *māɹu'l ward*) Rose-water. ماء السماء *māɹu's samāɹ*, Rain-water; ماء البحر *māɹu'l bahr*, Sea-water; ماء النهر *māɹu'n nahr*, River-water; ماء البئر *māɹu'l biɹr*, Well-water; ماء العین *māɹu'l ɛayn*, Spring-water; ماء الثلج *māɹu's salj*, Snow-water; ماء البرد *māɹu'l barad*, Hail-water (the seven kinds of water with which the Muhammadans may legally purify themselves). بیت الماء *baytu'l māɹ*, A water-closet. رجل ماء *rajulun māɹun*, A watery-hearted man. طریق ما *tariki mā*, An aqueduct.

A مآبر *maɹābir*, (pl. of مئبار *miɹbār* or مئبارة) Needle-cases. (pl. of مئبر *miɹbar*) Detractions.

A مآبض *maɹābiz*, (pl. of مأبض *maɹbiz*) Tendons of the hams.

A ماءة *māɹat*, Water. Slanderous (woman).

A مآتم *maɹātim*, (pl. of مأتم) Mournings.

A مآجل *maɹājil*, (pl. of مأجل) Ponds, ditches.

A مآخذ *maɹākhiz*, (pl. of مأخذ *maɹkhaz*) Baits for catching game.

A مآدب *maɹādib*, (pl. of مأدبة *maɹdaba* or *maɹdubat*) Feasts, entertainments to which one is invited.

A مآدیر *maɹādīr*, (pl. of مأدور) Ruptured.

A مآذن *maɹāzin*, (pl. of مئذنة *miɹzanat*) Towers of mosques, minarets.

A مآرب *maɹārib*, (pl. of مأربة *maɹraba*, *maɹri*, or *maɹrubat*) Things necessary to be done.

A مآرین *maɹārīn*, (pl. of مئران *miɹrān*) Lairs of wild beasts.

A مآزم *maɹāzim*, (pl. of مأزم *maɹzim*) Narrow places, passes.

A مآزیب *maɹāzīb*, (pl. of مئزاب *miɹzāb*) Water-courses, pipes, conduits.

A مآسد *maɹāsid*, (pl. of مأسدة *maɹsadat*) Places abounding in lions (اسد *asad*).

A مآکم *maɹākim*, (pl. of مأکمة *maɹkamat*) Prominent hips.

A مآل *maɹāl*, (v. n. of آل for اول) Returning, retiring. Being carried back, failing. A place whither one returns.

A مآلي *maɹālī*, (pl. of مئلاة *miɹlāt*) Handkerchiefs which women hold in their hands when weeping.

A مآود *maɹāwid*, Misfortunes.

A مائي *māɹiy*, Watery, aqueous.

A مآب *maɹāb*, (pl. of مآوب *maɹāwib*) (v. n. of آب for اوب) Returning. (A noun of place, of which there are great numbers in Arabic, as well as of nouns of time and of instrument, which begin with the letter م). A receptacle, repository, centre or point to which any thing returns, or a place in which it is contained. Such words are chiefly used in composition: as, عزت ماب *ʻiz-zat-maʼāb*, Seat of magnificence, residence of glory; (also, simply) magnificent, illustrious. بلاغت ماب *balāghat-maʼāb*, Eloquent.

A مأباة *maʼbāt*, (fem. of مأبى *maʼba'*) Abominable. Water which a camel refuses to drink.

A ما باقي *mā bākī*, The remainder, rest.

A مأبد *maʼbid*, Place, mansion. Name of a place.

A مأبض *maʼbiz*, (pl. مآبض *maʼābiz*) The back or sinewy part of the knee-joint, the hamstring. The inside of the elbow of a camel.

A مأبلة *maʼbalat*, A place full of camels.

A مأبوت *maʼbūt*, Hot in constitution, burning with indignation. Troubled with lumbago.

A مأبور *maʼbūr*, (An animal) in whose food a needle (ابرة *ibrat*) is concealed. Stung by a scorpion. Suspected. Reproached.

A مأبورة *maʼbūrat*, (A female palm-tree) sprinkled with the male flowers and rendered fruitful.

A مأبوض *maʼbūz*, Tied. Injured in the tendon of the thigh, and having the leg contracted.

A مأبول *maʼbūl*, A well surrounded by a parapet. Gotten (as colts, hair, or milk from camels).

A مأبولة *maʼbūlat*, (A camel) set at liberty from old age. (A camel) drawn and set apart for breeding and for milking.

P مابون *mābūn*, Infamous; a catamite. Name of a disease.

A مأبون *maʼbūn*, Suspected. Infamous. A wretch held in abhorrence. One who suffers himself to be abused contrary to nature.

A ما به الابتهاج *mā bihi'l ibtihāj*, That in which there is joy.

A مآبي *maʼābīy*, Pestiferous. امراض مآبية *amrāzi maʼābīya*, Pestilential diseases.

A مابين *mā bayn*, (or مابيني *mā baynī*) An interval, interstice, space between two bodies. Both sides. Between. Among.

P ماپروين *mā-parwīn*, The herb zedoary.

A مات *māta*, (fut. يموت *yamūtu*, يمات *yamātu*, and يميت *yamītu*) He died, he is dead. He reposed. He slept. He became old and worn.

T P مات *māt*, Astonished, amazed, confounded, perplexed. Conquered, subjected, reduced to the last extremity (especially at chess), receiving shāh māt, or check mate. P مات كردن *māt kardan*, To confound. To check mate.

A مأتاة *maʼtāt*, A coming, drawing near. اتيت الامر من مأتاته *ataytu'l amra min maʼtātihi*, I set about the business in the best manner.

A مأتة *maʼattat*, (v. n. of اتّ) Overpowering in argument. Breaking the head.

A ماتّة *māttat*, (pl. موات) Honour, respect. Cause, occasion: means, way of conciliating favour.

A ماتح *mātih*, A drawer of water.

P ماترنگ *mātirang*, A kind of lizard.

A ماتع *mātiʻ*, Long. Preponderating (scale of a balance). Well-twisted (rope). Excellent. Very red and excellent (wine).

A ما تقدم *mā takaddam*, What is gone before. The past, antiquity. P در ما تقدم *dar mā takaddam*, In the first place.

P ماتم *mātam*, Grief, mourning. A bitch. طعام ماتم *taʻāmi mātam*, A funeral-banquet. لباس ماتم *libāsi* (or خرقهٔ *khirkaʼi*) *mātam*, Mourning-apparel.

A مأتم *maʼtam*, (pl. مآتم *maʼātim*) A misfortune. An assembly of female mourners, beating their breasts, tearing their hair, face, or garments, and making a melancholy noise, on account of any misfortune, as the death of a friend. It also, sometimes, implies a promiscuous meeting of men or women on any festive occasion.

P ماتم پرسی *mātam-pursī*, Oblations, funeral-obsequies. Compliments of condolence.

P ماتم زده *mātam-zada*, Melancholy, almost dead. A mourner.

P ماتمكده *mātam-kada*, House of mourning.

P ماتم كنان *mātam-kunān*, Mourners.

P ماتمي *mātamī*, Mourning, clad in sable.

P ماتورنگ *māturang*, A lizard, land-crocodile (called in Arabic ضبّ *zabb*).

A مأتوناء *maʼtūnāʼ*, (pl. of اتان *atān*) She-asses.

A مأتى *maʼta'*, Face, appearance. That part of any thing (which can be approached or handled). A place to which one comes, a rendezvous.

A مأتيّ *maʼtīy*, (the passive participle being used in the sense of the active) Coming, about to come. وعده مأتيّ *waʻduhu maʼtīy*, His promise (namely God's) is at hand, or will be fulfilled in due season.

A مأثاة *maʼsāt*, Whisper, detraction, slander.

A مآثب *maʼāsib*, (pl. of مئثب *miʼsab*) Short swords. Plain grounds. Rising lands. Rivulets.

A ماثد *māsid*, A spy, scout, observer.

A مآثر *maʼāsir*, (pl. of مأثرة *maʼsarat*) Glories, excellencies. Signs, memorials. Illustrious acts. Histories, traditions. Places of efficacy. عساكر ظفر مآثر *ʻasākiri zafar-maʼāsir*, Victorious armies.

A مأثرة *maʼsarat* or *maʼsurat*, (pl. مآثر *maʼāsir*) Glory, nobility, greatness, hereditary honour.

A ماثل *māsil*, Obliterated vestiges of a house. مثل ماثل *misli māsil*, Extremely like.

A ماثلة *māsilat*, A lamp-stand. A lighted lamp.

A مأثم *maʼsam*, (v. n. of اثم) Sinning. Punishing for crimes. Iniquity. *Maʼsim*, Punishment.

A مأثمة *maʼsamat*, Iniquity.

A مأثور *maʼsūr*, Recorded, handed down by tradition. Remarkable, memorable. Noble. A history, saying, tradition. (A sword) having a glittering surface, or whose back is made of soft steel, and its edge of male steel; also an hereditary sword. المأثور *al maʼsūr*, Name of a sword said to have been forged by demons.

A مأثوم *maʼsūm*, Guilty or suspected (person).

A مأثية *maʼsiyat*, Whisper, detraction, slander.

P ماج *māj*, The moon. An historian. ماج و موج *māj u mūj*, Kissing and licking (as a cat does her kittens).

A مأج *maʼj*, Bitter, brackish (water). Foolish. Agitated, disturbed. Battle, slaughter. Agitation.

A ماجّ *mājj*, Slavering (old man or camel). A fool. احمق ماجّ *ahmak mājj*, A weak, slavering old man.

A ماجد *mājid*, (A man) conspicuous for honour, nobility, glory. Eminently beneficent and humane. شريف ماجد *sharīf mājid*, Most glorious, noble.

A ماجرا *mā jarā*, (or ماجري *mā jara'*) An accident, event, occurrence, adventure, thing past, state, condition, circumstances.

A ماجريات *mā jarayāt*, Events of past ages.

A ماجشون *mājushūn*, A kind of ship. A coloured stuff. (See ماجوشون *majūshūn*).

A ماجعة *mājiʻat*, A whore.

A مأجل *maʼjal*, (pl. مآجل *maʼājil*) A place where water lies. A pond, ditch.

A ماجل *mājil*, Water at the foot of a mountain or in a valley. A meeting-place at the gate of Mecca.

A ماجن *mājin*, (pl. مجّان *mujjān*) Licentious, insolent, careless and indifferent as to what one says or does, bold, impudent.

P ماجو *mājū*, A gall-nut.

A مأجوج *maʼjūj*, Magog, son of Japhet. That part of Eastern Tartary which borders on China.

A مأجور *maʼjūr*, Recompensed, paid, remunerated. A sort of vessel. A flower-pot.

A ماجوشون *mājūshūn*, (from P ماه گون *māh-gūn*) (Like the moon) A ship. A kind of dyed cloth.

P ماچ *māch*, A kiss. A bitch. A beast of burden. A ball of paste boiled amongst soup.

P ماچان *māchān*, Leaning upon. Remaining, stopping. پاي ماچان *pāy-māchān*, A bitch. A ball of paste boiled amongst soup. Asking pardon for not knowing the lesson. (In Persia a custom prevailed, that when a boy could not say his lesson he was obliged to buy something, on which the other boys feasted in a recumbent posture while he continued standing and asking pardon).

P ماچخ *māchikh*, Study, labour, exertion.

P ماچوچه *māchūcha*, A cup with a spout for pouring medicine down a child's throat.

P ماچين *māchīn*, The Emperor of China.

A ماح *māh*, The yoke; also, white of an egg.

A ماحة *māhat*, A court or inner quadrangle.

A ماحش *māhish*, A glutton. Gorged with food. Burning, blistering.

A ما حصل *mā hasal*, Any thing collected. The harvest; harvest of fruit-trees and the like. Profit, income. Result, upshot (of discussion, &c.)

A ماحض *māhiz*, One who possesses or longs for pure milk, unmixed with water (محض *mahz*).

A ما حضر *mā hazar*, Whatever is ready or prepared in haste (particularly victuals).

A ماحط *māhit*, (A year) of little rain.

A ماحق *māhik*, (pl. مواحق *mawāhik*) Intense (heat); hot (day); heat (of summer). Keen (sword).

A ماحل *māhil*, An informer. (A country or season) barren from want of rain. Changed, altered in body, emaciated. Avaricious, sordid; destitute of a single good quality.

A ماحوز *māhūz*, A certain fragrant herb.

A ماحي *māhī*, Obliterating, defacing; who or what erases, expunges, or defaces. A name of Muhammad. Mecca.

P A ماخ *mākh*, Adulterated gold or silver. A perfidious man: a coward, scoundrel. Despicable. An old man.

P ماخان *mākhān*, A title of the Emperor of China. Name of a village near مرو *marv*.

P ماخچي *mākhchī*, A horse between an Arab and a Turkī, commonly called مجنّس *mujannas*. An ambling nag. A pack-horse.

A مآخذ *ma,ākhiz*, Nets or other implements by which birds are caught.

A مأخذ *ma,khaz*, Bait, or whatever animals are taken with. A place where any thing is taken or derived. A receptacle. Source, origin. اخذ مأخذه *akhaza ma,khazahu*, He took entire possession.

A ماخرة *mākhirat*, (pl. مواخر *mawākhir*) (A ship) ploughing the ocean, cutting the water with a noise. A cut-water, shear-water.

A ماخض *mākhiz*, (pl. مواخض *mawākhiz* or مخّض *mukhkhaz*) (A woman, camel, or sheep) in labour, enduring the pangs of birth. Pregnant (ewe).

A ماخط *mākhit*, One who strips the caul from the head of a new-born camel.

A ماخل *mākhil*, Fugitive.

A ما خلا *mā khalā*, Besides, save and except.

A ما خلق الله *mā khalaka'llāh*, That which God has created, *i.e.* the world, all sorts of men or animals.

P ماخن *mākhan*, Impure. Vile, naughty. False.

A مأخوذ *ma,khūz*, Taken, occupied; held (opinion).

P ماخور *mākhwur*, A profligate assembly, company of drunkards. A tavern, pot-house, sot's hole. A gambling-house.

A ماخور *mākhūr*, (pl. مواخر *mawākhir* and مواخير *mawākhīr*) (from P ميخور *may-khwur*) A tavern, gaming-house, or brothel, or whatever attracts that way. A frequenter of taverns.

G ماخوليا *mākholiyā*, Melancholy, madness.

A مآخير *ma,ākhīr*, Hinder or extreme parts.

P ماد *mād*, (from مادر *mādar*) A mother.

A مأد *ma,d*, (v. n. of مأد) Waving to and fro (a young pliant branch). Being young, soft, and succulent (a bough). Tender, soft (branch or plant), delicate (youth). Water before it springs up. ثأد مأد *sa,dun ma,dun*, Easy, soft (place).

A مادّ *mādd*, Who or what extends or prolongs. A wire-drawer.

A مادام *mā dām*, (or P مادامكه *mā dām ki*) (or ما داميكه) During, whilst, so long as, until that.

A مآدب *ma,ādib*, (pl. of مأدبة *ma,dabat* or *ma,dubat*) Feasts, entertainments.

A مأدبة *ma,dabat* or *ma,dubat*, (pl. مآدب *ma,ādib*) A feast, entertainment to which one is invited.

A مأدة *ma,dat*, Soft, tender, delicate (girl).

A مادّة *māddat*, (pl. موادّ) Continued augmentation. Matter. Article, point, subject, argument.

P مادچين *mād-chīn*, A loop or ouch.

A مادح *mādih*, A praiser, encomiast.

A مادخ *mādikh*, Great, excellent, precious.

P مادر *mādar*, A mother. مادر آب و آتش *mādari āb u ātish*, (Mother of water and fire) Who sheds tears of grief. مادر باغ *mādari bāgh*, The earth. A garden. مادر بخطا *mādar ba khutā*, A term of abuse. اقبال مادرزاد *ikbāli mādar-zād*, Fortune, prosperity from the cradle.

A مادر *mādir*, One who plasters with clay. Name of a man proverbial for his avarice.

P مادر اندر *mādar-andar*, A stepmother.

P مادر دخت *mādar dukht*, Mallows.

P مادرزاد *mādar-zād*, Innate, congenital, sucked in with the mother's milk. كور مادر زاد *kūri mādar-zād*, Blind from one's birth.

P مادر زادي *mādar-zādī*, Birth.

P مادرزن *mādar-zan*, A wife's mother.

P مادرندر *mādarandar*, A stepmother.

P مادره *mādira*, A country in the west, Madeira?

P مادري *mādarī*, Maternal.

P مادگي *mādagī*, Female nature, feminality.

P مادندر *mādandar*, A stepmother.

A مأدور *ma,dūr*, (pl. مآدير *ma,ādīr*) Ruptured.

A مأدوم *ma,dūm*, (Bread) dressed or eaten with meat or fish. اطعمتك مأدومي *at,amtuka ma,dūmī*, I have put a sop for you in my victuals, *i.e.* I have made you all the apology in my power.

P ماده *māda*, A female. مادهٔ شير *mādaʼi sher*, A lioness. When affixed to a noun it denotes the female, as the word "she" prefixed in English: as, خرس ماده *khirs-māda*, A she-bear. سگ ماده *sag-māda*, A she-dog, a bitch.

A ماده *mādih*, (pl. مدّه) A praiser, commender.

P ماده سگ *māda-sag*, (She-dog) A bitch.

P مادگان *mādagān*, (pl. of ماده *māda*) Females.

P ماده گاو *māda-gāv*, A cow.

A مادّي *māddiy*, Material. علّت مادّيه *'illati māddiya*, A material cause.

P ماديان *mādiyān*, A mare.

A مآدير *ma,ādīr*, (pl. of مأدور *ma,dūr*) Ruptured.

P مادينه *mādīna*, A female in general.

A ماذ *māz*, Good-natured, gay, jovial.

P ماذر *māzar*, A mother.

P ماذريون *māzariyūn*, A Persian plant 5 or 6 feet high, bearing green berries like capers, which, being preserved in vinegar, are excellent for the dropsy.

A ماذل *māzil*, Weak, languid. One quite content and satisfied to relinquish any thing.

A مأذنة *ma,zanat*, (vulg. *mi,zanat*) A tower belonging to a mosque, from which the crier (مؤذّن *mu,azzin*) proclaims the hour of prayer.

A مأذون *ma,zūn*, Dismissed, suffered to depart. Licensed, permitted, allowed. Pained in the ear (اذن *uzn* or *uzun*). A privileged slave.

A ماذيّ *māziy*, New, white, pure, excellent honey. Arms or armour. A smooth coat of mail. ماذي مشار *māziy mushār*, White honey, for the procurement of which one has had recourse to assistance.

A ماذيانات *māziyānāt* or *māzayānāt*, Places through which water flows, water-courses. Grass growing about rivulets.

A ماذيّة *māziyat*, A woman. Mild, pleasant wine. A soft breast-plate or corslet. A shining coat of mail.

P مار *mār*, A serpent. A beating or striking. An accountant. An account-book, register. Sick, unwell. A mother. Name of the governors of Georgia. It is also sometimes used for ميار *mayār*, Bring not. مار افعي *māri af,a'*, A viper. مار بدست ديگري گرفتن *mār ba dasti dīgare giriftan*, To take the snake by another's hand, (met.) To employ another in any perilous business. مار پلاس *māri palās* or *mār-palās*, A lizard. مار خوردن *mār khwurdan*, To devour a snake, (met.) To suffer grief. مار در پيراهن *mār dar pīrāhan*, A snake in the sleeve, (met.) A neighbouring foe. مار دو زبان *māri du zabān*, A double-tongued serpent, *i.e.* a hypocrite. مار شكم سوراخ *mari shikam-sūrākh*, A musical pipe with seven stops. مار ضحّاكي *māri zahhākī*, A chain, fetter. مار قهقهه *māri kahkaha*, A basilisk. مار مصري *māri misrī*, An Egyptian spear. مار نه سر *māri nuh sar*, The nine heavens.

A مأر *ma,r*, (v. n. of مأر) Exciting enmities, instigating one against another. Filling (a leathern bottle). (v. n. of مئر) Meditating hostility. *Ma,ar*, (v. n. of مئر) Becoming corrupt (a wound).

A مار *mār*, (from the Syriac) A lord. A saint. مار يعقوب *mār ya,kūb*, Name of a heretical teacher of Christianity, whose followers in the East are called Jacobites to this day. مار سرجيس *mār sarjis*, Saint Serjius.

A مارّ *mārr*, A passer, walker, goer. Any one, some person. That which passes away, the past. مارّ البيان *mārru'l bayān*, The before-mentioned, the above-explained.

P مارا *mārā*, Us. To us.

P ماراب *mārāb*, Recent good fortune.

P مار اسپند *mār ispand*, (ماراسپندان *mār ispandān*, مار اسفند *mār isfand*, or ماراسفندان *mār isfandān*) The twenty-ninth day of the Persian month. Name of an angel.

P مار افسا *mār-afsā*, (مار افسار *mār-afsār*, مار افسان *mār-afsān*, or مار افساي *mār-afsāy*) A tamer or charmer of serpents.

P ماران *mārān*, (pl. of مار *mār*) Serpents. Smiths.

A مأرب *ma,rab*, The time or place for any necessary business. *Masrib*, A small place between Sanā and Hazramawt in Yaman, famous for salt.

P ماربالشي *mār-bālishī*, An asp.

A مأربة *masrabat, masrubat*, or *masribat*, (pl. مآرب *masārib*) Any thing necessary to be done. Necessity, indigence; (whence the proverb) مأربة لاحفاوة *masrabat lā hafāwat*, Necessity is not importunity, *i.e.* necessity has no law.

P ماربين *mārbīn*, Name of a district consisting principally of gardens near Ispahān.

P مارپا *mār-pā*, Having feet like a serpent.

P مارپیچ *mār-pech*, Circumvolution.

P مارتن *mār-tan*, Having a body like a serpent.

P مارتول *mārtol*, (PORT. Martello) A hammer.

A مارج *mārij*, Flame without smoke.

A مارجيّ *mārijīy*, (A Christian) perverse in religion.

P مارچوبه *mār-choba*, Asparagus. A kind of grass (so called from its resemblance to a snake).

A مارخ *mārihh*, Flowing, current. Who or what causes to flow or run.

A مارخة *mārikhat*, Name of a certain woman who used to assume airs of excessive modesty until she was discovered one day grubbing in a grave: hence the proverb, هذا حياء مارخة *hazā hayāsu mārikhat*, This is Mārikhat's delicacy (for you).

P مارخوار *mār-khwār*, The wild ox. A kind of wild sheep.

A مارد *mārid*, (pl. مردة *maradat*) Contumacious, stubborn, rude, insolent, proud. High, elevated, lofty. Name of a certain fortress; also of a man.

P ماردي *mārdī* or *māridī*, Red.

P ماردين *māridīn*, City and fort in Mesopotamia.

A مأرز *masriz*, An asylum, lurking-place.

P مارسار *mār-sār*, Name of the tyrant Zahhāk.

P مارسان *mārisān*, An hospital, infirmary.

P مارستان *māristān*, A place abounding with serpents (مار *mār*). An hospital or infirmary (a contraction of بيمارستان *bīmaristān*).

P مارش *mārash*, Name of an old idol-temple.

A مارض *māriz*, Sick, infirm, diseased.

A مارع *māriʿ*, A place full of grass and fodder.

A مارعة *māriʿat*, Name of a king and father of a tribe, whose descendants were called موارع.

A مارغ *māriġh*, A fool.

P مارفش *mārfash*, Name of the tyrant Zahhāk.

A مارق *mārik*, An apostate.

A مارقة *mārikat*, Schismatics.

G مارقشيشا *mārkashīsā*, The marcasite.

P مارگزيدگي *mār-gazīdagī*, A snake-bite.

P مارگزيده *mār-gazīda*, Snake-bitten.

P مارگياه *mār-giyāh*, Asparagus.

P مارگير *mār-gīr*, A snake-catcher. A shrewd rogue.

P مارماهي *mār-māhī*, (Snake-fish) An eel.

P مارمهره *mār-muhra*, A stone found in the head or brain of a large serpent (sometimes black, sometimes ash-coloured, marked with three lines).

A مارن *mārin*, Limber and hard (spear). The nose, or the point or soft part of it.

P مارناك *mārnāk*, A place full of serpents.

P ماريدر *mārandar*, A mother-in-law.

P مارنه *mārina*, Goats'-beard (an herb).

P مارو *mārū*, A mother.

A P ماروت *mārūt*, Great. Name of a king. Name of an angel, and companion of هاروت *hārūt*.

A مارورة *mārūrat*, A soft, delicate girl, tremulous from fat. A black and bitter grain growing in wheat.

A مأروش *masrūsh*, Created, formed.

A مأروض *masrūz*, Troubled with a rheum or running at the nose. Worm-eaten (wood). Possessed by the demons called اهل الارض *ahlu'l arz*. Troubled with convulsions, or epilepsy.

A مأروضة *masrūzat*, Worm-eaten (wood).

A مأروط *masrūt*, (Leather) tanned or dressed with with the bark of the tree ارطى *arta'*; (a camel) fed with its fruit; extremely fond of it; or griped from eating too much of it.

P ماروغ *mārūgh*, A kind of puff or fungus.

A مأروق *masrūk*, (Corn) mildewed, smutty.

A ماروق *mārūk*, Blighted, mildewed, smutty (corn). Jaundiced (man).

A مأروك *masrūk*, An origin, root.

A مأرومة *masrūmat*, Handsome and well-made (girl). Firm-fleshed. Desert, desolate, empty (place).

P مارون *mārūn*, Name of a stone which, when dissolved in vinegar, is good for the eyes. Name of a medicine.

P ماره *māra*, An account. A seal, stamp.

P ماري *mārī*, Smitten, slain. Trod. A virgin.

A ماري *mārī*, A young bullock smooth and white. A kind of small narrow-striped cloak. Woollen breeches. A worn garment. A hunter of the bird called قطا *katā*.

P ماريانه *māriyāna*, A bit of sugar. A sweetmeat.

A مارية *māriyat*, White, shining (woman). A cow whose calf is sleek and white. A she-calf smooth and white. Name of the daughter of one Arkam, whose valuable ear-rings are proverbial. (She presented them to the Kaaba). Name of an Egyptian woman, by whom Muhammad had a son called ابراهيم *ibrāhīm*. A female of the bird called قطا *katā*. خذه و لو بقرطى مارية *khuzhu wa law bi hurtay māriyat*, Procure it, though with Māriyat's ear-rings, *i.e.* at any cost.

A ماريّة *māriyat*, The bird called katā.

P ماريره *mārīra*, A mother-in-law.

P ماز *māz*, A chink in a wall or door. A wrinkle. A gall or oak-apple. A purgative medicine. A plait, fold. A twist. One particle or ingredient in ink.

P مازار *māzār*, A druggist, a vender of simples. (for ميازار *mayazār*) Do not afflict.

A مازج *māzij*, One who mixes, mixer, mingler.

A مازح *māzih*, A joker, a jester.

A مآزر *masāzir*, (pl. of مئزر *mizar*) Aprons. Breeches, trowsers.

A مازِرأسك *māzi rassaka*, Stretch out your neck (pronounced when going to behead a man).

P مازريون *māzaryūn*, Mezereon, spurge-olive.

A مأزفة *maszifat*, (pl. مآزف *masāzif*) Excrement, human dung. Dirt, filth.

A مأزق *maszik*, A narrow place. A close-fought field of battle.

P مازل *māzil*, A mountain in Hindūstān.

A مأزل *maszil*, A narrow place, strait.

A مأزم *maszim*, (pl. of مآزم *masāzim*) A narrow place, pass (as between mountains, aut naturæ muliebris); a narrowness of fortune, difficulties in life. A field of battle. *Maszim*, (or مأزمان *maszimāni*) Name of a narrow pass between Mecca and Mina, and another between Muzdalifat and Mount Arafāt.

P مازن *māzan*, The back-bone. A groove in the back caused by fatness.

A مازن *māzin*, The eggs of ants. Name of the father of a tribe.

P مازند *māzand*, (or مازندر *māzandar*) (for مازندران *māzandarān*) Name of a country near the Caspian Sea, to the north of Gīlān.

P مازنين *māznīn*, Name of a man who built the fortress of سنگويه *sangūya*, in India, with the cooperation of a woman named مازينه *māzīna*.

P مازو *māzū*, A gall or oak-apple. One particle or ingredient in the composition of ink. The back-bone. A harrow. A roller.

A مأزوّ *maszūw*, Worn with labour and vexation.

A مأزورة *maszūrat*, (for موزورة *mawzūrat* for the sake of rhyming with مأجورة *masjūrat*) Laden with sin and guilt, criminal.

P مازون *māzūn*, A certain astringent medicament, or constringent lotion, used by women.

P مازه *māza*, The back-bone. The groove down the middle of the back.

P مازه‌در *māza-dar*, (or مازه درد *māza-dard*) A pain in the back, lumbago.

A مازي *māzī*, Separate, asunder.

P مازياره *māzyāra*, A sweet dish or confection.

P مازينه *māzīna*, The woman who assisted Māznīn in the erection of the fortress of Sangūyah.

P ماژ *māj*, Sport, play, mirth, merriment. ماژ و موژ *māj u mūj*, The cry of a mouse at the sight of a cat or a snake.

P ماژدر *mājdar*, A large serpent.

P ماژديستان *mājdīstān*, (in zand and Pāzand) Purity, freedom from sin.

P ماس *mās*, (for آماس) Tumour, swelling.

A مأس *mass*, (v. n. of مأس) Rubbing (a skin or hide). Breeding dissensions. Having much milk in the udder (a camel). Being large or deep (a wound). Being angry, enraged against.

A ماس *mās*, Light, fickle (man), one on whom advice or reproof is thrown away. A diamond.

A ماسّ *māss*, Contiguous, adjacent, touching.

Nearest (kindred). Important, urgent, pressing (business), demanding care and concern.

P ماساي *māsāy*, (for مياساي *mayāsāy*) Rest not.

A ماسبق *mā sabak*, What precedes or has preceded; any thing past, said, or done.

P ماست *māst*, Sour, coagulated milk. Mastich.

P ماستابه *māstāba*, (ماستاوه *māstāva*, ماستوا *māst-wā*, ماستبا *māst-bā*, ماستو *māstū*, ماستونه *māstūna*, or ماستينه *māstīna*) Butter-milk strained, thickened, and dried. A dish dressed with dried sour milk.

P ماست دان *māstdān*, A bottle for churning.

P ماست مايه *māst-māya*, Rennet for curdling.

A ماسح *māsih*, A comber. One who indulges much in venery. A liar. A land-measurer. One who curries. (An excresence on the callous part of a camel's breast) which galls the elbows, yet not so as to fetch blood.

A ماسحة *māsihat*, A comber, tire-woman.

A ماسخة *māsikhat*, Name of a celebrated maker of bows of the tribe of ازد *azd*.

A ماسخي *māsikhīy*, A bow-maker.

A ماسخيّات *māsikhiyāt*, Good bows (named from the maker).

A مأسدة *masadat*, (or ارض مأسدة *arz masadat*) A country abounding in lions. A lion's den. (pl. of اسد *asad*) Lions.

A ماسط *māsit*, Bad, brackish water; a species of plant; or any thing which purges the bowels.

A ماسك *māsik*, Holding; retentive. قوّت ماسكه *kūwati māsika*, The retentive faculty.

A ماسكة *māsikat*, An interwoven affinity or relationship. The caul on a new-born infant or colt.

A ماسلف *mā salaf*, Before-mentioned or done.

A مأسوّ *masūw*, Cured, healed (wound).

A ماسوا *mā sawā*, That which is over. Exterior, outside. Besides, moreover, save.

P ماسوچه *māsūcha*, A turtle-dove, wood-pigeon.

A مأسور *masūr*, Bound, imprisoned. Pained by a strangury (اسر *usr*), strangurious.

P ماسور *māsūr*, Any thing mixed.

P ماسوره *māsūra*, A weaver's reed.

A مأسوف *masūf*, Vexed, troubled, grieved, sad. غير مأسوف عليه *ghayr masūf ʿalayhi*, At whom no one has been vexed.

A مأسوكة *masūkat*, A woman circumcised badly.

A ماسئ *māsiʾ*, Fearless, forward, impudent.

A ماسي *māsī*, One who listens to no advice.

P ماسيدن *māsīdan*, To break out in blotches. To coagulate (as milk); to congeal. To lick.

A مآسيق *maʾāsīk*, (pl. of ميساق *mīsāk*) Birds flapping their wings when flying.

P ماش *māsh*, Pease. Pulse. ماش عطّار *māshi ʿattār*, Name of a small black grain. ماش هندي *māshi hindī*, A sort of vetch.

A ماش *māsh*, A small round green pulse. Mean, common household furniture. الماش خير من لاش *al māsh khayr min lāsh*, Shabby furniture is better than an empty house.

A مأش *mash*, (v. n. of مأش) Driving off, thrusting away. Shaving, grazing the ground (rain).

P ماشاد *māshād*, A woollen garment.

P ماش دارو *māsh-dārū*, Ground-pine.

SY ماشرا *māsharā*, A bloody swelling.

A ماشرة *māshirat*, Ground whose vegetation shakes through freshness.

P ماشرز *māsharz*, Forceps, pincers.

A ماشط *māshit*, One who combs; a comber.

A ماشطة *māshitat*, (pl. مواشط *mawāshit*) A tire-woman, comber, or dresser (of a bride). A clever woman, good manager.

A ماشل *māshil*, Lean, spare of flesh.

P ماشو *māshū*, A sieve, searce, bolting or ranging sieve. A spattle, ladle, skimmer. A coarse woollen garment.

P ماشوب *māshūb*, A sieve, searce. (for مياشوب *mayāshūb*) Do not distress yourself, be not disturbed.

P ماشور *māshūr*, Things mixed together.

A مأشورة *mashūrat*, Sawed, split (wood).

P ماشوره *māshora*, A reed used by weavers to wind their thread upon. A syphon, pipe, spout. Raw thread or yarn. Any thing mixed. A sort of game. ماشورهٔ عاج *māshorai ʿāj*, The neck of a mistress.

P ماشوه *māshuh*, A sieve.

P ماشه *māsha*, Tongs, smiths' forceps; pincers. A weaver's brush. A spade. A small weight. A twelfth of a تولچه *tūlcha*, weighing $2\frac{1}{2}$ مثقال *miskāl*. That part of a match-lock which holds the match.

P ماشي *māshī*, Any dish made of pease.

A ماشي *māshī*, (pl. مشاة *mushāt*) Rich in flocks. A goer, walker, traveller. On foot. A pedestrian. An informer, tale-bearer.

P ماشيا *māshiyā*, Wild tansy.

A ماشية *māshiyat*, (pl. مواشي *mawāshī*) Quadrupeds, Sheep, oxen, or camels. (A she-camel) having many colts. (A woman) having many children.

A مآشير *maʾāshīr*, (pl. of مئشار *mishār*) Saws. Knobs at the ends of locusts' tails: serrulations.

P ماشيوه *māshewah*, A sieve. A strainer.

P ماص *mās*, The moon.

A مأص *maʾas*, White and noble camels.

A ماصّ *māss*, A sipper, sucker. ويلي علي ماصّان بن ماصّان *wayli ʿala' māssāni bin māssān*, May my troubles and sorrows light on him!

A ماصّة *māssat*, A child's disease (hair growing on the back-bone, which, unless removed, prevents digestion).

A ماصدق *mā sadak*, That which is true. Any thing which demonstrates, confirms, or verifies.

A مأصر *masir* or *masar*, (pl. مآصر *maʾāsir*) A place of confinement, a prison.

A ماصر *māsir*, (A sheep) giving little milk. (pl. مصار *misār*) (A camel) which gives her milk slowly. Whatever separates or intercepts two objects.

A ماصع *māsiʿ*, Shining, glittering, glancing. Salt (water), small in quantity, and muddy. Going away, departing. Altered, changed. ماصعة الدرّ *māsiʿatu'd darr*, (A camel) whose milk diminishes or dries up.

A ماصل *māsil*, Small (present), little (milk).

A ماضح *māzih*, One who hurts another's character.

A ماضر *māzir*, (Milk) becoming sour. Extremely white.

A ماضغان *māzighāni*, (dual) Two veins in the jaw. The roots of the jaws.

A ماضغة *māzighat*, The jaw, that part whence the teeth grow. A fool.

A ماضويّ *māzawīy*, Relating to the past tense.

A ماضي *māzī*, (pl. f. ماضات *māziyāt*) Passing away; past. Dead. Swift, fleet, expeditious. Quick, clever, expert. Sharp, piercing (sword). The preterite. A lion. A sword. الماضي *al māzī*, The past, time past. الماضي ما يذكر *al māzī mā yuzkar*, Of the past nothing is mentioned. ماضي استمراري *māzī istimrārī*, The imperfect tense. ماضي بعيد *māzī baʿīd*, The preter-pluperfect. ماضي قريب *māzī karīb*, The preterperfect. ماضي العزيمة *māzi'l ʿazīmat*, Successful in his plans. ماضي مشكوك *māzī mashkūk*, The preterite subjunctive or doubtful preterite. ماضي مطلق *māzī mutlak*, Preterite positive or absolute past. فعل ماضي *fiʿli māzī*, The preterite tense. ام ماضيه وملل سالفه *umami māziya u milali sālifa*, The ancients, the people of former times.

A ماضيّ *māzīy*, Relating to the past tense.

A ماطخ *mātikh*, (A horse) that runs gently.

A ماطر *mātir*, (pl. مواطر) Raining, rainy.

A ماطع *mātiʿ*, Who eats with the fore-teeth.

A ماطل *mātil*, Name of a celebrated camel.

A مأطور *matūr*, A well situated near another. Water lying in a level spot, and directed towards a tree that it may not flow away, and be lost.

A مأطورة *matūrat*, A leathern milk-pail, whose rim (اطار *itār*) is made of wood.

A مأطوم *matūm*, Bound in the body, costive.

A ماعج *māʿij*, Swift-paced (ass).

A ما عدا *mā ʿadā*, That which is past. Besides, except. That which follows or remains; sequel, rest.

A ماعز *māʿiz*, (pl. مواعز *mawāʿiz*) A goat (male or female). Goats' leather. Strong, muscular. A man sinewy and strong-built. Shrewd, clever, and able to defend what is behind him.

A ماعض *māʿiz*, Angry, vexed, sick at heart.

A ماعون *māʿūn*, (pl. مواعين *mawāʿīn*) Any kind of household utensils, as kettles, pots, hatchets, or any thing of similar necessary use. That part of a man's effects which was dedicated to pious uses. Any thing whereby one is benefited. Obedience, submission to God. Kindness, good-will, favour, courtesy. Any thing refused and withheld. Rain. Water. Leather. اعطاك الماعون *aʿtāka'l māʿūna*,

He submitted to you. ضربها حتّي اعطت ماعونها *zarabaha hatta' aʿtat māʿūnaha*, He beat her till she mended her pace.

A ماعي *māʿī*, Tender, soft (meat).

A ماعية *māʿiyat*, (A woman) enraged and pouring forth invectives.

P ماغ *māgh*, A cormorant, having a black spot on the head. A kind of pigeon, greenish or reddish about the wings, breast, and tail. A mist, a fog.

A ماغية *māghiyat*, Pleasant-spoken (woman).

A ما فات *mā fāt*, That which is past.

A ما فوق *mā fawk*, Beyond, without, above, aforesaid. ما فوق الحدّ *mā fawka'l hadd*, That which is beyond all bounds.

A مأفوك *maʾfūk*, Weak, deficient in understanding, inverted, subverted. Unfortunate. Flattered by hope, credulous, sanguine (like weak men).

A مأفوكة *maʾfūkat*, (Land) wanting rain and yielding nothing.

A مأفول *maʾfūl*, Weak, silly, deficient.

A مأفون *maʾfūn*, Corrupted, tainted, rotten (meat or nut). Silly, deficient in understanding. Pleasing, surprising, and good for nothing. A vain-boaster.

P مافه *māfa*, The bar of a door.

A ما في البال *mā fi'l bāl*, (ما في الضمير *mā fi'z zamir*, or ما في الفؤاد *mā fi'l fuʾād*) That which is in the mind; intention, thought, design, reflection.

A ما في نفس الامر *mā fi nafsi'l amr*, What is in the thing itself, *i. e.* essence, substance, principle.

A مأق *maʾk*, (or ماق) The inner corner of the eye.

A ما قبل *mā kibal*, What precedes; antecedent.

A ماقة *māḳat*, The inner corner of the eye.

A مأقة *maʾakat*, (v. n. of مأق) Sighing, sobbing, breathing with difficulty. A sob. Anger.

A ماقت *māḳit*, A hater.

A مأقط *maʾkit*, A field of battle. Difficulty, straits in battle.

A ماقط *māḳit*, (A horse) unable to move from lassitude and attenuation. The freedman of a freedman. The straitest and narrowest part of a battle-field. (pl. مقط *mukut*) A halter or bridle. The rope of a bucket. A diviner who prognosticates by throwing flints and gravel. ساقط بن ماقط بن لاقط *sāḳit bin māḳit bin lāḳit*, A reproachful mode of expression.

P ماقوت *māḳūt*, Name of a sweetmeat.

A مأقوط *maʾkūt*, (Meat) dressed with اقط *akit*. Heavy, unwholesome.

A مآقي *maʾāḳī*, (pl. of مأقي *maʾḳi*) Inner corners of eyes.

A مأقا *maʾka'*, The inner corner of the eye.

A ماقي *māḳī*, (pl. مواقي *mawāḳī* or مآقي *maʾāḳī*) The outer or inner corner of the eye.

P ماكان *mākān*, Name of a certain judge. Name of a country.

P ماكاني *mākānī*, Native of Mākān. A short spear or javelin used by the natives of that country.

A ماكث *mākis*, Permanent, durable, abiding.

A ماكد *mākid*, (fem. ماكدة) Perennial, unfailing.

A ماكدة *mākidat*, Perpetual (spring of water). (A camel) which gives much milk.

A ماكدون *mākadūn*, Macedonia. Nicomedia.

P ماكر *mākir*, The day after to-morrow.

A ماكر *mākir*, (pl. مكرة *makarat*) A deceiver, cheat. A troop of camels laden with raisins.

A ماكس *mākis*, A collector of tithe or tribute.

P ماكسين *mākisīn*, A town in خابور *khābūr*.

A مآكل *maʾākil*, (pl. of مأكلة *maʾkalat*) Victuals, eatables. مآكل ومشارب *maʾākil u mashārib*, Meats and drinks, eatables and drinkables. P در ملابس و مآكل *dar malābis u maʾākil*, In clothes and food.

A مأكل *maʾkal*, (v. n. of اكل) Eating. Gaining.

A مأكلة *maʾkalat* or *maʾkulat*, Aliment, food, any kind of nourishment. A pantry, larder, buttery. شاة مأكلة *shātun maʾkulatun*, A sheep fit for food.

A مأكم *maʾkam* or *maʾkim*, (مأكمة *maʾkamat*, or *maʾkimat*, (pl. مآكم *maʾākim*) Protuberant hip.

P ماكو *mākū*, A weaver's shuttle.

P ماكول *mākūl*, A glutton. A collar. A grown-up youth.

A مأكول *maʾkūl*, Eaten, devoured. Meat, food, victuals, viands. Eatable, edible, esculent. Subjects, people.

A مأكولات *maʾkūlāt*, (pl. of مأكول) Eatables.

A مأكوم *maʾkūm*, (Ground) eaten bare. Sad, sorrowful. One who conceals his grief.

P ماكيان *mākiyān*, A hen, fowl. ماكيان بياباني *mākiyāni biyābānī*, Jungle-fowl. An Ethiopian hen. A woodcock. ماكيان زاغ رنگ *mākiyāni zāgh-rang*, Night. ماكيان بر در كردن *mākiyān bar dar kardan*, To be extremely avaricious.

A مآل *maʾāl*, (v. n. of آل for اول) Returning, retiring. Failing, being deficient. A boundary, goal, any place whence, after reaching it, one immediately returns. Centre, foundation, or substance. End, event, consequence, issue, tendency. مآل مقال *maʾāli maḳāl*, The substance or tendency of the words. احوال خيرمآل *ahwāli khayr-maʾāl*, Affairs having a happy issue or tendency; fortunate circumstances. افعال شقا مآل *afʿāli shaḳā-maʾāl*, Actions having miserable tendency. P ياران حقيقت مآل *yārāni hakīkat-maʾāl*, Sincere friends. بي مآل *bī maʾāl*, Absurd, groundless. نقش بي مآل *nakshi bī maʾāl*, Writings without solidity, trifling.

P مال *māl*, Quiet, rest, repose. Alike, resembling. A lottery. (in comp. from ماليدن *mālīdan*) Wiping. Rubbing. Crushing. رومال *rū-māl*, A handkerchief, face-wiper. عدو مال *ʿadū-mal*, Crushing foes, exterminating enemies.

A مال *māl*, (pl. اموال *amwal*) Riches, money, property, wealth, possessions, stock, goods, effects, estate. Flocks, herds, cattle. Any thing yielding a revenue to the state. Rent or revenue arising from land. The product of any number multiplied by itself: thus, 9 is the مال *māl* or square number of 3. (pl. مالة *mālat* and مالون *mālūn*) Rich, affluent. مال اخروي *māli ukhrawī*, Blessings of futurity. مال دنيوي *māli dunyawī*, Temporal goods. P مال تحصيل كردن *māl tahsīl kardan*, To acquire riches. To collect revenue. مال تلف كردن *māl talaf kardan*, To squander wealth. مال زنده *māli zinda*, Live stock, cattle, flocks. A مال صامت *māli sāmit*, Gold and silver. مال ميري *māli mīrī*, Royal revenue or domains. مال ناطق *māli nātik*, Live stock. Coined gold or silver. مال ناطق و مال صامت *māli nātik u māli sāmit*, Goods moveable and immoveable; also an estate animate or inanimate (as slaves, flocks, herds, and money, lands, or houses). مال و جهات *māl u jihāt*, Rent of the grounds. مال ومتاع *māl u matāʿ*, Money and effects. بيت المال *baytu'l māl*, A treasury, exchequer. Confiscated goods.

A مأل *maʾal*, (v. n. of مأل) Coming to pass suddenly and finding one unprepared. Corpulent.

A مالّ *māll*, Tired, wearied, disgusted.

A ما لا كلام *mā lā kalām*, Unspeakable, inexpressible, unutterable, ineffable.

P مالامال *māl-ā-māl*, Heaped, brimful.

P مآل انديشي *maʾāl-andeshī*, Forethought.

P مالانك *mālānak*, A red peach.

A ما لا نهايه *mā lā nihāya*, Infinite. امكنهٔ ما لا نهايه *amkinaʾi mā lā nihāya*, Houses innumerable.

P مال آور *māl-āwar*, (Carrying off wealth) A name given to Arabian pirates.

P مالاي *mālāy*, (for ميلاي *mayālāy*) Defile not.

A ما لا يطاق *mā lā yatāk*, Insupportable.

A ما لا يعني *mā lā yaʿnī*, Foolish, unmeaning.

A ما لا ينحلّ *mā lā yanhall*, Inexplicable.

P مالبخش *māl-bakhsh*, Name of the eighth day of the month.

P مالپرست *māl-parast*, A votary of mammon.

A مألة *maʾālat*, A being fat and thick.

A مألة *maʾlat*, (pl. مثال *miʾāl*) A meadow. A mill or wheel. *Maʾalat*, (v. n. of مأل) Coming to pass suddenly, and finding one unprepared.

A مالة *mālat*, (fem. of مال *māl*) Wealthy (lady). (pl. of مال *māl*) Rich, opulent. (pl. of مائل *māʾil*) Inclined, leaning to.

T مالته *mālta*, The island of Malta.

A مالج *mālaj*, (P ماله *māla*) A plasterer's trowel.

A مالح *mālih*, Salt (water). Salted (fish).

A مالخ *mālikh*, A fugitive.

P مالخانه *māl-khāna*, A treasury, storehouse.

P مال خاوند *māl-khāwand*, A man of property.

G مالخوليا *mālikholiyā*, Melancholy.

P مالداده *māl-dāda*, Bought with a price. A youth, slave.

P مالدار *māl-dār*, Rich, monied; a proprietor.

P مالداري *māl-dārī*, Opulence, wealth.

P مال زاده *māl-zāda*, A son of a whore; a pimp.

A مالازم *mālazim*, That which is necessary. P پرسش

مالزم *pursishi mā lazim*, Necessary inquiry.

P مال زمين *māl-zamin*, Land-security for debt.

P مالش *mālish*, A rubbing, kneading, polishing, furbishing, friction. Shampooing, tripsis. A furbishing-instrument.

P مالشگر *mālishgar*, A barber: one who scrubs or shampoos the bathers in a warm bath.

A مال ضامن *māl-zāmin*, Bondsman for the payment of rent or a debt.

A مال ضامني *māl-zāminī*, Security for rent or debt.

A مالطة *mālitat*, Malta.

A مالغ *māligh*, (pl. ملاغ *mullāgh*) Impure. A whoremonger.

A مال غيبي *māl-ghaybī*, Hidden or lost goods and treasure, which, when found, is the property of the state: treasure-trove.

A مألف *maʼlaf*, A place to which one is accustomed, and with which one is familiar. A leafy tree, the habitual resort of game. Society.

A مالق *mālak*, (from P مالة *māla*) An implement with which a husbandman smooths ploughed ground. A plasterer's trowel. *Mālik*, A flatterer.

A مالقة *mālakat*, Malaga, in Spain.

A مألك *maʼluk*, A mission, embassy.

A مالك *mālik*, (pl. املوك *umlūk*) A possessor, occupier, lord, master, proprietor, ruler. (pl. ملاك *mullāk* and مُلك *mullak*) A king. A pirate. Name of an angel. Name of the keeper of hell. A title of the Imām of Madina. مالك الحزين *māliku'l hazīn*, Name of a certain water-fowl. مالك دينار *māliki dīnār*, Name of a certain saint. P مالك زمين *māliki zamīn*, Lord of the soil. مالك شدن *mālik shudan*, To possess. مالك الملك بي همتا *māliku'l milki bī hamtā*, The Lord of the incomparable kingdom, *i.e.* God. A مالك يوم الدين *māliku yawmi'd dīn*, Lord of the day of judgment. ابو مالك *abū mālik*, Hunger. Old age. شجرة ابي مالك *shajarasi abī mālik*, Pearl-ashes, lye. امام مالك *imām mālik*, Name of one of the four great Muhammadan lawyers. P بي مالك *bī mālik*, Without owner, masterless.

P A مالكانه *mālkāna*, A sort of sweetmeat from seven kinds of nuts. A sweetmeat made from rice. A sort of date. *Mālikāna*, Like an owner, in the manner of an owner. An annual or monthly allowance paid to a زميندار *zamīn-dār* by the person who occupies his lands, whether it be the state or a جاگيردار *jāgīr-dār*. تصرّف مالكانه *tasarrufi mālikāna*, Complete possession, absolute dominion.

A مالكة *mālikat*, A queen. مالكة الزمان *mālikatu'z zamān*, Queen of the age. Name of Mahmūd Shah's empress.

A مألكة *maʼlu* or *maʼlakat*, Mission, embassy.

A مالكي *mālikī*, State of master, mastership.

A مالكيّ *mālikiy*, Royal, kingly.

A مالكية *mālikīyat*, Possession. Ownership.

P مالگانه *māl gāna*, Penis.

P مال گذار *māl-guzār*, A landholder, one who holds land under government. A tenant, subject.

P مال گذاري *māl-guzārī*, Land-revenue. The state of a renter. Assessed land.

A مالم *mā lam*, As long as not, whilst as yet not.

P مال مردم خور *māli mardum-khwur*, Consumer of the property of others; one who borrows and never pays.

P مال مست *māl-mast*, Purse-proud, boastful.

P مال مستي *māl-mastī*, Pride of wealth.

P مالمك *mālamk*, Barley-sugar.

P مالمكا *mālamkā*, A sweetmeat made of rice.

G مالنخوليا *mālankhūliyā*, Melancholy.

P مالندگي *mālandagī*, Friction.

A مألوس *maʼlūs*, (or مألوّ *maʼlūw*) (Leather) tanned with the bitter shrub الاء *alās*.

A مال واجب *māl wājib*, Revenue, rent, dues, estate. P مال واجب سركار *māl wājibi sarkār*, The revenue of the state.

P مالوالي *mālwālī*, A small Lybian lizard.

P مالور *mālwar*, Rich, opulent.

P مالوس *mālūs*, A green lizard. A sweetmeat.

A مألوس *maʼlūs*, Insane. Demoniacal. Foolish milk (which will not make butter).

A مألوع *maʼlūʻ*, Insane, mad, foolish.

A مألوف *maʼlūf*, Familiar, accustomed to live in friendship with. Habituated. Ordinary, customary. P مسكن مألوفش *maskani maʼlūfash*, His ordinary residence.

A مألوق *maʼlūk*, An ambassador. Name of a horse. *Maʼlūk* or *musawlak*, Mad, frantic, insane.

A مألوك *maʼlūk*, An ambassador, legate.

P مالول *mālol*, A grown-up lad. A glutton.

A مألولة *maʼlūlat*, Fatigued, wearied.

A مألوم *maʼlūm*, Sad, mournful, afflicted.

A مالون *mālūn*, (pl. of مال *māl*) Rich, monied.

A مألوه *maʼlūh*, Worshipped, adored, deified.

P مالوه *mālwa*, A province in central India.

P ماله *māla*, A trowel for plastering walls. Anything with which they smooth ground. A shoemaker or weaver's thread (of the fibres of a palm-tree). A harrow. Brimful. Friction.

A مالي *maʼālī*, (pl. of مِئْلاة *miʼlāt*) Handkerchiefs which women hold in their hands when weeping.

A مآليّ *maʼāliy*, Centrical. Belonging to a future life, or any place to which one necessarily returns.

A مالئ *māliʼ*, Filling; who fills, a filler.

P مالي *mālī*, Much, many, abundant.

A مالي *mālī*, Worth; the quality of becoming or constituting property. Of or belonging to the revenue. مالي و ملكي *mālī u mulkī*, Finance and government.

A مألّي *maʼlīy*, Tanned with the shrub الاء *alās*.

A ماليّ *māliy*, Pertaining to riches. Wealthy.

P ماليا *māliyā*, A tall slender tree, from which they make javelins.

A مآلية *maʼāliyat*, (fem. of مآليّ *maʼāliy*) Pertaining to a future life. امور مآليه *umūri maʼāliya*, Things which appertain to the next life.

A مالية *māliyat*, Opulence. Finance, exchequer.

G ماليخوليا *mālīkholiyā*, Melancholy, madness.

P ماليدن *mālīdan*, To rub, polish, furbish, smooth. To shampoo. To chafe. To box the ears. To knead. To grind. To incrust. To bedaub, anoint, besmear. To thrust at and wound. To move a knife backwards and forwards (as in slaughtering). To resemble. To plough. To throw (one) down.

P ماليده *mālīda*, Rubbed. Polished. Shampooed. Broken in pieces. Anointed. Ploughed. Cakes made with flour, milk, butter, and sugar.

P ماليز *mālīz*, (and مالين *mālīn*) A leech.

P مام *mām*, Mother, mamma.

P ماما *māmā*, Mother (old women are so called).

A مأماة *maʼmaʼat*, The bleating (of a lamb).

P ماماچه *māmācha*, A midwife.

P ماماڻي *māmāʼī*, Midwifery. ماماڻيِ زنان كردن *māmāʼīsi zanān kardan*, To deliver a woman; to receive the infant.

A مآمر *maʼāmir*, (pl. of مؤتمر *muʼtamir*) Muharrams.

A ما مضى *mā maza'*, That which is past. مضى ما مضى *maza' mā maza'*, That which is past is past, let bye-gones be bye-gones; speak not of the past.

P مامك *māmak*, A little mother.

A مأمل *maʼmal*, A place of hope.

A ماملك *mā malak*, All that one possesses.

A مأمن *maʼman*, A place of security. Name of a town in Irāk.

P مام ناف *mām-nāf*, A midwife.

P مام نافي *mām-nāfī*, Midwifery.

A مأموت *maʼmūt*, Fixed, appointed for, defined time. اجل مأموت *ajali maʼmūt*, An appointed term.

A مأمود *maʼmūd*, Boundary, term, end in view.

A مأمور *maʼmūr*, Fixed, defined, determined. Ordered, commanded. Any one to whom authority or orders are delegated; a commissary, plenipotentiary. Usage, established custom. حسب المأمور *hasba'l maʼmūr*, Agreeable to orders. مأمور به *maʼmūr bihi*, Ordered, commissioned, deputed. يوم المأمور *yawmu'l maʼmūr*, A day observed by the tribe of بني الحارث *banī'l hāris*.

A مأمورة *maʼmūrat*, Multiplied, grown numerous.

A مأموريّة *maʼmūriyat*, Command, order, commission. Submission to a mandate.

A ماموس *māmūs*, (or ماموسة) Fire: fire-place.

A ماموسة *māmūsat*, A foolish, unskilful woman.

A مأمول *maʼmūl*, Hoped for, expected. Hope.

A مأموم *maʼmūm*, Struck on the crown of the head, wounded in the dura mater, or in the brain. Hurt in the bunch (a camel). Whatever hurts the membranes of the brain.

P مامون *māmūn*, A kind of wild mint.

A مأمون *maʼmūn*, Rendered secure, preserved. Freed from, exempted. Firm, constant. An uncle by the mother's side. A person in whom confidence is placed, to whom one trusts. The great Almamūn.

son of Hārūn Ar'rashīd, and the seventh caliph of the house of Abbas. He reigned from A. D. 813 to 833. مأمون به maʼmūn bihi, Trusted, confided in.

A مأمونية maʼmūniyat, Name of a city in Irāk.

P ماموني‌ة māmūniya, Marchpane, sugared bread. A covering.

A مأموه maʼmūh, Pustulous (cattle). Disturbed in mind, bereft of reason.

P مامهستان māmahistān, Indian leaf (medicine).

P مامي māmī, A mother, matron.

A ماميثا māmīsā, Juice of a kind of poppy.

A مآمير maʼāmīr, (pl. of مؤتمر) Muharrams.

P ماميران māmīrān, Swallow-wort.

P مان mān, A lord. A family. Household furniture. Hereditary property, an heirloom. A house. Grief, melancholy; disease. Besides. Like, resembling. Agreeable. Eternal, perpetual. (for ما mā) We, us. Our. (imper. of ماندن māndan) Remain thou. Do thou resemble. Leave off, let alone, desist.

A مأن maʼn, (v. n. of مأن) Striking on the abdomen or lower belly. Carrying burdens or provisions (to others). Being cautious, wary, timid. Minding, regarding, attending to, caring for. Making provision for any undertaking. Preparing, getting ready, expediting. Searching, seeking; taking much trouble. Knowing. (pl. مؤون muʼūn) A ploughshare of wood or iron. The hypochondria.

A مان mān, A liar. A plough.

P مانا mānā, Alike, equal, resembling. Certainly. You would think or say. Forthwith, quickly, immediately. (in zand and Pāzand) A name of God.

A مانا mānan, Truly.

P مانافي mānāf, A midwife. The navel.

P مانافي mānāfī, Midwifery.

A مأنة maʼnat, (pl. مأنات maʼnāt and مؤون muʼūn) The hypochondria; navel, or the part of the belly surrounding it. Fat adhering to the peritoneum.

A مأنة maʼannat, A thing worthy of. A sure indication, an infallible sign or criterion.

A مانح mānih, A giver, bestower, liberal man.

P ماندگي māndagī, Fatigue, lassitude.

P ماندن māndan, To remain. To be redundant, superfluous. To be fatigued. To abandon, relinquish, leave, slight, neglect, dismiss. To place. To resemble. To dress, adapt. باز ماندن bāz māndan, To remain behind. پاي ماندن pāy māndan, To stand firm.

P مانده mānda, Remaining, left. Fatigued, tired, wearied. Permitting, dismissing. مانده شدن mānda shudan, To remain or stand still with fatigue. عمل مانده ʻamal-mānda, Unequal to any business from fatigue.

P مانستار mānistār, The universal spirit.

P مانستن mānistan, To resemble.

A مانع māniʻ, (pl. منعة manaʻat) A refuser, denier, forbidder, prohibiter. Close-fisted, avaricious. A stout defender of a fortress. Difficult of access, reserved. Impediment, obstacle, opposition, hindrance. مانعات رعاف و اسهال الدم māniʻāti ruʻāf u is-hāli'd dam, Styptics.

P مانك mānk, The moon. The sun.

P مانمن mānmin, (in zand) A drinking-cup.

P مانند mānand, Like, resembling. Resemblance. As, thus. دريا مانند daryā-mānand, Like the sea.

P مانداب mānandāb, The rainbow.

P مانند آباد mānand-ābād, The region برزخ.

P مانند mānanda, Like, resembling.

P مانو mānū, Echo. Voice, sound, rumour. The first month of the year according to the æra of Jalālu'd dīn.

A مأنوت maʼnūt, One who is envied.

P مانورك mānūrah, A lark. A duck. Name of a medicine.

A مأنوس maʼnūs, (or مأنوس به maʼnūsun bihi) Familiar, intimate. A companion, associate, friend. A domestic. Name of a man. مأنوس الاستعمال maʼnūs'l istiʻmāl, Any thing commonly used, trite, vulgar. P مشرّف و مأنوس شدن musharraf u maʼnūs shudan, To be favoured, honoured, respected. A سعادت مأنوس saʻādat-maʼnūs, Happy, the favourite of fortune. غزا مأنوس ghazā-maʼnūs, Inured to war, warlike.

P مانوسار mānūsār, One of the assassins of Dārā.

A مأنوسة maʼnūsat, Fire.

P مانوش mānūsh, Name of a mountain.

A مأنوف maʼnūf, Hurt in the nose (انف anf).

P مانوك mānūk, A lark. A large duck.

A مانويّ mānawīy, Manichœan, Manes' disciple.

P مانه māna, Household furniture. A house.

P ماني mānī, Thou remainest. Thou resemblest. Rare, uncommon. Name of a celebrated Persian painter, the founder of the sect of the Manichœans.

A ماني mānī, One who metes out or determines.

P مانيد mānīd, A sin, fault, failure. Omission. He is dead, at a stand-still (a phrase used at dice).

P مانيدن mānīdan, To remain. To resemble. To wander, err. To forget. To quit, forsake, let alone.

P مانيستار mānīstār, The soul of all.

A مأو maʼw, (v. n. of مأا for مأو) Extending, stretching (a hide or leathern bottle). Intensity, violence, severity. (pl. of مأوة maʼwat) Low grounds.

A مأوا maʼwa', A mansion, dwelling, abode, habitation. P مأوا گرفتن maʼwa' giriftan, To reside, make a settlement. A مأواي خواقين maʼwāyi khawāḳīn, The residence of the princes.

A مأواة maʼwāt, (v. n. of اوي) Being tenderly affected to, pitying, compassionating. A habitation.

A مآوب maʼāwib, (pl. of مآب maʼāb) Places to which one returns. Stages, resting-places.

A مؤوّب muʼawwab, Round, circular, compact. Muʼawwib, (Wind) blowing every day.

A مأوة maʼwat, Low ground.

A مآود maʼāwid, Misfortunes, evils.

P ماور māwar, (for مياور mayāwar) Bring not.

A ماوراء mā warāʼ, That which is behind, after. ماوراء النهر mā warāʼu'n nahr, That which is beyond (or behind) the river (Oxus), i. e. Transoxiana.

A مأوز maʼwaz, (A place) abounding in geese.

A مؤوّق muʼawwiḳ, Dilatory about one's food.

A ماوقع mā waḳaʻa, An accident.

A مؤولع muʼawlaʻ, Mad.

A مؤولق muʼawlaḳ, Insane, mad.

A مؤوّم muʼawwam, Large and ugly-headed.

A مأوي maʼwa' or maʼwī, A mansion. An asylum, refuge. Maʼwī, (or مأوي الابل maʼwi'l ibl) A place where camels are kept.

A مآويّ maʼāwīy, (pl. of مأويّة maʼwīyat) Mirrors.

A ماويّ māwīy, Any copy of verses, of which every distich ends in ما mā. Watery.

A مأوية maʼwiyat, (v. n. of اوي) Being touched, affected, commiserating.

A مأويّة maʼwīyat, A looking-glass. Name of a woman.

P ماه māh, The moon. A month, whether lunar or solar. Name of the twelfth day of every solar month. A mistress. (in Pahlevi) A city. A country. ماه آب māhi āb, Month of October. ماه بركوهان māhi barkohān, Name of a note of the bārbud. ماه بماه māh ba māh, From month to month, every month. ماه چارده شبه māhi chārdah shaba, The fourteenth day of the moon, i.e. full moon. ماه چو شاخ گوزن māhi chu shākhi gawazn, The new moon. ماه چهار هفته māhi chahār hafta, A term used to signify non-existent. ماه خرگهي māhi khargahī, The moon when surrounded by a halo, (met.) A mistress. ماه سي روزه māhi si roza, A moon thirty days old, i.e. very small, (met.) A delicate, weak, and sickly mistress. ماه سيام māhi siyām, (ماه كاشغر māhi kāshghar, ماه كش māhi kash, ماه مزوّر māhi muzawwar, ماه مقنّع māhi mukannaʻ, and ماه نخشب māhi nakhshab) A luminous appearance resembling the moon, produced from a well at the foot of mount Siyām by the juggler Mukanna every night during a period of four months. ماه سي شبه māhi sī shaba, An expression used to denote any thing annihilated, destroyed, vanished. ماه قصب پوش māhi kasab-posh, (or دوخته dokhta) A mistress arrayed in fine linen. ماه كاشغر māhi kāshghar, A beautiful Turkish damsel. ماه كنعاني māhi kanʻānī, (Moon of Canaan) Joseph, son of Jacob. ماه منجوق چتر māhi manjūk-chatr, A golden dome on a pavilion. ماه نو māhi nav, The new moon. The first month. ماه يماني māhi yamānī, The enlightened cheek of the most exalted of creatures, i. e. of Muhammad.

A ماه māh, A town or a large village. Water. ماه الفؤاد māhu'l fuʼād, (Watery-hearted) Cowardly. Stupid. ماه القلب māhu'l kalb, Foolish, stupid.

P ماهار māhār, A camel's halter, a bridle.

P ماه آفريد māh-āfrid, Name of a slave of Iraj.

P ماهان *māhān*, Name of a village dependent on Kirmān. (pl. of ماه *māh*) Moons, months.

P ماهانه *māhāna*, Monthly. Monthly wages.

P ماهاني *māhānī*, Name of a medicinal stone.

P ماه پار *māh-pār*, (Piece of the moon) Lovely.

P ماه پروار *māh-parwār*, (or پروين *parwīn*) Zedoary, a Chinese root like ginger, but perfumed.

P ماه پيكر *māh-paykar*, One with a face beautiful as the moon. ماه پيكر درفش *māh-paykari dirafsh*, An epithet of night.

A ماهة *māhat*, (v. n. of ماه for موه) Being full, overflowing with water (a well). Leaking (a ship). Silly, stupid (woman). (A well) which contains much water. Measles.

P ماهتاب *māh-tāb*, Moonlight, moonshine. The moon. The face of a mistress. A kind of firework. Breath, animal life.

P ماهتابي *māh-tābī*, A fire-work; blue light.

A ماهج *māhij*, Thin milk or fat.

P ماهچه *māhcha*, A little moon. A little gilded globe or crescent on the top of a flag-spear. A pin worn on the head or bosom. A gusset. A small weight, the twelfth part of a توچله *tūlcha*.

A ماهد *māhid*, Who spreads out. Name of God.

P ماهر *māhir*, (in zand and Pāz.) To-morrow.

A ماهر *māhir*, (pl. مهرة *maharat*) Acute, ingenious, sagacious, expert, cunning. Skilful in swimming. Master of any art.

P ماه رمه *māh rama*, Wimble, auger, trepan.

P ماهروزة *māh-roza*, An almanac, ephemeris. Date, day of the month.

P ماه فرفين *māh firfīn*, Zedoary.

P ماهگانه *māh-gāna*, (ماهگاني *māh-gānī* or *māhigānī*) A monthly pension; soldier's pay.

P ماه گرفت *māh-girift*, A lunar eclipse. A freckle or mole on a beautiful face.

A ماهل *māhil*, Who makes haste, or goes before.

P ماهلو *māhilū*, Stone-parsley. Jamaica pepper.

P ماهلوج *māhlūj*, Amomum.

A ماهن *māhin*, A domestic servant.

P ماهناك *māhnāk*, Enlightened by the moon. Moonlight.

P ماهو *māhū*, Ornament, decoration. A stick for driving camels. The name by which the princes of Sīstān are addressed.

A ماهو *mā huwa*, What is that? That which is.

P ماهوار *māhwār*, (or ماهوارة) Monthly stipend.

P ماهواري *māhwārī*, The revenue which is collected within a month. Monthly wages.

P ماهوبدانه *māhūbdāna*, (or ماهودانه) A cherry.

P ماهوبه *māhūba*, A title of the governor of Sīstān.

P ماهور *māhūr*, Name of a branch of music.

A مأهول *maʼhūl*, Inhabited, peopled.

P ماهويه *māhūya*, Name of a governor of Sīstān under Yazdagird, king of Persia.

P ماهه *māha*, Moonlight, a night illuminated by the moon and stars. A wimble, auger, gimlet. Pincers. A small weight, a twelfth of a توچله *tūlcha*. Monthly stipend.

P ماهي *māhī*, Lunar, monthly. A lunatic. A fish. The sign Pisces. ماهي گرفتن *māhī giriftan*, To fish. ماهي و چشمهٔ خضر *māhī u chashmaʼi khizr*, The tongue and mouth of a mistress.

A ماهي *māhī*, A pourer out of water. A Mede. *Mā hiya*, (fem.) That which is.

A ماهيّ *māhīy*, Watery. ماهيّ الفؤاد *māhīyu'l fuʼād*, Watery-hearted; cowardly, stupid.

P ماهيابه *māhiyāba*, The jelly of the fish called ماهي اشنه *māhī-ashna*, especially salted.

P ماهي اشنه *māhī-ashna*, A small kind of fish.

P ماهيان *māhiyān*, (pl. of ماه *māh*) Months. ماهيان و ساليان *māhiyān u sāliyān*, Months and years. (pl. of ماهي *māhī*) Fishes.

P ماهيانه *māhiyāna*, Monthly wages. Fish-jelly.

P ماهياوه *māhiyāwa*, Jelly of salted fish.

P ماهي بلورين *māhī-billawrīn*, A mistress's finger.

P ماهي پشت *māhī-pusht*, Fish-(hog-)backed.

A ماهيّة *māhīyat*, Quality, essence, value, intrinsic worth. Nature. State, condition, circumstances.

P ماهي توه *māhī-tawa*, A pan for frying fish.

P ماهيچه *māhīcha*, Slices of paste eaten in soup.

P ماهيچين *māhī-chīn*, A cormorant. A weir.

P ماهي خوار *māhī-khwār*, Piscivorous. An icthyophagist, fish-eater. A heron, crane.

P ماهي خورد *māhī khwurd*, A gudgeon: small fry.

P ماهي دان *māhīdān*, Fish-pond, store, stew.

P ماهي دانه *māhī-dāna*, A cherry.

P ماهي دندان *māhī-dandān*, A fish's tooth, of which the hilts of swords are made.

P ماهي ربيان *māhī-rabyān*, A shrimp.

P ماهي ريز *māhī-rez*, (or ريزه *reza*) An anchovy.

P ماهيز *māhīz*, The herb mullein.

P ماهيزاد *māhī-zād*, The row or spawn of fish.

P ماهي زرين *māhī-zarīn*, A sand-eel. A skink.

P ماهي زهره *māhī-zahra*, A poisonous yellow-flowering milk grass. (Thrown into water it intoxicates the fish and brings them to the surface).

P ماهي سپهر *māhī-sipihr*, The sign Pisces.

P ماهي سيم *māhī-sīm*, (or ماهي شيم *māhī-shīm*) A kind of small sturgeon. A shad.

P ماهي فروش *māhī-farosh*, A fishmonger.

P ماهي گرد *māhī-gird*, A turbot: sturgeon: shad.

P ماهي گول *māhī gol*, A carp.

P ماهي گير *māhī-gīr*, A fisherman. An otter.

P ماهي مار *māhī-mār*, (Fish-snake) An eel.

P ماهي مراتب *māhī-marātib*, Certain honours of which the privilege is especially conferred on princes and great nobles. They are denoted by the figure of a fish with other insignia (two balls), carried as ensigns upon elephants.

P ماهينه *māhīna*, Monthly pay or pension.

P ماي *māy*, Any stinging or biting animal, as serpents, leeches, &c. Name of a city in India, which, according to Castellus, was much celebrated for sorcery. Name of a king of India. (for ميأي *mayāy*) Do not come.

A مأي *maʼy*, (v. n. of مأي) Extending, stretching. Using diligence, straining every nerve. Going deeply into. Budding, beginning to shoot (a tree), putting forth leaves. Making with one's self a hundred. Whispering, and exciting thereby dissensions. *Miʼan*, (pl. of مائة *miʼat*) Hundreds.

P مايان *māyān*, We, us.

A مائة *miʼat*, (pl. مئات *miʼāt*, مئون *miʼūn*, and مأي *miʼa'*) A hundred. ابن المائة *ibnu'l miʼat*, A man a hundred years old (Son of a hundred).

A مائت *māʼit*, Dying. Moribund. موت مائت *mawti māʼit*, A hard, painful, lingering death.

A مائتان *miʼatāni*, du. of مائة *miʼat*, Two hundred.

A ما يتحلل *mā yataḥallal*, Whatever is dissolvable by liquefaction or concoction.

A مائج *māʼij*, Tossed by the waves. Stormy.

A ما يحتاج *mā yaḥtāj*, What is needed.

P مايخوش *māy-khwush*, Subacid.

A مائدة *māʼidat*, (pl. موائد *mawāʼid*) A table, especially one covered with victuals. A circle, circumference, circuit, orbit. P مائدهٔ خرگهي *māʼidaʼi khargahī*, The joys of Paradise.

P مائده سالار *māʼida-sālār*, (or مائده نه *māʼida-nih*) A table-decker, a sewer.

A مائر *māʼir*, (pl. ميّار *muyyār* and ميّارة *mayyārat*) Who brings grain from other countries for family-use or sale. A purveyor. (An arrow) light, and which strikes the mark.

A مائرة *māʼirat*, Flowing (blood).

A مائس *māʼis*, Who walks proudly, waving from side to side. A calumniator, a whisperer.

A مائع *māʼiʻ*, Melted, fluid. Liquor.

A مائعات *māʼiʻāt*, Liquids, fluids.

A مائعة *māʼiʻat*, A certain ottar or perfume exceedingly fragrant. Storax. Oil of myrrh. The forelocks of a horse long and flowing.

A ما يعرف *mā yuʻraf*, Whatever is known; all.

A مائق *māʼiḳ*, (pl. موقيٰ *mawḳa'*) Stupid, silly, mad, foolish. احمق مائق *aḥmaḳ māʼiḳ*, An arrant fool, sheer blockhead.

A ما يقرأ *mā yuḳraʼ*, What is read, legible.

A مائل *māʼil*, (pl. مالة *mālat* and ميّل *muyyal*) Inclining, inclined, propense, biased. Who takes delight in, affectionate, partial to, addicted. An eccentric orbit. مائل الخدّ *māʼilu'l khadd*, Wry-cheeked.

A مائلات *māʼilāt*, Women who walk with a swinging, flaunting, jaunty, or haughty air; or who swerve from obedience to God; or who wear their hair in the fashion called ميلاء *maylāʼ*.

A مائلة *māʼilat*, (pl. موائل *mawāʼil*) A (camel's) bunch. Large (sand-hill). Very branchy (tree). (A woman) waving gracefully when walking.

P مائلتر *māʼiltar*, More inclined.

A مأيمة *maʼyamat*, A cause of widowhood. الحرب مأيمة *al ḥarbu maʼyamat*, War destroys men, and bereaves women of their sons and husbands.

A مائن *māʼin*, A liar.

P مايندر *māyandar*, A stepmother.

A مأيوس *maʼyūs*, Desperate, hopeless. P مأيوس شدن *maʼyūs shudan*, To despair, lose hope.

P مايون *māyūn*, Name of Farīdūn's cow.

P مايه *māya*, Ferment, leaven. Root, origin, principle, essence. Foundation. Wealth, money, cash. A capital in trade, stock, principal. Semen virile. Measure. Quantity, amount. A woman. The female of any animal; and a female camel in particular. Name of Farīdūn's cow. A coat-button or loop. Name of a note in music. مايهٔ شب *māyaʼi shab*, Darkness of night. مايهٔ صدق *māyaʼi sidk*, Name of Abū bakr. مايه و سود *māya u sūd*, Principal and interest.

P مايه خوش *māya-khwush*, Sweet or agreeable to the taste.

P مايه دار *māya-dār*, Thick, solid, strong. Rich. Fermented (bread). (in Gīlān) Camp-followers.

P مايه ستاني *māya-satānī*, Investment.

P مايه شير *māya-shīr*, Oxygal (*i.e.* a preparation of sour milk and herbs) put amongst new milk, which sours and coagulates it.

P مايه گاو *māya-gāv*, A cow.

P مائي *māʼī*, We-ism, wegotism.

A مائيّ *māʼiy*, Watery, aquatic, aqueous. Of or belonging to the particle ما *mā*, What.

A مأبيّ *maʼyiy*, (A place) of unwholesome forage.

A مائئة *māʼiʼat*, (مائية *māʼiyat*, or مائية *māʼiyat*) A cat, an animal that mews.

A ماهيّة *māʼiyat*, Essence, quiddity, nature, quality.

P مائيم *māʼim* or *māʼem*, We are.

A مائين *miʼīna*, (pl. of مائة *miʼat*) Hundreds.

P مائي و مني *māʼī u manī*, Pride and egotism.

A مباءة *mabāʼat*, A dwelling, residence, habitation. The part of the womb where the fœtus lies. A spot where cattle lie round a watering-place. A resting-place of camels. A wild bull's haunt. A nest of wild bees.

A مباءشة *mubāʼashat*, (v. n. 3 of بأش) Taking and prostrating one without reason or resistance.

A مباجّة *mubājjat*, (v. n. 3 of بجّ) Sallying forth against, descending into the arena.

A مباح *mubāh*, Allowed. Lawful, allowable. Common property. Any indifferent action, whatever a person may do or let alone; being attended neither with praise nor blame.

A مباحات *mubāhāt*, (pl. of مباح *mubāh*) Indifferent, allowable (acts). Lawful pleasure, festivity.

A مباحتة *mubāhatat*, (v. n. 3 of بحت) Shewing sincere friendship. Acting openly with. Feeding (a beast) with the plant ضريع *zariʻ* pure and neat. Sincerity, purity.

A مباحث *mabāhis*, (pl. of مبحث *mabhas*) Places of inquiry or scrutiny. مباحث البقر *mabāhisu'l bakar*, (proverbially) A place whose situation is unknown. *Mubāhis*, A disputant.

A مباحثة *mubāhasat*, (v. n. 3 of بحث) Examining, searching. Disputing. A dispute, debate, wager.

A مباحيّة *mubāhīyat*, A being lawful.

A مباخر *mabākhir*, pl. of مبخرة *mabkharat*, Censers.

P مباد *mabād*, (and مبادا *mabādā*) Let it not be, by no means, away! God forbid! lest.

A مباداة *mubādāt*, (v. n. 3 of بدا for بدو) Manifesting, discovering (enmity) towards any one.

A مبادّة *mubāddat*, (v. n. 3 of بدّ) Bartering goods. Contributing to a general fund.

A مبادر *mubādir*, One who makes haste. A youth arrived at maturity.

A مبادرة *mubādarat*, (v. n. 3 of بدر) Making haste. Outstripping, getting before. Beginning. Attacking. Labouring. Haste, expedition.

A مبادلة *mubādalat*, (v. n. 3 of بدل) Changing. Exchange, barter. Retaliation, recompense. P مبادله كردن *mubādala kardan*, To exchange, barter.

A مبادهة *mubādahat*, (v. n. 3 of بده) Coming upon one suddenly.

A مبادي *mabādī*, Beginnings, origins.

A مباذأة *mubāzaʼat*, (v. n. 3 of بذأ) Talking obscenely. Immodesty, obscenity.

A مباذّة *mubāzzat*, An outstripping, a preventing.

A مباذرة *mubāzarat*, (v. n. 3 of بذر) Squandering.

A مباذل *mabāzil*, (pl. of مبذلة *mibzalat*) Everyday clothes.

A مباذنة *mubāzanat*, (v. n. 3 of بذن) Knowing. Confessing. Humbling one's self, submitting.

P مبار *mabār* or *mubār*, A pudding, sausage.

A مبارّ *mabārr*, (pl. of مبرّ *mabarr*) Benefits.

A مباراة *mubārāt*, (v. n. 3 of برا for برو) Opposing, contending. Separating peacefully (a man and wife). Equality.

A مبارأة *mubāraʼat*, (v. n. 3 of برأ) Dismissing a partner, dissolving partnership. Departing from, leaving. Divorcing, putting away a wife on friendly terms. A dissolution of marriage by mutual consent.

A مبارّة *mubārrat*, (v. n. 3 of برّ) Being beneficent, shewing kindness or dutifulness.

A مبارز *mabāriz*, (pl. of مبرز *mabraz*) Fields of battle. Privies. *Mubāriz*, Prepared, ready for war. A warrior, combatant, brave soldier, hero.

A مبارزة *mubārazat*, (v. n. 3 of برز) Sallying forth against, descending into the arena. War, battle. P مبارزت كردن *mubārazat kardan*, To war.

A مبارق *mabārik*, (pl. of مبرق) (Camels) which, with uplifted tails, give false signs of pregnancy.

A مبارك *mubārak*, Blessed. Happy, fortunate, auspicious. August. Sacred, holy. Welcome, well. مبارك الله *mubāraka'llāh*, Blessed of God. مبارك الدولة *mubāraku'd dawlat*, Blessed by fortune. مبارك فال *mubārak-fāl*, Of happy omen, prognosticating felicity. بقلة المباركة *baklatu'l mubārakat*, (The blessed pot-herb) Endive. الليلة المباركة *al laylatu'l mubārakat*, The middle night of the month Shaaban. P مبارك باد *mubārak bād*, May he be blessed or fortunate! مبارك بادي *mubārak bādī*, Congratulation. Benediction.

A مباركة *mubārakat*, (v. n. 3 of برك) (God) blessing (man), prospering (him). Blessing, wishing happiness to. Being assiduous, persevering. Long-eared wheat.

A مباركي *mubārakī*, A benediction. Good-fortune. Sanctity.

A مباركيّة *mubārakīyat*, Name of a certain fort.

A مبارم *mabārim*, (pl. of مبرم *mibram*) Spindles for distaffs.

A مبازجة *mubāzajat*, (v. n. 3 of بزج) Boasting, contending for pre-eminence.

A مبازمة *mubāzamat*, Resolution, enterprise.

A مبازنة *mubāzanat*, A bringing, adducing.

A مباسرة *mubāsirat*, (A she-camel) that thinks of the stallion before she is completely in heat.

A مباسطة *mubāsatat*, (v. n. 3 of بسط) Laying aside shyness, becoming free and easy. Cheerful conversation, mirth; the feast of reason and the flow of soul. Sauciness, unblushingness, impudence.

A مباسق *mabāsik*, (pl. of مبسق *mubsik*) Camels which have biestings in their udder before foaling.

A مباسلة *mubāsalat*, (v. n. 3 of بسل) Attacking one another furiously. Getting round (an enemy) to take advantage of him.

A مباسم *mabāsim*, (pl. of مبسم) The fore-teeth.

P مباش *mabāsh*, Be it not! Stay not. Lest; perhaps.

A مباشر *mubāshir*, A manager, superintendant, supervisor, inspector, commissary, deputy, factor, agent, plenipotentiary. A mare in want of the horse.

A مباشرة *mubāsharat*, (v. n. 3 of بشر) Directing, managing, superintending personally. Lying with, lying skin to skin. Announcing good news. Management. Superintendency, prefecture, agency, investiture with full power. A beginning. P مباشرت كردن *mubāsharat kardan*, To commence. To undertake, take the management of any thing.

A مباصرة *mubāsarat*, (v. n. 3 of بصر) Trying who shall see first. Endeavouring to spy; looking from a height. Watching.

A مباضعة *mubāzaʻat*, (v. n. 3 of بضع) Lying with.

A مباطشة *mubātashat*, (v. n. 3 of بطش) Seizing each other by force. Fighting in close combat. Applying a remedy.

A مباطنة *mubātanat*, (v. n. 3 of بطن) Taking secret counsel with any one.

A مباع *mubāʻ*, Exposed to sale.

A مباعدة *mubāʻadat*, (v. n. 3 of بعد) Removing far. Retiring. Separation, distance, removal; departure of one from another.

A مباعرة *mubāʻarat*, (v. n. 3 of بعر) Dunging upon her milker, whilst being milked (a camel).

A مباعلة *mubāʻalat*, (v. n. 3 of بعل) Toying with a spouse); receiving with caresses, agreeing happily (as married people). Taking a husband (بعل *baʻl*).

Intermarrying (tribes). Sitting with another.

A مباغاة *mubāghāt*, (v. n. 3 of بغي) Playing the whore. Treating (another) unjustly.

A مباغتة *mubāghatat*, (v. n. 3 of بغت) Attacking unawares. Happening, befalling unexpectedly.

A مباغضة *mubāghazat*, A hating of one another.

A مباغمة *mubāghamat*, (v. n. 3 of بغم) Speaking softly, gently to one another.

A مباكاة *mubākāt*, (v. n. 3 of بكى) Contending with, or rivalling in weeping. Weeping together.

A مباكرة *mubākarat*, (v. n. 3 of بكر) Coming to (any one) in the morning.

A مبال *mabāl*, The urinary passage, urethra.

A مبالاة *mubālāt*, (v. n. 3 of بلي) Caring for, heeding, minding, regarding. Consideration. قلة المبالاة *killatu'l mubālāt*, Inattention, indifference.

A مبالدة *mubāladat*, (v. n. 3 of بلد) Fighting or fencing with sword or single stick.

A مبالزة *mubālazat*, A taking any thing together.

A مبالصة *mubālasat*, (v. n. 3 of بلص) Rushing on.

A مبالطة *mubālatat*, (v. n. 3 of بلط) Striving or labouring in swimming. Fencing with sword or stick; cudgel-playing. Fleeing, running away from. Reproaching, disgracing. Coming down upon in war.

A مبالغ *mabāligh*, (pl. of مبلغ *mablagh*) Sums (of money). Perfections. *Mubālagh*, Exaggerated, carried to the highest pitch. *Mubāligh*, Diligent, pains-taking, who does any thing to excess.

A مبالغة *mubālaghat*, (v. n. 3 of بلغ) Endeavouring, using diligence. Straining every nerve, striving. Dwelling on a subject. Insisting, pressing, urging. Diligence, care, endeavour, effort, exertion. Exaggeration, amplification, intensity, excess. Superiority. Stress. P مبالغه نمودن *mubālagha namūdan*, To exaggerate. چندان مبالغه نيست *chandān mubālagha nīst*, 'Tis not of such vast importance.

A مبان *mubān*, Separated, divided.

A مباني *mabānī*, Edifices, fabrics, structures, buildings. Foundations. P تعمير مباني خيرات كردن *taɛmīri mabānīi khayrāt kardan*, To build or repair pious works (as caravanseras or hospitals).

A مباوأة *mubāwaʼat*, (v. n. 3 of بوأ for باء) Being equal, even, quits (in retaliation).

A مباوك *mubāwik*, A meddler in a neighbour's concerns.

A مباهاة *mubāhāt*, (v. n. 3 of بهي) Disputing for superiority in beauty or any other qualification. Boasting, contending for glory. Vain-glory, pride, arrogance. Glory, honour.

A مباهت *mubāhit*, A framer of lies.

A مباهتة *mubāhatat*, (v. n. 3 of بهت) Framing a lie (بهت *buht* or بهتان *buhtān*).

A مباهجة *mubāhajat*, (v. n. 3 of بهج) Disputing about beauty, boasting against. Conviviality.

A مباهرة *mubāharat*, A boasting, a glorying.

A مباهل *mabāhil*, (pl. of مبهلة *mubhalat*) She-camels turned loose without a mark. *Mubāhil*, (A she-camel) free from marks (of burning).

A مباهلة *mubāhalat*, (v. n. 3 of بهل) Cursing. Wishing mischief to one another. Execration.

A مباهي *mubāhī*, Glorious, exalted. Proud, vain.

A مبايضة *mubāyazat*, (v. n. 3 of باض for بيض) Contending with for whiteness (بياض *bayaz*).

A مبايعة *mubāyaɛat*, (v. n. 3 of باع for بيع) Making a contract of purchase or sale. Inaugurating. Saluting, acknowledging any one invested with authority. Plighting faith, promising obedience. Traffic.

A مباينة *mubāyanat*, (v. n. 3 of بان for بين) Departing from, relinquishing. Being separated, distinguished.

A مبت *mubitt*, One who pronounces an irrevocable divorce.

A مبتاع *mubtāɛ*, A buyer.

A مبتج *mubtajj*, (Cattle) whose sides are ready to burst from repletion.

A مبتدأ *mubtadaʼ*, (A thing) begun. Beginning, principle, or subject of a proposition. A noun put in the nominative. مبتدأ و خبر *mubtadaʼ u khabar*, Subject and predicate: substantive and adjective.

A مبتدر *mubtadir*, One who rushes to seize; one who flies to arms. One who overwhelms.

A مبتدع *mubtadaɛ*, Newly-invented, originated. A new invention. *Mubtadiɛ*, An inventor, innovator, author; a heretic, or broacher of new opinions. طائفهٔ مبتدعه *tāʼifaʼi mubtadiɛa*, A sect of heretics.

A مبتدي *mubtadī*, A beginner, commencer, young scholar, disciple just commencing to learn, tyro. A founder. مبتديا *mubtadiyan*, At first, in the beginning. Of his own accord.

A مبتذل *mubtazal*, Used every day, treated as of little value, common, hackneyed; contemptible, base. *Mubtazil*, Clad in an every-day garment. One who does his own servile work. صدق المبتذل *sidku'l mubtazal*, Deep-cutting (sword).

A مبتر *mubattar*, Docked; mutilated; incomplete.

A مبترد *mubtarid*, One who washes with or drinks cold water.

A مبترك *mubtarik*, (A camel) reclined on the brisket. Who lays any one on his breast. One who makes haste or runs fast.

A مبتري *mubtaraʼ*, Hewed (with an axe). *Mubtarī*, A hewer, a cutter of chips.

A مبتز *mubtazz*, A star by which prognostications are made at the birth of a child.

A مبتزل *mubtazal*, Burst (bud of palm-flower).

A مبتسر *mubtasir*, A doer, or one desirous of doing any thing unseasonably. A beginner. One who takes any thing whilst fresh.

A مبتسل *mubtasil*, A charmer of serpents receiving his hire.

A مبتسم *mubtasim*, A smiler, or gentle laugher.

A مبتشر *mubtashir*, A receiver of good news.

A مبتضض *mubtaziz*, One who does by degrees (that which he ought).

A مبتغا *mubtaghaʼ*, (or مبتغى *mubtaghaʼ*) What is required. Requisition; debt, duty, obligation.

A مبتغي *mubtaghī*, A lion.

A مبتغيات *mubtaghiyāt*, (pl.) Requisitions.

A مبتقل *mubtakil*, Pot-herb-eating (ass).

A مبتكر *mubtakir*, An early riser. One who arrives betimes. A receiver of first-fruits. Present from the beginning of the Muhammadan form of worship, and a hearer of the prefatory oration called خطبه *khutba*, in which they praise God, bless the prophet, and pray for the sovereign.

A مبتكرة *mubtakirat*, (A female) who bears a male at the first birth.

A مبتل *mubtil*, A palm-tree which has a shoot ready for transplanting.

A مبتّل *mubattal*, Finely-proportioned (camel).

A مبتل *mubtall*, One recovering from indisposition; convalescent. Moistened, watered, moist.

A مبتلا *mubtalaʼ*, Afflicted, sorely tried.

A مبتّلة *mubattalat*, (A woman) elegantly shaped, exquisitely proportioned.

A مبتلع *mubtalaɛ*, Swallowed. *Mubtaliɛ*, A swallower.

A مبتلي *mubtalaʼ*, Afflicted, unfortunate, tried, or inured to distress. *Mubtalī*, One who insists on an oath or a confession.

A مبتني *mubtanī*, A builder. One who causes to build. One who fattens. Founded, erected, built.

A مبتوتة *mabtūtat*, Divorced finally (wife).

A مبتورة *mabtūrat*, Docked.

A مبتهج *mubtahij*, Exultant; joyful, full of glee.

A مبتهر *mubtahar*, Publicly talked of (on the subject, especially, of an amour). *Mubtahir*, One who imputes falsely; or gives to any one the merit of what he does not deserve. Assiduous (in prayer); incessant (in talking).

A مبتهل *mubtahal*, Cursed. *Mubtahil*, A supplicator. Groaning (in prayer). One who imprecates or pours forth curses.

A مبتئس *mubtaʼis*, Sad, full of complaints against fortune. Loath, averse, unwilling.

A مبثوث *mabsūs*, Dispersed, scattered. Spread out. Published, divulged.

A مبثوثة *mabsūsat*, (pl. مبثوثات *mabsūsāt*) A thing divulged.

A مبثور *mabsūr*, Envied. Extremely rich.

A مبجّل *mubajjal*, Much esteemed. Venerable. *Mubajjil*, A reverer, honourer, venerator.

A مبحث *mabhas*, (pl. مباحث *mabāhis*) A time and place for disputation, study, or inquiry. Dissertation, investigation, debate.

A مبحثر *mubahsir*, (Milk) separated into particles, granulated, curdled.

A مبحر *mubhar*, Salt as the sea (بحر *bahr*).

A مبحزج *mubahzaj*, Water at boiling heat.

A مبخبخة *mubakhbakhat*, (A she-camel) large in

the inner cavities of the body.

A مبخر *mubakhkhar*, Perfumed. Vaporous. *Mubakhkhir*, Fumous. What makes the breath stink.

A مبخرة *mabkharat*, A cause of offensiveness of breath (as fasting, for instance). (pl. مباخر *mabākhir*) A censer for burning incense in.

A مبخزج *mubakhzaj*, Made to boil fiercely.

A مبخضة *mibkhazat*, A churn.

A مبخل *mubakhkhal*, Very avaricious.

A مبخلة *mabkhalat*, An object of avarice. A source of carefulness and solicitude (as children).

A مبخوت *mabkhūt*, Fortunate, happy.

A مبخور *mabkhūr*, Perfumed. Intoxicated.

A مبخوس *mabkhūs*, Unlucky. Blinded.

A مبخوص *mabkhūs*, Spare of flesh about the feet.

A مبخوصة *mabkhūsat*, (A she-camel) hurt in the fleshy part of the foot, and halting.

A مبخوق *mabkhūk*, One-eyed.

A مبدا *mabda'*, A wilderness, a desert.

A مبدأ *mabdaʼ*, (*mubdaʼ*, or مبدأة *mabdaʼat*) Beginning, original, origin, principle, source, head.

A مبدان *mibdān*, One that grows soon fat.

A مبدد *mubaddad*, Scattered, dispersed.

A مبدر *mubdir*, One upon whom the full moon (بدر *badr*) shines brightly.

A مبدع *mabdaʻ*, An invention, discovery, first production. Fiction. The place where any thing new is produced. *Mubdaʻ*, One whose beast is tired. Made void, abolished. *Mubdiʻ*, Who first hits upon, strikes out, produces. A creator, author, originator, inventor, founder. Who feigns or tells a lie. A heretic, heresiarch, leader of a new sect; innovator. (A beast) which halts or limps from fatigue.

A مبدعات *mabdaʻāt*, (pl. of مبدع *mabdaʻ*) Innovations (in a bad sense), revolutions, heresies.

A مبدل *mubdal*, Changed. المبدل منه *al mubdal minhu*, (in grammar) The word exchanged for something else.

A مبدّل *mubaddal*, Changed, altered. Exchanged. Turned into, metamorphosed.

A مبدّن *mubaddan*, Corpulent, thick, big-bellied.

A مبدو *mabdaw*, A desert place.

A مبدوء *mabdūʼ*, One on whom the small-pox begins to appear, pitted.

A مبدوح *mabdūh*, Extensive (plain), wide (area).

A مبدوع *mabdūʻ*, Name of a horse.

A مبدهة *mibdah*, An improvisatore. *Mubdah*, Extempore, irregular.

A مبدئ *mubdiʼ*, A beginner, one who does any thing first. An inventor. Who makes manifest. One of the names of God. مبدئ معيد *mubdiʼ muʻid*, Skilfully trained, well-broken (horse). An experienced warrior. Practised, well-versed.

A مبذر *mubazzir*, Prodigal, lavish, unthrift.

A مبذرق *mubazrik*, Very bashful. Guide, escort.

A مبذري *mubazzirī*, Prodigality, luxury.

A مبذقة *mubazzikat*, One who deals more in words than in deeds.

A مبذل *mibzal*, A worn-out garment. An every-day or working-garment.

A مبذلة *mibzalat*, (pl. مباذل *mabāzil*) An every-day or working-garment. A threadbare garment.

A مبذلخ *mubazlikh*, One who promises but does not perform.

A مبذم *mibzam*, Strong, robust (she-camel).

A مبذور *mabzūr*, Much.

A مبذوع *mabzūʻ*, Frightened, timorous.

A مبذول *mabzūl*, Expended, bestowed, lavished. A magnificent present. Acceptable. Name of a poet.

P مبر *mabar*, (imper. negat. of بردن *burdan*) Do not carry, bear, or receive.

A مبرّ *mubirr*, Strong. Provident, prudent. Superior to one's companions.

A مبرا *mabra'*, The place where a pen is cut (generally an inch or so from the point). *Mibra'*, A penknife. A razor. A hatchet; any sharp instrument.

A مبرّا *mubarra'*, Exempted, free, absolved, far removed from.

A مبراة *mibrāt*, A penknife. A knife with which they trim bows. A plane. A file, a rasp. *Mubrāt*, (A she-camel) which wears a nose-ring.

A مبرّات *mabarrāt*, (pl. of مبرّة) Good works.

A مبربر *mubarbir*, A lion.

A مبرّة *mabarrat*, (v. n. of برّ) Doing good. A public work (as an inn) built by pious Muhammadans. Beneficence. Dutifulness, obedience. Name of a hill near Madīna. *Mubarrat*, Sugar-candy broken to pieces with a hatchet.

A مبرت *mibrat*, (or مبرّت *mubarrat*) Sugar-candy.

A مبرّج *mubarraj*, (A garment) painted or wrought with figures or holes like eyes, or like a tower (برج *burj*). *Mubarrij*, A boaster of his own merits.

A مبرّح *mubarrih*, Severe, heavy, distressing. ضربه ضربا مبرّحا *zarabahu zarban mubarrihan*, He struck him a violent blow.

A مبرد *mabrad*, A refrigerative. (Land) hailed upon. *Mibrad*, A file. *Mubrid*, One who comes in the cool. A bringer of any thing cool, or a drinker of cooled liquor. Who or what cools. One who despatches a messenger (بريد *barīd*). A post-master. جئتك مبردا *jiʼtuka mubridan*, I came to you post (or in the cold weather).

A مبرّد *mubarrad*, Chilled. Allowed to cool. Name of a man. *Mubarrad* or *mubrad*, Struck with hail (برد *barad*), hailed upon. *Mubarrid*, Refreshing, cooling, refrigerative.

A مبردانة *mibridānat*. (See هبردانة *hibridānat*).

A مبردة *mabradat*, A thing cooling or cooled. A refrigerative, a refrigerant.

A مبرذن *mubarzin*, The owner of a dull hack.

A مبرّر *mubarrar*, Justified. *Mubarrir*, Who or what justifies. A sheep which has shining parts on the udder.

A مبرز *mabraz*, (pl. مبارز *mabāriz*) A field of battle. An amphitheatre. A privy. A march to battle. *Mubraz*, Published. *Mubriz*, A publisher.

A مبرسم *mubarsam*, Afflicted with a pleurisy.

A مبرّض *mubarriz*, One who squanders all.

A مبرطس *mubartis*, One who lets out camels and asses on hire. A broker.

A مبرطش *mubartish*, A broker, one who effects sales between buyer and seller.

A مبرطل *mubartil*, Long-shaped.

A مبرطم *mubartim*, Proud, haughty, irascible.

A مبرق *mabrak*, The time of the breaking forth of the dawn. *Mubrik*, (pl. مبارق *mabārik*) A camel shewing false signs of pregnancy.

A مبرقش *mubarkash*, Speckled, spotted, dappled.

A مبرقط *mubarkat*, Food saturated with oil.

A مبرقع *mubarkaʻ*, Veiled.

P مبرقع *mubarkiʻ*, Name of a note in music.

A مبرقعة *mubarkaʻat*, A white-headed sheep. *Mubarkiʻat*, A white spot on the forehead of a horse spreading over the face.

A مبرك *mabrak*, (pl. مبارك *mabārik*) A place where a camel reclines.

A مبركة *mubrikat*, Fire.

A مبرم *mibram*, (pl. مبارم *mabārim*, A spindle for a distaff. *Mubram*, Twisted, of two threads twined together. Cloth woven with such threads. Firm, strong, doubled. قضائ مبرم *kazāʼi mubram*, Irresistible fate. *Mubrim*, Strengthening. Urgent, wearisome, importunate. Morose. Insipid in conversation. A gatherer of the fruit of the عضاه *ʻizāh*. Who hollows out large stones for making cauldrons; or who hews those stones from a mountain.

A مبرنتئ *mubrantiʼ*, Short. Deceitful. Choleric, caring for nobody. Ready, prepared.

A مبرندة *mubarnadat*, Very plump (woman).

A مبرندع *mubrandiʻ*, One who contracts his face.

A مبرنشق *mubranshik*, Joyful, exulting.

A مبرّوة *mabrūwat*, (The ring برة *burat*) passed through the nose of a camel.

A مبرود *mabrūd*, Cooled. Cold. Struck with hail. (Bread) moistened with cold water.

A مبرور *mabrūr*, Purified, absolved. Accepted of God, pious. Fair, equitable (bargain).

A مبروز *mabrūz*, Produced, edited (book).

A مبروص *mabrūs*, Leprous. A leper.

A مبروض *mabrūz*, Impoverished by liberality.

A مبرهن *mubarhan*, Demonstrated, proved. Demonstrative, authentic, evident, manifest.

A مبري *mubra'*, (A camel) having the ring of copper or hair (برة *burat*) passed through the nose.

A مبرّي *mubarra'*, Free, exempted.

A مبريّ *mabrīy*, Cut, chipped, hewn.

A مبرئيل *mubarʼil*, Ready for mischief.

A مبزّج *mubazzaj*, Dressed, ornamented, beautified, *Mubazzij*, Who or what adorns or beautifies.

A مبزر *mibzar*, A bleacher's beetle.

A مبزغ *mibzagh*, A fleam, a lancet.

A مبزل *mibzal*, (or مبزلة *mibzalat*) A cullender, wine-strainer, filtre.

A مبزم *mibzam*, A tooth.

A مبزور *mabzūr*, Possessed of a numerous offspring.

A مبزول *mabzūl*, Split.

A مبزي *mubzī*, Powerful, able to overcome.

A مبسار *mibsār*, A palm-tree which bears dates that will not ripen, and are called بسر *busr*.

A مبساق *mibsāk*, Long-uddered (sheep).

A مبسام *mibsām*, Who smiles much, or simpers.

A مبسر *mubsir*, (A palm-tree) with unripe dates.

A مبشّرة *mubassirat*, A wind, forerunner of rain.

A مبسط *mabsat*, An open, spacious place. *Mibsat*, Any place where carpets or cushions are spread.

A مبسّط *mubassat*, Expanded, spread. *Mubassit*, One who spreads.

A مبسق *mubsik*, (pl. مباسق *mabāsik* or مباسيق) A camel with milk in the udder before delivery.

A مبسل *mubsal*, Given over to destruction.

A مبسّل *mubassal*, (A colocynth) eaten by itself and its flavour detested.

A مبسم *mabsam*, A smile. *Mabsim*, The mouth when smiling; the fore-teeth which then appear.

A مبسور *mabsūr*, Troubled with hemorrhoids.

A مبسوس *mabsūs*, (A mountain) crumbled to dust. Deprived of a part of one's property.

A مبسوط *mabsūt*, Spread, extended, expanded, dilated, stretched out. (The hand) outstretched (in prayer). A certain form of a (camel's) saddle (the reverse of مفروق *mafrūk*). عمارة مبسوطة السماط *ʿimārat mabsūtatu's sumāt*, An inn, caravansera, hospital in the East, where provisions are kept for poor travellers.

A مبشر *mubshar*, Exhilarated with good news. مؤدم مبشر *muaddami mubshar*, Prudent, judicious, behaving with propriety. Expert, skilful. Blending mildness with severity.

A مبشّر *mubashshir*, An announcer. A bearer of good news; an evangelist. P مبشر بنام *mubashshir ba nām*, A title of the Lord Jesus, as announcing (the advent of Muhammad) by name. It is generally supposed that Muhammad or his prompter mistook Paracletos, "Comforter," for Periclutos, "Very illustrious, or greatly praised," which is the meaning of the word محمد *muhammad*. المبشرات *al mubashshirāt*, (Winds) the harbingers of rain.

P مبشل *mabshal*, Do not hang up. Do not twist. Do not sleep.

A مبشور *mabshūr*, (An upper garment) handsomely cut out, and of a beautiful colour.

A مبشورة *mabshūrat*, (A woman) of a handsome figure and fine complexion.

A مبشوش *mabshūsh*, Of a cheerful countenance.

A مبشوغ *mabshūgh*, Wet with small, fine rain which does not flow.

P مبشول *mabshūl*, Do not be perplexed. Do not distress. Look not at. Acquaint not yourself with.

A مبصر *mabsar*, An evident, convincing proof. *Mubsar*, Lightsome, clear, shining. *Mubsir*, Who sees. Clear-sighted. Clear, manifest. Who renders intelligent. Middling, moderate (garment, talk, or pace). One who hangs a curtain before his door. A lion which sees and makes for his prey afar off.

A مبصّر *mubassar*, Clear, perspicuous. Made manifest. *Mubassir*, One who shews, renders quick-sighted, or causes to understand.

A مبصرة *mabsarat*, An evident, convincing proof; undoubted fact. *Mubsirat*, A visible sign or token.

A مبصري *mubsirī*, Foresight, prudence.

A مبضع *mibzaʿ*, A lancet. A veterinary surgeon's fleam. A penknife. A leather-cutter's paring-knife. *Mubziʿ*, One who carries goods for sale.

A مبطأة *mabtaat*, A hindrance, cause of delay.

A مبطان *mibtān*, A slave to his belly. Swelled with over-feeding.

A مبطبطة *mubatbitat*, A hen-partridge. Distant country.

A مبطّة *mibattat*, A lancet, a fleam.

A مبطخة *mabta* or *mabtukhat*, A melon-ground.

A مبطل *mubtal*, (or مبطّل *mubattal*) Abolished, annihilated. *Mubtil*, (or مبطّل *mubattil*) Who or what invalidates; frustrative; a defacer, destroyer.

A مبطّن *mubattan*, (A garment) elegantly lined. One whose belly is fallen in (from hunger). (A horse) white about the back and belly.

A مبطّنة *mubattanat*, Slender-waisted woman.

A مبطوش *mabtūsh*, Seized by force.

A مبطول *mabtūl*, Paralyzed. A paralytic.

A مبطون *mabtūn*, A distended belly. Pained by the cholic, griped in the belly (بطن *batn*).

A مبطئ *mubtiʾ*, Late, tardy. Lazy, slow. P ميوهٔ مبطئة *mīvaʾi mubtiʾa*, Late fruit.

A مبظّرة *mubazzirat*, A female circumciser.

A مبعار *mibʿār*, A sheep dunging whilst milked.

A مبعث *mabʿas*, Mission, embassy.

A مبعد *mibʿad*, A traveller, one who goes far from home. *Mubʿad*, Removed to a distance.

A مبعر *mabʿar*, The place which contains the dung, the rectum (of a beast). *Mabʿar* or *mibʿar*, A stable, fold, stall. A laystall.

A مبعرة *mabʿarat*, Fundament (of a beast).

A مبعوت *mabʿūt*, Sent. Raised.

A مبعوث *mabʿūs*, Sent. Raised (from the dead). Awakened.

A مبعوج *mabʿūj*, Cut open.

A مبعوض *mabʿūz*, Infested by gnats.

A مبغاة *mabghāt*, A way of asking or seeking.

A مبغبغ *mubaghbagh*, Mixed, confused. Near. *Mubaghbigh*, Near. Quick in doing any thing. A mixer: one who creates confusion.

A مبغض *mubghaz*, Hated, hateful.

A مبغوشة *mabghūshat*, Land wet by gentle rain.

A مبغوض *mabghūz*, Detested, hated. Odious. مبغوض جميع جهانيان *mabghūzi jamīʿi jahāniyān*, Hated of all men.

A مبغولاء *mabghūlāʾ*, (pl. of بغل *baghl*) Mules.

A مبغيّ *mabghīy*, Desired, wished, sought.

A مبقّ *mibakk*, Talkative.

A مبقرة *mabkarat*, A way, a path.

A مبقل *mubkal*, (Ground) producing herbs. *Mubkil*, (Plants) which are putting forth their leaves.

A مبقلة *mabkalat* or *mabkulat*, A garden of pot-herbs, a kitchen-garden.

A مبقّم *mubakkam*, Dyed with بقّم *bakkam* wood.

A مبقوث *mabkūs*, Abhorred. Confused: mixed.

A مبقور *mabkūr*, Split, burst in the belly.

A مبقوع *mabkūʿ*, Reproached, abusively addressed, or falsely spoken of.

A مبقّى *mubakkaʾ*, Preserved, remaining.

A مبقيات *mubkiyāt*, Horses which continue to run after others started with them have stopped.

A مبكار *mibkār*, Early ripe. Fertile (ground), quick in bearing.

A مبكّت *mubakkit*, A woman who bears alternately boys and girls. A striker (with sword or staff). One who terrifies (especially by reproaches). One who silences either by reproof or argument. One who receives or treats another ungraciously.

A مبكر *mubkir*, Early spring-rains. One who does any thing early in the morning.

A مبكّر *mubakkir*, A doer of any thing early in the morning. A traveller (especially in the night-time, or before break of day). Who or what causes to rise early. Active in the prosecution of business.

A مبكّع *mubakkiʿ*, A cutter in pieces.

A مبكّل *mubakkil*, One who mixes.

A مبكّم *mubakkim*, Mute, dumb. Silencing.

A مبكونة *mabkūnat*, Base, contemptible (woman).

A مبكي *mubkī*, Who or what forces to weep.

A مبكّى *mubakkaʾ*, Deplorable.

A مبكيّ *mabkīy*, Wept. مبكيّ عليه *mabkīy ʿalayhi*, Wept over, bewailed, mourned.

A مبلّ *miball*, Firm, resolute (opponent). *Muball*, A follower. A helper.

A مبلاس *miblās*, (also مبلام *miblām*) (A she-camel) silent with lust.

A مبلّت *muballat*, Well-composed or well-adapted (speech). مهر مبلّت *mahri muballat*, A marriage-portion settled in trust or suretiship.

A مبلج *mublij*, Shining and bright (dawn). Who or what renders clear.

A مبلح *mublih*, (A palm-tree) with unripe dates.

A مبلد *mublid*, An old cistern or pond.

A مبلس *mublis*, Despairing, desperate; broken-hearted, melancholy, wretched, silent with grief.

A مبلط *mublit*, One who lays flag-stones, a pavier. Ruinous, reducing to beggary. Importunate, troublesome; a beggar. *Mublit* or *mublat*, Reduced to poverty, beggared.

A مبلّط *muballat*, Paved, flagged (city). *Muballit*, A pavier.

A مبلع *mablaʻ*, The gullet, swallow. The hole of a privy or sink, gulley-hole. *Miblaʻ*, A glutton.

A مبلعة *mublaʻat*, A well, smooth, even on the inside, from the surface of the water to the parapet.

A مبلغ *mablagh*, (v.n. of بلغ) Being good and excellent. (pl. مبالغ *mabāligh*) A sum, ready money. Perfection. Quantity, price, produce; product or quotient in arithmetic. Much, many. Place of arrival. مبلغ مرقوم *mablaghi markūm*, The abovementioned sum.

A مبلغي *mablaghe*, A considerable sum.

A مبلق *muballak*, Planked with teak (the sides of a well dug in loose earth).

A مبلّل *muballil*, Screaming (peacock). A continual roarer. One who wets much.

A مبلم *mublim*, Swelling. Swollen (lip). Silent, dumb with lust (she-camel). (A she-camel) which has not taken the male.

A مبلندي *mublandī*, Hardy and fleshy (camel).

A مبلود *mablūd*, Stupid, stolid, ignorant.

A مبلوع *mablūʻ*, Swallowed.

A مبلوغ *mablūgh*, Involved in difficulties.

A مبلول *mablūl*, Moistened, watered, wetted.

A مبلي *mublī*, A wearer, tearer, consumer. An experimenter. A tempter. One who renders happy. A cleaner, purifier. One who has enough; content.

A مبلّي *muballī*, Who causes one to cover or to clothe. One who ties (a camel), without meat or drink, to the grave of (her) deceased master, that (she) might die and accompany him to the other world (a rite of the pagan Arabians). A wearer, tearer, consumer.

A مبلّيات *muballiyāt*, Women who stand round a camel tied to the grave of his deceased master and rend the air with their cries.

A مبليّة *mablīyat*, (A she-camel) tied to the grave of (her) deceased master (a pagan rite).

A مبنّ *mubinn*, One who stands or stops. (A hind's lying-place) impregnated with the smell of dung.

A مبناة *mabnāt* or *mibnāt*, A tanned hide spread out for sitting upon. A portmanteau. A veil.

A مبنّت *mubannit*, An inquirer, a querist. A person who tells all that he knows.

A مبنّج *mubannaj*, Drugged with بهنگ *bhang*. *Mubannij*, Piping (partridge). Giver of hog's bean.

A مبندق *mubandik*, A musqueteer, fusileer.

A مبنس *mubnis*, Who flees from, shuns evil.

A مبنّس *mubannis*, One who retires, stays behind.

A مبنّش *mubannish*, Remiss, careless.

A مبنّق *mubannik*, Who stands (in one place). A shortener, polisher (of a speech). An inventor of a lie. One who cuts (the back with a scourge). One who puts any thing round the neck. One who enlarges (a shirt) by inserting a gore. One who makes (a quiver) wide at top and narrow at bottom.

A مبنّك *mubannik*, A teller of family-secrets.

A مبنّن *mubannin*, One who keeps a sheep tied in order to fatten.

A مبنور *mabnūr*, Tried, proved, experienced.

A مبنیٰ or مبني *mabna* or *mabnī*, An edifice, fabric. A foundation. *Mubnī*, One who orders or causes to build. A fattener. مبنیٔ فساد *mubnīʼi fasād*, A transgressor, author of mischief.

A مبنّي *mubannī*, Who builds or rears (with expedition, and well). A builder.

A مبنيّ *mabnīy*, Built, constructed, formed, founded. (in grammar) Indeclinable (noun).

A مبنيّة *mabnīyat*, (fem.) Built. مبنيّة بالكسر *mabnīyat bi'l kasr*, Ending in كسر *kasr* or *i* short ـِ.

A مبوّا *mubawwaʼ*, Habitation, resting-place.

A مبوّب *mubawwab*, Divided into chapters. ابواب مبوّبة *abwāb mubawwabat*, Different, distinct doors or chapters.

A مبور *mibwar*, A stallion-camel that distinguishes whether the female is pregnant.

A مبوّش *mubawwish*, Mixed, confused.

A مبوّق *mubawwak*, Vain, foolish (speech).

A مبول *mibwal*, A vessel for holding urine, urinal, chamber-pot. *Mubwil*, Diuretic.

A مبوّل *mubawwil*, Provocative of urine, diuretic.

A مبولة *mabwalat*, Any thing diuretic. *Mibwalat*, A urinal, a chamber-pot.

A مبهاج *mibhāj*, A beautiful, jolly girl. Fat (camel's bunch).

A مبهّت *mubahhit*, Who or what astonishes, confounds, or distracts.

A مبهج *mubhij*, Joy-inspiring, recreative; cheering. (Ground) luxuriant in herbage, verdant.

A مبهّج *mubahhij*, A beautifier. Exhilarant, gladdening. Who looks on as, or declares, beautiful.

A مبهر *mubhir*, A producer of any thing admirable. Enriched after having been poor. Scorched by the noon-day sun. One who behaves sometimes well, sometimes ill. One who weds a woman of a short slender form, or good family (بهيرة *bahīrat*).

A مبهرج *mubahraj*, (A well) common to all. (Blood) which may be shed with impunity.

A مبهرم *mubahram*, Dyed with saffron.

A مبهز *mibhaz*, A beater, thruster, trampler.

A مبهّش *mubahhash*, Quickened (pace).

A مبهص *mubhis*, A prohibiter, binderer.

A مبهض *mubhiz*, Troublesome, afflictive.

A مبهل *mibhal*, Light, active. *Mubhil*, One who sets at liberty, or permits another to do what he pleases. One who caresses.

A مبهلة *mubhalat*, (pl. مباهل *mabāhil*) (A she-camel) turned loose without a mark.

A مبهم *mubham*, Shut (door). Occult, unknown. Doubtful, obscure, uncertain. Indeterminate. Silent, dumb. Unintelligible (speech). Any thing prohibited (as marriage between a brother and sister). اسم مبهم *ismi mubham*, The demonstrative pronoun. هذه الآية مبهمة *hāzihi'l āyatu mubhamatun*, This verse (of the Kur'ān) is general and indefinite. *Mubhim*, One who shuts (a door). Who keeps concealed. Who leaves (any thing) hid or unknown. A diverter from any thing.

A مبهّم *mubahhim*, Who separates or weans. Who remains or dwells (in a place). مبهّم البهم *mubahhimu'l baham*, Who weans lambs or kids.

P مبهن *mabhan*, A place of safety. One's native country or habitation. That part of a house where guests are received. Domestic affairs. The habitation of enchanters or fascinators. A tribe, family. Ancestors. Kindred.

A مبهوت *mabhūt*, Stupefied, confounded, astonished, struck dumb, mute with astonishment. Defamed, falsely accused.

A مبهور *mabhūr*, Fatigued, breathless.

A مبهوظ *mabhūz*, Heavy laden, tired.

A مبهوق *mabhūk*, Afflicted with leprosy, white morphew, tetter, or ringworm (بهق *bahak*).

A مبهي *mubhī*, One who renders uninhabitable (a house), who lays waste. An emptier (of a vessel). A tearer (of a garment or tent). Who keeps idle, and does not allow (a horse to travel or go to war).

A مبهّي *mubahhī*, An enlarger of a tent.

A مبهّيات *mubahhiyāt*, Aphrodisiacal medicines.

A مبيت *mabīt*, (v. n. of بات for بيت) Passing the night. A bed-chamber, or sleeping-place.

A مبيّت *mubayyit*, Who surprises (an enemy) by night. Who goes about (business) in the night. A talker, thinker, ponderer by night. One who renders possible, disposes, or prepares. One who peels (a palm-tree).

A مبيّتة *mubayyatat*, Married, housed (woman).

A مبيث *mubīs*, An examiner, scrutator.

A مبيح *mubīh*, One who discloses (a secret), opens (the mind). Who allows one to follow his inclination. A doer of any thing by common right. المبيح *al mubīh*, The lion.

A مبيّح *mubayyih*, Who makes one a confidant in a secret. A cutter and distributor (of meat).

A مبيخ *mubīkh*, A quencher, extinguisher.

A مبيد *mubīd*, A destroyer, ruiner. God.

A مبير *mubīr*, A ruiner. Ruinous, destructive.

P ميژه *mabīja*, Name of Afrāsyāb's daughter.

A مبيض *mabīz*, A place where a bird lays her eggs. *Mubīz*, A bleacher, fuller, whitener.

A مبيّض *mubayyaz*, White-washed, whitened. *Mubayyiz*, A whitener, bleacher, scourer, embellisher. Clad in white. A filler. An emptier.

A مبيضّ *mubyazz*, White.

A مبيضة *mubīzat*, (A woman) who brings forth fair or white children.

A مبيّضة *mubayyizat*, One who brings forth a white child. A Muhammadan sect so called because they wear white garments (opposed to the sect called مسوّدة *musawwidat*).

A مبيطر *mubaytir*, A veterinary surgeon.

A مبيع *mabīʻ*, (v. n. of باع for بيع) Selling.

Sold or bought. *Mubīʻ*, One who exposes to sale.

A مبيعي *mubīʻī*, Sold. Bought. Venal.

A مبين *mubīn*, Manifest, clear, distinct. A divider, separater, distinguisher, or explainer. امر مبين *amri mubīn*, An evident thing. دين مبين *dīni mubīn*, The true religion. *Mubyin*, A divider.

A مبيّن *mubayyan*, Declared, explained, illustrated. Separated, distributed under distinct heads. *Mubayyin*, Illustrative, explanatory. A declarer.

P مبيناد *mabīnād*, God forbid!

A مبيوع *mabyūʻ*, Sold. Bought. Venal. Purchaseable.

A مبيٌ *mubīʼ*, (fem. مبيئة) Difficult, severe.

P مپريش *mapriṡh*, Do not scatter.

P مت *mat*, Syrup of grapes or dates.

A مت *matt*, (v. n. of مت) Extending. Drawing water from a well without a pulley. Seeking an alliance, assaying to establish a connection.

A متء *matʼ*, (v. n. of متأ) Striking (with a stick). Stretching (a rope).

A متاٴم *mutāʼam*, Doubly-woven (cloth).

A متاٴمة *mutāʼamat*, A weaving of cloth double.

A متاب *matāb*, (v. n. of تاب for توب) Repenting, being converted from sin. Being moved with pity, relenting (as God to man). A place to which one returns.

A متأبب *mutaʼabbib*, Hoarse. Full of wonder.

A متابة *matābat*, A vowing of repentance.

A متأبت *mutaʼabbit*, Burning, glowing (coal).

A متأبد *mutaʼabbid*, Wild, frightened, flying. One who shuns society, a misanthrope. (A dwelling-place) deserted by inhabitants, resorted to by wild beasts. Freckled (by the sun).

A متأبس *mutaʼabbis*, Changed, disordered. Soft.

A متأبض *mutaʼabbiz*, One who binds the forefoot of a camel with a rope (the knee being bent to the shoulder or thigh). Bound by the cord اباض.

A متأبط *mutaʼabbit*, One who carries any thing under the arm. The wearer of a cloak or any other garment, with the right arm clear, ready for action, one end being thrown over the left shoulder.

A متابع *mutābaʻ*, Firm, strong. *Mutābiʻ*, Continued, following. A follower, imitator. Obedient.

A متابعة *mutābaʻat*, (v. n. 3 of تبع) Following. Imitating. Conforming one's self to, submitting, obeying. Giving every member its due. Doing any thing solidly and certainly. (A field) thoroughly fattening (a camel). Obsequiousness, obedience. متابعت و موافقت *mutābaʻat u muwāfakat*, Mutual conformity, concord, harmony, agreement.

A متأبق *mutaʼabbik*, Hid, concealed, lurking, latent. A denier, refuser. Abstinent. Conformable.

A متأبل *mutaʼabbil*, A mourner (as Adam for the death of Abel). One who abstains from a spouse (when mourning); one who leads a life of celibacy. A purchaser of camels (ابل *ibl*). (Camels) which feed on green herbage.

A متابلة *mutābalat*, (v. n. 3 of تبل) Seasoning (a pot) with herbs and spices (تابل *tābil* or *tābal*).

A متأبه *mutaʼabbih*, Haughty. Disobedient.

A متأبي *mutaʼabbī*, Refractory, disobedient.

A متات *matāt*, That by which water is drawn, or by which a connexion is formed.

A متأتب *mutaʼattib*, (A woman) clothed in the garment اتب *itb*. One who puts on a coat of mail. One who slings a bow upon his back. Armed for battle. Hardened, becoming obdurate. Crucified.

A متأتي *mutaʼattī*, Who or what arrives, meets by chance, comes on suddenly, surprises: happening. Mild in behaviour; kind, humane. One who conforms to society. Ready, disposed, prepared. Easy, expeditious (business).

A متأثث *mutaʼassis*, Wealthy, opulent.

A متأثر *mutaʼassir*, Touched, impressed. Afflicted, disturbed. A preferer. An esteemer, thinker.

A متأثل *mutaʼassil*, A chooser or receiver of the best of any thing. An accumulater of riches. One who is waxed great, and assumes airs of consequence. Who considers as noble or radical. A well-digger.

A متأثم *mutaʼassim*, Penitent. Careful in avoiding sin (اثم *ism*).

A متأجج *mutaʼajjij*, Burning, scorching. Angry.

A متاجر *matājir*, Wares, goods, merchandize.

A متاجرة *mutājarat*, The driving on of a trade.

A متأجل *mutaʼajjal*, Gathered into one place. *Mutaʼajjil*, Who arrives at an appointed term, or who reaches the mark (اجل *ajal*). Dammed up (water). Divided into herds, flocks, or bevies.

A متأجم *mutaʼajjim*, Scorching (sun, day, or fire). Angry.

A متاح *mutāh*, Determined, defined. يوم متاح *yawm mutāh*, The day of death.

A متّاح *mattāh*, Long (night). Striding (horse).

A متأحد *mutaʼahhid*, United; made one.

A متأخر *mutaʼakhkhir*, Delayed, deferred, retarded. One who retires or lags behind. The last. Modern. لسان متأخرين *lisāni mutaʼakhkhirīn*, The language of the moderns.

A متاخم *mutākhim*, Bordering (country).

A متاخمة *mutākhamat*, A bordering upon.

A متآخي *mutaʼākhī*, United in brotherhood.

A متأخي *mutaʼakhkhī*, One who acts or receives as a brother. Who studies attentively, pays attention.

A متأدب *mutaʼaddab* or *mutaʼaddib*, Well-bred. Learned.

A متأدد *mutaʼaddid*, (Misfortune) befalling any one. Strong, vehement; one who waxes stronger.

A متآدي *mutaʼādī*, Reciprocal in giving aid. Prepared for.

A متأدي *mutaʼaddī*, Prepared, ready, arranged. (A messenger) who arrives. A payer, performer.

A متأذن *mutaʼazzin*, Signified, published.

A متأذي *mutaʼazzī*, Injured, vexed, grieved.

A متاربة *mutārabat*, (v. n. 3 of ترب) Being coeval, cotemporary (ترب *tirb*). Being a friend or companion. Associating with one's equals.

A متأرض *mutaʼarriz*, Whatever occurs, meets, opposes, happens, or befals. Gravitating to the earth. Fixed to any country (ارض *arz*). Shaved, cropt (grass). Delayed. Contingent.

A متاركة *mutārakat*, A dismissing unmolested.

P متاره *matāra*, A flexible leathern drinking-bottle or cup used by travellers. An ewer from which they pour water when performing ablutions.

A متآزخ *mutaʼāzikh*, Dilatory, slow. One who stops by the way. One who draws back.

A متأزخ *mutaʼazzikh*, Who loiters, draws back.

A متأزر *mutaʼazzar*, Breeched. Begirt.

A متأزز *mutaʼazziz*, Violently-boiling (cauldron).

A متآزف *mutaʼāzif*, Short of stature. Adjacent (houses), contiguous (tents).

A متأزف *mutaʼazzif*, One who takes close or short steps. Narrow (place). Close, churlish (fellow).

A متآزق *mutaʼāzik*, (or متأزق *mutaʼazzik*) Reduced to difficulties, hard pressed (in battle).

A متأزل *mutaʼazzil*, Oppressed with anguish.

A متأزم *mutaʼazzim*, Tried by a season of uncommon scarcity (ازمة *azmat* or *azamat*).

A متآزي *mutaʼāzī*, Seated near one another.

A متأزي *mutaʼazzī*, One who retires, recedes, or abstains. A restrainer. Hindered. (An arrow) which hits fairly the mark.

A متاساة *mutāsāt*, (v. n. 3 of تسي obsolete) Hurting. Despising.

A متأسد *mutaʼassid*, Furious as a lion (اسد *asad*).

A متأسر *mutaʼassir*, One who seeks a pretext (for delay).

A متأسف *mutaʼassif*, Groaning. Anxious.

P متأسفانه *mutaʼassafāna*, Filled with grief and lamentation. Grievingly, lamentingly.

A متأسل *mutaʼassil*, One who bears a resemblance to (a father).

A متأسن *mutaʼassin*, Altered, changed, stinking (water). Affected (by the noisome vapour of a well). One who resembles (a father). A delayer. One who excuses himself or seeks for a pretence.

A متآسي *mutaʼāsī*, Reciprocal, mutual in assisting or in comforting.

A متأسي *mutaʼassī*, Patient. A receiver of consolation. A follower, imitator. Grieved, distressed.

A متأشب *mutaʼashshib*, Mixed, crowded, assembled from all quarters. Adhering (client to his patron). Mixed, intertwined (trees).

A متآصر *mutaʼāsir*, Neighbouring, contiguous.

A متأطر *mutaʼattir*, Bent.

A متأطم *mutaʼattim*, Inflamed with rage, angry. Agitated, raging (sea). Growing dark (night). One who restrains himself (from saying or doing). A snorer. Purring (cat).

A متاع *matāʻ*, (pl. امتعة *amtiʻat*) Merchandise, goods. Furniture. Clothes, effects. Utensils. Valuables. Any thing refuse, or of which one has the use for a little while. Membrum virile. Lead. Iron. Brass. Copper. Profit, gain, advantage, benefit, use, enjoyment, usufruct. متاع البيت *matāʿu'l bayt*, Household furniture. *Mutāʿ*, Vomited forth.

A متاعب *matāʿib*, (pl. of متعب *matʿab*) Difficulties, toils, vexations, afflictions, evils.

A متاعة *matāʿat*, (v. n. of متع) Being liberal, beneficent. Being ingenious, witty, or graceful.

A متاعيس *matāʿīs*, (pl. of متعوس *matʿūs*) Fallen, lost, perished.

A متأفن *muta-affin*, Injured, impaired, minished.

A متاق *mit-ak*, Vigorous, swift. Swift to do evil.

A متاقنة *mutākanat*, A sitting together.

A متأكد *muta-akkad*, Corroborated, strengthened, confirmed. Repeated. *Muta-akkid*, A confirmer, strengthener. Repeated.

A متأكر *muta-akkir*, A digger of a trench (called أكرة *ukrat*) for planting trees.

A متأكل *muta-akkil*, Eaten. Corroded, consumed. An eater, devourer. Glittering (sword).

A متالاة *mutālāt*, A following in succession.

A متألب *muta-allib*, Assembled, collected.

A متالّة *mutāllat*, (v. n. 3 of تلّ) Seeking a stallion (for one's mare).

A متالع *mutāluʿ*, Name of a mountain.

A متألف *muta-allif*, One who cultivates acquaintance, or conciliates good will of. An exerciser, teacher, or breaker in. Associated, conjoined, familiar, intimate. Fitting, agreed.

A متألق *muta-allik*, Flashing, shining, glancing (lightning). Dressed, adorned (woman). Trussed, tucked up. One who raises the head (especially when quarrelling, or with any bad design).

A متألم *muta-allim*, Afflicted, pained, grieved, vexed, troubled, sad. Discontented.

A متالي *matālī*, Camels not foaling till summer. (pl. of متلي *mutlī* and متلية *mutliyat*) Camels followed by their colts. *Mutālī*, Consecutive, a follower (especially one who accompanies another in a song in a high tone of voice).

A متاليات *mutāliyāt*, Things consecutive.

A متآم *mit-ām*, (A woman) used to bring twins. (A garment) woven with a double thread.

A متاءمة *mutā-amat*, (v. n. 3 of تأم) Weaving (a garment) with a double thread (as with silk and cotton). Having a twin-brother. Running course after course (a horse).

A متام *matāma*, How long? Until when?

A متأم *mit-am*, A woman who bears twins.

A متأمر *muta-ammir*, Raised to dominion. One who obtains or exercises sovereign power.

A متأمع *muta-ammiʿ*, Weak, inconstant.

A متأمل *muta-ammil*, Contemplative, thoughtful, meditative. Considerate. A careful examiner.

A متأمم *muta-ammim*, An assayist, trier. One who proposes to do any thing. Who receives as a mother (امّ *umm*), or supplies a mother's place. One who purifies or rubs his hands, face, and other parts of the body with sand or dust (agreeable to the Muhammadan law), where water cannot be procured, before engaging in religious exercises.

A متامّمة *mutāmamat*, (v. n. 3 of تمّ) Contending with in finishing or perfecting any thing.

A متأمن *muta-ammin*, Who confides in; secure.

A متأمّي *muta-ammī*, Buyer of a female slave.

A متان *mitān*, (pl. of متن *matn*) Hard and elevated spots of ground. Sides of backs or loins.

A متانة *matānat*, (v. n. of متن) Being firm, solid, fixed, constant. Being hard and high (ground). Firmness, solidity. Fortification, castle, stronghold. Obstinacy. A place where figs (تين *tīn*) grow.

A متانّة *mutānnat*, (v. n. 3 of تنّ) Instituting a comparison between two things.

A متأنث *muta-annas* or *muta-annis*, Of the feminine gender. A soother, caresser.

A متانخة *mutānakhat*, Opposition in battle.

A متأنس *muta-annis*, Tamed, familiarized. Domestic. A lion: or one which sees his prey afar.

A متأنف *muta-annif*, One who seeks, longs for, pursues, seizes, gets possession of (one after another). Hitherto ungrazed (field).

A متأنق *muta-annik*, Dainty, nice, squeamish.

A متأنن *muta-annin*, Pleasing, agreeable. One who studies, desires, or wishes any thing to be acceptable: who makes any one contented.

A متأنّي *muta-annī*, One who behaves with address and attention in any affair; patient and cool in doing business. One who waits, lingers, delays.

A متأوب *muta-awwab*, (v. n. 5 of آب for اوب) Arriving at night-time. *Muta-awwib*, One who arrives during the night. A comer in quest of water.

A متاوبة *mutāwabat*, (v. n. 3 of تاب for توب) Standing in another's stead.

A متاوج *mutāwaj*, That part of the head which is bound about by a fillet. *Mutāwij*, Crowned.

A متأود *muta-awwid*, Crooked, curved, bent. Troublesome, burdensome (business).

A متأوق *muta-awwik*, Averse, hanging back.

A متأول *muta-awwil*, An interpreter. First.

A متأوه *muta-awwih*, One who sighs, crying Ah!

A متأوي *muta-awwī*, Assembled. One who remains quietly at home. طير متأويات *tayri muta-awwiyāt*, Birds in flocks.

A متأهب *muta-ahhib*, Ready, prepared.

A متأهل *muta-ahhil*, One who marries a wife. A family-man. Worthy, proper, suited.

A متاهمة *mutāhamat*, (v. n. 3 of تهم) Arriving in that part of Arabia called Tihāmah.

A متأهه *muta-ahhih*, Sorrowful, apt to sigh.

A متأيب *muta-ayyab*, (v. n. 5 of آب for ايب) Arriving at night-fall. *Muta-ayyib*, One who arrives at night-fall.

A متأيد *muta-ayyid*, Strengthened, confirmed.

A متايزة *mutāyazat*, A contention for victory, superiority, or pre-eminence.

A متأيس *muta-ayyis*, Tender, softened.

A متايسة *mutāyasat*, (v. n. 3 of تاس for تيس) Taking in hand, managing. Procrastinating, delaying, spinning out. Repelling.

A متايعة *mutāyaʿat*, A hastening to do mischief.

A متائم *mutā-im*, (A horse) which renews a race.

A متأيم *muta-ayyim*, Unmarried (man or woman). Become a widow, widowed.

A متأيي *muta-ayyī*, One who establishes himself, or who tarries. One who fixes his mind on, or goes in quest of, the very thing or person (آية *āyat*).

A متائيم *matā-īm*, (pl. of متآم *mit-ām*) Double-woven (cloths).

A متبّ *mutibb*, Whatever enfeebles, enervates.

A متبادّ *mutabādd*, Engaged in attacking one another, man to man, in battle. One who takes an associate (بدّ *bidd*) in any thing.

A متبادر *mutabādir*, One who makes haste and endeavours to get the start. A riser. Emergent.

A متبادل *mutabādil*, Agreed to take turn about.

A متبادي *mutabādī*, Rustic, rural, wild.

A متبارّ *mutabārr*, Mutual in conferring benefits.

A متبارز *mutabāriz*, A champion who comes forth from the crowd to engage with his rival.

A متبارك *mutabārik*, Blessed (God), reverenced. Holy. Illustrious. Happy and comfortable.

A متبارئ *mutabāri-*, Engaged to release one another, or to dissolve partnership.

A متباري *mutabārī*, Mutually contentious, opposed to each other. Rival in dignity.

A متباريان *mutabāriyāni*, Day and night.

A متبازج *mutabāzij*, Boastful to each other.

A متبازي *mutabāzī*, Wide-stepping. One who shakes his hips in walking. One who glories in what he does not possess.

A متباشر *mutabāshir*, Reciprocal in communicating good news or joyful tidings.

A متباطئ *mutabāti-*, Dilatory, slow in travelling. One who lies on the side. Weak-minded. Careless.

A متباعد *mutabāʿid*, Absent. Distant, remote.

A متباغض *mutabāghiz*, Full of mutual enmity.

A متباغي *mutabāghī*, Insolent, rebellious, tumultuous towards or against one another.

A متباقي *mutabākī*, A residue, remainder.

A متباكّ *mutabākk*, Crowded, thronging.

A متباكي *mutabākī*, One who forces himself, or is forced to shed tears. One who shams weeping.

A متبالط *mutabālit*, Engaged in fencing.

A متباله *mutabālih*, One who feigns ignorance.

A متبالي *mutabālī*, A prover, trier, experimenter.

A متباهج *mutabāhij*, Gay, flowery (garden).

A متباهل *mutabāhil*, Mutual in execrating.

A متباهي *mutabāhī*, Boastful to each other.

A متبائ *mutabā-i*, Equally matched.

A متبايش *mutabāyish*, A receiver with another.

A متبايع *mutabāyiʿ*, United in a mutual covenant. Associated together in commercial transactions, as buyer and seller to one another.

A متبائن *mutabāʾin*, Distant from each other.

A متباين *mutabāyin*, Distinct, separate from one another. A link which joins separate bodies. (in arithmetic) Incommensurable.

A متبتل *mutabattil*, One who retires from the world on a religious account: a recluse.

A متبهج *mutabahhih*, Received into a house.

A متبحر *mutabahhir*, Very learned, deeply read, profound (like the sea, بحر *bahr*). Very rich.

A متبختر *mutabakhtir*, A pompous, strutting fellow.

A متبخر *mutabakhkhir*, A perfumer of his person.

A متبدد *mutabaddid*, Dispersed, scattered, wasted. امرأة متبددة *imraʾat mutabaddidat*, A lean woman.

A متبدع *mutabaddiʿ*, An innovator, an inventor, author. An arch-heretic, broacher of novelties.

A متبدل *mutabaddil*, Changed. One who changes, substitutes, inverts. A receiver of one thing in exchange for another.

A متبدي *mutabaddī*, A beginner. A dweller in the desert (بادية *bādiyat*). One who comes into view.

A متبذل *mutabazzil*, A doer of his own drudgery.

A متبّر *mutabbar*, Ruined, broken. *Mutabbir*, A destroyer, a breaker in pieces.

A متبرج *mutabarrij*, Fine, gay, showy in dress.

A متبرد *mutabarrid*, Collected, gathered (water). *Mutabarrad* or *mutabarrid*, Washed in cold water.

A متبرّر *mutabarrar*, Justified. *Mutabarrir*, Pious, devout, dutiful, obedient. True, just.

A متبرّز *mutabarriz*, One who goes abroad into the fields to ease nature.

A متبرّص *mutabarras*, (A field) eaten quite bare.

A متبرّض *mutabarriz*, A receiver (of any thing) by instalments. One who earns a scanty livelihood and fares meanly.

A متبرّع *mutabarriʿ*, One who supererogates or does voluntarily that which is not obligatory on him.

A متبرّك *mutabarrak*, Blessed, holy, sacred, sanctified, consecrated. Fortunate, happy, august. اماكن متبركه *amākini mutabarraka*, Holy mansions, sacred places. *Mutabarrik*, Resolved, determined, bent upon.

A متبرّم *mutabarrim*, Sated, wearied, irked.

A متبرّي *mutabarraʾ*, Freed, absolved. *Mutabarrī*, Free, clear. Interposed, intervenient: hinderer.

A متبزّل *mutabazzil*, Split, cleft, riven. One who taps or broaches.

A متبس *muttabis*, Dry, dried.

A متبسّر *mutabassir*, Cold (day). Benumbed, asleep (foot). (A wild bull) which roots up and devours the dry roots of plants.

A متبسّط *mutabassit*, Extended far and wide, spread abroad. Who ranges, or expatiates at large.

A متبسّل *mutabassil*, Stern, crabbed. A lion.

A متبسّم *mutabassim*, Smiling: one who smiles. Flashing (lightning).

A متبشبش *mutabashbish*, Joyous, merry, blithe.

A متبصبص *mutabasbis*, Tail-wagging (dog).

A متبصّر *mutabassir*, One who contemplates attentively; considerate, prudent, judicious. One who keeps a sharp look out for the new moon.

A متبصّل *mutabassil*, (Bark) formed like an onion (بصل *basal*), coat upon coat.

A متبضّض *mutabazziz*, One who recovers (a debt) by degrees, by little and little.

A متبضّع *mutabazziʿ*, Flowing, fluid (sweat). Cracked, split (skin).

A متبطّح *mutabattih*, Extensive (plain). (Water) diffused and widely-spread over a plain.

A متبطّل *mutabattil*, Bold, brave, courageous.

A متبطّن *mutabattin*, Interior, internal. One who places (any body) under his belly. One who pierces the middle of any thing, or understands the truth of any matter. One who walks through (a garden). Cattle pasturing at large.

A متبع *mutbiʿ*, A follower. Who causes to follow another, or who joins one thing to another. (A ewe, cow, or concubine) followed by her offspring.

A متّبع *muttabiʿ*, A follower. Diligent in seeking, importunate. A pursuer in battle or in exile. One who overtakes. A client. Under protection.

A متبعّث *mutabaʿʿis*, Easy-flowing (verse).

A متبعّص *mutabaʿʿis*, Put in violent motion, writhing, as a snake when trampled on.

A متبعّض *mutabaʿʿiz*, Divided into parts.

A متبعّل *mutabaʿʿil*, (A wife) obedient to her lord (بعل *baʿl*), or one who adorns herself for him.

A متبغثر *mutabaghsir*, Disordered, confused.

A متبغّض *mutabaghghiz*, Hostile, inimical; hater.

A متبغّم *mutabaghghim*, Bleating, lowing.

A متبغّي *mutabaghghī*, A seeker of a thing lost.

A متبقّر *mutabakkir*, Profoundly learned. Affluent. Open, wide. One who dwells in a town or village, his family still remaining in the country.

A متبقّل *mutabakkil*, (An ass) which feeds on pot-herbs (بقل *bakl*). One who goes out to gather herbs, or who feeds his cattle with them.

A متبكّر *mutabakkir*, One who goes before.

A متبكّل *mutabakkil*, One who speaks confusedly. One who overwhelms with blows or reproaches. A plunderer. An opposer, obstructer. Who walks haughtily, a strutting coxcomb.

A متبكّم *mutabakkim*, Faltering (speech).

A متبل *mutbal*, Seasoned with pot-herbs. *Mutbil*, Who or what impairs friendship. Whatever weakens, sickens, or grieves. One who seasons (a pot) with herbs and spiceries (تابل *tābil* or *tābal*).

A متبلتع *mutabaltiʿ*, Who affects grace or wit.

A متبلّج *mutaballij*, Bright (dawn). A smiler.

A متبلّح *mutaballih*, Fatigued, tired, jaded.

A متبلّخ *mutaballikh*, Proud, lofty.

A متبلّد *mutaballid*, Stupid, dull. One who claps the hands. Astonished, stupefied, vexed. Fallen on the ground. Arrived in an uninhabited region. One who takes possession of another's country.

A متبلّص *mutaballis*, (Cattle) which eat a field bare. One who causes a field to be eaten bare. One who asks for any thing privately. Covetous, desirous.

A متبلّغ *mutaballigh*, Contented with what one has. (A disease) which gains ground. One who labours to reach (a stage or halting-place).

A متبلّل *mutaballil*, Moistened, wet. A lion.

A متبلّه *mutaballih*, Ignorant, simple. One who shams ignorance or simplicity. One who wanders about without inquiring the way or taking a guide.

A متبن *matban*, A bin for straw (تبن *tibn*).

A متّبن *muttabin*, Dressed in the short breeches تبّان *tubbān*, which barely conceal the nakedness.

A متبّن *mutabban*, Dyed of a straw-colour. *Mutabbin*, Intelligent, sagacious. Who fixes the mind or eye, and sees clearly.

A متبنة *matbanat*, A straw or hay-loft.

A متبنّج *mutabannij*, Who boasts a noble race.

A متبنّك *mutabannik*, Stationary, firm, steady.

A متبنّي *mutabannaʾ*, Adopted (son). *Mutabanni*, One who adopts as his son; adoptive (father).

A متبوّأ *mutabawwaʾ*, The place in the womb which contains the fœtus. A place where a bull is kept. A spot where cattle lie about a watering-place.

A متبوّب *mutabawwab*, Appointed as doorkeeper. *Mutabawwib*, One who appoints a porter.

A متبور *matbūr*, Perishing, ruined.

A متبوّش *mutabawwish*, Mixed (crowd).

A متبوع *matbūʿ*, Followed, obeyed. A lord, chief, leader. متبوع امت *matbūʿi ummat*, A chief of the people, a high priest.

A متبوّع *mutabawwiʿ*, One who measures with a fathom (باع *bāʿ*). Long-stepped. Long (rope).

A متبوّق *mutabawwik*, Propagated (murrain).

A متبول *matbūl*, Sick, pining (heart).

A متبوّل *mutabawwil*, One who makes water. One who overwhelms with blows and abuse.

A متبهّج *mutabahhij*, Merry, gay, pleasant.

A متبهّر *mutabahhir*, Breathless from fatigue. Filled. Bright (cloud).

A متبهّش *mutabahhish*, Assembled, convened.

A متبهّم *mutabahhim*, Doubtful, uncertain. Hidden, concealed, unintelligible, not understood.

A متبهنس *mutabahnis*, A stately walker. A lion.

A متبيّتة *mutabayyitat*, A woman who has gotten a husband and home (بيت *bayt*), housed, settled.

A متبيّن *mutabayyin*, Whatever renders clear or manifest. Explained, illustrated. Clear, distinct.

A متتابع *mutatābiʿ*, Consecutive, successive, coming one after another. Uninterrupted, continual. Who does any thing often; falls into repeated errors; or staggers often (as a drunken man). A camel whose shoulder moves to and fro in walking. (A man) of an excellent understanding, and of general and extensive knowledge. Finely-shaped (horse). Straight, without knots (a branch). P سه روز متتابع *sih rozi mutatābiʿ*, Three following days. قوافل متتابع النزول *kawāfili mutatābiʿu'n nuzūl*, Troops or caravans alighting one after another.

A متتارك *mutatārik*, Mutual in abandoning, desisting, or withholding the hand.

A متتالع *mutatāliʿ*, One who walks with head erect and stretched-out neck, particularly from pride.

A متتالي *mutatālī*, One following another in regular succession. Consequent.

A متتام *mutatāmim*, Simultaneous in flocking to. Complete in number, perfect.

A متتايع *mutatāyiʿ*, One who rushes or plunges into (vice). Hasty, precipitate in doing any thing. (Wind) which carries off or scatters (dust or leaves). Ready to rise. Quarrelsome: self-opiniated. Vacillating (drunkard). A camel whose shoulder moves to and fro in walking. Quick in succession, distracting, embarrassing (affairs).

A متبّ *mutibb*, What weakens or debilitates.

A متبّب *mutabbib*, Ruinous, destructive.

A متتبّع *mutatabbiʿ*, Diligent in seeking. A searcher. Imitative; an imitator.

A متتحتح *mutatahtih*, Moved, put in motion.

A متترّب *mutatarrib*, Strewed with earth, soiled.

A مترتر *mutatartir*, Agitated, moved; reeling.

A مترّح *mutatarrih*, Grieved, made sad.

A متترّس *mutatarris*, Armed with a shield.

A مترّع *mutatarriʿ*, In haste to do evil.

A مترّف *mutatarrif*, Blessed with life's comforts.

A متتلّع *mutatalliʿ*, Who stretches forth the neck, or raises the head to see and hear any thing. One who goes before.

A متتلّي *mutatallī*, One who follows, pursues, and prosecutes a claim. Consecutive.

A متتمّم *mutatammim*, Split, apparent (fracture); also without separation. One who walks painfully from a broken bone. Like the tribe of تميم *tamīm*, in regard to climate, locality, or opinions.

A متنّخ *mutatannikh*, A sojourner.

A متتوّج *mutatawwij*, The wearer of a crown (تاج *tāj*), crowned.

A متتهته *mutatahtih*, A stammerer.

A متتهّم *mutatahhim*, Who arrives in Tihāma.

A متّى *matta'*, Matthew.

A متتيّع *mutatayyiʿ*, One who rushes headlong into mischief. Self-conceited, opiniated.

A متثابر *mutasābir*, Mutual in rushing upon.

A متثاقل *mutasākil*, Heavy, slow, sluggish. Gravitating towards the earth. One who grudges to do (any thing) and desists (from it). Cowardly, declining battle.

A متثاون *mutasāwin*, An insnarer of game or wild beasts; catching them on all hands. Crafty.

A متثائب *mutasāʾib*, Slothful. Negligent.

A متثبّت *mutasabbit*, Fixed, established, settled. A delayer. A performer, finisher.

A متثبّن *mutasabbin*, One who carries with both hands, in an apron or skirt of a garment (ثبنة *subnat*).

A متثلّم *mutasattim*, Obscene in talk. Tattered (garment). Dissolved in rags (meat, by overboiling). Ruinous, dilapidated (shallow well).

A متثعّم *mutasaʿʿim*, Agreeable, pleasant.

A متثفّي *mutasaffīʿ*, (A mean original) preventive of the achievement of noble actions.

A متثقّب *mutasakkib*, Bored. Worm-eaten (hide). One who drills holes. A kindler of a fire.

A متثلّل *mutasallil*, Ruined, overthrown.

A متثلّم *mutasallim*, Broken in the edges, notched, chipped (sword or earthen dish); pierced through the middle (a wall or vessel); chinky.

A متثمّل *mutasammil*, Who protects or supports others (especially in meat and drink); who manages the concerns of his dependants. A devourer, eater, or drinker; who or what absorbs or exhausts.

A متثنّي *mutasannī*, Folded, doubled; inflected, complicated. Who goes with the body bent. Long without breadth. Haughty-walking (woman).

A متثوّب *mutasawwib*, One who says his prayers a second time, and thereby fancies himself entitled to a reward (ثواب *sawāb*).

A متثوّر *mutasawwir*, Set in motion. Boiling.

A متثوّل *mutasawwil*, One who gets the better of. Reproachful, insolent; one who inflicts wounds by blows. Swarming (bees).

A متثئّب *mutasaʾʾib*, Indolent, yawning, oscitant. Employed to gain intelligence.

A متجاثي *mutajāsī*, Seated knee to knee. Seated on the knees.

A متجاحف *mutajāhif*, Engaged in fencing, cudgelling, or carrying off the ball in the game of shinty.

A متجادع *mutajādiʿ*, Mutual in quarrel, fighting.

A متجادل *mutajādil*, Mutually contentious.

A متجاذب *mutajāzib*, Mutual in pulling. Dragged.

A متجاذع *mutajāziʿ*, Weak (lamb or horse-colt).

A متجاري *mutajārī*, One who goes in company with another. Quarrelsome, contentious.

A متجازي *mutajāzī*, Importunate creditor, dun.

A متجاسر *mutajāsir*, Brave, magnanimous. Bold, audacious, fierce in contending. One who shakes a stick at another.

A متجاسرة *mutajāsirat*, Swift, active (she-camel).

A متجاعل *mutajāʿil*, One who fixes a price or wages. People taking a thing amongst them.

A متجافي *mutajāfī*, Indifferent or unconcerned. Unsettled. Separate, distant. Removed from its place. Inclined (to one side).

A متجالّة *mutajāllat*, Aged, old (woman).

A متجالد *mutajālid*, Employed in fighting, in fencing, or in sword-exercise together.

A متجالس *mutajālis*, Seated together.

A متجالل *mutajālil*, Disdainful, contemptuous. One who takes the finest and best.

A متجالي *mutajālī*, Mutual in making a disclosure of each other's condition.

A متجانب *mutajānib*, One who avoids, shuns.

A متجانس *mutajānis*, Homogeneous.

A متجانف *mutajānif*, Inclined.

A متجانن *mutajānin*, Apparently insane.

A متجاوب *mutajāwib*, Reciprocal in answering.

A متجاور *mutajāwir*, Neighbouring, nigh.

A متجاوز *mutajāwiz*, One who transgresses, exceeds, or goes beyond. Who passes by, or forgives. Insolent, extravagant.

A متجاول *mutajāwil*, Circumambulant (as two parties preparing to fight or to wrestle).

A متجاهد *mutajāhid*, Pains-taking; a striver.

A متجاهر *mutajāhir*, One who appears in public.

A متجاهل *mutajāhil*, One who pretends to be a fool or ignorant (جاهل *jāhil*); who shams stupidity.

A المتجبّر *al mutajabbir*, The lion.

A متجبّس *mutajabbis*, Pompous in walking.

A متجبّن *mutajabbin*, Curdled (milk), cheesy.

A متجحدر *mutajahdir*, (A bird) ready to fly.

A متجحّر *mutajahhir*, Sunk in the socket (eye).

A متجدّب *mutajaddib*, Droughty, barren (year). One who deems (a thing) irksome.

A متجدّد *mutajaddid*, Renovated, renewed. New, recent. Dry, milkless (udder).

A متجر *matjar*, Commerce. *Mutjir*, A trader.

A متّجر *muttajar*, A place of business. *Muttajir*, A trader. A medicine-taker.

A متجرة *matjarat*, A country or market where trade (تجارة *tijārat*) is brisk.

A متجرّد *mutajarrad*, (v. n. 5 of جرد, irregular) Being stripped. Nakedness, nudity. حسن المتجرّد *hasanu'l mutajarrad*, Beautiful when naked. *Mutajarrid*, Stripped. Level (ground). (See تجرّد).

A متجرّس *mutajarris*, A speaker.

A متجرّع *mutajarriʿ*, One who swallows his cares and griefs. One who swallows by sips or gulps.

A متجرّف *mutajarrif*, (A ram) which, having lost his fat, shakes with leanness. (See تجرّف.)

A متجرّم *mutajarram*, Falsely accused. *Mutajarrim*, Completed (year). Past (night). A false accuser. A transgressor. (See تجرّم *tajarrum*.)

A متجزّئ *mutajazziʾ*, Divided into parts (جزء *juzʾ*). Content, satisfied.

A متجسّد *mutajassid*, Incarnate, embodied. Corpulent, stout. غير متجسّد *ghayr mutajassid*, Incorporeal.

A متجسّس *mutajassis*, A close searcher, spy.

A متجسّم *mutajassim*, Corporeal, incarnate, incorporate. Large-bodied, corpulent. A chooser (from among other men). One who proposes or engages in any thing great or laudable. Who enters upon the ascent of a mountain, or the most difficult stage of any business. A chooser of a piece of land near a particular district.

A متجشّع *mutajashshiʿ*, Very greedy, covetous.

A متجشّم *mutajashshim*, Pains-taking.

A متجشّي *mutajashshī*, One who belches.

A متجضّم *mutajazzim*, A snatcher with the mouth.

A متجعّب *mutajaʻʻib*, Thrown prostrate. Dead.

A متجعجع *mutajaʻjiʻ*, One who throws himself on the ground from excess of grief.

A متجعّد *mutajaʻʻid*, Curly (hair). Wrinkled.

A متجعّر *mutajaʻʻir*, One who ties the rope جعار *jiʻār* round his waist when descending into a well.

A متجعّم *mutajaʻʻim*, Desirous of meat, greedy. Sounding (harp).

A متجفجف *mutajafjif*, Partly dried (garment).

A متجفّر *mutajaffir*, (A kid) four months old.

A متجلّب *mutajallib*, Clamorous, noisy.

A متجلجل *mutajaljil*, One who crosses a country. Shaken, tottering (foundation).

A متجلّد *mutajallid*, Stubborn, sturdy, hardy.

A متجلّس *mutajallis*, Seated (as a judge).

A متجلّف *mutajallif*, Lean, emaciated.

A متجلّق *mutajallik*, Open-mouthed (laugher).

A متجلّل *mutajallal*, Covered, clothed. Magnified. *Mutajallil*, Who overcomes, rises superior (in dignity). Seated on horseback. A taker of whatever is best or most illustrious.

A متجلّي *mutajallī*, Illuminated. Splendid. Displayed. Transfigured.

A متجمّد *mutajammad*, Congealed, frozen.

A متجمّر *mutajammir*, Assembled, met together. Encamped, stationed in the seat of war.

A متجمّع *mutajammiʻ*, Collected, congregated.

A متجمّل *mutajammil*, Comfortable, well off. One who adorns his person. An eater of melted fat.

A متجمّي *mutajammī*, Who draws himself together (under a covering). Congregated, assembled. A taker, hider.

A متجنّب *mutajannib*, One who recedes or retires from, who shuns or avoids. Polluted.

A متجنّث *mutajannis*, One who pretends to belong to another family. Kind, friendly. A bird that drops its wings and sits.

A متجنّح *mutajannih*, Inclined to one side.

A متجنّن *mutajannin*, Seemingly mad. Furious.

A متجنّنة *mutajanninat*, A country so covered with grass that the paths have wholly disappeared.

A متجنّي *mutajannī*, A false accuser. A gatherer of fruit.

A متجوّر *mutajawwir*, Laid prostrate, fallen on the side. Broken, routed.

A متجوّز *mutajawwiz*, One who does any thing slightly. Perfunctory, careless (in prayer). Loose in conversation. A conniver, winker.

A متجوّش *mutajawwish*, Slightly emaciated.

A متجوّع *mutajawwiʻ*, One who starves himself.

A متجوّف *mutajawwif*, Hollow. One who enters.

A متجوّق *mutajawwik*, Collected, assembled.

A متّجه *muttajih*, (A notion or idea) which enters the mind.

A متجهّز *mutajahhiz*, Prepared for, equipped.

A متجهّم *mutajahhim*, Stern, ungracious, crabbed.

A متّجي *muttajī*, (Dates) packed together.

A متجيّش *mutajayyish*, A mustered army (جيش *jaysh*). Agitated, fluttered (spirits).

A متح *math*, (v.n. of متح) Drawing out, extracting. Drawing (water) from a well. Advancing (the day). Breaking wind. Voiding (dung). Fixing her tail in the sand when laying her eggs (a locust). Throwing down. Cutting. Striking.

A متحابّ *mutahābb*, Bound by mutual love.

A متحاتّ *mutahātt*, Falling (leaf). Flayed, skinned, excoriated, scratched.

A متحاتن *mutahātin*, Like, equal, agreeing.

A متحاثّ *mutahāss*, Reciprocal in animating with desire, in instigating and egging on.

A متحاجّ *mutahājj*, Mutually disputatious.

A متحاجز *mutahājiz*, Intent upon opposing, hindering, or throwing obstacles in each other's way. Mutual in retreating.

A متحاجي *mutahājī*, Engaged in proposing questions, enigmas, or riddles to one another.

A متحادّ *mutahādd*, Mutual in resisting.

A متحادث *mutahādis*, Engaged in conversation, mutual discourse, or talk.

A متحارب *mutahārib*, Mutual in fighting.

A متحاسب *mutahāsib*, Engaged in reckoning.

A متحاسد *mutahāsid*, Envious of each other.

A متحاسي *mutahāsī*, Engaged in compotation.

A متحاشي *mutahāshī*, Separate, standing apart from each other.

A متحاصّ *mutahāss*, Employed in distributing portions (حصّة *hissat*) amongst themselves.

A متحاضّ *mutahāzz*, Reciprocal in stimulating.

A متحاقّ *mutahākk*, Mutually contentious.

A متحاقر *mutahākir*, Mean in one's own eyes.

A متحاكم *mutahākim*, Agreed to go together before the judge (حاكم *hākim*).

A متحالف *mutahālif*, Leagued, bound together by oath, covenant, league, or treaty (حلف *hilf*).

A متحالم *mutahālim*, Falsely meek, demure.

A متحالي *mutahālī*, Delicate, dainty (dame).

A متحامق *mutahāmik*, One who shams the fool.

A متحامل *mutahāmal*, (v. n. 6 of حمل, irregular) Putting up with, being patient. A place where the exercise of patience is needed. *Mutahāmil*, Who puts up with trouble, patient.

A متحامي *mutahāmī*, Cautious, heedful, wary.

A متحاور *mutahāwir*, Engaged in a dialogue.

A متحاوز *mutahāwiz*, Mutual in retreating.

A متحاوص *mutahāwis*, Quick-sighted, eagle-eyed. One who shews himself to be احوص *ahwas*.

A متحايص *mutahāyis*, A mixer, a mingler.

A متحبّب *mutahabbib*, Loving, fond, affectionate. Granulated. (See also تحبّب *tahabbub*.)

A متحبجر *mutahabjir*, Griped in the belly.

A متحبّس *mutahabbis*, Self-restrained.

A متحبّش *mutahabbish*, Congregated, met.

A متحترش *mutahatrish*, Assembled, met.

A متحتّك *mutahattik*, A short and quick stepper.

A متحتّم *mutahattam*, Needful. *Mutahattim*, One who prays for good, or augurs well for another. Joyous, light, blithe. An eater of broken bits (حتامة *hutāmat*): one who clears the table.

A متحجّر *mutahajjir*, Petrified. Stony. Purulent, mattery (wound). (See تحجّر *tahajjur*.)

A متحجّي *mutahajjī*, Stationary. Greedy.

A متّحد *muttahid*, United, made one.

A متحدّب *mutahaddib*, Benevolent, friendly.

A متحدّبة *mutahaddibat*, A woman who remains a widow that she may look after her children.

A متحدّث *mutahaddas*, A place of conversation, an assembly. *Mutahaddis*, A relater, historian. Any thing happening new.

A متحدّر *mutahaddir*, Fluent, flowing (humour in the eye, or water from a cloud).

A متحدّس *mutahaddis*, An inquirer: inquisitive.

A متحدّي *mutahaddī*, Temperate, abstemious.

A متّحديّة *muttahidīyat*, Singleness. Union.

A متحذّق *mutahazzik*, Wise; a wise man.

A متحذلق *mutahazlik*, Sharp, clever. A boaster.

A متحرّب *mutaharrib*, A lion.

A متحرّج *mutaharrij*, Penitent. One who abstains from wickedness. Escaped from straits.

A متحرّد *mutaharrid*, Separate, solitary, remote from friends.

A متحرّس *mutaharris*, Careful, cautious, watchful, wary, abstemious.

A متحرّف *mutaharrif*, Changed, inverted.

A متحرّفة *mutaharrifa*, A tax on people of particular trades, a professional tax.

A متحرّق *mutaharrik*, Burnt; inflamed.

A متحرّك *mutaharrik*, Moved; moving one's self; moveable. Accented with short vowels. غير متحرّك *ghayr mutaharrik*, Immoveable. قواي متحرّكه *huwayi mutaharrika*, Moveable powers.

A متحرّم *mutaharrim*, Forbidden, unlawful. Self-denying. Revered. A refugee. Robber, outlaw.

A متحرّي *mutaharrī*, A purposer, intender.

A متحزّز *mutahazziz*, Cut, notched.

A متحزّق *mutahazzik*, Covetous, close-fisted.

A متحزّم *mutahazzim*, Girt round the waist.

A متحزّن *mutahazzin*, Grieved, afflicted, sad.

A متحسّب *mutahassib*, A seeker of intelligence.

A متحسّر *mutahassir*, Sorrowful; regretful.

A متحسّس *mutahassis*, An explorer, examiner.

A متحسّف *mutahassif*, One who leaves nothing but eats up all.

A متحشّد *mutahashshid*, Convened, assembled.

A متحشّف *mutahashshif*, Clad in old raiment.

A متحشّم *mutahashshim*, Covered with blushes.

A متحصرم *mutahasrim*, Close-fisted.

A متحصّل *mutahassil*, A gatherer, acquirer.

A متحصّلات *mutahassilāt*, Productions, products.

A متحصّن *mutahassin*, Who retires to a stronghold and fortifies himself there. A refugee. Grown up to be a stallion (حصان *hisān*).

A متحصّنة *mutahassinat*, Chaste (woman).

A متحصّى *mutahassī*, Cautious, wary.

A متحطّم *mutahattim*, Broken. Hot with rage.

A متحظّي *mutahazzī*, Fortunate, favoured.

A متحف *muthaf*, Dedicated, given. *Muthif*, Giver of a present, maker of an offering (تحفة *tuhfat*).

A متحفّظ *mutahaffiz*, Vigilant, cautious, one who takes heed to himself. One who commits to memory, or recollects one by one.

A متحفّل *mutahaffil*, Met together, assembled.

A متحفّى *mutahaffī*, Transported, filled with joy. Humane, benevolent. Industrious.

A متحقّق *mutahakkak*, Verified, true, sure, certain. *Mutahakkik*, Certain, true. A verifier.

A متحكّك *mutahakkik*, Evil-designed.

A متحكّم *mutahakkim*, Lord paramount, sovereign.

A متّحل *muttahil*, One who makes an exception or saving clause.

A متحلّب *mutahallib*, Milked. Flowing (sweat).

A متحلحل *mutahalhil*, Removing or moved (from place to place). Dispersed, scattered, beat, carded, or teased (as cotton).

A متحلّق *mutahallik*, Seated in a circle (people). Halo-encircled (moon).

A متحلّل *mutahallil*, Melted, dissolved. Sick on returning from a journey. Exceptive in an oath. Released from an oath by an expiation.

A متحلّم *mutahallim*, A dreamer. One who pretends to have had a dream or a vision. One who strives to evince meekness and patience. Fat (camel, child, locust, or Lybian lizard).

A متحلّي *mutahalla'*, Adorned (especially with bracelets or other female ornaments). *Mutahallī*, One who decorates. One who finds (a thing) sweet.

A متحمّ *mutahham*, (or متحمّ اللون *mutahhamu'l lawn*) (A horse) of a dark or chesnut-colour.

A متحمة *muthamat*, A striped stuff of Yaman.

A متحمّة *mutahhamat*, Striped stuff from Yaman.

A متحمحم *mutahamhim*, Neighing (horse).

A متحمّد *mutahammid*, Praised. Commendable. One who lays another under obligation.

A متحمّر *mutahammir*, One who calls, or is called, an ass. A speaker of the Himyaritic dialect.

A متحمّس *mutahammis*, A steady resister. Intrepid (in battle). Unflinching (in religion).

A متحمّض *mutahammiz*, (A camel) which feeds on the salt and bitter plant حمض *hamz*.

A متحمّل *mutahammil*, The bearer of a burden. One who supports or suffers patiently. Capable of bearing. One who moves a camp. Affable, considerate, enduring.

A متحنّث *mutahannis*, One who abstains from or discards sin. A renouncer of idolatry.

A متحنّط *mutahannit*, Buried with sweet herbs.

A متحنّف *mutahannif*, A follower of the sect of حنيفة *hanīfa*, *i. e.* true, orthodox in religion. Self-circumcised. A renouncer of idolatry. Inclined to.

A متحنّك *mutahannik*, One who passes the turban-sash under his chin (حنك *hanak*).

A متحنّن *mutahannin*, Tender, full of pity.

A متحنّي *mutahannī*, Curved, bent.

A متحوّب *mutahawwib*, One who refrains from crimes. One who, from being rich, has become poor; and from being poor has again become rich.

A متحوّر *mutahawwir*, Quick, hasty. Passionate.

A متحوّز *mutahawwiz*, Coiled (serpent). Assembled. Retired, gone aside.

A متحوّس *mutahawwis*, Intrepid, bold, dauntless. Sorrowful, sad; querulous.

A متحوّش *mutahawwish*, Retired to a distance, absent, separated. Ashamed.

A متحوّف *mutahawwif*, One who chips away.

A متحوّي *mutahawwī*, Collected, contained, comprised. Round, circular.

A متحيّر *mutahayyir*, Astonished, stupefied, wondering. Amazed, thunderstruck. Dim (sighted). Wandering, driven here and there, erratic. Flowing water, whirling in an eddy. Filled with water. كوكب متحيّر *kawkabi mutahayyir*, A wandering star, a planet. P متحيّر شدن *mutahayyir shudan*, To be lost in amazement, to be thunderstruck.

A متحيّز *mutahayyiz*, Congregated. Coiled (serpent). A deserter to the enemy.

A متحيّش *mutahayyish*, Fearing, frightened. Hasty in running. Increased. Overflowing.

A متحيّض *mutahayyiz*, A woman who abstains from public prayer through ceremonial uncleanness.

A متحيّف *mutahayyif*, One who pares (any thing) round the edges.

A متحيّن *mutahayyin*, Elapsed, going by, past (time). Perished. One waiting for his meal.

A متخ *matkh*, (v. n. of متخ) Removing, extracting. Carrying off. Placing at a distance. Striking. Cutting. Being firm, fixed. Lying with. Fixing her tail in the ground when laying eggs (a locust). Voiding (dung).

A متّخ *mutikhkh*, One who puts acid or ferment (into a mass of paste). A good kneader.

A متخاتل *mutakhātil*, Reciprocal in cozening.

A متخادع *mutakhādiʻ*, One who affects to have been duped. Mutual in deceiving.

A متخاذل *mutakhāzil*, Averse from, disinclined to help each other. Weak in the leg.

A متخارج *mutakhārij*, (A company of fellow-travellers) who make up a common purse for the expenses of their journey. Mutual in dividing (one party taking the house, and the other the lands).

A متخازر *mutakhāzir*, One who looks through half-shut eyes in order to discern more accurately.

A متخاسي *mutakhāsī*, Employed in pelting each other with stones.

A متخاشي *mutakhāshī*, Timid, fearful, timorous.

A متخاصر *mutakhāsir*, Hand in hand in walking.

A متخاصل *mutakhāsil*, Mutually emulous in throwing the javelin, or in archery.

A متخاصم *mutakhāsim*, Disputatious, mutually contentious. An adversary, opponent in a law-suit.

A متخاصمين *mutakhāsimayn*, (obl. du. of متخاصمان *mutakhāsimāni*) Plaintiff and defendant.

A متخاطر *mutakhātir*, Engaged in betting.

A متخاطي *mutakhātī*, Apt to err or blunder.

A متخافّ *mutakhāff*, Active, nimble, light.

A متخافت *mutakhāfit*, A reader in a low tone.

A متخافف *mutakhāfif*, Light, agile.

A متخالّ *mutakhāll*, Mutually friendly.

A متخالج *mutakhālij*, Occupant of the mind.

A متخالس *mutakhālis*, Mutual in snatching.

A متخالع *mutakhāliʻ*, Separated, divorced (man and wife). Mutually perjured.

A متخالف *mutakhālif*, Opposed, opposite; adverse. عماد متخالف الابعاد *ʻimādi mutakhālifu'l abʻād*, Columns at opposite distances, *i. e.* facing each other.

A متخالل *mutakhālil*, Amicable, very friendly.

A متخامص *mutakhāmis*, Distant, retired, removed. The payer of a debt. Waning (night).

A متخاوش *mutakhāwish*, Lean.

A متخاوص *mutakhāwis*, One who winks to look more steadily.

A متخاوض *mutakhāwiz*, Remote, far distant.

A متخايل *mutakhāyal*, (fem. متخايلة *mutakhāyalat*) (Ground) overspread with luxuriant herbage.

A متخبّر *mutakhabbir*, A picker up of news.

A متخبّس *mutakhabbis*, A receiver of spoil.

A متخبّط *mutakhabbit*, A destroyer. Mad, silly. Possessed by the devil. A wanderer.

A متخبّق *mutakhabbik*, High, sublime, lofty.

A متخبّي *mutakhabbī*, A pitcher of a tent.

A متختّر *mutakhattir*, Muddled, fuddled.

A متختّم *mutakhattim*, The wearer of a seal-ring (خاتم *khātam*), or of a turban. A concealer. Silent.

A متخدّب *mutakhaddib*, Long, slim, weak-headed. Hasty, precipitate. Neither a fast nor slow walker.

A متخدّد *mutakhaddid*, Covered, closed. Lean.

A متّخذ *muttakhaz*, Taken. *Muttakhiz*, A taker, receiver, selecter, chooser, assumer, associater. A preparer, dresser (of victuals). A commencer.

A متخرّج *mutakharrij*, A successful and advanced student in polite literature.

A متخرّد *mutakharrid*, Modest, bashful, silent.

A متخرّص *mutakharris*, An utterer of falsehoods.

A متخرّق *mutakharrik*, Torn, pierced. Chinky. A liar. Open-handed, liberal. متخرّق السربال *mutakharriku's sirbāl*, One whose clothes have been torn by a long journey.

A متخرّقة *mutakharrikat*, A womb injured by the fœtus and which does not conceive in consequence.

A متخرّم *mutakharrim*, Who or what tears up by the roots, and cuts off. Bold in wickedness. Burst (stitch). Split. Of the sect called خرّمية

khurramīyat. (See also تخرّم *takharrum.*)

A متخزّب *mutakhazzib*, Swollen, tumid; fat.

A متخزّع *mutakhazziʿ*, A lagger behind, or deserter of his friends. A receiver of his share.

A متخزّل *mutakhazzil*, Hindered, let, leaving off (work). (A cloud) piled one part upon another. A slow, heavy walker.

A متخشّب *mutakhashshib*, (A camel) fed on sticks or dry fodder (خشب *khashab*).

A متخشخش *mutakhashkhish*, Rattling (arms), or rustling (papers). Concealed (amongst trees).

A متخشّع *mutakhashshiʿ*, Humble, subdued.

A متخشّل *mutakhashshil*, Thrown away; vile.

A متخشّم *mutakhashshim*, Spoiled, stale, stinking (meat). Drunk: a drunkard.

A متخشّن *mutakhashshin*, Become rough. Rugged. Clad in rough clothing. Rude in speech, uncivil.

A متخشّي *mutakhashshī*, Awed by, afraid of.

A متخصّر *mutakhassir*, One who prays in the night, and, when tired, places his hands against his sides.

A متخصّص *mutakhassis*, Appropriated, made one's own. Peculiarized. Specially noted.

A متخضخض *mutakhazkhiz*, Moved, stirred up.

A متخضّد *mutakhazzid*, Bent double.

A متخضرع *mutakhazriʿ*, Covetous.

A متخضرم *mutakhazrim*, Cream which will not turn into butter on account of the cold.

A متخضّع *mutakhazziʿ*, Humbled, subdued.

A متخطّر *mutakhattir*, (An arrow) passed beyond, or fallen wide of the mark.

A متخطرف *mutakhatrif*, One who walks with wide steps. Good-natured, liberal.

A متخطّف *mutakhattif*, A seizer, spoiler.

A متخطّي *mutakhattī*, Overstepped, crossed over (boundary). One who steps or over-strides.

A متخفّر *mutakhaffir*, Ashamed, extremely bashful. A refugee. One who asks for a guide (خفرة *khufarat*). A guardian, protector.

A متخفّس *mutakhaffis*, Thrown or fallen down. Asleep on one side.

A متخفّف *mutakhaffif*, Booted.

A متخلخل *mutakhalkhil*, Scattered, routed (army). (A woman) with rings upon her ancles.

A متخلّس *mutakhallis*, A seizer, snatcher.

A متخلّص *mutakhallis*, Saved, rescued, escaped.

A متخلّع *mutakhalliʿ*, Disjointed, separated, scattered. Addicted to drink. A shambling walker.

A متخلّف *mutakhallif*, Remaining or left behind. A promise-breaker. An opponent.

A متخلّق *mutakhallik*, A teacher of polite learning. One who perfumes himself with خلوق *khalūk*. An inventor of lies. Sedulous in adopting the habits of another.

A متخلّل *mutakhallil*, One who uses a toothpick (خلال *khilāl*) after eating. (See also تخلّل *takhallul*).

A متخلّي *mutakhallī*, Free, disengaged.

A متخم *mutkhim*, Heavy, indigestible (food).

A متخمّم *muttakhim*, Oppressed at the stomach, incommoded by indigestion.

A متخمة *matkhamat*, (Food) which turns upon the stomach and produces indigestion.

A متخمّر *mutakhammir*, Veiled (woman).

A متخمّط *mutakhammit*, Swollen with pride or anger. Imperious. A powerful conqueror. Stormy (sea). Noisy (stallion).

A متخنّث *mutakhannis*, Flexible, limber, lithe. Soft-spoken (like a woman).

A متخنّس *mutakhannis*, A backbiter. Concealed, absent. One that lags behind.

A متخنّشة *mutakhannishat*, A woman who has still some remains of youth.

A متخنطي *mutakhantī*, Indecent, obscene.

A متخوّت *mutakhawwit*, Diminished, impaired. One who visits time after time.

A متخوّس *mutakhawwis*, One whose flesh stands out with fat.

A متخوّص *mutakhawwis*, A receiver of gifts one after another.

A متخوّض *mutakhawwiz*, Compelled to, or who summons all his energies to ford (a river).

A متخوّع *mutakhawwiʿ*, A diminisher. One who blows his nose or vomits.

A متخوّف *mutakhawwif*, Terrified, impressed with fear. A diminisher, lessener.

A متخوّق *mutakhawwik*, Enlarged, widened. Separated, apart from each other.

A متخوّل *mutakhawwil*, An observer of signs. (See also تخوّل *takhawwul*).

A متخوّن *mutakhawwin*, One who attends to, or looks after. A loser.

A متخيّل *mutakhayyal*, (Ground) covered with luxuriant herbage. *Mutakhayyil*, One who imagines, suspects, or fancies (good or evil). Whatever answers to an idea conceived of it. Cloudy (sky). (Clouds) threatening rain. One who thinks highly, but falsely of himself. Fantastic, imaginary.

A متخيّلة *mutakhayyilat*, Imagination, fancy.

A متخيّم *mutakhayyim*, One who pitches his tent.

A متداعم *mutadāʿam*, Infamous: a catamite. *Mutadāʿim*, Accumulated and weighing down.

A متدابر *mutadābir*, Mutual in deserting, turning the back, or opposing.

A متداثر *mutadāsir*, Old (vestige).

A متداخل *mutadākhil*, Inserted, introduced within each other, dove-tailed, mortised, compact.

A متدارس *mutadāris*, A fellow-student.

A متدارك *mutadārak*, Continuous, uninterrupted. Verse in which two letters inflected with vowels occur between two which are quiescent; as in the feet متفاعلن *mutafāʿilun*, فعولن فعل *faʿūlun faʿal*, فعول فل *faʿūlu ful*. *Mutadārik*, One who has overtaken or gotten. Possessed of. What comprehends.

A متداعك *mutadāʿik*, Intermixed in battle.

A متداعي *mutadāʿī*, Engaged in disputes, contests, or mutual provocation. A propounder of riddles. Who approaches, menaces (as an enemy). (A wall) which threatens ruin. Who agrees to, or takes advice.

A متداف *mutadāff*, Mounted on each other.

A متدافع *mutadāfiʿ*, Employed in pushing and thrusting each other, or repulsing in battle.

A متدافن *mutadāfin*, Employed in burying one another; agreed in concealing amongst themselves.

A متدافي *mutadāfī*, (An overloaded beast) which totters. A taker in turn. Intelligent.

A متداق *mutadākk*, Close, exact in reckoning.

A متداكس *mutadākis*, Much. Ill-tempered.

A متداكي *mutadākī*, Thrusting, thronging.

A متدالح *mutadālih*, Two (or more) persons who carry a burden between them upon a stick.

A متدامج *mutadāmij*, Reciprocal in assisting.

A متدامل *mutadāmil*, Mutually reconciled.

A متداني *mutadānī*, Near, adjacent.

A متداول *mutadāwal*, Bandied to and fro. *Mutadāwil*, People who make a thing pass from hand to hand, or take turn and turn about. Current.

A متداولة *mutadāwalat*, (fem.) Common, known, customary, usual. *Mutadāwalatan*, Alternately.

A متداوم *mutadāwim*, One who renders perpetual. Who or what revolves.

A متداومة *mutadāwamat*, A circuit, circle.

A متداوي *mutadāwī*, One who doctors himself.

A متداين *mutadāyin*, Mutual in giving credit.

A متدبّر *mutadabbir*, One who considers attentively, or who understands well. Well regulated.

A متدبّق *mutadabbik*, Caught with birdlime.

A متدثّر *mutadassir*, Wrapped up in a cloak or in the upper garment called دثار *disār*. A vaulter on horseback. Leaping (stallion). Infamous.

A متدجّج *mutadajjij*, Armed at all points.

A متدحدر *mutadahdir*, (or متدحرج *mutadahrij*) Tumbled, rolled about, wallowing.

A متدحّي *mutadahhī*, Ambling, galloping (horse). Expanded, spread, extended.

A متدخدخ *mutadakhdikh*, Shrunk, shrivelled.

A متدخّل *mutadakhkhil*, Allowed to enter, introduced. Who or what enters by little and little. One who enters very busily into matters.

A متدخّن *mutadakhkhin*, Smoked. Discoloured by smoke. Smelling of smoke (دخان *dukhān*).

A متدرّج *mutadarrij*, Gradually advanced.

A متدرّع *mutadarriʿ*, Clad in mail or quilted vest.

A متدرّعة *mutadarriʿat*, (A woman) dressed in a shift, smicket, or smock (درع *dirʿ*).

A متدرّي *mutadarrī*, Insolent, domineering. One who conceals himself in order to deceive.

A متدع *muttadiʿ*, Quiet, steady. Mild, placid. One who complains of one limb, the rest of his body being well.

A متدغّر *mutadaʿʿir*, Blackish, variegated, dirty-coloured, discoloured (face).

A متدعكس *mutadaʿkis*, A leader of the dance

with joined hands (after the manner of the Magi).

A متدعي *mutadaʻʻī*, One who claims, pretender.

A متدفق *mutadaffik*, Wide-spread (water): shed.

A متدفن *mutadaffin*, Buried. Hid, concealed.

A متدکل *mutadakhil*, Haughty, disdainful, arrogant. A blandisher.

A متدلث *mutadallis*, One who rushes upon or into. Fallen on the face.

A متدلس *mutadallis*, Concealed. A little eater. (Cattle) which lick any thing in play. Entering into darkness.

A متدلف *mutadallif*, One approaching. A lion marching leisurely.

A متدلق *mutadallik*, (A torrent) rushing at once.

A متدلك *mutadallik*, One who rubs himself with a fragrant substance, or who rubs the body (as in washing). Fit, suitable, apt.

A متدلل *mutadallil*, Pleasant, jocular (fellow).

A متدلمس *mutadalmis*, Bald in front.

A متدله *mutadallih*, Insane, dement.

A متدلي *mutadallī*, Jocose, merry. Descended. Approached, near. Pendulous, hanging (from a tree).

A متدمر *mutadammir*, Perishing. Indignant.

A متدمع *mutadammiʻ*, Ready to shed tears.

A متدمل *mutadammil*, Manured, dunged (land).

A متدمن *mutadammin*, Defiled with ordure.

A متدنس *mutadannis*, Dirty, soiled, nasty, filthy. Bad-tempered. Blemished, tarnished (character).

A متدنئ *mutadanniʼ*, One who urges on to that which is low and base.

A متدني *mutadannī*, One who approaches or draws near by little and little.

A متدوم *mutadawwim*, One who expects, awaits.

A متدون *mutadawwin*, Mean, contemptible.

A متدوه *mutadawwih*, Corrupted. Changed, altered. Scarce of provisions. Waxed thick.

A متدهدم *mutadahdim*, Fallen, dropping out.

A متدهده *mutadahdih*, (or متدهدي *mutadahdī*) (A stone) rolled, tumbled over.

A متدهقن *mutadahkin*, Appointed chief of the husbandmen (دهقان *dihkān*). A cultivator.

A متدهكر *mutadahkir*, Tumbled, rolled. Rushing upon. Shaky, tremulous.

A متدهكم *mutadahkim*, One who rushes headlong (into a thing). Proud, insolent, domineering.

A متدهم *mutadahham*, Concealed. Contracted.

A متدهن *mutadahhin*, One who anoints his person with unguent (دهن *duhn*). Fat, unctuous.

A متدي *muttadī*, A receiver of money, as the expiation of homicide. (It is called دية *diyat*.)

A متديث *mutadayyis*, A pimp, pander.

A متدين *mutadayyin*, Orthodox, upright, firm in religion. A borrower, debtor. Indebted.

A متذاءب *mutazaʼib*, Any thing formed in the shape of a wolf (especially such a figure thrown before a she-camel, which makes her give suck to a colt not her own). (Wind) which blows every way, and veers to every point of the compass.

A متذابح *mutazābih*, Employed in cutting each other's throats.

A متذاكر *mutazākir*, Mindful of one another.

A متذامر *mutazāmir*, Strenuous in exciting one another to battle. Excited, roused.

A متذامم *mutazāmim*, Mutual in casting blame.

A متذاوق *mutazāwik*, A receiver of meat or drink. Mutual in receiving spear-wounds.

A متذائل *mutazāʼil*, Mean, despicable.

A متذايل *mutazāyil*, Low (condition).

A متذبذب *mutazabzib*, Put in motion.

A متذبلة *mutazabbilat*, (A woman) whose walk resembles that of a man.

A متذرع *mutazarriʻ*, A great talker. (See تذرع).

A متذري *mutazarrī*, Winnowed. Married into a high family. Mounted on the top or pinnacle.

A متذعب *mutazaʻʻib*, Terrified (by demons).

A متذعذع *mutazaʻziʻ*, Squandered (wealth).

A متذعر *mutazaʻʻir*, Terrified, frightened.

A متذعلب *mutazaʻlib*, Who slinks off secretly. Lightly clad. Laid down, reclining on the breast.

A متذقح *mutazakkih*, One who takes pains to shew himself a villain.

A متذقط *mutazakkit*, A taker by degrees.

A متذكر *mutazakkir*, A rememberer, recorder, recollector. One who remembers advice.

A متذكرة *mutazakkirat*, A masculine woman.

A متذلغ *mutazalligh*, Useless, unprofitable.

A متذلل *mutazallil*, Humble, suppliant: meek.

A متذمر *mutazammir*, Self-blamed (for neglect). Altered, changed. Angry. Threatful.

A متذمم *mutazammim*, Blushing, ashamed.

A متذنب *mutazannib*, One who allows the end (ذنب *zanab*) of the turban-sash to fall down the side or back of the head. One who takes the road.

A متذوق *mutazawwik*, A taster again and again.

A متذئ *muttaziʼ*, Chid, blamed, reproved.

A متذيل *mutazayyil*, Proud, stately, who lets his train (ذيل *zayl*) sweep the ground. One who wears an every-day garment. One who does his own servile work.

A متذيلة *mutazayyalat*, (Land) slightly rained on.

A متذيئ *mutazayyiʼ*, (Meat) dissolved by boiling, and falling from the bone. Putrid, ulcerated (flesh) separating from the bone. Swollen (face).

A متر *matr*, (v. n. of متر) Cutting off, amputating. Throwing. Stretching (a rope). Lying with. Voiding (dung).

A متر *mutirr*, A cutter. A banisher, driver into exile. One who throws away.

P مترا *matrā*, (in zand and Pāzand) Rain.

A مترابط *mutarābit*, Perennial, unfailing.

A مترابل *mutarābil*, Leonine, lion-like.

A متراجع *mutarājiʻ*, Returned, brought back.

A متراجم *mutarājim*, Engaged in flinging stones at one another.

A متراح *mitrāh*, (pl. متاريح *matārih*) (A camel) which soon ceases to give milk.

A متراخي *mutarākhī*, Dilatory, slow, relaxed.

A متراد *mutarādd*, Reciprocal in contending, driving, repelling. Agreed to dissolve a contract.

A مترادف *mutarādif*, Successive, uninterrupted, at the heels of one another. United by intermarriages. Synonymous. A verse terminating in two quiescent letters.

A متراس *mutarāss*, Mutually communicative of secrets.

A متراسل *mutarāsil*, Reciprocal in sending news, keeping up an epistolary correspondence.

A متراص *mutarāss*, Set in close array, adhering.

A متراصع *mutarāsiʻ*, Billing (sparrows).

A متراصف *mutarāsif*, Standing in a row or file.

A متراضخ *mutarāzikh*, Engaged in pelting one another (with stones).

A متراضي *mutarāzī*, Contented with each other.

A متراطن *mutarātin*, Engaged in conversing in a barbarous idiom, *i.e.* not in Arabic.

A متراغي *mutarāghī*, (Camels) braying together, some from one place, some from another.

A مترأف *mutaraʼʼif*, (or مترأم *mutaraʼʼim*) Compassionate, full of pity, tender, affectionate.

A مترافد *mutarāfid*, Mutual in giving help.

A مترافع *mutarāfiʻ*, Mutually agreed to refer a matter to an umpire or judge.

A مترافق *mutarāfik*, A fellow-traveller.

A مترافئ *mutarāfiʼ*, Unanimous, quite agreed. Mutual in helping: help-mate.

P متراك *matrāk*, Name of a lunar mansion.

A متراكب *mutarākib*, Piled one upon another. Firm, strong.

A متراكض *mutarākiz*, Simultaneous in making (horses) run towards any one.

A متراكل *mutarākil*, Mutual in kicking.

A متراكم *mutarākim*, Accumulated, heaped up.

A مترامي *mutarāmī*, Occupied in shooting together. (See also ترامي *tarāmī*).

A متراوح *mutarāwih*, Beneficent, benevolent, now giving with this hand, now with that.

A متراوغ *mutarāwigh*, Engaged in a struggle or wrestling together.

A متراهص *mutarāhis*, Firmly-rooted (rock).

A متراهن *mutarāhin*, Mutual in depositing stakes, pledges, or wagers.

A مترائي *mutarāʼī*, Who contemplate one another. One who stands opposite, who views himself (in a mirror). Optical. (A palm-tree) which exhibits dates of various kinds. (See ترائي *tarāʼī*).

A مترب *matrab*, (v. n. of ترب) Having much earth. Holding earth in the hand. Being covered with earth. Cleaving to the ground. Becoming poor. Suffering loss. *Mutrib*, (or مترب *mutarrib*) One who throws or sprinkles earth (تراب *turāb*).

A مترب *mutarrab*, Strewed, soiled with dust.

A مترّبب *mutarabbib*, Assembled. One who claims to be the owner. A bringer up, educator.

A متربة *matrabat*, Poverty, beggary.

A متربّث *mutarabbis*, Slow, tedious.

A متربّجة *mutarabbijat*, (A woman) affectionate and careful (of her children). Foolish.

A متربّح *mutarabbih*, Bewildered.

A متربّخ *mutarabbihh*, Loose, relaxed.

A متربّد *mutarabbid*, Cloudy (sky). Austere, crabbed. A lion.

A متربّص *mutarabbis*, One who expects and waits for. A forestaller, regrater.

A متربّض *mutarabbiz*, Laid prostrate, killed. One who crumbles bread into gravy.

A متربّع *mutarabbaع*, A spring-habitation, a place where cattle pasture in the spring. *Mutarabbiع*, Fattened with spring-grass. One who sits four-square.

A متربّق *mutarabbik*, One who suspends (any thing from the neck).

A متربّل *mutarabbil*, Leafy, verdant (tree). (See also تربّل *tarabbul*).

A متربّلة *mutarabbilat*, Fleshy-breasted (woman).

A متربّي *mutarabbī*, One who gives food and nourishment. One who educates. Educated, instructed, trained. A preserver (of fruits or roots). Preserved.

A مترتّب *mutarattib*, Firm, settled; ordered, established. Arranged. One who runs in, upon, or against; who springs or rises. Suffering, affected.

A مترتّل *mutarattil*, One who sings with a sweet voice. A slow reader or speaker.

A مترتّم *mutarattim*, One who binds a string round his finger to put him in mind of something.

A مترثّن *mutarassin*, Rouged, farded.

A مترّج *mutarraj*, Red, orange-coloured.

A مترجّح *mutarajjih*, Prevalent or preponderating. Moved to and fro in the air. Vibrative.

A مترجرج *mutarajrij*, Agitated, trembling, tottering, moving to and fro. Vibrative, oscillatory.

A مترجّز *mutarajjiz*, Loud, rumbling (thunder). Slow-moving (watery cloud). A singer of the kind of verse called رجز *rajaz*.

A مترجّف *mutarajjif*, Moveable, tremulous.

A مترجّل *mutarajjil*, One who goes on foot: a pedestrian. One who descends (into a well). (See ترجّل *tarajjul*).

A مترجم *mutarjam*, Interpreted, translated. *Mutarjim*, A translator, interpreter.

A مترجميّة *mutarjimīyat*, A translation.

A مترجّي *mutarajjī*, Hoping, full of hope.

A مترح *mutrih*, One who hears and sees constantly what is disagreeable.

A مترّح *mutarrah*, (A garment) dyed of a full deep colour. Anxious, painful (life). Small (stream). Sad, mourning. *Mutarrih*, One who makes sad.

A مترحرح *mutarahrih*, Straddling to stale.

A مترحّل *mutarahhil*, Mounted and ready to depart or emigrate. A traveller. One who presents what is disagreeable.

A مترحّم *mutarahhim*, Compassionate, merciful, tender, pitiful, moved to pity.

A مترحّي *mutarahhī*, Coiled up (serpent).

A مترخّص *mutarakhhhis*, One who obtains leave. One who takes with ease.

A متردّد *mutaraddid*, Repulsed, rejected, refused. Who opposes or resists; adverse. Comer and goer; saunterer, wanderer. Irresolute, ambiguous, perplexed, hesitating. Discomposed. Short, squat.

A متردّس *mutaraddis*, Fallen (into a well).

A متردّم *mutaraddam*, Part (of a garment) covered with a patch. *Mutaraddim*, Threadbare (garment). A patcher. Patched.

A متردّي *mutaraddī*, Fallen (into a well or from a mountain).

A متردّية *mutaraddiyat*, A sheep fallen from a height (whether killed or not). Veiled (girl).

P مترز *matriz*, A shield.

A مترز *mutriz*, Whatever hardens (as running, a horse's flesh). (A woman) who makes a hard solid mass (of paste).

A مترزّن *mutarazzin*, Honoured, revered. Firm, steady, stedfast, grave.

P مترس *matars*, Be not afraid. The bar of a door. A parapet of wood or earth, a palisade. A ninepin. A scarecrow.

A مترس *mitras*, (pl. متارس) A bolt, bar.

A مترّس *mutarris*, One who arms (himself or another) with a shield (ترس *turs*).

A مترسّب *mutarassib*, What deposits sediment.

A مترسة *mitrasat*, A shield, coat of mail, or thing) which defends.

A مترسّل *mutarassil*, One who does (any thing) leisurely. A letter-writer.

A مترسّم *mutarassim*, One who searches for the vestiges (of a house). One who studies or commits to memory.

A مترشّف *mutarashshif*, A sipper, a sucker.

A مترشّي *mutarashshī*, Mild, gentle, kind.

A مترص *mutras*, Firm. A well-poised scale. *Mutris*, (or مترّص *mutarris*) One who strengthens or confirms; one who rectifies or equals.

A مترصّد *mutarassid*, One who contemplates, or gazes at. A watcher, expecter, explorer. Vigilant.

A مترضّب *mutarazzib*, Who kisses (as a lover).

A مترضّح *mutarazzih*, Bruised, pounded, crushed.

A مترضّض *mutarazziz*, Broken into coarse lumps.

A مترضّي *mutarazzī*, One who contents and gives satisfaction. One who begs, or is anxious, that any thing may be acceptable.

A مترطّم *mutarattim*, One who keeps in his excrement, costive, constipated.

A مترع *mutraع*, Full. *Mutriع*, One who fills.

A مترّع *mutarriع*, Who shuts (a door).

A ذو مترعة *zū matraعatin*, (A man) neither making haste nor angry; calm, sedate.

A مترعّث *mutaraععis*, Decked with ear-rings.

A مترعرع *mutaraعriع*, Sprightly.

A مترعّظ *mutaraععiz*, One who tries to make a camel's load equal when it leans on one side.

A مترعّي *mutaraععī*, Pasturing, out at grass.

A مترغّب *mutaraghghib*, Expectant, waiting for.

A مترغّم *mutaraghghim*, Angry, in a passion.

A مترف *mutraf*, Blest with affluence, and allowed to enjoy himself without interruption. Left to himself, and doing what he pleases. Proud, haughty, acknowledging no superior. *Mutrif*, One who obstinately perseveres in disobedience. *Mutrif*, (or مترّف *mutarrif*) (Riches) seducing and ruining (a man). A bestower of the comforts of life.

A مترفّض *mutaraffiz*, Scattered, dispersed, and going off. Torn up, broken.

A مترفّع *mutaraffiع*, Lifted up, raised, proud.

A مترفّغ *mutaraffigh*, Who leads an easy life.

A مترفّق *mutaraffik*, Benevolent, friendly.

A مترفّه *mutaraffih*, One who lives a pleasant life.

A مترقّب *mutarakkib*, One who contemplates, observes. One who expects, desires, or wishes with a degree of avidity. A guardian.

A مترقرق *mutarakrik*, Inclined, disposed to leanness or obesity. Brilliant, shining, glistening.

A مترقّش *mutarakkish*, Decorated, adorned.

A مترقّص *mutarakkis*, Moved up and down.

A مترقّع *mutarakkaع*, Room for reproach and ridicule. *Mutarakkiع*, A gainer, or one who tries to gain.

A مترقّق *mutarakkik*, Compassionate, tender.

A مترقّن *mutarakkin*, Tinged with privet.

A مترقّي *mutarakkī*, Ascended. Advanced.

A متركّب *mutarakkab*, Inserted, infixed, mounted, set. *Mutarakkib*, Mounted one on another.

A متركّح *mutarakkih*, Tedious, slow, sluggish, dilatory. Seated at ease. Wide, roomy. Handy, expert.

A متركّل *mutarakkil*, One who sets his foot on any thing (as on a spade when digging).

A متركّن *mutarakkin*, Firm, strong, well-established. Grave, staid, steady, sedate.

A مترمرم *mutaramrim*, Silent, mute. One who moves the lips without speaking.

A مترمّز *mutarammiz*, One who speaks by signs. Tumultuous, disordered, confounded.

A مترمّع *mutarammiع*, Agitated (with passion). Defiled by his own ordure.

A مترمّق *mutarammik*, Who sips at intervals.

A مترمّل *mutarammil*, Widowed. Stained with gore. Mean, contemptible.

A مترمّم *mutarammim*, Dispersed, separated.

A مترمّي *mutarammī*, A shooter at a mark.

A مترنّح *mutarannih*, One who staggers (from drink). One who drinks a little.

A مترنّخ *mutarannihh*, One that sticks his claws in and adheres firmly. Weak, contemptible.

A مترنّق *mutarannik*, Troubled, muddy (water).

A مترنّم *mutarannim*, A singer, hummer, warbler. Cooing (dove).

A مترنّن mutarannin, Sonorous, resounding.

A مترنّي mutarannī, A lover who gazes without ceasing on his mistress.

A متروّح mutarawwih, (A plant) high, tall, shot upwards. (A tree) which has put forth leaves a second time. One who raises (a wind) with a fan. (Water) which has contracted a smell from a neighbouring substance. One who goes in the evening.

A متروّع mutarawwiɛ, Terrified, alarmed.

A متروّغ mutarawwigh, (A horse) rolling himself.

A متروك matrūk, Left, relinquished, abandoned. Rejected, abolished, obsolete, neglected, fallen into disuse. متروك الاستعمال matrūku'l istiɛmāl, Unusual, not practised, disused, obsolete. مال متروك māli matrūk, The estate of a person deceased.

A متروكات matrūkāt, Moveables, any thing left behind one (either when leaving a place or dying). Unnecessary baggage.

A مترهّب mutarahhib, One who dedicates himself to the service of God; one who leads the life of a monk (راهب rāhib). A threatener.

A مترهّل mutarahhil, Loose, soft, flabby.

A متري mutrī, One who does things successively, with intermissions between each.

A مترئّد mutaraɛɛid, Delicate (plant), tremulous from its own weight.

A متريّع mutarayyiɛ, (The vapour سراب sarāb) floating up and down and glittering. Shining (butter on the top of a pudding). Who delays or protracts. Assembled (people). Astonished. One who lubricates his body with unguents.

A متريّف mutarayyif, Arrived at a rich and fertile country (such as they denominate ريف rīf).

A متريّق mutarayyik, (The vapour سراب sarāb) shining on the sands of the desert.

A متز matz, (v. n. of متز) Voiding (excrement).

A متزاحف mutazāhif, (Antagonists) advancing mutually to fight each other.

A متزاحم mutazāhim, Crowded, squeezed together, thronging (people).

A متزائر mutazaɛɛir, Roaring, growling (lion).

A متزاور mutazāwir, Reciprocal in paying visits. Turned from, declined.

A متزاول mutazāwil, Fellow-worker, joint-labourer.

A متزايد mutazāyid, Increased, augmented, multiplied. Verbose, talkative.

A متزايغ mutazāyigh, Inclined towards one another.

A متزايل mutazāyil, Distant, departing. Transitory. Separated, removed from. Damaged. Decomposed. Scattered. Ashamed of.

A متزبّد mutazabbid, Foamy, frothy. Hasty in swearing. One who takes cream or butter.

A متزبّع mutazabbiɛ, Malignant, irate, furious.

A متزبّي mutazabbī, One who digs (a pit for a lion, زبية zubyat) and decoys (him into it).

A متزتّت mutazattit, Adorned (bride).

A متزجّي mutazajjī, Content (with little).

A متزحزح mutazahzih, Distant, absent.

A متزحّف mutazahhif, One who advances.

A متزحّل mutazahhil, One who departs, retires.

A متزحلف mutazahlif, Rolled. Retired.

A متزخّن mutazahhin, Slow, dilatory. Reluctant, unwilling, forced against one's will.

A متزخّر mutazahkhkhir, Full, swelling (sea).

A متزر muttazir, Criminal, faulty.

A متزرّر mutazarrir, (A garment) furnished with buttons (زرّ zirr), by which (it) may be fastened.

A متزرّي mutazarrī, A slanderer of his brother. One who reproves or rebukes.

A متزع muttaziɛ, Stedfast in self-controul.

A متزعزع mutazaɛziɛ, Shaken, agitated.

A متزعّم mutazaɛɛim, Teller of falsehoods, liar.

A متزغّم mutazaghghim, Who speaks in a rage.

A متزفّي mutazaffa', Timorous, frightened.

A متزقّم mutazakkim, Who swallows gradually. Extremely voracious. Who makes up mouthsful. One who drinks milk to excess.

A متزكّر mutazakkir, (A child) in good condition. One who grows, thrives. Full, filled (child's belly).

A متزكّي mutazakkī, Grown. An alms-giver.

A متزلّج mutazallij, Slidden. A toper (of wine).

A متزلّح mutazallih, Tasting; a taster.

A متزلّخ mutazallikh, Thrown down. Slidden down a declivity or a slippery place.

A متزلزل mutazalzal, Convulsed by an earthquake. *Mutazalzil*, Shaking, quaking.

A متزلّع mutazalliɛ, Cracked, chapped (hand).

A متزلّف mutazallif, One who advances, precedes, goes before. Separated, scattered.

A متزلّق mutazallik, Slidden, slipped, fallen down. Slippery. Sleek, florid, and well-liking. Smart, trim.

A متزمّر mutazammir, Piping (male ostrich).

A متزمزم mutazamzim, Braying (camel).

A متزمّل mutazammil, One who wraps up close, or hides himself in his garment.

A متّزن muttazin, A receiver of weighed or counted (money). (Verse) of a just measure, accurate.

A متزنتر mutazantir, A pompous walker.

A متزنّح mutazannih, One who carries himself above his condition. One who speaks freely, openly, also imperiously. A drinker of water time after time.

A متزنّخ mutazannikh, Haughty, proud-spoken.

A متزنّد mutazannid, Reduced to a dilemma, nonplused, unable to reply. Angry.

A متزندق mutazandik, Turned Guebre (زنديق zindīk), become a worshipper of fire; impious.

A متزنّر mutazannir, Begirt with a girdle or zone (زنّار zunnār). Slender, fine. Pounded small.

A متزوّج mutazawwij, Who takes a wife: wived.

A متزوّد mutazawwid, One who makes provision (زاد zād) for a journey.

A متزوّر mutazawwir, Roaring (lion).

A متزهّد mutazahhid, Pious, devout, religious.

A متزهلق mutazahlik, White: pure; bright. Fat.

A متزيّد mutazayyid, Increased, raised (price of provisions). One who affixes, or adds a commentary or supplement.

A متزيّق mutazayyik, (A woman) dressing, adorning; also who tinges (her) eyes with a collyrium.

A متزيّل mutazayyil, Dispersed, scattered.

A متزيّن mutazayyin, Dressed, adorned.

A متزيّي mutazayyī, Habited, garbed.

A متس mats, (v. n. of متس) Voiding excrement. Seeking (grass) in order to root (it) up.

A متسائل mutasāɛil, Reciprocal in asking.

A متسابق mutasābik, Engaged in contest for a wager. Mutual, reciprocal in taking precedency.

A متساتل mutasātil, Joined, connected, arriving, or following each other.

A متساجل mutasājil, Mutually boastful.

A متسارّ mutasārr, Reciprocal in communicating secrets (سرّ sirr).

A متسارع mutasāriɛ, Simultaneous in making haste. One who makes haste.

A متسافح mutasāfih, A fornicator.

A متسافد mutasāfid, Engendering (beasts).

A متسافط mutasāfit, Green, unripe (date).

A متساقب mutasākib, Near each other, adjacent.

A متساقط mutasākit, Fallen. One who throws himself into. Falling step by step.

A متساقي mutasākī, Mutual in giving drink.

A متساكر mutasākir, One who shams drunkenness.

A متسالف mutasālif, Connected by affinity, related by marriage (as the husbands of two sisters).

A متسالم mutasālim, At peace together.

A متسامح mutasāmih, Mutually indulgent.

A متسامع mutasāmiɛ, One who pretends to hear. Published, revealed. Hearing from each other.

A متسامي mutasāmī, Mutually ambitious for pre-eminence.

A متساند mutasānid, Assembled under different standards. One who leans or stays himself upon. Auxiliary to one another.

A متساور mutasāwir, Who attack or leap on one another. Manifest, apparent. One who shews himself.

A متساوق mutasāwik, (Camels) which follow each other. Quiet. Gregarious.

A متساوك mutasāwik, Tottering (lean cattle).

A متساوي mutasāwī, Equal, parallel, straight. متساوية الاضلاع mutasāwiyatu'l azlāɛ, Equilateral.

A متساهل mutasāhil, Easy toward each other.

A متساهم mutasāhim, Engaged in casting lots.

A متساير mutasāyir, Associated in travel.

A متسايف mutasāyif, Engaged in fencing.

A متسايل mutasāyil, Confluent (troops).

A متسبّخ mutasabbikh, Assuaged (heat).

A متسبسب mutasabsib, Flowing (water).

A متستّر mutasattir, Concealed, hidden. Veiled. Cautious. One who keeps (a thing) at a distance.

A متسجّم mutasajjim, Rainy (sky).

A متسحّب mutasahhib, Coquettish.

A متسحّج mutasahhij, Excoriated, scratched.

A متسحّر mutasahhir, One who rises or sets out before daybreak, and breakfasts at that early hour.

A متسحّن mutasahhin, One who sees a thing to be good, or who finds it so.

A متسخّر mutasakhkhir, A despiser, jeerer, mocker. One who compels (another) to obey. Obliged to work for nothing, angariated.

A متسخّط mutasakhkhit, Incensed. Discontented, considering as small. One who gives unseasonably. Disapproving. A disliker. Sharp, keen (glance).

A متسخّي mutasakhkhī, Unwillingly liberal.

A متسدّي mutasaddī, Ascending. Seated on the upper part. A follower. A weaver.

A متسرّب mutasarrib, Who creeps into a hole.

A متسربل mutasarbil, Dressed in a shirt, shift, or covering for the body (سربال sirbāl).

A متسرّر mutasarrir, A keeper of a concubine.

A متسرّع mutasarriع, Active, quick, hasty.

A متسرّم mutasarrim, Separate, divided.

A متسرمط mutasarmit, (Hair) thin and few.

A متسرول mutasarwil, In breeches, breeched.

A متسرّي mutasarrī, One who keeps privately a female slave. One who plumes himself on his liberality; anxious to shew his generosity.

A متسطّر mutasattir, Vain boaster, empty talker.

A متسّع mutsiع, What makes up the number nine. One who waters a camel on the ninth day.

A متّسع muttasaع, Wide place, widest part. *Muttasiع*, Large, broad, spacious. Dilated. Diffused (water). The contents of any place.

A متسعّب mutasaععib, Viscid, ropy, stringy (honey or syrup). Thick (phlegm or spittle).

A متسعّر mutasaععir, Lighted, flaming (fire).

A متسعسع mutasaعsiع, Grown old and decrepit. Ended (life). (See تسعسع tasaعsuع).

A متسفّر mutasaffir, About to take a journey.

A متسفّط mutasaffit, Imbued with: an imbiber.

A متسفّل mutasaffil, Descended. Brought low. Low, ignoble, mean.

A متسقّط mutasakkit, One who seeks for the worst part of any thing, or who hunts after faults. A picker-up of news by little and little.

A متسقّف mutasakkif, Roofed. Created bishop.

A متسقّي mutasakkī, Soaked, imbued: bibulous.

A متسكّع mutasakkiع, A wanderer, stroller.

A متسكّن mutasakkin, Poor, impoverished.

A متسلّب mutasallib, (A widow) in mourning.

A متسلّج mutasallij, A great drinker.

A متسلّح mutasallih, Cased in armour, armed.

A متسلسل mutasalsil, Joined, linked together. Water flowing like a chain. Badly-woven (cloth).

A متسلّط mutasallit, Despotic, absolute. Invested with paramount authority.

A متسلّع mutasalliع, Split, cracked, chapped.

A متسلّف mutasallif, A borrower. A receiver of money per advance for goods to be delivered.

A متسلّق mutasallik, A climber of a wall. Restless in bed from pain or grief.

A متسلّل mutasallil, A withdrawer, tarrier behind. Who or what slips out secretly and unobserved.

A متسلّم mutasallam, Delivered, consigned. *Mutasallim*, One who receives any thing delivered, and keeps it in possession. A vicar, a locum tenens, a lieutenant to the governor of a province, sent before to take possession for his superior, and manage affairs till his arrival. Who keeps in the right road.

A متسلّي mutasallī, Comforted, solaced.

A متّسم muttasim, One who sets a mark upon himself whereby he may be known; signed, sealed.

A متسمّت mutasammat, The front of a shoe from below the latchet forwards.

A متسمّج mutasammij, Who gives grudgingly.

A متسمّط mutasammit, Hung up, suspended.

A متسمّع mutasammiع, A hearer, listener.

A متسمّك mutasammik, Exalted, excellent.

A متسمّل mutasammil, One who drinks up the remains of water in a vessel. (See تسمّل tasammul).

A متسمّن mutasammin, Fattened, waxed fat.

A متسمّي mutasammī, Self-named. Called, named, denominated, designated. High.

A متسنّم mutasannim, Seated, perched upon. One who pounces on suddenly and unawares.

A متسنّه mutasannih, Several years old. Old, changed, corrupted, rotten. Mouldy (bread).

A متسنّي mutasannī, Old, corrupted. Changed, altered. One who stays many years. One who takes matters easily and quietly. (See تسنّي tasannī).

A متسوّخ mutasawwikh, Fallen (in the mire).

A متسوّد mutasawwid, A man who marries.

A متسوّر mutasawwir, A wearer of bracelets.

A متسوّق mutasawwik, A buyer, seller, trader. A frequenter of the market (سوق sūk), a market-man.

A متسوّك mutasawwik, Who uses a dentifrice.

A متسوّم mutasawwim, Distinguished by a mark or distinctive badge (سيما sīma') in battle.

A متسوّي mutasawwī, Straight. Even, level.

A متسهّل mutasahhil, Easy. Smooth.

A متش matsh, (v. n. of متش) Separating, dividing with the fingers. Milking (a camel) feebly. A defect in the sight. White specks on the nails.

A متشائم mutashāـim, One who considers as unfortunate or bad. A foreteller of evil. One who goes towards the left side of a person or thing.

A متشابر mutashābir, Separated from each other only by the breadth of a span (شبر shibr).

A متشابك mutashābik, Intricate (affair).

A متشابه mutashābih, Like, resembling. Conformable. Allegoric, parabolical. Intricate, difficult (a verse of the Kur'ān), of uncertain meaning.

A متشابهات mutashābihāt, (pl. of متشابهة mutashābihat) Similies, allegories, metaphors. Doubts, ambiguities, intricacies.

A متشابهة mutashābihat, (fem. of متشابه mutashābih), Like. Comparison, resemblance.

A متشاتم mutashātim, Full of mutual revilings.

A متشاجر mutashājir, Mutually hostile, contentious. (See also تشاجر tashājur).

A متشاحّ mutashāhh, Mutually tenacious.

A متشاخس mutashākhis, Discordant (men), unharmonious (music). (See also تشاخس tashākhus).

A متشاخص mutashākhis, Distinct, different, diverse, separate.

A متشادف mutashādif, Bent, curved (bow).

A متشارجات mutashārajāt, Girls of same age.

A متشارش mutashārish, Mutually hostile.

A متشارك mutashārik, Associated in partnership; a partner.

A متشازب mutashāzib, One who waits for or catches whatever he can get; every one for himself.

A متشازر mutashāzir, Regardant of each other askance or with half-shut eyes.

A متشاظي mutashāzī, Full of mutual revilings.

A متشاع mutashāع, A partner.

A متشاعر mutashāعir, One who pretends to be, or who fancies himself a poet; a poetaster.

A متشاغل mutashāghil, People who keep one another employed.

A متشافّ mutashāff, A drinker of the contents of a cup. A taker of the whole.

A متشاقّ mutashākk, Vexatious, troublesome to one another.

A متشاكس mutashākis, Mutually cruel, hostile.

A متشاكل mutashākil, Suitable, agreeable to one another.

A متشاكي mutashākī, Mutually querulous.

A متشامّ mutashāmm, Simultaneous in smelling at. Approximated.

A متشانّ mutashānn, Old, dried-up (leathern bottle). Shrivelled (skin). Commingled.

A متشاور mutashāwir, Engaged in consultation.

A متشاوس mutashāwis, One who looks through half-shut eyes, or screws his face from pride or anger.

A متشاوظ mutashāwiz, Reciprocal in cursing.

A متشاوف mutashāwif, A slighter. Fearful.

A متشاول mutashāwil, Reciprocal in spearing.

A متشايع mutashāyiع, Associated together, following each other. A partner.

A متشبّث mutashabbis, One who grasps strongly, or infixes his nails or claws.

A متشبّع mutashabbiع, Boasting, vain-glorious, priding himself on what he does not possess. One who pretends to be satisfied when he is not. One who eats often. Abundant, replenished. A diligent searcher, skilful hunter.

A متشبّك mutashabbik, Mixed, intermixed, intertwined, jumbled together.

A متشبّه mutashabbih, Similar, resembling.

A متشتّي mutashattī, One who winters.

A متشجّع mutashajjiع, Proud of his courage.

A متشح *mutshih*, A smiter (with a javelin).

A متشحط *mutashahhit*, (A wounded man) rolled or wallowing in his own blood.

A متشخص *mutashakhkhis*, Separated: distinct.

A متشدخ *mutashaddikh*, Broken (pate or apple).

A متشدد *mutashaddid*, Hard, strong. Severe. Difficult. Stingy, avaricious.

A متشدق *mutashaddik*, One who aims at, affects eloquence. Who mouths much in speaking.

A متشذر *mutashazzir*, One who passes the train of a garment through the legs and tucks it up to the breast. A lion.

A متشر *muttashir*, One who requests that his teeth may be sharpened and made thin by the female professor of this art.

A متشرب *mutasharrib*, Imbibing: what drinks up, bibulous. Spreading: contagious.

A متشرد *mutasharrid*, Dispersed, put to flight.

A متشرط *mutasharrit*, Attentive, regardful.

A متشرع *mutasharriɛ*, Skilled in law: orthodox.

A متشرف *mutasharrif*, Honoured. High-minded. Handsome. (See تشرف *tasharruf*).

A متشرق *mutasharrik*, Basking in the sun, exposed to the sun. Sun-beat.

A متشرك *mutasharrik*, A partner, sharer.

A متشرم *mutasharrim*, Ripped, torn.

A متشري *mutasharri*, A sectary.

A متشزر *mutashazzir*, Provoked, angry.

A متشزن *mutashazzin*, An opponent in a controversy. Prepared, ready. Rough, hard, thick.

A متشظي *mutashazzī*, Splintered, shivered.

A متشعب *mutashaɛɛib*, Divided, branched.

A متشعث *mutashaɛɛis*, Soiled with dust. Dispersed, scattered. A little eater. Matted (hair).

A متشعر *mutashaɛɛir*, Hairy (unborn fœtus).

A متشعل *mutashaɛɛil*, Kindled, lighted: fiery.

A متشغر *mutashaghghir*, (A camel) that travels well. Far gone in wickedness.

A متشفع *mutashaffiɛ*, An intercessor, advocate.

A متشفي *mutashaffī*, Appeased, pacified.

A متشق *muttashik*, One who cuts (meat) into long slices after (it) has been parboiled.

A متشقق *mutashakkak* or *mutashakkik*, Split into several parts. Vivid, glaring (lightning).

A متشكر *mutashakkir*, Grateful, thankful.

A متشكك *mutashakkik*, Doubting, scrupulous.

A متشكل *mutashakkal*, Formed. Produced. Transformed. Beautiful. Half-ripe (grape). *Mutashakkil*, Like, resembling.

A متشكي *mutashakkī*, A complainer, bemoaner, lamenter: querulous. Afflicted, pained, diseased.

A متشلشل *mutashalshil*, (A boy) making water drop by drop. (A sword) dripping with blood. (Urine) coming away drop by drop. Lean, spare.

A متشمت *mutashammit*, Disappointed of booty.

A متشمخر *mutashamkhir*, Proud, haughty.

A متشمر *mutashammir*, Prepared, become ready for. (A gum) sticking close to the roots of the teeth.

A متشمز *mutashammiz*, Contracted, knit (brow). Changed (colour of the face).

A متشمس *mutashammis*, Exposed to the sun. Strong, powerful. Very avaricious.

A متشمص *mutashammis*, One who restrains himself. Wrinkled, puckered, contracted, shrivelled. A horse whose paunch is loaded with green fodder.

A متشمل *mutashammil*, Covered, concealed. Dressed in over-alls, surtout, or upper coat.

A متشمم *mutashammim*, One who smells gently.

A متشنج *mutashannij*, Shrivelled, wrinkled.

A متشنع *mutashanniɛ*, Mounted on horseback. Armed: prepared for battle. (See تشنع *tashannuɛ*.)

A متشنف *mutashannif*, Decked with ear-rings.

A متشنن *mutashannin*, Old, worn out. Dried, shrivelled, wrinkled, wizened, shrunk, contracted.

A متشوذ *mutashawwiz*, Dressed in a turban.

A متشور *mutashawwir*, Ashamed.

A متشوش *mutashawwish*, Disturbed, disordered.

A متشوط *mutashawwit*, One who tires his (horse).

A متشوف *mutashawwif*, Combed, dressed (damsel). (See also تشوف *tashawwuf*).

A متشوق *mutashawwik*, Wishful, desirous.

A متشوك *mutashawwik*, Beset with thorns.

A متشوه *mutashawwih*, Altered: unrecognisable.

A متشهد *mutashahhid*, One who makes a profession of faith. (See تشهد *tashahhud*.)

A متشهل *mutashahhil*, Faded (complexion).

A متشهي *mutashahha'*, Desired, longed for. *Mutashahhī*, Desirous, eager, longing more and more.

A متشي *muttashī*, (A sick person) restored to health. Healed, consolidated (broken bone).

A متشيخ *mutashayyikh*, A pretender to, or an assumer of, the character of a شيخ *shaykh*, *i.e.* of an elder, a venerable or learned person.

A متشيط *mutashayyit*, Burnt, scorched, parched. Lean by reason of excessive venery.

A متشيطن *mutashaytin*, Devilish, satanical.

A متشيع *mutashayyiɛ*, A sectary of Aliy; sheah.

A متشيم *mutashayyim*, Entered (into). Like unto (a father). Grey, hoary.

A متصاب *mutasābb*, One who drinks the remains of water in a pot (صبابة *subābat*).

A متصابي *mutasābī*, Amorously inclined.

A متصات *mutasātt*, Fighting together.

A متصادف *mutasādif*, One who meets with.

A متصادق *mutasādik*, Mutually sincere, true.

A متصادم *mutasādim*, Struck together, clashed.

A متصارم *mutasārim*, Sundered, severed.

A متصاعب *mutasāɛib*, Difficult, hard, untractable, troublesome.

A متصاعد *mutasāɛid*, Superior, above. Difficult (thing). Ascended, on the move upwards.

A متصاغر *mutasāghir*, Little in one's own esteem.

A متصافح *mutasāfih*, Mutual in shaking hands.

A متصافق *mutasāfik*, Mutual in shaking hands on striking a bargain.

A متصافن *mutasāfin*, (A company of travellers) dividing amongst themselves (water in the desert).

A متصافي *mutasāfī*, Mutually honest, upright.

A متصالح *mutasālih*, At peace together.

A متصالخ *mutasālikh*, One who shams deafness.

A متصام *mutasāmm*, One who shams deafness.

A متصاول *mutasāwil*, Mutual in assaulting, leaping at, springing upon, attacking, assailing.

A متصايح *mutasāyih*, Mutual in crying aloud. Split, cracked (sword-sheath).

A متصبب *mutasabbib*, Poured out; falling.

A متصبح *mutasabbih*, An early comer, who arrives betimes. One who sleeps, amuses himself, or eats in the morning.

A متصبر *mutasabbir*, One who affects patience (صبر *sabr*), or who imposes a restraint on himself.

A متصبصب *mutasabsib*, Elapsed, well-nigh spent. Scattered; lost.

A متصبي *mutasabbī*, A gay deceiver.

A متصتع *mutasattiɛ*, One who goes to and fro. Irresolute, vacillating.

A متصتم *mutasattim*, A leaper, passer rapidly by.

A متصحف *mutasahhif*, An incorrect reader.

A متصدد *mutasaddid*, Facing, standing opposite.

A متصدر *mutasaddir*, Seated in the chief seat.

A متصدع *mutasaddiɛ*, Importunate, troublesome. Cleft, split, divided. Scattered.

A متصدف *mutasaddif*, Face-averted.

A متصدق *mutasaddik*, A giver or asker of alms.

A متصدي *mutasaddī*, One who turns away the face, opposes, or objects. One who attempts, presumes, dares, is intent upon. Any inferior officer of government, a clerk, accomptant.

A متصرخ *mutasarrikh*, One who roars: screamer.

A متصرف *mutasarraf*, Whatever is in one's power or possession. متصرف فيه *mutasarraf fīhi*, Possessed, used. غير متصرف *ghayr mutasarraf*, Out of one's power (as a bird in the air, or a fish in the water). *Mutasarrif*, A possessor, occupant, enjoyer, master. A taker. One who uses his own discretion. Guilty of embezzlement. Profuse, extravagant. Dexterous. Declined. قوت متصرفه *kūwati mutasarrifa*, The thinking faculty.

A متصرم *mutasarrim*, Cut off, rescinded. Dexterous, clever.

A متصعد *mutasaɛɛid*, High. Hard, difficult.

A متصعر *mutasaɛɛir*, Spherical. Wry (face).

A متصعصع *mutasaɛsiɛ*, Separated, divided, dispersed (especially those who quit the line of battle). Thinned, broken (rank). Timid, pusillanimous, cowardly, abject, dejected. One who loses (friends). Dissipating, disastrous (fortune).

A متصعلك *mutasaɛlik*, Poor, indigent. Moulted.

A متصف *muttasif*, Praiseworthy. Qualified, endued, marked with an epithet. Described. A describer. Mutually laudatory.

A متصفح *mutasaffih*, One who looks at the broad or outside of a thing. Searcher, examiner, inspector.

A متصفق *mutasaffik*, (A camel) that moves from side to side. Irresolute, vacillating. One who encounters, opposes, meets.

A متصل *muttasil*, Contiguous, adjoining, conjunct, near, continual. Conjunctive. One who accosts a person courteously. The letter و *waw*. نسب متصل *nasabi muttasil*, An unbroken line of ancestry.

A متصلاً *muttasilan*, Continually. Contiguously.

A متصلة *muttasilat*, An affixed pronoun.

A متصلصل *mutasalsil*, Loud, rumbling (thunder). Clattering, tinkling, jingling (ornaments).

A متصلع *mutasalliع*, (The sun) breaking forth from behind a cloud and reaching the meridian.

A متصلف *mutasallif*, A boaster, braggart.

A متصلق *mutasallik*, Crying (woman in labour). Wallowing (beast). Plunging in water.

A متصلي *mutasalla'*, (A stick) straightened by fire. *Mutasallī*, Burnt. Warmed (at the fire).

A متصمر *mutasammir*, One who exposes himself to the sun. Strong, powerful. Very avaricious. Imprisoned, confined, kept in durance.

A متصمع *mutasammiع*, Stained with blood, and sticking together (feathers of an arrow).

A متصنع *mutasanniع*, Adorned, decorated. One who shews off his skill. Anxious to pass off well. Specious; one whose words and actions agree not.

A متصنف *mutasannif*, Excoriated (lip). (A plant) ready to burst into leaf.

A متصوب *mutasawwib*, Heavy, falling (rain). High ground sloping downwards.

A متصوح *mutasawwih*, Divided, parted (hair).

A متصور *mutasawwar*, Imagined. *Mutasawwir*, An imaginer, conceiver. Considerate, reflective. (A blow or stab) which inclines or verges towards. Imagined. Imaginable, conceivable, possible.

A متصوع *mutasawwiع*, Dispersed (people). Dishevelled (hair).

A متصوف *mutasawwif*, Obscure, mystical (speech). A sufi, soph, or mystic.

A متصوق *mutasawwik*, (or متصوك *mutasawwik*) Bedaubed with one's own dung.

A متصون *mutasawwin*, Careful (of one's self).

A متصوي *mutasawwī*, Sloping.

A متصيد *mutasayyid*, Devoted to hunting.

A متصير *mutasayyir*, Who takes after his father.

A متصيف *mutasayyif*, A summer-sojourner.

A متضاجم *mutazājim*, Wry-mouthed. An opponent, resister.

A متضاحك *mutazāhik*, Laughing together.

A متضاد *mutazādd*, Mutually opposed, contrary.

A متضار *mutazārr*, Suited. Mutually injurious.

A متضارب *mutazārib*, Distracted, fighting together, beating one another.

A متضارس *mutazāris*, Uneven, skew (building).

A متضاعف *mutazāعif*, Increased to twice as much, doubled.

A متضاغط *mutazāghit*, Crowded, huddled.

A متضاغن *mutazāghin*, Full of mutual enmity.

A متضاف *mutazāff*, (A herd of camels running to water) pressing, crowding on one another.

A متضافر *mutazāfir*, Confederate, auxiliary.

A متضافط *mutazāfit*, Compact, firm (flesh).

A متضافن *mutazāfin*, Mutual in giving help.

A متضام *mutazāmm*, Joined, heaped, compact. Drawn towards, assembled round.

A متضايف *mutazāyif*, Near, close to the side. Narrow (river). (See تضايف *tazāyuf*.)

A متضايق *mutazāyik*, Narrow, straitened (in mind or place).

A متضائل *mutazāʼil*, Slender, small, contemptible.

A متضبب *mutazabbib*, Fat, short-necked (boy).

A متضبط *mutazabbit*, One who seizes by force.

A متضجر *mutazajjir*, Distressed, oppressed, injured, afflicted, lamenting. Restless.

A متضجع *mutazajjiع*, Indolent, sitting still.

A متضح *muttazih*, Manifest, evident, clear.

A متضحك *mutazahhik*, A laugher, mocker.

A متضحي *mutazahhī*, A diner in the forenoon.

A متضرب *mutazarrib*, Beaten. Agitated, disturbed, uneasy, shaking.

A متضرج *mutazarrij*, Stained with blood. Roseate (cheek). Wide-spread (lightning's flash).

A متضرر *mutazarrir*, Scattered. Injured, harmed, oppressed.

A متضرع *mutazarriع*, Humbled; a suppliant.

A متضرم *mutazarrim*, Kindled (fire or rage).

A متضع *muttaziع*, Humbled, lowly: lowered, disgraced. Mean, despicable, vile.

A متضعضع *mutazaعziع*, Submissive, one who humbles himself. A suppliant. Shaken, overthrown.

A متضعف *mutazaععaf*, Regarded as weak, obscure and contemptible. *Mutazaععif*, One who looks on as weak (ضعيف *zaعif*). Obscure, despised.

A متضلع *mutazalliع*, Filled, satiated, glutted.

A متضمخ *mutazammikh*, (A body) anointed with sweet ungnent.

A متضمد *mutazammid*, Bandaged (wound).

A متضمر *mutazammir*, Fallen away, wrinkled, shrunk, wizened (face). Slender about the middle.

A متضمن *mutazammin*, What comprehends, contains, includes. A surety, bondsman, sponsor.

A متضوج *mutazawwij*, Meandrous (river).

A متضور *mutazawwir*, One who throws himself from side to side in a conflict. One who writhes (from pain, &c.). (See تضور *tazawwur*.)

A متضوع *mutazawwiع*, (Musk) fragrant when stirred. (See تضوع *tazawwuع*.)

A متضوك *mutazawwik*, Besmeared (with one's own dung).

A متضوي *mutazawwī*, Any one standing in the dark, that, by the light of a fire, he may see people.

A متضيح *mutazayyih*, One who comes to a cistern after the greater part of the water has been drunk. Diluted, thinned (milk). A drinker of milk mixed with water (ضياح *zayāh*).

A متضيع *mutazayyiع*, Fragrant (musk).

A متضيف *mutazayyif*, Near setting (sun). Inclined. Become a guest (ضيف *zayf*).

A متضيق *mutazayyik*, Hemmed in, straitened.

A متطابق *mutatābik*, Suited, agreeable to.

A متطارش *mutatārish*, A feigner of deafness.

A متطارق *mutatārik*, (Camels) which follow one another and tread in each other's steps.

A متطأطئ *mutataʼtiʼ*, One who hangs his head. Low, trodden (ground).

A متطاعم *mutatāعim*, Billing (doves).

A متطاعن *mutatāعin*, Mutual in spearing.

A متطال *mutatāll*, Eager to see, on tip-toe.

A متطامن *mutatāmin*, Quiet. Confident.

A متطاوح *mutatāwih*, Engaged in throwing date-stones at each other.

A متطاوع *mutatāwiع*, Diligent. Laborious, painstaking. Humble, submissive, obedient, compliant.

A متطاول *mutatāwil*, Eager to see, on tip-toe. Lofty from pride. Victorious. Long.

A متطاهر *mutatāhir*, Cleansed, purified.

A متطاير *mutatāyir*, Scattered, flying about here and there. Sky-covering (cloud).

A متطب *mutatibb*, A practitioner in medicine.

A متطبب *mutatabbib*, A student of the art of medicine. A medical practitioner.

A متطبع *mutatabbiع*, Implanted by nature, innate. One who forces himself to do a thing contrary to his nature. Full, filled (river or cup).

A متطبق *mutatabbik*, Agreeable to, suitable.

A متطخطخ *mutatakhtikh*, Black. A black cloud. Clouds piled one upon another. Weak-sighted.

A متطرب *mutatarrib*, One who moves briskly from joy or pain. A singer. One who makes cheerful and exhilarates.

A متطرح *mutatarrih*, A tired, languid pace.

A متطرز *mutatarriz*, Embroidered (hem).

A متطرس *mutatarris*, Squeamish, dainty, fastidious, choice, nice, particular.

A متطرش *mutatarrish*, Convalescent.

A متطرف *mutatarrif*, (A camel) grazing at the edge of a field, and not mixing with the others.

A متطرق *mutatarrik*, Who opposes, meets, encounters, thwarts. A leader, conductor.

A متطرم *mutatarrim*, A stammerer, stutterer. A speaker in a low tone or whisper.

A متطعم *mutataععim*, A taster, trier, sipper.

A متطغم *mutataghghim*, One who shams ignorance or folly.

A متطفل *mutataffil*, An uninvited guest.

A متطلب *mutatallib*, Inquisitive. A seeker.

A متطلس *mutatallis*, Erased, cancelled.

A متطلع *mutatalliع*, One who looks at, waits for. Informed, apprized of. (See تطلع *tatalluع*.)

A متطلّق *mutatallik*, Culled, chosen. (See تطلّق.)

A متطلّي *mutatallī*, Anointed, smeared, daubed.

A متطمّس *mutatammis*, Obliterated, erased.

A متطّن *muttatin*, Accustomed to; frequenter.

A متطوّح *mutatawwih*, A wanderer, vagrant.

A متطوّع *mutatawwiʻ*, Obedient. A volunteer (in a holy war). A doer of works of supererogation.

A متطوّف *mutatawwif*, One who moves round.

A متطوّق *mutatawwik*, Adorned with a chain or a collar: collared.

A متطوّل *mutatawwil*, A favourer, benefactor.

A متطوّي *mutatawwī*, Coiled up (serpent).

A متطهّر *mutatahhir*, Purified, cleansed, washed. Sanctified.

A متطهّل *mutatahhil*, Stale, stinking (meat). Changed (colour or taste of water).

A متطهّم *mutatahhim*, One who loathes (food). Sated, wearied, tired, disgusted.

A متطيّب *mutatayyib*, Embalmed. Perfumed.

A متطيّخ *mutatayyikh*, Defiled, dirtied.

A متطيّر *mutatayyir*, Who views as a bad omen.

A متطيّن *mutatayyin*, Bedaubed with mire.

A متظالم *mutazālim*, Employed in injuring one another. Reciprocal in complaining of injuries.

A متظاهر *mutazāhir*, Joined back to back. Mutually auxiliary. One who throws (another) on his back (ظهر *zahr*).

A متظبظب *mutazabzib*, Slightly impressive.

A متظرّف *mutazarrif*, An affecter of elegance.

A متظرمطة *mutazarmitat*, Muddy, clayey (soil).

A متظفّر *mutazaffir*, Victorious, triumphant.

A متظلّل *mutazallil*, Shaded, over-shadowed.

A متظلّم *mutazallim*, Darkened, obscure. Injured, oppressed, aggrieved. A wronger. A complainer of wrongs. P متظلّم داد خواه *mutazallimi dād-khwāh*, An oppressed person demanding justice. A متظلّمين *mutazallimīn*, (pl. oblique) Accusers; complainers of wrong and injustice.

A متظنّن *mutazannin*, (or متظنّي *mutazannī*) One who thinks, opines, surmises, or suspects.

A متظهّر *mutazahhir*, A pronouncer of a formula of divorce upon his wife. Protected, propped up, backed. One who goes at noon.

A متع *matʻ*, (v. n. of متع) Advancing (as the day). Being tall, long. Dipping, preponderating (a scale). Enjoying, reaping the advantage. Carrying away. *Matʻ* or *mutʻ*, (v. n. of متع) Regarding (one) as a liar. Being elevated (the vapour سراب *sarāb*). Being tight (a rope). Being of a deep red (wine). Being liberal and beneficent. Being ingenious. Being graceful and elegant. *Mitaʻ* or *mutaʻ*, (pl. of متعة *mitʻat* or *mutʻat*) Fruits, advantages. Victuals sufficient. *Mattaʻa*, May (God) grant, or permit freely to enjoy!

A متعاتب *mutaʻātib*, Mutually recriminative.

A متعادّ *mutaʻādd*, In number over (10,000).

A متعادل *mutaʻādil*, Parallel to each other.

A متعادي *mutaʻādī*, Mutually hostile. Inconvenient (place). (See تعادي *taʻādī*).

A متعادية *mutaʻādiyat*, Stony (ground) full of hollows; uneven with stones or clods.

A متعارّ *mutaʻārr*, One who lies awake and rolls on his bed, howling and making a noise.

A متعارض *mutaʻāriz*, Contrary, opposed to each other. Engaged in imitating, or doing any thing like one another. Conflicting, contradictory.

A متعارف *mutaʻārif*, Well known to each other. Common usage.

A متعارفية *mutaʻārifiyat*, Celebrity, notoriety.

A متعازل *mutaʻāzil*, Remote, removed, retiring, receding, withdrawing from each other.

A متعازي *mutaʻāzī*, Reciprocal in consoling or exhorting to the exercise of patience.

A متعاسر *mutaʻāsir*, Difficult. Hard, firm. Mutually perplexed.

A متعاشر *mutaʻāshir*, Intimate, familiar, mixed.

A متعاشي *mutaʻāshī*, One who feigns blindness, ignorance, purblindness, or nyctalopia.

A متعاطف *mutaʻātif*, Inclined to each other.

A متعاطي *mutaʻātī*, One who takes any thing to eat or drink. Mutual in sending presents.

A متعاظل *mutaʻāzil*, Fastened together when coupling (dogs or locusts).

A متعاظم *mutaʻāzim*, Proud, haughty, pompous. Equal in greatness.

A متعاظي *mutaʻāzī*, Mutually injurious.

A متعاقب *mutaʻākib*, Successive, following, pursuing. Subsequent. Afterward. متعاقب الورود *mutaʻākibu'l wurūd*, Coming successively. ثمرات متعاقبة *samarāti mutaʻākiba*, Fruits following in their seasons.

A متعاقد *mutaʻākid*, Leagued, confederate.

A متعاقر *mutaʻākir*, Reciprocal in wounding or killing. Rival in hamstringing cattle.

A متعاقم *mutaʻākim*, Successive, alternate.

A متعاكر *mutaʻākir*, Mixed together pell-mell.

A متعاكس *mutaʻākis*, Inverted, turned.

A متعاكظ *mutaʻākiz*, Engaged in a contention for glory. Mutually contentious or boastful.

A متعال *mutaʻāl*, High, sublime. P خداي متعال *khudāyi mutaʻāl*, The most high God.

A متعالّ *mutaʻāll*, A hard camel-driver.

A متعالم *mutaʻālim*, Known to each other; known of all.

A متعالى *mutaʻālī*, High, lofty, exalted. One who draws near.

A متعامس *mutaʻāmis*, A feigner of ignorance.

A متعامش *mutaʻāmish*, Negligent, remiss.

A متعامل *mutaʻāmil*, United by commerce.

A متعامي *mutaʻāmī*, One who shams blindness.

A متعانق *mutaʻānik*, Mutual in embracing.

A متعاود *mutaʻāwid*, Returned home in a tumultuous manner (two contending parties).

A متعاور *mutaʻāwar*, Borrowed. *Mutaʻāwir*, Reciprocal, alternate in doing (any thing).

A متعاوض *mutaʻāwiz*, Acceptor of a substitute.

A متعاوك *mutaʻāwik*, Engaged in combat.

A متعاون *mutaʻāwin*, Leagued for mutual aid.

A متعاونة *mutaʻāwanat*, A middle-aged and strong woman.

A متعاهد *mutaʻāhid*, Confederate, covenanted.

A متعايب *mutaʻāyib*, (or متعاير *mutaʻāyir*) Employed in mutual upbraidings.

A متعب *mutʻab*, Fatigued, tired. *Mutʻib*, One who fatigues or overworks. Toilsome. A filler (of a vessel). Broken again (a bone, after having been consolidated). An owner of jaded cattle.

A متعبّب *mutaʻabbib*, Addicted to wine.

A متعبة *matʻabat*, A place of fatigue.

A متعبّد *mutaʻabbad*, A place of worship. *Mutaʻabbid*, Devout, religious overmuch. Refractory, stubborn (camel). One who fatigues by driving. One who receives as a servant (عبد *ʻabd*).

A متعبّدات *mutaʻabbadāt*, The ceremonies and sacrifices prescribed in the pilgrimage to Mecca.

A متعبّس *mutaʻabbis*, Frowning, crabbed, austere.

A متعبهل *mutaʻabhil*, Prevented. Not prohibited from any thing.

A متعة *mitʻat* or *mutʻat*, (v. n. of متع) Performing the ceremonies at Mecca, making the sacred visitation called عمرة *ʻumrat*. Taking a wife on the condition of dismissing her after a few days cohabitation. (pl. متع *mitaʻ* and *mutaʻ*) Use, enjoyment, advantage, benefit. A moderate supply of provisions, enough to live upon. Game or food which one is permitted to enjoy. A rope and a leathern bucket. *Mutʻat*, (v. n. of متع) Carrying away. A present to a woman divorced from her husband. A bucket, an urn. A rope for buckets. متعة الحج *mutʻatu'l hajj*, A performing of the sacred visitation called عمرة *ʻumrat* along with the pilgrimage. متعة الطلاق *mutʻatu't talāk*, Money and clothes given to a wife at the time of divorce.

A متعتّب *mutaʻattib*, Angry, scolding, chiding.

A متعتّت *mutaʻattit*, Inconstant, unstable in one's words.

A متعتّد *mutaʻattid*, Ready, skilful (in any art).

A متعتّق *mutaʻattik*, Quick, instantaneous.

A متعتّه *mutaʻattih*, One who feigns ignorance or stupidity. Confused, stupid, bereft of sense. (See تعتّه *taʻattuh*).

A متعتّي *mutaʻattī*, Proud, exorbitant.

A متعثّر *mutaʻassir*, A stutterer, stammerer.

A متعثّق *mutaʻassik*, Confused, mixed (clouds).

A متعثكل *mutaʻaskil* or *mutaʻaskal*, Very branchy and laden with clusters (palm-tree).

A متعثلب *mutaʻaslib*, Lean, in bad condition.

A متعجّب *mutaʻajjib*, Astonished, amazed. Filled with admiration. Wonderful, strange.

P متعجّبانه *mutaʻajjibāna*, Wondrous.

A متعجّج *mutaʻajjij*, (A house) full of smoke.

A متعجر *mutaʻajjir*, Wrinkled with fat (belly).

A متعجس *mutaʻajjis*, Proud, haughty.

A متعجّل *mutaʻajjil*, Hasty, one who seizes hastily. One who sends home milk to his friends before the milking is finished.

A متعجّن *mutaʻajjin*, (A camel) filled with fat.

A متعجّنة *mutaʻajjinat*, Fat (she-camel) that gives little milk. A crowd, multitude.

A متعجّه *mutaʻajjih*, One who feigns ignorance.

A متعدّد *mutaʻaddid*, Many, various. In number over (10,000). Ready, prepared, expeditious.

A متعدّي *mutaʻaddī*, Who or what passes by, or from one to another. Active, transitive, causal (verb). A transgressor, wicked wretch, scoundrel. (People) infected by a contagious disorder: dying one after another.

A متعذّر *mutaʻazzir*, Difficult, impossible. Stained, besmeared. Effaced (vestige). An apologist. Deserving of pardon. (See تعذر *taʻazzur*.)

A متعذّل *mutaʻazzil*, Patient under reproof.

A متعرّب *mutaʻarrib*, One who lives amongst, and becomes like an Arabian. Not a pure Arabian.

A متعرّج *mutaʻarrij*, Oblique, scalene (edifice).

A متعرّر *mutaʻarrir*, Scabby, mangy (camel).

A متعرّز *mutaʻarriz*, Troubled, perplexed.

A متعرّس *mutaʻarris*, Fond of his wife.

A متعرّش *mutaʻarrish*, A permanent resident.

A متعرّص *mutaʻarris*, Stayer, dweller, resident.

A متعرّض *mutaʻarriz*, An opposer, hinderer, withstander. One who causes pain or trouble. Averse.

A متعرّف *mutaʻarrif*, A pryer into another person's secrets, curious to know. One who confesses.

A متعرّق *mutaʻarrik*, (or متعرّم *mutaʻarrim*) One who picks a bone clean.

A متعزّب *mutaʻazzib*, Bachelor, unmarried.

A متعزّز *mutaʻazziz*, Rare, precious, excellent.

A متعزّق *mutaʻazzik*, Unkind, severe.

A متعزّل *mutaʻazzil*, Dismissed, cashiered, removed from office. Retired.

A متعزّي *mutaʻazzī*, Pertaining, belonging to. One who claims relationship (true or false).

A متعس *mutʻis*, (God) destroying (any one).

A متعسّر *mutaʻassir*, Difficult, impossible, intricate, hard to be explained. Pressing (necessity). متعسّر الحصول *mutaʻassiru'l husūl*, Difficult to be obtained, arduous. متعسّر المرور *mutaʻassiru'l murūr*, Difficult to pass, hard to be got over.

A متعسعس *mutaʻasʻis*, One who hunts or prowls by night. Prowling (wolf).

A متعسّف *mutaʻassif*, One who goes in darkness and uncertainty. A griper, oppressor, extortioner. Vexed at a loss.

A متعسّق *mutaʻassik*, Extremely desirous or greedy: a diligent seeker.

A متعسّقر *mutaʻashir*, Quick. Hard and patient.

A متعسّن *mutaʻassin*, Like (his father).

A متعشّب *mutaʻashshib*, Fed on, or fattened by green herbage or grass (عشب *ʻushb*).

A متعشّق *mutaʻashshik*, A lover, sweetheart.

A متعشّم *mutaʻashshim*, Dried up, withered.

A متعشّي *mutaʻashshī*, One taking his supper. Purblind at night.

A متعصّب *mutaʻassib*, Attached to one's people; helping them. (See also تعصّب *taʻassub*.)

A متعصّر *mutaʻassir*, Expressed, squeezed out (juice). A refugee.

A متعصّم *mutaʻassim*, Protected, kept safe.

A متعصّي *mutaʻassī*, Who beats off with a stick. Rebellious. Difficult, intricate (affair).

A متعطّر *mutaʻattir*, Perfumed, highly scented.

A متعطّش *mutaʻattish*, One who pretends to be athirst. Wishful, desirous, eager, curious.

A متعطّف *mutaʻattif*, Indulgent, favourably inclined. One who throws a cloak over himself.

A متعطّل *mutaʻattil*, Idle, unemployed.

A متعطّلة *mutaʻattilat*, Unadorned (woman).

A متعطّي *mutaʻattī*, One who begs a present.

A متّعظ *muttaʻiz*, Admonished. One who takes admonition in good part, or follows advice.

A متعظّم *mutaʻazzim*, Proud, haughty, stately.

A متعفّج *mutaʻaffij*, Obliquely moving (camel).

A متعفّر *mutaʻaffir*, Soiled with dust, dusty.

A متعفّف *mutaʻaffif*, Chaste, continent, abstemious. Studying to keep one's self pure.

A متعفّن *mutaʻaffin*, Putrid, stinking, noisome. Rotten (rope).

A متعفّي *mutaʻaffī*, Utterly demolished.

A متعقّب *mutaʻakkib*, Punished for faults.

A متعقّد *mutaʻakkid*, Consolidated, fastened together. Concreted. (See also تعقّد *taʻakkud*.)

A متعقّف *mutaʻakkif*, Crooked, curved, bent.

A متعقّل *mutaʻakkil*, Intelligent, wise, learned.

A متعقّم *mutaʻakkim*, A goer to and fro.

A متعكّب *mutaʻakkib*, Solicitous, anxious about.

A متعكّز *mutaʻakkiz*, Propped by crutch or staff.

A متعكّس *mutaʻakkis*, A crawler, as a viper.

A متعكّش *mutaʻakkish*, Twisted up (hair).

A متعكّظ *mutaʻakkiz*, Intricate, difficult, perplexed (business). (See تعكّظ *taʻakkuz*.)

A متعكّف *mutaʻakkif*, Crisp, curled (hair). Devoted. One who restrains himself.

A متعكّن *mutaʻakkin*, (A belly) wrinkled from fat.

A متعلّق *mutaʻallak*, A place where any thing may be suspended. An interest. *Mutaʻallik*, Belonging to, dependent upon, connected, touching, concerning. Sticking close. A kinsman. A dependant. Suspended, hanging to. Addicted, dedicated, attached. Possessed of a bare subsistence. ليس المتعلّق كالمتأنّق *laysa'l mutaʻallik ka'l mutaʻannik*, He who is dependent on a bare subsistence is not as he who may eat whatever he fancies.

A متعلّقات *mutaʻallikāt*, (pl. of متعلّقة *mutaʻallikat*) Dependencies, appurtenances, circumstances. Children, family, domestics.

A متعلّل *mutaʻallil*, A cajoler. One who offers a reason or excuse. (See تعلّل *taʻallul*.)

A متعلّم *mutaʻallim*, Taught, instructed. One who applies himself to learn. A learner, scholar, disciple. A teacher.

A متعلّي *mutaʻallī*, High. One who ascends gradually. (See تعلّي *taʻallī*.)

A متعمّج *mutaʻammij*, Tortuous in one's gait.

A متعمّد *mutaʻammid*, Serious, attentive, earnest.

A متعمرط *mutaʻamrit*, A robber who carries off all he can lay his hands on.

A متعمّس *mutaʻammis*, Perplexed, uncertain.

A متعمّق *mutaʻammik*, Carried far in a discourse. Spruce in dress, foppish.

A متعمّل *mutaʻammil*, Studious, pains-taking.

A متعمّم *mutaʻammim*, Dressed in a turban.

A متعمّن *mutaʻammin*, An abider, stayer.

A متعنّت *mutaʻannit*, One who seeks the fall, depression, or humiliation of another.

A متعنّد *mutaʻannid*, A seeker of another's ruin.

A متعنّك *mutaʻannik*, (Sand) difficult to pass.

A متعنّي *mutaʻannī*, Tired, jaded, fatigued.

A متعوب *matʻūb*, Fatigued: oppressed: vexed.

A متعوّث *mutaʻawwis*, Confounded; amazed.

A متعوّج *mutaʻawwij*, Bent, crooked, curved.

A متعوّد *mutaʻawwid*, Accustomed, used to.

A متعوّذ *mutaʻawwiz*, One who takes refuge.

A متعوّر *mutaʻawwir*, Mutual in borrowing.

A متعوس *matʻūs*, (pl. متاعيس) Fallen, perished.

A متعوّق *mutaʻawwik*, Averted, turned away from. Hindered, let.

A متعهّت *mutaʻahhit*, Neat, spruce, fastidiously so. Foolish, senseless, destitute of reason.

A متعهّد *mutaʻahhid*, Continually engaged in the same act. Attentive to.

A متعيّب *mutaʻayyib*, A reproacher, accuser.

A متعيّد *mutaʻayyid*, Cruel, unjust, tyrannical. Angry, enraged. A false accuser. A threatener.

A متعيّش *mutaʻayyish*, Possessed of a sufficiency to support life, who has just enough to live upon. Supported by his own industry.

A متعيّط *mutaʻayyit*, Barren for several years (camel). (See تعيّط *taʻayyut*.)

A متعيّل *mutaʻayyil*, Pompous in one's gait.

A متعيّن *mutaʻayyin*, Public, open, plain, manifest, conspicuous. Certain, determined, constituted, appointed, deputed. One who follows with the eye, pierces, influences, or fascinates with malignant looks. Pierced full of small holes (a leathern-bottle or bag). The same thing continually hanging over or adhering. New (leathern-bottle). One who receives (any thing) after a delay given.

A متعيّنة *mutaʻayyana*, A station, post, command.

A متغابن *mutaghābin*, Mutually fraudulent.

A متغابي *mutaghābī*, Heedless, remiss.

A متغازّ *mutaghāzz*, A disputant, combatant.

A متغازل *mutaghāzil*, Mutually engaged in amorous blandishments.

A متغاضي *mutaghāzī*, Negligent, inattentive.

A متغاط *mutaghātt*, Engaged in mutual ducking.

A متغاطس *mutaghātis*, Indifferent, unconcerned. Engaged in ducking one another.

A متغاطش *mutaghātish*, Who shams blindness.

A متغافل *mutaghāfil*, One who shams negligence.

A متغالب *mutaghālib*, Victorious in turns.

A متغالي *mutaghālī*, Lean, falling away (flesh). High, long, luxuriant (grass). High (price). Rival in archery.

A متغامز *mutaghāmiz*, Engaged in winking at one another.

A متغاني *mutaghānī*, Independent of one another.

A متغاور *mutaghāwir*, Mutually engaged in hostile excursions and free-booting.

A متغاوط *mutaghāwit*, Reciprocal in ducking.

A متغاوي *mutaghāwī*, Assembled from every quarter in order to perpetrate villainy.

A متغايب *mutaghāyib*, Absent.

A متغايد *mutaghāyid*, Bent double, flexible.

A متغاير *mutaghāyir*, Diverse, different.

A متغايظ *mutaghāyiz*, Enraged at one another.

A متغب *mutghib*, Murderous, destructive.

A متغبّر *mutaghabbir*, Begetter (of children).

A متغبّق *mutaghabbik*, One who milks at even.

A متغتغ *mutaghtigh*, Scarcely heard to speak.

A متغدّن *mutaghaddin*, A staggerer, totterer.

A متغدّي *mutaghaddī*, One who breakfasts. One who dines early.

A متغذّم *mutaghazzim*, Voracious. A cutter.

A متغذّي *mutaghazzī*, Nourished, fed upon.

A متغرّب *mutagharrib*, On foreign travel. Far distant. A comer from the west (غرب *gharb*).

A متغرّد *mutagharrid*, A songster, warbler.

A متغرّر *mutagharrir*, Boiling (water).

A متغرغر *mutagharghir*, One gargling his throat.

A متغزّل *mutaghazzil*, A writer of erotic poetry.

A متغس *mutghis*, Who or what renders wretched. Who or what throws down.

A متغسّل *mutaghassil*, Nice in his ablutions.

A متغشرم *mutaghashrim*, Hard, severe.

A متغشمر *mutaghashmir*, Angry, in a passion.

A متغشّي *mutaghashshī*, Who covers himself.

A متغصّب *mutaghassib*, Constrained.

A متغضّب *mutaghazzib*, Angered, enraged.

A متغضّر *mutaghazzir*, Declining, receding.

A متغضّض *mutaghazziz*, (or متغضغض *mutaghazghiz*) Diminished.

A متغضّف *mutaghazzif*, Flagging. (See تغضّف.)

A متغضّن *mutaghazzin*, Wrinkled, puckered.

A متغطرس *mutaghatris*, Angry, wrathful. Proud. Covetous. Stately in walking.

A متغطرف *mutaghatrif*, Haughty, stately.

A متغطّش *mutaghattish*, Dark night: dim (eye).

A متغطغط *mutaghatghit*, Raging, stormy (sea).

A متغطّي *mutaghattī*, Covered, hid.

A متغفّق *mutaghaffik*, All day (at the bottle).

A متغفّل *mutaghaffil*, Careless, negligent. One who affects to be careless or negligent.

A متغلّب *mutaghallib*, Dominant, powerful.

A متغلّت *mutaghallit*, One who takes (any thing) with indifference.

A متغلّج *mutaghallij*, Unjust, iniquitous.

A متغلّد *mutaghallid*, Quick, instant (poison).

A متغلّف *mutaghallif*, Perfumed, civeted.

A متغلّل *mutaghallil*, Perfumed with civet.

A متغم *mutghim*, Dyspeptic.

A متغمة *matghamat*, Food which turns upon the stomach, and produces indigestion.

A متغمّد *mutaghammid*, A concealer, a hider. (God) receiving into his mercy. (Water) which fills or saturates.

A متغمّر *mutaghammir*, Tinged with saffron (غمرة *ghumrat*). (See also تغمّر *taghammur*.)

A متغمّس *mutaghammis*, Plunged, immersed. Dyed. متغمّس في السواد *mutaghammis fi's sawād*, Arrayed in sable garments.

A متغمغم *mutaghamghim*, Affrighted (bull). Indistinct (speaker). Noisy (combatants).

A متغنّج *mutaghannij*, Coquettish (woman).

A متغنّم *mutaghannim*, One who looks upon and considers as prey. (See غنيمة *ghanīmat*).

A متغنّي *mutaghannī*, A singer. Polite, amorous. Contented. A praiser. A disparager.

A متغوّر *mutaghawwir*, Retired into a cavern. A descender into low grounds (غور *ghawr*).

A متغوّط *mutaghawwit*, Completely swallowed. One who goes down into a hollow to ease nature.

A متغوّل *mutaghawwil*, Of various hues. Destructive.

A متغيّب *mutaghayyib*, Absent, disappeared.

A متغيّر *mutaghayyir*, Disturbed, perplexed, stupefied. Altered, changed (for the better), amended. Mutable, inconsistent.

A متغيّظ *mutaghayyiz*, Angry, wrathful. Intensely hot (noon-tide).

A متغيّف *mutaghayyif*, (A tree) waving from side to side. Name of a horse.

A متغيّق *mutaghayyik*, Dark, dim (eye).

A متغيّل *mutaghayyil*, Thick, entangled (trees). One who lives constantly in a forest; a forester.

A متفاءل *mutafāʼil*, One who prognosticates from a name.

A متفاتح *mutafātih*, In private conversation.

A متفاتي *mutafātī*, One who consults a مفتي *muftī*, or man learned in the law.

A متفاجّ *mutafājj*, A straddler in walking.

A متفاجي *mutafājī*, Distant (time or space).

A متفاحش *mutafāhish*, An obscene talker.

A متفاخر *mutafākhir*, Mutually boastful.

A متفادي *mutafādī*, Mutual in ransoming.

A متفارّ *mutafārr*, Fugitive from one another.

A متفارص *mutafāris*, Employed by turns.

A متفاسح *mutafāsih*, One who makes room for another (in an assembly). Comfortably seated.

A متفاسد *mutafāsid*, Mutually alienated.

A متفاسي *mutafāsī*, Ready to break wind.

A متفاشغ *mutafāshigh*, Open, manifest.

A متفاصح *mutafāsih*, Pompously eloquent.

A متفاضل *mutafāzil*, Engaged in a dispute about excellence. Mutually ambitious of superiority.

A متفاقح *mutafākih*, Joined back to back.

A متفاقد *mutafākid*, In search of one another.

A متفاقس *mutafākis*, Engaged in pulling each other by the hair.

A متفاقم *mutafākim*, Great, weighty (affair).

A متفال *mitfāl*, Stinking-breathed (woman).

A متفالي *mutafālī*, Reciprocal in lousing.

A متفاني *mutafānī*, Destructive of each other (in war): mutually exterminatory.

A متفاوت *mutafāwit*, Distinct, separate, distant, different. Interrupted. (See تفاوت *tafāwut*.)

A متفاوض *mutafāwiz*, Associated. A partner.

A متفايد *mutafāyid*, Mutually beneficial.

A متفائل *mutafāʼil*, An augurer, diviner.

A متفتّت *mutafattit*, Broken in pieces, crumbled. Dropped off.

A متفتّح *mutafattih*, Opened, set wide open.

A متفتّش *mutafattish*, A searcher, examiner.

A متفتّغ *mutafattigh*, Broken, crushed.

A متفتف *mutaftif*, An idle fellow who saunters about and retails the sayings of women.

A متفتّق *mutafattik*, Split, cleft, unsewed.

A متفتّل *mutafattil*, Twisted (rope).

A متفتّي *mutafattī*, A lad with the air of a man.

A متفجّر *mutafajjir*, Freely flowing (water). Bright (morning). Generous, liberal.

A متفجّس *mutafajjis*, Lofty, haughty, proud.

A متفجّع *mutafajjiʻ*, Afflicted, sorrow-struck.

A متفحة *matfahat*, An apple-orchard.

A متفحّج *mutafahhij*, Seated with open legs.

A متفحّس *mutafahhis*, A pompous walker.

A متفحّش *mutafahhish*, Obscene or vain talker.

A متفحّص *mutafahhas*, Questioned, examined. *Mutafahhis*, An inquisitor, investigator, examiner.

A متفحّل *mutafahhil*, Decently clothed and well fed. Fruitless (tree). (See تفحّل *tafahhul*.)

A متفخّت *mutafakhkhit*, Astonished, astounded. One who has the gait of a dove (فاختة *fākhita*).

A متفخّذ *mutafakhkhiz*, Dilatory, laggard.

A متفخّر *mutafakhkhir*, Proud, vain-glorious.

A متفخّز *mutafakhkhiz*, Proud, lifted up, boastful.

A متفدّح *mutafazzih*, A quadruped ready to stale.

A متفر *mutfar*, (A field) grazed whilst the grass is yet short. *Mutfir*, One who has long hairs growing out of the nostrils. Budding (tree).

A متفر *muttafir*, Many, numerous; augmented.

A متفرّث *mutafarris*, Dispersed (people).

A متفرّثة *mutafarrisat*, Palpitating, fluttering, fainting (pregnant woman).

A متفرّج *mutafarrij*, One who looks, examines, walks about, or gazes around. A spectator. One who unbends in the company of friends.

A متفرّد *mutafarrid*, Alone, sole, by one's self.

A متفرّس *mutafarris*, A judger from signs or appearances. A physiognomist. One who pretends to be an expert horseman (فارس *fāris*).

A متفرّش *mutafarrish*, (A bird) which hovers with expanded wings in one place ready to alight.

A متفرّط *mutafarrit*, One who takes the lead.

A متفرّع *mutafarriɛ*, Produced, originated. Derived, propagated, branched out, ramifying. Very branchy (tree). Graffed. Belonging to, depending upon. A suitor for a lady of rank.

A متفرّعات *mutafarriɛāt*, Dependencies. Derivatives, pertinents, appurtenances.

A متفرّغ *mutafarrigh*, At leisure: vacant, empty.

A متفرّق *mutafarrak*, (v. n. 5 of فرق) Being divided, separated. A place of division and separation. *Mutafarrik*, Separate, distinct, different, divided, dispersed, scattered, confused, dissipated, ruined. متفرّقات *mutafarrikāt*, Scattered things.

A متفرّقة *mutafarrikat*, Horse-guards, spearmen, or archers attending a king when he travels.

A متفرقع *mutafarkiɛ*, One who makes a smacking noise with the fingers.

A متفرّقيّة *mutafarrikiyat*, Dispersion.

A متفرّك *mutafarrik*, A stumbler. A stammerer.

A متفرّي *mutafarrī*, Split, cut, divided. Separated. Flowing (fountain).

A متفسّح *mutafassih*, Spacious, roomy. One who makes room for. Comfortably and widely seated.

A متفسّخ *mutafassikh*, (Meat) done to rags. (See تفسّخ *tafassukh*.)

A متفشّج *mutafashshij*, One who sits straddlingly.

A متفشّغ *mutafashshigh*, Well-clad. (See تفشّغ).

A متفشّل *mutafashshil*, Running (water).

A متفشّي *mutafashshī*, Wide (wound). Prevalent, spreading (disease).

A متفصّح *mutafassih*, Eloquent, rhetorical. One who takes great pains to appear eloquent.

A متفصّد *mutafassid*, Fluent, flowing.

A متفصّم *mutafassim*, Broken, but unsevered.

A متفصّي *mutafassī*, Rescued (from oppression).

A متفضّج *mutafazzij*, Covered with grease.

A متفضّض *mutafazziz*, Broken (seal). Scattered.

A متفضّل *mutafazzil*, Excellent, eminent. One who pretends to, and assumes a superiority to his fellows. A benefactor. Clad daily in the same dress.

A متفطّر *mutafattir*, Split, cleft, divided.

A متفطّن *mutafattin*, Considerate, thoughtful.

A متفظّع *mutafazziɛ*, Shameful (business).

A متفغّم *mutafaghghim*, Expanded (flower).

A متّفق *muttafik*, Consenting, agreeing, consentient, agreed. Corresponding, concurring (testimonies). Confederated, conspired. United, uniform. Nearly related. An accomplice, conspirator. Happening. The fifth circle in prosody. متّفق عليه *muttaffik ɛalayhi*, Agreed on.

A متفقّح *mutafakkih*, Opened, expanded (flower). Ready (for mischief).

A متفقّد *mutafakkid*, Deprived of, or in search of a lost or missing object.

A متفقّر *mutafakkir*, One who digs a trench for palm-trees. A country full of holes and ditches.

A متفقّرة *mutafakkirat*, A country abounding in wells or ditches.

A متفقّس *mutafakkis*, Overturned, fallen on.

A متفقّع *mutafakkiɛ*, Withered, hard (plant).

A متفقّه *mutafakkih*, Skilled in the divine law.

A متفقّي *mutafakkī*, (A cloud) emptied of rain. (See تفقّو *tafakkuw*.)

A متفكّر *mutafakkir*, Contemplative, thoughtful; given to consideration; serious, pensive, grave. Amazed. قوّت متفكّرة *kūwati mutafakkira*, Contemplation, the reflecting power.

A متفكّك *mutafakkik*, Weakened (by insanity).

A متفكّكة *mutafakkikat*, (A mare) in want of the male.

A متفكّن *mutafakkin*, Penitent, contrite: grave.

A متفكّه *mutafakkih*, Astonished, amazed. Penitent, contrite. (See تفكّه *tafakkuh*.)

A متفل *mutfil*, What causes to smell disagreeably.

A متفلّت *mutafallit*, Escaped, liberated; free.

A متفلّج *mutafallij*, Cracked, chapped (foot).

A متفلّع *mutafalliɛ*, (or متفلّق *mutafallik*) Cleft.

A متفلّق *mutafallik*, Separated into particles from sourness (milk). (An egg) broken in pieces.

A متفلّك *mutafallik*, Round, spherical.

A متفلّل *mutafallil*, Broken, notched (sword or knife). Routed (host).

A متفنّق *mutafannik*, Delicately brought up.

A متفنّكة *mutafannikat*, Foolish, silly (woman).

A متفنّن *mutafannin*, Possessed of a variety of sciences, modes, ways, or arts.

A متفنّي *mutafannī*, Vicious.

A متفوّت *mutafawwit*, Escaped, passed by.

A متفوّق *mutafawwik*, (A colt) which sips or sucks milk by little at a time. One who carefully reads a little at a time. Superior. Comfortably off.

A متفوّل *mutafawwil*, One who augurs.

A متفوّه *mutafawwih*, One who opens his mouth to speak. A speaker.

A متفه *mutfah*, Obedient, tractable (camel).

A متفهّر *mutafahhir*, Opulent, wealthy.

A متفهّق *mutafahhik*, Diffused, widely-extended (lightning). Flowing (blood).

A متفهّم *mutafahhim*, One who understands by little and little. Intelligent.

A متفيهق *mutafayhik*, Diffuse in talk or prayer.

A متفيّد *mutafayyid*, Inflamed, burnt.

A متفيّظ *mutafayyiz*, One who pours out (his whole soul).

A متفيّل *mutafayyil*, Erroneous in his opinion. Fat. (See تفيّل *tafayyul*.)

A متفيهر *mutafayhir*, Breathless, tired (man or horse). In easy circumstances.

A متفيهق *mutafayhik*, Diffuse in speech.

A متقابل *mutakābil*, Opposite: face to face.

A متقاتل *mutakātil*, Mutually slaughterous.

A متقادع *mutakādiɛ*, Employed in spearing one another. (See تقادع *takāduɛ*.)

A متقادم *mutakādam*, (in law) Such a distance of time as suffices to prevent punishment. It operates somewhat similar to our statutory limitation. *Mutakādim*, Ancient, antique, prior to.

A متقاذف *mutakāzif*, (A horse) that gallops apace. Employed in pelting one another. Abusive.

A متقارّ *mutakārr*, Mutually agreed. At rest.

A متقارب *mutakārib*, Near to each other, proximate. A kind of poetical measure, in which the metre فعولن *faɛūlun* is repeated eight times, or فعولن فعولن فعول *faɛūlun faɛūlun faɛul*, Twice.

A متقاربيّة *mutakāribiyat*, Proximity.

A متقارش *mutakārish*, Intermixed in battle.

A متقارض *mutakāriz*, Mutual, reciprocal in bestowing praise or censure. (See تقارض *takāruz*.)

A متقارظ *mutakāriz*, Mutually encomiastical.

A متقارع *mutakāriɛ*, Engaged in casting lots.

A متقارن *mutakārin*, Joined, united together.

A متقاسم *mutakāsim*, Confederate, leagued, sworn to each other. Agreed to divide (property) amongst themselves.

A متقاصّ *mutakāss*, Mutual in retaliating.

A متقاصر *mutakāsir*, Unequal to the performance of a thing. One who pretends to be short.

A متقاصف *mutakāsif*, Dashed to pieces, wrecked (ship). Assembled, come together.

A متقاضي *mutakāzī*, An exacter or receiver (of payment of a debt); a dun. Importunate.

A متقاطر *mutakātir*, Whatever drops or trickles. Coming in a train, one after another.

A متقاطع *mutakātiɛ*, Parted from each other.

A متقاعد *mutakāɛid*, Sedentary, stationary, inactive. Whosoever abstains, desists, or recedes. (A garrison-soldier) exempted from joining the army.

A متقاعس *mutakāɛis*, A receder, one who hangs back. One whose back goes in and breast sticks out.

A متقافس *mutakāfis*, Engaged in rushing at and pulling one another's hair.

A متقافط *mutakāfit*, Mutually helpful (in coitu).

A متقالّ *mutakāll*, One who considers as small, few, or trifling (قليل *kalīl*). High (sun).

A متقامر *mutakāmir*, Engaged at a game of dice, or in play for a wager.

A متقاود *mutakāwid*, Lofty, towering.

A متقاول *mutakāwil*, Engaged in a chat.

A متقاوم *mutakāwim*, Up in arms mutually.

A متقاوي *mutakāwī*, One who bids against another. One who passes the night fasting.

A متقايل *mutakāyil*, Released from a contract

by mutual agreement.

A متقبّب mutakabbib, One who enters a dome, vault, arch, or alcove (قبّة kubbat).

A متقبّس mutakabbis, Slack, not stretched (rope).

A متقبّض mutakabbiz, (A lion) prepared to spring. One who restrains himself. (See تقبّض.)

A متقبّي mutakabbī, Dressed in the tunic قباء.

A متقتّر mutakattir, Armed, ready (for battle). Angry, enraged. (See تقتّر takattur.)

A متقتّق mutaktik, Swift, rapid (nocturnal journey in search of water).

A متقتّل mutakattil, Modest, compliant. Come about his business. (See تقتّل takattul.)

A متقحّز mutakahhiz, Rude, harsh-spoken.

A متقحزن mutakahzin, Thrown prostrate, fallen.

A متقحّل mutakahhil, Withered, dry-skinned (old man). Wretched and miserable.

A متقحّم mutakahhim, Violent, precipitant.

A متقدّد mutakaddid, Divided, dispersed. Split, cut. Dried. Ragged. Lean.

A متقدّر mutakaddir, Measured, proportioned. Pre-ordained. Ready, prepared.

A متقدّس mutakaddis, Purified, made holy.

A متقدّم mutakaddim, One who goes before or leads the way. One who approaches or stands before any person. Higher, more prominent (than any other). Excelling, superior (in bravery). Ancient, anterior, antique, past, preceding. An ancient, ancestor. A chief, president, principal, governor. An offering, present.

A متقدّما mutakaddaman, In old time, long ago.

A متقدّمين mutakaddamīn, The ancients.

A متقدّي mutakaddī, A lion. A pompous walker.

A متقذّر mutakazzir, A dirtier (of his clothes). Shunned by mankind on account of his nastiness. One who holds in abhorrence all filth and impurity.

A متقذّع mutakazziɛ, One who prepares mischief.

A متقرّب mutakarrib, One who approaches or fears (God). One who has free access to a king. A royal relation or favourite. Adjacent, near, allied to. (See تقرّب takarrub.)

A متقرّح mutakarrih, Ulcerated, eaten of sores. Prepared, ready.

A متقرّد mutakarrid, Separate, detached from the rest (a bit of a cloud).

A متقرّر mutakarrir, Confirmed, established. (See تقرّر takarrur.)

A متقرّش mutakarrish, Assembled together. Pure, clear of every thing improper. (See تقرّش.)

A متقرّط mutakarrit, Adorned with ear-rings.

A متقرّع mutakarriɛ, One who rolls over from side to side when laid down.

A متقرّف mutakarrif, Peeled (tree or scab).

A متقرفصة mutakarfisat, Wrapped (old woman).

A متقرّه mutakarrih, Squalid, dirty (fellow).

A متقرّي mutakarrī, Addicted to sacred reading; devout, holy, pious.

A متقزّح mutakazzih, Shot in every direction, ramified (plant).

A متقزّز mutakazziz, Averse from impurity; free from dirt and filth.

A متقزّع mutakazziɛ, (A horse) ready to run.

A متقسّط mutakassit, Engaged in making an equal distribution.

A متقسقس mutakaskis, A listener.

A متقسّم mutakassim, A scatterer. Scattered.

A متقشّر mutakashshir, Peeled, barked (tree).

A متقشّط mutakashshit, Clear, serene (sky).

A متقشّع mutakashshiɛ, Dispelled, scattered, disappearing, vanishing (clouds). Flabby, flaccid.

A متقشّف mutakashshif, Scantily fed and coarsely clad. One who cares nothing for dirt and filth.

A متقصّد mutakassid, Broken (spear). Dead.

A متقصّص mutakassis, A tracker of steps. One who remembers a speech or story (قصّة kissat).

A متقصّع mutakassiɛ, (A sore) full of matter.

A متقصّف mutakassif, Dashed in bits (ship).

A متقصّل mutakassil, Cut up, divided.

A متقصّم mutakassim, Broken.

A متقصّي mutakassī, Diligent in inquiring. One who gets to the end (قصوي kuswa').

A متقضّب mutakazzib, Cut, lopped, pruned. Long-rayed (sun).

A متقضّض mutakazziz, Pouncing (hawk).

A متقضّع mutakazziɛ, Cut, divided.

A متقضّي mutakazzī, Finished, ended. Extinct, annihilated. Pouncing (hawk).

A متقطّب mutakattib, Grim, truculent, austere.

A متقطّر mutakattir, Prepared (for battle). Sweetly-scented, perfumed. (See تقطّر takattur.)

A متقطّع mutakattiɛ, Cut into several parts. (Wine) diluted with (water).

A متقطّي mutakattī, (A full bucket) slow and tardy in ascending.

A متقعّد mutakaɛɛid, Unable or loth to do any thing. (See تقعّد takaɛɛud.)

A متقعّر mutakaɛɛir, Deep well. Carried far in a speech. (See تقعّر takaɛɛur.)

A متقعّط mutakaɛɛit, One whose hair curls much. Hard, strong, vehement.

A متقعّف mutakaɛɛif, Moved from its place. Fallen (wall). A mountain-slip.

A متقعفز mutakaɛfiz, Fallen prostrate.

A متقعقع mutakaɛkiɛ, Removed with noise. Distant (journey) taxing the traveller's strength.

A متقفّر mutakaffir, A follower, imitator.

A متقفّز mutakaffiz, Tinged with privet. Covered with a glove (قفّاز kuffāz), gloved.

A متقفّس mutakaffis, A leaper, hopper, skipper.

A متقفّط mutakaffit, Ready, prepared for business.

A متقفّع mutakaffiɛ, Contracted, wrinkled.

A متقفقف mutakafkif, One who trembles, whose teeth chatter with cold. Withered (grass).

A متقفّل mutakaffil, Stingy, close-fisted.

A متقفّي mutakaffī, A follower or tracker of another's steps: an imitator. (See تقفّي takaffī.)

A متقلّب mutakallib, Turned inside out; converted, inverted. Expert, dexterous in business.

A متقلّد mutakallid, Adorned (with a necklace). Girt (with a sword). One who carries (a spear).

A متقلّس mutakallis, Dressed in the high-crowned cap or turban, called قلنسوة kalansuwat.

A متقلّص mutakallis, Shrivelled, shrunken.

A متقلّع mutakalliɛ, Uprooted, displaced.

A متقلعف mutakalɛif, Riding an unbroke nag.

A متقمّر mutakammir, A winner at dice. A visitor by the light of the moon (قمر kamar).

A متقمّص mutakammis, Dressed in a shirt.

A متقمّع mutakammaɛ, The head and parts about the mouth (of a horse). Mutakammiɛ, (An ass) shaking his head and driving away the flies.

A متقمّم mutakammim, (A stallion) covering.

A متقمّن mutakammin, Kind, complaisant.

A متقن mutkin, One who manages with propriety: one who does (any thing) firmly and well.

A متّقن muttakin, Sure of, certain. Known.

A متقّن mutakkhin, One who waters (the ground) with thick, and muddy water.

A متقنّب mutakannib, Setting (sun).

A متقنّز mutakanniz, A hunter.

A متقنّص mutakannis, Fond of the chase: hunter.

A متقنّع mutakanniɛ, Dressed in coif or cap.

A متقوّب mutakawwib, Bald from an old scab. Excoriated. A serpent that has cast his slough.

A متقوّت mutakawwit, Nourished, maintained.

A متقوّح mutakawwih, Mattery, ichorous (sore).

A متقوّر mutakawwir, Writhing, coiled (snake). Elapsed (greater part of the night).

A متقوّس mutakawwis, Bowed, bent, curved. Arched (eyebrow). Armed with a bow (قوس kaws).

A متقوّض mutakawwiz, Routed, broken (army). Ruined (building). (See تقوّض takawwuz.)

A متقوّع mutakawwiɛ, A walker as if on thorns.

A متقوعس mutakawɛis, Broken, decrepit (old man). Desolate (house).

A متقوّف mutakawwif, One who checks another when speaking, desiring him to say this or that.

A متقوّل mutakawwil, A teller of lies of another.

A متقوّم mutakawwim, Of great value. Straightened, rectified, corrected.

A متقوّي mutakawwī, Strong, courageous.

A متقهقر mutakahkir, Retreated: retrograde.

A متقهّل mutakahhil, Poor, miserable. A man whose skin is dried upon his bones.

A متّقي muttakī, Abstinent, abstemious, temperate, sober. Cautious. God-fearing, pious.

A متقيّح mutakayyih, Purulent (sore).

A متقيّد mutakayyid, Diligent, pains-taking. One who imposes restraints on himself.

A متقيّض mutakayyiz, (A wall) fallen in ruin.

A متقيّظ mutakayyiz, Who passes the summer.

A متقيّل *mutakayyil*, One who drinks or sleeps at noon. Like, resembling. Collected (water).

A متقيّن *mutakayyin*, Decorated, adorned.

A متقيّئ *mutakayyiʼ*, One who vomits.

P متك *matk*, An orange.

A متك *matk*, (v. n. of متك) Cutting. A section, segment. A kind of plant whose juice they concrete. *Matk, mutk*, or *mutuk*, The proboscis or penis of a fly. The urethra of the penis; also the frœnum. A nerve in the breast or nipple. The clitoris, or its nerve. That which the female circumciser leaves. A pasty, pancake fried with eggs and herbs. A lily, iris, or narcissus. *Matk* or *mitk*, An orange.

A متك *mutukk*, A vein inside the penis at the lower part of the gland, and is latest in healing after circumcision.

A متّكأ *muttakaʼ*, A day-bed, couch, sofa, cushion, or any thing upon which people recline.

A متكاء *matkāʼ*, The clitoris. An uncircumcised woman; also one who is unable to retain her urine. A woman whose two passages have been made one.

A متكاءد *mutakāʼid*, Difficult, troublesome.

A متكابر *mutakābir*, Proud, haughty, affected.

A متكاتب *mutakātib*, Engaged in a mutual correspondence by letter. (See تكاتب *takātub*.)

A متكاتع *mutakātiʻ*, Successive, consecutive.

A متكاتم *mutakātim*, Reciprocal in concealing (one's secrets).

A متكاثر *mutakāsir*, Increased, multiplied. Mutually boastful about numbers or wealth.

A متكاثف *mutakāsif*, Thick, surcharged.

A متكادر *mutakādir*, A looker on attentively.

A متكاذب *mutakāzib*, Mutually false, lying.

A متكارم *mutakārim*, Honourable, pure.

A متكاره *mutakārih*, Unwilling, reluctant.

A متكاري *mutakārī*, One who takes on hire.

A متكاسل *mutakāsil*, Indolent, slothful.

A متكاشف *mutakāshif*, Mutually communicative of each other's failings.

A متكاصّ *mutakāss*, Thronging, crowded (folk).

A متكاظّ *mutakāzz*, Mutually hostile, inimical.

A متكافي *mutakāfī*, Equal, correspondent.

A متكاكئ *mutakākiʼ*, Short, dwarfish.

A متكالب *mutakālib*, Furious, rageful against one another.

A متكالم *mutakālim*, Engaged in conversation together after having been distant.

A متكامل *mutakāmil*, Entire, perfect, complete.

A متكاوح *mutakāwih*, Unkind, mutually injurious.

A متكاوس *mutakāwis*, Compressed, huddled together. (in poetry) A succession of four letters inflected with vowels, as ضربني *zarabanī*.

A متكاول *mutakāwil*, One who pretends to be short. One who hangs back or desists.

A متكاهل *mutakāhil*, Negligent, remiss. Lazy. Related to the tribe of كهلان *kahlān*.

A متكايد *mutakāyid*, Mutually deceitful, insidious.

A متكايس *mutakāyis*, Sagacious, quick. One who boasts of his sagacity.

A متكايل *mutakāyil*, Reproachful towards one another. Measuring to one another.

A متكبّب *mutakabbib*, Fallen prostrate, prone.

A متكبّد *mutakabbid*, Meridian (sun). Ready, prepared for. Thick (milk).

A متكبّر *mutakabbir*, Proud, haughty, arrogant. Lofty. A name of God.

P متكبّرانه *mutakabbirāna*, Haughtily, proudly.

A متكبكب *mutakabkib*, Wrapped up, muffled up in one's garment.

A متكبّئ *mutakabbaʼ*, Perfumed, scented.

A متكتّب *mutakattib*, Drawn up in squadrons.

A متكتّف *mutakattif*, High-shouldered. One who shrugs his shoulders (كتف *katif*) in walking.

A متكتّل *mutakattil*, Dwarf-paced.

A متكثّر *mutakassir*, Multiplied. Enriched. Who makes a great display of what he does not possess.

A متكثّم *mutakassim*, Mute with astonishment. Bent double. Hidden. Halted, pausing.

A متكحّل *mutakahhil*, Anointed with eye-powder.

A متكدّح *mutakaddih*, Scratched, clawed.

A متكدّر *mutakaddir*, Turbid; disturbed, afflicted.

A متكدّس *mutakaddis*, (A horse) going as if overloaded. (See تكدّس *takaddus*.)

A متكذّب *mutakazzib*, The inventor of a lie. One who takes pains to tell lies. One who charges with falsehood.

A متكرّب *mutakarrib*, Picker of the dates كرابة.

A متكرّج *mutakarrij*, Musty, mouldy (bread).

A متكردس *mutakardis*, Contracted, compressed.

A متكردم *mutakardim*, Terrified, running in fear.

A متكرّر *mutakarrir*, Reiterated, repeated. Irresolute, wavering. The letter ر *rā*.

A متكرسف *mutakarsif*, Inserted, dove-tailed.

A متكرّع *mutakarriʻ*, A performer of ablutions before prayer.

A متكرفس *mutakarfis*, Drawn together.

A متكرّم *mutakarrim*, One who makes pretensions to generosity. Honoured, praiseworthy.

A متكرّه *mutakarrih*, Fastidious, disgusted with. Crabbed, grim, hideous, sad.

A متكرّي *mutakarrī*, Asleep.

A متكسّب *mutakassib*, Bent on making money.

A متكسّر *mutakassir*, Broken in pieces.

A متكسّي *mutakassī*, Clothed in a camelot.

A متكشّح *mutakashshih*, Who lies with a woman.

A متكشّف *mutakashshif*, Uncovered, exposed.

A متكشّئ *mutakashshiʼ*, One who eats roast meat dry. (See تكشّؤ *takashshuʼ*.)

A متكعّب *mutakaʻʻib*, Swelling (bosom).

A متكعكع *mutakaʻkiʻ*, Timid, cowardly.

A متكعنش *mutakaʻnish*, One who plunges in.

A متكفّر *mutakaffir*, Armed, clad in armour.

A متكفّف *mutakaffif*, One who takes with outstretched hand (كفّ *kaff*).

A متكفّل *mutakaffil*, A surety, bail, bondsman. An officer who examines accounts and seals them.

A متكفّئ *mutakaffiʼ*, Pompous, stately walker.

A متكفّي *mutakaffī*, Tall (tree), long (grass).

A متّكل *muttakal*, One to whom aught is entrusted.

A متكلّح *mutakallih*, Incessantly-flashing (sky). Crabbed, grim, grinning, shewing the teeth.

A متكلّد *mutakallid*, Hard and thick.

A متكلّس *mutakallis*, A swift or hard runner.

A متكلّع *mutakalliʻ*, Assembled. Sworn.

A متكلّف *mutakallif*, A meddler in what concerns him not. Pains-taking, striving. One who attempts more than is required. A troubler.

A متكلّل *mutakallil*, Crowned. Whatever comprehends, encloses, covers. Slightly flashing (cloud).

A متكلّم *mutakallam*, A place for speaking. *Mutakallim*, A speaker, orator, declaimer; an advocate. A spokesman. *Mutakallim*, (or نفس متكلّم *nafsi mutakallim*) (in gram.) The first person. متكلّم مليح *mutakallimi malīh*, An eloquent orator.

A متكلّئ *mutakalliʼ*, One who delays payment, or asks for credit. (See تكلّؤ *takalluʼ*.)

A متكلّي *mutakallī*, A lagger in the rear.

A متكمّش *mutakammish*, Quick, expeditious Contracted, wrinkled, puckered (skin).

A متكمكم *mutakamkim*, Drest in a round cap.

A متكمّل *mutakammil*, Perfect, complete.

A متكمّم *mutakammim*, Covered. Stupefied.

A متكمّن *mutakammin*, Ambushed; lier-in-wait.

A متكمّه *mutakammih*, A wanderer, roamer.

A متكمّئ *mutakammiʼ*, (Ground) which hides from view. One who disapproves, dislikes.

A متكمّي *mutakammī*, Cased in armour. Brave.

A متكنّس *mutakannis*, Concealed in a cave. Entered into a tent, or the camel-litter hawda.

A متكنّع *mutakanniʻ*, Close-chained (prisoner).

A متكنّف *mutakannif*, Enclosing, hemming in.

A متكنّه *mutakannih*, Arrived at the summit, limit, or boundary (كنه *kunh*).

A متكنّي *mutakannī*, Described by a metonymy.

A متكوّر *mutakawwir*, Tucked up, ready for. Gathered. Fallen on the ground. Trickled.

A متكوّز *mutakawwiz*, Collected, assembled.

A متكوّس *mutakawwis*, Inverted, head-down.

A متكوّع *mutakawwiʻ*, Sprained, pained, dislocated in the wrist (كوع *kūʻ*).

A متكوّف *mutakawwif*, Belonging to Kūfa.

A متكوّل *mutakawwil*, Assembled (against).

A متكوّن *mutakawwin*, Become, brought into existence (كون *kawn*), bred, engendered. Shaken.

A متكوّه *mutakawwih*, Confused, disordered.

A متكوّي *mutakawwī*, Entered a narrow place.

A متكهّف *mutakahhif*, Caverned (mountain).

A متكهّن *mutakahhin*, A predicter, prophet.

A متّكئ *muttakiʼ*, Supported, propped. One who leans, reclines, or sits (epecially from the heels);

laid down to sleep.

P متكيدن *mutkīdan*, To murmur. To chide one in a muttering strain.

A متكيّس *mutakayyis*, Anxious to make a display of wit, though destitute of it.

A متكيّف *mutakayyif*, Described, defined in form and quality. One who blemishes or tarnishes.

A متكيّل *mutakayyil*, A lagger in the rear.

A متل *matl*, The act of moving, agitating.

A متلّ *mitall*, Any thing throwing one upon the ground. Hard, firm (spear); (a man or camel) strong in body. (A man) erect (in prayer). *Mutill*, One who binds or leads by the hand. Who distils, or causes any thing liquid to drop.

A متلائم *mutalāʼim*, Restored to favour. Healed.

A متلاحّ *mutalāhh*, Jealous of each other.

A متلاحز *mutalāhiz*, (People in a mob) upsetting one another. Thick, close together (trees).

A متلاحظ *mutalāhiz*, Mutually looking back.

A متلاحق *mutalāhik*, Successive, following in a continued series, reaching, touching. Added, augmented (one following another).

A متلاحك *mutalāhik*, Inserted, stuck close together, let into one another.

A متلاحكة *mutalāhikat*, Robust (she-camel).

A متلاحمة *mutalāhimat*, (A wound) inflicted on the fleshy part of the head, and which does not penetrate the pericranium. Close, impervious (woman), from extreme fleshiness.

A متلاحي *mutalāhī*, Disputatious, captious with one another, mutually abusive.

A متلازق *mutalāzik*, Contiguous, continued.

A متلاشي *mutalāshī*, Vanishing, annihilated; vain, of no moment, worthless. An inquirer, searcher.

A متلاطس *mutalātis*, Dashed together (waves).

A متلاطف *mutalātif*, Mutually benevolent.

A متلاطم *mutalātim*, Employed in buffeting one another. Compressed, battered, dashed together, agitated (as the waves).

A متلاعن *mutalāʻin*, Engaged in cursing or invoking maledictions on each other.

A متلاف *mitlāf*, Profuse, prodigal, lavish.

A متلافق *mutalāfik*, (A community) whose affairs are well-ordered.

A متلافي *mutalāfī*, Who understands, attains to.

A متلاقي *mutalākī*, Met together face to face.

A متلالي *mutalaʼlī*, Glittering, resplendent.

A متلاوم *mutalāwim*, Mutually recriminative.

A متلاوي *mutalāwī*, Agreed, of one opinion. Convened, assembled.

A متلاهي *mutalāhī*, Engaged in play, amusing one another, or in soothing care or grief.

A متلايس *mutalāyis*, Of an excellent disposition. Conniving, connivent.

A متلبّب *mutalabbib*, Girt about the waist. One whose skirt is tucked. Ready, prepared.

A متلبّث *mutalabbis*, Dilatory, tardy, tedious.

A متلبّد *mutalabbid*, Stationary, cleaving to the ground. Adhering, sticking together, feltered, impacted, matted (wool or hair); caked (dung).

A متلبّس *mutalabbis*, Clothed, clad, dressed. (Food) sticking to the hand.

A متلبّط *mutalabbit*, Lain down, rolling on the ground. Turned towards. Bewildered.

A متلبّك *mutalabbik*, Confused, intricate.

A متلبّن *mutalabbin*, Dilatory, tardy, tedious.

A متلتّخ *mutalattikh*, Stained, defiled.

A متلثلث *mutalaslis*, Uncertain, irresolute. Laid down, rolling on the ground.

A متلثّم *mutalassim*, One whose mouth is veiled.

A متلج *mutlij*, One who opens or keeps open. Who or what relaxes the mind or takes recreation.

A متّلج *muttalij*, One who enters, or allows to enter. Allowed to enter.

A متلجّج *mutalajjij*, A pretender, one who lays claim to any one's goods.

A متلجّف *mutalajjif*, One who digs down to water. Honey-combed through age (a well), and therefore tearing the leathern buckets which are let down.

A متلجلج *mutalajlij*, A stammerer, stutterer. Irresolute, vacillating. Shaking. A taker, receiver.

A متلجّم *mutalajjim*, Bridled (horse).

A متلجّن *mutalajjin*, Partial in washing the head.

A متلحّز *mutalahhiz*, Avaricious, narrow-minded. Tucked up for travelling or fighting. (See تلحّز.)

A متلحّف *mutalahhif*, One who takes or makes up a sheet (لحاف *lihāf*).

A متلحّق *mutalahhik*, Consecutive, in a line.

A متلحّي *mutalahhī*, One who passes the turban-sash under the chin (لحية *lihyat*).

A متلخّص *mutalakhkhis*, Explained, declared.

A متلد *mutlad*, Riches, hereditary wealth; slaves or cattle brought forth in the family and descending by way of heritage. A slave brought from a distance when a boy, and reared amongst the Muhammadans. *Mutlid*, Possessed of hereditary wealth; master of slaves or cattle bred in his own house.

A متلّد *mutallad*, Old, ancient. *Mutallid*, One who collects or assembles. Who wards off, prevents.

A متلدّد *mutaladdad*, The neck. *Mutaladdid*, One who looks right and left.

A متلدّم *mutaladdim*, (A garment) burst, torn. (A shoe) in want of a patch. (See تلدّم *taladdum*).

A متلدّن *mutaladdin*, Slow, tedious, dilatory.

A متلذّذ *mutalazziz*, Who delights in; relishes.

A متلذّع *mutalazziʻ*, An elegant and quick walker. One who looks right and left.

A متلزّج *mutalazzij*, Ductile, limber. Viscous, ropy. Partially washed (head), not clean.

A متلزّج *mutalazzih*, (A mouth) watery from eating pomegranates or plums.

A متلسّن *mutalassin*, Lent (camel's colt in order to suck). Flaming (fire).

A متلسّنة *mutalassinat*, A camel that takes a liking for another's colt. Camels set free.

A متلّص *mutallis*, One who softens or smooths.

A متلصّص *mutalassis*, A robber, freebooter.

A متلطّخ *mutalattikh*, Defiled, dirtied, soiled.

A متلطّط *mutalattit*, A denier (of a debt due).

A متلطّع *mutalattiʻ*, Toothless from age.

A متلطّف *mutalattif*, Kind, favourably inclined.

A متلطّم *mutalattim*, An apostate, a renegade. Dark, ash-coloured (face).

A متلطّي *mutalattī*, A watcher for his enemy.

A متلظلظ *mutalazliz*, Writhing, coiled (snake).

A متلظّي *mutalazzī*, Blazing, flamy (fire).

A متلع *mutliʻ*, Advanced (day). One who raises the head or stretches out the neck (to hear or look at any thing). A beautiful woman.

A متّلع *muttaliʻ*, Ignorant of any person's situation, particularly if dead or alive.

A متلعّب *mutalaʻʻib*, An incorrigible player.

A متلعثم *mutalaʻsim*, One who takes time, dilatory. One who examines well, attentive.

A متلعّجة *mutalaʻʻijat*, Hot, lascivious (woman).

A متلعذم *mutalaʻzim*, An eater, taster.

A متلعّس *mutalaʻʻis*, One who devours greedily.

A متلعّص *mutalaʻʻis*, Hard upon one.

A متلعّع *mutalaʻʻiʻ*, A plucker of buds of plants.

A متلعّف *mutalaʻʻif*, Ready to leap in or over.

A متلعلع *mutalaʻliʻ*, One who moves or rolls about. (Honey) viscous, running into a thread. (See تلعلع *talaʻluʻ*.)

A متلعلم *mutalaʻlim*, Slow, calmly diligent.

A متلعّي *mutalaʻʻī*, Concreted, candied (honey). Viscous and ropy (honey). (See تلعّي *talaʻʻī*.)

A متلغّب *mutalaghghib*, A remover, driver away. One who tires and fatigues.

A متلغّد *mutalaghghid*, Enraged, indignant, angry.

A متلغذم *mutalaghzim*, A furious eater, a glutton.

A متلغّف *mutalaghghif*, Prepared to leap.

A متلغّم *mutalaghghim*, One who moves the parts round the mouth when speaking.

A متلف *matlaf*, A dangerous place. A desert. *Mitlaf*, Profuse. *Mutlif*, A destroyer, ruiner. A consumer, prodigal.

A متلفّت *mutalaffit*, One who turns his head and embraces in one view all the circumstances.

A متلفّظ *mutalaffiz*, A pronouncer, articulator.

A متلفّع *mutalaffiʻ*, Covered, wrapped in a garment. Silvered with grey hairs. (See تلفّع *talaffuʻ*.)

A متلفّف *mutalaffif*, Wrapped in a garment.

A متلفّق *mutalaffik*, Joined, united.

A متلفّم *mutalaffim*, One whose mouth or nose is veiled with the veil لفام *lifām*.

A متلقّب *mutalakkib*, Titled, surnamed.

A متلقّط *mutalakkit*, A gatherer, picker up.

A متلقّع *mutalakkiʻ*, A prater, babbler.

A متلقّف *mutalakkif*, (or متلقّم *mutalakkim*) A camel that turns his fore-hoofs out in walking. A half-starved wretch who devours greedily.

A متلقن *mutalakkin*, Taught; a learner by heart. A picker up.

A متلقي *mutalakkī*, One who arrives, meets, or encounters, or visits. Conceiving (woman).

A متلكد *mutalakkid*, Joined, firm, compact. Coherent. (See تلكد *talakkud*.)

A متلكي *mutalakkī*, One who stops or delays.

A متلمج *mutalammij*, A taster. One who breakfasts or takes a whet. One who licks his lips.

A متلمخ *mutalammikh*, An obscene talker.

A متلمس *mutalammis*, One who asks again and again. كواه المتلمسة *kawa'hu'l mutalammisat*, He branded (or cauterized) him on the sore place.

A متلمظ *mutalammaz*, One who smiles. *Mutalammiz*, One who rolls the tongue about the mouth after eating to clear away any remains of meat.

A متلمظة *mutalammazat*, A mode of tying together the fore-legs of a camel so that they rub against one another.

A متلمع *mutalammiʻ*, A snatcher, seizer.

A متلمق *mutalammik*, A taster, eater.

A متلمئ *mutalammiʼ*, (The earth) covering, concealing. One who chooses for himself.

A متلمي *mutalammī*, Faded (colour). Of the colour of wheat.

A متلوث *mutalawwis*, Dirtied, stained, defiled.

A متلوص *mutalawwis*, Twisted, inverted.

A متلوط *mutalawwit*, Addicted to sodomy.

A متلول *matlūl*, Thrown prostrate. Plump, round, and sleek (bull).

A متلوم *mutalawwim*, Slow, dilatory, patient.

A متلون *mutalawwin*, Changeable, variable. Of different hues, various. P متلون شدن *mutalawwin shudan*, To be altered, to change colour.

A متلون مزاج *mutalawwin-mizāj*, Capricious.

A متلوه *mutalawwih*, Tremulous, flickering.

A متلوه العقل *matlūhu'l ʻakl*, Insane.

A متلوي *mutalawwī*, Bent, distorted. Face-averted. Scattered. Flashing.

A متلهب *mutalahhib*, Bright, blazing (fire).

A متلهث *mutalahhis*, (A dog) that lolls out his tongue from thirst. (A man) making haste, breathing hard.

A متلهثا *mutalahhisan*, Ardently, wishfully.

A متلهف *mutalahhif*, Agitated, grieved, sad.

A متلهق *mutalahhik*, Intensely white.

A متلهم *mutalahhim*, Who devours or gulps up.

A متلهن *mutalahhin*, One who takes a whet.

A متلهي *mutalahhī*, A player, sporter. Playful, sportive. Forgetful, negligent.

A متلي *mutlī*, (or متلية *mutliyat*) (pl. متالي *matālī*) A camel followed by her colt.

A متليات *mutallayat*, Camels with their young.

A متليث *mutalayyis*, Bold, fierce, lion-like.

A متلين *mutalayyin*, Gentle, placid, benign. Bland, fawning.

A متم *mutamm*, Something superadded to a measure already full. The place at which the navel is cut. *Mutimm*, A completer, perfecter. A woman with child, gone her full time. The full moon.

A متماءر *mutamāʼir*, Mutually boastful.

A متماتر *mutamātir*, (Sparks) which fly here and there. Engaged in pulling different ways.

A متماثل *mutamāsil*, Convalescent. Coequal.

A متماجد *mutamājid*, Contentious about glory.

A متماجع *mutamājiʻ*, (also متماجن *mutamājin*) Saucy, impudent, obscene amongst themselves.

A متماحك *mutamāhik*, Mutually litigious.

A متماحل *mutamāhil*, Long. Extensive (desert). Tall and tremulous. (A house) distant from other dwellings. Changed in body. امور متماحله *umūri mutamāhila*, Affairs long, tedious, and trying.

A متمادح *mutamādih*, Mutually laudatory.

A متمادخ *mutamādikh*, Great, excellent, precious. One who does every thing expeditiously. Disobedient. Lazy, laggard.

A متمادي *mutamādī*, One who perseveres in, continues, prolongs, or protracts. Lengthened out, protracted. Contentious, disputatious.

A متمار *mutamārr*, Occupied in wrestling.

A متمارس *mutamāris*, Distracted, quarrelsome, fighting themselves.

A متمارض *mutamāriz*, One who shams sickness.

A متماري *mutamārī*, Doubtful, uncertain of. Litigious, quarrelsome, disputatious.

A متماز *mutamāzz*, Separate, wide apart.

A متمازح *mutamāzih*, Engaged in mutual jesting.

A متمازي *mutamāzī*, Distinct. Separate, asunder.

A متماس *mutamāss*, Contiguous, in contact.

A متماسح *mutamāsih*, Sincere, upright towards each other. Striking hands in making a bargain.

A متماسك *mutamāsik*, Powerful. Holding fast.

A متماشق *mutamāshik*, Pulling different ways.

A متماشي *mutamāshī*, Walking out together.

A متماصع *mutamāsiʻ*, Engaged in fighting.

A متماطر *mutamātir*, (or متماظ *mutamāzz*) (A cloud) which pours forth rain one while, and ceases the next. Rained on in one place, but not in another.

A متماكس *mutamākis*, A bidder against another.

A متمالك *mutamālik*, Able; who has in his power.

A متمالئ *mutamāliʼ*, Unanimous. Assembled.

A متماوت *mutamāwit*, One who feigns to be dead. A hypocrite in religion.

A متماهك *mutamāhik*, Engaged in mutual quarrel.

A متمايح *mutamāyih*, Staggering (drunkard).

A متماير *mutamāyir*, Broken off (friendship).

A متمايط *mutamāyit*, Distant, absent, retired. Alienated from one another.

A متمايل *mutamāyil*, Waving from side to side.

A متماءن *mutamāʼin*, A hypocrite. False (lover).

A متمتة *matmatat*, The courting of an alliance.

A متمتع *mutamattiʻ*, Possessed of, enjoying, delighting in. One who remains at Mecca, and performs the solemnities (متعة *mutʻat*) there.

A متمثل *mutamassil*, A propounder of parables. One who applies a metaphor or adage. An imitator. Like, resembling. One who retaliates.

A متمجد *mutamajjid*, Glorified.

A متمجس *mutamajjis*, Become a fire-worshipper.

A متمحق *mutamahhik*, Effaced, abolished. Diminished, decreased, waned. Burned.

A متمحك *mutamahhik*, Morose, quarrelsome.

A متمحل *mutamahhil*, Sly, deceitful, insidious.

A متمخخ *mutamakhkhikh*, Who extracts marrow.

A متمخر *mutamakhkhir*, One who catches the wind at sea. One who turns his back to the wind.

A متمخش *mutamakhkhish*, Much shaken.

A متمخض *mutamakhkhiz*, Shaken (churning milk).

A متمخط *mutamakhkhit*, Who blows his nose. One who walks in a tottering, staggering way.

A متمخي *mutamakhkhī*, Abstinent, refraining, clear from. One who complains. Who asks pardon.

A متمدج *mutamaddij*, Extended, widened.

A متمدح *mutamaddih*, Boastful. A fisher for compliments. (See تمدح *tamadduh*.)

A متمدد *mutamaddid*, Extended, outstretched.

A متمدل *mutamaddil*, One who wipes himself with a napkin (منديل *mindīl*).

A متمدن *mutamaddin*, Rich, comfortably off.

A متمده *mutamaddih*, Boastful, vain-glorious.

A متمدهن *mutamadhin*, One who fills or receives a cruise of oil (مدهن *mudhun*).

A متمر *mutmir*, Rich in dates (تمر *tamr*).

A متمر *mutammar*, Fed with dates. Become dry (date). (A palm-tree) loaded with dry dates.

A متمرد *mutamarrid*, Stubborn, disobedient, rebellious. Beardless. One who outstrips, gets before.

A متمرس *mutamarris*, Mischief-maker. Rubbed.

A متمرص *mutamarris*, Fled, gone: pulled off.

A متمرض *mutamarriz*, Languid, dull, heartless.

A متمرط *mutamarrit*, Fallen off (hair).

A متمرع *mutamarriʻ*, Quick, expeditious. A seeker of pasture. One who moves his nose in a rage.

A متمرغ *mutamarragh*, A place where a horse rolls. *Mutamarrigh*, Wallowing (horse). Slippery (place). (See تمرغ *tamarrugh*.)

A متمرق *mutamarrak*, Dyed with saffron. *Mutamarrik*, (A horse) which is becoming fat.

A متمرمر *mutamarmir*, A trembler, totterer. Shaking. Quaking (sand).

A متمرن *mutamarrin*, Used, accustomed to. On the edge. Exceeding, much, excessive.

A متمرئ *mutamarriʼ*, A pretender to humanity.

A متمري *mutamarrī*, Adorned, decorated.

A متمزر *mutamazzir*, One who milks the stroakings. *Mutamazzir*, (or متمزز *mutamazziz*) One who sips or sucks by little and little.

A متمزع *mutamazziʻ*, Splitting with rage.

A متمزق *mutamazzik*, Torn, rent (garment).

A متمزمز *mutamazmiz*, Driven here and there, scattered. Seared. Moving preparatory to rising up.

A ممزن *mutamazzin*, Well-deserving. Accustomed, habituated. (See تمزن *tamazzun*.)

A متمسح *mutamassih*, One who rubs one thing against another. (See تمسح *tamassuh*.)

A متمسخ *mutamassikh*, Metamorphosed.

A متمسك *mutamassik*, Retentive, hold-fast, tenacious. One who holds back.

A متمسي *mutamassis*, Old, torn (garment).

A متمشر *mutamashshir*, Apparently rich. Verdant (leaf). (See تمشر *tamashshur*.)

A متمشش *mutamashshish*, One who gnaws the end of a bone and sucks the marrow.

A متمشع *mutamashshiʿ*, A remover of filth from himself. One who eats the whole contents of a dish.

A متمشق *mutamashshik*, Torn (garment). Retiring (night). Peeled, denuded.

A متمشي *mutamashshī*, Running, set a going.

A متمصر *mutamassir*, One who milks the afterings. One who milks with the thumb and fore-finger. Lost. A follower. Scattered. (See تمصر *tamassur*).

A متمصرة *mutamassirat*, Scattered (camels). A blaze on a horse's face, narrow in one part and broad in another.

A متمصص *mutamassis*, One who sucks or sips.

A متمضر *mutamazzir*, Like unto a Muzarite. Angry with the Muzarites (an Arabian tribe).

A متمضمض *mutamazmiz*, A rinser of his mouth.

A متمضي *mutamazzī*, Transmitted, passed by.

A متمطر *mutamattir*, (A horse) carried rapidly along. Name of a horse and of a mare. (See تمطر.)

A متمطط *mutamattit*, Yawning. (See تمطط.)

A متمطق *mutamattik*, A taster, licker. One who smacks his tongue against the palate.

A متمطمط *mutamatmit*, Extended. Thick, muddy.

A متمطي *mutamattī*, A strutter. Long (day).

A متمظع *mutamazziʿ*, Moving (shadow). Licking; a licker. One who delays or puts off.

A متمعد *mutamaʿʿid*, Fresh (date).

A متمعدد *mutamaʿdid*, Distant (habitation). Coarsely fed, and roughly clad.

A متمعر *mutamaʿʿir*, (Colour) changed (by anger). Falling (hair).

A متمعز *mutamaʿʿiz*, Contracted (brow).

A متمعص *mutamaʿʿis*, Griped in the bowels.

A متمعط *mutamaʿʿit*, Bald from sickness.

A متمعق *mutamaʿʿik*, Carried far in speech. Deep, profound. Bad-tempered.

A متمعك *mutamaʿʿik*, Wallowing (horse).

A متمعي *mutamaʿʿī*, Stretched, extended. Divulged (secret). Pompous, strutting.

A متمغص *mutamaghghis*, Griped in the belly.

A متمغط *mutamaghghit*, (A horse or a camel) which outstretches his fore-feet when running. (See تمغط *tamaghghut*).

A متمغي *mutamaghghī*, Soft, flabby (leather).

A متمقت *mutamakkit*, Mutually inimical.

A متمقس *mutamak-his*, Fainted, swooned.

A متمقس *mutamakkis*, Fainted, swooned.

A متمقق *mutamakkik*, A sipper at several times.

A متمك *mutmik*, (Pasture) which fattens.

A متمكث *mutamakkis*, Slow, tedious, dilatory.

A متمكر *mutamakkir*, Tinged with vermilion.

A متمكك *mutamakkik*, A sucker up of the whole. Hard upon a debtor.

A متمكمكة *mutamakmikat*, Short, squat (woman).

A متمكن *mutamakkin*, Powerful, possessed of great authority. Placed, established, inhabiting, residing, fixed, located. Firmly seated. An inhabitant. P متمكنان ولايت *mutamakkināni wilāyat*, Inhabitants of the country; peasants. A اسم متمكن *ismi mutamakkin*, A noun declinable in all three cases, a triptote. غير متمكن *ghayr mutamakkin*, Incapable of inflexion. متمكن امكن *mutamakkini amkan*, A diptote (or noun of two or three cases, see Arab. Grammar). متمكن مبني *mutamakkini mabnī*, An adverb or preposition.

A متمكي *mutamakkī*, Moist with sweat. (A horse) that scratches his eye against his knee.

A متملح *mutamallih*, A manufacturer or vender of salt (ملح *milh*). One who cries out well done!

A متملخ *mutamallikh*, One who tears out (an eye). Weak in the back.

A متملز *mutamalliz*, Rid, escaped (from any one). (See تملز *tamalluz*.)

A متملس *mutamallis*, Polished, smoothed, shining. Escaped, past. One who hangs back.

A متملص *mutamallis*, Escaped, set free.

A متملط *mutamallit*, Unfeathered (arrow).

A متملغ *mutamalligh*, One who shams folly.

A متملق *mutamallik*, Kind, gracious; a flatterer, fawner. Bland.

P متملقانه *mutamallikāna*, Soothingly, blandly.

A متملك *mutamallik*, Possessed of, made ruler.

A متملل *mutamallil*, Swift, quick in walking. Restless through pain. (See تملل *tamallul*.)

A متململ *mutamalmil*, Uneasy, restless in bed.

A متملي *mutamallis*, Crammed, filled.

A متملي *mutamallī*, Tedious, dilatory. One who enjoys life.

A متمم *mutmam*, Complete, perfect, entire.

A متمم *mutammam*, Over and above a medium. Name of a poet. *Mutammim*, A completer, perfecter, finisher. Who gives to one whatever he gains at dice. One whose gaming arrow wins time after time. A consumer, destroyer. One who runs to despatch a wounded man. One who hangs an amulet round the neck of an infant to protect it against fascination or enchantment. Split, burst, cracked. The complement of a circle (in mathematics).

A متمنع *mutamanniʿ*, One who refrains or holds back. Victorious, bold, triumphant. Firm, strong.

A متمنعان *mutamanniʿāni*, A young she-camel and a kid.

A متمنن *mutamannin*, Enfeebling: a weakener. Apparently weak and tired.

A متمني *mutamannī*, One who wishes, hopes, asks, or prays. A reader of manuscript. A liar. An inventor, feigner. (in gram.) The optative mood.

A متمنيات *mutamanniyāt*, Objects of desire.

A متموج *mutamawwij*, Boisterous, dashing, swelling, surgy, raging: overflowing, boiling over.

A متمور *matmūr*, Provided, stocked with dates.

A متمول *mutamawwil*, Rich, wealthy, opulent.

A متمون *mutamawwin*, Liberal to dependants.

A متمهد *mutamahhid*, Waxen powerful, able.

A متمهر *mutamahhir* Quick, ingenious, intelligent. (A lion) clever at tearing his prey.

A متمهص *mutamahhis*, Plunged (into water).

A متمهق *mutamahhik*, Frequent at (the wine).

A متمهك *mutamahhik*, One who adorns, decorates, or does (a thing) well and handsomely.

A متمهل *mutamahhil*, Gentle, deliberate, slow.

A متمهل *mutmahill*, Long, straight, and well-proportioned.

A متمهمه *mutamahmih*, Who desists, abstains.

A متمير *matmīr*, A pizzle (hard and stiff).

A متمئر *mutmaʾirr*, Long, strong (spear). Hard and stiff (pizzle).

A متميز *mutamayyiz*, Separated, distinguished. Distinct. Discriminating. Splitting with rage.

A متميس *mutamayyis*, A stately walker.

A متميع *mutamayyiʿ*, Melted; fluid, fluent.

A متمئل *mutmaʾill*, Tall. Erect, well-made.

A متن *matn*, (v. n. of متن) Striking on the side of the back. Striking, striking hard. Drawing out lengthwise. Travelling through a country. Castrating (a ram). Travelling (with any person) the whole day. Swearing. Stitching. Lying with. A severe blow. Marriage. (pl. متان *mitān*) A hard or elevated piece of ground. A steady, hard man. That part of an arrow from the feathers to the middle. One side of the back or loins. Text of a book. The middle (of a road). A fortress, castle, bulwark.

A متن *mutinn*, Remote, far distant.

A متناعش *mutanāʿish*, A lagger far behind.

A متناتف *mutanātif*, Plucked, falling (hair).

A متناتل *mutanātil*, Long, entangled (grass).

A متناثر *mutanāsir*, Scattered, fallen here and there. Sick. Moribund.

A متناثل *mutanāsil*, Poured forth.

A متناجث *mutanājis*, One who scatters.

A متناجع *mutanājiʿ*, One who dreams true.

A متناجخ *mutanājikh*, Dashing, splashing.

A متناجز *mutanājiz*, Mutually combative.

A متناجش *mutanājish*, Engaged in bidding against each other to raise the price; a sweetener.

A متناجل *mutanājil*, Combative, disputatious.

A متناجي *mutanājī*, Engaged in private chat.

A متناحب *mutanāhib*, Agreed together upon a time for combat or other matters.

A متناحر *mutanāhir*, Who fly at one anothers'

throats (نحر nahr). Facing (houses). Devious.

A متناد mutanādd, Dispersed, flying in disorder.

A متنادس mutanādis, Abusive of each other.

A متنادم mutanādim, Engaged in familiar talk. Seated together at a banquet of wine.

A متنادي mutanādī, Engaged in calling out to one another. Assembled, collected.

A متناذر mutanāẓar, A lion. *Mutanāẓir*, Mutual in admonishing or deterring.

A متنازع mutanāzaʻ, Disputed. متنازع فيه mutanāzaʻ fīhi, The thing disputed about, the subject of controversy. *Mutanāziʻ*, Engaged in a dispute among themselves. Seizing a thing together.

A متنازق mutanāzik, Mutually reproachful.

A متنازك mutanāzik, Reciprocal in spearing.

A متنازل mutanāzil, Descending together into the arena. Fighting together.

A متناسب mutanāsib, Similar, proportionate.

A متناسف mutanāsif, Engaged in private communications.

A متناسق mutanāsik, Arranged, closely joined.

A متناسل mutanāsil, Begotten in succession.

A متناسي mutanāsī, One who pretends to forget.

A متناشب mutanāshib, Joined, connected. Hanging, clinging together.

A متناشد mutanāshad, (A poem) rehearsed amongst people. *Mutanāshid*, Engaged in repeating verses together.

A متناشي mutanāshī, Overcome with wine.

A متناصح mutanasih, Mutual in admonishing.

A متناصف mutanāsif, Just, mutually equitable.

A متناضل mutanāzil, Emulous of each other in darting and shooting.

A متناطح mutanātih, Mutual in butting.

A متناطي mutanātī, Anxious to excel a rival. Engaged in bandying words.

A متناظر mutanāzir, Opposed, looking at one another face to face. (See تناظر tanāzur.)

A متناعم mutanāʻim, Benevolent; a benefactor. Tender, delicate.

A متناعي mutanāʻī, One who stimulates his comrade to vigorous exertion in battle by announcing the death of his friend.

A متناغر mutanāghir, One who shews dislike. A producer of something unknown or disapproved.

A متنافذ mutanāfiz, Engaged in a law-suit, going together before a judge.

A متنافر mutanāfir, Timid, fleeing in a panic. Going together before a magistrate.

A متنافز mutanāfiz, Leaping together.

A متنافس mutanāfis, Desirous, wishful, eager, particularly when competitory.

A متنافط mutanāfit, Scum-casting (boiling pot). One who eats burnt hair in a season of scarcity.

A متنافي mutanāfī, Engaged in, studious of, compassing each other's destruction, or driving each other away.

A متناقض mutanākiz, Contradictory. A promise-breaker. One who untwists a rope. One who demolishes a building.

A متناكث mutanākis, Discordant, inimical. Mutual in breaking promises.

A متناكح mutanākih, Allied by intermarriages.

A متناكد mutanākid, Mutually severe, harsh.

A متناكر mutanākir, One who shams ignorance. Mutually hostile.

A متناكف mutanākif, Engaged in exchanging words, or talking by turns.

A متناوب mutanāwib, Observant of time and turn in drawing water or any thing else.

A متناوح mutanāwih, Contrary, opposite (winds). Facing (two mountains).

A متناوش mutanāwish, One who puts forth his hand to take something. (See تناوش tanāwush.)

A متناول mutanāwal, Taken. Eaten. *Mutanāwil*, One who takes or carries off. An eater.

A متناولات mutanāwalāt, Viands.

A متناوم mutanāwim, One who feigns sleep.

A متناهب mutanāhib, Dust-raising (camel).

A متناهد mutanāhid, (Travellers) who make up a joint purse.

A متناهز mutanāhiz, Simultaneous in hastening, ambitious to get before each other.

A متناهض mutanāhiz, Reciprocal in assailing or preparing for battle.

A متناهي mutanāhī, Finished, terminated. Arrived at the utmost extreme, gaining any point. A comer or bringer of intelligence. Stagnating or regorging (water). Averse from any thing prohibited. Mutual in prohibiting or in checking. Provident, prudent, sagacious.

A متنايك mutanāyik, (An eyelid) closed in sleep. Fast asleep.

A متنائي mutanāī, Retired far asunder.

A متنبب mutanabbib, (Water) set a-flowing.

A متنبج mutanabbij, Swollen and high (bone).

A متنبز mutanabbiz, Scurrilous, abusive.

A متنبط mutanabbit, One who fetches or brings out. Like a نبطي nabatiy.

A متنبع mutanabbiʻ, Water flowing by degrees.

A متنبل mutanabbil, Possessed of, or bearer of, arrows. A taker. (See تنبل tanabbul.)

A متنبه mutanabbih, Waking from sleep. Circumspect, aware, animadverting, turning the attention towards, recollecting, remembering, diligent. One who receives advice, and profits by it.

A متنبئ mutanabbi, One who calls himself a prophet: a pseudo-prophet. Name of an Arabian poet.

A متنة matnat, A hard hill, high, rugged ground.

A متنتخ mutanattikh, One in whose head lice are sought and found.

A متنتن mutantin, One who abandons relations, and associates with strangers.

A متنثر mutanassir, Scattered.

A متنجث mutanajjis, A scrutinizer, examiner.

A متنجح mutanajjih, One who despatches easily; successful.

A متنجد mutanajjid, Borne off, taken. High.

A متنجز mutanajjiz, One who expedites (any thing) properly and successfully. (See تنجز tanajjuz.)

A متنجس mutanajjis, Polluted, defiled.

A متنجع mutanajjiʻ, Seeker of forage or water.

A متنجم mutanajjim, An astronomer. One who counts the stars from wakefulness or love.

P متنجن گوسپندي mutanjani gospandī, A kind of dish (pulaw) made of goats' flesh.

P متنجوشه mutanjūsha, Mint, spearmint.

A متنجي mutanajjī, One who seeks the highest ground. (See تنجي tanajjī.)

A متنحس mutanahhis, An examiner (into news).

A متنحل mutanahhil, A false pretender to.

A متنحنح mutanahnih, The repeater of a sound, as *ah ah*, to clear the throat.

A متنحى mutanahha', A place to turn to. A place of profit. *Mutanahhī*, Removed (from his place). Reclined.

A متنخ mutnikh, (Fat) oppressive to the stomach.

A متنخع mutanakhkhiʻ, One who spits.

A متنخل mutanakhkhil, A sifter. A picker, chooser of the best.

A متنخم mutanakhkhim, One who spits, hawks, or blows his nose.

A متنخنخ mutanakhnikh, Recumbent (camel).

A متنخي mutanakhkhī, Boastful, vain-glorious.

A متندح mutanaddih, Strayed from the fold.

A متندخ mutanaddikh, Vain, arrogant. One who pretends to be full.

A متندس mutanaddis, A searcher into news. Fallen on the ground, and laying the hand on the mouth. (See تندس.)

A متندل mutanaddil, One who uses a napkin.

A متندم mutanaddim, Penitent, contrite.

A متندي mutanaddī, Liberal beyond others. (A tree) glittering with dew. (See تندي tanaddī.)

A متنذر mutanazzir, Timorous, cautious.

A متنزر mutanazzir, One who claims relationship to the tribe of نزار nizār.

A متنزع mutanazziʻ, One who makes haste.

A متنزل mutanazzil, Slow in desending.

A متنزه mutanazzah, A charming, delightful place. *Mutanazzih*, Pure, free (from vice or stain).

A متنزي mutanazzī, Prone to evil.

A متنسب mutanassib, A claimer of relationship.

A متنسر mutanassir, Untwisted (rope). Fallen to pieces. (See تنسر tanassur.)

A متنسس mutanassis, A receiver (of good).

A متنسع mutanassiʻ, Loose (tooth).

A متنسف mutanassif, One who prostrates his rival in wrestling.

A متنسق mutanassik, Arranged, threaded.

A متنسك mutanassik, Pious, devout.

A متوّق *mutanawwik*, Neat, spruce (in dress).

A متنوّم *mutanawwim*, Sleepy. A dreamer.

A متنهنه *mutanahnih*, One who desists, refrains.

A متنيّب *mutanayyib*, Old, aged (she-camel). One who tears up grass by the root.

A متو *matw*, (v. n. of متا for متو) Stretching (a rope). Going quick.

A متواعص *mutawāʻis*, Assembling, crowding.

A متواتر *mutawātir*, Successively, one after another, distinctly (as chronologies, or quotations). Verse in which is found a moveable letter between two quiescents; as, مفاعيلن *mafāʻīlun*.

A متواثب *mutawāsib*, Mutual in rushing.

A متوأد *mutawaʼid*, Who advances by degrees.

A متوادّ *mutawādd*, Fond of, loving each other.

A متوادع *mutawādiʻ*, At peace together.

A متوارث *mutawāris*, Possessed of by inheritance.

A متوارد *mutawārid*, Successive, one following another, continued, consecutive.

A متوارك *mutawārik*, Seated on the buttock.

A متواري *mutawārī*, Withdrawn, lurking, absconding; concealed, retired.

A متوازف *mutawāzif*, Square with each other in reckoning. Equal in contributing.

A متوازن *mutawāzin*, Equal in weight.

A متوازي *mutawāzī*, Parallel (lines).

A متواصف *mutawāsif*, Engaged in mutually praising, describing, recounting, or relating.

A متواصل *mutawāsil*, Joined, fastened together: connected with one another. Arrived, come forth.

A متواصي *mutawāsī*, Engaged in commending, enjoining, or charging each other. (Grass) growing together.

A متواضخ *mutawāzikh*, Emulous of each other in giving water or in travelling.

A متواضع *mutawāziʻ*, Submissive, obedient, humble, respectful, affable, complimentary, complaisant. Distant.

P متواضعانه *mutawāziʻāna*, Respectfully.

A متواطح *mutawātih*, Engaged in fierce strife.

A متواطخ *mutawātikh*, Agreed among themselves to take (any thing).

A متواطد *mutawātid*, Steady, strong, permanent, solid. United in close succession.

A متواطس *mutawātis*, Agreed. High (billow).

A متواطئ *mutawātiʼ*, Agreed together.

A متواعد *mutawāʻid*, Bound to each other by mutual promises: promising to one another.

A متوافر *mutawāfir*, Abundant, copious, many.

A متوافق *mutawāfik*, Agreed, leagued, confederate. (in arithmetic) Commensurable.

A متوافي *mutawāfī*, Arrived in great number.

A متواقح *mutawākih*, Proud, insolent (to others).

A متواقص *mutawākis*, Like one short-necked.

A متواقع *mutawākiʻ*, Fallen o'er one another.

A متواقف *mutawākif*, Face to face (foes).

A متواكظ *mutawākiz*, Confused (business).

A متنغّم *mutanaghghim*, A low reader or singer.

A متنفّج *mutanaffij*, A vain boaster, bouncer.

A متنفّح *mutanaffih*, Intervenient, intermedial.

A متنفّخ *mutanaffikh*, One who blows with the mouth, or who makes the noise *ukh ukh*.

A متنفّذ *mutanaffiz*, Passed by or through.

A متنفّر *mutanaffir*, Averse, abhorring.

A متنفّس *mutanaffis*, Possessed of breath. An animal. Single. (See تنفّس *tanaffus*.)

A متنفّش *mutanaffish*, Erect (feather), bristled (hair). Soft within. (See تنفّش *tanaffush*.)

A متنفّض *mutanaffiz*, One who examines (a place) well to know what is there.

A متنفّط *mutanaffit*, Enraged, fired. Blistered.

A متنفّغ *mutanaffigh*, Blistered with labour.

A متنفّق *mutanaffik*, One who draws forth a mole from its hole, called نافقاء *nāfikā*.

A متنفّل *mutanaffil*, One who does more than the law requires. One who takes more of the spoil (انفال *anfāl*) than his companions.

A متنقّب *mutanakkib*, Covered with a veil.

A متنقّث *mutanakkis*, One who gains love, conciliates affection. One who makes haste.

A متنقّح *mutanakkih*, Fallen away in flesh.

A متنقّد *mutanakkid*, Ready-money paymaster.

A متنقّذ *mutanakkiz*, A rescuer, deliverer.

A متنقّر *mutanakkir*, An examiner, searcher.

A متنقّص *mutanakkis*, A disgracer, disparager.

A متنقّض *mutanakkiz*, Burst, split. (Blood) falling drop by drop. (See تنقّض *tanakkuz*.)

A متنقّل *mutanakkil*, Translated, transported; copied, portable. Refreshed with a crust or cake after a glass of wine. One who makes (any thing) a نقل *nakl*, or accompaniment to wine.

A متنقّي *mutanakkī*, A chooser, picker.

A متنكّب *mutanakkib*, One who avoids or shuns. Reclined, pitched. One who slings a quiver or bow across his shoulder. A name common to two poets.

A متنكّد *mutanakkid*, Grieved, afflicted.

A متنكّر *mutanakkir*, Disguised, altered, travesty, incognito. Changed for the worse.

A متنكّظ *mutanakkiz*, Twisted. Stingy. Distressed when on a journey.

A متنمّر *mutanammir*, Surly, sulky, growling.

A متنمّص *mutanammis*, One from whose face the hairs are plucked up: smooth-faced.

A متنمّل *mutanammil*, In motion like ants.

A متنمّي *mutanammī*, High-soaring (hawk).

A متنوّح *mutanawwih*, Shaken, waving, flapping.

A متنوّد *mutanawwid*, Shaken, waving (bough).

A متنوّر *mutanawwir*, Illuminated. One who sees (a fire) at a distance. Anointed with the depilatory unguent called نورة *nūrat*. Routed.

A متنوّع *mutanawwiʻ*, Various, of different kinds, sorts, or forms. One who walks before, proceeds on a journey. Shaken (tree). (Any thing) divided into different parts or qualities. Distant.

A متنسّم *mutanassim*, Who perceives, gets wind of. Fragrant, sweet-scented. (See تنسّم *tanassum*.)

A متنشّب *mutanashshib*, Fixed in the heart.

A متنشّر *mutanashshir*, Spread abroad.

A متنشّز *mutanashshiz*, Hard, severe. Ready.

A متنشّط *mutanashshit*, One who rides a horse, and dismounts when he is tired. Brisk, lively, active.

A متنشّغ *mutanashshigh*, A groaner inwardly.

A متنشّف *mutanashshif*, Bibulous, spongy.

A متنشّم *mutanashshim*, A beginner. Soft and gentle in seeking knowledge.

A متنشّئ *mutanashshiʼ*, One who rises to begin, who stirs about his business.

A متنشّي *mutanashshī*, One who perceives a smell, and becomes intoxicated.

A متنصّب *mutanassib*, Erect, upright, on the feet. Highly-raised (dust).

A متنصّح *mutanassah*, Well-sewed. Patched (garment). Well-watered (camel). *Mutanassih*, One who listens to advice. A sewer, patcher.

A متنصّر *mutanassir*, Turned Christian (نصرانيّ *nasrāniy*). One who endeavours to assist another.

A متنصّف *mutanassif*, A servant. (See تنصّف).

A متنصّل *mutanassil*, Absolved, acquitted, declared innocent. (See تنصّل *tanassul*.)

A متنصّي *mutanassī*, Married into a high tribe.

A متنضّح *mutanazzih*, One who exculpates himself. Who keeps himself clear. Bubbling (fountain).

A متنضّض *mutanazziz*, A praiser, approver. One who recovers a debt. (See تنضّض *tanazzuz*.)

A متنضّي *mutanazzī*, Whatever emaciates.

A متنطّس *mutanattis*, Curious, inquisitive, accurate, neat, nice, dainty. (See تنطّس *tanattus*).

A متنطّع *mutanattiʻ*, Attentive, industrious, pains-taking; a careful inspector. (See تنطّع.)

A متنطّف *mutanattif*, Decked with ear-rings. Tarnished, blemished. (See تنطّف *tanattuf*.)

A متنطّق *mutanattik*, A speaker. Girded.

A متنطنط *mutanatnit*, Distant, gone to a distance.

A متنظّر *mutanazzir*, One who grants a delay. One who waits, or expects. A beholder.

A متنظّف *mutanazzif*, Neat, nice, spruce, clean, delicate. Anxious to be neat and clean.

A متنظّم *mutanazzim*, Arranged, well-strung.

A متنعّل *mutanaʻʻil*, Fitted with shoes, shod.

A متنعّم *mutanaʻʻim*, Soft and delicate. Affluent, fortunate, an enjoyer of the delights and comforts of life. Salubrious, agreeable (country). An inquirer (for any person). One who walks barefoot. One who stretches every nerve, exerts himself to the utmost. A furious driver (of cattle).

A متنعنع *mutanaʻniʻ*, Distant, retiring. Agitated. Scattered. Tortuously moving.

A متنغّر *mutanaghghir*, Indignant, full of rage.

A متنغّش *mutanaghghish*, Tottering, nodding.

A متنغّص *mutanaghghis*, Uncomfortable (life).

A متنغّض *mutanaghghiz*, Moved, shaken (head).

A متواكف *mutawākif*, Declined, turned from.

A متواكل *mutawākil*, Trusting to, relying upon one another.

A متوالد *mutawālid*, Waxed numerous (seed).

A متوالي *mutawālī*, Continued, successive, consecutive, following one after another.

A متواليات *mutawāliyāt*, (pl.) Consequences.

A متوالية *mutawāliyatan*, Uninterruptedly.

A متواني *mutawānī*, Slow, tedious, dilatory, weak, feeble, tired, falling short.

A متواهب *mutawāhib*, Mutually bounteous.

A متواهس *mutawāhis*, One mending his pace.

A متواهق *mutawāhik*, A fellow-traveller. Equal, matched. Equal-paced.

A متوايل *mutawāyil*, Crying woe to one another.

A متوائم *mutawāʼim*, Harmonious (song).

A متوبّد *mutawabbid*, One who has a very malignant eye. Uncomfortable, leading a wretched life.

A متوبل *mutawbal*, Seasoned with herbs.

A متوتّح *mutawattih*, Little given (to wine).

A متوتّر *mutawattir*, Hard (sinew or neck).

A متوثّب *mutawassib*, One who rushes upon and seizes unjustly.

A متوثّق *mutawassik*, Firm, steady in business

A متوج *matūj*, Long (declivity). A well from which water may be drawn by the help of a pulley.

A متوّج *mutawwaj*, Crowned (as the king of the Persians, معمّم *muʻammam* implying turbaned, which was the practice of the Arabian princes). *Mutawwij*, One who crowns.

A متوجّد *mutawajjid*, Indisposed, unwell, complaining of sleeplessness, &c. Sad.

A متوجّر *mutawajjir*, A swallower (of medicine). One who sips water unwillingly.

A متوجّز *mutawajjiz*, A purchaser. One who transacts or seeks to do business, or sell his wares.

A متوجّس *mutawajjis*, One who hears and attends to a low sound.

A متوجّع *mutawajjiع*, Pained. Grieved for. A singer of the marsiya for the dead.

A متوجّن *mutawajjin*, Submissive; a suppliant.

A متوجّه *mutawajjih*, Turned, or going towards; a traveller. One who attends to, or favours. Inclined. Attentive. Bent (as an old man). Routed.

P متوجّه شدن *mutawajjih shudan*, To set out.

A متوجّئ *mutawajjiʼ*, One who inflicts a blow with the hand or a knife.

A متوجّي *mutawajji*, (A horse) hurt in the hoof.

A متوح *matūh*, A drawer of water. A well from which the water may be drawn without the help of a pulley. عقبة متوح *ʻakabat matūh*, The ridge of a long or extensive mountain.

A متوحّد *mutawahhid*, Singular, unparalleled, alone, unique. Sole, solitary. المتوحّد *al mutawahhid*, An epithet of God.

A متوحّش *mutawahhish*, Hungry, empty-bellied. Desolate, deserted. Scared away. Ready to decamp (as one scared or startled).

A متوحّل *mutawahhil*, Grown miry: bemired.

A متوخّم *mutawahhim*, Waxed warm (cattle).

A متوحّن *mutawahhin*, (A belly) become big. Contemptible. Perished.

A متوحّي *mutawahhī*, Quick, expeditious.

A متوخّم *mutawakhkhim*, Unhealthy, unwholesome, indigestible. Noisome.

A متوخّي *mutawakhkhī*, One who seeks what is right, who strives to please.

A متود *mutūd*, (v. n. of متد) Sojourning, tarrying, abiding.

A متودّد *mutawaddid*, Affectionate, loving.

A متودّر *mutawaddir*, Squandered, wasted (property). Fallen into difficulty.

A متودّس *mutawaddis*, Clad with verdure. One who feeds his flocks in the herbage وداس *widās*.

A متودّع *mutawaddiع*, Meek, quiet, placid. Pained in one limb. (See تودّع *tawadduع*.)

A متودّف *mutawaddif*, (A goat) on a hill-top. A searcher, inquirer after news.

A متودّن *mutawaddin*, Softened, smooth (hide).

A متودّئ *mutawaddiʼ*, (Intelligence) concealed and kept back. (See تودّؤ *tawadduʼ*.)

A متوذّف *mutawazzif*, A short stepper.

A متوذّل *mutawazzil*, One who cuts (meat) without dividing (it).

A متوذّن *mutawazzin*, Sly, crafty.

A متورّخ *mutawarrikh*, Moist, soft.

A متورّد *mutawarrid*, (Horsemen) arrived in troops. Coming to water. A lion.

A متورّس *mutawarris*, One who anoints his body with the plant ورس *wars*.

A متورّط *mutawarrit*, Fallen into trouble or ruin.

A متورّع *mutawarriع*, Continent, abstinent, keeping aloof. Rejected, repulsed.

A متورّق *mutawarrik*, (A camel) fed on leaves.

A متورّك *mutawarrik*, One who rests his buttock on his foot at prayer. (See تورّك *tawarruk*.)

A متورّم *mutawarrim*, Swollen.

A متورّن *mutawarrin*, One who rubs much oil. One who brings up delicately.

A متورّه *mutawarrih*, Stupid, unskilful.

A متورّي *mutawarrī*, Hidden, lurking; fugitive.

A متوزّر *mutawazzir*, Chosen to be vazīr. One exercising this office.

A متوزّع *mutawazziع*, A divider. Distributed.

A متوزّم *mutawazzim*, One who treads firmly.

A متوزّئ *mutawazziʼ*, Filled (leathern bottle).

A متوسّخ *mutawassikh*, Dirtied, soiled (clothes).

A متوسّد *mutawassid*, One who puts (a thing) under his head to serve as a pillow. (See توسّد.)

A متوسّط *mutawassit*, Seated in the midst. Midway. Gotten into the middle of. A mediator, umpire. Moderate, neither long nor short. One who takes the medium between good and bad. A writer who leaves the middle of the leaf blank.

A متوسّطة *mutawassitat*, Name of a sect.

A متوسّع *mutawassiع*, Seated at one's ease.

A متوسّف *mutawassif*, Excoriated, peeled. Moulted. (See توسّف *tawassuf*.)

A متوسّل *mutawassil*, Studious of obtaining nearness of access; or of recommending one's self to the divine notice and favour. An intercessor, mediator. A camel-stealer. One who confides in, or relies upon. Adjoining, conjoined.

A متوسّم *mutawassim*, Marked, characterized. A physiognomist. (See توسّم *tawassum*.)

A متوشّح *mutawashshih*, Girt with the belt وشاح *wishāh*, or with a baldrick.

A متوشّز *mutawashshiz*, Prepared (for mischief).

A متوشّع *mutawashshiع*, (A flock) scattered about right and left and feeding on a mountain. Numerous.

A متوشّغ *mutawashshigh*, An evil-doer.

A متوشوش *mutawashwish*, Agitated, moved.

A متوشّن *mutawashshin*, Diminished (water).

A متوشّي *mutawashshī*, Conspicuous (grey hair).

A متوصّب *mutawassib*, Sick, ailing, unwell.

A متوصّف *mutawassif*, Described, celebrated.

A متوصّل *mutawassil*, Desirous of becoming united. Joined, united: connected, related, depending on. Arrived. A dependant, connexion.

A متوصّم *mutawassim*, Broken down (by fever).

A متوضّأ *mutawazzaʼ*, A place where they wash before prayer: a lavatory. A privy.

A متوضّح *mutawazzih*, Open, clear, manifest, conspicuous. One who keeps in the middle of the road. One who does not enter into a crowd. Whitish (camel). The hypochondria.

A متوضّر *mutawazzir*, Nasty, greasy (dish).

A متوضّم *mutawazzim*, One who lies with.

A متوضّن *mutawazzin*, Mean, contemptible.

A متوضّئ *mutawazziʼ*, One who washes before prayer. Grown (boy or girl).

A متوطّد *mutawattid*, Firm, steady. Heavy.

A متوطّن *mutawattin*, An inhabitant, resident, native, dweller. One who applies, gives the attention to, fixes the mind upon.

A متوطّئ *mutawattiʼ*, One who treads under foot.

A متوع *mutūع*, (v. n. of متع) Being high and not yet begun to decline, being at its height (the day). Enjoying, reaping the fruits of.

A متوعّد *mutawaععad*, Terrified, frightened, alarmed. *Mutawaععid*, A threatener, menacer.

A متوعّر *mutawaععir*, Rough, uneven (road). Bewildered, confused. (See توعّر *tawaععur*.)

A متوعّل *mutawaععil*, Mounted on a hill.

A متوعّن *mutawaععin*, Waxed fat (camel or sheep). One who takes all.

A متوغّر *mutawaghghir*, Angry, hot with rage.

A متوغّل *mutawaghghil*, One who travels far.

A متوغّم *mutawaghghim*, Angry, enraged.

A متوغّن *mutawaghghin*, Intrepid in battle.

A متوفّد *mutawaffid*, Eminent, overtopping.

A متوفّر *mutawaffir*, Many, numerous, plentiful, copious, much, abundant, exuberant.

A متوفّز *mutawaffiz*, Restless on one's pillow.

A متوفّق *mutawaffik*, Successful, prosperous.

A متوفّىٰ *mutawaffa'*, Received to the mercy of God, deceased, dead, defunct. P توابع يار متوفّي *tawābiʻi yāri mutawaffa'*, The family of a deceased friend. A *Mutawaffī*, One who pays or receives the whole of what was due. God taking to himself the souls of the just. Dead, defunct.

A متوّق *mutawwak*, Desired, wished. Wistful.

A متوقّح *mutawakkih*, Overbearing, insolent.

A متوقّد *mutawakkid*, One who kindles. Kindled, lighted (flame). Sparkling, glittering. Quick, clever, witty. Easily excited.

A متوقّر *mutawakkir*, Respected. Gentle, patient.

A متوقّز *mutawakkiz*, Restless, unable to sleep.

A متوقّش *mutawakkish*, Shaking.

A متوقّص *mutawakkis*, Hard-paced (horse).

A متوقّع *mutawakkiʻ*, An expectant.

A متوقّف *mutawakkif*, Slow, tardy, delaying, lingering. One who waits for: persevering.

A متوقّل *mutawakkil*, Ascended, perched on a hill.

A متوقّم *mutawakkim*, A killer (of game). A terrifier. A rememberer. (See توقّم *tawakkum*.)

A متوقّن *mutawakkin*, Ascended, perched on a hill. One who takes pigeons in their nest.

A متوقّي *mutawakkī*, Timid, cautious.

A متوكّد *mutawakkid*, Standing. Prepared.

A متوكّر *mutawakkir*, Crammed, filled (bird's crop, lad's belly, or leathern bottle).

A متوكّز *mutawakkiz*, Filled. Ready for mischief. Propped, leaning. One who waits upon or to.

A متوكّف *mutawakkif*, One who minds, attends, waits upon, looks after. One who waits for another in hope of some advantage.

A متوكّل *mutawakkil*, Trusting in God, resigned to one's fate. One who confides in another, as feeling unable to manage his own affairs.

A متوكّن *mutawakkin*, A sojourner (anywhere).

A متوكّي *mutawakkiʻ*, Supported by (a staff).

A متولّد *mutawallid*, Begotten, born.

A متولّن *mutawallin*, One who cries for help.

A متولّه *mutawallih*, Amazed, stupefied: sad.

A متولّي *mutawallī*, Superintendant or treasurer of a mosque; an administrator or procurator of any religious or charitable foundation. A prefect, governor. One who turns his back, retires, or recedes; a fugitive. Near; a kinsman, a friend; who receives as such. P متولّي چيره زبان *mutawallī chīra-zabān*, The planet Mercury.

A متوّم *mutawwam*, Adorned with a necklace.

A متومّز *mutawammiz*, Brisk, leaping in walking.

A متومّق *mutawammik*, Received to friendship.

A متون *mutūn*, (v. n. of متن) Remaining (in a place). Text of a book (in opposition to scholia). (pl. of متن *matn*) Rugged hills. Sides of haunches.

A متوّه *mutawwih*, A destroyer. A confounder.

A متوهّث *mutawahhis*, Far gone into.

A متوهّج *mutawahhij*, Kindled, burning (fire). Glittering (gem). Diffused (odour).

A متوهّد *mutawahhid*, One who lies with.

A متوهّر *mutawahhir*, An interrupter (of a speaker). Far gone (night, winter). Slipped (sand-hill).

A متوهّز *mutawahhiz*, One who treads heavily.

A متوهّس *mutawahhis*, A slow, heavy walker.

A متوهّط *mutawahhit*, Sunk (in the mire).

A متوهّق *mutawahhik*, Extremely hot (gravel). One who interrupts a speaker.

A متوهّل *mutawahhil*, One who seeks to mislead.

A متوهّم *mutawahhim*, Thinker, imaginer, doubter.

A متوهّن *mutawahhin*, Weak, languid (affair).

A متوي *mutwī*, Dissipator, squanderer (of cash).

A متويّل *mutawayyil*, A detester, abhorrer.

A متة *math*, (v.n. of متة) Letting down (a bucket). Seduction. *Matah*, A close secret. A facility of being deceived, credulity.

P متّه *mata* or *matta*, A gimlet, wimble, auger. A moth. A weevil.

A متهاتر *mutahātir*, Mutually contentious, giving the lie to one another.

A متهاتم *mutahātim*, Contentious, quarrelsome.

A متهاتن *mutahātin*, Continuous, gentle rain.

A متهاجر *mutahājir*, Removed, separate from one another, mutually alienated.

A متهاجم *mutahājim*, An assailant.

A متهاجن *mutahājin*, (or متهاجي *mutahājī*) Mutually satirical.

A متهادّ *mutahādd*, Following in succession.

A متهادر *mutahādir*, (or متهادم *mutahādim*) Reciprocal in permitting murder to go unpunished.

A متهادن *mutahādin*, Right, well-arranged.

A متهادي *mutahādī*, Mutually liberal.

A متهارش *mutahārish*, Irritated (dogs).

A متهارط *mutahārit*, Mutually reproachful.

A متهارم *mutahārim*, One who feigns extreme old age or decrepitude.

A متهافت *mutahāfit*, (A crowd) rushing consecutively. Old, worn out. Fallen to pieces.

A متهاكل *mutahākil*, Disputatious, strifeful.

A متهالك *mutahālik*, Fallen. One who runs headlong to ruin. Engaged in destroying each other. Restless, full of tossings in bed. One who walks flippantly, and waves from side to side. Strong.

A متهام *mithām*, A frequent goer to Tihāmah.

A متهامس *mutahāmis*, Mutual in the communication of secrets.

A متهامش *mutahāmish*, Mixed pell-mell.

A متهانف *mutahānif*, An ironical smiler.

A متهاوش *mutahāwish*, Mixed (crowd, mob).

A متهاون *mutahāwin*, One who despises, neglects, or holds cheap. Negligent, incurious.

A متهاوي *mutahāwī*, Fallen upon each other.

A متهايج *mutahāyij*, Hand to hand in fight.

A متهايط *mutahāyit*, Convened, assembled.

A متهايئ *mutahāyiʻ*, Agreed together.

A متهبّب *mutahabbib*, Worn, rent (garment).

A متهبّج *mutahabbij*, Troubled with swellings.

A متهبّد *mutahabbid*, One who extracts, bruises, and boils seeds of the colocynth (هبد *habd*).

A متهبّش *mutahabbish*, Assembled, collected. One who toils for his family.

A متهبّل *mutahabbil*, A provider for his family.

A متهبهب *mutahabhib*, Shaken from side to side, tottering.

A متهبّي *mutahabbī*, Weak-sighted. One who shakes his hand; empty.

A متهتّر *mutahattir*, Ignorant.

A متهتّك *mutahattik*, Torn. Careless about honour, damaged in one's reputation.

A متهتّم *mutahattim*, Broken (front teeth).

A متهته *mutahtih*, One who gives himself to trifling pursuits. A stammerer, a stutterer.

A متهتّئ *mutahattiʻ*, Torn, cut, worn (coat).

A متهجّد *mutahajjid*, A watcher or riser at night, wakeful. Asleep at night.

A متهجّر *mutahajjir*, Like to one who has been obliged to make a هجرة *hijra, i. e.* to flee his country. One who travels in the heat of the day (هجير *hajīr*).

A متهجّس *mutahajjis*, Unleavened (bread).

A متهجّنة *mutahajjinat*, A palm-tree bearing fruit for the first time.

A متهجّي *mutahajjī*, One learning his alphabet.

A متهدّج *mutahaddij*, (A camel) fond of her colt. Unable to speak, struck dumb.

A متهدّد *mutahaddid*, A terrifier, threatener.

A متهدّك *mutahaddik*, A reproacher, terrifier.

A متهدكر *mutahadkir*, Satiated with milk so as to be overcome with drowsiness therefrom. Different sorts of milk mixed together. A leaper, jumper.

A متهدكرة *mutahadkirat*, Summer-made butter.

A متهدّل *mutahaddil*, Pendulous, dangling.

A متهدّم *mutahaddim*, Pulled down, ruined, destroyed, demolished, in ruins. Angry and menacing.

A متهدّمة *mutahaddimat*, A decrepit old woman or she-camel.

A متهدّي *mutahaddī*, Guided (by God) aright. One who finds the road, or right direction.

A متهذخرة *mutahazkhirat*, Flaunting (woman).

A متهذكر *mutahazkir*, Sated with milk. Glad. One whose flesh and bones shake when walking.

A متهذّئ *mutahazziʻ*, Burst (ulcer).

A متهرّر *mutaharrir*, Howling, whining (dog).

A متهرّش *mutaharrish*, Dispelled (cloud).

A متهرّع *mutaharriʻ*, (A spear) levelled at a foe.

A متهرّئ *mutaharriʻ*, (Meat) boiled to rags.

A متهرّي *mutaharrī*, A beater, a cudgeller.

A متهزّج *mutahazzij*, Twanging (bow-string).

A متهزّز *mutahazziz*, Shaken (tree by the wind).

A متهزّع *mutahazziʻ*, Quick, swift, expeditious. Austere, crabbed. (See تهزّع *tahazzuʻ*.)

A متهزم *mutahazzim*, (A stick) broken with a crash). Thunder. A thunder-cloud.

A متهزهز *mutahazhiz*, Rejoiced (heart).

A متهزئ *mutahazzi,*, A giber, sneerer, scoffer.

A متهسم *mutahassim*, Broken, split.

A متهسهس *mutahas-his*, Clashing (mail).

A متهشم *mutahashshim*, Favourably inclined. Broken. Weak, languid.

A متهشهش *mutahashhish*, Sprightly, lively.

A متهشهشة *mutahashhishat*, Loving (wife).

A متهضم *mutahazzim*, Injurious, unjustly hurtful.

A متهطر *mutahattir*, Dilapidated, ruined (well).

A متهطرس *mutahatris*, A stately walker.

A متهطل *mutahattil*, (or متهطلس *mutahatlis*) Convalescent. (A thief) who uses artifice in stealing.

A متهطلي *mutahatli*, Convalescent.

A متهقع *mutahakkiع*, Light, silly. (See تهقع.)

A متهقيل *mutahakkil*, Who treads heavily.

A متهقم *mutahakkim*, One who swallows large mouthfuls. Triumphant.

A متهكر *mutahakkir*, Amazed, astounded.

A متهككة *mutahakkikat*, (A woman near delivery) large-breasted and relaxed about the haunches.

A متهكم *mutahakkim*, Proud. (See تهكم.)

A متهكن *mutahakkin*, Penitent, sorrowful.

A متهلب *mutahallib*, Stripped of bristles.

A متهلز *mutahalliz*, One who has tucked up his skirts. Ready, prepared. A strutter.

A متهلس *mutahallis*, Attenuated, lean.

A متهلل *mutahallil*, Cheerful, exulting (countenance). Bright, flashing (cloud).

A متهم *mut-him*, One who goes into a sultry country. One who finds the air unhealthy. A thinker, conjecturer, doubter, or who suspects (falsely).

A متهم *muttahim*, Suspected, accused, arraigned. One who suspects.

A متهم *mutahhim*, Intense (heat). (A camel) which refuses to eat disagreeable pasture.

A متهمرش *mutahamrish*, Shaking, moving.

A متهمش *mutahammish*, Slow-flowing (spring).

A متهمط *mutahammit*, One who seizes unjustly.

A متهمع *mutahammiع*, One who shams weeping.

A متهمك *mutahammik*, Pains-taking.

A متهمم *mutahammim*, A seeker, searcher: louser.

A متهمئ *mutahammi,*, Torn, worn (coat).

A متهنج *mutahannij*, Quickened (fœtus).

A متهندم *mutahandim*, Properly adapted.

A متهنئ *mutahanni,*, Refreshed with food.

H متهوت *mat'hūt*, An occasional tax raised to disburse the expenses of repelling invasions and paying indemnities for robberies.

A متهود *mutahawwid*, Converted to repentance. Returned to duty. Turned Jew. Slow in talking.

A متهور *mutahawwir*, Violent, furious. Rash, inconsiderate. One who rushes upon, stumbles, or falls upon any thing by accident. Gone by, elapsed (greater part of winter, or of night). Ruined, fallen down.

P متهورانه *mutahawwirāna*, Rashly, bravely.

A متهوش *mutahawwish*, Mixed, jumbled.

A متهوع *mutahawwiع*, One who shams vomiting. Forced to vomit.

A متهوك *mutahawwik*, Astonished, stupefied. Falling into the pit of perdition. Fallen into difficulties from inattention.

A متهول *mutahawwil*, Scared at the figure of a wolf. One who wounds with a malignant eye.

A متهوم *mutahawwim*, Nodding (drowsy man).

A متهيب *mutahayyib*, Timid, fearful. Formidable. المتهيب *al mutahayyab*, (The dreaded) A lion.

A متهيث *mutahayyis*, A giver, bestower.

A متهيج *mutahayyij*, Raised (dust).

A متهير *mutahayyir*. (See متهور *mutahawwir*.)

A متهيض *mutahayyiz*, Twice-broken (bone).

A متهيع *mutahayyiع*, A tyrant, oppressor. One who hastens to do evil. Spread.

A متهيعر *mutahayعir*, Restless.

A متهيف *mutahayyif*, Exposed to the wind هوف.

A متهيل *mutahayyil*, Poured out.

A متهيم *mutahayyim*, Astonished.

A متهيئ *mutahayyi,*, Ready, prepared for.

A متهيئة *mutahayyi,at*, A camel that rarely fails to conceive after taking the male.

A متي *maty*, (v. n. of متي) Extending, drawing out. Travelling far. *Mata'*, In the middle. *Mata'* or *muta'*, When? When, if at any time. From. متى ما *mata' mā*, Whensoever. حتي متى *hatta' mata'*, (or الي متى *ila' mata'*) Till when? how long?

A متّى *matta'*, Matthew. When?

A متياح *mityāh*, A restless, turbulent man, meddler. Determined, predestined (affair).

A متياسر *mutayāsir*, One who apportions the flesh of a slaughtered camel. One who takes the left.

A متئام *mit,ām*, Twin-bearing (woman).

A متيامن *mutayāmin*, One who goes to the right. One who arrives in Yaman.

P متيت *matīt*, A weaver's comb.

A متيجة *mittījat*, Name of a city in Africa.

A متيح *mityah*, A meddler in a matter which concerns him not. Fallen into trouble or affliction. (A horse) which curvets or leans to a side. قلب متيح *kalb mityah*, A heart inclined towards every thing. *Mutyah*, Determined, defined, measured.

A متيخ *mittīkh*, Long and limber (branch).

A متيخة *matyakhat* or *mityakhat*, A branch of a palm-tree. Stalk of a bunch of dates.

A متيخة *mittīkhat*, The branch of a palm-tree. Stalk of a bunch of dates. A staff. A slender hammer.

A متئد *mutta,id*, One who goes to work gently.

A متئر *mut,ir*, One who fixes his eye upon. A striker (with a stick).

A متير *mutīr*, One who repeats often.

A متئس *mutta,is*, Despairing, despondent.

A متيس *mutayyis*, A breaker in of a horse.

A متيسر *mutayassir*, Easy, happily despatched (business). Cold (day). Ready.

A متيع *mutīع*, One vomiting again and again.

A متيفع *mutayaffiع*, A climber of a hill. Exalted.

A متيقظ *mutayakkiz*, Awake. Vigilant, attentive, prudent, alert.

A متيقن *mutayakkin*, Sure of, certain, certified. An explorer, examiner.

P متيل *mitel*, A lamp called پيه سوز *pih-soz*.

A متئم *mut,im*, Twin-bearing (woman).

A متيم *mutayyam*, Subdued, conquered by love. *Mutayyim*, A reducer to slavery or servitude. (Love) rendering (a man) obsequious (to his mistress).

A متما *mata'mā*, Whenever.

A متيمم *mutayammim*, One who uses sand when water is not to be had for performing ablutions. One who makes preparation.

A متيمن *mutayammin*. (See تيمن *tayammun*.)

A متين *matīn*, Strong (castle). Firm, solid, obstinate. Sententious. Text (of a book). قلعهٔ متين *kalع,a,i matīn*, A strong fortification.

P متين *mitīn*, A spade, a shovel.

A متيوساء *matyūsā,*, (pl. of تيس *tays*) He-goats.

A متيه *matyah*, A desert where one becomes lost.

A متيهة *matīhat*, *mutīhat*, or *matyahat*, A desert in which one loses one's self.

A متئ *mutta,i*, Quiet, meek, placid.

P مث *mas*, Syrup of grapes or dates.

A مثّ *mass*, (v. n. of مث) Wiping the (hands with a linen cloth, or rubbing them with herbs in order to clean them). Rubbing (the mustachios) with ointment or pomatum. Removing matter or proud flesh from a sore. Exuding (as a leathern bottle). Imbibing moisture.

A مثاب *masāb*, The place at the brink or parapet of a well where the water-drawer stands. The middle of a well, cistern, or pond; also the place into which the water runs from the reservoir or spring. A place of rendezvous where scattered people assemble. Wherever a hunter spreads his nets. A premium. *Musāb*, Rewarded. P عند الله مثاب شدن *ﺀinda'llāh musāb shudan*, To be recompensed by God; to receive a present.

A مثابة *masābat*, A place to which one returns again and again. A place where people assemble. An inn, caravansera. Where a hunter spreads his nets. The middle of a well where the water collects. The stone-work round a well. A step, degree, point. Manner, likeness. Extent.

A مثابتة *musābatat*, (v. n. 3 of ثبت) Knowing with certainty. Fixing, corroborating.

A مثابرة *musābarat*, A persevering in, sticking to.

A مثار *musār*, (Land) turned up with a plough.

A مثاعب *masāعib*, Canals, conduits.

A مثاغمة *musāghamat*, (v. n. 3 of ثغم) Kissing.

A مثافل *musāfil*, One who, having no milk, eats solids, as corn or herbs; a feeder on cerealia.

A مثافلة *musāfalat*, (v. n. 3 of ثفل) Sitting together, or keeping company with.

A مثافن *musāfin*, A familiar, intimate friend.

A مثافنة *musāfanat*, (v. n. 3 of ثفن) Sitting or keeping company with. Helping.

A مثافيد *masāfīd*, Lining for clothes.

A مثاقب *masākib*, (pl. of مثقب *miskab*) Wimbles, gimlets, augers, or other boring instruments.

A مثاقف *musākif*, Clever, intelligent.

A مثاقفة *musākufat*, (v. n. 3 of ثقف) Contending with (any one) in regard to skill and genius.

A مثاقيل *masākīl*, (pl. of مثقال *miskāl*) Weights. Gold coins of a certain weight. Provisions (especially made up into loads for travellers or armies). القى عليه مثاقيله *alka' ɛalayhi masākīlahu*, He asked him for provisions. He threw on him his provisions.

A مثاكل *masākil*, (or مثاكيل *masākīl*) (pl. of مثكل *muskil*) Bereaved (mothers).

P مثال *misāl*, A royal mandate.

A مثال *misāl*, (pl. امثلة *amsilat* and مثل *musul*) Similitude. Like for like; a requital, retaliation. Like, resembling. A command, order. (pl. مثل *musl* and *musul*) An example, model. History, fable, description. A form, figure, mode, manner, definite quantity. A bed, or any place on which one reclines. (in gram.) The conjugation of an assimilated verb. مثال بدر *misāli badr*, Resembling the full moon. عالم مثال *ɛālami misāl*, The region of fiction, the world of fancy. A dream, vision, P بي مثال *bī misāl*, (A عديم المثال *ɛadīmu'l misāl*) Incomparable. دريا مثال *daryā-misāl*, Like the sea.

A مثالب *masālib*, (pl. of مثلبة *maslubat* or *maslabat*) Vices, defects, faults. *Musālib*, (A horse) fed upon old pasturage called ثليب *salīb*, or the plant of that name.

A مثالة *masālat*, (v. n. of مثل) Standing erect. Being excellent.

A مثالث *masālis*, (pl. of مثلثة *maslisat*) Third strings of lutes.

A مثالج *masālij*, (pl. of مثلجة *maslajat*) Ice-houses. Snow-cellars.

A مثالي *misāliy*, Like, resembling.

A مثامنة *masāminat*, Name of eight kings of Himyar. *Musāmanat*, (v. n. 3 of ثمن) Agreeing together about a price.

A مثانة *masānat*, The bladder. The place which holds the fœtus.

A مثاني *masānī*, The first section (of the Kur'ān). Verses repeated to avert evil. Any number less than 200 verses of the Kur'ān. The knee and elbow-joints of cattle. (pl. of مثنى *masna'*) Second strings of lutes. The windings of a river. (pl. of مثناة *masnāt* or *misnāt*) Plaits, folds. المثاني *al masānī*, The whole Kur'ān.

A مثاورة *musāwarat*, A rushing impetuously.

A مثاوي *masāwī*, (pl. of مثوي *maswa'*) Hotels.

A مثاهات *musāhāt*, Conversation: conference.

A مثبت *musbat*, Bound about with the girth ثبات *sibāt*. Bed-ridden with disease, and unable to move. (in grammar) The affirmative verb. *Musbit*, One who establishes, fixes, confirms, ratifies, or gives a sanction to. Heavy, bed-ridden. Affirmative. One who knows with certainty. Continually tormenting (disease).

A مثبّت *musabbat*, Established, proved, confirmed, written. *Musabbit*, One who reduces to writing. A fixer, establisher, prover.

A مثبّج *musabbaj*, Confused and involved (speech or writing). *Musabbij*, One who confounds and obscures (writing).

A مثبّجة *musabbajat*, An owl. An eagle.

A مثبر *masbir*, An assembly, place where people meet and sit. Any place where sand breaks off. Any place where a woman or animal is delivered. A place of slaughter.

A مثبّر *musabbir*, One who keeps back.

A مثبط *musbit*, (A distemper) which leaves little or no interval from pain.

A مثبّط *musabbit*, Who or what diverts or hinders (from business).

A مثبنة *masbanat*, A bag in which women keep their mirrors and other toilette-articles.

A مثبور *masbūr*, Ruined. Imprisoned. Foolish.

A مثبّي *musabbī*. (See تثبية *tasbiyat*.)

A مثج *masj*, (v. n. of مثج) Mixing. Giving food. Giving liberally. Exhausting (a well).

A مثجّ *misajj*, An eloquent orator, or preacher.

A مثجّج *musajjaj*, (as وطب مثجّج *watbi musajjaj*) A bottle whose butter will not concrete in churning.

A مثجّر *musajjar*, Knotty, jointed (reed or cane). *Musajjir*, An enlarger, extender, or amplifier. One who sets water a-flowing.

A مثجّل *musajjal*, One who has a flagging, loose, pendulous belly. Capacious (bag).

A مثجم *musjim*, Incessantly and heavy (rain). Continuing, lasting.

A مثخبج *musakhbaj*, Flabby, loose in the flesh.

A مثخن *muskhin*, Enfeebling (wound). One who makes a great slaughter (of the enemy). One who strives or does to excess.

A مثخنة *muskhanat*, A thick, bulky woman.

A مثد *masd*, (v. n. of مثد) Hiding, concealing (amongst stones). Peeping through chinks, observing the motions of an enemy, or the actions of others. Appointing a spy.

A مثدّم *musaddam*, (A vessel) whose mouth is covered with a cloth (for straining).

A مثدن *musdan*, Afflicted with a bodily defect.

A مثدّن *musaddan*, Fleshy, corpulent, heavy. مثدّن اليد *musaddanu'l yad*, Short-handed, stingy.

A مثدّنة *musaddanat*, Fleshy, heavy (woman).

A مثراة *masrāt*, Whatever multiplies or increases (wealth, or causes ثروة *sarwat*).

A مثراد *misrād*, A stone, bone, or iron instrument with which cattle are slaughtered. Bread crumbled into broth.

A مثرب *musrib*, A blamer, chider, reprover. Very fat (wether). Stingy, avaricious.

A مثرّب *musarrab*, Mixed, confused. Chid. Ruined. *Musarrib*, One who folds up. A chider, rebuker, reprover. A mixer, corrupter.

A مثرثر *musarsir*, A babbler, prater. A glutton.

A مثرد *misrad*, A culinary vessel in which the pudding ثريد *sarīd* is prepared.

A مثرد *mussarad*, Slightly rained on (field).

A مثرّد *musarrid*, One who slaughters (cattle) with a stone, a bone, or a blunt instrument.

A مثرّر *musarrir*, A sprinkler and moistener.

A مثرطلا *musartilan*, Trailing on the ground.

A مثرطم *musartim*, (A ram) fat to the extreme.

A مثرم *musrim*, (A disease) rendering toothless.

A مثرنتي *musrantī*, Luxuriant. Fleshy (body).

A مثرنطي *musrantī*, Heavy-bodied (man).

A مثرود *masrūd*, (A wounded man) borne from the field. Crumbled. (A field) slightly wet with rain. Dyed (garment).

A مثري *musrī*, Rich, affluent. Fruitful (womb). (A cloud) which moistens and softens (the ground). Moist, irriguous (land).

A مثرّي *musarrī*, A moistener (of corn or cake). A sprinkler (of the earth). Clothed in a skin-garment. One who smites to the ground. (See تثرية.)

A مثط *mast*, A pressing of any thing to the ground with the hand.

A مثطّع *musattiɛ*, One who breaks; a breaker.

A مثطوع *mastūɛ*, Troubled with a rheum.

A مثع *masɛ* or *masaɛ*, (v. n. of مثع) Walking awkwardly (a woman). *Masaɛ*, An awkward gait in a woman.

A مثعاء *masɛāɛ*, An awkward air in walking in a woman. A stinking hyena.

A مثعب *masɛab*, (pl. مثاعب *masāɛib*) A canal, conduit. *Musɛib*, (Water) which flows through a pipe or canal.

A مثعر *musɛir*, One who observes or notices any novelty (as a spy or informer).

A مثعل *masɛal*, (A place) swarming with foxes (ثعلب *saɛlab*). *Musɛil*, Dense (crowd of water-drawers). Many (strangers or guests). Important and perplexed (business). Contrary, repugnant.

A مثعلب *musaɛlib*, (fem. مثعلبة *musaɛlibat*) A tract of country abounding in foxes (ثعلب *saɛlab*).

A مثعلة *masɛalat*, A country overrun with foxes.

A مثعنجر *musɛanjur*, Midst of the sea. كالقرارة في المثعنجر *ka'l karārat fi'l musɛanjar*, As a pond (compared) to the ocean. *Musɛanjir*, Flowing (blood or tears). A dish dripping with fat.

A مثعنكد *musɛaɛidd*, A soft, smooth-skinned youth.

A مثغثغ *musaghsigh*, Unable to speak plain.

A مثغر *musghar*, One whose milk-teeth have been cast. *Musghir*, (A child) getting, also shedding, the milk-teeth (ثغر *saghr*).

A مثغم **musghim**, A filler (of a vessel). (A head) white as the herb ثغام *saghām*. Who fills with joy, or inflames with rage. (A valley) producing the wild anise.

A مثغور **masghūr**, (A child) shedding teeth. Bruised in the mouth.

A مثغي **musghī**, One who makes (a sheep or a goat bleat). A giver (of any thing).

A مثفاة **misfāt**, A tripod-shaped branding-iron. A woman who has buried three or more husbands.

A مثفّاة **musaffāt**, A woman whose husband has two other wives. A woman who has buried three or more husbands.

A مثفار **misfār**, (A horse) which shakes the saddle backwards. Infamous (man).

A مثفان **misfān**, (A camel) chafing the side with the callous elbow-joint.

A مثفّد **musaffid**, One who lines (a coat of mail) with cloth.

A مثفر **misfar**, Infamous (man). *Musfir*, One who fits a leathern crupper (ثفر *safr* or *safar*) under the tail (of a horse). (A goat) kidding. One who gives a kick on the posteriors.

A مثفّر **musaffir**, Who drives or pricks forward.

A مثفرق **musafrik**, (Milk) not yet coagulated.

A مثفل **musfil**, Sediment-leaving (wine).

A مثفّل **musaffil**, One who eats (wheaten food) with milk. (See تثفيل *tasfīl*.)

A مثفن **musfin**, An intimate companion. Whatever renders (the hand) callous: indurating.

A مثفي **misfaʼ**, (or مثفّي *musaffaʼ*) A man who has buried three or more wives. *Musfī*, (or مثفّي *musaffī*,) One who puts (a kettle) on a trivet.

A مثفّية **musaffiyai**, Thrice-married (woman).

A مثقال **misḳāl**, (pl. مثاقيل *masāḳīl*) The weight of a thing. A gold coin. A weight of a dram and three-sevenths. A kind of flute. مثقال ذرّه *misḳāli zarra* (or حبّه *habba*) A very little thing.

A مثقالي **misḳālī**, A kind of linen or flax.

A مثقب **masḳab** or **misḳab**, A large, spacious road. *Misḳab*, (pl. مثاقب *masāḳib*) A wimble, or other boring instrument. Sagacious, penetrating. *Musḳib*, What makes bright; a kindler, illuminator.

A مثقّب **musaḳḳab**, Pierced. *Musaḳḳib*, One who perforates often, or pierces full of holes. The kindler of a fire. Conspicuous (grey hairs).

A مثقّبة **musaḳḳabat**, Pierced, bored (pearl).

A مثقّف **musaḳḳif**, A straightener (of a spear).

A مثقل **musḳal**, Weighed down with debt. Overloaded. *Musḳil*, Oppressive, distressing, painful (load, sleep, disease, or guilt). Pregnant (woman).

A مثقّل **musaḳḳal**, Oppressed, heavy laden. Rendered heavy, marked with tashdeed (a word). *Musaḳḳil*, Who overloads. One who renders or calls (a thing) heavy.

A مثقّلة **musaḳḳalat**, Heavily-laden (woman). A heavy stone for steadying a carpet, coverlet, &c.

A مثقوب **masḳūb**, Bored, drilled, perforated.

SY مثك **mask**, Liquorice.

A مثكال **miskāl**, Bereaved (mother).

A مثكل **muskil**, (pl. مثاكيل) Bereaved (mother).

A مثكلة **maskalat**, (A spear) which occasions bereavement. *Muskilat*, (A poem) written upon such a subject; an elegy.

A مثل **masl**, (v.n. of مثل) Punishing (one) quickly (as an example). Giving warning to others, by mutilating the nose, ears, and the like. Standing respectfully (before a superior). Sticking to the ground. Falling from one's place. Comparing, likening. Being like, equal to, resembling. *Misl*, Similitude. Alike, equal. مثل ذلك *misl zālik*, Like to this, the same with that. P مثل عطارد بودن *misli ʽuṭārid būdan*, To be an able minister, governor, or secretary, like Mercury. A مثله *misluhu*, Like him or it. *Masal*, (pl. امثال *amsāl*) A fable, tale, parable, apologue, proverb, adage, example, instance, case in point, comparison, simile, allegory, metaphor. Alike, equal, resembling. مثل سائر *masali sāʼir*, A current proverb. P مثل گفتن *masal guftan*, To relate pleasant stories, tell tales. A هذا مثله *hāzā masaluhu*, This resembles it, it is the same with that. *Musul*, (pl. of مثال *misāl*) Examples. Commands, orders. Beds, couches.

A مثلّ **musill**, One who orders a ruinous thing (ثلّة *sillat*) to be repaired. Rich in wool or sheep.

A مثلاً **masalan**, For example, for instance.

A مثلات **masalāt**, Proverbs. *Musulāt*, (pl. of مثلة *muslat* and *musulat*) Punishments.

P مثلا كه **masalā ki**, As if.

A مثلبة **maslabat** or **maslubat**, (pl. مثالب *masālib*) Injury, reproach, fault, blemish.

A مثلة **maslat** or **masulat**, A public or exemplary punishment. *Muslat*, (v. n. of مثل) Making an example of (a homicide) by mutilating (him) in the nose, ears, lips, or extremities, and leading (him) about the streets mounted on an ass. Being like, resembling. *Muslat* or *musulat*, Exemplary punishment.

A مثلّة **masallat**, A shade; a shady place, especially in the desert. A place where they water camels after being two days without drink.

A مثلث **maslas**, The third string of a lute. In threes. *Muslas*, Amounting to three. *Muslis*, Become three. An informer against his friend to the king (as affecting three, friend, sovereign, and self).

A مثلّث **musallas**, Made into three, or into a third. Triangular; a triangle. An aromatic wine (composed of new wine boiled to a third part, and then mixed with sweet herbs). Marked with three points, trebly pointed, as ث *sā*. Inflected with either of the three vowels *a, i, u*: as, مقبرة *makbarat, makbirat*, or *makburat*, A burial-place. An aromatic electuary. مثلّث النعمة *musallasu'n niʽmat*, The prophet Idris, as endued with three gifts, royalty, wisdom, and prophecy. مثلّث حادّ الزوايا *musallasi hāddu'z zawāyaʼ*, Acute-angled triangle. مثلّث قائم الزاوية *musallasi kāʼimu'z zāwiyat*, Right-angled triangle. مثلّث متساوي الاضلاع *musallasi mutasāwī'l azlāʽ*, Equilateral triangle. مثلّث متساوي الساقين *musallasi mutasāwī's sāḳayn*, Isosceles triangle. مثلّث مثلا *musallas maslā*, Allegorical fable. مثلّث مختلف الاضلاع *musallasi mukhtalifu'l azlāʽ*, Scalene triangle. مثلّث منفرج الزاوية *musallas munfariju'z zāwiyat*, Obtuse-angled triangle. *Musallis*, Triangular, triple. Who calls or makes three. A compounder of the aromatic electuary مثلّث *musallas*. (A date) one-third ripe. An informer against his friend to the king. The third horse (in a race).

A مثلثة **maslisat**, The third string of a lute.

A مثلّثة **musallasat**, (fem. of مثلّث *musallas*) Composed of three. Triangular. P مثلّثهٔ آبي *musallasaʼi ābī*, (or A مائي *māʼī*) The watery three, Cancer, Scorpio, and Pisces. مثلّثهٔ آتشي *musallasaʼi ātishī*, (or A ناري *nārī*) The fiery three, Aries, Leo, and Sagittarius. مثلّثهٔ بادي *musallasaʼi bādī*, (or هوائي *hawāʼī*) The airy three, Gemini, Libra, and Aquarius. مثلّثهٔ خاكي *musallasaʼi khākī*, The earthy three, Taurus, Virgo, and Capricorn.

A مثلج **muslij**, Snowy (day). Caught in the snow. One who does any thing in snowy weather. Who or whatever gladdens and cheers. (See اثلاج.)

A مثلجة **maslajat**, An ice-house, snow-cellar.

A مثلط **maslat**, A place where the liquid dung (ثلط *salt*) of an elephant is voided.

A مثلّع **musallaʽ**, (and مثلّغ *musallagh*) Unripe broken dates fallen from the palm-tree.

A مثلّل **musallil**, Collector, gatherer (of money).

A مثلوث **maslūs**, Any thing of which a third part has been taken. A three-threaded rope. Thrice-ploughed (land).

A مثلوثة **maslūsat**, A large water-bottle made of three skins, one within another.

A مثلوج **maslūj**, Snowed upon. Cold (water). مثلوج الفؤاد *maslūju'l fuʼād*, Cold-hearted, dull.

A مثلوجة **maslūjat**, A snowy place.

A مثلى **muslaʼ**, (fem. of امثل) Excellent (woman), best deserving of imitation. Most like the truth.

A مثليّة **misliyat**, Similitude, resemblance.

A مثمّ **masamm**, The place where they cut the navel of a horse. مثمّ مقمّ *misamm mikamm*, (or مثمّة مقمّة *misammatun mikammatun*) One who scrapes all together, good or bad; who eats of every thing. *Misamm*, Very pure. A keeper or guardian to one who has no keeper. One who strengthens the interests of a feeble tribe. One who impoverishes (or breaks the back) of him who has no helper (no back). *Musimm*, (A man) grown old.

A مثماث **masmās**, A confused affair. Motion, agitation. *Mismās*, (v. n. of مثمث Q) Disturbing, perplexing (any business). Moving here and there. Plunging head first into water. Feeding (a wick) with oil. Putting in motion. Giving a little rest.

A مثمة *masammat*, The place where they cut a horse's navel. *Misammat*, One who scrapes all together, good and bad. Who eats of every thing.

A مثمثة *masmasat*, (v. n. of مثمث Q) Disturbing, perplexing. Moving here and there. Seizing the whole. Exuding (a leathern-bag). Supplying (a wick) with oil.

A مثمج *musmij*, A maker of various-coloured vests.

A مثمجة *musmijat*, A female embroiderer.

A مثمر *musmir*, Fruit-bearing (tree). Loaded with ripe fruit (a tree). Opulent, increased in wealth. Fruitful, bearing plenty of fruit. Who multiplies or augments. (A leathern-bottle) which has particles of butter sticking to the side. غير مثمر *ghayr musmir*, Unfruitful, barren, sterile.

A مثمّر *musammir*, One who gathers leaves and fruit for cattle. Fruit in an incipient state appearing on the tree after the blossoms have dropt off. Opulent, become rich.

A مثمعد *musmaʿidd*, Handsome-faced.

A مثمغد *musmaghidd*, Fat (kid).

A مثمل *masmil*, An asylum, a place of refuge. *Musmil*, Pleasant (country). Frothy milk.

A مثمّل *musammal*, Deadly poison. *Musammil*, Frothy milk. The braying of an ass.

A مثملة *masmalat*, A large well or public cistern whence water may be drawn. *Mismalat*, Mud at the bottom of a well. A lock of wool used in anointing a scabby sheep. A basket of palm-leaves (for holding اقط *akit*). A shepherd's scrip.

A مثمن *musman*, Precious. *Musmin*, Consisting of eight. Sold. Who waters his camels on the eighth day. Who gives the full price for any thing.

A مثمّن *musamman*, Octangular, eight-sided, eight-fold. Distressingly hot, feverish. *Musammin*, One who makes in the form of an octagon.

A مثمنة *mismanat*, A bag, a wallet.

A مثمود *masmūd*, Water drawn off or drunk almost up by a great concourse of people. A man self-ruined by giving away his wealth. Exhausted, drained by women.

A مثمور *masmūr*, Abundant, plentiful (riches). (pl. مثمورون *masmūrūn*) Numerous (people).

A مثموغ *masmūgh*, Relaxed, enervated, flabby.

A مثموم *masmūm*, (A chink) stopped with ثمام.

A مثن *masn*, (v. n. of مثن) Hurting in the bladder, or in that part which holds the fœtus. Deceiving, cheating, giving a false account. *Masan*, (v. n. of مثن) Suffering from a complaint in the bladder, being unable to retain one's urine. Caruncles in women. *Masin*, Pained in the bladder.

A مثنّ *musinn*, (A man) worn out with age.

A مثناء *masnāʼ*, (A woman) unable to retain (her) urine; weak in the bladder.

A مثناة *masnāt*, A bending. A distich. Subtraction (in arithmetic). Power, strength. *Masnāt* or *misnāt*, (pl. مثاني *masānī*) A plait, fold, or bending. A tetrastic. Song, vocal music. A rope made of twisted hairs or wool. A book which, beside the Bible, contains Jewish chronicles; Mishna.

SY مثنان *masnān*, A species of mezereon.

A مثنط *musannit*, A divider, splitter, cleaver.

A مثنوي *masnawī* or *masnavī*, Rhyme, poetry composed of distichs corresponding in measure, each consisting of a pair of rhymes, and besides which the distichs have distinct poetical endings. This species of poetry is called مزدوج *muzdawaj* (or wedded). A book of moral doctrine written in this species of metre. P مثنوي خوان *masnavi-khwān*, One who recites aloud this book. A صاحب مثنوي *sāhib masnawī*, A writer of such moral poems.

A مثنوية *masnawīyat*, Weakness. Return.

A مثنىٰ *masnaʼ*, Two and two. (pl. مثاني *masānī*, The winding of a river. The second chord or string of a lute. A distich. Divided, separated. مثنىٰ الايادي *masnaʼl ayādī*, A benefit twice conferred. Portions remaining of a slaughtered camel distributed to those who had no share in the game of ميسر *maysar*.

A مثنّى *musannaʼ*, Doubled, two-fold. (A noun) of the dual number. (A letter) marked with two points, double-dotted (as ت *te*). A copy. The second. Junior or younger (as distinguished from the father of the same name). *Musannī*, Who makes two, a doubler. One who marks (a letter) with two diacritical points (as ت *te* or ي *ye*).

A مثنيّ *masnīy*, Doubled, bent, folded. (Cloth) of two threads. Twice-ploughed (land).

A مثوا *maswā*, (in construction) (for مثوىٰ *maswaʼ*) A habitation. اكرم مثواه *akrama maswāhu*, He received him hospitably.

A مثؤب *masʼub*, Lazy, slow.

A مثوب *muswib*, A recompenser, rewarder.

A مثوّب *musawwib*, Returned, converted. A repayer, returner of a loan.

A مثوبة *masūbat* or *maswabat*, A reward, recompense, remuneration.

A مثوّر *musawwir*, One who raises (dust), excites (tumults), levies (war). Who compels (camels) to rise. An examiner (of the Kur'ān to discover the true meaning of a passage). Tumultuous.

A مثورة *maswarat*, A country abounding in bulls.

A مثول *musūl*, (v. n. of مثل) Comparing, likening. Becoming like. Standing respectfully (before a superior). Sticking to the ground. Falling from one's place. Moving, removing.

A مثولات *musūlāt*, (pl. of مثلة *muslat* or *musulat*) Punishments.

A مثؤوط *masʼūt*, Troubled with a rheum.

A مثوىٰ *maswaʼ*, (pl. مثاوي *masāwī*) A dwelling, habitation, resting-place. An inn. ابو المثوي *abū'l maswaʼ*, A landlord, host. A guest. امّ المثوي *ummu'l maswaʼ*, The female occupant of a house. A landlady. *Muswī*, Name of Muhammad's spear.

A مثويّ *maswīy*, Buried.

A مثيّب *musayyab*, Deflowered, depucelated.

A مثير *musīr*, One who forces into a more violent motion. A plougher or turner up (of the ground). (Wind) driving (the clouds), or raising (a dust).

A مثيرة *musīrat*, A ploughing heifer.

A مثيل *masyal*, A country which abounds in the plant ثيل *sīl*. *Masīl*, Like. Excellent, choice. Great. *Musayl*, (dim. of مثل *misl*) Somewhat like. هذا مثيل هذا *hāzā musaylu hāzā*, This is something like that.

A مثؤوب *masʼūb*, Taken with a fit of yawning.

P مج *maj*, An historian. Name of a poet. The moon. Crooked.

A مجّ *majj*, (v. n. of مجّ) Spitting out (saliva or wine). (for P ماش *māsh*) A kind of pot-herb round and green. *Mujj*, Drops of honey upon stones.

A مجاءة *mujāʼat*, (v. n. 3 of جاء for جيأ) Contending and exceeding in frequency of coming.

A مجاب *mujāb*, Answered, replied to, accepted. مجاب الدعوة *mujābu'd daʿwat*, One favoured with answers to prayer. A proper name.

A مجابّة *mujābbat*, (v. n. 3 of جبّ) Boasting, exaggerating (about beauty or food).

A مجاثاة *mujāsāt*, (v. n. 3 of جثي) Sitting together knee to knee.

A مجاثي *mujāsī*, Seated knee to knee.

A مجاج *majāj*, A tree bent; or boughs cut therefrom. A bunch of dates (dry). A kind of mushroom. *Mujāj*, Saliva running from the mouth. Honey. Millet. مجاج العنب *mujāju'l ʿinab*, (Grape-spittle) Wine. مجاج المزن *mujāju'l muzn*, Rain. مجاج النحل *mujāju'n nahl*, Honey. خبز مجاجا *khabaza mujājan*, He baked bread from millet.

P مجاجنك *majājang*, (or مجاچنك) A dildo.

A مجّاح *majjāh*, Proud, pompous.

A مجاحر *majāhir*, (pl. of مجحر) Hiding-places.

A مجاحسة *mujāhasat*, (v. n. 3 of جحس) Pressing (as a crowd). Preventing, obstructing.

A مجاحشة *mujāhashat*, (v. n. 3 of جحش) Contending, fighting, pushing one another about.

A مجاحفة *mujāhafat*, (v. n. 3 of جحف) Squeezing, thronging (as a crowd). Going near, approaching.

A مجاد *mijād*, (v. n. 3 of مجد) Contending for glory; boasting. *Mujād*, Well-wrought.

A مجادّ *mujādd*, One who disputes a point of right. One who co-operates with another.

A مجاداة *mujādāt*, The act of asking a gift.

A مجادبة *mujādabat*, (v. n. 3 of جدب) Having a barren (year).

A مجادة *majādat*, (v. n. of مجد) Being conspicuous for honour, nobility, or glory.

A مجادّة *mujāddat*, (v. n. 3 of جدّ) Disputing a point of right. Opposing, being hostile.

A مجادعة *mujādaʿat*, (v. n. 3 of جدع) Wrangling, disputing, reproaching, reviling.

A مجادف *majādif*, (pl. of مجدف *mijdaf*) Birds' wings. Oars, sculls. Arrows.

A مجادل *majādil*, (pl. of مجدل *mijdal*) Castles, strong towers, citadels. *Mujādil*, Contentious, disputatious, quarrelsome.

A مجادلة *mujādalat*, (v.n.3 of جدل) Contending, disputing. Contention, dispute, altercation, conflict.

A مجاديح *majādīh*, as مجاديح السماء *majādīhu's samāʼ*, Certain stars in the twenty-eighth mansion of the moon.

A مجاديف *majādīf*, (pl. of مجداف *mijdāf*) Oars.

A مجاذبة *mujāzabat*, (v.n. 3 of جذب) Contending (with any one). Turning away, diverting.

A مجار *mijār*, (v. n. 3 of مجر) Exacting a profit in buying or selling. A fetter for a camel. *Mujār*, Protected, sheltered. A refugee.

A مجارّ *mujārr*, A vexer, tormenter.

A مجاراة *mujārāt*, (v. n. 3 of جري) Going or running with (another). Agreeing.

A مجارّة *mujārrat*, (v. n.3 of جرّ) Delaying, putting off (any one). Seeking out a person's faults.

A مجارحة *mujārahat*, A wounding one another.

A مجارزة *mujārazat*, (v. n. 3 of جرز) Jesting with each other almost in a railing tone.

A مجارع *majāriʻ*, Camels which only give a sip or draught (جرعة *jurʻat*) of milk.

A مجارف *mujārif* or *raf*, One who gains little.

A مجارم *majārim*, Commercial dealings.

A مجاري *majārī*, (pl. of مجرى *majra'*) Streams, currents. Canals, ducts. Accidents, events, occurrences, contingencies. Ends of words.

A مجاريع *majārīʻ*, (pl. of مجرع *mujriʻ*) (Camels which yield little milk.

A مجاز *majāz*, (v. n. of جاز for جوز) Passing by, through, or beyond. Way, road, passage. Metaphor, simile, allegory. A deceitful word or action. Feigned, insincere, political, worldly, superficial, profane (opposed to divine love). A road which is crossed over from one side to the other. (A place) planted with nut-trees. مجاز الزقاق *majāzu'z zukāk*, The Straits of Gibraltar. المجاز قنطرة الحقيقة *al majāz kantaratu'l hakīkat*, Allegory is a bridge to reality. ذو المجاز *zu'l majāz*, Name of a market held in pagan time three leagues from عرفة *ʻarafat*. *Mujāz*, Permitted, allowed; lawful, convenient.

A مجازًا *majāzan*, Metaphorically. Superficially. Insincerely, hypocritically.

A مجازاة *mujāzāt*, (v. n. 3 of جزي) Compensating, requiting. Compensation, requital of good or evil. P مجازات و مكافات كردن *mujāzāt u mukāfāt kardan*, To requite and recompense.

A مجازة *majāzat*, A metaphor. (A place) planted with nuts (جوز *jawz*). A road through a salt-marsh.

A مجازر *majāzir*, (pl. of مجزر *majzir* and مجزرة *majzirat*) Slaughter-houses (for camels).

A مجازفة *mujāzafat*, (v. n. 3 of جزف) Doing rashly. Guess, conjecture in buying or selling.

A مجازي *majāzī*, Metaphoric. Untrue, feigned, insincere. Political. Profane. Superficial. (pl. of مجزي *majza'*) Condign, merited punishments. *Mujāzī*, A recompenser.

A مجاسّ *majāss*, (pl. of مجسّة *majassat*) Pulses or parts felt.

A مجاساة *mujāsāt*, A being inimical, hostile to.

A مجاسد *majāsid*, (pl. of مجسد *mujsad*) (Cloths) well dyed. ذو المجاسد *zu'l majāsid*, Name of an individual, so called because he was the first who wore garments dyed with saffron.

A مجاع *majāʻ*, Hunger.

A مجّاع *majjāʻ*, One who eats abundantly of dates and milk. *Mujjāʻ*, Gruel, thin gruel.

A مجاعة *majāʻat*, (v. n. of مجع) Being impudent. (v. n. of جاع for جوع) Feeling hungry. Leavings of dates and milk. Mockery, ridicule. (pl. مجائع *majāʼiʻ*) A barren year. Hunger, want.

A مجّاعة *mujjāʻat* or *majjāʻat*, Fond of impudence. One who eats abundantly of dates and milk.

A مجاعلة *mujāʻalat*, (v. n. 3 of جعل) Bribing.

A مجافاة *mujāfāt*, (v. n. 3 of جفا for جفو) Lifting a thing from its place and setting it at a distance.

A مجافخة *mujāfakhat*, (v. n. 3 of جفخ) Boasting against, contending for glory.

A مجال *majāl*, Power, strength, ability, vigour, skill. Place, opportunity. Force. A circus. A field of battle. The place where a serpent lies coiled up; or the track left by it in crawling. P زبون و بي مجال *zabūn u bī majāl*, Weak and insufficient. A *Mijāl*, (pl. of مجلة *majlat*) Thin skins covering watery blisters or pustules.

A مجالّ *majāll*, (pl. of مجلّة *majallat*) Treatises on metaphysics or abstract sciences.

A مجالاة *mujālāt*, (v. n. 3 of جلا for جلو) Opposing, withstanding openly.

A مجالب *majālib*, (pl. of مجلبة *majlabat*) Attracting causes, allurements.

A مجالح *mujālih*, A lion. (pl. مجاليح *majālīh*) A camel which gives milk plentifully in winter. Years fatal to cattle.

A مجالحة *mujālahat*, (v. n. 3 of جلح) Opposing with vehemence. Behaving with haughtiness. Displaying enmity.

A مجالد *mujālid*, A proper name.

A مجالدة *mujāladat*, (v. n. 3 of جلد) Fighting with swords, fencing. Gladiature, sword-play.

A مجالس *majālis*, (pl. of مجلس *majlis*) Sessions. Assemblies, conversations. *Mujālis*, Seated with.

A مجالسة *mujālasat*, (v. n. 3 of جلس) Sitting with (another). An assembly, session.

A مجالطة *mujālatat*, (v. n. 3 of جلط) Opposing with address, circumventing.

A مجالعة *mujālaʻat*, (v. n. 3 of جلع) Wrangling, squabbling over drink at play, or in sharing a thing.

A مجالغة *mujālaghat*, (v. n. 3 of جلغ) Laughing with the teeth exposed. Fighting with drawn swords.

A مجالي *majālī*, (pl. of مجلى *majla'*) The fore parts of the head soonest liable to become bald.

A مجاليح *majālīh*, (pl. of مجالح *mujālih*) Camels which give milk plentifully in winter. Lions. Years fatal to cattle.

A مجاليد *majālīd*, (pl. of مجلد *mijlad*) Leathern straps with which hired mourners strike their cheeks. Camels yielding much milk.

A مجامخة *mujāmakhat*, (v. n. 3 of جمخ) Boasting against, contending for glory.

A مجامد *mujāmid*, A next-door neighbour.

A مجامر *majāmir*, (pl. of مجمر *mijmar*, *mujmar*, or مجمرة *mijmarat*) Censers. Chafing-dishes.

A مجامع *majāmiʻ*, (pl. of مجمع) Congregations.

A مجامعات *mujāmaʻāt*, (pl. of مجامعة *mujāmaʻat*) Carnal connexions. Adulteries, fornications. مجامعات دبريّة *mujāmaʻāti duburiya*, Sodomy.

A مجامعة *mujāmaʻat*, (v. n. 3 of جمع) Consenting, agreeing to. Lying with. Carnal commerce.

A مجاملة *mujāmalat*, (v. n. 3 of جمل) Treating kindly, humanely, courteously, politely. Making fair but hollow professions of friendship.

A مجّان *majjān*, Gratuitous. Abundant, sufficient. *Mujjān*, (pl. of ماجن *mājin*) Careless what they say or do. Bold, fearless, audacious, impudent.

A مجانّ *majānn*, (pl. of مجنّ *mijann*) Shields.

A مجّانًا *majjānan*, Gratis, gratuitously.

A مجاناة *mujānaʼat*, A falling flat upon.

A مجانبة *mujānabat*, (v. n. 3 of جنب) Being near or at the side (جنب *jamb*) of (a person). Going to a distance, flying, receding, retiring.

A مجانة *majānat*, (v. n. of مجن) Not caring what one says or does. Boldness, impudence.

A مجانّة *mujānnat*, Blackness (of the face).

A مجانس *mujānis*, Like, similar, homogeneous.

A مجانسة *mujānasat*, (v. n. 3 of جنس) Being akin, homogeneous. Making use of alliteration (تجنيس *tajnīs*) in a poem.

A مجانق *majānik*, (and مجانيق *majānīk*) (pl. of منجنيق *manjanīk*) Balistas. Battering-rams.

A مجاني *majānī*, Gains, advantages.

A مجانين *majānīn*, (pl. of مجنون *majnūn*) Madmen, maniacs. (pl. of منجنون *manjanūn* and منجنين *manjanīn*) Water-wheels. Times. Fortunes.

A مجاواة *mujāwāt*, A calling (camels) to water.

A مجاوب *mujāwib*, An answerer, a respondent. A speaker, proposer.

A مجاوبة *mujāwabat*, (v. n. 3 of جاب for جوب) Answering one another, conversing together.

A مجاودة *mujāwadat*, (v. n. 3 of جاد for جود) Vying with in liberality.

A مجاور *mujāwir*, Adjacent. A neighbour. Fixed to the temple, *i. e.* devoutly employed. The sweeper of a mosque. P مجاوران فلك *mujāwirāni falak*, The seven planets: Saturn, Jupiter, Mars, the sun, Venus, Mercury, and the moon. The fixed stars.

A مجاورة *mujāwarat*, (v. n. 3 of جار for جور) Being near. Keeping up a good correspondence with neighbours. Becoming a neighbour. Taking under protection as a client. Remaining in the temple devoutly employed. Neighbourhood. Intimacy.

A مجاوز *mujāwiz*, One who passes over, transgresses, exceeds bounds. Transitive (verb). مجاوز الحد *mujāwizu'l hadd*, Immoderate, excessive.

A مجاوزة *mujāwazat*, (v. n. 3 of جاز for جوز) Transgressing, exceeding. Forgiving, passing over (a fault). Passing by. Crossing over. Causing to pass by. Transition. A departure from.

A مجاوعة *mujāwaʻat*, (v. n. 3 of جاع for جوع) Hungering, being hungry.

A مجاولات *mujāwalāt*, Rounds (in boxing).

A مجاولة *mujāwalat*, (v. n. 3 of جال for جول) Going round (one another when fighting, boxing, or wrestling) to seize an advantage.

A مجاوي *mujāwī*, A caller (of camels) to water.

A مجاهاة *mujāhāt*, (v. n. 3 of جها for جهو) Boasting against, vying with in glorying.

A مجاهد *mujāhid*, A labourer, endeavourer, striver. A warrior (in the cause of religion).

A مجاهدات *mujāhadāt*, (pl. of مجاهدة *mujāhadat*) Holy wars. Conflicts, struggles. Inflictions.

A مجاهدة *mujāhadat*, (v. n. 3 of جهد) Fighting (especially against infidels, in defence of the faith).

A مجاهرة *mujāharat*, (v. n. 3 of جهر) Carrying on open hostilities, being an undisguised enemy. Calling to in a loud voice. Reproaching, reviling. Proclaiming, revealing.

A مجاهز *mujāhiz*, A wealthy merchant. مجاهز ارواح *mujāhizi arwāh*, A name of God; also of Muhammad. مجاهز كان *mujāhizi kān*, The sun.

A مجاهضة *mujāhazat*, (v. n. 3 of جهض) Preventing, keeping back. Causing to make haste.

A مجاهل *majāhil*, (pl. of مجهل) Trackless plains.

A مجاهلة *mujāhalat*, (v. n. 3 of جهل) Vying with in ignorance.

A مجاهيض *majāhiz*, (pl. of مجهض *mujhiz*) (Camels) casting their young.

A مجاهيل *majāhīl*, (pl. of مجهول) Unknown.

A مجاياة *mujāyaʼat*, (v. n. 3 of جاء) Trying to beat any one in frequency of coming. Comparing, confronting, collating. Agreeing, conforming.

A مجاياة *mujāyāt*, A facing, confronting.

A مجايتة *mujāyatat*, (v. n. 3 of جيت, not used) Calling (camels) to water; also checking (them) by the words جوت جوت *jawt jawt*.

A مجايضة *mujāyazat*, (v. n. 3 of جاض for جيض) Boasting against, contending for glory.

A مجائع *majāʼiʻ*, (pl. of مجاعة) Barren years.

A مجائل *majāʼil*, (pl. of مجال) Assemblies.

A مجبأة *majbaʼat*, (Ground) rich in mushrooms.

A مجبال *mijbāl*, Coarse-shaped (woman).

A مجبب *mujabbab*, (A horse) white from the knees downward. *Mujabbib*, A fugitive from battle.

A مجبة *majabbat*, A highway, clear road.

A مجبر *mujbar*, Compelled, forced. *Mujbir*, One who forces unwillingly. One who considers as entire; one who refers or ascribes to a renovation or recruiting. *Mujbir*, (or مجبر *mujabbir*) A setter of broken bones.

A مجبل *mujbil*, (A horse) digging up the ground with his feet. One who goes toward a mountain.

A مجبن *mujbin*, One who discovers (a person) to be a coward (جبان *jabān*). Coagulated (milk).

A مجبن *mujabbin*, One who imputes to cowardice. One who makes, calls, or considers as a coward.

A مجبنة *majbanat*, Rough, rugged ground. Whatever makes a man a coward (as children).

A مجبوب *majbūb*, One whose virile organs have been cut away; castrated. Thrown into a well.

A مجبوبة *majbūbat*, A wallet consisting of one skin sewed over another.

A مجبور *majbūr*, Constrained, forced. Consolidated (broken bone). Re-established after having been in distressed circumstances.

A مجبورة *majbūrat*, The city of Madīna.

A مجبوس *majbūs*, Willingly, promptly obeyed.

A مجبول *majbūl*, Formed by nature, innate. A great or large man.

A مجبه *mujabbih*, One who receives (any thing) ungraciously, or who treats with contempt.

A مجبي *mujbī*, A seller of corn yet unripe.

A مجبي *mujabbī*, Who bends the body downward; who stands with the hands on the knees; whose face touches the ground.

A مجتاب *mujtāb*, A passer by. Dressed in a shirt.

A مجتاح *mujtāh*, Ruinous, destructive: destroyer.

A مجتاز *mujtāz*, A traveller. Fond of escape.

A مجتاف *mujtāf*, Stinking, fetid (carcase).

A مجتب *mujtibb*, A traveller through, or a viewer of, cities. Dressed in a tunic (جبة *jubbat*).

A مجتبر *mujtabir*, A setter of broken bones.

A مجتبه *mujtabih*, A denier. A reprobater.

A مجتبى *mujtaba'*, Chosen. *Mujtabī*, A chooser. A collector.

A مجتحف *mujtahif*, A seizer, a plucker. One who takes up (pudding) with three fingers. One who exhausts a well.

A مجتدي *mujtadī*, One who begs a gift.

A مجتر *mujtarr*, Dragged, drawn. Ruminant.

A مجترح *mujtarih*, One who labours to gain.

A مجترر *mujtarir*, One who draws. Ruminant.

A مجترس *mujtaris*, One who gets, or tries to get.

A مجترم *mujtarim*, Guilty, criminal. An estimator by guess of the produce of a palm-tree. One who strips (a palm-tree) of (its) dates. One who labours for his family.

A مجترئ *mujtariʼ*, Bold, endued with fresh courage. المجترئ *al mujtariʼ*, (The bold) A lion.

A مجتز *mujtazz*, Clipped, shorn. *Mujtizz*, A clipper, shearer.

A مجتزر *mujtazir*, One who slaughters or skins (a camel). (See اجتزار *ijtizār*.)

A مجتزز *mujtaziz*, A cutter of (corn or dates). A sheepshearer. (See اجتزاز *ijtizāz*.)

A مجتزع *mujtaziʻ*, A cutter or breaker (of branches from a tree).

A مجتزم *mujtazim*, An estimator of the produce of (a palm-tree) by looking at it. A receiver, taker. A buyer (of the best sort).

A مجتزئ *mujtaziʼ*, Content, satisfied.

A مجتزي *mujtazī*, One who demands a recompense (جزاء *jazāʼ*) for his labour.

A مجتس *mujtiss*, (or مجتسس *mujtasis*) A toucher, handler, feeler. An inquirer after intelligence.

A مجتشئ *mujtashiʼ*, Disagreeing (country).

A مجتعل *mujtaʻal*, Effected, performed, come to pass. *Mujtaʻil*, A taker. A putter, placer, or layer of one thing upon another. A doer, performer. A constituter, appointer. A possessor. A beginner.

A مجتفي *mujtafī*, A tearer up, thrower away.

A مجتلب *mujtalib*, One who carries from place to place (especially slaves or cattle for sale); a dealer, drover. الدائرة المجتلبة *ad'dāʼiratu'l mujtalibat*, Name of a form of Arabian verse.

A مجتلط *mujtalit*, A snatcher.

A مجتلف *mujtalaf*, Reduced to indigence by a calamitous year. *Mujtalif*, An extirpator.

A مجتلل *mujtalil*, One who gathers (camel-dung for firing). A picker of the best.

A مجتمر *mujtamir*, A burner of aloes.

A مجتمع *mujtamaʻ*, A place where things are heaped or collected together. A place of meeting. *Mujtamiʻ*, Convened, assembled, come together. Agreed in opinion. (A man) arrived at full strength. مشى مجتمعا *masha' mujtamiʻan*, He walked fast.

A مجتن *mujtann*, (or مجتنن *mujtanin*) Covered.

A مجتنب *mujtanab*, Shunned, scorned. *Mujtanib*, Remote, far removed. One who abstains from, declines, shuns, flies. Polluted.

A مجتنح *mujtanih*, Inclined. (See اجتناح.)

A مجتنى *mujtana'*, Gathered (crop). *Mujtanī*, A gatherer (of a crop).

A مجتور *mujtawir*, Neighbouring, adjacent.

A مجتوي *mujtawī*, An abhorrer, detester, loather; out of humour with (a climate).

A مجتهد *mujtahid*, One who strives hard to acquire correct and sound views, pains-taking. The highest degree to which the learned in the law attain, and was formerly conferred by the colleges.

A مجتهر *mujtahir*, A cleaner (of a well). One who considers (any thing) as great or respectable. One who looks at (a woman) unveiled.

A مجثاث *mijsās*, (or مجثة *mijassat*) An iron tool for pulling up palm-shoots. A gimlet, an auger.

A مجثث *mujassis*, The metre مستفعلن فاعلاتن فاعلاتن *mustafʻilun fāʻilātun fāʻilātun*.

A مجثم *majsim*, Place of squatting or sitting.

A مجثمة *mujassamat*, (A bird or beast) confined

to one spot and shot at till killed.

A مجثي *mujsī*, Who or what causes to kneel.

A مجثئل *mujsa,ill*, Erect, upright, standing.

A مجج *majaj*, A relaxation of the jaws. The ripening of a grape. *Mujuj*, Drunkards. A bee.

A مجح *majh*, (v. n. of مجح) Being proud, boasting. *Majah*, Joy, gladness.

A مجح *mujihh*, Pregnant and near delivery.

A مجحد *mujhid*, Stunted (plant), not growing.

A مجحر *majhar*, (pl. مجاحر *majāhir*) A hiding-place, asylum, shelter, den. *Mujhir*, Who or what forces to take refuge. (See اجحار *ijhār*.)

A مجحظ *mujahhiz*, One who fixes the eyes on.

A مجحف *mujhif*, Who or what carries away, or goes off with. An approacher. Pressing.

A مجحفة *mujhifat*, A calamity, misfortune.

A مجحل *mujahhal*, Thrown on the ground. *Mujahhil*, Who throws another on the ground.

A مجحم *mujahhim*, A stedfast looker at.

A مجحن *mujhan*, Short (herb) stunted for want of watering. *Mujhin*, (or مجحن *mujahhin*) Stingy to domestics, half-starving them. One who feeds with unwholesome aliment.

A مجحود *majhūd*, Denied, unacknowledged.

A مجحوش *majhūsh*, Smitten, wounded on the side.

A مجحوف *majhūf*, Troubled with flux, fluxed.

A مجخر *mujahhkhir*, One who makes wide (the mouth of a well).

A مجخي *mujahhkhī*, Bent (old man). Far-spent (night). (See تجخية *tajkhiyat*.)

A مجد *majd*, (v. n. of مجد) Excelling in glory. Finding a pasture abounding in grass and feeding nearly to satiety (camels). Satiating, or nearly satiating (camels) with green pasture. Overcoming, excelling. Glory, grandeur, greatness, splendour, the honour derived from ancestors. Praise (to God). صاحب مجد *sāhib majd*, Glorious, magnificent. زيد مجده *zīda majduhu*, May his glory be increased!

A مجد *mujadd*, Renewed. *Mujidd*, Solicitous, laborious, diligent, pains-taking. (See اجداد *ijdād*.)

A مجداب *mijdāb*, Land seldom yielding well.

A مجداح *mijdāh*, The sea-shore.

A مجدار *mijdār*, A scarecrow.

A مجداف *mijdāf*, (pl. مجاديف *majādīf*) A bird's wing. An oar, a scull.

A مجدال *mijdāl*, Litigious.

A مجدب *mujdib*, Distressed from scarcity of provisions. Barren (ground). Scarce, barren (year).

A مجدح *mijdah*, A ladle or spatula with which they mix medicines or gruel. A cautery on the thigh of a camel. *Mijdah* or *mujdah*, The bull's eye (a star). *Mujdih*, A mixer up of a ptisan.

A مجدح *mujaddah*, (Wine) stirred with a stick.

A مجدد *mujaddad*, Renewed. Repaired. (Cloth) of different-coloured stripes. A poem devoid of a description of one's own feelings, and an eulogium from beginning to end. *Mujaddid*, One who renews or makes afresh. A weaver of a garment of many colours. One who cuts off a camel's udder.

A مجددا *mujaddadan*, Again, afresh, newly.

A مجدر *mujdar*, A country where small-pox rages. *Mujdar* or *mujdir*, Ground which abounds with the herb جدر *jadr*.

A مجدر *mujaddar*, Pitted with small-pox.

A مجدرة *majdarat*, Convenient, suitable, deserving, worthy, proper, fit. A country where the small-pox rages. انه لمجدرة ان يفعل *innahu la majdaratun an yafʻala*, Truly it is meet he should do (it).

A مجدع *mujdiʻ*, One who gives (to a child) unwholesome food.

A مجدع *mujaddaʻ*, Entirely eaten up (herbage). Crop-eared (ass). *Mujaddiʻ*, Who says to another, may your hand or nose be cut off!

A مجدف *mijdaf*, A bird's wing. An oar.

A مجدف *mujaddif*, Ungrateful for the blessings of God, blasphemous in the enjoyment of them. A blasphemer. مجدف عليه *mujaddaf ʻalayhi*, Stinted in his circumstances, destitute of the comforts of life.

A مجدل *majdal*, A troop or body of men. *Mijdal*, (pl. مجادل *majādil*) A strong castle, a fort or citadel. Litigious (an instrument of litigation).

A مجدوب *majdūb*, Drawn, extended, abstracted, attracted. Severe (year). Desolate, barren (country).

A مجدوح *majdūh*, Stirred (ptisan). Blood drawn from live cattle (which the pagan Arabians used to eat in times of scarcity).

A مجدود *majdūd*, Happy, fortunate. Dignified. Wealthy. Cut (cloth). One who has a celebrated ancestor (جد *jadd*).

A مجدور *majdūr*, Spotted with small-pox. Spare, lean. Fit, worthy, deserving.

A مجدوف *majdūf*, Cut, clipped. (A skin-bottle) lopped in the extremities. مجدوف الكمين *majdūfu'l kummayn*, Short-sleeved.

A مجدول *majdūl*, Slender-boned in the hands and feet. Firmly-twisted (rope).

A مجدولة *majdūlat*, Elegantly-limbed (girl). Slender (leg). Firmly-woven (coat of mail).

A مجدوه *majdūh*, Astonished, amazed.

A مجدي *mujdī*, A giver, sufficer. Bleeding (wound).

A مجذاء *mijzā,*, A long taper stick used in an Arabian game. A beak.

A مجذاف *mijzāf*, An oar.

A مجذافة *mijzāfat*, An oar.

A مجذام *mijzām*, One who decides or cuts short.

A مجذامة *mijzāmat*, One who decides or cuts short. One who suddenly breaks off friendship.

A مجذر *mujzir*, A wild cow possessed of a calf.

A مجذر *mujazzar*, (A man) short and thick at his extremities. (A camel) very fleshy about the joints and ends of the bones.

A مجذع *mujzaʻ* or *mujazzaʻ*, Inconstant, irresolute, unsteady.

A مجذف *mujzif*, Swift-flying (bird).

A مجذفة *mujzifat*, A short-stepping woman.

A مجذم *mijzam*, Afflicted with the disease جذام.

A مجذم *mujazzam*, Amputated. Leprous.

A مجذوب *majzūb*, Drawn, attracted. Torn or carried away, abstracted. Lessened, diminished. مجنون و عاقل مجذوب و كامل *majnūn u ʻākil, majzūb u kāmil*, The foolish and the wise, the defective and the perfect.

A مجذوذ *majzūz*, Cut or broken off. Abrupt, interrupted. عطاء غير مجذوذ *ʻatā,i ghayr majzūz*, Uninterrupted liberality.

A مجذوذي *majzūziy*, One who adheres to one man, depends on him alone for victuals, and is obnoxious to him on that account. One who, when travelling, never leaves his luggage.

A مجذور *majzūr*, Squared (in arithmetic).

A مجذوف *majzūf*, One whose feet are cut off.

A مجذوم *majzūm*, Leprous, infected with leprosy. Afflicted with elephantiasis (جذام *juzām*).

A مجذي *mujzī*, Firm, erect. (A young camel) fat about the bunch. A lifter up (of a stone).

A مجر *majr*, (v. n. of مجر) Purchasing a fœtus in the belly of a sheep or camel. Purchasing a male camel with the fœtus in the belly of a she-camel. Selling corn before ripe or in the ear for a like quantity of wheat by conjecture. Selling without weight or measure (dates hanging on a palm-tree). Playing at dice. Being thirsty. Much, many. A numerous army. Interest, usury. Understanding. Thirst. The fœtus of a camel or sheep. *Majar*, (v. n. of مجر) Filling (the belly) with water, yet not enough to quench the thirst. Becoming large in the ewe's belly (a fœtus). Unquenchable thirst.

A مجر *majarr*, A large beam on which the cross-beams rest. *Mijarr*, An instrument dragged along the ground to level it, a harrow. *Mujirr*, One who slits the tongue of a young camel to prevent its sucking. One who pierces with a spear and leaves it in the body. One who permits (a man) to do what he pleases. One who allows (a debtor) a respite. (A camel) which chews the cud. One who imitates a predecessor.

A مجرا *majra'*, A channel, canal, aqueduct. Track or course of a ship. Direction, aim. One day's journey; also a ship's way in twenty-four hours. P مجراي آب *majrāyi āb*, A water-course. The urethra, urinary passage. A مجراي ماء *majrāyi mā,*, A water-course. مجراي نهر *majrāyi nahr*, Bed of a river. P مجرا بستن *majrā bastan*, To point (a gun). مجرا كردن *majrā kardan*, To explain. A *Mujra'*, Made to flow, rendered current. Allowance, premium; deduction. Obeisance, respect, visit, audience.

A مجراز *mijrāz*, A barren waste.

A مجراشة *mujra,ashshat*, (Camels) fleshy and fat.

A مجرائي *mijrā,ī*, One who pays his respects, *i.e.* servants, ministers, or the like.

A مجرب *mujarrab*, Expert, skilled, versed, experienced. Proved, examined (as medicine), tested, assayed (as coin). A lion. *Mujarrib*, A trier, prover, experimenter, assayer.

A مجربذ *mujarbiz*, (or مجربذ القوائم *mujarbazu'l kawāʼim*) (A horse) that carries his head low, and places his hind-feet in the prints of his fore-feet.

A مجرة *majrat*, (A sheep) very big with young, and so lean as to be scarce able to stand.

A مجرّة *majarrat*, The galaxy or milky-way.

A مجرتان *majratāni*, Two accidents to which sheep are exposed, *i. e.* severity of seasons, and wandering or being lost in the night.

A مجرّح *mujarrih*, One who wounds severely.

A مجرّد *mujarrad*, Stript, bare, naked, denuded. Drawn (sword). Experienced, tried. Unmarried. Solitary, alone. Mere, only. The yard of any solid-hoofed animal. بمجرّد النظر *bi mujarradi'n nazr*, At a mere glance. P بمجرّد گمان *ba mujarradi gumān*, On a mere suspicion. A حسن المجرّد *hasanu'l mujarrad*, Beautiful when nude. *Mujarrid*, One who lays bare or strips naked.

A مجرّدات *mujarradāt*, (pl. fem. of مجرّد *mujarrad*) Incorporeal beings, angels.

A مجردان (مذ *muz*) *majradāni*, Two days or two months since.

A مجردب *mujardib*, One who claps his hands upon meat to prevent its being carried off the table.

A مجردح *mujardah*, Long-headed (boy).

A مجردل *mujardal*, Ready to fall.

A مجرّدي *mujarradī*, Solitude, solitariness.

A مجرّديّة *mujarradiyat*, Solitude. Nakedness.

A مجرّذ *mujarraz*, Experienced, proved, tried.

A مجرّر *mujarrir*, One who pulls very hard.

A مجرز *mujriz*, Lean, emaciated (she-camel).

A مجرّس *mujarras*, Expert, skilled, versed. *Mujarris*, A trier, prover, experimenter. A speaker.

A مجرع *mujriʻ*, A drinker, absorber (of water). (pl. مجاريع) A camel giving only a sip of milk.

A مجرّع *mujarraʻ*, (A rope) of which one of the threads is over-twisted. *Mujarriʻ*, One who causes to drink (water) or to forget (grief).

A مجرّف *mujarraf*, Stripped of all; one whose whole property has been swept away. *Mujarrif*, Whatever carries away (as a river part of its banks). One who pours out well.

A مجرفة *mijrafat*, A scavenger's wooden shovel.

P مجرگ *majarg*, Pressing (post-horses, carriages, or ships); compelling one to work without hire.

A مجرم *mujrim*, Culpable, criminal; a sinner.

A مجرّم *mujarram*, Entire, complete (year). *Mujarrim*, Who completes a year. Who comes out of.

A مجرمز *mujramizz*, A year wherein much rain falls after a great drought in the spring. Drawn together, shrunk.

A مجرن *mijran*, A place where dates are dried, a date-kiln. A great glutton.

A مجرّن *mujarran*, Made supple and pliable.

A مجرنثم *mujransam*, High, prominent (pubes).

A مجروح *majrūh*, Wounded. Reproached. Reprobated, confuted, convicted of false evidence.

A مجرود *majrūd*, Torn off, skinned, unbarked, peeled, denuded. (Ground) infested by locusts. Griped in the belly from eating locusts (جراد *jarād*).

A مجرور *majrūr*, Marked with جرّ *jarr*. Dragged.

A مجروز *majrūz*, (A field) bare after harvest.

A مجروس *majrūs*, Any letter of the alphabet except the soft ones (حروف لين *hurūfi lin*).

A مجروّش *mujrawwash*, Middling-sided.

A مجروف *majrūf*, (A camel) marked on the thigh.

A مجروم *majrūm*, Large-bodied.

A مجرّه *mujarrih*, A publisher, divulger.

A مجرهدّ *mujrahidd*, A fast goer. Long (night).

A مجرهم *mujarhim*, Keen, diligent, active.

A مجريٰ *majra'*, (v. n. of جري) Mooring (a ship). A ship's course. A place where any thing flows. The last letter of a word. The inflexion of the last consonant of a distich to which all the others rhyme. *Mujra'*, (v. n. 4 of جري) Causing to flow, allowing to proceed. Conjugated, declined. *Mujra'* or *majra'*, A place where any thing runs. *Mujrī*, Who causes to flow or run. An executor, one who causes any order to be obeyed. A name of God. A bitch with her puppies (جرو *jarw*), or a female wild beast followed by her young.

P مجري *mijrī*, A vessel in which drugs are kept.

A مجريّ *majrīy*, Declined (noun).

A مجرية *mujriyat*, A bitch with her whelps.

A مجرئشّ *mujraʼishsh*, Thick-sided.

A مجزّ *mijazz*, A sickle. Shears. *Mujizz*, (Grain, flock, or palm-tree) ready to cut or shear.

A مجزأ *majzaʼ*, *mujzaʼ*, (مجزأة *majzaʼat*, or *mujzaʼat*) (v. n. of جزأ) Contenting. Enriching. اجزأت عنك مجزأ فلان *ajzaʼtu ʻanka majzaʼa* (مجزأة *majzaʼat*, مجزأ *mujzaʼa*, or مجزأة *mujzaʼat*) *fulānin*, I did without you, I supplied your place.

A مجزّأ *mujazzaʼ*, Divided into portions.

A مجزاع *mijzāʻ*, Extremely impatient.

A مجزب *mijzab*, Outwardly moral and virtuous.

A مجزبز *mujazbaz* or *biz*, Hard-trotting (horse).

A مجزر *majzir*, (pl. مجازر *majāzir*) A slaughter-house or place (especially for camels). *Mujzir*, (A camel) for slaughter. One who gives a sheep or goat to be killed. A palm-tree with fruit ripe for gathering. Decrepit (man) in life's last stage.

A مجزرة *majzirat*, A slaughter-house for camels.

A مجزع *mujziʻ*, Who or what causes one to lament. Who or what strikes with terror. Who or what renders impatient.

A مجزّع *mujazziʻ*, (A cistern) which has little water in it. One who cuts meat in pieces. *Mujazziʻ* or *mujazzaʻ*, (Dates) two-thirds ripe. A date-stone rubbed until a part becomes white. Any thing wherein there is black and white.

A مجزفة *mizafat*, A fishing-net.

A مجزل *mujzil*, Liberal, a great giver.

A مجزم *mijzam*, Full (bottle).

A مجزّم *mujazzim*, A filler (of a bottle). A coward: weak. One who keeps silence. Shrewd, clever.

A مجزوء *majzūʼ*, Deprived of a portion.

A مجزور *majzūr*, Slaughtered (camel).

A مجزوز *majzūz*, Clipped, shorn, cut, mowed.

A مجزول *majzūl*, (The foot متفاعلن *mutafāʻilun*) cut down to متفعلن *mutfaʻilun* in the measure كامل *kāmil* (Perfect).

A مجزوم *majzūm*, Cut, amputated, broken off. Marked with the character جزم *jazm* ـْـ.

A مجزئ *mujziʼ*, Satisfying, sufficing (food). (A man) sufficient for whatever he is commanded.

P مجس *majas*, A place where an apothecary brays any thing.

A مجسّ *majass*, Any part felt: the pulse.

A مجسّة *majassat*, (pl. مجاسّ *majāss*) The pulse or any part felt. ضيّق المجسّة *zayyiku'l majassat*, Narrow in the chest.

A مجسد *mijsad*, Those parts of a garment which touch the body. *Mujsad*, (pl. مجاسد *majāsid*, Red. (Cloth) dyed with saffron.

A مجسّد *mujassad*, (Cloth) dyed with saffron. (A voice) harmonious, true, in tune. بروج مجسّدة *burūj mujassadat*, The four signs of Sagittarius, Pisces, Gemini, and Virgo.

A مجسطي *mijastī*, The title of Ptolemy's celebrated work on astronomy, so called by the Arabians, who, adding the article ال *al* to the Μεγιστή of the Greek title Σύνταξις Μεγιστή, thus form the word المجسطي *almijastī* or *almajistī*.

P مجسطي گشاي *mijastī-gushāy*, Able to explain the Mijasti.

A مجسّم *mujassam*, Rendered corporeal, clothed with a body, incarnate. Corpulent. Massy, solid. مجسّم ذا اثني عشر قاعدة *mujassam zā isnatay ʻashara kāʻida*, An equilateral pentagon. مجسّم عدس *mujassami ʻadas*, A lentiform body. مجسّم كثير القواعد *mujassam kasīru'l kawāʻid*, A solid polyhedron. مجسّم متساوي *mujassami mutasāwī*, A plain solid. مجسّم متساوي الاضلاع *mujassam mutasāwi'l azlāʻ*, An icosaedron. مجسّم متوازي السطوح *mujassam mutawāzi's sutūh*, A solid parallelopipedon. *Mujassim*, One who clothes with a body. One who renders large and corpulent.

A مجسوءة *majsūʼat*, Hard (ground).

A مجشّ *mijashsh*, (or مجشّة *mijashshat*) A hand-mill. *Mujishsh*, One who grinds into coarse pieces.

A مجشاب *mijshāb*, Gross victuals.

A مجشب *mijshab*, A piece of wood on which clothes are laid. A man, thick, stout, and courageous.

A مجشّب *mujashshab*, One who lives poorly.

A مجشر *mijshar*, A cistern from which no water is drawn.

A مجشّر *mujashshar*, (A flock) led far from home.

A مجشّرة *mujashsharat*, A herd of horses turned

out to pasture.

A مجشم *majsham*, A falcon's perch. *Mujshim*, One who causes to labour. A lion.

A مجشّم *mujashshim*, One who pays attention to any thing, pains-taking.

A مجشوب *majshūb*, Broken into large pieces. Coarse fare.

A مجشور *majshūr*, (A camel) troubled with the dry, husky cough جشرة *jushrat*.

A مجشوش *majshūsh*, Broken, coarsely pounded.

A مجشونة *majshūnat*, Active, bustling (woman).

A مجصّص *mujassas*, Plastered with lime. *Mujassis*, A plasterer. (A whelp) opening the eyes.

A مجضّض *mujazziz*, One who goes with a quick pace. Prepared to fight.

A مجظئرّ *mujza,irr*, A preparer of mischief; one who raises himself by villainy. Tall, strong.

A مجع *majɛ*, (v. n. of مجع) Being impudent, immodest. *Mijɛ*, Foolish, insane. One who, when set down, will hardly take the trouble to rise.

A مجعار *mijɛār*, (A man) of a dry nature.

A مجعب *mijɛab*, A powerful wrestler, who throws down his antagonists, but is not thrown down himself.

A مجعة *majɛat*, (v. n. of مجع) Eating dates with milk, or eating dates and drinking milk upon them. *Majɛat*, *mujɛat*, or *mujaɛat*, Foolish, ignorant. *Mijɛat*, *mujaɛat*, or *mijaɛat*, Foolish (woman). *Mujɛat* or *majɛat*, One who, when set down, can hardly rise. *Mujɛat*, *mujaɛat*, *majiɛat*, or *mijaɛat*, Immodest (woman).

A مجعثن *mujaɛsan*, Compact.

A مجعّد *mujaɛɛad*, Thick (pottage). *Mujaɛɛid*, One who curls hair.

A مجعر *majɛar*, The fundament of a bird.

A مجعرة *majɛarat*, Any thing which causes a drying up of the moisture of the body.

A مجعل *majɛal*, (v. n. of جعل) Putting, placing. Doing, constituting, appointing. *Mujɛil*, A fixer or payer of wages (جعل *juɛl*). One who takes a pot off the fire (with the cloth جعال *jiɛāl*). (A bitch) in heat. (Water) infected by dead beetles. (A country) swarming with beetles (جعل *juɛal*).

A مجعم *majɛam*, A refuge. *Mujɛim*, A tearer up.

A مجعول *majɛūl*, Constituted, affected. Made.

A مجعوم *majɛūm*, Destitute of appetite.

A مجفاة *mujfāt*, (Cattle) turned from pasture, not suffered to graze.

A مجفر *majfar*, Anti-aphrodisiacal (food). *Mujfar*, Large-bellied (horse). *Mujfir*, One who leaves off (work). A dismisser or abandoner (of a friend).

A مجفّر *mujaffar*, Stinking-bodied (man).

A مجفرة *majfarat*, (Food) which checks venery, anti-venereal. Fasting.

A مجفّف *mujaffaf*, Dried. *Mujaffif*, Desiccative.

A مجفّفة *mujaffifat* (pl. مجفّفات *mujaffifāt*) Any thing acrid which dries up. A desiccative.

A مجفل *mujfil*, Hard-blowing (wind).

A مجفّن *mujaffin*, Much addicted to venery.

A مجفوّ *majfūw*, (or مجفيّ *majfiy*) Injured.

A مجفنظ *mujfanizz*, On the point of death.

A مجكر *mujkir*, A haggler, stickler for a price.

A مجل *majl* or *majal*, (v. n. of مجل) Blistering or contracting serous pustules (as the hand from hard labour). Becoming hard and well (a hoof that had been cut by a stone). Collecting between the skin and the flesh (water). *Majl*, (pl. of مجلة *majlat*) Thin skins covering watery blisters. *Mijl*, Cattle swelled with repletion.

A مجلّ *mujill*, One who reveres, magnifies, or considers as illustrious and estimable. The produce of a single birth. Who gives much, or shews a great deal. (See اجلال *ijlāl*.)

A مجلّا *mujalla'*, Polished, furbished, rendered clear and bright. Illustrated, manifested.

A مجلاح *mijlāh*, Hardy (she-camel).

A مجلب *mujlib*, Clamorous, noisy. One who bends or goes towards. A follower and driver (of a horse). (A wound) covered with a thin skin whilst healing. One who covers (the wooden frame of a camel's saddle with moist leather). A helper. (See اجلاب *ijlāb*.)

A مجلّب *mujallib*, Very noisy. Loud (thunder).

A مجلبة *majlabat*, An attracting cause.

A مجلّبة *mujallibat*, A scold, a termagant.

A مجلة *majlat*, (pl. مجال *mijāl* and مجل *majl*) Thin skin covering a watery blister or pustule.

A مجلّة *majallat*, (pl. مجالّ *majāll*) A book (especially of abstract science).

A مجلجب *mujaljib*, Collected, thronged (camels).

A مجلجل *mujaljal*, Rumbling (thunder-cloud). Extremely clever, faultless. (A camel) that has attained his full strength. (A camel) around whose neck little bells are suspended. *Mujaljil*, Who vibrates with the hand or finger (the strings of an instrument). Thundering (cloud). Very loud-voiced, who can be heard to a great distance. A lord, prince, or powerful man. Bold, brave. Great, immense (numbers).

A مجلّح *mujallah*, Eaten up (pasture). *Mujallih*, Voracious.

A مجلخدّ *mujlakhidd*, One who throws or stretches himself upon the ground.

A مجلد *mijlad*, (pl. مجاليد *majālīd*) A leathern strap with which hired mourners strike their cheeks.

A مجلّد *mujallad*, (A book) bound in leather. A volume, tome. (A bone) whereon nothing is left save the skin. A certain quantity of a load known in weight and measure. A horse callous to the lash. *Mujallid*, A book-binder. A skinner, flayer (of a camel).

A مجلّدة *mujalladat*, One book; a bound volume. (A bone) covered only with skin.

A مجلّز *mujalliz*, One who folds, wraps round, strengthens the handle of a knife, by binding it with the nerve of a camel's neck. Who lays or lets down. One who stretches out.

A مجلس *majlas*, (v. n. of جلس) Sitting down. *Majlis*, (or مجلسة *majlisat*) (pl. مجالس *majālis*) An assembly, congregation, convention, congress, council, consistory, conference, convivial meeting, conversation. Time and place of assembling. A judgment-seat, tribunal. مجلس حكومت *majlisi hukūmat*, A judgment-hall. مجلس رقص *majlisi raks*, A ball-room; a ball. *Mujlis*, One who causes to sit down.

P مجلس افروز *majlis-afroz*, (Banquet-illuminating) Wax-lights. Wine. Name of a note in music.

A مجلسي *majlisī*, An assessor.

A مجلعبّ *mujlaɛibb*, Passing away; past. Wicked. A stream collecting much.

A مجلّف *mujallaf*, Destroyed, ruined. Any thing torn from the side of another. That of which something remains. (A man) whose cattle and effects are destroyed by a murrain or other calamity. *Mujallif*, (A severe season) destructive to cattle.

A مجلّل *mujallil*, (A cloud) which wets the earth generally. Whatever completely covers or envelopes.

A مجلنديٰ *mujlanda'*, Conquering; superior.

A مجلنظيٰ *mujlanza'*, Laid on the back with the feet raised.

A مجلوّ *majlūw*, Polished, splendid, bright. مرآت مجلوّة *mir,āti majlūwa*, A clean or clear mirror.

A مجلوب *majlūb*, (A slave) led about for sale.

A مجلوّة *majlūwat*, A bride with unveiled face.

A مجلوت *majlūt*, Lank about the buttocks.

A مجلود *majlūd*, (v. n. of جلد) Being light, nimble (man). Covered with hoar frost.

A مجلوز *majlūz*, Compact in the body. Sound in judgment.

A مجلوف *majlūf*, Peeled. Burnt (bread).

A مجلوم *majlūm*, Shaved, shaven.

A مجلوة *majlūh*, (A house or tent) destitute of door or curtain.

A مجلىٰ *majla'*, (pl. مجالى *majālī*) The fore part (of the head), which is most liable to become bald. *Mijla'*, Baldness from the forehead to the crown. *Mujlī*, A wanderer, exile. One who sends into exile. Eased of grief; liberated.

A مجلّيٰ *mujalla'*, Illustrated, manifested. Polished; furbished. Made clear, clean, or bright. *Mujallī*, A polisher. Looking with a keen eye (as an eagle at his prey). Who or what illustrates, explains, declares. A revealer of his thoughts. The horse which comes in first at a race.

A مجلّيات *mujalliyāt*, Detergent medicines.

A مجليق *mijlīk*, A laugher with open mouth.

A مجمّ *majamm*, The breast. واسع المجمّ *wāsiɛu'l majamm*, Wide in the chest. *Majamm* or *majimm*, The part of a well where the water lies. *Mujamm*, (A horse) set at liberty. *Mujimm*, Who fills (a measure), heaps (it) up. A giver of, or refresher with, rest. Approached, drawn near, present. (See اجمام *ijmām.*)

A مجمأ *majmas,* (A horse) marked with a plain white spot on the forehead.

A مجماج *majmāj,* Relaxed, enervated, flabby.

A مجمّة *majammat,* A cause of repose.

A مجمجة *majmajat,* (v. n. of مجمج Q) Confounding, not making distinct (letters). Stammering, telling a story in a confused manner.

A مجمد *mujmid,* One who refuses to engage in any competition or game from avarice. One who does little good. An umpire, arbitrator. One entering on the month جمادي *jumāda'.*

A مجمّد *mujammad,* Congealed, frozen.

A مجمر *mijmar,* (or مجمرة *mijmarat*) (pl. مجامر *majāmir*) A censer for incense, chafing-dish. Incense. P مجمر آتش *mijmari ātish,* A chafing-dish. The sun. مجمر نقرۀ پوش *mijmari nukra-posh,* The world. A *Mujmar,* (v. n. 4 of جمر) Making up, arranging (a fire). Incense. Wood of aloes. *Mujmir,* One who throws perfume in the fire. A perfumer of a garment. (A horse) leaping with the feet bound. The hard hoof of a horse.

A مجمّر *mujammir,* One who cuts away the pith of the palm-tree called جمّار *jummār.* Who throws the little stones or pebbles called جمار *jimār.*

A مجمرة *majmarat,* A smith's forge of clay.

A مجمّز *mujammiz,* One who rides a swift she-camel called جمّازة *jammāzat.*

A مجمع *majmaɛ* or *majmiɛ,* (pl. مجامع *majāmiɛ*) A place of assembly. A concourse, crowd, convention, congregation, meeting. A collection, heap, pile. A book of miscellanies, a magazine. مجمع النهرين *majmaɛu'n nahrayn,* Confluence of two rivers. *Mujmaɛ,* Collected, brought together. (Property) amassed, kept together. Resolved upon, undertaken, set about. Firm, decided, made up (opinion). *Mujmiɛ,* A collector, container. Who keeps secretly. A resolver, determiner. Barren (year). One who binds the udders of a camel round with a cloth.

A مجمّع *mujammaɛ,* Collected. Resolved, decreed. *Mujammiɛ,* Who collects diligently. Assembled for prayers on a Friday. A counter (of money).

A مجمعة *majmaɛat,* A place of meeting. A desert. A sand-hill. *Mujmaɛat,* The prayer called خطبه *khutba,* free from any gap, chasm, or flaw. فلاة مجمعة *falāt mujmiɛat,* A desert through which people travel in bodies (from fear of danger or losing the way).

A مجمعلة *mujamɛalat,* Knotty-fleshed (woman).

A مجمل *mujmal,* Collected into a small compass. A summary, compendium. *Mujmil,* One who collects what has been dispersed. One who sums up (an account). One who abounds in good actions. A melter of fat. An earnest seeker. Rich in camels.

A مجمّل *mujammil,* An adorner, beautifier, or able executer. One who, for a long while, keeps up a standing army.

A مجملاً *mujmalan,* In substance.

A مجمّم *mujammam,* One whose hair is brought together and tied in a knot.

A مجمّمة *mujammimat,* A woman who allows not her hair to hang down.

A مجموع *majmūɛ,* Collected, assembled, convened, contained. Clenched (fist). Content, tranquil. All, the whole, every one. مجموع بني آدم *majmūɛi banī ādam,* All the sons of Adam, mankind.

A مجموعا *majmūɛan,* Totally, on the whole.

A مجموعة *majmūɛat,* (fem.) Collected, assembled, contained. All, the whole. A collection, magazine, compendium, miscellany. A crowd, assembly. A tray. A compound perfume. A form in printing.

P مجموع دار *majmūɛ-dār,* One who checks or audits the account of the revenue-collector in each district (an Indian phrase). A record-keeper.

A مجمول *majmūl,* Predicate of a proposition.

A مجموم *majmūm,* Rested, refreshed, recruited.

A مجمهرة *mujamharat,* Firmly-built (she-camel).

A مجن *mujn,* (v. n. of مجن) Caring not what one says or does.

A مجنّ *mijann,* (pl. مجانّ *majānn*) A shield, a buckler. A lady's belt or leathern girdle. قلب له ظهر المجنّ *kalaba lahu zahra'l mijann,* He renounced his friendship. *Mujann,* Insane, frantic.

A مجنأ *mujnas,* A shield without any iron in it (so called from its convexity).

A مجنأة *mujnasat,* A grave.

A مجنب *majnab,* (v. n. of جنب) Leading at the side (a captive or a horse). *Majnab* or *mijnab,* Much, many, numerous, plentiful. *Mijnab,* A shield. A veil, curtain. The extreme parts of the countries bordering upon Arabia; also the frontiers of Arabia which march with them. A kind of door on which the gatherer of honey stands. A tool resembling a toothless comb. *Mujnab,* A shield. *Mujnib,* Foreign. Exposed to the south wind.

A مجنّب *mujannab,* (A horse) led at the side. *Mujannib,* One who leads (a horse or captive) at the side. Who or what renders averse, or causes to abstain. (A horse) whose foot turns inwards.

A مجنّبة *mujannabat,* Advance guard of an army.

A مجنّبتان *mujannibatāni,* The wings of an army.

A مجنّة *majannat,* Fury, insanity. A place where any thing is hid. A district haunted by demons. *Mijannat,* A shield. قلب مجنّته *kalaba mijannatahu,* He discarded shame, and did whatever he pleased, uncontrolled.

A مجنح *mujnih,* Inclining; one who gives a propensity towards, or a favourable opinion of.

A مجنّح *mujannah,* (In poetry) when, in the same distich or hemistich, words occur at the beginning and at the end which are anagrams to each other.

A مجنّد *mujannad,* Assembled, mustered (troops). *Mujannid,* One who assembles (an army).

A مجندل *mujandal,* Trampled, trodden. *Mujandil,* One who throws prostrate.

A مجنّز *mujanniz,* A layer of a corpse on a bier.

A مجنّس *mujannas,* Composed of different kinds. *Mujannis,* One who arranges in classes, or who classifies. One who renders homogeneous.

A مجنف *mijnaf,* Inclined, biased, leaning. *Mujnif,* One who deviates from the right way; unjust, unfaithful (in respect of a will or testament). One who detects such deviation.

A مجنّق *mujannik,* A hurler (of stones) from a balista (منجنيق *manjanīk*).

A مجنقة *majnakat,* (v. n. of مجنق Q) Hurling (stones) from a balista (منجنيق *manjanīk*).

A مجنّن *mujannin,* Maddening, dementating.

A مجنوب *majnūb,* (A horse) led by the side (جنب *jamb*), in opposition to مركوب *markūb,* which signifies one ridden. Affected with a pleurisy or pain in the side. Whatever is brought by the south wind (جنوب *janūb,* as rain, or change of air).

A مجنوبة *majnūbat,* A cloud propelled by the south wind.

A مجنوح *majnūh,* (A camel) whose ribs (جوانح *jawānih*) are broken by overloading.

A مجنوز *majnūz,* Covered. Collected. A corpse.

A مجنون *majnūn,* (pl. مجانين *majānīn*) Possessed by a demon. Foolish, insane, mad, dement, furious, outrageous. A fanatic. A maniac. A demoniac. Desperately in love. Tall (palm-tree). Name of a celebrated Eastern lover. مجنون وعاقل *majnūn u ɛākil,* The foolish and the wise.

A مجنونيّة *majnūnīyat,* Insanity. Demonianism.

A مجنّه *mujannah,* as طبق مجنّه *tabaki mujannah,* A tray, waiter, or dish made of Indian reeds.

A مجني *mujnī,* A gatherer of fruit. (A tree) which has ripe fruit ready for plucking. Ripe fruit. Ground abounding in fruits, corn, herbage, mushrooms, &c. Plentiful (herbage).

A مجنيّ *majnīy,* Gathered (fruit).

P مجو *majw,* A lentil.

A مجواب *mijwāb,* A cutting-instrument, knife.

A مجواد *mijwād,* The doer of an excellent thing; also the proclaimer or praiser of such an action.

A مجوب *mijwab,* An iron instrument for cleaving or tearing any thing asunder. Shears. A shield, buckler. A fire-grate. A chafing-dish.

A مجوّب *mujawwab,* (A field) partially watered by rain. *Mujawwib,* A bringer, bearer. One who makes a shirt open at the breast (جيب *jayb*).

A مجوبة *majūbat,* An answer.

A مجوجن *mujawjan,* Stinking water.

A مجوح *mijwah,* A universal destroyer.

A مجود *majūd,* Parched with thirst. (A field) well watered by rain. *Mujūd,* (v. n. of مجد) Finding a pasture plenteous in grass, and feeding almost to satiety (camels).

A مجوّد *mujawwad*, Smitten with love. Full of desire. Well made or done. *Mujawwid*, Learned, good. An elegant writer; a lover of learning, rhetorician, philologist. A player on an instrument. A singer, especially one who intones the Kur'ān. A payer (of money). Fast-going (horse).

A مجوّر *mujawwar*, Thrown down, levelled with the ground. *Mujawwir*, One who accuses of injustice. A beater. One who levels with the ground. One who throws down or away.

A مجوّز *mujawwaz*, Lawful, or deemed so: tolerated. *Mujawwiz*, One who holds, proves, or asserts to be lawful. One who dismisses, or permits to pass or go.

A مجوس *majūs*, (pl. of مجوسيّ *majūsiy*) Magi, fire-worshippers. Small-eared.

P مجوسی *majūse*, One worshipper of fire.

A مجوسيّ *majūsiy*, (or مجوسي *majūsī*) (pl. مجوس *majūs*) A fire-worshipper: a follower of Zoroaster.

A مجوسيّة *majūsiyat*, The religion of the Magi.

A مجوّع *mujawwiʿ*, One who allows (another) to hunger, or who famishes (him).

A مجوعة *majwaʿat*, Hunger, need, famine.

A مجؤف *majʾuf*, Timid, fearful.

A مجوف *majūf*, Thick, large-bellied.

A مجوّف *mujawwaf*, Hollowed. Concave, vaulted. Hollow, empty (fellow). (A horse) white or speckled about the belly. *Mujawwif*, One who hollows out or makes concave (اجوف *ajwaf*).

A مجوّق *mujawwak*, Crooked-jawed. *Mujawwik*, One who collects or assembles together. One who cries out to.

A مجول *mijwal*, A shield. A kind of small vest worn by girls. Ornamental rings (worn by women round their ankles). Good money. Silver. A silver crescent in the middle of a necklace. An amulet or any similar thing for averting evil. A white cloth held in the hand by him to whom the gaming arrows are given. The onager, wild ass. *Mujūl*, (v. n. of مجل) Blistering or contracting serous pustules (as the hand from hard labour).

A مجوّل *mujawwil*, A great traveller, vagrant.

A مجون *mujūn*, (v. n. of مجن) Not caring about what one says or does. Being hard and thick. Boldness, impudence, brazenness.

A مجؤوث *majʾūs*, Terrified.

A مجؤوف *majʾūf*, Terrified. Hungry.

A مجوهر *mujawhar*, Adorned, set with gems.

A مجوي *mujwī*, One who hangs a kettle.

P مجّه *mujja*, The plant برغست *barghast*, resembling spinage, generally found on the banks of running streams.

A مجهار *mijhār*, One who speaks openly, clearly.

A مجهاض *mijhāz*, (A camel) used to miscarry.

A مجهب *mijhab*, Shameless.

A مجهجه *mujahjah*, A lion.

A مجهد *mujhad*, Longed for, desired. *Mujhid*, One who overloads (a horse). A vexer, disturber, injurer. The owner of a tired and overloaded beast. A soaker, dissolver. Desirous of meat; one who eats much and often. Who does a thing violently. Very grey, hoary. A quick goer. (See اجهاد *ijhād*.)

A مجهدة *majhadat*, A scarce, distressing season.

A مجهر *mijhar*, Aloud, open, or clear speaker. *Mujhar*, Sonorous, clear, distinct (speech, tone). *Mujhir*, One who speaks openly and publicly. An intoner.

A مجهز *mujhiz*, Quick, sudden (death).

A مجهّز *mujahhaz*, Endowed. Despatched. *Mujahhiz*, A decker (of a bride), fitter out (of a traveller), furnisher (of a funeral).

A مجهش *mujhish*, A leaper, riser up. A trembler, fearer, dreader. One who orders to make haste. Ready to cry.

A مجهض *mujhaz*, An abortive camel's colt. *Mujhiz*, Overcoming, superior. One who causes to make haste or to retire quickly. A remover. (pl. مجاهيض *majāhīz*) Miscarrying (camel).

A مجهل *majhal*, A desert without way-marks (literally, a place of ignorance). *Mijhal*, (or مجهلة *mijhalat*) A piece of wood for stirring new wine. Ignorant. A lion.

A مجهلة *majhalat*, Any thing indicative of ignorance. A cause of ignorance (جهل *jahl*).

A مجهم *mujhim*, Entered upon the middle or latter part of the night. (A sky) without rain.

P مجّه وا *mujja-wā*, A dish made of the herb مجّه *mujja* or برغست *barghast*.

A مجهود *majhūd*, Oppressed with labour or vexation, fatigued. (Food) longed for. Work, labour, trouble, endeavour, study, care. Milk from which the butter has been extracted.

A مجهور *majhūr*, Cleansed, cleaned. (A well) built, frequented. Strongly pronounced. Any of the letters contained in the artificial words, ظل قوّ ربض اذغز جند مطيع *zil, kawwin, rabaz, izghaz, jund, mutiʿ*.

A مجهول *majhūl*, (pl. مجاهيل *majāhīl*) Unknown. The passive voice. *Majhūl* is a term applied to the letters و *wāw* and ي *yā*, when the former has the sound of "o" in "stone," and the latter that of "e" in "there." مجهول مطلق *majhūli mutlak*, Very indolent or useless. مجهول النسب و نا معلوم الحسب *majhūlu'n nasab wa nā maʿlūmu'l hasab*, Unknown by birth and profession (or character).

A مجهولی *majhūlī*, Ignorance.

A مجهوليّة *majhūliyat*, Name of a sect.

A مجهی *mujhī*, Open (road). Serene, cloudless (sky). (A tent) destitute of a curtain. Who or what comes out, apparent. Stingy, giving nothing.

A مجهّی *mujahhī*, An enlarger, extender.

A مجهية *mujhiyat*, (A woman) not conceiving, and going away from (her husband).

A مجی *majī*, (or مجيّ *majiy*) (v. n. of جاء for جيأ) Coming, arriving. Bringing. Arrival.

A مجيّأ *mujayyaʾ*, One who stools during coition. Premature in effusion or consummation.

A مجيّأة *mujayyaʾat*, A woman whose natural passages have become one from too frequent intercourse with men; burst. (There are, in Arabic, several words having this signification.)

A مجيب *mujīb*, One who listens to, grants, accepts, takes well, humours, complies with, consents, or gives an answer. Obedient. An auditor. Easily-milked (teat).

A مجيّب *mujayyib*, A maker of a جيب *jayb*, i.e. collar or breast (of a shirt or other garment).

A مجيح *mujīh*, Ruinous, destructive.

P مجيد *majīd*, A quick step.

A مجيد *majīd*, Glorious, honourable, noble. High, exalted. Sacred. ربّ مجيد *rabbi majīd*, Most glorious God. *Mujīd*, Possessed of a swift horse (جواد *jawād*). One who says or does any thing good or excellent. Near, at hand (death).

P مجيدن *majīdan*, To wash, clean. To fry. To seize, snatch. To pluck, twitch, pinch. To walk fast.

A مجير *mujīr*, A protector from oppression.

A مجيّر *mujayyar*, Small and deep (cistern); or one plastered with lime (جير *jayr*).

A مجيز *mujīz*, A permitter, giver of leave, approver. A granter of liberty, giver of quarter. A lord. A helper. A guardian of an orphan. A privileged slave, one allowed to trade. One who leaves behind, relinquishes. Who cuts off. Who allows to come and go. Who sends, transmits; dismisses; gives way; causes to penetrate. Passing away (life). One who undertakes to supply or refresh with water.

A مجيّش *mujayyish*, One who levies an army.

A مجيّض *mujayyiz*, Who declines, turns from.

A مجيع *majīʿ*, A dish of milk and dates. *Mujīʿ*, Starved. One who allows to starve.

A مجيف *mujīf*, Hollow. (A blow or stab) which penetrates to the interior. One who shuts.

A مجيل *mujīl*, One who causes to go round: who distributes in a circle, gives all around.

A مجيّم *mujayyim*, A writer of the letter ج *jīm*.

A مجينق *mujaynik*, (dim. of منجنيق *manjanīk*) A small balista.

A مجيء *majīʾ*, (v. n. of جاء for جيأ) Coming, arriving. Happening, coming to pass.

A مجيّ *majʾiy*, (A leathern bottle) sewed with a double seam on either side.

P مچاچنگ *machāchang*, A dildo.

P مچرگ *macharg*, Ordering to work gratuitously.

P مچفس *machafs*, Do not stick.

P مچك *machak*, A lentil. Mountain-almond.

P مچگان *muchagān*, Eyelashes.

T مچلکه *muchalka*, A bond, note of hand, agreement, recognizance, engagement, promise.

P مچه *mucha*, An eyelash.

P مچّه *muchcha*, Name of a wild pot-herb resembling spinage.

P مچچه وا *muchcha-wā*, Soup of the herb مچچه.

P مچيدن *machīdan* or *michīdan*, To walk with a pompous or graceful air. To see.

A مح *mahh*, (v. n. of مح) Being worn (garment). A worn-out old garment. *Muhh*, The yolk of an egg. The purest part of any thing.

P محابا *muhābā*, Caution, care. Kind behaviour. An abatement in price. Dissimulation. A market for small wares. بي محابا *bī muhābā*, Without respect (of persons or circumstances).

A محاباء *muhābā*, (or محاباة *muhābāt*) (v. n. 3 of حبا for حبو) Shewing respect of persons, winking at, conniving. Aiding. Distinguishing by special favour. Vying with in acts of liberality. Respect, regard. Friendship, affection. محاباة الحق *muhābātu'l hatīy*, Dregs or rind of Indian dates.

A محابّة *muhābbat*, (or محاببة *muhābabat*) (v. n. 3 of حبّ) Loving, shewing regard or friendship.

A محابر *mahābir*, (pl. of محبر) Ink-horns.

A محابس *mahābis*, (pl. of محبس) Coverlets.

A محابسة *muhābasat*, An imprisoning, confining.

A محابض *mahābiz*, (pl. of محبض *mahbaz*) Cross-sticks in a hive to which the combs are fixed.

A محابيب *mahābīb*, (pl. of محبوب *mahbūb* or محبوبة *mahbūbat*) Lovers. Friends. Mistresses.

A محابيس *mahābīs*, (pl. of محبوس) Prisoners.

A محاتة *mahātat*, (v. n. of محت) Becoming hard. Being very hot (a day).

A محاتنة *muhātanat*, (v. n. 3 of حتن) Being equal or well-matched.

A محاج *mihāj*, (v. n. 3 of محج) Granting delay for the payment of a debt. Delaying payment.

A محاجّ *mahājj*, (pl. of محجّة) Clear, open roads.

A محاجاة *muhājāt*, (v. n. 3 of حجا for حجو) Propounding riddles to each other.

A محاجّة *muhājjat*, (v. n. 3 of حجّ) Pleading a cause. Bringing proof or arguments (حجّة *hujjat*).

A محاجر *mahājir*, Secret places. (pl. of محجر *mahjir*) Sockets, environs, or corners of eyes. (pl. of محجر *mahjir* or *mihjar*) The environs of a town.

A محاجزة *muhājazat*, (v. n. 3 of حجز) Restraining, taking one from another (to prevent fighting).

A محاجف *muhājif*, One who uses a leathern shield (حجفة *hajafat*). An opponent, combatant.

A محاجفة *muhājafat*, (v. n. 3 of حجف) Opposing, hindering, repelling.

P محاجم *mahājim*, Name of a certain antidote.

A محاجم *mahājim*, (pl. of محجم *mihjam*) Cupping-glasses. (pl. of محجمة *mahjamat*) Parts to which the cupping-glass is applied.

A محاجن *mahājin*, (pl. of محجن *mihjan*) Clubs with curved heads.

A محاجي *muhājī*, A propounder of riddles.

A محاح *mahāh*, Sourish land. *Muhāh*, Hunger.

A محّاح *mahhāh*, A liar, a deceiver. One who soothes and pleases by fair words.

A محادّ *muhādd*, A hinderer, opposer. Contiguous, adjacent, bordering.

A محادّة *muhāddat*, (v. n. 3 of حدّ) Hindering, preventing, opposing, resisting. Enraging. Numbering. Adjoining, being contiguous.

A محادثة *muhādasat*, (v. n. 3 of حدث) Conversing, discoursing together. Polishing, furbishing. Conversation, narration.

A محادلة *muhādalat*, A wrestling, a striving with.

A محاديك *muhādika*, Go on prosperously.

A محاذاة *muhāzāt*, An answering to; a facing.

A محاذرة *muhāzarat*, (v. n. 3 of حذر) Being cautious of each other. Caution.

A محاذي *muhāza'*, Opposite.

A محاذير *mahāzir*, Cautions. Alarms.

A محار *mahār*, A place to which one returns. *Mahār*, (or محارة *mahārat*) A return, a coming back.

A محارب *muhārib*, A warrior, combatant.

A محاربة *muhārabat*, (v. n. 3 of حرب) Fighting, waging war. Opposing. War, battle, combat.

P محاربه كردن *muhāraba kardan*, (or جنگ و محاربه كردن *jang u muhāraba kardan*) To war, to fight.

A محارة *mahārat*, (pl. محارات *mahārāt*) A shell, or any thing similar (as a bone). The shoulder-joint. The palate. A turning-place. The hollow of the ear. The part lying between the excrescence نسر *nasr* and the fore part of the hoof. A sort of travelling-litter. A line, stripe. Side, tract, quarter.

A محارد *mahārid*, Lips of men, camels, or horses. *Muhārid*, (or محاردة) (A camel) giving little milk.

A محاردة *muhāradat*, (v. n. 3 of حرد) Having little milk (a camel). Being scarce of rain (a year).

A محارز *muhāriz*, Keeper, guardian, governor. محارز حصن *muhārizi hisn*, Governor of a fort.

A محارزة *muhārazat*, (v. n. 3 of حرز) Jesting, joking in a manner approaching to raillery and abuse.

A محارسة *muhārasat*, A keeping, preserving.

A محارشة *muhārashat*, (v. n. 3 of حرش) Exasperating, irritating, setting by the ears.

A محارضة *muhārazat*, (v. n. 3 of حرض) Continuing at, dwelling upon (any work). Darting at each other arrows untrimmed and pointless.

A محارف *muhāraf*, Unfortunate. Prohibited, debarred, excluded.

A محارفة *muhārafat*, (v. n. 3 of حرف) Being destitute of victuals; finding difficulty in buying any. Requiting, repaying. Being cut off from all comfort or enjoyment. Inserting into a wound the probe called محراف *mihrāf*.

A محارقة *muhārakat*, (v. n. 3 of حرق) Lying with (a woman) on (her) side.

A محارم *mahārim*, Things unlawful. Dangerous times. (pl. of محرّم *muharram*) Months of Muharram. (pl. of محرمة *mahramat* or *mahrumat*) Wives. محارم الليل *mahārimu'l layl*, Dangers of the night (by which the timid are deterred from travelling).

A محارن *mahārin*, (Bees) sticking to honey.

A محاريب *mahārīb*, Jewish oratories. High altars. Upper parlours.

A محاريم *mahārīm*, (pl. of محرّم) Muharrams.

A محارين *mahārīn*, Honeys. (pl. of محران *mihrān*) Cotton-seeds. Bees adhering to the cross-sticks in the hive.

A محاز *mahāz*, (v. n. of محز) Lying with.

A محازبة *muhāzabat*, (v. n. 3 of حزب) Confederating, joining one's self to a party (حزب *hizb*).

A محازّة *muhāzzat*, (v. n. 3 of حزّ) Endeavouring earnestly after. Curiously prying or using every effort to get a knowledge of.

A محازم *mahāzim*, (pl. of محزم *mahzim*) The girth-places in animals.

A محاسب *muhāsib*, A keeper or settler of accounts. An examiner, auditor of accounts. Engaged together in calculation.

A محاسبة *muhāsabat*, (v. n. 3 of حسب) Reckoning with, calling to account. Considering attentively. Computation, calculation, adjustment of accounts. Arithmetic. P محاسبه كردن *muhāsaba kardan*, To compute, make up, or settle accounts.

P محاسبه دار *muhāsaba-dār*, One whose accounts are under scrutiny.

P محاسبه طلب *muhāsaba-talab*, One demanding a settlement of accounts.

A محاسن *mahāsin*, (pl. of حسن *husn*) Good works, laudable actions, virtues, merits. Benefits. The comely parts of the body, personal charms. Beauties. The beard and mustachios, or whiskers.

A محاسنة *muhāsanat*, (v. n. 3 of حسن) Boasting, glorying of goodness or beauty.

P محاسن شماري *mahāsin-shumārī*, A funeral oration or eulogy.

A محاش *mahāsh*, Goods, effects, furniture. *Mahāsh* or *mihāsh* People of different tribes assembling and entering into a league or covenant around a fire. *Muhāsh*, Burnt (bread) or roasted meat.

A محاشّ *mahāshsh*, (pl. of محشّة) Podices.

A محاشاة *muhāshāt*, (v. n. 3 of حشي) Excepting (any thing) out of a number.

A محاشنة *muhāshanat*, (v. n. 3 of حشن) Speaking opprobriously, provoking by reproaches.

A محاشيّ *mahāshī*, Coarse, rough garments.

A محاشي *mahāshī*, (pl. of محشي *mihsha'*) Stuffings or pads used by women to give a swelling appearance to the breast or hips.

A محاص *mahās*, (v. n. of حاص for حيص) Turning away from, swerving. Fleeing.

A محّاص *mahhās*, Shining, flashing (lightning), glittering (vapour). A desert requiring much exertion to cross.

A محاصّ *muhāss*, One who divides a thing with another; who takes his حصّة *hissat* (share).

A محاصّة *muhāssat*, A dividing with another.

A محاصر *mahāsir*, The nearest roads. *Muhāsir*, A besieger. صفوف محاصرين *sufūfi muhāsirīn*,

The ranks (or lines) of the besiegers.

A محاصرة *muhāsarat*, (v. n. 3 of حصر) Surrounding, besieging, besetting, investing, beleaguring, sitting down before a fort. Circumscribing. A siege, circumvallation, blockade.

A محاض *mahāz*, (v. n. of حاض for حيض) Having her courses (a woman). *Mihāz*, (pl. of محض *mahz*) Milks unmixed with water.

A محاضة *muhāzzat*, (v. n. 3 of حضّ) Instigating, compelling (each one his companion).

A محاضر *mahāzir*, Comers to water. (pl. of محضر *mahzar*) Inhabited places, quarters. Public documents. *Muhāzir*, Ready, present; who stands before you.

A محاضرة *muhāzarat*, (v. n. 3 of حضر) Appearing before, or against, another; pleading against or arraigning one (before a judge). Conversing, discussing, disputing. Endeavouring to excel in number or strength. Overcoming and taking away another's right. Sitting opposite with joined knees. Selling fruits before they are ripe (*i. e.* disposing of future property for present wants, a thing forbidden by the Muhammadan law).

A محاضن *mahāzin*, (pl. of محضن *mahzan* or *mahzin*) The nests of hens sitting.

A محاط *mahāt*, An enclosure, fold. *Muhāt*, Surrounded. Comprehended. Known.

A محاطب *muhātib*, (A camel) eating thorns.

A محاظيّ *mahāziy*, (pl. of محظيّة *mahziyat*) Concubines, kept mistresses.

A محافاة *muhāfāt*, A disputing, a contending.

A محافد *mahāfid*, (pl. of محفد *mahfid*) Roots of camels' bunches. Stripes upon linen. Palaces.

A محافر *mahāfir*, (pl. of محفر *mihfar* or محفرة *mihfarat*) Spades, implements for digging.

A محافزة *muhāfazat*, (v. n. 3 of حفز) Sitting opposite another with joined knees. Being near.

A محافظ *muhāfiz*, A defender, keeper, guardian, commander, governor, warden. قوت محافظه *kūwati muhāfiza*, The retentive powers, memory.

A محافظة *muhāfazat*, (v. n. 3 of حفظ) Preserving, keeping in custody. Persevering in, being assiduous. Prohibiting, repelling. Being cautious, abstaining. Custody, preservation, guardianship, protection, observation. Shame, a sense of honour.

A محافل *mahāfil*, (pl. of محفل *mahfil*) Assemblies. *Muhāfil*, Careful of one's reputation.

A محافه *muhāfa*, (a corruption of محفّه *mihaffa*) A litter in which women travel.

A محاق *ma, mi*, or *muhāk*, Wane of the moon. The three last nights of the lunar month; the dark period between the old and the new moon, when she is seen neither morning nor evening.

A محاقّ *muhākk*, Cattle unproductive the past year, and which have not given milk. An opponent, antagonist at law.

A محاقّة *muhākkat*, (v. n. 3 of حقّ) Contending. Contention at law about one's own rights. Hostility.

A محاقل *mahākil*, (pl. of محقلة *mahkalat*) Sown fields, arable lands. *Muhākil*, A sower.

A محاقلة *muhākalat*, (v. n. 3 of حقل) Selling corn before being ripe or in the ear. Receiving winnowed or clean grain in payment. Letting a field for cultivation for a third or other part of the produce. The sale of corn before ripe or in the ear, in exchange for a like quantity of wheat by guess, which kind of sale was prohibited by Muhammad.

A محاكاة *muhākāt*, (in Persian محاكا *muhākā*) (v. n. 3 of حكي) Relating, telling. Resembling, being like. Imitating, mimicking, saying or doing the words or acts of another. Tying (a knot) firm.

A محاكة *mahākat*, A weaver's shop.

A محاكّة *muhākkat*, (v. n. 3 of حكّ) Opposing, resisting. Rubbing sides together.

A محاكدة *muhākadat*, A leaning upon, relying.

A محاكرة *muhākarat*, A litigating, a disputing.

A محاكمة *muhākamat*, (v. n. 3 of حكم) Citing before the judge (حاكم *hākim*).

A محاكي *muhākī*, An imitator, mimic, mocker. Talking (bird, as a parrot, starling, &c.).

A محال *mahāl*, (v. n. of محل) Informing against one before the king. Fraud, art, machination. A large pulley used in drawing water. The middle of the back, the vertebræ. Power. A kind of female ornament. (pl. of محالة *mahālat*) The joints of a camel's back. Large pulleys used for drawing water. *Mihāl*, (v. n. 3 of محل) Deceiving. Seeking to effect by stratagem. Displaying enmity. Litigating. Destroying. Endeavouring to deceive. Examining into, looking to the end of any business. Contending with another for superiority in strength. Management. Exertion, industry. Power, strength. Deceit, fraud. Dispute, contention. Enmity. Pain, punishment. Vengeance. Destruction. Michael, a proper name. *Muhāl*, Impossible, absurd. محال مطلق *muhāli mutlak*, Very difficult, absolutely impossible, quite absurd.

A محالّ *mahāll*, (pl. of محلّة *mahāllat*) Streets, squares, courts, wards, places, houses, districts, departments. Land or public fund producing a revenue to the government: as, P نمك محال *namak-mahāl*, Duties arising from salt. محال آلتمغا سركار *mahāli āltamghā sarkār*, Lands held in free gift from government. A (pl. of محلّ *mahall*) Places where one alights or rests. *Muhāll*, One who goes down with another to any place, who lives along with him.

A محالاة *muhālāt*, (v. n. 3 of حلي) Playing, jesting, joking with. Behaving kindly.

A محالات *muhālāt*, (pl. of محال) Impossibilities.

A محالبة *muhālabat*, (v. n. 3 of حلب) Milking together (with another). Assisting one another.

A محالة *mahālat*, (v. n. of محل) Being barren for want of rain. (pl. محال *mahāl* and محاول *mahāwil*) A large pulley for drawing water. Vertebræ of a camel's back. Machination, fraud, craft. Power. A plank or scaffold on which a plasterer stands. لا محالة *lā mahālata*, There is now no escape, it becomes necessary; of necessity; there is no remedy. Undoubtedly.

A محالّة *muhāllat*, (v. n. 3 of حلّ) Going down with another to any place; living together.

P محالدار *mahāl-dār*, An officer appointed under the cutwal (police-magistrate) for the prevention of crimes and abuses: a policeman: ward-beadle.

A محالف *muhālif*, A confederate, sworn ally.

A محالفة *muhālafat*, (v. n. 3 of حلف) Entering into an agreement, confirming by oath. Serving continually, diligently attending on.

A محالق *mahālik*, (pl. of محلق *mihlak*) Razors.

P محال گوئي *muhāl-gūī*, A talking of nonsense.

A محاليد *mahālīd*, Camels, whose milk goes off.

A محامّ *muhāmm*, Stedfast, constant.

A محاماة *muhāmāt*, (v. n. 3 of حمي) Prohibiting, commanding to abstain. Repelling, guarding, defending. Paying attention (to a guest).

A محامّة *muhāmmat*, (v. n. 3 of حمّ) Asking, requiring. Approaching, going near.

A محامد *mahāmid*, (pl. of محمدة *mahmidat*) Laudable actions or qualities.

A محامقة *muhāmakat*, (v. n. 3 of حمق) Assisting, abetting, countenancing in any act of folly.

A محامل *mahāmil*, (pl. of محمل *mahmil*) Those things which carry the loads on either side of a camel. Velvets, satins (especially those which are sent annually to the temple at Mecca). Camel-litters in which females travel. (pl. of محمل *mihmal*) Sword-belts. Baldricks. محامل الذكر *mahāmilu'z zakar*, Veins at the root, or the skin of the penis.

A محاملة *muhāmalat*, (v. n. 3 of حمل) Lifting up together, or conjointly.

A محامليّ *mahāmiliy*, A maker of those things wherein camels' loads are carried, and which are called محامل *mahāmil*.

A محانة *mahānat*, The bend of a river.

A محانث *mahānis*, Iniquitous, sinful events.

A محانق *mahānik*, (pl. of محنق) Lean (camels).

A محاني *mahānī*, (pl. of محنية *mahniyat*) Windings of a river. Curvatures, bends.

A محانيق *mahānīk*, Lean (camels). Fat (camels).

A محاوتة *muhāwatat*, (v. n. 3 of حات for حوت) Striving, contending with. Repelling, resisting. Consulting, deliberating, conferring together. Promising. Appointing a time and place for a sale.

A محاودة *muhāwadat*, (v. n. 3 of حاد for حود) Attacking frequently (fever).

A قلقت محاوره *kalikat mahāwiruhu*, His affairs were in confusion.

A محاورات *muhāwarāt*, (pl. of محاورة *muhāwarat*) Dialogues, conversations.

A محاورة *muhāwarat*, (v. n. 3 of حار for حور)

Holding a dialogue. Conversation, conference. A reply. Idiom, usage, common speech, phraseology. محاورهٔ بحث و جدل *muhāwara-i bahs u jadal*, A disputation, an animated discussion.

A محاوزة *muhāwazat*, (v. n. 3 of حاز for حوز) Conversing, mixing together. Treading, trampling. Commerce, business (with any one).

A محاوشة *muhāwashat*, (v. n. 3 of حاش for حوش) Instigating, exciting, provoking. Keeping out of the way of the rain of a thunder-cloud in whatever part it might chance to fall.

A محاوصة *muhāwasat*, (v. n. 3 of حاص for حوص) Looking amorously through half-shut eyes.

A محاوطة *muhāwatat*, (v. n. 3 of حاط for حوط) Leaving, quitting, retiring from. Coming round a person, seeking to obtain some advantage from him.

A محاول *mahāwil*, (pl. of محالة *mahālat*) Large pulleys for drawing water.

A محاولة *muhāwalat*, (v. n. 3 of حال for حول) Sharpening one's look, gazing steadily. Wishing, desiring, seeking.

A محاوي *mahāwī*, Collections, miscellanies.

A محاويج *mahāwīj*, Needy, indigent (persons).

A محايا *mahāyā'*, (pl. of محيا *mahyā'*) Times when, or places where, any one lives. Lives.

A محاياة *muhāyāt*, (v. n. 3 of حي) Resuscitating (a fire) by blowing. Nutriment for a child.

A محايدة *muhāyadat*, A shunning, an avoiding.

A محايص *muhāyis*, Diligent to entrap, astute, sly, guileful. Overpowering, overcoming.

A محايصة *muhāyasat*, (v. n. 3 of حاص for حيص) Seizing insidiously, overcoming by stratagem.

A محائض *mahāiz*, (pl. of محيضة *mahīzat*) Menstruous cloths.

A محايقة *muhāyakat*, A hating, an envying.

A محاينة *muhāyanat*, (v. n. 3 of حان for حين) Fixing certain (a time). Agreeing, bargaining by the hour, or time (حين *hīn*).

A محبّ *muhabb*, Beloved. *Muhibb*, One who loves, chooses, or prefers. Grain-producing (corn). Kneeling (camel). Distempered with fatigue or labour; short-breathed. Hurt, and lying down, and not rising until killed or cured. Restive, refractory (camel). A lover, friend. محبّ صادق *muhibbi sādik*, (or محبّ مخلص *muhibbi mukhlis*) A sincere friend (a mode of subscribing familiar letters).

A محبار *mihbār*, Quickly-producing (ground).

P محبّانه *muhibbāna*, Friendly, like a friend.

A محبّب *muhabbib*, One who makes a friend.

A محبّبة *muhabbabat*, The city of Madīna.

A محبّة *mahabbat*, Love, affection. Friendship, esteem, benevolence. محبّت مشاركه *mahabbatimushārika*, Mutual love. بالمحبّة *bi'l mahabbat*, Lovingly, affectionately. *Muhabbat*, The city of Madīna.

P محبّت آميز *mahabbat-āmez*, Friendly.

P محبّت نامه *mahabbat-nāma*, Friendly letter.

A محبجرّ *muhbajirr*, Thick.

A محبحب *muhabhib*, One who lives poorly.

A محبر *mihbar*, (pl. محابر *mahābir*) An ink-holder. *Muhbir*, A signer, marker. One who makes glad.

A محبّر *muhabbar*, Marked on the body with flea-bites. (Arrows) well-shaven and dight. Painted, printed (garment). *Muhabbir*, One who does (any thing) in an elegant and ornate style. Name of a certain Arabian poet.

A محبرة *mahbarat*, A cause of joy and gladness. *Mahbarat*, *mihbarat*, or *mahburat*, An ink-holder.

A محبّرة *muhabbarat*, (A sheep) in whose eye are black and white specks.

A محبرّة *mahburrat*, An ink-holder.

A محبرم *muhabram*, Pomegranate-soup.

A محبس *mahbas*, (v. n. of حبس) Keeping back, detaining. Imprisoning. Prohibition, hindrance. *Mahbis*, A prison. A pound, dam. *Mihbas*, An embroidered cover. Bed-furniture. A counterpane. *Muhbas*, Imprisoned. (A horse) bequeathed for pious uses. *Muhbis*, One who throws into prison. A devisor for pious uses, prohibiting alienation.

A محبّس *muhabbis*, One who lays a counterpane or coverlet on a bed. A detainer, preventer.

A محبّش *muhabbish*, A collector, gatherer.

A محبشة *muhbishat*, (A woman) who brings forth (a child) black as an Ethiop (حبش *habash*).

A محبض *mihbaz*, (pl. محابض *mahābiz*) A cross-stick in a bee-hive to which the combs are fixed; a stick with which they drive away the drones. A bow with which they separate cotton.

A محبّك *muhabbak*, Crisp or curly-haired. Striped (stuff).

A محبل *mahbal*, Time of conception; period of gestation. The first book. *Mahbil* or *mahbal*, The womb. The mouth of the womb. The vagina. *Muhbil*, One who impregnates: impregnating.

A محبّل *muhabbal*, Thick, bushy, curly (hair). A rope. *Muhabbil*, Productive of pregnancy.

A محبنطي *muhbantī*, Short, fat, big-bellied.

A محبنظي *muhbanza'*, Filled with rage, irate.

A محبوب *mahbūb*, Beloved, loved, liked, amiable. Affectionate. Lovely. Thrown into trouble. P محبوب قلوب عالميان *mahbūbi kulūbi ʻālamiyān*, Delight of mortal hearts. زر محبوب *zari mahbūb*, Purest gold. A امّ محبوب *umm mahbūb*, A serpent.

A محبوبة *mahbūbat*, (fem. of محبوب *mahbūb*) Beloved. A sweetheart, mistress, lovely woman. The city of Madīna.

A محبوبط *muhbawbat*, Ignorant, soon provoked.

A محبور *mahbūr*, Glad, happy. Marked on the skin by a flea-bite, &c. محبور الخاطر *mahbūru'l khātir*, Of a cheerful mind, good-humoured.

A محبوس *mahbūs*, Detained, arrested, confined, imprisoned. (A horse) bequeathed for pious uses.

P محبوسخانه *mahbūs-khāna*, A prison-house.

A محبوك *mahbūk*, Firmly woven. (A horse) strong, firm on his legs.

A محبول *mahbūl*, A wild beast for which a net has been laid, though it be not yet taken.

A محبون *mahbūn*, Dropsical.

A محبئنّ *muhbaʼinn*, Enraged, irate.

A محّة *muhhat*, The yolk of an egg.

A محت *maht*, (v. n. of محت) Enraging. Sultry (day). Hard. Vehement, excessive. (pl. محوت *muhūt* and محتاء *muhatā'*) Intelligent, ingenious, clever. Pure, sincere.

A محتات *mihtāt*, A palm-tree whose dates are scattered. *Muhtāt*, (A horse) compact, firmly knit.

A محتاج *muhtāj*, Necessitous, needy, indigent. In need of. محتاج اليه *muhtāj ilayhi*, The person or thing needed.

A محتاصة *muhtāsat*, Impervious (she-camel).

A محتاط *muhtāt*, Surrounded, besieged.

A محتال *muhtāl*, Subtle, crafty. A deceiver.

A محتالة *muhtālat*, A bawd, procuress.

A محتبس *muhtabas*, Contained, detained, imprisoned. *Muhtabis*, A restrainer, detainer. Refraining. Kept back, withheld. Strangurious. محتبس بنفسه *muhtabis bi nafsihi*, Possessed of self-controul.

A محتبك *muhtabak*, Well-woven. *Muhtabik*, A fastener, strengthener. One who draws his back and legs together with a bandage (حبكة *hubkat*).

A محتبل *muhtabal*, Caught in a net, netted. The foot-joint or pastern (of a horse). *Muhtabil*, One who hunts or catches with a net.

A محتبي *muhtabī*, One who binds or strings up his legs to his hams with a sash.

A محتتش *muhtatish*, Fierce, ready for fight.

A محتتن *muhtatin*, Correspondent, resembling.

A محتثث *muhtasas*, (or محتثّ *muhtass*) Instigated, excited. *Muhtasis*, An exciter, instigator.

A محتجّ *muhtajj*, An arguer, pleader, debater.

A محتجب *muhtajib*, Veiled, retired, secluded.

A محتجج *muhtajij*, A pleader of a cause. A bringer of proofs (حجّة *hujjat*).

A محتجر *muhtajir*, Stony (ground). One who constructs a chamber or closet (حجرة *hujrat*) for his own special use. (See احتجار *ihtijār*).

A محتجز *muhtajaz*, The girthing-place, the waist. *Muhtajiz*, One who fastens round the middle (a girdle or drawers). One who goes to حجاز *hijāz*, or Arabia Petræa. Assembled, gathered together.

A محتجزة *muhtajizat*, A palm-tree whose clusters of dates are in its centre.

A محتجم *muhtajam*, Swollen with blood. *Muhtajim*, One who applies the cupping-glass. A cupper. One who requires cupping.

A محتجن *muhtajin*, One who draws (a thing) towards himself with the hooked club محجن *mihjan*. One who scrapes (money) together and keeps (it).

A محتد *mahtid*, Root, origin. Nature.

A محتدّ *muhtadd*, Keen, vehement, fierce (in anger or in battle); precipitate, impetuous. Flight, escape, retreat. لا اجد منه محتدا *lā ajid minhu muh-*

taddan, I find no escape from it.

A محتدم *muhtadim*, Burning (fire); scorching (heat); scorchingly-hot (day). Filled with rage. (Blood) very red, inclining to black.

A محتذر *muhtazir*, Cautious, wary.

A محتذي *muhtazī*, An imitator, doing as another does. Fitted with shoes, shod.

A محيتر *muhtir*, Frugal, economical.

A محتر *muhattir*, One who provides a feast for the builders. One who fastens a skirt to a tent.

A محترب *muhtarib*, Engaged in mutual war.

A محترث *muhtaris*, A tiller, ploughman, husbandman. A gainer, earner.

A محترز *muhtariz*, Cautious, careful, wary.

A محترس *muhtaras*, Guarded. *Muhtaris*, One who guards against. A nocturnal sheep-stealer. محترس من مثله وهو حارس *muhtaris min mislihi wa huwa hāris*, One who defends himself from his fellow, whilst he is the more dangerous of the two.

A محترص *muhtaris*, Greedy. Pains-taking.

A محترف *muhtaraf*, A place where one earns by one's labour. *Muhtarif*, An artificer.

A محترفه *muhtarifa*, Tax on trades or professions. Duty on tea, paid by people of particular occupations.

A محترق *muhtarik*, Set on fire, burnt.

P محترق ساز *muhtarik-sāz*, Setting on fire.

A محترك *muhtarik*, One who sticks close to the withers (حارك *hārik*) of his camel.

A محترم *muhtaram*, Honoured, venerable, sacred, revered, respected. وزير محترم *wazīri muhtaram*, An honoured prime-minister. *Muhtarim*, One who maintains his honour (حرمة *hurmat*).

A محتزز *muhtaziz*, One who cuts in notches.

A محتزم *muhtazim*, Girt about with a rope. Tightly-girthed (horse). Clothed. Armed.

A محتزن *muhtazin*, Grieved, sad, amazed.

A محتسب *muhtasib*, A reckoner, a calculator, accountant. The superintendant of the police, who examines weights, measures, and provisions, and prevents unlawful games, drinking, and the like.

A محتسبي *muhtasibī*, Administration of the police, or the office of Muhtasib.

A محتش *muhattash*, Excited against.

A محتشد *muhtashid*, Prepared. One who withholds not aid, personal exertion, or money. Assembled together, present.

A محتشم *muhtasham*, Powerful, great, attended by many followers or clients. *Muhtashim*, Bashful (from respect).

A محتشي *muhtashī*, Filled, crammed, stuffed.

A محتشية *muhtashiyat*, (A woman) who wears artificial stuffings (called حشيّة *hashīya*) to give a protuberance to the bosom or hips.

A محتصد *muhtasid*, A reaper of corn.

A محتصر *muhtasir*, A lion.

A محتضر *muhtazar*, Nigh unto death, dying. *Muhtazir*, A hurter, injurer. One who comes in person, present. Arrived in town from the country or from a journey. Running (horse, youth, hind).

A محتضن *muhtazan*, Taken in the arms, embraced. Kept back (from business). The body, from the arm-pits to the short ribs. *Muhtazin*, One who takes in the arms, or embraces. A hinderer (from business). (A sheep) lying down.

A محتضئ *muhtazi'*, A kindler of a fire.

A محتطب *muhtatab*, A wood-pile, a place where wood for fuel is kept. *Muhtatib*, A gatherer of wood. (A camel) which feeds on dry thorns, twigs, or sticks. (See احتطاب *ihtitāb*.)

A محتظر *muhtazar*, Made up of branches into a fold for camels. *Muhtazir*, A builder of the fold called حظيرة *hazīrat*.

A محتظي *muhtazī*, Fortunate. Court-favourite.

A محتفد *muhtafid*, Sharp, keen (sword). Swift. Ready to serve and to obey.

A محتفر *muhtafar*, Dug, excavated, hollowed out. *Muhtafir*, A digger (of a well).

A محتفز *muhtafiz*, Tucked up and ready for work. (See احتفاز *ihtifāz*.)

A محتفظ *muhtafiz*, A preserver. Provoked to anger. Cautious.

A محتفف *muhtafif*, One who covers or wraps himself up (in a garment). One who eats whatever is on the table or in the pot. (See احتفاف *ihtifāf*.)

A محتففة *muhtafifat*, (A woman) who makes smooth (her face) by twitching out the hairs.

A محتفل *muhtafal*, A place or time of meeting; a council, assembly. *Muhtafil*, Assembled. One who takes care of, or gives attention to. (A channel) filled with water. Manifest. (See احتفال.)

A محتفن *muhtafin*, A seizer, a taker. A rooter up. (See احتفان *ihtifān*.)

A محتفئ *muhtafi'*, A tearer up, puller away of the papyrus plant (حفأ *hafa'*).

A محتفي *muhtafī*, Barefoot. A tearer up. A caresser. (See احتفاء *ihtifā'*.)

A محتقّ *muhtakk*, Straight stab, direct thrust.

A محتقب *muhtakib*, One who removes or puts away. One who stores up. (See احتقاب *ihtikāb*.)

A محتقد *muhtakid*, Deficient, failing (rain).

A محتقر *muhtakar*, Vile, base, mean. *Muhtakir*, One who looks upon as contemptible.

A محتقق *muhtakik*, Who hits fair and kills (prey). Slender, lank (horse). Wrangling, engaged in altercation. (See احتقاق *ihtikāk*.)

A محتقن *muhtakin*, One who labours under a retention of urine. (See احتقان *ihtikān*.)

A محتكر *muhtakir*, A forestaller, regrater.

A محتكك *muhtakik*, (A horse) rubbing (against a post). See احتكاك *ihtikāk*.)

A محتكم *muhtakim*, A ruler, a governor.

A محتكئ *muhtaki'*, One who ties a knot.

A محتكي *muhtakī*, Firm, steady, settled.

A محتلب *muhtalib*, A milker.

A محتلج *muhtalij*, A taker of his due.

A محتلز *muhtaliz*, A taker of his due.

A محتلط *muhtalit*, A swearer. Enraged, fiercely contentious. Quick, impetuous, restless. Confused in speech, disturbed in mind.

A محتلق *muhtalik*, A shaver (of the head).

A محتلل *muhtalil*, One who descends, alights off a journey, stays, and lives with.

A محتلم *muhtalim*, A dreamer. Polluted. Arrived at the age of puberty.

A محتمّ *muhtamm*, Solicitous, anxious, sad. Unable to sleep.

A محتمّة *muhtammat*, Sleepless (eye).

A محتمد *muhtamid*, Intensely hot (day). One who confers obligations.

A محتمس *muhtamis*, Pugnacious, fighting (cocks).

A محتمش *muhtamish*, Inflamed with rage. Rushing to battle, fighting (cocks).

A محتمل *muhtamal*, Suspected, conjectured. Suspicious, doubtful, possible, probable. Suffering patiently. Enraged. Kindled. *Muhtamil*, A taker up of a burden. One who takes upon himself. One who departs from the house. A buyer of a captive. Patient. Suspected, conjectured. Hoped for, probable. محتمل الضدّين *muhtamilu'z ziddayn*, Capable of a double (or contrary) interpretation.

A محتملات *muhtamilāt*, Suspicions. Possibilities.

A محتمي *muhtamī*, One who shuns or restrains himself; cautious, abstinent (sick man).

A محتنج *muhtanij*, Inclined. Bent.

A محتنك *muhtanik*, An overcomer, conqueror, subduer. A rooter up, extirpator. Expert, experienced, firm. (Locusts) devouring herbage. (See احتناك.)

A محتور *mahtūr*, One who sucks a very little at a time on account of scarcity.

A محتوش *mahtūsh*, Excited with joy and lively spirits. *Muhtawish*, (A band of hunters) driving in a body, frightening. Intercepting, surrounding.

A محتوم *mahtūm*, Fixed, decreed.

A محتوي *muhtawī*, Comprising; who or what comprises. A collector, assembler, comprehender, embracer, occupier.

A محتئ *muhta'*, Firm, well-made (horse).

A محثّ *muhiss*, An exciter, instigator. One who renders greedy.

A محثّة *mahassat*, An urging, spurring.

A محثّث *muhassis*, An instigator, inciter, urger. One who renders greedy.

A محثحث *muhas-his*, An instigator. Who shakes, wags. (Lightning) flashing, moving with velocity.

A محثل *muhsal*, Unwholesomely fed (suckling). *Muhsil*, Adverse (fortune).

A محثلة *muhsilat*, A mother who feeds her infant with unwholesome aliment.

A محثوّ *mahsūw*, Sprinkled, scattered (earth).

A محج *mahj*, (v. n. of محج) Flaying. Rubbing (a rope) to soften (it). Copulating. Churning. Rubbing one thing off another. Sweeping violently (wind). Lying.

A محجّ *muhijj*, One who sends to Mecca to perform the ceremonies of pilgrimage.

A محجأ *mahjas*, An asylum, place of refuge.

A محجاة *mahjāt*, Worthy, fit, proper (the same for all genders and numbers).

A محجاج *mihjāj*, Quarrelsome, litigious. A probe for a wound. An implement for levelling ground.

A محجام *mihjām*, One who recedes or hangs back exceedingly; a great coward.

A محجّب *muhajjab*, Separated by a curtain (حجاب *hijāb*). Veiled, secluded. Kept back.

A محجّة *mahajjat*, (pl. محاجّ *mahājj*) A highway, a straight road. Any thing established by proof. Thesis, proposition.

A محجحج *muhajhij*, A retreater or retirer. One who restrains himself from speaking.

A محجر *mahjar*, Any thing forbidden. *Mahjir* or *mihjar*, (pl. محاجر *mahājir*) A garden planted with trees. The socket, environs, or corner of the eye. An eye peeping out from under a veil, or through the folds of a turban. The environs of a town.

A محجّر *muhajjar*, (The moon) cloud-encircled. (A camel) marked with the cautery round the eye.

A محجل *muhjil*, One who binds with a tether the right fore-foot (of a camel).

A محجّل *muhajjal*, Sunk in the socket (the eye). Shining, splendid (applied to the blest in heaven). Marked white by the صرار *sirār* (the teat of a camel). (A horse) having one hind-foot white (if all the four are white it is expressed by محجّل الاربع *muhajjalu'l arbaʻa*; if the two hind and one fore, محجّل الثلاث *muhajjalu's salāsa*; if the hind right, محجّل اليمنى *muhajjalu'l yumna'*, the left, محجّل اليسرى *muhajjalu'l yusra'*).

A محجم *mihjam*, (pl. محاجم *mahājim*) A cupping-glass or horn. A lancet. Thin, fine. *Muhjim*, Pusillanimous. One who draws or diverts one from.

A محجمة *mahjamat*, (pl. محاجم *mahājim*) The part to which the cupping-glass is applied. *Mihjamat*, A cupping-glass or horn.

A محجن *mihjan*, (pl. محاجن *mahājin*) A book-headed club. *Muhjan*, Small and weakly (plant). *Muhjin*, The herb ثمام *sumām* coming into leaf.

A محجنة *mihjanat*, A curved stick, hooked club.

A محجوب *mahjūb*, Veiled, covered, retired, prevented going abroad. Modest. Blind from birth.

P محجوبه *mahjūba*, A bar for fastening a door. محجوبه احمد *mahjūbaʼi ahmad*, The hamza of احمد *ahmad*, *i.e.* the letter ا *alif*.

A محجوج *mahjūj*, Resorted to, sought after. The temple of Mecca. Purpose, intent, design.

A محجور *mahjūr*, Prohibited, forbidden. An inhibited slave.

A محجوز *mahjūz*, Foot-bound. Struck on the waist. Girded with a waistband.

A محجوف *mahjūf*, Pained in the root of the lower jaw.

A محجول *mahjūl*, White-footed (horse). Intercepted.

A محجوم *mahjūm*, Cupped (man). Stout, bulky (man). Muzzled (camel).

A محجى *muhjī*, Covetous, avaricious.

A محجيّ *mahjīy*, Enigmatical.

A محح *mahah*, (v.n. of مح) Being worn (a garment).

A محدّ *mahadd*, Flight, escape. لا محدّ *lā mahadd*, There is no flight or retreat, it becomes necessary. *Muhidd*, A sharpener. One who points the eye towards. A widow mourning (her husband).

A محدب *muhdib*, One who gives a propensity or kind inclination. Who makes hump-backed.

A محدّب *muhaddab*, Convex. *Muhaddib*, One who raises the back, or makes gibbous or convex.

A محدث *muhdis*, A fornicator. Polluted by any accident, and disqualified thereby for prayer. (God) causing (an event) to happen. Any thing new, strange, disagreeable, or iniquitous. One who affords a refuge to a criminal. A polisher, furbisher.

A محدّث *muhaddas*, Sound, judicious in relating or distinguishing the actions or sayings of Muhammad. An orthodox believer in Muhammadan traditions. *Muhaddis*, One who produces something new, an inventor, an innovator. A narrator, relater. A collector, compiler, reporter of Muhammadan traditions. A believer in tradition.

A محدّثات *muhaddasāt*, Histories, accidents.

A محدثة *muhdasat*, Any thing new, strange, disagreeable, or iniquitous.

A محدج *muhdij*, One who binds on the حدج *hidj* or camel-litter.

A محدّج *muhaddij*, Who looks stedfastly at.

A محدّد *muhaddad*, Terminated, bounded, limited. Pointed, peaked. Sharpened, whetted. *Muhaddid*, One who circumscribes, confines, or limits. (See تحديد *tahdīd*.)

A محدر *muhdir*, One who doubles up or hems the lower part of a garment. (See احدار *ihdār*.)

A محدّر *muhaddir*, Who or what causes to descend or to precipitate; precipitant.

A محدرج *muhadraj*, Smooth, sleek. A whip.

A محدس *mahdis*, A question, a demand. Intention, proposition, wish, desire.

A محدق *muhdik*, Who or what surrounds, encircles, goes round.

A محدّق *muhaddik*, Clear-sighted. Who or what surrounds or encircles.

A محدلة *muhdulat*, (A bow) curved at the end.

A محدلق *muhadlik*, One who rolls his eyes.

A محدود *mahdūd*, Limited, bounded, separated, terminated, defined, definite. Prohibited, debarred, excluded. Unfortunate. Punished, chastised, bastinadoed according to law.

A محدودات *mahdūdāt*, Legal punishments; bastinadoes.

A محدي *muhdī*, Pains-taking.

A محذاء *mihzās*, A reviler, reproacher.

A محذّر *muhazzir*, A threatener, inspirer of fear. An admonisher, warner, cautioner, prohibiter.

A محذرف *muhazrif*, Smooth, even (solid or cloven hoof). Full (vessel).

A محذل *muhzil*, Who or what makes the hair fall off, and produces a redness round the eyelids.

A محذلق *muhazlik*, One who displays or boasts of his own cleverness. A taker.

A محذلم *muhazlim*, Swift, quick-paced. One who fills a bottle. (See حذلمة *hazlamat*.)

A محذم *mihzam*, A sharp sword.

A محذوّ *mahzūw*, Predestinated, fore-ordained.

A محذور *mahzūr*, Formidable. Well-guarded.

A محذورة *mahzūrat*, (v. n. of حذر) Avoiding, shunning, fearing. A misfortune, calamity (as being a thing dreaded). War. Caution. Terror. A bugbear, scarecrow, hobgoblin. ابو محذورة *abū mahzūrat*, (Father of terror) Name of سمرة بن معير *samurat bin miʻyar*, the Mu'ezzin of Muhammad.

A محذوري *mahzūrī*, Caution. Warning.

A محذوف *mahzūf*, Taken away, cut off, elided (syllable from a word, or foot from a verse). Docked (horse). Mutilated. A bottle, wine-skin.

A محذوق *mahzūk*, Cut.

A محذي *muhzī*, A giver of a shoe (حذاء *hizās*). One who gives part of booty.

A محرّ *muhirr*, Warm, hot, sultry (day). The owner of thirsty camels.

A محراب *mihrāb*, (pl. محاريب *mahārīb*) The principal place in a mosque, where the priest prays to the people with his face turned towards Mecca; a kind of high altar. A parlour, hall, or upper chamber. The neck of a beast. The chief seat at an entertainment. The royal closet or chamber. Warlike. Angry. A field of battle. P محراب جمشيد *mihrābi jamshed*, The sun. Fire. The cup or mirror of Jam, Solomon, or Alexander the Great, which, according to the eastern fabulists, represented the whole world. محراب شكربوره *mihrābi shakarbūra*, A triangular kind of pasty made with sugar.

A محراة *mahrāt*, Worthy, fit, suitable.

A محراث *mihrās*, (or محرث *mihras*) A coal-rake or malkin for ovens. A plough.

A محراج *mihrāj*, Bitterly cold (night).

A محراف *mihrāf*, A surgeon's probe.

A محراق *mihrāk*, The cause of a fire (as lightning or a thunderbolt).

A محراك *mihrāk*, A poker for stirring a fire.

A محران *mihrān*, (pl. محارين *mahārīn*) Honey. A honey-comb. A bee adhering to the cross-stick in a hive. Cotton-seed.

A محرب *mihrab*, Warlike. *Muhrib*, One who shews the way (as a guide to plunder an enemy). One who stirs up (a battle). Flowering (palm-tree).

A محرّب *muharrab*, A lion. *Muharrib*, An exasperator. An instigator. A sharpener of spear-heads.

A محربة *mihrabat*, A warlike people.

A محربئة *muharbi-at*, (A country) abounding in chameleons (حرباء *hirbā*). Rough, rugged (ground).

A محرث *mihras*, A plough. *Muhras*, Overworked, lean (beast). One who overworks his beast.

A محرج *muhrij*, One who renders criminal or miserable. Who reduces to difficulties, or leads into sin. Who forbids or makes unlawful.

A محرّج *muharraj*, (A dog) dressed in a collar of small shells (called حرج *hirj*). *Muharrij*, One who reduces to straits, who presses hard upon. One who forbids or makes unlawful. One who takes an oath. One who decorates a collar with little shells.

A محرد *mahrid*, The withers of a horse. A place where a cut is made. *Muhrid*, Swift, rapid. One who makes or who does alone.

A محرّد *muharrad*, Bent, arched, curved. (A house) built of reeds (حرديّ *hurdīy*). *Muharrid*, A restrainer. One who angers. A bender, a twister.

A محرّر *muharrar*, Written, inscribed. Consecrated to God. محرّر دارم *muharraru dārimin*, A kind of serpent. *Muharrir*, A writer, accomptant. A giver of liberty. A modest, also a neat or graceful speaker. One who devotes to the service of God.

P محرّران فلك *muharrirāni falak*, The moon, Mercury, Venus, the sun, Mars, Jupiter, and Saturn.

A محرز *muhriz*, One who obtains a reward and enjoys the benefit of it. (A place) affording security. A strengthener. Cautious. Abstinent. ابو محرز *abū muhriz*, (Father Wary) A sparrow.

A محرّز *muharriz*, A careful preserver.

A محرزة *muhrizat*, Chaste (woman).

A محرزق *muharzak*, Straitened. Imprisoned.

A محرس *muhris*, One who remains in one place a whole age (حرس *hars*).

A محرّش *muharrish*, A provoker, exasperator. One who sets (men or dogs) by the ears.

A محرّص *muharris*, An exciter to greediness.

A محرض *mihraz*, A vessel in which they keep ashes of alkali (حرض *hurz* or *huruz*). *Muhraz*, Distracted (with love). *Muhriz*, (Love or grief) preying upon one. The begetter of a wretched progeny.

A محرّض *muharraz*, Lean from love or grief. Unable to rise. *Muharriz*, An instigator, exciter, provoker. A dyer (of a garment) with saffron. A dealer in ashes or alkali. (A garment) old and worn at the edges.

A محرضة *mihrazat*, A vessel in which they keep ashes or alkali.

A محرف *mahrif*, A place where one turns or moves about in. A place where one's gains are made. Deliverance from calamity. *Muhrif*, Well, in good condition, increased in wealth. One who makes (a camel) lean. One who toils for his family. One who requites good or evil.

A محرّف *muharraf*, Inverted, transposed. An anagram. Diagonal, slant. *Muharrif*, A transposer (of letters). An anagrammatist. A maker or mender (of a pen). One who accommodates his religion to his favourite lusts or worldly schemes. Who or what causes to turn aside.

A محرق *mihrak*, A file. *Muhrak*, Inflamed, burnt. *Muhrik*, A maker of the gruel or pottage حروقة *harūkat*. *Muhrik*, Giving warmth, burning.

A محرّق *muharrak*, Burned. Boiling (water). *Muharrik*, An incendiary. Whatever causes thirst. Name of a man; also of an idol.

A محرقة *muhrakat*, A burnt-offering, holocaust.

A محرقص *muharkas*, Close (texture).

A محرك *mahrak*, The upper part of the root of the neck. *Muhrik*, A mover, stirrer up, adviser.

A محرّك *muharrak*, (in grammar) A word inflected with two or more *fathas*: as, مطر *matar*, حسنة *hasanat*. *Muharrik*, A mover, inciter, persuader. Stimulant, motory. One who marks (a consonant) with a vowel. محرّك الفتنة *muharriku'l fitnat*, An exciter of sedition. محرّك فساد *muharriki fasād*, A promoter of mischief, tumult, insurrection, or war. قوّت محرّكه *kūvati muharrika*, Motive or moveable power.

A محرم *mahram*, Unlawful, forbidden. A spouse, consort, confidant, intimate friend. ذو محرم *zū mahram*, Any one to whom the حرم *haram* or women's apartments are open (as a father, or a son). ذو محرم *zū mahram*, (or رحم محرم *rahim mahram*) One with whom marriage is unlawful. P نا محرم *nā mahram*, A stranger, one who is not permitted to enter the haram. A *Muhrim*, A prohibiter, interdicter. Unlawful. One who cultivates peace and friendship. Intimate; admitted to the female apartments. Conscious, sensible. Entered on the sacred month Muharram, during which it is unlawful to fight. One who assumes the pilgrim's garb احرام *ihrām*. One who, having resolved on pilgrimage, lays himself under peculiar restrictions. A menstruous woman.

A محرّم *muharram*, Forbidden. Venerable, dignified. The sacred enclosure of Mecca. Untanned (hide). Stiff, not softened (bull's pizzle, used for a scourge). Semi-tractable (camel). The soft part of the nose. A bodice, that part of the dress in which the breasts are confined. (pl. محارم *mahārim*, محاريم *mahārīm*, and محرّمات *muharramāt*) Name of the first month of the Muhammadan year, during which fighting is prohibited. *Muharrim*, One who forbids, interdicts, or declares unlawful. One who binds fast (a scourge). One who dresses leather improperly. (See تحريم *tahrīm*.)

A محرمات *mahrumāt*, Inviolable things.

A محرّمات *muharramāt*, Things prohibited. Months of Muharram.

A محرمة *mahramat* or *mahrumat*, (pl. محرمات *mahrumāt* and محارم *mahārim*) Any thing venerable, sacred, inviolable, prohibited by God. Repulse, disappointment. A wife.

A محرمد *muharmid*, (A well) full of black mud.

A محرميّة *mahramīyat*, The state of being a confidant; intimacy, trust, confidence.

A محرن *mihran*, A bow for dividing cotton.

A محرنجم *muhranjam*, A great number, numerosity.

A محرنفزات *muhranfizāt*, Excellent (verses).

A محرنفش *muhranfish*, Swollen. Inflamed with rage. Ready for mischief.

A محروب *mahrūb*, Robbed, plundered.

A محروت *mahrūt*, The root of benzoin.

P محروث *mahrūs*, Root of the assafœtida.

A محروث *mahrūs*, Ploughed, tilled (ground).

A محروحة *mahrūhat*, (A woman) hit on the حرح.

A محرور *mahrūr*, Freed from being a slave. Hot, choleric, furious. Libidinous. Written. محرور المزاج *mahrūru'l mizāj*, Of a warm temperament.

A محروريّ *mahrūrīy*, Hot, choleric.

A محروس *mahrūs*, Guarded, preserved, kept. بيت محروس الحوالي *bayti mahrūsu'l hawālī*, A house guarded on all sides. ممالك محروسه *mamāliki mahrūsa*, Countries occupied by any sovereign.

A محروسة *mahrūsat*, A garrisoned city. A capital, the metropolis of an empire.

A محروص *mahrūs*, Greedily desired, coveted. (A pasture) grazed, cropped close.

A محروض *mahrūz*, Worse, viler. Reprobated.

A محروف *mahrūf*, Inverted, changed. Deprived of part of one's property.

A محروق *mahrūk*, Burnt, inflamed. One, the top of whose thigh is dislocated. A roasting-spit.

A محروقة *mahrūkat*, Fuel. A keen sword.

A محروم *mahrūm*, Prohibited, forbidden. Debarred, excluded (from hope or favour), frustrated, disappointed, repulsed: deprived of the support of life: unlucky, unable to earn any thing: unfortunate; spoiled, plundered. Prevented by shame from begging. Venerable.

A محرومي *mahrūmī*, Disappointment.

A محروميّة *mahrūmiyat*, Prohibition, frustration, disappointment.

A محرئ *mihra'*, Vulva.

A محري *maharī*, A dromedary.

A محريّ *mahrīy*, Worthy, suitable.

A محز *mahz*, (v. n. of محز) Lying with. Smiting on the breast with the fist.

A محزّ *mahazz*, A moment. A groove. A cut. *Mihazz*, Reproachful, cutting, severe in language.

A محزان *mihzān*, Grieved, sad.

A محزّب *muhazzib*, A distributor in parts, especially (of the Kur'ān) into sixty sections (احزاب *ahzāb*). A collector of troops, crews, or gangs.

A محزرة *mahzarat*, A guessing, an estimating.

A محزرق *muhazrak*, Confined, imprisoned.

A محزّز *muhazzaz*, Notched, serrated. *Muhazziz*, A notcher, engraver, borer.

A محزم *mahzim*, (pl. محازم *mahāzim*) The girth-place of an animal. *Mihzam* or *mihzamat*, A girth. *Muhzim*, One who girths (a horse).

A محزن *muhzan*, Sad, grieved, saddened. *Muhzin*, (or محزّن *muhazzin*) A causer of grief, an afflicter.

A محزّن *muhazzan*, Saddened, grieved.

A محزور *muhazwir*, Provoked to anger, enraged.

A محزوزي *muhzanzī*, Erect. Restless. Broken.

A محزوق *mahzūk*, Narrow-necked (water-pot).

A محزوم *mahzūm*, Packed, made into bales.

A محزون *mahzūn*, Vexed, afflicted, grieved.

A محزئل *muhzaïll*, Collected, heaped together.

A محس *mahs*, (v. n. of محس) Currying (leather).

A محسّ *mihass*, A curry-comb. *Muhiss*, A discerner, feeler, seer. A comber.

A محسا *mahsa'*, The mouth.

A محساب *mihsāb*, A banker's counter.

A محساة *mihsāt*, An ox used in drawing water.

A محسان *mihsān*, An instrument of doing good; a benefactor: beneficent.

A محسب *muhsib*, Sufficient. A satisfier. A frequent giver.

A محسّب *muhassab*, Propped with pillows. Honoured. Sufficed, supplied with a sufficiency. *Muhassib*, One who gives sufficiently, so as to cause the receiver to say حسبي *hasbī*, it is enough for me.

A محسبة *mahsabat* or *mahsibat*, (v. n. of حسب) Thinking, imagining. *Mihsabat*, A small pillow.

A محسّة *mahassat*, A cause of burning. *Mihassat*, A curry-comb.

A محسّد *muhassad*, Greatly envied. *Muhassid*, One who envies greatly.

A محسر *mahsar* or *mahsir*, The face. Nature. A place of experiment. The inner part or heart. كريم المحسر *karīmu'l mahsar*, Well-tried, proved. *Muhsir*, One who dims his sight by looking long. One who tires his camel.

A محسّر *muhassar*, Troubled, despised.

A محسرة *mihsarat*, A besom, broom, brush.

A محسّك *muhassak*, Extremely covetous.

A محسّل *muhassil*, One who does less than he ought. One who throws himself away.

A محسمة *mahsamat*, What cuts off or cauterizes.

A محسن *muhsin*, One who does good, and obliges; a benefactor. One who knows well. A proper name. كرماءُ محسنين *kuramāï muhsinīn*, Generous nobles.

A محسّن *muhassan*, Beautiful (face). *Muhassin*, Who acts properly. An approver.

A محسنات *muhsanāt* or *muhsināt*, Ladies, beautiful, fair, and chaste.

A محسنة *mahsanat*, Any thing conducive (to health and to comeliness). *Mahsinat*, Any thing good, fair, excellent.

P محسني *muhsinī*, Of or belonging to Muhsin. اخلاق محسني *akhlāki muhsinī*, Muhsin's Morals or Ethics (title of a book written in Persian).

A محسوب *mahsūb*, Computed, reckoned, carried to account.

A محسود *mahsūd*, Hated, envied.

A محسور *mahsūr*, Dim-sighted. Wearied, fatigued. One who sighs.

A محسوس *mahsūs*, Perceived, felt. Known. (A locust) scorched, nipped, or killed by the cold.

A محسوف *mahsūf*, Enriched, blessed with abundance. Clean (dates) picked from the refuse. Reprobated, discarded, contemptible.

A محسول *mahsūl*, Despised. Vile, useless, unavailable, unserviceable.

A محسوم *mahsūm*, (A child) badly fed, deprived of (its) nutriment.

A محش *mahsh*, (v. n. of محش) Burning, blistering (the skin). Peeling, drawing off the skin. Carrying off all before it (a torrent). Indulging to excess in eating or venery.

A محشّ *mahashsh*, A scythe. A place abounding with hay, also with any thing agreeable. *Mahashsh* or *mihashsh*, A hay-loft, sack, or other place where it is kept. A heap or collection of dung. *Mihashsh*, Bold, brave. One who kindles war, expert in warfare. A scythe, hay-sickle. A poker. *Muhishsh*, One who goes a foraging, or collects hay. (A woman) who has a withered fœtus in the womb. Dried, withered (hand). (See احشاش.)

A محشأ *mihshaï*, (or محشاء *mihshā*) (pl. محاشئ *mahāshiï*) A kind of coarse or shaggy garment; any covering which wraps round the body; breeches or drawers of white cloth. A white apron.

A محشاة *mahshāt*, The nethermost part of the belly, where the digested food lies ready to be excreted. The fat of the intestines of quadrupeds.

A محشّة *mahashshat*, Land abounding in hay. (pl. محاشّ *mahāshsh*) Podex. *Mihashshat*, A poker. A loft or place where hay (حشيش *hashīsh*) is kept.

A محشر *mahshar* or *mahshir*, Place of assembly; last judgment. Destruction of cattle by severity of a season.

A محشف *muhshif*, (A palm) producing bad dates.

A محشّف *muhashshif*, One who looks attentively through half-shut eyes.

A محشم *mahsham*, A place where a great man's retinue is assembled. *Muhshim*, A venerator, honourer. (See احشام *ihshām*.)

A محشّم *muhashshim*, One who puts in a rage, wrings, or says any thing which gives another pain; who causes to blush.

A محشن *muhshin*, One who makes (a bottle) stink by keeping any thing in it a long time.

A محشوّ *mahshūw*, Filled, stuffed, crammed.

A محشود *mahshūd*, A man whose nod is obeyed, to whose service people flock from all quarters.

A محشور *mahshūr*, Collected, congregated. Thickly-feathered (arrow). Large, stout.

A محشوش *mahshūsh*, Swollen-sided (camel).

A محشى *mahsha'*, The stomach and viscera. *Mihsha'*, (pl. محاشي *mahāshī*) Stuffings used by women to give a swelling appearance to the breast or hips (in modern phrase called a bustle).

A محشّى *muhashsha'*, Illustrated by marginal notes. *Muhashshi*, One who trims the edge of a garment with fringe or lace. Who or what causes to pant or puff. محشّية الكلاب *muhashshiyatu'l kilāb*, (A hare) making the hounds pant.

A محشيّ *mahshīy*, Stuffed, farced. Full, close, mealy, fleshy (date).

A محشئنّ *muhshaïnn*, Angry, enraged.

A محص *mahs*, (v. n. of محص) Running (a deer). Stamping, striking the ground with the feet. Throwing out the feet (as an animal when slaughtering). Making great exertions in going. Purifying (gold by fire). Voiding (dung). Polishing, furbishing. Flashing, shining (lightning). Flying from. (A horse) strong in body, hardy by nature. *Mahis*, Even, smooth-worn, slender (rope).

A محصّ *muhiss*, Who gives another his share (حصّة *hissat*). One who cashiers.

A محصاة *mahsāt*, Stony, gravelly ground.

A محصاف *mihsāf*, (A horse) which passes rapidly by and throws the gravel about.

A محصال *mihsāl*, An iron implement for shaving arrows, and making them smooth and dight.

A محصّب *muhassab*, The place where pilgrims throw pebbles in the valley of Mina. Covered with pimples, measly. *Muhassib*, One who strews with gravel, or throws sand into any place or thing.

A محصبة *mahsabat*, A pebbly, gravelly place.

A محصد *mihsad*, A reaping-sickle. *Muhsad*, Closely-twisted (rope). Any plant dried whilst standing and not yet cut. محصد الرأي *muhsadu'r raïy*, Of a clear, sound judgment. *Muhsid*, (Corn) ready for cutting. A strengthener. One who twists firmly (a rope).

A محصّد *muhassad*, Steady, firm in mind.

A محصر *muhsar*, Prohibited, hindered, prevented. Besieged, invested. Constipated, costive. *Muhsir*, A camel, the orifice of whose teats is very narrow. A besieger. A hinderer, preventer. Impedimental.

A محصّر *muhassar*, The tying-place of a shoe, the latchet.

A محصرة *mahsarat*, A perforated vessel whereon they lay new cheese to be strained and dried in the sun. *Mihsarat*, A small saddle or riding-cushion.

A محصرم *muhasram*, Of little estimation (a poet). Butter which will not unite on account of the cold. *Muhasrim*, Covetous.

A محصف *mihsaf* or *muhsif*, (A horse) running, passing swiftly by, and scattering the gravel as he goes. *Muhsif*, One who manages or settles any thing judiciously. One who twists firmly (a rope), or weaves well.

A محصل *muhsil*, (or محصّل *muhassil*) (A palm-tree) bearing green or unripe dates.

A محصّل *muhassal,* Collected, acquired, brought together. محصّل الكلام *muhassalu'l kalām,* (or محصّل كلام *muhassali kalām*) The sum or substance of a speech. *Muhassal,* (or محصّلاً *muhassalan*) Upon the whole, to sum up all, to conclude. *Muhassil,* A collector, gatherer, acquirer. A collector of revenue, tax-gatherer. A dun. A farmer of the customs. A man who collects mineral earth, and sifts it in search of gold. One who produces or makes manifest. A guard placed over a person as a restraint, to prevent his escape, or to enforce the payment of a demand. A reader; digester, one who gives the substance (of an oration).

P محصّلانه *muhassilāna,* Fees of the bailiff or tax-gatherer.

A محصّلة *muhassilat,* (A woman) who collects (mineral earth, and sifts it in search of gold).

A محصمة *mihsamat,* An iron mallet.

A محصن *mihsan,* A lock, bolt. A basket. *Muhsan,* Guarded, preserved. Chaste, continent. Wedded, married. *Muhsin,* A defender. Chaste, continent.

A محصّن *muhassan,* Surrounded by a wall. Fortified. *Muhassin,* One who fortifies, defends, or surrounds with a wall. A preserver, keeper. Chaste. Who marries a wife (so keeping himself chaste).

A محصنة *muhsanat,* (A woman) joined in matrimony. Kept from men. *Muhsanat* or *muhsinat,* Chaste, modest (woman). محصنة الفرج *muhsinatu'l farj,* Chaste (woman), who defends her honour.

A محصوب *mahsūb,* Pustulous, pimpled.

A محصود *mahsūd,* Cut, reaped. Harvest.

A محصور *mahsūr,* Besieged, beleagured, surrounded, shut or hemmed in. Restrained, compressed: bounded. Constipated, costive. (A camel) covered with the cushion حصار *hisār.*

A محصوري *mahsūrī,* Confinement, durance.

A محصوص *mahsūs,* Naked. Shaven (hair).

A محصوصل *muhsawsil,* One whose abdomen is prominent, as that of a pregnant woman.

A محصول *mahsūl,* (v. n. of حصل) Remaining over and above. Collected. Harvest, in-gathering, crop; the produce or sum of any thing. Profit. Tax, duty, excise, custom, postage.

A محصولات *mahsūlāt,* (pl. fem.) Corn, fruits.

P محصولدار *mahsūl-dār,* Fruitful, rich, fertile. An officer employed to prevent the clandestine removal of the produce.

A محصون *mahsūn,* Fortified, defended.

A محصئ *muhsiʼ,* Who causes to break wind.

A محصي *muhsī,* A numberer. A writer. Comprehending, knowing, acquainted with. Powerful.

A محصيّ *mahsīy,* Afflicted with gravel (حصاة *hasāt*) in the bladder, calculous.

A محض *mahz,* (v. n. of محض) Possessing milk unmixed with water. Giving pure milk to drink. Shewing sincere affection and good will. (pl. محاض *mihāz*) Milk unmixed with water. Pure, unmixed, unalloyed. Sincere love. Only, mere, simple. خير محض *khayri mahz,* Unalloyed good, the summum bonum. *Mahaz,* (v. n. of محض) Drinking pure milk. *Mahiz,* Possessed of pure milk. Greedy. Pure milk.

A محضأ *mihzaʼ,* (or محضاء) A coal-rake or poker.

A محضا *mahzan,* Merely, purely, solely, wholly.

A محضاج *mihzāj,* A poker for the fire. One who deviates from the road. A fuller's beetle.

A محضب *mihzab,* A coal-rake, malkin; poker. A fomenter of war or sedition. A frying-pan.

A محضج *mihzaj,* A poker for stirring the fire. One who deviates from the road.

A محضر *mahzar,* Presence, approach. Nearness. A regal court. An inhabited place. Persons present. A place where people meet or sit together. A place to which one returns for water. A register, the record of a court of judicature, the decree of a judge, the minute or attestation of a notary. Any document attested by a number of witnesses, attestation, testimony. Nature, temper, disposition. حسن المحضر *hasanu'l mahzar,* One who speaks well of the absent. كريم المحضر *karīmu'l mahzar,* Of a noble disposition. *Muhzir,* A macebearer, serjeant, beadle, or officer employed to cite before a judge: a summoner.

A محضرب *muhazrab,* Filled. *Muhazrib,* One who bends (a bow) greatly; twists hard (a rope); or distends (a bag) by filling.

A محضرم *muhazram,* A man who has lived half his life a Pagan and half a Muhammadan. *Muhazrim,* A bad pronouncer (of the vowels).

P محضر نامه *mahzar-nāma,* A summons to appear. A muster-roll, list of those present.

A محضّض *muhazzaz,* Anointed with the juice of box-thorn. *Muhazziz,* An exciter, provoker.

A محضن *mahzan* or *mahzin,* (pl. محاضن *mahāzin*) The nest of a hen sitting. *Muhzin,* A despiser, contemner, scorner. A defrauder of (a man's) right.

A محضنة *mihzanat,* A shallow dish made of clay for the use of pigeons.

A محضور *mahzūr,* Arrived at one's accustomed home. Spoiled, tainted, infected, or haunted by جنّ *jinn* (milk or sheep-fold).

A محضئ *mihzaʼ,* A forge built of clay.

A محضير *mihzīr,* (A horse) running much.

A محط *maht,* Snot.

A محطّ *mahatt,* The end of a period or sentence, a full point. The place where people deposit their baggage when lighting off a journey. An anchorage for shipping. *Mihatt,* (or محطّة *mihattat*) An iron or wooden instrument with which they draw figures (on leather): also with which the Arabs trace figures on their arms. Pustulous (face).

A محطب *mihtab,* A pruning-hook, a bill. *Muhtib,* Woody (place). (A vine) ready for pruning.

A محطرب *muhatrab,* Strong, firmly-built (man).

A محطم *mihtam,* A lion.

A محطّم *muhattim,* A great breaker.

A محطمر *muhatmir,* Enraged, full of anger.

A محطور *mahtūr,* Thrown prostrate.

A محطوط *mahtūt,* Lowered, abated. Lean (haunches). Troubled with a disease in which the spleen adheres to the side. محطوط القدر *mahtūtu'l kadr,* Depressed in dignity, lowered in rank.

A محظار *mihzār,* A sort of green fly.

A محظرب *muhazrab,* Firmly-twisted (rope). Hard in body. Narrow-minded.

A محظنبئ *muhzambiʼ,* A man soon angry.

A محظور *mahzūr,* Forbidden, unlawful. Confined, restricted.

A محظورات *mahzūrāt,* (pl. fem.) Illicit things.

A محظوظ *mahzūz,* Favoured by fortune, blest. Glad, cheerful, contented, pleased, delighted, happy. غير محظوظ *ghayr mahzūz,* Discontented, unhappy.

A محظئ *muhzaʼ,* Preferred. *Muhzī,* One who prefers or favours (one beyond others).

A محظئبّ *muhzaʼibb,* Fat. Choleric, soon angry. Full-bellied.

A محظيّة *mahzīyat,* (pl. محاظي *mahāziy*) The concubine of a married man.

A محفّ *muhiff,* One who neglects the hair, or allows it to become dishevelled. One who overloads (a horse). (See احفاف *ihfāf.*)

A محفار *mihfār,* A digging implement, spade.

A محفّة *mihaffat,* A species of travelling-litter or couch for the women, resembling the هودة *hauda,* but not arched.

A محفد *mahfid,* (pl. محافد *mahāfid*) Origin, race, lineage. A manger, crib. A king's palace. The lower part of a camel's bunch. Embroidery on a garment. *Mihfad,* A vessel for measuring corn. A manger. The hem of a garment. A basket. *Muhfid,* Fast-going (camel or ostrich). (A servant) running to do any thing. Who causes or orders to travel quick.

A محفر *mihfar,* (or محفرة *mihfarat*) (pl. محافر *mahāfir*) A digging implement, spade.

A محفّس *muhaffis,* Who moves himself in bed. Disjoined, separated. (A woman) adorning her legs with rings.

A محفّض *muhaffaz,* Very dry (ground). *Muhaffiz,* One who throws away. (See تحفيض *tahfīz.*)

A محفظ *muhfaz,* Provoked to anger. *Muhfiz,* Who or what provokes to anger.

A محفّظ *muhaffiz,* Who or whatever causes to commit to memory.

A محفظة *mahfazat,* A magazine, hoard. محفظة ادراك *mahfazaʼi idrāk,* Where any thing is perceived or kept in mind.

A محفّف *muhaffif,* A weaver (of a garment). Indigent, distressed. One who covers or wraps up (any thing) in a garment.

A محفل *mahfil* or *mahfal,* (pl. محافل *mahāfil*) A place or time of meeting: an assembly, congregation, council, convention, congress, society, chorus. A pulpit, tribunal. محفل قضا *mahfili kazā,*

A court of justice, tribunal of the Kāzī or judge.

A محفّل muhaffal, Adorned. Muhaffil, A decorator. A collector.

A محفّلة muhaffalat, (A sheep) left unmilked several days that (she) may appear to greater advantage when exposed to sale.

A محفن mihfan, Who can hold much in his hands.

A محفود mahfūd, A master, one served.

A محفور mahfūr, Dug, excavated. Carved. One whose teeth are hollow or worn. A mark, a stigma. Name of a town on the coast of the Mediterranean where carpets were made.

A محفوظ mahfūz, Guarded, protected, preserved, kept safe. Committed to memory.

A محفوف mahfūf, Girt, encompassed. Oppressed by poverty.

A محفي muhfī, One who makes bare the feet. Possessed of a beast with a worn hoof. One who neatly trims (his mustachios). Strict in inquiry, importunate in asking. Benevolent, friendly.

A محق mahk, (v. n. of محق) Abolishing, making void, cancelling, effacing, obliterating. Burning, scorching. Depriving of a blessing.

A محقّ muhikk, One who confirms and establishes. A speaker of the truth. (See احقاق ihkāk.)

A محقان mihkān, One who makes water after a long retention of urine.

A محقب muhkab, A fox. Muhkib, Barren, without ore (mine). Dry (season). One who allows another to ride behind him. One who conforms (his opinion) to that of others. (See احقاب.)

A محقد mahkid, Root, origin. Nature. Muhkid, Who causes hatred. One who searches for mines, but finds none.

A محقر muhkir, A despiser.

A محقّر muhakkar, Despised. Poor, low. A trifle. Muhakkir, A despiser.

A محقّرات muhakkarāt, Trifles.

A محقرة mahkarat, (v. n. of حقر) Being vile, contemptible. Regarding as such. Vileness, baseness.

A محقّرة muhakkarat, A despicable thing, a trifle.

A محقف mihkaf, Who neither eats or drinks.

A محقّق muhakkak, Ascertained, confirmed, authenticated, certified, notorious, known for truth. Firmly woven (cloth). A kind of writing. Muhakkik, A verifier, affirmer, confirmer. One who knows or regards as true. An asserter or teacher of truth, a philosopher. An appealer to the Kur'ān, and not to tradition. One who renders necessary.

P محقّقانه muhakkikāna, Truly, accurately.

A محقلة mahkalat, (pl. محاقل mahākil) Arable land; a sown field. A tilth.

A محقن mihkan, A churning-bottle or bag having thick milk, upon which they pour fresh milk. A clyster-pipe. Muhkin, One who restrains (urine). One who collects different kinds of milk that they may become sweet when blended together.

A محقنة mihkana, A syringe, clyster-pipe.

A محقوّ mahkūw, Griped in the belly. Indisposed in the hypochondria.

A محقور mahkūr, The letters جدّ قطب jaddu katbin.

A محقوق mahkūk, Worthy, fit, proper.

A محقون mahkūn, Retained, confined, kept in.

A محقيّ mahkīy, Indisposed in the hypochondria (حقو hakw). Griped in the belly.

A محك mahk, A brawl. Mahik, A wrangler.

A محكّ mihakk, A touchstone, a test. P محكّ زر ايمان mihakki zari imān, The touchstone of the gold of faith, i. e. the black stone at Mecca. محكّ زرّين mihakki zarrīn, A touchstone for gold. The black stone at Mecca. محكّ صبر mihakki sabr, The touchstone of patience.

A محكان mahkān, A brawler. Morose, fitful.

A محكد mahkid, Origin, root, principle. Refuge, asylum. Muhkid, One who leans against. One who hangs back.

A محكّك muhakkak, Rubbed. A scrubbing-post for scabby camels. Muhakkik, One who scratches very hard.

A محكل muhkil, Dark, doubtful, difficult (affair). An exciter (of mischief).

A محكم muhkam, Fortified, strengthened, firm, robust. Stuck fast, impeded, entangled. Clear, perspicuous, incontrovertible. Strong. Muhkim, A strengthener, fortifier.

A محكّم muhakkam or muhakkim, Wise, discreet. Unshaken during martyrdom. Muhakkim, A prohibiter, hinderer. One who invests with power and authority. An experienced old man.

A محكمات muhkamāt, (pl. fem. of محكم muhkam) Incontrovertible, plain, perspicuous, not ambiguous (verses of the Kur'ān); or such as have not been abrogated.

A محكمة mahkamat, A tribunal, a court of justice, town-house or hall. Muhkamat, (fem.) Firm. Clear, perspicuous (thing). Unrepealed, unabrogated (verse or chapter of the Kur'ān).

A محكّمة muhakkimat, Name of a sect.

A محكمي muhkamī, Firmness, strength.

A محكوك mahkūk, Erased, cancelled. Rubbed.

A محكوم mahkūm, Ordered, commanded. Empowered, ordained, invested with supreme power. Subjected, under command. Bridled, curbed (horse). A servant. محكوم به mahkūm bihi, The predicate of a proposition. محكوم عليه mahkūmun ʻalayhi, Judicially condemned. The subject of a proposition.

A محكّمون muhakkamūn also muhakkimūn, A name given to certain individuals, who chose death rather than apostatize.

A محكيّ mahkīy, Related, told. Written. محكيّ عنه mahkīyun ʻanhu, Told of him.

A محل mahl, (v. n. of محل) Injuring by slander. Laying snares, informing against any one (before the king). Being barren for want of rain (a season). Want of rain. Unprofitable, useless (person). Fraud, deceit, treachery. Dust. Adversity, straits, distress. Dearth, scarcity. (Land) dry and barren for want of rain. Mahil, Driven until exhausted by fatigue. Muhal, (pl. of محال mahāl) The joints of the back.

A محلّ mahall, (v. n. of حلّ) Descending, lighting off a journey, staying, dwelling. Any place where one resides; a building, house, mansion. A palace. A place, post, situation, station, district, quarter. A delay, deferring. Time, opportunity. Opportune, suitable, apropos. P محلّ صفا بخش mahalli safā-bakhsh, A pleasant, delightsome spot. A ذكر محلّ و ارادهٔ حال zikri mahall u irādaʼi hāl, A trope, the containing for the contained. غير محلّ ghayr mahall, Unworthy. في محلّ آخر fi mahalli ākhar, In another place. من محلّ آخر min mahalli ākhar, From another place. مرسل الى محلّ آخر mursal ila' mahalli ākhar, Sent to another place. Mahill, (v. n. of حلّ) Being due, necessary. The appointed term for payment of debt, or for making a sacrifice. A place of sacrifice. Muhill, (A woman) mourning the death of her husband (fixed by the Muhammadan law to 110 days, during which time she was not permitted to remarry). About to enter upon those months when fighting was permitted (after the expiration of the sacred months, during which war was forbidden). One wholly regardless of matters which are deemed sacred. Deserving of punishment. (A sheep) having milk after eating spring-grass. Lawful.

P محلّا muhallā, Small pieces of meat roasted and sprinkled with lemon-juice. A fried melon.

A محلاء mihlā, An iron instrument for scraping off hair or for flaying.

A محلاب mihlāb, A milking-pail.

A محلاءة mihlaʼat, An instrument for braying antimony, or for applying it to the eyes. An iron instrument for removing the dirt and hair from a hide.

A محلّات mahallāt, (pl. of محلّة mahallat) Streets, squares. Muhillāt, A kettle, mill, knife, hatchet, pitcher, dish, and fire-steel (as with those utensils a man may travel without the assistance of others).

A محلاج mihlāj, An iron instrument with which they separate cotton from the seeds. A baker's rolling-pin. Light (ass).

A محلال mihlāl, A place where people assemble and sit down.

A محلب mahlab, A kind of grain resembling cherry-stones growing in Azarbayjān (Armenia). Honey. حبّ المحلب habbu'l mahlab, A kind of aromatic or spice. Mihlab, A milking-pail. Muhlib, One who assists in milking, or allows another to milk. A helper. (See احلاب ihlāb.)

P محلب mihlab, Name of a fragrant tree, of which the people of Nahāwand make whip-handles.

A محلبة mahlabat, A place where the grain mahlab grows.

A محلة *mahlat*, Barren (ground).

A محلّة *mahallat*, A street or quarter of a city. A parish. An inn, station, any encampment or halting-place for travellers. *Muhillat*, A knoll which has room to hold one or two houses.

A محلّتان *muhillatāni*, (dual of محلّة *muhillat*) A pot and a hand-mill.

A محلج *mihlaj*, (or محلجة *mihlajat*) A table on which they separate cotton from the seed. *Mihlaj*, The axis of a pulley. Light (ass). *Muhlaj*, Ready (money).

A محلحل *muhalhal*, A prince or chief of a tribe. A man endued with bulk and valour.

A محلس *muhlas*, A journey on which one does not tire. ما هو الا محلس على الدبر *mā huwa illā muhlasun ȥala'd dabar*, He is made to stick to this business as close as a saddle-cloth to the camel's back. *Muhlis*, One who covers (a camel) with a cloth under the saddle. Rain falling incessantly in small drops. (See احلاس *ihlās*.)

A محلسة *muhlisat*, Land whereon the grass stands as thick as the pile of the carpet حلس *hils*.

P محل سراي *mahal-sarāy*, Women's apartments.

A محلط *muhlit*, Vehement in swearing.

A محلف *muhlif*, Who exacts an oath and binds one by it. A doubtful affair, about which people swear differently. غير محلف *ghayr muhlif*, Undoubted, pure, clear (colour). كميت محلف *kumayt muhlif*, A colour partly bay, partly chesnut. (See احلاف).

A محلّف *muhallif*, One who exacts an oath.

A محلفان *muhlifāni*, Two stars which rise before Canopus.

A محلق *mihlak*, (pl. محالق *mahālik*) An instrument of shaving; a razor. Hairy, shaggy (vest).

A محلّق *muhallak*, Scraped, shaven, shorn. (A date) two-thirds ripe. A shaving-place, a place in Mina where the pilgrims shave their heads. *Muhallik*, One who shaves (his head) much. Partially ripe (date). Lean (sheep). Not full (vessel).

A محلقة *mihlakat* A shaving-instrument, razor.

A محلقم *muhalkim*, Half-ripe (date).

A محلقن *muhalkin*, Dates two-thirds ripe.

P محل گوي *mahal-gūy*, An apposite speaker.

A محلّل *muhallal*, A place whither any one frequently goes. Lawful. A small matter. Water frequented and made muddy by camels. *Muhallil*, One who makes lawful. One who marries a thrice divorced woman that she may lawfully return to her former husband. One who solves, resolves, renders justice. A solvent. One who obtains leave to run in a race on which bets are laid, paying nothing if beaten, but gaining something if he outstrips the rest.

A محلّلات *muhallilāt*, Medicines which, by their subtilty, dissolve and dissipate any morbid and stagnate fluid; solvents.

A محلم *muhlim*, Dreaming. A dreamer.

A محلّم *muhallim*, One who renders meek and long-suffering, or who enjoins meekness.

A محلنكك *muhlankik*, Black, pitchy.

A محلوب *mahlūb*, Milked (animal). Tanned with the plant حلب *hullab* (a leathern bottle).

A محلوت *mahlūt*, Shaved, shaven.

A محلوج *mahlūj*, (Cotton) cleared of the seed.

A محلوس *mahlūs*, Skinny (female privities).

A محلوف *mahlūf*, Sworn. *Mahlūf*, (or محلوفة *mahlūfat*) (v. n. of حلف) Swearing.

A محلوفاء *mahlūfāȥ*, An oath. لا و محلوفائه *lā wa mahlūfāȥihi*, No, I swear it.

A محلوق *mahlūk*, Shaved, shaven.

A محلول *mahlūl*, Dissolved. Discussed (a medical phrase). Loosed, absolved. Permitted. Vacant, empty. Legitimate, lawful. A solution.

A محلولك *muhlawlik*, Black, pitchy.

A محلّه *mahalla*, (properly محلّة *mahallat*) A quarter, part of the town, district, division. Review, muster. The community.

P محلّه دار *mahalla-dār*, A police-officer under the cutwal.

A محلي *muhlī*, An anointer of the eyes. One who makes or discovers (a thing) to be sweet.

A محلّى *muhalla'*, Sweetened. Polished, adorned, dressed. Ornamented with jewels, elegant. Written out. Praised, commended. *Muhalli*, One who decorates the hilt or sheath of a sword. A sweetener. One who describes or portrays (a man) by (his) form, mien, or external appearance.

A محمّ *mihamm*, An iron or brazen vessel tinned, in which they warm water. *Muhimm*, A warmer (of water). A measurer, definer. Near, at hand. Whatever throws into a fever, or renders one concerned and anxious. One who makes black. A washer with cold and warm water. Hot, feverish. Infected with an epidemical fever. A kinsman.

A محماح بحباح *mahmāhi bahbāhi*, An exclamation denoting loss, destruction, or termination.

A محماصة *mihmāsat*, A dexterous female robber.

A محماق *mihmāk*, (A woman) frequently bringing forth foolish children.

A محمّة *mahammat*, Any object of aim or pursuit. The cause of fever. *Mahammat* or *muhimmat*, (A district) infected by an epidemical disorder, especially amongst camels: feverish (country). *Muhimmat*, A pressing necessity. Present, immediate want. Whatever brings grief.

A محمّج *muhammij*, One who contracts the eye to look more stedfastly; who looks earnestly at; whose eyes are sunk; who rolls the eyes in terror. Whose countenance changes with rage.

A محمح *mahmah*, (or محماح *mahmāh*) Light, flighty. Close, stingy, avaricious.

A محمحة *mahmahat*, (v. n. of محمح Q) Being sincere in friendship.

A محمحم *muhamhim*, Neighing (horse).

A محمد *mahmid* or *mahmad*, (v. n. of حمد) Praising. *Muhmid*, One who acts laudably, and deserves commendation.

A محمّد *muhammad*, Highly praised. Praiseworthy. A proper name, particularly that of the great Arabian pseudo-prophet, which, by Europeans, is variously spelt and pronounced, as Muhammad, Mahommed, Mahomet, Mahmut, Mehmet, Mahound, &c., &c. *Muhammid*, A great praiser.

A محمدة *mahmidat* or *mahmadat*, (v. n. of حمد) Praising. An illustrious or laudable action. Fame, renown. Praise, eulogy.

P محمدة ساز *mahmada-sāz*, One who returns thanks to, and praises God.

A محمّديّ *muhammadiy*, Muhammadan.

A محمر *mihmar*, (pl. محامر *mahāmir*) A pack-horse. An instrument for stripping off hair or a skin. One who will not give until after much importunity. Ignoble, base. *Muhmir*, A camel in whose belly the fœtus is doubled and does not come out till she is dead. A quick goer.

A محمّر *muhammar*, Called an ass. *Muhammir*, One who calls (another) an ass. One who speaks in the Himyarit dialect. One of the sect called Muhammirat. One who writes in red characters.

A محمرّ *muhmarr*, Red.

A محمّرة *muhammirat*, The sect of Alkhurrumiyah (opposed to مبيّضة *mubayyizat*).

A محمش *muhmish*, (or محمّش *muhammish*) One who puts in a passion. One who adds fuel to fire.

A محمّص *muhammas*, Parched (pea or vetch). *Muhammis*, A toaster (of pease or vetches).

A محمض *mahmaz* or *muhmaz*, A place where camels feed on the bitter plant called حمض *hamz*. *Muhmiz*, (Land) fruitful in bitter and saltish plants.

A محمطرة *muhamtarat*, (Camels) heavily laden.

A محمق *muhmik*, One who discovers folly in another, or exhibits signs of it himself. A woman, the mother of a foolish son. Lank (horse). A sufferer from a disease resembling the measles. A mare whose breed is not surpassed.

A محمقات *muhmikāt*, Light and misty (nights).

A محمقة *muhmikat*, (A woman) who brings forth a foolish son.

A محمل *mahmil*, (pl. محامل *mahāmil*) That by which any thing is supported. That which carries the two loads of a camel. A camel-litter in which females travel. Velvet, satin, cloth (especially that sent annually to the temple of Mecca). That in or on which any thing reliance can be placed. A basket in which grapes are carried to the drying-house. *Mihmal*, A sword-belt, baldrick. The fibres of a tree. *Muhmil*, One who loads, or helps to load. Dropping milk without conceiving (woman, camel).

A محمّل *muhammal*, Carried, borne. *Muhammil*, A bearer, a carrier (of a letter).

A محملق *muhamlik*, Open-eyed, staring.

A مُحَمِّم *muhammim*, A payer of the marriage-settlements after a divorce. Who blackens the face with coal. Black (head) after shaving. Bearded (youth). A fledgeling.

A مَحْمَنَة *mahmanat* or *muhminat*, (A place) abounding with a small species of tike.

A محمود *mahmūd*, Praised. Laudable. Name of a man. Name of an elephant mentioned in the Kur'ān.

A محمودة *mahmūdat*, (P محموده) Scammony.

A محمودي *mahmūdī*, A silver coin equal to about $8\frac{1}{2}$ pence English. An Afghān tribe.

A محموراء *mahmūrā*, (pl. of حمار *himār*) Asses.

A محموز *mahmūz*, Tart (wine). Sharp, brisk. محموز البنان *mahmūzu'l banān*, Strong, powerful.

A محموصة *mahmūsat*, Stolen (sheep).

A محموق *mahmūk*, Small-poxed or measled.

A محمول *mahmūl*, Loaded, freighted. Carried, borne. Tolerated, allowed. Fortunate in being mounted on a brisk mule. A fœtus.

A محمولة *mahmūlat*, A sort of dusky-coloured wheat, very prolific. A cargo, burden: lading.

A محموم *mahmūm*, Warmed. Thrown into a fever, feverish. Definite, decreed, determined.

A محمي *mahmī*, A lion. *Muhma'*, Heated (iron). *Muhmī*, A preserver, defender. A heater (of iron).

A محميّ *mahmīy*, Protected, guarded. Heated (iron). Feverish. A lion.

A محمية *mahmiyat*, (v. n. of حمي) Abstaining through a nice sense of honour. Protecting, guarding, defending. Debarring.

A محميّة *mahmīyat*, A protected city, *i.e.* a metropolis or other distinguished place.

A محن *mahn*, (v. n. of محن) Striking, lashing. Trying, proving, tempting. Wearing out (a garment). Giving, bestowing. Lying with. Cleaning (a well) from mud. Stripping off bark. Smoothing (leather). *Mahan*, Fatigue from being employed, or from travelling all day. Smooth, soft. *Mihan*, (pl. of محنة *mihnat*) Afflictions. P عالم پر محن *ālami pur mihan*, A world full of troubles.

A محنّا *muhanna'*, Bent, crooked, hooked.

A محنّب *muhannab*, (A horse) curved or bent in the loins and pastern. Bent double with age.

A محنة *mihnat*, (pl. محن *mihan*) Moil, toil, drudgery. Calamity, misfortune, affliction, misery, evil, inconvenience, sorrow, teen, perplexity, labour, trouble, sore trial, temptation. P محنتها كشيدن *mihnathā kashīdan*, To suffer misfortunes. A محنت دنيا *mihnati dunya'*, The cares of the world.

P محنت زده *mihnat-zada*, Distrest, wretched.

P محنت كش *mihnat-kash*, Afflicted: moiling.

P محنت كشي *mihnat-kashī*, Misery, suffering.

P محنت كشيده *mihnat-kashīda*, Oppressed.

A محنتي *mihnatī*, Laborious, difficult. Unfortunate. Tried by afflictions.

A محنث *muhnis*, One who renders wicked and perjured. One who leads from falsehood to truth. An infamous wretch.

A محنج *muhnij*, One who distorts; a wrester: a prevaricator, perjurer. (See احناج *ihnāj*.)

A محنجة *mihnajat*, An instrument, utensil, tool.

A محنذ *muhniz*, One who gives less water and more wine, or vice versâ.

A محنذي *muhanzī*, Reproachful, contumelious.

A محنش *mihnash*, One who toils and gains much. *Muhnish*, A hastener. One who makes recede.

A محنط *muhnat*, Dead. *Muhnit*, The plant رمث *rims* when come to maturity. A burier of the dead with odours (حنوط *hanūt*).

A محنّط *muhannit*, A burier of the dead with odours (حنوط *hanūt*). Ripe (plant رمث *rims*).

A محنظي *muhanzī*, Abusive, opprobrious.

A محنق *muhnak*, Filled with indignation. *Muhnik*, One who puts in a passion. Lean (ass from much beating). (See احناق *ihnāk*.)

A محنك *mihnak*, The string with which the palate of a new-born infant is rubbed. A farrier's twitch. *Muhnak*, Experienced, proved, tried. *Muhnik*, Who or what renders expert.

A محنّك *muhannak*, A child whose palate has been rubbed with bruised dates, honey, or any thing similar, that it may be excited to suck more willingly. Experienced, proved, tried. *Muhannik*, Improving (trial). (See تحنيك *tahnīk*.)

A محنوة *mahnuwat*, The bend of a river.

A محنوج *mahnūj*, Firmly-twisted (rope).

A محنوذ *mahnūz*, (A horse) thrown into a sweat by being exercised in the sun.

A محنوش *mahnūsh*, Bitten by a serpent; stung by a reptile. Driven against one's will. Obscure, mean, of no reputation. Instigated, stirred up.

A محنوك *mahnūk*, (An infant) whose palate (حنك *hanak*) has been rubbed with chewed dates or honey that it may be induced to suck.

A محنون *mahnūn*, Mad, insane. Possessed by an evil spirit. Epileptic.

A محني *muhnī*, Affectionate (mother who refuses a second marriage from a regard to her children).

A محنّي *muhanna'*, Bent, curved, hooked. *Muhannī*, A bender.

A محنّئ *muhanni'*, Who dyes his beard with privet.

A محنية *mahniyat*, (pl. محاني *mahānī*) The bend or winding of a river. Crooked, uneven (ground). A pail made of a camel's skin, a part of which being filled with sand dries, and then remains as a saucer, or as the scale of a balance.

A محو *mahw*, (v. n. of محا for محو) Erasing, cancelling, obliterating, defacing, annulling, effacing, annihilating. Being effaced and obliterated. Erasement, obliteration. Blackness upon the moon. Effaced, forgotten, erased, obliterated. Distracted with terror or grief, mad from love. P محو شدن *mahv shudan* (or گرديدن *gardīdan*), To be effaced.

A محواة *mahwāt*, A country full of serpents.

A محوال *mihwāl*, Extremely absurd.

A محوّب *muhawwib*, From rich become poor, and from poor waxed rich again.

A محوة *mahwat*, Erasure, obliteration, effacement (especially by rain). A shower. The west wind. Disgrace, shame. An hour.

A محوت *muhūt*, (pl. of محت *maht*) Very hot days. Pure, sincere. Intelligent, clever.

A محوج *mahūj*, Distant (hill). *Muhwij*, Poor, indigent. Who or what makes poor and needy.

A محوح *muhūh*, (v. n. of محّ) Being worn (dress).

A محور *mihwar*, The axis (of a pulley). An axle-tree (of wood or iron). The pin on which the tongue of a buckle turns. A branding-iron. A rolling-pin.

A محوّر *muhawwar*, (Bread) made round. Lined with red leather. Very white (flour). (A dish) whitened with grease. *Muhawwir*, Who makes white and bright. محوّر الثياب *muhawwiru's siyāb*, A bleacher, fuller.

A محورة *mahwarat* or *mahwurat*, An answer. *Mihwarat*, A baker's rolling-pin.

A محوّرة *muhwarrat*, A large wooden bowl greasy with butter and shining.

P محو شده *mahv shuda*, Effaced, obliterated.

A محوصل *muhawsal*, One whose abdomen is very prominent.

A محوّض *muhawwaz*, A small ditch for watering palm-trees. Built (reservoir). *Muhawwiz*, A maker of a reservoir (حوض *hawz*).

A محوضة *muhūzat*, (v. n. of محض) Being pure, unmixed, sound in nobility.

A محوّط *muhawwat*, Surrounded by a wall (حائط *hā'it*). *Muhawwit*, Who goes round or revolves. One who encloses with a fence. A guardian.

A محوق *mahūk*, Swept. Rubbed, smoothed. (A country) thin of herbage for want of rain.

A محوّق *muhawwak*, Large-glanded (man).

A محوقة *mihwakat*, A granary or barn-besom.

A محوكة *mahwakat*, A battle, conflict.

A محول *mahūl*, An informer, sycophant. Dry, barren, afflicted with dearth (soil). *Muhwil*, (A camel) bringing forth a male after a female, or vice versâ. (A child) one year old.

A محوّل *muhawwal*, Changed. Conferred. *Muhawwil*, A turner, changer, converter. (A camel) not conceiving. (See تحويل *tahwīl*.)

A محونة *muhūnat*, Abolition, obliteration. Deficiency, damage. An unlucky affair.

A محوّي *muhawwa'*, Adjacent (tents). *Muhawwī*, A seizer, apprehender.

A محويّ *mahwīy*, Collected, comprehended.

A محي *mahy*, (v. n. of محي) Erasing.

A محيا *mahya'*, Life. (pl. محايا *mahāya'*) The time when, or the place where, one lives. محياي و مماتي *mahyāya' wa mamātī*, My life and my death.

A محيّا *muhayya'*, The countenance, face, cheek. Created, saluted (king).

A محياة *mahyāt*, A place infested by serpents.

A محياص *mihyāṣ*, Narrow in the vulva.

A محيان *mihyān*, A time, period, season.

A محيث *muhīs*, One who turns up and examines the ground (in search of any thing).

A محيد *mahīd*, (v. n. of حاد for حيد) Turning away from. Bend, curvature. Asylum, place of refuge.

A محيّر *muhayyir*, One who amazes, astonishes.

A محيص *mahīṣ*, (v. n. of حاص for حيص) Turning away, swerving. Flying, escaping, retreating. Shining, glittering (helmet). Polished (spear). Strong (camel). An asylum, place of refuge.

A محيض *mahīz*, (v. n. of حاض for حيض) Having the courses (a woman). The menses. Vulva.

A محيضة *mahīzat*, A menstruous cloth.

A محيط *muhīt*, Who or what contains, surrounds, encircles, or embraces. One who comprehends, or knows; well acquainted with. Perishing. Periphery of a circle. محيط دائرة *muhīti dāʼira*, Circumference of a circle. محيط علما *muhītu ʻilman*, Who knows well. بحر محيط *bahri muhīt*, Ocean.

A محيعل *muhayʻil*, One who cries حيّ على الصلوة *hayy ʻala's salāt*, Come to prayer.

A محيّف *muhayyif*, One who takes any thing by the side or edge and lessens it.

A محيق *mahīk*, Slender, sharp-pointed (spear). Swept. Rubbed smooth.

A محيك *muhīk*, Who or what makes an impression, tells, or produces an effect. Penetrating, effective (sword or speech).

A محيل *muhīl*, A cheat, deceiver, knave, prevaricator. One year old. One who appoints another to receive a debt. (A woman or camel) bringing forth a male after a female, or vice versâ.

A محيلي *muhīlī*, Fraud, deceit, knavery.

A محيم *mihyam*, Acute, ingenious (boy).

A محين *muhyin*, One who stops (in a place). (See احيان *ihyān*.) *Muhīn*, A destroyer.

A محيّن *muhayyin*, One who fixes the time for milking. A destroyer.

A محيوس *mahyūs*, One whose father and mother were both born of a handmaid.

A محيي *muhyī*, (or محيية *muhyiyat*) A reviver, giver of life. (A camel) having lively colts. محيي الدين *muhyi'd dīn*, The reviver of religion. (See احياء *ihyāʼ*.)

A محيّي *muhayyī*, A reviver; hence one of the names of God. One who salutes or creates a king by pronouncing حيّاك الله *hayyāk allāh*, May God give you life!

P مخ *mukh*, Fire. A wasp. Adhesive, sticking. Do not adhere. Annihilated, reduced to nothing, vanished. *Makh* or *mukh*, A bridle or its bit, with which they break young or wild horses. *Mukh*, A date-tree. A wasp. A weevil.

A مخّ *makhkh*, Soft, smooth. Softness, flabbiness, flaccidness. *Mukhkh*, (pl. مخاخ *mikhākh* and مخخة *mikhakhat*) The brain, marrow; pulp; kernel. The purest or best part of any thing. Fat (of the eye). مخّ البيض *mukhkhu'l bayz*, Yolk of an egg.

A مخا *mukhā*, Moka, a sea-port of Arabia.

A مخابأة *mukhābaʼat*, (v. n. 3 of خبأ) Teasing by asking questions.

A مخابرة *mukhābarat*, (v. n. 3 of خبر) Letting land to another for part of the produce. Sowing land on condition of receiving part of the produce.

A مخابز *makhābiz*, (pl. of مخبزة) Bakehouses.

A مخابط *makhābit*, (pl. of مخبط *mikhbat*) Sticks with which leaves are knocked off a tree.

A مخابي *makhābī*, (pl. of مخبية *makhbiyat*) Places where things are laid up or concealed.

P مخات *mukhāt*, Turkomān musk (an herb).

A مخاتل *mukhātil*, A deceiver, cheat, cozener.

A مخاتلة *mukhātalat*, (v. n. 3 of ختل) Cheating, cozening, or endeavouring to do so.

A مخاتمة *mukhātamat*, A finishing, concluding.

A مخاتنة *mukhātanat*, (v. n. 3 of ختن) Connecting one's self by marriage.

A مخاتيم *makhātīm*, Measures for dry goods (usually marked with a seal).

A مخاخ *mikhākh*, (pl. of مخّ *mukhkh*) Marrows.

A مخاخة *mukhākhat*, Marrow, juice in bones.

A مخادّ *makhādd*, (pl. of مخدّة) Bolsters, pillows.

A مخادّة *mukhāddat*, (v. n. 3 of خدّ) Being enraged against, opposing, thwarting.

A مخادش *mukhādish*, A cat, a scratcher.

A مخادشة *mukhādashat*, (v. n. 3 of خدش) Excoriating. Scratching each other.

A مخادع *mukhādaʻ*, Deceived. *Mukhādiʻ*, A deceiver.

A مخادعة *mukhādaʻat*, (v. n. 3 of خدع) Deceiving, circumventing. Endeavouring to deceive. Abandoning, forsaking.

A مخادم *makhādim*, Ministers, servants, domestics, slaves. Eunuchs. Families.

A مخادنة *mukhādanat*, (v. n. 3 of خدن) Acting towards as a friend (خدن *khidn*).

A مخاديم *makhādīm*, (pl. of مخدوم *makhdūm*) Lords, masters, persons served or waited on.

A مخاذيل *makhāzīl*, (pl. of مخذول *makhzūl*) Mean men; rabble. Destitute, poor, indigent.

A مخارج *makhārij*, (pl. of مخرج *makhraj*) Times or places of going out. Expenses, outgoings, disbursements. The parts (of the mouth or throat) from which letters are uttered.

A مخارجة *mukhārajat*, (v. n. 3 of خرج) Gambling with the fingers, playing at the game called in Italy la morre. Agreeing with a servant to pay his wages monthly. Rebelling.

A مخارز *makhāriz*, Seams, sutures.

A مخارشة *mukhārashat*, (v. n. 3 of خرش) Scratching one another. Seizing and taking from another against his will.

A مخارص *makhāris*, Points of spears.

A مخارصة *mukhārasat*, A bartering, swoping.

A مخارط *makhārit*, (pl. of مخراط *mikhrāt*) Camels suffering from the disease خرط *kharat*.

A مخارف *mukhāraf*, Prohibited, debarred, excluded, disappointed.

A مخارفة *mukhārafat*, (v. n. 3 of خرف) Spending the autumn with. Bargaining with any one for the autumn-harvest (خريف *kharīf*).

A مخارم *makhārim*, (pl. of مخرم *makhrim*) Roads through rocky grounds. Beginnings of night. Brows of hills, the projecting summits of mountains. Openings of valleys betwixt mountains: places of egress.

A مخاريط *makhārīt*, (pl. of مخراط *mikhrāt*) Camels troubled with the complaint خرط *kharat*. Snakes which have cast their slough.

A مخاريق *makhārīk*, (pl. of مخراق *mikhrāk*) Twisted wreaths, with which they playfully strike one another when dancing.

A مخازاة *mukhāzāt*, (v. n. 3 of خزي) Disgracing, endeavouring to render another more ignominious than one's self.

A مخازق *makhāzik*, (pl. of مخزق *mikhzak*) Sticks or skewers tipped with pointed iron, used for transfixing dates or figs.

A مخازمة *mukhāzamat*, (v. n. 3 of خزم) Taking possession of a road, meeting, intercepting. Taking two roads but meeting at the same place.

A مخازن *makhāzin*, The nighest (roads). (pl. of مخزن *makhzan*) Storehouses, magazines.

A مخازي *makhāzī*, Ignominies, disgraces.

A مخاساة *mukhāsāt*, (v. n. 3 of خسا for خسو) Playing with nuts at odd or even.

A مخاسأة *mukhāsaʼat*, (v. n. 3 of خسأ) Throwing stones at one another.

A مخاشاة *mukhāshāt*, (v. n. 3 of خشي) Being afraid of each other. Rivalling any one in fearing. Dismissing unmolested.

A مخاشفة *mukhāshafat*, (v. n. 3 of خشف) Driving (camels) all night. Making a noise when striking (an arrow). Hastening to violate a treaty.

A مخاشنة *mukhāshanat*, (v. n. 3 of خشن) Behaving roughly or severely to.

A مخاصر *makhāsir*, (pl. of مخصرة *mikhsarat*) Wands or staves to lean upon. مخاصر الطريق *makhāsiru't tarīk*, The nearest road.

A مخاصرة *mukhāsarat*, (v. n. 3 of خصر) Taking (a companion) by the hand and walking together. Going different ways and meeting at the same place. Walking by the side.

A مخاصم *mukhāsim*, Adverse, contentious. An antagonist, opponent.

A مخاصمة *mukhāsamat*, (v. n. 3 of خصم) Contending. Enmity, altercation, opposition, struggle.

A مخاض *makhāz*, Camels amongst which the stallion has been turned loose until he has served them all. *Makhāz* or *mikhāz*, (v. n. of مخض) Labouring in the birth (a she-camel). Pains of labour. Camels in foal, or ten months gone. (pl. of مخاضة *makhāzat*) Fords. ابن مخاض *ibn makhāz*, A camel's colt entering into the second year.

A مخاضة *makhāzat*, (pl. مخاض *makhāz* and مخاوض) A ford, shallow place where people cross.

A مخاضة *mukhāzzat*, (v. n. 3 of خض) Making a bargain of sale or purchase. Returning like for like, compensating.

A مخاضرة *mukhāzarat*, (v. n. 3 of خضر) Selling fruit, corn, or pot-herbs before full-grown.

A مخاضعة *mukhāzaʻat*, (v. n. 3 of خضع) Speaking gently, politely, amorously (to ladies).

A مخاضنة *mukhāzanat*, (v. n. 3 of خضن) Soothing, coaxing with gentle, amorous words. Reviling each other outrageously.

A مخاط *mukhāt*, Snot. مخاط الشيطان *mukhātu'sh shaytān*, Atoms like cobwebs playing in the sun during the hottest part of the day.

A مخاطب *mukhātab*, One spoken to by another. The second person. Titled, named, styled. شخص مخاطب *shakhsi mukhātab*, The person spoken to. *Mukhātib*, A speaker, one who converses with or addresses another. The second person.

A مخاطبة *mukhātabat*, (v. n. 3 of خطب) Speaking. Speech, address, discourse, conversation.

A مخاطبيّة *mukhātabiyat*, A being addressed.

A مخاطة *mukhātat*, Sebestens.

A مخاطرة *mukhātarat*, (v. n. 3 of خطر) Hazarding a battle; laying bets, gaming, putting any thing at risk, throwing one's self in the way of danger, exposing to danger. Being near, obtaining sovereignty. Danger, peril, risk, hazard.

A مخاطم *makhātim*, (pl. of مخطم *makhtim*) Noses.

P مخاطه *mukhāta*, Sebestens.

A مخافة *makhāfat*, (v. n. of خاف for خوف) Dreading. (pl. مخافات) Fear, terror. Danger.

A مخافتة *mukhāfatat*, (v. n. 3 of خفت) Speaking softly, whispering to another; telling a secret, reading low or mutteringly. A low, whispering tone.

A مخافضة *mukhāfazat*, The act of depressing.

A معم مخال *muʻimmi mukhāl*, One who has celebrated uncles paternal and maternal.

A مخالاة *mukhālāt*, (v. n. 3 of خلي) Leaving, abandoning, letting alone. Wrestling with, endeavouring to throw down. Endeavouring to deceive.

A مخالّات *mukhāllāt*, (pl. of مخالّة *mukhāllat*) Demonstrations of friendship.

A مخالب *makhālib*, (pl. of مخلب *mikhlab*) Talons, claws of rapacious birds or beasts.

A مخالبة *mukhālabat*, A deceiving, a cajoling.

A مخالة *makhālat*, (v. n. of خال for خيل) Imagining, thinking. Presuming, being self-opiniative, proud. Having a vain persuasion or false opinion.

A مخالّة *mukhāllat*, (v. n. 3 of خلّ) Cultivating friendship, shewing an affection, doing a favour.

A مخالجة *mukhālajat*, (v. n. 3 of خلج) Affecting the mind with anxiety.

A مخالصة *mukhālasat*, (v. n. 3 of خلص) Acting candidly. Sincerity, candour, affection.

A مخالط *mukhālit*, A partner. A mixer.

A مخالطة *mukhālatat*, (v. n. 3 of خلط) Conversing, mixing together in society. Mixing with, meddling. Lying with. Worrying the flock (a wolf). Being perplexed (in mind), confused, insane. Giving a headache or crop-sickness. Conversation, commerce, intercourse. Mixture.

A مخالعة *mukhālaʻat*, (v. n. 3 of خلع) Desiring her husband to divorce her (a wife). Staking (one's garments) at play. Divorcement.

A مخالف *mukhālif*, Contrary, opposite, repugnant, adverse, dissentient, contradicting. An enemy. One who leans on his left foot, or who walks on one side. مخالف مال *mukhālifi māl*, Generous, munificent. P مخالفان امر الهي *mukhālifāni amri ilāhī*, Opposers of the divine command.

A مخالفة *mukhālafat*, (v. n. 3 of خلف) Opposing, resisting, thwarting. Visiting (a woman) in the absence of her husband or master. Accompanying, keeping close to. Repugnance, contradiction, opposition, contrariety, transgression, disobedience, contravention, rebellion, enmity. Discord. P مخالفت كردن *mukhālafat kardan*, To oppose, contradict, dissent from, confute, resist, disobey, rebel against. A المخالفة بين الرجلين *al mukhālafat bayna'r rijlayn*, Dancing.

P مخالف مال *mukhālif-māl*, One who crushes his opponents.

A مخالقة *mukhālakat*, (v. n. 3 of خلق) Shewing kindness or good will, being humane.

A مخالمة *mukhālamat*, A cultivating of friendship.

A مخالي *makhālī*, (pl. of مخلاة) Provender-bags.

A مخاليف *makhālīf*, (pl. of مخلاف) Cantons or districts into which Arabia Felix is divided.

A مخاليق *makhālīk*, (pl. of مخلوقة) Created things.

A مخامر *mukhāmir*, Latent, hidden (disease).

A مخامرة *mukhāmarat*, (v. n. 3 of خمر) Absconding, hiding one's self. Harbouring a secret grudge. Residing constantly (at a place). Abiding. Being near one another. Selling a free man as a slave. Mixing with, interfering in. Beclouding, disturbing (the mind). Giving a headache or crop-sickness.

A مخانة *makhānat*, (v. n. of خان for خون) Deceiving, acting treacherously.

A مخانق *makhānik*, (pl. of مخنق *mikhnak*) Chains for the neck, collars, necklaces.

A مخاوتة *mukhāwatat*, (v. n. 3 of خات for خوت) Stealing a look at, turning the face suddenly towards one.

A مخاوذ ملاوذ *mukhāwiz mulāwiz*, Difficult, intricate (affair).

A مخاوذة *mukhāwazat*, (v. n. 3 of خاذ for خوذ) Opposing, resisting. Agreeing with, conforming to.

A مخاوشة *mukhāwashat*, (v. n. 3 of خاش for خوش) Raising (one's side) to a height from the bed.

A مخاوصة *mukhāwasat*, (v. n. 3 of خاص for خوص) Shewing and conferring (applied to merchants when exchanging or fixing a price). Winking or shutting the eyes in order to look more steadily.

A مخاوض *makhāwiz*, (pl. of مخاضة *makhāzat*) Fords, shallows.

A مخاوضة *mukhāwazat*, (v. n. 3 of خاض for خوض) Making (a horse) ford a stream.

A مخاوف *makhāwif*, (pl. of مخافة *makhāfat*) Dangerous or dreadful places. Scarecrows.

A مخاوفة *mukhāwafat*, (v. n. 3 of خاف for خوف) Overcoming by intimidation.

A مخاخ *makhāʼikh*, Choice, excellent (camels).

A مخايرة *mukhāyarat*, (v. n. 3 of خار for خير) Being superior (to another).

A مخائل *makhāʼil*, Marks, indexes, signs.

A مخايلة *mukhāyalat*, (v. n. 3 of خال for خيل) Promising rain (a cloud). Opposing, contending, disputing for superiority.

A مخبّ *mukhibb*, One who makes a horse amble.

A مخبأ *makhbaʼ*, A place where any thing is hid.

A مخبأة *mukhbaʼat*, (A girl) kept closely concealed from view and yet unmarried.

A مخبّأة *mukhabbaʼat*, (A woman) kept strictly concealed.

A مخبّب *mukhabbib*, A deceiver, seducer.

A مخبّة *makhabbat*, Lowest part of a valley.

A مخبت *mukhbit*, Humble, submissive.

A مخبث *mukhbis*, A corrupter. One who associates with rascally company. Wicked, corrupt. Obscene, foul-mouthed.

A مخبثان *makhbasān*, Impure, wicked, corrupt. One whose companions are impure and corrupt.

A مخبثة *makhbasat*, Corruption, villainy. A cause of impurity or maliciousness.

A مخبخب *mukhabkhab*, Fat, handsome (camel).

A مخبر *makhbar*, The knowledge of any thing by evidence or declaration. The interior. A place of trial or probation. *Mukhbir*, An announcer, signifier, certifier, teller of news. مخبر صادق *mukhbiri sādik*, Bringer of sure news, true reporter.

A مخبّر *mukhabbir*, A giver of information.

A مخبراني *makhbarāniy*, One who knows any thing by report.

A مخبرة *makhbarat*, A water-closet. *Makhbarat* or *makhburat*, A place of trial. The knowledge of a thing. The interior of any thing.

A مخبز *makhbaz*, (or مخبزة) A bakehouse.

A مخبصة *mikhbasat*, A kind of ladle.

A مخبط *mikhbat*, (pl. مخابط *makhābit*) A stick with which a tree is stripped of its leaves. *Mukhbat*, Vexed. Sick. *Mukhbit*, One who hangs his head.

A مخبّط *mukhabbat*, Disordered in the intellect, disturbed. مخبّط للعقل *mukhabbit li'l ʻakl*, Disturbing the brain.

A مخبل *mukhbil*, One who lends (a horse) to go to war; also (camels, sheep) to receive in return part of the milk, hair, or wool.

A مخبّل *mukhabbal*, Epileptic, mad, insane, possessed by a demon. Mutilated in the extremities. Name of several poets. *Mukhabbil*, A corrupter. A depriver of a limb or of reason. Time; fortune.

A مخبور *makhbūr*, Nicely-seasoned (meat).

A مخبوز *makhbūz*, Baked (bread).

A مخبوط *makhbūt*, (A leaf) shaken from a tree. Troubled with a cold at the beginning of winter.

A مخبول *makhbūl*, Disturbed in mind. Epileptic.

A مخبون *makhbūn*, Doubled and sewed up (a garment). Concealed under the arm-pit or under the garment (the hand). (Provisions) laid up against a scarcity. (in poetry) A foot, whose second quiescent letter is dropt.

A مخبي *mukhbī*, (or مخبّي *mukhabbī*) One who pitches a tent (خباء *khibā*).

A مخبئنّ *mukhba*inn*, Shrunk, drawn together.

A مخّة *mukhkhat*, Marrow.

P مخت *mukht*, Hope.

A مخّت *mukhitt*, One who diminishes or damages. Ashamed, blushing.

A مختار *mukhtār*, Chosen, selected. Most excellent, supreme, highest. Absolute, independent. A chooser. A free agent. Invested with power and authority; a ruler, master. مختار حق *mukhtāri hakk*, Chosen of God (an epithet of Muhammad). انت بالمختار *anta bi'l mukhtār*, It is you to choose, the choice rests with you.

P مختار نامه *mukhtār-nāma*, Written power, a power of attorney.

A مختاري *mukhtārī*, Independence, authority.

A مختال *mukhtāl*, Self-important, haughty, vain, proud, looking round in self-admiration. (A cloud) which promises rain.

P مختاله *mukhtāla*, A deceiver, impostor.

A مختان *mukhtān*, Deceived.

A مختبأ *mukhtaba*, Place of concealment.

A مختبر *mukhtabar*, Proved. *Mukhtabir*, Expert.

A مختبز *mukhtabaz*, A bakehouse. *Mukhtabiz*, One who feeds with bread (خبز *khubz*). A baker.

A مختبس *mukhtabis*, Possessed of by conquest. A spoiler. A lion.

A مختبط *mukhtabit*, One who asks with importunity a favour for nothing. One who shakes the leaves off a tree.

A مختبل *mukhtabil*, Who or what impairs or depraves the mind. Restless.

A مختبئ *mukhtabi*, Hid, concealed, lurking. A hider, concealer.

A مختتم *mukhtatim*, A finisher, concluder.

A مختتن *mukhtatin*, Self-circumcised.

A مختتئ *mukhtati*, Absconding for fear or shame: timid. A deceiver. A seizer.

A مختثي *mukhtatī*, Broken by sorrow or disease. Deficient, defective. A vender of wares piecemeal.

A مختتئة *mukhtati*at*, Dreadful (desert), where neither sound is heard or landmark seen.

A مختدر *mukhtadir*, Closely concealed.

A مختدع *mukhtada'*, Deceived, circumvented. *Mukhtadi'*, A deceiver. An evil-wisher.

A مختدف *mukhtadif*, One who snatches hastily. One who cuts a garment.

A مختدم *mukhtadim*, One who serves himself. One who employs or seeks to employ as a servant.

A مختّر *mukhattir*, Intoxicating, fuddling (drink).

A مخترج *mukhtarij*, An extractor, drawer forth.

A مخترجة *mukhtarajat*, A she-camel equal to a full-grown male in size and strength.

A مخترش *mukhtarish*, A scratcher. One who seeks a provision for a family.

A مخترص *mukhtaris*, A framer of lies. One who puts (what he wants) into his wallet.

A مخترط *mukhtarit*, One who draws (a sword). One who strips the leaves from a branch, or grapes from a stalk, by drawing it through the hand.

A مخترع *mukhtara'*, Invented. Coined (word). *Mukhtari'*, An inventor, author. A commencer, founder. One who does any thing de novo. A defrauder, cheat. A cleaver. One who lends a riding-horse for a time.

A مخترعات *mukhtara'āt*, Inventions, novelties.

A مخترف *mukhtaraf*, Gathered (fruit). *Mukhtarif*, A gatherer of fruit.

A مخترق *mukhtarak*, The time or place of passing. A (ship's) course. A place whence or whither the wind blows. A desert, wilderness. *Mukhtarik*, One who passes by. Hard-blowing (wind). An inventor of a lie.

A مخترم *mukhtaram*, Removed by death. *Mukhtarim*, A destroyer, extirpator, snatcher, tearer off.

A مختزع *mukhtazi'*, Who or what tears (any one) away from his family.

A مختزق *mukhtazik*, Unsheathed (sword).

A مختزل *mukhtazil*, Separate, solitary. One who cuts, tears, separates, or throws away.

A مختزن *mukhtazan*, Stored, hoarded, preserved. *Mukhtazin*, One who keeps a secret. A hoarder of wealth. One who takes the shortest road.

A مختشب *mukhtashib*, A hewer out roughly (of a bow or arrow). A composer of careless, unpolished verses thrown off at once.

A مختشع *mukhtashi'*, Humble, humbled.

A مختصّ *mukhtass*, Appropriated, proper, peculiar, special, private. Chosen, selected, elected.

A مختصّان *mukhtassān*, (Pers. pl. of مختصّ *mukhtass*) Intimates, familiars, chosen friends.

A مختصر *mukhtasar*, Abbreviated, abridged, contracted. Mean, trivial, small. A compendium, epitome, digest. Title of a book. P مختصر كردن *mukhtasar kardan*, To abridge. A *Mukhtasir*, One who goes a little way. An abridger, epitomist. A taker (by the hand). (See اختصار *ikhtisār*.)

A مختصران *mukhtasarān*, (Pers. pl.) Mean, low-spirited persons.

A مختصف *mukhtasif*, A doubler or sewer (of a slipper). One who covers (his body) with leaves sewed together.

A مختصم *mukhtasim*, Engaged in altercation. A disputant, wrangler.

A مختصي *mukhtasī*, A gelder. One who castrates himself, a self-castrator.

A مختضب *mukhtazib*, Dyed, tinged. One who paints himself. A Pict.

A مختضر *mukhtazar*, Dead in the flower of his age. *Mukhtazir*, A reaper of green corn. (See اختضار.)

A مختضع *mukhtazi'*, Humble, depressed, submissive. One who passes quickly by.

A مختضم *mukhtazim*, A cutter, amputator. A giver. One who breaks wind. (A sword) which cuts (the scabbard).

A مختطّ *mukhtatt*, (or مختطط *mukhtatit*) One who draws a line or marks out. Downy-cheeked.

A مختطب *mukhtatib*, One who asks (a woman) in marriage. One who invites (another man) to marry, and offers (him) one of his family.

A مختطف *mukhtatif*, A snatcher, seizer, carrier off. Departing, quitting (fever).

A مختطي *mukhtatī*, A stepper, advancer.

A مختفض *mukhtafiz*, Who descends or alights.

A مختفضة *mukhtafizat*, Self-circumcised (girl).

A مختفق *mukhtafik*, (Vapour or lightning) in motion. Loud-blowing (wind).

A مختفي *mukhtafī*, Hidden: absconding, lurking. A bringer out, drawer forth, publisher. A digger up of dead bodies. A secret murderer.

A مختلّ *mukhtall*, Emaciated, attenuated. Corrupted; disturbed, confounded, confused, depraved; ruined (business by negligence). Indigent; in need. Tart, acid. A sewer together. Excessively thirsty.

A مختلب *mukhtalib*, A deceiver.

A مختلج *mukhtalaj*, Drawn, carried off. Weaned. Fleshless (face). One about whose origin people dispute. *Mukhtalij*, A drawer away, abstracter. Trembling. Winking.

A مختلس *mukhtalas*, Snatched, carried off. *Mukhtalis*, A seizer, drawer to himself, stealer.

A مختلط *mukhtalit*, Perplexed, confused (business). Obscure, unknown (genealogy). A camel whose flesh is interlarded with fat. Mixed. Fat. (See اختلاط *ikhtilāt*.)

A مختلع *mukhtali'*, A spoiler, robber.

A مختلعة *mukhtali'at*, (A woman) who asks her husband to grant her a divorce with her marriage-settlements. A libidinous woman.

A مختلف *mukhtalaf*, Conflicting (opinion); disagreement, contrariety of sentiment. تربيع مختلف *tarbī'i mukhtalaf*, An irregular quadrangular figure, a trapezium. *Mukhtalif*, Diverse, different, discordant, various. Intricate. Troubled with diarrhœa. Become the successor or representative (خليفة

khalifat). One who moves to and fro, or turns here and there. One who visits the wife of his friend in his absence. مختلفة الاضلاع *mukhtalifatu'l azlāʻ*, A scalene triangle. باصناف مختلفه *ba asnāfi mukhtalifa*, In different manners, multifarious. طوائف مختلفه *tawāʼifi mukhtalifa*, Various sorts of people.

A مختلق *mukhtalak*, Well-made, completely formed. Invented, fabricated. A lie, fiction. *Mukhtalik*, A deviser, forger (of a lie). Well-made, well-formed. Adapted, accommodated, suited, proper.

A مختلم *mukhtalim*, A chooser, selector.

A مختلون *mukhtalūna*, (pl. of مختلي *mukhtalī*) Mowers of hay, foragers, grass-cutters.

A مختلي *mukhtalī*, Sharp (sword). A forager. A lion.

A مختم *mikhtam*, A nut which, when rubbed smooth, they shoot off.

A مختّم *mukhattam*, Carefully sealed. (The leg of a quadruped) marked with the least white.

A مختمّ *mukhtamm*, A sweeper (of the house). A cleaner (of a well). A cutter.

A مختمر *mukhtamir*, Fermented. Fermenting (wine); leavening (dough). White-headed (sheep or horse).

A مختنث *mukhtanis*, One who turns down the mouth of a bottle in order to drink.

A مختنق *mukhtanak*, Narrow (place). *Mukhtanik*, Strangled, throttled. A horse, the blaze of whose forehead reaches to his chin.

A مختوّ *makhtūw*, (The fringe of a garment) twisted by way of ornament.

P مختوم *makhtūm*, A bear.

A مختوم *makhtūm*, Sealed. Finished, concluded. A dry-measure called صاع *sāʻ*. طين مختوم *tīni makhtūm*, Sealing-wax or clay. مختوم الابصار *makhtūmu'l absār*, Whose eyes are sealed, blind.

A مختون *makhtūn*, Circumcised.

A مختوي *mukhtawī*, Rendered weak in mind. A traveller (over a country). A striker of a spear into the belly (of a horse). A taker, seizer. (A wild beast) which steals and eats (a calf).

A مخثاء *mikhsāʼ*, A honey-gatherer's bag.

A مخثر *mukhsir*, One who leaves (butter) unmelted. (See اخثار *ikhsār*.)

A مخثعم *mukhasʻam*, A lion. Plump-faced, fleshy.

A مخثّم *mukhassam*, (or مخثّمة *mukhassamat*) Broad-toed (shoe). *Mukhassim*, Who makes broad.

A مخج *makhj*, (v. n. of مخج) Drawing, moving (a bucket) about in a well till (it) fills with water. Lying with.

A مخجخج *mukhajkhij*, One who draws his body together through fear; absconding, concealing one's self. Violent (wind). One who moves quick and leans to a side. One who lies with. One who conceals his thoughts.

A مخجل *mukhjil*, Who or what banishes sorrow. Astonishing, confounding. (A valley) luxuriant with herbage. *Mukhjil*, (or مخجّل *mukhajjil*) One who makes ashamed, or puts to the blush.

A مخخة *mikhakhat*, (pl. of مخ *mukhkh*) Marrows.

A مخدّ *mukhidd*, A furrow-maker; digger.

A مخدة *makhadat*, Aid, help, favour, protection.

A مخدّة *mikhaddat*, (pl. مخادّ *makhādd*) A bolster; pillow. A coulter.

A مخدج *mukhdaj*, (A camel fœtus) imperfectly formed. Deficient in the hand, *i.e.* avaricious, stingy. *Mukhdij*, (A she-camel) going the full time, yet bringing forth an imperfect fœtus. (A summer) having little rain.

A مخدّد *mukhaddid*, Shrivelled, wrinkled (flesh or skin). Lean, scraggy. Who or what makes lean. A splitter.

A مخدر *mukhdar*, Concealed behind a curtain. *Muhhdar* or *mukhdir*, (A lion) hidden by a thicket. *Mukhdir*, One who arrives on a rainy day. Quiet at home or in a nest. Who or what stupefies and benumbs the limbs.

A مخدّر *mukhaddar*, Veiled, concealed, kept in. *Mukhaddir*, Narcotic. Who keeps concealed.

A مخدّرات *mukhaddirāt*, Narcotics, anodynes.

A مخدّرة *mukhaddarat*, (or مخدرة *mukhdarat*) A matron, a virtuous lady (true to the marriage-bed, and always veiled when going abroad); a young virgin kept retired, behind the curtain. P مخدّرات پردهٔ عصمت *mukhaddarāti pardaʼi ʻismat*, Concealed behind the veil of chastity, *i.e.* modest women.

A مخدش *mikhdash*, The space between the shoulders of a camel, the withers.

A مخدّش *mukhaddish*, Who or what scratches very much with the nails. A cat. The space between the shoulders of a camel.

A مخدع *mikhdaʻ* or *mukhdaʻ*, A storehouse, place where any thing is laid up. *Mukhdiʻ*, A layer up, preserver. (See اخداع *ikhdāʻ*.)

A مخدّع *mukhaddaʻ*, Often circumvented in war, and thereby gaining experience. *Mukhaddiʻ*, A remarkable deceiver.

A مخدم *mikhdam*, A sharp sword. *Mukhdim*, One who orders to serve; one who gives a servant. One who begs or hires a servant (خادم *khādim*).

A مخدّم *mukhaddam*, Possessed of many domestics or followers. The tying-place of a lady's drawers at the ankle. (A horse) having white circles round the feet. *Mukhaddam*, (or مخدّمة *mukhaddamat*) That part of the foot where they bind the fetter خدمة *khadamat*.

A مخدود *makhdūd*, Cauterized (camel).

A مخدور *makhdūr*, Retired, kept behind the curtain. (A lion) concealed in a brake.

A مخدوع *makhdūʻ*, Cut in the vein اخدع *akhdaʻ*.

A مخدوم *makhdūm*, Served, waited on (by slaves or familiar spirits). A lord, master. A little boy, an infant. A eunuch. مخدوم كائنات *makhdūmi kāʼināt*, Lord of all beings, Omnipotence.

A مخدومي *makhdūmī*, My lord or master.

A مخدوميّة *makhdūmīyat*, The condition of being served or waited upon. Lordship.

A مخذي *mukhdī*, One who walks step by step.

A مخذرق *mukhazrik*, A fast goer. A filler (of a vessel). A sharpener (of a sword). One who has a fit of purging. One who mutilates the extremities.

A مخذّع *mukhazzaʻ*, Minced, chopped small, but without separation. Roast meat. (A tree) bitten or cut off at the top or extremities. *Mukhazziʻ*, A circumciser.

A مخذعة *mikhzaʻat*, A knife.

A مخذف *mikhzaf*, The handle of that by which the bow-case is united to the quiver.

A مخذفة *mikhzafat*, A stick slit at the end for throwing stones, a sling. Podex.

A مخذقة *mahhzakat*, The anus.

A مخذل *mukhzil*, (A doe) staying with her young.

A مخذّل *mukhazzil*, One who causes a breach between friends. A despiser. An abandoner.

A مخذم *mikhzam*, A sharp sword.

A مخذّم *mukhazzam*, Sharp, keen (sword). *Mukhazzim*, One who cuts in pieces.

A مخذول *makhzūl*, Abandoned, forsaken; disappointed, frustrated; contemptible, vile.

A مخذئ *mukhziʼ*, A humbler, tamer, one who renders obsequious (man or beast).

A مخر *mahhr*, (v. n. of مخر) Passing through the sea (a ship); ploughing it with a dashing noise. Cutting the waves (as a swimmer). Wearing away the axle-hole, playing in it (the axis of a pulley). Being copiously watered (land). Taking the choicest of household stuff. Incommoding a camel (abundance of milk), causing her to be milked much. Bringing water into grounds (for cultivation). بنات مخر *banātu makhr*, White clouds before summer.

A مخرّ *mukhirr*, Who causes to fall, or throws down. Who cuts (the hand) with a sword so that it drops off.

A مخراة *mahhraʼat*, (or مخراة *mahhrāt*) A privy.

A مخراش *mikhrāsh*, A hooked stick. A shoemaker's implement for marking leather.

A مخراط *mikhrāt*, (pl. مخاريط *makhārit*) A camel whose milk habitually comes away in a clotted state. A snake which casts its slough every year.

A مخراق *mikhrāk*, A man with a handsome figure, whether tall or not. A wild bull. A lord. Liberal. Expert, skilful. A twisted wreath, with which they playfully strike one another when dancing. هو مخراق حرب *huwa mikhrāk harbin*, He is active in battle, he fights valiantly.

P مخران *makhrān*, Name of a Christian monastery or church, so called after the architect.

A مخرب *mukhrib*, Who or what desolates or lays waste; a destroyer, desolater.

A مخرّب *mukharrab*, Corrupted (word). Slit-eared. *Mukharrib*, Who destroys all around, far and wide. مخرّب معمور *mukharribi maʻmūr*, A ravager of cultivated countries.

A مخربة *mukhribat*, An empty bee-hive. A she-camel left unfettered for the purpose of being milked.

A مخربص *mukharbis*, A man who is a subtile calculator, who enters into the minutiæ of things.

A مخربق *mukharbik*, A tearer (of a garment). One who cuts small, or minces. A corrupter, spoiler.

A مخربقة *mukharbakat*, (A woman) subject to syncope in coitu.

A مخرة *makhrat*, *mikhrat*, or *mukhrat*, A chosen, selected thing. Any thing issuing from the belly and smelling offensively.

A مخرت *makhrat*, A straight or right road.

A مخرج *makhraj*, (v. n. of خرج) Going out in a hostile manner, sallying forth against. (pl. مخارج *makhārij*) Time and place of going forth. An organ of excretion. A necessary, privy. Utterance, pronunciation, or rather the part from which a letter is uttered. P مخرج پس *makhraji pas*, The hinder vent, anus. *Mukhraj*, (v. n. 4 of خرج) Producing, drawing out, bringing forth. Expelling. Led out, ejected, exported, carried forth. Time and place of leading forth. *Mukhrij*, Expelling; an expeller. A leader forth, bringer, thruster, or digger out. One who pays tribute. One who hunts a black and white ostrich (called اخرج *akhraj*).

A مخرّج *mukharraj*, Instructed in learning and politeness. (A field) partly covered with herbage. (A year) partly barren, partly fruitful. *Mukharrij*, A tutor, instructor of youth. One who covers part of a tablet with writing, but not the whole.

A مخرد *mukhrid*, Bashful, silent, or speaking in a low voice from modesty. Inclined to laughter, raillery, or any thing ludicrous.

A مخردل *mukhardal*, Chopped small (meat). Prostrated. Epileptic. *Mukhardil*, Greatly shaken (palm-tree), yet having large unripe dates remaining upon it. A cutter (of meat) in small pieces.

A مخرز *mikhraz*, A shoemaker's awl.

A مخرّز *mukharraz*, Any insect whose wings look as if perforated with stitch-holes (خرزة *khurzat*).

A مخرّس *mukharris*, One who dresses or gives the food خرسة *khursat* to a woman in child-bed.

A مخرش *mikhrash*, A hooked stick. A shoemaker's implement for drawing lines on the leather.

A مخرّش *mukharrish*, (Corn) shooting forth its first ears.

A مخرشة *mikhrashat*, A shoemaker's implement for drawing lines on leather.

A مخرص *mikhras*, A spear, especially the head.

A مخرط *mikhrat*, A turner's lathe. *Mukhrit*, Who draws together (a purse). (pl. مخاريط *makhārīt*) (A camel or a sheep) troubled with a disease (خرط *kharat*) which coagulates their milk.

A مخرّط *mukharrit*, Aperient, cathartic (medicine).

A مخرطم *mukhartam*, (A boot) pointed at the toe. *Mukhartim*, One who strikes on the خرطوم *khartūm* (proboscis, trunk, nose, or snout).

A مخرّع *mukharraꜥ*, Changeable, capricious.

A مخرف *makhraf*, (v. n. of خرف) Gathering fruit in autumn. The date-picking. A fruit-garden. An avenue between rows of palm-trees. An open level road. *Mikhraf*, A basket into which the choicest dates are picked. *Mukhrif*, One who begins the autumn. (A she-camel) which brings forth a colt in the autumn (خريف *kharīf*).

A مخرفة *makhrafat*, A fruit-garden, orchard. An open road. A way through rows of palms; avenue.

A مخرفج *mukharfaj*, Wide, ample (garment). Copious (draught of milk).

A مخرفش *mukharfash*, Mixed.

A مخرق *makhrak*, An extensive desert without water. A stone beside a cistern, whereon they stand in drawing water. *Mukhrik*, A striker with astonishment, a confounder.

A مخرّق *mukharrak*, Rent, torn. *Mukharrik*, A render, tearer. A great liar.

A مخرقة *makhrakat*, (v. n. of خرق) Telling a lie. A twisted wreath, with which they playfully strike each other when dancing.

A مخرم *makhrim*, (pl. مخارم *makhārim*) The brow of a hill, the projecting summit of a mountain, a ness. The fore part of a torrent. *Mukhrim*, (Death) snatching (one) away.

A مخرّمة *mukharramat*, Crop-eared (sheep).

A مخرمد *mukharmid*, Fixed, assiduous. Silent, looking on the ground.

A مخرميّة *makhrimīyat*, Metempsychosis, transmigration of souls. A certain licentious sect.

A مخرنبق *mukhrambik*, Silent, mute. مخرنبق لينباع *mukhrambik li yambāꜥ*, One who fixes his eyes on the ground that he may spring on his adversary unawares.

A مخرنشم *mukhranshim*, Proud, high in his own opinion. Ill-coloured and emaciated. Contracted in the limbs.

A مخرنطم *mukhrantim*, Haughty, tossing the nose.

A مخرنقة *mukharnikat*, A country swarming with leverets (خرنق *khirnik*).

A مخروب *makhrūb*, Split. Wasted, plundered.

A مخروة *makh* or *mukhrusat*, A privy, jakes.

A مخروت *makhrūt*, Split in the nose or lip.

A مخرورق *mukhrawrik*, One who goes about on a camel. Light. Clever, dexterous.

A مخروز *makhrūz*, Sewn, stitched.

A مخروش *makhrūsh*, (A camel) marked with the oblong impression خراش *khirāsh*.

A مخروط *makhrūt*, Unbarked, peeled. Planed, turned in a lathe. Conical. One who has a long face and thin beard. Purged with green food (a camel).

A مخروّط *mukhrawwit*, Swift (camel).

A مخروطة *makhrūtat*, A cone. A beard, light upon the cheek, smooth at the point, and long.

A مخروطی *makhrūtī*, Conical, tapering.

A مخروعة *makhrūꜥat*, Furious (she-camel) Marked in the ear with the mark خرع *kharaꜥ*.

A مخروف *makhrūf*, Plucked, pulled, gathere(d) (dates). Watered by the autumnal rain.

A مخروق *makhrūk*, Disappointed, debarred fro(m) the comforts of life.

A مخروم *makhrūm*, (Verse) of the measure فعولن *faꜥūlun* reduced to عولن *ꜥūlun*, and مفاعلتن *m*(*u*)*fāꜥalatun* cut down to فاعلتن *fāꜥalatun*.

A مخري *makhra'*, Name of a village in Hijā(z) possessing villages and forts.

A مخزاب *mikhzāb*, Swollen with fat (camel).

A مخزاج *mikhzāj*, Covered with collops of fat.

A مخزّة *makhazzat*, The form of a hare.

A مخزّر *mukhazzir*, One who straitens.

A مخزرق *mukhazrik*, Fast, long-stepping (beast).

A مخزّع *mukhazziꜥ*, Who or what cuts.

A مخزق *mikhzak*, (pl. مخازق *makhāzik*) A kin(d) of wooden stick with a sharp iron head, which run(s) through several (dates) at once, kept by a date seller. The purchaser receives for his money as man(y) dates as he can spit, be they many or few.

A مخزّم *mukhazzam*, (A bird) whose bill is per(forated). *Mukhazzim*, Who puts on a خزامة.

A مخزن *makhzan*, A storehouse, storeroom, ma(gazine), treasury, granary, cellar. مخزن الاسرار *makh(zanu'l asrār)*, A repository or keeper of secrets.

A مخزول *makhzūl*, Broken-backed.

A مخزوم *makhzūm*, Pierced in the nose. (A bird) perforated in the bill. Name of the founder of a tribe.

A مخزون *makhzūn*, Stored up, hoarded.

A مخزي *mukhzī*, Who or what covers with sham(e) or ignominy. A despiser; a depressor, afflicter, ruine(r).

P مخستان *mukhistān*, A grove of palm-trees.

A مخسر *mukhsir*, A loser. Detrimental.

A مخسّر *mukhassir*, One who causes loss; inju(rious), detrimental. A seducer.

A مخسف *mukhsif*, One who discovers a spring in a rock flowing forth incessantly. Blind (eye).

A مخسّف *mukhassaf*, A lion.

A مخسّل *mukhassal*, Rejected, reprobated, wick(ed), vile, useless, unserviceable.

A مخسن *mukhsin*, One become ignominious af(ter) having been in high repute.

A مخسور *makhsūr*, Injured, damaged.

A مخسوع *makhsūꜥ*, Removed to a distance.

A مخسوف *makhsūf*, (A spring or well) dug in a rock and perennial.

A مخسول *makhsūl*, Rejected, reprobated. Useless, unserviceable.

A مخسي *mukhsī*, (or مخسّي *mukhassī*) A playe(r) at odd or even with nuts.

A مخشّ *mikhashsh*, Bold in the night-time. A(n) intrepid horse. Penis.

A مخشاة *makhshāt*, (v. n. of خشي) Fearing: fear.

A مخشخش *mukhashkhish*, A producer of soun(d) by the collision of hard bodies or dry substances.

as papers, new clothes, or arms.

A مخشع *mukhshiʻ*, A humbler, depressor.

A مخشف *makhshaf*, A frozen place. *Mikhshaf*, A lion. A meddler in any business. (A road-guide) fearless in the night, conducting with expedition. *Mukhshif*, (A doe) which has a fawn.

A مخشّف *mukhashshif*, One who breaks with violence. A road-guide. Troubled with the scab or scald, and going straddlingly on that account.

A مخشّل *mukhashshal*, Rejected, discarded. Adorned with jewels.

A مخشّم *mukhashsham*, Very drunk. *Mukhashshim*, Pungent, intoxicating, overpowering (smell).

A مخشّن *mukhashshin*, Irritating: exasperator.

A مخشنة *makhshanat*, (v. n. of خشن) Being rough.

A مخشوب *makhshūb*, Polished (sword). Unpolished (sword). Ill-dressed (meat). Bread without meat.

A مخشوش *makhshūsh*, A camel in whose nose the wooden ring خشاش *khishāsh* has been inserted.

A مخشول *makhshūl*, Rejected, discarded. Low, base, despicable.

A مخشوم *makhshūm*, Drunk, intoxicated.

A مخشّی *mukhashshī*, Fear-inspiring, terrific.

A مخشية *makhshiyat*, (v. n. of خشي) Fearing.

A مخصاب *mikhsāb*, Fertile, fruitful (land).

A مخصال *mikhsāl*, A reaping-hook, a sickle.

A مخصب *mukhsib*, (A country or people) fruitful, rich in produce. Plenteous (year).

A مخصّر *mukhassar*, Slender, thin. Slim or hollow (sole of a shoe). Narrow-wristed (hand). A man hollow and narrow in the middle (of the foot).

A مخصرة *mikhsarat*, (pl. مخاصر *makhāsir*) Any thing taken in the hand to lean upon (as a staff); or for a public speaker to lean upon (as a wand).

A مخصّص *mukhassis*, One who appropriates or makes his own. (See تخصيص *takhsīs*.)

A مخصف *mikhsaf*, A cobbler's awl. *Mukhsif*, A quick goer.

A مخصّف *mukhassif*, A strong and good sewer. Bad-tempered. One who makes great pretensions to what he is not entitled.

A مخصل *mikhsal*, A sharp sword.

A مخصوف *makhsūf*, (A shoe) made of several layers or soles of leather. Smooth (sky). Bi-coloured, black and white.

A مخصور *makhsūr*, Injured, damaged.

A مخصوص *makhsūs*, Peculiar, special, particular, proper, specific, belonging to. Private, domestic, intimate. Addicted, dedicated; peculiarly ascribed or attributed to. P مخصوص دم بودن *makhsūsi dam būdan*, To have only the last breath remaining in the body.

A مخصوصا *makhsūsan*, Specially, particularly.

A مخصوصيّة *makhsūsiyat*, Property, peculiarity, speciality. Friendship.

A مخصى *mahhsa'*, The place of castration.

A مخصيّ *makhsīy*, Gelded. A eunuch.

A مخض *makhz*, (v. n. of مخض) Churning (which is done by shaking milk in a leathern bag or bottle). Shaking any thing violently. Moving (a bucket) in a well (till it fills). Braying (a he-camel).

A مخّض *mukhkhaz*, (pl. of ماخض *mākhiz*) In travail, experiencing the pains of birth (women, camels, or sheep).

A مخضب *mikhzab*, A vessel in which colouring matter is kept, a dyeing vat.

A مخضّب *mukhazzab*, Tinged, dyed, imbued. *Mukhazzib*, One who colours or dyes well.

A مخضد *mikhzad*, A voracious eater.

A مخضّر *mukhazzar*, Verdant, made green. Blest. *Mukhazzir*, One who makes green.

A مخضرّ *mukhzarr*, Green, verdant.

A مخضرب *mukhazrab*, Eloquent.

A مخضرة *makhzarat*, A verdant spot.

A مخضرم *mukhazram*, Spurious, born of a concubine, one who knows not his father. A man who has lived half his life a Pagan and half a Muhammadan (such was the poet لبيد *labīd*). Held in little estimation. A mulatto, one born of a white father and a black mother. Water betwixt heavy and light. Insipid (meat). (Meat) difficult to be discovered, whether of a male or female animal. Uncircumcised.

A مخضرمة *mukhazramat*, Circumcised (woman). (A she-camel) mutilated in the upper part of the ear.

A مخضع *mukhziʻ*, One who humbles, abuses, makes submissive. (Old age) making one to stoop. One who accosts (a woman) in gentle, soft terms.

A مخضفة *mukhzifat*, Wine (as causing a man to break wind without blushing).

A مخضل *mikhzal*, Sharp (sword). *Mukhzal*, Easy, pleasant (life). *Mukhzil*, Soft, tender, delicate.

A مخضّل *mukhazzil*, Soft, tender, delicate.

A مخضلّ *mukhzall*, (A hillock or a knoll) wet with dew. Easy, pleasant (life).

A مخضم *makhzam*, Any thing eaten with the front-teeth. *Mukhzam*, Blest with the conveniences of life. *Mukhzim*, (Water) slightly brackish, drunk by cattle, though not by men.

A مخضّم *mukhazzam*, Abundantly blest with pleasures or conveniences of life.

A مخضن *mikhzan*, Who wears out his cattle by much labour.

A مخضوب *makhzūb*, Tinged, stained, dyed.

A مخضود *makhzūd*, (A tree) cleared of its thorns. Unable to rise.

A مخضوع *makhzūʻ*, Depressed, humbled. A vassal.

A مخضون *makhzūn*, Dismissed (manliness).

A مخضونة *makhzūnat*, Pregnant (woman).

A مخط *makht*, (v. n. of مخط) Being shot off, piercing through (as an arrow). Drawing (a sword or a bow). Blowing the nose. A short garment. The caul or membrane covering the head of a new-born camel. Ashes. A quick step. The resemblance of a son to his father. *Makhit*, (pl. امخاط *amkhāt*) A generous prince.

A مخطّ *mikhatt*, A style, or any instrument of iron or wood for writing or drawing lines; a ruler.

A مخطاط *mikhtāt*, Any rule for making straight lines. A tablet whereon a thing is drawn or written.

A مخطب *mukhtib*, (Game) which approaches, and presents its side to the hunter. Who calls (any body) to witness or sanction a marriage. (A gourd) becoming yellow, with green streaks.

A مخطر *mukhtir*, One who puts any thing into another's head. One who rushes into danger against an adversary, or goes out to fight him. One who puts (his estate) at hazard upon two gamesters. Equal (in dignity). آخر مخطر *ākhiru makhtarin*, The end of a treaty.

A مخطرب *mukhtarib*, A liar. One who bends (a bow) greatly. One who twists firmly (a rope). One who lives wretchedly.

A مخطرف *mukhatrif*, A fast walker, a taker of long steps. A striker (with a sword).

A مخطرفة *mukhatrifat*, Loose-skinned (woman).

A مخطّط *mukhattat*, (A garment) marked with stripes, striped. (A young man) whose beard begins to appear. Handsome, comely. *Mukhattit*, One who draws straight lines. One who weaves or marks cloths with stripes. One who draws lines well or writes elegantly. A little eater.

A مخطف *mukhtaf*, (A horse) clung in the belly. *Mukhtif*, (An arrow) which flies wide of the mark. Fallen or clung together.

A مخطل *mukhtil*, Indecent in talk.

A مخطم *makhtam*, A woman. A wife. *Makhtim* or *mikhtam*, The nose, snout, or beak.

A مخطّم *mukhattam*, Haltered (camel). Marked on the nose (a beast of burden). *Mukhattam* or *mukhattim*, Half-ripe dates streaked. *Mukhattim*, One who puts a halter (on a camel or horse). Who overcomes with words. Name of a poet.

A مخطوب *makhtūb*, Affianced, betrothed, promised. Entitled.

A مخطوبة *makhtūbat*, Affianced (lady).

A مخطور *makhtūr*, Imagined, conceived.

A مخطوط *makhtūt*, Striped, channelled, grooved.

A مخطوف *makhtūf*, Lank-bellied. (A camel) burnt with a mark shaped like the iron خطّاف.

A مخطوم *makhtūm*, Haltered (camel). (A camel) marked on the nose or face. مخطوم خطام او خطامين *makhtūmu khitāmin aw khitāmayn*, Marked with one mark or two marks.

A مخطئ *mukhti*, One who sins through mistake, without design: one who blunders, or acts improperly. One who sins intentionally.

A مخطي *mukhtī*, One who causes to step or go.

A مخفّ *mukhiff*, Light, easy, nimble. One who removes or alleviates another's burden. Possessed of light, active cattle.

A مخفار *mikhfār*, Extremely bashful (woman).

A مخفر *mukhfir*, Who sends with, or gives one a guide (خفرة *khufarat*). A promise-breaker.

A مخفّر *mukhaffir*, A patron, protector. A guide. One who puts to the blush.

A مخفس *mukhfis*, Soon inebriating (wine). An obscene talker.

A مخفّس *mukhaffis*, A mixer of water with wine.

A مخفّش *mukhaffish*, One who throws down and tramples on. One who cleaves to the ground. A desolater. Infirm (body).

A مخفض *makhfaz*, The place of circumcision in a female.

A مخفّض *mukhaffiz*, One who does (any thing) gently and lightly. (See تخفيض *takhfīz*.)

A مخفّف *mukhaffaf*, Alleviated, made light. Contemptible. (A consonant) having a short for a long vowel, or a *tashdīd* removed. هاءِ مخفّف *hāi mukhaffaf*, The gentle aspirate, as the ه *he* at the end of such Persian words as خانه *khāna*, &c., like the "h" in Messiah. *Mukhaffif*, Who alleviates, makes light. One who marks (a consonant) with a long vowel for a short one.

A مخفق *mikhfak*, A broad sword. *Mukhfik*, One who nods the head. (See اخفاق *ikhfāk*.)

A مخفقة *mikhfakat*, A scourge, or any thing twisted, with which they strike one another playfully when dancing.

A مخفوض *makhfūz*, Depressed, submissive. (in grammar) Marked with خفض *khafz*, *i.e.* a short *i*.

A مخفوضة *makhfūzat*, Circumcised (girl).

A مخفوع *makhfūع*, Insane. Afflicted with a burning pain from hunger.

A مخفوف *makhfūf*, Alleviated. (A consonant) marked with a short for a long vowel.

A مخفوق *makhfūk*, Affected with a palpitation of heart (خفقان *khafakān*). Mad.

A مخفيّ *makhfiy*, Hid, concealed, covered, occult, clandestine, private. Suppressed. Secretly.

A مخلّ *mukhill*, A disturber, interrupter, corrupter, spoiler. Who disappoints, does not pay, or perform. One who reduces to poverty. (A commander of a garrison) who neglects or starves his soldiers. Who carries off, goes away with. Who deserts, abandons (his station). Poor, destitute. Pricked, turned (wine). (A palm) which bears bad or unripe dates. One who leads his camels forth to pasture on the herb خلّة *khullat*. Any one whose camels are thus pasturing. (A camel) which feeds on the sweet plant خلّة *khullat*. مخلّ صلح *mukhilli sulh*, A disturber of the peace.

P مخلّا *mukhallā*, A dish made of brinjals and baked meat, which, together with a few slices of lemon, is eaten with thin cakes.

A مخلّا *mukhalla'*, Empty. Dismissed, set at liberty, repudiated, set free. مخلّا بالطبع *mukhalla' bi't tabع*, Unceremonious, easy, free.

A مخلاة *mikhlāt*, (pl. مخالي *makhālī*) A provender-bag hung round (a horse's) mouth, a nose-bag.

A مخلاط *mikhlāt*, A busy-body, meddler.

A مخلاف *mikhlāf*, One who never keeps his promise. (pl. مخاليف *makhālīf*) A township or district, such as those into which Arabia Felix is divided.

A مخلب *mikhlab*, (pl. مخالب *makhālib*) A nail, claw, hooked talon of a rapacious bird or beast. A reaping-sickle without teeth. *Mukhlib*, Leafy (vine). (Water) troubled with stiff, black mud.

A مخلّب *mukhallab*, Deceived. Deep-coloured, highly-painted (vest). *Mukhallib*, A deceiver.

A مخلبس *mukhalbis*, Who or what makes mad.

A مخلّة *mukhillat*, Ground growing خلّة *khullat*.

P مخلج *makhlaj*, Name of a herb which intoxicates any quadruped that eats of it.

A مخلخل *mukhalkhal*, That part of the leg on which the ornament خلخال *khalkhāl* is worn; the ankle. *Mukhalkhil*, One who strips a bone.

A مخلد *mukhlid*, Stationary, settled. Strongly attached. Inclined to. Rendering perennial.

A مخلّد *mukhallad*, (A man) favoured with a green old age, and still capable of serving. Eternal, durable, permanent. Adorned with ear-rings or bracelets. *Mukhallid*, Fixed, settled. One who gives perpetuity.

A مخلس *mukhlis*, Mixed (green and dry grass, or black and grey hair).

A مخلص *makhlas*, An asylum. A place of escape. A surname adopted by poets, which they generally introduced into the last couplet of the غزل *ghazal*, or ode. It also denotes this last couplet, which is sometimes called شاه بيت *shāh bayt*, or the royal distich. *Mukhlas*, Pure, unsullied. *Mukhlis*, Sincere, candid, pure, real, loyal, unfeigned. محبّ مخلص *muhibbi mukhlis*, A sincere friend, loving affectionately. (This is often used in letters, and is synonymous with most devoted, affectionate, humble servant.

A مخلّص *mukhallis*, A liberator, deliverer, saviour. One who demonstrates sincere affection.

P مخلصانه *mukhlisāna*, Sincere, friendly, candid. Sincerely, like a sincere friend.

A مخلصة *mukhlisat*, The seed or grain of a certain herb called توروز اوتي *tūrūz oti*.

A مخلط *mikhlat*, (or مخلط مزيل *mikhlat mizyal*) A busy-body, meddling, officious person.

A مخلّط *mukhallat*, Well mixed. *Mukhallit*, A mixer. A confounder, disturber, perplexer.

A مخلّع *mukhallaع*, Paralytic. Distant between the hips. Weak, loose, relaxed. Apparently mad or silly. In the metre called بسيط *basīt* (Simple), مستفعلن *mustafعilun*, changed to مفعولن *mafعūlun*. *Mukhalliع*, A remover, drawer forth. A straddler.

A مخلف *makhlaf*, Roads through the valley of Mina, by which pilgrims pass. *Mukhlaf*, Depraved, corrupted. *Mukhlif*, One who substitutes, causes to succeed or follow. A restorer, returner, replacer; mender (of a garment). A corrupter. Offensive, smelling disagreeably. Untrue to his word. One who stretches out his hand and claps it to his sword. One who draws water for his family. Dry (hay) which puts forth young herbage. One who removes the girth from before the sheath (of a camel). (Stars) obscured by clouds, yet not followed by rain. One who repairs a loss, and recruits himself. A camel ten years old. مخلف عام *mukhlifi عām*, A camel one year less. مخلف عامين *mukhlifi عāmayn*, Two years less. مخلف ثلاثة اعوام *mukhlifi salāsat aعwām*, One three years under ten. (See اخلاف *ikhlāf*.)

P مخلف *mukhlaf*, A young pigeon. A handsome lad.

A مخلّف *mukhallaf*, Deceived. Any thing left behind (when dead). *Mukhallif*, One who leaves behind. One who appoints a vicegerent or successor (خليفة *khalīfat*). One who turns the backside to (another) in contempt. One who ties a camel's teat that the milk may not run out.

A مخلّفات *mukhallafāt*, (pl. fem. of مخلّف *mukhallaf*) Heritages, effects bequeathed or left.

A مخلفة *makhlafat*, A willow-ground. A road. A place where travellers alight, a stage. Any thing which imparts to the mouth an offensive smell. *Mukhlifat*, A she-camel which gives signs of pregnancy when that is not the case.

A مخلق *mukhlak* or *mukhlik*, Thread-bare (garment). *Mukhlik*, One who wears out (a garment). Who puts a worn garment on another person.

A مخلّق *mukhallak*, Well-shaped, perfectly-formed. Neatly-finished (arrow). *Mukhallik*, One who forms well, completes, makes smooth or level. One who anoints with the spice called خلوق *khalūk*.

A مخلقة *makhlakat*, Any thing well adapted or fitted. Worthy, fit, proper.

A مخلوجة *makhlūjat*, (A spear) vibrated from right to left. A just opinion.

A مخلوط *makhlūt*, Mixed, confused, blended.

A مخلوع *makhlūع*, Rejected by friends. Deposed, cashiered. (A quadruped) affected with a twisted hough.

A مخلوف *makhlūf*, Troubled with dysentery.

A مخلوق *makhlūk*, Created, formed, produced, brought forth. Smoothed, polished (arrow). Worn (garment). (Verses of one man) falsely attributed to another.

A مخلوقات *makhlūkāt*, (pl. of مخلوقة *makhlūkat*) Creatures: created beings.

A مخلوقة *makhlūkat*, (pl. مخاليق *makhālīk*) A creature, a created thing.

A مخلوقيّة *makhlūkiyat*, Condition of a created being (reverse of خالقيّة *khālikiyat*, Creativeness).

A مخلول *makhlūl*, Perforated, bored. (A camel's colt) having the tongue slit, and so weaned. Patched. Lisping, childish language.

A مخلولق *mukhlawlik*, Plain, level, smooth. Worn out, effaced (vestige).

A مخلى *mikhla'*, A reaping-hook, a sickle for cutting fodder. *Mukhlī*, One who desolates, lays waste. One who empties or finds empty. Alone (with another); who retires to, or appoints one to meet in, a solitary place. Peculiar, happening singularly. (Ground) rich in forage. A feeder of cattle with it.

A مخلى *mukhalla'*, Dismissed, liberated, set free, left at liberty, let alone. *Mukhallī*, One who liberates, sets free.

A مخم *mukhimm*, Corrupted, stinking (meat).

A مخمة *mikhammat*, A besom, a broom.

A مخمج *mukhammaj*, Depraved in morals.

A مخمخة *makhmakhat*, Extracting marrow.

A مخمد *mukhmid*, Who or what quenches a fire, or allays the paroxysm of a fever. Quiet, silent.

A مخمر *mukhmir*, A coverer, concealer, suppressor (of evidence). One who leavens (dough). Who conceives or turns a thing in the mind. A giver of possession. One who enters. A hater. Neglective, regardless of. (A country) plentiful in wine.

A مخمر *mukhammar*, Fermented. Half-drunk (with wine). *Mukhammir*, One who leavens. A baker. A maker of wine. A concealer.

A مخمرة *mukhammarat*, (A woman) highly scented with perfume. White-headed and black-bodied (sheep).

A مخمس *mukhmis*, An owner of camels which water once in five days. جاؤا مخمس *jāu makhmasa*, They came in fives.

A مخمس *mukhammas*, Quintupled. Pentangular. A pentagon. A kind of verse of five lines. *Mukhammis*, The maker of a pentagon.

A مخمسة *mukhammasat*, A matter regarding the law of inheritance, about which five persons disagreed; namely, علي *ẕalīy*, عثمان *ẕusmān*, ابن مسعود *ibn masẕūd*, زيد *zayd*, and ابن عبّاس *ibn ẕabbās*. It related to a mother, sister, and grandfather.

A مخمصة *makhmasat*, (v. n. of خمص) Being hungry. Emaciating (hunger). Falling away (the belly). Hunger, wretchedness.

P مخمل *makhmal*, Velvet. مخمل گورگ *makhmali gorg*, (or مخمل گرگ *makhmali gurg*) A kind of velvet. مخمل دو خوابه *makhmali du khwāba*, Velvet with two faces.

A مخمل *mukhmal*, Plushy, pily (garment).

A مخمن *mukhammin*, A speaker by conjecture.

A مخمور *makhmūr*, Drunk, quite intoxicated. Crop-sick. Covered over.

A مخموس *makhmūs*, (A garment) of five cubits; a spear (so long). Five-thread (rope).

A مخمول *makhmūl*, Halt, lame.

A مخموم *makhmūm*, Swept. Imprisoned in a hen-coop. المخموم القلب *al makhmūmu'l kalb*, Free from hatred or envy.

P مخميدن *makhmīdan*, To clean cotton.

A مخن *mahhn*, (v. n. of مخن) Drawing water from a well. Weeping. Peeling, barking. Marriage. A short, active man. A tall man.

A مخنّ *mikhann*, A tall man. Fruitful (year).

A مخناث *mikhnās*, (A woman) broken down and bent double.

A مخناف *mikhnāf*, A worthless stallion, unable to propagate. A man whose palm-trees and land bear badly though sprinkled and cultivated by his own hands.

A مخنب *mukhnib*, Lame. Perished. A weakener. A destroyer. One who cuts.

A مخنبة *makhnabat*, Separation from kindred.

A مخنة *makhnat*, A short, active woman.

A مخنّة *makhannat*, The nose, or tip of it. A sound made through the nose. The narrowest place of a channel. The middle of a court or house. The entrance to a road. The embouchure of a stream from high ground. A privilege, right. An open high road. An evident proof, an argument. Aliment, food. The best pasture. مخنّة القوم *makhannatu'l kawm*, The sacred rights or privileges of the people. *Mikhannat*, A plentiful year.

A مخنتب *mukhantab*, Short-bodied, dwarfish.

A مخنث *mukhannas*, Bent. Weak, impotent, without power of propagation. A hermaphrodite. A fool, blockhead, knave, good-for-nothing fellow. Effeminate, abject, infamous. An old catamite. *Mukhannis*, One who bends.

A مخنثي *mukhannisī*, Sodomy.

A مخنجل *mukhanjil*, One who weds a silly woman.

A مخندق *mukhandik*, One who cuts a ditch (خندق *khandak*) as a means of defence.

P مخنده *makhanda*, Reptiles, serpents, insects. Creeping things, little beasts. *Mukhinda*, An undutiful, disobedient son. Joined, glued.

A مخنس *mukhnis*, One who leaves behind.

A مخنّشة *mukhannashat*, A woman about whom are still some remains of youth.

A مخنشل *mukhanshil*, Tremulous from age.

A مخنع *mukhniẕ*, A humbler, depressor.

A مخنّع *mukhannaẕ*, Tamed, broke in, quiet. *Mukhanniẕ*, One who cuts with a hatchet.

A مخنق *mukhnak*, That part of the neck where one is strangled. *Mikhnak*, (pl. مخانق *makhānik*) A collar, ornament, or chain for the neck.

A مخنّق *mukhannak*, Strangled. The part of the neck where strangulation takes place. مخنّق الخصر *mukhannaku'l khasr*, Slender-waisted (youth). *Mukhannik*, A strangler, hangman.

A مخنقة *mikhnakat*, Collar, ornament, neck-chain.

A مخنّن *mukhannin*, Plenteous (year).

A مخنوق *makhnūk*, Hanged, strangled.

A مخنون *makhnūn*, Mad, crazed.

A مخني *mukhnī*, Obscene (in speech), abusive. A destroyer, ruiner. (A meadow) full of herbage. (A locust) full of eggs. Long, protracted (season).

A مخوخ *mukhwikh*, (Water) hidden, and little.

A مخوّد *mukhawwid*, A quick goer. One who takes up (any thing, as a bit of meat).

A مخور *mukhūr*, (v. n. of مخر) Passing through the sea (a ship), ploughing it with a dashing noise. Cutting the waves (a swimmer). Wearing away the axle-hole so as to play loosely in it (the axis of a pulley).

A مخوّش *mukhawwish*, One who diminishes.

A مخوّص *mukhawwis*, A receiver (of a gift), though small. (Hoariness) appearing. (See مخوبص).

A مخوّصة *mukhawwisat*, (Ground) which produces thorny plants with split or jagged leaves.

A مخوض *makhūz*, Pregnant (sheep). *Mikhwaz*, A pole used in stirring wine.

A مخوّض *mukhawwiz*, One who fords (a river). One who mixes or stirs up.

A مخوط *mukhūt*, (v. n. of مخط) Penetrating, piercing (an arrow). Drawing (a sword). Making haste. Removing, taking away, snatching. Extending. Blowing the nose.

A مخوّع *mukhawwiẕ*, One who diminishes, detracts, or carries away. (A river) breaking down or eating away its banks. One who weakens (by beating). A payer (of a debt).

A مخوف *makhūf*, Dangerous, formidable, dreadful, horrible, frightful, tremendous.

A مخوّف *mukhawwaf*, Frightened, terrified, deterred. *Mukhawwif*, One who terrifies. Terrific.

A مخوفات *makhūfāt*, (pl. of مخوفة) Dangers.

A مخوفة *makhūfat*, (fem. of مخوف *makhūf*) Formidable, dreadful. Dangerous, infested (road).

A مخوّق *mukhawwik*, A dilater, enlarger.

A مخول *makhūl*, Marked with many moles on the body. *Mukhwil* or *mukhwal*, One who has celebrated maternal uncles (خال *khāl*).

A مخوّن *mukhawwin*, An accuser of perfidy. Who or what diminishes. One who tends upon.

A مخوّي *mukhawwī*, Cattle (waxed fat. (A camel) whose belly is distant from the ground when reclining. One who prepares food for a woman in child-bed. (See تخوية *takhwiyat*.)

A مخيالة *mikhyālat*, A cloud portending rain.

A مخيّب *mukhayyib*, One who endeavours to balk another in his expectations: frustrative.

A مخيخ *makhīkh*, (A bone) full of marrow.

A مخيخة *makhīkhat*, (A sheep) fat, full of marrow.

P مخيد *makhīd*, Any thing which creeps or moves on the belly, or jumps about. A flea. A bug. An undutiful son.

P مخيدن *makhīdan*, To tremble, be moved or agitated, slip, slide, shake. To creep on the belly. To adhere, stick close to. To jump. To extend, reach, touch; to pull or pluck. To stand on end (as the hair or plumage from terror or rage). To be undutiful, disobedient.

P مخيده *makhīda*, A creeping thing, reptile. (A son) undutiful, disobedient to his parents.

A مخير *makhīr*, Milk mixed with water.

A مخير *mukhayyar*, Left to free choice. Indifferent. A kind of coarse camelot or hair-cloth.

P مخيّر بازار *mukhayyar bāzār*, A bargain made on condition that the purchaser may, if he choose, return the goods within a certain time. A *Mukhayyir*, One who gives an option or choice. Bountiful, charitable, liberal. (dim. of مختار *mukhtār*) Partly a free agent.

P مخيز *makhez*, A spur.

A مخيّس *mukhayyas*, Subdued, humbled. A prison; name of a prison in Irāk built by Aliy. *Mukhayyis*, A subduer, humbler, conqueror.

A مخيّسة *mukhayyasat*, (Camels) fed for slaughter.

A مخيض *makhīz*, Churned (milk). *Mukhīz*, One who leads or drives (a horse) into water.

A مخيط *makhīt*, A place where a serpent creeps. Sewed (garment). *Mikhyat*, A needle.

A مخيط *mukhkhayt*, Sebestens.

P مخيطا *makhītā*, Sebestens.

A مخيف *makhīf*, (A wall) threatening to fall. *Mukhīf*, Fear-inspiring, terrible, formidable, dreadful. المخيف *al mukhīf*, The lion.

A مخيّف *mukhayyif*, Terrible. One who renders formidable. (See تخويف *takhwīf*.)

A مخيل *makhīl*, One who has many moles (on the face). Worthy, fit, suitable. *Mukhīl*, Proud, vain, arrogant. Apt, convenient, adapted, well made, properly disposed. (A cloud) threatening rain. Habituated, accustomed (to horses).

A مخيّل *mukhayyal*, Fancied, imagined. *Mukhayyil*, One who imagines, fancies, doubts, is deceived, conjectures from physiognomy, conceives a good omen. One who directs his suspicions towards. (A cloud) which, by previous thunder and lightning, promises rain. One who places the figure of a man near a camel's colt to frighten away the wolf. One who hangs back (from friends).

A مخيلة *makhīlat*, (v. n. of خال for خيل) Imagining, thinking. Imagination, opinion. Pride. Any thing from which a conjecture is formed. *Mukhīlat*, A natural aptitude. Clouds portending rain.

A مخيّلة *mukhayyalat*, Fancy, imagination.

A مخيم *mikhyam*, A gathering up of the swaths of corn. *Mukhīm*, One who pitches a tent.

A مخيّم *mukhayyam*, Tented. An encampment; camp. *Mukhayyim*, One who pitches a tent, or who enters a tent. A sojourner.

A مخيوط *makhyūt*, Sewed (garment).

A مخيول *makhyūl*, Marked much with moles.

P مد *mad*, Wire. The 6th day of a month.

A مدّ *madd*, (v. n. of مدّ) Extending, stretching, lengthening. Lifting up the eyes towards any object. Drawing. Granting a delay; bearing patiently. Being tall. Being high, advanced (the day). Increasing, swelling (a river). Manuring (land). Supplying, feeding. Helping, assisting. Adorning. Giving (camels) water sprinkled with meal called مديد *madīd*. Putting ink into a standish. Taking ink from the inkstand. A peculiar mode of writing certain words in accounts. Extension, prolonging, delaying. (pl. مدود *mudūd*) The flow of the tide. Abundance of water, a flood. (for مدّة *madda*) The mark ـٓ placed sometimes over آ *alif*, which gives it a long broad sound. حرف المدّ *harfu'l madd*, A letter of extension: as, ا after *fatha*, و after *zamma*, and ي after *kasra*. قدر مدّ البصر *kadru maddi'l basar*, As far as the eye can reach. مدّ و جزر *madd u jazr*, Flux and reflux (of the sea), tides. *Mudd*, (pl. امداد *amdād*, مددة *midadat*, and مداد *midād*) A certain dry-measure used in Egypt, Syria, and other parts, about two handsful, and weighing two ritls, or a ritl and a third. مدّ النبيّ *muddu'n nabiy*, One-fourth of a صاع *sāɛ*.

A مداء *midāɛ*, (v. n. 3 of مدي) Filling.

A مداءلة *mudāɛalat*, (v. n. 3 of دأل) Cheating, cozening, or endeavouring to do so.

A مدابّ *madābb*, (pl. of مدبّ *madabb*) Places where things flow or creep.

A مدابح *madābih*, (pl. of مدبّحة *mudabbihat*) Hump-backed (sand-hills).

A مدابر *mudābar*, Nobly descended, whether on the father or the mother's side. *Mudābir*, Hostile, inimical. One who makes unfortunate throws at dice, or draws an unlucky gaming arrow. Unlucky (throw).

A مدابرة *mudābarat*, (v. n. 3 of دبر) Opposing, being adverse to, carrying on hostilities. Forgetting or neglecting the interests of a friend. Having a galled back. Being very rich. Slitting the ears of camels or sheep, so that part hangs backward. (A sheep) slit in the ear, with part hanging down behind. Dying.

A مدابغ *madābigh*, (pl. of مدبغة *madbaghat*) Skins thrown into a tan-pit.

A مداجاة *mudājāt*, (v. n. 3 of دجا for دجو) Counterfeiting, dissembling, deceiving; wheedling, flattering. Neither refusing nor consenting. Neither binding nor setting free.

A مداجرة *mudājarat*, A flying away, running off.

A مداجنة *mudājanat*, (v. n. 3 of دجن) Feigning, dissembling, acting hypocritically.

A مداجي *mudājī*, One who harbours a grudge.

A مدّاح *maddāh*, An encomiast, panegyrist.

A مداحلة *mudāhalat*, (v. n. 3 of دحل) Deceiving, betraying, lying in wait. Outbidding at a sale (fraudulently to enhance the price). Throwing down in wrestling. Telling a fiction and concealing the truth. Injuring, oppressing.

A مدّاحي *maddāhī*, Panegyric, encomium.

A مداخل *madākhil*, (pl. of مدخل *madkhal*) Entrances, places of access. *Mudākhil*, One who undertakes or enters into any business. Intimate, interior. Wadding, stuffing. A high hill overhanging marshy ground.

A مداخلة *mudākhalat*, (v. n. 3 of دخل) Entering into, engaging or taking part in, intermeddling. Being intimate with. Undertaking (business). Becoming a proselyte (to a wrong belief). Being inward, innermost. Taking hold of one (an erroneous notion). Access, ingress.

A مداد *midād*, (v. n. 3 of مدّ) Extending, lengthening out. Dung, manure. Ink. A supply, a feeder (as oil for a lamp). A way, path, or religious sect. Similitude. (pl. of مد *mudd*) Certain dry-measures. مداد السموات *midādu's samāwāt*, The number of the heavens. مداد قيس *midādi kays*, A kind of game.

A مدّاد *maddād*, Long-striding (horse).

P مدار *madār*, Do not have or hold.

A مدار *madār*, A centre, a place of turning or returning, a boundary or goal. A place within which any thing revolves. An orbit. A pivot. The centre of the earth. A place where any one stops or stands; station, seat. مدار الجدي *madāru'l jady*, Tropic of Capricorn. مدار سرطان *madāri saratān*, Tropic of Cancer. مدار عليه *madār ɛalayhi*, That round which any thing turns. A pivot. مدار المهام *madāru'l mahāmm*, The minister, *i. e.* the centre of affairs. Name of a celebrated Mussulmān saint. عزت مدار *ɛizzat-madār*, Seat of glory; magnificent.

P مدارا *mudārā*, Humility. Civility, politeness. Dissimulation.

A مدارأة *mudāraɛat*, (v. n. 3 of درأ) Repelling one another. Treating courteously.

A مداراة *mudārāt*, (v. n. 3 of دري) Dissembling. Cheating. Treating kindly. Affability, courtesy, lenity, gentleness. Deceit, dissimulation, circumvention. Concord.

A مدارة *midārat* or *mudārat*, A skin cut in a circular form, and, when sewed, used in drawing water. An embroidered apron.

A مدارج *madārij*, Steps, degrees, ascents.

A مدارس *madāris*, (pl. of مدرسة *madrasat*) Colleges, academies, public schools. مدارس و بقاع *madāris u bikāɛ*, Colleges and monasteries. *Mudāris*, A doctor, reader, learned man. One who mixes with sin and defiles himself therewith. One who returns to bad habits which he had once abandoned.

A مدارسة *mudārasat*, (v. n. 3 of درس) Studying, giving or taking a lesson. Study.

P مدار كار *madār-kār*, Principal of affairs.

A مداركة *mudārakat*, (v. n. 3 of درك) Prosecuting without intermission. *Mudārikat*, (fem.) Insatiable in lust.

A مدارة *madārih*, (pl. of مدرة *midrah*) Princes, chiefs of families, military commanders.

A مداري *madārī*, (and مداريّ *madāriy*) (pl. of مدري *midra'*, مدراة *midrāt*, or مدرية *midriyat*) Horns. *Mudārī*, A dissembler.

A مدارم *madārim*, (pl. of مدرام *midrām*) Bedaubed with filth.

A مداس *madās*, A kind of rustic shoe. *Madās*, (or مداسة) A floor where grain is trodden out.

A مدّاسة *maddāsat*, The nose.

A مدّاش اليد *maddāshu'l yad*, Weak-handed.

A مداص *madāṣ*, A pearl-fishery. A place where a diver plunges. A descending into the water, or a coming upon any thing suddenly.

A مداعاة *mudāʻāt*, (v. n. 3 of دعا for دعو) Contending with. Provoking. Proposing riddles to each other, puzzling one another with questions. Demolishing, ruining, destroying.

A مداعبة *mudāʻabat*, (v. n. 3 of دعب) Playing together, jesting with another.

A مداعس *madāʻis*, (pl. of مدعس) Lances.

A مداعسة *mudāʻasat*, A fighting with a spear.

A مداعصة *mudāʻaṣatan*, Forcibly, perforce.

A مداعق *madāʻiḳ*, Water-courses (in valleys); channels hollowed out by torrents.

A مداعك *mudāʻik*, Quarrelsome, litigious.

A مداعكة *mudāʻakat*, (v. n. 3 of دعك) Contending, fighting. Rubbing, chafing. Being foolish, stupid.

A مداعلة *mudāʻalat*, (v. n. 3 of دعل obsolete) Circumventing one another.

A مداعي *madāʻī*, (pl. of مدعاة *madʻāt*) Invitations to banquets. *Mudāʻī*, One who calls out to; contentious, quarrelsome.

A مداعير *madāʻīr*, (pl. of داعرة *dāʻirat*) Palm-trees not taking the fructifying pollen; barren.

A مداعيق *madāʻīḳ*, (Horses) treading down men in a hostile incursion.

A مدّاغة *maddāghat*, (in Morocco) The temples.

A مداغشة *mudāghashat*, A petitioning, requesting, desiring greatly. A crowding one upon another (especially round a watering-place). A hasty watering, drinking a small quantity. A lying in wait, ensnaring, treachery.

A مداغصة *mudāghaṣat*, (v. n. 3 of دغص) Commanding to make haste. Instigating, urging.

A مداغل *madāghil*, Mid-channels or valleys.

A مدافاة *mudāfāt*, (v. n. 3 of دفي) Rushing upon, or killing (a wounded man).

A مدافّة *mudāffat*, (v. n. 3 of دفّ) Hastening to despatch (a wounded man).

A مدافع *madāfiʻ*, (pl. of مدفع *madfaʻ*) Canals, conduits. (pl. of مدفع *midfaʻ*) Cannons, pieces of ordnance. *Mudāfaʻ*, Resisted, opposed (chieftain). *Mudāfiʻ*, One who repels, averts, hinders, or molests.

A مدافعة *mudāfaʻat*, (v. n. 3 of دفع) Repulsing, defending one's self, resisting, averting, prohibiting, checking. Protracting, delaying, making tedious. Deferring payment of a debt.

A مدافى *madāfī*, (pl. of مدفاة) Warm regions.

A مداق *madāḳ*, A circus, field of battle, or place for single combat. The place where a serpent lies coiled up, or where it moves about.

A مداقّ *madāḳḳ*, (pl. of مدقّ *midaḳḳ*, مدقّة *madaḳḳat*, *midaḳḳat*, and مدقّ *muduḳḳ*) Instruments with which any thing is bruised. Wooden mallets used in dressing cotton; stockers for milling cloths. Subtilties, minutiæ.

A مداقّة *mudāḳḳat*, (v. n. 3 of دقّ) Calculating with accuracy, going minutely (through accounts with any one). Making flour (دقيق *daḳīḳ*).

A مداقيس *madāḳīs*, pl. of مدقس, Strong camels.

A مداقيع *madāḳīʻ*, Camels which, in pasturing, eat the grass clean off the ground.

A مداك *madāk*, (v. n. of داك for دوك) Braying small (colours, odours). A stone upon which such substances are brayed. *Mudāk* or *madāk*, A place abounding with cocks (ديك *dīk*).

A مداكأة *mudākaʼat*, (v. n. 3 of دكأ) Thronging, pressing, crowding one another.

A مدالاة *mudālāt*, (v. n. 3 of دلو or دلي) Behaving kindly. Curing a disease, applying a remedy.

A مدالث *madālis*, Fields of battle. مدالث الوادي *madālisu'l wādī*, The channel of a river.

A مدالسة *mudālasat*, (v. n. 3 of دلس) Deceiving, circumventing, acting darkly or fraudulently.

A مدالكة *mudālakat*, (v. n. 3 of دلك) Putting off (a creditor). Detaining lawfully.

A مدأم *midʼam*, Thronging, overpowering (army).

A مدام *mudām*, Perpetual, continual, perennial, unceasing, lasting long, fixed, established. Always. A continued but gentle rain. Wine. مدام الوقت *mudāmu'l waḳt*, Continually. دور مدام *dawri mudām*, Perpetual motion. P مست مدام *masti mudām*, Intoxicated with wine, drunk.

A مدامة *mudāmat*, Wine.

A مدامجة *mudāmajat*, A dissembling, flattering.

A مدامرة *mudāmarat*, A watching (all night).

A مدامسة *mudāmasat*, (v. n. 3 of دمس) Lying hid. Covering, concealing.

A مدامع *madāmiʻ*, The inner corners of the eye.

A مداملة *mudāmalat*, A treating with kindness.

A مدامي *mudāmī*, Eternal.

A مدان *madān*, Egyptian basil. Deeply in debt. المدان *al madān*, Name of an idol. *Mudān*, Judged, condemned. Deeply in debt.

A مدّان *maddān* or *muddān*, Deeply in debt. *Middān*, Salt water.

A مداناة *mudānāt*, (v. n. 3 of دنا for دنو) Coming between two things. Bringing near. Straining, binding hard (a fetter).

A مدانس *madānis*, Impurities.

A مدانيس *madānīs*, Squalid, sordid (fellows).

A مداواة *mudāwāt*, (or مداوا *mudāwā'*) (v. n. 3 of دوي) Curing a disease, remedying, administering to the sick. Bringing aid, assisting.

A مداورة *mudāwarat*, (v. n. 3 of دار for دور) Curing, adjusting, administering. Going round along with another. Watching one to see how he will manage a business.

A مداوسة *mudāwasat*, (v. n. 3 of داس for دوس) Trampling, treading upon each other.

A مداولة *mudāwalat*, (v. n. 3 of دال for دول) Giving riches and happiness (God). Causing (days) to revolve.

A مداوم *mudāwim*, Assiduous, persevering.

A مداومة *mudāwamat*, (v. n. 3 of دام for دوم) Being assiduous, constant, unremitting, persisting in. Assiduity, continuance, perpetuity.

A مداوي *mudāwa'*, One to whom remedies are applied, or assistance is brought; cured, healed. *Mudāwī*, A healer.

A مداهاة *mudāhāt*, (v. n. 3 of دهي) Dissembling, practising mutual deception on each other.

A مداهرة *mudāharat*, (v. n. 3 of دهر) Agreeing with any one for a long period (as مشاهرة *mushāharat* means, Agreeing by the month).

A مداهل *madāhil*, Horrible deserts.

A مداهن *madāhin*, (pl. of مدهن *mudhun*) Oil-bottles, cruses. *Mudāhin*, A hypocrite, liar, impostor.

A مداهنة *mudāhanat*, (v. n. 3 of دهن) Covering, acting hypocritically, dissembling. Varnishing over, cheating. Despising advice. Hypocrisy, lying, imposture.

A مداهي *mudāhī*, A dissembler, cheat, deceiver.

A مدائح *madāʼiḥ*, (pl. of مديح *madīḥ*) Laudable acts. Praises, encomiums.

A مدائن *madāʼin*, (pl. of مدينة *madīnat*) Cities. مدائن كسري *madāʼini kisra'*, The cities of Chosroes, *i.e.* Ctesiphon or Madaïn. In the reign of Noshiravān there were seven cities called Madaïn.

A مداين *mudāyin*, A creditor. A debtor.

A مداينة *mudāyanat*, (v. n. 3 of دان for دين) Lending, giving credit. Dealing in credit, owing one another, as debtor and creditor.

A مدائنيّ *madāʼiniy*, Of the city of Ctesiphon.

A مدائين *madāʼīn*, (pl. of مديان *midyān*) Those who lend much. Those who run deeply in debt.

A مدبّ *madabb* or *madibb*, (pl. مدابّ *madābb*) The place where any thing flows or creeps. مدبّ الصبا *madabbu's ṣibā'*, The place of one's birth or childhood. *Mudibb*, One who pushes (a child) on gently, pleasantly. One who governs with justice.

A مدباة *madbāt*, Land swarming with locusts.

A مدبّة *madubbat*, A country full of, or infested with, bears (دبّ *dubb*). A bear-garden.

A مدبّج *mudabbaj*, Ornamented with brocade. Illuminated (frontispiece of a book). Ugly, ill-shaped (in head and body). A sort of owl.

A مدبّح *mudabbiḥ*, A keeper at home. One who stoops. (See تدبيح *tadbīḥ*.)

A مدبّحة *mudabbiḥat*, Hump-backed (sand-hill).

A مدبر *mudbir*, One who retires. One who turns

his back. One whose affairs are in a bad train, who is retrograding in the world. (See ادبار *idbār.*)

A مدبّر *mudabbar,* Ably conducted, properly managed (business). A slave set at liberty after the death of his master. *Mudabbir,* A governor, rector, moderator, director, administrator. A master; a scribe. Prudent; ingenious. مدبّر امور جمهور *mudabbiri umūri jumhūr,* A minister or director of public affairs. مدبّر تدبير *mudabbiri tadbīr,* One who makes a declaration of freedom, to be established after his decease. P مدبّران فلك *mudabbirāni falak,* The planets Saturn, Jupiter, Mars, the sun, Venus, Mercury, and the moon.

A مدبّرات *mudabbirāt,* Angels. Powers. The commonalty.

A مدبري *mudbirī,* Adversity, ill-luck, misery.

A مدبّس *mudabbis,* A hider. Hidden.

A مدّبغ *muddabigh,* Tanned, dressed (skin).

A مدبغة *madbaghat,* (pl. مدابغ *madābigh*) A skin thrown into a tan-pit. *Madbaghat* or *madbughat,* A tan-pit.

A مدبق *mudbik,* Who causes any thing to stick close. Who glues.

A مدبّق *mudabbik,* Who takes (birds) with birdlime (دبق *dibk*).

A مدبوّ *madbūw,* (A field) eaten up by locusts.

A مدبوبة *madbūbat,* (A country) infested by bears.

A مدبور *madbūr,* Wounded, galled (especially in the back). Wealthy. Overtaken by a westerly wind (دبور *dabūr*) which blows towards night.

A مدبوش *madbūsh,* (A field) eaten up by locusts.

A مدبوغ *madbūgh,* Tanned (bag, skin-bottle).

A مدبول *madbūl,* Dressed, tanned. Manured (land). Made up into mouthsful.

A مدبأ *madba'* or *mudbī,* Full of small locusts or ants (دبا *daba'*).

A مدبّي *mudabbī,* A hider, concealer.

A مدبيّ *madbīy,* (A field) eat up by locusts.

A مدبية *mudbiyat,* (A country) abundant in small locusts or ants (دبا *daba'*).

A مدّة *maddat,* One extension or prolongation. *Middat,* Pus, matter. *Muddat,* A space of time, a long season. End, limit, term. A penful of ink. مدّت عمر *muddati ʿumr,* A lifetime. مدّة العمر *muddatu'l ʿumr,* During life. P مدّتي چند *muddate chand,* (or مدّتها *muddathā*) For a long space of time.

A مدثّر *mudassar,* (Stones) piled over a body slain.

A مدثّن *mudussin,* Flying (bird); or which hops from place to place. One which builds in a tree.

A مدّج *muddaj,* A certain sea-fish (called likewise مشقّ *mushakk*)

A مدجان *midjān,* Dark, murky (night).

A مدجّج *mudajjaj* or *mudajjij,* Cased in armour. A hedgehog. *Mudajjij,* Cloudy (sky).

A مدجدج *mudajdij,* Dark (night).

A مدجّل *mudajjal,* (A camel) well nigh covered with pitch. A sword covered with gold. *Mudajjil,* One who gilds with gold or silver so as to give the appearance of those metals.

A مدجن *mudjin,* Raining incessantly. Unintermittent (rain or fever). (See ادجان *idjān.*)

A مدجوم *madjūm,* Sad.

A مدجونة *madjūnat,* (A she-camel) accustomed to carry water for the purpose of irrigation.

A مدجّه *mudajjih,* Lurking (hunter).

A مدجي *mudjī,* Dark (night).

A مدح *madh,* (v. n. of مدح) Praising. Praise, eulogium, encomium, commendation; approbation, applause, recommendation. مدح نفس كسر مشعر *madhi nafs kasri mashʿar,* (معشر *maʿshar?*) Self-commendation breaks ceremony, *i. e.* is disgusting.

A مدحاة *midhāt,* A child's curricle, or any vehicle in which it is dragged along.

P مدح آور *madh-āwar,* A praiser, encomiast.

A مدحة *midhat,* (v. n. of مدح) Praising. Praise, encomium. A laudable action, any thing deserving commendation.

P مدح خوان *madh-khwān,* Eulogic: a eulogist.

A مدحرج *mudahraj,* Round. مدحرج البعر *mudahraju'l baʿr,* The coldest days in winter. *Mudahrij,* (pl. دهارج *dahārij*) A revolver.

A مدحص *madhas,* The nest of the katā.

A مدحض *mudhiz,* One who causes to slide. One who renders void or fruitless. One who turns (a die or lot) after being thrown.

A مدحضة *madhazat,* A slippery place.

A مدحق *mudhik,* A repeller, driver away.

A مدحقب *mudahkib,* Who throws behind him.

A مدحل *mudhil,* One who enters and hides in a crypt or cave, narrow at top and wide at bottom.

A مدحلط *mudahlit,* One speaking confusedly.

A مدحلم *mudahlim,* One who throws from a mountain or into a well.

A مدحمر *mudahmir,* A filler (of a bottle).

A مدحمل *mudahmil,* Who rolls on the ground. Who lays prostrate, or places under.

A مدحور *madhūr,* Driven to a distance.

A مدحوس *madhūs,* Troubled with a whitlow or abscess at the finger's end. (A house) full of people.

A مدحى *madha',* A place in the sand where an ostrich lays her eggs.

A مدخ *madkh,* (v. n. of مدخ) Assisting. Magnitude, grandeur. Complete aid or support.

A مدخاء *mudakhās,* (pl. of مديخ *madikh*) Excellent, precious, great.

A مدخدخ *mudahhdikh,* A subduer, humbler. A restrainer, prohibiter, averter. A demolisher, breaker. One who goes quick with short steps.

A مدّخر *muddakhar,* Sound (judgment).

A مدخرص *mudakhris,* One who explains.

A مدخصة *mudkhasat,* Fat, fleshy (young woman).

A مدخل *madkhal,* (v. n. of دخل) Going in, entering into. Entrance, access. A port, gate, porch, vestibule. The time or place of entering. A mode of conducting one's affairs. *Midkhal,* A key. *Mudkhal,* (v. n. 4 of دخل) Introducing, inserting. Introduced, sent, or let out. Spurious, illegitimate; worthless, base. An initiation into any art; an introductory treatise. The place of introduction. *Mudkhil,* One who introduces or inserts.

A مدّخل *muddakhil,* One who enters.

A مدخلي *madkhalī,* Entrance, admission.

A مدخمر *mudakhmir,* A filler (of a bottle). One who covers, veils, hides, conceals.

A مدخمس *mudakhmas,* Hidden, concealed. *Mudakhmis,* A dissembler.

A مدخن *madkhan,* A place where smoke issues. *Mudkhin,* Hard-grained (corn). Smoky (fire).

A مدّخن *muddakhin,* Smoky (fire).

A مدخّن *mudakhkhin,* Smoking (fire).

A مدخنة *midkhanat,* Chafing-dish, brazier, censer.

A مدخول *madkhūl,* Entered. Return, gain, profit. Lean, emaciated, labouring in mind.

A مدخولة *madkhūlat,* Rotten within (palm-tree). Married (woman).

A مدد *madad,* Assistance, aid, succour, support. A supply; a feeder. مدد الجيش *madadu'l jaysh,* Reinforcements of an army. P مدد كردن *madad kardan,* To assist, relieve, help, succour. To patronize. A *Mudud,* (pl. of مديد *madīd*) Extended, lengthened out. Tall.

A مددة *midadat,* (pl. of مدّ) Certain dry-measures.

P مدد جوئي *madad-joī* or *jūī,* Search for aid.

P مدد خواه *madad-khwāh,* One who asks aid.

P مدد رس *madad-ras,* An assistant, helper.

P مددگار *madadgār,* Assistant, protector, ally.

P مددگاري *madadgārī,* Assistance, help, aid.

A مدد معاش *madad maʿāsh,* Land granted in perpetuity under the royal seal.

A مدر *madr,* (v. n. of مدر) Making a tank waterproof by closing up the chinks with mud. *Madar,* (v. n. of مدر) Having the belly distended. A clod, piece of dry clay (of which they build walls). A distension of the belly or hypochondria. (equiv. to مدار *madār*) A centre. Cities, towns. اهل المدر و الوبر *ahlu'l madar wa'l wabar,* Towns-people and country-folk (people of houses and tents).

P مدر *madar,* Tear not, do not rend.

A مدرّ *mudirr,* A woman who whirls her spindle with velocity. Diuretic. (See ادرار *idrār*).

A مدراء *madrās,* (A woman) who has a large swelled belly. A hyena. بنو مدراء *banū madrās,* Town-folk.

A مدراة *midrāt,* A horn. A comb. A pin for fixing a woman's hair.

A مدرّات *mudirrāt,* Diuretics, urinatives.

A مدرار *midrār,* Very rainy (cloud).

A مدراس *midrās,* A college, academy, school.

A مدرام *midrām,* Bedaubed with filth.

A مدران *midrān,* Dirty. Soiled (hand or clothes). (A deer) which feeds on dry herbage.

A مدّرب *muddarib,* One who advances into an

enemy's country through the narrow mountain-passes (درب *darb*) from the regions of روم *rūm*.

A مدرّب *mudarrab*, Trained, expert, disciplined, inured to hardship. A lion. A camel accustomed to travel through mountainous straits. *Mudarrib*, One who inures. An exciter. Patient, endued with fortitude in war.

A مدربج *mudarbij*, Softened.

A مدربح *mudarbih*, One who runs off in terror. Who bends the back and submits.

A مدربخ *mudarbikh*, (A female pigeon) which bends or extends the back and submits (to the male). Submissive, bending (man).

A مدرة *madarat*, A single clod, a lump of dry clay (of which they build walls). A city, town. A country. مدرتي *madaratī*, My own town or village.

A مدرّة *mudirrat*, (A woman) who whirls (her) spindle with great velocity.

A مدرج *madraj*, A road by which one walks. *Mudrij*, One who rolls or folds up. (See ادراج).

A مدرّج *mudarrij*, One who rolls or folds up. Tormenting, troublesome. (See تدريج *tadrīj*.)

A مدرجة *madrajat*, A way, mode, manner, institution, procedure. A country where the Asiatic woodcock (درّاج *durrāj*) breeds.

A مدردب *mudardib*, One who runs off and looks back in terror. (See دردبة *dardabat*.)

P مدرس *madars*, Bar of a door. Scarecrow.

A مدرس *midras*, A book (as that by which one is taught). *Mudris*, A user, studier (of a book); an exerciser, teacher by reading.

A مدّرس *muddaris*, One who cons or reads.

A مدرّس *mudarras*, Experienced, well taught. *Mudarris*, An academical lecturer, doctor, professor, teacher, instructor, schoolmaster.

A مدرسة *madrasat*, (pl. مدارس *madāris*) An university, college, academy, public school.

A مدرع *midraʻ*, A short shirt of coarse wool. *Mudriʻ* or *mudarraʻ*, A piece of water around which the herbage has been eaten up and carried off.

A مدرّع *mudarriʻ*, (A man) who puts on a coat of mail, or (a woman) a shift (درع *dirʻ*). Preferred; excellent, clear.

A مدرعة *midraʻat*, A jerkin made of coarse wool. The seat of a saddle, of which the fore and hinder parts are visible.

A مدرعفّ *mudraʻiff*, Ready for a journey.

A مدرقع *mudarkiʻ*, One who flees, goes swiftly, runs from danger. A receiver of benefits from others, and who yet speaks of them with malevolence.

A مدرقل *mudarkil*, A quick goer. (See درقلة.)

A مدرك *mudrak*, Comprehended. مدرك و مدرج *mudrak u mudraj*, Comprehended and contained. *Mudrik*, One who comprehends or understands; comprehensive.

A مدركة *mudrikat*, One who comprehends or understands. (A girl) come to maturity. A protuberance between the shoulders; a rising made by the application of a cupping-glass. *Mudrikat*, (or قوّت مدركه *kūwati mudrika*) The understanding, intellectual powers; memory.

A مدركيّة *mudrikīyat*, Comprehensiveness, apprehensiveness, the faculty of comprehension.

A مدرّمة *mudarramat*, Compact or soft (coat of mail or kirtle).

A مدرمس *mudarmis*, Silent. A concealer.

A مدرمك *mudarmik*, A runner. (See درمكة.)

A مدرن *mudrin*, Dry (wood). (See ادران.)

A مدرنفق *mudranfik*, Hasty, quick in walking.

A مدرنقع *mudrankiʻ*, Swift of flight; a fugitive. One who receives benefits from others, yet speaks of them with malevolence.

A مدروس *madrūs*, Defaced, obliterated, indistinct. Worn out. A worn garment. Insane.

A مدروع *madrūʻ*, Partially eaten off (field).

A مدروك *madrūk*, Understood, apprehended.

A مدرة *midrah*, (pl. مدارة *madārih*) A prince, chief of a family, commander of an army; tribune. A spokesman. Glib-tongued. Nimble-handed.

P مدره باز *madara-bāz*, A retail-dealer.

A مدرهم *mudarham*, Monied, rich.

A مدرهمّ *mudrahimm* Aged and tottering.

A مدري *midraʼ*, (pl. مداري *madārī*) A horn; the horn of a young buck, hart, or doe. A spit. An instrument for parting the hair, a comb. A hair-pin.

A مدرئ *mudris*, (A camel) whose milk flows after colting.

A مدّري *muddarī*, A deceiver.

A مدريّ *madarīy*, A citizen (especially of Madar in Arabia).

A مدرية *midriyat*, A horn.

A مدريّة *madarīyat*, (Spears) armed with sharp horn heads, or heads of bone.

A مدس *mads*, (v. n. of مدس) Rubbing a skin.

A مدسج *mudsij*, (or مدسّج *mudassij*) An animalcule which spins a web like a spider.

A مدّسج *muddasij*, A spider.

A مدسر *midsar*, One who indulges much in venery.

A مدسع *madsaʻ*, A narrow place. The entrance into the gullet. *Midsaʻ*, A leader, conductor.

A مدسف *mudsif*, A pimp, pander.

A مدسق *mudsik*, A filler.

A مدسم *mudsim*, A stopper, corker (of a bottle).

A مدسوس *madsūs*, Hidden. Anointed with pitch.

A مدسّي *mudassī*, An exciter. A seducer, corrupter. A receiver (of tradition); a relater (of another's sayings).

A مدش *madsh*, (v. n. of مدش) Eating little. Giving little. Somewhat, any thing. *Madash*, (v. n. of مدش) Having the nerves of the hand flexible, with little flesh. Dimness of the eyes from heat or hunger. A slenderness of the fore-leg and celerity in travelling. The cutting of the feet (of a horse) by striking one against another. A redness and roughness of face.

A مدشاء *madshāʼ*, Flexible-handed (female).

A مدشة *madshat*, Lightness (of flesh).

A مدصدص *mudasdis*, A shaker of a sieve.

A مدّعا *muddaʻā*, (in construction) for مدّعیٰ *muddaʻaʼ*, Whatever is alleged, pretended, or meant. Desire, wish. Meaning, suit, view, object, scope. A complaint.

A مدعاة *madʻāt*, An invitation to a banquet.

A مدعاس *midʻās*, (pl. مداعس *madāʻis*) A stiff spear. A beaten path.

A مدعة *madʻat*, A cocoa-nut without the kernel, used as a drinking-vessel.

A مدعث *mudʻis*, A leaver of a residue. A chooser. A thief. A traveller to a far country.

A مدعثر *mudaʻsir*, A demolisher.

A مدعدع *mudaʻdaʻ*, Filled (dish). *Mudaʻdiʻ*, One who runs softly. Who fills a dish. (See دعدعة.)

A مدعّر *mudaʻʻar*, A dirty colour, especially of an elephant.

A مدعرم *mudaʻrim*, A runner with short steps.

A مدعس *madʻas*, A thing desired or desirable. Copulation. *Midʻas*, (pl. مداعس *madāʻis*) A lance; whoever pierces with it. A beaten road.

A مدعّس *mudaʻʻas*, A place in the desert where they dress victuals or bake bread. An oven. *Mudaʻʻis*, One who thrusts through with a spear.

A مدعسج *mudaʻsij*, Swift, quick-going.

A مدعسق *mudaʻsik*, One who rushes on others. (See دعسقة *daʻsakat*.)

A مدعص *mudʻas*, One whose feet are beat and scorched by the sun's heat. *Mudʻis*, (Heat) destructive (to any one).

A مدعق *mudʻik*, One who spurs his horse.

A مدعك *midʻak*, Quarrelsome, squabbling, litigious. A rubbing or polishing instrument.

A مدعكس *mudaʻkis*, (People) dancing with joined hands, after the manner of the Magi.

A مدعلج *mudaʻlij*, One who collects water (in a cistern). (See دعلجة *daʻlajat*.)

A مدعلق *mudaʻlik*, One who engages in business. One who goes over a matter and knows it.

A مدّعم *muddaʻim*, One who leans upon.

A مدعمس *mudaʻmas*, Concealed.

A مدعمص *mudaʻmis*, (Water) full of tadpoles.

A مدعن *mudʻan*, Bad-tempered. Ill-fed.

A مدعنكر *mudʻankir*, Suddenly rushing (torrent). A bringer of any thing shameful.

A مدعوّ *madʻūw*, Invited. Called, styled. مدعوّ له *madʻūwun lahu*, A person prayed for, or upon whom a benediction is pronounced.

A مدعوج *madʻūj*, Mad, insane.

A مدعوق *madʻūk*, Worn, beaten (path).

A مدعوك *madʻūk*, (A place) worn down by a multitude. Offensive and noisome from a stagnation of water or urine.

A مدعي *mudʻī*, One who adopts as his son.

A مدّعا muddaʻa', (in construction مدّعا muddaʻā) An intention, design, purpose, proposal, cause, reason, subject, object. مدّعا عليه muddaʻa' ʻalayhi, A criminal; the defendant in a suit at law. P مدّعاي بيان كردن muddaʻāyi bayān kardan, To explain one's pretensions, to open a cause. مدّعاي تأييد كردن muddaʻāyi taʼyīd kardan, To support pretensions, to prove an allegation. مدّعاي نو پيدا muddaʻāyi naw paydā, A new invention, fresh argument. تعلّل عليل و مدّعاي بي دليل taʻalluli ʻalīl u muddaʻāyi bī dalīl, A weak pretext, argument without proof. A *Muddaʻī*, An adversary in a lawsuit, prosecutor, plaintiff, suitor, claimant. A pretender, boaster (of birth or courage). One who challenges a rival to fight, announcing his own name and family. One who causes another not to be called by his real father.

A مدعىّ *madʻiy*, Spurious, of doubtful pedigree.

A مدغبج *mudaghbaj*, Imposthumated.

A مدغدغ *mudaghdagh*, Accused, impeached. A tickler. A pincher. (See دغدغة *daghdaghat*.)

A مدغّر *mudaghghar*, Dirty (colour).

A مدغرة *madgharat*, A fierce battle, whose characteristic is giddy boldness or temerity.

A مدغش *mudghish*, Who enters the dark.

A مدغص *mudghis*, An exasperator. A fighter.

A مدغفق *mudaghfik*, Plentiful (year), comfortable (life). (Rain) heavy at first. (See دغفقة.)

A مدغل *mudghil*, Hidden (place). A deceiver. A spoiler, marrer. (See ادغال *idghāl*.)

A مدغم *mudgham*, Concealed. Inserted (one letter in another). *Mudghim*, see ادغام *idghām*.

A مدّغم *muddaghim*, One who inserts (one letter into another).

A مدغمر *mudaghmar*, (or مدغمس) Concealed.

A مدغمش *mudaghmish*, A fast walker.

A مدغور *madghūr*, An infant whose palate has been raised with the finger.

A مدفّ *mudiff*, Consecutive, uninterrupted, successive. (See ادفاف *idfāf*.)

A مدفأة *madfaʼat*, A warm country. *Mudfaʼat*, Camels fat and hairy.

A مدفّأة *mudaffaʼat*, Camels fat and hairy.

A مدفاع *midfāʻ*, A camel which has biestings in the udder before birth.

A مدفان *midfān*, (A man or a camel) who goes where there is no occasion. Concealed (well). Worn out (leathern bottle or bag).

A مدفر *midfar*, Compact (host).

A مدفع *madfaʻ*, (v.n. of دفع) Pushing, thrusting, driving away, beating off. Any place through which water flows, a canal, conduit. *Midfaʻ*, (pl. مدافع *madāfiʻ*) Cannon, artillery. Any thing by which (an enemy) is repulsed.

A مدفّع *mudaffaʻ*, Repulsed, outcast. Abject, base, contemptible, poor. A guest sent on by one tribe to another. Noble, high-bred.

A مدفعة *madfaʻat*, A means of repelling.

A مدفّف *mudaffif*, (A camel's bunch) which overhangs both sides. A hastener. One who hastens to despatch (a wounded person).

A مدفق *mudfik*, Who empties at once.

A مدفّق *mudaffik*, One whose hands give freely.

A مدفن *madfan*, A place of burial.

A مدّفن *muddafan*, Covered, concealed. *Muddafin*, A concealer. (A slave) absconding, especially when afraid of being sold.

A مدفنس *mudafnis*, Heavy, scarce able to move.

A مدفوع *madfūʻ*, Repulsed, driven off.

A مدفوق *madfūk*, (Water) poured out.

A مدفون *madfūn*, Buried, interred, concealed, hid (treasure under ground).

A مدفئ *mudfiʼ*, One who gives away warm clothing. (See ادفاء *idfāʼ*.)

A مدفي *mudfī*, One who rushes upon and kills (a wounded man). (See ادفاء *idfāʼ*.)

A مدفئة *mudfiʼat*, (or مدفّئة *mudaffiʼat*) Camels fat and hairy. A number of camels.

A مدق *madk*, (v.n. of مدق) Breaking (a stone).

A مدقّ *midakk*, (*mudukk*, مدقّة *midakkat*, or *madakkat*) (pl. مداقّ *madākk*) An instrument in which any thing is bruised; a wooden mallet used in dressing cotton; an instrument with which corn is threshed; a washer or bleacher's beetle; the pestle of a mortar. *Mudikk*, One who bruises, or beats small, thin, and fine. (See ادقاق *idkāk*.)

A مدقاع *midkāʻ*, Covetous, greedy.

A مدقس *midkas*, (pl. مداقيس *madākīs*) Strong (camel). *Midaks*, Silk.

A مدقع *mudkiʻ*, Depressive (poverty). Whatever prostrates or lays flat. Lean, meagre. Swift. Fugitive. Cleaving to the ground.

A مدقّق *mudakkak*, Pounded, pulverized. *Mudakkik*, One who pounds well. Intimately acquainted with the minutiæ of things.

A مدقّقة *mudakkakat*, A dish made of meat minced or bruised, and formed into balls.

A مدقل *mudkil*, (A sheep) lean and slender-boned. (A palm) which bears bad dates.

A مدقم *mudkim*, Mulier laxo pudendo.

A مدقوق *madkūk*, Pounded, pulverized. Driven firmly into the ground.

A مدكّ *midakk*, Robust (man) treading firmly, and able to work.

A مدكّة *midakkat*, (A maid-servant) capable of much labour, a maid of all work.

A مدكدك *mudakdak*, (A place) worn down by a multitude. Noisome and offensive from a quantity of camel's dung and urine.

P مدكش *mad-kash*, A wire-drawing machine. A smith.

A مدكّك *mudakkak*, (A colocynth) eaten with dates or aught beside.

A مدكوبة *madkūbat*, A fierce battle.

A مدكوع *madkūʻ*, (A horse or camel) troubled with a cough or disease in the breast.

A مدكوك *madkūk*, Hectic, consumptive. Troubled with a hectic complaint. Low and flat in the hip-bone (a horse).

A مدكوكة *madkūkat*, Land free from slopes, and in which the plant رمث *rims* grows.

A مدل *madl*, Contemptible, despicable, mean, base. Thick milk. *Midl*, Small-bodied, slender.

A مدلّ *mudill*, More powerful, superior (to companions). (See ادلال *idlāl*.)

A مدلبة *madlabat*, A country fruitful in plane-trees (دلب *dulb*). A race of negroes or Ethiopians.

A مدلث *mudlis*, Who covers, clothes, hides.

A مدلج *madlaj*, A place or trough at the mouth of a well, into which the water, when drawn up, is poured. *Mudlij*, One who sets out in the beginning of the night. المدلج *al mudlij*, (or ابو مدلج *abū mudlij*) A hedgehog.

A مدّلج *muddalij*, One who travels towards the end of the night.

A مدلجة *madlajat*, A place or trough at the mouth of a well, into which the water, when drawn up, is poured. The lair of a wild beast. *Midlajat*, A pail in which milk is carried.

A مدلس *mudlis*, One who finds the plants ادلاس *adlās*. (A country) rich in such plants.

A مدلّس *mudallis*, A concealer of the faults of merchandise on sale. A producer of incomplete or false evidence (in support of an allegation).

A مدلّص *mudallis*, One who makes (a cuirass) bright and smooth. One who copulates externally.

A مدلظ *midlaz* or *midalz*, One who thrusts violently forward.

A مدلع *mudliʻ*, One who lolls out the tongue. Swag-bellied.

A مدّلع *muddaliʻ*, Lolled, lolling (tongue).

A مدلف *mudlif*, At high words with another.

A مدلك *midlak*, An instrument with which a thing is rubbed.

A مدلنظي *mudlanzī*, Fleshy, but firm.

A مدلوج *mudlūj*, A bracelet worn above the elbow, an armlet. An amulet fastened about that part of the arm against fascination.

A مدلوك *madlūk*, Puzzled by many questions. (A horse) with flat or lean buttocks. (A camel) worn out or weak in the knees with travelling.

A مدلول *madlūl*, Directed, guided right. Proved. Demonstration, proof.

A مدلّه *mudallah*, Insane, distracted with love, or who forgets what he has done, or what has been done to him. *Mudallih*, Infatuating, dementing.

A مدلهث *mudalhis*, One who outstrips.

A مدلهمّ *mudlahimm*, Dark (night). Pitchy black. Old, aged.

A مدلي *mudlī*, One who prepares an argument or proof (at law). (See ادلاء *idlāʼ*.)

A مدلّي *mudallī*, One who brings (a man) into a disagreeable predicament.

A مدم *mudimm*, One who behaves shamefully. The father of a deformed child.

A مدماجة *midmājat*, A turban, or its sash.

A مدماك *midmāk*, A row of stones in a wall. A carpenter's or mason's plumb-line.

A مدمّة *midammat*, A wooden harrow or rake.

A مدمّث *mudammis*, One who makes any thing (especially a bed) smooth and soft.

A مدمج *mudmaj*, An arrow used in drawing lots; also the lot drawn. A level road. *Mudmij*, One who rolls, wraps, or folds up.

A مدمّج *muddamaj*, (One thing) enclosed in, thrust into, or entangled with another.

A مدمّح *mudammih*, One who bows his head.

A مدمحق *mudamhik*, A starcher of linens.

A مدمحل *mudamhil*, One who makes to roll.

A مدمخق *mudamkhik*, Slow-paced, heavy.

A مدمد *madmad*, River. Rope. Knot on a rope.

A مدمدة *madmadat*, A fleeing, running away.

A مدمّش *mudammash*, Firmly inserted.

A مدمدم *mudamdim*, Enraged, inflamed, pouring out invectives.

A مدمّس *mudammas*, Contaminated, defiled. *Mudammis*, A hider, burier.

A مدمشق *mudamshak*, Slightly broiled.

A مدمع *mudmiʻ*, One who fills to the brim.

A مدمغ *mudmigh*, One who necessitates.

A مدمّغ *mudammagh*, Foolish. *Mudammigh*, One who makes a sop in the pan.

A مدمّق *mudammik*, An inserter of one thing into another. Who sprinkles dough with flour.

A مدمقس *mudamkas*, (A garment woven) with the silk دمقس *dimaks*.

A مدمك *midmak*, A baker's rolling-pin.

A مدمّل *mudammil*, Cicatrizing, incarnative.

A مدملج *mudamlaj*, Round and smooth.

A مدملق *mudamlak*, Smooth, worn (hoof).

A مدملك *mudamlak*, Smooth, polished (arrow). Round and smooth (stone).

A مدمّم *mudammam*, Shallow (well), the sides of which are plastered. *Mudammim*, One who anoints the outside of the eyelids.

P مدمومنتن *madmamūnitan*, (in zand and Pāzand) To fear, be afraid. مدمومنم *madmamūnam*, I feared. مدمومنيد *madmamūnid*, Fear ye.

A مدمن *mudmin*, Assiduous, incessant, frequent.

A مدمّن *mudammin*, One who gives leave. Befouling, dirtying. (See تدمين *tadmīn*.)

A مدموع *madmūʻ*, Cauterized under the eye.

A مدموغ *madmūgh*, Wounded in the brain (دماغ *dimāgh*). Foolish, stupid, brain-sick.

A مدموق *madmūk*, (A thing) inserted into another.

A مدموم *madmūm*, Red, dyed blood colour. Fat, plump (camel, limb). Laden.

A مدمومة *madmūmat*, Broken and mended (pot).

A مدمي *mudmī*, Who wounds till blood appears.

A مدمّى *mudamma'*, Very red, of a bright shining red. (An arrow) red with blood.

A مدن *mud* or *mudun*, (pl. of مدينة) Cities.

P مدن *madan*, Do not walk or run with a gay, lively air.

A مدنّ *mudinn*, A stayer, sojourner.

A مدنّح *mudannih*, Quiet, submissive.

A مدنّخ *mudannikh*, One who has bumps and depressions (on his head). Who keeps close at home. Obscene, indecent. (See تدنيخ *tadnīkh*.)

A مدنّر *mudannar*, (A horse) distinguished by more white than black spots. Stamped (gold coin). Rich in gold coin (دينار *dīnār*).

A مدنّس *mudannas*, Defiled, contaminated. *Mudannis*, A defiler, polluter, profaner.

A مدنف *mudnaf* or *mudnif*, Afflicted with a chronical distemper. *Mudnif*, Pale, setting (sun). (See ادناف *idnāf*.)

A مدنّق *mudannih*, Thin-faced from grief. One who looks intently. (See تدنيق *tadnīk*.)

A مدنقر *mudankir*, One who closely attends to minute or difficult and intricate matters.

A مدنقس *mudankis*, A promoter of discord. One who humbly lowers his head.

A مدنكس *mudankis*, One who stays at home, to the exclusion and neglect of public calls or duties.

P مدنگ *madang*, A wooden key. The teeth or wards of a lock. Bolting or barring a door.

A مدنئ *mudnis*, A committer of a fault.

A مدني *mudnī*, Who brings near, or approaches. (A she-camel) near the birth.

A مدّني *muddanī*, Approached, become near.

A مدنّى *mudanna'*, Abject, weak (man). *Mudannī*, One who causes to approach, brings near. A pursuer of trifles as well as of important matters.

A مدنيّ *madanīy*, Belonging to the town, or a citizen of, Madina. A citizen. Urbane, sociable.

A مدنية *mudniyat*, (A she-camel) near the birth.

A مدنيّة *madanīyat*, (fem. of مدنيّ *madanīy*) Revealed at Madīna (a chapter of the Kur'ān).

A مدواس *midwās*, An instrument for threshing corn. A polishing or smoothing-tool.

A مدوام *midwām*, A piece of wood used in stilling a boiling pot.

A مدوّح *mudawwih*, Lavish, prodigal, profuse.

A مدوخ *madūkh*, Quick in doing every thing.

A مدوّخ *mudawwikh*, A humbler, subjugator. A traveller, roamer, rambler.

A مدود *midwad*, (for مذود *mizwad*) A manger. *Mudūd*, (pl. of مدّ *madd*) Flows of tides. Floods.

A مدوّد *mudawwid*, Infected with worms (دود *dūd*). Seated in a swing, see-sawing (boy).

A مدوّر *mudawwar*, Round, circular. The world. *Mudawwir*, One who causes to turn in a circle. One who makes (any thing) round.

A مدوّرة *mudawwarat*, (Camels) which the keeper milks in a circle.

A مدوس *midwas*, A machine for threshing corn. A tool used in polishing or smoothing (a sword).

A مدوش *madūsh*, (v. n. of مدش) Giving little. Eating little. Somewhat, any thing.

A مدوّص *mudawwis*, One who descends or lets himself down from a height.

A مدوظ *madwuz*, One with whom you are angry.

A مدوف *madūf*, Macerated, steeped, soaked. (Musk) brayed. Dissolved (in water).

A مدوك *midwak*, A stone for braying; muller.

A مدوم *midwam*, A stick used in stirring or stilling a boiling pot.

A مدوّم *mudawwim*, A giver in perpetuity. A quieter, pacifier. (See تدويم *tadwīm*.)

A مدون *mudūn*, (v. n. of مدن) Abiding, tarrying (in any place). Coming to a city (مدينة *madīnat*).

A مدوّن *mudawwin*, A collector of poems into a book (such collection being called a ديوان *dīwān*).

P مدونه *madūnih*, (in zand and Pāz.) Paradise.

A مدووظ *madwūz*, One with whom you are angry.

A مدووف *madwūf*, Macerated, mixed. Dissolved (in water). (Musk) moistened and brayed.

A مدوي *mudwī*, Who or what diseases. Abundant (food).

A مدوّي *mudawwī*, Thundering (cloud). One who drinks milk covered with a thin scum. Concealed, hidden.

A مده *madh*, Praise, eulogium.

P مده *muda*, Sick, indisposed.

A مدّه *muddah*, (pl. of ماده *mādih*) Encomiasts.

A مدهامّة *mudhāmmat*, A garden, the plants of which are black from rankness. مدهامّتان *mudhāmmatāni*, Two paradises (in the Kur'ān) plentifully watered, and full of verdant plants.

A مدهدق *mudahdik*, Breaker (of bones). Cutter (of flesh). (Meat) turning over in a boiling pot.

A مدهدم *mudahdim*, Who throws down in confusion, and tumbles one thing over another.

A مدهش *mudhish*, (or مدهّش *mudahhish*) One who amazes, astonishes, or confounds.

A مدّهق *muddahak*, Broken in pieces. Squeezed, expressed. *Muddahik*, Joined, impacted (stones).

A مدهم *mudhim*, Saddening.

A مدهّم *mudahhim*, Blackening (fire).

A مدهمرة *mudahmarat*, Compact, round (woman).

A مدهمس *mudahmas*, Hid, concealed.

A مدهمق *mudahmak*, Soft, supple (nerve or string). Smooth, faultless (arrow). Cracked, split. Agreeable, entertaining (book). Ill-dressed (victuals). *Mudahmik*, A breaker. A cutter. A title given to a certain eloquent man. (See دهمقة.)

A مدهن *mudhin*, A glozer, deceiver. *Mudhun*, (pl. مداهن *madāhin*) An oil-bottle or cruise. An ointment-box. Any hollow excavated by a torrent. A hollow in a mountain in which rain-water collects.

A مدّهن *muddahin*, Greasy. Anointed.

A مدهّنون mudahhanūn, Persons about whom are the signs of wealth.

A مدهور madhūr, The land-produce, as distinguished from the salt, in Bengal.

A مدهورون madhūrūna, (or مدهور بهم madhūrun bihim) Visited by, or enduring, adverse fortune.

A مدهوش madhūsh, Astonished, astounded, amazed, confounded, confused, thunderstruck.

P مدهون madhūn, A tanned hide.

A مدهون madhūn, Anointed (beard). (A field) wet superficially with rain.

A مدهّي mudahhī, Who calls (any one) ingenious. A dishonourer. Who inflicts misfortune.

A مدي mudy, (pl. امداء amdāɛ) A kind of dry-measure used in Syria and Egypt. *Mada'*, A boundary, term, period, goal. A butt for archers. Distance, intervening space. The extent to which the eye can reach; ken. A species of tree. A film floating on stagnant water. مدى الايّام mada'l ayyām, At all times. قدر مدى البصر kadru mada'l basar, As far as can be seen. *Muda'*, *mada'*, or *mida'*, (pl. of مدية madyat, midyat, and mudyat) Large knives.

P مدي madī, (for مده madih) Do not give.

A مدئ mudiɛ, (fem. مدئة mudiɛat) Sick, diseased, ailing.

A مدىّ madīy, (pl. امدية amdiyat) A place enclosed with stones (especially a lake or a well). The conduit through which water flows from a reservoir. Water running from a cistern which stagnates and corrupts.

A مديان midyān, (pl. مدائن madāɛin and مداين madāyin) One who runs deep into debt. One who lends much.

A مدية mad, mid, or mudyat, (pl. مدي mad, mid, or muda') A large knife. The handle of a bow. *Mudyat*, A boundary, term.

A مديّث mudayyas, Broke in, tame, quiet.

A مديح madīh, (pl. مدائح madāɛih) A praiseworthy act. Praise.

A مديخ madīkh, (pl. مدخاء mudahhāɛ) Excellent, precious, great.

A مدّيخ middīkh, Excellent, precious, great.

A مديد madīd, (pl. مدد mudud) Long, extensive. Extended, lengthened out. Tall of stature. A kind of long measure in verse. Water on which meal is sprinkled and given to camels. Grass, forage, hay, straw.

A مدير mudīr, Who turns round, converts, surrounds. One who goes or drives round. The chief of a province.

A مديق madīk, (Cattle) loathing forage.

A مديّق mudaykk, (dim. of مدقّ mudukk) A little mortar.

A مديك madīk, (A place) plentiful in cocks.

A مديل mudīl, One who assists, and gives victory or good fortune (دولة dawlat).

A مديم mudīm, Troubled with a hemorrhage at the nose. (See also ادامة idāmat.)

A مديمة mudīmat, (Ground) watered by continual, gentle rain (ديمة dīmat).

A مدين madyan, Midian, a city in Arabia Petrea. The place of Jethro, called by the Arabians شعيب shuɛayb. *Madīn*, A debtor. A lion. A servant, a slave. Recompensed, requited. *Mudīn*, A recompenser, requiter. (See ادانة idānat.)

A مديّن mudayyin, Tolerant in religious matters.

P مدينا madīnā, (in zand and Pāzand) A city.

A مدينة madīnat, (pl. مدائن madāɛin, مدن mudun, and mudn) A city. A maid-servant. Madīna in Arabia, where Muhammad was buried, formerly called Yatrib. It is also named مدينة النبيّ madīnatu'n nabīy, (or المدينة النبوية al madīnatu'n nabawiyat) The city of the prophet, or simply المدينة al madīnat. مدينة السلام madīnatu's salām, The city of peace, *i.e.* Baghdād. انا ابن مدينتها ana' bnu madīnatihā, I am thoroughly acquainted with all that relates to her.

A مدينيّ madyanīy, A Midyanite. *Madīnīy*, An inhabitant of any other city than Madīna (as Baghdād, Isfahān, &c.). Town-bred (bird, &c.).

A مديون madyūn, Indebted, involved in debt.

A مديونة madyūnat, A maid-servant, handmaid.

A مدئيّ mudiɛ, Sick, ailing. What makes sick.

A مذ miz, muz, or muza, From, since (in a past sense). In (in a present sense). مذ يومان muz yawmāni, Since two days.

P مذ muz, A lord, a master (used in composition, as اسفندارمذ isfandārmuz).

A مذاء mizāɛ, (v. n. of مذي) Toying with (any one) until a seminal effusion occurs. A mixed and mirthful assembly of men and women. Panderism to one's own wife. (pl. of مذيّة maziyat) Women.

A مذّاء mazzāɛ, Addicted to مذي mazy.

A مذاءرة muzāɛarat, Refractoriness (in a wife).

P مذاب muzāb or mazāb, Melted.

A مذاب muzāb, Liquefied, liquid, melted. P لعل مذاب laɛli muzāb, (or ياقوت مذاب yākūti muzāb) A liquid ruby, *i.e.* red wine; implying also sweetness.

A مذأّب muzaɛɛab, (A boy) whose locks dangle over his forehead. (A pack-saddle) furnished with a bit of skin called ذؤابة zuɛābat.

A مذأبة mazɛabat, (A country) swarming with wolves (ذئب ziɛb).

A مذابح mazābih, (pl. of مذبح mazbah) Places of sacrifice: altars.

A مذابر muzābir, A goer, traveller.

A مذاخر mazākhir, The intestines, the lower part of the belly. The veins.

A مذاد mazād, A spacious, luxuriant meadow.

A مذار mizār, Tell-tale, tale-bearing (woman).

A مذارّ muzārr, Vicious (she-camel).

A مذارّة muzārrat, (v. n. 3 of ذرّ) Spiting her colt (a camel). Being vicious (a she-camel).

A مذارع mazāriɛ, (pl. of مذراع mizrāɛ) Districts which lie between a cultivated country and a desert. Legs (of beasts of burden). Palm-trees near houses.

A مذارعة muzāraɛat, (v. n. 3 of ذرع) Selling by the cubit or ell (ذراع zirāɛ). Mixing.

A مذارف mazārif, Lachrymal ducts.

A مذاريع mazārīɛ, (pl. of مذراع mizrāɛ) Districts lying between cultivated and desert lands. Feet of beasts of burden. Palm-trees near houses.

A مذّاع mazzāɛ, Chinky. One who cannot keep a secret. A liar. Perfidious. A promise-breaker. Unsteady, moving about (as a shadow). Qui semen genitale vel urinam emittit ante tempus.

A مذافّة muzāffat, (v. n. 3 of ذفّ) Hastening to despatch a wounded man.

A مذاق mazāk, (or مذاقة mazākat) (v. n. of ذاق for ذوق) Tasting. Taste. The palate. صاحب مذاق sāhib mazāk, A voluptuary; an epicure.

A مذّاق mazzāk, Insincere in love.

A مذاقنة muzākanat, (v. n. 3 of ذقن) Hemming in, reducing to straits.

A مذاكرة muzākarat, (v. n. 3 of ذكر) Remembering (one). Conferring together. Commemorating, recollecting. Conversation, conference.

A مذاكي mazākī, Six-year-old (horses).

A مذاكير mazākīr, (pl. of ذكر zakar) Penes.

A مذال mazāl, (v. n. of مذل) Being unable to keep a secret. *Muzāl*, The verse called كامل kāmil or بسيط basīt lengthened out in the last foot by two letters. Long (coat of mail).

A مذّال mazzāl, Restless in bed, a troublesome bed-fellow. Greatly addicted to مذي mazy.

A مذالة muzālat, An air-assuming maid-servant.

A مذامّ mazāmm, (pl. of مذمّة mazammat) Contemptible things.

A مذانب muzānib, (A mare) on the point of colting. A camel in the hindermost part of a herd.

A مذانبة muzānabat, (v. n. 3 of ذنب) Being near foaling (a mare).

A مذانّة muzānnat, (v. n. 3 of ذنّ) Questioning.

A مذاهب mazāhib, (pl. of مذهب mazhab) Ways by which one goes. Sects. Institutes. Gilded (thongs).

A مذاهنة muzāhanat, (v. n. 3 of ذهن) Disputing, contending, vying about genius (ذهن zihn).

A مذائر muzāɛir, Audacious, refractory (wife). (A camel) which deserts her new-born colt.

A مذاييع mazāyīɛ, (pl. of مذياع) Blabbers.

A مذبّ mazabb or mizabb, A keeper, defender, protector of his women or harem.

A مذبّب muzabbib, (A horseman) who travels fast and alone. A long thirst, in consequence of which one makes haste to a distant watering-place.

A مذبّة mazabbat, (A place) infested with flies (ذباب zubāb). *Mizabbat*, Any thing for driving away flies, a fly-flap.

A مذبح mazbah, (pl. مذابح mazābih) That part in the throat where they generally slaughter animals. An altar; any place where an animal is sacrificed. A field of battle; an amphitheatre, or any place where they fight and kill one another. The principal place in a mosque, where the priest prays for the people with his face turned towards Mecca; a kind of high altar. A Christian's library. A fissure in the earth about a span in size. *Mizbah*, A sacrificing or slaughtering knife.

A مذبح *muzzabih*, A slayer, slaughterer.

A مذبح *muzabbih*, One who leans forward so much that his head is lower than his posteriors.

A مذبذب *muzabzib* or *muzabzab*, (Any thing) hanging and floating in the air; suspended; fluctuating, hesitating, irresolute. بعض مذبذبين اهل تقليد *baẕzi muzabzabīni ahli taklīd*, Some irresolute people, imitators of others.

A مذبر *muzabbar*, Written. Finely-painted (garment). *Muzabbir*, A writer.

A مذبل *muzbil*, Whatever emaciates, shrivels, makes lean, languid, and weak; withering (blast).

A مذبوب *mazbūb*, Infested with flies, tormented by flies (ذباب *zubāb*). Furious, insane, mad.

A مذبوح *mazbūh*, Slaughtered, sacrificed, slain, killed. One whose throat is covered by a beard. Pure, lawful (food).

A مذبور *mazbūr*, Written.

A مذبول *mazbūl*, Dried, withered, shrivelled.

A مذح *mazah*, A chafing of the thighs, hips, or groins by violent exercise. Honey produced from pomegranate-flowers. A splitting of the testicles from rubbing against any thing.

A مذحذح *muzahzih*, A fast goer with short steps. Dust-scattering (wind).

A مذخ *mazakh*, Pomegranate-flower honey.

A مذخاة *mazhhāt*, (A country) without trees.

A مذخر *muzzakhir*, A horse that reserves his full speed till after the others have broke down.

A مذخور *mazkhūr*, Stored up, hoarded, collected.

A مذر *mazar*, (v. n. of مذر) Being addle (an egg), rotten (a nut). Being disordered, qualmish (the stomach). Being indisposed. شذر مذر *shazara mazara*, Dispersed (camels) straying up and down. *Mazir*, Rotten, addle, stinking (egg).

A مذراة *mizrāt*, A fan. A wooden-teethed instrument used in winnowing corn.

A مذراع *mizrāẕ*, (pl. مذارع *mazāriẕ* and مذاريع *mazārīẕ*) A district or a town between a cultivated country and a desert.

A مذرب *mizrab*, The tongue.

A مذرّب *muzarrab*, Sharpened, edged. Poisoned (sword). *Muzarrib*, A sharpener, whetter.

A مذرة *mazirat*, A rotten egg. A nasty woman.

A مذرّة *mizarrat*, An instrument for separating the grain from the straw, a flail, thrashel.

A مذرّح *muzarrah*, Watered (milk or honey). *Muzarrih*, One who rubs (meat) with cantharides (ذرّاح *zurrāh*) as a poison. (See تذريح *tazrīh*.)

A مذرع *muzriẕ*, One who measures by the ell, cubit, or arm. (See اذراع *izrāẕ*.)

A مذرّع *muzzariẕ*, One who puts forth his arms (ذراعان *zirāẕāni*) from beneath his vest.

A مذرّع *muzarraẕ*, (An animal) distinguished by shining black streaks upon the fore-legs. Wounded in the brisket, so that the fore-legs are stained with blood. A swift horse, one that enables his rider to pierce the game, so that the horse's fore-legs are stained by the blood of the game. One whose mother is nobler than the father. Strangled. *Muzarriẕ*, A strangler. One who confesses. One who stretches out the arms or hands when going along (as people when they have got good news to tell). (Rain) penetrating the ground to the depth of a cubit. (See تذريع *tazrīẕ*.)

A مذرّعة *muzarraẕat*, A female hyena striped on the fore-legs.

A مذرّف *muzarrif*, Shedding (tears). Exceeding, above (a hundred). (See تذريف *tazrīf*.)

A مذرق *muzrik*, Muting (bird).

A مذرّق *muzzarik*, A mixer up of antimony with the juice of the herb ذرق *zurak*.

A مذرّق *muzarrak*, (Milk) mixed with water.

A مذرقة *mazrakat*, (v. n. of مذرق Q) Throwing. *Muzrikat*, Land which produces the herb ذرق.

A مذروان *mizrawāni*, (dual) The prominent extremities of the buttocks. The extremes or horns of a bow. Both sides of the head.

A مذروب *mazrūb*, Sharpened, whetted.

A مذرور *mazrūr*, Pounded, pulverized. Scattered.

A مذروع *mazrūẕ*, Measured with ell or cubit.

A مذروف *mazrūf*, Shed, fallen (tear).

A مذري *mizra'*, A fan; also a pronged instrument for winnowing corn. *Muzrī*, see اذراء *izrāʼ*.

A مذرئ *muzriʼ*, A camel that lets her milk flow.

A مذرّي *muzarrī*, A scatterer. A ventilator. An encomiast. (See تذرية *tazriyat*.)

A مذع *mazẕ*, (or مذعة *mazẕat*) (v. n. of مذع) Telling one part and concealing another (of news or any transaction). Scattering (urine). Flowing at the tops of mountains (springs). Colouring, glossing over. Taking oath.

A مذعابّين *muzẕābbīn*, Flowing in a line, as the hairs of a hyena's mane.

A مذعان *mizẕān*, Docile, tractable (camel).

A مذعذع *muzaẕzaẕ*, A bastard. An adopted son. *Muzaẕziẕ*, A squanderer. A blab. (See ذعذعة.)

A مذعر *muzẕir*, A terrifier.

A مذعّرة *muzaẕẕarat*, Mad, furious (she-camel).

A مذعف *muzẕif*, A killer. Instant (death).

A مذعور *mazẕūr*, Frightened.

A مذعورة *mazẕūrat*, Mad, furious (she-camel). (A woman) in dread of being suspected.

A مذعوف *mazẕūf*, Poisoned (victuals). Drugged with poison (ذعف *zaẕf*).

A مذفّف *muzaffaf*, Light and swift (arrow). *Muzaffif*, One who hastens to despatch a wounded man.

A مذفورة *mazfūrat*, (A garden) fragrant with wild rue (ذفراء *zafrāʼ*).

A مذفوف *mazfūf*, Ready prepared, at hand.

A مذق *mazk*, (v. n. of مذق) Mixing (milk) with water. Shewing feigned (affection).

A مذقوط *mazkūt*, Stained with dung of flies.

A مذكار *mizkār*, (A woman) who bears male children. A trackless waste, which none but a bold man will assay to cross.

A مذكر *muzkir*, A remembrancer. (A woman) who bears male offspring (ذكر *zakar*). Hard, adverse (times). Dangerous (road), sore (calamity).

A مذّكر *muzzakir*, A rememberer. A reminder.

A مذكر *muzakkar*, Masculine. A male sword, *i.e.* made of bright, well-tempered steel (such as they supposed to have been made by the Genies). Hard, adverse (fortune). Dangerous (road). مذكر سماعي *muzakkari samāẕī*, A hen-pecked husband. *Muzakkir*, An adviser, admonisher, remembrancer. (See تذكير *tazkīr*.)

A مذكرة *mazkarat*, Any thing worthy to be remembered (especially sacred). Mention, relation. *Muzkarat*, Masculine (woman).

A مذكّرة *muzakkarat*, Masculine (woman). Sore (calamity).

A مذكوبة *mazkūbat*, A virtuous woman.

A مذكور *mazkūr*, Remembered, recorded, mentioned; expressed, related. مذكور الاوصاف *mazkūru'l awsāf*, Above described.

A مذكورات *mazkūrāt*, (pl. of مذكورة *mazkūrat*) Discourses, relations, matters mentioned. Sundry petty allowances made to the zamīndārs and others at the close of the accounts of the annual settlement (a term used chiefly in India).

A مذكوري *mazkūrī*, Independent talukdārs who paid their own rents to government. Recollection.

A مذكي *muzkī*, One who kindles a fire. One who appoints spies. (See اذكاء *izkāʼ*.)

A مذكّي *muzakkī*, (pl. مذاكي *mazākī*) Six-year-old horse. (See تذكية *tazkiyat*.)

A مذكية *muzkiyat*, (A cloud) frequently raining.

A مذل *mazl*, (v. n. of مذل) Being unable to keep (a secret). Being oppressed and wearied by the charge of a secret. Being liberal. Sleeping, being torpid (as the foot). Languor, torpor. مذل النفس *mazlu'n nafs* (or يد *yad*), Liberal. *Mizl*, Small-bodied (man), spare of flesh. *Mazal*, (v. n. of مذل) Being heart-sick, wearied, melancholy, and restless. *Mazil*, One who cannot keep a secret. Heart-sick, melancholy. Weak, feeble. Liberal.

A مذلّ *muzill*, Who renders vile or abject; who discovers one to be so. Debasing. A name of God.

A مذلّة *mazallat*, (v. n. of ذلّ) Being abject and submissive. Baseness, contempt. عير المذلّة *ẕayru'l mazallati*, A peg, pin, nail.

A مذلعبّ *muzlaẕibb*, Reclined, lying on the breast.

A مذلغ *mizlagh*, The penis.

A مذلق *muzlak*, Pronounced with the tip of the tongue. *Muzlik*, see اذلاق *izlāk*.

A مذلّق *muzallak*, Sharpened at the point. (Milk) mixed with water. *Muzallik*, One who makes sharp, or who renders ready or voluble in speech.

A مذلّل *muzallal*, Broke in, tame, quiet. A palm-tree whose clusters of dates are left on the tree. (A tree) whose fruits hang low within reach of the hand. *Muzallil*, A vilifier. A humbler, debaser. One who leaves clusters of dates on the tree.

A مذلول *mazlūl*, Humble, submissive.

A مذلي *mizla'*, Restless, unquiet (men).

A مذمّ *mizamm*, Motionless. *Muzimm*, Who becomes contemptible, despicable, vile, mean, base. Incapable of moving from weakness. Faulty, damaged, vitiated, despised on that account; suspected. (See اذمام *izmām*.)

A مذماة *muzmāt*, Game hit with a shot.

A مذماذ *mazmāz*, Loud-voiced, clamorous.

A مذمّة *mazammat*, (v. n. of ذمّ) Blaming. Blame, scorn, contempt, satire, abuse. Any thing deserving censure, fault. Right, justice, what is due. Protection. ذو مذمّة *zū mazammatin*, Heavy, burdensome. *Mazimmat*, Grief and shame (for the neglect of any duty). اخذتني منه مذمّة *akhazatnī minhu mazimmat* or *mazammat*, I was ashamed of him. اذهب مذمّتهم بشيء *azhib mazimmatahum bi shay-in*, Give them something. قضي مذمّته *kaza' mazammatahu* or *mazimmatahu*, He did him a favour from shame, or in fear of censure.

A مذمذة *mazmazat*, (v. n. of مذمذ Q) Lying.

A مذمذيّ *mazmaziy*, Ingenious, subtile, elegant. Jocular, good-natured.

A مذمّر *muzammar*, That which is between the shoulders. بلغ المذمّر *balagha'l muzammar*, It reaches to the shoulders, it presses heavily. *Muzammir*, One who thrusts his hand into the matrix of a camel to ascertain whether her foal in embryo be male or female. One who helps a camel to bring forth.

A مذمّم *muzammam*, Very much blamed.

A مذموم *mazmūm*, Despised, scorned. Mean, base, blameable.

A مذميذ *mizmīz*, A great liar.

A مذنب *miznab*, A ladle, spoon. A rivulet of water brought from one garden to another. *Muznib*, Criminal, faulty. A sinner.

A مذنّب *muzannib*, One who goes tail (ذنب *zanab*) foremost. (A camel) pained at delivery and extending her tail. (A date) ripening about the stalk.

P مذنگ *mazang*, A wooden key. Teeth of a key. Wards of a lock. Bar of a door.

A مذؤب *maz-ub*, One whose sheep are carried off by the wolf (ذئب *zi-b*). Attacked by a sore throat (ذئبة *zi-bat*).

A مذوب *mizwab*, A vessel for melting things.

A مذوّب *muzawwab*, Melted, liquefied. *Muzawwib*, One who decorates (a boy) with forelocks.

A مذوبة *mizwabat*, A ladle, a spoon.

A مذوح *mizwah*, One who compels, forces, or treats with severity.

A مذوّح *muzawwih*, Wasteful, unthrifty.

A مذود *mizwad*, The tongue. A manger. The horn of a bull.

A مذوّد *muzawwid*, A driver.

A مذؤم *maz-um*, Disgraced, blamed.

A مذؤوب *maz-ūb*, Afraid of the wolf (ذئب *zi-b*). One whose flocks have suffered by the wolf. Indisposed from a sore throat (ذئبة *zi-bat*).

A مذؤوف *maz-ūf*, Drugged with deadly poison.

A مذهب *maz-hab*, (v. n. of ذهب) Going, walking, passing along. (pl. مذاهب *mazāhib*) A sect, religious order. A religious opinion. Canon, law, rule, institution, regulation; rite, ceremony. Root, origin, principle. A way through which one goes. A place where they wash before prayer. P بد مذهب *bad-mazhab*, A miscreant. A *Muzhab*, Gilded. The Kaaba. A horse of a reddish dun colour. Name of a horse. A demon that causes one to splash and waste the water in the performance of ablutions. *Muzhib*, A remover, carrier away. A gilder.

A مذهّب *muzahhab*, Gilded. Worked with gold thread. *Muzahhib*, A gilder. A gold-embroiderer.

A مذهن *muzhin*, Who or what causes to forget, or draws away the attention.

A مذي *mazy*, (v. n. of مذي) Turning (a horse) to grass. Experiencing a seminal effusion from toying and playing. Water which flows from the mouth of a conduit out of a cistern. *Mazy*, (*mazī*, or مذيّ *maziy*) A seminal effusion, the effect of contact or lewd imaginations. P مذي آوردن *mazī āwardan*, To indulge in secret vicious practices; to onanise.

A مذياع *mizyā'*, (pl. مذاييع *mazāyī'*) Full of chinks, a blabber, revealer of secrets.

A مذئّب *muz-ib*, Afraid. One who adorns a boy with forelocks (ذؤابة *zu-ābat*).

A مذيب *muzīb*, A melter. Predatory. An able, skilful manager.

A مذيّة *maziyat*, (or مذية *mazyat*) (pl. مذيّات *maziyāt* and مذاء *mizā-*) A woman.

A مذيّخ *muzayyikh*, A humbler, subduer.

A مذيخة *mazyakhat*, Wolves.

A مذيد *muzīd*, One who helps to drive.

A مذيذ *mazīz*, A liar.

A مذئر *muz-ir*, An exasperator. A compeller. An exciter, instigator. (See اذآر *iz-ār*.)

A مذيع *muzī'*, A divulger, publisher. A robber, carrier off. (See اذاعة *izā'at*.)

A مذيق *mazīk*, (Milk) mixed with water.

A مذيل *mazīl*, Unable to keep a secret. Weak, feeble. Restless from bodily indisposition. Soft iron.

A مذيّل *muzayyal*, (A tent or robe) having a long flap or train (ذيل *zayl*). Clad in an every-day garment, and doing one's own servile work.

A مذيم *mazīm*, (and مذيوم *mazyūm*) Vitiated.

P مر *mar*, Measure, number. Calculation, computation. A symbol or counter used by the natives of the East, to facilitate the adding up of large sums, and set against every hundred according to some, and according to others against every fifty. Since, because, only, solely. A particle seldom used, placed by way of pleonasm before Persian nouns, denoting the genitive, dative, or accusative; and sometimes used as a particle of restriction. *Mir*, A friend.

A مرّ *marr*, (v. n. of مرّ) Passing through or by, departing. Persevering, continuing. Being subject to bile. Haltering (a camel). Rendering bitter. Diffusing over the surface of the ground. A rope. A mattock, spade, or shovel; also the handle. (pl. of مرّة *marrat*) Times, turns. مرّ الدهور *marru'd duhūr*, The lapse of ages. علي مرّ الدهور *'ala' marri'd duhūr*, Continually. جئته مرّا او مرّين *ji-tuhu marran aw marrayn*, I came to him once or twice. *Murr*, (pl. امرار *amrār*) Bitter. Myrrh. Bitterness. (pl. of مرّة *murrat*) Certain bitter trees or herbs.

A مرء *mar-*, (v. n. of مرأ) Tasting (food). Lying with. *Mar-*, *mir-*, or *mur-*, (pl. مرؤن *mar-una*) A man, the human species. A wolf. *Mara-*, (v. n. of مرئ) Resembling a woman in appearance or in talk, having a feminine carriage. Finding (victuals) wholesome and easy of digestion.

P مرا *marā*, To me. *Mirā*, Friendship. The sun. The world. An equal draught.

A مراء *mirā-*, (v. n. 3 of مري) Disputing. Doubting, suspecting.

A مراءاة *murā-āt*, (v. n. 3 of رأي) Feigning, acting hypocritically, making a false show.

A مراءة *marā-at*, (v. n. of مرؤ) Being easy of digestion (meat). Being salubrious. Digestion.

A مرأب *mir-ab*, A repairer, a mender.

A مرابأة *murāba-at*, (v. n. 3 of ربأ) Shunning. Observing, guarding. Being ware of, fearing.

A مراباة *murābāt*, (v. n. 3 of ربا for ربو) Being affable, courteous, civil, polite, or dissimulating.

A مرابحة *murābahat*, (v. n. 3 of ربح) Gaining, making a profit. Allowing a profit or advantage.

A مرابض *marābiz*, (pl. of مربض) Sheep-folds.

A مرابط *marābit*, (pl. of مربط *marbat* or *marbit*) Places where cattle are tied; stables, stalls. *Murābit*, Quiet, still. Posted on an enemy's frontier. One who appoints or despatches.

A مرابطة *murābatat*, (v. n. 3 of ربط) Hovering with a corps of cavalry about an enemy's frontier. Being patient and stedfast.

A مرابطين *murābitīn*, Name of an Arabian dynasty which reigned in Africa and Spain.

A مرابع *marābi'*, (pl. of مربع *marba'*) Spring-habitations.

A مرابعة *murāba'at*, (v. n. 3 of ربع) Assisting in lifting or placing a load by joining hands with another, applying the shoulders. Bargaining with one for the spring-season (like مصايفة *musāyafat*).

A مرابيع *marābīʿ*, (pl. of مرباع *mirbāʿ*) The first spring-rains.

A مرآة *mar'āt*, The looks, countenance. Worthy, deserving. في مرآة العين *fī mar'āti'l ʿayn*, (She is beautiful) in the look or eyes; appearing (beautiful) to the eye. *Mir'āt*, (pl. مرائي *marā'ī* and مرايا *marāya'*) A looking-glass, mirror.

A مرأة *mar'at*, A woman, wife. A she-wolf. The looks, countenance. Well adapted or fitted. Wholesomeness, digestibility.

A مرّات *marrāt*, (pl. of مرّة *marrat*) Times, turns. Several times, repeatedly.

A مراتب *marātib*, (pl. of مرتبة *martabat*) Steps. Grades. Degrees, gradations of rank. Watch-towers. Times. Affairs. Particulars.

A مراتج *marātij*, Narrow ways.

A مراتع *marātiʿ*, (pl. of مرتع) Meadows.

A مراث *marās*, The fundament of a horse.

A مراثي *marāsī*, (pl. of مرثية *marsiyat*) Dirges.

A مراجعة *murājahat*, (v. n. 3 of رجح) Contending with any one in estimating or guessing. Excelling, overcoming.

A مراجع *marājiʿ*, (pl. of مرجع *marjiʿ*) Lower parts of shoulders. *Murājiʿ*, (A woman) who returns to her friends on the death of her husband.

A مراجعة *murājaʿat*, (v. n. 3 of رجع) Returning. Replying. Returning from one journey to undertake another. Repeating, doing over and over again. Taking a woman home, or re-marrying one formerly divorced. P دستور مراجعت *dastūri murājaʿat*, Licence, dismission, permission to return.

A مراجل *marājil*, (pl. of مرجل *mirjal*) Cauldrons, pipkins, kettles. (pl. of ممرجل *mumarjal*) Cloths or garments admirably coloured or embroidered.

A مراجم *marājim*, Foul language.

A مراجمة *murājamat*, (v. n. 3 of رجم) Using all one's might in talking, running, or fighting. Warding off or averting.

A مراجيح *marājīh*, Heavily-laden (palm-trees). (Camels) which travel with a light, ambling pace. Mild and gentle (men).

A مراح *marāh*, A place to and from which people go in the evening. *Mirāh*, Cheerfulness, gladness. *Murāh*, A place where cattle are lodged at night.

A مراحل *marāhil*, (pl. of مرحلة *marhalat*) Stations, stages, days' journeys.

A مراحلة *murāhalat*, (v. n. 3 of رحل) Assisting in loading or in preparing (a horse) for a journey. Road-expenses.

P مراحل نشين *marāhil-nishīn*, A planet. A traveller.

A مراحم *marāhim*, (pl. of مرحمة *marhamat*) Compassions. Favours. Kindnesses, gifts. ارباب مراحم و اشفاق *arbābi marāhim u ishfāk*, Compassionate and merciful men.

A مراحي *marāha'*, (pl. of مرح) Lively, sprightly.

A مراحيض *marāhīz*, (pl. of مرحاض *mirhāz*) Washers' beetles.

A مراخاة *murākhāt*, (v. n. 3 of رخي) Making soft, loose, and relaxed. Being near delivery. Keeping at a distance from.

A مراخي *marākhī*, (pl. of مرخاء *mirkhā'*) (Mares or she-asses) of a long or quick pace.

A مراد *marād*, The neck. A place through which camels pass to and fro in pasturing. *Murād*, Wished, willed, signified. Desire, wish, will, intention, design, end, scope. About, nearly. فهو المراد *fahwa'l murād*, Then the object is attained. *Murād*, (or المراد *al murād*) A proper name, Morad or Amurath.

P مراد *mirād*, A stone which shews many colours when exposed to the sun, and to which wonderful properties are ascribed.

A مرّاد *marrād*, (pl. مراريد *marārīd*) The neck.

A مرادّ *marādd*, (pl. of مردّ *muridd*) Camels which drink oft, and are oppressed thereby.

A مراداة *murādāt*, (v. n. 3 of ردي) Fighting with stones. Soliciting. Diverting from, carrying away. Treating kindly. Affability, courtesy, gentleness.

A مرادات *murādāt*, (pl. fem. of مراد *murād*) Things desired. Desires, intentions, wishes.

P مراد بخش *murād-bakhsh*, Giver of one's desires.

A مرادة *marādat*, (v. n. of مرد) Exceeding all bounds in daring, disobedience, insolence, and pride.

A مرادّة *murāddat*, (v. n. 3 of ردّ) Repelling.

A مرادسة *murādasat*, (v. n. 3 of ردس) Striking one another with stones.

A مرادغ *marādigh*, (pl. of مردغة *mardaghat*) The parts lying between the neck and collar-bones. Fruitful, flourishing gardens. ذات مرادغ *zāti marādigh*, Fat (she-camel).

A مرادف *murādaf*, Followed. *Murādif*, Synonymous.

A مرادفة *murādafat*, (v. n. 3 of ردف) Riding upon one another (locusts). Following one another, succeeding. Carrying double (a horse). Acting as viceroy or vicegerent (ردف *ridf*).

A مرادي *marāda'*, (pl. of مرداء *mardā'*) Barren, sandy grounds which produce nothing. *Marādī*, Breeches, drawers. The legs of a camel or elephant. (pl. of مردي *mirda'*) Stones, missiles.

A مرادي *murādī*, Favourably, agreeably to one's wish. Change, small money. (pl. مراديات *murādiyāt*) Obtaining one's wishes.

A مراديّ *marādīy*, (pl. of مرديّ *murdīy*) Oars. *Murādīy*, Voluntary, spontaneous.

P مرار *marār*, A kind of white thorn.

A مرار *marār*, A kind of rope. *Mirār*, (v. n. 3 of مرّ) Being drawn out. Wrestling, striving to throw another on the ground. Going along with, accompanying. (pl. of مرّة *marrat*) Times, turns. مرارا *mirāran*, Often, frequently, many times; sometimes, now and then. ذات المرار *zātu'l mirār*, Many times. *Murār*, A species of bitter but choice tree or plant, which shrivels the lips and bares the teeth of camels when eating it: hence the grandfather of Amru'l kays was called آكل المرار *ākilu'l murār*.

A مرارة *marārat*, (v. n. of مرّ) Being bitter. Saying any thing disagreeable. Bitterness. (pl. مرائر *marā'ir*) The gall-bladder. مرارة الموت *marāratu'l mawt*, The bitterness of death.

P مراري *marārī*, A hempen-rope.

A مراري *marārī*, (pl. of مروراة) Barren deserts.

A مراريّة *mirārīyat*, Biliousness, bile.

A مراريد *marārīd*, (pl. of مرّاد *marrād*) Necks.

A مراز *marāz*, (or مرازة *marāzat*) Weight.

A مرازان *marāzāni*, Both breasts.

A مرازبة *marāzibat*, (pl. of مرزبان *marzubān*) Princes, satraps. Lord-marchers.

A مرازغة *murāzaghat*, (v. n. 3 of رزغ) Wrestling with one another. Spearing each other.

A مرازمة *murāzamat*, (v. n. 3 of رزم) Doing one thing immediately after another, as eating hastily mouthsful of different kinds of victuals. Eating one day meat, another honey or dates, and a third milk-dishes. Pasturing (a camel) in two fields alternately. Offering up thanks to God after a meal, or between every mouthful. Remaining long at home. Buying any thing at market which does not fill a dish or sack. Bringing together, uniting.

A مرازن *murāzin*, An inhabitant of the same house with another. One who alights at the same time with another.

A مرازنة *murāzanat*, (v. n. 3 of رزن) Dwelling in the same abode with another. Alighting together.

A مرازي *marāzī*, A medicine mixed with tutty.

A مرازيب *marāzīb*, (pl. of مرزاب *mirzāb*) Ships long and wide.

A مرازيح *marāzīh*, (Camels) worn out, decaying.

A مرآس *mir'ās*, A horse which bites the heads (رأس *ra's*) of others in running, or keeps ahead in fleetness. A camel lean except about the head.

A مراس *marās*, Strength. *Mirās*, (v. n. 3 of مرس) Managing (affairs), applying with great attention, involving one's self (in them). Struggling with; grappling. Applying a remedy, giving medicine. Strength, vigour.

A مرأس *mir'as*, (pl. مرائس *marā'is*) A horse which bites or kicks the heads of others whilst running before them. A leader, chieftain. A strong head.

A مرّاس *marrās*, Robust, potent. Long (night).

A مرأس *mura''as*, Lean except about the head.

A مراساة *murāsāt*, A swimming together.

A مراسب *marāsib*, (pl. of مرسب) Columns.

A مراسة *marāsat*, Hardness, vehemence, strength.

A مراسّة *murāssat*, (v. n. 3 of رسّ) Beginning along with another. Going together before a judge.

A مراسغة *murāsaghat*, (v. n. 3 of رسغ, not in use) Catching (an adversary in wrestling) by the wrist or the ankle (رسغ *rusgh* or *rusugh*).

A مراسل *murāsil,* One who sends a letter or message. A woman, who, when repudiated, or learning the death of her husband, dresses to allure another, and sends to him. An old woman, or one whose husband is dead. Hairy-legged (woman).

A مراسلة *murāsalat,* (v. n. 3 of رسل) Writing a letter, or sending a messenger to (another). Keeping up a correspondence. The letter or summons of a judge, a citation.

A مراسم *marāsim,* Marks, signs, vestiges, customs, usages. Laws, conditions, agreements, pactions, conventions, covenants, obligations, observances, duties, prescriptions. اداء مراسم تهاني *adāʻi marāsimi tahānī,* Paying compliments of congratulation. ايفاء مراسم *īfāʻi marāsim,* Fulfilling the laws, performing one's duty.

A مراسي *marāsī,* (pl. of مرساة *mirsāt*) Anchors. Ports, harbours, anchorages. القت السحاب مراسيها *alkati's sahābu marāsīha,* The clouds cast their anchors, *i.e.* remained stationary and poured forth rain.

A مراسيل *marāsīl,* (pl. of مرسل *mursal*) Traditions traced or referred immediately to the prophet. (pl. of مرسال *mirsāl*) Pleasant-paced camels.

A مراسيم *marāsīm,* (pl. of مرسوم *marsūm*) Edicts.

A مراش *mirāsh,* Vomiting. A vomit.

A مراشاة *murāshāt,* (v. n. 3 of رشا for رشو) Helping, assisting. Endeavouring to conciliate, soothing by presents. Conniving, favouring.

A مراشب *marāshib,* Clay with which they stop the mouths of wine-jars that the aroma escape not.

A مراشة *murāshat,* A small due, a trifling claim.

A مراشد *marāshid,* Straight roads. Firm resolutions, steady designs.

A مراشف *marāshif,* (pl. of مرشف *marshaf*) Places of sucking or sipping.

A مراشقة *murāshakat,* (v. n. 3 of رشق) Walking or travelling along with another.

A مراصد *marāsid,* (pl. of مرصد *marsad*) Places of observation, ambushes.

A مراصدة *murāsadat,* (v. n. 3 of رصد) Seizing an opportunity of invading or attacking.

A مراصع *marāsiʻ,* (pl. of مرصع *mursiʻ*) Palm-trees having young ones.

A مراض *marāz,* (pl. مرائض *marāʻiz*) A hard low-lying place holding water. *Mirāz,* (pl. of مريض *marīz*) Sick, diseased, ill. *Murāz,* Blight, destructive to fruits.

A مراضاة *murāzāt,* (v. n. 3 of رضي) Striving to please and be agreeable; contending who shall please most. Being pleased and satisfied with each other.

A مراضب *marāzib,* Sweet spittles.

A مراضخ *marāzikh,* (pl. of مرضخة *mirzakhat*) Stones with which they pound date-stone skins.

A مراضخة *murāzakhat,* (v. n. 3 of رضخ) Giving unwillingly. Throwing, or contending in throwing stones. Pelting one another with stones.

A مراضع *marāziʻ,* (pl. of مرضع *marzaʻ*) Teats, nipples. (pl. of مرضع *murziʻ*) Wet-nurses.

A مراضعة *murāzaʻat,* (v. n. 3 of رضع) Suckling (a child), either one's own or that of another. Delivering a child to a wet-nurse. Sucking a pregnant mother. Having a foster-brother.

A مراضىٰ *marāzā',* (pl. of مريض *marīz*) Sick.

A مراضيع *marāzīʻ,* (pl. of مرضع) Wet-nurses.

A مراط *mirāt,* An unfeathered arrow. (pl. of مريط *marīt*) Unfeathered arrows.

A مراطة *murātat,* What falls when combing or pulling out hairs: combings.

A مراطنة *murātanat,* (v. n. 3 of رطن) Addressing (another) in a barbarous tongue, *i.e.* in any language besides the Arabic.

A مراغ *mirāʻ,* Fat, grease.

A مراعاة *murāʻāt,* (v. n. 3 of رعي) Observing, regarding. Considering, reflecting; viewing attentively. Attending to, listening. Shewing pity and mercy. Taking care of, preserving, guarding, maintaining. Looking to the end of any affair. Contemplating any thing, especially the setting stars. Feeding, pasturing (along with another). Abounding in pasture (ground). Regard, respect.

A مراعة *marāʻat,* (v. n. of مرع) Abounding in good pasture (a valley).

A مراعز *murāʻiz,* A chider, reprover.

A مراعزة *murāʻazat,* (v. n. 3 of رعز) Being drawn together, wrinkled, or contracted.

A مراعف *marāʻif,* The nose and the environs. على رغم من مراعفه *ʻala' raghmin min marāʻifihi,* Against his inclination.

A مراعي *marāʻī,* (pl. of مرعى *marʻa'*) Pastures. *Murāʻī,* An observer, guardian, keeper. A supporter.

A مراغ *marāgh,* A (horse's) rolling-place.

A مراغب *marāghib,* Necessaries of life. Women perplexed, embarrassed about the means of living. *Murāghib,* Desirous, wishful, inclined, propense.

A مراغبات *murāghabāt,* (pl. of مراغبة *murāghabat*) Affections, desires, wishes, hankerings.

A مراغبة *murāghabat,* (v. n. 3 of رغب) Expressing a wish. Desire, wish, affection, propensity.

A مراغة *marāghat,* A place where (a horse) rolls himself about or sleeps. A she-ass that resists not the males. A steward or manager of an estate.

A مرّاغة *marrāghat,* One that tumbles or wallows.

A مراغم *murāgham,* A place of refuge. A fortress. Agitated, disturbed. *Murāghim,* Unwilling.

A مراغمة *murāghamat,* (v. n. 3 of رغم) Flying in a rage (at a spouse). Abandoning (friends or family), relinquishing. Carrying on a war openly with (any one). Being inimical, hostile.

P مراغه *marāgha,* Name of a city in Azarbayjān.

A مراغي *marāghī,* (Camels) giving frothy milk.

P مراغيدن *marāghīdan,* To roll or wallow.

A مرافاة *murāfāt,* (v. n. 3 of رفا for رفو) Agreeing. Consolidating, healing (as a wound). Being united, soldered.

A مرافأة *murāfaʻat,* (v. n. 3 of رفأ) Behaving mildly. Shewing respect, acting kindly.

A مرافد *marāfid,* (pl. of مرفد *mirfad*) Goblets, large bowls (generally filled on the arrival of strangers. *Murāfid,* Reciprocal, mutual in aiding.

A مرافدة *murāfadat,* (v. n. 3 of رفد) Assisting one another, affording mutual aid.

A مرافض *marāfiz,* The open parts of valleys through which streams run. High places.

A مرافع *murāfiʻ,* Mutually agreed to go together before a judge: referring a case to him.

A مرافعة *murāfaʻat,* (v. n. 3 of رفع) Citing before a judge, carrying on a law-suit, accusing, having recourse to justice. Having business or dealing with. Throwing into trouble and difficulty. Sparing, pitying, leaving alive or remaining. An action, law-suit. Statement of a case.

A مرافق *marāfik,* Sinks for carrying off foul water, drains for receiving rain-water. Privies. (pl. of مرفق *mirfak*) Elbows. *Murāfik,* A fellow-traveller, a fellow-companion.

A مرافقة *murāfakat,* (v. n. 3 of رفق) Travelling in company with. Assisting. Company, society.

A مرافيد *marāfīd,* Sheep whose milk never ceases.

A مراقّ *marākk,* (pl. of مرقّ *marakk*) The soft parts of the belly. مراقّ الدبّ الاكبر *marākku'd dubbi'l akbar,* The 17th star in the Great Bear.

A مراقاة *murākāt,* An acting circumspectly.

A مراقب *murākib,* A looker after, observer.

A مراقبة *murākabat,* (v. n. 3 of رقب) Guarding. Observation. Contemplation, meditation. Partiality. In the versification of مضارع *muzāriʻ* and مقتضب *muktazab,* the alternate occurrence of the measure مفاعيل *mafāʻīl* and مفاعيلن *mafāʻīlun.*

A مراقة *murākat,* Wool plucked out, pelt-wool. Herbage plucked up to give to a camel.

A مراقد *marākid,* (pl. of مرقد) Tombs. Beds.

A مراقعة *murākaʻat,* A drinking of wine frequently.

A مراقي *marākī,* (pl. of مرقاة) Steps, stairs.

P مراك *marāk,* Unlearned, foolish. Deceived by words. Played upon, ridiculed.

A مراكب *marākib,* (pl. of مركب *markab*) Carriages, vehicles, ships, horses: machines or animals by which people are borne from place to place.

A مراكبيّ *marākibīy,* A ship-master. A waggoner, a drayman.

A مراكض *marākiz,* The sides of a tank.

A مراكضة *murākazat,* A riding a race with.

A مراكل *marākil,* (pl. of مركل) Ways, roads.

A مراكي *marākī,* (pl. of مراكية *murākiyat*) Plants of the salt and bitter species called حمض *hamz.* *Murākī,* Perennial, firm, unfading.

A مراكية *murākiyat,* A kind of the حمض plant.

A مرام *marām,* (v. n. of رام for روم) Seeking anxiously. Desire, wish, intention, aim, purpose, design. A place of search. Ascent. حسب المرام *hasba'l marām,* Agreeable to one's desire.

A مراماة *murāmāt*, (v. n. 3 of رمي) Contending with in throwing the javelin or shooting arrows.

P مرام بخش *marām-bakhsh*, Satisfying desires.

A مرامر *murāmir*, Vain, false, idle, trifling. Soft, delicate, and tremulous. مرامربن مرّة *murāmiru'bn murrat*, Name of the inventor of the Arabic character now in use.

A مرامق *murāmik*, A person who cherishes little remains of regard for another.

A مرامقة *murāmakat*, (v. n. 3 of رمق) Glancing at. Being just kept alive. Doing business ill.

A مرامي *marāmī*, Flings, throws. Projectiles. Instruments of war by which stones or other missiles were projected to a distance. Turrets, battlements. Deserts, perilous places. مرامي الغربة *marāmī'l ghurbat*, The tossings of peregrination.

A مراميم *marāmīm*, Feathered arrows.

P مران *marān*, That (opposed to this). A particle seldom used, placed by way of pleonasm before Persian nouns, denoting the genitive, dative, or accusative. Drive not. *Murān*, A tall and slender tree from which they make arrows.

A مران *mirān*, (v. n. 3 of مرن) Giving false signs of pregnancy (a camel).

A مرّان *murrān*, A tree of which they make spears. (pl. of مرّانة *murrānat*) Hard and limber (spears).

A مراناة *murānāt*, (v. n. 3 of رنا for رنو) Treating kindly, being affable and courteous to one another.

A مرانة *marānat*, (v. n. of مرن) Being hard and smooth. Being accustomed (to any thing), continuing at, being assiduous about it. Becoming hard (as the hand with labour). Smoothness.

A مرّانة *murrānat*, (pl. مرّان) A spear somewhat hard and limber. A tree of which spears are made.

P مرانيه *murānaya*, Name of a diuretic herb, having leaves like those of jasmine.

A مراوح *marāwih*, (pl. of مروحة *mirwahat*) Fans.

A مراوحة *murāwahat*, (v. n. 3 of راح for روح) Doing (two things) alternately. Standing first (on one foot) and then on the other. Turning from side to side.

A مراود *murāwid*, A suitor, importunate wooer.

A مراودة *murāwadat*, (v. n. 3 of راد for رود) Asking, requiring, desiring, begging, soliciting, wooing. Wish, desire.

A مراوزة *marāwizat*, Natives of مرو *marv*.

A مراوضة *murāwazat*, (v. n. 3 of راض for روض) Endeavouring to conciliate, coaxing, soothing. Selling by description and not by sample.

A مراوغ *murāwigh*, Sly, cunning, astute.

A مراوغة *murāwaghat*, (v.n. 3 of راغ for روغ) Using art or fraud, deceiving. Wrestling, striving with.

A مراوفة *murāwafat*, The being kind and friendly.

A مراوق *murāwik*, One whose tent or portico (رواق *rawāk*) joins another's; next-door neighbour.

A مراوون *murāsūn*, (pl. of مرائي) Hypocrites.

A مراوي *marāwī*, (pl. of مروي *mirwa'*) Ropes for fastening loads on camels.

A مراهاة *murāhāt*, (v. n. 3 of رها for رهو) Speaking gently. Drawing near. Consenting, agreeing.

A مراهص *marāhis*, Ranks, degrees, dignities.

A مراهصة *murāhasat*, (v. n. 3 of رهص) Seizing an opportunity of pouncing upon a debtor.

A مراهق *murāhik*, (A lad) near the age of puberty. One who comes towards the end of an appointed time (especially to perform the ceremonies of Mecca).

A مراهقة *murāhakat*, (v. n. 3 of رهق) Approaching the age of puberty. Arriving at Mecca when the ceremonies of the pilgrimage are nearly finished.

A مراهم *marāhim*, (pl. of مرهم *marham*) Plasters.

A مراهن *murāhin*, A bettor, layer of wagers.

A مراهنة *murāhanat*, (v. n. 3 of رهن) Contending, depositing the bets (especially at a horse-race). Betting, wagering.

A مراهي *marāhī*, (pl. of مرهاة) Swift horses.

A مرأي *marsa'*, The looks. في المرأي *fi'l marsa'*, Apparently. بمرأيً منّي *bi marsan minnī*, Within sight of me. حسن المرأي *hasanu'l marsa'*, Good-looking (man). رأس مرأي *rassu mursan*, A long-beaked or snouted head. مرأيً *marsan*, Within sight.

A مرايا *marāya'*, The lacteal veins. (pl. of مرآة *mirsāt*) Looking-glasses. (pl. of مريّ *mariy*) (Camels) abounding in milk, which streams out on pressing the dug.

A مراياة *murāyasat*, (v. n. 3 of ريأ, not used) Fearing, avoiding. Watching.

A مرايحة *murāyahat*, Quiet, repose, ease, tranquillity. Joy on the certain acquisition of a thing.

A مرائر *marāsir*, (pl. of مرير *marīr*) Barren grounds. Long, slender, but firmly-twisted ropes. (pl. of مرارة *mararat*) Gall-bladders.

A مرائس *marāsis*, Strong heads. *Murāsis*, One who lags behind in battle. Fat only about the head.

A مرائض *marāsiz*, (pl. of مراض *marāz*) Hard low-lying places which hold water.

A مرايفة *murāyafat*, (v. n. 3 of راف for ريف) Suspecting, casting suspicion.

A مرائل *murāsil*, One who goes quick, like a young ostrich (رأل *rasl*).

A مرائي *marāsī*, (pl. of مرآة *mirsāt*) Looking-glasses. *Murāsī*, (pl. مراؤون *murāsūn*) A hypocrite.

A مربّ *marabb*, One who calls the people together. A house, mansion, residence, resort. A place full of herbage.

A مربأ *marbas*, (or مربأة *marbasat*) A hill, or high place whence any thing may be seen.

A مرباء *marbās*, A ladder, stairs.

A مرباب *mirbāb*, A place full of herbage.

A مرباذ *mirbāz*, One who makes many blunders in a speech: extremely talkative.

A مرباع *mirbāع*, (pl. مرابيع *marābīع*) A place yielding early spring-grass. A fourth of the plunder, which in Pagan times was the chief's share. (A camel) accustomed to bring forth a colt in the spring. (according to some) (A camel) delivered of her first colt. Of a middling stature.

A مربال *mirbāl*, (Ground) abounding in ربول.

A مربّب *murabbab*, Preserved in syrup. Brought up, educated. *Murabbib*, A bringer-up, a tutor. A maker of preserves or rob (ربّ *rubb*).

A مربّة *marabbat*, Rule, dominion. *Murabbat*, A preserve, confection.

A مربّت *murabbit*, A bringer-up (of a child). One who pats or soothes (an infant) to rest.

A مربج *murbij*, A begetter of dwarfish children.

A مربد *mirbad*, A camel-stable. A place where dates are dried.

A مربدّ *murbadd*, Ash-coloured.

A مربذ *murbiz*, A cutter off. (See ارباذ.)

A مربش *murbish*, Leafy (tree). Split.

A مربض *marbiz* or *marbaz*, (pl. مرابض *marābiz*) A fold or other place for sheep. The part in which the intestines lie. *Marbiz*, (v. n. of ربض) Bringing (cattle or sheep) into a fold, folding them.

A مربط *marbat* or *marbit*, A place where cattle are tied: a stable. *Mirbat*, (or مربطة *mirbatat*) A chain, ligament, string, rope; a bridle, halter, reins.

A مربطة *mirbatat*, A leathern thong with which they bind a camel's pack-saddle.

A مربع *marbaع*, (pl. مرابع *marābiع*) A spring-habitation, any place where one resides, or cattle pasture in that season. *Mirbaع*, A pole held by a man at each end, with which they lift burdens. *Murbaع*, Attacked by a quartan ague. *Murbiع*, A fever which returns every fourth day. A camel which foals in the spring, or is followed by her colt. The sail of a ship filled by the wind. (See ارباع.)

A مربّع *murabbaع*, Squared. Square, quadrangular. An epigram or song of four verses or four lines, a quatrain. P مربّع كردن *murabbaع kardan*, To square, make quadrangular. مربّع نشستن *murabbaع nishastan*, To sit cross-legged like a tailor (in the manner of the Asiatics). A عسكرمربّع *ٴaskari murabbaع*, A body of horse, squadron. P مربّع خانهٔ نور *murabbaع-khānasi nūr*, The Kaaba, or temple of Mecca. A *Murabbiع*, A maker of a quadrangular or square figure.

A مربعة *marbaعat*, (Ground) abounding with jerboas (يربوع *yarbūع*). *Mirbaعat*, A pole held by a man at each end, with which they lift burdens.

A مربّعة *murabbaعat*, Square (figure).

P مربّع نشين *murabbaع-nishīn*, A sweetheart.

A مربغ *murbagh*, Allowed to drink his fill. *Murbigh*, One who allows (camels) to drink at pleasure.

A مربّق *murabbak*, Larded (bread).

A مربوب *marbūb*, Educated. Possessed, in the power of another. (A leathern bottle) seasoned by a sweet confection to give it an agreeable flavour.

A مربوث *marbūs*, Hindered, let, prevented.

A مربوص *marbūs*, Waited for, expected.

A مربوط *marbūt*, Bound, fastened, tied. Spell-bound, impotent. Contained, inherent, depending upon. Polished, classical, and grammatical (language). Contented. Name of a village near Alexandria, the inhabitants of which are remarkably tall. تاء مربوطة *tāʼi marbūta*, Tā closed (ة). مربوط اللسان *marbūtu'l lisān*, Tongue-tied.

A مربوع *marbūʻ*, Attacked by a quartan ague (ربع *ribʻ*). Middle-sized (man).

A مربوعة *marbūʻat*, Land (watered by vernal rains).

A مربوق *marbūḳ*, Fast caught in a noose or lasso, entangled in a net or loop (ربقة *ribḳat*).

P مربويا *marbūyā*, (in zand and Pāz.) A sweet melon. (according to others) An island.

A مربأ *marbaʼ*, A place where one is brought up and educated. *Murbī*, Receiver of interest, usurer.

A مربّى *murabbaʼ*, Educated. Patronized. Preserved (fruit or ginger); a confection. *Murabbī*, A patron. An educator, a bringer up. A confectioner, preserver of fruits.

A مربيّ *marbīy*, Educated, brought up. Increased, multiplied.

A مربّيات *murabbayāt*, Confections, preserves made of the inspissated juice called رب *rubb*.

A مربئنّ *murbaʼinn*, Elevated, situated aloft.

A مرة *marat*, A she-wolf. A woman.

A مرّة *marrat*, (v. n. of مرّ) Being subject to bile. Haltering (a camel). Rendering bitter. Diffusing over the surface of the ground. (pl. مرّ *marr*, مرار *mirār*, مرر *mirar*, مرور *murūr*, and مرّات *marrāt*) One time or turn, once. One transit or passage. ذات مرّة *zāta marratin*, Once, one time (I met him). مرّة عن مرّة *marratan ʻan marratin*, One after another, again and again. مرّة جيش و مرّة عيش *marratan jaysh wa marratan ʻaysh* (or *ʻish*), Sometimes war and sometimes peace; now labour and now rest. مرّة المسلسلة *marratu'l musalsalat*, The constellation called Andromeda. *Mirrat*, Gall, bile. (pl. مرر *mirar*, and امرار *amrār*) Strength, hardiness of body; power, potency. The understanding. Firmness of mind, solidity of judgment. The twist of a rope. ذو مرّة *zū mirratin*, The archangel Gabriel. *Murrat*, (pl. مرّ *murr* and امرار *amrār*) A species of bitter tree or herb. ابو مرّة *abū murrat*, Father of bitterness or sorrow, *i.e.* the devil.

P مرت *mart*, Alive. *Murt*, Distracted, dispersed.

A مرت *mart*, (pl. امرات *amrāt* and مروت *murūt*) A solitude barren of all herbage. A man destitute of hair on his eyebrows.

A مرتأب *murtaʼab*, United. Covered over. Forgiven.

A مرتاج *mirtāj*, (pl. مراتج *marātij*) A bar, bolt, or instrument which shuts a door. A lane, slum, alley.

A مرتاح *murtāḥ*, The horse placed fifth in a race.

A مرتاش *murtāsh*, In good condition, in easy circumstances (whose nest is well-feathered).

A مرتاض *murtāz*, Exercised, disciplined.

A المرّتان *al murratāni*, Severity and bitterness. لقي منه المرّتين *lakiya minhu'l murratayn*, He received from him sorrow and bitterness.

A مرتّب *murattab*, Put in order, arranged; regulated, prepared. Garnished. مرتّب على الحروف *murattab ʻala'l ḥurūf*, Arranged alphabetically. *Murattib*, A setter in order, arranger, director.

A مرتبّ *murtabb*, A benefactor. One on whom favours are conferred.

A مرتبأ *murtabaʼ*, An observatory, watch-tower.

A مرتبان *martabān*, (or مرتباني *martabānī*) A vessel of the finest porcelain which poison cannot penetrate; a jar, pot, vessel.

A مرتبة *martabat*, (pl. مراتب *marātib*) A step, stair. A stage, story (of a house). A watch-tower on the summit of a hill. Office, employment, charge. Height. Dignity, rank of honour. Time. كمال مرتبه *kamāl martaba*, Perfectly, completely. P يك مرتبه *yak martaba*, Once, one time.

A مرتبث *murtabis*, Divided, scattered.

A مرتبس *murtabis*, Close, compact (flesh).

A مرتبط *murtabat*, Tied, bound. *Murtabit*, One who keeps (a horse) equipped for war.

A مرتبع *murtabaʻ*, A spring-habitation. *Murtabaʻ* or *biʻ*, Of a middling stature. (See ارتباع.)

A مرتبق *murtabiḳ*, Netted (deer). Entangled in any intricate business. (See ارتباق *irtibāḳ*.)

A مرتبن *murtabin*, One who ascends a high place.

A مرتبئ *murtabiʼ*, One who ascends a high place to take a view. (See ارتباء *irtibāʼ*.)

A مرتثّ *murtass*, Fallen down from weakness. (A wounded man) carried from the field.

A مرتثد *murtasid*, Seated upon bales of merchandise laid side by side, waiting for the beasts of burden destined to carry them.

A مرتج *murtaj*, Unable to pronounce. (A field) full of plants. Litharge, dross of silver.

A مرتجّ *murtajj*, Agitated, trembling, raging.

A مرتجح *murtajiḥ*, Moved backwards and forwards, up and down in the swing, or see-saw. Shaking (buttocks). Inclined.

A مرتجز *murtajiz*, Thundering. A composer or reciter of a poem written in metre called رجز *rajaz*. Name of a horse belonging to Muhammad (so called from the beauty of his neighing).

A مرتجس *murtajis*, Trembling (edifice). Thundering (sky). Braying (camel).

A مرتجل *murtajal*, Spoken extempore. *Murtajil*, One who seizes by the foot. An extempore speaker. A collector of many locusts for roasting. One who holds the stick زند *zand* between his hands and feet. (See also ارتجال *irtijāl*.)

A مرتجم *murtajim*, Accumulated, heaped up.

A مرتجي *murtajī*, Full of hope. Fearful.

A مرتحض *murtaḥiz*, Shamed, disgraced.

A مرتحل *murtaḥil*, Migratory.

A مرتخ *murtakhkhkh*, Overcharged with drink.

A مرتخش *murtakhish*, Agitated, shaking.

A مرتخص *murtakhis*, A valuer or buyer cheap.

A مرتدّ *murtadd*, An apostate, renegado.

A مرتدح *murtadaḥ*, Width, space, room, liberty.

A مرتدع *murtadiʻ*, (A garment) dyed with saffron, or perfumed with unguent. (An arrow) broken when hitting the mark. (A camel) of full age.

A مرتدغ *murtadigh*, Fallen into thin clay.

A مرتدف *murtadif*, One who rides behind another on horseback. A follower, comer after.

A مرتدي *murtadī*, Dressed in a long robe or cloak.

A مرتزق *murtazaḳ*, Riches, wealth, that whereby one is profited. *Murtaziḳ*, A stipendiary.

A مرتزم *murtazam*, Laid close to the ground, as it were glued to the earth.

A مرتسم *murtasam*, Painted, embroidered. *Murtasim*, Obedient to any prescription or law. One who prays to God, saying, الله اكبر *allāh akbar*, God is great. Religious. Venerable. Proud.

A مرتشي *murtashī*, Corrupted by presents, suborned, bribed. A taker of bribes (رشوة *rishwat*).

A مرتصف *murtasif*, One whose teeth are closely set. A lion.

A مرتصق *murtasiḳ*, (A nut) whose kernel is difficult to be separated from the shell.

A مرتضخ *murtazikh*, An inelegant speaker.

A مرتضى *murtazaʼ*, Agreeable. Chosen, approved. A title of Alīy. *Murtazī*, One who makes choice of, or approves. Content, satisfied.

A مرتضيّ *murtazīy*, Belonging to مرتضى *murtazaʼ*.

A مرتطم *murtatim*, Thrown (in the mud), stuck fast, and unable to get out. A troublesome, embarrassed business. (See ارتطام *irtitām*.)

A مرتع *martaʻ*, A meadow, spacious and luxuriant in spring-herbage. *Murtiʻ*, Fruitful, rich in produce, lacking nothing.

A مرتعث *murtaʻis*, Adorned with ear-rings.

A مرتعد *murtaʻid*, Trembling, dreading.

A مرتعس *murtaʻis*, Terrified, quaking.

A مرتعش *murtaʻish*, Trembling, frightened.

A مرتعص *murtaʻis*, Writhing (wounded serpent). Shaken (cloth). Vibrated (spear). (See ارتعاص.)

A مرتعي *murtaʻī*, Pasturing, feeding, grazing.

A مرتغب *murtaghib*, A supplicator, beseecher.

A مرتفد *murtafid*, A gainer, receiver of profit.

A مرتفع *murtafiʻ*, Elevated, exalted, high, aggrandized. Removed. Put in the nominative case. Preponderating (scale). (See ارتفاع *irtifāʻ*.)

A مرتفق *murtafaḳ*, A couch. An inn or caravansery. *Murtafiḳ*, Who leans on the elbow or a cushion. Full (cistern). Firm, solid, durable.

A مرتقب *murtaḳib*, A guardian, keeper. A watcher. A waiting expectant.

A مرتقش *murtaḳish*, Mixed in battle.

A مرتقع *murtaḳiʻ*, Attentive to, mindful.

A مرتقن *murtaḳin*, Tinged with saffron.

A مرتقى *murtaḳaʼ*, A place of ascent; ascent.

Murtaki, Ascended, borne upward.

A مرتك *martak*, Litharge of silver. One who speaks indistinctly (as a drunken man), although at other times eloquent.

P مرتك *murtak*, Litharge or dross of silver.

A مرتكّ *murtakk*, One who is reputed eloquent, but who, when he begins to speak, stammers. Relaxed and thin-marrowed (camel).

A مرتكب *murtakib*, Mounted; borne. One who engages in, attempts, perpetrates, commits (a crime). One who encounters.

A مرتكبة *murtakibat*, (A dish) quite full of bread and milk.

A مرتكز *murtakiz*, Beating (artery). Firm, steady, fixed. (See ارتكاز *irtikāz.*)

A مرتكس *murtakis*, Inverted, subverted. Precipitated. Collected in a crowd. (See ارتكاس.)

A مرتكض *murtakaz*, A reservoir (of water), a place where it is collected. *Murtakiz*, Disturbed, confused. (See ارتكاض *irtikāz.*)

A مرتكم *murtakim*, Heaped up, piled. مرتكم الطريق *murtakamu't tarīk*, The middle of the road.

P مرتكو *martakū*, A sparrow.

A مرتكى *murtaka'*, One in whom confidence is placed; faithful, trustworthy; a helper. A place of confidence. *Murtakī*, One who relies upon, trusts to. Firm, fixed, immoveable.

A مرتّل *murattil*, One who intones or pronounces a discourse with a clear, melodious voice.

A مرتمز *murtamiz*, Agitated (assembly).

A مرتمس *murtamis*, A plunger.

A مرتمض *murtamiz*, Ill at ease, sick at heart, sad. (See ارتماض *irtimāz.*)

A مرتمل *murtamil*, Defiled. Mean, base.

A مرتمم *murtamim*, An eater, devourer.

A مرتمي *murtamī*, Thrown, cast forth. A guard, watchman. هو مرتمٍ لنا *huwa murtamin lanā*, The advanced guard, forlorn hope, those who clear the way for an army.

A مرتنة *mirtanat*, (or مرتّنة *murattanat*) Bread kneaded with lard. Buttered (bread).

P مرتو *mar tu*, For thee, on thy account.

A مرتوم *martūm*, Bruised (nose). Broken-nosed.

A مرتوي *murtawī*, One whose thirst is quenched. Moistened. Thick, strong (rope or joint).

A مرتهس *murtahis*, Full (river). Crowding (people). (See ارتهاس *irtihās.*)

A مرتهش *murtahish*, A thin, limber bow that vibrates greatly. (See ارتهاش *irtihāsh.*)

A مرتهن *murtahan*, Pledged; a pledge, gage. *Murtahin*, A receiver of a pledge, a pawnee.

A مرث *mars*, (v. n. of مرث) Rubbing (dates) in order to peel (them). Steeping, softening, or dissolving (in water). Beating. Causing (a lamb or kid) to emit an offensive smell, as to excite the aversion of its dam. (An infant) mumbling and sucking (its fingers). *Maras*, (v. n. of مرث) Being gentle, patient, mild towards an opponent. *Maris*, Mild, gentle, patient towards an adversary.

A مرِّث *muriss*, The owner of a worn rope, or of old decayed furniture.

A مرثاة *marsāt*, (v. n. of رثي) Lamenting (any person), pronouncing a funeral eulogium. (pl. مراثي *marāsī*) A funeral-oration, elegy, dirge.

A مرثد *marsad*, A lion. A noble or magnanimous man. Name of a companion of Muhammad. Name of a king that reigned in Yaman 600 years.

A مرثط *mursit*, One who sits or rides languidly.

A مرثعنّ *mursaɛinn*, A low-skirted cloud.

A مرثم *marsim* or *mirsam*, The nose.

A مرثّم *murassam*, Wetted by gentle rain.

A مرثّن *murassan*, Watered by frequent showers.

A مرثود *marsūd*, (Goods) ranged side by side.

A مرثوم *marsūm*, Bruised or sore about the nose. Broken and bloody. (The foot of a camel) wounded by striking against a stone.

A مرثون *marsūn*, Watered by frequent showers.

A مرثية *marsiyat*, (v. n. of رثي) Lamenting (any one), pronouncing a funeral eulogium. An elegy, dirge. A funeral-oration sung during the Muharram in commemoration of the descendants of Aliy.

P مرثيه گرفتن *marsiya giriftan*, To sing a dirge or make a doleful noise in the manner of the female mourners in the East.

P مرثيه خوان *marsiya-khwān*, A repeater of the Marsiya. مرثيه خواني *marsiya-khwānī*, The repetition or singing of the Marsiya.

P مرج *marj*, Confines. Earth, ground, land. A field with raised borders for planting or sowing. Heel or wrist of a man, pastern of a beast. مرج پاي *marji pāy*, The foot towards the heel. *Marj* or *murj*, Name of a city in Kohistān.

A مرج *marj*, (v. n. of مرج) Sending to pasture, allowing (cattle) to feed at liberty. Mixing. (God) permitting (the seas) to flow and mingle together. A meadow, pasture. Confines, marches bordering upon an enemy's country. هرج مرج *harj marj*, Disturbance, mixture, confusion. *Maraj*, (v. n. of مرج) Mixing, confounding. Moving, playing (a wide ring on the finger). Being disturbed, perverse, confused, mixed, or confounded. One or more camels feeding without a keeper. Marshmallows.

A مرِجّ *murijj*, (A mare) near the birth.

A مرجأ *murjaɛ*, (pl. مرجؤن *murjaɛun* or مرجون *murjawn*) Delayed, put off.

A مرجاة *marjāt*, Hope.

P مرجاده *marjāda*, (or مرجاوه *marjāwa*) A skin stuffed with straw used for crossing rivers.

A مرجاس *mirjās*, A stone tied to a rope and let down into a well in order to move the mud, which being carried off by the flux, the remaining water becomes pure; also a stone with which they fathom the depth of a well, whether there is water in it or not.

A مرجام *mirjām*, (A camel) extending the neck when travelling, going with rapidity. An engine for casting stones, a balista. (A horse) making the dust fly.

P مرجان *marjān*, Life, soul. A step-son. A robust man. A small pearl. Coral.

A مرجان *marjān*, A kind of spring pot-herb. *Murjān*, The halibut. A kind of red coral.

P مرجان پرورده *marjān-parwarda*, The lip of a mistress. Grape-wine.

A مرجانة *marjānat*, A woman's name, Morgiana.

P مرجان دانه *marjān-dāna*, Coral-grain; a bead.

A مرجائيّ *murjāɛiy*, Of the sect مرجية *murjiyat*.

A مرجّب *murajjab*, Honoured, venerable. Propped (tree). Firm, established, solid. *Murajjib*, One who props the branch of a tree. (See ترجيب.)

A مرجّح *murajjah*, Most excellent, superior. *Murajjih*, One who gives that which preponderates, who more than compensates.

A مرجحنّ *murjahinn*, Heavy, ponderous (mill-stone, legion, or sword).

A مرجّز *murajjaz*, Measured prose without rhyme.

A مرجس *mirjas*, Braying (camel).

A مرجع *marjaɛ*, (v. n. of رجع) Bringing back, restoring. A return. Time or place of return. A place of reference. Refuge. Repetition. Ultimate object. *Marjiɛ*, (v. n. of رجع) Returning. Bringing back, restoring. A return (to God). (pl. مراجع *marājiɛ*) The lower part of the shoulder. *Murjiɛ*, Profitable (merchandise, journey, or voyage), such as yields a return.

A مرجعة *marjiɛat*, (v. n. of رجع) Returning.

A مرجف *murjif*, One who makes a noise. One who spreads false or seditious reports. المرجفان *al murjifāni*, (dual) The water-jug and ewer, which are handed round after dinner, and, by being struck against each other, announce the termination of the repast. المرجفون في المدينة *al murjifūn fi'l madīnat*, Propagators of seditious rumours in the city.

A مرجل *marjal*, (pl. of رجل *rajul*) Men. *Marjal* or *mirjal*, A kind of striped Arabian garment. *Mirjal*, (pl. مراجل *marājil*) A large cauldron, pot, kettle, or pipkin. A comb. *Murjil*, A woman who bears male offspring. (See ارجال *irjāl.*)

A مرجّل *murajjal*, (Cloth or tapestry) worked with human figures. Marked. Made of the skin of one leg, and full (bottle). (Locusts) which leave their marks upon fields. *Murajjil*, A strengthener. (See ترجيل *tarjīl.*)

A مرجم *mirjam*, Strong. (A horse) which makes the dirt fly when running.

A مرجّم *murajjam*, (A speech) liable to uncertainty or suspicion; any thing doubtful or rejected. *Murajjim*, One who strikes furiously with stones. (See ترجيم *tarjīm.*)

P مرجمك *marjamak*, A lentil.

P مرجو *marjū*, A lentil.

A مرجوّ *marjūw*, Hoped for, expected, sought.

A مرجوب *marjūb*, Revered, honoured.

A مرجوح *marjūh*, Preponderating, superior.

A مرجوحة *marjūhat*, A swing, a see-saw.

A مرجوحيّة *marjūhiyat*, Preponderance.

A مرجوسة *marjūsat*, Confusion, perplexity, pother.

A مرجوع *marjūʻ*, Returned, referred, brought back. An answer to a letter.

A مرجوعة *marjūʻat*, A reply to a letter.

A مرجول *marjūl*, Skinned from the foot to the head. Seized by the foot (رجل *rijl*). Tethered.

A مرجوم *marjūm*, Stoned. Execrable. The devil.

A مرجؤن *murjaʼuna*, (pl. of مرجؤ *murjaʼ*) Last. Delayed, suspended, put off.

A مرجونة *marjūnat*, A dry and hollow gourd wherein women keep their cotton; a calabash.

A مرجئ *murjiʼ*, (or مرجي *murjī*) One who delays doing what he promises.

A مرجيّ *marjīy*, Shaken, agitated. *Murjīy*, One who defers to do what he promises. Near her delivery.

A مرجئة *murjiʼat*, Near her delivery. *Murjiʼat*, (or مرجية *murjiyat*) Name of a sect who procrastinate, or think good works unnecessary, and faith sufficient. Name of a tribe.

P مرچ *marich*, Pepper.

A مرح *marh* or *marah*, The stitch-holes of a wallet. *Marah*, (v. n. of مرح) Being cheerful, sprightly, active (man or horse). Strutting about. Excessive joy, boisterous mirth. Frowardness, pride. *Marih*, (pl. مرحي *marha'* and مراحي *marāha'*) Exulting, immoderate in joy, sprightly.

A مرحاض *mirhāz*, (pl. مراحيض *marāhīz*) A place where rubbish or excrement is thrown. A privy. A washer or a bleacher's beetle. Water, especially a place where clothes are washed.

A مرحان *marahān*, (v. n. of مرح) Being corrupted, hurt (eye), and running copiously. Joyousness, gladness. Weakness.

A مرحب *marhab*, Amplitude, largeness. Spacious, wide. مرحباً و سهلا *marhaban wa sahlan*, (or مرحبا بك الله و مسهلاً *marhaban bika'llāhu wa mas-halan*) May God grant you amplitude and convenience! or, You are welcome, may your arrival be happy! (a form of salutation, for which they generally use simply مرحبا *marhaban*, Hail! welcome! God bless you! live for ever!) P مرحبا كردن *marhabā kardan*, To applaud, to clap the hands.

A مرحبة *marhabat*, (v. n. of مرحب Q) Saying, you are welcome.

A مرحة *mirhat*, Magazine, store (of currants, &c.).

A مرحض *murhaz*, Washed (garment).

A مرحضة *mirhazat*, The place or vessel in which they wash the body before the performance of religious ceremonies.

A مرحل *mirhal*, Robust, fit for travelling (camel). *Murhil*, A possessor of many she-camels fit for burdens. (See ارحال *irhāl*.)

A مرحّل *murahhal*, Ordered off, commanded to depart. A kind of garment marked with the figures of saddles. Saddled (camel). Unsaddled (camel). *Murahhil*, Who sends away, who orders to depart.

A مرحلة *marhalat*, (pl. مراحل *marāhil*) A day's journey. An inn or halting-place for travellers.

A مرحّم *murahham*, Very much pitied. *Murahhim*, Very merciful, full of pity.

A مرحمة *marhamat*, (pl. مراحم *marāhim*) Pity, compassion, mercy, clemency, favour. A present. P مرحمت كردن *marhamat kardan*, To have compassion. بي مرحمت *bī marhamat*, Unmerciful.

P مرحمت گستري *marhamat-gustarī*, The exercise of mercy.

A مرحوض *marhūz*, Washed. Thrown into a sweat by an attack of fever.

A مرحول *marhūl*, Saddled (camel).

A مرحوم *marhūm*, Pitied. One who finds pity. One whom God has taken into his mercy, the defunct of happy memory.

A مرحومة *marhūmat*, Defunct, deceased (woman). المرحومة *al marhūmat*, The city Madīna.

A مرحي *marha'*, A field of battle. (pl. of مرح *marih*) Sprightly, merry. *Marha'*, (or مرحيًّا *marahayyan*) is applied to an archer who hits a mark, as برحي *barha'* implies one who misses.

A مرحّي *murahhī*, A millwright.

A مرخ *markh*, (v. n. of مرخ) Anointing (the body with oil). Playing, jesting, joking. A kind of Arabian tree which emits fire when rubbed by another called عفار *ʻafār*. *Marikh*, Soft, limber (tree). One who anoints his body much.

A مرّخ *murrakh*, A wolf.

A مرخاء *markhāʼ*, (pl. مراخي *marākhī*) (A mare or she-ass) of a long pace. Swift, sprightly (she-camel).

A مرخة *murkhat*, (pl. مرخ) An unripe date.

P مرخشة *marakhsha*, Unhappy, unfortunate. Dying. *Markhisha*, A word.

A مرخّص *murakhkhas*, Permitted to leave, allowed (to depart). Licensed. P نا مرخّص *nā murakhkhas*, Unpermitted. Unlawful. Intoxicated. A *Murakhkhis*, One who gives leave. One who frees from trouble. One who renders easy or remiss.

A مرخم *murkhim*, (مرخمة *murkhimat*, or *murakhkhamat*) (A hen) sitting on eggs.

A مرخّم *murakhkham*, Abbreviated, contracted. Adorned with marble, marbled. *Murakhkhim*, A stone-cutter. A smooth, specious talker.

A مرخيّ *markhīy*, Loose, flowing.

P مرد *mard*, A man, hero. Brave, bold. A male. مرد اصلي *mardi aslī*, A nobleman. مرد آدمي *mardi ādamī*, A gentleman. مرد خدا *mardi khudā*, A man of God. A priest of the Magi. مرد غريب *mardi gharīb*, A foreigner. A stranger. مرد مردانه وار *mardi mardānawār*, Like a man of courage. مرد نبرد *mardi nabard*, A soldier, a man of war. مرد نيك نام *mardi nek-nām*, A celebrated man, one of illustrious reputation. *Murd*, He died. Dead, deceased. Stagnant. خرد مرد *khurd murd*, Extremely small or minute. *Murad*, A sickle. A myrtle.

A مرد *mard*, (v. n. of مرد) Rubbing or moulding (bread or medicines) with the hand. Softening, steeping, dissolving. Sucking, mumbling the nipple (an infant). Cutting. Driving, pushing. Rowing. Tearing to pieces the reputation (of another). The fruit of the اراك *arāk* tree, fresh, tender, and ripe. *Murd*, (pl. of امرد *amrad*) Leafless (trees). Beardless (youths). (Horses) having little hair about their heels. *Marad*, (v. n. of مرد) Becoming smooth, bare, bald, beardless. After having been beardless, getting a beard. Eating habitually dates softened and dressed in milk.

A مرّد *maradd*, (v. n. of ردّ) Returning, answering, reducing, restoring, remitting. Repelling, rejecting, throwing back (upon one). Reprobating, refuting. A place to which one returns. *Muridd*, (pl. مرادّ *marādd*) (A camel) whose udder is swollen in consequence of lying on wet ground. Long unmarried. Long on a journey. Libidinous. Angry. (The sea) rolling many waves. (A camel) which drinks often, and is oppressed with it. (A ewe) full of milk before yeaning.

A مرداء *mardāʼ*, (fem. of امرد *amrad*) Leafless, bare (tree). Barren, sandy ground producing nothing. Bright-faced (girl). (A mare) with no long hairs about the feet. Destitute of hair about the privities. *Muradāʼ*, (pl. of مريد *marīd*) Insolent, stubborn, obstinate, perverse.

P مرداب *mardāb*, An extensive and deep lake or pond. *Murdāb*, (Dead water) A backwater. Creek.

A مرداة *mirdāt*, A stone thrown; any thing which breaks or dashes to pieces (as a stone from a warlike machine). The upper millstone. A stone on which a lizard sits. Hardy (she-camel). A cloak.

P مرداد *murdād*, Name of a month. Name of an angel. Name of the 7th and 8th day of the month.

P مردار *murdār*, A dead carcase, carrion. Impure, dirty, polluted. Obscene.

P مردار خانه *murdār-khāna*, A point of the table in the game of نرد *nard*, whence it is not possible to extricate one's self; lurch, limbo.

P مردار خوار *murdār-khwār*, An eater of carrion. A carrion-crow or vulture.

A مردارسنج *murdār-sanj* (or مرداسنج *murdāsanj*) (from P مردار سنگ *murdār-sang*), Dross of lead.

A مرداريّة *mardāriyat*, Name of a sect.

A مرداس *mirdās*, A hard and broad substance with which any thing is smoothed. A stone with which they fathom the depth of a well to ascertain whether there be water in it or not. The head.

P مردآسا *mard-āsā*, Like a man, tall, manly.

P مرد اسفرم *mard isfiram*, A kind of wild myrtle from which a vermifuge medicine is prepared.

P مرداسنگ *murdāsang*, Litharge, dross of lead.

P مرداش *mardāsh*, History, narration. A garden.

P مردافكن *mard-afkan*, Overthrowing men, *i.e.* a hero, warrior, champion. Strong, heady wine.

A مردام *mirdām*, A worthless fellow or thing.

P مردان *mardān*, (pl. of مرد *mard*) Heroes, warriors. مردان علوي *mardāni ʿulwī*, The planets. Seven illustrious personages in the invisible world.

P مردانگي *mardānagī*, Manhood. Manliness, courage, prowess. عرصهٔ مردانگى *ʿarsaʼi mardānagī*, A field of battle. Arena, place of exercise.

P مردانه *mardāna*, Brave, manly. Courageously, vigorously. What belongs to a man (as male apartments, زنانه *zanāna* denoting the women's apartments). مردانه كردن *mardāna kardan*, To remove women from their apartments that men may enter.

P مرداني *mardānī*, Masculine (woman).

P مرداوزن *mard-avzan*, (Man-overthrowing) Brave, warlike. Generous, heady wine.

P مردباز *mard-bāz*, An adultress, strumpet.

P مردبازي *mard-bāzī*, Adultery, whoredom.

P مردبان *mardubān*, A staircase. A ladder.

P مردبچه *mard-bacha*, Son of a brave man.

A مردة *maradat*, (pl. of مارد *mārid*) Stubborn, obstinate, rebellious. Devils.

A مردّة *maraddat*, Return; profit, emolument.

A مردّد *muraddad*, Reprobated, ruined. Irresolute, perplexed in mind. Reiterated. *Muraddid*, One who drives to and fro. One who revolves in his mind. A repeller.

P مرديك *murdarek*, A kind of sand used by goldsmiths for polishing; small gravel. Hereditary effects left at death.

A مردس *mirdas*, Any hard and broad stone with which any thing is smoothed.

P مرد شناسي *mard-shināsī*, Knowledge of men.

P مردشوي *murd-shūy*, A washer of dead bodies.

A مردع *mirdaʿ*, (A dart) which has lost its head. One who loses his labour, who returns unsuccessful. (An arrow) with a small notch. Sluggish (seaman). Short. One on whose body remains of perfumed unguent (ردع *radaʿ*) are found.

A مردّع *muraddaʿ*, (A garment) perfumed with fragrant unguents (ردع *radaʿ*).

A مردغة *mardaghat*, (pl. مرادغ *marādigh*) That which is between the neck and collar-bone. The flesh or muscle between the top of the shoulder and the breast-bone. A fruitful, flourishing garden.

A مردف *murdif*, One who seats (another) behind him. (See ارداف *irdāf*.)

A مردقوش *mardakūsh*, (from P مرده گوش *murda-gosh*) Marjoram. Saffron. A kind of aromatic of a reddish black colour, with which women perfume their combs.

P مردك *mardak*, A little man, a manikin. A low fellow, puppy. Vile, base.

P مردگان *murdagān*, (pl. of مرده) The dead.

P مردگوش *mardgosh*, Marjoram.

P مردگي *mardagī*, Sodomy. *Murdagī*, Death.

P مردگير *mard-gīr*, A crooked-bladed weapon.

P مرد گيران *mard-gīrān*, Name of a festival celebrated by the ancient Persians during the five last days of the month اسفندارمد *isfandārmud*, at the close of the year, during which the women are permitted to rule the men and treat them as they please. A paper written at that season in the fields, as a charm against noxious insects.

A مردلة *mardalat*, (v. n. of مردل Q) Doing any thing carelessly, slovenly, or weakly.

P مردم *mardum*, A man. A polite, civilized man. Civil, humane. The pupil of the eye. مردم چشم *mardumi chashm*, The pupil of the eye.

A مردم *murdim*, Continued (watering or fever). Silent, quiescent.

A مردّم *muruddam*, Burst and mended, old and patched (garment). *Muraddim*, A repairer (of a garment). Who carries on and finishes his discourse.

P مردم آزار *mardum-āzār*, Man-tormenting.

P مردم آزاري *mardum-āzārī*, Oppression.

P مردم آميز *mardum-āmez*, Humane, polite.

P مردم آهنگ *mardum-āhang*, A sort of weapon.

P مردم خوار *mardum-khwār*, A cannibal.

P مردم خيز *mardum-khez*, Producing men.

P مردم در *mardum-dar*, (Man-tearing) Who or what tears to pieces and devours mankind.

P مردم زاد *mardum-zād*, A man, son of a man.

P مردمك *mardumak*, A little man, dwarf, manikin. A vetch, a pea. مردمك چشم *mardumaki chashm*, The pupil of the eye.

P مردم كش *mardum-kush*, A murderer.

P مردم گزا *mardum-gazā*, (Man-biting) A tyrant.

P مردم گيا *mardum-giyā*, A plant, the produce of China, said to resemble a man and woman, and to which many wonderful effects are attributed.

P مردم گياه *mardum-giyāh*, The mandrake.

P مردم نوازي *mardum-nawāzī*, Courtesy.

P مردمه *marduma*, The pupil of the eye.

P مردمي *mardumī*, Manliness, humanity, courtesy, politeness, bravery, civility, generosity.

A مردن *mirdan*, The spindle of a distaff. *Murdin*, Dark, obscure, shady. Stinking (sweat).

P مردن *murdan*, To die, expire. To be extinguished, go out. To be offered in sacrifice.

P مرد نا رسيده *mard-nā-rasīda*, Unblemished (virgin), who has not known a man.

A مردود *mardūd*, (v. n. of ردّ) Returning. Rejecting, repelling, confuting. Returned, restored. Rejected, thrown back, repulsed, excluded, reprobated, confuted. Long unmarried. One, the term of whose journey has been very long.

A مردودة *mardūdat*, A divorced woman returned to her father's house. A razor folded into the handle.

A مردوديّة *mardūdiyat*, Repulse, rejection.

P مردوس *mardūs*, A Damascus scallion.

A مردوس *mardūs*, (in Morocco) A locust.

A مردوع *mardūʿ*, Infected, tinctured, stained. Tinctured with saffron. One on whose body remains of perfumed unguent are discovered. Fallen back, relapsed (sick man).

A مردون *mardūn*, A kind of wasp. Patched.

P مرده *murda*, Dead, defunct. A corpse.

P مرده دل *murda-dil*, Cold-hearted, lifeless.

P مرده دلي *murda-dilī*, Lifelessness.

P مرده ري *murda-rī*, Effects of a dead person.

P مرده ريك *murda-rik*, Effects of a dead person. Useless, worthless, good for nothing.

P مرده سنگ *murda-sang*, Litharge of lead.

P مرده شو *murda-shū*, A washer of the dead.

P مرده فروش *murda-farosh*, Name of a caste whose business is to carry the dead.

P مرده گوش *murda-gosh*, Sweet marjoram.

P مرده وار *murdawār*, As dead, like one dead.

P مردي *mardī*, Manliness, virility, valour. Bold, brave, warlike. *Marde*, A man, a certain man.

A مردئ *mirdaʼ*, (pl. مرادي *marādī*) A stone thrown. Any thing which dashes to pieces (as a stone from a warlike machine). مردي الحرب *mirdaʼl harb*, A bold man, brave in war.

A مرديّ *mardīy*, Aimed at or struck with a stone. *Murdīy*, (pl. مراديّ *marādiy*) An oar.

A مرز *marz*, A softening (of bread) in water.

A مرذّ *murazz*, Wet with due, or with a gentle mizzling rain. *Murizz*, (A day) wetting with dew.

A مرذوذ *marzūz*, Wet with dew or small rain.

A مرذول *marzūl*, Reprobated, discarded.

A مرذئ *murzaʼ*, Tired, jaded. Thrown on the highroad. Exposed (boy).

A مرر *mirar*, (pl. of مرّة *marrat*) Times, turns. (pl. of مرّة) Bodily powers. Biles. Bitter things.

P مرز *marz*, A limit, border, boundary of a country. A region, district. A kind of intoxicating liquor; beer. A field with a raised border; land. Cultivated. Coition. *Marz* or *murz*, The hole of the fundament. *Murz*, A mouse.

A مرز *marz*, (v. n. of مرز) Pressing gently with the tips of the fingers without giving pain (when painful it is expressed by قرص *kars*). Disparaging, disgracing. Striking with the hand. Giving part (of a mass of leaven or paste).

P مرزا *mirzā*, A Persian title. When it is put after a proper name it usually means 'prince;' as, ابراهيم مرزا *ibrāhīm mirzā*, Prince Ibrahim: but when it appears before, it means a gentleman only; as, مرزا ابراهيم *mirzā ibrāhīm*, Mr. Ibrahim.

A مرزّأ *murazzaʼ*, (pl. مرزّؤون *murazzaʼūn*) Most beneficent, munificent. Those whose chiefs are dead.

A مرزاء *mirzāʼ*, A defamer, disparager, accuser.

P A مرزاب *mirzāb*, (pl. مرازيب *marāzīb*) A canal, conduit, water-pipe. A long ship, a man-of-war.

A مرزامة *mirzāmat*, Young, active, and sprightly (she-camel): also one quiet and that eats much.

P مرزان *murzān*, The narcissus.

P مرزان گوش *marzān-gosh*, Mouse-ear (a plant).

P مرزائي *mirzāī*, An under jacket with long loose sleeves and open cuffs.

P A مرزبان *marzbān*, *marzabān*, or *marzubān*, (pl. مرازبة *marāzibat*) A general of the confines, governor on the borders of a hostile country, lord-marcher, margrave, landgrave. A landed proprietor. مرزبان الزارة *marzubānu'z zaṛrat*, The lion.

A مرزبة *marzabat*, A way. Regimen, government. The office of مرزبان *marzubān*. *Mirzabat*, An iron rod. A blacksmith's sledge hammer.

A مرزبّة *mirzabbat*, A clod-crushing mallet.

A مرزبوم *marzubūm*, Confines of a hostile country. Any place where one resides. P هر مرزبوم *har marzubūm*, All countries, every where.

A مرزة *mirzat*, A piece of paste. *Mirzat* or *marzat*, (v. n. of مرز) Arriving at, acquiring plenty of. *Murzat*, A kite or kind of eagle.

A مرزّة *marazzat*, A rice-ground.

A مرزتان *marzatāni*, The two little protuberances just above the soft part of the ears.

A مرزح *marzah*, A long way to travel. Level ground. *Mirzah*, A vine-prop.

A مرزّز *murazzaz*, Polished (helmet), glazed (paper). (Meat) dressed with rice (رزّ *ruzz*).

P مرزغان *marzaghān*, (or مرزغن *marzaghan*) Hell. A chafing-dish. A burial-place.

P مرزگون *marzgūn*, The penis.

A مرزم *mirzam*, Name of three stars: one in the right shoulder of Orion; the second in the hind dexter foot of the Canis Major; and the third in the neck of Canis Minor. The two last are expressed by the dual المرزمان *al mirzamāni*. امّ المرزم *ummu'l mirzam*, The north; the wind. *Murzim*, A lion.

P مرزن *marzan*, A mouse.

A مرزنجوش *marzanjūsh*, Sweet marjoram.

P مرزنگوش *marzangosh*, Mouse-ear (an odoriferous plant). A white rose. Purslain. The ringlets of a mistress.

P مرزو *marzū*, (or مرزوي *marzūy*) A field with a raised border.

P مرزوان *marz* or *marzawān*, General of the confines, governor on the border of a hostile country.

P مرزوبوم *marzūbūm*, Limits or boundary of a country. A place where one resides.

A مرزوق *marzūk*, Supplied with food, fed. Happy, fortunate. Acquired by art. مرزوقات *marzūkāt*, Riches, estates.

A مرزوم *marzūm*, Broken down by disease.

P مرزة *marza*, A mouse. A lamp. A trowel. Origany.

P مرزة گوش *marza-gosh*, Mouse-ear (a plant).

A مرزئة *marziʼat*, (v. n. of رزأ) Receiving benefits. Diminishing, lessening. Injury, detriment, misfortune, evil.

A مرزيح *mirzīh*, A weak voice. A vine-prop.

P مرژ *marj* or *mirj*, Name of a fire-worshipper.

P مرس *mars*, Name of a man. Name of a fruit.

A مرس *mars*, (v. n. of مرس) Steeping, soaking, or dissolving (in water). Rubbing (dates) in the hand. Sucking the fingers (as an infant). Wiping the hands with a napkin. Slipping off the wheel and hitching between it and the cheek of the pulley (a rope). One who applies strenuously to any thing. هم على مرس واحد *hum ʿala' marsin wāhidin*, They are of the same sort or genus. *Maras*, (v. n. of مرس) Having the rope sticking fast between the cheek and the wheel (a pulley). (pl. of مرسة *marasat*) Ropes. *Maris*, Mode, habit, manner, fashion. One who fights bravely, or who applies vigorously to any thing.

A مرساة *mirsāt*, (pl. مراسي *marāsī*) An anchor.

A مرسال *mirsāl*, (pl. مراسيل *marāsīl*) Easy-going. A short arrow. Despatched. A messenger.

A مرسب *marsab*, (pl. مراسب *marāsib*) A column. Intelligent. Patient. *Mirsab*, The sword of Muhammad. One of the swords sent by Bilkīs as a present to Solomon.

A مرسة *marsat*, (v. n. of مرس) Soaking (dates) in water, and rubbing and softening (them) with the hand. *Marasat*, (pl. مرس *maras* and امراس *amrās*) A rope.

P مرست *marast*, May it not remain! perish it!

A مرسّع *murassiʿ*, (or مرسّعة *murassiʿat*) Troubled with a distemper in the eyelids.

A مرسّغ *murassagh*, Confused (idea, mind).

A مرسل *mursal*, Sent to others. Let loose. Allowed to fall (hair). An ambassador. A prophet, apostle. (pl. مراسيل *marāsīl*) (Any tradition) which a collector or reporter of traditions (محدّث *muhaddis*) relates to a تابعي *tābiʿīy*, or follower of Muhammad's associates, who, when quoting or repeating it, simply asserts, "The apostle of God said," without adducing the name of the صحابيّ *sahābiy* (companion of Muhammad to whom the prophet delivered the saying). نبيء مرسل *nabīʼi mursal*, The prophet sent, *i.e.* Muhammad. مرسل اليه *mursal ilayhi*, He to whom (any person or thing) is sent. *Mursil*, A sender (of an ambassador). One who unlooses (the hair); dismisses (a man), lets loose (a beast), lets fall (a blow), lets (a mouthful) descend (down his throat).

A مرسلات *mursalāt*, (pl. of مرسلة *mursalat*) (Women) sent. Letters, missives. المرسلات *al mursalāt*, Winds. Angels. Horses.

A مرسلة *mursalat*, (fem. of مرسل *mursal*) Sent. A letter. A necklace, that part of it which hangs down the bosom.

P مرسله بند *mursala-band*, A clasp for a necklace.

P مرسله پيوند *mursala-paywand*, A pen.

A مرسلين *mursalīn*, (oblique pl. of مرسل *mursal*) Prophets. Apostles. سيّد المرسلين *sayyidu'l mursalīn*, Prince of the apostles, *i.e.* Muhammad. شيخ المرسلين *shaykhu'l mursalīn*, Noah.

A مرسم *mirsam*, A particular sort of camel's pace.

A مرسّم *murassam*, Striped (cloth). مرسّم عليه *murassam ʿalayhi*, Ordered to keep close at home, under arrest.

A مرسن *marsin* or *marsan*, The middle of the camel's nose, across which the halter goes. The human nose, also the bridge or gristle. على رغم مرسنه *ʿala' raghmi marsinihi*, Against his inclination.

A مرسوم *marsūm*, Signed, marked, notified, described; prescribed. Accustomed. Persuaded. (pl. مراسيم *marāsīm*) A mandate. Pay, stipend, salary. مرسوم امان *marsūmi amān*, Royal letters of security. P مرسوم داغ وفاداري *marsūmi dāghi wafādārī*, Impressed with the mark of sincerity, *i.e.* faithful, religious, worthy of confidence or trust. بي مرسوم *bī marsūm*, Without pay, stipend, or salary.

P مرسوم خوار *marsūm-khwār*, A stipendiary.

A مرسون *marsūn*, Haltered (horse).

A مرسى *marsa'* or *mursa'*, A place where any thing stands firmly. A port, anchorage. *Mursa'*, (v. n. 4 of رسا for رسو) Causing to stand still. Confirmed, established, fixed. *Mursī*, (God) who causes to stand fast.

A مرسية *mursiyat*, Name of a city in the west.

A مرش *marsh*, (v. n. of مرش) Scratching with the nails. Rubbing or scraping with the ends of the fingers. Hurting, injuring by unkind words. Ground whose surface has been soaked by rain, or which, when rained upon, soon runs with water. *Marash*, The herb ladies' bed-straw.

A مرشاء *marshāʼ*, (fem. of امرش *amrash*) Evil, malignant. A wounding, biting animal. (Ground) abundant in produce.

A مرشّة *mirashshat*, An instrument (especially a weaver's instrument) with which they sprinkle.

A مرشح *mirshah*, (or مرشحة *mirshahat*) A saddle-cloth. *Murshih*, A camel attended by her young.

A مرشد *marshad*, The right way. A firm resolution. *Murshid*, A guide to the right way, *i.e.* to salvation. An instructor, director, monitor. *Murshid*, (or P مرشد راه *murshidi rāh*) A guide of the road.

A مرشدي *murshidī*, Instruction in religion.

A مرشف *marshaf*, (pl. مراشف *marāshif*) A place of sucking or sipping.

A مرشوش *marshūsh*, Sprinkled.

A مرص *mars*, (v. n. of مرص) Pressing with the hand (a woman's bosom). *Maras*, (v. n. of مرص) Outstripping others.

A مرصاد *mirsād*, A broad, open way. A place where an enemy is watched.

A مرصاع *mirsāʿ*, A boy's top or gig which be either throws from his hand or whips on the ground. A piece of wood used for flattening any thing.

A مرصافة *mirsāfat*, A hammer.

A مرصد *marsad*, A place of observation or lying in wait. *Mursid*, Land rained upon, and from which vegetation is looked for.

A مرصّص *murassas*, Covered with lead. Washed over with tin (رصاص *rasās*).

A مرصع *mursiع*, (pl. مراصع *marāsiع*) A palm-tree having young ones.

A مرصّع *murassaع*, Covered with gold, set with jewels. فرس مرصّع الثّنن *faras murassaعu's sunan*, A horse, the hairs of whose fetlock are entangled. P شمشير مرصّع *shamsheri murassaع*, A scimeter studded with gems. A *Murassiع*, A composer, arranger. One who works or sets (a garment or crown) with gold and precious stones.

P مرصّعينه *murassaعīna*, Set, studded.

A مرصق *mursak*, A nut whose kernel it is very difficult to separate from the shell.

A مرصن *mirsan*, An iron for branding cattle.

A مرصود *marsūd*, (A field) wet with one shower. (A star) whose station is known by observation.

A مرصوص *marsūs*, Soldered. Compact, firm, indissoluble. (A well) lined with lead (رصاص *rasās*). بنيان مرصوصة صدق و صفا *bunyāni marsūsaسi sidh u safā*, The fabric cemented by sincere love.

A مرصوف *marsūf*, Joined together (stones).

A مرصوفة *marsūfat*, Narrow, impervious (woman).

A مرصون *marsūn*, (A limb) marked with the cautery. A limb pricked with a needle, upon which woad is afterwards rubbed.

A مرض *marz*, (v. n. of مرض) Falling sick. A disease in the heart. Doubt. Darkness. Loss, detriment. Hypocrisy, deceit. Debility, languor, lukewarmness. *Maraz*, (v. n. of مرض) Falling sick. Being weak from overstraining (the eye). (pl. امراض *amrāz*) Disease, sickness, indisposition, malady, distemper. Hypocrisy. Doubt, unbelief. Loss, detriment. Darkness. Languour, debility. مرض جبلي *marazi jibillī*, (ذاتي *zātī* or اصلي *aslī*) A disease from nature. P مرض زهره *marazi zahra*, Jaundice. A مرض ساقط *marazi sākit*, The falling sickness, epilepsy. مرض عارض *marazi عāriz*, An accidental indisposition. مرض الموت *marazu'l mawt*, The last illness. *Mariz*, Sick, diseased. Pained at heart.

A مرضا *marzā*, (in regimen for مرضي *marza'*) (pl. of مريض *marīz*) Sick, infirm. مرضاي امّت *marzāyi ummat*, The weaker part of the nation.

A مرضاة *marzāt*, A being pleased, satisfied.

A مرضاح *mirzāh*, (or مرضاخ *mirzākh*) A stone with which they break date-stones, and the like.

A مرضافة *mirzāfat*, A hot stone thrown into milk in order to warm it.

A مرضّة *murizzat*, Thick milk. (Meat or drink) which throws one into a violent perspiration. *Murizzat* or *mirazzat*, Dates stoned and steeped in milk.

A مرضخة *mirzakhat*, (pl. مراضخ *marāzikh*) A stone with which they break the covering of dates.

A مرضع *marzaع*, A teat, a nipple. Any place sucked. *Murziع*, (pl. مراضع *marāziع* and مراضيع *marāziع*) (A mother) having a sucking infant or young. A wet-nurse.

A مرضوّ *marzūw*, Agreeable, acceptable.

A مرضوح *marzūh*, (A date-stone) crushed.

A مرضود *marzūd*, (Wares) piled on one another.

A مرضوض *marzūz*, Broken, pounded, crushed. (Ground) beaten and made hard with flints.

A مرضوف *marzūf*, (Meat) roasted on a hot stone. (A pot) set a boiling by throwing in this stone.

A مرضوفة *marzūfat*, The stomach or tripe of an animal cleaned, and used, for want of a pot, to cook food in on a journey.

A مرضوم *marzūm*, (A beast of burden) infirm, having the nerves contracted. Firmly built with stone.

A مرضون *marzūn*, (Stones) placed one upon another in a building or otherwise.

A مرضيٰ *marza'*, (pl. of مريض *marīz*) Sick, ill. دار المرضي *dāru'l marza'*, A hospital, infirmary.

A مرضيّ *marziy*, Agreeable, acceptable, any thing in which one takes a pleasure. Laudable. Will, assent, pleasure. سلطان مرضيّ الاخلاق *sultāni marzīyu'l akhlāk*, A monarch of excellent principles.

A مرط *mart*, (v. n. of مرط) Pulling out hairs. Collecting, making haste. Casting forth (excrement, or a fœtus). *Mirt*, (pl. مروط *murūt*) A kind of short shift (cloak or breeches) of wool or coarse silk. *Murt*, (pl. of امرط *amrat*) Hairless-cheeked (men). Thin-eyebrowed. Weak-eyed, watery-eyed. Light, active of body. *Marat*, (v. n. of مرط) Having the cheeks or other parts of the body smooth, without hairs. Having weak eyes. *Murut*, (An arrow) without wings.

A مرطب *martab*, Green, verdant (soil). *Murtib*, Humid, moist, wet. Fresh (date). (A field) abounding with green herbage. Laden with fresh dates (a palm-tree).

A مرطّب *murattib*, Who or what makes moist.

A مرطبان *martabān*, A glazed vessel.

A مرطبة *martabat*, Sweet (well) lying between saline (springs).

A مرطة *miratat*, Light-bodied (men). Thin-eyebrowed (men). Watery-eyed (men).

A مرطل *murtil*, Tall (man). Soft, gentle.

A مرطلة *martalat*, (v. n. of مرطل Q) Staining, bedaubing (with mud). Injuring by slander. Moistening (rain). Continuing to do any thing bad. Persevering in any work.

A مرطم *murtam*, Shut up, confined. Costive.

A مرطوب *martūb*, Moist, humoral. مرطوب المزاج *martūbu'l mizāj*, Of a humid complexion.

A مرطوم *martūm*, Confined, shut up.

A مرطومة *martūmat*, (A woman) suspected.

A مرطيٰ *marata'*, A pace, faster than تقريب *takrīb*, slower than اذهاب *izhāb*. Swift (she-camel).

A مرطيّ *martiy*, (A hide) tanned with arta-bark.

A مرطيس *martīs*, A blue medicinal stone.

A مرع *marع*, (v. n. of مرع) Anointing (the head) plentifully. Combing (the hair). Plenty of forage. *Murع*, (pl. of مرعة *murعat* or *muraعat*) Asiatic woodcocks. *Mariع*, One who wants or seeks fodder.

A مرعاة *marعāt*, Pasture, a meadow.

A مرعان *murعān*, (pl. of مرعة *murعat* and *muraعat*, Asiatic woodcocks.

A مرعبب *muraعbib*, Fat, whose dripping falls.

A مرعبة *marعabat*, A desert or any place striking with terror: any thing causing sudden fright.

A مرعبل *muraعbal*, Torn or worn (garment).

A مرعة *murعat*, Fat, grease. *Murعat* or *muraعat*, (pl. مرع *murع* and مرعان *murعān*) A species of the attagen, or Asiatic woodcock.

A مرعّث *muraععas*, A roost-cock having hairy plumage under his wattles. Furnished with ear-rings.

A مرعد *murعad*, (A high tumulus of sand) liable to roll down. *Murعid*, Thundering (cloud).

A مرعدد *muraعdid*, Importunate, urgent in proposing questions.

A مرعزّ *marعizz*, (*mirعizz*, مرعزاء *marعizā*, *mirعizā*, مرعزي *marعizza'*, or *mirعizza'*) Fine wool under the coarser hair of goats (of such the Cashmere shawls are made).

A مرعس *mirعas*, A low wretch who picks up a miserable subsistence from a dunghill.

A مرعش *marعash* or *murعash*, A kind of dove which flies high with sweeping circles.

A مرعل *mirعal*, A sharp sword.

A مرعّل *muraععal*, Best of cattle or other property.

A مرعوب *marعūb*, Terrified. Terrible.

A مرعوث *marعūs*, Held in little repute.

A مرعون *marعūn*, Indisposed and pained in the head by the heat of the sun. Weak, hanging down.

A مرعيٰ *marعa'*, (v. n. of رعي) Feeding, being pastured. Forage. Pasture. A piece of pasture.

A مرعيّ *marعiy*, Pastured; tended upon. Turned to graze. Governed. Guarded, observed. مصالح مرعيّه *masālihi marعīya*, Matters worthy of attention. P مرعي داشتن *marعī dāshtan*, To observe.

P مرغ *margh*, A species of grass of which animals are exceedingly fond. Name of a city. *Murgh*, A bird, fowl. The sun. A lump or branched stick of ginger. مرغ آب *murghi āb*, (or مرغ آبي *murghābī*) An aquatic bird, water-fowl. مرغ آذر افروز *murghi āzar-afroz*, The fire-kindling bird, *i. e.* the phœnix. A moth. مرغ آفتاب علم *murghi āftāb-عalam*, Fire. مرغ الهي *murghi ilāhī*, The spirit, reasonable soul. مرغ باغ *murghi bāgh*, The garden-bird, *i. e.* the nightingale. مرغ بام *murghi bām*, The nightingale. The turtle-dove. مرغ چمن *murghi chaman*, A forest-bird. The nightingale. مرغ خانگي *murghi khānagī*, A domestic fowl. مرغ خوش خوان *murghi khwush-khwān*, The nightingale. مرغ دل *murghi dil*, The heart, understanding. مرغ رنگين تاج *murghi rangīn-tāj*, The cock. A woodcock. مرغ روز *murghi roz*, The bird of day, the sun. مرغ زر *murghi zar*, The sun. A golden cup made in the form of a bird. مرغ زند خوان murghi zand-khwān, The nightingale. مرغ زيرك سار murghi zīrak-sār, Name of a black melodious bird; a starling. مرغ سحر murghi sahar, The morning-bird, *i.e.* the nightingale. The cock. The turtle-dove. A devout man who rises betimes. مرغ سحر خوان murghi sahar-khwān, The cock. The nightingale. The turtle-dove. مرغ سدرة murghi sidra, The angel Gabriel. مرغ سليمان murghi sulaymān, The bird of Solomon, *i.e.* the hoopoo. مرغ شب آويز murghi shab-āwez, Name of a bird which is said to suspend itself by the claws, and to cry حق حق hak hak the whole night, till the blood drops from its mouth. مرغ شب آهنگ murghi shab-āhang, (or مرغ شبخيز murghi shab-khez) The nightingale. مرغ شب و روز murghi shab u roz, The moon and sun. مرغ صبح خوان murghi subh-khwān, or شب خوان shab-khwān, The nightingale. The cock. مرغ طرب murghi tarab, The nightingale. A musician. A singer. A carrier-pigeon. مرغ عيسيٰ murghi ʿisa', A bat. مرغ فلك murghi falak, An angel. مرغ گوشت ربا murghi gosht-rubā, A kite. مرغ لب murghi lab, A word, speech. مرغ مطرب murghi mutrib, The nightingale. A musician. A singer. مرغ نامه murghi nāma, A carrier-pigeon. مرغ نامه آور murghi nāma-āwar, The hoopoo. A carrier-pigeon. A postman, courier. مرغ ياقوت پر murghi yākūt-par, An epithet of fire. مرغ اين انجير نيست murghi īn injīr nīst, He is not a bird for this fig, *i.e.* he is not a fit person for this undertaking. پيل مرغ pīl-murgh, (or فيل مرغ fīl-murgh) The turkey, or elephant-bird. شتر مرغ shutur-murgh, The ostrich, or camel-bird.

A مرغ margh, (v. n. of مرغ) Eating grass. Standing in the grass. Foaming at the mouth (a camel). Rolling in his pasture (a horse). Spittle, slaver. A collection of sheep-dung. A garden; particularly one abounding in plants. *Maragh*, (v. n. of مرغ) Being rolled in the dirt (reputation). *Marigh*, (Hair) which needs ointment.

A مرّغ murragh, Frothing young camels.

P مرغاب murghāb, Name of a river.

A مرغاة mirghāt, An instrument for taking off froth.

A مرغادّ murghādd, Enraged, returning no answer. Sick, infirm. One who gets not his fill of sleep. Confused, perplexed in mind, irresolute.

A مرغامة mirghāmat, A woman who provokes her husband, an instrument of provocation, a shrew.

P مرغان murghān, (pl. of مرغ murgh) Birds. مرغان اولي اجنحه murghāni ūlī ajniha, Winged birds. Angels. مرغان سدره murghāni sidra, (or مرغان عرشي murghāni ʿarshī) Angels. آب مرغان ābi murghān, A fountain between Shīrāz and Ispahān.

P مرغانه murghāna, A bird's egg.

A مرغب murghib, Opulent, affluent.

A مرغّب muraghghib, One who renders greedy.

P مرغباز murgh-bāz, A cock-fighter or feeder.

A مرغة marghat, A garden full of plants.

A مرغيث murghis, Who gives suck.

A مرغّث muraghghas, The place of the ring on the finger.

P مرغ دل murgh-dil, Chicken-hearted, timid.

P مرغز marghaz or marghuz, Name of a place.

P مرغزار marghzār, A place abounding with the grass مرغ margh; a verdant lawn, mead, meadow. مرغزار عقبيٰ marghzāri ʿukba', The amber heaven.

P مرغ زبانك murgh-zabānak, The produce of the plant called sparrows'-tongue.

P مرغزن marghazan, A burying-ground.

A مرغس murghis or murghas, One who enriches or benefits himself, and who lives luxuriously. Affluence, ample means, command of luxuries.

A مرغّش muraghghish, One who enriches and benefits himself, who lives in ease and luxury.

P مرغك murghak, A little bird, chicken. مرغك دانا murghaki dānā, The wise bird, *i.e.* the parrot.

A مرغم margham or marghim, The nose.

A مرغمة marghamat, (v. n. of رغم) Being soiled, dirtied. Nauseating, disliking. A kind of game.

P مرغوا marghawā or murghuwā, An evil; a bad situation; unfortunate omen. An imprecation.

A مرغوب marghūb, Desired, coveted. Desirable, amiable, lovely, estimable, excellent, beautiful.

A مرغوث marghūs, Teased by petitions.

A مرغوثة marghūsat, A female that is sucked.

A مرغوس marghūs, Happy, blest. Rich.

A مرغوسة marghūsat, (A woman) bearing many children. Confusion, perplexity.

P مرغول marghūl, (or مرغوله marghūla) Locks twisted, plaited, or curling. Crisp, curly hair. A fold, wrinkle. Noise, clamour. A sweet, melodious voice. A trill, shake, quaver. Alacrity, mirth, glee.

P مرغه murgha, An egg.

A مرغّي muraghghī, Unintelligible (word).

A مرفأ mar or murfaʾ, Station, mooring of a ship.

A مرفاق mirfāk, (A camel) whose elbow strikes his side. (A she-camel) pained by the binding of her dugs (which is done to prevent her being milked, or the colt from sucking); bleeding at the udder.

A مرفال mirfāl, One whose garments trail on the ground, and who swings the arms much in walking.

A مرفد mirfad, A large goblet, cup, or dish (generally filled on the arrival of strangers). Quilting, or any kind of stuffing used by women to give the hips a more prominent appearance. *Murfid*, A tumbler, a rope-dancer. A maker of stuffing for saddles. (See رفادة rifādat.)

A مرفش mirfash, A fan, ventilator. *Murfish*, Luxurious, intemperate in the use of women or in the pleasures of the table.

A مرفشة mirfashat, A shovel, spade.

A مرفّض muraffaz, Poured out. Scattered.

A مرفق marfak, marfik, or mirfak, (v. n. of رفق) Aiding, assisting. Being benign, gentle, easy. Advantage, gain, profit. The elbow. *Marfik*, A place upon which a person leans with the elbow. A gutter on a house-top.

A مرفقة mirfakat, A cushion, bolster, pillow, or any thing upon which a person leans.

A مرفّقة muraffakat, (A sheep) white to the elbows.

A مرفوّ marfūw, Darned.

A مرفوت marfūt, Broken, brayed, bruised.

A مرفوض marfūz, Rejected, thrown away. (A camel) turned loose to pasture at liberty.

A مرفوع marfūʿ, Exalted, raised, honoured. Redressed. Marked with the vowel point ـُ u. Highly-valued (garments); also such as are laid one over another. Arrived, brought near. A particular pace.

A مرفوعة marfūʿat, (A thing) brought near.

A مرفوغة marfūghat, Close, impervious (woman).

A مرفوق marfūk, Pained in the elbow.

A مرفّه muraffah, Quiet, tranquil, contented, happy, prosperous. مرفّه البال muraffahu'l bāl, (and مرفّه الخاطر muraffahu'l khātir) Contented in mind, easy at heart. مرفّه الحال muraffahu'l hāl, In easy circumstances. *Muraffih*, A giver of ease and quiet. (See ترفيه tarfīh.)

A مرق mark, (v. n. of مرق) Making plenty of broth. Piercing rapidly, transfixing with a spear. Pulling wool or pelt off a skin. Flesh sticking to skin which has been stripped off. The chant of men or women-singers, especially of the meaner rank (as strollers). A putrid skin. (pl. مروق muruk and امراق amrāk) A beard of corn. في مرقك fi markika, On thy account, for thy fault (has this misfortune overtaken him). *Mirk*, Stinking wool. *Murk*, Bald (wolves). *Marak*, (v. n. of مرق) Bearing nothing after having been fruitful (a palm). Becoming addle (an egg). Broth. Blight of corn.

A مرقّ marakk, (pl. مراقّ marākk) The soft part of the belly, or lobe of the ear. *Murikk*, Elegant (writer). Thin-hoofed (horse).

A مرقأة mar or mirkaʾat, A staircase or ladder.

A مرقاة markāt or mirkāt, (one being the name of the place, the other the name of the instrument) (pl. مراقي marākī) A staircase. The step of a staircase. The round of a ladder.

A مرقاق mirkāk, A baker's rolling-pin.

A مرقال mirkāl, Swift; prancing (she-camel).

A مرقب markab, (or مرقبة markabat) A watch-tower, or high place whence observation is made.

A مرقّب murakkab, That part of a hide drawn off the head and neck when skinning.

A مرقة marakat, A quantity or a kind of broth.

P مرقد markad, A soothing, quieting medicine.

A مرقد markad, A bed, sleeping-place. A sepulchre, tomb, grave. *Murkid*, Soporiferous, narcotic. A plain road.

A مرقدّي mirkidda', Expeditious, diligent, active (in business). One who begins to nod over his work.

A مرقسيّ *marhasīy*, Related to the tribe of بنو امرئ القيس *banū amrisi'l hays.*

P مرقشيشا *markashīshā*, The marcasite-stone.

A مرقص *murkis*, One who persuades to dance.

A مرقّط *murakkat*, Speckled, spotted.

A مرقّع *murakkaɛ*, Patched, mended, botched. Ragged, clad in rags. *Murakkiɛ*, A patcher, botcher.

A مرقعان *markaɛān*, (fem. مرقعانة) Foolish.

P مرقّع دار ابليسي *murakkaɛ-dāri iblīsī*, A diabolical sect. An agent for the devil. Sinful practices carried on under the mask of piety. Thou art a factor of Satan. Thou perpetratest wickedness under the garb of religion.

A مرقّق *murakkak*, Thinned, sharpened, whetted.

A مرقل *murkil*, (or مرقلة) Prancing (she-camel).

A مرقم *mirkam*, A pen, style for writing with.

A مرقوم *markūm*, Written, described, inscribed, computed. Above-mentioned, aforesaid. Sealed (letter). Marked, especially with orthographical points. (A cauterized horse) marked in the legs. P مرقوم كردن *markūm kardan*, To inscribe.

A مرقومة *markūmat*, Land having few plants.

P مرقون *markūn*, Name of a priest of the Magi who maintained the doctrine of three principles.

A مرقون *markūn*, Marked; written; aforesaid.

A مرقيّ *markīy*, Fascinated: guarded by magic.

A مرقيا الانف *markayā'l anf*, Sides of the nose.

A مرك *marik*, A rank old catamite.

A مركّ *murakk*, (Ground) wet with small rain.

A مركاح *mirkāh*, (A saddle) slipping backwards (from the back of a horse).

A مركب *markab*, (v. n. of ركب) Riding. Being carried or borne. (pl. مراكب *marākib*) A horse, camel, carriage, ship, or any thing in which one is carried. P مركب جم *markabi jam*, Solomon's vehicle, i.e. the wind. مركب جمام *markabi jamām*, A horse that quickly devours his corn.

A مركّب *murakkab*, Compounded, composed, mixed. (An animal) of a mixed breed. Placed, mounted, set (as a stone in a ring): fixed. A horse borrowed on condition that half the spoil be given to the lender. A mixture, compound. Ink. A kind of orange. Root, origin, the place where any thing is produced. جهل مركب *jahli murakkab*, Gross ignorance. كريم المركب *karīmu'l murakkab*, Of a noble origin. مركّب اسنادي *murakkabi isnādī*, (or مركّب تامّ *murakkabi tāmm*) A sentence complete in itself and independent.

A مركّبات *murakkabāt*, Compound medicines.

A مركز *markaz*, (vulg. *margiz*) A centre, centre of a circle. A place of residence, halting-place, military camp. P مركز خورشيد *markazi khwurshed*, The fourth heaven. The world. A مركز الدائرة *markazu'd dāsira*, Centre of a circle.

P مركز راين *markaz rāyan*, (in zand and Pāz.) Any number of crimes deserving of death.

A مركض *mirkaz*, A malkin or coal-rake. Chips, fuel. A tinder-box.

A مركضة *mirkazat*, The arm of a bow. A horse that kicks up the earth with his feet.

A مركضتان *mirkazatāni*, The two arms of a bow.

A مركل *markal*, (pl. مراكل *marākil*) A way, road. The side of a horse, that part touched by the spur or by the heel in riding. *Mirkal*, The foot.

A مركلان *markalāni*, (du.) Both sides of a horse.

A مركّلة *murakkalat*, Worn, beaten (path).

A مركن *mirkan*, A vessel, of earth or stone, in which clothes are washed, a wash-tub.

A مركّن *murakkan*, Large (udder); large-dugged.

A مركوّ *markūw*, A large and small cistern.

A مركوب *markūb*, Ridden (horse). (A carriage, animal, road) by or on which one travels. A spade.

A مركوز *markūz*, Fixed, fastened. Infixed, implanted. Hid, buried. Comprehended, concentered. Wish, desire.

A مركوض *markūz*, (A horse) put to his speed.

A مركوك *markūk*, Trimmed, neatly finished (leathern bottle).

A مركوم *markūm*, Piled, heaped, accumulated.

P مرگ *marg*, Death. فرشتهٔ مرگ *firishtasi marg*, The angel of death, called مرداد *murdād*. مرگ راحت رسان *margi rāhat-rasān*, Death bringing rest. مرگ طبعي *margi tabɛī*, A natural death. مرگ ماهي *margi māhī*, Any thing by which fish are intoxicated and caught. مرگ مفاجات *margi mufājāt*, Sudden death. مرگ موش *margi mosh*, Rats'-bane. Realgar. *Murg*, Snot.

P مرگامرگ *marg-ā-marg*, (or مرگامرگي *murg-ā-margī*) A plague, pestilence.

P مرگامرگي زدگي *marg-ā-margī-zadagī*, A being smitten with pestilence. مرگامرگي زده *marg-ā-margī-zada*, Smitten with pestilence.

P مرگامرگي ناك *marg-ā-margīnāk*, Pestilential.

P مرگو *murgū*, A sparrow.

P مرم *maram*, (for مرهم *marham*) A plaster.

A مرمّ *murimm*, Silent. (A camel) full of marrow. Inclined to play. (See ارمام *irmām*.)

A مرماة *mirmāt*, A small or weak arrow; also one with a broad point for learning to shoot. *Mirmāt* or *marmāt*, A cloven hoof; a substance growing in the division of a sheep's hoof.

A مرمّات الاخبار *muramma*ɛ*ātu'l akhbār*, False news, groundless reports.

A مرمّات *murimmāt*, Misfortunes, troubles.

A مرماخوز *marmākhūz*, (or مرماخوزي *marmākhūzī*) A species of merow.

A مرمار *marmār*, A juicy pomegranate without pulp. Soft, delicate, and tremulous.

A مرمارة *marmārat*, A soft and delicate girl tremulous from fat.

A مرماش *mirmāsh*, A woman who winks much with the eyes, or one who beautifies her eyes.

A مرمّة *marammat*, (v. n. of رمّ) Mending, repairing (a house). Cropping with the lips shoots of trees (a cow). Devouring. Reparation, repair. P مرمّت كردن *marammat kardan*, To mend, repair. A *Marammat* or *mirammat*, The lips of a cow or any animal dividing the hoof.

P مرمّت خواه *marammat-khwāh*, Wanting repair.

A مرمثة *murmisat*, (Land) producing رمث *rims*.

A مرمّد *murammad*, (Meat) laid upon the coals (to broil). (Bread) baked upon the ashes.

A مرمدّ *murmadd*, Blear-eyed.

P A مرمر *marmar*, Marble. A juicy pomegranate without pulp. Soft, delicate, and tremulous. A certain cut or fashion of a woman's dress.

A مرمرة *marmarat*, (v. n. of مرمر Q) Being angry. Letting (water) flow on the surface of the ground. Copious rain.

A مرمريت *marmarīt*, A sore calamity.

A مرمريس *marmarīs*, Evil, misfortune, sore calamity. Any thing slippery, shining, even, or smooth. Long (neck). Hard. Bare, unproductive (land).

A مرمس *marmas*, A grave, a tomb.

A مرمّش *murammash*, Blear-eyed.

A مرمض *marmiz*, A place for roasting meat.

A مرمّعات *murammaɛāt*, Idle reports.

A مرمّعة *murammiɛat*, A desert.

A مرمعلّ *murmaɛill*, A follower of the right road.

A مرمغلّ *murmaghill*, Tanned (hide).

A مرمقّ *murmakk*, (or مرمّق *murammak*) One who lives badly; in a mean, miserable condition.

A مرمل *marmal*, (v. n. of رمل) Running, going fast, between a walk and a run. *Mirmal*, A kind of small fetter. *Murmal*, Made of woven, plaited palm-leaves (a sofa). *Murmil*, A lion.

A مرمّل *murammal*, Well stirred up (dish of dates and butter. *Murammil*, A lion.

A مرمنة *marmanat*, A pomegranate-orchard.

A مرموثاء *marmūsā*, A confusion of things.

A مرموثة *marmūsat*, (A well) fenced with a wooden parapet or cover.

A مرمورة *murmūrat*, A soft girl tremulously fat.

A مرموز *marmūz*, Expressed by signs.

A مرموض *marmūz*, (A sheep) split and roasted in the skin on a hot stone covered with ashes.

A مرموع *marmūɛ*, Afflicted with lumbago.

A مرموق *marmūk*, Looked back on, glanced at.

A مرمول *marmūl*, Flimsily woven. Covered or strewed over with sand (رمل *raml*), sanded.

A مرمهزّ *murmahazz*, Any thing wished for. *Murmahizz*, Light, not heavy.

A مرمى *marma'*, An object shot at, game.

A مرميّ *marmīy*, Thrown, cast. المرميّ بالريبة *al marmīy bi'r ribat*, Suspected, thought badly of.

A مرمئدّ *murmasidd*, Passing by, proceeding. Quick of apprehension, skilful.

A مرميس *mirmīs*, A rhinoceros.

A مرن *marn*, (v. n. of مرن) Anointing the worn part of a camel's hoof. Dashing (on the ground). Fleeing from an enemy. Softened or smoothed leather. A soft fur garment. A kind of plant. The side. A present. Flight from an enemy. *Maran*, Two pieces of wood leaning against the trunk of a palm-tree, on which the man who watches them sleeps. *Marin*, Custom, mode, manner, usage, habit. Tumult, clamour. War, battle.

A مرنّ *murinn*, Twanging (bow), chirping (bird).

A مرنان *mirnān*, A stiff, hard, sounding bow.

A مرنب *marnab*, (A garment) woven with a mixture of hare's pile. (A country) abounding in hares (ارنب *arnab*). A large mouse.

A مرنباني *marnabāniy* or *murnabāniy*, (A garment) of the colour of a hare (ارنب *arnab*).

A مرنّة *murinnat*, A twanging bow. A bow.

A مرنج *maranj*, Name of a fort in Hindūstān.

A مرنّح *murannah*, The best aloes. A staggerer.

A مرنحة *marnahat*, The prow of a ship.

A مرنعة *marnaʻat*, The sound of a multitude of voices, either in mirth or brawling. Convenience, ease, comfort. Liberty. A fruitful season: flourishing garden or mead. Part of meat, drink, or plunder.

A مرنّق *murannak*, Broken-winged (bird). *Murannik*, Dim-sighted from hunger.

P مرنگ *marang*, Name of a fort in India.

P مرنگو *marangu*, A porcupine.

P مرو *marw*, Name of a fragrant herb. A fire-striking stone. Name of a city in Khurāsān. *Marav*, (the negative imper. of رفتن *raftan*) Go not.

A مرو *marw*, A species of hard white flints full of fire. A kind of fragrant herb.

A مرؤ *muruʼ*, (pl. of مريء *mariʼ*) Gullets.

P مروا *murwā*, A good omen. Prognostication of happiness. مرواي نيك *murwāyi nek*, A good omen. The twenty-second note of the barbud.

A مروأة *muruʼat*, The being brave and manly.

P مرواريد *marwārīd*, A pearl. مرواريد بستن *marwārīd bastan*, To be promoted to a new situation. To blush, be ashamed.

A مروان *marwān*, Name of the ninth caliph of the house of Abbās.

A مروّب *murawwab*, (or مروب *mirwab*) A vessel in which milk is left to thicken. A churn.

A مروة *marwat*, A single hard and white fire-flint. المروة *al marwat*, The mountain of Mecca, so called from its flints.

A مروءة *muruʼat*, (or مروّة *murūwat*) (v. n. of مرؤ) Being bold, masculine, manly, vigorous. Manhood, virility, fortitude. Human nature; humanity. Generosity, politeness. P بي مروّت *bī murūwat*, Inhuman, uncivil, rude, unpolished.

A مروت *marūt*, A solitude wholly destitute of vegetation. *Murūt*, (pl. of مرت) Desolate wastes.

A مروتة *murūtat*, Smoothness of ground. Scantiness of eyebrows. Scarcity of herbage.

A مروث *marwas*, The fundament of a horse.

A مروج *murūj*, (pl. of مرج *marj*) Meadows.

A مروّج *murawwaj*, Current, saleable. Usual. *Murawwij*, A seller (of merchandise). مروّج امتعة علوم *murawwiji amtiʻati ʻulūm*, A retailer of science.

A مروح *marūh*, Light, sprightly (horse). Excellent, admirably formed for shooting (bow). *Mirwah*, (pl. of مروحة *mirwahat*) Fans, ventilators.

A مروّح *murawwah*, Perfumed, highly scented. *Murawwih*, A perfumer, vender of perfumes.

A مروحة *marwahat*, (pl. مراويح *marāwīh*) A desert. A place that may be blown through. *Mirwahat*, (pl. مراوح *marāwih* or مروح *mirwah*) A fan.

A مروخ *marūkh*, Oil, unguent for the body.

P مروخوش *marw khwush*, Name of a sweet herb.

A مرود *marwad* or *murwad*, (v. n. 4 of راد for رود) Assisting, favouring; being benevolent, kind, easy. Going gently. Driving gently. A light, gentle, slow pace. *Mirwad*, A bodkin with which the collyrium is applied to the eyes. The iron axle of a pulley. A hinge or joint in a horse's bit. *Murūd*, (v. n. of مرد) Being accustomed, brooding over; being intent upon. Exceeding all bounds in wickedness, insolence, obstinacy, or pride. Obstinacy.

P مرود *murūd*, A pear. A guava.

A مرودة *murūdat*, (v. n. of مرد) Being bare, beardless. After having been beardless, getting a beard.

A مرودكة *mu* or *marawdahat*, Blooming (girl).

A مرور *murūr*, (v. n. of مرّ) Passing by, through, over, or across. Being borne along. Persevering, continuing. Departing, proceeding. Walking, marching. Elapsing. Passage, pass, avenue, transition, transit. (pl. of مرّة *marrat*) Times, turns. مرور زمان *murūri zamān*, Lapse of time. P مرور كردن *murūr kardan*, (or مرور و عبور كردن *murūr u ʻubūr kardan*) To proceed, pass, cross. مرور على البحر كردن *murūr ʻala'lbahr kardan*, To cross the sea.

P مرورا *marūrā*, To or for him.

A مروراة *marawrāt*, (pl. مروري *marawra'*, مروريات *marawrayāt*, and مراري *marārī*) A barren desert.

P مرورشك *marvrishk*, Seed of مرو *marv*.

P مرو رود *marv-rūd*, Name of a river.

A مروري *marawra'*, (pl. of مروراة) Deserts.

A مروريات *marawrayāt*, (pl. of مروراة) Deserts.

P مروريه *marwariya*, Wild endive. Bitter lettuce.

P مروز *murūz*, A people in هري *harī* or Aria.

A مروزي *marwaziy*, Belonging to the city of مرو.

A مروزية *marūziyat*, (in Morocco) Mutton dressed with honey, almonds, currants, saffron, and pepper.

A مروس *marūs*, A pulley, the rope of which sticks between the wheel and the cheek.

P مروسيدن *marosīdan*, To apply a remedy, give medicine. To be accustomed. To be afflicted.

P مروش *marosh*, Shine not, enlighten not.

A مروش *murūsh*, Scratches.

P مرو شاهجان *marv shāhjān*, (or مرو شهجان *marv shahjān*) The city of Marv in Khurāsān.

A مروص *marūs*, Swift (she-camel).

A مروض *marūz*, Broke in, trained (colt).

A مروط *murūt*, (pl. of مرط *mirt*) Short smocks of wool or silk.

A مروّع *murawwaʻ*, Endued with accuracy, sagacity, and penetration. An expert physiognomist. *Murawwiʻ*, Formidable, dread-inspiring.

A مروق *murūk*, (v. n. of مرق) Passing through and coming out on the other side (an arrow). (pl. of مرق *mark*) Beards, piles, or awns of an ear of corn.

A مروّق *murawwak*, Strained, racked, filtered. Bright, clear. Porticoed (house). P آب مروّق *ābi murawwak*, Clear, filtered water.

A مرول *mirwal*, Extremely slabbery (man). A bit of weak rope.

A مرون *marūn*, Conquered, subjected. *Murūn*, (v. n. of مرن) Being smooth and somewhat hard Being addicted to, persevering in.

A مرؤون *marʼun*, (pl. of مرء *marʼ*, *mirʼ*, or *murʼ*) Men

A مرونة *murūnat*, (v. n. of مرن) Being smooth and hardish. Softness, smoothness with pliantness.

A مرؤوس *marʼūs*, Hurt on the head (رأس *raʼs*). Large-headed. One whose lust is in his head. A subject, tenant. A common man.

P مروّة *murawwah*, A perfumer.

A مرويّ *mirwa'*, (pl. مراوي *marāwī*) A rope for fastening a load. *Murwī*, Thirst-quenching (water).

A مرويّ *marwiy*, Related, affirmed, told. Alleged in the words or on the faith of another. One whose thirst is quenched. *Marwiy* or *maraviy*, Belonging to the city of Marv. ثوب مرويّ *saubun marwiyun*, Cloth manufactured at Marv.

A مرة *marah*, (v. n. of مره) Being diseased (the eye) for want of collyrium. Being white within the eyelids (the eye). *Marih*, Spoiled, weak. مره الفؤاد *marihu'l fuʼād*, Sick, low, faint-hearted.

P مرّه *marra*, Calculation, number, measure.

A مرهاء *marhāʼ*, (fem. of امره *amrah*, pl. مره *murh*) (A woman) sore-eyed from neglecting to anoint with collyrium.

A مرهاة *mirhāt*, (pl. مراهي *marāhī*) Swift (horse).

A مرهب *murhib*, Appalling.

A مرهبل *murahbal* or *murahbil*, Unintelligible.

A مرهة *murhat*, Shining whiteness, brightness. A ditch filled with rain-water.

A مرهج *murhij*, Rain-portending (star).

A مرهصة *marhasat*, Dignity, high degree, rank.

A مرهّط *murahhat*, Swelled, swollen.

A مرهف *murhaf*, A sword thin and keen at the curve where the execution is done. Gaunt-bellied (horse).

A مرهق *murhak*, One whom others pursue in order to kill. Overtaken.

A مرهّق *murahhak*, One of whom a bad opinion is conceived, to whom madness or villainy is imputed. A man followed by others; one on whom they depend. One whom guests hang upon.

A مرهّل *murahhal*, Swollen.

A P مرهم *marham*, (pl. مراهم *marāhim*) A plaster, any dressing for wounds. Salve.

P مرهم بها *marham-bahā*, A surgeon's fee.

A مرهمة *marhamat*, A putting on of a plaster.

A مرهمس *murahmas*, Concealed, secret.

P مرهم نه *marham-nih*, Who applies a plaster.

A مرهوب *marhūb*, Dreadful, dreaded. A lion.

A مرهود *marhūd*, Weak, loose (concern). Remiss, doubtful, uncertain in carrying on business.

A مرهوص *marhūs*, (A horse) hurt in the feet by the stones and limping.

A مرهوف *marhūf*, Thin, slim, slender-bodied.

A مرهوك *marhūk*, Ground or bruised very small. Weak, silly, or perplexed (business).

A مرهوم *marhūm*, Watered by a gentle rain.

A مرهون *marhūn*, Pledged, pawned. مرهون منت *marhūni minnat*, Bound in gratitude.

A مرى *mariʼ*, Easy of digestion, wholesome (food). المرى *al mariʼ*, The gullet. هنئ مرئ *haniʼ mariʼ*, (or هنئ مرئ حميد *haniʼ mariʼ hamīd*) Easy of concoction or digestion.

A مري *mary*, (v. n. of مري) Milking, pressing the teats. Whipping or spurring (a horse) to increase (his) speed. Inflicting (blows). Drawing out. (A horse) striking (the ground) with the fore-feet (either from sprightliness or pain). Dissolving (a cloud) into rain (wind). Denying a debt or any thing which one knows.

P مري *mire*, Labour, diligence. Equality in power or rank. An agreement, league (particularly in mischief). Litigation, law-suit. Good news.

A مرّي *murra'*, (fem. of امرّ *amarr*) Bitter.

A مريّ *mariy*, (pl. مرايا *marāya'*) (A camel) full of milk, which flows on pressing the dug.

A مرّيّ *murriy*, A kind of sourish stomach-water for creating an appetite or promoting digestion. A kind of condiment eaten with bread.

A مرياء *maryāʼ*, Place of seeing, watch-tower.

A مرياع *miryāɛ*, (A she-camel) returning from pasturing alone. One which lets her milk flow.

G مريافلن *muryāfilun*, Millefoil.

A المريان *al murrayāni*, The colocynth and marine wormwood.

A مريب *murīb*, Doubtful, apocryphal. Suspected, scandalous. Sly, deceitful.

A مرية *miryat* or *muryat*, The gallopping of a horse, especially when urged by the spur. A copious effusion of milk from the udder of a camel. Doubt, ambiguity. Altercation, contention.

A مرّيّة *murrīyat*, Bitterness.

A مريّث *murayyas*, Dull, heavy (eyed).

A مريج *marīj*, Confused, involved, intricate (business). A limber twig of a palm-tree entering amongst the branches. (pl. امرجة *amrijat*) A small white bone in the middle of a horn.

T مرّيج *marrīj*, The river Ebrus in Thrace.

A مريح *marīh*, Shaken by the wind. Wet with rain (a garden).

A مرّيح *mirrīh*, (pl. مرّيحين) Sprightly, jovial.

A مريخ *marīkh*, (pl. امرخة *amrikhat*) A soft bone inside the horn of an animal.

A P مرّيخ *mirrīkh*, The planet Mars. A fire-brand, torch. Iron, steel. A long arrow with four wings or feathers, with which they shoot to a great distance. Litharge of silver. A fool. Soft, limber (tree). P مرّيخ آفتاب علم *mirrīkhi āftāb-ɛalam*, A blazing fire. مرّيخ زحل خوار *mirrīkhi zuhal-khwār*, The embers of a fire-brand. مرّيخ و كيوان ديدن *mirrīkh u kaywān dīdan*, To see Mars and Saturn, (met.) To see charcoal half-lighted in a chafing-dish. مرّيخ ذنب فعل *mirrīkh zanab-fiɛl*, (or مرّيخ ذنب فعل زحل سيما *mirrīkh zanab-fiɛli zuhal-simā*) Fetters for a horse.

A مريّخ *murayyakh*, Litharge of silver. A small bone in the inside of a horn.

P مرّيخ سلب *mirrīkh-salab*, Scarlet raiment. Clad in scarlet.

A مريد *marīd*, (pl. مرداء *muradāʼ*) Stubborn, obstinate, contumacious, perverse, disobedient, insolent, proud. A date softened and dressed in milk. *Murīd*, Desirous, willing. One who wills or is the author of any thing. A scholar, disciple, the obsequious follower of another. A studious man, philosopher, hermit, soph, santon.

A مرّيد *mirrīd*, Very stubborn.

A مريداء *muraydāʼ*, A thin membrane between the navel and pubes.

P مريدانه *murīdāna*, Like a scholar, scholar-like.

P مريدن *marīdan*, To freeze, congeal.

A مريدي *murīdī*, Scholarship, discipleship.

A مرير *marīr*, (pl. مرائر *marāʼir*) Robust, strong, Barren ground. Purpose, design, intention.

A مريّر *murayyar* or *yir*, Oppressed with fat.

A مريراء *murayrāʼ*, A black bitter grain found in wheat. A soft, delicate girl tremulous from fat.

A مريرة *marīrat*, The twist of a rope. A firmly-twisted rope. A rope long and slender. Greatness of soul. Resolution, determination; design, intention.

A مرّيرة *mirrīrat*, Design, intention.

P مريزبانك *murīzbānk* or *murī zabānak*, A kind of medicine, called likewise خوب كلان *khūb kalān*.

A مريس *marīs*, Steeped, soaked (date). Crumbled, grated, or sliced bread for putting in milk or broth. Any thing slippery and shining.

A مرئّس *muraʼʼis*, A fierce lion.

A مريش *marīsh*, Feathered, winged (arrow).

A مريّش *murayyash*, Feathered, winged (arrow). Hairy and fleshless (camel). Printed or embroidered (stuff). Weak-backed (man). (A camel-litter) held together by thongs of undressed leather.

A مريّشة *murayyashat*, Fleshless (she-camel).

P مريشم *maresham*, A plaster for a sore.

A مريض *marīz*, (pl. مراض *mirāz*, مرضى *marza'*, and مراضى *marāza'*) Sick, ill, infirm, diseased. مريض و صاحب فراش *marīz u sāhibi firāsh*, Sick and bed-ridden. قول مريض *kawli marīz*, A feeble expression. Unsound doctrine.

A مريضة *marīzat*, Sick (woman). Weak, dim (eye). Unhealthy (country). Slight (wind). Feeble and obscure (sun, this word being feminine).

A مريط *marīt*, (pl. امراط *amrāt* and مراط *mirāt*) Featherless (arrow). The part between the point of the fetlock and the hoof. A certain vein in the body, in the dual called مريطان *marītāni*.

A مريطاء *muraytāʼ*, A thin internal membrane reaching from the navel to the pubes. The part between the breast or navel and the pubes. A vein which swells when any one bawls. The part of the lower lip which is exposed. The mustachios. The part which surrounds the hair between the nether lip and the chin. The arm-pit.

A مريطى *murayta'*, The palate. The uvula.

A مريع *marīɛ*, (pl. امرع *amruɛ* and امراع *amrāɛ*) Fertile, abounding in grass and water (place).

A مريّغ *murayyagh*, Soiled with dust or earth.

A مرّيق *murrayk*, Saffron.

A مريّق *murayyak*, Delighted constantly with.

A مريقة *muraykat*, Broth made of acid milk.

A مرئلة *muraʼilat*, (A she-ostrich) having young.

A مريم *maryam*, (A woman) who loves the conversation of men with a pure affection. مريم عور *maryami ɛūr*, The branch of a vine in the autumn. ابن مريم *ibn maryam*, The son of Mary, *i.e.* Jesus Christ. ابو مريم *abū maryam*, A police-officer, tip-staff. بخور مريم *bukhūri maryam*, The herb sowbread. حضرت مريم *hazrati maryam*, The Virgin Mary.

A مرين *murīn*, (pl. مرينون *murīnūn*) One who loses many of his cattle by murrain.

A ابو مرينا *abū marīna'*, Name of a fish. بنو مرينا *banū marīna'*, Hiraites in Mesopotamia.

A مرينة *murīnat*, The lamprey.

A مريّة *murayyah*, (Vapour) shining and fading.

A مرئ *mariʼ*, Manly, strong, brave. Light, easy of digestion. (pl. امرئة *amriʼat* and مرؤ *muruʼ*) Gullet, meat-pipe. *Murayʼ*, (dim. of مرء *marʼ*) A manikin.

A مرئيّ *marʼiy*, Human. Related to امرؤ القيس *amruʼul kays* (a name common to several poets, and companions of Muhammad).

A مريئة *mariʼat*, Healthy, salubrious (country). *Murayʼat*, (dim. of مرأة *marʼat*) A little woman.

P مز *maz*, Suck thou.

A مزّ *mazz*, (v. n. of مزّ) Sucking. Hard, difficult. *Mizz*, Excellence. Measure, quantity. له مزّ عليك *lahu mizzun ɛalayka*, He excels thee. *Muzz*, (Wine or a pomegranate) having a mixture of sweet and acid. Sweet wine.

A مزّاء *muzzāʼ*, A kind of wine. Sweet wine.

A مزابر *muzaʼbar* or *muzaʼbir*, Hairy, shaggy, pily, plushy, covered with nap (as new cloth).

A مزأبق *muzaʼbak*, Washed or overlaid with quicksilver (زئبق *ziʼbak*), quicksilvered.

A مزابل *mazābil*, (pl. of مزبلة Dunghills.

A مزابنة *muzābanat*, (v. n. 3 of زبن) Selling without weight or measure (corn in the ear, or dates still hanging on the palm-tree). This is forbidden by the Muhammadan law, as depending on conjecture. Repelling, resisting one another.

A مزاة *muzāt*, Tyrants. Giants.

A مزاج *mizāj*, Temperament, complexion, constitution, habit of body, disposition, temper. A mixture, any thing mixed; whatever is mixed with wine. (interrogatively) How do you do? How is your health? مزاج شريف *mizāji sharīf*, A noble disposition, an excellent constitution. P مزاج گوهران *mizāji gawharān*, The elements. مزاج نا خوش *mizāji nā khwush*, Indisposition, malady. تيزمزاج *tez-mizāj*, Impatient, choleric. A محرور المزاج *maḥrūru'l mizāj*, Of a hot or fiery temperament. مستقيم مزاج *mustaḳīm-mizāj*, Serene, even, equable.

P مزاج دان *mizāj-dān*, Knowing the temperament. A confidant.

P مزاج گوي *mizāj-gūy* or *goy*, Complimentary.

P مزاجگير *mizāj-gīr*, Agreeable, suited to the temper, constitution, or taste.

A مزاح *mizāḥ*, (v. n. 3 of مزح) Playing, jesting with. A joke. *Muzāḥ*, (or مزاحة *muzāḥat*) (v. n. of مزح) Jesting with. A joke, jest, fun, frolic.

A مزّاح *mazzāḥ*, Playful, gay, jocose. A jester.

A مزاحرة *muzāḥarat*, The being inimical, hostile.

A مزاحف *mazāḥif*, (pl. of مزحف *mazḥaf*) Tracks of serpents. Parts where drops of rain fall. *Muzāḥaf*, (Verse) in which one letter between two others is dropped (so that they are brought together).

A مزاحكة *muzāḥakat*, A removing, putting away.

A مزاحم *muzāḥim*, Inconvenient, preventive, hindering, molesting. Impediment, obstacle. P مزاحم شدن *muzāḥim shudan*, To molest, to be troublesome. A ابو مزاحم *abū muzāḥim*, An elephant. A bull with broken horns. Name of the first Turkish commander who fought with the Arabians.

A مزاحمة *muzāḥamat*, (v. n. 3 of زحم) Hindering, preventing from taking effect: disturbing, pressing upon, especially in a crowd. Hindrance, prevention, impediment, let, obstruction, molestation. A crowd, mob, throng. Approaching to fifty.

A مزاخرة *muzākharat*, Boast, a glorying against.

P مزاد *mazād*, Name of a game.

A مزاد *mazād*, Auction, a selling to the highest bidder. (pl. of مزادة *mazādat*) Large water-bottles made of a double skin, and sometimes covered with a third. P مزاد كردن *mazād kardan*, To raise the price, bid above. A *Muzād*, Increased, augmented.

A مزادة *mazādat*, (pl. مزاد *mazād* and مزائد *mazā*ʾ*id*) A large water-bottle made of a double skin, and enclosed sometimes in a third, to prevent in warm countries the exhalation or evaporation of the water. A purse, bag, scrip, or any thing similar in which they carry provisions. A ewer.

A مزار *mazār*, (v. n. of زار for زور) Visiting. A place of visitation; hence a sepulchre, tomb, grave. Visitation, a visit. مزار سعادت مدار *mazāri saʿādat-madār*, The glorious sepulchre.

A مزارة *mazārat*, (v. n. of زار for زور) Visiting. (v. n. of مزر) Being strong, brave, and undaunted. Becoming firm (a date).

A مزارّة *muzārrat*, A biting (of one another).

P مزارستان *mazāristān*, A burying-ground.

P مزارسنگ *mazār-sang*, A tomb-stone.

A مزارع *mazāriʿ*, (pl. of مزدرع *muzdaraʿ* and مزدرعة *muzdaraʿat*) Sown fields, lands in tillage. *Muzāriʿ*, A sower.

A مزارعة *muzāraʿat*, (v. n. 3 of زرع) Giving a field to sow. Furnishing seed to sow.

A مزاريع *mazārīʿ*, (pl. of مزروع *mazrūʿ*) Things sown, seeds.

A مزاريق *mazārīḳ*, (pl. of مزراق *mizrāḳ*) Javelins, demi-lances.

A مزازة *mazāzat*, Food partly sweet, partly sour. Abundance, plenty.

A مزّاع *mazzāʿ*, A hedgehog.

A مزاعة *muzāʿat*, Any thing dropped (as particles of cotton when teasing).

A مزاعلة *muzāʿalat*, (v. n. 3 of زعل) Rendering brisk and lively. Shoving, displacing, tearing up.

A مزاعم *mazāʿim*, Matters of doubt or opinion.

A مزاعمة *muzāʿamat*, A crowding, thronging.

A مزاق *mizāḳ*, Very swift (she-camel).

A مزاكنة *muzākanat*, (v. n. 3 of زكن) Approaching, amounting nearly to. Sitting knee to knee, keeping company with. Remaining near to. Conjecturing, guessing.

A مزالف *mazālif*, (pl. of مزلفة *mazlafat*) Villages situated between deserts and cultivated districts. Steps, stairs.

A مزاملة *muzāmalat*, (v. n. 3 of زمل) Making the loads equal on both sides of a camel.

A مزامنة *muzāmanat*, (v. n. 3 of زمن) Appointing a time, agreeing with one by time (زمان *zamān*).

A مزامير *mazāmīr*, (pl. of مزمار *mizmār*) Flutes, psalteries. (pl. of مزمور *mazmūr*) Psalms, canticles.

A مزّان *muzzān*, Dressed, adorned.

A مزاناة *muzānāt*, (v. n. 3 of زني) Fornicating.

A مزانحة *muzānaḥat*, A contending in praise.

A مزاوجة *muzāwajat*, (v. n. 3 of زاج for زوج) Coupling, joining, marrying, wedding.

A مزاود *mazāwid*, (pl. of مزود *mizwad*, مزواد *mizwād*, and مزادة *mazādat*) Wallets in which provisions are carried. رقاب المزاود *riḳābu'l mazāwid*, Foreigners. Barbarians. Persians.

A مزاولة *muzāwalat*, (v. n. 3 of زال for زول) Remedying, curing. Wishing, desiring, seeking, asking.

A مزاهر *mazāhir*, (pl. of مزهر) Kinds of lutes.

A مزاهمة *muzāhamat*, (v. n. 3 of زهم) Approaching to (fifty). Quitting, leaving. Separation. Opposition, hostility. Approximation.

A مزايا *mazāyā*, (pl. of مزيّة *mazīyat*) Excesses. Excellencies.

A مزائد *mazāʾid*, (pl. of مزادة *mazādat*) Large water-bottles made of double skins.

A مزايدة *muzāyadat*, An increasing mutually.

A مزايلة *muzāyalat*, A departing from, quitting.

A مزاين *mazāyin*, (and مزايين *mazāyīn*) (pl. of مزّان *muzzān*) Dressed, adorned.

A مزبّ *muzibb*, Rich, opulent.

A مزبّب *muzabbib*, Wealthy, affluent.

A مزبد *muzbid*, Foaming (sea).

A مزبر *mizbar*, A pen, implement for writing.

A مزبراني *mazbarānīy*, (A man or lion) fat between the shoulders.

A مزبرة *mazbarat*, (A place) swarming with wasps, hornets, or bees (زنبور *zumbūr*). *Muzibrat*, (in Morocco) A pruning-knife.

A مزبرج *muzabraj*, Adorned, dressed.

A مزبّق *muzabbaḳ*, (Base coin) washed over with quicksilver (زئبق *ziʾbaḳ*) to make it pass current.

A مزبلة *mazbalat* or *mazbulat*, A dunghill. Any place where they throw the filth or sweepings of a house. A necessary. An osier basket (especially on a carriage).

A مزبور *mazbūr*, Written. Above-mentioned. مزبوران *mazbūrāni*, The two (persons) aforesaid.

A مزبورة *mazbūrat*, (A well) constructed of stones.

A مزبورون *mazbūrūn*, (pl.) The before-mentioned. اشقياءِ مزبورون *ashḳiyāʾi mazbūrūna*, The aforesaid robbers.

A مزبوق *mazbūḳ*, Plucked (beard).

A مزّة *mazzat*, Sweet wine. One suck. Wine of an agreeable sharp taste. *Muzzat*, Pricked wine, having a disagreeable acidity.

A مزج *mazj*, (v. n. of مزج) Mixing, diluting wine (with water). Attacking each other (men or dogs). *Mazaj* or *mizj*, Honey. A bitter almond.

A مزجّ *mizajj*, A short spear.

A مزجاة *muzjāt*, (fem. of مزجي *muzjaʾ*) A small matter, a thing of little value. Inconvenient, unfit. بضاعة مزجاة *biẓāʿat muzjāt*, A small capital in trade.

A مزجال *mizjāl*, An arrow yet unfurnished with head or wing.

A مزجرة *mazjarat*, A scarecrow.

A مزجل *mizjal*, A short spear.

A مزجوج *mazjūj*, (A bucket) not made round, but whose lips are sewed together.

A مزجور *mazjūr*, Repressed. Driven off.

A مزجيٰ *muzjaʾ*, Small, insignificant (thing).

A مزجّيٰ *muzajjaʾ*, (A ship) driven forward. *Muzajjī*, One who connects himself with strangers (to his family or tribe).

A مزح *mazḥ*, (v. n. of مزح) Playing, jesting. An ear of corn. Spikenard.

A مزحاف *mizḥāf*, Limping, tired (camel).

A مزحزح *muzaḥzaḥ*, Removed.

A مزحف *mazḥaf*, (pl. مزاحف *mazāḥif*) (A place) where serpents crawl. *Muzḥif*, (A fatigued horse) dragging his legs.

A مزحل *mazhal*, (v. n. of زحل) Declining, receding, departing from. A place to which one retires.

A مزحم *mizham*, Much pressed or thronged.

A مزحور *mazhūr*, (A miser) oppressed, groaning when asked to give any thing.

A مزخة *mazakhkhat*, The privities of a woman. *Mazakhkhat* or *mizakhkhat*, A woman.

A مزخرف *muzakhraf*, Ornamented, varnished. Deceitful. *Muzakhrif*, A deceiver, cheat, liar.

A مزخرفات *muzakhrafāt*, Idle tales, lies.

A مزخف *muzkhif*, Vain-glorious, proud.

A مزخلب *muzakhlib*, A buffoon, wag, one who ridicules or plays upon another.

A مزد *mazd*, (v. n. of مزد) Rubbing (bread) until (it) becomes soft. A mode of coition. Cold.

P مزد *muzd*, A reward, premium, salary, wages, hire. A goat. مزد دندان *muzdi dandān*, Money distributed to the poor at a time of feasting. Any thing valuable (as pelisses or a horse) presented after an entertainment. بمزد دادن *ba muzd dādan*, To let on hire.

A مزداة *mizdāt*, A little hole into which boys throw nuts in a kind of game.

A مزدان *muzdān*, Adorned, decorated.

A مزدبد *muzdabid*, Possessed of cream or fresh butter (زبد *zubd*).

P مزدبر *muzd-bar*, One who works for wages.

A مزدجر *muzdajir*, A prohibiter. Forbidden, repulsed. One who augurs from birds.

A مزدحم *muzdaham*, A thronged, crowded place. مكان مزدحم عليه *makanun muzdahamun ʿalayhi*, A crowded place. *Muzdahim*, Crowding. A crowd.

A مزدرد *muzdarid*, A swallower (of a mouthful).

A مزدرع *muzdaraʿ*, (or مزدرعة *muzdaraʿat*) A sown field. *Muzdariʿ*, A cultivator, sower.

A مزدري *muzdara'*, Despised. *Muzdarī*, A despiser. المزدري *al muzdarī*, The lion.

A مزدع *mizdaʿ*, Quick in doing any thing.

A مزدغ *mizdagh*, (or مزدغة) A pillow, bolster.

P مزدفان *mazdafān*, Name of a city where they make pottery.

A مزدفر *muzdafar*, A deep-fetched breath. The part from which a horse's neigh proceeds.

A مزدقان *mazdakān*, Name of a city in Kohistān.

P مزدك *mazdak*, Name of a heresiarch.

A مزدلف *muzdalif*, An approacher, bystander.

A مزدلفة *muzdalifat*, Name of a place near Mecca, between mount Arafāt and the valley of Mina.

A مزدوج *muzdawaj*, Coupled, united, wedded.

P مزدور *muzdūr*, A mercenary, hired labourer. مزدور ديو *muzdūri dev*, A hireling of the devil, *i.e.* one who engages in useless or injurious acts. A clerk in the exchequer.

A مزدور *muzdawir*, Visited.

P مزدوران *muzdūrān*, One who performs beneficent actions, builds hospitals, or caravanseras; one who is influenced by the hopes of an eternal reward, and is supposed to deserve it.

P مزدورانه *muzdūrāna*, Like a hired servant.

P مزدوري *muzdūrī*, Bodily labour. Wages, hire.

P مزدوري كردن *muzdūrī kardan*, To work for hire.

P مزده *muzda*, Reward, salary, wages, hire.

P مزدها *muzdahā*, (pl. of مزد *muzd*) Rewards.

P مزده بر *muzda-bar*, A mercenary, hireling.

A مزدهد *muzdahid*, One who esteems as moderate, who thinks (any thing) little (زهيد *zahīd*).

A مزدهر *muzdahir*, One who keeps (a thing) with care, being fond of it. (See ازدهار *izdihār*.)

A مزدهف *muzdahaf*, Carried away, abolished, ruined. *Muzdahif*, One who carries off. One who turns his face. A liar. (See ازدهاف *izdihāf*.)

P مزده گير *muzda-gīr*, A hirer.

A مزدهي *muzdaha'*, Vain, proud.

P مزر *mazr*, A kind of drink made from barley and millet, a species of beer or ale.

A مزر *mazr*, (v. n. of مزر) Sipping in order to taste. Filling (a leathern bottle) so that no inequality appears on the surface. Pinching gently. Being angry against. A very moderate draught. A polite, graceful, ingenious, witty man. *Mizr*, A fool. Root, origin. Beer made from barley or millet.

A مزراء *mizrāʾ*, A slanderer, detractor.

A مزراب *mizrāb*, A canal of water.

A مزراة *mazrāt*, A chiding, censuring, defaming.

A مزراف *mizrāf*, Swift (she-camel).

A مزراق *mizrāk*, A javelin, demi-lance. A camel that moves his load backwards.

A مزرّج *muzarraj*, Intoxicated with wine.

A مزرح *mazrah*, Low and even ground.

A مزرد *mazrad*, The gullet. *Mizrad*, A rope fastened round a camel's neck to prevent him bringing up his food when chewing the cud, and throwing it on his rider.

A مزرعة *mazraʿat*, *mazruʿat*, or *mazriʿat*, A field sown, or ready prepared for it. P مزرعهٔ خاك *mazraʿaʾi khāk*, The ground. Bodies of men or animals. The grave. مزرعهٔ دانه سوز *mazraʿaʾi dāna-soz*, (Grain-consuming field) The world.

P مزركش *muzarkash*, Made of gold-wire.

A مزرود *mazrūd*, Choked, squeezed (throat).

A مزرودة *mazrūdat*, (Coat of mail) of iron rings.

A مزروع *mazrūʿ*, Sown, cultivated. Seed.

P مزره *mazra*, A lamp or lamp-holder.

A مزرية *mazriyat*, Censure, chiding, defaming.

A مزرئم *muzraʾimm*, Costive, constipated. Contracted within itself.

A مزرئن *muzraʾinn*, Cold (morning).

A مزز *mazaz*, (v. n. of مزز) Becoming excellent and eminent. Quiet, calm procedure, slow movement. Abundance. Time.

A مزع *mazʿ*, (or مزعة *muzʿat*) (v. n. of مزع) Running swiftly; springing lightly. Separating cotton with the finger. A quick, light pace, between a walk and a run.

A مزعاج *mizʿāj*, A restless woman.

A مزعافة *mizʿāfat*, A serpent.

A مزعامة *mizʿāmat*, A serpent.

A مزعة *mizʿat*, Some cotton or feathers. *Muzʿat* or *mizʿat*, A bit of meat given to a hawk when training. Slice of meat, bit plucked off. Remains of water. A bit of grease. A little water, a draught.

A مزعج *muzʿij*, Startling.

A مزعزع *muzaʿzaʿ*, Strained, filtered.

A مزعف *muzʿaf*, Brackish (well). *Muzʿif*, Sudden death. Death-inflicting (sword).

A مزعفر *muzaʿfar*, Tinctured with saffron. Tawny (lion). A kind of pilaw. A kind of sweet beverage, made of water, flour, and honey.

A مزعق *mizʿak*, An implement for ploughing or turning up the ground. Rapid (journey). Strong, hard (pull at a bow).

A مزعم *mazʿam*, Matter of doubt or opinion. A thing on which no reliance can be placed.

A مزعمة *muzʿamat*, (A she-camel or ewe) full of fat; also destitute of fat.

A مزعوق *mazʿūk*, Terrified. Much salted (meat). (Ground) moistened with a shower.

A مزعّي *mazʿiy*, An informer, accuser, whisperer.

A مزغب *muzghib*, Downy, callow (little bird).

A مزغف *mizghaf*, Gluttonous, greedy.

A مزغئدّ *muzghaʾidd*, Enraged, angry.

A مزفّة *mizaffat*, A camel-litter, in which the bride is carried to her husband's house.

A مزفّت *muzaffat*, Pitched, anointed with pitch.

A مزفّر *muzaffar*, (or مزفّرة *muzaffarat*, A deep-fetched breath. One who breathes deeply.

A مزفور *mazfūr*, Strongly, firmly-jointed (horse).

A مزفوف *mazfūf*, Conducted, brought.

A مزفّي *mazfiy*, Timorous, frightened.

A مزق *mazk*, (v. n. of مزق) Tearing (cloth). Slandering, defaming. Muting (a bird). *Mizak*, A piece torn from cloth.

A مزقة *mazkat*, (v. n. of مزق) Tearing. *Mizkat*, A piece torn from any thing. *Muzkat*, Name of a little bird.

A مزقزق *muzakzak*, Finished with despatch.

A مزقّق *muzakkak*, Shorn, but not plucked (skin). Shorn, clipped, polled (head).

A مزققة *muzakkakat*, Large (she-camel).

A مزقوق *mazkūk*, Skinned from head to foot.

P مزكت *mazkat* or *mizkit*, A small mosque.

A مزكّن *muzakkin*, A physiognomer.

A مزكو *muzakkū* or *muzakū*, A sort of food.

A مزكوبة *mazkūbat*, Picked up (woman).

A مزكوت *mazkūt*, Filled (bottle). Thought upon, turned over in the mind. (A locust) full of eggs. Affected severely by cold.

A مزكوم *mazkūm*, Troubled with a rheum.

A مزكّي *muzakka'*, Purified. Cleared, justified. *Muzakkī*, One who purifies his possessions by consecrating a part thereof to pious uses.

P مزگ *mazg*, A bitter almond-tree.

P مزگت *mazgit*, A house of prayer, mosque.

P مزگه *mizga*, A foul wind. A dark sky.

P مزگی *mazagī*, Sweetness, flavour.

A مزلّ *muzill*, One who causes to slide.

A مزلاج *mizlāj*, A bar, bolt, or latch of a door opened by the hand. A lank-hipped woman.

A مزلاق *mizlāk*, A bolt or a bar of a door. (A mare) accustomed to slip her foal.

A مزلّة *mazillat*, (v. n. of زلّ) Slipping, sliding, falling. Blundering in speech. *Mazillat* or *mazallat*, A slippery place.

A مزلّج *muzallaj*, Few, small. One who introduces himself amongst, and associates with, those to whom he does not belong. Mean, inferior, vile. A miser. Spurious, mixed (grain).

A مزلّع *muzallaع*, One who has the skin torn off the foot.

A مزلعبّ *muzlaعibb*, A swollen, dashing torrent.

A مزلفة *mazlafat*, (pl. مزالف *mazālif*) A country mid-way between a desert and a cultivated district, between one watered and one without water.

A مزلق *mazlak*, A slippery place.

A مزلقة *mazlakat*, A slippery place. *Mizlakat*, The buttocks of a horse.

A مزلّل *muzallil*, Abundant in kind acts.

A مزلّم *muzallam*, Well-proportioned (horse). Smooth, straight, justly-formed (arrow or staff). Slit-eared. Light, active. Short, dwarfish. Ingenious, clever. Small-bodied (mountain-goat). Badly fed.

A مزلّمة *muzallamat*, Good-sized, portly (woman).

A مزلهمّ *muzlahimm*, Light, active.

A مزلئمّ *muzlaیimm*, Goer, traveller, passenger. One who advances bolt upright. Firm, durable.

A مزمار *mizmār*, (pl. مزامير *mazāmīr*) A flute, pipe, shawm, psaltery. A good voice for singing. مزمار الراعي *mizmāru'r rāعī*, Shepherds'-pipe.

A مزمجر *muzamjir*, Roaring (lion).

P مزمزان *mazmazān*, Sucking a little at a time.

A مزمزة *mazmazat*, (v. n. of مزمز Q) Shaking to and fro, putting in motion.

A مزمع *muzmiع*, Constant: resolved, intent upon.

A مزمّعة *muzammiعat*, Modus coeundi.

A مزمّل *muzammal*, Muffled up, concealed in one's garments. سورة المزمّل *sūratu'l muzammal*, Name of a chapter in the Kur'ān.

P مزمّل *muzammil*, A brass cock.

A مزّمّل *muzzammil*, One who wraps up and hides in his garments.

A مزمّلة *muzammalat*, An earthen jar, or any thing similar in which water is cooled, a chatty.

A مزمن *muzman*, Ruined, desolate, deserted. *Muzmin*, Lasting, of long continuance. Chronic, chronical. Paralytic.

A مزمور *mazmūr*, (pl. مزامير *mazāmīr*) A psalm, canticle. A pipe, flute. A song, singing.

A مزموقة *mazmūkat*, Plucked (beard).

A مزموم *mazmūm*, Reined (camel), bridled.

A مزمهجّ *muzmahijj*, (Pasture) beautifully green.

A مزمهرّ *muzmahirr*, Very angry. Very cold (day). Red (eye). Twinkling (star). Chattering (teeth).

A مزمهلّ *muzmahill*, Pure (water). Erect, set up.

A مزمئجّ *muzmaیijj*, Enraged.

A مزن *mazn*, (v. n. of مزن) Going where one likes. Shining, being clear (the countenance). Filling (a bottle). Praising, extolling, preferring. Praising (one) in the royal presence. Preceding. يوم مزن *yawmi maznin*, A day of flight from an enemy. *Muzn*, A cloud. A white cloud. A watery cloud. حبّ المزن *habbu'l muzn*, Hail. *Mazan*, Custom, habit. Situation, condition, state. Mode, manner.

P مزنا *miznā*, (in zand and Pāz.) A pair of scales.

A مزنة *muznat*, Part of a white cloud. Rain. ابن مزنة *ibnu muznata*, The new moon.

A مزنّج *muzannaj*, Small (gift or draught).

A مزنجة *maznajat*, Natives of Ethiopia, Zingies.

A مزنّد *muzannad*, Narrow (in mind), strait, tight (garment). Avaricious, tenacious, covetous, stingy. A bastard. *Muzannid*, A liar. (See ترنيد.)

P مزنده *mazanda*, A sucker. A sort of water-bottle. Any thing that may be sucked.

A مزنّرة *muzannarat*, Tall and jolly (woman).

A مزنگو *mazangū*, A porcupine which kills snakes without eating them.

A مزنّم *muzannam*, Small camels. (A camel) whose ears are slit and hang down. A bastard. An intruder into a society with which he is unconnected.

A مزنوق *maznūk*, (A horse) fastened with the cord or twitch called زناق *zunāk*. Name of a horse.

A مزنيّ *muzanīy*, Of the tribe of Muzaynat.

P مزو *mazū*, Food for the sick.

A مزواج *mizwāj*, (A woman) who marries often.

A مزواد *mizwād*, A traveller's provision-bag.

A مزوبر *muzawbar*, Nappy, shaggy (garment).

A مزوّج *muzawwaj*, Married, wedded, conjoined, associated. *Muzawwij*, One who joins (a man and woman) in wedlock, who splices (them).

A مزود *mizwad*, A traveller's provision-bag.

A مزوّد *muzawwad*, Stocked with provisions.

A مزور *mazūr*, Visited.

A مزوّر *muzawwar*, Adulterated, falsified; false. Crooked, oblique. A camel in whose brisket there is a crookedness, caused by the hand of the accoucheur in drawing him forth. Lie, falsehood. مزوّر فحوى *muzawwar fahwa'*, Falsified in sense. *Muzawwir*, A liar, knave, cheat, falsifier.

A مزوزكة *muzawzikat*, Quick, active (woman).

A مزوّق *muzawwak*, Painted, washed, stained. (Any iron substance) plated with gold or washed with quicksilver.

A مزون *mazūn*, (with the article ال *al*) The country of عمان *عumān* in Arabia. *Muzūn*, (v. n. of مزن) Going where one pleases.

A مزؤود *mazیūd*, Terrified. Timid, fearful.

A مزه *mazh*, (v. n. of مزه) Playing, jesting.

P مزه *maza*, Taste, savour, smack, relish. مزه داشتن *maza dāshtan*, To have a flavour. بي مزه *bī maza*, Insipid, tasteless, flavourless, vapid. خوش مزه *khwush-maza*, Well-flavoured, sweet, delicate.

A مزهد *muzhid*, (fem. مزهدة *muzhidat*) Poor, indigent. افضل الناس مؤمن مزهد *afzalu'n nās muیmin muzhid*, The best of men is a poor believer.

A مزهر *mizhar*, (pl. مزاهر *mazāhir*) A kind of lute struck with a bow. One who kindles a fire to attract guests.

A مزهف *mizhaf*, A ladle or spatula with which they mix medicines or gruel. *Muzhaf*, Carried off. A lie. *Muzhif*, A liar. (See ازهاف *izhāf*.)

A مزهق *muzhak*, Killed, destroyed. *Muzhik*, A murderer, destroyer. One who goes fast.

A مزهوّ *mazhūw*, Proud, elated, vain.

A مزي *mazy*, (v. n. of مزي) Being proud.

A مزيّ *mazīy*, Elegant. Ingenious, clever.

A مزيال *mizyāl*, An ingenious, witty, sprightly man. One who mixes in matters.

A مزيبر *muzaybar*, Shaggy, nappy (cloth).

A مزيّة *maziyat*, (pl. مزايا *mazāya'*) Excess, superabundance. Excellence.

A مزيت *mazīt*, (Food) dressed with oil (زيت *zayt*), especially with olive-oil.

A مزيج *mazīj*, A bitter almond.

A مزيح *mazīh*, Jocularity, merriment.

P مزيد *mazīd*, He sucked.

A مزيد *mazīd*, Increase, augmentation. مزيد فيه *mazīd fīhi*, Augmented, increased (conjugation: as, استنصر *istansara*, He demanded assistance, from نصر *nasara*, He assisted).

P مزيدن *mazīdan*, To taste, suck, sip. To crop with the lips.

P مزيده *mazīda*, Name of a game.

A مزير *mazīr*, (pl. امازر *amāzir*) Strong, bold, fearless, intrepid. Ready in the despatch of business. Polite, elegant.

A مزئر *muzیir*, Roaring (lion).

A مزيز *mazīz*, Excellent, eminent. Little, few. Hard, difficult. عزيز مزيز *عazīz mazīz*, Difficult.

A مزيقياء *muzaykiyāی*, A name given to a king of Yaman, who used to put on two new garments every day, and tear them at night, unwilling to wear them himself a second time, or to allow them to be worn by any one else.

A مزيل *mizyal*, An ingenious, witty, agreeable, sprightly man. *Muzīl*, One who takes away. A remover. فاقة مزيل الطاقه *fākaیi muzīlu't tāka*, Poverty enervating the powers. P گلاب مزيل الصدوع *gulābi muzīlu's sudūع*, Rose-water removing the headache.

A مزيّن *muzayyan*, Adorned, dressed, having the hair cut or dressed. *Muzayyin*, A dresser, especially a barber. (dim. of مزدان *muzdān*) Somewhat decorated, partially adorned.

A مزينة *muzaynat*, Name of an Arabian tribe.

A مزيّنة *muzayyinat*, A tirewoman.

A مزيوت *mazyūt*, (Food) dressed with oil (زيت *zayt*), especially olive-oil.

P مژ *maj*, Bent, bowed, crooked. *Muj*, The eyelashes. A dark cloud; any thing darkening the air.

P مژد *mujd*, The planet Jupiter. Joyful tidings.

P مژدقان *majdakān*, Name of a city in Kohistān.

P مژدك *majdak* or *mujduk*, Name of a pretended prophet, a native of Nīshāpūr, who appeared in the reign of Kubād, king of Persia, and father of Noshīrawān. He adopted the doctrine of the principles of light and darkness, and the worship of fire; and taught, moreover, the community of women and of property. Vast numbers embraced his opinions, amongst whom was the king himself. The impostor, however, was at length put to death in the reign of Noshīrawān with 80,000 of his followers.

P مژدگان *mujdagān*, Good news. Eyelashes.

P مژدگانی *mujdagānī*, Good news. A present for bringing good news.

P مژده *mijda* or *mujda*, Glad news, joyful tidings. Joy, gladness. مژده کردن *mijda kardan*, مژده آوردن *mujda āwardan*, or مژده دادن *mujda dādan*) To bring or announce good news, to give the first intelligence of any thing wished for. To give advice or counsel. مژده مرترا *mujda mar turā*, I give you joy; I congratulate you.

P مژدها *mujdahā*, (pl. of مژده) Glad tidings.

P مژده فرماي *mujda-farmāy*, (or رسان *rasān*) A messenger, bringer, or relater of good news.

P مژده‌گانی *mujdagānī*, A reward to a bringer of good news.

P مژده‌ور *mujdawar*, A bearer of good news.

P مژگان *mujagān* or *mijagān*, The eyelids or the hairs, the eyelashes.

P مژمژ *mijmij*, A meat-tainting fly. A gadfly.

P مژنگ *majang*, Disagreeableness. Deformity, ugliness. Effeminate. A sodomite.

P مژو *mijū*, Underwood-fuel in baths. A lentil.

A مژه *mija* or *muja*, The eyelid, the hair of the eyelid, an eyelash.

P مژيده *majīda*, A game like leap-frog.

P مس *mas*, A sort of fetter. Great, noble, sir, lord, master. *Mis*, Copper. مسهاي زراندود *mis-hāyi zar-andūd*, Gilded coppers, (metaphor.) Insincere professions of esteem or good-will. *Mus*, Hindrance, impediment.

A مسّ *mass*, (v. n. of مسّ) Touching, handling, feeling. Pressing, being urgent and important (business). Touch. مسّ من الجنون *massun mini'l junūn*, A touch of insanity. مسّ الحمّى *massu'l humma'*, A touch of fever. *Muss*, (in the dialect of Morocco) A penknife. A razor.

A مسأ *mas*, (v. n. of مسأ) Being froward, saucy. Keeping the middle of the road. Exciting discord. Delaying, proceeding slowly. Deceiving, circumventing. Being given to, persevering in. Deferring, putting off. Stilling (a boiling pot). Mollifying by gentle words. Being rent (a garment). The middle of a road.

A مساء *masā*, Evening. مساء امس *masā amsin*, Yesterday-evening. مسا الخير *masā'l khayr*, Good evening. صبح و مسا *subh u masā*, Morning and evening.

A مساءة *masā'at*, (v. n. of ساء for سوأ) Grieving, saddening. Displeasing, disgusting. Doing evil. Crime, vice. Slander, detraction.

A مسأب *mis'ab*, A skin in which they keep honey. A large leathern bottle; also the case in which it is kept. A great water-drinker.

A مسابّة *musābbat*, (v. n. 3 of سبّ) Speaking opprobriously, provoking by reproaches.

A مسابحة *musābahat*, A swimming along with.

A مسابع *masābiʻ*, (pl. of مسبعة *masbaʻat*) Countries swarming with beasts of prey (سبع *sabuʻ*).

A مسابعة *musābaʻat*, (v. n. 3 of سبع) Indulging in venery. Bragging of one's powers in this line. Obscene talk, ribaldry. Reproaching, abusing each other.

A مسابقة *musābakat*, (v. n. 3 of سبق) Getting the start in a race, surpassing, overcoming, excelling, straining every nerve against another; happening before. Overtaking, preceding.

A مساتاة *musātāt*, (v. n. 3 of ستا for ستو) Playing at a game where they kick on the backside.

A مساترة *musātarat*, A veiling, a concealing.

A مساتق *masātik*, (pl. of مستقة *mustakat*) Fur pelisses with long sleeves.

A مساتلة *musātalat*, A following in succession.

A مساجاة *musājāt*, (v. n. 3 of سجا for سجو) Touching, handling, feeling. Applying a remedy.

A مساجد *masājid*, The (seven) members with which adoration is paid; namely, the hands, knees, feet, and forehead. (pl. of مسجد *masjid*) Places of worship. Mosques. مساجد ومدارس *masājid u madāris*, Muhammadan mosques and colleges.

A مساجرة *musājarat*, A cultivating friendship.

A مساجلة *musājalat*, (v. n. 3 of سجل) Contending with another, emulating, rivalling in running or in drawing water.

A مسّاح *massāh*, (and مسّاح الارض *massāhu'l arz*) A geometrician. A land-measurer.

A مساحة *misāhat*, (v. n. of مسح) Measuring (ground). Measurement or survey of land. Mensuration. علم المساحة *ʻilmu'l masāha*, The science of measurement, geometry.

P مساحت دار *misāhat-dār*, A land-measurer.

A انتفخ مساحره *intafakha masāhiruhu*, He exceeded his limits.

A مساحلة *musāhalat*, (v. n. 3 of سحل) Going on the sea-shore (ساحل *sāhil*). Walking arm in arm.

A مساحن *masāhin*, Stones containing gold and silver ore. Stones on which swords are whetted.

A مساحنة *musāhanat*, (v. n. 3 of سحن) Meeting. Mixing agreeably together, cultivating a friendly intercourse. Examining the exterior form, or softness and beauty of the skin.

A مساحی *masāhī*, (pl. of مسحاة) Iron shovels.

A مساحيق *masāhīk*, (pl. of مسحاق *mis-hāk*) Thin cuticles or membranes covering the outside of the skull. (pl. of منسحق *munsahik*) Flowing (tears). مساحيق السماء *masāhīku's samā*, The membranes of heaven, *i.e.* thin clouds. مساحيق من الشحم *masāhīk mini'sh shahm*, The grosser parts of fat which adhere to the intestines.

A مساخفة *musākhafat*, (v. n. 3 of سخف) Abetting each other in folly.

A مسأد *mis'ad*, A bottle or skin in which they keep honey or butter.

A مساد *misād*, (pl. of مسد *masad*) Ropes made of the fibres of the palm-tree or other substance. هو احسن مساد شعر منك *huwa ahsanu misād shaʻarin minka*, He is sprucer about his hair than you.

A مسارّ *masārr*, (pl. of مسرّة *misarrat*) Whispering-trumpets, speaking-trumpets. *Musārr*, A teller of a secret (سرّ *sirr*).

A مسارب *masārib*, (pl. of مسربة) Pastures.

A مسارّة *musārrat*, A whispering in the ear.

A مسارح *masārih*, (pl. of مسرح *masrah*) Large and rich pastures.

A مسارره *musārarat*, The telling of a secret.

A مسارعة *musāraʻat*, A making haste.

A مسارقة *musārakat*, (v. n. 3 of سرق) Stealing a look at, turning the face suddenly towards.

A مساري *musārī*, A lion.

A مساريع *masārīʻ*, (pl. of مسراع) Very swift.

A مساس *masās*, Touch thou. *Lā masāsi*, Touch not. *Misās*, (v. n. 3 of مسّ) Touching. Lying with. Mutual contact. Coition. لا مساس *lā misās*, I will not touch or be touched.

A مساساة *musāsāt*, (v. n. 3 of سسو, not used) Despising, blaming, scoffing, railing at.

A مساطاة *musātāt*, An oppressing, treating harshly.

A مساطب *masātib*, (pl. of مسطبة *mastabat* or *mistabat*) Anvils. Benches, forms, seats long and wide. Concealed wells covered with earth.

A مساطر *masātir*, (pl. of مسطر *mistar*) Rulers.

A مساعاة *musāʻāt*, (v. n. 3 of سعى) Contending, striving (with another). Soliciting (a servant maid) to commit whoredom.

A مساعد *masāʻid*, (pl. of مسعد *masʻad*) Degrees of happiness. *Musāʻid*, Name of a man.

A مساعدة *musāʻadat*, (v. n. 3 of سعد) Helping. Favour, assistance, aid.

A مساعر *masāʻir*, (pl. of مسعر *misʻar*) Chips. Pokers for stirring the fire. Arm-pits and groins (of camels).

A مساعف *musāʻif*, Near, neighbouring, adjacent.

A مساعفة *musāʻafat*, (v. n. 3 of سعف) Helping, assisting, acting in a friendly manner. Going near.

A مساعي *masāʻī*, (pl. of مسعاة *masʻāt*) Endeavours, labours, laudable studies, works, attempts. مساعيء جميله *masāʻīʻi jamīla*, Virtuous efforts.

A مساعير *masāʻīr*, (pl. of مسعار *misʻār*) Pokers, pieces of wood with which the fire is stirred.

A مساغ *masāgh*, A passage, road, way.

A مساف *masāf*, Distance. The nose. *Musāf*, Dead (child).

A مسافاة *musāfāt*, (v. n. 3 of سفا for سفو) Charging (any one) with folly. Reviling, abusing, calling bad names.

A مسافة *masāfat*, Distance, interval, part of a road or journey. Space; a journey. A day's journey, as far as a loaded camel can travel with ease, *i.e.* eight parasangs. مسافت بمسافت *masāfat ba masāfat*, From stage to stage.

A مسافحة *musāfahat*, (v. n. 3 of سفح) Whoring. Whoredom, debauchery.

A مسافر *masāfir*, That part of a face which is uncovered. *Musāfir*, A traveller, passenger, temporary sojourner. P مسافران والا *musāfirāni wālā*, Holy men, travellers to heaven.

A مسافرة *musāfarat*, (v. n. 3 of سفر) Travelling. Dying. Being contrary (as one wind sweeping away what another brings). اصحاب مسافرت *as-hābi musāfarat*, Travellers.

P مسافر خانه *musāfir-khāna*, An inn.

A مسافع *musāfiʻ*, A whoremonger. One who makes a furious attack. A lion. One who embraces or hugs. A combatant, fencer.

A مسافعة *musāfaʻat*, (v. n. 3 of سفع) Flapping the wings (a bird).

A مسافهة *musāfahat*, (v. n. 3 of سفه) Railing at, reproaching. Charging (any one) with folly. Sitting down before a barrel, and drinking hour after hour without measure. Keeping on the road at a hard pace (a camel).

A مساق *masāk*, (v. n. of ساق for سوق) Driving. Impulse, momentum.

A مساقاة *musākāt*, (v. n. 3 of سقي) Letting a vineyard or palm-plantation for part of the produce.

A مساقط *masākit*, Places where things fall.

A مساقطة *musākatat*, (v. n. 3 of سقط) Throwing. Becoming deficient or languid; failing, breaking down (a horse when running). Reciting any thing alternately with another. Causing to fall.

A مساك *masāk* or *misāk*, Tenacity, avarice. *Maṣ mi*, or *musāk*, Any place that holds water. *Misāk*, Whatever fastens or makes fast, a fastener. Goodness.

A مساكاة *musākāt*, (v. n. 3 of سكو, not in use) Being importunate, troublesome, dunning.

A مساكات *musākāt*, Places which hold water.

A مساكة *masākat*, (v. n. of مسك) Holding (water) well (a leathern bottle). *Masākat* or *misākat*, Avarice, stinginess.

A مساكتة *musākatat*, (v. n. 3 of سكت) Bidding to keep silence. Keeping mutual silence. Vying with another in keeping silence.

A مساكن *masākin*, (pl. of مسكن *maskan* or *maskin*) Habitations. مساكن علما و مواطن فضلا *masākini ʻulamā u mawātini fuzalā*, The mansions of the learned and residence of men of science, *i. e.* universities, colleges. *Musākin*, An inhabitant.

A مساكنة *musākanat*, (v. n. 3 of سكن) Living in the same house with (any one).

A مساكين *masākīn*, (pl. of مسكين) The poor.

A مسال *musāl*, The side of a man's beard; the side from the neck to the haunch.

A مسالّ *masāll*, (pl. of مسلّة *misallat*) Large packing-needles.

A مسألة *masʼalat*, (pl. مسائل *masāʼil*) A question, query, proposition, problem.

A مسالة *masālat*, A handsome length of face.

A مسالح *masālih*, (pl. of مسلحة *maslahat*) Frontier-garrisons, forts at the entrance into a country.

A مسالخ *masālikh*, (pl. of مسلخ) Slaughter-houses.

A مسالف *masālif*, (pl. of مسلفة *mislafat*) Harrows. *Musālif*, A fellow-traveller. One who does things equal to another.

A مسالفة *musālafat*, (v. n. 3 of سلف) Travelling (with another); doing (any thing) equal (to him). Preceding.

A مسالق *masālik*, (pl. of مسلق) Ladders.

A مسالك *masālik*, (pl. of مسلك) Ways, paths.

A مسالم *musālim*, Cultivator of peace and amity.

A مسالمة *musālamat*, (v. n. 3 of سلم) Cultivating peace or friendship. P مسالمه كردن *musālama kardan*, To salute one another.

A مساليط *masālīt*, (pl. of مسلاط) Wards of a key.

A مساليق *masālīk*, (pl. of مسلوقة) Broths, soups.

A مسامّ *masāmm*, Holes. Chinks. The ducts or canals of the body. P مسامّ بيني *masāmmi bīnī*, The nostrils. A مسامّ الجسد *masāmmu'l jasad*, The pores of the body.

A مساماة *musāmāt*, (v. n. 3 of سمي) Boasting, contending for glory. Opposing, contending.

A مسامة *masāmat*, A broad thick piece of wood at the bottom of the two posts of a door. A wooden bar in front of a camel-litter.

A مسامح *musāmih*, Negligent, slow, lenient, easy.

A مسامحة *musāmahat*, (v. n. 3 of سمح) Acting with lenity, pardoning. Lenity, connivance, negligence. Languor, coolness. P مسامحه و قصور كردن *musāmaha u kusūr kardan*, (or مسامحه كردن *musāmaha kardan*) To neglect, to be careless.

A مسامر *musāmir*, One who attends evening conversations held by moonlight.

A مسامرة *musāmarat*, (v. n. 3 of سمر) Holding conversations by moonlight.

A مسامري *masāmarī*, (in Morocco) Seller of nails.

A مسامع *masāmiʻ*, (pl. of مسمع *mismaʻ*) Ears.

A مسامعة *masāmiʻat*, Descendants of مسمع *mismaʻ*, the father of a tribe.

A مساميح *masāmīh*, (pl. of سمح *samh* or مسماح *mismāh*) Beneficent, liberal, easy, meek, humane.

A مسامير *masāmīr*, (pl. of مسمار) Nails, spikes.

A مسانّ *masānn*, Aged (camels).

A مساناة *musānāt*, (v. n. 3 of سنا for سنو) Agreeing (with one) by the year (سنة *sanat*). Giving annually. Satisfying, soothing, making happy, acting kindly, humanely. Bearing fruit every other year.

A مسانّة *musānnat*, (v. n. 3 of سنّ) Following the female (a male camel) desirous of covering.

A مسانتة *musānatat*, (v. n. 3 of سنت) Exploring a country in search of herbage.

A مسانحة *musānahat*, (v. n. 3 of سنح) Coming on the left of the hunter (game).

A مساند *masānid*, (pl. of مسند *masnad*) Thrones. (pl. of مسند *musnad*) (Stories) attributed to, or allegations made on, the evidence of another; predicated. *Musānid*, (A camel) whose chest or forefend is prominent.

A مساندة *musānadat*, (v. n. 3 of سند) Assisting, helping. Compensating, requiting. In verse, pointing the ردف *ridf* with a vowel different from the other hemistich.

A مسانف *masānif*, (pl. of مسنف *musnif*) (Horses) taking the lead of the others.

A مسانهة *musānahat*, (v. n. 3 of سنه) Bargaining by the year. Giving annually. Bearing every other year (a palm-tree). A stipend, salary; a thing paid, promised, or agreed on by the year.

A مسانيد *masānīd*, (pl. of مسند *musnad*) Allegations made on the authority of others.

A مساواة *musāwāt*, (v. n. 3 of سوي) Equalling, levelling. Being equal to, like, comparing (one thing with another). Being worth. Equation, evenness, equality. P مساوات شدن *musāwāt shudan*, To be equal. To be neutral.

A مساودة *musāwadat*, (v. n. 3 of ساد for سود) Contending for dominion. Vying in blackness. Whispering in the ear. (A camel) eating or endeavouring to eat grass (when short and difficult to be cropt). Driving away (a lion). Circumventing.

A مساور *masāwir*, (pl. of مسورة *miswarat*) Leather cushions.

A مساورة *musāwarat*, (v. n. 3 of سار for سور) Assailing, springing upon another, committing an assault. Seizing the head.

A مساوعة *musāwaʻat*, (v. n. 3 of ساع for سوع) Doing or agreeing about (any thing) by the hour.

A مساوفة *musāwafat*, (v. n. 3 of ساف for سوف) Whispering in the ear, communicating a secret. Lying with. Delaying, putting off.

A مساوقة *musāwakat*, (v. n. 3 of ساق for سوق) Boasting against (any one) in the market-place. Contending with (another) about driving. Vying with in reference to the hardness of one's leg (ساق).

A مساوم *musāwim*, One who bids against another in order to enhance the price.

A مساومة *musāwamat*, (v. n. 3 of سام for سوم)

Bidding against, raising the price upon (another). Bidding, making an offer.

A مساوي *masāwī*, (pl. of مساءة *masāʼat*) Crimes. Reproaches, accusations. P مساوي كردن *masāwī kardan*, To slander. To criminate. A *Musāwī*, Equal, parallel, equivalent. Neutral, impartial.

A مساوئة *masāwiʼat*, (v. n. of ساء for سوأ) Grieving, saddening. Displeasing, disgusting. Doing evil.

A مساهاة *musāhāt*, A being careless, inaccurate.

A مساهرة *musāharat*, (v. n. 3 of سهر) Watching (with another). Keeping any one watching.

A مساهل *musāhil*, Negligent, careless: easy, indifferent. P مساهل شدن *musāhil shudan*, To be careless.

A مساهلة *musāhalat*, (v. n. 3 of سهل) Treating gently. Neglecting, acting in a loose, negligent manner. Negligence. P مساهلت كردن *musāhalat kardan*, To neglect; to connive at, overlook.

A مساهم *musāhim*, Concerting with. A companion, a second. A partner.

A مساهمة *musāhamat*, (v. n. 3 of سهم) Casting lots, drawing arrows (with any one).

A مساية *masāyat*, (v. n. of ساء for سوأ) Grieving, saddening. Displeasing, disgusting. Doing evil.

A مسائح *masāʼih*, (pl. of مسيحة *masīhat*) Ringlets. Bows.

A مسايرة *musāyarat*, A going along with.

A مسائف *masāʼif*, Years. Dearth, famine.

A مسايفة *musāyafat*, (v. n. 3 of ساف for سيف) Fencing, duelling, using the broad sword.

A مسائل *masāʼil*, (pl. of مسألة *masʼalat*) Questions. Propositions. Problems. (pl. of مسيل *masīl*) Channels through which water flows.

A مسائية *masāʼiyat*, (or مسايئة *masāyiʼat*) (v. n. of ساء for سوأ) Grieving, saddening. Displeasing, disgusting. Doing evil.

A مسايح *masāyih*, (pl. of مسياح) Sycophants.

A مسبّ *misabb*, Foul-mouthed, reproachful.

A مسبأ *masbaʼ*, (v. n. of سبأ) Buying wine to drink. Striking, lashing, flogging. Skinning. Burning, scorching. Taking by the hand, shaking hands. A way, a road.

A مسبار *misbār*, A surgeon's probe. A tent for a wound. A painter's brush, a pencil.

A مسبّب *musabbab*, Caused. Excellent, select. Reviled, reproached, execrated. *Musabbib*, One who gives cause, or occasions a reason. مسبّب الاسباب *musabbibu'l asbāb*, Causer of causes, *i. e.* God. مسبّب حقيقي *musabbibi hakīkī*, The true cause, *i. e.* God.

A ابل مسبّبة *ibil musabbabat*, Choice and splendid camels (because the beholder on seeing them exclaims in astonishment, قاتلها الله *kātalahā 'llāh*).

A مسبّة *masabbat*, A reviler of men.

A مسبت *musbit*, Soporific, narcotic. Still, motionless. Who enters on the Sabbath (سبت *sabt*).

A مسبّت *musabbit*, Abortion-producing (camel or sheep). Soporific, narcotic.

A مسبّتات *musabbitāt*, Opiates, hypnotics.

A مسبّج *musabbaj*, Wide, ample (garment).

A مسبّح *musabbah*, Strong, stout (cloak). *Musabbih*, A praiser of God; teller of his beads.

A مسبّحة *musabbihat*, The fore-finger.

A مسبحلل *musbahlil*, A full-grown whelp.

A مسبّد *musabbid*, One whose head is unwashed and unoiled.

A مسبرة *masbarat*, Form, shape, mode, manner. *Musbarat*, (v. n. of سبر) Probing to the bottom.

A مسبرت *musabrat*, Hairless (man).

A مسبرد *musabrid*, (A camel) which casts forth a hairless fœtus.

A مسبّط *musabbit*, (A camel or a sheep) which has cast her young.

A مسبطر *musabtir*, One who sees commands executed; an overseer, inspector, superintendent.

A مسبع *musbaʻ*, Left to one's self to do what one pleases. A bastard. One, whose mother being dead, is nursed by another. One whose paternal ancestors have been in servitude for four or five generations. One who, having been turned loose among wild beasts (سبع *sabuʻ*), has become like one of them. A seven-months' child.

A مسبعة *masbaʻat*, (pl. مسابع *masābiʻ*) (A country) swarming with lions and other ferocious beasts.

A مسبغ *musbigh*, Clad in a large coat of mail. (God) making complete and pouring down benefits.

A مسبّغ *musabbigh*, (A camel) which drops a foal already covered with hair.

A مسبغلّ *musbaghill*, Wide, shining (coat of mail).

A مسبكرّ *musbakirr*, A boy of a straight, elegant shape, either tall or middle-sized. Long (hair). Who stretches himself along. Who lies on the side.

A مسبل *musbil*, The sixth or fifth gaming arrow. Penis. The Lybian lizard. The month of Zū'l hijjat. One who allows his garment to trail along the ground through pride. *Musbil* or *musbal*, Long-mustachioed (man).

A مسبّل *musabbal*, A deformed, stinking old man. *Musabbil* or *musabbal*, Long-mustachioed.

A مسبنتأ *musbantaʼ*, Who has a long-shaped head.

P مسبند *mas* or *musband*, Unable to quit home.

A مسبوت *masbūt*, Dead. Enraptured, overjoyed, in an ecstacy, swooning, fainting. One whose head is shaved.

A مسبور *masbūr*, Handsomely formed, of a comely shape or appearance.

A مسبوط *masbūt*, Attacked by fever.

A مسبوعة *masbūʻat*, (A wild cow) whose young has been devoured by wild beasts (سبع *sabuʻ*).

A مسبوق *masbūk*, Outstripped in a race.

A مسبوك *masbūk*, Cast in a mould.

A مسبوه *masbūh*, Delirious from old age.

A مسبّه *musabbah*, An old dotard. Eloquent.

A مسبئرّ *musbaʼirr*, One who travels under cover of night.

A مسّة *massat*, A sort of game.

P مست *mast*, Drunk, intoxicated. Libidinous, lustful, wanton, furious. An animal in rut. مست خراب *masti kharāb*, Exceedingly intoxicated, dead drunk. مست خراب و آلودهٔ مي ناب *masti kharāb u ālūdaʼi mayʼi nāb*, Excessively drunk and polluted with neat wine. مست شدن *mast shudan*, To be inebriated. مست شراب غرور *masti sharābi ghurūr*, Intoxicated with the wine of temerity, *i. e.* rash. مست مدام *masti mudām*, (or مست مدمن *masti mudmin*) Perpetually drunk. *Must*, Trouble, distress of mind, complaint, lamentation. Root of galangale.

A مستأثر *mustaʼsir*, One who chooses or prefers.

A مستأجر *mustaʼjar*, Hired, rented. *Mustaʼjir*, A tenant, hirer, farmer, renter. A servant.

A مستأجل *mustaʼjil*, One who begs delay.

A مستأحد *mustaʼhid*, One who remains alone or separate. One who gives attention, who knows.

A مستأخد *mustaʼkhid*, One who hangs the head from badness of sight or from pain.

A مستأخذ *mustaʼkhiz*, One who hangs the head on account of badness of sight or from pain. Quiet, tranquil. Humble, submissive. Long hair.

A مستأخر *mustaʼkhir*, One who remains behind: a loiterer, lagger.

A مستأدب *mustaʼdib*, A cultivator of the belles lettres or humanities (ادب *adab*).

A مستأدي *mustaʼdi*, One who begs assistance, implores relief. A taker, exacter, extortioner.

A مستأذن *mustaʼzin*, One who asks leave.

P مستار *mastār*, Name of a fragrant but extremely bitter herb. *Mustār*, Wine new and acid.

A مستأرب *mustaʼrab*, Overloaded with debt. *Mustaʼrib*, Firmly-twisted (rope).

A مستأرض *mustaʼriz*, Rankling and mattery (sore). Sticking in or to the ground. فسيل مستأرض *fasīl mustaʼriz*, A shoot of a palm-tree taking root.

A مستأزق *mustaʼzak*, Narrow, confined.

A مستآس *mustaʼās*, One of whom a gift is asked, or whose society is sought after.

A مستأسد *mustaʼsad*, Excited, stimulated. *Mustaʼsid*, Bold, fearless, intrepid. One who rushes upon and attacks fiercely, like a lion (اسد *asad*). Full-grown (plant).

A مستأسر *mustaʼsir*, One who surrenders himself a prisoner or captive (اسير *asīr*).

A مستأشرة *mustaʼshirat*, (A lady) who calls (a female) to sharpen and make thin her teeth.

A مستأصل *mustaʼsal*, Extirpated, uprooted. *Mustaʼsil*, An extirpator. Firmly-rooted (plant).

A مستاف *mustāf*, A place smelled. The place of smelling: the nose.

A مستأكل *mustaʼkil*, One who takes (a thing) to eat. One who devours the weak, *i. e.* extorts from them their possessions.

A مستأكلة *mustaʼkilat*, Oppressors, devourers.

A مستأمر *mustaʼmir*, One who asks advice, takes counsel, and deliberates.

A مستأم *mustaʼmim*, One who regards as a mother (امّ *umm*). One who receives as high priest, or chief director of religious ceremonies (امام *imām*).

A مستأمن *mustaʼmin*, One who places confidence in. One who considers as faithful and sure. One who implores protection, and takes refuge.

A مستأمي *mustaʼmī*, A buyer or receiver of a handmaid (امة *amat*).

A مستأنس *mustaʼnis*, Accustomed, habituated. Tamed (wild beast). Familiar. One who looks or knows well. One who asks leave.

A مستأنف *mustaʼnaf*, New, recently passed (day). *Mustaʼnif*, A beginner, a commencer. An anticipator; anticipatory.

P مستانه *mastāna*, Intoxicated. Like a drunkard.

A مستأني *mustaʼnī*, Patient, waiting.

A مستأهل *mustaʼhil*, Worthy, suitable, apt, fit. One who takes or eats the fat of meat.

A مستبحر *mustabhir*, Wide-spread. Verbose, full of talk, extensive as the sea (بحر *bahr*).

A مستبدّ *mustabidd*, One who acts alone. Possessed of, or a claimant of, exclusive right or property.

A مستبدع *mustabdiع*, One who considers as new, original, or wonderful (بديع *badiع*).

A مستبدل *mustabdil*, Desirous to exchange. One who takes as a substitute (بدل *badal*).

A مستبذر *mustabzir*, Swift, passing rapidly along.

A مستبر *mustabir*, One who probes a wound.

A مستبرز *mustabriz*, One who calls forth, challenges, or makes (a person or thing) appear.

A مستبرئ *mustabriʼ*, Anxious to know the whole of a thing. (See also استبراء *istibrāʼ*.)

A مستبسل *mustabsil*, One who throws himself fearlessly into danger, regardless of his life.

A مستبشر *mustabshir*, Glad, rejoiced at good news. A communicator of good news.

A مستبصر *mustabsir*, One who considers attentively, searches into any thing occult. Acute, penetrating, circumspect. Open, manifest.

A مستبضع *mustabziع*, One who arranges his wares and exposes them to sale in a market. كمستبضع تمر الى هجر *ka mustabziعi tamrin ilaʼ hajar*, Like one sending dates for sale to Hajar (a part of Arabia where that fruit abounds. Coals to Newcastle).

A مستبطن *mustabtin*, One who places (a thing or person) under himself, especially under his belly, and holds (it or her) there. One who keeps a thing closely hidden. Whatever passes inside or lines.

A مستبعد *mustabعad*, Regarded as far off; difficult, unattainable. *Mustabعid*, Who deems a thing to be far off. Desirous of being at a distance.

A مستبعل *mustabعil*, (A place or a palm-tree) which has become a بعل *baعl*. A married man.

A مستبعي *mustabعī*, A borrower of a dog for the chase, or a horse for the course.

A مستبغي *mustabghī*, Desirous, wishful: a seeker.

A مستبق *mustabik*, One who excels, gets the start of, or endeavours to outstrip.

A مستبقى *mustabkī*, One who reserves, preserves, keeps alive, or leaves a remainder. Ashamed.

A مستبكي *mustabkī*, One who forces to weep.

A مستبل *mustabill*, Recovering, convalescent.

P مستبند *mustband*, One labouring under sorrow, distress of body or mind. Unable, on account of some circumstance, to leave his home.

A مستبهج *mustabhij*, Glad, joyful.

A مستبي *mustabī*, One who leads captive.

A مستبيت *mustabīt*, Poor (without a lodging).

A مستبيح *mustabīh*, An extirpator, destroyer. One who makes lawful. One who finds lawful.

A مستبيع *mustabīع*, Who commands a sale.

A مستبيل *mustabīl*, About to make water, or desirous to make water. One who causes to make water, and receives the urine in his hands; (hence the adage expressive of a brave man) يستبيل الاسد *yastabīlu'l asad*, He receives urine from the lion.

A مستبين *mustabīn*, Become evident. One who knows for certain, one who has a subject clear before him. مستبين مرسوم *mustabīni marsūm*, A term applied to all regular deeds and contracts.

A مستتبّ *mustatibb*, (Business) well arranged, in an excellent train.

A مستتبع *mustatbiع*, One who wishes to follow.

A مستتر *mustatar*, A hiding-place, a place of shelter. *Mustatir*, One who hides himself, or absconds. Careful, wary.

A مستتلي *mustatlī*, Who calls one to follow.

A مستتمّ *mustatimm*, A performer, finisher. One who wishes or desires any thing to be supplementary in number or quantity. Who asks for any thing to finish another, as wool to complete a web.

A مستثبت *mustasbit*, Patient, steady. Solicitous for stability (ثبوت *subūt*).

A مستثقل *mustashal*, Oppressed with sleep, disease, or guilt.

A مستثمد *mustasmid*, Drained, exhausted. One who seeks favours and benefits.

A مستثنيٰ *mustasnaʼ*, (and in regimen مستثنا *mustasnā*) Excepted from any common rule. Selected, excellent, extraordinary. *Mustasnī*, Who makes an exception from a general rule: exceptive.

A مستثيب *mustasīb*, One who asks for a reward (ثواب *sawāb*). One who demands restitution.

A مستثير *mustasīr*, An exciter, rouser, stirrer up.

A مستجاب *mustajāb*, Heard; accepted. Agreeable. مستجاب الدعوات *mustajābu'd daعwāt*, One whose prayers are answered.

A مستجاد *mustajād*, Regarded as good, approved.

A مستجدّ *mustajidd*, One who renews or renovates. One who considers as new. Clad anew.

A مستجدي *mustajdī*, An asker; a petitioner for a gift (جدا *jadaʼ*).

A مستجرّ *mustajirr*, One who submits to the guidance of another. A drawer, dragger.

A مستجرح *mustajrih*, Depraved, corrupt.

A مستجري *mustajrī*, One who takes (another) for his agent or deputy (جريّ *jarīy*).

A مستجزّ *mustajizz*, (Wheat) ready to cut.

A مستجعل *mustajعil*, (A bitch) in heat.

A مستجفي *mustajfī*, Who regards as hard, severe.

A مستجلب *mustajlib*, In need of, or requiring to be dragged from its place.

A مستجمر *mustajmir*, Encamped for a long time in an enemy's country. (See استجمار *istijmār*.)

A مستجمع *mustajmiع*, Met together. Desirous of assembling. (See استجماع *istijmāع*.)

A مستجنّ *mustajann*, Possessed of a demon. *Mustajinn*, Covered.

A مستجهل *mustajhil*, One who considers as ignorant, thinks lightly, despises. (See استجهال).

A مستجيد *mustajīd*, Who calls or finds (a thing) good (جيّد *jayyid*). A seeker of something good. Desirous of procuring a swift horse (جواد *jawād*).

A مستجير *mustajīr*, One who implores protection; a refugee. A suppliant.

A مستجيز *mustajīz*, Desirous of water for cattle or fields. One who asks leave or a gift.

A مستجيش *mustajīsh*, One who asks for troops.

A مستجيع *mustajīع*, One who is never seen except hungry, or appearing so.

A مستحاض *mustahāz*, Collected in a pond.

A مستحاضة *mustahāzat*, A woman who still suffers a loss of blood after that the period of the monthly discharge has elapsed.

A مستحال *mustahāl*, Crooked, distorted (bow). (A field) neglected for one or more years.

A مستحالة *mustahālat*, (A man) the end of whose leg is crooked.

A مستحبّ *mustahabb*, Loved, liked, approved. *Mustahibb*, Loving, affectionate; who holds dear.

A مستحثّ *mustahiss*, An exciter, urger onward.

A مستحجر *mustahjir*, Petrified, turned to stone.

A مستحدّ *mustahidd*, One who sharpens, a whetter. One who shaves off the hair of his privities. Incensed, enraged.

A مستحدث *mustahdas*, Discovered, found out. Novelty, invention. *Mustahdis*, One who learns news; or who discovers (a thing) to be new.

A مستحرم *mustahrim*, Sacred, inviolate.

A مستحسر *mustahsir*, Fatigued, tired.

A مستحسن *mustahsan*, Approved, laudable, beautiful, elegant. *Mustahsin*, One who regards as fair and good (حسن *hasan*); an approver.

A مستحصد *mustahsad*, Firmly-twisted (rope). *Mustahsid*, (Corn) ready for the sickle, requiring to be reaped. (See استحصاد *istihsād*.)

A مستحصر *mustahsir*, One who comprehends; or endeavours. A besieger. مستحصر مشكلات مسائل *mustahsiri mushkilāti masāʼil*, Desirous of

The title of the 37th caliph of the house of Abbās.

A مستعصي **mustaʻṣī**, Rebellious, sinful.

A مستعطي **mustaʻṭī**, A petitioner for a gift.

A مستعظم **mustaʻẓam**, Regarded as great. *Mustaʻẓim*, One who regards as great. (See استعظام.)

A مستعفّ **mustaʻiff**, Chaste, abstemious.

A مستعقب **mustaʻḳab**, A person or thing followed. *Mustaʻḳib*, A railer at any one, searcher into his faults. Following. (See استعقاب *istiʻḳāb*.)

A مستعكد **mustaʻkid**, Fat (lizard or camel). Crouching (game). (See استعكاد *istiʻkād*).

A مستعلب **mustaʻlib**, Stinking (meat).

A مستعلج **mustaʻlij**, Thick-skinned.

A مستعلف **mustaʻlif**, In want of provender.

A مستعلم **mustaʻlim**, Curious, anxious to know.

A مستعلي **mustaʻlī**, High, elevated. الحروف المستعلية *al ḥurūfu'l mustaʻliyat*, The letters صضطظ خغق.

A مستعمّ **mustaʻimm**, One who takes as a paternal uncle (عمّ *ʻamm*). Dressed in a turban.

A مستعمر **mustaʻmir**, A peopler, colonizer.

A مستعمش **mustaʻmish**, Who regards as a fool.

A مستعمل **mustaʻmal**, Applied, used, employed; current, not obsolete (word). Second-hand. *Mustaʻmil*, A user, employer.

A مستعند **mustaʻnid**, (A horse or camel) too strong for the reins. (See استعناد *istiʻnād*.)

A مستعنز **mustaʻniz**, Retired to one side.

A مستعهد **mustaʻhid**, A party to a covenant or treaty (عهد *ʻahd*). (See استعهاد *istiʻhād*.)

A مستعير **mustaʻīr**, A borrower. Alone. Shaped like an ass (عير *ʻayr*). مستعير الحسن *mustaʻīru'l ḥusn*, A kind of bird. (See استعارة *istiʻārat*.)

A مستعين **mustaʻīn**, One who asks assistance.

A مستغاث **mustaghās**, Called upon for help. Convoked. المستغاث به *al mustaghās bihi*, A person called upon. المستغاث عليه *al mustaghās ʻalayhi*, A defendant. المستغاث له *al mustaghās lahu*, Time, affair, occasion, emergency for which one is convoked.

A مستغثّ **mustaghiss**, One who dresses a wound, and makes it discharge matter.

A مستغدر **mustaghdir**, (A spot) become a ditch.

A مستغذي **mustaghẕī**, One who prostrates.

A مستغرب **mustaghrab**, Wonderful. Foreign. Rare. *Mustaghrab* or *mustaghrib*, A violent laugher. *Mustaghrib*, One who behaves in a strange, outlandish manner. Amazed.

A مستغرق **mustaghraḳ** or *mustaghriḳ*, Immersed, plunged, drowned. *Mustaghriḳ*, Who fills (any thing); comprehends the whole. Who employs his whole strength (about a work). A great laugher. مستغرق فسق و فجور *mustaghriḳi fisḳ u fujūr*, Plunged in vice and debauchery. (See استغراق.)

A مستغزر **mustaghzir**, One who gives somewhat in order to receive more.

A مستغشّ **mustaghishsh**, False, insincere, fraudulent. Who looks on one as such.

A مستغشي **mustaghshī**, One who wraps himself in a garment so as neither to be seen or heard.

A مستغفر **mustaghfir**, One who asks pardon.

A مستغلّ **mustaghall**, A farm or estate which produces corn (غلّة *ghallat*). *Mustaghill*, A receiver of corn or fruits. (See استغلال *istighlāl*.)

A مستغلب **mustaghlib**, (Herbage) full grown and entangled. Prevalent, predominant.

A مستغلظ **mustaghliẓ**, (An ear of corn) swelling with grains. One who declines buying (cloth) on account of (its) coarseness (غلظ *ghilaẓ*).

A مستغلق **mustaghliḳ**, One who makes a close bargain, by selling (any thing) on condition that (it) shall not be returned. Goods sold on these terms. Difficult to be understood, obscure (speech).

A مستغلقة **mustaghlaḳat**, A fortress.

A مستغمد **mustaghmid**, Covered, veiled, overcast.

A مستغني **mustaghnī**, Rich, independent, able to do without: boastful, proud, lofty, haughty, supercilious, disdaining. One who derives advantage. Content, satisfied, acquiescing.

A مستغيث **mustaghīs**, Complainant, plaintiff.

A مستغير **mustaghīr**, A plunderer. Fat. (See استغارة *istighārat*.)

A مستفاد **mustafād**, Benefited. Received, acquired. Understood, meant, intended. Required.

A مستفاض **mustafāẓ**, (or مستفاض فيه *mustafāẓun fīhi*) Diffused, divulged, revealed.

A مستفتر **mustaftir**, Led (horse).

A مستفتي **mustaftī**, A consulter of a مفتي *muftī*: one who demands a فتوي *fatwa'*.

A مستفحل **mustafḥil**, Serious, weighty (affair). (See استفحال *istifḥāl*.)

A مستفخذ **mustafkhiẕ**, Flap-eared. Quiet.

A مستفخر **mustafkhir**, A buyer of (any thing) splendid (فاخر *fākhir*). Proud, vain, conceited.

A مستفرخ **mustafrikh**, A pigeon that chooses a place where to hatch her young (فرخ *farkh*).

A مستفرد **mustafrid**, Alone in doing any thing. (See استفراد *istifrād*.)

A مستفرع **mustafriʻ**, One who commences a work. (See استفراع *istifrāʻ*.)

A مستفرغ **mustafrigh**, An emetic. One who puts forth all his strength.

A مستفرغة **mustafrighat**, (A camel) which yields milk in abundance. (A horse) at full speed.

A مستفرمة **mustafrimat**, (A woman) who uses the constrictive medicament or lotion فرمة *farmat*.

A مستفره **mustafrih**, One who procures an excellent or lively nag (فاره *fārih*).

A مستفزّ **mustafizz**, A despiser, scorner. An eradicator. (See استفزاز *istifzāz*.)

A مستفسر **mustafsir**, In need of explanation.

A مستفصّ **mustafiss**, One who extracts.

A مستفضل **mustafẓil**, Superfluous, redundant. One who leaves a residue. One who exacts of a debt more than what is due, an extortioner.

A مستفظع **mustafẓiʻ**, One who finds (an affair) to be difficult and disagreeable (فظيع *faẓīʻ*).

A مستفقهة **mustafḳihat**, The leader of a band of hired female mourners.

A مستفل **mustafil**, Low, descending.

A مستفلّ **mustafill**, One who takes a little out of a great deal.

A مستفلح **mustafliḥ**, One who escapes.

A مستفلي **mustaflī**, In need of lousing.

A مستفنّ **mustafinn**, One who distributes under various heads, genera, or classes (فنون *funūn*).

A مستفهم **mustafhim**, Desirous to understand.

A مستفيد **mustafīd**, (A student) anxious to profit in any science. Intent on the acquisition of wealth. One who imparts advantage. A gainer.

A مستفيض **mustafīẓ**, One who seeks plenty of water. Diffused, spread abroad. Favoured, obliged.

A مستفيق **mustafīḳ**, Very sleepy (man).

A مستفيه **mustafīh**, Gluttonous; who eats much after fasting.

A مستقبح **mustaḳbaḥ**, Disapproved. Inelegant. Odious. *Mustaḳbiḥ*, One who regards as ugly.

P مستقبل **mustaḳbal**, A figure well delineated.

A مستقبل **mustaḳbil**, One who advances to meet or greet. Future. Future tense of a verb. زمان مستقبل *zamāni mustaḳbil*, Time future.

A مستقبليات **mustaḳbiliyāt**, Future events. Future tenses.

A مستقة **mustaḳat**, (pl. مساتق *masātiḳ*) A fur garment having long sleeves. A bow or any thing similar with which a musical instrument is struck.

A مستقتل **mustaḳtil**, Anxious for, or fearless of, death; seeking to be killed.

A مستقدّ **mustaḳidd**, Continuous, persevering. Even, level. (See استقداد *istiḳdād*.)

A مستقدر **mustaḳdir**, One who beseeches (God) that (he) would providentially arrange (for good).

A مستقدم **mustaḳdim**, Very true, unquestioned. Preceding, going, or desirous of going before. Bold.

A مستقذر **mustaḳẕar**, Dirtied. Regarded as dirty. P جامهٔ مستقذر البطانه *jāmaʼi mustaḳẕaru'l biṭāna*, A garment dirty in the lining or the inside. A *Mustaḳẕir*, Who regards as dirty, or abominates.

A مستقرّ **mustaḳarr**, A permanent dwelling-place, settled abode. *Mustaḳirr*, One who has a fixed residence. Firmly fixed. Rested, reposed.

A مستقرع **mustaḳriʻ**, A borrower of a stallion. (A she-camel or cow) in want of the male. Hard (hoof). Smooth (tripe).

A مستقصّ **mustaḳiss**, Who asks (one) to retaliate. Anxious for retaliation (قصاص *ḳiṣāṣ*).

A مستقصي **mustaḳṣī**, Earnest, pains-taking, persevering. One who commits excess.

A مستقفل **mustaḳfil**, Avaricious.

A مستقلّ **mustaḳill**, (vul. *mustaḳil*) Peculiar, precise, express, special, particular. Absolute, despotic, independent. Competent. Invested with plenipotentiary powers. Stable, firm, durable. A taker up and carrier of the water-pot قلّة *kullat*. High, elevated (sky). Soaring (bird). Trembling, seized by a fever, tremor, or rage. (People) moving from a place, going all away. مستقل ناموس *mustakil nāmūs*, A particular law. مستقلّ مزاج *mustakilli mizāj*, Persevering.

A مستقلاً *mustakilan*, Absolutely, expressly.

A مستقلات *mustakilāt*, Peculiars.

A مستقوس *mustakwis*, Arched (eyebrow).

A مستقى *mustaka'*, A place for drawing water. *Mustakī*, A drawer of water.

A مستقيد *mustakīd*, Obsequious, submissive. A demander of retaliation (قود *kawad*); one who petitions a judge to punish a homicide with death.

A مستقيل *mustakīl*, Desirous that one should rescind (an agreement or bargain).

A مستقيم *mustakīm*, Right, straight. Erect, bolt upright. Faithful, true, loyal. Resolute. Well constituted, having a good tendency. Who marks his goods with the price. مستقيم القامة *mustakīmu'l kāmat*, Of a just proportion, of an erect figure. خط مستقيم *khatti mustakīm*, A right line.

P مستكار *mast-kār*, (or مستكاره *mast-kāra*) Any thing inebriating. One always drunk.

A مستكبر *mustakbir*, Proud, haughty. One who esteems as great and grand (كبير *kabīr*).

A مستكثر *mustaksir*, One who increases.

A مستكرم *mustakrim*, A searcher for, asker, finder, or doer of any thing generous or honourable. One who has attained rank and honours.

A مستكره *mustakrah*, Abominable, disagreeable. *Mustakrih*, Who abominates, detests. Who does any thing unwillingly. (See استكراه *istikrāh*.)

A مستكري *mustakrī*, A hirer, a renter.

A مستكشف *mustakshif*, Desirous of uncovering. Manifest.

A مستكفّ *mustakiff*, Assembled round (any thing) to look at (it). (See استكفاف *istikfāf*.)

A مستكفّات *mustakaffāt*, Fountains. Camels collected together.

A مستكفي *mustakfī*, One who desires (another) to do (a thing) effectually or sufficiently.

A مستكلب *mustaklib*, One who imitates the barking of a dog. (See استكلاب *istiklāb*.)

A مستكلئ *mustaklis*, Very grassy (land). One who begs a respite or delay.

A مستكمل *mustakmil*, A seeker after perfection.

A مستكنّ *mustakinn*, Concealed, covered.

A مستكنّة *mustakinnat*, Hatred, rancour.

A مستكوي *mustakwī*, In need of the cautery.

A مستكير *mustakīr*, One who makes haste. A carrier of a bundle (كارة *kārat*).

A مستكين *mustakīn*, Quiet, humble.

A مستل *mastal*, A narrow road.

A مستلب *mustalab*, Robbed, stripped, spoiled. *Mustalib*, A robber, spoiler. Name of the sword of Amr bin kulsūm.

A مستلبث *mustalbis*, One who thinks, regards as slow or dilatory (لابث *lābis* or لبث *labis*).

A مستلبن *mustalbin*, One who asks milk.

A مستلبئ *mustalbis*, A sucker of biestings.

A مستلجّ *mustalijj*, Obstinate in swearing. (See also استلجاج *istiljāj*.)

A مستلحق *mustalhik*, An adopter, taker. One who invites to union.

A مستلحم *mustalhim*, Broad (way). A follower. A lion. (See استلحام *istilhām*.)

A مستلذّ *mustalizz*, One who relishes.

A مستلزم *mustalzim*, A causer, producer, exacter, demander. Cause, principle, motive; author.

A مستلسم *mustalsim*, A seeker.

A مستلطف *mustaltif*, One who fastens (any thing) on his arm or to his side. (See استلطاف.)

A مستلطم *mustaltim*, Desirous of slapping.

A مستلعب *mustalɛib*, Anxious to play.

A مستلغي *mustalghī*, A listener to words.

A مستلفث *mustalfis*, One who comes to the end, or takes all. (See استلفاث *istilfās*.)

A مستلفج *mustalfaj*, Poor, bankrupt. Sinking and bereft of consciousness through fear. Lean, and cleaving to the ground from weakness.

A مستلقي *mustalkī*, Lying or laid supine.

A مستلهم *mustalhim*, Desirous of revelation.

A مستليح *mustalīh*, A hearer, listener. One who looks narrowly. Thirsty.

A مستلئم *mustalsim*, (A man) who marries into a mean or worthless family. Who has base-born or inglorious (sons-in-law). One who has a wicked (father). Who puts on a coat of mail (لأمة *lasmat*).

A مستليم *mustalīm*, Obnoxious to censure, accused.

A مستمتع *mustamtiɛ*, An enjoyer of fruit or advantage, a usufructuary. One who remains at Mecca and performs the solemnities there, combining حجّ *hajj* and عمرة *ɛumrat*.

A مستمجد *mustamjid*, Who or what contains much: or who wishes and takes much.

A مستمحض *mustamhiz*, One who asks for pure milk without water (محض *mahz*).

A مستمخر *mustamkhir*, One who faces the wind for refreshment.

A مستمخض *mustamkhiz*, (Milk) slow in acquiring the consistency of butter.

A مستمدّ *mustamidd*, A petitioner for aid against an enemy. One who takes a penful of ink.

A مستمرّ *mustamarr*, Firm, steady, lasting, durable. بعيد المستمرّ *baɛīdu'l mustamarr*, Unflinching, unblenching, unwearied in hostility. يوم نحس مستمرّ *yawmu nahsin mustamarrin*, A day of protracted evil fortune. Wednesday at the end of a month. *Mustamirr*, Continuing, persevering, persisting, lasting long. Constant, continual, abiding. Firm, powerful (incantation); or vain and passing away.

A مستمرئ *mustamris*, One who finds (food) wholesome and digestible.

A مستمسك *mustamsik*, One who apprehends seizes, holds fast. One who restrains himself.

A مستمشي *mustamshī*, A taker of a cathartic medicine. Troubled with a flux.

A مستمصل *mustamsil*, Aperient, purgative.

A مستمطر *mustamtar*, A conspicuous place. *Mustamtir*, In need of rain. One who prays for rain One who asks a favour (from a friend). Rained upon. Quiet, silent.

A مستمع *mustamiɛ*, A listener, hearer. مستمع مقال *mustamiɛi makāl*, A listener to words or speeches.

A مستمعا *mustamiɛan*, In order to hear.

A مستمعز *mustamɛiz*, Pains-taking.

A مستمكت *mustamkit*, Purulent (sore).

A مستمكل *mustamkil*, Marrying (man).

A مستمكن *mustamkin*, Firm, keeping his place. Powerful, able.

A مستملّ *mustamill*, Tired, disgusted.

A مستملح *mustamlih*, One who thinks (a thing) beautiful (مليح *malīh*).

A مستملي *mustamlī*, Who desires one to indite.

A مستمنّ *mustaminn*, One who asks a favour.

A مستمنح *mustamnih*, One who begs a gift.

P مستمند *mustmand*, Poor, wretched, miserable, unhappy, afflicted, melancholy, lamentable, plaintive. A poor, unfortunate man. A complainant.

P مستمندانه *mustmandāna*, Wretchedly, like a poor wight: belonging to poverty or distress.

A مستمهل *mustamhil*, Who craves a delay.

A مستمهي *mustamhī*, A breaker of the ranks.

A مستميت *mustamīt*, (A bold man) who exposes (himself) at the risk of his life, who courts death. Over head and ears (in business). A seeker in every way. Fat after having been lean. The white of an egg or pellicle which covers it.

A مستميث *mustamīs*, The white of an egg or a pellicle that covers it.

A مستميح *mustamīh*, One who asks for a gift, or begs intercession (ميح *mayh*).

A مستميز *mustamīz*, Separate, apart.

A مستميق *mustamīk*, Who regards as a fool.

A مستميل *mustamīl*, Very wealthy. Inclined. (See استمالة *istimālat*.)

A مستنّ *mustann*, A lion.

A مستناء *mustanās*, Sued for a gift.

A مستنام *mustanām*, A place where (water) lies.

A مستنبح *mustambih*, Who makes (a dog) bark.

A مستنبط *mustambit*, One who causes to overflow. One who acquires knowledge in the law by ingenuity and study. (See استنباط *istimbāt*.)

A مستنبل *mustambil*, One who asks for arrows. One who takes the best part (of a thing).

A مستنبئ *mustambis*, An inquirer (after news).

A مستنتر *mustantir*, One who pulls forth. One who forces out the last drop.

A مستنتل *mustantil*, One who precedes, goes

before the ranks. Prepared, ready to do.

A مستنتي *mustantī*, Thick, many (pimples).

A مستنسج *mustansij*, Loose, slackened, low-hanging (one side of a camel-load).

A مستنثر *mustansir*, Who draws water up the nostrils. Who sucks or attracts, and then ejects with great vehemence.

A مستنجث *mustanjis*, One who draws out. One who goes up to, meets, or follows.

A مستنجح *mustanjih*, Desirous of success.

A مستنجد *mustanjid*, One who implores help. Strong after weakness. Bold after fear.

A مستنجز *mustanjiz*, Desirous that one should fulfil his promise.

A مستنجع *mustanjiع*, Well, grown fat by meat well digested.

A مستنجل *mustanjil*, Moist, springy (land).

A مستنجي *mustanjī*, One who cuts up a tree by the roots. (See استنجاء *istinjāء*.)

A مستنحس *mustanhis*, One who asks news.

A مستنخب *mustankhib*, A chooser.

A مستنخج *mustankhij*, Soft, flaccid.

A مستند *mustanad*, Supported. A prop. *Mustanid*, One who leans against and supports himself.

A مستندص *mustandis*, One who obtains his right and due.

A مستندة *mustandih*, Right and straight.

A مستنزل *mustanzal*, Removed from office, degraded. A habitation. *Mustanzil*, One who sends or lets down. Who receives hospitably; or places in an inn or caravansera (منزل *manzil*).

A مستنسب *mustansib*, One who mentions the pedigree of any one. (See استنساب *istinsāb*.)

A مستنسخ *mustansikh*, A transcriber.

A مستنسر *mustansir*, Vulturish, vulturine.

A مستنسئ *mustansiء*, One who craves a delay for payment of a debt, or asks for sale on credit.

A مستنشأ *mustanshaء*, Hoisted (standard); erect (cairn or heap of stones to shew the road).

A مستنشد *mustanshid*, One who requests (another) to repeat verses or a poem.

A مستنشط *mustanshit*, Shrivelled (skin or hide).

A مستنشق *mustanshik*, One who snuffs up water.

A مستنشئ *mustanshiء*, A smeller, one who perceives by the smell. An inquirer (after news).

A مستنشي *mustanshī*, Sweetly scented. Drunk.

A مستنشئة *mustanshiءat*, A priestess; she-augur.

A مستنصت *mustansit*, Anxious for silence.

A مستنصح *mustansih*, Desirous of obtaining advice; a consulter. One who considers as a faithful admonisher (ناصح *nāsih*).

A مستنصر *mustansir*, One who asks aid.

A مستنصف *mustansif*, One who receives from another payment of a debt or what is due, both parties then remaining equal or quits.

A مستنصل *mustansil*, A drawer out, a producer. (Heat) which causes (the down of the thistle) to fall off. (See استنصال *istinsāl*.)

A مستنضض *mustanizz*, One who asks a favour.

A مستنطق *mustantik*, Engaged in conversation. (God) making rational, the bestower of the gift of speech. Desirous of speaking.

A مستنظر *mustanzir*, One who craves delay.

A مستنعت *mustanعit*, Who requests one to describe or distinguish by an epithet (نعت *naعt*).

A مستنفج *mustanfij*, Who or what excites wrath, or elicits displeasure.

A مستنفد *mustanfid*, An exhauster, evacuator. One who wastes his strength.

A مستنفر *mustanfar* or *mustanfir*, Frightened, flying (ass). (See استنفار *istinfār*.)

A مستنفض *mustanfiz*, One who pries in every nook and corner. (See استنفاض *istinfāz*.)

A مستنفق *mustanfik*, One who expends, lays out.

A مستنفه *mustanfih*, Reposed, rested.

A مستنقذ *mustankiz*, A rescuer, deliverer.

A مستنقش *mustankish*, A painter, a limner.

A مستنقص *mustankis*, (A purchaser) anxious to lower the price of an article.

A مستنقع *mustankaع*, (A place) where ablutions are made. (A place) where water stagnates. An udder which at milking-time is empty, and at other times full. Changed (colour). Soaked, dissolved (in water). Stagnant (water). *Mustankiع*, Stagnate (water). Become yellow (water in the body). Elevated (voice). On the point of going out (the last breath). (See استنقاع *istinkāع*.)

A مستنقه *mustankih*, One who perceives and understands. A seeker, inquirer, querist.

A مستنكح *mustankih*, One who marries. One who lies with.

A مستنكر *mustankar*, Ignored: disallowed, disapproved of. Disagreeable, displeasing. *Mustankir*, One who ignores, denies, disowns, disavows. Who inquires (of another) that which he does not know.

A مستنكف *mustankif*, Ashamed, indignant. Proud, haughty. (See استنكاف *istinkāf*.)

A مستنكه *mustankih*, One who desires (another) to breathe, in order to discover by the smell whether he has drank wine.

A مستنوق *mustanwik*, A plagiarist.

A مستنوك *mustanwik*, Foolish, stupid.

A مستنهج *mustanhij*, A follower of the steps of another. (A highway) made open, clear.

A مستنهر *mustanhir*, Flowing freely, widely spread, diffused. One who directs the course (of a river) through solid ground. A reprover.

A مستنهض *mustanhiz*, A rouser, an exciter, one who bids (another) rise to do (any thing).

A مستنئ *mustaniء*, Setting (star).

A مستنيح *mustanīh*, A wailer. A howler.

A مستنير *mustanīr*, Shining, glancing, sparkling. One who seeks for light. Who terrifies, and causes to run or flee. A conqueror, overcomer.

A مستنيس *mustanīs*, One who remains behind. A despiser. (See استناصة *istināsat*.)

A مستنيع *mustaniع*, One who precedes or takes the lead. Waving (branch).

A مستنيم *mustanīm*, A sleeper. One who pretends to be asleep. Who rests, acquiesces, trusts to.

P مستو *mastū*, A reptile. One who makes acknowledgment.

A مستوبد *mustawbid*, One who finds it hard to live, pinched with want. Unacquainted with a place.

A مستوبق *mustawbik*, Perishing.

A مستوبل *mustawbil*, Heavy, unwholesome (air or meat). One who discovers or who fancies (a country) to be unhealthy.

A مستوبئ *mustawbiء*, One who finds (a country) pestilential, infected, and unhealthy.

A مستوثر *mustawsir*, Who asks much (of any thing). Filled with admiration.

A مستوثق *mustawsik*, One who takes a bond or agreement (وثيقه *wasīka*). Solid, firm, steady, constant. Established, confirmed (authority).

A مستوثن *mustawsin*, Fat. (See استيثان.)

A مستوجب *mustawjib*, Who makes or judges to be necessary. One who condemns to death. Meriting, proper, worthy of. An author, cause, motive. مستوجب الثواب *mustawjibu's sawāb*, Deserving reward, meritorious. صلح و صلاح مستوجب الفلاح *sulh u salāhi mustawjibu'l falāh*, Peace and tranquillity, increasing prosperity. مستوجب السرور *mustawjibu's surūr*, Glad, rejoicing, giving joy.

A مستوجف *mustawjif*, Maddening (love).

A مستوحش *mustawhish*, Desert, desolate, dreary (place). Afflicted.

A مستوحل *mustawhil*, (A place) clayey or muddy.

A مستوخم *mustawkhim*, Heavy and unwholesome (climate or food).

A مستوخي *mustawkhī*, Who asks news.

A مستودع *mustawdaع*, Deposited, committed, commended. A person with whom, or a place where, any thing is intrusted or deposited. المستودع *al mustawdaع*, That part of Paradise where Adam and Eve were placed. The womb. The grave. *Mustawdiع*, Who desires any one to preserve any thing committed to his care. One who commits or recommends.

A مستودق *mustawdik*, (A mare) a horsing.

A مستودي *mustawdī*, (A man) who acknowledges (what he owes).

A مستور *mastūr*, Covered, concealed, hid, veiled. Whatever covers or veils. Good, honest, abstaining from what is unlawful. P مستور شدن *mastūr shudan*, To lie hid, be veiled, abscond, disappear, be suppressed.

A مستورة *mastūrat*, A chaste matron. تاج المستورات *tāju'l mastūrāt*, The crown of ladies or matrons (a title often given to sultanas or princesses).

A مستورخ *mustawrikh*, Wet (ground).

A مستورد *mustawrid*, Present, drawn near, at

hand, standing before. A bringer.

A مستورط *mustawrit*, Got into difficulty.

A مستوري *mastūrī*, Modesty.

A مستوري *mustawrī*, A striker of fire from steel.

A مستوزر *mustawzir*, Who chooses (any one) as a vizier or counsellor. Who carries away (any thing). (See استيزار *istīzār*.)

A مستوزع *mustawziʻ*, One who beseeches (God) to inspire (a person with any sentiment).

A مستوزي *mustawzī*, Self-opiniated. Erect.

A مستوسخ *mustawsikh*, Nasty, dirty.

A مستوسع *mustawsiʻ*, Broad, wide, ample.

A مستوسق *mustawsiḳ*, Assembled (camels).

A مستوسن *mustawsin*, Drowsy, sleepy, comatose.

A مستوشرة *mustawshirat*, (A woman) who asks that her teeth may be sharpened.

A مستوشع *mustawshiʻ*, A drawer of water.

A مستوشم *mustawshim*, Desirous that one should prick figures on your hand or other part of the body with a needle, in order to rub the punctures over with woad, indigo, or other colour.

A مستوشي *mustawshī*, One who touches a horse with his heel that he may quicken his pace. (See استيشاء *istīshāʼ*.)

A مستوصف *mustawsif*, One who asks for a medical prescription (وصف *wasf*).

A مستوصل *mustawsil*, Desirous of joining.

A مستوصلة *mustawsilat*, A woman who requests that another's hair may be added to eke out her own.

A مستوصي *mustawsī*, One who receives a charge, command, last will, or testament (وصيّة *wasiyat*).

A مستوضح *mustawziḥ*, Desirous that one should make any thing evident. One who endeavours to discover any thing distinctly, by holding the hand over the eyes to keep off the glare of light. An explainer, narrator.

A مستوضع *mustawziʻ*, Desirous of having (any thing) lowered (in price).

A مستوضم *mustawzim*, Injurious, hurtful.

A مستوطن *mustawtan*, A settled abode. *Mustawtin*, Accustomed to a place, naturalized.

A مستوطئ *mustawtiʼ*, One who finds any thing soft, agreeable, easy, convenient.

A مستوظف *mustawzif*, Who takes the whole.

A مستوعب *mustawʻib*, A taker (of the whole). One who cuts off almost the whole nose.

A مستوعر *mustawʻir*, One who finds or thinks (a way) rugged and difficult (وعر *waʻr*).

A مستوعل *mustawʻal*, A refuge on a rock to which the mountain-goat (وعل *waʻil*) repairs.

A مستوعي *mustawʻī*, Who cuts up by the root. A taker of the whole.

A مستوغل *mustawghil*, A washer of the arm-pit. One who washes his groins.

A مستوفد *mustawfid*, Seated on the ends of his toes. (See مستوفز *mustawfiz*.)

A مستوفر *mustawfir*, A taker or a payer of the whole or a deal of what is due.

A مستوفز *mustawfiz*, Seated on the toes, in a crouching attitude, ready to spring up. On the watch, prepared to take advantage.

A مستوفض *mustawfiz*, One who goes quick, runs, make haste. Who causes to make haste or drives up. One who sends (another) abroad, or who banishes. Scattered (camels).

A مستوفق *mustawfiḳ*, One who beseeches (God) to be propitious; and wishes to be directed by him. A director. A bringer of assistance.

P مستوفي *mustawfī*, The principal officer of a detachment. An examiner, auditor of accounts.

A مستوفي *mustawfī*, Many, much. A receiver of the whole of a thing due; a payer of the whole.

P مستوفي‌گري *mustawfīgarī*, Clerkship, audit.

A مستوقح *mustawḳiḥ*, Hard, callous.

A مستوقد *mustawḳad*, A fire-place or hearth. *Mustawḳid*, A kindler (of fire). Kindled.

A مستوقر *mustawḳir*, A receiver (of the produce of a palm-tree for food). Fattened (camel).

A مستوقع *mustawḳiʻ*, An expectant; held in expectation by hopes. (A sword) in need of sharpening.

A مستوقف *mustawḳif*, A stander. Who desires one to stand; also to stop or restrain another.

A مستوقه *mustawḳih*, Obedient, submissive.

A مستوكث *mustawkis*, One who breakfasts.

A مستوكح *mustawkiḥ*, Close-fisted, disinclined to give. Fat, thick (young bird).

A مستوكع *mustawkiʻ*, Well-sewed, water-proof, not leaky (leathern bottle). Strong (stomach).

A مستوكف *mustawkif*, One who lets the water fall in drops when making his ablutions.

A مستوكي *mustawkī*, Waxen fat. Full (leathern bottle). Costive, constipated.

A مستول *mastūl*, Shaven on the head. Stripped of flesh.

A مستولخ *mustawlikh*, Moist, wet (ground).

A مستولغ *mustawligh*, Careless about disgrace or reproof.

A مستولي *mustawlī*, One who overcomes, subdues, takes possession of, or surmounts. Powerful, predominant, paramount.

A مستوهب *mustawhib*, One who asks a gift.

A مستوهر *mustawhir*, Sure of (a thing), having examined (it) thoroughly. Mad, silly. Affrighted.

A مستوهل *mustawhal*, Timid. Weak, languid. *Mustawhil*, Timid.

A مستوي *mustawaʼ*, The common gender. A level spot. *Mustawī*, Equal, straight, direct, even, level. Completed, finished. Moderate. Ripe, mature, of full intellect. Temperate. On the top or summit. Who ascends (to heaven). Seated firmly on horseback. Conspicuous, apparent. Prevailing over. A possessor.

A مستويا *mustawiyan*, Equally, directly.

P مستة *musta*, Food given to hunting birds. Force, oppression. Grief, sadness. Name of a medicinal herb. *Masituh*, Do not dispute.

A مستة *mustih*, Large-buttocked (man).

A مستهام *mustahām*, Astonished, distracted, unsteady (mind). Insane from love.

A مستهان *mustahān*, Despised, abject, base.

A مستهتر *mustahtar*, Given to wine, and unconcerned about aught beside. Absorbed in frivolous pursuits, indifferent to the opinion of others; mad.

A مستهتك *mustahtik*, Regardless of any slur cast upon one's character.

A مستهجن *mustahjan*, Corrupt, mongrel. *Mustahjin*, One who regards as ugly and base.

A مستهدج *mustahdaj*, Haste, a making haste. *Mustahdij*, Quick, hasty.

A مستهدف *mustahdaf*, High, raised (pubes). *Mustahdif*, Elevated, erect (thing); high (target); prominent (buttocks). Broad (pillar).

A مستهدي *mustahdī*, Who seeks direction.

A مستهزئ *mustahziʼ*, A sneerer, scoffer, mocker.

A مستهش *mustahishsh*, A despiser. One who regards as light, nimble, or active.

A مستهضب *mustahzib*, Dry (ewe).

A مستهطع *mustahtiʻ*, One who stretches the neck straight out and lowers the head.

A مستهكم *mustahkim*, Proud, domineering.

A مستهل *mustahall*, Visible (new moon). *Mustahill*, Visible (new moon). Very rainy (cloud or sky). Squalling, crying (new-born infant). (A speaker) who raises or lowers his voice. One who draws a (sword). Cheerful, bright (countenance).

A مستهلك *mustahlik*, Ruinous, destructive. A consumer, squanderer (of money).

A مستهمّ *mustahimm*, Sorrowful. Solicitous anxious about the concerns of others.

A مستهنع *mustahniʻ*, Unable to reply.

A مستهنئ *mustahniʼ*, One who begs assistance. One who asks for a present.

A مستهيث *mustahīs*, One who abounds, who does much. A doer of mischief.

P مستي *mastī*, Drunkenness, intoxication. Wantonness, lust. The rutting season. Pride.

A مستيسر *mustaysir*, Easy, quick, expeditious; prepared, well disposed, arranged.

A مستيقظ *mustayḳiz*, Watchful, awake. Vigilant, provident. Rattling, jingling (necklace).

A مستيقن *mustayḳin*, One who knows for certain, sure of; who searches into, and explores.

A مستيمن *mustaymin*, Prosperous, acting or happening fortunately. Who adjures, desires, or causes another to take an oath (يمين *yamīn*).

P مستيمند *mustīmand*, Fettered. Name of a place in India whence salt is brought.

A مستيهر *mustayhir*, One who sticks to, perseveres in. An examiner, explorer. A barterer. One who knows for certain. Alarmed, stupefied.

A مستيئس *mustayʼis*, Despairing, desperate.

A مسجّة *misajjat*, A plasterer's wooden trowel.

A مسجح *musjih*, One who forgives, acquits.

A مسجد *masjad*, (pl. مساجد *masājid*) That part of the forehead which touches the ground in the adoration called سجده *sajda*. *Masjid* or *masjad*, (pl. مساجد *masājid*) A mosque, temple, place of worship. مسجد جامع *masjidi jāmiʻ*, (or simply جامع *jāmiʻ*) The great or general mosque, where prayers are said every Friday. المسجد الحرام *al masjidu'l harām*, (or مسجد شريف *masjidi sharīf*) The temple of Mecca. المسجد الاقصى *al masjidu'l akṣa'*, The temple of Jerusalem, or the Turkish mosque there. مسجد الخيف *masjidu'l khayf*, A shrine in the valley of Mina near Mecca.

A المسجدان *al masjidāni*, (du.) The two mosques, *i.e.* of Mecca and Madina.

A مسجر *misjar*, Chips for lighting an oven.

A مسجّر *musajjar*, Set loose, flowing (hair).

A مسجع *masjaʻ*, Intent, aim, design. A place of destination, whither one tends. Middle of the road.

A مسجّع *musajjaʻ*, Rhythmical prose. *Musajjiʻ*, One who speaks in rhythmical prose. (The Arabians consider it as a great beauty in oratory to make their periods similar in rhyme and cadence.)

A مسجف *musjif*, Dark (night). *Musjif*, (or مسجّف *musajjif*) One who lets drop (a curtain).

A مسجل *musjal*, Free, or permitted to all. (A time) when no one stood in fear of another.

A مسجّل *musajjal*, Proved, authenticated, and sealed by a judge. *Musajjil*, (A judge) who sets his hand and seal to any sentence or decision.

A مسجوح *masjūh*, Nature. Side, face, surface.

A مسجوحة *masjūhat*, Nature.

A مسجود *masjūd*, Adored, worshipped.

A مسجور *masjūr*, Swollen. The sea. (Pearls) threaded together in rows, and hanging equally down. Kindled, burning. Quiet, extinct. Milk diluted with water, the latter prevailing. بحر مسجور *bahr masjūr*, A swelling sea. The celestial waters.

A مسجوم *masjūm*, A she-camel that straddles when milked, and carries her head high. Flowing (tears, or the like).

A مسجومة *masjūmat*, (Land) watered by rain.

A مسجون *masjūn*, Imprisoned, incarcerated.

A مسجهرّ *musjahirr*, Shiny (water-cloud). White.

A مسجّي *musajji*, One who covers (a dead body) with a garment.

A مسجرّ *musjaʻirr*, Hard.

A مسح *mas-h*, (v. n. of مسح) Wiping. Drawing the hand over the surface of any liquid, or over the head, in order to wipe it. Handling, stroking, rubbing. Anointing. Cutting off. Striking. Being chafed (the thighs). Flattering, cajoling. Measuring (ground). Making (a camel) do his day's work; tiring (him), galling (his) back and emaciating (him). (God) creating any thing agreeable or beautiful; any thing deformed or hateful. A lie. مسح الرأس *mas-hu'r ra's*, A wiping of the head. مسح الرقبة *mas-hu'r rakabat*, A wiping of the neck (rites observed by the Muhammadans before engaging in prayer). مسح اللحي *mas-hu'l luha'*, A stroking of the beard (a practice among the Arabs on a reconciliation taking place). *Mis-h*, (pl. مسوح *musūh* and امساح *amsāh*) A coarse cloth of hair or wool, of which they make saddle-cloths for beasts of burden. A hair-cloth, sackcloth. The middle of a road. A highway. *Masah*, (v. n. of مسح) Hurting the hams by the friction of coarse raiment. The friction of the inside of the thighs.

A مسحّ *misahh*, (A horse) at full gallop. *Musihh*, Hard and dry (dates).

A مسحاء *mas-hāʼ*, (fem. of امسح *amsah*) (A woman) whose legs and hips are small, whose breasts are flat, and the sole of whose foot is even (not concave). Blind of an eye. Wandering, strolling, lying (female). Galled in the hams by the friction of a coarse garment. Red (earth). Lean (ground). (A place) level and covered with small gravel, where no plants grow.

A مسحاة *mis-hāt*, (pl. مساحي *masāhī*) A shovel, a spade, especially of iron.

A مسحاج *mis-hāj*, An ass running under full speed. A woman who swears much and breaks her oath.

A مسحة *mas-hat*, A little, somewhat. A way, path. *Mus-hat*, One unction.

A مسحت *mus-hat*, Riches dissipated. *Mus-hit*, A destroyer, extirpator. A gainer by injustice.

A مسحج *mis-haj*, An ass running below full speed. An ass that bites much. A file or rasp.

A مسحّج *musahhaj*, (An ass) bitten and excoriated by other asses.

A مسحّر *musahhar*, Fascinated, enchanted, amused, deluded by witchcraft. Endued with lungs or lights. In need of meat and drink. Hollowed, hollow.

A مسحسحة *musahsihat*, (A stab) which causes much blood to flow.

A مسحط *mas-hat*, (v. n. of سحط) Slaughtering expeditiously. Turning a lamb loose with its dam. Diluting (wine with water). Choking any one (food). The throat.

A مسحف *mas-haf*, A snake's track on the ground.

A مسحفة *mis-hafat*, An instrument by which the flesh is stripped from off the bone.

A مسحل *mis-hal*, A file. A plane. An eloquent orator. The tongue. A bridle, bit. A wild ass, onager. A ring on either side of a bridle-bit. Excessive liberality. A public whipper or executioner. A smart, active cup-bearer. A sieve. The mouth of a large water-bottle or wallet. Versed in the Kur'ān. A clean cotton garment. Intrepid, enterprising. One who does any thing alone. An aqueduct or spout from which the water rushes furiously. A bold resolution. A rope of a single twist. Heavy rain. A man's cheek. ركب مسحله *rakiba mis-halahu*, He spoke diffusively, readily, or eloquently. He followed his own erroneous courses.

A مسحلان *mis-halāni*, (dual) Two little rings about the bit or snaffle of a bridle. *Mus-hulān*, (or مسحلاني *mus-hulāniy*) Tall (youth), with long and lanky locks.

A مسحن *mus-hin*, (A horse) finely-shaped, in good condition, beautiful.

A مسحنة *mis-hanat*, An instrument with which any fragrant substance is brayed or stones broken.

A مسحنفر *mus-hanfir*, Wide, spacious, open (town). Intelligent, skilful (man). Straight (road).

A مسحنكك *mus-hankik* or *kak*, Jetty (hair).

A مسحوب *mas-hūb*, Dragged, drawn, trailed.

A مسحوت *mas-hūt*, (Riches) squandered away. مسحوت الجوف *mas-hūtu'l jawf*, Of an insatiable appetite. Oppressed with indigestion. Large-paunched.

A مسحور *mas-hūr*, Bewitched, enchanted, fascinated. Unwholesome (food). (A place) noxious by reason of excess of rain or scarcity of forage.

A مسحوط *mas-hūt*, (Wine) diluted with water.

A مسحوف *mas-hūf*, Consumptive (man).

A مسحوق *mas-hūk*, Brayed, bruised.

A مسحوقونيا *mas-hūkūniyā*, Dross of glass.

A مسحول *mas-hūl*, Small and contemptible. Even and spacious (place). Name of a camel.

A مسخ *muskh*, (v. n. of مسخ) Changing, metamorphosing into a more deformed shape (especially men into apes). Emaciating, galling (a camel's back) by excessive labour. Adopting the thoughts of any other, but changing some of his words: plagiarism. Rendering insipid. Ugly, mis-shapen, changed into a meaner form, metamorphosed.

A مسخاة *miskhāt*, A poker, any thing for stirring the fire. Chips, fuel.

A مسخّد *musakhkhad*, Pale, sallow, heavy, obtuse (man). Of a full and puffed habit of body.

A مسخر *mashkhar*, (v. n. of سخر) Ridiculing.

A مسخّر *musakhkhar*, Taken, subdued, conquered. *Musakhkhir*, One who compels to work for nothing, guilty of angariation. A taker (of a town). A subduer, breaker in.

A مسخرة *mashkharat*, A buffoon, fool, jester, droll, wag, facetious fellow. A man in masquerade. A pleasantry, any thing ridiculous or mirthful; sport.

P مسخره كردن *mashkhara kardan*, To ridicule or deride; to play the buffoon, to laugh at others; also to be laughed at.

P مسخرگي *mashkhargi*, Jest, buffoonery, fun.

A مسخّرين *musakhkhrīn*, (in Morocco) The bearers of the emperor's mandates from place to place.

A مسخط *mashkhat*, (v. n. of سخط) Waxing wroth, being angry. Indignation, fury, displeasure.

A مسخفة *mushkhifat*, (Ground) thin of herbage.

P مسخ كرده *maskh-karda*, Metamorphosed into a vile shape.

A مسخّم *musakhkham*, Filled with hatred.

A مسخن *muskhan*, Heated, hot (water).

A مسخّن *musakhkhan*, Hot, heated (water). *Musakhkhin*, Heating, calefactory, calefacient.

A مسخنة *miskhanat*, Cauldron, copper, boiler.

A مسخوت *maskhūt*, Smooth, bald, bare, shiny.

A مسخوط *maskhūt*, Transformed, metamorphosed. Hateful, disagreeable, odious. Incensed. مسخوط و مغضوب *maskhūt u maghzūb*, Odious (to God).

A مسخول *maskhūl*, Discarded, reprobated. Low. Weak. Unknown (star).

A مسخيّة *miskhiyat*, A sort of carpet.

A مسد *masd*, (v. n. of مسد) Twisting (a rope) well. Persevering, prosecuting diligently a journey. Tiring, wearying. حسنة المسد *hasanatu'l masd*, (A girl) well formed by nature. *Masad*, (pl. مساد *misād* or امساد *amsād*) The fibrous bark of the palm-tree; a rope made of it, or of any other substance firmly twisted. An iron axis.

A مسدّ *masadd*, A chink, hole. Name of a garden. *Musidd*, One who hits the nail on the head, who attains any end. One who acts rightly, or speaks reasonably.

A مسداة *misdāt*, An instrument or loom whereon a weaver stretches the warp.

A مسدّد *musaddad*, Well directed; rectified. One whose affairs are managed with judgment and success. *Musaddid*, One who directs properly. Who points (a spear) well.

A مسدّس *musaddas*, Composed of six. Verse consisting of six lines. Six-sided, hexagonal. Cubic. A cube, hexagon. مسدّس عالم *musaddasi ʿālam*, The six sides of the world, viz. up and down, fore and aft, right and left.

A مسدع *misdaʿ*, One who goes where he pleases. A road-guide.

A مسدّم *musaddam*, (A camel) allowed to range at liberty. Libidinous (stallion). (A stallion) muzzled to prevent his biting. Wide-spreading, diffused (water).

A مسدوح *masdūh*, Supine. Laid on the face.

A مسدود *masdūd*, Shut, closed, corked, plugged.

A مسدوم *masdūm*, Libidinous (stallion).

A مسدي *musda'*, (or مسدّي *musadda'*) (Cloth) fitted to the loom, stretched upon the warp.

A مسر *masr*, (v. n. of مسر) Drawing out, extricating from difficulties. Accusing, impeaching (people), or setting (them) together by the ears.

P مسر *masar*, Ice.

A مسرّ *musirr*, A concealer, hider, one who keeps private. A divulger, publisher.

A مسرأة *masraʾat*, Land full of locusts.

A مسراع *misrāʿ*, Very swift for good or evil.

A مسربة *masrabat*, (pl. مسارب *masārib*) A meadow, pasture. *Masrabat* or *musrabat*, The ring of the anus. A veranda or portico. *Masrubat*, Fine or soft hairs stretching from the breast to the navel.

A مسربخ *musarbakh*, Distant, remote.

A مسربطة *musarbatat*, A melon slender and long.

A مسرة *misrat*, An instrument (volume or roll) in which any secrets are contained.

A مسرّة *masarrat*, (v. n. of سرّ) Being cheerful. Making glad. Cheerfulness, gladness, joy. Briskness, liveliness, happiness. The extremities of odoriferous herbs. *Misarrat*, (pl. مسارّ *masārr*) A whispering-trumpet.

A مسرّج *musarraj*, Saddled (horse). Combed.

A مسرجة *masrajat* or *musrajat*, A lamp, a vessel holding oil and a wick.

A مسرح *masrah*, (pl. مسارح *masārih*) A wide pasture, pasturage. *Misrah*, A comb.

A مسرد *misrad*, A saddler's awl or needle.

A مسرّد *musarrad*, (Leather) strengthened by sewing. Woven (coat of mail). Stitched (leather).

A مسردبيّة *musardabīyat*, (from P سرداب *sardāb*) An ice-house: a place for keeping water cool.

A مسردح *musardah*, Turned loose, allowed to go where one likes.

A مسردق *musardak*, (A house) surrounded by the curtain سرادق *surādik*: (a tent) so screened.

A مسرّس *musarras*, Intricate, difficult to decipher. Compactly-bound (book).

A مسرط *masrat* or *misrat*, The gullet.

A مسرع *misraʿ*, Swift to do evil or good. *Musriʿ*, Quick, swift, nimble, expeditious.

A مسرف *musrif*, Extravagant, profuse, lavish.

A مسرق *musrih*, Short-necked.

A مسرمط *musarmat*, Long-bodied (camel).

A مسروّ *masruʾ*, Abounding in locusts' eggs.

A مسروّ *masrūw*, Overspread with small locusts.

A مسروب *masrūb*, Affected by tightness at the chest from inhaling the fumes of silver.

A مسروح *masrūh*, The vapour سراب *sarāb*.

P مسرود *masrūd*, An invocation. An incantation, fascination.

A مسرود *masrūd*, (Leather) strengthened by sewing. Perforated. Stitched. Woven (coat of mail).

A مسرور *masrūr*, Glad, joyful, cheerful, exulting, gay, happy. One whose navel-string is cut. Name of the headsman of the caliph Hārūn Ar rashīd.

A مسروف *masrūf*, Worm-eaten (timber).

A مسروق *masrūk*, Stolen, robbed. Surreptitious.

A مسرول *musarwal*, (A pied-horse) white-legged to the knees and houghs (dressed in stockings).

A مسرولة *musarwalat*, (A dove) plumaged about the legs and feet.

A مسرهج *musarhaj*, Firmly-twisted (rope).

P مسرهٔ چرخ *masirasi charkh*, The moon.

A مسرهد *musarhad*, Fat (camel's bunch).

A مسري *masra'*, (v. n. of سري) Travelling by night. The nocturnal journey to heaven said to have been made by Muhammad.

A مسط *mast*, (v. n. of مسط) Wringing (wet cloth). Striking with a scourge. Squeezing with the hand a leathern bottle, or the intestines, in order to force out their contents. Thrusting the hand into the matrix of a camel to extract the seed deposited there by a sorry sire. Purging, moving the bowels.

A مسطار *mistār* or *mustār*, New, also sour wine; heady wine. Raised (dust).

A مسطبة *mastabat* or *mistabat*, (pl. مساطب *masātib*) A long and wide bench, or rather a stone platform, raised two or three feet above the ground, on which the Orientals recline. A smith's anvil.

A مسطح *mistah*, An open place on a plain where corn or dates are dried. The pillar, pole, or other wooden work of a tent. A broad piece of wood fixed on a vine-prop. A large smooth stone surrounded by other stones in order to collect water. A baker's rolling-pin. A bread-plate or basket. A mat made of palm-leaves. A large frying-pan in which wheat is toasted. A traveller's water-pot.

A مسطّح *musattah*, Superficial; levelled (ground); level, even. An open plain. Broad, flat (nose). مسطّح الاوّل *musattahu'l awwal*, (and مسطّح الثاني *musattahu's sānī*) First term and second term (in mathematics). *Musattih*, Who equals or makes level.

A مسطر *mistar*, (pl. مساطر *masātir*) A geometrical rule by which right lines are drawn, a ruler. Parallel threads strained on a piece of pasteboard, used by those who copy manuscripts for ruling lines.

A مسطّر *musattar*, Written; a writing. *Musattir*, A writer; amanuensis. Appointed, delegated. Despotic, absolute.

A مسطع *mistaʿ*, Eloquent.

A مسطّع *musattaʿ*, (A camel) marked on the neck with an oblong figure.

A مسطّن *musattan*, Firmly-planted (column).

A مسطوح *mastūh*, Stretched supine. Killed.

A مسطور *mastūr*, Written, described, specified.

A مسطوع *mastūʿ*, Raised (dust). Diffused (odour). Spread (dawn).

A مسع *misʿ*, The north wind.

A مسعاة *masʿāt*, (pl. مساعي *masāʿī*) Study, pains. A laudable endeavour or act. Greatness, nobility, the ne plus ultra of glory and nobility.

A مسعار *misʿār*, (pl. مساعير *masāʿīr*) A poker, piece of wood with which fire is stirred. One who stirs up strife, a breedbate.

A مسعام *misʿām*, (or مسعامّ *musʿāmm*) Rapid (current of water).

A مسعّب *musaʿʿab*, Permitted, allowed; lawful.

A مسعد *musʿad*, Happy. Propitious. August. (This form is not admitted by the best authorities).

A مسعر *masʿar*, The thinnest part of a camel's tail. *Misʿar*, A poker with which the fire is stirred. A horse that throws his legs out wide, and is restless and impatient. Long (neck). Strong, vehement. مسعر الحرب *misʿaru'l harb*, A raiser of war, seditious man. *Musʿar*, Fixed, estimated, rated. *Musʿir*, One who stirs up war. *Musʿur*, The thinnest part of a camel's tail.

A مسعر musaʻʻir, A judge or administrator.

A مسعط musʻut or misʻat, An instrument by which sternutatives are injected. A snuff-box.

A مسعل masʻal, The throat; where one coughs.

A مسعن musaʻʻan, A big double-skin bucket.

A مسعود masʻūd, Happy, fortunate, rendered fortunate, prosperous, blessed; favourable; august.

A مسعودي masʻūdī, Happiness, prosperity.

A مسعور masʻūr, Scorched by the blast سموم samūm. Furious. Thirsty. Greedy of meat, although the belly be filled.

A مسعوع masʻūʻ, Mildewed, smutty (wheat).

A مسعوف masʻūf, (An infant) ulcerated on the head or face.

A مسعيّ masʻiy, A man who walks much, going here and there. Strong, indefatigable.

A مسغب musghib, Hungry.

A مسغّب musghabb, (or مسغّب musaghghab) Allowed, permitted.

A مسغبة masghabat, A being hungry. Hunger.

A مسغبل musaghbal, Easy (thing).

A مسغد musghad, (A camel's colt) filled with milk and fat.

A مسغم musaghgham, (or مسغم musgham) Well fed. A youth tenderly brought up, delicate, in a good habit of body.

A مسغوم masghūm, Well fed and plump (boy).

A مسف musaff, Changed (colour). Musiff, A weaver of mats from palm-leaves. Attentive to minute details. (See اسفاف isfāf.)

A مسفّح musaffih, One who does a thing that yields him no advantage.

A مسفر misfar, (A camel) strong for travelling. One who travels much.

A مسفرة misfarat, A besom, broom, brush. Musfirat, Red (she-camel).

A مسفّرة musaffarat, A clew or ball of thread.

A مسفسف musafsaf, Fine, sifted (flour). Musafsif, Mean, avaricious, a small giver. (Wind) which sweeps the ground and scatters the finer dust.

A مسفّط الرأس musaffatu'r ras, One whose head is shaped like the casket or box سفط safat.

A مسفك misfak, Talkative, verbose.

A مسفن misfan, A hatchet, axe, or planing-instrument. A spade or implement with which they rake over ground which has been sowed.

A مسفوح masfūh, Poured out. (A camel) sent forth. Extended, drawn forth. Ample, spacious. Coarse, thick.

A مسفور masfūr, Above-mentioned, specified.

A مسفوع masfūʻ, One whose eye is sunk in the socket. Viewed with a malignant eye.

A مسفوك masfūk, Shed, spilled (blood).

A مسفه musfah, (A channel or valley) full of water. Musfih, Tiresome (food) which obliges one to drink much. (See اسفاه isfāh).

A مسفّه musaffih, One who calls another a fool.

A مسفي musfī, A calumniator, tale-bearer. (Wind) which carries away the dust.

A مسقاب mishāb, A camel accustomed to bring forth males (سقب sakb).

A مسقاة mashāt or mishāt, A place or vessel from which a bird drinks. The part of the belly where water in dropsy collects. Mishāt, An utensil out of which water is poured or any thing is sprinkled.

A مسقار mishār, A date-tree whose juice flows.

A مسقاط mishāt, Accustomed to cast her young.

A مسقام miskām, Often sick, infirm, ailing.

A مسقب mishab, A camel that has brought forth a male (سقب sakb). Mushib, Near.

A مسقسق musaksik, One who ascends a tripos and recites verses alternately with another.

A مسقط maskat, (v. n. of سقط) Falling. The lower part of a tent or bird's wing. A place where sands break off. Mascat in Arabia. Maskat or maskit, A place, especially where any thing falls. مسقط الرأس maskitu'r ras, A native country (where one falls at birth). Muskit, A dam which casts her young. Who or what causes to fall, lowers, abases, debases; dishonouring, degrading.

A مسقطة maskatat, (v. n. of سقط) Falling. A patron, asylum, protection, refuge. Any act by which one is lowered in public estimation. A place where a sand-hill breaks off.

A مسقع miskaʻ, Eloquent, high-voiced.

A مسقّف musakkaf, Roofed, floored. Long, tall.

A مسقفف muskafiff, (Hair) dirty and staring.

A مسقم muskim, Who or what makes sick.

A مسقوط maskūt, Fallen (date).

A مسقوم maskūm, Sick.

A مسقويّ mashawiy, (or مسقّيّ mashiy) Corn well watered. (A field) watered by art or by a rill.

A مسقّيّ mashiy, Imbued, saturated, soaked.

A مسك mask, (v. n. of مسك) Seizing, holding fast, retaining, restraining. Supporting, sustaining. (pl. مسوك musūk) Leather, especially of lamb or kid. مسك البرّ misku'l barr, (or مسك الجنّ mishu'l jinn) Names of plants. Masak, A place which holds water. (pl. of مسكة masakat) Bracelets or ankle-rings of tortoiseshell or ivory. Misak, (pl. of مسكة mishat) Particles of musk. Musak, (pl. of مسكة muskat) Aliments (as keeping the body together). (pl. of مسكة musakat) Tenacious, avaricious. Musuk, Avaricious, stingy.

A P مسك misk, Musk. غاليه مسك ghāliya-mish, Civet. مسك صابوني mish-sābūnī, A musky soap-ball.

A مسكان muskān, An earnest-penny.

A مسكة maskat, A piece of leather. Mishat, A bit of musk. Muscadel wine. Muskat, That by which any thing is held. (pl. مسك musak) Food (as keeping together the body). An excellent understanding. Covetousness, stinginess. Good, goodness. Remains, residue. A well dug in hard ground, through which water does not subside. The hard ground itself. Masakat, A bracelet or ankle-ring of tortoiseshell or ivory. A well dug in hard ground; also the hard ground itself. The caul on the head of a new-born infant or colt. حسكة مسكة hasakatun masakatun, Strong, strenuous. Musakat, (pl. مسك musah) Avaricious. One who holds any thing in his gripe and will not part with it. Musukat, Stinginess.

A مسكت muskit, One who orders silence, or strikes dumb. One who ceases to speak.

A مسكّت musakkat, The last gaming arrow. Musakkit, Silencing, who or what puts to silence.

A مسكر muskir, Inebriating. Any intoxicating liquor. كلّ مسكر حرام kullu muskirin harāmun, Every thing intoxicating is forbidden.

A مسكّر musakkar, Made drunk, crop-sick.

A مسكرات muskirāt, Intoxicating drinks.

A مسكعة musakkiʻat, A country where one easily loses the way.

P مسكل miskal, A sort of Jew's harp.

A مسكن mashan or maskin, (pl. مساكن masākin) Dwelling, habitation, house. Muskin, Poor, miserable.

A مسكّن musakkin, An allayer, quieter. مسكّنات اوجاع musakkināti awjāʻ, Anodynes.

A مسكنة maskanat, Poverty, misery. Humility, modesty. مسكنت و ضراعت maskanat u zarāʻat, Humbleness and submission. اهل مسكنت ahli maskanat, Modest, humble.

A مسكوب maskūb, Poured out, shed. (Water) poured out and flowing over the ground's surface.

A مسكور maskūr, Intoxicated, drunken. Concealed, veiled (eye).

A مسكوك maskūk, Coined, struck. Studded with nails. مسكوك سكّة maskūk sikkasi..... Stamped with the die of.....

A مسكون maskūn, Habitable, inhabited. Pacified. غير مسكون ghayr maskūn, Uninhabited. ربع مسكون rubʻi maskūn, The four quarters of the world. P مسكون شدن maskūn shudan, To be pacified, to become pleased.

P مسكه maska, Fresh butter.

A مسكيّ miskiy, Musky. Dark, musk-coloured.

P مسكين mishīn, Musky, musk-coloured.

A مسكير miskīr, Very apt to be intoxicated.

A مسكين miskīn or maskīn, (pl. مساكين masākīn and مسكينون miskīnūn) Indigent, wretched, a pauper. Humble, suppliant. A poor man or woman, a beggar, miserable wretch.

A مسكينة miskīnat, Poor, indigent (woman). The city of Madīna.

A مسكيني maskīnī, Poverty, misery.

A مسكينيّة miskīniyat, Beggary.

P مس گر misgar, A coppersmith, worker in brass.

A مسل masl, A flowing, running. Masal, (pl. امسلة amsilat, مسل musul, and مسلان muslān) The channel of a torrent or flux of water. Musul, (pl. of مسيل *masīl*) Channels of streams.

A مسلاء *maslāʼ*, Melted butter.

A مسلاة *maslāt*, Consolation.

A مسلاخ *mislākh*, A skin, raw hide. A serpent's slough. A palm-tree whose dates drop whilst green.

A مسلاس *mislās*, (A palm) stript of its branches.

A مسلاط *mislāt*, The tooth or ward of a key.

A مسلاق *mislāk*, Eloquent, glib-tongued.

A مسلان *muslān*, (pl. of مسل *masal* and مسيل *masīl*) Places through which water flows.

A مسلب *muslib*, (or مسلّب *musallib*) Abortion-producing (woman or camel).

A مسلة *masalat*, (also مسئلة *masʼalat*) A question, proposition, problem. An action, thing.

A مسلّة *misallat*, (pl. مسالّ *masāll*) A large needle for sewing sacks.

A مسلّح *musallah*, Armed for war.

A مسلحبّ *muslahibb*, Broad, open, extended (road). Straight.

A مسلحة *maslahat*, (pl. مسالح *masālih*) A frontier-garrison, a fortification at the entrance into a country. Armed (men), warlike (people). Guards, guardians. A dangerous place, where it is necessary to carry arms (سلاح *silāh*).

A مسلخ *maslakh*, (pl. مسالخ *masālikh*) A place where they slaughter and skin (animals).

A مسلخمّ *muslakhimm*, Proud, refractory.

A مسلس *muslis*, Abortion-producing (camel).

A مسلسل *musalsal*, Enchained, linked, concatenated, sewed, or fastened together, coherent, successive, consecutive, placed in order. Badly-woven (cloth). Striped, painted (stuff).

A مسلط *musallat*, Appointed, set over. Conquered, subdued. *Musallit*, A governor, a ruler. P مسلط شدن *musallit shudan*, To overcome, rule over, be superior.

A مسلع *mislaʻ*, A leader or guide of men or cattle.

A مسلّع *musallaʻ*, Cleaved, split. A wild bullock, to whose tail are fastened pieces of the wood سلع *salaʻ* and عشر *ʻushar*, which being set on fire, generally made them run up a mountain (a superstitious ceremony among the Pagan Arabs, in order to obtain rain in a dry season). A piece of wood thus tied and kindled.

A مسلعف *musalʻaf*, Thick.

A مسلف *muslif*, (A woman) of five and forty.

A مسلفة *mislafat*, A harrow. Any instrument used in levelling ground. A plasterer's trowel.

A مسلق *mislak*, Eloquent. A scaling-ladder.

A مسلك *maslak* or *maslik*, Way, path, track. Passage. Institution, regulation. Series, line.

A مسلّك *musallak*, Lean, slim, thread-like paper.

A مسلكة *maslakat*, A border torn off a garment.

A مسلم *muslim*, A musulman, a true believer in the Muhammadan faith, a Moslem.

A مسلّم *musallam*, Consigned, intrusted, given in charge. Free, dispensed with, exempted from public burdens. Complete, sound, safe, entire, whole. Certain, secure. مسلّم الانصاف *musallammu'l insāf*, Tenacious of equity. طبيب مسلم دوا *tabībi musallam dawā*, An excellent physician, certain of curing. P سخنان مقرّر ومسلّم *sukhanāni mukarrar u musallam*, Words certain and true. مسلّم كردن *musallam kardan*, To grant a dispensation. A *Musallim*, One who keeps safe, preserves in liberty, or rescues. One who delivers (any thing to a person). One who submits to, and acquiesces in, the judgment of another. One who salutes, pronounces a benediction or salutation. One who blesses the memory (of the departed), saying, السلام عليه *as'-salām ʻalayhi*, Peace be with him! The herald of peace. The lieutenant of a new governor sent before him to take possession till his arrival.

P مسلمان *muslimān*, (Pers. pl. of A مسلم *muslim*) Orthodox believers, Mussulmāns, Moslems.

T P مسلمان *musulmān*, A musulman, believer.

P مسلماني *musulmānī*, Muhammadism.

A مسلمة *muslimat*, A Muhammadan woman.

A مسلمين *muslimīn*, (pl. oblique of مسلم *muslim*) Muhammadans, faithful; believers, Moslems.

A مسلنطح *muslantih*, A wide, open field.

A مسلنقي *muslankī*, Supine, laid on the back.

A مسلوب *maslūb*, Seized, snatched away. Spoiled, stripped. Erred. Forgotten. Robbed of one's senses.

A مسلوت *maslūt*, Shaved on the head. Stripped of flesh.

A مسلوخ *maslūkh*, Skinned, flayed (sheep). Galled, made raw. Finished (month).

A مسلوس *maslūs*, Insane, foolish.

A مسلوط *maslūt*, Thin of hair about the jaw.

A مسلوع *maslūʻ*, Afflicted with سلعة *silʻat*.

A مسلوعة *maslūʻat*, A highway, straight road.

A مسلوف *maslūf*, Levelled (ground): harrowed.

A مسلوق *maslūk*, Boiled. Name of a certain day observed by the Arabs.

A مسلوقة *maslūkat*, (pl. مساليق *masālīk*) Broth.

A مسلوك *maslūk*, Beaten, walked, trodden (path). Inserted, put into.

A مسلول *maslūl*, Unsheathed. Consumptive.

A مسلوم *maslūm*, Bitten by a serpent. (A hide) tanned with bark of the tree سلم *salam*.

A مسلوماء *maslūmāʼ*, Fruitful in *salam* trees.

A مسلهمّ *muslahimm*, Changed in colour.

A مسلّي *musallī*, One who solaces, or who makes content and happy. The third horse in a race.

A مسلئبّ *muslaʼibb*, Hard and plenteous rain.

A مسمّ *misamm*, One who eats all he can get hold of. *Musimm*, (A day) distressingly hot with a pestilential blast (سموم *samūm*).

A مسمّا *musammā*, Called, named.

A مسماة *mismāt*, A sandal made especially for climbing rocks in pursuit of the mountain-goat.

A مسمّات *musammāt*, Names, denominations.

P مساجنك *mas*, (*mismājang*, or مساچنك *masmāchang*) An artificial penis, a dildo.

A مسماح *mismāh*, Liberal, bountiful.

A مسمار *mismār*, (pl. مسامير *masāmīr*) A nail, pin, peg, stake. A skilful manager of camels.

A مسماريّ *mismāriy*, Clavated, nail-shaped.

A مسماس *mis* or *masmās*, A confused business.

A مسماك *mismāk*, A forked tent-pole.

A مسمّة *masammat*, as اهل المسمّة *ahlu'l masammat* or *musimmat*, Relations, friends, intimates.

A مسمح *masmah*, Width, breadth, amplitude.

A مسمدرّ *musmadirr*, Long and straight (road). Well-arranged (discourse).

A مسمرط *musamrat*, Long-headed.

A مسمسة *masmasat*, (v. n. of مسمس Q) Being disturbed, disordered. Confusion, intricacy.

A مسمّط *musammat*, (A royal mandate) having effect, efficacious, received, and obeyed everywhere. (in poetry) A poem in which the rhyme of one line is different from all the rest.

A مسمع *masmaʻ*, A place where any thing is heard, a place within hearing. *Mismaʻ*, (pl. مسامع *masāmiʻ*) The ear, organ of hearing. The ear of a bucket. The handle in the middle of a bucket, or of a basket for drawing up earth, to which the rope is fastened. Name of the father of a tribe. *Mismaʻ* or *masmaʻ*, The ear-hole. *Musmaʻ*, Made to hear. Accepted, approved, heard, listened to, attended to. Clever. *Musmiʻ*, One who makes to hear. A fetter, pinion, manacle.

A مسمعا *masmaʻan*, Within hearing.

A مسمّع *musammaʻ*, Fettered, or having a log tied to the neck. *Musammiʻ*, Obscene, foul-mouthed.

A مسمعة *musmiʻat*, A female singer.

A مسمعلّ *musmaʻill*, Long (camel).

A مسمغلّة *musmaghillat*, Long (she-camel).

P مسمقار *masmakār*, (مسمقران *masmakrān*, or مسمقورة *masmakūra*) Long birthwort.

A مسمقرّ *musmakirr*, Extremely hot (day).

A مسمكات *musmakāt*, Heavens, lofty skies.

A مسمن *musmin*, (fem. مسمنة) Naturally fat.

A مسمّن *musammin*, Fattening.

A مسمنة *musmanat*, (fem.) Naturally fat.

A مسمّنة *musammanat*, (fem.) Fat by art or care, fattened.

A مسمور *masmūr*, Fixed together with nails. Lean and spare, but having the bones and muscles firmly knit together. Checkered (life).

A مسمورة *masmūrat*, A wench firmly knit together and brawny.

A مسموط *masmūt*, (A kid) whose hair is scalded off with water, and prepared for roasting.

A مسموع *masmūʻ*, Heard. Audible.

A مسموك *masmūk*, Long. High. Strong (rope).

A مسموكات *masmūkāt*, Skies.

A مسمول *masmūl*, Blinded, knocked out (eye).

A مسموم *masmūm*, Killed or injured by poison. Infected (meat), poisoned (sword), envenomed (arrow). Venomous. (A day) distressingly sultry by the blowing of the hot wind سموم *samūm*.

A مسمّة *musammah*, Mad with love. A fool, idiot.

A مسمهج *musamhaj*, (A horse) middle-sized, with well-proportioned limbs.

A مسمهرّ *musmahirr*, Penis.

A مسمهلّ *musmahill*, Slender round the belly.

A مسمّى *musamma'*, Named, called, styled. Entitled, denominated. Inscribed. *Musammī*, One who gives a name; denominative.

A مسمّياً *musammiyan*, Nominally; by name.

A مسمألّ *musmaʼill*, Lank in the belly. Old, worn out (garment). Name of a bird.

A مسن *masn*, A flagellation, a stroke with a scourge. *Masan*, (v. n. of مسن) Being hard and thick. Fearlessness.

A مسنّ *misann*, A whetstone, an instrument for sharpening. *Musinn*, Aged, stricken in years.

A مسنّاة *musannāt*, A bank, mound, or dike.

A مسناع *misnāʻ*, A beautiful she-camel.

A مسناف *misnāf*, A camel which shakes forward or backward the saddle (which is fastened on by the strap called سناف *sināf*). A camel wearing the poitrel or breast-harness سناف *sināf*.

A مسنبة *masnabat*, Wickedness. Greediness.

A مسنبخ *musambakh*, One who travels at mid-day. Distant, remote.

A مسنّة *musinnat*, An aged female.

A مسنت *musnit*, Barren, unproductive (soil). Scarce, barren (season). Visited by a barren season.

A مسنّج *musannaj*, Striped (stuff).

P مسند *masnad*, A scoundrel, lying rascal.

A مسند *masnad*, (pl. مساند *masānid*) A throne. A large cushion on which they recline. A prop, support. مسند سلطان *musnadi sultān*, A royal throne. P مسند آسودگان *masnadi āsūdagān*, The grave. The world. مسند جم *masnadi jam*, The wind. در مسند عزت *dar masnadi ʻizzat*, On the throne of glory, glorious. A *Musnad*, (pl. مساند *masānid* and مسانيد *masānīd*) Attributed to, related, alleged (on the authority of another). Predicated. Reared, propped. Spurious, a bastard. Time, an age, fortune. The Himyaritic character, which differs from the common Arabic or Niskhi. (in gram.) The subject. مسند اليه *musnad ilayhi*, The subject of a proposition. مسند به *musnad bi-hi*, The predicate of a proposition. *Musnid*, Who causes to lean. One who makes an allegation on the authority of another.

P مسند آرا *masnad-ārā*, Adorning the throne, *i.e.* a king. مسند آراي قصر متين دين *masnad-ārāyi kasri matīni dīn*, The ornament of the throne of the impregnable palace of religion (a title given sometimes to a chief priest).

A مسنّدة *musannadat*, Propped up (faggots).

P مسند گاه *masnad-gāh*, A support, asylum.

P مسند نشين *masnad-nishīn*, Sitting on the throne, *i.e.* a reigning prince. مسند نشين شدن *masnad-nishīn shudan*, To sit upon a throne, to fill the chief seat, to reign.

A مسنديّ *musnadīy*, A follower of the مساند *masānid*, to the exclusion of the مراسيل *marāsīl* and مقاطيع *makātīʻ*. A proper name.

A مسنسن *musansan*, Beaten, trodden (road).

A مسنطل *musantal*, Weak in going; a stumbler. One who waves the head up and down, unable to keep himself still, paralytic. Large-bellied.

A مسنف *musnif*, (pl. مسانف *masānif*) (A horse) which takes the lead of the others.

A مسنفة *musnafat*, (A she-camel) whose saddle is bound by the girth called سناف *sināf*. *Musnifat*, A mare outstripping horses. A young she-camel ten months gone with foal, and whose udder swells. Barren (ground). Lean (she-camel).

P مسنگ *masang*, Unfair play at dice. Boast.

A مسنم *musnim*, (Ground) productive of the plant اسنام *isnām*.

A مسنّم *musannam*, (A hovel or grave) shaped like an ass's back. (A camel) turned loose and never ridden (allowed to get a hunch).

A مسنوّ *masnūw*, Watered (ground).

A مسنوت *masnūt*, An intimate companion who flies in a rage without reason.

A مسنون *masnūn*, Changed, altered in smell or colour. Fetid (mud). Smooth, clear (faced). Long-faced and long-nosed. Polished, sharpened (sword). (Land) eat bare of grass. Circumcised. Rendered legal, legalized, lawful, adopted into use. قاعدهٔ مسنونه *kāʻidari masnūna*, A canon or rule; in law an evangelical council.

A مسنّة *musannah*, Mouldy (bread).

A مسنيّ *masnīy*, Watered (ground).

A مسو *masw*, (v. n. of مسا for مسو) Being restive, stubborn (an ass). Extracting the seed from the uterus of a camel.

A مسوء *musūʼ*, (v. n. of مسأ) Being froward, saucy. Keeping the middle of the road. Exciting discord. Delaying, proceeding slowly. Deceiving, circumventing. Being given to, persevering in. Deferring, putting off. Stilling (a boiling pot). Mollifying by gentle words. Being rent (a garment).

A مسواط *miswāt*, A horse that requires the whip (سوط *sawt*) to make him gallop. A harrow. A spoon with which things are mixed.

A مسواك *miswāk*, A dentifrice, especially one made from a certain kind of tree.

A مسوّج *musawwaj*, Circularly-cut (garment).

A مسوجر *musawjar*, (A dog) with the log ساجور *sājūr* tied to his neck. (Hair) hanging down.

A مسوح *musūh*, (v. n. of مسح) Travelling, roaming. (pl. of مسح *mis-h*) Coarse cloths of hair or wool, of which they make saddle-cloths for beasts of burden. Highways. Sackcloths.

A مسوّد *musawwad*, An intestine filled with camel's blood, roasted and eaten; a black pudding. *Musawwid*, A chooser of a chief, lord, or prince. One who blackens or marks with black.

A مسودّ *muswadd*, Black (in the face, from grief).

A مسودة *maswadat*, Water upon which there is a yellow tint. *Muswidat*, A woman the mother of black children.

A مسوّدة *musawwadat*, (fem. of مسوّد *musawwad*) Blackened. A black thing. A note or memorandum-book, the first sketch, conception, or rough draught of any thing, with many blottings and corrections. *Musawwidat*, Name of a Muhammadan sect (the sect of Abbās), so called because they dressed in black.

A مسور *masūr*, Walked, trodden (road). Lived with (man). *Miswar*, A leathern cushion.

A مسوّر *musawwar*, Built (wall). Enclosed by a wall (سور *sūr*), walled. Adorned with bracelets (سوار *siwār*). The part encircled by a bracelet.

A مسورة *miswarat*, A leathern cushion.

A مسوس *masūs*, Brackish, not salt or fresh. Water which hands have touched. Water which allays excessive thirst. Whatever allays thirst. Pure, sweet water. The bezoar-stone.

A مسوّس *musawwis*, Worm-eaten (tree). (A tree) which breeds worms (سوس *sūs*).

A مسوط *miswat*, A ladle or spatula for mixing things. A certain imp which stirs men to anger.

A مسوّع *musawwaʻ*, Permitted, allowed; lawful.

A مسوّغ *musawwagh*, Permitted, allowed; lawful.

A مسوف *masūf*, Furious (stallion-camel). *Miswaf*, A scent-bottle, or box for holding perfumes.

A مسوّف *musawwif*, One who does what he likes without let, hindrance, check, or opposition.

A مسوّفة *musawwifat*, (A well) of which it is affirmed that water will surely be found in it: or whose water when smelled is nauseated. Disobedient (wife), who promises to do well and does not.

A مسوق *masūk*, Rudely and violently driven. *Miswak*, A stick or switch for striking a horse. *Muswik*, (A camel) which follows or presses on the game, enabling the hunter to catch it.

A مسوقة *miswakat*, A whip.

A مسوك *musūk*, (pl. of مسك *mask*) Skins of lambs or kids. هم في مسوك الثعالب *hum fī musūki 's saʻālib*, They are terrified.

A مسوّم *musawwam*, Signed, marked. Sent to pasture. حجارة مسوّمة *hijārat musawwamat*, Pebbles which have on them an impress like seals; or marked white and red. *Musawwim*, One who makes a mark. One who turns his horse loose to graze.

A مسوود *masʼūd*, Afflicted with سواد *suʼād*.

A مسووف *masʼūf*, Furious, rampant (he-camel).

A مسوون *muswūn*, (pl.) Well, healthy, entire.

A مسوّى *musawwa'*, Made level, even, and smooth. *Musawwī*, One who makes any thing even, level, and straight.

A مسهب *mus-hab* or *mus-hib*, A horse going with long steps; also going at full gallop. A blabber, a great talker. *Mus-hab*, Deprived of sense from love, fright, disease, or the bite of a serpent.

A مسهبة *mus-habat*, Deep (well), or one whose water is so sandy as to be undrinkable.

A مسهج *mas-haj*, A place where the wind blows. *Mis-haj*, A prater, babbler, trifling speaker. Eloquent, high-voiced.

A مسهّد *musahhad*, Rendered sleepless, roused.

A مسهف *mas-haf*, (Meat) creating (thirst).

A مسهك *mas-hak*, A violent wind or its current. *Mis-hak*, Light, active, fleet (horse). Eloquent, rapid in utterance.

A مسهكة *mas-hakat*, Current of a strong wind.

A مسهل *mus-hal*, Purged, troubled with a diarrhœa. *Mus-hil*, Laxative, aperient, purgative, cathartic. A purge (in India called a mussaul). مسهلات بلغم *mus-hilāti balgham*, Medicines which carry off phlegm, phlegmagogues. مسهلات سودا *mus-hilāti saudā*, Medicines which expel the bile, melanagogues. مسهلات صفرا *mus-hilāti safrā*, Medicines which expel bilious fœces, cholagogues.

A مسهّل *musahhal*, Lightened. Made easy, softened. *Musahhil*, A loosener, solvent.

A مسهم *mus-ham*, (A horse) of ignoble breed. Emaciated, lean (from love). *Mus-him*, Talkative.

A مسهّم *musahham*, A garment marked with stripes resembling arrows (سهم *sahm*). Plaited.

A مسهّمة *musahhamat*, (Camels) affected with the disease called سهام *suhām*.

A مسهوف *mas-hūf*, Tormented with an unquenchable thirst (سهاف *suhāf*).

A مسهوم *mas-hūm*, (A camel) affected by the disease سهام *suhām*. Scorched by the summer-heat.

A مسي *masy*, (v. n. of مسى) Extracting the prolific seed from the matrix of a camel. (Heat) wasting (flocks). Going an easy journey. Stroking (with the hand). *Misy* or *musy*, Evening. مسي امس *musyu amsin*, Yesterday evening.

A مسي *misī*, Made of copper. A sort of dentifrice or colouring for the teeth used in Hindūstān.

A مسئ *musīʼ*, A sinner, criminal, malefactor, evil-doer. Injurious.

A مسيّ *musayy*, (dim. of مسا) A little evening.

A مسيّا *musayyan*, As the evening began.

A مسياح *misyāh*, (pl. مسايح *masāyih*) A sycophant going about to sow dissensions.

A مسياع *misyāʻ*, (A she-camel) which goes to pasture without a keeper. One that leaves her colt for the wild beasts to eat. A camel badly looked after. A camel employed in the transport of wares. مسياع مضياع *misyāʻ mizyāʻ*, A prodigal, a spendthrift.

A مسياف *misyāf*, Bereaved (mother).

A مسيّانات *musayyānāta*, In the evening hours.

A مسيّب *musayyab*, Set at liberty. Given.

A مسيجة *masījat*, A thorn-fenced enclosure.

P مسيچه *musīcha*, A sort of bird white like a turtle or duck, but larger, making with its wings a hissing noise when flying.

A مسيح *masīh*, Smooth, bare. A rough towel. The bare part of a coin, either unstamped or where the impression has worn off. One who measures or travels much. Sincere. Sweat. A liar. Silver. Anointed. Wiped, cleaned. One who indulges much in venery. المسيح *al masīh*, The anointed, the Messiah, our Lord Jesus Christ. المسيح الدجّال *al masīhu'd dajjāl*, (or simply دجّال *dajjāl*) Antichrist. مسيح القدمين *masīhu'l kadamayn*, One whose feet are flat (not concave at the soles).

A مسّيح *missīh*, One who measures much. One who travels much. Antichrist.

A مسيّح *musayyah*, Striped (garment or locust). A highway from which many distinct lanes branch off. The wild ass.

P مسيحا *masīhā*, Christ, the Messiah. A Christian.

A مسيحانفس *masīhā-nafas*, Possessed of the breath of the Messiah (an expression used to imply a skilful physician; as if endowed, like the Messiah, with the power of recovering the sick or recalling the dead by a breath.)

P مسيحاوار *masīhāvār*, Christ-like: or a Christian.

A مسيحائي *masīhāʼī*, Christ-like. Of the Messiah. The office or works of the Messiah.

A مسيحة *masīhat*, A bow. A ringlet of hair.

A مسيحي *masīhiy*, Christian. Appertaining to Christ. ملت مسيحيّه *millati masīhiya*, The Christian religion. The Christian people.

A مسيخ *masīkh*, Metamorphosed, changed into a meaner shape. Deformed, ugly. Weak. Foolish. A monster. Tasteless, insipid (meat or fruit).

A مسيد *masīd*, (in Morocco) A school.

P مسيدن *masīdan*, To pluck, gather, cull. To wash, squeeze, wring, press, extort, wrench, twitch. To make haste, walk fast.

A مسير *masīr*, (or مسيرة *masīrat*) (v. n. of سار for سير) Going, walking, proceeding on a journey, travelling. A journey. مسيرة يوم *masīratu yawmin*, A day's journey.

A مسئر *musʼir*, One who leaves a remainder (of meat or drink, the same being called سؤر *suʼr*).

A مسيّر *musayyar*, (Cloth) woven with stripes (like thongs). A kind of sweetmeat. A journey. A pleasant or celebrated place, worthy of a traveller's curiosity.

A مسيس *masīs*, (or مسّيسى *missīsaʼ*) (v. n. of مسّ) Touching, handling, feeling. Touch.

A مسيط *masīt*, Impure water, especially at the bottom of a cistern. Clay, mud. A small stream. A stallion which covers to no purpose.

A مسيطة *masītat*, Impure water, especially at the bottom of a cistern. A small stream. A well of sweet water spoiled by bad water running into it. Water flowing between a well and a cistern and becoming fetid.

A مسيّطة *musayyitat*, A small stream.

A مسيطر *musaytir*, A keeper, guardian, governor, commander, inspector. Invested with authority.

A مسيعة *misyaʻat*, A plasterer's trowel.

A مسيف *musīf*, Girt with, or bearing a sword. Deprived of a child by death, bereaved (father).

A مسيّف *musayyaf*, (Coin) plain on the sides, free from any impression.

A مسيفة *masīfat*, (pl. of سيف *sayf*) Swords.

A مسيك *masīk*, Avaricious, tenacious, close-fisted. Hard ground which holds water. Food. An excellent understanding.

A مسّيك *missīk*, Avaricious, tenacious, close-fisted. (A bottle or bag) which holds water well.

A مسيكة *masīkat*, (Ground) of a solid stratum, which holds water, and does not allow it to percolate.

A مسيل *masīl*, (pl. مسائل *masāʼil*, مسل *musul*, امسلة *amsilat*, and مسلان *muslān*) A channel. A flux or stream of water.

A مسئلة *masʼalat*, (v. n. of سال) Asking, praying.

A مسيلمة *musaylimat*, Name of a famous impostor, to whom the epithet كذّاب *kazzāb*, "liar," is usually affixed.

P مسين *misīn*, (or مسينه *misīna*) Made of copper.

A مسؤد *masʼūd*, Afflicted with the disease سؤاد.

A مسئول *masʼūl*, Asked, begged, desired, demanded, interrogated. A petition: any thing sued for. مسئول عنه *masʼūl ʻanhu*, (Any person or thing) inquired after.

A مسئولات *masʼūlāt*, Questions, queries.

A مسيئ *musīʼ*, A sinner, evil doer.

A مشّ *mashsh*, (v. n. of مشّ) Milking (a camel), but leaving part in the udder. Taking (any thing) by little and little. Rubbing (the hands), cleaning or wiping (them) of grease. Mixing or rubbing (any thing) until (it) dissolves. Gnawing the extremity of a bone, in order to suck out the marrow. Litigation, law-suit.

A مشا *mashaʼ*, A yellow carrot or similar plant.

A مشاء *mashāʼ*, (v. n. of مشى) Being remarkable for a numerous offspring (a woman). Laxative, aperient (medicine).

A مشّاء *mashshāʼ*, A fast goer, a vigorous walker. An informer. (A camel) going well, unfatigued. (A she-camel) affected with a white speck on the eye.

A مشاءاة *mushāʼat*, (v. n. 3 of شأو for شأا) Going before, preceding. Getting the start of.

A مشاءة *mashāʼat*, (v. n. of شيء) Being willing: wishing, desiring.

A مشاءمة *mushāʼamat*, (v. n. 3 of شأم) Sitting on the left hand. Going to the left. Arriving in Syria.

A مشابر *mashābir*, (pl. of مشبر *mashbar* and مشبرة *mashbarat*) Notches or other marks upon an ell-measure, to mark the half-yard, quarter, &c. A low-lying stream into which water flows from every part.

A مشابه *mashābih*, (pl. of شبه *shabah*) Resemblances, forms, figures, pictures, images. *Mushābih*, Like, resembling.

A مشابهات *mushābahāt*, (pl. of مشابهة *mushābahat*) Similitudes, semblances. Doubtful or different things.

A مشابهة *mushābahat*, (v. n. 3 of شبه) Resembling. Similitude, resemblance. Comparison of things similar. Probability.

A مشابيه *mashābīh*, (pl. of شبه) Resemblances.

A مشاة *mishāt*, (pl. مشائي *mashāʼī*) A vessel by which they take mud out of wells.

A مشاة *mushāt*, (pl. of ماشي *māshī*) Walkers, pedestrians. Spies, whisperers.

A مشاتاة *mushātāt*, (v. n. 3 of شتا for شتو) Agreeing with (another) for the winter (شتاء *shitāʼ*): doing any thing during that season.

A مشاتغ *mashātigh*, Dangerous places; perils.

A مشاتمة *mushātamat*, (v. n. 3 of شتم) Reviling, abusing one another. Rudeness, reproachfulness.

P مشاتمه كردن *mushātama kardan*, To rail at.

A مشاجب *mashājib*, (pl. of مشجب *mishjab*) Wooden clothes-horses.

A مشاجة *mushājjat*, (v. n. 3 of شج) Fighting; breaking or endeavouring to break another's head.

A مشاجر *mashājir*, (pl. of مشجر *mishjar*) The wooden works of camel-litters open at top.

A مشاجرة *mushājarat*, (v. n. 3 of شجر) Resisting, opposing, controverting. Gnawing a tree (an animal). Pasturing, tending cattle.

A مشاحة *mushāhhat*, (v. n. 3 of شح) Acting in an avaricious, grasping manner (towards any one). Litigation, altercation.

A مشاحذة *mushāhazat*, (v. n. 3 of شحذ) Lifting and twisting (her) tail much (a camel in travail).

A مشاحن *mushāhin*, Troublesome (enemy). Heretical. An innovator.

A مشاحنة *mushāhanat*, A hating of one another.

A مشاخسة *mushākhasat*, (v. n. 3 of شخس) Endeavouring, but unsuccessfully, to mend a broken dish.

A مشاخلة *mushākhalat*, (v. n. 3 of شخل) Behaving sincerely, treating with pure affection.

A مشاد *mushād*, Carried up, built.

A مشادة *mushāddat*, (v. n. 3 of شد) Opposing, resisting. Seizing or contending with vehemence.

A مشادن *mashādin*, or مشادين *mashādīn*, (pl. of مشدن *mushdin*) (Does) whose young are full grown.

A مشادة *mashādih*, Employments, engagements which distract and confound.

A مشار *mashār*, (v. n. of شار for شور) Taking (honey) from a hive. A hive of bees. *Mushār*, Signified, indicated. مشار اليه *mushār ilayhi*, Abovementioned, aforesaid, touched upon before, related above. A person or thing consulted. ماذيّ مشار *māziy mushār*, White honey, in the gathering of which assistance has been rendered.

A مشاراة *mushārāt*, (v. n. 3 of شري) Making a contract of purchase or sale. Quarrelling, disputing.

A مشارب *mashārib*, (pl. of مشرب *mashrab*) Dispositions. (pl. of مشربة *mashrabat* and *mashrubat*) Dining-rooms, parlours. Places whence water is fetched. (pl. of مشربة *mishrabat*) Drinks, things in general which are potable. Drinking-vessels.

A مشاربة *mushārabat*, (v. n. 3 of شرب) Drinking with or to another.

A مشارة *mashārat*, (v. n. of شار for شور) Taking (honey) from a hive. Fatness and comeliness. (pl. مشاور *mashāwir* and مشائر *mashāʼir*) Part of a sown field.

A مشارّة *mushārrat*, (v. n. 3 of شرّ) Injuring (another), being malignant or adverse.

A مشارجات *mushārijāt*, (Girls) of the same age.

A مشارجة *mushārajat*, (v. n. 3 of شرج) Resembling one another.

A مشارز *mushāriz*, Malicious, ill-disposed. Sharp (iron instrument), cutting whatever passes across it.

A مشارزة *mushārazat*, (v. n. 3 of شرز) Contending, striving, disputing, litigating. Being malignant, bad-tempered.

A مشارسة *mushārasat*, A giving hard treatment.

A مشارطة *mushāratat*, (v. n. 3 of شرط) Stipulating with each other, entering into mutual conditions.

A مشارع *mashāriʻ*, (pl. of مشرع *mashraʻ* and مشرعة *mashraʻat*) Streets, broadways.

A مشارف *mashārif*, Arabian villages on the banks of the Euphrates rich in pastures. Eminences, high places.

A مشارفة *mushārafat*, (v. n. 3 of شرف) Contending with concerning nobility or glory. Being near. Hanging over, impending.

A مشارق *mashārik*, Eastern places.

A مشارك *mushārak*, Common, shared in common. Mutual, reciprocal. *Mushārik*, An associate, partner. A wind close to the north-east.

A مشاركة *mushārakat*, (v. n. 3 of شرك) Entering into partnership. Being partner. Co-partnership. Community, society, association, participation, communication, correspondence. مشاركت دينيّه *mushārakati dīniya*, Religious fellowship.

P مشارة *mashāra*, A border round a sown field.

A مشاريط *mashārīt*, (pl. of مشراط *mishrāt*) Beginnings of things. Surgeons' lancets or scarificators.

P مشاش *mashāsh*, A decoction of honey poured upon a plate to harden. Piss not.

A مشاش *mushāsh*, Soft earth. Soul, mind, nature, disposition, temperament. Light, active, dextrous, expert in serving. Root, origin. (pl. of مشاشة *mushāshat*) Tops of marrow-bones, the ends sucked.

A مشاشة *mushāshat*, (pl. مشاش *mushāsh*) The head of a soft bone which may be gnawed. Hard ground wherein clean wells are dug, and which always remain full. The inside of the ground. A road through loose earth and soft stones. A mountain wherein are land-springs.

A مشاط *mishāt*, (pl. of مشط *mushut* or مشّط *mushutt*) Combs.

A مشاطأة *mushātaʼat*, (v. n. 3 of شطأ) Walking opposite on different sides of a stream.

A مشاطة *mishātat*, The art of combing. *Mushātat*, Hairs which fall in combing; hair-combings.

A مشّاطة *mashshātat*, A comber, waiting-maid, bride-dresser, or tire-woman.

A مشاطّة *mushāttat*, (v. n. 3 of شطّ) Receding from what is right and true. Striving to exceed in injustice. Contending with any one in going far away.

A مشاطر *mushātir*, A next-door neighbour.

A مشاطرة *mushātarat*, (v. n. 3 of شطر) Halving. Being next-door neighbour. Milking with one teat.

P مشّاطگي *mashshātagī*, Art of attiring a bride.

A مشاطن *mushātin*, One who draws up a bucket with a couple of ropes.

A مشاع *mushāʻ*, Divulged. Common to all. Undistributed (portion).

A مشاعبة *mushāʻabat*, (v. n. 3 of شعب) Removing far off. Dying.

A مشاعة *mashāʻat*, A being divulged, published.

A مشاعر *mashāʻir*, Holy places at Mecca. The five senses or inlets of knowledge. *Mushāʻir*, A poetaster, petty poet.

A مشاعرة *mushāʻarat*, (v. n. 3 of شعر) Contending with, or excelling in poetry. Lying or sleeping together under one inner garment. A meeting of poets.

A مشاعل *mashāʻil*, (pl. of مشعل *mashʻal*) Lanterns. Torches. Flames, lights, splendours. (pl. of مشعلة *mashʻalat*) Places for lanterns or fires.

A مشاعليّ *mashāʻiliy*, An executioner.

A مشاغب *mushāghib*, An evil-doer. A defamer. A stirrer up of mischief. ذو مشاغب *zū mashāghib*, Seditious, troublesome; breedbate.

A مشاغبة *mushāghabat*, (v. n. 3 of شغب) Injuring. Defaming. Squabbling, raising tumults.

A مشاغرة *mushāgharat*, (v. n. 3 of شغر) Contracting the double treaty of marriage called شغار *shighār*. Joining together to oppress one (two men).

A مشاغل *mashāghil*, Employments.

A مشافر *mashāfir*, (pl. of مشفر *mishfar* or *mashfar*) Lips of camels or men.

A مشافعة *mushāfaʻat*, (v. n. 3 of شفع) Asking of one another the right of pre-emption of property adjoining their own.

A مشافل *mashāfil*, (pl. of مشفلة) Tripes.

A مشافه *mushāfih*, A speaker face to face.

A مشافهة *mushāfahat* (v. n. 3 of شفه) Bringing near. Speaking to one's face, lip to lip.

P مشاق *mushāk*, A servant, domestic.

A مشّاق *mashshāk*, A practiser.

A مشاقّ *mashākk*, (pl. of مشقّة *mashakkat*) Afflictions, inconveniences, hardships.

A مشاقاة *mushākāt*, (v. n. of شقا for شقو) Applying one's self to, persevering in any thing with much trouble. Opposing, contending. Disputing about misery (شقاء *shakāʼ*).

A مشاقة *mushākat*, Whatever falls from hair or wool when combed, combings.

A مشاقة *mushākkat*, (v. n. 3 of شقّ) Contending, quarrelling, opposing. Contention, opposition.

A مشاقحة *mushākahat*, (v. n. 3 of شقح) Railing at, reproaching one another. Being crabbed, austere.

A مشاقذة *mushākazat*, (v. n. 3 of شقذ) Being hostile, inimical, hating one another.

A مشاقر *mashākir*, Sand sliding down into low-lying ground. The hardest kind of sand. Places where the plant عرفج *ʻarfaj* grows.

A مشاكرة *mushākarat*, (v. n. 3 of شكر) Beginning to converse or tell a story. Evincing gratitude (شكر *shukr*), shewing that one is grateful.

A مشاكسة *mushākasat*, (v. n. 3 of شكس) Being peevish, crabbed, difficult.

A مشاكل *mushākil*, Resembling; suitable, apposite, convenient. مشاكل و موافق *mushākil u muwāfik*, Suitable and convenient.

A مشاكلة *mushākalat*, (v. n. 3 of شكل) Agreeing with, suiting. Resembling, favouring. Resemblance, conformity.

A مشاكهة *mushākahat*, (v. n. 3 of شكه) Resembling, being like. Being near, neighbouring. Being a friend, companion, or cotemporary.

A مشال *mushāl*, Raised, lifted up, cocked.

A مشامّ *mashāmm*, The smell. The palate. ديار شام جنّت مشام *diyāri shāmi jannat-mashām*, The country of Damascus redolent of Paradise.

A مشأمة *mashʼamat*, The left hand or side. Any place towards the left.

A مشامّة *mushāmmat*, (v. n. 3 of شمّ) Smelling one another. Approaching, appearing in sight (of an enemy). Looking at, prying into, snuffing.

A مشامع *mashāmiʻ*, (pl. of مشمعة) Candlesticks.

A مشان *mishān*, A rapacious wolf. A clamorous, impudent woman. Name of a mountain. *Mushān*, A kind of date. *Mushān* or *mishān*, A sweet kind of fresh date.

A مشانب *mashānib*, Sweet, fresh mouths.

A مشانقة *mushānakat*, (v. n. 3 of شنق) Mixing one's flocks or goods with those of another.

A مشاوب *mushāwab*, (pl. مشاوب *mashāwib*) A case or covering for a glass-bottle.

A مشاوذ *mashāwiz*, (pl. of مشوذ) Turbans.

A مشاور *mashāwir*, (pl. of مشارة *mashārat*) Parts of a sown field. *Mushāwir*, A counsellor, senator. مشاورين *mushāwirīn*, (oblique pl.) Counsellors.

A مشاورة *mushāwarat*, (v. n. 3 of شار for شور) Consulting, asking advice. Counsel, consultation, deliberation, conference.

A مشاوس *mushāwis*, (or مشاوش *mushāwish*) Water in a deep well, scanty and scarcely discernible.

A مشاوظة *mushāwazat*, (v. n. 3 of شاظ for شوظ) Abusing one another, calling one another ill names.

A مشاولة *mushāwalat*, (v. n. 3 of شال for شول) Elevating, raising, lifting. Attacking one another with spears.

A مشاويذ *mashāwīz*, (pl. of مشواذ) Turbans.

A مشاهاة *mushāhāt*, A resembling, taking after.

A مشاهة *mashāhat*, (A place) full of sheep.

A مشاهد *mashāhid*, (pl. of مشهد *mashhad*) Places where people assemble. Sacred. *Mushāhad*, Seen, witnessed, beheld. *Mushāhid*, One who sees, views, or contemplates; a spectator.

A مشاهدة *mushāhadat*, (v. n. 3 of شهد) Seeing, contemplating. Sight, vision, contemplation, speculation, ocular demonstration. Revelation. A testimony. مشاهدات غيبيّة *mushāhadāti ghaybīya*, Contemplations or visions of future, absent, or invisible things. مشاهده كردن *mushādada kardan* (or نمودن *namūdan*), To see, witness, contemplate, behold, look at, consider.

A مشاهرة *mushāharat*, (v. n. 3 of شهر) Bargaining by the month (شهر *shahr*). Paying monthly. Monthly wages. Allowances to zamīndārs.

A مشاهلة *mushāhalat*, (v. n. 3 of شهل) Reproaching, railing at one another. Injuring each other.

A مشاهير *mashāhīr*, (pl. of مشهور *mash-hūr*) Celebrated, notorious.

A مشايعة *mushāyahat*, (v. n. 3 of شاح for شيح) Being diligent, striving (in business). Taking heed to one's self, abstaining. Fighting.

A مشائخ *mashāʼikh*, (pl. of شيخ *shaykh*) Aged men. Sheiks. Elders, doctors, priors, abbots, holy persons, dervishes.

A مشائخي *mashāʼikhī*, Sanctity, piety.

A مشائر *mashāʼir*, (pl. of مشارة *mashārat*) Parts of a sown field.

A مشايصة *mushāyasat*, A contention for glory. Mutual distance or aversion.

A مشايع *mushāyiʻ*, A follower, adherent.

A مشايعة *mushāyaʻat*, (v. n. 3 of شاع for شيع) Following, adhering to. Assisting. Calling (camels or sheep) when lagging behind.

A مشائم *mashāʼim*, Disastrous, unfortunate things. (pl. of مشيمة *mashīmat*) Membranes in which fœtuses are wrapped, secundines.

A مشائن *mashāʼin*, Shameful things, vices.

A مشائي *mashāʼī*, (pl. of مشآة *mishʼāt*) Baskets by which they raise mud out of wells.

A مشائية *mashāʼiyat*, (v. n. of شاء for شيئ) Willing, wishing, desiring.

A مشايط *mashāyiṭ*, (pl. of مشياط *mishyāt*) (Camels) which soon fatten.

A مشائيم *mashāʼīm*, Unlucky (persons).

A مشبّ *mishabb*, (A sheep or ox) in his prime. An old ox. *Mushibb*, A lion.

A مشبّج *mushabbah*, Peeled, skinned. A stout, coarse, rough garment.

A مشبر *mashbar*, (or مشبرة *mashbarat*) (pl. مشابر *mashābir*) A notch or mark set upon an ell or yard-measure to shew the half, quarter, &c. A low-lying stream into which water falls.

A مشبرق *mushabrak*, (Cloth) badly woven and cut. From every surrounding part.

A مشبرم *mushabram*, Any particle frayed and fallen from a rope or string; flue.

A مشبع *mushbaʻ*, Saturated, sated, satiated. مشبع العقل *mushbaʻu'l ʻakl*, Of full intellect.

A مشبّك *mushabbak*, Latticed, grated, netted, reticulated. مشبّك قلعه *mushabbak-kalʻa*, A censer. The sky.

A مشبل *mushbil*, (A lioness) with her young.

A مشبّم *mushabbam*, Gagged (kid); muzzled.

A مشبوب *mashbūb*, Grown up, adult. Stirred, blazing (fire). (A beautiful object) which excites love or admiration.

A مشبوح *mashbūh*, One whose arms are wide apart. Large-boned. Broad in the arms.

A مشبورة *mashbūrat*, Liberal, generous (woman).

A مشبوك *mashbūk*, Caught, fixed, entangled.

A مشبّه *mushabbah*, Obscured, ambiguous, intricate. Compared, likened. Like, resembling. مشبّه به *mushabbah bihi*, That whereunto a thing is likened.

A مشبيّ *mashbīy*, (or مشبي *mushbī*) The father of an intelligent lad.

P مشت *masht*, Abundant, full, overflowing. Thick, gross, coarse. Name of a town near Ghaznīn. *Musht*, The fist. A blow with the clenched fist. A handful. A handful of people, a few. A hammer. Root of galangale. Little, mean. He rubbed. Rubbed. مشت آب *mushti āb*, A gulp of water. مشت آتشي *mushti ātishi*, A handful of fire, (met.) Tyrants. Fire-worshippers. مشت خاك *mushti khāk*, A handful of earth. The terrestrial ball, the world. Man. مشت زدن *musht zadan*, To strike the fist, to box.

A مشتّ *mushitt*, A disperser; separator.

A مشتا *mashta'*, Winter-quarters. Caverns.

A مشتاة *mashtāt*, Winter-quarters.

A مشتار *mushtār*, A gatherer of honey.

P مشتا سنگ *mushtā-sang*, A stone with a hole by way of handle, either held in the hand or thrown when fighting. The stone of a sling.

P مشت افشار *musht-afshār*, A soft kind of gold capable of being moulded by the hand. A small golden scent-box held by great people in the hand. New wine (called مسطار *mustār*).

A مشتاق *mushtāk*, Full of desire, wishing, longing, anxious to see an absent friend.

P مشتاقانه *mushtākāna*, Desirous of seeing.

A مشتاقي *mushtākī*, Vehement desire, longing.

A مشتبك *mushtabik*, Perplexed, intricate, intermixed, mixed, confused. Latticed, grated, reticulated, made like a net (شبكة *shabakat*).

A مشتبه *mushtabih*, Obscure, doubtful, intricate.

A مشتبهات *mushtabihāt*, Obscure, ambiguous (sentences). Doubtful, intricate (affairs).

A مشتبهة *mushtabihat*, An ambiguous matter.

A مشتّت *mushattat*, Separated, divided, scattered.

A مشتجر *mushtajir*, A disputant, squabbler.

A مشتدّ *mushtadd*, Waxed strong, potent.

A مشتدح *mushtadah*, Facility, convenience, ability of doing any thing.

A مشتدخ *mushtadikh*, Broken (hollow thing).

A مشتدق *mushtadik*, Wry-mouthed in speaking.

A مشترط *mushtarit*, One who fixes a condition.

A مشترف *mushtarif*, Erect, upright, standing up. Tall (horse).

A مشترك *mushtarak*, Shared. Common, paying tribute to two masters (as in the case with some frontier-towns). Common to many. حسّ مشترك *hissi mushtarak*, Common sense. لغت مشتركه *lughati mushtaraka*, A word of many significations, common to many senses. P شكار مشتركست *shikār mushtarakast*, The game is in common. A *Mushtarik*, A partner in trade, associate, accomplice. Common to many. Complex. Synonymous. One who talks to himself; a misanthrope.

P مشت رند *musht-rand*, (or مشت رنده *musht-randa*) A carpenter's plane, hand-plane.

P مشترو *mushtrū*, A kind of mezereon.

A مشتري *mushtara'*, Bought. *Mushtarī*, A buyer, purchaser. The planet Jupiter. A kind of bird.

A مشتريّ *mushtariy*, Relating to a buyer (مشتري).

P مشت زن *musht-zan*, Boxer, bruiser, pugilist.

P مشت زني *musht-zanī*, Fisticuffs, boxing.

P مشت سنگ *musht-sang*, Sling-stone: missile.

A مشتعل *mushtaǎal*, Kindled, set on fire.

A مشتغر *mushtaghir*, Far-advanced (into the desert). Proud, overbearing. Numerous, many, that cannot be numbered. Large, vast (account). Difficult, intricate (affair).

A مشتغل *mushtaghil* or *mushtaghal*, Employed, occupied, engaged, busied.

P مشتفشار *mushtafshār*, A soft kind of gold capable of being worked in the hand like wax. New wine.

A مشتفي *mushtafī*, Convalescent.

A مشتق *mushtakk*, Derivative, derived (as one noun from another). اسم مشتق *ismi mushtakk*, A derivative noun. اسم غير مشتق *ismi ghayr mushtakk*, A primitive, underived noun.

A مشتقق *mushtakik*, One who derives (one noun from another). A taker of a half. A squabbler, brawler.

A مشتكر *mushtakir*, Violent, stormy (wind). (See اشتكار *ishtikār*.)

A مشتكل *mushtakil*, Doubtful, obscure, difficult.

A مشتكي *mushtaka'*, Any thing complained of. Suspected. *Mushtakī*, Pained, or complaining of a pain. A complainer, lamenter.

A مشتّم *mushattam*, Grim (lion).

A مشتمة *mashtamat* or *mashtimat*, (v. n. of شتم) Reproaching, reviling, cursing, vilifying.

A مشتمر *mushtamir*, Diligent, pains-taking.

A مشتمل *mushtamil*, Whatever surrounds, embraces, comprehends, contains, comprises.

P مشتن *mushtan*, To rub.

P مشتنگ *mushtang*, A thief, robber. Poor.

P مشتو *mushtū*, A sort of red clay (گل *gil*) or red flower (گل *gul*).

P مشتواره *mushtwāra*, As much as can be held in the hand: a handful. A handful of wheat or barley in the ear. A small joiner's plane.

A مشتور *mashtūr*, One whose eyelids are weak and inverted.

A مشتوم *mashtūm*, Reproached, reviled, cursed, treated contumeliously.

A مشتوي *mushtawa'*, A place for cooking.

P مشته *mashta*, Selling any thing by trick and artifice. *Mushta*, A wooden instrument with which they strike the bow-string when preparing cotton for spinning. An oblong piece of wood or bone used by shoemakers in smoothing the soles. The handle of any tool or weapon.

A مشتهر *mushtahar* or *mushtahir*, Proclaimed. Called, named. Famous. *Mushtahir*, One who celebrates, proclaims abroad.

A مشتهي *mushtaha'*, Longed for, lusted after: desirable. *Mushtahī*, One who loves, wishes, desires, longs for, hankers after.

A مشتهيات *mushtahiyāt*, (pl. fem.) Desires, wishes, appetites. مشتهيات نفسانيّه *mushtahiyāti nafsāniya*, Carnal desires.

P مشتي *mushtī*, A garment of fine cloth. Fine cloth of cotton or silk. A handful. A small number or quantity, a few. مشتيء آتشي *mushtīi ātishī*, Tyrants, oppressors. Fire-worshippers. مشتيء خاك *mushtīi khāk*, The world. A handful of people. مشتيء زياد *mushtīi ziyād*, Adverse, dissentient, opponents. Poor, contemptible. مشتيء شرار *mushtīi sharār*, Stars, planets. مشتيء غبار *mushtīi ghubār*, A company of persons. The earth.

A مشتّي *mushattī*, Sufficient for the winter.

A مشج *mashj*, (v. n. of مشج) Mixing. Disturbing. *Mashāj* or *mashij*, (pl. امشاج *amshāj*) Mixtures.

A مشجاذ *mishjāz*, A sling for stones.

A مشجب *mishjab*, A three-legged piece of wood on which they hang clothes, a clothes-horse.

A مشجّب *mushajjib*, Coarse, homely (in diet).

A مشجّج *mushajjaj*, Broken-skulled. Split (post).

A مشجر *mashjar*, (A place) planted with trees, a grove. *Mishjar*, A camel that browses upon trees. A three-footed piece of wood upon which they hang clothes. A bleacher's block. *Mishjar* or *mashjar*, The wooden frame-work of a camel-litter. A smaller kind of travelling vehicle and open. *Mushjir*, (Ground) which produces trees. Abundant in trees.

A مشجّر *mushajjar*, (A garment) figured with trees and leaves. Any thing after the fashion of a tree.

A مشجرة *mashjarat*, (Ground) planted with, or abounding in, trees (شجر *shajar*).

A مشجع *mashjiǎ*, Stark mad.

A مشجّع *mushajjiǎ*, Courage-inspiring.

A مشجوّ *mashjūw*, Sad, grieved, melancholy.

A مشجوب *mashjūb*, Perished, destroyed.

A مشجوج *mashjūj*, Wounded in the pate, broken-headed. Split (post).

A مشجوع *mashjūǎ*, Excelled in intrepidity.

A مشح *mashah*, A chafing of the inside of the thighs by walking, or of the hams by a rough garment.

A مشحاذ *mish-hāz*, A spacious hillock. Level ground. The summit of a mountain.

A مشحج *mish-haj*, The wild ass.

A مشحذ *mish-haz*, A whetstone. A hard driver.

A مشحشح *mushahshah*, Worthless, good for little.

A مشحط *mash-hat*, (v. n. of شحط) Diluting (wine or milk). Being distant, absent. Retiring, receding. Outstripping, getting the start of. Slaughtering (a camel). Being estimated beyond the value. Propping (a palm-shoot). Stinging (a scorpion). Filling (a vessel). Voiding dung. Chirping (a bird). *Mish-hat*, A vine-prop.

A مشحّم *mushahham*, (Bread) baked or stuffed with lard (شحم *shahm*), larded. *Mushahhim*, One who has much fat in the house, or has fat camels.

A مشحنزر *mush-hanzir*, Prepared to reproach or revile. A slow grower.

A مشحنظر *mush-hanzir*, Prominent-eyed.

A مشحون *mash-hūn*, Filled, charged. Full. Freighted (ship). Driven back. P دل صفا مشحون *dili safā-mash-hūn*, A heart replete with purity; also of content or happiness.

A مشحئنّ *mush-haǐnn*, Provoked, enraged.

P مشخ *mashkh*, An example, a copy to write after; an exercise.

P مشخش *mashakhsh*, Do not trip or stumble.

A مشخّص *mushakhkhas*, Ascertained, certain. Stipulated, agreed. A fine, amercement.

A مشخل *mishkhal* or مشخلة *mishkhalat*, A strainer.

A مشخلبة *mashkhalabat*, (in Irāk) A white spheric shell, resembling a pearl; a necklace made of such shells strung on the fibres of the palm-tree; also a girl wearing such necklace.

P مشخنه *mushakhna*, A kind of sweetmeat.

A مشخوص *mashkhūs*, Disturbed, disquieted.

A مشخئنّ *mushkhaǐnn*, Enraged, angry.

A مشدح *mashdah*, Vulva.

A مشدخ *mishdakh*, Any implement for breaking.

A مشدّخ *mushaddakh*, Broken (head). Burst by pressing (date). Decollated. The place of decollation.

A مشدّد *mushaddad*, Strengthened. Tied together. A letter marked with the sign of duplication ّ, called تشديد *tashdīd*.

A مشدن *mushdin*, (pl. مشادن *mashādin* and مشادين *mashādīn*) (A doe) mother of a grown fawn.

A مشدود *mashdūd*, Bound, tied, fastened, begirt.

A مشدونة *mashdūnat*, (A girl) kept at home till past her bloom.

A مشدوه *mashdūh*, Astonished, amazed, thunderstruck. Employed.

A مشذب *mishzab*, A pruning-hook.

A مشذب *mushazzab*, Lopt, pruned. Tall, well-shaped, and handsome (man). Long-bodied (horse).

A مشر *mishr*, Very ruddy (man). *Mashar*, (v. n. of مشر) Putting forth green and tender branches or suckers about the root (a tree). One who goes with a graceful, sprightly air. اذهبه مشرا *azhabahu masharan*, He reviled, ridiculed, disparaged him.

A مشراص *mishrās*, A crooked iron slightly pricking an ass between the shoulders.

A مشراط *mishrāt*, (pl. مشاريط *mashārīt*) A lancet or scarificator. A beginning. Make, structure.

A مشراق *mishrāk*, A place exposed to the sun.

A مشرب *mashrab*, (v. n. of شرب) Drinking. Imbibing. A reservoir of water, or any place out of which they drink. Water. A beverage. (pl. مشارب *mashārib*) Nature, temper, humour. Sect, religion. لطيف مشرب *latīf-mashrab*, Of an amiable disposition, affable, good-natured.

A مشرّب *musharrab*, Mixed, deeply imbued. The letters ر *r*, ز *z*, ض *z*, ظ *z*, and ذ *z*.

A مشربة *mashrabat* or *mashrubat*, (pl. مشارب *mashārib*) A dining-room, parlour. A banquet. A veranda, portico, or gallery. A window. A place whence they fetch water. A handful of water. Soft ground; also verdant. *Mishrabat*, A drinking-vessel.

A مشرة *mashrat*, An ear beautifully shaped. Raiment, dress. A leaf ere it has become green and rough. A shoot resembling a palm-leaf from about the roots of the tree عضاة *ɛizāt*, and of many other trees; also a soft, tender branch or twig. Name of a bird. ما احسن مشرة الارض *mā ahsana mashratu'l arz*, How beautiful is the face of the ground! امرأة مشرة الاعضاء *imraɛat mashratu'l aɛzā*, A woman who has quenched her thirst.

A مشرّج *musharraj*, Drawn (purse-string).

A مشرجع *musharjaɛ*, Lengthened, elongated. A sledge-hammer or a square block of wood rounded or bevelled at the edges.

A مشرجعة *musharjaɛat*, A long hammer.

A مشرح *mashrah*, Privities of a female.

A مشرّح *musharrah*, (Meat) cut into bits.

A مشرّر *musharrar*, (Meat) dried in the wind.

A مشرّز *musharraz*, Tied together. Intricate, mazy.

A مشرس *mushris*, The owner of camels which feed on the thorny shrub شرس *shirs*.

A مشرسة *mushrisat*, A place where the dwarfish thorny mountain-shrub شرس *shirs* grows.

A مشرسفة *musharsafat*, White-sided (sheep).

A مشرشر *musharshir*, A lion.

A مشرط *mishrat*, A lancet or fleam.

A مشرطح *mushartih* or *mushartah*, A traveller, a wanderer over the earth.

A مشرع *mushraɛ*, Levelled, pointed (spear).

A مشرعة *mashraɛat* or *mashruɛat*, A place where cattle are watered.

A مشرف *mashraf*, (pl. مشارف *mashārif*) An eminence, high place. *Mushraf*, A tower or lofty building on an eminence. *Mushrif*, Imminent, impending, overhanging. Erect, upright, tall, high. Near, at the point of. One who raises or ennobles. An examiner, inspector, observer. An officer in a treasury who authenticates accounts and writings.

A مشرّف *musharraf*, Exalted, honoured, ennobled. (A house) ornamented with pinnacles, turrets, or battlements. A margin, brink, edge.

A مشرفيّ *mashrifiy* or *mashrafiy*, Belonging to, or produced in, the villages of مشارف *mashārif*.

A مشرق *mashrik*, The east, sun-rising. P مشرق گشاده زال زر *mashrik-gushāda-zāli zar*, Dawn. Sunrise. A *Mushrik*, Bright, shining.

A مشرّق *musharrak*, (Meat) dried in the sun. (A garment) dyed red. Plastered red (edifice). An oratory, place dedicated to prayer. The mosque of Khayf. The market of Taif. *Musharrik*, One who dries (meat) in the sun. One who turns to, or verges towards, the east (شرق *shark*).

A مشرقان *mashrikāni*, (dual) The east and west. The summer and winter solstices. بعد المشرقين *buɛdu'l mashrikayn*, The distance between the east and west. The distance between Cancer and Capricorn.

A مشرقة *mashrakat*, *mashrikat*, or *mashrukat*, A place where they sit to bask in the sun.

A مشرقيّ *mashrikiy*, Oriental, eastern.

A مشرك *mushrak*, Shared. A thing common to many. *Mushrik*, One who makes a partner, admits into partnership. One who believes in a plurality of gods, a polytheist, idolater, pagan. One who talks to himself like a mopish, melancholy man.

A مشرّك *musharrak*, Shared. Common to many. (A shoe) furnished with latchets or strings (شراك).

A مشركيّ *mushrikiy*, A polytheist, idolater, pagan.

A مشركين *mushrikīn*, (pl. of مشرك) Infidels.

A مشرمط *musharmit*, Ragged (garment).

A مشروب *mashrūb*, Drunk; imbibed; potable.

A مشروبات *mashrūbāt*, (pl. fem.) Drinkables.

A مشروح *mashrūh*, Explained, declared, illustrated. Above-mentioned. Wine or any beverage. The vapour called سراب *sarāb*. P برمنوال مشروح *bar minwāli mashrūh*, In the aforesaid manner.

A مشروحا *mashrūhan*, Agreeably to the explanation, circumstantially.

A مشروسة *mashrūsat*, Scabby-lipped (camels).

A مشروص *mashrūs*, Cut.

A مشروط *mashrūt*, Cut open. Agreed upon, stipulated. Pledged, under obligation. Conditional. Contingent. (in India) A settled revenue of ten per cent. allowed to the zamindārs. (Lands or grants) appropriated in whole or in part to particular uses.

A مشروطات *mashrūtāt*, Contingencies.

A مشروع *mashrūɛ*, Begun, commenced. Legal, just, prescribed by law. Levelled, pointed (spear). A kind of cloth of silk and cotton mixed, in which Muhammadans are allowed to pray.

A مشروف *mashrūf*, Excelled in nobility.

A مشروم *mashrūm*, Split in the nose.

P مشرونيتن *mashrūnitan*, (in zand) To gather.

A مشرهف *mushrahiff*, One whose hair is dishevelled. Barefoot. Pale, pallid.

A مشريق *mishrīk*, A place where they sit exposed to the sun. (A door) pervious to the rays of the rising sun. The door of repentance in heaven.

A مشش *mashash*, (v. n. of مش) Having a cartilaginous excrescence on the pastern (a horse); the excrescence itself. A white speck coming on the eye of a camel.

A مشقّص *mushiss*, (A camel) scarce of milk.

A مشط *masht*, (v. n. of مشط) Combing. Mixture. دائم المشط *dāɛimu'l masht*, A fawner, flatterer. *Masht*, *misht*, *musht*, *mashit*, *mushut*, or *mushutt*, (pl. امشاط *amshāt* and مشاط *mishāt*) A comb. مشط الذئب *mushtu'z zib*, Name of a plant. مشط الراعي *mushtu'r rāɛī*, Shepherd's comb, the teasle. *Musht*, A mark impressed upon camels. The shoulder-blade. Small bones in the upper part of the feet. The instrument by which the web is stretched in working. The cover of a jar. *Mashat*, (v. n. of مشط) Having collops of fat upon his sides (a camel). Becoming hard from labour, or having a thorn run into it (the hand).

A مشطّب *mushattab*, Furrowed (sword-blade). Striped (garment). (Ground) hollowed by the flux of water. A stuffed and quilted saddle-cloth.

A مشطة *mashtat*, A comb made of box-wood. *Mishtat*, Mode or style of combing. مشطة الرجل *mishtatu'r rijl*, The upper part of the foot.

A مشطوب *mashtūb*, Grooved (sword-blade). Swollen with fat (loins or buttocks of a horse).

A مشطور *mashtūr*, Halved, bi-sected, divided in two. Bread smeared over with condiment. In the verse called رجز *rajaz*, three parts out of six dropped.

A مشظ *mashz*, (v. n. of مشظ) Choosing a country (for one's residence). Snatching. A piece of a thorn sticking in the skin. *Mashz* or *mashaz*, (v. n. of مشظ) Being hurt (in the hand) by a sharp thorn or any thing similar. Having galled thighs. Having his sinews seen through the skin (a horse). *Mashiz*, Pierced in the hand with a thorn or splinter.

A مشظة *mashzat*, Any thing obscure: doubtful intelligence. *Mishzat*, A splinter, chip, fragment.

A مشظّظ *mushazzaz*, Erect and stiff.

A مشظف *mishzaf*, A talker little to the purpose.

A مشع *mashɛ*, (v. n. of مشع) Collecting, acquiring, gaining. Seizing, drawing away, carrying off. Travelling leisurely. Milking (sheep). Teasing (cotton). Striking (with a rope). Eating (a cucumber). Emitting (urine or sperm).

A مشعال *mishɛāl*, (pl. مشاعيل *mashāɛīl*) A leathern vessel placed upon four feet, in which the Nomade Arabs keep their palm-wine.

A مشعانّ *mushɛānn*, One with dishevelled hair.

A مشعب *mashʿab*, A path, covered way, by-road. A mark impressed on a camel. مشعب الحق *mashʿabu'l hakk*, The way of truth. *Mishʿab*, An instrument with which they mend broken vessels. A gimlet, a boring instrument.

A مشعّب *mushaʿʿab*, Patched. Marked with the sign شعب *shiʿb*.

A مشعّبة *mushaʿʿabat*, (A dish) mended with several pieces.

P مشعبدان حقهٔ سبز *mushaʿbidāni hukkaʿi sabz*, The sun and moon. The planets.

A مشعبذ *mushaʿbiz*, A juggler, conjurer.

A مشعة *mishʿat*, A bit of teased cotton.

A مشعّث *mushaʿʿas*, (in versification) When one of the two inflecting vowels of the foot وتد *watad* has been dropped.

A مشعر *mashʿar*, (pl. مشاعر *mashāʿir*) A place dedicated to religious ceremonies, or where sacrifices are offered. The rites of the temple of Mecca. Trees growing in smooth ground, affording shelter in winter and shade in summer. External sense (as hearing or seeing). المشعر الحرام *al mashʿaru'l* (or *al mishʿaru'l*) *harām*, Muzdalifa. *Mushʿir*, One who signifies, indicates, makes sign, or gives information; whatever denotes or bears marks of. Hairy, shaggy.

A مشعراني *mushʿarānīy*, Hairy.

A مشعرة *mashʿarat*, A rendezvous of poets.

A مشعشع *mushaʿshaʿ*, (Shade) light, not dense. Mixed, diluted (wine).

A مشعل *mashʿal*, A torch, flambeau, lantern. A fire-grate. A light-house. *Mishʿal*, (pl. مشاعل *mashāʿil*) A leathern vessel placed upon four feet, in which the Scenite Arabs keep their palm-wine. A strainer. *Mushʿal*, Kindled, lighted. *Mushʿil*, One who kindles (a fire). An incendiary. Numerous and scattered (swarm of locusts).

A مشعلة *mashʿalat*, (pl. مشاعل *mashāʿil*) Any place for a lantern or fire. *Mushʿilat*, Scattered, dispersed (army). Scattered (locusts).

P مشعلچي *mashʿalchī*, A torch-bearer.

P مشعله *mashʿala*, A lantern, link, torch, flambeau. مشعلهٔ خاوري *mashʿalaʿi khāwarī*, (روز *roz*, or صبح *subh*) The world-illuminating sun. مشعلهٔ گيتي فروز *mashʿalaʿi gītī-furoz*, The world-illuminating sun. An epithet of Muhammad.

A مشعنب *mushaʿnab* or *mushaʿnib*, (A ram) whose horns are bent backward over the head.

A مشعوذ *mushaʿwaz*, Bewitched, enchanted, fascinated: deceived by conjuring or magical arts. *Mushaʿwiz*, A juggler, conjurer.

A مشعور *mashʿūr*, (مشعورة *mashʿūrat*, or مشعوراء *mashʿūrāʾ*) (v. n. of شعر) Knowing, perceiving, understanding, noticing, remarking.

A مشعوف *mashʿūf*, Desperately in love. Foolish, mad, crazed. Terrified.

A مشعون *mashʿūn*, Dishevelled (hair). مشعون مجنون *mashʿūn majnūn*, Insane.

A مشغ *mashgh*, (v. n. of مشغ) Eating (a cucumber) slowly, leisurely. Striking. Stigmatizing, reproaching, reviling. *Mishgh*, Red earth, ruddle.

A مشغب *mishghab*, Riotous; a mischief-maker.

A مشغة *mashghat*, A piece of worn cloth, rag. A lump of clay into which they fix thorns, and, when dry, use it as a card for dressing flax.

A مشغزب *mushaghzib*, One who trips up his rival in wrestling.

A مشغل *mushghal*, Busied, occupied, employed. *Mushghil*, One who busies himself.

A مشغلة *mashghalat*, (pl. مشاغل *mashāghil*) Business, employment, occupation. Pastime. A place of business. A school.

A مشغنب *mushaghnab* or *mushaghnib*, (A goat) whose (horns) bend backwards.

A مشغوف *mashghūf*, Inflamed with love, distraught, foolish, frantic, mad.

A مشغول *mashghūl*, Busied, occupied, employed, wholly dedicated to, diligent, anxious about.

A مشغولي *mashghūlī*, Occupation, employment.

A مشغوم *mashghūm*, A camel abounding in milk.

A مشفار *mishfār*, The lip of a camel.

A مشفترّ *mushfatirr*, Trembling with horror. One whose skirts are tucked up. Diligent, prepared for business, alert, despatchful. One whose hair stands on end. Erect. Raised (dust).

A مشفّح *mushaffah*, Disappointed in every thing.

A مشفر *mishfar* or *mashfar*, (pl. مشافر *mashāfir*) The lip of a camel (though sometimes applied to men). Prohibition. Strength. Vehemence. A district of ground or of sands.

A مشفّر *mushaffir*, Narrow, scanty (subsistence).

A مشفشف *mushafshaf* or *mushafshif*, Weak, foolish, light, hasty. Bad-tempered, vicious. Tremulously sensitive, jealous.

A مشفق *mushfik*, Kind, gracious, pitiful, compassionate, sympathetic, tender. Timid, fearful.

A مشفّق *mushaffak*, Small (present). Badly woven.

P مشفقانه *mushfikāna*, Mercifully, pitifully.

A مشفلة *mishfalat*, (pl. مشافل *mashāfil*) Tripe.

A مشفوع *mashfūʿ*, Furious, insane. United, paired.

A مشفوف *mashfūf*, Clear, pellucid, diaphanous.

A مشفوه *mashfūh*, (A well or a dish) surrounded by a throng. A man who requires to be importuned with questions before any thing can be elicited from him. Little, few, exhausted.

A مشق *mashk*, (v. n. of مشق) Piercing suddenly with a spear; striking, beating, lashing, or eating with velocity. Tearing. Writing, drawing the letters. Combing. Chafing the skin (a new garment). Drawing (a thong) every way in order to stretch it. Leaving more meat than what one has eaten. Eating gently. Eating up the best parts (of forage). Being tall and slender (a girl). Milking a little. An example, a copy to write after; an exercise. Practice, usage, use. Red-dyeing earth, ruddle. Modus coeundi. *Mishk*, Red-dyeing earth, ruddle. Spare, lean. *Mushk*, (pl. of امشق *amshak*) Chafed between the thighs. *Mashak*, (v. n. of مشق) Being galled between the thighs (a man). *Mishak*, (pl. of مشقة *mishkat*) Locks, tufts of wool.

A مشقّ *mashakk*, A nick, slit, cranny, opening.

A مشقأ *mashkaʾ*, The parting of the hair on the head. *Mishkaʾ*, A comb.

A مشقا *mishkaʾ*, A comb.

A مشقاء *mashkāʾ*, (fem. of امشق *amshak*) Galled between the thighs. *Mishkāʾ*, A comb.

A مشقأة *mishkaʾat*, A comb: bodkin for the hair.

A مشقة *mashkat*, The mark of a tethering rope on the leg of an animal. Width, space between the legs of an animal. A crack in the hoof. A bad scratch. *Mishkat*, (pl. مشق *mishak*) A tuft of wool. Hair-combings, wool-combings. A torn garment. *Mushkat*, A chafe-gall between the thighs, and a liability to it from their form.

A مشقّة *mashakkat*, (v. n. of شقّ) Being difficult and troublesome. Throwing into difficulties. *Mashakkat* or *mishakkat*, Inconvenience, trouble, labour, pains, toil, affliction, adversity, pain, distress, misfortune.

A مشقّر *mushakkar*, A leathern water-bottle. A large cup or goblet.

A مشقص *mishkas*, An arrow with a broad long point for shooting wild beasts.

A مشقّص *mushakkis*, A butcher.

A مشقّق *mushakkak*, Cracked, split.

A مشقوح *mashkūh*, Reprobated, cursed.

A مشقوق *mashkūk*, Split, cleft, riven.

P مشقوليه *mashkūliya*, Wāmik's mother-in-law.

A مشقي *mashkī*, Acquired by practice.

A مشقي *mishkaʾ*, A comb.

P مشك *mashk*, A sheep-skin tanned or not, especially for carrying butter-milk or water. مشك چرمي *mashki charmī*, Vulva. *Mushk* or *mishk*, Musk. مشك اذفر *mushki azfar*, The finest kind of musk. مشك بلاد *mushki bilād*, Civet. مشك تاتاري *mushki tātārī*, Musk of Tartary. مشك تبت *mushki tubt* or *tabut*, Musk of Tibet (of a very superior quality). مشك تركماني *mushki turkmānī*, Root of the cyperis (an Indian plant like ginger, having, when chewed, the virtues of saffron). مشك دواني *mushki dawānī*, A fire-arrow. مشك زمين *mushki zamīn*, Musk of the earth, galangale. مشك نافه *mushki nāfa*, Exquisite musk. موي مشك بوي *mūyi mushk-būy*, Hair scented with musk. مشك بستن *mushk bastan*, To tie the hands behind the back.

A مشكّ *mashakk*, A place of joining.

A مشكاة *mishkāt*, A hole in the wall not quite through, a niche (in which a lamp is placed).

A مشكار *mishkār*, (Cattle) full of milk.

P مشكبار *mushk-bār*, Diffusing musk. Lock, curl, or ringlet of a mistress.

P مشك بيد *mushk-bīd,* Flower of the willow.

P مشك دانه *mushk-dāna* or *mishk-dāna,* Name of a fragrant berry which they bore and pass through with a thread. Name of the 22d note of the barbud.

P مشكدر *mashk-dar,* Name of an animalcule which eats holes into a leathern bottle.

P مشكدم *mushk-dām,* A black singing bird.

P مشكدوز *mashk-doz,* A leathern-bottle stitcher.

P مشكر *mashikar,* Do not hunt.

A مشكر *mushkir,* (An udder) full of milk.

A مشكرة *mashka* or *mushkirat,* Grass which causes a great increase of milk. *Mushkirat,* Milky (herb).

P مشكسار *mushk-sār,* (or مشكسارة *mushk-sāra*) (A place) sweetly smelling, perfumed with musk.

P مشكفام *mushk-fām,* Musk-coloured: black, jetty. The locks of a mistress.

P مشك فروشان *mushk-faroshān,* Venders of musk, (metaphorically) Polite, amiable men.

P مشك فشان از قفا *mushk-fishān az kafā,* Who emits a fragrant smell from the mouth in speaking.

P مشكك *mushkak,* Galangale. A field-mouse.

A مشكك *mushakkak,* Thrown into doubt.

P مشكل *mashkul,* A thief, a robber.

A مشكل *mushkil,* Difficult, hard, painful; intricate. Doubtful, obscure, ambiguous. A difficulty.

مشكل التسخير *mushkilu't taskhīr,* (A town) hard to be taken.

A مشكّل *mushakkal,* Formed. Well-shaped. Beautiful, handsome.

A مشكلات *mushkilāt,* (pl. fem.) Difficulties.

P مشكل پسندان *mushkil-pasandān,* Those who are fond of difficulties.

A مشكلة *mushkilat,* (fem. of مشكل) Difficult, obscure. A doubtful proposition, problem.

P مشكل كشا *mushkil-kushā,* Solver of difficulties.

P مشكمالي *mushk-mālī,* Name of the twenty-fourth note of the barbud.

P مشك موي *mushk-moy,* Black-haired.

P مشكن *mashkan,* Do not break. Be not impetuous or severe. Be not disturbed.

P مشكناب *mushk-nāb,* Exquisite musk.

P مشكنافه *mushk-nāfa,* A musky-smelling plant.

P مشكنك *mushkinah,* A bird about the size of a partridge, generally found on the banks of rivers. A ditch, a low-lying place.

P مشكو *mashkū,* A small leathern bag or bottle. *Mushko,* (*mashko,* or مشكوي *mushkoy*) A palace built by Khusraw Parvez, king of Persia, in which he lived with his consort Shīrīn. A temple, shrine of an idol. The female apartments in a palace. An upper chamber, gallery, or balcony on the top of a house. A garden.

A مشكوّ *mashkūw,* Complained of.

A مشكور *mashkūr,* Thanked. Praised. Acknowledged, rewarded. Worthy of thanks or praise, laudable, agreeable, acceptable. Liberated. اللفت المشكور *al liftu'l mashkūr,* (in Morocco) A large kind of rape-root.

A مشكوري *mashkūrī,* Reward. Thanking.

P مشكوفه *mashkūfa,* (or مشكوفي *mashkūfī*) A confection of almonds and sugar.

A مشكوك *mashkūk,* Doubted, doubtful, uncertain, problematical. Run through with a spear.

P مشكول *mashkūl,* A small water-bottle or bag.

A مشكول *mashkūl,* A verse in which the second and seventh letters are dropped; as when فاعلاتن *fāʿilātun* is reduced to فاعلات *fāʿilātu.*

P مشكوله *mashkūla,* A little water-vessel. *Mushkūla* or *mishkūla,* A small bit of musk.

P مشكويه *mashkoya,* An idol-temple. The princesses' apartments. Name of a note in music.

P مشكوئي *mashkoʾī,* Name of a note in music.

P مشكي *mushkī,* Dark bay, verging to black.

A مشكي *mushkī,* One who pacifies, or who stills a complaint (شكاية *shikāyat*).

A مشكيّ *mashkīy,* Complained of. Suspected.

P مشكيدن *mushkīdan,* To gnaw. To murmur.

P مشكيزة *mashkīza,* A small water-bottle.

P مشكين *mushkīn,* Musky. Black, dark, jetty.

مشكين وفادار *mushkīni wafā-dār,* The narcissus.

P مشكين چاه *mushkīn-chāh,* (مشكين چه *mushkīn-chah,* or مشكين جو *mushkīn-jav*) A mole on the face of a mistress.

P مشكين ختام *mushkīn-khitām,* (Wine) of a musky flavour.

P مشكين سنان *mushkīn-sinān,* (Black points of spears) The eyelashes of a mistress.

P مشكين فام *mushkīn-fām,* Black-coloured.

P مشكينك *mushkīnah,* A kind of sweetmeat.

P مشكين كلاه *mushkīn-kulāh,* (or كله *kulah*) A black cap. The raven locks of the fair.

P مشكين مهره *mushkīn-muhra,* The earth.

P مشگ *mashg,* A milk-bottle or water-bottle made of a sheep-skin *Mishg,* Musk.

A مشل *mashl,* A little milking.

A مشلّ *mishall,* Active in serving; social, cheerful, friendly. An ass that pursues (the female).

A مشلّح *mushallah,* Stripped. An antechamber in a bath where the bathers leave their clothes; the stripping-room. *Mushallih,* A stripper.

A مشلشل *mushalshal,* Distilling, dropping.

P مشلوز *mishshalawz,* A sweet-pulped apricot.

A مشلول *mashlūl,* Dried, withered (hand).

A مشلّي *mushalla',* Slender.

A مشليق *mishlīk,* A laugher with open mouth.

A مشمّ *mushimm,* Averse, alienated.

A مشمال *mishmāl,* The outward covering of the body, a wrapper.

A مشمّت *mushammat,* Created, saluted (king). *Mushammit,* One who blesses or congratulates.

A مشمخرّ *mushmahhirr,* A high mountain.

A مشمذ *mishmaz,* A turban-sash.

A مشمّر *mushammir,* One who tucks up his apron or trousers. Alert, active, expeditious. Expert.

A مشمرج *mushamraj,* Reared with care.

A مشمرق *mushamrak,* Cut, burnt in bits (garment).

A مشمّس *mushammas,* Exposed to the sun.

A مشمش *mashmash* or *mishmish,* An apricot.

P مشمشا *mashmashā,* (in zand) A kind of apricot.

A مشمشة *mashmashat,* A steeping of medicine (in water). Lightness, agility, swiftness.

A مشمّع *mushammaʿ,* Waxed, smeared with wax. Wax-cloth, cerecloth.

A مشمعة *mashmaʿat,* (v. n. of شمع) Playing, jesting. A joke. *Mishmaʿat,* A candlestick.

A مشمعلّ *mushmaʿill,* A sprightly she-camel. Long (camel). Tall, light, and elegant (man). Sharp, sour (milk).

A مشمل *mishmal,* A short sword worn under the garment. *Mishmal,* (or مشملة *mishmalat*) A garment of coarse velvet which quite covers the body.

A مشموط *mashmūt,* Mixed.

A مشموع *mashmūʿ,* Ambergrised (musk).

A مشمول *mashmūl,* Comprehended, contained, surrounded. Common, universal. Blown upon or shaken by the north wind (شمال *shamāl* or *shimāl*). Refrigerated, cooled (wine). (Wine) cold to the taste. (A man) of an excellent disposition.

A مشموم *mashmūm,* Smelled. Perfumed, odoriferous, musky, fragrant. Tried, proved. Musk.

A مشمئزّ *mushmaʾizz,* Terrified, horror-stricken.

A مشن *mashn,* (v. n. of مشن) Striking gently (with a sword or scourge). Scratching, excoriating, grazing the skin. Lying with. Rubbing with the hand in order to make smooth. Giving.

A مشنأ *mashnaʾ,* (v. n. of شنأ) Hating. (sing. and pl. mas. and fem.) Ugly, deformed in countenance, disagreeable, although liked. A hater of mankind, a misanthrope.

A مشناء *mishnāʾ,* Hated by all.

A مشناة *mashnaʾat,* (v. n. of شنأ) Hating.

A مشنة *mashnat,* An excoriation, scratch. A broad wound but not deep.

P مشنج *mishanj,* A meat-fly. *Mushanj,* A grain.

A مشنّج *mushannaj,* Wide, ample, roomy.

A مشنّخ *mushannakh,* A palm cleared of prickles.

A مشنّط *mushannat,* Roasted (meat).

A مشنّف *mushannaf,* Decked (with ear-rings).

A مشنّق *mushannak,* Cut into slices, as a cake dressed with oil amongst meat.

A مشنقة *mashnakat,* A hanging-place, gallows.

A مشنگ *mashang,* A thief or robber. A kind of rope. *Mushang* or *mashang,* A sort of grain.

مشنگ تلخ *mashangi talkh,* A bitter pea.

P مشنگك *mashangak,* A thief. *Mushangak,* A species of grain.

P مشنو *mishnav,* Listen not.

A مشنوّ *mashnūw,* Hated, detested.

A مشنوء *mashnūʾ,* Hated, disliked (though fair).

A مشنوءة *mashnūʾat,* (v. n. of شنأ) Hating.

A مشنوع *mashnūʿ*, Notorious, well-known.

A مشنوفة *mashnūfat*, (A woman) decked with a nose-jewel: (a camel) with a rein through the nose.

A مشنوق *mashnūḳ*, (A camel) reined up tight. Hanged. Tall (man).

A مشنيّ *mashnīy*, Hated, disliked.

A مشو *mashw*, Aperient, laxative (medicine).

P مشو *mashav*, (imper. of شدن *shudan*) Be not thou. *Mashū*, (imper. of شستن *shustan*) Do not wash. *Mushū*, Pease.

A مشوّ *mashūw*, Aperient, laxative (medicine).

A مشواذ *mishwāz*, (pl. مشاويذ) A turban.

A مشوار *mishwār*, (v. n. of شار for شور) Offering (cattle) for sale; riding (a horse) backwards and forwards by way of shewing him off to a buyer. A place where horses are exposed to sale. A piece of wood to which the combs in a hive are fastened, or with which the honey is taken out. The string of a large bow, with which they beat cotton. The inside of any thing; also the outside. Fatness. The cud. The yard (of a horse).

A مشوارة *mishwārat*, A bee-hive.

A مشواع *mishwāʿ*, Chamber of oven or furnace.

A مشوال *mishwāl*, A stone which is lifted up as a trial of strength.

A مشوذ *mishwaz*, A turban. A king, lord.

A مشور *mashūr*, Adorned, decorated. Gathered (honey). *Mishwar*, A piece of wood with which the honey is taken out. A prism.

A مشوّر *mushawwar*, Saffron-dyed (garment).

A مشورة *mashwarat*, Counsel, consultation, advice. P مشورت كردن *mashwarat kardan*, To consult, deliberate. مشورت طلب كردن *mashwarat talab kardan*, To ask advice. A اهل مشورة *ahli mashwara*, A counsellor, one of the counsel.

A مشوز *mashūz*, Unsteady, restless, and timid.

A مشوش *mashūsh*, A napkin. Any thing with which the hand is wiped.

P مشوش *mushūsh*, Oil beat into a consistency with the white of an egg.

A مشوّش *mushawwash*, Disturbed, distressed, uneasy, perplexed. Confused, intricate, embroiled. مشوّش الرقوم *mushawwashu'r rukūm*, Confused writing. (An old woman) wrinkled (with age). Melancholy; uncertain. *Mushawwish*, Rough and dangerous (sea).

A مشوع *mashūʿ*, Rapacious (wolf).

A مشوف *mashūf*, Bright (money). Dressed, adorned (with various-coloured wool, &c.) Anointed with pitch (a camel). Furious, raging (stallion). مشوف معلم *mashūf muʿlam*, Bright stamped coin.

A مشوق *mashūḳ*, Full of desire. (A leathern bottle) reared against a wall.

A مشوك *mashūk*, Infected with the disease called شوكة *shawkat*. *Mushwik*, Thorny (tree).

A مشوكة *mushwikat*, Thorny (tree or land).

A مشول *mishwal*, A small sieve. A small sickle. *Mushūl*, (v. n. of مشل) Being spare (flesh).

A مشوم *mashūm*, Unfortunate. Marked with a mole. P مشوم اختر *mashūm-akhtar*, Born under an unlucky planet; ignoble.

A مشؤمة *mashʼumat*, Unlucky (woman).

A مشؤوز *mashʼūz*, Unsteady, restless, and timid.

A مشؤوف *mashʼūf*, Frightened, terrified, timid.

A مشؤوفة *mashʼūfat*, (A foot) ulcerated below.

A مشؤوم *mashʼūm*, (pl. مشائيم) Unfortunate.

A مشوّه *mushawwah*, Deformed, disfigured, ugly-shaped. Viewed with a malignant eye.

A مشوي *mushwī*, One who roasts meat, or prepares it for dressing. (See اشواء *ishwāʼ*.)

A مشويّ *mashwīy*, Roasted. Missed by a stone.

A مشهبر *mushahbar*, Large (headed).

P مشهد *mash-had*, The city of Tūs, in Khurāsān, together with the adjacent village Sanābād.

A مشهد *mash-had*, A burying-place for those especially who have been killed in fighting for religion, and therefore a place of holy visitation. A place where people meet. مشهد معطّر و مرقد منوّر *mash-hadi muʿattar u marḳadi munawwar*, The holy sepulchre. *Mush-had*, Slain for religion's sake; a martyr. Slain without any mulct or fine being paid. *Mush-hid*, A witness. One who calls for or brings evidence. Standing before. (A woman) present with her husband.

A مشهدة *mash-hadat* or *mash-hudat*, A place where people meet.

A مشهّر *mushahhar*, Embroidered (upper-garment).

A مشهّرة *mushahharat*, Name of a horse.

A مشهود *mash-hūd*, Attested, proved. Witnessed. Friday. The resurrection. The day of عرفة *ʿarafat*.

A مشهودة *mash-hūdat*, Prayer. Evening-prayer. Morning-prayer.

A مشهور *mash-hūr*, Drawn, brandished (sword). (pl. مشاهير *mashāhīr*) Public, notorious, well-known. Published, divulged, conspicuous. Celebrated, illustrious, noted, famous, glaring. مشهور عالم و معلوم بني آدم *mashhūri ʿālam u maʿlūmi banī ādam*, Published to the world, and known to the sons of men.

A مشهوم *mash-hūm*, Struck with terror. Quick, clever, witty.

A مشهّي *mushahhī*, Lust-exciting.

A مشي *mashy*, (v. n. of مشي) Walking, going. Driving. Being directed in one's march, finding one's way. Being rich in cattle. A looseness, flux, purging. مشيا على الاقدام *mashyun ʿala'l ikdām*, Trusting to his feet (he went). مشيا علي وجه *mashyan ʿala' wajhin*, To go upon the face, *i. e.* to behave with humility, to approach as a suppliant. P مشي علي وجه البحر كردن *mashy ʿala' wajhi'l bahr kardan*, To sail on the face of the sea.

A مشيّ *mashīy*, Aperient, purgative (medicine).

P مشيا *mashyā*, (in zand and Pāzand) Butter made of sheep's milk.

A مشيّأ *mushayyaʼ*, Weak, corrupt. Discordant.

A مشياط *mishyāt*, (A she-camel) soon fattening.

A مشياع *mishyāʿ*, Who discovers or blabs all.

P مشيب *mashīb*, Do not be distressed.

A مشيب *mashīb*, Grey hair, hoariness.

A مشيئة *mashīʼat*, (or مشيّة *mashīyat*) Will, pleasure. Will of God, fate. Strength. Puberty.

A مشية *mishyat*, A mode of walking. Gait. Walking. Direction.

A مشيج *mashīj*, (pl. امشاج) Mixed. A mixture.

A مشيح *mushīh*, One who approaches and keeps off any one who may be behind him. Diligent. Strong and fleet (camel). Broad and prominent-chested (camel).

A مشيحي *mashīha'*, Diligence in the expediting of business. Mixture, confusion.

A مشيخاء *mashyukhāʼ*, (مشيخة *mashyakhat*, or *mashīkhat*) (pl. of شيخ *shaykh*) Seniors, elders, sheiks, old men, princes, presidents, prelates, doctors.

A مشيد *mashīd*, Plastered.

A مشيّد *mushayyad*, Plastered. High-raised (edifice). Firm, solid, strengthened. P آستان مشيّد الاركان *āsitāni mushayyadu'l arkān*, The palace raised upon lofty columns or strong pillars, *i. e.* the Ottoman Porte. A *Mushayyid*, An architect.

A مشيّدة *mushayyadat*, High-raised (edifices).

A مشير *mushīr*, Pointing; any thing that points. A counsellor, senator.

A مشيرة *mushīrat*, The index or fore-finger.

A مشيّز *mushayyaz*, Red-striped (long cloak).

A مشيط *mashīt*, Combed (hair).

A مشيع *mashīʿ*, Filled (vessel). *Mishyaʿ*, Malevolent. Worthless. Avaricious.

A مشيّع *mushayyaʿ*, Bold, strenuous. Hasty. Accompanied, followed.

A مشيعة *mashīʿat*, A bit of teased cotton. *Mishyaʿat*, A box or basket of palm-leaves in which women keep their sewing cotton.

A مشيق *mashīḳ*, (A garment) worse for the wear. Gaunt-bellied (horse). Spare, lean.

A مشيم *mashīm*, Marked with a black mole. (pl. of مشيمة *mashīmat*) Secundines, after-births.

A مشيمة *mashīmat*, (pl. مشيم *mashīm* and مشائم *mashāʼim*) The membrane which enwraps the fœtus in the womb, and comes along with the birth. مشيمة عالم *mashīmaʼi ʿālam*, The sun. The sky.

A مشين *mashīn*, Villainous, worthless.

A مشيّن *mushayyan*, Stately, dignified.

A مشيوخاء *mashyūhāʼ*, Diligence, expedition in any work. Mixture. A difficult business. A work in which expedition is manifested. *Mashyūhāʼ*, (or مشيوحا *mashyūha'*) (Land) abounding in Pontic wormwood.

A مشيوخاء *mashyūkhāʼ*, (pl. of شيخ *shaykh*) Venerable men, elders, sheiks, persons conspicuous for their piety and learning.

A مشؤوز *mashʼūz*, Unsteady, unquiet.

A مشؤوم *mashʼūm*, Unfortunate, ill-omened.

A مشيوم *mashyūm*, Marked with a black mole.

A مشيئة *mashī-at*, (v. n. of شيئ) Willing, wishing, desiring. Desire, will.

A مص *mas*, (for مصنف *musannif*) An author.

A مص *mass*, (v. n. of مص) Sucking, sipping.

A مصاءكة *musā-akat*, (v. n. 3 of صئك) Seizing, or vehemently contending with.

A مصاب *mis-ab*, One who drinks much water, who quenches thirst.

A مصاب *musāb*, Afflicted, hurt. Insane, possessed. Low-spirited. Struck (as an arrow upon the mark). Happened. Found. An affection of the mind. A sugar-cane.

A مصاباة *musābāt*, (v. n. of صبا for صبو) Inverting (a sword) to sheath it; (a spear) to strike with it; (or as a camel, the lips) to drink. Causing (a building) to lean. Making verses without much point or meaning in them.

A مصابة *musābat*, (v. n. 4 of صاب for صوب) Injuring, hurting, afflicting. A misfortune, calamity.

A مصابح *masābih*, (pl. of مصباح *misbāh*) Goblets from which they drink in the morning.

A مصابر *musābir*, Patient towards one's fellows.

A مصابرة *musābarat*, (v. n. 3 of صبر) Exercising patience (towards one another). Endurance.

A مصابية *musābiyat*, A calamity, misfortune.

A مصابيح *masābīh*, (pl. of مصباح *misbāh*) Lanterns. The heavenly luminaries. Cups from which they drink in the morning.

A مصاتة *musāttat*, A debating, a wrangling.

A مصاحات *musāhāt*, Skins of lambs or kids stuffed and placed before the dams to induce them to let their milk flow freely; tulchans.

A مصاحب *musāhib*, A companion, associate, friend. The favourite of a prince. An aid-de-camp. Gentle and tractable after having been stubborn and refractory.

A مصاحبة *musāhabat*, Company, familiarity, society. *Mushāhibat*, A female friend.

A مصاحر *musāhir*, One who in the desert attacks his companion, yet openly, not unawares.

A مصاحرة *musāharat*, (v. n. 3 of صحر) Doing (any thing) plainly, publicly, and openly.

A مصاحف *masāhif*, (pl. of مصحف *mas, mis,* and *mus-haf*) Books, volumes. Kur'āns.

A مصاخ *mussākh*, A plant coated like an onion.

A مصاخبة *musākhabat*, A reproving sharply.

A مصاخد *masākhid*, Noon-tide heats.

A مصاخف *masākhif*, (pl. of مصخفة) Spades.

A مصاد *masād*, The top or most inaccessible part of a mountain. (pl. امصدة *amsidat* and مصدان *musdān*) A high mountain.

A مصاداة *musādāt*, (v. n. 3 of صدا for صدو) Counterfeiting, dissembling, wheedling, flattering. Covering, hiding. Opposing, resisting.

A مصادر *masādir*, (pl. of مصدر *masdar*) Sources. Infinitives, (more properly) verbal nouns.

A مصادرة *musādarat*, (v. n. 3 of صدر) Fining, mulcting, amercing. Requiring, demanding. Spoiling, plundering. A mulct (for manslaughter).

A مصادع *masādiɛ*, (pl. of مصدع *masdaɛ*) Level paths through rough grounds. (pl. of مصدع *misdaɛ*) Arrows having long and broad heads.

A مصادغة *musādaghat*, (v. n. 3 of صدغ) Going side by side, and step for step. (See مداراة *mudārāt.*)

A مصادف *musādif*, Who finds, meets, falls on.

A مصادفة *musādafat*, (v. n. 3 of صدف) Meeting, encountering, finding, lighting on. Happening, occurring, taking place. An encounter.

A مصادقة *musādakat*, (v. n. 3 of صدق) Being friendly, cultivating friendship. Sincere and mutual friendship, veracity, sincerity.

A مصادمة *musādamat*, (v. n. 3 of صدم) Striking. Beating one another. Collision, blow, knock, shock of combatants.

A مصار *misār*, (pl. of مصور *masūr*) (Camels) which give their milk slowly.

A مصار *masārr*, Intestines.

A مصارة *musārat*, A place where a horse is made to gallop.

A مصارة *musārrat*, (v. n. 3 of صر) Forcing or detaining against the will.

A مصارح *musārah*, Clear, open. *Musārih*, One who discloses.

A مصارحة *musārahat*, (v. n. 3 of صرح) Doing (any thing) openly. Disclosing.

A مصارحة *musārahatan*, Openly, before another.

A مصارع *masāriɛ*, (pl. of مصرع *masraɛ*) Arenas, rings for wrestling-matches. *Musāriɛ*, A wrestler.

A مصارعة *musāraɛat*, (v. n. 3 of صرع) Wrestling, endeavouring to throw down. A contest, struggle. P دم مصارعت كردن *dami musāraɛat kardan*, To dare or presume to contend (with another).

A مصارف *masārif*, (pl. of مصرف *masraf*) Expenses, disbursements. Changes, vicissitudes.

A مصارمة *musāramat*, (v. n. 3 of صرم) Separating one from another, cutting, abandoning.

A مصاري *masārī*, (or مصاري *masāriy*) (pl. of مصري *misriy*) Town (asses).

A مصاريع *masārīɛ*, (pl. of مصراع *misrāɛ*) Folding-doors. Hemistichs.

A مصاريف *masārīf*, (pl. of مصروف *masrūf*) Expenses, disbursements, outlays, costs.

A مصارين *masārīn*, (pl. of مصران *musrān*) The intestines which receive the chyle.

A مصاص *musās*, The choicest part (of property). A species of plant. مصاص قومه *musāsu kawmihi*, The flower of his people, of an excellent origin.

A مصاص *massās*, A sucker.

A مصاصة *musāsat*, What is sucked: small thing.

A مصاطب *masātib*, (pl. of مصطبة *mistabat*) Benches, stone platforms, estrades upon which the people of the East recline.

A مصاعب *masāɛib*, Difficulties.

A مصاعد *masāɛid*, (pl. of مصعد) Ascents, steps.

A مصاعرة *musāɛarat*, (v. n. 3 of صعر) Turning the face obliquely, making wry faces in contempt.

A مصاغ *musāgh*, Cast (gold-chain or jewellery).

A مصاف *musāff*, (pl. of مصف *masaff*) Ranks. Fields of battle. P درروز مصاف *dar rozi masaff*, In the day of battle. A *Musāff*, Ranged opposite.

A مصافاة *musāfāt*, (v. n. 3 of صفا for صفو) Behaving, sincerely acting with pure affection towards (any one), making (him) your friend. Pure friendship, sincerity.

A مصافات *musāffāt*, Wars, battles.

A مصافه *musāffat*, (v. n. 3 of صف) Appearing before one another in opposition, especially in battle-array. Standing in a row or rank. Sitting over against each other on opposite benches.

A مصافح *musāfih*, One who fornicates with any woman, bond or free, gentle or simple.

A مصافحة *musāfahat*, (v. n. 3 of صفح) Taking by the hand, joining or shaking hands.

A مصافق *musāfik*, (A camel) that lies first on one side, then on the other.

A مصافقة *musāfakat*, (v. n. 3 of صفق) Turning (the side), changing or shifting a position. Labouring in the birth (a she-camel). Putting on two garments, the one over the other.

A مصافي *masāfī*, (pl. of مصفى *misfa'* or مصفاة *misfāt*) Strainers. *Musāfī*, A sincere, beloved friend.

A مصاقبة *musākabat*, (v. n. 3 of صقب) Being opposite and near.

A مصاقل *masākil*, (pl. of مصقلة *miskalat*) Polishing instruments.

A مصالة *masālat*, (v. n. of صال for صول) Being proud, insolent, perverse, unjust. *Musālat* or *masālat*, Whatever drops from a jar or exudes from a wound. The serum or whig of milk.

P مصالح *masālih*, Spicery, drug, ingredient; a compound of various drugs and spices.

A مصالح *masālih*, (pl. of مصلحة *maslahat*) Affairs. Employments, occupations. Materials. Glory.

A مصالحة *musālahat*, (v. n. 3 of صلح) Making peace together. Reconciliation, pacification.

A مصالي *masālī*, (pl. of مصلاة) Bird-nets.

A مصاليق *masālīk*, Great stones. Light camels.

A مصام *masām*, (and مصامة *masāmat*) A place where a horse stands.

A مصامد *masāmid*, (or مصاميد *masāmīd*) Camels whose milk fails not in cold or in dearth.

A مصامص *musāmis*, Compact, well-built (horse). Pure. Eminent for birth, dignity, merit. Pious.

A مصان *masān*, A den. *Musān*, Guarded, preserved. Laid up.

A مصان *massān*, One who sucks cattle from avarice; hence, يا مصان *yā massān* (fem. يا مصانة *yā massānat*) is used as a term of reproach.

A مصانع *masāniɛ*, (pl. of مصنع *masnaɛ*) Structures, buildings, forts, cisterns, tanks, &c. *Musāniɛ*

One who endeavours to conciliate.

A مصانعة *musānaʻat*, (v. n. 3 of صنع) Endeavouring to conciliate, soothing (by presents). Not putting forth his whole strength in running (a horse). Dissembling, feigning. Bribery.

A مصاوب *masāwib*, (pl. of مصوبة *masūbat*) Accidents of fortune.

A مصاولة *musāwalat*, (v. n. 3 of صال for صول) Endeavouring to insult, striving who shall be most insolent, or assault most furiously.

A مصاهاة *musāhāt*, A mounting or riding on the middle of a horse's back (صهوة *sahwat*).

A مصاهرة *musāharat*, (v. n. 3 of صهر) Forming a matrimonial alliance, marrying into a family. Affinity, connexion.

A مصائب *masāʼib*, (pl. of مصيبة *musībat*) Shocks of fortune, afflictions, calamities.

A مصاية *musāyat*, A little phial. The large crop of a bird.

A مصايحة *musāyahat*, (v. n. 3 of صاح for صيح) Calling to any one, crying aloud to one another.

A مصائد *masāʼid*, Hunter's nets, snares.

A مصائر *masāʼir*, (pl. of مصور *masūr*) (Camels) which give their milk slowly.

A مصائص *masāʼis*, (pl. of مصوص *masūs*) (Women) greedy in the enjoyment of a man; suckers.

A مصائف *masāʼif*, (pl. of مصيف *masīf*) Summer-residences.

A مصايفة *musāyafat*, (v. n. 3 of صاف for صيف) Bargaining with any one for the summer (صيف).

A مصبّ *masabb*, A place to which water flows.

A مصباح *misbāh*, A light, lantern, lamp, torch. Broad arrow or spear-head. A she-camel that rises not up to pasture till after sun-rise. Cup, goblet.

A مصبح *masbah*, The place and time of morning. *Misbah*, A cup from which they drink in the morning. *Musbah*, The morning. A passing of the morning. The place where one is in the morning.

A مصبع *masbaʻ*, (or مصبعة *masbaʻat*) Pride.

A مصبغ *musbigh*, A palm-tree whose dates have begun to acquire a ripe tint.

A مصبّغ *musabbagh*, Tinged, stained, dyed.

A مصبغة *masbaghat*, A dyeing-house.

A مصبوّ *masbūw*, Blown on by the east wind.

A مصبوب *masbūb*, Poured out. Gone, obliterated, effaced.

A مصبور *masbūr*, Taken and kept to be put to death.

A مصبورة *masbūrat*, A solemn oath.

A مصبوع *masbūʻ*, Proud, arrogant, haughty, lofty.

A مصبوغ *masbūgh*, Dyed, tinged, imbued with.

A مصبي *musbī*, (and مصبية *musbiyat*) (A woman) who has children, especially boys (صبيّ *sabīy*). One who renders frantic with love.

A مصّة *mussat*, Choicest part (of property).

A مصت *mast*, (v. n. of مصت) Lying with. Extracting the prolific seed from the uterus of a camel.

A مصتّم *musattam*, Completed, perfected, made perfect. A closed valley. A turn-again lane.

A مصتيت *mistīt*, Sharp, penetrating, knowing.

A مصح *mas-h*, (v. n. of مصح) Going. Being broken off, finished. Distilling, dropping (dew). Snatching, seizing. Being old and worn out (a garment). Losing its colour (a plant). Being diminished, drying up (a camel's milk). Healing, curing (the diseased). Decreasing (a shadow).

A مصحّ *musihh*, One whose family or flocks are healthy and sound (صحيح *sahīh*).

A مصحاب *mis-hāb*, Obedient, docile, tractable.

A مصحاة *mis-hāt*, A cup, a silver goblet.

A مصحب *mus-hab*, Hairy (bottle or bag). Mad, lunatic. *Mus-hib*, Gentle and tractable after having been stubborn and refractory. Right, straight. One who marches onwards without halting. (Water) covered with a green film. (A man) whose son has attained the age of puberty, and who resembles him. *Mus-hib* or *hab*, A man full of strange imaginings.

A مصحّة *masahhat* or *masihhat*, A wholesome thing; any thing conducive to health (as occasional abstinence or regular exercise).

A مصحّح *musahhah*, Mended, emended, corrected, made accurate. Cured, made whole. *Musahhih*, A mender. An emendator. A verifier.

A مصحر *mus-hir*, One who goes forth into the desert (صحراء *sahrāʼ*). A lion.

A مصحصح *musahsih*, One who talks folly; one engaged in trifles, a trifler. Sincere in friendship.

A مصحف *mus-haf*, *mas-haf*, or *mis-haf*, (pl. مصاحف *masāhif*) A book, volume. A page, written leaf. المصحف *al mus-haf*, The Kur'ān. P مصحف بغلي *mus-hafi baghlī*, A small pocket-Kur'ān. مصحف ياقوت *mus-hafi yākūt*, The Kur'ān written in the character Yākūtī.

A مصحّف *musahhaf*, Mis-spelt, wrongly written, inaccurate, incorrect. When words are used, which, upon the changing the diacritical or the vowel-points, have meanings diametrically opposite.

A مصحنة *mis-hanat*, A large pan or dish.

A مصحوب *mas-hūb*, Accompanied, associated. مكتوب محبّت مصحوب *maktūbi mahabbat-mas-hūb*, Letters accompanied with demonstrations of affection. مكتوب تهديد مصحوب *maktūbi tahdīd-mas-hūb*, Threatening letters.

A مصحية *mus-hiyat*, Serene, clear (sky).

A مصخ *maskh*, (v. n. of مصخ) Drawing, taking any thing, especially the leaves of the plant ثمام *sumām*. Changing, metamorphosing.

A مصخدة *mashhadat*, (pl. مصاخد) Mid-day heat.

A مصخر *mushhir*, Rocky (place).

A مصخفة *mishkhafat*, (pl. مصاخف) A spade.

A مصد *masd*, (v. n. of مصد) Lying with. Giving milk. Sucking saliva. Sucking (the mother). Humbling, debasing, degrading. Thunder. Intense cold. Heat. A high, steep mountain. *Masad*, Intense cold. A high hill.

A مصداق *misdāk*, Whatever verifies: a verifier

A مصدام *misdām*, Bold, brave, capable (literally an instrument) of giving hard knocks and blows.

A مصدان *musdān*, (pl. of مصاد) High mountains.

A مصدة *masdat*, Refreshing coolness. Rain.

A مصدح *misdah*, One who cries aloud, clamorous.

A مصدر *masdar*, (pl. مصادر *masādir*) Origin, source, spring, theme. The noun of action of the Arabic verb. A departure. A return. A place from whence one returns. مصدر ميميّة *masdari mīmiya*, A noun of action formed by a م *mīm* marked with a fathah. *Musdir*, The month of جمادي الاولى.

A مصدّر *musaddar*, Strong in the breast (صدر *sadr*). One whose sweat falls on his breast. (A sheep or horse) white on the throat or sticking-place. Black-breasted (sheep), the rest of the body being white. Swift (horse), outstripping others. (An arrow) thick from the middle to the point. The first of the gaming arrows without any mark on it. A lion. A wolf.

A مصدريّ *masdarīy*, Belonging to a source, or the infinitive; having the sense of the verbal noun.

A مصدريّة *masdariyat*, A certain duty levied on merchants (in Turkey, and other countries).

A مصدع *masdaʻ*, (pl. مصادع *masādiʻ*) A level path through rough grounds. *Misdaʻ*, Eloquent (orator). Clever, intelligent. (pl. مصادع *masādiʻ*) An arrow having a long and broad head.

A مصدّع *musaddaʻ*, Troubled with a headache (صداع *sudāʻ*). *Musaddiʻ*, One who cleaves asunder. The sword of Zuhayr. Whatever makes the head to ache; cephalalgic.

A مصدّغ *musaddagh*, Marked by a hot iron.

A مصدغة *misdaghat*, A pillow.

A مصدق *masdak* or *misdak*, (in comp. with ذو *zū*, as) ذو مصدق *zū masdakin* or *zū misdakin*, Bold, dauntless. Swift (horse) unfailing in the course.

A مصدّق *musaddik*, A verifier, affirmer. One who believes another. A receiver or collector of alms, or whatever is due to God. One who bestows; also one who asks an alms.

A مصّدّق *mussaddik*, (for متصدّق) A giver of alms.

A مصدور *masdūr*, Derived. Issued, despatched. Pained in the breast (صدر *sadr*).

A مصدوع *masdūʻ*, Troubled with headache.

A مصدوغ *masdūgh*, (A camel) branded on the temple (صدغ *sudgh*) by a hot iron.

A مصدوق *masdūk*, Verified, true. Believed.

A مصدوقة *masdūkat*, A thing verified, truth.

A مصدوم *masdūm*, Bruised, knocked.

A مصر *masr*, (v. n. of مصر) Milking with the tips of the three fingers, or with the thumb and fore-finger only. Milking all that is in the udder. Afterings. *Misr*, (pl. امصار *amsār*) A city, a town; a tract or region. Egypt; also its metropolis Cairo. (pl. مصور *musūr*) A limit, boundary, any thing which separates two objects. Any thing intervenient (as a curtain). A sword. A sheath, case, or repository. Red clay. P مصر زليخا پناه *misri zulaykhā-panāh*, The human body, the residence of the soul.

A مصرّ *musirr*, One who perseveres, continues, sticks close to any thing. (See اصرار *isrār*.)

A مصرّاة *musarrāt*, (A sheep) left unmilked in order that the milk may increase.

A مصراح *misrāh*, A non-grazing camel.

A مصراد *misrād*, Able to resist cold. Soon sensible of cold. (An arrow) which flies rapidly and penetrates. A country destitute of trees or vegetation.

A مصراع *misrāȝ*, (pl. مصاريع *masārīȝ*) One leaf of a folding-door. A hemistich.

A مصراعان *misrāȝāni*, Two first lines of a poem.

A مصران *musrān*, (pl. of مصير *masīr*) The intestines which contain the chyle. مصران الفار *musrānu'l fār*, A kind of bad date. المصران *al misrāni*, The two cities, *i.e.* Kūfa and Basra.

A مصرب *misrab*, A vessel in which milk is put to turn sour.

A مصرّة *masarrat*, Urinary and alvine passages. *Musirrat*, (A camel) that emits milk sparingly.

A مصرح *musarrih*, Serene, cloudless (day). One who tells plainly. (See تصريح *tasrīh*.)

A مصرّحة *musarrahatan*, Openly, plainly.

A مصرخ *musrikh*, A giver of aid, an assistant.

A مصرد *musrad*, Missing (arrow).

A مصرّد *musarrad*, Given in a small quantity. *Musarrid*, One who gives little.

A مصرع *masraȝ*, (v. n. of صرع) Throwing down, prostrating. (pl. مصارع *masāriȝ*) A place where any one is thrown down. An arena for wrestlers. *Misraȝ*, A hemistich, a line of a poem.

A مصرّع *musarraȝ*, Prostrated, thrown down (in great numbers). *Musarriȝ*, One who throws down with violence. (See تصريع *tasrīȝ*.)

A مصرعان *misraȝāni*, (dual) Folding-doors.

A مصرف *masraf*, Expense, disbursement, cost, charge. اخذ و مصرف *akhz u masraf*, Receipt and expenditure. *Masrif*, Any place where money is spent. A place of turning. Deliverance (from calamity). *Musrif*, Prodigal, spendthrift.

A مصرم *masrim*, A place narrow and rapid. *Misram*, A crooked knife used in polishing distaffs. A bill. *Musrim*, A pauper with a large family. The owner of a herd of camels.

A مصرّمة *musarramat*, (A she-camel) having a dug cut off, in order that, by the milk being stopped, she may acquire strength.

A مصرور *masrūr*, Nipped, cut up by cold. Put in a purse, pursed. Narrow (hoof of a horse).

A مصرورة *masrūrat*, (A camel) tied over the dugs with the string صرار *sirār*.

A مصروع *masrūȝ*, Prostrated. Seized with epilepsy, epileptic. P مصروع خاوري *masrūȝi khāwari*, The sun at its rising and setting.

A مصروف *masrūf*, Turned, changed. Inflected, conjugated. (pl. of مصاريف *masārīf*) Expended, employed. Unmixed (wine). غير مصروف *ghayr masrūf*, Partially declined.

A مصروفة *masrūfat*, Wine drunk, quaffed.

A مصروم *masrūm*, Pruned, lopped.

P مصري *misrī*, Pen. Sword. Treacle. A plant.

A مصري *misrīy*, An Egyptian; (a native) of Cairo. A citizen. Egyptian sugar. (pl. مصاري *masārī* and مصاريّ *masārīy*) Town (ass). P مصري مار *misrī-mār*, An Egyptian spear.

A مصط *mast*, (v. n. of مصط) Extracting from a camel's matrix the lymph of a mongrel stallion.

A مصطاد *mustād*, A hunter. A lion.

A مصطار *mustār*, Wine. *Mustār*, (or مصطارة *mustārat*) Sour wine.

A مصطاف *mustāf*, One who passes the summer (any where). A summer-residence.

A مصطبّ *mustabb*, Poured out, infused.

A مصطبة *mistabat*, (or مصطبه *mistaba*) A long and wide bench or stone-platform raised two feet from the ground, on which the people of the East recline. A tavern.

A مصطبح *mustabih*, One who takes a morning draught. One who lights a lamp.

A مصطبر *mustabir*, One who displays patience. A follower. (See اصطبار *istibār*.)

A مصطح *mistah*, A desert without herbage. A place made level for treading out corn.

A مصطخب *mustakhib*, Clamorous, noisy.

A مصطخد *mustakhid*, One who stands upright in the sun.

A مصطخم *mustakhim*, Erect, standing up.

A مصطدم *mustadim*, Dashing together.

A مصطرّ *mustarr*, Narrow (horse's hoof).

A مصطرب *mustarib*, One who collects milk (in a vessel), pours in some, time after time, and leaves it to grow sour.

A مصطرد *mustarid*, Angry, choking with rage.

A مصطرع *mustaraȝ*, A place for wrestling. *Mustariȝ*, A wrestler.

A مصطرف *mustarif*, Busy, active, bustling.

A مصطع *mistaȝ*, Eloquent.

A مصطفّ *mustaff*, Placed in a row, ranged in order. Assembled, convened.

A مصطفق *mustafik*, Shaken, vibrating.

A مصطفويّ *mustafawīy*, Belonging to Mustafa.

A مصطفى *mustafa'*, Chosen, elected. A man's name, particularly a name of Muhammad.

A مصطفيّ *mustafīy*, Belonging to مصطفى.

A مصطكا *mastaka'*, (*mustaka'*, or مصطكاء *mastakāȝ*) Gum-mastic.

A مصطلب *mustalib*, One who extracts fat or grease (صلب *salab*) from bones.

A مصطلح *mustalah*, Idiomatic, phraseological, metaphoric. (See اصطلاح *istilāh*.)

A مصطلق *mustalik*, One who has a fine musical voice. Name of a tribe of heretics.

A مصطلم *mustalim*, An eradicator, uprooter.

A مصطلي *mustalī*, One warming himself at a fire.

A مصطنع *mustaniȝ*, A receiver (of a benefit). Who confers (a benefit). (See اصطناع *istināȝ*.)

A مصطهر *mustahir*, A melter. One who eats the fat and marrow of a bone (صهارة *suhārat*).

A مصع *masȝ*, (v. n. of مصع) (A horse) lashing (his tail). Striking (another) with a sword or whip. Striking three or four strokes. Sprinkling with cold water (the dugs of a camel). Passing rapidly by. Running fast. Departing, going off (cold). Losing her milk (a camel). Voiding dung (a bird). Shooting out dung when going in fear or haste. Losing one's courage. Moistening (a cistern) with a little water. (A mother) bringing forth (young). Flashing, glancing (lightning). Departing, travelling (by land). *Masȝ* or *masiȝ*, Robust, warlike (man). One who strikes with a sword. One who strikes playfully with a twisted wreath. An old man panting for breath. *Musaȝ* or *musȝ*, (pl. of مصعة *musȝat* and *musaȝat*) Green birds. Fruits of the Indian thorn. مصع العصفور *musaȝu'l ȝusfūr*, A cock-sparrow.

A مصعاد *misȝād*, A rope or any thing by which one climbs a palm-tree. A scaling-ladder.

A مصعب *musȝab*, A stallion. A stallion that has never yet been ridden or borne burdens. A refractory camel. *Musȝib*, The owner of a stubborn, refractory camel.

A مصعة *musȝat* or *musaȝat*, (pl. مصع *musȝ* and *musaȝ*) Name of a green bird. Fruit of the tree lycium.

A مصعتج *musaȝtaj*, Bolt-upright. Straight and polished.

A مصعتل *musaȝtal*, One who has a long head.

A مصعد *masȝad*, Place of rising. An ascent. A step, ladder, stair. *Musȝad*, Raised. *Musȝid*, Ascending.

A مصعّد *musaȝȝad*, (Wine) distilled, burnt, refined, sublimated, or rectified by fire.

A مصعر *musȝar*, Painful and difficult (nocturnal journey in search of water).

A مصعفق *musaȝfik*, Lean-bodied.

A مصعلك *musaȝlak*, One who has a round (head).

A مصعّن *musaȝȝan*, Pointed and pricked (ear).

A مصعنب *musaȝnab*, Oblong-headed. Compact, compressed. Turned in.

A مصعنج *musaȝnaj*, Polished (arrow). Round.

A مصعنفر *musȝanfir*, Quick, expeditious. (An ass) running away through fear.

A مصعوف *masȝūf*, Trembling with fear or cold. seized with a shivering fit (صعفة *saȝfat*).

A مصغبة *masghabat*, Hunger, need.

A مصغّر *musaghghar*, (A noun) put into the diminutive form. *Musaghghir*, A diminisher.

A مصغرة *musghirat*, (Ground) which produces short plants or stunted herbage.

A مصغوراء *masghūrāȝ*, (pl. of صغير *saghīr*) Little, small, low.

A مصغى *musgha'*, Inclined to one side. *Mus-ghi*, One who lends an ear.

A مصف *masaff*, (pl. مصاف *masāff*) A place where ranks are drawn up. A battle-field: battle.

A مصفاة *misfāt*, A strainer, colander.

A مصفح *musfah*, Broad. One, the sides of whose head are flat and forehead prominent. Inclined, crooked, wry. Inverted. One who has the bridge of the nose level. Flat and elongated (head). A heart in which faith and hypocrisy are united. Smooth, handsome (face). Sixth gaming arrow. مصفحاً *musfahan*, (He struck) with the broad side.

A مصفح *musaffah*, Overlaid with plates. Broad.

A مصفحة *musaffahat* also *musaffihat*, A sword. *Musaffahat*, (A sheep) left unmilked in order that she may shew a large udder.

A مصفر *musfir*, Empty-handed, destitute.

A مصفر *musaffar*, Starved, pale-faced. مصفر استه *musaffiru istihi*, One who farts aloud.

A مصفر *musfarr*, Yellow.

A مصفرة *musaffirat*, Those whose colours or badge is yellow.

A مصفعاني *masfaɛāniy*, One who takes cuffs patiently. A boxer, one who gives slaps or cuffs.

A مصفور *masfūr*, One who has a collection of bile or yellow water in the belly, dropsical. Hungry.

A مصفوف *masfūf*, Drawn up, ranged in a row.

A مصفى *misfa'*, A strainer.

A مصفى *musaffa'*, Strained, racked, clarified, clear. *Musaffi*, A purifier, clearer.

A مصقر *musakhar*, Hard (dates) softened by pouring upon them the honey of others.

A مصقع *miskaɛ*, Eloquent. One possessed of a clear and distinct enunciation, and free from stammer.

A مصقل *mishal*, A smooth shell, or any thing used in polishing. Eloquent (preacher or orator).

A مصقلة *mishalat*, (pl. مصاقل *masākil*) An instrument with which a thing is polished, glazed, or furbished; a shell used for that purpose.

A مصقور *mashūr*, Struck, hit.

A مصقوعة *maskūɛat*, (Ground) covered with hoar-frost (صقيع *sakīɛ*).

A مصقول *mashūl*, Polished, furbished.

A مصك *masakk*, (An ostrich) the joints of whose legs smite each other, knock-kneed. *Misakk*, Strong, firmly-built (man or horse). A lock, bar, or bolt.

A مصكة *misakkat*, Strong, stout (she-ass).

A مصل *masl*, (v. n. of مصل) Suppurating (a wound). Falling in drops. (Milk) being put into a vessel made of palm-leaves that the whey may be strained through it. Making the soft cheese called اقط *akit*. Withdrawing (a part of any thing due). Injuring, hurting (flocks). Wasting or squandering one's property. The whey or scum of milk which is strained off when making اقط *akit*.

A مصلا *musalla'*, An oratory, a place of prayer. A mosque. A mat for saying prayers upon.

A مصلاع *maslāɛ*, Small-armed (woman).

A مصلاة *maslāt*, (Ground) abounding in the herbage صليان *silliyān*. *Maslāt* also *mislāt*, (pl. مصالي *masālī*) A net for catching game.

A مصلات *mislāt*, Brisk, active in doing.

A مصلاد *mislād*, A camel which has foaled, but is milkless.

A مصلادة *mislādat*, (A she-camel) scarce of milk.

A مصلاق *mislāk*, Very noisy (orator).

A مصلال *mislāl*, Clay dried and hard, which yields a ringing or tinkling sound.

A مصلب *musallab*, (A garment) marked or woven with the sign of the cross (صليب *salib*). *Musallib*, (A date) hardened or dried. (See تصليب.)

A مصلة *misallat*, A strainer, vessel for racking.

A مصلت *mislat*, (A man) brisk and active in doing any thing. *Muslat*, Drawn (sword).

A مصلح *musluh*, Prepared, rectified. *Muslih*, One who adjusts, trims, gives a finish. A reformer, corrector, rectifier, restorer. A mediator, arbiter, pacifier, reconciler. Healthy, wholesome.

A مصلحة *maslahat*, (pl. مصالح *masālih*) An affair, business, subject. Employment, transaction, occupation. An urgent occasion. Benevolence, kindness, peace, goodwill. Welfare, that which is best, a prudent measure, advisable thing. Advice.

P مصلحت دادن *maslahat dādan*, To give advice. مصلحت ديدن *maslahat dīdan*, To regard as advisable, to deem prudent. مصلحت بين *maslahat-bīn*, Expert, intelligent, versed in affairs.

P مصلحت گذار *maslahat-guzār*, A chargé d'affaires. Expert, intelligent.

A مصلخم *muslakhimm*, Steep (mountain). Strong, sharp, penetrating.

A مصلد *muslid*, Milked into a greasy dish, which prevents (milk) from frothing.

A مصلصل *musalsal*, Rolling, pealing (thunder). Illustrious, of noble pedigree. *Musalsil*, Noisy (ass).

A مصلطح *musaltah*, Broad, wide.

A مصلف *muslif*, (A husband) whom his wife, though obsequious and attentive, cannot please.

A مصلفح *musalfah*, Broad (head).

A مصلق *mislak*, Eloquent.

A مصلقع *musalkiɛ*, Poor, penniless.

A مصلل *musallil*, Illustrious in rank, a prince. Fruitful (shower). A shoemaker. Noisy, jingling.

A مصلم *musallam*, Earless (naturally).

A مصلحمة *musalmahat*, (A girl) thin of hair.

A مصلوب *maslūb*, Suspended, hanged, crucified, gibbeted. Marrow, fat. مصلوب عليه *maslūbun ɛalayhi*, Seized with a burning fever.

A مصلوق *maslūk*, (Water) long stagnant and befouled by cattle.

A مصلهب *musalhib*, Tall (man).

A مصلى *musalla'*, Prayed. Merciful, propitious (God). An oratory, pulpit. A carpet for praying upon. Name of a place much celebrated by the poet Hāfiz. *Musalli*, One who prays. A preacher. Holy, righteous. Second (horse) in a race (because his head touches the haunches (صلا *sala'*) of the first).

A مصلى *masliy*, Roasted, toasted, burnt, scorched.

A مصم *musimm*, Deaf. One who discovers to be deaf. One who deafens. The maker of a stopple (صمام *simām*).

A مصماد *mismād*, (pl. مصامد *masāmid* and مصاميد *masāmīd*) A camel which ceases not to give milk notwithstanding cold and scarcity.

A مصمت *musmat*, Closed. (A door or lock) closing softly, without noise. Solid, not hollow. (A horse or cloth) of one colour. (A thousand) complete. حروف مصمتة *hurūf musmatat*, All the letters in the alphabet except مربنفل. *Musmit*, Silent (sick man). (See اصمات *ismāt*.)

A مصمت *musammat*, (A thousand) complete. *Musammit*, Silent. A silencer.

A مصمد *musmad*, Solid, not hollow.

A مصمد *musammad*, Sought for (a house), which one wishes to arrive at. Hard and firm (thing).

A مصمرط *musamrat*, Long-headed.

A مصمص *musamis*, Compact, well-built (horse).

A مصمصة *masmasat*, (v. n. of مصمص Q) Sipping, tasting with the tip of the tongue. Washing.

A مصمع *musammaɛ*, Pointed-eared (wild buck).

A مصمعات *musammaɛāt*, Cows lean with thirst.

A مصمعة *musammaɛat*, Bread crumbled and heaped up to a point.

A مصمعد *musmaɛidd*, A lion.

A مصمغ *musammagh*, (Ink) thickened with gum.

A مصمغة *musmighat*, (A sheep) with clotty milk.

A مصمغد *musmaghidd*, Swollen, either from distemper or fat.

A مصمق *musammik*, Astonished, amazed; abstaining from meat and drink.

A مصمقر *musmakirr*, Hot. Sultry (day).

A مصمم *musammam*, Fixed, concluded, determined. Resolute. *Musammim*, Resolved, intent upon. (See تصميم *tasmīm*.)

A مصمئك *musmaɛikh*, (Ground) moist with rain. (A sky) even and disposed to rain.

A مصمئلة *musmaɛillat*, A misfortune, evil.

A مصن *musinn*, Furious, boiling with rage.

A مصنب *misnab*, Very fond of صناب *sināb*.

A مصنبع *musambaɛ*, Oblong (in the head).

A مصنتع *musantaɛ*, Hollow. One who has a large forehead and thin hollow cheeks.

A مصندل *musandal*, Perfumed with sandal.

A مصنطل *musantil*, One who hangs his head.

A مصنع *masnaɛ*, (pl. مصانع *masāniɛ*) A cistern, receptacle for rain-water. A structure.

A مصنعة *masnaɛat* or *masnuɛat*, (pl. مصانع *masāniɛ*) A cistern. An entertainment prepared for a friend. Any strongly-built edifice; a fort.

A مصنف *musannaf*, Composed (book). (A tree) consisting of dry and green parts. *Musannif*, A composer, author, editor. مصنّف الاصل *musanniful'asl*, The author of an original (of any translated book).

A مصنّفات *musannafāt*, Books, works, compositions. P از مصنّفات حافظ *az musannafāti hāfiz*, From the works of Hāfiz.

A مصنق *musnik*, One who takes care of camels. Skilful in the management of camels.

A مصنوع *masnūʻ*, Made, formed, prepared, invented. Artificial.

A مصنوعات *masnūʻāt*, pl. fem., Created things; creatures. مصنوعات الهی *masnūʻāt ilāhī*, Creation. مصنوعات بنّا *masnūʻāti bannā*, The works of builders.

A مصنوعی *masnūʻī*, Artificial.

A مصواء *maswāʼ*, The posteriors. A woman lank in the thighs or hips.

A مصوات *miswāt*, One who cries aloud, a shouter. Any one. ما بالدار مصوات *mā bi'd dār miswāt*, There is no sound in the house, *i.e.* nobody at home.

A مصوان *miswān*, A bow-case.

A مصوب *miswab*, A spoon.

A مصوبة *masūbat*, An accident, misfortune.

A مصوّت *musawwit*, One who cries aloud. A shouter. Noisy.

A مصوح *musūh*, (v. n. of مصح) Going. Carrying away, removing (a disease). Being broken off, finished. Being worn (a garment). Distilling, dropping (dew). Being firmly rooted, so as to defy the tweezers (hair upon a horse's heel). Being diminished, drying up (a camel's milk). Fading (as a plant). Decreasing (as a shadow).

A مصوخة *masūkhat*, (A ewe) relaxed about the root of the udder.

A مصور *masūr*, (pl. مصار *misār* and مصائر *masāʼir*) (A camel) which gives her milk slowly. (A camel or goat) which yields but little milk. *Musūr*, (pl. of مصر *misr*) Large cities. Environs. اشتری الدار بمصورها *ishtara'd dāra bi musūrihā*, He bought the house with its precincts.

A مصوّر *musawwar*, Formed. Painted. Sculptured. *Musawwir*, One who forms or figures. A painter, limner. A sculptor.

A مصوّری *musawwarī*, The art of painting.

A مصوص *masūs*, (pl. مصائص *masāʼis*) A dish made of boiled meats, especially young pigeons, fowls, or other birds dressed in vinegar. Viri avida (mulier). Sperma de glande absorbens (vulva).

A مصوصة *masūsat*, Lean, emaciated (woman).

A مصوصی *musawsī*, as المصوصی *al musawsī*, One of the winter days called العجوز *al ʻajūz*.

A مصوع *masūʻ*, Timid, faint-hearted. *Musūʻ*, (v. n. of مصع) Going off, diminishing (as the milk of a camel, or cold weather). Going off (cold weather).

A مصوغ *masūgh*, Cast, molten. Harmonious.

A مصول *miswal*, Any liquid in which the colocynth-fruit is soaked to take off its bitterness. *Musūl*, (v. n. of مصل) Dividing (water from milk).

A مصولة *miswalat*, A besom, broom, brush.

A مصوّلة *musawwalat*, Winnowed and heaped.

A مصومد *musawmid*, Gross, rude, rugged, rough.

A مصومعة *musawmaʻat*, Bread crumbled small and heaped up to a point.

A مصون *masūn*, (or مصوون *maswūn*) Guarded, kept safe, laid up, preserved, defended. Recondite.

A مصهّب *musahhab*, Bits of meat laid in a row for roasting. Wild beasts mingled together.

A مصهر *mus-hir*, Near.

A مصهرج *musahraj*, (A cistern) of rough stones, or rough cast with mortar (صاروج *sārūj*).

A مصياف *misyāf*, (Ground) refreshed plentifully with summer-rains. (A camel) accompanied by her colt. A man who does not marry because he is growing grey. (Land) behind in its vegetation.

A مصيب *musīb*, (An arrow) which hits the mark. Good or fortunate (counsel).

A مصيبة *musībat*, (pl. مصائب *masāʼib*) A misfortune, disaster, calamity, affliction, evil, misery, ill, trouble, adversity. Agony.

A مصيد *masīd*, Taken by hunting. *Misyad*, A net.

A مصيدة *misyadat* also *masīdat*, A net, or any hunter's implement for catching fish or game.

A مصير *masīr*, (v. n. of صار for صير) Becoming. Inclining to. Place of destination, goal; residence, receptacle, reception. (pl. امصرة *amsirat* and مصران *musrān*) The intestine which receives the chyle. سریر معدلت مصیر *sarīri maʻdilat-masīr*, The royal throne, the residence of equity. تدبیر شقا مصیر *tadbīri shakā-masīr*, A pernicious counsel.

A مصيرة *musayrat*, A small city, a town.

A مصيص *masīs*, Moist earth or sand.

A مصيصة *masīsat*, A saucer, dish, or plate.

A مصيطر *musaytir*, A keeper, guardian, governor appointed to some office or post of authority. A commander, inspector, notary.

A مصيف *masīf*, A summer-house, villa, country-residence. (A camel) accompanied by her colt. A winding water-course.

A مصيّف *musayyif*, Sufficient for the summer.

A مصيفة *masīfat*, (Ground) watered by summer-rains. (A camel) accompanied by her colt.

A مصيقل *musaykal*, Polished, furbished.

A مصيوف *masyūf*, Watered by summer-rain.

A مصيون *masyūn*, Kept, preserved: safe, well.

A مضّ *mazz*, (v. n. of مضّ) Grieving, afflicting. Making (the mouth or eye) smart (vinegar or collyrium). Sucking, sipping strongly. Hot, burning collyrium. A stone in an old well. مضّ الضرب *mazzu'z zarb*, One who inflicts a painful blow. *Mizz*, No, not at all (but implying (yes).

A مضاء *mazāʼ*, (v. n. of مضي) Being transported, carried far (in any affair). Being bold. ابو المضاء *abū'l mazāʼ*, A horse. *Muzāʼ*, (v. n. of مضي) Cutting (a sword). The penetrancy or power of penetrating or piercing: keenness. Quick, expeditious.

A مضاءلة *muzāʼalat*, (v. n. 3 of ضؤل) Shewing one's figure as small and contemptible (ضئيل *zaʼīl*).

A مضابّ *mazābb*, (pl. of مضبّة *mazabbat*) Tracts of country swarming with Lybian lizards.

A مضابث *mazābis*, Claws (of a lion). Fists.

A مضابحة *muzābahat*, (v. n. 3 of ضبح) Calling ugly and shameful. Abusing one another to the face. Abhorring, detesting.

A مضابئة *muzābiʼat*, A large heavy sack, which conceals the bearer who carries it.

A مضاجّة *muzājjat*, (v. n. 3 of ضجّ) Exciting a tumult, raising a clamour. Quarrelling.

A مضاجر *mazājir*, (pl. of مضجر *muzjir*) Wearisome, irksome, troublesome.

A مضاجرة *muzājarat*, A reducing to straits.

A مضاجع *mazājiʻ*, (pl. of مضجع *mazjaʻ*) Beds, sleeping-places. Places where rain falls. اذا قرّت المضاجع *izā karrati'l mazājiʻ*, When the beds are still, *i.e.* the dead of night. *Muzājiʻ*, A bed-fellow.

A مضاجعة *muzājaʻat*, A sleeping along with.

A مضاجير *mazājīr*, (pl. مضجر *muzjir*) Wearisome, irksome, troublesome.

A مضاحاة *muzāhāt*, (v. n. 3 of ضحا for ضحو) Coming to (one) in the forenoon (ضحی *zuha'*).

A مضادّ *muzādd*, An opponent, antagonist.

A مضاداة *muzādāt*, An opposing, resisting.

A مضادّة *muzāddat*, (or مضاددة *muzādadat*) (v. n. 3 of ضدّ) Being adverse, repugnant, contrary. Opposition. Antipathy.

A مضارّ *mazārr*, (pl. of مضرّة *mazarrat*) Injuries.

A مضارب *muzārib*, A combatant, fencer.

A مضاربة *muzārabat*, (v. n. 3 of ضرب) Fighting, fencing, getting the better by beating. Contending with another in striking. Selling the goods of another for half the profit. Being distracted amongst themselves. Partnership. A battle, combat, conflict.

A مضارة *muzārat*, The whey or whig (of milk).

A مضارّة *muzārrat*, (v. n. 3 of ضرّ) Hurting, harming, injuring each other. Being jealous. Taking two or three wives. Quarrelling.

A مضارج *mazārij*, (pl. of مضرج *mizraj*) Threadbare, every-day garments. Clippings, cloth-pollings.

A مضارحة *muzārahat*, (v. n. 3 of ضرح) Speaking opprobriously, provoking by reproaches. Contending in throwing the javelin. Being near; shewing propinquity.

A مضارسة *muzārasat*, (v. n. 3 of ضرس) Fighting, carrying on mutual hostilities.

A مضارع *muzāriʻ*, Like. The aorist tense.

A مضارعة *muzāraʻat*, (v. n. 3 of ضرع) Being like, resembling. A compact betwixt two persons, one a proprietor of land, and the other the cultivator, by which it is agreed that whatever the land yields shall belong to both in such proportion as may be there determined.

A مضاض *muzāz*, Pure, sincere. A sort of tree. Water brackish and undrinkable.

A مضاضة *mazāzat*, (v. n. of مضّ) Grieving on account of some misfortune.

A مضاعف *muzāʿaf*, Doubled. A duplicate. (in grammar) A reduplicate verb, *i.e.* whose second and third letter are alike: as, مدّ *madda*, He extended. A quadriliteral verb, whose letters are repeated: as, زلزل *zalzala* (unlike دحرج *dahraja*).

A مضاعفة *muzāʿafat*, (v. n. 3 of ضعف) Doubling. Adding twice as much to any thing so that it becomes trebled. Weaving (a coat of mail) with a double texture of rings. (fem. of مضاعف *muzāʿaf*) Doubled. (A coat of mail, hauberk, or habergeon) made with a double texture of rings.

A مضاغ *mazāgh*, (v. n. of مضغ) Chewing (meat). Chewed or masticable. Mastication. Somewhat. ليّن المضاغ *layyinu'l mazāgh*, Easy of mastication.

A مضاغة *muzāghat*, Chewed (thing).

A مضّاغة *muzzāghat*, Foolish. A fool.

A مضاغط *mazāghit*, (pl. of مضغط *mazghat*) Grounds full of low places in which water collects.

A مضاغطة *muzāghatat*, (v. n. 3 of ضغط) Hindering, preventing, pressing upon.

A مضاف *muzāf*, Annexed, added, related. One who is added to others (especially to those with whom he has no natural connection. Surrounded in battle. (A district) surrounded by war. Spurious, adopted. A refuge, asylum. One who asks for a leathern bottle. One who maintains his footing towards his enemies. (in gram.) A noun placed in regimine or construction: as, غلام زيد *ghulāmu zaydin*, The boy of Zayd (غلام *ghulām* being called مضاف *muzāf* or المضاف *al muzāf*, The governing noun; and زيد *zaydin*, styled المضاف اليه *al muzāf ilayhi*, The noun governed). P مضاف كردن *muzāf kardan*, To annex, add.

A مضافات *muzāfāt*, (pl. f. of مضاف) Additions.

A مضافرة *muzāfarat*, An assisting one another.

A مضامّة *muzāmmat*, A heaping, accumulating.

A مضامير *mazāmīr*, (pl. of مضمور) Adjuncts.

A مضامين *mazāmīn*, (pl. of مضمون) Contents. Significations. Future fœtuses in the loins of a sire.

A مضاناة *muzānāt*, (v. n. 3 of ضني) Resisting, opposing. Enduring any evil with all its consequences. Taking upon one's self the trouble of another person's concerns.

A مضاوي *mazāwī*, Skylights.

A مضاهاة *muzāhāt*, (v. n. 3 of ضهي) Resembling (another). *Muzāhāt*, (or مضاهأة *muzāhaʾat*) Assistance, aid; benignity, benevolence.

A مضاهبة *muzāhabat*, (v. n. 3 of ضهب) Reviling, reproaching one another.

A مضائغ *mazāʾigh*, (pl. of مضيغة *mazīghat*) Meats sticking to the bones. Muscles. Sinews whipt about the horns of a bow.

A مضائف *mazāʾif*, Sides (of a river or valley).

A مضائق *mazāʾik*, (pl. of مضيق *mazīk*) Arduous, difficult affairs, straits, difficulties.

A مضايقة *muzāyakat*, (v. n. 3 of ضاق for ضيق) Hemming in, reducing to straits. Oppressing. Oppression. Difficulty. Penury, scarcity, want, necessity, distress. Moment, consequence, significance. P مضايقه كردن *muzāyaka kardan*, To bid one do more than he can. To make a difficulty.

A مضبّ *muzibb*, Bold, shameless. Strong, hardy.

A مضبأ *mazbaʾ*, A lurking-place.

A مضباة *mazbāt*, A hole for baking bread in. *Muzbāt*, Bread baked under the ashes.

A مضبّب *muzabbab*, Hooped (vessel). (A door) barred or covered with an iron plate. *Muzabbib*, One who catches the Lybian lizard (generally done by pouring water into their holes, which forces them out with the tail foremost).

A مضبّة *mazabbat*, (pl. مضابّ *mazābb*) A country abounding in Lybian lizards. (pl. of ضبّ *zabb*) Lybian lizards.

A مضبث *mizbas*, A lion.

A مضبّر *muzabbar*, Firm, compact (camel). A lion.

A مضبعة *mazbaʿat*, The fleshy part of the arm under the arm-pit in front. (pl. of ضبع *zabuʿ* or *zabʿ*) Hyenas.

A مضبّعة *muzabbaʿat*, (A she-camel) whose breast projects far before the fore-legs. *Muzabbiʿat*, Lewd (female), opening her own privities.

A مضبوث *mazbūs*, (A camel) branded, marked with the brand ضبثة *zabsat*.

A مضبوحة *mazbūhat*, The flint of a tinder-box.

A مضبور *mazbūr*, Firm in body, compact.

A مضبوط *mazbūt*, Possessed, occupied. Held. Governed, regulated, controlled, checked, restrained. Tamed. Moderated, disciplined. Committed to memory. Firm, strong, solid. (Land) rained on. P مضبوط كردن *mazbūt kardan*, To fortify, strengthen.

A مضبوطى *mazbūtī*, Strength, durability.

A مضبوع *mazbūʿ*, Devoured by hyenas.

A مضبون *mazbūn*, Tried, afflicted. Impaired in constitution by disease. Paralytic. Clear (water).

A مضبوءٌ به *mazbūʾ bihi*, Thrown on the ground, made to cleave to the earth.

A مضبئ *muzbiʾ*, Silent, taciturn. One who keeps a thing concealed within his breast.

A مضّة *mazzat*, A woman unable to endure that which displeases her. Sour milk.

A مضجر *muzjar*, Languid, vexed in mind. *Muzjir*, (pl. مضاجر *mazājir* and مضاجير *mazājīr*) Wearisome, troublesome, irksome. An annoyer.

A مضجع *mazjaʿ*, (pl. مضاجع *mazājiʿ*) A place of repose. A bed. A place of slaughter. A battle-field. The grave.

A مضجور *mazjūr*, Depressed, dispirited.

A مضجوع *mazjūʿ*, Weak in mind.

A مضح *mazh*, (v. n. of مضح) Diminishing or traducing (the reputation of another). Repelling, driving off. Being scattered about (camels). Sweating, oozing (a leathern bottle). Darting rays (the sun).

A مضحاة *mazhāt*, A sunshine place.

A مضحاك *mizhāk*, Laughing, merry (woman).

A مضحك *mazhak*, The part where the teeth appear in laughing. *Muzhak*, Ridiculed, derided. *Muzhik*, Ridiculous, droll, causing laughter. A mime, buffoon. Who laughs at or ridicules.

A مضحكات *muzhikāt*, (pl. of مضحكة *muzhikat*) (or مزاح و مضحكات *mizāh u muzhikāt*) Jests, jokes, buffooneries; sayings or doings exciting laughter.

A مضحكة *mazhakat*, Humour, fun, drollery. *Muzhikat*, Facetious, jocular (woman).

A مضحل *mazhal*, A place of little water.

A مضحى *muzhī*, One who is early in the forenoon (ضحى *zuha'*), or does any thing at that time.

A مضخ *mazkh*, A perfuming of one's body.

A مضخّة *mizakhkhat*, A tube from which they squirt water. A squirt, syringe.

A مضخم *mizkham*, Who strikes or dashes against with violence. A noble and corpulent man.

A مضد *mazd*, (for ضمد *zamd*) A binding of the head. *Mazad*, Malevolence, hatred.

A مضر *mazr* or *mazar*, (v. n. of مضر) Becoming acid, pricking the tongue (milk or wine). Becoming white. *Mizr*, A shedding of blood with impunity. خضرا مضرا *khizran mizran* or *khaziran maziran*, With impunity, unrevenged (was his blood shed). خذه خضرا مضرا *khuzhu khaziran maziran*, Take it fresh and tender. *Mazir*, Sour, acid. Very white. مضر بن نزار *muzar bin nizār*, Name of the father of an Arabian tribe.

A مضرّ *muzirr*, Offensive, noxious, pernicious, hurtful. One who has a large daily income. (A man) who has two wives. (A woman) whose husband has another wife. Approaching, near.

A مضراب *mizrāb*, An instrument for striking. A musical bow. One who strikes much.

A مضرار *mizrār*, Frightened, fleeing, refractory (mare, camel, or woman).

A مضرب *mazrab*, (v. n. of ضرب) Departing travelling (by land). Roaming in search of prey, provisions, or gain. Flying (as a bird) in quest of food. A sword. The edge of a sword. A bone full of marrow, and worth the breaking. A place where any thing is struck, fixed, or planted. The time of a camel's being covered. A field of battle. A place of encampment. *Mazrib*, The time or the place where a stallion covers. The chief part of a sword, about a span from the point. A place of striking. A sword. مضرب عسلة *mazribu ʿasalatin*, Origin, stock, kind. Pedigree. Property. ما يرمّ منها مضرب *māyurimmu minhā mazrib*, There is no marrow in it, *i.e.* it is a lean sheep. *Mizrab*, (pl. مضارب *mazārib*) An instrument for striking. A plectrum. One who strikes often. A large tent. *Muzrib*, Who causes to be struck. (A serpent) remaining immoveable in a place.

A مضرّب *muzarrab*, Sewed, stitched, lined with

cotton (a garment). *Muzarrib,* An exciter of disturbances, a raiser of tumults.

A مضربة *mazrabat,* Hairs or cotton-thread rolled into a clew or hank. A sword. The edge of a sword. *Mazribat,* The principal part of a sword, that which gives the blow. A sword. The edge of a sword.

A مضرّة *mazarrat,* (pl. مضارّ *mazārr*) Detriment, damage, injury, hurt, harm, inconvenience. *Muzirrat,* (A woman) whose husband has another wife: a rival wife. (Clouds) hanging near the earth.

A مضرج *mizraj,* (pl. مضارج *mazārij*) A threadbare every-day dress. Cloth-polling or clipping.

A مضرّج *muzarraj,* Bloody, tinged of a bloody colour, gory. *Muzarrij,* A lion.

A مضرح *mazrah,* (Long-winged) hawk. A white vulture.

A مضرحيّ *mazrahīy,* A noble and generous lord. Long. White. Long-winged (hawk). A white vulture.

A مضرّس *muzarras,* (A place) full of rough and unequal stones, resembling dogs' teeth. (A well) built up with stones. A kind of coloured vest, embroidered stuff, having the figures of teeth. Tried and proved by use or experiment. *Muzarris,* (Experience in war) rendering (one) skilful in tactics. (A lion) which chews the flesh of his prey without swallowing it.

A مضرط *muzrit,* (or مضرّط *muzarrit*) Who causes one to break wind. One who makes a noise with the mouth in derision. A scorner, mocker. مضرّط الحجارة *muzarritu'l hijārat,* Violent and strong, causing the stones to fart.

A مضرغطّ *muzraghitt,* Excessively thick. Fat and good for nothing.

A مضرم *muzram,* Kindled.

A مضروب *mazrūb,* Beaten, struck, stampt, hammered, forged. Pitched (tent). Affixed, appointed, determined. Used, idiomatic, proverbial. (in arith.) Multiplied. Covered with hoar-frost. Kind, species.

A مضروبة *mazrūbat,* A flagellation. A wheal.

A مضروجة *mazrūjat,* (An eye) with a wide opening.

A مضرور *mazrūr,* Damaged, injured.

A مضروس *mazrūs,* (A place) full of rough and unequal stones, like dogs' teeth; gravelly.

A مضروسة *mazrūsat,* (A well) regularly built up with stones from the bottom to the top.

A مضري *muzrī,* (or مضرّي *muzarrī*) Who trains (a dog to hunting), and sets (him) on to attack prey.

A مضريّة *muzarīyat,* The Modarites or Mozarites, an Arabian tribe (whose war-signs were red, those of Yaman being yellow).

A مضرئزّ *muzraʼizz,* Stingy towards one's self.

A مضز *muzizz,* Passionate, testy, bad-tempered. Covetous. Bitten.

A مضض *mazaz,* (v. n. of مضض) Grieving, being pained (on account of some misfortune). Affliction, misfortune. Sour milk.

A مضط *muzt,* (for مشط *musht*) A comb.

A مضطبث *muztabis,* A lion.

A مضطبن *muztabin,* Who carries under the arm.

A مضطجع *muztajaʻ,* Any thing for reclining or reposing upon; a bed. *Muztajiʻ,* Laid down, reclining on the side.

A مضطحي *muztahī,* One who does any thing, or who arrives in the forenoon (ضحى *zuha'*)

A مضطرّ *muztarr,* Reduced to difficulties, made desperate, forced by necessity, distressed, afflicted.

A مضطرب *muztarib,* Agitated, moved, disturbed, confounded, afflicted, anxious, fluctuating, staggering, tottering, nodding, distracted, tormented, chagrined. Wavering or prevaricating (evidence). Long and straight (spear). Erect, upright (man). مضطرب العنان *muztaribu'l ʻinān,* Routed, fleeing away singly.

A مضطرح *muztarah,* Rejected, thrown aside.

A مضطرم *muztarim,* Kindling, blazing (fire). Conspicuous (hoariness), advancing (old age).

A مضطغن *muztaghin,* Prone to hatred. One who takes in or under the arms.

A مضطلع *muztaliʻ,* Able, powerful, equal to.

A مضطمّ *muztamm,* Contracted. Accumulated. Composed. Added, attributed, inserted.

A مضطمر *muztamir,* Slender or clung in the belly. (A pearl) small round the middle.

A مضطهد *muztahad,* Constrained, forced, subdued. *Muztahid,* One who subjects, subdues, or compels. A lion.

A مضطئل *muztaʼil,* Slender, small, contemptible.

A مضعف *muzʻaf,* Blind. *Muzʻif,* One who has debilitated cattle. One weakly mounted. One whose property is multiplied. One whose trade is wide and extensive. *Muzʻif* or *muzʻaf,* One deserving of double.

A مضعّف *muzaʻʻaf,* Debilitated. Doubled, multiplied. Lined (garment). *Muzaʻʻif,* One who regards as weak. (See تضعيف *tazʻīf.*)

A مضعّفة *muzaʻʻafat,* (Ground) sprinkled with gentle rain.

A مضعوف *mazʻūf,* Doubled. Weakened, enfeebled. Blind.

A مضغ *mazgh,* (v. n. of مضغ) Chewing. *Muzagh,* (pl. of مضغة *muzghat*) Pieces of meat.

A مضّغ *muzzagh,* Minutiæ, detail, trifles.

A مضغبة *mazghabat,* (Ground) fruitful in cucumbers, or in a pot-herb like asparagus.

A مضغة *muzghat,* (pl. مضغ *muzagh*) A piece of meat (or any thing filling the mouth), gobbet. A lump (of flesh, or the fœtus in the womb). A morsel, fragment. A glutton; an ill-bred person. مضغة من جسد البشر *muzghatun min jasadi'l bashar,* The human heart.

A مضغط *mazghat,* (pl. مضاغط *mazāghit*) A low tract of ground with holes in which water lodges.

A مضفّر *muzaffar,* (Hair) plaited in three braids.

A مضفور *mazfūr,* Plaited, twisted: braided.

A مضفوف *mazfūf,* (Water) much sought after, contended for by many. Poor, destitute, reduced, impoverished by excessive liberality.

A مضلّ *muzill,* Who causes or permits (one) to err, who leaves in an error. A seducer. A loser. (See اضلال *izlāl.*)

A مضلّة *mazallat, mazillat,* or *mizallat,* A country where one easily strays and loses one's self.

A مضلع *muzliʻ,* Heavy, causing to incline to one side (a burden). Strong, equal to. Weak in the sides, unfit for carrying loads.

A مضلّع *muzallaʻ,* Woven in the shape of ribs. (A bridle) marked with stripes. (Cloth) partly woven, partly not.

A مضلّل *muzallal,* One bereft of reason, and who perseveres in an error. One who keeps not good faith. الملك المضلّل *al maliku'l muzallal,* A name of Imrau'l Kays.

A مضلوعة *mazlūʻat,* A bow in whose wood is curvature and straightness, whilst the whole resembles that part which is called كبد *kabid.*

A مضمار *mizmār,* A large plain or place for exercises; also a field of battle. A space of forty days, during which a horse has a more than ordinary allowance of food, in order to fatten him; the place where a horse is so fed. The utmost speed of a horse in a race.

A مضماض *mazmāz* or *mizmāz,* A washing or rinsing of the mouth. *Mizmāz,* Active, light, nimble (man). Burning.

A مضمان *mizmān,* A pregnant camel.

A مضمحلّ *muzmahill,* Disappearing, vanishing; cancelled, defaced, carried off, dispersed.

A مضمّخ *muzammakh,* Copiously perfumed.

A مضمر *muzmar,* Concealed. Conceived (in mind); understood. A place of concealment. *Muzmir,* Who conceives or imagines. (See اضمار *izmār.*)

A مضمّر *muzammar,* Lean, lank, attenuated. *Muzammir,* What makes lean, attenuates, emaciates.

A مضمرط *muzmarat,* Wrinkled (in the face).

A مضمضة *mazmazat,* (v. n. of مضمض Q) Washing (the mouth), rinsing (a vessel). Being affected (the eyes) slightly by drowsiness.

A مضمّن *muzamman,* (A poem) comprehending the verses of another poet; also a verse or word depending upon the following word or verse to be fully intelligible.

A مضموم *mazmūm,* Added, joined. Compressed, drawn in. (A letter) marked with *zamma* ـُ.

A مضمومات *mazmūmāt,* (pl. fem.) Additions, accumulations.

A مضمون *mazmūn,* (pl. مضامين *mazāmīn*) Sense, signification, meaning, contents (of a letter). (A hand) folded across, and concealed under the armpit, or under the garment. A fœtus in the loins of his sire. مضمون خطاب *mazmūni khitāb,* The subject of discussion. خلاصهٔ مضمون *khulāsaʼi maz-*

mūn, The substance of the contents.

A علق مضنة *ɛilku mazannatin* or *mazinnatin*, Any thing precious.

A مضنوك *maznūk*, Troubled with a rheum.

A مضنون *maznūn*, Preserved with avaricious care. Civet, musk.

A مضنونة *maznūnat*, The well Zamzam.

A مضنىٔ *muzna'*, Emaciated. *Muzni*, Emaciating (disease).

A مضنیٔ *muzniɛ*, (A man) with many cattle.

A مضنئة *muzniɛat*, Prolific (woman).

A مضوّ *muzūw*, (v. n. of مضى) Passing by, going away. Being carried far (in any thing).

A مضواء *muzawāɛ*, A preceding, a going before.

A مضور *muzūr*, (v. n. of مضر) Becoming acid, pricking the tongue (milk or wine). Becoming white.

A مضوز *mazūz*, Aged (she-camel).

A مضوضئ *muzawziɛ*, (or مضوضیّ *muzawzīy*) (A man) calling aloud.

A مضوف *mazūf*, (Any thing) to be dreaded.

A مضوفة *mazūfat*, Need. Care, anxiety.

A مضؤود *mazɛūd*, Troubled with a rheum.

A مضؤوك *mazɛūk*, Troubled with a rheum.

A مضهّب *muzahhab*, (Meat) cut and half-roasted.

A مضهود *mazhūd*, Subdued; constrained.

A مضىٔ *maza'*, It is past. مضى سبيله *maza' sabīlahu*, He died. He pursued his own plan. مضىٔ ما مضىٔ *maza' mā maza'*, Let what is past be past, let bygones be bygones; let us speak no more of it.

A مضیّ *muzīy*, (v. n. of مضى) Passing, going by. Being carried far into. Pace. الى مضىّ الحول *ila' muzīyi'l hawl*, To the expiration of the year.

A مضياع *mizyāɛ*, A prodigal, spendthrift.

A مضير *mazīr*, Acid, sour (milk). Very white.

A مضيرة *mazīrat*, A kind of soup or broth made of sour milk; and sometimes with fresh milk.

A مضيض *mazīz*, (v. n. of مضّ) Afflicting, grieving. Grieving on account of some misfortune. Drinking and compressing the lips (a she-goat).

A مضيع *muzīɛ*, Rich in farms or estates (ضيعة *zayɛat*). One who dissipates or squanders. One who frustrates or makes void.

A مضيّع *muzayyiɛ*, A prodigal, spendthrift.

A مضيعة *mazyaɛat*, A place of danger or destruction. *Mazīɛat*, Perdition. دار مضيعة *dāri mazīɛa*, The house of perdition.

A مضيغة *mazīghat*, (pl. مضيغ *mazīgh* and مضائغ *mazāɛigh*) That part of the jaw-bone which projects under the ear. Flesh adhering to the bone. A muscle. A piece of flesh under that part of the fore-leg of a horse called ناهض *nāhiz*. A sinew bound round the horn or extreme part of a bow.

A مضيف *muzīf*, One who bends or causes to incline. The master of a feast. (See اضافة *izāfat*.)

A مضيفة *mazīfat* or *mazyufat*, Any thing formidable. Grief, sadness, care.

A مضيق *mazīk*, A narrow place, pass, strait. A difficult affair.

A مضيّق *muzayyak*, Straitened, narrowed, pinched.

A مضيم *mazīm*, Injured, oppressed, defrauded.

A مضيوح *mazyūh*, Chequered with joy and grief.

A مضئود *mazɛūd*, Troubled with a rheum.

A مضىٔ *muziɛ*, Bright, shining, luminous.

A مطّ *mat*, for مطلوب *matlūb*, The thing intended.

A مطّ *matt*, (v. n. of مطّ) Extending. Raising the eyebrows, *i.e.* being proud. Drawing up (a bucket). Pointing, talking with the fingers.

A مطء *matɛ*, (v. n. of مطأ) Lying with.

A مطا *mata'*, (pl. امطاء *amtāɛ*) The back. A yawning, gaping, oscitation. Favour, protection. A split branch of a palm-tree, with which things are hooped together.

A مطاء *mitāɛ*, (pl. of مطو *matw*) Split branches of palm-trees, with which they hoop or fasten things together. (pl. of مطو *mitw*) Clusters of dates.

A مطابّة *mutābbat*, (v. n. 3 of طبّ) Applying a remedy, physicking, treating medically, curing.

A مطابخ *matābikh*, (pl. of مطبخ) Kitchens.

A مطابق *mutābik*, Conformable, suitable, equal, agreeable to, consonant with, answering to.

A مطابقة *mutābakat*, (v. n. 3 of طبق) Being uniform, equal, agreeing with. Applying one thing to another, to fit them, fitting, matching. Putting on two shirts. Going with short steps, as with bound feet. Placing the hind-feet in the footsteps of the fore-feet (a horse when walking). Adopting a custom, mode, or habit. Conformity, congruity, uniformity, proportion. Similarity, sameness, equality. Antithesis.

A مطابنة *mutābanat*, (v. n. 3 of طبن) Making deep (a pit for keeping fire in, to prevent it from dying away). Being conformable, agreeing with.

A مطاحن *matāhin*, (pl. of مطحان) Mills.

A مطّاخ *mattākh*, Stupid, foolish. Proud, puffed up.

A مطادة *matādat*, A widely-extended desert.

A مطار *matār*, Large-mouthed (well). Sprightly, fleet (horse). *Mutār*, Forced to fly. Broken, split.

A مطّار *mattār*, Swift (horse).

A مطارب *matārib*, (pl. of مطرب *matrab* and مطربة *matrabat*) Divided and narrow ways. Name of a district in Yaman.

A مطارة *matārat*, (A country) abounding in birds (طائر *tāɛir*). Name of a mountain. *Matārat* or *mutārat*, A wide-mouthed well.

A مطارح *matārih*, (pl. of مطرح *matrah*) Places. مطارح الزرع *matārihu'z zarɛ*, Sown fields.

A مطارحة *mutārahat*, (v. n. 3 of طرح) Talking together, holding a conference, bandying words to and fro. Propounding. Conference, conversation.

A مطاردة *mutāradat*, (v. n. 3 of طرد) Attacking one another furiously. Opposition, mutual attack.

A مطارف *matārif*, (pl. of مطرف *mutraf*) Square-cut garments of coarse stuff ornamented with a border. مطارف الثري *matārifu's sary*, The garments of opulence.

A مطارق *matārik*, (pl. of مطرقة *mitrakat*) Sledge-hammers. *Mutārak*, Having one thing above another, as a double slipper, or two garments.

A مطارقة *mutārakat*, (v. n. 3 of طرق) Putting on (two garments), the one over the other. Sewing together (two soles).

A مطارنة *matārinat*, (pl. of مطران *matrān* or *mitrān*) Metropolitans, archbishops.

A مطاريق *matārīk*, Pedestrians. Camels following each other when approaching water. (pl. of مطراق *mitrāk*) (Things) consecutive and similar (to each other). جاءت مطاريق *jāɛat matārīka*, They came one after another.

A مطاسب *matāsib*, Concealed water. Running, dashing water.

A مطاط *matāt*, Camel's milk thick and sour. *Mitāt* or *mutāt*, Long (back).

A مطاع *mutāɛ*, Obeyed. One who is, or ought to be, obeyed. P فرمان جهان مطاع *farmāni jahān-mutāɛ*, A mandate obeyed by all the world.

A مطاعم *matāɛim*, (pl. of مطعم *matɛam*) Meats, eatables. مطاعم و مشارب *matāɛim u mashārib*, Meats and drinks.

A مطاعمة *mutāɛamat*, The billing (of doves).

A مطاعن *matāɛin*, (pl. of مطعن *mitɛan*) (or مطاعين *matāɛīn*, pl. of مطعان *mitɛān*) (Enemies) who pierce furiously with spears.

A مطاف *matāf*, (v. n. of طاف for طيف) Appearing (as a spectre). A place round which they walk in procession in religious ceremonies.

A مطافل *matāfil*, (or مطافيل) (pl. of مطفل *mutfil*) (Hinds) attended by their young or near the birth.

A مطال *mitāl*, (v. n. 3 of مطل) Hammering, flattening (iron). Extending, prolonging. Putting off (the payment of a debt).

A مطّال *mattāl*, One who makes or hammers helmets. One who puts off payment (of a debt).

A مطالب *matālib*, (pl. of مطلب *matlab*) Questions, demands, petitions, propositions, requisitions.

A مطالبة *mutālabat*, An asking, a requiring.

A مطالبیّ *matālibīy*, A deceiver, a cheat.

A مطالة *mitālat*, The art of hammering helmets.

A مطالع *matāliɛ*, (pl. of مطلع *matlaɛ*) The places of (the stars' rising). *Mutāliɛ*, Considerate, attentive. One who exposes or offers any thing for inspection, or to be read. P مطالع شدن *mutāliɛ shudan*, To contemplate, read, study.

A مطالعة *mutālaɛat*, (v. n. 3 of طلع) Considering, turning the attention to. Writing to any one to apprise him. Exhibiting (any thing) to inspection, or to be read. Consideration, contemplation. Reading, study. A glance. A perusal. A letter. مطالعة كتب *mutālaɛaɛi kutub*, The reading of books.

A مطالق *matālik*, (pl. of منطلق *muntalik*) Dismissed, set at liberty. Departing.

A مطالي *matālī*, Places where wild beasts rear

their young.

A مطامح *matāmih*, (pl. of مطمح *mutmah*) Sights, spectacles.

A مطامع *matāmiɛ*, Things longed for, objects coveted and hankered after.

A مطامنة *mutāmanat*, (v. n. 3 of طمن) Being quiet, secure, at rest. A lowering of the back, and a making of it level.

A مطامير *matāmīr*, (pl. of مطمورة *matmūrat*) Caverns or subterraneous store-rooms for grain.

A مطانب *matānib*, (pl. of مطنب *matnab*) The shoulders, the parts between the shoulder-blades and the neck. *Mutānib*, A neighbour whose tent ropes (طناب *tanāb* or *tināb*) touch your own.

A مطانزة *mutānazat*, (v. n. 3 of طنز) Ridiculing, bantering, jeering, gibing one another.

A مطاوح *matāwih*, Dangerous parts. Places into which any thing is thrown.

A مطاوحة *mutāwahat*, (v. n. 3 of طاح for طوح) Contending in throwing, throwing at each other.

A مطاود *matāwid*, Places of peril and danger.

A مطاوع *mutāwiɛ*, Acquiescing, obedient, compliant, submissive. A recipient: as, from معلّم *muɛallim*, A teacher, comes متعلّم *mutaɛallim*, One who submits to be taught; a learner. The latter word is the مطاوع *mutāwiɛ* of the former. مطاوع العرض *mutāwiɛu'l ɛarz*, (or عراض *ɛurāz*) Broad.

A مطاوعة *mutāwaɛat*, (v. n. 3 of طاع for طوع) Consenting, agreeing, accommodating one's self to. Consent. Submission. The sense of the fifth conjugation; as, obeying, submitting to, accepting, or acquiescing in the sense of the second; as, تأدّب *taɛaddub*, A submitting or consenting to be taught; تعلّم *taɛallum*, A submitting to receive knowledge; learning. P مطاوعت كردن *mutāwaɛat kardan*, To agree, consent, shew obedience. To accommodate.

A مطاول *matāwil*, (pl. of مطول) Ropes, halters.

A مطاولة *mutāwalat*, (v. n. 3 of طال for طول) Disputing about length, excellence, or strength. Delaying payment or a promise. Procrastination.

A مطاوي *matāwī*, (pl. of مطويّ *matwa'*) Folds (of a book), wrinkles (in the belly), plies (in the intestines), coils (of a serpent).

A مطاهر *matāhir*, (pl. of مطهرة *matharat* and *mitharat*) Vessels with spouts, from which they pour water when making ablutions. Dentifrices. *Mutāhar*, Purified, pure, holy. *Mutāhir*, A purifier.

A مطاهرة *mutāharat*, A purifying, cleansing.

A مطايا *matāya'*, (pl. of مطيّة) Horses, mules.

A مطائب *matāɛib*, Best, choicest (ripe dates).

A مطايبة *mutāyabat*, (v. n. 3 of طاب for طيب) Jesting, playing, joking together: joke, pleasantry.

A مطايرة *mutāyarat*, (v. n. 3 of طار for طير) Putting to flight, making fly.

A مطائط *mutāɛit*, Long (back).

A مطبّخ *mutabbakh*, Fat and full of flesh.

A مطبخ *matbakh*, A kitchen, a place for cooking. *Mitbakh*, Any cooking-instrument, as a spit or pot.

A مطّبخ *muttabakh*, Cooked. A place for cooking, a kitchen. *Muttabikh*, A cook. Who takes or prepares any thing for dressing.

A مطبّخ *mutabbikh*, Growing (boy). A boy, youth. A young crocodile or Lybian lizard.

A مطبخيّ *matbakhīy*, Culinary, belonging to a kitchen. A cook, a clerk of the kitchen.

A مطبع *matbaɛ*, A place where any thing is stamped or printed. A printing-office.

A مطبعة *matbaɛat*, A printing-press or office.

A مطّبعة *mutabbaɛat*, Heavily-laden (she-camel).

A مطبق *mutbak*, Covered with a lid. Folded together. Agreed, suited to, fitted. *Mutbik*, Incessant (fever). Continued (madness). (See اطباق.)

A مطبّق *mutabbak*, Complicated, multiplied, double. (Clouds) overspreading or wetting the whole earth. *Mutabbik*, (A sword) which separates the joints (مصمّم *musammim* implying, cutting through bones). Penetrating, hitting (the nail on the head. Continual, unintermitting (disease). Clever. One who manages properly, easily, well. (Clouds) overspreading or wetting the whole earth.

A مطبقة *mutbakat*, (fem. of مطبق *mutbak*) Folded, covered. الحروف المطبقة *al hurūfu'l mutbakat*, The letters ص *sād*, ض *zād*, ط *tā*, and ظ *zā*. *Mutbikat*, Continual (fever).

A مطبّل *mutabbal*, Drum-shaped.

A مطبوب *matbūb*, Fascinated, bewitched.

A مطبوخ *matbūkh*, Dressed, cooked. Boiled. Boiling, fermenting. Dressed silk. مطبوخ في الماء *matbūkh fi'l māɛ*, Seethed in water.

A مطبوع *matbūɛ*, Struck, stamped, impressed. Coined. Formed by nature. Natural, innate. Agreeable, acceptable, worthy, laudable. Celebrated. Defiled, contaminated, disgraced. Of a well-proportioned shape. مطبوع القلب *matbūɛu'l kalb*, Agreeable to the heart. مجموعهٔ مطبوعه *majmūɛaɛi matbūɛa*, An excellent collection.

A مطبئنّ *mutbaɛinn*, Quiet, secure, content.

A مطثّة *mitassat*, A battledore, bat, racket.

A مطجّن *mutajjan*, Fried in a pan (طاجن *tājan*).

A مطح *math*, (v. n. of مطح) Striking (with the hand). Lying with.

A مطحان *mithān*, A mill. (A viper) coiling itself in a circle.

A مطحانة *mithānat*, A mill. A little dish.

A مطحّة *mitahhat*, The hinder part of a sheep's hoof; or an excrescence hanging from it which rubs against the ground.

A مطحر *mithar*, A bow which sends the arrow far. An arrow which flies far. A lion. حرب مطحر *harb mithar*, A battle in which the combatants knock each other about. *Muthar*, (An arrow-head) made long.

A مطحرة *mitharat*, Fierce (war). A spear.

A مطحلب *mutahlib* or *mutahlab*, (Water) covered with a green scum called طحلب *tuhlub*.

A مطحنة *mathanat*, A bakehouse. A mill where they grind. *Mithanat*, A mill. A little dish.

A مطحوّ *mathūw*, Wide-spread (shade, arbour).

A مطحول *mathūl*, Splenetic. Full (vessel). Hurt in the spleen (طحال *tihāl*).

A مطحوم *mathūm*, Full, replete.

A مطحون *mathūn*, Ground, crushed in a mill.

A مطحّي *mutahhī*, (A vegetable) which grows and covers the face of the ground.

A مطحيّ *mathīy*, Wide-spread (shade, arbour).

A مطخ *mathh*, (v. n. of مطخ) Eating, devouring (much). Licking (honey). Drawing (water in a bucket). Striking (with the hand). Sullying, tarnishing (the reputation of another). A remainder of dirty water in the bottom of a cistern. مطخ مطخ *mitikh mitikh*, Mere nonsense! fictions! (applied to people when telling absurdities or lies).

A مطخّة *mitahhhat*, A piece of wood used by boys at play; a bat, battledore, racket.

A مطخرر *mutakhrar*, Weak, feeble.

A مطر *matr*, (v. n. of مطر) Travelling over, crossing (a country). Filling (a leathern bottle). Going fast (a horse). Descending with rapidity (a bird). Raining. لا ادري من مطر به *lā adrī man matara bihi*, I know not who has taken it. (pl. امطار *amtār*) A skin filled with oil. *Mutr*, Custom, fashion, usage. An ear of millet. *Matar*, (v. n. of مطر) Raining. (pl. امطار *amtār*) Rain. مطر طيّب الاثر *matari tayyibu'l asar*, A salutary rain. *Matir*, Rainy (day).

A مطرّ *mutirr*, (Anger) bursting forth without provocation. Pompous, stately in walking.

A مطرّا *mutarra'*, Fresh. Perfumed. Polished.

A مطراب *mitrāb*, (or مطرابة *mitrābat*) One who moves with alacrity from joy or sorrow.

A مطرّاة *mutarrāt*, Perfumed, scented, spiced (wash for the head).

A مطراف *mitrāf*, (A she-camel) requiring frequent change of pasturage; roaming about.

A مطراق *mitrāk*, (pl. مطاريق *matārīk*) (One thing) following (another) and resembling (it).

P مطرّاگر *mutarrāgar*, One who smoothes or glazes linens, silks, or clothes. A calendrer.

A مطران *matrān* or *mitrān*, An archbishop.

A مطرب *matrab*, (and مطربة *matrabat*) (pl. مطارب *matārib*) A divided or narrow way. A by-lane leading into a high road. *Mutrib*, A musician, minstrel. A singer. Who or what causes to dance and skip about for joy.

A مطرة *matrat* also *matirat*, Manner, custom, usage. *Matarat*, A large leathern water-bag. The middle of a cistern. *Matirat*, (A woman) constantly cleaning her teeth, careful in being neat.

A مطرّة *mutirrat*, Manner, custom, usage.

A مطرح *matrah*, A place, station, post, situation, foundation; a place where any thing is thrown.

A place of reverbation or echo. *Mitrah*, Far-sighted (eye). A stallion whose seed falls far short of the womb. *Mutrah*, Thrown away, rejected.

A مطرّح *mutarrah*, Laid prostrate, at full length. Extensive, long (building).

A مطرخمّ *mutrakhimm*, Choice, handsome (youth). Proud. Angry. Reclining on the breast.

A مطرد *mitrad*, A short hunting-spear.

A مطرد *muttarid*, Unimpeded, flowing freely, and in a straight and onward course.

A مطرّد *mutarrad*, Long (day). Driven away.

A مطردة *matradat*, A cause or means of driving away. *Matradat* or *mitradat*, A highway, a king's road. *Mitradat*, A damp cloth with which an oven is cleaned, a malkin.

A مطرّز *mutarraz*, (A garment) ornamented with a lace or fringe (طراز *tirāz*). *Mutarriz*, A worker of lace or fringe for garments, a laceman.

P مطرف *mitraf*, A veil, a curtain.

A مطرف *mutraf*, (pl. مطارف *matārif*) A kind of garment of coarse silk ornamented with a border. *Mutrif*, Newly-acquired (wealth).

A مطرّف *mutarraf*, New. Days lately past. Beginning, commencement. (A horse) having his head and tail white or black, and the rest of his body different. (A sheep) having the tail black, the rest of the body being white. Rhyming (prose). *Mutarrif*, (An army) attacking the wing or outskirts (طرف *taraf*) of the enemy.

A مطرفسة *mutarfisat*, Cloudy (sky).

A مطرق *mitrah*, A rod for beating cotton or wool. Name of a camel. *Mutrah*, A shield formed of several coats of leather. *Mutrih*, One whose eyelids are relaxed, and who naturally looks on the ground. Low, ignoble.

A مطرّق *mutarrik*, (A woman or camel) in labour.

A مطرقة *mitrahat*, A smith's hammer. A rod for teasing cotton or wool. *Mutrakat* or *mutarrakat*, (A shield) consisting of different coats of leather.

A مطرمذ *mutarmiz*, A vain-boaster, one who talks much but performs not. Inexperienced, unversed.

A مطروح *matrūh*, Thrown, flung, cast. Rejected, dejected, abject. An infidel. Distant (place). (in Morocco dialect) A remainder (in subtraction).

A مطرود *matrūd*, Banished, persecuted, driven off to a distance. مآل المطرود *maʻālu'l matrūd*, Refuge of the destitute. مردود و مطرود *mardūd u matrūd*, Rejected and cast off.

A مطرور *matrūr*, Whetted, sharpened (knife). Furbished (sword).

A مطروف *matrūf*, One whose eyes are not steadily fixed upon any object. (Eyes) hurt by any thing which makes them water.

A مطروفة *matrūfat*, A woman who looks from her husband (towards other men). (Ground) fertile in the plant نصيّ *nasiy*.

A مطروق *matrūh*, (A man) weak, feeble in intellect. (Water) defiled with the dung or urine of cattle. (Fodder) wet with rain after being dry. Flabby, flaccid.

A مطروقة *matrūhat*, (A she-goat) marked in the middle of the ear.

A مطرهفّ *mutrahiff*, A comely, well-made man.

A مطرهمّ *mutrahimm*, Well-made (youth). Untractable (camel), unused to the halter.

A مطري *mutrī*, One who praises to excess. One who makes fragrant.

A مطرّي *mutarra'*, (and in regimine مطرّا *mutarrā*) Perfumed, scented with aromatics. Polished, glazed, calendered, made to look new.

A مطرير *mitrīr*, An impudent, noisy woman.

A مطز *matz*, The venereal act.

A مطس *mats*, (v. n. of مطس) Giving a blow, box, slap. Voiding (dung) at a single effort.

A مطسّس *mutassis*, A roamer through cities.

A مطسع *mitsaʻ*, Skilful, intelligent (guide).

A مطشوشة *matshūshat*, (Land) wet with rain.

A مطع *matʻ*, (v. n. of مطع) Travelling, wandering, not to be found. Eating with the fore-teeth.

A مطعام *mitʻām*, Hospitable; giving food.

A مطعان *mitʻān*, (pl. مطاعن *matāʻin* or مطاعين *matāʻīn*) One who stabs much with a spear.

A مطعم *matʻam*, Eating. Food. *Mitʻam*, One who eats much and greedily. *Mutʻam*, Fed, supported in the necessaries of life. *Mutʻim* or *mutaʻʻim*, One who feeds, gives to eat, one who maintains or entertains others.

A مطّعم *muttaʻam* or *ʻim*, A camel full of marrow.

A مطعّم *mutaʻʻim*, (Milk) having a fine flavour from the bag into which it has been put. (A camel, male or female) fat and full of marrow.

A مطعمة *mutʻamat*, A bow. *Mutʻimat*, A bow (as providing meat for its owner). The larynx or top of the windpipe.

A مطعمتان *mutʻimatāni*, A bird's two fore-talons.

A مطعن *matʻan*, Obnoxious to reproach or chiding. *Mitʻan*, (pl. مطاعن *matāʻin*) One who pierces his enemy with a spear.

A مطعوم *matʻūm*, Any thing eatable.

A مطعومات *matʻūmāt*, Eatables.

A مطعون *matʻūn*, Transfixed with a spear, speared. Infected with the pestilence (طاعون *tāʻūn*). Accursed, damned; reprehended, chidden.

A مطغمش *mutaghmish*, One who darts a sly look from a blemish in the eye. Weak, feeble. Hidden, secret.

A مطغي *mutghī*, Insolence-inspiring.

A مطفّ *mutiff*, Happening, falling out. Possible. Near knowing, ware of. (See اطفاف *itfāf*.)

A مطّفح *muttafih*, One who skims (a pot).

A مطفّح *mutaffih*, Who fills to the brim.

A مطفحة *mitfahat*, A ladle, skimmer.

A مطفرش *mutafrish*, Weak-sighted.

A مطفّف *mutaffif*, One who does not fill a vessel, giving unfair measure. (See تطفيف *tatfīf*.)

A مطفل *mutfil*, (pl. مطافل *matāfil* and مطافيل *matāfīl*) (A mother) having an infant or young along with her. (A severe night) killing young animals with cold.

A مطفي *mutfiʼ*, (or مطفّي *mutaffiʼ*) One who extinguishes, an extinguisher. مطفي الجمر *mutfiʼu'l jamr*, Extinguishing the glede (name of the fifth or the fourth of the days called العجوز *al ʻajūz*). مطفي الرضف *mutfiʼu'r razf*, Adversity, calamity (especially such as effaces the remembrance of former calamities. مطفئة الرضف *mutfiʼatu'r razf*, Whatever extinguishes a fire (as a bit of melted fat, or the venom of a serpent crawling by). حدس لهم بمطفئة الرضف *hadasa lahum bi mutfiʼati'r razf*, He slaughtered for them a lean sheep which would extinguish the fire ere it were cooked.

A مطق *matak*, A disease which attacks a palm.

A مطقة *mathat*, Sweetness.

A مطل *matl*, (v. n. of مطل) Hammering, flattening, drawing out (iron). Melting, casting, forging. Extending, prolonging; putting off (the payment of a debt). *Mutl*, Reprieve, respite. A little water poured or dropping from a bottle.

A مطلّ *mutall*, (Blood) unpunished, shed with impunity. Rained upon gently. *Mutill*, Uncertain, fluctuating (business). Impending, overhanging. (God) suffering blood to be shed with impunity.

A مطلا *mitla'*, (or مطلاء *mitlāʼ*) (pl. مطالي *matālī*) Soft level ground producing the plant عضاة *ʻizāh*. A narrow channel for water.

A مطلّا *mutalla'*, Gilded, covered with gold.

A مطلاع *matlāʻ*, (in Morocco) A large adze.

A مطلاق *mitlāh*, A camel going to water. (A man) frequent in divorcing (his wives).

A مطلب *matlab*, A question, demand, request, petition. Intention, purpose, proposition, wish, desire, pursuit, motive. Effect. P هم مطلب *hammatlab*, Having the same desire, *i. e.* a rival, competitor. A *Mutlib*, One who gives orders to be asked. A granter of any thing petitioned. Far distant (forage or water). (See اطلاب *itlāb*.)

A مطّلب *muttalib*, A seeker.

A مطلبة *matlabat*, A question, proposition. An intention.

A مطلة *matlat* or *matalat*, The dirty remainder of water in the bottom of a reservoir. *Mutlat*, A little water flowing from a leathern bottle.

A مطلحبّ *mutlahibb*, Long, extended.

A مطلسم *mutalsam*, Armed with a talisman.

A مطلع *matlaʻ*, The beginning of a poem. *Matlaʻ* or *matliʻ*, (v. n. of طلع) Arising, appearing (as the sun or stars). The place of rising (especially of the stars). P از مطلع تا مقطع *az matlaʻ tā mahtaʻ*, From beginning to end. A *Mutliʻ*, One who reveals or causes to understand. (See اطلاع *itlāʻ*.)

A مطّلع *muttalaʻ*, Able, sufficient, powerful, equal

to. Lifted up or made to ascend. Coming, about to come. A place to which one comes, or whither any thing tends or is directed. A place which one ascends, or from whence one descends or looks down. The day of the resurrection. *Muttaliʻ*, One who penetrates, inspects, and looks into (affairs). Apprized. One who considers and wishes to explore the intention or opinion of another. Strong, violent, oppressive. High. P مطّلع شدن *muttaliʻ shudan*, To perceive, penetrate, see distinctly, be fully informed of.

A مطلّع *mutalliʻ*, One who fills a measure.

A مطلعة *matlaʻat*, A high place, watch-tower. *Mutliʻat*, (A palm-tree) towering above the rest.

A مطلف *mutlif*, A giver, bestower. One who permits, makes great allowance, passes over a great deal. Unrevenged (blood).

A مطلق *mutlak*, Absolute, universal, principal, supreme. Free, exempt, unrestrained. Indefinite. Wholly, not in the least, never, entirely, altogether. A course or race-ground for horses. مطلق العنان *mutlaku'l ʻinān*, Free, having the reins loose. خير مطلق *khayri mutlak*, The chief good, summum bonum. قادر مطلق *kādiri mutlak*, Omnipotent (God), powerful. وكيل مطلق *wakīli mutlak*, A plenipotentiary. مطلقا *mutlakan*, Absolutely, properly, simply, quite, altogether. *Mutlik*, A perient, cathartic. (See اطلاق *itlāk*.)

A مطلّق *mutallak*, Recovered from the pain caused by the bite of a serpent. One whose grief is mitigated. Divorced. *Mutallik*, A divorcer. One who engages in a horse-race. A giver, a bestower.

A مطلنفى *mutlanfī*, Crouching (hunter).

A مطلنفئ الشرف *mutlanfiʼu'sh sharaf*, (A camel) having a compressed or flat bunch.

A مطلوب *matlūb*, Demanded, called, exacted, required, sought, wanted, needed. The thing desired. Wish, intention. Name of a place. P چهرهٔ مطلوب *chihraʼi matlūb*, The appearance of any thing wished for.

A مطلوبة *matlūbat*, (Any thing) sought, wished.

A مطلوح *matlūh*, Empty-bellied.

A مطلوس *matlūs*, Cast into prison, imprisoned.

A مطلوقة *matlūkat*, Agonized by the pains of parturition. Divorced (woman).

A مطلول *matlūl*, (Blood) shed with impunity. Moistened with dew (طلّ *tall*), bedewed.

A مطلّى *mutalla'*, A sufferer from severe and continued illness. Imprisoned without hope of escape. *Mutallī*, One who smears with pitch. An attendant on the sick. A reviler. A singer.

A مطلي *matlīy*, Tied, bound. Anointed, smeared.

A مطليق *mitlīk*, A man who frequently divorces his wives; frequent in طلاق *talāk*.

A مطمار *mitmār*, A mason's plumb-line. A man in tattered garments. Form, figure, face. هو على مطمار ابيه *huwa ʻala' mitmāri abīhi*, He resembles his father in person and disposition.

A مطماع *mitmāʻ*, (A woman) who excites desire (طمع *tamaʻ*) in a man, but gives no opportunity.

A مطمأنّ *mutmaʼann*, Rested, reposed. The place where one rests.

A مطمح *mutmah*, Raised up, turned upwards (the sight). A show, spectacle. A theatre. مطمح نظر *mutmah nazar*, Regarding, with a view to. A butt for archers. *Mutmih*, Who raises his eyes or looks up.

A مطمخرّ *mutmahirr*, Filled (vessel).

A مطمر *mitmar*, A mason's plumb-line. اقم المطمر يا محدّث *akimi'l mitmar yā muhaddis*, Tell your tale in a straightforward manner, O story-teller!

A مطمرة *mutmirat*, A dangerous affair.

A مطمّرة *mutammarat*, Long, strong-built, and hardy (she-ass). *Mutammirat*, Dangerous (affair).

A مطمس *mutmas*, Blinded, blind.

A مطمطة *matmatat*, (v. n. of مطمط Q) Being slow in writing or talking.

A مطمع *matmaʻ*, (or مطمعة *matmaʻat*) A thing desired or desirable. *Mutmaʻ*, Longed for, wished, desired. *Mutmiʻ*, Whatever excites a longing desire (طمع *tamaʻ*), or inspires hope.

A مطمعة *matmaʻat*, What sets one a-longing.

A مطملة *mitmalat*, A rolling-pin.

A مطمور *matmūr*, Stored (grain). Troubled with toothache.

A مطمورة *matmūrat*, (pl. مطامير *matāmīr*) A subterraneous cavern in which they lay up corn.

A مطموس *matmūs*, Blind, bereft of sight. Erased, effaced, obliterated. مطموس العين *matmūsu'l ʻayn*, Antichrist (as being one-eyed).

A مطموع *matmūʻ*, Greedily desired, coveted.

A مطمول *matmūl*, Bloody (arrow). Rolled out (leaven). Smeared (with blood, pitch, &c.).

A مطموم *matmūm*, Closely shorn (head). One who has much hair.

A مطمّه *mutammah*, Long, tall.

A مطمئنّ *mutmaʼinn*, Quiet, secure, content, acquiescing, safe, enjoying repose and ease. Low and level (country).

A مطناب *mitnāb*, Numerous (host).

A مطنب *matnab*, The shoulder, that place between the shoulder-blades and the neck. *Mutnib*, (A river) flowing a great way.

A مطنّب *mutannab*, (A tent) stretched by ropes.

A مطنزة *matnazat*, Men ridiculous in their behaviour. Worthless, good for little.

A مطنف *mutnif*, One who stands upon a pinnacle or a mountain's top, or on the coping of a wall. One possessed of a coping on his wall, or of a slab, projection, or pent (طنف *tanf*) over his door.

A مطنّف *mutannaf*, Suspected. Inwardly bad.

A مطنفسة *mutanfisat*, Cloudy (sky).

A مطو *matw*, (v. n. of مطا for مطو) Going quick. Exerting one's self in travelling. Travelling with for a long time. Extending. Associating (with a friend). Forming a connexion (with a woman), lying with (her). Yawning. Opening (the eyes). Eating fresh moist dates on the stalk. *Matw* or *mitw*, (pl. مطاء *mitāʼ*, امطاء *amtāʼ*, and مطىّ *matīy*) Any thing long, especially split branches of palm-trees, with which they hoop or fasten things together. *Mitw*, Alike, resembling. A companion, peer, equal. (pl. مطاء *mitāʼ*) The stalk of a bunch of dates. The ear of millet or panic.

A مطواء *mutawāʼ*, Extension, stretching, prolongation. Oscitation, yawning.

A مطواح *mitwāh*, A staff.

A مطواع *mitwāʻ*, Obedient, obsequious.

A مطوة *matwat*, An hour.

A مطوّح *mutawwih*, A thrower. (See تطويح.)

A مطوّد *mutawwad*, Distant, far off.

A مطور *mutūr*, (v. n. of مطر) Travelling, perambulating (a country). Going fast, being borne rapidly along (a horse). Filling (a leathern bottle).

A مطوّس *mutawwas*, Elegant, ornamented.

A مطوع *mutūʻ*, (v. n. of مطع) Wandering, travelling about, so as not to be found. Eating with the fore-teeth.

A مطوّع *mutawwiʻ*, A volunteer, especially in a sacred war. مطوّعة *mutawwiʻat*, A nation engaged in a sacred war as volunteers without conscription.

A مطوّف *mutawwaf*, Distant, remote.

A مطوّق *mutawwak*, Ornamented with a collar, collared. ميم مطوّق *mīmi mutawwak*, Penis.

A مطوّقة *mutawwakat*, A ring-dove. A large vessel with a neck like that of the ring-dove.

A مطول *matūl*, One who delays payment of a debt, or the performance of a promise. *Mitwal*, (pl. مطاول *matāwil*) A rope. Penis.

A مطوّل *mutawwal*, Extended, prolonged, elongated, continued. Tall, lengthy.

A مطويٌ *matwa'*, (pl. مطاوي *matāwī*) Leaf or fold of a book. A wrinkle (in the belly), ply (in the intestine).

A مطويّ *matwīy*, Folded, complicated, twisted up. (A well) built up, lined (with stones, &c.). Resolved on, undertaken. Employed, busied.

A مطهر *mathar*, Place of purification. Purgatory. *Mithar*, An instrument for cleansing or purifying.

A مطهّر *mutahhar*, Purified, cleaned, pure, holy. روضهٔ مطهّره *rawzaʼi mutahhara*, The pure garden, *i. e.* the tomb of Muhammad.

A مطهرة *matharat*, A cause of purity or cleanliness. السواك مطهرة للفم مرضاة للربّ *as siwāk matharat li'l fam, murzāt li'r rabb*, A dentifrice is the means of cleansing the mouth, (and) a thing agreeable to the Lord. *Mitharat* or *matharat*, (pl. مطاهر *matāhir*) A vessel having a spout, from which they pour water when performing ablutions, a ewer. A dentifrice. A house in which ablutions are made.

A مطهريّة *mathariyat*, Purity, cleanness.

A مطهّم *mutahham*, Complete, perfect. Plump.

round (face or man). Beautiful, comely. Fat and unsightly. Lean.

A مطى *mata'*, (pl. امطاء *amtāɛ*) Extension, prolongation. The back.

A مطى *matiy*, (pl. of مطيّة) Beasts of burden.

A مطيّب *mutayyab*, Spiced, perfumed, aromatized. Name of one of Muhammad's sons. حلف المطيّبين *hilfu'l mutayyabayn*, Name of a certain treaty between two Arabian tribes. *Mutayyib*, Whatever imparts an aroma, aromatic, odorous.

A مطيبة *matyabat*, Any thing sweet, agreeable.

A مطيّبة *mutayyabat*, The city of Madīna.

A مطيّة *matiyat*, (pl. مطايا *matāya'*, مطيّ *matiy*, and امطاء *amtāɛ*) A horse, beast of burden.

A مطيّح *mutayyah*, Vicious, spoiled. Worthless.

A مطيّخ *mutayyakh*, Vicious, corrupt, naught. Bedaubed with pitch.

A مطير *matyar*, Flight. كلّ مطير *kull matyar*, On every side. *Matīr*, Rained upon. *Mutayr*, A drop of rain. Name of a man.

A مطيّر *mutayyar*, Fresh. A stick, or green bough. (A vest) painted with the figures of birds (طير *tayr*). عود مطيّر *ɛūdi mutayyar*, The wood of aloes, especially split or broken for perfuming.

A مطّيري *muttayra'*, A prayer for (to be used by?) children when in want of rain.

A مطيشة *matīshat*, (in the dialect of Morocco) A beam suspended for the purpose of swinging.

A مطيطاء *mutaytāɛ*, (*matītā*, or مطيطى *matīta'*) A pompous, stately manner of walking with a stretching forth of the hands.

A مطيطة *matītat*, Thick water at the bottom of a cistern.

A مطيع *mutīɛ*, Obedient, submissive, obsequious. P مطيع شدن *mutīɛ shudan*, To submit. مطيع كردن *mutīɛ kardan*, To subject, render obsequious.

A مطيف *mutīf*, Who or whatever surrounds, encompasses, and encloses.

A مطيق *mutīk*, One who gives power, or confers ability (طاقة *tāḳat*). Able, powerful.

A مطيلق *mutaylik*, (or مطيليق *mutaylīk*) (dim. of منطلق *muntalik*) Somewhat loosened or relaxed.

A مطين *matīn*, Covered with clay, clayed (roof).

A مطيّن *mutayyan*, Plastered over. *Mutayyin*, One who delights to dabble in clay (طين *tīn*).

A مظّ *mazz*, (v. n. of مظّ) Despising, slighting, scorning. Stripping off bark. The pomegranate, also a wild kind of it. Dragons' blood, a gum. The expressed juice of the roots of the tree ارطى *arta'*.

A مظاءبة *muzāɛabat*, (v. n. 3 of ظأب) Being allied (to another), as those who have married sisters.

A مظاءرة *muzāɛarat*, (v. n. 3 of ظأر) Hiring or receiving a nurse. Taking a child to suckle (a nurse). Having the relationship of foster-brother subsisting between them (two persons).

A مظاءمة *muzāɛamat*, (v. n. 3 of ظأم) Being allied to each other (men who have married sisters).

A مظارير *mazārīr*, (pl. of مظرور) Sharp stones.

A مظاظ *mizāz*, (v. n. 3 of مظّ) Contending, striving, disputing. Being malignant and injurious.

A مظاظة *mazāzat*, Strength of body. Roughness, harshness, inhumanity, violence of temper. *Muzāzat*, (v. n. of مظّ) Contending, striving, litigating.

A مظالّ *mazāll*, (pl. of مظلّة *mizallat*) Shades. Tents, pavilions. Parasols.

A مظالفة *muzālafat*, (v. n. 3 of ظلف) Concealing one's footsteps by walking upon hard ground.

A مظالم *mazālim*, (pl. of مظلمة *mazlamat*) Oppressions, tyrannies, aggrievances. ذكر بعض مظالم تيمور *zikri baɛzi mazālimi tīmūr*, The mention of some of the cruelties of Tamerlane.

A مظالمة *muzālamat*, An oppressing; oppression.

A مظانّ *mazānn*, (pl. of مظنّة *mazinnat*) Places where things are supposed to be.

A مظاهر *mazāhir*, (pl. of مظهر *mazhar*) Objects, spectacles. *Muzāhir*, A protector, defender, backer, supporter, assistant. A representer.

A مظاهرة *muzāharat*, (v. n. 3 of ظهر) Assisting, protecting, supporting. Putting on two garments, one over the other. Saying to a wife, عليّ انت كظهر امّي *ɛalayya' anti ka zahri ummī*, Thou art to me as the back of my mother (a formula of divorce).

A مظبظب *muzabzab*, Afflicted with fever.

A مظرّب *muzarrab*, Hard (hoof, nail, claw).

A مظرّة *mazarrat*, A place abounding in sharp stones. *Mizarrat*, (v. n. of ظرّ) Cutting out a flint-stone. Slaughtering (a camel) with a sharp stone, or any thing else. A fire-emitting flint-stone.

A مظرور *muzrūr*, (pl. مظارير *mazārīr*) A stone, especially one round and sharp.

A مظع *mazɛ*, (v. n. of مظع) Making (a bow-string) supple and flexible.

A مظعة *mazɛat*, The remainder, latter part, or concluding portion of a discourse.

A مظفار *mizfār*, Fortunate, always successful. Tweezers.

A مظفر *muzfar*, Scratched with the nails (ظفر *zufr* or *zufur*), clawed. Rendered triumphant.

A مظفّر *muzaffar*, Rendered victorious, accustomed to conquer, superior, fortunate. August. A conqueror. A horse from whose extremities a little has been cut away. مظفّر و منصور *muzaffar u mansūr*, A conqueror, triumpher. المظفّر دائما *al muzaffar dāɛiman*, Ever victorious. P مظفّر شدن *muzaffar shudan*, To be made victorious, to gain a victory, to conquer. مظفّر گشتن سلطان *muzaffar gashtani sultān*, The king's becoming victorious.

A مظفّرون *muzaffarūn*, Name of a dynasty which reigned in Persia from A.D. 1317 to 1395.

A مظفور *mazfūr*, Affected with a web in the eye.

A مظفوف *mazfūf*, (Water) much sought after, contended for by many. Empty-handed (man).

A مظلام *mizlām*, Dark, mysterious (affair).

A مظلّة *mizallat*, A parasol. *Mizallat* or *mazallat*, A tent, pavilion.

A مظلّف *muzallaf*, Endued with a cloven foot (ظلف *zilf*). Increased, augmented.

A مظلّل *muzallal*, Shaded. A parasol-stick.

A مظلم *muzlim*, Blackish green (plant). Jetty (hair). Dark (night). Dark, mysterious (affair). One who enters into, or walks in, darkness. Very evil, unlucky, disastrous (day).

A مظلّم *muzallam*, A pelican. A crow. Grass which has received no rain.

A مظلمة *mazlimat*, Oppression, tyranny, cruelty, injustice, iniquity. A requisition of justice. Justice.

P مظلمه كار *mazlima-kār*, Injurious, tyrannical.

A مظلوف *mazlūf*, Hurt in the hoof or nail.

A مظلوم *mazlūm*, Injured, oppressed. Seized forcibly. Upturned (earth). Mild, gentle, modest. Milk drunk off before it becomes thick. P من مظلومم نه ظالم *man mazlūmam, na zālim*, I am sinned against, not sinning.

P مظلومانه *mazlūmāna*, Like an injured man.

A مظلومة *mazlūmat*, (Land) never yet ploughed.

A مظلومى *mazlūmī*, Oppression, misery.

A مظمأ *mazmaɛ*, A thirsty spot.

A مظماء *mizmāɛ*, Very thirsty (man).

A مظمائيّ *mazmaɛiy*, (A field) watered by rain from heaven (not by irrigation).

A مظمظة *mazmazat*, A swinging to and fro.

A مظميّ *mazmiy*, (A field) watered by rain, (not by rivulets, canals, or art).

A مظنّة *mazinnat*, Opinion, thought. Suspicion, conjecture. (pl. مظانّ *mazānn*) The place where any thing is supposed to be.

A مظنون *maznūn*, Thought, suspected, opined.

A مظواة *mazwāt*, (Ground) producing plentifully the plant ظيّان *zayyān*.

A مظؤورة *mazɛūrat*, (A camel) taken as a nurse (ظئر *ziɛr*) to another's colt.

A مظوّي *muzawwa'*, (Leather) dressed or tanned with the leaves of the plant ظيّان *zayyān*.

A مظه *mazh*, The act of travelling, traversing.

A مظهر *mazhar*, An ascent, step, ladder, or stair. A place where any spectacle is represented; a theatre, amphitheatre, stage. مظهر احسان و الطاف *mazhari ihsān u altāf*, Deemed worthy of grace and favour. مظهر جلال الهى *mazhari jalāli ilāhī*, The object of the divine power, *i.e.* any person, place, or thing which has been the object of Almighty vengeance. مظهر عداوت *mazhari ɛadāwat*, Odious, held in detestation. *Muzhar*, Displayed, manifested. هاى مظهر *hāɛi muzhar*, The sensible aspirate; as in پادشاه *padshāh*, A king, فربه *farbih*, Fat (not as in جامه *jāma*, A robe). *Muzhir*, One who manifests, shews, displays. A comer or goer at noonday (ظهر *zuhr*). Possessed of a number of riding-camels (literally of backs).

A مظهّر *muzahhar*, Strong in the back. Thrown behind the back, rejected, discarded. *Muzahhir*,

One who comes at noon. (See تظهير *tazhīr.*)

A مظهريّة *mazhariyat*, State of being the object.

A مظىّ *muzayy*, (Leather) tanned with the leaves of the plant ظيّان *zayyān*.

A مظياة *mazyāt*, (Land) rich in the ظيّان plant.

A مظيّن *muzayyan*, Tanned with ظيّان leaves.

A مع *maɛ* or *maɛa*, With, together with, in the company of. (It denotes confederacy and favour, likewise opposition and hostility). Notwithstanding. مع ان *maɛ an*, Although, notwithstanding. مع كل هذا *maɛa kull hāzā*, With all this, notwithstanding, still. مع هذا *maɛ hāzā*, Beside.

A معا *maɛan*, Along with, together. At once.

A معّ *maɛɛ*, A being melted.

A معاء *muɛāɛ*, The mewing (of a cat).

A معاب *maɛāb*, (or معابة *maɛābat*) (pl. معائب *maɛāɛib*) A vice, reproach, fault, blemish.

A معابّة *muɛābbat*, Contest for glory or increase.

A معابد *maɛābid*, (pl. of عبد *ɛabd*) Servants, slaves. (pl. of معبد *maɛbid*) Places of worship.

A معابر *maɛābir*, (pl. of معبر *maɛbar*) Passes, ferries, fords. (pl. of معبر *miɛbar*) Ferry-boats.

A معابل *maɛābil*, (pl. of معبلة *miɛbalat*) Arrow-heads broad and long.

A معابير *maɛābīr*, The timbers of a ship to which the anchor is attached.

A معاتب *muɛātab*, Reprehended, chidden. غير معاتب *ghayr muɛātab*, Blameless, irreproachable. *Muɛatib*, A chider, expostulator.

A معاتبة *muɛātabat*, (v. n. 3 of عتب) Expostulating (especially lovers or friends). Chiding, reproving. Reprehension, expostulation.

A معاتّة *muɛāttat*, (v. n. 3 of عتّ) Contending. Animosity, altercation.

A معاتيق *maɛātīk*, (pl. of معتوق *maɛtūk*) Emancipated, set free, manumitted.

A معاث *maɛās*, A way, path, passage. A wide, open space. Rule, institution.

A معاثّة *maɛāssat*, A trill, shake, quaver.

A معاثر *maɛāsir*, Stumbling-blocks.

A معاج *maɛāj*, (v. n. of عاج for عوج) Stopping, staying. Continuing, allowing to remain. Pulling a (camel's) head to one side with the reins. Retiring, receding.

A معاجاة *muɛājāt*, (v. n. 3 of عجا for عجو) Fostering (an infant), allowing (it) to suck a nurse, not (its) mother. Feeding a child bereaved of its mother. Delaying to suckle an infant beyond the stated time.

A معاجرة *muɛājarat*, (v. n. 3 of عجر) Scampering (a horse when frightened).

A معاجز *muɛājiz*, One who opposes, thwarts, bears malice, or endeavours to weaken and cripple.

A معاجزة *muɛājazat*, (v. n. 3 of عجز) Departing and nobody overtaking. Preceding, excelling, getting the start in any business. Inclining towards. Contending for superiority and precedency.

A معاجلة *muɛājalat*, (v. n. 3 of عجل) Making haste to inflict punishment. Hurrying a debtor, demanding instant payment.

A معاجيج *maɛājīj*, Violent, blustering (winds).

A معاجيل *maɛājīl*, Short roads, by which any one may speedily make a cross cut.

A معاجين *maɛājīn*, (pl. of معجون) Electuaries.

A معاد *maɛād*, Place or state to which one returns. A return. The other world. Paradise. The resurrection (the body being then supposed to return to its pristine state). Pilgrimage. Mecca. P شاه بهشتي معاد *shāhi bihishtī-maɛād*, The prince destined for paradise, *i.e.* the deceased king. معاد ساختن *maɛād sākhtan*, To apply to. To rub.

A معاداة *muɛādāt*, (v. n. 3 of عدا for عدو) Detesting, being inimical, hostile. Contending in running. Passing from one to another; seeking immediately (one thing after another). Passing through one to another (as piercing two animals with one shot). Seizing or lifting up by the hair. Enmity, hostility, hatred, animosity.

A معادّة *muɛāddat*, (v. n. 3 of عدّ) Numbering, enumerating. Tormenting (one) with the pain called عداد *ɛidād*. Making mutual preparations for war.

A معادل *muɛādil*, Equal, equivalent, alike, resembling, comparable, opposed to. Just. P بي معادل *bī muɛādil*, Unparalleled, incomparable. اي عادل بي معادل *ay ɛādili bī muɛādil*, O incomparable judge!

A معادلة *muɛādalat*, (v. n. 3 of عدل) Being equal, equivalent to. Making equal. Measuring, estimating. Turning back, retiring. Riding in company in the litter called كجاوه *kajāwa*. Hesitating or remaining in doubt with regard to two matters. Equalizing. Being crooked. Stopping, delaying, halting. Equilibrium, equality. Justice.

A معادن *maɛādin*, (pl. of معدن *maɛdin*) Mines, quarries. P معادن آهن ونقره وطلا *maɛādini āhan u nukra u tilā*, Mines of iron and silver and gold.

A معاذ *maɛāz*, A refuge, asylum. *Maɛāz*, (or معاذة *maɛāzat*) (v. n. of عاذ for عوذ) Taking refuge, fleeing (to God), in any misfortune. معاذ الله *maɛāza'llāh*, (or معاذة الله *maɛāzata'llāh*) God forbid! Heaven defend me!

A معاذة *maɛāzat*, An amulet, charm.

A معاذب *maɛāzib*, (pl. of معذب *maɛzab*) Strips of cloth worn round the waist by wailing women.

A معاذرة *muɛāzarat*, (v. n. 3 of عذر) Making a false and inadmissable excuse. Apologizing mutually.

A معاذير *maɛāzīr*, (pl. of معذار *miɛzār*) Coverings, veils. Proofs, demonstrations. Excuses.

A معار *miɛār*, A horse that swerves with his rider. *Muɛār*, Lent. (A horse) let loose, started. Lean, slender, gaunt. Rat-tailed (horse). Fat.

A معاراة *muɛārāt*, (v. n. 3 of عري) Riding (a horse) bare-backed (عري *ɛury*), without a saddle.

A معارة *maɛārat*, Crossness, badness of temper.

A معارّة *muɛārrat*, (v. n. 3 of عرّ) Making a noise (as the ostrich). Being slow and dilatory: delaying.

A معارج *maɛārij*, (pl. of معرج) Ladders, steps.

A معارزة *muɛārazat*, (v. n. 3 of عرز) Being adverse, averse. Angering, irritating one another. Opposing, resisting, thwarting. Shunning, avoiding. Corrupting, vitiating, spoiling. Being contracted, wrinkled.

A معارض *muɛāriz*, An adversary, competitor, opponent. P مانع و معارض شدن *māniɛ u muɛāriz shudan*, To oppose, prevent.

A معارضة *muɛārazat*, (v. n. 3 of عرض) Going side by side, and step for step. Doing equal with another, exactly what the other has done. Opposing, resisting, thwarting. Collating (books). Falling in with, joining a funeral procession. Walking on the edge of a road. Bringing the female and exposing her to the male. Retiring to a side, giving place, going away. Opposition, contradiction. عن معارضة *ɛan muɛārazatin*, (She brought forth a son) illegitimately. ابن المعارضة *ibnu'l muɛārazat*, An unlucky gaming arrow.

A معارف *maɛārif*, (pl. of معرف *maɛraf*) Faces, hands, and other parts of women displayed. Known, acquaintances. Definite nouns. (pl. of معرفة *maɛrafat* or *maɛrifat*) Sciences. معارف شهر *maɛārifi shahr*, The nobles or notables of the city.

P معارف پرداز *maɛārif-pardāz*, Versed in science.

A معارك *maɛārik*, (pl. of معركة *maɛrakat*) Fields (of battle). معارك قتال *maɛāriki kitāl*, Fields of battle: amphitheatres. *Muɛārik*, A veteran in war.

A معاركة *muɛārakat*, (v. n. 3 of عرك) Fighting, especially hand to hand, jostling one another in battle. Conflict, combat.

A معاري *maɛārī*, The face, feet, or hands of a girl (as being most exposed to view). Beds. Places bare of vegetation.

A معاريج *maɛārīj*, (pl. of معراج) Ladders, stairs.

A معاريض *maɛārīz*, Parables, or like sayings.

A معاز *miɛāz*, The goat-species.

A معّاز *maɛɛāz*, An owner of goats.

A معازّة *muɛāzzat*, (v. n. 3 of عزّ) Overpowering (by words). Contending about price or glory.

A معازف *maɛāzif*, (pl. of معزف *miɛzaf* or معزفة *miɛzafat*) Musical instruments.

A معازق *maɛāzik*, (pl. of معزق *miɛzak* and معزقة *miɛzakat*) Fans, winnowing machines. Implements for turning up the ground.

A معازل *maɛāzil*, (pl. of اعزل *aɛzal*) Unarmed. (pl. of معزل *maɛzil*) Places of retirement.

A معازلة *muɛāzalat*, A retiring from battle.

A معازيل *maɛāzīl*, (pl. of معزال *miɛzāl*) Shepherds who retire from the others at pasture. Weak. Foolish. Unarmed, spearless.

A معّاس *maɛɛās*, Bold, intrepid, valiant.

A معاسرة *muɛāsarat*, (v. n. 3 of عسر) Shewing a bad temper, creating difficulty.

A معاش *maɛāsh*, (v. n. of عاش for عيش) Living. Life, living, livelihood, subsistence. A place where one lives. كفاف معاش *kafāfi maʻāsh*, Victuals; viands. Salary, wages, income, sufficient for subsistence. A kind of sour curd. P بد معاش *bad-maʻāsh*, Wicked, a bad liver.

A معاشر *maʻāshir*, (pl. of معشر *maʻshar*) Companies, congregations, coteries. *Muʻāshir*, A companion, intimate friend, messmate.

A معاشران *muʻāshirān*, (Pers. pl.) Intimates.

A معاشرة *muʻāsharat*, (v. n. 3 of عشر) Contracting friendship, entering into alliance, associating, conversing. Conversation, familiarity, society, living, eating, and drinking together.

A معاشقة *muʻāshakat*, A loving one another.

A معاشيب *maʻāshib*, (pl. of معشاب *miʻshāb*) (Lands) rich in green pasture (عشب *ʻushb*).

A معاصاة *muʻāsāt*, (v. n. 3 of عصا for عصو) Fighting with sticks, playing at quarter-staff or single-stick. Rebelling against, opposing. Rebellion, defection.

A معاصر *maʻāsir*, Places of confinement. (pl. of معصر *miʻsar*) Presses (for wine or olives). *Maʻāsir*, and معاصير *maʻāsīr*) (pl. of معصر *muʻsir*) Marriageable (girls). *Muʻāsir*, Cotemporary, coetaneous.

A معاصرة *muʻāsarat*, A being cotemporary with.

A معاصم *maʻāsim*, (pl. of معصم *miʻsam*) Wrists.

A معاصي *maʻāsī*, (pl. of معصية *maʻsiyat*) Sins, crimes. *Muʻāsī*, Rebellious, criminal.

A معاضبة *muʻāzabat*, (v. n. 3 of عضب) Repelling.

A معاضة *muʻāzzat*, A biting one another.

A معاضد *maʻāzid*, (pl. of معضد *miʻzad*) Bracelets, armlets. Tools used in felling trees. *Muʻāzid*, An assistant, helper.

A معاضدة *muʻāzadat*, (v. n. 3 of عضد) Helping one another. Assistance, mutual aid.

A معاضيل *maʻāzīl*, (Ewes) obstructed in the birth.

A معاطاة *muʻātāt*, (v. n. 3 of عطا for عطو) Labouring for, serving. Giving. Submitting.

A معاطب *maʻātib*, (pl. of معطب *maʻtab*) Perilous places. Dangers, perils.

A معاطس *maʻātis*, (pl. of معطس) Noses.

A معاطش *maʻātish*, (pl. of معطش *maʻtash*) Stated times when (camels) become thirsty. (pl. of معطشة *maʻtashat*) Thirsty lands with no water.

A معاطشة *muʻātashat*, A contending about thirst.

A معاطف *maʻātif*, Bending-places, sinuosities (of a stream or valley).

A معاطفة *muʻātafat*, (v. n. 3 of عطف) Shewing kindness and affection towards one another.

A معاطل *maʻātil*, Those parts on which female ornaments are worn.

A معاطن *maʻātin*, (pl. of معطن *maʻtin*) Places where cattle lie down near water. Pearl-fisheries.

A معاطي *maʻātī*, (or معاطيّ *maʻātīy*) (pl. of معطاء *miʻtāʼ*) Munificent, liberal in giving.

A معاظة *muʻāzzat*, (v. n. 3 of عظّ) Biting one another. Calling one another bad names. Leading a miserable life. Exertion, vehemence in battle.

A معاظلة *muʻāzalat*, (v. n. 3 of عظل) Inserting or foisting the verses of another amongst one's own. Sticking fast together (dogs and locusts).

A معاعاة *muʻāʻāt*, (v. n. of عاعي Q) Calling to sheep. Shouting to one another.

A معاف *muʻāf*, Absolved, excused, forgiven, pardoned, condoned, spared, dispensed with, exempted from, free, privileged.

A معافاة *muʻāfāt*, (v. n. 3 of عفا for عفو) Restoring to, or preserving in, health (God). Defending from harm. Rendering one free from care, concern, and anxiety. Safety, health, security.

A معافر *maʻāfir*, Name of a country, and of a family of Hamdān Arabians. *Muʻāfir*, A slow walker. One who endeavours to obtain any thing by caresses; a coaxer, cajoler. One who follows a caravan, and eats their leavings.

A معافرية *maʻāfirīyat*, Linen cloth made at معافر

A معافزة *muʻāfuzat*, (v. n. 3 of عفز) Toying with each other (husband and wife).

A معافسة *muʻāfusat*, (v. n. 3 of عفس) Straining, compressing, grasping. Handling or treating gently. Kicking on the backside.

A معافقة *muʻāfakat*, (v. n. 3 of عفق) Deceiving, circumventing. Applying a remedy, curing. Ravaging a flock (a wolf).

P معاف گاه *muʻāf-gāh*, A free or sacred place. A sanctuary.

P معاف نامه *muʻāf-nāma*, Letter of affranchisement, charter of immunity from tribute or taxes.

A معافى *muʻāfa'*, Well, free from pain. *Muʻāfī*, Immunity, privilege, exemption. Exempt from the payment of rent or tax.

A معاقب *muʻākab*, Followed: overtaken. Punished, chastised. *Muʻākib*, A follower, one who comes behind. A punisher. One who does any thing alternately with another.

A معاقبة *muʻākabat*, (v. n. 3 of عقب) Coming behind, following at the heels of. Punishing, chastising. Changing (turns) with another, doing duty alternately. Riding by turns. Making gain or plunder. In poetry, an alternate dropping of the ن *nūn* and ي *ye* in مفاعيلن *mufāʻīlun*, but never of both at once. *Muʻākibat*, (Camels) feeding now on salt herbage, and now on sweet herbage.

A معاقة *maʻākat*, (v. n. of معق) Being deep (well).

A معاقد *maʻākid*, (pl. of معقد *maʻkad* and معقد *maʻkid*) Knots. Places where things are tied. *Muʻākid*, Confederated, bound.

A معاقدة *muʻākadat*, (v. n. 3 of عقد) Entering into an alliance or confederacy. A tying or knotting together. A league.

A معاقر *muʻākir*, One who contends (with another). Assiduous. One who sticks close to the bottle.

A معاقرة *muʻākarat*, (v. n. 3 of عقر) Contending (with another), either before a judge upon important subjects, or in reproaches and satire. Shunning each other. Being assiduous, attentive, sticking close to. Remaining continually in the butt (wine). Drinking (wine) incessantly or immoderately. Choosing distance and solitude. Boasting against another in respect of hamstringing (camels).

A معاقصة *muʻākasat*, (v. n. 3 of عقص) Overpowering by words. Seeking mutually to overcome.

A معاقل *maʻākil*, (pl. of معقل *maʻkil*) Refuges, asylums. (pl. of معقلة *maʻkulat*) Expiations of murder; parts remaining to be paid of such composition. هم على معاقلهم الاولى *hum ʻala' maʻākilihimi'l ūla'*, Their expiatory fines for murder remain the same as they were in Pagan times; *i.e.* they keep to the customs of their ancestors.

A معاقلة *muʻākalat*, (v. n. 3 of عقل) Disputing (with another) for superiority of genius. Equalling, being worth. Valuing (a woman) at the third part (of a man) in a composition for bloodshed.

A معاقم *maʻākim*, (pl. of معقم *maʻkim*) Joints in horses or other solid-hoofed animals (as the knee or pastern). Dorsal vertebræ from the withers to the root of the tail.

A معاقمة *muʻākamat*, (v. n. 3 of عقم) Disputing, calling names. Fighting, quarrelling. Altercation.

A معاك *maʻāk*, (v. n. of عاك for عوك) Gaining (a livelihood). Fleeing unto, taking refuge. Lifting and carrying on the head or back. Taking upon one's own neck. Institution, regulation, rite. A sect, religious order. A refuge, asylum. Possibility, probability.

A معاكة *maʻākat*, (v. n. of معك) Being quarrelsome, litigating. Being foolish, stupid.

A معاكّة *muʻākkat*, A turning, inclining, bending.

A معاكد *maʻākid*, (pl. of معكد) Places of refuge.

A معاكسة *muʻākasat*, A contradicting.

A معاكظة *muʻākazat*, (v. n. 3 of عكظ) Hammering. Extending, prolonging, granting delay.

A معاكيس *maʻākis*, (pl. of معكوس) Poor.

A معال *muʻāl*, High; higher (part).

A معالاة *muʻālāt*, (v. n. 3 of علا for علو) Being above in the upper part, superior to. Exalting one (God). Publishing, announcing. Retiring, receding to one side. Placing over, lifting upon. Coming into that part of High Arabia called عالية *ʻāliyat*.

A معالة *maʻālat*, Forage, provender. Evil, mischief.

A معالّة *muʻāllat*, (v. n. 3 of علّ) Being milked at mid-day (a camel).

A معالج *muʻālaj*, Cured. Prepared. Cooked. *Muʻālij*, One who dresses or cooks. A physician.

A معالجة *muʻālajat*, (v. n. 3 of علج) Applying a remedy (to a distemper), healing, curing. Adjusting or managing (any affair). Dressing, cooking, preparing. Grasping, holding fast, handling. Striking with a sword. Remedy, cure. Dispute.

A معالف *maʻālif*, (pl. of معلف) Mangers, cribs.

A معالق *maʻālik*, (pl. of معلق) Small crocodiles.

A معالم *maʻālim*, (pl. of معلم *maʻlam*) Signs,

direction-posts. Vestiges. Signals, banners. Badges. Beaten roads. Colleges, schools, seminaries. معالم الدين *maʻālimu'd dīn*, Dogmas of religion.

A معالمة *muʻālamat*, (v. n. 3 of علم) Disputing with on science or superiority of knowledge.

A معالنة *muʻālanat*, (v. n. 3 of علن) Acting openly with a person, or with one another.

A معالي *maʻālī*, (pl. of معلاة *maʻlāt*) Eminences. High matters. معالي الامور *maʻālī'l umūr*, High matters. دامت معاليه *dāmat maʻālīhu*, May his grandeur be eternal! من معالي *min maʻālī*, From above.

A معاليق *maʻālīk*, A species of palm-tree. (pl. of معلاق *miʻlāk*) Strings, &c., whereby things are suspended: suspenders, braces.

A معامسة *muʻāmasat*, (v. n. 3 of عمس) Veiling and concealing (hostility). Whispering in the ear. *Muʻāmisat*, A woman who veils herself in her youth, and never violates her honour.

A معامع *maʻāmiʻ*, Wars, battles, tumults, seditions. Injuries, oppressions. Great, important matters. Leagues, confederations.

A معامل *muʻāmil*, One who deals fairly and lives happily with others. A fellow-workman, co-worker.

A معاملات *muʻāmalāt*, Domains. Dealings.

A معاملة *muʻāmalat*, (v. n. 3 of عمل) Trading, negociating. Bargaining with, dealing. Giving hard treatment. Taxing one to labour beyond his strength. Business, trade, commerce, traffic, affair, negociation, contract, correspondence, agreement; usury, interest. اهل معامله *ahli muʻāmala*, Men of business. A tradesman. P حسن معامله كردن *husni muʻāmala kardan*, To be in good correspondence, to live happily with another. A صورت معامله *sūrati muʻāmala*, Dissimulation, fiction. Feignedly, for form's sake.

A معاملي *muʻāmilī*, One who, by any kind of work, seeks a living here and there for his family.

A معامي *maʻāmī*, Blind deserts, *i. e.* without culture, inhabitants, or signs of roads.

A معان *maʻān*, A stage, halting-place. Waters. Name of a place in Syria.

A معاناة *muʻānāt*, (v. n. 3 of عني) Taking good care (of one's property), managing (it) well. Following, attending to (trade or craft), mixing in commercial dealings. Resisting, opposing. Enduring any evil with all its consequences. Afflicting, causing trouble.

A معانة *maʻānat*, Aid, assistance, succour, help. *Muʻānat*, (v. n. of عان for عون) Assisting, helping.

A معانّة *muʻānnat*, (v. n. 3 of عنّ) Opposing, resisting.

A معاند *muʻānid*, Obstinate, stubborn, refractory, contumacious, disobedient, opiniative.

A معاندة *muʻānadat*, (v. n. 3 of عند) Sticking close to. Requiting. Opposing, being stubborn, contrary, adverse, repugnant. Shunning, avoiding, quitting (one another). Obstinacy, opposition. Assiduity, perseverance.

A معانشة *muʻānashat*, (v. n. 3 of عنش) Hugging one another. Pulling by the neck in battle.

A معانق *muʻānik*, One who throws the arms round another's neck, who hugs and embraces him.

A معانقة *muʻānakat*, (v. n. 3 of عنق) Embracing, hugging one another close in friendship or in fight. An embrace. معانقات صدريّه *muʻānakāti sadrīya*, Embracing breast to breast.

A معاني *maʻānī*, (pl. of معنى *maʻna'*) Significations, senses. Sublime realities, spiritual matters.

A معانيق *maʻānīk*, (pl. of معناق *miʻnāk*) Fine-necked (horses). Hillocks in advance of sand-hills.

A معاواة *muʻāwāt*, A crying to (barking dogs).

A معاود *muʻāwid*, Accustomed, habituated, used to. One who returns often to the same thing. Sedulous, assiduous, strenuous. A brave man, champion.

A معاودة *muʻāwadat*, (v. n. 3 of عاد for عود) Returning to a former habit or action, relapsing. Making a habit or custom (عادة *ʻādat*). Attacking with intermissions (as the ague). Pressing by repeated questions. Exercising, examining. Being assiduous, attentive, diligent. P معاودت ساختن *muʻāwadat sākhtan*, To return.

A معاورة *muʻāwarat*, (v. n. 3 of عار for عور) Making or marking a weight or measure agreeable to standard. Doing (a thing) with another by turns and in rivalry. Lending. Borrowing from one another.

A معاوز *maʻāwiz*, (pl. of معوز *miʻwaz*) Old worn-out every-day clothes. Swaddling-bands for the hands and feet of a child in the cradle.

A معاوصة *muʻāwasat*, (v. n. 3 of عاص for عوص) Wrestling, struggling, trying to throw down.

A معاوضة *muʻāwazat*, (v. n. 3 of عاض for عوض) Returning like for like, compensating, giving a substitute. P معاوضت كردن *muʻāwazat kardan*, To barter, to exchange.

A معاول *maʻāwil*, (pl. of معول *miʻwal*) Pointed instruments with which they split stones.

A معاومة *muʻāwamat*, (v. n. 3 of عام for عوم) Bearing fruit every second year (a palm-tree). Agreeing with (any one) by the year (عام *ʻām*). Selling corn whilst growing; or allowing an increase of the debt to obtain a delay of payment (practices forbidden by the Muhammadan law).

A معاون *muʻāwin*, Assisting: an assistant.

A معاونة *muʻāwanat*, (v. n. 3 of عان for عون) Helping one another. Aiding, assisting. Aid, assistance, help, succour, subsidy, supply. Favour, grace.

A معاوية *muʻāwiyat*, A fox's whelp. A bitch in heat. A man's name. ابو معاوية *abū muʻāwiyat*, The cheeta, ounce, or hunting-panther.

A معاهد *maʻāhid*, (pl. of معهد *maʻhad*) Places often frequented. Monuments. Things well done. *Muʻāhid*, One who plights his faith, confederate. Tributary, subject.

A معاهدة *muʻāhadat*, (v. n. 3 of عهد) Entering into an alliance, conspiring, confederating, covenanting. Swearing mutually. Attending to, looking after, managing. An agreement, confederacy, alliance, association, stipulation, bargain, treaty. معاهدهٔ نكاح *muʻāhadaʼi nikāh*, Marriage-contract.

A معاهر *muʻāhir*, A whorish woman.

A معاهرة *muʻāharat*, (v. n. 3 of عهر) Going a whoring. Following evil ways and thieving. *Muʻāhirat*, A whorish woman.

A معاي *maʻāy*, Tired, jaded (camels).

A معايا *maʻāya'*, Tired jaded (camels).

A معاياة *muʻāyāt*, (v. n. 3 of عيّ) Meddling with, undertaking any business which one is unable to manage. Stammering, speaking unintelligibly.

A معائب *maʻāʼib*, (pl. of معاب *maʻāb* and معابة *maʻābat*) Faults, blemishes.

A معاثر *maʻāsir*, Faults, blemishes.

A معايرة *muʻāyarat*, (v. n. 3 of عار for عير) Making or marking a weight or measure agreeable to standard. Reproaching. Dividing, apportioning. Seeing, examining.

A معايش *maʻāyish*, (pl. of معيشة *maʻīshat*) Victuals, provisions: necessaries. Allowance. معايش دنيويّه *maʻāyishi dunyawīya*, Worldly matters.

A معايشة *muʻāyashat*, A living together.

A معاين *muʻāyan*, Seen, made public: manifest.

A معاينة *muʻāyanat*, (v. n. 3 of عان for عين) Beholding, contemplating, seeing face to face. Sight. Being a father's or mother's brother.

A معبأ *maʻbaʼ*, Way. Sect. Rule, law, canon.

A معبأة *miʻbaʼat*, A menstruous cloth.

A معبد *maʻbad*, A place of worship. *Miʻbad*, A shovel, rake, hoe. *Muʻbad*, Received as a servant.

A معبّد *muʻabbad*, Beaten (path). Firmly-driven (stake). Honoured. Subjected, subdued. Tame, quiet, gentle, submissive. (A camel) anointed (with pitch). A country destitute of vestige or water. *Muʻabbid*, A worshipper.

A معبدة *maʻbadat*, (pl. of عبد) Servants, slaves.

A معبّدة *muʻabbadat*, Pitched (ship).

A معبر *maʻbar*, A pass, ferry, ford. P معبر پرخطر *maʻbari pur khatar*, A dangerous pass. A *Miʻbar*, (pl. معابر *maʻābir*) A ferry-boat, ponton. A bridge. *Muʻbar*, Fully-feathered (arrow). (A boy) not yet circumcised though attaining the age of puberty. (A sheep) left a year unshorn. (A camel) abounding in hair). *Muʻbir*, One who leaves sheep unshorn for a whole year. (Sheep) abounding in wool, or (a camel) in hair.

A معبّر *muʻabbar*, Interpreted (dream). *Muʻabbir*, An interpreter of dreams.

A معبرة *muʻbarat*, Uncircumcised (girl). (A camel) which has not brought forth for three years, and these have been hard times with her. Unshorn (ewe). A woman from whom mattery water flows. يا ابن المعبرة *yā ibnu'l muʻbarat*, A term of reproach.

A معبّرة *muʻabbarat*, Complete, perfect (bow).

A معبّل *muʻabbil*, A possessor of arrow-heads

broad and long.

A معبلة *mizbalat*, A broad and long arrow-head.

A معبود *maẕbūd*, Adored, worshipped: a god.

A معبوداء *maẕbūdā*, (pl. of عبد) Servants, slaves.

A معبودية *maẕbūdiyat*, State of being worshipped.

A معبوط *maẕbūt*, Rent (garment).

A معبهلة *muẕabhalat*, (Camels) unattended.

A معت *maẕt*, (v. n. of معت) Rubbing or smoothing (a skin).

A معتاد *muẕtād*, Accustomed, wonted. Custom, habit, use. P معتاد شدن, To be accustomed.

A معتاط *muẕtāt*, One that fails to conceive for several years although not barren.

A معتاق *miẕtāk*, One who makes a horse gallop. One who hunts with vehemence or speed.

A معتب *maẕtab*, (v. n. of عتب) Chiding, reproaching. *Muẕtab*, Turned back. *Muẕtib*, Troublesome. (See اعتاب *iẕtāb*.)

A معتبة *maẕta* or *maẕtibat*, Reproachful speech.

A معتبد *muẕtabid*, One who takes as a servant.

A معتبر *muẕtabar*, Honoured, esteemed, revered. Creditable, respectable. Confidential, trustworthy. P معتبر شدن *muẕtabar shudan*, To be in high reputation. A *Muẕtabir*, Respectable, worthy of consideration. (See اعتبار *iẕtibār*.)

A معتد *muẕtad*, Prepared, set in order, ready.

A معتدّ *muẕtadd*, Numbered, counted, computed.

A معتدر *muẕtadir*, Heavy (rain). Moist, irriguous (place). Abundant (water).

A معتدل *muẕtadil*, Moderate, well-proportioned. Temperate, tolerable, neither cold nor hot. Equal, even, just.

A معتدي *muẕtadī*, Iniquitous. Inimical.

A معتذب *muẕtazib*, One who lets the ends of the turban-sash hang over the shoulders.

A معتذر *muẕtazir*, One who excuses himself. A complainer. (See اعتذار *iẕtizār*.)

A معتذل *muẕtazil*, One who blames himself, or allows himself to be blamed.

A معتذلات *muẕtazilāt*, Sultry (days).

A معترّ *muẕtarr*, Poor, indigent. One who does not ask for what he wants.

A معترس *muẕtaris*, Scattered.

A معترش *muẕtarish*, A maker of the bower or arbour عريش *ẕarish*. (See اعتراش *iẕtirāsh*.)

A معترص *muẕtaris*, Playful. Jocose. Throbbing, quivering (skin).

A معترض *muẕtariz*, Opposing, interposing, transverse, hindering. Parenthetic. One who goes sideways. جمله معترضه *jumla muẕtariza*, A parenthesis. (See اعتراض *iẕtirāz*.)

A معترف *muẕtarif*, One who acknowledges and confesses. Or who shews and points out.

A معترق *muẕtarak*, Spare of flesh on the bones.

A معترك *muẕtarak*, A field of battle. *Muẕtarik*, Pressing on one another in battle. (See اعتراك).

A معتري *muẕtarī*, Who or what surprises, comes suddenly upon; or who approaches to ask a favour. (See اعتراء *iẕtirā*.)

A معتزل *muẕtazil*, Seceder, dissenter, separatist.

A معتزلة *muẕtazilat*, A sect of Muhammadan schismatics, an offset of the sect قدرية *kadarīyat*.

A معتزلي *muẕtaziliy*, Dissenter, separatist, seceder.

A معتزم *muẕtazim*, One who gives his whole attention; pains-taking, constant, steady, firm. A lion. (See اعتزام *iẕtizām*.)

A معتزي *muẕtazī*, Related, denominated (truly or falsely), belonging to any one.

A معتسر *muẕtasir*, One who takes part (of a son's effects) without his consent. (See اعتسار *iẕtisār*.)

A معتسف *muẕtasif*, One who deviates or declines from the road. Exorbitant, unreasonable, exacting, extortionate.

A معتسم *muẕtasim*, One who buys or puts on old shoes or boots. (See اعتسام *iẕtisām*.)

A معتش *muẕtashsh*, (or معتشش *muẕtashish*) Nest-building (bird). A carrier of little provision.

A معتشي *muẕtashī*, One who begins a journey in the evening. (See اعتشاء *iẕtishā*.)

A معتصب *muẕtasib*, Patient, content (with any thing). Turbaned. (See اعتصاب *iẕtisāb*.)

A معتصر *muẕtasar*, Squeezed. Old age, decrepitude. Long life, duration. A place of refuge. كريم المعتصر *karimu'l muẕtasar*, Liberal, munificent when applied to. *Muẕtasir*, One who does his business. One whose urine and excrement are obstructed. (See اعتصار *iẕtisār*.)

A معتصف *muẕtasif*, A gainer, intent on gain.

A معتصم *muẕtasam*, A place of refuge. *Muẕtasim*, A servant. معتصم بالله *muẕtasim bi'llāh*, A title assumed by the son of Hārūn Arrashīd, the 8th caliph of the house of Abbās. (See اعتصام.)

A معتصي *muẕtasī*, One who leans on a staff (عصا *ẕasa'*). Who uses (a sword) for a staff. Who cuts a staff from a tree. Hard (date-stone).

A معتضد *muẕtazid*, A petitioner for justice, a plaintiff. معتضد بالله *muẕtazid bi'llāh*, Name of the 16th caliph of the house of Abbās.

A معتفد *muẕtafid*, One who shuts himself up to die of hunger (a custom with the Pagan Arabians in times of scarcity). Believing, sure, certain.

A معتفر *muẕtafir*, Soiled with dust. Powerful. (A lion) snatching away (a man). One who throws on the ground. (See اعتفار *iẕtifār*.)

A معتفس *muẕtafis*, (People) in commotion.

A معتفص *muẕtafis*, An extorter (of a debt).

A معتفق *muẕtafih*, (A lion) attacking (his prey) with impetuosity. Engaged in fencing.

A معتفي *muẕtafī*, One who approaches to ask a favour, or what is just or due. (See اعتفاء *iẕtifā*.)

A معتق *muẕtak*, Manumitted, liberated. Emancipated (slave). *Muẕtih*, A liberator of slaves.

A معتّق *muẕattak*, Old, ancient, antique.

A معتقب *muẕtakib*, Who detains (a man). One who detains goods sold till the price is paid.

A معتّقة *muẕattakat*, Old wine. A kind of perfume.

A معتقد *muẕtakid*, A believer. A faithful friend. A support, protector. A servant. An acquirer (of money or lands). Very hard and firm.

A معتقدات *muẕtakadāt*, (pl. fem.) Things believed or deemed credible; articles of faith.

A معتقر *muẕtakar*, (Meat) cut and dried in the sun. *Muẕtakir*, Hurt (camel), galled on the back.

A معتكب *muẕtakib*, Raised (dust).

A معتكد *muẕtakid*, Necessary.

A معتكس *muẕtakis*, Inverted, upside down.

A معتكف *muẕtakaf*, A place of retirement for devotional purposes. *Muẕtakif*, One who is continually at prayer in the temple. Attentive to religious duties.

A معتكل *muẕtakil*, Obscure, intricate, doubtful (matter). (See اعتكال *iẕtikāl*.)

A معتكم *muẕtakim*, One who makes equal loads on each side of a camel. (See اعتكام *iẕtikām*.)

A معتل *miẕtal*, One who draws violently.

A معتلّ *muẕtall*, Weak, sick, infirm. A word in which either of the letters و *wāw* or ي *yā* (called debiles or weak) makes a part. معتل العين *muẕtallu'l ẕayn*, A verb whose medial radical letter is infirm, called concave; as, قال *kāla* (for قول *kawala*).

A معتلث *muẕtalis*, An adopted son, the putative son of one not his own father.

A معتلج *muẕtalij*, Engaged in a struggle. Dashing (waves). Very grassy (spot).

A معتلط *muẕtalit*, Pugnacious. Seditious.

A معتلفة *muẕtalifat*, A midwife.

A معتلق *muẕtalik*, In love with: a lover.

A معتلن *muẕtalin*, Divulged, published.

A معتلي *muẕtala'*, A lion.

A معتمّ *muẕtamm*, The wearer of a turban; turbaned. Full-grown (plant). A field long-grassed.

A معتمد *muẕtamad*, Pursued, resolved, purposed. *Muẕtamad*, (or معتمد عليه *muẕtamad ẕalayhi* or اليه *ilayhi*) One in whom confidence is placed. Confidential, faithful, trustworthy. آدم معتبر و معتمد *ādami muẕtabar u muẕtamad*, An estimable and trustworthy man. *Muẕtamid*, One who rests or leans upon. A believer. Resolved, determined.

A معتمر *muẕtamir*, A visitor. One in pursuit.

A معتمل *muẕtamil*, One who keeps himself employed. (See اعتمال *iẕtimāl*.)

A معتمي *muẕtamī*, A lion.

A معتن *muẕtin*, Severe to a debtor.

A معتنز *muẕtaniz*, Inclined, leaning. Far-going.

A معتنش *muẕtanish*, One who throws his arms round another's neck in fighting. Injurious, oppressive. An unjust seizer.

A معتنف *muẕtanif*, Indirect, inconvenient (road).

A معتنق *muẕtanak*, The place where the necks (اعناق *aẕnāk*) of mountains peep out above a mist.

A معتني *muẕtanī*, Diligent, pains-taking.

A معتور *mugtawir*, Reciprocal in taking a thing by turns, or in passing it from hand to hand.

A معتوق *maɛtūk*, (pl. معاتيق) Emancipated.

A معتول *muɛtawil*, A weeper, wailer.

A معتوه *maɛtūh*, Weak in mind, insane, delirious, deficient in intellect, stupid. Quick, intelligent.

A معتوي *muɛtawī*, One who makes a loud and hideous noise or howl. (See اعتواء *iɛtiwāʼ*.)

A معته *muɛattah*, Intelligent, sensible, rational, moderate. Crazy and irrational.

A معثرة *maɛsarat*, A cause of offence.

A معثكل *muɛaskil*, (A camel-litter) decorated with dangling locks of wool (عثكولة *ɛushūlat*).

A معثلب *muɛaslab*, A fallen-in or filled-up ditch; that especially called نؤي *nuʼy*, dug round a tent for receiving the rain-water. Bent double with old age. *Muɛaslib*, Loose, unsteady (business).

A معثن *muɛassan*, One whose beard is thick at the point.

A معثون *maɛsūn*, Smoked, spoiled by smoke.

A معج *maɛj*, (v. n. of معج) Going swiftly (an ass). Striking its head against the mother's udder when going to suck, and turning its mouth obliquely to catch the dug (a camel's colt). Stirring the bodkin in the collyrium-box. Copulating. Striking with a sword. Battle, conflict. Agitation. *Maɛij*, (for معي *maɛī*) With me.

A معجّ *muɛijj*, (A day) of violent wind and dust.

A معجاز *miɛjāz*, A road.

A معجب *maɛjab*, A place for wonder or admiration. *Muɛjab*, Admired by others. Surprised, pleased, delighted. *Muɛjib*, One who is pleased with and admires himself. Pleasing, agreeable, affording pleasure, or surprise.

A معجّب *muɛajjab*, Admirable, wonderful, stupendous. *Muɛajjib*, Surprising, astonishing.

A معجبة *maɛjabat*, A place, cause, subject, or reason for wonder or admiration.

A معجة *maɛjat*, The beginning of any thing. The flower of youth.

A معجر *miɛjar*, A cloth worn by women to preserve their head-dress from being soiled by the unguent or pomatum of their hair. A kind of sack, made of the fibres of the palm-tree. P معجر زرنيخ *miɛjari zirnīkh*, Autumnal leaves. Yellow flowers. Streaks of dawn. معجر غاليه گون *miɛjari ghāliya-gūn*, Night (the veil of the colour of civet).

A معجرد *muɛajrid* or *muɛajrad*, Naked.

A معجرم *muɛajram*, Knotty (yard). Any thing intricate and knotty. A camel's bunch.

A معجز *maɛjaz* or *maɛjiz*, Weakness, impotence. *Muɛjiz*, One who finds or esteems as weak and impotent. A miracle (as demonstrating the weakness of an adversary). Any thing which incapacitates.

A معجّز *muɛajjaz*, Weak. Large-buttocked.

A معجزات *muɛjizāt*, (pl. of معجزة) Miracles.

A معجزة *maɛjazat* or *maɛjizat*, (v. n. of عجز) Being weak and feeble. Leaving undone what ought to be done. Being sluggish and negligent. Weakness, infirmity; impotency, defect. A place where nothing is to be earned. *Muɛjizat*, A miracle. معجزهٔ مسيح *muɛjizaʼi masīh*, A miracle of Jesus, i. e. the resuscitation of the dead. A table which descended from heaven at the command of Jesus.

P معجزنشان *muɛjiz-nishān*, Marvellous, miraculous, signalized by wonders.

P معجزنما *muɛjiz-namā*, Displaying wonders. ساحر معجزنما *sāhiri muɛjiz-namā*, A magician performing miracles.

A معجس *maɛjis*, The handle of a bow.

A معجل *muɛjal*, Done in haste. A camel's colt brought forth before the time and yet surviving. *Muɛjil*, A camel prematurely delivered of a colt which survives. A camel leaping or curvetting when the rider puts his feet in the stirrup. An early palm-tree. A cow having a calf (عجل *ɛijl*).

A معجّل *muɛajjal*, Done in a haste. Hastened, executed with despatch. *Muɛajjil*, Who hastens or causes to make haste. A camel which curvets the moment the rider puts his foot in the stirrup. A shepherd who sends milk home to his family before the milking is quite finished. One who gives a wife part of a dowry in advance. A camel delivered before the time of a colt which survives.

A معجّلاً *muɛajjilan*, In haste.

A معجم *maɛjam*, (in comp.) as صلب المعجم *sulbu'l maɛjam*, Respectable in himself, venerable, grave.

A معجم *muɛjam*, (v. n. 4 of عجم) Pointing (a letter). Locked or barred (door). Pointed. Marked with diacritical points (to distinguish letters of the same shape, whose difference of sound proceeds merely from punctuation: as, د *dāl* and ذ *zāl*, ب *bā* and ت *tā*; ذ *zāl* being called ذال معجم *zāli muɛjam*, (or more commonly *zāli muɛajjam*) and د *dāl* being named دال مهمله *dāli muhmala*; and so with regard to the rest. The alphabet arranged according to the order of the letters, *alif*, *be*, *te*, &c. (in contradistinction to the ابجد *abjad*).

A معجمة *maɛjamat*, Fat and able to travel (she-camel). Fatness. Power, strength. Sufficiency of strength to travel.

A معجور عليه *maɛjūr ɛalayhi*, Stripped of all his property by beggars.

A معجوز *maɛjūz*, Wearied by importunate begging.

A معجوف *maɛjūf*, Lean (camel). Rusty, unpolished (sword).

A معجون *maɛjūn*, Kneaded. An electuary, medicine, confection, jelly, paste. P معجون سرشته *maɛjūni sirishta*, Any medicine pulverized and mixed up with honey or inspissated juice.

P معجون كش *maɛjūn-kash*, A spoon or similar instrument for taking an electuary from a jar.

P معد *maɛd*, The plant satyrion.

A معد *maɛd*, (v. n. of معد) Travelling, perambulating. Drawing or seizing (any thing) rapidly. Carrying off (any thing). Striking in the stomach. Biting flesh with the front teeth. Becoming spoiled. Swift (camel). Fresh (pot-herb or fruit). Thick, large, corpulent, rough, gross. Thickness, coarseness. ثعد معد *saɛd maɛd*, Fresh, ripe (dates). رطبة معدة *rutabat maɛdat*, A fresh, moist date. *Maɛid* or *miɛad*, (pl. of معدة *maɛidat* or *miɛdat*) Stomachs.

A معدّ *maɛadd*, (dual معدّان *maɛaddāni*) The side. The belly. Flesh under the shoulder. A vein in that part of a horse about the fore-shoulder, and under the mane. That part of the back on which the sides of the saddle press. Name of a man, the son of Adnān and father of the Arabians. *Muɛadd*, Prepared, disposed, set in order, arranged. Computed. Counted, numbered. *Muɛidd*, One who prepares, disposes in order. One who reckons (amongst the dead).

A معدان *maɛdān*, (A man) of a capacious stomach.

A معدّان *maɛaddān*, The part of the saddle where the flaps join.

A معدة *maɛidat* and *miɛdat*, (pl. معد *maɛid* and *miɛad*) The human stomach, paunch. P معده تنگ كردن *miɛda tang kardan*, To guttle, to cram to repletion. داروي معده *dārūyi miɛda*, A stomachic. A سوء معده *sūʼi miɛda*, A disorder in the stomach. ضعف معده *zaɛfi miɛda*, Weakness of stomach. مسدود معده *masdūd-miɛda*, Obstructed in the stomach.

A معدكة *miɛdakat*, A mallet for beating cotton.

A معدل *maɛdil*, Place of turning, return, retreat.

A معدّل *muɛaddal*, Rectified, adjusted. *Muɛaddil*, Just, temperate. (See تعديل *taɛdīl*).

A معدّلات *muɛaddalāt*, The corners of a house.

A معدلة *maɛdalat* or *maɛdilat*, (v. n. of عدل) Administering justice. Justice, equity, rectitude.

A معدم *muɛdim*, One who deprives or annihilates. Destitute, poor. (See اعدام *iɛdām*.)

A معدن *maɛdin* or *maɛdan*, (pl. معادن *maɛādin*) A mine, quarry. The place of any thing, especially where it remains fixed. معدن الفضل والكلام *maɛdinu'l fazli wa'l kalām*, The mine of learning and eloquence (applied to judges and priests). *Miɛdan*, A pointed hammer for breaking stones.

A معدّن *muɛaddan*, (A torn bucket) patched at the bottom. *Muɛaddin*, A quarryman, a miner.

A معدنيّ *maɛdanīy*, Mineral, metallic. Metal. عصير معدني *ɛasīri maɛdani*, Mineral juice.

A معدوّ *maɛdūw*, Maltreated (as an enemy).

A معدود *maɛdūd*, Numbered, told, counted, reckoned, computed. الايّام المعدودات *al ayyāmu'l maɛdūdāt*, The three days of تشريق *tashrīk*. P نا معدود *nā maɛdūd*, (A غير معدود *ghayr maɛdūd*) Unnumbered, untold. P معدودي چند *maɛdūde chand*, A few, a limited number.

A معدوس *maɛdūs*, Troubled with the pustules عدسة *ɛadasat*.

A معدول *maʻdūl*, Distorted, wrested. Quiescent or silent و *wāw*, *i.e.* when written but scarcely pronounced, as in خوان *khwān*, A table. A place of turning, return, or retreat.

A معدوم *maʻdūm*, Wished for but not found, non-existent, lost. Poor, needy. موجود الاسم معدوم الجسم *manjūdu'l ism maʻdūmu'l jism*, Known by name, but inexistent by nature.

P معده انبار *miʻda* or *maʻida-ambār*, A glutton.

A معدى *muʻda'*, Transit, pass, passage. ما لي عنه معدى *mā lī ʻanhu muʻda'*, There is no pass for me (to escape) from him. *Muʻdī*, Contagious.

A معدّي *muʻaddī*, Transitive.

A معديّ *maʻdiy*, Injuriously treated.

A معدّيّ *maʻaddiy*, Of the tribe of معدّ *maʻadd*. لبسة معدّيّة *libsat maʻaddiyat*, Coarse clothing.

A معديّة *maʻdiyat*, (or معدّيّة *muʻaddiyat*) (in the dialect of Morocco) A raft, float.

A معديكرب *maʻdikarib*, Name of a warrior.

A معذار *miʻzār*, A covering. An excuse.

A معذب *maʻzab*, (pl. معاذب *maʻāzib*) A strip of cloth tied about the waist by wailing women.

A معذّب *muʻazzab*, Hindered, let, prevented. Tormented, chastised, punished. Afflicted, vexed. *Muʻazzib*, A tormentor, punisher. Afflictive.

A معذج *miʻzaj*, Malignant. A slanderer. Jealous.

A معذِر *muʻzir*, Apologist. Deserving of excuse.

A معذّر *muʻazzar*, Circumcised. A circumcision-feast. That part of the jaws over which the bridle passes, the cheek. The side of a spear-head. *Muʻazzir*, One who cuts off the foreskin. A maker of a false excuse, unworthy of pardon. One who makes a true apology, or admissable excuse. (See تعذير *taʻzīr*.)

A معذرة *maʻzirat* or *maʻzurat*, (v. n. of عذر) Excusing. *Maʻzarat*, *maʻzirat*, or *maʻzurat*, Excuse, apology.

P معذرت خواه *maʻzirat-khwāh*, One who excuses another and makes his apology. معذرت خواه عجزهٔ امّت *maʻzirat-khwāhi ʻajzaʼi ummat*, The apologiser for the infirmities of the people (*i. e.* Muhammad).

P معذرت خواهي *maʻzirat-khwāhī*, Excuse.

A معذّل *muʻazzal*, Prodigal, blamed for too great profusion. *Muʻazzil*, A chider, reprover.

A معذلج *muʻazlaj*, Full (leathern bottle). *Muʻazlij*, Handsome, healthy (boy).

A معذور *maʻzūr*, Disappointed. Helpless, imperfect. Troubled with an inflammation in the throat. Excused. Excusable. Circumcised. P معذور باد *maʻzūr bād*, Let it be pardoned, excuse me! معذور داشتن *maʻzūr dāshtan*, To excuse.

A معر *maʻar*, (v. n. of معر) Being thin (hairs or feathers). Falling off (hair or nails). *Maʻir*, One who loses his hair. One whose nails have dropped. (Ground) thin of herbs. Thin of feathers. (A boot) which has lost its hair. A miser, a good-for-nothing fellow. A bad disposition.

A معرّا *muʻarra'*, (in reg. for معرّي *muʻarra'*) Denuded, naked, stripped bare, bald. Pure, free.

A معراء *maʻrāʼ*, (Bald) forehead.

A معراة *maʻrāt*, That part of a girl which is exposed to view, as the face, hand, or foot. A place which produces nothing.

A معراج *miʻrāj*, (pl. معاريج *maʻārīj*) A ladder, step, staircase, ascent. ليلة المعراج *laylatu'l miʻrāj*, The night of ascent (when the Muhammadans suppose their prophet to have ascended through the seven stages of heaven into the presence of God). معراج حضرت عيسیٰ *miʻrāji hazrat ʻīsa'*, The ascension of the Lord Jesus.

A معرار *miʻrār*, A scabby palm bearing bad dates.

A معراس *miʻrās*, The new moon.

A معراض *miʻrāz*, An unfeathered arrow, thin at each end, and thick in the middle. The argument of a discourse.

A معرب *maʻrib*, A fine Arabian horse. *Muʻrab*, Declined. المعرب *al muʻrab*, (in gram.) A triptote. *Muʻrib*, Indicative. (A horse) descended from a noble Arabian breed, without any mixture. One possessed of such horses. No one (at home).

A معرّب *muʻarrab*, Made Arabic or Arabian. The form which a foreign word assumes, or in which it appears, when adopted into Arabic.

A معربد *muʻarbid*, A drunken man who hurts his pot-companion. Bad-tempered and quarrelsome.

A معرة *muʻrat*, A reddish colour. *Maʻirat*, A place destitute of herbage.

A معرّة *maʻarrat*, A crime, fault, trespass. A mulct, an expiation for the shedding of blood. Perfidy, treachery. Name of a star beside the milky-way. A fight betwixt armies without the permission of the commander. The change of colour in the face of an angry man. *Maʻarrat*, (or معرّة النعمان *maʻarratu'n nuʻmān*) A city in Syria.

A معرتن *muʻartan*, (Leather) dressed with the plant عرتن *ʻartan*.

A معرج *maʻraj*, (v. n. of عرج) Climbing (a ladder). Becoming high. *Muʻraj* or *miʻraj*, A ladder, step, staircase (place or means of ascent).

A معرّج *muʻarraj*, Curvilineally striped (vest).

A معرس *miʻras*, A clever and judicious driver (of cattle), driving them when they are brisk and lively, and halting when they are tired. *Muʻras* or *muʻarras*, Any place to which travellers retire at the latter part of the night, in order to refresh and repose a little before continuing their journey. *Muʻris*, Engaged, but who has not taken his wife.

A معرّس *muʻarras*, (A house) roofed in the manner described under عرس *ʻars*. *Muʻarris*, One who alights at the end of the night. A traveller. A seller of the young camel عرس *ʻars*.

A معرّش *muʻarrash*, Propped, trained (vine).

A معرّص *muʻarras*, (Flesh) exposed in a court-yard to dry; (meat) cut in bits and laid on the embers, mixed with ashes, and badly roasted. A camel whose back is subjugated, but whose head is not.

A معرض *maʻraz*, Occasion, contingency, occurrence; place of meeting. *Miʻraz*, Robes for young girls. A wrapper containing stuffs offered for sale. *Muʻriz*, One who makes broad, clear, apparent, or conspicuous. One who borrows from everybody that comes in his way: or who turns a deaf ear to all who would dissuade him from borrowing. One who borrows fearlessly from all and everybody without paying again. Fearless in doing any thing. Averse, abhorring, turning away.

A معرضاً *muʻrizan*, From every quarter. طأ معرضاً حيث شئت *taʼ muʻrizan haysa shiʼta*, Tread wherever you will (all is in your power).

A معرّض *muʻarraz*, (Sheep) impressed with the mark عراض *ʻirāz*. (Meat) insufficiently dressed. A quadruped. A broad brand on the buttocks of a quadruped. *Muʻarriz*, A circumciser of boys.

A معرضة *muʻrizat*, Grassy land where cattle may find pasturage.

A معرف *maʻraf*, (pl. معارف *maʻārif*) The face, and other parts (of a woman) which are displayed (as the hands).

A معرّف *muʻarraf*, Made known. Marked, notified, rendered definite. A place on Mount Arafāt where they perform certain religious ceremonies. *Muʻarrif*, Who or what makes known, distinguishes, or gives notice. One who introduces; a chamberlain, master of the ceremonies.

A معرفة *maʻrafat*, That place of the neck whence the mane grows. A cock's comb. *Maʻrifat*, (v. n. of عرف) Knowing. Knowledge, acquaintance. Science, learning. Art, skill, craft. Whatever conduces to ease of mind in one protected with reference to his protector. Account, cause, reason, means, by, by means of, through. To the care of; in charge of. اهل معرفت *ahli maʻrifat*, Learned, accomplished, intelligent. P پر معرفت *pur maʻrifat*, Full of knowledge or skill. بمعرفت او *ba maʻrifati u*, With his knowledge, by his means, through him. A المعرفة *al maʻrifat*, (or حرف معرفت *harfi maʻrifat*) The definite article ال *al*, The.

A معرفةً *maʻrifatan*, Definitively, expressly.

A معرفتي *maʻrifatī*, Knowledge, acquaintance.

A معرق *maʻrak*, (v. n. of عرق) Gnawing or picking (a bone). *Muʻrak*, (Wine) dashed with a little water. High-bred (sire). Possessed of the remains of any quality or disposition (good or bad).

A معرّق *muʻarrak*, Lean, having little flesh on the bones. (Wine) somewhat diluted. معرّق الخدّين *muʻarraku'l khaddayn*, Meagre-jawed.

A معرقب *muʻarkab*, Houghed (quadruped).

A معرقة *muʻrikat*, (or معرّقة *muʻarrikat*) Name of a road into Syria, formerly travelled by Kuraysh.

A معرك *maʻrak*, (معركة *maʻrakat*, or *maʻru-*

kat, معركهٔ جهاد *maʻrakaʼi jihād*, (P معركهٔ كارزار *maʻrakaʼi kārzār*) A field of battle. An amphitheatre for gladiators or prize-fighters. *Muʻrik*, A menstruous woman.

A معركة *miʻrakat*, A menstruous cloth.

P معركه گير *maʻraka-gīr*, A rope-dancer.

A معرمض *muʻarmiz*, (Water) covered with the green substance عرمض *ʻarmaz* or عرماض *ʻirmāz*.

A معرّن *muʻarran*, (A spear) whose head is well fastened with a nail or stud.

A معرنفط *muʻranfit*, The privities of a woman.

A معروّ *maʻrūw*, Seized with an ague. Longing for any thing that one has disposed of.

A معرور *maʻrūr*, Contaminated. (A camel) troubled with the ulcers called عرّ *ʻurr*. Struck by the cold. One who has received something which will not remain with him.

A معرورة *maʻrūrat*, (Cattle) whose milk is affected by malignant eyes. Impregnated (she-camel).

A معرورك *muʻrawrak*, Intermixed (sands). Close and compactly-built (man).

A معروش *maʻrūsh*, Shaded by a tree, or by any thing similar. (A vine) propped by wooden work. Covered (well). Large-sided (camel). (A bit of wood) continuing lighted. معروشات وغير معروشات *maʻrūshāt wa ghayr maʻrūshāt*, (Gardens) made by art and by nature. *Muʻarwash*, Seated in the shade of a tree, or any thing similar.

A معروض *maʻrūz*, Offered, presented, exposed. Related. Laid crosswise, transverse. (A camel) branded with a mark crosswise. An exposition, explanation, representation, petition, exhibition. P معروض داشتن *maʻrūz dāshtan*, To represent.

A معروف *maʻrūf*, Known, celebrated, famous, notorious. Lawful, proper, suitable. Ulcerated in the palm of the hand. Kindness, good-will, courtesy, favour, benefit. Obedience to God. The active voice of a verb. The letters و *wāw* and ي *yā* are said to be *maʻrūf* when the former has the sound of "ū" in "rude," as نور *nūr*, Light; and the latter that of "ī" in "police," as نير *nīr*, A yoke. Name of Ibn Muskān, builder of the Kaaba. بالمعروف *bi'lmaʻrūf*, Justly, uprightly, courteously.

A معروفة *maʻrūfat*, Land which yields in abundance the plant عرف *ʻarf*.

A معروق *maʻrūk*, Somewhat diluted (wine). معروق العظام *maʻrūku'l ʻizām*, Lean, having little flesh on the bones.

A معروك *maʻrūk*, (Water) thronged by people.

A معروكة *maʻrūkat*, (Land) trodden and bare.

A معرون *maʻrūn*, (A leathern bottle or bag) tanned or prepared with عرنة *ʻirnat*. Hurt in the nose by the wood عران *ʻirān*.

A معريّ *maʻra'*, (pl. معاري *maʻārī*) The part (of a girl) exposed to view, as the face, hand, or foot. A bare place, producing nothing. *Muʻra'*, (A palm-tree) given up to common use.

A معرّي *muʻarra'*, Naked, stripped, bare, denuded, bald. Deprived of, exempted, pure, free from. Ungoverned (noun), in the nominative case. (A poem) destitute of ترفيل *tarfīl*, اذالة *izālat*, and اسباغ *isbāgh*. (Female privities) furnished with a fleshy excrescence.

A معز *maʻz*, (v. n. of معز) Separating (sheep from goats). (pl. معيز *maʻīz*) A goat. (pl. of ماعز *māʻiz*) Goats. (pl. of امعز *amʻaz* and معزاء *maʻzāʼ*) Hard (grounds). *Maʻz* or *maʻaz*, The goat-species. *Muʻz*, Hard, stony places. *Maʻaz*, (v. n. of معز) Being rich in goats. Hardness (of soil).

A معزّ *muʻizz*, One who honours or worships.

A معزاء *maʻzāʼ*, (fem. of امعز *amʻaz*) (Ground) of a hard consistence. *Miʻzāʼ*, The goat-species.

A معزاب *miʻzāb*, One who goes with his cattle to pasture at a great distance from other men.

A معزابة *miʻzābat*, A man who goes with his cattle to pasture at a great distance from other men. A man long unmarried, an old bachelor. An old maid.

A معزاز *miʻzāz*, Very ill, dangerously sick.

A معزال *miʻzāl*, (pl. معازيل *maʻāzīl*) One who separates himself from others, either to pasture cattle, to avoid misfortunes or any thing disagreeable. One who, from niggardly motives, refuses to mix with gamblers. Weak, foolish. Unarmed, spearless.

A معزب *muʻzib*, One who has camels feeding far off. One in search of distant pasture.

A معزّب *muʻazzab*, (A flock) led far from home. Driven or conducted far from home.

A معزبة *miʻzabat*, A handmaid. A wife.

A معزّبة *muʻazzibat*, A wife.

A معزّز *muʻazzaz*, Corroborated, strengthened. Honoured, dignified, magnified, revered, glorious, honourable, venerable, magnificent.

A معزف *miʻzaf*, (or معزفة *miʻzafat*) (pl. معازف *maʻāzif*) A musical (especially stringed) instrument.

A معزق *miʻzak*, (and معزقة *miʻzakat*) (pl. معازق *maʻāzik*) A fan, winnowing machine. An implement with which the ground is turned up, where the plough cannot be used.

A معزل *maʻzil*, (pl. معازل *maʻāzil*) A place of retirement or of separation. في معزل *fī maʻzilin*, Alone, apart, separated, at a distance.

A معزم *maʻzam* or *maʻzim*, (v. n. of عزم) Undertaking, applying the mind.

A معزّم *muʻazzim*, Enchanter, exorcist, charmer.

A معزوزة *maʻzūzat*, Hard (ground). (Land) wet with rain. القمح معزوزة *al kamh maʻzūzat*, (in Morocco) A kind of wheat.

A معزوقة *maʻzūkat*, (Ground) turned up by the agricultural implement معزق *miʻzak*.

A معزول *maʻzūl*, Displaced, deposed, removed, dismissed, turned out, deprived of dignity, degraded, cashiered, set apart. P معزول كردن *maʻzūl kardan*, To displace, turn out, dismiss from office.

A معزولاً *maʻzūlan*, Without employment.

A معزولى *maʻzūlī*, Abdication. Deposition, dismissal. P معزولي دفتر *maʻzūlī-daftar*, An office for the examination and adjustment of dismissed officers' accounts.

A معزوم *maʻzūm*, Resolved on, purposed, intended.

A معزهل *muʻazhal*, Well-fed. Turned loose to pasture without a keeper.

A معزيّ *miʻza'*, The goat-species. A herd of goats.

A معزّي *muʻazzī*, A comforter, condoler.

A معزيّ اليه *maʻzīy ilayhi*, Alluded to. *Miʻzīy*, Avaricious.

A معس *maʻs*, (v. n. of معس) (A currier) rubbing violently (leather). Lying with. Despising. Piercing with a spear. (The camel has no) milk.

A معسّ *maʻass*, Any thing sought or asked after. A place where any thing is sought.

A معساء *miʻsāʼ*, Marriageable (girl).

A معساة *maʻsāt*, Worthy, suited, fitted.

A معساج *miʻsāj*, (A camel) stretching out the neck when travelling.

A معسر *miʻsar*, A rigid exactor of debt. *Muʻsir*, Poor, needy.

A معسرة *maʻsarat* or *maʻsurat*, Difficulty. *Muʻsirat*, A travailing woman in hard labour.

A معسطل *muʻastal*, Incoherent (speech).

A معسف *miʻsaf*, Oppressive, iniquitous. Erring, out of the way.

A معسكر *muʻaskar*, Encamped (army). A place of encampment, a camp. *Muʻaskir*, One who encamps or exercises troops. An officer who marks out camps. A commander.

A معسّل *muʻassal*, (Ginger) preserved, compounded, or mixed up with honey (عسل *ʻasal*).

A معسلة *maʻsalat*, A hive of bees, bees'-nest.

A معسلط *muʻaslat*, Mixed. Incoherent.

A معسم *maʻsim*, A place or state of desire.

A معسور *maʻsūr*, Difficult. A difficulty.

A معسورات *maʻsūrāt*, Difficulties, misfortunes.

A معسول *maʻsūl*, Dressed with honey, honied.

A معسون *maʻsūn*, (in Morocco) An intoxicating drink made of حشيشة *hashīshat*, honey, and spices.

A معسية *muʻsiyat*, A camel concerning which there is a doubt if she have milk or not.

A معش *maʻsh*, The act of rubbing gently.

A معشّ *maʻashsh*, A request, demand, petition. Intention, wish, desire.

A معشاب *miʻshāb*, (pl. معاشيب) Grassy (land).

A معشار *miʻshār*, The tenth part, tithe. (A camel) yielding an abundance of milk.

A معشب *muʻshib*, (A field) luxuriant in grass.

A معشّة *maʻashshat*, Rough, rugged, hard ground.

A معشر *maʻshar*, (pl. معاشر *maʻāshir*) A company, troop. A society, or body of men. The wife, children, or family of a man. Men and genies.

A معشّر *muʻashshar*, A decagon. معشّر متساوي الاضلاع *muʻashshar mutasāwi'l azlāʻ*, An equilateral decagon. One whose camels have brought forth, or are near it, or are in the state called عشار *ʻishār*.

A معشر معشر *maʻshara maʻshara*, By, or in tens.

A معشش *muʻashshash*, Nestled. A nest in a tree. A place for birds' nests (عش *ʻushsh* or *ʻashsh*).

A معشف *muʻshif*, One before whom is placed food of which he has never partaken, and of which he does not eat. A camel fresh from pasture, that has not yet tasted hay, date-stones, or barley.

A معشق *maʻshak*, Love.

A معشوش *maʻshūsh*, Diminished, small.

A معشوق *maʻshūk*, Loved, beloved. A beloved object. P معشوق تنگدل *maʻshūki tang-dil*, (or سنگدل *sang-dil*) A hard-hearted mistress. The world.

A معشوقة *maʻshūkat*, A mistress.

A معشوقي *maʻshūkī*, A being loved. The state or condition of a beloved object. Loveliness.

A معشوقية *maʻshūkiyat*, Loveliness.

A معص *maʻas*, (v. n. of معص) Having a distortion in the foot or hand. Limping, halting. Being put out (the finger). A twist in the tendon of the foot. A cramp in the foot or tendon of the leg, or bodily inconvenience from over-walking. White and noble (camels).

A معصار *miʻsār*, An instrument for crushing or squeezing, a press.

A معصال *miʻsāl*, A hooked pole, with which they pull down branches. A curved club or bandy.

A معصب *muʻassab*, Lank in the belly from hunger. Reduced to poverty by an unfavourable season. *Muʻassib*, One who binds his head with a fillet. One who ties a girdle about himself when pinched with hunger. Poor, indigent. One whose camels have perished from famine. A lord, a master.

A معصر *maʻsar*, as كريم المعصر *karīmu'l maʻsar*, One who shews liberality when asked. *Miʻsar*, (pl. معاصر *maʻāsir*) An instrument with which any thing is pressed, a press. *Muʻsir*, (pl. معاصر *maʻāsir* and معاصير *maʻāsīr*) Marriageable (girl).

A معصر *muʻassar*, An asylum, refuge.

A معصرات *muʻsirāt*, Clouds pressed or pouring down rain.

A معصرة *maʻsarat*, A place where things are pressed. *Miʻsarat*, A press (for grapes or olives).

A معصف *muʻsif*, Violent (wind). (A place) fruitful in corn and full of straw.

A معصفة *muʻsifat*, Violent (wind).

A معصفر *muʻasfar*, Dyed with saffron.

A معصل *miʻsal*, Severe upon a debtor.

A معصل *muʻassil*, An arrow which is distorted, or swerves in its flight. Any missile which deflects.

A معصم *miʻsam*, The wrist, the bracelet-place.

A معصوب *maʻsūb*, Tied. Very hungry. Nervous, brawny, firm. (A ram) castrated by compression. One whose body is elegantly shaped, in just symmetry. An elegant sword. In poetry when مفاعلتن *mufāʻilatun* is made مفاعيلن *mufāʻīlun*.

A معصوبة *maʻsūbat*, Elegantly-formed (girl).

A معصور *maʻsūr*, Pressed out, squeezed.

A معصوم *maʻsūm*, Defended, preserved. Innocent. An infant, a little boy. A proper name.

A معصومي *maʻsūmī*, Innocence. Chastity.

A معصومية *maʻsūmiyat*, Innocence. Infancy.

A معصية *maʻsiyat*, (v. n. of عصي) Rebelling, disobeying. Disobedience, rebellion, defection. Sin.

A معصيل *miʻsīl*, A curved club, bandy, shinty.

A معض *maʻz* or *maʻaz*, (v. n. of معض) Being angry, vexed, sick at heart. Being difficult, troublesome (business). *Maʻiz*, Angry, vexed, sick at heart.

A معض *maʻazz*, A place where any thing may be seized or held. ما لي في هذا الامر معض *mā lī fī hāzā'l amri maʻazz*, There is nothing in this affair on which I can lay hold or get a bite; *i. e.* I have no opportunity of understanding it. *Muʻizz*, Who has camels pasturing on عض *ʻizz*.

A معضاد *miʻzād*, An armlet or ornament for the upper arm. A strap, or any thing similar, with which one is struck on the upper part of the arm. An implement like a sword for cutting trees, a bill. A huge knife wherewith a butcher severs bones.

A معضد *miʻzad*, An ornament for the upper arm, *i. e.* between the shoulder and elbow, an armlet. A sword-like implement used in felling trees, a bill.

A معضد *muʻazzad*, A garment whose sleeves are ornamented with figures or borders. *Muʻazzid*, Dates ripening on one side.

A معضدة *miʻzadat*, A scrip worn at the side.

A معضض *muʻazzaz*, (An ass) bitten by others.

A معضل *muʻzal*, Difficult, obscure, hard to understand. *Muʻzil*, Deep, designing, malicious (fellow). Strong, muscular, powerfully-built (man). *Muʻzil*, (or معضل *muʻazzil*) (A woman) who has a painful birth. (A hen) which lays with difficulty.

A معضل *muʻazzil*, Narrow, confined (house). (A country) too strait for its inhabitants.

A معضلات *muʻzilāt*, Difficulties, troubles; arduous affairs, intricacies, perplexing questions.

A معضوب *maʻzūb*, Weak, unable to move.

A معضود *maʻzūd*, (A tree) felled with the instrument معضاد. Pained in the upper part of the arm.

A معضوض *maʻzūz*, Bitten, seized by the teeth.

A معضهة *muʻzihat*, (Land) fruitful in عضاه.

A معط *maʻt*, (v. n. of معط) Extending. Drawing (a sword). Lying with. Bringing forth (a woman). Plucking hair. Breaking wind. Putting off (payment of a debt). Being without hair (the body). *Muʻt*, (pl. of امعط *amʻat*) Bald wolves, hairless from disease. Barren; barren (sands). (Robbers) resembling wolves. *Maʻat*, (v. n. of معط) Being bare, bald, without pile. Losing his coat (a wolf). Being impure, wicked, flagitious. Smoothness of body, without hairs. *Maʻit*, Bald (wolf).

A معطاء *maʻtāʼ*, (fem. of امعط *amʻat*) Bare (country), destitute of vegetation. Bald (woman). Nastiness. Secret parts. Grief, melancholy. *Miʻtāʼ*, (pl. معاطي *maʻātī* and معاطي *maʻātiy*) A liberal giver (an instrument of liberality).

A معطار *miʻtār*, (A man or woman) highly perfumed. Strong and handsome (she-camel).

A معطارة *miʻtārat*, Perfumed, scented (woman). High-bred and excellent (she-camel).

A معطاش *miʻtāsh*, An owner of thirsty camels.

A معطال *miʻtāl*, (A woman) without necklace or other ornaments, seldom wearing any.

A معطب *maʻtab*, (pl. معاطب *maʻātib*) A dangerous place. Peril, danger. *Muʻtib*, Frugal, economical, parsimonious in household expenses.

A ابو معطة *abū muʻtat*, (Father baldness) A wolf.

A معطر *muʻtir*, Strong, handsome (she-camel).

A معطر *muʻattar*, Perfumed, scented, fragrant.

P معطر ساز *muʻattar-sāz*, Perfuming. A perfumer.

A معطرة *muʻtirat*, Excellent (she-camel).

A معطرة *muʻattarat*, Very handsome (she-camel). Perfumed, scented (woman).

A معطس *maʻtas* or *maʻtis*, (pl. معاطس *maʻātis*) The nose (the sneezing-part).

A معطس *muʻattas*, One whose nose has been rubbed in the dirt. Made to sneeze. *Muʻattis*, Sternutative (medicine); a sternutatory.

A معطش *maʻtash*, (pl. معاطش *maʻātish*) The stated time when camels become thirsty.

A معطش *muʻattash*, Imprisoned, incarcerated.

A معطشة *maʻtashat*, (pl. معاطش *maʻātish*) Dry ground, destitute of water; a thirsty land.

A معطف *miʻtaf*, A loose upper garment wrapped round the body. A sword. سهل المعطف *sahilu'l miʻtaf*, (A horse) obedient to the rein and going well.

A معطف *muʻattaf*, Bent much, curved (bow). Very favourably inclined.

A معطفة *muʻattafat*, (A camel) made tenderly affected, and giving milk plentifully when her colt, or its effigy or tulchan (as it is called in Scotland), is brought to her. Bent, inclined (thing).

A معطل *muʻattal*, Abandoned, deserted, uninhabited, unfrequented, neglected, fallen into disuse, obsolete, antiquated, voided, annihilated, annulled, disabled, powerless, destitute, empty, useless, vain, idle, of no account. Out of employ. (Land) uncultivated and without inhabitants. (Camels) without a keeper. (A well) whence no water is drawn, the inhabitants being dead or departed. P معطل كردن *muʻattal kardan*, To cancel. A *Muʻattil*, One who denies or, would abolish, the Creator, and who regards divine institutions and ordinances as vain.

P معطل گاه *muʻattal-gāh*, A neglected spot.

A معطلي *muʻattalī*, Neglect. Delay.

A معطن *maʻtin*, (pl. معاطن *maʻātin*) A spot where camels or sheep lie round a watering-place. A pearl-fishery.

A معطوش *maʻtūsh*, Overcome by thirst.

A معطوط *maʻtūt*, Overpowered, beat, conquered.

A معطوف *maʻtūf*, Turned, twisted, distorted,

bent, curved. Joined, coupled, connected by the copulative particle و or ف. In the sentence زيد و عمرو *zayd u ʻamr*, Zayd is the معطوف *maʻṭūf*, and Amr the معطوف عليه *maʻṭūf ʻalayhi*. P معطوف كردن *maʻṭūf kardan*, To turn (the reins). To conjoin.

A معطوفة *maʻṭūfat*, (A bow) very much bent. A peculiar bow used in shooting at targets.

A معطون *maʻṭūn*, (A hide) steeped for tanning; macerated with dung and salt to fetch off the hair. Spoilt and rotten (hide).

A مُعطى *muʻṭa'*, Given, presented. *Muʻṭī*, A giver, bestower. هل انت معطيه *hal anta* (or انتم *antum*) *muʻṭīhu*, Dost thou (or do you) give it?

A معطير *miʻṭīr*, (A man or woman) highly perfumed or scented. Red (she-camel) whose sweat emits an aroma.

A معظظ *muʻaẓẓiẓ*, (An arrow) swerving and devious in its flight.

A معظل *muʻẓil*, (A place) plenteous in trees.

A معظم *muʻẓam*, The greater part, or better sort (of any thing). The mass or major part. Primary (argument). معظمات بلاد *muʻẓamāti bilād*, The chief cities.

A معظّم *muʻaẓẓam*, Honoured, great, respectable.

A معظمة *muʻẓamat*, A heavy disaster.

A معظوم *maʻẓūm*, Boned (weaned camel's colt), *i. e.* the bone (عظم *ʻaẓm*) in his mouth broken to prevent him sucking.

A معظومة *maʻẓūmat*, (fem.) Fond of a large penis.

A معظئل *muʻẓaill*, (A spot) plentiful in trees.

A معفاج *miʻfāj*, A fuller's beetle. An evil-doer. *Miʻfāj*, (and معفجة *miʻfajat*) A staff, club.

A معفاص *miʻfāṣ*, Bad-tempered (girl).

A معفاق *miʻfāḳ*, Frequent in visiting, often going to and fro.

A معفج *miʻfaj*, A fool; a man incapable of talking or acting rationally. A staff, club.

A معفرت *muʻafrat*, Possessed by an عفريت.

A معفس *maʻfis*, A joint.

A معفّص *muʻaffaṣ*, Dyed black with gall-nuts.

A معفو *maʻfū*, (or معفوّ *maʻfūw*) Absolved, pardoned, condoned, forgiven.

A معفور *maʻfūr*, (or *maʻfūrat*) Dull (market).

A معفورة *maʻfūrat*, (Ground) eaten bare.

A معفوس *maʻfūs*, Imprisoned. Despicable, contemptible, cared little about. Dressed slovenly.

A معفون *maʻfūn*, Putrid, noisome, stinking.

A معفّي *muʻaffī*, A companion, one equal in every thing, and independent of any favour.

A معق *maʻḳ*, (v. n. of معق) Drinking greedily, swilling. Sweeping every thing away (a torrent). Distance. Depravity of disposition. A disorder of the stomach. Sharp wine. (pl. امعاق *amʻāḳ*) A wide-extended desert. Ground destitute of every plant. Whatsoever is swept away by a current. *Muʻḳ*, Distance.

A معقّ *muʻiḳḳ*, Pregnant (mare); one in foal.

A معقاب *miʻḳāb*, A woman used to bring forth alternately a boy and a girl. A part of a house where they lay dried grapes.

A معقاد *miʻḳād*, A thread on which beads are strung, those especially hung as amulets round the necks of children to defend them from fascination.

P معقار *miʻḳār*, Plum-tree gum.

A معقار *miʻḳār*, Galling (saddle).

A معقاص *miʻḳāṣ*, A sheep with a crooked horn. A girl of the worst disposition.

A معقب *miʻḳab*, A woman's veil for the head or face. An ear-ring. One who is appointed successor to the high priest. A skilful driver. *Muʻḳib*, (One star) rising immediately after another. (A son) succeeding (his father).

A معقّب *muʻaḳḳab*, Turned out of a tavern to make room for a superior. *Muʻaḳḳib*, One who follows close at the heels. A procrastinator. One who delays, keeps back, or retards.

A معقّبات *muʻaḳḳibāt*, The angels of the night and day, who alternately succeed one another and pronounce سبحان الله *subḥāna'llāh*, Praise be to God! (Camels) standing one behind another in order to drink in rotation.

A معقّة *maʻaḳḳat*, (v. n of عقّ) Being stubborn, undutiful, disobedient (to parents): undutifulness.

A معقد *maʻḳad*, The place of tying a knot. *Maʻḳid*, (pl. معاقد *maʻāḳid*) A place where a knot is tied. A kind of mantle. معقد الازار *maʻḳidu'l izār*, Near in rank and station.

A معقّد *muʻaḳḳad*, Much entangled or involved, intricate, knotty. (A speech) obscure, perplexed, difficult to be understood. An oath, the violation of which requires expiation: one which cannot be violated without perjury. *Muʻaḳḳid*, An enchanter, magician, one who binds by spells.

A معقر *miʻḳar*, One who galls the back of his beast by over-work. *Miʻḳar* or *muʻḳir*, (A saddle) hurting a horse's back. *Muʻḳir*, Possessed of much land or other possessions (عقار *ʻaḳār*).

A معقرب *muʻaḳrab*, Crooked, twisted. Strong, compactly built. Invincible. A powerful assistant. A twisted head of hair. *Muʻaḳrib*, (A place) where many scorpions (عقرب *ʻaḳrab*) are bred.

A معقرة *maʻḳarat*, A place infested by scorpions.

A معقص *miʻḳaṣ*, A crooked arrow, or one whose point is broken: one whose shaft has been taken out, straightened, and replaced.

A معقّف *muʻaḳḳaf*, Crooked, curved.

A معقل *maʻḳil*, Refuge, asylum. A man's name.

A معقلة *maʻḳulat*, (pl. معاقل *maʻāḳil*) The mulct of atonement for bloodshed. That which is necessary to the expiation of murder. ضمد من معقلة *ẓamad min maʻḳulat*, Any part remaining to be paid of such composition. *Muʻḳalat*, Expiated (blood).

A معقم *maʻḳim*, (pl. معاقم *maʻāḳim*) A joint in horses or other solid-hoofed animals (as the knee or pastern). A knot on reeds or straw.

A معقود *maʻḳūd*, Bound, tied, fastened, fixed. Tied in a knot. Reared, curved (dome or arch). Struck, concluded, made (bargain). Firmness of judgment. معقود اللسان *maʻḳūdu'l lisān*, Tongue-tied. معقودة القراء *maʻḳūdatu'l ḳirāʼ*, Strong-backed (she-camel). بناء معقود *bināʼ maʻḳūd*, A building wherein are ties or curves, as doorways.

A معقور *maʻḳūr*, Cut, wounded. Hamstrung.

A معقوف *maʻḳūf*, Crooked, bent, bended.

A معقوفة *maʻḳūfat*, A sheep whose foot is bent by the disease عقاف *ʻuḳāf*.

A معقول *maʻḳūl*, (v. n. of عقل) Being intellectual, endowed with reason. Understanding, perceiving. Reasonable, probable, just, pertinent, apposite, to the purpose, approved, acceptable. Intelligible, perceptible. Formed in wisdom; good, nice, choice. Verse in which the fifth foot is dropped. Bound. Detained. Strengthened, fortified.

A معقولات *maʻḳūlāt*, Probabilities, words or things consistent with reason.

A معقوليّة *maʻḳūliyat*, Reasonableness.

A معقوم *maʻḳūm*, Dry, withered (joint). Barren (womb). Addle, unprolific (loins of man).

A معقومة *maʻḳūmat*, Barren (womb).

A معقّي *muʻaḳḳī*, Hovering round any thing from a height (as an eagle over his prey).

A معك *maʻk*, (v. n. of معك) Rubbing (leather). Rolling (one upon the ground). Giving a signal (for fighting or litigation). Delaying, demurring, procrastinating. Being foolish, stupid. *Maʻik*, One who delays paying a debt or performing a promise. Quarrelsome, squabbling. Foolish, stupid.

A معكّ *miʻakk*, (A horse) requiring the lash after having run a little way. Litigious, quarrelsome.

A معكاء *miʻkāʼ*, Fat (camels); also numerous, the head of one being close to the tail of another.

A معكاد *miʻkād*, Hard and rough (she-camel).

A معكد *maʻkid*, An asylum, sanctuary.

A معكل *maʻkal*, Detention, restraint, durance. A place where (a man) is kept bound. *Miʻkal*, A needle; a sewing implement used by shepherds.

A معكم *miʻkam*, Corpulent, but firm in flesh.

A معكّنة *muʻakkanat*, (A girl) wrinkled in the belly from fat (from عكنة *ʻuknat*, A wrinkle).

A معكود *maʻkūd*, Fixed, assiduous, constant, persevering. Possible. Detained, arrested, imprisoned. Unfailing (food).

A معكوس *maʻkūs*, Inverted, reversed, turned upside down, preposterous. Poor.

A معكوش *maʻkūsh*, Collected.

A معكوف *maʻkūf*, Detained, confined, stopped, embargoed. Combed, dressed, plaited (hair).

A معكوك *maʻkūk*, Shut up, confined (camel).

A معكوكاء *maʻkūkāʼ* or *muʻkūkāʼ*, Grief, sorrow, evil. Tumult, row. Raised, flying dust.

A معكوكة *muʻkūkat*, Abundance (of wealth). A

great number (of camels).

A معكوم *maʻkūm*, Turned away, diverted.

A معكي *maʻkā'*, Many (camels).

A معل *maʻl*, (v. n. of معل) Seizing, carrying off, abstracting. Drawing out quickly a camel's colt from the matrix. Diverting (one from a design). Hastening (business). Corrupting, breaking off. Spoiling. Defaming, disparaging. Splitting (a beam). Falling foul on. Gelding (an ass). Making haste, going fast. *Maʻil*, Swift, quick.

A معلّ *muʻall*, Sick, ailing, infirm.

A معلا *muʻallā'*, Exalted, elevated, sublime.

A معلاة *maʻlāt*, (pl. معالي *maʻālī*) The attainment of nobility and dignity. A cemetery at Mecca.

A معلاق *miʻlāk*, (pl. معاليق *maʻālīk*) A drop, pendent, ear-ring. That to or by which such things are suspended, as a hook. The ear of a bucket. The tongue. *Miʻlāk*, (or ذو معلاق *zū miʻlāk*, Vehement in language, hot in disputation.

A معلّب *muʻallab*, (A camel) marked along the neck. *Muʻallib*, A maker of boxes, milk-pails, &c.

A معلبة *muʻlibat*, (or معلّبة) Nasty (she-camel).

A معلّس *muʻallas*, Experienced, tried (man).

A معلّسة *muʻallasat*, (A she-camel) which in temper and motion resembles the male.

A معلسط *muʻalsat*, Incoherent, rambling (talk).

A معلط *maʻlat*, The part of (a camel's) neck which is branded with a mark crosswise.

A معلّط *muʻallat*, Robust, strong, hardy. Impure, wicked. Extremely subtle.

A معلف *maʻlaf*, A place where food is given to cattle, a crib, manger, cratch, stable, stall, boose. Certain stars disposed in a circular and scattered form. *Miʻlaf*, A sack with provender hung round the neck of a horse, a nose-bag.

A معلّف *muʻallaf*, Fatted, crammed, stall-fed.

A معلق *maʻlak*, (pl. معالق *maʻālik*) A small crocodile. *Miʻlak*, A small milk-pail.

A معلّق *muʻallak*, Suspended, hung up, pendulous, hanging, dangling. That by which (a bow) is suspended. A road. A beam to which the pulley of a well is fastened. The pulley of a well. The bucket-rope. A large bucket. Love, attachment.

A معلّقات *muʻallakāt*, (pl. of معلّق *muʻallak*), and particularly applied to denote the seven famous Arabic poems hung up in the temple of Mecca.

A معلقة *maʻlukat*, An expiatory fine for manslaughter. ذو معلقة *zū maʻlakatin*, One who hangs upon every body he meets.

A معلّقة *muʻallakat*, A woman not having a husband, nor courted to be a wife; hanging on hand.

P معلّق زن *muʻallak-zan*, A dancer, tumbler. An infamous fellow, sodomite. Quick at prayers.

A معلكس *muʻalkis*, Thick, bushy, and jetty (hair). Accumulated (sand). (Dry grass) thickly collected together. Irresolute.

A معلكم *muʻalkam*, A strong camel.

A معلّل *muʻallal*, Endued with a cause. *Muʻallil*, One who drinks or who plucks fruit again and again. Who soothes and quiets (a child). One who by excuses puts off the tax-gatherer. The sixth of the winter-days called العجوز *al ʻajūz*.

A معلم *maʻlam*, A sign, mark, milestone, direction-post. A law, precept. Suspicion, conjecture. A place where any thing is supposed to be. That whereby a thing is proved or demonstrated. A straight or even place. A flat country, in which nothing but way-marks are to be seen. *Muʻlam*, Distinguished by a particular mark or badge. *Muʻlim*, One who distinguishes garments by a particular mark. Conspicuous for intrepidity in battle.

A معلّم *muʻallam*, Taught, instructed, trained, disciplined (as a man, horse, hound, or falcon). Marked; striped or spotted. *Muʻallim*, A schoolmaster, preceptor, professor, tutor. معلّم اوّل *muʻallimi awwal*, The first master; (amongst the learned) Aristotle; (in vulgar cant) The devil. معلّم و متعلّم *muʻallim u mutaʻallim*, Teacher and scholar.

A معلّمة *muʻallamat*, (fem. of معلّم *muʻallam*) Taught. A hunting-dog. *Muʻallimat*, A school.

P معلّم خانه *muʻallim-khāna*, A school.

A معلّميّة *muʻallimīyat*, Instruction.

A معلن *muʻlin*, A revealer, divulger, publisher.

A معلنجم *muʻlanjim*, Heaped up (sand).

A معلنداة *muʻlandāt*, Remedy, help, escape.

A معلندد *muʻlandad* or *muʻlandid*, Flight, escape. *Muʻlandid*, Way, means, access. A country without pasture or water.

A معلنكس *muʻlankis*, Thick, bushy (hair). Jet-black (hair). Heaped together (sand). Thickly collected together (dry stuff). Irresolute.

A معلنكك *muʻlankik*, Thick, bushy (hair).

A معلوب *maʻlūb*, Open, clear, trodden, beaten (road). (A sword) around whose haft the sinew of a camel's neck has been firmly whipped.

A معلوجاء *maʻlūjāʼ*, (or معلوجى *maʻlūjā'*) (pl. of علج *ʻilj*) Those who go over from barbarians to the Arabians. Religious proselytes. Wild asses. Stewards, bailiffs.

A معلّوط *muʻallawat*, The place on a (camel's) neck which is branded crosswise.

A معلوف *maʻlūf*, Fed, fatted. Stall-fed.

A معلوق *maʻlūk*, Hung, suspended. One at whose throat a leech is sticking, leeched. *Muʻlūk*, That to which, or from which, any thing is suspended.

A معلول *maʻlūl*, Caused, produced. Appeased, soothed. Distempered, indisposed. Weakened, diluted (wine). Partaken of, partly eaten (food).

A معلوم *maʻlūm*, Known, distinguished. Celebrated, famous, remarkable, notorious, signalized. Clear, evident, certain, obvious, apparent. The active voice of a verb. Money, stamped coin. P معلوم شدن *maʻlūm shudan*, To be known, evident, conspicuous. معلوم كردن *maʻlūm kardan*, To certify, mark, signify, or give information, make known. To know, discover.

A معلومات *maʻlūmāt*, (pl. fem. of معلوم *maʻlūm*) Things known, sciences. الايّام المعلومات *al ayyāmu'l maʻlūmāt*, The ten known days, *i.e.* Ten days in the last month of the year, called ذو الحجّة *zū'l hijja*, when the pilgrims visit Mecca.

A معلومي *maʻlūmī*, Knowledge, information.

A معلوميّة *maʻlūmīyat*, State of being known.

A معلهج *muʻalhaj*, Foolish. Vile, abject. The issue of a noble father by a slave mother. (A horse) bred from an Arabian sire and a half-bred dam.

A معلهز *muʻalhaz*, Raw (meat).

A معلهزة *muʻalhazat*, Lean, scraggy (sheep).

A معلهص *muʻalhas*, Badly-dressed (meat).

A معلي *muʻlī*, An elevator, exalter, raiser.

A معلّى *muʻallā'*, Elevated, exalted, sublime, eminent. The seventh gaming arrow. P درگاه معلّى *dargāhi muʻallā'*, The sublime Porte. A رفيع و معلّى *rafīʻ u muʻallā'*, High and elevated. *Muʻallī*, An elevator, exalter. A milker at the right side.

A معمّ *miʻamm*, Universal (in good deeds or in genius). *Muʻamm* or *muʻimm*, One who has many and celebrated paternal uncles (عمّ *ʻamm*).

A معمّا *muʻammā'*, An enigma.

A معمار *miʻmār*, (or معماريّ *miʻmāriy*) An architect. An overseer of buildings. P معمار كارخانهٔ قدرت *miʻmāri kār-khānaʼi kudrat*, God, the supreme architect of power.

A معمد *muʻmad*, Long, tall, lofty, high.

A معمّد *muʻammad*, (A tent) supported, propped by columns. Sick with love. Heart-broken. Baptized. وشيٌ معمّدٌ *washyun muʻammadun*, A kind of painting. *Muʻammid*, A baptizer, baptist.

A معمر *maʻmar*, A large mansion abounding with water and provender. *Muʻmar*, Cultivated. (Any thing) given towards the support of life.

A معمّر *muʻammar*, Blest with long life. Happy. *Muʻammir*, Who renders habitable and populous.

A معمرط *muʻamrit*, (A robber) carrying off all.

A معمّس *muʻammas* or *mis*, Obscure (affair).

A معمع *maʻmaʻ*, A woman tenacious of her property, and giving away nothing. Acute, clever, sharp, quick. ذو معمع *zū maʻmaʻ*, Very patient and skilful in the management of affairs.

A معمعان *maʻmaʻān*, Excessive heat. Very hot.

A معمعانيّ *maʻmaʻānīy*, Extremely hot.

A معمعة *maʻmaʻat*, The cracking noise of fire amongst reeds. Sound of the arms of combatants. Battle, conflict. A travelling in sultry weather. Expedition in business. Heavy rain abrading the ground. A crying مع مع *maʻ maʻ* continually.

A معمعيّ *maʻmaʻiy*, One who is on the conqueror's side and follows his fortunes. (Money) inscribed with مع مع *maʻ maʻ*.

A معمقة *maʻmakat*, (v. n. of معمق Q) Being soft and easy. Retaining, imprisoning. Mastering, subjecting. Sucking the udder vehemently.

A معمل mu'mal, Beaten, trodden, used (road).

A معمّم mu'ammam, Adorned with a turban (عمامة 'imāmat), turbaned; (hence) A prince, chief; a king of the Arabians. (A horse) having a white crown or forelock. White-headed (horse).

A معمّمة mu'ammamat, (A sheep) white on the upper part of the forehead.

A معمود ma'mūd, Sick with love.

A معموداني ma'mūdāniy, A baptist.

A معموديّة ma'mūdiyat, Baptism: baptismal water.

A معمور ma'mūr, Cultivated, inhabited, peopled. Flourishing (exchequer). Well-appointed (army). Delightfully built. Full, abundant. Affluent, prosperous. P معمور و آباداني گاه ma'mūr u ābādānī-gāh, A pleasant and cultivated country. معمور كردن ma'mūr kardan, To cultivate, restore, preserve, enlarge, render pleasant or habitable. A البيت المعمور al baytu'l ma'mūr, A certain house in the sky facing the temple of Mecca. غير معمور ghayr ma'mūr, Uninhabitable, desert. معمورهٔ عمرو ليث ma'mūra-i 'amr lays, The building of Amr Lays, a name of the city of Shīrāz (Amrlaystown).

A معموري ma'mūrī, A flourishing condition, fulness (of the treasury), efficiency (of the army).

A معموريّة ma'mūriyat, Habitableness.

A معمول ma'mūl, Made. Prepared; dressed. Customary, established. (Drink) diluted with milk and honey. Action, operation. Usage, established custom. (in grammar) Governed.

A معموم ma'mūm, Turbaned.

A معمّى mu'amma', An enigma. An acrostic, obscure, occult, mysterious verse or saying.

A معن ma'n, (v. n. of معن) Going very fast (a horse). Setting (water) a-flowing. Being well watered and coming to maturity (a plant). Acknowledging, admitting baseness of spirit. (A thing) easy to be done. Any thing whereby one is benefited. Expeditious (man in business). Long. Short. Many. Few. Goat's leather. Water. Ingratitude. معن بن زائدة ma'n bin zā'idat, Name of a man celebrated for his liberality. Mu'un, (pl. of معين ma'īn) Flowing waters.

A معنّ mi'ann, A preacher. One who intermeddles in affairs in which he has no concern. Opposing, contradictory.

A معنا ma'na', (and معناة ma'nāt) Sense, meaning. The title or lettering of a book.

A معناق mi'nāq, (pl. معانيق ma'ānīk) (A horse) with a fine neck (عنق 'unk, 'unuk, or 'unah).

A معنان mu'nān, A water-course in a valley.

A معناوي ma'nāwiy, Significant, real, true.

A معنّب mu'annab, Thick and long. Thick (pitch). Tall (man). Plump-cheeked, fleshy, corpulent. Mu'annib, A gatherer or bringer of grapes.

A معنبر mu'ambar, Perfumed with amber (عنبر 'ambar). Changed, altered.

A معنة ma'nat, A thing of no consequence. ما له سعنة و لا معنة mā lahu sa'nata wa lā ma'nata, He possesses nothing.

A معنّة mi'annat, Stubborn, disobedient woman.

A معنت mu'nat, (A bone) set after a fracture.

A معنج mi'naj, An opposer, hinderer, withstander.

A معنجد mu'anjad, Prone to anger, hot.

A معنذب mu'andib, Enraged, angry.

A معنذر mu'andir, Heavy (rain).

A معنز mu'annaz, Small-headed. Spare of flesh, lean, lank (in the face). Bearded like a goat.

A معنق mu'nik, Rugged and high ground in the midst of a plain. High (watch-tower).

A معنّقات mu'onnihāt, Long (mountains).

A معنقة ma'nakat, A country uninhabitable from sterility. Any curved or unequal projection from stones. Mi'nakat, (pl. معانيق ma'ānīk) A collar or any thing similar round the neck. A small hill in front of a heap of sand (like a neck).

A معنّقة mu'annikat, A kind of insect.

A معنك mi'nak, A large bar or bolt. A lock.

A معنّم mu'annam, Dyed, tinged (finger).

A معنّنة mu'annanat, A girl, twisted, distorted.

A معنوز ma'nūz, Unfortunate, distressed.

A معنوشة ma'nūshat, Long (neck).

A معنون ma'nūn, Insane, lunatic. Impotent, fascinated, bewitched, or judicially declared to be so. Mu'anwan, (A book) marked with a title or inscription (عنوان 'unwān).

A معنوي ma'nawiy, Significant. True, real, intrinsic, essential, absolute. Spiritual. (in grammar) Flowing from the sense (opposed to لفظي lafẓiy, Verbal). معارف معنويّة ma'ārifi ma'nawiya, The speculative sciences.

A معنى ma'na', (or معنيّ ma'niy) Sense, meaning, signification, import, drift, reality. Virtue, efficacy. Spirituality. A thing, any thing. A subject. صورة بلا معنى sūratun bilā ma'na', Form without substance. عالم معنى 'ālami ma'na', The spiritual world. علم معنى 'ilmi ma'na', Rhetoric. P بي معني bī ma'nī, Without meaning, vain, foolish.

A معنيً ma'nan, Really, in fact. لفظاً و معنيً lafzan wa ma'nan, In word and meaning.

A معنّى mu'anna', Fatigued, oppressed, careworn. An ignoble, poor-blooded stallion that is kept in the stable. Detained long in captivity. A camel whose bunch is cloven.

A معنيّ ma'niy, Taking care of, careful, anxious, much concerned about (any thing). Intent, design.

A معنية ma'niyat, Sense, reality.

A معو ma'w, Dates ripe or ripening on the tree. A fissure in a camel's under-lip.

A معوان mi'wān, One who aids effectually.

A معوة ma'wat, A single date ripe on the tree. A half-dried date.

A معوّج mu'awwaj, Bended, curved. Mu'awwij, A bender. An inlayer with ivory (عاج 'āj).

A معوجّ mu'wajj, Crooked, curved, bent.

A معوجّة mu'wajjat, Crooked (staff).

A معود ma'ūd, Afflicted with a disease. Visited (sick man). Mu'ūd, (v. n. of معد) Carrying off.

A معوّد mu'awwad, Exercised, trained. Mu'awwid, A trainer, teacher (of dogs to hunt).

A معوذ mi'waz, An amulet, or any thing for averting evil. Mu'wiz, (A mare, camel, or doe) which has recently brought forth.

A معوّذ mu'awwaz, The place of a horse's neck where the amulets are hung. A camel which moves not from his place. A camel's pasture near a house. Mu'awwaz or mu'awwiz, Herbage growing at the roots of thorns, or in rough places where cattle cannot crop it. Mu'awwiz, One upon whom are suspended amulets made of dead men's bones, fetid rags, or other kinds of filth. Name of a man.

A معوّذتان mu'awwizatāni, A name given to the two last chapters of the Kur'ān.

A معور mi'war, The covering of a cradle. Mu'wir, Dangerous (place), infested by robbers.

A معوز mi'waz, (or معوزة) (pl. معاوز ma'āwiz) A garment for daily use. Mu'wiz, Poor, distressed.

A معوشة ma'ūshat, Food, livelihood.

A معوضة ma'ūzat, A thing given for another; equivalent, compensation.

A معوق mu'wik, Sleepy, nodding (man). Hungry.

A معوّق mu'awwak, Detained, delayed, hindered, kept back (from battle). Mu'awwik, One who diverts or hinders from business. A detainer.

A معوكة ma'wakat, A battle, combat.

A معول ma'ūl, Overcome, exhausted (patience). Mi'wal, A pointed instrument with which they split stones. Mu'wal, Bewailed. معول عليه mu'wal 'alayhi, Lamented over, bewailed.

A معوّل mu'awwal, (v. n. 2 of عال for عول) Leaning, relying upon. A place of confidence. A helper, or one relied upon for help. Mu'awwil, One who trusts, a confider.

A معون ma'ūn, (pl. of معونة) Helps, favours.

A معونة ma'ūnat or ma'wanat, Aid, assistance, favour, protection. صاحب المعونة sāhibu'l ma'ūnat, A police-magistrate.

A معوود ma'wūd, Visited (by disease). Visited (sick man); tended by a physician or nurse.

A معويّ mi'awiy, Intestinal.

A معه ma'ahu, With him, together with.

A معهد ma'had, A place which one frequents, in which he does any thing often. A place to which one always returns, whithersoever one may have gone. A monument.

A معهّد mu'ahhad, Partially visited by rain.

A معهود ma'hūd, Agreed, established, fixed, determined, appointed, resolved, promised, accustomed. Known, certain, distinguished, celebrated, confirmed, bound. Seen. Watered by early spring-rains (a field). شيء معهود shay'i ma'hūd, A known or undoubted thing. مسكن معهود *maskani maʿhūd*, Accustomed abode, customary habitation.

A معي *maʿy* or *miʿa'*, (pl. أمعاء *amʿāʾ*) An intestine, a gut. المعى الاعور *al miʿa'l aʿwar*, The blind gut, cœcum. *Miʿa'*, A channel through which water flows to low ground, or from field to field. Soft ground between two hard grounds. معى الفار *miʿa'l fār*, A bad species of date.

A معيار *miʿyār*, The mark or standard of money, weight, or measure. Touchstone, assay-balance.

A معياص *miʿyāṣ*, One who makes difficulties in regard to whatever any person ask him for.

A معيان *miʿyān*, Who looks stedfastly with malignant eye. A leader of the people. One who looks out for water and straw for his tribe.

A معيب *maʿīb*, Vicious, reproached with vice. Vice, disgrace, blemish.

A معيبات *maʿībāt*, (pl. fem. of معيب) Vices.

A معيبة *maʿyabat*, Place or object of dishonour.

A معيّة *maʿiyat*, Conjunction, society, association, co-existence. Favour, affection, partiality. *Muʿayyat*, (dim. of معاوية *muʿāwiyat*) A little bitch in heat.

A معيد *muʿīd*, Skilful, clever, experienced, able, powerful. (God) the restorer or bringer again. A lion. A stallion which covers frequently. مبدئ معيد *mubdiʾ muʿīd*, Broke in, well-trained (horse). One who has fought many battles with the infidels.

A معيديّ *muʿaydiy*, (dim. of معدّيّ *maʿaddiy*) Of the tribe of Maadd.

A معيذ *muʿīẕ*, (A mare, camel, or doe) which has recently brought forth.

A معير *miʿyar*, Misfortune. ابنة معير *ibnatu miʿyar*, Misfortune. *Muʿīr*, A lender.

A معيّر *muʿayyar*, A kind of figured silk, with spots resembling the eyes of the wild ass (عير *ʿayr*).

A معيرة *maʿīrat*, Disgrace, infamy.

A معيز *maʿīz*, Goat-species. (pl. of معز) Goats.

A معيش *maʿīsh*, (v. n. of عاش for عيش) Living. Life. A place where one lives.

A معيشة *maʿīshat*, (v. n. of عاش for عيش) Living, leading a life. (pl. معائش *maʿāʾish*) Food, any thing belonging, to needful for life. المعيشة الضنك *al maʿīshatu'z zank*, The punishment of the grave.

P معيشت اندوز *maʿīshat-andoz*, Getting a living.

A معيص *maʿīṣ* or *maʿyaṣ*, A thick grove.

A معيق *maʿīḳ*, Small. عميق معيق *ʿamīḳ maʿīḳ*, Deep (river).

A معيل *maʿīl*, (v. n. of عال for عيل) Wanting, being indigent, helpless, destitute. Rendering necessitous. Tiring, exhausting. Frustrating. *Muʿīl*, Possessed of a numerous family or household (عيال *ʿiyāl*). A lion. A leopard. A wolf.

A معيم *muʿīm*, Long (day).

A معين *maʿīn*, (Water) flowing over the surface of ground. Pure, clear (water). (Water) which bursts forth when dug for. Touched or struck on the eye. Viewed with a malignant eye. Fascinated. A rhomb. شبيه المعين *shabīhu'l maʿīn*, A rhomboid. *Muʿīn*, An assistant. المعين *al muʿīn*, (God) the defender.

A معيّن *muʿayyan*, Fixed, determined, settled, appointed, specified, destined, assigned, declared, expressed, certified, stationed. Tesselated, variegated by squares. (A bull) black between the eyes. A certain famous bull. A rhomb. شبيه بالمعيّن *shabih bi'l muʿayyan*, A rhomboid. غير معيّن *ghayr muʿayyan*, Undetermined, inexplicable.

A معيوب *maʿyūb*, Vicious, defective, faulty, blemished. Sprained. Disfigured. Opprobrious, dishonoured, stigmatized, infamous.

A معيوة *muʿaywat*, (dim. of معاوية *muʿāwiyat*) A little bitch in heat.

A معيوراء *maʿyūrāʾ*, (pl. of عير *ʿayr*) Asses.

A معيون *maʿyūn*, Touched or struck on the eye. Viewed with a malignant eye. Fascinated. (Water) pure and flowing bursting out when dug for.

A معيوه *maʿyūh*, (A country) whose cattle are distempered and corn blighted.

A معي *muʿyī*, Tired, jaded.

A معيّ *maʿyiy*, Of the intestines, intestinal.

A معيية *muʿayyat*, A little bitch in heat. *Muʿyiyat*, Tired, jaded (camels).

P مغ *magh*, Depth. A channel, bed of a river. *Migh*, (contraction of ميغ *megh*) A cloud. *Mugh*, One of the Magi, worshipper of fire, infidel, pagan. A Christian monk. A tavern-keeper. An ox's horn.

A مغاء *maghāʾ*, The mewing (of a cat).

A مغاب *maghāb*, (v. n. of غاب for غيب) Being absent. Slander, detraction; any thing secretly whispered of an absent person (implying truth however, as بهتان *buhtān* expresses a false accusation). Absence. Concealment, invisibility.

A مغابّة *maghābbat*, End, issue, final success.

A مغابصة *mughābaṣat*, (v. n. 3 of غبص) Attacking or seizing unawares, rushing suddenly on.

A مغابن *maghābin*, Groins. Arm-pits.

P مغاث *maghās*, Root of the wild pomegranate.

A مغاث *mighās*, (v. n. 3 of مغث) Rubbing one another. Contending, litigating. Altercation, animosity. *Mughās*, A kind of medicinal root purgative and emetic.

A مغاثة *mughāsat*, (Land) refreshed by rain.

A مغاثير *maghāsīr*, (pl. of مغثور *mughsūr*) Esculent juices thick as honey, extracted from the plants ثمام *sumām*, عشر *ʿushar*, and رمث *rims*.

A مغاداة *mughādāt*, A coming in the morning.

A مغادرة *mughādarat*, (v. n. 3 of غدر) Leaving, forsaking. Remaining.

A مغاذّ *mughāzz*, (A camel) averse from water.

A مغار *maghār*, The covert of a deer. A cavern. *Mughār*, (v. n. 4 of غار for غور) Rushing upon, plundering, making a foray. Depredation, plunder. Twisted (rope). A cavern.

A مغارّ *mughārr*, (pl. مغارّ *maghārr*) (A she-camel) running in terror, and, in consequence, having little milk. A close-fist, avaricious.

A مغاراة *mughārāt*, (v. n. 3 of غرا for غرو) Joining (two things), subjoining, annexing, adding. Litigating, disputing with.

A مغارب *maghārib*, (pl. of مغرب) Wests.

A مغاربة *maghāribat*, (pl. of مغربيّ *maghribiy*) Westerns, natives of Western Africa or Morocco.

A مغارة *maghārat* or *mughārat*, A den, a cave. A cavern, grotto. A ditch, trench.

A مغارّة *mughārrat*, (v. n. 3 of غرّ) Having a diminution of milk from terror (a camel). Billing (as turtles). Giving food to his mate (a turtle-dove). Being languid (market). Not properly performing the sacred inflexions ركوع *rukūʿ* or سجود *sujūd* in prayer. Deficiency.

A مغارز *maghāriz*, (pl. of مغرز *maghraz* or *maghriz*) Bases, bottoms, seats.

A مغارس *maghāris*, (pl. of مغرس *maghras*) Nursery-grounds. (figuratively) Women, wives.

A مغارضة *mughārazat* (v. n. 3 of غرض) Leading out (camels) to water in the morning.

A مغارف *maghārif*, (pl. of مغرف *mighraf*) Excellent, swift (horses). (pl. of مغرفة *mighrafat*) Ladles, skimmers.

A مغارم *maghārim*, (pl. of مغرم) Debts.

A مغاريد *maghārīd*, (pl. of مغرود *mughrūd*) Sorts of mushrooms.

A مغازّة *mughāzzat*, (v. n. 3 of غزّ) Outstripping, getting before.

A مغازر *mughāzir*, One who parts with something to receive more in return.

A مغازرة *mughāzarat*, (v. n. 3 of غزر) Giving somewhat to receive more in return.

A مغازل *maghāzil*, Women's spindles. The teeth of a certain threshing-instrument.

A مغازلة *mughāzalat*, (v. n. 3 of غزل) Soothing, flattering a beloved object, especially by amorous verses or speeches. Approaching (forty).

A مغازليّ *maghāziliy*, A maker of distaffs.

A مغازي *maghāzī*, (pl. of مغزي *maghzaʾ*) Camps, battles. Military virtues or qualities.

A مغاسل *maghāsil*, (pl. of مغسل *maghsal*) Bathing-places or vessels, especially for dead bodies.

A مغاشّ *mughāshsh*, One who makes haste.

A مغاشّة *mughāshshat*, (v. n. 3 of غشّ) Accelerating, despatching (work), making haste.

A مغاص *maghāṣ*, (v. n. of غاص for غوص) Diving in search of any thing. A place where a diver plunges. The top of the leg.

A مغاض *maghāẓ*, (v. n. of غاض for غيض) Decreasing (as water or the price of provisions). Diminishing or causing to decrease.

A مغاضب *mughāẓib*, Angry with one's own kinsfolk, tribe, or nation, and forsaking them.

A مغاضبة *mughāẓabat*, (v. n. 3 of غضب) Putting in a passion, irritating one another. Being angry with one another.

A مغاضنة *mughāzanat*, (v. n. 3 of غضن) Wrinkling about the eyes, either from weakness, age, or anger. Closing or contracting the eyes.

A مغاطّة *mughāttat*, A ducking one another.

A مغافر *maghāfir*, (and مغافير *maghāfīr*) (pl. of مغفار *mighfār*, مغفير *mighfīr*, مغفر *mighfar*, *mughfur*, and مغفور *mughfūr*) Esculent juices, of the consistency of honey, extracted from the plants ثمام *sumām*, عشر *ʻushar*, and رمث *rims*.

A مغافصة *mughāfasat*, (v. n. 3 of غفص) Attacking or seizing unawares, rushing suddenly upon.

P مغاك *maghāk*, A ditch, furrow, pit, low place. Hell. Deep. مغاك ظلمت *maghāki zulmat*, (or مغاك ظلمت خاك *maghāki zulmati khāk*) The earth. The human body. مغاك غار *maghāki ghār*, The grave. مغاك هولناك *maghāki hawlnāk*, A dreadful cavern.

P مغاكچه *maghākcha*, A little pit. A dimple.

P مغاكي *maghākī*, Depth. A hollow.

A مغال *maghāl*, (v. n. of غال for غول) Destroying. *Mighāl*, (pl. of مغلة *maghlat*) Sheep which lamb twice in a year. *Mughāl*, (An infant) sucking the milk of a woman when pregnant, or when cohabiting with a man.

A مغالاة *mughālāt*, (v. n. 3 of غلا for غلو) Throwing or shooting (a javelin or arrow) with the utmost force). Bidding against, raising the price upon another. Buying (meat) at a high price.

A مغالبة *mughālabat*, (v. n. 3 of غلب) Contending with (another) for victory or superiority. Overpowering, overcoming.

A مغالة *maghālat*, (v. n. of مغل) Informing against, accusing, slandering, whispering. Perfidy, fraud.

A مغالث *mughālis*, One who fights hand to hand, or presses upon (a foe) in battle.

A مغالثة *mughālasat*, (v. n. 3 of غلث) Fighting hand to hand, battling with an enemy.

A مغالطة *mughālatat*, (v. n. 3 of غلط) Leading one another into error (غلط *ghalat*).

A مغالظة *mughālazat*, (v. n. 3 of غلظ) Hating one another. Thickness, grossness, rudeness of temper. Enmity.

A مغالق *maghālik*, (or مغاليق *maghālīk*) (pl. of مغلق *mighlak*) Gaming arrows (particularly winning ones). Locks, bolts.

A مغالقة *mughālakat*, (v. n. 3 of غلق) Betting, laying a wager.

A مغامّة *mughāmmat*, (v. n. 3 of غم) Rendering each other sad and melancholy.

A مغامر *mughāmir*, One who encounters dangers without fear or care, who throws himself into the thick and throng of any thing.

A مغامرة *mughāmarat*, (v. n. 3 of غمر) Fighting hand to hand, without fear of death.

A مغامز *maghāmiz*, Faults, blemishes.

A مغامسة *mughāmasat*, (v. n. 3 of غمس) Ducking one another. Involving one's self in war, rushing headlong into battle.

A مغامض *maghāmiz*, (pl. of مغمض *maghmaz*) Very low parts of the earth.

P مغان *mughān*, (pl. of مغ *mugh*) Christian fraternities of monks, who are by the Muhammadans placed, in this sense, on a footing with the pagans or worshippers of fire. A beautiful girl. A wine-cellar. Name of a district in Azarbayjān.

A مغانم *maghānim*, (pl. of مغنم *maghnam*) Spoils.

P مغانه *mughāna*, Any thing which relates to the Mughs or worshippers of fire.

A مغاني *maghānī*, Songs. Singing women. (pl. of مغنى *maghna'*) Pleasant houses, the abodes of mirth. Mansions.

A مغاوث *maghāwis*, Waters.

A مغاور *mughāwir*, A warrior, one who makes frequent excursions to lay waste and plunder.

A مغاورة *mughāwarat*, (v. n. 3 of غار for غور) Making a hostile excursion against, contending with.

A مغاولة *mughāwalat*, (v. n. 3 of غال for غول) Destroying. Taking the lead together. Making haste together.

A مغاياة *mughāyāt*, (v. n. 3 of غي) Overshadowing with their swords.

A مغايبة *mughāyabat*, (v. n. 3 of غاب for غيب) Being absent from each other. Speaking of the absent.

A مغائر *maghā,ir*, (pl. of مغارة *maghārat*) Caves.

A مغاير *mughāyir*, Contrary, repugnant, adverse. مغاير صلح *mughāyiri sulh*, Contrary to the peace.

A مغايرة *mughāyarat*, (v. n. 3 of غار for غير) Exchanging, bartering (merchandise).

A مغايطة *mughāyatat*, Controversy, disagreement.

A مغايظة *mughāyazat*, A putting in a passion.

A مغائير *maghā,ir*, (pl. of مغيار) Jealous (men).

A مغبّ *mughibb*, (A friend) who visits every third day. One who intermits (any thing) for two days. (A camel) which drinks every alternate day. Stinking, stale (meat). A lion.

A مغبار *mighbār*, A camel yielding milk abundantly after they that brought forth at the same time have ceased to do so. A dusty palm-tree.

A مغبّة *maghabbat*, End, issue, termination.

P مغبچه *mugh-bacha*, The son of a fire-worshipper or tavern-keeper. A noviciate in a monastery.

A مغبر *mughbir*, A raiser of dust. Raining much. One who strains every nerve to perform any thing.

A مغبرّ *mughbarr*, One whose hair and beard are dusty, dirty, and squalid.

A مغبّرة *mughabbirat*, Name of a class continually engaged in praising God; and who, by their manner of reading the Kur'ān, excite in the souls of men a desire after heavenly things.

A مغبطة *maghbatat*, (Ground) covered with thick, entangled herbage.

A مغبن *maghbin*, The groin. The arm-pit.

A مغبور *mughbūr*, A kind of gum extracted from the plants ثمام *sumām*, عشر *ʻushar*, and رمث *rims*.

A مغبوض *maghbūz*, Odious, hated.

A مغبوط *maghbūt*, Happy, prosperous, fortunate, blest. Emulated, envied, or imitated by others.

A مغبوطة *maghbūtat*, Any thing coveted. Wealth.

A مغبون *maghbūn*, Deceived. Cheated, gulled, imposed upon, defrauded, injured. Weak in mind.

A مغبية *mughbiyat*, Raining small rain.

A مغتاب *mughtāb*, A slanderer of the absent.

A مغتاظ *mughtāz*, Inflamed with rage.

A مغتاط *mughtāt*, (A womb) unfruitful, unproductive, though not absolutely barren.

A مغتاظ *mughtāz*, Angry, enraged.

A مغتال *mughtāl*, Fat, jolly (youth). Strong, nervous (arm).

A مغتبط *mughtabit*, In easy circumstances. Happy, cheerful.

A مغتبق *mughtabak*, (v. n. 8 of غبق) Drinking wine in the evening. A place where wine is drunk.

A مغتذر *mughtazir*, One who prepares the food called غذيرة *ghazīrat*.

A مغتذم *mughtazim*, A glutton.

A مغتذي *mughtazī*, Nourished, fed with.

A مغترف *mughtarif*, One who sips with the hand.

A مغتزل *mughtazal*, A slender rope. *Mughtazil*, A spinner (of cotton).

A مغتزي *mughtazī*, One who wills, intends, designs, proposes, purposes. Who has one intimate among many companions.

A مغتسل *mughtasal*, Cold water, or any thing one washes with. Washing-water. A washing-place. A place where dead bodies are washed. *Mughtasil*, One who washes. One who perfumes himself. (A horse) bathed in sweat.

A مغتضر *mughtazar*, Dying young and healthy.

A مغتلّ *mughtall*, Oppressed with thirst. Longing for, favourably inclined to.

A مغتلف *mughtalif*, One who procures a sheath. One whose hair is scented with civet (غالية *ghāliyat*).

A مغتلم *mughtalim*, Furious, raging (stallion).

A مغتلمة *mughtalimat*, Libidinous, lewd (woman).

A مغتلي *mughtalī*, Quick, going rapidly.

A مغتمّ *mughtamm*, Sad, gloomy, melancholy.

A مغتمر *mughtamir*, Overflowing, drowning (water). One who tinges with the liniment called غمرة *ghumrat*. Wheat with the husk upon it. (A palm-tree) which imbibes much water. Drunken (man).

A مغتمز *mughtamiz*, A reproacher, traducer.

A مغتمس *mughtamis*, What subsides or sinks to the bottom. Equally tinged (hand).

A مغتمص *mughtamis*, A despiser, detractor.

A مغتمض *mughtamiz*, A conniver: connivent. Drowsy, dosy.

A مغتمط *mughtamit*, Superior, one who overpowers (with words). (See اغتماط *ightimāt*.)

A مغتنم *mughtanam*, Regarded as an invaluable prize (غنيمة *ghanīmat*). *Mughtanim*, Who considers as prey. Enriched, endowed with abundance, possessing, enjoying.

A مغتهب *mughtahib*, A traveller in the dark.

A مغث *maghs*, (v. n. of مغث) Macerating, dissolving (medicine in water). Striking gently. Injuring the reputation of another. Submersion, drowning. A battle, fighting. Vanity, folly, play. An evil. *Maghis*, A strong wrestler. One who can floor his antagonist.

A مغثر *mighsar*, (and مغثور *mughsūr*) (pl. مغاثير *maghāsīr*) An esculent juice, of the consistency of honey, extracted from the plants ثمام *sumām*, عشر *ʻushar*, and رمث *rims*.

A مغثري *mughasrī*, (Water) up to the brim. Grassy, verdant (spot).

A مغثمر *mughasmar*, Unsifted wheat. Coarse, flimsy cloth. *Mughasmir*, Iniquitous, oppressive.

A مغثوم *maghsūm*, Mixed.

A مغج *maghj*, (v. n. of مغج) Passing by, going, walking, running.

P مغچه *mughcha*, Soreness under the arms.

P مغد *maghd*, A mandrake. A brinjal or egg-plant. A medlar. A small kind of mushroom.

A مغد *maghd*, (v. n. of مغد) Living luxuriously. Being long and luxuriant (herbage). Sucking (the dam). Rendering delicate and soft (luxurious living). Plucking the fruit of the تنضب *tanzub*. Becoming fat. Sucking. Having to do (with a girl). Plucking hairs pulled from the middle of a horse's brow, that white ones may grow in their room. Tender, soft, delicate. Fleshy and succulent (camel). Any thing thick and long. The mandrake. A fruit resembling the cucumber. A large bucket. *Maghad*, (v. n. of مغد) Growing fat.

A مغدّ *mughidd*, Enraged (man). (A camel) having the plague (غدّة *ghuddat*).

A مغداد *maghdād*, (or مغدان *maghdān*) The city of Baghdād. *Mighdād*, Much enraged, perpetually in a passion (man or woman).

A مغدر *maghdar* or *dir*, Perfidious. A traitor.

A مغدرة *mughdirat*, Dark (night).

A مغدف *mighdaf*, An oar.

A مغدود *maghdūd*, (A camel) infected with plague.

A مغدودن *mughdawdan*, Tender, delicate, lithe, limber (shrub). Delicate (youth).

A مغذمر *mughazmir*, A chief, a leader. One who commits things which he has learned from one, and teaches another. One who waives his own right in favour of another. One who follows his own inclination, good or bad. One who, unresisted, passes a righteous or unrighteous sentence.

A مغر *maghr*, (v. n. of مغر) Travelling quick, crossing a country in haste. *Maghar*, A dark, opaque, reddish colour.

A مغرب *maghrib*, The west, either of the heavens or earth. The western countries; Hesperia, Africa, Barbary, or Morocco. صلوٰة المغرب *salātu'l maghrib*, Evening-prayer. *Mughrab*, Whitish. White about the edges. White-eyebrowed (man or beast). Morning, dawn. *Mughrib*, Exciting wonder.

A مغرّب *mugharrab*, Far distant. *Mugharrib*, One who goes towards the west. *Mugharrib* or *mugharrab*, Distant, remote.

A مغربان *maghribān*, The beginning of sunset. The west. *Maghribāni*, (dual of مغرب *maghrib*) West and east.

A مغرّبة *mugharribat*, A strange, foreign, outlandish thing. Foreign news.

A مغربل *mugharbal*, Sifted, passed through a sieve or searce. Killed and swollen (body). Low, base, ignoble. Departing (possessions).

A مغرّبون *mugharribūn*, Persons in whose race there is a mixture of the جنّ *jinn*.

A مغربيّ *maghribīy*, (pl. مغاربة *maghāribat*) Western. African. Native of Morocco.

A مغربيّة *mughribīyat*, Strangeness, foreignness.

A مغربين *maghribayni*, (oblique of مغربان *maghribāni*) (The two wests) West and east.

A مغرة *maghrat*, (Rain) beneficial; also light or weak. *Maghrat* or *magharat*, Red clay or earth. *Magha* or *mughrat*, A dark, opaque, reddish colour.

A مغرّد *mugharrid*, A singer, warbler, songster. *Mugharrid* or *mugharrad*, Distant, remote.

A مغرّر *mugharrir*, Thoughtless, giddy, heedless: one who exposes himself to danger.

A مغرز *maghraz* or *maghriz*, (pl. مغارز *maghāriz*) A root, base, bottom, seat. *Mughriz*, (Ground) fruitful in the bog-rush غرز *gharaz*.

A مغرّز *mugharriz*, (A locust) fixing its tail in the ground (when laying).

A مغرض *maghriz*, (pl. مغارض *maghāriz*) The side of (a camel's belly) under or behind the ribs.

A مغرّض *mugharraz*, Emptied, exhausted.

A مغرف *mighraf*, (pl. مغارف *maghārif*) Swift (horse) in the race. Swift (horseman).

A مغرفة *mighrafat*, (pl. مغارف *maghārif*) A ladle.

A مغرق *mughrak* or *mugharrak*, Gilded or ornamented with silver (a sword-hilt or bridle). *Mughrik*, Engulphing, drowning.

A مغرّق *mugharrak*, Plunged in water.

A مغرم *maghram*, Debt. *Maghram* or *mughram*, A debt which must be paid. *Mughram*, Desirous, wishful. Given up to love. Drowned in debt, a prisoner for debt. Liable, exposed to. A mulct, fine.

A مغرندي *mughrandī*, Conquering, superior. One who overpowers by strength or by opprobrious language.

A مغروّ *maghrūw*, Glued, covered with glue (غرا *ghara'* or غراء *ghirāʼ*). An arrow. A spear.

A مغرود *mughrūd*, A kind of mushroom.

A مغروداء *maghrūdāʼ*, Land rich in mushrooms.

A مغرور *maghrūr*, Deceived, deluded, buoyed up with vain hopes. Proud, arrogant, presumptuous, haughty, self-conceited.

A مغروري *maghrūrī*, Haughtiness, arrogance.

A مغروس *maghrūs*, Planted, set (tree, shrub).

A مغروسة *maghrūsat*, Confusion, broil: mixture.

A مغروض *maghrūz*, Rain-water.

A مغروف *maghrūf*, Clipped, shorn, polled.

A مغروق *maghrūk*, Immersed, drowned, sunk.

A مغريٰ *mughra'*, Excited, stirred up. Greedy. *Mughrī*, One who excites, stirs up, or eggs on.

A مغريّ *maghrīy*, (or مغرّيٰ *mugharra'*) Glued.

P مغز *maghz*, Brain. Fat. Marrow. Kernel, pith, pulp, chief substance or essence of any thing. Pride, arrogance. مغز بادام *maghzi bādām*, Bleached almonds. مغز بردن *maghz burdan*, To talk much. To give the headache. مغز پشت *maghzi pusht*, The spinal marrow. مغز تر کردن *maghz tar kardan*, To speak, talk. مغز جوز *maghzi jawz*, Peeled walnuts. مغز در سر کردن *maghz dar sar kardan*, To keep silence (to keep the brain in the head). مغز روشن *maghz-roshan*, (Clearing the brain) Snuff.

A مغزّ *mughizz*, (A cow) with a painful gestation.

A مغزار *mighzār*, (A sheep) rich in milk.

P مغزدار *maghz-dār*, Marrowy. Kernelled, kernelly. Pithy, containing pith or brain.

A مغزر *mughzar*, Possessed of many camels, or of camels yielding much milk. *Mughzir*, (Sheep) rich in milk, or (a plant) in leaves.

A مغزرة *mughzirat*, A plant of which cattle are fond, and which makes them give much milk.

A مغزل *maghzal*, An amorous verse or speech. *Mighzal*, *maghzal*, or *mughzal*, A spinning-spindle. *Mughzil*, (A doe) with a young one (غزال *ghazāl*).

A مغزور *maghzūr*, Plentifully watered with rain.

A مغزول *maghzūl*, Spun.

A مغزيٰ *maghza'*, A field of battle, war, an expedition against infidels. Intent, scope, drift, meaning.

A مغزية *mughziyat*, (A woman) whose husband is on military service. (A camel) gone with young a month over the year. An ass slow in conceiving.

P مغزين *maghzīn*, A kind of sweetmeat.

P مغزينه *maghzīna*, The brain.

A مغس *maghs*, (v. n. of مغس) Piercing with a spear. Feeling, handling. *Maghs* or *maghas*, (v. n. of مغس) Being griped. Cholic, gripes.

P مغستان *mughistān*, A palm-plantation.

A مغسّس *mughassis*, New-gathered but bad (date).

A مغسل *maghsal* or *maghsil*, (pl. مغاسل *maghāsil*) A bathing-place or vessel, especially for dead bodies. *Mighsal*, That with which any thing is washed. (A stallion-camel) which covers (or a man who cohabits) much, but ineffectually.

A مغسلة *maghsilat*, Name of certain ground at Madīna where clothes are washed.

A مغسوس *maghsūs*, (A camel) affected with the disease غساس *ghusās*. Newly-gathered but worthless (date).

A مغسوسة *maghsūsat*, A she-cat. A palm-tree whose dates are ripe but destitute of sweetness.

A مغسول *maghsūl*, Washed, cleaned.

A مغشم *mighsham*, Intrepid. Headstrong. Conceited, self-opiniated, following one's own fancies.

A مغشوش *maghshūsh*, Adulterated, falsified, deceitful. Insincere. مغشوش طبيعت *maghshūsh-tabīʻat*, Deceitful by nature, a cheat.

A مغشّى *mughashsha'*, Embroidered.

A مغشىّ *maghshīy*, Surprised, taken unawares. مغشىّ عليه *maghshīy ʻalayhi*, Fainted away.

A مغص *maghs* or *maghas*, Cholic, gripes. *Maghas*, The best species of camels. Heavy.

A مغصوب *maghsūb*, Seized by force; ravished.

A مغضب *mughzab*, Provoked to anger, irritated. *Mughzib*, One who provokes to anger; irritant.

A مغضبة *maghzabat*, (v. n. of غضب) Being angry, in a rage. Anger, rage, wrath.

A مغضّة *maghazzat*, Meanness. Defect, deficiency.

A مغضر *mughzir*, Affluent, well off.

A مغضف *mughzif*, Dark (night). Weak, flaccid, pendulous. (A palm-tree) whose fruit is not good.

A مغضّن *mughazzan*, Wrinkled. Folded, plaited.

A مغضوب *maghzūb*, Irritated, incensed. Afflicted with small-pox. مغضوب عليه *maghzūbun ʻalayhi*, Odious, one against whom anger is felt.

A مغضوث *maghzūs*, Disturbed, perplexed.

A مغضور *maghzūr*, Affluent, well off.

A مغضي *mughzī*, Dark (night).

A مغط *maght*, (v. n. of مغط) Extending, stretching (any thing elastic). Exerting one's strength to draw (a bow).

A مغطش *mughtish*, Dark (night). (God) making (night) dark.

A مغطغط *mughatghit*, Bubbling, wallopping (pot).

A مغطل *mughtil*, Very dark (cloud).

A مغطّى *mughatta'*, Covered, concealed, hidden.

A مغظغظة *mughazghazat* or *mughazghizat*, Furiously-boiling (pot).

A مغفار *mighfār*, (مغفر *mighfar*, or *mughfur*) (pl. مغافر *maghāfir* and مغافير *maghāfīr*) An esculent vegetable substance of the consistency and taste of honey, but of a strong smell.

A مغفر *mighfar*, Mail or network of steel worn under the cap or hat; also a protection for the face worn in battle. *Mughfir*, (pl. مغفرات *mughfirāt*) A wild she-goat, the mother of a kid (غفر *ghufr*).

A مغفرة *maghfirat*, (v. n. of غفر) Pardoning, condoning, forgiving, remitting sins, absolving. Remission, forgiveness. A wild she-goat, the mother of a kid called غفر *ghufr*. P سلطان مغفرت آشيان *sultāni maghfirat-āshyān*, The prince whose sins are forgiven, the deceased monarch. A *Mighfarat*, Mail or network of steel worn under the cap. *Mughfirat*, A wild she-goat, the mother of a kid.

A مغفق *maghfik*, A place of return.

A مغفّل *mughaffal*, Destitute of genius, attention, or presence of mind. Negligent, careless, thoughtless, heedless, incurious, ignorant. Dull, stupid.

A مغفلة *maghfalat*, Hairs growing between the under-lip and the chin.

A مغفور *maghfūr*, Pardoned, forgiven. (or مغفور له *maghfūrun lahu*) One whose sins are forgiven, the pious defunct. Relapsed (sick man). *Mughfūr*, (pl. مغافير *maghāfīr*) An esculent juice, of the consistency of honey, extracted from the plants ثمام *sumām*, عشر *ʻushar*, and رمث *rims*.

A مغفوراء *maghfūrāʼ*, (Ground) producing مغافير.

A مغفير *mighfīr*, (pl. مغافير *maghāfīr*) An esculent vegetable substance resembling honey.

P مغكده *mugh-kada*, A tavern. A fire-temple.

P مغل *maghl*, Sleep, rest. *Mughul*, The Great Mogul, emperor of Hindūstān. The Moguls, Tartars, natives of Tūrān, Scythia, or Transoxiana. The Georgian Christians.

A مغل *maghl*, (v. n. of مغل) Accusing, whispering against, slandering. *Maghl* or *maghal*, The milk of a pregnant animal. *Maghal*, (v. n. of مغل) Eating earth along with grass and being griped thereby (cattle). Giving suck whilst pregnant. Being diseased (the eye).

A مغلّ *mughill*, A traitor, deceiver. (Land) fruitful in grain and produce (غلّة *ghallat*).

A مغلاء *mighlāʼ*, An arrow discharged with the utmost force.

A مغلاة *mighlāt*, A long throw of a dart. A light arrow. ناقة مغلاة الوهق *nākatun mighlātu'l wahak*, A she-camel running away very fast, and avoiding the noose which one tries to throw over her.

P مغلاج *magh-lāj*, or مغلاغ *magh-lāgh*, A trap-ball.

A مغلاط *mighlāt*, One who blunders much.

A مغلاق *mighlāk*, A lock, bar, bolt, or any instrument for fastening a door.

P مغلاك *mughlāk*, Wretched, poor, contemptible. A poor man, religious mendicant.

A مغلب *maghlab*, Victory, dominion, power.

A مغلّب *mughallab*, Often conquered or defeated. (A poet) the conqueror of his cotemporaries, and acknowledged by them as superior.

A مغلبة *maghlabat*, Victory, power, conquest.

A مغلة *maghlat*, (pl. مغال *mighāl*) A sheep or goat bringing forth twice in one year. The belly-ache in cattle. Wickedness, mischief, violence. *Maghilat*, Cattle griped from eating earth with the young herbage.

A مغلّة *mughallat*, The fruits of the earth.

A مغلج *mighlaj*, (A horse) going or running well. (An ass) which drives the female before him.

P مغلچين *mughalchīn*, A fine black eye.

A مغلصمة *mughalsamat*, (fem.) Tied by the neck.

A مغلطة *maghlatat*, An improper question, liable to mistake or misapprehension. A labyrinth.

A مغلّظ *mughallaz*, Severe, heavy (mulct for bloodshed). Solemn, binding (oath). Very foul, impure, offensive. *Mughalliz*, Whatever renders coarse, strong, or offensive (غليظ *ghalīz*).

A مغلغل *mughalghal*, (or مغلغلة *mughalghalat*) A letter or message borne from country to country.

A مغلق *mighlak*, A lock, bolt. (pl. مغاليق *maghālīk* or مغالق *maghālik*) Any of the arrows used in games of chance. The seventh gaming arrow. *Mughlak*, Shut, closed, fastened (door). Abstruse, abstract, obscure, difficult.

P مغلگاه *maghl-gāh*, A sleeping-place.

A مغلم *mughlim*, Libidinous. A pederast.

A مغلمى *mughlimā*, Unnatural lust for boys.

A مغلنبي *mughlambī*, One who conquers another, and thereupon becomes great.

A مغلندف *mughlandif*, (or مغلنظف *mughlanzif*) Very dark, close, shady.

A مغلوب *maghlūb*, Conquered, overcome. مغلوب خوف و هراس *maghlūbi khawf u hirās*, Struck with dread and confusion. مغلوب و مقهور *maghlūb u mak-hūr*, Overcome and subjected. غير مغلوب *ghayr maghlūb*, Unconquered, invincible.

A مغلوبة *mughlūbat*, Thickly-planted (garden).

A مغلوبيّة *maghlūbiyat*, Subjugation; the state and condition of being conquered; vassalage.

A مغلوث *maghlūs*, Mixed. (Bread) made of wheat and barley. Seasoned with the flavour of dates (a leathern bottle).

A مغلوق *maghlūk*, Shut, barred, locked, bolted. (A skin) tanned with the herb غلقة *ghalkat*. *Mughlūk*, A bolt, bar, or lock.

A مغلول *maghlūl*, One whose hands are tied to the neck. Pilloried. Fettered. Oppressed with thirst.

A مغلولبة *mughlawlibat*, Thickly-planted (garden).

A مغلي *mughlī*, One who makes dear, finds or considers dear, buys or sells dear (غالي *ghālī*).

P مغلي قندز *mughulī kunduz*, Tartar children. Fearless, intrepid. Bloodthirsty.

A مغليم *mighlīm*, (fem. مغلمة) Lustful.

A مغمّ *mughimm*, Intensely hot, suffocating (day). Melancholy (day). (A country) abundant in plants.

A مغمّج *mughammaj*, (Water) without sweetness.

A مغمد *mughmad*, Sheathed (sword).

A مغمّر *mughammar*, Inexperienced. *Mughammir*, One who throws himself into the thickest and most thronged part. Silly, foolish. (See تغمير.)

A مغمز *maghmaz*, Any thing liable to detraction or misconstruction. A state or place of desire; also of reproach or stabbing.

A مغمض *maghmaz*, Very low ground.

A مغمّض *mughammaz*, Obscure, unintelligible. *Mughammiz*, Who goes over and knows a matter.

A مغمّضات *mughammizāt*, Sins which an intelligent man commits knowingly.

A مغمغة *maghmaghat*, (v. n. of مغمغ Q) Chewing (meat) partially. Speaking obscurely. Moving (a garment about in water when washing it). Thrusting (his) muzzle into a pot (a dog). Moistening (sliced bread) with fat. Mixing. Being mixed. Mixture, confusion. A weak and bad business.

A مغمل *mighmal*, Greedy in eating dirt. *Mughmil*, A woman who gives suck whilst pregnant, or who bears every year, and conceives afresh before the child is weaned.

A مغمّم *mughammim*, (A cloud or sea) full of water.

A مغمود *maghmūd*, Sheathed (sword).

A مغمور *maghmūr*, Overwhelmed. Obscure, mean, abject, unknown, without rank or dignity.

A مغموز *maghmūz*, Accused. Suspected.

A مغموص عليه *maghmūsun ع alayhi*, One who is reproached on account of religion.

A مغموق *maghmūk*, Full grown and nearly ripe (date). (A camel) diseased in the loins.

A مغمول *maghmūl*, Mean, obscure. Unknown. Covered over with bed-clothes in order to get a sweat. (Green fruits or herbs) put under straw in order to ripen. Macerated (hide) in order to get the hair off. Heaped up (herbage).

A مغموم *maghmūm*, Afflicted, sad, melancholy. Beclouded, overcast. Troubled with cold in the head.

P مغمومه *maghmūma*, Fried brinjals.

A مغمون *maghmūn*, Put under ground.

A مغميّ عليه *mughman* (or مغميّ *maghmīyun*) ع*alayhi*, Fainted away, fallen into a swoon.

A مغنّ *mughinn*, (A valley) resonant with the buzzing of flies. (A valley) rich in herbage.

A مغناة *maghnāt* or *mughnāt*, (v. n. of غني) Supplying the place of another; acting as well as he did.

A مغناج *mighnāj*, Attractive, lovely, coquettish.

A مغناطيس *maghnātīs*, (مغنطيس *maghnatīs*, or مغنيطيس *maghnītīs*) The magnet or loadstone.

P مغند *mughund*, (or مغنده *mughanda*) Every thing which makes an excrescence on the body, as a wen, swollen gland, strained sinew, wind pent up in any limb; a callous protuberance from a broken bone; the cicatrice of a wound. A horse-market. Any thing mixed or confused.

P مغندگي *mughundagī* or *mughandagī*, A protuberance, lump, bump, or swelling.

A مغنم *maghnam*, Spoil, plunder, booty. Any thing acquired without labour.

A مغنمة *mughnamat*, (or مغنّمة *mughannamat*) Many (sheep), numerous (flocks).

P مغنود *maghnūd*, Sleeping, asleep. Fainting.

A مغنوظ *maghnūz*, One who labours under great affliction, even to the point of death, sorely grieved.

A مغنى *maghna'*, (pl. مغاني *maghānī*) A pleasant mansion, the abode of cheerfulness. Ability to do without. Remedy. Flight, escape. Worthy, fit. *Mughnī*, Who or what supplies the place of, excuses, or dispenses with; independent. غير مغني *ghayr mughnī*, Not dispensing, not independent.

A مغنّي *mughannī*, A singer.

A مغنّية *mughanniyat*, A female musician, singer.

P مغنيسا *maghnīsā*, A black earth brought from a mountain in Kāshān. A coloured stone very soft, used by glass-makers.

A مغو *maghw*, The mewing (of a cat).

A مغواة *mighwāt*, A country in which one is very liable to lose one's way.

A مغوّاة *mughawwāt*, (pl. مغوّيات *mughawwayāt*) A ditch made for decoying and catching wild beasts. A country where one is liable to stray.

A مغوار *mighwār*, A warrior, one who makes many excursions (غارة *ghārat*) to lay waste and plunder an enemy's country: engaged in forays.

A مغوثة *maghūsat*, A succouring, an assisting.

A مغوّس *mughawwas*, (A palm) stript of thorns.

P مغوشا *mughūshā*, A sect of the Magi.

P مغوشك *mughūshak*, Christian monks. Magi.

A مغوّصة *mughawwasat*, A woman who persuades her husband that she is menstruous when not.

A مغول *mighwal*, A long small sword. A long spear-head. A piece of iron inserted within a whip. A man's name. ذات مغول *zāt mighwal*, (A horse) swift, outstripping all others.

P مغول *mughol*, A Mogul.

A مغوي *mughwī*, One who causes to err.

A مغويّ *maghwīy*, Free, at liberty. Empty-bellied.

A مغي *maghy*, (v. n. of مغي) Speaking pleasantly, clearly, and openly. Softness or laxity of leather. A praising of any one for qualities which he does not possess (either in jest or in earnest).

P مغي *mughī*, The religion of the Magi.

A مغيار *mighyār*, (pl. مغائير *maghā'ir*) Jealous.

P مغياز *maghyāz* or *mighyāz*, A small gratuity over and above the regular hire.

A مغيال *mighyāl*, Entangled, leafy, shady (tree).

A مغيب *maghīb*, (v. n. of غاب for غيب) Being absent or hidden. Absence. Setting (of the sun). *Mughīb* or *mughyib*, (A woman) having an absent (غائب *ghā'ib*) husband.

A مغيّب *mughayyab*, Hidden, invisible.

A مغيّبات *mughayyabāt*, (pl. fem.) Mysteries, secrets, concealed things.

A مغيبة *mughībat*, (A woman) whose husband is absent (غائب *ghā'ib*).

A مغيّبة *mughayyabat*, A mystery, secret.

A مغيث *maghīs*, (A field) watered by rain. Corn laid by the rain. *Mughīs*, Who gives aid, auxiliary.

A مغيثيّة *mughīsīyat*, A college at Baghdād.

A مغير *maghīr*, Watered by rain. (Milk) red, mingled with blood. *Mughīr*, One who makes a predatory incursion, a spoiler, plunderer.

A مغيّر *mughayyar*, Changed, altered. *Mughayyir*, Variable, changeable.

A مغيربان *mughayribān*, (pl. مغيريانات) Setting of the sun, when just beginning to go down.

A مغيرة *maghīrat*, Watered ground. *Mughīrat*, Light horsemen, when making a plundering excursion into an enemy's country.

A مغيض *maghīz*, A place of little (water).

A مغيظ *maghīz*, Incensed.

A مغيل *mughyal*, Suckled (infant) whilst the mother is pregnant or cohabiting with a man. *Mughil* or *mughyil*, (A woman) so suckling an infant.

A مغيّل *mughayyal*, Fixed and settled among thorns and bushes (غيل *ghīl* or *ghayl*): a bushman.

P مغيلان *mughaylān*, (for امّ غيلان *umm ghaylān*) Egyptian or Arabian thorns, different from acacia. خار مغيلان *khāri mughaylān*, The thorn of this tree, in imitation of which caltrops are made. مغيلان باستان *mughaylān bāstān*, (or مغيلان گاه *mughaylān-gāh*) The world. Time. Fortune.

A مغيوب *maghyūb*, Absent, hid, invisible.

A مغيوث *maghyūs*, (A field) wetted with rain.

A مغيور *maghyūr*, (A field) rained upon.

A مفاء *mufā'*, A servant, a slave.

A مفآد *mif'ād*, A poker. A spit.

A مفاتح *mafātih*, (pl. of مفتح *miftah*) Keys.

A مفاتحة *mufātahat*, (v. n. 3 of فتح) Beginning to converse or tell a story. Bidding for any thing but without making a deposit. Going (together) before a judge or arbiter. Carnal connexion.

A مفاتكة *mufātakat*, (v. n. 3 of فتك) Carrying on open hostilities, being an undisguised enemy. Rushing on, attacking, falling foul upon together. Keeping (any one). Assiduous, unremitting. Bidding and making a deposit.

A مفاتيح *mafātīh*, (pl. of مفتاح *miftāh*) Keys.

A مفاجّا *mufājjan*, (Going) with toes turned out.

A مفاجأة *mufāja'at*, (v. n. 3 of فجأ) Falling upon any thing unexpectedly, rushing upon unawares, and snatching. Accosting. P مرگ مفاجات *margi mufājāt*, Sudden death.

A مفاجاة *mufājāt*, A sudden surprise.

A مفاجة *mafājat*, Foolish, stupid (man).

A مفاجر *mafājir*, (pl. of مفجرة *mafjarat*) Large channels or valleys through which water runs.

A مفاجئ *mufāji'*, One who comes unexpectedly. المفاجئ *al mufāji'*, The lion (the surpriser).

A مفاحشة *mufāhashat*, (v. n. 3 of فحش) Bandying ribaldry (فحش *fuhsh*) between each other.

A مفاحص *mafāhis*, (pl. of مفحص *mafhas*) Nests of the قطا *katā*. *Mufāhis*, A pryer into the secrets and failings of his neighbour.

A مفاحصة *mufāhasat*, (v. n. 3 of فحص) Inveighing against, prying into secrets and faults.

A مفاخذة *mufākhazat*, (v. n. 3 of فخذ) Assembling tribes. Sitting knee to knee.

A مفاخر *mafākhir*, (pl. of مفخرة *mafkharat*) Ornaments. Glories. Illustrious actions. مفاخر الاماثل و الاقران *mafākhiru'l amāsil wa'l akrān*, The eminent amongst their peers (officers of state). *Mufākhir*, Glorious. Vain-glorious.

A مفاخرة *mufākharat*, (v. n. 3 of فخر) Boasting against, contending for glory. Arrogance.

A مفاخزة *mufākhazat*, (v. n. 3 of فخز) Bragging, boasting, glorying against each other.

A مفأد *mif'ad*, (مفآد *mif'ād*, or مفأدة *mif'adat*) (pl. مفائد *mafā'id*) A poker, or any thing used in stirring an oven. A spit.

A مفاداة *mufādāt*, (v. n. 3 of فدي) Ransoming.

A مفأرة *mafʼarat*, (A country) abounding in mice.

A مفارخ *mafārikh*, Birds' nests, places where the young or chicks (فرخ *farkh*) are hatched.

A مفارزة *mufārazat*, (v. n. 3 of فرز) Breaking off, interrupting. Settling accounts (with a partner), dissolving partnership.

A مفارش *mafārish*, Carpets. Wives. كريم المفارش *karīmu'l mafārish*, One who weds honourable or respected wives.

A مفارصة *mufārasat*, (v. n. 3 of فرص) Observing rotation, doing any thing alternately with another.

A مفارطة *mufāratat*, (v. n. 3 of فرط) Contending, endeavouring to get a superiority over another. Finding, meeting with.

A مفارع *mafāriʻ*, (pl. of مفرع *mifraʻ*) Arbiters, umpires. Peace-makers.

A مفارق *mafārik*, (pl. of مفرق *mafrak* and *mafrik*) Crowns of heads where the hair parts. Places where roads branch off. Faces, aspects.

A مفارقة *mufārakat*, (v. n. 3 of فرق) Quitting, leaving. Separation, alienation, absence.

A مفاركة *mufārakat*, (v. n. 3 of فرك) Leaving, dismissing, giving up.

A مفارم *mafārim*, Astringent medicaments, constrictive lotions used by women.

A مفازة *mafāzat*, Flight. Escape, deliverance. (pl. مفاوز *mafāwiz*) A place where one obtains a victory; also whither people fly; and likewise where they perish: hence, A desert without water.

A مفازع *mufāziʻ*, Terrified, frightened.

A مفازعة *mufāzaʻat*, Act of frightening, terrifying.

A مفاسد *mafāsid*, (pl. of مفسدة *mafsadat*) Evils.

A مفاشغة *mufāshaghat*, (v. n. 3 of فشغ) Slaughtering a camel's colt and bringing another for her to take a liking to.

A مفاشقة *mufāshakat*, (v. n. 3 of فشق) Attacking suddenly, falling upon unexpectedly.

A مفاصل *mafāsil*, (pl. of مفصل *mafsil*) Joints. Any gravelly spots between two mountains where the water is clear and cold. Spots lying between mountains and sands. وجع مفاصل *wajaʻi mafāsil*, A pain in the joints.

A مفاصلات *mafāsilāt*, Joints of the fingers, &c.

A مفاصلة *mufāsalat*, (v. n. 3 of فصل) Breaking off. Closing accounts. Dissolving partnership. Distance, interval, space, separation.

A مفاض *mufāz*, Large, diffusive, extended. Ample, profuse. Even, on a level. مفاض فيه *mufāzun fīhi*, (A speech) lengthened out. مفاض البطن *mufāzu'l batn*, One whose breast and belly are equally prominent.

A مفاضة *mufāzat*, Wide, roomy (coat of mail or woman). Large-bellied (woman).

A مفاضح *mafāzih*, (pl. of مفضحة) Disgraces.

A مفاضخ *mafāzikh*, Jars for holding grape-juice.

A مفاضل *mafāzil*, (pl. of مفضل *mifzal*) Every-day clothes.

A مفاضلة *mufāzalat*, A contending for excellence.

A مفاطنة *mufātanat*, (v. n. 3 of فطن) Attending to (any one) in order to understand (him). Displaying acumen to one another.

A مفاطير *mafātīr*, (pl. of مفطر *muftir*) Those who breakfast.

A مفاغمة *mufāghamat*, (v. n. 3 of فغم) Kissing.

A مفاقر *mafākir*, Poverties, miseries. سدّ الله مفاقره *sadda'llāhu mafākirahu*, May God end his poverty, or enrich him!

A مفاقمة *mufākamat*, (v. n. 3 of فقم) Lying with.

A مفاقهة *mufākahat*, (v. n. 3 of فقه) Disputing, discussing a point in religion, law, or science.

A مفاكهة *mufākahat*, (v. n. 3 of فكه) Jesting (with another), being merry, facetious, joyous.

A مفالتة *mufālatat*, A coming upon unexpectedly.

A مفالذة *mufālazat*, (v. n. 3 of فلذ) Casting words upon each other.

A مفاليج *mafālīj*, (pl. of مفلوج) Paralytics.

A مفأم *mifʼam*, (and مفآم *mifʼām*) (A camel) fat between the shoulder-blades. *Mufʼam*, (or مفأّم *mufaʼʼam*) Enlarged (camel's pack-saddle).

A مفاناة *mufānāt*, (v. n. 3 of فني) Treating kindly. Quieting, giving rest.

A مفانذة *mufānadat*, Act of urging, pressing.

A مفانق *mufānik*, Easy, delicate (life).

A مفانقة *mufānakat*, (v. n. 3 of فنق) Treating indulgently, pampering.

A مفانكة *mufānakat*, (v. n. 3 of فنك) Eating up the whole, sticking close to it, without shame.

A مفاوز *mafāwiz*, (pl. of مفازة *mafāzat*) Places whither people fly. Deserts.

A مفاوصة *mufāwasat*, (v. n. 3 of فاص for فوص) Explaining; explanation. Clearness, distinctness.

A مفاوض *mufāwaz*, Equal (partnership).

A مفاوضة *mufāwazat*, (v. n. 3 of فاض for فوض) Having business (with another), consulting or explaining any thing (with him). Causing to flow. Going or running with another. Agreeing. An epistle, a letter (from a superior to an inferior). Conversation. Partnership. A rejoinder. Equality.

P مفاوضه شدن *mufāwaza shudan*, To be a companion or equal to another. مفاوضه كردن *mufāwaza kardan*, To return, make retribution, recompense.

A مفاوضةً *mufāwazatan*, Reciprocally, alternately.

A مفاوهة *mufāwahat*, (v. n. 3 of فاه for فوه) Talking together. Boasting against.

A مفاويق *mafāwīk*, (pl. of مفيق *mufīk* and مفيقة *mufīkat*) Camels having milk in their udders between two milkings.

A مفاهاة *mufāhāt*, A talking with. A boasting.

A مفاهر *mafāhir*, Flesh of the breast.

A مفائد *mafāʼid*, (pl. of مفأد *mifʼad*, مفأاد *mifʼād*, and مفأدة *mifʼadat*) Sticks for stirring the fire; pokers. Spits.

A مفايشة *mufāyashat*, Boast, menace, vaunting threat in battle. Contention for superiority.

A مفائل *mufāʼil*, One who divides the heaps of soil in the game فئال *fiʼāl*.

A مفائلة *mufāʼalat*, (v. n. 3 of فأل) Playing at the game فئال *fiʼāl*.

A مفايلة *mufāyalat*, (v. n. 3 of فال for فيل) Being weak in mind, erring in opinion or conjecture. Imbecility, folly. A game at which boys play.

P مفت *muft*, Gratuitously, without payment, gratis. مفت خوار *muft-khwār*, A parasite, one who eats for nothing.

A مفتاح *miftāh*, (pl. مفاتيح *mafātīh*) A key, or any instrument with which a door is opened. A mark made upon the thigh or neck.

A مفتأد *muftaʼad*, (Bread) baked under the ashes; also the place where it is baked.

A مفتّت *mufattat*, Broken to bits, crumbled, comminuted. *Mufattit*, Who or what crumbles or breaks in pieces.

A مفتّتات *mufattitāt*, Lythontriptics.

A مفتتح *muftatah*, Opened. Commenced, begun. Taken (city). *Muftatih*, Conqueror, taker (of a city).

A مفتتن *muftatin*, Fallen into temptation. A trier, tempter. Bereft of property and reason.

A مفتجر *muftajar*, A sandy place.

A مفتح *maftah*, A storehouse, cellar. A treasury. *Miftah*, (pl. مفاتح *mafātih*) A key.

A مفتّح *mufattah*, Open. Taken (town). *Mufattih*, A conqueror, taker of towns. Deobstruent.

A مفتّحات *mufattihāt*, Medicines which remove obstructions, deobstruents.

A مفتخر *muftakhir*, Boastful. Splendid, gorgeous, sumptuous. P مفتخر و مباهي شدن *muftakhir u mubāhī shudan*, To glory, boast, vaunt.

A مفتدى *muftadaʼ*, Redeemed. *Muftadī*, One who ransoms himself, a self-redeemer.

A مفترس *muftaris*, (A lion) tearing (prey).

A مفترش *muftarish*, A tracker. A treader, trampler. (See افتراش *iftirāsh*.)

A مفترص *muftaris*, Seizer (of an opportunity).

A مفترط *muftarit*, One who loses a son before he has attained the age of puberty.

A مفترع *muftariʻ*, A ravisher, deflowerer.

A مفترغ *muftarigh*, One who pours out (water for or upon himself).

A مفترق *muftarik*, Dispersed, scattered.

A مفترم *muftarim*, A woman who ties on the menstruous cloth فرام *firām*.

A مفتري *muftarī*, Liar, slanderer: knave, rogue. Clad in a fur dress (فرو *farw*).

A مفتّش *mufattish*, An inquisitor, commissary, examiner, superintendant, censor, syndic, visitor.

A مفتصد *muftasid*, One who opens a vein.

A مفتصع *muftasiʻ*, A lad who draws back the foreskin over the gland. One who forces (from a debtor that which he owes).

A مفتض *muftazz*, The taker of a maidenhead.

A مفتضح *muftazih*, Disgraced, exposed to infamy. Infamous. Evident, apparent.

A مفتعل *mufta͑al*, Made, framed, invented. A stupendous or arduous deed.

A مفتعّل *mufta͑ill*, Badly-trimmed (arrow).

A مفتق *maftah*, The opening (of a shirt).

A مفتقد *muftakad*, Missed, inquired after.

A مفتقر *muftakir*, Reduced to poverty.

A مفتّل *mufattal*, Twisted.

A مفتلة *maftalat*, A circular piece of wood put on a spindle to give it a steady motion when spinning.

A مفتلت *muftalat*, Suddenly snatched away, dying unexpectedly. *Muftalit*, An extempore speaker.

A مفتلذ *muftaliz*, One who takes a portion.

A مفتلط *muftalit*, Seized suddenly.

A مفتلق *muftalik*, Strange, wonderful, marvellous (speaker or runner).

A مفتلي *muftalī*, One who weans. Who educates. A keeper, guardian.

A مفتن *muftan*, Tempted, seduced to evil, drawn into sedition. Charmed, bewitched. Mad, insane. Assayed, standard (money). *Muftin*, A tempter, seducer, who leads astray.

A مفتّن *mufattan*, (Gold) tried by the fire, or (a man) by temptations. Thrown into disorder, excited to sedition or any thing bad. Burnt.

A مفتوت *maftūt*, Broken, crumbled. Cleft.

A مفتوح *maftūh*, Opened. Occupied, taken (town). Subdued. (A letter) marked with the vowel فتحه *fatha* ـَ *a*. Diluted (colour). جمله قلاع مفتوحه *jumla kilā͑i maftūha*, All the castles taken.

A مفتوق *maftūk*, Ruptured.

A مفتول *maftūl*, Twisted.

P مفتول سر *maftūl-sar*, Wry-headed.

A مفتون *maftūn*, (Gold) tried in the fire. Drawn into sedition. Seduced into evil. Insane, fascinated, charmed, mad with love. Deserted by his reason and property. Experiment, trial, proof.

A مفتي *muftī*, Wise. One whose sentence has the authority of the law, an expounder of the Muhammadan law; the muftī or head law-officer amongst the Turks (above a قاضي *kāzī*, or judge). Name of a certain measure.

A مفثّة *mafassat*, Multitude, plenty, abundance. كثير مفثّة *kasīru mafassatin*, Abundant in hospitality.

A مفج *mafj*, (v. n. of مفج) Being foolish.

A مفجّ *mufijj*, Protuberant, rounded, convex (hoof of a horse).

A مفجر *mafjar*, A place where water gushes out. *Mufjir*, Present at day-break (فجر *fajr*).

A مفجرة *mafjarat*, (pl. مفاجر *mafājir*) A wide channel through which a torrent runs. Level ground along which a river runs.

A مفجوع *mafjū͑*, Oppressed, overwhelmed.

A مفحش *mufhish*, Obscene in talk, ribaldish.

A مفحص *mafhas*, A nest of the bird قطا *katā*.

A مفحم *mufham*, Unable to repeat verses. Silenced, unable to reply.

A مفخّر *mufakhkhar*, Glorified, glorious, exalted.

A مفخرة *mafkha* or *mafkhurat*, A thing in which a man glories, or which gives him pre-eminence.

A مفخّم *mufakhkham*, Magnified, great, glorious, illustrious. Broad, openly pronounced.

A مفخوذ *mafkhūz*, Hurt in the thigh.

A مفدر *mufdir*, Anti-aphrodisiacal (diet).

A مفدرة *mafdarat*, A place frequented by mountain-goats. Anti-aphrodisiacal (diet). *Mafdarat* or *mafdurat*, (pl. of فدر *fadar*) Aged or full-grown mountain-goats.

A مفدغ *mifdagh*, Any implement for breaking.

A مفدغم *mufadgham*, Full-faced (man).

A مفدم *mufdam*, (Cloth) dyed of a full or unmixed red. Full and thick (colour). *Mufdam* or *mufaddam*, (A water-pot) covered with a lid or stopple.

A مفدّمة *mufaddamat*, Muzzled (ox).

A مفدوح *mafdūh*, Oppressed with debt.

A مفذّ *mufizz*, A ewe which brings forth but one lamb at a birth.

A مفذاذ *mifzāz*, (A sheep or camel) accustomed to bring forth only one at a time.

A مفرّ *mafarr* or *mafirr*, (v. n. of فرّ) Fleeing away. *Mafirr*, An asylum, whither one flies for refuge. *Mifarr*, Generous (horse), ready for flight, on which one may easily escape.

A مفرّات *mufirrāt*, (Days) which bring news.

A مفراح *mifrāh*, Glad, exulting, joyous, fain.

A مفراد *mifrād*, (A she-camel) pasturing alone.

A مفراش *mufrāsh*, (in the idiom of Morocco) A sack in which a bed is laid up.

A مفراص *mifrās*, Shears for cutting silver or iron.

A مفرج *mufraj*, One who has no near relations or patron. The upper part of the mouth, the palate. Slain (man), and found far from a town. *Mufrij*, A good archer, but sometimes missing. (A hen) having chickens (فرّوج *farrūj* or *furrūj*).

A مفرّج *mufarraj*, Large, wide, opened, cleft, sundered, divided. A comb. One whose elbow is distant from the side or arm-pit.

A مفرجن *mufarjan*, Curried (horse).

A مفرح *mufrah*, Poor, oppressed with debt. An obscure man, known neither from birth nor from connections. One whose debts must be paid from the public treasury. Found killed between two towns. *Mufrih*, Exhilarant.

A مفرّح *mufarrih*, Exhilarating, who or what makes cheerful. A species of exhilarating medicine, in which rubies are an ingredient. مفرّح قلب *mufarrihi kalb*, Rejoicing the heart.

A مفرخ *mufrikh*, (A bird) having young.

A مفرخة *mufrakhat*, A bird's nest.

A مفرد *mufrad*, Single, simple, alone, solitary, unique. Sent alone, without a companion. بمفرده *bi mufradihi*, Alone, by himself. *Mufrid*, One who engages in or does any work alone. One who singles out. One who sends an ambassador. A woman who brings forth one child.

A مفرّد *mufarrad*, (Gold) set with or separated by the pearls called فريد *farīd* or فرائد *farā͗id*. *Mufarrid*, A Muhammadan lawyer. One who retires to lead a solitary religious life. One who has outlived all his cotemporaries and children. One who travels alone, his beast his sole companion.

A مفردة *mufradat*, Simple. The minor term in logic. Singular number. مفردات الطبّ *mufradātu 't tibb*, Simples in medicine.

A مفردخ *mufardakh*, Large, thick, and soft.

A مفردس *mufardas*, Large (breast).

P مفرد سوار *mufrad-suwār*, Who rides alone.

P مفرس *mafras*, Ornaments suspended from the ceiling.

A مفرّس *mufarras*, Adopted into the Persian.

A مفرسخ *mufarsakh*, Wide (breeches).

A مفرسن *mufarsan*, Fleshy about the face.

A مفرش *mifrash*, A coverlet, counterpane. A travelling-bag, a sac-de-nuit.

A مفرّش *mufarrash*, Bunchless (camel). (A bed) spread on the ground. *Mufarrish*, One who spreads (a carpet, &c.). One who paves a house with flag-stones. (Corn) which extends its leaves along the ground.

A مفرشة *mifrashat*, A saddle-cloth laid upon a camel's saddle.

A مفرّشة *mufarrishat*, A skin-wound on the head, without any fracture.

A مفرص *mifras*, Shears for cutting silver or iron.

A مفرض *mifraz*, A tool for cutting or notching.

A مفرضخ *mufarzakh*, Infirm, weak.

A مفرط *mufrat*, Left, deserted, forgotten. Sent before. Hastened. (A cistern) full, overflowed with water. *Mufrit*, One who exceeds bounds. Transcendent, transcendental. Excessive.

A مفرطح *mufartah*, Broad and flat.

A مفرطم *mufartam*, Pointed (boot).

A مفرع *mifra͑*, (pl. مفارع *mafāri͑*) Arbiters, peace-makers. *Mufra͑*, Broad (in the shoulder-blades). *Mufri͑*, Descending. لقيت فلانا فارعا مفرعا *lakītu fulānan fāri͑an mufri͑an*, I met so-and-so, one of us ascending, the other descending.

A مفرغ *mufragh*, (A ring) cast in a mould, founded, so that the joining is not perceptible.

A مفرّغ *mufarragh*, Empty. *Mufarrigh*, One who pours out. An emptier (of a vessel).

A مفرغة *mufraghat*, A ring solid, not hollow.

A مفرق *mafrak* or *mafrik*, (pl. مفارق *mafārik*) The place where the hair parts. The crown of the head. A place where a road separates into many. *Mufrik*, The mother (camel) of a dead colt. Lean (man). Fat (man).

A مفرّق *mufarrak*, Scattered. *Mufarrik*, One who separates, scatters, or divides. One who inspires with fear. مفرّق النعم *mufarriku 'n naʻam*, Separating flocks, *i.e.* the animal called ظربان *zaribān* (stinkard), because he disperses sheep when he gets amongst them.

A مفرقة *mafrikat*, A place where two ways meet.

A مفرقم *mufarkam*, One who slowly grows old. Badly fed.

A مفرّك *mufarrak*, (A man) hated by women.

A مفرّكة *mufarrakat*, (A woman) hated by men.

A مفركح *mufarkah*, One whose buttocks are high and prominent.

A مفروج *mafrūj*, Split, cracked, broken.

A مفروح *mafrūh*, Glad, exulting, rejoicing.

A مفروز *mafrūz*, Dispersed, separated. A Nazarite. (Cloth) having an elegant border. (Land) given in fee. Mended, sewed (garment).

A مفروش *mafrūsh*, Expanded, spread. Paved, flagged. A carpet.

A مفروض *mafrūz*, Cut off. Cut, nicked, notched. Divinely appointed, ordained by God, necessary to be observed. الصلوات المفروضة *as' salawātu'l mafrūzat*, The (five daily) prayers appointed, and considered as of perpetual obligation.

A مفروضات *mafrūzāt*, The commands of God.

A مفروغ *mafrūgh*, Discharged. Cut short.

A مفروق *mafrūk*, Separated, divided.

A مفروك *mafrūk*, Rubbed (ear of corn). Cracked with the fingers (louse). Dyed deeply. (A camel) whose shoulder is cut, and the nerve inside of whose upper-lip is split.

A مفره *mufrih*, (or مفرّهة *mufarrihat*) (A she-camel) bringing forth a brisk and lively colt.

A مفري *mufrī*, One who adjusts, arranges, rectifies. (See افراء *ifrā'*.)

A مفرّي *mufarra'*, (fem. مفرّاة) Covered with fur.

A مفزع *mafzaʻ*, An asylum. *Mufzaʻ*, Terrified, terror-stricken. *Mufziʻ*, Terrifying, horrible.

A مفزّع *mufazzaʻ*, Timorous, terrified. Brave.

A مفزعة *mafzaʻat*, Any thing which is a cause of terror (فزع *fazaʻ*). An asylum.

A مفزور *mafzūr*, High-backed or breasted (man).

A مفسا *mafsa'*, The anus (wind-letting part).

A مفسد *mufsid*, Mischievous, pernicious, destructive, corruptive, vitiating. A corrupter, depraver, destroyer, author of evil, malefactor, seditious man, breed-bate, mischief-maker.

A مفسدة *mafsadat*, An evil, pernicious thing, tending to disturb or corrupt (reverse of مصلحة).

A مفسّر *mufassar*, Explained, commented on. *Mufassir*, A commentator, expositor, or interpreter. مفسّرين *mufassirīn*, (obliq. pl.) Commentators.

A مفسّلة *mufassilat*, An artful, trickish woman, who evades the caresses of her husband under pretence of being menstruous or from other pretext.

A مفسوء *mafsuʼ*, Weak, broken-backed. One hollow-backed, protuberant-breasted, flat-hipped. One whose buttocks seem in pain when he walks.

A مفسوخ *mafsūkh*, Broken, dissolved.

A مفسوخيّة *mafsūkhīyat*, A rupture. Nullity.

A مفسود *mafsūd*, Corrupted, spoiled.

A مفسول *mafsūl*, (A man) of the worst kind.

A مفشّ *mufishsh*, Provocative of eructation.

A مفشغ *mifshagh*, One who accosts his friend with something disagreeable. Who checks or brings under. *Mufshigh*, That which has little good in it.

A مفشل *mifshal*, The covering of a camel-litter. One who chooses a foreign wife in the hope of having a vigorous, healthy offspring.

A مفشّي *mufashshī*, Wind-expelling.

A مفشّيات *mufashshiyāt*, Carminatives.

A مفصح *mufsih*, Clear. Eloquent. (A day) without cloud or cold. (See افصاح *ifsāh*.)

A مفصد *mifsad*, A lancet, fleam.

A مفصل *mafsil*, (pl. مفاصل *mafāsil*) A joint, juncture, articulation, the space between the joints. A space between two sand-hills, especially gravelly, where limpid water collects. A heap of flints. *Mifsal*, The tongue.

A مفصّل *mufassal*, Distinct, partitioned (as a bracelet, which between every two pearls has a larger gem or one of a different kind). Divided, separated, particularized, detailed. Fully described; separate, distinct, clear, ample. Cut off (as a garment). The subordinate divisions of a district (in contradistinction to the term صدر *sadr*, which implies the chief seat of government, or of the collectors of the public revenue). The Kur'ān from الحجرات *al hujurāt* (name of the 49th chapter) to to the end. *Mufassil*, One who enlarges upon, amplifies. One who distinguishes, who divides into parts.

A مفصّلاً *mufassalan*, Distinctly, minutely, prolixly, diffusively, in detail.

A مفصوخ *mafsūkh*, Cheated, gulled, imposed upon.

A مفصود *mafsūd*, One whose vein has been opened; bled, blooded.

A مفصول *mafsūl*, Separated, detached.

A مفصوم *mafsūm*, Broken without separation of the parts. Demolished, overthrown (house, tent).

A مفضاة *mufzāt*, A woman whose two passages have been made one by frequent cohabitation.

A مفضاج *mifzāj*, Thick, corpulent, soft.

A مفضاض *mifzāz*, A mallet, clod-crusher.

A مفضال *mifzāl*, Pre-eminent in beneficence; literally, an instrument of liberality.

A مفضّة *mifazzat*, A maul for crushing clods.

A مفضحة *mafzahat*, Reproach: disgrace, scandal.

A مفضخة *mifzakhat*, A stone with which unripe dates may be bruised. Capacious (bucket).

A مفضّض *mufazzaz*, Plated with silver, silvered.

A مفضغ *mifzagh*, One who distorts the corners of the mouth, and speaks indistinctly. One who takes pains to be eloquent, and commits blunders.

A مفضل *mifzal*, An every-day garment. One who excels greatly. *Mufzil*, One who leaves something redundant or remaining.

A مفضّل *mufazzal*, Excelling greatly, eminent in virtue and beneficence. Preferred. In the phrase زيد اعلم من بكر *zaydun aʻlamu mim bakrin*, Zayd is more learned than Bakr; Zayd is the مفضّل *mufazzal*, and Bakr the مفضّل عليه *mufazzal ʻalayhi*.

A مفضلة *mifzalat*, An every-day garment.

A مفضوح *mafzūh*, Exposed to infamy, shamed.

A مفضوخ *mafzūkh*, Bruised, crushed (date).

A مفضوض *mafzūz*, (Tears) profusely shed.

A مفضول *mafzūl*, Overcome, conquered.

A مفطّح *mufattah*, Broad (head).

A مفطر *muftir*, (pl. مفاطير *mafātīr*) One who breaks a long fast.

A مفطوح *maftūh*, Broad, wide (head).

A مفطوم *maftūm*, Weaned.

A مفظع *mufziʻ*, Base, shameful (affair).

A مفعاة *mafʻāt*, (A place) full of vipers.

A مفعّاة *mufaʻʻāt*, A (she-camel) branded with a mark in the form of a viper. The brand itself.

A مفعول *mafʻūl*, Made, done. Acted. Abused contrary to nature; a pathick. Passive voice. Accusative case. (in gram.) Governed. اسم مفعول *ismi mafʻūl*, Passive participle. المفعول به *al mafʻūlu bihi*, The object of a transitive verb. المفعول لاجله *al mafʻūlu li ajlihi*, Dative case. المفعول له *al mafʻūlu lahu*, Accusative case. المفعول معه *al mafʻūlu maʻahu*, Ablative case.

A مفعوليّة *mafʻūliyat*, The condition of the accusative case, accusativeness. The condition of the passive voice, passiveness, passivity.

A مفغرة *mafgharat*, A spacious district. A hole in a mountain smaller than a cave.

A مفغم *mufgham*, Excited; greedy.

A مفقاس *mifkās*, A crooked stick or bit of wood used in snaring birds, a springe.

A مفقاص *mifkās*, A knob at the end of a mace, capable of smashing every thing it strikes.

A مفقر *mufkar*, Impoverished. *Mufkir*, Strong and able to bring to pass. Strong in the فقارة *fakārat* or vertebræ (as a colt able to be ridden).

A مفقّر *mufakkar*, (A sword) notched on the side or back. Rough (sword). Equal to whatever one is commanded to do.

A مفقرة *mafkarat*, Poverty.

A مفقع *mufkiʻ*, Depressing (poverty), such as makes (one) crouch to the earth.

A مفقّع *mufakkaʻ*, Sharp-pointed (boot).

A مفقّعة *mufakkiʻat*, A black bird with white at the root of its tail.

A مفقلة *mifkalat*, A kind of winnowing machine.

A مفقود *mafkūd*, Disappeared, and concerning whom it is not known whether he be living or dead: lost, missing. Missed, regretted. Unfortunate, destitute, deprived, frustrated.

A مفقور *mafkūr*, Broken-backed. (A camel) pierced in the nose. Perforated, dug through.

A مفقوص *mafkūs*, Broken (egg).

A مفقّي *mufakkiء*, Earth-furrowing (torrent).

A مفكّر *mufakkir*, One who thinks deeply.

A مفكّرة *mufakkirat*, The thinking faculty.

A مفكّك *mufakkak*, Untied, unloosed.

A مفكوك *mafkūk*, Liberated, unloosed, manumitted. Pardoned. Open, not united by *tashdīd*.

A مفكول *mafkūl*, Trembling, tremulous.

A مفكه *mufkih*, (or مفكهة *mufkihat*) (A camel) that gives thick milk.

A مفلاق *miflāk*, Mean, despicable, destitute.

A مفلّج *mufallaj*, One whose fore-teeth are wide apart. Perplexed, paralysed, lame, bad (business).

A مفلح *muflih*, Prosperous, happy. A peasant.

P مفلحان *muflihān*, Name of a river. (Pers. pl. of A مفلح *muflih*) Villagers, husbandmen.

A مفلس *muflis*, Insolvent, bankrupt. Poor.

A مفلّس اللون *mufallasu'llawn*, Dapple-coloured, like fish-scales (فلس *fals*). (See تفليس *taflīs*.)

A مفلسي *muflisī*, Insolvency, bankruptcy.

A مفلطح *mufaltah*, Broad, flat (head). Spread out (snare).

A مفلّع *mufallaء*, (A water-bottle) sewed with thongs of leather.

A مفلفل *mufalfal*, (Wine) pungent as pepper. (A garment) embroidered as with cloves of pepper (فلفل *fulful* or *filfil*). Crisp (hair). Seasoned, spiced (meat). Well-tanned (leather).

A مفلق *muflik*, Wonderful (poet).

A مفلّق *mufallak*, Dried (peach) which separates from the stone.

A مفلقة *maflakat* or *muflakat*, Any thing strange and portentous. A misfortune.

A مفلّك *mufallik*, Swelling-breasted (girl). A bitch in heat. (See تفليك *taflīk*.)

A مفلّل *mufallal*, (A blade or head of a sword or spear) notched or teethed like a saw; serrated.

A مفلوج *maflūj*, Paralytic, palsied.

A مفلوذ *maflūz*, Forged of excellent steel.

A مفلوس *maflūs*, Shining like a fish-scale.

A مفلوق *maflūk*, (A camel) marked with the mark فلقة *falkat* under the ear.

P مفلوك *maflūk*, Unfortunate. Poor, indigent.

A مفلوك *maflūk*, Swelling-breasted (girl).

A مفلول *maflūl*, Broken, notched, chipped (sword).

A مفلهد *mufalhad*, A stout, fat, handsome youth who has arrived at puberty.

A مفلي *muflī*, (and مفلية *mufliyat*) A mare having a yearling colt, or one that has been weaned.

A مفنّ *mifann*, (A man) who utters wonderful things. One who speaks in flowery language.

A مفناة *mafnāt*, A country that agrees well with those that visit it.

A مفناق *mifnāk*, Delicately brought up (girl).

A مفنخ *mifnahh*, One who subdues his foes.

A مفنّد *mufnid*, Weak in mind. An old dotard.

A مفنّد *mufannid*, A reproacher, upbraider.

A مفنشخ *mufanshikh*, Sleepy and falling.

A مفنشل *mufanshil*, One who scatters or dishevels. Fearless.

A مفنشئاً *mufanshiءan*, Fearlessly, menacingly.

A مفنع *mifnaء*, Highly esteemed, of good repute.

A مفنّنة *mufannanat*, A malignant old woman. A camel which appears ten months gone with young.

A مفني *mufnī*, Ruinous, destructive, wasteful.

A مفواد *mifwād*, One who lays out his wealth freely and usefully (an instrument of usefulness).

A مفؤد *mafءud*, Heartless, dispirited. Roasted (meat). (Bread) baked under the ashes. Wounded in the heart (فؤاد *fuءād*). Sick at heart.

A مفوّدجة *mufawdajat*, Straight-horned (sheep).

A مفوّض *mufawwaz*, Committed or entrusted to the care of, consigned, delivered, recommended. Submitted for opinion.

A مفوّف *mufawwaf*, (A garment) thin, dyed, or striped with white: a garment in general.

A مفوّق *mufawwak*, Notched (arrow).

A مفوود *mafءūd*, (Bread) baked under the ashes. Smitten in the heart (فؤاد *fuءād*). Heartless, lifeless.

A مفوّه *mufawwah*, Loquacious. Very eloquent (orator or oration). Aromatic (wine). A glutton. (Cloth) dyed with the roots of the herb madder.

A مفوّي *mufawwa'*, Dyed with madder. (fem. مفوّاة *mufawwāt*) (Land) which grows madder.

A مفهاق *mifhāk*, (A well) full of water.

A مفهوت *mafhūt*, Confounded, astonished.

A مفهوم *mafhūm*, Understood, perceived, comprehended. The contents, tenor, or sense of a letter.

A مفيء *mufīء*, A patron or a master, one who affords shade and shelter (فيء *fayء*).

A مفياة *mafyaءat* or *mafuyaءat*, A shady place, a place built for giving shade (فيء *fayء*).

A مفياد *mifyād*, One who expends largely but usefully (an instrument of usefulness).

A مفيد *mufīd*, Useful, profitable, salutary. Who acquires wealth and bestows it liberally and usefully.

A مفيص *mafīs*, Flight, avoiding. A place of escape, flight, or refuge.

A مفيض *mufīz*, A shedder (of tears), pourer out (of water). A giver. مفيض البركات *mufīzu'l barakāt*, Any thing producing affluence; a bestower of abundant blessings.

A مفيق *mufīk*, Wonderful, marvellous (poet). *Mufīk*, (and مفيقة *mufīkat*) (pl. مفاويق *mafāwīk*) A camel having milk in her udder between the times of milking.

A مفيوءة *mafyūءat*, (fem.) Shaded. A bower, arbour; a place impenetrable to the sun's rays.

A مفيولاء *mafyūlāء*, Young elephants.

A مقّ *makk*, (v. n. of مقّ) Splitting (the branch of a female palm) to inject the male flowers.

A مقّاء *makkāء*, (fem. of أمقّ *amakk*) Long-bodied (mare). Lean (thigh). Distant (country).

A مقأب *mikءab*, A great drinker.

A مقابح *makābih*, (pl. of مقبحة *makbahat*) Offences, offensivenesses, odiums.

A مقابحة *mukābahat*, (v. n. 3 of قبح) Reviling, reproaching, calling one another ugly names.

A مقابر *makābir*, (pl. of مقبرة *makbarat*) Cemeteries, grave-yards, tombs.

A مقابل *mukābal*, Of noble parentage on both sides. *Mukābil*, Opposite, over against, fronting. One who puts himself opposite, or looks towards, or meets. One who confronts, comptrols, collates, or compares (one copy of a book with another). P مقابل شدن *mukābil shudan*, To be opposite, meet, be confronted, compared, contrasted, or comptrolled.

A مقابلة *mukābalat*, (v. n. 3 of قبل) Facing, standing over against. Looking towards. Comparing, collating (one book) with another, confronting. Meeting face to face. Opposing, resisting. Recompensing. Bending the tongue of a shoe-latchet. Slitting a (sheep's) ear, and letting a part hang forward. Supplying (a shoe) with the thong called قبال *kibāl*. Opposition. Opposite quarter. Comparison, comptrol, collation, examination. Contrast. Exchange, reciprocation, equality, retrospection. A book of comptrol. Contradistinction. A counterpart, duplicate. Tablets, memorandum-book. (A sheep) whose ears are slit, part hanging forward (opposed to مدابرة *mudābarat*). P مقابله كردن *mukābala kardan*, To compare, collate, confront, contrast.

A مقابلة *mukābalatan*, Before, in presence of.

A مقابيح *makābīh*, (pl. of مقبوحة *makbūhat*) Crimes, vices, misdemeanors, infamous actions.

A مقاتة *makātat*, (v. n. of مقت) Hating.

A مقاتعة *mukātaءat*, A fighting, contending with.

A مقاتل *makātil*, (pl. of مقتل *maktal*) Places of death. *Mukātil*, A soldier, combatant who seeks to kill. Internecine, murderous.

A مقاتلة *mukātalat*, (v. n. 3 of قتل) Fighting, trying to kill. Cursing. Excluding from good. Battle, conflict, slaughter, carnage. مقاتلة عظيمة *mukātalaءi ءazīma*, A great and bloody battle. *Mukātilat*, Men ready for war or carnage.

A مقاتية *makātiyat*, (or مقاتوة *makātiwat*) (pl. of مقتوي *maktawī*) Servants.

A مقاثب *makāsib*, Presents, gifts.

A مقاحلة *mukāhalat*, (v. n. 3 of قحل) Being assiduous, fixed to, persevering in.

A مقاحم *makāhim*, Places of danger, perils.

A مقاحمة *mukāhamat*, (v. n. 3 of قحم) Rushing furiously upon. A hostile attack, furious charge.

A مقاحيد *makāhīd*, (pl. of مقحاد *mik-hād*) Large-bunched she-camels.

A مقاد المهر *makādu'l muhr*, The right or off side.

A مقاداة *mukādāt*, (v. n. 3 of قدي) Opposing, contending. Equalling.

A مقادة *makādat*, (v. n. 3 of قاد for قود) Lending. Guidance, conduct. اعطاه مقادته *aءtāhu makādatahu*, He gave him the reins, he submitted to him.

A مقادر *mukādar*, Narrow, confined (house).

A مقادرة *mukādarat*, (v. n. 3 of قدر) Measuring one thing on another. Doing exactly like another.

A مقادسة *makādisat*, (pl. of مقدسيّ *makdasīy*) Natives of the holy city Jerusalem.

A مقادم *makādim*, The fore parts.

A مقادير *makādīr*, (pl. of مقدار *mikdār*) Quantities. Spaces. Measures. Decrees, fates.

A مقاديم *makādīm*, (pl. of مقدم *mukdim*, *mukaddam*, or مقدام *mikdām*) The fore parts. ركب مقاديمه *rakiba makādīmahu*, He fell prostrate.

A مقاذاة *mukāzāt*, A recompensing, repaying.

A مقاذحة *mukāzahat*, A reviling, a reproaching.

A مقاذعة *mukāzaʻat*, (v. n. 3 of قذع) Bandying ribaldry from one to another. Calling bad names, reviling, abusing.

A مقارّ *makārr*, Depths, deep recesses.

A مقارأة *mukāraʼat*, (v. n. 3 of قرأ) Reading along with (another). Teaching to read.

A مقارب *mukārab*, Moderate, tolerable (in price, size, &c.). *Mukārib*, Near, neighbouring. Tolerable, moderate. Mid-way, between good and evil.

A مقاربة *mukārabat*, (v. n. 3 of قرب) Drawing near, approaching. Shewing propinquity or neighbourhood. Speaking gently or soothingly in order to deceive. Taking short steps. Lifting the leg. Letting alone excess, and aiming at what is just and right. Preparing, making ready. Taking the middle of the road. Bidding against. Proximity.

A مقارّة *mukārrat*, (v. n. 3 of قرّ) Resting. Becoming firm, settled, strengthening one's interest (with another). Being present (at prayer).

A مقارحة *mukārahat*, (v. n. 3 of قرح) (Coming) face to face, before, from the opposite side.

A مقارض *makāriz*, Places where the water-drawer is obliged to descend into the well on account of the paucity of water. Ground thinly sown. Large wine-vessels.

A مقارضة *mukārazat*, (v. n. 3 of قرض) Requiting, restoring, compensating. Entering into partnership and trading with another's capital.

A مقارع *makāriʻ*, (pl. of مقرعة *mikraʻat*) Whips, lashes. *Mukāriʻ*, Conquered. A conqueror. A prince, leader. An adversary.

A مقارعات *mukāraʻāt*, Blows, contusions.

A مقارعة *mukāraʻat*, (v. n. 3 of قرع) Beating one another (combatants). Casting lots.

A مقارف *makārif*, (pl. of مقرف *mukrif*) Born of a slave father and free mother. (Horses) from a mean sire by a blood mare.

A مقارفة *mukārafat*, (v. n. 3 of قرف) Mixing (with sin), defiling one's self (with it). Commingling. Having to do (with one's wife). Drawing near, approaching.

A مقارن *mukārin*, Associated, connected, related, allied, familiar, intimate, domesticated. Simultaneous with. Near.

A مقارنة *mukāranat*, (v. n. 3 of قرن) Living in society, being intimate. Being in conjunction (as two stars). Collating. Tying up two things together. Eating two dates at once. Rendering (one) successful or unfortunate (a star). Conjunction, connection, companionship, familiarity. Proximity.

A مقاري *makārī*, Summits of hillocks. Pots.

A مقارئ *mukāriʼ*, An alternate reader.

A مقاريب *makārīb*, (pl. of مقرب *mukrib*) (Women, mares, or sheep) near the birth.

A مقاريح *makārīh*, Five-year-old horses.

A مقاريض *makārīz*, (pl. of مقراض) Shears.

A مقّاس *makkās*, Able to repeat poetry at will.

A مقاساة *mukāsāt*, (v. n. 3 of قسا for قسو) Becoming callous with regard to any evil, and enduring it with all its inconveniences. Enduring, suffering.

A مقاسحة *mukāsahat*, (v. n. 3 of قسح) Drying.

A مقاسم *makāsim*, (pl. of مقسم *maksim*) Places of division or distribution. *Mukāsim*, A coparcener.

A مقاسمة *mukāsamat*, (v. n. 3 of قسم) Dividing (with another), admitting (him) to a share. Taking one's own share. Causing (one) to swear fidelity. Swearing, declaring on oath. Partition.

A مقاص *makās*, A rafter, joist, king-post, into which other beams are inserted. Shears, scissors.

A مقاصّ *makāss*, (Mares) apparently in foal.

A مقاصاة *mukāsāt*, (v. n. of قصو) Going far off. Contending which shall go to the farthest distance.

A مقاصّة *mukāssat*, (v. n. 3 of قصّ) Retaliating. Making equal, balancing (accounts).

A مقاصد *makāsid*, Designs, enterprises, machinations, great attempts or undertakings. Thoughts; aims, desires; wishes, wants, inclinations.

A مقاصر *makāsir*, (pl. of مقصرة *maksarat*) The later hours of the evening, a mixture of darkness with light. هو مقاصري *huwa mukāsirī*, His villa (قصر *kasr*) faces mine: my country-neighbour.

A مقاصير *makāsīr*, The later hours of evening, a mixture of darkness with the light. Sides. (pl. of مقصورة *maksūrat*) Private apartments for women.

A مقاضاة *mukāzāt*, (v. n. 3 of قضي) Going together before a judge or arbiter (قاضي *kāzī*).

A مقاضمة *mukāzamat*, (v. n. 3 of قضم) Taking by little and little. Buying or selling in small quantities, retailing.

A مقاط *mikāt*, A cord with which a sheep's legs are tied when slaughtered. Swaddling-clothes. A small strongly-twisted rope.

A مقاطّ *makātt*, (pl. of مقطّ *mikatt*) Pieces of bone on which they nib writing-reeds or pens.

A مقاطر *makātir*, (pl. of مقطر *maktar*) Drops.

A مقاطرة *mukātarat*, (v. n. 3 of قطر) Going and coming. Weighing one hamper, and taking the others without weighing, supposing them all alike.

A مقاطع *makātiʻ*, (pl. of مقطع *maktaʻ*) Places of cutting. Sections (especially pauses in the Kur'ān). Fords, passes, passages of rivers. The hinder or extreme parts. Custom-houses, or any other places where public imposts or taxes are paid.

A مقاطعة *makātiʻat*, Any places where public taxes are received. Impost, custom. *Mukātaʻat*, (v. n. 3 of قطع) Being disunited, estranged. Deciding (any thing with another). Contending with another whose sword is sharpest (اقطع *aktaʻ*).

A مقاطل *makātil*, (pl. of مقطلة *miktalat*) Iron cutting-instruments.

A مقاطيع *makātīʻ*, (pl. of مقطوع *maktūʻ*) Cut off. Stragglers.

A مقاظ *makāz*, A place for passing the hottest part of summer called قيظ *kayz*.

A مقاعد *makāʻid*, (pl. of مقعد *makʻad*) Places in the market where people sit. Benches, seats. Backsides. Camps. *Mukāʻid*, A doe, a bird, or whatever comes behind another. A guardian, keeper, preserver.

A مقاعدة *mukāʻadat*, (v. n. 3 of قعد) Sitting down by (another). *Mukāʻidat*, A woman. A kind of floor-cloth or carpet on which they sit. A sack full of provisions, especially dried flesh and biscuit. A roundish heap of sand.

A مقاعس *makāʻis*, (or مقاعيس *makāʻīs*) (pl. of مقعنسس *mukʻansis*) Strong, hard. *Mukāʻis*, One who recedes from a treaty or oath.

A مقال *makāl*, (v. n. of قال for قيل) Taking a nap at noon. A word. An opinion, sentence. فعل و مقال *fiʻl u makāl*, Actions and words.

A مقالة *makālat*, (v. n. of قال for قول) Speaking, saying. A word, discourse, saying, opinion, sentence, adage, proverb.

A مقالّة *mukāllat*, (v. n. 3 of قلّ) Giving little (قليل *kalīl*). Doling out water scantily.

A ضاقت عليه مقالده *zākat ʻalayhi makāliduhu*, (or مقاليده) His affairs pressed sorely upon him.

A غرض المقالعة *gharazu'l mukālaʻat*, The target by which archers first learn to shoot, and which, for the convenience of the tyro, is fixed low.

A مقالم *makālim*, Prominent joints of cane-spears.

A مقالي *makālī*, (pl. of مقلاة *miklāt*) Frying-pans.

A مقاليت *makālīt*, (pl. of مقلات *miklāt*) Bereaved mothers.

A مقاليد *makālīd*, (pl. of مقلاد or مقلد) Keys.

A مقام *makām*, (v. n. of قام for قوم) Staying, stopping, halting, resting, residing (in any place). Place of residence, dwelling, mansion. Stay, halt. Post, station, office. State, dignity, condition. A royal court. The halting of an army. The presence of God in judgment. A musical tone. صاحب مقام *sāhib makām*, Raised to honour, dignified. Skilled in musical sounds. قائم مقام *kāʼim makām*, Locum tenens. The vicegerent, the Kaimacam, or governor of Constantinople, who is also the lieutenant of the Grand Vizier. P مقام بمقام *makām ba makām*, From tone to tone, through every mode. From place to place. A مقام مصلاّ *makāmi musallā*, Name of a place where Abraham prayed. ما يقوم مقامه

mā yakūmu makāmahu, That which stands in the place of. P مقام كردن *makām kardan,* To settle, remain, halt. A *Mukām,* (v. n. of قام for قوم) Staying, stopping, reposing, resting. Time or place of rising, standing, or remaining. A stay, halt. A successor appointed in another's room.

A مقاماة *mukāmaʿat,* (v. n. 3 of قما), or مقاماة *mukāmāt,* (v. n. 3 of قما for قوم) Suiting, agreeing with.

A مقامات *makāmāt,* (pl. of مقامة *makāmat*) Sittings, conversations held at those assemblies. Compositions recited on those occasions. Musical modes, of which there are twelve. Degrees. مقامات رضوان *makāmāti rizwān,* The eighth heaven. اهل مقامات *ahli makāmāt,* Eminent in dignity. Musical.

A مقامة *makāmat,* A meeting, assembly, sitting, session. *Mukāmat,* (v. n. 4 of قام for قوم) Perpetuating, keeping up. Staying, reposing, resting.

A مقامح *mukāmih,* (A camel) which throws up his head and refuses to drink when distempered or when the water is too cold.

A مقامحة *mukāmahat,* (v. n. 3 of قمح) Tossing up (his) head and refusing to drink (a camel). *Mukāmihat,* (Camels) which so toss the head.

A مقامر *mukāmir,* An antagonist at play, or in laying wagers.

A مقامرة *mukāmarat,* A playing at dice.

A مقامس حوتا *mukāmis hūtan,* One who dives against a fish, (metaph.) Rash enough to compete with his superior.

A مقامسة *mukāmasat,* (v. n. 3 of قمس) Contending with another who shall plunge or dive. Rivalling a fish in diving.

A مقامع *makāmiʿ,* (pl. of قمعة *kamaʿat*) Gadflies, which in hot weather torment camels. (pl. of مقمعة *mikmaʿat*) Iron instruments with which they strike the heads of elephants, or wooden instruments for striking the heads of men.

A مقامق *mukāmik,* Who speaks from the bottom of his throat.

A مقامي *makāmī,* Local.

A مقاناة *mukānāt,* (v. n. 3 of قني) Being convenient, accommodated, advantageous to, agreeing with, suiting. Being perpetual, continual, perennial. Mixing together.

A مقانب *makānib,* Wild dogs trained to hunt.

A مقانع *makāniʿ,* (pl. of مقنع *maknaʿ*) Valid evidences. (pl. of مقنع *miknaʿ* or مقنعة *miknaʿat*) Veils.

A مقاواة *mukāwāt,* (v. n. 3 of قوي) Contending with (another) for superiority in power or strength (قوة *kūwat*). Giving, presenting.

A مقاود *makāwid,* (pl. of مقود) Leading-reins.

A مقاوس *mukāwis,* One who starts horses at a race. One who institutes a comparison.

A مقاوسة *mukāwasat,* (v. n. 3 of قاس for قوس) Comparing (two things). Corresponding with, resembling (as one man another). Running (with others) in a place of exercise.

A مقاول *makāwil,* (pl. of مقول *mikwal*) Tongues. Kings of the Himyarit Arabs. *Mukāwil,* Engaged in conversation.

A مقاولة *makāwilat,* (pl. of مقول *mikwal*) Kings of the Himyarit Arabs. *Mukāwalat,* (v. n. 3 of قال for قول) Conversing. Agreement, compact.

A مقاوم *mukāwim,* An adversary, one who rises up against another, an antagonist. One who stands near a person. مقاوم الشتاء *mukāwimu'sh shitāʾ,* Winter-resisting, perennial (plant).

A مقاومة *mukāwamat,* (v. n. 3 of قام for قوم) Opposing, resisting, withstanding. Standing front to front; standing near. Opposition, resistance.

A مقايسة *mukāyasat,* (v. n. 3 of قاس for قيس) Running a race on the course. Instituting a comparison or analogy between (two things). Agreeing with, answering to in measure or comparison.

A مقايضة *mukāyazat,* (v. n. 3 of قاض for قيض) Exposing merchandise to sale. Exchanging, bartering, giving an equivalent.

A مقايظة *mukāyazat,* (v. n. 3 of قيظ) Agreeing with for the midsummer-season called قيظ *kayz.*

A مقائل *makāʾil,* (pl. of مقيل *makīl*) Places where people take their siesta.

A مقايلة *mukāyalat,* (v. n. 3 of قال for قيل) Returning like for like.

A مقائيد *makāʾīd,* (pl. of مقيّد *mukayyad*) Fettered (men or camels). Bonds, fetters.

A مقباس *mikbās,* A spark of fire, or a small quantity taken to kindle a greater.

A مقبّب *mukabbab,* Vaulted, arched. Slender, lank, collapsed (abdomen).

A مقبحة *makbahat,* (pl. مقابح *makābih*) Any thing offensive and deserving of reproach.

A مقبر *makbar,* (v. n. of قبر) Burying.

A مقبرة *makba, makbi, makbu,* or *mikbarat,* (pl. مقابر *makābir*) A burying-ground, burial-place.

A مقبريّ *makbariy* or *makburiy,* Belonging to a sepulchre or burying-ground. *Makburiy,* Name of a class of reporters of traditions. A dweller amongst the tombs.

A مقبس *mukbis,* One who begs fire for any one. (See اقباس *ikbās.*)

A مقبص *mikbas,* A barricado, goal, or starting-place; particularly a rope stretched before the horses when drawn up for a race, which being dropt was the signal for starting. على المقبص *ʿala'l mikbas,* Straight and true.

A مقبض *makbaz,* (*makbiz, mikbaz,* مقبضة *makba, makbi,* or *mikbazat*) The hilt or handle (of sword or bow). The handle of a spade. Handle, occasion.

A مقبقب *mukabkab,* A lion. *Mukabkib,* The fourth year from the present.

A مقبل *mukbal,* Placed over against, looking towards. Fat. *Mukbil,* Prosperous, fortunate. Favouring (fortune). Approaching, advancing towards one, nearly arrived.

A مقبّل *mukabbal,* Kissed. A person or place kissed. Patched (garment). *Mukabbil,* Kissing.

A مقبلة *mukbilat,* Approaching (night).

A مقبوّ *makbūw,* Contracted, drawn together.

A مقبوب *makbūb,* Slender, lank (abdomen).

A مقبوح *makbūh,* Reprobated, cursed. Laid aside. Debarred from good.

A مقبور *makbūr,* Buried. Enveloped, involved.

A مقبوض *makbūz,* Taken, seized, occupied, possessed, held, received, preserved. Restricted, contracted, bound. Constipated. Imprisoned. Dead. A styptic.

A مقبول *makbūl,* Accepted, admitted, approved. Taken in good part. Agreeable, acceptable, pleasing. One of the faithful. Patched (garment). A mistress. P مقبول قلوب عالميان *makbūli kulūbi ʿālamiyān,* Dear to men's hearts, agreeable to all.

A مقبوليّة *makbūliyat,* Agreeableness, acceptableness. Agreement. Orthodqxy.

A مقبيّ *makbiy,* Fat, greasy.

A مقبئنّ *mukbaʾinn,* Contracted within itself. Absent, left, or lagging behind.

A مقة *mikat,* (v. n. of ومق) Loving. Love.

A مقت *makt,* (v. n. of مقت) Hating. Hatred. نكاح المقت *nikāhu'l makt,* The odious marriage (*i.e.* when any one married his step-mother after the death of his father, a custom which prevailed amongst the Pagan Arabians).

A مقتاد *muktād,* Yielding, tractable, obedient.

A مقتب *muktib,* One who saddles a camel. One who swears roundly.

A مقتبّ *muktabb,* Amputated (hand).

A مقتبس *muktabas,* Quoted. *Muktabis,* One who receives, acquires, borrows, or quotes (light, fire, or science) from, or imparts (them) to, another.

A مقتبل *muktabal,* In the flower (of youth).

A مقتّت *mukattat,* (Oil) mixed with odours, scented (oil). *Mukattit,* One who imbues (an ointment) with odours. An informer, slanderer.

A مقتتل *muktatal,* Killed by love. Slain by a demon. *Muktatil,* Engaged in fighting.

A مقتني *muktanī,* A taker or hirer of a servant.

A مقتحم *muktahim,* One who plunges rashly (into a business). Setting (star). A despiser. (See اقتحام).

A مقتدا *muktadā,* (for مقتدي *muktadaʾ*) Followed, imitated; imitable. مقتداي ناس *muktadāyi nās,* A chief whom others follow, especially in prayer; hence a prelate, priest, or exemplary person.

A مقتدح *muktadih,* Who strikes fire from a flint. Who drinks soup from a pot. Arranger, manager.

A مقتدر *muktadar,* Compact, round. *Muktadir,* Powerful, strong, able. One who boils in a pot (قدر *kidr*). The middle of any thing.

A مقتدي *muktadī,* An imitator, follower.

A مقتر *muktir,* Frugal, parsimonious, economical (in domestic expense). Poor. A saddle of a convenient moderate size and sitting nicely.

A مقتّر *muhattar*, Fragrant, odoriferous. *Muhattir*, Frugal, parsimonious, economical.

A مقترب *muktarib*, Approaching, brought near. (A promise) shortly to be performed.

A مقترة *muktirat*, Aloe-perfuming (woman).

A مقترت *muhtarit*, One who takes every thing to himself that he can lay his hand upon.

A مقترح *muktarih*, One who asks or solicits with importunity, inproperly, unnecessarily. A speaker or repeater of verses extempore. A doer of any thing never done hitherto. (See اقتراح *iktirāh*.)

A مقترض *muktariz*, A borrower: getting in debt.

A مقترع *muktariع*, Chosen for a stallion.

A مقترف *muktaraf*, Recently purchased. *Muktarif*, A gainer. A transgressor. Arraigned, accused.

A مقترن *muktarin*, Associated. Following immediately. A friend, ally.

A مقتري *muktarī*, One who intends, designs, endeavours, strives, pursues, follows. A traveller from country to country. One who receives (a friend) hospitably.

A مقتسر *muktasir*, One who forces unwillingly.

A مقتسط *muktasit*, (or مقتسم *muktasim*) Engaged in dividing (wealth among themselves).

A مقتسم *muktasim*, Mutual in swearing. A schismatic. A divider.

A مقتشب *muktashib*, One who earns to himself praise or censure.

A مقتشر *muktashir*, Naked, stripped.

A مقتصّ *muktiss*, A relater (of a speech truly). One who takes revenge (قصاص *kisās*) for a past injury, or who desires (another) to retaliate.

A مقتصد *muktasid*, One who keeps the middle. Of a moderate temperament of body or mind; neither gross nor slender; neither profuse nor parsimonious; neither quick nor slow. One who gives his attention to writing poetry. A hypocrite, atheist.

A مقتصر *muktasar*, Abbreviated, abridged. A compendium, summary, epitome. *Muktasir*, Addicted (to any thing), content with that alone, and not exceeding or leaving it. مقتصر علي ازار *muktasir ع̣ala' izārin*, Content with breeches (to cover the nakedness).

A مقتضا *muktazā*, (in construction for مقتضىٰ *muktaza'*) Exacted, required, needed. Exigency, necessity. A craving, requirement. Drift, scope. مقتضاي مودّت و مخالصت *muktazāyi mawaddat u mukhālasat*, That which friendship and good correspondence requires. P بر مقتضاي شرع شريف *bar muktazāyi sharع̣i sharīf*, According to law.

A مقتضب *muktazab*, Pruned, lopped. Rude, inexperienced; untaught, awkward, clumsy. (Verse) spoken extempore. A kind of verse. A poem destitute of the transition from a description of the writer's feelings to the eulogy of the person addressed.

A مقتضىٰ *muktaza'*, Exacted, required, conformable. Drift, scope. *Muktazī*, An exacter, demander. Leading to, producing, demanding, requiring.

A مقتضيّات *muktaziyāt*, Exigencies, events, necessary consequences. Conjectures.

A مقتطع *muktataع̣*, Cut.

A مقتعد *muktaع̣ad*, A beast or place on which a person sits. *Muktaع̣id*, Mounted, seated, riding upon.

A مقتعل *muktaع̣al*, Rough-hewn (arrow).

A مقتفر *muktafir*, A follower (of footsteps).

A مقتفل *muktafil*, Close-fisted, avaricious.

A مقتفىٰ *muktafa'*, Preferred, set over. (An oration) rythmically composed. مقتفىٰ به *muktafa' bihi*, Honoured (guest). *Muktafī*, One who follows (another). One who chooses any thing for his own peculiar use.

A مقتل *maktal*, (pl. مقاتل *mahātil*) Place of slaughter. Place of death, *i.e.* any part of the body, which, being wounded, causes death.

A مقتّل *mukattal*, Tried, proved. Quiet, gentle, subdued. Conquered by love. *Mukattil*, *mukittil*, or *mukuttil*, Engaged in combating, fighting together.

A مقتلع *muktalaع̣*, Torn up, drawn out. *Muktaliع̣*, One who removes, tears up. Uprooted.

A مقتلف *muktalaf*, Uprooted.

A مقتنّ *muktann*, Erect, upright.

A مقتنص *muktanas*, Hunted. *Muktanis*, Hunter.

A مقتنىٰ *muktana'*, (in regim. مقتنا *muktanā*) Possessed. *Muktanī*, An acquirer, possessor.

A مقتول *maktūl*, Killed, slain, slaughtered.

A مقتوي *maktawī*, (pl. مقتوون *maktawūna*, مقاتوة *mahātiwat*, and مقاتية *mahātayat*) A servant, domestic, slave. *Muhtawī*, Waxed strong. (See اقتواء.)

A مقتوين *maktawīn* or *maktawayn*, (mas. and fem. sing. and pl.) A domestic, one especially who serves for victuals.

A مقتىٰ *makta'*, (v. n. of قتا for قتو) Serving well (a domestic). A servant who serves for his victuals.

A مقتيّ *maktiy*, Married to his father's widow. A son born of such a marriage.

A مقثئنّ *muktasinn*, Erect, upright.

A مقثأة *maksaat*, A cucumber-bed.

A مقثّة *makassat*, Multitude, plenty, abundance. A broad piece of wood used by children at play.

A مقثرد *muksarid*, Possessed of many sheep and much furniture (قثرد *kasrad*, *kusrud*, or *kisrid*).

A مقثعلّ *muhsaع̣ill*, Rough, ill-polished (arrow).

A مقثؤة *mahsuat*, A cucumber-bed.

A مقحاة *mik-hāt*, A wooden shovel or spade.

A مقحاد *mik-hād*, Large-bunched (she-camel).

A مقحام *mik-hām*, A he-camel rushing in amongst the females with no one to guide him.

A مقحدة *mak-hadat*, Root of a camel's bunch.

A مقحط *mik-hat*, A horse not easily tired with running. *Muk-hat*, Barren (year).

A مقحفة *mik-hafat*, A fan for winnowing.

A مقحقح *mukahkih*, A hard night's journey in search of water.

A مقحم *muh-ham*, A camel changing the fore-teeth and those next to them in the same year. An Arab born in the desert. Weak. Compelled by famine to emigrate.

A مقحوّ *mak-hūw*, (or مقحيّ *mak-hiy*) (A medicine) made of anthemis or camomile (قحوان *kuhwān*).

A مقحوز *mak-hūz*, Repelled, rejected, driven back.

A مقحوط *mak-hūt*, Afflicted with scarcity.

A مقحوف *mak-hūf*, One whose skull is cut.

A مقدّ *makadd*, A road. A level country. *Mikadd*, An iron instrument for cutting into oblong strips (قدّ *kadd*), or for dressing leather.

A مقداح *mikdāh*, A fire-steel.

A مقدار *mikdār*, Quantity. Space. Measure, dimension. Power, strength.

A مقدام *mikdām*, (or مقدامة *mikdāmat*) Very bold, dauntless, animated. Fierce against an enemy. A kind of date.

A مقدّة *mahaddat*, Name of a place noted for its wine. A road.

A مقدح *mikdah*, A large spoon or ladle. A steel, flint, tinder-box.

A مقدحة *mikdahat*, A fire-steel. A ladle, skimmer.

A مقدّد *mukaddad*, Well cut (garment). Flesh cut into oblong slices for future use, jerked.

A مقدّر *muhaddar*, Predestined, predetermined, decreed by God, prescribed, fated. Understood, (not expressed). Fate, destiny. *Mukaddir*, God, the predestinator. An architect, projector, designer. P حضرت خداوند مقدّر الآجال *hazrati khudāwandi mukaddiru'l ājāl*, The Divine Majesty, the predestinator of death. مقدّر بها *mukaddiri bahā*, An appraiser, one who affixes a price.

A مقدرة *makdarat*, Fate, destiny. Divine Providence prevailing over all. *Makda*, *makdi*, or *makdurat*, (v. n. of قدر) Being able, waxing strong, prevailing. Power, strength, ability. ذو مقدرة *zū makdurat*, Endowed with power, strong, powerful.

A مقدس *makdis*, A holy place. بيت المقدس *baytu'l mahdis*, Jerusalem.

A مقدّس *muhaddas*, Sanctified, consecrated. Holy. بيت المقدّس *baytu'l mukaddas*, Jerusalem. Name of a mosque at Damascus. بردۀ مقدّس الاستار *burdaï mukaddasu'l astār*, The sacred mantle or pall. *Muhaddis*, One who sanctifies or consecrates. A Christian presbyter or monk. A Jew.

A مقدّسة *muhaddasat*, (fem. of مقدّس *mukaddas*) Sanctified, holy. الارض المقدّسة *al arzu'l mukaddasat*, The holy land.

A مقدسيّ *makdasiy*, (pl. مقادسة *mahādisat*) A native of Jerusalem.

A مقدشو *makdishū*, Name of a town between Zanguebar and Abyssinia.

A مقدّع *muhaddaع̣*, Full of wrinkles or folds.

A مقدعة *mikdaع̣at*, A staff.

A مقدم *makdam*, (v. n. of قدم) Coming, arriving (off a journey). Arrival. A place from which one arrives. مقدم سعادت مدار *makdami saع̣ādat-*

madār, The auspicious arrival. مقدم الحاجّ *makdama'l hājj*, On the arrival of the pilgrims. *Mukdam*, The time or crisis of advancing or taking the lead. Boldness, enterprise, endeavour, diligence. جرئ المقدم *jari*ʼ*u'l mukdam*, Bold and animated. *Mukdim*, Intrepid, attacking an enemy with courage. Who gives or inspires spirit or courage. Diligent, laborious, careful, solicitous. Who orders to approach. Who orders to go before. Who administers an oath. A centurion. The fore part of a camel's saddle. (pl. مقاديم *makādim*) The anterior or inner corner of the eye, *i.e.* that which is next to the nose (the other being called موٴخر *mu*ʼ*khir*). The part of the face fronting one.

A مقدّم *mukaddam*, Placed before. Preferred. Antecedent, prior, preceding. Sent before. A leader, commander. The advanced guard. The major proposition of a syllogism. A superior officer of the revenue in a village. The fore part of any thing, especially of a camel's saddle. A species of fine silk cloth used for turbans and sashes. The inner corner of the eye. The part of the face fronting one. مقدّم و تالي *mukaddam u tālī*, Antecedent and consequent, subject and predicate. P مقدّم داشتن *mukaddam dāshtan*, To prefer. A *Mukaddim*, Who places before and gives the preference. Preliminary, introductory, preceding.

A مقدّماً *mukaddaman*, Firstly, before all things. Anciently, long before this, previously.

A مقدّمات *mukaddamāt*, Premises, pre-requisites.

A مقدمة *mukdimat*, The fore part of a camel's saddle. A sort of comb.

A مقدّمة *mukaddamat*, An affair, matter, case, business, subject; cause, suit, law-suit. The front, fore part, advanced guard. The fore part of a camel's saddle. The preamble (to a speech); preface (to a book); premises (in an argument); major proposition of a syllogism. Prelacy, primacy. First of all, in the first place. مقدّمة الجيش *mukaddamatu'l jaysh*, (or مقدّمهٔ جيش *mukaddama*ʼ*i jaysh*) The advanced guard of an army. P مقدّمهٔ خون *mukaddama*ʼ*i khūn*, A case of blood or murder. A *Mukaddimat*, The van of an army. A mode of combing forwards. The forelock. The forehead. The commencement or first of any thing. (A camel) that has not yet produced.

A مقدّمي *mukaddamī*, An allowance made to the Mukaddam.

A مقدود *makdūd*, (A man) of a fine stature.

A مقدور *makdūr*, Predestined, decreed. Fatal. Fate. Possibility, power, whatever one is able to do. حسب المقدور *hasbu'l makdūr*, According to (one's) ability.

A مقدوع *makdūʻ*, Who refrains from calling out.

A مقدونية *makdūniya*, Macedonia.

A مقديّ *makadīy*, Wine from honey; mead.

A مقدّيّ *makaddīy*, (A wine) so named from a city in Syria.

A مقدّيّة *makaddīyat*, A kind of stuff.

A مقذّ *makazz*, That part of the hind-head between the ears where the hair terminates. *Mikazz*, A knife, or any instrument used in cutting feathers for winging an arrow.

A مقذاف *mikzāf*, An oar.

A مقذحرّ *mukzahirr*, Ready for perpetrating mischief, for fighting or reviling. One who is always angry, whose nostrils swell with rage.

A مقذّذ *mukazzaz*, Of a middle stature and an elegant shape. Cut and handsomely-fashioned (ear). One whose hair is cut or dressed.

A مقذّذة *mukazzazat*, Not tall (woman).

A مقذر *makzar*, Shunned by mankind on account of impurity, an object of disgust.

A مقذع *mukziʻ*, Defamatory (verse).

A مقذعرّ *mukzaʻirr*, One habitually prepared to act wickedly, to kill, or to revile.

A مقذعلّ *mukzaʻill*, Swift, expeditious.

A مقذف *mikzaf*, An oar.

A مقذّف *mukazzaf*, Very corpulent. Cursed, execrated, driven off.

A مقذوذ *makzūz*, One whose hair is clipped or dressed. Cut (hair). Trimmed.

A مقذوذة *makzūzat*, Circularly cut and handsomely-shaped (ear). Root, origin.

A مقذيّ *makzīy*, Troubled with a mote in the eye.

A مقذيّة *makzīyat*, An eye with a mote in it.

A مقر *makr*, (v. n. of مقر) Striking (one upon the neck) with a stick (so as to fracture the bone without breaking the skin). Steeping (salt fish in vinegar). Juice of aloes. Poison. Any thing acid. *Makar*, (v. n. of مقر) Being bitter. Being sour (milk). *Makir*, Bitter. Acid. The aloe. Poison.

A مقرّ *makarr*, Residence, dwelling, mansion, habitation, station, seat, place of rest or quiet. مقرّ الرحم *makarru'r rahim*, Fundus uteri. *Mukirr*, One who establishes, confirms, settles. One who asserts, affirms, or avers. One who makes confession. A deponent. One who acknowledges the right of another upon himself. Who or what refreshes, cools, or bathes (the eye). P مقرّ شدن *mukirr shudan*, To confess, acknowledge.

A مقرأ *mukra*ʼ or *makra*ʼ, Name of a place in Yaman where mines of cornelian exist.

A مقراء *mikrā*ʼ, Extremely hospitable.

A مقراة *makrāt*, A place to which rain-water flows from different quarters. *Mikrāt*, A lady who entertains very hospitably. Hospitable (cup) with which guests are received.

A مقرّأة *mukarra*ʼ*at*, A woman, the termination of whose courses is waited for, she being confined on that account.

A مقراص *mikrās*, A knife curved at the end.

A مقراض *mikrāz*, Shears, scissors. Snuffers.

P مقراضة *mikrāza*, A forked arrow. A kind of sweetmeat.

P مقراضي *mikrāzī*, Curiously cut out with scissors.

A مقراع *mikrāʻ*, A mallet or hammer for breaking stones. (A camel) pregnant from a single covering.

A مقرب *makrab*, A short road. *Mukrab*, Esteemed, honoured. Kept near. (A horse) of high blood. (A camel) girthed ready for mounting. *Mukrib*, (pl. مقاريب *makārīb*) Near the birth (a woman, mare, or sheep).

A مقرّب *mukarrab*, Approximated. Admitted, allowed to approach. Nearly related. A cherubim. مقرّب الخدمة *mukarrabu'l khidmat*, Confidential servants. P مقرّبان الاهي *mukarrabāni ilāhī*, Beloved, nearest to God. مقرّبان حضرت *mukarrabāni hazrat*, The king's relations, the royal blood. *Mukarrib*, An offerer, sacrificer.

A مقربة *makrabat*, A short road. *Makrabat*, *makribat*, or *makrubat*, Relationship, propinquity. *Mukrabat*, (A woman) had in honour. A she-camel girthed for riding. Noble (mare) kept in the stable and not allowed to be turned out to pasture.

A مقرّبون *mukarrabūn*, (oblique مقرّبين *mukarrabīn*) Cherubims. Relations, nearest kindred.

A مقرّة *makarrat*, A watering-trough. A small water-pot (in Yaman).

A مقرتب *mukartab*, A foul feeder. Badly fed.

A مقرّح *mukarrih*, Caustic. Vesicatory, epispastic. مقرّحات *mukarrihāt*, Medicines which serve to raise blisters: vesicatories, blisters.

A مقرّحة *mukarrahat*, The commencement of freshness and succulence (in dates). (Camels) ulcerated in the mouth, and hence hanging the jib.

A مقردح *mukardah*, The eleventh (horse) in a race.

A مقرّر *mukarrar*, Established, confirmed, ratified, agreed upon, fixed, settled. Ascertained, undoubted, certain, infallible, unquestionable. Appointed. Tribute, tax, impost, duty. P مقرّر كردن *mukarrar kardan*, To ratify, approve, confirm. A *Mukarrir*, A giver of rest. An establisher, confirmer. One who lays on a tax. One who forces to confess. A relator, narrator. مقرّر دعوي *mukarriri daʻwa'*, An advocate, counsellor, pleader.

A مقرّري *mukarrarī*, Fixed tenure in perpetuity.

P مقرّري دار *mukarrarī-dār*, A holder of a Mukarrarī-tenure.

A مقرزم *mukarzam*, Base, contemptible.

A مقرّشة *mukarrishat*, A barren year.

A مقرّص *mukarras*, Round, circular (stud).

A مقرض *mukriz*, A lender, usurer. ابن مقرض *ibn mikrazin*, The weasel which destroys pigeons.

A مقرضب *mukarzib*, A starving fellow who gobbles up all that is set before him.

A مقرّط *mukarrat*, Adorned with ear-rings.

A مقرطس *mukartis*, Mark-hitting (arrow).

A مقرطم *mukartam*, Patched (boot), hard at the toe, and capable of breaking a stone.

A مقرع *mikraʻ*, A vessel for holding dates. *Muk-*

raǥ, One who, after a sound drubbing, lifts his head.

A مقرعبّ mukraǥibb, Hanging the head in wrath.

A مقرعة mikraǥat, (pl. مقارع) A whip, scourge.

A مقرّعة mukarriǥat, A strong woman or female.

A مقرعم mukarǥaj, Long, tall in body.

A مقرف makraf, A place where any thing is uprooted. *Makrif*, Any part (of a tree) stript of the bark. Any part (of a tree) from which gum has been extracted. *Mukraf*, Accused. *Mukrif*, Born of a slave father and a free mother. (A horse) of a mean sire from a blood mare. An accuser. Ruddy.

A مقرفل muharfal, (Food) spiced with cloves.

A مقرقم mukarkam, Whatever grows not. (An infant) not thriving at the breast, ill-fed, stunted.

A مقرم makram, (v. n. of قرم) Eating languidly (a child), nibbling (a camel). *Mikram*, Tapestry worked with stripes or figures. *Mukram*, A stallion-camel of great value, and exempted for that reason from labour; also one fatted for slaughter. Made a lord or prince. قرم مقرم *karmun mukramun*, A prince, lord, man of rank.

A مقرمة mihramat, A veil embroidered with figures. Bed-clothes. A dormitory.

A مقرمد mukarmad, (A house) built of tiles, bricks, or stones (قرميد *kirmīd*); also raised high. (A garment) anointed with saffron.

A مقرمط mukarmat, Short, contracted.

A مقرن makran, A bar across the neck of two oxen yoked to the plough; a yoke. *Mihran*, That which unites one thing with another. *Mukrin*, One who has no companion in ploughing. One who gives power. A helper. Able, adequate, competent.

A مقرّن muharran, Yoked with many others.

A مقرّنة mukarranat, Small adjacent hills.

A مقرنذح mukranzih, Prepared for mischief.

P مقرنس muharnas, A lofty circular building or parlour decorated with pictures, to which one ascends by a winding or spiral staircase. A kind of turban. Various-coloured.

A مقرنس muharnas, (A sword) made in the shape of a ladder. (A falcon) seated on his perch.

A مقرنشع mukranshiǥ, Erect, raised. Glad, rejoiced at good news. Ready prepared (for mischief).

A مقرنص muharnas, (A hawk) kept for hunting.

A مقرنصف mukransif, Swift, quick. A lion.

A مقرنف muharnaf, (Food) spiced with cloves.

A مقرنفط mukranfit, Exceedingly angry, swollen with rage. The privities of a female.

A مقرنفل mukranfal, (Meat) spiced with cloves.

A مقرنئ muharna', Horned (snake). (A leathern bottle) tanned with the plant قرنوة *karnuwat*.

A مقرؤ mahrus, Read: legible, readable.

A مقرّو mahrūw, Read: legible, readable.

A مقروء mahrūs, Read, legible.

A مقروة mahrūwat, A ewe whose neck is fixed in a yoke to prevent her sucking her own teat.

A مقروح mahrūh, Ulcerated. Beaten (path).

A مقرور makrūr, Affected with, or smitten by, cold (قرّة *kirrat*); chilled. Cold (day). Refreshed.

A مقروري makrawriy, Long-backed.

A مقروص makrūs, Cut.

A مقروض makrūz, Cut. Lent. That which a camel brings up when chewing the cud. Burdened with debt (قرض *karz* or *kirz*).

A مقروضي makrūzi, A person in debt.

A مقروظ makrūz, (Leather) tanned or dressed with the fruit of the acacia (قرظ *karaz*), or tanned or dyed with the leaves of the tree سلم *salam*.

A مقروع makrūǥ, Chosen to be a stallion. A prince, chief of a people, master of a family. Marked on the leanest part of the leg or on the middle of the nose (a camel). Beaten, struck.

A مقروف makrūf, Suspected. Blamed, reproved. Slender, graceful, thin, and slim.

A مقروم mahrūm, Marked by a cut in the nose.

A مقرون makrūn, Conjoined, fastened, adhering, bound together; connected, related; near, neighbouring. One who has close eyebrows. (In verse) when three consecutive consonants are moveable or have vowels, and the fourth is quiescent or gezmated; as, متفا *mutafā* (in متفاعلن *mutafāǥalun*), or علتن *ǥalatun* (in متفاعلتن *mutafāǥalatun*). In متفا *mutafā* and علتن *ǥalatun* two cords (سبب *sabab*) are joined together (مقرون *mahrūn*). سعادت مقرون *saǥādat-makrūn*, Happy, august, united with felicity. فعل لفيف المقرون *fiǥli lafīfu'l makrūn*, A verb having two weak letters joined (as شوي).

A مقرونيّة makrūniyat, Conjunction, proximity. مقرونيّة بالاجابة *makrūniyat bi'l ijāba*, Ready (or a readiness) to hear or grant a request.

A مقرويّ makrawiy, Long-backed.

A مقريّ makra', A place in which water is collected. *Mikra'*, One who entertains hospitably. The hospitable cup with which guests are welcomed. *Mukrī*, One who orders to read.

A مقرئ mukris, One who causes or orders to read. The reader or minister of a mosque.

A مقريّ makrīy, Read, legible.

A مقزّح mukazzah, A tree resembling the fig.

A مقزحة mikzahat, A vessel in which they keep spiceries or seasoning (قزح *kizh*) for the pot.

A مقزّع muhazzaǥ, Swift, nimble, light, active. (A horse) prepared to run. One appointed solely to carry good news. One who has thin (hair) and divided in several places. (A horse) thin of hair in the forelocks.

A مقزعلّ muhzaǥill, Posted on an insecure eminence. Quick, expeditious in every thing.

A مقس maks, (v. n. of مقس) Plunging, dipping (a thing) into water. Filling (a water-bottle). Flowing (water). Breaking. Reciting poetry. *Makas*, (v. n. of مقس) Fainting, being indisposed.

A مقساة maksāt, Any thing that causes hardness or obduracy. الذنب مقساة للقلب *az zamb maksātun li'l kalb*, Sin hardens the heart.

A مقسط muksit, Just, equitable, impartial.

A مقسم maksam or miksam, Part, portion. *Muksim*, A place of partition. *Muksam*, Sworn. An oath. A place where they swear. *Muksim*, One who swears (by God).

A مقسّم mukassam, Divided, distributed. Scattered. Possessed of a beautiful (face). Beautified. Sad, sorrowful. *Mukassim*, A divider, distributor. A disperser, scatterer.

A مقسوح maksūh, Dried.

A مقسوم maksūm, Distributed, divided. Quotient.

A مقش mukishsh, One who makes haste, who goes away with rapidity.

A مقشّب mukashshab, Mixed (nobility), doubtful, apocryphal (in birth or reputation).

A مقشر mikshar, Importunate, teasing.

A مقشّر mukashshar, Barked, skinned, peeled. Round. *Mukashshir*, A peeler, barker, skinner.

A مقشعرّ mukshaǥirr, (pl. قشاعر *kashāǥir*) One who trembles or thrills with horror.

A مقشقش mukashkish, One recovering (from scab, mange, measles, or small-pox). One who returns from apostacy or hypocrisy.

A مقشقشتان mukashkishatāni, The two chapters of the Kur'ān entitled, يا ايّها الكافرون *yā ayyuhā'l kāfirūna* and الاخلاص *al ikhlās*.

A مقشم maksham, A pasture. Death.

A مقشوّ makshūw, (or مقشور) Peeled, barked.

A مقشورة makshūrat, A woman whose face is scratched or peeled in order to give her a clear and ruddy complexion.

A مقشيّ makshīy, Peeled, barked, skinned.

A مقص mikass, Shears, scissors. *Mukiss*, (pl. مقاص *makāss*) (A mare) apparently pregnant. A retaliator, one who demands قصاص *kisās*.

A مقصال miksāl, Sharp (sword). Ready (tongue).

A مقصّان mikassāni, Two blades of scissors.

A مقصّب mukassab, Curled, twisted (hair). *Mukassib*, One who guards the towns on the frontier. Milk which has cream floating on the surface.

A مقصبة maksabat, A bed or place where reeds or canes (قصب *kasab*) grow.

A مقصد maksad, Intent, desire, will. Intention, design, aim, end, enterprise. Place of destination or tendency. *Muksad*, Dead of a sudden disease.

A مقصّد mukassad, Of a moderate temperament of body or mind.

A مقصدة maksadat, A woman sought after or courted on account of her elegance of figure. A woman inclined to be short.

A مقصر maksir or maksar, Evening. Twilight. End of the evening. *Maksir*, Less, faulty, deficient, short of. *Muksir*, (Water) round which cattle pasture. Aged (sheep or goat).

A مقصّر mukassar, Deficient, defective, coming short. *Mukassir*, A fuller. One who fails in his duty.

A مقصرة maksarat, (pl. مقاصير makāsir) A mixture of darkness and light; evening. *Miksarat*, A fulling-hammer, or beetle used by fullers, washers, or bleachers. A fuller or bleacher's block.

A مقصّص mukassas, One whose forelocks are cut.

A مقصّع mukassaʻ, Sharp (sword).

A مقصل miksal, Sharp (sword or tongue).

A مقصمل mukasmil, A lion. A shepherd who uses his staff much.

A مقصوّ maksūw, Crop-eared.

A مقصود maksūd, Intended, proposed, desired, wished, sought. Intention, design, aim, view, purpose, drift, desire, scope, object. مقصود كن فكان maksūdi kun fakān, The purpose (of Him who said) "Be, and it was," (an epithet of Muhammad).

A مقصور maksūr, Abridged, curtailed, diminished, confined, restricted. Deficient, defective, insufficient, unequal to, impotent. Shortened (as when جلفار julfār is written جلفر julfar). الف مقصوره alifi maksūra, Short ا alif, sometimes written: as, عصا ʻasa', A staff; but more frequently taking the form of ي with a small ا alif placed above: as, in the word بشريٰ bushra', Glad tidings.

A مقصورة maksūrat, (pl. مقاصير makāsir) The most sacred place (in a temple), the part appropriated to the Imām, or officiating minister. A closet, or any retirement (in a house), to which only the master has access; a sanctum sanctorum. A large, fortified, or protected house. (A woman) kept at home. The ornamented chamber where the bride sits. Near, neighbouring. Edge (of a plate).

A مقصورةً maksūratan, In the next degree of kin.

A مقصوص maksūs, Cut. (A bird) clipped in the wings. مقصوص له maksūsun lahu, Punished, retaliated on him.

A مقصوع maksūʻ, (A boy) who thrives not on his food, stunted in his growth.

A مقصىٰ muksa', (A camel or sheep) the tips of whose ears have been cut off. Remote, removed.

A مقصيّ maksīy, (A camel or a sheep) the tips of whose ears have been cropped.

A مقضاب mikzāb, A pruning-hook. (Ground) producing plenty of clover (قضب kazb).

A مقضب mikzab, Pruning-hook. Sharp (sword).

A مقضبة makzabat, A place where clover grows. A place where trees grow of which bows are made.

A مقضم makzam, Any thing eaten by the front teeth: hence, food in a moderate quantity.

A مقضوض makzūz, Large gravel. Food mixed with gravel, gritty.

A مقضيّ makzīy, Finished, settled. Perfected, completed. Decreed. P مقضيّ المرام شدن makzīyu'l marām shudan, To obtain the completion of one's wishes. A علىٰ مقضيّ الفؤاد ʻala' makzīyi'l fuʼād, According to the heart's desire.

A مقط makt, (v. n. of مقط) Breaking (the neck). Binding with a small rope. Putting in a furious passion. Throwing (a ball) on the ground and catching (it) at the rebound. Prostrating, throwing down. Striking (with a stick or with a small firm-twisted rope). Treading (as a bird). Adjuring (by the faith). Twisting lightly. A hard twist of a rope. Vehemence, severity, hardness. *Mukt*, (pl. امقاط amkāt) A rope or gin for catching birds. (pl. of ماقط mākit) Buckets, ropes. Halters, bridles. *Makit*, Born in the sixth or seventh month.

A مقطّ makatt or mikatt, The part where the cartilages of the ribs terminate. *Mikatt*, A piece of bone on which they nib their writing-reeds or pens.

A مقطار miktār, Water-dropping (cloud).

A مقطاع miktāʻ, Unsteady in friendship, apt to give the cut. (A well) soon drained of water.

A مقطّب mukattib, One who frowns, knits his brows, and puts on a grim, frowning, austere look.

A مقطّة mikattat, Bone on which they nib pens.

A مقطر miktar, A chafing-dish, fire-pan, censer.

A مقطّر mukattar, Allowed to fall drop by drop. Distilling, dropping, trickling. ماء مقطّر mā'i mukattar, (P آب مقطّر ābi mukattar) Distilled water.

A مقطرة miktarat, A chafing-dish. A censer. Wooden shackles, the stocks.

A مقطرن mukatran, Besmeared with pitch.

A مقطع maktaʻ, (v. n. of قطع) Cutting, amputating. Dividing. A cut; place of separation. Pass of a river, ford. A pause in the Kur'ān. Interruption, an abrupt breaking off. (pl. مقاطع makātiʻ) A place where sand breaks off, or where any thing ends and leaves off. Cesura or pause in reading verse. مقطع كلام maktaʻi kalām, An interruption in speech. مقطع الحقّ maktaʻu'l hakk, The point where a judicial sentence hits the truth. That whereby falsehood is exploded. *Miktaʻ*, (pl. مقاطع makātiʻ) Shears for cutting cloth or silver. Any cutting-instrument. *Muktaʻ*, Torn (from friends). One who is passed by when his companions are honoured with gifts. One who has no ديوان dīwān. A man who loves not women. (A camel) weak and tired with covering, or broken down with leanness. A place where a river is crossed, or a ditch excavated. حروف مقطعة hurūfi muktaʻa, Cut or separate letters, i.e. abbreviations, or letters put for words, as صلعم salʻam. *Muktiʻ*, Prevented from continuing a journey, especially a pilgrimage to Mecca. Silenced, overcome in argument.

A مقطّع mukattaʻ, Cut into several pieces. Cut out, shaped. Well-dressed. Well-shaped, beautiful. Short, dwarfish. Disjoined. (Iron heads) made for arms (as arrows, spears, and the like). مقطّع الاسحار mukattaʻu'l (or mukattiʻu'l) as-hār, (fem. مقطّعة الاسحار mukattaʻatu'l (or mukattiʻatu'l) as-hār) A hare (because her own lungs or those of the hounds often burst in running).

A مقطّعات mukattaʻāt, Small garments, especially made of coarse silk. Narrow (cloths). Short (poems). Printed stuffs.

A مقطعة maktaʻat, Whatever cuts down or carries off (as fasting does sensual desires).

A مقطّعة mukattaʻat, (Wine) diluted with water.

A مقطف miktaf, A hamper.

A مقطّفة mukattafat, A short man, a dwarf.

A مقطقط mukatkat, Small about the head.

A مقطّل mukattal, Cooked.

A مقطلة miktalat, An iron cutting-instrument.

A مقطم miktam, A nail, claw, talon.

A مقطّم mukattam, Name of a hill in Egypt.

A مقطنة maktanat, A cotton-plantation.

A مقطوب maktūb, Mixed (wine).

A مقطور maktūr, Dropped, fallen in drops. Besmeared with pitch. (Land) moistened with rain.

A مقطورة maktūrat, (Camels) tied by the string قطار kitār, one behind another.

A مقطوط maktūt, Dear (provision), high (price or assize of victuals).

A مقطوطعات muktawtiʻāt, (or مقطوعات maktūʻātin) (The horses came in) gallopping singly.

A مقطوع maktūʻ, Cut, amputated. Mutilated, disabled. Separated, unconnected, interrupted, intercepted, broken off, abrupt. Agreed upon, adjusted, concluded, arranged. Deficient, carried off, removed. A straggler. A bargain, price agreed upon. Afflicted with an asthma, troubled with a shortness of breath. (in prosody) A verse terminating in a foot called وتد watad, as فعل faʻal deprived of its letter and becoming فع faʻ. مقطوع الذنب maktūʻu'z zanab, Wanting the tail, docked. مقطوع العضو maktūʻu'l ʻuzw, Maimed, lame in any member. مقطوع به maktūʻun bihi, Prevented from it, i.e. pursuing a journey. جرف مقطوع jurfi maktūʻ, An abrupt precipice.

A مقطوف maktūf, Gathered (fruit).

A مقطول maktūl, Cut. Killed.

A مقطئرّ muktaʻirr, Passionate.

A مقع makʻ, (v. n. of مقع) Drinking eagerly. Abusing, reviling. Suspecting.

A مقعار mikʻār, One who moves his mouth much in speaking, a mouther. Deep and capacious (bowl).

A مقعاص mikʻās, A lion that kills instantly.

A مقعالّة mukʻāllat, (A stone) standing erect, but not fixed in the ground.

A مقعّب mukaʻʻab, Cup-resembling (hoof of a horse, or depressed navel, Canticles vii. 2).

A مقعبل mukaʻbal, One whose toes turn in much.

A مقعثلّ mukʻasill, Rough, ill-polished (arrow).

A مقعد makʻad, (v. n. of قعد) Sitting down, resting. A seat, chair, carpet, cushion. (pl. مقاعد makāʻid) Hips, buttocks, anus. مقعد القابلة makʻadu'l kābilat, Very near. *Mukʻad*, Lame, crippled, obliged to sit, unable to stir. (The breasts of a girl) beginning to swell. Flat-nosed. A poem which has a foot dropped and halts in every verse. Name of a man who used to feather arrows. An eaglet or young vulture. A vulture caught by a poisoned bait for the use of his feathers. *Muk̤ʻad*, (or مقعّد *muk̤aʻʻad*) A veteran soldier exempted from further military duty.

A مقعدات *muk̤ʻadāt*, Frogs. Young katā birds ere they have begun to rise from the ground.

A مقعدان *muk̤ʻadān*, Name of a tree not browsed.

A مقعدة *mak̤ʻadat*, The place of sitting. A seat. The buttocks. A basis. *Muk̤ʻadat*, A hamper made of palm-leaves. A well excavated, but no water appearing, therefore abandoned.

A مقعدد *muk̤aʻdad*, An eaglet or young vulture. A vulture caught by an envenomed bait, and deplumed thereby.

A مقعّر *muk̤aʻʻar*, Excavated. Hollow, concave. Deep, profound. The concave surface of a sphere. مقعّر الصدر *muk̤aʻʻaru's sadr*, Hollow in the breast.

P آيينۀ مقعّر *āyīnaʼi muk̤aʻʻar*, A concave mirror.

A مقعص *mik̤ʻas*, A lion that kills instantly.

A مقعّط *muk̤aʻʻat*, A burden high above a camel's back. *Muk̤aʻʻit*, Rigid in exacting a debt.

A مقعطة *mik̤ʻatat*, A turban-sash, wreath.

A مقعقع *muk̤aʻk̤aʻ*, (Ground) dry and echoing. *Muk̤aʻk̤iʻ*, A shaker of gaming arrows with a rattling noise.

A مقعنسس *muk̤ʻansis*, (pl. مقاعس *mak̤āʻis* and مقاعيس *mak̤āʻīs*) Strong, firm, hard.

A مقعوصة *mak̤ʻūsat*, (A sheep) troubled with the distemper called قعاص *k̤uʻās*.

A مقعوطة *muk̤ʻūtat*, Dung rolled by a beetle.

A مقعى *muk̤ʻī*, Seated or squatting with the buttocks resting on the heels.

A مقفّا *muk̤affā*, (for مقفّى *muk̤affa'*) Rythmically composed (oration).

A مقفار *mik̤fār*, A desert without herbage or water.

A مقفر *muk̤fir*, Ruined, desolate, desert.

A مقفّز *muk̤affaz*, (A horse) whose fore-legs are white to the knees like stockings; stockinged.

A مقفّص *muk̤affas*, (A garment) striped after the fashion of a bird-cage (قفص *k̤afas*).

A مقفّع *muk̤affaʻ*, Contracted, shrunk. One who has shrivelled (and contracted hands). *Muk̤affiʻ*, One who habitually hangs his head.

A مقفعة *mik̤faʻat*, A ferula with which children are corrected.

A مقفل *muk̤fal*, (or مقفّل *muk̤affal*) Bolted, locked (door). Close-handed, stingy.

A مقفول *mak̤fūl*, Locked, bolted (door).

A مقفى *muk̤fa'*, Preferred before, set over. *Muk̤fī*, One who prefers, or gives the preference. One who selects or appoints. (See اقفاء *ik̤fāʼ*.)

A مقفّى *muk̤affa'*, (An oration) rythmically composed, rhyming. *Muk̤affī*, One who sends after, in the track of, or who causes to follow.

A مقفّى *mak̤fīy*, Killed by an incision or blow on the back of the head or neck (قفا *k̤afa'*).

A مقق *mak̤ak̤*, The length of a horse.

A مققة *mak̤ak̤at*, Sucking kids. Ignorant (men).

A مقل *mak̤l*, (v. n. of مقل) Beholding, looking at. Immerging (a thing) in water till (it) is covered. Putting (a stone) into a vessel in order to distribute water equally (this is done where there is any apprehension of scarcity of water when travelling through deserts; on which occasion, in order to proportion with justice the allowance for men and camels, they put a stone into the measuring vessel, which they just cover over with water, and so serve the caravan with impartiality). Striking. Bottom of a well. A particular mode of suckling or feeding young animals (when afraid that a young camel should drink too much they give it by little and little out of the palms of the hands). *Muk̤l*, Fruit of the dwarf or wild palm-tree called دوم *dawm*. Frankincense. Bdellium, a fragrant Arabian gum-tree. *Muk̤al*, (pl. of مقلة *muk̤lat*) The black parts of the eye.

P مقل *muk̤l*, A heavy iron mace. A medicine for driving away love. An aromatic mixture of aloes, amber, sandal, and other ingredients. Gum.

A مقلّ *muk̤ill*, Poor, indigent, possessing little.

A مقلاء *mik̤lāʼ*, The club or bandy with which the قلة *k̤ulat* is struck in an Eastern game. مقلاء القنيص *mik̤lāʼu'l k̤anīs*, Name of a dog.

A مقلاة *mik̤lāt*, (pl. مقالي) A frying-pan.

A مقلات *mik̤lāt*, (A woman) with no surviving offspring. (A camel) conceiving once and no more.

A مقلاد *mik̤lād*, (pl. مقاليد *mak̤ālīd*) A key. A treasury, magazine.

A مقلاص *mik̤lās*, (A camel) fattening in summer.

A مقلاع *mik̤lāʻ*, A sling (for stones). A pickaxe or implement for stocking up the ground.

A مقلاعة *mik̤lāʻat*, A sling.

A مقلاق *mik̤lāk̤*, Restless (man or woman).

A مقلب *mik̤lab*, A spade, or any similar instrument with which ground is dug or turned over.

A مقلّب *muk̤allib*, A turner. مقلّب القلوب *muk̤allibu'l k̤ulūb*, (God) the converter of hearts.

A مقلة *mak̤lat*, A stone put into a vessel in order to distribute water equally. *Muk̤lat*, The eyeball. (pl. مقل *muk̤al*) The black, also the white of the eye. The pupil of the eye. The middle of any thing. سواد المقلة *sawādu'l muk̤lat*, The pupil of the eye, (met.) Any thing very dear to one. ابن مقلة *ibn muk̤lat*, Name of a celebrated calligrapher, the inventor of sundry kinds of Arabic writing; such as the ثلث *suls*, توقيع *tawk̤īʻ*, نسخ *naskh*, ريحان *rayhān*, رقاع *rik̤āʻ*, and محقّق *muhak̤k̤ak̤*.

A مقلتة *mak̤latat*, A place of danger. Danger.

A مقلد *mik̤lad*, (pl. مقالد *mak̤ālid*) A key. A crooked instrument with which they twist straw or hay into ropes. A forage-sack. A measure for dry goods. A staff with a crooked head.

A مقلّد *muk̤allad*, Imitated, mimicked, represented; imitable. The place to which a sword is suspended from the shoulder. The lower part of the neck where the necklace goes. Adorned with a necklace or chain. (A horse) so ornamented when conqueror in a race. *Muk̤allid*, (A woman) adorning herself with a necklace. A ludicrous imitator, mimic, mime, mummer, buffoon.

A مقلّدات *muk̤alladāt*, Poems extant from age to age.

A مقلّس *muk̤allis*, A mime, a mummer; or he who beats the Arabian drum دف *daf*, and meets or goes before kings and other great men with that and other musical instruments on triumphal occasions.

A مقلّص *muk̤allas*, Habitually prepared for a journey. *Muk̤allis*, (A horse) having long projecting legs, and of a quick pace.

A مقلع *muk̤laʻ*, (v. n. 4 of قلع) Abstaining, desisting. *Muk̤liʻ*, (A ship) rigged with sails.

A مقلعة *muk̤liʻat*, Rigged (vessel).

A مقلعطّ *muk̤laʻitt*, Fleeing away, frightened. One whose hair is much curled or crisped.

A مقلفع *muk̤alfaʻ*, Dirty (wool).

A مقلّل *muk̤allal*, (A sword) with a pommel.

A مقلم *mik̤lam*, A camel's sheath.

A مقلّم *muk̤allam*, Pared (nail). Armed (battalion). Unmarried, single (woman). مقلّم الظفر *muk̤allamu'z zufr*, One whose nails have been cut; contemptible, despicable.

A مقلمة *mik̤lamat*, A pen-case.

A مقلّمة *muk̤allamat*, Unmarried (woman).

A مقلوّ *mak̤lūw*, Fried, cooked in a frying-pan.

A مقلوب *mak̤lūb*, Turned, inverted, converted. Subverted, overturned. (A camel) troubled with the distemper قلاب *k̤ulāb*. مقلوب القلب *mak̤lūbu'l k̤alb*, Perverse-hearted. مقلوب مستوي *mak̤lūb mustawī*, A word or a sentence which may be read backward or forward (as درد; or in English, madam), a palindrome.

A مقلوبة *mak̤lūbat*, The ear.

A مقلود *mak̤lūd*, Twisted (rope or bracelet).

A مقلوع *mak̤lūʻ*, Eradicated, torn up, removed from its place. Removed from office, cashiered. (A horse) marked with white under the saddle. Troubled with the thrush.

A مقلوف *mak̤lūf*, Unbunged (barrel).

A مقلوفة *mak̤lūfat*, (pl. مقلوفات *mak̤lūfāt*) A hamper full of dates (used in Bahrayn).

A مقلوم *mak̤lūm*, Pared, clipped. مقلوم الظفر *mak̤lūmu'z zufr*, Abject (whose nails are cut).

SY مقلونيا *mak̤lūniyā*, A long cucumber.

A مقلهفّ *muk̤lahiff*, Thick, long, dishevelled, and high-standing (hair).

A مقلى *mik̤la'*, A frying-pan. The stick, bandy, bat, or racket with which the ball (قلة *k̤ulat*) is struck in the game of hockey or shinty.

A مقليّ *mak̤līy*, Fried in a pan.

A مقلية *mak̤liyat*, (v. n. of قلي) Hating.

SY مقليسا *mak̤līsā*, Seed of wild rue.

A مقمّ *mik̤amm*, (A man) eating whatever is set

before him.

A مقمأة *makmaʼat*, A place upon which the rays of the sun shine not.

A مقمار *mikmār*, A palm-tree bearing white unripe dates.

A مقمّة *mikammat*, A besom, broom. *Mikammat* or *makammat*, The mouth or lips of a bull, or of any animal dividing the hoof.

A مقمجر *mukamjir*, A bow-maker.

A مقمر *mukmir*, (or مقمرة) A moon-shine night.

A مقمطر *mukamtar*, (Milk) turned by rennet.

A مقمعة *mikmaʻat*, (pl. مقامع *makāmiʻ*) An iron hooked instrument with which they strike the head of an elephant when training or guiding him. A club, mace, or any thing similar with which a man's pate is broken.

A مقمعدّ *mukmaʻidd*, One who although spoken to most energetically remains untractable and disobedient. One, the upper part of whose belly is prominent, and the lower part shrunk and collapsed.

A مقمقة *makmakat*, (v. n. of مقمق Q) Speaking from the bottom of the throat.

A مقمل *mikmal*, Waxen rich after having been poor. *Mukmil*, Breeding lice; pediculous.

A مقمن *makman*, (or مقمنة *makmanat*) Convenient, apt, worthy, fit, suitable, becoming, proper.

A مقموءة *makmuʼat*, A spot inaccessible to the sun.

A مقمور *makmūr*, Beaten at dice. Evil, wickedness.

A مقموط *makmūt*, Bound hand and foot.

A مقموع *makmūʻ*, Conquered, subdued. (A herd of camels) stripped of their choicest ones. Troubled with indigestion (قمع *kumaʻ*).

A مقمئنّ *mukmaʼinn*, Shrunk, wrinkled.

A مقناب *miknāb*, The claw of a lion.

A مقناة *maknaʼat*, (*maknuʼat*, or مقناة *maknāt*) A place on which the sun shines not.

G مقناطيس *miknātīs*, The loadstone.

A مقنب *miknab*, The claw of a lion. A troop, especially of horse, from thirty to forty, or three hundred. A hunter's bag in which he carries his game.

A مقنبع *mukambiʻ*, Long-shaped.

A مقنثع *mukansiʻ*, Large-bearded (man).

A مقند *mukannad*, (or مقندي *mukanda'*)(Any thing) dressed with sugar-candy. (Wheat or barley-meal) dressed with candied sugar (قند *kand*).

A مقنّر *mukannir*, Corpulent and ugly. One who wears a turban loose and awry.

A مقنّش *mukannash*, Liberal, profuse (household-expenditure).

A مقنطر *mukantar*, Perfect, complete. Arched.

A مقنطرات *mukantarāt*, Circles parallel with the horizon. Bridges. Arches.

A مقنطرة *mukantarat*, A hundred pounds weight.

A مقنطرة *mukantaratan*, By talents.

G مقنطيس *miknatīs*, The loadstone.

A مقنع *maknaʻ*, Sufficient, satisfactory, valid, legal (evidence). *Miknaʻ*, (and مقنعة *miknaʻat*)(pl. مقانع *makāniʻ*) A coif of fine linen about two cubits long, open before, worn by the Arabian women at home and abroad. *Muknaʻ*, One whose teeth are bent inward. *Mukniʻ*, One who lifts up the eyes to heaven in devotion or humility.

A مقنّع *mukannaʻ*, Covered with a helmet of iron. قمر المقنع *kamaru'l mukannaʻ*, A certain luminous appearance in the sky, which was produced by the art of a thaumaturgist named Mukanna.

A مقنعة *maknaʻat*, Riches. *Muknaʻat*, A shepherd's pipe. *Mukniʻat*, A high-voiced she-camel.

A مقنّف *mukannaf*, Large (shield of leather).

A مقنفش *mukanfish*, Slovenly in dress, or disgusting in appearance.

A مقنّن *mukannin*, An institutor. مقنّن قوانين عدل و احسان *mukannini kawānīni ʻadl u ihsān*, Author of the institutions of justice and clemency.

A مقنوة *maknuwat*, (or مقنؤة *maknuʼat*) A place not exposed to the sun.

A مقنود *maknūd*, Dressed with sugar-candy.

A مقنور *mukanwir*, Corpulent and ugly. One who wears a turban loose and awry.

A مقني *muknī*, A spearman.

A مقنّي *mukannī*, Skilful in finding water. مقنّي الارض *mukannī'l arz*, The hoopoo.

A مقو *makw*, (v. n. of مقا for مقو) Polishing (a sword). Cleaning (the teeth). Sucking violently (a camel's colt). Guarding. Custody.

A مقوال *mikwāl*, Loquacious, talkative, verbose (man or woman; literally, a talking-instrument).

A مقود *makūd*, A horse or camel led in the hand and not ridden. *Mikwad*, (pl. مقاود *makāwid*) Reins, a bridle, halter, that by which an animal is led.

A مقوّد *mukawwad*, Led. A long mountain.

A مقوّر *mukawwar*, Bedaubed with pitch.

A مقورّ *makwarr*, Slender-flanked (horse).

A مقوس *mikwas*, A quiver. A bow-case. A barrier, starting-post: the rope stretched before horses when starting at a race. A course, race-ground.

A مقوّض *mukawwaz*, Demolished, taken down.

A مقوط *mukūt*, A being very lean and emaciated.

A مقوّق *mukawwak*, One on whose head there is a large bald place.

A مقوقس *mukawkis*, A bird resembling a pigeon with a black and white ring round the neck. Name of the king of Egypt and Alexandria. Name of the kings of India.

A مقول *makūl*, (originally مقوول *makwūl*) Said, above-mentioned. What is said. A word, any thing spoken before. *Mikwal*, (pl. مقاول *makāwil* and مقاولة *makāwilat*, The instrument of talking, the tongue. Very talkative (man or woman). A king, especially of the Himyarite Arabians (a dictator). ذو مقول جري *zū mikwali jarī*, Glib-tongued.

A مقوّل *mukawwal*, Repeated again and again.

A مقوم *mikwam*, A plough-tail or handle.

A مقوّم *mukawwam*, Appointed, set over. Straightened. Valued, appraised. *Mukawwim*, One who rectifies, constitutes, adjusts, arranges, or directs.

A مقوود *makwūd*, (A horse or camel) led by the hand (not ridden).

A مقوول *makwūl*, Said, spoken, above-mentioned.

A مقوي *mukwī*, Possessed of a strong beast of burden. Strong (horse). One who descends into a desert. One whose provisions have all run out.

A مقوّي *mukawwa'*, Strengthened. Suspected. Reproached with, accused of. A case, especially one of a circular oblong shape, in which they carry rolls of papers. *Mukawwī*, Corroborative. A strengthener, confirmer, fortifier. A comforter. P مقوّيات دل *mukawwiyāti dil*, Cordials. A مقوّيات دماغ *mukawwiyāti dimāgh*, Cephalics. مقوّيات كبد *mukawwiyāti kabid*, Hepatics. مقوّيات معدة *mukawwiyāti miʻda*, Tonics. مقوّيات للباءة *mukawwiyāt li'l bāʼat*, Aphrodisiacks, stimulants.

A مقه *makah*, Grey or blue (colour of the eye). A disease of the eye, caused by a want of collyrium.

A مقهاء *mak-hāʼ*, (fem. of امقه *amkah*) Blue-eyed (woman). Water-coloured (wine).

A مقهر *muk-har*, Subdued, defeated, conquered.

A مقهنب *mukahnib*, One ever at the water.

A مقهور *mak-hūr*, Conquered, subdued, vanquished. Oppressed, vexed. (Flesh) caught by the fire and emitting moisture.

A مقي *maky*, (v. n. of مقى) Polishing (a sword); scouring (a bason). Guarding. *Maka'*, (v. n. of مقي) Cleaning (teeth).

A مقيّء *mukayyiʼ*, Vomitive (medicine).

A مقياس *mikyās*, Quantity, measure. A measuring-instrument, the nilometer of Egypt. The hand of a watch or a dial.

A مقية *mukyat*, Inner corner of the eye.

A مقيت *makīt*, Hated. *Mukīt*, Powerful. One who maintains in victuals and takes care of. A guardian, keeper, inspector. A witness. على كلّ شيء مقيت *ʻala' kulli shayʼin mukīt*, (God is) the guardian of every thing.

A مقيّد *mukayyad*, (pl. مقاييد *makāyīd*) Bound, fixed. Fettered. Determined. Attentive, solicitous, dedicated to, diligent. Written, noted, registered, signed, marked. That part of the leg which is enclosed by the fetter, the ankle. A place where a camel is fettered and then left. Verse in which the حرف رويّ *harfi rawiy* is silent. بنو مقيّد *banū mukayyad*, Scorpions. P مقيّد شدن *mukayyad shudan*, To give attention, to study, take care of. A مقيّدة الحمار *mukayyadatu'l himār*, A stony, burnt-up country.

A مقيّدي *mukayyadi*, Bondage. Close attention.

A مقيّر *mukayyar*, Daubed over with pitch.

A مقيس *makīs*, Compared. Comparison.

A مقيّس *mukayyas*, Embroidered, ornamented. Analogous.

A مقيسرة *mukaysirat*, Aged (camels).

A مقيض *makīẓ*, The part of the egg touched by the shell. The place where an egg is laid.

A مقيضة *makīẓat*, (A well) full of water.

A مقيظ *makīẓ* or *makyaẓ*, A summer-residence.

A مقيّظ *mukayyiẓ*, Sufficient for the hot season.

A مقيظة *makīẓat*, Plants remaining green till midsummer, or hot season called قيظ *kayẓ*.

A مقيعس *mukayʻis*, (or مقيعس *mukayʻis*) (dim. of مقعنس *mukʻansis*) Moderately strong.

A مقيل *makīl*, (v. n. of قال for قيل) Taking a nap at mid-day or a little before. Any place where one reposes then, a dormitory. The grave.

P مقيل *mukīl*, A dish of wheat, barley, vetches, lentils, beans, peas, and scarlet beans, eaten on the tenth day of Muharram.

A مقيّل *mukayyil*, Who gives to drink at noon.

P مقيلبا *mukīl-bā*, A kind of spoon-meat, composed of pounded flesh, sheep's chitterlings, chopped small, the fat of a sheep's tail, mixed up with onions, wheat, rice, vetches, lentils, beans, scarlet-beans, turnips, beet, leeks, and carrots, and eaten on the tenth day of Muharram.

A مقيم *mukīm*, A dweller, resident, inhabitant. Fixed, assiduous, constant, persevering. P مقيم شدن *mukīm shudan*, To dwell. To persevere. مقيم منزل هفتم *mukīmi manzili haftum*, The planet Saturn.

P مقيمي *makīmī*, Brokerage.

A مقيّن *mukayyin*, A decorator, adorner.

A مقيّنة *mukayyinat*, The tire-woman of a bride.

A مقيء *mukīʼ*, An emetic.

A مقيّئ *mukayyiʼ*, Emetical, vomitive.

A مقيئات *mukīʼāt*, Emetics.

P مك *mak*, (imp. of مكيدن *makīdan*) Suck thou. One who sucks. *Mak* or *muk*, A short spear, halberd, javelin.

A مكّ *makk*, (v. n. of مكّ) Sucking. Diminishing, destroying. Voiding (excrement). Suction.

A مكا *makā'*, (v. n. of مكا for مكو) Swelling (as the hand) with labour. The hole of a fox or hare.

A مكاء *mukāʼ*, (v. n. of مكا for مكو) Hissing. Whistling (a bird or man, especially on his fingers). Being exposed and breaking wind (posteriors).

A مكّاء *mukkāʼ*, (pl. مكاكي *makākī*) A kind of small bird whistling in gardens.

P مكاب *makāb*, Do not dig, do not search for. Reluctance.

A مكابحة *mukābahat*, (v. n. 3 of كبح) Reviling, reproaching, abusing one another.

A مكابدة *mukābadat*, (v. n. 3 of كبد) Waxing callous with regard to evil, and enduring it with all its inconveniences. Labour, toil.

A مكابرة *mukābarat*, (v. n. 3 of كبر) Lifting up. Contending. Haughtiness, contention. مكابرهٔ و عناد *mukābara u ʻinād*, Contention and stubbornness. جدل و مكابره *jadal u mukābara*, Altercation and pride.

A مكابسة *mukābasat*, An assaulting one another.

A مكابلة *mukābalat*, (v. n. 3 of كبل) Putting off payment of a debt. Deferring to purchase a house adjoining to that which one possesses, in order that, after being bought by another, he may recover it at law by right of pre-emption (an evil practice).

A مكابين *makābīn*, (pl. of مكبونة *makbūnat*) Short-legged, big-bellied, slender-boned (horses).

A مكاتب *makātib*, (pl. of مكتب *maktab*) Schools. *Mukātab*, A slave self-ransomed (written off).

A مكاتبة *mukātabat*, (v. n. 3 of كتب) Corresponding by letter. (A slave) giving a certain sum of money to his master for liberty; literally, writing off his slavery.

A مكاتعة *mukātaʻat*, (v. n. 3 of كتع) Fighting, assaying to kill. Driving or keeping away from any thing good.

A مكاتلة *mukātalat*, (v. n. 3 of كتل) Fighting. Cursing, damning, keeping (any one) from happiness.

A مكاتمة *mukātamat*, A concealing (of one's secret).

A مكاتيب *makātīb*, (pl. of مكتوب *maktūb*) Letters. Writings. خليطهاي مكاتيب *khalītahāyi makātīb*, Letter-bags.

A مكاثبة *mukāsabat*, (v. n. 3 of كثب) Approaching, drawing nigh.

A مكاثرة *mukāsarat*, (v. n. 3 of كثر) Disputing about multitude. Asking (from any person) much (water) to drink. Copiousness.

A مكاثمة *mukāsamat*, (v. n. 3 of كثم) Approaching. Interfering, mixing, or having business with.

A مكاحل *makāhil*, (pl. of مكحل *mik-hal*) Pins, bodkins for anointing the eyes with collyrium. (pl. of مكحلة *muk-hulat*) Culverins. Muskets.

A مكاد *makād*, (and مكادة *makādat*) (v. n. of كاد for كود) Being near, or all but (doing). Being hardly able (to do).

A مكادمة *mukādamat*, (v. n. 3 of كدم) Being unable to bite herbage (cattle).

A مكاذبة *mukāzabat*, (v. n. 3 of كذب) Considering as false, regarding as a liar.

A مكّار *makkār*, Cheat, knave, impostor, deceiver.

A مكارات *mukārāt*, A hiring out, letting on hire.

A مكاربة *mukārabat*, (v. n. 3 of كرب) Being near (happening). Preparing for.

A مكاردة *mukāradat*, A driving off one another.

A مكارزة *mukārazat*, (v. n. 3 of كرز) Running to any place and hiding there. Fleeing from. Endeavouring to get the start of another. Disabling.

A مكارم *makārim*, (pl. of مكرمة *makrumat*) Laudable or generous actions of noble, honourable men. Excellencies, virtues. Favours, benefits. Miracles.

A مكارمة *mukāramat*, (v. n. 3 of كرم) Contending, vying with about honour, nobility, or bounty.

A مكارون *mukārūn*, (pl. of مكاري) Camel-hirers.

A مكاره *makārih*, Inconveniences, misfortunes, accidents. Disagreeable things.

A مكاري *mukārī*, (pl. اكرياء *akriyāʼ* and مكارون *mukārūn*) One who lets out camels, horses, or mules. A muleteer. A camel-leader.

A مكّاري *makkārī*, Cheating, knavery, roguery.

P مكاس *makās*, Do not diminish. *Mukās*, Earnest endeavour, intense exertion, importunity. Toll, tribute, custom. A toll-gatherer; a tithe-collector.

A مكاس *makās*, A place where a serpent coils itself up. *Mikās*, (v. n. 3 of مكس) Bidding against each other. P مكاس كردن *mikās kardan*, To bid against another, to raise the price.

A مكاساة *mukāsāt*, A contending for glory.

A مكاسب *makāsib*, (pl. of مكسب) Earnings.

A مكاسحة *mukāsahat*, A drinking hard together.

A مكاسر *mukāsir*, Near, neighbouring. A neighbour, one whose house, or the skirt of whose tent (كسر *kasr*), is in juxtaposition with one's own.

A مكاسرة *mukāsarat*, (v. n. 3 of كسر) Contending or vying with in breaking. Consternation.

A مكاسي *mukāsanī*, (in the dialect of Morocco) Servants of the royal household.

P مكاسه *mukāsa*, A village held free by a Poligar on condition of his protecting the property of passengers (an Indian term).

A مكاسير *makāsīr*, (pl. of مكسور) Things broken.

A مكاشحة *mukāshahat*, (v. n. 3 of كشح) Having a secret grudge against.

A مكاشر *mukāshir*, Opposite. جاري مكاشري *jārī mukāshirī*, My neighbour lives over against me (as though he were grinning at me).

A مكاشرة *mukāsharat*, (v. n. 3 of كشر) Laughing or grinning (at one) with shut teeth.

A مكاشفة *mukāshafat*, (v. n. 3 of كشف) Acting openly (with). Shewing open enmity, persecuting. Displaying (any thing). Revelation, apocalypse.

A مكاظّة *mukāẓẓat*, (v. n. 3 of كظّ) Endeavouring to get into the thick of the fight.

A مكاعمة *mukāʻamat*, (v. n. 3 of كعم) Kissing. Lying within one garment (with a woman).

A مكافأة *mukāfaʼat*, (v. n. 3 of كفأ) Recompensing, requiting. Answering exactly. Being equal, like, resembling. Observing, watching, guarding. Repelling, warding off. Spearing alternately.

A مكافاة *mukāfāt*, (v. n. 3 of كفي) Compensating. Recompense, retribution, compensation.

A مكافتة *mukāfatat*, (v. n. 3 of كفت) Getting the start in a race, surpassing, overcoming, excelling. Dying suddenly.

A مكافحة *mukāfahat*, (v. n. 3 of كفح) Disclosing, laying open. Looking in the face and speaking to. Kissing with unveiled lips. Fighting with drawn swords. Altercation, strife, battle.

A مكافرة *mukāfarat*, A denying one his due.

A مكافل *mukāfil*, A neighbour. A sworn ally.

A مكافئ *mukāfiʼ*, (commonly *mukāfī*) Equal, like another in any quality that admits comparison.

A مكافئتان *mukāfaʼatāni*, (or *mukāfiʼatāni*) Equal in age, &c. (two sheep).

A مكافيف *makāfīf*, (pl. of مكفوف) Blind.

A مکاك mukāk, Sucked.

A مکاکة mukākat, Marrow. Any thing sucked.

A مکّاکة makkākat, A handmaid.

P مکاکفت makākaft, Pain, trouble, misfortune.

A مکاکي makākī, (pl. of مکّاء mukkā) Small birds whistling in gardens. (pl. of مکّوك makkūk) Measures which contain three کیلجات kaylajāt.

A مکاکیك makākīk, (pl. of مکّوك makkūk) Measures containing three کیلجات kaylajāt.

A مکال makāl, (v. n. of کال for کیل) Measuring (corn). Mukāl, Fat, tallow.

A مکالبة mukālabat, (v. n. 3 of کلب) Feeding on thorns (a camel). Being malignant, hurting one another. Suffering from want.

A مکالحة mukālahat, (v. n. 3 of کلح) Not declining from her mansion (the moon).

A مکالمة mukālamat, (v. n. 3 of کلم) Talking together. Conversation, dialogue, conference. P مکالمه کردن mukālama kardan, To discourse, reason.

A مکامة mukāmat, A married woman.

A مکامرة mukāmarat, (v. n. 3 of کمر) Contending, vying with (another) regarding the size of his gland (کمر kamar).

A مکامعة mukāmaȥat, (v. n. 3 of کمع) Lying within one garment with. Drawing to one's self.

A مکامن makāmin, (pl. of مکمن) Ambushes.

A مکامیح makāmīh, (Camels) near the birth. Camels travelling all night, so as to reach water early in the morning.

A مکان makān, (pl. امکنة amkinat and اماکن amākin) A place. A habitation, house, dwelling. Dignity. مکان خفي makāni khafī, A secret place. مکان رفیع makāni rafīȥ, A high place. Exalted dignity. مکان قریب makāni karīb, A near place. The grave. Makāna, In place of, instead of. قتله مکانه katalahu makānahu, He slew him on the spot.

A مکّان makkān, One who sucks his cattle from avarice, so as not to be overheard in milking them.

A مکانات makānāt, (pl. of مکانة makānat) Places. Dignities, posts of honour.

A مکانة makānat, (v. n. of مکن) Occupying rank and station near a monarch. Being firmly settled. A place. Authority, dignity. An office at court. Slowness, sedateness, gravity. Design, purpose, intention. (in the dialect of Morocco) A watch.

P مکاندار makān-dār, Owner of a place. The fakīr who occupies any particular station. A watchman.

A مکانس makānis, (pl. of مکنسة) Besoms.

A مکانفة mukānafat, An assisting mutually.

A مکانيّ makāniy, Relating to place, local.

A مکاواة mukāwāt, A railing (at one another).

A مکاوحة mukāwahat, (v. n. 3 of کاح for کوح) Railing at one another. Abusing each other face to face. Conquering in fight.

A مکاوسة mukāwasat, A throwing prostrate.

A مکاهاة mukāhāt, A contending for glory.

A مکاهلة mukāhalat, (v. n. 3 of کهل) Being married. Being advanced in age, getting on in life.

A مکاهنة mukāhanat, (v. n. 3 of کهن) Conniving, winking at. Helping one another, or giving gifts without recompense. Inclining towards one another. Respect, regard.

A مکائد makāīd, Frauds.

A مکایدة mukāyadat, The act of circumventing.

A مکایسة mukāyasat, (v. n. 3 of کاس for کیس) Contending about sagacity or ingenuity. Using cunning in buying or selling.

A مکایصة mukāyasat, (v. n. 3 of کاص for کیص) Managing (affairs), applying with great attention, involving one's self (in them).

A مکایلة mukāyalat, (v. n. 3 of کال for کیل) Measuring to one another. Doing or saying as another had said or done. Railing at, reviling.

A مکائیل makāīl, Dry or liquid-measures.

A مکبّ mikabb, (and مکباب mikbāb) One who looks much upon the ground, one who mostly hangs his head. Mukibb, Prone, inclined. Who or what causes one to hang his head; depressing.

A مکبّبة mukabbabat, Brown, large-eared wheat.

A مکبّة mikabbat, A cover, Mukabbat, (in Morocco) A spinning-wheel, a reel.

A مکبّح mukabbah, Sublime, high, lofty. Proud.

A مکبر makbir, (v. n. of کبر) Being of an advanced age. A great age.

A مکبّر mukabbar, Undiminished (noun).

A مکبرة makbarat or makburat, A great age.

A مکبّس mukabbis, Weak-eyed by nature. Base, ignoble. One who rushes headlong upon men and overwhelms them.

A مکبّل mukabbal, Fettered. Imprisoned.

A مکبن mukban, Firm, strong (in the vertebræ).

A مکبوث makbūs, Stinking, tainted (meat).

A مکبود makbūd, Hurt or diseased in the liver.

A مکبوراء makbūrā, (pl. of کبیر kabīr) Grandees. Great.

A مکبول makbūl, Fettered: prisoner, captive.

A مکبون makbūn, (A camel) troubled with the disease کبان kubān. Short-legged, slender-boned, and big-bellied (horse). One whose hands have become hard from work. مکبون الاصابع makbūnu'l asābiȥ, Thick-fingered.

A مکبونة makbūnat, (pl. مکابین makābīn) Short-legged, big-bellied, and slender-boned (horse). Quick, nimble (woman).

A مکّة makkat, A place of great concourse: Mecca in Arabia, where Muhammad was born.

A مکت makt, (v. n. of مکت) Abiding in a place.

A مکتاف miktāf, A horse hurt in the shoulder (کتف katif) by the saddle.

A مکتام miktām, A camel which does not cock her tail in token of being pregnant.

A مکتب maktab, (pl. مکاتب makātib) A place or time of writing. A writing-school. Muktab, Taught. (A leathern bottle) fastened with a thong, or closed at the mouth. Muktib, A writing-master.

A مکتّب mukattab, Written, registered, enrolled, inscribed. (Cavalry) drawn up in squadrons. A bunch (of grapes) of which part is eaten.

A مکتبت muktabit, Grieved, sad, melancholy.

P مکتب خانه maktab-khāna, A writing-school.

P مکتب دار maktab-dār, A schoolmaster.

A مکتتب muktatab, Written. Reviewed, numbered. Muktatib, A writer. One who ties fast (a leathern bottle).

A مکتتم muktatim, Hidden, concealed. A concealer. Clouds without thunder.

A مکتحل muktahil, (Ground) verdant with early plants. One whose eyes are tinged with collyrium (کحل kuhl). Fallen into misfortunes.

A مکترب muktarib, Afflicted, grieving, sad.

A مکترث muktaras, Heeded, cared about. Muktaris, Solicitous, anxious about. Afraid.

A مکتري muktarī, A hirer, taken on hire.

A مکتز muktazz, Shrunk (with cold).

A مکتسب muktasib, An acquirer, gainer. Studious, attentive, assiduous.

A مکتسر muktasir, A breaker, bruiser.

A مکتسع muktasiȥ, (A dog) clapping his tail between his legs. (A stallion) whisking his tail from side to side.

A مکتسعة muktasaȥat, (A sheep) bitten by a venomous reptile called البرصة الوحرة al barsatu'l waharat, so that one side of her udder dries.

A مکتسي muktasī, Clothed, clad, dressed. One who dresses himself.

A مکتظ muktazz, Distended with repletion, oppressed with too much meat, and unable to breathe. (A channel) filled with water, almost stagnating.

A مکتع muktaȥ, (An opinion or counsel) agreed upon, united, and strong.

A مکتعا muktiȥan, (He came walking) quickly.

A مکتّف mukattaf, Pinioned.

A مکتفل muktafil, One who makes a cushion (کفل kifl) for a camel's bunch. One who appoints or delegates.

A مکتفئ muktafi, One who turns (a vessel) head downwards. Content, satisfied.

A مکتفي muktafī, Content. Complete, perfect, significant (sentence).

A مکتل miktal, A basket or vessel containing fifteen صاع sāȥ.

A مکتّل mukattal, Short. Compressed together. Round, circular. Fat, corpulent (man).

A مکتلئ muktali, Cautious, apprehensive of, shunning. Sleepless, watching, on one's guard. (A seller) who takes credit instead of ready money.

A مکتلي muktalī, Pained in the kidneys.

A مکتّم mukattam, Concealed, closely hidden.

A مکتمن muktamin, Concealed (grief).

A مکتنّ muktann, Hidden, concealed. Become white. The haunt or lurking-place of a wild beast.

A مكتنز *muktaniz*, Compact, close, full.

A مكتنف *muktanif*, Who or what surrounds, blockades, besieges, encloses, hedges. A helper.

A مكتنه *muktanih*, One who reaches the summit, or who arrives at the end (كنه *kunh*).

A مكتني *muktanī*, Called or known by the figure metonymy (كناية *kināyat*); styled, dubbed.

A مكتوب *maktūb*, Written. Sewn or stitched together. A letter, writing, scripture. (in the dialect of Morocco) A sack or bag in which any thing is kept. The letters ميم *mīm*, نون *nūn*, and واو *wāw*. المكتوب *al maktūb*, The scriptures, the sacred writings. مكتوب محبّت *maktūbi mahabbat*, (or مكتوب مودّت اسلوب *maktūbi mawaddat-uslūb*), Friendly letters, letters of compliment.

A مكتوتب *muktawtib*, Swollen with repletion.

A مكتوف *maktūf*, Hooped (vessel). Pinioned.

A مكتوم *maktūm*, Hidden, concealed.

A مكتومة *maktūmat*, An unguent, of which saffron forms an ingredient. The well Zamzam.

A مكتهل *muktahil*, Of mature age; grey. Full-grown, flourishing plant. Flowerful (garden).

A مكتهلة *muktahilat*, White-headed (sheep).

A مكتهي *muktahī*, Standing in front of another for the purpose of asking a question.

A مكتئب *mukta,ib*, Dark (ashes). Sad, sorrowful.

A مكتئنّ *mukta,inn*, Restless. Uneven.

A مكث *maks*, *miks*, *muks*, or *makas*, (v. n. of مكث) Delaying, waiting, expecting. Delay. على مكث *ʻala' muks*, With delay, at intervals.

A مكثار *miksār*, Talkative, a great talker.

A مكثان *muksān*, Delay.

A مكثر *muksir*, Rich, wealthy, opulent.

A مكثّر *mukassir*, One who augments or multiplies. (in grammar) The plural number.

A مكثرة *maksarat*, Any thing augmentative.

A مكثّعة *mukassiʻat*, (A woman) thick-lipped, or whose gums are turgid with blood.

A مكثوب *maksūb*, Inserted, infused. Poured out. Collected. Inverted (quiver). Charged, attacked.

A مكثور عليه *maksūr ʻalayhi*, Much frequented. Greatly urged, thronged by creditors, dunned.

A مكثي *maksī*, Tardy.

A مكثير *miksīr*, Very talkative.

A المكحالان *al mik-hālāni*, Two bones in the hips; also two in the fore-legs of a horse.

A مكحل *mik-hal*, (or مكحال *mik-hāl*) A bodkin with which they apply the collyrium to the eye.

A مكحّل *mukahhal*, Painted or anointed, especially with black lead or a preparation of the powder of tutty, which is applied to the eyes.

A مكحلة *mukahlat*, (in the idiom of Morocco) A culverin. A musket. *Muk-hulat*, (pl. مكاحل *ma-kāhil*) A box in which they keep collyrium or sulphuret of antimony (كحل *kuhl*).

A مكحول *mak-hūl*, Anointed with collyrium. Name of a servant of Muhammad; of a certain lawyer; also of a horse.

A مكد *makd*, (v. n. of مكد) Remaining or stopping. Diminishing (as the milk of a camel). *Mikd*, A comb. *Muhd*, (pl. of مكود *makūd*) Camels always abounding in milk.

A مكدّ *mikadd*, A comb. *Mukidd*, Pains-taking.

A مكداء *makdā*, (A camel) always abounding in milk. (A camel) whose milk never fails.

A مكدّح *mukaddah*, Scratched, clawed (face). (An ass) raw from the bites of other asses.

A مكدّر *mukaddar*, Rendered muddy or turbid. Disturbed, afflicted, vexed. Anxious, sullen.

A مكدّرات *mukaddarāt*, (pl. fem.) Disturbances, afflictions, distressful events.

P مكدّرساز *mukaddar-sāz*, A disturber, troubler.

A مكدّل *mukaddal*, Turbid. Disturbed, afflicted.

A مكدم *makdam*, A place for search. كدم في غير مكدم *kadama fī ghayr makdamin*, He sought in a place improper for search.

A مكدّم *mukaddam*, Bit, taken with the teeth.

A مكدنة *mukdanat*, Fleshy, bunched (she-camel).

A مكدوبة *makdūbat*, White, fair (woman).

A مكدود *makdūd*, Trodden, trampled (ground).

A مكدوه *makdūh*, Beclouded. Afflicted, sad.

A مكدّي *mukaddī*, Nipping, withering. Painful.

A مكديّة *makdīyat*, Close, impervious (woman).

P مكديطس *makdītus*, Name of Wāmik's father.

A مكذب *mukzib*, One who eggs on or compels (another) to tell a lie. One who detects and exposes a falsehood, or who accuses of lying.

A مكذّب *mukazzib*, A camel that takes the male without conceiving (giving the lie).

A مكذبان *makzabān*, (or مكذبانة) A liar.

A مكذبة *makzabat* or *mukzubat*, A lie.

A مكذوب *makzūb*, Noted as a liar. A lie.

A مكذوبة *makzūbat*, Weak, feeble (woman). A lie.

A مكر *makr*, (v. n. of مكر) Plotting. Deceiving. Colouring with ruddle, or with the tree called مكر *makr*. Irrigating (land). Fraud, plot, machination. Duplicity. Malice, malignity. Plumpness in the legs. A whistling noise. The noise of a lion breathing. Red earth. (pl. مكور *mukūr*) A species of dust-coloured tree or plant. فراخ المكر *firākhu'l makr*, The fruit of this tree. *Makar*, (v. n. of مكر) Being red.

A مكرّ *makarr*, A field of battle, a place of combat. *Mikarr*, An assailant. (A horse) fit to make an onset; a charger.

A مكراف *mikrāf*, (A male ass) accustomed to smell the urine of the female.

A مكرام *mikrām*, One who pays men honour; literally, an instrument of honouring.

P مكر آميز *makr-āmez*, Deceitful.

P مكران *makrān* or *mukrān*, Name of a city and country in Irān.

A مكرب *mikrab*, A plough. *Mukrab*, Sinewy (joint). Firmly-tied (rope). Compact (building or joint). Thrown into straits. *Mukrib*, Speedy, quick.

A مكربات *mukrabāt*, Camels or horses brought in cold weather to the tent-door that they may be warmed by the smoke.

A مكربة *mukrabat*, A bucket with a rope tied to the middle to preserve the long rope from being wetted and rotting.

A مكربس *mukarbas*, One with a compressed head.

A مكربلاً (جاء يمشي *jāʻa yamshī*) *mukarbalan*, He came walking slowly, as if through stiff clay.

A مكرة *makrat*, A leg, thick, yet elegant in shape. Spoiled clover. One plant called مكر *makr*. A fresh pulled but bad date. A hard date approaching the state called رطب *rutab*. *Makarat*, (pl. of ماكر *mākir*) Deceivers, cheats.

A مكرّة *mikarrat*, (A camel) which comes twice a day to be milked.

P مكر چكر *makar chakar*, Fraud and subterfuge.

A مكردح *mukardah*, Humble, suppliant. Mean in one's own estimation.

A مكردس *mukardas*, Of a compact, firm, hard body. Bound hand and foot.

A مكرّر *mukarrar*, Repeated, reiterated. The letter ر *rā*. P مكرّر كردن *mukarrar kardan*, To repeat, confirm by repetition. شكر مكرّر *shakari mukarrar*, (P گل مكرّر *guli mukarrar*) Conserve of roses.

A مكرّز *mukarraz*, Worthless, avaricious.

A مكرس *mukras*, A chain or necklace formed of rows of pearls, with large ones inserted at intervals between the smaller.

A مكرّس *mukarras*, Short-bodied, fleshy, sleek, and succulent. A chain or necklace formed of rows of pearls, with large ones inserted at intervals between the smaller.

A مكرّشة *mukarrashat*, The paunch of a camel stuffed with meat and fat, a haggess. *Mukarrishat*, A slice of a melon.

A مكرص *mikras*, A leathern milk-pail.

A مكرع *mukraʻ*, (A horse) strong in the legs.

A مكرعات *mukraʻāt*, A palm-tree planted in or near water. *Mukriʻāt*, Camels which hold their heads over the fire, and blacken their necks.

A مكرفح *mukarfah*, Deformed, disfigured.

A مكركس *mukarkas*, One whose mother, paternal or maternal grandmother, or maternal great-grandmother was a slave. Bound, fettered.

A مكرم *makrum*, The deeds of a generous, noble, honourable man. Land favourable to vegetation. يا مكرمان *yā makramānu*, O illustrious or most honourable man! *Mukram*, (v. n. of كرم) Honouring. Honour, respect. Honoured, noble. Generous, liberal. *Mukrim*, One who honours.

A مكرّم *mukarram*, Honoured, respected, revered. Noble, august, illustrious, venerable. Liberal, generous. Holy, sacred. P وجود مكرّمش *wujūdi mukarramash*, His sacred or august person. A حجر مكرّم *hajari mukarram*, The revered stone, *i.e.* the philosopher's stone.

A مكرمة makrumat, (pl. مكارم makārim) Honour, glory, dignity, nobility, liberality, greatness. The actions of a generous, noble, and honourable man. Generosity, bounty. Clemency, grace, goodness. Ground favourable to vegetation. P مكرمت گستر makrumat-gustar, Diffusing beneficence, gracious, liberal. A Mukramat, Generous, noble.

A مكرنف mukarnif, A broad, thick nose. One who gathers dates from the trunks of the branches called كرانيف karānīf.

P مكرنه makrana, Goats'-beard, an herb.

A مكروب makrūb, Sad, oppressed with grief.

A مكرود makrūd, Cut, trimmed (mustachio).

P مكرونتن makrūnitan, (in zand and Pāzand) To take, to receive.

A مكروه makrūh, Hated, odious, detestable, abominable, execrable, disgusting, obscene. (in a milder sense) Improper, unbecoming, distasteful, unpleasant. P مكروه داشتن makrūh dāshtan, To hate, abhor.

A مكروهات makrūhāt, Abominations, shameful acts, odious, dirty, or detestable things.

A مكروهة makrūhat, Force, severity.

A مكره mukrah, Compelled, forced.

A مكرهة makra or makruhat, (v.n. of كره) Hating, abhorring, loathing. Aversion, abhorrence, disgust.

A مكرهفّ mukrahiff, (Clouds) piled one above another. (Hair) high, heaped up. Stiff (penis).

A مكري mukra', Hired.

A مكرّي mukarrī, Slow-paced (camel).

A مكزّ mukizz, Whatever brings ague.

A مكزوبة makzūbat, A mixture of white and black hairs.

A مكزوز makzūz, Much affected by cold, agueish.

A مكس maks, (v. n. of مكس) Offering a price, bidding at a sale. Accumulating money. Collecting tribute, tolls, taxes, or tithes. Creating confusion and bother at a sale. Inflicting damage, detriment, and loss. Lowering, bating a price. Oppressing. (pl. مكوس mukūs) Customs, duties, tribute, market-dues. An extra fee. Decrease, detriment. Oppression, tyranny.

P مكس makis, Duties, fees, tolls, dues.

A مكساب miksāb, A gainer, winner.

A مكسال miksāl, Sluggish, lazy. (A girl) delicately brought up, who scarce moves from (her) seat. (This is considered as an accomplishment).

A مكسب maksab or maksib, A place of gain. Maksab, (maksib, or مكسبة maksibat) Gain, acquisition.

P مكست mikast, A particle placed after a word to heighten the sense; شكست مكست shikast-mikast, He broke (it) quite, he dashed (it) all to pieces.

A مكسّح mukassah, Barked, skinned, peeled.

A مكسحة miksahat, Besom, broom: snow-shovel.

A مكسر maksar, A sort of charcoal. عود طيّب المكسر ʿūd tayyibu'l maksar, Excellent aloe-wood. Maksir, A place of fracture. A place of trial, testing, or proving. Root, origin, stock.

A مكسّر mukassar, Broken. The broken or irregular plural in Arabic. A river whose reaches flow. Mukassir, One who breaks in pieces; who routs an enemy.

A مكسّع mukassaʿ, Unmarried (man). One who abstains from venery.

A مكسل miksal, A string hanging from a bow for dividing cotton. (A family) having few illustrious ancestors. Muksil, (A channel) receiving a flux of water from neighbouring grounds or reservoirs.

A مكسوّ maksūw, Clothed, dressed, clad.

A مكسوب maksūb, Gained, gotten, earned.

A مكسوح maksūh, Exceedingly lame (camel).

A مكسور maksūr, Broken. A consonant marked with the vowel kasra ـِ i. A fraction in arithmetic.

A مكسوس maksūs, Broken (bread).

P مكش makash, Do not draw. Makish, Suction.

A مكشح mikshah, (or مكشاح mikshāh) An axe, hatchet. The edge of a sword.

A مكشوح makshūh, Branded under the short ribs. Name of a certain valiant man.

A مكشوط makshūt, Flayed (camel). Taken off, removed (horse-cloth).

A مكشوف makshūf, Uncovered, unveiled, discovered, disclosed, displayed, revealed; open. مكشوف العورة makshūfu'l ʿawrat, Whose nudity is exposed. مكشوف القلب makshūfu'l kalb, Open-hearted.

A مكظّظ mukazzaz, (or مكظوظ makzūz) Oppressed with labour.

A مكظوم makzūm, Checked, restrained (anger). Vexed, sad.

A مكعّب mukaʿʿab, Of a square or cubic form. (Cloth) dyed with square figures. (Cloth) compactly folded. Swelling (bosom). A geometrical cube. Mukaʿʿib, (A girl) with a swelling bosom. Swelling (bosom).

A مكعّبة mukaʿʿabat, A palm-leaf basket.

A مكعبر mukaʿbar or mukaʿbir, Name of two poets, the one Arabian, the other Persian.

A مكعر mukʿir, (A camel) becoming fat in the bunch. Urged, spurred, making haste.

A مكعطل mukaʿtal, Who stretches the body or expands the nails.

A مكعّل mukaʿʿil, One swollen with rage, or one who wags his backside.

A مكعنب mukaʿnab, A goat whose horn is twisted in a circle.

A مكعوم makʿūm, Muzzled (camel).

A مكفاة makfāt, A sufficiency.

A مكفال mikfāl, Large-hipped.

A مكفت mukfit, One who puts on two coats of mail with an intermediate garment.

A مكفخ mikfakh, Strong (man). Firm (column).

A مكفّر mukaffar, (or مكفر mukfar) One who receives no thanks from those he has served, one whose favours are unacknowledged. Closely and firmly cased in iron. Mukaffir, Armed, mailed.

A مكفن mukfan, One who has neither salt, milk, nor any thing to eat with bread.

A مكفّن mukaffan, Shrouded, wrapped in a winding-sheet (كفن kafan).

A مكفوّ makfū, Changed (colour). Bent inwards.

A مكفور makfūr, (Ashes) covered with dust blown.

A مكفوف makfūf, Closed, drawn together (purse-string). (pl. مكافيف makāfīf) Blind. A particular foot in versification, in which the seventh quiescent letter is dropped. بينهم عيبة مكفوفة baynahum ʿaybatun makfūfatun, There is something concealed as a close treaty between them.

A مكفوفة makfūfat, (Cloth) turned in, hemmed.

A مكفول makfūl, Terror-stricken, trembling.

A مكفوء makfūʾ, Inverted, upset (vessel).

A مكفهرّ mukfahirr, Thick and black (cloud). Any thing compact, composed of several parts piled together. (A face) thin of flesh. Gross, shameless, unblushing. Austere, stern, crabbed. Dusky-coloured. Hard and inaccessible (mountain).

A مكفئ الظعن mukfiʾu'z zaʿn, One of the winter-days called ايّام العجوز ayyāmu'l ʿajūz.

A مكفيّ makfīy, Sufficient. Comfortable, well off (in regard to food and clothing).

P مكل makil, A leech.

A مكل mukul or makil, (A well) exhausted of water. Mukul, (pl. of مكول makūl) Wells containing little mud.

A مكلأ mukallaʾ, (A place) sheltered from the violence of the wind. A mooring, dock, anchorage, or harbour. A river's bank.

A مكلأة maklaʾat, Land fruitful in herbage.

A مكلّب mukallab, Fettered (captive). Mukallib, A trainer of dogs (كلب kalb).

A مكلبة maklabat, Procurement, panderism.

A مكلة maklat or muklat, Little thin black mud in a well. A drop at the bottom of a well or vessel.

A مكلث miklas, Persevering, pushing, active.

A مكلثم mukalsam, Fat about the face, chubby.

A مكلثمة mukalsamat, Plump-faced (woman).

A مكلّس mukallas, Calcined. Covered with lime (كلس). Mukallis, A lime-burner, maker of mortar.

A مكلع mukliʿ, Dirty (vessel).

A مكلّف mukallaf, Pimpled, freckled. Excellent, choice. Well-made, elaborate, elegant.

A مكلفة mukalfat, (in Morocco) A wasting fever.

A مكلّل mukallal, Crowned. Ornamented with jewels. Edged, bordered. (Clouds) surrounded or appearing crowned with other clouds. (A cloud) bright with lightning. Mukallil, Diligent, studious, intent upon, pains-taking.

A مكلّلة mukallalat, (A garden) planted round with flowers (forming, as it were, a crown).

A مكلندد muklandid, (or مكلندي muklandī) Hard, rough (place).

A مكلنزز muklanziz, Hard, strong, severe.

A مكلوب maklūb, Attacked by hydrophobia;

maddened by the bite of a rabid dog (كلب *kalb*).

A مكلوم *maklūm*, Wounded, hurt.

A مكلهز *muklahizz*, Contracted, compressed, drawn in, shrunk, shrivelled.

A مكلئ *mukliʼ*, (Land) fruitful in forage.

A مكلّى *mukalla*,' (A dog) wounded by a cow's horn in the narrow part of his body or flank.

A مكليّ *makliy*, Pained or hurt in the kidneys.

A مكلئز *muklaʼizz*, Contracted, shrunk, drawn together. A camel whose girth is loose.

A مكمأة *makmaʼat*, A place full of mushrooms.

A مكماكة *makmākat*, Short, squat, squab (woman).

A مكمّة *mikammat*, Any thing covering the muzzle of an ass (as a nose-bag). A harrow, or implement for covering over seed cast into the ground.

A مكمتل *mukamtal*, Compact-bodied (camel).

A مكمخ *mukmah*, High, lofty, proud.

A مكمكة *makmakat*, (v. n. of مكمك Q) Sucking up the whole of any thing. Going with a rolling, wabbling gait.

A مكمل *mikmal*, Consummate, perfect (either in excellence or villainy).

A مكمّل *mukammal*, Perfected, complete, consummate. Most excellent.

A مكمن *makman*, (pl. مكامن *makāmin*) An ambush. A concealed place.

A مكمنة *makmanat*, A treasury.

A مكموءة *makmuʼat*, A place full of mushrooms.

A مكمود *makmūd*, Saddened, inwardly grieved.

A مكمور *makmūr*, (pl. مكموراء *makmūrāʼ*) One who has a large gland (كمرة *kamarat*). Hurt in that part when circumcised.

A مكمورة *makmūrat*, (A woman) married, one that has known man.

A مكموم *makmūm*, (A tree) whose fruit begins to appear. (A camel) muzzled that he may not bite. A camel's colt covered over that he may get strength. (A date) enveloped in the husk.

A مكمون *makmūn*, Hid, concealed. (An eye) troubled with the disease كمنة *kumnat*.

A مكمّه *mukammah*, One whose eyes have not been opened.

A مكمهل *mukamhal*, A cotton-pod with its seeds.

A مكن *makn*, (v. n. of مكن) Laying eggs (a lizard). *Makn* or *makin*, Eggs of lizards or locusts.

A مكنّ *mukann*, Hid, concealed, stored in the mind.

A مكناء *mukanāʼ*, (pl. of مكين *makīn*) Firmly fixed, established by custom. High in rank or office.

A مكنات *makināt*, (pl. of مكنة *makinat*) Eggs (of birds), lizards, or locusts. على مكناتهم *ʻalaʼ makinātihim*, Firmly-established (men).

A مكناسة *miknāsat*, (or مكناسة الزيتون *miknāsatu'z zaytūn*) Name of a place in Morocco.

A مكنان *maknān*, A kind of plant.

A مكنب *miknab* or *muknib*, Callous (hoof, claw, nail). *Muknib*, (A hoof) becoming callous.

A مكنة *miknat* or *muknat*, Power, strength, force, virtue. *Makinat*, One egg of a lizard, locust, or similar animal. (pl. مكن *makin* and مكنات *makināt*) The lodging-place of a bird.

A مكنّة *mukannat*, (A girl) secluded and kept out of the sight of men.

A مكنثر *mukansir*, Thick, coarse, fleshy (face).

A مكنّر *mukannir*, One who wears a turban loose. Thick, corpulent. Deformed, hideous, stinking.

A مكنّس *mukannis*, A besom-maker or vender.

A مكنسة *miknasat*, A besom, brush, broom.

A مكنع *muknaʻ*, (A bucket) whose mouth is brought near to a pond to be filled. Shrivelled or contracted; also whose hand has been amputated.

A مكنّع *mukannaʻ*, One who has the hand wrinkled, withered, fractured, or amputated.

A مكنّف *mukannaf*, Every where surrounded or enclosed. Raised (pie). Large-bearded.

A مكنّفة *mukannafat*, (A beard) rough on the sides of the face.

A مكنور *maknūr*, One who wears a turban loose. Thick, corpulent. Deformed, hideous, stinking.

A مكنوز *maknūz*, Hid, laid up in a treasury.

A مكنوس *maknūs*, Swept (house). Treasured.

A مكنوسة *maknūsat*, (A camel's hoof) smooth in the hollow, having no hairs.

A مكنون *maknūn*, Hidden, concealed, laid up. Secret. درّ مكنون *durri maknūn*, A fine pearl.

A مكنونة *maknūnat*, The well Zamzam. Secluded (girl).

A مكنيّ *makniy*, (or مكنّأ *mukannaʼ*) Designated by the rhetorical figure metonymy, surnamed, nicknamed, styled, dubbed.

A مكنثب *muknaʼibb*, Coarse, thick, stout, short.

A مكو *makw*, (v. n. of مكا for مكو) Breaking wind. Whistling (as a bird, or as a man on his fingers). Being exposed and breaking wind (anus). (pl. امكاء *amkāʼ*) A hare's form. A fox's cover.

P مكو *mako*, A weaver's shuttle. Name of a species of solanum (nigrum ?)

A مكواة *mikwāt*, A hot instrument with which they cauterize or mark the skin, a cauter.

A مكوارة *mikwārat*, A turban.

A مكوة *makwat*, Podex.

A مكوتعا *mukawtiʻan*, Expeditiously.

A مكوث *mukūs*, Delay.

A مكود *makūd*, (pl. مكد *mukd*) (A camel) always abounding in milk; also having little. *Mukūd*, (v. n. of مكد) Remaining or stopping. Diminishing (a camel's milk).

A مكوّذ *mukawwiz*, Girt with a girdle or sash about the loins, breeched to the groin.

A مكور *mikwar*, A camel's saddle. *Makūr*, A cheat, knave, impostor. *Mikwar*, A turban. *Mukūr*, (pl. of مكر *makr*) Frauds, machinations, impostures. Dusty plants.

A مكوّر *mukwarr*, *mikwarr*, or *makwarr*, Shameful, base, low, wicked, obscene, impudent. Short, dwarfish, and broad. Talkative. A camel's saddle.

A مكورة *mikwarat*, A turban.

A مكورّى *makwarraʼ*, Mean, worthless, shameful, base, obscene. Talkative. Broad, squat, dwarfish. A large lump of dung.

A مكوريّ *makwariy* also *mikwariy*, A large tip of the nose. *Makwariy*, *mikwariy*, or *mukwariy*, Worthless, despicable, mean. Talkative. Broad, wide. A dwarf. Shameful; base, obscene.

A مكوّز *mukawwaz*, One who has a long (head).

A مكوس *mikwas*, A tool with which they notch millstones. *Mukūs*, (pl. of مكس *maks*) Tolls, dues.

A مكوّس *mukawwas*, Name of an ass.

P مكوك *makok*, A weaver's shuttle.

A مكّوك *makkūk*, A drinking-cup made in the form of a ship. (pl. مكاكيك *makākīk* and مكاكي *makākī*) A measure containing a صاع *ṣāʻ* and a half; or half a رطل *riṭl*; or half a ويبة *waybat*; or three كيلجات *kaylajāt*.

A مكوكب *mukawkib*, Glittering, starlike.

A مكوكى *mukawkaʼ*, Who has little good in him.

A مكول *makūl*, (pl. مكل *mukul*) A well which contains little water, and is allowed to rest in order that the water may collect. *Mukūl*, (v. n. of مكل) Containing little mud (a well).

A مكوليّ *makūliy*, Base, sordid, avaricious.

A مكون *makūn*, (A locust, lizard, or any similar animal) that has laid its eggs.

A مكوّن *mukawwin*, A creator.

A مكوئدّ *mukwaʼidd*, Tottering (old man).

A مكوئلّ *mukwaʼill*, Short-bodied.

A مكهمل *mukahmal*, All, entire.

A مكّيّ *makkiy*, (fem. مكّيّة *makkiyat*) A native of Mecca. Revealed at Mecca (a chapter of the Kur'ān, of which seventy are said to have been revealed at Mecca, and forty-four at Madina).

P مكياز *mikyāz*, Beardless youth. Infamous boy.

A مكيال *mikyāl*, A measuring-instrument or vessel, either for dry goods or liquids.

A مكيان *mikyān*, A security, surety, bail.

P مكيب *makīb*, (imperat.) Do not turn from the right road; do not depart from that resolution. Be not seduced. Do not mislead.

A مكيث *makīs*, Grave, sedate. P مكيث كردن *makīs kardan*, To tarry.

A مكّيثى *mikkīsaʼ*, (or مكّيثاء *mikkīsāʼ*) Delay.

A مكيد *makīd*, (v. n. of كاد for كيد) Laying snares, plotting mischief and fraud.

A مكيدة *makīdat*, Deceit, fraud, stratagem.

P مكيدن *makīdan*, To suck.

P مكيس *makīs*, Duties, fees, taxes, toll, impost. *Mukīs*, Earnest endeavour, intense exertion.

A مكيّس *mukayyas*, Ingenious, sagacious, prudent, cunning, sharp, shrewd.

A مكيّف *mukayyaf*, Qualified, designated.

P مكيك *makīk*, A weaver's shuttle.

A مكيل *makīl*, (v. n. of كال for كيل) Measuring

(corn). Measured. *Makīl,* (or مكيلة *makīlat*) A measuring-instrument or vessel, either for dry goods or liquids.

A مكين *makīn,* (pl. مكناء *mukanā*) An inhabitant, dweller. Firmly fixed, well-established. Grave, authoritative, in a high station. Master of the house.

A مكينة *makīnat,* Slowness, sedateness, gravity. Design, purpose, intention.

A مكيول *makyūl,* Measured.

P مگ *mag,* Name of a people inhabiting the shores of Aracan. (zand and Pāz.) A tree. A palm.

P مگر *magar,* But. Unless, except, only, if it is not. Perhaps, by chance, haply. Moreover. Nay.

P مگرد *magard,* Turn or convert not; return not.

P مگس *magas,* A fly. A freckle. The sight of a gun. A kind of Indian corn. مگس انگبين *magasi angubīn,* (or مگس عسل *magasi ʻasal*) A bee. مگس پرانيدن *magas parānīdan,* Whisking the flies (from off the goods), a phrase for dulness of market.

P مگس ران *magas-rān,* A fan, a flyflap.

P مگس راني *magas-rānī,* Flyflapping, fanning.

P مگس ريدة *magas-rīda,* Dirtied by flies.

P مگسك *magasak,* A little fly, a gnat.

P مگس گير *magas-gīr,* A cobweb. Any thing for keeping the flies off. An insect of the spider-kind. A white worm found in gardens and in the dung of cattle.

P مگس ناك *magasnāk,* Infested with flies.

P مگس وار *magaswār,* Like a fly.

P مگسي *magasī,* Fly-bitten (colour). Freckled.

P مگل *magal,* A frog. *Magil,* A leach.

P مل *mil,* Hair. *Mul,* Wine. Spirituous liquor. A pear. A guava.

A مل *mall,* (v. n. of مل) Basting (a garment slightly before the second sewing, called كف *kaff*). Laying (meat or bread) on ashes or coals to roast or bake. Making (a bow or arrow supple by fire). Walking fast. Tiring one (a journey). Making (one) weary and restless. Tired, weary, jaded, languid, satiated, sated. A live coal.

A ملأ *malʼ,* (v. n. of ملأ) Filling. Assisting. *Milʼ,* Any thing that fills another; fulness. ملأ الفم *milʼu'l fam,* A mouthful. ملأ كف *milʼ kaf,* A handful. اعطني ملأه و ملأيه و ثلاثة املائه *aʻṭinī milʼahu wa milʼayhi wa salāsata amlāʼihi,* Give me it once, and twice, and thrice full. *Malaʼ,* (v. n. of ملئ) Being full. (pl. املاء *amlāʼ*) A body of men, assembly, meeting, mote, parliament, crowd; people. Deliberation, consultation for mutual assistance. Nobility, high rank, superiority. Nobles, angels. Disposition, habit, manners. Opinion. Desire, concupiscence. ملأ اعلى *malaʼi aʻla',* The sublime assembly, court of heaven. على ملأ الناس *ʻala' malaʼi'n nās,* Before men, in the sight of all.

A ملا *mala',* Time, either of day or night. A desert.

A ملا *mullā,* A schoolmaster, doctor. (cor. of ملواح *milwāh*) A decoy-bird. Learned.

A ملاء *malāʼ,* (or ملاءة *malāʼat*) (v. n. of ملأ) Being full of riches, wealthy, opulent. Wealth, opulence. *Milāʼ,* (pl. of مليء *malīʼ*) Opulent, wealthy. (pl. of ملآن *malʼān*) (Cups) full (of water). *Mulāʼ,* Heaviness from repletion. Rheum, defluxion. (pl. of ملاءة *mulāʼat*) Women's veils. Tents made of a single piece of cloth.

A ملأء *mulaʼāʼ,* (pl. of مليء *malīʼ*) Opulent.

A ملاءة *malāʼat,* (v. n. of ملأ and ملؤ) Being rich. Being troubled with a rheum and stuffiness. *Mulāʼat,* (pl. ملاء *mulāʼ*) A tent of one piece of cloth. An outer covering. Heaviness from repletion.

A ملأم *milʼām,* One who is the advocate and patron of low, base, avaricious fellows (لئيم *laʼīm*).

A ملاءمة *mulāʼamat,* (v. n. 3 of لأم) Consenting, being of accord. Agreeing with any one (food). Adjusting differences (betwixt people), uniting (them) together in peace.

A ملآن *malʼān,* (A cup) full (of water).

A ملاب *malāb,* A species of aromatic resembling خلوق *khalūk.* Saffron.

P ملابار *malābār,* Malabar in India.

A ملابس *malābis,* (pl. of ملبس *malbas*) Garments. ملابس و ماكل *malābis u maʼkal,* Clothes and food. *Mulābis,* One who mixes or holds intercourse with.

A ملابسة *mulābasat,* (v. n. 3 of لبس) Mixing in, transacting (business). Knowing (a man) inwardly. Commerce, intercourse.

A ملابئ *mulābiʼ,* (A camel) near the birth.

A ملاة *malāt,* (pl. ملا *mala'*) A desert, a plain. Any piece of stuff of a simple surface without a seam.

A ملأة *malʼat* or *milʼat,* (v. n. of ملأ) Filling. *Milʼat,* The manner in which any thing is filled. *Milʼat* and *mulʼat,* Heaviness (from repletion). *Mulʼat,* Defluxion, rheum. A swelling in a camel from long confinement after a journey.

A ملاتب *malātib,* Threadbare waistcoats.

A ملاث *malās,* (pl. ملاوث *malāwis,* ملاوثة *malāwisat,* and ملاويث *malāwīs*) A man or family distinguished for nobility.

A ملاثمة *mulāsamat,* (v. n. 3 of لثم) Kissing.

A ملاجّة *mulājjat,* (v. n. 3 of لج) Litigating, disputing. Drawing out a dispute to a great length.

A ملاح *milāh,* Wind driving a ship. A veil, awning, shield, &c. A horse's provender-bag. The head of a spear. The blowing of the south wind after the north. Chilliness of the ground caused by rain. The suckling of a child. Dressing the matrix of a camel. (pl. of ملح *milh*) Salts. Brackish wells. (pl. of مليح *malīh*) Beautiful. *Mulāh,* (pl. ملاحون *mulāhūn*) Elegant, pretty, good.

A ملاح *mallāh,* A seaman, sailor, mariner, boatman. A pilot. A manufacturer or vender of salt. One habitually engaged or who seeks to amend, correct, and put straight. (in the dialect of Morocco) Any place inhabited by Jews. P ملاح سفينه گذار *mallāhi safīna-guzār,* A skilful pilot. A *Mullāh,* (pl. ملاحون *mullāhūn*) Agreeable, elegant, good. A salsuginous plant, sea-purslain.

A ملاحاة *mulāhāt,* (v. n. 3 of لحي) Disputing, debating. Opposing, litigating.

P ملاحان *mallāhān,* (pl. of A ملاح *mallāh*) Seamen.

A ملاحة *malāhat,* (v. n. of ملح) Being salt (water). Being good, agreeable, or elegant. Beauty of the mouth. Beauty, elegance, goodness, excellence, fineness, delicacy. P ملاحة بي همتا *malāhaʼi bī hamtā,* Peerless beauty. A *Milāhat,* Navigation. Seamanship, the profession of a sailor.

A ملاحة *mallāhat,* A salt-pit, salt-pan, or any place whence salt (ملح *milh*) is procured.

A ملاحج *malāhij,* Straits, narrow places.

A ملاحد *mulāhid,* Crooked, false, insincere, hypocritical. Impious, heretical; a heretic.

A ملاحدة *mulāhadat,* (v. n. 3 of لحد) Acting hypocritically or indirectly. *Mulāhidat,* Heretics.

A ملاحز *malāhiz,* Straits.

A ملاحس البقر *malāhisu'l bakar,* A desert, unknown place (uncertain where one is).

A ملاحظة *mulāhazat,* (v. n. 3 of لحظ) Looking askance at each other through the outer corner of the eye. Looking attentively, contemplating, remarking. Contemplation, consideration, view, notice. P ملاحظه شدن *mulāhaza shudan,* To be seen, viewed, inspected, glanced at.

A ملاحف *malāhif,* (pl. of ملحف *milhaf* and ملحفة *milhafat*) Sheets, coverlets. Outer garments.

A ملاحفة *mulāhafat,* (v. n. 3 of لحف) Being assiduous, sticking closely one to another. Assisting.

A ملاحك *malāhik,* Straits, difficulties.

A ملاحكة *mulāhakat,* (v. n. 3 of لحك) Being inserted and adhering firmly; being let into one another (as the vertebræ or joints of the back).

A ملاحم *malāhim,* Fleshy parts. (pl. of ملحمة *malhamat*) Bloody battles. *Mulāham,* Added, annexed, joined. Firmly-twisted (rope).

A ملاحمة *mulāhamat,* (v. n. 3 of لحم) Joining, causing to stick together.

A ملاحنة *mulāhanat,* (v. n. 3 of لحن) Displaying quickness and intelligence one towards another. Bandying talk. Evincing talent in comprehending the meaning of what is said.

A ملاحي *mallāhī,* The profession of a seafaring man. A manufactory of salt.

A ملاحيّ *mulāhīy* or *mullāhīy,* A species of oblong grape. A kind of fig. The اراك *arāk*-tree white and red and of a dark white.

A ملاحيّة *mallāhīyat,* The nautical art. Navigation. Seamanship.

P ملاخ *malākh,* Malacca. Name of a drug.

A ملاخ *mallākh,* Fugitive; who oft absconds.

A ملاخاة *mulākhāt,* (v. n. 3 of لخي) Being friendly, cultivating friendship, dealing courteously with one another. Opposing, contradicting, disagreeing.

Endeavouring to conciliate, soothing by presents. Irritating, setting by the ears. Lying, colouring with falsehoods. Whispering, calumniating.

A ملاخبة *mulākhabat*, (v. n. 3 of خلب) Boxing, bruising, slapping, or cuffing one another.

A ملاخة *malākhat*, (v. n. of ملخ) Abstaining from covering (a horse). Being insipid (meat).

P ملاخه *malākha*, Malacca.

A ملادّة *mulāddat*, (v. n. 3 of لدّ) Litigating, pleading (for another). Driving off, thrusting away.

A ملادس *malādis*, (pl. of ملدس *mildas*) Large stones with which date-stones are broken.

A ملاذ *malāz*, An asylum, refuge, protection, defence, stronghold. A protector. ملاذ الفقراء *malāzu'l fukarā*, Refuge of the poor.

A ملّاذ *mallāz*, A liar, one whose word and actions do not correspond. Self-opiniated. Unsound in friendship. Swift (wolf).

A ملاذّ *malāzz*, (pl. of ملذّ *malazz*) Delights.

A ملاذانيّ *malāzāniy*, A liar; a pretended friend.

A ملاذبة *mulāzabat*, (v. n. 3 of لذب) Staying, stopping, standing still.

A ملاز *malāz*, Asylum, place of refuge.

A ملّاز *mallāz*, A wolf.

A ملازة *malāzat*, (A place) abounding with almonds (لوز *lawz*), an almond-grove.

A ملازّة *mulāzzat*, (v. n. 3 of لزّ) Adhering, being joined or connected with (any person).

A ملازم *mulāzim*, One who embraces another round the neck. Assiduous, diligent, attentive, attached to, persevering, inseparable, adhering firmly. Continually attending or serving (domestic). (in gram.) Invariable. A servant. P ملازم درگاه *mulāzimi dargāh*, (or ملازم سلطان *mulāzimi sultān*) An attendant upon a king or his court; a courtier. A ملازم لغلطه *mulāzim li ghalatihi*, Wedded to his own errors. P ملازمان سرکار *mulāzimāni sarkār*, The attendants of the state or government; the servants of a great man.

A ملازمة *mulāzamat*, (v. n. 3 of لزم) Being assiduous, fixed to, persevering in. Serving continually. Attendance. Dependence. Assiduity, diligence. Service, paying respects to a superior. Continual personal attendance upon, or watch over, a debtor set at liberty from prison. P ملازمت کردن *mulāzamat kardan*, To be assiduous, to be diligent, to assist, serve.

A ملازمی *mulāzimī*, Service. Attendance.

P ملازه *malāza*, (*mulāza*, or ملاژه *malāja*) The uvula of the throat; top of the windpipe. The palate. The bone to which the tongue is connected.

A ملازیب *malāzīb*, pl. of ملزاب, Very avaricious.

A ملاسة *malāsat*, (v. n. of ملس) Being sleek, smooth, and bare. Smoothness, sleekness.

A ملّاسة *mallāsat*, A roller for the ground.

A ملاسنة *mulāsanat*, (v. n. 3 of لسن) Railing against. Arguing, discussing.

A ملاس *milās*, A smooth white stone. جارية ذات شماس و ملاس *jāriyat zāt shimās wa milās*, A lass, light, slippery, forward, and fearless. يا ابن ملّاس *yā ibna mallās*, A term of reproach.

A ملاصق *mulāsik*, Contiguous, adjoining, neighbouring. A companion, attendant.

A ملاصقة *mulāsakat*, (v. n. 3 of لصق) Adhering, being joined to. Being contiguous. Contiguity.

A ملاط *milāt*, The side (of a camel's bunch). Clay, mud, or mortar, with which they build or plaster walls. ابن ملاط *ibnu milātin*, The new moon. ابنا ملاط *ibnā milāt*, The two shoulders or two arms of a camel.

A ملاطث *malātis*, Parts rubbed or bruised by carrying or striking. *Mulātis*, A collector.

A ملاطس *malātis*, (pl. of ملطس *miltas* or ملطاس *miltās*) Stones with which date-stones are crushed.

A ملاطف *mulātif*, Courteous, polite, civil, affable, humane. Pleasant, facetious.

A ملاطفة *mulātafat*, (v. n. 3 of لطف) Behaving courteously, shewing favour reciprocally. Courtesy, politeness, favour, kindness, benignity. A letter. P ملاطفت کردن *mulātafat* (also ملاطفه *mulātafa*) *kardan*, To caress, to favour.

A ملاطمة *mulātamat*, (v. n. 3 of لطم) Slapping, buffeting, cuffing, boxing (one another).

A ملاع *malāɛ*, An unfrequented desert. عقاب ملاع *ɛukābi malāɛ*, The eagle of the desert, which feeds on field-mice, called in Persian موش خوار *mūsh-khwār* (used to imply a thing very rare).

A ملاعب *malāɛib*, (pl. of ملعب *malɛab*) Jests, pleasantries. ملاعب الريح *malāɛibu'r rīh*, Currents of wind. *Mulāɛib*, A player, jester. ملاعب ظلّه *mulāɛibu zillihi*, Name of a bird which endeavours to catch its own shadow in the water.

A ملاعبة *mulāɛabat*, A playing, joking, toying.

A ملاعجة *mulāɛajat*, (v. n. 3 of لعج) Being oppressive, giving great pain or affliction.

A ملاعق *malāɛik*, (pl. of ملعقة) Spoons.

A ملاعن *malāɛin*, (pl. of ملعنة *malɛanat*) Dwellings. Privies. Things which bring down curses.

A ملاعنة *mulāɛanat*, (v. n. 3 of لعن) Execrating, cursing (one another). Giving a decision, pronouncing sentence (a judge).

A ملاعين *malāɛīn*, (pl. of ملعون) Cursed.

A ملّاغ *mullāgh*, (pl. of مالغ) Whoremongers.

A ملاغدة *mulāghadat*, (v. n. 3 of لغد) Taking by the hand against (a person's) will, and restraining (him) from what he wishes to do.

A ملاغفة *mulāghafat*, (v. n. 3 of لغف) Meeting, encountering, finding. Kissing.

A ملاغم *malāghim*, The outer parts of the mouth within reach of the tongue (generally covered with froth in camels).

A ملاق *malāk*, A trowel, harrow, roller, or any instrument for smoothing walls, earth, and the like.

A ملّاق *mallāk*, A flatterer.

A ملاقاة *mulākāt*, (v. n. 3 of لقي) Meeting, encountering, falling on. Conversing. A meeting, interview, introduction. Conversation. P ملاقات کردن *mulākāt kardan*, To meet, encounter.

A ملاقح *malākih*, Winds which drive the clouds, shake and fructify the trees. (pl. of ملقح *mulkih*) Stallions. (pl. of ملقحة *mulhakat*) (Camels) in foal.

A ملاقس *mulākis*, Who calls one by any nickname. One who exercises patience towards his fellow.

A ملاقسة *mulākasat*, (v. n. 3 of لقس) Giving one another opprobrious or ridiculous names.

A ملاقطة *mulākatat*, (v. n. 3 of لقط) Being similar, or corresponding with in an opposite direction (as two houses built on the same plan on different sides of a street). Lifting up all his four feet at once (a horse).

A ملاقعة *mulākaɛat*, (v. n. 3 of لقع) Disputing, contending (in speech), endeavouring to excel (in oratory), or to overpower (with words). Disputation.

A ملاقي *malākī*, (pl. of ملقى *malka'* and ملقاة *malkāt*) Ramifications at the head of the womb. *Mulākī*, Who encounters, joins, meets, converses.

A ملاقيح *malākīh*, (pl. of ملقوحة *malkūhat*) Fœtuses in the bellies (of camels). Mothers. Sperms in the loins of sires.

A ملأك *malɛak*, An angel (as sent by God). Embassy, mission. An epistle.

A ملاك *malāk*, Self-possession. Marriage-contract, espousals. *Malāk* or *milāk*, That by which any thing subsists, is contained, or held together. Power, possessions. ملاك الجسد *malāku'l jasad*, The heart (as keeping the body in existence). *Milāk*, Marriage-contract, espousals. (A she-camel) following the males. Clay, mud. (pl. ملك *mulk* or *muluk*) The fore or hind-foot of a horse.

A ملّاك *mullāk*, (pl. of مالك *mālik*) Kings.

A ملأكة *malɛakat*, Embassy, mission. A letter.

A ملاكة *malākat*, Possession. ما له مولى ملاكة دون الله *mā lahu mawla' malākatin dūn allāh*, None can possess him but God.

A ملاكد *mulākid*, One who makes a fetter which gave pain in walking sit more easy. One who, on account of a fetter, is unable to walk comfortably.

A ملاكيع *malākīɛ*, Impure water which comes with the birth.

A ملال *malāl*, (v. n. of ملّ) Being tired, wearied, vexed. Sadness, vexation, affliction, anguish, languor.

A ملال *mulāl*, Heat of a fever in the bones. Feverish perspiration. Pain in the back. Restlessness in bed (from grief or sickness). The wooden part of a sword-hilt. Handle or middle of a bow.

A ملالة *malālat*, (v. n. of ملّ) Becoming tired, fatigued, weary, languid, vexed. Weariness, ennui. Affliction, sadness. Wearied.

A ملام *malām*, (v. n. of لام for لوم) Reproving, blaming. Reproach, reprehension, reviling, rebuke, accusation, blame: disgrace: opprobrium, malediction. ذلّ و ملام *zull u malām*, Contempt and ignominy.

A ملأم *malʼam*, Deserving of reproof. *Malʼam*, (*milʼam*, or ملآم *milʼām*) The advocate, patron, or apologist of low, base, sordid fellows (لئيم *laʼim*).

A ملأم *mulaʼʼam*, Clad in a coat of mail.

A ملأمان *malʼamān*, Deserving of reproof.

A ملأمة *malʼamat*, (v. n. of لؤم) Being covetous, mean, blameable, ignoble, or sordid.

A ملامة *malāmat*, (v. n. 3 of لام for لوم) Reproaching, reproving, blaming. (pl. ملاوم *malāwim*) Reprehension, reproach, rebuke, censure. Criticism. Contumely. ملامت نفس *malāmati nafs*, Self-reproach. P ملامت كردن *malāmat kardan*, To accuse, reproach, reprove, blame, revile.

P ملامت زده *malāmat-zada*, Censured, blamed. Accused. Criminated.

P ملامت گر *malāmatgar*, A censurer, blamer.

P ملامت ناك *malāmatnāk*, Blameable.

A ملامتي *malāmatī*, Reproached, reprehensible. A kind of Muhammadan monk who conceals his devotions, makes no parade of any thing good, and hides nothing bad.

A ملامج *malāmij*, The interior sides round the mouth. The outer parts of the mouth within reach of the tongue.

A ملامح *malāmih*, (pl. of لمحة *lamhat*) Distinguished features, particularly such as resemble those of others: as, ملامح من ابيه *malāmih min abīhi*, Having features like his father.

A ملامخة *mulāmakhat*, (v. n. 3 of لمخ) Boxing, slapping one another.

A ملامسة *mulāmasat*, (v. n. 3 of لمس) Handling, feeling. Lying with. The conjugal act. A practice in the markets of obliging those who handled another's goods to purchase them at a price fixed: "touch and take" (which is forbidden by the Muhammadan law).

A ملامظ *malāmiz*, Environs of mouth and lips.

A ملامل *mulāmil*, Swift (ass).

A ملآن *malʼān*, (A cup) full (of water). *Milʼān*, (for من الآن *mini'l ān*) Henceforth, from now.

P ملان *malān*, Do not shake or scatter. A stranger.

A ملآنة *malʼānat*, (fem.) (A cup) full (of water).

A ملاني *malānī*, Comparison or adjustment.

A ملاني *mullānī*, The wife of a Mulla; a learned woman; a schoolmistress.

A ملاواة *mulāwāt*, (v. n. 3 of لوي) Twisting and coiling up, hiding itself (a serpent).

A ملاوة *ma, mi*, or *mulāwat*, A long space of time.

A ملاوث *malāwis*, (and ملاوثة *malāwisat*) (pl. of ملاث *malās*) Men, families, or tribes distinguished for nobility.

A ملاوذ *malāwiz*, (pl. of ملاذة *malāzat*) Red China silks. Breeches, trowsers. Aprons.

A ملاوذة *mulāwazat*, (v. n. 3 of لاذ for لوذ) Flying for refuge to one another. Taking for a protection or fortress. Using art or fraud. Wrestling against. Opposing, contradicting.

A ملاوصة *mulāwasat*, (v. n. 3 of لاص for لوص) Looking slyly through the chinks of doors. Looking on all sides. Purposing to fell a tree, and examining it on every side to see where it is best to begin.

A ملاوطة *mulāwatat*, Commission of sodomy.

A ملاوعة *mulāwaʻat*, A discolouring (by the sun).

A ملاوم *malāwim*, (pl. of ملامة) Reproofs.

A ملاومة *mulāwamat*, A blaming one another.

A ملاويث *malāwīs*, Noble men or tribes.

P ملاه *malāh*, A bulrush.

A ملاهاة *mulāhāt*, (v. n. 3 of لها for لهو) Drawing near, approaching. Being nigh. Disputing, contending, litigating. Being fit for weaning (a child).

A ملاهسة *mulāhasat*, (v. n. 3 of لهس) Running (to meat) like a famished man. Running to any thing with impetuosity, and overturning others in the way.

A ملاهي *malāhī*, (pl. of ملهى *milha'*) Instruments of music, implements of play. Any kinds of ludicrous or wanton pastimes prohibited by law. P ترك ملاهي كردن *tarki malāhī kardan*, To abandon amusements forbidden by divine law.

A ملأى *malʼa'*, (fem. of ملآن) Full (bucket).

P ملاي *malāy*, Speak not. Complain not. Defile not.

A ملايثة *mulāyasat*, (v. n. 3 of ليث, not in use) Resembling a lion (ليث *lays*). Attacking with intrepidity. Boasting of valour.

A ملايس *mulāyis*, Slow, tardy, dilatory.

A ملائك *malāʼik*, (and ملائكة *malāʼikat*) (pl. of ملك *malak* or ملأك *malʼak*) Angels.

P ملائك پي *malāʼik-pay*, Of happy footstep.

A ملايلة *mulāyalat*, A bargaining with (any one) by the night (ليل *layl*).

A ملائم *malāʼim*, Practices deserving of censure. Reproofs, censures. *Mulāʼim*, Wholesome, suitable. Mild, gentle, affable, easy, tame, submissive, docile, placid, benign, quiet, peaceable; tender, delicate. Soft, smooth, even. Agreeable or conforming to, just.

A ملايمة *mulāyamat*, (instead of ملاءمة *mulāʼamat*) (v. n. 3 of لأم) Being concordant, reconciling, making peace (between enemies). Agreeing with, doing good. Gentleness, softness, smoothness, delicacy, tenderness, humanity, tractability. Evenness. P ملايمت كردن *mulāyamat kardan*, To act humanely, affably. To soften, smooth; to sooth.

A ملاينة *mulāyanat*, (v. n. 3 of لان for لين) Acting gently, soothing. Being soft and smooth.

A ملبّ *mulabb*, (or ملبب *mulbab*) (A horse) provided with a poitrel or breast-armour.

A ملبد *mulbad*, A lion. (A horse) having a felt-cloth under the saddle. Packed close together: felted, impacted. *Mulbid*, A camel whisking his tail round his buttocks. A lion.

A ملبس *malbas*, Whatever one enjoys, or wishes the enjoyment of. انّ فيه لملبسا *inna fīhi la malbasan*, There is in him something agreeable, he is not supercilious. There is nothing of old age about him. *Malbas* also *milbas*, A garment, vest, robe. اعرض ثوب الملبس *aʻraza sawba'l malbas*, (*milbas*, or *mulbis*) One very generally suspected. *Mulbis*, Dark, doubtful, or intricate.

A ملبّس *mulabbas*, Clothed, dressed. Made elegant. Confused, mixed, embroiled. *Mulabbis*, A mixer or compounder. A concealer of the truth. A deceiver, fraudulent dealer.

A ملبّق *mulabbak*, Thick (cake) mixed or softened with fat.

A ملبلب *mulablib*, A he-goat that rattles in rut.

A ملبن *malban*, Lactarian (herbs) increasing the milk of sheep. *Milban*, A vessel into which they milk or carry milk. A milk-pail. A milk-strainer. A mould for making brick (لبن *labin*). A thing in which bricks are carried; hod. *Mulbin*, Milch (ewe).

A ملبّن *mulabban*, (A brick) made of clay and burnt. A preparation of plums dried, the juice of grapes, nuts, and almonds, put up in the form of sausages or lozenges.

A ملبنة *malbanat*, Lactarian herbage increasing the milk of cattle. *Milbanat*, A ladle, skimmer, spatula. *Mulbinat*, Milch (ewe).

A ملبوب *malbūb*, Ingenious, intelligent. (A horse) furnished with a poitrel. Those three letters of the Arabic alphabet whose initial and final in pronunciation are the same; namely, ميم *mīm*, نون *nūn*, and واو *wāw*.

A ملبوج *malbūj*, Thrown prostrate.

A ملبوس *malbūs*, Clothed, clad, dressed. Clothes already worn, wearing apparel.

A ملبوسات *malbūsāt*, Garments, clothes.

A ملبوط *malbūt*, Troubled with a rheum (لبطة *labtat*) in the head. Thrown down.

A ملبون *malbūn*, (A horse) brought up or fed with milk. Drunk with milk (that of the camel having an inebriating quality).

A ملبئ *mulabbiʼ*, (A sheep) having biestings, called لبأ *libaʼ*, in the udder.

A ملّة *mallat*, (v. n. of ملّ) Loathing. Languor, fatigue. Warm ashes, or a furrow made in them. Feverish perspiration. Hot sand. A burning coal or billet. خبز ملّة *khubz mallat*, Bread hot from the ashes. ذو ملّة *zū mallatin*, Fatigued, tired, languid. *Millat*, Religion, faith, creed. A nation, people. An expiatory fine for murder. ملّت مسيحيّه *millati masīhīya*, The Christian religion; Messiah's people. *Mullat*, The first sewing or basting of a garment.

A ملت *malt*, A putting in motion, hard shaking.

A ملتاث *multās*, Intricate, perplexed.

A ملتاح *multāh*, Changed, altered.

A ملتاع *multāʻ*, Pained with love or grief.

A ملتاق *multāk*, Attached. Sincere, intimate. Independent. (See التياق *iltiyāk*.)

A ملتب *miltab*, One who sits quiet at home.

A ملتبد *multabid*, Caked, matted, feltered.

A ملتبس *multabis*, Obscure, doubtful, intricate,

perplexed, entangled (thing). Ambiguity.

A ملتبط *multabit*, Astonished. Disturbed. Sticking close to. (See التباط *iltibāt.*)

A ملتبك *multabik*, Mixed, confused, jumbled.

A ملتبن *multabin*, One who sucks her own milk.

A ملتبية *multabiyat*, Equality of rank with each other. Partnership, association.

A ملتثق *multasik*, Made wet, moistened.

A ملتثم *multasam*, Kissed. A place kissed. *Multasim*, One whose mouth is covered with a veil or fillet for the mouth (لثام *lisām*).

A ملتج *multajj*, Deep-furrowed, billowy (sea).

A ملتجا *multaja*, Place of refuge. A protector.

A ملتجة *multajjat*, Black (eye). Green (field).

A ملتجئ *multaji*, One who flies to, or takes refuge with. A supplicant, petitioner, refugee.

A ملتجي *multajī*, One who connects himself with those to whom he has no relation.

A ملتحب *multahib*, A goer in a broad road.

A ملتحج *multahaj*, A place of refuge. *Multahij*, A compeller, forcer. Difficult, perplexing. One who flies to, and takes refuge.

A ملتحد *multahad*, An asylum. A protector. *Multahid*, Inclined towards. An apostate.

A ملتحس *multahis*, One who receives (a debt).

A ملتحص *multahis*, A forcer, compeller. One who restrains or keeps back. (See التحاص *iltihās.*)

A ملتحف *multahif*, Covered, or who covers himself with an upper garment or wrapper (لحاف *lihāf*).

A ملتحم *multahim*, Closed, healed (wound). Fierce, raging (battle).

A ملتحي *multahī*, Bearded (youth).

A ملتخ *multakhkh*, Confused, disturbed. Full of drink. Luxuriant, entangled (herbage).

A ملتخي *multakhī*, (A babe) fed with pap.

A ملتدّ *multadd*, Flight, escape. Inclined. A taker of medicine, poured in at the corner of the mouth.

A ملتدم *multadim*, Disturbed, put in commotion. (A woman) striking (her) breast when mourning.

A ملتذّ *multazz*, One who relishes. Name of a pleasant garden near Madīna, the pleasaunce.

A ملتذع *multazig*, Hot, painful (wound).

A ملتزج *multazij*, Close, adhering closely.

A ملتزق *multazik*, Adhering, coalescing, joined.

A ملتزم *multazim*, Constrained, compelled. Convicted. Conjunct, necessarily following, attached to. A tenant, hirer, farmer; a toll-gatherer. Name of a place between the door of the temple of Mecca and the black stone. P ملتزم شدن *multazim shudan*, To be compelled.

A ملتسق *multasik*, Adhering. Convex.

A ملتصب *multasib*, Narrow (way).

A ملتصق *multasik*, Adhering, adhesive.

A ملتطّ *multatt*, Scented with musk. Veiled (woman). Concealing, covering.

A ملتطم *multatim*, Dashing (waves).

A ملتظي *multazī*, Burning, flaming (fire).

A ملتعج *multagij*, Heated, restless, unsettled from anxiety or grief.

A ملتعجة *multagijat*, (A woman) raging with lust.

A ملتعن *multagin*, Reciprocal in cursing. Just in invoking on himself.

A ملتفّ *multaff*, (fem. ملتفّة *multaffat*) Entangled, intricate, luxuriant. (A garden) containing (such herbs). Close (plumage). Plump. Heaped up (dust). Wrapped up in one's garments.

A ملتفت *multafat*, Esteemed, looked upon, considered with great respect. *Multafit*, One who bends himself, who leans or looks back; who turns the head aside. One who takes care of, who has an eye over. Attentive. Esteeming.

A ملتفم *multafim*, One who ties a fillet (لفام *lifām*) over the nose.

A ملتقا *multakā*, A place of meeting.

A ملتقص *multakis*, One who pursues subtilties or minutiæ.

A ملتقط *multakit*, One who collects from all quarters. One who falls unexpectedly upon any thing not sought for. One who picks up a foundling (لقيط *lakīt*). (See التقاط *iltikāt.*)

A ملتقع *multakag*, Changed, altered (colour).

A ملتقم *multakim*, A swallower of a mouthful.

A ملتقى *multaka'*, A place of meeting. Confluence of two rivers, meeting of seas (as of the White and Black Seas at the Thracian Bosphorus, or the Straits of Constantinople). *Multakī*, One who comes before, into the presence, or meets another.

A ملتكّ *multakk*, A drunkard dried up with drunkenness. (See التكاك *iltikāk.*)

A ملتمس *multamas*, Asked, importuned. *Multamis*, One who begs, prays, supplicates, beseeches.

A ملتمط *multamit*, Who takes his due.

A ملتمظ *multamiz*, One who throws quickly into his mouth. (See التماظ *iltimāz.*)

A ملتمع *multamig*, Splendid, shining, glancing, brilliant. Who draws towards himself, who seizes or attracts. P ملتمع شدن *multamig shudan*, To change or disappear (as colour). To shine.

A ملتمم *multamim*, A visitor. One who alights. Round (stone).

A ملتمى *multama'*, (also ملتما *multama*) Changed, lost (colour).

A ملتمئ *multami*, One who takes what is in a dish.

P مل تنك *mul-tunuk*, (or مل تنگ *mul-tang*) One who is soon overcome by wine.

A ملتوت *maltūt*, (Barley-meal) moistened.

A ملتوث *multawis*, Confused, perplexed (business). Who curls (hair with tongs). Dilatory, slow. Fat. Strong. (See التياث *iltiyās.*)

A ملتوح *multawih*, Thirsty. Flashing (lightning). Visible (star).

A ملتوخ *multawikh*, Mixed. Leavened.

A ملتوط *multawit*, One who adopts (as a son). Adhesive, sticking to. (See التياط *iltiyāt.*)

A ملتوم *multawim*, Blamed, reprehended.

A ملتوي *multawī*, Crooked, oblique, distorted. Squinting. Perverse. Delaying, spinning out. Protracted, postponed. (See التواء *iltiwā.*)

A ملتهب *multahib*, Kindled, burning (fire).

A ملتهث *multahis*, One who lolls his tongue from thirst or fatigue.

A ملتهف *multahif*, Flaming, burning (fire).

A ملتهم *multaham*, Changed (colour). *Multahim*, A swallower up quickly, and at once. (An infant) that exhausts (the breast).

A ملتهي *multahī*, Playing, playful.

A ملتئم *multa'im*, Joined, consolidated, healed.

A ملث *mals*, (v. n. of ملث) Soothing, caressing, coaxing, cajoling; making many promises without any intention of performing. Hindering, keeping back. A slight blow. Languor, weakness in running. *Mals* or *malas*, Beginning of the night, crepuscule, twilight, or a little after it. *Malsa*, In the beginning of the night (I went to him). *Mils*, Unsatisfied with venery.

A ملثّ *muliss*, Importunate. One who remains or dwells. Continuous (rain).

A ملثة *mulsat*, The beginning of night, a little after twilight.

A ملثم *milsam*, Stone-striking (hoof).

A ملثوم *malsūm*, (A hoof) hurt by stones.

A ملج *malj*, (v. n. of ملج) Seizing the mother's nipple with (its) mouth; sucking (as an infant). *Mulj*, The stone of the wild date called مقل *mukl*. *Malaj*, (v. n. of ملج) Ceasing to flow (a camel's milk), and being succeeded by a saltish kind of liquor. Eating a wild date, or chewing the stone. *Muluj*, Sucking kids.

A ملجأ *malja*, (v. n. of لجا) Taking refuge. An asylum, place of refuge, retreat; security, support. A resting-place. ملجاي خواقين *maljāyi khawākin*, The refuge or support of kings. ملجاي نوح *maljāyi nūh*, The mountain جودي *jūdī* (Ararat), on which Noah's ark is supposed to have rested.

A ملجاب *miljāb*, A feathered, pointless arrow.

A ملجاذ *miljāz*, (Cattle) cropping pot-herb tops.

A ملجان *maljān*, (A man) who sucks his camels from avarice.

A ملجم *muljam*, Bridled.

A ملجون *maljūn*, Shaken (leaves) mixed with meal, date-stones, or barley (food for camels).

P ملچخ *milchakh*, A stone for a sling.

P ملچكا *malchakā*, Wish, will, desire, inclination.

A ملح *malh*, (v. n. of ملح) Salting, seasoning (fish or a pot). Giving suck, or offering one (milk). Feeding (flocks) with salsuginous herbage, different from حمض *hamz*. Traducing, slandering. Increasing in rapidity (the flapping of a bird's wing). Scalding (a sheep). *Milh*, (pl. ملحة *milhat*, ملاح *milāh*, املاح *amlāh*, and ملح *milah*) Salt. Salt, salsuginous, or brackish (water). A draught of milk from the breast. Learned men. Beauty. Science. Fatness. Protection. An oath. ملح الصناعة *milhu's sināʿat*, (or as some write it, though perhaps erroneously, ملح الصاغة *milhu's sāghat*, Goldsmiths' salt) Artificial salt, borax. ملحه علىٰ ركبته *milhuhu ʿala' rukbatihi*, Faithless in his promise (his salt upon his knee). *Malah*, An unnatural swelling in the hough or in the pastern of cattle. Whiteness mixed with black. *Milah*, (pl. of ملح *milh*) Salts. Brackish waters. *Mulah*, (pl. of ملحة *mulhat*) Narratives, stories, pleasant, agreeable tales.

A ملحّ *mulihh*, Importunate in asking questions; urgent in begging, pressing one's suit.

A ملحاء *malhās*, (fem. of املح *amlah*) (A sheep) variegated with black and white wool. Very blue or grey (eyed). A great body of horsemen, especially with white arms or armour. Leafless (tree). (A night) white with dew or hoar-frost. Best, most convenient. The middle of the back, between the haunch and the hip.

A ملحاح *milhāh*, Urgent, importunate in begging. (A she-camel) that departs not from the cistern). A camel's saddle hurting his back. رحيً ملحاح *rahan milhāh*, A millstone grinding heavily.

A ملحاق *milhāh*, An excellent she-camel which none can outstrip.

A ملحان *malhān* or *milhān*, Winter-months or days white with hoar-frost or snow. The months called جمادي الآخرة *jumūda'l ākhirat* and كانون آخر *kānūni ākhir*.

A ملحب *milhab*, An instrument with which any thing is cut off, scraped, or peeled. Slanderous, reviling. A calumniator.

A ملحّب *mulahhab*, Cut in pieces. Beaten or open (road).

A ملحة *malhat*, The midst of the sea, the abyss. *Milhat*, An oath. Protection. (pl. of ملح *milh*) Salts. Brackish waters. *Mulhat*, (pl. ملح *mulah*) A narrative, story, tale, relation, pleasant fable. A blue or a grey colour, white mixed with black. Reverence, fear, dread. Gravity, authority. A blessing.

A ملحج *malhaj*, A place of refuge, asylum.

A ملحد *mulhad*, A tomb or grave, in the side of which a niche has been cut. A niche in the side of a grave. *Mulhid*, A heretic, pagan, unbeliever, one who denies the resurrection of the dead. A deist. Impious, iniquitous. One who renounces the faith.

A ملحس *malhas*, (v. n. of لحس) Licking (a dish). *Milhas*, Covetous, greedy, grasping. Bold, fearless.

A ملحص *malhas*, An asylum.

A ملحف *milhaf*, (and ملحفة *milhafat*) (pl. ملاحف *malāhif*) The outer covering of the body, a wrapper. *Mulhif*, Importunate, urgent.

A ملحق *mulhak*, Added, joined, annexed, appended. Attributed. Coherent, adherent, belonging to. Correlative. Adopted. (in grammer) A quadriliteral verb formed from a triliteral: as, شملل *shamlala* from شمل *shamala*, بيطر *baytara* from بطر *batara*. *Mulhik*, Reaching, touching, overtaking.

A ملحقات *mulhakāt*, (pl. fem. of ملحق *mulhak*) Additions, appendices, supplements. Towns taken from an enemy and incorporated with or annexed to the empire.

A ملحلح *mulahlah*, A lord, chief of a family.

P ملحم *malham*, Silk cloth.

A ملحم *mulham*, One who lives upon wild-fowl or other game. Adopted, joined to a people. A kind of cloth or garment. *Mulhim*, A weaver. One who gives flesh (لحم *lahm* or *laham*) to eat.

A ملحّم *mulahham*, Fleshy, corpulent. *Mulahhim*, One who makes fleshy.

A ملحمة *malhamat*, (pl. ملاحم *malāhim*) A bloody battle. Peace. Restoration, arrangement (of affairs).

A ملحوب *malhūb*, Beaten (path). Peeled (timber). Cut lengthwise. Name of a place.

A ملحود *malhūd*, (A grave) in the side of which a niche has been dug. The niche itself.

A ملحوس *malhūs*, Sucked, licked. Lean, skinny.

A ملحوظ *malhūz*, Looked at kindly, viewed with affection, regard, or respect. Contemplated, thought of.

A ملحوظات *malhūzāt*, (pl. fem. of ملحوظ *malhūz*) Thoughts, meditations, agitations of mind.

A ملحوم *malhūm*, Killed, slain.

A ملحون *malhūn*, Erroneous.

A ملحيّ *malhīy*, Traduced; blamed. Disgraced. Displaced. Peeled (timber).

A ملخ *malkh*, (v. n. of ملخ) Going stoutly, travelling far. Being much addicted (to trifles). Drinking his own urine (a goat). Seizing or catching with the teeth and dragging. Being knocked up with covering (a stallion). Being folded, doubled, bent. Being broken to pieces. Corruption of meat. Coition. The gambols of a horse.

P ملخ *malakh*, A locust. ملخ آبي *malakhi ābi*, (or ملخ دريائي *malakhi daryāʾī*, A sea-locust, *i.e.* a shrimp. ملخ پياده *malakhi piyāda*, A grasshopper. A small locust whose wings are not yet grown.

A ملخّب *mulakhkhab*, Buffeted. Worsted, beat.

P ملخچ *malakhch*, Name of an herb which intoxicates such animals as eat of it.

A ملخص *mulkhas*, (A camel) examined in the eye to ascertain if she be fat enough to be slaughtered.

A ملخّص *mulakhkhas*, (or ملخّص التفصيل *mulakhkhasu't tafsīl*) Succinctly related. Extracted, abridged. Clearly and plainly told.

P ملخودن *malkhūdan*, To card cotton.

A ملخيٰ *milkha'*, A gallipot for holding drugs. A snuff-box. The skin of a marine animal which excites sneezing.

A ملد *mald*, (v. n. of ملد) Stretching. Tender, delicate, soft, limber. The sylvan demon غول *ghūl*. *Malad*, (v. n. of ملد) Shaking. Being joyous and cheerful. Softness, tenderness. Youth. A wavering, a tottering. Freshness and lustre of the face.

A ملداء *maldās*, Tender, delicate (girl).

A ملدام *mildām*, Stone for breaking date-stones.

A ملدان *maladān*, (v. n. of ملد) Shaking. Being cheerful and joyous. Youth. Freshness and lustre of the countenance.

A ملدانيّة *muldāniyat*, Tender, delicate (girl).

A ملدس *mildas*, A stone with which they break date-stones or apricot-stones. A man treading firm. Powerful in venery.

A ملدّس *muladdas*, Mended or patched.

A ملدغ *mildagh*, A slanderer, calumniator.

A ملدم *mildam*, A stone with which they break date-stones as food for cattle. Foolish, slow, and heavy. امّ ملدم *umm mildam*, A fever.

A ملدّم *muladdam*, Mended, patched.

A ملدود *maldūd*, A patient, into the corner of whose mouth medicine is poured; drenched.

A ملدوغ *maldūgh*, Stung by a scorpion. Bitten by a serpent.

A ملذ *malz*, (v. n. of ملذ) Lying, saying one thing and doing another. Rubbing upon the hand. Piercing (with a spear). Throwing out the feet to the utmost of his power in running (a horse). Swiftness in running. *Malaz*, A mixture of darkness.

A ملذان *malazān*, (or ملذانيّ) A pretended friend.

A ملذّذ *mulazzaz*, Delicious.

A ملذم *mulzam*, Addicted, inflamed, excited, rendered greedy. Encouraged, stimulated.

A ملز *malz*, (v. n. of ملز) Going away with any one. Remaining behind. *Maliz*, Muscular (man).

A ملزّ *milazz*, (A man) assiduous, industrious, diligent in any thing he undertakes. Very litigious.

A ملزاب *milzāb*, Extremely avaricious.

A ملزام *milzām*, Forceps, pincers which hold firmly, a vice. A press.

A ملزز *mulazzaz*, Of a compact, firm, hardy body. Brawny, sinewy, muscular.

A ملزّق *mulazzak*, Not firmly adhering.

A ملزم *milzam*, A needle-maker's or furbisher's vice. A press. A vice. *Mulzam*, Conjoined, driven together, annexed, inseparable. Convinced, convicted, condemned.

P ملزوق *malzūk*, Clammy, sticky, cohesive.

A ملزوم *malzūm*, Inseparable, connected, affixed. Belonging to.

A ملزون *malzūn*, (A well) thronged by men.

A بعته الملزيّ *biʿtuhu'l malaza'*, I sold it unconditionally, out and out.

A ملس *mals*, (v. n. of ملس) Driving furiously. Being sleek and shining. Castrating (a ram). Smoothing. Soothing, coaxing. Mixture of darkness and light, *i.e.* twilight. ملس الظلام *malsa'z zalām*, (I came to him) in the beginning of the twilight.

P ملسا *milsā*, A stretched rope, or a piece of wood, on which any thing is hung.

A ملساء *malsās*, (fem. of املس *amlas*) Smooth,

bare. Delicate wine gliding smoothly down the throat. Acid milk with which pure milk is diluted.

A ملسد *milsad*, (A camel's colt) sucking much.

A ملسع *milsaع*, A skilful guide.

A ملسّع *mulassaع*, Stopping, not going away.

A ملسّعة *mulassaعat*, One who remains constantly in one place, and never moves abroad. *Mulassiعat*, A crowd standing in one spot.

A ملسّق *mulassah*, Adopted.

A ملسلس *mulaslas*, Striped and painted cloth.

A ملسن *milsan*, A stone placed at the door of a house as a trap for wild beasts.

A ملسّن *mulassan*, (A shoe) sharp-pointed like the tongue. Possessed of divine eloquence in speaking or disputing, gifted with a tongue (لسان *lisān*).

A ملسّنة *mulassanat*, Sharp-pointed (shoe). (A woman) whose foot is long and pointed as a tongue.

A ملسوع *malsūع*, Stung by a serpent or scorpion.

A ملسون *malsūn*, A liar. One whose tongue (لسان *lisān*) has been cut out.

A ملسى *malasa'*, Swift, fleet (she-camel). Smooth, bare. ملسي و لا عهدة *malasa' wa lā عuhdata*, (He got) clear off, and returned not. انار ملسي *anāri malasa'*, A species of pomegranate large and juicy.

A ملش *malsh*, (v. n. of ملش) Searching, groping with the hand as if feeling for something.

A ملص *mals*, (v. n. of ملص) Voiding excrement. *Malas*, (v. n. of ملص) Falling out of the hand from slipperiness. *Malis*, Slippery (rope) which cannot be held with a tight grasp.

A ملصاب *milsāb*, (A sword) fast in the sheath.

A ملصة *malisat*, A sea-tortoise, a turtle.

A ملصّة *malassat* or *mulissat*, (A country) infested by robbers (لصّ *liss*, *lass*, or *luss*).

A ملصق *mulsah*, Adopted (son). Conjoined, heaped together, united, glued, fastened, fixed.

A ملصّق *mulassak*, Adopted (son).

A ملصقة *mulsahat*, Narrow and fleshy (woman).

A ملصوق *malsūk*, Adhering, joined.

A ملط *malt*, (v. n. of ملط) Plastering (a wall). Bringing forth an abortion. Shaving. *Milt*, (pl. املاط *amlāt* and ملوط *mulūt*) A thief, or one who appropriates to himself whatever comes in his way. One of unknown parents. غلام ملط خلط *ghulāmi milt khilt*, A boy born of obscure or of mixed parentage. *Malat*, (v. n. of ملط) Having no hairs on the body. Being thin-bearded.

A لاطّ ملطّ *lātt mulitt*, One who is filthy himself, and whose companions are filthy.

A ملطاء *miltāء*, (or ملطاة *miltāt*) A thin membrane between the flesh of the head and the bone. A wound penetrating to the brain.

A ملطاس *miltās*, A stone with which they break date-stones. An iron instrument for breaking stones.

A ملطاط *miltāt*, An oil-mill or press. Handle of a hand-mill. A mason's trowel. Top, also projection from the side of a mountain. Margin of a river or valley. Sea-shore. The head. Skin of the head. A wound in the head laying open the skull, or penetrating to the brain. One part or side of the head; also an excrescence or inequality in that part of a camel's head. A beaten path.

A ملطة *multat*, (v. n. of ملط) Having no hairs on the body. Being thin-bearded.

A ملطس *miltas*, (pl. ملاطس *malātis*) An instrument resembling معول *miعwal*, but broader. A stone with which they break date-stones. The hard hoof of a horse or camel.

A ملطّف *mulattif*, An attenuant.

A ملطّفات *mulattifāt*, Attenuating medicines.

A ملطم *maltam*, (The cheek of a horse) distinguished by a mark which is continued from the forehead. الملطمان *al maltamāni*, The two cheeks (as the parts which are slapped or buffeted). *Miltam*, A floor-cloth, especially made of leather.

A ملطّم *mulattam*, Smitten or buffeted (face). Ignoble, worthless, covetous. White (cheek).

A ملطوخ *maltūkh*, Bedaubed; in a dirty plight.

A ملطوط *maltūt*, (A shield) thrown on the face.

A ملطوم *maltūm*, Slapped on the cheek, buffeted. White-faced (horse).

A ملطه *malta*, The island of Malta.

A ملطى *milta'*, A wound penetrating to the brain. *Malata'*, A kind of (horse's) pace.

A ملطية *malatyat*, Name of a city in Mesopotamia. *Multiyat*, A wound reaching the pericranium.

A ملظّ *mulazz*, Necessary to be done. *Mulizz*, Very importunate in asking.

A ملظاظ *milzāz*, Very importunate in asking.

A ملظّة *mulizzat*, A legation, embassy, mission, missive, epistle.

A ملع *malع*, (v. n. of ملع) Skinning (a sheep), beginning at the neck. Travelling quick and lightly. A conspiracy, confederacy, or plan of operations against an enemy. *Muluع*, (pl. of مليع *maliع*) Large extents of level sterile ground. Barren deserts.

A ملعب *malعab*, A play, pastime, or show; a theatre or place for any similar exhibition.

A ملعبة *mulعibat* or *milعabat*, A little garment without sleeves which boys wear at play.

A ملعط *malعat*, Plants, herbage, pasturage, grazing-ground, that especially which is round the tents.

A ملعّظة *mulaععazat*, A tall, plump girl.

A ملعقة *milعakat*, (pl. ملاعق *malāعik*) A spoon. A ladle, skimmer, spatula.

P ملعقه تراش *milعaka-tarāsh*, A ladle-maker.

P ملعم *malعam*, A plaster.

A ملعّن *mulaععan*, Cursed, execrated, damned.

A ملعنة *malعanat*, (pl. ملاعن *malāعin*) The beaten part of a road. A dwelling. Whatever brings down a curse. A privy. Excrement.

A ملعوب *malعūb*, (The mouth of a babe) emitting saliva. A trick played off upon any one, a hoax.

A ملعون *malعūn*, (pl. ملاعين *malāعīn*) Cursed, damned, accursed, execrated, detestable, excommunicated, driven out of society, shut out from mercy. الشجرة الملعونة *ash' shajaratu'l malعūnat*, The tree zakkūm, the damned or infernal tree.

A ملغ *milgh*, (pl. املاغ *amlāgh*) A foolish fellow speaking obscenely.

A ملغاة *malghāt*, (v. n. of لغا for لغو) Blundering in speech. Talking triflingly and nonsensically.

A ملغز *mulghiz*, An enigmatist, punster.

A ملغفة *malghafat*, A knot of daring robbers.

A ملغم *malgham*, An emollient poultice or unguent for sores (especially warm).

A ملغوس *mulaghwas*, Crude, raw, undressed fat.

A ملف *milf*, (in the Morocco dialect) Cloth.

A ملفّ *milaff*, Any thing in which people wrap themselves when going to sleep, a blanket, bedding, night-garments.

A ملفج *mulfaj*, A pauper, bankrupt.

A ملفّط *mulaffat*, Swollen, puffy, blistered.

A ملفّف *mulaffaf*, Wrapt, folded. A milk-bottle.

A ملفّق *mulaffak*, False (narrative); a lie.

A ملفوظ *malfūz*, Thrown out, rejected. Uttered, pronounced, spoken, expressed. Those thirteen letters of the Arabic alphabet which for their enunciation require three letters; namely, الف *alif*, جيم *jīm*, دال *dāl*, ذال *zāl*, سين *sīn*, شين *shīn*, صاد *sād*, ضاد *zād*, عين *عayn*, غين *ghayn*, قاف *kāf*, كاف *kāf*, and لام *lām*. Annals.

A ملفوف *malfūf*, Wrapt up, involved, enclosed; folded (letter). Collected. An enclosure. An envelope. Cabbage.

A ملق *malk*, (v. n. of ملق) Obliterating, defacing. Washing (clothes). Sucking the dam (a camel's colt). Lying with. Striking (with a stick). Going, travelling fast. *Malak*, (v. n. of ملق) Flattering, soothing, making insincere professions. Falling from the finger (a ring). Love, mildness, soothing, flattery, blandishment. A canter. A gallop. Fresh and quickly sprouting verdure. Level ground. *Malik*, Bland, insincere. (A horse) on whose paces one cannot rely. Swift (horse). Weak.

A ملقّا *mulakka'*, Thrown into, tossed; hitting, lighting upon.

A ملقاة *malkāt*, (pl. ملاقي *malāki*) A ramification at the head of the womb. *Mulkāt*, (fem.) A thing used and thrown away.

A ملقاط *milkāt*, A pen. Tweezers. A spider; cobweb.

A ملقاع *milkāع*, An obscene, impudent woman.

A ملقّب *mulakkab*, Surnamed, nicknamed, entitled. *Mulakkib*, A giver of nicknames.

A ملقة *malakat*, A smooth stone. *Malikat*, Bland (woman).

A ملقح *mulkih*, (pl. ملاقح *malākih*) A stallion-camel. One who fecundates a palm-tree.

A ملقّح *mulakkah*, (A female palm-tree) sprinkled with the male flowers. Experienced (man).

A ملقحة *mulkahat*, (pl. ملاقح *malākih*) Pregnant

(woman or camel). *Mulkihat,* (Wind) making a cloud to descend in fructifying showers.

A ملقط *milkat,* Instrument for picking up.

A يا ملقطان *yā malkatānu,* O thou fool!

A ملقعة *milkaʿat,* Impudent, foul-mouthed, obscene (woman).

A ملقلق *mulaklak,* Acute, quick, restless (eye).

A ملقو *malkūw,* Afflicted with the disease لقوة.

A ملقوحة *malkūhat,* (pl. ملاقيح *malākīh*) A mother. The fœtus in the belly (of a camel); or what is in the loins of the stallion.

A ملقوط *malkūt,* Collected, picked up. A foundling.

A ملقوم *milkawm,* (for من القوم *mini'l kawm*) From the tribe or from the people.

A ملقى *malkaʾ,* A place. The abode of a female mountain-goat. A man who has experienced much good and ill-fortune. (pl. ملاقي *malākī*) A ramification in the head of the womb. *Mulkaʾ,* Brought down (by a fever). A place where any thing is thrown. A man who has seen much good and much evil. *Mulkī,* A thrower.

A ملقى *mulakkaʾ,* Thrown, tossed. A man who has seen much good and much evil.

A ملقيّ *malkīy,* Thrown, tossed into; hitting, lighting upon. One who has seen much good and evil fortune, who has been much tossed about.

A ملك *malk,* (v. n. of ملك) Kneading (dough). Possessing, having dominion. Filling, saturating (water). Marrying, taking a wife. Restraining (a woman) from marriage. Following the dam (a full-grown colt). Wealth, any thing which one possesses or enjoys. Water. A place of pasture and water. A well. (pl. املاك *amlāk*) A king. Bondage, slavery, thraldom. ملك الولي *malku'l walīy,* A woman, a wife (as being the riches of the husband). *Malk, milk,* or *mulk,* The middle, also the boundary of a road. *Milk,* (v. n. of ملك) Possessing, having dominion. Reigning. Marrying. Filling any one (water). A kingdom, dominion, possession; property, right. Bondage, servitude. Water. A place of pasturage and water. A well. ملك يدك *milku yadika,* Whatever is in thy possession. ملك الطريق *milku't tarīk,* The middle of the road. The margin or boundary of the road. *Mulk,* (v. n. of ملك) Possessing, having dominion. Marrying. A kingdom. Royalty. Power, dominion. Possession in lands, patrimony, heritage, property. Glory, magnificence. Little water. Pasturage. Bondage, servitude. A pen. The feet of a horse. الملك *al mulk,* (or ملك الملكوت *mulku'l malakūt*) The sensible, likewise the invisible world. P ملك ارشي *mulki arashī,* The country of Irān. ملك فربه كردن *mulk farbih kardan,* To strengthen an empire. A *Mulk* or *muluk,* (pl. of ملاك *milāk*) The feet of horses. *Malak,* (for ملأك *malʾak*) (pl. ملائكة *malāʾikat,* ملائك *malāʾik,* and املاك *amlāk*) An angel. Possession of a place. Pasture and water. That by which any thing subsists. A grain which resembles a French bean. ملك الموت *malaku'l mawt,* The angel of death, called عزرائل *ʿizrāʾīl.* ملك امر *malaki amr,* Water. *Malik,* (pl. ملوك *mulūk*) A king. A title of honour conferred by the sovereigns of Egypt on prime-ministers or generals. A pirate. ملك متعال *maliki mutaʿal,* (الملك الاعلى *almaliku'l aʿlaʾ,* ملك ذو الجلال *maliki zū'l jalāl,* ملك ودود *maliki wadūd,* ملك القدوس *maliku'l kuddūs,* and ملك مالك الملك *maliki māliku'l mulk*) God Almighty, the most high and mighty King, the glorious King, the benevolent Sovereign, the sacred Lord, the King of the kings of kingdoms, or the Lord of lords. P ملك نيم روز *maliki nīmroz,* Adam. Muhammad. Rustam Zāl. A title of the governors of Sīstān. A *Muluk,* Possession.

P ملك *milk,* White specks growing at the roots of the nails. A straight road. *Mulk,* A black grain like a French bean.

A ملّك *mullak,* (pl. of مالك *mālik*) Kings.

P ملكا *malkā,* (in zand and Pāzand) A king.

A ملكا *malkā,* The leader of a Christian sect.

A ملكاء *mulakāʾ,* (pl. of مليك *malīk*) Kings.

A ملكات *malakāt,* (pl. of ملكة *malakat*) Possessions. Habits, principles. Qualities.

P ملكان *malkān,* The father of خضر *khizr.*

P ملكانيّه *malkānīya,* A sect of Christians which attributes divinity to the Virgin Mary.

P ملك آوازه *malak-āwāza,* Far-famed.

A ملكبة *malkabat,* Fleshy, fat (she-camel).

A ملكة *milkat,* Property, possession. *Malakat,* (v. n. of ملك) Possessing. Possession, rule. Servitude. A benevolent and liberal manner of behaving to servants. An acquired habit or principle. *Malikat,* A queen. Quickness of apprehension, strength of intellect. ملكة الكبري *malikatu'lkubraʾ,* Queen-consort. *Mulukat,* The feet of a horse.

A ملكد *milkad,* A mallet or similar thing.

P ملكدار *milk-dār* also *mulk-dār,* A landholder. Rich in possessions.

P ملك داري *mulk-dārī,* Government.

A ملكذب *mil kazib,* (for من الكذب *mini'l kazib*) From the lie, or from the false.

A ملكعان *malkaʿān,* Abject, mean: a sensualist.

P ملكك *mulkak,* (or ملكل *mulkal*) Mallows.

A ملكّك *mulakkak,* Firm-fleshed.

P ملك گيري *mulk-gīrī,* Government.

A ملكم *milkam,* (or ملكّم *mulakkam*) Hard (camel's hoof) which breaks the stones.

A ملكّم *mulakkam,* Patched (boot).

A ملكّمة *mulakkamat,* A cake pressed flat.

A ملكوت *malakūt,* (or ملكوة *malkuwat*) Empire, dominion, power, authority, magnificence. Angels, spirits. الملكوت *al malakūt,* (or عالم ملكوت *ʿālami malakūt*) The invisible, contemplative, or intelligent world; the heavenly court, hall of angels.

P ملكوتا *malkūtā,* (in zand and Pāzand) A paramount sovereign.

P ملكوس *malkūs,* Name of a wicked person on whose account the deluge was sent, according to a notion of the ancient Persians.

A ملكوم *malkūm,* Name of a well at Mecca.

A ملكي *milkīy,* Imperial, royal, belonging to empire. Civil, pertaining to the country. A farmer. مصالح ملكيّه *masālihi milkīya,* Public affairs. *Mulkīy,* Proper, peculiar, hereditary. *Malakīy,* Angelic. Royal. Orthodox; who follows the religion of the king. الملكيّة *al malakīyat,* A sect of those principles called Malakites.

A ملكيّة *milkīyat,* Property. Possession, use.

A ملكي صفات *malakī-sifāt,* Of angelic temper.

A ملل *malal,* (v. n. of ملّ) Being weary, languid, vexed. A mark behind the ear. *Milal,* (pl. of ملّة *millat*) Religions, sects. Peoples, nations.

A ملم *malam,* Worthless.

A ملمّ *milamm,* Who assembles his relations or domestics. *Mulimm,* Vehement. Hard, firm, strong. Who approaches to puberty.

A ملماء *milmāʾ,* (for من الماء) From the water.

P ملماز *malmāz,* A yellow dye for cloth.

A ملمّة *mulimmat,* An accident, misfortune.

A ملمّج *mulammaj,* Supple, smooth (spear).

A ملمذ *milmaz,* A liar. A pretended friend.

A ملمس *malmas,* The touch. A part touched. Body or skin.

A ملمع *milmaʿ,* A bird's wing. *Mulmiʿ,* (A mare, ass, doe, or lioness) having swelling udders with black dugs. (A sheep) moving the tail in a particular manner, shewing that she is pregnant.

A ملمّع *mulammaʿ,* (A horse) of different colours; hence, the Turkish language, as being a mixture of Arabic, Persian, and Turkish. A poem, the hemistichs or distichs of which are written in Persian and Arabic alternately, and which is allowable as far as ten distichs in each language. Bright; gilded; plated.

A ملمعة *mulmiʿat,* (Ground) covered with withering and whitish plants. (A sheep) which moves her tail in a certain manner denoting that she is pregnant.

P ملمّع كار *mulammaʿ-kār,* A gilder, plater. A hypocrite, dissembler, traitor.

P ململ *malmal,* Muslin.

A ململة *malmalat,* Swiftness.

A ململم *mulamlam,* Collected, brought together into one. Dense (host). Round and hard (stone).

A ململمة *mulamlamat,* An elephant's trunk.

A ململي *malmalaʾ,* Swift (she-camel).

A ملمؤة *malmuʾat,* A repository, a place in which any thing is found. A net, snare.

A ملموس *malmūs,* Smoothed (pack-saddle), freed from crookedness, unevenness, and inequality.

A ملموسات *malmūsāt,* Tangible things.

A ململ *mulmul,* A bodkin for applying collyrium to the eye. An iron style for writing with.

The pizzle of a fox or camel.

A ملموم *malmūm*, Collected together. Round. Insane, crazy.

P ملميز *malmīz*, A certain yellow dye.

P ملنجيدن *milinjīdan*, To attract, draw up; hang.

G ملنخوليا *malankhūliyā*, Melancholy.

P ملند *muland*, One who listens, or is attentive and obedient. Much talking.

P ملنگ *malang*, A man barefoot and bare-headed, ecstasied; a religious enthusiast.

A ملو *malw*, A going quick, running violently.

A ملواح *milwāh*, (A horse) soon becoming thirsty. A woman speedily becoming lean and thin. Tall, slender. (A woman) with broad shoulder-blades and restless. (An owl) fastened by the foot in order to lure a hawk.

A ملوان *malawānī*, (du. of ملا *mala'*) Day and night.

A ملوّب *mulawwab*, Crooked, bent (iron).

A ملوة *mal, mil,* or *mulwat*, A long space of time. *Milwat*, Some time, a good while, a whole age.

A ملوث *milwas*, A man, family, or tribe distinguished for nobility.

A ملوّث *mulawwas*, Stained, defiled, nasty.

A ملوحة *mulūhat*, (v. n. of ملح) Being salt (as water). Being beautiful. Saltness, brackishness.

A ملوخ *mulūkh*, (v. n. of ملخ) Being knocked up with covering (a horse).

P ملوخيا *mulūkhiyā*, A kind of marshmallow.

A ملوذ *milwaz*, A pretended friend. A liar.

A ملوذة *milwazat*, Asylum, refuge, stronghold.

A ملوّز *mulawwaz*, Stuffed with almonds. Beautiful (face). Almond-shaped, resembling almonds.

A ملوس *malūs*, Long-necked (camel) which always take the lead.

A ملوسة *mulūsat*, (v. n. of ملس) Being sleek, soft, smooth, bare. Smoothness, sleekness.

A ملوّص *mulawwas*, (A dish) made of unground wheat, honey, and water.

A ملوط *mulūt*, (v. n. of ملط) Thieving. Being born of unknown parents. (pl. of ملط *milt*) Thieves or worthless fellows. Born of unknown parents.

A ملوظ *milwaz*, A stick or scourge.

A ملوغة *malūghat*, (fem.) Foolish, low, obscene.

A ملوغي *mulūghī*, (in the dialect of Morocco) A jester, droll, merry fellow.

A ملوف *malūf*, (Forage) wet with rain.

A ملوك *mulūk*, (pl. of ملك *malik*) Kings.

P ملوكا *malūkā*, The head of a Christian sect.

P ملوكانه *mulūkāna*, Royal, princely, like a king. خوانچهٔ طعام ملوكانه *khwānchaʼi taʻāmi mulūkāna*, A trayful of viands fit for a king: royal dainties.

A ملوكة *mulūkat*, Possession. Servitude.

A ملوكيّ *mulūkīy*, Royal, regal, kingly.

A ملول *malūl*, Fatigued, tired. Sick, languid. Melancholy, vexed, sad, dejected, out of spirits.

P ملول شدن *malūl shudan*, To be afflicted.

A ملولا *malolā*, Vexation, grief, affliction, sadness, melancholy.

A ملولب *mulawlab*, An instrument or style with which collyrium is applied to the eyes.

A ملولة *malūlat*, (m. f.) Sad, afflicted. Wearied.

A ملولي *malūlī*, Weariness, disgust.

A ملوم *malūm*, Reprehended, accused.

A ملوّن *mulawwan*, Coloured, of various colours.

SY ملونيا *mulūniyā*, A long melon.

A ملوّي *mulawwa'*, Distorted, crooked.

A ملويّ *malwīy*, Twisted (rope). Plaited (bracelet). Distorted.

P ملّه *malla*, A piece of nankeen.

A ملهب *milhab*, Extremely fair.

A ملهّب *mulahhab*, Cloth not saturated with dye.

P ملهتي *malhatī*, Liquorice.

A ملهّج *mulahhaj*, Sleepy, drowsy, unable to work.

A ملهّد *mulahhad*, Much beaten. Trodden under foot. Injuriously or iniquitously used.

A ملهز *milhaz*, A giver of a box under the ear.

A ملهّق *mulahhak*, Made white, whitened.

P ملهم *malham*, (for مرهم) A salve, plaster.

A ملهم *milham*, Gluttonous. *Mulham*, Inspired. *Mulhim*, An inspirer.

A ملهوّ *malhūw*, Played, amused.

A ملهوب *malhūb*, Kindled, inflamed.

A ملهوت *malhūt*, Name of the fish which Muhammadans imagine supports the world.

A ملهوز *malhūz*, Marked with the first appearance of grey hairs (half-grey being اشمط *ashmat*, and white hairs اشيب *ashyab*). Compact in body. Seared on the cheek-bone under the ear.

A ملهوف *malhūf*, Injured, oppressed, afflicted, sighing, sad, distressed. ملهوف القلب *malhūfu'l kalb*, Pained at heart.

A ملهوق *mulahwik*, A vain-boaster.

A ملهيٰ *milha'*, Any instrument used in play or by way of recreation; likewise a musical instrument, or the art of performing. *Mulhī*, A mimic, buffoon, jester, one who affords amusement.

A مليٌّ *malīy*, Opulent, wealthy.

A ملّى *mulla'*, A cake well baked.

A مليّ *maliy*, A portion of an age. A long hour.

A مليًّا *maliyan*, For a long while.

A ملياح *milyāh*, (A horse) soon thirsty.

A ملياع *milyāʻ*, (A she-camel) soon thirsty; also one running before others and then returning.

P مليبار *malībār*, Malabar in India.

A مليت *millīt*, Leaf of the مرخ *markh*-tree.

A مليث *milyas*, Strong, powerful.

A مليّث *mulayyas*, (A man) corpulent, flabby, and slow-paced. Base, contemptible.

A مليج *malīj*, A suckling. Great, illustrious.

A مليح *malīh*, (pl. ملاح *milāh* and املاح *amlāh*) Beautiful. Agreeable, sweet, charming. Salt water (well). Saltish (fish). مليح الكلام *malīhu'l kalām*, Eloquent, agreeable. ابو المليح *abū'l malīh*, A lark.

P مليح گوي *malīh-gūy*, Eloquent, charming speaker.

A مليخ *malīkh*, Insipid (meat); weak, corrupt. Slow in coition.

A مليز *malīz*, A place of refuge, asylum.

A مليس *mullīs*, (in the Morocco dialect) A plum.

A مليساء *mulaysā*, Acid milk, with which pure milk is diluted. Mid-day. The time between sunset and the evening-prayer. The month of Safar. A month between the close of the hot weather and the winter (a kind of Indian summer). A little household furniture. Name of a fort in Taif.

A مليص *malīs*, (v. n. of ملص Voiding excrement. An abortion.

A مليط *malīt*, (A fœtus) without hair. Featherless (arrow). An abortion.

A مليع *malīʻ*, (pl. ملع *muluʻ*) A barren desert: level and sterile ground. Swift (she-camel or horse).

A مليق *malīk*, An abortion.

A مليقة *malīkat*, An ink-stand furnished with cotton, silk, or any thing similar.

A مليك *malīk*, (pl. ملكاء *mulakā*) A king. A pirate. مليك النحل *malīku'n nahl*, King of the bees.

A مليكة *mulaykat*, Name of a company or body of people. A page, leaf, folio.

A مليل *malīl*, (Bread) baked under the ashes. (Meat) dressed amongst hot ashes called ملة *mallat*. Beaten or marked (road). *Mulayl*, A crow.

A مليّل *mulayyal*, Long and dark (night).

A مليلة *malīlat*, The heat of a fever penetrating to the bones.

A مليم *malīm*, Reproved, blamed. *Mulīm*, An accuser, censurer, blamer. Reprehensible, deserving censure. ربّ لائم مليم *rubba lāʼimin mulīmun*, Many a censurer is deserving of censure.

P ملي ميدان *malī maydān*, Apparent, public.

A مليّن *mulayyan*, Softened, soothed, pacified, pleased. Favourable. *Mulayyin*, Softening, emollient. A lenitive, laxative.

A ملينة *malyanat*, A soft thing laid under the head. ذو ملينة *zū malyanatin*, Placid, mild, amiable, lenient, engaging.

A مليه *malīh*, (for مليح) Good, beautiful.

A مليٌّ *malīʼ*, (pl. ملاء *milāʼ*, املاء *amliʼā*, and ملاء *mulaʼā*) Rich, wealthy, affluent, opulent.

A مليّيث *mulayyis*, (or مليبيث *mulayyis*) Very hairy and full of flesh (camel).

A مّ *mam*, (a contraction of ممنوع *mamnūʻ*) Inadmissible. (and of مسلّم *musallam*) Granted.

A ممّا *mimmā*, (or مّمّ *mimma*) (for من ما *min mā*) From or of that which. From what cause.

A مماءاة *mumāʼāt*, (v. n. 3 of ماي) Acting or computing by hundreds (مائة *miʼat*; as مؤالفة *muʼālafat*, implies numbering by thousands الف *alf*).

A مماءرة *mumāʼarat*, (v. n. 3 of مأر) Committing mutual hostilities. Boasting against or defying (another). Exasperating each other. Being, making, or becoming equal (in any thing).

A مماءنة *mumāʼanat*, (v. n. 3 of مأن) Giving

attention to. Worthy, deserving of.

A ممات *mamāt*, Place or time of death. Death. *Mumāt*, Mortal. Obsolete, disused (verb).

A مماتكة *mumātakat*, (v. n. 3 of متك, not in use) Contracting, engaging to give marriage-portions to each other.

A مماتن *mumātin*, Great, distant (journey).

A مماتنة *mumātanat*, (v. n. 3 of متن) Retiring a great way off. Putting off.

A مماثل *mumāsil*, Alike, resembling, equal, similar, identical. Comparable. A name for any of the five conjugations فعّل *faʻʻala*, فاعل *fāʻala*, افعل *afʻala*, تفعّل *tafaʻʻala*, and تفاعل *tafāʻala*. P مماثل شدن *mumāsil shudan*, To resemble. A غير مماثل *ghayr mumāsil*, Dissimilar. A name for any of the seven conjugations انفعل *infaʻala*, افتعل *iftiʻala*, افعلّ *ifʻalla*, استفعل *istafʻala*, افعالّ *ifʻālla*, افعوعل *ifʻawʻala*, افعوّل *ifʻiwwala*.

A مماثلة *mumāsalat*, (v. n. 3 of مثل) Being like, resembling. Resemblance, similitude, allusion.

A مماجدة *mumājadat*, (v. n. 3 of مجد) Contending for glory (مجد *majd*). Boasting, glorying in.

A مماجرة *mumājarat*, (v. n. 3 of مجر) Taking usury in buying and selling.

A مماجعة *mumājaʻat*, (v. n. 3 of مجع) Sneering, ridiculing; being petulant, impudent, saucy; talking obscenely amongst themselves.

A مماجن *mumājin*, (A camel) not conceiving though oft covered.

A مماجنة *mumājanat*, (v. n. 3 of مجن) Playing the whore (a mare), not standing to the first leap.

A مماحجة *mumāhajat*, A delaying of payment.

A مماحك *mumāhik*, Quarrelsome. A brawler.

A مماحكة *mumāhakat*, (v. n. 3 of محك) Litigating, suing at law. Disputing, wrangling.

A مماحلة *mumāhalat*, (v. n. 3 of محل) Dealing fraudulently one with another. Contending with for superiority in strength. Enmity, animosity.

A مماخطة *mumākhazat*, (v. n. 3 of مخط) Forcing the female to lie down (a stallion-camel).

A مماداة *mumādāt*, (v. n. 3 of مدي, not used) Bearing with, tolerating, granting a delay. Filling.

A ممادّة *mumāddat*, (v. n. 3 of مدّ) Extending, stretching. Prolonging. Deferring payment.

A مماذاة *mumāzāt*, (v. n. 3 of مذي) Playing and toying together (men and women). Pandering to one's own wife.

A مماذق *mumāzik*, Untrue in love or friendship.

A مماذقة *mumāzakat*, (v. n. 3 of مذق) Shewing a pretended regard or feigned love.

A مماراة *mumārāt*, (v. n. 3 of مري) Disputing, contending with, quarrelling, opposing. Doubting, suspecting. Contention, opposition.

A ممارّة *mumārrat*, (v. n. 3 of مرّ) Wrestling, twisting one's self round (another), throwing (him) on the ground. Going along with another.

A ممارث *mamāris*, (pl. of ممرث *mimras*) Patient, mild towards (adversaries).

A ممارزة *mumārazat*, (v. n. 3 of مرز) Applying a remedy, remedying, curing.

A ممارس *mumāris*, Devoted, addicted. Studious.

A ممارسة *mumārasat*, (v. n. 3 of مرس) Managing (affairs), applying with great attention, involving one's self (in them). Handling, manipulating. Remedying, curing. Trying, testing. Close application to study.

A ممارطة *mumāratat*, (v. n. 3 of مرط) Pulling the hair. Tearing, scratching with the nails.

A ممارن *mumārin*, (A she-camel) not conceiving, being covered unseasonably.

A ممارنة *mumāranat*, (v. n. 3 of مرن) Giving false signs of pregnancy (a camel).

A ممازّة *mumāzzat*, (v. n. 3 of مزّ) Retiring. Removing. Setting a distance between two persons.

A ممازجة *mumāzajat*, (v. n. 3 of مزج) Glorying against any one, contending about glory. Mixing together. Muddling, stupefying.

A ممازحة *mumāzahat*, (v. n. 3 of مزح) Playing, sporting, jesting (with another).

A ممازقة *mumāzakat*, (v. n. 3 of مزق) Endeavouring to outstrip (in a race).

A ممازهة *mumāzahat*, A playing together.

A ممأس *mimʼas*, Swift. A calumniator, whisperer.

P مماس *mumās*, Low (place), a ditch.

A مماسّ *mumāss*, Touching, tangent, contiguous.

A مماسّة *mumāssat*, (v. n. 3 of مسّ) Touching (another). Lying with. Contact. Touch.

A مماسحة *mumāsahat*, (v. n. 3 of مسح) Coaxing.

P مماش *mumāsh*, A hoe. Low, not high.

A مماشاة *mumāshāt*, A walking along with.

A مماشقة *mumāshakat*, (v. n. 3 of مشق) Striving with in drawing or reproaching.

A مماصعة *mumāsaʻat*, A fighting with swords.

A مماضغة *mumāzaghat*, (v. n. 3 of مضغ) Enraging (any one) in a combat.

A مماطل *mumātil*, One who delays payment.

A مماطلة *mumātalat*, (v. n. 3 of مطل) Deferring payment. Being dilatory in performing a promise.

A مماظّة *mumāzzat*, (v. n. 3 of مظّ) Contending, striving, disputing. Being malignant and injurious.

A مماعك *mumāʻik*, One who delays payment.

A مماعكة *mumāʻakat*, A delaying, putting off.

A مماغثة *mumāghasat*, (v. n. 3 of مغث) Rubbing one another. Contending, litigating. Altercation, animosity.

A مماقسة *mumākasat*, (v. n. 3 of مقس) Contending in diving. Rivaling a fish in diving.

A مماكس *mumākis*, One who bids against another at a sale; an unfair, roguish, haggling fellow.

A مماكسة *mumākasat*, (v. n. 3 of مكس) Bidding against another. Bating, lowering a price, haggling. Acting like a niggard.

A مماكل *mumākil*, One who collects all together.

A ممال *mamāl*, (v. n. of مال for ميل) Inclining, having a propensity; declining, deviating from. Propensity, inclination. *Mumāl*, Inclined. (The vowel فتحه *fatha*) sounded like كسر *kasr*.

A ممالأة *mumālaʼat*, (v. n. 3 of ملأ) Assisting.

A ممالثة *mumālasat*, (v. n. 3 of ملث) Acting hypocritically, dissembling. Playing, joking, toying.

A ممالحة *mumālahat*, (v. n. 3 of ملح) Eating another's salt as a pledge of friendship. Confiding mutually. Sucking (milk) together.

A ممالخة *mumālakhat*, (v. n. 3 of ملخ) Flattering, soothing. Playing together.

A ممالطة *mumālatat*, (v. n. 3 of ملط) Repeating half a verse which another finishes.

A ممالغة *mumālaghat*, A jesting obscenely.

A ممالقة *mumālakat*, A flattering, soothing.

A ممالك *mamālik*, (pl. of مملكة *mamlakat*) Kingdoms, provinces, dominions, states, regions. Estates, possessions, crown-lands. A kingdom, realm, empire, dominion. ممالك محروسه *mamāliki mahrūsa*, (or ممالك محروسهٔ عثمانيّه *mamāliki mahrūsaʼi ʻusmāniya*) The Ottoman empire, or the protected dominion of Osmān.

A ممالیط *mamālīt*, (pl. of مملط *mumlit*) (Camels) which bring forth hairless colts.

A مماليك *mamālīk*, (pl. of مملوك *mamlūk*) Servants, slaves, either purchased or taken in war. Mamalukes. اقلّ المماليك *akallu'l mamālīk*, The lowest of slaves, humblest of servants.

A مماناة *mumānāt*, (v. n. 3 of مني) Granting a delay. Extending, drawing out, prolonging. Expecting. Repaying. Treating courteously. Coming or riding behind another. Riding in turns. Rendering necessary, compelling.

A ممانّة *mumānnat*, (v. n. 3 of منّ) Helping one: going and coming repeatedly on his affairs.

A ممانح *mumānih*, (A camel) which gives milk when others have ceased. Continual, incessant (rain).

A ممانحة *mumānahat*, A weeping perpetually.

A ممانع *mumāniʻ*, A hinderer, an opposer: one who forbids, impedes, obstructs. Rebellious.

A ممانعة *mumānaʻat*, (v. n. 3 of منع) Preventing, forbidding, prohibiting, driving away, repelling. Prohibition, obstruction, obstacle, repulse.

A مماني *mumānī*, A cuckold, pimp to his own wife.

A مماوتة *mumāwatat*, (v. n. 3 of مات for موت) Exercising patience towards (any one).

A مماهرة *mumāharat*, (v. n. 3 of مهر) Contracting, engaging to give marriage-portions (مهر *mahr*).

A ممايحة *mumāyahat*, The act of mixing together.

A ممايرة *mumāyarat*, (v. n. 3 of مار for مير) Resembling (another), doing any thing in the same manner, imitating, mimicking.

A ممايلة *mumāyalat*, (v. n. 3 of مال for ميل) Conciliating, causing to incline to one another. Making a hostile incursion on one another.

A ممتاد *mumtād*, One who gives, or who asks for a present.

A ممتار *mumtār*, Sent in quest of provisions.

A ممتاز *mumtāz*, Chosen, distinguished, select. Eminent, excellent, illustrious. Separate, distinct.

A ممتثل *mumtasil*, Obedient, obsequious, obeying orders; a follower or observer (of religion, law, or custom). An imitator. (See امتثال *imtisāl*.)

A ممتحط *mumtahit*, Running. One who draws a sword. (See امتحاط *imtihāt*).

A ممتحش *mumtahish*, Burnt, scorched.

A ممتحق *mumtahik*, Abolished, obliterated. Burnt. Diminished, perished. Clean.

A ممتحك *mumtahik*, Morose, surly, angry.

A ممتحن *mumtahan*, Experienced, tried. Skilful. *Mumtahin*, One who tries, proves, examines, and weighs (words). (God) opening and enlarging (the heart of man).

A ممتخر *mumtakhir*, One who chooses the best, gives a preference to, takes the choicest part of any thing. One who sucks the marrow out of a bone. (A horse) standing facing the breeze to inhale it.

A ممتخض *mumtakhiz*, (Milk) shaken in the churn; or (a fœtus) stirring in the belly.

A ممتخط *mumtakhit*, One who blows his nose. One who draws a sword. One who draws a bow with the whole strength. Who extracts, shakes out; who seizes (what is in another's hand).

A ممتدّ *mumtadd*, Extended, prolonged, protracted, stretched.

A ممتدح *mumtadih*, A praiser. Wide, spacious (country). Blown out (side, waist, hypochondria).

A ممتدر *mumtadir*, One who takes up a clod.

A ممتدش *mumtadish*, A seizer, snatcher.

A ممتدي *mumtadī*, One who draws out.

A ممتذق *mumtazih*, (Milk) diluted with water.

A ممترز *mumtariz*, A vilifier, calumniator.

A ممترس *mumtaris*, Rubbed against. Mute, dumb, unable to speak at the time of contest.

A ممترش *mumtarish*, One who snatches or shakes out of the hand of another. One who labours, studies, endeavours.

A ممترط *mumtarit*, A snatcher. A collector.

A ممترق *mumtarik*, (An arrow) passing through.

A ممتري *mumtarī*, Doubtful about (a thing). Who or what forces out. (See امتراء *imtirāʼ*.)

A ممتزج *mumtāzij*, Mingled, mixed, compounded. Accustomed, used to, agreeing with one's constitution (مزاج *mizāj*).

A ممتسح *mumtasih*, Who draws a sword.

A ممتسخ *mumtasikh*, Who draws (a sword).

A ممتسغ *mumtasigh*, Retired to one side.

A ممتسك *mumtasik*, Holding fast.

A ممتسل *mumtasil*, Who draws a sword.

A ممتسي *mumtasi*, Thirsty.

A ممتش *mimtash*, A thief, a robber.

A ممتشط *mumtashit*, Combed. One who combs himself. One who allows the hair to fall.

A ممتشع *mumtashiʻ*, A spoiler, snatcher, seizer. One who draws a sword. (See امتشاع *imtishāʻ*.)

A ممتشق *mumtashik*, One who draws a sword. A snatcher. A cutter. Who milks the udder dry.

A ممتشل *mumtashil*, Who draws a sword.

A ممتشي *mumtashī*, One whose flocks (ماشية *māshiyat*) are very healthy and prolific.

A ممتصخ *mumtasikh*, One who strips off.

A ممتصر *mumtasir*, One who milks with the tips of his fingers. (See امتصار *imtisār*.)

A ممتصع *mumtasiʻ*, Travelling (horse). One who departs on a journey.

A ممتطخ *mumtatih*, High, swollen (river).

A ممتطل *mumtatil*, One who delays a term of payment. (A plant) growing long.

A ممتطي *mumtatī*, Who uses as a beast of burden.

A ممتّع *mumattiʻ*, A user, an enjoyer.

A ممتعد *mumtaʻid*, A seizer, snatcher.

A ممتعض *mumtaʻiz*, Angry. Difficult.

A ممتعل *mumtaʻil*, Who snatches hastily.

A ممتغط *mumtaghit*, Drawn. Who draws (a sword). High, full (day).

A ممتقط *mumtakit*, Who brings out.

A ممتقع *mumtakaʻ*, Changed (colour).

A ممتقل *mumtakil*, Who dives again and again.

A ممتكر *mumtakir*, Coloured with red earth.

A ممتلّ *mumtill*, One who passes swiftly by. One who puts bread on the ashes to bake. One who embraces a sect or creed (ملّة *millat*).

A ممتلج *mumtalij*, Who sucks milk.

A ممتلح *mumtalih*, Who mixes falsehood with truth.

A ممتلخ *mumtalakh*, Bereft of sense. *Mumtalikh*, One who draws, pulls out, or extracts.

A ممتلذ *mumtaliz*, A receiver of a gift.

A ممتلس *mumtalas*, Gone, lost (sight).

A ممتلط *mumtalit*, A seizer, snatcher.

A ممتله *mumtalih*, One losing his wits.

A ممتلئ *mumtaliʼ*, Filled, replete, heaped, full.

A ممتنح *mumtanah*, Enriched (with wealth) by God. *Mumtanih*, A receiver of a present: a beneficiary. A giver of riches.

A ممتنع *mumtaniʻ*, Prohibited. Impossible. One who abstains from or desists. A strong lion. Inaccessible (mountain). Strong, generous, bold. ممتنع العلاج *mumtaniʻu'l ʻilāj*, Incurable. ممتنع الوصول *mumtaniʻu'l wusūl*, Inaccessible.

A ممتنعات *mumtaniʻāt*, Impossibilities.

A ممتهج *mumtahaj*, Drawn (blood).

A ممتهك *mumtahik*, In the flower of youth.

A ممتهن *mumtahin*, Who receives as a servant. One who enters into service. (See امتهان *imtihān*.)

A ممثل *mumsil*, One who punishes by way of example; who kills a homicide in retaliation.

A ممثّل *mumassal*, Pictured, represented.

A ممثون *mamsūn*, Pained in the bladder.

A ممجّد *mumajjad*, Glorified, glorious.

A ممجر *mumjir*, Twin-bearing (woman).

A ممجرة *mumjirat*, (or ممجر *mumjir*) A sheep or a camel lean from having an overgrown fœtus in the womb. A woman advanced in pregnancy and unable to rise. *Mumjirat*, (The year) when the sheep or camel is so affected.

A ممجّط *mumajjat*, One who vacillates from tallness of stature.

A ممجمج *mumajmaj*, Shaky, tremulous (buttock).

A ممجّن *mumajjan*, Extended, protracted (road).

A ممحاة *mimhāt*, A cloth for wiping the privities.

A ممحال *mimhāl*, Barren, smitten with dearth.

A ممحش *mumhash*, Burnt (bread). *Mumhish*, Burning, blistering.

A ممحشة *mumhishat*, Barren, burning (year).

A ممحّص *mumahhas*, Strong, hardy (horse).

ممحّصة الذنوب *mumahhisatu'z zunūb*, (A woman) clear of faults.

A ممحل *mumhil*, (Earth) parched for want of rain.

A ممحّل *mumahhal*, Long, lengthened out. (Milk) losing its sweetness, growing sour.

A ممحلة *mamhalat*, A milk-bottle made of the skin of a sucking lamb.

A ممحوّ *mamhūw*, Obliterated, defaced.

A ممحوص *mamhūs*, Polished, shining, glittering (spear). Strong (camel). Firm-fleshed.

A ممحوض *mamhūz*, Pure, unmixed, unalloyed.

A ممحيّ *mamhīy*, Effaced, obliterated.

A ممخّ *mumikhkh*, Long, tedious (affair). (A bone) full of marrow (مخّ *mukhkh*).

A ممخّة *mumikhkhat*, Fat, full of marrow (sheep).

A ممخرق *mumakhrak*, Dispersed (crowd).

A ممخض *mimkhaz*, A leathern bottle churn.

A ممخضة *mimkhazat*, A churn.

A ممخّن *mumakhkhan*, (A road) made hard and smooth by treading.

A ممخوض *mamkhūz*, Churned (milk).

A ممدّ *mumidd*, An extender, prolonger, protracter. A helper, furnisher of supplies.

A ممدّح *mumaddah*, Lauded, greatly extolled.

A ممدّد *mumaddad*, Stretched (tent with cords).

A ممدّر *mumaddar*, Plastered with clay.

A ممدرة *mimdarat* or *mamdarat*, A place whence they take pure clay (مدر *madar*).

A ممدّرة *mumaddarat*, Fat (camels).

A ممدوح *mamdūh*, Praised, celebrated, famous, laudable, commendable.

A ممدوحات *mamdūhāt*, Laudable acts or things.

A ممدود *mamdūd*, Extended, protracted, lengthened out. Marked with the sign *madda* ~.

A ممدّة *mumaddah*, Praised, lauded, eulogised.

A ممذقرّ *mumzakirr*, Milk divided into its lacteous and serous particles, which on being shaken unite. A man of a mixed race.

A ممذل *mimzal*, A pimp to one's own wife.

A ممذوق *mamzūk*, (Milk) mixed with water.

A ممذئلّ *mumzaʼill*, Astonished, disturbed in mind. Bad-tempered.

A ممرّ *mamarr*, (v. n. of مرّ) Departing, passing

by, proceeding. Pass, passage, transit, ford. Account, cause. A canal. ممرّ الزمان *mamarru'z zamān*, Lapse of time. ممرّ ناس *mamarri nās*, The transit of man, *i.e.* Death. A beaten path. Twisted firmly (rope). *Mumirr*, One who, having made a young refractory camel apparently quiet, holds fast by the tail, and fixes his feet firmly on the ground, that he may not drag him if he tries to escape.

A ممراج *mimrāj*, (A camel) accustomed to abort. (A man) whose affairs are in confusion.

A ممراح *mimrāh*, Active, sprightly (horse). Land quickly producing. (An eye) shedding many tears.

A ممراض *mimrāz*, One often sick.

A ممراط *mimrāt*, (A palm-tree) whose dates usually drop off. Swift (camel).

A ممراع *mimrāع*, Fertile, cultivated (place).

A ممرث *mimras*, (pl. ممارث *mamāris*) Patient, mild towards an adversary.

A ممرّثة *mumarrasat*, (Land) wet by gentle rain.

A ممرجل *mumarjal*, (pl. مراجل *marājil*) A garment remarkable for its colour and figures. Marked with the figure of a cauldron (مرجل *mirjal*).

A ممرح *mimrah*, Active, sprightly (horse).

A ممرّح *mumarrah*, Trained, fruit-bearing (vine).

A ممرّد *mumarrad*, Lengthened (building).

A ممرض *mumriz*, An attendant on the sick.

A ممرط *mumrit*, (A palm) whose dates drop off. Swift (camel).

A ممرع *mumriع*, Fruitful, rich in provender. One who has sheep well fed.

A ممرعز *mumarعaz*, (A garment) made of goats' hair or other fine hair.

A ممرّغ *mumarrigh*, A wallower on the ground.

A ممرغة *mimraghat*, The blind gut.

A ممرّق *mumarrik*, A singer. Particles of butter like locusts' eyes floating in milk.

A ممرّن *mumarran*, Of a rigid (countenance).

A ممروت *mamrūt*, (Land) barren, destitute of herbage by reason of a superabundance of moisture.

A ممرور *mamrūr*, Troubled with bile, bilious. Filled (leathern bottle).

A ممروس *mamrūs*, Steeped. Rubbed (date).

A ممرئ *mumri*, Wholesome, digestible (food). A she-camel retaining the seed of the male.

A ممري *mumrī*, In a proper train (business). A camel retaining the seed of the male.

A ممرية *mumriyat*, A cow followed by a calf of a brilliant white colour.

A ممزّق *mumazzak*, (v.n. 2 of مزق) Tearing. Torn.

A ممزوج *mamzūj*, Tempered, mixed. شراب ممزوج *sharābi mamzūj*, Wine diluted (with water).

A ممزوق *mamzūk*, Torn, rent.

A ممساس *mamsās*, Light, not heavy.

A ممسح *mimsah*, A liar.

A ممسك *mumsik*, Who holds, contains, retains, seizes. One who restrains himself (from speaking). Avaricious, stingy, parsimonious. Economical. A miser, niggard. A horse that has one fore and one hind-foot white on the same side.

A ممسّك *mumassak*, (A garment) perfumed with musk. (A medicine) mixed with musk.

A ممسكة *mumsakat*, (A horse's leg) possessed of white; also destitute of white.

A ممسوح *mamsūh*, Cleaned, wiped. Polished, furbished. Anointed. Characterized by a plain face or level superficies. A rough cheek or towel.

A ممسوخ *mamsūkh*, Changed, metamorphosed into a deformed shape. (A horse) lank-buttocked.

A ممسوخة *mamsūkhat*, Meagre-hipped (woman).

A ممسود *mamsūd*, Excellently or elegantly formed by nature, well knit in the bones.

A ممسوس *mamsūs*, Touched. Tangible. Furious. (Water) partly sweet and partly brackish.

A ممسىٰ *mumsa'*, (v. n. 4 of مسى) Being evening, becoming evening. A monk's cell. The place where the evening is past. *Mumsī*, Late in the evening. One who comes or does any thing in the evening.

A ممشاة *mamshāt*, A causeway, path by which one walks. *Mumshāt*, Propagated (religion).

A ممشش *mimshash*, A thief, robber, stealer.

A ممشط *mimshat*, A comb.

A ممشّق *mumashshak*, Dyed with red earth.

A ممشل *mimshal*, One who milks leisurely.

A ممشوط *mamshūt*, Combed. (A camel) marked with the sign مشط *musht*. Tall and slim (man).

A ممشوق *mamshūk*, Thin, lean, spare (man). Slender-waisted (horse). Long and slender (penis).

A ممشوقة *mamshūkat*, (A girl) of an elegant form.

A ممشول *mamshūl*, Meagre in the thighs.

A ممشىٰ *mamsha'*, (v. n. of مشى) Walking. *Mamshi* or *mamsha'*, A privy. *Mumshī*, One who observes (the law). (See امشاء *imshā*.)

A ممصال *mimsāl*, (A sheep) whose milk separates from the serum before being churned.

A ممصّر *mumassar*, Coloured with red clay.

A ممصطك *mumastak*, Mixed with gum mastich.

A ممصل *mimsal*, A press, strainer, or cauldron used by dyers. *Mumsil*, (A woman) bringing forth an abortion. (A sheep) whose milk separates from the serum before being churned.

A ممصمصة الذنوب *mumasmisatu'z zunūb*, (A woman) clear of crime.

A ممصور *mamsūr*, (A horse) put to his speed.

A ممصوص *mamsūs*, Slender (horse's pastern).

A ممصوصة *mamsūsat*, Lean, emaciated (woman).

A ممضّ *mumizz*, Hot, burning (collyrium).

A ممضغة *mamzaghat*, Mastication. Root of jaw.

A ممضوّ عليه *mamzūwun عalayhi*, (Business) cleverly managed, properly executed.

A ممضوغ *mamzūgh*, Masticated, chewed.

A ممضىٰ *mumza'*, Subscribed, authenticated. An authentic writing. ممضىٰ و مسجّل *mumza' u musajjal*, Signed and sealed.

A ممطر *mamtar*, (*mimtar*, or ممطرة *mimtarat*) A woollen cloak to protect one from the rain (مطر *matar*). *Mumtir*, Rainy (day).

A ممطّعة *mumattaعat*, A camel whose udder is full and flows with milk.

A ممطور *mamtūr*, Wetted with rain (مطر *matar*), rained upon. One who rubs the teeth much.

A ممطول *mamtūl*, Hammered. Extended. Put off (creditor).

A ممظّح *mumazzah*, Praised.

A ممعد *mimعad*, A wolf that steals rapidly along.

A ممعّز *mumaععaz*, Hard-skinned (man).

A ممعّط *mumaععit*, Very tall.

A ممعك *mimعak*, One who puts off payment.

A ممعود *mamعūd*, Disordered in the stomach.

A ممعور *mamعūr*, Austere, frowning with rage.

A ممعوق *mamعūk*, Disordered in the stomach.

A ممعول *mamعūl*, Gelded (ass).

A ممعون *mamعūn*, Succulent, juicy (grass).

A ممغار *mimghār*, (A sheep) accustomed to give milk mixed with blood. A palm bearing red dates.

A ممغر *mimghar*, A palm-tree bearing red dates. *Mumghir*, (A sheep) giving milk mixed with blood.

A ممغّر *mumaghghar*, Coloured with the red earth مغرة *maghrat*. *Mumaghghir*, (An unripe date) of the colour of مغرة *maghrat*.

A ممّغط *mummaghit*, Tall (man).

A ممغل *mimghal*, Desirous of eating earth. *Mumghil*, (A woman) bearing a child every year, and conceiving before the weaning of the former infant.

A ممغوث *mamghūs*, Warmed. Attacked by fever. Definite, determined. Corn beaten down by the rain.

A ممغوص *mamghūs*, Griped, troubled with cholic.

A ممقر *mumkir*, Acid, bitter. A well containing little water. Milk.

A ممقوت *mamkūt*, Hated, held as an enemy.

A ممقور *mamkūr*, Steeped in brine, salted (fish).

A ممقوع *mamkūع*, Hit. Reviled. Suspected.

A ممكار *mimkār*, A palm-tree accustomed to bear hard, unripe dates.

A ممكر *mumakkir*, A regrater, forestaller.

A ممكل *mimkal*, A pond containing little water. A well wherein is water.

A ممكلة *mamkulat*, Exhausted (well).

A ممكن *mumkan* or *mumakkan*, Confirmed, established. *Mumkin*, Possible. (A lizard) full of eggs. (A lizard) which has its eggs under it. (A valley) producing the plant مكنان *maknān*. ممكن الدخول *mumkinu'd dukhūl*, Accessible. P ممكن شدن *mumkin shudan*, To be possible.

A ممكنات *mumkināt*, Possibilities.

A ممكور *mamkūr*, (A lion) besmeared with the blood of his prey. Coloured with red earth.

A ممكورة *mamkūrat*, Handsome-legged, firm-fleshed, and well-built (woman).

A ممكوك *mamkūk*, Sucked, especially marrow.

A ممكولة *mamkūlat*, Exhausted (well).

P ممل *mumul*, A blemish in the eye.

A ممّل *mumall*, Beaten (path); worn (thing). *Mumill*, One who wearies: wearisome.

A مملاص *mimlās*, (A woman) apt to miscarry.

A مملاط *mimlāt*, (A camel) generally bringing forth camels without hair.

A مملان *mimlān*, The first king of Azarbayjān.

A مملّح *mumallah*, Salted.

A مملحة *mamlahat*, A salt-work. *Mimlahat*, A salt-cellar.

P مملخت *mamlakht*, A shoe or slipper.

A مملّس *mumallas*, Smooth, bare, sleek, slippery.

A مملص *mumlis*, Miscarrying (woman).

A مملط *mumlit*, (pl. مماليط *mamālīt*) (A camel) bringing forth a hairless colt.

A مملق *mimlak*, A plasterer's trowel. *Mumlik*, Poor, destitute.

A مملّك *mumallak*, Put into one's possession (property). Enriched, made possessor. A king. *Mumallik*, One who constitutes (another) possessor; who puts in possession.

A مملكة *mamlukat*, *mamlakat*, or *mamlikat*, (v. n. of ملك) Possessing, having dominion, holding. *Mamlakat* or *mamlukat*, An empire, a kingdom, realm, dominion, country, province, district, possession. Regal power, grandeur, magnificence. P مملكت راندن *mamlakat rāndan*, To sway the sceptre. A عبد مملكة *ʿabdun mamlakatun*, *mamlikatun*, or *mamlukatun*, A purchased slave, or captive born of free parents (one born a slave being called عبد قنّ *ʿabdu kinnin*). *Mamlukat*, Centre of the kingdom.

P مملكت پناه *mamlakat-panāh*, Asylum or defender of the kingdom, *i.e.* the king.

P مملكت پناهي *mamlakat-panāhī*, Defence of the kingdom, *i.e.* royal authority, empire.

A مملوّ *mamlūw*, Full, filled, replete. Indisposed through repletion.

A مملوء *mamlūʾ*, Filled. Indisposed from repletion. Troubled with rheum or cold in the head.

A مملوح *mamlūh*, Salted.

A مملوحات *mamlūhāt*, Salted meats. Pickles.

A مملوس *mamlūs*, (Castrated) boy.

A مملوق *mamlūk*, (or مملوق الذكر *mamlūku'z zakar*) (A horse) young, unpractised, new at covering.

A مملوك *mamlūk*, Well-kneaded (dough). Possessed, in one's power. (pl. مماليك *mamālīk*) A purchased slave or captive. A white slave, a Mamaluke. غلام مملوك *ghulāmi mamlūk*, A slave-boy.

A مملوكة *mamlūkat*, Empire, dominion.

A مملوكي *mamlūkī*, Servile condition, servitude.

A مملوكية *mamlūkiyat*, Slavery. Captivity.

A مملول *mamlūl*, (Bread) baked under the ashes.

A مملئ *mumliʾ*, A ewe supposed to be with young, yet having only water in the uterus.

P ممن *mamin*, (in zand and Pāzand) What?

A ممن *miman*, (contracted from the prep. من *min* and the pron. من *man*) Than him who.

A ممنأة *mamnaʾat*, (or ممناة *mamnāt*) Black earth.

A المُمنّان *al muminnāni*, Day and night.

A ممنح *mumnih*, (A camel) near the birth.

A ممنوّ *mamnūw*, Sought after.

A ممنوع *mamnūʿ*, Prohibited. Forbidden, restrained. (in grammar) Deprived of tanwin and of all variation in inflection (as ذكري *zikra'*). فاكهة ممنوعة *fākihat mamnūʿat*, Forbidden fruit.

A ممنوعة *mamnūʿat*, (pl. ممنوعات *mamnūʿāt*) A forbidden thing.

A ممنون *mamnūn*, Obliged, who has received a favour. Diminished, broken off. Reckoned up, computed. Robust, strong. Weak. The utmost of one's power. The best of whatever one has. اجر غير ممنون *ajri ghayr mamnūn*, Eternal rewards. P ممنون كردن *mamnun kardan*, To favour, oblige.

A ممنوني *mamnūnī*, Obligation.

A ممني *mumnī*, (and ممنية *mumniyat*) (A she-camel) whose pregnancy cannot be ascertained within fifteen days after her taking the male.

A ممنيّ *mamniy*, Tried, proved. Guided, favoured, prospered.

P ممول *mamul*, Do not delay.

A ممولا *mamolā*, A wagtail (motacilla).

A مموم *mamūm*, Pleuritic or small-pocked.

A ممون *mamūn*, Maintained in food and raiment.

A مموّه *mumawwah*, Gilded, washed over with gold. Falsified, adulterated, insincere.

A ممهاء *mimhāʾ*, (A camel) giving thin milk.

A ممهّد *mumahhad*, Levelled, smoothed. Disposed, arranged. Well-laid (foundation). Luke-warm (water). *Mumahhid*, One who lays a foundation.

A ممهر *mumhir*, (A mare) followed by a colt.

A ممهّك *mumahhik*, In the flower of youth or vegetation. Of a tall, incompact shape. Swift, wide-stepped (horse).

A ممهل *mumhil*, Slow, granting delay.

A ممهوّ *mamhūw*, Thin, watery (milk).

A ممهوج *mamhūj*, Flabby, pendulous-bellied.

A ممهور *mamhūr*, Signed, sealed.

A ممهورة *mamhūrat*, Dowered, portioned (woman).

A ممهوك *mamhūk*, A great blunderer in talk.

A مميت *mumīt*, Who or what causes death: mortal, fatal, deadly. (A camel) which has lost her colt.

A مميز *mumayyaz*, Distinguished. Discerned. *Mumayyiz*, Judicious, discriminating; a discerner.

A مميل *mamīl*, (v. n. of مال for ميل) Inclining, having a propensity. Deviating, swerving. Inclination, propensity, bias.

A مميلة *mumīlat* (A woman) who wins men's hearts, or moves her veil aside to shew her face and hair.

A ممئيّ *mamʾiy*, (pl. ممئيون *mamʾiyūn*) Made a hundred (مائة *miʾat*).

P من *man*, I. Me. A weight which varies according to the custom of the country, from 40 to 84lbs. The heart. The hole of a balance through which the tongue plays. A heap or a pile of any thing. از من *az man*, From, or than me. اين از آن منست *in az āni manast*, This is mine.

A من *man*, (pron. of com. gender, singular and plural) He who, she who, they who. Who? Whosoever, whatsoever, every one (either interrogatively or not). Some one, any one, a certain person. من طلب غلب *man talaba ghalaba*, He who asks, prevails; he who searches, finds (a proverb).

A من *min*, From. Of. For. On. Than, more than. By. Besides. In comparison of. On the part of, on account of, by reason of. A part of, some. Like, resembling, of the sort of, as, after the manner of. Without, against. Namely, to wit. It is sometimes expletive. من اجل *min ajli*, For which reason. من اجل ذالك *min ajli zālik*, On that account. من اجلك *min ajlika*, On thy account. من آخر *min ākhir*, Behind, at the back. من الآن *mini'l ān*, Henceforth, after this, from this time forward. من امم *min amam*, From the neighbourhood, near at hand; soon. من اين *min ayn*, (also من حيث *min hays*) Whence. من اي وجه كان *min ayyi wajhin kāna*, In whatever manner, in every shape, however. من بعد *mim baʿd*, After, hereafter; presently; never, in no shape. من بعد ما *mim baʿda mā*, After that. من تحت *min tahta*, From below. من دون *min dūn*, Besides, except. من الصبح *mini's subh*, Since morning. من الصباح الى الرواح *mini's sabāh ila'r rawāh*, From the morning till the evening. من طرف *min taraf*, Apart. من غير ان *min ghayr an*, Notwithstanding, although, nevertheless. من فوق *min fawk*, From above. من قبل *min kabl*, Formerly. من قبل ان *min kabl an*, Heretofore. من كل وجه *min kulli wajhin*, (or من كل وجوه *min kulli wujūh* and من كل الوجوه *min kulli'l wujūh*) In every manner, in all respects. من محل *mim mahal*, From elsewhere. من المهد *mini'l mahd*, From the cradle. من وجه محبّ و من وجه عدوّ *min wajhin muhibb wa min wajhin ʿadūw*, In one respect a friend, in another an enemy. من هنا *min hunā*, (or من هناك *min hunāk*) Hence. من هنا و هنا *min hunā wa hunā*, On every side. P هيچ من بعد *hech mim baʿd*, Never hereafter. A من اوّل يوم *min awwal yawm*, From the first day. من اوّله الى آخره *min awwalihi ilaʾ ākhirihi*, From the first of it to the last. من سنة *min sanatin*, During a whole year. من شهر *min shahr*, For a whole month (I have not seen him). من القوم *mini'l kawm*, (We assisted him) against his people. ما جاءني من احد *mā jāʾanī min ahadin*, There came not one to me. رجس من الاوثان *rijsun mini'l awsān*, An abomination of idols. ثوب من حرير *sawbun min harīr*, A garment of silk. من ربّي *mir rabbī*, From my Lord.

A منّ *mann*, (v. n. of من) Fatiguing (as a journey; (a rider) tiring (a camel). Depriving of strength. Breaking or cutting (a rope). Diminishing, withholding. Being deficient, defective. Being benevolent, benign, propitious, favourable. Conferring a benefit (on any person). Manna, a species of honey-dew gathered from plants. (pl. امنان *amnān*) A pair of scales. A measure for dry goods. Very fine dust. Weakness. A weight of 40 sers, a maund. A weight of about 2lbs. One whom nobody invites. منّ سلوي *manni salwa'*, The manna and quails (of the Israelites). *Minn*, Beneficence, grace, favour. بمنّه وجوده *bi minnihi wa jūdihi*, By His (God's) grace and goodness (or bounty).

A منأ *manʻ*, (v. n. of منأ) Steeping, soaking (a hide for tanning).

P منا *manā*, (in zand and Pāzand) Open, displayed, wide, spacious.

A منا *mana'*, Death. (pl. امناء *amnāʻ*, امني *amnī*, منيّ *muniy*, and *maniy*) A weight of two pounds. A pair of scales. A measure for dry goods. Divine decree. A part of any thing opposite to another part. Intention, design. (by poetic license for منازل *manāzil*) Mansions. داري منا داره *dārī manā dārihi*, My dwelling (is) opposite his dwelling.

A مناب *manāb*, (v. n. of ناب for نوب) Supplying the place (of another), doing any thing for him; acting as a locum tenens. Lieutenancy, vicegerency. The place where any one is, or acts as, a substitute. A road leading to water.

A منابأة *munābaʻat*, (v. n. 3 of نبأ) Announcing (any thing to another). Leaving off a habit. Giving up an acquaintance.

A منابت *manābit*, (pl. of منبت *mambit*) Places where plants naturally grow, their habitat.

A منابذة *munābazat*, (v. n. 3 of نبذ) Throwing (one thing to another). Saying, Throw the cloth to me, or I will throw it to you (a kind of contract in buying and selling). Recoiling mutually (two parties in battle). Carrying on a war openly. Retiring from an adversary in battle.

A منابر *manābir*, (pl. of منبر) Pulpits, rostra.

A منابزة *munābazat*, A calling one another names.

A منابض *manābiz*, (pl. of منبض *mimbaz*) Bows with which they separate cotton.

A منابع *manābiʻ*, (pl. of منبع) Fountains.

A منابلة *munābalat*, (v. n. 3 of نبل) Contending, endeavouring to excel in dexterity or archery.

A منات *manāt*, One weight of two pounds. One of the three chief idols of the pagan citizens of Mecca (the others being اللات *allāt* and عزّي *ʻuzza'*).

A منات *manāt*, (pl. of منة *manat*) What females?

A مناترة *munātarat*, (v. n. 3 of نتر) Speaking or calling with a loud voice.

A مناتين *manātīn*, (pl. of منتين) Stinking (men).

A مناث *manʻas*, (v. n. of نأث) Being distant, far off. Purposing, striving. *Munʻas*, Removed to a distance from his friends.

A مناجاة *munājāt*, (v. n. 3 of نجي) Telling a secret. Acting or speaking privately with another. Prayers, recommendations. An address to the Deity.

A مناجح *manājih*, (pl. of منجح *munjih*) Happy, prosperous, fortunate, successful in business.

A مناجد *manājid*, (pl. of منجد *minjad*) Broad gold necklaces, adorned with jewels and pearls, hanging below the breasts. *Munājid*, A defender, assistant. One who fights a battle.

A مناجدة *munājadat*, (v. n. 3 of نجد) Assisting, aiding. Going near. Fighting.

A مناجذ *manājiz*, (pl. of جلذ *julz*) Moles.

A مناجز *munājiz*, A champion; one who goes forth to the place of combat.

A مناجزة *munājazat*, (v. n. 3 of نجز) Preparing for battle, descending into the place of combat.

A مناجل *manājil*, (pl. of منجل *minjal*) Sickles.

A مناجيب *manājīb*, (pl. of منجاب) Feeble men. Polished arrows without point or feather.

A مناجيح *manājīh*, (pl. of منجح) Fortunate.

A مناجيق *manājīk*, (pl. of منجنيق *manjanīk*) Warlike engines for casting stones, balistæ.

A مناجين *manājīn*, (pl. of منجنون *manjanūn*) Wheels for raising water from rivers or wells, or used in watering gardens.

A مناح *manāh*, (v. n. of ناح for نوح) Mourning (a deceased husband).

A منّاح *mannāh*, A giver, bestower.

A مناحبة *munāhabat*, (v. n. 3 of نحب) Citing or bringing an adversary (before a judge). Contending for glory, boasting one against another. Depositing bets at a horse-race.

A مناحة *manāhat*, A house of mourning.

A مناحدة *munāhadat*, (v. n. 3 of نحد, not used) Entering into an agreement, covenanting.

A مناحس *manāhis*, Unfortunate (things).

P مناخ *manākh*, Close. Open.

A مناخ *munākh*, A place where a camel lies down. One's quarters.

A مناخر *manākhir*, (pl. of منخر) Nostrils.

A مناخسة *munākhasat*, (v. n. 3 of نخس) Flowing or being poured into one another (cisterns, pots).

A مناخل *manākhil*, (pl. of منخل *munkhul*) Sieves.

A مناخليّ *manākhiliy*, A sieve-maker.

A مناداة *munādāt*, (v. n. 3 of ندا for ندو) Calling to one, invoking, convoking, proclaiming. Boasting against another. Disclosing (a secret). Sitting down by, or being with another in an assembly. Lying open (the way). Seeing, knowing (any thing). A proclamation. P منادات كردن *munādāt kardan*, To proclaim, to make a proclamation.

A منادّة *munāddat*, The act of opposing, resisting.

A منادسة *munādasat*, (v. n. 3 of ندس) Contending in piercing with a spear. Calling one another nicknames. Walking or travelling in emulation.

A منادغة *munādaghat*, (v. n. 3 of ندغ) Soothing, cajoling. Talking amorously and politely together.

A منادم *munādim*, A companion, intimate.

A منادمة *munādamat*, (v. n. 3 of ندم) Being a confidential or pot-companion. Conviviality.

A منادي *manādī*, Proclamations. P منادي كردن *manādī kardan*, To make a proclamation. A *Munādī*, A crier, herald, proclaimer. A small drum that is beat about to notify or proclaim any thing. منادي اسلام *munādīʻi islām*, One who calls to prayers, a muezzin.

A مناديح *manādīh*, A desert.

A مناديل *manādīl*, (pl. of منديل) Towels, napkins.

A منادر *manāzir*, Admonishers, exhorters.

A منادرة *manāzirat*, Men of the tribe of منذر.

A منار *manār*, A candlestick, lamp, lantern. A lighthouse. A lofty turret joining the Muhammadan mosques, from which the crier calls the people to prayers (as they use no bells). A kind of fish destructive to ships. A march-stone or boundary-mark, a way-stone or direction-post. A clear, open road. ذو المنار *zū'lmanār*, Surname of Abraha, king of Arabia Felix, who is said to have first erected such posts when going to war, as directions for his return through deserts and uninhabited districts.

A منارة *manārat*, (pl. مناور *manāwir* and منائر *manāʻir*) A candlestick, lamp. A lighthouse. A slender lofty turret from whose projecting balcony the people are called to prayers; a minaret.

A منازّة *munāzzat*, (v. n. 3 of نزّ) Trying to overpower by words. Victory. Contention.

A منازع *manāziʻ*, Competitions, disputes. *Munāziʻ*, Contentious, litigious, opposed to, refractory.

P منازعان *munāziʻān*, Adverse parties, competitors.

A منازعة *munāzaʻat*, (v. n. 3 of نزع) Contending (against another), opposing, litigating. Having a strong propensity, longing for, inclining towards. Bordering upon, being contiguous, touching. Contest, litigation, controversy, altercation, fierce strife.

A منازف *manāzif*, (pl. of منزفة *minzafat*) Small buckets at the end of cross-poles for drawing water.

A منازقة *munāzakat*, (v. n. 3 of نزق) Reviling one another, being scurrilous. Drawing near.

A منازل *manāzil*, (pl. of منزل *manzil*) Mansions, halting-places, inns, caravanseras. Days' journeys, stages in travelling. منازل فراغ *manāzili firāgh*, Delightful dwellings, pleasant retreats. منازل القمر *manāzilu'l kamar*, Mansions of the moon (twenty-eight in number). منازل متباينه *manāzili mutabāyina*, Apartments not adjoining. منازل ملازمه *manāzili mulāzima*, Adjoining tenements; such as are in the same house.

P منازل شناسان *manāzil-shināsān*, Ascetics.

A منازه *manāzih*, (pl. of منزهة) Pleasant places.

A منازيح *manāzīh*, (Men) removed far off.

A مناسب *munāsib*, Corresponding, adapted to, conformable, proportioned, agreeing with, analogous, congruous, just, fit, proper, suitable, pertinent. Related to. P مناسب شدن *munāsib shudan*, To be suitable, to correspond with. A مناسب مقام *munāsibi makām*, (or مناسب المقام *munāsibu'l makām*) Adapted to a place, filling any office

A مناغضة *munāghazat*, (v. n. 3 of نغض) Thronging, crowding on one another in a narrow pass.

A مناف *manāf*, Name of a pagan Arabian idol. عبد مناف *ʻabdu manāf*, Name of an Arabian tribe.

A مناف *minsaf*, One who strives. Fortunate.

A منافاة *munāfāt*, (v. n. 3 of نفى) Dispelling. Repelling, driving each other off: repulse, opposition.

A منافث *munāfis*, A whisperer in another's ear.

A منافثة *munāfasat*, (v. n. 3 of نفث) Talking to.

A منافج *manāfij*, Cushions or pads with which women make a false swell of the hips; bustles.

A منافحة *munāfahat*, (v. n. 3 of نفح) Pleading or carrying on a law-suit (for another). Quarrelling, squabbling face to face. Revealing: discovery. Looking at, speaking to. Kissing with naked lips.

A منافخ *manāfikh*, (pl. of منفخ *minfakh*) Bellows.

A منافد *munāfid*, Most obstinate in litigation.

A منافدة *munāfadat*, (v. n. 3 of نفد) Citing before a judge, contending, opposing, going to law.

A منافذ *manāfiz*, (pl. of منفذ *manfaz*) Passages.

A منافرة *munāfarat*, (v. n. 3 of نفر) Contending for honour or nobility before a judge. Emulation.

A منافسة *munāfasat*, (v. n. 3 of نفس) Blowing, breathing. Aspiring to. Competing with. Envying.

A منافصة *munāfasat*, (v. n. 3 of نفص) Trying who can squirt his urine to the greater distance.

A منافطة *munāfatat*, (v. n. 3 of نفط) Throwing up scum (a boiling pot).

A منافع *manāfiʻ*, (pl. of منفعة *manfaʻat*) Gains, profits. Advantages, emoluments. Fruits, benefits. Valuable uses, useful purposes. منافع دارين *manāfiʻi dārayn*, The good things of both worlds. منافع دنيا و آخرت *manāfiʻi dunyaʼ u ākhirat*, The good things of this world and the next. منافع دنيويه *manāfiʻi dunyawīya*, Worldly advantages or interests. P مزارع پر منافع *mazāriʻi pur-manāfiʻ*, Fruitful fields.

A منافعة *munāfaʻat*, A deriving advantage.

A منافق *munāfik*, A hypocrite, dissembler, atheist. An enemy. Atheistic, impious. Hypocritical.

P منافقانه *munāfikāna*, Hypocritically, impiously.

A منافقة *munāfakat*, (v. n. 3 of نفق) Making a hole; or going into its hole (the jerboa). Acting hypocritically. Hypocrisy; impiety, atheism.

A منافي *munāfī*, Repugnant, contrary. منافي المروة *munāfiʼl murūwat*, Repugnant to humanity.

A منافيّ *manāfiy*, Related to the Arabian tribe of عبد مناف *ʻabd manāf*. (عبديّ *ʻabdiy* would be the more regular form, but منافيّ *manāfiy* has been substituted to avoid ambiguity).

A مناقب *manākib*, (pl. of منقبة *mankabat*) Virtues, abilities. سير و مناقب *siyar u manākib*, Virtues and good manners.

A مناقبة *munākabat*, (v. n. 3 of نقب) Meeting unexpectedly. Finding (water) when unlooked for.

A مناقحة *munākahat*, (v. n. 3 of نقح) Taking the management of any business. Fighting and quar-

nāsafa, or P بطريق مناصفه *ba tarīki munāsafa*) Equally, in halves.

A مناصيب *manāsīb*, (pl. of منصوب *mansūb*) Positions of the men on a chess-board.

A مناضحة *munāzahat*, (v. n. 3 of نضح) Defending one's self. Putting to a distance.

A مناضخة *munāzakhat*, (v. n. 3 of نضخ) Sprinkling one another (with water).

A مناضلة *munāzalat*, (v. n. 3 of نضل) Contending (with one) in throwing the javelin. Defending, excusing, pleading a cause.

A مناط *manāt*, Distance. مناط الثريا *manātuʼs surayyaʼ*, Distant as the Pleiades. *Munāt*, A man, beast, or place to which a thing is suspended or added. فيض مناط *fayz-munāt*, Bountiful.

A مناطاة *munātāt*, (v. n. 3 of نطا for نطو) Weaving in a particular manner by throwing clues to one another (women). Contending, litigating. Disputing about length. Delaying payment, or a promise.

A مناطبة *munātabat*, (v. n. 3 of نطب) Setting (men or dogs) together by the ears.

A مناطحة *munātahat*, A meeting in battle. Battle.

A مناطق *manātik*, (pl. of منطق) Girdles, belts.

A مناطقة *munātakat*, (v. n. 3 of نطق) Talking together. Discussing. Bestowing reason or speech.

A مناطل *manātil*, Presses (for wine or olives).

A مناظر *manāzar*, (in the dialect of Morocco) A spying-glass. *Manāzir*, (pl. of منظرة *manzarat*) Spectacles, public or theatrical exhibitions, aspects, appearences. Objects of sight. Conspicuous places. *Munāzir*, Like, resembling. A disputant, opponent.

A مناظرة *munāzarat*, (v. n. 3 of نظر) Disputing. Resembling. Making one thing to resemble another. Disputation, struggle, strife, contest.

A مناظم *manāzim*, (pl. of نظم *nazm*) Orders, rows. The orderly course (of human affairs).

A مناع *manāʻi*, Prevent thou.

A منّاع *mannāʻ*, A hinderer, refuser, denier.

A مناعة *manāʻat*, (v. n. of منع) Being inaccessible. Inaccessibility. A fort or inaccessible place.

A مناعف *manāʻif*, Summits of mountains.

A مناعفة *munāʻafat*, (v. n. 3 of نعف) Stopping up (a road), intercepting. Opposing, resisting.

A مناعم *munāʻim*, Gentle, soft, smooth, tender, delicate (plant). Benevolent, kind.

A مناعمة *munāʻamat*, (v. n. 3 of نعم) Affirming a thing to be so. Binding fast, tying (a rope). Enjoying the conveniences of life. Doing good to, bestowing plenty on. A benefaction. Pleasure, delight, a comfortable life. Delicate (woman) well fed and in good health.

A مناعي *manāʻī*, (pl. of منعى) News of a death.

A مناغاة *munāghāt*, (v. n. 3 of نغى) Speaking gently or soothingly (as a lover to his mistress, or a mother to her child). Singing (a bird). Approaching, being near. (A mountain) being high (as the heavens). Opposing, contending.

with propriety.

A مناسبة *munāsabat*, (v. n. 3 of نسب) Resembling. Being analogous, bearing a proportion to. Being related. Proportion, connexion, relation, comparison. Suitableness, convenience. Propriety, aptness, fitness. P بي مناسبت *bī munāsabat*, Out of proportion, disproportioned, inconvenient, absurd, impertinent.

A مناسخة *munāsakhat*, The death of one of the heirs before the partition of the inheritance. Inheritance, especially of indivisible property. Revolutions of time, succession of ages.

A مناسقة *munāsakat*, (v. n. 3 of نسق) Following one another secretly, imitating.

A مناسك *manāsik*, (pl. of منسك *mansik*) The ceremonies and sacrifices prescribed in the pilgrimage to Mecca.

A مناسم *manāsim*, (pl. of منسم *mansam* or *mansim*) Feet of camels or ostriches. Marks, traces, paths. Modes, manners.

A مناسمة *munāsamat*, (v. n. 3 of نسم) Perceiving by the smell of the breath. Whispering.

A مناسيب *manāsīb*, (pl. of منسوب *mansūb*) Amatory (verses) written in praise of a mistress.

A مناسيف *manāsīf*, (Camels) tearing up grass.

A مناشب *manāshib*, Small bad dates.

A مناشدة *munāshadat*, (v. n. 3 of نشد) Praying, adjuring, causing to swear (by God). Conjuring one as in the presence of God. Repeating verses to each other.

A مناشف *manāshif*, (pl. of منشف) Napkins.

A مناشير *manāshīr*, (pl. of منشور *manshūr*) Royal mandates, patents, or diplomas.

A مناص *manās*, (v. n. of ناص for نوص) Moving one's self. Retiring, declining, flying from. Lagging behind. Delaying. Refuge, asylum, retreat.

A مناصاة *munāsāt*, (v. n. 3 of نصا for نصو) Taking hold of another's forelocks (ناصية *nāsiyat*) when fighting. Touching, joining.

A مناصب *manāsib*, (pl. of منصب *mansib*) Offices, dignities. (pl. of منصب *minsab*) Trevets, or things similar, whereon pots are placed. *Munāsib*, An adversary, opponent.

A مناصبة *munāsabat*, (v. n. 3 of نصب) Conspiring against, laying snares for. Preparing war.

A مناصّة *munāssat*, The harassing a debtor.

A مناصحة *munāsahat*, (v. n. 3 of نصح) Advising sincerely. Mutual sincerity.

A مناصرة *munāsarat*, (v. n. 3 of نصر) Assisting one another. Mutual assistance.

A مناصع *manāsiʻ*, (pl. of منصع *mansaʻ*) Conferences, assemblies, sessions. Necessaries, privies.

A مناصف *manāsif*, (pl. of منصف *mansaf*) Servants. Clever tricks.

A مناصفة *munāsafat*, (v. n. 3 of نصف) Dividing into two equal parts. Halving with another. *Munāsafatan*, (على طريق مناصفه *ʻalaʼ tarīki mu-*

relling face to face.

A مناقدة *munākadat*, A contending, disputing.

A مناقر *manākir*, (pl. of منقر *munkur*) Wells dug in hard ground, narrow-mouthed and full of water.

A مناقرة *munākarat*, A bandying words to and fro.

A مناقش *munākish*, A disputant.

A مناقشة *munākashat*, (v. n. 3 of نقش) Entering minutely into calculation with another. Quarrelling. Contention, dispute.

A مناقض *munākiz*, Contradictory, contrary.

A مناقضة *munākazat*, (v. n. 3 of نقض) Contradicting. Contradiction. Opposition. Repugnance.

A مناقع *manākiʿ*, Places wherein water collects.

A مناقف *munākif*, A swordsman.

A مناقفة *munākafat*, (v. n. 3 of نقف) Striking with a sword, or breaking a head.

A مناقل *manākil*, (pl. of منقل *minkal*) Quick-trotting (horses). *Munākil*, Quick-trotting (horse).

A مناقلة *munākalat*, (v. n. 3 of نقل) Conversing, telling stories to one another. Trotting well, picking up his feet nimbly (a horse). Going well over stones, placing the feet properly and going fast (a horse). Passing the cup round. A banquet, the circulation of the glass. Volubility of tongue. Conversation, story-telling.

A مناقيب *manākīb*, (pl. of منقب *minkab*) Instruments with which they tap for dropsy, trocars.

A مناقير *manākīr*, (pl. of منقار *minkār*) Birds' beaks. Pointed instruments used by smiths. (pl. of منقر *munkur* and *minkar*) Trays or troughs used in making wine.

A مناكب *manākib*, (pl. of منكب *mankib*) Shoulders. المناكب *al manākib*, Four feathers in a bird's wing after those called القوادم *al kawādim*.

A مناكح *manākih*, Marriages. Women.

A مناكحات *munākahāt*, Nuptials, marriages.

A مناكحة *munākahat*, (v. n. 3 of نكح) Marrying.

A مناكدة *munākadat*, (v. n. 3 of نكد) Behaving harshly to: giving pain, perplexing.

A مناكرة *munākarat*, (v. n. 3 of نكر) Disputing, fighting; contention. Contending with another about quickness and cunning (نكر *nakr* or *nukr*).

A مناكيد *manākīd*, Avaricious (men).

A مناكير *manākīr*, (pl. of منكر *munkar*) Iniquitous things. Intelligent, cunning.

A منال *manāl*, Mode, manner, way, disposition.

A منام *manām*, Bed, dormitory. Dream, sleep.

A منامة *manāmat*, A bed. Bed-clothes. Velvet, satin. A shop, warehouse.

A منامس *munāmis*, A confidant. One who lies concealed in a hunter's lurking-place.

A منامسة *munāmasat*, (v. n. 3 of نمس) Communicating a secret. Hiding himself, going into the lurking-place called ناموس *nāmūs* (a hunter).

A منامله *munāmalat*, The pace of a man in fetters.

A منانى *manāni*, (du. of من *man*) What two men?

A منّان *mannān*, Beneficent, benign, propitious (applied especially to Omnipotence).

A منأنأ *munaʾnaʾ*, Weak, infirm. Timid. One who rolls about the pupil of the eye.

A منأنأة *munaʾnaʾat*, (v. n. of نأنأ Q) Being weak in mind, and confused or unsteady (in counsel). Being impotent, unequal to what one undertakes or ought to perform. Prohibiting, restraining. Nourishing, bringing up well.

A منّانة *mannānat*, (A woman) rich, liberally endowed, married for her fortune (and, as it were, heaping favours on her husband, or laying him under obligations, منّة *minnat*).

A مناوءة *munāwaʾat*, (v. n. 3 of ناأ for نوأ) Disputing with, opposing another (in good humour or in enmity), glorying against.

A مناواة *munāwāt*, (v. n. 3 of نوي) Rising (upon another), opposing, competing with.

A مناوبة *munāwabat*, (v. n. 3 of ناب for نوب) Doing by turns. Punishing. Alternate succession.

A مناوة *ma* or *mināwat*, Recompense, retribution.

A مناوحة *munāwahat*, (v. n. 3 of نوح) Opposing (as winds). Lamenting to another (a woman).

P مناور *manāwar*, Name of a city in Tartary, and of an idol-temple.

A مناور *manāwir*, (pl. of منارة *manārat*) Lamps, lanterns, lighthouses. Lofty turrets adjoining Muhammadan mosques, minarets.

A مناورة *munāwarat*, (v. n. 3 of نار for نور) Deriding, ridiculing, treating with contumely.

A مناوشة *munāwashat*, (v. n. 3 of ناش for نوش) Approaching (an enemy); attacking (a foe in battle).

A مناوصة *munāwasat*, (v. n. 3 of ناص for نوص) Struggling, endeavouring to escape (as a deer caught in a toil, which draws it closer). Managing affairs, applying with great attention. Catching hold of each other in combat.

A مناولة *munāwalat*, The act of giving, offering.

A مناومة *munāwamat*, (v. n. 3 of نام for نوم) Contending who shall sleep most.

A مناهبة *munāhabat*, (v. n. 3 of نهب) Reproaching, cutting (in discourse). Straining against, endeavouring to outstrip each other (race-horses).

A مناهج *manāhij*, (pl. of منهج) Open roads.

A مناهدة *munāhadat*, (v. n. 3 of نهد) Drawing lots, especially with the fore-fingers; gaming (with another). Rising up (against an enemy); opposing or fighting hand to hand.

A مناهزة *munāhazat*, (v. n. 3 of نهز) Approaching; running after game. Obtaining an opportunity. Approaching puberty (a boy). Anticipating, pre-occupying, studying an occasion.

A مناهضة *munāhazat*, (v. n. 3 of نهض) Rising against, opposing, attacking. Battle, combat.

A مناهل *manāhil*, (pl. of منهل *manhal*) Places where any body stops. Watering-places. قطّاع المناهل *kuttāʿu'l manāhil*, Writers who take an account of watering-places.

A مناهمة *munāhamat*, (v. n. 3 of نهم) Sighing and lamenting together.

A مناهىّ *manāhīy*, (pl. of منهىّ *manhīy* or منهيّة *manhīyat*) Prohibited things. Sins, crimes.

A مناهيج *manāhīj*, (pl. of منهاج) Open roads.

A مناهيم *manāhīm*, (pl. of منهام *minhām*) (She-camels) obedient to the word.

A منايا *manāyaʾ*, (pl. of منيّة *maniyat*) Deaths.

A منائح *manāʾih*, (pl. of منيحة *manīhat*) Profitable, serviceable, beneficial. منائح افاده *manāʾihi ifāda*, Beneficial, advantageous.

A منائر *manāʾir*, (pl. of منارة *manārat*) Lighthouses. Lanterns. Turrets, spires, minarets.

A منايرة *munāyarat*, Evil, mischief.

A منبت *mambit*, (for *mambat*) (pl. منابت *manābit*) A place where plants grow, their habitat. *Mumbit*, A pot-herb sprouting, growing, vegetating; (land) fertile in plants, vegetables, or fruits.

A منبتّ *mumbatt*, Obliged to break off a journey.

A منبتر *mumbatir*, Destitute of offspring.

A منبتل *mumbatil*, Separated, cut off, disunited.

A منبثّ *mumbass*, Fainted away.

A منبج *mambaj* or *bij*, Name of a place in Syria. *Mimbaj*, One who promises but performs not.

A منبجّ *mumbajj*, (Cattle) having the belly swelled with eating too much.

A منبجانىّ *mambajānīy*, Of, or made at, Mambij.

A منبجس *mumbajis*, (Water) gushing forth.

A منبذة *mimbazat*, A pillow.

A منبر *mimbar*, A pulpit, a high chair, reading-desk. A shelf. A counter. P منبر آلودگان *mimbari āludagān*, The bodies of wicked and atheistical men. منبر نه پايه *mimbari nuh-pāya*, The ninth heaven, the throne of God.

A منبّر *munabbar*, (fem. منبّرة *munabbarat*) (A verse or poem) ending in *hamza* ـٔ.

A منبسط *mumbasit*, Dilated, extended. Of an open, cheerful countenance; rejoicing, exultant. One who lays aside modesty or shame, who looks with audaciousness.

A منبض *mambiz*, The place where the heart beats. *Mimbaz*, A bow for beating cotton.

A منبطح *mumbatih*, Lying outstretched on the stomach. Wide (river). Flat (hoof).

A منبع *mambaʿ*, (pl. منابع *manābiʿ*) Fountain, spring, source, origin. A gush of water, jet-d'eau. منبع فساد *mambaʿi fasād*, Source of evil, *i.e.* wine.

A منبعث *mumbaʿas*, A place whence water gushes forth. *Mumbaʿis*, Origin, cause, that from which any thing proceeds. Excited; sent. Going quick. Spurting (blood).

A منبعج *mumbaʿij*, Heretical, anathematized.

A منبعق *mumbaʿik*, Liberal. Very rainy (cloud). Verbose. (See انبعاق *imbiʿāk*.)

A منبغي *mumbaghī*, Desired, required, requisite. Agreeing with, suitable, convenient.

A منبّق *munabbak* or *munabbik*, (Trees) disposed in a straight line, planted in a row.

P منبك *mimbak*, Broom for making besoms.

A منبكي *mumbakī*, Forced to shed tears.

P منبل *mambal*, A pedlar. A vagrant. Lazy, idle. One not to be believed or trusted. *Mumbal*, One who denies or disapproves. Far out of the road.

P منبل دارو *mambal-dārū*, Name of a plant.

A منبلط *mumbalit*, Remote, distant.

A منبلق *mumbalik*, Clear, distinct (way).

P منبلي *mambalī*, Idleness, laziness. Unworthiness. Bad faith.

A مُنَبَّن *munabban*, Partly eaten (bunch of grapes).

A منبوت *mambūt*, Growing, made to grow.

A منبوذ *mambūz*, Spurious, supposititious, thrown on the highway. Foundling, bastard. What is not eaten as being lean. (A tomb) separate from others.

A منبور *mambūr*, (Verse) ending in hamza ـُ.

A منبوش *mambūsh*, Uprooted, drawn out.

A منبوه *mambūh*, Celebrated, known.

A منبه *mumbah* or *mumbih*, Forgotten.

A منبّه *munabbih*, An admonisher, awakener. An alarm-bell or clock.

A منبهة *mambahat*, (Any thing) rendering (a man) celebrated. Whatever tends to admonish, awaken, warn, or give information. *Mumbihat* or *mumbahat*, Any necessary business forgotten.

A منة *manat*, (fem. of من *man*) What (woman)?

A منّة *minnat*, (v. n. of منّ) Conferring a favour. Obligation, favour, courtesy, grace. Kindness or service done to any one. Praise, thanks. Humble and earnest supplication. A reproaching, twitting, casting in the teeth of benefits conferred. المنّة لله تعالي و تقدس *al minnat li'llāh taʻālā' wa takaddas*, Praise be to God the most high and holy. P منّت داشتن *minnat dāshtan*, To hold as a favour. منّت كردن *minnat kardan*, To confer; also to ask, a favour. منّت نهادن *minnat nihādan*, To lay under obligations, to confer favours. بي منّت *bī minnat*, Disinterested. A *Munnat*, Strength. Weakness.

A منتاب *muntāb*, A visit paid time after time.

A منتاخ *mintākh*, (منتاش *mintāsh*, or منتاف *mintāf*) Tweezers; any hair-twitching instrument.

A منتاف *mintāf*, A short-stepping camel.

A منتاق *mintāk*, Prolific (woman).

A منتان *manatāni*, (du. of منّة) What two females?

A منتأي *muntaʻa'*, A distant place. A ditch dug round a tent to keep off rain-water.

A منتبث *muntabis*, One who digs with the hand. Who reveals a secret. (See انتباث *intibās*.)

A منتبج *muntabij*, Swollen (bone).

A منتبذ *muntabiz*, Retired to one side. A maker of the drink نبيذ *nabīz*. (See انتباذ *intibāz*.)

A منتبر *muntabir*, Throbbing (artery). Blistered (hand). Mounted on a pulpit (منبر *mimbar*).

A منتبل *muntabil*, A killer. Killed, dead. One who snatches or carries off at once quickly.

A منتبه *muntabih*, Awake. Watchful, attentive.

A منتثر *muntatir*, Drawn, dragged.

A منتتش *muntatish*, (Grain) swelling with moisture, and beginning to germinate.

A منتتف *muntatif*, Torn up. Plucked, twitched. Flowing or falling down or off.

A منتتم *muntatim*, An obscene speaker.

A منتثر *muntasir*, Scattered, dispersed. One who sneezes or forces (by breathing hard) water or any thing out of the nostrils.

A منتثل *muntasil*, One who muds (a well).

A منتثم *muntasim*, Obscene in talk.

A منتج *mantij*, The period of birth, time of bringing forth. *Muntaj*, Brought forth, born; drawn out; concluded. A native-place. P چه منتج *chi muntaj*, What is to be thence concluded? A *Muntij*, Who brings forth. Any thing causing or producing.

A منتجب *muntajab*, Chosen, elect, choice. *Muntajib*, Who peels (a tree). A picker, chooser, selector.

A منتجة *mintajat*, The backside.

A منتجث *muntajis*, One who draws out. One who goes in the track of. (See انتجاث *intijās*.)

A منتجع *muntajaʻ*, A place where those live who go in search of forage. *Muntajiʻ*, A forager, who goes in quest of fodder, pasture, or sown fields. Who waits upon one to ask a favour.

A منتجعون *muntajiʻūna*, (Men) foraging.

A منتجف *muntajif*, One who draws out. One who drains (a sheep) of her milk. (See انتجاف.)

A منتجل *muntajil*, Become manifest, conspicuous, evident. One who departs or passes by. (See انتجال.)

A منتجم *muntajim*, Appearing, rising (star). Going off (rain or cold). Vanishing (cloud).

A منتجئ *muntajiʻ*, Who looks with evil eye.

A منتجي *muntajī*, Who chooses (one) to communicate a secret to (him). (See انتجاء *intijāʻ*.)

A منتحب *muntahib*, One who weeps bitterly and laments loudly. One who breathes hard and sobs.

A منتحة *mintahat*, The anus.

A منتحر *muntahar*, Plain, open (road). *Muntahir*, One who cuts his own throat, a self-murderer. Adhering tenaciously; taking one another by the throat (نحر *nahr*).

A منتحل *muntahil*, One who falsely assumes to himself the merit of another's verses or sayings. A professor (of a religious creed).

A منتحي *muntahī*, Who goes towards (any person), seeking (him). Inclining to one side (as loads). One who turns (the face towards any place).

A منتخب *muntakhab*, Chosen. Selected; a selection. Timid, cowardly. *Muntakhib*, One who selects, chooses the best.

A منتخبات *muntakhabāt*, Extracts, selections.

A منتخص *muntakhis*, (Flesh) falling off.

A منتخط *muntakhit*, Who blows the nose. Like.

A منتخع *muntakhiʻ*, (Clouds) pouring down rain. One who goes far (from home).

P منّتدار *minnat-dār*, Under obligation, obliged.

A منتدب *muntadib*, Who listens and attends to. (God) propitious, granting prayers. (See انتداب.)

A منتدح *muntadah*, A spacious tract of country. Amplitude, capacity, ability (of doing any thing).

A منتدي *muntada'*, An assembly, place of daily conference, meeting, conference. *Muntadī*, Assembled, present in any congregation or meeting.

A منتذر *muntazir*, One who makes a vow.

A منترّ *muntarr*, A post-horse that picks up his feet quickly or travels fast.

A منتزح *muntazah*, Distance. *Muntazih*, Far, distant, remote.

A منتزع *muntazaʻ*, Pulled up. *Muntaziʻ*, A remover, tearer away, plucker up. Torn or dug up, eradicated. One who restrains himself, abstains from, refuses, desists, or renounces.

A منتزه *muntazah*, A place of recreation.

A منتسأ *muntasaʻ*, A long stroll, great distance.

A منتسب *muntasib*, Named, denominated, related to, allied, connected by blood.

A منتسج *muntasaj*, Woven. *Muntasij*, (Water or sand) marked with transverse wavings when blown upon obliquely by the wind.

A منتسخ *muntasakh*, Transcribed. *Muntasikh*, One who obliterates or effaces. A copier, transcriber.

A منتسر *muntasir*, (A wound) becoming raw. (Cloth or paper) wearing, going to pieces by degrees.

A منتسف *muntasaf*, Altered (colour) from terror. *Muntasif*, One who uproots, who destroys from the foundation. A speaker in a whispering voice.

A منتسق *muntasik*, Arranged, disposed in order. Adhering in a regular series or row (نسق *nasak*).

A منتشب *muntashib*, Fixed, inherent. A gatherer (of wood). (See انتشاب *intishāb*.)

A منتشر *muntashir*, Published, propagated, divulged, diffused, dispersed, wide-spread. Spirting about, scattered. (Trees) putting forth leaves, expanding. Long (day). Stiff (yard); libidinous (man). Camels pasturing at a distance from their keeper.

A منتشط *muntashit*, One who scales (a fish). One who pulls a knot. (See انتشاط *intishāt*.)

A منتشع *muntashiʻ*, One who inhales (drugs) by the nose. One who pulls out.

A منتشف *muntashaf*, Changed (colour). *Muntashif*, One who drinks new frothing milk.

A منتشل *muntashal*, (Meat) taken out of a pot with the hand or with a fork. *Muntashil*, One who so takes meat.

P منّت شناس *minnat-shināṣ*, Grateful.

A منتشي *muntashī*, Fragrant. Drunk.

A منتصّ *muntass*, Raised, lifted up, standing. Drawn together, shrunk. (See انتصاص *intisās*.)

A منتصب *muntasib*, Erect, set up; placed, exposed. Pointed with the vowel fathah ـَ *a*.

A منتصح *muntasih*, One who listens to advice and improves upon it.

A منتصر *muntasir*, A conqueror; superior to an

enemy. Liberated; one who extricates himself.

A منتصف *muntasaf*, The middle. *Muntasif*, Mid-day. Who keeps the middle. One who adjusts (any thing). Who gets or gives what is just. A taker of the whole of a debt. (See انتصاف *intisāf.*)

A منتصل *muntasil*, (A spear) without a head.

A منتصي *muntasa'*, The upper part of two valleys or channels. *Muntasī*, Long (hair). High (mountain). A chooser, selector.

A منتضح *muntazih*, Starting (tear). One who sprinkles his privities with water after prayer.

A منتضخ *muntazakh*, Sprinkled (water).

A منتضد *muntazid*, Stationary, in one place.

A منتضف *muntazif*, Sucking (camel's colt).

A منتضل *muntazil*, Engaged in a contest for glory. One who takes out, off, or away. One who chooses (an arrow from a quiver, or a man from a crowd). (See انتضال *intizāl.*)

A منتضي *muntazī*, One who draws (a sword). One who wears out (a garment). (See انتضاء.)

A منتطح *muntatah*, A place of butting. الجاثم في منتطح الكبشين *al jāsim fī muntatahi'l kabshayn*, Seated between two rams butting (in jeopardy).

A منتطق *muntatik*, Rare, precious, incomparable. One who leads (a horse) at his side. (See انتطاق *intitāk.*)

A منتظر *muntazir*, One who expects with impatience; a tarrier. P منتظر شدن *muntazir shudan*, To wait with anxiety. To be in expectation of.

A منتظم *muntazam*, A place where things are strung. *Muntazim*, Ordered, arranged, placed in rows, joined together, threaded (as pearls). One who regulates or places in order. A piercer, transfixer (with a spear). رسول منتظم الكلام *rasūlun muntazimu'l kalām*, An eloquent ambassador, arranging well his words.

A منتعت *muntaʿit*, (A horse) outstripping others.

A منتعش *muntaʿish*, One who stands on the feet, who rises after a fall. Convalescent.

A منتعص *muntaʿis*, Angry. A heavy walker. Who rises after a fall.

A منتعظ *muntaʿiz*, Stung with lust, ruttish.

A منتعف *muntaʿaf*, The boundary between a plain and mountainous or stony ground. *Muntaʿif*, Conspicuous (horseman). Perched on a high place. (See انتعاف *intiʿāf.*)

A منتعفة *muntaʿifat*, Lax, pendulous (ear).

A منتعل *muntaʿil*, Shod. A pedestrian. One who sows hard ground. (See انتعال *intiʿāl.*)

A منتغ *mintagh*, An accuser, slanderer.

A منتف *munattaf*, Plucked, picked clean.

A منتفج *muntafij*, Swelling, high, prominent (side). Proud, haughty. Roused, started (game).

A منتفخ *muntafikh*, Swollen. Advanced (day).

A منتفد *muntafad*, A wide extent, distance. Independence. Liberty, space, facility. *Muntafid*, Who empties or carries all off. A milker. Inclined to one side, seated in a stooping posture.

A منتفذ *muntafaz*, Amplitude, capacity, facility, convenience, opportunity.

A منتفش *muntafish*, Swollen, soft-bellied. A bird ruffling its plumage, or a cat bristling up its hair.

A منتفشة *muntafishat*, (A girl) with (hair) uncombed and dishevelled. (A nose) flattened on the face.

A منتفض *muntafiz*, Shaken (tree): beaten (garment). Green (leaf). (See انتفاض *intifāz.*)

A منتفع *muntafiʿ*, One who uses, enjoys, has the advantage, profit, or use of any thing: benefited, advantaged, profited. A gainer.

A منتفق *muntafik*, A goer in a narrow road. A field-mouse making its hole (نافقاء *nāfikāʾ*).

A منتفل *muntafil*, One who does more than is required, who repeats prayers of supererogation.

A منتفي *muntafī*, Repulsed, rejected, removed. Dissipated, destroyed. Retired to one side.

A منتق *mantak*, That part of a (horse's) belly which touches the ground when he is laid down.

A منتقب *muntakib*, (A woman) covering her face with the veil نقاب *nikāb*.

A منتقث *muntakis*, One who extracts the marrow (from a bone). Who examines (any thing). Expeditious, doing a thing quickly.

A منتقد *muntakad*, Separated (good coin from bad), told, summed up. *Muntakid*, One who discerns or picks the good from bad money. A receiver of ready money. Growing (boy).

A منتقر *muntakir*, Dug. An examiner. A chooser, culler. Who gives a preference to, or invites, one before others. One whose eyes are sunk in the sockets. (See انتقار *intikār.*)

A منتقز *muntakiz*, A sheep suffering from the disease نقاز *nukāz*. A paltry giver.

A منتقش *muntakash*, Engraved, carved. Enchased. Painted. *Muntakish*, One who orders a seal to be engraved. One who extracts a thorn from the foot. (See انتقاش *intikāsh.*)

A منتقص *muntakis*, Diminished, decreased, deficient. An injurer or diminisher. (See انتقاص.)

A منتقض *muntakaz*, Untwisted (rope), demolished (structure), violated (agreement).

A منتقع *muntakaʿ*, Changed (colour). *Muntakiʿ*, One who slaughters (a camel to entertain guests).

A منتقف *muntakif*, One who cuts open (a colocynth). One who takes or draws out.

A منتقل *muntakil*, Moveable, migratory.

A منتقم *muntakim*, One who punishes or takes revenge. (God) the punisher, avenger.

A منتقه *muntakih*, Convalescent. One who understands well.

A منتقى *muntaka'*, Selected. *Muntakī*, One who selects. One who takes marrow from a bone.

P منتك *mantak*, Broom for making besoms.

A منتكب *muntakib*, One who shoulders his quiver or bow. Fallen into trouble (نكبة *nakbat*).

A منتكت *muntakit*, Fallen on the head.

A منتكث *muntakis*, Dissolved; untwisted (rope). Broken (faith), violated (agreement). Emaciated. One who turns from one business to another.

A منتكس *muntakis*, Inverted, head-downwards.

A منتكش *muntakish*, Who cleans out a well.

A منتكف *muntakif*, Exposed to a shower, and enduring it till it has ceased. (See انتكاف *intikāf.*)

A منتكي *muntakiʿ*, A receiver (of what is due).

A منتمي *muntamī*, (A hawk) soaring from height to height. Related to, of the same family.

A منتن *mun*, *mintin*, or *muntun*, Stinking, fetid.

P منت نهنده *minnat-nihinda*, One who confers many favours, and lays under numerous obligations.

P منتو *mantū*, A piece of sheep's tripe sewed up and stuffed with rice and other condiments.

P منتوجه *mantūja*, A kind of hyacinth.

A منتور *muntawir*, One who anoints his hairy parts with the depilatory unguent نورة *nūrat*.

A منتوط *muntawit*, Suspended, hung up. Far distant (house). One who lends (a camel) to carry provisions. (See انتياط *intiyāt.*)

A منتوف *mantūf*, Plucked. منتوف الذنب *mantūfu'z zanab*, Rat-tailed.

A منتوي *muntawī*, One who proposes where to go, or fixes upon (a caravansera, stage, or halting-place) where (he) intends to stop on a journey.

A منتها *muntaha'*, Terminated, concluded.

A منتهب *muntahab*, (Goods) plundered. *Muntahib*, One who carries off or who snatches away; a seizer, plunderer. Boldly-going (horse).

A منتهر *muntahir*, (A vein) bleeding copiously, not to be stanched. Loose (belly).

A منتهز *muntahiz*, One who seizes (an opportunity). Immoderate, excessive, rude (in laughing). A youth near puberty.

A منتهشة *muntahishat*, (A sorrowing woman) who scratches her face and disfigures herself.

A منتهض *muntahiz*, One who rises up.

A منتهك *muntahik*, A violater of honour, virtue, or respect. One who fatigues or emaciates.

A منتهى *muntaha'*, Finished, terminated, ending. End, conclusion, term, boundary, extremity. Prohibited. منتهى الجموع *muntaha'l jumūʿ*, The extreme of plurals, or plural of plurals. منتهاي طلب *muntahāyi talab*, (منتهاي مراد *muntahāyi murād*, or منتهاي مقصود *muntahāyi mahsūd*) Extent of wishes, height of desire, intent of a petition. *Muntahī*, One who brings to a conclusion, or comes to the end; ceased, stopped. One who has finished his studies, learned.

A منتين *mintīn*, (pl. مناتين) Fetid, stinking.

A منثار *minsār*, A palm-tree having unripe dates dropping off.

A منثة *minassat*, A rag for rubbing in ointment.

A منثجا *minsajan*, (He went out) to ease nature.

A منثجة *minsajat*, The fundament.

A منثدق *munsadik*, Engaged in deeds of plunder, spoil, and rapine.

A منثر *minsar*, Talkative.

A منثر *munassar*, Scattered (abundantly). Weak, languid, good for nothing.

A منثرّ *munsarr*, (A horse) which moves (his) feet swiftly.

A منثقب *munsakib*, Perforated, pierced, bored.

A منثلم *munsalim*, Broken, notched (sword).

A منثني *munsanī*, Averse. Bent, folded.

A منثور *mansūr*, Scattered, strewed. A violet. Winter gillyflower. Wild pepper. كلام منثور *kalāmi mansūr*, Prose. منظوم و منثور *manzūm u mansūr*, Verse and prose.

P منج *manj*, Rhubarb. *Minj*, A seed. *Munj*, A bee. A yellow bee; hornet, wasp. A gad-fly. Any thing bad. The carcase of a poor feeble ass. A bitter almond-tree. Name of a village.

A منج *manj*, Two or three dates sticking together. A kind of intoxicating seed. *Munj*, A kind of green pulse smaller than a pea.

A منجا *manja'*, Any high place where one may escape a flood.

A منجاب *minjāb*, Peeled, barked. Tanned with the bark of the acacia and of other trees. (pl. مناجيب *manājīb*) (A woman) bearing heroic sons. A weak man. A polished arrow wanting point and feathers. A poker; implement for stirring a fire.

A منجاة *manjāt*, Flight, escape. A place to which people flee.

A منجار *minjār*, Name of a boy's game.

A منجاش *minjāsh*, One who rouses wild beasts and makes them pass by where the hunter lurks.

A منجب *munjib*, One who begets a heroic son: also a timid or degenerate one. Generous.

A منجبة *munjibat*, (A woman) bearing excellent progeny.

A منجبر *munjabir*, Restored to soundness.

A منجح *munjih*, (pl. مناجيح *manājīh* or مناجح *manājih*) Of good judgment, excellent in advising; fortunate in one's affairs, successful.

P منجخ *minjahh*, A stone for a sling.

A منجخ *munajjihh*, One who coughs.

A منجد *minjad*, (pl. مناجد *manājid*) A broad golden necklace richly ornamented with jewels, which hangs down below the breasts. A small rope.

A منجّد *munajjad*, Proved, tried, experienced (man). Prepared, adorned.

A منجدة *minjadat*, A whip or switch. A piece of wood in a camel's saddle.

A منجدل *munjadil*, Fallen on the ground.

A منجّذ *munajjaz*, Experienced in the ways of the world, taught by painful experience; sage, sagacious.

A منجذب *munjazib*, Drawn, dragged, snatched.

A منجذر *munjazir*, Ebbed (tide).

A منجر *manjar*, Unswerving (purpose). *Minjar*, A furious driver.

A منجرّ *munjarr*, Drawn, dragged.

A منجرة *manjarat*, (in Morocco) A dockyard. *Minjarat*, A hot stone for warming water.

A منجرد *munjarid*, Extended, lasting long. Smoothed, sleek, bare. (See انجراد *injirād*.)

A منجرف *munjarif*, Swept away.

A منجز *munjiz*, A performer (of promises). Expeditious, ready. A purgative medicine. (See انجاز.)

P منج زراوشان *munj zirāwishān*, Safflower-seed.

A منجزم *munjazim*, Cut, amputated. Abrupt (business); broken off (negociation). Broken (bone). Gezmated (letter), marked with jazm ـْـ.

A منجّس *munajjis*, One upon whom are suspended amulets made of dead men's bones, fetid rags, or other kinds of filth.

A منجش *minjash*, A strap sewed between two large pieces of leather. One who discovers another's faults and traduces him.

A منجعف *munjaꜥif*, Thrown prostrate.

A منجعل *munjaꜥil*, Placed, deposited.

A منجف *minjaf*, A basket. Dung.

A منجفل *munjafil*, Departed, (shadow, night). Gone, moved rapidly off.

P منجك *manjak*, A juggler's trick, which consists in making particles of gravel fly from out of a bowl filled with water. A rising up. A cradle. *Munjak*, A little bee. The clove-gillyflower.

P منجل *minjal*, A large beam pierced with holes through which they pass chains with large stones suspended to them (they are used in a peculiar manner in trials of strength).

A منجل *minjal*, (pl. مناجل *manājil*) A reaping-hook, a sickle. (A spear-head) making a large wound. Luxuriant and entangled (corn). (A man) having many children. (A camel) striking a fungus with his foot. Any thing with which boys' writing-tablets or slates are cleaned and the characters obliterated.

P منجلاب *manjalāb*, Polluted water (in which a dog or carrion has been thrown). A sink or sewer for carrying off dirty water from baths.

A منجلع *munjaliꜥ*, Uncovered, discovered.

A منجلي *munjalī*, Conspicuous, apparent (as God to man). Departed. (See انجلاء *injilās*.)

A منجليق *manjalīk*, A balista.

A منجم *manjam*, A mine. An open road. *Manjim* or *minjam*, A prominent bone in the foot, the ankle-bone. *Minjam*, The handle or eye of a balance in which the tongue or needle vibrates.

A منجّم *munajjam*, Calculated or determined by the aspect of the stars. Lent for a certain given time. *Munajjim*, An astronomer, astrologer, almanack-maker.

A منجمد *munjamid*, Congealed. Pent up.

A منجمع *munjamiꜥ*, Gathered from every part.

A منجمله *minjumla*, Among, among all; in all; from among; totally. Upon the whole.

A منجنون *manjanūn*, (or منجنين *manjanīn*) (pl. مناجين *manājīn*) A wheel for raising water from rivers or wells, or used in watering gardens and fields. Time. Fortune.

G منجنيق *manjanīk*, (*minjanīk*, منجنزق *manjanzuk*) (pl. منجنيقات *manjanīkāt*, مجانق *majānik*, and مجانيك *majānīk*) A warlike engine, catapulta, balista, sling. A pulley, machine for raising great weights. It is also written منجنيك.

A منجنيقي *manjanīkiy*, An inventor, maker, or user of the machine منجنيق *manjanīk*.

P منجو *manjū*, A lentil, a kind of pulse.

A منجوّ *manjuw*, Dismissed, set free; escaped.

A منجوب *manjūb*, (A leathern bottle) tanned or dressed with the bark of the acacia or other trees. Leather so prepared. A large cup or goblet, or, in general, a capacious vessel. *Munjawib*, Dispersed, cleared off (as clouds).

A منجود *manjūd*, Afflicted, distressed in mind. Perishing, annihilated, destroyed.

A منجور *manjūr*, Planed, hewn, cut, chipt.

A منجورة *manjūrat*, A water-wheel.

A منجوز *munjawiz*, One who recedes, declines from, retires. A deserter to the enemy.

A منجوف *manjūf*, Broad or broad-headed (arrow). Capacious (vessel). Spacious (cavern). (A he-goat) prevented from gendering by a piece of leather called نجاف *nijāf*. Disabled from venery. A coward.

A منجوق *manjūk*, The ball or spear-head of a banner gilded. A flag hoisted on a turret as a signal for public prayer. A parasol. A crown, globe, or any ornament on the top of a tower.

A منجول *manjūl*, (A skin) drawn off an animal, beginning at the hough.

A منجي *munajja'*, Name of a sword.

P منجير *manjīr* or *munjīr*, A latticed enclosure erected before a door, generally in an oblique direction, that the apartments may not be viewed from without. Musk of Trebizond.

A منح *manh*, (v. n. of منح) Giving, presenting; giving away milk, hair, or young (of a camel), but with a view to return the dam.

A منحاة *manhāt*, A winding channel. The path of a camel trained to draw water. اهل المنحاة *ahlu'l manhāt*, Distant people, unconnected by relationship, strangers. *Munhāt*, Stout (bow). Large-bunched (camel).

A منحار *minhār*, One who slaughters many (camels); hence, liberal, magnificent (these being considered as the highest species of entertainment amongst the Arabians).

A منحاز *minhāz*, The pestle of a mortar.

A منحاص *minhās*, A tall, slender woman.

A منحّب *munahhib*, Quick (walk or journey).

A منحة *minhat*, A gift. A portion of camels' or sheeps' milk which another is allowed to draw, but afterwards to restore the animal. The animal itself. Any thing lent in general.

A منحت minhat, A hatchet, adze, or plane.

A منحّت munahhat, Pared (hoof).

A منحجز munhajiz, Who hangs back. A goer to, or comer from, حجاز hijāz, in Arabia.

A منحدر munhadar, munhudur, or munhudur, Sloping, low-lying (place). Munhadir, One who descends a declivity, or goes into low grounds. Sloping (place). Foundering (ship).

A منحر manhar, A place where they slay animals for sacrifice. The part for neck-ornaments.

A منحرد munharid, Dispersed. Solitary, alone. Fallen (star).

A منحرف munharaf, A trapezium. شبيه بالمنحرف shabīh bi'l munharaf, A trapezoid. Munharif, Changed, inverted. One who declines or turns from. Swerved. The letter ل lām.

A منحّزة munahhizat, (A she-camel) troubled with the complaint نحاز nuhāz.

A منحسّ munhass, Torn up or away. Fallen, shed (tooth).

A منحسر munhasir, Naked, nude, uncovered.

A منحسم munhasim, Cut, lopt, amputated.

A منحصّ munhass, (Hair) fallen; docked (tail).

A منحصر munhasir, Surrounded, besieged, beleagured, blockaded, pressed, hemmed in, confined to, restricted. Contained, comprehended. Numbered.

A منحطّ munhatt, Handsome (shoulder), as being low. Munhitt, Falling, let down, descending. (Provisions) falling (in price). (A camel) become master of the reins and rushing towards a precipice.

A منحطة munhatat, (Horses or camels) seized with the distemper نحطة nahtat.

A منحف munhaf, Rendered lean, emaciated.

A منحلّ munhall, Loosed (knot).

A منحمق munhamik, Become mean, vile, contemptible. Blunted (sword). Worn (garment). Flat, dull (market).

A منحنى munhana', The bend of a valley or river. Munhanī, Flexible, crooked, bent. Lean, decrepit.

A منحوت manhūt, Cut out, hewn (as a column or pillar). Pared: chipped. An image, statue, or piece of sculpture; workmanship of the statuary.

A منحور munhūr, The throat, gorge, or place for neck-ornaments.

A منحوز manhūz, (A camel) troubled with the disease نحاز nuhāz. Munhawiz, Retired, departed.

A منحوس manhūs, Unfortunate, unhappy. منحوس الحال manhūsu'l hāl, In a wretched plight.

A منحوش munhawish, Terrified, flying.

A منحوض manhūz, Firm-fleshed, plump. Lean, emaciated. Thin, sharp (point of spear or arrow).

A منحوطة manhūtat, (Horses or camels) troubled with the disease نحطة nahtat.

A منحوف manhūf, Lean, slim, slender.

A منحول manhūl, (Verse of one author) falsely attributed to another.

A منحوي munhawī, Rolled together: coiled.

A منخاب minkhāb, Weak, worthless.

A منخار minkhār, (A woman) breathing hard through the nostrils as if furious in the act of venery.

A منخاس minkhās, A spur, goad.

A منخاق munkhāk, Widely-extended. Deep.

A منخبة mankhabat, Podex.

A منخدر munkhadir, Veiled, close kept (woman).

A منخدع munkhadiع, Deceived, cheated.

A منخر mankhar, minkhir, munkhur, mankhir, or minkhar, A nostril.

A منخّربة munakhrabat or munakhribat, Worm-eaten (tree).

A منخرط munkharit, Subdued. Constrained. Rash, precipitate. (See انخراط inkhirāt.)

A منخرع munkhariع, Split, broken in pieces. Enfeebled. Dislocated. Displaced.

A منخرق munkharak, (Any place) through which the wind blows. A blast or breath of wind. Munkharik, Torn, lacerated. منخرق السربال munkhariku's sirbāl, One whose clothes are torn (by travel).

A منخرم munkharim, Split, notched.

A منخزع munkhaziع, Cut. Bent double with old age and weakness.

A منخزق munkhazik, Transfixed, pierced: enfiled.

A منخزل munkhazil, Broken; abrupt. Ceasing.

A منخسف munkhasif, Blinded (eye). Eclipsed.

P ماه منخسف māhi munkhasif, The moon eclipsed.

A منخع mankhaع, The articulation of the head and neck to the first dorsal joint.

A منخفس munkhafis, Spoiled, stinking (water).

A منخفض munkhafaz, A depressed part. Munkhafiz, Depressed, subjected. (in grammar) Marked with كسر kasr ـِ i. الحروف المخفضة al hurūfu'l munkhafizat, The letters, except ضغط خفق.

A منخل munkhal or munkhul, A sieve, searce.

A منخنث munkhanis, Folded, bent: flaccid.

A منخنس munkhanis, Who lags, keeps behind.

A منخنق munkhanik, Self-strangled.

A منخوب mankhūb, Cowardly. Emaciated.

A منخوت mankhūt, Removed, displaced. منخوت الفؤاد mankhūtu'l fuاād, Fearful, chicken-hearted. Munkhawit, Darting, pouncing (hawk).

A منخور munkhūr, A nostril.

A منخوس mankhūs, (A camel) scabby about the tail, or having a fissure under his arm-pit. Lean.

A منخوش mankhūsh, Lean.

A منخوع mankhūع, Slaughtered by a gash made as deep as the neck-bone.

A منخول mankhūl, Sifted (grain), skreened (gravel).

A منخى munkhī, Excessive vanity or pride.

A منخيّ mankhīy, Puffed with pride, vain-glorious.

P مند mand, A species of jet or black amber. (a possessive particle added to words in Persian, synonymous with the prefix ذو zū in Arabic) Endowed with, possessed of, having: as, خردمند khiradmand, Possessed of understanding, judicious.

A مندّ munidd, One who disperses (camels).

A منداس mindās, Light, active (woman).

A منداص mindās, A foolish, frivolous woman. Meagre-hipped (woman). A troublesome, insolent fellow. An immodest woman. Mundās, One who attacks privately; who propagates any thing bad.

P منداور mandāwar, Name of a country.

A مندب mundib, One who exposes himself to dangers. Large (scar). باب المندب bābu'l mandib, (Gate of tears) Babelmandel.

P مندبور mandbūr, Unfortunate, unhappy.

A مندبئ mindaba', Quick, ready, nimble.

A مندجر mundajir, Loose, flexible (rope).

A مندح mandah, A spacious place.

A مندخ mindakh, One who does not care what he says, or what is said of him.

A مندخل mundakhil, One who enters.

A مندر mundir, One who subtracts (from an account). One who makes (a thing) fall. One who draws forth (his money).

A مندرج mundarij, Comprehended, contained, collected, inserted. Enrolled, registered. Involved within itself, coiled or rolled up. Perishing (family), become extinct.

A مندرجه mundarija, Contents.

A مندرس mundaris, Obliterated. Worn out.

A مندرع mundariع, One who approaches. Quick. Dislocated (bone). Filled (belly). Emerging (moon from behind a cloud).

A مندسّ mundass, Hid, buried.

P مندش mandish, A carpet, a rug.

A مندعص mundaعis, Dissolved (dead body).

A مندعي mundaعī, Responsive. A respondent.

A مندغ mindagh, Satirical, sarcastic.

A مندغة mindaghat, White specks appearing on the nails. (See منسغة minsaghat.)

A مندف mindaf, (and مندفة mindafat) A large bow bent, the string of which they beat with a mallet in separating or teasing cotton; also the mallet.

A مندفع mundafiع, Beat, trampled upon. Driven away, expelled, repulsed, removed. Carried far (in a story). Swift (horse). Far-gone. Arrived unexpectedly. Given, delivered, surrendered.

A مندفق mundafik, Wide-spread, outpoured.

A مندفن mundafin, (A well) filled up, covered over with a part of itself. Concealed.

A مندقّ mundakk, Brayed (in a mortar). Battered (city-wall). Knocked at (door).

P مندك mandak, Badness of markets, difficulty of sale.

A مندكّ mundakk, Levelled (height, hollow).

A مندكم mundakim, Who thrusts himself in.

P مندل mandal, An enchanter's circle described on the ground, in which they sit when endeavouring to conjure up demons or spirits.

A مندل mandal, A boot. Wood of aloes. Name of a town in India, whence the best kind is brought.

Mindal, An active man, suddenly snatching any thing. A yard erect. A towel, napkin. A towel with which one is girded. A table-cloth.

A مندل *mundall*, Guided, led. Poured, spread.

A مندلث *mundalis*, Who rushes upon or into. Who goes quick, who passes rapidly by. Self-opiniated. Who walks bolt upright.

A مندلص *mundalis*, (A slippery thing) sliding out of the hand: lubricous.

A مندلع *mundaliʻ*, Protruded (tongue). Prominent, flagging (belly). Drawn (sword).

A مندلف *mundalif*, A lion marching leisurely.

A مندلق *mundalik*, One who precedes and outstrips in going or running. Whatever protrudes or slips out (as a gut) from the belly, (or a sword) from the sheath. (A torrent, or a body of horse) overwhelming (people).

P مندله *mandala*, Wood of aloes. A magic circle traced on the ground. *Mandila*, A kind of silken stuff.

A مندلي *mandalīy*, (or المندلي *al mandalīy*) Of the city of Mandal, especially wood of aloes.

A مندم *mandam*, Repentance (especially late).

A مندمة *mandamat*, That of which one repents. A cause of repentance.

A مندمج *mundamij*, Round, smooth. Inserted and sticking fast. Compact.

A مندمس *mundamis*, One who enters (a bath, cavern, or prison).

A مندمق *mundamak*, An entrance, place where one enters. *Mundamik*, One who enters abruptly or without leave. Falling from its place. Concealed (hunter).

A مندمل *mundamil*, Healed (wound or sore).

P مندو *mandū*, Name of a city in Hindūstān.

A مندوب *mandūb*, Lamented, celebrated in a funeral oration. Beloved. Name of a famous horse. Name of a place.

A مندوحة *mandūhat*, A wide, extensive place. Extension. Facility, ability.

P مندور *mandūr*, Sad, afflicted. Miserable, unfortunate, unhappy. Avaricious. A fly.

A مندوسة *mandūsat*, A beetle.

A مندوغ *mandūgh*, Gently rubbed.

A مندوف *mandūf*, Carded or teased (cotton). Struck with a bow, bowed.

A مندول *mundawil*, A mover or roamer from place to place. Loose (belly). Alvine (excretions) coming forth. (Any thing) adhering when touched.

P مندوور *mandwūr*, Unfortunate, miserable, excluded from the divine favour. Sorrowful.

P منده *manda*, A pitcher, especially a broken-handled one. Dulness of markets. Bread.

A مندهن *mundahin*, One who anoints himself.

A مندّي *munadda'*, Moistened. The place where camels pasture between the first and second drinking. A place where horses are watered.

A منديات *mundiyāt*, Disgraces, affronts.

A مندية *mundiyat*, A word applied to a coward, by which he feels himself disgraced.

P منديش *mandesh*, Be not anxious or thoughtful. Name of a fortress in Khurāsān.

A منديل *mandīl* or *mindīl*, A towel, a napkin. A table-cloth. *Mindīl*, A wreath, sash, turban-cloth, or any thing rolled round the head of a man or woman. A handkerchief, whether thrown round the neck or worn stuck in the girdle. A mantle.

A منذ *munzu* or *minzu*, (contraction from من *min* and اذ *iz*) From, since (in a past sense). In (in a present sense). لقيته منذ يومان *lakītuhu munzu yawmāni*, I met him two days ago. منذ يوم الخميس *munzu yawmi'l khamīs*, Since Thursday.

A منذر *munzir*, An admonisher, adviser. One who puts in fear. ابو المنذر *abū'l munzir*, A cock. بات بليلة بن منذر *bāta bi laylati'bn munzir*, He passed a restless night. المنذر *al munzir*, Name of a prince of the Arabians; also of his tribe.

A منذور *manzūr*, Promised, vowed, dedicated.

A منربة *manrabat*, Detraction, slander.

A منز *minazz*, Ricketty, unsteady. A cradle.

A منزاف *minzāf*, (A goat) whose milk has stopped.

A منزجر *munzajir*, Rebuked, rebuffed, put down.

A منزحة *minzahat*, A bucket, or any thing for drawing water.

A منزرب *munzarib*, Lurking (hunter).

A منزرق *munzarik*, Dilatory, lagging. Laid supine. Flying, passing (arrow).

A منزع *manzaʻ*, A place of drawing. *Minzaʻ*, An arrow by which any thing is removed or pulled up. A man who pulls hard.

A منزّع *munazzaʻ*, Pulled up (herbage).

A منزعة *manzaʻat*, The end or design of any thing, action, or counsel; the place to which one hastens or returns. The end or interruption of a draught. A stone upon which one stands near a well to draw water. A bow whose string is far distant from the handle. طيّب المنزعة *tayyibu'l manzaʻat*, (Wine) which leaves a pleasant smack on the palate. *Manzaʻat* or *minzaʻat*, Care, solicitude. *Minzaʻat*, A ladle-shaped stick with which they gather honey.

A منزعج *munzaʻij*, Displaced, removed.

A منزغ *minzagh*, (and منزغة) A slanderer.

A منزغة *minzaghat*, A tuft of feathers; also an iron wire brush, with which bakers brush their bread.

A منزف *munzaf* or *zif*, Drunk, stupid. Weak.

A منزفة *minzafat*, (pl. منازف *manāzif*) A small bucket at the end of a cross pole for drawing water.

A منزل *manzal* or *manzil*, (v. n. of نزل) Descending or alighting (as a stranger or guest). *Manzil*, (pl. منازل *manāzil*) A caravansera, inn, or place for the accommodation of travellers; a house, hotel, lodging, mansion, habitation, dwelling. A mansion of the moon. A day's journey. A stage in travelling or in the divine life. Boundary, end, limit, goal, place of destination. A post-office, a stage where post-horses are furnished. Rank, dignity. Three stars in the tail of the Great Bear. P منزل جان *manzili jān*, The world above. The human body. A منزل حزن *manzili huzn*, (or P منزل خاكي *manzili khākī*) The world. P منزل نبهره فريب *manzili nabahra-firīb*, The world. Time. Fortune. منزل گرفتن *manzil giriftan*, To halt, encamp. A *Munzal*, (v. n. 4 of نزل) Causing (one) to alight, giving (him) a hospitable reception. The mode itself. Made to alight. Sent down (angel or revelation). *Munzil*, One who causes to alight, who receives hospitably. (See انزال *inzāl*.)

A منزلة *manzilat*, A house of accommodation for travellers. A step. A post of honour, dignity, rank, station, condition. A watering-place. بمنزلة *bi manzilat*, In the place, in lieu, in loco. In reference to. في منزلة اخ *fī manzilati akh*, In the capacity of a brother, like a brother.

P منزل خانه *manzil-khāna*, A post-house.

P منزل شناس *manzil-shinās*, A holy man.

A منزلق *munzalik*, Sliding; slippery; liable to slide.

P منزلگاه *manzil-gāh*, (and منزلگه *manzil-gah*) A day's journey. An inn.

A منزم *minzam*, A tooth.

A منزّم *munzamm*, Bound, tied, fastened.

A منزوع *manzūʻ*, Greedy, addicted to.

A منزور *manzūr*, Little, small. Importuned, urged, pressed to give.

A منزوع *manzūʻ*, Torn up, eradicated.

A منزوف *manzūf*, Weakened by loss of blood. Inebriated, stupid. Parched with thirst. Exhausted (well). Nonplused in argument.

A منزول *manzūl*, Troubled with a rheum (نزلة *nazlat*). *Munzawil*, Perishing, falling, decaying.

A منزوّ *manzūʻ*, Addicted, dedicated.

A منزوي *munzawī*, Solitary, recluse; a hermit. Shrivelled, puckered (leather).

A منزّه *munazzah*, Exempted from, free. Pure, blameless, holy.

A منزهة *manzahat*, (pl. منازه) A pleasant place.

A منزي *munzī*, Wishful, inclined to.

A منزيّ *manzīy*, Exhausted, dried up.

A منس *manas*, Cheerfulness, briskness, joy.

A منسأة *mansaʼat*, (v. n. of نسأ) Delaying, giving credit, selling on credit. Driving (camels) by shouting to them. *Mansaʼat*, (*minsaʼat*, منساة *mansāt*, or *minsāt*) A staff, a shepherd's crook.

A منساح *minsāh*, A broom, besom, or fan.

A منساق *munsāk*, Near, nigh. A follower. A kinsman. (A mountain) shelving off lengthwise.

A منسبة *mansabat*, (v. n. of نسب) Praising (a mistress) in verse.

A منسبت *munsabit*, Perfectly ripe (date).

A منسبك *munsabik*, Molten (silver).

A منسة *mansat*, Old, aged (female).

A منسّة *minassat*, A rod, staff.

A منسطع *munsatiʻ*, Diligent, prompt, expeditious.

A منسج *mansij* or *mansaj*, A weaver's shop. A workshop. *Minsaj*, The instrument by which the web is stretched when working. A weaver's loom. That part of a horse about the fore-shoulder and under the mane.

A منسجر *munsajir*, Loose, flowing hair. Following without interruption.

A منسجل *munsajil*, (Water) poured forth. Written or signed (by a judge).

A منسحب *munsahib*, Trailed on the ground.

A منسحط *munsahit*, Falling (out of the hand) from slipperiness. Slipping down a pole.

A منسحق *munsahik*, Worn by friction. Reduced to powder, crumbled to dust. Widened. (pl. مساحيق *masāhik*) Flowing (tear).

A منسحل *munsahil*, Smoothed, polished, bright. Diffusive (orator). Drawn back (skin).

A منسدّ *munsadd*, Closed, stopped, shut (hole).

A منسدر *munsadir*, Loose (woman's hair). One who goes quick, who makes haste.

A منسدل *munsadil*, Loose, flowing, pendulous (woman's hair, veil, or robe).

A منسدم *munsadim*, Healed (wound).

A منسر *mansir*, A troop of horse from 30 to 40, or 40 to 60, or 100 to 200. The advanced guard of an army, the van. *Mansir* or *minsar*, The beak of a rapacious bird (منقار *minkār* being the bill of any other bird).

A منسرب *munsarib*, (A fox) creeping (into his hole). Very long.

A منسرح *munsarih*, One who throws off his clothes, who strips naked. Extended on the back. One who stretches out the feet. Flowing, gliding, creeping. Moving to and fro. (A camel) going swiftly. A kind of verse.

A منسرحة *munsarihat*, Swift, quick (she-camel).

A منسري *munsarī*, Dispelled (grief, fear).

A منسطح *munsatih*, One who stretches himself out, lying on the back motionless.

A منسع *minsaʻ*, The north wind.

A منسعة *minsaʻat*, Ground quickly producing.

A منسغة *minsaghat*, A tuft of feathers; also something similar of iron wire, with which bakers brush or make marks upon their bread.

A منسف *minsaf*, A fan for winnowing corn. *Minsaf* or *mansif*, The mouth or muzzle of an ass.

A منسفة *minsafat*, An instrument for undermining walls.

A منسفر *munsafir*, Bare, destitute.

A منسفق *munsafik*, Quite open (door).

A منسفك *munsafik*, Shed (blood or tear).

A منسّق *munassak*, Joined in order.

A منسك *mansak*, (v. n. of نسك) Being religious, devoted to the service of God. A frequented place. *Mansak* or *mansik*, (pl. مناسك *manāsik*) A place of sacrifice, especially in the valley of Mina near Mecca. The rites and ceremonies attending those sacrifices, or religious worship in general.

A منسكب *munsakib*, Outpoured, flowing, fluid (water); shed, gushing (blood).

A منسل *mansil*, Generation, progeny. *Munsal*, Begotten, generated. *Munsil*, (A bird) moulting; (a camel) changing his coat. (Garments) falling off or flowing down. (An animal) near the time for changing its hair or feathers. (A plant) shooting out, putting forth, and throwing off. One who precedes (others).

A منسلّ *munsall*, One who withdraws himself stealthily. What falls off or drops from the middle.

A منسلب *munsalib*, Swift in going.

A منسلخ *munsalakh*, The end of a month. *Munsalikh*, Drawn off (skin). Finished (month).

A منسلق *munsalik*, (An eye) afflicted with the disease سلاق *sulāk*.

A منسلك *munsalik*, Joined, enrolled in, added.

A منّ سلوي *mann salwa'*, Manna (and) quails (food of the Israelites in the wilderness).

A منسلي *munsalī*, Shaken off (fear or sadness).

P منسم *mansim*, Name of a plant which they mix up with perfumes.

A منسم *mansim*, A mark, sign. Way, road, path. Mode, manner, opinion. Face, aspect. Sect. The foot of a camel. من اين منسمك *min ayn mansimuka*, Whence come you?

A منسّم *munassim*, Enlivener, vivifier, animator.

P منسنو *mansunū*, The elect, chosen of God.

A منسوب *mansūb*, Related, belonging, relative, connected, allied. Noted. Denominated from his family, derived from another, surnamed. Attributed, ascribed, charged, imputed, addicted to, depending upon, chargeable. (pl. مناسيب *manāsīb*) Amorous (verse) in praise of a mistress. منسوب كردن *mansūb kardan*, To charge, attribute.

P منسوبه *mansūba*, Adjustment, arrangement, happy contrivance, position, or posture. The game of chess. The seventh game of نرد *nard*.

A منسوج *mansūj*, Woven. منسوجات *mansūjāt*, Things weaved; gold-wrought garments.

P منسوج باف *mansūj-bāf*, A weaver of gold-wrought garments.

A منسوخ *mansūkh*, (fem. منسوخة *mansūkhat*) Cancelled, obliterated, abolished, abrogated.

A منسوق *mansūk*, Joined in order.

A منسوك *mansūk*, (fem. منسوكة *mansūkat*) Smooth-skinned or sleek-coated (horse). Manured (field). Purified, washed, cleaned (thing).

A منسوّ *mansūʼ*, Delayed, protracted.

A منسي *munsī*, Who causes one to forget.

A منسيّ *mansīy*, Forgotten, buried in oblivion, neglected, omitted. Hurt in the nerve نسا *nasa'*.

P منش *manish*, Greatness of soul, magnanimity, authority, gravity, dignity. Liberality. Nature, genius. Constitution, temperament, disposition, good-nature, cheerfulness, content. The heart. Pride, arrogance. Desire, wish. منش زدن *manish zadan*, (كردن *kardan*, or گشتن *gashtan*), To nauseate, to have a disordered stomach.

A منشأ *manshaʼ*, A place where any one grows up; one's native soil. Principal, beginning, origin, source, spring, motive. Allusion. Exordium, or argument of any composition. *Munshaʼ*, Hoisted (standard), raised high. Erect (stone or stake). One who grows; tall (girl).

A منشأة *munshaʼat*, A ship with sails hoisted.

A منشات *munshāt*, Compositions, writings.

A منشار *minshār*, A saw. A wooden pronged-instrument for winnowing corn. The sword-fish.

A منشاريّ *minshārīy*, Serrate, sawed.

A منشاص *minshās*, (A woman) disobedient to her husband in not admitting him into her bed.

A منشاف *minshāf*, (A camel) sometimes abounding in milk and sometimes destitute.

A منشال *minshāl*, A flesh-hook or fork with which they take meat out of a pot.

A منشب *manshab*, Any thing which adheres (especially bad). *Minshab*, A net, gin, noose, snare. (pl. مناشب *manāshib*) A small worthless date.

A منشّب *munashshab*, (A garment) painted with the figures of arrows (نشّاب *nushshāb*).

A منشبة *manshabat*, Live or dead stock.

A منشبل *munshabil*, Slow-flowing or gliding.

A منشتّ *munshatt*, Separated, distinct, dispersed, scattered.

A منشتر *munshatir*, (An eye) whose lashes are either inverted, wide asunder, or loose.

A منشد *munshid*, One who makes a sign, points to, or informs (where any thing is lost). One who asks information about any thing lost. A reciter (of verses), an improvisator. A satirist.

A منشدي *munshadī*, A reciter (of verse) in a loud voice. A learner of erudition, or any thing elegant, from another.

A منشر *munshar*, Diffused, scattered. *Munshir*, (God) the reviver, bringer to life.

A منشّر *munashshar*, Spread open, unfolded, diffused, scattered.

A منشرج *munsharij*, Split, gaping, open.

A منشرح *munsharih*, Cheerful, rejoicing.

A منشرق *munsharik*, Split, cracked (bow).

A منشرم *munsharim*, Split, slightly cut.

A منشط *munshit*, Possessed of sprightly (نشيط *nashīt*) horses or domestics.

A منشع *manshaʻ*, (v. n. of نشع) Tearing away with violence. Putting any thing into the mouth of an infant. Instructing, teaching. (See نشوع *nushūʻ*). *Minshaʻ*, A box in which they keep snuff, or any thing for clearing the brain.

A منشعب *munshaʻib*, Divided (way or branches). Branching (road or tree). Scattered.

A منشعل *munshaʻil*, Kindled, flaming.

A منشغة *minshaghat*, A medicine-chest.

A منشف *minshaf*, (pl. مناشف) A towel.

A منشّف *munashshif*, Imbibing; absorbent.

A منشق *manshak*, The nose or nostril. *Munshik*, One who puts (medicine) into the nostrils.

A منشقّ *munshakk*, Split. (See انشقاق.)

P منش گردا *manish-gardā*, A nausea, loathing. A fainting-fit.

P منش گشته *manish-gashta*, Distempered, indisposed, sick.

A منشل *minshal*, A flesh-hook or fork with which they take meat out of a pot.

A منشلة *manshalat*, The place of the ring on the little finger.

A منشم *manshim* or *mansham*, Name of a certain perfume hard to pound. A certain poisonous plant called قرون السنبل *kurūnu's sumbul*. *Manshim*, A fruit black and stinking. Carpo-balsam. Name of a certain vendress of perfumes at Mecca.

A منشمر *munshamir*, A pompous walker. One who prepares with diligence and expedition for any thing. Quick-going (horse).

A منشمل *munshamil*, One who prepares for doing any thing. (See انشمال *inshimāl*.)

P منشن *manishin*, Nature, disposition, temperament. Gravity, magnificence, high-mindedness.

A منشوب *manshūb*, Adhering, fixed.

A منشور *manshūr*, Diffused, spread open or abroad, divulged. Published (book). One whose affairs are in disorder. A royal mandate, diploma, patent, or privilege not sealed or stamped with the royal signet. (A man) of extensive business. Divided, cut with a saw. A prism. P منشور نويسان باغ *manshūr-navīsāni bāgh*, Nightingales, larks, &c.

A منشورة *manshūrat*, A noble, bountiful lady.

A منشوش *manshūsh*, (An unguent) thickened with perfumes.

A منشوع *manshūʿ*, Addicted; wishful.

A منشوغ *manshūgh*, (A child) drenched with medicine. Wishful, desirous, greedy.

A منشوي *munshawī*, Roasted.

A منشي *munshī*, A writer, author, secretary, tutor, or language-master. A composer in prose. منشيء فلك *munshīʾi falak*, The planet Mercury.

P منشي *manishī*, Constitutional, natural.

P منشيا *manshiyā*, (in zand and Pāzand) The minister of a fire-temple.

A منشئات *munshaʾāt*, Literary compositions.

P منشيدن *manshīdan*, To nauseate, loathe.

P منشي گري *munshīgarī*, Business of a munshī.

A منصاح *munsāh*, Water overflowing the surface of the ground.

A منصال *mansāl*, A body of troops smaller than مقنب *miknab*. *Minsāl*, An oblong stone with which any thing is bruised.

A منصب *mansib*, A turning-place. *Mansib* or *mansab*, A principle, origin. (pl. مناصب *manāsib*) Dignity, office, ministry, magistracy. A high place; a place where any thing is erected. P از منصب عزل كردن *az mansib ʿazl kardan*, To deprive of, or dismiss from, an employment. A *Minsab*, (pl. مناصب *manāsib*) A trivet or any thing similar on which a pot is placed. *Munsab*, Pained, indisposed. Wearied, fatigued. *Munsib*, One who fatigues. Oppressive, vexatious (anxiety).

A منصّب *munassab*, (Dust) moistened and adhering together. Evenly set (row of teeth). Laid one upon another (stones).

A منصبّ *munsabb*, Poured out, diffusing itself. Smitten with love. Sloping (ground).

A منصبة *mansabat*, Trouble, labour, toil, care. The discharging of an office, performance of duty.

P منصبدار *mansib-dār*, Appointed to office under government. Invested with dignity, official. A magistrate, a man in office.

A منصبغ *munsabigh*, Tinged, dyed, immersed, dipped. Baptized.

A منصبن *munsabin*, Returned, receded, departed.

A منصّة *manassat*, The marriage-chamber or bed (richly ornamented). A theatre. *Minassat*, A raised seat highly decorated, on which the bride is exhibited to public view.

A منصح *minsah*, (or منصحة *minsahat*) A needle.

A منصدع *munsadiʿ*, Separated. Cleft, rent.

A منصرح *munsarih*, Clear, plain, transparent.

A منصرف *munsaraf*, (v. n. 7 of صرف) Turning one's self, receding, departing. Place of departure. *Munsarif*, Converted, turned back, receding, departing, deviating. Rebellious. Related to. Declinable (noun).

A منصرم *munsarim*, Cut (rope).

A منصع *mansaʿ*, (pl. مناصع *manāsiʿ*) A privy. A company, an assembly.

A منصف *mansaf*, (pl. مناصف *manāsif*) A domestic. The middle or the half of the way. *Minsaf*, A domestic. *Munsif*, Discreet. Just, equitable. A judge-advocate. (in India) A district or village-judge. An arbiter. One who gives a half.

A منصّف *munassaf*, (Wine) boiled down to one-half. Half-ripe (date). *Munassif*, One who wraps a turban round the head.

P منصفانه *munsifāna*, Candidly, equitably.

A منصفة *man* or *minsafat*, A female servant.

A منصفق *munsafik*, Turned back. Shut, closed, covered. Depressed.

P منصف نهاد *munsif-nihād*, Just, equitable.

A منصل *munsul* or *munsal*, A sword. منصل الاسنّة *munsilu'l asinnat*, (or منصل الالّ *munsilu'l all*) The month Rajab (during which the spear-heads were taken off).

A منصلت *munsalit*, Brisk, active, bustling (man). Sharp and glittering (sword).

A منصمي *munsamī*, Poured upon.

A منصوب *mansūb*, Erected, planted, set up, constituted, excited, fixed, established, appointed, named for. Promoted to dignity. Substituted. Marked with the vowel point fatha ـَ *a*. (ingram.) Governed. Collocation; the situation of the men on a chess-board. Dignity.

P منصوبه *mansūba*, Intention, will, desire. Contrivance. The sixth of the seven games of نرد *nard*.

P منصوبه باز *mansūba-bāz*, Considerate, foreseeing, prudent, sagacious, ingenious.

A منصوح *mansūh*, Advised, counselled.

A منصوحة *mansūhat*, Well-watered (land), and producing herbage so thick as to touch each other.

A منصور *mansūr*, Aided, defended, protected (by God), triumphant. *Mansūr*, (or منصورو مظفّر *mansūr u muzaffar*) Victorious, conquering. *Mansūr*, (or المنصور *almansūr*) Name of the second caliph of the house of Abbās.

A منصورة *mansūrat*, Name of several towns.

A منصوص *mansūs*, Manifested, declared. منصوص و معروف اهل حال *mansūs u maʿrūfi ahli hāl*, Manifested and known to one skilled in the business.

A منصيل *minsīl*, A long stone for bruising.

A منضا *munzaʾ*, Emaciated with travelling.

A منضاج *minzāj*, A roasting-spit.

A منضج *munzaj*, Well-cooked, thoroughly dressed (meat). *Munzij*, Suppurative.

A منضّج *munazzij*, (pl. منضّجات *munazzijāt*) (A camel) not bringing forth for a year. Suppurative.

A منضجات *munzi*, or *munazzijāt*, Suppuratives.

A منضجع *munzajiʿ*, Reclined on a bed or on the ground (especially on the side).

A منضحة *minzahat*, (or منضخة) A giraffe.

A منضّد *munazzad*, (Carpets or blankets) laid one upon another. Well-set (pearls).

A منضرج *munzarij*, Split. (See انضراج.)

A منضرح *munzarih*, Widely different (word and deed). Distant. Thrown aside.

A منضف *minzaf*, One who breaks wind loud.

A منضفر *munzafir*, (Ropes) twisted together.

A منضمّ *munzamm*, Contracted, heaped, joined, added, inserted. (A pearl) slender in the middle.

A منضمر *munzamir*, Flexible after effusion (yard).

A منضود *manzūd*, (Carpets, blankets, and the like) laid one upon another.

A منضور *manzūr*, Florid, blooming, beautiful, verdant. P منضور شدن *manzūr shudan*, To flourish, to be verdant.

A منضى *munzaʾ*, Attenuated with travelling.

A منطاد *muntād*, Lofty, high-raised (edifice).

A منطب *mintab*, (or منطبة) Strainer, cullender.

A منطبة *mantabat*, Foolish, stupid. A fool.

A منطبخ *muntabikh*, Cooked, boiled, dressed.

A منطبع *muntabiʿ*, Tamed, trained. Obedient, tractable. Yielding, malleable, (metal). Printed.

A منطبق *muntabik*, Fitting, equal, even.

A منطرح *muntarih*, Thrown prostrate, floored.

A منطرد *muntarid*, Driven away, thrust out.

A منطسم *muntasim*, Obliterated, defaced.

A منطّف *munattaf*, (fem. منطّفة *munattafat*) Charged with a shameful crime, accused. Decked with ear-rings.

A منطفى *muntafiʼ*, Extinguished. Extinct.

A منطق *mantik*, (v. n. of نطق) Speaking, pronouncing, articulating. An oration. Eloquence. *Mantik*, (or علم منطق *ʻilmi mantik*) Logic, reasoning. *Mintak*, The female garment نطاق *nitāk*. A girdle, zone, belt, sash. منطق البروج *mintaku'l burūj*, The celestial girdle, the zodiac.

A منطّق *munattak*, (A mountain) encircled round the middle with clouds, the top being clear. (Sheep) marked with red chalk round the short-ribs.

A منطقة *mintakat*, A girdle. منطقة البروج *mintakatu'l burūj*, (or منطقة ذات البروج *mintakaʼi zātu'l burūj*) The celestial girdle, *i.e.* the zodiac. منطقهٔ مبروده *mintakaʼi mabrūda*, Frigid zone. منطقهٔ محروقه *mintakaʼi mahrūka*, Torrid zone. منطقهٔ معدّله *mintakaʼi muʻaddila*, Temperate zone.

A منطقي *mantikīy*, Logical, dialectic.

A منطقيّات *mantikīyāt*, Dialectics.

A منطلس *muntalis*, Secret, mysterious.

A منطلق *muntalik*, Dismissed, freed, set at liberty, departing, going away; loosened, relaxed. Open, cheerful.

A منطوح *mantūh*, Butted by the horns of a ram, and hurt or killed. (A ram) butted to death.

A منطوع *mantūʻ*, Changed (colour). *Muntawiʻ*, Obedient, tractable, ductile.

A منطوف *mantūf*, Suspected. Criminated.

A منطوق *mantūk*, Said, spoken, articulated.

A منطوي *muntawī*, Folded, wrapped.

A منطيق *mintīk*, Extremely eloquent. A woman whose petticoat is stuffed so as to give her a prominence round the hips.

A منظار *minzār*, A mirror, looking-glass.

A منظر *manzar*, (v. n. of نظر) Looking, beholding. Countenance, face, aspect, visage, looks. A spectacle, stage-play, theatre, scene. A tower, lofty building, palace. An object of sight. Any thing looked at, agreeable or disagreeable. P منظر چشم *manzari chashm*, Pupil of the eye. منظر نيم خايه *manzari nīm-khāya*, The sky. A dome. A كريه المنظر *karīhu'l manzar*, Ill-looking, ugly. *Munzar*, Waited for. Listened to. Cast behind.

A منظرانيّ *manzarānīy*, Beautiful of face.

A منظرة *manzarat*, (v. n. of نظر) Looking at, beholding. A place where one may have an extensive prospect. Spectators. Any thing looked at, agreeable or otherwise. The face, countenance.

A منظريّ *manzarīy*, Beautiful of face.

A منظّف *munazzaf*, Cleaned, purified, purged.

A منظلم *munzalim*, Oppressed, wronged.

A منظم *munzim*, (A fish or lizard) marked with the lines نظامان *nizāmāni*.

A منظّم *munazzam*, Arranged, in excellent order, placed in a row. *Munazzim*, (A fish) marked with the line نظام *nizām*.

A منظور *manzūr*, Looked at, seen, visible. Admired. Chosen, approved of, admitted, accepted, agreeable, acceptable. P منظور شدن *manzūr shudan*, To be seen, to go in sight. منظور كردن *manzūr kardan*, To approve, admit, or accept. منظور نظر *manzūri nazar*, Chosen, agreeable to the sight, beloved. A mistress. P منظور نظر خواص وعوام شدن *manzūri nazari khawāṣ u ʻawām shudan*, To be seen by nobles and plebeians, *i.e.* to be conspicuous.

A منظورة *manzūrat*, A misfortune. (A woman) reproached with vice.

A منظوريّة *manzūrīyat*, State of being seen.

A منظوم *manzūm*, Joined, threaded. Arranged in order. Metrical, versified, poetic. A large flight of locusts. Three stars in Orion. The Pleiades. The star called the Bull's-eye.

A منظومة *manzūmat*, Rhyme. Any thing placed in a series, row, line, or order. P منظومهاي اهالى پسند *manzūmahāyi ahālī-pasand*, Verses approved by judges. A منظومهٔ زواهر *manzūmaʼi zawāhir*, A string of pearls.

A منع *manʻ*, (or, as used, *manaʻ*) (v. n. of منع) Forbidding, repelling, counteracting, inhibiting, rejecting, withholding, refusing, preventing, denying, dissuading. Making a hamza light (as when سبأ *sabaʼ* becomes سبا *saba'*). Prohibition, hindrance, obstacle, preventive, refusal, opposition. (pl. منوع) A crab. P منع كردن *manaʻ kardan*, To restrain.

A منعاة *manʻāt*, News of any one's death.

A منعام *minʻām*, Very beneficent.

A منعب *minʻab*, (A horse or camel) going fast, swift, excellently; stretching out the head when running like a crow. A foolish, clamorous, noisy man.

A منعة *manʻat* or *manaʻat*, Difficulty of access. *Manaʻat*, Dignity. (pl. of مانع *māniʻ*) Hinderers, prohibiters. Difficult of access, grave, reserved (men).

A منعثق *munʻasik*, Confused, mixed (clouds).

A منعثل *munaʻsil*, (A horse) that throws his feet about, or when he lifts them, appears to be drawing them out of mud.

A منعجد *munʻajid*, Sharp, angry.

A منعجف *munʻajif*, Lean (camel).

A منعدل *munʻadil*, One who deviates from.

A منعدم *munʻadim*, Destroyed, annihilated, annulled, demolished, ruined, extinct, lost, missed, disappeared. P منعدم كردن *munʻadim kardan*, To deface, destroy, annihilate.

A منعدي *munʻadī*, Contagious. Men dying one after another of pestilence or any contagion.

A منعرج *munʻaraj*, Bent. Bend (of a river). *Munʻarij*, Bent, turned, inflected. Sloping (sun).

A منعزق *munʻazik*, Bad-tempered.

A منعزل *munʻazil*, Separated, removed to a distance. Retired, sequestered. Deprived of office, removed from ministry or from a government.

A منعش *munʻashsh*, Patched (shirt).

A منعصب *munʻasib*, Grown strong, hard, firm.

A منعصر *munʻasir*, Pressed, squeezed: expressed.

A منعصم *munʻasim*, Preserved, defended, kept.

A منعط *munʻatt*, Torn (garment).

A منعطف *munʻataf*, The bend of a valley or river. *Munʻatif*, Bent, doubled, curved.

A منعظ *munʻiz*, Whatever causes a priapism. (A vulva) wide open through lust.

A منعفر *munʻafir*, Soiled with, or rolled in, dust.

A منعفق *munʻafak*, A place of departure or of turning back. *Munʻafik*, Carried rapidly on (in business). Bent, curved. Led away from water.

A منعق *munʻakk*, Split. Dispersed, dispelled (cloud). (Lightning) gleaming like a sword. (See انعقاق *inʻikāk*.)

A من عقب *min ʻakib*, Behind, after.

A منعقد *munʻakid*, Tied, knotted. Bound. Agreed upon, concluded (peace, marriage, bargain). Piled up, cumulated (cloud). منعقد اللسان *munʻakidu'l lisān*, Tongue-tied.

A منعقر *munʻakir*, Galled in the back. Wounded in the feet (camel or horse with a sword), hamstrung. Cut off. Cut, lopped (palm-tree). Detained, bound.

A منعكس *munʻakis*, Reflected, reversed (as a figure in a mirror or water): contrary, inverse.

A منعكف *munʻakif*, Curled (hair).

A منعل *manʻal*, (and منعلة *manʻalat*) Hard ground. *Munʻal*, (A palm-sucker) torn from the parent stock. (A horse) marked with white in the hinder part of the pastern. Shod with shoe, slipper, or sandal (نعل *naʻl*). Hard-hoofed (horse).

A منعم *munʻam*, Benefited. منعم عليه *munʻam ʻalayhi*, Benefited; a recipient of bounty. *Munʻim*, Beneficent, liberal, generous, gracious. A benefactor. منعم حقيقي *munʻimi hakīkī*, The true benefactor, *i.e.* God. *Munʻum*, A besom, broom.

A منعّم *munaʻʻam*, Delicate (woman), in good health or excellent condition. Rich. Mild, soothing (speech).

A منعّمة *munaʻʻamat*, Delicate (woman), in good health or condition. Mild, soothing (speech). Benefit, recompense. A pleasant, delightful life.

A منعمد *munʻamid*, Supported by pillars.

A منعمل *munʻamil*, Made, done, performed.

A منعميّة *munʻimīyat*, Bestowment.

A منعوت *manʻūt*, Qualified by an adjective. Described.

A منعوش *manʻūsh*, (A corpse) laid on a bier.

A منعوي *munʻawī*, Distorted, bent, twisted.

A منعى *manʻa'*, (pl. مناعي *manāʻī*) The news of any one's death. Abstinence. Hindrance, prevention. Confinement, durance.

A منعيّ *manaʻīy*, Fond of crab-fish (منع *manʻ*).

A منغار *minghār*, (or منغر *munghir*) A sheep accustomed to give red or bloody milk.

A منغدل munghadil, Large and loose-headed.

P منغر manghur, (or منغرك manghurah) A small copper coin, a farthing. *Munghur*, (or منغرك munghurah) A large goblet.

A منغرف mungharif, Cut, clipped, shorn.

A منغس munghass, Plunged, immersed. Driven away (as a cat) by the cry غس غس *ghass ghass*.

A منغسل munghasil, Washed. Flowing.

A منغص munaghghas, (A life) rendered miserable, irksome, and melancholy. *Munaghghis*, Who or what renders (a person's life) unhappy.

A منغض munghizz, A winker. Winking (eye).

A منغضف munghazif, One who gets amongst dust. (A well) falling to ruins.

A منغط munghatt, Immersed (in water). One who dives or plunges himself.

A منغفق munghafah, A place of departure.

A منغفي munghafi, Broken.

A منغل munghall, Entering, inserted.

A منغلق munghalik, Shut up or against; closed.

P منغله manghala, A sort of game.

A منغم munghamm, Shut, stopt, closed, covered (mouth or nostril). Haltered (camel). Sorrowful.

A منغمر munghamir, Sunk, plunged.

A منغمض munghamiz, One who winks; a winker.

A منغوط munghawit, Bent, curved (stick).

A منغوي munghawī, Deceived. Fallen. Bent.

A منغير min ghayr, Involuntarily, accidentally.

A منف manf, Memphis in Egypt.

A منفاخ minfākh, Bellows.

A منفاص minfās, (or منفاض minfāz) A woman who laughs much. A woman who often makes water in bed.

A منفاق minfāk, One who spends much.

A منفت munfatt, Crumbled.

A منفتح munfatih, Open (door). Disjoined.

A منفتحة munfatihat, The letters except صضطظ.

A منفتق munfatik, Split, broken, cleft. (Misfortune) overtaking (any one).

A منفتقة munfatikat, Deflowered. Wide, roomy (woman). منفتقة بالكلام *munfatikat bi'l kalām*, Talkative (woman).

A منفتل munfatil, Twisted (rope). Turned (from any design or resolution): receding.

A منفث munfass, Broken.

A منفج munfajj, (A bow) wide between the string and the handle.

A منفجر munfajar, A road through sands. A place where water gushes forth and flows freely. *Munfajir*, Let loose, broached, flowing (water). (Dawn) beginning to diffuse itself. A displayer (of magnificence and liberality). (Night) dispelled by dawn. Dawn. (Evils) crowding from all quarters.

P منفجي munfajī, Open (gate or door).

A منفح minfah, A meddler, busybody.

A منفحة minfahat, A yellow curdling substance from the stomach of a sucking lamb or kid, rennet.

A منفخ minfakh, (pl. منافخ manāfikh) Bellows.

A منفخت munfakhit, Pierced (roof).

A منفد munfid, One who exhausts or carries off. Destitute of provisions, poor. Dry (well).

A منفدي munfadī, Redeemed, ransomed.

A منفذ manfaz, (pl. منافذ manāfiz) A place through which any thing passes or penetrates; a hole, passage, vent, outlet. *Munfiz*, One who causes to pass, pervade, or be received.

A منفر munfir, Who terrifies and puts to flight. One who gives victory, who salutes as conqueror. An assistant. Possessed of frightened camels.

A منفرث munfaras, (in compos. with بها *bihā*) as منفرث بها *munfaras bihā*, Fainting (pregnant woman). *Munfaris*, Burst (belly or liver).

A منفرج munfarij, Tranquil, contented, happy, free from care or grief. Cracked, split, separated, distant. Open, gaping. منفرجة *munfarijat*, (or منفرجة الزوايا *munfarijatu'z zawāya'*) Obtuse-angled (mathematical figure).

A منفرد munfarid, Simple. Alone, solitary, singular, unique. منفردا *munfaridan*, Separately, solely, singly.

A منفرق munfarik, Distinct, separate, dispersed.

A منفرك munfarik, Rubbed. Skinned, barked.

A منفزر munfazir, Torn, ragged (garment).

A منفس manfas, Much desired (thing). Vent, breathing-hole, mouth. *Munfis*, Much desired (object). *Munfis* or *munfas*, Many, much (wealth).

A منفسح munfasah, Open, expanding (place). *Munfasih*, Joyous, delighted, expanded (heart). Convenient, commodious (lodging-place for cattle).

A منفسخ munfasikh, Dissolved, broken off (contract, marriage, &c.). Excommunicated.

A منفسد munfasid, Corrupted.

A منفسق munfasik, (A ripe date) bursting from its skin.

A منفش المنخرين munaffashu'l minkharayn, One who has wide nostrils.

A منفص munfass, Gone out, departed, separate.

A منفصد munfasid, Flowing, fluid.

A منفصع munfasiʻ, Protruded (glans penis).

A منفصل munfasal, A place of separation. *Munfasil*, Dissected. Separated, disjoined, distinct, cut off; weaned, driven from the mother. One who departs. Disjunctive.

A منفصم munfasim, Broken without separation.

A منفصي munfasī, Escaped, released.

A منفض minfaz, A fan, ventilator. *Munfiz*, Impoverished (people). (See انفاض *infāz.*)

A منفضج munfazij, One, the roots of whose hair are moist (with sweat), but not flowing. Visible (horizon). Burst (wound); open (navel). Leaking (skin-bottle). Loose, disordered, distracted (affair).

A منفضح munfazih, Detected in villainy and exposed to infamy, rendered ignominious.

A منفضخ munfazikh, Bruised (camel's bunch). Burst (sore). Leaky (bucket). Who weeps bitterly.

A منفطر munfatir, Split, cracked, splitting.

A منفطم munfatim, Prohibited; cautious. Desisted. Arrived at the end.

A منفع munfiʻ, A seller of walking-sticks.

A منفعة manfaʻat or manfiʻat, (pl. منافع manāfiʻ) Emolument, profit, gain, advantage. Use.

P منفعت كردن manfaʻat kardan, To do good.

P منفعت گيري manfaʻat-giri, A getting good.

A منفعل munfaʻil, Made, done, performed. Disturbed, afflicted. Bashful, ashamed.

A منفغر munfaghir, Open (mouth), expanding, full-blown (flower).

A منفق munfik, One who lays out money. One who easily and readily disposes of his goods.

A منفقق munfakk, Open, separated, disjoined.

A منفك munfakk, Dislocated, removed from a place. Separate, distinct: alienated.

A منفل munfil, One who gives liberally, more than is necessary. (A leader) who gives up the whole plunder (to his soldiers). One who, with a hatchet, cuts the tragacanth as food for camels.

A منفل munfall, Broken, notched (edge).

A منفلت munfalit, Escaped, set at liberty.

A منفلق munfalik, Split, broken in pieces.

A منفوخ manfūkh, Inflated, tumid, swollen, swelled in the belly, fat.

A منفور manfūr, Abhorred, shunned. Conquered, overcome. P منفور شدن *manfūr shudan*, To be detested.

A منفوس manfūs, Born. An infant whose mother is still in child-bed. Much desired (thing).

A منفوش manfūsh, Plucked, teased (cotton or wool). Coloured (lock of wool).

A منفوض manfūz, Shaken. Trembling with horror. Shaking with ague, agued.

A منفوطة manfūtat, Blistered (hand).

A منفوق munfawik, Broken, notched (arrow).

A منفوه manfūh, Timid, cowardly.

A منفه munaffah, Lazy, tired (camel).

A منفهق munfahik, Wide-spread, diffused (lightning or water). Abounding.

A منفهم munfahim, Perceived, understood.

A منفي manfiy, Negative. Rejected. Banished.

A منفئن munfaʼinn, The same as يفن *yafan*.

A منقاب minkāb, A pipe, a tube.

A منقاد minkād, A bird's beak. An instrument for assaying gold and silver coin. *Munkād*, Obedient, submissive, tractable. Soft, yielding (soil).

A منقادة minkādat, Ground soft and trodden.

A منقادية munkādiyat, Obedience.

A منقار minkār, (pl. مناقير manākīr) Beak of a bird. A pointed iron instrument used by smiths. Point, toe of a boot. منقار النجار *minkāru'n najjār*, A carpenter's chisel. منقار الرحى *minkāru'r raha'*, A tool for notching millstones. منقارقار *minkāri kār*, Nib of a pen. P منقار كبوتر *minkāri kabūtar*,

Bill of a dove. منقار گل *minkāri gil*, The tongue.

A منقاش *minkāsh*, Pincers. Tweezers.

A منقاص *munkāṣ*, Eradicated.

A منقاض *munkāẓ*, (A tree) cleft lengthwise.

A منقاف *minkāf*, The beak of a bird. The bone of a shell-fish, used in polishing. A kind of lizard.

A منقال *minkāl*, Quick-trotting (horse).

A منقب *mankab*, A road through mountains or over rough grounds. A pass, passage. A street. That part of the belly near the navel where they tap for the dropsy. *Minkab*, The instrument with which that operation is performed, a trocar. A road through hard and rough ground.

A منقّب *munakkib*, An examiner, scrutinizer.

A منقبة *mankabat*, A path through mountains. A narrow way between houses. A wall, enclosure. A bridge. Any thing in which a man glories, or which confers on him pre-eminence. Glory.

A منقبض *munkabiz*, Contracted within itself, shrunk, wrinkled, drawn together. Fast-going.

A منقبع *munkabiʿ*, (A bird) retiring (to her nest). Concealed.

P منقبه *mankaba*, Art, science. A cobbler. Sole of the foot.

A منقح *munkih*, One who empties (a bone) of the marrow. A polisher of verse. One who sells the ornaments of his sword, and other things similar, when forced by necessity in scarce seasons.

A منقّح *munakkah*, Made manifest, clear. *Munakkih*, One who extracts marrow. Who sharpens the wit. A pruner, lopper of superfluities.

A منقحم *munkahim*, One who plunges in with impetuous temerity. Fallen into difficulties.

A منقدّ *munkadd*, Split, cut longwise.

A منقدة *minkadat*, A sherd with which they peel and clean walnuts.

A منقدر *munkadir*, Predestined, made necessary, created. Exact in measure.

A منقدع *munkadiʿ*, Averse from, hanging back.

A منقذ *munkiz*, A deliverer, redeemer, rescuer.

A منقذم *munkazim*, Swift; one who makes haste.

A منقر *minkar*, A pointed hammer used in digging, hollowing, or cutting stones, a pick. *Minkar* or *munkur*, (pl. مناقير *manākīr*) A tray or trough used in making wine. *Munkir*, Milk extremely acid. *Munkur*, (pl. مناقر *manākir*) A well dug in very hard ground, with a narrow mouth and full of water. A watering-cistern or trough.

A منقّر *munakkar*, One whose eyes are sunk in the sockets.

A منقرد *munkarid*, Fixed, settled in a place.

A منقرض *munkariz*, Cut, notched; corroded. Extinct (family, race). Consumed, elapsed (time).

A منقرع *munkariʿ*, Rolling from side to side: restless. Precious, dear. Stopped, desisting.

A منقز *munkiz*, One who drinks pure water called نقز *nakiz*. One who kills (an enemy), or causes him to be killed. Possessed of cattle afflicted with the distemper نقاز *nukāz*. One who acquires (especially by births) the kind of sheep called نقز *nakaz*.

A منقسم *munkasim*, Divided into parts (قسم *kism*), as a book into chapters.

A منقش *minkash*, Pincers, tweezers.

A منقّش *munakkash*, Painted, stained, printed, speckled. Embroidered. *Munakkish*, A painter, printer, stainer. An embroiderer. An engraver.

A منقشة *minkashat*, A pencil, painter's brush.

A منقّشة *munakkishat*, Skull-fracturing (wound), and causing exfoliation.

A منقشر *munkashir*, Peeled, barked. Round.

A منقشع *munkashiʿ*, Scattered (cloud), dispelled (grief).

A منقصة *mankaṣat*, Loss, defect, deficiency.

A منقصف *munkaṣif*, Broken. Who or what goes off, retires, passes by, or flees away.

A منقصل *munkaṣil*, Cut.

A منقصم *munkaṣim*, Broken to bits, separated.

A منقضّ *munkazz*, (A hawk) darting on his prey. (Cavalry) charging (a foe). (A wall) falling down, or threatening ruin. Setting (star).

A منقضب *munkazib*, Cut, separated. (A star) passing, leaving its place.

A منقضع *munkaziʿ*, Retired far, gone away.

A منقضف *munkazif*, Moved (from its place).

A منقضي *munkazī*, Finished, completed. Annihilated, extinct. Elapsed, passed.

A منقّط *munakkat*, Marked with points: dotted.

A منقطع *munkataʿ*, A place where (any thing) finishes or breaks off. Extremity (of a sand-hill or valley). منقطع به *munkataʿ bihi*, Unable to prosecute a journey (from the weakness of one's beast or from any other cause). *Munkatiʿ*, Broken (rope). Abrupt, broken off, separated, disjoined, finished, ceased, terminated, extinct, perishing, exterminated. (Sour milk) separated into particles. A recluse. Disabled. منقطع القرين *munkatiʿu'l karīn*, Unequalled, unrivalled, incomparable, matchless. غير منقطع *ghayr munkatiʿ*, Uninterrupted.

A منقطعة *munkatiʿat*, (White on a horse's forehead) reaching from the nostrils to the eyes.

A منقع *mankaʿ*, The sea, bed of the ocean. (pl. مناقع *manākiʿ*) Any place where water collects, remains, or stagnates. As much water as is sufficient for a draught. Legal, unobjectionable, competent (witness). *Minkaʿ*, A vessel in which medicines are steeped or soaked. منقع البرم *minkaʿu'l burm*, A place where a pot or cauldron is laid up. *Munkaʿ*, Pickled, preserved (fruit). Good, wholesome, cool (water) quenching thirst. Cooling butter-milk. Steeped (thing). Strong (poison). A wine-measure of about eighteen gallons. A worn cloth taken to pieces to be woven a second time; shoddy. A small stone cistern. Any thing left in the bottom of a stone kettle. *Munkuʿ*, A small kettle in which milk and dates are dressed for children.

A منقعة *mankaʿat*, A place where water collects or stagnates. *Minkaʿat*, A vessel wherein medicines are soaked. *Minkaʿat* or *munkaʿat*, A stone vessel in which children's food is dressed.

A منقعر *munkaʿir*, (A tree) uprooted and falling down. Fallen on the ground.

A منقعط *munkaʿit*, One whose hair is very curly. Assiduous, attentive to business.

A منقعف *munkaʿif*, (A thing) moved from (its) place. (A wall) tumbling down.

A منقف *mankaf*, Any thing unequal, roughnesses remaining in planed wood. *Munkaf*, (A man) having prominent (bones). *Munkif*, One who splits (a colocynth) and takes out (the core). One who holds out a bone that another may extract (the marrow). (Locusts) filling (a valley) with eggs.

A منقفش *munkafish*, (A spider) drawing up his legs together, or entering his hole.

A منقفشة *munkafishat*, Shrivel-skinned (reptile).

A منقفع *munkafiʿ*, Prohibited. Hanging back.

A منقفل *munkafil*, Bolted, locked. منقفل اليدين *munkafilu'l yadayn*, A gripe-fist, miser.

A منقل *mankal*, A boot or shoe worn or mended. A way through a mountain. *Minkal*, (A camel) drinking twice. (pl. مناقل *manākil*) Quick-trotting (horse), that picks up his feet nimbly. *Munkal*, Well-made (shoe). (A sheep) going from meadow to meadow. Narrated, told, alleged. *Munkil*, One who patches shoes and boots. One who roves from pasture to pasture.

A منقلا *munkalā*, A deputy, ambassador.

A منقلب *munkalab*, (v. n. 7 of قلب) Being turned. Inversion. A place of turning. A place of returning. Issue, upshot. *Munkalib*, Turned, changed, converted, perverted, inverted, averted.

P منقلب شدن *munkalib shudan*, To be turned.

A منقلبات *munkalibāt*, (pl. fem.) A name given to the cities of the plain which were overthrown in the time of Lot, viz. سدوم *sudūm*, صبغة *sabghat*, غمرة *ghumura*, رمادر *rumādar*, and صعدة *saʿdat*.

A منقلة *mankalat*, A day's journey, or the space travelled. A halting-place. A way through mountains. A sort of game.

A منقّلة *munakkilat*, (A wound) fracturing the skull, and producing an exfoliation. (The fine for such is fifteen camels).

A منقلع *munkaliʿ*, Torn up, uprooted, extracted.

P منقله *munkula*, A chafing-dish.

A منقمح *munkamih*, (A camel) raising the head and refusing to drink any more.

A منقمس *munkamis*, Dipt (in water). Setting (star).

A منقمع *munkamiʿ*, Subdued, tamed, subjected. Low, mean. One who enters a house privately.

A منقوب *mankūb*, Bored, perforated, hollowed, dug. Smitten with the scab, scabby.

A منقود *mankūd*, Ready money.

A منقور *mankūr*, Hollowed, excavated.

A منقوز *mankūz*, (fem. منقوزة *mankūzat*) (Sheep) troubled with the distemper نقاز *nukāz*.

A منقوش *mankūsh*, Painted, printed, stained, coloured. Embroidered. Engraved. (A branch) dotted with ripe dates.

A منقوشة *mankūshat*, (A skull-wound) requiring that parts of the bone should be taken out.

A منقوص *mankūs*, Damaged, defective, diminished, shortened. Verse characterized by عصب *ʻasb* and كفّ *kaff*.

A منقوض *mankūz*, Untwisted. Demolished.

A منقوط *mankūt*, Spotted, dotted, marked with a diacritical point, as ذ *zāl*, ز *zayn*. A composition in which all the letters have diacritical points.

A منقوع *mankūʻ*, Steeped, soaked: an infusion.

A منقوف *mankūf*, Worm-eaten (trunk of a tree). Slender. Active and light of flesh. Lean, thin-faced (man), pale, infirm, weak, thin-necked (camel). Split (colocynth). Reddish (eye).

A منقول *mankūl*, Said, narrated, recounted. Copied, transcribed. Personal property of every description: moveables. Technical.

A منقولة *mankūlat*, A mended, patched boot.

A منقه *munkih*, Who raises from sickness.

A منقهل *munkahil*, Weak, falling down.

A منقي *munkī*, Fat, and having bones full of marrow. A chooser.

A منقّى *munakka'*, Cleaned, purged, purified. A species of dried grapes or raisins. *Munakkī*, One who cleans corn; or who cleans out a well. Purifying, cleansing.

A منقيّ *mankīy*, A road.

A منكب *mankib*, (pl. مناكب *manākib*) The shoulder; also that part of the arm next to it. The corresponding part in animals. A track. High ground. A chief, leader, general.

A منكبّ *munkabb*, Stooping, down-faced, prone.

A منكّتة *munakkitat*, A date beginning to ripen.

A منكثب *munkasib*, Heaped up (sand). Inserted, thrust, or poured into.

A منكدر *munkadir*, Quick, swift, hastening. Falling (star). Precipitant, rushing headlong. طريق المنكدر *tarīku'l munkadir*, The road of Yamāmat to Mecca.

A منكر *munkar*, Denied, unacknowledged, ignored, disowned. Unknown. Disallowed, unlawful (opposed to معروف *maʻrūf*). Wicked, bad, iniquitous. A disagreeable, iniquitous thing. Iniquity. (pl. مناكير *manākīr*) Intelligent, cunning. An angel, who, together with another named نكير *nakīr*, is supposed to examine the spirits of the departed in the tomb. *Munkir*, One who denies, rejects, disapproves, ignores, repudiates, takes ill, or feels disobliged: averse, disapproving. One who places no confidence in another, but disbelieves what he professes. Disabling (wound). Ungrateful. P منكر شدن *munkir shudan*, To deny a promise, retract one's word.

A منكّر *munakkar*, Indeterminate, indefinite.

A منكرات *munkarāt*, Iniquitous, unlawful, disagreeable things. منكرات الموت *munkarātu'l mawt*, The pains of death.

A منكرة *munkarat*, A prodigy, unheard-of thing.

A منكرث *munkaris*, Cut (rope). Consumed.

A منكرس *munkaris*, Who falls, or rushes headlong on: who precipitates himself into.

A منكرم *munkarim*, Honoured. Glorified.

A منكس *munakkas*, Inverse, with head inverted. *Munakkis*, (A horse) not holding up his head, especially in a race; also one unable to follow the others.

A منكسر *munkasir*, Broken. Broken in spirit. Fragile, frail. Put to flight, routed (enemy). Flaccid, pendulous (ear). منكسر الحال *munkasiru'l hāl*, In a distressed situation. P منكسر دلان *munkasir-dilān*, (pl.) Heart-broken.

A منكسف *munkasif*, Eclipsed (sun or moon).

A منكش *minkash*, An examiner, scrutinizer.

A منكشح *munkashih*, Scattered, dispersed. Retiring (from water).

A منكشط *munkashit*, Open, naked. Dispelled (fear).

A منكشف *munkashif*, Discovered, uncovered, revealed, published, displayed. Illustrated.

A منكص *mankas*, (v. n. of نكص) Departing, retiring, desisting from timidity. *Munkas*, Retired, gone to one side.

A منكّص *munakkas*, A place of return, gain, or profit. Retired, gone to one side.

A منكظة *mankazat*, Effort, exertion. Haste, speed.

A منكع *munkaʻ*, Flat-nosed. One who retires.

A منكّع *munakkaʻ*, Flat, flattened (nose).

A منكّف *munakkif*, (A camel) having the glands of the head called نكفات *nakafāt* protuberant.

A منكفّ *munkaff*, One who departs or retires.

A منكفت *munkafit*, Averse, departing from his resolution. Wrinkled, contracted. Lean (horse). Assembled (people).

A منكفس *munkafis*, Twisted, distorted, coiled.

A منكفئ *munkafi'*, Retired. Changed (colour).

A منكل *mankal*, A rock. *Mankal* or *mankil*, Whatever brings on a man punishment and chastisement. *Minkal*, Any thing that inspires fear.

A منكلّ *munkall*, One who smiles and just shews the teeth. (Lightning) which flashes slightly, so as to distinguish black from white. Blunted (sword).

A منكلت *munkalit*, Contracted. Shed, spilt.

A منكمش *munkamish*, Swift, hastening.

A منكمي *munkamī*, Lurking, hidden, concealed.

P منكو *mankū*, The water of life.

A منكوب *mankūb*, Afflicted, miserable. Hurt in the feet by stones. Subdued. Crooked or uncertain (road).

A منكوث *mankūs*, Untwisted (rope).

A منكوحة *mankūhat*, A married woman.

A منكود *mankūd*, Small (present).

P منكور *mankūr*, Name of a mountain in the desert of Kipchāk, where there is a spring, which, though very small, yields as much water as can be taken away.

A منكور *mankūr*, Denied. Ignored.

A منكوز *mankūz*, Thrown, beaten, trodden on.

A منكوس *mankūs*, Inverted. Read backwards. Suffering from a relapse. Preposterous (birth), i.e. with the feet foremost. Head downwards, topsy turvy. A figure in geomancy.

A منكوسة *mankūsat*, A bow, the lower extremity of which naturally grew out of the branch (considered a blemish).

A منكوف *mankūf*, (fem. منكوفة *mankūfat*) (A camel) troubled with the tumour نكاف *nukāf*.

A منكوه *mankūh*, Stinking-breathed (from indigestion).

P منكوه *ma nikūh*, Revile not, blame not.

A منكيّ *mankiy*, Killed. Wounded.

P منگ *mang*, A die, dice. A game at dice. A gamester. A gaming-house. Custom, habit; rule, law, regulation. Boast, brag, vanity. Cheating, fraud, deception. A robber, highwayman. Rhubarb. The henbane-plant. Herbs, grass. Yawning, oscitation. A mode of making the joints crack. *Ming*, A water-pipe, conduit. *Mung*, A black intoxicating grain. A bee.

P منگك *mangak*, Dice. Boasting, bragging.

P منگل *mangul*, A robber. A wart.

P منگلور *mangalor*, Mangalore in Mysore.

P منگلوس *mangalūs*, Name of a place famous for white elephants.

P منگله *mangala*, Name of a place noted for fine elephants. *Mangula*, Name of a wild herb. A strap or thread by which any thing is hung.

P منگوا *manguwā*, A dice-player. Name of a man.

P منگور *mangūr*, A mountain in Kipjāk.

P منگوش *mangosh*, An ear-ring.

P منگیا *mangi* or *mangyā*, Dice. Gaming-house.

P منگیاگر *mangiyāgar*, A dice-player, gamester.

P منگیدن *mangīdan*, To mutter in a rage. *Mangīdan* or *mungīdan*, To speak through the nose.

A منلا *manlā*, A judge, lord. A doctor of laws.

P منلاك *man* or *munlāk*, A poor, wretched man.

P منم *manam*, I am.

A منمّ *minamm*, A tale-bearer, calumniator.

A منماص *minmās*, Tweezers.

A منمجّ *munmajj*, (Wine or saliva) ejected (from the mouth). (Ink) dropping (from a pen).

A منمحس *munmahis*, Elapsed. Escaped from an eclipse. Abated, subsided (swelling).

A منمحي *munmahī*, Erased, obliterated. Clean.

A منمّر *munammar*, Dappled, spotted, speckled.

A منمرط *munmarit*, (Hair) fallen off.

A منمص *minmas*, Tweezers.

A منمّغ *munammagh*, Mixed. Sociable.

A منمّق *munmik*, Stoneless (date).

A نمل minmal or munmil, A slanderer. *Munmal*, (or منمل munammal, A closely-written hand.

A منمّل munammal, Raised, exalted.

A منمّل munmall, Fallen or dropt out. One who steals away.

A منمّلة munammalat, Restless (woman).

A منملس munmalis, Polished, made bare, bright, shining. Liberated, escaped. Retired, desisted. (Sight) snatched away.

A منملص munmalis, Escaped, slipped away.

A منملق munmalik, Smooth, slippery, shining. Freed, fallen out, escaped.

A منمنم munamnam, Painted, striped (garment).

A منمول manmūl, (Food) gnawed by ants (نمل *naml*). The tongue.

A منمهّل munmahill, Erect and stiff.

A منن minan, (pl. of منّة minnat) Claims, obligations. ذو المنن zū'l minan, Possessed of (many) claims, *i.e.* God.

A مننة minanat, A spider. A she-tortoise.

P مننگ manang, A sort of rush, of which they make brooms.

P منن و عنن manan u ʿanan, More particularly.

A منو manw, (v. n. of منو for منا) Proving, trying. Understanding, comprehending. Measuring. *Manū*, (acc. منا manā, oblique مني manī) Who?

P منو manav, Do not move or complain. *Manū* or minū, Paradise. High, sublime.

A منواع minwāʿ, A weaver's beam.

A منوال minwāl, A loom. A weaver's beam. A weaver. Mode, manner, rule, form, constitution, disposition, frame, texture. Propriety, decency, duty, office. على هٰذا المنوال ʿala' hāzā'l minwāl, In this manner, according to this fashion. هم على منوال واحد hum ʿala' minwālin wāhidin, They are of one disposition; they are similar in genius and manners. منوالك ان تفعل كذا minwāluka an tafʿal kazā, It behoves you to do that.

A منوة munwat, A space of ten or fifteen days after a camel has been covered, during which it is uncertain whether she has conceived or not.

A منوّرة munūwat, Desire; a wished-for object.

A منوّج mansuj, Turned, twisted, distorted.

P منوچهر minū-chihr, Of a heavenly countenance. Of high degree. Name of the son of ايرج īraj, and seventh king of the Peshdādian dynasty; also name of an ancient chief.

A منوح manūh, (A camel) giving milk in winter.

A منودل munawdil, An old man tottering with infirmity, feeble in the limbs.

A منور manwar, Name of a place or mountain. ذات منور zātu manwarin, A palpable blow, a throw or shot conspicuous to all.

A منوّر munawwar, Illuminated, enlightened, elucidated, explained, illustrated, clear, splendid, bright, brilliant. منوّر القلب munawwaru'l kalb, Of an enlightened heart; serene, intelligent. P منوّر كردن munawwar kardan, To illuminate. A *Munawwir*, An illuminator. Illuminative. (See تنوير.)

A منوّس munawwis, (A date) becoming black at the extremity.

P منوشان manoshān, Name of one of the governors of Persia in the reign of Kay Khusraw. Cause not thou to drink.

A منوط manūt, Dependent, fastened, bound, belonging to, attached, tied. Admitted, allowed entrance, adopted.

A منوع manūʿ, A hinderer, preventer, refuser. *Munūʿ*, (pl. of منع manʿ) Crabs.

A منوّق munawwak, Trained, broke in (camel). (A female palm) sprinkled and fructified by the male-flowers. Placed in order, ranged in a row.

A منول minwal, A weaver's beam.

A منوّم munawwim, Narcotic, soporific, sedative.

A منون manūn, Time, age. Death, fate. One who confers many favours, and lays under many obligations. One who upbraids very much with benefits conferred. A wealthy woman married on account of her dowry, and who lays her husband under many obligations. A liar. (in the dialect of Morocco) A yellow kind of melon. *Manūna*, (pl. of من man) What persons?

A منوّن munawwan, Marked with تنوين tanwīn.

A منونة manūnat, Reproachful, one who upbraids or casts in the teeth. One who confers many favours, and lays under numerous obligations. A spider.

A منؤوشة mansūshat, Lean (she-camel).

A منوي manawīy, Belonging to the idol مناة.

P منه manah, The lower jaw, the chin.

A منها minhā, (literally, From that) Deduction, subtraction. P منها ساختن minhā sākhtan, To subtract (in arithmetic).

A منهأ munhaʾ, Half-dressed meat.

A منهاة manhāt, Intelligent, prudent (man).

A منهاج minhāj, An open road; a wide street; highway. حجاج هدايت منهاج hujjāji hidāyat-minhāj, Pilgrims on the right road.

A منهاض munhāz, (A bone) broken anew after having been set and knit.

A منهاع munhāʿ, Prone, hastening to evil.

A منهال minhāl, One who irritates or provokes greatly. A heap of sand continually rolling or sliding down. Great munificence. The grave. Very liberal. *Munhāl*, Poured out under a certain measure.

A منهام minhām, (pl. مناهيم manāhīm) (A she-camel) obedient to the word.

A منهائي manhāʾī, Forbidding, prohibition. *Minhāʾī*, Subtracted, deducted. Unassessed land.

A منهب minhab, Swift (horse), beating others. *Munhib*, One who gives to be plundered.

A منهبص munhabis, Immoderate in laughter.

A منهبط munhabit, Depressed, falling.

A منهت munhit or minhat, Roaring: a roarer. المنهت al munhit or al minhat, A lion.

A منهتك munhatik, Torn, cut. Careless and unconcerned about one's character.

A منهج manhaj, Road, highway: way, manner. P منهج فرمان برداري manhaji farmān-bardārī, The path of obedience.

A منهّد munahhid, Swelling-breasted (girl).

A منهدّ munhadd, Broken, rent (as a mountain by an earthquake).

A منهدغ munhadagh, A sip of spoon-meat.

A منهدم munhadam, Symmetrically formed. *Munhadim*, Demolished, destroyed.

A منهدن munhadin, One who relaxes (from study, or from any plan or resolution).

A منهر manhar, A place excavated by a flux of water. The pipe of a conduit or reservoir, through which the water runs. A gutter or conduit by which water is brought into a fort. *Munhir*, One who digs till he arrives at water. Who lets (blood) flow. (A vein) bleeding excessively, so as not to be stopt. One who enlarges, widens. A maker of a deep or large wound. A doer of any thing in the day-time. (A horse) relaxing his speed. One who obtains nothing good. (See انهار inhār.)

A منهرة manharat, A place in a court-yard of a house where rubbish is thrown; a dust-hole.

A منهريج munharij, Overcome by beer or wine.

A منهز munhaz, The outside (of a well), the station of a camel when employed in drawing water for the purpose of irrigating fields or gardens.

A منهزع munhaziʿ, Broken, pounded, crumbled.

A منهزم munhazim, Put to flight, running away, discomfited in battle. Pressed inwards, rendered hollow by pressure. (A stick) broken with a loud crash. P منهزم ساختن munhazim sākhtan, To rout. منهزم و تار و مار كردن munhazim u tār u mār kardan, To rout, defeat, disperse. A منهزماً munhaziman, Dispersedly, like defeated men.

A منهس manhas, A place out of which one eats. *Minhas*, A lion.

A منهشم munhashim, Broken. Weak, languid (camel). Withered (herb).

A منهصر munhasir, Beaten, trampled, or trodden. Drawn, attracted. Bent, twisted.

A منهضّ munhazz, Bruised, crumbled, pounded.

A منهضم munhazim, Wrapt close, not appearing from the buds (palm-flower). Well-digested (food).

A منهفت munhafit, Depressed. Diminished.

A منهفك munhafik, One who errs and blunders much. One who goes totteringly, weakly, languidly.

A منهقع munhakiʿ, Hungry. Gaunt-bellied.

A منهك munhakk, Overcome with wine. Expanded in the birth (about the flanks). (A camel) reclining on the ground.

A منهكّة munhakkat, (A woman) bringing forth with difficulty.

A منهل manhal, (v. n. of نهل) Drinking, quenching the thirst; drinking the first draught. A watering-place in a field, a horse-pond. A halting-place in the desert. A draught that quenches thirst. A tomb, sepulchre, tumulus, grave. Extremely munificent. Great munificence. *Munhil*, One who drinks. One who has camels satisfied with drinking. One who inflames with rage.

A منهلّ *munhall*, (Rain) descending with great violence. (Eyes) flowing with tears.

A منهلت *munhalit*, Gone far. Forgetful. Heedless, inattentive.

A منهلك *munhalik*, One who throws himself into danger, or in the way of destruction.

A منهمّ *munhamm*, Melted (fat or hailstone). Pining, wasted with age, grief, or care. Waxed old.

A منهمة *manhamat*, A carpenter's shop.

A منهمر *munhamir*, (Water) poured out, flowing. Destroyed, falling to ruin. Stripped (branch).

A منهمز *munhamiz*, Squeezed, pressed. Hamzated.

A منهمس *munhamis*, Hidden, concealed.

A منهمك *munhamik*, Laborious, pains-taking.

A منهمل *munhamil*, (An eye) suffused with tears.

A منهوب *manhūb*, Snatched away by force.

A منهوس *manhūs*, Lean (man). منهوس القدمين *manhūsu'l kadamayn*, Spare of flesh on the soles of the feet.

A منهوش *manhūsh*, Oppressed with poverty and misfortune. Tired with travelling. Slender. منهوش القدمين *manhūshu'l kadamayn*, One whose feet have little flesh upon them.

A منهوك *manhūk*, Debilitated, afflicted with continued disease. In the metre called رجز *rajaz*, when two-thirds of the verse have been taken away and one-third is left. *Munhawik*, Astonished, stupefied. Fallen into difficulties from inattention.

A منهوم *manhūm*, Very greedy (of food, money, or science).

A منهي *munhī*, One who announces news. P منهيان ربع مسكون *munhiyāni rubʿi maskūn*, The planets Saturn, Jupiter, Mars, the sun, Venus, Mercury, and the moon.

A منهّي *munahhī*, One who forbids or warns.

A منهيّ *manhīy*, Forbidden.

A منهيات *manhīyāt*, Unlawful, forbidden things.

A مني *many*, (v. n. of مني) Defining, apportioning. Trying, proving, afflicting. A seminal effusion. *Muny*, (v. n. of مني) Being tried and proved. (pl. of منيّ *manīy* and منية *manyat*) Seminal fluids. *Manaʾ*, Death. The Divine decree. Measure, quantity. Design, intention. *Minaʾ*, Name of a valley nigh unto Mecca where sacrifices are offered up. The seminal fluid (of man or woman). *Munaʾ*, (pl. of منية *munyat*) Desires, wishes, aspirations.

P مني *manī*, Presumption, boasting, egotism. Egoism, or that sufficiency in himself and independence of other beings which is peculiar to the Deity.

A منيّ *manīy*, (pl. مني *muny*) The seminal fluid of man or woman. *Manīy* or *munīy*, (pl. of منا *manaʾ*) Weights of two pounds.

A منيب *munīb*, A copious rain. A favourable spring-season. Master, patron. Client, constituent.

A منية *manyat*, (pl. مني *muny*) Seminal fluid. *Munyat*, (in Egypt) A village. *Munyat* or *minyat*, (pl. منى *munaʾ*) Wish, desire. منية الناقة *munyatu'n* (or *minyatu'n*) *nākat*, The wish for the camel, *i. e.* fifteen days after she has been covered, when it is uncertain whether she is pregnant or not.

A منيّة *manīyat*, (pl. منايا *manāyaʾ*) Death, fate. Any thing definite in time and manner. The providence of God. بحيرة المنيّة *baḥīratu'l manīyat*, Sea of Tiberias. بنت المنيّة *bintu'l manīyat*, Echo.

A منيح *manīḥ*, A giver. An arrow entitled to nothing. An arrow borrowed, because regarded as lucky. An arrow entitled to a prize.

A منيحة *manīḥat*, (pl. منائح *manāʼiḥ*) (A she-camel) lent in order to be milked. An animal whose wool, milk, or young one is given without being required again.

A منيخ *munīkh*, A lion.

P منيد *maned*, Ye are to me: as, هوادار منيد *hawā-dāri maned*, Ye are well-wishers to me.

A منيذا *munayzan*, (dim. of منذ *munz*) From.

A منير *munīr*, Shining, splendid, illuminating.

A منيّر *munayyar*, Thick (skin). (A garment) marked with a double stripe.

P منيژه *maneja*, Name of Afrāsyāb's daughter.

A منيع *manīʿ*, Inaccessible, impregnable.

A منيف *minsaf*, Diligent, pains-taking.

A منيف *munīf*, Eminent, exalted, high, lofty.

A منيم *munīm*, One who appeases, quiets, or lulls to sleep.

A منين *manayn*, (ob. of منان *manāni*) What two? *Manīn*, Weak. A weak rope. A strong man. Dust.

A منّيني *minnīnaʾ*, (v. n. of منّ) Conferring a benefit. A reproaching or casting in the teeth.

P منيوش *manyosh*, Do not hearken, listen not.

A منيوكة *manyūkat*, (A woman) lain with.

A منيئة *manīʾat*, An untanned, but soaked hide. A tan-pit.

P مو *maw*, The mewing of a cat. *Mū* or *mo*, Hair. A crack in a cup. Exactness, precision. موي زنگي *mūyi zangī*, The hair of an Ethiop. موي سفيد *mūyi safed*, White or grey hairs. مو دادن *mū dādan*, (or مو فرستادن *mū firistādan*) To send a hair in a letter (a mode by which a despairing inamorato apprises a lady, to whom he cannot gain access, of his emaciated condition). پرمو *pur-mū*, Hairy, full of hair. سنبل مو *sumbul-mū*, One who has hair like the hyacinth, odoriferous, and gently waving. مسكين مو *miskīn-mū*, Having musky ringlets, fragrant, and black, like that perfume.

A مو *mū*, The herb spignell.

A موء *mūs*, (or مواء *muwāʾ*) Mewing (of a cat).

A مواءلة *muwāʾalat*, (v. n. 3 of وأل) Endeavouring to fly, hastening in order to escape.

A مواءمة *muwāʾamat*, (v. n. 3 of وأم) Consenting, agreeing, doing the like. Disputing, contending for glory.

A موابذة *mawābizat*, (pl. of موبذ *mawbaz*) Priests of the Magi. موابذة الحلّ والعقد *mawābizatu'l hall wa'l ʿahd*, Lords of loosing and binding, able critics.

A موابلة *muwābalat*, Assiduity, attention.

A موات *mawāt*, Lifeless. A desert, waste ground from which a man can derive no profit, and not owned. The dead; corpses. *Muwāt*, Death.

A مواتاة *muwātāt*, (v. n. 3 of اتي) Consenting, agreeing with, stipulating. Obeying, being obsequious. Favouring, helping.

A مواتر *muwātir*, (A camel) which first puts down one knee and then the other in kneeling (a practice extremely incommoding to the rider).

A مواترة *muwātarat*, (v. n. 3 of وتر) Prosecuting or doing (any thing) at intervals (مداركة *mudārakat* implying whatever is pursued without intermission); fasting every alternate day. Putting down one knee after another when kneeling (a camel). Bringing (books), despatching (letters) one after another.

A مواتنة *muwātanat*, Assiduity, fixedness.

A مواتي *muwātī*, Flexible (bow).

A مواثبة *muwāsabat*, (v. n. 3 of وثب) Leaping or rushing upon (one another).

A مواثر *mawāsir*, (pl. of ميثرة *mīsarat*) Whatever things are thrown over the saddle to make the seat more easy. Outer garments.

A مؤاثرة *muʾāsarat*, (v. n. 3 of اثر) Choosing, preferring. Causing to follow or come in the track.

A مواثق *mawāsik*, Agreements, covenants. *Muwāsik*, Confederate.

A مواثقة *muwāsakat*, (v. n. 3 of وثق) Entering into a confederacy.

A مؤاثم *muʾāsim*, One who, having gone, comes not back.

A مواثمة *muwāsamat*, (v. n. 3 of وثم) Running a race, contending in swiftness. Exercising mutual patience.

A مؤاثي *muʾāsī*, A malevolent adversary.

A مواثيق *mawāsīk*, (pl. of ميثاق *mīsāk*) Agreements, confederacies, pacts, compacts.

A موّاج *mawwāj*, Stormy, billowy, surgy.

A مواجب *mawājib*, Salaries, pensions, rewards, hires. Rights, dues, wages. Places for wrestlers.

A مواجبة *muwājabat*, A rendering obligatory.

A مؤاجرة *muʾājarat*, (v. n. 3 of اجر) Paying the hire for labour. Hiring, making an agreement, contracting for labour. Letting out on hire.

A مؤاجلة *muʾājalat*, (v. n. 3 of اجل) Hindering, detaining, throwing obstacles in the way.

A مواجلة *muwājalat*, (v. n. 3 of وجل) Being afraid of. Contending or vying with in being afraid.

A مواجهة *muwājahat*, (v. n. 3 of وجه) Meeting face to face, coming before (another); beholding, confronting; conferring; laying (one thing with another). Presence, appearance. Opposition of two stars or planets. مواجهة *muwājahatan*, (or بالمواجهة *bi'l muwājaha*) Before, in presence of.

A مواجير *mawājīr*, (pl. of ميجار) Clubs, beetles.

A مواحف *mawāhif*, Places where (camels) lie.

A مواحق *mawāhik*, (pl. of ماحق) Sharp swords.

A مواحلة *muwāhalat*, (v. n. 3 of وحل) Rolling (one) in the mire (وحل *wahl*), bemiring.

A مؤاحنة *mu,āhanat*, (v. n. 3 of احن) Being inimical, malevolent. Hatred, dislike, enmity.

A مواحيد *mawāhīd*, (pl. of ميحاد) Single objects (as hillocks) separated from other similar objects.

A مؤاخاة *mu,ākhāt*, (v. n. 3 of اخا for اخو) Entering into a brotherhood. Fraternity, brotherly love; intimate friendship.

A مؤاخذ *mu,ākhaz*, Chastised, punished, reprehended, reproved, rebuked, taken to task.

A مؤاخذة *mu,ākhazat*, (v. n. 3 of اخذ) Taking satisfaction, retaliating, calling to account. Chastising, blaming, reproaching, reproving, rebuking.

A مواخر *mawākhir*, (pl. of ماخرة *mākhirat*) (Ships) ploughing the ocean with noise, or advancing and receding with one wind. (pl. of ماخور *mākhūr*) Taverns, gaming-houses, or brothels.

A مؤاخرة *mu,ākharat*, (v. n. 3 of اخر) Postponing, delaying. Putting behind. Rejecting.

A مواخض *mawākhiz*, (pl. of ماخض *mākhiz*) Travailing (women, camels, or sheep).

A مواخمة *muwākhamat*, (v. n. 3 of وخم) Comparing notes (with another) to see who suffered most from indigestion or who is heavier.

A مواخير *mawākhīr*, (pl. of ماخور *mākhūr*) Taverns. Frequenters of taverns.

A موادّ *mawādd*, (pl. of مادّة *māddat*) Matters, points. موادّ صلح *mawāddi sulh*, Articles of peace.

A موادّة *muwāddat*, (v. n. 3 of ودّ) Loving one another. Mutual love or esteem.

A موادع *mawādiʻ*, (pl. of ميدع) Every-day clothes.

A موادعة *muwādaʻat*, (v. n. 3 of ودع) Quieting, reconciling, returning to favour, making peace.

A مؤادمة *mu,ādamat*, (v. n. 3 of ادم) Being united in friendship and amity.

A مؤادي *mu,ādī*, Strong, powerful. Accoutred.

A مؤاراة *mu,ārāt*, (v. n. 3 of اري) Tying up a beast to feed in the same stall (آريّ *āriy*) with another.

A موارات *muwārāt*, (v. n. 3 of وري) Hiding. Burying.

A مؤارب *mu,ārib*, A cunning fellow, deceiver.

A مؤاربة *mu,ārabat*, (v. n. 3 of ارب) Conquering, overcoming. Deceiving.

A مواربة *muwārabat*, (v. n. 3 of ورب) Conquering, overpowering. Acting basely (with a friend), endeavouring to circumvent him.

A موارة *muwārat*, Wool which fall from a sheep dead or alive. Whatever falls from wool when plucked or teased.

A موّارة *mawwārat*, Easy-paced (she-camel).

A مؤارخة *mu,ārakhat*, (v. n. 3 of ارخ) Dating.

A موارد *mawārid*, (pl. of مورد *mawrid*) Passes, entrances. Places where people descend; stations. Places where they draw water. موارد الهلك *mawāridu'l hulk*, Fatal expeditions. موارد مطروقه *mawāridi matrūka*, Turbid or befouled waters. مصادر و موارد *masādir u mawārid*, Places where learned men meet. موارد و مداخل *mawārid u madākhil*, (and موارد و مدارج *mawārid u madārij*) Passages, entrances, and exits, ingress and egress.

A مواردة *muwāradat*, (v. n. 3 of ورد) Coming to a watering-place together.

A موارع *mawāriʻ*, Men of the tribe of مارعة.

A موارعة *muwāraʻat*, (v. n. 3 of ورع) Discoursing, conferring, conversing, consulting with.

A مؤارف *mu,ārif*, Adjoining, adjacent, nigh unto, contiguous; an immediate neighbour.

A مؤارفة *mu,ārafat*, (v. n. 3 of ارف) Being adjacent to, bordering upon, being separated by the same marches.

A موارق *muwārik*, Near.

A موارقة *muwārakat*, A being near, approaching.

A موارکة *muwārakat*, (v. n. 3 of ورك) Passing (a mountain).

A مؤارنة *mu,āranat*, (v. n. 3 of ارن) Glorying, boasting, vaunting. (A bull) longing for and following (a cow).

A مواريث *mawārīs*, (pl. of ميراث) Heritages.

A موّاز *mawwāz*, A vender of banana-fruit.

A مؤازاة *mu,āzāt*, (v. n. 3 of ازي) Being parallel, opposite, equi-distant; proportioned, equal to.

A موازاة *muwāzāt*, (v. n. 3 of وزي) Answering, being opposite unto. Coming from any quarter.

A موازج *mawāzij*, (or موازجة *mawāzijat*) (pl. of موزج *mawzaj*) Boots.

A مؤازر *mu,āzir*, A helper, assistant.

A موازر *muwāzir*, The bearer of a load.

A مؤازرة *mu,āzarat*, (v. n. 3 of ازر) Assisting. Answering to, corresponding with, being equal to. Supporting each other by being entangled together (stalks of standing corn). Equality in measure. Strength. Assistance, support.

A موازرة *muwāzarat*, (v. n. 3 of وزر) Governing for a sovereign or chief, being lieutenant or vizier.

A موازفة *muwāzafat*, (v. n. 3 of وزف) Expending equally with, contributing to a common purse.

A موازنة *muwāzanat*, (v. n. 3 of وزن) Comparing (two things). Compensating, requiting. Being equivalent, equalling. Being opposite to, corresponding with. Facing. An equilibrium.

A مؤازي *mu,āzī*, Parallel, exactly opposite, and resembling one another. Equal, nearly, about.

A موازين *mawāzīn*, (pl. of ميزان *mīzān*) Balances, scales.

P مواسا *muwāsā*, Ease, rest. Benevolence, favour.

A مواساة *muwāsāt*, (for مؤاساة *mu,āsāt*) (v. n. 3 of اسى) Doing good, benefiting. Giving one a pattern or exemplar. Condoling with; reviving by consolation, encouraging.

A مواساة *muwāsāt*, (v. n. 3 of وسي) Assisting.

A مواسق *mawāsik*, (or مواسيق *mawāsīk*) (pl. of واسق *wāsik*) Pregnant (camels).

A مواسقة *muwāsakat*, (v. n. 3 of وسق) Opposing (another); resembling, being equal to, or of the same weight.

A مواسم *mawāsim*, (pl. of موسم *mawsim*) Places where pilgrims assemble at Mecca. The fairs there held. (pl. of ميسم *mīsam*) Branding-irons.

A مواسمة *muwāsamat*, (v. n. 3 of وسم) Disputing in point of beauty.

A مواسي *mawāsī*, (pl. of موسى *mūsa'*) Razors.

A مواسيق *mawāsīk*, (pl. of واسق) (Camels) in foal.

A مواشط *mawāshit*, (pl. of ماشطة *māshitat*) Tire-women, combers or dressers (of brides).

A مواشظة *muwāshazat*, (v. n. 3 of وشظ) Rubbing or pressing each other's privy member against each other's belly (two lewd fellows).

A مواشك *muwāshik*, One who goes fast.

A مواشكة *muwāshakat*, A travelling fast.

A مواشل *mawāshil*, Places.

A مواشي *mawāshī*, (pl. of ماشية *māshiyat*) Quadrupeds, especially camels, sheep, cows, calves, and other similar cattle.

A مواشير *mawāshīr*, (pl. of ميشار *mīshār*) Saws.

A مواشيق *mawāshīk*, The teeth of a key.

A مواصة *muwāsat*, Dirty water in which any thing has been washed.

A مؤاصر *mu,āsir*, Near, neighbouring. Friends, companions. جار مؤاصر *jāri mu,āsir*, One whose tent (tent-peg, اصار *isār*) joins another's.

A مؤاصرة *mu,āsarat*, (v. n. 3 of اصر) Being near. Pitching a tent next to another's.

A مواصفة *muwāsafat*, (v. n. 3 of وصف) Buying or selling any thing by description (not by sample). بيع المواصفة *bayʻu'l muwāsafat*, A sale by description (not by sample).

A مواصل *mawāsil*, Ligaments. Certain musical instruments.

A مواصلة *mawāsilat*, Natives of Mesopotamia. *Muwāsalat*, (v. n. 3 of وصل) Being constantly with another; enjoying a beloved object. Doing (any thing) incessantly, without interruption. Conjunction, adhesion, copulation, enjoyment. Interview.

A مؤاضّ *mu,āzz*, Parturient. One who makes haste, or gets the start.

A مواضاة *muwāzaʻat*, (v. n. 3 of وضا) Contending with (another) who is cleanest after performing ablution, vying with in cleanness.

A مواضخة *muwāzakhat*, (v. n. 3 of وضخ) Contending with about drawing water. Rivalling in leaping or moving forwards.

A مواضع *mawāziʻ*, (pl. of موضع *mawziʻ*) Places. Villages. Occurrences.

A مواضعة *muwāzaʻat*, (v. n. 3 of وضع) Wagering, depositing the bets. Leaving, abandoning (a sale). Consenting, assenting. Communicating to each other their respective opinions.

A مواضين *mawāẓīn*, (pl. of ميضنة *mīẓanat*) Sacks made of palm-leaves.

A مواطأة *muwāṭaʼat*, (v. n. 3 of وطئ) Emulating, doing equal with. Repeating the last syllable of a verse. Consenting, agreeing (with another).

A مواطر *mawāṭir*, (pl. of ماطر *māṭir*) Rains.

A مواطن *mawāṭin*, (pl. of موطن *mawṭin*) Countries, native dwellings, habitations. Battle-fields. The stations at Mecca.

A مواطئ *mawāṭiʼ*, (pl. of موطئ *mawṭiʼ*) Footsteps, prints of feet. Footstools.

A مواظب *muwāẓib*, Assiduous, persevering. Constant, incessant. مواظبا *muwāẓiban*, Assiduously, continually.

A مواظبة *muwāẓabat*, (v. n. 3 of وظب) Persevering, being assiduous, sticking close to, minding, attending to. Perseverance, continuance, assiduity.

A مواظفة *muwāẓafat*, (v. n. 3 of وظف) Consenting, agreeing to. Governing for a king or chief. Being assiduous, sticking close to.

A مواعد *mawāʻid*, (pl. of موعدة *mawʻidat*) Places of promise.

A مواعدة *muwāʻadat*, (v. n. 3 of وعد) Promising, plighting faith, appointing time and place. Vying with any one in making promises or threats.

A مواعز *mawāʻiz*, (pl. of ماعز *māʻiz*) Goats.

A مواعسة *muwāʻasat*, (v. n. 3 of وعس) Making a long or forced journey, especially in the night-time. Contending with another in walking. Walking over soft and sandy places. Travelling with a long step and stretched-out neck (a camel).

A مواعظ *mawāʻiẓ*, (pl. of موعظة *mawʻiẓat*) Exhortations, counsels, sermons, homilies. مواعظ و نصائح *mawāʻiẓ u naṣāʼiḥ*, The same.

A مواعظة *muwāʻaẓat*, (v. n. 3 of وعظ) Admonishing, exhorting. Preaching. Instruction.

A مواعيد *mawāʻīd*, (pl. of موعودة) Promises.

A مواعين *mawāʻīn*, (pl. of ماعون) Pots, kettles, &c.

A مواغ *muwāgh*, The mewing (of a cat).

A مواغدة *muwāghadat*, (v. n. 3 of وغد) Imitating, doing the same as another in play; taking equal steps. Moving with an equal pace (a she-camel).

A موافاة *muwāfāt*, (v. n. 3 of وفي) Going on pilgrimage. Coming, approaching, arriving.

A موافق *muwāfiḳ*, One who consents, agrees, approves. Conformable, agreeable, consonant, congruous, suiting, apt, expedient, like, similar, resembling. Equitable. Prosperous, favourable, propitious. P بادموافق *bādi muwāfiḳ*, A favourable wind.

A موافقة *muwāfaḳat*, (v. n. 3 of وفق) Being conformable, consenting, suiting, approving, judging expedient or convenient. Meeting, striking against, stumbling upon, encountering. Imitating, seconding. Conformity, agreement, unanimous consent, concordance, concord, correspondence, consent, sympathy, unanimity, analogy. بحكم الموافقة *bi ḥukmi'l muwāfaḳa*, From a similarity (of their manner, genius, and the like).

A موافقية *muwāfiḳīyat*, Suitableness, congruity.

A مواقة *muwāḳat*, (v. n. of ماق for موق) Being stupid, silly, careless. Perishing. Folly.

A مواقت *mawāḳit*, Stated times or places. Watches, dials.

A مواقتة *muwāḳatat*, (v. n. 3 of وقت) Mentioning or prescribing a fixed time (وقت *waḳt*).

A مواقذ *mawāḳiẕ*, (pl. of موقذ *mawḳiẕ*) Extremities, prominent bones (as of the elbow, knee, heel, or shoulder).

A مواقر *mawāḳir*, (pl. of موقر *mūḳar* and موقرة *mūḳarat*) (Trees) laden with fruit. Heavy laden. Pregnant (women).

A مواقع *mawāḳiʻ*, Accidents, occurrences, contingencies. مواقع الغيث *mawāḳiʻu'l ghays*, Places where rain falls.

A مواقعة *muwāḳaʻat*, (v. n. 3 of وقع) Rushing on (the enemy), attacking (in battle), fighting. Lying with. Assault, attack, conflict.

A مواقف *mawāḳif*, (pl. of موقف) Stations, posts.

A مواقفة *muwāḳafat*, (v. n. 3 of وقف) Standing (for another). Assisting, aiding. Standing in a place with another transacting business. Asking one to stop and pause.

A مواقي *mawāḳī*, (pl. of ماقي) Inner corners of eyes.

A مواقيت *mawāḳīt*, (pl. of ميقات) Stated times.

A مواقير *mawāḳīr*, pl. of ميقار, Loaded (palm-trees).

A مواكب *mawākib*, (pl. of موكب *mawkib*) Troops, legions, armies. مواكب كواكب *mawākibi kawākib*, Legions of stars.

A مواكبة *muwākabat*, (v. n. 3 of وكب) Riding (with another) (especially on a camel); trying who rides fastest. Being assiduous, diligent, and persevering (in any thing). *Muwākibat*, Wide-stepping, fast-going (she-camel).

A مواكدة *muwākidat*, (A she-camel) which goes very quick. Tired (she-camel).

A مؤاكرة *muʼākarat*, A giving land to sow.

A مواكظة *muwākaẓat*, (v. n. 3 of وكظ) Sticking close to, being constantly engaged about.

A مواكعة *muwākaʻat*, (v. n. 3 of وكع) Treading (as the cock a hen).

A مواكفة *muwākafat*, (v. n. 3 of وكف) Opposing an enemy in battle, assaulting him.

A مؤاكل *muʼākil*, Mess-mate, fellow-commoner.

A مواكل *muwākil*, Weak, unequal to any business, and therefore intrusting it to another.

A مؤاكلة *muʼākalat*, (v. n. 3 of اكل) Eating together; eating with one another.

A مواكلة *muwākalat*, (v. n. 3 of وكل) Trusting (to one another); having mutual confidence. Going heavily (a horse).

A مؤاكمة *muʼākamat*, Large-hipped (woman).

A موالاة *muwālāt*, (v. n. 3 of ولي) Being a lover, friend, assistant. Continuing or following without intermission. Restoring (any person to his office). Separating (sheep) by way of distinction. Friendship, love, affection. Mutual amity. Patronage, clientage. Continuation. Mutual necessity.

A موألة *mawʼalat*, A place of refuge.

A موالج *mawālij*, Places into which one enters.

A موالد *mawālid*, (pl. of مولد) Travailing (women).

A موالس *muwālis*, A deceiver.

A مؤالسة *muʼālasat*, (v. n. 3 of الس) Being perfidious, unfaithful.

A موالسة *muwālasat*, (v. n. 3 of ولس) Relating (a thing) obscurely and ambiguously. Dissembling, acting hypocritically. Fraud, treachery.

A مؤالفة *muʼālafat*, (v. n. 3 of الف) Agreeing with any one by the thousand (الف *alf*). Rendering familiar, accustoming, habituating.

A موالفة *muwālafat*, (v. n. 3 of ولف) Being familiar. Coming together. Being near. Claiming relationship.

A موالون *muwālūn*, (pl. of موالي) Helpers.

A موالي *mawālī*, (pl. of مولى *mawlaʼ*) Lords, princes. Judges. موالي العظام *mawālī'l ʻiẓām*, Great, wise judges. *Muwālī*, An assistant, defender.

A مواليا *muwāliyan*, In a continued series.

A مواليد *mawālīd*, (pl. of مولد *mūlid*) (Women) in travail. (pl. of مولود *mawlūd*) Sons. مواليد ثلاثة *mawālīdi salāsa*, (or P مواليد سه گانه *mawālīdi sih-gāna*, The three kingdoms of nature, animal, vegetable, and mineral.

A موأم *muwaʼʼam*, Large-headed and deformed.

A مؤام *muʼāmm*, Approaching near. Clear, evident. Consenting, agreeable.

A مواماة *muwāmaʼat*, A consenting, agreeing to.

A مؤمة *mawʼamat*, An iron helmet without any clasps to connect it with the coat of mail.

A مؤامة *muʼāmmat*, A being near, approaching.

A مؤامر *muʼāmir*, One who consults, asks counsel.

A مؤامرة *muʼāmarat*, A consulting, advising.

A موامي *mawāmīy*, (pl. of موماء *mawmāʼ* or موماة *mawmāt*) Deserts.

A مواميس *mawāmīs*, (pl. of مومسة *mūmisat*) Immodest (women).

A موانات *muwānāt*, (v. n. 3 of وني, not used) Doing (any thing) with equal torpor and fatigue.

A موانحة *muwānaḥat*, (v. n. 3 of ونح) Consenting to, agreeing with.

A مؤانس *muʼānis*, Familiar, accustomed to.

A مؤانسة *muʼānasat*, (v. n. 3 of انس) Cultivating an intimacy, keeping company, conversing, living under the same roof with. Custom, familiarity, society, intimacy, companionship, fellowship.

A موانع *mawāniʻ*, Impediments, hindrances.

A مؤاوبة *muʼāwabat*, (v. n. 3 of آب for اوب) Striving against another in travelling.

A مواهب *mawāhib*, (pl. of موهبة *mawhabat*)

Ditches. (pl. of موهبة mawhabat or mawhibat) Gifts.

A مواهبة muwāhabat, A contending in liberality.

A مواهة muwāhat, Beauty of countenance.

A مواهسة muwāhasat, A going very quick.

A مواهقة muwāhakat, (v. n. 3 of وهق) Emulating, imitating, doing as another. Extending the neck in travelling (a camel).

A مواهيب mawāhib, (pl. of موهوب mawhūb) Things presented.

A موائد mawāʼid, (pl. of مؤيد muʼyid) Great events; mishaps. (pl. of مائدة māʼidat) Tables, especially covered with meats.

A مؤايدة muʼāyadat, (v. n. 3 of آد for ايد) Strengthening, infusing fresh vigour, assisting.

A مؤايسة muʼāyasat, A driving to desperation.

A موائل mawāʼil, pl. of مائلة, Bending (branches).

A مؤبات muʼabāt, Shameful, disgraceful things.

P موباف mū-bāf, A hair-ribbon.

P موبد mūbid, mawbad, or mūbad, A worshipper of the sun, one of the Magi, Pārsis, or Guebres, especially one of their priests. A doctor, philosopher, any man of great wisdom whose sayings are quoted. One who administers justice; a judge, especially of the Jews. A vazir, a counsellor of state. Name of the husband of Vīsa.

A مؤبد muʼabbad, Eternal, perpetual.

A مؤبدة muʼabbadat, Untractable (she-camel).

A موبذ mawbaz, (mūbiz, mūbaz, and موبذان mūbazān) (pl. موابذة mawābizat) A priest or learned doctor of the Magi.

A مؤبر muʼabbar, Made fruitful. Muʼabbir, One who fructifies the female palm-tree by sprinkling over it the male flowers.

A موبر muwabbar, (A female palm-tree) sprinkled with the flowers of the male.

P موبرج mūbarij, (in Shīrāz) Berberis.

A مؤبش muʼabbish, A collector, mixer. One who hears or pronounces a confused speech.

A مؤبط muʼabbit, (God) humbling (any one).

A موبق mawbik, (v. n. of وبق) Perishing. A dangerous or fatal place. A prison. The valley of Gehenna, where they sacrificed children to Moloch. A time or place of promise. An interstice, interval, whatever separates two things, or proves destructive. Mūbak, Destroyed, ruined. Imprisoned.

A موبل mawbil, A staff. A bundle of faggots.

A مؤبل muʼabbal, Rich in camels. Name of a poet in Spain. ابل مؤبلة ibilun muʼabbalatun, Camels acquired. Camels drawn and picked out for breeding and milking. Muʼabbil, One who procures camels (by birth or otherwise). One who fattens. A mourner bewailing (one dead).

P مو بمو mū ba mū, Hair by hair. Countless.

A مؤبن muʼabbin, A traducer, censurer, calumniator. A follower of another's steps. An observer. One who praises and bewails (the dead). One who bleeds an animal in order to dress and eat the blood (a practice in Arabia in scarce times).

A موبوءة mawbūʼat, (A land) much afflicted with the pestilence (وباء wabaʼ).

A موبول mawbūl, Watered by a heavy shower.

A مؤبه muʼabbih, One who recals to memory. One who reverences, honours, magnifies.

A موبئ mūbiʼ, Little and exhausted (water).

A مؤبي muʼabbī, Who calls (any one) father.

A موبئة mūbiʼat, (A land) afflicted with plague.

A موت mawt, (v. n. of مات for موت) Dying. Resting, reposing, sleeping. Waxing old. Death.

P موت گرفتن mawt giriftan, To brave death.

A موتا mawtā, (in construction for موتي mawta') The dead.

A مؤتاب muʼtāb, One who returns or comes.

P موتاب mū-tāb, A hair-rope maker.

A موتاد mawtād, (for معتاد muʼtād,) Quantity.

A موتان mūtān or mawtān, A deadly distemper amongst cattle. موتان الفؤاد mawtānu'l fuʼād, (fem. موتانة الفؤاد mawtānatu'l fuʼād) Stupid and foolish. Mawatān, Dead stock (as houses or lands). Uncultivated land.

A مؤتب muʼattab, Crooked, bent, distorted, wry (in the back, eye, or nail). Muʼattib, Clothed with the garment called اتب itb.

A مؤتبثة muʼtabisat, A bottle filled with milk and left to swell.

A مؤتبض muʼtabiz, Injured in the tendon of the thigh (اباض ibāz), and having the leg contracted. مؤتبض النسا muʼtabizu'n nasa', A crow.

A مؤتبل muʼtabil, Unsteadily seated on a camel, riding badly. Careless in pasturing camels.

A مؤتة muʼtat, Name of a place east of Damascus, where swords were formerly made.

A موتة mūtat, A fainting-fit, in which the subject is apparently dead, but returns to life. Madness. Epilepsy.

A مؤتثجة muʼtasijat, (Land) abundant in forage.

A مؤتثئ muʼtasiʼ, Indisposed to eat, not hungry. One who has eaten much, and when thirsty is unable to quench his thirst with water.

A مؤتثي muʼtasī, Who over-eats till he is thirsty.

A مؤتجر muʼtajir, Hired; a hired servant. A receiver of wages (اجرة ujrat).

A مؤتخذ muʼtakhiz, A taker, receiver, selector, chooser. One who prepares (victuals). A beginner. Humble, submissive. (See ائتخاذ iʼtikhāz.)

A مؤتد muʼattad, Libidinous (man).

A موتر mūtar, Strung (bow).

A مؤتر muʼtarr, One who causes to make haste.

A مؤترق muʼtarik, Sleepless, unable to sleep.

A مؤترك muʼtarik, Arrived at perfection (the tree اراك arāk), i. e. when become thick and firm, and its first fruit come to maturity; numerous and entangled (trees of this species).

A مؤتري muʼtarī, Honey-baking (bee).

A مؤتزر muʼtazar, The girding-place, the waist. Muʼtazir, One who puts on the breeches ازار izār.

A موتزم mūtazam, Earth, ground.

A مؤتسي muʼtasī, An imitator: who takes after.

A مؤتشب muʼtashab, Of a mixed race, not pure. Muʼtashib, Mixed (people).

A مؤتشر muʼtashir, Who asks one to sharpen or thin his teeth (a female profession in Arabia).

A مؤتشي muʼtashī, (A broken bone) set and become sound.

A مؤتض muʼtazz, Compelled, forced.

A مؤتعد muʼtaʼid, One who recieves, or is gratified by a promise.

A موتعد mūtaʼid, What threatens mischief.

A مؤتفظ muʼtafiz, Necessary.

A مؤتفك muʼtafik, Overthrown (by an earthquake). A liar.

A مؤتفكات muʼtafikāt, The cities of the plain overthrown in the time of Lot. Winds blowing from different points, and promoting the earth's fertility.

A مؤتقط muʼtakit, One who uses a substitute (as flour and unripe grape juice) for اقط akit. A maker of the new cheese اقط akit.

A مؤتك muʼtakk, Boiling, raging. Hot (day). (See ائتكاك iʼtikāk.)

A مؤتكل muʼtakil, Eaten, corroded, worn (horn or tooth of an animal). Enraged.

A موتلخة mūtalikhat, Ground thickly covered.

A موتلع القلب mūtalaʼu'l kalb, Disturbed, agitated, chicken-hearted.

A مؤتلف muʼtalif, United, associated, familiar.

A مؤتلي muʼtalī, A swearer, taker of an oath.

A موتم mūtim, (pl. مياتيم mayātīm) A mother of fatherless children.

A مؤتم muʼtamm, Taken for a leader, model, guide, or exemplar. Muʼtimm, A follower, imitator. One who chooses as a leader or president.

A مؤتمر muʼtamir, Obsequious, submissive, obedient. One who follows what is agreeable to the mind. Who consults or asks advice. The last of the days called ايام العجوز ayyāmu'l ʼajūz. (pl. مامر maʼāmir and مامير maʼāmīr) The first month of the Muhammadan year called محرم muharram.

A مؤتمن muʼtaman, Believed. A curator, any person trusted in whom one is safe and secure. One of the titles of God. Muʼtamin, One who trusts to, confides in, or devolves his affairs to the management of another.

A موتن mūtin, (and موتنة mūtinat) (A woman or any female) that brings forth her young with the feet foremost.

A مؤتنب muʼtanib, One with no desire for food.

A مؤتنف muʼtanaf, A place yet ungrazed. جارية مؤتنفة الشباب jāriyat muʼtanafatu'sh shabāb, A young girl approaching to the age of puberty. Muʼtanif, One who sets about (a thing) from the beginning: beginner. Approaching, arriving; future.

A موتود mawtūd, Driven (stake).

A موتور *mawtūr*, Negligent in revenging a friend's death; or unable to do it, though desirous.

A مؤتول *muʼtawil*, One who administers or manages well, who arranges properly.

A موتون *mawtūn*, Hurt in the vein وتين *watīn*.

A مؤتوي *muʼtawī*, One who receives hospitably. Tender, compassionate, moved, condoling, pitying.

P موته جنگلي *mawta jangalī*, The root of a species of grass.

A موتيٰ *mawta'*, (pl. of ميّت *mayyit*) Deceased, defunct: the dead.

A مؤتي *muʼtī*, A bringer, adducer.

A موث *maws*, (*mawas*, or موثان *mawasān*) (v. n. of ماث for موث) Mixing. Soaking, steeping, dissolving (in water).

A موثبان *mawsabān*, One who delays an expedition; sedentary, indolent (king).

A موثّخ *muwassakh*, Weak, flaccid, flabby.

A مؤثر *muʼsir*, A chooser. One who prefers another's interest to his own.

A مؤثّر *muʼassar*, Penetrated, affected. *Muʼassir*, Whatever penetrates or impresses; efficacious.

A مؤثّف *muʼassaf*, Short of stature, squat, fleshy, juicy, and corpulent. *Muʼassif*, One who supports on a tripod; one who puts (the pot) on a trivet.

A مؤثفة *muʼsafat*, (A pot) placed on a trivet.

A موثق *mawsik*, (v. n. of وثق) Trusting, confiding in, relying upon. A treaty, compact. *Mūsak*, Bound, tied, firmly knit together.

A موثّق *muwassak*, Gifted with a strong constitution of body. Trusted, confided in, relied upon.

A موثقة *mawsakat*, (v. n. of وثق) Trusting to.

A مؤثّل *muʼassal*, Firmly rooted. Of a noble race. مال مؤثّل *māli muʼassal*, A principal sum; a capital in trade.

A مؤثم *muʼsim*, Who or what compels or induces (any one) to commit a sin or crime (اثم *ism*).

A مؤثّم *muʼassim*, An accuser, reproacher.

A موثن *mūsin*, One who bestows liberally. A taker of much (wealth) or many (cattle).

A موثوءة *mawsuʼat*, (or موثوّة) Sprained (hand).

A موثوجة *mawsūjat*, Loosely-woven (cloth).

A موثوخ *mawsūkh*, Weak, flabby.

A موثوغة *mawsūghat*, (A cake, a pancake, or dough) folded into several plies.

A موثوق *mawsūk*, Tied, fastened. Firm, constant. P ياران موثوق بهم *yārāni mawsūkun bihim*, Faithful friends.

A موثول *mawsūl*, Conjoined, sticking, adhering.

A موثونة *mawsūnat*, Vile, base, mean (woman).

A موثيّ *mawsīy*, Sprained (hand).

A موج *mawj*, (v. n. of ماج for موج) Being agitated (as the sea), rolling in billows. Being tumultuous (men). Deviation from the right way. (pl. امواج *amwāj*) A wave, surge, billow. Whim, caprice. موج نسيم *mawji nasīm*, A cooling squall.

A مؤوّج *muʼj*, (v. n. of مأج) Moving (the knee-pan) backward and forward.

P موجان *mūjān*, A beautiful, languishing eye.

A موجب *mūjab*, Affirmative (proposition). *Mūjib*, Who or what renders necessary or obligatory. Cause, motive, reason, account. An acceptor, receiver. The month Muharram. P موجب اطمئنان قلوب آدميان *mūjibi itmiʼnāni kulūbi ādamiyān*, The cause of tranquillity to the hearts of men. موجب عبرت كردن *mūjibi ʻibrat kardan*, To give as an example. A عمل خير موجب الثواب *ʻamali khayri mūjibu's sawāb*, A good action, worthy of a reward. من غير موجب *min ghayr mūjib*, Without reason or fault. موجب السائلين *mūjibu's sāʼilīn*, A hearer or receiver of petitions. بلا موجب *bilā mūjib*, Without a cause.

A موجّب *muwajjib*, One who eats once only in twenty-four hours. A camel having biestings coagulated in the udder.

A موجبات *mūjibāt*, (pl. fem.) Causes.

A موجبة *mūjibat*, A thing of great importance, whether good or bad, great virtue or vice as deserving of reward or punishment in the world to come. The rewards or punishments of eternity. (in logic) An affirmative proposition (opposed to سالبة *sāliba*).

A موجة *mawjat*, One wave. Vigour of youth.

A مؤجة *muʼujat*, (v. n. of مؤج) Being bitter and brackish (water).

A مؤجّج *muʼajjij*, One who inflames or kindles. Who or what makes (water) salt or bitter.

A موجح *mūjah*, (Cloth) of a thick texture. A smooth hide, shining skin. A refuge, asylum.

A مؤجد *muʼjad*, Strengthened, firm, compact, strong (in teeth or claws); firmly-tied (knot); strongly-built (house); thick, well-wrought (cloth). *Muʼjid*, Who or what strengthens, invigorates, restores, or reinstates (after sickness or poverty).

A موجد *mūjid*, An author, causer.

P موج دار *mawj-dār*, Wavy, undulatory. Grained (as Morocco leather).

A موجدة *mawjidat*, (v. n. of وجد) Flying in a passion. Seeking a pretence to assault or chide.

A مؤجدة *muʼjadat*, Strong, compact (she-camel). مؤجدة القري *muʼjadatu'l kara'*, (A she-camel) strong about the withers and firm in the bunch.

A مؤجر *muʼjir*, One who hires, lets to farm, or rents. (A woman) who prostitutes herself, who plays the whore. One who sets or replaces (a broken or dislocated bone). One who repays.

A موجر *mūjir*, Who obliges (any one) to hear what is disagreeable to him. Who strikes (a spear) into the mouth or breast.

A مؤجّر *muʼajjir*, A maker of bricks or tiles (آجرّ *ājurr*). A recompenser, rewarder.

A موجز *mūjaz*, Epitomized. *Mūjaz* or *mūjiz*, Brief (epistle). A compendium, epitome, summary. كلام موجز *kalāmi mujaz*, A compendious discourse.

P موج زن *mawj-zan*, Boisterous, billowy.

A موجع *mūjiʻ*, Painful (blow).

A موجف *mūjaf*, Agitated. *Mūjif*, A driver of camels at the pace called وجف *wajf*.

A موجل *mawjal*, (v. n. of وجل) Being afraid (of another). Fear. *Mawjil*, A ditch where water stagnates. A dreadful place.

A مؤجّل *muʼajjal*, Collected, assembled. Payment deferred. A place where water collects. مال مؤجّل *māli muʼajjal*, Money laid up against a certain time. *Muʼajjil*, One who cures a pain in the neck (اجل *ijl*), who applies medicine to it. One who collects (water) into one place. Who defers, gives a delay, but fixes a time. A book containing the appointed term or limit of any thing.

A موجلة *mawjalat*, A dreadful place.

A موجّن *muwajjan*, Prominent-cheeked (man).

A موجوء *mawjūʼ*, Struck with the hand or a knife. Castrated (goat) by crushing of the sinews.

A موجوب *mawjūb*, Rendered necessary. غير موجوب *ghayr mawjūb*, Unnecessary. Illegitimate.

A موجوح *mawjūh*, Rejected. Shut, closed (door).

A موجود *mawjūd*, Found. Present, existing, standing before. Ready at hand. Brought into existence. Review, muster. P موجود شدن *mawjūd shudan*, To be present.

A موجودات *mawjūdāt*, Creatures, existences, beings. Things present. Ready money, cash, specie. (in Indian statistics) The unmeasured or unpartitioned part of a pergunnah in which there are sundry partners.

A موجونة *mawjūnat*, A decorated bridal chamber.

A موجوه *mawjūh*, Struck on the face.

A موجّه *muwajjah*, Approved, acceptable, agreeable. Suitable. Uniform, congruous, placed regularly. Conspicuous for excellence; of great authority. (A man) with a bunch on the back and breast. Double-faced (cloth). قضاياي موجّهه *kazāyāyi muwajjaha*, Propositions or judgments agreeable to reason. *Muwajjih*, (or موجه *mūjih*) One who raises to dignity or renders respectable.

A موجيٰ *mawja'*, Fast-going (she-camel), whose girth slips through the inequality of the motion of her fore and hind-feet.

P موچينه *mū-chīna*, Tweezers.

A موحد موحد *mawhada*, (or موحد موحد *mawhada mawhada*) Singly and separately. *Mūhid*, (A sheep) bringing forth one (lamb).

A موحّد *muwahhad*, Single-pointed (as ب *be*).

A مؤحّد *muʼahhid*, (or موحّد *muwahhid*) One who professes his belief that there is one (God), orthodox: a unitarian.

A موحر *mūhir*, (The reptile وحرة *wahrat*) infecting (meat or drink) with venom.

A موحش *mūhish*, Dismal, causing sadness, disastrous, afflicting. Terrible, dreadful. Desert, uninhabited (country). Destitute of provisions, hungry, starving. One who finds (a country) desolate.

A موحّش *muwahhish*, A desolater.

A موحف *mūhif*, Unblemished (man). Uncomfortable (fold for camels).

A موحل *mawhal*, (v. n. of وحل) Falling into thin soft clay or sludge. Being miry, consisting of mire. *Mawhil*, Mire, sludge; or a place full of it.

A موحوش *mawhūsh*, Overrun with wild beasts.

A موخ *mawkh*, The subsidence (of anger).

P موخ *mūkh*, A standard, an ensign.

A مؤخذ *muʼakhkhaz*, Taken, snatched, seized. Retaliated on, called to account. Fascinated. Soured.

A مؤخر *muʼkhar* or *khir*, The hind part of a saddle.

A مؤخر *muʼakhkhar*, The hinder part of any thing, the posteriors. مؤخّر العين *muʼakhkharu'l ʻayn*, The outer angle of the eye. *Muʼakhkhar* or *muʼakhkhir*, Posterior, consequent. Delayed, procrastinated, left behind. The following or latter part. The hinder part (of a saddle). *Muʼakhkhir*, One who keeps back, or puts things in their proper places; hence, a name of God.

A مؤخرة *muʼkharat* or *muʼkhirat*, The hinder part of a saddle. مؤخرة العين *muʼkhiratu'l ʻayn*, The outer angle of the eye.

A مؤخّرة *muʼakhkharat* or *muʼakhkhirat*, The hinder part of a saddle. The consequent (in opposition to the antecedent). The end, epilogue.

A موخف *mūkhif*, A kind of dish prepared with the new cheese called اقط *akit*, on which, after sprinkling it with water, they pour fresh dates, butter, or broth. Water mixed with clay. Woollen or silken stuff in the loom. A four-square carpet to lie upon. Foolish, stupid. A baker.

A موخمة *mawkhamat*, Any thing unwholesome, injurious to the stomach. An unhealthy country. (Meat) corrupting in the stomach.

A موخوط *mawkhūt*, Wounded deeply; struck with the edge of a sword. Sprinkled with a few white hairs.

A موخوم *mawkhūm*, Troubled with indigestion.

A مؤخّي *muʼakhkhī*, One who prepares a ring, rope, or tethering-peg. (See تأخية *taʼkhiyat*.)

P مود *mūd*, An eagle of whose feathers they mount arrows.

A مودّ *miwadd*, One who loves greatly.

A مودّأة *muwaddaʼat*, A dangerous or infested place, especially a desert.

A مؤدب *muʼdib*, An inviter to a feast.

A مؤدّب *muʼaddab*, Chastised. Learned, instructed. Well-bred, polite, civil, modest, courteous. *Muʼaddib*, A chastiser, chider. One who teaches the belles-lettres, who educates well. An instructor, teacher, preceptor. One who invites to a feast.

A مودّة *mawaddat* or *miwaddat*, Friendship, love. Benevolence. A book. A letter. P مودّت كردن *mawaddat kardan*, To love, to discover a regard for. A مكتوب مودّت *maktūbi mawaddat*, Friendly letters. A love-letter.

A مودع *mūdiʻ*, Submissive. (See ايداع *īdāʻ*.)

A موددة *mawdidat*, Love, friendship.

A مودع *mūdaʻ*, Easy, obedient (horse).

A مودق *mawdik*, A place. A place where any thing drops.

A مؤدم *muʼdim*, A peace-maker, renewer, or strengthener of friendship or love. Who prepares fish or any thing to be eat with bread. مؤدم مبشر *muʼdam mubshar*, One who unites the softness of the inner with the roughness of the outer skin. Practised, experienced in business.

A مودن *mūdan*, (or مؤدن *muʼdan*) Puny, thin, weakly (boy). Short, dwarfish.

A مودوسة *mawdūsat*, (Ground) covered with young herbage.

A مودوع *mawdūʻ*, Left, let alone. Quiet, manageable (horse). Modesty, softness, gentleness, placidness. عليك بالمودوع *ʻalayka bi'l mawdūʻ*, Behave modestly, be quiet.

A مودون *mawdūn*, Short or contracted in the shoulders, neck, or hands. A small date-basket or other repository. Puny, thin, weakly (boy). Steeped, wetted, soaked. Name of a horse.

A مؤدي *muʼdī*, Conducive. A helper, assistant, succourer. Prepared for a journey. Armed, or otherwise properly prepared. Strong, powerful.

A مودي *mūdī*, Perishing, lost. A lion. Kind, beneficent, bountiful. مودي اليه *mūdan ilayhi*, Benefited, obliged.

A مؤدّي *muʼaddaʼ*, Payed. Performed. Led, brought. *Muʼaddī*, Who causes to happen, who brings or adduces; leading to, conducive. A payer, performer of what is due. A cause, motive.

A مؤذّن *muʼazzin*, The public crier, or muezzin, who assembles the people to prayers by proclamation from a minaret or tower of a mosque. (See also تأذين *taʼzīn*.)

A مؤذنة *muʼzanat*, Name of a bird.

A مؤذي *muʼzaʼ*, Afflicted, pained. *Muʼzī*, Noxious, troublesome, vexatious, hurtful, pernicious.

P موذي گري *mūzīgarī*, Troublesomeness.

A مور *mawr*, (v. n. of مار for مور) Moving, being agitated, fluctuating. Being put in commotion (dust). Moistening (medicine). Plucking or teasing (wool or cotton) with the fingers. Flowing on the surface of the ground. Oscillating crosswise. Arriving in نجد *najd*. A wave, surge, billow. Agitation, commotion. Any thing soft. A way, track, beaten, or level path. The coast of Yaman, north of Zabīd. *Mūr*, Dust in motion.

P مور *mūr*, (by some *mor*) An ant, emmet, pismire. An emblem of poverty and weakness. Rust. عساكر مور شمار *ʻasākiri mūr-shumār*, Any army numerous as ants. گور پرمار و مور *gori pur mār u mor*, A tomb full of serpents and ants. همچو موري بي زور *hamchu mori bī zor*, Weak as an ant, like an ant, without strength.

A موراق *mūrākh*, Ripening (date).

A موراك *mīwrāk*, Fore part of a camel's saddle.

P مورامون *mūrāmūn*, A wild carrot.

A مؤرب *muʼrib*, Victorious over.

A مؤرّب *muʼarrab*, Bound, tied. Much, many, copious. *Muʼarrib*, Who fastens or draws tight (a knot). A fulfiller, performer. One who comprehends within limits.

A مورة *mūrat*, Wool which falls off a sheep dead or alive; pelt wool.

A مورث *mūras*, Appointed heir. Hereditary possession. *Mūris*, One who makes (a person) an heir. Cause, author. قبائح مورث الفضائح *kabāʼihi mūrisu'l fazāʼih*, Transgressions which entail ignominy.

A مؤرّث *muʼarris*, One who lights a fire. An exciter of discord.

A مؤرّج *muʼarraj*, Easily excited. A lion. *Muʼarrij*, A raiser of tumults, rebellion, sedition, or war. A disturber of the peace, exciter of faction, breedbate. المؤرّج *al muʼarrij*, Name of a man.

P مورجان *mūrjān*, Name of a mountain in Persia where there is a famous spring which flows exactly in proportion to the quantity of water required.

P مورچال *mūrchāl*, An intrenchment for besieging a fortified place.

P مورچانه *mūrchāna*, Rust of iron.

P مورچه *mūrcha*, A little ant, emmet, pismire. The waving lustre of a sword. Rust. A small black glass. A poor, weak, contemptible fellow. A battery. مورچه پي زدن *mūrcha pay zadan*, To pluck up the beard by the root. مورچهٔ عنبرين *mūrchaʼi ʻambarīn*, The sprouting beard of a youth.

P مورچه ناك *mūrchanāk*, Swarming with ants.

A مورخ *mūrikh*, One who softens (leaven).

A مؤرّخ *muʼarrakh*, Dated. Chronicled. *Muʼarrikh*, (or مورّخ *muwarrikh*) Who dates (a letter); who marks the time of any event. A chronologer, chronicler, annalist, historian. اكثر مورّخين *aksari muwarrikhīn*, Most historians.

A مورّخ *muwarrakh*, Fixed, defined by a time.

P مورخانه *mūrkhāna*, Small black ants. Rust.

P مورد *mord*, Myrtle. The ringlets of a mistress. A seal; a ring.

A مورد *mawrid*, (pl. موارد *mawārid*) A place of arrival, descending, alighting, or appearing. A place through which one passes; access, entrance, passage, approach. Station, quarters. A road to water.

A مورّد *muwarrad*, Rose-coloured (garment).

P مورداسپرم *mord-isparam*, Name of a fragrant flower with leaves like the myrtle.

P موردانه *mordāna*, (for مورددانه *mord-dāna*) Myrtle-seed. Seed of a kind of mezereon.

A موردة *mawridat*, A highway. A drinking-place.

A مورس *mūris*, (The thistle ورس *wars*) turning yellow. Leaf-bearing (tree). (See ايراس.)

A مورّس *muwarras*, (Cloth) dyed with ورس *wars*.

A مؤرّس *muʼarris*, One who asks or uses the

assistance of another. Turned farmer.

P مورش *mūrish*, Small shells or glass beads. A place before a shop where goods are exposed to sale. An estrade raised a little above the ground for sitting upon, especially on the outside of a house. The back-bone. مورش سيمين *mūrishi sīmīn*, Silver beads resembling pearls.

A مؤرّش *mu*,*arrish*, One who kindles a fire. An exciter (of sedition), raiser (of a rebellion).

A مؤرض *mu*,*riz*, Productive of a heaviness or stuffing of the head (ارض *arz*).

A مؤرّض *mu*,*arriz*, One who causes land to be grazed. A rigid faster. (See تأريض *ta*,*rīz*.)

A مؤرط *mu*,*rit*, (Sandy grounds) which produce the tree ارطى *arta'*.

A مورع *mūriꜥ*, What separates (two things).

A مؤرّف *mu*,*arrif*, One who places a stone or other boundary-mark (ارفة *urfat*) for dividing lands. One who knots (a rope).

A مورق *mawrak*, Maurice (a proper name). *Mūrik*, Leafy (tree). Opulent (man).

A مؤرق *mu*,*rik*, Who renders wakeful.

A مؤرّق *mu*,*arrak*, Prevented from sleeping, kept awake. *Mu*,*arrik*, Who or what renders (any one) wakeful or sleepless.

A مورّق *muwarrik*, A scribe.

A مورقة *mawrakat*, Any thing which increases wealth and prosperity.

A مورك *mawrik*, The fore part of a camel's saddle, whereon the rider places his foot. Outer (shoe). The outer sole of a shoe. *Mūrik*, One who neither has nor claims any thing.

A مؤرك *mu*,*rik*, One who alights or remains at a spot abounding in اراك *arāk*-trees.

A مورّك *muwarrak*, Blameless, innocent.

A مؤرّك *mu*,*arrik*, One who adorns (a place) with a throne (اريكة *arīkat*).

A موركة *mawrikat*, The fore part of a camel's saddle, on which the rider rests his foot when tired. Outer (shoe). The outer sole of a shoe. *Miwrakat*, The fore part of a camel's saddle. A cushion whereon the rider sits.

A مورم *mawrim*, The place of the gum where the grinders grow.

A مؤرّم *mu*,*arram*, (A head) large in the fore part. (An egg) big at one end.

A مورّم *muwarram*, Swelled, swollen. A great detachment of an army making a nocturnal excursion. Bulky (man).

P مور ملخ *mor-malakh*, Thick as ants or locusts.

A مؤرنب *mu*,*arnab*, (A garment) woven with a mixture of hare's pile. *Mu*,*arnib*, (A country) abounding in hares (ارنب *arnab*).

A موروث *mawrūs*, Hereditary, possessed by paternal succession. مال موروث *māli mawrūs*, Hereditary wealth, patrimony.

A موروثي *mawrūsī*, The state of being hereditary. Hereditary.

A مورود *mawrūd*, Seized with the paroxysm of a fever. Descended to, arrived at. مورود ورد *mawrūdi wird*, The place where one alights off a journey. Celebrated by every tongue.

A مورور *muwarwir*, Thoughtless, giddy, who exposes himself to danger.

A موروك *mawrūk*, Outward (sole of a shoe), that which presses the ground.

P موري *mūrī*, An earthen pipe joined to an aqueduct. A water-course, channel, gutter. Shoemakers' black. A kind of silken stuff. Small shells or glass beads. Name of a country in Turkistān.

A موري *mūrī*, One which strikes fire.

A مؤرّي *mu*,*arrī*, One who makes a tethering-peg (آريّة *ārīyat*) for a quadruped. (See تأرية *ta*,*riyat*.)

P موريانه *mūriyāna*, Rust, especially that which cannot be polished, eating (a thing) full of holes.

P موريه *mūriya*, A vinegar-cruet.

A موز *mawz* or *mūz*, Banana, plantain-fruit.

A موزّة *mawazzat*, (A country) abounding in geese.

A موزج *mawzaj*, (from P موزه *mūza*) (pl. موازجة *mawāzijat* and موازج *mawāzij*) A boot.

P موزدونتن *mawzdūnitan*, (in zand) To sell.

A مؤزّر *mu*,*azzir*, One who covers (his body) with the breeches ازار *izār*. A confirmer, strengthener. نصر مؤزّر *nasrun mu*,*azzarun*, Powerful and sufficient assistance.

A مؤزّرة *mu*,*azzarat*, A sheep whose legs are black, as if covered with dark trowsers (ازار *izār*).

A مؤزّز *mu*,*azziz*, Pealing (thunder), noisy (mill); (boiling water) murmuring. (See تأزيز *ta*,*zīz*.)

A موزع *mūzaꜥ*, Instigated, urged, set on.

A موزّع *muwazzaꜥ*, Divided. Scattered, dispersed. *Muwazziꜥ*, A divider, distributor.

A مؤزلة *mu*,*zilat*, (or مؤزّلة *mu*,*azzilat*) A year bringing scarceness with it.

A موزن *mawzan*, A place for weighing.

A موزور *mawzūr*, A criminal, a malefactor, one laden with crimes (وزر *wizr*).

A موزورة *mawzūrat*, A crime, sin, fault.

A موزوز *muwazwiz*, A singer, chanter, songster.

A موزوع *mawzūꜥ*, Held back, restrained.

A موزوم *mawzūm*, Deprived of part of one's property.

A موزون *mawzūn*, Weighed. Well adjusted, balanced (as an account). (Verse) which consists of an exact number of feet. (Money) of just standard. Good, sweet, excellent, agreeable. Modulated (sound), harmonious. موزون وزنة *mawzūni waznaꜥi*, Weighed at the weight of .... P كلام نا موزون *kalāmi nā mawzūn*, Ill-chosen words, disagreeable speech.

A موزونة *mawzūnat*, A silver coin current in Morocco of the value of twenty-four فلس *fulus*. Short and intelligent (woman).

P موزه *mūza*, A boot. A stocking. موزه نهادن *mūza nihādan*, (To put up one's boots) To give over travelling, to stay at home. موزه درگل *mūza dar gil*, (Boot in the mud) A difficult business. *Mūza* or *mawza*, A kind of sweetmeat.

P موزه بالين *mūza-bālīn*, (Boot-cushion) Soft lining in the heel of a shoe or boot.

P موزه پوشيده *mūza-poshīda*, Booted.

P موزه دوز *mūza-doz*, A bootmaker.

P موزه گير *mūza-gīr*, A horse biting his rider.

A مؤزي *mu*,*za'*, Oppressed with toil and vexation. *Mu*,*zī*, Afflictive. A maker of the conduit or pipe ازاء *izāꜥ*. One who benefits, enriches, or multiplies. One who repays. Afraid.

P موژ *moj*, A pond, tank. *Mūj*, Grief, sorrow.

P موژان *mojān*, A narcissus; hence, a beautiful eye, looking languishingly and amorously, and having a mole at the side.

P موژه *moja*, A pond, tank. *Mūja*, Sorrow, grief, affliction. Name of a sweetmeat.

A موس *maws*, A shaving of the hair. *Mūs*, A graving-tool, pen-knife. A scalpel. A razor.

A مؤس *ma*,*us*, A whisperer, talebearer.

P موسا *mūsā*, A companion. An easy, good, or agreeable work. Monthly pay.

A موسائي *mūsāꜥī*, Judaism (religion of Moses).

A موسب *mūsib*, (or مؤسّب) Fleecy (ram).

P موسترده *mū-suturda* or *mūsturda*, One whose poll is shaved. A calender monk, shaveling. Bald.

A موسج *mūsij*, Name of a town in Tihāmah.

P موسخ *mūsakh*, Threads worn by Brahmans.

A موسّخ *muwassakh*, Dirtied. *Muwassikh* or *mūsikh*, One who dirties or soils (a garment).

A موسد *mūsid*, One who sets (a dog) at game. Quick, fast, rapid.

A موسر *mūsir*, (pl. مياسير) Opulent, wealthy.

A مؤسّر *mu*,*assir*, One who ties, presses close.

A مؤسّس *mu*,*assas*, Founded, built. *Mu*,*assis*, Who lays a foundation: a founder. A strengthener.

A موسط *mūsat*, The middle of a house.

A موسع *mūsaꜥ*, Rich, able, powerful.

A موسّع *muwassaꜥ*, Large, ample; enlarged.

A مؤسف *mu*,*sif*, One who makes melancholy; an afflicter. One who provokes to anger.

P موسقار *mūsikār*, (موسقدان *mūsikdān*, or موسقيدان *mūsikīdān*) A musician. Music. ارباب موسقار *arbābi mūsikār*, Musicians.

A موسقة *mūsikat*, Fruitful, loaded (palm-tree).

G موسقي *mūsikī*, Music. ارباب علم موسقي *arbābi ꜥilmi mūsikī*, Skilled in music, musicians.

A مؤسّل *mu*,*assal*, Pointed, sharp (spear).

A موسم *mawsim*, Time, season. Place of meeting. The season when the pilgrims assemble at Mecca; the place marked out for their meeting; the people who assemble them; the fairs then and there held: hence, the word monsoon. P موسم بهاري *mawsimi bahārī*, Season of spring. موسم گل *mawsimi gul*, Season of roses.

A موسن *mūsin*, (fem. موسنة) Noisome (well),

causing (one) to faint with its noxious vapours.

P موسنج *músanh*, Tobacco of Tartary (black).

A موسوس *muwaswis*, One who speaks or mutters to himself. موسوس سودائي *muwaswisi sawdā,ī*, A moody, melancholy man.

A موسوق *mawsūk*, Freighted, loaded (vessel).

A موسوم *mawsūm*, Marked, signed, impressed, branded. Characterized. Noted, stigmatized. Named, called. (A coat of mail) adorned with agates, &c., round the bottom. موسوم بالخير *mawsūm bi'l khayr*, Marked with excellence, having good signs.

A موسومة *mawsūmat*, (Ground) watered by spring-rains, or producing spring-grass.

A موسونة *mawsūnat*, Idle, sluggish (woman).

A موسوي *mūsawiy*, Mosaic, belonging to Moses.

P موسه *mūsa* or *mawsa*, A bee. A wasp.

A موسى *mūsa'*, Moses. A razor. The apex of the crest of a helmet. كتاب موسى *kitābi mūsa'*, The book of Moses, the Pentateuch.

A موسىّ *mūsiy*, Mosaical, Mosaic.

P موسيچه *mūsīcha*, Wood-pigeons, ring-doves. A swallow or martin. A finch.

P موسيقار *mūsīkār*, Pipes made of unequal reeds. Pandean pipes. A bird whose bill is perforated with holes, through which it emits a musical sound.

G موسيقي *mūsīkī*, Music.

A موش *mawsh*, The gleaning (of a vine).

P موش *mūsh*, A mouse. A chaffinch. موش پرنده *mūshi paranda*, (Flying-mouse) A squirrel. موش دشتي *mūshi dashtī*, (or موش صحرائي *mūshi sahrā,ī*, A field-mouse, a mole (especially one with a red back, a white belly, a long tail, white at the extremity, with short fore-feet. It leaps rather than runs. The Arabians hunt and eat it). موش كور *mūshi kūr*, A blind mouse, mole. A bat. *Mosh*, Grief, sorrow, cry, lamentation.

A موشان *mūshān*, A kind of sweet fresh date.

A مؤشّب *mu,ashshab*, (A man) of a mixed race. *Mu,ashshib*, An irritator, exciter of discord. One who entangles.

P موشبازي *mūsh-bāzī*, A sort of firework.

A موشّح *muwashshah*, Clad with any thing, especially obliquely, as a scarf or baldrick from the shoulder to the opposite side. Ornamented. (Verses) arranged so that the initials of each line being put together form some word or verse, an acrostic.

A موشّحات *mūshahāt*, A sort of odes.

A موشّحة *muwashshahat*, (A sheep) streaked with white on the sides.

P موش خوار *mūsh-khwār*, An eagle that lives upon field-mice.

P موش دربندي *mūsh darbandī*, A plant growing in Darband, which the natives bruise and form into little bougies, and use as an eye-salve. It is also good for the gout and swellings.

P موش دندان *mūsh-dandān*, (Mouse's tooth) A mode of staining or printing.

A مؤشّر *mu,ashshar*, Notched, jagged, teethed like a saw, serrate, serrated. Thinned. جعل مؤشّر العضدين *ju,ali mu,ashsharu'l ,azudayn*, A beetle with serrulated claws. *Mu,ashshir*, One who cuts in jags or notches; a maker of serrulations. One who sharpens the teeth; or who thins them.

P موشك *mūshak*, A mole. A musk-rat. A bat. A squib. موشك پرّان *mūshaki parrān*, A squirrel.

P موشكا *mūshkā*, Name of a Jewish doctor.

P موشكاف *mū-shikāf*, (Hair-splitting) Minute, small, scarcely visible. A critic, subtle reasoner. One who performs with the greatest nicety.

P موشكافي *mū-shikāfī*, Criticism.

P موشك دواني *mūshak-dawānī*, Seditiousness.

P موشگر *moshgar*, A woman hired to eulogize the dead, and with others to cry and wail.

P موشگير *mūsh-gir*, A bird that feeds on field-mice. A sparrow-hawk.

A موشل *mūshil*, A diminisher (of another's fortune). (See ايشال *īshāl.*)

A موشم *mūshim*, (Ground) which begins to be covered with grass. (See also ايشام *īshām.*)

A موشّم *muwashsham*, Grassy (place).

P موشناك *mūshnāk*, Full of mice.

A موشور *mawshūr*, A prism.

A موشيّ *mawshiy*, (or موشّى *muwashsha'*) Painted, printed, coloured (cloth).

A موص *maws*, (v. n. of ماص for موص) Washing gently. Rubbing with the hand. Preparing by thrice washing (the seeds of the colocynth). Straw.

A موصب *mūsib*, Sick. (See ايصاب *īsāb.*)

A موصّب *muwassab*, Much distempered; exposed to ailments, abounding in pains.

A موصة *mawsat*, One washing.

A مؤصد *mu,sad*, (A door) shut, a little way open. Covered. نار مؤصده *nāri mu,sada*, Fire equally piled up on all sides.

A موصّد *muwassad*, A curtain behind which women sit. The female apartments.

A موصّدة *muwassadat*, A girl's small shift.

A موصل *mawsil*, The place where two ropes are joined or tied. That part of a camel between the thigh and the root of the tail. *Mawsil*, (or dual الموصلان *al mawsilāni*) Name of a city and district which joins Mesopotamia to Babylonia, situated on the western bank of the Tigris, opposite to the spot where Nineveh was supposed to have stood. *Mūsil*, Leading to, joining. A carrier, bearer.

A مؤصل *mu,sil*, A comer in the evening.

A مؤصّل *mu,assal*, Radical, fixed, firm. اصل مؤصّل *asl mu,assal*, Firmly rooted, of an old family; of unblemished honour. *Mu,assil*, Taking root, become firm. One who ennobles or calls noble.

A موصّل *muwassal*, Happily arrived, joined. Acquired, attained.

A موصوف *mawsūf*, Praised, celebrated, commendable, laudable. Endowed. Qualified, described, distinguished, characterized. Before-mentioned, aforesaid. A noun substantive qualified by an adjective.

A موصوفيّة *mawsūfiyat*, Qualification.

A موصول *mawsūl*, Joined, coupled, arrived. Attained, collected. A relative pronoun. Tax. Collection. A kind of musical pipe. A kind of stinging bee. اسم موصول *ismi mawsūl*, A regular pronoun. جواب موصول *jawābi mawsūl*, A correlative pronoun.

A موصى *mūsa'*, Commanded by last will. موصى به *mūsa' bihi*, A legacy, bequest. موصى له *mūsa' lahu*, A legatee. *Mūsī*, One who makes a will or bequeaths; a testator.

A موصّى *muwassa'*, Appointed tutor or guardian.

A موصية *mūsiyat*, A testatrix.

A موضح *mūzih*, An explainer, manifester. Appearing clear, coming in sight. (A man) who begets fair children.

A موضّح *muwazzih*, An explainer, manifester.

A موضحة *mūzihat*, A wide, open wound exposing the whiteness of the bone.

A موضع *mawza,* or *mawzi,*, (v. n. of وضع) Placing, laying down. (pl. مواضع *mawāzi,*) A place, site, situation, post. A village, hamlet, township, district. Occasion, occurrence, conjuncture. *Mūzi,*, (A camel) feeding on the plant حمض *hamz*.

A موضّع *muwazza,*, Enervated, enfeebled, broken down, worn out, overcome, impotent.

A موضعة *mawzi,at*, Love, friendship.

A موضوع *mawzū,*, (v. n. of وضع) Placing, laying down. Losing in trade. Making haste, going quick. Placed, situated. Fixed, assigned. (A camel) compelled to keep in his pasture. Deposited, laid up for preservation. Modulated (voice or sound). Injured, affected by losses. Site, position. Subject (of a speech), object. موضوع علم *mawzū,i ,ilm*, The object of science. حسن الموضوع *hasanu'l mawzū,*, Well-going, quick-paced.

A موضوعة *mawzū,at*, Contradictory (stories). Camels left to graze in the night without a keeper.

A موضون *mawzūn*, Doubled, folded together. Made of any thing doubled or twisted.

A موضونة *mawzūnat*, (A coat of mail) made of double-linked rings. (Any thing) worked or set with gems and gold.

A موطأ *mawta,*, A footstep, print of a foot. A footstool. A sock or wrapper for the feet.

A موطّأ *muwatta,*, Trampled, trodden. Spread out, made soft and level. موطّأ الاكناف *muwattasu'l aknāf*, Possessed of authority, influential. A generous, courteous, affable man. Humane, hospitable. موطّأ العقب *muwattasu'l ,akib*, (A king) having many followers or attendants.

A موطّد *muwattad*, Firmly united; made solid.

A مؤطّم *mu,attam*, Defended. اطم مؤطّم *utmi mu,attam*, A castle strongly fortified.

A موطن *mawtin*, (pl. مواطن *mawātin*) Habitation, mansion, place of residence, house, home, dwelling, birth-place. An encampment; battle-field, place of martyrs. Martyrdom.

A موطوء *mawtūʼ*, Beaten, trodden, trampled on.

A موطوءة *mawtuʼat*, Travellers, tramps.

A موطود *mawtūd*, Fastened, made strong and firm, or heavy.

A موطئ *mawtiʼ*, A footstep, foot-print.

A موظف *muwazzaf*, Allowed a fixed pay or pension (وظيفه *wazīfa*). Ordained, limited. *Muwazzif*, One who orders a daily stipend.

A موظوب *mawzūb*, (fem. موظوبة *mawzūbat*) Exposed to repeated losses in property or cattle.

A موظوبة *mawzūbat*, (A place) wholly bare of grass, from much grazing or being often sat on.

A موعب *mūʻab*, Collected. (A nose) cut clean off. جدع موعب *jadʻu mūʻab*, A deformed mutilation of the nose. *Mūʻib*, One who collects all he can.

A موعة *mawʻat*, Early youth.

A موعث *muwaʻʻas*, Difficult, capricious (man). Difficult (road).

A موعد *mawʻid*, (or موعدة *mawʻidat*) (v. n. of وعد) Predicting, foretelling any future event. Promising. A promise; the time or place of a promise or threat. Agreement. P موعد كارزار *mawʻidi kārzār*, The place and time appointed for a battle.

A موعظة *mawʻizat*, (v. n. of وعظ) Admonishing. Advice, admonition. An address to the Deity. P موعظه كردن *mawʻiza kardan*, To admonish, exhort, by holding out future reward or punishment.

A موعلة *mawʻilat*, A female mountain-goat. (pl. of وعل *waʻl*) Mountain-goats.

A موعوث *mawʻūs*, Deficient in dignity or spirit.

A موعود *mawʻūd*, (or موعودة *mawʻūdat*) (v. n. of وعد) Predicting, auguring, or prognosticating any thing good. Promising. Promised, predicted, predestined. اجل موعود *ajali mawʻūd*, Predestined or unavoidable death.

A موعوك *mawʻūk*, Enfeebled, weakened by fever.

A موعيّ *mawʻiy*, Well-knit in the wrist or ankle.

P موغ *mūgh*, A Magian or fire-worshipper.

P موغان *mūghān*, (pl. of موغ *mūgh*) Fire-worshippers. Name of a city in Azarbayjān.

P موغ بد *mūgh-bad*, A high priest of the Magi.

A موغل *mūghil*, One who enters a place hastily.

A موفد *muʼfid*, Tardy, late.

A موفر *muwaffar*, Luxuriant, plentiful, abundant, copious, redundant, impossible to be collected. Poetic measure in which elision is allowed though not made.

A موفّف *muʼaffif*, One who cries uph! fy! pho!

A موفق *muwaffak*, (Meat and drink) taken by little and little. Favoured. *Muwaffik*, One who directs, prospers, seconds. A public reader. والله الموفق المعين *wa'llāhu'l muwaffiku'l muʻīn*, It is God who prospers and assists (a phrase put frequently after the preface of a book; and sometimes at the end of a volume).

A موفّل *muʼaffal*, Weak.

P موفلون *mūflūn*, Melilot.

A موفور *mawfūr*, Complete, perfect, entire, luxuriant, copious, full, ample, numerous, many, abundant, plenteous, much. Poetic measure in which elision is lawful though not made. سعي موفور *saʻyi mawfūr*, Great endeavour, extreme diligence, much labour or fatigue. محصولات موفورة *mahsūlāti mawfūra*, Abundant produce, luxuriant harvests.

A موفي *mūfī*, A fulfiller (of an engagement).

A موفيّ *mawfiy*, Satisfied, paid, performed.

A موفية *muwaffiyat*, The city of Madīna.

P موفيون *mūfiyūn*, A kind of poison.

A موق *mawk*, (v. n. of ماق for موق) Perishing. Being cheap, trifling (a bargain). *Mūk*, (v. n. of ماق for موق) Being stupid, foolish, careless. Perishing. Folly, stupidity. (pl. امواق *amwāk*) A large boot worn over another of thinner leather. A winged pismire. Dust. The inner corner of the eye.

A مؤق *muʼk*, (or موق *mūk*) (pl. آماق *āmāk* and اماق *amʼāk*) The inner corner of the eye (لحاظ *lihāz* denoting the corner next the temples). (pl. آماق *āmāk*) Low-lying (ground). *Muʼuk*, (v. n. of ماق for موق) Being foolish, careless. Perishing.

A موقت *mawkit*, Place (fixed) by any given time. Time (specified) for any appointed place.

A موقّت *muwakkat*, Fixed or restricted to a certain definite time. Appointed (hour). *Muwakkit*, An observer of times or hours. A person in the Muhammadan mosques, who observes the exact hour when the people are to be assembled to prayers, and gives notice accordingly to the crier.

A موقّح *muwakkah*, Taught by misfortunes.

A موقد *mawkid*, A fire-hearth, grate, where they kindle a fire. *Mūkad*, Kindled, blazing (fire).

A موقذ *mawkiz*, (pl. مواقذ *mawākiz*) An extremity, point, or prominent bone (as of the elbow, knee, heel, or shoulder).

A موقّذة *muwakkazat*, (A she-camel) hurt in the udder by the rope صرار *sirār*; or whose udder is enlarged by the feeble sucking of her colt.

A موقر *mawkir*, A plain at the foot of a mountain. *Mūkar*, Loaded, carrying a heavy burden. Pregnant (woman). (pl. مواقر *mawākir*) (A tree) loaded with fruit. Oppressed, weighed down. Reduced to poverty. *Mūkir*, (A tree) laden with fruit. Oppressive. One who reduces to poverty.

A موقّر *muwakkar*, Honoured, revered, respected, venerable. Experienced, proved, intelligent, acquainted with the world. *Muwakkir*, An honourer, reverencer, respecter. One who quiets (a horse). Who makes or calls grave, modest, or respectable.

A موقرة *mūkarat*, (fem.) (pl. مواقر *mawākir*) (A tree) loaded with fruit. (A woman) heavily pregnant. *Mūkirat*, (A tree) laden with fruit.

A موقّرة *muwakkarat*, (A tree) laden with fruit.

A موقّس *muwakkas*, Scabby (camel).

A موقع *mawkiʻ*, A place where any thing falls. Accident, contingency, occurrence, vicissitudes of fortune. Proper, fit, suitable. (pl. مواقع *mawākiʻ*) The falling of a star; the place where a star sets or rain falls. *Mūkiʻ*, Adverse (fortune).

A موقّع *muwakkaʻ*, Sharpened (sword or knife). Bruised with a hammer. Beaten (path). Worn out with misfortunes, oppressed with evils. (A camel or ass) galled on the back. A decree, statute, mandate. *Muwakkiʻ*, One who strikes with a hammer. A writer of a توقيع *tawkīʻ* or letters patent. One who sharpens (a knife or a sword). موقع الوطاء *muwakkiʻu'l watʼ*, Lightly treading, going nimbly.

A موقعة *mawkaʻa* or *mawkiʻat*, A place where rain drops. A place where a bird lights or rests.

A موقّعة *muwakkaʻat*, Polished, sharpened (point of a spear).

A موقف *mawkif*, A station, a post, any place where one remains; especially where they celebrate the pilgrimage-solemnities at Mecca; called also Mount عرفات *ʻarafāt*. The site of the last judgment. The eye. Whatever is exposed to the view of another. The climax of eloquence. موقفان *mawkifāni*, Two cavities about the small ribs or hypochondria of a horse. Two veins near the fundament, which, if wounded, prove mortal. حسنة الموقفين *hasanatu'l mawkifayn*, (A woman) with a handsome face and foot, or fine eyes and hands.

A موقّف *muwakkaf*, (A horse) having the pasterns or that part of his feet white which corresponds to the wrist in man; having his ears variegated with white. (An ass) having a round impression made by a hot iron on the shoulders and fore-legs. (A bull or goat) having the fore-legs of a reddish colour, different from the rest of the body. Experienced, knowing (man). Tardy, slow. A gaming arrow. *Muwakkif*, One who causes (any body) to stand or to remain in a place. A detainer, preventer, hinderer.

P موقلون *mūklūn*, The herb melilot.

A موقن *mūkin*, Certain of. A supposer.

A موقوت *mawkūt*, Restricted to a certain time. وقت موقوت *wakti mawkūt*, An appointed hour.

A موقود *mawkūd*, Kindled.

A موقوذ *mawkūz*, Beaten. At the point of death.

A موقوذة *mawkūzat*, (A sheep) killed with a club.

A موقور *mawkūr*, Heavy (ear). Cracked (bone).

A موقوس *mawkūs*, Scabby (camel).

A موقوص *mawkūs*, One whose neck is broken.

A موقوط *mawkūt*, Pained, oppressed with a blow.

A موقوع *mawkūʻ*, Sharpened, (sword or knife) on a whetstone, keen, acute. (A hoof) worn or hurt on the stones. Occurred.

A موقوف *mawkūf*, Left or bequeathed for pious uses, consecrated to God. Delayed, stopped, deferred, postponed, put off, suspended, relinquished, dismissed, discontinued. Established, determined, fixed, supported. Belonging or restricted to, dependent upon, suspended by or from. Quiescent (having no vowel). A legacy, bequest. موقوف عليه *mawkūf ɛalayhi*, (A word) paused on.

A موقوفي *mawkūfī*, Discontinuance, suspension.

A موقوم *mawkūm*, Much grieved, very sad.

A موقومة *mawkūmat*, (Ground) bare and trodden.

A موقونة *mawkūnat*, (A girl) kept at home.

A موقى *mawka'*, (pl. of مائق *māɪik*) Foolish, brainless, stupid.

A موق *mūkiɪ*, Outer or inner corner of the eye.

A موقّى *muwakka'*, One very much dreaded. One whom every body shuns. Bold, strenuous.

A موقّي *mawkīy*, One who is feared.

P موك *mūk*, The sting of an insect.

A موكب *mawkib*, An army, forces, large detachment, either of horse or foot; choice body of troops; lifeguards; large cavalcade, riding especially on camels. A kind of pace. P موكبيان سحر *mawkibiyāni sahar*, Certain angels which are said to have attended Muhammad in his ascent to heaven on the night called ليلة المعراج *laylatu'l miɛrāj*. *Mūkib*, see ايكاب *īkāb*.

A موكّب *muwakkib*, A ripening, blackening date.

A موكّت *muwakkit*, Ripening (date).

A موكّد *muɪakkad*, Confirmed, corroborated, strengthened. Redoubled. Efficacious, powerful, strong. P موكّد شدن *muɪakkad shudan*, To be confirmed. *Muɪakkid*, (or موكّد *muwakkid*) One who confirms, strengthens, binds close, connects. Who redoubles or reiterates. Confirmatory. Immediate. Energetic.

A موكّداً *muɪakkadan*, Confirmatively, repeatedly, to the utmost.

P موكده *mūkada*, Absolute.

A موكل *muɪkal*, Supplied with food, fed. *Muɪkil*, One who gives or offers to eat. One who slanders and ruins another's reputation.

A موكّل *muwakkal*, Appointed guardian, commissary, superintendant. A vicegerent, substitute, deputy. The keeper of a prisoner. The demon supposed to guard treasure buried in the earth. *Muwakkil*, One who appoints a lieutenant, deputy, substitute, factor, or agent (وكيل *wakīl*); one who delegates power.

A موكّل *muɪakkil*, Eating, pasturing; fed. A giver of victuals or a livelihood.

A موكّمة *muɪakkimat*, Large-hipped (woman).

A موكن *mawkin* or موكنة *mawkinat*, A bird's nest.

A موكوت *mawkūt*, Care-worn, anxious, sad.

A موكول *mawkūl*, Committed, entrusted.

A موكوم *mawkūm*, Very unhappy, tortured in mind, melancholy.

A موكومة *mawkūmat*, (Ground) bare and trodden.

A مول *mawl*, (v. n. of مال for مول) Being rich (especially in flocks). Giving away one's property. *Mūl*, A spider.

P مول *mol*, Delay. Repentance. Remaining behind, desisting. A thief. A gallant, paramour. A bastard. A wink, signal with the eye.

A موّل *mawwil*, Rich, wealthy.

A مولا *mawlā*, A slave. *Mawlā* or *mullā*, A judge, magistrate of a large city. A lord, master; and sometimes Omnipotence. مولا اسفل *mawlā asfal*, The inferior mawlā or the client. مولا اعلى *mawlā aɛla'*, The superior mawlā or the patron. مولانا فلان *mawlānā fulān*, My lord judge (such-a-one). مولاناي مزبور *mawlānāyi mazbūr*, Our lord afore-mentioned. This title, مولانا *mawlānā*, is given to judges and prefects even by the king.

A مولاة *mawlāt*, A lady of rank. A freed woman or manumitted slave. A female slave.

P مولامول *mol-ā-mol*, A tedious delay.

A مولائي *mawlāɪī*, Judgeship, lordship.

A موءلّب *muɪallib*, An instigator. (See تأليب.)

A مولة *mūlat*, (pl. مول *mūl*) A spider.

A مولج *mawlij*, A place wherein a thing enters or collects.

A مولد *mawlid*, (v. n. of ولد) Bringing forth children (a woman). Nativity, birth. A birthplace. Time of birth. *Mūlid*, (pl. موالد *mawālid* or مواليد *mawālīd*) (A woman) travailing in birth.

A مولّد *muwallad*, Procreated, begotten. Educated, brought up. Invented, coined. Not sufficiently examined, uncertain (proof). A foreigner; not genuine Arabian (man, saying, or writing). *Muwallid*, A begetter, procreator, generator. An educator, bringer up. (The Muhammadans aver that the expression انت نبيّي وانا ولّدتك *anta nabīyī wa ana' wallattuka*, Thou art my prophet, and I have brought thee up, has been corrupted and changed by the Christians into بنيّي *bunayyī*, My son, and I have begotten thee.)

A مولّدة *muwalladat*, (fem. of مولّد *muwallad*) Born amongst Arabians. (A thing) recently invented. Inventions of poets. *Muwallidat*, A midwife.

P مولش *molish*, Expectation, delay.

A مولع *mūlaɛ*, Excited. Wishful, desirous, passionately fond of, dedicated or addicted to, greedy.

A مولّع *muwallaɛ*, Shining, splendid. (A horse or bull) marked with oblong white and black spots; hence, a language composed of various tongues, as the Turkish interlarded with Persian and Arabic.

A مولغ *mūligh*, One who causes to lap.

A موءلف *muɪlif*, One who renders familiar, accustoms, uses, or associates. Familiarized. One who makes a thousand (الف *alf*). (See ائلاف.)

A موءلّف *muɪallaf*, Conciliated, won over, united. Composed, published (book). Completed, made up (thousand). *Muɪallif*, One who completes the number of 1000 (الف *alf*). Become 1000, made up that number. One who joins two things together. One who collects together. A compiler, composer, author, editor. موءلّف الاصل *muɪallifu'l asl*, An original author.

A موءلّفات *muɪallafāt*, Compositions, writings.

A موءلّل *muɪallal*, Pointed, pricked (ear). *Muɪallil*, One who sharpens or gives a point.

A موءلم *muɪlim*, Painful, afflictive, dolorific.

P مول مول *mol mol*, Stay, stay.

P مولنجه *mūlanja*, A corn-destroying insect, weevil.

P مولو *mūlū*, A trumpet made of a horn, used by fakīrs. Small bells used as music.

A مولوج *mawlūj*, Afflicted, tried by misfortune. Troubled with toothache (ولجة *wālijat*).

A مولود *mawlūd*, Generated, born. A son. Birthday, nativity. مولود عيسى *mawlūdi ɛīsa'*, The nativity (of the Lord) Jesus.

A مولوق *mawlūk*, Affected with a touch of insanity.

A مولولة *mawlūlat*, Bawling, noisy (woman).

A مولوي *mawlawīy*, Judicial, belonging to a judge or magistrate. A doctor of the Muhammadan law. An assistant lawyer. A learned man. Divine, religious, belonging to God. A dervish, Muhammadan monk. P كلاه مولوي *kulāhi mawlavī*, A kind of high woollen cap worn by them. مولوي خانه *mawlavī-khāna*, A convent of dervīshes.

A مولويّة *mawlawīyat*, A resemblance to, or equality with, a prince, lord, master, or benefactor.

A موله *mūlah*, A spider. (Water) set a-flowing over a plain.

A مولّه *muwallah*, (A child) separated from its mother (in captivity). (Water) set a-flowing over sown fields.

A مولى *mawla'*, (pl. موالي *mawālī*) A king, prince, sovereign, lord, master, judge, magistrate; one who liberates (slaves). God. A slave, servant, freedman or manumitted slave. A follower, client. A benefactor, helper. One benefited. A companion, confederate, partner. A father's brother. A son. A son-in-law. A sister's son. A cousin. A neighbour. A sworn friend. A lover. A citizen. A stranger. A visitor, guest.

A موءلي *muɪlī*, One who takes an oath.

P مولي *mūlī*, One who has a lover. Name of a diuretic plant. Delay. An ogler.

P موليان *mūliyān*, Robbers, plunderers.

P موليدن *molīdan*, To delay, hesitate, deliberate. To be languid, impotent, deficient. To loathe, conceive a disgust, be tired of. To slide. To arm. To adorn one's self with ornaments. To deplore, weep. To turn back. To cause to turn back.

P موم *mūm* or *mom*, Wax. A wax-candle. موم كردن *mom kardan*, To melt (as a candle its wax).

A موم *mūm*, An instrument used in weaving. A shoemaker's instrument. Pleurisy. Malignant small-pox. Wax.

A موماء *mawmāɪ*, (or موماة *mawmāt*) A desert.

P موم آيين *mūm-āyin*, A mummy.

A مؤمّت *mu*,*ammat*, Full and equally distended. Suspected, accused.

P موم جامه *mom-jāma*, Waxcloth, cerecloth.

A مؤمّد *mu*,*ammad*, Terminated, finished. Empty, completely drained (water-bottle).

P موم دل *mom-dil*, Tender-hearted.

A مومر *mu*,*mir*, Who multiplies, makes numerous.

A مؤمّر *mu*,*ammar*, Invested with office, appointed to government. Defined, bound, limited. Marked, signed, impressed. Conquered, subdued. A spear when the head is fixed on. امير مؤمّر *amīri mu*,*ammar*, A general appointed to command. *Mu*,*ammir*, One who gives the command, who appoints a chief or governor (امير *amīr*).

P موم روغن *mom-rawghan*, Wax and oil mixed.

A مومسة *mūmisat*, Unchaste, impudent (woman).

A مؤمّل *mu*,*ammal*, The eighth horse in a race. *Mu*,*ammil*, Hoping. One who holds out hope.

A مؤمن *mu*,*min*, Believing, faithful, orthodox. (God) protecting, or the protector. A Musulmān weaver. (pl. مؤمنون *mu*,*minūna*, and obl. مؤمنين *mu*,*minīna*) The orthodox, the faithful. امير المؤمنين *amīru'l mu*,*minīn*, Commander of the faithful, a title adopted by the caliph Omar.

A مؤمنات *mu*,*mināt*, The faithful (women).

A مومّوت *mawmūt*, Determined (by measure, manner, or time).

A مومور *mawmūr*, Known, measured, defined.

A مّوموق *mawmūḳ*, Beloved.

P موّمول *mūmūl*, A disease affecting the eye.

A مؤمه *mu*,*mah*, Troubled with the pustules called اميهة *amīhat*.

P مومي *momī*, Waxen; of the colour of wax. (applied to chintz) Prepared after stamping by covering the flowers with wax to prevent their being spoiled by other colours afterwards applied.

A مومئ *mūma'*, (or مومئ اليه *mūma' ilayhi*) Pointed out. Above-mentioned. P ايلچيء مومئ اليه *ilchi*,*i mūma' ilayhi*, The ambassador before-named. A *Mūmī*, Who consents, who nods assent.

A P موميا *mūmiyā*, A mummy. The substance with which mummies are preserved.

P مومياي *momiyā*,*ī*, Name of a medicine.

A مون *mawn*, (v. n. of مان for مون) Furnishing with necessaries; maintaining, feeding. *Mūn*, (or المون *al mūn*) (in Morocco) A heap of stones thrown into the sea to make a port; a breakwater.

A مونة *mawnat*, Provisions, daily food.

A مؤنة *ma*,*unat*, (v. n. of مان for مون) Maintaining, feeding. Provisions. A wallet, saddle-bags, any thing equal to another in weight or quantity. A load, a weight. Trouble, molestation. مؤنة كافي *ma*,*unat kāfī*, Provisions sufficient.

A مؤنث *mu*,*nis*, Who brings forth a female.

A مؤنّث *mu*,*annas*, Feminine, of the feminine gender. An effeminate wretch. Any thing fragrant (as saffron) with which clothes are dyed.

A مؤنس *mu*,*nis*, A companion, intimate friend. A solacer, comforter. Thursday. ابو مؤنس *abū mu*,*nis*, (Father Sociable) A wax-light.

A مؤنّس *mu*,*annis*, A companion of Muhammad.

A مؤنسات *mu*,*nisāt*, Arms which one is accustomed to wear.

A مؤنسة *mu*,*nisat*, Name of a city in Mesopotamia near نصيبين *nasibīn*.

A المؤنسيّة *al mu*,*nisīyat*, A village near Thebes.

A مؤنض *mu*,*niz*, One who leaves meat raw, or not well-dressed.

A مونع *mūniʻ*, Ripe.

A مؤنف *mu*,*nif*, Uncropped, ungrazed (meadow).

A مؤنّف *mu*,*annaf*, Led forth to fresh pasture. (A spear-head) sharpened at the point.

A مؤنيق *mu*,*nik*, Pleasing, agreeable.

A مؤنّق *mu*,*annik*, An admirer.

A مؤنمل *mu*,*namil*, One whose finger-ends (انامل *anāmil*) are short, thick, and stumpy.

P مونه *mūna*, Temperament, constitution.

A مؤني *mu*,*nī*, A retainer, detainer, or forcer. A procrastinator, deferrer, retarder, delayer; who does any thing in a slow or hesitating manner.

A مؤوء *ma*,*ūs*, (for مأووء *ma*,*wūs*) (Leather) tanned with the shrub or tree آء *ā*,*s*. A cat mewing.

A مؤوّب *mu*,*awwib*, (Wind) blowing all day.

A مؤود *ma*,*ūd*, Oppressed with heaviness.

A مؤوّد *mu*,*awwid*, Who bends, makes crooked.

A مؤودة *maw*,*udat*, (A girl) buried alive.

A مؤوس *ma*,*ūs*, A whisperer, breedbate.

A مؤوف *ma*,*ūf*, Blighted, smutty (corn).

A مؤوّق *mu*,*awwik*, A despiser. (See تأويق.)

A مؤول *mu*,*ūl*, (v. n. of مال for مول) Being rich (especially in cattle).

A مؤوّل *mu*,*awwil*, One who brings back. An explainer, interpreter. (See تأويل *ta*,*wīl*.)

A مؤولة *mu*,*ūlat*, (v. n. of مال) Being fat and bulky.

A مؤوّم *mu*,*awwam*, One with a big, ugly head.

A مؤون *mu*,*ūn*, (pl. of مأن *ma*,*n*) Ploughshares. (pl. of مأنة *ma*,*nat*) Hypochondria.

A مؤونة *ma*,*ūnat*, Provisions. A load. Weight.

A مووه *mu*,*ūh*, (v. n. of ماه for موه) Being full and overflowing (a well). Springing a leak, filling with water (a ship). Offering water to drink.

A موويّ *mawawiy*, (Verse) ending in ما *mā*.

A موه *mawh*, (v. n. of ماه for موه) Being full and overflowing (a well). Making water, leaking (a ship). Mixing. Giving water to drink.

A موهب *mawhib*, A present, gift. *Mūhab*, Ready, presented, unbought (victuals). A present. *Mūhib*, One who accepts a present. Permanent, perpetual. Ready, prepared. Able.

A موهبة *mawhabat*, (v. n. of وهب) Giving, granting, conceding. A cloud which rains wherever it happens to be. *Mawhabat* or *mawhibat*, A gift. (pl. مواهب *mawāhib*) A hollow on a mountain wherein water collects. A small pond.

A موهة *mūhat*, Clearness, beauty of face.

A موهّز *muwahhaz*, One who treads hard.

A موهّص *muwahhas*, (A man) endowed with a good constitution, or a firm, compact body.

A بنو موهصى *banū mawhasa'*, Slaves.

A مؤهل *mu*,*hil*, Who makes (one) worthy. Who admits into one's family.

A مؤهّل *mu*,*ahhil*, Who makes worthy, proper.

A موهن *mawhin*, Part, about half of the night. *Mūhin*, Who or what weakens, enfeebles, debilitates.

A موهوب *mawhūb*, Given, presented, conferred. موهوب له *mawhūbun lahu*, One on whom something is bestowed, or to whom a gift is made.

A موهودي *mawhūdī*, A garment with sleeves which reach the ground.

A موهوص *mawhūs*, (A man) of a good (constitution), firm, compact (body), with the joints of the bones well knit together.

A موهوم *mawhūm*, Imagined, fancied, opined, thought. Suspected, supposed, surmised. Imaginary.

A موهون *mawhūn*, Enervated, weakened.

A موهوهة *muwahwihat*, (A woman) shaking from repletion or corpulence.

A موهيّ *mawhīy*, Torn, lacerated.

P موي *mūy* or *moy*, Hair of the head. Pile (of cloth or carpets). Hair, down, first plumage of birds. *Moy*, Weep thou. موي از كف بر آمدن *mūy az kaf bar āmadan*, Hair growing from the palm of the hand, (metaph.) An impossibility. موي بر بستن *mūy bar bastan*, To be prepared, to make ready. موي خمير *mūyi khamīr*, Ease, facility. موي مستعار *mūyi mustaʻār*, Borrowed locks, artificial curls. موي نهاني يا زهار يا عانه *mūyi nihānī*, or *zihār* or *ʻāna*, Hair of the pubes. موي و خمير *mūy u khamīr*, (or موي و روغن *mūy u rawghan*) Expressions signifying any thing easy to be done.

A مويّ *muwayy*, (for مويه *muwayh*) Little water.

P موي‌ار *mūy-ār*, Wearing long hair, hairy.

P مويان *moyān*, Weepers, mourners. *Mūyān* or *moyān*, (pl. of موي *mūy* or *moy*) Hairs.

A موئبات *mu*,*ibāt*, Shameful, scandalous (jobs).

A موئبة *maw*,*ibat*, Disgrace, shame, ignominy.

P مويتاب *mūy-tāb*, A hair-rope maker.

P مويتراشي *mūy-tarāshī*, A cutting off the hair of a person to be adopted.

P موي تونتن *mūytūnitan*, (in zand) To count.

P مويچينه *mūy-chīna*, Tweezers.

P موي خوشه *mūy-khosha*, Beards of corn.

A مؤيد *mu*,*yid*, Assisted, victorious. *Mu*,*yid*, (pl. مايد *ma*,*āyid*) A strengthener, a helper. (pl. موائد *mawā*,*id*) Large, weighty. Evil, misfortune.

A مؤيّد *mu*,*ayyad*, Confirmed, fortified, assisted. *Mu*,*ayyid*, One who confirms, increases in strength, strengthens, corroborates, or aids.

A مؤيّر *mu*,*ayyir*, An indulger in venery.

P موي رفتگي *mūy-raftagī*, Baldness, loss of hair.

P موي رفته *mūy-rafta*, Bald.

P موي ريخته *mūy-rekhta*, Bald, moulted, that has shed his coat, or cast his feathers.

P مويز *mawīz*, Dried grapes, raisins.

P مويز آب *mawīz-āb*, An acid and inebriating drink made from dried grapes and water.

P مويزك *mawīzak*, A certain black grain.

P مويزه *mawīza*, A kind of woodbine.

P مويژ *mawīj*, Red paint used by women.

A مؤيّس *muʼayyis*, One who drives to despair.

P موي شكاف *mūy-shikāf*, The Indian hyacinth. (figuratively) The ringlets of the fair.

A مويشي *maweshī*, A herd or drove of oxen.

P موي كن *mūy-kan*, (Hair-extracting) Tweezers.

P موي كنان *mūy-kanān*, Tearing the hair.

P موي گياه *mūy giyāh*, The hairy grass; Indian spikenard.

A موئل *mawʼil*, A refuge, an asylum. A place where a current stops.

A مويل *muwayl*, The month Rajab. *Muwayl* and *muwayyil*, (dim. of مال *māl*) Little wealth.

A مؤيّل *muʼayyil*, A master of flocks.

A مؤيّم *muʼayyim*, Widowing (God).

A مؤيمة *muʼyimat*, (A woman) blest with abundance, but destitute of a husband.

P موي ميان *mūy miyān*, Long hair flowing down the back.

P موين *mūyin*, Made of hair.

P مويندي *moyandī*, Skill, art, dexterity.

P مويه *moya*, Weeping, lamentation.

A مويه *muwayh*, (or مويهة *muwayhat*) (dim. of ماء *māʼ*) A little water.

P مويه زال *mūya-zāl*, Name of a note in music.

P مويه‌گر *moyagar*, A weeper.

P موبي *mūyī*, Made of fur or hair. جامهٔ موبي *jāmaʼi mūyī*, A garment trimmed with fur.

P موييدن *moyīdan*, To weep and cry aloud. To lament the dead. To milk.

P موئين *mūʼīn*, Twisted or made of hair. Slender as hair.

P موبينه *mūyīna*, Made of fur. A big drum.

P مه *ma*, A pen. A sand-hill. No, not (with the imperative). مه رس *ma ras*, Do not arrive. *Mah*, The moon. مه نو *mahi naw*, New moon. مه بدر *mahi badr*, Full moon. *Mih*, Great. Principal. The forehead. A fog, mist.

A مه *mah*, (for ما *mā*) What? *Mah* or *mahin*, (and مه مه *mah mah*) Desist! abstain!

A مهّ *mahh*, (v. n. of مهّ) Dealing gently with, being kind and easy to.

P مها *mahā*, Crystal. *Mihā*, Great.

A مها *maha'*, (pl. of مهاة *mahāt*) Wild cows.

A مهاء *mahāʼ*, Crookedness. Defect, blemish.

A مهاب *mahāb*, Formidable (place). *Muhāb*, Awful, revered (man); dreaded (thing).

A مهابّ *mahābb*, (pl. of مهبّ *mahabb*) Quarters whence the wind blows.

P مه آباد *mah-ābād*, Name of the most ancient prophet who was sent to Persia, and author of a book called Dasātīr.

A مهابة *mahābat*, (v. n. of هاب for هيب) Fearing, being in awe of. Reverence, fear, dread. Majesty, gravity, awe, greatness, authority.

A مهابذة *muhābazat*, (v. n. 3 of هبذ) Running, making haste, being swift in running or flying.

A مهابل *mahābil*, (pl. of مهبل *mahbil*) Wombs, or the lower parts of them.

A مهاة *mahāt*, (pl. مها *maha'*, مهوات *mahawāt*, and مهيات *mahayāt*) A wild cow. Crystal, a bit of crystal. The sun. *Muhāt*, (pl. مهى *muha'*) The seed of the male in the womb of the female.

A مهاتاة *muhātāt*, (v. n. 3 of هتي) Conceding, granting. Concession, grant, present.

A مهاترة *muhātarat*, (v. n. 3 of هتر) Speaking opprobriously, provoking by reproaches.

A مهاتكة *muhātakat*, A travelling in the dark.

A مهاجاة *muhājāt*, A reviling, cursing, reproaching, satirizing in verse, lampooning each other.

A مهاجر *muhājir*, A fugitive, one who abandons his country, especially on account of public calamity or persecution. Obscene, disgusting (talk).

A مهاجرة *muhājarat*, (v. n. 3 of هجر) Abandoning one's friends, fleeing from country to country on account of persecution. Desertion, flight. Separation, distance.

A مهاجزة *muhājazat*, (v. n. 3 of هجز) Saying a thing privately, telling a secret, whispering.

A مهاجلة *muhājalat*, (v. n. 3 of هجل) Contending (with another) in drinking or forcing water. Travelling through low grounds.

A مهاجي *muhājī*, Mutually satirical.

A مهاجين *mahājīn*, (or مهاجنة *mahājinat*) (pl. of هجين *hajīn*) Those whose fathers are free, but their mothers slaves.

A مهاد *mihād*, (pl. امهدة *amhidat* and مهد *muhud* or *muhd*) A bed, sofa, chair, throne, or any place on which one sits or reclines. A cradle. A floor, pavement firm beneath the tread. A flat country, valley. A waste. A prop, stay, support. A place or state which any one prepares for himself. P سلطان نيك نهاد عالي مهاد *sultāni nīk-nihādi ʻāli-mihād*, The magnanimous prince; the prince on the throne endowed with illustrious qualities.

A مهاداة *muhādāt*, (v. n. 3 of هدي) Gratifying one another with gifts, making mutual presents. Going staggeringly with another, walking between two, supported by them on account of weakness.

A مهادنة *muhādanat*, (v. n. 3 of هدن) Making peace or cessation of arms. Truce, peace.

A مهاذبة *muhāzabat*, The doing (a thing) quickly.

A مهاذيب *mahāzīb*, Quick-moving (camels).

P مهار *mahār*, Reins, a bridle.

A مهار *mahār*, (v. n. of مهر) Excelling in any art or profession. *Mihār*, A piece of wood put through a perforation in the nose of a camel to guide him by. (pl. of مهر *muhr*) Horse-colts.

A مهاراة *muhārāt*, (v. n. 3 of هري) Ridiculing, jeering, gibing one another.

A مهارة *mahārat*, (v. n. of مهر) Excelling in any art or profession. Subtlety, acuteness, genius, skill, excellence. *Mihārat*, (pl. of مهر *muhr*) Horse-colts.

A مهارّة *muhārrat*, (v. n. 3 of هرّ) Detesting, expressing abhorrence (of one) before (his) face.

A مهارش *muhārish*, One who sets (men or dogs) by the ears. مهارش العنان *muhārishu'l ʻinān*, (A horse) swift and obedient to the rein.

A مهارشة *muhārashat*, (v. n. 3 of هرش) Setting (men or dogs) by the ears. Dallying, toying.

A مهارق *mahārik*, (pl. of مهرق *muhrak*) Polished papers. Books, writings, papers, diplomas.

P مهار گسستگي *mahār-gusistagī*, Unruliness.

P مهار گسسته *mahār-gusista*, Headstrong, unruly.

A مهاري *mahāra'*, (or مهاريّ *mahāriy*) (pl. of مهريّة *mahrīyat*) Excellent camels, so named from مهر *mahr*, the father of a tribe.

A مهاريس *mahārīs*, Mortars.

A مهازل *mahāzil*, Years of scarcity.

A مهازلة *muhāzalat*, (v. n. 3 of هزل) Being careless, remiss, jesting, trifling, playing.

A مهازيل *mahāzīl*, (pl. of مهزول) Lean, emaciated.

A مهاشاة *muhāshāt*, A playing, jesting with.

A مهاصاة *muhāsāt*, A breaking of the back.

A مهاصريّ *muhasiriy*, Striped stuff of Yaman.

A مهاضاة *muhāzāt*, (v. n. 3 of هضو, not in use) Considering as foolish or contemptible, despising.

A مهافاة *muhāfāt*, A being obsequious, attentive.

A مهاكاة *muhākāt*, A holding cheap, despising.

A مهال *mahāl*, Formidable, dreadful (place). Delay, pause, respite. *Muhāl*, Poured out (earth or sand), overflowing.

A مهالاة *muhālāt*, A terrifying, frightening.

A مهالبة *mahālibat*, Descendants of one مهلّب *muhallab*, a poet, and father of a tribe.

A مهالّة *muhāllat*, (v. n. 3 of هلّ) Agreeing with by the month, or from new moon to new moon.

A مهالسة *muhālasat*, The whispering a secret.

A مهالك *mahālik*, (pl. of مهلكة *mahlikat*) Dangerous places, perils, precipices, deserts.

A مهامّ *mahāmm*, (pl. of مهمّ *muhimm*) Serious affairs, momentous business, important transactions. مهامّ جمهور *mahāmmi jumhūr*, Business of the nation. اهمّ مهامّ *ahammi mahāmm*, The affair of affairs, the most important of all concerns, indispensable business.

A مهامة *mahāmat*, A desert.

A مهامرة *muhāmarat*, (v. n. 3 of همر) Sweeping off, taking the largest part.

A مهامز *mahāmiz*, (pl. of مهمز *mihmaz*) Spurs.

A مهامسة *muhāmasat*, A private conference, whispering conversation.

A مهامشة *muhāmashat*, A making haste together.

A مهامه *mahāmih*, (pl. of مهمه *mahmah* and مهمهة

mahmahat) Extensive deserts.

A مهاميز *mahāmīz*, (pl. of مهماز *mihmāz*) Spurs.

P مهان *mihān*, (pl. of مه) The great: grandees.

A مهان *muhān*, Despised, slighted; abject, base.

A مهانة *mahānat*, (v. n. of هان for هون) Being despicable, contemptible, abject. Baseness, meanness, a contemptible state.

A مهانغة *muhānaghat*, (v. n. 3 of هنغ) Soothing, flattering (a beloved object), especially by amorous verses or speeches.

A مهانفة *muhānafat*. (v. n. 3 of هنف) Smiling ironically (a woman). Playing, joking, toying.

P مهانل *mahānul*, (or مهانول *mahānūl*) Opium.

A مهاواة *muhāwāt*, (v. n. 3 of هوي) Contending, disputing, litigating. Going fast, increasing in speed. Treating kindly. Soothing, flattering. Playing, trifling, now offering a thing, now drawing it back.

A مهاوة *mahāwat*, (v. n. of مهو) Being thin and watery (milk or butter).

A مهاودة *muhāwadat*, (v. n. of هاد for هود) Doing (any thing) repeatedly. Making peace, truce, or cessation of arms. Conciliating, causing to incline to each other. Promising, plighting faith, appointing time and place.

A مهاوش *mahāwish*, Unjustly acquired wealth. Stolen cattle or other plunder. من اصاب مالاً من مهاوش اذهبه الله في نهابر *man asāba mālan min mahāwish, azhabahu'llāh fī nahābir*, A proverb equivalent to, "What is gotten over the devil's back, is spent under his belly."

A مهاوشة *muhāwashat*, (v. n. 3 of هاش for هوش) Mixing, interfering with.

A مهاونة *muhāwanat*, A favouring of one's self.

A مهاوي *mahāwī*, (or مهاويّ *mahāwīy*) (pl. of مهوي *mahwa'*, مهواء *mahwāʼ*, and مهواة *mahwāt*) Gorges, ravines between two mountains.

A مهاه *mahāh*, Beauty. The lustre of any thing fresh and new. Any thing easy or tolerable. A vain thing. Beautiful.

A مهاهة *mahāhat*, A thing easy to be done.

A مهاياة *muhāyāt*, Partition of usufruct.

A عليه مهاياة *ʻalayhi muhāyaʼat*, An affair in which many are jointly concerned.

A مهايث *muhāyis*, One who receives much.

A مهايثة *muhāyasat*, (v. n. 3 of هاث for هيث) Disputing about multitude. Asking much.

A مهايجة *muhāyajat*, (v. n. 3 of هاج for هيج) Exciting, stirring up. Firing with rage. Fighting, killing. Battle, contest, fierceness.

A مهائص *mahāʼis*, (pl. of مهيص *mahyas*) Places where birds mute and deposit guano.

A مهايطة *muhāyatat*, (v. n. 3 of هاط for هيط) Calling out, making a noise. Being near.

A مهائع *mahāʼiʻ*, (pl. of مهيع *mahyaʻ*) Open (roads).

A مهبّ *mahabb*, (pl. مهابّ *mahābb*) A breathing-hole, vent. A place whence or whither the wind blows. *Muhibb*, Who awakes or arouses from sleep.

A مهباب *mihbāb*, Libidinous (stallion). A goat that rattles much at rutting-time.

A مهبّج *muhabbaj*, Heavy, slow, dull.

A مهبرج *muhabraj*, Bad, uneven (bow-string).

A مهبط *mahbit*, A place by which one descends. *Muhbit*, Who or what throws down, precipitates. Who or what lessens, lowers, or abates (a price).

A مهبع *muhbiʻ*, An owner of colts of the last foaling (such colts being called هبع *hubaʻ*).

A مهبل *mahbil* or *mahbal*, The womb, that part of it where the fœtus is lodged. The neck or orifice of the uterus. The straight gut. A pass through a country. مهبل الهوا *mahbilu'lhawa'*, A mountain-path from top to bottom. *Mihbal*, Nimble, active.

A مهبّل *muhabbal*, (A son) lost by death. Corpulent, fleshy. Plump-faced. Cursed, anathematized.

A مهبوت *mahbūt*, Weak, timid, languid.

A مهبوش *mahbūsh*, Collected, scraped together.

A مهبوط *mahbūt*, Lean, emaciated by disease.

A مهبول *mahbūl*, Bereaved.

P مهپارگان *mah-pāragān*, (pl.) Fair as the moon.

P مه پاره *mah-pāra*, A piece of the moon. A mistress. A month.

P مه پرستان *mah-parastān*, Lovers.

A مهتّ *mihatt*, Glib-tongued, talkative.

P مهتاب *mah-tāb*, Moonlight, moonshine, full moon, splendour of the moon. The moon. A kind of firework. مهتاب پیمودن *mah-tāb paymūdan*, To measure moonshine, *i.e.* to engage in any vain undertaking, to build castles in the air.

P مهتابي *mah-tābī*, Belonging to, or bright as, the moon. A kind of fireworks. An open high terrace.

A مهتاض *muhtāz*, One whose bone has been broken after having been set.

A مهتاف *muhtāf*, Thirsty (man).

A مهتبّ *muhtabb*, Libidinous (stallion).

A مهتبد *muhtabid*, One who gathers or breaks the colocynth (هبد *habd*): or who takes out the seeds and boils it to weaken the bitterness of it.

A مهتبر *muhtabir*, A cutter (with a sword).

A مهتبش *muhtabish*, Assembled, convened.

A مهتبل *muhtabil*, A liar. (See اهتبال *ihtibāl*.)

A مهتتش *muhtatish*, Irritated (dog, wild beast).

A مهتجّ *muhtajj*, Insolent, outrageous.

A مهتجل *muhtajil*, One who conceives or brings forth any thing new.

A مهتجم *muhtajim*, Who milks dry (an udder).

A مهتجن *muhtajin*, Who marries a girl too young.

A مهتجنة *muhtajinat*, A female palm-tree bearing fruit for the first time.

A مهتجون *muhtajūna*, (pl. of مهتجي) Satirists.

A مهتجي *muhtajī*, Mutually satirical.

A مهتدي *muhtadī*, Directed, conducted, led (into the way of salvation). Guided aright. (See اهتداء.)

P مهتر *mihtar*, Greater. Elder. Prince, lord, chief, governor. A sweeper, a menial who removes filth. A groom. مهتر رخت *mihtari rakht*, Keeper of the wardrobe, valet. A head-servant who superintends the packing of travelling-furniture.

A مهتر *muhtar*, Delirious with old age. One who speaks dotingly, foolishly, blunderingly.

P مهتراني *mihtarānī*, (fem. of مهتر *mihtar*) A female remover of filth. A female innkeeper.

P مهترائي *mihtarāʼī*, Chiefship. Seniority.

A مهترع *muhtariʻ*, A breaker (of aloe-wood).

P مهتري *mihtarī*, Dominion, grandeur.

A مهتزع *muhtaziʻ*, Swift. Brandished, flourished (sword), vibrative, vibratory (spear).

A مهتزم *muhtazim*, (A horse) making a noise when running. (See اهتزام *ihtizām*.)

A مهتشّ *muhtashsh*, Affable, agreeable, benign.

A مهتشم *muhtashim*, Submissive. (See اهتشام.)

A مهتصر *muhtasir*, A lion. (See اهتصار.)

A مهتضب *muhtazib*, Verbose. (See اهتضاب.)

A مهتضم *muhtazam*, Forced. Defrauded, injured.

A مهتقع *muhtakaʻ*, Changed colour. *Muhtakiʻ*, (A mean disposition) which restrains, prevents, and keeps (one) back from achieving any illustrious action. (See اهتقاع *ihtikāʻ*.)

A مهتكع *muhtakiʻ*, Submissive. (See اهتكاع.)

A مهتلس *muhtalas*, Weak (in mind).

A مهتلك *muhtalik*, One who throws himself into danger. One who never resolves on a thing, but people hem him in. One in quest of forage and water who loses his way. مهتلكين *muhtalikin*, (pl.) Foragers who have lost their way.

A مهتمّ *muhtamm*, Anxious, concerned.

A مهتمج *muhtamij*, Debilitated, enervated by heat. Withered, shrivelled (face).

A مهتمر *muhtamir*, Gallopping (horse).

A مهتمش *muhtamish*, Mixed. (See اهتماش.)

A مهتمط *muhtamit*, One who injures, defrauds (another) of his right. A slanderer, detractor.

A مهتمل *muhatmil*, A whisperer, a defamer.

A مهتني *muhtaniʼ*, A skilful manager.

A مهتور *muhtawir*, Going to ruin; perishing.

A مهتوش *mahtūsh*, (A dog) irritated, instigated, set after game.

P مهتوك *mahtūk*, Dead, defunct.

A مهج *mahj*, (v. n. of مهج) Sucking (the teat). Lying with. Looking beautiful after a disease.

A مهجة *muhjat*, Life, soul, spirit. Heart's blood.

A مهجد *muhjid*, Asleep. (See اهجاد *ihjād*.)

A مهجر *muhjir*, One who goes abroad and travels in the heat of the day. Beautiful, elegant, excellent, noble, superior. Fat (camel) yet travelling well. Spreading (palm-tree). Great, numerous. (See اهجار.)

A مهجّر *muhajjir*, One who repairs betimes to the house of prayer.

A مهجرة *muhjirat*, Vain, foolish, indecent, obscene (speech); an execration. Spreading (palm-tree). Handsome (she-camel).

A مهجع *mihjaʻ*, Senseless, foolish. Careless. *Muhjiʻ*, Who allays (his hunger).

A مهجل mahjil, The womb, or that part of it where the fœtus is lodged. A water-course. Muhjil, One who permits (camels) to go slower. One who widens or enlarges (a thing). One who loses (money).

A مهجلة muhjalat, Large-bellied and flabby (woman). Burst (woman).

A مهجم muhjim, (God) removing a distemper. (See also اهجام ihjām.)

A مهجن muhjin, Possessed of many white camels of an excellent kind. (A stallion) impregnating (a young she-camel).

A مهجنة mahjanat, (مهجني mahjana', or مهجناء mahjunā) Worthless, good-for-nothing persons.

A مهجنة muhajjanat, (A camel) not allowed to be covered for the first time except by a stallion of her own breed. (A female palm-tree) fecundated for the first time.

A مهجو mahjūw, Satirized, lampooned.

A مهجور mahjūr, Separated, cut off. Left, forsaken, abandoned, rejected, repudiated. Delirious, foolish (speech), nonsensical (stuff). (A stallion camel) whose head is tied to the saddle.

A مهجوري mahjūrī, Separation, absence.

A مهجوس mahjūs, Ambiguous, perplexed.

A مهجوم mahjūm, Falling, ruinous (house). (A tent) whose cords are loosened.

A مهجه mahcha, A little moon. An ornament on the top of an ensign-staff. A round bit of wood perforated with a circular hole for receiving the upper end or head of a tent-pole.

P مهد mahd, An auger, wimble. A certain root from which pearl-ashes are made.

A مهد mahd, (v. n. of مهد) Making (a bed), spreading equally. Attending to one's affairs and gaining. (pl. مهود muhūd) A cradle, couch, swing. A tract of level ground. من المهد mini'l mahd, From the cradle. مهد نفس موسي mahdi nafs-mūsa', The ark of bulrushes in which the infant Moses was exposed. مهد مينا mahdi mīnā, The sky. Muhd, (pl. امهاد amhād and مهدة mihadat) A piece of ground prominent or hollow; also plain and level. Muhud or muhd, (pl. of مهاد mihād) Beds.

A مهدّ mihadd, Talkative (man).

A مهدأ mahdas, Part of the night (a third).

A مهداء mihdās, Accustomed to give presents.

A مهدأة mahdasat, Condition, estate.

A مهداج mihdāj, Shrill-voiced (camel).

A مهدّب muhaddab, Fringed (silken garment).

A مهدة muhdat, A piece of ground prominent or hollow; also plain and level. Mihadat, (pl. of مهد muhd and مهدة muhdat) Patches of ground prominent or hollow; also plain and level.

A مهدد mahdad, A woman's name.

A مهدر muhdar, (Blood) shed with impunity.

A مهدّر muhaddir, Braying (camel). كالمهدّر في العنّة ka'l muhaddir fi'l ʿunnat, Like a camel braying in the pen kept apart from the females (said of one who makes a noise without doing any thing).

A مهدرة mahdarat, Small fore-teeth.

A مهدفة muhdifat, Fleshy (woman).

P مهدم mahdum, A pigeon with a black body and white tail.

A مهدم muhdim, Libidinous (she-camel).

A مهدن muhdin, (A horse) that abates or conceals his speed.

A مهدنة mahdanat, Quiet, tranquillity.

A مهدود mahdūd, Demolished, ruined.

A مهدوش mahdūsh, Instigated, irritated (dog).

A مهدوم mahdūm, Destroyed, demolished, levelled with the ground. Thick (milk). Giddy in sailing. مهدوم الاساس mahdūmu'l asās, Totally ruined, destroyed to the very foundation.

A مهدومة mahdūmat, (Land) wet with gentle rain.

A مهدي mihda', A plate or any thing similar in which an offering or a present is made. A man or woman who makes frequent offerings or presents. Muhda', Offered, presented, dedicated.

A مهديّة mahdīyat, A bride carried home to her husband's house. A present, gift.

P مهديّة mahdīya, Name of a city in the west.

A مهذار mihzār, Delirious, raving, doting (woman). Mihzār, (or مهذارة mihzārat) Delirious, raving, doting. A dotard.

A مهذّب muhazzab, Good, sincere, upright, free from vice. Improved. Polite. Adorned, trimmed.

A مهذر mihzar, Delirious, doting.

A مهذف mihzaf, Quick, active, expeditious.

A مهذم mihzam, Sharp, keen (sword).

A مهر mahr, (v. n. of مهر) Contracting, engaging by writing to make a settlement on a wife. Excelling in any art or profession. (pl. مهور muhūr) A marriage-portion or gift settled upon the wife before marriage. Muhr, (pl. امهار amhār, مهار mihār, and مهارة mihārat) A horse-colt. The firstling (of a horse or other aninal). (pl. مهرة miharat) A bone in the upper part of the breast. The fruit of the colocynth. Muhar, (pl. of مهرة muhrat) Joints of the breast; or gristles of the ribs.

P مهر mihr, The sun. Love, friendship, affection, kindness. Mercy, pity. The month of September. The sixteenth day of every month. Death. A mandrake. A red stone. A gilded ball fixed on a canopy or a standard. Name of a fire-temple. Name of an angel. Name of a village in Hindūstān. مهر خاوران mihri khāwarān, Name of the poet انوري anwarī. مهر شريعت mihri sharīʿat, An epithet of Muhammad. مهر و محبّت و ودّ و الفت mihr u mahabbat u widd u ulfat, Love, and friendship, and affection, and benevolence. Muhr or muhur, A seal, seal-ring. A gold coin current in India for about 1l. 16s. The cautery, or the instrument which makes the impression; also the mark made upon cattle by way of distinction. Virginity of a daughter. مهر جم muhri jam, (مهر خم muhri khum, or مهر فم muhri fam) Silence. مهر دهان روزه داران muhri dahāni roza-dārān, An epithet of the sun during the month of Ramazān. مهر زدن muhr zadan, To seal. مهر شدن muhr shudan, To be suspended, deferred. مهر كردن muhr kardan, To suspend, defer. مهر سليمان muhri sulaymān, The seal of Solomon; also the knot of Solomon, being two triangles interbraced, which they suppose to have a cabalistical virtue. مهر نبوّت muhri nubūwat, The seal of prophecy impressed on the shoulder of Muhammad. مهر نره muhri nara, Glans penis. Muhr, (or مهر مريم muhri maryam) (The knot of Mary) A kind of herb.

P مهرا mihrā, Name of the daughter of the governor of Kābul and mother of Rustam.

A مهرّأ muharras, Well-dressed or boiled.

P مهراب mihrāb, Name of a champion of Tūrān. (See مهرا mihrā.)

A مهرات muhrāt, (pl. of مهرة muhrat) Fillies.

P مهراز mihrāz, (in Morocco) A mortar.

A مهراس mihrās, (pl. مهاريس mahārīs) A mortar in which any thing is bruised. An oblong stone trough in which they perform their ablutions before prayer. A man fearing nothing in the night-time. A camel bulky and slow. A voracious camel.

P مهراسفند mihr isfand, Name of the twenty-ninth day of every month in the solar year; also of the angel presiding over that day.

A مهراع mihrāʿ, as المهراع al mihrāʿ, The lion.

A مهراق mah or muhrāh, Poured out, diffused.

P مهران mihrān, Name of a great river. Name of a learned man. Name of a king.

A مهرانه muhrāna, A fee exacted by the Kāzī from the Muhammadans at weddings.

A مهرب mahrab, (v. n. of هرب) Fleeing, running away. Flight. A place to flee unto. Mihrab, A wooden instrument moved to and fro by a sower. Muhrib, Timid, fearful.

P مهربان mihrbān, Benevolent, beneficent, kind, affectionate, friendly, compassionate, favouring, loving: propitious. A preserver, defender. A friend.

P مهرباني mihrbānī, Friendship, friendliness, kindness. A sort of stuff of an extremely delicate texture. Name of a note in music. مهرباني كردن mihrbānī kardan, To favour, to shew friendship.

P مهرباني كرده شده mihrbānī karda shuda, Pitied.

A مهرة mahrat, The name of the founder of an Arabian tribe. Muhrat, A female colt, a filly. A bone in the upper part of the breast. A small shell or pearl used as a philtre by women. (pl. مهر muhar) A joint in the breast; or the gristle of the ribs. لم تعط هذا الامر المهرة lam tuʿti hāza'l amra'l miharata, You have not gone the right way to work in this matter. Maharat, (pl. of ماهر māhir) Masters, skilful men in any art or profession. مهرة فنّ حديث maharasi fanni hadīs, Celebrated collectors or expounders of the sayings (of Muhammad). *Miharat*, (pl. of مهر *muhr*) Bones in the upper parts of the breast. Colocynth-fruits.

A مهرّت الاشداق *muharratu'l ashdāk*, (A dog) having a wide, gaping mouth.

A مهرج *mihraj*, (A horse) running much or fast.

P مهرجان *mihrjān* or *mahrajān*, The autumnal equinox. The autumn. فصل مهرجان *fasli mahrajān*, The autumnal season. A festival celebrated in Persia in the month of September.

A مهرجة *mahrajat*, (v. n. of مهرج Q, a verb coined from P مهرجان *mahrajān*) Presenting (a sweetmeat) at the autumnal equinox.

P مهر خوان *mihr-khwān*, A title, an address (used particularly in India); as, آصف خان *āsaf-khān*, اسلام خان *islām-khān*, &c.

P مهردار *muhr-dār*, Keeper of the seals.

P مهردهان *muhr-dahān*, Taciturnity. A fast.

P مهردهانان *muhr-dahānān*, Those who fast.

A مهرزق *muharzak*, Shut up in prison.

P مهرزن *muhr-zan*, A sealer.

A مهرع *muhraʿ*, Trembling from terror, anger, or weakness. المهرع *al muhriʿ*, The lion.

A مهرق *muhrak*, (pl. مهارق *mahārik*) A shell used in smoothing or glazing paper. A tableman for playing draughts or backgammon. Glazed paper: A leaf, page. A book, writing. A desert; level ground.

A مهرقان *mahra*, *muhra*, or *muhrukān*, The sea.

P مهرگان *mihrgān*, Autumn. (See مهر *mihr*.) مهرگان بزرگ *mihrgāni buzurg*, Name of a note in music. مهرگان خاصه *mihrgāni khāsa*, Name of the twenty-first day of the month مهر *mihr*. مهرگان خردك *mihrgāni khurdak*, (or مهرگان کوچك *mihrgāni kūchak*) Name of a note in music. مهرگان عامه *mihrgāni ʿāma*, Name of the sixteenth day of the month مهر *mihr*.

P مهرگاني *mihrgānī*, Autumnal. Autumnal produce. Name of the twenty-fifth note of the barbud.

P مهرگيا *mihr-giyā*, (or مهرگياه *mihri giyāh*) A mistress, the face of a sweetheart. The mandrake. The plant turnsole. A fresh fruit, from the root of which a delicious juice is extracted. Chemists; those especially who search after the philosopher's stone. The down on the cheek of a youth. Kings.

A مهرم *mahram*, (or مهرمة *mahramat*) Decrepitude, imbecility of old age.

P مهرماني *mihrmānī*, Name of the twenty-fifth note of the barbud.

P مهرماه *mihrmāh*, Name of the seventh month of the solar year.

A مهرنفة *muharnifat*, (A female) crying in a low sobbing voice, and weeping silently.

P مهرو *mah-rū*, Moon-faced, beautiful.

A مهروء *mahrūʾ*, Affected by intense cold.

P مهروبان *mahrūbān*, Name of a town in Persia.

A مهرود *mahrūd*, (Cloth) dyed yellow.

A مهرودة *mahrūzat*, equiv. to ممصّرة *mumassarat*.

A مهرور *mahrūr*, (A camel) troubled with a flux or watery tumour between the skin and flesh.

A مهرورق *muhrawrik*, (Rain) poured forth.

A مهروع *mahrūʿ*, Fallen on the ground. Seized with madness.

A مهروءن *mahraʾun*, Hurt by intense cold.

P مهره *muhra*, A kind of small shell resembling pearls; concha veneris. Glass or coral-beads. A stone found in the head of a serpent. A shell used for giving a smoothness and a glossiness to paper. An iron or bone polishing-instrument. A rubber. Glossiness (of paper). A chessman, a tableman, counter for playing any game, as backgammon or draughts. Dice. A smith's hammer. مهرهٔ پشت *muhraʾi pusht*, The back-bone. مهره تاج *muhra-tāj*, Any thing hollow which is blown like a trumpet. مهرهٔ جاندارو *muhraʾi jān-dārū*, Bezoar-stone. مهرهٔ خاك *muhraʾi khāk*, (or مهرهٔ گلين *muhraʾi gilīn*) Terrestrial globe. Human body. مهره در جام افگندن *muhra dar jām afgandan*, To throw the pebble into the cup (a signal for mounting on horseback). مهره در ششدر بودن *muhra dar shash dar būdan*, To be fast in prison. مهره در طاس افگندن *muhra dar tās afgandan*, To break wind. مهره در گردن جمع شدن *muhra dar gardan jamʿ shudan*, To break the neck. مهرهٔ ديوار *muhraʾi dīwār*, Plaster, incrustation, or ornament of a wall. مهرهٔ زر *muhraʾi zar*, The world-illuminating sun. مهرهٔ سيم *muhraʾi sīm*, (or مهرهٔ سيمابي *muhraʾi sīmābī*) Moon and stars. مهرهٔ لاجورد *muhraʾi lājaward*, The sky. مهرهٔ مشكين *muhraʾi mushkīn*, The earth. مهره و حقّه *muhra u hukka*, (Cup and ball) Earth and heaven. مهرهاي تسبيح *muhrahāyi tasbīh*, A string of beads, rosary. مهرهاي فلك *muhrahāyi falak*, The stars. خرمهره *kharmuhra*, Trappings for mules ornamented with small shells. كاغذ مهره كردن *kāghid muhra kardan*, To glaze or smooth paper. مهرهاي سيمابي *muhrahāyi sīmābī*, The stars.

P مهره دار *muhra-dār*, Polished, glazed, glossy.

P مهره زن *muhra-zan*, A polisher.

P مهره سنگ *muhra-sang*, An onyx, especially one black and white found in Arabia.

P مهري *mihrī*, A psaltery, sackbut. A kind of lute. P *Muhrī*, A drain, a gutter. P *Muhurī*, (or مهرّي *muharrī*) Any writer or under-clerk among the natives of Bengal.

A مهرّأ *muharraʾ*, Well-dressed, boiled (meat).

A مهريّ *mahrīy*, (pl. مهاري *mahāraʾ*) A camel bred in the tribe of Mahrat.

A مهريّة *mahrīyat*, (pl. مهاري *mahāraʾ* and مهاريّ *mahārīy*) A particular species of Arabian camel. A red kind of wheat.

A مهريق *muhrīk*, One who pours out.

A مهز *mahz*, (v. n. of مهز) Keeping back, driving off. Striking on the breast with the fist.

A مهزأة *mahzaʾat*, (v. n. of هزأ) Laughing at, mocking, jeering.

A مهزاق *mihzāk*, (A woman) who laughs immoderately, and remains not still in a place.

A مهزام *mihzām*, A tower. A piece of wood on the end of which boys in play put fire (whence, يلعبون مهزاما *yalʿabūna mihzāman*, They play at that game). A poker or brand with which they stir the fire. A short staff or rod.

A مهزر *mihzar*, Cheated, cozened, defrauded.

A مهزرق *muhazrak*, Shut in prison, imprisoned.

A مهزع *mihzaʿ*, A pestle with which they pound in a mortar. A lion crushing his prey. One who breaks every tree.

A مهزور *mahzūr*, Driven off, expelled.

A مهزول *mahzūl*, (pl. مهازيل *mahāzīl*) Emaciated (especially with age).

A مهزوم *mahzūm*, Routed, put to flight. Divided, separated, torn (from one's family).

P مهست *mahist*, Weighty, heavy.

A مهش *mahash*, (v. n. of مهش) Burning. Being burnt. Scratching with the nails. Shaving (her) face (a woman).

A مهشاء *mahshāʾ*, (or مهشام *mihshām*) (A she-camel) soon becoming lean.

A مهشار *mihshār*, (A camel) conceiving at once.

A مهشوم *mahshūm*, Broken. Routed.

P مهشيد *mah-shed*, Moonlight. The moon.

A مهصاء *mahsāʾ*, (Ground) bare of herbage.

A مهصار *mihsār*, (or مهصر *mihsar*) (A lion) breaking to pieces his prey.

A مهصل *muhsal*, Thick, bulky (ass).

A مهصم *mihsam*, A lion.

A مهصور *mahsūr*, Bent, curved, bowed down.

A مهصوص *mahsūs*, Trampled on. Broken.

A مهصهصة *muhas-hisat*, A thief's eye at night.

A مهصير *mihsīr*, (A lion) crushing his prey.

A مهضم *muhazzam*, Slim (waist). Reeden (pipe).

A مهضوض *mahzūz*, Broken, bruised, pounded.

A مهضوم *mahzūm*, Collapsed, shrunken (belly). Close, compressed (as the two divisions of a cloven foot). Reeden (flute). المهضومة *al mahzūmat*, An aromatic made with a mixture of musk and unguentary nuts.

A مهضهضة *muhazhizat*, (A woman) troublesome to her neighbours.

A مهطع *muhtiʿ*, One who keeps the eyes fixed on the ground in silence from modesty or humility. (A camel) naturally low in the neck.

A مهطول *mahtūl*, Wet with incessant rain.

A مهع *mahaʿ*, A change of colour in the face produced by some fearful event.

A مهفّفة *muhaffafat*, Slender-waisted, merry, and jovial (girl).

A مهفّك *muhaffak*, A blundering fellow.

A مهفوت *mahfūt*, Astonished, amazed.

A مهفهفة *muhafhafat*, Slender-waisted, merry, and jovial (woman).

A مهق *mahk*, (v. n. of مهق) Running. *Mahak*,

Greenness of water. Blue colour of eyes.

A مهقاء *mahkā*, (fem. of امهق *amhak*) White, without any mixture of red or glossiness. Blue or grey (eye). (A fountain) of green water.

A مهقوع *mahkūʿ*, (A horse) marked with a circle of hairs on the breast.

P مهك *mahk*, Liquorice. *Muhak*, A wart.

A مهك *mahk*, (v. n. of مهك) Grinding (aromatics) into a fine powder. Tiring, wearing out with excessive venery. Polishing, smoothing. Travelling fast (camels). *Mahak*, (v. n. of مهك) Being addle, unfruitful (a stallion's loins).

A مهكة *mah* or *muhkat*, Youth; maturity of youth.

A مهكر *mahkar*, (or مهكرة *mahkarat*) A place for wonder or admiration.

A مهكوك *mahkūk*, Worn down by rubbing. Impudent, saucy. Unable to keep in wind or dung.

A مهل *mahl*, (v. n. of مهل) Anointing (a camel) with the liquid pitch called خضخاض *khazkhāz*. The pus of dead bodies. *Mahl* or *mahal*, (v. n. of مهل) Going quietly, doing any thing by degrees, slowly, easily. Quiet, leisure. Delay, respite. على مهله *ʿala' mahlihi*, Leisurely, by degrees. لا مهل *lā mahla*, No delay. *Muhl*, Any kind of mineral or metal, especially melted brass or iron. Mother or dregs of oil. Liquid pitch. Pus, matter. Poison, venom. A bit of coal or ashes dropping from bread. *Mahal*, Quiet, leisure, delay, calm procedure, slow movement. Progress, advancement. Ancestors. Corruption of a dead carcase.

A مهلاً *mahlan*, Fair and softly, give a little time.

A مهلب *muhallab*, Name of a poet. *Muhallib*, The coldest days in the middle of January.

A مهلة *mah*, *mih*, *muh*, or *mahalat*, The pus of dead bodies. *Muhlat*, Thin or melted pitch. Delay, putting off, deferring, retarding; respite, time, leisure. Provision or preparation made for any approaching event. A delay granted for an appointed time or term. اخذ على فلان المهلة *akhaza ʿala' fulānin al muhlata*, He took precedence of So-and-so (in age or in good-breeding).

P مهلقا *mah-likā*, Fair as the moon, beauteous.

A مهلك *muhlak*, Destroyed, ruined. *Muhlik*, Destructive, killing, fatal, deadly, pernicious.

A مهلكة *mahlakat*, *mahlikat*, or *mahlukat*, A dangerous place, precipice. A desert. *Mahlikat*, (v. n. of هلك) Dying, perishing.

A مهلل *muhallal*, Bent, curved in the form of the new moon; crescent-shaped, semi-lunar. (A camel) humpbacked from leanness.

P مهلند *mahland*, An Indian sword.

A مهلوب *mahlūb*, (A horse) the hairs of whose tail have been plucked out: rat-tailed.

A مهلوس *mahlūs*, Stupid, silly. Lean. Consumptive. مهلوس العقل *mahlūsu'l ʿakl*, Bereft of reason.

A مهلوسة *mahlūsat*, Skinny (woman).

A مهلهل *muhalhal*, Delicately-composed (verse). Thinly or finely-wrought (cloth). *Muhalhil*, A maker of fine, subtle, or delicate verses. Name of Amru'l Kays.

A مهمّ *muhamm*, Oppressed with care, sad. *Muhimm*, Great, important, necessary, urgent, serious, momentous (business). P مهمّ شدن *muhimm shudan*, To be of great consequence, to urge, press.

A مهما *mahmā*, As often as, so many times as, whensoever. Whenever. Wherever. How often? When? مهما امكن *mahmā amkana*, In whatever it may be possible, whenever it can, as often as possible.

A مهمّات *muhimmāt*, (pl. fem. of مهمّ *muhimm*) Necessary things, matters of grave importance. Expeditions. Studies, cares, endeavours. مهمّات سفر *muhimmāti safar*, Needful provisions for a journey.

A مهمار *mihmār*, Verbose, talkative.

A مهماز *mihmāz*, (pl. مهاميز *mahāmīz*) A spur.

A مهمام *mahmāmi*, Nothing remains (in answer to ابقي عندكم شيء *a baka' ʿindakum shay*, Have you any thing left?)

P مهمان *mihmān*, A guest. A son-in-law.

P مهمان پرور *mihmān-parwar*, Hospitable.

P مهمان پروري *mihmān-parwarī*, Hospitality.

P مهمان خانه *mihmān-khāna*, (or مهمان سراي *mihmān-saray*) An inn, caravansera, or any place where travellers are lodged and entertained. A hospitable hall. A hospital, hospice. An almshouse. The world.

P مهمان دار *mihmān-dār*, A hospitable or courteous man. One who has the charge of receiving and entertaining guests. A host. An officer appointed to receive and entertain an ambassador.

P مهمانداري *mihmān-dārī*, Hospitality, a waiting upon guests.

P مهماني *mihmānī*, An entertainment, banquet, feast. Hospitality. مهماني كردن *mihmānī kardan*, To prepare a feast, to give مهماني عام *mihmānīi ʿām*, A general entertainment to all ranks (مهمانيء خاص *mihmānīi khās* implying a banquet to which only select friends are invited). مهمانيء ختنه *mihmānīi khutna*, A circumcision-feast. مهمانيء عروس *mihmānīi ʿarūs*, A marriage-feast.

A مهمّة *mahammat*, (v. n. of همّ) Keeping (one) in an anxious state of mind (a thing). *Muhimmat*, An important affair, about which one grows anxious.

P مهمترين *muhimtarīn*, Most important, necessary above all.

A مهمر *mihmar*, Verbose, talkative.

P مهمرد *mih-mard*, A great man. Head man of a ward, judge of the market. Master of the horse.

A مهمز *mihmaz*, (pl. مهامز *mahāmiz*) A spur.

A مهمزة *mihmazat*, A goad, or instrument of wood, or pointed with iron (for driving asses).

A مهمّق *muhammak*, Bruised barley.

A مهمل *muhmal*, Allowed to range at liberty. Not used, obsolete, of no signification; spoken without meaning; (a word) used improperly: neglected. A letter without a diacritical point, unpointed; as, د *dāl* or ر *rā* with respect to ذ *zāl* or ز *zayn*, the former being called دال مهملة *dāli muhmala*, the latter ذال معجمة *zāli muʿjama*. (in grammar) Not governing (opposed to عامل *ʿāmil*). *Muhmil*, Negligent, careless, remiss, indifferent, unconcerned.

A مهمسلج *muhamlaj*, Convenient, manageable (business). Tractable, easy-paced (pack-horse).

A مهموز *mahmūz*, Alif ا *hamzated*, *i.e.* marked with *hamza* ـٔ. (A poem or verse) ending in hamza.

A مهموس *mahmūs*, Hidden, concealed. Feebly pronounced (letter).

A مهموسة *mahmūsat*, Those letters of the alphabet which are contained in the artificial words, حثه شخص فسكت *hassahu shakhsun fasakata*.

A مهموص *mahmūs*, Agitated, disturbed (at heart).

A مهموك *mahmūk*, Relaxed, hanging down.

A مهمول *mahmūl*, Shed, fallen, dropt (tear).

A مهموم *mahmūm*, Grieved, sad, low, melancholy.

A مهمه *mahmah*, An extensive desert.

A مهمهة *mahmahat*, (v. n. of مهمه Q) Checking, chiding, rebuking, driving off. Preventing, hindering. (pl. مهامه *mahāmih*) An extensive desert. A barren wilderness.

P مهميز *mihmīz* or *mahmīz*, A spur. مهميز كردن *mihmīz kardan*, To spur (a horse).

P مهميز خور *mihmīz-khwur*, A horse that will bear the spur, dull, thick-skinned.

A مهن *mahn* or *mihn*, (v. n. of مهن) Serving, waiting upon (as a domestic). Striking, distressing, injuring. Drawing (a garment). Lying with. Milking (a camel) at her return from watering.

A مهنأ *mahnaʾ*, Easy, light, wholesome. Any thing acquired without trouble.

A مهنّأ *muhannaʾ*, Received with congratulations, or deserving of them.

A مهناء *muhanāʾ*, (pl. of مهين *mahīn*) Contemptible, abject. Weak in judgment. Little, few. Unfruitful (stallions).

P مهناك *mahnāk*, Bright (moon), at the full.

P مهنانه *mahnāna*, An ape, a monkey.

A مهنب *mihnab*, Intensely silly.

A مهنة *mahnat*, (v. n. of مهن) Serving. Service. *Mihnat*, *mahnat*, *mahanat*, or *mahinat*, Skilfulness in doing any thing (specially adroitness as a servant).

A مهنّد *muhannad*, (A sword) of Indian steel.

A مهندس *muhandis*, (or مهندز *muhandiz*) (a word coined from the P اندازه *andāza*) A geometrician. A maker of subterraneous aqueducts. A measurer, land-measurer. مهندس فلك *muhandisi falak*, An astronomer. The planet Saturn.

A مهندسيّ *muhandasiy*, Constructed with mathematical exactness (هندسة *handasat*).

A مهندم *muhandam*, Prepared with due regard to rule and proportion (P اندام *andām*).

A مهنوء *mahnūʾ*, (A camel) daubed with pitch.

A مهنوع *mahnūʿ*, (A camel) marked with هنعة.

A مهنون *mahnūn*, Strong. Fat. Made to weep.

A مهنّأ *muhanna'*, Received with gratulations.

A مهنّي *muhanniع*, One who congratulates.

A مهو *mahw*, (v. n. of مهو for مها) Striking hard. Thin, watery milk. A thin or sharp sword; and shining when brandished. Pearls. A whitish stone. A ripe date. A violent blow. Cold. Name of the father of an Arabian tribe.

A مهواء *mahwāع*, A space between two mountains, or any thing similar, gap. The atmosphere.

A مهواة *mahwāt*, Air, sky, atmosphere.

A مهوات *mahawāt*, (pl. of مهاة) Wild cows.

P مهوار *mahwār*, Like the moon. Monthly.

P مهوارة *mahwāra*, A monthly stipend.

A مهواع *mihwāع*, A shout in battle.

A مهوأنّ *muhwaعann* or *عinn*, A large plain; extensive desert. Custom, usage. Part of the night.

A مهوب *mahūb*, Awful, revered (man). Formidable (place). A lion.

A مهوبرة *muhawbarat* or *muhawbirat*, Hairy (ear). *Muhawbirat*, Very fleshy (she-camel).

A مهوة *mahwat*, Tenuis genitura.

A مهود *muhūd*, (pl. of مهد *mahd*) Cradles.

A مهوّد *muhawwad*, (fem. مهوّدة *muhawwadat*) Gentle (singing). Turned Jew, judaised.

P مهور *mahwar*, The selenites in Arabia (having a number of shining white spots, which increase and decrease with the moon).

A مهور *muhūr*, (v. n. of مهر) Excelling in any art or profession. (pl. of مهر *mahr*) Dowries, marriage-portions, or gifts settled on wives before marriage.

A مهوّس *muhawwas*, Struck with fury, demented. *Muhawwis*, Dementating. An alchymist.

A مهوّسي *muhawwisī*, Alchymy.

P مهوش *mahwash*, Like the moon. Beautiful as the moon. A sweetheart.

A مهوع *mihwaع*, A shout in battle.

A مهوك *mahūk*, A slender, limber bow.

P مهول *mahūl*, A gin for catching birds.

A مهول *mahūl*, (in comp. with هول *hawl*) as, هول مهول *hawlun mahūlun*, Great terror.

A مهوّل *muhawwil*, Terrific, horrible. One who exacts an oath by fire. (See تهويل *tahwīl*).

A مهوّن *muhawwin*, One who makes light or easy.

P مهوند *mahwand*, Name of a place in India famed for its salt.

A مهوي *mahwa'*, A space between two mountains, or the like; a gap, gorge. A precipice.

A مهويّ *mahwīy*, Desired, loved, liked, wished.

A مهوئنّ *muhwaعinn* or *muhwaعann*, A wide extent of low land.

A مهه *mahah*, (v. n. of مهه) Being smooth. Smoothness. The lustre of any thing fresh or new. Smooth. Any thing easy or supportable. Hope. A vain thing. Intention, design. Pendulousness. Time. Languor, slowness. (See also مهل *mahal.*)

A مهي *mahy*, (v. n. of مهي) Pouring much water upon any thing. Making thin, sharpening (a shoemaker's knife). The full speed of a horse: a giving him plenty of rein. *Muha'*, (pl. of مهاة *muhāt*) Aquæ admissariorum.

P مهي *mahī*, A kind of crystal, which, when hung round the neck, is supposed to facilitate parturition. *Mihī*, Greatness. Seniority.

A مهيّأ *muhayya'*, (or حاضر ومهيّا *hāzir u muhayya'*) Disposed in order, prepared, arranged, ready.

P مهيّا داشتن *muhayya' dāshtan*, To keep ready.

A مهيات *mahayāt*, (pl. of مهاة) Wild cows.

A مهياج *mihyāj*, (A camel) sooner thirsty than others. (A she-camel) longing for (her) home.

P مهياز *mihyāz*, Name of a wrestler of Tūrān.

A مهياف *mihyāf*, Fine-necked (camel). Soon or extremely thirsty (man or she-camel).

P مهياوة *mahyāwa*, Jelly of fish dried in the sun. Any condiment eaten with bread.

A مهيب *mahīb*, Formidable, terrible, fearful, awful; severe; grave, revered. المهيب The lion.

A مهيبة *mahyabat*, A cause of fear and dread.

A مهيّج *muhayyij*, Stimulant, inciting.

A مهيدئة *muhaydiعat*, (dim. of مهدأة) Condition.

P مهير *mahīr*, The moon.

A مهيرة *mahīrat*, Free and dowered (woman).

A مهيص *mahyas*, (pl. مهائص *mahāعis*) A place where birds mute. A deposit of guano.

A مهيض *mahīz*, (A bone) broken anew after having been set.

A مهيع *mahyaع*, (pl. مهائع) A broad, open road.

A مهيق *mahīk*, A far country, distant ground. An impression made lengthwise. A mark of the rubbing of the foot.

A مهيك *mahīk*, A stallion that impregnates not.

A مهيل *mahīl*, Formidable, dreadful (place). (Heaped-up dust or sand) poured out, flowing down.

A مهيم *mahyam*, (supposed to be abbreviated from ما هذا يا امر *mā hāza' yā amr*, What is this, O man!) How do you do? how is your health? what has happened to you?

A مهيمن *muhayman*, Safe, secure, protected. A name of God. *Muhaymin* or *muhayman*, A protector, defender from fear and danger. One who says 'amen' to any thing, *i.e.* confirms it by his testimony, a witness, evidence. المهيمن *al muhaymin*, A name of God. مهيمن الاعلي *muhayminu'l aعla'*, The most high God, Omnipotence.

A مهين *mahīn*, (pl. مهناء *muhanāع*) Contemptible, abject. Weak in judgment. Unfruitful (stallion). Little, few. Acid (milk) biting the tongue. *Muhīn*, A despiser, contemner. Ignominious, degrading (punishment).

P مهين *mihīn*, Greater, greatest. Elder born. Fine, subtle, thin. Like, equal. Name of a woman.

P مهينا *mahīnā*, A month. Monthly pay.

P مهينا دار *mahīnā-dār*, A monthly servant.

P مهين دوز *mihīn-doz*, A tailor, a performer of any fine needle-work.

P مهينة *mihīna*, Greater, greatest. Eldest.

A مهيوم *mahyūm*, Thirsty from disease. Astonished, confused, wandering from love or other cause.

P مهيوة *mahyawa*, Any thing eaten with bread. Eggs or rows of fish. Meat dressed with medicinal herbs, prepared with vinegar, and dried in the sun; also preserved with aromatic herbs, vinegar, salt, or in any other manner.

A مهيّي *muhayyī*, An arranger or preparer.

P مي *may*, Grape-wine. Rose-water. Spirituous liquor. A goblet. مي ِ سوسن *mayi sūsan*, Liquorice-wine. مي ِ ناب *mayi nāb*, Neat wine. *Mī*, A particle fixed to Persian verbs, and generally indicating the present or preterite imperfect tense. It is also prefixed to the continuative imperative: as, ميرو *mī rav*, Keep on going.

P ميا *mayā*, A woman's name. (the negative imperative of آمدن *āmadan*, To come) Do not come.

A ميائسة *muyāعasat*, (v. n. 3 of يئس) Rendering desperate, filling with despondency.

A ميابسة *muyābasat*, (v. n. 3 of يبس) Drying.

A مئات *miعāt*, (pl. of مائة *miعat*) Hundreds.

A مياتيم *mayātīm*, (pl. of موتم *mūtim*) (Mothers) left with fatherless children.

A مياثر *mayāsir*, (pl. of ميثرة *mīsarat*) Things thrown over a saddle to make the seat more easy. Outer garments. مياثرالحمر *mayāsiru'l humr*, Persian vehicles of silk (prohibited by the Muhammadan law).

A مياثق *mayāsik*, (or مياثيق *mayāsīk*) (pl. of ميثاق *mīsāk*) Agreements, treaties.

A ميّاح *mayyāh*, (fem. ميّاحة *mayyāhat*) A walker with a graceful, haughty, flaunting air.

A مياحة *miyāhat*, (v. n. of ماح for ميح) Making a present. Deprecating, interceding.

A ميادات *muyādāt*, (v. n. 3 of يدي) Recompensing; giving like for like; retaliating. Delivering from hand to hand, or out of your own to another's.

A ميّادة *mayyādat*, A negro or mulatto girl.

A ميادين *mayādīn*, (pl. of ميدان *maydān* or *mīdān*) Camps, plains. Race-grounds, courses.

A ميازين *mayāzīn*, (pl. of مئذنة) Minarets.

A مئار *miعār*, An exasperating of each other.

A ميّار *mayyār*, One who brings grain from other countries for family-use or sale. *Muyyār*, (and ميّارة *mayyārat*) (pl. of مائر *māعir*) Purveyors, victualers, caterers.

A ميّاس *mayyās*, A pompous walker waving from side to side. A lion. A wolf.

A مياسر *mayāsir*, The left side.

A مياسرة *muyāsarat*, (v. n. 3 of يسر) Being mild, gentle, humane. Turning to the left (with fellow-travellers).

P مياسطو *mayāstū*, Name of a fire-temple.

A مياسم *mayāsim*, (pl. of ميسم *mīsam*) Hot irons with which they brand cattle. Marks so made.

A مياسير *mayāsir*, (pl. of موسر *mūsir*) Opulent, wealthy. (pl. of ميسور *maysūr*) Prosperous (affairs).

A مياسيق *mayāsīk*, (pl. of ميساق *mīsāk*) Birds flapping their wings when flying.

A مياسين *mayāsīn*, (pl. of ميسان *mīsān*) Sparkling stars in Orion.

A مياط *miyāt*, (v. n. of ماط for ميط) Driving away; repulsing. Avoiding, retiring from. A violent push upon the breast.

A ميّاط *mayyāt*, Idle, lazy. An idler, sporter.

A مياطين *mayātīn*, (pl. of ميطان) Race-grounds.

A مياعطة *muyāʻatat*, (v. n. 3 of يعط, not used) Crying "the wolf!" Giving warning of the approach of an enemy.

A ميّافارقين *mayyāfārikīn*, Name of a place.

A مياكيد *mayākīd*, Straps with which the fore parts of camels' saddles are held together.

A مئال *miʼāl*, (pl. of مألة) Meadows. Mills.

A ميّال *mayyāl*, Waving. Very affectionate.

P ميامار *mayāmār*, Reckon not, calculate not.

A ميامن *mayāmin*, The right side. (pl. of يمن *yumn*) Prosperities; benedictions. *Muyāmin*, One who is on the right side.

A ميامنة *muyāmanat*, (v. n. 3 of يمن) Praying for a blessing on another, pronouncing a benediction. Turning to the right (with fellow-travellers). Going to Yaman or Arabia Felix.

A ميامين *mayāmīn*, (pl. of ميمون) Fortunate.

P ميان *miyān*, Waist, loins. Middle, centre. Money-bag, scrip. Sheath, scabbard. Among, between, mean. ميان بربستن *miyān bar bastan*, To gird the waist. ميان لشكريان *miyāni lashkariyān*, Amidst the soldiers. ازميان برافتادن *az miyān bar uftādan*, To be lost, to disappear. درميان آوردن *dar miyān āwardan*, To produce, shew, bring into the middle, introduce. يك روز درميان *yak roz dar miyān*, One day between, every alternate day.

A مئان *muʼān*, A giving attention to.

A ميّان *mayyān*, A liar.

P ميان بالا *miyān-bālā*, Of middle stature.

P ميان بسته *miyān-basta*, Ready, loin-girded.

P ميان بند *miyān-band*, Begirt. A belt, girdle; waistband of drawers or trowsers.

P ميان پاي *miyān-pāy*, Infamous boy. Penis.

P ميان تهي *miyān-tihi*, Empty within; hollow.

P ميانجي *miyānjī*, A mediator, arbitrator, go-between, broker. A schoolmaster. Arbitration. ميانجي كردن *miyānjī kardan*, To arbitrate, mediate.

A ميانجيّ *miyānijiy*, Native of Miyāna.

P ميانجي گر *miyānjīgar*, A mediator.

P ميانجي گري *miyānjīgarī*, Mediation. ميانجي گري نمودن *miyānjīgarī namūdan*, To mediate.

P ميان خالي *miyān-khālī*, Hollow within.

P ميان دار *miyān-dār*, A mediator, procurator, middle-man, broker.

P ميان سر *miyān-sar*, The crown of the head. A female ornament like a small crown adorned with gems worn on the head.

P ميان سرا *miyān-sarā*, (or سراي *sarāy*) Middle; square, court of a house; space between tents.

P ميان سرائي *miyān-sarāʼī*, A kind of grape which grows abundantly in Khurāsān.

P ميان قد *miyān-kad*, Of a middle stature.

P ميان كاواك *miyān-kāwāk*, Hollow within.

P ميانگي *miyānagī*, Middle, half. Mediation.

P ميانگين *miyāngīn*, The centre.

P ميانه *miyāna*, The middle. The middle pearl in a string. Middle-sized. An interstice. Mediation. A sort of covered litter. Name of a city. *Miyānih*, A town in Azarbayjān.

P ميانه حال *miyāna-hāl*, Middling, neutral.

P ميانه روي *miyāna-ravī*, Moderation, economy. A middle course.

P ميانه قد *miyāna-kad*, Of middle stature.

P مياني *miyānī*, A cod-piece.

A ميانين *miyānīn*, Middlemost.

A مياوم *muyāwim*, One who agrees by the day (يوم *yawm*). Daily. Lasting long.

A مياومة *muyāwamat*, (v. n. 3 of يوم) Transacting business in the day-time, bargaining by the day (يوم *yawm*). Hiring for a certain number of days (مشاهرة *mushāharat* implying taking by the month, شهر *shahr*).

A مياه *miyāh*, (pl. of ماء *māʼ*) Waters. مياه جاري *miyāhi jārī*, Running waters, rivers, currents.

A ميبة *maybat*, (from P مي به *may-bih*) A kind of medicine made from quince-juice.

A مئبر *miʼbar*, A needle-case. A sting. (pl. مابر *maʼābir*) Detraction. A secret grudge or hatred (as being caused by slander). Whatever is thrown upon arable grounds or palm-trees to render them fruitful. Fine sand.

A مئبرة *miʼbarat*, Slander. A sowing of dissension. A needle-case. The first sprouting of the dwarf palm-tree called دوم *dawm*.

A ميبّس *muyabbis*, Drying; desiccative.

A ميبل *maybal*, A whip made of twisted leather thongs fastened to a stick. *Mībal*, A thick stick.

A مئبل *miʼbal*, A thick stick.

A ميبلة *maybalat*, A whip of twisted thongs.

P مي پخته *may-pukhta*, (in Arabic turned into ميبختج *may-bukhtaj*) Wine boiled down to a consistency. Syrup of dates and grapes.

P مي پرست *may-parast*, Addicted to wine.

A ميت *mayt*, (pl. ميتون *maytūn*) Dead. A corpse. جماعت ميت *jamāʻati mayt*, A funeral.

A ميّت *mayyit*, (pl. اموات *amwāt*, موتي *mawta'*, or ميّتون *mayyitūn*) Dead. Dying, moribund.

A مئتاء *miʼtāʼ*, A boundary, goal, winning-post (at a race). A public road, highway. The meeting of several roads. Contiguity, conjunction, especially in a straight line. Liberal, attentive to reward. داري بمئتاء داره *dārī bi miʼtāʼi dārihi*, My house is contiguous to his house.

A مئتان *miʼtān*, A woman accustomed to bring forth children with the feet foremost.

A مئتبة *miʼtabat*, A kind of square female shift without bosom or sleeves.

A ميتة *maytat*, Carrion. Unclean cattle of which no tithes are paid. *Maytat*, (or ميّتة *mayyitat*) Dead (woman). *Mītat*, Death. Manner of dying.

A مئتّة *maʼittat*, Victory in a suit at law.

T ميت تاريخي *mayt-tārīkhī*, An epitaph.

A ميتخة *mītakhat*, A staff, stick, cudgel, club.

A ميتد *mītad*, (or ميتدة *mītadat*) A mallet for driving piles or tent-pins.

P ميتر *mītar*, Name of a wrestler.

A ميتّم *muyattim*, (Maker of orphans) Death.

A ميتمة *maytamat*, (pl. of يتيم *yatīm*) Orphans.

P ميتو *mītū*, A kind of club, having a head resembling wings, with sharp edges.

A ميتون *maytūn*, Brought forth with the feet foremost, preposterously born. (pl. of ميت) Dead.

A ميّتون *mayyitūn*, (pl. of ميّت) Dead. Dying.

P ميته *mīta*, A moth.

A ميتيّ *maytīy*, Belonging to the dead.

P ميتين *metīn*, A hoe, pick: stonemason's chisel.

A ميث *mays*, (v. n. of ماث for ميث) Dying. Steeping, soaking, dissolving (in water). *Mīs*, (pl. of ميثاء *maysāʼ*) Soft, level grounds.

A ميّث *mayyis*, Soft, smooth.

A ميثاء *maysāʼ*, (pl. ميث *mīs*) Soft, level ground. *Misāʼ*, A mallet, maul. An anvil.

A ميثاق *mīsāk*, (pl. مواثيق *mawāsīk*, ماياثق *mayāsik*, and مياثيق *mayāsīk*) A promise, agreement, bargain, compact, confederacy, alliance, league. A testament. عهد وميثاق *ʻahd u mīsāk*, Agreements, articles, and conditions (of peace).

A مئثب *miʼsab*, (pl. مآثب *maʼāsib*) A short sword or other instrument with which one rushes upon another. Plain ground. Mountainous ground. A rivulet. Name of a place in the city of Madina, bequeathed by Muhammad to the poor.

A ميثب *mīsab*, Level ground. Hilly ground. One who leaps or springs on. Sedentary.

A مئثرة *miʼsarat*, An iron instrument with which they scrape the soles of camels' feet, that their impressions on the ground may appear more distinctly.

A ميثرة *mīsarat*, (pl. مواثر *mawāsir* and مياثر *mayāsir*) Any thing thrown over a saddle to make the seat more easy. An outer garment. A pad or saddle-cloth. A Persian vehicle of silk or brocade (prohibited by the Muhammadan law). The skin of a lion or other wild beast.

A ميثم *mīsam*, (A camel's foot) treading hard on or scraping the ground.

A ميج *mayj*, Mixture, confusion, perplexity.

A ميجار *mījār*, (pl. مواجير *mawājīr*) A kind of curved stick or shinty. (See صولجان *sawlajān*.)

A ميجاز *mījāz*, Compendious, laconic.

A ميجر *mayjar*, (or ميجرة *mayjarat*) A spoon or

any vessel from which medicine is poured into the (corner of the) mouth: a drenching-horn.

A میجمة *mijamat*, A girdle. A large beetle or mallet. An anvil.

A میجنة *mijanat*, (pl. مواجن *mawājin*) A mallet, hammer. A wooden instrument used by washers.

P میجو *mijū*, A lentil. Pease.

P میچانیدن *michānīdan*, To cause to fry.

P میچودن *michūdan*, To fry. To snatch, carry off. To effect.

A میح *mayh*, (v. n. of ماح for میح) Going down into a well to fill one's pitcher. Walking with elegance. Making a present. Interceding for, deprecating. Cleaning the teeth or extracting spittle with the dentifrice مسواك *miswāk*. The gait of a duck. Profit, gain, advantage. *Mīh*, A bad sour sort of date.

A میحاد *mīhād*, (pl. مواحید *mawāhīd*) One thing (as a hillock) separate from others. A series of units.

A میحال *mīhāl*, Michael (a Christian name).

A میحوحة *mayhūhat*, A walking elegantly.

A میخ *maykh*, A walking pompously.

P میخ *mekh*, A nail. A pin, peg. A tent-pin or pole. A hook, tenter, crook. A wedge. A little broach or spit. A coiner's die. An ingot of gold or silver, from which they cut the pieces to be struck. Caps, fillets, or mitres (which adhere closely to the head). Urine. میخ درم *mekhi diram*, (or میخ دیناري *mekhi dīnārī*) A steel die for coining.

A میخار *mīkhār*, A palm-tree bearing fruit to the last lopping, and to the end of winter. Very dilatory.

P میخانه *may-khāna*, A wine-celler, tavern.

P میختن *mekhtan*, To make water.

P میخ دوز *mekh-doz*, Nailing. Nailed up, closed. میخ دوز کردن *mekh-doz kardan*, To nail, to fasten with nails.

A میخط *mīkhat*, Who or what enters.

P میخ قدم *mekh-kadam*, Lame, unable to stir.

P میخک *mekhak*, A small nail, a tack. A clove.

P میخکده *mekh-kada*, A mint.

P میخ کوب *mekh-kob*, A mallet for driving piles, pegs, or tent-pins. A pile-driver.

P مي خوار *may-khwār*, (or خواره) A wine-drinker.

P مي خوارگي *may-khwāragī*, Wine-bibbing.

P میخور *may-khwur*, A wine-drinker, sot, wine-bibber. An earthen jug for holding wine.

P میخوش *may-khwush*, Subacid. Sapid, sweet.

P میخي *mekhī*, A kind of breastplate. A dervish's habit closely stitched. میخي چند *mekhe chand*, A few nails.

P میخي روپیّه *mekhī rūpayya*, A plugged rupee.

A مید *mayd*, (v. n. of ماد for مید) Inclining. Being crooked. Growing. Being moved, agitated. Walking airily, with a swinging, swaggering gait. Visiting. Lying. Collecting (provisions) and carrying them (to others). Being dizzy (from drink or from the motion of a ship). Becoming damp and changing colour (wheat). Quivering, playing with a tremulous motion (the vapour سراب *sarāb*). A boundary, terminus, goal. *Mayda*, Besides, except. Because. مید ان *mayda an*, Because that, seeing that. Except that.

A میدا *maydā*, Because, on account, for the sake of. Opposite.

A میداء *mīdāʼ*, Quantity, product: measure. End, extremity. Sides of a road. Distance. میداء داره *mīdāʼ dārihi*, (بمیداء داره *bi mīdāʼi dārihi*, or بمیدا داره *bi mīdaʼ dārihi*) Opposite his house.

A میداعة *mīdāʻat*, An every-day garment.

P مي دان *maydān*, A wine-glass. *Mīdān*, Know.

A میدان *maydān* or *mīdān*, (pl. میادین *mayādīn*) An open field without buildings, an extensive plain. A race-ground, or any place for exercises or walking. A field of battle. War, battle, combat. میدان اغبر *maydāni aghbar*, The earth. P میدان بسر آمدن *maydān ba sar āmadan*, The termination of life. The arrival of the day of judgment. میدان خاك *maydāni khāk*, The earth. The body of men or of animals. A میدان عاج *maydāni ʻāj*, A sheet of blank paper. P میدان گشاده یافتن *maydān gushāda yāftan*, To live comfortably and merrily. A *Mayadān*, (v. n. of ماد for مید) Inclining. Being crooked. Being moved (any thing), agitated (a branch). Walking airily, jauntily, with a swinging, swaggering gait.

P میداني *maydānī*, A person who precedes a general or vazir and proclaims his titles. A kind of hookah used by fakīrs. Flour made into dough for the preparation of sweetmeats.

A میدة *maydat*, A table covered with viands.

P میدخ *mīdakh*, A grey horse. A stubborn horse.

A میدع *maydaʻ*, A small sea-fish. *Mīdaʻ*, A bag or place in which clothes are laid up. Enough to enable one to live without work. Disagreeable, offensive (speech). ما له میدع *mā lahu mīdaʻun*, He possesses nothing. *Mīdaʻ*, (or میدعة *mīdaʻat*) (pl. موادع *mawādiʻ*) Every-day, working-garment.

P میدن *mīdan*, To be new. To sift, clean. To incline the mind.

P میده *mayda*, The finest flour. Bread of fine flour unmixed with bran. A kind of sweetmeat. میده کردن *mayda kardan*, To grind flour. To pulverize. *Mīda*, A chaste woman.

P میده سالار *mayda-sālār*, A baker.

P میده نه *mayda-nih*, A table-decker, sewer.

A میدئ *mīdaʼ*, End, extremity.

A میديّ *maydiy*, Hurt in the hand. One whose hand (ید *yad* or یدي *yady*) has been amputated. (A deer) caught in a gin by the fore-foot (مرجول *marjūl* denoting one taken by the hind-foot).

P میدیارم *maydiyārim*, The fifth period, of eighty days, in which living creatures were created.

P میدیوزرم *mīdyūzaram*, A period of forty-five days, in which, according to the notion of the ancient Persians, God created the heavens.

P میدیوسمه *midyūsama*, The second period, consisting of sixty days, when the waters were created.

A میذنة *mīʼzanat*, A turret; a minaret or tower adjoining the Muhammadan mosques, whence the crier summonses the people to prayer. A cloister.

A میر *mayr*, (v. n. of مار for میر) Providing food for one's family; bringing corn from a distance. Moistening, wetting, and rubbing (a medical powder).

P میر *mīr*, An emperor, prince, lord, governor, chief, leader. The head of a family. A title by which the Sayyids or descendants of the family of Muhammad are called. (in comp.) Dying. میرآتش *mīr-ātish*, Chief of the fireworks or artillery, master of the ordnance. میرآتشي *mīr-ātishī*, The office of میرآتش *mīri ātish*. میرآخور *mīri ākhwur*, (or میرآخر *mīr-ākhur*) Master of the horse. میرآش *mīri āsh*, One who calls people to meat. میربکاول *mīri bakāwul*, A house-steward. میرعاشقان *mīri ʻāshikān*, The herb house-leek. میرعدل *mīri ʻadl*, Superintendant of the courts of justice. میرعرض *mīri ʻarz*, Superintendant of petitions. میرعلم *mīr-ʻalam*, (or میر لوا *mīri liwā*) The royal standard-bearer. میرعمارت *mīri ʻimārat*, Superintendant of the buildings, master of the works. میرقافله *mīri kāfila*, Commander of a caravan. میرکلام *mīri kalām*, An eloquent orator. میرمال *mīri māl*, Crown-lands. Master of the treasury. میرمجلس *mīri majlis*, Master of the ceremonies. میرمنزل *mīri manzil*, Overseer of the halting-places. Quarter-master-general. میرمیدان *mīri maydān*, A brave champion. میرهشت بهشت *mīri hasht bihisht*, A title of رضوان *rizwān*, the door-keeper of Paradise. میرهفتمین *mīri haftumīn*, Lord of the seventh (heaven), *i. e.* the planet Saturn.

A مئر *maʼir*, Serious and disastrous (business). *Maʼir* or *miʼar*, A breedbate, a mischief-maker. *Miʼar*, (or میر *miyar*) (pl. of مئرة *miʼrat*) Enmities. Slanders.

A مئرّ *miʼarr*, (A man) much addicted to venery.

A میراث *mīrās*, (pl. مواریث *mawāris*) Heritage, succession, patrimony. P میراث خوردشدن *mīrās-khwur shudan*, (میراثدن، میراثیدن *mīrāsidan*, *mīrāsdan*, میراث زدن *mīrās zudan*, or میراث خوردن *mīrās khwurdan*, To take possession of an inheritance.

P میراث خور *mīrās-khwur*, An heir.

A میراثن *mīrāsan*, A singing-girl (of a caste who sing only before women).

A میراثي *mīrāsī*, Hereditary, inherited. A singer (of a caste which follows that profession from generation to generation). A hereditary right to cultivate the soil, or to hold village-offices (in India).

P میراثي دار *mīrāsī-dār*, A holder of a meerasee right; hence, village-servants whose offices are hereditary.

A میراص *mīrās*, A woman who stools in coitu.

A مئران *miʼrān*, (pl. مآرین *maʼārīn*) A lurking-place, haunt, or den for wild beasts.

P ميران *mīrān*, A portion paid to the head of a department out of the fees received by the inferior officers. ميران قضا *mīrān kazā*, The kāzī's dues or fees. (They are now abolished).

P ميرانيدن *mīrānīdan*, To cause to die. To kill. To mortify.

P ميراو *mīrāv*, The superintendant of a river or other public reservoir for watering fields (when water is allowed to run through a certain opening for a time specified).

P مير بار *mīr-bār*, Master of the hall of audience.

P مير بحر *mīr-bahr*, A collector of port-duty: harbour-master. An overseer of boats.

P مير بحري *mīr-bahrī*, Admiralty. Port-dues.

P مير بخشي *mīr-bakhshī*, Paymaster-general.

A مِرَّة *mi-rat*, Enmity. Slander, calumny.

A ميرة *mīrat*, Corn brought from a distance.

P ميرتن *mīr-tan*, One who makes himself great.

P مير توزك *mīr-tūzak* or *tozak*, Master of the ceremonies. A marshal.

P ميرداد *mīr-dād*, A president, chief judge. A portico or place where those who solicited offices paid their respects to their patrons.

P ميرده *mīr-dah*, A commander of ten, decurion. A tithing-man. A head, chief of the mace-bearers.

P ميرديني *mīrdīnī*, A kind of violet. A kind of silk of which women make inner garments.

P ميرزا *mīr-zā*, A prince; son of a great lord, noble cavalier, knight. A gentleman. A writer, scribe.

P ميرسامان *mīr-sāmān*, Head-steward.

P ميرسين *mīrsīn*, A myrtle-tree.

P مير شكار *mīr-shikār*, Master of the hunt, and trainer of hawks: grand falconer. A bird-catcher. (metaphorically) A pimp.

P مير صد *mīr-sad*, A centurion.

A ميركة *mīrakat*, The place where a fatigued person puts down the foot. A cushion on which they ride. The fore part of a camel's saddle.

P ميرواري *mīrwārī*, Fees levied at ferries.

A ميروق *mayrūk*, (Standing corn) struck with a blight (يرقان *yarakān*). Jaundiced (man).

P ميروك *mīrūk*, A small ant.

P ميره *mīra*, Master of a family. Concord, unanimity. Meat, provision, victual, food.

P ميري *mīrī*, Belonging to a prince. The royal treasury. Land-tax. P A winner at play. (among schoolboys) He that first comes to the master to say his lesson.

P ميريدن *mīrīdan*, To be nipt, frost-bitten.

P ميري مال *mīrī-māl*, The royal revenue.

P ميرين *mīrayn*, Name of the son-in-law of a Roman emperor. Name of Khusraw and of the Amīr Hasan Dahlavī.

A ميز *mayz*, (v. n. of ماز for ميز) Separating, distinguishing, discerning. Preferring, exalting. Departing, removing from place to place. *Mīz*, Very muscular (man).

P ميز *mez*, A stranger, a guest. Preparations for entertaining a guest. A chair on which they eat their dinner. Urine. One who makes water. A table. Discrimination, discernment.

P ميزاب *mīzāb*, Canal, aqueduct, spout, drain.

A مئزاب *mi-zāb*, (Arabic form of P ميزاب *mīzāb*).

P ميزاد *mīzād*, Nuptials, pleasure, joy. A feast.

A P ميزان *mīzān*, (pl. موازين *mawāzīn*) A balance, pair of scales. The celestial sign Libra. Measure, metre, rhyme, verse, prosody. Quantity. Rule, method. A syllogism. استقام ميزان النهار *istakāma mīzānu'n nahār*, The scales of the day are even, *i.e.* it is noon. A عين ميزان *ʻayni mīzān*, Eye of the balance, *i.e.* the perpendicular bars between which the tongue vibrates. لسان الميزان *lisānu'l mīzān*, Tongue of the balance. P نو روز ميزان *naw-rozi mīzān*, The autumnal equinox.

P ميزبان *mezbān*, A landlord, master of the house or of a feast, one who hospitably entertains strangers; a host. A caravansera, or place where travellers lodge.

P ميزبان گستري *mezbān-gustarī*, Hospitality.

P ميزباني *mezbānī*, Hospitality. Housekeeping. ميزباني كردن *mezbānī kardan*, To use hospitality.

P ميزد *mayazd* or *mīzad*, A banquet of wine, marriage-feast, entertainment: pleasure, high living, festivity, jollity, mirth. *Mezad*, He makes water.

P ميزده *may-zada*, Overcome with wine. Indisposed, upset by excessive drinking.

P ميزر *mayzar*, A turban.

A مئزر *mi-zar*, (pl. مازر *ma-āzir*) A veil. Breeches, trowsers. An apron.

P ميزك *mezak*, Urine. A little rain. A mixture; mixed, entangled, intricate things.

P ميزمان *mezmān*, (for ميزبان *mezbān*) A host.

P ميزه *mīza*, The middle of a saddle.

P ميزيدن *mezīdan*, To make water. To mix. To be hard, frozen. *Mayzīdan*, To suck. To taste.

P ميژد *mījad*, A mistress, concubine.

P ميژك *mījak*, A murmuring, muttering.

P ميژو *mījū*, A lentil; pease, pulse.

A ميس *mays*, (v. n. of ماس for ميس) Walking flauntingly, airily, jauntingly, or with an elegant air. Afflicting with numerous maladies (God). Being hard and thick. A kind of large tree. A large kind of vine; also of grapes.

A ميساب *mīsāb*, A date nearly ripe.

A ميساق *mīsāk*, (pl. مياسيق *mayāsīk* and مئاسيق *ma-āsīk*) A bird flapping his wings when flying.

A ميسان *maysān*, (pl. مياسين *mayāsīn*) A glittering star. Name of a star in Orion. One who walks in a stately manner. The night of Badr. Name of a village between Basrah and Wāsit. *Mīsān*, Sleepy, drowsy. ميسانة الضحى *mīsānatu'z zuha'*, (A woman) very drowsy at breakfast-time (or luncheon). *Mayasān*, (v. n. of ماس for ميس) Walking flauntingly, airily, jauntily.

P ميسي *mesī*, The leprosy. Leprous.

A ميسر *maysar*, A sort of plant. *Maysir*, The camel which the Pagan Arabians used to purchase on credit. (They then slaughtered him and divided the carcase into eight-and-twenty, or into ten parts, for which they drew lots with gaming arrows, called ازلام *azlām*. The expense was defrayed by those who drew blanks.) Dice, cards, or any game of hazard prohibited by the Muhammadan law.

A ميسّر *muyassar*, Facilitated, rendered easy, feasible, practicable, favourable, and happy (by Omnipotence). Attained, attainable, procurable, obtainable. Ready, prepared. A dish made of eggs and meat. *Muyassir*, One who facilitates, renders easy, gives success. (A man) possessed of sheep which give plenty of milk.

A ميسرة *maysarat*, The left side, left wing of an army. ميمنة ميسرة *maymana maysara*, Right and left. Fortunately and unfortunately; right and wrong. *Maysarat*, *maysirat*, or *maysurat*, Opulence, prosperity. Ease, facility.

A ميسم *mīsam*, (pl. مواسم *mawāsim* and مياسم *mayāsim*) A hot iron with which they brand cattle. The mark so made. The impression (on a coin). Any characteristic mark. Root, origin. Beauty. ذات ميسم *zāt mīsam*, Beautiful (woman).

A ميسور *maysūr*, (v. n. of يسر) Being easy. (pl. مياسير *mayāsīr*) Facilitated, made easy, prosperous, going on successfully. Prosperous, affluent. قول ميسور *kawlun maysūr*, An easy, *i.e.* a kind word.

A ميسورات *maysūrāt*, Prosperous affairs.

A ميسوسن *may-sūsan*, A lotion which women use in washing their heads.

A ميسون *maysūn*, Handsome, well-made (youth).

P ميسيدن *mīsīdan*, To wash. To stroke, soothe. To milk.

A ميش *maysh*, (v. n. of ماش for ميش) Mixing (intelligence), *i.e.* telling one part and concealing another. Mixing half of what is in the udder, and letting the rest remain. A mixture of wool and hair; also of sheep and goat milk.

P ميش *mesh*, A sheep. A ram. The sign Aries.

P ميشا *meshā*, (or ميشاني) The plant houseleek.

A مئشار *mi-shār*, (pl. مآشير *ma-āshīr*) A saw. A knob at the end of a locust's tail.

A ميشار *mīshār*, (pl. مواشير *mawāshīr*) A saw. The jagged or serrated part of a locust's leg.

P ميشانه *mīshāna*, Name of the first woman.

P ميش بهار *mesh-bahār*, Ox-eye (a plant). Houseleek. A cloud.

A ميشة *mayshat*, A passing through (a land).

P ميشته *mīshta*, A Jewish doctor.

P ميشتي *mīshtī*, A kind of silken stuff.

P ميش چشم *mesh-chashm*, One having sheep's eyes, *i.e.* of a dark grey colour. A blockhead.

P مي ء شعري فش *may-i shiʻra' fash*, Red wine.

P ميش ماده *mesh-māda*, A ewe.

A ميشمة *mishamat*, A woman who punctures her posteriors with indigo by way of ornament.

P ميش مرغ *mesh-murgh*, A bustard.

P ميشناي *mishnāy*, Name of an herb.

P ميشو *mishū*, A vetch.

A ميشوم *mayshūm*, Unfortunate, unlucky, ill-omened, inauspicious. Perverse, execrable.

P ميشه *misha*, Name of the first man.

U ميشى *mishī*, A kind of leather, chamois.

A مئشير *mi*ₛ*shīr*, Active, lively, sprightly (horse, camel, or woman).

P ميشين *meshīn*, Belonging to sheep. A dressed sheep's skin.

P ميشينه *meshīna*, A flock of sheep.

A ميضاء *mīzā*ₛ, A vessel from which they pour water when performing their ablutions.

A ميضأة *mīza*ₛ*at*, A place for performing sacred ablutions. A jug or vessel with a spout, from which they pour water when making religious ablutions.

A ميضانة *mīzānat*, A basket, pannier, hollowed gourd or calabash serving the same purpose.

A ميضنة *mīzanat*, (pl. مواضين *mawāzīn*) A thing in the form of a sack made of palm-leaves.

A ميط *mayt*, (v. n. of ماط for ميط) Beating off, repulsing, pushing forward. Putting to a distance. Being far distant, retiring, receding. Railing, chiding. Wandering from the right path, being wicked, deviating from justice. Oppressing. Augmentation, increase. Power. Something, somewhat.

A مئط *ma*ₛ*it*, (or ميّط) Increase, augmentation.

A ميطاء *mīṭā*ₛ, Low land between high lands.

A ميطان *mīṭān*, The extremity of any thing. A race-ground, especially the starting-post (the winning-post being expressed by ميتاء *mītā*ₛ and ميداء *mīdā*ₛ). *Mayatān*, (v. n. of ماط for ميط) Being far off, retiring, receding. Placing at a distance.

A ميطدة *mīṭadat*, An instrument with which they beat clay floors to make them hard and smooth, a beetle; also one for driving piles into the ground.

A ميظب *mīzab*, A stone sharp as a knife.

A ميع *may*ع, (v. n. of ماع for ميع) Flowing over the surface of the ground. Melting (as fat). Running (a horse).

A ميعاد *mī*ع*ād*, Place or time of a promise. Return, anniversary. يوم الميعاد *yawmu'l mī*ع*ād*, Day of promise, *i.e.* the resurrection.

A ميعاس *mī*ع*ās*, Soft ground. Soft sand. A road.

A ميعة *may*ع*at*, The flowing of any thing poured out. Mirth, joy. The beginning of a horse's gallop. Morning. Bloom of youth. A certain perfume exceedingly fragrant. Storax. Oil of myrrh. Gum of the quince-tree. A certain tree from whose kernel the liquid ميعة *may*ع*at* is expressed, and whose bark forms the dry ميعة *may*ع*at*. ميعة النشاط *may*ع*atu'n nashāt*, The bloom of youth.

P ميغ *megh*, A cloud. Fog, mist. ميغ گاه *megh-gāh*, The place where the pilgrims encamp at Mecca.

A ميغر *mīghar*, (or ميغرة) A certain fixed time.

P ميغناك *meghnāk*, Cloudy; misty, foggy.

A ميفاء *mīfā*ₛ, Projecting, appearing above, sticking out. The lid or cover of an oven. A large hearth for baking bread. A kiln for burning brick. High ground.

A ميفاة *mīfāt*, An eminence, high ground.

A ميفاض *mīfāz*, Swift (she-camel, she-ostrich).

A ميفاق *mīfāķ*, Convenient season, opportunity.

A مئفر *mi*ₛ*far*, Active, ready to serve.

P مي فروش *may-farosh*, A vintner.

A ميفعة *mayfa*ع*at*, Highness of ground.

A ميفوخ *mayfūkh*, Hurt on that part of the head called يافوخ *yāfūkh*.

A ميفىً *mīfa'*, An eminence, high ground. The cover or lid of an oven. A brick-kiln. A hearth for baking bread.

A مئق *ma*ₛ*iķ*, A boy sobbing, and breathing with difficulty.

A ميقاب *mīķāb*, One who drinks much water. Foolish (woman), or one esteemed so. A woman who brings forth foolish children. (A woman) wide about the privities (whence بنو الميقاب *banū'l mīķāb* is a term of reproach). سير الميقاب *sayru'l mīķāb*, Incessant journey day and night.

A ميقات *mīķāt*, (pl. مواقيت *mawāķīt*) A stated time. A place appointed for a certain time or action. ميقات الحاجّ *mīķātu'l ḥājj*, The place where the pilgrims assemble, whence they proceed to perform the solemnities at the temple of Mecca.

A ميقاد *mīķād*, (A steel) which soon strikes fire.

A ميقار *mīķār*, (pl. مواقير *mawāķīr*) Loaded, carrying a heavy burden.

A ميقاف *mīķāf*, A wooden ladle, or any thing for stirring a pot and stilling its boiling.

A ميقان *mīķān*, One who credits all he hears.

A ميقب *mīķab*, A white shell, concha veneris.

A ميقع *mayķa*ع, A complaint resembling measles, incident and fatal to young camels.

A ميقعة *mīķa*ع*at*, A place where a falcon generally lives: a perch, roost. A mallet, smiths' hammer. A washer or bleacher's beetle. A wooden block, on which they beat cloths with that beetle. A whetstone for swords, knives, and the like. A file.

A ميقف *mīķaf*, A wooden ladle, or any thing for stirring a pot and stilling its boiling.

A ميقوظ *mayķūz*, Wakened, roused from sleep.

A مئكال *mi*ₛ*kāl*, An instrument for eating with (as spoons, or even forks where they are known).

A ميكال *mīkāl*, (ميكائيل *mīkā*ₛ*īl*, or ميكائين *mīkā*ₛ*īn*) Michael.

P ميكده *may-kada*, A tavern. A wine-cellar.

A ميكع *mīka*ع, Thick and firm (leathern bottle). (pl. of ميكعة *mīka*ع*at*) Ploughshares.

A ميكعة *mīka*ع*at*, A ploughshare.

A مئكلة *mi*ₛ*kalat*, A kind of small travelling-kettle used by the Scenite Arabs and gypsies. A small dish holding enough for three persons.

P ميگ *mayg*, A locust.

P ميگزد *mī-gazad* or *may-gazad*, A banquet of wine. A marriage-feast or any entertainment: pleasure, festivity, jollity, mirth. The banqueting-house of kings and other great men.

P ميگسار *may-gusār*, A wine-drinker.

P ميگك *maygak*, A locust. A small locust.

P ميگندر *mīgandar*, or ميگنده *mīganda*, Stinking.

P ميگون *may-gūn*, Wine or ruby-coloured, reddish. Auburn, fair. Somewhat rusty.

A ميل *mayl*, (v. n. of مال for ميل) Inclining, leaning. Deflecting, deviating. Setting (as the sun). Inclination, tendency, penchant, bias, impulse, affection, love, benevolence. ميل شمس *mayli shams*, Sunset. P ميل كردن *mayl kardan*, To love, to have an inclination or partiality for. ميل نمودن *mayl namūdan*, To incline. A *Mīl*, (pl. اميال *amyāl* and ميول *muyūl*) A mile (used generally for an English or Italian mile, though often for a German mile or French league). A mile of four thousand cubits. As far as the eye can reach, ken. A mile-stone or direction-post. A column, an obelisk. A wooden club for exercising the arms, dumb-bells. A goal. The axletree of a carriage. A surgeon's probe. A bodkin, skewer, or wire for anointing the eye with collyrium. A pointed iron style, used in writing on palm-leaves. Water, or a hot iron with which they take away the eyesight. P ميل كشيدن *mīl kashīdan*, To blind. To drive to a distance. ميل فرش *mīli farsh*, A weight laid on the edge of a counterpane or a carpet to prevent the wind from entering below. A *Mayal*, (v. n. of ميل) Inclining with the body to one side, from any natural defect. An inclination to one side wryness, obliquity. *Miyal*, (pl. of ميلة *mīlat*) Times.

A مئل *ma*ₛ*il*, A fat, bulky man.

A ميّل *mayyil*, Rich, wealthy, monied. *Muyyal*, (pl. of مائل *mā*ₛ*il*) Inclined, biassed.

A مئلّ *mi*ₛ*all*, Swift (horse).

A ميلاء *maylā*ₛ, (fem. of اميل *amyal*) (A woman) inclined to one side. Large (heap of sand). Very branchy (tree). Crooked-bunched (she-camel). A mode of rolling the sash round the turban; also of combing hair without curling or twisting.

A مئلاة *mi*ₛ*lāt*, (pl. مآلى *ma*ₛ*ālī*) A handkerchief tied round the waist, which a woman holds in her hand when crying and weeping.

P ميلاد *mīlād*, Name of a city. Name of a champion of Iran.

A ميلاد *mīlād*, Nativity, birth-day.

P ميلاميل *mīl-ā-mīl*, From mile to mile, step by step. Continuation, succession. All, the whole. Mixed together.

P ميلان *maylān*, Name of a philosopher.

A ميلان *mayalān*, (v. n. of مال for ميل) Inclining towards, being propense. Deviating. Loving.

Inclination, affection, regard, respect.

P ميلاو *milāv*, A pupil, apprentice, servant.

P ميلاوه *milāwa*, Drink-money given to a servant over and above his hire. Good news.

A ميلاة *milāh*, (A she-camel) excessively fond of the male. Distracted from excess of affection, frantic at the loss of a child. A violent wind.

A مئلب *mi،lab*, Swift, quick, active.

A ميلة *mīlat*, (pl. ميل *miyal*) Time.

A ميلع *mayla،*, Tall, long. Swift, quick-paced (camel). Moveable, waving to and fro; in perpetual motion. A barren waste.

A ميلغ *mīlagh*, (or ميلغة *mīlaghat*) A vessel from which a dog laps or eats his food.

A ميلق *maylak*, Swift, nimble, quick.

A مئلق *mi،lak*, Foolish, insane. A man, at one time sane, and at another time crazy.

A ميلولة *maylūlat*, An inclining, leaning, bias.

P ميله *mīla*, Name of a place in Turkistān where a battle was fought by Mahmūd Ghaznavī.

A ميله *mīlah*, A desert, barren plain.

A ميلي *maylī*, Willingly, of one's own free will and inclination.

P ميلي *mīlī*, A cat.

A ميم *mīm*, The letter م *m*, which stands for 40. Pure, neat wine. A well. ميم كاتب *mīmi kātib*, Blind. ميم مطوّق *mīmi mutawwak*, Penis.

P ميم *mayam*, A note in music. My wine.

A مئمّ *mi،amm*, A guider, leader. A camel that leads the troop (acting as an امام *imām*).

A ميماس *mīmās*, The Orontes.

A ميمّم *muyammam*, Possessed of all he wishes.

A ميمّن *muyamman*, Fruitful (year). Whoever or whatever brings a blessing and prosperity.

A ميمنة *maymanat*, The right side or hand. The right wing of an army. Fortune; prosperity, happiness. P مانهٔ همايون ميمنت مقرون *nāma،i humāyūni maymanat-makrūn*, August, imperial, or royal letters or mandates.

P ميمند *maymand*, A town in Ghaznīn.

A ميموم *maymūm*, Plunged into the sea; engulphed in the mighty deep. Encroached upon and overflowed by the sea (يمّ *yamm*).

P ميمون *maymūn*, A baboon, ape, monkey. A slave. Name of a certain creeping-plant.

A ميمون *maymūn*, (pl. ميامين *mayāmīn*) Fortunate, happy, prosperous, august, auspicious. Penis.

A مي مي *mi، mi،*, The bleat of a lamb or fawn.

A ميميّ *mīmiy*, Possessing the letter م *mīm*.

P ميميز *mīmīz*, Dried grapes, raisins.

A مين *mayn*, (v. n. of مان for مين) Lying. Ploughing (the ground). (pl. ميون *muyūn*) A lie.

P بي مين *bī mayn*, Without a lie.

TART. مين *mīn*, (for من *man*) I, me.

P مينا *mīnā*, A glass globule or bead, a false gem of a blue colour. Bluestone, caustic. A blue colour. A stone resembling lapis lazuli, with which they tinge silver. Vitriol; essence of vitriol. Alchymy. Enamel. Concha veneris. A goblet, glass, decanter. Heaven, sky, the azure vault. Name of a fort between Lār and Hormuz. مينا كردن *mīnā kardan*, To enamel.

A مينا *mīna'*, (or ميناء *mīnā،*) A port, haven, harbour. An anchoring-ground, anchorage.

A ميناء *mīnā،*, A glass gem.

P مي ناب *may-nāb*, Pure wine.

A مئناث *mi،nās*, (A woman) who brings forth only girls. An effeminate wretch. Blunt (sword).

A ميناثة *mīnāsat*, (Ground) luxuriant in herbage, fruitful in pot-herbs. Blunt (sword).

P مينار *mīnār*, A tower, turret, steeple, spire, minaret. An obelisk.

A مئناس *mi،nās*, Name of a woman.

A مئناف *mi،nāf*, One who travels early in the night. A shepherd who has no pasture ungrazed.

P مينا فام *mīnā-fām*, Azure, cerulean.

P مينا كار *mīnā-kār*, An enameller.

P مينا كاري *mīnā-kārī*, Enamel.

P ميناگر *mīnāgar*, An alchymist.

P مينان *mīnān*, Conflux, confluence. A plum.

P ميناي *mīnā،ī*, Enamel.

A مئنّة *ma،innat*, A sign, note, mark. Worthy, fit.

P مينك *mīnak*, A herb whence brooms are made.

P مينو *mīnū*, Heaven. An emerald. White or blue glass. A glass gem. Hair. مينوي خاك *mīnūyi khāk*, The grave.

P مينو باد *mīnū-bād*, Wine. Name of a city existing in Zahhāk's time.

P مينو پيوند *mīnū-paywand*, Beautiful.

P مينوس *mīnūs*, Name of a certain king, who, after having been reduced to poverty and distress, was restored to royalty.

P مينه *mīna*, A plum.

A ميني *mīna'*, A glass bead. A port, a haven.

P ميو *mev*, Hair. A vine. A fruitful branch.

P ميواد *mīvād*, (for ميبايد *mībāyad*) It behoveth.

A ميوجات *mīwajāt*, (pl. of P ميوه *mīva*) Fruits.

P ميوران *maywarān*, Odoriferous herbs and flowers, with which they adorn the festive board, part of which was presented to every guest as he entered, together with a health or toast.

A ميؤس *may،us*, Desperate. A desperate man. ميؤس منه *may،us minhu*, Despaired of.

A ميوس *mayūs*, A pompous walker, one who moves, waves, or swaggers from side to side.

A ميول *muyūl*, (v. n. of مال for ميل) Inclining to the west (the sun). Keeping the middle of the road. (pl. of ميل *mīl*) Miles. Milestones.

A ميولة *muyūlat*, Inclination, propensity, bias.

A ميون *mayūn*, A liar. *Muyūn*, (pl. of مين) Lies.

A مئون *mi،ūn*, (pl. of مائة *mi،at*) Hundreds.

P ميوه *mīva* or *mayva*, Fruit. ميوهٔ باغ مرادم *mīva،i bāghi murādam*, The fruit of the garden of my desire. ميوهٔ دل *mīva،i dil*, (Fruit of the heart) Word, language. Poetry. A beloved child. ميوهاي گوناگون *mīvahāyi gūn-ā-gūn*, Fruits of many kinds.

P ميوه خانه *mīva-khāna*, A fruit-shop or loft.

P ميوه دار *mīva-dār*, Fruitful, laden with fruit. درخت ميوه دار *dirakhti mīva-dār*, A fruitful tree.

P ميوه فروش *mayva-farosh*, A fruiterer.

P ميوه ناك *mīvanāk*, Laden with fruit.

A مئويّ *mi،awiy*, Centesimal. Hundredth.

P ميويژه *mīwīja*, The convolvulus.

P ميوينه *mīvīna*, Tree-loppings in early spring.

A ميه *mayh*, (v. n. of ماه for ميه) Being full and overflowing with water (a well). Giving water to drink. Leaking, making water (a ship). Gilding (a sword).

P ميه *miya*, A moth eating a garment.

A ميّه *mayyih*, Full of water (well or ship).

A ميهة *mayhat*, (v. n. of ماه for ميه) Being full, overflowing (a well). Filling, leaking (a ship).

P ميهمان *mihmān*, A guest.

P ميهمن *mihman*, A family, race, tribe. Hereditary possessions.

P ميهن *mihan*, One's native soil, home. Wife and children. People, tribe, kindred. Hereditary possessions, moveable and real. Good nature. Fresh butter. Sheep's milk.

A مئيد *ma،īd*, Soft, delicate.

A مئير *ma،īr*, Lain with (woman). Difficult (affair). *Mi،yar*, (A man) much addicted to venery.

A مئيف *ma،īf*, Blighted, smutty (corn).

A ميقن *muyaykin*, (dim. of موقن *mūkin*) Almost certain about, partly sure of.

A مئين *mi،īn*, (pl. of مائة *mi،at*) Hundreds.

ن

ن *nūn*, The twenty-fifth letter of the Arabic alphabet, and the twenty-ninth of the Persian. In arithmetic it expresses 50; and in almanacs it denotes the conjunct aspect of the stars. Before ب *be*, پ *pe*, and م *mīm*, it should be pronounced as م *m*. Before ر *rā*, ل *lām*, م *mīm*, و *wāw*, and ي *ye*, it takes the sound of the following letter with the sign of reduplication *tashdīd* ـّ, as من ربّ *mir' rabbin*, من ليل *mil 'layl*, &c.

In Persian ن *nūn* may be changed to م *mīm*, as بام *bām* for بان *bān*. *Na* or *ni* at the beginning of a word implies negation. When final after ت *te* or د *dāl*, ن *n* is a sign of the infinitive mood: as, آمدن *āmudan*, To come; رفتن *raftan*, To go. It stands sometimes in the place of است *ast*, Is: as, خوشن *khwushan* for خوشست *khwushast*, نيكن *nekan* for نيك است *nek ast*, It is good. It is used to form the relative noun: as, ريمن *rīman*, Filthy, from ريم *rīm*, Filth: also as a pleonasm; as, پاداشن *pādāshan* for پاداش *pādāsh*, Recompense.

P نا *nā*, Water. A chider, rebuker. Rebuke, reproof.

(for ناو nāv) A ship. (for ناي nāy) A pipe, reed. The throat. A negative or privative particle, prefixed to nouns in Persian, equivalent to *ir*, *in*, *un*, &c. in English: as, ناپايدار *nā pāy-dār*, Inconstant. See other examples in the alphabetical order. At the end of a word it implies place, as in پهنا *pahnā*, A broad part; تيزنا *teznā*, A sharp part; درازنا *darāznā*, Oblong.

A نا *nā*, (when affixed to nouns is the possessive pronoun) Our, ours: as, كتابنا *kitābunā*, Our book. (when annexed to verbs it is the personal pronoun) We: as, ضربنا *zarabnā*, We struck; or us; as, ضربنا *zarabanā*, He struck us.

P نا آباد *nā ābād*, Ruined, depopulated.

A نأات *na*s*āt*, Groaning, sighing: a groaner. النأات *an' na*s*āt*, A lion.

A نـأاج *na*s*āj*, (or النأاج *an' na*s*āj*) The lion.

P نا استاد *nā ustād*, Unskilful, awkward.

P نا استادي *nā ustādī*, Unskilfulness.

P نا استوار *nā ustuwār*, Unsteady. Perfidious.

P نا آشنا *nā āshnā*, Unacquainted, unknown.

P نا آشنائي *nā āshnā*i*, Unacquaintance.

P نا التفاتي *nā iltifātī*, Inattention, slight.

P ناامید *nā umed* or *ummed*, Desperate, desponding, hopeless.

P نا اميدي *nā umedī*, Despair.

P نا آميزگار *nā āmezgār*, Unsociable.

P نا انبان *nā-ambān*, A bagpipe.

P نا انديش *nā andesh*, Clear, evident. Requiring no thought.

P نا انصافي *nā insāfī*, Injustice.

G نا اوس *nā us*, A church. A fire-temple.

P نا اهل *nā ahl*, Incapable. Unfit, unworthy. هر نا اهل و نادان *har nā ahl u nā dān*, Every incapable and ignorant person.

P ناب *nāb*, Pure, clear, limpid. Genuine, unmixed, unadulterated, neat. Mere, sincere. Similar, resembling. A furrow in the buttocks of a horse or camel from fat. مي ناب *may*i* nāb*, (or بادهٔ ناب *bāda*i* nāb*, Neat wine. Pure wine.

A نـاب *nāb*, (pl. انيب *anyub*, انياب *anyāb*, نيوب *nuyūb*, انابيب *anāyīb*) A cheek-tooth, grinder. A canine tooth. (pl. انياب *anyāb*, نيوب *nuyūb*, نيب *nīb*) An aged she-camel. A prince, chief, head, or master of a family.

P نابالغ *nā bāligh*, Under age, unripe, immature.

P ناباي *nā bāy*, Impossible, absurd.

P نابايست *nā bāyist*, Improper, unlawful.

P نابائستن *nā bā*i*stan*, To be odious, offensive.

A نابت *nābit*, Growing, germinating.

A نابتة *nābitat*, (pl. نوابت *nawābit*) Any thing that grows. Young progeny of man or beast.

A نابجة *nābijat*, Evil, misfortune. A kind of food made of milk mixed with camel's hair.

A نابح *nābih*, A barker.

A نابخة *nābihhat*, (pl. نوابخ *nawābikh*) A speaker, especially on high and abstruse subjects. Proud. Misfortune. Distant (country).

P نابخرد *nā bakhirad*, Unwise.

P نابخشنده *nā bakhshanda*, Indisposed to give.

P نابدان *nābdān*, (for ناودان) A canal, gutter.

P نابرجا *nā bar jā*, Out of place. Ill-timed, impertinent, inconvenient, improper, vain, foolish.

P نا برهندسه *nā bar handasa*, Ungeometrical.

P نا بسود *nā bisūd*, Not used, quite new.

P نا بسي *nā basī*, Nonexistence.

A نابض *nābiz*, Anger. Beating (artery), throbbing (pulse). A thrower, darter.

A نابع *nābi*ع, Bursting out, overflowing (well, fountain, or rivulet).

A نابغة *nābighat*, (pl. نوابغ *nawābigh*) A man of magnificence or of exalted rank. A name common to several Arabian poets.

A نابك *nābik*, High, eminent, lofty (place).

P نا بكار *nā ba kār*, Useless, unserviceable. A vagabond, idler, stroller, lazy, worthless fellow, belonging to no profession or religion. Bad, wicked.

P نابكاري *nā ba kārī*, Villainy.

A نابكة *nābikat*, High (ground).

P نابل *nābil*, A quiver.

A نابل *nābil*, (pl. نبّل *nubbal*) An archer, darter, thrower. Skilful in shooting arrows. One who has or makes arrows. Skilful, ingenious, dextrous, clever. *Nābul*, Name of a man, Nabal.

A نابلس *nābulus*, Name of a town in Palestine.

P نابنوا *nā bi nawā*, Lost, fruitless, of no use.

P نا بود *nā būd*, Annihilated, reduced to nothing, disappeared. That never existed. Ruined. A bankrupt. Non-existence. نابود كردن *nā būd kardan*, To make disappear, annihilate. نابود و ناپيدا شدن *nā būd u nā paydā shudan*, To be dispersed, vanish.

P نا بودمند *nā būdmand*, Ruined, wholly destitute; a bankrupt.

A نابه *nābih*, (pl. نبه *nabh*) Celebrated (man). Grave, important (affair). ابن نابه *ibni nābih*, Great, held in high estimation.

P نابهره *nā bahra*, Great, choice, excellent. Ignoble, mean, abject. Unsaleable (goods). Base (coin). Covered, concealed.

P نا بهنجار *nā bahanjār*, Irregular. Wicked. كار نابهنجار *kāri nā bahanjār*, A bad action.

P نا بي *nā bī*, (for نا بينا) Blind, not seeing.

A نابئ *nābi*s, Elevated, convex. (A man or a stream) which comes from an opposite quarter.

A نابي *nābī*, (pl. نبيّ *nubīy*) High ground.

A نابية *nābiyat*, A bow distant from the string.

P نا بين *nā bīn*, Weak-sighted, seeing bad.

P نا بينا *nā bīnā*, Blind.

P نابينائي *nā bīnā*i*, Blindness.

P نـابيوسان *nā bayūsān*, Expectation, hope. Sudden, unawares, unexpected.

P نا پاك *nā pāk*, Impure, unclean, polluted, filthy, defiled. Lewd, licentious.

P ناپاكي *nā pākī*, Impurity, uncleanness, defilement, dirt. Licentiousness, lewdness.

P ناپايدار *nā pāy-dār*, Inconstant, frail, unsteady, fickle, not durable, unstable, transitory, momentary.

P ناپاينده *nā pāyanda*, Transient, fleeting.

P نا پخته *nā pukhta*, Uncooked.

P نـا پديد *nā padīd*, Invisible, inconspicuous, not to be found, vanished, private, concealed.

P ناپديدگي *nā padīdagī*, Obliteration, invisibility.

P نا پروا *nā parwā*, Intrepid, fearless, inconsiderate, thoughtless, heedless, restless. Without wish or desire. Occupied, fully employed. Weak. Astonished, confounded, stupefied.

P نا پروائي *nā parwā*i*, Occupation, employment.

P نا پرهيزگار *nā parhezgār*, Careless, incautious, negligent, inattentive to health. Unchaste.

P نـا پرهيزگاري *nā parhezgārī*, Licentiousness. Carelessness, a want of due attention to health.

P نا پسند *nā pasand*, (or نا پسنديده *nā pasandīda*) Unchosen, disapproved of, reprobated. Disagreeable, displeasing, offensive, odious. Enormous. نا پسند داشتن *nā pasand dāshtan*, (or شمردن *shumurdan*) To abhor, detest, disapprove, dislike. نا پسنديده شدن *nā pasandīda shudan*, To disgust, to be disapproved.

P نا پسندي *nā pasandī*, Disagreeableness. Unwillingness.

P ناپگار *nāpigār*, Filthy, vile.

P نـا پيدا *nā paydā*, Unborn, that has never existed, not to be found. Vanished.

P نا پيراسته *nā payrāsta*, Untanned, undressed.

A نأات *na*s*āt*, A lion.

A نأت *na*s*t*, (v. n. of نأت) Roaring, bellowing loudly and much. Envying.

A نات *nāt*, (for ناس *nās*) Men.

P ناتاب *nā tāb*, Weak, infirm.

A ناتج *nātij*, Who brings forth, breeds; a breeder.

P ناتدبير *nā tadbīr*, Unthinking. Resourceless.

P ناتراشيده *nā tarāshīda*, (or ناتراش) Unshaved, unsmoothed, unlicked. Unpolite, uncultivated.

P ناتربيت *nā tarbiyat*, Uneducated.

A ناترة *nātirat*, (A bow) snapping the string.

P ناترس *nā tars*, Fearless. Severe, hard-hearted.

A ناتف *nātif*, A kind of sweetmeat.

A ناتق *nātik*, One who raises. One who spreads. (A woman) who has many children, fruitful. Who splits open or looses. Fire-striking (tinder-box or stick). (A horse) which shakes his rider. (A she-camel) soon conceiving. Far distant. The ancient name of the month رمضان *ramazān*.

P ناتمام *nā tamām*, Imperfect, unfinished.

P ناتمامي *nā tamāmī*, Imperfection.

P نـاتوان *nā tuwān*, Weak, impotent, infirm, powerless, feeble, frail. پير ناتوان *pīri nā tuwān*, A decrepit, weak old man. ناتوان شدن *nā tuwān shudan*, To become infirm, unable. ناتوان كردن *nā tuwān kardan*, To debilitate, enfeeble.

P ناتوانائي *nā tuwānā*i*, Inability, weakness.

P ناتوان بين *nātuwān-bīn*, Envious, malevolent.

P ناتواني *nā tuwānī*, Weakness, ailment.

A ناتئ *nātiʼ*, Swelling, prominent, projecting.

A ناتي *nātī*, Swelling, swollen (member). High.

A نأث *naʼs*, (v. n. of نأث) Being distant, far off. Purposing, striving.

A ناثر *nāsir*, A speaker or writer in prose. (A sheep) coughing, sneezing. (A sheep) which voids something from the nose resembling a worm.

P ناج *nāj*, A pine. A cypress.

A نأج *naʼj*, (v. n. of نأج) Groaning in prayer. Hooting (an owl). Lowing (an ox). *Naʼaj*, (v. n. of نأج) Eating slowly.

P ناجاي *nā jāy*, Deficiency in produce.

P ناجائز *nā jāʼiz*, Unlawful, unsuitable.

P ناجايگاه *nā jāy-gāh*, Ill-timed. Misplaced.

A ناجح *nājih*, Easy, expeditious, quick, rapid (journey). Hard travelling. Prosperous.

A ناجخ *nājikh*, One who makes a noise when coughing. (The sea) resounding with the dashing of the waves. The beating of the sea on the shore.

A ناجد *nājid*, Stupid, silly. A stammerer.

A ناجذ *nājiz*, (pl. نواجذ *nawājiz*) The wisdom-tooth. عضّ على ناجذه *ʻazza ʻala' nājizihi*, He attained his full strength (his wisdom-tooth).

A ناجر *nājir*, Sultry (month). The month Rajab, Safar, or any summer-month.

P ناجرمك *nājurmak*, Sitting in an idol-temple. Name of an anchoret. A Christian church.

A ناجز *nājiz*, Present, ready, prompt. Ready money, cash. ناجزا بناجز *nājizan bi nājiz*, Readily, promptly, expeditiously.

P ناجز انجام *nājuz anjām*, Endless. Ad infinitum.

A ناجس *nājis*, Incurable (disease).

A ناجش *nājish*, One who rouses wild beasts, and makes them pass by where the hunter lurks.

A ناجع *nājiʻ*, Wholesome, thirst-quenching.

A ناجعة *nājiʻat*, (Men) going out a foraging, or seeking to better their condition.

A ناجل *nājil*, A parent, sire. High-bred (horse).

A ناجلين *nājilayn*, (obl. du. of ناجل) Parents.

P ناجنبان *nājumbān*, Immoveable, not in motion.

P ناجنس *nā jins*, Ignoble, rude, uncivil.

P ناجو *nājū*, The pine-tree.

P ناجود *nājūd*, A cup, full or empty.

A ناجود *nājūd*, A large cup, goblet, or vessel from which lesser ones are filled. Saffron. Blood.

A ناجه *nājih*, Entering an unhealthy country.

A ناجي *nājī*, One who escapes. Swift. Free, liberated, excused. A deliverer. An epithet of Noah. الناجي *an' nājī*, Elect, predestined, saved. A name common to several persons.

A ناجية *nājiyat*, A swift she-camel running away with the rider. بنو ناجية *banū nājiyat*, Name of an Arabian tribe.

A ناجين *nājīn*, (pl. obliq. of ناجي) Escaping.

P ناچار *nā chār*, Remediless. Helpless, destitute, abandoned, poor, miserable, forlorn, distressed. Forced by necessity, constrained. Necessary, indispensible. By force, against the inclination.

P ناچاري *nā chārī*, Helplessness, destitution.

P ناچاق *nā chāk*, Unsound, indisposed, lean.

P ناچاويده *nā chāwīda*, Unmasticated.

P ناچخ *nāchakh*, A battle-axe. A halbert. A double-pointed spear. A short javelin.

P ناچسپان *nā chaspān*, Unworthy. Inconvenient, impertinent. Disproportioned.

P ناچيده *nā chīda*, Ungathered.

P ناچيز *nā chīz*, A trifling, silly thing, of no consequence, insignificant. Destroyed, ruined. Nothing.

P ناچيزي *nā chīzī*, Smallness. Insignificance. Nullity, nothingness.

A ناحاة *nāhāt*, A side, a quarter.

A الناحران *an' nāhirāni*, (and الناحرتان *an' nāhiratāni*) Two nerves or veins in the throat or jaws. Two of the short ribs.

A ناحرة *nāhirat*, (pl. نواحر *nawāhir*) The last day and night of the lunar month.

A ناحز *nāhiz*, (A camel) diseased in the lungs and troubled with a cough; one which has a callosity on the knees and the middle of the breast. A long tract of ground.

A ناحس *nāhis*, Scarce, disastrous (year).

A ناحص *nāhis*, A one-year-old wild she-ass.

A ناحط *nāhit*, One who coughs much.

P نا حفاظ *nā hifāz*, Not to be restrained or kept back from what is evil or improper.

P ناحق *nā hak* or *hakk*, False, untrue: unjust, unlawful. Injurious. Injury. Falsity. Unjustly. عمل ناحق *ʻamali nā hak*, An iniquitous action.

P ناحق شناس *nā hak-shinās*, Ungrateful, inequitable, having no notions of right or justice.

A ناحل *nāhil*, Lean (camel). Thin (sword).

A ناحي *nāhī*, Inclined, tending towards. (pl. نحاة *nuhāt*) A grammarian.

A ناحية *nāhiyat*, (pl. نواحي *nawāhī*) A country, territory, district; tract, coast, shore. A side, quarter.

P ناخ *nākh*, The navel.

P ناخاست *nā khāst*, Unable to rise.

P ناخاسته *nā khāsta*, Unleavened, unfermented.

P ناخدا *nā khudā*, (No God) An atheist, impious wretch. The master or the commandant of a ship, a captain; a supercargo. A seaman.

P ناخدا ترس *nā khudā-tars*, Not fearing God.

A P ناخذا *nākhuzā*, (ناخذاي *nākhuzāy*, ناخذاه *nākhuzāh*, or ناخذاة *nākhuzāt*) (pl. نواخذة *nawākhizat*) A shipmaster. A seaman. A supercargo.

A ناخر *nākhir*, (fem. ناخرة *nākhirat*) Worn hollow (carious bone). Sonorous (thing hollow and pervious to the wind). (pl. نخر *nukhur*) A hog trained up to hunting and falling upon the prey. One, single. لا ناخربها *lā nākhira bihā*, There is nobody at home, there is nothing in it.

P ناخردمند *nā khiradmand*, Unwise.

A ناخس *nākhis*, The scab round a camel's tail; also a fissure under his arm-pit. A young mountain-goat. دائرة الناخس *dāʼiratu'n nākhis*, A circular appearance of hairs on the upper part of the buttocks of a horse, and stretching towards the nerves of the thigh (regarded as a blemish).

P ناخسته *nākhista*, A slender rope.

A ناخص *nākhis*, Emaciated, shrivelled, wrinkled, wizened (old woman).

A ناخع *nākhiʻ*, Knowing, intelligent.

P ناخفته *nā khufta*, Uncoagulated.

P ناخفراه *nā khafrāh*, A sailor, shipman.

A ناخل *nākhil*, One who sifts, a sifter. ناخل الصدر *nākhilu's sadr*, Sincere, faithful (adviser).

P ناخلف *nā khalaf*, Degenerate, ignoble, spurious, villainous, dastardly. Wicked, vicious (boy).

A ناخم *nākhim*, A skilful singer or player.

P ناخن *nākhun*, A nail, talon, claw. ناخن آفتاب *nākhuni āftāb*, Fire. The nail of a mistress. ناخن بدندان *nākhun ba dandān*, Vexation, regret, disappointment. Afflicted, grieved. Astonished, confounded. ناخن بويا *nākhuni boyā*, (ناخن پريان *nākhuni pariyān*, ناخن خوش *nākhuni khwush*, or ناخن ديو *nākhuni dev*) Perfumed nails. ناخن خامه *nākhuni khāma*, The nib of a pen. ناخن روز *nākhuni roz*, The world-illuminating sun. ناخن بر دل زدن *nākhun bar dil zadan*, To tamper with the constitution. ناخن چيدن *nākhun chīdan*, (تراشيدن *tarāshīdan*, or گرفتن *giriftan*) To pare the nails. ناخن زدن *nākhun zadan*, To stir up strife.

P ناخنان *nākhunān*, Callosities, hard parts.

P ناخن بر *nākhun-bur*, (ناخن برا *nākhun-burā*, or ناخن براي *nākhun-burāy*, ناخن تراش *nākhun-tarāsh*, and ناخن گير *nākhun-gīr*) A small knife or scissors for paring the nails.

P ناخن پال *nākhun-pāl*, A whitlow.

P ناخن پيراي *nākhun-payrāy* or *perāy*, Scissors for the nails. A barber.

P ناخن خواره *nākhun-khwāra*, An imposthume under the root of the nail, a whitlow. A disease in the hoof of a horse.

P ناخنه *nākhuna*, A nail, claw. A cataract in the eye. An instrument used to strike the strings of a lute with, a bow. ناخنۀ چشم شب *nākhunaʼi chashmi shab*, The new moon.

P ناخواست *nā khwāst*, Unsolicited, undesired. Trampled.

P ناخوانده *nā khwānda*, Unread. Unlearned. Uninvited, unbidden.

P ناخواه *nā khwāh*, Unwilling, constrained, against the will. Unwillingly, constrainedly.

P ناخواهان *nā khwāhān*, Unwelcome: uncalled for.

P ناخواهاني *nā khwāhānī*, Abstinence, indifference.

P ناخوب *nā khūb*, Not good, bad.

P نا خورش *nā khwurish*, Victuals remaining at the bottom of a pot and sticking to it.

P ناخوست *nā khwust*, A place beat with the

feet, or smoothed (as sown ground with a harrow).

P ناخوستن *nākhwustan*, To trample under foot.

P نا خوش *nā khwush*, Bad, wicked. Indisposed, unhappy. Displeased. Unpleasant, harsh, disagreeable. Unwilling. ناخوش آمدن *nā khwush āmadan*, To be disapproved of.

P ناخوش آواز *nā khwush-āwāz*, One who has a harsh and disagreeable voice.

P ناخوش كردار *nā khwush-kirdār*, An evil-doer.

P ناخوشگوار *nā khwush-guwār*, Difficult of digestion; unwholesome (meat).

P ناخوشمش *nā khwushmish*, (or ناخوشمنش *nā khwush-manish*) Loathing, nausea. Nauseating. Detestable.

P ناخوشنود *nā khwushnūd*, Discontented.

P ناخوشي *nā khwushī*, Indisposition, bad health or constitution. Disagreeableness, bitterness. Fret. Displeasure. Depravity, villainy.

P ناخون *nākhūn*, (for ناخن *nākhun*) A nail.

A ناد *naʼād*, (or نادي *naʼāda'*) Evil, calamity.

A ناد *naʼd*, (v. n. of ناد) Exuding, pouring out water abundantly (ground). Envying. Overtaking one (calamity). Envy. Ground from which water flows.

A ناد *nādd*, Whatever is necessary for the support of life. One who flees or scampers away.

P نادار *nā dār*, Insolvent, indigent, poor, without possession. A poor ryot, or cultivator.

P نادار باقي *nādār-bākī*, A balance due by poor ryots (a revenue-term in India).

P ناداري *nā dārī*, Poverty, insolvency, indigence. Incapacity.

P ناداشت *nā dāsht*, Poor, moneyless. Impudent, indecent. Faithless. Name of a sect of beggars. (See شاخشانه *shākh-shāna.*)

P ناداشتي *nā dāshtī*, Poverty. Bankruptcy. Shamelessness, indecency. Irreligion, impiety.

P نادان *nā dān*, Ignorant, silly, unlearned, simple, rude. نادان ده مردگوي *nā dāni dah mard-gūy* (or *goy*), An ignorant, prating fellow.

P نادانستگي *nā dānistagī*, Ignorance.

P نادانسته *nā dānista*, Ignorantly, unknowingly, unwittingly. Incognito, unknown.

P ناداني *nā dānī*, Ignorance, simplicity, idiotism. Infatuation. Incapacity. ناداني كردن *nā dānī kardan*, To act foolishly or ignorantly. نادانيم *nā dāniyam*, My ignorance.

A نادّة *nāddatan*, In all directions.

A نادر *nādir*, Singular, rare, uncommon, unusual, wonderful, excellent, precious. Projecting. Rarely. نادر الحسن *nādiru'l husn*, Of uncommon beauty. نادر الوقوع *nādiru'l wukūʻ*, Of rare occurrence.

A نادرا *nādiran*, Rarely, perchance.

P نا در برابر *nā dar bar-ā-bar*, Impertinent, irrelevent, incongruous, unconnected.

A نادرة *nādirat*, (pl. نوادر *nawādir*) An uncommon thing, a rarity, a curiosity. An incomparable man, phœnix of the age, rara avis. Strange, uncommon, obsolete (speech). An unexpected accident, any thing that surprises.

P نادرست *nā durust*, Not right or true, false. Imperfect; impertinent, incongruous.

P نادرستي *nā durustī*, Falsehood. Unsoundness.

P نادرشاه *nādir shāh*, Name of a king of Persia who reigned from A.D. 1736 to A.D. 1747.

P نادره پرسي *nādira-pursī*, Inquiry about rare and extraordinary matters.

P نادره دان *nādira-dān*, Acute, intelligent, learned, knowing rare, mysterious things.

P نادره كار *nādira-kār*, Doing any thing extraordinary. An excellent artificer.

A نادري *nādirī*, A rarity.

A نادف *nādif*, A cotton-dresser.

P نادل چسپ *nā dil-chasp*, Disliked.

A نادم *nādim*, (pl. ندام *nidām* and ندّام *nuddām*) Penitent, sorry for. Bashful, ashamed, abashed.

P نادم شدن *nādim shudan*, To be sorry, to repent.

P نادمساز *nā dam-sāz*, Discordant, dissonant.

P نادهنده *nā dihanda* or *dihinda*, Not paying what is due. Stingy, not giving.

A نادي *naʼāda'*, Evil, calamity, misfortune.

A نادي *nādī*, One who calls or convokes. A council, assembly, mote, congregation, or place of meeting. A crier. (Camels) pasturing between two drinkings.

A نادية *nādiyat*, (A she-camel) pasturing between two drinkings. (A palm-tree) far from water. (pl. ناديات *nādiyāt*) Beginnings (of things).

P ناديدگي *nā dīdagī*, Poverty, bankruptcy.

P ناديدني *nā dīdanī*, Not to be seen; invisible, imperceptible. Unfit to be looked upon.

P ناديده *nā dīda*, Unseen. Not seeing. One who has seen little; inexperienced. Vile, abject, base.

A ناذر *nāzir*, The city of Mecca.

A ناذع *nāziʻ*, Flowing, fluent (sweat or water).

P نار *nār*, A pomegranate. نار رباب *nāri rubāb*, (or رُبّاب *rubbāb*) A kind of sour pomegranate. نار شيرين *nāri shīrīn*, Name of a note in music. نار فارسي *nāri fārsī*, Name of a very deadly poison. نار هندي *nāri hindī*, Name of a fruit resembling the quince (called in India بل *bil*). نار باغ سينه *nāri bāghi sīna*, A nipple, dug, teat.

A نار *nār*, (pl. انوار *anwār*, نيران *nīrān*, نور *nūr*, نيار *niyār*, انورة *anwirat*, and نيرة *niyarat*) Fire. Hell. (Hell, or the infernal region, is supposed by the followers of Muhammad to consist of seven strata, distant from each other a journey of a thousand years, being severally the appropriate abode of a distinct class of sinners. Commencing with the uppermost, the names of these dismal regions are, جهنّم *jahannam*, لظي *laza'*, جحيم *jahīm*, سعير *saʻīr*, سقر *sakar*, حطمة *hutamat*, and هاوية *hāwiyat*). A mark made by burning. Mind, intellect; counsel, advice. اهل النار *ahlu'n nār*, The damned. P نار افشاندن *nār afshāndan*, (To scatter fire) To shed hot tears.

P ناراست *nā rāst*, Not right. Untrue, false. Adulterated. A fault, error.

P ناراض *nā rāz*, (or ناراضي *nā rāzī*) Dissatisfied, discontented, displeased.

P ناراي *nā rāy*, Inconsiderate, injudicious, indiscreet. Unbelieving.

P ناربا *nār-bā*, Meat drest with pomegranate.

P نارين *nār-bun*, The pomegranate-tree.

P نارپستان *nār-pistān*, A round swelling breast, of the form of a pomegranate. A female who has firm round breasts.

P نارپوست *nār-post*, Cinnamon.

P نارجيل *nārjīl*, A cocoa-nut. The Persian pipe for smoking through water. The cocoa-nut tree.

A نارجيل *naʼrijīl*, A cocoa-nut.

P نارخو *nār-khu*, (*nār kho*, or نارخوي *nār-khoy*) The flower of the pomegranate. Fiery-tempered.

P نارخوك *nārkhūk*, Opium, theriac.

P نارد *nārad*, The tike or dog-louse. The sting of a gnat. A miser. Spikenard. (for نيارد *nayārad*) He does not bring. He cannot, he is unable.

P ناردان *nārdān*, The juice, also the grains of the pomegranate. Syrup of pomegranates, also of dried grapes. A chafing-dish. ناردان افشاندن *nārdān afshāndan*, To shed tears of blood.

P ناردانهٔ دشتي *nār-dānaʼi dashtī*, The seed of the wild pomegranate.

P ناردنگ *nārdang*, Victuals dressed with pomegranate-syrup.

P نارده *nārda*, A gnat. A tike, dog-louse.

A P ناردين *nārdīn*, Spikenard.

P نارس *nā ras*, Unripe.

P نا رسا *nā rasā*, Unworthy, unfit. Ill-bred.

P نارسائي *nā rasāʼī*, Incapacity, unworthiness, unfitness: unskilfulness. Unmannerliness, ill-breeding.

A نارسة *nārisat*, The best sort of dates.

P نارست *nārast*, (for نيارست) He was not able.

P نارسيده *nā rasīda*, Not arrived. Unripe, immature, not arrived at perfection or puberty. Sour. Destitute, unfortunate.

P نارفته *nā rafta*, Not gone. Immoveable.

P ناركند *nār-kand*, A grove of pomegranates.

P ناركوك *nārkūk*, A kind of opium.

P ناركيوا *nār-kīwā*, Head of the black poppy.

P نارگيل *nārgīl*, Fruit of the cocoa-palm; cocoanut. The Persian pipe for smoking through water.

P نارگيو *nār-gīv*, Head of the white poppy.

P نارمشك *nār-mushk*, An Indian fruit resembling the pomegranate; the flowers of which, when they fall, are fragrant; the best being of a whitish colour mixed with red. A smith's forge.

A P نارنج *nāranj*, (or نارنگ *nārang*) An orange. نارنج دلاويز و ترنج عطر آميز *nāranji dil-āwez, wa turunji ʻatar-āmez*, A beautiful, odoriferous orange.

P نارنجي *nāranjī* or *nārinjī*, Orange-coloured.

P نارنگي *nārangī*, Orange-coloured. Name of

a fruit smaller than an orange and sweeter. The absence of colour.

P نارو *nārū*, A sweetly-singing bird resembling the nightingale. A thread which comes forth from a tumour in the body incident to strangers in some parts of Persia.

P ناروا *nār-vā*, Victuals dressed with pomegranates. Heat. *Na ravā*, Not current or passable. Unsaleable. Inadmissible, prohibited. Unworthy. نا روا شدن *nā rawā shudan*, To be unsaleable.

P ناروان *nārvān*, Sour cherry, morel. *Nā ravān*, Base, not current. Stagnant. Inanimate, immoveable. Dull, flat (market). A tall shady tree.

P نارواني *nā rawānī*, Dulness of trade, difficulty of disposing of goods, unsaleableness.

P نارور *nārvar*, (A girl) with round swelling breasts, of the form of the pomegranate.

P نارون *nārvan*, A very lofty kind of tree which gives much shade, the sour cherry. Name of a wood. *Nārwan* or *nārwun*, The pomegranate-tree. *Nārawan*, Soft, smooth. Fresh. The tall, erect branch of a tree shaken by the wind. The elm-tree; a tree called likewise طبرخون *tabarkhūn*.

P ناروند *nārvand*, Name of a tall, elegant tree.

P ناروه *nārūh*, Name of a bird resembling the nightingale. *Nārūh* or *nārwa*, Tongue of a balance.

P ناره *nāra*, The tongue of a pair of scales. A thick rope. A stone weight against which any thing is weighed. A groan. ناره قبّان *nāra kabbān*, The handle, also tongue of a balance.

P ناري *nārī*, A garment.

A ناريّ *nāriy*, Fiery, full of fire. Hellish.

A ناريّة *nāriyat*, State, nature, or force of fire.

P ناريدن *nārīdan*, To hunt, to take. To wax great. To be lengthened out.

P نارين *nārīn*, Fresh, shining, clear, polished, elegant, adorned. نارين قماش *nārīn-kumāsh*, A beautiful stuff.

P ناز *nāz*, Blandishments, soothing or endearing expressions used by lovers, or by parents to children, fondling, coquetry, amorous playfulness, feigned disdain. Pride, consequential airs. Softness, elegance, gracefulness. Beneficence. Dissimulation. Delicacy, softness. Young, fresh, tender, newly sprung up. A wild pine-tree, cypress, or box. نازنو روز *nāzi naw-roz*, Name of a note in music. ناز و نياز كردن *nāz u niyāz kardan*, To supplicate, to entreat soothingly.

P نازاد *nā zād*, Barren.

P نازان *nāzān*, Sporting, toying (as lovers).

P نازايندگي *nā zāyandagī*, Female sterility.

P نازاينده *nā zāyanda*, Barren, unprolific.

P نازائيده *nā zāʼida*, A female that has not brought forth young.

P نازبالش *nāz-bālish*, A pillow, bolster, cushion.

P نازبالين *nāz-bālīn*, A pillow, bolster, cushion. A kind of pillow for the armhole. (Ezek. xiii. 18).

P نازبردار *nāz-bardār*, One who bears another's whims; a flatterer.

P نازبرداري *nāz-bardārī*, Flattery.

P نازبو *nāz-bo*, The herb ocymum pilosum.

P نازبوي *nāz-boy* or *būy*, The herb basilicum.

P نازپرور *nāz-parwar*, (نازپرورد *nāz-parward*, or نازپرورده *nāz-parwarda*) Delicately brought up. A spoilt child.

P نازپري *nāz parī*, Name of the daughter of the king of Khwārazm, married to Bahrāmgūr.

A نازح *nāzih*, Distant (town). Exhausted (well).

A نازش *nāzish*, Dissimulation, blandishment. Glory, exaltation, eminence, boasting. Importunity.

A نازع *nāziʻ*, (A male or she-camel) longing for its ordinary pasture or habitation. One who makes haste. One who excites divisions. The devil. (pl. نزّاع *nuzzāʻ*) A foreigner, stranger.

A نازعات *nāziʻāt*, Stars. Bows. Name of a chapter in the Kur'ān. النازعات *an'nāziʻāt*, Angels who seize and carry off the souls of the wicked; (figuratively) soldiers.

P نازك *nāzuk*, Thin, slender, subtle, tender, delicate, fragile, light, elegant. Clean, neat, ornamented. Facetious, gracious, genteel. Beloved object, mistress. Bread baked of fine flour and butter.

P نازك ادا *nāzuk-adā*, (The nightingale) with the sweet notes.

P نازك اندام *nāzuk-andām*, Delicately formed in every limb.

P نازك بدن *nāzuk-badan*, Delicate (an epithet of a mistress). A species of jujube. A certain red flower. A flower resembling the purple amaranth.

P نازك تهيگاه *nāzuk-tihī-gāh*, Slender-waisted.

P نازك خلق *nāzūk-khulk*, Of a delicate or yielding disposition.

P نازك مزاج *nāzuk-mizāj*, Of a delicate complexion or habit of body.

P نازكننده *nāz-kunanda*, See نازنين *nāzanīn*.

P نازك وجود *nāzuk-wujūd*, Delicate of body.

P نازكي *nāzukī*, Tenderness, softness, delicacy.

A نازل *nāzil*, One who descends, dismounts, alights, or arrives at. P نازل شدن *nāzil shudan*, To alight, to descend. نازل كردن *nāzil kardan*, To cause to descend or dismount.

A نازلة *nāzilat*, (pl. نوازل *nawāzil*) A disaster, calamity, misfortune (as descending from heaven). A defluxion of humours, rheum, disorder.

P نازنده *nāzanda*, (or نازنين *nāzanīn*) Delicate, elegant, delightful, delicious, amiable, agreeable, beloved. Dissembling, feigning (in a good sense), pretending to be angry when pleased (as lovers). اوقات نازنين *awkāti nāzanīn*, Precious hours. زن نازنين *zāni nāzanīn*, An amiable woman. A mistress, a sweetheart. محبوب نازنين *mahbūbi nāzanīn*, A beloved object.

P نازو *nāzū*, A cat. Name of a melodious bird. A turtle-dove.

P نازور *nā zor*, Weak, without strength.

P نازوري *nā zorī*, Weakness.

P نازون *nāzūn*, A kind of hard tree.

A نازه *nāzih*, (pl. نزهاء *nuzahāʼ*) Pure, chaste, temperate. نازه النفس *nāzihu'n nafs*, Pure. One who lives apart from society, a recluse: a puritan.

P نازيب *nā zīb* or *zeb*, Ugly, inelegant.

P نازيبا *nā zībā* or *zebā*, Ugly, unseemly, ungraceful, unbecoming, disfigured. Plain.

P نازيبائش *nā zebāʼish*, Ugliness, plainness.

P نازيبائي *nā zebāʼī*, Ugliness.

A نازية *nāziyat*, A deep dish. Hot. Cold. Passion, vehemence, impetuosity.

P نازيدن *nāzīdan*, To dissemble (as lovers); to counterfeit, to feign, coquet; to assume a graceful or haughty air. To boast of wealth. To emulate, rival, envy. To use well, to indulge, behave humanely, wink at another's errors. To enjoy the conveniencies or comforts of life, to live agreeably; to feel a momentary pleasure; to be constantly in spirits, always happy.

P ناژ *nāj*, Pine, box, cypress. Yawning.

P ناژو *nājū*, A pine-tree.

P ناژون *nājūn*, A juniper-tree.

P ناژه *nāja*, The tongue of a balance.

P ناژين *nājīn*, A certain tree, large and leafy, bearing pods in which gnats are found in great numbers.

A ناس *nās*, Men, mankind, human beings. Angels, demons, genii. Any thing suspended from the roof of a house. Name of the father of a tribe. مقتداي ناس *muktadāyi nās*, A priest, prelate.

A ناسّ *nāss*, Who checks or cries (to a camel). Dry (bread). Thirsty (bird). A species of ape.

P ناساز *nā sāz*, Dissonant, discordant, out of tune. Obscene, rude, uncivil. آهنگ ناساز *āhangi nā sāz*, Discordant sounds. An absurd proposition.

P ناسازكار *nā sāz-kār*, Rendering dissonant or absurd. Unfortunate. Dissentient.

P ناسازكاري *nā sāz-kārī*, Discordance, absurdity, dissension. ناسازكاري كردن *nā sāz-kārī kardan*, To dissent, disagree.

P ناسازنده *nā sāzanda*, Ineffectual, inoperative.

P ناسازوار *nā sāzwār*, Refractory, discordant.

P ناسازواري *nā sāzwārī*, Discordance, dissonance. Dissension. Refractoriness. ناسازواري نمودن *nā sazwārī namūdan*, To disobey.

P ناسازي *nā sāzī*, Opposition, contradiction, discordance, ill-behaviour. Dissimulation.

P ناساماني *nā sāmānī*, Disorder; unruliness.

P ناسپاس *nā sipās*, Ungrateful, unthankful. Disagreeable. Undiscriminating. ناسپاسي *nā sipāsī*, Unthankfulness, ingratitude.

P ناسپال *nāspāl*, Rind of the pomegranate.

A ناسّة *nāssat*, Dry bread. الناسّة, Mecca.

P ناستاد *nāsitād*, Name of a district.

P ناستوده *nā sutūda*, Vile, abject, mean, low, base, foolish, stupid, worthless, wicked.

A ناسج *nāsij*, A weaver. A composer; a maker of an oration. ناسج الحيل *nāsiju'l hiyal*, A hatcher of conspiracy or treachery.

P ناسخ *nāsikh*, A kind of silken stuff woven with gold or silver.

A ناسخ *nāsikh*, One who abolishes, obliterates, erases, cancels. A verse of the Kur'ān which abrogates what has been said before. Abrogated. A copier of a book, an amanuensis. A transformer.

P ناسرايش *nā sarāyish*, Talking by signs, and not by the voice.

P ناسره *nāsara*, (or ناسزه *nāsaza*) Money bad, not passable, uncurrent coin; a thing which passes with difficulty. A sown field.

P ناسزا *nā sazā*, Unworthy, improper, impertinent, foolish, indecent; unmerited.

A ناسع *nāsiʻ*, Longneck: uncircumcised (woman).

A ناسعة *nāsiʻat*, (A woman) who has long a back, belly, or clitoris.

P ناسفته *nā sufta*, Not perforated, unbored, whole. Thin, not dense. درّ ناسفته *durri nā sufta*, An unbored pearl. An unblemished maid.

P ناسك *nāsik*, Name of the founder of a Hindū sect. Name of an infidel people, or one unsteady in their religious opinions.

A ناسك *nāsik*, Devoted to God or virtue.

A ناسكة *nāsikat*, (Ground) green, rained upon.

P ناسگاليده *nā sigālida*, Unthought of.

A ناسل *nāsil*, Dropping, moulting (hair, feather).

A ناسلة *nāsilat*, Lean (thigh).

A ناسم *nāsim*, Sick, at the last gasp.

P ناسنج *nāsinj*, A fine kind of cloth, called the cloth of paradise, ornamented with gold, silver, and silk embroidery.

A ناسوت *nāsūt*, Human nature, humanity.

A ناسوتيّ *nāsūtiy*, Worldly. Human.

P ناسور *nāsūr*, An incurable wound. Fistula.

A ناسور *nāsūr*, (pl. نواسير *nawāsīr*) A disease in the corner of the eye; one in the gums, and one in the podex, attended by a constant running.

P ناسوري *nāsūrī*, The throat, gullet.

A ناسئ *nāsiʼ*, (pl. نسأة *nasaʼat*) Fat. One who gives the names, arranges the order of the months.

A ناسي *nāsī*, Forgetting, forgetful. One who defers the pilgrimage to Mecca. P ناسي شدن *nāsī shudan*, To forget.

P ناسيدن *nāsīdan*, To be born with a bad disposition. To be lame or mutilated from the birth. To be lean.

A نأش *naʼsh*, (v. n. of نأش) Accepting, receiving, taking (any thing to eat). Seizing by force. Deferring, delaying. Rising up. Springing upon, making an onslaught.

P ناش *nāsh*, Lamentation, plaint, wailing.

P ناشاد *nā shād*, Cheerless, joyless, low-spirited, dissatisfied, displeased, hippish.

P ناشادي *nā shādī*, Dulness, displeasure.

P ناشايست *nā shāyist*, Improper.

P ناشايستگي *nā shāyistagī*, Impropriety.

P ناشايسته *nā shāyista*, Unworthy, improper, indecent, indecorous, illicit. ناشايسته حركات *nā shāyista harakāt*, Shameful or unlawful actions, misdeeds, crimes, sins.

A ناشب *nāshib*, Sticking, inherent. A man who has arrows (نشّاب *nushshāb*).

A ناشبة *nāshibat*, (Any thing) adherent, sticking fast. (pl. of ناشب *nāshib*) Furnished with arrows. ناشبة المحال *nāshibatu'l mahāl*, A pulley.

P ناشپاتي *nāshpātī*, The common pear.

P ناشتا *nāshitā*, Hungry, having an empty stomach. Fasting. Breakfast. A foreigner, stranger. (Any thing) received on credit. (The price) of any thing to be paid. Equal. ناشتا شكستن *nāshitā shikastan*, To breakfast.

P ناشتاب *nāshtāb*, Fasting, abstinence.

P ناشتاخورده *nāshitā-khwurda*, Taken on an empty stomach, eaten fasting.

P ناشتا شكن *nāshitā-shikan*, Breakfast.

P ناشتائي *nāshitāʼī*, Fasting, hunger. A breakfast, whatever one eats after a long fast. ناشتائي شكستن *nāshitāʼī shikastan*, To breakfast.

P ناشدني *nā shudanī*, Impossible, impracticable.

A ناشر *nāshir*, One who disperses, scatters, diffuses, divulges. Who brings to life. One who pricks his ears. One who saws, a sawyer.

A ناشرة *nāshirat*, (Ground) verdant with herbage at the end of summer. (pl. نواشر *nawāshir*) A vein, nerve, or tendon of the arm, especially interior.

A ناشز *nāshiz*, Beating (pulse) when indisposed, or (heart) from fear. Stubborn (woman).

P ناشسته *nā shusta*, Unwashed. طفل ناشسته *tifli nā shusta*, A new-born babe not yet washed.

A ناشص *nāshis*, Rude, uncivil, contradicting. Angry. Stubborn (woman) who dislikes her husband.

A ناشط *nāshit*, Brisk, active, lively, and well-fed (horse). (A wild bull) going out, and running from place to place. Absurd (question). A path turning to the right or left from the high road.

A ناشطات *nāshitāt*, Stars moving from one place to another in the heavens. Angels receiving the souls of true believers. Believing souls, which quit the body with joy and alacrity.

A ناشع *nāshiʻ*, High. Prominent, projecting.

A ناشغ *nāshigh*, One who makes a noise in the throat as if about to faint.

P ناشك *nāshik*, A debtor.

P ناشكري *nā shukrī*, Unthankfulness.

P ناشكيب *nā shikīb*, Impatient.

P ناشكيبا *nā shikībā*, Impatient, unsteady.

P ناشكيبائي *nā shikībāʼī*, Impatience.

P ناشگفته *nā shigufta*, Unblown, unexpanded (flower). ابكار ناشگفته *abkāri nā shigufta*, Unblemished virgins.

A ناشلة *nāshilat*, Lean (thigh). A light, slender sword. Water newly drawn from the well.

P ناشنا *nāshinā*, Even in number, equal.

P ناشناس *nā shinās*, Not recognising, acknowledging, or owning. Ignorant, rude. A rustic.

P ناشناسا *nā shināsā*, Unknown, not to be recognized. Ignorant.

P ناشناسائي *nā shināsāʼī*, Ignorance.

P ناشناسي *nā shināsī*, A refusing to recognise. Ignorance. Rusticity. A rustic.

P ناشنوا *nā shinavā*, Deaf. Unwilling to listen.

P ناشنوائي *nā shinavāʼī*, Deafness. An unwillingness to listen.

P ناشنيدني *nā shanīdanī*, Not fit to be heard.

P ناشنيده *nā shanīda*, Unheard.

A ناشئ *nāshiʼ*, (pl. نشء *nashʼ* or *nashaʼ*) Who or what grows. A boy or girl starting into youth. (pl. ناشئة *nāshiʼat*) Any thing arising, appearing, or produced in the night.

A ناشئة *nāshiʼat*, (v. n. of نشأ) Growing, increasing, growing up amongst. The first hour of night or day; also any hour at which one rises. Beginning. Any thing arising, appearing, or produced in the night-time. A rising or starting repeatedly from sleep. The first sprouting of young herbage.

P ناشيرين *nā shīrīn*, Not sweet. Disagreeable, sour (face). Insipid (meat). Depraved, not good.

A ناصاة *nāsāt*, The forelocks.

P ناصاف *nā sāf*, Unclean, dirty.

A ناصب *nāsib*, One who erects, sets up, fixes, plants, places, constitutes. Fatigued, laborious, painful (life). Wearying, vexatious (care and solicitude). (A particle) which requires a word to be inflected with the vowel نصب *nasb*.

A ناصبيّة *nāsibīyat*, (with the article ال *al*) The enemies of Alīy.

A ناصح *nāsih*, (pl. نصّح *nussah* and نصّاح *nussāh*) A monitor, counsellor, adviser, sincere friend, faithful minister. Any thing pure (as honey). ناصح الجيب *nāsihu'l jayb*, Sincere, free from guile. *Nāsih*, (or ناصحيّ *nāsihīy*) A tailor.

A ناصر *nāsir*, (pl. نصّار *nussār*, نصر *nasr*, *nusar*, and انصار *ansār*) A defender, assistant, helper, deliverer, ally. (God) the giver of victory. (pl. نواصر *nawāsir*) A canal; any channel through which water runs, that especially made by a torrent, and coming from a distance: the feeder of a main stream. A hill two miles in length.

A ناصرة *nāsirat*, Nazareth in Galilee.

A ناصع *nāsiʻ*, Pure, clear (colour): as, ناصع ابيض *nāsiʻ abyaz*, (or ناصع البياض *nāsiʻu'l bayāz*) Pure white, snowy.

A ناصف *nāsif*, (pl. نصف) A domestic servant.

A ناصفة *nāsifat*, (pl. نواصف *nawāsif*) A channel, or the middle part through which water runs; also a stone in mid-stream.

A ناصل *nāsil*, (A beard) losing its dye.

P ناصواب *nā sawāb*, Not right, bad. Unwholesome. هرزه وُ ناصواب *harza u nā sawāb*, Vain and false (words).

P ناصور *nāsūr*, An old wound. A callosity.

A ناصي *nāsī*, Highly raised (camel in a pasture).

A ناصية *nāsiyat*, (pl. نواصي *nawāsī*) A forelock. Appearance, bearing, manner, purport. غضر الناصية *ghaziru'n nāsiyat*, Gifted with fine forelocks; fortunate, lucky, prosperous, happy. P ناصيه داران پاك *nāsiya-dārāni pāk*, Angels. Holy men, saints.

A ناضّ *nāzz*, Possible, practicable, feasible. Easily accomplished (business). Gold or silver money.

A ناضب *nāzib*, Far distant, wide (plain).

A ناضج *nāzij*, Ripe (fruit): well-dressed (meat).

A ناضح *nāzih*, (A camel) which draws water.

A ناضحة *nāzihat*, (pl. نواضح *nawāzih*) A she-camel trained to water ground.

A ناضد *nāzid*, One who lays things side by side.

A ناضر *nāzir*, Florid, vivid, bright. Water-moss. اخضر ناضر *akhzaru nāzir*, Of a bright green.

A ناضف *nāzif*, One who breaks wind much.

A ناضل *nāzil*, A warrior, champion.

A ناطب *nātib*, A strainer, colander.

A ناطح *nātih*, Butting (ram). (Game) coming in front of one. Meeting in full career (two birds or beasts). (pl. نواطح *nawātih*) Adversity. الناطح *an'nātih*, The horns of the ram, *i.e.* Two bright stars in the head of Aries. ليس له ناطح ولا خابط *laysa lahu nātihun wa lā khābitun*, He has neither what butts or stumbles, *i.e.* sheep or camel.

A ناطر *nātir*, (a foreign word) (pl. نطّار *nuttār*, نطراء *nutarāʼ*, and نطرة *natarat*) The keeper of a vineyard or palm-garden. The servant at a bath.

A ناطس *nātis*, An examiner, searcher: a spy.

A ناطع *nātiʻ*, One who eats with the fore-teeth. Whatever strikes the palate with a smacking noise. بياض ناطع *bayāzi nātiʻ*, Pure whiteness.

A ناطف *nātif*, A confection, especially one white and hard, made of the root عسلج *ʻusluj*, boiled long with new wine, sugar, and other ingredients.

A ناطفيّ *nātifiy*, A vender of ناطف *nātif*.

A ناطق *nātik*, Speaking. A speaker. Perspicuous (book). Rational (animal). Live stock. The waist. غير ناطق *ghayr nātik*, Dumb, irrational. حيوان ناطق *hayawāni nātik*, A rational animal: man. حيوان غير ناطق *hayawāni ghayr nātik*, An irrational animal: a beast.

A ناطقة *nātikat*, Faculty of speech. Waist. طوطيء ناطقه *tūtiʼi nātika*, A talking parrot.

A ناطل *nātal* or *nātil*, (pl. نياطل *nayātil*) A wine-measure. Wine. *Nātil*, Any thing remaining in a measure. One draught of wine, water, or milk. ما ظفرت بناطل *mā zafirtu bi nātil*, I have obtained nothing.

P ناطل *nātil*, A weight of seven pounds; also one of two and a-half drachms.

P ناطلب *nā talab*, Uncalled.

A ناطور *nātūr*, (pl. نواطير *nawātīr*) The keeper of a vineyard or palm-plantation. One who keeps a look out from the mast-head.

A ناطوري *nātūrī*, A watch set over sown fields.

A ناظر *nāzir*, A seer. A superintendant, inspector, observer, supervisor, guardian, spectator, keeper, purveyor, commissary. An officer employed in a judicial court superior to all peons, or bailiffs; a sheriff. The eye, or the black speck in the eye. Sight, vision. The lachrymal duct in the nose. A bone from the forehead to the roots of the nose. ناظر بيوتات *nāziri buyūtāt*, Superintendant of household expenses. P ناظر شدن *nāzir shudan*, To look, behold, observe. ناظر در سراي *nāziri dar sarāy*, A servant of the royal household posted at the gate of the palace to take an account of servants absent from their posts. شديد الناظر *shadīdu'nnāzir*, Clear of suspicion, who looks with his full eyes. احمر ناظر *ahmaru nāzirun*, Of a bright red.

A ناظران *nāzirāni*, Lachrymal ducts from the inner corner of the eye down each side of the nose.

A ناظرة *nāzirat*, (pl. نواظر *nawāzir*) The eye. Sight, vision. Reading, studying.

P ناظره خواني *nāzira-khwānī*, Reading (in opposition to repeating by heart).

A ناظم *nāzim*, A composer, arranger, adjuster. A governor, regulator. The chief officer of a province, in whose hands the protection of the country and the execution of the laws are entrusted. A poet. (A fish or lizard) marked with the lines نظامان *nizāmāni*. (A hen) full of eggs. ناظم اشعار *nāzimi ashʻār*, A composer of verses, a poet.

A ناظور *nāzūr*, A watchman, a watcher.

A ناظورة *nāzūrat*, Looked at or revered above all others, as respectable and venerable.

A ناعبة *nāʻibat*, Swift (she-camel).

A ناعجة *nāʻijat*, White (she-camel), one especially which they ride when hunting wild-cattle. Plain, level (ground).

A ناعس *nāʻis*, Sleepy, drowsy, lethargic.

A ناعصة *nāʻisat*, Assistance, aid. A helper. اسد بن ناعصة *asadu bin nāʻisat*, Name of an ancient Christian poet.

A ناعط *nāʻit*, (pl. نعط *nuʻut*) One who eats ungracefully, who swallows one half of a mouthful, and lets the other drop on his plate, or throws it away. One who travels to a great distance. Name of a district in Arabia Felix, of a mountain near Sanāa, and of a castle.

A ناعظ *nāʻiz*, Stiff, erect, rigid (yard).

A ناعفة *nāʻifat*, A loose, pendulous, flagging ear. اخذ ناعفة القنة *akhaza nāʻifata'l kunnat*, He climbed the mountain-top by an easy ascent.

A ناعق *nāʻik*, (pl. نعقة *naʻakat*) Croaking (raven).

A الناعقان *an' nāʻikāni*, Two stars in Orion.

A ناعل *nāʻil*, One who wears shoes or slippers; one who has many of them. Hard, solid (hoof). The onager or wild ass.

A ناعم *nāʻim*, Soft, easy, gentle, tender, delicate. Soft (silk). Easy (temper), cheerful (countenance).

A ناعمة *nāʻimat*, A garden, meadow. Delicate (woman), well fed and healthy.

A ناعور *nāʻūr*, A vein spirting out blood, not to be stopt. The sail of a mill. A water-mill.

A ناعورة *nāʻūrat*, (pl. نواعير *nawāʻīr*) A mill, especially that which is turned by weight of water, by the wind, or by cattle, for raising water from a well or river (so named from the sound it makes). A water-wheel. A water-bucket or pitcher. The nose, also the division of the nostrils.

A ناعوظ *nāʻūz*, One who produces a priapism.

A ناعي *nāʻī*, One who announces another's death. News of any person's death.

A ناعية *nāʻiyat*, (pl. of ناعي *nāʻī*) Those who bring intelligence of a person's death.

P ناغ *nāgh*, The elm-tree.

P ناغست *nāghist*, An Indian fruit resembling the pomegranate, the flowers of which, when they fall, are fragrant.

P ناغشت *nāghisht*, Ethiopian pepper.

A ناغض *nāghiz*, In motion, one following another (as clouds). Cartilage of the shoulder-blades.

P ناغوش *nāghosh*, Diving and remaining under water: plunging the head into water.

P ناغول *nāghūl*, Steps, a ladder, staircase, trap-door on the roof of a house.

P ناغيست *nāghīst*, Name of a scarlet seed good for the liver and stomach.

A نأف *naʼf*, (v. n. of نئف) Striving, using exertion. Being fortunate. *Naʼaf*, (v. n. of نئف) Eating (meat). Quenching (thirst). Loathing.

P ناف *nāf*, The navel, nave, middle of any thing. A round cushion. ناف ارض *nāfi arz*, (ناف خاك *nāfi khāk*, ناف زمين *nāfi zamīn*, or ناف عالم *nāfi ʻālam*) The navel of the earth, *i.e.* Mecca, or the Kaaba. ناف زدن *nāf zadan*, To cut the navel-string. ناف برخوشي زدن *nāf bar khwushī zadan*, To cut the navel-string cheerfully. (If, at the moment of performing this operation, the midwife be in a lively mood, they suppose that the child will be of a gay and cheerful temper; and if the contrary, they think the child will be of a dull and gloomy disposition, which they express by the phrase, ناف برغم زدن *nāf bar gham zadan*). ناف سپر *nāfi sipar*, The navel or centre boss of a shield. ناف شب *nāfi shab*, Midnight. در ناف شهر *dar nāfi shahr*, In the middle of the city. ناف هفته *nāfi hafta*, The middle of the week, *i.e.* Tuesday.

A نافث *nāfis*, A conjurer blowing or puffing when making incantations or playing tricks.

A نافثة *nāfisat*, Incantation, conjurer's trick.

A نافج *nāfij*, Thick, coarse (voice).

A نافجة *nāfijat*, (pl. نوافج *nawāfij*) Beginning or rise of a thing (as of a violent wind or rain). A cloud fraught with rain. The short ribs. A daughter. (from P نافه *nāfa*) A bag of musk.

A نافخ *nāfikh*, One who blows or puffs: a blower. نافخ ضرمة *nāfikhu zaramatin*, Blowing into flame.

A نافذ *nāfiz*, One who penetrates, passes, gets through, or executes. (A royal edict) having effect, received, or obeyed every where. Quicksilver. Worn, beaten, travelled (road). اميرِ نافذ الامر *amīri nāfizu'l amr*, A prince whose commands all obey. نافذ الكلمتين *nāfizu'l kalimatayn*, One whose words are penetrating, one from whose "yes" and "no" there is no appeal; absolute, despotic. P سوراخ نافذ *sūrākhi nāfiz*, A hole quite through.

A نافر *nāfir*, (pl. نفر *nafr*) Timid, flying. Stiff, erect. Sneezing (sheep). Conquering; a victor. A governor, a commander.

A نافرة *nāfirat*, Kinsmen, near relations.

P نافرجام *nā farjām*, Ineffectual, inconclusive, of bad tendency. A trifling or useless thing; a shameful action. Little, diminutive, small. سخنِ نافرجام *sukhuni nā farjām*, (or كلامِ نافرجام *kalāmi nā farjām*) Foolish, unmeaning words.

P نافرمان *nā farmān*, Disobedient, stubborn.

P نافرماني *nā farmānī*, Disobedience. نافرماني كرده *nā farmānī karda*, Uncommanded.

P نافرهخته *nā farhakhta*, Rude, unmannerly, ill-bred. Ugly. Rudeness, ill-manners. Ugliness.

A نافس *nāfis*, One who looks with a malignant eye. Name of the fifth gaming arrow.

A نافض *nāfiz*, Trembling, tremor. *Nāfiz*, (or النافض *an' nāfiz*) (A fever) attended with tremor.

A نافطة *nāfitat*, A sheep. A she-goat. Blistered (hand). (Cattle) driving any thing out of the nose. ما له عافطة ولا نافطة *mā lahu ʿāfitatun wa lā nāfitatun*, He has nothing.

A نافع *nāfiʿ*, Salutary, wholesome, good, useful, profitable, advantageous, assisting. Ridding of, freeing from (spoken of medicine). Name of a freedman who belonged to Muhammad. Name of a prison built by Alīy. P نافع شدن *nāfiʿ shudan*, To do good, to assist, to make use of.

A نافق *nāfiḳ*, Saleable, finding a ready sale.

A نافقاء *nāfiḳāʾ*, (pl. نوافق *nawāfiḳ*) The hole of a field-mouse (with ten or a dozen entrances).

A نافقة *nāfiḳat*, A bag or bladder of musk.

A نافلة *nāfilat*, (pl. نوافل *nawāfil*) A voluntary act of religion, the observance of which is not positively enjoined. A work of supererogation. Supererogatory prayers. Religious merit. An extraordinary gift. Children of children. Plunder, booty.

A نافوخ *nāfūkh*, Liquorice-root.

P نافه *nāfa*, A bag or bladder of musk. The belly, or skin of the belly of any animal. A pod, cod. نافۀ آف *nāfaʾi āf*, The navel of the musk-deer. نافۀ آهو *nāfaʾi āhū*, The musky ringlets of the fair. نافۀ مشك *nāfaʾi mushk*, A bladder of musk. Navel-bag of the musk-deer or goat. نافۀ مشك يافتن *nāfaʾi mushk yāftan*, To find a bladder of musk, (metaph.) To get a great name.

A نافه *nāfih*, Lazy, sluggish (camel). A coward.

P نافه بوي *nāfa-boy* or *būy*, One who has stinking breath. A tale-bearer, whisperer, slanderer.

P نا فهم *nā fahm*, Not understanding.

A نافي *nāfī*, Negative. Who rejects. Rejected.

A ناق *nāḳ*, Pustules or excrescences in the hand. The grooves or wrinkles between the roots of the little finger and thumb, or any thing similar in the other parts of the body, as in the interior bend of the elbow-joints. (pl. of ناقة *nāḳat*) She-camels.

P ناقابل *nā ḳābil*, Incapable: silly. Insufficient.

A ناقبة *nāḳibat*, An ulcer in the side.

P ناقبول *nā ḳabūl*, Not consenting. Loathing. Unpleasant, disagreeable, unacceptable.

A ناقة *nāḳat*, (pl. ناق *nāḳ*, نوق *nūḳ*, انوق *anwuḳ*, انؤق *anʾuḳ*, اونق *awnuḳ*, اينق *aynuḳ*, نياق *niyāḳ*, ناقات *nāḳāt*, انواق *anwāḳ*, ايانق *ayānik*, and نياقات *niyāḳāt*) A she-camel. One pustule. الناقة *an' nāḳat*, Certain stars in the form of a camel.

A ناقد *nāḳid*, One whose business it is to examine coin and ascertain its goodness. An assayer. Clever in the despatch of business.

P ناقر *nāḳir*, A harp, psaltery.

A ناقر *nāḳir*, One who strikes or hollows out. (An arrow) penetrating the mark.

A ناقرة *nāḳirat*, Adversity, evil, misfortune, calamity. Argument, proof, reason. Controversy.

A ناقز *nāḳiz*, Poor, trifling (present).

A ناقس *nāḳis*, Acid, sour.

A ناقص *nāḳis*, Deficient, defective, imperfect, unfinished. Mutilated. Inexpert. (in gram.) Defective (verb, as غزا *ghazaʾ* or رمى *ramuʾ*). ناقص العقل *nāḳisu'l ʿaḳl*, (or ناقص عقل *nāḳis ʿaḳl*) Deficient in judgment; silly, stupid.

A ناقض *nāḳiz*, One who breaks forcibly or untwists. One who violates or rescinds.

A ناقط *nāḳit*, The servant of a freedman.

A ناقع *nāḳiʿ*, (Venom) which penetrates or lodges in the body. Newly-drawn (blood). Wholesome (water), quenching thirst.

A ناقف *nāḳif*, One who breaks the head.

A ناقل *nāḳil*, One who transports from place to place. A porter, carrier. A reporter, relater. A copier. A painter, delineator. ناقلِ ورقه *nāḳili waraḳa*, (ناقل الورقة *nāḳilu'l waraḳat*, ناقلِ صحيفه *nāḳili sahīfa*, or ناقلِ مكتوب مودّت *nāḳili maktūbi mawaddat*) The bearer of these letters or presents.

A ناقلة *nāḳilat*, (pl. نواقل *nawāḳil*) Inconstant (fortune). Temporary or migratory inhabitants. A copy. A translation.

A ناقم *nāḳim*, A kind of date. A reprover, rebuker, chider. A requiter, recompenser.

P ناقور *nāḳūr*, Celebrated, renowned.

A ناقور *nāḳūr*, A trumpet (such especially as the angels are said to blow at the last (day).

P ناقوره *nāḳūra*, A drinking-vessel.

A ناقوس *nāḳūs*, A thin oblong piece of wood, struck with a flexible rod called وبيل *wabīl*, used by the Eastern Christians to summon the congregation to divine service, a kind of wooden gong (church-bells not being allowed in Muhammadan countries).

P ناقوسي *nāḳūsī*, Name of a mode in music. The twenty-sixth note of the barbud.

A ناقه *nāḳih*, (pl. نقّه *nukkah*) Weak after sickness. Contemptible. Intelligent, able to understand.

P ناك *nāk*, Adulterated. Adulterated musk or ambergris. Mixed, moistened. Stained, polluted. Inaccurate. A sort of musky herb. A sweet juicy pear. The uvula. The jaw. A kind of alligator. Affixed to nouns, in Persian, it denotes affection or abundance: as, خشمناك *khishmnāk*, Inflamed with anger; دردناك *dardnāk*, Affected with pain; طربناك *tarabnāk*, Cheerful, joyous; ميوناك *mīvanāk*, Laden with fruit, fruitful. ناكِ بالا *nāki bālā*, Upper jaw. ناكِ پائين *nāki pāʾīn*, Under jaw.

A ناكاج *nākāj*, (the Arabic form of P ناگاه *nāgāh*) Suddenly, unawares, unseasonable, late. At once.

P ناكارگي *nā kāragī*, Idleness. Uselessness.

P ناكاره *nā kāra*, Useless, worthless. Idle, lazy.

P نا كاسته *nā kāsta*, Undiminished, unaltered (regard). ماهِ نا كاسته *māhi nā kāsta*, Full moon.

P ناكام *nā kām*, Unwilling. Disagreeable. Hopeless, remediless. Disappointed, discontented. ناكام شدن *nā kām shudan*, (or بودن *būdan*) To reject, refuse.

P ناكامي *nā kāmī*, Disappointment.

A ناكب *nākib*, One who bows down, bends, declines, turns from.

A ناكت *nākit*, (A camel) rubbing the hair off his side with a distorted elbow.

P ناكتخدا *nā-katkhudā*, A pilot. A ship-master.

A ناكح *nākih*, One who marries. A man in the act of venery. A stallion. A married woman.

A ناكحة *nākihat*, A married woman, a wife.

P ناكدخدا *nā kad-khudā*, One not a family-man. A bachelor. An unmarried woman. A widow.

P ناكدون *nākdawn*, Asparagus.

P ناكردگار *nā kirdigār*, Ignorant, unskilful.

P ناكردني *nā kardanī*, Not fit or improper to be done. Impracticable, unachievable.

A ناكز *nākiz*, (pl. نواكز *nawākiz*) (A well) containing little water, exhausted.

P ناكس *nā kas*, Unmanly, worthless, unworthy, mean, base, ignoble, vile. Sordid, avaricious; abject, illiberal. A lown. Cowardly, timid, degenerate. A man of light character, of no consequence. Nobody. Impotent, emasculated. A pederast.

A ناكس *nākis*, (pl. نواكس *nawākis*) Mean, humbled, depressed, hanging the head.

P ناكسي *nā kasī*, Meanness, abjectness, worthlessness, villainy, infamy. Impotency, cowardice, timidity. Avarice, stinginess.

A ناكف *nākif*, One who refuses from modesty or shame; who disdains. A coward.

A ناكل nākil, Weak. A coward. One who prevaricates in oath, who uses subterfuge.

P ناكند nākand, A colt.

P ناگاه nā gāh, Suddenly, unexpectedly. All at once, unawares. Unseasonably. Ill-timed.

P ناگاه گير nāgāh-gīr, Taking, seizing unawares.

P ناگرفت nā girift, Suddenly, unexpectedly.

P ناگرويدن na girawīdan, To disbelieve, be impious. ناگرويده nā girawīda, Unbelieving, infidel. Disobedient. Disbelieved.

P ناگزر nā guzir, (or ناگزران guzirān) Impotent, helpless, reduced to extremities, necessary.

P ناگزير nā guzīr, Impossibility to dispense with.

P ناگفته nā gufta, Not spoken, unsaid.

P ناگوار nā guwār, (and ناگوارد nā guwārd) Undigested, indigestible, unpalatable, unwholesome, unacceptable. Irksome. Unarranged. Indigestion. Indisposed, digesting badly.

P ناگوارائي nā guwārāʼī, (or ناگوارندگي nā guwārandagī) Unwholesomeness, unhealthiness.

P ناگواره nāguwāra, Undigested. Any thing lost. Unwholesome water.

P ناگواريدگي nā guwārīdagī, Unwholesomeness. Indigestibility.

P ناگواريدن nāguwārīdan, (or ناگواليدن nā guwālīdan) To crack (as the skin with intense cold or heat), to chap (as the lips), to become yellow (as herbs) from dryness.

P ناگور nā guwar, (or ناگورد nā guward) Undigested. Unwholesome, indigestible.

P ناگوهر nā gawhar, Accident (philosophically).

P ناگه nā gah, (or ناگهان nā gahān, ناگهانه nā gahāna, or ناگهاني nā gahānī) Suddenly, all at once. Unexpected, sudden, unforeseen, unawares, fatal. بلاي ناگهانه balāyi nāgahāna, Sudden misfortune.

A نأل naʼl, (naʼal, or نألان naʼalān) (v. n. of نأل) Going, jumping, or skipping along, and moving the head upward. Shaking the head when trotting (a horse). Behoving. Envying.

P نال nāl, A slender yellow reed. A writing-reed. A hollow reed. A tube, pipe. A gun-barrel. Sugar-cane. A solid reed of which they make arrows. The threads or pith inside of a writing-reed. Tip of the tongue. A small stream. A small cistern. A large river. Lamentation. Name of a small melodious bird. (in comp.) Lamenting, complaining.

A نال nāl, (v. n. of نال for نول) Giving, bestowing. Obtaining. (pl. انوال anwāl) Liberal. Any thing acquired. A gift.

P نالان nālān, Lamenting. One who laments. Lamentable. Name of a mountain. نالان كردن nālān kardan, To lament, groan, sigh. گريان و نالان giryān u nālān, Weeping and lamenting.

P نا لائق nā lāʼik, Improper, unsuitable, unfit, unworthy, inconvenient. Improperly, unsuitably.

A نالة nālat, (v. n. of نال for نول) Obtaining, acquiring (a good thing). A court-yard. The area of the temple of Mecca, the sacred enclosure.

P نالش nālish, A groan, lamentation, complaint, exclamation. نالش كردن nālish kardan, To exclaim, complain, lament. عرض نالش گردانيدن ɛarzi nālish gardānīdan, To lodge a complaint.

P نالكس nālkis, The coping of a wall.

P ناله nāla, A small river, canal. Complaint, lamentation. نالۀ عندليب nālaʼi ɛandalīb, The plaint of the nightingale. ناله كردن nāla kardan, To sigh, lament, complain. نالۀ ناي رويين nālaʼi nāyi royīn, The blast of a brazen trumpet.

P ناله كنان nāla-kunān, Uttering complaints.

P ناليدن nālīdan, To lament, complain, grieve.

P ناليش nālīsh, Sigh, groan. Humility, submission.

P نام nām, A name. Fame, reputation, renown. نام از شكم افتادن nām az shikam uftādan, To be lost, annihilated. نام بد nāmi bad, A bad name. نام بر آوردن nām bar āwardan, To become famous. نام بر يخ زدن nām bar yakh zadan, To write one's name upon the ice. To erase. To forget. نام بنام nām ba nām, Name by name, expressly, particularly. نام دادن nām dādan, (also نام نهادن nām nihādan) To give a name, to nominate. نام زدن nām zadan, To pronounce a name. نام كشيدن nām kashīdan, To revile, call names, reproach. نام نامي nāmi nāmī, An exalted name. نام نيك nāmi nek, A good name, a clear or illustrious reputation. بد نام bad-nām, Infamous. نيك نام nek-nām, Famous, celebrated, of good reputation.

P ناماْمول nā maʼmūl, Unlooked, unhoped for.

P نام آور nām-āwar, Illustrious. Famous, in high repute.

P نا مبارك nā mubārak, Unfortunate, inauspicious, execrable.

P نام بردار nām-bardār or burdār, Well known.

P نام برده nām-burda, One whose name has been before mentioned, aforesaid. Celebrated, famous.

A نأمة naʼmat, A musical tone, melody. Singing. اسكت الله نأمته ashkata' (or اسكن askana') llāh naʼmatahu, May God silence his gamut!

A نامة nāmat, A chink, a cranny.

A نامّة nāmmat, Vital motion. Sound. اسكت الله نامّته ashkata'llāh nāmmatahu, May God extinguish his life!

P نا متصوّر nā mutaṣawwir, Not to be imagined, inconceivable.

P نا متناهي nā mutanāhī, Infinite. Divine. عنايت نا متناهي ɛināyati nā mutanāhī, Divine favour.

P نا متوقّع nā mutawakkiɛ, Unexpected.

A ناماجات nāmajāt, (pl. of نامه nāma) Letters.

P نام جو nām-jo, Seeking fame, ambitious.

P نام جوي nām-joy, Intrepid, warlike, magnanimous. Name of the tenth day of the month according to the era of Jalālu'd dīn.

A نا محدود nā mahdūd, Unlimited, boundless. Innumerable. Infinite.

P نا محرم nā mahram, A stranger, one not allowed to enter the women's apartments.

P نا محرميّت nā mahramiyat, The not being permitted to enter the haram. The not being confidential; the not being consulted; the not being in the secret.

A نا محصور nā mahsūr, Immense, infinite, unbounded. اموال نا محصور amwāli nā mahsūr, Vast riches, endless wealth, boundless resources.

P نا محضور nā mahzūr, Not present, absent.

P نا مخصوص nā makhsūs, Not peculiar or special.

P نامدار nām-dār, Renowned, celebrated, illustrious, famous, noted, glorious. درميان نامداران ممالكستان dar miyāni nām-dārāni mamālik-satān, Amongst the illustrious princes, conquerors of countries. نامدارترين nāmdārtarīn, Most illustrious.

P نامداري nām-dārī, Fame, celebrity.

P نامراد nā murād, Dissatisfied, disappointed, frustrated. Unfortunate, disconsolate. Miserable, wretched. Compelled, forced.

P نامرادي nā murādī, Disappointment. Dissatisfaction. An unwelcome thing.

P نامربوط nā marbūt, Unconnected. Impertinent, mal-à-propos.

A نامرة nāmirat, A net in which a sheep is enclosed to decoy a wolf. An iron hook baited with flesh for catching wolves.

P نامرد nā mard, Unmanly, a coward. Impotent. Covetous.

P نامردانه nā mardāna, Unmanly.

P نامرد سازي nā mard-sāzī, A rendering impotent (by witchcraft or spells).

P نامردم nā mardum, Unmanly, worthless, mean, base, ignoble.

P نامردمي nā mardumī, Rudeness.

P نامردي nā mardī, Cowardice, baseness. Effeminacy, impotence.

P نامرضي nā marzī, Unacceptable, detestable, disapproved, worthless.

P نا مرعي nā marɛī, Unobserved, unattended to.

P نامرغوب nā marghūb, Unwished for, unsought, vile. وضع نامرغوب wazɛi nā marghūb A mean or impertinent action.

P نامزد nām-zad, Named (for an office), nominated, appointed, declared, destined. Betrothed. A betrothed virgin.

P نامزروع nā mazrūɛ, Unsowed (field).

P نامساعد nā musāɛad, Unaided.

P نامستحسن nā mustahsan, Worthless, deformed, censurable, disapproved of.

P نامستحق nā mustahak, Unworthy, undeserving.

A نامستعدّ nā mustaɛidd, Inapt, stupid.

P نامسعود nā masɛūd, Inauspicious, unfortunate, unhappy.

P نامسموع nā masmūɛ, Not to be heard, inadmissible. Unheard.

P نامشخّص nā mushakhkhas, Inconstant, variable.

P نامشغول nā mashghūl, Inattentive. Unemployed.

A نامصة nāmisat, A tire-woman, one who twitches

the hairs from the face.

P نامضبوط *nā mazbūt*, Insolent, ungovernable.

P نامطبوع *nā matbūʻ*, Unacceptable, disagreeable, unpleasant, repugnant to nature, unnatural. Cruel. Worthless.

P نامعتدل *nā muʻtadil*, Intemperate, exorbitant.

P نامعتمد *nā muʻtamad*, Not trustworthy.

P نامعدود *nā maʻdūd*, Unnumbered, innumerable.

P نامعروف *nā maʻrūf*, Unknown, incognito.

P نامعقول *nā maʻkūl*, Improbable, absurd, impertinent, improper, unreasonable, inconvenient. نامعقول حركت *nā maʻkūl harakat*, (or وضع نامعقول *wazʻi nā maʻkūl*) An improper action.

P نامعلوم *nā maʻlūm*, Unknown. Uncertain.

P نامعيّن *nā muʻayyan*, Indefinite, undefined.

P نامغلوب *nā maghlūb*, Unconquered.

P نامفروق *nā mafrūk*, Inseparable, undivided.

P نامقبول *nā makbūl*, Unacceptable, disagreeable, displeasing. نامقبول و ناپسنديده شدن *nā makbūl u nā pasandīda shudan*, To be disagreeable and disapproved of.

A نامل *nāmil*, A secret defamer, slanderer.

P ناملاطف *nā mulātif*, Ungracious, unpolite.

P ناملائم *nā mulāʼim*, Incongruous, unsuitable, inconvenient, improper. Severe, hard, austere.

A نأملة *naʼmalat*, (v. n. of نأمل Q) Walking in fetters. The pace of one in fetters.

A نامله *nāmilat*, Beaten paths. Travellers going in different ways.

P ناميّزي *nā mumayyizī*, Indiscrimination.

P نامناسب *nā munāsib*, Indecent, impertinent, incongruous, improper, unsuitable.

P ناموافق *nā muwāfik*, Differing, adverse, absurd, disagreeing, contrary, opposite.

P ناموجّه *nā muwajja*, Disapproved, disagreeable.

P نامور *nāmwar* or *war*, Celebrated, renowned.

A نامور *nāmūr*, Blood. A kind of iron hook baited with flesh for catching wolves.

A نامورة *nāmūrat*, A net in which a sheep is enclosed to decoy a wolf.

P ناموري *nāmwarī*, Reputation, fame, celebrity.

P ناموزون *nā mawzūn*, Unweighed. Discordant, unrythmical, badly composed (verse or prose). Ill-made or dressed.

A ناموس *nāmūs*, Reputation, fame, renown, esteem, honour. Dignity. Law. Divine decrees or judgments. Disgrace, reproach, shame. Voice, sound, noise, clamour. War, battle. The master of a house, the proprietor of a mansion. The lurking-place of a hunter. Hidden fraud, concealed deceit. Angels. The female part of a family. A net. The den of a lion. A participator of another's secrets. Cunning, sagacious. One who insinuates himself by flattery and address. A flea. A calumniator, informer. The muster-roll of an army. Intense study. The angel Gabriel (called also ناموس الاكبر *nāmūsu ʼlakbar*, The great secretary). ناموس عبراني *nāmūsi ʻibrānī*, The Judaical law. اصحاب وقار و ناموس *as-hābi wakār u nāmūs*, Lords of authority and estimation.

A ناموسة *nāmūsat*, A lion's den.

P ناموس گاه *nāmūs-gāh*, A field of battle.

A ناموسيّة *nāmūsīyat*, A housing.

P ناموية *nāmūya*, A faithful wife.

P نامه *nāma*, A writing, letter, epistle. A diploma. A history, work, book. Exemplar, model, type. A mirror, looking-glass. A flood, torrent. The character called تعليق *taʻlīk*. نامهٔ اعمال *nāmaʼi aʻmāl*, The book of works (a book of the actions of mankind, supposed to be kept by guardian or observing angels, to be produced at the day of judgment). نامهٔ چهارم *nāmaʼi chahārum*, The fourth book, *i.e.* the Kur'ān, as succeeding to the Pentateuch, Psalms, and Gospel. نامهٔ خاقاني *nāmaʼi khākānī*, Imperial or royal letters. نامهٔ دلكشا *nāmaʼi dil-kushā*, A heart-rejoicing letter. نامهٔ همايون *nāmaʼi humāyūn*, August letters, imperial mandates. نامهٔ همايون ملاطفت مشحون مصادقت نمون سعادت مقرون *nāmaʼi humāyūni mulātafat-mashhūni musādakat-numūni saʻādat-makrūn*, August, most gracious, most benevolent, imperial letters or mandates. امان نامه *amān-nāma*, A safe-conduct, passport. تسليت نامه *tasliyat-nāma*, Consolatory letters, or letters of condolence. راضي نامه *rāzī-nāma*, Acquittance. ساعت نامه *sāʻat-nāma*, An hour-book, *i.e.* a watch or dial. شهادت نامه *shahādat-nāma*, Certificates, attestations. شاه نامه *shāh-nāma*, The history or mirror of kings, the celebrated epic poem of Firdawsī. فتح نامه *fath-nāma*, (or ظفر نامه *zafar-nāma*) Letters announcing victory. A book of triumphs (the name of a history of Tamerlane in Persian, and of several other books. See ظفر *zafar* and فتح *fath*.) فراست نامه *farāsat-nāma*, (محبّت نامه *mahabbat-nāma*, or عهد نامه *ʻahd-nāma*) Friendly, affectionate letters. همايون نامه *humāyūn-nāma*, The august history, a Turkish translation of the Persian 'Anwāri Suhaylī,' a paraphrase of Pilpay's Fables.

P نامه آور *nāma-āwar*, Letter-carrier, postman.

P نامه دان *nāmadān*, A letter-case, portfolio.

P نامهربان *nā mihrbān*, Unfriendly. نامهربانيها *nā mihrbānīhā*, Unkindnesses.

P نامه ور *nāmawar*, Letter-bearing. كبوتر نامه ور *kabūtari nāmawar*, A carrier-pigeon.

P نامي *nāmī*, Illustrious, celebrated. Celebrity, notoriety. A book, letter, diploma.

A نامي *nāmī*, Growing; whatever grows.

A نامية *nāmiyat*, A creature. Any thing created by God. Stalk or stem (of grapes). Growth, vegetation. قوّت نامية *kūwati nāmiya*, Power of growth.

P ناميدن *nāmīdan*, To name, nominate, call, give mention, express a name. To grow, increase. To chap (as the lips).

P نا ميسّر *nā muyassar*, Impossible, difficult.

A نان *nān*, Bread. A loaf. A light round cake. A pikelit, a muffin. نان آبي *nāni ābī*, Bread kneaded with water. نان آتش روي *nāni ātish-rūy*, The world-illuminating sun. نان پختن *nān pukhtan*, To bake bread. نان پخته *nāni pukhta*, Baked bread. نان تلخ *nāni talkh*, Stale, old bread. نان تهي *nāni tihī*, Bread alone, dry bread. نان حادثه خام بودن *nāni hādisa khām būdan*, To meet with a disappointment. نان حلال *nāni halāl*, Bread earned by honest labour. Obedience, worship, devotion. نان خرچنگ *nāni kharchang*, The moon. نان خطائي *nāni khatāʼī*, A kind of sweetmeat. نان خميري *nāni khamīrī*, Leavened bread. نان در انبان نهادن *nān dar ambān nihādan*, To put bread in the wallet; to get ready for a journey. نان در جامه كردن *nān dar jāma kardan*, To put bread upon the cloth, *i.e.* to sprinkle cloth with water and bread, or starch. نان رباط *nāni ribāt*, Bread given in monasteries. نان زرّين *nāni zarrīn*, (The golden loaf) The sun. نان سفيد فلك *nāni safedi falak*, (or نان سيمين *nāni sīmīn*) The moon. نان سوخته *nāni sokhta*, Burnt bread. نان شيرين بودن *nāni shīrīn būdan*, A failure, a want of bread. نان فطيري *nāni fatīrī*, Unleavened bread. نان فيروز خاني *nāni fīroz-khānī*, A loaf of bread weighing a من *man*. نان كشكين *nāni kashkīn*, Bread made of bean-meal, barley-meal, and wheaten-flour. نان كلاغ *nāni kulāgh*, Name of an herb growing in marshy places. Camomile-flowers. Crows'-foot. نان گلاج *nāni gulāj*, A Persian cake made of flour, honey, and sesame-oil; also one made of the finest flour, white of egg, and refined sugar. نان لاكو *nāni lākū*, A kind of bread made in Gīlān. نان مشوش *nāni mashūsh*, A thin sort of cake, over which they pour syrup and the white of egg. نان نهاري *nāni nahārī*, Breakfast. نان وقف *nāni wakf*, Bread given in charity. نان و پارچه *nān u pārcha*, Food and raiment. نان و نمك *nān u namak*, Bread and salt, *i.e.* hospitality, or any benefit received from another. نان و نمك خائني *nān u namak-khāʼinī*, Perfidious, ungrateful, treacherous to a host or a master, a bread-and-salt traitor. نان و نمكدان شكستن *nān u namakdān shikastan*, A phrase used to imply, to eat forbidden fruit.

P نانا *nānā*, A maternal grandfather.

A نأنأ *naʼnaʼ*, One who frequently rolls the black part of the eye. Weak, infirm, timid.

A نأناء *naʼnāʼ*, Weak, infirm. Timid.

A نأنأة *naʼnaʼat*, (v. n. of نأنأ Q) Being weak in mind, feeble in judgment. Being unequal to a thing, doing less than one's duty. Forbidding, averting. Nourishing, feeding well. Weakness. The feeble beginnings of Islām.

P نان با *nān-bā*, Broth with crumbs. A baker.

P نان بائي *nān-bāʼī*, A bread-seller.

P نان پاره *nān-pāra*, A piece of bread.

P نان پز *nān-paz*, A baker. چوب نان پز *chūbi*

(or *chobi*) *nān-paz*, A baker's rolling-pin.

P نان‌پزي *nān-pazī*, Trade of a baker, baking.

P نان جامه *nān-jāma*, A servant for his victuals.

P نانجوي *nān-joy*, A beggar. A worldling.

P نان چاشت *nān-chāsht*, Bread eaten at noon.

P نان چين *nān-chīn*, An instrument for drawing bread from an oven.

P نان خواه *nān-khwāh*, Aniseed (in some places it seems to mean caraway-seed), which they frequently bake in bread on account of its flavour and stomachic qualities. Bishop's weed, ammi. One who begs his bread.

P نان خورش *nān-khwurish*, A sourish kind of stomach-water for creating an appetite and promoting digestion. Meat or fish eaten along with bread. نانخورش خانه *nān-khwurish-khāna*, Vinegar made from grapes.

P نان روغني *nān-raughanī*, Bread mixed with, or dipped into, boiled butter. Buttered toast.

P نان ريزه *nān-reza*, A crumb. A slice of bread.

P نانكار *nān-kār*, (Indian phrase) Lands granted to zamindārs, chowdries, and talookdārs, as a maintenance for them, even after their removal from their stations; hereditary, and consequently alienable. A cess to defray the household expenses of a governor.

P نانكاري *nān-kārī*, Belonging to نانكار *nān-kār*.

P نانكش *nānkish*, Juniper-berry. Pistachio-nut.

P نان كور *nān-kūr*, Ungrateful, base, worthless.

P نانگواه *nān-gawāh*, Aniseed.

P نان مخور *nān makhwur*, (Eat not bread) Frugal, parsimonious.

P نانمش *nānimash* or *nānamish*, A thing unseen, out of sight. Deviation from the road.

P نانمشيدن *nānamshīdan*, To meet with continual disappointments, to fail in the attainment of one's desire.

P نانو *nānū*, A little song or a story which mothers repeat while rocking their children to sleep; lullaby. A cradle. (for نانوا *nānwā*, A baker.

P نانوا *nānwā*, A baker. Food made of bread.

P نانوائي *nānwāī*, Art of baking bread, baking.

P نانوخيه *nānūkhiya* or *nānūkhaya*, Aniseed.

P نا نهاده *nā nihāda*, Not placed or fixed.

P نانيوشان *nāniyūshān* or *nānayūshān*, Sudden, unawares, without notice. Unheard.

P ناو *nāw* or *nāv*, A trough. A pipe for carrying off the rain from the roof of a house. The passage through which the meal or flour runs when grinding. Any thing long and hollow. The sluice of a mill-dam. A river, channel, aqueduct, canal. A cistern. The furrow or groove down the middle of a man's back or the loins of a horse; also in a grain of wheat and a date-stone. A hole. A crack, chink. A baker's rolling-pin. A frying-pan. A cauldron, kettle, pot. An easy, graceful air in walking. A boat, small ship.

A ناو *nasw*, (v. n. of نأا for ناو) Going far.

P ناوارث *nā wāris*, Friendless, patronless, without a protector. Without an heir, heirless.

P ناواقف *nā wākif*, Unskilled, inexperienced.

P ناواقفيت *nā wākifīyat*, Inexperience.

P ناوانيدن *nāwānīdan*, To crook, bend. To fatigue. To cause to be engraved.

P ناوچه *nāwcha*, A mould in which ingots of gold and silver are cast. A little boat.

P ناودان *nāwdān* or *nāwidān*, A canal, aqueduct, mill-dam, or the force of water which drives the mill-wheel. The passage through which the meal or flour runs when grinding.

P ناور *nāwar*, Possible.

P ناوران *nāwarān*, Things possible, possibilities.

P ناورد *nāward*, Battle, combat. March.

P ناوردگاه *nāward-gāh*, A battle-field.

P ناورفرتاش *nāwar-fartāsh*, Whose existence is possible.

P ناوژه *nāwja*, A little boat; a trough.

P ناوس *nāwus*, A cemetery of the Magi. A fire-temple.

P ناوسار *nāwsār*, The main beam of a mill turned by a water-wheel. A canal for watering gardens.

P ناوسند *nā wasand*, Not approved, disagreeable. Poor, weak, lean.

P ناوسيد *nāwasīd*, Poor, weak, lean.

P ناوك *nāwak*, A small arrow. An arrow flying swift and directly to the mark. An arrow with which they shoot birds, made of a reed, with a notch on the side. A tube through which an arrow is projected. A cross-bow. A reed, or any thing similar, naturally or artificially hollow. The feeder of a mill. A canal. The groove down a man's back. A reed-bed. A bee's sting. A ploughshare. Nimble, expeditious. (dim. of ناو *nāw*, q. v.) ناوك سحري *nāwaki saharī*, Execrations poured forth early in the morning. ناوك قلبي *nāwaki kalbī*, A sigh from the heart. A satire, lampoon.

P ناوك انداز *nāwak-andāz*, An archer. ناوك انداز ادب *nāwak-andāzi adab*, A schoolmaster.

P ناوميد *nā umed*, (or *nā ummed*) Hopeless.

P ناوناوان *nāwnāwān*, A pompous walker.

P ناووس *nāwūs*, (in modern orthography ناوس *nāmus*) A temple of the fire-worshippers.

A ناووس *nāwūs*, A burying-place of the Magi.

P ناوه *nāwa*, A boat. A kneading-trough, hutch, or bin; any thing similar used by a baker or a maker of plaster. The groove down a man's back. The passage through which the meal or the flour runs when grinding. A tube through which an arrow is projected. The body (as containing the soul). A canal, lake. A kettle, cauldron, pot. An old veil or curtain. A stick for scratching the back. Name of a place. ناوه محراب *nāwa-mihrāb*, A little chapel; the place where the priest stands when praying.

A ناوي *nāwī*, (pl. نواء *niwāa*) Fat (camel).

A ناوية *nāwiyat*, Fat (she-camel).

P ناويدن *nāwīdan*, To hollow out a stone or a piece of wood. To slumber, begin to sleep. To weep, lament, complain. To walk with a pompous or graceful air. To be bent. To be tired.

P ناويژه *nāwīja*, Thick, dense. Opaque, impure. Blemished. Mixed, adulterated.

P ناه *nāh*, Noxious exhalations from the ground.

A ناه *nāh*, Abstinent, averse, refraining from.

P ناهار *nāhār*, Unknown, incognito, strange. (for نا آهار *nā āhār*) Fasting, eating nothing.

P ناهاري *nāhārī*, A light breakfast. ناهاري كردن *nāhārī kardan*, To breakfast.

A ناهب *nāhib*, A seizer, snatcher, spoiler.

A ناهت *nāhit*, The throat.

A ناهج *nāhij*, A finder or pointer out of the way.

P ناهد *nāhid*, Venus. A cultivated garden.

A ناهد *nāhid*, (A girl) with swelling breasts. Swelling (breast). Any thing raised. A lion.

A ناهدة *nāhidat*, A girl with swelling breasts.

P ناهدا *nāhidā*, The planet Venus. Name of the mother of Alexander the Great.

A ناهر *nāhir*, White grapes.

A ناهز *nāhiz*, One who approaches, draws near.

A ناهض *nāhiz*, A young bird whose wings are full and prepared to fly. A protuberant muscle or piece of flesh in the upper part of the arm or fore-leg of a horse. Rising up.

A ناهضة *nāhizat*, Sons of the same father by different mothers rising against or opposing one another. Servants, domestics, as rising up to obey.

A ناهق *nāhik*, Braying (ass), neighing (horse). (pl. نواهق *nawāhik*) The place in the throat whence these sounds proceed. ناهقان *nāhikānī*, Two prominent bones in the cheeks of solid-hoofed animals.

A ناهك *nāhik*, One who strives, endeavours.

A ناهل *nāhil*, (pl. نواهل *nawāhil*, نهال *nihāl*, نهل *nahal*, and نهول *nuhūl*) (A camel) drinking the first draught, yet still dry. Thirsty. Who or what quenches thirst. Hungry.

A ناهلة *nāhilat*, A crowd pressing to the cistern.

P ناهمتا *nā hamtā*, Incomparable, unparalleled. Dissimilar, dissonant, opposite, repugnant.

P ناهموار *nā hamwār*, (or ناهمواره *nā hamwāra*) Unequal, uneven, rough, having protuberances, irregular, capricious, froward, perverse. Unworthy, incongruous, unbecoming, inconvenient, disproportioned. اطوار ناهموار *atwāri nā hamwār*, Unworthy, indecent actions. روزگار ناهموار *rozgāri nā hamwār*, Inconstant fortune.

P ناهمواري *nā hamwārī*, Inequality, unevenness. Inconvenience.

P ناهنجار *nā hanjār*, Rough, uneven, untoward.

P ناهنجاري *nā hanjārī*, Impropriety, deviation from right, frowardness, disobedience.

P ناهوا *nā hawā*, Unequalled, incomparable.

A ناهور *nāhūr*, A cloud.

P ناهوش *nā hosh*, Suddenly.

P ناهي *nāhī*, The planet Venus.

A ناهي *nāhī*, (pl. نهاة *nuhāt*) A prohibiter, forbidder, interdicter. هذا رجل ناهيك من رجل *hāzā rajulun nāhīka mi'r rajulin*, This is a man that will suffice you (you cannot desire a better). ناهيك ان *nāhīka an*, Let it suffice you that.

A ناهية *nāhiyat*, Interdict, prohibition. Any thing forbidden. هي ناهيتك من امرأة *hiya nāhiyatuka min imra*ₛ*atin*, Let that woman suffice thee.

P ناهيد *nāhīd*, Name of the mother of Alexander the Great. *Nāhīd*, (and ناهيدة *nāhīda*) (The planet) Venus. A girl with a swelling bosom. A cultivated, flourishing garden.

P ناي *nāy*, A reed, pipe. A flute, flagelet, fife. A reed played upon by the dervishes. The throat. Pride, vain-glory. Name of a fort. ناي بيني *nāyi bīnī*, The nostrils, the passage of the nose. ناي تركي *nāyi turkī*, A trumpet, clarion. ناي زدن *nāy zadan*, To play on the flute, to pipe. ناي گلو *nāyi gulū*, The wind-pipe. ناي لوس *nāyi los*, (or ناي لوش *nāyi losh*) Name of a musical instrument. ناي و نوش *nāy u nosh*, Music and wine. صورناي *sūr-nāy*, A fife, flagelet, crooked trumpet, clarion.

A نأي *na*ₛ*y*, (v. n. of نأي) Being far distant. Making a trench round a tent to keep off the rain-water. A ditch so cut round a tent. Distance.

P نا ياب *nā yāb*, Rare, not to be found, scarce. Unattainable. Undiscoverable.

P ناي انبان *nāy-ambān*, A bagpipe.

A نائب *nā*ₛ*ib*, (pl. نوب *nawb*) A lieutenant, viceroy, vicegerent, substitute, deputy; the deputy of a judge. (pl. نوب *nūb*) A bee. Any thing copious or plentiful. Contingency, event. A penitent, one converted from sin. P نايب تنگري *nā*ₛ*ibi tingrī*, God's vicegerent, *i.e.* a caliph, an emperor. A نائب مناب *nā*ₛ*ib munāb*, A vicegerent.

P نايبان *nāybān*, A flute-player. A pigeon.

A نائبة *nā*ₛ*ibat*, (An ague) returning periodically. (pl. نوائب *nawā*ₛ*ib*) Accident, misfortune, calamity, disaster.

A نائجات *nā*ₛ*ijāt*, Noisy (owls or reptiles).

P نايچ *nāyich*, A pipe, flute, fife.

P نايچه *nāycha*, A small reed, especially one used by weavers. A hookah-snake. نايچه بند *nāycha-band*, A hookah-snake maker. نايچه بندي *nāycha-bandī*, Hookah-snake making.

A نائح *nā*ₛ*ih*, (pl. نوح *nawh*) A weeper, mourner.

A نائحة *nā*ₛ*ihat*, (pl. نوائح *nawā*ₛ*ih*, نائحات *nā*ₛ*ihāt*, نوح *nawh*, انواح *anwāh*, and نوّح *nūwah*) Weeping, lamenting. A hired female mourner.

A نائخة *nā*ₛ*ikhat*, A distant country.

A نائر *nā*ₛ*ir*, Bright, clear, shining, luminous.

P نايز *nāyir*, A small tube. A kind of rhythm.

A نائرة *nā*ₛ*irat*, (pl. نوائر *nawā*ₛ*ir*) Fire, heat, warmth, inflammation, flame. Enmity, hatred. A fire-place. Charcoal. (Ground) whose plants are yellow from drought.

P ناي زن *nāy-zan*, A flute-player, fifer, piper.

P ناي زني *nāy-zanī*, Piping.

P نايزة *nāyiza*, (or نايژة *nāyija*) A tube. A syphon, pipe, or spout of a ewer or alembic. The throat. Any hollow-stemmed plant with joints upon it, a stalk of corn; kex. The urethra. Membrum virile. A small reed. A weaver's spindle. A reed upon which weavers wind their thread. The knots on a reed or stalk. A lance or a javelin. An instrument with which they spread or scrape money together. The trickling or dropping of water. نايژة كردن *nāyija kardan*, To drop water.

A نائص *nā*ₛ*is*, Who raising his head, runs off.

A نائط *nā*ₛ*it*, A thick vein running up the back.

A نائع *nā*ₛ*i*ₑ, (pl. نياع *niyā*ₑ) Thirsty. Tottering from hunger. جائع نائع *jā*ₛ*i*ₑ *nā*ₛ*i*ₑ, Starved.

A نائك *nā*ₛ*ik*, One who indulges in venery.

P نايكسان *nā yaksān*, Unequal, dissimilar.

A نائل *nā*ₛ*il*, (v. n. of نال for نول) Giving liberally, bestowing. One who arrives at, obtains, acquires. A taker. Whatever any person obtains; a gift. Munificence, liberality. P نائل شدن *nā*ₛ*il shudan*, To accomplish one's wish, obtain, carry off.

A نائلة *nā*ₛ*ilat*, Name of a woman, and an idol.

A نائم *nā*ₛ*im*, (pl. نيام *niyām*, نوّم *nūwam*, نيّم *nuyyam*, or *nīyam*, نوّام *nūwām*, نيّام *nuyyām*, and نوم *nawm*) One who sleeps or slumbers; asleep. Sleepy, quiet (night). A dormitory. P نائم شدن *nā*ₛ*im shudan*, To sleep, to be asleep.

A نائمة *nā*ₛ*imat*, (pl. نوّم *nūwam* and نيّم *nuyyam*) Sleeping (woman). Death. A serpent.

P ناي مشك *nāy-mashk*, (or مشكك) A bagpipe.

P ناي نبرد *nāy-nabard*, A trumpet.

P ناي نواز *nāy-nawāz*, A piper.

P ناي نوازي *nāy-nawāzī*, Piping.

P نايه *nāya*, A reed, pipe, tube.

A نائه *nā*ₛ*ih*, High, eminent, magnificent.

P نائي *nā*ₛ*ī*, A flute-player. Refined sugar.

P نائيدن *nāyīdan*, To boast, brag, glory.

A نبّ *nabb*, (v.n. of نبّ) Behaving haughtily. Rattling at rutting-time (a he-goat). Running.

A نبء *nab*ₛ, (v. n. of نبأ) Being exalted, projecting, eminent, superior or above (others). Looking back upon, considering, reflecting. Going from country to country. Producing (from the ground). Growling in a low key (a dog). Announcing.

A نبأ *naba*ₛ, News, a thing related, announced.

A نباء *nibā*ₛ, (v.n.3of نبأ) Announcing to another. Removing to a distance, dropping acquaintance.

A نبآء *nuba*ₛ*ā*ₛ, (pl. of نبيء *nabī*ₛ) Prophets.

A نباب *nubāb*, (v. n. of نبّ) Rattling at rutting-time (a he-goat). Running.

A نبأة *nab*ₛ*at*, A low voice. The barking, growling, or snarling of a dog.

P نبات *nabāt*, (or نبات شكر *nabāt-shakar*) Fine sugar, white, candied, refined.

A نبات *nabāt*, (v. n. of نبت) Growing, germinating. An herb, vegetable; grass. Vegetation. Down, hair. علم نبات *ᶜilmi nabāt*, The science of plants, *i.e.* botany.

A نباتات *nabātāt*, (pl. of نبات *nabāt*) Herbs, simples, plants, vegetables. Sweetmeats.

A نباتة *na* or *nubātat*, Grass. Vegetation.

P نباتناك *nabātnāk*, Verdant, grassy (ground).

A نباتيّ *nabātiy*, Vegetable. A botanist, herbalist.

A نباتية *nabātīyat*, Vegetables, herbs, plants.

P نباج *nabāj*, Two women wedded to one man.

A نباج *nabāj*, (pl. of نبجة *nabajat*) Hillocks. *Nubāj*, The loud or hoarse barking of a dog. Rumble of the belly, breaking wind. Name of a town in the desert.

A نبّاج *nabbāj*, Hoarse, loud, deep-voiced (dog). Barking, baying (dog). A ladle, spatula.

A نبّاجة *nabbājat*, The buttocks. كذبت نبّاجته *kazabat nabbājatuhu*, He broke wind.

A نباجيّ *nubājiy*, Gruff, deep-voiced (dog).

A نباح *nibāh* or *nubāh*, (v. n. of نبح) Barking (a dog), bleating (a goat or stag). Hissing (a serpent). *Nubāh*, A lion's roar. The bark of a dog.

A نبّاح *nabbāh*, Loud, noisy, bawling. A barker. (pl. of نبّاحة *nabbāhat*) Mecca shells (of which they make necklaces). *Nubbāh*, The hoopoo.

A نبّاحة *nabbāhat*, A kind of Mecca shell, of which they make necklaces. Barking (bitch).

A نبّاخ *nabbākh*, (Leaven) turning sour.

A نباخي *nabākhī*, (pl. of نبخاء *nabkhā*ₛ) High grounds soft and loose, mixed with stones.

P نبادا *nabādā*, Let it alone, may it never be.

A نباديد *nabādīd*, (as طير نباديد *tayr nabādīd*) Scattered birds. *Nabādīda*, Scatteringly, dispersedly.

A نبّاذ *nabbāz*, Vender of the wine نبيذ *nabīz*.

A نبار *nibār*, (pl. of نبر *nibr*) Short-bodied, ill-looking, mean. Tikes or similar insects: gad-flies.

A نبّار *nabbār*, Eloquent. Clamorous.

P نبارش *nabārash*, Disobedience. A piece of timber used as a prop to the roof of a house, or for shoring up a tottering wall.

A نباريس *nabārīs*, (pl. of نبراس *nibrās*) Lanterns. النباريس *an' nabārīs*, Certain wells in Arabia.

P نبازي *nabāzī*, A mistress.

A نبّاش *nabbāsh*, A digger, especially of graves. A plunderer of the dead, stripper of grave-clothes.

A نبّاض *nabbāz*, A feeler of the pulse, physician.

A نباطى *nabāṭī*, (نباطيّ *nabātiy*, *nibātiy*, or *nubātiy*) A Nabathean.

A نبّاعة *nabbā*ₑ*at*, Buttocks. كذبت نبّاعتك *kazabat nabbā*ₑ*atuka*, Thou didst break wind.

P نباغ *nabāgh*, Two women married to one man, rival wives. The end of a thread.

A نباغ *nubāgh*, Dust raised by a mill.

A نبّاغ *nabbāgh*, Scales on the head, scurf, dandriff. One who comes out.

A نباغة *nubāghat*, Meal, flour. Scurf on the head.

A نبّاغة *nabbāghat*, The backside. Schismatics. Dusty (road). *Nubbāghat*, Scurf, dandriff.

A نباك *nibāk*, (pl. of نبكة *nabkat*) Hillocks.

A نبال *nabāl*, Knowledge, genius, skill. Readiness, preparation, aptitude. Apparatus, equipment. *Nibāl*, (pl. of نبل *nabl*) Arrows. (pl. of نبيل *nabīl*) Ingenious. Excellent.

A نبّال *nabbāl*, One who has or makes arrows. Skilful in archery. Cased in armour.

A نبالة *nabālat*, (v. n. of نبل) Excelling in genius or skill. Being great and excellent. Darting, shooting arrows. Apparatus, equipment. *Nibālat*, The art of making arrows. *Nubālat*, (v. n. of نبل) Being ready for any thing. Apparatus, equipment.

A نباوة *nabāwat*, The higher part of ground. *Nibāwat*, Prophecy, the prophetical office or gift.

A نباه *nabāh*, Famous, noble. High, overhanging.

A نباهة *nabāhat*, (v. n. of نبه) Being noble, renowned. Nobleness, nobility.

A نبائت *nabā,it*, (pl. of نبيتة *nabītat*) Branches of فلجان *faljān*.

P نبايد *na bāyad*, It is not required or proper.

A نبائر *nabā,ir*, (pl. of نبيرة *nabīrat*) Grandsons.

A نبائل *nabā,il*, (pl. of نبيلة) Beautiful. Great.

A نبّة *nabbat*, An offensive smell.

A نبت *nabt*, (v. n. of نبت) Growing, germinating, sprouting (as herbage); vegetating, bringing forth. Bringing forth herbage (the earth). Grass, vegetation.

A نبتة *nibtat*, Growth. Place of vegetation.

P نبتر *nabtar*, Hairy circles on the forehead or neck of a horse, which are esteemed excellent marks; whilst on the breast and under the arm-pits they are thought blemishes.

A نبتل *nabtal*, Strong. Hard, vehement. Name of a place. A man's name.

A نبث *nabs*, (v. n. of نبث) Digging (a well or ditch) with the hands. Cleaning a well. Laying open (any thing concealed). Uprooting (vegetables). Anger, rage. *Nabas*, A mark, vestige.

A نبج *nabj*, (v. n. of نبج) Coming out of the shell (a partridge). Oakum, the fibry tops of the papyrus, or similar thing, with which they caulk ships. *Nubuj*, Sacks for corn or hay, especially black.

A نبجان *nabjān*, Threatening, commination.

A نبجة *nabajat*, A hill, heap, tumulus.

A نبح *nabh*, (v. n. of نبح) Barking. Bleating (a goat or deer). Hissing (a serpent).

A نبحاء *nabhā,*, Bleating (doe).

A نبخ *nabkh*, Blisters on the hand from hard labour. Root of the papyrus, which the Egyptians and others chew. *Nabkh* or *nabakh*, Small-pox.

A نبخاء *nabkhā,*, (pl. نباخىٰ *nabākhā'*) High ground soft and loose, mixed with stones.

A نبخة *nabkhat*, A sulphur-match for lighting a fire. *Nabkhat* or *nubkhat*, A point. *Nabkhat* or *nabakhat*, The papyrus, used in caulking ships.

A نبذ *nabz*, (v. n. of نبذ) Beating (as an artery or the pulse). Throwing (any thing) from the hand. Pressing wine. Making malt-liquor or beer. (pl. انباذ *ambāz*) A small quantity, some (money, herbage, rain). *Nubaz*, (pl. of نبذة *nubzat*) Small portions

A نبذان *nabazān*, The beating (of pulse, artery).

A نبذة *nabzat* or *nubzat*, A shore, tract, side. Somewhat, a small portion, particle (of information), brief sketch, glance at. *Nabzatan*, Aside, in a separate place (he sat down).

A نبذرة *nabzarat*, A dissipating and squandering of money improperly.

A نبر *nabr*, (v. n. of نبر) Elevating, exalting, raising up. Raising the voice, shouting. Growing (a boy). Checking, chiding. Overpowering, overcoming in words. Marking (a letter with hamza ـٔـ). Digging hastily; piercing with a spear, and drawing it out again violently. Shameless, unblushing. *Nibr*, (pl. انبار *ambār* and نبار *nibār*) Short-bodied, deformed, hideous, mean-looking. A tike or any similar insect which infests cattle, causing the parts over which they crawl to swell: a gad-fly. A fly. A wild beast of prey. (pl. انبار *ambār*) A granary, storehouse, warehouse. *Nubar*, Large mouthsful.

A نبراس *nibrās*, A lantern, lamp, candle, light. A spear. The iron head of a spear.

A نبرة *nabrat*, Any thing high. A swelling on the body. A raising of the voice from the bass to the treble notes in song. A shriek of terror. The orthographical mark hamza ـٔـ. The middle of the groove on the upper lip.

P نبرد *nabard*, Battle, engagement, war, contest. Bold, valiant. نبرد كردن *nabard kardan*, To contend.

P نبرد آزما *nabard-āzmā*, A veteran, warrior.

P نبرد پيشه *nabard-pesha*, Inured to war.

P نبردگاه *nabard-gāh*, A battle-field.

P نبرده *nabarda*, Warlike, brave. Chosen.

P نبريده *na burīda*, (in Arabic corrupted into نبريج *nabrīj*) A castrated ram with wool unshorn.

A نبز *nabz*, (v. n. of نبز) Surnaming. Reproaching. Pointing, nodding, beckoning. Defamation. *Nibz*, The upper bark of the palm-tree. *Nabaz*, (pl. انباز *ambāz*) A surname. A nickname. *Nabiz*, Contemptible, despicable.

A نبزة *nubazat*, One who gives many nicknames.

P نبزه *nabza*, A surname.

A نبس *nabs*, (or نبسة *nubsat*) (v. n. of نبس) Speaking. Hastening, making haste. Moving one's self. ما نبس بكلمة *mā nabasa bi kalimatin*, He uttered not a word. *Nubus*, Speakers. Those who make haste.

P نبس *nabas*, (or نبّس *nabbas*) A daughter's son or daughter.

P نبسه *nabasa*, (or نبّسه *nabbasa*) A daughter's son or daughter. A son's son or daughter.

A نبش *nabsh*, (v. n. of نبش) Discovering or digging up what has been buried (as treasures or dead bodies). Gaining, acquiring. Aiming at without hitting. Drawing forth (a story or narrative). *Nibsh*, A species of very hard pine. *Nabash*, A camel having a mark on the sole of the foot, by which his impression is known on the ground.

P نبشت *nibisht*, Writing. He wrote.

P نبشتن *nibishtan*, To write. To describe.

P نبشته *nibishta*, Written. A book. نبشته شدن *nibishta shudan*, To be written or described.

P نبشلد *nabashlad*, It does not adhere.

A نبص *nabs*, (v. n. of نبص) Speaking. Small pot-herbs just beginning to grow.

A نبصاء *nabsā,*, Sounding, twanging (bow).

A نبصة *nabsat*, One word.

A نبض *nabz*, (v. n. of نبض) Beating, throbbing (as pulse or artery). Making (a bowstring) vibrate or twang. Flashing lightly (lightning). Motion, the beating of an artery. The pulse. P نبض گير شدن *nabz-gīr shudan*, To feel the pulse. A فؤاد نبض *fu,ādun nabzun, nabazun*, or *nabizun*, A courageous spirit. ما به حبض و لا نبض *mā bihi habazunwa lānabazun*, No motion or spirit is in him or it. *Nabaz*, (v. n. of نبض) Beating, throbbing (artery).

A نبضان *nabazān*, (v. n. of نبض) Beating (as an artery). Making (a bowstring) vibrate or twang. Flashing gently (lightning).

A نبضة *nabzat*, One pulsation.

A نبط *nabt*, (v. n. of نبط) Springing up (water). Drawing water from a well. *Nabat*, (v. n. of نبط) Having white hairs under the arm-pit (a horse). The first water which bursts forth when digging a well. Depth, deep reflection. Nabatheans, a people inhabiting the low countries between Arabian and Persian Irāk. *Nabat* or *nubt*, White hairs on a horse's breast, belly, or under the arm-pit.

A نبطاء *nabtā,*, (A sheep) white on the thigh.

A نبطة *nubtat*, The first water which bursts forth when digging a well. White under the belly or arm-pit of a horse.

A نبطىّ *nabatīy*, A Nabathean.

A نبع *nabʿ*, (v. n. of نبع) Springing or bursting from a fountain (water). A kind of tree growing on the summit of a mountain, from which they make bows and arrows. The thill or shaft of a waggon. ماء نبع *mā,i nabʿ*, Flowing or spring-water. لو اقتدح بنبع لأورى *law iktadaha bi nabʿin la awra'*, Were he to use friction with the wood نبع *nabʿ*, he would certainly strike fire (spoken of a very clever man. This wood contains no fire in it).

A نبعة *nabʿat*, A certain kind of mountain-tree, of which they make arrows.

A نبغ *nabgh*, (v. n. of نبغ) Appearing, becoming manifest, divulging. Springing up, bursting forth. Going out against. Becoming a good poet, though not naturally so. Being extended, diffused in the world. Flying from the head (scurf). Flying about (the finest flour). The dust or powder flying round a mill.

A نبغة *nabaghat*, Middle of a crowd. Flour.

A نبق *nabk*, Writing. Sweet farina in the heart of a palm-branch, of which they make a wine. *Nabk*, *nibk*, or *nabik*, Fruit of the tree سدر *sidr*.

A نبقة *nabikat*, The fruit of the lot-tree.

P نبك *nabk*, The oozing of water through the bank of a river.

A نبك *nabk* or *nabak*, (pl. of نبكة *nabkat* or *nabakat*) Hills or tumuli with sharp tops and reddish; undulating grounds.

A نبكة *nabakat* or *nabkat*, (pl. نبك *nabk*, *nabak*, نباك *nibāk*, and نبوك *nubūk*) A hillock or tumulus with a pointed top, and sometimes reddish. A country of hill and dale, undulating.

A نبل *nabl*, (v. n. of نبل) Darting, shooting (one) with an arrow. Shooting arrows for people. Giving arrows (to another). Excelling (another) in the goodness of arrows, or in shooting them; also in skill or genius. Eating by degrees; also giving (another victuals) by little and little at a time, by way of soothing or keeping (him) obedient. Travelling hard. Equipping, fitting out (a camel). Watering (a camel). Driving (a camel) violently. (pl. انبال *ambāl*, نبال *nibāl*, and نبلان *nublān*) An Arabian arrow. Arabian arrows. Small stones. Apparatus, whatever is necessary to equip a man for any thing. *Nubl*, Excellence, greatness; ingenuity, knowledge, genius. Apparatus, equipment. *Nabal*, Excellent, ingenious, skilful. Generous. Great (ones). Small (ones). (pl. of نبيل *nabīl*) Excellent. Large stones or turfs. Small flint-stones, with which the Muhammadans clean themselves after voiding urine and fœces. *Nubal*, (pl. of نبلة *nublat*) Affairs of importance, events of consequence. Gifts. Small stones used in cleansing the organs of excretion and generation.

A نبّل *nubbal*, (pl. of نابل *nābil*) Archers.

A نبلاء *nubalāʼ*, Intelligent, clever (men).

A نبلان *nublān*, (pl. of نبل) Arabian arrows.

A نبلة *nablat*, White ivy. One Arabian arrow. A present. (pl. of نبيل *nabīl*) Excellent. Ingenious. *Nablat* or *nublat*, A thing of great moment. *Nublat*, A reward, requital, compensation. (pl. نبل *nubal*) A gift. A mouthful. Apparatus, preparation, readiness. Ingenuity, knowledge, genius. *Nabalat*, (fem. of نبل *nabal*) Excellent, skilful, ingenious.

P نبناد *nabnād*, Circumspection, innocence.

A نبنبة *nabnabat*, (v. n. of نبنب Q) Being long in doing a thing, but doing it well. Being delirious (in coitu). Rattling at rutting-time (a goat).

A نبو *nabw*, (نبوّ *nubūw*, and نبوة *nabwat*) (v. n. of نبا for نبو) Retiring, receding. Being distant, remote (one thing from another). Becoming blunt (as a sword from a blow). Becoming dim (the eyesight). Falling short of the mark (an arrow). Being disagreeable (mansion), inconvenient, uneasy (bed). Being unable to rest (in bed). Being repulsive, disagreeable to behold.

A نبوء *nubuʼ*, (v. n. of نبأ) Being high, exalted, eminent, superior, or above (others). Going from one country to another.

A نبوة *nabwat*, Higher part of ground.

A نبوّة *nubūwat*, Prophecy.

A نبوت *nubūt*, (v. n. of نبت) Appearing, beginning to swell (a girl's breasts).

A نبوح *nubūḥ*, The clamour or noise of a crowd. The barking of dogs. A multitude, mob. Glory.

A نبوخ *nubūkh*, (v. n. of نبخ) Souring (leaven).

A نبور *nabūr*, Buttocks, podex.

A نبوض *nubūẓ*, (v. n. of نبض) Flowing down upon low grounds (water).

A نبوط *nubūt*, (v. n. of نبط) Springing up, bursting forth (water).

A نبوع *nubūʻ*, (v. n. of نبع) Springing up.

A نبوغ *nubūgh*, Appearance, manifestation.

A نبوك *nubūk*, (pl. of نبكة *nabkat* and *nabakat*) Pointed hills.

A نبويّ *nabawīy*, Prophetical.

A نبه *nabh*, (pl. of نابه *nābih*) Known, celebrated. *Nubh*, Intelligence, perception. An awakening from sleep. Vigilance, resisting sleep, watchfulness. Any thing perceived, seen, comprehended. *Nabah*, (v. n. of نبه) Recollecting, perceiving, recalling to memory. Understanding, comprehending. (Cattle) lost, and found by chance or unlooked for. Any thing discovered after an attentive search. A nobleman, a distinguished personage or personages. *Nabah* or *nabih*, Known, celebrated, notorious.

A نبها *nabahan*, Unexpectedly, unlooked for.

A نبهرج *nabahraj*, (from P نبهره) Bad money.

P نبهره *nabahra*, Bad money; goods which will not sell; any thing that does not pass current. Low, vile, base. Poor; a poor person, a pauper. Great. Covered, concealed.

A نبيء *nabīʼ*, A way, path (especially clear, open). A high or conspicuous place. Who migrates from place to place (applied particularly to Muhammad's going from Mecca to Madina).

P نبي *nubī* or *nibī*, Word of God, Kur'ān.

A نبيّ *nabīy*, (pl. انبياء *ambiyāʼ*) A prophet. A way. The higher part of ground. *Nubayy*, A minor prophet. *Nubīy*, (v. n. of نبا for نبو) Becoming dull-sighted. A tray made of palm-leaves. (pl. of نابي *nābī*) High grounds.

A نبيب *nabīb*, (v. n. of نبّ) Rattling (a he-goat at rutting-time). Running.

A نبيّة *nabīyat*, A table, plate, table-mat, or similar thing made of palm-leaves. (fem. of نبيّ *nabīy*) A prophetess.

A نبيت *nabīt*, The name of a tribe in Yaman. خبيت نبيت *khabīt nabīt*, Mean, despicable.

A نبيتة *nabītat*, (pl. نبائت *nabāʼit*) A branch of the tree فلجان *faljān*.

A نبيث (خبيث *khabīs*) *nabīs*, Malignant.

A نبيثة *nabīsat*, The earth or mud at the bottom of a well or in the bed of a river.

A نبيج *nabīj*, The barking of a dog. A kind of food made of milk mixed with camels' hair.

A نبيح *nabīḥ*, (v. n. of نبح) Barking (a dog). Bleating (a goat or deer). Hissing (a serpent).

A نبيخة *nabīkhat*, A bit of sulphur, or a sulphureous match for lighting a fire. Papyrus, with which, like oakum, they caulk ships.

P نبيد *nubed*, Good news.

A نبيذ *nabīz*, Thrown. (pl. انبذة *ambizat*) Wine. A kind of drink made of dates or raisins. نبيذ جو *nabīzi jaw*, (Barley-wine) Beer, ale, malt-liquor.

A نبيذة *nabīzat*, Lean, and which is not eaten.

P نبير *nabīr*, A son's son. A grandchild.

A نبير *nabīr*, A cheese. *Nubayr*, Cunning, skilful, sagacious.

P نبيره *nabīra*, A grandson, a grandchild, a son's son. Hidden, concealed.

P نبيسه *nabīsa*, A son's son.

A نبيص *nabīs*, (v. n. of نبص) Twittering (a sparrow). Making a noise with the lips, which makes the male tread the female. The noise itself.

A نبيط *nabīt*, (pl. انباط) A Nabathean Arab.

A نبيغ *nabīgh*, A shaking of a branch of the male palm over the female to fructify it.

A نبيقة *nabīkat*, A large twig or spur of a vine; a large tear or exudation of gum.

A نبيل *nabīl*, (pl. نبال *nibāl*, نبل *nabal*, and نبلة *nablat*) Excellent, ingenious, skilful. Skilful in shooting arrows. Generous. Great, large, corpulent. Good, beautiful. A standard, ensign.

A نبيلة *nabīlat*, (fem.) Beautiful. Great, excellent. A carcase.

A نبيّون *nabīyūna*, (pl. of نبيء *nabīʼ*) Prophets.

A نبيه *nabīh*, Celebrated, famous, noble.

A نبيء *nabīʼ*, (pl. انبياء *ambiyāʼ*, نباء *nubaʼāʼ*, انباء *ambāʼ*, and نبيّون *nabīyūna*) A prophet. A messenger from God. One who goes from place to place. A clear, open road. A high place. Crooked.

A نبيّء *nubayyiʼ*, (dim. of نبيء *nabīʼ*) A little or obscure prophet.

A نبيّئة *nubayyiʼat*, (dim. of نبوّة *nubūwat*) A little prophecy. نبيّئة مسيلمة *nubayyiʼatu musaylimata*, The insignificant prophecy of Musaylimat, known by the title of الكذاب *al kazzāb*, The liar.

P نپراش *naprāsh*, The faculty of resolving problems with ease.

P نپک *napak*, Ready-handed, dextrous.

P نپور *napūr*, A kind of trumpet.

P نپي *nupe* or *nipe*, Word of God, Kur'ān.

A نتّ *natt*, A swelling (of the nostrils) with rage.

A نتاء *natʼ*, (v. n. of نتأ) Being exalted, eminent, superior, prominent; appearing, getting out, being produced. Growing up, being marriageable (a girl). Swelling (as a wound or sore).

A نتاج *nitāj*, (v. n. of نتج) Helping (cattle) to bring forth. Birth. Breed. The breeding season.

P نتاس *nitās*, Good. Healthy. Cheerful, gay, merry, pleasant, courteous, polite, affable, kind.

P نتاسيدن *nitāsīdan*, To be well, happy, pleased, and contented; to pass one's time pleasantly.

A نتّاش *nuttāsh*, The meanest or basest of mankind. Cheats, knaves, jugglers, impostors.

A نتاف *nutāf*, (and نتافة *nutāfat*) What falls when plucking out any thing. Hair plucked off.

A نتاق *nitāk*, (A house) situated opposite another.

A نتانة *natānat*, (v. n. of نتن) Stinking.

A نتائج *natāʼij*, (pl. of نتيجة *natījat*) Births. Conclusions, syllogisms, consequences, substances. غنم نتائج *ghanam natāʼij*, Sheep of the same year. غنمي نتائج *ghanamī natāʼij*, My flock was born all in the same year.

A نتّة *nuttat*, A small hollow in a smooth stone.

A نتح *nath*, (v. n. of نتح) Evaporating. Perspiring, exuding, emitting any kind of moisture. Causing to sweat. Sweat. Moist (earth). Fat, filth from a leathern butter-bottle.

A نتخ *nathh*, (v. n. of نتخ) Drawing, dragging, pulling. Tearing (as a bird of prey his food). Drawing, extracting (a thorn from the foot or a tooth). Weaving (a garment). Fixing (the eyes upon).

A نتر *natr*, (v. n. of نتر) Drawing (a bow) with vigour. Snatching, pulling roughly, carrying off. Tearing (cloth with nails or teeth). Pressing the glans penis after pissing. Piercing, stabbing with vehemence. Harsh or passionate speech. Importunity, teasing. Severity, rigour, violence, force. Weakness, debility, languor, indolence in labour. *Natar*, Corruption, perdition, loss, ruin.

A نترة *natrat*, One penetrating stroke. A speech which galls or pierces the heart.

A نتش *natsh*, (v. n. of نتش) Pulling out (a thorn) with pincers. Tearing (flesh). Extorting, receiving. Gaining. Striking, kicking, driving, thrusting. Secretly injuring (any one), slandering. Emptying (a well), taking out fetid mud. Gain, acquisition. *Natash*, The first sprouting of plants. The tip or first point, either of the blade or root. The herb gromwell.

A نتغ *natgh*, (v. n. of نتغ) Disgracing, dishonouring. Slandering, accusing falsely.

A نتف *natf*, (v. n. of نتف) Pulling out, twitching (hairs or feathers). Drawing smartly (a bow). *Natif*, (A crow) with a part of the wing pulled off. *Nutaf*, (pl. of نتفة *nutfat*) Whatever things are plucked or twitched with the fingers (as herbs).

A نتفة *nutfat*, (pl. نتف *nutaf*) Whatever is plucked or twitched with the fingers (as herbage). A gift. *Nutafat*, One who is superficially learned; one who has culled a little knowledge.

P نتفتر *nutaftar*, Name of the herb ياز *yāz*.

A نتق *nath*, (v. n. of نتق) Moving, shaking. Skinning. Drawing up (a bucket) from a well. Having a numerous offspring. Speaking, articulating (a woman).

P نتك *nath*, A saddle-belt. A difficult thing.

A نتك *nath*, (v. n. of نتك) Drawing, dragging, or seizing by violence. Pulling out (hair). Pressing or rapping (the organ of generation) in order to squeeze out any remains of urine.

A نتل *natl*, (v. n. of نتل) Drawing forward or towards one's self, attracting. Driving or frightening away with the voice. Chiding, reproving, railing. Emptying (a wallet). Going before one's companions (when proceeding in a line or row). Short, dwarfish. *Natl* or *natal*, An ostrich's egg, which they fill with water, and bury in the desert.

A نتلان *natalān*, (v. n. of نتل) Going before one's comrades (when proceeding in a line).

A نتن *natn*, A smelling badly. Stink, funk.

A نتوّ *nutūw*, The swelling (of a limb or member).

A نتوء *nutūʼ*, (v. n. of نتأ) Being exalted, eminent, superior, prominent; appearing, getting out, being produced. Growing up, being marriageable (a girl). Swelling (a wound or sore).

A نتوب *nutūb*, (v. n. of نتب) Swelling, being prominent (the breasts).

A نتوج *natūj*, (A mare or camel) pregnant and near the birth. (Cattle) bringing forth, or near it.

A نتوح *nutūh*, (v. n. of نتح) Evaporating, perspiring, exuding. Emitting moisture. Gums of trees.

A نتوض *nutūz*, (v. n. of نتض) Being affected by ringworm, dry scab, or similar disease.

A نتوع *nutūʻ*, (v. n. of نتع) Flowing gently (blood) from a wound, (water) from a fountain, (or sweat) from the body.

A نتوق *nutūk*, (v. n. of نتق) Producing many children (a woman). Becoming filled with fat.

A نتول *nutūl*, (v. n. of نتل) Going before one's companions (when proceeding in a line).

A نتيت *natīt*, The noise of a boiling pot, or fermentation of wine. (A nostril) swelling with rage.

A نتيجة *natījat*, (pl. نتائج *natāʼij*) A fœtus, offspring, birth, of the same year with another. Sum or substance. Result, issue, fruit, effect, consequence, what necessarily follows. The conclusion (of a syllogism). Retribution, reward. P نتيجهٔ سنگ *natījaʼi sang*, Fire. Iron. Copper. Gold. Silver. The ruby. A نتيجهٔ فؤاد *natījaʼi fuʼād*, Intent of the heart. نتيجهٔ كلام *natījaʼi kalām*, Substance of a speech. On the whole, in a word. نتيجهٔ لازم الاحتياج *natījaʼi lāzimu'l ihtiyāj*, A conclusion drawn from undeniable premises. مطلوب صحيح و نتيجهٔ صريح *matlūbi sahīh u natījaʼi sarīh*, The real intention and evident consequence.

P نتيجه بخش *natīja-bakhsh*, Fulfilling the desire, causing to succeed, giving a result.

A نتيجي *natījīy*, Deductive, deducible.

A نتيف *natīf*, (A camel) whose hair has been pulled or fallen off (so as to require some pitch).

P نتيل *natīl*, Fraud, imposture.

A نتيلة *natīlat*, Cause, means. (See وسيلة).

A نثّ *nass*, (v. n. of نثّ) Divulging, publishing. Anointing, dressing (a wound). Sweating, exuding. A wall moist and sweating. غثّ نثّ *ghassun nassun*, Bad (speech).

A نثا *nasa'*, What is said of one (commendatory or otherwise).

A نثاث *nisās*, Ointment for a wound. Whatever one is anointed with.

A نثّاث *nussās*, Slanderers of the absent.

P نثار *nisār*, Money which is thrown amongst the people at marriages or on other festive occasions. (in comp.) Scattering, strowing. درنثار *dur-nisār*, Scattering pearls, *i.e.* eloquent. جواهر نثاري تحقيق شدن *jawāhir-nisāri tahkīk shudan*, To strow the gems of certainty and truth, *i.e.* to relate any thing true.

A نثار *nisār*, (v. n. of نثر) Scattering, dispersing. Using many words, being diffuse in speech. Having a numerous offspring. Offering, exhibiting, presenting. A scattering, dispersion. A sacrifice. P نثار شدن *nisār shudan*, To be killed. نثار كردن *nisār kardan*, To scatter. A *Nusār*, Any thing dispersed or strown about.

A نثارة *nusārat*, Any thing scattered. Crumbs falling from a table, which are picked up and eaten as an act of piety.

P نثارچين *nisār-chīn*, One who catches or gathers the money thrown amongst the people at marriages and other festivities.

P نثاريدن *nisārīdan*, To scatter (money, &c.).

A نثال *nisāl*, Money or things scattered.

A نثالة *nusālat*, Earth taken out of a well.

A نثت *nasat*, (v. n. of نثت) Stinking (meat).

A نثج *nasj*, (v. n. of نثج) Striking with a knife. Pushing out the fundament, and voiding its contents. *Nisj*, Timid, cowardly, worthless. *Nusuj*, Buttocks.

A نثد *nasad*, (v. n. of نثد) Being still, calm, quiescent. Growing (a mushroom).

A نثر *nasr*, (v. n. of نثر) Dispersing, scattering. Employing many words, being diffusive in speech. Having a numerous offspring. Drawing off (a coat of mail). Blowing with violence any thing disagreeable out of the nostrils; sneezing (as cattle, عطس *ʻats* being applied to men). Scattered. An oration, prose-composition. *Nasar*, Any thing falling or scattered. *Nasir*, Talkative, verbose.

A نثرة *nasrat*, A sneeze, sternutation, or coughing of animals. The division or space between the mustachios under the nose; that part in a lion. The root of the nose; the inside of the nose and the parts adjacent. A large coat of mail easily put on. النثرة *an' nasrat*, Two small stars in the nose of the Lion; the eighth mansion of the moon.

A نشط *nast*, (v. n. of نشط) Squeezing, pressing

(any thing) on the ground until (it) become quite flat. Protruding through the ground (a plant). Coming forth (a mushroom). Rendering heavy. Repose. A herb that has burst through the ground.

A نثل *nasl*, (v. n. of نثل) Throwing earth (out of a well), cleaning (it). Taking arrows (from a quiver), or provision (from a bag), emptying (them). Throwing off or putting on (a coat of mail). Putting minced or sliced meat (into a pot). Voiding dung (a solid-hoofed animal). *Nasal*, A ditch, furrow from which the earth is dug.

A نثلة *naslat*, A large coat of mail. The division or space between the mustachios under the nose.

A نثم *nasm*, (v. n. of نثم) Talking indecently.

A نثنثة *nasnasat*, (v. n. of نثنث Q) Sweating profusely. Exuding (a leathern bottle). Wiping.

A نثو *nasw*, A divulging. A scattering.

A نثور *nasūr*, A woman who bears many children. (A sheep) sneezing, and casting from the nose something like a worm. (A sheep) which has dugs with large orifices. *Nusūr*, (v. n. of نثر) Reposing, resting.

A نثوط *nusūt*, Quiet, rest, repose.

A نثول *nasūl*, (A woman) who puts chopt meat into a pot.

A نثي *nasy*, A publishing, blazing abroad.

A نثيّ *nasīy*, Sprinklings, droppings from a rope whilst water is being drawn.

A نثيث *nasīs*, (v. n. of نثّ) Exuding, sweating. Being divulged (news).

A نثيثة *nasīsat*, Sweating of a leathern bottle.

A نثير *nasīr*, (v. n. of نثر) Sneezing (as beasts). Sternutation in beasts (عطاس *ʻutās* being used for human beings).

A نثيل *nasīl*, Dung. A solid-hoofed animal.

A نثيلة *nasīlat*, Earth taken out of a well. Remains. Fat flesh.

P نج *naj* or *nuj*, The inside of the mouth.

A نجّ *najj*, (v. n. of نجّ) Running, producing matter (a sore). Being quick, making haste.

A نجأ *najs*, A looking with a malignant eye.

A نجا *naja'*, (v. n. of نجا for نجو) Looking at intently to hurt with a malignant eye. Excoriating, skinning, peeling. A skin. Wood, timber: branch of a tree; rod, staff, stick. Timbers of a camel's saddle. High ground, to which the water does not reach. النجاك النجاك *an' najāka an' najāka*, Flight! Flight! escape for your life.

A نجاء *najās*, (v. n. of نجا for نجو) Escaping, being liberated, set free, emancipated. Making haste, outstripping, being swift or expeditious. An asylum, place of refuge. النجاءك النجاءك *an' najāsaka an' najāsaka*, Flight! Flight! escape for your life. *Nijās*, (v. n. 3 of نجا for نجو) Doing (any thing) privately (with another); telling a secret. (pl. of نجو *najw*) Clouds which have shed their rain. (pl. of نجيّ *najīy*) Confidants.

A نجابة *najābat*, (v. n. of نجب) Being generous, liberal, high-minded. Being excellent (a she-camel). Generosity, nobleness.

A نجأة *najsat*, An earnest or importunate look.

A نجاة *najāt*, (v. n. of نجا for نجو) Escaping. Liberation, freedom, salvation, escape, flight. A swift-going camel. (pl. نجا *naja'*) Avidity. Envy. High ground to which the water does not reach. Ground from whose trees bows and wands are cut. Branch of a tree. A mushroom, fungus. P نجات شدن *najāt shudan*, To escape, get to a place of safety. To obtain freedom. نجات كردن *najāt kardan*, To set at liberty, save, rescue.

A نجّاث *najjās*, An examiner, inquisitor.

A نجاح *najāh*, (v. n. of نجح) Happening fortunately. Being easy. Being victorious and triumphant. Good success. P نجاح ساختن *najāh sākhtan*, To gain a victory.

A نجاحة *najāhat*, Patience.

A نجاخ *nujākh*, The sound of coughing.

A نجّاخة *najjākhat*, (A woman) who sweats, and wipes off moisture. A woman windy in coitu.

A نجاد *nijād*, A sword-belt. (pl. of نجد *najd*) High grounds. Carpets, mats, floor-cloths, cushions, or any thing similar. طلّاع نجاد *tallāʻu nijād*, One who thinks exaltedly, who meditates great things. طويل النجاد *tawīlu'n nijād*, Tall (man).

A نجّاد *najjād*, A maker of cushions and beds. One equal or superior to what he undertakes, who manages business with propriety and expedition.

A نجادة *najādat*, (v. n. of نجد) Being bold, courageous, magnanimous. Being grieved, deeply distressed. Fortitude, magnanimity. Battle. Affliction, misfortune. Calamity. Terror.

P نجار *najār*, Red paint for the face, rouge.

A نجار *nijār* or *nujār*, Nature. Colour. Estimation, reputation. Root, origin. Diversity.

A نجّار *najjār*, A carpenter. النجّار *an' najjār*, An Arabian tribe of Ansārs.

A نجارة *nijārat*, Carpentry, the carpenter's craft. *Nujārat*, Wood-shavings.

A نجاري *najāra'*, Thirsty (camels).

A نجّاري *najjārī*, Carpenter's craft, carpentry.

A نجاريّة *najāriyat*, Name of a sect.

A نجازة *najāzat*, A gift.

A نجاسة *najāsat*, A being dirty: nastiness, dirt.

A نجاش *nijāsh*, A strap or belt sewed between two larger pieces of leather.

A نجّاش *najjāsh*, A hunter.

A نجاشة *nijāshat*, A being quick, expeditious.

A نجاشيّ *najāshīy*, One who starts game and drives it towards the hunter. *Najāshīy*, (نجاشي *najāshī*, or *nijāshī*, or with the article النجاشيّ *an' najāshīy*) A title of the kings of Ethiopia.

A نجاع (شجاع *shujāʻ*) *nujāʻ*, Bold, strenuous.

A نجاف *nijāf*, (v. n. of نجف) Tying a piece of leather under a goat's belly to prevent him gendering. The piece of leather itself. A woollen jerkin. A bolt. The threshold of a door; also a heel which revolves in a socket in the lintel and threshold, and serves the purpose of a hinge. (pl. of نجف *najaf*) High grounds to which water does not reach.

A نجال *nijāl*, (pl. of نجل *najl*) Waters flowing over the surface of the ground. (pl. of انجل *anjal*) Long. Large. Broad. Large-eyed.

A نجّام *najjām*, An astronomer, astrologer.

A نجامة *nijāmat*, Consulting the stars, astrology.

A نجاوة *najāwat*, An extensive district.

A نجائب *najāsib*, (pl. of نجيبة *najībat*) Excellent (she-camels). The chief passages (of the Kur'an).

A نجاية *najāyat*, A being liberated, escaping.

A نجب *najb*, (v. n. of نجب) Peeling (a tree). Liberal, noble, generous. *Najab*, Bark of a tree; also the root or hardest part of the trunk. *Nujub*, (pl. of نجيب *najīb*) Excellent, noble.

P نجب *najab*, Bark or rind of any plant, but especially that of the cassia of Arabia.

A نجباء *nujabās*, (pl. of نجيب) Excellent, noble.

A نجبة *nujabat*, (pl. انجاب *anjāb*) Noble, generous; a hero. The flower of a nation.

A نجبيّ *najabīy*, (A bag) tanned with acacia-bark.

A نجث *najs*, (v. n. of نجث) Asking assistance, imploring help. Examining, investigating. Exciting to mischief, leading astray. *Nujs* or *nujus*, (pl. انجاث *anjās*) A breast-plate, a cuirass. A man's house. The purse of the heart, pericardium. *Najis*, An examiner or inquisitor.

A نجح *nujh*, (v. n. of نجح) Happening fortunately, having one's wishes accomplished. Being victorious and triumphant. Being easy, expeditiously transacted. Good success, victory, triumph.

A نجخ *najkh*, (v. n. of نجخ) Boasting. Digging (a well). Raising a storm (a setting star). Hurling down a portion of a mountain-steep in the midst of a valley (a torrent).

A نجد *najd*, (v. n. of نجد) Overcoming, conquering. Proving, making an experiment. Knowing, discerning. Flowing with sweat (the body). The breast, bosom. (pl. انجد *anjud*, انجاد *anjād*, نجاد *nijād*, نجود *nujūd*, and نجد *nujud*) High ground; an open or high road, especially to higher ground; the higher part of Arabia towards Babylon (the lower being تهامة *tihāmat*). (pl. نجود *nujūd* and نجاد *nijād*) A carpet, cushion, pillow, couch, or such like furniture. Quick, expeditious. Expert, ingenious, industrious. Bold, animated, especially where others despond. Skilful (guide). Victory, superiority. Excess. Grief, anguish. A place destitute of trees. A kind of thorny shrub. *Najad*, (v. n. of نجد) Sweating with labour or anxiety. Being tired. Being dull from fatigue. Grief, anguish, fatigue, lassitude. An impediment in speech. Sweat. Stupidity, folly. *Najid* or *najud*, (pl. انجاد *anjād*) Bold, brave, strenuous, especially where others despond. *Najud*, The higher regions of Arabia. *Nujud*, (pl. of نجد *najd*) High grounds. (pl. of نجود *najūd*) Lengthy, tall, and long-necked (she-asses and she-camels). Elegant and intelligent (women). (pl. of نجيد *najīd*) Bold, brave, strong.

A نجداء *nujadā*, (pl. of نجيد) Strong and brave.

A النجدات *an' najadāt*, Certain schismatics.

A نجدة *najdat*, (v. n. of نجد) Being bold. Fortitude, boldness. Magnanimity. A battle. Affliction, misfortune. Terror, flight. Severity.

A نجديّ *najdīy*, Bold, brave, strong.

A نجذ *najz*, (v. n. of نجذ) Biting hard, or chewing with the cheek-teeth. Speaking bitterly. Importuning, urging.

A نجر *najr*, (v. n. of نجر) Planing (wood). Warming (water) by placing (it) upon or throwing into (it) a hot stone. Driving (camels) fast. Giving a fillip on the head with the knuckle of the middle finger. Dragging, drawing, hauling, pulling. Copulating. Mixing flour and butter amongst new milk, preparing the dish نجيرة *najīrat*. Making a roof of wood with no admixture of reeds. Nature, origin, root. Dignity, estimation. Colour. Variation, diversity. Inconstancy. Purpose, intention, aim, design. Heat. The territory of Mecca and Madīna. *Najar*, That excessive thirst with which men are seized in Arabia from drinking sour milk; or cattle from eating a kind of wild bitter seed (which proves often mortal).

A نجران *najrān*, The wood or socket in which the hinge of a door turns. Thirsty. Name of a town in Arabia Felix, of another near Damascus, and of a third between Kūfa and Wāsit.

A نجرة *najirat*, (or نجرى) Thirsty (camels).

A نجز *najz*, (v. n. of نجز) Performing (business), fulfilling (a promise). هو على نجز حاجته *huwa ʿala' najzi* (or *nujzi*) *hājatihi*, He is on the point of accomplishing his business. *Najaz*, (v. n. of نجز) Being performed (a promise), being finished (a business or discourse); being at the end of a journey. Perishing, being ruined; vanishing. Being present, in readiness.

A نجس *najs, najis, nijs, najas*, or *najus*, Dirty, filthy, nasty, squalid. *Najas*, (v. n. of نجس) Being dirty, filthy. Dirtiness, filth, dung.

A نجش *najsh*, (v. n. of نجش) Rousing (a wild beast); exciting, stirring up, agitating. Raising the price of any thing at a sale by praising or overbidding. Driving together (scattered camels). Investigating, examining. Collecting. Being swift. Causing to pass through. Wishing to extract. Examination, investigation. Extraction.

A نجع *najʿ*, (v. n. of نجع) Giving (to a camel) meal sprinkled with water.

A نجعة *nujʿat*, (pl. نجع *nujaʿ*) A feeding, foraging, or search for fodder.

A نجف *najf*, (v. n. of نجف) Hewing out, smoothing, polishing (an arrow). Milking (a sheep) well. Cutting down or pulling up (a tree) by the roots. *Najaf*, (pl. نجاف *nijāf*) High ground to which water does not reach; a high ridge in the middle of a channel left dry by the stream. A hill, hillock, tumulus, or any thing projecting above the level of the ground. Bark of the plant صليان *silliyān*. Name of a place in which is the tomb of Alīy. *Nujuf*, Old leathern bottles. (pl. of نجيف *najīf*) Broad-headed arrows.

A نجفة *nujfat*, A small quantity, a little. *Najafat*, High ground to which water does not reach, especially long and steep. A bank, dam, or mound for impounding water. نجفة الكثيب *najafatu'l kasīb*, A heap of sand blown together by the wind, and sharp at top.

P نجك *najak*, A kind of battle-axe.

A نجل *najl*, (v. n. of نجل) Throwing, driving, or scattering about. Hitting. Splitting. Doing work. Cleaning his writing-tablet or slate, effacing the letters (a boy). Producing, begetting. Making manifest or conspicuous, bringing out. Piercing with a spear, making a large wound. Skinning (an animal), beginning at the houghs. Kicking one down. Injuring, hurting. Leading or taking out. Becoming green with herbage (ground). Being full of springs (ground). Race, family, stock, progeny, son. The young of an animal. A father. Water bursting from the earth and stagnating. Flowing water. Hard travelling. Work. A great collection or heap. A rapid pace. A vast multitude. An open road, highway. A cleaning of tablets, obliteration of writing. *Nujl*, (pl. of انجل *anjal*) Long. Wide. Broad. Large-eyed. (pl. of نجيل *najīl*) Certain bitter plants. *Najul*, (v. n. of نجل) Having wide-opening eyelids. A great width of eye. Those who carry dung to mix with clay for making brick.

A نجلاء *najlā*, (fem. of انجل *anjal*) Long. (A stab) which makes a great wound. Broad and spacious (area). Large (eye).

A نجلة *najlat*, (v. n. of نجل) Kicking down.

P نجم *najm*, A cloth spread out for catching the money thrown about on an occasion of public rejoicing. *Najm*, (or نجمة) Fruit of the tamarisk.

A نجم *najm*, (pl. انجم *anjum*, انجام *anjām*, نجوم *nujūm*, and نجم *nujum*) A star, planet. Fortune. A prediction from observations of the stars. Horoscope, calculation of nativity. The star under which one is supposed to be born. A certain or a true origin. Pension, stipend, salary. Appointed or predetermined time. Any plant without a stalk or trunk, as grass. Root, origin. النجم *an' najm*, The Pleiades. The polar star. نجم ازهر *najmi azhar*, A beautiful star. نجم سائر *najmi sāir*, (or نجم السيّار *najmu's sayyār*) The wandering star, *i.e.* a planet (in opposition to the fixed stars); also a comet. ليس لهذا الحديث نجم *laysa lihāza'l hadīs najm*, There is nothing certain in that intelligence, there is no foundation for it.

A نجمة *najmat* or *najamat*, Name of a plant or a grass. ذو النجمة *zu'n najmat*, An ass.

A نجنجة *najnajat*, (v. n. of نجنج Q) Moving, shaking (a man). Purposing to do a thing, but without taking pains or making effort. Forbidding, preventing, hindering. Thinking carelessly, injudiciously, or irresolutely (about any thing). Driving (camels) a second time to the watering-place. Moving about from fear. Assembling in crowds in the meadows, and then going to water (men). Doing or writing over again the letter ر *rā*.

P نجند *najand*, Unhappy, sorrowful, miserable.

A نجو *najw*, (v. n. of نجا for نجو) Escaping. Farting. Going out of the body (urine, excrement, or wind). Communicating a secret to another. Breathing in another's face. Bidding any one breathe in your face to discover what he has been drinking. Evacuating the body. Skinning (a camel). Felling (a tree), or lopping (the branches). (pl. نجاء *nijā*) A cloud pouring down rain. A skin when taken off. Excrement of a beast. Wind from the body.

A نجوء *naju*, One who looks with an evil eye.

A نجواء *nujawā*, Yawning.

P نجوان *najwān*, Saffron.

A نجوة *najwat*, High ground, a hill.

A نجوج *najūj*, Swift, expeditious.

A نجوخ *najūkh*, Noisy, boisterous (sea).

A نجود *najūd*, (pl. نجد *nujud*) A woman of an intelligent mind and elegant shape. (A she-ass or she-camel) which has a high or long neck. (A camel) going swift, outstripping others; also abounding with milk, giving it plentifully; (a camel) kneeling on high ground. (A wild ass) not conceiving. *Nujūd*, (v. n. of نجد) Being manifest, clear. (pl. of نجد *najd*) High countries or roads. Household furniture, carpets, couches, cushions, pillows, or floor-cloths.

A نجوع *najūʿ*, Wholesome, salubrious (water). Water mixed with flour or meal given to camels. نجوع الصبيّ *najūʿu's sabīy*, The drink or aliment of infants, *i.e.* milk. *Nujūʿ*, (v. n. of نجع) Digesting well (victuals); agreeing (as medicine with men, and pasture with cattle). Producing a good effect (an exhortation). Being well off; (any thing) turning out advantageously, fortunate. Giving (a camel) water mixed with meal. Going in quest of forage or water. Approaching (any person) in order to do him good or receive benefit.

A نجوم *nujūm*, (v. n. of نجم) Appearing, rising (a star). Paying at stated periods, or by instalments. Budding (a horn). Coming up, appearing above the ground (wheat). (The first stage is called نجوم *nujūm*; then تفريخ *tafrīkh*, Branching or tillering; تقصيب *taksib*, Coming into stalk; اعصاف *iʿsāf*, Putting forth the blade or the flag;

سنبلة *sambalat*, Coming into ear; احباب *ihbāb*, Corning; الباب *ilbāb*, Kernelling; اسفاء *isfāʼ*, Bearding; افراك *ifrāk*, Fitness for rubbing; and, finally, احصاد *ihsād*, Fitness for reaping). Coming out (any new doctrine or heresy). (pl. of نجم *najm*) Stars. نجوم الاخذ *nujūmu'l akhz*, Mansions of the moon, of which there are twenty-eight; certain stars in the moon's orbit, of which the Arabian astronomers made use in their observations. اهل نجوم *ahli nujūm*, An astronomer, astrologer. علم نجوم *ʻilmi nujūm*, Astronomy, astrology.

A نجوميّ *nujūmiy*, Astronomical. An astronomer. An astrologer.

A نجوؤ *najūʼ*, A looker with a malignant eye.

A نجويٰ *najwa'*, (v. n. of نجا for نجو) Communicating a secret. Breathing in any one's face. A secret, any clandestine action or conversation. (pl. انجية *anjiyat*) A partner in a secret. Tellers of secrets.

A نجه *najh*, (v. n. of نجه) Chiding, repelling, frightening away by calling out; repulsing contemptuously; receiving superciliously or with disdain. Rising above, excelling, outstripping. Entering a country unsuited to one's constitution.

A نجيئ *najiʼ*, A looker with malignant eye.

A نجيّ *najiy*, (v. n. of نجا for نجو) Communicating a secret. (pl. انجية *anjiyat*) A confidant, partner in a secret. A secret.

A نجيء *najiʼ*, A looker with a malignant eye.

A نجيب *najīb*, (pl. انجاب *anjāb*, نجباء *nujabāʼ*, and نجب *nujub*) Generous, excellent, noble, praiseworthy, honourable. A hero. A volunteer. Excellent (she-camel). A certain class of Indian soldiers who are distinguished by a peculiar dress. نجيب الطرفين *najību't tarafayn*, Noble on both sides (father and mother).

A نجيبة *najībat*, (pl. نجائب) Choice (she-camel).

A نجيّة *najiyat*, Swift (she-camel).

A نجيث *najīs*, A secret. A butt for archers, especially a mound of earth. Slow. A kind of pot-herb.

A نجيثة *najīsat*, Earth thrown out of a well. The divulged or discovered part (of any news, especially the worst). Endeavour, aim, scope.

A نجيج *najīj*, (v. n. of نجّ) Flowing (blood from a wound, or pus from a sore). Making haste.

A نجيح *najīh*, Fortunate or sound (advice); just (opinion). Prosperous (man). Hard (journey).

A نجيحة *najīhat*, A patient soul.

A نجيخة *najīkhat*, Butter adhering to the sides of a vessel in which it is made.

A نجيد *najīd*, (pl. نجد *nujud* and نجداء *nujadāʼ*) Bold, brave, strong. Sad, vexed, in anguish. النجيد *an' najīd*, The lion.

P نجير *najīr*, Starch or paste used by weavers, shoemakers, or bookbinders. Fruit of the tamarisk-tree.

A نجيرة *najīrat*, Recompense. Water warmed with a hot stone. Butter mixed with milk or flour. The roof of a house made of wood without any admixture of reeds, &c. A short plant. لانجرنّ نجيرتك *la anjuranna najīrataka*, is equivalent to لاجزينّ جزاءك *la ajziyanna jizāʼaka*.

A نجيرم *najīram*, Name of a quarter in Basrah, the birth place of sundry learned men.

A نجيز *najīz*, Present, ready.

A نجيس *najīs*, Incurable (disease). Dirty.

A نجيش *najīsh*, A hunter.

A نجيع *najīʻ*, A mixture of dry pounded leaves, flour, and water, which they put into a camel's mouth. Blackish blood from the interior part of the body. Wholesome, salubrious.

A نجيف *najīf*, (pl. نجف *nujuf*) Broad-headed (arrow). An old leathern bottle.

P نجيل *najīl*, Fruit of the tamarisk-tree.

A نجيل *najīl*, (pl. نجل *nujl*) Name of a plant or herb, or a broken leaf of it.

A نجيئ *najīʼ*, A looker with a malignant eye.

P نچاس *nachās*, The cork-tree.

P نچک *nachak*, A kind of battle-axe.

A نحّ *nahh*, A stimulating, urging onward.

A نحاء *nihāʼ*, (pl. of نحي *nihy*) Leathern bottles for keeping butter. Earthen milk-vessels. Broad-headed arrows.

A نحاة *nahāt*, A side, tract, quarter. اهل النحاة *ahlu'n nahāt*, Distant people, foreigners, no relations. *Nuhāt*, A large bow. (pl. of ناحي *nāhī*) Inclined, tending towards. Grammarians.

A نحات *nahāt*, Nature.

A نحاتة *nuhātat*, A chip, shaving; planings.

A نحاحة *nahāhat*, Patience. Liberality. Avarice.

A نحاريّة *nahārīyat*, Name of a sect.

A نحاز *nahāz*, A long tract of country. *Nuhāz*, A disease in a camel's lungs. *Nuhāz* or *nihāz*, A root, origin.

A نحاس *nahās*, *nihās*, or *nuhās*, Sparks flying from iron or copper when hammering. Brass, melted brass. Fire. *Nuhās*, Smoke without flame. *Nuhās* or *nihās*, Nature, origin. كريم النحاس *karīmu'n nihās*, Of a noble disposition.

P نحاس *nihās*, Bits of leather put between the soles of shoes, the better to exclude water.

A نحّاس *nahhās*, A worker in brass, a brasier. A coppersmith.

A نحاسيّ *nahāsiy*, Brazen, copper. معادن نحاسي *maʻādini nahāsī*, (or نحاس *nuhās*) Copper mines.

A نحاشة *nihāshat*, Burnt bread.

A نحاض *nihāz*, Large masses of flesh.

A نحاضة *nahāzat*, Great fleshiness of body.

A نحاط *nuhāt*, A sobbing, secret sighing.

A نحّاط *nahhāt*, Proud.

A نحاف *nihāf*, (pl. of نحيف *nahīf*) Thin, lean.

A نحافة *nahāfat*, (v. n. of نحف) Being lean, thin, and spare naturally. Leanness, want of flesh.

A نحام *nuhām*, A reddish goose-like bird.

A نحّام *nahhām*, One who breathes hard, who sighs from the bottom of his heart. A miser. A lion. A kind of red water-fowl. النحّام *an' nahhām*, Name of a horse.

A نحانحة *nahānihat*, Avaricious men, misers.

A نحائر *nahāʼir*, (pl. of نحير *nahīr*) Stuck, slaughtered (camels).

A نحائز *nahāʼiz*, (pl. of نحيزة *nahīzat*) Natures.

A نحب *nahb*, (v. n. of نحب) Vowing, devoting, consecrating. Walking, going, travelling (especially quick). Being diligent, assiduous, attentive, careful. Crying excessively, weeping aloud, howling. Playing at dice. Wagering and depositing the bets (especially at a horse-race). Dying. An hour, time. Death, fate, last breath. Sleep. Soul, spirit. A cough. A vow. Space of time, long season. Great danger or fear. Exalted dignity. An important affair. Design, aim, purpose. A heavy weight or great bulk. Demonstration, proof. Grief, distress. Necessity. Vehemence. A large camel. Fatness. هو علیٰ نحب *huwa ʻala' nahbin*, He travels expeditiously. قضیٰ نحبه *kaza' nahbahu*, He is dead.

A نحباة *nahbāt*, Funeral laments, chants, dirges.

A نحبة *nuhbat*, A lot which is cast.

A نحّة *nuhhat*, (or نحح *nahah*) (v. n. of نحّ) Having a hoarse voice.

A نحت *naht*, (v. n. of نحت) Smoothing, planing, shaving, rasping, scraping any thing to make it fit. (Hard travel) emaciating (camels). Throwing down in wrestling. Lying with. Sharp, clear, cold, keen frost. Nature.

A نحر *nahr*, (v. n. of نحر) Hurting the throat. Slaughtering, sticking (cattle), cutting their throats. Being opposite (as one house to another). Standing erect with a stretched-out breast whilst at prayer, having the face turned towards the قبله *kibla*, and the right hand placed upon the left. (pl. نحور *nuhūr*) The throat, the upper part of the breast where the necklace is fixed. Beginning of the day, month, or new moon. مسجد النحر *masjidu'n nahr*, Name of a mosque at Mina. يوم النحر *yawmu'n nahr*, The day of sacrifice, being the tenth of the month ذو الحجّة *zū'l hijjat*, when the pilgrims assemble at Mecca. *Nihr*, Industrious, intelligent, expert, skilful, knowing, experienced.

A نحراء *nuharāʼ*, (or نحري *nahra'*) (pl. of نحير *nahīr*) Stuck, slaughtered (camels).

A نحرة *nahrat*, The first day of the new moon; also the last. صحرة نحرة *sahratan nahratan*, Before the eyes, clearly, plainly, visibly.

A نحرير *nihrīr*, Industrious, intelligent, skilful, knowing, expert, experienced.

A نحز *nahz*, (v. n. of نحز) Shaking, striking, repelling. Pounding in a mortar. Beating with the fist on the breast. *Nahiz*, Coughing (camel).

A نحس *nahs*, (v. n. of نحس) Oppressing. Tiring, making miserable. A sinister aspect of the stars. A bad omen. Misfortune. A cold wind blowing from the west. Dark and mysterious (affair). Dust scattered high in the air. (pl. نحوس *nuhūs*) Unlucky, bad, inauspicious. *Nahas*, (v. n. of نحس) Being unlucky, ill-fated (a day). *Nahis*, Unlucky (day), ill-fated (man). *Nuhas*, Three days after those called درع *duraʿ*.

A النحسان *an' nahsāni*, The two unlucky ones; namely, the planets Saturn and Mars.

A نحص *nahs*, A one-year-old wild she-ass. *Nuhs*, Bottom of a mountain. اصحاب نحص الجبل *as-hābu nuhsi 'l jabal*, Those slain at the battle of احد *uhud*.

A نحض *nahz*, (v. n. of نحض) Laying bare or stripping (the flesh off a bone). Urging, pressing, being importunate. Making sharp or thin (the head of a spear). Flesh, especially when compact.

A نحضة *nahzat*, (pl. نحوض *nuhūz* and نحاض *nihāz*) Large masses of flesh.

A نحط *naht*, A sob or secret crying. The hard breathing of an overloaded horse or camel. The hem, or sound made by a washer or fuller when beating cloths with a beetle. A chiding, checking. A repulse given to one who asks.

A نحطة *nahtat*, A disease in the chest, to which horses and camels are subject.

A نحفاء *nuhafāʿ*, (pl. of نحيف) Thin, lean, spare.

A نحل *nahl*, (v. n. of نحل) Attributing, imputing (to one the verses or sayings of another). Reproaching, reviling. A free gift. Any thing given. Lean, thin. The new moon. Bees. *Nuhl*, (v. n. of نحل) Presenting (a gift). Granting (to a woman her marriage-gift, portion, or settlement), especially voluntarily. A gift, donative.

A نحلان *nuhlān*, A present, gift, donative.

A نحلة *nahlat*, One bee. *Nihlat* or *nuhlat*, An appointment of a marriage-portion. A gift. A law-suit. Pretension, claim. The religion of the Magi. *Nihlatan*, Of one's own accord, voluntarily.

A نحلى *nahla'*, (pl. of ناحل *nāhil* or نحيل *nahīl*) Lean (camels). *Nuhla'*, A gift.

A نحلي *nahlīy*, Keeper of bees, bee-master.

A نحم *nahm*, (v. n. of نحم) Coughing; hemming and hawing. Groaning, sobbing. Growling (a leopard). *Naham*, (equiv. to نعم *naʿam*) Yes.

A نحّم *nihamm*, Who groans, sobs, sighs very much.

A نحمان *nahmān*, (v. n. of نحم) Coughing; hemming and hawing. Groaning.

A نحمة *nahmat*, A cough.

A نحن *nahnu*, We. نحن نفسنا *nahnu nafsunā*, We ourselves.

A نحنحة *nahnahat*, (v. n. of نحنح Q) Hemming, clearing the throat. Grumbling (the belly). Repulsing with contempt.

A نحو *nahw*, (v. n. of نحا for نحو) Going towards (another); seeking, aiming at, hitting (him). Leaning on one side. Inclining over one's bow. Changing, turning. Casting back. Aim, intent, design. (pl. انحاء *anhāʿ* and نحوّ *nuhūw*) Way, path, tract. Mode, manner, sort. النحو *an' nahw*, (pl. نحوّ *nuhūw* and نحيّ *nuhīy*) Grammar, syntax, etymology, inflection, declension. Literal speech, according to the rules of grammar. *Nahwa*, As, like, about, towards, near. كنحو *kanahwa*, Agreeable to.

A نحواء *nuhawāʿ*, A tremor, yawning, stretching.

A نحور *nuhūr*, (pl. of نحر *nahr*) Throats, sticking-places in animals: hence, frontiers, approaches. Beginnings of days, months, or new moons.

A نحوس *nahūs*, Bad, ill, unfortunate.

A نحوسة *nuhūsat*, (v. n. of نحس) Being unfortunate, unlucky (the day). A bad presage, unhappy accident, misfortune. Inauspiciousness. P داروي نحوست *dārūyi nuhūsat*, A scorbutic medicine.

A نحوص *nahūs*, An ass having no colt, and without milk. A she-camel too fat to conceive. *Nuhūs*, (v. n. of نحص) Being very fat. Paying (another) what is due.

A نحوض *nuhūz*, (v. n. of نحض) Being attenuated. (pl. of نحضة *nahzat*) Large masses of flesh.

A نحول *nuhūl*, (v. n. of نحل) Being emaciated, lean. Leanness, dryness.

A نحويّ *nahwīy*, Pertaining to grammar; grammatical. A grammarian.

A نحي *nahy*, (v. n. of نحي) Churning (milk). Putting to a distance. Directing the eye towards. *Nihy*, *nahy*, or *naha'*, (pl. انحاء *anhāʿ*, نحيّ *nahīy*, and نحاء *nihāʿ*) A leathern bottle in which they put up butter. An earthen vessel for holding milk. A broad-headed arrow. A kind of soft, moist date.

A نحيّ *nahīy*, Camels removed to one side. *Nuhīy*, (pl. of نحو *nahw*) Grammars.

A نحيب *nahīb*, (v. n. of نحب) Weeping excessively, crying aloud, howling, shrieking.

A نحيّة *nahīyat*, (in comp. with القوارع *al kawāriʿ*) نحيّة القوارع *nahīyatu'l kawāriʿ*, One whom misfortune threatens.

A نحيت *nahīt*, (v. n. of نحت) Crying out, lamenting. Shaved, pared. Nature. A comb. Flux, looseness in the belly. (A camel) emaciated by hard travel. (A camel) having the edges of his hoofs worn. A stranger who mixes amongst other people. A roar, bellow. A cold sigh. Vile, mean.

A نحيتة *nahītat*, Nature. Cry, lamentation. A cold sigh. A looseness in the belly.

A نحيح *nahīh*, (v. n. of نحّ) Rumbling (the belly). شحيح نحيح *shahīh nahīh*, Miserly, covetous.

A نحير *nahīr*, (pl. نحرى *nahra'*, نحراء *nuharāʿ*, and نحائر *nahāʾir*) (A camel) slaughtered, stuck in the throat. The last night of the month.

A نحيرة *nahīrat*, The first or last day of the month. The last night of the month.

A نحيزة *nahīzat*, Nature. Way, mode, manner, habit, custom. A kind of flap fastened round the lower part of a tent. Rough ground. A long slip of country, not less than a mile. A narrow road leading out of a main road to an open plain.

A نحيس *nahīs*, Scarce, disastrous (year). Unlucky (day).

A نحيص *nahīs*, A camel fat and not conceiving.

A نحيض *nahīz*, Firm-fleshed, plump (thigh). Emaciated, lean, fleshless. Thin, sharp (spear-head).

A نحيط *nahīt*, (v. n. of نحط) Sobbing, crying secretly. The hard breathing of an overloaded beast.

A نحيف *nahīf*, (pl. نحاف *nihāf*) Lean, spare, meagre, slim, weak, slender. P نحيف كردن *nahīf kardan*, To make lean, attenuate.

A نحيفي *nahīfī*, Leanness, spareness.

A نحيل *nahīl*, Lean (camel). Slender (waist).

A نحيم *nahīm*, (v. n. of نحم) Groaning. Coughing; hemming and hawing. Growling (a panther).

P نخ *nakh*, A carpet beautiful on both sides, having a long pile. A small carpet with a short pile. A raw thread of yarn of any sort. A rank of soldiers and the like. A little, few. Name of an evil spirit in Māzandarān. A ploughshare. *Nukh*, Following one step by step.

A نخّ *nakhkh*, (v. n. of نخّ) Travelling with great expedition. Driving violently. Making (a camel) lie down by crying اخ اخ *ikh ikh*. The camels which are made to kneel before the officer appointed to collect the tithes of cattle for religious uses. An oblong carpet. *Nukhkh*, Marrow.

A نخاخة *nakhākhat*, Marrow.

P نخاره *nakhāra*, Fasting.

A نخاريب *nakhārīb*, (pl. of نخروب *nukhrūb*) Fissures in stones. Cells in honeycombs.

A نخاس *nakhās*, A thong sewed betwixt two pieces of leather. *Nikhās*, A bit of wood with a hole in the middle inserted into an axle-hole which has become too wide from much wear: a bush, box.

A نخّاس *nakhkhās*, A seller of captives, or cattle taken as plunder. A driver. An appraiser of cattle.

A نخاسة *nakhāsat* or *nikhāsat*, The sale of cattle or of slaves. *Nikhāsat*, A bit of wood hollow in the centre inserted into an axle-hole, which by wear had become too wide; a bush.

A نخاع *na*, *ni*, or *nukhāʿ*, Spinal marrow.

A نخاعة *nukhāʿat*, Phlegm, spittle, mucus, snot.

A نخاف *nikhāf*, (pl. انخفة *ankhifat*) A boot.

A نخالة *nukhālat*, Grain, or any thing sifted; also what remains in the sieve, siftings. Bran. Scurf.

A نخامة *nukhāmat*, Phlegm, mucus.

A نخانيق *nakhānīk*, (pl. نخنوق *nukhnūk*) Low parapets around wells. Nooks inside of wells.

A نخاورة *nakhāwirat*, (pl. of نخوار *nikhwār*) Noble, elevated.

A نخب *nakhb*, (v. n. of نخب) Extracting, drawing, or tearing out. Biting. Lying with (a woman), having a carnal connection in a peculiar manner. Podex, anus. A copious draught, that especially which is drank to the health of a friend. *Nakhb*, *nakhab*, or *nakhib*, (pl. نخب *nukhub*) Timid, fearful, pusillanimous. *Nukhab*, (pl. of نخبة *nukhbat* or *nukhabat*) Chosen, selected. *Nukhub*, (pl. of نخب *nakhib*, *nikhabb*, and نخيب *nakhib*) Cowards.

A نخب *nikhabb* or *nikhibb*, Timid, fearful.

A نخبة *nakhbat*, The buttocks. *Nukhbat*, A copious draught, that especially which is drunk to the health of a friend. *Nukhbat* or *nukhabat*, (pl. نخب *nukhab*) Chosen, selected. Better. A good or chosen thing. Cowardly, dastardly.

A نخة *nakhkhat*, A servant, slave. (Females) brought up in houses. Camel-drivers. Uncertain news. Gentle rain. The dīnār which the tithe-collector, from his receipts, takes for himself. A dīnār, a gold coin. *Na*, *ni*, or *nukhkhat*, Wine. *Na* or *nukhkhat*, Working oxen. Shepherds.

A نخت *nakht*, (v. n. of نخت) Extracting, drawing, or tearing out. Finishing a speech for any one. Taking a date or two out of a wallet. Inquiring, prying into. Pecking.

A نخج *nakhj*, (v. n. of نخج) Shaking a bucket in a well to fill it. Lying with. A flux of water, torrent. The sound made by it (striking upon the banks of the channel). Breaking wind.

P نخجد *nakhjad*, (or نخچد *nakhchaz*) Dross of iron. Iron. Very hard bread made of millet. A hard stone with which any thing is pounded or bruised. A tickling or scratching with the fingers.

P نخچ *nakhch*, Broom for making besoms.

P نخچل *nakhchul* or *nakhchal*, Pinching.

P نخچند *nakhchand*, Slag or dross of iron.

P نخچوان *nakhchuwān*, A city of Armenia.

P نخچير *nakhchīr*, Hunting, the chase. Prey, game, a wild beast. A mountain-goat. A hunter. The place of hunters. نخچير شدن *nakhchīr shudan*, To be hunted. نخچير كردن *nakhchīr kardan*, (or نخچير افكندن *nakhchīr afkandan*) To hunt, take game.

P نخچيرگان *nakhchīr-gān*, (or نخچيرگاني *nakhchīr-gānī*) Name of the last note of the barbud.

P نخچيرگاو *nakhchīr-gāw*, Name of a note in music.

P نخچيرگاه *nakhchīr-gāh*, Chase, hunting-ground.

P نخچيرگير *nakhchīr-gīr*, (نخچيروان *nakhchīrwān*, or نخچيروال *nakhchīr-wāl*) A hunter. شير نخچيرگير *sheri nakhchīr-gīr*, A prey-hunting lion.

P نخچيز *nakhchīz*, Twisted, contracted, shrunk. A twisting.

P نخچيل *nakhchīl*, Pinching.

A نخر *nakhr*, (v. n. of نخر) Snorting, or making a similar noise through the nostrils. Putting the hand into (a camel's) nostril and scratching it to induce her to give milk freely. *Nakhar*, (v. n. of نخر) Being rubbed, worn, putrefied, and scattered. *Nakhir*, Worn, rubbed to pieces; pierced (carious bone). Any thing hollow, pervious to the wind, and making a sound. *Nukhur*, (pl. of ناخر *nākhir*) Hogs trained to hunt.

P نخرا *nakhrā*, Trick, artifice, joke, waggery, coquetry, deceit, sham, pretence.

P نخراز *nukhrāz*, A belwether.

P نخراس *nukhrās*, A goat, kid.

A نخربة *nakhrabat*, Boring of wood (by a worm).

A نخرة *nakhrat*, (v. n. of نخر) Blowing hard (the wind). *Nukhrat*, A violent blast of wind; storm. The nostril. *Nukhrat* or *nukharat*, Tip of the nose (of man, camel, horse, or dog).

A نخروب *nakhrūb*, (pl. نخاريب *nakhārīb*) A fissure in a stone. A hole. A cell in a honeycomb.

A نخروش *nakhrawish*, Excited, pugnacious (dog).

P نخري *nakhirī*, A first-born child.

A نخز *nakhz*, (v. n. of نخز) Striking, wounding with an iron instrument. Paining by harsh language.

P نخز *nakhuz*, First.

P نخزار *nukhzār*, (or نخزان *nakhzān*) A goat, kid.

A نخزة *nukhzat*, A prick, puncture, hole.

P نخزين *nakhuzin*, The first.

P نخس *nakhs*, Paleness from grief, loss of colour. Leanness.

A نخس *nakhs*, (v. n. of نخس) Cutting, plucking. Pricking, pressing (with the finger). Driving, pushing backward or forward. Spurring, goading. Mending a pulley by inserting a narrower ring (called a bush) into an axle-hole which has been worn too wide.

A نخسة (ابن *ibnu*) *nikhsatin*, A bastard.

P نخست *na khast*, He wounded not. *Nukhust*, Beginning, principle. The first. At first.

P نخست زاد *nukhust-zād*, (or زاده) Eldest son.

P نخست زادي *nukhust-zādī*, Primogeniture.

P نخستگي *nukhustagī*, First-fruits. Priority.

P نخستين *nukhustīn*, The first.

A نخش *nakhsh*, (v. n. of نخش) Becoming lean and emaciated. Exciting. Shaking, causing to move. Vexing, annoying. A violent motion or driving. An injury, detriment. A peeling, taking off the bark. A scratch. A taking away of the best and choicest part of any thing. Part of cattle or other wealth. *Nakhash*, (v. n. of نخش) Becoming old and worn out at the bottom.

P نخشب *nakhshab*, Name of a city in Turkistān, where they say there is a well named چاه نخشب *chāhi nakhshab*, from which an appearance of the moon, called ماه نخشب *māhi nakhshab*, was produced by a noted magician named مقنع *mukannaʻ*.

A نخشبي *nakhshabīy*, Native of Nakhshab.

P نخشة *nakhsha*, Proof, demonstration.

P نخشيدن *nakhshīdan*, To break the head, split the skull.

A نخص *nakhs*, (v. n. of نخص) Becoming lean with age, emaciated, shrivelled. (Old age) emaciating. *Nakhas*, (v. n. of نخص) Wasting away (flesh).

A نخط *nakht*, (v. n. of نخط) Blowing (the nose). Coming suddenly upon. *Nukht*, The spinal marrow. The water contained in the membrane which encloses the fœtus. *Nukht* or *nakht*, Men, mankind. *Nukhut*, (improperly *nukhkhat*) Those who tilt with spears, as amusement or trial of prowess.

A نخع *nakhʻ*, (v. n. of نخع) Acknowledging, owning (a debt). Oversticking (an animal in slaughtering), touching the spinal marrow. Blowing the nose. Taking off part of the skin (of a sheep), and thrusting the knife deep in order to draw the heart's blood. Having a sincere affection for (another), giving (him or her) excellent counsel. *Nakhaʻ*, (v. n. of نخع) Flowing in the tree (sap). *Nukhuʻ*, (pl. of نخاع *nakhāʻ*, *nikhāʻ*, or *nukhāʻ*) Spinal marrows.

A نخف *nakhf*, (v. n. of نخف) Breathing aloud, as if sneezing (a she-goat). The noise made in blowing the nose.

A نخفة *nakhfat*, A hollow on a mountain-top.

P نخكلا *nakhkala*, A hard nut.

P نخگلوي *nakhgulūy*, Narrow-necked (vessel).

P نخل *nakhl*, A tree. A festoon, thyrsus, rod upon which flowers, interspersed with paper of different colours, are tied round to give it the appearance of a natural branch.

A نخل *nakhl*, (v. n. of نخل) Sifting (meal). Separating or choosing the best. Filtering. (pl. نخيل *nakhīl*) The palm-tree (and often used for a young tree of any kind), a plant. A species of female dress or ornament.

P نخلبند *nakhl-band*, A maker of artificial flowers. A gardener. One who moulds figures of trees or fruits in wax.

P نخلبندي *nakhl-bandī*, A plantation.

A نخلة *nakhlat*, One palm-tree. Name of a valley in Hijāz between Mecca and Tāif. ذو النخلة *zū'n nakhlat*, Jesus the Messiah. نخلة محمود *nakhlasi mahmūd*, Certain palm-trees in Mecca. Name of a palm-plantation.

P نخلستان *nakhlistān*, A palm-plantation.

P نخله *nakhla*, A walking-staff. A shoe.

P نخم *nakhm*, A cloth supported by sticks, in which they catch sugar, sweetmeats, or money thrown amongst the crowd on marriage-ceremonies and other public festivities.

A نخم *nakhm*, (v. n. of نخم) Playing. Singing well. *Nakhm* or *nakham*, (v. n. of نخم) Blowing the nose, spitting. *Nakham*, (v. n. of نخم) Being tired. Tiring. Fatigue.

A نخمة *nakhmat*, Beauty, elegance. Phlegm, spittle, mucus.

A نخنخة *nakhnakhat*, (v. n. of نخنخ Q) Removing, putting to a distance. Travelling fast. Making (a camel) kneel.

A نخنوق *nukhnūk*, (pl. نخانيق *nakhānīk*) A low parapet about a well. A nook within a well.

A نخوار *nikhwār*, (pl. نخاورة *nakhāwirat*) Noble, haughty, elevated. Mean, cowardly.

A نخوبة *nakhūbat*, Posteriors, buttocks.

A نخوة *nakhwat*, (v. n. of نخا for نخو) Boasting. Carrying one's self haughtily. Praising. Pride, haughtiness, consequential airs; pomp. P نخوت پيشه *nakhwat-pesha*, (نخوت فروش *nakhwat-fa-*

rosh, نخوت کش nakhwat-kash, or نخوت کیش nakhwat-kesh) Given to pride, proud, haughty, pompous, self-important.

P نخود nukhūd, A vetch, pulse.

P نخود آب nakhūd-āb, (Vetch-water) A decoction of meat with vetches (given in cases of syphilis).

A نخور nakhūr, (A camel) giving no milk unless they tickle her nostril.

A نخورش nakhwarish, (A dog) scratching much; hurtful, dangerous. A whelp in continual motion.

A نخوريّ nakhwariy, Having a large orifice in the dugs. Large-mouthed. Big-bellied.

A نخوس nakhūs, A young mountain-goat.

P نخوش nakhosh, (Not-dry) A kind of wild vine.

A نخوص nukhūs, (v. n. of نخص) Becoming attenuated with age, emaciated, and shrivelled.

P نخهم nakhuham, (for نخواهم nakhwāham) I wont.

A نخيب nakhīb, Timid, fearful, cowardly.

A نخيجة nakhījat, Thin butter remaining in the churn after the more solid had been taken out.

A نخيخة nakhīkhat, Butter which adheres to the sides of the churn.

P نخير nakhīr, (or نخيز nakhez) Ignoble, mean, abject, base, worthless. An ambush, lurking-place. A nursery-ground.

A نخير nakhīr, A snoring, snorting: the noise itself.

P نخيرگاه nakhīr-gāh, An ambuscade.

P نخيري nakhīrī, A first-born child.

P نخيز nakhez, Defective. Coarse. Common, low. An ambush. A branch stuck in the ground that it may take root.

P نخيزگاه nakhez-gāh, An ambush, lurking-place.

A نخيس nakhīs, A pulley whose axle-hole is worn too wide, and mended by inserting a narrower ring or bush. The place of a horse round which the surcingle or belt is fastened.

A نخيسة nakhīsat, Goats' milk mixed with that of a sheep. Acid milk mixed with sweet.

A نخيط nakhīt, (v. n. of نخط) Defaming, disparaging, reviling. Carrying one's self proudly and overbearingly.

A نخيف nakhīf, (v. n. of نخف) Sneezing, or making a sound resembling it. A sound resembling laughing and crying through the nose.

A نخيل nakhīl, A palm-tree. A palm-grove. (pl. of نخل nakhl) Palm-trees.

A نخيلة nukhaylat, Nature. Advice. Name of a place in Babylonian Irāk where the caliph Alīy was murdered by the schismatics. Name of a female slave liberated by Ayisha.

P ند nad, Increase, abundance. Bent.

A ندّ nadd, (v. n. of ندّ) Fleeing, running away, scampering off. Alike, resembling. A high heap of clay, earth, or sand. A perfume composed of musk, ambergris, and the wood of aloes; or simply of ambergris. Nidd, (pl انداد andād) An image, idol. Like, resembling. An equal, peer, friend. An enemy, rival. Scented with ambergris.

A ندأ nads, (v. n. of ندأ) Throwing (meat) into the fire. Putting (meat) under the ashes. Frightening. Throwing on the ground. Ascending, coming upon, being visible. Abhorring. Making a furrow in hot ashes.

P ندا nidā, The sixth of a farsang; half a mile.

A نداء nidās, (v. n. of ندا for ندو) Calling to one. Convoking, proclaiming. Glorying, boasting. Sitting (with any one). Seeing and knowing. Lying open (a road). Proclamation, edict. Sound, voice, clamour. A call, or voice from heaven.

P ندا کردن nidā kardan, To make proclamation, proclaim, announce, divulge, publish. A حرف ندا harfi nidā, The interjection of calling, the vocative. Nudās, Vociferation. (pl. of ندأة nudasat) Parts of many scattered plants.

A ندابة nadābat, A being quick, clever, intelligent.

A ندأة nadsat or nudsat, Abundance of wealth. The rainbow. A halo, circle round the sun or moon. Redness of the clouds at the rising or setting of the sun. Nudsat, A streak in a piece of meat of a different colour from the rest. Any thing stuffed into the matrix (of a camel) to induce her to take a liking to the colt of another. Nudsat or nudasat, (pl. نداء nudās) One part of many scattered plants. Nudasat, The rainbow.

A نداة nadāt, The inside of a horse's thigh.

A ندّاف naddāf, A cotton-dresser.

A ندّافي naddāfī, Business of a cotton-dresser.

A ندام nidām, (v. n. of ندم) Being a confidential friend or pot-companion. (pl. of نادم nādim) Penitents. (pl. of نديم nadīm) Pot-companions, good fellows at carousals.

A ندّام nuddām, (pl. of نادم nādim) Penitents.

A ندامة nadāmat, (v. n. of ندم) Repenting. Repentance, contrition, penitence, regret.

A ندامى nadāma', (pl. of ندمان nadmān) Pot-companions. Nudāma', (pl. of ندمان) Penitents.

A نداوة nadāwat, Moisture of ground.

A ندائد nadāsid, (pl. of نديدة nadīdat) Equals, rival women.

A ندب nadb, (v. n. of ندب) Lamenting or mourning (the dead). Making a funeral-oration or encomium. Calling one (to do any thing). Instigating, impelling. Sending. Being swift (a horse). Having a scar (the back). (A man) active, expeditious in doing any thing. (pl. ندوب nudūb and ندباء nudabās) Swift (horse). (pl. of ندبة nadbat) Scars of wounds. Nadab, (v. n. of ندب) Becoming covered with a scurf, scab, or cicatrice (a wound). Danger. A bet, stake, wager. Archery. The brandishing or throwing of a javelin. Name of a tribe. ندبنا يوم كذا nadabunā yawma hazā, Our commencement of archery was on such a day.

P ندب nadab, A term at the game of نرد nard.

A ندباء nudabās, (pl. of ندب nadb) Swift (horses).

A ندبة nadbat, (pl. ندب nadab, انداب andāb, and ندوب nudūb) The scar of a wound. A hoof or nail which is constantly changing. Name of a woman. Nudbat, Plaint, lamentation. A funeral-oration, elegy. Eloquent (Arabian). Name of a celebrated woman called امّ خفاف ummu khufāf.

A ندح nadh (v. n. of ندح) Enlarging. Nadh or nudh, (pl. انداح andāh) A spacious tract of country. Amplitude, plenty, multitude. Nidh, Any thing appearing high and seen from an eminence. Burden, heaviness.

A ندحة na or nudhat, A spacious tract of country.

A ندخ nadhh, A driving, dashing. Arrival.

A ندد nadad, Scattered (camels).

A نُدداء nudadās, (pl. of نديد) Equals, rivals.

A ندر nadr, (v. n. of ندر) Falling. Remaining alone.

A ندرة nadrat, One particle of gold in the mine. A quick fart. Nadrat or nadarat, On such a day (I met him). Nudrat, Oddness, singularity, rareness.

A ندري nadara', (في ندري fī nadara', الندري an' nadara', or في الندري fī'n nadara') After a few days, or a few days ago (I met him). مائة ندري misat nadara', A hundred-fold.

A ندس nads, (v. n. of ندس) Piercing with a spear. Kicking. Throwing (on the ground). Treating with contumely, reproaching. Averting, diverting, leading (out of the road). Conceiving (a false opinion of). One who hears well, even the lowest sound. Nads, nadis, or nadus, Intelligent, sharp, crafty, cunning. Nadas, (v. n. of ندس) Being intelligent, crafty. Understanding, cunning, skill.

A ندش nadsh or nadash, (v. n. of ندش) Inquiring into, investigating. Dividing, separating, carding (cotton).

A ندص nads, (v. n. of ندص) Going out (one thing from another). Nadas, (v. n. of ندص) Being burst (an abscess), and discharging (its) contents.

A ندع nads, Bastard marjoram.

A ندغ nadgh, (v. n. of ندغ) Poking with the fingers. Piercing (with a spear or with words). Acting wrong, injuring. Nadgh or nidgh, Wild marjoram. The best honey.

A ندغة nudghat, Whiteness upon the nails.

A ندف nadf, (v. n. of ندف) Separating (cotton) with the string of a large bow, which they strike with a kind of hammer. Striking (a lyre), playing on any musical instrument. (Clouds) pouring down (rain). Snowing. Moving the feet quick (a horse). Driving (a horse) violently. Eating. Drinking or lapping water by snatches (as a wild beast). Milking with two fingers.

A ندفان nadafān, (v. n. of ندف) Picking up (his feet) nimbly (a horse).

A ندفة nudfat, A small quantity of milk.

P ندفي كردن nadfī kardan, To divide (cotton).

A ندل nadl, (v. n. of ندل) Transporting from place to place. Receiving, picking out, choosing, seizing. Drawing (a bucket) out of a well. Taking (dates out of a basket) with the hands joined. Voiding (dung). Dirt, filth. ندل الثعالب nadlu's saɛālib, Swiftness, celerity. Nadal, (v. n. of ندل) Being dirty (the hand). Nudul, Servants who attend a banquet.

A ندم nadm, Ingenious, clever, witty. Nadam, (v. n. of ندم) Repenting. Penitence. A mark.

A ندماء nudumāɛ, (pl. of نديم nadīm) Companions, familiars, pot-companions, boon-companions.

A ندمان nadmān, (pl. ندامى nadāma') A pot-companion. (pl. ندامى nudāma') Penitent. (pl. of نديم nadīm) Pot-companions, jolly fellows at a drinking-bout.

A ندمانة nadmānat, A female pot-companion.

A ندماني جذيمة nadmānay jazīmat, Two stars near the pole (called فرقدان farkadāni).

A ندو nadw, (v. n. of ندا for ندو) Calling (a council), convoking. Assembling (a congregation). Being capacious, holding, containing (a place of meeting). Being present at an assembly. Separating, being scattered. Being liberal. Being noble, excellent (camel). Being pastured (camels) between two waterings. Passing from a bitter or salt to a sweet pasture. A heavy thing, weight, burden.

A ندوب nudūb, (v. n. of ندب) Being scarred (the back). (pl. of ندب nadb) Swift (horses). (pl. of ندبة nadbat) Scars.

A ندوبة nudūbat, (v. n. of ندب) Being scarred.

A ندوة nadwat, A council, assembly, convocation, congregation, mote, crowd. A daily meeting. دار الندوة dāru'n nadwat, The hall of convocation (in Mecca). Nudwat, A place where camels drink.

A ندوّة nudūwat, Moisture.

A ندود nudūd, A scampering away, running off.

A ندور nudūr, (v. n. of ندر) Falling. Falling (as one thing out of another and coming into view). Becoming leafy and verdant (trees or plants). Being alone, solitary. Ascending, arising. Farting in another's presence. Trying, proving. Dying.

A ندوس nadūs, (A she-camel) choosing, or content with, a scanty or bad pasture.

A ندوص nudūs, (v. n. of ندص) Going out (one thing from another). Projecting, being prominent, starting out (the eye of a strangling person).

A ندة nadh, (v. n. of ندة) Chiding. Checking (camels) by crying to (them); also driving or collecting (them) together.

P ندة anda, sometimes inda (a termination, which, when added to the second person of the imperative, forms a noun of agency), as, خوان khwān, Read or sing thou; خوانندة khwānanda, A reader; دة dih, Give thou; دهندة dihinda, Giving: a giver.

A ندهة nadhat or nudhat, Affluence, a great deal of wealth (whether live or dead stock). Twenty sheep or similar cattle). A hundred camels. A thousand pieces of money.

A ندي nada', (v. n. of ندي) Being moist, humid, wet. Disliking, detesting, nauseating, abhorring. (pl. انداء andāɛ and اندية andiyat) Moisture, rain, wetness (of ground), day-dew (سدي sada' denoting night-dew). A pleasing-smelling vapour. Fresh fodder. Term, time, period; interval, space, as far as a person can be heard when hallooing. Fat, tallow. Munificence. A gift. Nadī, Moist. Nadī, (or ندي الكف nadi'l kaf) Liberal, generous.

A نديّ nadīy, A congregation, council, assembly. One who calls with a loud voice, who halloos. Liberal, munificent.

A نديان nadyān, Succulent, juicy (tree).

A نديب nadīb, Scarred (back or wound).

A ندية nadiyat, Wet (ground).

A نديد nadīd, (v. n. of ندّ) Running away (a camel). (pl. ندداء nudadāɛ) Like, equal. A rival.

A نديدة nadīdat, (pl. ندائد nadāɛid) An equal, a rival (woman).

A نديف nadīf, (Cotton) beaten or bowed.

A نديم nadīm, (or نديمة nadīmat) (pl. ندماء nudamāɛ, ندام nidām, and ندمان nudmān) A pot-companion, boon-companion, intimate friend, privy counsellor, confidant. A king's fool, jester, or buffoon.

A نديئ nadīɛ, The rainbow. Ruddiness of the clouds at sunrise or sunset. Dough laid on the ashes to bake. Meat laid on the fire to roast.

A نذّ nazz, (v. n. of نذّ) Making water.

A نذارة na or nizārat, Exhortation, dehortation, admonition with threat. Fear, terror, dread.

A نذّال nuzzāl, (pl. of نذيل) Mean, despicable.

A نذالة nazālat, (v. n. of نذل) Being of the meanest rank, despicable. Vileness, baseness.

A نذخ nazkh, Rapid travelling (of an ass).

A نذر nazr, (v. n. of نذر) Vowing. Devoting, presenting, dedicating to God. Frightening, alarming, warning, inspiring dread of an enemy. Putting (one) in the van of an army (as if to victimize him). (pl. نذور nuzūr and نذر nuzur) A vow, promise made to God. A gift, any thing offered or dedicated. A present or offering from an inferior to a superior. An interview. A mulct of atonement for a wound. P نذر كردن nazr kardan, To vow. To make an offering. A Nazr, nuzr, or nuzur, Dehortation, commination, warning, menace, advice accompanied with threats. Nuzr, The skin of a wild date. Nazar, (v. n. of نذر) Being aware of, and on one's guard. Nuzur, Terror. (pl. of نذر nazr) Vows, promises made to God. (pl. of نذير nazīr) Devoted to God, Nazarites. Prophets, preachers sent to alarm the wicked.

A نذراء nuzarāɛ, (pl. of نذير) Fear-inspirers.

A نذر امام nazr imām, Presents given in memory of the Imāms Hasan and Husayn.

P نذرانة nazrāna, Fees paid to government as an acknowledgment for a grant of land or any public office. Gifts offered or received when people of rank meet, or pay their respects to a prince. A kind of tribute.

P نذر درگاة nazr-dargāh, An endowment in land to places of worship among the Muhammadans.

A نذري nuzra', Admonition, dehortation. Fear.

A نذع nazɛ, The flowing (of sweat or water).

A نذل nazl, (pl. انذال anzāl and نذول nuzūl) A low, mean, abject man.

A نذلاء nuzolāɛ, (pl. of نذيل) Vile, abject, men.

A نذور nuzūr, (v. n. of نذر) Vowing. (pl. of نذر nazr) Vows, promises made to God. Mulcts of atonement for wounds.

A نذول nuzūl, (pl. of نذل or نذيل) Base, vile.

A نذولة nuzūlat, (v. n. of نذل) Being of the meanest rank, vile, and despicable.

A نذيذ nazīz, A making water. Spittle, mucus.

A نذير nazīr, (pl. نذر nuzur) A messenger of bad news. A prophet or preacher (sent to terrify the wicked), an apostle, legate. Naked, bare. Grey hair, hoariness. Devoted to God, a Nazarite. Commination, dehortation, advice accompanied with a threat. The twang of a bow. Terrified. النذير an' nazīr, The admonisher, i.e. Muhammad. النذير العريان an' nazīru'l ɛaryān, The faithful prophet, he who delivers the naked truth.

A نذيرة nazīrat, Any thing dedicated to God in consequence of a vow, especially children (as the child Samuel or Sampson). The first line of an army (as devoting themselves), the forlorn hope.

A نذيل nazīl, (pl. نذلاء nuzalāɛ and نذّال nuzzāl) A vile, abject man.

P نر nar, Male, masculine. Membrum virile. Rough. A stallion. Sordid, abominable, filthy, detestable, ugly. A wave. A bunch. A hillock. The main branch of a tree. A hermaphrodite. Name of the father of سام sām. نر دادن nar dādan, To give the male (to a female). نرانگشتي nar-angushtī, (or انگشت نر angushti nar) The thumb.

P نرا narā, A small wall raised as a skreen.

A نرّاد narrād, A player at the game of نرد nard.

P نراك narāk, Always, for ever.

A نرجس narjis or narjas, The narcissus.

P نرجل narajul, A silken cloth made in Abyssinia.

P نرخ nirkh, Tax, tariff, price. Assize of provisions established by the magistrates. Currency. Beauty, elegance. Grace, splendour. نرخ بازار nirkhi bāzār, Market-price. نرخ نهادن nirkh nihādan, To fix an assize, tariff, or duty upon commodities; to publish such regulation.

P نرخبندي nirkh-bandī, Rate. Price-current.

P نرخ داروغة nirkh-dārogha, Clerk of the market, who regulates the price of grain, &c.

P نرخنامة nirkh-nāma, A price-current.

P نرخي nirkhī, He who fixes the price-current, an appraiser, assigner, assizer.

P نرد nard, Chess, draughts, backgammon, tables, dice. Trunk of a tree. مهرة نرد muhrasi nard,

A chessman, tableman.

A نرد *nard*, Chess, draughts, tables, dice. A sack wide at bottom and narrow at top, made of palm-leaves, and strengthened by fibres which stands erect, into which they put fresh dates to be transported to distant places. A kind of medicinal ointment.

P نردبان *nardubān*, A staircase, steps, ladder, especially a scaling-ladder.

P نردك *nardak*, An enigma. (dim. of نرد *nard*, q.v.)

A نرز *narz*, A withdrawing, absconding from fear.

P نرزد *narzad*, (for نيارزد *nayarzad*) It is not worth.

A نرس *nars*, Name of a town in Babylonia where stuffs are made.

P نرسك *narask*, A lentil.

P نرسي *narsī* or *nursī*, A name of several kings of Persia. The son of Gūdarz, one of the Ashkāniyan kings.

A نرسيّ *narsiy*, A cloth made at Nars.

A نرسيان *nirsiyān*, The best kind of dates.

A نرش *narsh*, A taking of any thing in the hand (to eat).

P نرك *narak*, A bone found in the root of a tiger's tail, which, when brayed in a mortar, is used for various medicinal purposes.

P نرگ *narg*, A ring formed by hunters for enclosing game.

P نرّگان *narragān*, Impudent, importunate mendicants, sturdy beggars.

P نرگاو *nar-gāw*, *gāo*, or *gāv*, A bull.

P نرگدا *nar-gadā*, Impudent, shameless, sturdy beggars; audacious fellows. Outrageous.

P نرگس *nargis*, A narcissus (to which the poets frequently compare the eyes of beautiful women); also a kind of yellow flower. نرگس مخمور *nargisi makhmūr*, An epithet applied to the eyes of a mistress (intoxicated narcissus). نرگس نيم خواب *nargisi nīm-khwāb*, The eye of a mistress. نرگس و گل *nargis u gul*, The eye and ear of one's beloved.

P نرگسدان *nargisdān*, A pot in which they put a narcissus; a place where it grows.

P نرگسه *nargisa*, The figure of a narcissus carved in ivory or bone and placed on the roof of a house. The stars. The Pleiades. نرگسهٔ سقف چرخ *nargisaʼi sakfi charkh*, The Pleiades.

P نرگسي *nargisī*, Belonging to a narcissus. A sort of cloth; also of food.

P نرگه *narga*, A circle formed by hunters. A house, square tent. Order, series, row, line, rank. An assembly.

P نرم *narm*, Soft to the touch. Smooth, sleek. Mild, gentle, easy. Silly. Fine. Defective. The bass part of music. نرم و درشت *narm u durusht*, Smooth and rough. نرم كردن *narm kardan*, To soften, mitigate, soothe, reconcile, pacify. نرم رفتن *narm raftan*, To go softly, gently, pleasantly.

P نرمادگي *nar-mādagī*, A bolt, kind of lock.

P نرماده *nar-māda*, Male and female; hermaphrodite. A bolt, bar, and staple. A vice, screw. A hinge. نرمادهٔ در *nar-mādaʼi dar*, The bolt and staple of a door.

P نرم آهن *narm-āhan*, (Soft-iron) Lazy, indolent, idle. Weak, infirm, impotent.

P نرم بر *narm-bur*, Name of a carpenter's and blacksmith's tool. A flatterer, wheedler.

P نرم بيز *narm-bīz* or *bez*, A fine sieve.

P نرم پاي *narm-pāy*, Name of a creature in India with legs thin and lithe like leathern straps.

P نرم چشم *narm-chashm*, Of a stern look.

P نرم خو *narm-kho* or *khū*, Soft-natured.

P نرم دست *narm-dast*, A fine kind of stuff.

P نرم دل *narm-dil*, Tender-hearted, gentle.

P نرم رو *narm-rav*, Gentle, tractable (horse).

P نرمسار *narm-sār*, Kind, meek, forbearing.

P نرم شانه *narm-shāna*, Weak, lazy; obedient.

P نرمغت *narmaght*, A swing, a see-saw.

A نرمق *narmak*, (P نرمه *narma*) Soft, smooth.

P نرم گردن *narm-gardan*, (Soft-neck) Obedient.

P نرم گردني *narm-gardanī*, Submission, obedience.

P نرم لگام *narm-lugām*, Docile, tractable: obedient.

P نرم نرم *narm narm*, Softly, gently.

P نرمود *narmūd*, (or نرموده) A swing, see-saw.

P نرمودن *narmūdan*, To swing. To vacillate.

P نرموره *narmūra*, Any thing thick, coarse, rough, uneven, or untrimmed. A walnut. A swing.

P نرمه *narma*, Soft. نرمهٔ گوش *narmaʼi gosh*, Lobe of the ear. نرمهٔ سر كودك *narmaʼi sari kūdak*, The soft part of the head of a new-born infant.

P نرمي *narmī*, Softness, smoothness, sleekness. Gentleness, mildness. نرمي نمودن *narmī numūdan* or *namūdan*, To behave meekly or tamely.

P نرميّت *narmīyat*, Softness.

P نرميش *nar-mesh*, (Male-sheep) A ram.

A نروة *narwat*, A certain thin white stone.

P نروك *narūk*, Name of a root of which the tiger is very fond.

P نرول *narūl*, An officer who takes charge of forfeited estates.

P نره *nara*, (or نرّه *narra*) Male. Penis. Trunk of a tree. A wave. Wards of a key. A hermaphrodite. A beggar. Rough, rude. Filthy, sordid. Ugly, abominable. Name of the father of سام *sām*. نره بر آوردن *nara bar āwardan*, To unsheath, to draw (a gelding, stallion). نرّهٔ آب *narraʼi āb*, A wave.

P نرّه ديو *narra-dev*, An execrable demon.

P نرّه گاو *narra-gāw* or *gāo*, A bull.

P نري *narī*, Penis. Virility, masculineness. The masculine gender. A dressed sheep-skin.

P نريم *narīm*, (or نريمان *narīmān*) Name of a famous hero of Persia, son of قهرمان *kahramān*, father of سام *sām*, grandfather of زالزر *zālzar*, and great-grandfather of رستم *rustam*: all champions in the ancient Persian histories, poems, and romances.

P نرينه *narīna*, Male, masculine. Virility. فرزند نرينه *farzandi narīna*, A male child.

A نزّ *nazz*, Brisk, light, active (man), incessantly on the move. Acute, ingenious, witty. Many. Liberal, munificent. (An ostrich) running from place to place. *Nazz* or *nizz*, Water springing up.

A نزأ *nazʼ*, (v. n. of نزأ) Spreading dissensions, instigating men to fight. Rushing upon. Forcing or exciting. Repelling, removing, diverting from.

P نزا *nazā*, A mound, enclosure.

A نزاء *nazāʼ*, A leap. *Nazāʼ* or *nizāʼ*, (v. n. of نزا for نزو) Leaping, mounting (as the male on the female). *Nuzāʼ*, (v. n. of نزا for نزو) Leaping, making an assault. Having a strong propensity, inclining towards. A disease incident to sheep, causing them to leap and blissom until they die.

A نزّاء *nazzāʼ*, Prone (to evil). One who assaults his pot-companions.

A نزاب *nuzāb*, (v. n. of نزب) Calling to the female, rattling (as a buck at rutting-time).

P نزار *nizār*, Thin, slim, slender. Lean, spare. Flesh without fat. Weak. كلك نزار *kilki nizār*, A slender reed or pen.

A نزار *nizār*, Name of the father of an Arabian tribe. Nizārites descended from him. (pl. of نزر *nazr*) Little, few. Insipid.

A نزارة *nazārat*, (v. n. of نزر) Being small, mean, vile. Smallness, exility. Gait.

P نزاري *nizārī*, Leanness, slenderness.

A نزاز *nizāz*, Addicted (to evil).

A نزازة *nazāzat*, March, gait.

A نزاع *nizāʻ*, (v. n. of نزع) Hastening (homeward or to any accustomed place). Retiring, desisting. (v. n. 3 of نزع) Disputing, contending, litigating. Dispute, contention, altercation, controversy, litigation, law-suit. ما به النزاع *mā bihiʼn nizāʻ*, The subject of dispute. P قطع نزاع كردن *katʻi nizāʻ kardan*, To decide a controversy.

A نزّاع *nuzzāʻ*, (pl. of نازع *nāziʻ*) Foreigners.

A نزاعة *nazāʻat*, (v. n. of نزع) Hastening (homeward or to any accustomed place). Retiring, desisting. Dispute, controversy, law-suit, litigation.

A نزّاغ *nazzāgh*, A malevolent slanderer.

A نزاق *nizāk*, (v. n. of نزق) Reproaching, railing at, reviling one another. Approaching. Very swift (she-camel).

A نزّاك *nazzāk*, A defamer, slanderer.

A نزاكة *nazākat*, (a word coined from P نازك *nāzuk*) Elegance, softness, tenderness, politeness. P بي نزاكت *bī nazākat*, Inelegant. Ill-bred. Ill-dressed, slovenly, slatternly.

A نزال *nizāl*, (v. n. 3 of نزل) Alighting from horseback, descending into the arena to fight (with another). Combat, fight. *Nazāli*, Descend into the arena to combat.

A نزّال *nuzzāl*, (pl. of نازل *nāzil*) Those who descend or dismount. Valiant heroes.

A نزالة *nazālat*, (v. n. of نزل) (Ground) being overflowed by a slight rain (from the hardness of the soil). *Nizālat*, A journey. *Nuzālat*, Sperma genitale quod emittitur.

A نزانز *nuzāniz*, Choice, excellent (stallion).

A نزاه *nizāh*, (pl. of نازه) Pure, chaste, temperate.

A نزاهة *nazāhat*, (or نزاهية *nazāhiyat*) (v. n. of نزه) Lying at a distance from water, being remote from the sea, and free from miasmata (land). Being removed from all evil and annoyances. Being cheerful and pleasant (a country). Pleasantness (of a place). Solace, recreation. Delectableness. Spotlessness, purity of life.

A نزائع *nazāʼiʻ*, (pl. of نزيعة *nazīʻat*) (Women) married into a foreign family. (Horses or camels) brought from another country and pining to return, having the maladie de pays.

A نزب *nazb*, (v. n. of نزب) Bleating (as deer, especially the stag). *Nazab*, A surname, nickname.

A نزّة *nazzat*, (fem. of نزّ) Swift, brisk (she-camel). *Nizzat*, Desire, lust.

A نزج *nazj*, (v. n. of نزج) Dancing.

P نزج *nazaj*, A city called ارمنية *armaniya*.

A نزح *nazh*, (v. n. of نزح) Exhausting nearly (a well) of water. Having their wells distant or exhausted (a people). Being far distant from home. Being nearly exhausted (a well). *Nazah*, A well emptied of the greatest part of the water. Muddy water. *Nuzuh*, A well having little water. An exhausted well. Distant.

P نزد *nazd*, Near, about, with, A side. نزد من *nazdi man*, My side, at my side, near or with me. از نزد من *az nazdi man*, From near me, at my side, with me, in my possession. نزد آب آمدن *nazdi āb āmadan*, To draw near to water.

P نزديك *nazdīk*, Near, neighbouring, hard by, close to. Vicinity. نزديك آمدن *nazdīk āmadan*, To come near, to approach, advance towards. نزديك آوردن *nazdīk āwardan*, To bring near, to apply, put together, lead towards, bring or present before. نزديك رسيدن *nazdīk rasīdan*, To arrive, reach. نزديك رفتن *nazdīk raftan*, To go near. نزديك شدن *nazdīk shudan*, To approach. To be near. نزديك كردن *nazdīk kardan*, To lead towards, to cause to approach. نزديك تپ *nazdīki tap*, Fit of ague or fever. در نزديك *dar nazdīk*, Near, in the neighbourhood.

P نزديك تك *nazdīk-tak*, Shallow (well or river).

P نزديكي *nazdīkī*, Nearness, neighbourhood, vicinity, approach. Intimacy.

A نزر *nazr*, (v. n. of نزر) Being importunate, impertinently urgent. Being roused and excited. Being quick and expeditious. Commanding. Regarding as small. Despising. Being little, small, few. Little, small; moderate, low-priced, cheap. Tasteless. A swelling in a camel's udder. An affair, business. *Nazran*, Late, slowly. *Nazar*, (v. n. of نزر) Being little small; cheap, low-priced; mean, vile. *Nuzur*, A phantom, ghost, spectre. عن نزر *ʻan nuzurin*, Face to face.

A نزرة *nazirat*, Unprolific (woman), having little milk, or aught else which she should have.

A نزع *nazʻ*, (v. n. of نزع) Removing, carrying off, pulling up, tearing out. Taking (the hand) out of the bosom. Drawing up (a bucket). Drawing (a bow). Drawing water. Resembling (a father. Being in the agonies of death. The agonies of death. نزع روح *nazʻi rūh*, (or P روان *rawān*) The last breath. *Nazaʻ*, (v. n. of نزع) Being bald round the temples. Baldness.

A نزّع *nuzzaʻ*, (A ewe) wanting the male.

A نزعاء *nazʻāʼ*, (fem. of انزع *anzaʻ*) Bald about the temples (زعراء *zaʻrāʼ* is more correct). *Nuzaʻāʼ*, (pl. of نزيع *nazīʻ*) Foreigners.

A نزعة *nazʻat* or *nazaʻat*, A bald place round the temples. A kind of herb. *Nazaʻat*, A path through mountains. A convenient place for any thing, especially for an arrow. (pl. of نازع *nāziʻ*) Archers drawing their bows. Those who can redress themselves at law. عاد السهم الى النزعة *ʻāda's sahm ila'n nazaʻat*, The right reverted to those to whom it was due (literally, the arrow returned to those who discharged it).

A نزغ *nazgh*, (v. n. of نزغ) Sowing dissensions. Reproaching, stabbing (with bitter words); slandering, reviling (the absent); saying any thing bad.

A نزف *nazf*, (v. n. of نزف) Exhausting (a well) entirely of water. Failing (as blood). Becoming weak from the loss of blood. Being exhausted, dried up (tears). Flowing fast (blood). Being deficient (in mind), losing the senses, being stupefied, drunk. Losing a cause, failing in an argument. نزف الرحم *nazfu'r rahim*, A flooding in women. *Nuzf*, A failure of water in a well. The drawing out or exhaustion of the water of a well. *Nazaf*, (v. n. of نزف) Being exhausted, dried (tears). *Nazif*, Enfeebled by loss of blood. *Nuzaf*, (pl. of نزفة *nuzfat*) Small quantities of water, blood, or wine.

A نزّف *nuzzaf*, (Veins) not emitting blood.

A نزفة *nuzfat*, (pl. نزف *nuzaf*) A small quantity of water, blood, or wine.

A نزق *nazk*, (v. n. of نزق) Leaping (as a horse upon the mare). Running fast, outstripping. *Nazk* or *nazak*, (v. n. of نزق) Being precipitate, prone to anger, rash. Being filled to the brim (a pond or vessel). Being variable, moveable, volatile, inconstant, unsteady; levity, volatility. *Nazak*, Neighbouring (place). *Nazik*, Light, flighty, rash. نزق الحقاق *naziku'l hikāk*, A disputant about trifles.

A نزك *nazk*, (v. n. of نزك) Piercing with a javelin. Taunting, accusing falsely, reviling unjustly. *Nizk*, The hip or haunch-bone. *Nazk* or *nizk*, The male Lybian lizard. *Nuzak*, A defamer, slanderer.

P نزگ *nazag*, A lentil.

A نزل *nazala*, (fut. ينزل *yanzilu*) He descended. He travelled.

A نزل *nizl*, Joined, compressed, brought together. *Nuzl*, (pl. انزال *anzāl*) Any thing provided for the entertainment of strangers. Augmentation, redundancy, increase of meat or bread when cooked. Sperma genitale. Hospitality. The place where pilgrims or other strangers alight or are entertained; also what is given to them. *Nazal*, (v. n. of نزل) Being plentiful (an entertainment). Being strong and clean (growing corn). Being troubled with a catarrh. Rain. Abundance, gain, profit. Provisions; any thing provided for the entertainment of strangers. *Nazil*, A hard soil, through which rain does not subside. (A place) where one often descends or goes. Joined, compressed, close (handwriting). *Nuzul*, Any thing provided for a guest. Increase, enlargement of food or bread when dressed. Meat richly or excellently dressed; abundance, plenty, richness of agricultural produce. A gift. A mansion, hospitable dwelling. A company of visitors. (pl. of نزيل *nazīl*) Strangers, foreigners.

A نزلات *nazalāt*, Catarrhs, rheums. *Naza* or *nazilāt*, Right disposition, sound, good arrangement.

A نزلة *nazlat*, One descent. نزلة اخرى *nazlatun ukhra'*, A second descent. ارض نزلة *arzun nazlatun*, Land well-cultivated. *Nazlat* or *nuzlat*, Descent or defluxion of humours, rheum, catarrh. *Nazilat*, (pl. نزلات *nazilāt*) Hard (soil), not drinking in rain.

P نزم *nazm* or *nizm*, A mist, a fog, a vapour.

A نزم *nazm*, A severe bite.

A نزنزة *naznazat*, A shaking, nodding (of the head).

A نزو *nazw*, (v. n. of نزا for نزو) Leaping upon, assaulting. Mounting and overpowering (wine). Rising in price (corn).

A نزوء *nuzuʼ*, (v. n. of نزأ) Spreading dissensions, instigating (men) to fight.

A نزوم *nuzūm*, (v. n. of نزا for نزو) Leaping on, assaulting. Sparkling from an admixture of water (wine).

A نزوان *nazawān*, (v. n. of نزا for نزو) Leaping. Making an assault, or attacking one's pot-companions. Twisting or turning the body. Being sharp. Receding, retiring. Power, violence, vehemence. The pain or irritation of a disease.

A نزوة *nazwat*, A kind of thin white stone (with which they strike fire). Short, dwarfish (woman).

A نزوح *nazūh*, (A well) having little water, or one whose water has been exhausted. Distant. *Nuzūh*, (v. n. of نزح) Exhausting nearly (a well). Being far distant (home).

A نزور *nazūr*, Not prolific (woman), having little milk or any thing else which she ought to have. (A camel) which conceives with difficulty, or will hardly take the male; also one which has an affection for a strange colt, her own being dead. *Nuzūr*, (v. n. of نزر) Being little, small, and mean.

A نزورة *nuzūrat*, A being small, mean, vile.

A نزوز *nuzūz*, (pl. of نزّ) Waters springing up.

A نزوع *nazūʻ*, Shallow (well), the water of which

may be reached (by the hand). Full of desire. *Nuzūg*, (v. n. of نزع) Coming to an end, retiring, desisting (from any thing). Resembling (parents). Drawing (a bow or bucket). Running at full speed (a horse). Going. Hastening homeward, wending one's way to any accustomed place.

A نزوف *nazūf*, (A well) whose water may be drawn by the hand.

A نزوق *nuzūḳ*, (v. n. of نزق) Leaping on, mounting. Running fast, outstripping.

A نزول *nuzūl*, (v. n. of نزل) Descending. Alighting, sojourning (as a stranger). Inhabiting, encamping. Happening, befalling (as misfortunes to mankind). Going down, falling, perishing. Arriving at Mina near Mecca, where sacrifices are offered up. A descent, alighting. A cataract in the eye. P نزول آب *nuzūli āb*, A swelling of the testicle, which (excepting in the case of a blow or of hernia) is universally ascribed to the descent of water. It therefore comprehends hydrocele, hernia humoralis, and schirrus. A درجات نزول *darajāti nuzūl*, Degrees of descent (in consanguinity).

A نزه *nazh*, (v. n. of نزه) Driving (camels) a great way (from water). Restraining (one's self from any thing improper). Pleasant (place). Spotlessness, purity of life. *Nazh*, (or نزه الفلاة *nazhu'l falāt*) Part (of a desert) far from water and pasturage. *Nazh* or *nizh*, Pure, chaste, temperate. *Nazih*, Far distant (place).

P نزه *nazah*, The roof of a house. Timber used for covering a roof, shingle. A chink through which air may pass. The oozing of water through a bank.

A نزهاء *nuzahās*, (pl. of نازه *nāzih*) Pure, chaste.

A نزهان *nazahān*, (v. n. of نزه) Leading (camels) far (from water).

A نزهة *nazhat* or *nazihat*, A place far from water or pasture; also from marshes or corruption of the air. *Nuzhat*, Distance. Pleasure, delight, joy, cheerfulness. Pleasantness (of a place). Ornament. *Nazihat*, Delightful (country).

P نزهت افزا *nuzhat-afzā*, Increasing delight.

P نزهت پذير *nuzhat-pazīr*, Recreated, pleased. Adorned.

P نزهتگاه *nuzhat-gāh*, A pleasant place.

A نزيّ *naziy*, Prone (to evil). One who assaults his pot-companions.

A نزيب *nazīb*, (v. n. of نزب) Rattling (a stag) when in want of the doe.

A نزيّة *nazīyat*, A deep dish. A cloud.

P نزيج *nazīj*, A horse of parade or state led before a great man.

A نزيح *nazīh*, Far distant, very wide.

P نزيدن *nazīdan*, To draw out, extract.

A نزير *nazīr*, Small, moderate. Little, few.

A نزيز *nazīz*, (v. n. of نزّ) Running or passing with rapidity; also crying (a deer). Rattling at rutting-time (a goat). Exuding, pouring out water abundantly, being full of land-springs (ground). Separating, becoming detached. Being hard and firm. Vibrating (as a bow-string when shooting). Full of desire, lustful. Brisk, active. Light, volatile, moveable. Joyous, jovial. Addicted (to evil).

A نزيع *nazīg*, Shallow (well). Foreign. Far distant. Gathered, collected (fruit). A foreigner, stranger. One whose mother was a captive.

A نزيعة *nazīgat*, (pl. نزائع *nazāsig*) Excellent (horse, she-camel, or camels), such as they carry to other countries. A fine (woman) carried to be married amongst strangers (to improve the breed).

A نزيف *nazīf*, Debilitated by loss of blood. Inebriated, stupid. Parched with thirst. Feverish.

A نزيكات *nazīkāt*, Worst of (men or goats).

A نزيل *nazīl*, A stranger, foreigner: visitor, guest. Perfect. Plentiful or magnificent (entertainment).

P نزيم *na* or *nizīm*, Cloud; mist. *Nizīm*, A deluge.

A نزيم *nazīm*, A handful of pot-herbs.

A نزيه *nazīh*, Far-distant (place). Remote from the sea, or from fens, and free from miasmata (land). Free from every thing objectionable; pure.

A نزيهة *nazīhat*, A country distant from marshes, fens, or foul air.

P نژ *naj*, What draws out or extracts. The wards of a key.

P نژاد *nijād*, Family, origin, root, or principle. Seed, descent, extraction. Noble, born of a distinguished race. بد نژاد *bad-nijād*, Ignoble, base-born. پاك نژاد *pāk-nijād*, Of a good family, nobly born. اسب تازي نژاد *asbi tāzī-nijād*, An Arab horse.

P نژاده *nijāda* or *najāda*, Family, origin, root, principle. Radical, original, generous, noble.

P نژد *nijd*, A great man. A master, preceptor. Sad, glum.

P نژغار *najghār*, Noise, shout, exclamation.

P نژم *nijm* or *nujm*, Cloud; fog, mist; a low-hanging vapour obscuring the surface of the ground: darkness. Noise, shouting, clapping of hands. Vexation, sadness, anguish. Inundation, deluge.

P نژمند *nijmand*, Venerable. Anxious, afflicted.

P نژمودن *najmūdan*, To scum, to clarify.

P نژند *nijand* or *najand*, Formidable, terrible, tremendous. Venerable, revered. Astonished, stupid. Altered, changed (by grief or age), sad, cast down. Angry. A considerable merchant. A learned preceptor. An old man of authority and experience, one that may be trusted. Faithful. Turbid, muddy, obscure. Ugly, lean, thin, withered. Timid, weak, infirm; bearing, or unable to repel an injury. An unjust person, wicked man, sinner; one who injures or oppresses. Abhorred, abominable. Low (ground). (in astronomy) The lower apsis in an eccentric orbit (opposed to اوج *awj*).

P نژندي *nijandī*, Sadness, gloom, melancholy.

P نژنك *najnak*, A gin, trap, snare.

P نژه *najah*, A very slender branch of a tree. A hunter's arrow. A thin plate of gold or silver cut in the form of the leaves of flowers, and occasionally sprinkled upon the heads of bridegrooms. Name of a fixed star. Wood with which they cover the roofs of houses. *Nijah*, Timid, troubled, vexed. Venerable, revered, awful.

P نژيدن *najīdan*, To draw forth, extract.

P نژيم *nijīm*, Vapour, mist, darkness.

P نس *nas*, A shade, arbour, bower. A house. *Nus*, The circumference or environs of the mouth. Intellect, judgment, understanding. The beard. Vulva. A slippery place.

A نس *nas*, A vein, a sinew.

A نسّ *nass*, (v. n. of نسّ) Driving, checking, or crying to (camels). Being dishevelled (hair). Going on rapidly or perseveringly (in any affair). Approaching to water. Dryness.

A نسء *nass*, (v. n. of نسأ) Driving or checking (camels) by crying to them. Being wanton (a doe), frisking (round the male). Throwing the month Muharram on into Safar. Driving away (cattle) from the trough. Delaying, protracting, giving time. Giving credit (for any thing sold). Selling on credit. Allowing (camels) to become extremely thirsty. Beginning to fatten (sheep). Guarding (as God does man), prolonging life. Beginning to grow (as an animal's coat) after the former had dropt off. Mixing, mingling. Mixing (milk) with water; offering it or wine to one. Having a stoppage of the menses beyond the usual time (a woman), and thence supposing herself pregnant. Licking her newly-dropt fawn (a doe). Striking with a staff. The beginning of fat or corpulency. Generous wine promoting cheerfulness. A new camel's coat. Thin, watery milk. امرأة نسء *imrasatun nassun*, A woman supposed to be pregnant from the stoppage of the menses. *Nass*, *niss*, or *nuss*, A woman who fancies herself to be with child, or whose pregnancy appears. *Niss*, One who mixes or converses with. نسء نساء *nissu nisāsin*, An entertainer of ladies, one fond of their society.

P نسا *nasā*, A place to which the sun's rays never penetrate. Dead. *Nisā*, The flesh and bones of any dead animal. Name of two cities in Khurāsān.

A نسا *nasa'*, (dual نسوان *nasawāni* and نسيان *nasayāni*) (pl. انساء *ansās*) A nerve or tendon extending from the hip to the heel; also a disease affecting it; sciatica.

A نساء *nasās*, (v. n. of نسأ) Granting a delay for the payment of a debt. Length (of life). *Nisās*, Woman, the female sex; a lady.

A نساب *nisāb*, Connection, relation.

A نسّاب *nassāb*, Skilful in genealogies.

A نسّابة *nassābat*, Skilful in genealogies, an able genealogist: a registrar of pedigrees.

A نسأة *nassat*, (v. n. of نسأ) Supposing (herself) pregnant from the stoppage of her courses (a woman). *Nussat*, Delay, a putting off the payment of a debt. باعه بنسأة *bāʿahu bi nussatin*, He sold or he bought it upon credit. *Nasasat*, (pl. of ناسئ *nāsiʾ*) Fat. Those who give names to and arrange the order of the months.

A نسّاج *nassāj*, A weaver. A maker of coats of mail with iron rings. A composer, inventor. A liar.

A نساجة *nisājat*, The weaving art.

A نساح *nusāh*, Rubbish, stalks, date-fragments.

P نسار *nasār*, A place impervious to the sun's rays. An arbour, canopy, bower, shade, shadow.

A نسارِيّة *nusārīyat*, An eagle.

A النسّاسة *an' nassāsat*, Mecca.

A نساسيف *nasāsīf*, (pl. of نسّاف *nussāf*) Birds resembling swallows.

A نساطرة *nasātirat*, Nestorians.

A نساف *nisāf*, (pl. of نسيفة) Pumice-stones.

A نسّاف *nussāf*, (and نساسيف *nasāsīf*) A kind of bird resembling a swallow.

A نسافة *nusāfat*, Chaff which flies off when winnowing. The froth of milk.

A نسّاك *nussāk*, (pl. of ناسك) Religious, devout.

A نساكة *nasākat*, (v. n. of نسك) Being religious, devoted to God. Piety, morality, virtue.

A نسال *nusāl*, Feathers or hairs falling from birds and animals. Gossamer, down flying off from withered plants.

A نسالة *nusālat*, Hairs or feathers falling from animals or birds when moulting.

A نسام *nisām*, (pl. of نسيم) Gentle breezes.

A نسامة *nasāmat*, (v. n. of نسم) Spirting forth water (ground). Striking with the foot (a camel). Changing, turning.

A نسانس *nasānis*, A satyr. An ourang-outang. She-marmosets, female chimpanzees.

A نساوة *nisāwat*, (v. n. of نسي) Forgetting.

A نسائج *nasāʾij*, (pl. of نسيجة) Webs, wefts.

A نسائس *nasāʾis*, (pl. of نسيسة) Detractions.

A نسائك *nasāʾik*, (pl. of نسيكة) Sacrifices.

A نسائم *nasāʾim*, (pl. of نسيم) Breezes, gales.

A نسب *nasab*, (v. n. of نسب) Mentioning the lineage of any one; denominating him by his family-name. Referring (to any one); deriving (one thing from another). Praising (a mistress) in verse. (pl. انساب *ansāb*) Genealogy (especially in the paternal line); lineage, race, stock, family, house. A patronymic or family-name. نسب و حسب *nasab u hasab*, Genealogy and acquirements. ذو نسب *zū nasab*, Related, a relation, one of the family. مجهول النسب *majhūlu'n nasab*, Of unknown family.

P نسب پذير *nasab-pazīr*, A pretender, claimant.

P نسب پذيري *nasab-pazīrī*, Pretendership.

A نسبة *nisbat*, (v. n. of نسب) Mentioning the lineage (of any one). Referring (to any one), deriving one thing from another. Relation, respect, regard, attribute, reference. Affinity, connection. ياء نسبت *yāʾi nisbat*, The affix ي denoting kindred and relationship (in Arabic words with, and in Persian words without, *tashdīd*. *Nisbat* or *nusbat*, Lineage, stock, race, extraction, relationship on the father's side. *Nisbatan*, (P بانسبت *bā nisbat*) Relatively, in respect of, in regard to.

P نسبت كردن *nisbat kardan*, To ascribe to, impute. كسي را بدروغ نسبت كردن *kasērā ba durogh nisbat kardan*, To accuse or charge a person with a lie. A *Nasabat*, Proportion.

A نسبتي *nisbatī*, Related, having reference to. Related by marriage, connected. A wife's brother.

P نسبنامه *nasab-nāma*, Pedigree, descent. A genealogical tree.

P نسبو *nasbū*, A slippery place. Plain, smooth.

P نسبوت *nasbūt*, Judgment, discrimination. The faculty of judging between good and bad.

P نسبه *nisba*, A course of bricks in a wall.

A نسبيّ *nasbiy*, Related to, of the blood.

P نسپار *naspār*, Place where they press grapes.

P نسپه *nispuh*, A layer or course of bricks or clods in a wall.

P نستاك *nistāk*, A twist of the guts, gripes.

P نستر *nastar*, A narcissus. The dog-rose. Name of a monk of Persia cotemporary with Noshīravān.

P نستردن *nastardan*, A narcissus.

P نسترن *nastaran*, A narcissus. The dog-rose; the white rose of India. A flower-garden. Clover. A kind of cloth.

P نسترون *nastarūn*, A narcissus. Dog-rose.

A نستعليق *nastaʿlīk*, (from نسخ *naskh* and تعليق *taʿlīk*) A kind of Persian writing (or characters).

A نستق *nustuk*, A servant.

P نستك *nistak*, Very fine spun cotton.

P نستم *nistam*, A place of sitting down or abiding. A nest.

P نستوه *nastūh*, Brave, warlike. Contentious, quarrelsome, pugnacious. Rude, harsh, rough, morose, churlish. Name of a champion of Irān.

P نستهن *nastahan*, The brother of Pīrān Wīsah.

A نسج *nasj*, (v. n. of نسج) Weaving (cloth). Lying, giving a false colouring. Marking (as the wind does sand or water) with long furrows or waves (when blowing lengthwise and crosswise). Composing, making verses. Texture. نسج العنكبوت *nasju'l ʿankabūt*, A cobweb. *Nusuj*, Carpets on which they kneel at prayer.

A نسح *nas-h*, (v. n. of نسح) Blowing, sweeping (dust). Rubbish, stalks of dates; any thing similar at the bottom of a vessel or hamper. *Nasah*, (v. n. of نسح) Coveting.

A نسخ *naskh*, (v. n. of نسخ) Transcribing (a book), copying. Cancelling. Obliterating, defacing, abrogating (a law), repealing (one by another), annulling, rejecting, breaking, confuting. Transforming into an ugly shape. Turning the contents of one hive into another. The modern Arabic character. *Nusakh*, (pl. of نسخة *nuskhat*) Examples. ناسخ نسخ تواريخ سلف *nāsikhi nusakhi tawārīkhi salaf*, The writers of the exemplars or annals of ancient times, *i.e.* ancient historians.

A نسخة *nuskhat*, (pl. نسخ *nusakh*) Exemplar, prototype, archetype, a copy or model whence any thing is taken. A manuscript-copy. A physician's recipe. A prescription of ingredients for any composition. P نسخه كردن *nuskha kardan*, To transcribe.

P نسخجات *nuskhajāt*, (pl. of نسخه) Books.

P نسخه نويسي *nuskha-navīsī*, Recipe-writing.

P نسخي *naskhī*, A mode of writing.

A نسخية *nusakhīyat*, Distant (city).

A نسر *nasr*, (v. n. of نسر) Tearing (flesh) with the beak (a hawk). Shaving, erasing, flaying, denuding. Slandering. Wounding. Rankling (as a wound). Taking a little food. (pl. انسر *ansur* and نسور *nusūr*) A vulture. An eagle. (pl. نسور *nusūr*) A piece of hard dry flesh like a date-stone on the upper interior part of the hoof of a sheep. The frog of a horse's foot. نسر طائر *nasri tāʾir*, The constellation called the Eagle. النسر الواقع *an' nasru'l wāḳiʿ*, The falling vulture, *i.e.* the Lyre (another constellation). جناح النسر *janāhu'n nasr*, Elecampane. النسر *an' nasr*, Name of an Arabian idol.

P نسر *nasar*, Shade, shadow. The shadow of a mountain or high cap. A hut or wooden shed on the top of a mountain. A shady place. A place impervious to the sun's rays. *Nisar*, A canopy.

P نسرد *nasrud*, *nasurd*, or *nusurd*, A hunter.

P نسرم *nasram*, Name of an idol, of a female figure, in a temple at Bāmeān.

A نسري *nasrī*, Aquiline.

A نسرين *nasrayn*, (oblique dual of نسر *nasr*) The constellations of the Eagle and the Lyre. *Nisrīn*, Name of a flower.

P نسرين *nasrīn*, A wild rose. Name of an island where amber is found.

A نسس *nusus*, Bad roots or origins.

A نسط *nast*, (v. n. of نسط) Thrusting the hand into the matrix of a mare and extracting therefrom the seed of a low-bred stallion. Wringing (a wet cloth). Striking (with a whip). *Nusut*, Those who extract the fœtus in a bad or preposterous birth.

A نسطاس *nistās*, A proper name.

A نسطور *nustūr*, Nestorius, who appeared in the time of the caliph Māmūn.

A نسطوريّ *nastūrīy*, Nestorian. A Christian.

A نسطورية *nus* or *nastūrīyat*, Nestorian sect.

A نسع *nasʿ*, (v. n. of نسع) Being bare of the gums and loose (the teeth). Having such teeth. Dropping from the gums (the front teeth). Being crook-backed, having crooked teeth; having a collapse of belly. Travelling. *Nisʿ*, The north wind. A kind of twisted thong. A strap with which they bind a camel's pack-saddle. The wrist-joint. *Nusʿ* or *nisʿ*, (pl. of نسعة *nisʿat*) Twisted thongs.

A نسعة *nisʿat*, (pl. نسع *nusʿ*, *nisʿ*, انساع *ansāʿ*

and نسوع *nusūʻ*) A thong twisted with a broad plat. A thong with which they bind a camel's pack-saddle.

A نسعيّة *nasʻiyat*, Northern (wind).

A نسغ *nasgh*, (v. n. of نسغ) Striking (with rod or lash). Brushing (as a baker his bread) with a bunch of feathers. Pricking especially certain figures upon the skin with a needle, and then rubbing them over with woad, indigo, or any thing similar which makes an indelible impression. Stabbing (with reproaches). Travelling, wandering. Being loose (the teeth). Diluting (wine or milk) with water. *Nusgh*, The young sproutings of lopt-trees. Water flowing out of a tree that has been cut.

A نسف *nasf*, (v. n. of نسف) Pulling down (an edifice) to the foundation. Tearing up grass by the roots (a camel). Bruising, pounding small, and scattering. Winnowing (corn). Biting. Bedaubing, plastering. Wiping (the hands). *Nisaf* or *nusuf*, (pl. of نسيفة *nasīfat*) Blackish pumice-stones with which they clean the feet.

A نسفان *nasfān*, Full, overflowing (vessel).

A نسفة *nas, nis, nus*, or *nasafat*, A kind of black pumice-stone with which they clean the feet.

A نسفيّ *nasafīy*, Native of Nasaf.

A نسق *nask*, (v. n. of نسق) Putting in order, making (a speech) coherent, connecting it judiciously. Threading (pearls). *Nasak*, Order, method, series. Arrangement, management. Connection. Style, mode of writing. Well-connected (oration). Strung together (pearls, beads). A well-set row of teeth. (A mouth) with well-set, even teeth. النسق *an' nasak* or *nusuh*, The constellation Orion. حروف النسق *hurūfu'n nasak*, The letters و *wāw* and ف *fā*; also the words ثمّ *summ*, او *aw*, ام *am*, حتّى *hatta'*, بل *bal*, لا *lā*, امّا *ammā*, لكن *lākin*. نسقاً *nasakan*, In rows or ranks (as men or trees).

P نسق *nasak*, Conformable. Manner, habit, order.

A نسقان *naskāni*, Two stars near الفكّة *al fakkat*, one on the right, the other on the left.

P نسك *nask*, A lentil. Name of a triangular thorny plant. *Nusk*, A section or part of the Zand (of which there are twenty-one).

A نسك *nask*, (v. n. of نسك) Cleaning (a garment), washing with water. Rendering (saltish ground) sweet and wholesome. Persevering in a correct line of conduct. *Nusk, nask, nisk*, or *nusuk*, (v. n. of نسك) Being religous, devout; virtuous, dedicating, or sacrificing to God. Divine worship, adoration. Every thing due to God. *Nusk* or *nusuk*, A victim, sacrifice. *Nasak*, A frequented place. *Nusak*, A kind of bird. *Nusuk*, The blood of a victim. (pl. of نسيكة *nasikat*) Sacrifices, victims.

P نسكا *naskā*, The earth, ground.

P نسكبا *nask-bā*, Lentil-broth.

A نسكة *naskat*, (v. n. of نسك) Being religious, devoted to the worship of God.

P نسكنج *naskanj*, A tickling, pinching.

A نسل *nasl*, (v. n. of نسل) (An animal) begetting or bringing forth (many young). Changing (the feathers), moulting. Casting (the coat). Running fast. Slipping from off the shoulders (a cloak). Losing one's wits. (pl. انسال *ansāl*) Offspring, progeny, lineage, pedigree, genealogy, descendants, descent, relationship, stock, race, breed, caste, family. نسل ادهم *nasli adham*, Wine made from black grapes. *Nasal*, (v. n. of نسل) Making haste, running fast. Milk flowing spontaneously from the dug; also from a green fig.

A نسلان *nasalān*, (v. n. of نسل) Making haste (in running). Slipping off the shoulders (a cloak).

A نسليّ *naslīy*, Of family.

A نسم *nasam*, (v. n. of نسم) Blowing gently (wind), breathing (as odours). Changing, corrupting (in smell). A kind of green and swift-flying bird. The scent of milk. The smell of grease. Beginning, commencement, exordium. The first blast of wind, that especially which is the forerunner of a gale. A defaced or indistinct path. (pl. انسام *ansām*) Respiration. A gentle breeze. (pl. of نسمة *nasamat*) Souls, spirits. Men.

A نسمان *nasamān*, (v. n. of نسم) Blowing gently (wind), breathing (perfume).

A نسمة *nasamat*, Breathing, respiration. An asthma. (pl. نسم *nasam* and نسمات *nasamāt*) A man. A purchased slave.

P نسميل *nasmīl*, Congruous, agreeing, suiting. One who fixes his residence anywhere.

A نسناس *nasnās* or *nisnās*, A kind of ape, a marmoset; an ourang-outang, satyr, fawn. A monstrous race of men or demons who have only one leg and one arm, and move by leaping. قرب نسناس *karabun nasnāsun*, A swift nocturnal journey in quest of water. قطع الله نسناسه *kataʻa'llāhu nasnāsahu*, May God efface his vestiges! ناقة ذات نسناس *nākatun zātu nasnāsin*, A she-camel with remains of strength for travelling.

A نسنسة *nasnasat*, (v. n. of نسنس Q) Flying rapidly (a bird). Driving or calling out to camels. Being weak. Blowing cold (wind).

P نسو *na* or *nisū*, Slippery, smooth, bright (mirror, sword). نسو كردن *nasū kardan*, To polish, smooth, brighten.

A نسوء *nasuʼ*, A woman supposed pregnant.

A نسوان *niswān*, Women, ladies.

A نسوانيّ *niswānīy*, Feminine, womanly.

P نسوبار *nasūbār*, (in zand and Pāz.) Fasting.

A نسوة *naswat*, (v. n. of نسي) Forgetting. Neglect or abandonment (of work). One draught of milk. *Niswat* or *nuswat*, Women (the singular in use is مرءة *marʼat*, A woman).

A نسوج *nasūj*, (A she-camel) going or trotting fast and throwing the load on her withers. One which carries a burden steadily.

P نسود *nasūd*, Soft, smooth, slippery.

P نسودي *nasūdī*, The agricultural class, or the third of the four orders, into which Jamshed, king of Persia in ancient times, divided his subjects.

A نسور *nusūr*, (pl. of نسر *nasr*) Eagles. Vultures. Pieces of flesh hard and dry between the hoofs of sheep, or on the frog of a horse's foot.

A نسوس *nusūs*, Dryness.

A نسوع *nusūʻ*, (v. n. of نسع) Being bare (the gums). Being loose (the teeth). Having such teeth. Being crooked-backed, having crooked teeth; having the belly fallen in. Travelling. Length. (pl. of نسعة *nisʻat*) Twisted thongs with which they bind camels' pack-saddles.

A نسوف *nasūf*, (pl. مناسيف *manāsīf*) (A camel) tearing up grass by the roots. (A horse) moving the feet near the ground when running: one that brings his elbows near the girth. Long and difficult (ascent of a mountain). *Nusūf*, (v. n. of نسف) Biting. Mark of a bite.

A نسول *nusūl*, (v. n. of نسل) Changing (the feathers), moulting. Shedding his coat (a horse). Dropping off. Falling, slipping off (garments).

A نسولة *nasūlat*, (A female) kept for breeding.

A نسون *nisūn*, Women, the female sex.

A نسويّ *niswīy*, Womanly, feminine, female.

A نسها *nasahā*, Veiny.

P نسهانتن *nas-hānitan*, (in zand & Pāz.) To cook.

A نسي *nasy*, (v. n. of نسي) Hurting the nerve of the thigh called نسا *nasa'*. Striking upon the vein نسا *nasa'*. *Nisy*, (v. n. of نسي) Forgetting. Neglecting, omitting. *Nisy* or *nasy*, (pl. انساء *ansāʼ*) A thing forgotten or unworthy to be remembered. Amenstruous cloth thrown away. Any thing thrown away or dropt as useless. *Nasa'*, (v. n. of نسي) Suffering in the nerve نسا *nasa'*, being troubled with sciatica. *Nasī*, Troubled with sciatica.

A نسيء *nasīʼ*, Thin, watery milk. Credit. An embolism of a month, or rather the throwing on of one, as محرّم *muharram* into صفر *safar*.

A نسيّ *nasīy*, One who is not numbered with others, as despised or unworthy. Forgetful. Intercalary days of a lunar year.

A نسياء *nasyāʼ*, (A woman) pained in the nerve نسا *nasa'*, troubled with sciatica.

A نسيًا منسيًّا *nasyan mansīyan*, By forgetfulness and neglect.

A نسيان *nasyān*, Forgetful. *Nisyān*, (v. n. of نسي) Forgetting. Leaving, abandoning. Forgetfulness. Oblivion. Lethargy.

P نسيان *nisyān*, Opposition, contradiction.

A نسيب *nasīb*, (v. n. of نسب) Celebrating (a mistress) in verse. Conformable, corresponding. Related to another. High in rank or birth. Erotic, amatory poetry. نسيب ناسب *nasīb nāsib*, Polished amatory verse.

A نسئة *nus* or *nisʼat*, Purchase or sale on credit. بعته بنسئة *biʻtuhu bi nusʼatin*, I sold it on credit.

A نسيّة *nusayyat*, (dim. of نسوة) Little women.

A نسيج *nasīj*, Woven. Incomparable, sole, unique. A weaver.

A نسيجة *nasījat*, A web, any thing woven. Across (as one wind to another).

P نسيچ *nasīch*, A kind of silken stuff embroidered with gold. Weak in mind, foolish. Pleased with one's self.

A نسيخة *nasīkhat*, Distant (city).

P نسيدن *nasīdan*, To put, place, leave.

P نسيرم *nasīram*, A place where the sun shines not. A window. A skylight.

A نسيس *nasīs*, The last breath, remains of life. Great diligence, excessive labour or study, vigorous effort. Extreme hunger. Nature, innate disposition, natural form. Two veins in the brain. بلغ منه نسيسه *balagha minhu nasīsuhu* or نسيسته *nasīsatuhu*, He is almost dead.

A نسيسة *nasīsat*, (pl. نسائس *nasāʼis*) Detraction, slander, private malicious whispering. The moisture of a burning billet exuding at the end out of the fire. Nature, quality, temperament.

A نسيغ *nasīgh*, Perspiration, sweat.

A نسيف *nasīf*, A secret, any thing spoken in a whisper. The mark of a bite of an ass. The mark left in running a race.

A نسيفة *nasīfat*, (pl. نسف *nisaf*, نساف *nisāf*, and نسف *nusuf*) A kind of blackish pumice-stone with which they rub the feet. Black burnt stones.

A نسيق *nasīḳ*, Joined in order.

A نسيك *nasīk*, Gold and silver.

A نسيكة *nasīkat*, (pl. نسك *nusuk* and نسائك *nasāʼik*) A sacrifice, victim. An ingot of gold or silver.

A نسيل *nasīl*, Melted honey separated from the wax. Feathers or hairs falling from animals.

A نسيلا *nasīlā*, Veined. Of good breed.

A نسيلة *nasīlat*, Offspring. A wick. Honey.

P نسيله *na* or *nusīla*, A string or troop of horses.

A نسيم *nasīm*, (v. n. of نسم) Breathing gently (wind, odours). Gentle breeze, zephyr, fragrant air, spicy gale. Breath. Perspiration. نسيم سحر *nasīmi sahar*, Morning-breeze. P نسيم عنبرشميم *nasīmi ʻambar-shamīm*, A gale sweet as ambergris.

P نسيمن *nasīman*, (in zand) Prayer, worship.

P نسيه *nasiya*, Delay, adjournment, respite, credit. به نسيه خريدن *ba nasiya kharīdan*, To buy on credit.

A نسيء *nasīʼ*, Delayed, deferred. Delay. A selling on credit. النسيء *an' nasīʼ*, A month which the Pagan Arabians kept holy instead of another: as, صفر *safar* for محرّم *muharram*, in order that three months, during which they were prohibited from fighting, might not follow one another. (In old times they lived almost entirely on plunder, and a tedious peace was distressing.)

A نسيئة *nasīʼat*, Delay, respite; credit.

P نش *nash*, Shade, a shady place. The shadow of a lofty cap. *Nush*, Alike, resembling, equal. Phlebotomy. A wild pine-tree.

A نشّ *nashsh*, (v. n. of نشّ) Driving gently. Mixing. A weight of twenty درهم dirhams, dirhems, or drachmas.

A نشء *nashʼ*, (v. n. of نشأ) Growing, increasing; growing up, being educated (amongst others). Creating. Rising, being high (as a cloud). A high cloud, or one beginning to gather. (pl. نشأ *nashaʼ*) A young camel. (pl. of ناشيء) Youths. Young women.

A نشأ *nashaʼ*, (pl. of نشء *nashʼ*) Young camels. (pl. of ناشيء *nāshiʼ*) Youths. Young women.

A نشا *nasha'*, An agreeable smell. A headache or crop-sickness (from over-drinking). (pl. of نشاة *nashāt*) Young trees. (for نشاستج *nashāstaj*) Starch.

A نشاء *nashāʼ*, (v. n. of نشأ) Growing, increasing; growing up (amongst). Being borne upward (a cloud). Creating. Starch. An agreeable smell.

A نشاءة *nashāʼat*, (v. n. of نشأ) Appearing, being produced. Growing. Any thing produced or growing. Creating.

A نشّاب *nashshāb*, An arrow-maker. *Nushshāb*, (pl. of نشّابة *nushshābat*) Arrows.

A نشّابة *nashshābat*, Archers. *Nushshābat*, An arrow, especially a Persian arrow, made of wood; an Arabian one, being a reed, is called سهم *sahm*.

P نشابور *nishābūr*, (or نشاپور *nishāpūr*) One of the capitals of Khurāsān. The word is said to imply the city of Shāpūr. Name of a note in music.

A نشأة *nashʼat*, (v. n. of نشأ) Growing. Appearing, being produced. Being borne upward (a cloud). Creating. Any thing produced, growing. Creature. نشأة الاولى *nashʼatu'l ūla'*, First creation. نشأة الاخري *nashʼatu'l ukhra'*, Last creation.

A نشاة *nashāt*, (pl. نشا *nasha'*) A young tree.

A نشات *nashāt*, A creature. Any thing produced or growing. Appearing, growing.

A نشاتين *nashātayn*, This world and the next.

A نشّاح *nashshāh*, Full and trickling (bottle).

P نشاختن *nishākhtan*, (or نشاخيدن *nishākhīdan*) To fix in the ground. To establish, strengthen, appoint, specify.

P نشاخور *nashā-khwur*, A person who takes intoxicating drugs, a drunkard.

A نشاد *nishād*, (v. n. 3 of نشد) Praying, beseeching, conjuring.

A نشادر *nushādir* or *nishādir*, Sal-ammoniac.

A نشارة *nushārat*, Sawdust.

P نشاره *nishāra*, Rotten wood falling to powder.

P نشاريدن *nishārīdan*, To scatter, bestow gifts.

A نشاز *nashāz*, A high place. *Nishāz*, (pl. of نشز *nashz*) High places.

A نشاستج *nashāstaj*, (from P نشاسته) Starch.

P نشاستن *nishāstan*, To cause to sit, place, seat.

P نشاسته *nishāsta*, Starch. Placed, seated.

A نشّاشة *nashshāshat*, Salsuginous ground, producing no grass.

A نشاص *nashāṣ*, Persons of the same age. A crowd of young girls. Equal herds (of horses or camels). *Nishāṣ* or *nashāṣ*, (pl. نشص *nushus*) A high, towering cloud.

A نشاصيّ *nashāṣīy*, (A horse) whose buttocks or other extremities are prominent.

A نشاط *nashāt*, (v. n. of نشط) Being brisk, lively, sprightly. Growing fat with excellent pasture (a horse). Cheerfulness, gladness, glee, joy, exultation, triumph, briskness, pleasure. *Nishāt*, (pl. of نشيط *nashīt*) Brisk, cheerful, lively.

A نشاطي *nashāṭī*, Cheerful, brisk, lively, saucy.

A نشاعة *nushāʻat*, Any thing torn up with the hand and thrown away.

P نشاف *nishāf*, Dryness in the mouth from extreme hunger.

A نشاف *nishāf*, (pl. of نشفة *nashfat*) Black pumice-stones with which they rub the feet.

A نشّاف *nashshāf*, One who dips bread into the pot, and eats it slily by himself. P كاغذ نشّاف *kāghizi nashshāf*, Blotting-paper.

A نشافة *nushāfat*, Froth of new milk. Bilge-water.

A نشّافة *nashshāfat*, A napkin.

A نشاقي *nashāḳa'*, Deer or other game caught by the neck in the hunters' toils.

P نشاك *nashāk*, (in zand and Pāzand) Sugar.

A نشّال *nashshāl*, One who dips a sop in the pot and eats it alone.

P نشان *nishān*, A sign, signal, mark, character, seal, stamp, impression, annotation, index. A butt, target (for archers). A trail. An ensign, flag, banner, standard, colours. Family-arms, armorial bearings. The letter of a prince. A goal, term, boundary. A cicatrice, scar. Part, portion, share; chance, lot. (in comp.) Fixing, planting, establishing, allaying, impressing: as, شاه نشان *shāh-nishān*, Establishing a king; حرارت نشان *harārat-nishān*, Allaying heat. خاطر نشان *khātir-nishān*, Impressing the mind. نشان شير و خورشيد *nishāni sher u khwurshed*, The order of the Lion and Sun. نشان كردن *nishān kardan*, To impress, make a mark, sign, or signal. To make an annotation. To resemble. نشان نهادن *nishān nihādan*, To betroth, affiance, or marry a woman by giving her a ring. خاطرنشان *khātir-nishān*, A memorial, remembrance.

P نشان بردار *nishān-bardār*, A standard-bearer.

P نشان دار *nishān-dār*, A standard-bearer, ensign, cornet. Marked, signed. Possessing armorial bearings.

P نشاندگي *nishāndagī*, Insertion, plantation.

P نشاندن *nishāndan*, To mark, delineate, place one thing upon another, in order to make an impression or ornament. To fix in the ground (a stone or stake) by way of signal; to insert; to plant (a tree). To shake (garments). To follow one, to attend, to dog. To quench (a fire) with water, to extinguish. To wipe, clean. To sit, or cause to sit. To prescribe business, to constitute, appoint; to put in order, place. To take aim.

P نشاندهٔ *nishānda*, Planted. نشاندهٔ دستي *nishānda-i dastī*, Planted with (his) own hand.

P نشانستن *nishānistan*, To place, seat, make sit.

P نشانگاه *nishān-gāh*, A butt, target. A goal.

P نشانگر *nishāngar*, One who makes a mark. A pair of compasses. Keeper of the seals.

P نشانه *nishāna*, A butt for archers. A mark, sign, impression.

P نشانه انداز *nishāna-andāz*, Hitting the mark, unerring. A marksman.

P نشاني *nishānī*, A mark, sign, token. Signature. A token of remembrance.

P نشانيدن *nishānīdan*, To mark, impress. To quench thirst.

P نشاور *nishāwar*, Name of a river in Persia.

P نشايد *nashāyad*, It does not suit; it is disagreeable, improper, or inconvenient.

A نشائيّ *nashāiy*, A maker or vender of starch.

A نشب *nashb*, (v. n. of نشب) Sticking to, being necessary. *Nashab*, (v. n. of نشب) Adhering tenaciously, being fixed firmly. Leaving off, desisting, giving over. Wealth in slaves, cattle, land, live or dead stock. A tree of which they make bows.

A نشبة *nushbat*, (v. n. of نشب) Adhering tenaciously, being firmly fixed. Adhesion, tenacity. A man who sticks close to a thing. A wolf. Name of a man. *Nashabat*, Wealth in live or dead stock.

P نشبره *nishbara*, Part of the food which cattle keep in their mouths to ruminate. A shade.

P نشبيل *nashbil*, Laying one's hands on a thing. Suspending. Sewing or joining two things together.

P نشپيل *nashpīl* or *nishpīl*, A net. A fishing-hook. A hook for hanging any thing up. A hooked pole for pulling down the boughs of fruit-trees.

P نشت *nasht*, Destroyed, ruined, spoiled, lost, perished; withered. Weak, lazy, languid. *Nisht* Well, good, healthy.

P نشتر *nishtar*, A lancet, fleam. A trocar. A canine tooth. نشتر زدن *nishtar zadan*, To apply the lancet, to lance.

P نشتر زده *nishtar-zada*, Lanced.

P نشتن *nishtan*, To sit. To remain.

P نشتو *nashtū*, Name of a man.

P نشتي *nishtī*, Goodness; weal. How are you?

A نشج *nashj*, (v. n. of نشج) Crying, sobbing. Braying (an ass). Shaking, trilling, quavering (a singer). Croaking (a frog). Making a noise (like a boiling pot, or a bottle when decanting). *Nashaj*, (pl. انشاج *anshāj*) An aqueduct, canal, water-course.

A نشح *nashh*, (v. n. of نشح) Drinking, though not sufficient to quench thirst. Drinking enough. Watering (horses). *Nushuh*, Drunkards.

P نشخار *nush* or *nishkhār*, What ruminant animals throw up to be chewed: the cud.

P نشخوار *nishkhwār* or *nushkhwār*, (نشخور *nishkhwur* or نشخوره *nishkhwura*) Chewing the cud. The cud. نشخوار كردن *nushkhwār kardan*, (or زدن *zadan*) To chew the cud, ruminate.

P نشخوار زننده *nishkhwār-zananda*, Ruminant.

A نشد *nashd*, (v. n. of نشد) Seeking (any thing lost). Knowing, recollecting. Giving information to the owner of a thing lost. Asking, inquiring, beseeching for Gods's sake, saying (to one), I conjure you by God! نشدك بالله *nashdaka bi'llāh*, I conjure thee for God's sake!

A نشدان *nishdān*, (v. n. of نشد) Seeking (any thing lost). Asking, inquiring, beseeching for God's sake. Giving information to the owner of a thing lost.

A نشدة *nishdat*, (v. n. of نشد) Seeking (any thing lost). Asking, inquiring, beseeching for the love of God. Giving information to the owner of a thing lost. A sound, noise, voice. Verses which are desired to be repeated.

A نشر *nashr*, (v. n. of نشر) Spreading (a table or carpets); expanding, extending, diffusing. Publishing (news). Dispersing, scattering, strewing. Reviving, recalling to life. Coming to life (one dead). Being scattered (leaves). Putting forth leaves (a tree). Pricking up the ears. Cutting with a saw. Being verdant at the end of summer (ground), being covered with a fresh crop. Blowing on a cloudy day (wind). Averting evil (from another), arming (him) with a talismanic charm. The scab. The first appearance of young herbage. Withering grass refreshed by rain. Life. A fragrant smell. The smell of a woman's breath. The stench of the arm-pits after sleeping. Men scattered without a leader. نشرت الريح *nasharati'r rīh*, The wind blew on a cloudy day. P نشرخوان كردن *nashri khwān kardan*, To cover a table. A *Nashr* or *nashar*, Diffused (wind) scattering clouds and causing rain. *Nushr* or *nushur*, (pl. of نشور *nashūr*) Diffused (winds) scattering clouds and causing rain. *Nashar*, (v. n. of نشر) Being afflicted with a contagious scab (camels). Scattered. Men scattered without a leader. A nocturnal dispersion of sheep pasturing without a shepherd. اللهمّ اضمم نشري *allāhumma azmum nasharī*, An ejaculatory prayer. *Nushur*, Sponte effluens viri sperma.

A نشرة *nushrat*, An amulet, preventive, charm to drive away madness or disease. P نشرهٔ طفلان *nushra-i tiflān*, Any thing written with saffron on the tablets of children for averting evil.

P نشرم *nashram*, A place impervious to the sun.

A نشري *nashra'*, (Camels) troubled with a spreading and contagious scab.

A نشز *nashz*, (v. n. of نشز) Ascending, sitting, standing on a high place. (pl. نشوز *nushūz*, انشاز *anshāz*, and نشاز *nishāz*) A high place. *Nashaz*, A high place. Height of situation. An old man, but sound in body. *Nashiz*, Soft and flaccid.

P نشست *nishast*, He sat down. Sitting. Session. نشست برخاست *nishast bar khāst*, Good-breeding, etiquette, politeness. نشست كردن *nishast kardan*, To sit down. شتر نشست *shutur-nishast*, Sitting or riding a camel. A riding-camel.

P نشستگاه *nishast-gāh*, (or گه *gah*) A place on which one sits. The time or place of sitting. A dwelling, habitation, residence. Buttocks.

P نشستن *nishastan*, To sit down, recline. To sink, settle down, precipitate. To dwell, inhabit. To settle upon (as dust). To remain. To extinguish. To be extinguished.

P نشستن گاه *nashastan-gāh*, The time or place of washing. *Nishastan-gāh*, A place on which one sits. The buttocks.

P نشستني *nishastanī*, Whatever one is carried upon (as a horse, camel, vehicle, or ship). Any place or thing in which one sits.

P نشسته *nishasta*, Sitting. Who sits or resides. (Dust) settled upon (any thing). برهم نشسته *barham nishasta*, Collected together, accumulated, heaped, piled up. فرو نشسته *faro nishasta*, Low, depressed, humble. Sitting in a low place.

A نشص *nushus*, (pl. of نشاص) Towering clouds.

A نشط *nasht*, (v. n. of نشط) Going out (of a place). Carrying one from place to place (anxiety). Pulling (a bucket) briskly (out of a well) at one draught without the aid of a pulley. Putting (a knot) on a rope. Biting (a serpent). *Nushut*, Those who untwist a rope in order to twist it a second time.

A نشظ *nashz*, A carrying off rapidly.

A نشع *nashą*, (v. n. of نشع) Tearing up or carrying off by violence. Putting any thing into the mouth of an infant. Instructing, teaching. Making a noise in the throat.

A نشغ *nashgh*, (v. n. of نشغ) Making a noise in the throat, as one going to faint; also in grief or any other violent emotion. Suggesting or teaching (a speech). Flowing (water). Piercing. Pouring (medicine) down a child's throat. Drinking (water) from the hand.

A نشّغ *nushshagh*, (pl. of ناشغ *nāshigh*) Those who make a noise in the throat.

A نشف *nashf*, (v. n. of نشف) Going away, perishing. (A garment) imbibing (perspiration), or a cistern (water), or paper (ink). Sinking into the ground (water). *Nishf*, *nashaf*, *nishaf*, and *nushaf*, (pl. of نشفة *nash*, *nish*, *nush*, and *nashafat*) Black, burnt-looking pumice-stones. *Nashaf*, Ground imbibing water, or the water so sucked up.

A نشفة *nashfat*, A clout with which rain-water is sucked up and wrung out into a vessel. *Nashfat*, *nishfat*, *nushfat*, or *nashafat*, (pl. نشف *nashaf*, *nishf*, *nishaf*, *nushaf*, and نشاف *nishāf*) A pumice-stone for rubbing the feet. *Nishfat* or *nushfat*, A little remaining in the bottom of a vessel. Whatever is taken with a ladle out of a boiling pot and sipped hot. *Nushfat*, Froth of new milk. *Nashi-*

fat, Ground which imbibes water.

A نشق *nashk*, (v. n. of نشق) Smelling (any thing fragrant); snuffing up (medicine or perfume). Being caught and entangled in a toil (a deer). Odour, perfume. مكروه النشق *makrūhu'n nashk*, Of a disagreeable flavour or smell. *Nashik*, One who embarrasses himself in affairs from which he cannot extricate himself.

A نشقة *nushkat*, A rope which they tie round the neck of brutes.

P نشك *nashk*, A pomegranate. A wild pine. *Nashk* or *nashik*, Dragons'-wort, an herb. A hard fruitless tree. Tooth of elephant, hog, or serpent.

P نشكرد گازران *nashkardi gāzurān*, A sponge.

P نشكرده *nishkar*, *nishkur*, or *nushkurda*, A shoemaker's knife. A graving-tool, scraper.

P نشكنج *nishkunj*, Pinching. Tickling, twitching.

P نشكنجيدن *nishkunjīdan*, To pinch, nip, twitch.

P نشگرده *nishgir* or *garda*, A cobbler's knife.

A نشل *nashl*, (v. n. of نشل) Pulling away or carrying off with violence. Taking (meat out of a cauldron) with the hands, with a flesh-hook, or any thing but a ladle. Taking up meat or a bone in the hand, and eating or gnawing it. Lying with. Dressing meat without aromatics, spiceries, or pot-herbs. *Nashil*, One who takes meat out of the pot with his hands, with a flesh-hook, or any thing but a ladle.

P نشل *nashal*, Sticking, glueing. Suspending, hanging up. Being hung up. Suspension. A fish-hook.

P نشليدن *nashlīdan*, To hang up, be suspended.

A نشم *nasham*, (v. n. of نشم) Being marked with black and white specks. A kind of tree of which they make bows. *Nashim*, (A bull) marked with black and white spots. (fem. نشمة *nashimat*) Stinking (hand with cheese or grease).

P نشمن *nashman*, Fortune. A seat. A throne. *Nishmin*, A people, nation, tribe, family.

P نشمين *nashmīn*, A native country.

A نشناش *nashnāsh*, Light and active (in the arm). Salsuginous, barren (ground).

A نشنشة *nashnashat*, (v. n. of نشنش Q) Making a bubbling noise when boiling (water). Flaying, skinning very rapidly. Rattling, sounding (a coat of mail). Pluming himself (a bird), and scattering (his) feathers. Gobbling (meat) in haste. Driving on, urging forward, pushing onward. Repelling, driving off. Agitating, putting in violent motion. Pulling off (clothes). Shaking or pulling any thing out of a vase. Loosing down (drawers). Lying with. The noise of a boiling pot. *Nishnishat*, (equiv. to شنشنة *shinshinat*) Nature, temper, disposition. A part, portion. A stone. نشنشة من اخشن *nishnishat min akhshana*, A stone from a mountain.

A نشنشيّ *nashnashīy*, Light, active in the arm.

P نشنيدني *nashnīdani*, Unfit to be heard.

P نشنيده *nashnīda*, Who hears not; unheard.

A نشو *nashw*, (v. n. of نشا for نشو) Inquiring whence (news) comes. Being intoxicated. Making a habit or custom, returning to a thing repeatedly. Being indisposed from the scent of the shrub عضاه *ʻizāh* (camels).

A نشوء *nushuʼ*, (v. n. of نشأ) Increasing, rising, growing up (as a boy). Springing, sprouting, being produced. Being raised (a cloud). A vegetive, vegetable. Vegetation.

P نشو *nushū*, Plain, level, smooth, slippery.

A نشوء *nushūʼ*, (v. n. of نشأ) Creating. Living. Growing up. P نشويافتن *nushū yāftan*, To grow up.

P نشوا *nashwā*, Oxyacanth-fruit. Wild plum.

P نشواد *nashwād*, Name of a hero of Tūrān.

P نشوار *nishwār*, Ruminating. A man's name.

A نشوار *nishwār*, Food which a ruminating animal keeps in the mouth to chew. A stall for cattle.

P نشوارة *nishwāra*, Frankincense. A shade.

A نشوان *nashwān*, Intoxicated.

A نشوب *nushūb*, (v. n. of نشب) Adhering tenaciously; becoming fixed, inherent. (pl. of نشب *nashab*) Riches in slaves, cattle, lands, in live or dead stock.

A نشوة *nashwat*, (v. n. of نشا for نشو) Examining (into intelligence). Intoxication. Odour, perfume; thing smelt. An orange of the same year. *Nash*, *nish*, or *nushwat*, (v. n. of نشا for نشو) Perceiving (an agreeable smell); smelling to (any thing). Being overcome with wine, crop-sick. Making a habit or custom of any thing, returning to it repeatedly. Ailing from the smell of the shrub عضاه *ʻizāh* (cattle). *Nishwat*, Inquiry into news.

A نشوح *nashūh*, A little water. *Nushūh*, (v. n. of نشح) Drinking, yet not so as to quench the thirst. Drinking enough. Watering (horses).

A نشور *nashūr*, (pl. نشر *nushr* and *nushur*) (Wind) diffused, scattering clouds, and causing rain. *Nushūr*, (v. n. of نشر) Rising from the dead, reviving. Receiving vernal showers and putting forth vegetation (ground). Recalling to life. Resurrection. بعث و نشور *baʻs u nushūr*, The day of resurrection, the rising and the resurrection. يوم النشور *yawmu'n nushūr*, The day of resurrection.

A نشورة *nashwarat*, (v. n. of نشور Q) Keeping a little food in the mouth to chew (ruminating camel).

P نشوره *nishwara*, Frankincense.

A نشوز *nushūz*, (v. n. of نشز) Catching upon the horn and throwing on the ground. Being disobedient to her husband (a woman), provoking him to use her ill. Being angry and ill-treating his wife (a man). Being greatly moved, boiling (the soul). (pl. of نشز *nashz*) High places.

A نشوص *nashūs*, Straight, upright (spear). *Nushūs*, (v. n. of نشص) Being high (a cloud). Being put out of its place, disturbed. Being torn away from home or country. Projecting (as a tooth). Being disobedient (a woman), and averse from her husband. Provoking to anger. Boiling (with rage). Piercing with a spear. Leading, drawing, or taking out. Being agitated (the heart).

A نشوط *nashūt*, A deep well, whence a bucket cannot be easily or quickly drawn out. A fish which is generally eaten salted.

A نشوظ *nushūz*, (v. n. of نشظ) Germinating, just appearing, vegetating, sprouting.

A نشوع *nashūʻ*, One who breathes hard. *Nashūʻ* or *nushūʻ*, A medicine swallowed or snuffed up. Whatever drives back the breath. *Nushūʻ*, (v. n. of نشع) Suggesting (a speech to another), putting it into his mouth; teaching, making him understand it. Recovering at the point of death.

A P نشوغ *nashūgh*, A medicine which is taken in the mouth, or snuffed up.

A نشوف *nashūf*, A she-camel giving milk before the birth, and then ceasing.

A نشوق *nashūk*, A medicine snuffed up.

A نشول *nushūl*, (v. n. of نشل) Being lean (the thigh). Drawing (a thing) out with haste. Lying with.

P نشو نما *nashw numā*, Growing up.

P نشوه *nashwa*, Drunkenness. *Nishwa*, The mixture of any ingredients to form a composition, especially medicine, as antidotes against venom; treacle. Exhilaration from wine.

P نشوه بخش *nashwa-bakhsh*, Inebriating.

A نشوى *nashwa'*, Name of a place in Azarbayjān.

P نشوي *nashwī*, The city of نخچوان *nakhchawān*.

P نشي *nashī*, A porcupine, hedgehog.

A نشيان *nashyān*, One who inquires after or learns any news: one who obtains the earliest information. Drunk, intoxicated.

P نشيب *nishīb*, A descent, declivity. Low, hollow. نشيب زمين *nishībi zamīn*, Lowness of ground, slope of any place. نشيب و فراز *nishīb u firāz*, Descent and ascent.

P نشيب فراز *nishīb farāz*, Up and down. The ups and downs of life. Profit and loss; the advantages and disadvantages of any affair.

P نشيبگاه *nishīb-gāh*, A descent; low place.

A نشيّة *nashīyat*, A smell perceived or felt.

A نشيج *nashīj*, (v. n. of نشج) Crying, sobbing, weeping, being choked.

A نشيد *nashīd*, Verses which people recite alternately. A raising of the voice.

P نشيد *nished*, Song, poetry.

P نشيدن *nishīdan*, To put, to place.

A نشير *nashīr*, An apron worn by girls; zone, belt, girdle. Unthreshed grain in a barn.

P نشيره *nashīra*, Frankincense.

A نشيش *nashīsh*, (v. n. of نشّ) Failing, drying up, being exhaled or absorbed in the ground (water). Making a hissing noise (meat when roasting, or a hot iron immersed in water). The noise of any thing boiling. Barren, salsuginous (ground).

A نشيص *nashīs*, Straight, upright (spear).

Bread baked of dough and properly leavened.

A نشيط *nashīt*, Brisk, cheerful, frisky. One who has sprightly horses or cheerful domestics. Name of a certain architect. النشيط *an' nashīt*, A horse (especially swift and spirited).

A نشيطة *nashītat*, Booty which a soldier plunders on his route before arriving at the destined place of expedition. (Camels) hired, and driven beyond their strength, or the agreement made with their owner.

P نشيل *nashīl*, Hanged, suspended.

A نشيل *nashīl*, Meat dressed alone, without pot-herbs, spiceries, and the like. Milk whilst milking. Water just drawn from the well. (Meat) taken out of the pot with the hand or a fork. A thin sword.

A نشيلا *nashīlā*, Intoxicating.

P نشيم *nishem*, A bird's nest. A resting-place.

P نشيمن *nisheman*, A seat, bench, stool, chair. A settlement, mansion; one's native country. A bird's nest. نشيمن ديو *nisheman-dev*, The world.

P نشيمه *nashīma*, Raw hides used for sword-belts and the like.

P نشين *nishīn*, The north pole. The outward covering of a cushion. The skin inside the anus. (in composition) Sitting, sitting down or along with. An associate. A successor. صفّه نشين *suffa-nishīn*, (or اورنگ نشين *awrang-nishīn*) Sitting on a throne, *i.e.* a reigning prince. كشتي نشين *kashtī-nishīn*, Sailing, sitting in a ship. گوشه نشين *gosha-nishīn*, Sitting in a corner, *i.e.* solitary. ويرانه نشين *werāna-nishīn*, Inhabiting a desert; hermit.

P نشيننده *nishīnanda*, Sitting; seated.

P نشيو *nishīv*, Steep. A declivity, descent.

A نشيّ *nashīy*, A cloud just appearing.

A نشيئة *nashī'at*, A rising again and again from bed. The foundation or bottom of a cistern or watering-trough: a stone placed at the bottom of it. Earth raised behind the stones or wall of a cistern. Any thing produced or growing. A moist date.

A نصّ *nass*, (v. n. of نصّ) Elevating, raising. Placing one thing upon another (especially furniture). Causing (a bride) to sit on a bridal throne. Manifesting, demonstrating, exhibiting. Referring or submitting any thing to the opinion of others. Going or driving fast, getting the utmost (out of a camel). Interrogating close, examining an evidence. Moving (especially the nose in anger). Appealing to a king, referring to the highest authority. Appointing. The term (of full age). Quick, smart (pace). History, tradition. Demonstration, proof. The Kur'ān. نصّ كريم *nassi karīm*, An oracle, mandate, or text of the Kur'ān.

A نصا *nasw*, (v. n. of نصا) Raising, lifting up. Checking, crying out to (a camel). Taking hold of the forelocks.

A نصاء *nisā*, (v. n. 3 of نصا for نصو) Taking hold of (another's) forelocks when fighting. Touching, joining.

A نصاب *nisāb*, (v. n. 3 of نصب) Conspiring against (any one), laying snares for (him). Root, origin, principle. A certain estate or number of cattle, for which a tax is paid (as 200 dirhems, or five camels). The bladder of a fish. A return. Capital, principal, property. (pl. نصب *nusub*) Handle (of a knife). Setting of the sun. Dignity; fortune. نصاب الصبيان *nisābu's sibyān*, (lit. The capital stock of children) Title of an Arabic vocabulary with a Persian translation in rhyme. صاحب نصاب *sāhib-nisāb*, High in dignity, fortunate. افادت نصاب *ifādat-nisāb*, Learned (instructor).

A نصّاب *nassāb*, Sly, cunning, plotful.

A نصاح *nisāh*, (pl. نصح *nus-h* and نصاحة *nisāhat*) A thread in a needle.

A نصّاح *nassāh*, A tailor. *Nussāh*, (pl. of ناصح *nāsih*) Counsellers, advisers. Sincere friends.

A نصاحات *nisāhāt*, Hides. Ropes with nooses placed for catching monkeys.

A نصاحة *nasāhat*, (v. n. of نصح) Advising, giving counsel. *Nisāhat*, (pl. of نصاح *nisāh*) Threads.

A نصاحية *nasāhiyat*, An advising, giving counsel.

A نصّار *nassār*, A name common amongst the Arabians. *Nussār*, (pl. of ناصر *nāsir*) Assistants.

A نصاري *nasāra'*, (in construction نصارا *nasārā*) (pl. of نصران *nasrān*) Christians, Nazarenes.

A نصّاص *nassās*, One who draws up (the nose).

A نصاعة *nasā'at*, (v. n. of نصع) Being pure, bright (colour); very white, snow-coloured.

A نصاف *nisāf* or *nasāf*, (v. n. of نصف) Serving (as a domestic).

A نصافة *nisāfat* or *nasāfat*, (v. n. of نصف) Serving (as a domestic). Taking half.

A نصال *nisāl*, (pl. of نصل) Points, spear-heads.

A نصائب *nasā'ib*, Stones built round a cistern, the interstices of which are filled with clay.

A نصائح *nasā'ih*, (pl. of نصيحة *nasīhat*) Counsels, advices, admonitions. P نصائح پر مصالح *nasā'ihi pur masālih*, Salutary advice, admonitions full of safety. نصائح صالحهٔ پيران *nasā'ihi sāliha'i pīrān*, The sound admonitions of the aged.

A نصب *nasb*, (v. n. of نصب) Erecting, establishing, fixing, planting, elevating, exalting, rearing. Playing tricks upon, plotting. Removing. Striving. Driving camels and singing or humming a certain tune. Bringing down, making low. Declaring war. Indisposing, distempering, wearying (as sickness). Opposing (an enemy). Bearing hatred. Travelling languidly, with a slow, fatigued pace. Leaving off, giving over. Marking a consonant with the vowel fatha ـَ *a*. (pl. انصاب *ansāb*) Any thing erected, as a stature, image, or idol. A milestone, direction-post. A butt, goal, boundary, end, extremity. A net spread for game. Disease, calamity. Perfection, accuracy of rhythm in a poem. The vowel fatha ـَ *a*, which, in the construction or formation of a word, is called فتح *fath*; but in inflexion or declension is called نصب *nasb*. نصب العرب *nasbu'l 'arab*, A delicate species of Arabian music, softer than حداء *hidā*. نصب العين *nasba'l* or *nusba'l 'ayn*, In full view. اهل النصب *ahlu'n nasb*, The enemies of Alīy. P نصب كردن *nasb kardan*, To settle, fix, appoint. A *Nisb*, Part, portion, lot; good fortune. *Nusb* or *nusub*, A sign, military standard. An idol. Evil, calamity. Sickness, disease. *Nasab*, (v. n. of نصب) Becoming fatigued. Labouring, toiling, striving. Having erect horns. A sign-post. Grief, trouble, affliction, sadness. *Nasib*, Sick, diseased, pained. *Nusub*, A milestone, a direction-post. A signal. An idol. (pl. of نصاب *nisāb*) Handles, hafts, hilts.

A نصباء *nasbā*, (fem. of انصب *ansab*) (A she-goat) having erect horns or a stretched-out breast.

A نصبة *nasbat*, Opposition, resistance to a hostile attack. *Nusbat*, A ship's mast. A raised column.

A نصّة *nassat*, A hen-sparrow. *Nussat*, A plaiting of the hair. The hair on a woman's forehead.

A نصت *nast*, (v. n. of نصت) Keeping silence.

A نصتة *nustat*, Silence.

A نصح *nus-h*, (v. n. of نصح) Advising, giving counsel. Being sincere. Sewing (a garment). Drinking sufficiently. Watering a country (rain) until it is quite covered by vegetation. (pl. of نصاح *nisāh*) Threads in needles ready for sewing.

A نصّح *nussah*, (pl. of ناصح *nāsih*) Monitors. Sincere friends.

A نصحاء *nusahā*, (pl. of نصيح *nasīh*) Faithful. Faithful admonishers or advisers.

A نصر *nasara*, (fut. ينصر *yansuru*) He aided.

A نصر *nasr*, (v. n. of نصر) Succouring, helping. Rescuing, delivering (from evil). Supplying, feeding (as a tributary stream). Giving. Watering (the earth) plentifully (rain). Assistance, aid. Victory. A gift, present. A helper. Name of the founder of an Arabian tribe. (pl. of ناصر *nāsir*) Helpers, assistants. نصر من الله *nasrun min allāh*, Victory from God. *Nusar*, Helpers.

A بخت نصّر *nukhtu nassar*, Nebuchadnezzar.

A نصراء *nusarā*, pl. of نصير, Assistants: defenders.

A نصران *nasrān*, (pl. نصاري *nasāra'*) A Christian, Nazarene. Name of a town in Syria.

A نصرانة *nasrānat*, (pl. نصاري *nasāra'*) A Christian woman. (Used only by Muhammadans.)

A نصرانيّ *nasrānīy*, A Christian. Belonging to Christianity. (A word not used by Christians.)

A نصرانيّة *nasrānīyat*, A Christian woman. النصرانيّة *an' nasrānīyat*, Christianity.

A نصرة *nusrat*, Assistance, help, defence, efficient aid. Victory.

P نصرت جو *nusrat-jo*, Seeking victory, warlike.

P نصرت گستر *nusrat-gustar*, Victorious.

A نصريّ *nasrīy*, Triumphal, victorious.

A نصريّون *nasrīyūn*, Name of a sect.

A نصع *nasع, nisع*, or *nusع*, A kind of white cloth or leather. *Nisaع*, A piece of leather on which they sit, or on which they play at draughts.

A نصف *nasf*, (v. n. of نصف) Reaching to the middle of any thing. Taking the half of what is in a cup. Going through the half (of the Kur'ān). Arriving at middle-age. Reaching to the middle of the thigh (a garment). Serving (as a domestic). Being about mid-day. A half. Middle-aged. *Nisf*, (v. n. of نصف) Taking half, halving. The half. (A man, men, or woman) of a middle stature or age. نصف آخر *nisfi ākhar*, The last half. نصف النهار *nisfu'n nahār*, In the middle of the day; noon. نصف الليل *nisfu'l layl*, Midnight. P در نصف الليل *dar nisfu'l layl*, In the middle of the night. در نصف طريق *dar nisfi tarīk*, In the middle of the journey. A *Nusf*, (pl. انصاف *ansāf*) Half. *Nusf* or *nusuf*, (pl. of نصف *nasaf*) Middle-aged (women). *Nasaf*, Justice, equity. (pl. انصاف *ansāf* and نصفين *nasafīn*) Middle-aged (man). (pl. انصاف *ansāf*, نصف *nusuf*, and *nusf*) (A woman) advanced in years, about forty or fifty. (pl. of ناصف *nāsif*) Domestics, servants.

A نصفان *nasfān*, Half-full (vessel).

A نصفانصف *nisf-ā-nisf*, Half, dividing in two, cutting through the middle, being in the middle.

A نصفة *nasfat*, Justice, equity. An equitable transaction. *Nasafat*, Middle-aged.

A نصفى *nasfa'*, (fem. of نصفان) Half-full (vessel).

P نصفي *nisfī*, A sort of wine-goblet. A kind of astrolabe. Bad silver, base coin. Name of a musical instrument.

A نصل *nasl*, (v. n. of نصل) Being firmly fixed in any thing (an arrow). Infixing an arrow. (pl. انصل *ansul*, نصال *nisāl*, and نصول *nusūl*) The point of a spear, sword, or knife. The head with what it contains. The crown of the head. The hind-head. A prominence or little bump behind the ears. That which the plant بهمى *buhma'* puts forth from the pod. A thread whilst spinning. Length of neck in camels or horses. معول نصل *miعwalun naslun*, A pick-axe deprived of its handle or heft.

A نصلان *naslān*, An iron point of a spear or a knife. A sword-blade without the handle.

A نصلة *naslat*, The crown of the head.

A نصمة *nasmat*, An idol.

A نصناص *nasnās*, (A snake) writhing much, in perpetual motion.

A نصنصة *nasnasat*, (v. n. of نصنص Q) Moving, shaking (any thing) that (it) may settle down into (its) place. Moving (one's tongue). Moving (himself) on (his) knees when preparing to rise from the ground (a camel).

A نصو *nasw*, (v. n. of نصا for نصو) Seizing (one), especially by the forelocks. Extending and drawing out the forelocks. Allowing the forelocks (of a dead person) to grow. Opening, exposing to view. Joining, being united (one desert to another). The belly-ache, or twisting of the bowels.

A نصوح *nasūh*, True, constant, sincere (repentance). A faithful friend. Well sewed. توبهٔ نصوح *tawbaعi na* or *nusūh*, Sincere, unrelapsing penitence.

A نصور *nasūr*, A helper. *Nusūr*, (v. n. of نصر) Assisting, helping, succouring (the oppressed).

A نصوص *nusūs*, (pl. of نصّ *nass*) Demonstrations, proofs, evidences.

A نصوع *nusūع*, (v. n. of نصع) Being pure, lively (colour). Being very white, snow-coloured. Being manifest, clear, evident, conspicuous. Quenching one's thirst. Bringing forth (as a mother). Acknowledging and paying (a debt).

A نصوف *nusūf*, (v. n. of نصف) Having dates partly red and partly green (a palm-tree).

A نصول *nusūl*, (v. n. of نصل) Losing (its) dye (the hair or beard). Losing (its) head (a spear). Losing its virus (a venomous bite). Falling off (a nail or hoof). Being firmly fixed in any thing (an arrow). (pl. of نصل *nasl*) Spear-heads.

A نصيّ *nasīy*, A species of white thistle. (pl. of نصيّة *nasīyat*) Most excellent, choicest.

A نصيب *nasīb*, (pl. انصباء *ansibāء* and انصبة *ansibat*) A part, portion. Chance, lot. Good fortune. Fate, destiny. A spread net. A prize (in a lottery). A fish-pond. P نصيب شدن *nasīb shudan*, To have the fortune (to gain any thing), to be destined. بي نصيب شدن *bī nasīb shudan*, To be frustrated, to be deprived of. To be unfortunate.

A *Nusayb*, Name of a poet.

A نصيبة *nasībat*, A thing erected for a signal.

P نصيبدار *nasīb-dār*, A partaker; one who receives what he is entitled to by lot.

P نصيبداش *nasīb-dāsh*, A companion in fortune, having the same fate or lot.

A نصيبون *nasībūn*, Nasībīn in Mesopotamia.

P نصيبه *nasība*, A lot, fortune.

P نصيبه وار *nasībawār*, Fortunate.

A نصيبيّ *nasībīy*, A native of Nasībīn.

A نصيبين *nasībīn*, Nisibis in Mesopotamia.

A نصيبينيّ *nasībinīy*, Belonging to Nasībīn.

A نصيّة *nasīyat*, (pl. نصيّ *nasīy*, انصاء *ansāء*, and اناصي *anāsī*) A chosen thing, the best sort (of people, camels, or the like).

A نصيتة *nusaytat*, Silence.

A نصيح *nasīh*, Faithful. (pl. نصحاء *nusahāء*) An adviser, a monitor.

A نصيحة *nasīhat*, Counsel, advice, exhortation, admonition, reprimand; a sermon. An advertisement, precaution. Moral. P نصيحت كردن *nasīhat kardan*, To exhort, admonish. نصيحت آميز *nasīhat-āmez*, Mixed with good advice. نصيحت پذير *nasīhat-pazīr*, Listening to good advice.

P نصيحت گر *nasīhatgar*, Admonisher, adviser.

A نصيحه *nasīha*, An office for revenue-papers.

A نصير *nasīr*, (pl. انصار *ansār*) An assistant, defender, ally, helper.

A نصيريّ *nusayrīy*, One who believes in the divinity of Alīy.

A نصيص *nasīs*, (v. n. of نصّ) Crackling (as meat laid upon the coals). Boiling (a pot). Quick, smart (pace). A number (of men).

A نصيع *nasīع*, Pure, clear.

A نصيف *nasīf*, Half. A woman's veil; a man's turban, or any covering for the head. (A striped garment) of two colours. A certain measuring instrument or vessel. *Nusayf*, (dim. of نصف *nasaf*) A little middle-aged woman.

A نصيل *nasīl*, (Wheat) threshed and cleared of chaff. The joint under the jaw between the head and neck. Crown of the head. The palate, and the under part of the mouth opposite to it. Beak (of a bird), snout (of a beast), tip (of the nose). An arrow. A small excrescence of flesh in women. An axe. A stone about a cubit in length with which they bruise any thing.

A نضّ *nazz*, (v. n. of نضّ) Flowing gently (water). Exuding (through any vessel). Oozing from the end of a lighted stick (sap). Moving the wings (a bird). Bursting from fulness (a bottle). Becoming possible. Gold or silver money. A little water. Detestable (thing). (See also اظهار *izhār*.)

A نضّاح *nazzāh*, One who draws water by means of a camel, and drives him with it towards a palm-plantation. Strong, far-shooting (bow).

A نضّاحة *nazzāhat*, Any thing allowed to fall drop by drop into the mouth. A kind of aromatic. Who or what throws to a great distance.

A نضاخ *nizākh*, (v. n. 3 of نضخ) Sprinkling water on one another.

A نضّاخ *nazzākh*, Copious (rain).

A نضّاخة *nazzākhat*, Plentifully-flowing (fountain). A cameleopard, giraffe.

A نضار *nazār*, Gold and silver. *Nizār*, (pl. of نضر *nazr*) Golds, silvers. *Nuzār*, Gold. A bead of pure fossile gold. Purest or best part. The tamarisk-tree with long erect branches; also a mountain-species that keeps green without water. *Nuzār* or *nizār*, A wood of which they make vessels. قدح نضار *kadahi nuzār*, A cup made of this wood.

A نضارة *nazārat*, (v. n. of نضر) Flourishing, being green (as a tree). Verdancy, verdure. Beauty, lustre, brightness, freshness, floridness, pleasingness. The tamarisk-tree.

A نضاض *nizāz*, That which is distilled drop by drop. A gift. (pl. of نضيض *nazīz*) Small quantities of milk or water. *Nuzāz*, The best (sort of people).

A نضّاض *nazzāz*, (A serpent) in perpetual motion, whose bite is instant death.

A نضاضة *nuzāzat*, A remainder of water. نضاضة الولد *nuzāzatu'l walad*, The last or youngest child.

A نضّاضة *nazzāzat*, (A serpent) in perpetual motion, whose bite is instant death.

A نضال *nizāl,* (v. n. 3 of نضل) Contending in throwing the javelin. Defending, excusing (any one), pleading (his) cause. A battle.

A نضّال *nuzzāl,* (pl. of ناضل *nāzil*) Warriors.

A نضائض *nazāʼiz,* (pl. of نضيض *nazīz*) Small quantities of water. (pl. of نضيضة *nazīzat*) Small rains. Sounds made by meat when frying on hot stones. ذات نضائض *zāt nazāʼiz,* Thirsty (camels) that cannot be satisfied.

A نضّة *nazzat,* Gold or silver money.

A نضج *nazj* or *nuzj,* (v. n. of نضج) Ripening (as dates). Going over the year without foaling (a camel). Being near ready (meat dressing). Suppuration.

P نضج يافته *nazj-yāfta,* (Meat) cooked, dressed.

A نضح *nazh,* (v. n. of نضح) Sprinkling (a house) with water, or (the thigh with urine). Shooting (at one), sprinkling (him) with arrows. Slightly quenching thirst, giving a sprinkling (to cool the tongue). Drinking enough, completely satisfying the thirst. Drawing water, also watering (palm-trees) by the assistance (of a camel). Exuding, transmitting water (a leathern bottle or other vessel). Emptying out (a date-basket). Pouring forth tears (the eye). Averting (evil) from any one. Returning. Opening and putting forth its buds (a tree). Beginning to fill (ears of corn). Some part. *Nazah,* (pl. انضاح *anzāh*) A watering-trough, a cistern. *Nuzuh,* (pl. of نضيح *nazīh*) Watering-troughs.

A نضحيّ *nuzahīy,* A far-shooting bow.

A نضخ *nazkh,* (v. n. of نضخ) Scattering, dispersing, sprinkling. Shooting at (with arrows), scattering (them) amongst an enemy. Being half-satisfied with water. Bursting (as water) from a fountain. Boiling or bubbling up (water). Remains of perfume upon garments.

A نضخة *nazkhat,* One shower.

A نضد *nazd,* (v. n. of نضد) Spreading (carpets) one over another. *Nazad,* (pl. انضاد *anzād*) Noble, illustrious, eminent. Nobility, ancestral eminence. Carpets, cushions, or other similar furniture laid one upon another; a throne, bed, or couch covered with them; the best of such furniture. Fat (she-camel).

A نضر *nazr,* (v. n. of نضر) Endowing with beauty and every ornamental excellence (God). (pl. نضار *nizār* and انضر *anzur*) Gold or silver. *Nizr,* A wife. *Nazar,* (v. n. of نضر) Flourishing, being green (a tree). Freshness of countenance. Brightness, beauty.

A نضرة *nazrat,* Brightness, splendour, beauty. Freshness of countenance. Opulence, affluence, fortune. Pleasure.

A نضريّ *nazarīy,* Of the Jewish tribe نضير *nazīr.*

A نضف *nazf,* (v. n. of نضف) Sucking the udder dry. Serving (as a domestic). Breaking wind. *Nazaf,* Wild marjoram. *Nazif,* Unclean, nasty.

A نضفان *nazafān,* A side.

A نضل *nazl,* (v. n. of نضل) Darting, shooting with bow and arrow; conquering at that exercise. *Nazal,* (v. n. of نضل) Being lean, fatigued (camel).

A نضم *nazm,* Good wheat.

A نضمة *nazmat,* A grain of good wheat.

A نضناض *naznāz,* (A serpent) in perpetual motion, whose bite is instant death.

A نضنضة *naznazat,* (v. n. of نضنض Q) (A serpent) moving (the tongue).

A نضو *nazw,* (v. n. of نضا for نضو) Pulling (the garments off another), stripping. Drawing (a sword). (One horse) outstripping (others), bursting from a troop or herd, hurrying along. Flying rapidly (as an arrow), and going beyond the mark. Travelling, passing (through a country or desert). Going down, subsiding (a swelling). Drying up (water). *Nazw,* (or نضوّ *nuzūw*) (v. n. of نضا for نضو) Going off from the beard, head, hands, or feet (dye). *Nizw,* (pl. انضاء *anzāʼ*) An emaciated camel or other beast, especially with fatigue. A worn, tattered garment. The wood of an arrow without point, and much worn. The iron part of a bridle without the leather.

A نضوب *nuzūb,* (v. n. of نضب) Flowing, running, descending, sinking (water in the earth). Being sunk in the socket (the eye of a she-camel). Being distant (desert). Being sore and adverse (fortune). Dying. Being diminished, scarce (produce).

A نضوة *nizwat,* (fem.) Emaciated (she-camel).

A نضوح *nazūh,* A species of aromatic. Any thing which they pour in the mouth, as medicine. (A bow) which shoots to a great distance. *Nuzūh,* A drawing of water by the assistance of cattle.

A نضود *nazūd,* A fat she-camel.

A نضور *nuzūr,* Brightness, beauty.

A نضوض *nazūz,* Leaky (well). A well whose water comes in small quantities.

A نضي *nazy,* (v. n. of نضي) Drawing (a sword). Wearing (a garment) threadbare.

A نضيّ *nazīy,* Cattle emaciated with extreme labour. An arrow without a head or feathers. A gaming arrow newly polished but not used. That part of a spear or arrow from the handle or feather to the head. The head of an arrow or javelin. The back of the neck with the bone or joints from the ears to the shoulders. Virga virilis. *Nuzīy,* (v. n. of نضا for نضو) Starting from a troop, outstripping other horses. Going through, passing beyond (an arrow). Pulling off (a garment). Drawing (a sword). Travelling, passing through cities and stations. Going off, (the colour of privet)

A نضيج *nazīj,* Ripe (fruit). Well-cooked (meat). نضيج الرأي *nazīju'r raʼy,* Matured in judgment.

A نضيح *nazīh,* (pl. نضح *nuzuh*) A watering-trough.

A نضيحة *nazīhat,* A kind of medicine or aromatic which they put into the mouth. Far-shooting (bow).

A نضيد *nazīd,* Piled one upon another.

A نضيدة *nazīdat,* A cushion, a pillow.

A نضير *nazīr,* Gold or silver. Florid, vivid, splendid, bright. Name of a Jewish tribe that dwelt at Khaybar.

A نضيض *nazīz,* (v. n. of نضّ) Flowing gently. Exuding, sweating. Oozing from the end of a lighted stick (sap). Becoming possible. Bursting from fulness (a bottle). (pl. نضائض *nazāʼiz* and نضاض *nizāz*) A small quantity of milk or water. Lean (man). جاؤا باقصىٰ نضيضهم و نضيضتهم *jāʼu bi akṣaʼ nazīzihim wa nazīzatihim,* They came the whole company of them.

A نضيضة *nazīzat,* (pl. انضّة *anizzat* and نضائض *nazāʼiz*) A little rain. The crackling sound of meat when put upon hot stones. Gentle (wind). A wind which brings rain. Water gliding softly. A crowd, a company. Thirst. ذات نضيضة *zāt nazīzat,* Thirsty camels that cannot be satisfied.

A نضيف *nazīf,* Filthy, nasty, dirty.

A نطّ *natt,* (v. n. of نطّ) Extending, stretching. Tying fast. Travelling (over a country). Raving, doting, talking nonsense.

A نطّاء *nattāʼ,* (fem. of انطّ *anatt*) Far distant.

A نطاب *nitāb,* The head. Neck or jugular-vein. (v. n. 3 of نطب) Setting (men or dogs) by the ears.

A نطاة *natāt,* (pl. انطاء *antāʼ*) The stalk of an unripe date. Branches whence the clusters hang. The fortress of Khaybar.

A نطّاح *nattāh,* Butting (ram).

A نطّار *nuttar,* A scarecrow amongst corn. (pl. of ناطر) Keepers of vineyards or palm-gardens.

A نطارة *nitārat,* The charge of a vineyard or palm-garden.

A نطاسيّ *nitāsīy* or *natāsīy,* Intelligent, ingenious, learned, skilful, accurate. A physician.

A نطّاط *nattāt,* Delirious; idle talker, dotard.

A نطاع *nitāʼ,* Tents. Land. Country.

A نطّاع *nattāʼ,* One who sets on a table half-eaten bread. Extremely careful in gathering up food in the table-cloth نطع *nitʼ.*

A نطاعة *nutāʼat,* A half-eaten mouthful on table.

A نطاف *natāf,* (v. n. of نطف) Flowing (water). *Nitāf,* (pl. of نطفة *nutfat*) Clear waters.

P نطاف *nitāf,* A falconer's glove.

A نطافة *natāfat,* (v. n. of نطف) Being suspected of, or tainted by, vice. *Nitāfat,* (v. n. of نطف) Flowing (as water). *Nutāfat,* A little water remaining in a bottle.

A نطاق *nitāk,* (pl. نطق *nutuk*) A girdle, zone. A kind of female garment, being a cloth fastened round the waist, the outer fold reaching to the knees, the interior to the ground. P نطاق كهكشان *nitāki kahkashān,* The milky-way. ذات نطاقين *zāt nitākayn,* Name of اسماء *asmāʼ,* daughter of Abū bakr.

A نطّاق *nattāk,* A great talker.

A نطاقان *nitākāni,* Duo labra vulvæ.

A نطانط *natānit,* (pl. of نطنط *natnat, nitnit,* or نطناط *natnāt*) Tall (men), long (things).

A نطب *natb,* (v. n. of نطب) Striking or twitching (any one's) ears with the fingers.

A نطثرة *natsarat*, (v. n. of نطثر Q) Having the stomach overloaded with fat meat.

A نطح *nath*, (v. n. of نطح) Butting with the horns, goring. النطح *an' nath*, The two horns of the ram, *i. e.* the two bright stars in the head of Aries.

A نطخ شرّ *nitkhu sharrin*, The author of mischief, a wretch.

A نطر *natr*, (v. n. of نطر) Keeping guard, watching a vineyard or palm-garden. The charge or care of a palm-garden.

A نطراء *nutarā*, (or نطرة *natarat*) (pl. of ناطر *nātir*) Keepers of vineyards or palm-gardens.

A نطرون *natrūn*, Nitre. Natron. Borax. Native alkaline salt.

A نطس *nats*, *natis*, or *natus*, Intelligent, ingenious, learned, skilful, accurate. *Natas*, (v. n. of نطس) Excelling in learning, intelligence, and ingenuity. *Natis*, Extremely careful in avoiding every thing impure. *Nutus*, Skilful physicians. Persons extremely nice and careful in keeping clear from all impurity.

A نطسة *nutasat*, A man nice in dress, victuals, speech, superstitiously attentive to his ablutions.

A نطش *natsh*, Bodily constitution, strength.

A نطشان (عطشان *ʿatshān*) *natshān*, Thirsty.

A نطط *nutut*, (pl. of انطّ *anatt*) Distant journeys.

A نطع *nitʿ*, *natʿ*, *nataʿ*, and *nitaʿ*, (pl. انطاع *antāʿ* and نطوع *nutūʿ*) A sheet of dressed leather, which they spread as a table or table-cloth; also one upon which they play at chess or draughts; or on which a criminal sits to be decapitated. *Nitʿ* and *nitaʿ*, (pl. نطوع *nutūʿ*) The fore part of the palate; also its corrugations. *Nutuʿ*, Those who have wide jaws; or who grin, twist, or open wide their mouths.

A نطعيّة *nitʿīyat*, The letters pronounced by the pressure of the tongue on the fore part of the palate; viz. ت *te*, د *dāl*, and ط *to*.

A نطف *natf*, (v. n. of نطف) Flowing (water). Accusing, suspecting, impeaching. Pouring (water). *Nataf*, (v. n. of نطف) Being suspected of, or tainted by, vice or crime. Being spoiled (a thing). Being hurt by a wound penetrating to the brain. Having a pestilential swelling in the belly; also a deep wound or galling on the back (a camel). Having the stomach overloaded with meat (a man). Being troubled with an indigestion. A vice, corruption, evil. A species of distemper, for which a man is cauterized with a hot iron. A sore on a camel's back. *Natif*, Deeply wounded in the head. A camel diseased as above. Unclean, impure. Suspected of vice. *Nutaf*, (pl. of نطفة *nutfat*) Spermata genitalia. Seas, clear waters. (pl. of نطفة *nutafat*) Ear-rings.

A نطفان *natafān*, The flowing (of water).

A نطفة *nutfat*, (pl. نطاف *nitāf* and نطف *nutuf*) Clear water, whether little or much, lymph. A little water remaining in a bottle. The sea. (pl. نطف *nutaf*) Sperma hominis. *Nata* or *nutafat*, (pl. نطف *nutaf*) An ear-ring. A small pure pearl.

A النطفتان *an' nutfatāni*, The two seas, as the Eastern and the Western, Mediterranean and Red Sea, Persian Gulph, and Sea of China.

A نطفون *natifūna*, (pl. of نطف *natif*) Impure, unclean. Suspected of vice.

A نطق *nutk*, (v. n. of نطق) Speaking, pronouncing, articulating. A word, speech, articulation, pronunciation. P بستگیء نطق *bastagiʾi nutk*, Silence, speechlessness. A *Nutuk*, Parts of a mountain which overtop others. (pl. of نطاق *nitāk*) Female drawers or trowsers.

A نطل *natl*, (v. n. of نطل) Pressing (grapes), squeezing out (wine). Sprinkling (the head of a sick person) with water. What is got from pressed grapes after the first wine. The skin of the grape having its taste. *Nitl*, Dregs or remains of wine.

A نطلاء *natlā*, An evil, misfortune.

A نطلة *nutlat*, What any one takes out of the mouth of a leathern bottle. One draught (of water).

A نطم *natm*, Full, good wheat.

A نطنط *natnat*, (*nitnit*, and نطناط *natnāt*) (pl. نطانط *natānit*) Tall, long.

A نطنطة *natnatat*, (v. n. of نطنط Q) Extending, stretching. Being very long (a journey). Performing a long journey. Lying far off (a country).

A نطو *natw*, (v. n. of نطا for نطو) Drawing out, laying down (the warp) in a loom. Being absent, far distant. Being silent.

A نطوع *nutūʿ*, (pl. of نطع *natʿ*, *nitʿ*, *nataʿ*, and *nitaʿ*) Sheets of leather used as table-cloths. (pl. of نطع *nitʿ*) The fore parts of the palate.

A نطوف *natūf*, Rainy (night), till morning.

A نطوفة *nutūfat*, (v. n. of نطف) Being suspected of, or tainted by, vice.

A نطوق *nutūk*, (v. n. of نطق) Speaking.

A نطول *natūl*, Warm water medicinally prepared, and poured from a vessel slowly over the head; an embrocation. *Nutūl*, (v. n. of نطل) Pouring forth an embrocation.

A نطيّ *natiy*, Distant (place).

A نطيح *natīh*, (Game) coming in front of one. Butted by a ram, killed with the blow. Hateful, detestable, despicable. (A horse) having two circular spots on his forehead (a blemish).

A نطيحة *natīhat*, (A beast) gored to death.

A نطّيس *nittīs*, A physician. Skilful.

A نطيش *natīsh*, Motion.

A نطيط *natīt*, (v. n. of نطّ) Fleeing, running away. Remote, distant.

A نطيلق *nutaylik*, (dim. of انطلاق *intilāk*) A short absence.

A نظار *nizār*, Physiognomy, sagacity, penetration. *Nazāri*, Wait thou.

A نظّار *nazzār*, Noble-spirited, sharp-eyed (horse). A scrutinizer. بنو النظّار *banū'n nazzār*, A tribe of Arabians. *Nuzzār*, Spectators.

A نظارة *nazārat*, Inspection, superintendancy, administration. A walking and a looking about. Cleanliness, purity, abstinence from any thing gross (an idiom, technical language peculiar to lawyers).

A نظّارة *nazzārat*, Spectators.

P نظّارگی *nazzāragī*, Seeing, looking at; sight. (pl. نظّارگیان *nazzāragiyān*) A spectator, beholder.

A نظاره *nazāra* or *nazzāra*, Sight, view, look.

P نظاره کنان *nazāra-kunān*, Shewing.

P نظاره گاه *nazāra-gāh*, A pleasant prospect.

P نظّاريّ *nazzāriy*, A superior kind (of camel).

A نظافة *nazāfat*, Cleanness, neatness, purity.

A نظام *nizām*, (v. n. of نظم) Joining in a row, stringing (pearls). Arranging, governing, regulating. Adorning. Making verses. Having the lines نظامان *nizāmāni* (a lizard or fish). Order, disposition, arrangement. (pl. نظم *nuzum*) A string of pearls or beads, or that upon which they are strung. Composition of verses. Custom, habit, mode, way of life, institution. Heaped up sands. The right way, right line. (pl. انظمة *anzimat*, اناظم *anāzim*, and نظم *nuzum*) Foundation, basis, constitution. نظام العالم *nizāmu'l ʿālam*, Governor of the world, administrator of public affairs (a title given by the king and others to the Grand Vazir). نظام الملك *nizāmu'l mulk*, The administrator (literally, the good order) of the empire.

A نظّام *nazzām*, A stringer of pearls.

A نظامان *nizāmāni*, (dual of نظام *nizām*) Two lines of a white colour running from the head to the tail of a crocodile or fish.

A نظامة *nazāmat*, A string of eggs, or the egg-bed of a fowl. *Nizāmat*, Administration of justice, government, arrangement, regulation.

P نظامی *nazāmī*, Name of a famous poet.

A نظاميّة *nazāmiyat*, A college in Baghdād.

A نظائر *nazāʾir*, (pl. of نظيرة *nazīrat* and نظورة *nazūrat*) Those who are looked upon or revered above all others; eminent, venerable, or respectable men. Nobles, grandees, chief men. Like, similar. *Nazāʾira*, (Counting cattle) by pairs, two and two.

A نظائف *nazāʾif*, (pl. of نظيف) Clean (things).

A نظر *nazr*, (v. n. of نظر) Expecting, waiting for. Delaying, granting a delay or respite. Selling on credit. *Nizr*, Like, resembling. *Nazar*, (v. n. of نظر) Looking at, beholding, seeing, gazing upon, viewing, turning the eyes or the mind towards, scanning. Attending to: considering, pondering, weighing, measuring, rating, valuing, estimating. Defending, helping, assisting. Expecting, waiting. Predicting, presaging, divining. Being tenderly affected towards. Selling upon credit. Deciding, judging, passing sentence. Exercising authority. Being situate over against (as one house to another). Exhibiting to the eye her plants (the earth). Sight, vision, view: look, glance. An oversight. Doubt, uncertainty, perplexity. Neighbours. نظر امعان *nazari imʿān*, Attentive consideration, a look of attention. نظر بعيد *nazari baʿīd*, A prospect. نظر ثاني *nazari sānī*, A review or second examination of recruits at which they are finally past. Revisal of a writing or book. نظر مكرّر *nazari mukarrar*, Review, revisal. P نظر انداختن *nazar andākhtan*, To cast a glance. از نظر راندن *az nazar rāndan*, To drive out of (one's) sight, to expel. A اهل نظر *ahli nazar*, Sagacious, penetrating. حيّ نظر *hayyu nazar*, A town or village closely adjoining to another. ديوان النظر *dīwānu'n nazar*, A council-board. مصلح النظر *maslahu'n nazar*, The herb mullein.

A نظراء *nuzarāʾ*, (pl. of نظير *nazīr*) Equals, likes.

A نظرات *nazarāt*, Looks. Appearances.

A نظران *nazarān*, (v. n. of نظر) Seeing, looking at, viewing, scanning.

P نظر انداز *nazar-andāz*, Cast off, out of sight.

P نظر باز *nazar-bāz*, One who plays with or deceives the eyes. An ogler. A juggler.

P نظر بازي *nazar-bāzī*, Ogling. Illusion.

P نظر بند *nazar-band*, Strictly watched (without imprisonment). Fascination of conjurors.

P نظر بندي *nazar-bandī*, Confinement.

A نظرة *nazrat*, One look, glance. An apparition. Fascination, malignant eye, look of a demon; deformity, vice, defect. Ugliness or change of countenance. Pity, mercy. A fainting-fit, swoon. Fear. Awe. نظرهٔ اولى *nazrai ūla'*, (or نظرة الاولى *nazratu'l ūla'*) The first glance, at first sight. *Nazirat*, Delay, respite, space granted. Credit.

P نظرگاه *nazar-gāh*, Place of sight. A theatre or place where any spectacle is exhibited. The tomb of a prophet or holy man.

A نظرنّة *nizrann, nizrinn*, or *nuzrunnat*, (A woman) who sees not really what she thinks she sees.

A بنو نظري *banū nazara'*, (or نظّري *nazzara'*) Those who gaze upon women, and speak to them politely, gently, and soothingly.

A نظريّ *nazarīy*, Speculative, notional, ideal.

A نظم *nazm*, (v. n. of نظم) Joining (pearls) in a row. Composing (verses). Order, arrangement. A string (of pearls). Poetry, verse. A large flight (of locusts). Three stars in Orion. نظم و نسق *nazm u nasak*, Order and arrangement. *Nuzum*, (pl. of نظام *nizām*) Strings of pearls. Bases, constitutions of things.

A نظمي *nazmī*, A composer, arranger. A poet.

A نظور *nazūr*, One who attentively looks at another he likes. *Nazūr*, (or نظورة *nazūrat*) (pl. نظائر *nazāʾir*) One who is looked upon or revered above all others, a venerable or respectable man.

A نظورة *nazūrat*, First line or van of an army.

A نظير *nazīr*, (pl. نظراء *nuzarāʾ*) Alike, resembling, equal to. نظير الشيء *nazīru'sh shay*, Looking towards or opposite to a thing. نظير السمت *nazīru's samt*, (or النظير *an' nazīr*) The Nadir or point of the lower hemisphere, in opposition to the vertical point Zenith. مجلس جنّت نظير *majlisi jannat-nazīr*, An assembly resembling paradise. P بي نظير *bī nazīr*, Incomparable, peerless, matchless.

A نظيرة *nazīrat*, (pl. نظائر *nazāʾir*) One who is looked upon or revered above all others, a venerable or respectable man. The first line or van of an army. A similitude, comparison, example, specimen.

A نظيف *nazīf*, Pure, clean. Alkali, or the ashes. نظيف السراويل *nazīfu's sarāwīl*, Chaste.

A نظيم *nazīm*, A path through mountains distinguished by a string of little pools lying nigh unto each other. That to which syllables of similar endings answer. A trench in which suckers of palm-trees are planted. Well-arranged (assembly).

A نعّ *naʿʿ*, Weak, languid (man).

A نعاء *nuʿāʾ*, The mewing of a cat. *Naʿāʾi*, Announce his death.

A نعاب *nuʿāb*, (v. n. of نعب) Croaking (a raven); crowing (a cock); also other birds.

A نعّابة *naʿʿābat*, Swift (she-camel)

A نعابع *naʿābiʿ*, Those parts (of a camel's body) where the sweat flows.

A نعاتة *naʿātat*, (v. n. of نعت) Being swift, fleet (a horse). Being qualified, praised, celebrated.

A نعاج *niʿāj*, (pl. of نعجة *naʿjat*) Ewes, especially of the species of sheep called ضأن *zaʾn*. Wild cows, especially white.

A نعار *nuʿār*, (v. n. of نعر) Making a sound through the nose. Bursting with a gushing noise (blood from a vein). Roaming through cities.

A نعّار *naʿʿār*, A vein spirting out blood. Rebellious, seditious, disobedient. Clamorous, noisy. Cunning, sly.

A نعّارة *naʿʿārat*, Noisy, impudent (woman).

A نعاس *nuʿās*, Somnolency, drowsiness, lethargy.

A نعّاس *naʿʿās*, Sleepy, drowsy, comatose.

P نعاس زده *nuʿās-zada*, Lethargic, comatose.

A نعاعة *nuʿāʿat*, (pl. نعاع) Fresh, tender herbage.

A نعاف *niʿāf*, (pl. of نعف *naʿf*) Declivities of mountains, slopes of valleys.

A نعاق *nuʿāk*, (v. n. of نعق) Calling out to, checking (sheep). Croaking (a raven).

A نعال *niʿāl*, (pl. of نعل *naʿl*) Shoes, slippers. Horse-shoes. Clogs. Pattens.

A نعاليّ *niʿālīy*, A shoe or sandal-maker.

A نعام *naʿām*, An ostrich. The ostrich-species. A desert, solitude. A direction-post set up in the desert. Yes. نعام عين *naʿām* (*niʿām*, or *nuʿāma*) *ʿaynin*, For the gratification of.

A نعامة *naʿāmat*, A cross-beam over two upright posts, to which the bucket is suspended for drawing water from a well. A swipe for raising water; a crane for lifting great weights. A drawer of water at a well. Any conspicuous structure on a hill or eminence. A stone projecting from a well. An elevated banner. A direction-post erected in the desert. An ostrich. A high road. A desert, solitude. The leg-bone. The sole of the foot. The brain (of a horse). The membrane of the brain. The muzzle (of a horse). Self, soul. A title of the sovereigns of حيرة *hīrat*. A crowd, a meeting, assembly. Delight, joy, gladness. Honour. A camel's saddle, and what is under it. A sudden victory. Darkness. Ignorance. Name of seven different horses. نعامة عين *naʿāmata ʿaynin*, For the gratification of. شالت نعامته *shālat naʿāmatuhu*, He died. He was light. He became calm after being angry.

A نعامى *nuʿāma'*, The south wind. The south-east wind. نعاماك *nuʿāmāka*, As far as you can reach, as much as you can. نعامى عين *nuʿāma' ʿaynin*, For the gratification of.

A نعانع *naʿāniʿ*, Flounces, furbelows, or similar things fastened to the girdle by way of ornament.

A النعائم *an' naʿāʾim*, The twentieth mansion of the moon, being eight stars in a circular position, of which four are called الصادرة *as' sādirat*, the other four الواردة *al wāridat*.

A نعب *naʿb*, (v. n. of نعب) Croaking (a raven). Crowing (a cock). Moving the head or neck when vociferating. Giving notice of the hour of prayer (as the muezzin from the minaret or tower of a mosque). Going quick, with a corresponding motion of the head (a camel). Violent (wind). *Nuʿub*, (pl. of نعوب *naʿūb*) Swift (she-camels).

A نعبان *naʿabān*, (v. n. of نعب) Croaking (a raven). Crowing (a cock).

A نعت *naʿt*, Epithet, description. An adjective noun. Praise, eulogium, encomium. (A horse) outstripping others in a race. نعت النبيّ *naʿtu'n nabīy*, The praise of the prophet (which, after the praises of God, is inscribed at the beginning of many books; a kind of invocation). *Naʿat*, (v. n. of نعت) Making pretensions to great speed. Being elaborately described, qualified, or praised.

A نعتة *naʿtat*, (A horse) outstripping others in a race. *Nuʿtat*, The highest dignity.

A نعث *naʿs*, The act of taking, receiving.

A نعثل *naʿsal*, The male (hyena). A doting, weak old man. Name of a man remarkable for a very long beard; hence applied to any man with such a beard. Name of a certain Jew.

A نعثلة *naʿsalat*, Collection, congregation, meeting. Folly. The feeble pace of a decrepit old man. The strut of one who goes with the feet wide and inverted; or of one who walks with a haughty air, and swings the body and feet.

A نعج *naʿaj*, (v. n. of نعج) Being very white, shining bright. Being fat. Being indisposed after eating mutton. *Naʿij*, Unwell from eating mutton.

A نعجات *naʿajāt*, (pl. of نعجة *naʿjat*) Ewes.

A نعجة *naʿjat*, (pl. نعاج *niʿāj* and نعجات *naʿa-*

jāt) A ewe. A wild cow, particularly a white one.

A نعر *naɛr*, (v. n. of نعر) Opposing, resisting, thwarting. Refusing. Flocking together in a tumultuous, disorderly manner. Coming, approaching. Rising up to do any thing, exerting one's self. *Naɛar*, (v. n. of نعر) Being infested by gad-bees or horse-flies (especially in the nose). *Naɛir*, Unable to rest in a place. (An ass) stung in the nostril by a gad-fly. *Nuɛar*, The early fruit of the tree اراك *arāk*. An embryo, imperfect, unformed (ass-foal). A wind which makes a noise in the nose. A blue fly.

A نعرة *naɛrat*, (v. n. of نعر) Bursting with a gushing noise (blood from a vein). Roaming through cities. Clamour, cry, vociferation, great noise, roar; sound made by the nostrils. نعرة النجم *naɛratu'n najm*, The blowing of a wind, with great heat, about the rising of a star. P نعرة زدن *naɛra zadan*, (or بر آوردن *bar āwardan*) To raise a cry. A *Nuɛrat* or *nuɛarat*, The root of the nose, or the inside of it. *Naɛarat* or *nuɛarat*, An affair to which one gives attention. Pride, arrogance. *Nuɛarat*, A large blue fly which infests asses and horses, the gad-bee, horse-fly, bree. The fruit of the tree اراك *arāk*. Imperfect, unformed (ass-foal).

P نعرة زنان *naɛra-zanān*, Uttering loud cries.

A نعرى *naɛra'*, Clamorous (woman).

A نعس *naɛs*, (v. n. of نعس) Sleeping, slumbering. Somnolency. Softness, weakness in body or mind. Dulness of markets, when goods are not bought, nor exposed to sale.

A نعسان *naɛsān*, (little used) Sleepy, drowsy.

A نعسة *naɛsat*, One sleep, slumber, nap, snooze.

A نعش *naɛsh*, (v. n. of نعش) (God) exalting (any one). Repairing the broken fortune of any one. Eulogizing the dead. Lifting up (the eyes). A bier with a dead body (when empty it is called سرير *sarīr*). A litter in which a sick person is carried. A catafalque whereon a royal corpse is laid. A piece of wood, with a notch or a piece of cloth at the end of it, for catching young ostriches. Permanency, duration. Life. بنات نعش *banāti naɛsh*, The constellation of the Bear, as well الكبري *al kubra'*, The Greater, as الصغري *as' sughra'*, The Lesser. They are both called the Bier; the three stars which go before the Bier being called بنات *banāt*, and every individual star ابن نعش *ibn naɛsh*.

P نعشيله *naɛshīla*, A fowl fricaseed with onions, vetches, and eggs.

A نعص *naɛs*, (v. n. of نعص) Eating herbage (a locust). *Naɛas*, A leaning from side to side. Curvature, crookedness. Inversion.

A نعض *naɛz*, (v. n. of نعض) Finding, obtaining. *Nuɛz*, Name of a thorny tree, of whose wood they make dentifrices, and whose bark is used in tanning hides.

A نعط *nuɛut*, (pl. of ناعط *nāɛit*) Ungraceful eaters. Travellers to a great distance. Ill-bred, unpolished.

A نعظ *naɛz* or *naɛaz*, (v. n. of نعظ) Rising, becoming erect (the yard). *Naɛiz*, Hot, prurient (vulva).

A نعف *naɛf*, (pl. نعاف *niɛāf*) The declivity of a mountain, slope of a valley. The fore part and the narrow of a sand-hill. نعاف نُعَّف *niɛāfun nuɛɛafun*, Ascents or descents, declivities of a mountain.

A نعفة *naɛfat*, A shoe-strap striking the top of the foot on the outside. *Naɛafat*, A strap hanging from behind a camel's saddle. A kernel or tumour in the flesh. The hairy plumage of a cock; also his wattles and comb.

A نعق *naɛk*, (and نعقان *naɛakān*) (v. n. of نعق) Calling out (to sheep), checking (them). Croaking (as a raven).

A نعل *naɛl*, (v. n. of نعل) Shoeing (a horse). Giving shoes. (pl. نعال *niɛāl*) A shoe, sandal, or any thing which defends the feet of man or beast, a woman's buskin, clog, patten. A horse-shoe. A hoof. A base fellow that may be trodden upon like the ground. Hard and barren ground shining with sand and gravel. The ferule at the end of a sword-sheath, of silver or iron. A nerve twisted round the horns of a bow; the membrane which covers the whole back of a bow. A ploughshare. A wife. A fish with a large jowl. P نعل افكندن *naɛl afkandan*, To throw off the horse-shoe, *i.e.* to ride or run fast. To lag behind, break down. نعل بستن *naɛl bastan*, To shoe (a horse). نعل در آتش *naɛl dar ātish*, Restlessness, perturbation, uneasiness. نعل شام *naɛli shām*, The moon. The morning-breeze. نعل كهنه بحلوا دادن *naɛli kuhna ba halwā dādan*, To give an old shoe in exchange for sweetmeats (a custom which prevails in certain parts of the world). نعل و داغ *naɛl u dāgh*, A scar made by enthusiasts on the breast in the form of a horse-shoe. نعل واژگون *naɛli wājgūn*, A matter kept secret from people. A *Naɛal*, (v. n. of نعل) Being shod, putting on shoes.

P نعلبند *naɛl-band*, A smith, farrier.

P نعلبندي *naɛl-bandī*, New-shoeing a horse. A light tribute.

P نعل بها *naɛl-bahā*, Money given to foreign troops to abstain from plunder and devastation.

A نعلة *naɛlat*, A shoe, slipper.

P نعلتراش *naɛl-tirāsh*, (or ساز *sāz*) A maker of buskins, shoes, clogs, or slippers.

P نعل زده *naɛl-zada*, Shod. A horse prepared for a journey.

P نعلك *naɛlak*, (or نعلكي) A kind of goblet.

A نعلّي *naɛliy*, In the form of a horse-shoe.

A نعلين *naɛlayn*, (dual) A pair of shoes of a particular kind, *i.e.* with wooden soles; a clog, patten.

P نعلين دوز *naɛlayn-doz*, A clog-maker.

A نعم *naɛm*, (v. n. of نعم) Coming barefoot. *Naɛm*, (for *naɛam*) (pl. انعام *anɛām* and اناعم *anāɛim*) Cattle feeding (especially camels or sheep). نعم عين *naɛma* (*nuɛma*, or *nuɛam*) *ɛaynin*, For the gratification of. *Naɛma*, *niɛma*, *nuɛima*, or *niɛima*, Hail! welcome, O most excellent (man or woman)! نعم الرجل زيد *niɛma'r rajulu zaydun*, Good is the man Zayd. *Nuɛm*, (pl. انعم *anɛum*) Prosperity, good fortune. Delight. Name of a woman, Naomi. *Naɛam*, (v. n. of نعم) Being green and succulent (a branch). (pl. انعام *anɛām* and نعمان *nuɛmān*) Cattle feeding (especially camels or sheep). *Naɛam* or *naɛim*, Yes, thus, it is so, very well. فبها و نعم اما *fa bihā wa naɛam ammā*, It's all very well, but . . . . *Naɛim*, Soft, easy, convenient, gentle. Tender, delicate. *Niɛam*, (pl. of نعمة *niɛmat*) Benefits, favours. Pleasure, comfort, blessings (of life). Meats, viands, victuals. P نعم گوناگون *niɛami gūnāgūn*, Meats of different kinds, every sort of good things.

A نعمّا *niɛimmā*, Hail! O excellent! دقًا نعمًّا *dakkan niɛimman* or *niɛamman*, Bruising or braying small, reducing to subtle powder.

A نعماء *naɛmāɛ*, A boon, blessing, favour. A helping hand. الحمد لله علي نعمائه *al hamdu li'llāh ɛala' naɛmāɛihi*, Praise be to God for His benefits!

A نعمات *niɛamāt*, (pl. of نعمة *niɛmat*) Conveniences. Riches.

A نعمان *nuɛmān*, Blood. Name of the kings of حيرة *hīrat* in Arabia, especially of the last. Name of an island in the Arabian Gulf. (pl. of نعم *naɛam*) Cattle feeding. شقائق النعمان *shakāɛiku'n nuɛmān*, The anemone.

A نعمة *naɛmat*, Convenience, ease. Affluence, wealth. Tenderness, delicacy. واسع النعمة *wāsiɛu'n naɛmat*, Abounding in riches. نعمة عين *naɛmata* (*nuɛmata*, or *niɛmata*) *ɛaynin*, For the gratification of. *Niɛmat*, (pl. نعم *niɛam*, انعم *anɛum*, نعمات *niɛamāt*, and *niɛimāt*) The hand. Graciousness, beneficence, a benefit, boon, blessing, favour. A kind, helping hand. Riches, good things. Delight, pleasure, joy. ولي نعمت *wali niɛmat*, A benefactor.

P نعمت پرست *niɛmat-parast*, A Mammonist.

P نعمت خور *niɛmat-khwur*, Enjoying favour.

P نعمتكده *niɛmat-kada*, Paradise.

P نعمتي *niɛmati*, Good things, comforts, riches. Iron on the sole of a shoe.

A نعمى *nuɛma'*, Graciousness, beneficence. A benefit. A kind, helping hand. Delight, pleasure, joy. A thing which gratifies the eye. Ease, quiet. نعمى عين *nuɛma' ɛaynin*, For the gratification of.

P نعنا *naɛnā*, Mint.

A نعناع *naɛnāɛ*, Mint, spearmint.

A نعنع *naɛnaɛ* or *nuɛnuɛ*, Mint, spearmint. *Nuɛnuɛ*, A tall man. Long and slender (penis). Flabby in body, tottering, shaking. Long and narrow (rima); also flabby.

A نعنعة *naɛnaɛat*, A hesitation in speaking; pronouncing ن *na* instead of ل *la*. Limberness of a pizzle after being stiff. *Nuɛnuɛat*, Crop of a bird.

A نعو *naʿw*, A circle under the nose. A crack or slit on the upper lip of a camel. A fissure or crack in the hoof of a horse. The opening in the hinder part of the hoof. Fresh and moist dates.

A نعوب *naʿūb*, (pl. نعب) Swift (she-camel).

A نعوت *nuʿūt*, (pl. of نعت *naʿt*) Encomiums. Adjectives.

A نعوج *nuʿūj*, (v. n. of نعج) Being very white.

A نعوذ بالله *naʿūẕu bi'llāh*, (in sing. اعوذ بالله *aʿūẕu bi'llāh*) Let us fly to God (from any thing wicked)! نعوذ بالله من ذلك *naʿūẕu bi'llāh min zālika*, God preserve us from that! نعوذ بالله من الشيطان الرجيم *naʿūẕu bi'llāh mini'sh shayṭāni'r rajīm*, God defend us from Satan the accursed! (which is often made to rhyme with بسم الله الرحمن الرحيم *bi'smi'llāhi'r rahmāni'r rahīm*, In the name of God, the gracious, the merciful!) نعوذ بالله من شرور انفسنا *naʿūẕu bi'llāh min shurūri anfusinā*, God protect us from the wickedness of ourselves!

A نعور *naʿūr*, A vein spirting out blood. Distant (design). (Wind) bringing a cooling blast in sultry weather, and a warm breeze in cold weather.

A نعوس *naʿūs*, (A she-camel) giving much milk (she is then inclined to sleepiness).

A نعوظ *nuʿūẓ*, (v. n. of نعظ) Becoming stiff and erect (the yard).

A نعوف *naʿūf*, Loose, pendulous, flagging (ear).

A نعومة *nuʿūmat*, (v. n. of نعم) Being soft and flexible. Affording repose. Softness, smoothness.

A نعي *naʿy*, (or نعيان *nuʿyān*) (v. n. of نعى) Announcing the death of any one. Exposing (another's faults).

A نعيّ *naʿīy*, (v. n. of نعي) Announcing the death of any one. Exposing (another's faults). A bearer of the tidings of any one's death. News of any one's death.

A نعيب *naʿīb*, (v. n. of نعب) Croaking (a raven). Crowing (a cock).

A نعيبة *naʿībat*, Tribute payed into the treasury of the emperor of Morocco from the different provinces of the empire.

A نعيت *naʿīt*, (or نعيتة *naʿītat*) (A horse) outstripping others in a race.

A نعير *naʿīr*, (v.n. of نعر) Making a sound through the nose. Bursting with a gushing noise (blood from a vein). Roaming through cities. A clamour, shout, vociferation (especially in a tumult or in battle). نعير الهم *naʿīru'l hamm*, Provident, thinking upon distant affairs.

A نعيف ضعيف *naʿīfun ẓaʿīfun*, Weak.

A نعيق *naʿīk*, (v. n. of نعق) Calling out to, checking (sheep). Croaking (a raven).

A نعيلة *nuʿaylat*, (dim. of نعل) A small shoe.

A نعيم *naʿīm*, Ease, quiet, tranquillity, pleasure, affluence, delicate living, luxury, any thing good which we enjoy. نعيم الله *naʿīmu'llāh*, The benefits, favours, or grace of God. نعيم الدنيا *naʿīmu'd dunya'*, The conveniences and luxuries of life. نعيم عين *naʿīma ʿaynin*, For the gratification of. *Naʿīm*, (or جنّت نعيم *jannati naʿīm*) The paradise of delights. ابو نعيم *abū nuʿaym*, White bread.

P نعيم پاك *naʿīm-pāk*, Works of piety.

A نغّار *naghghār*, Bleeding (wound).

A نغّاز *nughghāz*, Slanderers, seditious; breedbates, mischief-makers.

A نغاش *nughāsh*, A very dwarfish man.

A نغاشة *nughāshat*, Name of a bird.

A نغاشيّ *nughāshiy*, A very dwarfish man.

A نغّاض *naghghāẓ*, (One thing) moving after others. Thick and wrinkled. نغّاض البطن *naghghāẓu'l batn*, Wrinkled in the belly.

P نغاغ *naghāgh*, Rare and excellent things. The joints of the neck. A drinking-vessel.

P نغاك *naghāk*, A fine cotton-thread. *Nighāk*, A blockhead, fool, stupid fellow. A rogue. A bastard.

P نغام *naghām*, Particles of dust floating in the air. *Naghām* or *nighām*, Ugly, ill-favoured; dark-complexioned.

A نغانغ *naghānigh*, (pl. of نغنغ *nughnugh*) Isthmuses or divisions between throats and windpipes; the flesh thereabouts.

A نغب *naghb*, (v. n. of نغب) Sucking up, absorbing, swallowing (spittle or single draughts). Sipping (as a bird). *Nughab*, (pl. of نغبة *nagh* or *nughbat*) Quantities. Draughts. Shameful acts.

A نغبة *naghbat*, One draught (of water). Hunger. Destitution. *Nughbat*, The quantity taken in a single draught. A shameful action.

A نغبق *nughbuk*, Foolish, insane.

A نغبقة *naghbakat*, The grumbling of horses' bellies. *Naghbakat*, (or نغبوقة *nughbūkat*) Noise made by a horse's yard in the sheath.

A نغبوق *nughbūk*, Name of a bird.

A نغبول *nughbūl*, Name of a bird and plant.

A نغت *naght*, A pulling of the hair.

A نغث *naghs*, A sore and lasting evil.

P نغچه *nighcha*, A weazel. A kind of lizard.

A نغر *naghr*, (v. n. of نغر) Tickling (the throat of a child). Drinking much water. *Naghar*, A salt-water spring. *Naghar*, (or نغران *nagharān*) (v. n. of نغر) Boiling with rage, being indignant bursting with smothered passion. Boiling (as a pot), boiling over. Contracting her hinder parts and travelling on (a camel). Being plentiful and redundant (water). *Naghir*, Angry, passionate. *Nughar*, (pl. نغران *nighrān*) A nightingale. Young sparrows. A sparrow with a red beak. A species of asses, or the males of them. A fœtus making a noise in the womb.

A نغران *nighrān*, (pl. of نغر) Nightingales.

A نغرة *naghirat*, Jealous (woman). *Nugharat*, A kind of sparrow with a red beak.

A نغرقة *nughrukat*, A lock of hair twisted but not plaited.

P نغروچ *nughrūch*, A rolling-pin.

P نغز *naghz*, Beautiful. Good, sincere, excellent; pure, clear. Swift, nimble. Rare, surprising.

A نغز *naghz*, A sowing dissensions. A tickling.

P نغزتر *naghztar*, More rare. Very uncommon.

P نغزك *naghzak*, Rare, strange. The mango.

P نغزي *naghzī*, Rareness, choiceness.

P نغزيدن *naghzīdan*, To become good.

A نغش *naghsh*, (or نغشان *naghashān*) (v. n. of نغش) Shaking, being loose (in its place). Nodding (the head). Moving, being tremulous (a bird). Inclining or leaning towards. Agitation, commotion.

A نغص *naghas*, (v. n. of نغص) Being disappointed in one's hopes, unable to perform what was expected or is necessary. Breaking off when drinking (a camel). Bringing camels to a cistern to drink, and driving them away before they are filled. Being disturbed in his draught (a camel), being driven from the well that another may drink. *Naghis*, (Wine) which is cut off from the drinkers before they are full.

A نغض *naghẓ*, (v. n. of نغض) Being moved. Vacillating. Chattering (as the teeth of a child when loose). Moving, setting in motion. Being dense (clouds), pressing upon one another. Pulling a strong camel from between two at the watering trough, that a weaker one may get near to drink. One who moves his head and totters in walking. *Naghẓ* or *nighẓ*, A male ostrich. A herd of ostriches. *Naghẓ* or *nughẓ*, The cartilage of the shoulder-blades. *Naghaẓ*, (v. n. of نغض) Shaking (the head in admiration). Being moved, shaking, vacillating.

A نغض *nughghaẓ*, Large pulley for drawing water.

A نغضان *naghaẓān*, (v. n. of نغض) Being moved (the head). Shaking, moving, staggering (a tooth, saddle, or animal travelling).

A نغضل *naghẓal*, Lazy, heavy (post-horse).

A نغط *nughut*, Tall men.

A نغظلة *naghẓalat*, Slow running. A shaking of the body right and left in walking.

A نغف *naghaf*, (v. n. of نغف) Being troubled with many of the worms called نغف *naghaf* (a camel). Small worms which infest the noses of camels and sheep; likewise a white worm which is found in macerated date-stones; also one which comes out of a beetle. The dry mucus of the nose.

A يا نغفة *yā naghfata*, A word used in contempt.

A نغفتان *naghafatāni*, (dual of نغفة *naghafat*) The two extremities of the upper jaw-bones, the motion of which is said to occasion sneezing.

A نغل *naghl*, A bastard. (A man) of a mean race. A skin spoiled in the tanning. *Naghal*, (v. n. of نغل) Being marred and spoiled (as leather whilst tanning); rotting, becoming full of holes. Being bad, villainous (intention). Having an aversion. Being in a bad state (a wound). Fomenting discord. Discord (occasioned by whispered slander). *Naghil,* A bastard. Rotten leather. (A man) of a mean race.

P نغل *naghil,* An enclosure, fold for cattle not covered over. Den (of a wolf), hole (of a fox).

A نغلة *nughlat,* Rottenness of leather in tanning. *Naghilat,* Rotten (nut).

P نغم *naghm,* Making a hole, digging out, making hollow.

A نغم *naghm* or *nagham,* (v. n. of نغم) (Reading or singing) in a low voice. Sipping, swallowing draughts. A low tone of voice. *Nugham,* (pl. of نغمة *nughmat*) Single draughts of water.

A نغمة *naghmat* or *naghamat,* A soft, sweet voice. A musical sound or tone. Melody, song, modulation, trill, shake. نغمهٔ عنقا *naghma-i ʿankā,* Name of a note in music. *Nughmat,* (pl. نغم *nugham*) One draught (of water).

P نغمه پرداز *naghma-pardāz,* (زن *zan,* ساز *sāz,* سراي *sarāy,* or كش *kash*) Singer, warbler, musician.

P نغن *naghan,* The hollow of the navel. Anise, which they sometimes sprinkle over dough when making bread.

P نغنخلان *naghankhalān,* (نغنخواد *naghnakhwād,* نغنخوالان *naghnakhwālān,* نغنخوايين *naghankhwāyīn,* or *naghnkhwāyīn*) Anise.

P نغنغ *naghnagh* or *nughnugh,* A large Transoxianian measure containing four ass-loads.

A نغنغ *nughnugh,* (pl. نغانغ *naghānigh*) The isthmus or division between the throat and the windpipe; the flesh adjacent to the throat. That part in the throat of a camel which moves up and down when he chews the cud. Foolish, silly; weak. Carnosa vulva.

A نغنغة *naghnaghat,* (v. n. of نغنغ Q) Being affected in the نغنغ *nughnugh.*

P نغنويدن *naghanwīdan,* To be restless, not able to sleep.

A نغو *naghw,* A speaking softly.

A نغوة *naghwat,* A musical tone or sound.

P نغوسه *naghosa,* Breaking the heart. Consolation, solace.

P نغوشا *naghoshā,* (*nighoshā,* or نغوشاك *naghoshāk*) A sect of infidels, applied chiefly by the Muhammadans to the Jews and fire-worshippers, and their religious ceremonies. One who turns from one religion to another; a Sabean. Name of an idol.

P نغوشاكيدن *naghoshākīdan,* To change one's religion.

P نغوشه *naghosha,* A breaking of the heart. Administration of comfort, solace. Listening, hearing.

A نغوض *naghūz,* A large-bunched camel. *Nughūz,* (v. n. of نغض) Being moved (the head). Shaking, tottering, staggering (a saddle, tooth, or animal travelling).

P نغوك *nighok,* A Jew. A fire-worshipper. An idolater.

P نغول *naghol,* An excavation made in the ground or side of a hill for sheltering cattle. *Nighol,* A staircase. The covering of a staircase. A trap-door on the roof of a house. *Nughol,* Deep, hollow. A long way. Profoundly versed in any art.

A نغولة *nughūlat,* (v. n. of نغل) Becoming corrupt (a thing newly born).

P نغوله *naghola,* The curling locks of the fair.

P نغولي *nugholī,* Depth.

A نغي *naghy,* A speaking intelligibly.

A نغية *naghyat,* First rumour of any thing before it is confirmed. A musical tone or sound.

A نغير *nughayr,* (dim. of نغر *nughar* and نغرة *nugharat*) Small birds with red beaks.

A نغيق *naghīk,* (v. n. of نغق) Croaking (a raven). (A camel) that brays in a low voice at intervals.

A نغيل *naghīl,* (fem. نغيلة) A bastard.

A نف *naff,* (v. n. of نف) Sowing (ground). Taking dry medicines.

A نفاء *nafāʼ,* (or نفاة *nafāt*) Refuse, worst part.

A نفأة *nufʼat,* (pl. نفأ *nufaʼ*) A segment of a plant. An enclosure of the best pasture.

A نفاث *naffās,* One who blows, a blower.

A نفاثة *nufāsat,* Whatever is spit out of the mouth, especially after rubbing the teeth. The breathing of one who has a pain in the chest. بنو نفاثة *banū nufāsat,* Name of a people.

A نفّاثة *naffāsat,* A female blower. نفّاثة في العقد *naffāsat fi'l ʿukad,* A female who blows upon the knots; a witch, sorceress.

A نفّاج *naffāj,* Proud, haughty, pompous, arrogant, presuming.

A نفاجة *nifājat,* A square patch of cloth put under the sleeve or cuff.

A نفّاجة *nuffājat,* A gusset let into a shift.

A نفاح *nufāh,* (v. n. of نفح) Diffusing fragrance (a perfume).

A نفّاح *naffāh,* Beneficent. Fragrant. A husband.

A نفاخ *nufākh,* A swelling of the belly.

A نفّاخ *nuffākh,* A flatulent tumour.

A نفّاخة *naffākhat,* A blister. *Nuffākhat,* A bubble floating on water. The bladder of a fish.

A نفاد *nafād,* (v. n. of نفد) Vanishing, perishing: being cleared, finished. Exhaustion. Death, destruction, annihilation.

A نفاذ *nafāz,* (v. n. of نفذ) Penetrating, pervading, piercing (any thing aimed at) and coming out on the other side. Arriving, coming, being brought (as a letter). Passing, leaving behind. Penetration. Escape from an enemy. Obeyed (order). The vowel kasra ـِ *i* written under the letter ه *he* when used as an affixed pronoun: as, تجرّد المجنون من كسائه *tajarrada'l majnūn min kisāʼihi,* The madman stripped himself of his clothes.

A نفّاذ *naffāz,* Whatever penetrates or passes; efficacious, efficient.

A نفار *nifār,* (v. n. of نفر) Being terrified, frightened, and running away (an animal). Going out (to do any thing). Fugaciousness, fugacity.

A نفارة *nufārat,* Plunder carried off by a conqueror; effects seized by a magistrate. Dominion, empire, authority, command, sway.

A نفارية *nufāriyat,* (with عفارية *ʿufāriyat*) as عفارية نفارية *ʿufāriyat nufāriyat,* Any thing gigantic, stupendous, terrible.

A نفارير *nafārīr,* Sparrows.

A نفّاز *nuffāz,* Diversion of jumping, leap-frog.

A نفاس *nifās,* (v. n. of نفس) Being precious, esteemed valuable. Child-birth, labour, bringing forth. A woman for forty days after child-birth. *Ni* or *nufās,* (pl. of نفساء *nufasāʼ*) Travailing women.

A نفاسة *nafāsat,* (v. n. of نفس) Being precious, exquisite. Esteeming (a thing) highly, and being sparing of (it). Envying (one), and deeming him unworthy. Bringing forth (a woman). Costliness.

A نفّاش *nuffāsh,* (Camels) pasturing at night without a keeper.

A نفاص *nifās,* (v. n. 3 of نفص) Trying who can make water the furthest. *Nufās,* A diabetes incident to sheep, often mortal.

A نفاض *nafāz,* The trembling of an ague or fever. *Nafāz* or *nufāz,* Scarcity of provisions on a journey. *Nifāz,* (pl. نفض *nufuz*) Breeches worn chiefly by boys. A cloth on which they shake the leaves of the Egyptian thorn or other trees. ما عليه نفاض *mā ʿalayhi nifāz,* He is naked, he has no garment. *Nifāz* or *nufāz,* Any thing that falls by shaking (as leaves or fruit from trees).

A نفاضة *nufāzat,* Any thing that falls by shaking (as leaves or fruit from trees). (equivalent to نفاثة *nufāsat*) Whatever is spit out of the mouth, especially after rubbing the teeth.

A نفاط *nafāt* or *naffāt,* Naphtha, bitumen, or a place where it is found in great plenty. A lamp, match, candle, torch. *Nifāt,* (v. n. 3 of نفط) Throwing up scum (a boiling pot).

A نفّاط *naffāt,* A brazen warlike instrument, from which an explosion is made by the means of naphtha. A preparer of naphtha.

A نفّاطة *naffātat,* A warlike engine for shooting forth naphtha.

A نفاطير *nafātīr,* (pl. of نفطورة *nuftūrat*) First spring-grasses. Scattered pastures or forage.

A نفاع *nafāʿ,* Profit, advantage, utility, use.

A نفّاع *naffāʿ,* Useful; one who does good.

P نفاغ *nifāgh,* A large cup, especially made of the skull of an animal or of bone. Imprecation, curse.

A نفافي *nafāfī,* (pl. of نفّي *naffaʼ*) Tables on which they sift polenta or barley-meal.

A نفاق *nafāk,* (v. n. of نفق) Being saleable (goods). Being brisk (market). *Nifāk,* Hypocrisy. (pl. of نفقة *nafakat*) Expenses, disbursements. اهل نفاق *ahli nifāk,* A hypocrite. P كلام نفاق انجام *kalāmi nifāk-anjām,* Hypocritical words.

A نفال *nifāl,* (pl. of نفل *nafal*) Plunders, spoils, especially those taken from the enemies of the faith.

Gifts, presents.

P نفام *nafām*, Darkish, blackish. Ugly. Bad.

A نفانف *nafānif*, (pl. of نفنف *nafnaf*) Valleys between mountains. The walls (of a house). The parts about (the liver).

A نفاوة *nufāwat*, Worst or refuse of a thing.

A نفاية *nafāyat* or *nufāyat*, Refuse, worst part.

P نفايه داشتن *nafāya dāshtan*, To reject, discard.

A نفائج *nafā*ʼ*ij*, (pl. of نفيجة *nafījat*) Bows.

A نفائح *nafā*ʼ*ih*, (pl. of نفيحة *nafīhat*) Strong, far-shooting (bows).

A نفائس *nafā*ʼ*is*, (pl. of نفيسة *nafīsat*,) Precious things. Delicacies. Much wealth. *Nafā*ʼ*is*, (or نفائس بهيّة *nafā*ʼ*isi bahiya*) Exquisite viands.

A نفائض *nafā*ʼ*iz*, Lean camels. Camels wandering or travelling. Those who throw pebbles to learn if any enemy or misfortune awaits them.

P نفايه *nafāya*, A dark colour. Black, turbid.

P نفت *naft*, Naphtha. Combustible matter.

A نفت *naft*, (v. n. of نفت) Swelling from milk or water poured over it (flour). *Naft*, (or نفتان *nafatān*) (v. n. of نفت) Being enraged, swelling with passion. Boiling (a pot), running over. Sticking to the sides of a pot (broth).

P نفت انداز *naft-andāz*, Firing artillery. A maker of fireworks.

P نفتغ *naftagh*, A measure.

P نفتي *naftī*, Of a dark green colour.

A نفث *nafs*, (v. n. of نفث) Blowing (as a necromancer when making incantations or playing tricks). Spitting (especially venom as a serpent). Pouring out blood (a vein or wound). Pronouncing (verse), delivering (an oracle). نفث الدم *nafsu'd dam*, A spitting of blood. نفث الشيطان *nafsu'sh shaytān*, (Devil's spittle) Poetry.

A نفثة *nafsat*, A magic puff. Whistling of winds.

P نفج *nafj*, Writing-paper.

A نفج *nafj*, (v. n. of نفج) Coming forth from the egg (a chick). Bouncing forth (a hare). Blowing stiffly (wind). Increasing, augmenting (wealth). (A woman's breasts) heaving up (her shift). *Nufuj*, (pl. of نفّيج *niffīj*) Strangers coming amongst others. Slow, dull (persons). امرأة نفج الحقيبة *imra*ʼ*atun nufuju'l hakībat*, A large-hipped woman.

A نفجة *nufjat*, A gore inserted in a shift.

A نفح *nafh*, (v. n. of نفح) Breathing or diffusing odour. Blowing (the wind). Striking (with a sword). Moving, setting (hair) in motion. Giving, bestowing. Bleeding (a vein). نفح روح *nafhi rūh*, The Holy Spirit which the angel Gabriel blew into the sleeve of the Virgin Mary, according to the Mussulmān belief. نفح نسيم *nafhi nasīm*, Breathing as the zephyrs. *Nafah*, Remote (design).

A نفحان *nafahān*, A breathing or diffusing odour.

A نفحة *nafhat*, One puff, gust, or breath of wind. A fragrant gale. Reputation. A gift. A part or mode of punishment. One draught of pure milk.

P نفحات نسائم چمن *nafahāti nasā*ʼ*imi chaman*, The fragrant air of the meads.

A نفخ *nafkh*, (v. n. of نفخ) Blowing, puffing (with the mouth). Sounding, winding (a horn). Inspiring, breathing into. Breaking wind. Bright, clear, advanced (as the day towards the meridian). Pride, vain-glory. Swelling, flatulency. Rupture, hernia. ذو نفخ *zū nafkh*, Proud, swelling (man). P نفخ صور كردن *nafkhi sūr kardan*, To wind a horn. To blow the last trump. A *Nufukh*, Full of juvenile vigour.

A نفخاء *nafkhā*ʼ, High ground, soft and loose, mixed with stones. The upper part of the leg-bone.

A نفخة *naf*, *nif*, or *nufkhat*, A windy tumour.

A نفد *nafad*, (or نفدان *nafadān*) (v. n. of نفد) Vanishing, being dissipated (wealth). Becoming empty of water and drying up (a well). Losing their provisions or stock (people).

A نفذ *nafz*, (v. n. of نفذ) Penetrating, pervading, passing, piercing quite through and coming out at the other side. Perception or intimate knowledge. *Nafaz*, The penetrating power. Free course.

A نفر *nafr*, (v. n. of نفر) Being frightened and running away. Going out of the valley at the time of the ceremonies at Mecca (this takes place on the second day after the festival). Being erect. Being divided, separated, scattered. Frightening. Victory. A crowd or body of men to which one belongs, especially fleeing or going together (to any one), or taking the precedency (in any thing). (pl. of نافر *nāfir*) Timid, runners away in fear. يوم النفر *yawmu'n nafr* or *nafar*, The day on which the pilgrims depart from Mina. *Nifrun*, (in comp. with عفر *ʻifrun*) as عفر نفر *ʻifrun nifrun* or *ʻafirun nafirun*, Any thing immense, awful, terrible, or gigantic. *Nafar*, (pl. انفار *anfār*) A number of men from three to ten. Any corps or society to which one belongs. A person, especially of the common people; a common soldier. A groom, servant. P نفر ضامن *nafar-zāmin*, Bail for personal appearance.

A نفّر *nuffar*, Frightened (fawns or women).

A نفرات *nafarāt*, (pl. of نفر) Troops of soldiers.

A نفراج *nifrāj*, (or نفراجة *nifrājat*) Pusillanimous, cowardly, base.

A نفران *nafarān*, (v. n. of نفر) Running away terrified (an animal).

A نفرة *nafrat*, Flight, terror. Abomination, aversion, horror. A crowd or body of men, especially flying or emigrating from any place. A body of men from three to ten. Kindred, near relations, associates. P نفرت داشتن *nafrat dāshtan*, To abhor, hold in abomination. نفرت كردن *nafrat kardan*, To fly from. A *Nufrat*, Dominion, command, authority, magistracy. *Nufrat* or *nufarat*, An amulet hung round the neck of a child to defend it against malignant eyes.

A نفرج *nifrij*, Timid, cowardly.

A نفرجاء *nifrijā*ʼ, Pusillanimous, cowardly, base.

A نفرجة *nafrajat*, (v. n. of نفرج Q) Talking much. *Nifrijat*, Cowardly, timid; a run-away.

P نفروج *naf* or *nufrūj*, A kind of rolling-pin.

P نفري *nafrī*, (or نفرين *nafrīn*) A curse.

A نفري *nafarī*, Service, profession (particularly that of a groom). A giant. A demon.

A نفريت (عفريت *ʻifrīt*) *nifrīt*, (عفرية نفرية *ʻifriyat nifriyat*, or عفريتة نفريتة *ʻifrītat nifrītat*) Gigantic; a giant.

A نفريج *nifrīj*, Loquacious, verbose.

P نفريدن *nafrīdan*, To execrate, curse, abominate.

P نفرين *nafrīn*, Detestation, abhorrence, execration. Imprecation, curse, opprobrious words, reproaches; treating with contumely or ridicule; holding out the fingers at, either before the face or behind the back; imprecating with held-up hands. Terror. Weeping, lamentation. نفرين كردن *nafrīn kardan*, (نفرين دادن *nafrīn dādan*, or نفريدن *nafrīdan*) To curse, execrate, imprecate. To abominate; to avoid. To be frightened. To take offence at another's words and fly in a passion.

P نفرين كنا *nafrīn-kunā*, One who execrates.

P نفرينيدن *nafrīnīdan*, To stink, smell badly.

A نفزان *nafazān*, (v. n. of نفز) Bounding (a doe).

A نفس *nafs*, (pl. نفوس *nufūs*) Breath, animal life. Soul, spirit, self. Body, blood, flesh. A person, individual, substance, essence, individual thing itself. Concupiscence, carnal or inordinate desire, sensuality. Truth, reality. The eye. A malignant eye. Mind, thought. Will, pleasure, desire. Grandeur, magnificence, pomp. Pride. Vice, fault, blemish. Disgrace, shame. The divine displeasure; punishment, chastisement, torment. One dose; a certain quantity of the herb قرظ *karaz*, with which they tan leather. نفس الامر *nafsu'l amr*, Essence, soul, or foundation of any thing. في نفس الامر *fī nafsi'l amr*, In fact, in truth. نفس امّارة *nafsi ammāra*, (or توقان نفس *tawkāni nafs*) Inordinate appetite, concupiscence. نفس سبعي يا لوّامة *nafsi sabʻī* or *lawwāma*, Irascibility or promptitude to the vindictive passions. نفس سائلة *nafsi sā*ʼ*ila*, Flowing blood. P ضبط نفس كردن *zabti nafs kardan*, To restrain one's passions, to overcome the lust of the flesh. A نفس عن نفس *nafsun ʻan nafsin*, One soul instead of another. نفس مطمئنّة يا نفس ملكي *nafsi mutma*ʼ*inna* or *nafsi malakī*, Benevolence. نفس ناطقة *nafsi nātika*, Reason. نفس نفيس *nafsi nafīs*, The precious soul. P نفس واپسين *nafsi wāpasīn*, The last breath. A بنفسه *bi nafsihi*, He himself. حليم النفس *halīmu'n nafs*, Of a meek spirit. *Nafas*, (v. n. of نفس) Envying. Esteeming (a thing) highly, being sparing or tenacious of (it). Being highly esteemed, much desired (a thing). (pl. انفاس *anfās*) Breath, respiration. A draught which quenches thirst. A long winded speech. Amplitude, ease, liberty. P نفس زدن *nafas zadan*, To breathe. نفس شمار زدن *na-*

fas shumār zadan, To hold the breath a long time as a penance. نفس كردن *nafas kardan*, To take breath, to pause. نفس گل *nafasi gul*, The empyrean heaven. A آخر نفس *ākhar nafas*, The last breath. ذو نفس *zū nafas*, Sufficient and agreeable (drink). صادق نفس *sādik nafas*, True, truth-speaking. ضيق النفس *ziku'n nafas*, (P تنگ نفس *tang-nafas*) Asthma, difficulty of respiration. انت في نفس من امرك *anta fī nafasin min amrika*, Be at ease in your affairs, do what you please. *Nufus* or *nufs*, (pl. of نفساء *nufasās*) Women in labour.

A نفسا *nafsan*, Willingly.

A نفساء *nufasās*, *nafsās*, or *nafasās*, (du. نفساوان *nufasāwāni*) (pl. نفساوات *nufasāwāt*, نفاس *nifās*, *nufās*, نفس *nufus*, *nufs*, and نوافس *nawāfis*) A woman in labour. A woman who has borne a child within forty days, or one not yet recovered after child-birth.

P نفسآباد *nafas-ābād*, The lungs, chest.

P نفساني *nafsāni*, Lewd, sensual. Spiritual, vital.

A نفسانيّة *nafsānīyat*, Sensuality, carnality, luxury, pride, pomp.

A نفسة *nufsat*, Delay, respite, breathing-time.

P نفس تنگ *nafas-tang*, Twinkling of an eye.

P نفس دراز *nafas-darāz*, Long-winded, prolix.

A نفسي *nafasī*, An instant.

A نفسيّ *nafsiy*, Carnal, sensual. Desirable. Spiritual, vital.

A نفش *nafsh*, (v. n. of نفش) Plucking or teasing (wool or cotton) with the fingers. (Camels) feeding in the night-time without a keeper (if straying in the day-time the word is همل *hamal*). *Nafash*, Wool. A plentiful year.

A نفص *nafs*, (v. n. of نفص) Speaking fast.

A نفصة *nufsat*, A violent flux of blood.

A نفض *nafz*, (v. n. of نفض) Shaking (a tree or garment). Shaking or causing (one) to tremble (an ague or fever). Having one's provisions spent. Being prolific (camels). Having many children (a woman). Putting forth ears (corn), or clusters (a vine). Fading partially (colour). Examining if safe (a place) all around. Reading (the chapters of the Kur'ān). *Nifz*, Bees' excrements. Parts (of dead bees) in the combs. Honey mixed with myrtle, with which they besmear a hive in order to entice the bees to make honey. *Nafaz*, Any thing falling from a tree (as leaves or fruit). Grape-stones sticking one within another. *Nufuz*, (pl. of نفاض *nifāz*) Breeches.

A نفضاء *nufazās*, The trembling of the body (in an ague). Partial rain.

A نفضة *nufzat*, Partial rain. *Nufzat* or *nufazat*, The trembling of the body (in an ague). *Nafazat*, A reconnoitering party, spies, scouts.

A نفضى *nafazā'*, (or نفضّي *nifizzā'*) Motion, agitation, tremor.

A نفط *naft*, (v. n. of نفط) Being angry, boiling with rage. *Naft* or *nift*, Naphtha, bitumen, liquid naphtha. Gunpowder. *Naft* or *nafat*, (v. n. of نفط) Being covered with pustules or blisters (as the hand with hard labour).

P نفط انداز *naft-andāz*, Casting forth naphtha (from fire-ships). A maker of fireworks. Engineer.

A نفطة *naftat*, *niftat*, or *nafitat*, Blisters. Pustules, pimples, small-pox. *Nafutat*, The ear. The outside or flap of the ear. *Nafitat*, Blistered (hand). *Nufatat*, A person soon angry; apt to explode.

A نفطورة *nuftūrat*, (pl. نفاطير *nafātīr*) The first spring-herbage; scattered forage.

P نفطي *naftī*, Anointed with bitumen.

A نفطيّ *naftīy*, Consisting of naphtha.

A نفطيّة *naftīyat*, Hurlers of naphtha.

A نفع *nafʿ*, (v. n. of نفع) Being useful, profitable, beneficial, availing. Gain, profit, advantage, emolument, interest. Avail. P سلطان نفع رسان *sultāni nafʿ-rasān*, A beneficent prince, one who confers benefits. A *Nifʿ* or *nifaʿ*, (pl. of نفعة *nifʿat*) Patches of leather sewed on a traveller's bag. *Nufʿ*, (pl. of نفوع *nafūʿ*) Useful, good-doing (men).

A نفعة *nafʿat*, (pl. نفعات *nafaʿāt*) A staff, rod. *Nifʿat*, (pl. نفع *nifʿ* and *nifaʿ*) A piece of leather sewed to each side of a traveller's scrip or bag.

A نفغ *nafgh*, (v. n. of نفغ) Having pustules or blisters on the hand from hard labour. Swelling from hard work (the hand).

A نفق *nafk*, (v. n. of نفق) Quitting its hole (a field-mouse). *Nafak*, (v. n. of نفق) Perishing, failing, dying (provisions, money, cattle), being deficient. A narrow, indistinct road. A hole, lurking-place. A mouse-hole. نفق الجري *nafiku'l jary*, (A horse) that soon spends himself in running, and comes speedily to a halt.

A نفقة *nafakat*, (pl. نفقات *nafakāt* and نفاق *nifāk*) The necessary expenses for living, expenditure, disbursement. Stipend, salary, maintenance. P نفقه خوردن *nafaka khwurdan*, To expend. نفقه كردن *nafaka kardan*, To defray the expenses of living. To maintain (a person), to give (him) a pension. A *Nufakat*, The hole of a field-mouse or mole (which has generally ten or a dozen entrances).

A نفكة *nafakat*, The root of the bone of the chin. A lump behind the ear.

A نفل *nafl*, (v. n. of نفل) Presenting with a gift or plunder. Giving an extraordinary gift. Swearing. A voluntary act of religion, the observance of which is not prescribed: a work of supererogation. Cold. A gift. *Nafal*, (pl. انفال *anfāl* and نفال *nifāl*) Plunder, especially taken from the enemies of the faith. Spoil, prey. A present, donation. A kind of clover-grass. *Nufal*, The three first nights of the month (the days being called غرر *ghurar*).

P نفل *nufal*, A place in the fields or desert where men and animals rest in the winter.

A نفناف *nafnāf*, A valley between mountains.

A نفنف *nafnaf*, A valley between mountains. The air between heaven and earth. The steep-down, perpendicular descent of a mountain like a wall. The side of a well or wall from top to bottom. A desert. (pl. نفانف *nafānif*) The walls (of a house). The parts about the liver.

A نفو *nafw*, The act of driving away.

A نفوة *nafwat* or *nifwat*, The worst part of any thing. *Nifwat*, Driven away, outcast.

A نفوت *nafūt*, (A pot) boiling over.

A نفوح *nafūh*, (A camel) giving milk without being milked. Strong, far-shooting (bow).

A نفوذ *nafūz*, One who penetrates, passes, gets through, or executes (business). *Nufūz*, (v. n. of نفذ) Penetrating, piercing through, pervading.

A نفور *nafūr*, Frightened, scared, fleeing. One who abhors or nauseates; averse. P بيزار و نفور شدن *bīzār u nafūr shudan*, To abominate, nauseate, fly from. A *Nufūr*, (v. n. of نفر) Being frightened and running away (an animal). Going out of the valley of Mina at the performance of the ceremonies at Mecca. Going about (any business). Being inflamed and swollen (the eye). Swelling (as the skin or any other part). يوم النفور *yawmu'n nufūr*, The day on which the pilgrims depart from Mina.

A نفورة *nufūrat*, Dominion, empire, command, magistracy. Affinity. Kinsmen, paternal relations.

A نفوز *nafūz*, Bounding (doe).

A نفوس *nufūs*, (pl. of نفس *nafs*) Souls, selves.

A نفوش *nufūsh*, (v. n. of نفش) Feeding in the night-time without a keeper (camels or sheep). Possessing the produce of a fruitful season. Drawing meat towards you in order to eat.

A نفوض *nafūz*, Fruitful, prolific (woman). *Nufūz*, Recovery from sickness, convalescence.

A نفوع *nafūʿ*, Useful, beneficent (man).

A نفوغ *nufūgh*, (v. n. of نفغ) Being blistered by hard labour: swelling from hard work (the hand).

A نفوق *nufūk*, (v. n. of نفق) Perishing, failing, or dying (provisions, money, or cattle). Being excoriated (a wound).

P نفول *nafūl* or *nufūl*, The leg, shank.

A نفوه *nufūh*, (v. n. of نفه) Being dejected, cowardly, lazy, slow. Submission after disobedience.

A نفه *nafh*, (v. n. of نفه) Being jaded, sluggish, and weak (a camel).

A نفّه *nuffah*, (pl. of نافه) Lazy, slow (camels).

A نفي *nafy*, (v. n. of نفي) Prohibiting, interdicting, proscribing. Denying, disowning, disavowing. Driving about (as wind the dust). Carrying down foam, leaves, &c. (a torrent). Driving away or abandoning (as a father his son). Banishing, exiling. Being afar off, retiring apart. Being rejected or banished. Spreading out (coin) to separate the good from the bad. Pouring down its contents (a cloud). Negation. A threat. The negative imperative. Prohibition, proscription. *Nufa'*, A round table made of palm-leaves.

A نفأ naffa', (pl. نفافي nafāfī) A table on which they sift polenta or barley-flour.

A نفيّ nafīy, Negative. Rejected, disowned, abandoned, turned out of doors (by a father). Rubbish blown round the root of a tree. Drops of water falling from a rope whilst being drawn out of a well. Gravel scattered by the feet of a gallopping horse. Refuse, filth, rubbish. Froth or scum of a boiling pot. Annihilation, non-existence. Part of an army scattered or loitering about the wings or rear; camp-followers; the meaner sort of attendants. A shield made of palm-leaves. A threat. The negative attribute (in logic). نفيّ المطر nafīyu'l matar, Bespattered by the rain.

A نفيان nafayān, (v. n. of نفي) Driving about (as wind the dust). Spreading out (coins) to separate the good from the bad. Pouring forth its contents (a cloud). Drops of rain flying about. Dust or leaves blown about the root of a tree.

A نفية nafyat, A table made of palm-leaves, on which they spread اقط akit to dry. *Nifyat*, Driven away, outcast. *Nufyat*, A round table made of palm-leaves, without feet, which they place on the ground and eat off.

A نفيّة nafīyat, A round table of palm-leaves, without feet, from which they eat, or whereon they spread new cheese to dry.

A نفيتة nafītat, Coarse food made of meal sprinkled with milk or water (eaten in a scarcity).

A نفيث nafīs, (Blood) poured from a wound.

A نفّيج niffīj, (pl. نفج nufuj) One who interposes to reconcile differences, or who neither reconciles or promotes discord.

A نفيجة nafījat, A bow.

A نفّيح niffīh, A meddler, busy-body.

A نفيحة nafīhat, Strong (bow) shooting far. A bit of the tree نبع nabع.

A نفيخ nafīkh, Appointed to blow the fire.

A نفيذ nafīz, Who or what pierces, penetrates, or pervades. (A royal edict) received and obeyed.

P نفير nafīr, A kind of musical instrument. A brazen trumpet. A fife, flute. The shrill note of the fife. طبل و نفير tabl u nafīr, Drum and fife. نفير نامه nafīr-nāma, A general order in writing for assembling an army.

A نفير nafīr, (v. n. of نفر) Going (about any business). One who goes before. A body (of men), especially from three to ten. A crowd or body of men, especially flying or emigrating from any place. نفير عامّ nafīri عamm, A general rising or expedition; the publishing of the Arrière-ban, a general summons of the nobility to appear in arms with their troops. يوم النفير yawmu'n nafīr, The day on which the pilgrims depart from Mina to Mecca. *Nufayr*, (dim. of نفر nafar) A very small number of persons.

P نفيرندن nafīrandan, To be good, beautiful.

P نفيري nafīrī, A kind of trumpet.

A نفيز nafīz, (or نفيزة nafīzat) Butter in the churning-bottle floating in small particles.

A نفيس nafīs, (fem. نفيسة nafīsat) Precious, delicate, exquisite. A precious or wished-for object, whatever one receives with a short-breathing eagerness. Great riches.

A نفيش nafīsh, Scattered furniture.

A نفيص nafīs, Sweet or fresh water.

A نفيضة nafīzat, An advanced post, spy, scout.

A نفّيضي niffīza', Motion. Tremor.

A نفيط nafīt, (v. n. of نفط) Sneezing, or forcing any thing out of the nose (a goat). Being blistered from hard work (the hand). Boiling over (as a pot). Being enraged. Squalling (a child). Speaking what is not understood. Breaking wind. Troubled with pustules or blisters.

A نفيطة nafītat, Blistered (hand).

A نفيعة nafīعat, Gain, profit, advantage, benefit.

A نفيف nafīf, The girth of a camel's saddle.

A نق نق nuk nuk, A word commanding a Jew-butcher to strip the fat from the flesh.

A نقا naka', (pl. انقاء ankās and نقيّ nukīy) A heap of sand. The bone of the arm. Any bone containing marrow. بنات النقا banātu'n naka', (or شحمة النقا shahmatu'n naka') A kind of animalcule living in the sand. *Nuka'*, (pl. of نقاوة nukāwat) The best parts of things.

A نقاء nakās, (v. n. of نقي) Being good, pure, sifted, cleaned. Cleanness; purity; innocence. Pure, clean. *Nikās*, (v. n. of نقي) Meeting, encountering. *Nukās*, (pl. of نقاوة nukāwat) The best or selectest parts of things. (pl. of نقيّ nakīy) Clean, pure, excellent.

A نقاءة nakāsat, (v. n. of نقي) Being clean, sifted, good, excellent.

A نقاب nikāb, (v. n. of نقب) Meeting unexpectedly. Finding by chance (water) unlooked for. A woman's veil. A signal, sign, mark. A very learned man. The belly. A road through rugged grounds. (pl. of نقب nukb) Scabs. نقاب خضرا nikābi khazrā, The vault of heaven. P نقاب نيلي nikābi nīlī, (The sable veil) Night.

A نقّاب nakkāb, A sapper, miner. An examiner, inquirer, scrutinizer.

A نقابة nakābat, (v. n. of نقب) Being or becoming chief, magistrate, or leader of the people. *Nikābat*, Tribunitial or magisterial dignity.

A نقاة nakāt, Best part of corn (or dates) when sifted or cleaned. *Nukāt*, Refuse of sifted corn.

A نقاث nakāsi, A hyena.

A نقاخ nukākh, Cold, pure, sweet water. Sweet and refreshing sleep.

A نقّاخ nukkākh, The back part of the head towards the ears. A lump on the top of the ear.

A نقاد nikād, (or نقادة nikādat) (pl. of نقد nakad) Certain kinds of sheep of a bad sort.

A نقّاد nakkād, A cambist who knows at once good from bad money. Prompt, ready. An adept. A shepherd of the sheep called نقد nakad.

A نقار nikār, (v. n. 3 of نقر) Stabbing with reproaches, railing at, expostulating sharply with. Bandying words. Expostulation. (pl. of نقرة nukrat) Caverns. Particles of gold or silver.

A نقّار nakkār, A piercer or a striker with the beak. Whoever or whatever pecks or notches.

A نقارة nukārat, As much as a bird takes up in its bill or pecks at once, a beakful.

A نقارچي nakārchī, A beater of the kettle-drum.

P نقارخانه nakār-khāna, A band of music. The place at the porch of a palace where the drums are beaten at stated intervals.

P نقاره nakāra or nakkāra, A kettle-drum.

A نقاري nakārī, A beater of the kettle-drum.

A نقاز nukāz, An ulcerous distemper incident to cattle, which makes them jump till they die.

A نقّاز nakkāz or nukkāz, A species of bird. Young sparrows.

A نقاسة nikāsat, Reproach, ridicule, sarcasm, irony. A nickname.

A نقّاش nakkāsh, A painter, stainer, embroiderer, gilder (of books). A sculptor, carver, engraver. A draughtsman.

A نقاشة nikāshat, The art of painting, staining, embroidering, or engraving.

A نقّاشي nakkāshī, Drawing, painting; graving. نقّاشي كردن nakkāshī kardan, To paint. To carve.

A نقاصة nakāsat, Sweetness, purity (of water).

A نقّاض nakkāz, One who hurts the back (of a pack-horse), who throws on a burden with violence. A heavy, back-breaking, creaking load. A breaker (of an agreement). Name of a certain Musulmān doctor. *Nukkāz*, Name of a plant.

A نقاضة nukāzat, The untwisted part of a rope, especially of goats' hair: whatever falls from it.

A نقاط nikāt, (pl. of نقطة nuktat) Points, dots. Scattered bits of fodder, patches of grass.

A نقّاط nakkāt, Who marks with points or dots.

A نقاع nikāع, (pl. of نقع nakع) Dusts. Hard places where waters stagnate.

A نقّاع nakkāع, Proud, conceited; a vain boaster.

A نقاعة nukāعat, A liquid in which any thing has been soaked, a decoction.

A نقاف nikāf, (v. n. 3 of نقف) Striking with a sword or breaking the head of another. Prudent, attentive. (See also نقاب nikāb.) اليوم قحاف و غدا نقاف al yawm kihāf wa ghadā nikāf, To-day cups, and to-morrow business.

A نقّاف nakkāf, Prudent, attentive, or curious (man), one who questions accurately, who inquires eagerly. A bloody robber, killing all he meets.

A نقّافة nakkāfat, (A woman) importunate, teasing with questions.

A نقّاقة nakkākat, A (female) frog.

A نقال *nikāl*, (v. n. of نقل) Allowing (camels) to drink once and again. (v. n. 3 of نقل) Trotting well (a horse). Conversing, telling stories one to another. Drinking water and eating fodder once or twice without any one pasturing him (a camel). (pl. of نقل *nakl* or *nikl*) Mended boots. (pl. of نقلة *naklat*) Short and broad-headed spears.

A نقّال *nakkāl*, Swift, quick-trotting (horse). A transporter. A mimic, actor, player.

A نقّالي *nakkālī*, Acting, mimicking.

A نقام *nakām* or *nikām*, Muddy (water). *Nikām*, Salted.

A نقانق *nakānik*, (pl. of نقنق *niknik*) Ostriches.

A نقاوة *nakāwat* or *nukāwat*, (v. n. of نقي) Being cleaned, sifted, good, and choice. Purity, cleanness. (pl. نقا *nuka'* or نقاء *nukā*) The best or selected part of any thing. *Nukāwat*, (pl. نقاوي *nakāwa'*) A kind of plant used in washing.

A نقاوي *nakāwa'*, (pl. of نقاوة *nukāwat*) Plants of the حمض *hamz* species, used in washing linens.

A نقاهة *nakāhat*, Recovery from disease, convalescence. Weakness, feebleness, languor.

A نقايا *nakāya'*, (pl. of نقاية *nukāyat*) Choicest parts of things cleaned or sifted.

A نقاية *nakāyat*, (v. n. of نقي) Being cleaned, sifted. Being good and excellent. *Nukāyat*, (pl. نقايا *nakāya'* and نقاء *nukā*) The choicest part of any thing cleaned. Refuse of a thing (as chaff).

A نقائذ *nakāiz*, (pl. of نقيذة *nakīzat*) Horses taken from the enemy.

A نقائص *nakāis*, (pl. of نقيصة *nakīsat*) Imperfections, bad qualities, vices, blemishes.

A نقائض *nakāiz*, (pl. of نقيضة *nakīzat*) Contradictions. Damages, injuries.

A نقائع *nakāiʿ*, (pl. of نقيعة *nakīʿat*) Camels or other cattle slaughtered for the entertainment of strangers. نقائع الموت *nakāiʿu'l mawt*, The feasts of death, *i.e.* mankind.

A نقائل *nakāil*, (pl. of نقيلة *nakīlat*) Patches of leather for mending boots or shoes.

P نقب *nakb*, A rabbit's burrow. A subterraneous excavation, a mine, gallery. An implement of miners or thieves for piercing walls. نقب زن *nakb-zan*, A miner, any one using such an instrument.

A نقب *nakb*, (v. n. of نقب) Digging (through a wall). Tapping (for the dropsy). Inquiring after news. Relating or retailing (news). Mending (boots), patching a hole. Requiting any one (misfortune). Going from place to place. Lifting his feet towards his belly (a horse). A way through mountains. The scab. An ulcer in the side. *Nukb*, (pl. انقاب *ankāb* and نقاب *nikāb*) The scab. *Nahab*, (v. n. of نقب) Having the feet worn bare, smooth, and perforated below (a camel). Being torn or worn (a boot). Going from place to place seeking an asylum. *Nukab*, Parts of the scab scattered here and there.

A نقباء *nukabā*, Princes, leaders, tribunes.

A نقبة *nikbat*, A mode of veiling the face. *Nukbat*, A hole. Scab, or parts of it, scattered here and there. A garment worn round the middle; breeches. Colour. The face. Rust.

A ثقة نقة *sikat nikat*, Trusty, confidential.

A نقت *nakt*, An extracting of marrow.

A نقث *naks*, (v. n. of نقث) Emptying (a bone) of the marrow. Tearing up, and carrying from place to place. Inquiring into. Mixing, confounding, (a discourse, as meats are mixed together). Injuring, hurting (by words). Making haste, doing any thing expeditiously, going out quickly.

A نقثلة *naksalat*, (v. n. of نقثل Q) Going in a drawling, feeble pace, and raising the dust.

A نقح *nak-h*, (v. n. of نقح) Extracting (the marrow from a bone). Unbarking, peeling. Clearing away excrescences (from the stem of a palm-tree). A white summer cloud. *Nakah*, Pure sand.

A نقخ *nakhh*, (v. n. of نقخ) Smiting, piercing. Striking (the head), penetrating to the brain.

A نقخة *nakakhat*, Sluggish, fat (she-camel).

A نقد *nakd*, (v. n. of نقد) Glancing (the eye upon any thing). Counting out or paying (in ready money). Separating the good from bad coin. Choosing the best of any thing. Poking the finger into a walnut. Peeling (nuts). Striking with the bill (a bird, particularly a net or trap). Biting (a serpent). Ready money, prompt payment, cash. (Coin) of a just standard. P نقد جان *nakdi jān*, (or نقد روان *nakdi rawān*) The spirit. Current coin. نقد شش روزه *nakdi shash roza*, The world with all it contains. A نقد و جنس *nakd u jins*, Money and goods. P با وجه نقد *bā wajhi nakd*, With ready money. A *Nikd* or *nukd*, A boy who does not grow or thrive on his food. *Nukd*, *nakad*, *nakid*, or *nukud*, A kind of tree. *Nakad*, (v. n. of نقد) Being peeled, excoriated (the hoof of a horse). Being broken or worn down (a tooth). (A boy) not growing or thriving, whose food does not agree with (him). (pl. نقاد *nikād* and نقادة *nikādat*) A species of ugly short-legged sheep (peculiar to بحرين *bahrayn* in Arabia; whence the proverb, اذلّ من النقد *azall mini'n nakad*, Meaner than such sheep. *Nakid*, Peeled (hoof).

A نقدا نقد *nakdā nakd*, Prompt payment.

A نقدة *nikdat*, Caraway (seeds).

P نقد گير *nakd-gīr*, A bribe-taker. A worldling.

A نقديّ *nakdīy*, Ready (money). Belonging to ready money. A monied man.

P نقدي گماشته *nakdī-gumāshta*, A subordinate in a treasury.

P نقدينه *nakdīna*, Ready cash.

A نقذ *nakz*, (v. n. of نقذ) Saving, delivering, rescuing. Safety. Rest. نقذا لك *nakzan laka*, A formula pronounced when one is slipping or falling. *Nakaz*, (v. n. of نقذ) Fleeing, escaping. Liberated, rescued. ما له شقذ ولا نقذ *mā lahu shakaz wa lā nakaz*, He has nothing.

A نقر *nakr*, (v. n. of نقر) Striking. Turning the point of the tongue against the palate and making a whistling noise. Smacking (the thumb and middle finger). Hollowing, excavating, chiseling (stone or wood). Graving, writing upon stone. Piercing with the beak (as a bird her eggs). Stabbing with reproaches, railing at, scolding. Pecking (grain) with the bill. Inviting some to the exclusion of others. Blowing the trumpet ناقور *nākūr*. A smack with the lips, to make a horse quicken his pace. A smacking noise made by the thumb and middle finger. *Nikr*, A small groove in a date-stone whence the stalk grows. *Nakar*, (v. n. of نقر) Growing angry, becoming enraged. Being distempered in the feet (a sheep). Loss of property. اعوذ بالله من العقر و النقر *aʿūzu bi'llāh mini'l ʿakar wa'n nakar*, God preserve me from misfortune! *Nakir*, Enraged, angry. *Nukar*, (pl. of نقرة *nukrat*) Caverns, small round cavities.

A نقرة *nakrat*, Somewhat (used only negatively). A hollow groove in a date-stone whence the stalk grows. One smack with the fingers. *Nikrat*, A bandying of words to and fro. *Nukrat*, A cavern, cavity, hollow (especially small, as in the lower part of the hind-head, socket of the eye, or foramen ani). A place where a bird lays her eggs. (pl. نقر *nukar* and نقار *nikār*) A round hollow in the ground. (pl. نقار *nikār*) Melted gold or silver; an ingot. Gold or silver coin, money. *Nakirat*, (A sheep) distempered in the feet. High ground rising out of low-lying ground. *Nukarat*, A disease in the feet or side of a sheep.

A نقردة *nakradat*, Continuance in a place.

P A نقرس *nikris*, Gout (especially with swelling in the feet or hands). Death, destruction. A sore calamity. An omen, portent. A skilful and attentive road-guide. An excellent physician. A female ornament or head-dress resembling a rose.

P نقره *nikra*, Caraways. *Nukra*, Silver. A numbness in the limbs. Any thing white. نقرهٔ خام *nukrai khām*, Pure, virgin silver. Purity, softness, delicacy. نقرهٔ خنگ زرتشتي *nukrai khing zartushtī*, The sun. نقرهٔ شاخدار *nukrai shākhdār*, Silver (pure), plate.

A نقري *nakra'*, An especial and exclusive invitation (opposed to جفلي *jafala'*). *Nakara'*, Defamation. بنات نقري *banātu nakara'*, Women who abuse and rail at every one who passes by.

A نقريس *nikrīs*, A skilful physician. An expert road-guide.

P نقرئي *nukraī*, Made of silver, silver.

A نقز *nakz*, (v. n. of نقز) Bounding (as a deer or kangaroo). *Nikz*, The worst species of cattle. *Nukz*, A well. *Nahaz*, A surname, nickname. *Nakaz* or *nakiz*, The worst part of any thing remaining after the best has been taken away. Poor, lean cattle. Low, base men. *Nakiz*, Pure, fresh, sweet water. A surname, nickname.

A نقزان *nakazān*, The bounding (of a doe).

A نقس *naks*, (v. n. of نقس) Striking (especially the wooden gong ناقوس *nākūs*). Railing at, reproaching. Vice, failing, fault. Reproach, satire. The scab. *Niks*, (pl. انقاس *ankās* and انقس *ankus*) Writing-ink.

A نقش *naksh*, (v. n. of نقش) Painting, printing, staining of two or more colours. Embroidering. Carving, engraving. Lying with. Pulling out (a sting, thorn, hair). Clearing (a place) of thorns (where sheep are to recline). Striking (clusters of dates) with thorns to make them ripen quicker. Doing any thing attentively and expeditiously. Publishing, divulging, exposing. Having ripe dates (a branch). Dry dates put into a vessel and sprinkled with water. Painting, embroidery; a picture, drawing, portrait, map, plan. A pip on a card, a dot on a die. Venery. A lucky throw at dice. A bit of gum, less than صعرور *sug-rūr*. نقش بحرام *nakshi ba harām*, (or نقش حرام *nakshi harām*) A well-made person, but good for nothing. P نقش بر آب زدن *naksh bar āb zadan*, To write upon the water, (met.) To obliterate. نقش بر آب كشيدن *naksh bar āb kashīdan*, To draw figures on the water, (met.) To engage in unprofitable pursuits. نقش بستن *naksh bastan*, To design, fashion, make, create. To limn, portray. نقش بي غبار *nakshi bī ghubār*, Cries of the oppressed. نقش پرگار كن *nakshi pargār-kun*, All created things. نقش پرمور *nakshi parmūr*, The comb of honey, a bee-hive. نقش خاك گوهري *nakshi khāki gawharī*, The portrait or figure of a noble and upright man. نقش دوختن *naksh dokhtan*, To embroider. نقش ديوار *nakshi dīwār*, Thunderstruck, confounded (so as to appear like a picture on the wall. نقش قندهار *nakshi kandahār*, An alluring, ravishing object. A نقش كالحجر *naksh ka'l hajar*, (or more properly كالنقش في الحجر *ka'n naksh fi'l hajar*) Like an engraving on stone, *i.e.* indelible. نقش كل *nakshi kul*, The throne of God. P نقش نيك *nakshi nek*, Happy but fleeting days. پر نقش و نگار *pur naksh u nigār*, Full of paintings and ornaments. A *Nuksh*, Ripe dates, but moist, not dried.

P نقش آباد *naksh-ābād*, Ardent spirits.

P نقش بازي *naksh-bāzī*, Cunning.

P نقشبان *nakshibān*, A city in ارّان *arrān*.

P نقشبند *naksh-band*, A painter, embroiderer. One who adorns. نقشبند حوادث *naksh-bandi hawādis*, An epithet of God.

P نقشبندي *naksh-bandī*, The art of painting or embroidery. *Naksh-bandī*, (or نقشبنديه *naksh-bandiya*) Certain rites or ceremonies of the Soofies.

P نقش پرداز *naksh-pardāz*, A painter.

P نقش پيوند *naksh-paywand*, A limner.

P نقشجهان *nakshijihān*, (or نقشوان *nakshu-wān*) Name of a city in Armenia.

P نقش زياد *naksh-ziyād*, Any thing existing only in name. A kind of game with dice.

A نقشة *naksha*, A portrait, model, map, plan.

A نقص *naks*, (or نقصان *nuksān*) (v. n. of نقص) Diminishing, injuring. Being defective, damaged. Defect, deficiency, wastage, diminution, decrease, detriment, damage, loss, want, blemish, injury, prejudice, mischief (نقص *naks*, in general, implying, In quality, and نقصان *nuksān*, In quantity). دخل عليه نقص في عقله *dakhala ʿalayhi naksun fī ʿak-lihi*, There is a defect in his understanding. P نقصان آوردن *nuksān āwardan*, To cheat, defraud, entail loss.

A نقض *nakz*, (v. n. of نقض) Demolishing, dissolving, undoing, untwisting. Violating (an agreement), breaking (faith). Dissolution. Violation, rupture. P نقض پيمان *nakzi paymān*, Violation of agreement, breach of treaty. A *Nikz*, (pl. انقاض *ankāz*) A male or she-camel emaciated with fatigue. Untwisted, undone. Demolished. Emaciated. Ground broken into many hillocks by mushrooms piercing through. The piping of chickens, young ostriches, or quails. The cry of a scorpion or crocodile. The croaking of a frog. The sound made by an eagle or a hawk. Bees' excrements, or dead insects fallen into honey. The cracking noise made by pulling the joints of the fingers. Honey, which, with myrtle, they rub on a hive to induce bees to make honey. *Nikz* or *nakaz*, A rope untwisted to be re-twisted, or a garment unravelled to be re-spun. (pl. انقاض *ankāz* and نقوض *nukūz*) The surface of the earth upheaved by mushrooms. *Nukz*, Part of a demolished building. *Nakaz*, Taken down, demolished (building). *Nukaz*, A mode of wrestling.

A نقضة *nikzat*, A she-camel lean from travel.

A نقط *nakt*, (v. n. of نقط) Marking (a letter) with the diacritical points. *Nukat*, (pl. of نقطة *nuktat*) Points, dots. Patches of grass.

A نقطة *nuktat*, (pl. نقط *nukat* and نقاط *nikāt*) A point, a dot. A geometrical point. A spot, stain. A dot, a pip or spot upon a die. A diacritical point upon some of the consonants. A part of any thing. A little fodder separated from the rest. Choice wealth. نقطهٔ اعتدال *nuktaʾi iʿtidāl*, Equinoctial colure. نقطة الاعتدال الربيعي *nuktatu'l iʿtidāli'r rabīʿiy*, Vernal equinoctial point. نقطة الاعتدال الخريفي *nuktatu'l iʿtidāli'l kharīfiy*, Autumnal equinoctial point. نقطه بنقطه *nukta ba nukta*, From point to point, punctually. نقطهٔ حسّي *nuktaʾi hissī*, A tangible point. نقطهٔ دائره *nuktaʾi dāʾira*, Point of a circle. Muhammad. P نقطهٔ روشنتر پرگار *nuktaʾi ro-shantar-pargār*, The pole. Centre of the world. Muhammad. نقطهٔ زرّين *nuktaʾi zarrīn*, The sun. A نقطة سمت الرأس *nuktatu samti'r raʾs*, The vertical point. نقطهٔ سويدا *nuktaʾi suwaydā*, Heart's core. نقطهٔ عرضي *nuktaʾi ʿarazī*, An imaginary point. P نقطهٔ گل *nuktaʾi gil*, Centre of the earth. Terrestrial globe. A نقطة المقابلة *nuktatu'l mukā-balat*, An opposite point. نقطة المنقلب الشتوي *nuk-tatu'l munkalabi'sh shatawiy*, Brumal or winter solstitial point. نقطة المنقلب الصيفي *nuktatu'l mun-kalabi's sayfiy*, Summer solstitial point. P نقطهٔ نه دائره *nuktaʾi nuh dāʾira*, Centre of the earth. Muhammad.

P نقطه دار *nukta-dār*, Dotted. Marked with a diacritical point (as ز *ze* or ش *shīn*).

A نقع *nakʿ*, (v. n. of نقع) Flowing into any place and stagnating (water). Steeping, soaking (in water), putting (any thing medicinal) into (it). Abounding (death). Killing. Being raised (a sound). Making a continued noise or bawling, hallooing. Tearing, slitting (the breast of a garment). Quenching (thirst). Believing (intelligence). Slaughtering (a camel to entertain guests); whence ميلوا ننقع لكم *mīlū nankaʿ lakum*, Turn in, we'll treat you well. Provoking (with reproaches). A flat, level country. (pl. نقاع *nikāʿ* and نقوع *nu-kūʿ*) Raised dust; a cloud of dust. An ostrich's cry. (pl. نقاع *nikāʿ* and انقع *ankuʿ*) A place where water stagnates, hard clay soil which it cannot penetrate. Saliva in the mouth. A rent in the breast or collar. Slaughter. (pl. انقع *ankuʿ*) Stagnant water.

A نقعاء *nakʿāʾ*, A flat, level country.

A نقف *nakf*, (v. n. of نقف) Striking violently (on the head) with a spear or stick and penetrating nearly to the brain. (A bird) breaking (her eggs). Splitting (a colocynth), taking away (the rind or core). Straining, clearing. Diluting (wine) with water. *Nikf* or *nakf*, A young bird coming out of the shell. *Nukf*, (pl. of نقيف *nakīf*) Worm-eaten (trunks of palm-trees).

A نقفة *nakafat*, A hollow on a mountain-top.

A نقل *nakl*, (v. n. of نقل) Transporting, carrying from one place to another. Transplanting. Moving, making a move at chess. Translating (from one language into another). Transcribing, copying. Imitating. Mimicking, acting. Relating, telling. Repairing, mending (a boot). Patching, mending (a garment). Putting a leather sole on a camel's foot when hurt. Transportation, translation. History, narrative, relation, report, account, theme, tale, story. A copy, duplicate. Whatsoever is carried; a burden. The transitive or active signification of a verb. Affability, mildness, softness, easy good-nature. P نقل كردن *nakl kardan*, To transport from place to place. To die. To translate. To relate. To mend. نقل اثقال كردن *nakli askāl kardan*, To carry loads from one place unto another. نقل ماتم *nakli mātam*, Sweetmeats sent round at a funeral. A نقل مكان *nakli makān*, Emigration. The first stage of a journey, or halting-place at a very little distance, where they remain some time to collect what may have been forgotten of the requisites for travelling. The first stage is often made long before they really mean to set off, for the sake of seizing a lucky moment to commence a journey in. Transmigration. P شراب نقل کردن *sharāb nakl kardan*, To pour wine from one vessel into another. A *Nakl, nikl*, or *nakal*, (pl. انقال *ankāl* and نقال *nikāl*) A worn and patched boot or shoe. *Nakl* or *nukl*, Any thing given at entertainments along with wine, as fruits or sweetmeats. *Nukl*, Presents sent with much pomp by a bridegroom to his bride before marriage. Emigration. Whispering, slander. P نقل خواجه *nukli khwāja*, A small grain resembling black pepper, but which within is white and sweet. A نقل مجلس *nukli majlis*, A buffoon, fool, jester. Sport, play, pleasantry, buffoonery. *Nakal*, A feather taken from one arrow and put on another. A stony place with trees. Volubility of tongue, readiness of reply, repartee. A distemper in the sole of a camel's foot, rendering it necessary that it be tied up. Stones held in the hand for breaking nuts or pounding drugs. *Nakil*, Stony with trees. (A man) ready in answer. *Nukal*, The fourth, fifth, and sixth nights of a month.

P نقل *nukul*, A shelter for cattle made in the ground or on a hill's side. Hollow, deep. Bottom.

A نقلاً *naklan*, Traditionally.

A نقلاء *nukalā*, (pl. of ناقل *nākil*) Transporters. Relators.

A نقلب *naklab*, Name of a people in Arabia who profess the Christian religion.

P نقل بند *nakl-band*, A compiler of narratives.

A نقلة *naklat*, (pl. نقال *nikāl*) A short and broad-headed spear. *Niklat*, (A woman) not asked in marriage, as being advanced in years. *Nuklat*, Removal from one place unto another; departure, migration: a roving life. Detraction, slander. *Nakalat*, Sound of running water. (pl. of ناقل *nākil*) Writers. نقلةُ احوال *nakalaẞi ahwāl*, Historians.

P نقلدان *nukldān*, A fruit or sweetmeat-plate.

P نقل نويسي *nakl-narīsī*, Copying.

A نقلي *naklī*, Fictitious. Copied, transcribed.

A نقليّ *nakliy*, A vender of dried fruits. Imitated, copied, transcribed.

A نقم *nakm*, (v. n. of نقم) Being angry. Chiding, reproving, checking, reproaching. Punishing, taking private revenge. Hating, disapproving. Voraciousness. *Nakam*, Middle of the road. *Nakim* or *nikam*, (pl. of نقمة *nakmat, nikmat*, or *nakimat*) Punishments, revenges.

A نقمات *nakimāt*, (pl. of نقمة) Punishments.

A نقمة *nakmat, nikmat*, or *nakimat*, (pl. نقم *nakim* and *nikam*) Punishment, revenge, vengeance. *Nikmat*, Hatred. A distemper. Vehemence, hardness, severity.

A نقنق *niknik*, (pl. نقانق *nakānik*) An ostrich. Timid, flying. Light, not heavy.

A نقنقة *naknakat*, (v. n. of نقنق Q) Being deeply sunk in the socket (the eye). Clucking (as a hen). Croaking (as a frog). The croaking of a female frog.

A نقو *nakw*, (v. n. of نقا for نقو) Extracting marrow from a bone. *Nakw* or *nikw*, (pl. انقاء) The bone of the arm. Any bone containing marrow.

A نقواء *nakwā*, (pl. of نقيّ *nakiy*, irregular) Clean. Sifted, cleaned, selected things. Small-boned (woman).

A نقوان *nakawāni*, Two heaps of sand.

A نقوة *nakwat*, The best, sifted or selected part. Refuse, siftings.

A نقود *nukūd*, (pl. of نقد *nakd*) Sums of ready money. P نقود نا محدود *nukūdi nā mahdūd*, Untold ready money.

A نقوش *nakūsh*, A sort of shrub. *Nukūsh*, (pl. of نقش *naksh*) Pictures. Engravings. Inscriptions. Dots on dice, pips on cards.

A نقوض *nukūz*, (pl. of نقض *nikz*) Surfaces of grounds perforated by mushrooms.

A نقوع *nakūʿ*, Any thing diluted or dissolved in water, to make medicines or drink: an infusion. A preparation of pure water and different kinds of perfumes. Cold and sweet (water). Brackish (water). نقوع اذن *nakūʿ uzunin*, Credulous, disposed to believe implicitly all he hears. نقوع زبيب *nakūʿi zabīb*, An infusion of raisins. *Nukūʿ*, (v. n. of نقع) Flowing into one place and stagnating (water). Abusing, defaming. Being raised (a noise or dust). Believing. Abounding (death). Recovering health. Killing a sheep or camel to entertain a guest. (pl. of نقع *nakʿ*) Raised (dusts).

A نقول *nukūl*, (pl. of نقل) Narratives, copies.

A نقوه *nukūh*, (v. n. of نقه) Recovering (from an indisposition), though still weak. Understanding, finding out.

A نقه *nakah*, (v. n. of نقه) Recovering (from sickness), though still weak. Understanding, perceiving. *Nakih*, Intelligent.

A نقّه *nukkah*, (pl. of ناقه *nākih*) Convalescents. Intelligent.

A نقي *naky*, (v. n. of نقي) Taking marrow out (of a bone). Giving marrow to eat. *Niky*, (v. n. of نقي) Meeting. (pl. انقاء *ankā*) Marrow. The fat part of the eye.

A نقيّ *nakiy*, (pl. نقاء *nikā* and نقواء *nakwā*) Clean, pure, excellent, exquisite. Finest and whitest flour. *Nukiy*, (pl. of نقا *naka'*) Heaps of sand.

A نقيب *nakīb*, (pl. نقباء *nukabā*) A chief, leader. An intelligent person. One acquainted with the genealogies of a people. A servant whose business it is to proclaim the titles of his master, and to introduce those who pay their respects to him. One equal in rank to a corporal. (A dog) the top of whose throat is pierced that he may not bark loud. The tongue of a balance. A pipe or flute. P نقيبان بار *nakībāni bār*, Angels.

A نقيبة *nakībat*, Soul, mind; intellect, understanding, penetration. Nature. Counsel, advice, instruction. The success of any thing. (A she-camel) with large teats. ميمون النقيبة *maymūnu'n nakībat*, Of a noble disposition or excellent understanding.

A نقيبي *nakībī*, The chief magistracy.

A نقيّة *nakiyat*, (fem. of نقيّ *nakiy*) Pure, clean. A word, saying, discourse.

A نقيذة *nakīzat*, (pl. نقائذ *nakāʾiz*) A horse taken from an enemy. A coat of mail. A married woman.

A نقير *nakīr*, Hollowed (wood or stone). A trough made of a hollowed palm-tree, in which they make a strong wine from dates. Poor and despised. Few, little. A tree pierced with holes, which serve as a ladder. (pl. انقرة *ankirat*) A canal, trough, tray. A hollow dug in the ground, or in a stone. A small groove in a date-stone, from which the stalk grows. A black fly. Nature, origin, kind, species. *Nakīr*, (or حقير نقير *hakīr nakīr*) Extremely poor. نقير و قطمير *nakīr u kitmīr*, Minutely. كريم النقير *karīmu'n nakīr*, Of a noble race, of an excellent origin. لا فتيل ولا نقير *lā fatīla wa lā nakīr*, Not a particle, nothing. ليس في نقير *lays fī nakīr*, It is of no value.

A نقيش *nakīsh*, Scattered furniture. Similitude, resemblance, effigy, symbol. Like, resembling. A fellow, equal.

A نقيص *nakīs*, Sweet or pure water. A fragrant aromatic, a perfume. Defective, deficient, faulty, vicious. شخص نقيص *shakhsi nakīs*, A vicious person.

A نقيصة *nakīsat*, (pl. نقائص *nakāʾis*) Imperfection, defect, vice, bad quality. Disgrace, slander. P نقيصه گفتن *nakīsa guftan*, To disparage.

A نقيض *nakīz*, Destruction of a work, demolition of a building. Contrary, opposite, reverse, reversed, inverted, adverse, inimical. The sound made by a loose saddle or load upon a camel. The sound of the string of a harp or bow, &c.; also of cracking the joints of the fingers. The creaking of a pulley. The sound made by the air when rushing out of a cupping-glass. The cry of an eagle.

A نقيضة *nakīzat*, A competition between two poets, when one repeats a line or lines, to which the other makes an extemporary contradictory reply. A road through mountains.

A نقيط *nakīt*, The servant of a freedman.

A نقيع *nakīʿ*, Good, wholesome, cool (water), which quenches thirst. Steeped, soaked. An infusion. Brackish (water). Standing water. Cooling (whey). Wine made of steeped grapes, raisins, or dates without boiling. A trough in which they steep dates. (pl. انقعة *ankiʿat*) (A well) overflowing with water. Clamour, loud voice. (A man) born of a foreign mother.

A نقيعة *nakīʿat*, (pl. نقائع *nakāʾiʿ*) A camel or other cattle killed for the entertainment of strangers. Preparations made for marriage-ceremonies, or the reception of guests when coming off a journey.

A نقيف *nakīf*, (pl. نقف *nukf*) (The trunk of

the palm-tree) eaten by the worms. Split (colocynth).

A نقيق nakīk, (v. n. of نق) Croaking (a frog or raven); clucking (a hen); mewing (a cat). The sounds made by those animals. It also expresses the cries of other animals, as scorpions.

A نقيل nakīl, Foreign (man). A traveller. A torrent, especially one rushing down from a rainy country to another (as from Abyssinia to Egypt). A way. A peculiar pace of a horse. (pl. of نقيلة nakīlat) Patches of leather for mending boots.

A نقيلة nakīlat, (pl. نقيل nakīl and نقائل nakāʼil) A patch of leather with which they mend a boot, or sole a camel's hoof. The interior fleshy part of the arm. Foreign (woman). ابن نقيلة ibn nakīlat, A stranger. A traveller.

A نقيمة nakīmat, Nature, disposition. ميمون النقيمة maymūnu'n nakīmat, Of a happy disposition.

A نقيه nakīh, Faint, feeble, weak.

P نك nak, Behold! Green vitriol. Nuk, A bird's bill.

A نكأ nakʼ, (v. n. of نكأ) Taking the scab off a sore before it is healed. Killing or wounding (an enemy). Paying (debt), performing (what is due).

P نكاب nakāb, Green vitriol; vitriol in solution. Nikāb, A stocking, glove, or muff. A falconer's glove. News, intelligence. A figure drawn by a pencil or wrought with a needle.

A نكابة nikābat, (v. n. of نكب) Being set (over others) as leader or tribune.

A نكأة nakaʼat or nukaʼat, The reddish top or flowers of the plant طرثوث turṡūs. زكأة نكأة zukaʼat nukaʼat, Who pays a debt without delay.

A نكات nikāt, (pl. of نكتة nuktat) Points, conceits, witticisms, quaint phrases, epigrams.

A نكات nakkāt, A reviler, detractor.

A نكاث nukāṡ, Pustules about a camel's mouth.

A نكاثة nukāṡat, The fibry particles, left in the mouth, of the stick used as a dentifrice. The worn parts at a rope's end.

A نكاح nikāḥ, (v. n. of نكح) Marrying. Lying with. Matrimony, marriage. Conjugal intercourse. A dowry. P نكاح كردن nikāḥ kardan, (or عقد نكاح كردن ʻakdi nikāḥ kardan) To marry, take a wife. A حجت نكاح hujjati nikāḥ, A marriage-contract signed by a judge. اسرع من نكاح ام خارجة asraʻ min nikāḥi ummi khārijat, Speedier than marriage (in the tribe) of Umm Khārijat (where, it would seem, such matters were quickly arranged).

A نكّاح nakkāḥ, One who marries many wives, a polygamist. Potent in venery.

A P نكاحي nikāḥī, Matrimonial. Married woman.

A نكارة nakārat, (v. n. of نكر) Being acute, clever, subtle. Being hard, difficult. Craft, cunning, skill.

P نكاره nakāra, Worthless, useless. Invalid.

A نكاز nakkāz, (pl. نكازات nakkāzāt and نكاكيز nakākīz) A most dangerous serpent stinging but not biting (it appears to have no mouth, the head and the tail being equally small, and the difference hardly to be distinguished).

P نكاس nakās, (in zand and Pāz.) A look, glance.

A نكاس nikās, The demand which the superior makes to the farmer for his accounts. A daily fair for cattle. Nukās, A relapse.

P نكاف nikāf, A falconer's glove.

A نكاف nukāf, A tumour rising in the throat of a camel (often fatal), also a lump behind the ear.

A نكاكيز nakākīz, (pl. of نكاز nakkāz) Serpents of a very dangerous kind.

A نكال nakāl, Exemplary punishment, chastisement. A public and ignominious exposure.

P نكال nikāl, A coal.

A نكالة nakālat, Punishment, torture.

A نكاية nikāyat, (v. n. of نكى) Killing, wounding, injuring. Thinking evil, devising mischief. A wound, injury, slaughter.

P نكائي nikāʼī, Goodness; welfare. Beauty.

A نكب nakb, (v. n. of نكب) Inverting (a quiver). Pouring out the contents of a vessel. Throwing down or away. Hurting the foot (a stone). Breaking, injuring any one (fortune). Turning out of the way, declining from. (pl. نكوب nukūb) Affliction, adverse fortune. Position, disposition. Nukb, (pl. of نكباء nakbāʼ) Winds blowing obliquely. These are four, viz. الازيب al azyab, The south-east wind; الصابية as ṣābiyat, North-east; الجربياء al jirbiyāʼ North-west; and الهيف al hayaf, South-west. Nakab, (v. n. of نكب) Breaking, injuring any one (fortune). Turning out of the way, declining from. Having a pain in the shoulders, being slip-shouldered. A hurt or disease in (a camel's) shoulder, which causes him to halt. Nakab, Lamed by a stone in the foot.

A نكباء nakbāʼ, A side wind. A north-east wind.

A نكبة nakbat, (v. n. of نكب) Breaking, injuring any one (ill-fortune). (pl. نكبات nakabāt) Adversity, calamity, misfortune, affliction. Bad health. Ignominy, contempt. Nukbat, A heap of corn in a barn unmeasured and unweighed.

P نكبتخانه nakbat-khāna, The residence of contempt, i.e. a mean habitation.

A نكبتي nakbatī, Contemptible, miserable, wretched, worthless.

A نكت nakt, (v. n. of نكت) Poking the ground with the end of a stick and leaving there a mark. Being restless, jumping, and prancing (a horse). Piercing and tumbling head over heels. Nukat, (pl. of نكتة nuktat) Witticisms.

A نكتة nuktat, (pl. نكات nikāt or نكت nukat) A subtle or quaint conceit, nice or metaphysical distinction, mystical signification, quaint saying, pithy sentence. A point. An impression made with the tip of the finger, or with a stick on the ground. Spots or rust upon a mirror. P نكتهٔ بادي nuktaʼi badī, Agreeable, charming words, such as delight the heart. Empty boast, falsehood. نكته گرفتن nukta giriftan, To separate, make nice distinctions. To take by the handle. خطاب نكته آميز khiṭābi nukta-āmez, A speech full of subtleties.

P نكته بين nukta-bīn, A caviller.

P نكته پرور nukta-parwar, (or طبع نكته پرداز tabʻi nukta-pardāz) An acute genius.

P نكته پيوند nukta-paywand, Subtle, ingenious.

P نكته چين nukta-chīn, A caviller, carper.

P نكته سنج nukta-sanj, A weigher of words, an orator.

P نكته سنجي nukta-sanjī, The weighing, or nice distinction, of words or minute objects.

P نكته شناس nukta-shināṣ, (or نكته دان nukta-dān) Sagacious, understanding subtleties or mysterious meanings.

P نكته گذار nukta-guzār, Witty, clever.

P نكته گوي nukta-goy, Eloquent: epigrammatic.

P نكته گير nukta-gīr, A caviller, carper: critic.

A نكث niks, (v. n. of نكث) Loosing, untwisting (a rope). Separating, dividing, branching out (the fibrous particles of a certain stick which is used as a dentifrice). Breaking (an agreement). Rebelling. A taking to pieces of the worn cloth of a garment or tent to be re-woven. Name of a man.

A نكح nakaha, (fut. ينكح yankahu) (Sleep) overcame (his eyes). (Rain) lay (on the ground).

A نكح nak-h, Genitale arvum. Venery. A woman joined in matrimony. Nik-h, (النكح an'nik-h, or an'nuk-h) A word used by the betrothed party in betrothing a young girl. Nuk-h or nik-h, Marriage. Nukah, A polygamist.

A نكحة nukahat, One who marries many wives, a polygamist. Lecherous.

A نكخ nakhh, (v. n. of نكخ) Striking on the throat with fist or spear.

A نكد nakd, (v. n. of نكد) Croaking with all his might (a raven). Refusing, denying, withholding, or giving sparingly. Nakd or nukd, A small gift. Calamity. Nakd, nakad, or nakid, (pl. انكاد ankād and مناكيد manākīd) Miserable, avaricious (fellow), niggardly. Sinister. Of a bad disposition. Nukd, (pl. of نكداء nakdāʼ) (Camels) which give much or little milk. Nakad, (v. n. of نكد) Being wretched, miserable (life). Containing little water (a well). Trouble, wretchedness of life. Importunity.

A نكداء nakdāʼ, (pl. نكد nukd) (A camel) having no young remaining alive, and therefore giving plenty of milk; also one dry.

A نكر nakira, (fut. ينكر yankaru) He denied.

A نكر nakr, Understanding, sagacity, cunning. ما اشدّ نكره mā ashadda nakrahu, How shrewd he is! Nukr, An iniquitous, disagreeable, inconvenient (thing). بنكر bi nukrin, Incognito. Nukr or nukur, (v. n. of نكر) Not knowing or acknowledging, ignoring, denying. Reprobating, rejecting, repudiating. Nakar, (v. n. of نكر) Being ignorant of, not knowing. Being penetrating, ingenious, skilful, shrewd, sagacious, prudent, crafty. *Nakir*, An indefinite noun. *Nakir, nakur*, or *nukur*, (pl. انکار *ankār*) Ingenious, shrewd. Ignorant. *Nukur*, An important or difficult affair. A disagreeable, iniquitous thing. Ingenious, cunning (woman).

A نکراء *nakrāʼ*, Clever (woman). Subtlety of genius. A disagreeable, iniquitous thing. *Nakarāʼ*, Manner, mode. Affliction, calamity.

A نکرة *nakrat*, Subtlety of genius. *Nakarat*, Ignorance. *Nakirat*, Undetermined, unrestricted, indefinite (noun). Evil, misfortune. Ignorance. Any humours carried off by medicine. Blood or pus running from a wound; the bloody flux. A green film which comes out with the fœtus. اسهل فلان نکرةً *as-hala fulānun nakiratan*, So-and-so laboured under such distemper.

A نکز *nakz*, (v. n. of نکز) Striking. Driving away, beating back, repulsing, trampling upon. Stinging with the nose (a serpent which has apparently no mouth). Fixing the sharp point of any thing in the ground. Retiring from fear. *Nikz*, Any thing vile and worthless. Remains of marrow left in a bone. *Nakaz*, (v. n. of نکز) Being empty, dry (a well). *Nukuz*, (pl. of نکوز *nakūz*) Empty (wells).

P نکژده *nakajda*, An earthen cup or jar.

A نکس *naks*, (v. n. of نکس) Inclining downward, inverting, placing topsy turvy. Reading backward (especially a chapter of the Kurʼān). (Food, &c.) causing a disease to return. تعسا له و نکسا *taʻsan lahu wa naksan* or *nuksan*, May he be so visited! *Niks*, (pl. انکاس *ankās*) Weak, unable to rise to any thing honourable. (An arrow) broken at the notch. A spear whose head is broken at the bottom, so that it may be used as well as the point. A bow, the lower extremity of which naturally grew out of the branch (considered a blemish). A preposterous birth. *Nuks*, A relapse. P نکس کردن *nuks kardan*, To relapse into distemper. A *Nukus*, Stooping old men.

P نکس *nakas*, (for ناکس *nā kas*) Vile, sordid.

A نکش *naksh*, (v. n. of نکش) Emptying (a well), taking out fetid mud. Finishing, bringing to a close, extirpating. Consuming (herbage).

A نکص *naks*, (v. n. of نکص) Departing, retiring, desisting through timidity from something good.

A نکظ *nakz*, (v. n. of نکظ) Rendering (any one's business) troublesome. *Nakz*, (*nakaz*, or نکظة *nakazat*) (v. n. of نکظ) Being diligent, expeditious. *Nakaz*, A causing to make haste. Excessive hunger.

A نکع *nakʻ*, (v. n. of نکع) Removing away quickly. Repelling, beating off, driving away. Detaining what is due, or giving it. Abstaining, refraining, failing. Milking (cattle) hastily. Kicking on the backside. Annoying, vexing by overmuch despatch. *Nakʻ, nakiʻ*, or *nukaʻ*, (A man) of a blackish red colour. *Nakaʻ*, (v. n. of نکع) Having a reddishness on the nose with an excoriation. The reddishness itself. *Nukaʻ*, A red colour. *Nukuʻ*, (pl. of نکوع *nakūʻ*) Short-bodied (women).

A نکعة *nakʻat*, A kind of plant resembling the طرثوث *tursūs*. *Nakaʻat*, The red fruit of the نقاوی *nukāwaʼ*, and of another tree. Gum of the tragacanth. The tip of the nose. A dark reddish-coloured man. *Nakaʻat* or *nukaʻat*, The reddish top of the طرثوث *tursūs*, or of another plant having a flower like the amaranth, used in dyeing. *Nakiʻat*, A ruddy woman. Very red (lip). *Nukaʻat*, A man who has an excoriated, reddish nose. هکعة نکعة *hukaʻat nukaʻat*, A fool, one who remains always at home.

A نکف *nakf*, (v. n. of نکف) Penetrating (rain), enduring (it) while it lasts (whence لا ینکف *lā yunkafu*, (The rain) cannot be borne; (the sea) cannot be fathomed). جیش لا ینکف *jayshun lā yunkafu*, An innumerable army. Discovering (the impression of a camel's foot on a plain, after having in vain sought for it over rugged grounds). Wiping with the finger (the tears) from the cheek. Declining, turning away from. *Nakf* or *nakaf*, (v. n. of نکف) Disdaining, refusing, rejecting. *Nakaf*, (v. n. of نکف) Being free, exempted. Being pained (the hand). (pl. نکفة) Tubercles or kernels between the ears and the roots of the lower jaws.

A نکفة *nakfat, nukfat*, or *nakafat*, (du. نکفتان *nakfatāni*) The root of the bone of the chin. *Nakafat*, (pl. نکف *nakaf*) A tubercle or kernel between the ear and root of the lower jaw.

A نکل *nikl*, (pl. انکال *ankāl*) A chain, fetter, manacle, collar. A fetter of fire. A bridle, reins; the iron bit of a bridle. A particular kind of bridle used by couriers. A tried, bold, or experienced man; a bulwark against an enemy. *Nukl*, An example, punishment. That which brings punishment. *Nakal*, (v. n. of نکل) Receiving chastisement. Robust (man) of tried bravery. Excellent (horse). A bucket rope. النکل علی النکل *an nakal ʻala'n nakal*, A brave man on a gallant steed.

P نکل *nikil* or *nakl*, A youth whose beard begins to grow.

A نکلة *nuklat*, An example, punishment. That which brings punishment. A bulwark.

A نکمة *nakmat*, Calamity, affliction.

A نکنکة *naknakat*, A craving hard for debt. The correction of any work.

P نکو *nikū* or *niko*, Good, beautiful: a good thing.

A نکوب *nukūb*, (v. n. of نکب) Straying, declining, turning away (from the right way). Preceding, as a chief or leader. Blowing (intermediate winds, as N E., S E., N W., or S W.). (pl. of نکب *nakb*) Adversities.

P نکو خواه *nikū-khwāh*, A well-wisher.

A نکور *nukūr*, (v. n. of نکر) Not knowing or acknowledging, ignoring, denying. Reprobating, rejecting.

A نکوز *nakūz*, (pl. نکز *nukuz*) (A well) containing little water. *Nukūz*, (v. n. of نکز) Flowing down upon low ground, or sinking into the earth (water).

P نکو سیر *nikū-siyar*, Of good disposition.

A نکوص *nukūs*, A departing, desisting from fear.

A نکوع *nakūʻ*, Short-bodied (woman).

A نکول *nukūl*, (v. n. of نکل) Retiring, flying through timidity from something good. Retreating from an enemy. Abstaining, refraining (from swearing).

P نکونام *nikū-nām*, Of good repute.

P نکونتن *nakūnitan*, (in zand and Pāz.) To kill.

P نکوه *nakūh*, One who hunts for faults, an evil-speaker. A false-accuser, slanderer.

P نکوهش *nakūhish* or *nikūhish*, Reproach, chiding, rebuking, blame, scorn, contempt, rejection.

P نکوهنده *nikūhanda*, An accuser, traducer, despiser, blamer, contemner.

P نکوهیدگی *nikūhīdagī*, Contempt, reproach.

P نکوهیدن *nakūhīdan* or *nikūhīdan*, To despise, slight, reject, blame, treat with contempt, speak ill of, slander, reproach, complain of another. To disregard religious duties.

P نکوهیده *nakūhīda* or *nikūhīda*, Despised, rejected. Blamed, scorned. Spoken ill of. افعال نکوهیده *afʻāli nikūhīda*, Unworthy actions.

P نکوئی *nikūʼī*, Goodness. A good thing. لطف و نکوئی *lutf u nikūʼī*, Graciousness and goodness.

A نکه *nak-h*, (v. n. of نکه) Breathing into the face or the nostrils of another. Being intensely hot (the sun). Smelling another's breath.

A نکه *nukkah*, Tired (camels) unable to bray.

A نکهة *nak-hat*, Smell of the breath. Odour.

P نکهت *nuk-hat*, Perfume, odour.

P نکهه *nak-ha*, The string of a paper-kite.

A نکیب *nakīb*, A circle round a camel's hoof.

A نکیباء *nukaybāʼ*, (dim. of نکباء *nakbāʼ*) A little side wind. النکیباء *an' nukaybāʼ*, The north-east wind. نیحة النکیباء *nayyihatu'n nukaybāʼ*, The south-west wind.

A نکیثة *nakīsat*, A serious and important business. Soul, spirit. Breach of promise. The utmost effort. Power, strength. Nature, temper, disposition.

A نکیر *nakīr*, (v. n. of نکر) Repudiating, reprobating. Being ignorant of, not knowing. Denying. Hateful, detestable, odious, disagreeable. Changed for worse. Any thing spoilt, fallen to decay. A change, alteration. Strong, impregnable (fortress). One of two angels supposed by the Muhammadans to try the departed in the tomb.

A نکیف *nakīf*, Glanders. ذات نکیف *zātu nakīf*, Name of a place in Arabia. یوم نکیف *yawmu nakīf*, A battle fought there, in which Kuraysh defeated Banī Kinānat.

P نگ *nag*, The roof of the mouth, palate.

P نگار *nigār*, A picture, portrait, effigy, or idol. Figures stained on the hands and feet with a dye extracted from the colouring shrub حنا *hinā*. A beautiful woman, mistress, sweetheart. (Imp. and partic. of نگاریدن nigārīdan) Paint thou; painting. An idea. Adorned with different colours. نگار خاطر nigāri khātir, Impression on the mind. نگار عالم nigāri ɛālam, (or نگار روزگار nigāri rozgār) Idol of the world, marvel of beauty, beloved by all. پر نقش و نگار pur naksh u nigār, Full of pictures.

P نگارخانه nigār-khāna, (or نگارستان nigāristān) A picture-gallery. The house of the celebrated eastern painter and impostor Mānī.

P نگارش nigārish, Writing; painting, drawing.

P نگارش نامه nigārish-nāma, A letter, epistle.

P نگار علم nigār-ɛalam, An elegant border.

P نگار گرد nigār-gird, A round edge or hem.

P نگارنده nigāranda, A painter, stainer: writer.

P نگاریدن nigārīdan or نگاشتن nigāshtan, To paint, embroider, draw, pourtray, delineate, or write.

P نگارین nigārīn, Embellished. A beloved object. نگارین کردن nigārīn kardan, To adorn.

P نگاشته nigāshta, Written. Painted, stained. Pourtrayed. Embroidered.

P نگاف nigāf, A glove.

P نگال nigāl, A coal, a live coal.

P نگاه nigāh, Look, aspect; a beholding. Observation, watching, keeping watch, taking notice. A glance. Custody, care, caution. نگاه تند nigāhi tund, A severe look, frown.

P نگاهبان nigāhbān, A guard, guardian, keeper. A petty officer of government.

P نگاه بانی nigāhbānī, Custody, guard. نگاهبانی کردن nigāhbānī kardan, To guard, preserve.

P نگاه چران nigāh-charān, One who goes with half-shut eyes, inattentive to surrounding objects.

P نگاه دار nigāh-dār, A guardian, conservator.

P نگاه داشت nigāh-dāsht, He guarded. Observation, watch. Custody, preservation. Any thing committed to care or guardianship. A keepsake.

P نگاه داشتن nigāh dāshtan, To observe, regard. To keep, maintain, guard, preserve, look after. To enlist.

P نگاهیدن nigāhīdan, To behold. A deposit.

P نگاهي کردن nigāhī kardan, To behold.

P نگر nagar, A grape-stone.

P نگران nigrān, One who looks, beholds, expects. نگران باش nigrān bāsh, Be ready, prepare yourself. نگران شدن nigrān shudan, To expect, to be on the look out.

P نگراني nigrānī, Expectation.

P نگرستن nigaristan, (or نگریستن nigarīstan) To behold, look at, observe. To turn the eye towards. بکسي نگرستن ba kase nigaristan, To look at any one.

P نگرش nigarish, Sight, look, observation.

P نگریدن nigarīdan, To view, see, look.

P نگزرد nagzirad, (or نگزیرد nagzīrad) There is no help for it, there is no remedy.

P نگژده nagajda, An earthen drinking-cup.

P نگل nagl or nigil, A youth whose beard begins to grow.

P نگندن nigandan, To quilt, to sew in an ornamental way.

P نگنده niganda, A particular kind of ornamental sewing, counterpoint, embroidery. Any thing hidden, particularly treasure. نگنده کردن niganda kardan, To sew with long stitches, baste.

P نگوسار nigū-sār, Inverted, turned upside down. Ruined. One who hangs his head from shame. A low-bodied beast of burden.

P نگون nigūn, Turned, inverted, hanging down. Upside down.

P نگونبخت nigūn-bakht, Unfortunate, hapless.

P نگون سار nigūn-sār, One who hangs the head from shame. Inverted. نگون سار کردن nigūn-sār kardan, To overturn.

P نگونساري nigūn-sārī, A hanging of the head.

P نگون طالع nigūn-tāliɛ, Unlucky.

P نگون طشت nigūn-tasht, The sky.

P نگه nigah, A look, glance. Observation. Guardianship.

P نگهبان nigahbān, A keeper, guard, watchman. نگهبان قلعه nigahbāni kalɛa, Garrison of a castle.

P نگهباني nigahbānī, Guard, custody, guardianship. Observation, watching.

P نگهدار nigahdār, A guardian.

P نگه دارنده nigah-dāranda, A keeper.

P نگه داره nigah-dāra, Guard, keeper, observer.

P نگهداري nigah-dārī, Observation. Keeping (a secret).

P نگه داشت nigah-dāsht, He regarded. He observed. Any thing committed to another's care.

P نگهداشتن nigah dāshtan, (or کردن kardan) To behold, to observe. To take care of.

P نگیسا nigīsā, A musician of Khusraw Parwez.

P نگین nigīn, (or نگینه nigīna) A ring, especially the seal-ring of a prince. A precious stone set in a ring.

P نگین دان nigīndān, The collet, *i.e.* that part of a ring in which the precious stone is set.

P نگین ساي nigīn-sāy, An engraver of seals. A polisher of gems.

A نل nal, Take, carry off (any thing good).

P نلچ nalch, Pus from a boil or wound.

P نلسك nilisk, (or نلشك) In debt, a debtor.

P نلك nalk or nilk, The medlar. The medlar-tree. *Nilk*, A dried plum. Seed of fenugreek. Understanding, knowledge.

A نلك nulk or nilk, A plane-tree. A medlar.

A نلكة nilkat or nulkat, A single medlar.

P نلكس nilkas, The coping of a wall.

P نلم nalm, Good, fair, fine.

P نلند naland, A spade or shovel.

A نلنل nulnul, A weak, cowardly man.

P نله رو nala rū, Wild spikenard.

P نم nam, Moisture. Dew. Tears.

A نمّ namm, (v. n. of نمّ) Calumniating, publishing (the sayings or actions of others) in order to create animosities. Telling or propagating falsehoods. Diffusing a smell, being fragrant (musk). Motion. Breath. (pl. انمّاء animmāɛ) Calumniator, whispering slanderer. *Numm*, Calumniators.

A نمأ namɛ or namaɛ, Small lice, nits. Small sheep.

P نما namā or numā, (in comp.) Shewing, pointing out. An index. ره نما rah-numā, Shewing the way; a guide. کشور خوشنما kishwari khwush-numā, A pleasant country.

A نماء namāɛ, (v. n. of نمي) Growing, increasing. Becoming full or deep-coloured (especially red). Rising (water). Rising (as the price of provisions). Growing fat. Being picked up (any saying).

A نماة namāt, (pl. نمي nama') A small ant.

A نمّاة nummāt, One piece of money.

P نماد namād, He shewed. One who shews or points out.

P نمار namār, A hint, glance, intimation.

A نمار nimār, (pl. of نمر namir) Leopards.

P نماران namārān, Signs, hints, intimations.

A نمارة nimārat, (pl. of نمر namir) Leopards, pards, panthers.

A نمارق namārik, (pl. of نمرق namrak, rik, or ruk) Pads placed between a rider and his saddle.

P نماز namāz, Prayers, those especially prescribed by law (which are repeated five times a day). Adoration, worship. Devotion, ministry, service. Obedience. نماز بامداد namāzi bāmdād, Morning-prayers said before dawn; نماز پیشین namāzi peshīn, Mid-day prayers; نماز خفتن namāzi khuftan, Prayers before going to bed, two hours or more after sunset; نماز دیگر namāzi dīgar, Afternoon-prayers; نماز شام namāzi shām, Evening-prayers, vespers (immediately after sunset); altogether being called پنج وقت نماز panj wakti namāz, The five hours of prayer. نماز کردن namāz kardan, (or نماز گذاردن namāz guzārdan) To say one's prayers, to attend divine service. قدّاس نماز kuddās-namāz, The holy prayers; mass, as celebrated by Eastern Christians.

P نمازگاه namāz-gāh, A place of prayer (a building generally erected without the walls of a town. It is square, and stands on a pediment three or four feet above the level of the ground. Public service is performed here chiefly on great occasions; as during a pestilence, or famine, or a scarcity of water, or the marching of an army to battle. It is often erected amidst gardens). The principal place in a mosque, where the priest prays with the people with his face turned towards Mecca.

P نمازگذار namāz-guzār, One who prays.

P نمازي namāzī, A praying person. Relating to prayers. Devout, or in the constant habit of praying. Clean, pure, fit for prayer.

A نمّاس nammās, A calumniator, whisperer.

A نماص *nimās*, A thread in a needle. *Numās*, (pl. نمص *numus* and انمصة *anmisat*) A month. نماصًا *numāsan*, During a month (I saw him not).

A نماط *nimāt*, Coverings. Housings.

P نماك *namāk*, Custom, habit, fashion. Beauty, ornament.

A نمال *nimāl*, (pl. of نمل *naml*) Ants.

A نمّال *nammāl*, A whisperer, slanderer, censurer.

A نمّام *nammām*, A calumniator, accuser, whisperer. A kind of wild thyme or betony. A medicine.

A نمامة *namāmat*, Mint.

A نماميُ *namāma'*, (pl. of نميّ) Monies, coins.

A نمّامي *nammāmī*, Calumniation.

P نماي *na* or *numāy*, A shewer, exhibiter.

P نمايان *na* or *numāyān*, Appearing, apparent. Bold (as a picture). نمايان شدن *numāyān shudan*, To appear, be shewn, come in sight. نمايان كردن *numāyān kardan*, To shew, demonstrate.

P نمايش *numāyish* or *namāyish*, Appearance, face, form, figure. Vision, sight, development; an apparition, spectre, phantom. نمايش آب *numāyishi āb*, Semblance of water on a sandy plain.

A نمائم *namāsim*, (pl. of نميمة) Detractions.

P نماينده *numāyanda* or *namāyanda*, One who shews. Showy, striking.

P نماييدن *nu* or *namāyīdan*, To shew, exhibit.

A نمّة *nammat*, A female calumniator. *Nimmat*, One ant. One louse.

A نمت *namt*, A kind of fruit-bearing herb.

P نمتك *namath*, A wild plum. *Namtuh*, A medlar. *Numuth*, A red substance resembling coral.

P نمج *namj*, Broom. Bulrushes.

P نمچ *namch*, Dew, humidity, moisture.

P نم خورده *nam-khwurda*, Injured by moisture.

P نمد *namad*, Felt. A garment of coarse cloth. A cloak worn during rain. A rug or coarse carpet on which they sit. Membrum virile. نمد در آب داشتن *namad dar āb dāshtan*, To deceive, plot, lay snares. نمد در بر *namad dar bar*, With a coarse cloak or garment over the shoulders.

P نمدار *nam-dār*, Moist, humid.

P نمدان *namdān*, Vulva mulieris.

P نمد پاره *namad-pāra*, A piece of coarse felt.

P نمد پوش *namad-posh*, Clad in woollen or felt.

P نمدزين *namad-zīn*, A coarse woollen saddle-cloth. A cushion stuffed with wool or sand. A saddle stuffed on the upper part, to prevent the rider being galled. (The modern name is تگلتو *tagaltū*).

P نمد ساز *namad-sāz*, A felt-manufacturer.

P نمد مال *namad-māl*, A felt-maker.

P نمديده *nam-dīda*, Bathed in tears, weeping.

P نمدين *namadīn*, Made of felt. Woollen. كلاه نمدين *kulāhi namadīn*, A cap of felt.

A نمر *namr*, (v. n. of نمر) Climbing (a mountain). *Nimr*, Name of a man. *Numr*, Name of a place in Huzayl. *Numr* or *numur*, (pl. of نمر *namir*) Leopards. *Namar*, (v. n. of نمر) Being full of spots, or spotted like a pard. Being dappled (a cloud). Being angry, surly, growling, ill-humoured, of a bad disposition. *Namir*, (pl. انمر *anmur*, انمار *anmār*, نمر *numur*, *numr*, نمار *numār*, نمارة *nimārat*, and نمور *numūr*) A leopard. A panther. Wholesome (water). Pure, perfect (esteem). Many, much. Name of the founder of an Arabian tribe. (pl. of نمرة *namirat*) Bits of a cloud. *Numar*, (pl. of نمرة *numrat*) Spots of divers colours.

A نمراء *namrās*, (fem. of انمر *anmar*) Dappled (cloud), spotted like a leopard. Dapple-grey (mare).

A نمرة *numrat*, (pl. نمر *numar*) A spot of any colour soever. *Namirat*, (fem. of نمر *namir*) Spotted like a leopard. A dappled cloud. (pl. نمر *namir*) A small part of a cloud. A kind of cloak marked with black and white lines; a woollen Arabian garment of different stripes. A net in which a sheep is enclosed to decoy a wolf. A kind of iron hook baited with flesh to catch wolves. Name of a place in Arafāt near Mecca, or the mount whereon are the stones called انصاب *ansāb*.

A نمرق *namrah*, (*nimrih*, *numruh*, نمرقة *namrahat*, *nimrikat*, or *numrukat*) A small cushion or pillow, especially placed between a rider and his saddle. A horse or camel-cloth.

A نمرقة *nimrikat*, A cloud having wide openings, and giving little rain.

P نمرود *namrūd* or *numrūd*, Nimrod, a king, who is said to have cast Abraham into the fire.

A نمريّ *namarīy*, Resembling a leopard, leopard-like. Of the tribe of نمر *namir*.

A نمس *nams*, (v. n. of نمس) Concealing (a secret). Making (one) a confidant. *Nims*, The ichneumon or Egyptian weasel, which kills the crocodile. *Nums*, (pl. of انمس *anmas*) Dark-coloured. The bird قطا *katā*. *Namas*, (v. n. of نمس) Being spoilt, rancid (butter or oil).

P نمس *numus*, A weasel.

P نمش *namsh*, Fraud, deceit, artifice, cunning. A kind of food or dish made of milk, whipt cream.

A نمش *namsh*, Lines conspicuous on the hands or face. A gathering or scraping together of any thing on the ground, as done by an idling, trifling fellow. An eating up by locusts of whatever is on the ground. A lie. Any thing spoken or published with a bad intention. *Namash*, (v. n. of نمش) Being marked with points of different colours. Spots or marks on the skin (as of leprosy, morphew, or freckles). The lines in paintings or engravings. *Namish*, Spotted with black and white, freckled. (A sword) marked with lines on the blade. (A camel's foot) making uncommon marks on the ground.

P نمشته *namishta*, Faith, belief, confidence.

P نمشك *namshak*, Coriander, pepperwort. *Nimishk*, Milk milked upon sour milk. Cream. Butter.

P نمشيدن *namshīdan*, To succeed, obtain one's wish, prosper.

A نمص *nams*, (v. n. of نمص) Pulling the hairs out of the face. *Nims*, A kind of plant. *Namas*, Small hairs like wool. Fine, thin hairs like the yellow down upon an unfledged bird. Thinness of hair. Thin hairs on the eyebrows. Short feathers. A kind of plant of which they make trays and lids. *Numus*, (pl. of نماص *numās*) Months.

A نمط *namat*, (pl. انماط *anmāt* and نماط *nimāt*) A mode, manner of acting. A covering, blanket, coverlet. The outside of any coverlet or carpet. A woollen cloth or housing thrown over a camel-litter. A wicker basket, bandbox, calabash, or any thing similar in which a woman puts her work or linen. A society, company of men, club. على نمط واحد *ʿala' namatin wāhidin*, In one manner, uniformly.

P نمطی *namatī*, A bed, a covering.

A نمطيّ *namatīy*, A maker or seller of coverlets.

A نمغة *namaghat*, Top of a mountain or of the head. The bregma of an infant's skull palpitating just after birth. The first, also the middling class (of people). A great number of cattle.

A نمق *namh*, (v. n. of نمق) Striking (one upon the eye) with the open hand. Giving a mouthful (to a hawk). Writing or dictating (a book). *Namah*, The middle of a road.

A نمقة *namakat*, The currency of an article, its facility of being disposed of.

P نمك *namak*, (by some *nimak*) Salt. Spirit, animation. Bread, subsistence. نمك زدن *namak zadan*, To salt, sprinkle with salt. نمك انگيزيدن *namak angezīdan*, (or ريزيدن *rezīdan*) To shed tears. نمك سياه *namaki siyāh*, (or نمك هندي *namaki hindī*) Salt of bitumen. نمك شيشه *namaki shīsha*, Dross of glass.

P نمك پرور *namak-parwar*, One who eats another's salt, *i. e.* a servant.

P نمك پرورده *namak-parwarda*, Brought up or supported at the expense of another.

P نمكت *namakt*, Dew, moisture.

P نمكچش *namak-chash*, A taste, specimen.

P نمك چشي *namak-chashī*, The first feeding of a child about six months of age, attended with certain ceremonies.

P نمك حرام *namak-harām*, Untrue to (his) salt: ungrateful, faithless, perfidious, disloyal. Disobedient. Evil, wicked.

P نمك حلال *namak-halāl*, Faithful, loyal, true.

P نمك حلالي *namak-halālī*, Fidelity, loyalty.

P نمك خوار *namak-khwār*, Eating salt.

P نمكدان *namakdān*, A salt-cellar. The mouth of a mistress. نمكدان شكستن *namakdān shikastan*, (To break the salt-cellar) To be ungrateful.

P نمك ريز *namak-rez*, Scattering salt.

P نمكزار *namakzār*, (or نمكسار) A salt-pan.

P نمك زده *namak-zada*, Salted.

P نمكزي *namakzī*, A dish made of honey, flour, and butter (or mutton-fat), with pistachio-nuts, sprinkled with white sugar-candy.

P نمك سود *namak-sūd*, Salted: hung beef.

P نمك شناس *namak-shinās*, Grateful: loyal.

P نمكين *namakīn*, Salted, salt, saline, brackish. Witty, poignant, sarcastic. Handsome, beautiful.

P نمكينه *namakīna*, A food prepared of soured curds, with salt, coriander-seeds, &c.

P نمكيني *namakīnī*, Saltness. Agreeableness.

P نمگيره *nam-gīra*, (Dew-catching) A canopy.

P نمگين *nam-gīn*, Moist, wet, humid.

A نمل *naml*, (v. n. of نمل) Slandering, backbiting. (pl. نمال *nimāl*) An ant. A kind of St. Anthony's fire; an ulceration on the side of the body, any kind of blisters from burning. رقية النمل *rukyatu'n naml*, The amulet of the ant (by which they mean a woman may adorn herself with every kind of ornament, but must not disobey her husband). *Numl*, An ant. *Namal*, (v. n. of نمل) Being asleep and helpless (the hand). Climbing (a tree). Quickness, haste, expedition. *Namil*, Brisk, prancing, spirited (horse). Quick, nimble, ready (handed). (pl. انمال *anmāl*) Slanderous. A new-born infant, in whose hand they put an ant (accompanying the ceremony with a wish that he may be prudent and industrious). نمل الاصابع *namilu'l asābiɛ*, One who imitates every thing he sees; an ingenious workman. *Namul*, *numal*, or *numul*, An ant.

A نملان *namalān*, (v. n. of نمل) Climbing (a tree). A looking down from an eminence. Quickness, haste, expedition.

A نملة *namlat*, One ant. A secret mixture of much falsehood with some truth. A crack in the hoof of a horse. An ulceration on the side of the body, any kind of blisters from burning, erysipelas. *Namlat*, *nimlat*, or *numlat*, Malignant and clandestine whispering or defamation. *Numlat*, Disquietude, restlessness; incessant motion. A remainder of water in a cistern. *Namilat*, (A place) swarming with ants.

P نمله *namla*, Full (especially of trouble).

A نملي *namla'*, Restless (woman).

A نمم *numam*, A kind of tree.

P نمناك *namnāk*, Moist, dank, damp. Dewy.

P نمناكي *namnākī*, Moistness, humidity.

P نمنك *numunk*, A red substance like coral.

A نمنم *nimnim*, A mark left by the wind on sand. *Nimnim*, (*numnum*, or نمنمة *nimnimat*) White specks on the nails (of youths).

A نمنمة *namnamat*, (v. n. of نمنم Q) Painting, printing. Making lines (upon the sands). Dressing, ornamenting, embellishing with fiction.

A نمنيم *nimnīm*, A mark left by the wind on sand.

A نمو *namw*, (v. n. of نما for نمو) Raising (a fire) and making (it) burn brisker. Growing fat (a man). Rising (water). Being elevated.

A نمو *numūw*, (v. n. of نما for نمو) Growing, increasing. Becoming full or deep-coloured (black or red). Raising (a fire) and making (it) burn brisker. Growing fat (a man). Rising (water). Being elevated. Quoting sayings of another (as deserving credit). Vegetation, growth, increase. P نمو يافتن *numū yāftan*, To grow up.

P نمود *namūd* or *numūd*, He shewed. An index, guide. Appearance. Proof. Apparent, public, glaring, shewn, exhibited, famous, prominent. سعادت نمود *saɛādat-namūd*, Happy, august.

P نمودار *namūdār*, (or نمودش *namūdish*) Exemplar, proof, symbol, specimen, representation, imitation, model, copy. Appearing, exhibiting. Argument. Visible. Noted, famed. Like, after the manner. نمودار شدن *namūdār shudan*, To appear.

P نموداري *namūdārī*, Publicity. A compensation for not having lands ascertained by actual measurement (an Indian phrase).

P نمودج *namūdaj*, (A نموذج *namūzaj*) An exemplar, model, specimen.

P نمودن *nu* or *namūdan*, To shew, demonstrate, cause to appear, exhibit; to declare. To appear, seem.

P نموداني *namūdanī*, An apparition.

P نموده *numūda* or *namūda*, Exhibited, shewn. Appeared.

P نمودي *namūdī*, Appearance, shew.

A نمور *numūr*, (pl. of نمر *namir*) Pards.

P نموزج *numūzaj*, (or نموزش) A throne, seat.

P نموسك *namūsak*, (نموشك *namūshak*, or *numūshak*) A small kind of partridge.

P نموك *namūk*, A butt for archers.

A نموم *namūm*, A calumniator. One who adorns a tale with falsehood.

P نمون *namūn* or *numūn*, A guide; index. رهنمون *rah-namūn*, A road-guide. نصيحت نمون *nasīhat-namūn*, Shewing documents; an adviser.

P نمونه *namū*, (*nimū*, *numūna*, نمويه *namū*, or *numūya*) Sample, example, specimen, type, form, pattern. A muster. Like, resembling. Tasting before. A taster. Deformed, ugly. Inverted, upside down. Incomplete, defective, useless. Idle, slothful, worthless.

A نمه *namah*, Astonishment, confusion, dismay.

A نمي *namy*, (v. n. of نمي) Relating, allying (one to his father). Growing fat. Rising (water). Being picked up (any saying). *Namy*, (and نمي *numīy*) (v. n. of نمي) Growing, increasing; rising (as the price of provisions). Becoming deeper (dye). Attributing a thing (to any one) as the author. Raising (a fire) and making (it) burn. Lifting up and putting (one thing upon another). *Nama'*, (pl. of نماة *namāt*) Small ants.

P نمي *namī*, Coolness. Moistness, dampness.

A نمي *numma'*, (or نمي *nummīy*) Any one, any body. (pl. نمامي *namāma'*) Money, nummus, coin (that especially in which there is brass or tin). The scale of a balance. Fraud, perfidy. Enmity. Vice, defect. Nature, genius (of man), substance, essence.

A نمية *namiyat*, (v. n. of نمي) Growing. Becoming deeper (dye). Two opposite skeins of thread, which they wind up together into clews.

A نمية *nummīyat*, The female ringdove.

P نميج *namīch*, A seat, chair, throne.

P نميد *namīd*, Moist. *N'umīd*, Hopeless. Bad, wicked. Miserable.

P نميدن *namīdan*, To grow moist. To incline towards, have an inclination or desire for. *N'umīdan*, To despair.

P نميده *namīda*, Inclined, turned towards. Moist with dew. *N'umīda*, Hopeless, despairing.

P نميدي *n'umīdī*, Hopelessness, despair.

A نمير *namīr*, Wholesome (water), easy of digestion. Pure (friendship, esteem). Many, much. *Numayr*, Name of the father of a tribe.

P نميرا *namīrā*, Explanation, interpretation, commentary.

A نميص *namīs*, Plucked (hair). (Grass) cropt by a sheep's mouth, and, being half-cut, grows again.

A نميقه *namīka*, A letter, writing.

A نميلة *namīlat*, Detraction, slander, whisper.

A نميمة *namīmat*, (pl. نمائم *namāɛim*) Detraction, slander, calumny; whispering in the ear. The sound of a pen when writing. The noise of a quiver. A low whisper.

P نميمه كار *namīma-kār*, A slanderer.

A نميمي *namīmīy*, Slanderous, sycophantic.

A نن *nun*, (for نون *nūn*) The letter ن *n*.

A نن *nann*, A small hair.

A نندل *nandul* or *nindul*, The nightmare. *Nindil*, A thing of great moment.

A نندلان *ninda*, *nindi*, or *nindulān*, Nightmare. *Nandalāni*, (dual) The two teats.

P ننگ *nang*, Honour, reputation, estimation. Disgrace, infamy, ignominy. Base, shameful. Battle, dispute. A hermaphrodite. (in zand and Pāzand) A hen. ننگ داشتن *nang dāshtan*, To blush, be ashamed, disdain. حفظ ناموس و ننگ كردن *hifzi nāmūs u nang kardan*, To defend one's honour and good name. فارغ از نام و ننگ *fārigh az nām u nang*, Destitute of reputation and of honour. كفاري بي ناموس و ننگ *kuffāri bī nāmūs u nang*, Infidels without reputation or honour.

P ننگسار *nangsār*, Changing from a good to a worse form, transmigration, metamorphose.

P ننگنامه *nang-nāma*, A history of wars. Prose or verse written in the way of irony or satire.

P ننگين *nangīn*, Ugly, deformed, faulty. Naked.

P ننهيدن *nunhīdan*, To cover, hide, conceal.

P نو *naw*, A hero, brave man. Crying, weeping. Motion, action, trembling. Name of a note in music. *Naw*, *nau*, *nav*, *nū*, or *no*, New, fresh. نو باده *naw bāda*, New wine. نو بهار *naw-bahār*, The spring. نو سن و سال *naw-sin u sāl*, A youth. نو و كهن *naw u kuhan*, New and old. ماه نو *māhi naw*, The new moon.

A نوء *naws*, (v. n. of ناء for نوأ) Rising with difficulty, striving to rise (with a heavy load). Oppressing any one and making him stoop (a heavy load). Falling down (especially when heavy laden). Setting in the west (as a star) in the twilight, another rising opposite to it in the east. Going far away. A gift. (pl. انواء *anwāʻ* and نوآن *nuʻān*) A star, especially one belonging to the twentieth mansion of the moon, which sets in the morning when the star رقيب *rakīb* is rising (whence the Arabians prognosticate rain and tempest).

P نوا *nawā*, A sum of money sent to an invader to save the country from plunder. Largest and best of any thing. The leg. A hop, skip, or jump. A name of the Moguls. Name of a fire-worshipper. Voice, sound, modulation, song. A certain musical tone or mood. Name of a musical instrument. Riches, opulence, wealth, plenty. Profit, advantage, gain, usefulness, interest. A happy life. A splendid situation; prosperity. Content. Food, sustenance. Provisions for a journey. Apparatus, furniture, material. Grief, pain. An army. Point of a thing. History. Separation, disunion. Wariness, caution. Information. A pledge (either for a debt or when wagering); a wager, stakes. A pawned garment. Fettered. A prisoner, captive. A foot-band. Grains, seeds, or stones of fruit. Fortune, chance. Order, arrangement, constitution. A parrot. Writing. A son; a grandson. نواي مرغان *nawāyi murghān*, Songs of birds. نواي جان *nawāyi jān*, A risking of one's life. نواي چكاوك *nawāyi chakāwak*, Name of a note in music. نواي خاركن *nawāyi khār-kan*, (or خاركند *khār-kand*) Name of a note in music. بي نوا *bī nawā*, Without food, helpless, unfortunate.

A نواء *niwāʻ*, (v. n. 3 of ناً for نوأ) Disputing with, opposing, glorying against. (pl. of ناوي *nāwī*) Fat (camels, mares, or women).

A نوآن *nuʻān*, (pl. of نوء) Settings of stars.

A نوّاب *nawwāb*, A guard of soldiers. *Nūwāb*, (pl. of نائب *nāʻib*) Vicegerents, deputies, lieutenants, governors. A nabob.

P نو آباد *naw-ābād*, Newly peopled, recently colonized, or cultivated.

A نوابت *nawābit*, Raw, inexperienced youths. Good-tempered and handsome young men. (pl. of نابت *nābit*) Plants, vegetables.

A نوابخ *nawābikh*, (pl. of نابخة *nābikhat*) Proud. Pompous talkers.

A نوابع *nawābiʻ*, Places of the body whence perspiration flows (especially of camels), pores.

A نوابغ *nawābigh*, (pl. of نابغة) Men of magnificence and rank. Surnames of several poets.

A نوابك *nawābik*, (pl. of نابك) High (places).

A نوّابي *nawwābī*, Deputyship. A kind of cloth. Relating to a nabob.

P نوابين *nawābīn*, A successful wish. Disposed. Flourishing, florid, gay. A flower.

A نواة *nawāt*, (v. n. of نوي) Intending, proposing. (pl. نوي *nawaʼ*) One date-stone. A weight of five درهم *dirham*; also of three, and of three and a-half dirhams. Twenty, also ten, in number. An ounce of gold, or four pieces of gold coin.

A نواتج *nawātij*, (pl. of ناتج *nātij*) Fruitful, prolific. مواشي نواتج *mawāshīʻi nawātij*, Prolific cattle.

A نواتي *nawātī*, (pl. of نوتاة) Short, dwarfish.

A نواتيّ *nawātīy*, (pl. of نوتيّ *nūtīy*) Sailors.

A نواجب *nawājib*, Pure, unmixed. Nobles.

A نواجد *nawājid*, Long streaks of fat in meat. Bits of cotton adhering together.

A نواجذ *nawājiz*, (pl. of ناجذ) Wisdom-teeth.

P نواجست *nawājast*, (or نواجسته *nawājasta*) A vineyard newly planted.

A نواجل *nawājil*, (Camels) feeding on the plant نجيل *najīl*, or on its broken leaves. ابو نواجل *abū nawājil*, Name of a place on the Red Sea.

A نواجي *nawājī*, (pl. of ناجية *nājiyat*) Swift she-camels running away with their riders.

A نواح *nuwāh*, (v. n. of ناح for نوح) Mourning (one defunct). Complaining; a complaint.

A نوّاح *nūwāh*, Environs, district, tract, coast, shore.

A نوّاحة *nawwāhat*, A hired female mourner.

A نواحر *nawāhir*, (pl. of ناحرة *nāhirat*) The last days and nights of a lunar month.

A نواحل *nawāhil*, Swords thin by much use.

A نواحي *nawāhī*, (pl. of ناحية *nāhiyat*) Environs, borders, suburbs. Coasts. Parts adjacent. Territories. P نواحي نشين *nawāhī-nishīn*, Dwelling on a coast.

P نواخانه *nawā-khāna*, A prison.

P نواخت *nawākht*, He caressed. Caresses, blandishment. Singing, trying or tuning the voice or an instrument. Making an essay, tasting.

P نواختن *nawākhtan*, To soothe, caress, treat humanely or kindly, gratify, fulfil the wishes of another. To praise, flatter, extol, magnify by words or actions. To give presents. To use as a brother or friend. To play upon any instrument. To sing, to strike up a loud noise.

P نواخته *nawākhta*, Protected, reared, cherished, caressed. Good works. Presents, favours.

A نواخذة *nawākhizat*, (pl. of ناخذاة *nākhuzāt*) Commanders of vessels. Supercargoes.

P نواخسته *nawākhasta*, A garden or orchard newly planted.

P نواد *nawād*, A hole in the ground for concealing treasure. Injury, loss. The tongue, speech. Calculation.

A نواد *nuwād*, (v. n. of ناد for نود) Being moved, shaken. Tottering, nodding (from drowsiness).

A نوادة *nawādat*, A place in Yaman remarkable as being the burial-place of the patriarch Shem.

A نوادر *nawādir*, (pl. of نادرة *nādirat*) Rare things, rarities, wonders. نوادر الكلام *nawādiru'l kalām*, Unusual phraseology, uncommon language.

A نوادس *nawādis*, Levelled (spears).

P نوادشه *nawādsha*, Clay, rubbish.

P نواده *nawāda*, A grandson, a son's son. A dear child. نواده پسرينه *nawāda pisarīna*, A son's son. نواده دخترينه *nawāda dukhtarīna*, A daughter's son.

A نوادي *nawādī*, Accidents, events. Flying, fugitive (camels). Fragments of date-stones flying off when broken.

P نوار *nawār* or *nuwār*, A broad border round a tent; also a piece sewed above a seam to strengthen it. A cable. A belt for man or beast. Innocent.

A نوار *nawār*, (v. n. of نار for نور) Being terrified, fleeing away, abhorring, spurning. (pl. نور *nūr*) Timid (woman), dreading suspicion. Innocent, beyond the reach of calumny. (A cow) flying the bull. (A mare) in want of, but dreading the stallion. *Niwār*, (v. n. of نار for نور) Being frightened and fleeing away.

A نوّار *nūwār*, Flowers, especially white. Blossoms.

A نوارا *niwārā*, A boat. A kind of boat.

A نوّارة *nūwārat*, One flower. A white blossom.

P نوارس *nuwāris*, A kind of long cucumber.

P نواره *nawāra*, A boat. An establishment of boats kept up at Dacca for the defence of the coast.

P نوارهان *nawārahān*, A present made to a poet, musician, or messenger of good news.

P نواريدن *nawārīdan*, To bolt without chewing.

P نواز *nawāz*, One who caresses, soothes, or flatters. A performer on a musical instrument. Caresses, blandishments. Comfort, satisfaction. بنده نواز *banda-nawāz*, Humane towards servants. غريب نواز *gharīb-nawāz*, Kind to strangers. بربط نواز *barbut-nawāz*, Tuning a lute or harp; a player on that instrument.

P نوازاده *nawā-zāda*, A grandson.

P نوازان *nawāzān*, One who caresses, soothes. A performer on a musical instrument. A singer.

P نوازش *nawāzish*, Caresses, blandishments, soothing, kindness, politeness, courtesy. A trying to sing, a tuning the voice. Beating or blowing a musical instrument. A musical instrument. نوازش كردن *nawāzish kardan*, To caress, soothe.

P نوازشات *nawāzishāt*, (pl. of نوازش) Caresses.

P نوازش گر *nawāzishgar*, One who caresses.

P نوازش گري *nawāzishgarī*, Kind usage.

P نوازش نامه *nawāzish-nāma*, Polite, complimentary letters.

A نوازل *nawāzil*, (pl. of نازلة *nāzilat*) Misfortunes, calamities. Colds, rheums.

P نوازندگي *nawāzandagī*, The playing on an instrument. Flattering, caressing.

P نوازنده *nawāzanda*, A flatterer, caresser. A player upon an instrument.

P نوازي *nawāzī*, Clemency, courtesy, kindness.

P نوازيدن *nawāzīdan*, To soothe, caress. To play on a musical instrument.

A نوّاس *nawwās*, Waving, agitated. Pendulous.

P نواسا *nawāsā*, A grandson.

P نوا ساز *nawā-sāz*, Making prisoner.

P نواستن *nawāstan*, To contend.

P نواسته *nuwāsta*, Bricks laid close (in building). A brick-wall. Tiles; heaps or piles of them.

P نواسه *nawāsa*, A grandchild, daughter's child.

P نواسی *nawāsī*, A granddaughter.

A نواسیّ *nawāsiy*, (or النواسیّ *an' nawāsiy*) A kind of white grape.

A نواسیر *nawāsīr*, (pl. of ناسور *nāsūr*) Running sores in the corners of eyes.

P نواش *nuwāsh*, Melon, cucumber: garden-fruit.

P نواشتن *nawāshtan*, To labour, struggle, strive, exert one's self. To be wrinkled, contracted.

P نواشته *nuwāshta*, A brick-wall. Bent, crooked.

A نواشر *nawāshir*, (pl. of ناشرة *nāshirat*) Veins. Arm-muscles. Wings. نواشر ناشرة *nawāshiri nāshira*, Outstretched wings.

A نواشط *nawāshit*, (pl. of ناشط *nāshit*) Absurd, impertinent (questions).

A نواشغ *nawāshigh*, Channels through which streams run down to a valley.

P نواشه *nuwāsha*, Clay or building-cement.

A نواصب *nawāsib*, The enemies of Aliy.

A نواصر *nawāsir* (pl. of ناصر *nāsir*), and نواصف *nawāsif* (pl. of ناصفة *nāsifat*), Gutters, gullies by which water runs down a valley.

A نواصي *nawāsī*, (pl. of ناصية *nāsiyat*) Forelocks. Eminent men (the forelocks of the nation).

A نواضح *nawāzih*, (pl. of ناضحة *nāzihat*) She-camels trained to water ground.

A نواضر *nawāzir*, (pl. of ناضر *nāzir*) Green.

A نواطب *nawātib*, Cloths through which any thing is strained.

A نواطح *nawātih*, (pl. of ناطح *nātih*) Adversities.

A نواطل *nawātil*, (pl. of ناطل) Wine-measures.

A نواطير *nawātīr*, (pl. of ناطور *nātūr*) Keepers of vineyards or palm-gardens. Guardians of citadels.

A نواظر *nawāzir*, (pl. of ناظرة *nāzirat*) Eyes.

A نواعير *nawāʻīr*, (pl. of ناعور *nāʻūr* or ناعورة *nāʻūrat*) Water-mills. Water-wheels. Water-buckets.

A نوافث *nawāfis*, (pl. of نافثة) Juggling tricks.

A نوافج *nawāfij*, (pl. of نافجة *nāfijat*) Beginnings or origins of any thing.

A نوافذ *nawāfiz*, The avenues whereby joy or grief are conveyed to the soul, and which are said to be the ear, nose, mouth, and fundament.

A نوافز *nawāfiz*, Feet (of horses).

A نوافس *nawāfis*, (pl. of نفساء) Women in labour.

A نوافش *nawāfish*, (Camels) feeding in the night-time without a keeper.

A نوافق *nawāfiḳ*, (pl. of نافقاء) Holes of field-mice.

A نوافل *nawāfil*, (pl. of نافلة *nāfilat*) Spontaneous acts of devotion not prescribed by law, works of supererogation.

A نوّاق *nawwāḳ*, Sagacious, experienced, fit for any thing. A breaker in of camels (ناقة *nāḳat*).

A نواقر *nawāḳir*, Reproaches, imprecations. Striking, cogent, knock-down arguments.

A نواقز *nawāḳiz*, Feet (of horses).

A نواقل *nawāḳil*, (pl. of ناقلة *nāḳilat*) Vicissitudes of fortune. Tribes (of Arabs) roaming from place to place. Tribute carried from city to city.

A نواقيس *nawāḳīs*, (pl. of ناقوس *nāḳūs*) Wooden gongs, which serve the Christians in the East to summon their congregations to prayer (bells not being allowed by the Muhammadans).

A نواقيسيّ *nawāḳīsiy*, Beater of the ناقوس *nāḳūs*.

A نواكة *nawākat*, The being foolish. Folly.

A نواكز *nawākiz*, (pl. of ناكز *nākiz*) Wells emptied, nearly exhausted.

A نواكس *nawākis*, (pl. of ناكس *nākis*) Hangers of the head.

P نواگر *nawāgar*, A singer, musician. One who reads a book from beginning to end. One who does a thing thoroughly.

A نوال *nawāl*, A present, gift, benefit. Fortune. A lot, portion. Mode, dimension, measure; a given weight. What is proper or convenient: the right way. Office, duty, any thing that ought to be performed. عمّ نواله *ʻamma nawāluhu*, His liberality is universal. نوالك ان تفعل كذا *nawāluka an tafʻala kazā*, It is your duty; you ought to do that. ليس هذا بالنوال *laysa hāzā bi'n nawāl*, That is not right or true.

A نوالة *nawālat*, A present, gift, donation. A brothel. A cellar. A cottage. A mat.

P نواله *nawāla* or *nuwāla*, A part of any victuals kept for one absent, or set down before an unexpected guest. A dish of meat. A mouthful, morsel. The wadding of a gun. Whatever one carries home from an entertainment. Listening. دوست نواله *dosti nawāla*, A trencher-friend, parasite.

P نواله بر *nawāla-bar*, One who carries away provisions. *Nawāla-bur*, A knife, carving-knife.

P نواليدن *nawālīdan*, To complain, cry. To shake, tremble.

A نوام *nuwām*, Drowsiness.

A نوّام *nawwām*, One who sleeps much, a great sleeper. *Nūwām*, (pl. of نائم *nāʼim*) Sleepers.

P نو آموز *naw-āmūz* or *āmoz*, A learner, noviciate. Inexperienced. A young falcon learning to hunt. Fond of new things. One who learns any thing new, or from the beginning. One who comes to perfection in any study.

P نو آموزنده *naw-āmozanda*, A writing-master.

A نوامي *nawāmī*, (pl. of نامية) Growing things.

A نواميس *nawāmīs*, (pl. of ناموس *nāmūs*) Hunters' lurking-places.

P نوامين *nawāmīn*, First-fruits. Any thing rare, new, and seen for the first time.

A نوآن *nuʼān*, (pl. of نوء *nawʼ*) Stars. Setting stars.

P نوان *nawān*, One who walks with a waving motion, or who moves see-saw, whilst reading or meditating. Tremulous. Feeble, weak, lean. The messenger of good news. A horse between a cream-colour and a chesnut. Intelligence, information. Direction. Prey, plunder. Reading. A reader, writer, learned man, doctor. Crying, weeping, complaining. Bent, crooked, doubled. Old (opposed to new). Aware, wary, prudent, intelligent.

P نوانزده *nuwānzdah*, Nineteen.

P نوانيدن *nawānīdan*, To cry, lament, weep. To cause to cry. To shake, tremble, be agitated. To cause to shake. To be aware or wary. To warn, inform, certify.

P نوآورد *naw-āward* or *no-āward*, An invention, new publication, any thing new.

A نواوير *nawāwīr*, (pl. of نوّار) White flowers.

A نوّاهة *nawwāhat*, A hired female mourner.

A نواهد *nawāhid*, Swelling-breasted (girls).

A نواهض *nawāhiz*, Large strong camels.

A نواهق *nawāhiḳ*, (pl. of ناهق *nāhiḳ*) Prominent bones in the cheeks of solid-hoofed animals. The places in the throats of asses which produce the braying sounds.

A نواهل *nawāhil*, (pl. of ناهل *nāhil*) (Camels) taking their first draught. Hungry camels.

A نواهي *nawāhī*, (pl. of نهي *nahy* or ناهية *nāhiyat*) Prohibitions, things forbidden by law.

P نواي *nawāy*, The side of the face, cheek.

A نؤي *nuʼa'*, A ditch or a trench cut round a tent to keep off the rain-water.

A نوائب *nawāʼib*, (pl. of نائبة *nāʼibat*) Accidents, revolutions of fortune, adversities, troubles, calamities. Extraordinary aids beyond the established contributions.

A نواية *nawāyat* or *niwāyat*, (v. n. of نوي) Becoming fat (a camel).

A نوائح *nawāʼih*, (pl. of نائحة *nāʼihat*) Weeping, wailing (women).

A نوائر *nawāʼir*, (pl. of نائرة *nāʼirat*) Enmities, hatreds. Fires.

A نوائع *nawāʼiʻ*, Waving (branches).

P نو آينده *naw-āyanda*, A new comer.

P نوائي *nawāʼī*, Voice, sound, melody. Riches, affluence, plenty, opulence. اهل نوائي *ahli nawāʼī*, One with a fine voice. A good musician; musical.

P نواييدن *nawāyīdan*, To cry, lament, weep, complain. To walk pompously. To swing to and fro.

P نو آيين *naw-āyin*, Things newly made or never before seen; novelties, wonders. A new fashion. One who introduces a new fashion. Adorned, decorated. The decorations of a house.

A نوب *nawb*, (v. n. of ناب for نوب) Supplying the place (of another), being a vicar, vicegerent, lieutenant, or nabob. Befalling (as misfortune). Being near. Returning. Being converted to God; being obedient, performing assiduously every religious duty. Descent, falling. Nearness. Success.

Event, accident. Cause of any business or evil. Strength, force. Any place distant a day and night's journey. (pl. of نائب *nāʼib*) Vicegerents. *Nūb*, The Nubians in Ethiopia. (pl. of نائب *nāʼib*) Bees. *Nuwab*, (pl. of نوبة *nawbat* and *nūbat*) Periods, turns. Accidents of fortune.

P نوباده *naw-bāda*, New wine.

P نو باره *naw-bāra*, First-fruits.

P نوبامون *nawbāmūn*, The ox of king Farīdūn.

P نوبان *nūbān*, A king's son.

P نوباوه *naw-bāwa*, First-fruits, early fruit. Any thing new, curious, or agreeable to the eye.

A نوبة *nawbat*, (v. n. of ناب for نوب) Supplying the place (of another). (pl. نوب *nuwab*) A period, time, turn, revolution; any thing done periodically. A guard which is relieved; keeping watch, relieving guard. Drums beating at the gate of a great man at certain intervals. A sentinel, watchman. Vicissitude. Degree, pitch, weight. A crowd of people. Descent, falling. A circuit. Occasion, opportunity. P نوبت تب *nawbati tab*, Paroxysm of a fever. A *Nūbat*, Accident, calamity, misfortune. Period, time, turn. Nubia, part of Ethiopia.

A نوبة *nūbatan*, Alternately, successively.

P نوبت *nawbat* or *nobat*, A very large kettle-drum, struck at stated hours. A large state-tent for giving audience. Security, safety. Opportunity. Guard, protection.

P نوبتخانه *nobat-khāna*, A watch-tower. A guard-house. The music-gallery.

P نوبتگه *nawbat-gah*, A place where a tent is pitched. An orchestra, music-gallery.

P نوبتي *nawbatī*, He who beats the kettle-drum called نوبت *nawbat*. The grand tent of audience. The tent in which the نوبت *nawbat* is kept. A led horse. One turn. One guard.

P نوبر *naw-bar*, Fresh fruits newly ripe. A damsel whose breasts begin to shew.

P نوبشتن *nūbishtan*, To preserve, spare.

P نوبك *nūbak*, A vine-twig or shoot.

P نوبندجان *nawbandajān*, A city in Persia.

P نوبه *nawba*, First-fruits. *Nūba*, Complaint, moan. Bark of the wild pine. Pith of a tree. Nubia.

P نوبهار *naw-bahār*, The spring-quarter. Name of a fire-temple.

P نوبهاري *naw-buhārī*, Name of a note in music. Name of the 27th note of the barbud.

A نوبي *nūbaʼ*, Seasonable spring-rain.

A نوبيّ *nūbīy*, One Nubian.

P نوبيخ *nawbīkh*, Ivy.

P نوبيدن *nūbīdan*, To roll, wallow (as a horse).

P نوپان *nūpān*, A wicker basket.

P نوپيدا *naw-paydā*, New, newly produced.

A نوت *nawt*, A staggering from weakness.

A نوتاة *nawtāt*, (pl. نواتي) Short, dwarfish.

P نوتاش *nawtāsh*, Constant, eternal, everlasting.

A نوتيّ *nūtīy*, (pl. نواتيّ *nawātīy*) A seaman.

A نوج *nawj*, Hypocritical behaviour.

A نؤج *nawuj*, Violent (wind). *Nuwuj*, Travel.

P نوج *nūj*, (or نوچ *nūch*) A pine-tree.

P نوجبه *nawjaba*, Inundation, flood. An angel.

A نوجة *nawjat*, A whirlwind.

A نوجر *nawjar*, Any ploughing-implement.

P نوجوان *naw-jawān*, A young man, lad, youth.

P نوجواني *naw-jawānī*, Prime of life, youth.

P نوچكي *nawchagī*, Newness, freshness.

P نوچه *nawcha*, A youth, a young man.

A نوح *nawh*, (v. n. of ناح for نوح) Lamenting, complaining, moaning. Mourning a deceased relative. Plaint, moan. The plaintive note of a dove. Rhyme, rhythmical oration; a company of people uttering together a rhythmical oration. *Nawh*, (or نوّح *nūwah*) (pl. of نائحة *nāʼihat*) Female mourners. *Nūh*, Noah.

P نوح *nūh*, Ivy.

A نوحة *nawhat*, Lamentation, moan, wail over the dead (by female mourners). P نوحه كردن *nawha kardan*, To wail (as hired mourners). To milk.

P نوحه گر *nawhagar*, One who laments. A hired mourner. One who milks.

P نوحه گري *nawhagarī*, Lamentation.

P نوحيدن *nawhīdan*, To weep, lament.

P نوخ *nūkh*, Plaint, moan, lamentation.

P نوخاسته *naw-khāsta*, New-risen, *i.e.* a youth, young man. دلاوران نوخاسته *dilāwarāni naw-khāsta*, Youthful warriors.

A نوخة *nawkhat*, A stopping, standing still.

P نوخط *naw-khat*, A youth whose mustachios are just appearing. نوخطي عالم *naw khatīʼi ʻālam*, Early spring-grass.

P نوخيدن *nawkhīdan*, To lament, weep.

P نوخيز *naw-khez*, New-risen, fresh, tender.

A نود *nawd*, (or نودان *nawadān*) (v. n. of ناد for نود) Being moved, agitated, waving, tottering, nodding (from drowsiness).

P نود *nūd*, A beloved son. *Nawad*, The posteriors. Ninety. He trembles. نود بار *nawad bār*, Ninety times.

A نؤد *naʼud*, Misfortune, disaster, calamity.

A نودأة *nawdaʼat*, (v. n. of نودأ Q) Running.

P نوداران *nawdārān*, (or نوداراني *nawdārānī*) Drink-money, over and above stipulated wages. Any thing given to a poet, or to the servant who brings a present, or to a messenger of good news.

A نودان *nawadān*, The to-and-fro motion of the Jews in their schools.

P نودد *nawdad*, A fold.

P نودر *nawdar*, Any thing new and strange. Name of the son of منوچهر *minū-chihr*.

P نودران *nawdarān*, Servants, apprentices.

P نودرانه *nawdarāna*, Drink-money.

P نودره *nawdara*, A beloved offspring. Bold, warlike. Folded up, rolled together, creased. A mode of stitching. A border sewed on a garment.

P نودساد *nūdsād*, Any honourable profession or employ. A bias to the useful and praiseworthy.

A نودل *nawdal*, The breast.

A نودلة *nawdalat*, (v. n. of نودل Q) Being pendulous, hanging. Tottering with age.

P نو دولت *naw-dawlat*, An upstart, parvenu.

P نوده *nawda*, Air, atmosphere. Bold. *Nawada*, A grandchild. Beloved offspring.

A نوذخ *nawzakh*, Timid, abject. A coward.

A نور *nawr*, (v. n. of نار for نور) Shining. Impressing a mark by burning. Being frightened, flying in horror from any thing. Frightening (a female), causing (her) to run away with fear. Seeing a fire at a distance. Turning the back, being put to flight. (pl. انوار *anwār*) The blossom of a tree, a flower (especially when white). *Nūr*, (pl. انوار *anwār* and نيران *nīrān*) Light, rays of light; splendour, illumination. An epithet of God. One who enlightens (applied as an epithet to Muhammad). Knowledge. Truth. Quicksilver. (pl. of نار *nār*) Fires. (pl. of نؤور *naʼūr* and نوار *nawār*) Timid (women or fawns). Mares dreading the stallion. نور الهي *nūri ilāhī*, Divine light. نور ايمان *nūri īmān*, Light of the faith. P نورچشم *nūri chashm*, (or ديده *dīda*) Light of the eyes; a beloved child. نور ساده *nūri sāda*, Pure light, without any mixture of darkness. A نور عذرا *nūri ʻazrā*, The light of Jesus and Mary. P نور گسترانيدن *nūr gustarānīdan*, To display, lay open. To turn to. To do good. نور نخستين *nūri nakhustīn*, (نور پسين *nūri pasīn*, or A نور مبين *nūri mubīn*) Muhammad.

A نورا *nūrā*, Depilatory.

P نور اسپهبد *nūr ispahbud*, (اسپهود *ispahwud*, اسفهبد *isfahbud*, اسفهود *isfahwud*) Rational soul.

P نور افشان *nūr-afshān*, Light-diffusing.

P نوراني *nūrānī*, (pl. نورانيان *nurāniyān*) Serene, light, clear, bright, luminous. Serenity, brightness.

A نورانيّة *nūrānīyat*, Light, splendour, brightness, luminousness.

P نوراور *nawrāwar*, A copper vessel.

P نوراهان *nawrāhān*, A present, gift. Good news.

P نور بخش *nūr-bakhsh*, Light-bestowing.

A نورة *nawrat*, One blossom. *Nūrat*, A mark impressed by a hot iron. Quick lime; also a medicament made of it and arsenic for taking out hairs by the roots. A liniment of pitch, with which they bedaub camels for the scab. Name of a sorceress.

A نورج *nawraj*, A ploughshare. An instrument (of wood or iron) for beating out the corn. The vapour called سراب *sarāb*.

A نورجة *nawrajat*, Whispering, tale-bearing, detraction. Hesitation, fluctuation in opinion.

P نورد *naward*, A ply, fold, wrinkle, twist. A crease. A scroll. Any thing folded and round. The hem or any thing sewed round the edge of a garment. Ready money. A brute. Battle, combat, quarrel, law-suit. A gift, present. A weaver's beam, upon which he rolls the cloth. Worthy, convenient, proper, excellent. Approved, acceptable, agreeable. Like, resembling, equal, of the same stature, breadth, weight, or measure. (in composition) Going round, surrounding, travelling over. A traveller. Collected, gathered, gained. سمندِ رہ نورد *samandi rah-naward*, A horse that can travel well. سیّاحِ جہان نورد *sayyāhi jahān-naward*, A traveller who has gone round the world. صحرا نورد شدن *sahrā-naward shudan*, To scour the country round. *Nord*, Original name of the city of Gāzur.

A نوردجة *nawardajat*, (from P نوردہ *nawarda*, Plaited) Wicker-work.

P نوردن *nawardan*, To fold, twist. To crease. A weaver's beam, on which he rolls the cloth.

P نوردناك *nawardnāk*, Wrinkled, creased.

P نوردہ *nawarda*, A daughter's son. A shirt, shift. The body of a shirt. Any written attestation signed by a judge. Twisted, plaited, folded, coiled. Creased. نوردۂ پیراهن *nawarda-i pīrāhun*, Any kind of border sewed round a shirt.

P نوردیدن *nawardīdan*, To fold, crease. To twist. To travel, walk, wander, stray. To render nameless, to remove any mark of distinction. To omit, leave undone. To pass by or over, to slight.

P نوردیدہ *nawardīda*, Folded: creased: twisted.

P نورس *naw-ras*, Young, fresh, tender, recent.

P نورستہ *naw-rasta*, A young shoot, sapling.

P نورسیدہ *naw-rasīda*, New, fresh, germinating.

P نورگستر *nūr-gustar*, Light-diffusing.

P نورنجہ *nawranja*, A lake, pool. Name of a city.

P نورند *nūrand*, A translation.

P نوروز *naw-roz*, New-year's day (according to the Persian calendar; being that on which the sun enters Aries). (This is called عامّہ *ʿāmma*, or General; and the sixth of the same month خاصّہ *khāssa*, Special, or بزرگ *buzurg*, Great. Both of these days, as well as those which intervened, were celebrated by feasts, the liberation of prisoners, and the like. نوروز بزرگ *naw rozi buzurg*, Name of a note in music. نوروز خردك *naw rozi khurdak*, (or نوروز كوچك *naw rozi kūchak*) Name of a note in music. نوروز سلطاني *naw rozi sulṭānī*, The true astronomical vernal equinox.

P نوروزیہ *nawroziya*, A new-year's gift.

P نورہ *nawra*, Wood for roofing. *Nūra*, A depilatory unguent made of arsenic and quick-lime.

P نورهان *naw-rahān*, (or نورهاني *naw-rahānī*) A present brought from a journey. A poem recited by a strolling bard or minstrel. Good news. A present made to a poet.

A نوريّ *nūrīy*, Splendid, bright, clear. An epithet of Abū'l Husayn, a celebrated preacher.

P نوريتہ *nūrīta*, Imagined, conceived, thought.

A نورين *nūrayn*, (oblique dual of نور *nūr*) Both lights, *i.e.* the sun and moon; also the eyes. ذو النورين *zū'n nūrayn*, Name of the caliph Othmān.

P نوز *noz*, (for هنوز *hanoz*) Now. A pine-tree.

P نوزاد *naw-zād*, Newly born. Name of a village in Khurāsān.

P نوزادہ *naw-zāda* or *no-zāda*, Recent or lately born. نوزادگان چمن *naw-zādagāni chaman*, Sprouts, shoots, buds, blossoms.

P نوزائندہ *naw-zāinda*, (or نو زائیدہ *naw-zāīda*) Recently-delivered (female).

P نوزدہ *nūzdah*, Nineteen.

P نوزدهم *nūzdahum*, The nineteenth.

P نوژ *noj*, A pine-tree.

P نوژان *nūjān*, A dreadful, terrifying voice.

P نوژن *nojan*, A pine-tree.

P نوژندہ *nawjanda*, Who or what produces an effect, who or what causes.

P نوژہ *nūja*, The collar of a garment.

A نوس *naws*, (and نوسان *nawasān*) (v. n. of ناس for نوس) Driving (camels). Being moved to and fro, shaken. Flowing down the back (hair).

P نوس *nos*, The rainbow. Mimicry, the burlesque imitation of a person's voice.

P نوسپاس *nū sipās*, (for ناسپاس) Ungrateful.

P نوستن *nawistan*, To groan.

P نوستہ *nosta*, Noise in the throat by one crying.

P نوسہ *nosa*, The mirage. The rainbow.

P نوسیرہ *nawsīra*, Debate, dispute, controversy.

A نوش *nawsh*, (v. n. of ناش for نوش) Taking; seizing (the beard or the hair). Searching, inquiring. Going, proceeding forward. Bringing near. Rising quickly.

A نؤش *nausush*, Robust, strong, victorious. One who seizes any thing forcibly.

P نوش *nūsh* or *nosh*, (in comp.) Drink thou. Drinking. A drinker. A drink, draught. Any thing drank, especially sweet, agreeable, and wholesome. Honey. Treacle. An antidote against poison. The water of life or immortality. Life. Sweetness. Sweet. Pleasing, agreeable. Consonant, harmonious. The wild pine. A present, reward. Name of a fire-temple. Name of the fifth day of the month according to the æra of Yazdagird. Hear thou! hearken thou! The sense of hearing. A listener. *Nawash*, A present. A recompense. *Nawish*, Writing. Predestination.

P نوشا *noshā* or *nūshā*, A drinker.

P نوشابہ *noshāba*, The water of life. Name of the queen of بردع *bardaʿ*.

P نوشاد *nawshād*, Name of a city famous for the beauty of its inhabitants.

P نوشادر *nawshādur*, Sal-ammoniac (used in tinning and soldering).

P نوش آذر *nosh-āzar*, The second of the seven famed fire-temples in Persia. Name of a champion.

P نوشانوش *nosh-ā-nosh*, With full cups, with repeated bumpers.

P نوشانیدن *noshānīdan*, To cause to drink.

P نوشاہ *naw-shāh*, A bridegroom.

P نوش باد *nosh-bād*, (or نوش بادہ *nosh-bāda*) Name of a note in music.

P نوشت *nosht*, A draught, potation. A drinker. *Nawasht*, He twisted, folded, or creased. Dragonwort. *Niwisht*, He wrote. Writing. نوشت خدا *niwishti khudā*, The prescience of God, divine predestination.

P نوشتجات *nuwishtajāt*, Writings.

P نوشت خواند *nivisht-khwānd*, Epistolary correspondence, reading and writing.

P نوشتن *noshtan* or *nūshtan*, To drink. *Nawashtan*, To fold, twist, coil. *Nawishtan* or *nuwashtan*, To go far away. To groan. *Nivishtan* or *nuwishtan*, To write. To preserve, to spare.

P نوشتہ *nawashta*, Folded, coiled, twisted. *Niwishta*, Written, described. A writing.

P نوشخور *nosh-khwur*, The fifth day of the month according to the æra of Jalālu'd dīn.

P نوشدارو *nosh-dārū*, Treacle; antidotes of every kind. Wine. Name of an electuary.

P نوشروان *noshirwān*, (نوشیروان *nawshīrvān*, *noshīrwān*, or نوشین روان *noshīn-rawān*) Name of a king of Persia, in whose reign Muhammad was born, A.D. 578. Just. The archangel Gabriel.

P نوشگفتہ *naw-shigufta*, New-blown (rose) beginning to expand. نوشگفتۂ بامداد *naw-shigufta-i bāmdād*, Break of day, dawn. غنچۂ نوشگفتہ *ghuncha-i naw-shigufta*, A rose-bud.

P نوش گیا *nosh-giyā*, Name of an antidote.

P نوش لبینا *nosh-lubīnā*, Name of a musical note.

P نوشنجہ *noshanja*, Wholesome, digestable.

P نوشندہ *noshanda*, A drinker. نوشندۂ شربت مودّت *noshanda-i sharbati mawaddat*, A drinker of the nectar of love.

P نوشو *naw-shav*, New, recent, fresh.

P نوشہ *naw shah*, A young king. A bridegroom, son-in-law. *Nosha*, Fortunate, happy, prosperous. Sweet, cheerful. Sweetness, goodness. Affliction, sadness. Distracting cares. The rainbow. نوشہ کردن *nosha kardan*, To flatter.

P نوشیدگي *noshīdagī*, A drinking; a draught.

P نوشیدن *noshīdan*, To drink; take. To digest.

P نوشین *noshīn*, Sweet, pleasant. Easy of digestion. To be listened to; audible.

P نوشین بادہ *noshīn-bāda*, Wine which flows pleasantly down the throat. Name of the twenty-eighth note of the barbud.

P نوشین روان *noshīn-rawān*, Sweet life.

P نوشینہ *noshīna*, Pleasant wine. Name of a note in music.

A نوص *naws*, (v. n. of ناص for نوص) Retiring, retreating, declining, shunning, flying from, escaping. Remaining behind. Delaying. Moving one's self. Raising one's self up, rising to do any thing. Taking refuge. A wild ass.

A نوصان *nawasān*, A moving one's self.

A نوصة *nawsat*, One lotion or washing.

A نوض *nawz*, (v. n. of ناض for نوض) Travelling, perambulating. Moving any thing in order to draw it out (as a tent-pin). Drawing or letting out (water). Having many clusters (a vine). Shining, flashing (lightning). Motion, a waving, shaking in the air. The rump-bone, root of the tail. (pl. انواض *anwāz*) The suture or joining-place of the buttocks with the back (especially in a camel). (pl. انواض *anwāz* and اناويض *anāwiz*) High ground. A place or opening by which water flows.

A نوط *nawt*, (v. n. of ناط for نوط) Suspending, appending. Being troubled with a pestilential swelling (a camel). (pl. انواط *anwāt* and نياط *niyāt*) Any thing hung up or appended to another. A parcel hung or placed between the two larger trusses or loads carried on each side by a camel. A hamper in which they carry dates, hanging it to a camel's load. The interstice between the buttocks and loins of beasts. *Nūt*, (pl. of نياط *niyāt*) Strings (of a bow or bottle) by which they are hung up.

A نوطة *nawtat*, A hamper in which they carry dates, hanging it to a camel's load. Hatred, rancour, malice. A kind of pestilential bubo, to which camels are subject; they break out in the breast, groin, neck, and belly. A bird's crop. A place high above water. The part between back and buttock. A grove thickly planted with acacias and tamarisks.

A نوع *nawɛ*, (pl. انواع *anwāɛ*) Species, kind, sort, manner, mode (جنس *jins* signifying a genus). Request, petition. A leaning or waving from side to side in walking. The darting of an eagle upon his prey. نوع انسان *nawɛi insān*, Mankind. نوع بشر *nawɛi bashar*, The human race. نوع جفا *nawɛi jafā*, A kind of vexation, any thing perplexing. P نوع ديگر *nawɛi dīgar*, Another kind. A نوع فراغ *nawɛi firāgh*, A little rest. نوع و جنس *nawɛ u jins*, Species and genus. *Nūɛ*, Thirst (hence the imprecation رماه الله بالجوع و بالنوع *ramāhu'llāh bi'l jūɛ wa bi'n nūɛ*, (or simply جوعا نوعا *juɛān nūɛan*) May God strike him with hunger and thirst!)

A نوعا *nawɛan*, Somewhat, in some manner.

A نوعة *nawɛat*, Fresh fruit.

P نو عروس *naw-ɛarūs*, A newly-married bride. نو عروسان چمن *naw-ɛarūsāni chaman*, Young shoots, opening flowers.

P نو عنان *naw-ɛinān*, New to the bridle.

A نوعيّ *nawɛīy*, Constituting a species, specific.

P نوغ *nogh*, A place near the desert of Kipchāk.

A نوف *nawf*, (v. n. of ناف for نوف) Hanging (over), appearing (above). Being broad and long. Sucking (a teat). (pl. انواف *anwāf*) A camel's bunch (especially of the larger kind). The clitoris (which is usually cut off). A suck from the breast. A cry (especially of the hyena).

P نوف *nūf*, Echo from a mountain. Hollow place or cavern. Noise of a multitude. Howl of a dog.

P نوفاغ *nūfāgh*, Name of a city.

P نوفتم *nūftam*, I may not fall.

P نوفر *nūfar* or *nawfar*, Water-lily, nenuphar.

A نوفل *nawfal*, The sea. A munificent man. A present. A handsome youth. Male hyena. Whelp of a wild beast. A jackal. Adversity. Name of a man.

A نوفلة *nawfalat*, A salt-pit, a place whence salt is brought. A kind of woollen veil worn by the Arabian women.

P نوفه *nūfa*, A loud noise, clamour; the confused noise of a multitude of men or animals.

P نوفيدن *nūfīdan*, To resound as an echo, or the confused noise of men and animals. To cry with a loud voice, roar, bray. To move, stir, shake, wag. To be disturbed.

A نوق *nūḳ*, (pl. of ناقة *nāḳat*) She-camels. *Nawaḳ*, A reddish white.

A نوقة *nūḳat*, Skill, dexterity. *Nawaḳat*, Jew-butchers who take the fat from the flesh.

P نوك *nawk* or *nok*, A point, tip, end. Beak of a bird. Tips of eyelashes. نوك زبان *noki zabān*, Tip of the tongue. نوك قلم *nawki kalam*, (or نوك خامه *nawki khāma*) Point or nib of a pen.

A نوك *nūk*, (pl. of انوك *anwak* and نوكاء *nawkāɛ*) Foolish men or women. *Nūk* or *nawk*, Folly. *Nawak*, (v. n. of نوك) Being foolish, stupid.

A نوكاء *nawkāɛ*, Foolish, stupid (woman).

P نوكار *naw-kār*, Young in business.

P نوكال *nūkāl*, Deception.

P نوكدار *nok-dār*, Pointed.

P نوكدخدا *naw kad-khudā*, A new housekeeper. A bridegroom.

P نوكر *nawkar* or *nūkar*, A servant. A dependant. *Nūkar*, Name of a king.

P نوكرده *nawkarda*, A grandson.

P نوكري *nawkarī*, Service, attendance, inferiority.

P نوكري پيشه *nawkarī-pesha*, One who lives on employment. A servant.

P نوك ريز *nawk-rez*, A dip of ink.

A نوكىٰ *nawka'*, (pl. of انوك) Foolish people.

P نوكيلا *nokīlā*, Sharp-pointed.

P نوگان *nūgān*, (*nawgān*, or عيد نوگان *ɛīdi nawgān*) An anniversary, encænia, commemoration.

P نوگفاره *nawgufāra*, A talkative man.

P نوگند *nogand*, Newly sprung up.

P نوگواره *nawguwāra*, A talkative fellow.

P نوگيوش *nūgiyūsh*, Name of the king of the island طرطانيوش *tartāniyūsh*.

A نول *nawl*, (v. n. of نال for نول) Giving, presenting, being liberal. Folding, twisting. A gift, present. Manner, mode. (pl. انوال *anwāl*) A weaver's beam. Office, duty, whatever one ought to perform. A channel full of water. Freight. نولك ان تفعل كذا *nawluka an tafɛala kazā*, You ought to do thus. *Nūl*, A race of Negroes.

P نول *nol*, The outer part of the mouth. A beak, bill. A spout. The neck of a bottle. Any thing on which one leans or is supported. A whirlpool, vortex. نول مرغ *noli murgh*, The beak or bill of any bird, especially a goose.

A نولة *nawlat*, One largess or gift. Somewhat. A kiss. النولة *an' nawlat*, The area of the temple of Mecca, that which surrounds الحرم *al haram*, or sacred enclosure. *Nūlat*, Any thing obtained, a gift.

G نولون *nawlūn*, Freight.

P نوله *nūla*, Speech, a word.

A نوم *nawm*, (v. n. of نام for نوم) Beating (any one) in sleeping, oversleeping (him). Sleeping, falling asleep. Sleeping (as a silkworm) after casting the skin. Being still, not sounding (the ankle-ring called خلخال *khalkhāl* being closely filled with flesh). Being dull (market). Being still (the wind). Being extinguished (a fire). Being calm (sea). Being dead (sheep). Being worn (a garment). Acquiescing, submitting. Sleep, slumber. (pl. of نائم *nāɛim*) Sleepers. نوم دائم *nawmi dāɛim*, A perpetual sleep. *Nuwam*, Sleepy. Comatose.

A نوّم *nūwam*, (pl. of نائم *nāɛim* or نائمة) Sleepers.

A نومان *nawmān*, Name of a plant. يا نومان *yā nawmānu*, O sleepy! O indolent!

A نومة *nūmat* or *nuwamat*, Mean, obscure. *Nuwamat*, Somnolent, sleepy. Careless, inactive.

P نو مسلمان *naw musulmān*, One who sets about a thing properly.

P نو ملازم *naw-mulāzim*, A raw recruit, novice.

P نوملازمي *naw-mulāzimī*, Noviciate.

P نوميد *nawmed*, (or نوميذ *nawmez*) Hopeless. نوميد شدن *nawmed shudan*, To be desperate, lose hope, despair. نوميد گردانيدن *nawmed gardānidan*, To drive to desperation, render desperate.

P نوميدن *nūmīdan*, To sleep, dose, rest.

P نوميدي *nawmedī*, (or نوميذي *nawmezī*) Despair. Disappointment, ill-luck.

P نون *nūn*, Dimple in the chin. Trunk of a tree. Firm, fixed in a place. The eyebrow. Greatness, magnificence, opulence, prosperity. (for اكنون *aknūn*) Now.

A نون *nūn*, (pl. نونات *nūnāt*) The letter ن *n*. (pl. نينان *nīnān* and انوان *anwān*) A fish. The sharpest part of a sword. A sword. Riches, prosperity. An inkholder. ذو النون *zū'n nūn*, The prophet Jonah (as being swallowed by a fish). ذو النون *zū'n nūn*, (and ذو النونين *zū'n nūnayn*) Two famous swords so called.

A نونة *nūnat*, One fish. A dimple in a boy's chin. A true or right word. Name of a woman.

P نوند *nawand*, A courier, messenger, newsman. A well-going or ambling horse or mule. A horse. Swift, quick-going. Rue. Echo, loud noise. A searcher, seeker, inquirer. A deceiver. A man of quick conception. Name of a place; of a mountain; and of a champion of Irān.

P نونداك *nawnadāk*, Suddenly, unexpectedly.

P نوندول *nawandūl*, A son's son.

P نونده *nawanda*, A swift horse. Swift, active,

nimble. Rue. One who moves or trembles. One who calls out for help. Acute, ingenious, quick of apprehension. *Nuwanda*, Any thing newly produced.

P نونندة *nūnanda*, Acute, ingenious, quick.

A نَوْنُوءٌ *nusnus*, Weak, infirm. Timid.

P نونة *nūna*, A pit in the chin.

P نونهال *naw-nihāl*, A young tree.

P نونياز *naw-niyāz*, Any thing newly produced. A beginner, tyro, novice.

P نوّو *nasū*, A fresh date.

A نووج *nasūj*, A blowing wind. *Nusūj*, (v. n. of ناج) Travelling.

A نوود *nasūd*, Evil, misfortune, calamity.

A نوور *nasūr*, Woad used in dyeing blue. Indigo. The smoke of tallow, which, when rubbed over figures pricked on the skin, previously touched with woad or indigo, makes the colour green. A fossil like antimony with which they sprinkle the gums. (pl. نور *nūr*) Timid (woman), dreading suspicion.

A نووش *nasūsh*, Strong, robust. One who snatches or seizes a thing with violence.

A نوول *nasūl*, One who goes friskingly, prancing with a peculiar nod of the head; shaking the body (trotting horse or hyena).

A نووم *nasūm*, Somnolent; one who sleeps much.

A نوويّة *nawawiyat*, (Camels) fed on date-stones.

A نوه *nawh*, (v. n. of ناه for نوه) Being exalted. Raising the head and hooting (an owl). Buzzing (a stinging insect). Growing (as a plant). Satiating cattle (herbage). Being eminent, magnificent, generous. Being strong, firm, courageous. Abstaining, refraining from, having nothing to do with. *Nawh* or *nūh*, Aversion, abstinence.

P نوه *nūh*, Nine. *Nawa*, A grandchild. New.

A نوّة *nūwah*, (for نوّح) Female mourners.

A نوهة *nawhat*, What one eats at once, a meal.

A نوي *nusy* or *nusa'*, (pl. آناء *ānās*, انآء *ansās*, نُوِيّ *nusiy*, and نِيّ *nisiy*) A ditch made round a tent to keep off the rain-water.

A نوي *nawa'*, Intention, purpose. Mode, manner. Absence, distance. Any place to which a traveller goes. A house. Departure, a travelling from place to place. The place of circumcision in a girl. (pl. of نواة *nawāt*) Date-stones.

P نوي *navi*, Newness, freshness, novelty. *Niwe* or *nuwe*, The Kur'ān.

A نوِيّ *nawiy*, A companion of like sentiments. *Nuwiy* or *niwiy*, (pl. of نوي *nawa'*) Date-stones.

A نويان *nūyān*, A prince, king's son (chiefly used by the Tartars and Turks). A wicker-basket.

A نويب *nuwayb*, (dim. of ناب *nāb*) A small dog-tooth.

P نويچ *nawech*, Ivy, woodbine.

P نويد *nawed*, Happy tidings, good news. The gospel. A present to the bringer of good news. Reward, recompense. Equity, justice. Vow, promise. Entertainment, feast, hospitality. Part of the provisions of a feast which the guests carry away. Power, strength. Reproaching, reviling. نويد دادن *nawed dādan*, To promise. *Nuwed*, Mirth. Good news. Any thing which affords pleasure. Invitation to a feast. Promise of a lucrative situation. *Noyad*, He trembles. He complains. He weeps.

P نويدن *nawīdan*, To sleep, slumber, rest little or badly. To move, especially when rising from a place. To shake, tremble, stagger. To complain. To invite to a feast. To make or become new.

P نويدة *nawīda*, Tottering. Complaining.

A نويرة *nuwayrat*, (dim. of نار *nār*) A little fire.

P نويس *navīs*, Writing, describing. A writer. زود نويس *zūd-navīs*, A quick writer.

P نويساندن *navīsāndan*, (or نويسانيدن *navīsānīdan*) To cause to write or describe.

P نويستن *nawīstan*, To write.

P نويسندگي *nawīsandagī*, Writing.

P نويسندة *nawīsanda*, A writer, scribe, clerk, accountant.

P نويسة *nuwīsa*, The rainbow.

P نويش *navīsh*, (in comp.) Writing; a writer.

P نويشتن *navīshtan* or *nuvīshtan*, To write.

P نويشة *nuwīsha*, Blandishments. نويشة كردن *nuwīsha kardan*, To caress. To ask. To deprecate.

A نويص *nawīs*, (v. n. of ناص for نوص) Moving one's self. Strength, the power of moving one's self.

P نويك *nūyak*, A time, turn, period. A pipe, flute. A vine-twig or sucker.

P نويل *nawīl*, The front, forehead.

P نويم *nawīm*, Only, merely. بنويم ديدن شناخت *ba nawīmi dīdan shinākht*, By only seeing he knew.

A نويم *nawīm*, Negligent, careless. Obscure.

P نوين *nawīn* or *nuvīn*, A prince, a king's son. The most excellent of any thing.

P نويندة *nūyanda*, Acute, ingenious, quick.

P نوية *nūya*, A sucker at the root of a tree. A tender shoot. Sap. Plaint, lamentation, moan.

P نوييدن *nūyīdan*, To cry aloud, lament.

P نويين *nūyīn*, (in the Khwārazm dialect) Son of a king, prince. A commander of 10,000.

P نة *na*, (sometimes, in poetry, *nah*) No, not, neither, not yet. *Na* added to words denotes fitness: as, پادشاهانة *pādshāhāna*, Befitting a king; بزرگانة *buzurgāna*, Befitting a great man. *Nih*, (from نهادن *nihādan*) Placing; one who places or applies. A town, city; whence is said to be derived نشاپور *nishāpūr* for نة شاپور *nihi shāpūr*, The city of Shāpūr. داغ نة *dāgh-nih*, Marking with scars. مرهم نة *marham-nih*, One who applies a plaster. قدم نة *kadam-nih*, Fixing or placing the feet. قدم نة زيارت شدن *kadam-nihi ziyārat shudan*, To visit. *Nuh*, Nine. The nine orifices of the human body. نة بام *nuh bām*, The nine heavens. (Synonymous to which are the following: نة پاية *nuh pāya*, نة پدر *nuh pidar*, نة پردة *nuh parda*, نة حجرة *nuh hujra*, نة حصار مينا *nuh hisāri mīnā*, نة خراس *nuh kharās*, نة رواق *nuh rawāk*, نة سپهر *nuh sipihr*, نة شهر بالا *nuh shahri bālā*, نة صحيفة گردون *nuh sahīfasi gardūn*, نة طارم *nuh tāram*, نة طبق *nuh tabak*, نة قصر *nuh kasr*, نة كاخ *nuh kākh*, نة مقرنس *nuh mukarnas*). نة پاية *nuh pāya*, A pulpit. نة پدر *nuh pidar*, The seven planets with the dragon's head and tail. نة حجرة *nuh hujra*, The haram of Muhammad. نةُ *nasi*, Thou art not.

A نها *nahs*, (v. n. of نهيٌ) Being filled, replenished. Being half-raw, ill-dressed (meat).

A نها *niha'*, Glass: a phial.

A نهاء *nihās*, A small mound, dam, or receptacle for rain-water. A white stone softer than marble. A sort of glass-bead. Glass. End, limit, extremity. A kind of medicine which grows in the fields. (pl. of نهي *nahy*) Ditches. *Nihās*, The rising (of water); advancing (of the day). (pl. نهاة *nuhāt*) A phial, jug. *Nuhās*, A number (of a hundred men).

A نهاءة *nahāsat*, (v. n. of نهيٌ) Being half-raw, ill-cooked, insufficiently-dressed (meat).

A نهاب *nihāb*, (pl. of نهب *nahb*) Spoils.

A نهّاب *nahhāb*, A plunderer, spoiler. النّهّاب *an' nahhāb*, The lion.

A نهابر *nahābir*, Hell. (pl. of نهبرة *nuhburat*) High sand-hills. Ditches and hollows amongst heaps of sand. Dangerous places, perils, precipices.

A نهابير *nahābīr*, Dangerous places, perils, precipices. (pl. of نهبورة *nuhbūrat*) Ditches or hollows amongst heaps of sand. High sand-hills.

A نهاة *nuhāt*, (pl. of نهاء *nihās*) Phials, jugs. (pl. of ناهي *nāhi*) Prohibitors.

A نهات *nuhāt*, (v. n. of نهت) Bellowing, roaring, lowing; shout, cry, murmur.

A نهّات *nahhāt*, Roaring (lion); braying (ass); blowing or breathing hard, groaning (man).

P نهاد *nahād*, Nature, disposition, temperament. Manner, custom. آتش نهاد *ātish-nahād*, Of a fiery quality; inflammable. *Nihād*, (third pers. pret. and verbal noun of نهادن *nihādan*) He placed. Placing, position, posture. Nature, form, habit, constitution of the body. Stature. Quality, essence. Mind, heart. Manner; prescribed mode, custom. Description. Vestige, mark, sign. A structure. Family, stock, race. Dregs, dung. Young (horse or cow). Fear. Untamed, wild. بد نهاد *bad-nihād*, Wicked, cruel. پيش نهاد *pesh-nihād*, Institution, profession. سلاطين نيك نهاد *salātīni nek-nihād*, Princes of noble dispositions. صادق نهادان امّت *sādik-nihādāni ummat*, Good-hearted people.

A نهاد *nuhād*, Quantity, number (of 100).

P نهادگي *nihādagī*, Habit, form, constitution, nature, quality. Holiday-clothes. The shew-bread.

P نهادن *nihādan*, To place, put, lay upon, collocate. To appoint. To apply, administer. To build. To copulate. گام نهادن *gām nihādan*, To step, walk, go. گردن نهادن *gardan nihādan*, To bow the neck, submit. خودرا بمستي نهادن *khwudrā ba masti ni-*

kādan, To counterfeit intoxication.

P نهاده *nihāda*, Placed. Appointed.

P نهاديدن *nahādīdan*, To fear, to dread.

P نهار *nahār*, Much, many. Diminution. A goat. A black water-fowl with white spots on the head. (for ناهار *nāhār*) Fasting. *Nihār*, An idol. Detriment, loss. *Nihār* or *nahār*, Fear, dread, apprehension. Consumption, a wasting of the body.

A نهار *nahār*, (pl. انهر *anhur* and نهر *nuhur*) The day from sunrise to sunset. The diffusion of light, making things visible. (pl. انهرة *anhirat* and نهر *nuhur*) A young bustard (or قطا *katā*). A male owl or bustard. نهار لامع الانوار *nahāri lāmiʻu'l anwār*, A day shining with light; a bright day. ليلاً و نهاراً *laylan wa nahāran*, By night and by day.

P نهارة *nahāra*, A light breakfast.

P نهاري *nahārī*, Much, many. Breakfast. A kind of bit or bridle.

P نهاريدن *nahārīdan*, To breakfast. *Nihārīdan* or *nahārīdan*, To waste, decay, fall away. To be terrified, to be afraid (as boys of a schoolmaster).

P نهاز *nihāz*, Fear, dread. *Nuhāz* or *nahāz*, A large castrated he-goat, with spreading horns and long legs, that leads the flock. Any person or animal followed by others.

A نهاز *nuhāz*, Measure, quantity.

A نهّاز *nahhāz*, An ass extending his neck to run.

A نهازة *nihāzat* or *nuhāzat*, Quantity, number.

P نهازيدن *nihāzīdan*, To dread, fear, apprehend.

A نهّاس *nahhās*, A lion. The sparrow-hunter.

A نهاض *nihāz*, Paths up a mountain-steep. *Nuhāz*, The highest and steepest parts of a road.

A نهاق *nuhāh*, (v. n. of نهق) Braying (an ass).

A نهاكة *nahākat*, (v. n. of نهك) Overcoming, conquering. Fatiguing, emaciating (with labour), afflicting; attenuating (as disease). Wearing (a garment) till it becomes threadbare. Eating fast. Greatly injuring (reputation). Taking much pains. Being strong, vigorous.

P نهال *nihāl*, A young plant, shoot, sucker cut from a tree to be planted separately; any plant or herb transplanted; growing from the root of a tree. Carpet, cushion, mattress, bedding. Chase, game.

A نهال *nihāl*, (Camels) drinking and quenching their thirst.

P نهالچه *nihālcha*, A quilt, wrapper, coverlet.

P نهال گاه *nihāl-gāh*, (or گه *gah*) A lurking-place for hunters. A place for hunting.

P نهاله *nihāla*, A lurking-place for hunters. A hunting-place. Chase, game. A scarecrow set up to drive beasts into the hunter's toils. A young shoot or sucker. A carpet.

P نهاله گاه *nihāla-gāh*, (or نهاله گه *nihāla-gah*) A hunting-place. A lurking-place for hunters.

P نهالي *nahālī*, (or نهالين) A species of small carpet with a short pile. A mattress for sleeping on.

P نهالين *nahālīn*, A cushion.

A نهام *na, ni*, or *nuhām*, A blacksmith. A carpenter. *Nuhām*, A kind of bird, an owl. A monk.

A نهّام *nahhām*, A lion. Middle of an open road.

A نهامة *nahāmat*, (v. n. of نهم) Being voracious and insatiable, Gluttony. A lion.

A نهامي *na, ni*, or *nuhāmīy*, A blacksmith. A carpenter. *Nihāmīy*, An easy, plain road. *Ni* or *nuhāmīy*, An abbot, a prior.

P نهامين *nahāmīn*, A blacksmith.

P نهان *nihān*, Hid, concealed, occult. Prudently, secretly. نهان داشتن *nihān dāshtan*, To conceal, hide, suppress. نهان شدن *nihān shudan*, To be concealed. نهان و آشكاره *nihān u āshkāra*, (Things) private and public.

P نهان پيكران *nihān-paykarān*, Angels, spirits, invisible beings.

P نهانچه *nihāncha*, A concealed, secret thing.

P نهانخانه *nihān-khāna*, (or نهان دره *nihān-dara*) A cabinet, closet, private room. A hole dug in the ground for sitting in during the hot weather, or in which they store up corn. A place where rubbish or filth is thrown.

P نهان دار *nihān-dār*, A concealer.

P نهاندان *nihāndān*, A granary, warehouse, storehouse, cellar. A wardrobe, closet.

P نهاني *nihānī*, Privately, secretly. A secret. Concealment. Secret, privy. Occult, clandestine. اندام نهاني *andāmi nihānī*, The privy member. اتّفاق نهاني *ittifāki nihānī*, A private confederacy, league.

P نهانيچه *nihānīcha*, Privately, secretly.

A نهاوة *nahāwat*, (v. n. of نهو) Being filled. Being half-raw, not sufficiently dressed (meat).

A نهاوش *nahāwish*, Oppressions. Afflictions. Iniquities.

P نهاوند *nih-āwand* or *nah-āwand*, Name of a city in Persian Irāk. Name of a mountain nigh to that city. A species of musical mode or song.

P نهاوندي *nihāwandī*, Name of a note in music.

P نهاويدن *nahāwīdan*, To be afraid (as boys of the master).

A نهاية *nahāyat*, (v. n. of نهو) Being very intelligent. *Nihāyat*, The extremity of a wooden curb put on a camel's nose; also a cradle or other wooden frame on which the load (of a camel) rests. End, extremity, term, goal, boundary, butt. Excess. Very much, extreme, exquisite, excessive, stupendous. Remarkable, at the utmost. بلغ نهايته *balagha nihāyatahu*, He hit the mark, he gained his end. نهاية الامر *nihāyatu'l amr*, The end of the matter, finally, on the whole, to conclude. But, however, notwithstanding, nevertheless (which are also expressed by نهايت *nihāyat* and نهايتي *nihāyatī*). الى غير النهاية *ila' ghayri'n nihāyat*, Ad infinitum. P بي نهايه *bī nihāya*, (or بي نهايت *bī nihāyat*) Infinite, without end, endless. Excessive.

A نهب *nahb*, (v. n. of نهب) Seizing, snatching, spoiling, carrying off. Reproaching, cutting (with words). Seizing by the heel (as a dog). A mode of kicking. (pl. نهاب *nihāb*) Rapine, plunder, spoil.

P نهب كردن *nahb kardan*, (or نهب و غارت كردن *nahb u ghārat kardan*) To plunder and carry off.

P نهبانيدن *nuhbānīdan*, To make beautiful.

A نهبة *nahbat*, Rapine, spoil, plunder.

P نهبت *nuhbat*, The division of the signs of the zodiac into nine parts, and assigning of a star to each division. Immensely great, exceeding measure.

A نهبرة *nahbarat*, Long, meagre; at the point of death. *Nuhburat*, A ditch or hollow amongst heaps of sand. Danger; a dangerous place.

A نهبل *nahbal*, Old (man).

A نهبلة *nahbalat*, (v. n. of نهبل Q) Growing old. A languid pace like that of an aged person. An old woman. Large (she-camel).

A نهبور *nuhbūr*, A mountain of sand.

A نهبورة *nuhbūrat*, (pl. نهابير *nahābīr*) A hollow amongst heaps of sand. Danger; a dangerous place.

A نهبوغ *nuhbūgh*, A French bean. Name of a bird. A kind of ship, long and swift (called دونيج *dūnij*).

P نهبه *nuhbah*, The understanding.

P نهبهره *na bahra*, Exceeding bounds or measure, excessive. *Nuhbahra*, The division of the signs of the zodiac into nine parts, and the assigning of a star to each division.

A نهبي *nuhba'*, Plunder.

A نهترة *nahtarat*, Invention of a lie against.

A نهثرة *nahsarat*, Pace, step, manner of going.

A نهج *nahj*, (v. n. of نهج) Pointing out (the way), making clear, prescribing, giving directions. Following or keeping the road. Lying open (a road). Wearing (a garment) out. Being worn out. A high road, beaten path. Way, manner. P بنهجيكه *ba nahje ki*, In a manner that. A *Nahaj*, (v. n. of نهج) Breathing hard, being asthmatic. Asthma.

P نهجيز *nahjīz*, A fold, plait, twist. A twisting.

P نه خوش *na khwush*, The wild vine.

A نهد *nahd*, Any thing elevated. High, fleshy, well-shaped (horse). Generous, well-born (man), tending to any thing great. A lion. A breast which begins to swell. *Nahd* or *nihd*, What is equally contributed by travellers for expenses on the road. *Nahd* or *nahad*, (v. n. of نهد) Raising one's self up, springing on (a foe). *Nuhd*, (pl. of نهداء *nahdā*) Plump-breasted (girls).

A نهداء *nahdā*, A mountain or heap of sand. Plump-breasted (girl).

A نهدان *nahdān*, (A vessel) three parts full.

A نهدة *nahdat*, Thick fresh butter.

P نه ده *nuh dah*, Ornament, decoration.

A نهر *nahr*, (v. n. of نهر) Causing (a river) to run. Digging until water is met with. Flowing, especially over the surface of ground (water). Prohibiting, checking, chiding, crying to (cattle). *Nahr* or *nahar*, (pl. انهار *anhār*, نهور *nuhur*, نهر *nuhur*, and انهر *anhur*) A river, stream, flowing canal.

نهر السلام *nahru's salām*, The river Tigris. *Nuhr*, (pl. of نهر *nahr* and *nahar*) Rivers. *Nahar*, Amplitude, space, facility, convenience. *Nahir*, One who does any thing in the day-time, especially making an excursion against the enemy. Wide (river). White grapes. نهار نهر *nahāri nahir*, A clear day. *Nuhur*, (pl. of نهر *nahr* and *nahar*) Rivers. (pl. of نهار *nahār*) Days. Young katās or bustards. Male owls or bustards.

A نهرة *nahrat*, An invitation. Spoliation, rapine.

A نهرج *nahraj*, Wide (road).

A نهرجة *nahrajat*, (v. n. of نهرج Q) Lying with.

P نهروالە *nahrwāla*, A name of Guzerat in India.

P نهروان *nahrawān*, Name of a city.

P نهره *nahra*, An instrument for separating butter from whey. A churn, whether of wood or skin. نهره كوس *nahra-kos*, A churn-staff.

A نهريّ *nahrīy*, Fluviatic, belonging to a river.

A نهز *nahz*, (v. n. of نهز) Striking, beating off, repulsing. Shaking a bucket (in a well) in order to fill it. Moving or shaking (the head); carrying it high and projecting the breast (as a camel). Striking with the head (the udder of the mother). Being near, nigh. Quantity, number. *Nahiz*, A lion.

A نهزة *nuhzat*, An occasion, an opportunity. Plunder, booty.

A نهس *nahs*, (v. n. of نهس) Biting, eating, or plucking out with the fore-teeth; biting (as a serpent). *Nuhas*, The sparrow-hunter (a bird).

A نهسان *nihsān*, (pl. of نهس) Sparrow-hawks.

P نهستن *nihistan*, To put, place. To leave.

A نهسر *nahsar*, A wolf. The whelp of a wolf and a hyena. Nimble, swift. Voracious, carnivorous.

A نهسرة *nahsarat*, (v. n. of نهسر Q) Cutting flesh. Eating food.

A نهسك *nahsak*, A wild carrot.

A نهش *nahsh*, (v. n. of نهش) Biting (a serpent). Biting (especially with the front teeth). Oppressing, reducing to poverty (misfortune). *Nahish*, Swift, nimble-footed. (A camel) making with his feet a different mark on the ground from others.

A نهشة *nahshat*, A bite.

P نهشتن *nihashtan*, To put, place. To leave.

P نهشل *nahshal*, A wild carrot.

A نهشل *nahshal*, A wolf. A hawk. Aged, tottering with age. Name of a man.

A نهشلة *nahshalat*, (v. n. of نهشل Q) Growing old. Biting in sport and play. Riding on a borrowed camel. Eating as one famished.

P نهصد *nuh sad*, Nine hundred.

A نهض *nahz*, (v. n. of نهض) Raising one's self, rising up (to do any thing against any person). Sprouting up, growing (as a plant). Cresting up, and spreading the wings (a bird when about to fly). (pl. انهض *anhuz*) That part in a camel between the upper and lower part of the shoulder. Iniquity, injury, cruelty, oppression.

A نهضة *nahzat*, A rising up, departure, march.

P نهضت سلطان بسوي دهلي *nahzati sultān ba sūyi dihlī*, The departure of the king towards Dehli.

A نهضل *nahzal*, Old (man): aged (vulture, hawk).

A نهط *naht*, A piercing with a spear.

A نهف *nahf*, Astonishment, amazement, stupor.

P نهفت *nihuft*, He hid. Concealment. Covered, concealed. A king's private chamber. A secret place in a wall for hiding money. A certain mode or species of music.

P نهفتگي *nihuftagī*, Concealment. Any thing occult or hid.

P نهفتن *nihuftan*, To hide, conceal, cover. To lie concealed, abscond, lie hid. To be beautiful.

P نهفته *nihufta*, Covered. Concealed, hidden. Private. Privately, covertly, secretly.

P نهفته نياز *nihufta-niyāz*, A private petitioner.

P نهق *nahḳ*, Parsley chiefly from fenny grounds.

A نهق *nahḳ*, Name of a bird. A plant resembling the wild herb rocket. The herb rocket.

P نهك *nahk*, Less, least. Lean, meagre. Being given to wine. Thirst. Quenching thirst.

A نهك *nahk*, (v. n. of نهك) Committing excess in any thing. Conquering, overcoming. Putting to the torture. Eating fast. Afflicting (as a fever). Weakening any one (drink). Wearing constantly the same garment. Milking an udder quite dry. Drinking up entirely (liquor). Ruining, or greatly injuring (the reputation of another). *Nahah*, (v. n. of نهك) Fatiguing, attenuating, afflicting (as a fever). Being emaciated, labouring under an unremitting malady.

A نهكة *nahkat*, The pain of a disease. Languor, weakness. Excessive severity in the infliction of punishment. *Nahakat*, (v. n. of نهك) Afflicting, weakening (as a fever).

P نهل *nahl*, Name of a champion of Tūrān.

A نهل *nahal*, Meat, any eatable. The first drinking of camels (then they recline, and afterwards drink again, which is called علل *ʻalal*). (pl. of ناهل *nāhil*) Camels thirsty, and quenching the thirst. *Nahal* or *nahl*, (v. n. of نهل) Drinking for the first time, taking his first draught (a camel). Being thirsty. Being saturated with drink.

A نهلان *nahlān*, (A camel) which drinks the first time. One which drinks but is still dry. Who quenches the thirst.

A نهلة *nahlat*, Camels come to the cistern to take their first draught.

A نهلى *nahla'*, Camels taking the first draught.

A نهم *nahm*, (v. n. of نهم) Checking (camels) by calling to them, or making them go faster. Roaring (a lion). Braying (an elephant). Crying to, or threatening. Throwing pebble-stones, or any thing similar. *Nuhm*, Satan. Name of an idol formerly worshipped by the tribe of مزينة *muzaynat*; also the worshippers of that idol. *Naham*, (v. n. of نهم) Being gluttonous, voracious. Gluttony, insatiable appetite. *Nahim*, Greedy, hungry-eyed. A glutton.

P نهم *nuhum*, The ninth.

P نهمار *nahmār*, (or نهماز *nahmāz*) Great, large, immense, out of proportion, immeasurable, endless. A very wonderful thing. A serious and difficult affair. All, altogether.

A نهمة *nahmat*, (v. n. of نهم) Calling out (to camels) to mend their pace. Attaining one's object. Being very keen (desire). Great avidity or desire. Necessity, need, lack. A roar, loud cry.

P نهم چرخ *nuhum charkh*, The ninth heaven.

P نهنبان *nuhum*, (*nahum*, *nihambān*, نهنبن *nuham*, *nahum*, or *nihamban*) Lid of pot or furnace.

P نهنبيدن *nihambīdan*, To cover, stop up.

P نهنبيده *nihambīda*, Hid, covered, concealed.

P نهنج *nihinj*, A flour-sack of hair or wool.

P نهندره *nihandara*, A store, warehouse, treasury.

P نهنگ *nahang*, (by some *nihang*) A crocodile, alligator. A shark. A water-dragon or similar monster. A sword. A pen. The sky. Time, fortune, the world. نهنگ دشتي *nahangi dashtī*, The land-crocodile, *i. e.* the skink. نهنگ زير خفتان *nahangi zīri khaftān*, (or نهنگ سياه *nahangi siyāh*) A glittering sword. نهنگ فلك *nahangi falak*, The signs Cancer and Pisces. نهنگان نيام *nahangāni niyām*, Swords in the scabbard.

P نهنگ سبز *nahang-sabz*, An Indian sabre.

A نهنه *nahnah*, Fine cloth.

A نهنهة *nahnahat*, (v. n. of نهنه Q) Hindering, making desist by shouting. Scaring (the wolf).

A نهوّ *nahūw*, A prohibitor, forbidder. Prudent.

A نهوء *nuhūʼ*, (and نهوءة *nuhūʼat*) (v. n. of نهيء) Being half-raw, not sufficiently dressed (meat).

A نهود *nuhūd*, (v. n. of نهد) Rising up or springing (upon an enemy). Swelling (as the breasts of a girl). Having round, plump breasts (a girl). Extolling, magnifying, making, or esteeming great (a gift). Passing on at all events.

A نهودة *nuhūdat*, (v. n. of نهد) Being full of flesh, tall, and beautiful (a horse).

P نهوده *nuhūda*, Female ornaments, trinkets.

P نهور *nuhor*, The eye. Sight. An angry look.

A نهور *nuhūr*, (pl. of نهر *nahr* or *nahar*) Rivers.

A نهوس *nahūs*, A lion.

A نهوض *nahūz*, One who rises up. *Nuhūz*, (v. n. of نهض) Raising one's self, rising up (against any one, or to do him honour). Cresting up or spreading the wings (as a bird preparing to fly). Sprouting up, growing (a plant).

A نهوع *nuhūʻ*, (v. n. of نهع) Retching, but having no acid humour on the stomach to bring up.

A نهوك *nahūk*, Strong, bold, brave (man).

A نهول *nuhūl*, Those who drink for the first time and are still thirsty. Those who quench their thirst.

A نهي *nahy*, (v. n. of نهي) Prohibiting, forbidding. Arriving, reaching. Giving over, leaving off. Prohibition, interdict. Prudence, sagacity, knowledge. نهي الغائب *nahyu'l ghāʼib*, (or نهي الحاضر *nahyu'l hāzir*) The prohibitive or negative imperative. هذا رجل نهيك من رجل *hāzā rajulun nahyuka min rajulin*, This man will suffice you. *Nahy* or *nihy*, (pl. انهي *anhī*, انهاء *anhāʼ*, نهيّ *nuhīy*, and نهاء *nihāʼ*) A pond, ditch. *Nahī*, (pl. نهين *nahīna*) Intelligent. *Nuha'*, Intellect. (pl. of نهية *nuhyat*) Understandings. Interdicts.

A نهيّ *nahīy*, (pl. of انهياء *anhiyāʼ*) Intelligent. Forbidden. *Nuhīy*, (pl. of نهي *nahy* and *nihy*) Ditches, ponds.

P نهيب *nahīb* or *nihīb*, Fear, terror. Grief. Anxiety. Anguish. Haste, expedition. نهيب زد شدن *nahīb-zad shudan*, To be terror-stricken.

P نهيبه *nahība*, Fear. Spoliation (of infidels).

A نهيبي *nuhhay* or *nuhayba'*, Plunder, spoil, booty.

P نهيبيدن *nahībidan*, To fear, dread. To frighten.

A نهية *nihyat*, Extremely fat (she-camel). *Nuhyat*, An interdict, prohibition; any thing forbidden. (pl. نهى *nuha'*) Intelligence, knowledge, prudence. End. Extremity. A hole in the head of a pin or peg.

A نهيّة *nahīyat*, (fem.) Fat, bulky (she-camel).

A نهيت *nahīt*, A lion's roar: bray of ass: shout.

A نهيد *nahīd*, Thick, also thin (butter).

A نهيدة *nahīdat*, A dish made of the mucilaginous part of boiled colocynth-grains mixed with flour.

P نهيدن *nahīdan* or *nihīdan*, To place, put, lay, leave. To consider, reflect on. To grieve.

A نهير *nahīr*, Affluent. Copious, much, many.

A نهيرة *nahīrat*, (A camel) abounding in milk.

A نهيق *nahīḳ*, (v. n. of نهق) Braying (an ass).

A نهيك *nahīk*, Bold, strong, strenuous. Painstaking. Sharp, penetrating (sword). Fierce, fell (lion). Of a handsome form or noble disposition. Strong (camel), and fierce, and dangerous. *Nahīk* or *nuhayk*, A kind of flea.

P نهيك *nuh-yak*, A ninth part, one of nine.

A نهيم *nahīm*, (v. n. of نهم) Checking (camels) by calling to them to quicken their pace. Urging onward (a horse). Roaring (a lion), grunting (an elephant). Chiding, threatening. A glutton.

P نهيو *nihīv*, Fear, dread, terror.

A نهيء *nahīʼ*, (Meat) half-dressed.

P ني *nay*, A pipe, tube, flute, fife. A reed, cane, pen. The windpipe, throat, gullet. نيء شكر *nayʼi shakar*, A sugar-cane. نيء هندي *nayʼi hindī*, A bamboo. *Nay* or *ne*, No, not, neither, nor.

A نيّ *nayy*, (v. n. of نوي) Becoming fat (a camel). Fat, tallow, fatness. *Nīy*, Raw (flesh). Fatness.

A نيء *nayʼ*, (v. n. of نيءٌ) Being ill-dressed, half-raw (meat).

P نيا *niyā*, A grandfather. Maternal uncle. Elder brother. A sheath. Power, greatness.

A نياء *niyāʼ*, (v. n. of نيءٌ) Being raw (flesh). Rawness, crudity.

P نياب *niyāb*, A sheath, scabbard. A vessel.

A نيابة *niyābat*, Turn, period. Order, rank. Vicegerency, deputyship. Succession. *Niyābatan*, Virtually, really. In the right of another.

P نيابت دار *niyābat-dār*, A lieutenant, deputy.

P نيابه *nayāba*, A time, a turn.

A نياح *niyāh*, (v. n. of ناح for نوح) Lamenting, moaning. Bemoaning (the loss of a husband).

A نياحة *niyāhat*, (v. n. of ناح for نوح) Bemoaning (a husband). Lamentation, complaint, moan.

A نيار *niyār*, (pl. of نار *nār*) Fires.

P نيارست كرد *nayārast kard*, He could not do (it). نيارست ساخت *nayārast sākht*, He could not make (it) effectual.

P نياري *nayārī*, A mistress with whom one is deeply in love.

P نياز *niyāz*, Indigence, poverty, necessity. Petition, supplication, prayer. Inclination, wish, longing appetite. Greediness. Dearness, scarcity. A friend. A gift, present. A thing dedicated. Needy, wishful. A petitioner. Sound, whole. Rough. نياز كردن *niyāz kardan*, To pray or beg submissively. نياز گذاشتن *niyāz guzāshtan*, To give, bestow. بي نياز *bī niyāz*, Content, wanting no assistance.

P نيازارم *nayāzāram*, I will not or do not afflict. I will not or do not sorrow.

P نياز آميز *niyāz-āmez*, Suppliant, begging.

A نيازك *nayāzik*, (pl. of نيزك) Short spears.

P نيازگار *niyāzgār*, A suppliant, petitioner.

P نيازمند *niyāzmand*, Indigent, supplicating. نيازمند شدن *niyāzmand shudan*, To want, to be in need. To petition, beg, supplicate.

P نيازمندي *niyāzmandī*, Necessity, indigence. Supplication.

P نيازومند *niyāzūmand*, Indigent; a suppliant.

P نيازي *niyāzī*, A lover. A friend. A mistress. Name of a tribe of Afghāns.

P نيازيان *niyāziyān*, The needy. Lovers.

P نيازيدن *nayāzīdan*, Not to want or desire; not to covet. Not to stretch out the hand to take. Not to throw. Not to complain. *Niyāzīdan*, To ask, beg a thing necessary, supplicate. To observe.

P نيازيده *nayāzīda*, One who does not stretch forth his hand (to any thing). *Niyāzīda*, Ill-discharged (arrow). Inharmonious (voice). Badly-told (story).

A نياصة *niyāṣat*, A moving of one's self.

A نياط *niyāt*, (pl. انوطة *anwitat*, انواط *anwāt*, and نوط *nūt*) A long tract of desert ground. The string of a bow or bottle, by which they are hung up. Heart-strings. The heart. The great liver-vein which goes through the body. An artery in the back. (pl. of نوط *nawt*) Things hung up or pendulous. النياط *an' niyāt*, Two stars, one on each side of the Scorpion's heart. مقطعة النياط *muḳattiʼatu'n niyāt*, A hare.

A نياطل *nayātil*, (pl. of ناطل) Wine-measures.

A نياع *niyāʼ*, (pl. of نائع *nāʼiʼ*) Thirsty. جياع نياع *jiyāʼ niyāʼ*, Hungry, famished (persons).

A نياف *niyāf*, High (castle); long and tall (male or she-camel).

A نيّاف *nayyāf*, Long-bunched (camel).

A نياق *niyāḳ*, A giving delight, the exciting of admiration. (pl. of ناقة *nāḳat*) She-camels. (pl. of نيق *nīḳ*) Tops, ridges of mountains.

A نياقات *niyāḳāt*, (pl. of نياق) She-camels.

A نيّاك *nayyāk*, Much addicted to venery. A jackass. نيّاك الهواء *nayyāku'l hawāʼ*, The kestril-hawk.

P نياگان *niyāgān*, (pl. of نيا *niyā*) Grandsires.

P نيام *niyām*, A sheath, scabbard, case. The womb. A sinew. A bandage for a broken limb. The plough-tail or handle. The middle of a sword or of any thing else. An amulet, charm against sorcery. نيام چشم *niyāmi chashm*, The eyelid.

A نيام *niyām*, (v. n. of نام for نوم) Sleeping, falling asleep. Sleeping (as a silkworm) after casting the skin. Sleep, slumber. *Niyām*, (or نيّام *nuyyām*) (pl. of نائم *nāʼim*) Sleepers, persons asleep.

P ني انبا *nay-ambā*, A house made of reeds.

P ني انبان *nay-ambān*, A bagpipe.

P نيايش *niyāyish*, Benediction, blessing. Praise. Friendship, affection.

P نيايشگري *niyāyishgarī*, Praising.

A نيب *nayb*, (v. n. of ناب for نيب) Striking on the canine-tooth. Breeding a canine-tooth. *Nīb*, (pl. of ناب *nāb*) Aged (she-camels).

P نيب *nīb*, A particle sometimes added to words without altering the sense.

P نيپال *nepāl* or *naypāl*, Name of a country to the north of Bengal, whence good musk is brought.

P نيء پنج *nayʼi panj*, A horse under five years old.

A نيّة *nīyat*, (or نية *niyat*) (v. n. of نوي) Intending, proposing, aiming at. Preserving, guarding (God). Throwing away date-stones. *Niyat*, Intention, intent, purpose, design. Resolution, will. Desire, wish. Object or end of deliberation. An institution. Distance. نيّة خير عاقبة خير *niyat khayr ʼāḳibat khayr*, To a good design, good success.

A نيت *nayt*, A nodding from age or weakness.

A نيتون *naytūn*, Name of a stinking tree.

A نيثران *naysurān*, Loquacious, talkative.

P نيچه *naycha*, A tube, a small pipe. The tube or snake of the Indian apparatus for smoking tobacco, called a hookah. نيچه بند *naycha-band*, A maker of hooka-snakes. نيچه بندي *naycha-bandī*, The trade of a naycha-band.

A نيح *nayh*, The induration of a bone after it has been soft. *Nayh*, (or نيحان *nayhān*) The waving of the branch of a tree.

A نيّح *nayyih*, Hard and solid (bone).

A نيّحة *nayyihat*, (One wind) blowing opposite to another (distinct from نسيجة *nasījat*, which implies a cross wind).

A نيدر *naydar*, Name of the city of Madīna.

P نيدفه *naydafa*, The place in the waistband of

the drawers through which the string passes which fastens them. A piece inserted between the thighs of the breeches.

A نئدل *niʼdil*, Calamity, mishap: grave affair.

A نيدل *nīdul*, The nightmare.

P نيدلان *naydalān*, The nightmare. Epilepsy. A pipe, flute.

A نئدلان *niʼda, niʼdi*, or *niʼdulān*, Nightmare.

A نيدلان *nīdulān, nīdalān*, or *nīdilān*, Nightmare.

A نيده *nīdah*, Indian thorn.

A نير *nayr*, (v. n. of نار for نير) Marking (cloth) with a border of a different colour. *Nīr*, (pl. انيار *anyār*) A border of a different colour from the garment. (pl. انيار *anyār* and نيران *nīrān*) A yoke for coupling oxen. The hem or fringe of a garment. The woof of a web. Thread tied together. A reed. A plain track, or open road. A furrow or rut on the highway; also the way-side. ذو نيرين *zū nīrayn*, (Cloth) marked with two borders. (A man) of double strength. ذات نيرين *zātu nīrayn*, Old (she-camel) with some remains of strength.

A نيّر *nayyir*, Bright, clear. Shining, luminous. The sun. The moon. نيّراعظم *nayyiri aʻzam*, The greater luminary, *i.e.* the sun.

P نيرا *nīrā*, (in zand and Pāzand) Fire.

A نيران *nīrān*, (pl. of نار *nār*) Fires. (pl. of نور *nūr*) Flames, lights, rays, flashes. (pl. of نير *nīr*) Yokes. Hems or fringes of garments. Woofs of a web.

A نيرب *nayrab*, Detraction, slander. Strong, hardy, smart, active (man). Wickedness, evil. *Nayrab*, (or ذو نيرب *zū nayrab*) Worthless, malignant (fellow).

A نيربة *nayrabat*, (v. n. of نيرب Q) Whispering, calumniating, backbiting. Mixing or confounding (words). Weaving. Marking (as the wind does sand or water with long furrows or scores).

A نيربي *nayrabaʼ*, Evil, misfortune, calamity.

A نيرة *niyarat*, (pl. of نار) Fires. Rays, flashes.

A نيّرة *nayyirat*, A palpable blow, throw, or shot conspicuous to all. A sorceress, female fascinator.

A نيرج *nayraj*, A ploughshare. A threshing-instrument of wood or iron. A whisperer, slanderer. An excellent she-camel. Swift. Haste.

P نيرج *nīraj*, Any thing marcid or withered.

A نيرجة *nayrajat*, (v. n. of نيرج Q) Being irresolute, hesitating, wavering, fluctuating in opinion. Lying with. Talebearing, detraction, slander.

A نيرزة *nayrazat*, (v. n. of نيرز Q, derived from the Persian نو روز *naw roz*) Bringing a new-year's gift.

P نيرزد *nayarzad*, Is not worth.

P نيرك *nīrak*, Fascination, fraud. Talisman.

P نيرم *nayram*, Narīmān father of Sām.

P نيرنج *nīranj*, Magic, necromancy, enchantment. A talisman. Fraud, deceit, stratagem. History. One who recites histories. An exorcist, a necromancer. Fascination.

A نيرنجات *nīranjāt*, Incantations, fascinations.

P نيرنگ *nīrang* or *nayrang*, Fascination, incantation, magic, sorcery, deception. Deceit, pretence. Origin, root. The first rude sketch of a picture. A miracle; any thing new. فرنگ پر نيرنگ *firangi pur nīrang*, The wily Franks.

P نيرنگ ساز *nayrang-sāz*, Magician, juggler.

P نيرنگ سازي *nayrang-sāzī*, Deceit, subtlety.

P نيرنگي *nayrangī*, Magic. Deceitfulness.

P نيرنود *nīrnūd*, A discovery made by thought.

P نيرو *nīrū*, Strength, power. Possibility, probability. Manure. نيروي بازو *nīrūyi bāzū*, Strength of arm. نيرو دادن بسرگين *nīrū dādan ba sargīn*, To hearten (land) by manure, to manure. نيرو گرفتن *nīrū giriftan*, To acquire strength, to wax powerful.

A نيروز *nayrūz*, (from P نوروز) New-year's day.

P نيروفر *nīrūfar*, Nenuphar, the water-lily.

P نيرومند *nīrūmand*, Powerful: rich, prosperous.

P نيرومندي *nīrūmandī*, Power, strength.

P نيره *nīra*, An earthen churning-vessel.

P نيريز *nīrīz*, A town famous for the manufacture of muskets. Name of a note in music.

A ذو النيرين *zūʼn nīrayn*, Doubly strong (man).

A نيّرين *nayyirayn*, (dual oblique of نيّر *nayyir*) Both luminaries, sun and moon.

P نيز *nīz*, Also, likewise, even, too. Again. Afterwards.

P ني زار *nayzār*, A reed-bed, cane-plantation.

A نيزب *nayzab*, A buck. An ox.

A نيزج *nayzaj*, The privities of a female when the clitoris is long and erect.

A نيزك *nayzak*, (P نيزه *neza*) A javelin.

P نيزك *nezak*, A javelin, short spear, demi-lance.

P ني زن *nay-zan*, A piper, fifer, flutist.

P نيزه *neza*, A short spear, demi-lance, javelin, dart, pike. A piece of reed from which pens are made. A standard, ensign. نيزهٔ آتشين *nezaʼi ātishīn*, The sun's rays when rising or setting. نيزه بكف *neza bakaf*, The sun illuminating the world. نيزهٔ خطّي *nezaʼi khattī*, A straight spear.

P نيزه باز *neza-bāz*, A spearman. A jouster.

P نيزه بازي *neza-bāzī*, A throwing of the spear.

P نيزه بردار *neza-bardār*, A spearman.

P نيزه دار *neza-dār*, Armed with a spear, spearman.

P نيزه زن *neza-zan*, A spearman.

P نيزه گر *nezagar*, A spearmaker.

P نيزه گري *nezagarī*, The art of making spears.

P نيژ *nīj*, Convolvulus. Ivy. Ardent love.

P نيژه *nīja*, Frankincense, perfume. A parasitical plant.

P نيسابور *nīsābūr*, The capital of Khurāsān.

P نيساري *nīsārī*, A soldier. The military, or second of the four orders into which Jamshed, an ancient Persian monarch, divided his subjects.

P نيسان *naysān*, Like, resembling. *Nīsān*, Discord, opposition. A false promise, a lie; the time when a promise is broken.

P نيسان *naysān*, A Syrian month which corresponds to April. قطرات نيسان *katarāti naysān*, Drops of spring-rain, which they believe to produce pearls if they fall into shells, and venom if they drop upon serpents.

A نيسب *naysab*, Vestiges. A track made by ants. *Naysab*, (or نيسبان) A straight or plain road.

A نيسبة *naysabat*, (v. n. of نيسب Q) Whispering, acting as a tell-tale (between two persons).

P نيسبه *nīsba*, A layer, course of turf in a wall.

P نيست *nīst*, It is not. Nought. Annihilation. نيست كسي *nīst kase*, There is nobody. نيستم *nīstam*, I am not. نيستيد *nīsted*, You are not. نيست شدن *nīst shudan*, To perish, to be annihilated. نيست كردن *nīst kardan*, To dissipate, squander. نيست گردانيدن *nīst gardānīdan*, To demolish, destroy, ruin, annihilate, kill.

P نيستان *naystān*, A canebrake, reed-bed. A sugar-plantation, field of sugar-cane.

P نيست كن *nīst-kun*, Annihilate thou. An annihilator.

P نيسته *nīsta*, Nought, nothing. There is not.

P نيستي *nīstī*, Nullity, non-existence. Annihilation, ruin, destruction, destitution. Thou art not.

A نيسم *naysam*, A defaced path. A gentle breeze. The smell of milk or grease. A swift kind of bird green about the upper part.

P نيسو *nīsū*, (or نيسويا *nīsūyā*) A lancet.

A نيسون *nīsūn*, Anise.

P نيش *nesh*, The sting (especially of a venomous animal). A sharp point. A lancet, scalpel, probe. A puncture. A sign, signal, mark. An ensign, banner. A kind of date. Poison. نيش زدن *nesh zadan*, To sting, prick.

A نيش *nīsh*, (in Morocco) An apricot.

P نيشابور *nīshābūr*, Name of a city in Khurāsān.

P نيشاپورك *nīshāpūrak*, Name of a note in music.

P نيشان *nīshān*, A sign, spot, mark.

P نيشتر *neshtar*, A lancet.

P نيشتن *nīshtan*, (for نوشتن *nivishtan*) To write.

P نيش زن *nesh-zan*, A stinger. An incendiary. One who inflames disputes, a tell-tale.

P نيش زني *nesh-zanī*, The exciting of quarrels.

P نيشك *neshak*, A debtor.

P نيشكر *nay-shakar*, Sugar-cane. نيشكر خطّ *nay-shakari khatt*, (or خدّ *khadd*) The first appearance of a beard.

P نيشمن *nīshmin*, (in zand and Pāz.) A woman.

P نيشو *nīshū*, A kind of plum. A lancet. A flute.

P نيشه *naysha*, A small reed. A pipe, flute, bagpipe. *Nīsha*, A kind of plum.

A نيص *nays*, A gentle motion. A hedgehog.

A نيض *nayz*, The pulse. Pulsation.

A نئضل *niʼzil*, A misfortune: a portent, prodigy.

A نيط *nayt*, (v. n. of ناط for نيط) Being far off, distant. The last breath; death. Dead. A funeral. Heart-strings. رماه الله بالنيط *ramāhuʼllāh biʼn nayt*, May God pierce his heart-strings! *i.e.* slay him.

A نيّط *nayyit*, A well whose waters flow in at the sides (not from the bottom).

A نيّطة *nayyitat*, A camel sent for provisions.

A نئطر *ni'tir*, Evil, calamity, misfortune. A shrewd, clever fellow.

A نيطرون *naytarūn*, Borax.

A نيطل *naytal*, A large urn or bucket. A very subtle man. One who has long genitals. Wine. A wine-measure. *Naytal* and *nītal*, A misfortune.

P نيطل *nītal*, A weight of seven drachmas.

A نئطل *ni'til*, A sore calamity. A subtle fellow.

A نيع *nayʻ*, Inclination, leaning, waving.

A نيّف *nayyif*, (or نيف *nayf*) Excess, surplus, redundancy. Some (from one to three). Any number between one decimal and another. Excellence, goodness, beneficence. عشره و نيّف *ʻashara wa nayyif*, Upwards of ten.

P نيفا *nefā*, A breeches-belt, the part of the drawers through which the string runs to tie them round the loins with.

A نيفق *nayfak*, Open or loose part of breeches.

P نيفه *nefa*, A place at the top of the drawers through which the string passes which fastens them. A breeches-belt or strap. White cloth or fine linen. A square wrapper in which wearing-apparel is folded up. Belly-skin of any animal. Fur of any animal. A fox. نيفه سست كردن *nefa sust kardan*, (To loosen the waistband) To prepare to rest one's self.

A نيق *nīk*, (v. n. 4 of انق, irreg.) Delighting, exciting admiration. Pleasure, complacency. (pl. نياق *niyāk*, انياق *anyāk*, and نيوق *nuyūk*) The summit of a mountain.

A نيّق *nayyik*, One who lives delicately.

A نيقة *nīkat*, Delicacy in eating. Elegance in clothes. Neatness in executing any thing.

A نيك *nayk*, A lying with. Coition.

P نيك *nek*, Good, beautiful, excellent. Lucky, much, many. Very, exceedingly. نيك و بد *nek u bad*, Good and bad. *Nayak*, (dimin. of ني *nay*) A small reed or pen.

P نيكا *nekā*, Good, beautiful, elegant.

P نيك اختر *nek-akhtar*, Of good star, lucky.

P نيك اختري *nek-akhtarī*, Goodness of fortune.

P نيكان *nekān*, (pl. of نيك *nek*) Good (men).

P نيك انديش *nek-andesh*, A well-wisher.

P نيك باز *nek-bāz*, Virtuous, of good actions.

P نيكبخت *nek-bakht*, Fortunate, august, happy, blest. Of good disposition.

P نيك پاك *nek-pāk*, Virtuous.

P نيك پوست *nek-post*, Of the best leather.

P نيكتر *nektar*, Better. نيكترين *nektarīn*, Best.

P نيك تن *nek-tan*, Sleek-skinned (horse).

P نيك خصلت *nek-khaslat*, Of good habits.

P نيكخو *nek-khu*, (*nek-khū*, *nek-kho*, or نيكخوي *nek-khūy*) Of good dispositions or habits; humane, polite, good-natured, well-bred.

P نيكخواه *nek-khwāh*, Well-wishing, benevolent, affectionate, friendly, faithful, grateful. نيكخواهي *nek-khwāhī*, Benevolence.

P نيك خوئي *nek-khū'ī*, Kindness, humanity.

P نيك ديانت *nek-diyānat*, Pious, devout.

P نيك ذات *nek-zāt*, Of good breed or temper.

P نيك رو *nek-rav*, Good-paced (horse).

P نيك سگال *nek-sigāl*, Benevolent.

P نيك سيرت *nek-sīrat*, Virtuous, moral.

P نيك فال *nek-fāl*, Of happy omen.

P نيك فرجام *nek-farjām*, Of happy end.

P نيك قال *nek-kāl*, Well-spoken.

P نيك كار *nek-kār*, Well-doer. Beneficent.

P نيك كردار *nek-kirdār*, Beneficent.

P نيك گوي *nek-goy*, (or *gūy*) Eloquent.

P نيك محضر *nek-mahzar*, Good-natured.

P نيك مرد *nek-mard*, A good man.

P نيك منظر *nek-manzar*, Handsome, comely.

P نيكنام *nek-nām*, A good name, celebrity. Having a good name: famous, renowned, celebrated.

P نيكنامي *nek-nāmī*, Reputation, a good name (said to be حيات ثانيه *hayāti sāniya*, A second life).

P نيك نفس *nek-nafs*, Of a virtuous soul.

P نيك نهاد *nek-nihād*, Of good disposition.

P نيك نيّت *nek-nīyat*, Well-intentioned.

P نيكو *nekū* or *neko*, Good. Beautiful, elegant. Much. Well. Excellently, elegantly. نيكو آمدن *nekū āmadan*, To please, appear beautiful. نيكو داشتن *nekū dāshtan*, To approve, esteem. نيكو كردن *nekū kardan*, To behave beneficently, do well. زن نيكو دهن *zani nekū-dahan*, A woman with a charming mouth or sweet breath.

P نيكو آداب *nekū-ādāb*, Well-mannered, polite.

P نيكو بخت *neko-bakht*, Fortunate, happy.

P نيكو حال *neko-hāl*, In a good situation. In excellent health.

A نيكور *naykūr*, Unknown (road).

P نيكو رو *neko-rav*, Fleet, going well. *Neko-rū*, Of beautiful countenance.

P نيكو روي *neko-ravī*, Fleetness.

P نيكو سير *nekū-siyar*, Well-disposed.

P نيكو كار *neko-kār*, A benefactor. Benevolent.

P نيكو كاري *neko-kārī*, Benevolence.

P نيكو معامله *nekū-muʻāmala*, A fair dealer.

P نيكو نيّت *nekū-nīyat*, Well-intentioned.

P نيكو نيّتي *nekū-nīyatī*, Good intention.

P نيكويان *nekūyān*, The good, the virtuous.

P نيكوئي *nekū'ī*, Elegance. Goodness. A benefit, kindness, favour, gift. نيكوئي كننده *nekū'ī kunanda*, Beneficent.

P نيكي *nekī*, Goodness, piety, virtue, probity. Charitableness, beneficence. Beauty, elegance.

P نيگوهر *ne gawhar*, Accident (philosophically).

A نيل *nayl*, (v. n. of نال for نيل) Obtaining, acquiring, taking, reaching. Being munificent, liberal. Whatever one acquires. A gift. P نيل كردن *nayl kardan*, To obtain, get at. To give, bestow.

AP نيل *nīl*, The river Nile. The indigo-plant. A blue colour, indigo (with that and the gall of an ox the pilgrims mark their arms). A fumigation of wild rue. P نيل خم آسمان *nīli khumi āsmān*, (or نيل فلك *nīli falak*) Blackness of the sky. A bad presage, sinister accident.

P نيلاب *nīlāb*, The river Attock or Indus.

P نيل اندود *nīl-andūd*, (or نيل فام *nīl-fām*) Azure, blue, cerulean. Livid, obscure.

P نيلپر *nīlupar*, The water-lily.

A نيلة *naylat*, Whatever any one obtains.

A نيلج *nīlaj*, (from P نيله *nīla*) The dried juice or sediment of the indigo-plant. Indigo.

P نيلفر *nīlufar*, The water-lily.

P نيلك *nīlak*, (dim. of نيل *nīl*) A little blue, blueish. Blue, as the fingers with cold. Pinching.

P نيلگاو *nīl-gāw*, The white-footed antelope of Pennant, and antelope picta of Pallas.

P نيلگري كردن *nīlgarī kardan*, To cause grass to grow.

P نيلگون *nīl-gūn*, A blue colour, cerulean. The face of the heavens. A cloud fraught with rain. بحر نيلگون *bahri nīlgūn*, The Black or Euxine Sea. نيلگون پردها *nīlgūn-pardahā*, (نيلگون خيام *nīlgūn-khayām*, or نيلگون وطا *nīlgūn-witā*) The sky.

P نيلم *nīlam*, A sapphire.

A نيلنج *nīlanj*, Smoke of fat which stains green.

P نيلوبرگ *nīlūbarg*, (نيلوپر *nīlūpar*, نيلوپل *nīlūpal*, نيلوفر *nīlūfar*, and نيلوفل *nīlūfal*) The water-lily. جشن نيلوفر *jashni nīlūfar*, A festival held on the seventh day of خرداد *khurdād*.

A نيلوفر *naylūfar*, The water-lily.

P نيله *nīla*, Dried juice or sediment of the indigo-plant. Blue. A colour in horses or mules.

A نيليّ *nīlīy*, Belonging to the Nile. Blue, livid, blackish.

P نيلي بحر *nīlī-bahr*, (نيلي پرده *nīlī-parda*, نيلي حقّه *nīlī hukka*, or نيلي دوائر *nīlī-dawā'ir*) The sky.

P نيم *nīm*, A half. The middle. A sort of tree in India whose leaves are good in cases of wounds. نيم تسليم *nīmi taslīm*, Half a salutation, made by placing the hand on the breast and stooping the head. A complete salutation (تمام تسليم *tamāmi taslīm*) is made by putting the hand to the ground and raising it to the forehead. نيم شب *nīmi shab*, Midnight. گندم نيم برشته *gandumi nīm-burushta*, Green wheat half-toasted in the ears.

A نيم *nīm*, Any thing good, the comforts or conveniences of life. A familiar friend, in whom one trusts. A soft garment. Velvet, satin. A coat of mail. A worn-out jacket made of a skin. Night-clothes. Bed-clothes. Marks resembling steps made by the wind on sand. Name of a tree of which they make arrows.

A نيّم *nuyyam* or *niyam*, (pl. of نائم *nā'im*) Sleepers. (pl. of نائمة *nā'imat*) Sleeping (women).

P نيماد *nīmād*, Judgment, discrimination.

P نيم آستين *nīm-āstīn*, An upper robe with

half sleeves, often made of gold and silver tissue.

P نيم اشكني *nīm-ishkanī*, A kind of sweetmeat.

P نيم بدست *nīm-bidist*, Half a span. The distance between the point of the thumb and tip of the extended fore-finger. A small pillow.

P نيم برش *nīm-burush*, (or نيم برشت *nīm-burusht*) A poached egg (half-boiled).

P نيم بسمل *nīm-bismil*, Half-slaughtered.

P نيم پارچه *nīm-pārcha*, Hemiplegy.

P نيم پخت *nīm-pukht*, Parboiled. Half-ripe.

P نيم پخته *nīm-pukhta*, Parboiled.

P نيم پر *nīm-pur*, Half-full.

P نيم پرتو *nīm-partav*, Half-shining, *i.e.* the moon or stars when giving a feeble light.

A نيمة *nīmat*, Sleep, slumber. A night's lodging. A manner of sleeping. Supineness, negligence.

P نيم تاج *nīm-tāj*, An ornamental head-dress for a spouse.

P نيمترك *nīmtark*, A helmet. *Nīmtarah*, A low voice.

P نيم تن *nīm-tan*, (or نيم تنه *nīm-tana*) The Creator. A short garment or shirt; a vest worn by the eastern monks, called Calendars, which reaches to the lower part of the belly.

P نيم ته *nīm-tih*, Half a load. Divided in two.

P نيم جان *nīm-jān*, Half-dead (with fright).

P نيم جوان *nīm-jawān*, A middle-aged man. An unbroke horse.

P نيم جو سنگ *nīm-jaw-sang*, The weight of half a grain.

P نيم جوش *nīm-josh*, Coddled.

P نيم چاشت *nīm-chāsht*, Breakfast: lunch.

P نيم چرخ *nīm-charkh*, A kind of bow.

P نيمچه *nīmcha*, A short upper garment. A small, little, or short sword, musket, or bow.

P نيم چهره *nīm-chihra*, (or نيم تن *nīm-tan*) A species of imaginary being, having half a face, one eye, one arm, one foot: it is male and female; the male having the right hand, foot, &c., the female the left: when united they resemble one human figure: when separate they are supposed to run with amazing velocity on one foot, and are considered as very dangerous and cruel.

P نيم خانۀ مينا *nīm-khāna-i mīnā*, The sky.

P نيم خايه *nīm-khāya*, A cupola, dome. The vault of heaven.

P نيم خواب *nīm-khwāb*, Half-asleep, dozing.

P نيم خورد *nīm-khwurd*, (or نيم خورده *nīm-khwurda*) Half-eaten or gnawed, what is left on the plates after meals, the remains of victuals, orts. Toasted wheat.

P نيم دست *nīm-dast*, A small cushion, pillow.

P نيم دينار *nīm-dīnār*, The lip of a mistress.

P نيم راست *nīm-rāst*, Name of a musical note.

P نيم راضي *nīm-rāzī*, Half-satisfied.

P نيم راه *nīm-rāh*, Half-way, mid-way.

P نيم رخ *nīm-rukh*, (or نيم رخساره *nīm-rukhsāra*) A half-face, a side-face, a profile.

P نيم رس *nīm-ras*, Half-ripe.

P نيم رنگ *nīm-rang*, A secondary or heterogeneous colour.

P نيم رو خاكي *nīm-rū-khākī*, Lying with one side of the face on the ground.

P نيمروز *nīm-roz*, Mid-day. Name of the province of Sīstān. A species of money. Name of a note in music. The twenty-ninth of the barbud. پادشاه نيمروز *pādshāhi nīm-roz*, The sun. Muhammad. سلطان نيمروز *sultāni nīm-roz*, The prince of the meridian, *i.e.* the sun.

P نيم روزه *nīm-roza*, Of half a day.

P نيم زال *nīm-zāl*, A middle-aged woman.

P نيم سال *nīm-sāl*, A middle-aged man.

P نيم سفته *nīm-sufta*, Half-bored. An unfinished speech. Covered over, hidden. A gentle trickling or exudation.

P نيم سوخته *nīm-sokhta*, (or نيم سوخت *nīm-sokht*) A piece of burnt cloth. Half-burnt.

P نيم سوز *nīm-soz*, Half-roasted, scorched.

P نيم شكري *nīm-shakarī*, A sweetmeat.

P نيم فسرده *nīm-fusurda*, Half-frozen.

P نيم كار *nīm-kār*, Half-used, worn.

P نيم كاره *nīm-kāra*, An apprentice. A hired servant. A thing unfinished, incomplete.

P نيم كاسه *nīm-kāsa*, A kind of semi-globular wooden dish.

P نيم كوز *nīm-kūz*, Hump-backed (man).

P نيم گرم *nīm-garm*, Milk-warm, lukewarm.

P نيملاتوتيا *nīm-lātūtiyā*, Blue vitriol.

P نيملحظه *nīm-lahza*, An affair of a moment. Half a moment.

P نيم لنگ *nīm-ling*, A case for a bow. A quiver. A bow. As much as a beast of burden carries on one side, half an ass-load. Good, well, fair, handsome.

P نيم مرده *nīm-murda*, Half-dead.

P نيم مست *nīm-mast*, Half-drunk.

P نيم نيزه *nīm-neza*, Short spear, demi-lance.

P نيمو *nīmū*, A stone found in the gall-bladders of cows. Any antidote taken out of animals.

P نيمور *nīmūr*, Membrum virile.

P نيمه *nīma*, A half. Hemiplegy. A half or short under-garment. A lady's veil, through which only the eyes are seen. نيمۀ راه *nīma-i rāh*, Mid-way. نيمۀ دينار *nīma-i dīnār*, The lip of a mistress. نيمه كردن *nīma kardan*, To half-fill. بدو نيمه شدن *ba du nīma shudan*, To be parted in twain.

P نيمه آستين *nīma-āstīn*, Half-sleeved. A kind of jacket.

P نيمه پر *nīma-pur*, Half-full.

P نيمه شام *nīma-shām*, Evening.

P نيمه قنديل *nīma-kindīl*, The new moon.

P نيمه كرده *nīma-karda*, Half-filled, half-done.

P نيم هلال *nīm-hilāl*, The lip of a mistress.

P نيناد *nīnād*, Patience.

P ني ناك *naynāk*, Abounding in hollow reeds.

A نينان *nīnān*, (pl. of نون *nūn*) Fishes.

P ني نواز *nay-nawāz*, A piper.

A نينوفر *naynūfar*, A water-lily, nenuphar.

A نينوي *nīnawa'*, Nineveh.

P نينوي *nīnuwī*, Nineveh. Fresh butter.

P ني نهاوندي *nay-nihāwandī*, Name of a black and bitter medicinal cane.

SY نينيا *nīniyā*, Anise.

P نيو *nev*, Intrepid, bold, brave, warlike; a hero, champion. A canal, aqueduct, mill-dam. The tube through which the meal or flour runs when grinding. *Nayū*, Straight. *Niyū*, A kind of cinnamon. Intelligent, prudent, learned. Warlike. Power, strength. An instrument.

A نيوء *nuyū*, (or نيوأة *nuyūat*) (v. n. of نيء) Being half-raw or only half-dressed (meat). Rawness.

P نيواد *nevād*, Courage.

P نيوار *niwār*, The sky, atmosphere.

P نيواره *newāra*, A rolling-pin.

A نيوب *nuyūb*, (pl. of ناب *nāb*) Canine-teeth. Aged she-camels. Princes, chiefs.

A نيّوب *nayyūb*, An aged she-camel. The leader of the people, head of a family.

P نيوباريدن *nayawbāridan*, Not to fill, throw in, or swallow.

P نيوتش *nīvtash*, Venery.

P نيوتور *nīvtūr*, Pride, arrogance, vain-glory.

P نيور *nīvar*, Beings, creatures. The universe. نيور نيوار *nīvari nīvār*, Productions of the sky, such as rainbows, meteors, comets, snow, rain, and the like.

P نيوراد *nīvrād*, Order, method, arrangement.

P نيوساد *niyūsād*, Eternal, perpetual.

P نيوسوم *nīvsūm*, An insatiable appetite.

P نيوش *niyosh*, Listen. A listener. Attention.

P نيوشا *niyoshā*, A listener. One who retains any thing in his memory. One who does any thing of great importance.

P نيوشنده *niyo* or *niyūshanda*, A listener.

P نيوشه *niyūsha* or *niyosha*, Attention, listening. Weeping with sobbing. A listener, eaves-dropper. نيوشه كردن *niyūsha kardan*, To listen, hear, play the eaves-dropper.

P نيوشيدن *niyūshīdan* or *niyoshīdan*, To lend an ear, listen, hear. To weep and sob. To read. To hope for any thing. To murmur, sob, cry silently. To seek, investigate, examine.

P نيوشيده *niyūshīda*, Heard. Hearsay.

P نيوشين *niyūshīn*, To be listened to.

A نيوق *nuyūk*, (pl. of نيق) Tops of mountains.

P نيوك *niyūk*, A bride.

P نيومرد *nev-mard*, A warlike man. Prudent, wise.

P نيوند *nīwand*, Understanding. *Nīwand*, (or نيوند مريم *nīwandi maryam*) A kind of wild rue.

P نيونديدن *niyūndīdan*, To mix. To rush upon, shew courage.

P نيوه *neva*, Crying, lamentation, grief. نيوۀ چمينه *neva-i chamīna*, The power which the soul has to quit the body and to return to it.

A نيه *nayh*, (v. n. of ناه for نيه) Being high. Causing surprise. Giving pleasure.

A نيّ *niy*, (pl. نيّ *niȳy*) A trench cut round a tent to keep off rain-water.

A نيّ *nī*, Raw or half-cooked flesh.

P نيي *nayī*, A player on the flute.

A نيّ *naiy*, Distant.

A نييب *nuyayb*, (dim. of ناب *nāb*) Petty chiefs.

A نئيت *naīt*, (v. n. of نأت) Roaring, bellowing loudly. Envying.

A نئيج *naij*, (v. n. of نأج) Blowing and whistling (the wind). The blowing of the wind with a loud or hissing noise.

A نئيشاً *naīshan*, At length, lastly. نئيشاً من النهار *naīshan mini'n nahār*, At the end of the day.

A نئيط *naīt*, (v. n. of نأط) Crying. Breathing hard. The hard breathing of an overloaded beast.

A نئيل *naīl*, (v. n. of نأل) Going, jumping, or skipping along, and moving the head upward; shaking the head when trotting. Behoving. Envying.

P نييل *nayīl*, A flag, standard. Large and fat. Good, handsome, elegant. Prudent, intelligent.

A نئيم *naīm*, (v. n. of نأم) Groaning, breathing hard. Lamenting. Twanging (a bow-string). Roaring (a lion). Bleating (a deer). A weak, gentle voice.

P نئين *naīn*, Made of reeds, reeden. Not this.

و

و *wāw*, (وا *wā*, or واو *wāw*, in Persian *vāv*) The twenty-sixth letter of the Arabic, and the thirtieth of the Persian alphabets. In arithmetic it denotes 6; and in the Ephemerides it is the character for Friday and the sign Libra.

This letter is sometimes a consonant; when it is one of the labial letters, having the sound of the English *w* or *v*. It is also one of the حروف علّت *hurūfi ɛillat*, or weak letters; when it serves with the vowel-point ضمّه *zamma* and فتحه *fatha*, written over the preceding consonant, to form the long vowels *o*, *ū*, and *aw*, or *au*. The و being homogeneous with ضمّه *zamma*, when a quiescent و immediately follows that vowel it only prolongs its sound, and the result is a simple long vowel. That vowel may be either *o*, as in "more," and *ou* in "though," or *ū*, as in "rule," and *ou* in "through." The former is called مجهول *majhūl* (Unknown, concealed), either because it does not occur in the Arabic language, or because the sound of ضمّه *zamma* is obscured by an admixture of فتحه *fatha*. It is also called واو فارسي *wāwi* or *vāvi fārsī*, or اعجمي *aɛjamī*, *i.e.* Persian *wāw*. The latter, from its occurring in Arabic, and exhibiting the full sound of ضمّه *zamma*, is called معروف *maɛrūf*, (Known). When quiescent و *wāw* follows a letter having the vowel فتحه *fatha*, (واو ساكن ما قبل مفتوح *wāwi sākini mā kabl maftūh*) it forms the diphthong *aw* or *au*, like the words "our, owl;" as, يوم *yawm*, A day. After the vowel كسر *kasr* it rarely occurs.

In certain instances و *wāw*, though written, is not pronounced. Thus (1) in the words دو *du*, "two;" تو *tu*, "thou;" چو *chu*, "when;" &c., the sounds are simply those of ضمّه *zamma* without prolongation, as in this line of Nazāmī, چو تو گر كسي باشد آنهم توئي *chu tu gar kase bāshad, ān ham tuī*, where the first syllable is short. This is called واو بيان ضمّه *wāwi bayāni zamma*. (2) After خ *khe*, moveable by زبر *zabar*, (or sometimes by زير *zīr* and پيش *pesh*) on the one hand; and the letters ا *alif*, د *dāl*, ر *re*, ز *ze*, س *sīn*, ش *shīn*, ن *nūn*, ي *ye*, ه *he*, or پ *pe*, quiescent, on the other; the sound of و *wāw* is often entirely lost; and the letter خ *khe* is pronounced as if it were moveable by a short vowel, differing in some degree from the sounds of زبر *zabar*, زير *zīr*, and پيش *pesh*, but invariably approaching to that of پيش *pesh*. The letter و *wāw* in this situation receives neither a vowel-point nor a quiescent mark, and is termed واو معدوله *wāwi maɛdūla*, واو اشمام ضمّه *wāwi ishmāmi zamma* (or رسمي *rasmī*); that is, *wāw* applied in an unusual manner; or *wāw* used for the purpose of varying the sound of the preceding vowel. The following are examples: خواب *khwāb*, Sleep; خود *khwud* or *khwad*, Self; خور *khwur*, The sun; خوزم *khwazm*, Vapour; آبخوست *āb-khwust*, An isle, islet; خوش *khwush*, Pleasant; آخوند *ākhwund*, A teacher; خوي *khway*, Perspiration; خويش *khwesh*, Own; خوهل *khwahl*, Crooked; خوپله *khwapla*, A fool.

It is changed (1) Into ا *alif*; as, قال *kāla* for قول *kawala*, He spoke. (2) Into ت *te*; as, اتّعد *ittaɛada*, He accepted a promise for اوتعد *iwtaɛada*. (3) Into م *mīm*; as, فم *fam* for فو *fū*, The mouth. (4) Into ن *nūn*; as, صنعانيّ *sanɛāniy* for صنعاويّ *sanɛāwiy*, A native of Sanāa. (5) Into ء *hamza*; as, قائل *kāil* for قاول *kāwil*, A speaker. (6) Into ي *ye*; as, ايقاد *īkād* for اوقاد *iwkād*, Kindling a fire. (7) Into ب *be*; as, نبشتن *nibishtan* for نوشتن *niwishtan*, To write. (8) Into ف *fe*; as, يافه *yāfa* for ياوه *yāra*, Nonsense. (9) Into پ *pe*; as, پام *pām* for وام *wām*, Debt. Colour.

In Persian it serves (1) as a substitute for او *u*; as, ورا گفتم *warā guftam* for اورا گفتم *urā guftam*, I told him. (2) Annexed to nouns, to form diminutives without being pronounced; as, شيخو *shaykh*, A little old man, from شيخ *shaykh*; پسرو *pisar*, A little boy, from پسر *pisar*. In this manner it is used also to express endearment and compassion. (3) To denote an indefinite relation; as, آبو *ābū*, A water-lily, from آب *āb*, Water. هندو *hindū*, A Hindoo, from هند *hind*. (4) To denote congruity or suitability (ملازمت *mulāzamat*); as, تو وُ حلوا وُ مزعفر، من و خرما وُ عدس *tu u halwā u muzaɛfar, man u khurmā u ɛadas*, Sweetmeats and food dressed with saffron *are suitable to* you; dates and pulse *are fit* for me. (5) Redundant, and mostly prefixed to يا *yā* and ليكن *lekin*. It also occurs in the middle of a word; as, نيازومند *niyāzūmand*, (for نيازمند *niyāzmand*) Necessitous. A petitioner. Sometimes it is used to fill up, or to eke out measure (اشباع *ishbāɛ*); as, for كمال *kamālu*, they write كمالو *kamālū*.

P و *wa* is a conjunction; and when inserted between two verbs proceeding from the same person, it assumes the sound of the vowel ضمّه *zamma*, applicable to the final letter of the verb which precedes it: as, رفت و آمد *raft u āmad*, He went and came; نشست و برخاست *nishast u barkhāst*, He sat down and rose up. Also between two nouns dependent on the same verb: as, باغ وخانه را خريدند *bāgh u khānarā kharīdand*, They bought the garden and the house; بزرگ وكوچك جمع شدند *buzurg u kūchak jamɛ shudand*, Great and small were assembled. After a word ending in mute ه *he* (هاي مخفف *hāi mukhaffaf*), or in ا *alif* or و *wāw* quiescent, it assumes the sound of soft ء *hamza* moveable by ضمّه *zamma*; as, تو وُ طوبي *tu u tūba'*, Thou and the Tūba (tree); سينه وُ پا وُ دست *sīna u pā u dast*, Breast, hand, and foot. At the beginning of a sentence, or when the letter which precedes it is silent, the و *vāv* must take the vowel فتحه *fatha*: as if one person should say, من بخراسان ميروم *man ba khurāsān mī ravam*, I am going to Khurāsān, and another should add وبعراق هم *wa ba ɛirāk ham*, and to Irāk also: or one should say, سلام عليكم *salām ɛalaykum*, Peace be on you! to which another should reply, وعليكم السلام *wa ɛalaykumi's salām*, And upon you be peace!

A و *wa*, And. Too, also. As, whilst, yet. With, in company with, together. By (in swearing). Whilst. Then. There. Or. For, but, although. Perhaps. Many, often. والسلام *wa's salām*, (and والدعا *wa'd duɛā*) And may there be health, then farewell (a formula of salutation put sometimes at the end of letters). والّا *wa illā*, But, besides. والله *wa'llāh*, By God! والله العظيم *wa'llāhi'l ɛazīm*, By the great God! وربّك *wa rabyika*, By thy Lord! وامّا *wa ammā*, But. والحاصل *wa'l hāsil*, Upon the whole. ولكن *wa lākin*, But.

P وا *wā*, Fire. Distant. (for با *bā*), With. When added to some nouns it signifies dressed victuals: as, گندم وا *gandum-wā*, A dish made with wheat. In composition وا *wā* signifies *again*, as واگفت *wā guft*, He spoke again; *back*, as وا داد *wā dād*, He gave back; *open*, as دررا واكن *darrā wā kun*, Open the door; *off* or *away*, as وا بريدن *wāburīdan*, To cut off or away. It is used to express the cry of one in great pain; also as an interjection of wonder and surprise, and it is sometimes redundant. See other examples in alphabetical order.

A وا *wā*, Holla! hark ye! Alas!

A وآة *wa·āt*, The female of the wild ass.

P وا استادن *wā istādan*, To stand back. To stop, cease, desist. وا استادن بچيزي *wā istādan ba chīze*, To insist upon a thing. وا استادن برچيزي *wā istādan bar chīze*, To be deficient in doing any thing, to omit somewhat (with در *dar* instead of بر *bar*, it signifies, To hesitate, to delay).

A وآل *wi·āl*, (v. n. 3 of وأل) Endeavouring to flee, hastening to any place in order to escape.

A وآم *wi·ām*, (v. n. 3 of وأم) Consenting, agreeing, doing the like. Disputing, contending for glory.

A وا امّياه *wā ummayāh*, Alas! O mother.

A وأب *wa·b*, (v. n. of وأب) Being contracted together. Blushing, being ashamed. A blush, modesty. Strong, well-formed (horse-hoof). A large camel. A capacious drinking-cup. *Wa·ab*, (v. n. of وئب) Being angry.

P وابا *wābā*, Intellect, understanding.

A وأبة *wa·bat*, A hollow in a stone containing water. A deep well.

A وابر *wābir*, Some one, any one. ما بها وابر *mā bihā wābir*, There is nobody there.

P وا بردن *wā bardan*, To flatten a lump of dough.

P وا برون كردن *wāburūn kardan*, To elevate.

P وابريدن *wā burīdan*, To cut off. وا بريده شدن *wā burīda shudan*, To be cut off, end, finish.

P وابس *wābas*, Only. *Wābis*, Scarcely, hardly.

P وا بستگان *wā bastagān*, (pl. of وا بسته *wā basta*) Domestics, dependants, connexions, adherents.

P وابستگي *wā bastagī*, Connexion, obligation.

P وا بستن *wā bastan*, To bind back. To tie, fasten. To refer. وا بستن بقومي *wā bastan ba kawme*, To refer (one) to a nation, *i.e.* to call (him) a native of such a country.

P وا بسته *wā basta*, Bound. Restrained. Related, connected, depending on. A man-servant; a dependant, adherent. وا بسته بودن *wā basta būdan*, To be bound, depend upon, stand.

A وابصة *wābisat*, Fire. Credulous. A man's name.

A وابط *wābit*, Weak, timid, cowardly.

A وابل *wābil*, A heavy shower with large drops.

A وابلة *wābilat*, The top of the shoulder-blade, the coracoid process. The head of the thigh-bone. A bone in the knee-joint. The flesh of the thigh close and firm. The young of a camel or sheep.

A وابن *wābin*, Any body.

P وا پرسيدن *wā pursīdan*, To ask again, inquire, examine.

P واپس *wāpas*, Behind, back, back again, afterwards, then, again. Returning, refunding. Restitution. Grief, torment. واپس استادن *wā pas istādan*, To stand back, loiter by the way. واپس افتاده *wā pas uftāda*, Fallen behind; a loiterer. واپس افگندن *wā pas afgandan*, (or واپس انداختن *wā pas andākhtan*) To procrastinate, delay. واپس آمدن *wā pas āmadan*, To come back, return. واپس بردن *wā pas burdan*, To send or carry back. واپس دادن *wā pas dādan*, To give back. واپس داشتن *wā pas dāshtan*, To detain, retard. واپس رفتن *wā pas raftan*, To retire, go back, recede. واپس گرفتن *wā pas giriftan*, To receive again, resume. واپس ماندن *wā pas māndan*, To remain behind, stay back. واپس نشستن *wā pas nishastan*, To sit down, to sit together. To agree, be well adapted.

P واپستن *wā pastan*, (or واپس جستن *wā pas justan*) To leap back. To sit behind.

P واپسته *wāpasta*, Joined. A friend, companion.

P واپسين *wā pasīn*, The last, posterior, hindmost, or latter. دم واپسين *dami wā pasīn*, The last breath. تا دم واپسين *tā dami wā pasīn*, Until the last breath. روز واپسين *rozi wā pasīn*, The last day, the day of judgment. سحر واپسين *sahari wā pasīn*, The time after dawn.

P واپكيدن *wā pakīdan*, (وابكيدن *wā bakīdan*, or واپيكيدن *wā pīkīdan*) To cover the mouth or face. To throw any thing out of the mouth with violence, to squirt out water, or blow in derision.

A وأة *wa·at*, A female wild ass.

P وات *wāt*, A letter, word. A fur-garment.

P واتر *wātar*, Farther off.

P واتگر *wātgar*, One who makes garments of skins, a furrier. A poet, story-teller. Name of a river.

A واتل *wātil*, (A man) filled with drink.

P واتم *wātam*, (in Ispahān for گفتم *guftam*) I said.

A واتن *wātin*, Perennial, perpetual, fixed in a place. Living or running (water).

P واتوختن *wā tokhtan*, To repay, weigh back.

A واثق *wāsik*, Confiding, secure, depending upon. Firm, solid, strong, robust.

A واثن *wāsin*, Perennial, perpetual. Water continually flowing.

P واج *wāj*, Speak, say.

P وأج *wa·j*, Extreme hunger.

P واجار *wājār*, (equiv. to بازار *bāzār*) A market.

A واجب *wājib*, Necessary, obligatory, binding. Expedient, proper, worthy, convenient, fit. Right, due, just, reasonable. Monthly pay. Killed, slain. واجب الاتّباع *wājibu'l ittibāᶓ*, Worthy to be obeyed. واجب الادا *wājibu'l adā*, Necessary to be discharged (duties). واجب الاذعان *wājibu'l iẕᶓān*, Necessary to be heard. واجب الامتثال *wājibu'l imtisāl*, Necessary to be performed. واجب التعذير *wājibu't taᶓzīr*, Punishable. واجب التعظيم *wājibu't taᶓzīm*, Worthy of respect and attention. واجب الرعاية *wājibu'r riᶓāyat*, Deserving to be honoured or obeyed. P واجب شدن *wājib shudan*, To behove. A واجب الصلب *wājibu's salb*, Meriting the gallows. واجب العرض *wājibu'l ᶓarz*, Fit to be represented. A written representation or petition. واجب القتل *wājibu'l katl*, Deserving death. واجب القضا *wājibu'l kazā*, Necessary to be done over again (when not properly done at the first). P دست واجب القطع *dasti wājibu'l katᶓ*, A hand which it is proper to amputate, or that deserves to be cut off. A واجب النظر *wājibu'n nazar*, Respectable, worthy of regard. جناب واجب الوجود *janābi wājibu'l wujūd*, God (whose existence is necessary, *i.e.* self-existent). بالواجب *bi'l wājib*, Necessarily, deservedly.

A واجبات *wājibāt*, (pl. fem. of واجب *wājib*) Necessary things, whatever is proper, expedient, or requisite to be done. اهمّ واجبات دينيّه *ahammi wājibāti dīniya*, The most necessary or important points relative to religion.

A واجبي *wājibī*, That which is expedient. Salary, stipend.

A واجد *wājid*, An inventor, finder. Ivy.

P واجده كردن *wājuda kardan*, (or وا جدا كردن *wā judā kardan*) To separate, sort, distinguish.

A واجز *wājiz*, Brief. Epitomized (speech).

A واجس *wājis*, (A thing) occurring to the mind.

P واجستن *wā justan*, To inquire (after the absent). To search (for any thing lost).

A واجف *wājif*, Palpitating (heart).

A واجل *wājil*, Timid, afraid.

A واجلة *wājilat*, Timid, bashful (woman).

A واجم *wājim*, Sad, grim. Afflicted, silent, fixing the eyes on the ground from pain, rage, or vexation.

P وا چسپيدن *wā chaspīdan*, To grow to, adhere.

P وا چيدن *wā chīdan*, To pick out, collect. To remove wrinkles from the face. وا چيدن پنبه *wā chīdani pamba*, To separate or tease cotton.

A واحد *wāhid*, (pl. واحدون *wāhidūn*) One, individual, single, sole, unique, singular. (pl. وحدان *wuhdān* and احدان *uhdān*) Pre-eminent. واحد الاحدين *wāhidu'l ahadīn*, The one of ones, an incomparable man. واحد بعد واحد *wāhid baᶓda wāhid*, One after another. واحد حقيقي *wāhidi hakīkī*, The true unity (God). واحد دهره *wāhidu dahrihi*, The phœnix of his age, incomparable. واحد شاهد *wāhid shāhid*, God is my witness. (metaphorically) Giving, bestowing. واحد و اثنين *wāhid wa isnayn*, One or another, one or two. حتّى الي الواحد *hatta' ila'l wāhid*, Almost every one. طعام واحد *taᶓāmun wāhidun*, One kind of food. في موضع واحد *fī mawzaᶓi wāhid*, In one and the same place, in one place, in some place. كلّ واحد *kullu wāhidin*, Every one. واحدا *wāhidan*, Apart, separately. واحدا واحدا *wāhidan wāhidan*, One by one, separately, singly.

A واحدون *wāhidūn*, (pl. of واحد) Ones, units.

A واحدي *wāhidī*, Any one.

A واحديّة *wāhidīyat*, Name of a Muhammadan sect. Unitarianism.

A واحرزي *wā haraza'*, Stop! beware! be prudent! (you have enough).

A واحسرتاه *wā hasratāh*, Alas!

A واحف *wāhif*, Luxuriant, plentiful (herbage). Full-feathered (wing). A big bucket, two of whose handles having been cut off it is suspended by two.

A واحم *wāhim*, Sad and silent.

P واخ *wākh*, Rectitude, verity, truth. Sure, true, certain, right. A conjecture, especially approaching to certainty. The dawn. The east, or place of the dawn. A transverse beam or bow, used (by wheelwrights) in boring or turning. A particle of applause or approbation.

P وا خانيدن *wā khānīdan*, To cause to pick or tease cotton.

P واختر *wākhtar*, The east.

P واخچي *wākhchī*, A horse with a pack-saddle. A despiser.

A واخد *wākhid*, (A camel) taking wide, quick steps.

P واخريدن *wā kharīdan*, To buy; to re-purchase. To redeem.

P وا خواندن *wā khwāndan*, To substitute one word metonymically for another.

P واخوردن *wā khwurdan*, To take care or think of. To perform by labour. To pity.

P واخيدن *wākhīdan*, To beat or tease (cotton), to separate and clean it. To separate, pull to pieces.

P واد *wād*, A son. (for باد *bād*) Air, wind.

A وأد *waʼd*, (v. n. of وأد) Digging a grave, and burying a daughter alive (a pagan Arabian custom). A loud sound or voice. The braying of a camel.

P وا داد *wā dād*, He gave back, he restored. (or وادار *wādār*) Despising, denying, prohibiting.

P وا دادن *wā dādan*, To give back, restore, return.

P وادارنگ *wādārang*, An orange.

P وا داشتن *wā dāshtan*, To keep back, restrain, retain, check, prohibit, inhibit, oppose, avert. To hide, conceal.

P وادخ *wādikh*, A vine-bud.

A وادس *wādis*, (A plant) springing up.

A وادع *wādiʻ*, One who leaves or lets alone. Mild, gentle, tame, placid, quiet. وادعا *wādiʻan*, Placidly, tranquilly, without importunity or trouble.

A وادق *wādik*, Iron. Sharp (sword).

A وادك *wādik*, Fat, corpulent (man).

P وا دوختن *wā dokhtan*, To sew together.

P وا دوسيدن *wā dosīdan*, To adhere, stick.

P وادة *wāda*, Root, foundation, origin, source. Loud in one's own praises.

A وادي *wādī*, (with tanwīn واد *wādin*) (pl. اوداء *awdāʼ*, اودية *awdiyat*, اوداة *awdāt*, and اوداية *awdāyat*) A valley; low-lying ground. An oasis, or green fertile spot in a desert. A desert. Channel of a river. A river. A corner. Depth. A reed-bed, cane-plantation. وادي ايمن *wādīʼi ayman*, The wilderness through which the children of Israel were led. وادي الحشر *wādīʼl hashr*, The valley of the last judgment. P واديء خاموشان *wādīʼi khāmoshān*, A burial-ground. A وادي عروس *wādī ʻarūs*, Name of a valley on the road to the Kaaba. وادي الكبير *wādīʼl kabīr*, (The Great River) The Guadalquivir in Spain.

P واديىاب *wādiyāb*, Killed, reduced to nothing.

P واديان *wādyān*, (for باديان *bādyān*) Fennel.

P واديج *wādīj*, Large boots or stockings, such as couriers wear. A trellis, vine-prop. A vine-bud, the place whence the grape sprouts. A place where they hang up grapes. A jar in which they make grape-vinegar.

P واديخ *wādīkh*, A vine-bud, the part where the grape shoots.

P وا ديدن *wā dīdan*, To gaze at, look again.

P وازارنگ *wāzārang*, The herb baum.

A واذر *wāzir*, One who leaves or relinquishes.

A وآر *wiʼār*, The spades of clay-diggers. *Wuʼār*, (pl. of وؤرة *wuʼrat*) Fires. Fire-hearths.

P وار *wār*, (in composition) Having, possessing, endowed with; as, اميد وار *umedwār*, Full of hope, hoping. Like, resembling, in the manner of; as, بيخود وار *bī khwudwār*, Like one beside himself; ذرّه وار *zarrawār*, Like an atom. Fit, suiting, befitting; as, شاه وار *shāhwār*, Worthy of, befitting a king; درّ شاه وار *durri shāhwār*, A royal pearl worthy of a king. (for بار *bār*) A time, turn, or portion of time; as, يك وار *yak wār*, One time, once; وارها *wārhā*, Often, many times. A load, burden; as, خروار گندم *kharwāri gandum*, An ass-load of wheat. Quantity, proportion, measure; as, يك جامه وار *yak jāmawār*, A quantity sufficient for a garment. Custom, mode, manner, rule, law, regulation. Much; repeated, reiterated. Love.

A وأر *waʼr*, (v. n. of وأر) Terrifying, frightening. Throwing into evil. Making a hearth for a fire.

P واران *wārān*, The elbow.

P وا راندن *wā rāndan*, To till. To equal, make adequate. To drive off, repel, chase away.

P وارتگاه *wārat-gāh*, The dawn. The east.

P وارث *wāris*, (pl. ورثة *warasat*) An heir. Master, lord, owner. One who survives all his friends. One who manages another's affairs. A name of God. P وارث شدن *wāris shudan*, To inherit. بي وارث *bī wāris*, Heirless. وارث داوٗد *wārisi dāʼud*, David's heir, *i.e.* Solomon.

P وارخ *wārakh*, Beam. Elbow. Viper. Lizard.

P وارخد *wārahhd*, Weak, poor, miserable.

A وارد *wārid*, (pl. ورّاد *wurrād*) One who comes, arrives, approaches. One who descends or enters into; who goes to water. (A fever) seizing one. One who joins. Present. A bringer of tidings. Long, hanging down, straight (hair). A modern author. A guest. Preceding, going before. Cited. Brave, warlike. Event, result. Tawny-coloured (lion). Long-haired. Dangling-lipped. Long-nosed. A road. P وارد شدن *wārid shudan*, To arrive. A وارد و صادر *wārid u sādir*, A comer and goer. A guest, a traveller. واردين و صادرين *wāridīn u sādirīn*, Comers and goers.

A واردات *wāridāt*, (pl. fem. of وارد *wārid*) Things coming in, *i.e.* produce, revenue, or rent. Events, accidents, contingencies. Conjuncture.

P وار داشتن *wār dāshtan*, To raise up, exalt.

P واردان *wārdān*, A rolling-pin. A large sack.

A واردة *wāridat*, A body of cattle or men at a watering-place. A road within a road.

P واردن *wārdan*, A baker's rolling-pin. Whatever they wet a rolling-pin with that the dough may not adhere to it. A midwife.

P واردين *wārdīn*, A midwife.

A وارس *wāris*, (A leaf) turning yellow.

P وارستادن *wāristādan*, To rise or stand up.

P وارستگي *wā rastagī*, Liberation. Humility.

P وارستة *wā rasta*, Humble. Escaped, saved.

P وا رسيدن *wā rasīdan*, To receive, attain, arrive at. To obtain information.

A وارش *wārish*, One who takes meat, eats, or comes uninvited to a feast.

P وارغ *wāragh*, A trellis. *Wārigh*, *ragh*, or *rugh*, A dam, dike, weir. Solder. *Wārugh*, Belching.

A وارف *wārif*, Ample, long, extensive. Green, fresh, verdant.

P وارف *wāruf*, A fan, ventilator. Any thing stuffed with straw to serve the purpose of a table.

P وا رفتن *wā raftan*, To wander, walk about.

A وارق *wārik*, Becoming leafy; green, flourishing, verdant.

A وارقة *wāraka*, Leaf of tree or book; a letter.

A وارك *wārik*, One who neither has, nor claims any thing. *Wārik*, (or واركة *wārikat*) That part of a camel's saddle whereon the rider lays his foot.

P واركار *wārkār*, Melon-ground. Kitchen-garden; part of a garden. A plant without an erect stalk (as cucumber or melon). A hut in a vineyard.

P وارم *wāram*, A painful swelling.

A وارم *wārim*, Swelling, swollen.

P وارن *wāran* or *wārin*, The elbow. *Wārun*, Topsy-turvy.

P وارنج *wāranj*, The elbow.

P وارنگ *wārang*, A long crooked cucumber. A large lemon or orange-tree.

P وارو *wārū*, Any thing stuffed with straw and made to answer the purpose of a table. A fan.

P واروغ *wārūgh*, A belch, eructation.

P وارون *wārūn*, (or وارونة *wārūna*) Inverted, turned upside down. Unfortunate.

P وارة *wāra*, Like, resembling. Lord, master, owner. A row, series. Manner, custom; law, rule. Time, turn, season, juncture. Much, a large quantity.

P وا رهانيدن *wā rahānīdan*, To deliver, free.

A وارهة *wārihat*, Spacious (house).

P واري *wārī*, Like; as, گل واري, Rose-like.

A واري *wārī*, Sharp, subtle, and excellent (musk). Fat (meat). Fire-emitting (stick زند *zand*).

A وارية *wāriyat*, A disease on the lungs. Fat (she-camel).

P واريج *wārij*, The part of the branch whence the grape grows.

P واريخ *wārīkh*, The elbow. A vine-prop.

P واريدن *wāridan*, To swallow. To stick to.

P وارين *wārin*, Going quick. The elbow.

P وارينه *wārina*, Like.

P واز *wāz*, A desisting, giving over, suspending, relinquishing, letting alone, abandoning, deserting, renouncing, taking no care of. (for باز *bāz*) Open. Back. Again.

P وازدن *wā zadan*, To cover, to hide. To beat, tease, or separate (cotton).

A وازر *wāzir*, (fem. وازرة *wāzirat*) One bearing a burden (وزر *wizr*). Laden with crimes, criminal.

A وازع *wāziʻ*, (pl. وزعة *wazaʻat*) A prince; a prefect, governor, magistrate. The leader of the line of an army; preventing confusion. A dog, especially the guardian of a house or of sheep.

P وازغ *wāzagh*, Cuttings of palm-trees. A trellis. *Wāzigh*, Bread made from the fibrous integument of the palm-tree.

P وازگون *wāzgūn*, Inverted.

A وازن *wāzin*, (Money) of just weight.

P وازنج *wāzinj*, A shout, a loud noise.

P وازنيج *wāznīj*, A swing, see-saw, a common Persian amusement, especially on holidays.

P وازيج *wāzīj*, A vine-branch. Any thing from which grapes are suspended. Any place in which grapes are hung up. A vine-prop. A vine-bud, the place whence the grape sprouts.

P وازيخ *wāzīkh*, Hot, scalding.

P وازيدن *wāzīdan*, To declare one's condition to another.

P وازيره *wāzīra*, Time.

P وازينج *wāzīnj*, Crying out, crying hey hey to animals, vociferating.

P واژ *wāj*, Inverted. Money extorted by a more powerful monarch from a weaker.

P واژغ *wājagh* or *wājugh*, Cuttings of palm-trees. *Wājugh*, A rope made of palm-tree fibre; coir.

P واژگون *wājgūn*, (or واژگونه *wājgūna*) Inverted, preposterous, backwards, contrary, reversed, opposite. Unfortunate.

P واژون *wājūn*, (or واژونه *wājūna*) Inverted, turned upside down. Unfortunate, unlucky.

P واژه *wājah*, (in zand and Pāzand) A word.

P واژيان *wājyān*, The great, upper ranks.

P واژيدن *wājīdan*, To tell one's condition, or state of health.

P واس *wās*, An ear of wheat or barley.

P وا ساختن *wā sākhtan*, To supply one's need.

P وا ستاندن *wā satāndan*, To resume, take back.

P واسر شدن *wā sar shudan*, To relapse.

A واسط *wāsit*, The middle. A mediator. A brideman, marriage-broker, match-maker. A tooth. Name of a city between Kūfa and Basra; and other half-way towns. The fore part of a camel's saddle.

A واسطة *wāsitat*, The middle or largest pearl, jewel, or bead in a necklace or bracelet. Any thing intermediate. A female-mediator. A bridemaid. Motive, cause, reason, occasion. Account, sake. Means. The fore part of a camel's saddle. واسطهٔ عقد نجوم *wāsitaʼi ʻikdi nujūm*, The sun. P بواسطهٔ باران *ba wāsitaʼi bārān*, By reason of the rain. بواسطهٔ اينست *ba wāsitaʼi īnast*, Hence it is.

A واسطى *wāste*, On account of. *Wāstī*, A reed, pen.

A واسطىّ *wāsitīy*, Belonging to the city of Wāsit. قلم واسطي *kalami wāsitī*, The best sort of writing-reed from that city.

A واسع *wāsiʻ*, Ample, large, capacious, spacious, wide, roomy. Liberal. A name of God. واسع الفضل *wāsiʻu'l fazl*, Of enlarged beneficence, *i.e.* God. واسع مذهب *wāsiʻ-mazhab*, Of a wide conscience, *i.e.* lax in religious duties or morals.

A واسق *wāsik*, (pl. وساق *wisāk*, مواسق *mawāsik*, and مواسيق *mawāsīk*) Pregnant (camel).

A واسل *wāsil*, Devout, religious. Necessary, proper. Desirous of, anxious for.

A واسلة *wāsilat*, Royal favour, patronage. Dignity. Propinquity, affinity.

P وا سوخت *wā sokht*, An impassioned style.

P واسه *wāsa*, A butterfly. A moth flying about the candle.

P واش *wāsh*, Forage, food for cattle.

P واشامه *wāshāma*, A veil. A tiara; a kind of head-dress worn by Persian monks, made of white wool or camels' hair.

A واشج *wāshij*, Intermixed, interlaced.

A واشجة *wāshijat*, An interwoven relationship.

P وا شدن *wā shudan*, To be open. To be free or clear. To be dissipated, to vanish. To be separated or disjoined. To retire; to go off (as grief). واشدن تاري *wā shudani tārī*, The dispelling of darkness. آسمان از ابر وا شده *āsmān az abr wā shuda*, The sky cleared of clouds. پهن وا شدن *pahn wā shudan*, To spread wide, extend in breadth. To be far separated; having wide intervals.

A واشرة *wāshirat*, A woman whose profession is to thin and sharpen the teeth.

A واشق *wāshik*, One who goes or passes by. A little milk. Lost. Name of a man and dog. (for باشق *bāshik*) A sparrow-hawk.

P (بيع *bayʻ*) وا شكافتن *wā shikāftan*, To act as broker.

P واشكرده *wāshkarda*, Made, formed, prepared, ready. Quick, light, active, brisk.

P واشگونه *wāsh-gūna*, Inverse, upside down.

A واشل *wāshil*, High (mountain), whence water trickles. One who receives a small portion, poor.

P واشم *wāshim*, Name of a river and town.

A واشمة *wāshimat*, A female who pricks figures on the hands or other parts of the body and rubs in woad or indigo.

P واشنگ *wāshing*, A peace-officer. A watchman; chief of the watchmen.

A وا شوقا *wā shawkā*, O would!

P واشه *wāsha*, Darkness covering the fields towards break of day. A sparrow-hawk or merlin.

A واشي *wāshī*, (pl. وشاة *wushāt*) A whisperer, slanderer, informer. (A man) having a numerous offspring. One who explores a mine in search of gold. A coiner, master of the mint. A weaver.

A واشية *wāshiyat*, A woman with many children.

A واص *waṣṣ*, A striking (the ground).

A واصب *wāsib*, Eternal (punishment).

A واصبا *wāsiban*, Perpetually, continually.

A واصبة *wāsibat*, Extensive (desert).

A واصف *wāsif*, A praiser. A describer.

P واصفان *wāsifān*, (pl. of A واصف) Describers.

A واصل *wāsil*, One who joins, meets, or arrives. Arrived, met. Joined, connected, coupled. What is collected (of the public revenue). Name of a man. واصل باقي *wāsil bākī*, Collections and balances. P واصل كردن *wāsil kardan*, To cause to arrive, to join. واصل گرديدن *wāsil gardīdan*, To reach, arrive at.

A واصلات *wāsilāt*, The total collected under every description (a revenue-term in India).

A واصلة *wāsilat*, (pl. وواصل *wawāsil*, afterwards changed to اواصل *awāsil*) A woman who adds her own or other false hair to another's head.

A واصي *wāsī*, Contiguous, uninterrupted. An executor.

A واصية *wāsiyat*, (Ground) whose plants are growing close together.

A واضح *wāzih*, Evident, manifest, clear, apparent, undoubted. Whitish (camel). الواضح *al wāzih*, The morning-star. حجت واضحه *hujjati wāziha*, Evident proof, undeniable argument.

A واضحات *wāzihāt*, Evidences, incontrovertibilities, things clear as noon-day.

A واضحة *wāzihat*, Clear, evident (thing). The front-teeth which appear in laughing.

A واضع *wāziʻ*, One who puts, places, establishes. Inventor, founder, author. (A woman) without a veil. One who conceives a little before menstruation. A camel feeding on sour grass. واضع القانون *wāziʻu'l kānūn*, (or واضع الناموس *wāziʻu'n nāmūs*) A legislator.

A واضعة *wāziʻat*, A lewd woman. (Camels) feeding on the salt and bitter shrub ضعة *zaʻat*.

A واضىٔ *wāziʼ*, Clean.

A وأط *waʼt*, (v. n. of وأط) Visiting. Exciting, stirring up. Being excited or stirred up. Battle, combat. Perturbation, agitation.

A وأطة *waʼtat*, Deep place (of water). High land.

A واطد *wātid*, Firm, solid, steady.

A واطئة *wātiʼat*, Dates falling from the tree. Travellers, trampers. A beaten road.

A واعد *wāʻid*, (A cloud) portending rain. (A horse) promising speed, or one course after another. (A day) promising heat or cold.

A واعدة *wāʻidat*, (Ground) promising a crop.

P واعدي *wāʻide*, An appointed time.

A واعر *wāʿir*, Rough, rugged, uneven (place).

A واعظ *wāʿiz*, Preacher, exhorter, admonisher.

A واعي *wāʿī*, A guardian.

A واعية *wāʿiyat*, (A woman) retaining any thing by memory. Attentive (ear). Clamour, noise.

A واغر *wāghir*, Enraged, fretting.

P واغل *wāghil*, Victuals ready dressed.

A واغل *wāghil*, One who goes to a drinking-party uninvited. Weak, not firm.

P واف *wāf*, A nightingale. A singer.

A وافد *wāfid*, (pl. وفود *wufūd*, وفد *wafd*, اوفاد *awfād*, and وفّد *wuffad*) An approacher, comer on a mission. An ambassador. (A camel, or the bird katā) preceding the troop.

A وافدان *wāfidāni*, (or الوافدان *al wāfidāni*) The cheeks, or their prominent parts which stick out during mastication. غاب وافداه *ghāba wāfidāhu*, He grew old or decrepit.

A وافدون *wāfidūn*, (pl. of وافد *wāfid*) The chief men of a city; rulers, officers, peers.

A وافر *wāfir*, Abundant, plentiful, exuberant, copious, luxuriant; much, many. Rich, opulent, wealthy. Ample, large (garment). Long (bearded). الوافر *al wāfir*, A species of verse whose cæsura is مفاعلتن *mufāʿalatun* six times repeated. وافرا *wāfiran*, Sufficiently, enough.

A وافرة *wāfirat*, (fem.) Rich. الوافرة *alwāfirat*, A large fat ram's tail. A long ear. A long slice of fat. The world. This life. امّ وافرة *ummu wāfirata*, The world.

P وا فروختن *wā farokhtan*, To sell, sell again.

A وافل *wāfil*, Full-grown, full-sized (reed).

A وافه *wāfih*, The minister of a church.

A وافي *wāfī*, Sincere, honourable, faithful to promises or engagements. Complete, perfect, entire, full (weight), just (measure). Plentiful, copious, numerous, many. It is also equivalent to ذو *zū* or صاحب *sāhib*. الوافي *al wāfī*, An Arabian drachm and four دوانيق *dawānīk*.

A وافية *wāfiyat*, (fem. of وافي *wāfī*) Full, perfect. الوافية *al wāfiyat*, Full weight or measure. الطاف وافيه *altāfi wāfiya*, Many favours. سورة الوافية *sūratu'l wāfiyat*, First chapter of the Kur'ān.

P واق *wāk*, A fabulous tree whose fruit resembles various animals which make a noise. A frog. The croak of a frog. A kind of bird.

A واقح *wākih*, Hard (hoof or nail).

A واقذ *wākiz*, One who throws prostrate.

A واقصة *wākisat*, A station on the road to Mecca.

A واقع *wākiʿ*, Falling. Befalling, happening, arriving, occurring, appearing, intervening. Lying, situated. Real, true. A bird descending from the air. Necessary. Transitive (verb). واقع حال *wākiʿ hāl*, State of the case, the thing as it happened. P واقع شدن *wākiʿ shudan*, To happen. واقع كردن *wākiʿ kardan*, To happen. A غير واقع *ghayr wākiʿ*, Untrue, false. A neuter verb. في الواقع *fiʾl wākiʿ*, Very true, very right, certainly, in reality. النسر الواقع *an' nasru'l wākiʿ*, The falling vulture, *i.e.* the constellation of the Lyre. واقعا *wākiʿan*, In fact, really, actually happening thus.

A واقعات *wākiʿāt*, Accidents. Occurrences. Intelligence.

A واقعة *wākiʿat*, Accident, misfortune. A grievous calamity. Battle, encounter, conflict. Death. Occurrence, news, intelligence. Strong, bold, brave. A dream, vision. الواقعة *al wākiʿat*, The day of judgment. P واقعه شدن *wākiʿa shudan*, To die.

P واقع نويس *wākiʿ-navīs*, (or واقع نگار *wākiʿ-nigār*) A news-writer, an intelligencer.

P واقعه ديده *wākiʿa-dīda*, A man of experience.

P واقعه طلب *wākiʿa-talb*, Rebellious, seditious, mutinous, treacherous, villainous.

A واقعي *wākiʿī*, Real, actual, true. Right, proper, completely. Truth. The essence, the soul, or foundation of any thing.

A واقعيّة *wākiʿiyat*, Reality. Existence.

A واقف *wākif*, One who stands, stops, remains, or stays. Informed, aware. Knowing, sensible, intelligent, versed in, experienced, expert, skilful, learned. A testator, one who leaves any thing by last will. P واقف شدن *wākif shudan*, To know, understand. واقف حال يا كار *wākif hāl yā kār*, Experienced, intelligent; a connoisseur.

P واقف كاري *wākif-kārī*, Experience, knowledge.

A واقفيّة *wākifiyat*, Experience, knowledge, intelligence, information.

A واقم *wākim*, The castle of Madīna. حرّة واقم *harrat wākim*, A street near the castle.

P واقواق *wākwāk*, A tree which grows in some of the Indian islands, to the height of about a hundred cubits, having leaves like shields, of a sea-green colour, and fruit resembling a human head, with ears, eyes, nose, and the rest. When agitated by the wind it bends its branches to the ground, making the sound wāk wāk, whence it is named.

A واقه *wākih*, The minister of a church.

A واقي *wākī*, A preserver, defender, guardian, protector. (A saddle) saving (not galling) a beast's back. Cautious in setting his foot on the ground for fear of hurting it. الواقي *alwākī*, The bird صرد *surad*.

A واقية *wākiyat*, (v. n. of وقي) Taking care of, preserving, guarding, keeping one's self or garments clean. An ounce. (pl. اواقي *awākī*) A female protector or defender.

P واك *wāk*, Name of a water-fowl, in Arabic called واق *wāk*.

P واكاويدن *wā kāwīdan*, To inquire, examine.

A واكبة *wākibat*, Standing (woman); firm, steady.

A واكت *wākit*, (A camel) rubbing the hair off the side with a distorted elbow.

A واكر *wākir*, A bird entering her nest.

P وا كردن *wā kardan*, To seize, carry off, lay waste. To shut up close, to cover. To open. To remove, carry off. To pull up, extract, draw away. جدا وا كردن *judā wā kardan*, To separate, scatter.

A واكز *wākiz*, A striker.

P وا كشادن *wā kushādan*, To open.

P وا كشاده *wā kushāda*, Open, plain. واكشاده شد در سخن *wā kushāda shud dar sukhan*, He was free-spoken, he spoke openly.

P وا كشتن *wā kushtan*, To kill in return.

P (سر خم *sari khum*) وا كشودن *wā kushūdan*, To open the head of a jar or barrel.

P وا كشيدن *wā kashīdan*, To pull back. To protract. To extract. To stretch or hold out.

A واكظ *wākiz*, One who beats off or drives away.

A واكل *wākil*, Slow, sluggish (horse), that leans against his fellow and requires the whip.

A واكن *wākin*, Seated, lying on. Sitting (bird).

A واكنات *wākināt*, Sitting (pigeons).

P (باهم *bāham*) وا كوفتن *wā koftan*, To strike against one another. وا كوفته شدن *wā kofta shudan*, To rub or cut (as the feet of a horse).

P وا كويدن *wā kawīdan*, To examine or search (either in disputing or in digging for a thing).

P واگذاشتن *wā guzāshtan*, To leave. واگذاشتن كار بخداي *wā guzāshtani kār bakhudāy*, Committing a business to God.

P و اگر *wa agar*, And if, but if, however.

P وا گردانيدن *wā gardānīdan*, To invert. To turn back.

P واگرديدن *wā gardīdan*, To be inverted, reversed, turn the fore-side backward. To return.

P وا گرفتن *wā giriftan*, To take away, remove.

P و اگرنه *wa agarna*, Otherwise, if not.

P وا گفتن *wā guftan*, To reproach, revile.

P وال *wāl*, A whale, large fish. Name of a river.

A وال *wāl*, (v. n. of وأل) Flying to, taking refuge. Escaping. A place of refuge.

P والا *wālā*, Exalted in dignity or in mind, eminent, respectable, high, sublime, majestic, grave. Power. A friend. Friendship. A kind of silken stuff. شاه والا سرير *shāhi wālā-sarīr*, The king of the exalted throne, *i.e.* powerful. رسول والا منزلت *rasūli wālā-manzilat*, The most sublime prophet.

A و الا *wa illā*, If not, otherwise. But, yet, still, however, nevertheless, notwithstanding. Unless.

P والا جاه *wālā-jāh*, Of elevated dignity.

P ولاد *walād*, Incrustation or plastering of a wall; its white or pictured superficies. (In the East they often powder the walls with gold-dust). A mud-building. A large brick for building. A wall of brick or stone. A row of stones in a structure. A foundation. An edifice; also the front or side of it. Roof or covering of a house. The form or frame-work of a dome or cupola.

P والادگر *wālādgar*, One who lays rows of bricks or stones in a wall, a builder.

P والا شان *wālā-shān*, Of elevated rank.

P والا قدر *wālā-kadr*, Of high dignity.

P والا مناقب *wālā-manākib*, Of exalted virtues.

P والا منش *wālā-manish*, Of exalted nature.

P والان *wālān*, Fennel. A pack-saddle. Brave.

P والانه *wālāna*, A sore, a wound.

P والائي *wālāʼī*, Exaltation, greatness.

A والب *wālib*, One who enters, goes into.

A والبة *wālibat*, A young shoot of corn. Corn shot up a second time. Children, young ones. والبة الابل *wālibatu'l ibl*, The young of a camel.

A وألة *waʼlat*, Dung of sheep and camels collected and sticking together. Camels' dung and urine. A dunghill.

A والة *wālat*, Sweepings. Chips. Basil.

A والث *wālis*, Everlasting (evil). Heavy, oppressive (debt).

A والج *wālij*, Who or whatever enters.

A والجة *wālijat*, Grief seizing one. Inward pain, gripes. An abscess. Adversity, misfortune. Afflicted, tried by misfortunes. Troubled with toothache.

A و الحاصل *wa'l hāsil*, Upon the whole.

A والد *wālid*, A parent. A father. A mother. Pregnant (sheep). P والد بهشت آشياني *wālidi bihisht-āshyānī*, (His) father, whose rest is paradise, *i.e.* (his) deceased father.

A والدان *wālidāni*, (obl. والدين *wālidayn*) Parents.

A والدة *wālidat*, (generally والده *wālida*) A mother. والده سلطان *wālida sultān*, Queen-mother.

P و الدعا *wa'd duʻā*, Adieu! farewell!

A والع *wāliʻ*, (pl. ولعة *walaʻat*) A liar, teller of falsehoods. ولع والع *walʻun wāliʻun*, A bouncing lie. اتّلع فلانا والعه *ittalaʻa fulānan wāliʻuhu*, His business is a mystery to me; I know not if he be living or dead.

A والعة *wāliʻat*, Any thing which obstructs.

P والغانه *wālghāna*, (or والغونه *wālghūna*) Rouge.

A والله *wa'llāh*, And God. والله اعلم *wa'llāh aʻlam*, God is most wise. والله الموفق المعين *wa'llāhu'l muwaffiku'l muʻīn*, By the favour and assistance of God (placed after the exordium or preface of a book, praying for divine aid in finishing the work). *Wa'llāhi*, By God!

P والوچانيدن *wālūchānīdan*, To mimic, to imitate the words and actions of another.

P واله *wāla*, A kind of silken cloth. Cloth naturally white without bleaching. The false appearance of water on a sandy plain. Lamentation. Diligence in business.

A واله *wālih*, (fem. والهة *wālihat*) Astonished, stupefied, confounded, dejected, dispirited, driven to despair, distracted with terror or grief, mad from love. An idiot; a lover.

A والي *wālī*, A prince, governor of a province. One who exercises jurisdiction or authority, a chief magistrate. P واليء سپهر پنجم *wālīʼi sipihri panjum*, The planet Mars. واليان قرمان *wāliyāni karmān*, The princes or governors of Carmania.

P واليس *wālis*, Name of an intimate of Alexander the Great.

P واليگري *wāligarī*, Lordship, authority.

P وام *wām*, Debt, loan. Credit. Lending. Borrowing. The dawn. (in composition denotes) Colour, form, or likeness. وام زمين *wāmi zamīn*, The atoms of earth of which the human body is composed. وام خواستن *wām khwāstan*, To borrow, to beg a loan. وام دادن *wām dādan*, To lend, give credit. وامت گذار *wāmat guzār*, Pay thy debt. وام گذاريدن *wām guzārīdan*, To pay a debt. وام گرفتن *wām giriftan*, To borrow.

A وأم *waʼm*, Warm (house). Broad-bodied, broad.

A و امّا *wa ammā*, As for.

P وا ماندگان *wā māndagān*, (pl. of وا مانده *wā mānda*, Tired. وا ماندگان بيت *wā māndagāni bayt*, Those who remain at home.

P وا ماندگي *wā māndagī*, Openness, exposure.

P وا ماندن *wā māndan*, To remain, lag behind, especially from fatigue. To remain suspended in opinion, to hesitate, desist. To lie open, to be exposed.

P وا مانده *wā mānda*, Fatigued and loitering behind. Open, exposed to view.

A وأمة *waʼamat*, An equal, peer, or companion. One who does and imitates the acts of another.

P وامخواه *wām-khwāh*, A creditor, dun, who demands or exacts payment of a debt. Importunate.

P وامدار *wām-dār*, A debtor. A creditor.

P وامران *wāmirān*, Swallow-wort.

P وامستان *wām-satān*, A debtor. A creditor.

A وامق *wāmik*, Enamoured; a lover. The lover of عذرا *ʻazrā*. A word used in the game of نرد *nard*.

P وامي *wāmī*, In debt; distressed, unfortunate.

A وامئة *wāmiʼat*, A ruinous misfortune. ذهب ثوبي فما ادري وامئته *zahaba sawbī fa mā adrī wāmiʼatahu*, My garment is gone: I know not what has taken it.

P وان *wān*, Like, equal. Name of a city. (an affix denoting) A keeper, guardian: as, دروان *darwān*, A porter, guard of a gate; رزوان *razwān*, Keeper of a vineyard; گله وان *galawān*, A shepherd, herdsman; فيل وان *fīlwān*, An elephant-keeper.

A وأن *waʼn*, Broad, large, wide.

A و ان *wa in*, Although, notwithstanding.

P وانج *wānj*, A lentil.

P وانساز *wānsāz*, (or وانسانه) A pair of compasses.

P وانسان *wān-sān*, Of that sort or manner.

A وا نفساه *wā nafsāh*, Alas! my soul.

A وانك *wānik*, A bird sitting on her eggs. Seated, leaning, reclined.

A و ان كان *wa in kāna*, Although it be.

P وانكونتن *wānkūnitan*, (in zand & Pāz.) To take.

P وانگرستن *wānigaristan*, To look back. To stare.

A و ان لم *wa in lam*, And if not, although not. و ان لم يكن *wa in lam yakun*, Although he were not.

P وا نمودن *wā numūdan* or *namūdan*, To shew again, to produce a confirmation. To shew off.

P وا نهادن *wā nihādan*, To fix. To put down the feet. To replace.

A واني *wānī*, Torpid, languid, fatigued. Cowardly, base.

A واو *wāw*, (pl. واوات *wāwāt*) The name of the letter و. The colour of water. التشهّد بواوين *at'tashahhud bi wāwayn*, The attestation with the double wāw, *i.e.* اشهد ان لا اله الا الله و اشهد ان محمّداً عبده و نبيّه *ashhadu an lā ilāha illā'llāh, wa ashhadu an muhammadan ʻabduhu wa nabīyuhū*, I profess there is no god but God, and I profess that Muhammad (is) his servant and prophet.

A وأوأ *waʼwaʼ*, The yell of a jackal.

A واويّ *wāwiy*, Containing the letter واو *wāw*.

A واويلا *wāwaylā*, Exclamation, cry, lament.

P واه *wāh*, Fy! pho! Bravo! admirable!

A واه *wāh*, (or واهاً *wāhan*) (an interjection of admiration) O! wonderful! excellent! واها لهُ ما اطيبه *wāhā lahu mā atyabahu*, O how excellent it is! (also an interjection of pain) Oh! alas!

P واها *wāhā*, (pl. of وا *wā*) Meats, dishes.

A واهب *wāhib*, A giver, a bestower. Liberal, generous, munificent. واهب الآمال *wāhibu'l āmāl*, The granter of desires. P واهب بي منت *wāhibi bī minnat*, Disinterestedly liberal, who giveth liberally and upbraideth not (the Deity). A واهب الحاجات *wāhibu'l hājāt*, Bestower of necessaries, *i.e.* God. واهب العطايا *wāhibu'l ʻatāyā*, Bestower of bounties (God). واهب الوجود *wāhibu'l wujūd*, Giver of existence.

A واهج *wāhij*, Blazing (fire).

P وا هش آمدن *wā hush āmadan*, To recover from ebriety. وا هشي آمده *wā hushī āmada*, Recovered from intoxication.

A واهف *wāhif*, One who has care of a temple.

A واهلة *wāhilatin*, Before all things.

P واهم *wā ham*, Together with, in one. Equally, in the same manner. Backward. Wrinkled, contracted. Wrapt up. Crooked. Equipage, accoutrement. A badger, grey, or brock. واهم آمدن *wā ham āmadan*, To assemble together. To be spoiled. واهم جسته *wā ham jasta*, Leaping backward. Bent, curled.

A واهم *wāhim*, Who thinks, imagines, or fancies. قوت واهمه *kūwati wāhima*, Imagination, fancy.

A واهما *wāhiman*, Erroneously.

A واهن *wāhin*, Weak, silly, feeble, enervated.

A واهنة *wāhinat*, Weak, silly (woman). The lowest rib of the breast, a short rib. The bone of the arm. The strong rib of a horse nearest the breast. The cervical vertebræ. Flatulencies about the veins of the neck, shoulders, and arms (to which old people are subject).

A واهي *wāhī*, Weak. Torn. Easily dissolved or broken. A cold, insipid word. مقدّمات واهيه *muhaddamāti wāhiya*, Weak, ill-founded premises.

A واهيات *wāhiyāt*, Absurdities, fiddle-faddle.

P واي *wāy*, A well having a flight of steps down

to the bottom. Losing one's way, deviating: seduced. An interjection of pain or threatening. Oh! fy! away! woe to you! alas! واي بوي *wāy ba vay*, Woe be to him!

A واي *waʼy*, (v. n. of وأي) Promising. Being surety for. A promise. Imagination, opinion. A multitude, a number of men. *Waʼa'*, The onager or wild ass (especially when fat). A swift and strong beast of burden.

P وايا *wāyā*, The object of a wish, desire, or inclination; necessary, wanted. Open.

P وا يافتن *wā yāftan*, To understand.

A واياواي *wāyāwāy*, The uproar of combatants.

A وأية *waʼyat*, A large saucer or pot.

P وايج *wāyij*, A trellis, prop for a vine.

A واثر *wāʼir*, Timid, frightened.

P وايزك *wāyzak*, A spark of fire.

P وايست *wāyist*, Occasion, want.

A وا يوسفاه *wā yūsufāh*, Alas! for Joseph.

P وايه *wāya*, A part, portion, lot. Cheerfulness, delight, pleasure, taste. The mind. Occasion, want, wish, desire. Need, necessity.

P وايه گير *wāya-gīr*, One who participates in pleasure. Want, wish, desire. Clever, learned.

P وائي *wāʼī*, Necessary.

A وائية *wāʼiyat*, A large saucer and pot.

P وايبج *wāyīj*, A trellis for training a vine.

P وايبدن *wāyīdan*, Necessity, obligation.

A وبّ *wabb*, (v. n. of وبّ) Preparing, especially to make an onset in battle.

A وبأ *wabʼ*, (v. n. of وبأ) Arranging, drawing up. Yearning (as a camel towards her colt). Infecting or filling with the plague. Beckoning to any one, or pointing out any thing with the finger. *Wabaʼ*, (v. n. of وبئ) Being infected with the plague (a village). (pl. اوباء *awbāʼ*) Plague, pestilence, or any epidemical disease.

A وبا *waba'*, Plague, pestilence.

A وباء *wabāʼ*, (v. n. of وبئ) Being infected with the plague (a village). (pl. اوبئة *awbiʼat*) Plague, pestilence. Cholera.

A وباءة *wabāʼat*, (v. n. of وبئ) Being afflicted with any pestilential disorder. Beckoning (to any one).

A وبار *wabār*, Name of a sandy desert in Arabia. The third of the winter-days called العجوز *al ɛajūz*. *Wibār*, A kind of salsuginous herb. *Wibār*, (or وبارة *wibārat*) (pl. of وبر *wabr*) Animals smaller than cats, of a dusky colour, without tails.

P وبا رسيدگي *wabā-rasīdagī*, Visitation by plague.

P وبا رسيده *wabā-rasīda*, Visited by plague.

P وباسك *wabāsak*, Yawning.

A وبّاص *wabbās*, Bright-coloured. The moon.

A وباطة *wabātat*, Cowardice, timidity.

A وبّاعة *wabbāɛat*, The opening in the crown of the head of a new-born child. Buttocks. كذبت وبّاعته *kazabat wabbāɛatuhu*, He broke wind.

A وبّاغة *wabbāghat*, The backside. كذبت وبّاغته *kazabat wabbāghatuhu*, He broke wind.

A وبال *wabāl*, (v. n. of وبل) Being heavy and unwholesome (air). An unhealthy climate or atmosphere, any thing painful. Heaviness. Cholera. A crime, sin, fault. Punishment. Harshness, severity. Painful, vexatious.

A وبالة *wabālat*, A being heavy and unhealthy.

A وبت *wabt*, (v. n. of وبت) Abiding, staying.

A وبخة *wabkhat*, A reproof, reprimand.

A وبد *wabd* or *wabad*, A hollow or furrow on a mountain. *Wabad*, (v. n. of وبد) Being enraged at. Being indisposed; leading a miserable, laborious, or starving life. Being worn (a garment). One in a wretched situation. A large family in narrow circumstances. Largeness of family, and smallness of means. Shame, modesty. Anger. Heat. A vice, fault, defect, blemish. *Wabid*, Hungry, famished. One who has a malignant eye.

A وبر *wabara*, (fut. يبر *yabiru*) He abode.

A وبر *wabr*, (pl. وبور *wubūr*, وبار *wibār*, and وبارة *wibārat*) An animal smaller than a cat, of a dusky colour, without a tail. One of the five days called العجوز *al ɛajūz*. *Wabar*, (v. n. of وبر) Having much hair (a camel). (pl. اوبار *awbār*) The hair, wool, or flue of camels, goats, hares, or other animals of a soft kind. اهل الوبر *ahlu'l wabar*, The Nomades, or wild Arabs (because they live in tents of goats' hair, in contradistinction to اهل المدر *ahlu'l madar*, The Arabians who dwell in towns or houses of clay). *Wabir*, Hairy, furry (camel or hare).

A وبراء *wabrāʼ*, (fem. of اوبر *awbar*) Hairy (she-camel). A sort of plant. A kind of woolly fungus.

A وبرة *wabrat*, (fem. of وبر *wabr*) An animal smaller than a cat, of a dusky colour, without a tail. One of the wintry days called عجوز *ɛajūz*. *Wabirat*, Hairy (she-camel).

P وبردك *wabardak*, A riddle, enigma.

P وبس *wabs*, Resembling.

A وبش *wabsh* or *wabash*, White specks upon the nails. A kind of ulcerous corroding scab marked with black and white points. *Wabash*, (v. n. of وبش) Being marked black and white (a scabby camel). (pl. اوباش *awbāsh*) A crowd, mob of the lower people. *Wabish*, (A camel) marked with black and white spots from a corroding scab.

A وبص *wabs*, (v. n. of وبص) Shining, flashing (lightning). Opening the eyes (a whelp). Being luxuriant with herbage (ground). *Wabas*, Agility, briskness, sprightliness. *Wabis*, Nimble, frisky (horse), with sparkling eyes.

A وبصان *wabsān* or *wubsān*, An Arabian month, called also ربيع الآخر *rabiɛu'l ākhir*.

A وبط *wabt*, (v. n. of وبط) Being cowardly, timid, wavering, weak, undetermined (opinion). Entangling, incumbering, restraining. Giving a paltry portion. Deposing from dignity, degrading. Opening, laying open (a wound). *Wabat*, (v. n. of وبط) Being weak and cowardly.

A وبغ *wabgh*, (v. n. of وبغ) Reproaching, treating opprobriously. *Wabagh*, The scales of the head. A disease which corrupts camels' hair. *Wabigh*, Troubled with scales on the head, scurfy.

A وبغة *wabaghat*, A crowd: middle of a crowd.

A وبق *wabak*, (v. n. of وبق) Perishing, dying.

A وبل *wabl*, (v. n. of وبل) Pursuing hard, hunting close. Striking (with a stick). Raining heavily. Being heavy and unwholesome. A shower with large drops. *Wubul*, (pl. of وبيل *wabīl* or وبيلة *wabīlat*) Unwholesome (pastures).

A وبلة *wabalat*, Heaviness of air or meat, unwholesomeness. A desire for the male (in a ewe).

A وبلي *wabala'*, (A she-camel) giving much milk after the first gush.

A وبنة *wabnat*, Hunger. Harm, hurt, damage.

A وبوبة *wabwabat*, (v. n. of وبوب Q) Preparing, especially to make an onslaught.

A وبور *wubūr*, (pl. of وبر *wabr*) Animals smaller than cats, dusky-coloured, without tails.

A وبوط *wubūt*, (v. n. of وبط) Being weak (an opinion), cowardly (the spirit).

A وبوق *wubūk*, (v. n. of وبق) Perishing, dying.

A وبول *wubūl*, (v. n. of وبل) Being heavy and unwholesome (the air).

A وبه *wabh*, Intelligence, prudence. Magnificence, greatness, pomp, pride. *Wabh* or *wabah*, (v. n. of وبه) Considering attentively, perceiving, understanding, minding, regarding, attending to.

A وبئة *wabiʼat*, (or وبيئة *wabīʼat*) (A country) afflicted with plague or other epidemy.

A وبيص *wabīs*, (v. n. of وبص) Flashing (lightning). Opening the eyes (a whelp). Being luxuriant with herbage (ground).

A وبيصة *wabīsat*, Flame, fire.

A وبيل *wabīl*, Unhealthy, unwholesome. Dangerous, hurtful. Heavy, severe, vehement (blow, thwack, or torment). A thick staff. A stick with which they beat the wooden bell or gong ناقوس *nākūs*. A supple rod or twig. A beetle used by bleachers or washers of clothes. A bundle of rods. ابيل علي وبيل *abīl ɛala' wabīl*, An aged man (leaning) on a staff.

A وبيلة *wabīlat*, (pl. وبل *wubul*) Unhealthy (country). A club, bludgeon. A bundle of rods, grass, or hay.

P وپاراي *wapārāy*, The planet Venus.

P وپرش *waprish*, Colour.

P وپس *wa pas*, Like, resembling.

P وت *wat*, Fur, peltry: fur-garment. A word.

A وتّ *watt* or *wutt*, The cooing of doves.

A وتأ *watʼ*, (v. n. of وتأ) Walking sluggishly.

A وتا *wata'*, Pus, matter. Black viscous mud.

A وتاحة *watāhat*, Lowness of price.

A وتار *witār*, (v. n. 3 of وتر) Prosecuting or doing any thing at intervals.

A وتاوت *watāwit*, Evil suggestions, counsels.

A وتائر *watāʼir*, (pl. of وتيرة *watīrat*) Ways, tracks, or paths near mountains.

A وتب *watb*, (v. n. of وتب) Sitting firm in a place, remaining immoveable, steady, fixed.

A وتّة *wuttat*, The cooing of doves.

A وتح *watḥ*, (v. n. of وتح) Making a small present. *Wath*, (*watah*, *watih*, or وتح وعر *wath waʼr*) Small in quantity, low-priced. *Watiḥ*, Low (fellow).

A وتحة *watahat*, A little. لا وتحة Nothing.

A وتخ *watkh*, A beating with a stick.

A وتخة *watakhat*, Mire, dirt, clay. Fear. Any thing.

A وتد *watd*, (v. n. of وتد) Driving (a stake). A stake. *Watad* or *watid*, (pl. اوتاد *awtād*) A stake or peg driven into the ground or into a wall. A wooden club. (in prosody) A foot consisting of three consonants, of which two are inflected with vowels, and one quiescent. When the two first letters have vowels, and the last is marked with jazm, as in لقد *lakad*, it is called وتد مجموع *watad majmūʻ*; but when the two moveable letters are separated by one gezmated, as in قبل *habla*, it is called وتد مفروق *watad mafrūk*. وتد واتد *watadun wātidun*, A stake firmly fixed in the ground.

A وتدان *watidāni*, Two prominences within the ear. The two sides of the back or loins.

A وتر *watr*, (v. n. of وتر) Prosecuting, terrifying, promoting evil, fomenting enmity, prompting to revenge. Defrauding. Making an even number odd. Separating, setting apart. Inflicting any thing disagreeable and disgusting. Stringing (a bow). Offering special and voluntary prayers. The ninth day of the month ذو الحجّة *zuʼl hijjat*. *Watr* or *witr*, A unit. An odd number. Malevolence, thirst for revenge. *Witr*, Special, voluntary prayers repeated by the Muhammadans, and not enjoined by the فرض *farz* nor سنّة *sunnat*. The day on which the ceremonies of the pilgrimage are performed at mount Arafāt. One, single, alone. وترا وترا *witran witran*, Singly, separately. *Watar*, (pl. اوتار *awtār*) String of bow, harp, lute. The string by which a bow is hung up. A chord. (pl. of وترة *watarat*, q. v.).

A وترة *watarat*, The septum of the nose; also the edge of the nostril. The frenum of the prepuce; also of the tongue. The round compassing muscle of the arse-gut of a horse. The space between the tip of the nose and the mustachios. The skin between the thumb and the fore-finger; also between any two fingers. The cartilage of the upper part of the ear. That part of a house which is supported alone by pillars. The choicest part of any thing. A nerve in the back. That part of a bow whence the arrow is let fly.

A وتري *watraʼ*, Separately, singly.

A وتز *watz*, (in Yaman) A kind of tree.

A وتش *watsh*, Small, contemptible. The dregs of the people.

A وتشة *watashat*, Weak. Worn down with disease, at the point of death.

A وتغ *watagh*, (v. n. of وتغ) Committing a crime, being culpable. Perishing. Being foolish, ignorant. Being lascivious and indulging in solitary vice (a woman). Ruin. Blame, reprehension. Stupidity, weakness of mind. A crime. An error in speech. Pain.

A وتغة *watighat*, Lascivious (female).

P وتك *watak*, A quail.

P وتكژ *watkaj*, A grape-stone or seed.

P وتگر *watgar*, A furrier, maker of fur-garments.

A وتل *wutul*, (pl. of اوتل *awtal*) (Men) full or drunk with wine or other liquor. Full, sated (people).

A وتن *watn*, (v. n. of وتن) Hurting the heart-vein وتين *watīn*. *Wutun*, (pl. of وتين *watīn*) Veins by which the heart is suspended, heart-strings.

A وتنة *watnat*, A being perpetual. Opposition.

P وتنگ *watang*, A bunch of grapes.

A وتوحة *wutūhat*, A being little and low-priced.

A وتون *wutūn*, (v. n. of وتن) Being perpetual. Running continually (water).

A وتي *wataʼ*, Running sores.

A وتيح *watīh*, Small in quantity and low-priced.

A وتيرة *watīrat*, A way, path, track (especially near a mountain). A long narrow strip of ground. Mounds of earth in a prismatic form. A grave. White earth. That part of a house or tent which is supported alone by pillars or poles. The partition between the nostrils. The cartilage of the top of the ear. The skin between the thumb and fore-finger; also between any two fingers. A white spot on the forehead of a horse. A rose (especially red). Mode, manner, custom, habit. Detention. Intermission from labour. Delay, tediousness, hindrance, slowness, languor. Patience. Malevolence, a thirst for revenge. Defect, blemish. A consequence, any thing following. The nerve under the tongue; also one in the back, and another in the anus. Whatever surrounds any thing, a wrapper, husk. The groove in an Arabian bow, from which the arrow flies. A loop by which the bow is suspended to learn them to shoot straight. A prison. A ring by which they learn to use the lance (like the quintain or tilting-block of olden time). A decimal.

P نيك وتيره *nek-watīra*, Of good disposition.

A وتين *watīn*, (pl. وتن *wutun* and اوتنة *awtinat*) The vein by which the heart is suspended.

A وثأ *wasʼ*, (v. n. of وثأ) Rendering soft. Bruising (flesh by a blow); hurting the flesh, but not the bone; dislocating a bone without breaking it. Spraining (the hand). A bruise, a sprain. *Wasaʼ*, (or وثاء *wasāʼ*) (v. n. of وثئ) Being dislocated or sprained (the hand).

A وثاب *wisāb*, (v. n. of وثب) Assaulting, assailing; leaping, springing, rushing (on another). *Wisāb*, Seats. A throne. A bed, couch. Mansions. وثاب الملائكة *wisābuʼl malāʼikat*, The mansions of angels, *i.e.* heaven.

A وثّاب *wassāb*, A jumper, springer, caperer.

A وثابة *wasābat*, An assault, one attack.

A وثاءة *wasāʼat*, A blow which hurts the flesh without breaking a bone. A sprain.

A وثاجة *wasājat*, (v. n. of وثج) Being thick, dense. Abundance of flesh, fleshiness.

A وثار *wasār* or *wisār*, A soft thing. A soft carpet, covering, or upper garment. A treading, or a softening by treading. *Wisār*, (pl. of وثيرة *wasīrat*) (Women) agreeably plump and full of flesh.

A وثارة *wasārat*, (v. n. of وثر) Being fleshy, soft. Being reduced to a soft consistency. Being soft by beating or treading upon. Fatness, corpulency, abundance of fat.

A وثاق *wasāk* or *wisāk*, A ligature, chain, rope, or any fastening. *Wisāk*, (v. n. 3 of وثق) Entering into a confederacy, stipulating, pledging one's faith. Captivity. A camp. (pl. of وثيق *wasīk*) Firm, solid, constant.

P وثاق *wisāk*, A house, lodge, hut, hovel. A chamber, lodgings. وثاق پيرزن *wisāki pīr-zan*, The old woman's cottage which she refused to sell (a refusal of course religiously respected), when Noshiravān, king of Persia, would have bought it to make room for a palace he was about to build.

A وثاقة *wasākat*, Firmness, fixedness.

A وثام *wasām*, (v. n. of وثم) Making the feet bleed (a stone).

A وثائر *wasāʼir*, (pl. of وثيرة) Plump (women).

A وثائق *wasāʼik*, (pl. of وثيقة *wasīkat*) Trusts.

A وثب *wasb*, (or وثبان *wasabān*) (v. n. of وثب) Assaulting, assailing, leaping, or springing (upon another). (in the dialect of Himyar) Sitting.

A وثبات *wasabāt*, Assaults, attacks, irruptions.

A وثبة *wasbat*, A spring, leap. Boldness. Nobleness. Generosity. Multitude. Departure.

A وثبي *wasabaʼ*, (A woman) who jumps much.

A وثخة *wasakhat*, Moisture, wetting, watering.

A وثر *wasr*, (v. n. of وثر) Softening by beating, treading upon. Covering frequently, but in vain (a camel). Made soft. A kind of garment worn by young girls among the Scenite Arabs, made of slips of leather. A leathern garment round the waist, cut in thongs of four fingers' breadth. An outer garment. Short breeches, *i.e.* without legs. A kind of waistcoat or shirt made soft. *Wasr* or *wasir*, Soft, trodden upon. *Wisr*, A soft bed or carpet. A saddle-cloth. وثر علي وثر *wasrun ʻalaʼ wisrin*, Coitus supra mollem lectum. *Wasir*, Made soft.

A وثغ *wasgh*, (v. n. of وثغ) Breaking (the head). Inducing a camel to suckle another's colt by the stratagem وثيغة *wasīghat*.

A وثغة *wasghat*, A small quantity (of rain).

A وثف *wasf*, An underpropping (of a kettle).

A وثق *wask*, Confidence, trusting in.

A وثقي *waskaʼ*, (fem. of اوثق *awsak*) Very firm.

A وثل *wasal*, A rope made of وثيل *wasīl* (coir).

A وثم *wasm*, (v. n. of وثم) Running. Breaking, bruising, pounding, treading upon. Spurning the ground with his hoofs (a horse). (A stone) hurting (the foot) so that (it) bleeds. Collecting. *Wasam*, (v. n. of وثم) Producing little vegetation (ground). Scarcity, paucity.

A وثن *wasan*, (pl. وثن *wusun* and اوثان) An idol.

A وثني *wasaniy*, An idolater, pagan, heathen.

A وثوب *wusūb*, (v. n. of وثب) Assaulting, assailing, leaping, jumping, springing, rushing on.

A وثوق *wusūḳ*, (v. n. of وثق) Confiding in, trusting to. Confidence, dependence, reliance. Strength, firmness, stedfastness.

A وثي *wasaʼ*, A bruise, sprain. *Wusaʼ*, Pains.

A وثيب *wasīb*, (v. n. of وثب) Assaulting, assailing, leaping, springing, rushing.

A وثئة *wasiʼat*, Dislocated, sprained, hurt (hand).

A وثيج *wasīj*, Thick, dense. Firm-fleshed.

A وثيخة *wasīkhat*, A bunch of different kinds of fresh herbs. Small bones mixed with fat. Clay ground. Thick milk.

A وثير *wasīr*, (Dough) softened by kneading. A soft bed. A saddle-cloth. An upper outer garment. A linen cloth in which garments are wrapped. A pad in front of a saddle. The skin of a rapacious animal. Any thing to sit on, or to be borne upon, made of brocade or silk. Softened. Trodden.

A وثيرة *wasīrat*, (pl. وثائر *wasāʼir* and وثار *wisār*) (A woman) agreeably plump, full of flesh, fit or agreeable for lying with.

A وثيغة *wasīghat*, A small quantity (of rain). A figure resembling a camel's colt, made of woollen or cotton, which they place before her to make her give milk or suckle the young of another as her own; a tulchan. Different kinds of grass luxuriantly entangled in the spring. (A cake) folded in several plies.

A وثيق *wasīḳ*, (pl. وثاق *wisāḳ*) Firm, solid, strong, steady, constant. حجت وثيقه *hujjati wasīḳa*, A judicial decree. عهد وثيق *ʻahdi wasīḳ*, Firm covenant.

A وثيقة *wasīḳat*, (v. n. of وثق) Trusting to. Being firm, steady, solid. Firmness, solidity. Confidence, faith. Confederacy, compact, treaty, promise, engagement, writing, obligation, bond, written agreement. (Ground) abundant in herbage.

A وثيل *wasīl*, The fibres of the trunk of the palm-tree; a rope made of those fibres: coir. A hempen rope. A weak rope of a bucket. Weak, flaccid. Weakly (young deer). An old tree.

A وثيم *wasīm*, Firm-fleshed.

A وثيمة *wasīmat*, A large heap of corn, grass, or fodder. Stones, gravel.

A وثيئة *wasīʼat*, Dislocated, sprained (hand).

A وج *wajj*, Galangale. The yoke upon the neck of a ploughing-ox. Celerity. The bird قطا *ḳaṭā*. An ostrich. Name of a valley in Taif.

A وجأ *wajʼ*, (v. n. of وجأ) Striking (with a knife or the hand), giving a slap with the palm. Beheading. Bruising the testicles of a goat between two stones. Failing, drying (water). Lying with. *Wajʼ* or *wajaʼ*, Bad (water).

A وجا *wajaʼ*, (v. n. of وجى) Having a thin, worn hoof. Soreness of feet from travelling barefoot.

A وجاء *wajāʼ*, Bad (water). *Wijāʼ*, (v. n. of وجأ) Castrating (a goat) by crushing his testicles. (pl. اوجية *awjiyat*) A small truss or bundle of clothes. A portmanteau.

A وجاب *wajāb*, (for ايجاب *ījāb*) Ratifying a purchase, knocking (an article) down (to the buyer). *Wijāb*, (v. n. 4 of وجب) Rendering necessary, making obligatory. (pl. of وجب *wajb*, Large bottles of goats' skins. Places where water stagnates.

A وجّاب *wajjāb*, (or وجّابة) Cowardly, timid.

A وجأة *wajʼat*, (A well) destitute of water.

A وجاح *wajāḥ*, A quantity of water just covering the bottom of a reservoir. Smooth stones. ادنى وجاح *adnaʼ wajāḥin*, The first thing, at first sight. *Wajāḥ*, *wujāḥ*, or *wijāḥ*, A veil, covering.

A وجاد *wijād*, Places where waters stagnate.

A وجاذ *wijāz*, (pl. of وجذ *wajz*) Cavities in mountains wherein water collects: tarns.

A وجار *wajār* or *wijār*, (pl. اوجرة *awjirat* and وجر *wujur*) A den (of a hyena). A herd of hyenas. Part of the banks of a river carried off by the water.

P وجارش *wijārish*, (in zand and Pāzand) Consumption, weakness, leanness.

A وجازة *wajāzat*, (v. n. of وجز) Being ready, short, brief, laconic. Readiness. Agility.

A وجاع *wijāʻ*, (pl. of وجع *wajaʻ*) Pains, aches.

A وجاعى *wajāʻaʼ*, (pl. of وجعة *wajiʻat*) Pained, afflicted (women). *Wujāʻaʼ*, (pl. of وجع *wajiʻ*) Pained, afflicted (men).

A وجال *wijāl*, (pl. of وجل *wajil*) Timid.

A وجالة *wajālat*, (v. n. of وجل) Being full of years.

A وجاه *wijāh*, (v. n. 3 of وجه) Comparing one (thing) with another. Presence, opposition, fronting, face to face. Measure, quantity. وجاه الف *wijāhu alfin*, Amounting to a thousand. وجاهاً *wijāhan*, *wujāhan*, or *wajāhan*, Before, in presence of, fronting, face to face. وجاهك *wijāhaka*, *wajāhaka*, or *wujāhaka*, Fronting, facing thee.

A وجاهة *wajāhat*, (v. n. of وجه) Being honourable and high in authority. Presence, aspect, respect, appearance. Position. Dignity, authority. Beauty, comeliness.

A وجب *wajb*, (v. n. of وجب) Palpitating (the heart). Setting (the sun). Repelling. Being sunk deep in the socket (the eye). A marriage contracted by depositing a pledge or token. A bet or stake at a race. Timid, pusillanimous. Foolish. (pl. وجاب *wijāb*) A large bottle made of goat's skin. A she-camel whose biestings coagulate in the udder.

P وجب *wajab*, A span, nine inches. وجب كردن *wajab kardan*, To measure by the span, to span.

A وجبان *wajabān*, Palpitation (of the heart).

A وجبة *wajbat*, (v. n. of وجب) Falling or stumbling with a great noise; the sound made by it. Dying. اكل وجبة *akala* (or حلب *halaba*) *wajbatan*, He eat (or milked) once a day (only).

A وجج *wujuj*, A swift ostrich.

A وجح *wajḥ*, (v. n. of وجح) Being manifest, visible, open, public. *Wajaḥ*, A cave, cavern, den.

A وجد *wajd*, (v. n. of وجد) Being enraged at, taking occasion to quarrel with or chide (another). Being melancholy. Being transported, in an ecstasy of love. Ecstasy, excessive love. Wildness, transport (in love or grief). (pl. وجاد *wijād*) A place in which water stagnates. P وجد كردن *wajd kardan*, To move about in an ecstasy. آهنگ وجد و سماع *āhangi wajd u samāʻ*, The harmony of love and music. A *Wajd*, *wijd*, or *wujd*, (v. n. of وجد) Having enough, being wealthy, opulent, rich. Opulence. *Wajd* or *wujd*, (v. n. of وجد) Discovering, procuring, finding, recovering (any thing lost or searched for).

A وجدان *wajdān*, Ecstasy. *Wijdān*, (v. n. of وجد) Recovering (any thing lost), discovering, finding. *Wujdān*, pl. of وجيد *wajīd*, Level, plain grounds.

A وجدة *wijdat*, (v. n. of وجد) Having enough, being rich. Opulence, wealth.

A وجذ *wajz*, (pl. وجذان *wijzān* and وجاذ *wijāz*) A cavity in a mountain where water collects. A cistern, reservoir, pond, or trough. *Wajiz*, (A place) containing much water.

A وجر *wajr*, (v. n. of وجر) Making (one) hear that which is disagreeable. Putting medicine into the mouth (of a child), giving a drench. A cavern in a mountain. *Wajar*, (v. n. of وجر) Fearing, being afraid of. *Wajir*, Timid, trembling. *Wujur*, (pl. of وجار *wajār*) Hyenas' dens.

P وجر *wajar*, The decree of a judge.

A وجراء *wajrāʼ*, (fem. of اوجر) Timid (female).

A وجرة *wajrat* or *wajarat*, (pl. اوجار *awjār*) A hole dug to entrap wild beasts. *Wajirat*, Timid, trembling (woman).

P وجرگر *wajargar*, A chief, interpreter of the law, a chief justice, mufti.

A وجز *wajz*, (v. n. of وجز) Being ready, short, laconic. Ready at giving. Nimble, active. Epitome, compendium. Abridged, epitomised, brief.

P و جز آن *wa juz ān*, Et cetera.

A وجس *wajs*, A soft voice, a low sound (particularly the noise of a man with a girl when overheard by another). Tremor, palpitation, terror (arising from any sound).

A وجسان *wajsān*, Fear, trepidation, or startle (caused by noise).

A وجع *wajaʻ*, (v. n. of وجع) Being pained. (pl. اوجاع *awjāʻ* and وجاع *wijāʻ*) Disease, pain, ache. Complaint, mourning. وجع الآذان *wajaʻuʼl āzān*, Ear-ache. وجع الاسنان *wajaʻuʼl asnān*, Toothache. وجع الظهر *wajaʻu'z zahr*, Back-ache, lumbago. وجع مفاصل *wajaʻi mafāsil*, A pain in the joints, rheumatism. *Wajiʻ*, (pl. وجعون *wajiʻūna*, وجعى *wajʻa'*, and وجاعى *wujāʻa'*) Full of pain, aching. امّ وجع الكبد *ummu wajiʻi'l kabid*, A certain plant good for liver-disease.

A وجعاء *wajʻā*, The backside.

A وجعة *wajiʻat*, Afflicted, pained (woman).

A وجعى *wajʻa'*; (pl. of وجع *wajiʻ*) Pained.

A وجف *wajf*, (v. n. of وجف) Tottering, staggering, being in commotion, palpitating. A particular pace (of a horse or camel).

A وجل *wajl*, (v. n. of وجل) Exceeding or beating another in terror and alarm. *Wajal*, (v. n. of وجل) Being afraid or cautious (of another). Fear, terror, apprehension. *Wajil*, (pl. وجال *wijāl* and وجلون *wajilūna*) Timid, fearful, cowardly.

A وجلاء *wajlā*, (fem. of اوجل) Timid (woman).

A وجلة *wajilat*, Timid, timorous (woman).

A وجم *wajm*, (v. n. of وجم) Being afflicted and silent; fixing the eyes upon the ground from pain, rage, or vexation. Abhorring, detesting. Striking on the breast with the fist. (A man) of the worst kind or meanest rank. The face. وجم سوء *wajmu sawʻin*, A bad man. *Wajam*, (pl. اوجام *awjām*) Drowsiness, somnolency. A heap of stones, a lofty cairn, said to be the work of عاد *ʻād*. Any thing erected in the desert as a direction for travellers. Avaricious, despicable. Thin or small of body. *Wajim*, Sad, grim. Afflicted, silent, and fixing the eyes upon the ground from pain, rage, vexation, or intense grief.

A وجمة *wajmat*, One meal. A falling flat on the face when eating. *Wajamat*, A reviling of men. Disgrace, ignominy, scorn.

A وجن *wajn*, (v. n. of وجن) Beating (cloth, as a fuller or washer). Throwing (on the ground), prostrating. Flinging to a distance. Contusion, blow. ما ادري اي من وجّن الجلد هو *mā adrī ayyu man wajjana'l jilda huwa*, I do not know what he is.

A وجناء *wajnā*, A strong, firm-fleshed she-camel. A large-cheeked she-camel.

A وجنة *waj, wij, wuj*, or *wajinat*, (pl. وجنات *wajnāt*) A prominent or chubby cheek.

P وجنك *wajnak*, The bill of a bird.

A وجوب *wajūb* or *wujūb*, (v. n. of وجب) Being necessary. Being necessary (to do or to suffer any thing). Repelling. *Wujūb*, (v. n. of وجب) Being firm, fixed, settled, confirmed (a sale). Setting (as the sun). Being sunk deep in the socket (the eye). Dying. Necessity, obligation, duty. Debt.

A وجوبة *wujūbat*, (v. n. of وجب) Being timid, cowardly. Being a fool. Timidity, cowardice.

A وجود *wujūd*, (v. n. of وجد) Discovering, procuring, finding, recovering (any thing lost or searched for). Being found, existing, or beginning to exist. Invention. Existence, substance, essence, body, person, individual. Trunk of a tree. Penis. (pl. of وجد *wijd*) Riches. (pl. of وجد *wajad*) Ecstasies. P وجود پذير شدن *wujūd-pazīr shudan*, To come to light, to appear, be published or produced. با وجود *bā wujūd*, Chiefly. Notwithstanding. Through, in consequence of. A صاحب وجود *sāhib-wujūd*, Existing. Eminent. P وجود ساز معادن *wujūd-sāzi maʻādin*, An epithet of the sun.

A وجور *wajūr*, A thing disagreeable to the ear. *Wajūr* or *wujūr*, A medicine (put in the mouth).

A وجوز *wujūz*, (v. n. of وجز) Being ready, short, brief, laconic (in speech). Readiness, promptitude.

A وجوف *wujūf*, A tottering, a staggering.

A وجول *wujūl*, Old men, doctors.

A وجوم *wujūm*, (v. n. of وجم) Being afflicted, vexed, silent with grief or anger. Being sultry (the day).

A وجوه *wujūh*, (pl. of وجه *wajh*) Faces, aspects. Chiefs (of a country, city, or society). من كلّ وجوه *min kull wujūh*, In every shape, entirely, every way.

P وجه *wajh*, The price (of any thing). Debt, obligation. Expense, disbursement.

A وجه *wajh*, (v. n. of وجه) Smiting on the face. Turning the face to. Becoming more respectable than another in the eyes of people. (pl. اوجه *awjuh*, وجوه *wujūh*, and اجوه *ujūh*) Face, visage; aspect, countenance. Effigy. Presence, appearance, shape, semblance, surface. Front, fore part. The side (of any thing). Mode, manner, reason, ratio, method, cause, means, way, plan. Wages, salary, money. Maidenhead. Essence, substance. Honour, authority. Veneration, respect. Dignity, nobility, greatness, high rank. Respectable, dignified, honourable. (pl. وجوه *wujūh*) A prince, chief, leader. A little water. The aspect of a star. Style, manner, design, bearing, purpose, drift (of a speech). A wish. Beginning, commencement (of an age). Essence, reality; the individual thing itself. Satisfaction, good pleasure, favour. وجه احسن *wajhi ahsan*, A good manner. وجه ارض *wajhi arz*, Surface of the ground. وجه تسميه *wajhi tasmiya*, Cause of giving any particular name, etymology of words. وجه حال *wajhi hāl*, Mode of living, state of circumstances. وجه كرايه *wajhi kirāya*, Ground-rent, lodging-charges. وجه كفاف *wajhi kafāf*, Enough of provisions. وجه معاش *wajhi maʻāsh*, Maintenance, subsistence. بوجه من الوجوه *bi wajhin mini'l wujūh*, By all manner of means. P بروجه اجمال *bar wajhi ijmāl*, By way of abridgment. بروجه تعجيل *bar wajhi taʻjīl*, Hastily, expeditiously. A بوجه شرعي *bi wajhi sharʻī*, In a legal manner. P دروجه مشروح *dar wajhi mashrūh*, In the manner (above) explained. A لوجه الله *li wajhi'llāh*, For God's sake. من وجههم *min wajhihim*, Immediately on their arrival, before they had rested. علم وجه *ʻilmi wajh*, Physiognomy. على وجه *ʻala' wajh*, According to the mode. في وجه اجمل *fī wajhi ajmal*, In an excellent method. *Wijh* or *wujh*, A side. *Wajah*, A little water. *Wajuh*, Respectable, dignified.

A وجها *wajhā*, Allowance, pension, salary.

A وجها *wajhan*, Apparently, seemingly. وجها من الوجوه *wajhan mini'l wujūh*, In no shape.

A وجهاء *wujahā*, (pl. of وجيه *wajīh*) Respectable, dignified. Princes, chiefs.

A وجهة *wij* or *wujhat*, Side, part. Mode, manner.

A وجى *waja'*, (v. n. of وجى) Having a thin, worn hoof (a horse). Castrating. Discovering one to be avaricious and worthless. Soreness in the feet from travelling barefoot. *Waji*, (A horse) worn in the hoof.

A وجىّ *wajīy*, (A horse) hurt in the hoof. Avaricious, worthless.

A وجياء *wajyā*, (A mare) hurt in the hoof.

A وجيب *wajīb*, (v. n. of وجب) Palpitating.

A وجيبة *wajībat*, Purchase-money paid by instalments. A thing agreed to be bought and delivered to the buyer. Pension, stipend, daily allowance.

A وجيج *wajīj*, Thick, stoutly-woven (cloth).

A وجيد *wajīd*, Level, plain (ground).

A وجيرة *wajīrat*, Timid, fearful (woman).

A وجيز *wajīz*, Brief, short, laconic. Epitomized. كلام وجيز *kalāmi wajīz*, A short, pithy discourse.

A وجيع *wajīʻ*, Painful. Pained. Patient.

A وجيف *wajīf*, (v. n. of وجف) Palpitating (the heart). Tottering, staggering. A particular pace (of a horse or camel).

A وجيل *wajīl*, A hollow where water stagnates.

A وجيم *wajīm*, Sultry, intensely hot (day).

A وجيمة *wajīmat*, Blighted, smutty (corn).

A وجين *wajīn*, Hard, rugged ground. Side of a mountain. Bank of a river.

A وجيه *wajīh*, (pl. وجهاء *wujahā*) Of a noble presence, respectable, and dignified (man). Handsome, comely. Specious. A prince, chief. Beads worn as preservatives against fascination. Cloth with a double face. A child brought forth with the arms, or a colt with the fore-feet, foremost.

A وجيهة *wajīhat*, Beads or similar things hung about the body as preservatives against fascination.

A وجيء *wajīʻ*, Castrated (goat) by crushing.

A وجيئة *wajīʻat*, A cow. A dish made of bruised locusts, to which they add butter or oil; one made of dates stoned, with milk or butter poured over.

P وچر *wachar*, Decree of a judge. A prophet.

P وچرگر *wachargar*, A judge. A prophet.

A وح *wah*, Used in crying to kine.

A وحّ *wahh*, A tent-pole or pin. Name of a poor man; whence the proverb, افقر من وحّ *afkar min wahh*, Poorer than Wahh.

A وحاء *wahā*, Swiftness, haste, expedition.

A وحاب *wuhāb*, A camel's distemper.

A وحاة *wahāt*, Noise, distant roll of thunder.

A وحاد *wuhād*, Ones. *Wuhāda*, One by one.

A وحادة *wahādat*, A being unequalled, unique.

A وحاشي *wahāsha'*, (pl. of وحشان *wahshān*) Sad.

A وحاف *wihāf*, (pl. of وحفة *wahfat*) Black stones. Sounds, voices.

A وحافة *wahāfat*, (v. n. of وحف) Being long and luxuriant (herbage or black hair).

A وحافي *wahāfa'*, (pl. of وحفاء *wahfā'*) Lands full of black stones.

A وحام *wihām*, (pl. of وحمي *wahma'*) Longing (women). *Wihām* or *wahām*, (v. n. of وحم) Longing (as a pregnant woman). Being difficult and untractable (a pregnant animal). The longing of a pregnant woman for any particular food.

A وحامي *wahāma'*, (pl. of وحمي) Longing women.

A وحج *wahaj*, (v. n. of وحج) Fleeing for refuge. An asylum, a refuge.

A وحجة *wahajat*, Low ground, a hollow.

A وحد *wahd*, (v. n. of وحد) Being single, alone, or incomparable. Sole, alone, separate. Solitary (wild beast). (A person) of an unknown tribe or family. Solitude. جلس وحده *jalasa wahdahu*, He sat alone. رأيته وحده *ra'aytuhu wahdahu*, I saw him alone. هو عيير وحده *huwa ʻuyayru wahdihi*, (or جحيش وحده *juhayshu wahdihi*) He is a whimsical, self-opiniated fellow (spoken in censure). هو نسيج وحده *huwa nasīju wahdihi*, He is a singular man (spoken in praise). انت وحد *anta wahdun*, (or انت وحدك *anta wahduka*) Thou alone. هو وحده *huwa wahduhu*, He only. له وحده *lahu wahduhu*, To him singly. علي وحدهما *ʻala' wahdihimā*, (or وحديهما *wahdayhimā*) By their two selves. هم وحدهم *hum wahduhum*, Them only. علي وحده *ʻala' wahdihi*, Separately, alone, by himself. *Wahad* or *wahid*, Sole, alone, separated. Unique, incomparable.

A وحدان *wuhdān*, (pl. of واحد *wāhid*) Ones, single (numbers or things). Pre-eminent.

A وحدانية *wahdānīyat*, Unity, singularity. Belief in the unity of God. Unity (attribute of God).

A وحدة *wahdat*, (v. n. of وحد) Being single, alone, solitary. Unity. Solitariness. *Wahidat*, Alone, single (woman).

A وحر *wahr*, Indignation, concealed hatred. *Wahar*, (v. n. of وحر) Eating viands over which the venomous reptile وحرة *waharat* has crawled. Being poisoned by the aforesaid reptile (food). Boiling with rage, fostering hatred and rancour. (pl. of وحرة *wahrat* and *waharat*, q.v.). *Wahir*, Filled with anger; rancorous.

A وحرة *waharat*, (v. n. of وحر) Harbouring malice in the heart. An animal resembling a lizard, of a red colour, which adheres to the ground, and poisons meat or any thing it touches (severe vomiting and purging are the first symptoms attending those who are affected by it). (A woman) of a dark complexion, squab and contemptible, or ruddy and dwarfish. Dwarfish (camel).

A وحرمي *wa harma'*, Assuredly, verily.

A وحش *wahsh*, (v. n. of وحش) Throwing away (cloak, arms, or spear) in flight. Desert, desolate. Hungry. Unsavoury. Distraction, madness. (pl. وحوش *wuhūsh* and وحشان *wuhshān*) A wild beast, a fierce, shy, untamed animal. Game. حمار وحش *himāru wahshin*, The onager or wild ass. وحش اصمت *wahshi ismit*, A desert, solitude. بات وحشا *bāta wahshan*, He slept in the desert, *i.e.* he was starved with cold or hunger. بقر الوحش *baharu'l wahsh*, The wild ox.

A وحشان *wahshān*, (pl. وحاشي *wahāsha'*) Sad, melancholy. *Wuhshān*, (pl. of وحش *wahsh*) Wild, untamed animals.

A وحشة *wahshat*, A desert, solitude, or dreary place. Waste, desert, comfortless, gloomy (country). Wildness, fierceness. Fear, dread, terror, horror. Sadness, solitariness, dreariness. Grief, care. نفرت و وحشت *nafrat u wahshat*, Fear and horror.

P وحشت آميز *wahshat-āmez*, Unpleasant.

P وحشت انگيز *wahshat-angez*, Frightful.

P وحشتناك *wahshatnāk*, Frightful, dreary.

A وحشيّ *wahshīy*, (fem. وحشيّة *wahshīyat*) Wild (man or beast). Shy. Fierce, savage, untractable, uncivil. The right side of a thing; also the left or offside (the near side being called انسيّ *insīy*); the outside which may be joined to another; the outside (of a bow, feet, or hands). The interior, inside (of a bow). حمار وحشيّ *himārun wahshīy*, A wild ass.

A وحشيّة *wahshīyat*, A strong wind which gets under one's clothes.

P وحشي مزاج *wahshī-mizāj*, Savage. Misanthropic, shy, unsociable.

A وحص *wahs*, (v. n. of وحص) Dragging on the ground. A pimple on the face of a pretty woman.

A وحصة *wahsat*, Cold. اصبحت و ليس بها وحصة *asbahtu wa laysa bihā wahsatun*, I experienced there (or then) no cold.

A وحف *wahf*, (v. n. of وحف) Throwing one's self on the ground, lying down. Approaching, making up to. Alighting. Going fast. Plentiful, luxuriant (herbage). (A wing) full of feathers. *Wahf* or *wahaf*, Much and beautiful (black hair).

A وحفاء *wahfā'*, Red earth. (pl. وحافي *wahāfa'*) Ground covered with black stones.

A وحفة *wahfat*, (pl. وحاف *wihāf*) A black stone. A sound, voice, noise.

A وحل *wahl*, (v. n. of وحل) Rolling (one) in the mire. Mud. *Wahal*, (v. n. of وحل) Falling in the mire. (pl. اوحال *awhāl* and وحول *wuhūl*) Black adhesive clay, slime, ooze, mud, mire.

A وحم *wahm*, (v. n. of وحم) Going towards, aiming at, making for. *Waham*, (v. n. of وحم) Longing (as a pregnant woman). The longing of a woman with child; also the particular thing longed for. Any strong desire. Appetitus venerei congressus. The sound of a bird's flying.

A وحمي *wahma'*, (pl. وحام *wihām* and وحامي *wahāma'*) Longing (pregnant woman).

A وحن *wahan*, (v. n. of وحن) Falling into the mire.

A وحنة *wahnat*, Slippery and adhesive clay.

A وحواح *wahwāh*, (or وحوح *wahwah*) Nimble, agile, quick, active (man). Strong, robust. Barking or howling (dog).

A وحوح *wahwah*, A sort of bird.

A وحوحة *wahwahat*, (v. n. of وحوح Q) Making a hoarse noise. Breathing upon the fingers in extreme cold.

A وحود *wuhūd*, (or وحودة *wuhūdat*) (v. n. of وحد) Being sole, unique, incomparable.

A وحوش *wuhūsh*, (pl. of وحش *wahsh*) Wild beasts. P وحوش بيابان *wuhūshi biyābān*, The wild beasts of the desert. Savages. Satyrs.

A وحوفة *wuhūfat*, (v. n. of وحف) Being long and luxuriant (herbage or black hair).

A وحول *wuhūl*, (pl. of وحل *wahal*) Thin clays.

A وحي *wahy*, (v. n. of وحي) Indicating. Suggesting. Revealing. Writing. Making haste. Revelation, any thing (divine) suggested, inspired, or revealed (by vision or otherwise). (pl. وحيّ *wuhīy*) A book, writing, epistle. Clamour, murmur, noise of a crowd. وحي رباني *wahyi rabbānī*, Divine revelation (that especially which Muhammad gave out he received by the angel Gabriel). وحي قلب *wahyi kalb*, The (divine) inspiration of the heart. *Waha'*, A sound, noise. A great prince. A king, monarch. A falcon. Swiftness, haste.

A وحيّ *wahīy*, Quick, swift, nimble. Sudden (death). *Wuhīy*, (pl. of وحي *wahy*) Things revealed, revelations. Noises.

A وحيد *wahīd*, (fem. وحيدة *wahīdat*) Alone, unique, single, singular. Sole, separated. وحيد دهر *wahīdi dahr*, Phœnix of the age. وحيد العصر *wahīdu'l ʻasr*, The nonpareil of the age.

A وحيدة *wahīdatan*, Only, singly.

A وحيش *wahīsh*, A wild beast. Untamed.

A وحيف *wahīf*, Name of a place at Mecca, where dead bodies were formerly thrown.

A وحيم *wahīm*, Hot, sultry (day).

A وخّ *wakhkh*, Purpose, design. Pain, agony.

A وخاء *wikhā'*, (v. n. 3 of اخا for اخو) Choosing for a brother, behaving as a brother.

A وخاءة *wikhā'at*, (v. n. of اخا for اخو) Behaving as a brother.

A وخّاد *wakhkhād*, (A camel) taking wide and quick steps.

A وخاش *wikhāsh*, (pl. of وخش) Vile, worthless.

A وخاشة *wakhāshat*, Badness, baseness, vileness.

A وخام *wakhām*, An unhealthy country, one whose vegetation is unwholesome. *Wikhām*, (pl. of وخم *wakhm*) Heavy, disagreeable men. (pl. of وخم *wakhim*, وخوم *wakhūm*, or وخيم *wakhīm*) Heavy, hurtful (meats). Oppressed with indigestion.

A وخامة *wakhāmat*, (v. n. of وخم) Having an indigestion, or the stomach overloaded (with meat). Being heavy and indigestible (meat). Indigestion.

Hurtfulness, noxiousness, badness, injury, harm, evil.

A وخامى *wakhāmā'*, (pl. of وخم *wakhim*, وخوم *wakhūm*, and وخيم *wakhīm*) Troubled with indigestion. Heavy and disagreeable men.

P وخچي *wakhchī*, A date-stone.

A وخد *wakhd*, (or وخدان *wakhadān*) (v. n. of وخد) Throwing out the feet in the manner of an ostrich (a camel). Taking wide and quick steps. That mode of walking.

P وخر *wakhar*, A place.

A وخز *wakhz*, (v. n. of وخز) Striking slightly but not piercing (with a spear or similar weapon). Pulling up, tearing out, removing. Growing grey (as hairs, though still mixed with black). Making a honey-cake. Any thing small or few. وخزا وخزا *wakhzan wakhzan*, (They came) four and four, by fours.

P وخش *wakhsh*, A beginning, commencement. Name of a city. *Wakhash*, A disease in the feet of asses, which makes them lame.

A وخش *wakhsh*, (pl. اوخاش *awkhāsh* and وخاش *wikhāsh*) (A person or thing) of the worst kind. The dregs of the people.

P وخشت *wakhshat*, The fifth of the five embolismal days formerly added to the Persian year.

P وخشور *wakhshūr* or *wukhshūr*, A prophet, an apostle (especially Muhammad).

P وخشوربند *wakhshūr-pand*, (وخشور بند *wakhshūr-band*, or وخشور نهاد *wakhshūr-nihād*) Any law established by divine authority.

P وخشي *wakhshī*, A garment of fine texture.

P وخشيرك *wakhshīrak*, Khurāsān-wormwood.

P وخشينه *wakhshīna*, A white bird which appears in gardens in the spring. Any thing white. Break of day.

A وخض *wakhz*, (v. n. of وخض) Piercing (with a knife or a spear), but not penetrating mortally. (Hoariness) coming (upon one).

A وخط *wakht*, (v. n. of وخط) Mixing, sprinkling (any one) with a few white hairs (hoariness). Going quick. Entering. Wounding deep. Penetrating slightly. Striking with the best part of the sword-edge. In trade losing sometimes, and sometimes gaining. Creaking (as a shoe).

A وخف *wakhf*, (v. n. of وخف) Striking marshmallows until they become viscous. Becoming viscous (marshmallows). Making evil mention of any one. Foolish, silly.

A وخفة *wakhfat*, A leather purse or bag.

A وخم *wakhm*, (v. n. of وخم) Suffering more than another from indigestion. (pl. اوخام *awkhām* or وخام *wikhām*) Heavy and disagreeable (man). *Wakhm* or *wakhim*, (pl. اوخام *awkhām*) Troubled with indigestion. Heavy and unwholesome (meat). *Wakham*, Hemorrhoids, to which she-camels are subject. *Wakhim*, (pl. وخامى *wakhāmā'*) Heavy, disagreeable (man).

A وخمة *wakhma* or *wakhimat*, Unhealthy country. *Wakhamat*, (A she-camel) troubled with emerods.

A وخمة *wakhma*, Bad, unwholesome food.

A وخنة *wakhnat*, Mischief, spoil, damage.

A وخواخ *wakhwākh*, Weak, silly, impotent, lazy, slothful. Cowardly. One who has a loose, flagging belly. A soft or withering date.

P وخ وخ *wakh wakh*, Particles of exclamation, indicative of pleasure or surprise.

A وخوخة *wakhwakhat*, Cry of a certain bird.

A وخود *wakhūd*, A wide and quick-stepper.

A وخوشة *wukhūshat*, (v. n. of وخش) Being of the worst kind, being bad, vile, base.

A وخوص *wukhūs*, Motion.

A وخوم *wakhūm*, (pl. وخام *wikhām*, وخامى *wakhāmā'*, and اوخام *awkhām*) A heavy, disagreeable man. Troubled with indigestion. An unhealthy country. *Wukhūm*, A suffering from indigestion.

A وخومة *wukhūmat*, (v. n. of وخم) Having an indigestion, or the stomach overloaded with meat. Being heavy and indigestible (meat). Indigestion.

A وخي *wakhy*, (v. n. of وخى) Intending, tending, going, or proceeding (right). Going neither fast nor slow. Studying (carefully). *Wakhy* or *wakha'*, (pl. وخيّ *wakhīy* or *wukhīy*) Aim, design, resolve. A journey. A traveller, a courier. The right way. Any road by which one goes.

A وخيد *wakhīd*, A quick manner of walking.

A وخيز *wakhīz*, A honey-cake.

A وخيض *wakhīz*, Pierced, wounded.

A وخيفة *wakhīfat*, Marshmallows beaten till they have become viscous.

A وخيم *wakhīm*, Heavy, unwholesome, noxious, hurtful, disastrous, injurious. (pl. وخام *wikhām*) A heavy, disagreeable man. (pl. اوخام *awkhām*) Pained with indigestion. وخيم و شوم *wakhīm u shūm*, Noxious and healthy.

A وخيمة *wakhīmat*, An unhealthy country.

P ود *wad*, A learned, wise friend. Warm, hot.

A ودّ *wadd*, (v. n. of ودّ) Loving, liking. Being desirous or delighting to do. One who loves to excess. A lover, friend. Lovers, friends. Love, friendship. (for وتد *watd*) A pile, pin, post, pole. Name of an Arabian idol. الودّ *al wadd*, Name of a mountain. بودّي ان تكون كذا *bi waddī an takūna kazā*, It is in my wish that it may happen. P مهر و محبّت و ودّ و الفت *mihr u mahabbat u widd u ulfat*, Love, friendship, benevolence, and intimacy; the most intimate union or regard. A *Widd*, A lover, friend. *Wudd*, (v. n. of ودّ) Loving, liking. Wishing to do (any thing). Love, friendship. A lover, a friend. Name of an Arabian idol.

A وداج *widāj*, The jugular vein in a horse.

A وداد *wa*, *wi*, or *wudād*, Love, friendship. وداد و اتّحاد *wadād u ittihād*, Love and unity.

A ودادة *wadādat*, Love, friendship.

A وداس *widās*, Herbage just beginning to cover the surface of the ground.

A وداع *wadāʻ* or *widāʻ*, Adieu, farewell. Any benediction pronounced on taking leave, parting. الوداع *al widāʻ*, Farewell. P وداع گفتن *widāʻ guftan*, To bid farewell.

A وداعة *wadāʻat*, (v. n. of ودع) Going on a journey. Being quiet, mild, placid. Quiet, bodily ease, comfortable circumstances. A deposit, trust.

P وداع نامه *widāʻ-nāma*, Farewell-letters.

A وداعيّ *widāʻīy*, Valedictory.

P وداغ *wadāgh*, Fire.

A وداف *wudāf*, The penis (because it occasionally drops, as in a gleet, &c.).

A وداق *wadāk*, (v. n. of ودق) Wanting the male (a mare or ass). *Widāk*, Heat, lust. Sharp (sword).

A ودان *widān*, (v. n. of ودن) Moistening, steeping, soaking. Paying great attention to (a bride).

A ودائع *wadāʼiʻ*, (pl. of وديع *wadīʻ*) Agreements, covenants. (pl. of وديعة *wadīʻat*) Deposits.

A ودب *wadb*, A bad state, an evil case.

A ودج *wadj*, (v. n. of ودج) Bleeding (a horse) in the neck. Adjusting any difference. *Wadaj*, (pl. اوداج *awdāj*) The jugular vein of a horse, where they generally let blood. Cause, occasion, means.

A ودجان *wadajāni*, (dual of ودج *wadaj*) The two jugular veins. Two brothers, peers, equals.

A ودحة *wadahat*, (or وتحة) Somewhat, aught.

P ودخين *wadhkhīn*, A long-necked animal, having teeth, but no eyes, which is said to be fond of living in salt and dirty water.

A ودداء *wudadāʼ*, (pl. of وديد) Friends, lovers.

A ودر *wadr*, The being drunk to insensibility.

A ودس *wads*, (v. n. of ودس) Being hid, concealed. Concealing. Going away. Beginning to look green with young herbage (ground). Beginning to address every one without completing. Grass beginning to cover the surface of the ground. ما احسن ودسها *mā ahsana wadsahā*, How beautiful its herbage!

A ودش *wadsh*, Depravity, mischief, ruin.

A ودص *wads*, (v. n. of ودص) Telling or talking in an indistinct, low, muttering voice.

A ودع *wadʻ*, (v. n. of ودع) Placing, depositing. Laying up, enwrapping (one garment within another). Leaving at liberty, permitting, allowing one to do what he pleases. Laying aside. Bidding adieu, taking leave. Abandoning. A grave, tomb, or enclosure round it. *Wadaʻ*, (pl. of ودعة *wadaʻat*) Shells, conchæ veneris. ذات الودع *zātu'l wadaʻ*, The ark of Noah. The temple of Mecca. An idol. *Wadʻ* or *wadaʻ*, The jerboa.

A ودعاء *wudaʻāʼ*, (pl. of وديع) Mild, meek.

A ودعة *wadʻat* or *wadaʻat*, (pl. ودعات *wadaʻāt*) A small white shell (hung round the necks of children and cattle as a defence against fascination).

A ودف *wadf*, (v. n. of ودف) Melting, falling in drops (fat). Pouring in drops. Giving little.

A ودفة *wadfat*, A meadow verdant with herbage. *Wadafat*, The clitoris. The shrub صليان *silliyān*. The flower نصيّ *nasiy*.

A ودق *wadk*, (v. n. of ودق) Dropping, distilling (as the heavens), falling (rain). Approaching, drawing near, and seizing. Being possible, in one's power. Finding repose. Being loose and purging (the belly). Being sharp (a sword). Swelling, being prominent (the navel). Being familiar, on intimate terms. Rain, especially incessant. Face, aspect, side. ذات ودقين *zātu wadkayn*, A misfortune attacking a man from two quarters. *Wadk* or *wadah*, Any kind of red speck on the eye. *Wadah*, (v. n. of ودق) Being affected by a red pimple (the eye). A pimple on the eye, ear, or other part of the body. *Wadak*, (or ودقان *wadakān*) (v. n. of ودق) Wanting the male (a mare or ass).

A ودقة *wadikat*, (An eye) red with the pimple ودق.

A ودك *wadak*, (v. n. of ودك) Being fat and greasy (the hand). The melted fat of meat, dripping. The interior fat. Name of the mother of Zahhāk. ودك الجفان *wadaku'l jifān*, Gumminess about the eyelids. ذو ودك *zū wadakin*, Corpulent (man). *Wadik*, Fat (meat).

A ودل *wadl*, The shaking of a bottle to churn.

A ودن *wadn*, (v. n. of ودن) Moistening, steeping, soaking. Paying great attention (to a spouse), making (her) comfortable. Shortening. Striking with a stick. Bringing forth a puny boy.

A ودناكسي *wadnāksī*, (or الودناكسي *al wadnāksī*) (in the dialect of Morocco) A white kind of fig extremely delicious.

A ودود *wadūd*, Loving, friendly, affectionate. Beloved. ودود و ولود *wadūd u walūd*, Affectionate and prolific (wife). الملك الودود *al maliku'l wadūd*, The loving King, *i.e.* God.

A ودوق *wadūk*, Libidinous (mare or ass). *Wudūk*, (v. n. of ودق) Approaching, drawing near. Being possible, feasible. Raining. Being sharp (a sword). Swelling. Being prominent (the navel).

A ودوك *wadūk*, A fat cock or hen.

A وده *wadh*, (v. n. of وده) Prohibiting, hindering, keeping back. *Wadah*, (v. n. of وده) Being hindered, desisting.

A ودهاء *wadhāʼ*, Fair, comely (woman).

A ودي *wady*, (v.n. of ودي) Paying a mulct or a compensation for manslaughter. Preparing to stale or cover (a horse). Voiding something after having made water. Giving access, causing to approach. Promoting, advancing. Whatever is voided after having made water. P ودي انداختن *wady andākhtan*, To unsheath or draw (as a stallion). A *Wadaʼ*, Death, destruction, murder.

A وديّ *wadiy*, Whatever is voided after having made water. A young palm-tree or shoot.

A وديّة *wadiyat*, One young palm-tree or shoot.

A وديد *wadīd*, (pl. وداء) A lover or friend.

A وديس *wadīs*, Dry, withering (plant).

A وديع *wadīʻ*, Quiet, placid, obedient, mild, meek, tame. Well-broke, manageable (horse). (pl. ودائع *wadāʼiʻ*) An agreement, covenant.

A وديعة *wadīʻat*, (pl. ودائع *wadāʼiʻ*) A deposit, trust, whatever is committed to another's charge. Rain (as the deposit of the clouds). Subjects (as committed to the charge of the king). P وديعت حيات سپردن *wadīʻati hayāt sipurdan*, To resign one's life, to die.

A وديفة *wadīfat*, A verdant mead.

A وديق *wadīk*, (A mare or ass) wanting the male.

A وديقة *wadīkat*, Intense heat. Lust. A place bearing pot-herbs and grass.

A وديك *wadīk*, A fat cock or hen.

A وديكة *wadīkat*, A fat hen. Flour moistened with dripping.

A ودين *wadīn*, Steeped, wetted, soaked.

A وذأ *wazʼ*, (v. n. of وذأ) Accusing, reproaching, treating opprobriously. Despising. Checking, chiding. Being dim (the eye). A disagreeable speech.

A وذاب *wizāb*, Paunch, stomach. The intestines, into which they pour milk, which curdles forthwith. The handles of a wallet.

A وذأة *wazʼat*, Casualty, calamity, disease.

A وذاة *wazāt*, Detriment; injurious thing.

A وذاح *wazāh*, A drab going after slaves.

A وذارة *wuzārat*, A bit of cloth cut from the middle of a larger.

A وذاع *wizāʻ*, (Water) flowing over the surface of the ground. Any thing flowing over a large smooth stone.

A وذاف *wuzāf*, Membrum virile.

A وذالة *wazālat*, A piece of meat, especially not cut out by a butcher in the common way.

A وذام *wizām*, Tripes with the intestines.

A وذائل *wazāʼil*, (pl. of وذيلة *wazīlat*) Pieces of polished silver. Mirrors, looking-glasses.

A وذائم *wazāʼim*, (pl. of وذيمة *wazīmat*) Offerings, especially of cattle sacrificed at Mecca.

A وذح *wazh*, (v. n. of وذح) Collecting and driving (cattle). *Wazah*, (v. n. of وذح) Having filth and sweat adhering to the fleece (a sheep). (pl. وذح *wuzh*) Sweat or grease adhering to the wool of sheep. A concretion of dung, urine, and sweat (adhering to the tails and groins of cattle). An excoriation or heating between the thighs.

A وذحة *wazahat*, A little sweat and dung adhering to a sheep's groin and tail. Somewhat, a little.

A وذر *wazr*, (v. n. of وذر) Cutting, wounding. Cutting (meat) in pieces. *Wazr* or *wazar*, (pl. of وذرة *wazrat* and *wazarat*) Pieces of meat without bones. Clitores. Glandes. Penes.

A وذرة *wazrat*, Clitoris. Glans penis. يا ابن شامّة الوذرة *yā ibna shāmmati'l wazrat*, O thou son of a whore! *Wazrat* or *wazarat*, A small piece of meat without bone, or a broad piece cut off; a rasher. *Wazirat*, Stinking (female). *Wazirat*, (or كثيرة الوذر *kasīratu'l wazr*, Thick-lipped (woman).

A الوذرتان *al wazratāni*, (dual) The two lips.

A وذع *wazʻ*, The running, flowing (of water).

A وذف *wazf*, The running (of melted fat).

A وذفان *wazfān*, One who makes haste. Near.

A وذفة *wazafat*, Clitoris.

A وذلة *wazalat* or *wazilat*, A woman; an old servant maid; one with small hips. *Wazilat*, Active (servant).

A وذم *wazam*, (v. n. of وذم) Having the rope وذمة *wazamat* broken (a bucket). The rope which runs between the ears or handles of a leathern bucket. A wart or excrescence. Excrescences, warts in the uterus of a camel, which prevent her breeding. Penis cum testiculis.

A وذماء *wazmāʼ*, Barren (woman).

A وذمة *wazamat*, The fat tripe, the intestines.

A وذواذ *wazwāz*, Quick, active in walking.

A وذوذة *wazwazat*, (v. n. of وذوذ Q) Passing along (a wolf). Haste, expedition.

A وذي *wazy*, A vestige, mark, scratch.

A وذية *wazyat*, Pain, disease. Defect, blemish. Little water. Cold weather. ما به وذية *mā bihi wazyat*, He is faultless.

A وذيلة *wazīlat*, (pl. وذيل *wazīl* and وذائل *wazāʼil*) A piece of polished silver. A looking-glass. A slice of fat from a camel's bunch or sheep's tail. An active, notable, and talkative maid-servant with small hips.

A وذيمة *wazīmat*, (pl. وذائم *wazāʼim*) An offering, especially of cattle, sacrificed at the temple of Mecca; the cattle so offered.

P ور *war* or *var*, A board upon which boys are taught to write. Heat. (for و اگر *wa agar*) And if. (for بر *bar*) On, upon. The breast, chest. When added to nouns, it implies possession: as, پيشور *peshavar*, An artificer, one possessing art. تاجور *tājwar*, Crowned. جانور *jānvar*, Having life: a living creature, animal, beast. رهور *rahwar*, Possessing the road, *i.e.* a traveller. سخنور *sukhanvar*, Having words, a speaker. هنرور *hunarvar*, Clever, skilful. But whenever an accumulation of consonants threatens, then, in order to lighten the word, the و *va* or *wa* is sounded *ū*; as in رنجور *ranjūr*, Sick; سمجور *sumjūr*, Houseless poor; گنجور *ganjūr*, A treasurer; مزدور *muzdūr*, A hireling, &c.

A ورّ *warr*, The hip-bone. The produce of a fruitful season.

A ورأ *warʼ*, (v. n. of ورأ) Driving off, repelling. Being filled with food.

P ورا *warā*, (for اورا *urā*) Him, to him.

A وراء *warāʼ*, What is behind or beyond; also what is before. A son's son; grandchildren, posterity. The latter part. After, behind. Beyond. Before. Besides, except. من وراء *min warāʼ*, Behind, on the hinder part. ما وراء النهر *mā warāʼu'n nahar*, The country beyond the river, *i.e.* Transoxiana, Tartary, or Tūrān beyond the Oxus. P در وراي پردهٔ خفا *dar warāyi pardaʻi khafā*, Behind the veil of secrecy. در وراي ظهر احباب *dar warāyi zahri ahbāb*, Behind friends' backs.

A وراثة *wirāsat*, (v. n. of ورث) Receiving by inheritance, inheriting. Heritage, hereditary right.

A وراد *wirād*, (pl. of ورد *ward*) Roses. Rosy.

A ورّاد *warrād*, A gardener. One who waters cattle. *Wurrād*, (pl. of وارد *wārid*) Those who water cattle.

A ورادة *warādat*, (v. n. of ورد) Being of a bay colour (a horse).

P ورا رود *warā rod*, (or ورا زود *warā zod*) Behind or beyond the river, Transoxiana, Turkistān.

P وراز *wurāz* or ورّاز *warrāz*, A large hog. A boar.

P وراستاد *warāstād* or *istād*, One's lot, portion from providence. Allowance of meat and clothing.

P وراستادن *war istādan*, To rise up or stand.

A وراشين *warāshīn*, (pl. of ورشان) Queests.

A وراط *wirāt*, (v. n. of ورط) Gathering together scattered camels, in order to be numbered by the tithing-man. Separating those which are in a body. Concealing one's camels in another's herd, or in another field, that the tithe-gatherer may not see them. Fraud, deceit. (pl. of ورطة *wartat*) Precipices, places of danger. Whirlpools.

A وراع *warāʻ*, (or وراعة *warāʻat*) (v. n. of ورع) Being timid, terrified. Being cautious, especially in doubtful points, afraid of doing any thing unlawful or sinful. Being moderate, pious, modest, temperate, continent. Being weak, small, slender.

P وراغ *warāgh*, Glow, light, flame of fire.

A ورّاف *warrāf*, Verdant, of a bright green.

A وراق *warāk*, The surface of the ground verdant with herbage. *Wirāk*, The season when trees come into leaf. (pl. of ورق *wark*) Stamped moneys.

A ورّاق *warrāk*, A writer, copyist, transcriber. A cutter of paper. A monied man.

A وراقة *wirākat*, The profession of a copyist or transcriber. The art of cutting out paper.

A وراقى *warākī* or *warākaʼ*, (pl. of ورقاء *warkāʼ*) She-wolves. Hen-pigeons.

A وراك *wirāk*, (pl. ورك *wurk* and *wuruk*) A cushion placed on the fore part of a camel's saddle and doubled under. The part of a camel-saddle on which the rider rests his foot; the cloth spread over it. An ornamented cloth for the fore part of a camel's saddle (called مورك *mawrik*). Embroidered work, with tufts of coloured wool, with which the part of the saddle where the hips rest is covered.

P ورام *warām*, Any deficiency of weight or measure for which a deduction is made. Light and easy. Name of a city in Persia.

P ورانبر *warāmbar*, On that or the other side.

A ورانية *warāniyat*, The anus, backside.

A ورايا *warāyaʼ*, The creatures of God.

P وراي پست و بلند *warāyi past u baland*, The invisible world.

A ورائد *warāʼid*, (pl. of وريد) Jugular veins.

A ورب *warb*, The den of a wild beast. (pl. أوراب *awrāb*) The mouth of the hole of a field-mouse or scorpion. The membrane between the ribs or fingers. The space between the index and thumb. An interpolation. A member, joint. Buttocks. Hips. *Wirb*, Industry, skill, ingenuity, art, cunning. *Warab*, (v. n. of ورب) Being corrupt and degenerate (stock). *Warib*, Corrupt. Loose or low-hanging (cloud).

A وربة *warbat*, A member. The fundament.

P وربند *war-band*, The poitrel of a horse.

P ورپوشنه *war-poshna*, (or ورپوشه *war-posha*) A woman's mantle or veil.

A ورّة *warrat*, Base and contemptible (woman). The hip-bone.

P ورت *wart* or *wurt*, Naked. *Warat*, (for ورتو *war tu* or و اگرتو *wa agar tu*) If thou.

P ورتا *wartā*, (in zand and Pāzand) A rose.

P ورتاج *wartāj*, Great. Mallows. The nenuphar; or a water-plant which turns its leaves always towards the sun. A fire-worshipper; a worshipper of the sun. A quail.

P ورتافتن *wartāftan*, To kick, tread on. To bend.

P ورتج *wartaj*, A quail.

P ورتيج *wartīj*, A quail. Threshold, sill.

A ورث *wars*, Any thing recent or fresh. *Wirs*, (v. n. of ورث) Receiving by inheritance, succeeding as heir.

A ورثة *warasat*, (pl. of وارث *wāris*) Heirs.

A ورثه *warsa*, A heritage.

P ورج *warj*, An area round a house. *Warj* or *wirj*, Greatness, largeness; grandeur, pomp. Worth, value. Office, dignity, charge, rank. Step, degree. Hard. A digging, rooting up. *Wiraj*, Galangale.

P ورجستگي *warjastagī*, A pustulous eruption.

P ورچه *warchi*, (for واگرچه) Although.

P ورخ *warkh*, Name of an herb used in diseases of the eye.

A ورخ *warkh*, A kind of tree. *Warakh*, Softness, thinness of leaven (from too much water).

P ورخاستن *warkhāstan*, To rise, stand up.

A ورخة *warikhat*, (Ground) covered with luxuriant herbage.

P ورخج *warakhj*, (or ورخچ *warakhch*) Impure, filthy, hideous, abominable, unsightly.

P ورخچي *warakhchī*, Foulness, ugliness.

P ورخش *warkhash*, Beginning of a work. Name of a city in the district of بلخ *balkh*.

P ورخوردن *warkhwurdan*, To see; meet, find.

A ورد *ward*, (pl. ورد *wurd*, وراد *wirād*, and اوراد *awrād*) A rose. A flower. Leaf of a flower, petal. Any flowering tree or shrub. Saffron. Brave, warlike. Rosy. A roan-coloured horse. A tawny lion. Name of one of the seven horses which Muhammad is said to have possessed. ورد الابيض *wardu'l abyaz*, White rose. Narcissus. P ورد چيني *wardi chīnī*, Rose of Jericho, or dog-rose. A ورد الحمار *wardu'l himār*, Ox-eye. ورد الحمير *wardu'l hamīr*, Piony, or ass-rose. ورد دفلي *wardi diflaʼ*, Rododaphne-rose. ورد الزينة *wardu'z zīnat*, Marsh-mallows. ورد مضاعف *wardi muzāʻaf*, The hundred-leaf rose. ابو الورد *abū'l ward*, (Father of the rose) Penis. *Wird*, Continual motion or employment, incessant labour, daily use, practice; a task. Approach, access (to water). Watering cattle; also the time and place. A halting-place, stage. A section of the Kur'ān. A quantity of water. Rosy. A legion, cohort, or detachment of an army. A body of men and cattle at a watering-place. A bevy of birds. Thirsty (persons). A fever, the day on which it begins. P ورد زبان *wirdi zabān*, Speaking perpetually, a fluency of speech. A *Wurd*, (pl. of ورد *ward*) Rosy. Roses.

P ورد *wird*, A disciple, pupil, apprentice.

P ورداشتن *war dāshtan*, To exalt.

P وردان *wardān*, A rolling-pin. An apartment open in front. *Wirdān*, A wart. (pl. of ورد *wird*) Pupils, apprentices.

A بنات وردان *banāt wardān*, Certain reptiles.

P وردانه *wardāna*, A rolling-pin. An axle-tree.

A وردة *wardat*, One rose. A single flower. Ruin, destruction. (fem. of ورد *ward*) Rosy, roseate. عشيّة وردة *ʻashiyat wardat*, A rosy-coloured evening-sky. *Wurdat*, A dun colour.

P وردك *wardak*, Paraphernalia of a bride, what a woman brings to her husband's house.

P وردنه *warduna*, A rolling-pin. An axle-tree.

P وردوك *wardūk*, The effects of a bride. *Wardūk*, (or وردوكه *wardūka*) A thatched house or hut.

P ورده *warda*, A pigeon living among rocks. A pigeon-house, especially a turret. A stick with which they force pigeons to take wing (on the flight of these birds they often lay great wagers).

A وردي *wardiy*, Rosy. A slave. وردية الشميم *wardiyatu'sh shamīm*, The odour or ottar of roses, of a rosy smell.

P ورديج *wardīj*, A quail.

A ورذ *warz*, A delaying, proceeding slowly.

P ورز *warz*, Gain, profit, acquisition. Custom, habit. Trade, art, craft. Art of tanning. Growing corn. A sown field. Agriculture. A field having a raised border round it. Minced meat. The river Oxus. Transoxiana. (in comp.) Gaining, acquiring; learning; accustomed to, conversant with. Sowing. آب ورز *āb-warz*, A swimmer. اخلاص ورزان *ikhlās-warzān*, Persons accustomed to sincerity.

P ورزاو *warzāv*, A ploughing-ox.

P ورزد *warzad*, He studies, he labours.

P ورزرود *warzrod*, The Oxus. Turkistān.

P ورزش *warzish*, Custom, habit, exercise, use, study, labour, exertion. Gain. Abstinence, sobriety.

P ورزكار *warz-kār*, A farmer, ploughman.

P ورزكن *warzkun*, A flagon of water.

P ورز گاو *warz-gāv*, An ox for ploughing.

P ورزگر *warzgar*, Workman: farmer, ploughman.

P ورزگن *warzagan*, A pitcher full of water.

P ورزم *warazm*, Fire.

P ورزة *warza*, Acquiring, accomplishing. Agriculture. Art, trade, profession. A cultivator.

P ورزي *warzī*, A tiller of the land, labourer.

P ورزيدن *warzīdan*, To sow a field. To accustom one's self, to acquire and cultivate a habit. To boast, glory. To labour, endeavour, study. To acquire, gain. To be a faithful observer of religious duties. To blow. To ply. To exercise, perform, practise. انحراف ورزيدن *inhirāf warzīdan*, To decline, avoid, turn away. To swerve, deviate, deflect. To rebel, revolt. تغافل ورزيدن *taghāful warzīdan*, To be negligent, inattentive. سكونت ورزيدن *sukūnat warzīdan*, To take up one's residence. كينه ورزيدن *kīna warzīdan*, To cherish hatred.

P ورزيدة *warzīda*, Sown. Assiduous, industrious, laborious. Very experienced. Any thing which has been very much handled, and thereby become smooth (as leather).

P ورژ *waraj*, Galangale, or sweet cane.

P ورس *wars* or *waras*, A blacksmith's or farrier's twitch. A bit of wood put through a camel's nose. Rope-fetters. A thread. *Wurs*, The wild cypress.

A ورس *wars*, Saffron. A plant resembling sesame, peculiar to Arabia Felix, of which they make غمرة *ghumrat*, a kind of yellow wash for the face, used by the Arabian ladies, and also by the men. *Waras*, (v. n. of ورس) Being covered with a green smooth moss (a rock in water).

P ورسا *warsā*, A starling or stare.

P ورساخيدن *warsākhīdan*, To lick.

P ورساز *warsāz*, Ingenious, clever, acute. Graceful, neat, elegant. A performer on a musical instrument. Name of a place and of a country.

P ورستاد *warastād*, A stipend, a pension.

P ورستان *warastān* or *waristān*, The disciples or followers of a prophet or saint.

P ورسن *warsan*, Fetters. A rope, a cord.

P ورسنگ *warsang*, Strange, wonderful, curious; respectable, worthy of consideration. Esteem, honour, reverence, respect. A makeweight.

A ورسيّ *warsiy*, A species of yellowish red pigeon. An excellent kind of wood for making arrows. (See نضار *nuzār*.)

P ورسيج *warsīj*, Ceiling, roof. Floor: threshold.

A ورش *warsh*, A dish made with milk. *Warash*, (v. n. of ورش) Being brisk, nimble, and sprightly (a camel). Cholic, gripes. *Warish*, (A camel) brisk, cheerful, nimble, sprightly, eager to run.

P ورش *warash*, A turtle-dove, wood-pigeon.

P ورشاد *warashād*, A stipend, pension.

A ورشان *warashān*, (pl. ورشان *wirshān* and واراشين *warāshīn*) A turtle-dove, wood-pigeon.

A ورشة *warishat*, Swift, eager (she-camel).

P ورشتن *warashtan*, To wash.

P ورشك *warshak*, A bit of cloth, or little bag in which they put medicine and drugs.

P ورشنان *warashnān*, The disciples or followers of any prophet.

P ورشيم *warshīm*, Sort; division, part, section.

A ورص *wars*, The laying of an egg at once.

A ورض *warz*, (v. n. of ورض) Laying an egg at once, without difficulty (a hen). Voiding soft dung by a single effort.

A ورطة *wartat*, (pl. وراط *wirāt*) A precipice, labyrinth: any danger or difficulty in which one is embarrassed. A whirlpool. A clay-marsh, in which an animal sinks and cannot get out. Destruction, ruin. Any thing low, hollow, depressed. The anus. A well. Any thing frightful or dangerous, whence one can hardly escape. A level and pathless country. ورطهٔ هلاكت *wartaï halākat*, The gulf of perdition. A fatal precipice.

P ورطوري *wartūrī*, Name of a mountain-plant with many medicinal qualities. Wild leek.

A ورع *wareʿ* or *waraʿ*, (v. n. of ورع) Being timid, cautious. Refraining from any thing doubtful (in religious points), being scrupulous and apprehensive of doing wrong. Being modest, pious, chaste, and temperate. *Wurʿ* or *wuruʿ*, (v. n. of ورع) Being small, slender, and weak. *Waraʿ*, Timidity, cowardice. Abstinence from any thing doubtful. The fear of God. Temperance, chastity. (pl. اوراع *awrāʿ*) Small, slender. Weak, deficient. *Wariʿ*, Timid, scrupulous. One who fears God. Cautious, chaste. Small, slender, weak, deficient.

A ورعة *wareʿat* or *wurʿat*, (v. n. of ورع) Being timid, afraid, cautious, especially in doubtful points, fearing to do any thing unlawful or sinful. Being moderate, pious, modest, temperate, continent. Being weak, small, slender.

P ورغ *wargh* or *warigh*, A mound, a dam, or weir for confining water. A ditch. A weasel. Light, splendour. *Wurugh*, Darkness, obscurity. Agitation, mental distress, chagrin.

P ورغا *warghā*, (or ورغارة) An indolent swelling.

P ورغست *warghast*, Name of a plant resembling spinage growing on the banks of rivers.

P ورغشت *warghasht*, Clear, open. A sort of herb.

P ورغلانيدگي *war ghalānīdagī*, Incitement, instigation. Seduction.

P ورغلانيدن *warghalānīdan*, To seduce, invite, debauch. To join. To desire. To prevail.

P ورغن *warghan*, An indolent swelling. Any round protuberance on the body.

A ورف *warf*, (v. n. of ورف) Being broad, long, and extensive (a shadow). Being fresh and verdant (a plant). The extremes or edges of the liver.

P ورّفان *warrafān*, An intercessor, mediator.

A ورق *wark*, (v. n. of ورق) Stripping (a tree) of its leaves. Coming into leaf (a tree). *Wark*, *wirk*, *wurk*, *warak*, or *warik*, (pl. اوراق *awrāk* and وراق *wirāk*) Coin, stampt money. *Wurk*, (pl. of اورق *awrak*) Years without rain. *Warak*, A leaf of a tree or of paper. Paper cut out into any shape. Blood dropping from a wound, making a round or leafy figure on the ground. A card. A slice. The sail of a ship. Young men in the bloom of youth or prime of life. A living creature. The beauty or pleasantness of the world. Weak men (falling like the leaves). Pus dropping from a wound. Any thing trodden or broken under the feet of animals. Wealth in money or camels. P ورق آفتاب *waraki āftāb*, The cheek of a mistress. ورق باد *waraki bād*, The tongue. A ورق التوت *waraku't tūt*, Mulberry-leaf. ورق الخيال *waraku'l khayāl*, Name of an intoxicating drug (cannabis sativus). P ورق گردانيدن *warak gardānīdan*, To change (love for hatred, or the contrary). A *Warik*, Leafy. Vile, avaricious, low, sordid.

A ورقاء *warkāa*, Brown, tawny, dusky-coloured (she-wolf or pigeon). (pl. وراقي *warāka'* and *warākī*) A she-wolf. A female pigeon.

A ورقاويّ *warkāwiy*, Of a dusky colour.

A ورقة *warkat*, A blemish in a bow from the knot by which it was united to the branch. Vile, avaricious. Liberal (woman). *Wurkat*, A blackish colour inclining to white. *Warakat*, One leaf. A letter, billet, schedule, paper. Vile, avaricious. Noble, generous. ورقهٔ وداد *warakaï widād*, Friendly letters. حامل ورقت *hāmili warakat*, The bearer of these presents. *Warikat*, Low, sordid (woman).

P ورق داغي *warak-dāghī*, Written paper.

P ورق نيل *warak-nīl*, A plant, of which women make a decoction for dyeing the eyebrows black.

P ورقة *warka*, The lover of گل شاه *gul-shāh*.

A ورقي *warake*, A single leaf.

A ورك *wark*, (v. n. of ورك) Placing (any thing) near the haunch or hip. Resting, reclining on one's haunch. *Wark*, *wirk*, or *warik*, (pl. اوراك *awrāk*) The hip or haunch-bone. Buttocks, haunches. The knotty part of a branch. *Wark* or *warik*, A crowd, collected company. *Wirk*, The side of a bow, the part along which the string goes. A bow made of the lower part of a tree. *Wurk* or *wuruk*, (pl. of وراك *wirāk*) Ornamental cloths for that part of a saddle where the hip rests. *Warak*, The hip-bone. The lower part of a branch.

P ورك *warak*, A thorn used for heating ovens.

P وركا *warkā*, A falcon. A kind of pigeon.

A وركاء *warkāa*, (fem. of اورك *awrak*) Large-hipped (woman). Name of Abraham's birth-place.

P وركار *warkār*, Busy, occupied. Every kind of fruit not produced from a tree, as melons, cucumbers, gourds, &c.

P وركاك *warkāk*, A rapacious bird of the kite-species (in Arabic called صرد *surad*).

P وركالوج *warkālūj*, A broken finger.

P وركانة *warkānat*, Large-hipped (woman).

P وركتا *warkatā*, (in zand and Pāzand) A bone.

P وركردن *war kardan*, (for بركردن *bar kardan*) To extol, exalt, raise high. To pull up, tear out, extirpate. To throw away. To prop, support. To burn, set fire to.

P وركرده *war karda*, Kindled, set on fire.

P وركك *warkak*, A falcon which eats carrion.

P وركوه *warkoh*, Name of a city in Irāk.

A وركي *warka'* or *wirka'*, Root, origin, stock.

P وركا *wargā*, A black grain growing in corn.

P وركار *wargār*, Fruits produced twice a year.

P وركاه *wargāh*, A kind of hawk. A ditch, pool, or marsh. A stove in a bath.

P وركشتن *wargashtan*, To subvert. To be ruined.

P وركو *wargo*, Speak thou. Name of a city.

P وركوش *wargosh*, (or وركوشي *wargoshī*) An ear-ring with a long drop. Lobe of the ear.

P وركه *wargah*, A beam, joist, rafter.

A ورل *waral*, (pl. ورلان *wirlān*, اورال *awrāl*, and ارول *arwul*) An animal of the lizard-kind, with a broad head, a rough skin of a reddish yellow, swift of foot, with envenomed teeth, and a sting-tail.

P ورل ماهي *waral-māhī*, A newt, eft, asker.

P ورم *waram*, (for واكرمن *wa agar man*) And if I.

A ورم *waram*, (v. n. of ورم) Swelling, becoming inflated (the skin). Shooting, growing high (a plant). Being angry, enraged, being distended with rage (the nose). (pl. اورام *awrām*) A tumour, swelling, imposthume.

P ورمال كردن *warmāl kardan*, (or ورمال زدن *warmāl zadan*) To run away in terror.

P ورماليدن *warmālīdan*, To tuck up the skirt and sleeves of one's garment. To run away.

P ورماندگي *warmāndagī*, Colic from indigestion or repletion.

P ورمن *warman*, (in zand and Pāzand) He.

P ورنا *warnā* or *wurnā*, A youth. Good, fair. A turtle-dove, blue-coloured pigeon. Wheat.

P ورناس *wurnās*, Careless, indolent, senseless.

P ورنام *warnām*, A surname. ورنام نهادن *warnām nihādan*, To surname.

P ورنامه *warnāma*, Superscription of a letter.

P ورنان *warnān*, Useful, advantageous. A mediator.

A ورنة *warnat*, Name of the month ذو القعدة.

A ورنتل *warantal*, A calamity. *Warantal*, (or ورنتلي *warantala'*) An important affair.

P ورنج *waranj*, Greedy, gluttonous, avaricious.

P ورنجن *waranjan*, (or ورنجين *waranjīn*) A ring of gold or of silver worn by women on their wrists and ankles: a bracelet or anklet.

P ورنجه *waranja*, Name of a famous general.

P ورند *warand*, A spider and its web.

P ورنداز *warandāz*, Sketching or doing any thing roughly. Taking the measure of garments.

P ورنشستن *war nishastan*, To mount on horseback, or in a carriage. To embark on board-ship.

P ورنگ *warang*, A patch. A darning.

P ورنه *war na*, And if not, otherwise.

P وروار *warwār*, (also ورواره) A royal seat or throne. An open gallery or balcony on a house-top.

A ورواقي *warwākiy*, Dusky coloured.

A ورود *wurūd*, (v. n. of ورد) Being present, appearing, entering, descending, alighting, approaching (to drink). Attacking (as a fever). Approach, entrance, descent, arrival. A watering. (pl. of وريد *warīd*) The jugular veins on each side of the neck.

A ورودة *wurūdat*, (v. n. of ورد) Being bay-coloured (a horse).

A ورور *warwar*, The bee-eater (a bird).

A ورورة *warwarat*, (v. n. of ورور Q) Sharpening (the sight), looking keenly. Talking rapidly.

P وروره *warwara*, Pontic mouse. Squirrel.

A وروري *warwariy*, Weak-sighted.

A وروش *wurūsh*, (v. n. of ورش) Taking, devouring (food). Being greedy. Going uninvited to a feast. Instigating, setting against. Attending to the details and minutiæ of a thing.

A وروع *warūʿ* or *wurūʿ*, (v. n. of ورع) Being timid, terrified, cautious, especially in doubtful points, fearing to do any thing unlawful or sinful. Being moderate, pious, modest, temperate, continent. *Wurūʿ*, (v. n. of ورع) Being weak, small, slender.

P وروغ *wurogh*, Eructation. Darkness. Trouble.

A وروف *wurūf*, (v. n. of ورف) Being long and broad (a shadow).

A وروك *wurūk*, (v. n. of ورك) Lying on the side, the hip touching the ground. Striking on the hip. Resting his chin on the hip of the female (a male ass). Remaining, staying, dwelling. Turning the hip (ورك *warak*) when going to dismount. Being equal to any business, succeeding.

A وره *warah*, (v. n. of وره) Being foolish, stupid. Blowing violently (wind). Being fat (a woman). Awkwardness; a want of skill. Folly, stupidity. Insolence.

A ورهاء *warhāʾ*, Silly, foolish (woman). Violent, whiffling, and unsteady (wind). *Warhāʾ*, (or ورهة *warihat*) (A cloud) full of rain.

A ورهة *warihat*, Fat (woman).

A ورهرهة *warahrahat*, Foolish, stupid (woman).

P ورهم *warham*, Harsh words.

P ورهمين *warhamīn*, (or ورهين *warhīn*) Hard bread; bread baked of wheat and barley.

A وري *wary*, (v. n. of وري) Corrupting, eating away (the inside of the body). Hurting (any one) in the lungs. Emitting sparks of fire (the stick زند *zand*). Being kindled (a fire). Being plentiful and thick (marrow) in a bone. Being lodged within the skin (matter). Being fat. Fat meat. Pus, corrupted matter in the body. A large ulcer full of, or running with, matter. *Wara'*, A disease on the lungs. Men, mortals. ما ادري ايّ الوري هو *mā adrī ayyu'l wara' huwa*, I do not know who (or what kind of a man) he is.

A وريّ *wariy*, A stick (زند *zand*) which emits sparks. Fat, fleshy. *Wuriy*, (v. n. of وري) Emitting sparks of fire (the stick زند *zand*).

P وريا *waryā*, A large iron hammer.

P وريب *warīb*, Any thing preponderating, as the load on one side of a horse. Part of any thing, especially prominent or projecting. *Wurīb* or *wirīb*, Crooked, curved.

A وريّة *waryat*, Tinder. Touchwood.

A وريّة *wariyat*, (fem. of وريّ *wariy*) Fat.

A وريخة *warīkhat*, Moist or watered ground. Leaven rendered thin or soft.

A وريد *warīd*, (and حبل الوريد *hablu'l warīd*) (dual وريدان *warīdāni*, pl. اوردة *awridat*, ورود *wurūd*, and وارئد *warāʾid*) The jugular vein on either side of the neck.

P ويريز *wirīz*, A particular gum. Cassia.

A وريزة *warīzat*, A vein reaching from the stomach to the liver.

A وريس *warīs*, Dyed with the plant ورس *wars*.

P وريستاد *warīstād*, A foot, footstep.

A وريع *warīʿ*, Abstinent, abstemious, chaste.

A وريعة *warīʿat*, Name of a horse.

A وريف *warīf*, (v. n. of ورف) Being long, broad, and widely extended (a shadow). Being fresh and green (a plant). A quick pace. Spacious (country).

A وريق *warīk*, Leafy. *Wurayk*, (dim. of اورق *awrak*) Somewhat of a dusky colour.

A وريقة *warīkat*, (fem. of وريق) Leafy (tree).

A وريهة *warīhat*, Fat (woman).

A وريّئة *wurayyiʾat*, (dim. of وراء *warāʾ*) A little before or behind. A little beyond.

P وز *waz*, (for واز *wa az*) Again. From hence.

A وزّ *wazz*, A goose.

A وزأ *wazʾ*, (v. n. of وزأ) Drying (flesh). Repelling one another. *Wazaʾ*, (v. n. of وزئ) Being firm and robust.

A وزّاب *wazzāb*, Cunning, crafty (thief).

A وزارة *wizārat* or *wazārat*, The dignity of vazīr, minister, or privy counsellor, vizierate, premiership. وزارت عظمي *wizārati ʿuzma'*, The office of prime-minister or grand vazīr.

A وزاغ *wizāgh*, (pl. of وزغة) Lizards. Frogs.

A وزام *wizām*, Velocity.

A وزّام *wazzām*, Fleshy, muscular.

P وزان *wazān*, Blowing (wind). باد وزان آسا *bādi wazān-āsā*, Like a violent wind.

A وزان *wizān*, Opposite, over against.

A وزّان *wazzān*, One who weighs, a weigher.

A وزانة *wazānat*, Prudence, sagacity.

A وزاوزة *wazāwizat*, Light, volatile, inconstant (man). One who wags his hips when walking.

A وزر *wazr*, (v. n. of وزر) Filling up (a gap). Conquering. (in the passive form) Being oppressed with guilt. *Wazr* or *wizr*, (v. n. of وزر) Bearing (a burden), supporting, sustaining. Committing a crime, sinning. *Wizr*, (pl. اوزار *awzār*) A burden, load: any thing heavy or oppressive. Weight, heaviness. A crime, sin, fault. Arms, especially what one carries. A large bundle of clothes: a bale, a pack. *Wazar*, A mountain or any place of refuge, an asylum. A fortification.

A وزراء *wuzarāʼ*, (pl. of وزير *wazīr*) Vazīrs, privy counsellors, ministers of state. وزرائ عظام ذوي الاحترام و وكلائ فخام عاليمقام *wuzarāʼi ʻizāmi zawi'l iḥtirām, wa wukalāʼi fikhāmi ʻālī-maḥām*, Illustrious vazīrs endowed with honour, and magnificent vicegerents of exalted dignity (titles given to ministers of state).

P وزرانتن *wazrānitan*, (in zand and Pāz.) To go.

P وزرگ *wuzurg*, (for بزرگ *buzurg*) Great, large.

P وزش *wazish*, The blowing of the wind.

A وزع *wazʻ*, (v. n. of وزع) Restraining, checking, prohibiting. Bringing (soldiers) together, allowing the front to mix with the rear.

A وزعة *wazaʻat*, (pl. of وازع *wāziʻ*) Governors, prefects. Captains, generals. Guards, those whose duty it is to keep people off, and to prevent confusion.

P وزغ *wazagh*, A frog. A species of lizard, which lives upon scorpions and is poisonous.

A وزغ *wazagh*, A shaking, a tremor. A vicious, worthless fellow. Sick, prostrate by disease. (pl. of وزغة *wazaghat*) White lizards.

A وزغان *wizghān*, (pl. of وزغة *wazaghat*) Lizards.

A وزغة *wazaghat*, (pl. وزغ *wazagh*, اوزاغ *awzāgh*, وزغان *wizghān*, وزغ *wizagh*, and ازغان *izghān*) A kind of lizard called سامّ ابرص *sāmm abras*.

P وزغشت *wazghasht*, Name of an herb.

A وزف *wazf*, (v. n. of وزف) Urging or ordering to make haste. Making haste.

P وزق *wazak*, A frog. Galangale, sweet cane.

A وزك *wazk*, (v. n. of وزك) Making haste, or walking badly (a woman). Being languid in coitu.

P وزك *wazak*, A frog. A lizard. A towel. A particular tree which bears no fruit, of which it is said, that, if a man happens to swallow a leech, if he drinks some of the expressed juice of its leaves the animal will immediately be thrown up again.

A وزم *wazm*, (v. n. of وزم) Paying one's debts. Eating only once a day. Adding a little to a little. Breaking the edge (of a sword or earthen vessel). A bunch of pot-herbs. Quantity. Whatever is done or happens seasonably. Flesh carried by an eagle to her nest.

A وزمة *wazmat*, (v. n. of وزم) Losing part of one's property. Lying on one's face in eating. Quantity.

P وزمه *wazma*, Winter. وزمه باد *wazma-bād*, A wind which begins to blow about the end of winter.

A وزن *wazn*, (v. n. of وزن) Weighing exactly. Adjusting. Weighing out (to any one) money, telling (it) by just weight. Examining. Making (verses) according to just measure. Guessing by the eye the produce of a palm-tree. Paying (tribute). Applying (the mind to any thing), and habituating one's self (to it). (pl. اوزان *awzān*) Weight, measure. Metre, poetic measure. A shekel. A weight of a مثقال *miskāl*. Reflux of the sea. Reputation, esteem, honour. Examination. Proper mode, just proportion. (pl. وزون *wuzūn*) A large measure of dates, such as can hardly be lifted from the ground. (Money) of just weight. Opposite, over against. الوزن *al wazn*, Name of a star which rises before Canopus. راجح الوزن *rājiḥu'l wazn*, Extremely intelligent. وزن سبعة *waznu sabʻatin*, The weight of seven (a title or name). *Wazna*, Opposite, over against.

P وزن *wazan*, One who goes friskingly, briskly, cheerfully. *Wizan*, A tree of which bows are made.

A وزنة *waznat*, A weight. A talent, a shekel. Short and intelligent (woman). *Wiznat*, A certain measure, or mode of weighing.

P وزندار *wazn-dār*, (Money) of just weight.

P وزنگ *wazang*, A little bit of cloth, patch.

A وزني *waznī*, Heavy, weighty.

A وزواز *wazwāz*, Volatile, light, inconstant (man). Nimble, active. One who walks with a peculiar motion of the hips. Short in body. Name of a bird.

A وزوب *wuzūb*, The flowing of water.

A وزوز *wazwaz*, Death. A broad plank upon which they hurl earth from high to low grounds.

A وزوزة *wazwazat*, (v. n. of وزوز Q) Moving the hips in a peculiar manner when walking. Going with short steps and a peculiar motion like a dwarf. Springing or leaping upon, attacking. Lightness, celerity, alacrity.

A وزوع *wazūʻ*, (v. n. of وزع) Restraining, checking, prohibiting. Exciting, urging. Inspiring.

A وزون *wuzūn*, (pl. of وزن *wazn*) Large measures of dates, as can scarcely be lifted from the ground.

A وزي *wazy*, (v. n. of وزي) Being assembled. *Wazaʼ*, A short-bodied man, dwarf. A strong ass.

P وزيدن *wazīdan*, To blow as the wind. To grow (as herbage or hair).

P وزيدنگاه *wazīdan-gāh*, Airy site, windy place.

P وزير *wazer*, Turmeric.

A وزير *wazīr*, (pl. اوزار *awzār* and وزراء *wuzarāʼ*) A vizier, counsellor of state, minister, vicegerent, or lieutenant of a king (as bearing the weight of government). A helper, assistant. A porter. An eater. وزيراعظم *wazīri aʻzam*, The grand vizier, prime-minister. P وزيرچپ *wazīri chap*, An officer of government.

P وزيري *wazīrī*, A kind of fig.

A وزيري *wazīrī*, The office of minister of state, vizierate, viziership, premiership. P وزيري نمودن *wazīrī namūdan*, To discharge the office of vazir.

A وزيف *wazīf*, (v. n. of وزف) Making haste, travelling fast. A quick pace.

A وزيم *wazīm*, A bunch of pot-herbs. Quantity, proportion. A date-bud wrapt round with a palm-leaf, which improves the quality. Remainder of broth, or any thing similar. Roast meat. Corpulent, fleshy, firm-bodied (man). *Wazīm*, (or وزيمة *wazīmat*) Meat dried, bruised, and eaten with any thing fat (especially flesh of crocodiles and locusts).

A وزيمة *wazīmat*, A bundle of pot-herbs.

A وزين *wazīn*, Weighty, ponderous. An accurate weigher. A ground or bruised colocynth. وزين الرأي *wazīnu'r raʼy*, Prudent, sagacious.

A وزّين *wazzīn*, A goose.

P وژ *waj*, Anger, indignation, rage. Malice, malignity. The herb galangale.

P وژخ *wajkh*, Galangale, sweet cane. A span.

P وژده *wajda*, Any thing poured out.

P وژن *wajan*, Density, grossness.

P وژنگ *wajang*, A fringe, edging. A little piece of cloth, patch. *Wujang*, A thin kind of bark of a liver-colour bound round that end of an arrow to which the point is made fast. Fringe, edge, ornament sewed to the border of a garment. A patch.

P وژنين *wajnīn*, Watery camel's milk.

P وژول *wujūl*, Taste and relish of savoury food or soup. Broth, soup. The shin-bone of a sheep, ankle-bone. Noise, uproar, tumult. Violence. Climate, country.

P وژولنده *wujūlanda*, One who excites to mutiny or rebellion; a promoter of war and discord.

P وژوليدن *wujūlīdan*, To entice, instigate, seduce. To excite, to promote quarrels and disputes. To quench thirst. To blow (as the wind).

P وژوه *wajūh*, Dropping of rain from eaves.

P وژه *waja*, A span.

P وژيدن *wajīdan*, To measure with a span.

P وس *was*, Enough, sufficient. Much. How.

A وسّ *wass*, A substitute.

A وسّاج *wassāj*, (in comp. with عسّاج *ʻassāj*) (as وسّاج عسّاج *wassāj ʻassāj*) Quick-going (camel).

A وساد *wisād*, (*wasād*, *wusād*, and وسادة *wisādat*) (pl. وسد *wusud* and وسائد *wasāʼid*) A cushion, pillow, couch, or day-bed. A throne. وسادك لعريض *wisāduka la ʻarīzun*, Your pillow is very broad (implying, you are much addicted to sleep), or your head is very large (indicating stupidity).

A وساطة *wasātat*, Mediation, arbitration. Medium. Mediocrity in point of quality.

A وساع *wasāʻ*, An excellent horse, that goes fast, with long steps. Quick, active in doing any thing. Noble, honourable. *Wisāʻ*, (pl. of وسيع *wasīʻ*) Wide, roomy, ample, spacious.

A وسّاع *wassāʻ*, Wide-stepping (camel).

A وساعة *wasāʻat*, (v. n. of وسع) Going with a wide step, or with a cubit's space between each. Being of a generous breed.

A وساق *wisāk*, (pl. of واسق) (Camels) in foal.

A وسالة *wasālat*, Channel, medium, means.

A وسام *wasām*, (v. n. of وسم) Being beautiful, handsome, elegant. *Wisām*, A mark with which cattle are branded. (pl. of وسيم *wasīm* and وسيمة *wasīmat*) Handsome-faced (men or women).

A وسامة *wasāmat*, (v. n. of وسم) Being beautiful, elegant, handsome. Beauty.

A وساوس *wasāwis*, (pl. of وسوسة *waswasat*) Suggestions. Temptations. وساوس شيطان *wasāwisi shaytān*, The temptations of the devil.

A وسائد *wasāïd*, (pl. of وساد) Cushions, pillows.

A وسائط *wasāïṭ*, (pl. of وسيطة *wasīṭat*) Means, intermediate links.

A وسائل *wasāïl*, (pl. of وسيلة) Causes, means.

A وسب *wasb*, (v. n. of وسب) Being grassy, abounding in herbage (ground). (pl. وسوب *wusūb*) A piece of wood which they put over the bottom of a well to prevent the sand from moving about. *Wisb*, Plants, herbs. *Wasab*, (v. n. of وسب) Being dirty and filthy. Dirt, filth.

P وستا *wastā*, Fire. A commentary on the zand or the book of Zoroaster. Praising, glorifying God.

P وستازند *wastāzand*, A title of the Zand.

P وستان *wastān*, Sleeping on the back. One who sleeps on his back.

P وسترك *wastrak*, (*wastark*, or وسترنگ *wastrang*) The red button of a rose, which remains after the leaves have dropt off. Marshmallows.

P وستي *wastī*, Translation, explanation.

A وسخ *wasakh*, (v. n. of وسخ) Being dirty (a garment). (pl. اوساخ *awsākh*) Dirt, nastiness. Earwax. وسخ الكوارير *wasakhu'l kawārīr*, Bees-wax. *Wasikh*, Dirty, nasty.

A وسد *wusud*, (pl. of وساد) Pillows, cushions.

P وسّد *wussad*, Coral.

A وسط *wasṭ*, (v. n. of وسط) Sitting amongst many people, penetrating into the middle of a crowd. وسط القوم *wasṭa'l kawm*, (He sat) in the midst of the people. *Wasaṭ*, (pl. اوساط *awsāṭ*) Middle, centre. The waist. Centrical. Any thing of a middling sort, neither elegant nor ugly. Right, just, proper, suitable. Just, equitable. Exquisite, excellent. Magnificent, opulent. وسط السماء *wasaṭu's samāʼ*, The ecliptic. في الوسط *fi'l wasaṭ*, In the middle. في وسط الشتاء *fī wasaṭi'sh shitāʼ*, In mid-winter.

A وسطى *wusṭa'*, Middle (finger). Middling, neither long nor short (speech). The middle one of the five daily prayers appointed by the Muhammadan law. الاصبع الوسطى *al iṣbaʻu'l wusṭa'*, The middle finger. الصلوة الوسطى *as salātu'l wusṭa'*, The mid-day prayer.

A وسع *wasʻ*, *wisʻ*, or *wusʻ*, Power, ability. Opportunity, ease, conveniency of doing. Opulence. Capacity, capability of holding. Eloquence.

A وسعة *wusʻat*, Latitude, amplitude, spaciousness, space. Convenience, opportunity, ease, leisure.

A وسف *wasf*, A crack appearing in the thighs and buttocks of a camel when growing fat, which afterwards becomes general in him.

P وسفاد *wisfād*, Much, many.

A وسق *wasḳ*, (v. n. of وسق) Gathering together, heaping up, collecting (as tears in the eyes). (Night) involving (in darkness). (Robbers) driving together or driving off (camels) in the night. Conceiving, becoming pregnant, having the matrix closed. *Wasḳ* or *wisḳ*, (pl. وسوق *wusūḳ* or اوسق *awsuḳ*) A load of corn weighing 60 صاع *ṣāʻ*. A camel-load. A freight.

P وسكرده *washarda* or *wisharda*, Active, expert, industrious; one who does any thing speedily. Powerful, strong.

A وسم *wasm*, (v. n. of وسم) Marking with a hot iron, branding (man or beast). Describing, delineating. Excelling in beauty. (pl. وسوم *wusūm*) The mark left by a hot iron. Sign, mark, brand. A name. P وسم دادن *wasm dādan*, To brand, mark.

A وسماء *wusamāʼ*, (pl. of وسيم *wasīm*) Handsome, comely, beautiful.

A وسمة *wasmat*, (*wasimat*, or P وسمه *wasma*) Leaves of woad or indigo-plant; also their juice. Indigo, with which they paint the skin or dye cloth.

P وسمه پوش *wasma-posh*, Dressed in clothes stained or dyed with وسمه *wasma*.

P وسمه دار *wasma-dār*, Stained with وسمه *wasma*.

A وسميّ *wasmīy*, Spring-rain. Spring-grass.

P وسن *wasan*, Dirty, filthy. Filth, defilement.

A وسن *wasan*, (v. n. of وسن) Slumbering, beginning to sleep. Fainting from the putrid exhalation of a well. Slumber, sleep. Drowsiness. A nap, snooze. (pl. اوسان *awsān*) Need, want. ما له همّ و لا وسن الّا ذا *mā lahu hammun wa lā wasanun illā zā*, He has no business or care, but this alone. *Wasin*, Drowsy. Indisposed from the noisome exhalation of a well.

P وسناد *wasnād*, Many. Full, abundant.

A وسنان *wasnān*, Sleepy, slumbering, dozing.

A وسنة *wasnat* or *wasanat*, Sleep. Slumber, drowsiness. *Wasinat*, Drowsy (woman).

P وسنگ *wasang*, Name of a plant or herb growing in rocky places and fragrant as a lemon.

A وسنیٰ *wasna'*, Idle, sluggish, drowsy (woman).

P وسني *wasnī* or *wusnī*, Two women married to one husband: a rival wife.

P وسو *wusū*, Leaning upon, supporting one's self. The circumference of the mouth.

A وسواس *waswās*, Any thing suggested to the mind. An evil inspiration. A low voice or sound (of hunters or dogs). The rattling of a necklace, jingle of ear-rings, or any thing similar; the rustling of silk. The noise of a tree moved by the wind. الوسواس *al waswās*, Satan, the tempter. *Wiswās*, (v. n. of وسوس Q) Suggesting, hinting (one's own thoughts or the devil). A diabolical suggestion, black inspiration; temptation of the devil.

A وسواسي *waswāsī*, Doubtful, distracting. Apprehensive.

A وسواسيّ *waswāsīy*, Melancholy, morbid.

A وسوب *wusūb*, (pl. of وسب *wasb*) Pieces of wood put over the bottom of a well to keep the sand from moving about.

A وسوج *wasūj*, (with عسوج *ʻasūj*) (as وسوج عسوج *wasūj ʻasūj*) Quick-going (camels).

A وسوسة *waswasat*, (v. n. of وسوس Q) Inspiring, suggesting (one's own mind or Satan). Whispering any bad, injecting. Talking to one's self, muttering. A suggestion, instinct. (pl. وساوس *wasāwis*) A suggestion or persuasion of the devil. Conscience. Temptation.

P وسوسه انداز *waswasa-andāz*, One who injects evil suggestions: suggestive of evil.

A وسوط *wasūṭ*, A kind of hair-tent. A small tent made of hair. A camel which fills the pail. A camel which they load on the head and back, but never fetter. A camel which goes with young forty days over the year.

A وسوق *wusūḳ*, (pl. of وسق) Camels' loads.

A وسوم *wusūm*, (pl. of وسم *wasm*) Marks burnt upon the skin, brands.

P وسه *wasa*, Power. Wood; handle; staff.

A وسيج *wasīj*, (v. n. of وسج) Travelling with a certain quick pace (a camel). A hasty step.

P وسيط *wasīṭ*, A city between Kūfa and Basrah.

A وسيط *wasīṭ*, Middle. A mediator, arbiter, umpire. Highest in rank, dignity, or kind.

A وسيطة *wasīṭat*, Water which gets the better of the mud.

A وسيع *wasīʻ*, (pl. وساع *wisāʻ*) Ample, wide, roomy, capacious, extensive. An excellent, fast-going, long-stepping horse.

A وسيق *wasīḳ*, Rain. A driving, urging on.

A وسيقة *wasīḳat*, Camels driven in a body.

A وسيلة *wasīlat*, (pl. وسيل *wasīl* and وسائل *wasāïl*) Propinquity, affinity. Cause, means, occasion, conjuncture. A prop, shore, support, aid. That which unites, connects, or effectuates. Whatever conciliates the favour of a prince or other person; as a present, or merit. Dignity. Royal favour, patronage.

P وسيله *wasīla*, A herd, flock. Cause, means, help. بو سيله *ba wasīla*, Through, by the intervention.

P وسيله دار *wasīla-dār*, A client, dependant.

P وسيله داري *wasīla-dārī*, Clientage.

A وسيم *wasīm*, (pl. وسماء *wusamāʼ* and وسام *wisām*) Beautiful, handsome, elegant, comely. Distinguished by a scar or mark on the body. A mark.

A وسيمة *wasīmat*, (pl. وسام) A beautiful woman.

P وش *wash* or *vash*, Good, excellent, choice, beautiful, fair. The end of a turban-sash hanging loose. A rich kind of satin. Name of a city in Turkistān. A particle of similitude added to nouns: as, قمروش *kamarvash*, Moon-like; غنچه وش *ghunchavash*, Like a rose-bud.

A وشاء *washāʼ*, Opulence, wealth. (pl. of وشي *washy*) Certain kinds of stuffs.

A وشاة *wushāt*, Coiners of gold. (pl. of واشي *wāshī*) Spies, whisperers.

A وشاح *wishāh* or *wushāh*, (pl. وشح *wushh*, *wushuh*, اوشحة *awshihat*, and وشائح *washāʼih*) A belt or girdle of leather adorned with jewels, worn by ladies round their waists. A string of pearls, and one of other jewels, plaited together. A baldrick.

A وشاحة *wishāhat*, A sword.

P وشادن *wishādan*, (in zand and Pāz.) To open.

A وشاق *washāḳ*, Lost. Passing, going by. A little milk.

P وشاق *wishāḳ*, Good news, or any present made on that account. A single garment, without lining or quilting. A lynx or ounce. An approved slave. A pious son. An attendant on a mendicant. A female slave or servant. وشاقان چمن *wishāḳāni chaman*, Rose-bushes. Young plants, shoots, suckers.

A وشاك *wishāk*, (v. n. 3 of وشك) Going fast. Quickness, expedition.

A وشام *wishām*, (pl. of وشم *washm*) Figures pricked on the hands and other parts of the body with a needle and rubbed with woad or indigo, which leaves an indelible impression.

P وشاني *washānī*, Gold, three-tenths of which is alloy, formerly coined in Khurāsān.

A وشايات *wishāyāt*, Whisperings.

A وشاية *wishāyat*, (v. n. of وشي) Playing the spy, whispering, informing against, accusing. Multiplying (as offspring).

A وشائج *washāʼij*, (pl. of وشيجة) Roots of trees.

A وشائح *washāʼih*, (pl. of وشاح *wishāh* or *wushāh*) Belts of leather adorned with jewels and worn by ladies. Baldricks.

A وشائز *washāʼiz*, Well-stuffed cushions.

A وشائظ *washāʼiẓ*, (pl. of وشيظة *washīẓat*) Bits of solid bone.

A وشائع *washāʼiʻ*, (pl. of وشيعة *washīʻat*) Reeds round which weavers roll their threads.

A وشائق *washāʼiḳ*, (pl. of وشيقة *washīḳat*) Long slices, strips of meat parboiled and dried: rashers.

A وشب *washb*, Any thing bad, coarse, and thick. (Fruit) with a thick rind. *Wishb*, (pl. اوشاب *awshāb*) A crowd.

P وشت *washt*, Goodness. Good, beautiful. Whistling, smacking, or making any noise with the lips contracted. The confines or marches of an enemy's country. The galling of horses' backks. Dancing. A dancer.

P وشتا *washtā*, Alive. Life.

P وشتمونتن *washtamūnitan*, (in zand and Pāzand) To eat and drink.

P وشتن *washtan*, To dance. A dance, especially a kind of circular motion peculiar to the eastern monks or dervishes.

P وشتي *vashtī*, Beauty, goodness. Esther, ch. i.

P وشتيدن *wushtīdan*, To make a sound with the lips (when watering horses).

A وشج *washj*, (v. n. of وشج) Becoming mixed together (as the roots or branches of trees). Being complex, existing in various ways (relationship). *Wushj*, (from P وشك *wushk*) The gum of the plant بدران *badrān*.

A وشح *wushh* or *wushuh*, (pl. of وشاح *wishāh*) Belts or girdles of leather adorned with jewels, worn by the ladies round their waists.

A وشحاء *washhāʼ*, White-streaked she-goat.

A وشخ *washkh*, Weak; bad. A little basket in which they put up dates.

A وشخة *washakhat*, Any thing of palm-leaves.

A وشر *washr*, (v. n. of وشر) Sawing. Sharpening (her) teeth (a woman). *Wushur*, Sharpness or thinness of teeth. Teeth of a scythe or sickle.

P وشرك *washrak*, A piece of cloth in which they enclose drugs and medicines.

A وشز *washz* or *washaz*, A high place. Any thing one trusts to or leans upon. Haste, expedition. Place of refuge, asylum. Adversity, poverty, distress. A strong camel travelling well. علی وشز *ʻala' washazin*, On the road, making haste.

A وشظ *washẓ*, (v. n. of وشظ) Breaking a piece off a bone. Making firm (an axe) by putting a piece of wood between the iron and handle. A small company advancing or joining themselves (to others).

A وشع *washʻ*, (v. n. of وشع) Mixing a medicine to be swallowed or snuffed up. (Grey hairs) appearing upon any body. Growing up, shooting (green grass from the roots of dry grass). Going up, climbing (a mountain). The flowers of potherbs. The balsam-tree. *Wushuʻ*, A spider's web.

A وشغ *washgh*, (v. n. of وشغ) Scattering urine. Small and moderate (thing).

P وشفنگ *washfang*, Purslain.

A وشق *washḳ*, (v. n. of وشق) Cutting (parboiled meat) into oblong slices. Piercing. Making haste. Scattered forage.

P وشق *washaḳ*, A fox-like animal, found in Turkistān, from whose skin fur-garments are made.

A وشق *wushshaḳ*, Gum-ammoniac.

P وشقدار *washaḳ-dār*, (or وشقي *washaḳī*) A leader of horses of state, without riders.

A وشك *washk* or *wushk*, (v. n. of وشك) Being expeditious (business): proceeding rapidly. Despatch (of business), celerity, expedition.

P وشك *wushk*, Gum of the plant بدران *badrān*.

A وشكان *wash, wish*, or *wushkān*, (v. n. of وشك) Proceeding rapidly (business). Celerity, expedition. *Washkāna*, Quickly, expeditiously, fast as possible.

P وشكدانه *wushk-dāna*, Juniper-berries.

P وشكردن *washkardan*, To labour diligently, work well, be industrious. To die.

P وشكرده *washkarda* or *wushkirda*, One to whom you trust. Business committed to those you can depend upon. Experienced, expert, skilful. Swift. Of bright or acute parts. Quick at work. Wealthy, having the thoughts centered in riches. A petition. An assembly, congregation. Residence in any place. *Wishkarda*, Active, enterprising. Strong, powerful.

P وشكرديدن *washkardīdan*, (or وشكريدن *washkarīdan*) To execute with expedition.

P وشكل *wishkal*, A ram.

P وشكله *washkila*, (or وشگله *washgala*) A grape-stone separated from the fruit.

P وشكليدن *washkulīdan*, To shew dexterity.

P وشكنه *washkana*, The penis.

P وشكول *wishkūl, washkūl*, or *wushkūl*, Active, expert, dexterous. Activity, dexterity, expertness.

P وشكوليدن *washkūlīdan*, To execute promptly, skilfully, and well.

A وشل *washl*, (v. n. of وشل) Flowing, running, dropping slowly (water). Being weak, poor, and needy. Supplicating. *Washal*, (pl. اوشال *awshāl*) A small quantity of water, especially running or dropping from a height. A few drops of tears. Much water. Many tears. Reverence, awe, fear.

A وشلان *washalān*, (v. n. of وشل) Flowing, running, or dropping slowly (water). Being weak, poor, and needy. Supplicating.

P وشم *washm*, A sign, mark. Steam of a pot. Fog, mist, haze. A picture, portrait. *Wushm*, A quail.

A وشم *washm*, (v. n. of وشم) Pricking figures on the hands and other parts of the body with a needle, and rubbing the punctures with woad or indigo, which leaves an indelible impression. (This practice is chiefly in use amongst the wild Arabs, as amongst our own sailors, and is considered as highly ornamental: it is also done by pilgrims to Jerusalem.) (pl. وشوم *wushūm* and وشام *wishām*) Figures of the above on the body. The first appearance of herbage above ground. A line of a different colour on the fore-leg of a wild cow.

A وشمة *washmat*, One drop of rain. One word.

P وشمك *washmak*, A leather shoe. A treadle.

P وشمموننتن *washmamūnitan*, (in zand) To hear.

P وشن *washn*, Name of a reputed prophet. *Washan*, Stained, painted, bedaubed. Stain, pollution.

A وشن *washn*, High ground. Thick, bulky (camel).

P وشناب *wishnāb*, (for وشنه آب) Cherry-wine.

P وشناد *washnād*, Plenteous, abundant. A heap or abundance of any thing.

A وشنان *washnān, wishnān*, or *wushnān*, The herb or ashes of alkali; barilla.

P وشنگ *washang*, An iron instrument for extracting the seeds from the cotton. A heap of cucumbers or melons.

P وشنگه *washnaga* or *washanga*, Penis.

P وشنه *washna*, Neighing of horses. *Wishna*, A cherry. وشنه آب *wishna-āb*, Cherry-water.

P وشني *washnī*, Red, rouge used as a cosmetic.

A وشواش *washwāsh*, Slender, light, nimble,

active (man, camel, or ostrich).

A وشوشة *washwashat*, (v. n. of وشوش Q) Giving in a small quantity. Confusion of speech. Alacrity, levity, activity. A confused speech.

A وشوشي *washwashiy*, Active (in the arm).

A وشوع *washūʻ*, A medicine, swallowed or snuffed up. Straggling mountain-herbs.

A وشوغ *washūgh*, A medicine either swallowed or snuffed up.

P وشوق *washūk*, A kind of sewing, embroidery.

A وشول *washūl*, Milch (she-camel). *Wushūl*, (v. n. of وشل) Being weak and needy (a man). Weakness. Poverty.

A وشوم *wushūm*, (pl. of وشم *washm*) Figures pricked on the hand or body. Stripes on the fore-legs of the wild cow.

A وشوي *washawiy*, Signed, marked, stampt, printed (stuff).

P وشه *washa*, Gum-ammoniac, assafœtida. A sort of medicine.

A وشي *washy*, (v. n. of وشي) Painting, printing, staining, dyeing (cloth or stuff). Lying, colouring a story with falsehoods. Breeding. Multiplying, becoming very numerous (offspring). Reporting to the king, informing against. The colour or painting of a garment. Embroidery. The lustre of a sword-blade inlaid with golden or other figures. Something shining in a vein of metallic ore. (pl. وشاء *wishāʼ*) A kind of stuff.

P وشي *washī* or *washshī*, Ruddiness, redness. A kind of silken stuff manufactured at وش *wash*.

P وشيان *washyān*, Compensation, reward.

A وشيج *washīj*, Intermixture of relationship. A tree of which spears are made, the ash.

A وشيجة *washījat*, Root of a tree. Fibres of a palm or similar tree, which are twisted between boards into ropes for binding up cut-down corn. A crowd, mob, rabble.

A وشيظ *washīz*, A bit of gristle at the end of a bone. A mixed assembly; people of different tribes. Servants, followers. Stupid, dull. Harsh-tempered.

A وشيظة *washīzat*, A mob, a rabble. A hard solid bit of bone, an excrescence from another. A bit of wood for repairing a broken bowl.

A وشيع *washīʻ*, A course of palm-leaves, or any thing similar, laid on the top joists of a house, and fastened with ثمام *sumām*. The tent of a chief, higher than, and overlooking, the rest. A hedge of thorns or of other trees round gardens. A tree withered and fallen down. A beam or plank, especially at a well, on which the person stands who draws water. A weaving-instrument called حف *haff*. A kind of mat made of ثمام *sumām*. Withered leaves or dry branches falling from a tree. The embroidered border of a garment.

A وشيعة *washīʻat*, The reed around which weavers roll their threads. What goes round the shuttle. A clew; wool, or any thing wound up into clews or hanks. A sprinkling of hoariness. A stripe on the stuff called برد *burd*. A streak of dust.

A وشيق *washīk*, (or وشيقة *washīkat*) (pl. وشائق *washāʼik*) Meat parboiled and dried, or cut into strips and dried. A rasher.

A وشيك *washīk*, Expeditious, quick, brisk, active (man or woman).

A وشيمة *washīmat*, A thing said with a deceitful or bad design. Wickedness, evil. Enmity, grudge.

P وشينه *washīna*, A cuirass.

P وشيه *washya*, A jest, a joke.

A وص *wass*, A firm, solid way of doing.

A وصا *wasaʼ*, (v. n. of وصئ) Being dirty.

A وصاء *wasāʼ*, (or وصاءة *wasāʼat*) (v. n. of وصي) Having plants growing close together.

A وصاب *wisāb*, (and وصابي *wasāba'*) (pl. of وصب *wasib*) Sick, indisposed, ailing.

A وصاة *wasāt*, A command, charge, will, testament. Counsel, advice, exhortation. (pl. وصا *wasa'*) A branch of palm-trees, with which things are sewed or loads fastened.

A وصاد *wassād*, A weaver.

A وصاف *wassāf*, One who describes ably, or who praises. One who writes a medical prescription. A man's name.

A وصافة *wasāfat*, (v. n. of وصف) Being of a proper age for a servant. Serving. Attendance, readiness, activity in serving.

A وصافي *wassāfiy*, Related to وصاف *wassāf*.

A وصال *wisāl*, (v. n. 3 of وصل) Being united in friendship, society, or confederacy. Being annexed, connected, adhering. Doing (any thing) without interruption. Being continually (with any one). Meeting, interview, conjunction, arrival, attainment, fruition, enjoyment of any desired object. Collection. Death.

A وصاوص *wasāwis*, Small veils worn by girls. Stones upon hard and high grounds.

A وصايا *wasāya'*, (pl. of وصية *wasiyat*) Precepts, commandments. Testaments, wills. وصاياء الله *wasāyāʼu'llāh*, The commandments of God; the decalogue. وصاياي حسنه *wasāyāyi hasana*, Excellent admonitions. The words of a last will.

A وصاية *wasāyat*, Whatever is ordered; a commandment, mandate, testament. Counsel, advice. A branch of a palm-tree with which a load is fastened. *Wusāyat* or *wisāyat*, The office of administrator.

A وصائف *wasāʼif*, (pl. of وصيفة *wasīfat*) Girls fit for service.

A وصائل *wasāʼil*, (pl. of وصيلة *wasīlat*) Camels which, having borne ten colts, are exempted from all further labour. Striped stuffs of Yaman.

A وصب *wasb*, The space between the fore-finger and ring-finger. *Wasab*, (v. n. of وصب) Being sick. (pl. اوصاب *awsāb*) Disease, indisposition. *Wasib*, (pl. وصاب *wisāb* and وصابي *wasāba'*) Sick.

A وصخ *wasakh*, Filth, dirt, nastiness.

A وصد *wasd*, (v. n. of وصد) Standing firm. *Wasad*, Texture, weaving. *Wusud*, (pl. of وصيد *wasīd*) Thresholds.

A وصر *wisr*, A compact, a contract. The title-deeds of an estate. A writing or sentence signed by a judge. A voucher.

A وصرة *wasarrat*, The written and signed sentence of a judge. A compact, contract. Title-deeds.

A وصع *wasʻ*, (v. n. of وصع) Enclosing, covering, comprehending. The chirping of a sparrow or of the young ones. *Wasʻ* or *wasaʻ*, (pl. وصعان *wisʻān*) A certain bird smaller than a sparrow.

A وصف *wasf*, (v. n. of وصف) Describing, declaring, rehearsing. Writing a medical prescription, prescribing. Praising. Description, narrative, expression of qualities. Praise, encomium. Attribute, epithet, quality, property. A medical prescription. Merit, virtue, worth. وصف تركيب *wasfi tarkīb*, A compound participle; the adjective of a compound noun: as, نما *namā* in رهنما *rah-namā*, Shewing the way. وصف مذموم *wasfi mazmūm*, A blameable quality. اسم وصف *ismi wasf*, An adjective.

A وصفاء *wusafāʼ*, (pl. of وصيف *wasīf*) Lads fit for service.

A وصل *wasl*, (v. n. of وصل) Joining together, coupling, fastening. Giving. Being united in friendship, society, or confederacy. Repairing, mending (a garment). Meeting, union. Conjunction, attachment, enjoyment of the society of friends; whatever joins or couples. (pl. اوصال *awsāl*) A seam, joint, joining, articulation, joint of bones. Appendage. A thing resembling, or that must be connected with, another (as one boot or shoe). Liberality. Goods, traps. الف الوصل *alifu'l wasl*, The alif of union, *wasla*. حرف الوصل *harfu'l wasl*, The letter which follows the روي *rawiy*, as in the word اخاطبه *ukhātibuh*, the ب *be* is the روي *rawiy*, and the ه *he* is the *wasl*. ربيع الوصل *rabiʻu'l wasl*, The season of fruition, *i.e.* autumn. ليلة الوصل *laylatu'l wasl*, The last night of the moon (the conjunction of the old with the new). هذا وصل هذا *hāzā waslu hāzā*, This is fellow to or fits that. *Wisl* or *wusl*, (pl. اوصال *awsāl*) A bone that breaks not, or one which is not intermixed with another bone. The articulation of two bones. *Wusal*, (pl. of وصلة *wuslat*) Hinges, joints, knuckles, seams.

A وصلة *waslat*, (v. n. of وصل) Arriving. *Wuslat*, (pl. وصل *wusal*) Conjunction. A link or bond of union. A hinge, joint, knuckle, seam.

A وصله *wasla*, (for فصله *fusla*) Segment, section.

A وصلي *wasalī*, A piece of wood, pasteboard, slate, or parchment, on which children learn to write.

A وصلي *wasliy*, Copulative, conjunctive. An æra computed from the death of Muhammad.

A وصم *wasm*, (v. n. of وصم) Breaking (without separation of parts), bruising; cleaving (wood), yet leaving the parts adhering. Binding quickly. Scorning, upbraiding, reproaching, accusing. A rupture, crack, fissure. (pl. وصوم *wusūm*) A knot in wood. Reproach, disgrace, blemish. *Wasam*, Disease.

A وصمة *wasmat*, Reproach, disgrace. A crime, sin, fault, blemish. *Wusmat*, Torpor, languor, weakness. One crack or fissure.

A وصنة *wasnat*, A bit of cloth.

A وصواص *waswās*, An opening in a veil through which a woman may peep. A small veil worn by girls. Gravel upon hard ground.

A وصوب *wusūb*, (v. n. of وصب) Being continual, perpetual, perennial. Being firm, constant, steady; assiduous, attentive (to business). Managing, administering well.

A وصوص *waswas*, An opening in a veil through which a woman may see.

A وصوصة *waswasat*, (v. n. of وصوص Q) Looking through an aperture in a veil. Peeping through eyes nearly closed. Opening the eyes (a whelp). Veiling (herself) closely (a woman).

A وصوف *wusūf*, (v. n. of وصف) Going fast.

A وصول *wusūl*, (v. n. of وصل) Arriving. Arrival. Union with, or enjoyment of, a wished-for object. Collection. Acquisition. عند الوصول *ʻinda'l wusūl*, (or لدي الوصول *ladayi'l wusūl*) On (his) arrival; when (he) arrives. وصول باقى *wusūl bākī*, Arrear, uncollected balance.

A وصولي *wusūlī*, That may be realized or collected.

A وصوم *wusūm*, (pl. of وصم *wasm*) Disgraces. Knots in wood. Ruptures, secret cracks.

A وصى *wasy*, (v. n. of وصي) From being exalted, being abased. Becoming weighty from being light. Being closely united. Joining together, coupling. Having plants growing together (ground).

A وصيّ *wasīy*, (v. n. of وصي) Having plants growing close together (ground). (pl. اوصياء *awsiyāʼ*) Who commands, bequeaths, or recommends any thing. A testator. An executor, administrator. A guardian, tutor (of children or pupils). (pl. of وصية *wasiyat*) Palm-branches stripped of their leaves, with which any thing is sewed. الوصىّ *al wasīy*, Seth, son of Adam.

A وصيّة *wasīyat*, (pl. وصىّ *wasīy*) A branch of a palm-tree stript of leaves, with which any thing is sewed. (pl. وصايا *wasāyā'*) A precept, mandate, charge, command. A last will or testament. P وصيّت كردن *wasiyat kardan*, To command by will, to devise, bequeath. To charge.

P وصيّت نامه *wasiyat-nāma*, Last will, testament.

A وصيد *wasīd*, A threshold. A portico or area before a door. A fold for cattle built of stone upon a mountain. A mountain. The cave of the seven sleepers (see كهف *kahf* and رقيم *rakīm*). Close, narrow. One who is twice circumcised. Short-stalked (plant). A fold, enclosure made of boughs.

A وصيدة *wasīdat*, A stone enclosure or pen for sheep or cattle (حظيرة *hazīrat* implying one constructed of wood or branches).

A وصيرة *wasīrat*, A compact, a contract. The written and signed sentence of a judge. A voucher. The title-deeds of an estate.

A وصيع *wasīʻ*, The chirping of a sparrow. A young sparrow.

A وصيف *wasīf*, (pl. وصفاء *wusafāʼ*) A servant boy or girl. A lad fit for service.

A وصيفة *wasīfat*, (pl. وصائف) A servant girl.

A وصيل *wasīl*, One who comes in and goes out with any one. Intimate (friend). الوصيل *alwasīl*, A serjeant, a lictor (hence alguazil, in Spanish).

A وصيلة *wasīlat*, (pl. وصائل *wasāʼil*) A cause, any thing which arrives, happens, or is productive of consequences. A sword. Fertility, abundance, plenty, cheapness. A clew or hank of thread. Society, company. Benignity; politeness. A company of fellow-travellers. Cultivation, habitableness. An extensive district. A striped Arabian cloth. An edifice erected from religious motives, a pious foundation. A sheep whose lamb, if male, was sacrificed by the pagan Arabs to their idols; if female, it was preserved; and if both of male and female, none of them were sacrificed: if a sheep, after bringing forth six times female twins, lambed a male and female, the male was spared on account of its mother, which was then considered as free, and was no more milked. A she-camel in the same situation, after having brought ten colts. (See سائبة *sāʼibat*.)

A وصيم *wasīm*, The space between the ring-finger and the little finger.

A وضّ *wazz*, Necessity, violence, compulsion. Distress of mind, perplexity.

A وضأ *wazʼ*, (v. n. of وضأ) Excelling another in cleanness and nicety in making sacred ablutions.

A وضاء *wizāʼ*, (or وضّاء *wuzzāʼ*) (pl. of وضيءٌ *wazīʼ*) Neat, nice, clean, cleanly.

A وضاءة *wazāʼat*, (v. n. of وضأ) Being clean. Cleanness, neatness. Clearness of complexion.

A وضاح *wazāh*, Evident, manifest, clear.

A وضّاح *wazzāh*, Clean, fair, handsome (man). Clear, evident, manifest. Spotted with the leprosy. The day. بكر وضّاح *bikri wazzāh*, The first prayer in the morning. عظم وضّاح *ʻazmi wazzāh*, A boy's game, in which they search for a white bone cast into a dark place.

A وضاخ *wizākh*, (v. n. 3 of وضخ) Contending with in leaping, walking, or drawing water.

A وضاضئ *wazāzīʼ*, Clean, neat (persons).

A وضّاع *wazzāʻ*, A compiler, composer.

A وضاعة *wazāʻat*, (v. n. of وضع) Becoming mean and low; letting (one's self) down. Being an adopted son. Being lowered, let down, degraded. Humility, humiliation.

A وضائح *wazāʼih*, (pl. of وضيحة *wazīhat*) Cattle feeding (as sheep or camels).

A وضائع *wazāʼiʻ*, (pl. of وضيعة *wazīʻat*) The carriages or baggage of people on a journey. Military stations or garrisons. Soldiers marching (from place to place). Hostages. Books, the depositaries of the sayings of the wise. وضائع الملك *wazāʼiʻu'l mulk*, Fixed taxes to be paid by the subjects.

A وضّائين *wuzzāʼīn*, Clean, neat (persons).

A وضح *wazah*, (pl. اوضاح *awzāh*) A bracelet, necklace, or ornament for the ankle or any other part of the body (particularly of silver). Good coin. Light, lustre, splendour (of the dawn or moon). White (especially on the forehead or feet of a horse). White hair, hoariness. Milk. Leprosy. The best part of the road. A certain kind of young green herbage. Virtue, merit.

A وضحة *wazahat*, A she-ass.

A وضخ *wazkh*, The filling of a bucket half-full.

A وضر *wazar*, (v. n. of وضر) Being greasy (a dish). Being stained with saffron. (pl. اوضار *awzār*) The smell of tainted meat. The corrupted part of fat or milk. Dirty water, with which dishes or bottles have been washed. A stain from saffron. Marks left by a pitch-plaster. *Wazir*, Bedaubed with the fat of meat, greasy. Stained with saffron.

A وضراء *wazrāʼ*, A mark impressed on the neck of camels of the tribe of بني فزارة *banī fazārat*. A large stone projecting from a mountain.

A وضري *wazraʼ*, (fem.) Bedaubed with the fat of meat. Anointed with saffron. A large rock projecting from a mountain.

A وضع *wazʻ*, (v. n. of وضع) Placing or laying down upon. Establishing or laying a foundation, building. Composing, writing (a book). Inventing. Depositing (any thing with another) to keep. Removing (a burden or any thing with the hand). Remitting part of a debt. Taking away, removing (sin). (A woman) laying aside (her veil). Deposing (from any dignity), degrading. Depressing, humbling. Humbling (one's self). Suffering losses in trade. Conceding, granting. Going fast. Cutting off (the head). Bringing forth a child. Opening (a book). Grazing on the plant حمض *hamz* without quitting the spot (a camel). Making camels keep their pasture. Situation, position, imposition, disposition, condition, state, gesture, action, conduct, manner. Mode of living or acting. Operation, performance, procedure. A literary composition. Subtraction, deduction, abatement. Stature. P وضع كردن *wazʻ kardan*, To invent. وضع اساس كردن *wazʻi asās kardan*, To lay a foundation. وضع بناي جامع كردن *wazʻi bināyi jāmiʻ kardan*, To lay the foundations of a mosque. وضع پسنديده *wazʻi pasandīda*, A laudable act. A وضع حمل *wazʻi haml*, Childbirth, delivery. Abortion, miscarriage. P وضع حمل كردن *wazʻi haml kardan*, To lay down a burden, *i.e.* to bring forth. A وضع خمس *wazʻi khums*, Fixing the fifth part (of the spoils as the property of the king). P وضع قدم كردن *wazʻi kadam kardan*, To place or fix the feet. A وضع منّت *wazʻi minnat*, The conferring of an obligation. وضع و حالت *wazʻ u hālat*, (or وضع وحركت *wazʻ u harakat*) Conduct and situation; action and motion. P بيضه وضع كردن *bayza wazʻ kardan*, To lay an egg. رهين وضع كردن *rahin wazʻ kardan*, To pledge, pawn, bet, wager. A وضعاً و قولاً *wazʻan wa kawlan*, With gestures and words, or with words and actions. *Wuzʻ*, (v. n. of وضع) Bringing forth (a woman). Conceiving a little before menstruation. Travelling fast (a camel). A fœtus conceived.

A وضعة *wazʻat* or *wizʻat*, Situation, position, posture.

A وضعيّ *wazʻiy*, Relating to form, position, or posture; positive.

A وضف *wazf*, (v. n. of وضف) Going fast.

A وضم *wazm*, (v. n. of وضم) Placing (meat) on a mat or board that (it) may not be soiled. Laying the board or mat وضم *wazam* (under meat). Coming down upon, making a descent on. *Wazam*, (pl. اوضام *awzām* and اوضمة *awzimat*) A mat, board, or any thing similar whereon meat is placed to be kept clean. تركهم لحماً علي وضم *tarakahum lahman ʻala' wazamin*, He left them as meat on a a mat, *i. e.* he trounced them finely.

A وضمة *wazmat*, A crowd, body of men, especially of the same tribe. A body of men, from 200 to 300.

A وضن *wazn*, (v. n. of وضن) Placing close together, or one upon another, doubling, interlacing. Plaiting, weaving a girth or surcingle for the hawda. *Wuzun*, (pl. of وضين *wazin*) Girths, surcingles.

A وضوح *wuzūh*, (v. n. of وضح) Being clear, evident, manifest. Making a brilliant display of milk (a camel). Evidence, proof. Clearness, distinctness.

A وضوخ *wazūkh*, Water filling a pipe or bucket half-way.

A وضوع *wuzūʻ*, (v. n. of وضع) Going fast, travelling quick. Cutting off (the head). Humbling one's self. Taking away, removing (sin).

P وضوگاه *wuzū-gāh*, A place where they wash before prayer. A lavatory. A piscina.

A وضوء *wazūʼ*, Water used for performing ablutions. *Wazūʼ* or *wuzūʼ*, A sacred ablution (performed before prayer, and which consists in washing, first the hands, then the mouth inside, then throwing water on the forehead, washing the whole face, the arms, and lastly the feet). P وضو ساختن *wuzū sākhtan*, To wash, especially the whole body, as a purification from sin or defilement.

A وضيح *wazīh*, Evident, manifest, plain, clear.

A وضيحة *wazīhat*, Cattle which are pastured.

A وضيع *wazīʻ*, Ignoble, plebeian, mean, base, low. A deposit, any thing given into the custody of another. Moist dates preserved in earthen jars. شريف و وضيع *sharīf u wazīʻ*, Noble and plebeian.

A وضيعة *wazīʻat*, (v. n. of وضع) Depositing (any thing) with (another). Grazing on the plant حمض *hamz* near water without leaving the spot (camels). Losing (in trade, making a bad market). Any thing lowered, abated, or deducted. A military colony, frontier-garrison. Troops, whose names are given to places and towns, the inhabitants of of which are not expected to fight. Tax, tribute, or toll paid to the king. (pl. وضائع *wazāʼiʻ*) Any baggage belonging to travellers. A book in which are inscribed the sayings of wise men. Bruised wheat eaten with melted butter. Spurious; a bastard. A certain salt and bitter plant. (A camel) anxious for salt and bitter herbage. Injury, contumely. اصحاب وضيعه *as-hābi wazīʻa*, People who take up their quarters in places abounding in the plant حمض *hamz*, and feed their camels there.

A وضيعي *wazīʻī*, Baseness, meanness.

A وضيمة *wazimat*, A body of men, from 200 to 300. A small number who surprise a greater. A funeral-banquet. A quantity or pile of forage.

A وضين *wazīn*, (pl. وضن *wuzun*) Interlaced, entangled. Folded, doubled. The girth, belt, or surcingle of the hawda or camel-litter. The poitrel, also the girth of a camel's saddle; any broad straps of leather doubled. قلق وضينها *kaliha wazīnuhā*, Her girth rattled (through her leanness).

A وضيّ *wazīʼ*, (pl. اوضياء *awziyāʼ* and وضاء *wizāʼ*) Clean, neat, pure.

A وطّ *watt*, The note of a swallow or martinet. Creaking noise made by a burden when carrying.

A وطأ *watʼ*, (v. n. of وطئ) Trampling, treading (under foot). Putting the foot to the ground, or making an impression with it. Arranging, disposing in order. Making (a bed) smooth and soft. Lying with. Taking under the arm. Low ground.

A وطاء *watāʼ*, Low ground. *Watāʼ* or *witāʼ*, An uncovering, unveiling (opposed to غطاء *ghitāʼ*). *Witāʼ*, (v. n. 3 of وطئ) Rivalling, doing any thing equal. Consenting, agreeing (with another). Repeating the last syllable of a verse.

A وطاءة *watāʼat*, (v. n. of وطؤ) Being beaten, trodden, trampled on. Being equal, level, easy, and soft (the ground or a bed). A treading, a trampling. Softness, smoothness (of a bed).

A وطاب *witāb*, (pl. of وطب *watb*) Leathern bottles in which they put milk. صفرت وطابه *safirat witābuhu*, His bottles became empty, *i. e.* he died or was slain.

A وطأة *watʼat*, A footstep, impression of the foot. Violence, compulsion. A violent assault, forcible squeeze, gripe, or seizure. *Wataʼat*, Travellers, trampers. A beaten path.

A وطّاس *wattās*, A shepherd.

A وطاوط *watāwit*, (or وطاويط *watāwīt*) (pl. of وطواط *watwāt*) Swallows.

A وطائد *watāʼid*, The foundations (of a house). Trivets for pots, pot-irons.

A وطب *watb*, (pl. اوطب *awtub*, وطاب *witāb*, اوطاب *awtāb*, and pl. of pl. اواطب *awātib*) A leathern bottle in which they put milk. Severe, hard-hearted, or insolent (man). A large breast. الوطب *al watb*, (A man) going barefoot.

A وطباء *watbāʼ*, Large-breasted (woman).

A وطث *wats*, (v. n. of وطث) Treading firmly. A violent stamp, tread, or kick on the ground.

A وطح *wath*, (v. n. of وطح) Repelling imperiously. Knocking away the filth وطح *wath*. *Wath* or *watah*, Filth which adheres to the cloven feet of cattle, or the claws of fowls.

A وطد *watd*, (v. n. of وطد) Establishing, confirming. Joining, consolidating, causing to stick. Rendering heavy. Being firm, solid, perpetual, perennial. Making a deep impression, planting or fixing in the ground. Levelling, making (a place) convenient (for any thing). Walking, marching, moving. Treading upon, stamping, wearing down, kicking, trampling under foot. Ramming hard, making (ground) solid. Rolling (a stone against a cave) in order to shut up the entrance. Despising. *Watid*, Firm, steady, solid; strengthened.

A وطدة *watdat*, A tread, trampling, stamping.

A وطر *watar*, (pl. اوطار *awtār*) A necessary or important thing, a thing which lies at heart. Necessity. قضي وطره *kaza' watarahu*, He accomplished his object.

A وطس *wats*, (v. n. of وطس) Striking hard with one's boot. Breaking to pieces.

A وطش *watsh*, (v. n. of وطش) Relating any thing in part. Giving (any thing to another). Repelling, thrusting away. Striking. Speaking obscurely and indistinctly.

A وطط *wutut*, Persons weak in mind or body.

A وطف *watf*, (v. n. of وطف) Hanging low (the skirts of a cloud). *Wataf*, Much hair on the eyebrows or lids. The fruitfulness, softness, and out-pouring of a cloud.

A وطفاء *watfāʼ*, (A cloud) full of rain; raining much and long; or raining a short time.

A وطفة *watfat*, A small quantity of hair.

A وطم *watm*, (v. n. of وطم) Treading, trampling (under foot). Letting fall (a veil or curtain).

A وطن *watn*, (v. n. of وطن) Abiding, dwelling. *Watn* or *watan*, (pl. اوطان *awtān*) A country, dwelling, residence, abode, wherever one lives, native or not. Home. A place where cattle are tied up, a stall. وطن اصلي *watani aslī*, (or وطن حقيقي *watani hakīkī*) A true, real, or native country. The original country, *i. e.* heaven. P وطن گرفتن *watan giriftan*, To make (any place) one's country, to fix one's residence. A وطن مألوف *watani maʼlūf*, Fixed residence, accustomed place of abode. P ترك وطن كردن *tarki watan kardan*, To abandon one's country. A حبّ الوطن من الايمان *hubbu'l watan mini'l īmān*, Love of country (is an article) of religion (a saying of Muhammad).

P وطن دشمن *watan-dushman*, A traitor.

P وطن دوست *watan-dost*, A patriot: patriotic.

P وطنگاه *watan-gāh*, Place of one's abode, home.

A وطنيّ *wataniy*, Belonging to one's country.

A وطوءة *wutūʾat*, A treading, a trampling.

A وطواط *watwāt*, (pl. وطاوط *watāwit* or وطاويط *watāwīt*) A mountain-swallow, martinet. Loud-voiced, noisy. (A man) having a voice resembling this swallow. A fast talker. A bat, rere-mouse. A frog. A timid, languid man. وطواط البحر *watwātu'l bahr*, A flying fish. ابصر في الليل من الوطواط *absar fi'l layl mini'l watwāt*, Clearer-sighted at night than the bat.

A وطواطيّ *watwātiy*, Timid, languid. Talkative.

A وطوءة *wutuʾat*, (v. n. of وطئ) Being even, level, easy, and soft (ground or a bed).

A وطوطة *watwatat*, Imbecility, fear. The voice of a man resembling the note of a swallow. A quick, rapid articulation.

A وطيّ *watiy*, Trodden under foot. Well broke in.

A وطيد *watīd*, Firm, fixed, steady. Made heavy.

A وطيرة *watīrat*, Manner, way, habit, custom.

A وطيس *watīs*, A furnace, an iron oven. Importance of business. الآن حمي الوطيس *al ān hamiya'l watīs*, The oven is now heated, *i.e.* The war is now raging.

A وطيسة *watīsat*, Importance of a business.

A وطيء *watīʾ*, Trodden under foot. Equal, easy, soft, smooth (ground or bed).

A وطيئة *watīʾat*, A kind of sack in which a traveller carries dried flesh and biscuit. A dish made of bruised date-kernels with milk.

A وظائف *wazāʾif*, (pl. of وظيفة *wazīfat*) Pensions. Stipends, rations, daily allowances. Agreements, contracts. Duties, daily tasks. اهل وظائف *ahli wazāʾif*, Pensioners, stipendiary soldiers.

A وظب *wazb*, A trampling, treading on.

A وظبة *wazbat*, The vulva of mares or other animals that divide not the hoof.

A وظر *wazar*, (v. n. of وظر) Being fat and full of flesh. *Wazir*, Fat, corpulent in the belly and thighs.

A وظف *wazf*, (v. n. of وظف) Shortening the leg-bands (of a camel), and hurting in the shank. Striking the shank. Following. *Wuzuf*, (pl. of وظيف *wazīf*) Shanks, cannon-bones in horses. Rations, daily allowances, stipends. Agreements, contracts.

A وظوب *wuzūb*, (v. n. of وظب) Being assiduous, persevering. Minding, attending to.

A وظيف *wazīf*, (pl. اوظفة *awzifat*, and وظف *wuzuf*) The thinnest part of (a horse's or camel's leg), the shank or cannon. (A man) strong in travelling, especially over rough grounds. موصل الوظيف *mawsilu'l wazīf*, The fetlock-joint, which connects the shank and pastern. جاءت على وظيف *jāʾat ʿala' wazīfin*, They followed one another.

A وظيفة *wazīfat*, (pl. وظائف *wazāʾif* and وظف *wuzuf*) A pension, stipend, salary, soldiers' pay, allowance of provisions, commons (by the day, month, or year). Any thing stipulated or agreed upon. A task, religious duty. Employment, post, office. Use, purpose. P قطع وظيفه كردن *katʿi wazīfa kardan*, To withdraw a pension.

P وظيفه خور *wazīfa-khwur*, A pensioner.

A وعّ *waʿʿ*, A jackal.

A وعاء *wiʿāʾ* or *wuʿāʾ*, (pl. اوعية *awʿiyat* and اوعاء *awʿāʾ*) A sheath, case, repository, or place where any thing is laid up. A pod, capsule.

A وعاب *wiʿāb*, Wide spaces of ground.

A وعارة *waʿārat*, (v. n. of وعر) Being little, few. Being rough, rugged, uneven.

A وعاط *wiʿāt*, A red or yellow rose.

A وعّاظ *wuʿʿāz*, (pl. of واعظ *wāʿiz*) Preachers.

A وعاف *wiʿāf*, Hard grounds where water lies.

A وعاق *wuʿāk*, (v. n. of وعق) Making a noise in (his) belly or sheath (a horse). The grumbling noise of a horse's belly when trotting.

A وعام *wiʿām*, (pl. of وعم *waʿm*) Lines or veins in a mountain different in colour from the rest.

A وعان *wiʿān*, (pl. of وعنة) Hard grounds.

A وعاوع *waʿāwiʿ*, Strong, brave, bold (men). The first who come to the succour of combatants.

A وعب *waʿb*, (v. n. of وعب) Taking the whole. Wide roads. Highways.

A وعث *waʿs*, (v. n. of وعث) Being difficult to travel on (a road). Leanness. Soft earth or sands into which the feet easily sink. A broken bone. Capricious-tempered. *Waʿs* or *waʿis*, A difficult road. *Waʿas*, (v. n. of وعث) Being broken (the hand).

A وعثاء *waʿsāʾ*, Difficulty (in travelling).

A وعثة *waʿisat*, Corpulent, fleshy, fat (woman).

A وعد *waʿd*, (v. n. of وعد) Promising. Auguring or prognosticating any thing good. Threatening. Exceeding (any one) in promising. A promise. A threat.

A وعدة *waʿdat*, (pronounced وعده *waʿda*) A promise, vow. Any determined, appointed, certain time or term. A stated period for the discharge of a debt, or the payment of a sum of money. Agreement, bargain. P وعده كردن *waʿda kardan*, (or نمودن *namūdan*) To promise, agree, engage.

P وعده براي *waʿda-barāy*, The performance of an agreement.

P وعده بندي *waʿda-bandī*, Stated dates on which to discharge a debt or pay money.

P وعده جاي *waʿda-jāy*, Place of promise.

A وعده خلاف *waʿda-khilāf*, A false contract. One who does not keep his promise.

P وعده شكن *waʿda-shikan*, A promise-breaker.

P وعده فراموش *waʿda-farāmosh*, Forgetful of one's promise.

P وعده گاه *waʿda-gāh*, Time of promise.

A وعده وعيد *waʿda waʿīd*, Evading a promise.

A وعده وفا *waʿda-wafā*, Keeping one's promise.

A وعر *waʿr*, (v. n. of وعر) Prohibiting, preventing. Being filled with wrath and hatred. (pl. اوعر *awʿur*, وعور *wuʿūr*, and اوعار *awʿār*) Rocky, unequal, uneven, rugged. قليل وعر *kalīlun waʿrun*, A small matter, a little. وعر المعروف *waʿru'l maʿrūf*, Scanty in doing good. رجل وعر المعروف *rajulun waʿru'l maʿrūf*, A man who does little good, scant in acts of kindness. *Waʿr* or *waʿar*, (v. n. of وعر) Being rough, difficult to ascend (a mountain or other broken ground). Being intricate (a question). *Waʿir*, A rugged place, declivity, any thing rough. وعر معر *waʿir maʿir*, Difficult (verse).

A وعز *waʿz*, (v. n. of وعز) Making a sign, nodding, beckoning, commanding, charging.

A وعس *waʿs*, Name of a tree of which they make musical instruments. A vestige. A trampling. A sandy plain difficult to pass over. *Wuʿs*, (pl. of اوعس *awʿas*) Soft and sandy (places).

A وعساء *waʿsāʾ*, (fem. of اوعس *awʿas*) Soft, sandy (plain). A soft, sandy soil of a high exposure, producing herbs which are eaten raw.

A وعظ *waʿz*, (v. n. of وعظ) Admonishing, exhorting. Preaching. Giving warning respecting future punishment. Advice, exhortation, admonition: a sermon, oration, homily. P وعظ كردن *waʿz kardan*, To preach, exhort, advise, sermonize.

A وعف *waʿf*, Hard ground where water lies.

A وعق *waʿk*, (v. n. of وعق) Being quick, making haste. *Waʿk* or *waʿik*, Bad-tempered, morose, refractory, stubborn, touchy, capricious.

A وعقة *waʿkat*, Bad-tempered, morose. Moroseness, badness of disposition.

A وعك *waʿk*, (v. n. of وعك) Weakening, emaciating (as a fever). Rolling in the dust (dogs their prey). Being still (the wind). Febrile pain or debility. Intense heat; a suffocating calm without a breath of wind. *Waʿk* or *waʿik*, Emaciated by fever or fatigue.

A وعكة *waʿkat*, A pressing on one another, as of camels when running to water. A violent fall when running. A field of battle, an amphitheatre or place of combat. A fierce battle. Intense heat without a breath of air.

A وعل *waʿl*, (v. n. of وعل) Looking down from an eminence. (pl. اوعال *awʿāl* and وعول *wuʿūl*) Noble. A prince. An asylum. The month شوّال *shawwāl*. ما لي من ذلك وعل و وعن *mā lī min zālika waʿlun wa waʿnun*, To me that is unavoidable. *Waʿil*, (*waʿl*, and sometimes *wuʿil*) (pl. اوعال *awʿāl*, وعول *wuʿūl*, وعل *wuʿul*, and موعلة *mawʿilat*) The ibex or mountain-goat. *Waʿil*, (pl. اوعال *awʿāl* and وعلان *wiʿlān*) The eighth Arabian month, called also شعبان *shaʿbān*. Noble. Powerful. هم عليه وعل واحد *hum ʿalayhi waʿlun wāhidun*, They all assembled or rose against him. *Wuʿul*, (pl. of وعل *waʿl* or *waʿil*) Mountain-goats.

A وعلان *wiʿlān*, (pl. of وعل) Months of Shaabān.

A وعلة *waɛlat*, The handle of a flagon or ewer. A button-loop. A stone or any thing projecting from a mountain. An inaccessible part of a mountain. *Waɛilat*, The female of the mountain-goat.

A وعم *waɛm*, (v. n. of وعم) Addressing the inmates of a house morning and evening, "Health and happiness to you!" (pl. وعام *wiɛām*) A line or vein in a mountain different in colour from the rest.

A وعن *waɛn*, White barren ground. Asylum.

A وعنة *waɛnat*, (pl. وعان *wiɛān*) Hard ground, rocks. White barren ground. An asylum. Vestiges of an ant's nest. Lines on, or veins in, a mountain.

A وعواع *waɛwāɛ*, A voice, sound, noise; murmur of a crowd. Howl of a dog, yell of a jackal. A man with a disagreeable voice. A watch, guard. A multitude. Talkative, prating.

A وعوثة *wuɛūsat*, Softness of earth or sand into which the feet easily sink.

A وعور *wuɛūr*, (v. n. of وعر) Being difficult to ascend (a mountain). Checking, hindering. (pl. of وعر *waɛr*) Rugged, steep, difficult (places).

A وعورة *wuɛūrat*, (v. n. of وعر) Being rough, rugged, and difficult to ascend. Being few and small. Steepness and ruggedness.

A وعوع *waɛwaɛ*, Eloquent, rhetorical. A jackal. A fox. A desert. A watch, guard. Weak.

A وعوعة *waɛwaɛat*, (v. n. of وعوع Q) Shaking violently. Murmuring, making a noise. The howl or bark of a dog, wolf, hyena, or similar animal.

A وعوعيّ *waɛwaɛiy*, Ingenious, witty, clever.

A وعوف *wuɛūf*, Weakness of sight.

A وعول *wuɛūl*, (pl. of وعل *waɛl* and *waɛil*) Mountain-goats. Nobles. Princes.

A وعي *waɛy*, (v. n. of وعى) Preserving, collecting, treasuring, or laying up; custody, preservation. Holding. Remembering, retaining (any saying). Repressing, containing one's self. Being restored, set crookedly (a broken bone). Collecting (as pus in a sore). Pus, matter. Flight, escape. A place of refuge. *Waɛy* or *waɛa'*, Clamours, confused noises. The cry of dogs. *Waɛa'*, (v. n. of وعي) Calling aloud, crying out.

A وعيّ *waɛiy*, Powerful, strong (horse).

A وعيب *waɛīb*, Spacious (mansion). Extreme, utmost. ركض وعيب *rakzun waɛībun*, A great leap. A strong effort.

A وعيد *waɛīd*, (v. n. of وعد) Threatening, predicting any thing bad. Promising any thing good. Threat, commination. The braying of a he-camel.

A وعير *waɛīr*, Rugged, rough, uneven (place).

A وعيق *waɛīk*, (v. n. of وعق) Making a grumbling or flapping noise (the belly or sheath of a horse). The noise itself.

P وغا *waghā*, War, battle, tumult. A tiger.

A وغاب *wighāb*, (pl. of وغب) Large sacks.

A وغادة *waghādat*, (v. n. of وغد) Being servile, menial. Being weak, enervated, mean, base, foolish.

A وغب *waghb*, (pl. اوغاب *awghāb* and وغاب *wighāb*) A large sack. Pots, pans, dishes, and other meaner kind of household furniture. A large strong camel. (fem. وغبة *waghbat*) Foolish, stupid; weak in body and mind.

A وغبة *waghabat*, Foolish, stupid.

P وغد *waghd*, A fruit called in India brinjāl.

A وغد *waghd*, (pl. اوغاد *awghād*, وغدان *wughdān*, or *wighdān*) A servant, domestic, one especially who serves for victuals. A boy. One of the gaming arrows, especially a blank. The fruit of the brinjāl. Vile, base. Weak in body. A fool.

A وغدان *wugh* or *wighdān*, (pl. of وغد *waghd*) Servants, especially those who serve for victuals.

A وغر *waghr*, (v. n. of وغر) Being sultry (as mid-day). *Waghr* and *waghar*, (v. n. of وغر) Being angry, enraged, indignant, having a private grudge. Hatred, rancour, enmity. Indignation, rage. A tumult, the noise of an armed host.

A وغرة *waghrat* or *wagharat*, Scorching heat. Hatred, rancour.

P وغزن *wughzun*, A burial-ground.

P وغست *waghast*, Apparent, visible, plain.

P وغستن *waghastan*, To make evident, clear.

A وغف *waghf*, (v. n. of وغف) Walking fast, running. Weakness in the eyes. A piece of leather tied under the belly of a goat (to prevent him from drinking his own urine, or impregnating the female).

A وغل *waghl*, (v. n. of وغل) Going into a company of wine-drinkers (especially uninvited). That which one drinks on that occasion. Tares growing amongst corn eat by pigeons. A man of a low condition; a vagabond, slave, silly fellow, unfit for any thing. One who falsely pretends to high birth. Luxuriant and entangled foliage. One who goes uninvited to a drinking-party. A drinking-party to which any one goes uninvited. A place of refuge, an asylum. Flight, escape. ما لي عن هذا الامر وغل *mā lī ɛan hāzā'l amr waghl*, For me, there is no escape from this business. *Waghl* or *waghil*, One who takes bad nourishment.

A وغم *waghm*, (v. n. of وغم) Telling (news) ill-authenticated. (pl. اوغام *awghām*) Malevolence, hatred, when deeply fixed in the mind. Force, violence. War, battle. Soul, self. Heavy. Foolish.

A وغنة *waghnat*, A wide wine-jar.

A وغوبة *wughūbat*, A being large and thick.

A وغودة *wughūdat*, (v. n. of وغد) Being servile, menial. Being weak, enervated, mean, and base.

P وغوغ *waghwagh*, The croak of a frog.

A وغوف *wughūf*, Weakness, dimness of sight.

A وغول *wughūl*, (v. n. of وغل) Penetrating, entering (into a thicket) and hiding. Going to a distance.

A وغى *wagha'*, A battle. *Wagha'* or *wigha'*, Tumult, noise, clamour, especially of an army.

A وغية *waghyat*, A small portion, particle, bit.

P وغيج *waghīj*, A ditch, pool, marsh.

A وغير *waghīr*, Milk warmed by puting into it a hot stone. Hot water. (Meat) dressed upon a hot stone. Boiled milk, milk-meats.

A وغيرة *waghīrat*, Milk heated by a hot stone. Milk-meats.

A وغيره *wa ghayruhu*, Et cetera.

P وغيش *waghesh*, Many, much, abundant, large, broad, wide. Grief, anguish.

A وغيق *waghīk*, The noise made by a horse's yard coming out of the sheath, or a noise proceeding from his belly when running.

A وفاء *wafāɛ*, (v. n. of وفي) Performing a promise, keeping an engagement. Sufficing. Performance of a promise, observation of good faith, fidelity, sincerity. Fulfilment. A security of sale. A sufficiency, a completing or filling up. Conclusion, end, completion. Length, duration. P وفا كردن *wafā kardan*, To perform a promise, satisfy, fulfil. A مات فلان و انت بوفاء *māta fulānun wa anta bi wafāɛin*, Such a one is dead, and thou art alive.

P وفا بيگانه *wafā-bīgāna*, Faithless.

P وفا پرست *wafā-parast*, Faithful, sincere.

P وفا پيوست *wafā-paywast*, Faithful, sincere, constant, performing engagements.

A وفاة *wafāt*, Death, decease, demise. P وفات يافتن *wafāt yāftan*, To die.

P وفا دار *wafā-dār*, Trusty, true, faithful.

P وفا داري *wafā-dārī*, Fidelity, sincerity.

A وفادة *wifādat*, (v. n. of وفد) Coming, arriving as an ambassador. The arrival of an ambassador.

A وفار *wifār*, Hairs reaching below the ears.

A وفارة *wafārat*, (v. n. of وفر) Being full, complete, whole, entire. Being much, copious, abundant. Abundance, exuberance, copiousness.

A وفاز *wifāz*, (pl. of وفز *wafz* or *wafaz*) Hastes.

P وفا سگال *wafā-sigāl*, (or وفا خواه *wafā-khwāh*) Benevolent, affectionate, a real well-wisher. ياروفا سگال *yāri wafā-sigāl*, A sincere friend.

A وفاض *wifāz*, A piece of leather put under a handmill. A place containing or retaining water. (pl. of وفضة *wafzat*) Leathern quivers. Scrips. خاوي الوفاض *khāwī'l wifāz*, Empty in wallet.

A وفاع *wifāɛ*, The stopple of a bottle.

A وفاق *wifāk*, (v. n. 3 of وفق) Consenting to, agreeing. Suiting, becoming. Turning out well. Meeting, encountering. Consent, assent, agreement, concord, harmony, good understanding, conformity. A plot, confederacy, conspiracy. جزاء وفاق *jazāɛi wifāk*, A suitable recompense.

A وفاهة *wafāhat*, The superintendence of a church. The daily allowance of a minister of a church.

A وفائي *wafāɛī*, Fidelity, sincerity. P بيوفائي *bī wafāɛī*, Breach of faith, want of fidelity.

P وفتوك *waftūk*, Tiger-skin spread over a throne.

A وفد *wafd*, (v. n. of وفد) Arriving, coming (as an ambassador to a king). The top of a sandy hill. Comers. (pl. of وافد *wāfid*) Crowds.

A وفّد *wuffad*, (pl. of وافد *wāfid*) Those who arrive. Ambassadors.

A وفر *wafr*, (v. n. of وفر) Becoming full, complete, entire, numerous, copious, abundant. Filling, completing, making plentiful. Sparing (a person's reputation), not reviling. Returning (a gift). (pl. وفور *wufūr*) Plenty, abundance; affluence, opulence. Full, complete, entire, numerous, copious, abundant. Complete, perfect (leathern bottle).

A وفراء *wafrā*, (fem. of اوفر *awfar*) More plentiful. Full. Large (ear or leathern bottle). (Ground) abounding in herbage.

A وفرة *wafrat*, (pl. وفار *wifār*) The hair reaching below the ear. (See جمّة *jummat* and لمّة *limmat*). *Wafrat* or *wafirat*, Plenty, abundance. وفرت و كثرت *wafrat u kasrat*, Superfluity and exuberance.

P وفره *wafra*, A weaving-instrument.

A وفز *wafz* or *wafaz*, (pl. اوفاز *awfāz*) Haste, expedition. A high place. هو على وفز *huwa ʿala' wafazin*, He is on the road, or in haste.

A وفض *wafz* or *wafaz*, (v. n. of وفض) Making haste, running. (pl. اوفاض *awfāz*) Expedition, despatch. *Wafaz*, (pl. اوفاض *awfāz*) Any thing on which flesh is cut.

A وفضة *wafzat*, (pl. وفاض *wifāz*) A leathern quiver. A shepherd's scrip or traveller's bag, in which provisions are carried. The groove on the upper lip between the mustachios.

A وفع *wafʿ*, A lofty building. A cloud which gives promise of rain. *Wafaʿ*, (or وفعة *wafaʿat*) (pl. وفعان *wifʿān*) A boy from puberty to twenty years of age.

A وفعة *wafʿat*, A bit of rag in which borrowed fire is carried. The stopple of a bottle. A basket made of palm-leaves.

A وفق *wafk*, (v. n. of وفق) Finding (a thing) to be convenient and useful. Useful, apt, convenient (thing). A sufficiency; a quantity just sufficient, where nothing overflows or is redundant. Opportunity, convenient season. P وفق كردن *wafk kardan*, To accommodate one's self (to the times). بروفق *bar wafk*, In accordance with, agreeably to.

A وفل *wafl*, (v. n. of وفل) Unbarking, peeling. Any thing small or few.

A وفنة *wafnat*, Paucity, fewness.

A وفود *wufūd*, (v. n. of وفد) Coming, arriving (as an ambassador to a king). Arrival. (pl. of وافد *wāfid*) Comers. Ambassadors.

A وفور *wufūr*, (v. n. of وفر) Being full, complete, copious, abundant. Multitude, plenty, abundance. (pl. of وفر *wafr*) Full, complete, universal.

A وفه *wafh*, The superintendence of a church.

A وفهيّة *wafhiyat*, Prelacy, or high church-dignity. Ecclesiastical law, discipline, or precept.

A وفى *wafa'*, High ground.

A وفيّ *wafiy*, Entire, whole, complete. Just (weight). Full (measure). Much. *Wufiy*, (v. n. of وفي) Being full, entire, abundant. Being equal to a miskāl in weight (a dirham).

A وفيعة *wafiʿat*, Stopple of a phial. A basket or hamper made of palm-leaves. A pen-wiper. A lock of wool used in anointing a scabby (camel).

A وفيق *wafik*, A companion, friend.

A وق *wakk*, The note of the bird صرد *surad*.

A وقاء *wakā*, or *wikā*, That by which any thing is kept or preserved. ابن وقاء *ibni wakā* or *wikā*, The bird صرد *surad*. Name of a man. لازم الوقاء *lāzimu'l wakā*, Worthy of being preserved.

A وقاح *wakāh*, (pl. وقح *wukuh*) Hard (hoof). Shameless, brazen, unblushing. وقاح الذنب *wakāhu'z zamb*, Daring in the perpetration of crime. وقاح الذنب *wakāhu'zzanab*, Inured to much riding.

A وقاحة *wakāhat*, (v. n. of وقح) Being hard (a hoof). Being impudent, barefaced: impudence.

A وقاد *wikād*, Fuel for fire. Name of an isle.

A وقّاد *wakkād*, One who kindles. Skilful, knowing, intelligent. Bright, lucid, burning. Fiery.

A وقار *wakār*, (v. n. of وقر) Being quiet, calm, modest, mild, sedate, grave. Modesty, mildness. Sedateness, gravity. Majesty, authority, dignity. Prudent, modest, mild, sedate. اهل وقار *ahli wakār*, (P با وقار *bā wakār*) Majestic, of authority. بي وقاري *bī wakārī*, Want of gravity, unsteadiness.

A وقارة *wakārat*, Quietness, modesty, gravity.

A وقاط *wikāt*, (pl. of وقيط *wakīt*) Large hollows in mountains or hard lands where water collects.

A وقاع *wikāʿ*, (v. n. of وقع) Rushing upon (an enemy), attacking (in battle), fighting. Copulation. (pl. of وقيعة *wakīʿat*) Cavities in which water collects, tarns. *Wakāʿi*, A round mark burnt on the hips of horses.

A وقّاع *wakkāʿ*, Slanderous, malevolent (man). *Wukkāʿ*, Slanderous and malevolent (men).

A وقّاعة *wakkāʿat*, Slanderous, malevolent (man).

A وقاف *wikāf*, (v. n. of وقف) Standing (for another), aiding, assisting. Opposing, resisting. Asking one to stop and pause.

A وقّاف *wakkāf*, Tardy, dilatory. One who refrains from fighting.

A وقام *wikām*, A sword. A scourge, stick, or any instrument which inflicts pain. A rope.

A وقامة *wakāmat*, Subjugation. Shameful repulse.

A وقاه *wukāh*, The minister of a church.

A وقاهية *wakāhiyat*, The dignity of a bishop or other headship.

A وقايا *wakāya'*, (pl. of وقيّة *wukiyat*) Weights of seven miskāls. Weights of forty dirhams.

A وقاية *wakāyat* or *wikāyat*, A cloth worn by women to preserve their head-dress from being soiled by the unguent or pomatum of their hair. *Wakāyat*, *wikāyat*, or *wukāyat*, That by which any thing is kept or preserved. *Wikāyat*, (v. n. of وقي) Taking care of, preserving, keeping (one's person or garments) clean. Custody, guardianship, precaution. نون الوقاية *nūnu'l wikāyat*, The guarding ن or ن interposed between a verb and an affixed pronoun of the first person singular, to prevent the verb from being taken for a noun: as, حسبني *hasabanī*, It sufficed me; حسبي *hasabī*, My reputation. P وقايت كردن *wikāyat kardan*, To guard, preserve, defend.

A وقائز *wakāʾiz*, Rows of stones laid down for a pavement.

A وقائص *wakāʾis*, Tops of neck-joints.

A وقائع *wakāʾiʿ*, (pl. of وقيعة *wakīʿat*) Accidents, events. Engagements, battles. Hollows in mountains wherein water collects. وقائع و حوادث *wakāʾiʿ u hawādis*, Accidents and events.

P وقائع نگار *wakāʾiʿ-nigār*, Intelligencer.

P وقائع نگاري *wakāʾiʿ-nigārī*, The office of an intelligencer.

P وقائع نويس *wakāʾiʿ-navīs*, An imperial historiographer.

P وقايه *wukāya*, A silken or linen veil which reaches to the feet (worn by the eastern ladies when abroad; that which they wear at home does not hide the face, nor come lower than the knee).

A وقب *wakb*, (v. n. of وقب) Being concealed. Being eclipsed (the moon). Standing. Turning towards, going towards. A furrow, hollow, or well in a mountain or stone in which water collects, especially about a fathom or two in depth. The axle-hole of a pulley. The hollow immediately above the eye of a horse. The socket of the eye; any hollow in the body. Foolish. Low, mean. Absence, concealment. *Wakb*, (or وقبة *wakbat*) (v. n. of وقب) Entering. Becoming eclipsed (the moon). Setting (the sun). Coming on (darkness); assailing (misfortune). Approaching. Happening opportunely.

A وقبة *wakbat*, A hollow in a pudding, into which they pour sauce, or in a stone holding water. The orifice of the ear. A large shady niche in a wall. A bee-hive or nest.

A وقبيّ *wukbīy*, Companion of fools or low men.

A وقت *wakt*, (v. n. of وقت) Appointing a time. (pl. اوقات *awkāt*) Time, season, hour, especially fixed for doing any thing. Opportunity. Adversity, distress. P وقت بوقت *wakt ba wakt*, From time to time. وقت بيوقت *wakt bī wakt*, Constantly, perpetually. وقت روز *wakti roz*, Time of battle. A وقت المسا *waktu'l masā*, Evening-tide. وقت معلوم *wakti maʿlūm*, Fixed time, *i.e.* the hour of death. P وقت نازك *wakti nāzuk*, Delicate times. وقت نا وقت *wakt nā wakt*, Occasionally, without any stated time. A وقت وقت *wakt wakt*, (or وقتا *waktan*) Sometimes. بوقتها *bi waktihā*, Presently, immediately. P بي وقت *bī wakt*, Untimely, ill-timed. دروقت *dar wakt*, Immediately. دروقت حاجت *dar wakti hājat*, In time of need. A للوقت *li'l wakt*, (or لوقته *li waktihi*) Opportunely, in time. يوم وقت معلوم *yawmi wakti maʿlūm*, The day of judgment. P خوش وقت *khwush-wakt*, Pleased.

P وقت بينا *wakt-bīnā*, Observing time.

P وقت شناس *wakt-shinās*, An astronomer, an astrologer, one who knows times and seasons.

P وقتها *wakthā*, At times, ever and anon.

A وقتي *waktīy*, Whilst, when.

P وقت ياب *wakt-yāb*, Finding an opportunity.

A وقتئذ *wakta-izin*, Immediately, then.

P وقتي كه *wakte ki*, Whensoever, at what time. تا وقتي كه *tā wakte ki*, As long as. اندك وقتيرا *andak wakterā*, After a short time.

A وقح *wuk-h* or *wukuh*, (v. n. of وقح) Being hard (a hoof). Impudence. *Wakah*, (v. n. of وقح) Being hard (a hoof). Being shameless, impudent (a man). Impudence, arrogance, audacity. *Wakih*, Impudent, immodest, shameless. *Wukuh*, (pl. of وقاح *wakāh*) Hard hoofs or nails.

A وقد *wakd* or *wakad*, (v. n. of وقد) Being lighted, burning (a fire). The heat of fire. *Wakad*, Fire.

A وقدان *wakdān*, (v. n. of وقد) Being lighted, burning (a fire).

A وقدة *wakdat*, Excessive heat. The middle, the fifteenth, also tenth day of the month.

A وقذ *wakz*, (v. n. of وقذ) Beating with violence, almost to death. Throwing (one) on the ground. Leaving (one) fatigued or sick. Quenching, calming, quieting. Overcoming one (as sleep).

A وقر *wakr*, (v. n. of وقر) Burdening. Being deaf (the ear). Making deaf. Splitting or breaking (a bone). Sitting. Deafness, heaviness of hearing. Malevolence, hatred, rancour. A fissure or a cut in the leg. A hollow in a mountain, stone, or bone. The socket of the eye. *Wikr*, (pl. اوقار *awkār*) Weight. A heavy burden (carried by an ass or a mule, وسق *wisk* implying a camel's load). *Wakur*, Mild, modest, grave, sedate.

A وقرات *wakarāt*, Impressions, signs, marks.

A وقرة *wakrat*, (v. n. of وقر) Being lamed by a stone sticking in the foot (a horse). The lameness itself, or a blemish of that kind. A crack or hollow in a mountain or a bone. A hole in a stone wherein water collects. وقرة في صخرة *wakrat fi sakhrat*, One upon whom misfortunes make but little impression.

A وقري *wakra'*, Loaded (beast of burden).

A وقري *wakariy*, A shepherd. Rich in flocks, especially by births. An owner of asses. A denizen of a large city.

A وقس *waks*, (v. n. of وقس) Excoriating, laying bare (a sore), taking off the scab. Attacking a camel, diffusing itself (the scab). Suspecting one of adultery or fornication. The scab. Obscenity, turpitude, baseness, the mention of any thing shameful.

A وقش *waksh*, (v. n. of وقش) Becoming effaced (vestiges). A kind of herb. Name of a town in Yaman. *Waksh*, (*wakash*, وقشة *wakshat*, or *wakashat*) Motion. The murmur of people in motion; the sound of any thing moved. Chips for lighting a fire.

A وقص *waks*, (v. n. of وقص) Breaking the neck (of any body). Being broken (neck). Knocking, bruising. Shaking, jolting his rider (a camel). Blemish, defect, detriment, decrease. *Waks* or *wakas*, (in prosody) A uniting of اضمار *izmār* and خبن *khabn*. *Wakas*, (v. n. of وقص) Being short (the neck). Shortness of neck. Chips or sticks for burning. (pl. اوقاص *awkās*) Any number under ten and above five, in relation to the taxing of cattle for sacrifice (supposing the owner to be assessed to the value of a sheep for every five oxen; whatever number he has above five and under ten pays nothing).

A وقط *wakt*, (v. n. of وقط) Striking (one), and weighing him down. Treading (a cock). Oppressing one (milk). A large hollow in a mountain or hard ground where water collects.

A وقطان *wiktān*, (pl. of وقيط *wakīt*) Hollows in mountains or hard grounds where water collects.

A وقظ *wakz*, (v. n. of وقظ) Striking to the ground. Leaving one weak and sick. Being constantly intent upon any thing. A small cistern or watering-trough fed by a large reservoir.

A وقع *wakʿ*, (v. n. of وقع) Provoking, irritating. Leading or throwing (one) into battle. Sharpening (a sword, knife, or spear). Branding the thigh of a horse with the mark وقاع *wakāʿi*. Being carried with celerity, let loose, set at liberty. Blow, shock, collision. Respect, regard, consideration, attention. A high place, a projecting part of a mountain. *Wakʿ* or *wakiʿ*, A cloud promising rain. A thin cloud. وقع في يده *wukiʿa fi yadihi*, He became contemptible. He was sorry. *Wukʿ*, Places full of hollows where water collects. *Wakaʿ*, (v. n. of وقع) Having (bare feet) hurt by stony ground. Being worn thin (a horse's hoof). Nakedness of feet. Rocks, stones. *Wakiʿ*, Foot-sore from travelling over rough ground.

A وقّع *wukkaʿ*, Falling, alighting (birds).

A وقعات *wakaʿāt*, Accidents. Battles.

A وقعة *wakʿat*, Battle, combat, engagement, with shock succeeding shock. A blow. Contingence, occurrence. الوقعة *al wakʿata*, Once, all at once. *Wikʿat*, A (bird's) manner of alighting. *Wakaʿat*, One stone.

A وقف *wakf*, (v. n. of وقف) Standing, stopping, staying, halting, waiting. Remaining in the same place. Making a pause in reading. Being intent (upon any thing), endeavouring fully to understand (it). Checking, stopping, pulling, or keeping back. Making (a horse) stand still. Stilling (a boiling pot) by a dash of cold water. Detaining (one at home). Ministering in a Christian church. Giving one any thing to consider, apprizing. Bequeathing for pious uses (as habitations for the poor, and books for the use of learned men). Such bequest or legacy. Continence, abstinence. A horse white about the thinnest part of his legs. Tranquillity, firmness, constancy. A prison, restraint. Punctuation. A pause. A bracelet of ivory. Any rim (as iron or horn) surrounding a shield. P وقف كردن *wakf kardan*, To dedicate, consecrate.

A وقفة *wakfat*, Delay. A sinew whipt round a bow to strengthen it.

A وقفه *wakfa*, Delay. Choaking, stopping, retarding, respite, vacancy.

A وقفي *wakfi*, Belonging to a pious bequest.

A وقفيّة *wakfīyat*, The book wherein bequests are registered.

A وقل *wakl*, (v. n. of وقل) Climbing (a mountain). Lifting up one foot, and standing firm on the other. (pl. اوقال *awkāl*) A dwarf palm-tree (the fruit of which is called مقل *mukl*); also its fruit when dry (when fresh it is called بهش *bahsh*). *Wakal*, A stone, rock; stones, rocks. The stumps of lopt branches, by which they climb up palm-trees. *Wakal*, *wakil*, or *wakul*, (A she-goat) standing on the summit of a rock. *Wakil* or *wakul*, (A horse) going well over rocks or up a hill.

P وقل *wuhl*, A medicine called مقل *mukl*.

A وقلة *waklat*, (pl. وقول *wukūl*) A single dwarf palm-tree, the fruit of which is called مقل *mukl*. The kernel of that fruit. *Wakalat*, Small-headed (man).

A وقم *wakm*, (v. n. of وقم) Prohibiting, preventing, restraining, checking, drawing the reins. Repulsing with contempt or violence. Oppressing, afflicting, grieving. Stilling (a boiling pot). Breaking, subduing, subjecting. Being trodden (ground) and made bare of herbage by grazing.

A وقنة *wuknat*, (pl. وقنات *wuknāt*) A bird's nest. A cavern. A little pit.

P وقواق *wakwāk*, Name of an island; also of a mountain where gold is said to be found in such plenty that the inhabitants make all their utensils of it; where the monkeys are taught to fetch wood and sweep the houses; and where there is a tree, the fruit of which resembles men and other animals.

A وقواق *wakwāk*, Timid, pusillanimous. Name of a country north of China. Name of a tree from which inkstands are made.

A وقواقة *wakwākat*, Talkative, loquacious.

A وقوب *wukūb*, (v. n. of وقب) Setting, sinking below the horizon (the sun). Being eclipsed (the moon). Sunset. Absence, concealment.

A وقوحة *wukūhat*, (v. n. of وقح) Being hard (a hoof). Being shameless, impudent, brazen-faced.

A وقود *wakūd*, (v. n. of وقد) Being kindled, burning (a fire). Fuel for fire. Heat of fire. *Wukūd*, (v. n. of وقد) Being kindled, burning (a fire). Heat of fire. A burnt-offering.

A وقور *wakūr*, Grave: prudent, modest, mild, sedate.

A وقورة *wukūrat*, A sitting, remaining at home.

A وقوع *wukūʿ*, (v. n. of وقع) Falling (into, or from its place). Falling, alighting (a bird). Falling (a spring-shower). Being necessary, obligatory. Being firm, fixed, settled, confirmed. Kneeling (a camel). Lying down (a sheep or a dog). Happening, occurring. Accident, contingency, occurrence, event. Death, destruction. Evidence. Falling, alighting birds. نادر الوقوع *nādiru'l wukūʿ*, Seldom happening, of rare occurrence.

A وقوعي *wukūʿī*, Reality.

A وقوف *wukūf*, (v. n. of وقف) Standing still (a horse). Remaining in the same place. Checking, stopping, pulling, or keeping back. Stilling the boiling of a pot by a dash of cold water. Giving one any thing to consider, apprizing. Being intent upon (a thing), endeavouring to understand it. Making a pause (in reading or speaking). Ministering in a Christian church. Experience, knowledge, practice; sense, understanding, wisdom. Notice, information. Conflict, engagement. A pause. Stagnation. (pl. of واقف *wākif*) Standers, bystanders. اهل وقوف *ahli wukūf*, (or صاحب وقوف *sāhib wukūf*) Experienced, skilful, intelligent. P بي وقوف *bī wukūf*, Unskilful. وقوف يافتن *wukūf yāftan*, To obtain a knowledge, receive information.

P وقوف دار *wukūf-dār*, Informed of, knowing.

A وقوفيّة *wukūfīyat*, Experience, knowledge.

A وقوقة *wakwakat*, Barking of dogs. Chattering or chirping of birds.

A وقول *wukūl*, (v. n. of وقل) Ascending (a mountain), standing on the summit (a she-goat). (pl. of وقلة *wahlat*) Kernels of the fruit مقل *mukl*.

A وقه *wakah*, (v. n. of وقه) Listening to, obeying.

A وقهة *wak-hat*, Obedience, attention to duty.

A وقي *wahy*, (v. n. of وقي) Taking care of, preserving, protecting, keeping one's self or garments clean. وقاه الله *wakāhu'llāh*, May God preserve or protect him!

A وقيّ *wakīy*, One who keeps (a thing) out of harm's way. Kept safe from injury or defilement. سرج وقيّ *sarjun wakiyun*, A saddle which galls not a (horse's) back. *Wukīy*, (v. n. of وقي) Being safe from injury. Protection, preservation. Abstinence, chastity. (pl. of وقيّة *wukayyat*) Ounces.

A وقيب *wakīb*, Noise of a yard in the sheath.

A وقيّة *wakīyat*, A weight of 2¼lbs. *Wukīyat*, (pl. وقايا *wakāyaʾ*) A weight of seven miskāls and forty dirhams.

A وقيح *wakīh*, Impudent, barefaced.

A وقيد *wakīd*, Fuel. Heat of fire.

A وقيديّة *wakīdīyat*, A species of goat.

A وقيذ *wakīz*, Prostrate, thrown down. Slow, inactive. Heavy, dull. Dangerously ill, at the point of death. A sheep killed by a stick.

A وقير *wakīr*, A large hollow on a mountain or a hole in a stone containing water. A flock of sheep or goats (about five hundred). A flock, with the shepherd, his dog, and his ass. Split (bone). Prudent, wise. Grave, quiet. Loaded with debts. فقير وقير *fakīr wakīr*, Poor.

A وقيرة *wakīrat*, A large mountain-tarn.

A وقيط *wakīt*, (pl. وقطان *wiktān*, وقاط *wikāt*, and اقاط *ikāt*) A large hollow in a mountain or hard ground where water collects. One whose sleep flies from him, so that he becomes heavy and spiritless. Pained, oppressed with a blow or grief. يوم الوقيط *yawmu'l wakīt*, A day on which a memorable battle was fought amongst the Arabs.

A وقيظ *wakīz*, Immoveable, unable to rise.

A وقيع *wakīʿ*, Sharpened, whetted (sword, knife). Worn (as a hoof by the stones). (A place) having many hollows filled with water.

A وقيعة *wakīʿat*, (pl. وقائع *wakāsiʿ*) An accident, action, battle, combat, engagement, event. The shock or brunt of a battle. A hamper or basket made of palm-leaves in which clothes are kept. (pl. وقاع *wikāʿ* and وقائع *wakāsiʿ*) Any cavity in which water collects (less than وقيط *wakīt*). Slander, disparagement. (Ground) not imbibing water. وقيعة الاثنين *wakīʿatu'l isnayn*, A fight between two, a duel. (See وفيعة *wafīʿat*.)

A وقيفة *wakīfat*, A mountain-goat beset by dogs and hunters, and forced to flee to the rocks.

A وقّيفى *wikkīfaʾ*, (v. n. of وقف) Ministering in a Christian church.

P وك *wak*, A frog.

A وكّ *wakk*, A spurning, repulsing.

A وكأ *wakʾ*, (v. n. of وكأ) Leaning on a staff. Crying (as a camel in labour).

A وكاء *wikāʾ*, (v. n. of وكي) Binding or stopping the mouth of a bottle. A chain, or any thing fastening the mouth of a bottle or the cover of a vessel. Any vessel whose head is covered over. An avaricious man.

A وكّاب *wakkāb*, One who mourns much and often. Name of a poet of the tribe of هذيل *huzayl*.

A وكاث *wi* or *wukās*, A hasty meal. Breakfast.

A وكاد *wikād*, (pl. وكائد *wakāsid*) A leathern belt (especially one used to tie a cow when milking).

A وكّار *wakkār*, A prancer, ambler, runner.

A وكاعة *wakāʿat*, (v. n. of وكع) Being firm and hard (a leathern bottle, skin-garment, horse, or the heart). Being base, ignoble.

A وكاف *wikāf* or *wukāf*, The stuffing of a pack-saddle (for an ass).

A وكال *wikāl*, (v. n. 3 of وكل) Trusting to one, having mutual confidence. Going heavily (a horse). *Wi* or *wakāl*, Slowness, sluggishness (of a horse).

A وكالة *wakālat* or *wikālat*, Vicegerency. The office of substitute, agent, administrator, or plenipotentiary; embassy, agency, deputation. The business of a وكيل *wakīl*: attorneyship.

P وكالت نامه *wakālat-nāma*, A plenipotentiary commission, full powers. An ambassador's credentials. A power of attorney.

P وكانا *wakānā*, Part of a cluster of dates or bunch of grapes.

A وكاية *wikāyat*, A walking-stick, a prop.

A وكائد *wakāsid*, (pl. of وكاد *wikād*) Thongs, straps for tying and fastening.

A وكب *wakb*, (v. n. of وكب) Being erect, straight. Making a gradual progress. Being assiduous. *Wakab*, Dirt, filth. Blackness of ripe dates.

A وكبان *wakabān*, A gradual progress.

A وكت *wakt*, (v. n. of وكت) Making an impression. Filling. A small thing, scarcity. A walk taken with short steps. Calumny, accusation. Labour expected from a half-free servant.

A وكتة *waktat*, A point. A white speck in the black part of the eye. *Wuktat*, That part of a tinder-box where the fire is struck.

P وكته *wukta*, A point or dot.

A وكح *wak-h*, (v. n. of وكح) Treading hard. *Wukuh*, Plump chickens or other young birds.

A وكد *wakd*, Any thing which one wishes to do and is solicitous about. *Wukd*, Study, endeavour. An act or deed. Power, strength.

P وكده *wakada*, (in zand and Pāz.) A female.

A وكر *wakr*, (v. n. of وكر) Entering its nest (a bird). Giving an entertainment on completing a house. Prancing (a horse). Jumping, leaping (a boy). Being swift of foot (a she-camel); also short and corpulent. Filling (a bottle or vessel). Striking on the nose with the fist. A prancing or ambling pace. (pl. اوكر *awkur*, اوكار *awkār*, وكور *wukūr*, and وكر *wukar*) A bird's nest (in a tree). *Wakar*, A prancing or ambling pace. *Wukar*, (pl. of وكر *wakr*) Birds' nests.

A وكرة *wakrat*, A nest. *Wakrat* or *wakarat*, A feast given on the finishing of a house. *Wukrat*, A cistern. A descent to water in order to drink.

A وكريٰ *wakaraʾ*, A prancing or ambling pace. Short of stature and corpulent (she-camel). Swift (she-camel). Firmly-treading (woman).

A وكز *wakz*, (v. n. of وكز) Striking with the fist (about the chin). Beating off, repelling, driving away. Digging, piercing, stabbing. Running. Filling. A dance. Besides.

A وكس *waks*, (v. n. of وكس) Being diminished, deficient. Losing (in trade). Diminishing, injuring. Defect, detriment, diminution. The entrance of the moon into an unlucky constellation. The lunar mansion in which the moon is eclipsed. Remains of matter in a wound. When blood or part of the skull falls in upon the dura mater or membrane of the brain.

P وكشك *wakshak*, The mastich-tree.

A وكظ *wakz*, (v. n. of وكظ) Beating off, thrusting away. Being intent on, persevering.

A وكع *wakʿ*, (v. n. of وكع) Striking, stinging (a scorpion), biting (a serpent). Striking the udder of a sheep (a lamb when sucking). Bruising (the nose). Rebuking, silencing. Squatting for the cock to tread (a hen). Falling through disease (a camel). *Wakaʻ*, A protuberance formed by the great toe resting upon the next one.

A وكعاء *wakʻāʼ*, (A woman) whose big toe leans upon the next one, so as to form a protuberance. (A woman) pained, filled with pain. Foolish (woman). The backside.

A وكف *wakf*, (v. n. of وكف) Running (as the eaves of a house with rain-water). Event, accident, issue, success. A sheet of dressed leather, which they spread as a table or table-cloth; also one upon which they play at chess or draughts. *Wakaf*, (v. n. of وكف) Being bent; inclining. Practising iniquity. Being culpable and blemished. Being weak. (pl. اوكاف *awkāf*) Injustice, partiality, deviation, excess. Crime, fault; stain, spot. The side of a mountain. A vein. Corruption, weakness. Difficulty, distress. Low-lying gravelly ground. Weight, gravity. An upper parlour constructed over the door-way or projecting part of a house. Sweat.

A وكل *wakl*, (v. n. of وكل) Entrusting (one's affairs to another). Acknowledging one's own weakness, and confiding (in God). Being weak (a beast). *Wakal*, Weak, unequal to; one who commits his business to another to execute.

A وكلاء *wukalāʼ*, (pl. of وكيل *wakīl*) Lieutenants, vicegerents, deputies, ministers, commissaries, delegates. Attorneys. وكلائ دولت *wukalāʼi dawlat*, Ministers of state. وكلائ طرفين *wukalāʼi tarafayn*, The plenipotentiaries of both sides.

A وكلة *wukalat*, Weak, incapable, and who therefore commits his business to another to execute.

A وكم *wakm*, (v. n. of وكم) Teasing, vexing, making sad. Becoming sad, afflicted, sorrowful, vexed. Treading down or eating up (pasture). Subduing, taming. Saluting. *Waham*, (v. n. of وكم) Being sad. Solicitude.

A وكمة *wakmat*, (fem.) Thick, filled, saturated.

A وكن *wakn*, (v. n. of وكن) Sitting (as a bird upon her eggs). Making great progress, going quick. A sitting, session. A nest on a mountain or in a wall. *Wukn*, (pl. of وكنة *wuknat*) Birds' nests.

A وكنة *waknat*, *wiknat*, *wuknat*, or *wukunat*, (pl. اوكن *awkun*, وكن *wukn*, and وكون *wukūn*) A nest on a mountain or in a wall. Any thing on which a bird perches.

A وكواك *wakwāk*, Timid, cowardly. One who goes with a trotting or ambling pace.

A وكواكة *wakwākat*, Large-hipped (woman).

A وكوب *wakūb*, (A doe) going quick with stretched-out neck. *Wukūb*, (v. n. of وكب) Being assiduous, attentive (to business). Gradual progress.

A وكود *wukūd*, (v. n. of وكد) Stopping, standing still. Intending, purposing. Overtaking, reaching. Tying (a knot). Fastening (a saddle).

A وكور *wukūr*, (v. n. of وكر) Entering its nest (a bird). Jumping, leaping (a boy). Filling (a vessel). (pl. of وكر *wakr*) Nests.

A وكوع لكوع *wakūʻ lakūʻ*, Worthless, base.

A وكوف *wakūf*, (A she-camel) full of milk.

P وكوك *wakwak*, The bark of a dog.

A وكوكة *wakwakat*, (v. n. of وكوك Q) Trotting. Flight (from battle). The cooing of a dove.

A وكول *wukūl*, (v. n. of وكل) Entrusting one's affairs to another, relying upon him.

A وكون *wukūn*, (v. n. of وكن) Sitting (as a bird upon her eggs). (pl. of وكنة *wuknat*) Nests.

A وكي *waky*, (v. n. of وكي) Binding or stopping the mouth of a vessel.

A وكيت *wakīt*, Information against any one, whispering, accusation. Lie, falsehood.

A وكيد *wakīd*, Strong, firm, solid.

A وكير *wakīr*, (or وكيرة *wakīrat*) A feast given on finishing a house, or to a stranger.

A وكيع *wakīʻ*, A belwether or leader of a flock. Hard, firm. Strong, unleaky (bottle); hardy, unsweating (horse). Hard (heart). قلب وكيع *kalbi wakīʻ*, A heart having eyes and ears, *i.e.* attentive to every thing. وكيع لكيع *wakīʻ lakīʻ*, Worthless, base, ignoble.

A وكيف *wakīf*, (v. n. of وكف) Running (as the eaves of a house with rain-water).

A وكيل *wakīl*, (pl. وكلاء *wukalāʼ*) An ambassador, agent, deputy, vicegerent, lieutenant, commissary, factor, administrator, representative. An attorney, pleader, counsellor (at law). A governor, protector. God. وكيل خرج *wakīli kharj*, Master of a house, host, purveyor. وكيل الدعوا *wakīlu'd daʻwaʼ*, An advocate, counsellor, proctor, agent, or attorney at law. وكيل سلطنت عليّه *wakīli saltanati ʻaliya*, The administrator of the powerful empire, *i.e.* prime-minister. P وكيل كردن *wakīl kardan*, To substitute, to declare one your representative, to appoint an ambassador. A وكيل مطلق *wakīli mutlak*, A plenipotentiary, procurator-general, absolute vicegerent.

A وكيلي *wakīlī*, The office of a wakeel.

P وگال *wugāl*, A live coal.

P وگر *wagar*, (for واگر *wa agar*) And if, although.

P وگرنه *wa gar na*, (for واگرنه *wa agar na*) Otherwise. And if not.

P ول *wal*, A flower. A blossom. A vine-bud. *Wil*, Independent, one's own master.

P ولا *wilā* or *walā*, A thing, business. Time.

A ولاء *walāʼ*, Kindred, relationship. Assistance. A kingdom. Sovereignty. Authority, power. Nearness. The right and power exercised over one lately set free. Freedom, liberty. Friendship, love. Assistants, friends. *Wilāʼ*, (v. n. 3 of ولى) Continuing, following without intermission. Helping, befriending. Sovereignty. Separating (sheep) by way of distinction. Continuation. على الولاء *ʻala'l wilāʼ*, In uninterrupted succession, continuously.

A ولاءة *walāʼat*, Government, authority, jurisdiction. Friendship, love.

A ولاة *wulāt*, (pl. of والى *wālī*) Governors, presidents. Judges. Lords.

A ولّاج *wallāj*, One who enters briskly.

P ولاد *walād*, Silken-stuff.

A ولاد *wilād*, (v. n. of ولد) Bearing children (a woman). Nativity, birth-day. Child-birth.

A ولادة *wilādat*, (v. n. of ولد) Bearing children. Birth. يوم الولادة *yawmu'l wilādat*, Birth-day.

P ولاده *wilāda*, A round bit of wood fastened to a spindle's neck to prevent the thread coming off.

A ولّاذ *wallāz*, Swift (wolf). A liar, who promises but performs not. Self-opiniated. Insincere in friendship.

A ولّاس *wallās*, A wolf.

A ولاف *wilāf*, (v. n. of ولف) Flashing incessantly (lightning). Running (as a horse) and putting down both the fore-feet at once. Coming one after another (people). Becoming familiar, intimate. (v. n. 3 of ولف) Being accustomed. Being joined, united. Claiming relationship. Familiarity, friendship, society.

P ولانه *walāna* or *wilāna*, A wound.

P ولاني *wulānī*, New wine.

P ولاو *wilāv*, Divided, scattered about, separated.

A ولايا *walāyaʼ*, (pl. of وليّة *walīyat*) Pack-saddles, or saddle-cloths. Governments, jurisdictions.

A ولاية *walāyat*, (v. n. of ولي) Helping, assisting. Governing. *Walāyat* or *wilāyat*, (v. n. of ولى) Being master of, controlling. Receiving any thing purchased or agreed for. Government, jurisdiction, dominion, power, authority. A province. *Wilāyat*, An inhabited country, dominion, district. (In India, *wilāyat* usually means England or Europe). ولايت قالوا بلى *wilāyati kālū balaʼ* or *balī*, Faith, religious belief. A covenant made with God by Adam and his seed. See Kur'ān, ch. vii. Sale in loc.

P ولايت ستان *wilāyat-satān*, A friend of God, saint, prophet (one who takes the kingdom).

A ولايتي *wilāyatī*, European, foreign.

A ولايتي خط *wilāyatī-khat*, A kind of Persian Nastalik hand.

A ولائح *walāʼih*, (pl. of وليحة *walīhat*) Corn-sacks.

A ولائد *walāʼid*, (pl. of وليدة) Girls. Handmaids.

A ولت *walt*, (v. n. of ولت) Diminishing. Diminution, defect, detriment.

A ولث *wals*, (v. n. of ولث) Striking (with a stick). Writing or ratifying (an agreement, especially one weak and not binding). An agreement, compact, confederacy (especially involuntary, accidental, and not durable). A faint promise. Moderate (rain). A remainder of wine in a bottle, water in sandy ground, or leaven on a baker's board. A blow. A beating. Vile, base. Weak in body. Remains or vestiges of ophthalmia. Manumission promised to a slave after his master's death in the following form: انت حرٌّ بعد موتي *anta hurrun baʿda mawtī,* Be thou free after my death.

P ولج *walaj, walj,* or *wilj,* A quail.

A ولج *walaj,* A way through sands. *Wulaj,* A young eagle. *Wuluj,* Streets, squares. Shores, coasts. Ladles or similar utensils in which honey is gathered.

A وَلَجَة *walajat,* (pl. اولاج *awlāj*) A cavern or similar place into which passengers retire to shelter themselves from rain. The bend of a river or valley. *Wulajat,* (in comp. with خرجة *khurajat*): as, وُلَجَة خُرَجَة *wulajat khurajat,* Restless, unquiet, moving from place to place, going in and out.

P ولچ *walach, walch,* or *wilch,* A quail.

A ولح *walh,* The overloading (of a camel).

A وخة *walikhat,* (Land) covered with luxuriant herbage.

A ولد *wald, wild, wuld,* or *walad,* (pl. اولاد *awlād,* ولدة *wildat,* الدة *ildat,* ولد *wuld, wild,* and *wald*) A son, offspring. Sons. ولد الزناء *waladu'z zināʾ,* A bastard. An earth-worm. *Wuld,* (pl. of ولد *walad*) Sons, children. (pl. of ولود *walūd*) Prolific, teeming. *Walad,* The offspring (of the brute creation) so long as they are unable to feed themselves. فلان ولد فلان *fulān waladi fulān,* Such a one, the son of such a one. مال و ولد *māl u walad,* Substance and children; things most highly prized.

A ولدان *wildān,* (pl. of وليد *walīd*) Sons, children. Servants.

P ولدان *waladān,* (pl. of A ولد *walad*) Sons.

A ولدة *wildat,* (pl. of ولد) Sons, children.

A ولذ *walz,* Speed, expedition. Motion.

A ولس *wals,* (v. n. of ولس) Relating any thing obscurely, ambiguously, and enigmatically. Perfidy, fraud. *Walas,* (or ولسان *walasān*) (v. n. of ولس) Going quick with a stretched-out neck (a camel).

A ولع *walʿ,* (or ولعان *walaʿān*) (v. n. of ولع) Telling a lie. Restraining, hindering, prohibiting, forcing. Becoming light and contemptible. Taking (what belongs to another). *Walaʿ,* (v. n. of ولع) Desiring eagerly; being given to, intent upon. The eager desire of one intent upon any thing.

A ولعة *walaʿat,* (pl. of والع *wāliʿ*) Liars. *Wulaʿat,* Desirous, greedy of what belongs not to one.

A ولغ *walgh,* (*wulgh,* or ولغان *walaghān*) (v. n. of ولغ) Thrusting his muzzle into a pot and lapping (a dog), sipping (a fly).

A ولغة *walghat,* A small bucket.

P ولغونه *wulghūna,* Rouge used by ladies.

A ولف *walf,* Incessant flash (of lightning).

A ولق *walk,* (v. n. of ولق) Being expeditious, active. Being ready at falsehood. Persevering in a journey or a lie. Piercing slightly. Striking (with a sword).

A ولقة *walakat,* (pl. ولقات *walakāt*) A blow.

A ولقى *walakā,* A prancing, springing pace. Swift (she-camel). عدا الولقى *ʿadā'l walkā,* (The camel) ran with springiness.

A ولكن *wa lākin,* But, nevertheless.

A ولم *walm* or *walam,* A saddle-girth, surcingle. A fetter; tether. A belt or rope passing from the poitrel to the crupper of a camel.

A ولمة *walmat,* A complete collection, whole.

P ولمشك *walmashk,* Mastick-tree or fruit.

A ولو *wa law,* At least; and if; even if, though, even should. اولم و لو بشاة *awlim wa law bi shātin,* Give a marriage-feast, if only with one sheep.

A ولوال *walwāl,* Anxiety. Anguish, vexation. The cry of one weeping or threatening. A large male owl. *Wilwāl,* (v. n. of ولول Q) Howling, lamenting, crying. Wail, lamentation.

P ولوالي *walwālī,* (in the dialect of Samarkand) Sheeps' chitterlings stuffed with meat and spices.

A ولوب *wulūb,* (v. n. of ولب) Arriving at, reaching. Entering. Going quick, making haste.

A ولوج *wulūj,* (v. n. of ولج) Creeping (into a hole), flying (to a den). ولوج و خروج *wulūj u khurūj,* Ingress and egress.

A ولود *walūd,* Prolific, teeming.

A ولودة *wulūdat,* Generation. Nativity.

A ولوديّة *walūdiyat* or *wulūdiyat,* Iniquity, inhumanity, vexation, importunity, trouble. Littleness, tenderness of age.

A ولوع *walūʿ,* (v. n. of ولع) Desiring eagerly, being given to, intent on. Desire, avidity. Greedy.

A ولوغ *walūgh,* Any thing tasted or sipt. *Wulūgh,* (v. n. of ولغ) Lapping (a dog), sipping (a fly).

A ولوف *walūf,* (Lightning) flashing incessantly.

A ولولة *walwalat,* (v. n. of ولول Q) Howling, lamenting, crying. Twanging (a bow-string). Wail, lamentation. Tumult, noise, confused murmur. P ولولهٔ تفنگ *walwalaʾi tufang,* The explosion of a musket. ولولهٔ كوس و نفير *walwalaʾi kos u nafīr,* Clang of drum and trumpet.

A ولويّ *walawiy,* (Rain) falling rapidly.

P وله *wala* or *walla,* Force, violence. Blandishment. Anger, rage. A distressed lover.

A وله *walah,* (v. n. of وله) Being frightened. Being sad, afflicted, sorrowful, distracted, or impatient from love or grief. Fear. Terror, grief, perturbation of mind, stupor.

A ولهان *walhān,* Astonished, stupefied, confounded, dejected, distracted with terror or grief, mad with love. *Walahān,* (v. n. of وله) Being sorrowful, distracted, impatient from love or grief.

P وله زده *walah-zada,* A lover hardly used and ill-treated. *Wala-zada,* Angry, passionate, furious.

A ولهى *walhā,* (fem. of ولهان *walhān*) (A woman) astonished, stupefied, distracted with love, fear, or grief. Name of a demon that excites persons to scatter the water about very much in making their ablutions.

A ولي *waly,* (v. n. of ولي) Being near, neighbouring, contiguous, joining. Being wet with successive showers (ground). Shower following shower. Nearness. و ما يليه *wa mā yalīhu,* And what adjoins it; the parts adjacent. *Wulā',* (pl. of وليا *wulyā'*) Near. Excellent (women).

P ولي *wale,* (for وليك *wa lek* or وليكن *wa lekin,* from A ولكن *wa lākin*) But, yet, however, for all that.

A وليّ *waliy,* A favourite of God or the king. A sincere friend. A helper, guardian, defender. A prince, lord, president, governor, judge. Nigh, adjoining, hard by. A servant, slave. Like. Holy. (pl. اولية *awliyat*) Shower following shower. وليّ بعيد *waliy baʿīd,* A guardian of a more distant degree than a father, brother, or uncle. وليّ جنايت *waliy jināyat,* The next of kin entitled to exact retaliation for offences. وليّ الجود *waliyu'l jūd,* Lord of liberality, *i.e.* God. P ولي خدا *waliʾi khudā,* A friend of God, a holy man. A وليّ الدم *waliyu'd dam,* The next of kin entitled to be the avenger of blood. ولي عهد *waliʾi ʿahd,* Heir apparent, destined or acknowledged successor. A vicegerent. P ولي عهد كردن *waliʾi ʿahd kardan,* To nominate or declare a successor to a kingdom. A ولى عهدي *wali ʿahdī,* Heritage, the state of being an heir apparent. Deputyship. AP ولي كامل *waliʾi kāmil,* A perfect saint. ولي نعمت *waliʾi niʿmat,* (or وليّ النعم *waliyu'n niʿam*) The lord of beneficence, *i.e.* the master of a feast, the landlord. A benefactor, lord, master. A title of respect by which a father is addressed.

A وليا *wulyā',* (fem. of اولي *awlā'*) More excellent.

A وليّة *waliyat,* (pl. ولايا *walāyā*) Government, jurisdiction. A province. A woollen saddle-cloth, or any thing put under it. Provisions set apart by a woman for any expected guest.

A وليجة *walījat,* An intimate, confidential friend (especially not of one's own people). Near, adjacent.

A وليحة *walīhat,* (pl. وليح *walīh* and ولائح *walāʾih*) A corn-sack. A large basket or hamper.

A وليخ *walīkh,* A linen cloth or garment.

A وليخة *walīkhat,* (Ground) covered with luxuriant herbage. Thick milk. Thin mud, clay.

A وليد *walīd,* (pl. ولائد *walāʾid* or ولدان *wildān*) A son, lad, child. A servant. امّ الوليد *ummu'l walīd,* The mother of children, *i.e.* a hen.

A وليدات *wulaydāt,* (dim. of لدة *lidat*) Little cotemporaries.

A وليدة *walīdat,* (fem. of وليد *walīd*) (pl. ولائد) A girl. A handmaid. Born amongst the Arabians.

A وليدون *wulaydūna,* (dim. of لدة *lidat*) Little cotemporaries.

P وليس *walīs,* (or وليسه *walīsa*) Good, fair.

A وليع *walīʿ,* Unblown flowers of palm-trees.

A وليعة *walīʿat,* A branch of the tribe of Kindat.

A وليف *walīf,* (v. n. of ولف) Flashing incessantly (lightning). Running, and putting down both the fore-feet at once (a horse). Coming one after another (people). Being familiar, intimate.

(Lightning) flashing incessantly.

A وليقة *walīkat*, A dish of flour, butter, or milk.

P وليك *walek*, (or وليكن *wa lekin*) But.

A وليمة *walīmat*, (pl. ولائم *walāʼim*) A banquet. A marriage-feast. وليمة الختان *walīmatu'l khitān*, A circumcision-feast.

P ولين *wilīn*, Ringworm, dry scab.

A وليات *wulyayāt*, pl. of وليا, Excellent (women).

A وماء *wamāʼ*, (v. n. of ومأ) Making a sign. A nod, sign.

A ومّاج *wammāj*, properly ومّاح *wammāh*, Vulva.

A ومّاح *wammāh*, Fissure of the female privities.

A ومحة *wamhat*, A mark made by the sun.

A ومخة *wamkhat*, A smarting, cutting reproof.

A ومد *wamad*, (v. n. of ومد) Being extremely hot (night). Boiling with rage. Intense heat in a still, sultry night. Anger, passion, rage. Nocturnal dew rising from the sea. *Wamid*, Hot, warm, also dewy (night).

A ومدة *wamadat*, Intense heat of a still, sultry night. Anger. *Wamidat*, Hot and dewy (night).

A ومذة *wamzat*, Pure, unmixed whiteness.

P ومر *wamar*, Besides, moreover.

A ومز *wamz*, (v. n. of ومز) Moving (the nose in anger), or making a signal with the nose.

A ومس *wams*, A rubbing smooth, excoriating.

A ومشة *wamshat*, A white mole on the face.

A ومض *wamz*, (and ومضان *wamazān*) (v. n. of ومض) Gleaming, flashing slightly (lightning) (when spreading wide it is called خفو *khafw*; when it seems to pierce the clouds in perpendicular bolts it is expressed by عقيقة *ʻakīkat*).

A ومطة *wamtat*, Prostration from fatigue.

A ومعة *wamʻat*, A large rolling wave. A rush, flush, or gush of water.

A ومغة *wamghat*, A single long hair.

A ومق *wamk*, (v. n. of ومق) Loving, liking. Love.

A ومكة *wamkat*, Amplitude, space. Liberty.

A ومه *wamh*, (v. n. of ومه) Being excessively hot (the day).

A ومهة *wamhat*, The purest part, or the liquefaction of any thing.

P وميدن *wamīdan*, To cut into small pieces. To splice or join a broken rope without a knot. To be hollowed, excavated, or dug out. To rub. To blow into, puff up.

A وميض *wamīz*, Slight flash (of lightning).

P ون *wan*, Like, resembling. Pure. Sincere. A kernelled fruit, called in Arabic الحبّة الخضراء *al habbatu'l khazrāʼ*. But, yet, however. (in Kathay) Ten thousand years.

A ونّ *wann*, Weakness, languor, fatigue, labour. A musical instrument struck with the finger, a cymbal. Name of a city.

P ونا *wanā*, A turtle-dove, wood-pigeon.

A وناء *wanāʼ*, Labour, toil. Languor, lassitude.

A وناة *wanāt*, Torpid, languid (woman), slow in rising or sitting. Mild, gentle, tame (female). A pearl.

P ونانه *wanāna*, A kind of round cake.

P ونج *wanj*, A sparrow. *Wanaj*, Ugly. Unpleasant, morose.

A ونج *wanaj*, A stringed instrument; a lute.

P ونجنك *wanjnak*, Sweet-basil.

P وند *wand*, Experiment, proof. Labour, toil. Praise. A vessel, vase, cup. *Wand* (in forming possessives) is used for مند *mand*, as دولتوند *dawlatwand* for دولتمند *dawlatmand*, Rich, a rich man.

P وندا *wandā*, (in zand and Pāz.) A wish, desire.

P وندانه *wan-dāna*, The fruit ون *wan*.

P وندسار *wandsār*, The centre of a circle.

T وندك *wanadik*, Venice. Venetian state.

P وندوندید *wandwandīd*, 7th book of the Zand.

P ونده *wanda*, Cresses.

P ونديداد *wandīdād*, Sixth book of the Zand.

P ونديدن *wandīdan*, To labour, to toil.

P ونديدوزند *wandīdūzand*, 9th book of the Zand.

P ونژد *wan-jad*, Gum of the ون *wan*-tree.

A ونع *wanaʻ*, A small thing, a little.

A ونك *wank*, A residence (among relations).

P ونك *vanak*, An animal smaller than a cat, of a dusty colour, without a tail.

P ونكول *wankūl*, Wanting, necessary, required.

P ونكه *wanki*, Nay, but.

P ونگ *wang* or *wing*, Empty, empty-handed, poor, destitute. Echo, noise. Ugly.

A ونم *wanm*, (v. n. of ونم) Muting (a fly).

A ونمة *wanamat*, Dung or mark of a fly.

P ونمشك *wanmashk*, Gum of the tree بن *ban*.

P وننگ *wanang*, A line upon which they hang grapes. The top of a bunch of grapes; also the stalk. The tendril of a vine.

A وني *wany*, (v. n. of وني) Leaving off, ceasing. Tucking up (the sleeve). هو لا يني يفعل كذا *huwa lā yanī yafʻalu kazā*, He ceases not to do so. *Wany* or *wanaʼ*, (v. n. of وني) Being sluggish, dull, heavy, slothful, listless. *Wanaʼ*, Languor, lassitude, listlessness. Labour, toil.

A ونيّ *wunīy*, (v. n. of وني) Being sluggish, dull, heavy, listless.

A ونية *wanyat*, A pearl. A string of pearls. A sack. *Wanyat* or *winyat*, (v. n. of وني) Being torpid, languid, slothful, slow, fatigued. Delay, slowness, languor, lassitude. بلا ونية *bilā winyat*, Without delay.

P ونيزد *wanīzad*, (or ونيژد *wanījad*) Gum of the tree ون *wan*.

A ونيم *wanīm*, (v. n. of ونم) Muting (a fly). The excrement or mark of a fly.

A وو *wāw*, The letter و.

P ووا *wawā*, A good omen, happy presage.

A وؤرة *wuʼrat*, (pl. وآر *wuʼār*) A fire. A hearth.

A وؤول *wuʼūl*, (v. n. of وأل) Taking refuge. Getting off safe.

P وه *wah*, Strange! Would to God! Alas! Ho! have a care!

A وه *wah*, O rare! excellent! Ah! alas!

A وهّ *wahh*, Grief, sadness. *Wahhin*, Fy!

A وهّاب *wahhāb*, (and وهّابة *wahhābat*) A giver, one who bestows. Liberal, munificent. An epithet of God. وهّاب العطايا *wahhābu'l ʻatāyaʼ*, (God) the bestower of benefits.

A وهّابيّة *wahhābiyat*, Extreme liberality.

A وهّاج *wahhāj*, Burning, flaming; raging.

A وهاد *wihād*, (pl. of وهدة *wahdat*) Valleys, low grounds. تلال و وهاد *tilāl u wihād*, Hills and dales.

A وهازة *wihāzat*, The step of a modest woman, her elegant, unaffected manner of walking.

A وهّاس *wahhās*, A lion. A proper name.

A وهّاص *wahhās*, A liberal giver.

A وهاط *wihāt*, (pl. of وهطة) Low grounds.

A وهافة *wihāfat*, (v. n. of وهف) Having charge of a temple. *Wihāfat* or *wahāfat*, The office of a person who has charge of a temple.

A وهّام *wahhām*, Suspicious, distrustful.

A وهب *wahb*, (v. n. of وهب) Excelling in a contest concerning liberality. *Wahb* or *wahab*, (v. n. of وهب) Giving, bestowing. Pardoning, forgiving. *Wahab*, A gift.

A وهبي *wahbī*, Bestowed by God.

A وهت *waht*, A pressing, squeezing, thumping.

A وهتة *wahtat*, Low ground. A hard fall.

A وهث *wahs*, (v. n. of وهث) Being diligent, assiduous, most attentive. Trampling under foot.

A وهج *wahj*, (or وهجان *wahajān*) (v. n. of وهج) Burning (as fire). *Wahaj*, The heat of fire.

A وهد *wahd*, (pl. أوهد *awhud* and وهدان *wuhdān*) or وهدة *wahdat*, (pl. وهاد *wihād*) A valley, hollow, declivity.

P وهر *wahr*, (or وهره) Name of a country.

A وهر *wahr*, (v. n. of وهر) Bringing (one) into a scrape from which (he) cannot extricate (himself). *Wahar*, The scorching rays of the sun reflected from the ground, and floating on the surface like a vapour.

A وهز *wahz*, (v. n. of وهز) Trampling upon, beating (a path). Cracking (a louse) between the nails. Striking one with the feet or with the fist. Repelling. Exciting, stimulating. A short corpulent man; hardy, square-built.

A وهس *wahs*, (v. n. of وهس) Going quick. Behaving haughtily or injuriously to friends. Bruising, breaking. Trampling, treading under foot. A secret. Detraction, slander. Machination, perfidy.

P وهشت *wahshat*, Name of the fourth embolismal day added to the Persian year.

A وهص *wahs*, (v. n. of وهص) Breaking (especially any thing soft or hollow within). Treading under foot. Throwing with violence, dashing on the ground. Castrating.

A وهصة *wahsat*, (or وهضة) Ground low, circular.

A وهط *waht*, (v. n. of وهط) Breaking. Trampling hard upon. Being weak and enervated. Stabbing. Leanness, meagreness. A large company of men. A great quantity of the plant عرفط *ɛurfut* or عشر *ɛushar*, or a place where it grows. Name of a garden in Taif, formerly belonging to عمرو بن العاص *ɛamr bini'l ɛās.* (pl. of وهطة *wahtat*) Low grounds.

A وهطة *wahtat*, Low ground.

A وهف *wahf*, (v. n. of وهف) Putting forth leaves (a tree), flourishing (as plants). Having the care of a temple. Being shaken by the wind (a tree). Approaching, drawing near. Presenting itself, appearing. Happening.

P وهفت *wahift*, Name of one of the embolismal days added to the Persian year.

A وهفيّة *wuhfiyat* or *wihifīyat*, The office of one who has the charge of a temple.

A وهق *wahk*, (v. n. of وهق) Restraining, hindering. *Wahk* or *wahak*, (pl. اوهاق *awhāk*) A noose thrown to catch men or animals, a lasso. A long rope for tethering cattle.

A وهل *wahl*, (v. n. of وهل) Applying one's mind to any thing, though wishing to do another. Conjecturing, supposing. Afraid, timid, frightened. *Wahal*, (v. n. of وهل) Being weak, timid, terrified. Committing an error, making a slip. Forgetting, blundering. Fear, terror. Mistake. Forgetfulness. *Wahil*, Languid. Frightened, trembling.

P وهل *wuhl*, Any coniferous tree.

A وهلة *wahlat*, Fear, terror. اوّل وهلة *awwala wahla* or *wahalatin*, First, before all, first of all.

A وهم *wahm*, (v. n. of وهم) Thinking, turning any thing in one's mind, imagining, persuading one's self; conceiving a false idea. Pretending to do (one thing), when wishing or purposing to do another. Mind, sense. (pl. اوهام *awhām*) Opinion, conjecture. Suspicion, doubt, scruple, caution. Fear, distrust. Anxiety, apprehension. Malevolence. (pl. وهم *wuhm* and وهوم *wuhūm*) A wide or clear road, highway. A large tractable camel. A large-bodied man. P وهم كردن *wahm kardan*, To imagine, suspect. A قوّت وهم *kūwati wahm*, The intellectual faculty, power of imagination. لا وهم من كذا *lā wahma min kazā*, It is inevitable or necessary. *Waham*, (v. n. of وهم) Making a mistake (in reckoning). Wishing ill. *Wuhum*, (pl. of وهم *wahm*) Highways. Large men. Large tractable camels.

P وهمناك *wahmnāk*, Frightened, fearful, trembling; suspicious, scrupulous. Terrific.

P وهمنش *wahmanish*, (in zand and Pāzand) Any one whose heart is right with God.

A وهمي *wahmīy*, Imaginary, conjectural.

A وهن *wahn*, (v. n. of وهن) Weakening, enervating. Entering on the midnight hour. Midnight, or the hour after it. Short and thick (man). A thick-bodied camel. *Wahn* or *wahan*, (v. n. of وهن) Being weak, unequal to. Weakness, imbecility. *Wuhn*, (pl. of واهن *wāhin*) Weak, enervated.

A وهنانة *wahnānat*, Languid, slow-rising (woman).

P وهنگ *wihang*, A ring on a rope, by means of which they fasten burdens upon camels. A wooden stirrup. A noose for catching man or beast, a lasso. A fattening grain which women eat. A single draught of water.

A وهواه *wahwāh*, Brisk, active, lively (horse). Growling (lion). A male ass in want of the female.

A وهوب *wahūb*, Liberal, munificent.

A و هو حيّ *wa huwa hayy*, And he (still) living.

A وهوم *wuhūm*, (pl. of وهم *wahm*) Highways. Large men. Large tractable camels.

A وهوه *wahwah*, Brisk, active, lively (horse).

A وهوهة *wahwahat*, (v. n. of وهوه Q) Roaring, growling (as a lion). Braying softly (an ass). Barking low (a dog). Exclaiming, lamenting (a woman). A sound in the throat (of a horse) just after neighing.

A وهي *wahy*, (v. n. of وهي) Being broken, torn, burst, split (a leathern bottle). Being rotten and falling to pieces (a rope). Being ruinous, threatening to tumble (a wall). Bursting its fastenings and dropping to pieces (any thing). Being scattered (a cloud). Being foolish and blundering (a man). Being destitute of abilities or reputation, becoming worthless. (pl. وهيّ *wuhīy* and اوهية *awhiyat*) A rent, fissure, crack.

A وهية *wahyat*, A crevice, crack, rent.

A وهيّة *wahīyat*, A large pearl. A fat young camel for slaughter. *Wuhayyat*, (dim. of وهي *wahy*) A small fissure.

A وهيج *wahīj*, Heat, sultriness. A blaze.

A وهيدة *wuhaydat*, A little hollow.

A وهيسة *wahīsat*, A dish made of locusts dried and bruised, and eaten plain or with fat.

A وهيف *wahīf*, (v. n. of وهف) Producing leaves, flourishing (a tree). Beginning to look green and gay (a plant). Being shaken by the wind (a tree). Approaching, coming near. Presenting itself, appearing. Happening.

A وهين *wahīn*, An overseer of hired servants.

P وي *way*, A part, quantity. A fold. Woe! Ah! alas! ده وي *dah-way*, Ten fold. صد وي *sad-way*, A hundred fold. (for او *u*) He. ويرا *wayrā*, (for اورا *urā*) Him, to him. *Wī*, Root, origin. O thou! (for بي *bī*) Without; as, وي عيب *wī ɛayb*, (or بي عيب *bī ɛayb*) Faultless.

A وي *way*, O! strange! wonderful! Fy on (you)! woe to (you)! ويك *wayka*, Woe be to thee!

A وياك *wiyāka*, (for اياك *iyāka*) Thee.

A وئال *wiɛāl*, (v. n. 3 of وأل) Endeavouring to fly, hastening to (any place) in order to escape.

A ويب *wayb*, Fy upon, woe to (you)!

A ويبة *waybat*, A measure of 22 or 24 مدّ *mudd*.

P ويتر *waysar* or *waysir*, A white rose.

A ويج *wayj*, The wooden sock of the plough.

P ويجك *wījak*, Pure, clear.

A ويح *wayh*, Oh! (in pity). Woe be to (you)! Bravo! well done! ويحك *wayhak*, O fortunate!

A ويخ *waykh*, Woe be to (you)!

P ويد *wīd* or *wayd*, Lost. Little, few, not much. Aid, help, remedy. Any thing of an astringent or styptic quality. *Wed*, The Hindū Scriptures.

P ويدا *wīdā* or *waydā*, Little, not much, few. Lost. Found, recovered, come to light. Pain, sorrow.

P ويدانك *wedānak*, Unconnected. Not brought to a conclusion.

P ويدستر *wīdastar*, The beaver.

P ويدن *wīdun* or *waydan*, To seek for help, to apply a remedy. To lose. To seek.

P ويده *way* or *wīda*, One who seeks a remedy.

P ويدي *wīdī*, (or ويذي *wīzī*) The leprosy.

P ويديدن *waydīdan*, To be lost. To diminish, injure. To seek and apply a remedy.

P وير *wīr*, Mind, intellect, reason. Interrogation. Recollection; by heart. A friend. A groan, lamentation. Custody, preservation. Name of a village. *Wer*, A fool.

A وئر *waɛir*, Very dry (place), very thirsty (land).

P ويرا *wayrā*, (for اورا *urā*) Him, to him. *Wīrā*, One who remembers, a learner. A lord. A keeper.

P ويراف *wīrāf*, The father of the prophet Ardā.

P ويران *wīrān wayrān*, or *werān*, Desert, desolate, ruined, depopulated. ويران كردن *werān kardan*, To lay waste, destroy, depopulate.

P ويرانگر *werāngar*, Ruinous, destructive.

P ويرانه *wīrāna* or *werāna*, Desolate. A solitude, a place full of ruins.

P ويراني *wīrānī*, *wayrānī*, or *werānī*, Desolation, depopulation, dilapidation, ruin.

P ويرج *wīraj*, Galangale, sweet-scented flag.

P ويردي *wīrdī*, Given, bestowed.

P ويرو *wīrū*, (or ويرو ويرا *wīrū wīrā*) Recollection.

P ويروير *wīrwīr*, Frequent interrogation.

P ويره *wayra*, Any plant not having an upright stem (as a melon); any parasitical plant, ivy. Fy!

P ويري *wīrī*, The leprosy. Cloth.

P ويژ *wej*, (or ويژه *weja*) Sincere, unmixed; pure, clear. The purest part of any thing. Neat wine. دوست ويژه *dosti weja*, A sincere friend. روغن ويژه *rawghani weja*, Purified fat or butter. شير ويژه *shīri weja*, Unmixed milk.

P ويژش *wejish*, Sanctification, holiness, purity.

P ويژگان *wejagān*, Intimate, chosen friends.

P ويژگي *wejagī*, Purity.

P ويژيدن *wejīdan*, To purify, clarify.

A ويس *ways*, Indigence. Any thing one desires. Exclamation of pity or approbation. Woe be to you!

P ويس *wīs*, Like. Name of the mistress of رامين.

P ويسه *wīsa*, Good. Abomination. Like, resembling. Name of the mistress of رامين *rāmīn*. Name of the father of پيران *pīrān*, Afrāsyāb's commander-in-chief. ويسه داشتن *wīsa dāshtan*, To detest. ويسه كردن *wīsa kardan*, To render abominable.

P ويشانيدن *wīshānīdan*, To assemble, convoke.

P ويشل *wayshal*, Name of a disease.

P ويشه *wesha*, A forest, wood. *Wīsha*, Ivy.

P ويشيدن *weshīdan*, To assemble. To make a bed, spread a cloth.

P ويشيدة *weshīda*, Spread out, made (bed). Exalted, raised. Twisted, involved.

A ويك *wayka* or *wayk*, Woe to you! Don't you see?

P ويك *wīk*, Bravo! Fy! out upon! Oh! (an interjection of pity).

P ويكان *waykān*, Oh! alas!

A ويكأنّ *waykasann*, Do you not see?

A ويل *wayl*, (v. n. of ويل) Paining, afflicting. Woe to (you)! fy upon (you)! An affliction, misfortune. Punishment, torment. Reprisals, revenge. The gate of hell; also name of a valley, river, or well there. ويلي *waylī*, Woe is me! ويلك *waylaka*, Woe to thee! ويله *waylahu*, Woe to him! ويلاً له *waylan lahu*, Woe betide him! ويل وائل *wayli wāsil*, (ويل وئل *wayli wasil*, or *wayli wasil*) A very great misfortune.

P ويل *wīl* or *wayl*, Victory, success, happy issue. Superiority. Bravo!

P ويلان *welān*, Any thing having a beginning and an ending, but no middle; incomplete.

P ويلانج *waylānj*, Sweet.

A ويلاه *waylāhu*, Alas! for him.

A ويلة *waylat*, Woe! alas! Disgrace, ignominy.

P ويل كش *wayl-kash*, Vindictive.

A ويلمة *waylimat* or *waylumat*, Sly, cunning.

A ويلمّة *waylummat*, (for ويل لامّه *waylun li ummihi*) Woe to his mother!

A ويله *waylih* or *luh*, Cunning, shrewd (man).

P ويله *wīla*, Victory; fortitude. Clamour, great noise. A clew of cotton thread.

P ويم *wīm*, A wash for walls.

A ويمة *waymat*, Suspicion, detraction, whispering.

A وين *wayn*, Black grapes.

P وين *wīn*, Black grapes. Colour.

A وينة *waynat*, A single black grape.

P ويند *wīnad*, (for بيند *bīnad*) He sees.

P ويندانك *venadānak*, A bladder of musk.

P ويو *wayo* or *wiyo*, A bride.

A ويه *wayh*, (*wayhi*, and ويها *wayhan*) Come on! along! away then! (a particle of invitation). Wo be to you!

P ويهند *wayhand*, Name of a city in Kandahār.

A وئيب *wasib*, (fem. وئيبة) Deep (cauldron).

A وئية *wasiyat*, A fine pearl. Wide and deep (sack, cauldron, or dish). Large she-camel. A woman who keeps close at home.

A وئيد *wasīd*, (A girl) buried alive. A loud sound or voice. A slow, gentle pace.

A وئيدة *wasidat*, (A girl) buried alive.

P وييس *wiyis*, Like, resembling.

A وئيصة *wasisat*, A crowd, company, body. ما ادري ايّ الوئيصة هو *mā adri ayyu'l wasisat huwa*, I do not know who he is.

A وئيل *wasīl*, (v. n. of وأل) Taking refuge. Getting off safe.

ه

ه *he* or *hā*, (called هاءِ هوّز *hāsi hawwaz* or هاءِ مدوّرة *hāsi mudawwara*, Round *hā*) The twenty-seventh letter of the Arabic alphabet, and the thirty-first of the Persian, is a guttural, and slightly aspirated, as the "h" in "hope." It signifies five in arithmetic. In almanacks it denotes Thursday, and the sign Virgo; also the planet Venus, and the moon when bright. At the end of Arabic words it is the affixed pronoun, "him, his, it:" as, كتابه *kitābuhu* nom., *kitābahu* accus., His book; في كتابه *fī kitābihi*, In his book. It is interchangeable with ج *jīm*, ح *he*, خ *khe*, ف *fe*, ك *kāf*, و *wāw*, ي *ye*.

When ه *he* is marked with two points, ة or ة, the sign of the feminine noun in Arabic, it is pronounced *t*, and called تاءِ گرد *tāsi gird*, Round *t*: and in the construction of Persian words is written with ت, or the ه is written without the points and not sounded: as, هدايت *hidāyat*, (or هدايه *hidāya*) (Arabic, هداية *hidāyat*) Guidance, direction. ه *hi* is sometimes written for هي *hiya*, She.

In Persian, ه *he* is of two kinds; manifest or sounded (ظاهر *zāhir*), and concealed or mute (مخفيّ *makhfiy*). The former is enunciated whether preceded by *fatha*, *zamm*, or *kasr*: as, ره *rah*, A road; اندة *anduh*, Grief; فربه *farbih*, Fat; رهها *rahhā*, Roads; اندهها *anduhhā*, Griefs; گرهها *girihhā*, Buttons; كوهها *kohhā*, Mountains. In the diminutive it is marked with fatha: as, رهك *rahak*, A little road; اندهك *anduhak*, A trifling sorrow; گرهك *girihak*, A small button. When taking the اضافت *izāfat* it is marked with kasr: as, رهِ من *rahi man*, My road; اندوهِ من *andūhi man*, My sorrow; گرهِ من *girihi man*, My button.

Mute ه *he* (as "h" in "Messiah") is fourfold:

(1) It is added to nouns bearing a resemblance or relationship to another object: as, دهنه *dahana*, An orifice, from دهن *dahan*, The mouth; دسته *dasta*, A handle, from دست *dast*, The hand; دندانه *dandāna*, The tooth (of a saw), from دندان *dandān*, A tooth; زبانه *zabāna*, The tongue (of a balance), from زبان *zabān*, The tongue.

(2) To form the past active participle, or the simple passive participle: as, كشته *kushta*, Having slain, or slain; گفته *gufta*, Having said, or said; خفته *khufta*, Asleep; مرده *murda*, Dead.

(3) To specify time, at the end of the words سال *sāl*, Year; ماه *māh*, Month; روز *roz*, Day; and شب *shab*, Night: as, يكساله *yak-sāla*, Yearling; دماهه *du-māha*, Bi-monthly; هر روزه *har roza*, Daily; چهارشبه *chahār-shaba*, Quadri-nocturnal, every fourth night.

(4) هاءِ بيان فتحه *hāsi bayāni fatha* merely denotes that the vowel of the preceding consonant is fatha: as, جامه *jāma*, A garment; خانه *khāna*, A house; دانه *dāna*, Grain; كاشانه *kāshāna*, A cottage. In the plural of such words the ه *he* is dropped: as, خانها *khānahā*, Houses; جامها *jāmahā*, Garments: but in the plural of such as denote living beings it is changed to گ *gāf*; as, زنده *zinda*, Living, pl. زندگان *zindagān*; آهوبره *āhū-bara*, A fawn, pl. آهوبرگان *āhū-baragān*. In the diminutive it is also changed to گ *gāf*: as, جامگك *jāmagak*, A little garment. When taking the اضافت *izāfat* it is changed to soft hamza (همزهٔ ملينه *hamzasi mulayyina*): as, خانهٔ من *khānasi man*, My house; بندهٔ من *bandasi man*, My servant. It is also dropped in كرا *kirā*, the dative case of كه *ki*, Who? and is sometimes redundant; as, انبان *ambān*, (or انبانه *ambāna*) A granary.

P ها *hā*, Have a care! be ready! Here! behold! Whether? is it so! A slap on the face. White on a bird's face. The plural of things inanimate; as, سنگ *sang*, A stone; سنگها *sanghā*, Stones: and sometimes of animated beings; as, مرغ *murgh*, A bird; مرغها *murghhā*, Birds. Although ان *ān* is the sign of the plural in animated beings, their members are made plural by ها *hā*: as, دستها *dasthā*, Heads; پايها *pāyhā*, Feet; سرها *sarhā*, Heads (but chieftains سران *sarān*).

A ها *hā*, (the third person sing. of the affixed pronoun) Her, to, of, from, or by her. (fem. pl. هاءات *hāsāt*) The name of the letter ه. (هاءُ *hās* masc., هاءِ *hāsi* fem., هاءا *hāsā* dual masc. and fem., هاؤا *hāsu* pl. masc., هاءن *hasna* pl. fem.) Lo! behold! take! هاك *hāka*, (fem. *hāki*) Here for thee! (dual هاؤما *hāsumā* or هاكما *hākumā*) Do you two take! (pl. masc. هاؤم *hāsum* or هاكم *hākum*, pl. fem. هاؤنّ *hāsunna* or هاكنّ *hākunna*) Behold for you! do you take! *Hā* is also a particle of swearing: as, لا ها الله *lā ha'llāhi* Not, by God!

A هاء *hāsa*, (fut. يهاء *yahāsu* and يهيء *yahīsu*) He was handsome and of a respectable appearance.

A هاء *hās*, (fem. هاء *hāsi*, pl. هاؤ *hāsu*) Take!

A هاء *hāsi*, (fem. هائي *hāsī*, dual هائيا *hāsiyā*, pl. m. هاؤوا *hāsū*, pl. f. هائين *hāsīna*) Give! grant!

A هاب *hāb*, A serpent. In driving camels, as هاب هاب *hāb hāb* (*hābi* being the word for horses).

A هابدة *hābidat*, (pl. هوابد *hawābid*) A woman who gathers colocynths or the seeds thereof.

A هابذة *hābizat*, Swift, quick (she-camel).

A هابر *hābir*, (A blow) which cuts asunder and divides, so that one part falls.

A هابش *hābish*, One who collects much.

A هابشة *hābishat*, A crowd just assembled.

A هابط *hābit*, Falling, descending; a faller.

A هابي *hābī*, Covered or filled with small flying dust. الهابي *al hābī*, The dust of the tomb.

P هابيغي *hābīghī*, Real, true.

A هابيل *hābīl*, Abel, Adam's son.

A هات *hāti*, (fem. هاتي *hātī*, dual هاتيا *hātiyā*, pl. masc. هاتوا *hātū*, pl. fem. هاتين *hātīna*) Give!

grant! let it be so!

A هاتا *hātā*, (or هاتاك *hātāka*) She. This.

A هاتان *hātāni*, (dual) These two (females).

A هاتر *hātir*, (used with هتر *hitr*) (as هتر هاتر *hitr hātir*) The talk of a doting, raving fellow.

A هاتف *hātif*, One who cries aloud. An encomiast, praiser. A voice from heaven, or from an invisible speaker. A secret monitor, guardian angel.

A هاتل *hātil*, (pl. هتّل *huttal*) (A cloud) raining incessantly, but small.

A هاتن *hātin*, (pl. هتّن *huttan*) (A cloud) raining incessantly, but small rain.

A هاتيك *hātīka*, She. This.

A هاجة *hājat*, A female frog.

A هاجّة *hājjat*, (An eye) sunk in the socket.

A هاجد *hājid*, Asleep, sleeping. Wakeful.

A هاجر *hājar*, Hagar the mother of Ishmael. *Hājir*, Elegant, excellent (thing). Delirious, speaking foolishly or deliriously. Name of a tribe.

A هاجرة *hājirat*, Vain, foolish. Obscene, profane, or malevolent discourse. (pl. هواجر *hawājir*) The sultry afternoon-heat.

A هاجريّ *hajiriy*, An architect. A townsman. A citizen of Hajar in Arabia Felix. Good, excellent.

A هاجس *hājis*, (A thing) recurring to mind.

A هاجشة *hājishat*, A crowd recently collected.

A هاجع *hājiع*, (pl. هجّع *hujjaع* and هجوع *hujūع*) Asleep, sleeping.

A هاجل *hājil*, A sleep. One who travels oft.

A هاجن *hājin*, A girl married prematurely. Any animal brought too early to the male. A tinder-box not striking fire at once.

A هاجنة *hājinat*, A female palm-tree bringing forth fruit for the first time.

A هاجي *hājī*, A satirist. One who spells.

P هاچيدن *hāchīdan*, To seize, carry off. To dry, wither. To be, or to grow cold.

A هاد *hād*, (v. n. of هيد) Frightening. Checking, chiding. Oppressing the spirits. Amending, correcting. Turning, diverting. A word used in calling to a camel. Moving, disturbing. ما له هيد و لا هاد *mā lahu haydun wa lā hādun*, He does not move. ما يقال له هيد ولا هاد *mā yuḳālu lahu haydun wa lā hādun*, He is not denied nor contradicted in any thing.

A هادّ *hadd*, Sound, especially the roaring or murmuring of the sea. A noise, which heard on the sea-shore indicates an approaching earthquake.

A هادّة *häddat*, Thunder.

P هادخت *hādukht*, Name of a chapter of the Zand.

A هادر *hādir*, One who permits the effusion of blood with impunity. Vile, contemptible. Useless. Extinct. Braying (camel). (Milk) turning thick at top when it sours.

A هادرة *hādirat*, (Ground) covered with full-grown herbage. Braying (she-camel).

P هادرويش *hā darwish*, A desert in Turkistān.

A هادف *hādif*, One who enters, who approaches. A stranger. هل هدف اليكم هادف *hal hadafa ilayhum hādifun*, Came any one to you?

A هادفة *hādifat*, A body, crowd of people.

A هادل *hādil*, (A camel's colt) hanging an ulcerated lip. Pendulous (lip). Pendulous-lipped.

A هادم *hādim*, A demolisher, marrer, destroyer. هادم اللذات *hādimu'l lazzāt*, (Death) the destroyer of (man's) pleasures.

P هادوري *hādūrī*, Name of a sect of beggars.

P هادوريان *hādūriyān*, (pl. of هادوري *hādūrī*) Bold, sturdy beggars, destitute vagrants whom the police keep off the roads.

P هادي *hādī*, A kind of stone, which whoever keeps by him, the dogs will not bark at him.

A هادي *hādī*, (pl. هداة *hudāt*) A director, leader, guide. A wild bull that precedes the herd. A bell-wether, or any leader of a herd or flock. The neck of a horse; also his loin or croup. A handle (of a mill). A lion. The neck. Beginning of any thing; fore part, or that which first appears. Head or point of an arrow. الهادي *al hādī*, An ox in the centre of a threshing-floor, round which the other oxen move when treading out the grain. هادي السبيل *hādī's sabīl*, (or هادي الطريق *hādī't tarīk*) The guide to the way (of salvation), *i.e.* God. هاديء سبل *hādīi subul*, A guide of the ways, *i.e.* Muhammad. هاديء مهدي غلام *hādīi mahdī ghulām*, Name of Muhammad.

A هادية *hādiyat*, The leader of a flock (as mentioned above). A rock appearing above water. A stick, staff. A horse's neck, or the fore part of it.

A هاذ *hāz*, A kind of tree.

A هاذا *hāzā*, This. (See هذا *hāzā*.)

A هاذة *hāzat*, One tree of the هاذ *hāz* kind.

A هاذر *hāzir*, Hot, sultry (day).

P هاذل *hāzil*, Midnight; also the beginning or remainder of the night.

P هار *hār*, A row, rank, line, string. A string of pearls. A necklace. A wreath, chaplet. A pearl. Any thing well arranged. The neck; the bones in the neck of any animal. A piece of wood put through a perforation in a camel's nose to guide him by. Excrement. Putrid flesh. Astonished, stupefied. Unfortunate, distressed. Foolish. Silent.

A هار *hār*, Weak with age or infirmity.

A هارّ *hārr*, The squalling of a cat.

A هاران *hārān*, Haran, Terah's son, brother of Abraham and father of Lot.

A هارب *hārib*, (pl. هرّاب *hurrāb*) Flying. A fugitive. One who returns from watering. P هارب شدن *hārib shudan*, To fly, to shun. A ما له قارب ولا هارب *mā lahu kārib wa lā hārib*, He has nothing, he is of no account (one whom none approaches and none shuns, neither esteemed nor feared).

P هارپا *hār pā*, Name of a prickly little fish.

P هارد *hārad*, Name of the 25th of the month.

P هارش *hārish*, Vanity, vain-glory, boasting.

A هارموز *hāramūz*, The great king of Persia.

G هارو *hārū*, Hero, the mistress of Leander.

A P هاروت *hārūt*, Name of an angel, who, together with another named ماروت *mārūt*, having severely censured mankind before the throne of God, they were sent down to earth in human shapes to judge of the temptations to which man was subject. They could not withstand them: they were seduced by women, and committed every species of iniquity; for which they were suspended by the feet in a well in Babylon, where they are to remain in great torment till the day of judgment.

P هاروت فن *hārūt-fan*, A skilful magician.

P هاروتي *hārūtī*, Magic, incantation, sorcery.

P هارون *hārūn*, Aaron, brother of Moses. A refractory horse. Chief, leader. A messenger, courier. Helplessness, indigence. Astonishment. Amazement. هارون الرّشيد *hārūn ar'rashīd*, The fifth caliph of the house Abbās, and twenty-fourth from Muhammad. He reigned from A. D. 786 till 808.

P هارون آستانهٔ گردون *hārūni āsitānaــi gardūn*, The courier of the court of heaven, (met.) The moon.

P هارونيدن *hārūnīdan*, To be at a loss, confounded, distracted.

P هاري *hārī*, A doer of every kind of dirty work, a sweeper.

A هاري *hārī*, Tumbled down, ruined. Weak.

P هاز *hāz*, A curling lock.

A هازّ *hāzz*, Shining, glittering (star).

A هازباء *hāzibāع*, (هازبي *hāziba'*, *hāzibī*, or هازبيّ *hāzibīy*) A species of fish.

A هازبانية *hāzubāniyat*, A horn, antennæ, or feeler (of an insect).

A هازبيّة *hāzibīyat*, A kind of fish.

A هازل *hāzil*, Facetious. A joker, jester.

A هازم *hāzim*, One who depresses, oppresses, or puts to flight.

A هازمة *hāzimat*, Misfortune, calamity.

P هاژ *hāj*, Clamour, loud exclamation, sound. Afflicted, mournful, penitent. Astonished. Stock-still with amazement. Stupid. Poor. Abject, vile, bad. Ugly. Silent from love.

P هاژو *hāju*, (and هاژه *hāja*) Astonished, stupefied. Abject, vile, poor. Ugly.

P هاژوييدن *hājūyīdan*, To be distracted, at a loss, confounded.

P هاژيدن *hājīdan*, To weep, cry. To look.

P هاس *hās*, Too, alas, likewise. Dread, fear.

A هاشمة *hāshimat*, A wound or contusion breaking a bone without shivering it.

A هاصّة *hāssat*, The eye of an elephant.

A هاصر *hāsir*, (A lion) tearing (his prey).

A هاضب *hāzib*, Wetting rain. Rain falling in large drops.

A هاضم *hāzim*, Soft, loose. Digestive. Purgative.

A هاضوم *hāzūm*, Medicine, or any thing promoting digestion. Liberal. A lion.

A هاطل *hātil*, Incessant and small (rain).

A هاع *hāʻ*, Greedy. Covetousness, avarice, meanness, baseness. Cowardice, timidity. هاع لاع *hāʻ lāʻ*, Timid, cowardly. Weak.

A هاغية *hāghiyat*, A foolish woman. A beautiful woman.

A هافة *hāfat*, (A she-camel) soon thirsty.

A هافي *hāfī*, Starving, famished (man).

A هاقّ *hākk*, Frequent and impetuous in coitu.

A هاقل *hākil*, A male mouse.

P هاك *hāk*, (in zand and Pāz.) A bird's egg.

A هاك *hāka*, Take!

P هاكره *hākra*, (or هاكله *hākla*) A stutterer.

P هاكول *hākūl*, Ratsbane.

P هال *hāl*, Quiet, firmness, establishment. Patience. The goal in the game of bandy or shinty. The lesser cardamom.

A هال *hāl*, (for آل *āl*) Posterity. Spread, scattered (sand). The vapour سراب *sarāb*. *Hāli* or *hālin*, Used in calling to or driving camels.

A هالب الشعر *hālibu'sh shaʻr*, The coldest days of winter.

A هالبة *hālibat*, Rainy (night).

A هالة *hālat*, (pl. هالات *hālāt*) A halo round the moon. Name of the wife of Abdu'l mutallib.

A هالج *hālij*, One who has many confused and inexplicable dreams.

A هالط *hālit*, Long, entangled (corn). Loose in the belly.

A هالع *hāliʻ*, Very impatient. Swift-paced (ostrich).

A هالك *hālik*, (pl. هلكي *halka'*, هلّك *hullak*, هلّاك *hullāk*, and هوالك *hawālik*) Perishing, in the state of being destroyed or killed. Destructive.

P هالك شدن *hālik shudan*, To perish.

A هالكة *hālikat*, Gluttonous, given to excess.

A هالكيّ *hālikiy*, A blacksmith. A polisher.

P هالوجين *hālūjīn*, A swing.

A هالوك *hālūk*, A mouse. A sort of the طرثوث.

P هاله *hāla*, A halo round the moon. A bad fellow, corrupter, destroyer, author of evil. Colour. At ease, at rest; quiet, easy. A sort of wood of which they make lamp-wicks.

P هاله وار *hālawār*, Circularly (like a halo).

A هام *hām*, (pl. of هامة) Owls. Heads. Chiefs.

P هامال *hāmāl*, Of the same mind, unanimous, similar, uniform. A companion, equal, peer.

P هامان *hāmān*, Name of Abraham's brother. Name of Pharaoh's vazīr.

P هاماور *hāmāwar*, (or هاماوران) Syria. Yaman.

A هامة *hāmat*, (pl. هام *hām*) An owl. The head of any animal. The chief of a people, family, or tribe. A horse.

A هامّة *hāmmat*, (pl. هوامّ *hawāmm* and هميم *hamīm*) A stinging reptile. Beasts, cattle. نعم الهامّة *niʻmu'l hāmmat*, A horse.

A هامج *hāmij*, A remainder of any thing jumbled together. Great, intense. همج هامج *hamaji hāmij*, Excessive hunger.

A هامد *hāmid*, Worn. Obsolete. Black, changed, withered (plant). Barren (place). Extinct (fire).

A هامر *hāmir*, (A cloud) pouring down rain.

P هامراه *hām-rāh*, A companion, fellow-traveller.

P هامرز *hāmarz*, (in Pehlevi) Rise up.

A هامرز *hāmarz*, A Persian king.

A هامز *hāmiz*, A defamer (male or female).

A هامش *hāmish*, (foreign) Margin of a book.

P هامل *hāmil*, Unanimous, like, uniform.

A هامل *hāmil*, (pl. هوامل *hawāmil*) (A camel) feeding at large night and day.

A هاملة *hāmilat*, Camels feeding at large night and day.

P هامن *hāmun*, A plain; hard level ground.

P هاموار *hāmwār*, (or هامواره *hāmwāra*) Smooth, even, level. Always, continually. Eternity, perpetuity.

A هاموم *hāmūm*, The melted fat of a camel's bunch. A camel whose bunch is melted.

P هامون *hāmūn*, A plain: level ground. A desert. دشت و هامون *dasht u hāmūn*, A desert and extensive plain. هامون نورد *hāmūn-naward*, A traveller of the desert.

P هامي *hāmī*, Distracted, astonished.

P هاميان *hāmyān*, A long purse.

P هان *hān*, Truly, yes. Make haste! Know! Have a care! Let it not be!

A هانّة *hānnat*, The interior fat of the eye. Strength, vigour in a camel. Remains of marrow.

A هانذا *hānazā*, Behold!

A هانع *hāniʻ*, (pl. هنّع) Humble, submissive.

P هانه *hāna*, Is it not?

P هاني *hānī*, (in Pehlevi) Sit down.

A هانئ *hāniʼ*, A domestic servant.

P هاو *hāw*, Used when charging an enemy.

P هاوش *hāwush*, (or هاوشت *hāwusht*) (in zand and Pāzand) A disciple or follower of a prophet. Attached, dependant.

P هاون *hāwan*, A mortar. Vulva. *Hāwin*, (in zand and Pāz.) The first of the five daily prayers.

A هاون *hāwan* or *hāwun*, A mortar.

P هاون دسته *hāwan-dasta*, Pestle and mortar.

P هاون كوب *hāwan-kob*, A pounder in a mortar. A maker of ink.

A هاوون *hāwūn*, (pl. هواوين *hawāwīn*) A mortar.

A هاوي *hāwī*, A locust. Fallen headlong.

A هاويّ *hāwiy*, Aerial, airy, windy.

A هاوية *hāwiyat*, The nethermost hell. A deep, dark place, gulf, pit-fall. Locusts. (A woman) deprived of her children. Air, sky.

P هاويه بند *hāwiya-band*, Hell-closing.

P هاويه مثال *hāwiya-misāl*, Hell-like, infernal.

A هاه *hāh*, A tip-cat. A threat. Laughter.

A هأها *haʼhaʼ*, A laugher, giggler.

A هأهاء *haʼhāʼ*, (or هأهأة *haʼhaʼat*) (v. n. of هأهأ Q) Calling (camels) to (their) provender by saying the words هئ هئ *hiʼ hiʼ*. Checking (camels) by the words هأ هأ *haʼ haʼ*. Laughing. *Haʼhāʼ*, A laugher.

A هاهنا *hāhunā*, Here. Hither.

A هاي *hāy*, O! ah! alas! Well done! strange!

P هاياهاي *hāyāhāy*, The cries of mourners.

P هاياهوي *hāyāhūy*, Shout of joy and festivity.

A هائب *hāʼib*, Timid, timorous, afraid, fearful.

A هائج *hāʼij*, Furious, raging, rampant. Anger, rage. Dry, withered (herbage). الهائج *al hāʼij*, A furious, mettlesome stallion in a state of excitement.

A هائجة *hāʼijat*, (Ground) whose herbage or pot-herbs are turning yellow from want of moisture. Dry (ground).

A هائد *hāʼid*, Repentant, returning to duty.

A هائر *hāʼir*, Tumbled down, ruined, falling into misfortune; crumbling into ruins.

A هائع *hāʼiʻ*, Liquid, melted (lead). Dark (night). *Hāʼiʻ*, (or هائع لائع *hāʼiʻ lāʼiʻ*) Timid, languid, cowardly. جائع هائع *jāʼiʻ hāʼiʻ*, Hungry and voracious.

A هائعة *hāʼiʻat*, A horrible noise, fearful sound.

A هائف *hāʼif*, Very thirsty.

A هائفة *hāʼifat*, (Camels) turning their open mouths to the wind from intense thirst.

A هائل *hāʼil*, Terrible, horrible, frightful. Huge, large. One who lets out or pours forth (flour or sand). (Sand) poured forth. واقعةٌ هائلة *wākiʻaʼi hāʼila*, A dreadful accident.

A هائم *hāʼim*, Astonished, confused, wandering, distracted, furious, from love or any other cause.

P هاينه *hāyina*, Destitute, helpless. Doubtless.

A هايهات *hāyahāt*, (or هايهان *hāyahān*) Off!

P هاي هاي *hāy hāy*, Quick, quick! Cries of the distressed.

P هاي هوي *hāy hūy*, Noisy mirth, festivity, conviviality. Make haste! be quick! Hue and cry.

P هائينه *hāʼīna*, (or هائنه) Always. Certainly.

A هب *hab*, Grant it, allow it to be so. Fear thou.

P هب *hib*, (in zand and Pāzand) Leave alone.

A هبّ *habb*, (v. n. of هبّ) Awaking, rising (from sleep). Blowing with violence (wind). Being active, brisk, nimble, swift (a camel). Coming. Beginning, setting about a thing. Calling the male to the female. Cutting. Being shaken or brandished (a sword). Departing, being absent, or lying hid a while. Being routed, fleeing away.

A هباء *habāʼ*, (or هباب *habāb*) Dust, especially the finer particles which fly about, and are only conspicuous in the sun's rays. (pl. اهباء *ahbāʼ*) (A man) of little understanding. P هبا كردن *habā kardan*, To reduce to powder, to annihilate. To exhale, evaporate.

A الهباءة *al habāʼat*, A part of Arabia. يوم الهباءة *yawmu'l habāʼat*, A battle fought there (near the walls of Madīna).

A هباب *hibāb*, (v. n. of هبّ) Being brisk, swift. Rattling at rutting-time (a he-goat).

A هبّاب *habbāb*, Violent, blustering (wind).

A هباة *habāt*, Name of a place within the tribe of Ghatafān, where a battle was fought.

A هبات *hibāt*, (pl. of هبة *hibat*) Gifts.

A هبّار *habbār*, Sharp (sword). A very hairy monkey. الهبّاران *al habbārāni*, Two Syrian months called كانون *kānūn* (December and January).

A هبارك *hubārik*, Grown up (youth), of age.

A هبارية *hubāriyat*, Flocks of wool, or the down which falls from feathers.

A هباريّة *hubārīyat*, (Wind) raising and sweeping along the dust.

A هبّاش *habbāsh*, One who acquires or collects, who scrapes together for his family.

A هباشة *hubāshat*, A crowd. A herd.

A هباع *hibāʿ*, (pl. of هبع *hubaʿ*) (Asses' colts) of the last birth.

A هباقع *hubākiʿ*, Short, dwarfish, and compact.

P هباك *habāk*, Top of a mountain. Crown of the head. The dyeing matter of gum-lac.

A هبال *habāl*, Name of a tree.

A هبّال *habbāl*, One who searches or watches to catch or to deceive. A hunter. One who lays snares for man or beast.

A هبالة *habālat*, Search, endeavour; petition.

A هبانق *hubānik*, A boy, a servant.

A هبانيق *habānīk*, Boys.

A هبائب *habāʾib*, (A garment) torn to pieces.

A هباية *hubāyat*, The bark of a tree.

A هبب *hibab*, A worn or tattered garment. (pl. of هبّة *hibbat*) Rags, tatters.

A هبة *hibat*, (v.n. of وهب) Giving, bestowing. Pardoning, forgiving. (pl. هبات *hibāt*) A gift, a present. P هبت كردن *hibat kardan*, To give, bestow. A *Hubat*, Provision for any undertaking.

A هبّة *habbat*, (v. n. of هبّ) Rattling at rutting-time (a he-goat). *Habbat* or *hibbat*, An hour; a short time before dawn; any space of time; a year. هبّة الشهر *habbatu'sh shahr*, The remainder of a month. *Habbatan*, At once, in a moment. هبّة من الدهر *habbatan mini'd dahri*, A short space, a good while, some time. *Habbat* or *hibbat*, (v. n. of هبّ) Cutting. *Hibbat*, The penetrancy of a sword, its power of piercing and entering into. (pl. هبب *hibab*) A rag, tatter. Ecstasy.

A هبت *habt*, (v. n. of هبت) Descending. Striking, beating down.

A هبتة *habtat*, Weakness of mind; cowardice, baseness; dotage, madness, silliness. A stroke, blow.

A هبتر *habtar*, Short-bodied; a dwarf.

A هبج *habj*, (v. n. of هبج) Striking (with a stick). *Habaj*, A sort of tumour on a camel's udder.

A هبد *habd*, (v. n. of هبد) Gathering, bruising, or boiling the seeds of the colocynth; serving them up before any one. The wild gourd, or its seed.

P هبد *habad*, A piece of board used to level the surface of a new-ploughed field.

A هبذ *habz*, (v. n. of هبذ) Running, making haste, being swift of foot. Flying fast (a bird).

A هبر *habr*, (v. n. of هبر) Cutting (meat), cutting off (a piece). Pausing at the beginning of a verse in reading the Kur'ān (a practice disapproved of). Flesh. Painful (blow). (A blow) which divides, so that a part falls off. (pl. هبور *hubūr* or *hubr*) Level or low ground or sands. *Hubr*, Refuse which falls from flax. A grape-stone. (pl. of هبر *habr*) Level or low grounds or sands. *Habar*, (v. n. of هبر) Being full of flesh (a camel). *Habir*, Very fleshy (camel). هبر وبر *habir wabir*, A very fleshy and hairy camel. *Hubur*, (pl. of هبير *habīr*) Level or low grounds, especially amongst hills.

P هبر *habar*, The pus and matter of a sore.

A هبّر *hibirr*, Cut off, separated from the rest.

A هبراء *habrāʾ*, Very fleshy (she-camel).

A هبرة *habrat*, A shell used to avert the effect of a malignant eye. A charm used by women to secure the affections of men. A piece of flesh without bone. *Habirat*, Very fleshy (she-camel).

A هبرج *habraj*, A light, quick pace. One who walks proudly, or in a disordered manner. Garments painted or dyed with different colours. A bull. An old deer. *Habraj* or *hibrij*, Large and fat.

A هبرجة *habrajat*, The painting of a garment. A haughty or disordered step.

A هبردانة مبردانة *hibirdānat mibirdānat*, Bread crumbled into broth, cold, compact, even, and round.

A هبرزيّ *hibriziy*, Pure gold. A new gold coin. Beautiful. Elegant Persian bracelet. Handsome boot. A lion. امّ الهبرزيّ *ummu'l hibriziy*, A fever.

A هبرقيّ *habrakiy* or *hibrikiy*, A blacksmith. A goldsmith. A maker, artificer, smith. A mountain or wild bull.

A هبرك *habrak*, (A youth) grown up, of age. Full, complete (youth).

A هبركة *habrakat*, A soft, delicate girl.

A هبركع *habarkaʿ*, A dwarf; short-bodied.

A هبركل *habarkal*, A lusty handsome youth.

A هبرمة *habramat*, Voraciousness, gluttony. Loquacity, babbling, garrulity.

A هبرون *habrūn*, Hebron in Palestine.

A هبرية *hibriyat*, Scales or scurf on the head. Flocks falling from cotton, or down from feathers.

A هبز *habz*, (v. n. of هبز) Cutting (meat), cutting off a piece. Waxing fat (a camel).

A هبزان *habazān*, (v. n. of هبز) Dying, especially suddenly.

A هبس *habas*, The violet. A kind of wild thyme or betony. The herb ox-eye. Mallows.

A هبش *habsh*, (v. n. of هبش) Collecting, scraping together. Overtaking, reaching, finding. Acquiring, carrying home. A painful blow.

A هبص *habas*, (v. n. of هبص) Being brisk, cheerful, active. Lying eagerly in wait (for game). Being greedy (about to eat), with a degree of flurry. Alacrity, cheerfulness. Haste. *Habis*, Brisk, active.

A هبصى *habasaʾ*, A brisk, quick pace.

A هبط *habt*, (v. n. of هبط) Sending, letting, or throwing down, precipitating. Lowering or beating down (a price). Attenuating, emaciating (as disease). Entering. Causing to enter. Striking, shaking (any thing). Decrease. A fall into evil or misfortune.

A هبطة *habtat*, Level, low, sloping (ground).

A هبع *habaʿ*, (v. n. of هبع) Coming suddenly from all quarters (men). Stretching out the neck (as a camel or ass) when going quick; beginning to do so (a colt). *Hubaʿ*, (pl. هبعات *hubaʿāt* and هباع *hibāʿ*) A camel's colt of the last birth, or end of the breeding season (ربع *rubaʿ* implying, of the first or beginning of the season).

A هبعان *habaʿān*, (v. n. of هبع) Beginning to stretch out (his) neck (a camel's colt).

A هبعة *hubaʿat*, (fem. of هبع *hubaʿ*) (pl. هبعات *hubaʿāt*) Camels' colts of the last birth.

A هبقع *habkaʿ*, Short and compact; dwarfish.

P هبك *habak*, The palm of the hand.

A هبكة *hubakat*, Foolish. Loose earth into which the feet sink.

A هبل *habal*, (v. n. of هبل) Being deprived by death (a mother of her children). Bereavement. اهتبل هبلك *ihtabala habaluka*, It becomes thee, it is proper for thee. *Habil*, (A wolf) lying on the watch. *Hibil*, Corpulent, aged (man, camel, or ostrich). *Hubal*, Name of an ancient idol in the temple of Mecca. Name of the father of the Kelibite tribe of Arabians.

A هبلّ *hiball*, Heavy-bodied, slow. Old. *Hiball* and *hibill*, Corpulent and tall (man).

A هبلات *hubalāt*, Descendants of Hubal.

A هبلس *hiblis*, (There is not) any one, nobody (at home).

A هبلع *hiblaʿ*, A bandog of the breed called هبلع سلوقيّ *salūkiy*; or simply, a dog. *Hiblaʿ*, (هبلّع *haballaʿ*, or هبلاع *hiblāʿ*) A glutton; one who has a wide throat; a devourer of large mouthfuls.

A هبلّق *haballak*, A dwarf.

A هبلّى *hibillaʾ*, A haughty or strutting pace.

A هبليس *hiblīs*, Some one, any one.

A هبنق *hubnuk*, A boy, a servant.

A هبنّق *habannak*, A dwarf. A fool.

A هبنقة *habnakat*, The act of sitting on the inside of the thighs.

A هبنّقة *habannakat*, Name of a man.

A هبنقع *habankaʿ*, Proud; foolish. Fond of talking with women. One who begs with a stick in his hand. One who does not stir when once seated.

A هبنقعة *habankaʿat*, A mode of sitting on the point of the toes, with the thighs joined together, and the legs diverging from each other. A camel that hangs the lip.

A هبنّك *habannak*, Foolish, silly. Weak, languid. One who acts fraudulently; who goes about whispering slander.

A هبنكة *habannakat*, Slothful, knavish, cowardly. Foolish, weak, languid (woman).

A هبنوق *hubnūk*, A boy, a servant.

A هبنوقة *hubnūkat*, A flute, pipe, psaltery.

A هبنيق *habnīk* or *hibnīk*, A boy, a servant.

A هبو *habw*, Name of a tribe.

A هبوّ *hubūw*, (v. n. of هبا for هبو) Being raised and flying in the air (dust). Dying. Running off.

A هبوب *habūb*, A wind which blows hard and raises the dust. *Hubūb*, (v. n. of هبّ) Awaking, breaking from sleep. Blowing furiously (the wind).

A هبوبة *habūbat*, Strong, dust-raising (wind).

A هبوة *habwat*, Dust. Darkness.

A هبور *habūr*, A spider. *Hubūr*, (pl. of هبر *habr*) Low grounds or sands. Large stones on hills.

A هبّور *habbūr*, A small ant.

A هبوز *hubūz*, (v. n. of هبز) Dying, and suddenly.

A هبوط *habūt*, A steep or sloping place. *Hubūt*, (v. n. of هبط) Descending from a height. Decreasing, falling (price). Reducing, lowering prices. Emaciating any one (sickness). Descent, declivity. P هبوط كردن *hubūt kardan*, To go down, descend.

A هبوع *hubūʿ*, (v. n. of هبع) Coming suddenly from all quarters. Stretching out the neck (a camel or ass) going quick; beginning to do so (a colt).

A هبوغ *hubūgh*, (v. n. of هبغ) Sleeping.

A هبول *habūl*, Bereaved (mother).

A هبون *habūn*, A spider.

A هبهاب *habhāb*, The vapour called also سراب *sarāb*, mirage. A kind of boy's game. Swift.

A هبهب *habhab*, A wolf light and swift.

A هبهبة *habhabat*, (v. n. of هبهب Q) Rattling at rutting-time (a he-goat). Slaughtering, sacrificing. The motion of the vapour سراب *sarāb*, or mirage. Swiftness. A checking, driving, or crying (to cattle). Waking, watchfulness. Swift.

A هبهبي *habhabiy*, Quick-going (camel). A shepherd, pastor. A he-goat that leads the flock. A skilful camel-driver, one who sings well to them (which these animals are very fond of, and travel in consequence with a rapid pace). Excellent (servant). A butcher. Light, slight. Swift.

A هبهبيّة *habhabiyat*, Light, active (she-camel).

P هبه نامه *hiba-nāma*, Testament, deed of gift.

A هبي *habi*, Used in calling to a horse to back.

A هبّى *hubba'*, (Stars) concealed by dust.

A هبيّ *habayy*, A young boy. *Habiy*, A little girl.

A هبيب *habīb*, (v. n. of هبّ) Blowing (the wind). Awaking, rising from sleep. Rattling (as a he-goat).

A هبيّة *habayyat* or *habiyat*, A young girl.

A هبيت *habīt*, Cowardly, timid.

A هبيج *habīj*, A deer with two oblong lines on the side different in colour from the rest.

A هبيّج *habayyaj*, A youth healthy and vigorous.

A هبيّخ *habayyakh*, A young boy, a youth full of health and vigour. Languid, relaxed. Worthless. A fool. A large river or channel.

A هبيّخة *habayyakhat*, A young girl full of juice. A woman giving suck. A haughty air in walking.

A هبيّخى *habayyakha'*, A haughty air in walking.

A هبيد *habīd*, The bitter gourd or its seed.

A هبير *habīr*, (A blow) which divides, so that a part falls off. Level or low ground or sands. Pudenda. (pl. هبر *hubur* and اهبرة *ahbirat*) Level or low ground, especially amongst hills.

A هبيرة *hubayrat*, A hyena. A hyena's whelp. A man's name. ابو هبيرة *abū hubayrat*, The male frog. امّ هبيرة *ummu hubayrat*, A female frog.

A هبيرةً *hubayratan*, At no time, never.

A هبيط *habīt*, Lean, slender, meagre, emaciated by disease. Lean (she-camel).

A هبيل *habīl*, Abel, son of Adam.

A هبينغ *habaynagh*, Foolish.

A هبينق *habaynak*, A boy, a servant.

P هبيون *habyūn*, (or هپيون *hapyūn*) Opium.

P هپاك *hapāk*, Top or crown of the head.

P هپد *hapad*, An agricultural implement for levelling ploughed ground, a harrow.

P هپر *hapar*, The pus or matter of a sore.

A هتّ *hatt*, (v. n. of هتّ) Relating (any thing) readily and with propriety. Tearing (the garments). Breaking, dashing to pieces. Pouring out. Laying or throwing down, deposing from any dignity; causing to lose rank or reputation. Drawing, stripping off (the leaves of a branch). Drawing out the thread in spinning (a woman). A fracture.

A هتء *hatʾ*, (v. n. of هتأ) Striking. *Hatʾ*, (*hitʾ*, هتاء *hitāʾ*, or هتأة *hatʾat*) Time; an hour, especially of the night. *Hataʾ*, (v. n. of هتئ) Being bent. Eating (meat). A fissure, rent, tear, crevice.

A هتّات *hattāt*, Ready in speech; talkative.

A هتار *hitār*, (v. n. 3 of هتر) Speaking opprobriously, provoking by reproaches.

A هتاف *hutāf*, (v. n. of هتف) Exclaiming, calling to one. Praising. Complimenting (a lady) on (her) beauty.

A هتّافة *hattāfat*, Twanging (bow-string).

A هتّاك *hattāk*, Violater, ravisher, profaner.

A هتامة *hutāmat*, Fragment, bit, broken piece.

A هتان *hātāni*, (du. of هذه *hāzihi*) These two.

A هتّان *hattān*, Glib-tongued; ready speaker. (A cloud) pouring forth small but incessant rain.

A هتر *hatr*, (v. n. of هتر) Tearing, cutting, breaking. Tearing (one's) reputation, slandering, defaming. Impairing the intellect, making (one) a dotard (old age). *Hitr*, (pl. اهتار *ahtār*) A lie. An idle, foolish speech. A blunder, slip of the tongue, mistake. A wonderful thing: portent, omen, prodigy. The first half of the night. A misfortune. هتر هاتر *hitri hātir*, The speech of a silly dotard. A wonder of wonders. هتر اهتار *hitri ahtār*, Cunning, shrewd, knavish. *Hutr*, Folly, mental aberration from age, disease, or grief.

A هترة *hatrat*, Ridiculous folly, stupidity.

A هترك *hatrak*, A lion.

P هتشه *hatsha*, Ice.

A هتع *hatʿ*, An approaching quickly.

A هتف *hatf*, (v. n. of هتف) Cooing (a dove). Calling (to one), exclaiming. *Hataf*, A noise, sound.

A هتفى *hatafa'*, Twanging (bow-string).

A هتك *hatk*, (v. n. of هتك) Tearing (a veil or curtain), so as to discover those who were concealed. Violating, ravishing. Dishonouring, disgracing, defaming. Revealing, discovering. هتك حجاب عصمت *hatki hijābi ʿismat*, A tearing of the veil of chastity. P هتك عرض كردن *hatki ʿirz kardan*, To defame. A *Hutk*, Midnight. *Hatik*, Levity, affront, disrespect. *Hitak*, The membrane which envelopes the head of a new-born child.

A هتكة *hutkat*, A rent in a veil or curtain. An hour of the night. Slander, defamation. A reproach, disgrace.

A هتل *hatl*, (or هتلان *hatalān*) (v. n. of هتل) Raining incessantly (the sky), pouring down one gentle shower after another. Flowing from the eyes (tears). *Hatil*, (A cloud) which drops a gentle rain.

A هتّل *huttal*, (Clouds) letting fall a gentle but incessant rain.

A هتلان *hatalān*, A gentle, incessant rain.

A هتلى *hatla'*, Name of a plant.

A هتم *hatm*, (v. n. of هتم) Smiting (one) on the mouth, and dashing out (his) front-teeth. *Hatam*, (v. n. of هتم) Losing the fore-teeth, having them struck out.

A هتماء *hatmāʾ*, A woman whose front-teeth have dropped out, edentate.

A هتمرة *hatmarat*, Loquacity, talkativeness.

A هتملة *hatmalat*, A speaking low, muttering.

A هتمنة *hatmanat*, Loquacity.

A هتن *hatn*, (v. n. of هتن) Pouring forth a continued rain (the sky); raining awhile, then ceasing, and afterwards re-commencing; raining gently but without interruption. *Hutun*, (pl. of هتون *hatūn*) and هتّن *huttan*, (pl. of هاتن *hātin*) (Clouds) which drop rain without intermission.

A هتنان *hatanān*, A pouring down continued rain.

A هتو *hatw*, (v. n. of هتا for هتو) Breaking, crushing with the foot.

A هتوء *hutūʾ*, (or هتوء *hutūʾ*) Fissure, rent, crevice.

A هتوف *hatūf*, Twanging (bow-string).

A هتول *hutūl*, A raining gently but incessantly.

A هتون *hatūn*, (pl. هتن *hutun*) (A cloud) dropping rain incessantly. *Hutūn*, (v. n. of هتن) Dropping without intermission (rain).

A هتهات *hathāt*, Ready, voluble, talkative.

A هتهتة *hathatat*, (v. n. of هتهت Q) Speaking readily, with propriety. Crying هت هت *hat hat* to (a camel) drinking. A fracture.

A هتيء *hitʾ*, (هتيء *hatīʾ*, هتياء *hityāʾ*, or هتي *haty*) A part (of the night has passed).

A هتيان *hatayān*, Small camels. Mean, contemptible men. Verboseness. Quilting, stuffing.

A هتيكة *hatīkat*, Disgraceful exposure.

A هتيمة *hatīmat*, The smaller حمض shrubs.

A هث *hass*, A lie.

A هثاث *hassās*, A liar.

A هثرمة *hasramat*, Talkativeness.

A هثم *hasm*, (v. n. of هثم) Pounding into powder. Giving frequently and liberally of one's property. *Husum*, Round sand-hills rolling down.

A هثملة *hasmalat*, Corruption. Confusion, mixture. Whispering.

A هثمنة *hasmanat*, Loquaciousness.

A هثهاث *has-hās*, Swift, expeditious. Confused. Dusty (country or city). A liar.

A هثهثة *has-hasat*, (v. n. of هثهث Q) (Clouds) pouring down fast (rain or snow). Kicking or treading upon with vehemence. Being unjust (a judge). Ruling with tyranny. Being confounded, mixed.

P هج *haj*, A straight and erect position. Preparation for an expedition. Erecting any thing in the manner of a spear, holding it perpendicular.

A هج *haj*, Used in calling to a dog.

A هجّ *hajj*, (v. n. of هجّ) Demolishing (a house). *Hujj*, A yoke on the neck of an ox.

A هجء *hajـ*, (v. n. of هجأ) Being satisfied (hunger). Eating, filling (the belly). Stopping (camels) in order to graze. *Hajaـ*, (v. n. of هجئ) Being very keen (hunger). Business that has been broken off.

A هجاء *hijāـ*, (v. n. of هجا for هجو) Satirizing, ridiculing, railing at, lampooning, laughing to scorn. Dividing into syllables, spelling. Satire, bitter words, reproach. Form, figure. حرف هجاء *harfu hijāـin*, A letter of the alphabet. على هجاء هذا *ʿala' hijāـi hāzā*, In this manner. P هجا كردن *hijā kardan*, To connect the letters, to syllable, spell. To compose a satire, to ridicule.

A هجاة *hajāt*, A frog.

A هجأة *hujaـat*, Foolish, stupid. A fool.

A هجاج *hajāj*, A quick pace. *Hajāja* or *hajāji*, A conceited or stubborn man. One who restrains others from any thing.

A هجاجة *hajājat*, Foolish (man). Dust.

A هجاجيك *hajājayka*, Have a care! refrain from!

A هجار *hijār*, A bow-string. A ring at which the Persians were used to shoot. A chain. A diadem. A rope which ties the foot of a camel to his girth.

A هجارس *hajāris*, (pl. of هجرس *hijris*) Foxes or their cubs. Calamitous times.

A هجّاس *hajjās*, A lion on the listen.

A هجاع *hajāʿ*, (erroneously for هجاج *hajāj*) A conceited or stubborn man.

A هجال *hijāl*, (pl. of هجل *hajl*) Large plains. (pl. of هجيل *hajīl*) Low, level grounds.

A هجّالة *hajjālat*, A widow.

A هجان *hijān*, Noble and excellent (woman). Base, wicked (fellow). Good, fertile (ground). The better class of people. Excellent white (camel or camels). (pl. of هجينة *hajīnat*) The daughters of free fathers and slave mothers.

A هجّان *hujjān*, (pl. of هجيج *hajīj*) Lines drawn by a conjuror on the ground.

A هجانة *hajānat*, Goodness, excellence, nobility of birth. *Hijānat*, (v. n. of هجن) Being born of a slave mother from a free father. Foulness, baseness.

A هجاوة *hajāwat*, Heat, sultriness (of the day).

P هجاور *hajāwar*, An assembly of people. Name of a country famous for handsome people.

A هجاهج *hujāhij*, Thick, gross.

A هجائن *hajāـin*, (pl. of هجان *hijān*) White and noble (camels). (pl. of هجينة *hajīnat*) The daughters of free fathers and slave mothers.

A هجائي *hijāـiy*, Relating to the alphabet, alphabetical. الحروف الهجائية *al hurūfu'l hijāـiyat*, The letters of the alphabet.

A هجب *hajb*, A driving. Celerity. A threshing.

A هجد *hajid*, A word used in calling to a horse.

A هجّد *hujjad*, (pl. of هجود *hajūd*) Those who pray by night.

A هجدم *hijdam*, A word for urging on a horse.

P هجده *hajdah*, (for هشتده *hashtdah*) Eighteen. هجده هزار *hajdah hazār*, Eighteen thousand.

P هجدهم *hajdahum*, The eighteenth.

A هجر *hajr*, (v. n. of هجر) Separating, dividing, or cutting off. Leaving, abandoning, deserting friends or country. Speaking deliriously (as a sick man). Abstaining from venery during Ramazān or Lent. Fastening one end of a rope round a camel's foot, and the other at the saddle-girth. Separation, disjunction, desertion of country or friends. Absence. Mid-day, or the more sultry time of the day which follows it. Beautiful, elegant. Generous, liberal. Good, excellent. A halter, a bridle. (pl. اهجار *ahjār*) Fruitful (country). هجر النهار *hajra'n nahār*, At mid-day. ما لقيته عن هجر *mā lakaytuhu ʿan hajrin*, I have not met him for an entire year, or during the whole of the week, or since his absence. *Hijr*, Superior, super-excellent. Excellent (camel). *Hujr*, (v. n. of هجر) Doting, raving, talking nonsense (in sleep or sickness). Dotage. Trifling conversation, idle garrulity. A foolish or improper speech. *Hajar*, Name of a tract of country in Arabia called بحرين *bahrayn*; (according to others) that part of Bahrayn which borders on نجد *najd*. Name of the capital of Bahrayn. Name of a city in Yaman and of a village near Madina. كمبضع تمرالى هجر *ka mubziʿi tamrin ila' hajar*, Like one carrying dates for sale to Hajar (where they are found in the greatest abundance; Coals to Newcastle). *Hajir*, Elegant, excellent. One who walks weakly, as if weighed down. *Hujur*, (pl. of هجير *hajīr*), Large cisterns for watering cattle.

A هجرا *hajran*, (A tree growing) thick and long.

A هجّر *hijirr*, Flight to villages or towns.

A هجراء *hajrāـ*, Foolish, shameful, improper conversation. Power, ability.

A هجران *hijrān*, (v. n. of هجر) Cutting off. Departing, being separated from, or not frequenting friends; leaving one's country. Separation, disjunction, remoteness, distance from friends.

A هجرة *hajrat*, One year. *Hijrat* or *hujrat*, Departure from one's country and friends, separation of lovers or friends. الهجرة *al hijrat*, The Hajira, or flight of Muhammad from Mecca to Madina, which, in the reign of the caliph Omar, was ordered to be considered as the Muhammadan æra. سنة الهجرة *sanatu'l hijrat*, The year of the Hijra. قديم هجرة *kadīmu hijratin*, An old man. الهجرتان *al hijratāni*, The two flights or emigrations, *i.e.* the one above-mentioned, and the other of many Muhammadans to Ethiopia. ذو الهجرتين *zū'l hijratayn*, One who made both these migrations.

A هجرس *hijris*, (pl. هجارس *hajāris*) A fox, or the cub of a fox; also another animal smaller than a fox, which prowls about in the night. A bear. An ape, monkey, baboon. Worthless, avaricious. Small (rain) freezing into hail or hoar-frost.

A هجرع *hajraʿ* or *hijraʿ*, Foolish, insane. Long, tall; thin, meagre. Long and lame. A light, swift hunting dog, a greyhound.

A هجريّ *hijriy*, Of, or according to, the Muhammadan æra. *Hajariy*, Native of Hajar.

A هجريا *hijrīya'*, Manner, custom.

A هجز *hajz*, The passing of a thought in the mind. A low unintelligible voice; any thing muttered.

A هجزع *hijzaʿ*, A coward.

A هجس *hajs*, (v. n. of هجس) Coming into mind. Averting, driving from. Whatever one recollects or thinks of. Whatever passes in one's mind. Instinct. A low unintelligible voice; any thing muttered.

A هجش *hajsh*, (v. n. of هجش) Pushing or driving gently. Irritating, exciting, stirring up. Desiring, longing for.

A هجشة *hajshat*, A rising up, going away.

A هجع *hajaʿa*, (fut. يهجع *yahjaʿu*) He slept.

A هجع *hajʿ*, (v. n. of هجع) Satisfying (hunger). *Hijʿ*, *hajiʿ*, or *hujaʿ*, Senseless, thoughtless, careless.

A هجّع *hujjaʿ*, (pl. of هاجع *hājiʿ*) Sleepers.

A هجعة *hajʿat*, A gentle sleep, a slumber in the beginning of the night. Night-watches. *Hijʿat*, A manner of sleeping. *Hijʿat* or *hujaʿat*, Senseless, foolish, careless.

A هجعمة *hajʿamat*, Boldness, audacity.

A هجف *hajaf*, (v. n. of هجف) Being hungry. Being loose and flabby (the body). Falling here and there by disease and death.

A هجفّ *hijaff*, An old ostrich. Stupid, lazy, slow (man or ostrich). Large-bellied.

A هجفان *hajfān*, Thirsty.

A هجفة *hijfat*, A side, part, tract, or quarter moist and wet. *Hajifat*, Thin, lean (woman).

A هجفجف *hajafjaf*, One with a capacious belly.

A هجل *hajl*, (v. n. of هجل) Looking slily askance. Throwing, hurling (the cane-spear). (pl. اهجال *ahjāl*, هجال *hijāl*, هجول *hujūl*, and هجلات *hajalāt*) A large plain, valley, or wood between mountains. *Hujul*, Unbeaten, unused (road).

A هجم *hajm*, (v. n. of هجم) Driving in, forcing to enter. Urging on, thrusting forward, driving away. Being still and quiet, keeping silence. Breaking down, overthrowing (a house). Being subdued and weakened (disease). Exhausting (by milking). Being deeply sunk in the socket (the eye). Sweating. Making the eyes close in sleep. Sweat, perspiration. *Hajm* or *hajam*, (pl. اهجام *ahjām*) A cup, capacious bowl or goblet.

A هجمة *hajmat*, Assault, onset, attack. Rigour or severity of winter. Sultry heat of summer. A herd of camels, from forty to a hundred.

A هجن *hajn*, (v. n. of هجن) Being married too young (a girl). Bearing fruit for the first time (a female palm-tree). *Hujun*, (pl. of هجين *hajīn* or هجينة *hajīnat*) Sons or daughters of free men by slave women.

A هجناء *hujanāʼ*, (or هجنان *hujnān*) (pl. of هجين) Men whose fathers are free and mothers slaves.

A هجنة *hujnat*, (v. n. of هجن) Having a free father and slave mother. Turpitude, baseness, blemish. Bad language. Loss of learning. Worthless men.

P هجند *hajand*, An herb which, when boiled, is given to cattle.

A هجنس *hijans*, Heavy.

A هجنع *hajanna‛*, (fem. هجنعة *hajanna‛at*) Long and thick. Bald (old man). Bald (male ostrich) with strength yet remaining. A camel's colt dropped in the hottest part of the year.

A هجنف *hajannaf*, Tall and wide.

P هجنم *hajnam*, (in zand and Pāzand) I give.

A هجو *hajw*, (v. n. of هجا for هجو) Satirizing, lampooning, reproaching, blaming. Joining (letters) in syllables, spelling. Satire, lampoon, pasquinade. P هجو كردن *hajw kardan*, To satirize. A هجو مليح *hajw malīḥ*, Seeming praise, but real satire; irony.

A هجوء *hujūʼ*, (v. n. of هجأ) Being satisfied (hunger). Eating, filling (the belly). Stopping (camels) in order to graze.

A هجود *hajūd*, (pl. هجود *hujūd* and هجّد *hujjad*) One who says nightly prayers. *Hujūd*, (v. n. of هجد) Sleeping in the night. Waking, watching. Laying the curved part of the neck on the ground (a camel). Sleep.

A هجور *hujūr*, (v. n. of هجر) Tying (a camel) with one end of the rope round (his) feet and the other to the saddle-girth.

A هجوريّ *hajūriy*, A noonday-meal, lunch.

A هجوع *hujū‛*, (v. n. of هجع) Sleeping, especially at night. Being satisfied (hunger). Sleep, slumber. Sleepers.

A هجول *hujūl*, A roomy woman. A whore. *Hujūl*, Flowing (tears). (pl. of هجل *hajl*) Wide plains.

A هجوم *hajūm*, (Wind) blowing down a house. One who enters suddenly. Introduced. *Hujūm*, (v. n. of هجم) Attacking, invading, charging, assaulting, rushing upon suddenly. Falling (a house). Entering without leave. Introducing. Coming on (winter). Exhausting (the udder) by milking. Being deeply sunk in the socket (an eye). An assault, attack, effort; impetuosity.

A هجونة *hujūnat*, (v. n. of هجن) Having a free father and slave mother. Turpitude, deformity.

A هجهاج *hajhāj*, Timid, flying in terror. (A camel) braying loud. Cruel, unfeeling. Long, tall. Stupid, foolish. A misfortune.

A هجهاجة *hajhājat*, Stupid, foolish.

A هجهج *hajhaj*, Used in calling to sheep. Hard, sterile ground. *Hujahij*, A ram. Water drank.

A هجهجة *hajhajat*, (v. n. of هجهج Q) Shouting aloud to drive off (the lion), or checking (a camel) by calling out هيج *hij*. The shout of the Kurds at the onset of a battle.

A هجي *hajy*, (v. n. of هجي) Being uncovered, lying open. Being deeply sunk (a camel's eye).

A هجي *hajī*, Spelling.

A هجيج *hajīj*, (v. n. of هجّ) Demolishing (a house). A long country that hurries travellers forwards. A deep valley. Heat (of fire). (pl. هجّان *hujjān*) A line drawn by a conjurer on the ground.

P هجيد *hajed*, (in zand and Pāzand) Give ye.

P هجيدن *hajīdan*, To grow dry.

P هجير *hajīr*, Name of the son of Kāran bin Kāwa. *Hujīr*, Good, fair, select, choice.

A هجير *hajīr*, Meridian, noon, mid-day. (pl. هجر *hujur*) A large and capacious cistern or trough for watering cattle. Dry herbs, of a salt and bitter kind, broken and left by cattle. Thick and rough (wild ass). A large cup. A stallion, weak, languid from frequent covering. Thick (milk).

A هجيرة *hajīrat*, The meridian, mid-day. *Hujayrat*, (dim. of هجرة *hajrat*) An entire year.

A هجّيرة *hijjīrat*, Manner, custom.

A هجّيرى *hijjīra'*, (v. n. of هجر) Raving, doting (in sleep or sickness). Manner, custom. ما زال ذاك هجّيراه *mā zāla zāka hijjīrāhu*, That never ceased to be his custom.

A هجيسة *hajīsat*, Milk spoiled, or turning sour.

A هجيع *hajī‛*, A third, a fourth, or a smaller part of the night.

A هجيل *hajīl*, (pl. اهجال) Low level ground.

A هجيمة *hajīmat*, Milk put into a new churning-bottle but not thickening. Milk becoming thick before it be shaken.

A هجين *hajīn*, (pl. هجن *hujun*, هجناء *hujanāʼ*, هجنان *hujnān*, مهاجين *mahājīn*, and مهاجنة *mahājinat*) A man born of a free father and a slave mother. A horse got by an Arabian sire from a foreign dam. A mean-blooded pack-horse. Base, sordid. Milk not pure.

A هجينة *hajīnat*, (pl. هجن *hujun*, هجائن *hajāʼin*, and هجان *hijān*) A woman born of a free father and slave mother.

P هچ *hach* or *huch*, A halbert stuck in the ground. A thing fixed in the ground, standing bolt upright.

P هچكارا *hichkārā*, Useless, bad.

P هچيدن *hachīdan*, To vex, grieve, irritate, injure, molest. To gape, yawn. To reel, stagger (as sheep). To seize, carry off. To flay a sheep.

A هخ *hikh*, The noise in expectorating.

A هدّ *hadd*, (v. n. of هدّ) Breaking, demolishing, ruining. Being weak. A thick, hoarse voice; the braying of a camel. The last stage of old age. Liberal. A generous man. لهدّ الرجل *la hadda'r rajulu*, Hail! welcome! O most excellent man. فلان يهدّ *fulānun yuhaddu*, So-and-so is a strong, brave fellow. *Hadd* or *hidd*, (pl. هدّون *haddūn* or *hiddūn*) Weak (hence, a threat, انّي لغير هدّ *innī la ghayru haddin*, However weak I may be (I will humble you). هدّك من رجل *haddaka* (or *haddika*) *mir rajulin*, This is a man sufficient for thee. *Haddi*, Used when an ass drinks.

A هدأ *hadʼ*, (v. n. of هدأ) Reposing, resting, remaining (in a place). Dying. A state, condition. Habit, mode of life. *Hadʼ* or *hudʼ*, A part of the night, a third of it. *Hadaʼ*, (v. n. of هدئ) Bending inwards. Being crook-backed. A protuberance. A slight depression in a camel's bunch produced by frequent overloading.

A هدآء *hadʼāʼ*, A she-camel whose bunch is flattened by overloading.

A هدّاءة *huddāʼat*, A slender horse.

A هداب *hidāb*, (pl. of هدب *hadab*) Small leaves of plants somewhat resembling hair.

A هدّاب *huddāb*, The small leaf of a certain plant resembling hair. Impotent, languid, slow. هدّاب النخل *huddābu'n nakhl*, Palm-tree branches.

A هدابد *hudābid*, Very thick milk.

A هدءة *hadʼat*, Part (of the night), as far as a third. هدأة ليلة *hidʼatu laylatin*, Food for a night.

A هدأة *hadaʼat*, A kind of running pace.

A هداة *hadāt*, An instrument. *Hudāt*, (pl. of هادي *hādī*) Guides.

A هداج *hudāj*, The tremulous gait of an old man.

A هدّاج *haddāj*, (An old man) running tremulously.

A هدادة *hadādat*, Timid, cowardly.

A هداديك *hadādayka*, Slowly, by degrees, fair and softly, give a little time.

A هدار *hadār*, Name of the birth-place of Musaylimat the pretender (styled الكذّاب *al kazzāb*).

A هدّار *haddār*, A multitude plundering and committing every kind of enormity.

A هداريس *hadārīs*, Misfortunes.

A هدافة *hudāfat*, Corpulency, fleshiness.

A هداكر *hudākir*, Delicate, in good health.

A هدال *hadāl*, Branches hanging down. *Hidāl*, (pl. of هدالة *hadālat*) Crowds.

A هدالة *hadālat*, A crowd. A species of tree.

A هدام *hudām*, Giddiness when sailing.

A هدامیٰ *hadāma'*, Ruttish (she-camels).

A هدان *hidān*, Foolish. Slow, lazy. Timid.

A هدانة *hudānat*, Peace, tranquillity. A truce.

A هداوي *hadāwa'* or *wī*, (pl. of هديّة) Gifts.

A هداهد *hadāhid*, Gentleness, courtesy. (pl. of هدهد *hudhud*, *hudahid*, and هداهد *hudāhid*) Whoops, houps, puets. (pl. of هدهدة *hadhadat*) Whispers, murmurs. Brayings of camels. Cooings of doves. *Hudāhid*, A hoopoe, puet.

A هداهيد *hadāhīd*, The voices of demons and genies. (pl. of هدهد *hudhud*, *hudahid*, and هداهد *hudāhid*), Houps, hoopoes, puets.

A هدايا *hadāya'*, (pl. of هديّة *hadiyat*) Gifts, presents. P هداياي شاهانه *hadāyāyi shāhāna*, Royal gifts, presents worthy of a king. A هداياي فاخره *hadāyāyi fākhira*, Costly gifts.

A هداية *hidāyat*, (v. n. of هدي) Making known, guiding, directing. Leading one into the right road (in a literal or religious sense). Preceding, going before. A guide or direction to the right way or to the road of salvation. Name of a law-treatise.

A هدب *hadb*, (v. n. of هدب) Milking (a camel). Cutting. Gathering fruit. Impotent, slow. *Hadab*, (v. n. of هدب) Having long eye-lashes (the eye). Having long pendulous boughs (a tree) (pl. اهداب *ahdāb* and هداب *hidāb*) The small hair-like leaf of a plant (such as the tamarisk or cypress). The hairy or tufted branch (of a palm-tree). هدب العين *hadabu'l ʿayn*, The eye-lash. *Hadib*, a lion. *Hudub* or *hudb*, The hairs of the eye-lids. Scalloped or fringed edges of garments.

A هدبّ *hudubb*, Impotent, weak, languid, slow.

A هدباء *hadbās*, (fem. of اهدب *ahdab*) (A tree) having long hanging branches (like the larch). Long-eyebrowed or eyelashed (female).

A هدبة *hudb* or *hudubat*, One eyelash. *Hadabat*, One leaf resembling hair. *Hudabat*, A sort of bird.

A هدبد *hudabid*, Very thick milk. A weakness of sight and running at the eye. Purblindness during the night. A kind of black gum. Weak-sighted.

A هدبّس *hadabbas*, A male tiger, or his whelp.

A هدبل *hidabl*, Hairy. One whose hair is uncombed or dishevelled. Slow, tardy.

P هدبه *hadba*, A species of centipede.

A هدّة *haddat*, Noise of a falling wall, or the like.

A هدجان *hadajān*, Tremulous gait of an old man.

A هدجة *hadajat*, The cry of a camel to her colt.

A هدجدج *hadajdaj*, Trembling-paced (man).

A هدد *hadad*, A thick, hoarse, gruff voice.

A هدر *hadr*, (v. n. of هدر) Being shed or allowed to be shed with impunity (blood). Being long and luxuriant (herbage). Suffering (blood) to be shed unrevenged. Cooing (as a dove). Braying in the throat (as a camel). Boiling (wine). Appearing, bursting forth (palm-flowers). *Hidr*, Heavy, slow (man). *Hadar*, (v. n. of هدر) Being shed or allowed to be shed unrevenged (blood). Boiling (wine). Contemptible, vile. دماؤهم هدر *dimāʾuhum hadarun*, The slaughter of those is permitted to all. ذهب دمهم هدرا *zahaba damuhum hadaran*, Their blood was shed with impunity.

A هدرة *ha*, *hi*, or *hudarat*, Worthless (man, men).

A هدس *hadas*, (in Yaman) A myrtle-tree.

A هدغ *hadgh*, The breaking (a hollow substance).

A هدف *hadf*, (v. n. of هدف) Entering. Approaching (fifty). Being weak, lazy, and torpid. *Hidf*, Corpulent. *Hadaf*, (pl. اهداف *ahdāf*) A butt or mark for archers. Any thing elevated or placed high. A mountain, a hill of sand. A lofty building. Heavy, stupid, worthless. Sleepy. A word used in calling sheep to be milked. هل هدف اليكم هادف *hal hadafa ilaykum hādifun*, Did any body come to you? (especially strangers).

A هدفة *hidfat*, A crowd. A cluster of houses.

A هدك *hadk*, (v. n. of هدك) Ruining, demolishing, levelling with the ground.

A هدكر *hudukir*, A woman moving her flesh and bones when walking. Thick milk.

A هدكرة *hadkarat*, (v. n. of هدكر Q) Taking what is within one's reach.

A هدكورة *hudkūrat*, (fem.) Corpulent, plump. Graceful in darting amorous glances.

P هدگير *hadgīr*, An island in the Indian sea.

A هدل *hadl*, (v. n. of هدل) Allowing (any thing) to hang loose. Dropping (his) nether lip when ulcerated (a camel). Cooing (a turtle-dove). Seizing a camel (an ulcer). *Hidl*, Thick milk. بنو هدل *banū hidlin*, Certain Syrian Jews who dwelt at Madīna. *Hadal*, (v. n. of هدل) Being long-lipped (a camel). Hanging (a camel's lip). *Hadil*, Long-lipped (camel).

A هدلاء *hadlās*, (fem. of اهدل) Hanging (lip).

P هدل زنگي *hadal zangī*, Turbith-root.

A هدلق *hidlik*, Relaxed. (A camel) having the corners of the mouth wide. A hair-seive.

A هدلقة *hidlikat*, Hair on a camel's nether jaw.

A هدلوغة *hudlū* or *hidlawghat*, Ugly and foolish.

A هدلیٰ *hadla'*, Pendulous, hanging (lip).

A هدم *hadm*, (v. n. of هدم) Ruining, demolishing, levelling with the ground, laying waste. Breaking the back. Ruin, destruction. *Hadm* or *hadam*, Blood shed with impunity. *Hidm*, (pl. اهدام *ahdām* and هدم *hidam*) A worn or patched garment. An old boot. A decrepit old man. *Hadam*, (v. n. of هدم) Longing for the male (a she-camel). Any thing falling into a well from the side. دماؤهم هدم *dimāʾuhum hadamun* or *hadmun*, Their blood may be shed with impunity. *Hadim*, An old catamite. A destroyer.

P هدمان *hadmān*, Depriving one's self of a thing to bestow it upon another.

A هدمة *hadmat*, Small rain. Part (of wealth). *Hadamat*, (v. n. of هدم) Longing for the male (a she-camel). *Hadimat*, (pl. هدامیٰ *hadāma'* and هدمة *hidamat*) Libidinous (she-camel).

A هدمل *hidaml*, Slow. A high hill or heap. *Hidaml* or *hidmil*, A worn or torn garment. *Hidmil*, One who has much hair and dishevelled. Old, of long continuance.

A هدملة *hadmalat*, (v. n. of هدمل Q) Tearing one's clothes. *Hidamlat*, A sandy soil abounding with trees. Ancient times. A crowd of people.

A هدن *hidn*, Plenty, fertility. *Hudun*, (pl. of هدان *hidān*) Foolish. Lazy, slow.

A هدنة *hadnat*, Small, gentle rain. *Hudnat*, Peace. A truce. Quiet, tranquillity.

P هدنج *hadanj*, (or هدنگ) A white or gray horse.

A هدوّ *hadūw*, A road-guide.

A هدوء *hudūs*, (v. n. of هدأ) Resting or remaining in a place. Quiet, rest, tranquillity (especially of the night). Part (of the night), a third (of it).

A هدوج *hadūj*, Quick-boiling (pot): loud (wind).

A هدود *hadūd*, Plain ground. The steep declivity of a mountain. *Hudūd*, (v. n. of هدّ) Breaking, demolishing; a fracture.

A هدور *hudūr*, (v. n. of هدر) Being long and luxuriant (herbage). Falling, giving way (the lungs) in consequence of severe beating.

A هدون *hudūn*, (v. n. of هدن) Resting. Quieting. Soothing and quieting (as a mother her child). Killing. Burying. Living in affluence and quiet. Quiet, tranquillity.

A هدّون *haddūn* or *hiddūn*, (pl.) Weak.

P هده *hula*, Just, true. Profit, advantage. Truth. بي هده *bī huda*, False, vain. Speaking foolishly.

A هدهاد *hadhād*, Name of the father of Bilkīs.

A هدهد *hadhad*, The noise or voice of demons. *Hudhud*, Any bird that calls out much. *Hudhud* or *hudahid*, (pl. هداهد *hadāhid*) The houp, hoopoo, or puet. A dove which cooes much.

A هدهدة *hadhadat*, (v. n. of هدهد Q) Cooing (as a dove). Braying (as a camel). Moving, rocking, or soothing (a child) to make (it) sleep. Suggesting to the mind, presenting to the fancy. Letting (a thing) down from top to bottom. (pl. هداهد *hadāhid*) A whisper, murmur. The cooing of a dove. The braying of a camel. A lullaby.

P هدي *hady*, A corn-field watered by rain.

A هدي *hady*, (v. n. of هدي) Guiding right, directing. Pointing out the way (home, or to any other place). Leading a bride home to her husband. Finding the way. Being directed in the right way. Institution, mode of living, habit. Cattle carried to Mecca to be sacrificed. A bride. (pl. of هدية *hadyat*) Institutions. Methods in business. هدي هديه *hada' hadyahu*, He followed his steps, he imitated his manners. ما لي هدي ان كان كذا *mā lī hadyun in kāna hazā*, May I have no cattle to sacrifice if the case be so. *Huda'*, (v. n. of هدي) Directing, guiding. Direction into the right road, or into the way of salvation. The way of salvation. A straight road. A day.

A هديّ *hadīy*, Cattle carried to Mecca to be sacrificed. A captive. A bride conveyed to her husband's home. Any thing honourable, venerable, or precious.

A هديء *hadīs*, A part of the night.

A هديّا *hudayya'*, Alike, equal.

A هدية *hadyat*, One animal offered in sacrifice at Mecca. *Hadyat* or *hidyat*, Institution, custom; any situation in which one is. خذ في هديتك *khuz fī hidyatika*, Keep to your plan in saying or doing. نظر هدية امره *nazara hidyata amrihi*, He saw the (proper) method of managing the affair. ما احسن هديته *mā ahsana hidyatuhu*, How admirably does he regulate his conduct! *Hadyat*, *hidyat*, or *hudyat*, Conduct, method (in business). *Hidyat*, (v. n. of هدي) Guiding in the right way.

A هديّة *hadīyat*, (pl. هدايا *hadāya'*, هداوي *hadāwa'*, or *hadāwī*) A present, especially one offered to superiors. One animal offered in sacrifice at Mecca. An offering on the altar. The price of a Kur'ān. A bride. P هديّهٔ دندان *hadiyaṣi dandān*, Money distributed to the poor after a feast. A هديّة القدوم *hadiyatu'l kudūm*, A present to a prince or a friend on their arrival. P هديّه كردن *hadiya kardan*, To make a present.

A هديد *hadīd*, (v. n. of هدّ) Falling with a crash (a wall). A thick, hoarse voice. A tall man.

A هدير *hadīr*, (v. n. of هدر) Cooing (a pigeon). Braying (a camel). Being long and luxuriant (grass).

A هديل *hadīl*, (v. n. of هدل) Cooing, mourning (as a turtle-dove). A pigeon, a dove. A young pigeon or any bird which dies of thirst, or is carried off by a rapacious bird.

A هديم *hadīm*, Remainder grass of the former year.

P هدينه *hadīna*, A ladder.

A هذّ *hazz*, (v. n. of هذّ) Cutting or reading quickly. Who or what cuts quickly, very sharp.

A هذء *hazs*, (v. n. of هذأ) Cutting off at a blow, amputating. Putting (a foe) to flight. Making (one) hear what is disagreeable. Falling, stumbling oft.

A هذا *hāzā*, This (man or thing). هذا اليوم *hāza'l yawm*, To-day, now, at present, in these times. اش هذا *ash hāzā*, What is this! لاجل هذا *li ajli hāzā*, On this account, wherefore. لهذا *li hāzā*, Therefore, for that reason. مثل هذا *misl hāzā*, In this manner, thus, so.

A هذأ *hazas*, A perishing with cold.

A هذاء *huzās*, Dotage, delirium (in sleep or fever).

A هذّاء *hazzās*, Doting, raving (fellow).

A هذّاءة *hazzāsat*, Doting, raving, delirious.

A هذابة *hazābat*, (v. n. of هذب) Being swift.

A هذأة *hazsat*, A shovel, spade, mattock, pick-axe.

A هذاذ *hazāz*, A cutting quickly; reading fast.

A هذّاذ *hazzāz*, Whoever cuts quickly. (A camel) which precedes or gets before others.

A هذاذيك *hazāzayka*, Stand back! Keep off! هذاذيك و بذاذيك *hazāzayka wa bazāzayka*, Here and there.

A هذار *hazzār*, Delirious; a vain, idle talker.

A هذارم *huzārim*, (and هذارمة *huzārimat*) One who reads or speaks fast.

A هذاريف *hazārīf*, (pl. of هذروف) Quick, swift.

A هذّاف *hazzāf*, Quick, expeditious. Sharp.

A هذاك *hāzāka*, He. That.

A هذاليل *hazālīl*, (pl. of هذلول *huzlūl*) Hillocks.

A هذام *huzām*, Sharp (sword). Bold, strong.

A هذان *hāzāni*, (dual of هذا *hāzā*) These two.

A هذاهذ *hazāhiz*, Those who say all they meet are their friends or servants. Sharp, cutting quickly.

A هذب *hazb*, (v. n. of هذب) Cutting. Pruning palm-trees of the hairy fibres called ليف *lif*. Cleaning, purifying, making free from admixture. Adapting, fitting. Making a confused noise (people). Running, flowing. Being swift (a man or beast). *Hazab*, Purity, integrity. Brightness.

A هذخرة *hazkharat*, (v. n. of هذخر Q) Walking with graceful, jaunty air, or flauntingly (a woman).

A هذذ *hazaz*, (v. n. of هذّ) Cutting, or reading quickly. Hastening, accelerating.

A هذر *hazr*, (v. n. of هذر) Doting, reasoning absurdly, talking idly. *Hazar*, (v. n. of هذر) Being pre-eminently nonsensical and frivolous (talk). Delirium, insanity; loquacity, frivolous garrulity, nonsense. *Hazir* or *hazur*, Delirious, foolish in speech.

A ذو هذرات *zū hazarāt*, One who is cozened in buying and selling.

A هذربان *huzrubān*, Active in serving; ready in speech.

A هذربة *hazrabat*, (v. n. of هذرب Q) Being loquacious, speaking easily.

A هذرة *hazirat*, Delirious, doting (woman). *Huzarat* or *huzurat*, A vain, idle talker.

A هذرفة *hazrafat*, Celerity, expedition.

A هذرمة *hazramat*, (v. n. of هذرم Q) Reading or speaking easily and fast.

A هذرمى *hazrama'*, (A woman) full of rage; clamorous, and raising a disturbance.

A هذروف *huzrūf*, (pl. هذاريف) Quick, swift.

A هذريان *hizriyān*, Delirious, foolish in speech. Easy, quick in speaking, reading, or serving.

A هذف *hazif*, Quick. Sharp.

A هذلان *hazalān*, (v. n. of هذل) Going fast.

A هذلبة *hazlabat*, Agility, celerity.

A هذلة *hazlat*, A quick short-stepped gait.

A هذلمة *hazlamat*, A quick step.

A هذلوغ *huzlūgh*, Thick-lipped.

A هذلول *huzlūl*, (pl. هذاليل *hazālīl*) A little hill, hillock, heap of sand. Fine sand. A small channel of a river. A thin cloud. Rain appearing in the sky just before it descends. The beginning of the (night). The remainder of the night. Blight of corn. A light, active man. A light or slender arrow. A wolf. A tall and hardy horse.

A هذليّ *huzalīy*, Pertaining to هذيل *huzayl*.

A هذم *hazm*, A cutting quick. Fast eating.

A هذملة *hazmalat*, A going with short steps.

A هذو *hazw*, (v. n. of هذا for هذو) Being delirious, raving in speech, from distemper or other cause. Shaking, brandishing (a sword).

A هذوذ *hazūz*, Quick-cutting, very keen (knife).

A هذوف *huzūf*, A going fast, a making haste.

A هذه *hāzihi*, (or هذي *hāzī*) This. She.

A هذهاذ *hazhāz*, Keen, sharp (knife). قرب هذهاذ *karabun hazhāzun*, A nocturnal journey distant and difficult, when travelling rapidly to water.

A هذي *hazy*, (v. n. of هذي) Being delirious, raving, talking nonsense, from disease or other cause.

A هذيّا *hāzayya'*, (dim. of هذا *hāza'*) The little he or this.

A هذيان *hazayān*, (v. n. of هذي) Being delirious, raving, talking nonsense. Vain, useless words. هذيان محرور *hazayāni mahrūr*, The delirium of one in a fever. P هذيان پاش *hazayān-pāsh*, Scattering nonsense, speaking idly.

A هذيرى *huzayriba'*, Manner, custom, habit.

A هذيل *huzayl*, Name of an Arabian tribe.

P هر *har*, Every, all. Each. Any. A noxious grain amongst corn. هر احد *har ahad*, Every one. هر آن كه *har ān ki*, Every one who. هر آن چه *har ān chi*, Every thing that. هر بار *har bār*, Every time, at all times, always, as often as, whensoever, at whatever time, for as much as, if so be. هر جنس *har jins*, Every kind, of all sorts. هر چند كه *har chand ki*, Although, notwithstanding, how much soever. هر چه *har chi*, Whatsoever. هر چه باد باد *har chi bād bād*, Whatever must be must be, follow what will, whatever is the consequence. هر دايما *har dāyimā*, Perpetually, always, continually. هر دم *har dam*, Every moment, always. هر روز *har roz*, Every day, daily. هر زمان *har zamān*, (or هر وقت *har wakt*) Every time, at all times, continually. هر سال *har sāl*, Every year, annually. هر شي *har shay*, Every thing. هر گاه كه *har gāh ki*, Every time that, whensoever. هر كس *har kas*, (and هر فرد *har fard*) Every one, every bit. از هر طرف *az har taraf*, From every side. *Har*, (in zand and Pāzand) An agent, a doer. *Hir*, Used in calling sheep together. Cloud, fog. Ice. A groan. A pimple, pustule. *Hur*, Fear. Departure.

A هرّ *harr*, (v. n. of هرّ) Abhoring, detesting. Eating the grapes هرور *hurūr*. Voiding dung. Flowing freely (dung) till (the camel) dies. Making (a dog) whine (the cold). Twanging (a bow-string). Being bad-tempered. Whining (a dog). Drying, withering, growing hard and prickly (the head of a thistle). A word used in crying to camels. *Hirr*, A driving or a calling of sheep, especially to water. (pl. هررة *hirarat*) A ram-cat. Name of a woman. لا يعرف هرًّا من برّ *lā yaʿrifu hirran min birrin*, He knows not bad from good. *Hurr*, (v. n. of هرّ) Being troubled with flux, or a distemper producing it (a camel). Much water or milk. A lion.

A هرء *hars*, (v. n. of هرأ) Speaking with gross impropriety or obscenity. Killing (a chilling blast). Being intensely cold (wind). Dressing meat till the flesh separates from the bone. *Hars* or *hurs*, (v. n. of هرئ) Being boiled (meat) till it dissolves or falls from the bone. *Huras*, Loquacious.

P هرا *harā*, A trifling, incoherent speech, foolish words. One who speaks indecently. *Hirā*, Name of the city of هرات *hirāt*.

P هرّا *harrā*, Horse-furniture; gold and silver ornaments or trappings. The myrobalan. *Harrā* or *hurrā*, Voice, sound; the roar of a lion. *Hirrā*, Noise of trickling water. *Hurrā*, Fear. Splendour.

A هراء *hirās*, The young shoot of a palm-tree. A demon which suggests bad dreams. *Hurās*, A long, stupid, incoherent discourse. Verbose doting.

A هرّاء *harrās*, A vender of cloths made at Herāt.

A هراءة *harāsat*, (v. n. of هرأ) Being intensely cold (wind), killing.

A هرّاب *hurrāb*, (pl. of هارب *hārib*) Fugitives.

A هرابذة *harābizat*, (pl. of هربذ *hirbiz*) The attendants on a fire-temple.

P هرات *hirāt*, Good fortune. A man of good fortune. *Hirāt*, (A هراة *harāt*), One of the capital cities in Khurāsān, Herat.

A هرّات *harrāt*, (or الهرّات *al harrāt*) A lion.

G A هراتقي *harātikīy*, A heretic.

A هراثم *hurāsim*, A lion.

A هرّاج *harrāj*, Fast-running (horse). An auction, outcry, roup.

A هرّاجة *harrājat*, A crowd of people speaking confusedly all together.

A هراجيل *harājīl*, Tall (men). Large, fat, and full of flesh (camels).

A هرار *hirār*, (v. n. 3 of هرّ) Detesting, expressing abhorrence of any one before his face. *Hurār*, (v. n. of هرّ) Being troubled with a flux, or any distemper causing it (a camel). The flux itself. A tumour between the skin and flesh.

A هرّار *harrār*, Very noisy. الهرّار *al harrār*, The star called the Falling Eagle; also the heart of the Scorpion. The first and last Syrian months called كانون *kānūn*, *i.e.* December and January. الهرّاران *al harrārāni*, Both those stars and both those months.

A هرّارة *harrārat*, Overflowing with tears (eye).

P هرارزده *hurār-zada*, (A camel) troubled with a watery humour between the skin and flesh. Fluxed.

A هراس *harās*, A kind of thorny tree bearing fruit like the plant nabik. *Hurās*, Voracious (lion).

P هراس *hirās*, Terror, fear, dread. Confusion, amazement. A scarecrow placed in a garden to frighten away birds or beasts. علامت هراس *ʿalāmati hirās*, Signs of fear. هراس كردن *hirās kardan*, To terrify.

A هرّاس *harrās*, A vender or preparer of a sort of pottage called هريسة *harīsat*. Voracious (lion).

P هراسا *hirāsā*, Timid, fearful. A scare-crow.

P هراسان *hirāsān*, Frightened, fearing, dreading, timid. Frightening. هراسان شدن *hirāsān shudan*, To dread.

P هراسندگان *hirāsandagān*, Penitents; men endued with the fear of God, God-fearing men.

P هراسه *harāsa* or *hirāsa*, Terror. A scarecrow. *Hirāsa*, Any thing used to cause fear.

P هراسيدن *hi* or *harāsīdan*, To fear, dread, be cautious. To defend, preserve. To terrify.

P هراسيده *hirāsīda*, Terrified, frightened.

P هراش *harāsh*, A vomit, vomiting.

A هراش *hirāsh*, (v. n. 3 of هرش) Setting (men or dogs) together by the ears. Romping.

P هراشيدن *harāshīdan*, To vomit.

G هراطقة *harātikat*, Heretics.

A هراع *hurāʿ*, A tremulous but quick pace.

A هراعلة *harāʿilat*, Mean, worthless (men).

A هراقة *hirāhat*, The act of pouring out (water).

A هراكل *hurākil*, Big, bulky (man or camel).

A هراكلة *harākilat*, Large fish, sea-dogs, or other sea-animals, especially large behind. The flowing of the sea, much sea-water.

A هرامس *hurāmis*, A fierce lion.

A هراميت *harāmīt*, Clean wells.

A هراميل *harāmīl*, (pl. of هرمول *hurmūl*) Hairs or feathers remaining on the head or other parts of the body. (Hairs) fallen off, shed.

P هران *har ān*, Every.

A هرانع *harāniʿ*, Roots of the طرثوث *tursūs*.

P هراني *harānī*, A cauldron, kettle.

P هرانيد *harānīd*, True nature; truth, reality.

P هرآوا *harāwā*, (or هرآواز *har-āwāz*) A nightingale, or rather a bird peculiar to the East which sings all notes.

A هراوة *hirāwat*, (pl. هراوي *harāwā'*, هريّ *hirīy*, or *hurīy*) A staff, club, mace. هراوة الاعزاب *hirāwatu'l aʿzāb*, The bachelor's staff, *i.e.* A horse bequeathed for bachelors to ride (on forays) in order to raise money for procuring a wife.

P هراول *harāwal*, Vanguard. Running footman.

P هراهر *hirāhir*, A cloud of dust raised by the wind. The roaring of wild beasts.

A هراهر *hurāhir*, Much milk or water. A lion.

P هراي *harāy*, Religion, sect. (See هرا *harā*.)

P هرآئنه *har-āsina*, (or هرائينه *har-āsīna*) Destitute, helpless. Doubtless, undoubtedly, certainly, assuredly, inevitably, infallibly, necessarily. Always, ever, in every way, by all means, at all events. Clear, evident. Fit, proper, necessary.

A هرب *hurb*, The thin caul of fat covering the intestines of animals. *Harab*, (v. n. of هرب) Flying, running away, absconding. Sinking (as part of a stake in the ground). Growing old. Flight.

P هرباب *har bāb*, Every chapter, subject, or topic. All sciences. Every circumstance.

P هربابي *harbābī*, Master of all knowledge.

P هرباس *harbās*, A wooden club.

P هرباسب *har bāsb*, Each of the seven planets, *i.e.* Saturn, Jupiter, Mars, the sun, Venus, Mercury, and the moon.

A هربان *harbān*, A fugitive. *Harabān*, (v. n. of هرب) Fleeing away, running off.

A هربجة *harbajat*, A slovenly way of doing.

P هربد *hirbad*, A priest or judge of the worshippers of fire. A servant who lights the fires in the tombs of the Magi.

A هربذ *hirbiz*, (pl. هرابذة *harābizat*) The priest or keeper of a temple of fire. One of the chief priests or wise men of that religion.

A هربذة *harbazat*, An ambling, shuffling gait.

A هربذي *hirbazā'*, A haughty, strutting walk. The camel's pace when leaning to one side.

A هربع *hurbuʿ*, Active thief. Stealthy wolf.

P هربنگ *hurbang*, A noxious weed found among wheat in the spring, said to stupefy those who eat it.

A هربوغ *hurbūgh*, A certain esculent vegetable.

P هربه *harba*, A chameleon.

P هرپاسبان *har pāsbān*, The seven planets.

A هرّة *hirrat*, (pl. هرر *hirar*) A she-cat.

A هرت *hart*, (v. n. of هرت) Tearing (a garment). Dishonouring, defaming. Boiling (meat) till (it) falls to rags. *Harat*, (v. n. of هرت) Being broad, wide (corners of the mouth). Being burst (a woman). الهرت *al harit*, The lion.

P هرتوز *hartūz*, Truthfulness, veracity.

P هرته *harta*, A sheath or vessel containing any thing. *Hartih*, On all sides, everywhere.

A هرث *hirs*, A worn garment.

A هرثم *harsam*, A lion.

A هرثمة *harsamat*, The tip of the nose (especially of a dog); the black division between the nostrils of a dog. The space between the nose and the lip. The groove on the upper lip. A lion. A man's name.

P هرج *harj*, Confines of an enemy's country.

A هرج *harj*, (v. n. of هرج), Being copious, superabounding in any thing. Speaking a great deal confusedly and incoherently. Being tumultuous, seditious, destroying one another. Lying with. Running much or well (a horse). Leaving (a door) open. Tumult, sedition, confusion. Slaughter. هرج مرج *harj marj*, (or هرج و مرج *harj u marj*) Tumult, confusion, anarchy, chaos. *Hirj*, Foolish, silly, feeble (man). *Haraj*, (v. n. of هرج) Being uneasy from excessive heat, or when besmeared with pitch.

P هرجا *har jā*, Every place, everywhere.

A هرجاب *hirjāb*, Tall (man). Name of a place.

P هرجاكه *har jā ki*, Everywhere that, wherever.

P هرجاگرد *har-jā-gard*, A vagrant.

A هرجان *harjān*, A kind of wild almond. زيت الهرجان *zaytu'l harjān*, Oil of almonds.

P هرجائي *harjāʼī*, Of, belonging to, existing in every place. Ubiquitous. Unsettled, variable, desultory, inconstant in love or friendship. A vagabond; stroller. هرجائي نهاد *harjāʼī-nihād*, Ungrateful, inconstant in love.

A هرجبّ *hirjabb*, Long, tall (man).

A هرجة *hirjat*, Light or slight (bow).

A هرجشة *hirjishat*, An old she-camel.

A هرجيع *harjaʻ*, Lame.

A هرجف *hirjaff*, Weak and soft (man).

A هرجل *hurjul*, One who goes with long steps.

A هرجلة *harjalat*, (v. n. of هرجل Q) Travelling with a disordered step. A disordered pace.

P هرچند *har chand*, How much soever, although. Whensoever. هرچند كه *har chand ki*, Notwithstanding, although, how much soever that. هرچند بيشتر *har chand beshtar*, The more, how much the more. هرچند تنگتر بهتر *har chand tangtar bihtar*, The narrower the better. هرچند زودتر *har chand zūdtar*, As quick as possible, the sooner the better.

P هرچه *harchi*, Whatsoever. Whosoever. هرچه بادا باد *har chi bādā bād*, Let what will happen. هرچه زودتر *harchi zūdtar*, As quick as possible.

P هرحال *har hāl*, Howsoever.

A هرد *hard*, (v. n. of هرد) Tearing (reputation or a garment). Boiling or stewing (meat) to a jelly. Being so stewed (meat). Being able to accomplish (any thing) or to make (it) answer. Tumult, sedition; rip and tear. *Hird*, A man of the meanest sort. A she-ostrich. *Hurd*, Saffron. Certain dyeing roots. A kind of bole or red clay.

P هرد *harad*, Turmeric.

A هرداء *hirdāʼ*, A species of plant.

A هردبة *hardabat*, A heavy run.

A هردبّة *hirdabbat*, An old woman. (A man) with a swollen body and a timid mind.

A هردجة *hardajat*, Speed in walking.

A هردشة *hirdishat*, (An old woman, she-camel, or sheep) worn out with age.

P هردل *hardal*, A small black plum. A small black grain growing amongst corn; darnel.

P هردل عزيز *har-dil-ʻazīz*, Dear to every heart, beloved by all, popular.

P هردم *har dam*, Every moment. هردم خيالي *har-dam-khayāle*, Whimsical. Capricious.

P هردو *har du*, Both. هردو عالم *har du ʻālam*, Both worlds, this life and the next.

P هردود *hardūd*, An island in the Indian sea.

P هردوم *hardūm*, The river Jordan.

A هردي *hirdaʼ*, A kind of plant.

A هرديّ *hurdīy*, Dyed with هرد *hurd* roots.

A هرديّة *hurdīyat*, A girdle of rushes tied round a fence made of reeds.

P هرديگي چمچه *har dege chamcha*, A sponger, one who hangs on others for a maintenance.

A هرر *harar*, (v. n. of هرر) Being of a bad disposition. *Hirar*, (pl. of هرّة) She-cats, queen-cats.

A هررة *hirarat*, (pl. of هرّ *hirr*) Tom-cats.

P هرروزه *har roza*, Daily, quotidian.

P هرز *harz*, Vain, futile, idle. A place where water stagnates.

A هرز *harz*, (v. n. of هرز) Dying, perishing. A violent blow or squeeze with the hand.

P هرزجه *harzaja*, A dish made of neats' fat guts.

P هرزوات *harzawāt*, Trifles, falsehoods.

A هرزوقي *hurzūhaʼ*, A prison.

P هرزه *harza*, Vain, futile, frivolous, absurd, nonsensical. Trifles, bagatelles, nonsense.

P هرزه چانگي *harza-chānagī*, Babble, prate.

P هرزه چانه *harza-chāna*, A babbler, chatterer.

P هرزه خاي *harza-khāy*, (or هرزه خوار *harza-khwār*) A prating fellow. هرزه خايان نميمت شعار *harza-khāyāni namīmat-shiʻār*, The idle talkers accustomed to slander, detractors.

P هرزه دراي *harza-darāy*, A prater, babbler.

P هرزه درائي *harza-darāʼī*, Prate, babble, chatter.

P هرزه كار *harza-kār*, A trifler.

P هرزه گرد *harza-gard*, A gossip.

P هرزه گوي *harza-goy* or *gūy*, A foolish, prating fellow, an idle talker. هرزه گويان عالم *harza-goyāni ʻālam*, The babblers of the times.

P هرزه گوئي *harza-gūʼī* or *goʼī*, Babble, chatter.

P هرزه ملاي *harza ma lāy*, Talk no nonsense.

P هرزيد *harzīd*, Aid, help, assistance.

P هرژفدك *harjafdah*, A kind of herb. Castor.

P هرس *hars*, The wooden roof of a house. *Hirs*, Biestings in the udder.

A هرس *hars*, (v. n. of هرس) Thumping, bruising violently. Contusion, severe blow. Voracity, gluttony. A cat. *Haras*, (v. n. of هرس) Eating voraciously. *Haris*, Strong, voracious (lion). Worn (garment). A cat.

P هرساله *har-sāla*, Annual, yearly.

A هرسة *harisat*, (Land) fruitful in هراس *harās*.

P هرسو *har sū*, Every side.

P هرسه دختر *har sih dukhtar*, (All three daughters) Three stars in the Great Bear.

P هرسه نوع *har sih nawʻ*, The three kingdoms of nature, animal, vegetable, and mineral.

P هرش *hirsh*, Poison. *Harash*, Biestings.

A هرش *harash*, (v. n. of هرش) Being bad (the disposition). *Harish*, Foolish, stupid, indolent. Unfeeling, cruel, rough.

A هرشبّة *hirshabbat*, An old woman.

A هرشفة *harshafat*, (v. n. of هرشف Q) Drinking gently. Drying up (cotton in an ink-stand).

A هرشفّة *hirshaffat*, An old woman. A cloth in which they receive rain-water, which they squeeze into a leather bag or bottle (in very dry seasons). Dry cotton in an inkstand. An old bucket.

A هرشمّ *hirshamm*, A soft stone. A mountain of light soil, easily dug.

A هرشمّة *hirshammat*, Hard ground. A sheep abounding in milk.

A هرشن *hirshin*, Wide-mouthed.

P هرشه *harsha*, Ivy; convolvulus.

A هرص *haras*, (v. n. of هرص) Being corroded with the scab. The scab. Worms.

P هرصورت *har sūrat*, Every appearance, or way.

A هرض *harz*, (v. n. of هرض) Tearing (a garment). *Haraz*, The scab corroding the body from extreme heat.

A هرط *hart*, (v. n. of هرط) Detracting, slandering, tearing (reputation) to pieces. Being careless (in speech). *Hart* or *hirt*, Lean meat resembling dry mucus. *Hirt*, (pl. اهراط *ahrāt* and هروط *hurūt*) An old she-camel or sheep. A rich man. *Hirat*, (pl. of هرط *hirt* and هرطة *hirtat*) Old sheep.

A هرطال *hirtāl*, Long, tall.

A هرطة *hirtat*, (pl. هرط *hirat*) Foolish, timid (woman). An old sheep.

P هرطرز *har tarz*, Every manner.

A هرطمان *hurtumān*, *hurtamān*, or *hartamān*) A grain betwixt wheat and barley, good for coughs and dysentery. Oats.

A هرع *harʻ*, (v. n. of هرع) Driving apace. *Haraʻ*, (v. n. of هرع) Flowing fast. Celerity, speed. A quick flux, a rapid stream. A tremulous, hasty step. *Hariʻ*, Hot, flowing fast (blood). (A man) prone to weeping.

A هرعة *harʻat* or *haraʻat*, A small louse. *Haraʻat*, A kind of animalcule different from a louse. *Hariʻat*, Lewd (woman).

A هرف *harf*, (v. n. of هرف) Praising extravagantly (from wonder or ignorance). Producing an early crop (a palm). لا تهرف ما لا تعرف *lā tahrif mā lā taʻrif*, Praise not what thou knowest not.

A هرق *hirk*, Old or worn cloth or garment.

A هرقل *hirakl* or *hirkil*, Heraclius. *Hirkil*, A sieve, a searce.

P هركار *har kār*, Every business.

P هركاره *har-kāra*, (Of all work) A cauldron, a kettle, cooking-pot. A bucket. An attendant upon men of rank in India. An out-door servant employed to go on errands; running footman, messenger.

P هركجا *har kujā*, Wherever.

P هركدام *har kudām*, Whichever, whosoever.

P هركش *harkush*, A sentinel, picquet.

A هركلة *harkalat*, The haughty strut of a proud man. *Harkalat*, *hirahlat*, and *hurahilat*, (A female) of a noble disposition, elegant form, and gait.

A هركولة *hirkawlat*, A woman moving the hips when walking. A woman of a noble disposition, elegant form, and gait.

A هركيل *hirkīl*, (A woman) of a noble disposition, elegant form, and gait.

P هرگ *hurg*, Idiot, fool, simpleton; mad-cap.

P هرگاه *hargāh*, Whenever, wherever. Constantly.

P هرگز *hargiz*, Ever, always. Continually. Perpetually. Eternal, durable. هرگزنه *hargizna*, Never.

P هرگزي *hargizī*, Perpetuity. Eternal.

P هرگله *hargala*, A herd of horses.

P هرگونه *har gūna*, Every kind.

P هرگوني *har gūnī*, Skilful, clever.

P هرم *harm*, Name of a plant of the species called حمض *hamż*. Purslain. ذو الهرم *zū'l harm*, Property in Taif which belonged to Abdu'l Muttalib and Abū Sufyān. يوم الهرم *yawmu'l harm*, A battle famous among the Arabians. *Haram*, (v. n. of هرم) Being old and decrepit. Old age, imbecility, decrepitude. (pl. اهرام *ahrām*) An Egyptian pyramid. Name of a place in Yaman containing famous buildings erected by the Himyarite kings. *Harim*, (pl. هرمون *harimūn* and هرمي *harma'*) A decrepit old dotard. Soul; intellect, understanding.

A هرماس *hirmās*, A lion rushing upon men. A young panther.

P هرماس *hurmās*, A bad guide, an evil spirit.

P هرمان *hirmān*, A long life, old age.

A هرمان *hurmān*, Intellect. ما له هرمان *mā lahu hurmān*, He has no understanding.

A هرمة *harmat*, One plant of the kind called حمض *hamż*. ابن هرمة *ibnu harmatin*, The son of an old man or woman. *Harimat*, Old and decrepit (woman). A lioness.

P هرمز *hurmuz*, Ormuz, a city and isle in the Persian gulf. Name of a king of Persia who reigned A.D. 272. The planet Jupiter. God. Name of the first day of the month; also of the angel presiding over that day.

A هرمزان *hurmuzān*, The potentate of Persia.

A هرمزة *harmazat*, (v. n. of هرمز Q) Being extinguished (a fire). Chewing (a mouthful) slowly. A discourse which one conceals from a friend. The meanness of a worthless or avaricious man.

P هرمزد *hurmuzd*, Hormuzd, the name of a king. God. Name of the first day of the month. Name of an angel. The planet Jupiter. Thursday.

P هرمزده *hurmizda*, (or هرمزده خدا *hurmizda-khudā*) God.

A هرمزيّ *hurmuziy*, Pertaining to Rām Ormuz.

P هرمس *hurmus*, (and هرمست *hurmust*) Hermes Trismegistus. The first day of the month. Name of an angel. The planet Jupiter.

A هرمسة *harmasat*, Austerity of countenance. Tumult, confused noise, clamour.

A هرمطة *harmatat*, A tarnishing of reputation.

A هرمّع *harammaʿ*, Prone to weep, easily made to cry. Agility, celerity, swiftness.

A هرمل *hirmil*, An old she-camel. An old woman, enervated, but naturally hasty.

A هرملة *harmalat*, (v. n. of هرمل Q) Pulling up or cutting (hair). Being worn with age, and losing her faculties (a woman). Being spoiled and marred (work).

P هرموز *hurmūz*, Name of a city in Karamania: also of an island and city in the Persian Gulf.

A هرمول *hurmūl*, (pl. هراميل *harāmīl*) Some hairs or feathers remaining on the head.

A هرمولة *hurmūlat*, A rent in the lower part of an old shift or garment.

P هرمهي *har mahī*, Of every night, nightly.

A هرمىٰ *harma'*, Decrepit (woman). Dry wood. (pl. of هرم *harim* or هرمة) Decrepit (men or women).

A هرميس *harmīs*, Hermes Trismegistus. *Hirmīs*, A fierce lion. A rhinoceros. A buffalo.

A هرنبز *harambaz*, (هرنبزان *harambazān*, or هرنبزانيّ *harambazāniy*) Sharp. A jumper, springer, caperer.

P هرند *hirand*, Name of a river in Georgia.

A هرنصانة *hirinsānat*, A kind of ship-worm.

A هرنصة *harnasat*, The crawl of an هرنصانة.

A هرنع *hurnuʿ*, A small louse.

A هرنعة *hirniʿat*, A large louse.

A هرنفة *harnafat*, A laughing feebly.

A هرنكس *harankas*, A dangerous thing, a fatal distemper from air or pasture (attacking cattle).

A هرنوة *harnuwat*, (هرنويّ *harnuwiy* or هرنوي *harnawa'*) An herb growing in the clefts of sand-hills. The fruit of the wood-aloe tree. Grain smaller than pepper, very yellow, and of a fragrance like aloe-wood.

P هرنوت *harnūt*, Fraud, deceit. Evil-speaking.

A هرنوع *hurnūʿ*, A small, also large louse.

P هرنيد ساو *harnīd-sāv*, Name of a political treatise ascribed to the prophet مه آباد *mah-ābad*.

P هرنيز *hirnīz*, (in zand and Pāzand) Establishment, stability. Appointment. Consignment.

P هرنيه *harniya*, A vessel shaped like a cucumber in which they warm water.

P هرو *harv*, Brave, warlike, intrepid.

A هرو *harw*, A striking with a stick.

A هروء *hurūʾ*, (v. n. of هرئ) Being thoroughly dressed (meat).

P هروانگه *harwānagah*, An hospital.

P هروانه *harwāna*, An hospital. Pain, torture, the rack. Name of a mountain.

A هروت *harūt*, (or الهروت *al harūt*) The lion.

P هروتوم *harotom*, Seed of fleawort.

A هرور *hurūr*, Grapes fallen from the bunch.

A هروزة *harwazat*, A dying, a perishing.

A هروط *hurūt*, (pl. of هرط *hirt*) Old she-camels.

P هروقتي *har wakhtī*, Common, of every-day use.

P هروك *harwak*, Name of Khusraw Parvez.

P هروكيدن *hurūkīdan*, To fear.

P هرول *hirwul*, A grain like a French bean.

A هرولة *harwalat*, (v. n. of هرول Q) Trotting, going moderately, especially after galloping. Making haste (to pay one's respects).

P هروم *harūm*, Name of a wrestler, and city.

A هروم *harūm*, Malignant, bad (woman).

P هروهل *harwahal*, Sediment, caput mortuum.

P هروي *hiravī*, A native of هرات *hirāt*. Hiravī was one of the dialects of Persia, but is now obsolete.

A هرويّ *harawiy*, A native of هراة *harāt*.

P هرّه *hurra*, The backside. Name of an intoxicating plant growing amongst corn.

A هرهار *harhār*, Much water. A foolish laugher, a laugher at any thing trifling. Lean flesh. Much milk. A lion.

A هرهر *harhar*, The noise of running water. *Hirhir*, A she-camel past having young. An old sheep.

A هرهرة *harharat*, (v. n. of هرهر Q) Calling (sheep) to water. Moving, shaking, agitating (any thing). Transgressing, being unjust, oppressing. A vain, foolish horse-laugh. The bleating of sheep. The roaring of lions. The confused noise which the natives of India used to make in battle.

P هرهفت *har haft*, Seven things used by women in adorning their persons: privet, woad, rouge, ceruse, antimony, gold-leaf, and civet; or (according to some) a patch on the face. Ornament, dress. Adorned, dressed. The narcissus.

A هرهور *hurhūr*, Water running copiously and with great noise. An old sheep. Grapes falling from the bunches. A kind of ship. Much water or milk.

A هرهير *hirhīr*, A kind of fish. A dangerous kind of serpent.

A هري *hary*, (v. n. of هري) Striking with a stick. *Hury*, (pl. اهراء *ahrāʾ*) A royal or public granary.

P هري *harī*, A field watered by the rain. *Hirī*, The city of Harāt, Aria, or Rai.

A هريّ *hiriy* or *huriy*, (pl. of هراوة *hirāwat*) Staves, clubs, walking-sticks.

A هريء *harīʾ*, Overboiled (meat).

P هريار *haryār*, A redundant tooth.

A هرياع *hiryāʿ*, A leaf shaken by the wind.

A هريّة *harīyat*, Coldness, chilliness.

A هريت *harīt*, Broad, wide (especially about the mouth). A blabbing fellow, one who tells every secret; one who speaks shamefully, improperly, or obscenely. Short-cheeked (horse). Burst, abused (woman). A lion.

P هرير *harer*, A doer, maker.

A هرير *harīr*, (v. n. of هرّ) Abhorring, detesting. Whining (as a dog with cold); a dog's whine.

A هريرة *hurayrat*, (dim. of هرّة *hirrat*) A little cat, a kitten. ابو هريرة *abū hurayra*, Name of one of the companions of Muhammad, so called from a favourite kitten which he had. His real name was عبد الرحمن بن صخر *ʿabdu'r rahmān bin sakhr*. Many are the traditions recorded by this personage.

A هريس *harīs*, (fem. هريسة *harīsat*) Bruised.

A هريسة *harīsat*, A kind of thick pottage made of bruised wheat boiled to a consistency; to which they add meat, butter, cinnamon, and aromatic herbs.

A هريصة *harīsat*, A ditch, pool, pond.

A هريعة *harīʿat*, A certain small tree with slender branches.

P هريك *har yak*, Every one, each.

P هرين *hurīn*, Awful sound; wild beasts' roar.

P هرّين *harrīn*, A voice, noise, sound.

P هريو *hirīv*, The city of هرات *hirāt*.

P هريوة *hireva*, Gold coin. Gold mixed with alloy. An immodest woman. Belonging to the city of Hirāt.

A هريئ *hariʼ*, (Cold) fatal to man or beast.

P هز *hiz*, Limber. Loose, flabby. *Huz*, Tribute. Daily expense; provisions daily dealt out to servants.

A هزّ *hazz*, (v. n. of هزّ) (Wind) shaking (a tree).

A هزء *hazʼ*, (v. n. of هزأ) Breaking. Killing with cold. Shaking, setting in motion. Dying. *Huzʼ*, (v. n. of هزأ) Laughing at, mocking, jeering. Ridicule, irony, satire. *Hazaʼ*, (v.n. of هزئ) Dying.

A هزابر *hazābir*, (pl. of هزبر *hizabr*) Lions. *Huzābir*, A lion.

A هزأة *huzʼat*, Ridiculous (fellow), any one laughed at, laughing-stock, butt. *Huzaʼat*, A wag, ridiculer.

P هزار *hazār*, A thousand. A bird called the thousand voices, having an uncommon variety of melodious notes; a species of nightingale. A term employed in the game of نرد *nard*. هزاران هزار *hazārān hazār*, Thousands and thousands. سنابل هزار دانه *sanābili hazār dāna*, Ears containing a thousand grains.

P هزار اسب *hazār asb*, A fort in Khurāsān.

P هزار اسپند *hazār ispand*, Wild rue.

P هزار آستين *hazār āstīn*, (Thousand-sleeved, *i.e.* bay or creek) The sea.

P هزار افشان *hāzār afshān*, Bryony.

P هزاران *hazārān*, Thousands. A thousand. A nightingale. A word used in the game of نرد *nard*.

P هزار آوا *hazār-āwā*, (or آواز *āwāz*) (The bird) of a thousand notes; nightingale.

P هزاربز *hazār buz*, Name of a fort in Khurāsān.

P هزارپا *hazār-pā*, Scolopendra, millipede, palmer-worm of a dangerous kind.

P هزارپسر *hazār-pisar*, Name of a medical grass.

P هزار تابه *hazār-tāba*, (Thousand-ray) Sun.

P هزار تو *hazār to* (or توي *toy*) The second stomach of beasts (as being in many divisions).

P هزارچشان *hazār-chashān*, White vine. Bryony.

P هزارچشمه *hazār-chashma*, A cancer (disease).

P هزار خانه *hazār khāna*, The second stomach of beasts, the tripe.

P هزارداستان *hazār-dāstān*, (or هزاردستان *hazār dastān*) (Teller of) a thousand tales, *i.e.* the nightingale (to which they sometimes prefix بلبل *bulbul*).

P هزاردانه *hazār dāna*, The thousand-grain (ear), the hundred-leaf (flower). Beads for saying prayers, on counting of which they repeat the praises, names, or attributes of God; as الحمد لله *al hamdu li'llāh*, Praise be to God! الله اكبر *allāh akbar*, God is great.

P هزار رخشان *hazār-rakhshān*, Bryony.

P هزارستون *hazār-sutūn*, (Thousand columns) Name of a celebrated palace in Persepolis.

P هزارسفند *hazārisfand*, Wild rue. A kind of medicine.

A هزارف *huzārif*, A swift ostrich.

P هزار گائيده *hazār-gāʼida*, A common whore.

P هزارميخ *hazār-mekh*, A dervish's habit closely stitched. The starry firmament.

P هزار ميخي *hazār mekhī*, A common strumpet.

P هزارة *hazāra*, A tribe of Affghāns. A double flower. A divided stream or jet d'eau (like that of a watering-pan).

P هزارها *hazārhā*, Thousands.

P هزاري *hazārī*, What relates to a thousand. The command of a thousand. يك هزاري *yak hazārī*, A man who receives a thousand rupees per month salary. A commander of gunmen.

P هزارينه *hazārīna*, Impure, unrefined gold. Pure gold.

A هزاز *hazzāz*, The bird called a wagtail.

A هزاع *hizāʻ*, One remaining (arrow in a quiver).

A هزّاع *hazzāʻ*, A lion tearing his prey.

P هزاك *huzāk* or *hazāk*, An idiot. Unlearned, ignorant, foolish, stupid, mean, contemptible. Any one easily deceived by another's words. Proud, self-conceited. Ugly. An extensive garden supposed to have formerly belonged to Kay Kāwus, the second Persian king of the Peshdādian dynasty.

A هزال *hazāl* or *huzāl*, (v. n. of هزل) Being extenuated through age. *Huzāl*, Lean. Leanness.

A هزّال *hazzāl*, A droll.

A هزالة *huzālat*, A jest, joke, play. Pleasantry, sprightliness, cheerfulness.

A هزامج *huzāmij*, A continued sound.

A هزامل *hazāmil*, Confused, inarticulate sounds.

P هزاهز *hazāhiz*, A quaking from fear. Seditious.

A هزاهز *hazāhiz*, Seditions, tumults, intestine wars. *Huzāhiz*, Copious and flowing (water). Swift, active.

A هزائم *hazāʼim*, (pl. of هزيمة *hazīmat*) Wells overflowing. Lean beasts. Flights, routs, dispersions.

A هزبر *hizbar* also *hizabr*, (pl. هزابر *hazābir*) A lion. Thick, strong, hard. P هزبران وغا *hizbarāni waghā*, The lions of the field, heroes.

P هزبرانه *hizabrāna*, Lion-like. Resembling brave warriors.

A هزبرة *hazbarat*, (v. n. of هزبر Q) Cutting.

A هزبري *hizabrī*, Fierceness.

A هزبلة *hazbalat*, A being depressed by poverty.

A هزبليلة *hazbahlat*, Any thing, somewhat.

P هزبه *huzba*, Flower of the meadow-saffron.

A هزّة *hizzat*, Alacrity, cheerfulness, exultation. Cheerfulness, alacrity in bestowing a gift. The murmuring of a boiling pot. Reverberation, peal of thunder. A pace peculiar to a camel.

A هزج *hazaj*, (v. n. of هزج) Shaking, trilling (a singer). Modulation, shaking, trilling. Any consecutive thread of discourse. الهزج *al hazaj*, A species of verse.

P هزد *hazad*, The beaver.

P هزد گند *hazad-gund*, Testicles of the beaver.

A هزر *hazr*, (v. n. of هزر) Striking with a stick, particularly in a violent manner on the back and sides. Banishing, driving away. Throwing prostrate. Giving largely. Laughing. Making haste about any necessary business. Selling dear. Falling suddenly or rushing into. Purchasing without thought or care. *Hizr*, Deceived, defrauded, cozened. Foolish, simple. Strong, vehement.

A هزرات *hazarāt*, (pl. of هزرة *hazrat*) Blows.

A هزراف *hizrāf*, A swift ostrich.

A هزربة *hazrabat*, Agility, levity. Celerity.

A هزرة *hazrat* or *hazarat*, Thin earth. One blow, one beating. ذو هزرات *zū hazarātin*, (or فيه هزرات *fīhi hazarāt*) Cozened, cheated, gulled.

A هزرفة *hazrafat*, (v. n. of هزرف Q) Going fast, being quick. *Hizrifat*, An old woman or she-camel.

A هزرقة *hazrakat*, A ridiculous horse-laugh.

A هزروج *hazrūj*, Root of the طرثوث *tursūs*.

A هزروف *hizrawf* or *huzrūf*, A swift ostrich.

A هزروفة *hizrawfat*, An old woman or she-camel.

A هزروقي *huzrūka'*, A prison.

A هزع *huzaʻ*, A prey-tearing lion.

A هزف *hazf*, (v. n. of هزف) Easily blowing away (wind).

A هزفّ *hizaff*, Swift, flying away. Long-feathered. Slow, heavy, stupid.

A هزق *hazak*, Alacrity, cheerfulness. *Hazik*, Loud and repeated peals of thunder.

A هزقة *hazikat*, A woman full of spirits, who laughs much, and cannot rest in a place.

A هزل *hazl*, (v. n. of هزل) Making lean, emaciating. Having lean cattle. Losing one's cattle. Becoming poor. Joking, jesting. A jest, playfulness. P كلام هزل آميز *kalāmi hazl-āmez*, A facetious discourse, mixed with wit and humour. A *Hazl* or *huzl*, (v. n. of هزل) Being lean, and emaciated with age. A *Hazil*, Jocose, sportful.

A هزلاج *hizlāj*, A swift wolf.

A هزلاع *hizlāʻ*, A mongrel whelp of a he-wolf and she-hyena lank about the thighs. A proper name.

A هزلّج *hazallaj*, Swift (ostrich).

A هزلجة *hazlajat* Confusion in speaking.

A هزلّع *hazallaʻ*, Swift, quick.

A هزلعة *hazlaʻat*, (v.n. of هزلع Q), Passing, withdrawing one's self. Coming out from concealment.

P هزل گو *hazil-gū* or *go*, An idle talker.

A هزلي *hazla'*, (pl. of هزيل) Thin. Serpents.

A هزليات *hazlīyāt*, Jest, pleasantries.

A هزم *hazm*, (v. n. of هزم), Putting to flight, routing, dispersing. Depressing, crushing. Pressing (an apple) and leaving a mark. Twanging (a bow-string). Defrauding. Digging a well. Inclining, being favourably inclined. Fragments of dry thorns. Low ground. Thin clouds, not watery. (pl. of هزمة *hazmat*) Hollows made by pressure. *Hazam*, The sound or twang (of a bow-string). *Ha-*

zim, Thick, incessant (rain). (A pot) boiling furiously. A tractable horse.

P هزم *hizam*, Wood.

P هزمان *hazmān*, (for هرزمان) Every time.

A هزمة *hazmat*, The pit in the stomach. (pl. هزم *hazm*, and هزوم *huzūm*) Any cavity made by pressure (as in an apple).

A هزمجة *hazmajat*, A confusion of voices. A speech delivered without proper pauses.

A هزمرة *hazmarat*, (v. n. of هزمر Q), Agitating violently, moving with rapidity. Incommoding, molesting. Forcing one to act against his will.

A هزمل *hazmal*, Confused, inarticulate noise.

A هزنبر *hazambar*, (or هزنبران *hazambarān*) Cunning. Sharp-headed. Malignant, of a bad disposition.

A هزنبز *hazambaz*, (or هزنبزان *hazambazān*) A jumper. Sharp. Bad-tempered.

A هزنبزانيّ *hazambazāniy*, Sharp-witted, clever.

A هزنوغ *huznūgh*, (or هرنوغ *hurnūgh*) A kind of esculent root resembling the plant طرثوث *tursūs*.

A هزو *hazw*, (v. n. of هزا for هزو) Travelling.

P هزو *hazū*, A courageous, valiant man.

A هزؤ *huzu‚*, (or هزوء *huzū‚*) (v. n. of هزأ) Laughing at, mocking, jeering. Derision, mockery, ridicule. Irony.

P هزوان *hazwān*, The tongue; speech.

A هزوّر *hazawwar*, Weak.

A هزوع *huzūʻ*, (v. n. of هزع) Making haste.

A هزوم *hazūm*, Twanging (bow-string). *Huzūm*, The latter part (of the night). (pl. of هزم *hazm*) Fragments of dry thorns. (pl. of هزمة *hazmat*) Hollows made by pressure, dents.

A هزهاز *hazhāz*, Copious and flowing (water). Bright, glittering, waving (sword). Name of a dog.

A هزهز *huzhuz*, Deep (well). *Huzhuz* or *huzahiz*, Copious and flowing (water). *Huzahiz*, Swift, active, brisk.

A هزهزة *hazhazat*, (v. n. of هزهز Q) Moving. Subduing, mastering, bringing into subjection. Sedition, tumult, intestine war.

A هزيج *hazīj*, Part of the night.

A هزيد *ha zayd*, (for ازيد *a zayd*) Is Zayd?

A هزير *hazīr*, Expelled, driven back.

A هزيرة *huzayrat*, (dim. of هزرة *hazrat*) Very lazy.

A هزيز *hazīz*, (v. n. of هزّ) Making (camels) brisk and travel fast (by singing to them). Falling (a star). Sound. The whisper or murmur of the winds, especially through trees. The roll of thunder.

A هزيع *hazīʻ*, A third, fourth, or smaller portion of the night. Foolish, ignorant, silly.

A هزيل *hazīl*, Thin and lean.

A هزيم *hazīm*, Loud-neighing (horse). Sound of thunder. Incessant, heavy (rain).

A هزيمة *hazīmat*, (v. n. of هزم) Routing, putting to flight. (pl. هزائم *hazā‚im*) Rout, defeat, dispersion. A well overflowing with water. Lean cattle.

P هزيمت خوردن *hazīmat khwurdan*, (also يافتن *yāftan*) To experience a defeat, to be routed.

P هزيمت يافته *hazīmat-yāfta*, Put to flight.

A هزيمي *hazīmatī*, Routed. A fugitive.

A هزّيمى *hizzīma'*, Flight, rout, defeat.

P هزينه *hazīna*, Expenditure, disbursement, household expenses. Daily, continual. A treasury.

P هژده *hajdah*, (for هشتده *hashtdah*) Eighteen.

P هژهار *hajhār*, A superfluous tooth which prevents a horse from thriving on his food.

P هژيدن *hajīdan*, To dry, wither.

P هژير *hajīr*, (*hujīr*, or هژيره *hajīra*) Dignity, whatever commands respect. Beautiful, good, agreeable, acceptable, praiseworthy. Swiftness of foot. Acuteness of genius.

A هس *hus*, Used in crying to sheep.

A هسّ *hass*, (v. n. of هسّ) Pounding small. Breaking. Talking to one's self. Suggesting, hinting (as one's own thoughts).

A هساد *hisād*, (pl. of هسد *hasad*) Lions.

A هساهس *hasāhis*, Mutterings, whisperings. Nocturnal walkings. Voices or whispers of demons.

A هسب *hasb*, Enough, sufficiency.

P هسبت *hasbat*, A foreigner; unknown.

P هست *hast*, Is, exists, remains. Existence, being. هست شدن *hast shudan*, To be, become, happen. هست كردن *hast kardan*, To give being, to create, produce.

P هست استا *hast astā*, A magician, conjuror.

P هستان *hastān*, Is, exists. Existence.

P هستبر *hastabr*, The star called the Dragon.

P هست بود *hast būd*, (What is, was) A rent-roll.

P هستره *hastara*, A kind of vehicle formed of wood and reeds for carrying bricks, earth, &c.

P هست كن *hast-kun*, The Creator.

P هستن *hastan*, To be, exist, subsist.

P هستو *hastū*, The stone of fruit. Truth, justice, rectitude. One who gives his consent to, confesses or acknowledges, a thing.

P هست و بود *hast u būd*, (Is and was) The present actual state of the revenue compared with former years (an Indian phrase). Rent-roll.

P هستودان *hastūdān*, A king of Azarbayjān.

P هسته *hasta*, Fruit-stone or kernel. Existent.

P هستي *hastī*, Being, existence, entity, world, created beings. Wealth, riches. Self-conceit, self-love. هستيء صرف *hastī‚i sirf*, Pure, independent, absolute existence.

P هستيدن *hastīdan*, To be, to exist. To agree, suit, be worth, turn to account.

A هسد *hasad*, A lion. Strong, strenuous.

P هسر *hasar*, Ice.

A هسرة *husrat*, Friends, relations, uncles.

A هسع *hasʻ*, (v. n. of هسع) Making haste.

P هسك *hasak* or *hask*, An instrument for separating corn from the chaff, a fan, ventilator.

A هسم *hasm*, (v. n. of هسم) Breaking (especially a thing dry and hollow). *Husum*, Caustics.

A هسهاس *has-hās*, A butcher. (A shepherd) grazing sheep all night. Any one who wakes all night in doing any thing. Expeditious (journey, especially in the night, through the deserts, to water).

A هسهسة *has-hasat*, (v. n. of هسهس Q) Muttering, whispering. Rustling. A whispering tone. The rattling (of a necklace, of other jewels, or armour), the noise of (a man) moving in the night, especially when lying amongst leaves. The surface of water, which, being ruffled by a gentle breeze, flows like a chain.

P هسير *hasīr*, Ice.

A هسيرة *husayrat*, (dim. of هسرة *husrat*) Relations, uncles (paternal and maternal).

A هسيس *hasīs*, Broken in large pieces. Crumbled bread. A whisper, any thing uttered in a low tone.

P هش *hash*, Motion, departure. Mud, clay. *Hish*, The team of the plough to which oxen are fastened. *Hush*, Understanding, mind. Care, attention, study. Death. هش داشتن *hush dāshtan*, To be intelligent, learned, prudent. طبيب عيسوي هش *tabībi ʻīsawī-hush*, A physician skilful as Jesus.

A هشّ *hashsh*, (v. n. of هشّ) Beating (the leaves) off trees with a stick, especially as food for cattle. (A horse) which perspires much. Soft (bread). Light, nimble, cheerful, brisk. Easy polite, humane. انا به هشّ بشّ *ana' bihi hashshun bashshun*, I am extremely glad of it; I wish it with all my heart. اطعمه هشا مشا *atʻamahu hashshan mashshan*, He fed him well. هشّ المكسر *hashshu'l maksir*, Easy, affable in receiving petitions or in doing business.

A هشاش *hashāsh*, Joy, exultation, cheerfulness. Lightness. Soft (bread).

A هشّاش *hashshāsh*, Cheerful. Easy, polite, humane. (A leathern bottle) leaky from thinness.

A هشاشة *hashāshat*, (v. n. of هشّ) Being light, nimble, cheerful, brisk. Being easy, polite, humane. Gladness, joy, cheerfulness, lightness. Softness.

A هشام *hishām*, Beneficence, liberality.

P هشپلك *hushpulak*, A sound made with the ends of two fingers applied to the mouth by those who fly pigeons.

P هشت *hasht*, Eight. هشت بهشت *hasht bihisht*, The eight paradises. *Hisht*, A hiss, whistle, or noise made with the lips.

P هشتاد *hashtād*, Eighty. پير هشتاد ساله *pīri hashtād sāla*, An old man of eighty; octogenarian.

P هشتادم *hashtādum*, The eightieth.

P هشت باغ *hasht bāgh*, (هشت بستان *hasht bustān*, هشت مرعي *hasht marʻa'*, هشت ماوي *hasht marʻa'*, and هشت هيكل رضوان *hasht haykali rizwān*, The eight heavens.

P هشتده *hashtdah*, Eighteen.

P هشتدهان *hashtdahān*, Aloe-wood. Mallows.

P هشتدهم *hashtdahum*, The eighteenth.

P هشت ساله *hasht-sāla*, Eight years old.

P هشت سو *hasht-sū*, Eight-sided, octangular.

P هشتصد *hashtsad*, Eight hundred.

P هشتگان *hashtagān*, (or هشتگانه *hashtagāna*) Eight each; in eights.

P هشت گنج *hasht ganj*, The eight treasures of خسرو پرويز *khusraw parvez*, namely: 1. گنج عروس *ganji ʻarūs*; 2. گنج باد آورد *ganji bād-āward*; 3. گنج ديبهٔ خسروي *dībaʼi khusravī*; 4. گنج افراسياب *ganji afrāsyāb*; 5. گنج سوخته *ganji sokhta*; 6. گنج خضرا *gānji khazrā*; 7. گنج شاد آورد *ganji shād-āward*; 8. گنج بار *ganji bār*.

P هشت گوشه *hasht gosha*, An octagon.

P هشتم *hashtum* (or هشتمي *hashtumi*) Eighth.

P هشت منظر *hasht manzar*, The eight heavens. The zodiac, with the orbits of Saturn, Jupiter, Mars, the sun, Venus, Mercury, and the moon.

P هشتن *hishtan*, To dismiss, leave, let fall. To hang, suspend. To roll round, involve.

P هشت و مشت *husht u musht*, Wrestling and boxing.

P هشتويش *hashtiwesh*, Name of the fifth supplemental day added to the Persian year.

P هشته *hishta*, Relinquished, let go. Hanging loose. فروهشته *faro hishta*, Flowing (hair).

P هشتيدن *hashtīdan*, To whistle, hiss, or make any noise with the lips. To preserve, keep.

P هشت يك *hasht-yak*, An eighth.

P هشدار *hush dār*, Attend, be careful.

P هشده *hashdah*, Eighteen.

A هشر *hashr*, (v. n. of هشر) Milking out the whole contents of a camel's udder. Thinness, slenderness, weakness, softness. Lightness.

A هشرة *hashrat*, Sauciness, petulance. Ingratitude. Pomp, pride. *Hashirat*, (A tree) which soon loses its leaves.

P هشستن *hashistan*, To abandon, leave, dismiss.

P هشفيفل *hashfīful*, Wild carrot.

A هشم *hashm*, (v. n. of هشم), Breaking (any thing) not solid, (as the nose, a bone, or an egg). Breaking a bough (wind). Honouring, esteeming highly. *Hashim*, Liberal, munificent. *Hushum*, Soft mountains, easy to be dug. Milkers.

A هشمة *hashmat*, نفس مشاش الجبل الكذّانة *nafsu mushāshi'l jabali'l kazzānat*. *Hashamat*, A mountain-goat.

A هشمشمة *hashamshamat*, A lion.

P هشن *hashan*, Care, study.

P هشنگ *hashang*, A poor helpless wretch.

P هشو *hashū*, Marrow. *Hushū*, Understanding, ready wit, ingenuity. A fortification.

P هشوار *hushwār*, Prudent, intelligent.

A هشور *hashūr*, (A tree) soon losing its leaves.

A هشوش *hashūsh*, (A sheep) very milch.

A هشوشة *hushūshat*, The softening (of bread).

P هشومند *hushūmand*, Prudent, intelligent.

P هشونش *hashūnash*, The fifth day added to the Persian year.

A هشهاش *hashhāsh*, Liberal, kind, excellent.

A هشهشة *hashhashat*, Putting in motion, shaking.

P هشيار *hushyār*, Intelligent, prudent. Cautious. Abstemious, sober. هشيار ساز *hushyār-sāz*, Rendering wise; restoring one to their senses (after being intoxicated).

P هشياري *hushyārī*, Prudence.

P هشيدن *hishīdan*, To dismiss, let fall, let go, leave. To hang, suspend.

A هشيرة *hushayrat*, (dim. of هشرة *hashrat*) A moderate degree of petulance.

A هشيش *hashīsh*, Gentle, humane, affable. Weak and flaccid. Soft (bread).

A هشيلة *hashyalat*, Aged and fat (she-camel). *Hashīlat*, A horse or camel taken from the owner without his consent, but returned to him when the journey is over: a thing pressed for public service.

P هشيله *hashīla*, Domestic or sea-fowls dressed with pease, beets, and eggs.

A هشيم *hashīm*, Broken, bent. Dry, withered, brittle. Dry forage, chips, stubble. Weak, flaccid, frail.

A هشيمة *hashīmat*, (A place) full of dry trees.

هشيمة الكرم *hashīmatu'l karam*, Liberal, munificent.

P هشيوار *ha* or *hushīwār*, Intelligent, prudent.

A هصّ *hass*, (v. n. of هصّ) Breaking, bruising (particularly any thing hollow). Treading upon.

A هصّار *hassār*, A prey-crushing lion.

A هصّام *hassām*, A lion.

A هصاهص *husāhis*, A strong and black man.

A هصر *hasr* (v. n. of هصر) Driving, beating off. Drawing, attracting, bringing near. Bending (a branch). Breaking (without cracking or bending). A fracture. *Hasir* or *husar*, A lion tearing his prey.

A هصرة *has* or *hasarat*, A kind of philtre or fascination. *Husarat*, (or الهصرة *al husarat*) A lion.

A هصم *hasm*, A breaking. *Husam*, A lion.

A هصمصم *hasamsam*, A lion.

A هصو *hasw*, A growing old.

A هصور *hasūr* or *haswar*, A prey-breaking lion.

A هصورة *haswarat*, A lion.

A هصهاص *has-hās*, Of sparkling eyes.

A هصهص *hus-hus*, A strong black man.

A هصهصة *has-hasat*, (v. n. of هصهص Q) Squeezing, pressing with the hand. Defaming, accusing.

A هصيص *hasīs*, Beaten, broken, bruised, trodden down. The tremulous light (of fire).

A هضّ *hazz*, (v. n. of هضّ) Breaking. Pounding. Walking well. Instigating, exciting. Travelling fast (camels). A fracture, amputation, bruise.

A هضّاء *hazzāʼ*, A crowd. A troop of horse.

A هضاب *hizāb*, (pl. of هضبة *hazbat*) Showers which consist of large drops. Long, steep, and inaccessible mountains, separate from others.

A هضاة *hizāt*, The forelocks. A she-ass.

A هضّاض *hazzāz*, (A stallion) breaking necks.

A هضاضة *hazāzat*, Any thing broken.

A هضّام *hazzām*, Digestive. Medicine or aught similar promoting digestion. Liberal. A lion.

A هضائم *hazāʼim*, (pl. of هضيمة *hazīmat*) Meats dressed for a funeral entertainment.

A هضب *hazb*, (v. n. of هضب) Raining incessantly. Speaking much; being loquacious and noisy. Walking at a slow, sluggish pace. *Hizab*, (pl. of هضبة *hazbat*) Rains falling in large drops. Mountains, ranges of hills.

A هضبّ *hizabb*, (A horse) perspiring greatly. Strong, robust.

A هضبة *hazbat*, (pl. هضب *hizab*, هضاب *hizāb*, هضبات *hazabāt*, and اهاضيب *ahāzīb*) Rain consisting of large drops. A mountain spread over a large surface of ground. A high, steep, inaccessible mountain, separated from all others. A mountain consisting of a single rock.

A هضل *hazl*, (v. n. of هضل) Pouring forth oratory or verse. Much.

A هضلاء *hazlāʼ*, Possessed of long teats.

A هضم *hazm*, (v. n. of هضم) Breaking. Digesting (food), concocting. Attacking, invading, entering suddenly upon. Injuring, oppressing, defrauding, seizing the property of another. Bearing patiently. Digestion. Any aromatic substance. Oppression, injury, loss. هضم اوّل *hazmi awwal*, The first concoction. P هضم كردن *hazm kardan*, To digest. To embezzle. A قابل هضم *hābili hazm*, Digestible. Tolerable. *Hazm* or *hizm*, (pl. اهضام *ahzām* and هضوم *huzūm*) A plain, extensive and lying low; the bottom of a valley, channel, or sea. *Hazam*, (v. n. of هضم) Being slender (the waist), being shrunk or collapsed (the belly). Being straight, and without curve (the ribs of a horse). Slenderness round the waist; a shrinking in the belly (of man or beast). (pl. اهضام *ahzām*) A kind of aromatic substance. *Huzum*, (pl. of هضوم *hazūm*) Liberal (hands).

A هضماء *hazmāʼ*, Gaunt-bellied (mare).

A هضوبة *huzūbat*, One shower by which a field is wet enough.

A هضوم *hazūm*, (Medicine) which helps digestion, peptic. Liberal, beneficent. (pl. هضم *huzum*) Liberal (hand). A lion. *Huzūm*, (pl. of هضم *hazm*) Plains. Bottoms of valleys or of seas.

A هضهاض *hazhāz*, (A stallion) breaking the necks of others.

A هضهضة *hazhazat*, (v. n. of هضهض Q) Breaking in pieces, pounding.

A هضيب *hazīb*, (A ewe) giving little milk.

A هضيج *hazīj*, Little (boys).

A هضيض *hazīz*, Broken, bruised (thing).

A هضيم *hazīm*, Injured, oppressed. Slender-waisted (woman). Shrunk, lank (belly). Forced. A pipe or flute (especially of reed). Contracted, turned in (cow's hoof). (Palm-flowers) wrapt close, not appearing from the buds.

A هضيمة *hazīmat*, Injury, oppression; iniquity. Wrath. (pl. هضائم *hazāʼim*) Meat dressed for a funeral entertainment.

A هضيمي hazīmiy, Fit for a funeral-feast.

A هطاء hattās, (fem. of اهط ahatt) (A she-camel) patient of labour and travelling well.

A هطال hattāl, Constantly dropping (cloud).

A هطاهط hutāhit, A horse.

A هطر hatr, (v. n. of هطر) Striking. Killing (a dog) with a stick.

A هطرة hatrat, The humble manner in which a poor man begs.

A هطط hutut, Ruined or perishing men.

A هطع hatꜥ, (v. n. of هطع) Running in terror. Looking at (any thing) with fixed eyes.

A هطف hatf, (v. n. of هطف) Milking. Raining. The noise made in walking. *Hatif*, Thick rain.

A هطق hatak, A quick pace.

A هطل hatl, (v. n. of هطل) Raining incessantly. Raining at intervals, pouring out showers with large drops. Making a horse sweat profusely (a race). Travelling languidly (a camel). Flowing with tears (the eye). Incessant and small rain. An uninterrupted flow of tears. *Hitl*, A wolf. A robber, thief. A fool. Fatigued (camel). *Hutl*, (Rain) which continues night and day. *Hatil*, (pl. هطل huttal) Constantly dropping (cloud or rain).

A هطل huttal, (pl. of هاطل) Incessant rains.

A هطلاء hatlās, (Rain) continuing night and day.

A هطلان hatalān, (v. n. of هطل) Raining at intervals, shower following shower.

A هطلس hatlas (or هطلس hatallas) A thief. A highway-robber. A wolf.

A هطلع hatallaꜥ, Great (cloud). Numerous (army). Tall and corpulent (man).

A هطلى hatla', Slow-going (she-camel). *Hatla'* or *hatala'*, Camels going in droves without a driver.

A هطو hatw, A throwing, casting away.

A هطوع hutūꜥ, (v. n. of هطع) Running in terror. Looking at (a thing) with fixed eyes.

A هطهطة hat-hatat, The neighing of a horse. Expedition in travelling or in working.

A هطى huta', A wrestling, throwing down. A violent blow.

A هطيع hatīꜥ, A broad highway.

A هعة haꜥꜥat, (v. n. of هع) Vomiting, puking.

A هع هع huꜥ huꜥ, The noise made in vomiting.

P هف haf, A weaver's shop, sley, or reed.

A هف haff, (v. n. of هف) Whistling (as the wind). *Hiff*, A cloud without water. A comb without honey, or containing little. A light or empty thing. An empty, light, shallow, insignificant fellow, a sorry scrub. Corn not reaped in time, the grains of which are shaken out. *Haff* or *hiff*, A species of small fish. A large kind of tadpole.

A هفا hafa', A slight rain soon over.

A هفاة hafāt, Manner, custom. A gentle shower soon over.

A هفات hafāt, Foolish, insane. *Hufāt*, (v. n. of هفت) Flying or fluttering about as any thing light. Being depressed, lowered, set down. Being thinned, made small. Speaking rashly or impertinently without foundation or proof.

A هفاف haffāf, Light, active, nimble. Sprightly and prancing (ass). Light, fit for flight (bird or feather). Cool, peaceful, but not perpetual (shade). Thin, transparent (linen or vest). Shining, splendid.

A هفافة haffāfat, Gentle, light (wind). Bright, glancing (eye).

A هفان haffān or hiffān, A woman's name.

A (جاء على) هفانه (jāꜥa ꜥala') hiffānihi, He came after him, following his steps.

A هفة hiffat, One small fish. A big tadpole.

P هفت haft, Seven. *Hift*, The first degree of dryness after being wet. *Huft*, Foolish, void of understanding. Plain, level ground. A single gulp or draught of any liquor.

A هفت haft, (v. n. of هفت) Flying or fluttering about (as any thing light). Being depressed, lowered, set down. Being thinned, made small. Speaking rashly or impertinently without foundation or proof. An extensive valley. Rain spreading all around. Extreme insanity, egregious folly.

P هفت آبا haft ābā, The seven heavens.

P هفت اختان haft ukhtān, The seven planets.

P هفتاد haftād, Seventy.

P هفتاد كشتي haftād kushtī, The seventy kinds of diseases incident to living creatures.

P هفتادم haftādum, The seventieth.

P هفتاد و دو شاخ haftād u du shākh, A phrase denoting the seventy-two nations and different forms of religion upon earth; also seventy-two modes of chanting the Kur'ān.

P هفتاد و دو كشتي haftād u du kushtī, Seventy-two kinds of religion on earth.

P هفت اژدها haft ajdahā, The seven planets.

P هفت آسيا haft āsyā, The orbits in which the seven planets revolve.

P هفت اصل haft asl, (Seven roots) The seven earths. The seven climates.

P هفت اقليم haft iklīm, The seven climates.

P هفت الوان haft alwān, Different kinds of meats. Food sent from heaven for Jesus Christ; bread, salt, fish, vinegar, honey, butter, and cresses.

P هفت اندام haft andām, The seven members of the body, namely, the head, breast, belly, hands, and feet; or, the head, hands, sides and feet. The aorta or the great artery, called in Arabic نهر البدن nahru'l badan, The river of the body.

P هفت اورنگ haft awrang, The constellation of the Great Bear. The seven heavens.

P هفت آينه haft āyina, (or هفت آيينه haft āyīna) The seven planets.

P هفت ايوان haft aywān, The seven heavens.

P هفت باز haft bāz, A companion, partner.

P هفت بام haft bām, The seven heavens.

P هفت بانو haft bānū, The seven planets.

P هفت برادران haft birādarān, The seven brothers, *i.e.* seven stars in the Great Bear.

P هفت برگ haft barg, Heptaphyllous. Mezereon.

P هفت بنا haft binā, (or بنيان bunyān) The seven heavens (literally, seven structures).

P هفت پدر haft pidar, (Seven fathers) The seven planets. The seven heavens.

P هفت پر ثريا haft pari surayyā, The smallest star in the Pleiades.

P هفت پرده haft parda, The seven heavens. The seven notes of the gamut. *Haft parda*, (هفت حجلهٔ نور haft hajlaꜥi nūr, or هفت راه haft rāh) The seven tunics of the eye, namely, صلبيه salbīya, (sclerotic), مشيميه mashīmīya (choroid), شبكيه shabakīya (retiform), عنكبوتيه ꜥankabūtīya (arachnoid), عنبيه ꜥinabīya (uveous), قرنيه karnīya (corneous), and ملتحمه multahima (conjunctiva).

P هفت پرگار haft pargār, The seven heavens.

P هفت پوست haft post, The seven heavens.

P هفت پير haft pīr, The seven masters in reading the Kur'ān, نافع nāfiꜥ of Madina, ابن كثير ibn kasir of Mecca, ابو عامر abū ꜥāmir of Basra, ابن عامر ibn ꜥāmir of Damascus, عاصم ꜥāsim, حمزة hamza (or همزة hamza), and كسائي kisāꜥī of Kūfa.

P هفت پيكر haft paykar, The seven heavens. The seven planets.

P هفت تنان haft tanān, The seven sleepers. Certain pious individuals for whose sake the world is kept in existence.

P هفت جوش haft josh, A metal compounded of iron, antimony, lead, gold, tin, copper, and silver.

P هفت چتر آبگون haft chatri āb-gūn, The seven heavens.

P هفت چشم چرخ haft chashmi charkh, (or هفت چشم خراس haft chashm kharās) The planets.

P هفت حال haft hāl, Always, continually.

P هفت حرف آبي haft harfi ābī, The seven watery letters: ج jīm, ز zā, ك kāf, س sīn, ق kāf, ث sā, and ظ zā.

P هفت حرف آتشي haft harfi ātishī, The seven fiery letters: ا alif, ه he, ط to, م mīm, ف fe, ش shīn, and ذ zāl.

P هفت حرف استعلا haft harfi istiꜥlā, The seven high letters: خ khā, ص sād, ض zād, غ ghayn, ط to, ق kāf, and ظ zā.

P هفت حرف خاكي haft harfi khākī, The seven earthy letters: د dāl, ح hā, ل lām, ع ꜥayn, ر rā, خ khā, and غ ghayn.

P هفت حرف هوائي haft harfi hawāꜥī, The seven airy letters: ب be, و wāw, ي yā, ن nūn, ص sād, ت tā, and ض zād.

P هفت خاتون haft khātūn, The seven planets.

P هفت خراس haft kharās, (or هفت خروار كوس haft kharwār kos) The seven heavens.

P هفت خزينه haft khazīna, The seven inner

parts, namely, the stomach, liver, lungs, heart, gall, spleen, and kidneys. The seven heavens.

P هفت خضرا *haft khazirā*, The seven heavens.

P هفت خط *haft khat*, The seven lines (on the cup of جم *jam*, viz. خط جور *khati jawr*, خط بغداد *khati baghdād*, خط بصرة *khati basra*, خط ازرق *khati azrak*, خط اشك *khati ashk*, خط كاسه گر *khati kāsagar*, and فرودينه *farodīna*). The seven climes.

P هفت خليفه *haft khalīfa*, The stomach, liver, lights, heart, gall, milt, and kidneys. Soul, reason, sight, hearing, taste, smell, and touch. Forehead, palms of hands, knees, and points of the great toes.

P هفت خم *haft khum*, The seven heavens.

P هفتخون *haft khūn*, (or هفتخوان *haft khwān*) A sevenfold slaughter. Seven places where the champion Rustam pitched his tent.

P هفت دادران *haft dādarān*, The seven stars in the Bear called بنات النعش *banātu'n naȝsh*.

P هفت دانه *haft dāna*, A kind of dish composed of seven different sorts of fruits and herbs dressed with syrup, which, on the tenth day of the month محرم *muharram*, they distribute in Persia to neighbours and to the poor, in commemoration of the death of حسين *husayn*, son of the caliph علي *ȝaliy*.

P هفت دختر خضرا *haft dukhtari khazirā*, (or هفت در *haft dur*) The seven planets.

P هفت در هفت *haft dar haft*, The seven articles of a lady's toilet, namely, privet, antimony, woad, rouge, ceruse, gold leaf, and civet. The seven planets, or seven climes. Seven by seven, forty-nine.

P هفت دريا *haft daryā*, The seven seas.

P هفت دگان *haft dugān*, The seven climates.

P هفت دور *haft dawr*, Seven revolutions or cycles, said to consist of 1000 years each, and each depending on one of the planets.

P هفتده *haftdah*, Seventeen. Adorned. *Haft dih*, The seven heavens. The seven climes.

P هفتدهم *haftdahum*, The seventeenth.

P هفت راه *haft rāh*, The seven tunics of the eye.

P هفت رخشان *haft rakhshān*, Seven planets.

P هفت رصد *haft rasad*, The seven climates.

P هفت ركعهٔ ادكن *haft ruhȝaȝi adkan*, The seven earths.

P هفت رنگ *haft rang*, The seven colours which are referred to the planets, namely, black to Saturn, brown to Jupiter, red to Mars, yellow to the sun, white to Venus, blue to Mercury, and green to the moon. A species of beautiful Indian rose of many colours. Painting or embroidery. Female-ornaments.

P هفت رنگي *haft rangī*, Capricious. Artful.

P هفت زرده *haft zarda*, A kind of narcissus.

P هفت زمين *haft zamīn*, The seven climates.

P هفت سقف *haft sakf*, The seven heavens.

P هفت سلطان *haft sultān*, The seven princes, namely, the Sultan of Khurasān, Sultan ابراهيم ادهم *ibrāhīm adham*, Sultan بايزيد بسطامي *bāyazīd bastāmī*, Sultan ابو سعيد ابو الخير *abūsaȝīd abū'l khayr*, Sultan محمود غازي *mahmūd ghāzī*, Sultan سنجر ماضي *sanjar māzī*, and Sultan اسمعيل ساماني *ismaȝīl sāmānī*. The seven planets.

P هفت شمع *haft shamaȝ*, The seven planets.

P هفتصد *haft sad*, Seven hundred.

P هفت طارم *haft tāram*, The seven heavens.

P هفت طبق *haft tabak*, (Seven stories or strata) The seven heavens. The seven earths.

P هفت طفل جان شكر *haft tifli jān-shikar*, The seven planets.

P هفت علفخانه *haft ȝalaf-khāna*, (or هفت فرش *haft farsh*) The seven climates.

P هفت فرش *haft farsh*, The seven earths.

P هفت فرشتهٔ ايام هفته *haft farishtaȝi ayyāmi hafta*, The seven archangels, اورياٴيل *ūriyāȝīl*, جسدياٴيل *jasdiyāȝīl*, شماٴيل *shamāȝīl*, رفاٴيل *rafāȝīl*, عناٴيل *ȝanāȝīl*, جبراٴيل *jabrāȝīl*, and عزراٴيل *ȝazrāȝīl*.

A هفت فعل قلوب *haft fiȝli kulūb*, The seven verbs of the heart, namely: زعمت *zaȝamtu*, I supposed; وجدت *wajattu*, I found; رأيت *raȝaytu*, I saw; علمت *ȝalimtu*, I knew; خلت *khiltu*, I fancied; ظننت *zanantu*, I thought; حسبت *hasibtu*, I reckoned.

A هفتق *haftak*, (from P هفته *hafta*) A week.

P هفت قلعهٔ مينا *haft kalȝaȝi mīnā*, The seven heavens.

P هفت قلم *haft kalam*, The seven pens or styles of writing: ثلث *suls*, محقق *muhakkak*, توقيع *tawkīȝ*, ريحان *rayhān*, رقاع *rikāȝ*, نسخ *naskh*, تعليق *taȝlīk*.

P هفتك *haftak*, A fourth of the Kur'ān.

P هفت كار *haft kār*, Cloth of seven colours.

P هفت كحلي *haft kuhlī*, The seven heavens.

P هفت كرة *haft kura*, The seven heavens.

P هفت كشور *haft kishwar*, The seven climes.

P هفت كهنه *haft kuhna*, The seven old ones, viz. friend, associate, book, wine, bath, sword, china.

P هفتگانه *haftgāna*, In sevens.

P هفت گاه *haft gāh*, The seven heavens. The seven climates.

P هفت گره *haft girih*, The seven heavens: seven planets: seven climates.

P هفت گنبد *haft gumbad*, The seven heavens. Seven cupolas built by بهرام گور *bahrām gūr*.

P هفت گنجينه *haft gunjīna*, Gold, silver, tin, lead, iron, copper, and mountain-brass.

P هفت گوشه *haft gosha*, A heptagon.

P هفت گيسودار *haft gīsūdār*, The seven heavens. The seven planets.

P هفتم *haftum*, (or هفتمين *haftumīn*) Seventh.

P هفت مجمرة *haft majmara*, Planetary orbits.

P هفت محراب فلك *haft mihrābi falak*, The seven planets.

P هفت محيط *haft muhīt*, The seven heavens. The sea of China, Western Ocean, Mediterranean, sea of Tiberias, Euxine, Caspian, and of Khwārazm.

P هفت مرد *haft mard*, The seven sleepers. Certain pious persons for whose sake the world is kept.

P هفت مشعله *haft mashȝala*, The planets.

P هفتم كشور *haftum kishwar*, The seventh climate, *i. e.* that of Hindūstān.

P هفت مندل *haft mandal*, The seven heavens.

P هفت منزل *haft manzil*, The seven heavens.

P هفت مهرهٔ زرين *haft muhraȝizarrīn*, (or هفت نژاد فلك *haft najād falak*) The seven planets.

P هفت نطع *haft nataȝ*, The seven earths.

P هفت نقطه *haft nukta*, The seven planets. Decoration.

P هفت نوبتي چرخ *haft nawbatī charkh*, The seven planets.

P هفت نيم خايه *haft nīm khāya*, (or هفت والاي خضرا *haft wālāyi khazirā*, The seven heavens.

P هفت واد *haft-wād*, (Seven sons) Name of a man.

P هفتوانه *haftwāna*, A sort of food.

P هفتوت *haftūt*, (from A هفوة *hafwat*) Error, blunder, crime, offence, fault.

P هفت وجوه صرف *haft wujūhi sarf*, The seven kinds of verbs in Arabic grammar, called صحيح *sahīh*, Sound, as كتب *kataba*, He wrote; مضاعف *muzāȝaf*, Reduplicated, as مد *madda*, He extended; مثال *misāl*, Assimilated, as وجد *wajada*, He found; ناقص *nākis*, Defective, as غزا *ghaza'*, He fought, or as رمى *rama'*, He shot; لفيف *lafīf*, Doubly imperfect, as وقى *waka'*, He preserved, or شوي *shawa'*, He roasted; مهموز *mahmūz*, Hamzated, as أمر *amara*, He commanded; اجوف *ajwaf*, Concave, as قال *kāla* (for قول *kawala*) He said, or باع *bāȝa* (for بيع *bayaȝa*) He sold.

P هفتورنگ *haft warang*, Constellation of the Bear. هفتورنگ مهين *haftwarangi mihīn*, Ursa Major. هفتورنگ كهين *haftwarangi kihīn*, Ursa Minor.

P هفت و شش *haft u shash*, The seven planets. The six sides, viz. below and above, right and left, before and behind.

P هفت و نه *haft u nuh*, Seven and nine (articles of a lady's toilet and dress); namely, حنا *hinnā*, وسمه *wasma*, سرمه *surma*, سرخي *surkhī*, سفيداب *safedāb*, زرك *zarak*, غاليه *ghāliya*; and سرآويزه *sar-āweza*, گوشواره *gosh-wāra*, سلسله *silsila*, حلقهٔ بيني *halkaȝi bīnī*, گلوبند *gulū-band*, بازوبند *bāzū-band*, دست برنجن *dast-baranjan*, انگشتر *angushtar*, and خلخال *khalkhāl*.

P هفت و هشت *haft u hasht*, High words, litigation. The howl of a dog.

P هفته *hafta*, A week, se'nnight, hebdomad.

P هفته دوست *hafta-dost*, A week's acquaintance, a slight acquaintance, inconstant friend.

P هفت هزاري *haft hazārī*, The command of seven thousand.

P هفت هشت *haft hasht*, Abuse, idle talk.

P هفت هفت *haft haft*, In sevens.

P هفت هيكل *haft haykal*, The seven heavens. The seven earths. Amulets, charms.

P هفت يك *haft yak*, One of seven, a seventh.

P هفدانه *hafdāna*, A kind of food.

P هفده *hafdah*, (for هفتده *haftdah*) Seventeen.

P هفده سالگی *hafda sālagī*, Seventeen years (of age).

P هفدهم *hafdahum*, The seventeenth.

A هفو *hafw*, (v. n. of هفا for هفو) Being hungry. Excessive hunger. Light, active (man). Stray (camels). *Hafw*, (هفوان *hafawān* or هفوة *hafwat*) (v. n. of هفا for هفو) Falling, slipping, blundering. Being swift, running with velocity (as a deer). Being hungry. Moving, fluttering (the wings), flying (as a bird). *Hafw*, (or هفوّ *hufūw*) (v. n. of هفا for هفو) Prosecuting any thing (in one's thoughts). Flying through the air (flocks of wool or feathers). Shaking (the wind). Exulting, rejoicing.

A هفوة *hafwat*, Error, blunder, offence, fault.

P هفوش *hafwash*, Rice cooked by steam.

A هفهاف *hafhāf*, Light (feather). Thin, transparent (linen or dress). Gaunt-bellied. Thirsty.

P هفه رفه *hafa rafa*, Ornament, decoration.

P هفهف *hafhaf*, The bark of a dog.

A هفهفة *hafhafat*, (v. n. of هفهف Q) Being long and slender-bodied, like a branch.

A هفيّة *hiffīyat*, The office or duty of one who has charge of a temple.

A هفيتة *hafītat*, A number (of people) running to swell a crowd. Men wasted from scarcity of food.

A هفيف *hafīf*, (v. n. of هفّ) Whistling (as the wind). Being tranquil, placid, quiet. Being light and active. Going away. Shining. The whistling of the wind. A quick step, rapid progress.

A هقّ *hakk*, (v. n. of هقّ) Working, exhausting by excessive venery.

A هقاع *hukāʿ*, Indolence, torpor, distraction of mind caused by grief or distemper.

A هقالس *hakālis*, (pl. of هقلّس *hakallas*) Bad, malicious (as wolves or foxes).

A هقب *hakb*, Amplitude, width, largeness. *Hikab*, Used in calling to horses.

A هقبّ *hikabb*, Large-bodied and tall (ostrich). Wide in the throat.

A هقبقب *hakabkab*, Hard and strong.

A هقرة *hukrat*, A disease among sheep.

A هقز *hakz* or *hikz*, Cloth of red wool with a mixture of silk.

A هقط *hakat*, Swiftness. *Hikit*, Used in calling to horses.

A هقع *hakaʿ*, (v. n. of هقع) Lying down when in heat (a she-camel). *Hakiʿ*, Unable to rise.

A هقعة *hakʿat*, A circle of hairs on a horse's breast, or where the rider's foot touches (which are reckoned blemishes). Any white spot on the left side of a horse. الهقعة *al hakʿat*, Three bright stars near one another in the head of Orion, which mark the fifth mansion of the moon. *Hakiʿat*, (A she-camel) lying down when in want of the male. *Hukaʿat*, One who reclines much and maintains a recumbent posture amongst others.

A هقف *hakaf*, A moderate appetite.

A هقق *hukuk*, Men frequent in venery.

A هقل *hikl*, A young ostrich. A tall, lazy fellow. *Hakil*, Hungry.

A هقلّس *hakallas*, (pl. هقالس *hakālis*) Famished and lean (wolf). Of a bad disposition. A fox.

A هقم *hakam*, (v. n. of هقم) Being very hungry, starving. *Hakim*, Hungry, starving.

A هقمّ *hikamm*, A glutton. The sea.

A هقو *hakw*, (v. n. of هقا for هقو) Being delirious, raving in speech. Speaking shamefully, addressing (any one) in foul language.

A هقوّر *hakawwar*, Long, large-sized. A fool.

A هقوغ *hukūgh*, (v. n. of هقغ) Being languid, emaciated from disease or hunger.

A هقهاق *hak-hāk*, Expeditious in business.

A هقهقة *hak-hakat*, (v. n. of هقهق Q) Travelling fast. A quick and a hard pace in travelling. Bringing a small present to a tribe.

A هقي *haky*, (v. n. of هقى) Corrupting in morals.

P هك *hak*, Full. Hail.

A هكّ *hakk*, (v. n. of هكّ) Striking (with a sword). Breaking wind gently. Voiding dung (a bird). (Wine) conquering or intoxicating. Wearing down by rubbing. Falling in (a well). Lying with a woman much and often. Drawing out (milk). A repeated stabbing with a sword or spear. Great rain. (pl. هككة *hakakat* and اهكاك *ahkāk*) One who labours in mind. Dung of ostrich or bustard. *Hukka*, He was made to fall, he was thrown down.

A هكارس *hakāris*, Frogs.

A هكاع *hukāʿ*, Cough. Sleep after toil. Lust.

A هكاعيّ *hukāʿīy*, Libidinous.

A هكب *hakb* or *hakab*, Derision, ridicule.

P هكچه *hukcha*, Agitation of the throat in hysterics and the like. Hiccough.

A هكذا *hākazā*, In this manner, thus.

A هكر *hakr*, *hikr*, or *hakar*, (v. n. of هكر) Admiring, being filled with wonder. Astonishment, wonder. *Hakr* and *hakar*, A deep sleep. Admiration, amazement. *Hakar*, (v. n. of هكر) Slumbering. *Hakir*, Wondering, astonished. *Hakir* or *hakur*, Sleepy.

P هكري *hukrī*, A field watered only by rain.

A هكع *hakaʿ*, (v. n. of هكع) Being impatient and helpless. Being submissive and modest.

A هكعة *hakiʿat*, A she-camel languishing for the male. *Hukaʿat*, A fool.

A هكف *hakaf*, Speed in running or walking.

P هكك *hikak*, A machine somewhat resembling the camel-litter in which women travel. *Hukak* or *hikak*, Hiccough.

A هككة *hakakat*, (pl. of هكّ) Troubled in mind.

P هكل *hukal*, A white egg-like fungus.

A هكلّس *hakallas*, Strong, vehement.

A هكم *hakim*, A malignant intermeddler.

A هكوع *hukūʿ*, (v. n. of هكع) Being quiet, lying down, taking rest, reposing; reclining (as an ox) in the shade, during the heat of the day. Falling flat on the ground, or lying upon it. Diffusing darkness (night). Coughing (a camel). Being broken again after having been set (a bone).

A هكوك *hakūk*, Impudent. Hasty.

A هكوّك *hakawwak*, Impudent, shameless. Hasty, precipitate. Fat, corpulent. Hard, rough ground. A plain, level country.

P هكوي *hakwī*, Distracted, distressed. *Hakwi*, Grape-wine. Irresolution, hesitation, fluctuation.

P هكه *hika*, A kind of sling.

P هكّه *hukka*, Hiccough.

A هكهاك *hak-hāk*, Much addicted to venery.

P هكهك *huk-huk*, Hiccough, hiccup.

A هكهكة *hak-hakat*, A being libidinous.

A هكيك *hakīk*, Lessened, worn by rubbing. Effeminate, abject, infamous. The dung of a bustard.

P هگاه *hagāh*, Whether?

P هگل *hagal*, A fungus or mushroom.

A هل *hal*, (interrogation) Perhaps? Whether or not? Indeed, aye, yes. It is not, there is not. هل لك فيه *hal laka fīhi*, Whether or not have you (any business) there? هل لك في كذا *hal laka fi kazā*, Have you need of such a thing? هل من اله غير الله *hal min ilāhin ghayra'llāh*, Is there any god beside God? *i.e.* There is no god but God.

P هل *hil*, Leave alone. Cardamoms. *Hul*, The side under the arm. The embrace.

A هل *hala*, (in comp. with حيّ *hayya'*) as حيّ هل *hayya' hala*, Come on then! well! حيّ هلك *hayya' halaka*, Come on thou! حيّ هل الصلوة *hayya' hala's salāt*, Come to prayers.

A هلّ *hall*, (v. n. of هلّ) Falling heavily (rain). Appearing (the new moon). Shouting for joy. Thin (cloth). Delicate (verses). *Hill*, The beginning of a month, the appearance of the new moon. (A woman) wearing the same garment every day.

P هلا *halā*, Observe! take care! beware!

A هلا *halā*, Hola! bravo! well done! take care! let alone! beware! Come along! draw near. Yes, thus, it is so. A word used to frighten horses; or to quiet a mare when taking the horse. Is it not?

A هلّا *hallā*, Come on. Why not?

A هلّاب *hallāb*, Rainy (year). The coldest winter-days in the middle of January. *Hallāb* (or هلّابة *hallābat*) A cold wind accompanied with rain.

A هلابة *hulābat*, The dirty water which comes away with the secundine.

A هلابج *hulābij*, Thick milk.

A هلابع *hulābiʿ*, Corpulent. Cowardly, rascally. Mean, base. Gluttonous, voracious. A wolf.

A هلاتة *hulātat*, The membrane which comes with a new-born lamb.

A هلاث *hulās*, Languor, feebleness.

P هلاج *halāj*, Cotton.

P هلاجين *halājīn*, A swing or see-saw.

A هلاس *hulās*, Consumption, decay.

P هلاشم *halāsham*, An ugly, disagreeable thing.

A هلاع *hulāʿ*, Cowardice.

A هلاك *halāk*, (v. n. of هلك) Perishing. Falling down. Being lost. Being greedy, addicted to excess. Perdition, destruction, ruin. Slaughter, death. Lost, fatigued. P هلاك شدن *halāk shudan*, To be ruined. To die, perish. هلاك كردن *halāk kardan*, To destroy, overwhelm, drive to destruction.

A هلّاك *hullāk*, (pl. of هالك *hālik*) Lost, perishing. Those who pay repeated visits to obtain favours. Foragers who have missed their way.

A هلاكة *halākat*, Perdition, ruin, destruction.

P هلاك شده *halāk-shuda*, Perished, ruined.

A هلاكي *halākī*, Perdition, destruction, ruin.

A هلال *halāl* or *hilāl*, The beginning of a shower. *Hilāl*, (v. n. 3 of هل) Agreeing (with one) by the month, or from month to month, or new moon to new moon. (pl. اهلّة *ahillat* and اهاليل *ahālīl*) The new moon; also the moon on the wane, especially the first and last two or three days; the moon being called قمر *kamar* the rest of the month. The point of a spear; a two-headed hunting-spear. A male serpent. Slough of a snake. A mill or millstone broken in the middle or at the extremities. That part of the upper-leather in the toe of a shoe which touches the ground. A mark like a crescent burnt on a camel. A little water, especially in the bottom of a well. A ring of wine at the bottom of a decanter, heel-taps. One shower. Dust. Stones placed in rows in pavements. A white semi-circle at the root of the nails. A hoop round a hogshead. A piece of iron or wood which connects the curved timber of a camel's saddle. A lean camel. A date-stone protuberant in the middle. An instrument used in hamstringing asses (from its semilunar form). A handsome lad. Name of a tribe. هلال معنبر *hilāli muʿambar*, The eyebrow of a mistress.

P هلال ابرو *hilāl-abrū*, With eye-brows arched like the new moon, semilunar, crescent-shaped.

P هلال واري *hilālwārī*, Crescent-shaped.

P هلالوس *halālūs*, Fraud, deceit,

P هلالوش *halālūsh*, Riot, clamour, squabble.

A هلالى *hilālī*, Novilunar. Belonging to or resembling the new moon; semilunar. A kind of arrow with a crescent-shaped head. A segment of a circle. Name of a celebrated poet.

A هلام *hulām*, A dish made with veal. Veal-jelly. Almonds dressed in vinegar. Broth of سكباج *sikbāj* cooled and strained from the grease.

P هلانيدن *hilānīdan*, To abandon, dismiss.

A هلاهل *halāhil*, *halāhal*, or *halāhul*, Mortal, deadly. (Cloth) of a thin texture. Fine, delicate (verses). Deadly poison. ذو هلاهل *zū halāhilin*, A species of Arabian medicine. *Hulāhil*, Abundant and limpid water.

P هلاهلا *halāhalā*, Easy.

A هلاهلة (ذو *zū*) *hulāhilat*, A sort of medicine.

A هلب *halb*, (v. n. of هلب) Stripping (a horse's tail) of the long hairs, plucking bristles. Wetting with a continuous rain (the sky). Prosecuting his journey, continuing his course (a horse). Treating contumeliously, satirizing. *Hulb*, Hairs of horses' tails. Bristles of hogs or similar animals. *Halab*, Hirsuteness, hairiness. *Halib*, Name of ابو قبيصة *abū kabīsat*, who was bald, but whose hair grew after Muhammad with his hand had rubbed his head.

A هلباء *halbāʾ*, (fem. of اهلب *ahlab*) Hairy, bristly. The podex, and hairs around it. هلبة هلباء *halbat halbāʾ*, Calamitous accident, great misfortune.

A هلباجة *hilbājat*, Thick milk. Gross, foolish, stammering, gluttonous; a man in whom every thing bad is centered.

A هلبة *hulbat*, Severity of winter. Hard times, adverse fortune. One horse-hair, or hog's bristle.

A هلبّة *hulubbat*, The severity of winter.

A هلبج *hulabij*, Thick milk.

A هلبس *halbas*, (or هلبسيس *halbasīs*) One with whom you could converse (is not in the house).

A هلبسيس *halbasīs*, (or هلبسيسة *halbasīsat*) A small quantity, the least part (is not for you). Clothes or ornaments (she has none). These words are only used negatively.

A هلبع *hulabiʿ*, Greedy, gluttonous. A corpulent man. Cowardly, rascally. Unclean. A wolf.

A هلبوث *hilbaws*, Foolish, stupid. A stammerer.

P هلبه *hulba*, Stature, posture, figure.

A هلّة *hallat*, One shower. A lamp. هلّة بلّة *hallat ballat*, Somewhat, any thing (is not to be found). *Hillat*, The beginning (of a month).

A هلت *halt*, (v. n. of هلت) Stripping off the skin. Uprooting. Bark of a tree.

A هلتات *hultāt*, A crowd, body of men rising and departing on a journey.

P هلتاك *haltāk*, Snow.

A هلتى *halta'*, A species of plant.

A هلثاء *halsāʾ* or *hilsāʾ*, A noisy crowd.

A هلثاءة *halsāʾat* or *hilsāʾat*, Languor, feebleness. A noisy crowd.

A هلثة *hulsat*, A crowd of noisy people.

A هلثى *halsa'*, A crowd of noisy persons.

A هلج *halj*, (v. n. of هلج) Telling incredible stories. *Hulj*, Confused, uninterpretable dreams.

A هلجاب *hiljāb*, A large kettle, a cauldron.

A هلد *hald*, An attack (of fever).

A هلدم *hildim*, A garment made of bits of cloth sewed together. A coarse woollen cloth put under a saddle to imbibe the sweat.

P هلدن *hildan*, To dismiss, abandon.

P هلده *halda*, A kind of corn.

A هلس *hals*, (v. n. of هلس) Attenuating, emaciating (as disease). Being attenuated. Abundant good. Leanness, meagreness. Consumption, phthisy. *Hulus*, (Persons) recovering from sickness, weakly.

P هلش *halsh*, Name of a carrion-eating bird.

A هلص *halz*, A pulling, tearing up.

A هلطة *haltat*, Doubtful news.

A هلطوس *hiltaws*, A small fly.

A هلع *halaʿ*, (v. n. of هلع) Being extremely impatient, or dastardly. Great impatience; shameful cowardice. Avarice. *Haliʿ*, Very impatient. *Hulaʿ*, Greedy (wolf).

A هلّع *hillaʿ*, A kid.

A هلعة *hulaʿat*, Impatient. Soon hungry.

A هلّعة *hillaʿat*, A female kid.

A هلّغف *hillaghf*, One who totters or shakes.

A هلفوف *hulfūf*, Very hairy.

SY هلفيفا *halfīfā*, A kind of endive.

A هلق *halk*, (v. n. of هلق) Making haste.

A هلقام *hilkām*, Tall, large-sized. A lion.

A هلقامة *hilkāmat*, A glutton.

A هلّقت *hillakt*, Intense hunger.

A هلّقس *hillaks*, Great (hunger). Bulky (man).

A هلّقف *hillakf*, A dull, heavy fellow.

A هلقم *hilkim*, Old (woman). Strong, tall, big. Large-mouthed, big-jawed. *Hulakim*, A glutton.

A هلقّم *hilkamm*, A glutton. A large portly chief of a tribe. An owner of camels.

A هلقمة *halkamat*, (v. n. of هلقم Q) Swallowing a mouthful. Eating much.

A هلقى *halaka'*, A prancing, dashing pace.

A هلك *halk*, (v. n. of هلك) Ruining, leading to destruction. *Hulk*, (v. n. of هلك) Perishing, dying. Destruction, ruin, perdition. Shipwreck. لاذهبنّ فامّا هلك وامّا ملك *la azhabanna fa immā halkun* (or *hulkun*) *wa immā malkun* (or *mulkun*), I will surely go, be it to death or to victory. *Halak*, Any thing fallen down. A steep place, precipice. Whatever lies between each earth to the seventh. The carcase of a perished animal. The space between the top of a mountain and the bottom, or between any two objects. (pl. of هلكة *halakat*) Years of destructive scarcity. هلكت هلك *halakta huluka*, You are entirely ruined.

P هلك *halak* or *hilak*, The hiccough. *Hulak*, A kind of sling for casting stones at an enemy.

A هلّك *hullak*, (pl. of هالك) Lost, ruined, perished.

A هلكاء *halkāʾ*, Destruction, ruin. هلكة هلكاء *halkat halkāʾ*, A fatal calamity, great destruction.

A هلكان *halkān*, Confounded, tired, wearied.

A هلكة *hilkat*, (pl. هلك *hilak*) A low or fallen (creature). *Halakat*, Destruction, ruin. (pl. هلك *halak* and هلكات *halakāt*) A year of great scarcity.

A هلّكس *hillaks*, Intense (hunger). Very corpulent (man). *Hillaks*, (or هلكس *hilkis*) Mean, vile; of bad morals or temper.

A هلكون *halakūn* or *hilakūn*, Barren ground. Land not rained upon for a long time.

A هلكى *halka'*, (pl. of هالك) Ruined, perished.

A هلكين *halakīn*, (Land) not rained on for an age.

A هلل *halal*, (v. n. of هل) Being timid, cowardly. The beginning of rain, or the noise of falling rain.

Spiders' webs; and the brain of an elephant (as being supposed poisonous). (pl. of هلّة hallat) Rains.

P هلل hulul, Juice of buckthorn.

A هلم halam, A reply to the call هلمّ halumma. *Hulum*, Wild bucks, chevrils.

A هلّم hilamm, Weak, relaxed. *Halumma*, (also هلمّ لك halumma laka) Come on! approach! draw near! هلمّ كذا halumma hazā, Tell me, shew me, or grant me that. (This word is used by some tribes for all numbers; others use the dual and plural as in other nouns). الام اهلمّ ilāma ahalummu, (or لا اهلمّه lā ahalummahu) For what should I come! I will not give that. (This they say in answer to لك هلمّ الي كذا laka halumma ila' hazā, Come thou to this; or هلمّ كذا halumma hazā, Give or grant me that). جاد بهلمّه jāda bi halummihi, He obeyed his call.

A هلمّان hilimmān, Plenty (of bread or money).

A هلمطة halmatat, A taking, collecting.

A هلمّع halammaʻ, Prone to weeping.

A هلممة halmamat, A calling any one.

P هلموت halamūt, A kind of wild beet-root.

P هلناك halnāk, Snow. Sour clotted milk, strained and sun-dried for winter-use.

P هلندور halandūr, (or هلندوز halandūz) Trefoil.

A هلنقص halankas, A dwarf.

P هلنند halanand, Idle, good for nothing.

P هلو hulū, A kind of peach. A swing.

A هلواع hilwāʻ, (or هلواعة hilwāʻat) (A she-camel) travelling well and obedient to the driver.

A هلواعة hilwāʻat, Greedy, Frightened, fleeing away sharply and briskly.

A هلوب halūb, (A woman) fond of, and often approaching her husband; also disliking him, and keeping at a distance.

P هلوچين hulūchīn, A swing or see-saw.

P هلوزون halavzūn, Painting, decoration on the walls of a house, fresco.

A هلوع halūʻ, Very impatient, fretful. Greedy.

A هلوعة halwaʻat, A travelling fast.

A هلّوف hillawf, Thick, heavy, corpulent. Large-bearded. Very hairy. Large-bellied. Impatient, fretful. Stupid, foolish. Useless, unprofitable. An old man. A liar, lying. A large beard. A cloudy day. An old camel.

A هلّوفة hillawfat, A large beard.

A هلوك halūk, A modest woman, obedient to her husband. A whore, adultress, lascivious woman. A man quick at انزال inzāl. *Hulūk*, (v. n. of هلك) Perishing, dying. Falling down, dropping off.

P هله hala, Let alone! desist! be quiet! have done! But, still, yet; at length, however, whatever it is. هله كردن hala kardan, To advance, assail, storm.

P هلهال halhāl, A sieve.

A هلهال halhāl, (Cloth) of a thin texture. Fine, delicate (verses).

A هلهل halhal, Mortal poison or venom. Cloth of a thin texture. Delicate verses. *Hulhul*, Snow.

P هلهل halahil, Deadly poison.

P هلهلا halhalā, Poison.

A هلهلة halhalat, (v. n. of هلهل Q) Weaving (cloth) of a thin texture. Passing (flour) through a fine sieve. Raising and falling (the voice) alternately. Calling out هلا halā to (a horse). Tarrying, waiting for, granting a delay. Being scarcely able (to overtake), being very near (accomplishing).

P هلهله halhala, Shrill cries of exultation in women, which they evince by crying out لي لي lī lī.

P هلهليون halhalyūn, The medlar-tree.

P هلي hily, Leave alone, dismiss.

A هلّي hulla', The voice of one bidding a horse come near. Joy after grief.

A هلياع hilyāʻ, (more correctly هلياغ hilyāgh) The whelp of a savage beast. Male porcupines.

A هلياغ hilyāgh, The young of certain wild beasts. A male hedgehog.

P هلياك halyāh, Thin milk, thickened by boiling, and hardened or dried.

A هلّيان hilliyān, as ذهب بالهلّيان zahaba bi'l hilliyān, (or بذي هلّيان bi zi hilliyān) He went to an unknown place.

P هليانه halyāna, Fumitory.

A هليب halīb, The coldest days in January.

A هليّة hulayyat, (dim. of هل hal) Perhaps.

P هليجو halīju, (in zand and Pāzand) A plum.

P هليدن hilīdan, To dismiss, abandon, quit, leave. To omit. To place.

P هليسه halīsa, An oar.

P هليش halīsh, Name of a carrion-eating bird.

P هليك halek, (in zand and Pāz.) A small apricot.

A هليل hulayl, (dim. of هل hal) Perhaps.

A هليلة halīlat, Ground wet with rain surrounded by land not so wet.

P هليله halīla, The myrobalan or citron-tree. هليلهٔ زرد halīlaʼi zard, Yellow myrobalans. هليلهٔ سياه halīlaʼi siyāh, Black myrobalans. هليلهٔ كابلي halīlaʼi kābulī, Chebulic myrobalans.

A هليم halīm, Adhering, joined. Adhesive.

P هليو halīv, hal, or hilyū, A rubbish-basket.

P هليوم halyūm, (or هليون halyūn) Asparagus.

A هليون hilyawn, Asparagus.

P هليوي hilevī, A boy's game with nuts.

P هليه hulya, Stature. Woman. Fenugreek.

P هم ham, Also, likewise, in the same manner, equally, even, same. Together, with, both, one another, other. Mutual. All. Whether. Either. (in comp.) Fellow: as, همشهر ham-shahr, A fellow-citizen. باهم bā ham, Together with. درهم رفته darham rafta, Entangled.

A هم hum, (pl. of هو huwa, He) They, them.

A همّ hamm, (v. n. of همّ) Keeping (one) in an anxious state of mind (any thing). Turning (a thing) anxiously in the mind, meditating, purposing. Oppressing, overloading (abundance). Creeping (an insect). Milking. Melting (fat). Causing (one) to melt away or decay (as disease). Hushing (an infant) to sleep. (pl. هموم humūm) Grief, care, solicitude. Purpose, design. Any thing turned anxiously in the mind. Worn out by age. هذا رجل همّك من رجل hāzā rajulun hammuka mir rajulin, This is a man sufficient for you. *Himm*, (pl. اهمام ahmām) A decrepit old man.

A هم‌ء hamʼ, (v. n. of هما) Tearing, wearing out (a garment). *Himʼ*, (pl. اهماء) A worn garment.

P هما hamā, A shower, rain. *Humā*, A bird peculiar to the East: it is supposed to fly constantly in the air, and never to touch the ground: it is looked upon as a bird of happy omen; and that every head it overshades will in time wear a crown. It commonly denotes a bird of paradise, phœnix, large royal eagle, or pelican. هماي لامكان humāyi lā makān, The eagle without a fixed abode (as supposed to be always flying). هماي بيضهٔ دين humāyi bayzaʼi dīn, An epithet of Muhammad.

A هما hamā, Verily, truly, indeed.

P هماپايه humā-pāya, Illustrious.

P هماد hamād, All, whole.

P همادي hamādī, The whole. Completeness.

P هماديان hamādiyān, All, every one, every thing. The entire works of an author.

A همادي hamāziy, A swift camel. Velocity. Excessive heat. A heavy rain.

P همار hamār, Number, quantity, measure.

A همّار hammār, Talkative. Rainy (cloud).

P همارا hamārā, (or هماره) Always, constantly. A plain, level ground, equal. Number, quantity.

A همّاز hammāz, A defamer.

P هماس humās, Friend, partner, companion.

A همّاس hammās, A lion tearing his prey.

P هماش hamāsh, Astonied. Mean, base.

P هم آشيان ham-āshyān, Of the same nest.

P هم آغوش ham-āghosh, Locked in each other's arms. هم آغوشي ham-āghoshī, Embrace.

P همال hamāl or humāl, Alike, equal, resembling. Coequal, cotemporary, A companion, equal, peer; a friend, confidant.

A همال himāl, Camels allowed to pasture at large night and day.

A همّال hummāl, Loose, withered, flabby. A country left uncultivated on account of war.

A هماليج hamālīj, (pl. of هملاج himlāj) (Horses) tractable, going quietly or slowly on the road.

A هماليل hamālīl, Remains of forage. Weakly (birds, especially rapacious). Torn garments.

A همام hamām, (v. n. of همّ) Making a hoarse noise in the throat. (in comp. with لا lā) لاهمام lā hamāmi, I do not care, I think not of it, it is of no importance. *Humām*, (pl. همام himām) A great king, a hero, magnanimous prince, liberal, magnificent man. A lion. Melted fat of a camel's bunch. Water which has run from melted snow.

A همّام *hammām*, A slanderer, whisperer. The third of the days of cold.

P همّام *hummām*, Name of a Trebizond poet.

A همامة *hamāmat*, A waxing old and frail.

P همامه *humāma*, A tree whose branches resemble gold, the fruit being of a musky flavour.

A همامي *humāmi*, Heroic, magnificent.

P همان *ham ān*, Only, solely. Self-same, all one, one and the same, even that, that very. In this manner, exactly so, thus, equally. Always, continually. همان لحظه *hamān lahza*, Immediately, straightway, all at once, that very moment. *Humān*, Who contracts friendship with another.

P همانا *hamānā*, Certainly, surely. Apparently. Again, the same thing repeated, ditto, as before. Alike, resembling. Immediately, all of a sudden. A phantom, spectre. Opinion, imagination. هماناكه *hamānāki*, At the same time that.

P هماندم *hamāndam*, That very moment. At that moment, all at once, immediately, suddenly.

P همانست *hamānast*, It is even that.

P همانگه *hamāngah*, As soon as, or ever.

P همانند *hamānand*, (for هم مانند *ham-mānand*) Resembling one another.

P هماواز *ham-āwāz*, Singing in tune or in unison with another; speaking in the same tone of voice. Harmonious. Of the same voice, sound, or note.

A هما و الله *hamā wa'llāh*, Indeed! by God!

P هماور *hamāwar*, Alike, equal, resembling, similar. A school-fellow; a fellow-servant (from هم *ham*, Same, آور *āwar*, Master). Syria and Yaman.

P هماوران *hamāwarān*, Syria. Yaman. Name of a king.

P هماورد *hamāward*, A rival.

P هماون *hamāwan*, A mountain in Irān.

P هماويز *ham-āwez*, An equal, rival.

A هماهم *hamāhim*, Cares.

P هماهنگ *hamāhang*, (or هم آهنگ *ham-āhang*) Agreeing, of the same inclination, harmonious, concordant. هماهنگ شدن *hamāhang shudan*, To be in concord or tune.

P هماهنگي *hamāhangī*, Harmony, concord.

P هماي *hamāy*, Name of a boy's game played with nuts. *Humāy*, Humāy, a queen of Persia, grandmother to Dārāb II. or Darius Codomannus, overthrown by Alexander. Name of a sister of Isfandyār. Name of a daughter of بهمن *bahman*. Name of a daughter of the Emperor of Constantinople married to بهرام گور *bahrām gūr*. Name of the lover of همايون *humāyūn*. A standard bearing a figure of the bird هماي *humāy*, Phœnix or eagle.

P هماي آزاد *humāy-āzād*, Daughter of Bahman, married to her father, after the law of Zardusht.

A هماىٔم *hamā,im*, Frail old women.

P همايون *humāyūn*, Blessed, sacred, fortunate, august, royal, imperial. Name of several kings. Name of the mistress of هماي *humāy*. علم همايون خاقاني *'alami humāyūni khāhānī*, The august imperial standard. نامهٔ همايون *nāma,i humāyūn*, Royal letters, commissions. همايون نامه *humāyūn-nāma*, Pilpay's fables. (See بيد پاي *bīd-pāy*.)

P همايون گاه *humāyūn-gāh*, The royal palace.

P همائي *humā,ī*, Fortunate. Phœnix-like.

A همايين *hamāyīn*, (pl. of هميان *himyān*) Long purses, scrips. Large buttocks.

P همبار *ham-bār*, Who bears an equal burden, or toils equally with another; a companion in oppression, labour, or affliction.

P همباز *ham-bāz*, A playmate; associate.

P همبازي *ham-bāzī*, Association.

P همبر *ham-bar*, Like. A friend, companion.

P همبري *ham-barī*, Conformity, equality, likeness. A fit, a match. Companionship.

P همبزم *ham-bazm*, Of the same society, associating together. A convivial companion, one who sits with others at a feast. همبزم شدن *ham-bazm shudan*, To live, eat, drink, or converse together.

P همبستر *ham-bistar*, Bed-fellow; of same pillow.

P همبندي *ham-bandī*, The connexion. Subjection, confinement, government.

P همبوي *ham-boy*, Of the same disposition or habits. Name of a woman who rescued her brother from the hands of Zahhāk.

P هم پا *ham-pā*, A companion. A protector.

P همپاي *ham-pāy*, A fellow-traveller. همپاي دم سيّال *ham-pāyi dami sayyāl*, The companion of bloodshed (the devil).

P همپايه *ham-pāya*, A colleague. Of equal dignity and rank. Illustrious.

P همپائي *ham-pā,ī*, A social walk.

P همپشت *ham-pusht*, A companion, assistant.

P همپشتي *ham-pushtī*, Aid. همپشتي كردن *ham-pushtī kardan*, To assist, back, second, support.

P همپهلو *ham-pahlū*, An equal, peer, partner.

P هم پياله *ham-piyāla*, A pot-companion.

P همپيشه *ham-pesha*, Of the same craft.

P همپيله *ham-pīla*, Of the same weight.

P هم پيمان *ham-paymān*, Confederate.

A همّة *himmat*, (pl. هماىٔم *hamā,im*) A decrepit old woman or man. *Himmat* or *hammat*, (pl. همم *himam*) Inclination, desire, resolution, intention, design; mind, thought, attention, care. Magnanimity. Power, strength, ability. Auspices, grace, favour. P همّت كردن *himmat kardan*, To endeavour, to design. A هذا رجل همّتك من رجل *hāzā rajulun hammatuka mir rajulin*, Here is a man sufficient for thee.

A همت *hamt*, (v. n. of همت) Disappearing, sinking in fat or in broth (crumbled or sliced bread).

P همتا *hamtā*, Equal, resembling. A fellow, an equal. بي همتا *bī hamtā*, Incomparable, peerless.

P همتازيانه *ham-tāziyāna*, A companion at a horse-race, or on a marauding excursion.

P همتائي *hamtā,ī*, Equality.

P همترازو *ham-tarāzū*, Of equal weight.

A همتع *humtu'*, Gathered fruit of the تنضب.

P همتك *ham-tak*, A fellow-traveller.

P همتلميذ *ham-talmīz*, A school-fellow.

A همج *hamj*, (v. n. of همج) Drinking at one draught as much as satisfies thirst (a camel). *Hamaj*, Small gnats which infest the nostrils or eyes of cattle. Old crippled sheep. Lean sheep. Abject, low, or foolish men. A little fly. A thing of no use. A mean manner of living, either in conduct or in eating. Hunger. همج هامج *hamaji hāmij*, Severe hunger, starving.

P همجا *hamjā*, Reproach. Injury, oppression.

P همجاي *ham-jāy*, (or همجائي *ham-jā,ī*) A fellow-citizen or countryman. Friendship, nationality.

A همجة *hamajat*, One gnat. One lean sheep.

P هم جنب *ham-jamb*, Sitting together; friend.

P همجنس *ham-jins*, Homogeneous. Consubstantial.

P همجنسي *ham jinsī*, Homogeneousness.

P همجنگ *ham-jang*, Battle-field. Fellow-soldier.

P هم جوار *ham-jiwār*, Townsman, neighbour.

P همجي *hamjī*, A small fly. A beetle.

P هم چشم *ham-chashm*, One's equal. هم چشمي كردن *ham-chashmī kardan*, To contend, vie with.

P همچنان *hamchunān*, In that manner, in the same manner, exactly like, so, still. همچنانچه *ham chunānchi*, As, same manner as, in like manner. همچنانكه *hamchunānki*, In the same manner as.

P همچند *hamchand*, Only, so many.

P همچنين *hamchunīn*, In this manner, thus, in like manner, in the very same manner.

P همچو *hamchu* (or همچون *hamchūn*) Like, such, such like, as, thus, so, even as, as if.

P همحال *ham-hāl*, A companion, one in the same station of life, a partner. همحال شدن *ham-hāl shudan*, To be in partnership, or intimate.

P همحجره *ham-hujra*, Of the same chamber.

P همخانگي *ham-khānagī*, Cohabitation. همخانگي كردن *ham-khānagī kardan*, To live along with.

P همخانه *ham-khāna*, A fellow-lodger, companion, partner. A spouse, husband and wife. هم خانهٔ مسيح *ham-khāna,i masīh*, The sun (whose place is in the fourth heaven, or heaven of Jesus).

P همخدمت *ham-khidmat*, A fellow-servant.

P همخوابگي *ham-khwābagī*, A sleeping together. همخوابگي كردن *ham-khwābagī kardan*, To sleep together.

P همخوابه *ham-khwāba*, A bed-fellow: spouse.

P همخواه *ham-khwāh*, One who asks the same thing, or at the same time. A fellow-citizen.

P همخوند *ham-khwund*, (for هم خداوند *ham-khudāwand*) A fellow-student, or servant. Contrary, adverse, inimical. A large bench upon which people recline.

P همخوي *ham-khoy* or *khūy*, Of the same disposition, temper, or habits.

A همد *hamd* or *humd*, (v. n. of همد) Being worn (a garment), torn or cut along the folds.

P همداستان *ham-dāstān*, Of the same advice. Telling the same story. An intimate friend, an inseparable companion. A confidant, secretary. Conformable, agreeable. Obedient. Contented, thankful. Contentment, thankfulness.

P همداستاني *ham-dāstānī*, Taxes, tribute.

P همداماد *ham-dāmād*, A son-in-law; each of those who have married two or more sisters; kindred by marriage.

P همدامان *ham-dāmān*, Married to the sister of another's wife.

P همدان *hamadān*, A city and district in Persia.

P هم دبستان *ham-dabistān*, A school-fellow.

A همدة *hamdat*, Apoplexy.

P هم درد *ham-dard*, A partner in sorrow, a fellow-sufferer. Sympathetical.

P هم دردي *ham-dardī*, Sympathy.

P هم دست *ham-dast*, A partner, companion, associate, accomplice. One who sits or converses with another. Of equal strength, power, or greatness.

P همدستان *ham-dastān*, Hand in hand. (pl. of همدست *ham-dast*) Partners, associates.

P هم دگر *ham-digar*, Together.

P همدل *ham-dil*, Unanimous, of the same opinion. Sympathetic. A cordial friend. Unanimously.

P همدلي *ham-dilī*, Sympathy.

P همدم *ham-dam*, Breathing together, *i.e.* an intimate companion, friend, or spouse. One (fisher for pearls) who can hold his breath for the same time as another. A goblet of wine.

P همدمي *ham-damī*, Friendship, familiarity.

P همدوش *ham-dosh*, An equal, companion.

P همدهي *ham-dihī*, Of the same village.

P همديگر *ham-dīgar*, Both, each.

P همديوار *ham-dīwār*, Having the same wall, *i.e.* a neighbour, neighbouring.

P همديهي *ham-dīhī*, A fellow-villager.

P همذات *ham-zāt*, Co-existent, consubstantial.

A همذان *hamazān*, A mode of walking which leaves foot-marks on the ground. A city built by Hamazān, son of Peleg, son of Shem, son of Noah.

A همذانيّ *hamazāniy*, Verbose, loquacious. A confused, disordered pace.

A همر *hamr*, (v. n. of همر) Ruining, demolishing, laying waste. Teasing, incommoding a camel (abundance of milk). Being poured out. Talking much. Pouring (water). Milking out all that is in the udder. Giving away part (of one's wealth). Making (the earth) shake (with) his feet (a horse). *Hamir*, Thick, gross, fat. A great hill of sand.

P هم راد *ham-rād*, Of equal liberality, munificence, or courage.

P همراز *ham-rāz*, Knowing each other's secrets. A confidant, intimate friend.

P همرافته *hamrāfta*, Understood, perceived.

P همراه *ham-rāh*, A fellow-traveller. With, along with. همراه من *ham-rāhi man*, Along with me.

P همرهي *ham-rāhī*, Society on the road, fellow-travelling. همراهي كردن *ham-rāhī kardan*, To travel in company.

A همرة *hamrat*, One shower. One breaking of a branch of a tree. A species of philtre or fascination. One burst of passion.

A همرّج *hamarraj*, Acute, sagacious, enterprising.

A همرجان *humrujān*, A confused hum of men.

A همرجة *hamrajat*, (v. n. of همرج Q) Being intricate and confused (a story), or relating (a story) in such a manner. Mixture, confusion. Speed. Lightness. A confused noise of human voices. Vain, false.

A همرجل *hamarjal*, Swift. Swift, excellent (camel).

A همرجلة *hamarjalat*, A choice she-camel.

P همرس *ham-ras*, Money, specie, cash.

A همّرش *hammarish*, An old woman. A camel abounding in milk. Name of a bitch.

A همرشة *hamrashat*, Commotion, tumult.

P همرف شده *hamraf-shuda*, (or همرو شده *ham-rū-shuda*) (A horse) rising five-year old.

P همرقّاص *ham-rakkās*, Dancing together.

P همركاب *ham-rikāb*, A stirrup-fellow, one who rides alongside of another.

P همرنگ *ham-rang*, Of the same colour, complexion, nature, or disposition.

P همرو *ham-rav*, A fellow-traveller. *Ham-rū*, Face to face. همرو شدن *ham-rū shudan*, To appear before; to be placed opposite, face to face. To be of full age (as a horse five years old).

P همروزگار *ham-rozgār*, Cotemporary.

P همرويندة *ham-royanda*, Full grown.

P همرة *ham-rah*, (for همراه) Fellow-traveller.

P همرهي *ham-rahī*, Fellowship in travel.

A همرئ *hamara'*, A noisy, foul-mouthed woman.

A همز *hamz*, (v. n. of همز) Squeezing (in the hand), or as (a cat) does (a mouse), treading upon. Impelling, driving, spurring, goading, or striking. Piercing, pricking, biting. Breaking. Dashing upon the ground, prostrating. Marking (a letter) with the sign *hamza* ـٔـ. Accusing, defaming, detracting. Beckoning with the eye. همز الشيطان *hamzu'sh shaytān*, Madness, demoniacal possession.

A همزات *hamazāt*, Instigations (of Satan).

P همزاد *ham-zād*, Born together, congenital. Twin, of equal age. A cotemporary, playmate. A جنّ *jinn*, or familiar spirit, said to be produced at the birth of every child, and to accompany him through life. A sharer of provisions on a journey.

P همزانو *ham-zānū*, Sitting with another; knee to knee; living together. A companion, associate.

P همزانوئي *ham-zānūī*, Close intimacy.

P همزبان *ham-zabān*, Of the same language.

A همزة *hamzat*, The sign hamza, or letter أ *alif*. همزهٔ بين *hamzasi bayn*, A hamza substituted for a و or ي. همزهٔ مسمار *hamzasi mismār*, A crooked nail. *Hamazat*, (pl. همزات *hamazāt*) A suggestion of the devil. *Humazat*, One who defames or reproaches (especially a person present).

P هم زلف *ham-zulf*, A wife's sister's husband.

P همزمان *ham-zamān*, Cotemporary.

A همزئ *hamaza'*, Stiff, stout (bow). Loud (wind).

A همس *hams*, A gentle noise. Any thing clandestine or concealed. The slightest noise imaginable made by the feet. The sound of muttering or breathing hard. Pressure. A breaking. Mastication with a compression of the lips. A journey with little or no intermission for a day and night.

P همساز *ham-sāz*, Unanimous. A friend, correspondent, confederate; of the same family.

P همسال *ham-sāl*, Of the same year or age.

P همسان *ham-sān*, Resembling each other.

P همسايگان *ham-sāyagān*, Neighbours.

P همسايگي *ham-sāyagī*, Neighbourhood. Neighbourship, neighbourliness.

P همساية *ham-sāya*, Under the same shade, *i.e.* neighbouring, neighbour. همسايهٔ مسيح *ham-sāyasi masīh*, The sun (whose seat is the fourth heaven).

P همسايه نوازي *hamsāya-nawāzī*, Friendly terms with neighbours.

P همسبق *ham-sabik*, Schoolfellow, class-fellow.

P همسدة *hamsada*, Name of a spirit which incites to good acts.

P همسر *ham-sar*, Of the same head, *i.e.* equal in height, age, or of the same authority; also of the same rank or profession; an associate. A spouse.

P همسري *ham-sarī*, Equality, evenness.

P هم سفر *ham-safar*, A fellow-traveller. همسفران جاهل *hamsafarāni jāhil*, (Ignorant fellow-travellers) The human soul and body.

P همسفرگي *ham-sufragī*, Commensality, fellowship of table. همسفرگي كردن *ham-sufragī kardan*, To mess together.

P همسفرة *ham-sufra*, Sitting at the same table; messmate, fellow-commoner; a convivial companion. A boarder.

P هم سن *ham-sin*, Of equal age, a playfellow.

P همسنگ *ham-sang*, Of the same weight.

P همسود *hamsūd*, The red jujube. The red button of a rose.

P همسيراز *hamsīrāz*, A translation.

A همش *hamsh*, (v. n. of همش) Entering (one within another). Shaking, moving. A collection. A bite. A peculiar manner of milking. Much talking. *Hamish*, Dexterous, clever with his fingers.

P همشپتمهديم *hamshpatamahdīm*, The sixth period of the creation, 75 days, in which God created man.

A همشة *hamshat*, The noise of locusts shut up and moving to and fro in a narrow place.

P همشراب *ham-sharāb*, A pot-companion.

P هم شكل *ham-shakl*, Like, resembling.

P همشكم *ham-shikam*, Uterine (brother).

P همشوي *ham-shūy*, A rival wife.

P همشهري *ham-shahrī*, A fellow-townsman.

A همشي *hamasha'*, A noisy, talkative woman.

P همشير *ham-shīr*, Of the same milk, *i.e.* a uterine or a foster-brother or sister.

P همشيرگي *ham-shīragī*, A suckling with another.

P همشيرة *ham-shīra*, A foster-brother. A sister (by the mother only, or a foster-sister). همشيرة زاده *ham-shīra zāda*, A nephew by the sister.

P همشين *hamshīn*, (for همنشين *ham-nishīn*) One who sits or converses with another.

A همص *hams*, (v. n. of همص) Eating one's flesh. Throwing, prostrate. Conquering, overcoming. Killing.

P همصحبت *hum-suhbat*, Of the same society, an associate. همصحبت شدن *ham-suhbat shudan*, To converse, debate, associate.

P همصحبتي *ham-suhbatī*, Fellowship.

A همط *hamt*, (v. n. of همط) Defrauding one of his due, injuring, oppressing. Striking hard. Trampling. Devouring, eating voraciously. Talking audaciously. Seizing with violence, plundering. Mixing truth with falsehood.

P هم طبق *ham-tabak*, A messmate.

A همع *hamʿ*, (or همعان *hamaʿān*) (v. n. of همع) Shedding tears. Flowing (as a liquid thing), falling (as dew). *Hamiʿ*, (A cloud) pouring out rain.

P همعقد *ham-ʿakd*, United, tied together.

P همعنان *ham-ʿinān*, With equal reins, *i.e.* riding alongside of another. A companion, equal, associate, friend, peer.

P همعهد *ham-ʿahd*, Coeval, cotemporary. Joined, allied: adopted brother, united by friendship.

A همغ *hamgh*, A breaking (of the head).

A همق *hamik*, Soft herbage, easily eaten; a great deal of dry herbs, grass, or hay.

A همق *himakk*, Foolish, disturbed, confused.

A همقاق *hamkāk* or *humkāk*, A grain growing on mountains, which, when parched, they eat as a strengthener, or a stimulative to venery.

P هم قد *ham-kad*, Of equal stature.

P همقدح *ham-kadah*, A pot-companion.

P همقدر *ham-kadr*, Equivalent, of an equal price, value, dignity, or power.

P همقدم *ham-kadam*, A companion. An attendant. A footman.

P همقريه *ham-karya*, A fellow-villager.

A همقع *humakiʿ*, (or همّقع *hummakiʿ*) Foolish. Fruit of certain plants.

P هم قوم *ham-kawm*, Of the same tribe.

A همقي *himakka'* or *himikka'*, (He walked) waving from side to side.

A همقيق *hamkīk*, Name of a plant.

A همك *hamk*, (v. n. of همك) Launching (any one) into an affair. Plunging into.

P همكار *ham-kār*, A fellow-workman.

P همكاسه *ham-kāsa*, A convivial or pot-companion. A fellow-commoner, boarder.

P هم كفو *ham-kufū*, Of the same family.

P هم كلام *ham-kalām*, Intercourse. Engaged in conversation.

P همكن *ham-kan* or *ham-kun*, A companion in toil or travel.

P هم كنار *ham-kinār*, Embracing.

P همكنيت *ham-kunyat*, Of the same patronymic.

P همكيش *ham-kesh*, A co-religionist.

P همكين *hamkīn*, Fellow-labourer or traveller.

P همگان *hamagān*, (pl. of همه *hama*) All.

P هم گپ *ham-gap*, A gossip.

P همگر *hamgar*, A weaver. Relation, affinity.

P همگنان *hamginān*, All. A company. Homogeneous. Equals.

P هم گوشه *ham-gosha*, Of the same species. A neighbour.

P همگي *hamagī*, All, the whole: entirety. از همگيء زنان *az hamagī-i zanān*, Of all women.

A همل *haml*, (v.n. of همل) Shedding tears. Raining incessantly. Being left to themselves to graze where they please night and day (camels). *Himl*, An Arabian garment of coarse stuff. Mended clothes. An old tent made of hair. *Hamal*, (Camels) allowed to feed at large night and day. (Water) flowing freely without impediment. The fibres called ليف *līf*, torn from the trunk of the palm-tree: coir.

A همّل *hummal*, (Camels) feeding at large.

A هملاج *himlāj*, (pl. هماليج *hamālīj*) Tractable, going quietly or slow (a horse on the road). (A sheep) having no marrow from leanness.

A هملان *hamalān*, (v. n. of همل) Shedding tears. Raining incessantly.

A هملجة *hamlajat*, Easy pace of a pack-horse.

P هملخت *ham-lakht*, A kind of shoe. The sole of a shoe. هملخت دوز *hamlakht-doz*, A cobbler.

A هملس *hamallas*, Strong-legged, able walker.

A هملطة *hamlatat*, A taking, a collecting.

A هملّع *hamallaʿ*, Swift (camel), that travels fast and takes wide steps. A wolf. Treacherous, deceitful, inconstant in friendship.

A هملقة *hamlakat*, Swiftness, celerity, haste.

A هملي *hamla'*, (Camels) pasturing night and day without a keeper.

A همم *himam*, (pl. of همّة *himmat*) Intentions, resolves. Cares, anxious wishes. Favours. Decrepit old women.

P هم مذهب *ham-mazhab*, A co-religionist.

P هم مشرب *ham-mashrab*, Like-tempered.

P هم مصلحت *ham-maslahat*, Confederate.

P هم معني *ham-maʿna'*, Synonymous.

P هم مكتب *ham-maktab*, A schoolfellow.

P هم نام *ham-nām*, A namesake.

P همنبر *hamambar*, Alike, resembling. Good.

P همنبرد *ham-nabard*, A fellow-labourer.

P هم نداء *ham-nidā*, Singing in concert.

P هم نسل *ham-nasl*, Of the same breed.

P همنشين *ham-nishīn*, One who sits or converses with another, a companion. All living creatures.

P هم نشيني *ham-nishīnī*, Concession.

P همنفس *ham-nafs*, A friend, intimate companion. *Ham-nafas*, Consonant, harmonious.

P هم نمك *ham-namak*, A messmate.

P هم نواله *ham-nawāla*, A messmate.

A همو *hamw*, The flowing (of tears).

P همو *hamu*, (for هم او *ham u*) He also.

P هموا *hamwā*, Desire, intention, wish.

P هموار *hamwār*, Plain, equal, level. An even place or thing, Lenient, behaving gently or tenderly to another. Clear, melodious (intonation). Proportionable, well-made. Suitable, worthy, fit. Always, constantly, continually. Perpetual. هموار كردن *hamwār kardan*, To level, smooth, make plain. نا هموار *nā hamwār*, Uneven. Unsuitable, disproportioned, indecent, absurd, unworthy. Discordant.

P همواره *hamwāra*, Always, continually.

P هموثاق *ham-wisāk*, Associated, confederated, joined in alliance or conspiracy.

A همود *humūd*, (v. n. of همد) Being extinguished (fire, together with all its heat). Being worn, torn, or cut along the folds (a garment). Being destitute of rain and vegetation, being dead, producing nothing at all (land). Death.

P همورد *hamūrad*, The joists of the roof.

P هم وزن *ham-wazn*, Of the same weight.

A هموس *hamūs*, A prey-rending lion. Soft-treading (lion). One who travels much or fast at night.

A هموع *hamūʿ*, Flowing, fluent. *Humūʿ*, (v. n. of همع) Shedding tears. Flowing (as any thing liquid). Falling (as dew).

P هموقت *ham-wakt*, At the same time. Of the same age.

A همول *humūl*, (v. n. of همل) Raining gently, but incessantly. Shedding tears.

A همولة *humūlat*, (Camels) pasturing night and day without a keeper.

A هموم *hamūm*, (A well) abounding with water. (A cloud) raining copiously. A reed shaken by the wind. A she-camel going well. *Humūm*, (pl. of همّ *hamm*) Cares, afflictions, anxieties.

A همومة *humūmat*, A waxing old and frail.

P همون *hamūn*, In this manner, exactly so, thus. همون جا *hamūn jā*, That same place.

P همه *hama*, All, the whole, every, each, every thing. An assault, attack. با همه *bā hama*, With all.

A همهام *hamhām*, A great king. A hero, magnanimous prince, liberal man. A lion. *Hamhāmi*, There is nothing remaining.

A همهامة *hamhāmat*, A large troop of camels.

P همه جا *hama-jā*, Everywhere.

P همهجي *hamajī*, A beetle.

P همه ساله *hama sāla*, Alway, for ever.

A همهم *himhim*, Braying (ass). A lion.

A همهمة *hamhamat*, (v. n. of همهم Q) Making

a hoarse noise in the throat (as an elephant, or ox). A low voice, whisper, murmur. (A mother) hushing her infant to sleep.

A همهوم *humhūm*, A lion.

A همهومة *humhūmat*, A large troop of camels.

A همهيم *himhīm*, A lion. Braying (ass).

A همى *hamy*, (v. n. of همى) Falling. *Hamy* (or همى *humīy*) (v. n. of همي) Flowing (water or tears). Weeping, shedding tears. Wandering (flocks).

P همي *hamī*, Patient, modest. *Hamī* (for مي *mī*) A particle prefixed to some tenses of the Persian verb, more particularly to the present and preter-imperfect; as, همي پرسد *hamī pursad*, He asks.

P همياز *hamyāz*, A friend, companion.

A هميان *himyān*, (pl. همايين *hamāyīn*) A long purse or scrip, especially hung at the side. A girdle, belt. The string of the breeches or drawers. له هميان *lahu himyān*, He has large buttocks. *Hamayān*, (v. n. of همي) Flowing (water or tears). Shedding tears. Wandering here and there (a flock).

P هميج *hamīj*, A young deer, slender-bodied. (A deer) having two lines on the back, of a different colour from the rest of the body. (A deer) troubled with the gripes or any other distemper which makes the face thin. Tormented by gnats.

P هميجان *hamījān*, In the same manner.

P هميد *hamīd*, Thus, in the same manner, in this way. A fault, suspicion, accusation (especially false). Foolish, stupid.

A هميد *hamīd*, (or الهميد *al hamīd*) Tribute or tax, to be paid, as entered in the public books.

P هميدون *hamīdūn*, Now, at this moment. Always, perpetually. Suddenly. Such, in this manner. In the same place. Care, endeavour. Favour.

A همير *hamīr*, Handsome, beautiful (female deer).

A هميرة *hamīrat*, A decrepit old woman.

A هميروي *hamī ravī*, Thou goest. Goest thou?

P همیز *hamez*, (or همين *hamen*), (in zand) Summer.

A هميز *hamīz*, Bold, keen, penetrating (man).

A هميس *hamīs*, Noise made by the motion of the feet of camels (scarcely audible).

A هميسع *hamaysaʻ*, Strong, robust, not to be thrown down. Long, tall.

P هميشك جوان *hamīshak-jawān*, Houseleek.

P هميشگى *hamīshagī*, Eternity, perpetuity.

P هميشه *hamīsha*, Always, continually, perpetually. Anciently, having no beginning. هميشه بهار *hamīsha-bahār*, Ox-eye, a species of camomile.

A هميع *himyaʻ*, Sudden death.

A هميغ *hamyagh*, The مغد *maghd*-tree. *Himyagh* Sudden death.

A هميم *hamīm*, Small rain. Sour milk kept in a bottle or churn for drinking, not for making butter. (pl. of هامّة *hāmmat*) Reptiles.

A هميمة *hamīmat*, Small rain. A gentle gale. Any thing about which one is anxious.

P همين *hamīn*, Only, solely, neither more nor less, even this, this same, equally, so, in the same manner. همين ساعت *hamīn sāʻat*, This self-same hour. همين طور *hamīn tawr*, This same manner, by a parity of reasoning.

P همينك *hamīnak*, Behold now! lo here he is! This moment. All.

P هن *han*, Gratitude, obligation, thanks. *Hin*, (in the Shīrāz-dialect) (for هست *hast*) Is, exists.

A هن *han*, Some (man). ياهن *yā hanu*, O thou man! (come hither). *Han*, (dual هنان *hanāni*, هنتان *hanatāni*, هانان *hānāni*, and هنوان *hanawāni*, pl. هنون *hanūna*) A thing, small matter, somewhat. Pudendum muliebre. *Hin* (for ان *in*) If.

A هنّ *hann*, (v. n. of هنّ) Weeping, deploring, crying lamentably. Crying to (her) colt in an affectionate manner (a camel). *Hunna*, (fem.) They.

A هنء *hans*, (v. n. of هنأ) Anointing, bedawbing (a camel) with pitch. Giving, bestowing, presenting; maintaining, supporting any one, especially by the month. Pasturing freely in a field of pot-herbs without being satiated. Being joyful, glad, merry. Saying "May you prosper!" *Hans* or *hins*, (v. n. of هنأ) Being wholesome (meat), agreeing well (with one). Preparing (food) well. Causing (food) to agree with one (health). *Hins*, A present. Part of the night. An anointing with pitch. The pitch with which they anoint a camel.

A هنأ *hanas*, (v. n. of هنئ) Pasturing in a field of herbs without being satisfied. Rejoicing. Digesting well food.

A هنا *hana*, (for انا *ana*) I. *Hunā*, Here. A pastime, play. Name of a place. يوم هنا *yawmu hunā*, On the first day.

A هنّا *hannā*, Here. من هنّا و هنّا *min hannā wa hannā*, Here and there, on every side.

A هناء *hināʼ*, (v. n. of هنأ) Anointing (a camel) with pitch. Aiding, assisting. Liquid pitch for anointing a scabby camel. A cluster of dates the fruit of which has been eaten.

A هناءة *hanāʼat*, (v. n. of هنئ or هنؤ) Being light, wholesome, and digestible (meat). Happening, arriving without trouble or difficulty.

A هنابذ *hanābiz*, (pl. of هنبذة *hambazat*) Serious, important, weighty, and difficult affairs.

A هنابير *hanābīr*, High hills of sand. A place of destruction. Hell.

A هنأة *hanʼat*, (v. n. of هنأ) Preparing (food) well. *Hanaʼat*, (v. n. of هنئ or هنؤ) Being light, wholesome, and digestible (meat).

A هناة *hanāt*, (pl. هنوات *hanawāt*) A calamity.

A هنات *hanāt*, (pl. of هنة *hanat*) Certain women. Small things. Rimæ mulierum. يا هنات *yā hanāt*, O women! come hither. فيه هنات *fīhi hanāt*, In him there are bad qualities.

A يا هناتاه *yā hanātāhu*, O two women hither!

A هنادسة *hanādisat*, (pl. of هندوس) Skilful.

A هنادك *hanādik*, (pl. of هندكي) Hindūs.

A هنادكة *hanādikat*, Indians, Hindūs.

A هناف *hināf*, A smile (especially ironical).

A هناك *hunāka*, (هنّاك *hannāka*, or هنالك *hunālika*) There, in that place.

P هنام *hunām*, (in ancient Persian) Stature, figure, form of the body, symmetry, arrangement.

A بنو هنام *banū hinnām*, Name of a tribe of Jinns.

A ياهنان *yā hanāni*, Hither, O you two men!

A هنانة *hunānat*, The interior fat of the eye. Fat, strength, vigour (in a camel). Remains of marrow.

A هنانيه *hanānayh*, (in comp. with يا *yā*) as يا هنانيه *yā hanānayh*, O you two women!

A هناه *hanāhu* (with يا *yā*) as يا هناه *yā hanāhu*, O thou! come hither.

P هناهين *hanāhīn*, The noise of people talking together, or an army, horse and foot, on the march.

A هناي *hanaʼ*, (Cattle) fed with herbs, but in a small quantity, getting just a snatch.

P هنائش *hināʼish*, Effect, impression.

A هنب *himb*, Name of a man, a catamite, expelled by Muhammad. *Hanab*, Carelessness, simplicity, folly (applied especially to a woman).

A هنباء *hambāʼ*, Foolish, unskilful (woman).

A هنّباء *hunnabāʼ*, Simple, foolish, unskilful (woman). Foolish, insane (man).

P هنباز *ham-bāz*, A companion, partner.

A هنباغ *himbāgh*, Extreme hunger.

P هنبان *hambān*, A wallet. Soft leather.

A هنبتة *hambatat*, Slowness, delay. Languor.

A هنبثة *hambasat*, An important or difficult affair. Confusion in speech.

A هنبذة *hambazat*, A weighty, difficult affair.

P هنبر *hambar*, Fair, handsome, good.

A هنبر *himbir*, An ass's colt. امّ الهنبر *ummu'l himbir*, A she-ass. ابو الهنبر *abū'l himbar*, A male hyena. امّ الهنبر *ummu'l himbar*, A female hyena. *Himbir* or *hinabr*, A hyena.

A هنّبر *hinnabr*, A horse. A bull. Spoilt leather; the edges of a skin. A hyena.

A هنبرة *himbarat*, A she-ass. *Himbirat*, A she ass-colt.

A هنبسة *hambasat*, Inquiry into news.

A هنبص *himbis*, Weak, wretched, contemptible. *Humbus*, Large-bellied.

A هنبصة *hambasat*, A low laugh scarcely audible.

A هنبض *humbuz*, Large-bellied.

A هنبع *humbuʻ*, A sort of girl's head-dress.

A هنبعة *humbuʻat*, A hyena-like pace.

A هنبغ *humbugh*, Extreme hunger. Dust which flies about with the least motion. A lion. A foolish, weak woman.

A هنبغة *hambaghat*, (v. n. of هنبغ Q) Hungering. Flying about (dust).

A هنبلة *hambalat*, (v. n. of هنبل Q) Going like a lion. The limping pace of a hyena.

A هنبي *hanabaʼ*, Silly (woman).

A هنّبي *hunnabaʼ*, Simple, foolish, unskilful (woman). Foolish, insane (man).

A هنة *hanat*, Aught. A certain woman. Rima.

A هنت *hant*, (for هنة *hanat*) A small matter, somewhat. A certain woman. (for انت *anta*), Thou. يا هنتاه *yā hantāhu*, (يا هنتانيه *yā hanatāniyah* or يا هناتوه *yā hanātūh*, Oh woman! oh both women! and oh women! (come hither).

A ياهنتان *yā hanatāni*, Hither. O two women!

A هنتبة *hantabat*, A relaxing, growing languid.

P هنج *hanj*, Extracting, drawing. Casting, throwing, flinging. Concord, harmony. Riches. Harmonious, agreed.

P هنجار *hanjār* or *hinjār*, A mason's rule, any string or instrument used by builders in laying stones straight, a plumb-line, a level. A straight road. An unbeaten path, by-path. Way, rule, law. Habit, custom. Conduct. Going on a road-side: taking a cross-cut by a by-path. Colour. Vexation, grief.

P هنجاره *hanjāra*, Sad, afflicted.

P هنجاريدن *hanjārīdan*, To travel on, by, or near the road, or on the side of it.

P هنجام *hanjām*, Out of employ; a vagrant, lazy, idle, good-for-nothing fellow.

P هنجك *hinjak*, A pot-herb eaten boiled.

A هنجل *hunjul*, Heavy.

P هنجمك *hinjamak*, An herb which is given to cattle boiled.

P هنجيدن *hanjīdan*, To draw out, bring forth. To pull up. To yawn, stretch. To flay a sheep. To vex, grieve, molest, injure, irritate, try, tempt.

P هند *hand*, (for اند *and*) (They) are. Way, road, manner, law, custom, usage.

A هند *hind*, A hundred (camels), or a few more or less. Two hundred. India. The Hindū people. (pl. اهند *ahnud*, اهناد *ahnād*, and هنود *hunūd*) A woman's name. مراة الهند *mirātu'l hind*, (in the dialect of Morocco) A telescope.

A هندابة *hindābat*, Any one (is not at home).

A هندات *hindāt*, Hindas (women's names).

A هنداز *hindāz* or *handāz*, (from P اندازه *andāza*) A certain quantity or determinate measure.

A هندام *handām*, (from P اندام *andām*) Stature. Symmetry, just proportion.

A هندب *hindab*, Endive, succory.

A هندباء *hindabā*, (*hindibā* or هندبي *hindiba'*), Endive. هندباى برّي *hindabāi barrī*, Wild endive.

A هندباة *hindabāt*, A single endive.

A هندبيّ *handabiy*, Verbose, loquacious.

P هنديد *hindbed*, Endive.

A هندس *hindis*, Intrepid, fierce (lion). Skilful, experienced, sagacious (man).

P هندسان *hindusān*, (for هندوستان) Hindūstān.

A هندسة *handasat*, (from P اندازه *andāza*) Skill in the construction of subterraneous aqueducts. Geometry. اهل الهندسة *ahlu'l handasat*, Geometricians.

P هندستان *hindustān*, India.

P هندسه *hindisa*, Numeration by the letters of the alphabet. A cypher. Arithmetic.

A هندسيّ *handasiy*, (fem. هندسيّة *handasiyat*) Geometrical. P آداب هندسيان *ādābi handasiyān*, The geometrical science.

A هندكي *hindikiy*, (pl. هنادك *hanādik* or هنادكة *hanādikat*) Indian, Hindū.

A هندلع *hundaliʿ*, A small sort of pot-herb.

A هندليق *handalīk*, Talkative, verbose.

P هندمند *hindamand*, Name of a river in Sīstān.

P هندو *hindū*, An Indian. Black. A servant. A slave. A robber. An infidel. A watchman. A mole on the cheek of a mistress. هندوي باريك بين *hindūyi bārīk-bīn*, The planet Saturn. (Synonymous to which are these: هندوي پير *hindūyi pīr*, هندوي چرخ *hindūyi charkh*, هندوي سپهر *hindūyi sipihr*, هندوي گنبذ گردان *hindūyi gumbazi gardān*).

P هندوان *handawān*, Name of the fort of Balkh.

P هندوانه *hinduwāna*, A pumpkin, water-melon.

A هندوانيّ *hindawāniy* or *hundawāniy*, Made of Indian steel. (A sword) of an excellent edge.

P هندوبار *hindūbār*, Hindūstan. An ink-horn.

A هندوس *hundūs*, (pl. هنادسة *hanādisat*) Experienced, skilful.

P هندوستان *hindūstān*, India, Hindūstān.

P هندوستاني *hindūstānī*, Belonging to Hindūstān; the language of that country, Hindūstānī.

P هندوستانيت *hindūstāniyat*, Ease, indulgence.

P هندووي *hindūwī*, (or هندوي *hinduwī*) An Indian. Indian; the Indian language, Hindee.

P هندوي *hunduwī*, A bill of exchange.

P هندوي اژدها *hinduwī-ajdahā*, An Indian sword.

P هندوي دريا نشين *hinduwī daryā-nishīn*, Writing, manuscript.

A هندويل *handawīl*, Gross, large, and flabby.

P هندي *hinde*, One Indian. *Hindī*, Any thing Indian, or belonging to India. A sword of Indian steel. *Hundī*, A bill of exchange.

A هنديّ *hindiy*, Indian, pertaining to the Hindūs.

P هنديان *hundiyān*, (or هنديawan هندياون *hundiyāwan*) Commission on bills of exchange.

P هندي نژاد *hindī-nijād*, Born in India.

P هنر *hunar*, Skill, science, knowledge, ingenuity, art, industry, excellence, virtu. Profession. A bill of exchange.

P هنر بند *hunar-band*, Clever, skilful.

P هنرپرور *hunar-parwar*, A lover, cultivator, patron, or encourager of science. A virtuoso.

P هنرپروري *hunar-parvarī*, Cleverness, skilfulness, genius, abilities. Virtuosoship.

P هنرپيشه *hunar-pesha*, An artist. Skilful.

P هنردار *hunar-dār*, Skilful, knowing, clever.

P هنرمند *hunarmand*, Learned, excellent, skilful, industrious. معمار هنرمند *miʿmāri hunarmand*, A skilful architect. هنرمندانه *hunarmandāna*, Skilfully.

P هنرمندي *hunarmandī*, Skilfulness, skill.

P هنرور *hunarwar*, Skilful, clever.

A هنزمن *hinzamn*, (from P انجمن *anjuman*) A crowd, a company.

A هنشنش *hanashnash*, Light, not heavy.

A هنع *hanʿ*, (v. n. of هنع) Bending, folding, doubling. Submitting, humbling one's self unto. A shortness of neck of a reddish white deer. *Hanaʿ*, (v. n. of هنع) Being buck-necked. The natural bend of the body. The concave curve in the neck of a camel, or ostrich, and other long-necked beasts and birds.

A هنّع *hunnaʿ*, Humble, submissive (men).

A هنعاء *hanʿā*, Short, contracted (hillock). (An ostrich) which has a contracted and bent neck.

A هنعة *hanʿat*, A mark burnt on the right side of a camel's neck. Five stars in the left shoulder of Orion; the sixth mansion of the moon, distinguished by two bright stars in the feet of Gemini; also the name of several other stars in the Milky Way, and of eight in the form of a bow, called Brachium Leonis.

A هنق *hanak*, Affliction, grief, trouble, restlessness from grief: fidget.

A هنقب *hankab*, A dwarf; short-bodied.

P هنگ *hang*, Understanding, intellect. Majesty, authority. Dignity, gravity. Purpose, design, institution. A wave. A cavern, cleft in the rock. Quantity or weight of any thing. Sympathy. Strength, power, ability. Many, much, abundant. Keeping, guarding. Acute, intelligent. A tribe, family. An army, soldier. A stroke, blow, collision, wound, hurt. Defluxion, rheum, cold. A draught of water. *Hing*, Prosperity, happy times. A pain in the bowels. Assafœtida. Intellect. *Hung*, Provisions. Power, strength.

P هنگار *hangār*, (or هنگارد) Haste. Vehemence.

A هنگام *hangām*, Time, hour, season. An assembly. هنگام ننگ و نبرد *hangāmi nang u nabard*, Time of battle. از هنگام سحر تا هنگامهٔ شام *az hangāmi sahar tā hangāmai shām*, From morning until evening. آن هنگام *ān hangām*, That time, then. بي هنگام *bī hangām*, Untimely, ill-timed, out of season. درهنگام شام *dar hangāmi shām*, In the evening.

P هنگامه *hangāma*, A convention, assembly, meeting of merchants. A place for any kind of play or entertainment. Noise, tumult, commotion, confusion, riot, disorder, crowd, throng. هنگامهٔ طفلان *hangāma-i tiflān*, The world. هنگامه كردن *hangāma kardan*, To make a noise, to raise a disturbance.

P هنگامه گير *hangāma-gīr*, A rope-dancer. Tumultuous, uproarious.

P هنگامي *hangāmī*, Temporal; ephemeral; animals which shortly appear and disappear, as insects.

P هنگفت *hanguft* or *hunguft*, Thick, dense, coarse. Much, abundant. Cloth of a plain, equal, or firm texture. A kind of female upper garment. A bed counterpane quilted with cotton.

P هنگه *hanga*, A place for any entertainment.

P هنگيدن *hangīdan*, To be troubled, muddy.

A هنم *hanam*, A species of date.

A هنمة *hinnamat*, A kind of philtre used by women. A dwarf. Short or deformed in body.

P هنمد *hanmad*, Green substance upon water.

A هننة *hinanat*, A sort of hedgehog.

A هنو *hinw*, Time, season.

A هنوات *hanawāt*, (pl. of هنت *hant*) Small things. (pl. of هناة *hanāt*) Calamities.

A هنوان *hanawāni*, (dual of هن *han*) Two things. Two men.

P هنوبر *hunūbar* (or هنوبرة *hunūbara*) A palm-tree with one trunk.

P هنوتاس *hanūtās*, Spirits which surround the throne of God.

A هنود *hunūd*, (pl. of هند *hind*) Indians, Hindūs. Hindas (Arabian women's names).

P هنوز *hanūz* or *hanoz*, Yet, still, further, just now, at present, hitherto, to this very time, until now. Not yet.

A (يا *yā*) هنوك *hanūka*, O thou! (come here).

A هنون *hanūn*, (pl. of هن *han*) Small things.

A يا هنون *yā hanūna*, (or هنوناه *hanūnāhu*) O ye men! come hither.

P هنوند *hanwand*, Shame, modesty, bashfulness.

P هنه *ha na*, Is it not? whether?

A هني *hany*, (v. n. of هني) Doing.

A هنئ *hanīʼ*, (Meat) light, easy of digestion, pleasant. Any thing possessed or acquired without trouble. كلوا هنيا مريا *kulū hanīʼan marīʼan*, Eat ye with a good digestion. حالة هنئة *hālat hanīʼat*, An agreeable condition.

A (يا *yā*) هني *hanyi*, O my son! come hither.

P هني *hunī*, A funnel.

A هنيّ *yā hanayya'*, O you my two sons! come hither. *Yā hanīya'*, O you my children! come hither.

P هنيار *hanyār*, (or هنيان) A consort, partner.

A هنيّة *hunayyat*, A small thing, a trifle.

A هنيت *hanaytu*, (for فعلت *faʻaltu*) I did.

A هنيدة *hunaydat*, A hundred camels. A hundred of any thing.

P هنير *hunīr*, Good, beautiful. Excellence, beauty.

P هنيز *honez*, Hitherto, thus far, as yet, until now. Is it not yet? Is it not also? در هنيز *dar hanez*, Whilst yet.

A هنيزة *hanīzat*, Trouble, affliction.

A هنيع *hanīʻ*, Crooked and short-necked (man).

A هنين *hanīn*, (v. n. of هنّ) Crying affectionately to (her) colt (a camel). Weeping, wailing, lamenting. *Hunayn*, (dim. of هن *han*) Small rima.

A هنيهة *hunayhat*, (dim. of هنة *hanat*) A trifle.

A هنيئة *hunayʼat*, A small thing, a trifle.

P هو *haw*, White or red pus. A bloody swelling. The moon. A cloud; fog, mist. *Hū*, A sigh. Ah! alas! Ho! mind!

A هو *huwa*, He. He is. A name of God. هو الله المستعان *huwa'llāhu'l mustaʻān*, He is God, whose assistance we implore. هو الله الغنيّ المغني المعين *huwa'llāhu'l ghanīyu'l mughni'l muʻīn*, He is God, the rich, the enricher, the helper. هو المعين المتعال *huwa'l muʻīnu'l mutaʻāl*, He is the exalted assistant. هو العزيز *huwa'l ʻazīz*, He is glorious. It is often written at the top of a letter, where in Europe they used formerly to put the sign of the cross. As a pronoun, it is often put for the substantive verb كان *kāna* in every tense.

A هوّ *haww*, A side. A window.

A هوء *hawʼ*, (v. n. of هاأ for هوأ) Aspiring, tending upwards. Thinking (either good or bad). Rejoicing at. Design, purpose. Delight. بعيد الهوء *baʻīdu'l hawʼ*, One who revolves in the mind distant or important objects. *Hawʼ* or *hūʼ*, Opinion, mind, thoughts.

A هوأ *hawaʼ*, A thinking anxiously about.

P هوا *havā*, Name of a village in Dāmaghān, where there is a remarkable well.

A هوا *hawa'*, Affection, favour, love, mind, desire.

A هواء *hawāʼ*, (pl. اهوية *ahwiyat*) Air, atmosphere, ether, the space between heaven and earth. Wind, gentle gale. Sound, voice, tone, air of music, a song. Any thing empty. P هواي تند *hawāyi tund*, A storm, tempest. Ambition; vanity. A coward. هواي نفساني *hawāyi nafsānī*, (or هوا و هوس *hawā u hawas*) Lust, concupiscence, sensuality, luxury. هواي خفتانپوش *hawāyi khaftān-posh*, (or هواي سنجابي *hawāyi sinjābī*) A cloudy sky. سنبل هوا *sumbul-hawā*, (or پوش هوا *posh-hawā*) A dark or cloudy atmosphere. كشاده هوا *kushāda-hawā*, An open or serene sky. A *Hiwāʼ*, (v. n. 3 of هوي) Soothing, flattering, cajoling. Playing, trifling, now offering a thing and now drawing it back.

A هوّاءة *hūwāʼat*, A deep valley, low ground.

P هوابد *hawābid*, (pl. of هابدة *hābidat*) Women who gather colocynths or their seeds.

P هوا پرست *hawā-parast*, A worshipper of the air, i.e. vain, given to vanity (ambition or sensuality).

A هواة *hawāt*, Air, ether, atmosphere.

A هواجر *hawājir*, Sultry afternoon-heats.

A هواجس *hawājis*, (pl. of هاجسة) Thoughts.

A هواجم *hawājim*, Assaults, shocks, brunts.

P هوا جوي *hawā-joy* or *jūy*, A lover.

P هواخواه *hawā-khwāh*, Vain, desirous of vanities, ambitious, fond of pleasure. A friend, well-wisher.

P هوا خواهي *hawā-khwāhī*, Well-wishing.

P هوادار *hawā-dār*, Airy, having or following the wind. A friend. A lover, well-wisher. Saucy. Flighty. Dispersed in air, given to the winds. The seat placed on an elephant to ride in. زلف هوادار *zulfi hawā-dār*, Ringlets waving in the wind.

P هواداري *hawā-dārī*, Affection, liking.

A هوادة *hawādat*, (v. n. of هود) Making peace. Inclining. Softness. Inclination. Indulgence, licence, leave. That from which good is hoped for.

A هوادج *hawādij*, (pl. of هودج) Camel-litters.

A هوادر *hawādir*, Braying camels: cooing doves.

A هوادي *hawādī*, A crowd, a multitude. (pl. of هادي *hādī*) Beginnings of night. Necks of horses. The first that appear in sight of a herd of camels.

A هوارة *hawārat*, Destruction, annihilation.

A هوارم *hawārim*, (pl. of هارم *hārim*) (Camels) feeding on the shrub هرم *harm*.

P هواري *hawārī*, A large tent. An audience-chamber. Unseasonable, ill-timed. Foolish, ignorant.

P هوازد *hawā-zad*, Spring, force, impulse of air.

P هوازدگي *hawā-zadagī*, Chill, chilliness, cold.

P هوازده *hawā-zada*, Chilled, cooled.

P هوازه *hawāza*, Suddenly, at once, unawares.

P هوازي *hawāzī* or *hiwāzī*, An audience-chamber. Suddenly, all at once, without notice.

A هواس *hiwās*, Lust, heat.

A هوّاس *hawwās*, Libidinous. الهوّاس A lion.

A هوّاسة *hawwāsat*, A lion. Strong, intrepid.

P هواسيدن *hawāsidan*, To convene, assemble. To have chapt or pale lips (from heat or fear).

P هواسيده *hawāsida*, A pale, livid lip.

A هواشات *huwāshāt*, (pl. of هواشة) Crowds. Herds of camels mixed together. Ill-gotten riches.

A هواشة *huwāshat*, A crowd of men, or a number of camels, especially in confusion.

A هواصر *hawāsir*, (pl. of هاصر) Prey-tearing lions.

A هواع *huwāʻ*, (v. n. of هاع for هوع) Vomiting spontaneously. A vomit. Any thing vomited. (pl. هواعات *huwāʻāt* and اهوعة *ahwiʻat*) Name of the month ذو القعدة *zu'l kaʻda*.

A هوافي *hawāfī*, Strayed (camels).

A هوّاك *hawwāk*, Astonished, stupefied.

A هوّاكة *hawwākat*, An evil smell.

A هوالس *hawālis*, (Persons) light of body.

A هوالك *hawālik*, (pl. of هالك *hālik*) Perishing.

A هوام *huwām*, Excessive thirst. Madness.

A هوّام *hawwām*, A lion.

A هوامّ *hawāmm*, (pl. of هامّة *hāmmat*) Reptiles. Serpents. Insects. هوامّ الارض *hawāmmu'l arz*, The reptiles of the earth. P هوامّ ضرر رسان *hawāmmi zarār-rasān*, Noxious reptiles.

A هوامع *hawāmiʻ*, Flowing (tears).

A هوامل *hawāmil*, (pl. of هامل *hāmil*) Camels feeding at large night and day.

A هوامي *hawāmī*, Stray (camels).

A هوان *hawān*, (v. n. of هان for هون) Being contemptible. Contempt, scorn. Meekness, mildness. Languid.

A هواوين *hawāwīn*, (pl. of هاوون *hāwūn*) Mortars.

A هواهي *hawāhī*, Trifles, ridiculous actions, sayings, or things.

A هواهية *hawāhiyat*, A very deep well. Cowardly.

A هواي *hawāya'*, My wish.

P هوائي *hawāʼī*, Airy, windy. Idle, vain, capricious, licentious; a votary of pleasure. Ambitious. Flighty. Vain, idle, rash, trifling talk. A rocket. Income not derived from any fixed source. Blue, cerulean, azure, sky-coloured.

A هوائيّ *hawāïy*, Airy, windy.

A هوب *hawb*, Foolish, loquacious. The heat of fire. *Hawb* or *hūb*, Distance. تركته في هوب دابر *tarahtuhu fī hawbin* (or *hūbin*) *dābirin*, I left him no one knows where.

A هوبجة *hawbajat*, Low and level ground. The end of a valley where water collects. A pond towards which water is directed.

A هوبر *hawbar*, A very hairy ape. The panther, or beast called cheeta; also its whelp. A lily, or the purple kind of it.

P هوبر *hobar*, The shoulder, armpit, side. Aid.

P هوبره *hawbara*, Distracted. *Hobara*, A bustard.

P هوبسيا *hobasyā*, (in zand and Pāz.) A tooth.

P هوبه *hoba*, The shoulder. Aid, protection.

P هوپمن *hopman*, (in zand and Pāz.) The face.

A هوّة *hūwat*, (v. n. of هوي) Ascending, being raised. Air, atmosphere. The letter ي *ye*. A deep valley, cavern, hollow, or ditch.

A هوتة *hū* or *hawtat*, (pl. هوت *huwat*) Low land.

A هوثة *hawsat*, Thirsty (woman). Thirst.

A هوج *hūj*, (pl. of هوجاء *hawjā*) Winds blowing down tents. *Hawaj*, Extreme folly or levity. Haste, precipitation.

A هوجاء *hawjā*, (fem. of اهوج *ahwaj*) A camel going precipitately. Tall, foolish, precipitate. (pl. هوج *hūj*) Violent (wind) blowing down tents or buildings.

P هوجره *hūjara*, Shepherd's staff. Bugloss.

A هوجل *hawjal*, Swift (camel). A skilful or active road-guide. A heavy, dull, tall, stupid man. A slow, languid step. An immodest woman. A roomy woman. A solitude, desert without direction-posts, or signs of a road; also having many uncertain or perplexing paths. Uneven ground. A long night. A propensity to sleep. A ship's anchor.

A هوجلة *hawjalat*, (v. n. of هوجل Q) Travelling over level or low-lying ground.

P هوخ *hokh*, (هوخت *hokht*, or هوخست *hokhst*) The temple of Jerusalem.

P هوختن *hokhtan*, (also هوخيدن *hokhīdan*) To draw out, unsheathe. To report. To prophecy. To singe. To labour. To receive justice.

A هود *hawd*, (v. n. of هاد for هود) Repenting, returning to one's duty. Turning Jew. *Hūd*, (pl. of هائد *hāïd*) Penitents. The Jews. Name of a prophet; (so the Arabians called the patriarch Heber) whence, those to whom a prophet is sent are called قوم هود *kawmi hūd*, The people of Hūd. *Hawad*, (pl. of هودة *hawadat*) Camels' bunches.

P هود *hod*, Tinder. Scorched, singed cloth.

A هودة *hawadat*, (pl. هود) A camels' bunch.

A هودج *hawdaj*, A litter carried by a camel, in which the Arabian ladies travel: it is made of wood, or cloth stretched upon a frame, and is either open or covered at top; also any canopy, veil, or curtain, which conceals women when travelling. A seat to place on an elephant's back.

A هودجة *hawdajat*, (v. n. of هودج Q) Being high (a camel's bunch).

P هودر *hawdar*, Scab, mange. A pustule, pimple, felon, bile. *Hodar* or *hawdar*, Ugly, ill-favoured.

P هودش *hawdash*, A pustule, a scab.

A هودع *hawdaʻ*, An ostrich.

A هودك *hawdak*, Fat.

P هودل *hūdil*, Astronomical observations.

P هودل بند *hūdil-band*, A calculator of, or one who draws up, astronomical tables.

P هوده *hoda*, Truth. True, just, right. Old.

A هوذا *hūzā*, Behold! lo!

A هوذة *hawzat*, (pl. هوذ *huwaz*) A man. A species of bird, the قطا *katā* (one of the tetraonidæ or grouse-family).

P هوذر *hūzar*, Ugly, ill-favoured.

A هوذلة *hawzalat*, (v. n. of هوذل Q) Being quick (in going). Being shaken, vacillating in running (the body). Being shaken (a bucket). Scattering (as a camel his urine). Being weak and languid in venery. Making water in the air.

A هور *hawr*, (v. n. of هار for هور) Falling down (as a mound, wall, or any building). Conceiving an opinion, suspecting, thinking about. Throwing down, tumbling one over another, ruining, demolishing. Killing. Impelling. Driving forward. Driving back or away, averting. Deceiving. (pl. اهوار *ahwār*) A pool, lake, marsh, or quagmire into which one easily sinks. A flock of sheep, especially when numerous, and tumbling one over another.

P هور *hor*, The sun. The moon. A star. Name of a star which is seen once in a thousand years. Fortune. A horoscope, nativity. Red, ruddy. A cloud, fog. Suffocation from the vapour of a well.

A هورات *hawrāt*, Dangers, destructions.

A هورة *hawrat*, A dangerous place. *Hūrat*, Suspicion, thought.

P هورخش *horakhsh*, The sun.

P هورش *hawrash* or *rish*, A bile, felon, sore.

A هورع *hawraʻ*, A light, forward woman.

P هورمز *hormuz*, (or هورمزد *hormuzd*) Name of an angel. The first day of the solar month. The planet Jupiter. Name of the grandson of Isfandyār.

A هورورة *hawarwarat*, (A woman) perishing.

P هوز *hūz*, A sharp sound from metal.

A هوز *hūz*, Creatures, men. ما في الهوز مثلك *mā fi'l hūz misluka*, There is not among men your equal. ما ادري اي هوز هو *mā adrī ayyu hūzin huwa*, I know not what kind of man he is.

A هوّز *hawwaz*, One of the artificial words composed of the letters of the alphabet. (See ابجد *abjad*.) Name of a Himyarite king.

P هوزان *hozān*, A narcissus in bloom.

A هوزب *hawzab*, A vulture. A strong camel.

P هوزرش *hawzarish*, A malignant boil or sore.

P هوز مشير *hūz mashīr*, The province of Ahwāz.

A هوزن *hawzan*, Dust. Name of a bird.

P هوژه *hūja*, A small bird (in Arabic صعوة *saʻwa*).

A هوس *haws*, (v. n. of هاس for هوس) Bruising, beating. Breaking. Going about or wandering in the night-time (as cattle when pasturing); going slow, step by step, and feeding as they go. Driving (camels) gently. Eating voraciously. Wasting, destroying (as a wolf the flock). A mode of walking. *Hawas*, Desire, lust, concupiscence, inordinate appetite. Ambition. Curiosity. A sort of madness. P هوس كردن *hawas kardan*, To desire eagerly, to endeavour to procure, to aspire, long, have a fancy for. A *Hawis*, Libidinous.

P هوس *hos*, Lust. *Hūs*, Intellect, mind.

A هوسان *hawasān*, (v. n. of هاس for هوس) Going about or wandering in the night-time. Going slowly, step by step (as a lion).

P هوس باز *hawas-bāz*, Indulging inclination.

A هوسة *hawisat*, Libidinous (she-camel).

P هوسرب *hosurub*, (in zand) A good name.

P هوسكار *hawas-kār*, (or گار *gār*) Inclined.

P هوسناك *hawasnāk*, Wishful. Curious.

A هوسى *hawsaʼ*, Devourers, consumers.

P هوسين *hūsīn*, A die, dice.

P هوش *hawsh*, Pomp, pride. *Hosh*, Understanding, judgment, intellect; the mind, the soul. Destruction, perdition, ruin, death; any thing which causes death or ruin. Poison. باهوش *bā hosh*, Intelligent, judicious, prudent, wise. Wary, sensible. بي هوش *bī hosh*, Foolish, insane. Unwary, insensible. واهوش رفتن *wā hosh raftan*, (or بي هوش شدن *bī hosh shudan*) To faint, to swoon away, to be deprived of sense. بهوش آمدن *ba hosh āmadan*, To return to one's senses (after intoxication or fainting). بهوش بودن *ba hosh būdan*, To take care, to be provident, wary, cautious.

A هوش *hawsh*, A crowd, immense multitude. الهوش الهائش *al hawshu'l hāïsh*, A great multitude. *Hawash*, (v. n. of هوش) Being tumultuous, mixed, confused. Being small (the belly).

P هوشا *hoshā*, Idle, lazy, indolent, slow. Fat of a sheep's tail. Extended forward, straight. Perfect.

A هوشات *hawashāt*, (pl. of هوشة) Tumults.

P هوشاز *hoshāz*, (or هوشازه *hoshāza*) Excessive thirst of cattle.

P هوشازيدن *hoshāzīdan*, To be exceedingly thirsty (cattle).

P هوشاشدن *hoshāshudan*, To move or tumble about, restless (as a sick person in bed); to be troubled in mind. To recover from a swoon, from intoxication, or insanity; to awake from sleep.

P هوشان *hūshān*, (or هوشاني) The Epiphany.

P هوش باخته *hosh-bākhta*, Senseless, silly.

P هوشبر *hosh-bar*, Depriving of sense or understanding. بادهٔ هوشبر *bādaï hosh-bar*, Wine which deprives one of reason.

A هوشة *hawshat*, A tumult; crowd, mob (as in a market-place). Confusion, disorder. Commotion.

Insurrection, sedition.

P هوشكش *hosh-kash*, An inebriating electuary made of hemp-leaf: hence, wine, or any thing which intoxicates or distracts the senses.

P هوشمند *hoshmand*, Prudent, wary, wise, canny.

P هوشمندي *hoshmandī*, Understanding.

P هوشنگ *hoshang* or *hūshang*, Name of the second king of Persia, of the Peshdādian dynasty. His father was سيامك *siyāmak*; his grandfather كيومرث *kayūmars*. Wisdom, prudence, intellect.

P هوشني *hūshnī*, Name of an herb.

P هوش واژن *hosh-wājan*, A trance.

P هوشيار *hosh-yār*, Prudent, wise, canny. Sober, not intoxicated. Wary, aware, cautious, vigilant.

P هوشياري *hosh-yārī*, Prudence, caution, vigilance, wakefulness, watchfulness. Sobriety.

P هوشيدن *hoshīdan*, To understand.

A هوع *hawʻ*, (v. n. of هاع for هوع) Being light. Grieving. Meditating an attack upon each other. Vomiting without any effort. A vomit. A strong but improper desire. *Hawʻ* or *hūʻ*, Enmity, hatred.

A هوغ *hawgh*, Abundant, much, many.

A هوف *hawf* or *hūf*, A hot wind. A cold wind. *Hūf*, An empty, slothful, good-for-nothing fellow. A fool, an oaf. A coward. The skin of an egg. A hot, dry wind, &c. (See هيف *hayf*.)

A هوفة *hūfat*, A crowd, mob, meeting.

P هوقار *hūkār*, A heron.

A هوكة *hawkat*, An assembly, a crowd.

A هوك *hawk* or *hiwakk*, Silly, foolish, with a mixture of reason. *Hawak*, (v. n. of هوك) Being foolish, silly. Folly.

A هوكة *hūkat*, A ditch, pit, hole. *Hawikat*, Salsuginous, noisome (ground).

P هوگان *hawgān*, A brass kettle or pot.

P هوگويك *hogūyak*, A bird which is said to suspend itself by the claws, and all night to cry *hak, hak*.

P هوگيك *hoguyak*, An unripe melon.

A هول *hawl*, (v. n. of هال for هول) Terrifying, striking with horror. Seeing many confused colours (a drunken man). (pl. اهوال *ahwāl* and هوول *huwūl*) Fright, terror. Any thing terrible attacking one. A figure in the shape of a human head close to the pyramids of Egypt, the sphinx (supposed by the unlettered natives to have been placed there as a talisman). هول هائل *hawli hāʼil*, A dreadful fright. هول الجنان *hūluʼl janān*, Brisk, skittish.

P هول *hol*, High, lofty. True, just. Straight.

A هؤلاء *haʼulāʼ*, These.

A هولة *hawlat*, Terror. Any thing terrible attacking a person. *Hūlat*, A sacred fire before which the pagan Arabians used to swear; so called because they sometimes threw privately into it a kind of salt, which making a sudden explosion, terrified often a perjured witness, and made him tell truth. A woman dazzling the eyes with her beauty. Self-love or admiration.

P هولس *hūlis* or *hūlas*, Life, soul, spirit.

P هولشك *hūlishk*, A thick, dense, contemptible, mean fellow. One who habitually befouls himself.

A هولع *hawlaʻ*, Swift.

P هولك *hawlak*, A blister on the hands or feet. Ruin, destruction, A dried grape, raisin. *Holak*, A game with nuts.

P هولناك *hawlnāk*, Terrible, dreadful, horrible, frightful, terrifying, dangerous, perilous.

P هولناكي *hawlnākī*, Dreadfulness.

A هولول *hawalwal*, A light, nimble, active man.

P هولي *hawlī*, A colt that has not been backed. *Hūlī*, Name of a Hindu festival.

A ابو الهولى *abūʼl hūlaʼ*, A sphinx. A talisman or charm for driving away spiders. Name of a poet.

A هوم *hawm*, Low grounds. هوم المجوس *hawmuʼl majūs*, A kind of jessamine from which a diuretic medicine is prepared.

P هوم *hūm*, Name of a tree resembling the tamarisk. Name of a descendant of Farīdūn.

P هومات *hūmāt*, Dull, heavy, doltish, silly.

P هومان *hūmān*, The brother of Pīrānwīsah.

A هومة *hawmat*, A desert, solitude.

P هون *hawn*, A ploughed field full of clods and stones. *Hūn*, The gold coin called by Europeans pagoda, current at Madras. An affirmative particle.

A هون *hawn*, (v. n. of هان for هون) Being light, smooth, easy. Resting, remaining quiet. Giving rest, making easy. Quiet, tranquillity. Mildness, modesty, gentleness, tameness. Base, despicable. على هونك *ʻalaʼ hawnika*, At your conveniency. يمشي هونا *yamshī hawnan*, He walks gently. *Hūn*, (v. n. of هان for هون) Being vile, mean, base, contemptible. Baseness, meanness. A contemptible state. Created beings, creatures. عذاب الهون *ʻazābuʼl hūn*, Ignominious punishment.

A هونة *hawn* or *hūnat*, Rested, reposed: quiet, gentle.

P هونگ *hawang*, Bunches of fruit hung up to dry.

P هوو *hūw*, Either of two women engaged by one man. A rival wife.

A هوول *huwūl*, (pl. of هول *hawl*) Terrors, frights. Frightful things.

A هوه *hūh*, Timid, cowardly. *Huwah*, He. *Hiwah*, Mallows.

A هوهاءة *hawhāʼat*, A fool.

A هوهاة *haw* or *hūhāt*, A fool. A well whose water lies at a great depth, and no means of getting at it.

A هوهة *hūhat*, Timid, cowardly.

P هوه جوه *hawah jūh*, Melilot.

P هوهو *hūhū*, An owl. A dove.

A هوي *hawy*, (v. n. of هوي) Gaping (a spear-wound. *Hawaʼ*, (v. n. of هوي) Loving, desiring, wishing for, hankering after. (pl. اهواء *ahwāʼ*) Desire, love, inclination, will, wish (good or bad). Desired, wished. Loved; a beloved object. *Hawī*, One who loves, desires, or wishes.

P هوي *hūy*, Fear, dread. Breath. A sigh. A word used in exciting attention.

A هويّ *hawiy*, (v. n. of هوي) Ascending. An ascent. *Hawiy* or *huwiy*, (v. n. of هوي) Falling, descending from a height. Flying downwards (as a hawk upon his prey). Being extended or upraised (the hand). Catching a gentle sound (the ear). Blowing (the wind). Dying. Part (of the night). A hissing or tingling in the ear. *Huwiy*, Descent. *Hawayya*ʼ, My desire.

A هويان *hawayān*, (v. n. of هويٰ) Falling, descending from a height. A fall.

A هويّة *hawiyat*, Desire. An object of desire. A deep well. *Huwiyat*, (Divine) essence. Existence, it-ism.

A هويجة *huwayjat*, A small frog.

P هويد *hawīd*, The territory of Samarcand. *Hawīd* or *huwayd*, Camels' packsaddles.

P هويدا *huwaydā*, Clear, evident, open, manifest, conspicuous. Pale. Clearly, publicly. هويدا شدن *huwaydā shudan*, To appear, be evident. هويدا كردن *huwaydā kardan*, To make appear; to publish, divulge. هويدا سخن *huwaydā-sukhun*, Intelligible in speech, easily understood.

P هويدائي *huwaydāʼī*, Clearness, manifestation.

P هويدك *huwaydak*, Name of a heresiarch.

P هوير *huwīr*, One who hopes.

A هويس *hawīs*, Thought. Any thing revolved in the mind.

A هويشة *hawīshat*, A mixed crowd.

P هويه *hūya*, A shoulder. Aid, protection.

P هه *hah*, The sound of the breath. هه كردن *hah kardan*, To breathe in the face of another.

A هه *hah*, (Remembering any thing) verily, truly. Woe be to you! Fy upon you! Take care what you do! Ha! ha! ha!

A هةّ *hahh*, (or ههّة *hahhat*) (v. n. of هةّ) Stammering, being tongue-tied.

A ههنا *hāhunā*, Here.

P هي *hay*, Ho! hark ye! holla! Have a care! softly! touch it not! Oh! alas! Bravo! Is, exists. Existence.

A هي *hiya*, (or هيَ *hiya*) She. She is.

A هيّ *hayy*, (also هيّ بن بيّ *hayyuʼbnu bayyin*) The unknown son of an unknown father. يا هيّ *yā hayya*, Strange! wonderful! ah! alas!

A هيّء *hayyiʼ*, Of a handsome exterior.

A هيا *hayā*, Ho! holla! hark ye!

A هيآت *hayʼāt*, (pl. of هيأة) External forms.

A هيّاب *hayyāb*, (and هيّابة *hayyābat*) Timid, fearful. Feared, dreaded.

A هيأة *hayʼat*, (v. n. of هاء for هيأ) Being prepared, ready. Face, countenance, aspect, exterior form. State, quality. Mode, style, fashion. The form, figure, or aspect of the heavens. Astronomy. *Hiʼat*, (v. n. of هاء) Longing for, desiring.

A هيّاة *hayyāt*, A business, an affair.

A هياج *hiyāj*, (v. n. of هاج for هيج) Being

raised (dust), excited (anger). Exciting, stirring up. Being thirsty. Being in a rage. Boiling (blood). Battle. يوم الهياج *yawmu'l hiyāj*, Day of carnage.

A هيار *hayār*, Fallen down, ruined.

A هيّار *hayyār*, Weak.

P هياسه *hayāsa*, A girth, a surcingle.

A هياط *hiyāt*, (v. n. 3 of هيط) Crying, being noisy. Approach, nearness.

A هياطل *hayātil*, (or هياطلة *hayātilat*) A Scythian or Indian race that was formerly powerful.

P هياطله *hayātala*, Name of a city.

P هياع لياع *hiyāʻ liyāʻ*, Violent (wind).

A هياف *hiyāf* or *huyāf*, (v. n. of هاف for هيف) Opening their mouths to inhale the hot wind هوف *hūf* from excess of thirst (camels). Violent thirst.

P هياك *hayāk*, Mind, soul, spirit.

A هياكل *hayākil*, (pl. of هيكل *haykal*) Giants, colossal figures. Forms, spectres. Palaces, temples.

P هياكيدن *hayākīdan*, To run mad as a dog, to be seized with canine madness.

A هيال *hayāl*, Sand or the like poured out.

P هياليدن *hayālīdan*, To fear, to dread.

A هيام *hayām* or *huyām*, (pl. هيم *huyum*) Sand which one cannot grasp in the hand on account of its fineness. *Hiyām*, (pl. of هيمان *haymān*) Thirsty (camels). *Huyām*, (v. n. of هام for هيم) Thirsting exceedingly. Wandering about like a madman, from love or any other cause. Insanity from love. Excessive thirst.

A هيّام *huyyām*, Lovers. Mutterers to themselves.

A هيّان *hayyān*, A word used to designate any one unknown. هيّان بن بيّان *hayyānu' bnu bayyān*, The unknown son of an unknown father.

A هياه *hayāh*, A name for the devil.

P هياهو *hayāhū*, Clamour, shouts in battle.

A هيب *hayb*, (v. n. of هاب for هيب) Fearing, standing in awe of, dreading.

P هيب *heb*, (in zand) End of any business.

A هيّب *hayyib*, Timid, fearful.

A هيبان *haybān*, Formidable.

A هيّبان *hayyabān*, Extremely timid. Light. Smooth. The earth. A shepherd. A coward. A he-goat. Foam about a camel's mouth. *Hayyabān* or *hayyibān*, Terrified, timid, cowardly.

A هيبة *haybat*, Fear, timidity, panic. Respect, reverence, awe. Awfulness, gravity. Sternness, severity. Dignity, majesty, grandeur.

P هيبتوار *haybatwār*, Venerable, awful, majestic.

A هيبليّ *haybaliy*, A Christian monk.

A هيئة *hiʼat*, External form of any thing. The form of the heavens. Astronomy. Carriage, bearing, manner, appearance, aspect, feature.

P هيت *hīt*, Tumult, clamour, strife.

A هيت *hīt*, Low ground. Name of an infamous catamite banished from Madīna by Muhammad. *Hayta, hayti, haytu*, or *hīta*, Come hither! approach! هيت لك *hayta laka*, (or هيت لكم *hayta lakum*) Approach thou! or approach you!

A هيتاء *hītāʼ*, A part of the night.

P هيتال *haytāl*, Free from taxes. Strong, powerful. The countries ختلان *khatlān* and بدخشان.

P هيتان *haytān* or *hītān*, A lie. False, untrue.

A هيتكور *haytakūr*, Sleepy (by day and night).

A هيتم *haytam*, A kind of salt and bitter plant.

A هيث *hays*, Motion. *Hays*, (or هيثان *haysān*) (v. n. of هاث for هيث) Giving a small quantity, bestowing little. A small present. Taking proper care of cattle. Injuring.

A هيثة *haysat*, (equiv. to هيشة *hayshat*) A crowd.

A هيثم *haysam*, A young eagle or vulture. A reddish, soft, or even sand-hill. A plain, level country.

P هيج *hayj*, Right, straight. Tearing up. Instigation. Reverence, authority, majesty. *Hij*, A three-pronged corn-fork.

A هيج *hayj*, (v. n. of هاج for هيج) Raising (dust). Being in a rage. Boiling (blood). Being raised (dust), excited (anger). Thirsting (a camel). Withering (a plant). Windy, rainy, or cloudy (day), or one of battle. *Hīj*, Used in calling out to camels.

A هيّج *hayyij*, Raised (dust). Roused (anger).

A هيجاء *hayjāʼ*, or هيجا *hayjaʼ*, War, battle, combat.

A هيجان *hayajān*, (v. n. of هاج for هيج) Being raised (dust), excited (anger). Vehemence, violence. A pain or swelling in the eye.

A هيجبوس *hayjabūs*, A tall, foolish, hasty, harsh-tempered, peevish, testy, pettish fellow.

A هيجفل *hayjafil*, (A bow) shooting easily.

A هيجمان *hayjumān*, A large pearl.

A هيجمانة *hayjumānat*, A pearl. A spider.

P هيچ *hech*, Nothing, a mere trifle. Lost, annihilated. Never, at no rate, on no account, at all. (in composition, without a negative, implies, *some, any*; and with a negative, expressed or understood, *not any, none.*) هيچ اصلاً *hech aslan*, In no shape, in no respect. هيچ چيز *hech chīz*, Nothing at all. هيچ نگفت *hech na guft*, He said nothing at all.

P هيچكاره *hech kāra*, Unsuccessful in one's labours. هيچكارهٔ همه كار *hech kāraʼi hama kār*, Unfortunate in every thing.

P هيچ كس *hech kas*, Somebody. Nobody; low, vile.

P هيچگاه *hech gāh*, Every, any time.

P هيچگونه *hech gūna*, In any form or manner.

P هيچمدان *hech madān*, Perfectly ignorant.

P هيد *hayd*, An instrument for winnowing corn.

A هيد *hayd*, (v. n. of هاد for هيد) Moving, disturbing, driving off. Frightening. Oppressing the spirits. Amending, correcting, restoring. Turning, diverting. Checking, chiding. Propelling. Disturbed. ايّام هيد *ayyāmu haydin*, The days of a fatal epidemic which raged in the time of paganism. هيد ما لك *hayda mā laka*, How do you do? *Hayd* or *hīd*, Used in calling to camels.

A هيدان *haydān*, Cowardly. Covetous, avaricious. الهيدان والزيدان *al haydān wa'z zaydān*, Known and unknown (as when charity is distributed promiscuously to known people or strangers).

A هيدب *haydab*, Impotent, weak, languid, slow. Scalloped or fringed edges of garments. A low-hanging cloud full of rain, or the skirt of it. A continued flowing of tears. Pendula pubes mulieris.

A هيدبى *haydabaʼ*, A hard horse's pace.

A هيدبيّ *haydabiy*, A very talkative man.

P هيدخ *haydakh*, A fine spirited young horse, difficult to be broke (especially about three years old). The bridle of a spirited horse.

A هيدكر *haydakur*, Corpulent, plump (woman).

A هيدكور *haydakūr*, Corpulent, plump (woman); also one young, lusty, and graceful in darting amorous glances, or who hides herself in order to allure. Thick milk. هيدكور الاساطين *haydakūru'l asātīn*, Firmly placed on pillars (house).

A هيدكورة *haydakūrat*, Stout, plump (woman).

A هيدلة *haydalat*, A kite. A driving of camels with singing.

A هيذار *hayzār*, (or هيذارة) A foolish talker.

A هيذام *hayzām*, Bold, strong. A glutton.

A هيذبى *hayzabaʼ*, A certain quick pace of a horse.

P هيذ خرمن *hayzi khirman*, A winnowing fan.

A هيذم *hayzam*, Quick, swift.

A هير *hayr* or *hīr*, North wind. Part of night.

P هير *her*, Fire. Humility, obedience.

A هيّر *hayyir*, The north wind. Part (of the night). One who plunges rashly into any business.

P هيراد *hīrād*, Appearing fresh and healthy.

P هيربد *her-bud*, A priest of a fire-temple. A judge of the Magi. A fire-worshipper. An ascetic.

A هيرة *hayrat*, Plain, level, smooth ground.

A هيردان *hayrudān*, A robber. A sort of plant.

P هيرسا *hersā*, One who in the course of his life has had no connection with woman.

A هيرط *hayrat*, Soft, loose, flaccid.

A هيرع *hayraʻ*, Light, inconstant (woman). Weak, cowardly, and worthless. A fool. (Wind) blowing with velocity and whirling aloft the dust.

A هيرعة *hayraʻat*, A shepherd's pipe made of a reed. The dust of the battle-field. A sylvan demon. A libidinous woman.

P هيرك *hīrak*, A kid. A young camel.

P هيرمند *hermand*, Humble, obedient. A priest of the Magi. Name of a river in the country of نيمروز *nīm roz*. A name of گشتاسب *gushtāsb*.

A هيرون *hayrūn*, A sort of date.

P هيرون *hīrūn*, A kind of cane.

P هيري *hīrī*, A species of violet.

P هيز *hīz*, A utensil used in baths for drinking or pouring water on the body. An infamous boy.

P هيزان *hīzān*, A beam, joist.

A هيزب *hayzab*, Sharp, strong. Fierce and strong (lion).

A هيزعة *hayzaʻat*, Fear. Tumult. The noise of combatants.

A هيزلة *hayzalat*, A beast of burden.

A هيزم *hayzam*, Hard, strong. A lion.

P هيزم *hezam*, Wood, timber. A staff, a stick. هيزم سوختني *hezami sokhtanī*, Fire-wood, fuel.

P هيزم كش *hezam-kash*, A carrier of wood, woodman. One who sets wood in order on the fire. هيزم كش ديو *hezam-kashi dev*, A hireling of the devil, *i.e.* a mischievous person, a breed-bate.

P هيزن *hīzan*, A beam, joist.

P هيزه *hīza*, A corn-fork.

P هيزينه *hīzīna*, A cylinder or rolling-stone, for consolidating and smoothing the clay-roofs of houses to keep out rain.

A هيس *hays*, (v. n. of هاس for هيس) Taking or receiving (any thing) in a great quantity. Walking, going. Treading down, trampling upon, beating to pieces. Dispersing, putting to flight (an army). A plough; any instrument for cultivating ground. *Haysi*, Cheer up! be of good courage! success to you!

A هيش *haysh*, (v. n. of هاش for هيش) Being in commotion, roused. Spoiling, laying waste. Collecting. Being talkative, verbose. Milking gently. A collection. (See هيج *hayj*.)

P هيش *hesh*, Nothing. A kind of linen stuff made in India. A ploughshare. A huge elephant (male or female).

A هيشة *hayshat*, Tumult, sedition: a mob. A chameleon.

P هيشت *hīsht*, A lance, a javelin.

P هيشتن *hīshtan*, To dismiss, leave, let fall, or hang loose. To roll round, to revolve.

A هيشر *hayshar*, Soft, loose, relaxed, weak. A wild artichoke. A tree growing in sand. Poppy.

A هيشوم *hayshūm*, A kind of tree.

A هيص *hays*, (v. n. of هاص for هيص) Throwing away, ejecting (as a bird muting). The dung of a bird. Violence. A contusion on the neck.

A هيصار *haysār*, A lion breaking his prey.

A هيصر *haysar*, A lion.

A هيصم *haysam*, A lion breaking in pieces his prey. A strong man. A kind of smooth stone.

A هيصمّية *haysamīyat*, Name of a branch of the sect كرامية *karāmīyat*.

A هيصور *haysūr*, A lion breaking his prey.

A هيض *hayz*, (v. n. of هاض for هيض) Breaking (a bone) again before (it) is quite consolidated. Making raw (a wound). Causing (one) to relapse into a distemper. (A propensity to sleep) rendering (one) lethargic. Muting (a bird). Disease upon disease. The dung of birds.

A هيضاء *hayzāʼ*, A crowd, multitude.

A هيضة *hayzat*, (v. n. of هاض for هيض) Being unwholesome and indigestible (food). A disease after a disease. A relapse into distress of mind or body. Cholera morbus; flux and vomit together.

P هيضه زدن *hayza zadan*, To vomit and purge.

A هيضل *hayzal*, A numerous army: armed body.

A هيضلة *hayzalat*, A stout middle-aged woman. A camel abounding in milk. An aged and fat she-camel. Clamour of the people. An armed body.

A هيضمان *hīzamān*, Horse-radish.

A هيط *hayt*, (v. n. of هاط for هيط) Calling out, crying, vociferating, being tumultuous. Noise, uproar, tumult, commotion.

A هيطل *haytal*, A fox. A small body of men making an excursion against an enemy. Name of a district beyond the Oxus.

A هيطلة *haytalat*, A cauldron of brass.

A هيع *hayʻ*, (v. n. of هاع for هيع) Being melted (lead). Vomiting by force. Being spread out. Being covetous. Being mean, feeble, or cowardly. Being impatient. Hungering. Longing for water.

A هيعان *hayaʻān*, (v. n. of هاع for هيع) Being timid, cowardly. Hungering.

A هيعة *hayʻat*, The flowing of any thing on the surface of the ground. Any thing obscene. Covetousness, avarice. Meanness, baseness. Weakness. Any horrible voice or terrifying sound.

A هيعرة *hayʻarat*, (v. n. of هيعر Q) Being restless, unable to remain quiet in one place. An impudent, inconstant, headstrong woman. Levity, inconstancy. The monster called غول *ghūl*.

A هيعرون *hayʻarūn*, An old woman. Misfortune.

A هيعوعة *hayʻūʻat*, (v. n. of هاع for هيع) Vomiting, puking. A vomit.

A هيف *hayf*, (v. n. of هاف for هيف) Running away (a servant). Excessive thirst. A hot, dry, south-west wind blowing from Yaman. *Hayf* or *hayaf*, (v. n. of هيف) Being slender round the waist, being clung or contracted in the belly. *Hīf*, (pl. of اهيف *ahyaf* and هيفاء) Slender-waisted.

A هيفاء *hayfāʼ*, (fem. of اهيف *ahyaf*) Slender-waisted (woman). Gaunt-bellied (mare).

A هيفان *hayfān*, Thirsty. *Hayafān*, Very thirsty.

A هيفك *hayfak*, Foolish (woman).

A هيق *hayk*, Thin and long. A (male) ostrich.

A هيقعة *haykaʻat*, The clashing of swords in battle. The noise of hard and dry substances struck one against another.

A هيقل *haykal*, A (male) ostrich. Lybian lizard.

A هيقلة *haykalat*, A certain mode of walking.

A هيقم *haykam*, A tall (male) ostrich. The vast ocean. Roar of the sea. Noise of swallowing.

A هيقمانيّ *haykumānīy*, Long, tall.

P هيكل *haykal*, A figure, image, face, form, stature or shape of the body. A temple of idolaters. An amulet or talisman inscribed with magic figures, hung round the body, as a defence against fascination or misfortune. هيكل بستن *haykal bastan*, To die. دلاوران قوي هيكل *dilāwarāni kawī-haykal*, Warriors of formidable appearance.

A هيكل *haykal*, A long or tall horse. A palace, stately edifice. A spring-habitation. An idol-temple. A christian church. A monastery. Any thing large-sized. A giant. A tall plant. هيكل رضوان *haykali rizwān*, The form of the heavens. P هيكل خاكي غبار *haykali khākī-ghubār*, The human body.

A هيكلة *haykalat*, (v. n. of هيكل Q) Being large and tall. A tall, big woman.

P هيكله *haykala*, Name of an herb.

A هيكوك *haykūk*, Silly, foolish with shrewdness.

P هيكر *haygar* also *haygir*, A brown horse with black tail and mane.

A هيل *hayl*, (v. n. of هال for هيل) Letting fall, or pouring out (flour or sand) without measure. Sands poured out. Sand, earth, or flour rolling down. Great affluence, abundance, plenty. Wind.

P هيل *hel*, The lesser cardamoms.

P هيلا *haylā*, A sparrow-hawk, merlin.

P هيلاج *haylāj*, The material body.

A هيلان *hayalān*, Sand or any thing similar poured out. Name of an Arabian tribe.

A هيلة *haylat*, Name of a goat that used to give milk to those who maltreated her, and to butt those kind to her. *Hīlat*, Terrors. A fearful business.

P هيلج *haylij*, The master of a family.

A هيلع *haylaʻ*, Weak.

P هيلك *haylak*, Small pebbles or gravel thrown amongst stones when building. The superficies of a wall; the interstices filled up with cement, between the rows of stones in a building.

A هيللة *haylalat*, (v. n. of هيلل Q) Saying لا اله الا الله *lā ilāha illa'llāh*, No god but God.

A هيلكون *haylakūn*, A toothless sithe or sickle.

A هيلمان *haylamān* or *haylumān*, Much wealth, great abundance, many cattle. Sand. Wind.

P هيلوي *hay* or *hīlūy*, A game played with nuts.

P هيله *hayla*, Master of a family, householder. *Hīla*, A hurricane. Stratagem.

P هيليدن *hīlīdan*, To dismiss, to leave.

A هيم *haym*, (v. n. of هام for هيم) Falling in love with a woman. هيم الله *haymu'llāh*, By God! *Hīm*, Thirsty (men or camels) *Huyum*, (pl. of هيام *hayām*) Sands which cannot be grasped in the hand by reason of their fineness.

P هيم *hayam*, (I) am, (I) exist, (I) live.

A هيماء *haymāʼ*, (A she-camel) distempered from drinking bad water. The disease itself. A desert without water.

A هيمان *haymān*, (pl. هيام *hiyām*) Thirsty (camel). Mad, insane. Enamoured. *Hayamān*, (v. n. of هام for هيم) Falling in love with a woman.

A هيمرة *haymarat*, A decrepit old woman.

P هيمستان *hemistān*, A wood. A wood-pile.

A هيمع *haymaʻ*, Sudden (death), Quickly executed (slaughter). Name of a tree.

A هيمنة *haymanat*, (v. n. of هيمن Q) Saying Amen. Covering (her) young with (her) wings (a bird). Guarding, protecting, watching over.

P هيمه *hema*, Fire-wood, fuel. Humble. هيمه

ترفروختن *hemaṣi tar farokhtan*, To sell wet fire-wood: to deceive, impose upon. *Hema* or *hayma*, Soup made of minced meat.

P هيمه ريز *hema-rez*, A bit or chip of wood.

P هيمه زفت *hema-zaft*, A thick plank or block (whereon butchers cut up their meat). The stocks.

P هيمه شكن *hema-shikan*, A breaker of wood.

P هيمه كش *hema-kash*, A carrier of wood.

A هيمي *hayma'*, (fem. of هيمان *haymān*) Thirsty.

A هين *hayn*, (and هيّن *hayyin*) (pl. اهوناء *ah-wināṣ* and اهيناء *ahyināṣ*) Quiet, easy, gentle. Modest. Vile, despicable. Any thing light and easy.

P هين *hīn*, Have a care! Make haste! Lo! behold! Thus, in this manner. One, only. A torrent, a flux of water. Speaking.

P هينا *hīnā*, A sword of the finest steel.

A هينام *haynām*, An unintelligible discourse.

P هيناهين *hīnāhīn*, Haste, expedition. Be quick.

A هينة *hay* or *hīnat*, Convenience, ease, facility. علي هينتك *ṣala' hīnatika*, (Go) at your leisure.

P هيند *hīnd*, (for هند *hind*) India.

A هينغ *haynagh*, A woman wholly shameless, exposing her nakedness to everybody: also one who laughs immoderately.

A هينم *haynam*, A low tone of voice. Cotton.

A هينمة *haynamat*, A low tone of voice. Reading the Kur'ān in a low tone. A certain pot-herb.

A هينوم *haynūm*, An unintelligible discourse.

A هينون *haynūna*, (pl. of هين) Easy, quiet (men).

A هيؤ *hayuṣa*, (fut. يهيؤ *yahyaṣu*) He wore a respectable appearance.

A هيوب *hayūb*, Formidable, dreaded. Timid.

A هيوع *huyūṣ*, (v. n. of هاع for هيع) Being timid, cowardly. Being hungry.

A هيوف *hayūf*, Very thirsty.

A هيول *hayūl*, A particle of dust seen floating in the rays of the sun.

G هيولي *hayūla'*, (or هيّولي *hayyūla'*) Matter. The first principle of every thing material. The first sketch of a picture or sculpture. Cotton.

A هيّولانيّ *hayyūlāniy*, Material.

A هيوم *hayūm*, Astonished, wandering about as a madman from love or any other cause.

P هيون *hayūn*, A camel of burden, the one that carries the hawdah. Any large animal. A horse.

P هيوند *hīwand*, Purity, chastity, continence.

A هيه *hayh*, One who retires or is driven away on account of the dirtiness of his garments. هيه هيه *hīh hīh*, Away! away! begone! Well done! bravo! encore! *Hiyah*, She.

A هيهات *hayhāt*, An extensive desert. هيهات هيهات *hayhāt hayhāt*, (or هيهاه هيهاه *hayhāh hayhāh*) Begone! away!

A هيهان *hayhān*, (هيهاه *hayhāh*, هايهات *hā-yihāt*, هايهان *hāyihān*, تهايهات *tahāyihāt*) varied in fifty-seven ways, the same as هيهات *hayhāt*.

P هي هي *hay hay*, A large goblet filled with wine which is drunk off at the end of a repast.

P هي *hayī* or *hiyī*, Essence, existence.

A هيء *hīṣi*, Used in calling one to eat or drink.

A هيئة *hīṣat*, (v. n. of هاء for هيأ) Desiring. State, quality, form, external appearance. علم هيئت *ṣilmi hīṣat*, Astronomy.

A هيئ *hayīṣ*, (or هيّئ) Respectable-looking.

ي

ي *yā* or *ye*, (called ياء حطّي *yāṣi hutti* or ياء مثنّات تحتاني *yāṣi musannāti tahtānī*, Yā doubly dotted below) The twenty-eighth and last letter of the Arabic alphabet, and the thirty-second and last of the Persian. In arithmetic it expresses ten; and in the almanacks it is the character for Jupiter and the sign Aquarius. Like ا *alif* and و *wāw*, this letter is also one of the حروف علّت *hurūfi ṣillat*, or letters of weakness (مدّ *madd*, Extension, or لين *līn*, Softness), being, like the English *y*, sometimes a consonant and sometimes a vowel. In the former case it has the sound of *y* in *youth*. As a vowel, it serves, when preceded by the mark كسر *kasr*, to form the long vowel ī or *ea* (as sounded in "police", and in "meat," and in "tear" of the eye; or *e* or *ea*, as sounded in "where", and "wear," and "tear"); and with فتحه *fatha*, the diphthong *ay* (as sounded in "aye," "aisle," "eye," "buy"). The first is called ياء معروف *yāṣi maṣrūf*, Known yā: the second ياء مجهول *yāṣi majhūl*, Unknown yā: and the third ياء ساكن ما قبل مفتوح *yāṣi sākin mā kabl maftūh*, Quiescent *yā* preceded by the vowel *a*. It is considered homogeneous with كسر *kasr*; and a quiescent ي *yā* never follows the vowel ضمّه *zamma*.

It is changed in Arabic, (1) into ء *hamza*, as بائع *bāṣiṣ* for بايع *bāyiṣ*, A seller; (2) into ا *alif*, as باع *bāṣa* for بيع *bayaṣa*, He sold; (3) into و *wāw*, as طوبي *tūba'* for طيبي *tība'*, Agreeable; (4) into ت *tā*, as اتّسر يتّسر *ittasara, yattasiru*, for ايتسر ييتسر *ītasara, yaytasiru*, He played, or he may play, with dice; (5) into ج *jīm*, as فقيج *fu-kaymaj* for فقيمي *fukaymī*, One of the tribe of فقيم *fukaym*. It is the substitute of ب *be* in ثعالي *saṣā-lī* for ثعالب *saṣālib*, Foxes: of و *wāw* in ميزان *mīzān* for موزان *miwzān*, Scales; and of س *se* in خامي *khāmī* for خامس *khāmis*, Fifth. It is employed to form the feminines in verbs: as, تقومين *takūmīna*, Thou shalt arise; قومي *kūmī*, Arise thou; and in nouns, as حبلي *hubla'*, Pregnant; عطشي *ṣatsha'*, Thirsty; ذكري *zikra'*, Mention. It also forms the diminutive; as, رجيل *rujayl*, A little man; and is used in forming the dual and plurals both regular and irregular.

In Persian it is sometimes substituted for ا *alif*, as يرمغان *yarmaghān* for ارمغان *armaghān*, A present; and for ه *he*, as شايگان *shāyagān* for شاهگان *shāhagān*, Like a king. When the substantive verb ام *am* or its inflexions are combined with the words كه *ki*, چه *chi*, or نه *na*, the ه *he* is often rejected, and the ا *alif* changed into ي *ye*, making كيست *kīst*, چيست *chīst*; نيست *nīst*, كيم *kiyam*; نيم *nayam* for كه است *ki ast*, Who is it? چه است *chi ast*, What is it? نه است *na ast*, It is not; كه ام *ki am*, Who am I? نه ام *na am*, I am not.

It follows the first of two nouns (to denote that the second is in the genitive case) if ending in ا *alif* or *wāw*; as, ميوها *mīvahā*, Fruits; ميوهاي شيرين *mīvahāyi shīrīn*, Sweet fruits.

The uses of the *yāṣi maṣrūf* are: 1. (نسبتي *nisbatī*) To express relation or connexion; as, هندي *hindī*, Belonging to India, Hindee; فارسي *fārsī*, Belonging to Persia, Persian, Persic. In Arabic the ي *yā* which forms the relative adjective requires the character *tashdīd* ّ or sign of reduplication, as ارضيّ *arziy*, Earthy, from ارض *arz*, Earth; مصريّ *misriy*, Egyptian, from مصر *misr*, Egypt. But Arabic adjectives, when used by Persian authors, are considered as Persian, and do not take tashdīd. Thus, لطف ربّانيّ *lutfun rabbānīyun* or اللطف الربّانيّ *al lutfu'r rabbānīyu*, Divine grace, becomes in Persian, لطف ربّاني *lutfi rabbānī*.

2. (خطابي *khitābī*) The affixed pronoun of the second person singular; as, گفتي *guftī*, Thou spakest; عالمي *ṣālimī*, Thou art wise: and in this case will be changed into hamza after the gentle aspirate, or the letter ي; as, آمدهٔ *āmadaṣi*, Thou hast come; كهٔ *kiṣi*, Who art thou? چهٔ *chiṣi*, What art thou? نهٔ *naṣi*, Thou art not; آدمي ء *ādamīṣi*, Thou art a man.

3. (ياء مصدر *yāṣi masdar*) Forming the verbal or abstract noun: زربخشي *zar-bakhshī*, The act of bestowing gold; نيكي *nekī*, Goodness; بدي *badī*, Badness; دانائي *dānāṣī*, Wisdom.

4. (لياقت *liyākat*) Expressing fitness; as, كشتني *kushtanī*, Deserving of being killed; سوختني *sokhtanī*, Fit to be burned.

5. (متكلّم يا القابي *mutakallim* or *alkābī*) Expressing in Arabic the pronoun of the first person singular; as, ربّي *rabbī*, My lord; ضربني *zurabanī*, He struck me: and after مقصوره ا *alif maksūra*; as, عصاي *ṣasa'ya'*, My staff. It is also used as a mark of intensive superlative; as, احمري *ahmarī*, Most exceedingly red.

6. (فاعل *fāṣil*) Affixed to nouns, shewing an actor or agent; as, جنگي *jangī*, A warrior; حكمتي *hikmatī*, A man of science.

7. (مفعول *mafṣūl*) Also affixed to nouns, expressing the object of some act; as, سندي *sanadī*, Established by authority; لعني *laṣnatī*, Cursed; دستخطّي *dast-khattī*, Signed.

8. (مشابه *mushābih*) Implying similitude, or assumption of character; as in these lines of Nazāmī:

زاغ بفرّ تو همائی کند
zāgh ba farri tu humāʼī kunad;
سرکه رسد پیش تو پائی کند
sar ki rasad peshi tu pāʼī kunad.

"The crow, from thy magnificence, imitates the humā. The head that approaches thee acts the part of a foot."

9. It is sometimes used to eke out measure (اشباع *ishbāʻ*); as when كمالي *kamālī* is put for كمال *kamāli*.

Of *yāʼi majhūl*, The uses are—1. (تنكير يا وحدت *tankīr* or *wahdat*) Expressing unity or the indefinite article *a*: as, مردي *marde*, A man, one man. كتابي ازكتب خانه بيار *kitābe az kutub-khāna biyār*, Bring *a book* (no matter what book) from the library. This is sometimes applied to express excess; as in this expression of *Hāfiz*, عشق آفتي است *ʻishk āfate ast*, Love is one (*i.e.* a very great) mischief. Sometimes, on the other hand, it signifies diminution or contempt; as,

هست خاكي كه بآبي نخرد طوفان را
Hast khāke ki ba ābe na kharad tūfānrā.

"There is a *little earth* which esteems the universal deluge less than the *smallest drop* of water."

On the other hand, it is sometimes used to denote veneration; as, زيد مردي است *zayd marde ast*, Zayd is a *man*, *i.e.* eminent for all the qualities that may become a man.

After the gentle aspirate (هاى مخفف *hāʼi mukhaffaf*) the indefinite ي is changed to hamza: as, بندهٔ *bandaʼe*, A slave; ديوانهٔ *dīwānaʼe*, A madman. Also after the proper names of men celebrated for a certain attribute, it converts these into epithets significant of such attribute: as, فرعوني *firʻawne*, A Pharaoh, or proud man; حاتمي *hātime*, A Hātim, or liberal man.

2. (صفت *sifat*) Affixed to nouns, supplies the place of the demonstrative pronoun *that*; and has necessarily in the same sentence the relative كه *ki*, either closely attached or at some distance. This Kāim says—

دميكه با قدّ دلجوي تو نگاه كنم
dame ki bā haddi dil-jūyi tu nigāh kunam;
ز پا در افتم و بي اختيار آه كنم
zi pā dar uftam u bī ikhtiyār āh kunam.

"*That instant*, when I look upon thy heart-alluring form, I lose my stability, and sigh without self-controul."

3. (استمراري *istimrārī*) Affixed to the preterite of verbs, to convey the idea of perpetuity, or continued action: as, زيد هر روز نزد من آمدي *zayd har roz nazdi man āmade*, Zayd *continued to visit* me daily. With the optative and conditional conjunction كاش *kāsh*, and اگر *agar*, it comes in place of مي *me* of the imperfect; as in these lines of Shaykh Awhadu'd dīn—

گر مونس و همدمي دمي يافتمي
gar mūnis u ham-dame dame yāftame;
زو چاره و مرهمي همي يافتمي
zū chāra u marhame hame yāftame;
از آتش دل سوختمي سر تا پا
az ātishi dil sokhtame sar tā pā;
در ديده اگرنمي نمي يافتمي
dar dīda agar name name yāftame.

"If I *had* for a short time *possessed* an affectionate friend, I *should have found* in him a remedy and a plaster. I *should have been consumed* from head to foot in the fire of my heart, if I *had not found* moisture in my eyes." In the second and fourth instances above, the final *yā* appears redundant, as the مي *me* and هي *hame* are also preserved. Mawlawī Rūm says—

نقره ؤ زر گرنه بودندي نهان
nukra ʼu zar gar na būdande nihān;
پرورش كي يافتندي زيركان
parwarish kay yāftande zīrakān.

"If silver and gold *were not* concealed, how *should* the wise *obtain* the means of subsistence?"

كاش كه سعادت شهادت در يافتمي
kāsh ki saʻādati shahādat dar yāftame;

"Would that I *had* obtained the happiness of martyrdom."

4. (زائد *zāʼid*) Redundant after a quiescent ا *alif*: as, بكشاي *bukshāʼe* for بكشا *bukshā*, Open thou!

P يا *yā*, Or. O! If, unless. Either. يا خود *yā khwud*, O certainly! undoubtedly! يا بخت يا تخت *yā bakht yā takht*, Either a throne or a winding-sheet! victory or a glorious death! (like the saying of Nelson, A coronet or Westminster Abbey).

A يا *yā*, Milk remaining in the breast of a woman. (pl. يايات *yāyāt*) The letter ي *yā*. O! يا الله *yā allāh*, O God! يا ليت *yā layta*, Would to heaven! I wish to God! يا ليتني *yā laytanī*, O would that I! يا ويلتي *yā waylatī*, O! woe is me.

P ياء *yāʼ*, A nick at the end of a bow in which the string goes.

A يأاعي *yaʼāʼī*, (pl. of يؤيؤ *yuʼyuʼ*) Kestrels, inferior kinds of hawks that cannot be trained.

P ياب *yāb*, Face, countenance. Non-existent. Lost, perished. Vain, futile, frivolous, fruitless, abortive, unprofitable. The contracted participle of يافتن *yāftan*, To find, used in a compound form: as, كام ياب *kām-yāb*, Who finds what he desires, *i.e.* fortunate, happy, powerful. بارياب *bār-yāb*, Admitted at court. A courtier. ره ياب شدن *rah-yāb shudan*, To find the way.

P يابا *yābā*, Finding.

P يابان *yābān*, A desert; a place far from cities.

P ياباني *yābānī*, Wild, desert.

P يابر *yābir*, A fee, a fief, charity-lands.

A يابس *yābis*, (pl. يبس *yabs*) Dry, naturally dry. يابس مزاج *yābis-mizāj*, Of a dry temperament.

P يابنده *yābinda*, A finder, discoverer.

P يابو *yābū*, A pony, nag, cob. A pack-horse. A draught-horse.

P يابه كردن *yāba kardan*, To ask, to beg.

P يابيدن *yābīdan*, To find. To get.

P ياتش *yātish*, A guard stationed at a palace-gate.

P ياتش خانه *yātish-khāna*, A guard-house.

P ياج *yāj*, The game of tip-cat.

A ياجوج *yājūj*, One who runs up and down.

A يأجوج *yaʼjūj*, One who kindles a fire. A mover of sedition. Gog. The people of Eastern Scythia, beyond Imaus. يأجوج و مأجوج *yaʼjūj wa maʼjūj*, Gog and Magog.

A ياجور *yājūr*, A brick.

P ياختن *yākhtan*, To draw (a sword). To strike. To throw. To disclose. To ask, inquire.

P ياخته *yākhta*, Drawn (sword). Taught, educated. A chamber. Wine. A small wine-jar. Like, resembling.

P ياختي *yākhtī*, He drew out. He designed. He threw. He disclosed. He was drawing out, &c. Thou drewest out, &c.

P ياد *yād*, Remembrance, recollection, memory. Watching, watchfulness. A picture, painting, figure, image. ياد جناب مولا *yādi janābi mawlā*, Remembrance or invocation of God. ياد دادن *yād dādan*, To remind. ياد كردن *yād kardan*, (ياد داشتن *yād dāshtan*, or ياد گرفتن *yād giriftan*) To remember, recollect, make mention, keep in memory, be mindful. To learn, get by heart. ببدي ياد كردن *ba badī yād kardan*, To speak ill of, or recollect any thing bad of another. بياد آمدن *ba yād āmadan*, To come in mind. بياد آوردن *ba yād āwardan*, To recollect, call to mind. بياد بودن *ba yād būdan*, To dwell on the mind, to remain fixed in the memory.

P يادار *yādār*, Remember, bear in mind.

P ياداشتي *yādāshtī*, Empty-handed, poor. Avaricious, stingy.

P ياد دار *yād-dār*, Remember, keep in remembrance. Mindful, remembering. One who remembers or recollects.

P ياد داشت *yād-dāsht*, (or ياداشت *yā dāsht*) A memorandum, a memorial, a note. Recollection.

P ياد ده *yād-dih*, A reminder: remindful.

P ياد دهي *yād-dihī*, Reminiscence.

P يادر *yādar*, The twelfth of the month Tīr.

P يادزشت *yād-zisht*, (for *yādi zisht*) Calumny, recollecting or relating any thing bad of another.

P يادست *yādast*, It is remembered. A kind of game in which certain words are used, which if one person does not pronounce upon receiving something from another, he loses.

P ياد كار *yād-kār*, (ياد گار *yādgār*, and ياد كرد *yād-kard*) Any thing given as a memorial, a valuable present to a mistress or friend. A souvenir, keepsake. A monument, any thing memorable, worthy of remembrance, or which recalls a person or thing to memory.

P يادگاري *yādgārī*, Remembrance.

P ياد گيرنده *yād-giranda*, One who learns or retains any thing by heart.

P يادندان *yādandān*, All the kings of the world.

P يادہ *yāda*, A bribe to a judge; whatever is given for the performance of any unlawful act. The retentive faculty.

P يار *yār*, A friend, lover, companion, comrade. An assistant, defender. A mistress. Strength, power. A pestle. يار جان *yāri jān*, An intimate friend. يار غار *yāri ghār*, A companion in a cave, *i.e.* an intimate friend, confidant. A name of Abū bakr. يار وفادار *yāri wafā-dār*, A sincere friend, constant lover. يار شدن *yār shudan*, To contract friendship, to be friendly.

A يارّ *yārr*, (حارٌّ يارٌّ *hārrun yārrun*, or حرّان يرّان *harrānun yarrānun*) Hot, scorching, scalding.

P يارا *yārā*, (the final ا *alif* being in lieu of يا *yā* or اي *ay*, prefixed, as, يا يار *yā yār* or اي يار *ay yār*) O friend! Boldness, courage. Strength, force, power of resistance. A wound. Occasion.

P يارابہ *yārāba*, Rape-root; bread made of it.

P يار اسپند *yār ispand*, (also يار اسفند *yār isfand*) Isfandyār, son of Gushtāsb.

P ياران *yārān*, A friend. A polite, well-spoken man; a jovial, agreeable companion. Purposing, resolving. (pl. of يار *yār*) Friends. Followers, clients. ياران شدن *yārān shudan*, To contract friendship, to be friendly. صحبت ياران *suhbati yārān*, A jovial company, a meeting of friends.

P يارانہ *yārāna*, Friendly.

P ياراي *yārāy*, O friend!

A يارب *yā rabb*, O Lord! O God!

A يارّة *yārrat*, Fire.

P يارج *yāraj*, The heart. A bracelet.

P يارد *yārad*, (the third person sing. fut. of يارستن *yārastan*) He will inculcate good morals. He will be able. What is in one's hand or power, whatever is possible or can be performed.

T ياردم *yārdum*, (Tartaric) Assistance.

P يار رس *yār-ras*, A helper. Aid, help.

P يارستن *yārastan*, To inculcate good morals, teach politeness, educate well. To be modest or bashful. To be able. To stretch out the hand. To tyrannize over.

P يارسہ *yārasa*, A bat or rere-mouse.

P يارش *yārish*, Friendship, love.

P يارغو *yārghū*, Strife, contention, litigation; whatever disturbance happens amongst men. A court of justice.

P يارغوچي *yārghūchī*, Strife. An arbitrator.

P يارفروشي *yār-faroshī*, Approval, assent.

A يارق *yārak*, (from P يارہ) A broad bracelet.

P يارك *yārak*, A little friend, a sort of friend. The membrane that encloses a fœtus. A child's caul. An idle, boasting fellow. A mode of singing usual among debauchees in بدخشان *badakhshān*.

P ياركي *yārakī*, Power, strength, ability.

P يارم *yāram*, A half.

P يارمند *yārmand*, Friendly. An assistant. Possessed of friends.

P يارمندي *yārmandī*, Aid, assistance. يارمندي كردن *yārmandī hardan*, To render assistance.

P يارنامہ *yār-nāma*, A good act, good name.

P يارند *yārand*, Detestation, abhorrence. Imprecation, curse. Contumely, ridicule. They are able.

A ياروقية *yārūkiyat*, A village near Aleppo.

A ياروج *yārūj*, A sword. An arrow, javelin, spear, or dart.

P ياروي *yārūy* or *yārway*, A wound.

P يارہ *yāra*, A broad ornamental bracelet. A collar for the neck. A glove, gauntlet. The wrist. A wound. Power, strength. Measure, quantity. A certain aperient medicine. A bold, also a shrewd man. Friendship. Necessity. Tax, toll, revenue.

P يارہ گير *yāra-gīr*, A tax-gatherer, collector of revenue. A receiver of bribes.

P ياري *yāre*, A friend. A certain friend. *Yārī*, Friendship, intimacy. Assistance, aid. Favour. Power. The wives of two brothers. Two women engaged to the same man: a rival wife. ياري كردن *yārī kardan*, (ياري دادن *yārī dādan*, or ياريدن *yārīdan*) To assist, help, favour, benefit, serve, do good offices, befriend. To abet. To be able.

P ياريگر *yārīgar*, A helper, ally, assistant.

P ياري گري *yārīgarī*, Help, assistance.

P ياز *yāz*, A countryman, peasant, rustic. Yawning, stretching. Stretching out the hand to take any thing. A tree extending its branches. Growing. Measuring, mensuration. A cubit, the distance from the elbow to the tip of the finger. A measurer. A step. Intention, design. One who intends or purposes. The spring.

P يازاب *yāzāb*, (or يازابہ) A kind of pickle.

P يازان *yāzān*, One who intends or endeavours to acquire any thing. A measurer.

P يازدن *yāzidan*, To extend the hand to take any thing. To long for. To be exalted. To gape, yawn. To intend, endeavour, design.

P يازدہ *yāzdah*, Eleven.

P يازدهم *yāzdahum*, The eleventh.

P يازش *yāzish*, Gaping, yawning. Desire, will, wish. Growth, extension. Stature. Form, shape, figure. Length.

A يازع *yāzi'*, One who prohibits, averts, keeps off.

P يازند *yāzand*, Figure, form, appearance.

P يازندہ *yāzanda*, A purposer, resolver, wisher.

P يازہ *yāza*, Yawning, stretching. Trembling.

P يازي *yāzī*, A husbandman, peasant, rustic.

P يازيدگي *yāzīdagī*, Oscitation, yawning, a yawn.

P يازيدن *yāzīdan*, To yawn, gape, oscitate, stretch out the arms. To embrace. To grow up. To wish, desire, long for, design, purpose.

P يازہ *yāja*, Foolish words, any thing trifling, futile, vain. A vagabond. A foolish fellow that knows not what he does.

A يأس *yaʼs*, (v. n. of يأس) Despairing. Knowing. Being apparent, manifest. Despair, desperation, hopelessness, despondency. A desperate thing. *Yaʼas*, A consumption.

P ياس *yās*, The jasmine. Fear, terror.

A ياس *yās*, (or يس *yās*) (supposed to be a contraction of ياانسان *yā insānu*, O man! or يا سيّد *yā sayyidu*) O Lord!

P ياسا *yāsā*, (or ياسہ *yāsa*) (Tartar words), A royal mandate, edict, proclamation. A law; code of laws, those especially made by order of Changīz Khān. Capital punishment. چوب ياسا *chūbi* (or *chobi*) *yāsā*, The bastinado.

P ياساق *yāsāk*, The Moghul code. Explanation, investigation, arranging. Drawing up an army. Explanation of a doubt, rectification of an error. Prohibition. Chastisement. شمشير ياساق *shamshīri yāsāk*, (and چوب ياساق *chobi yāsāk*) The sword or staff of correction; those with which criminals are punished by sentence of the judge.

P ياسان *yāsān*, Fit, proper. Name of a prophet.

A يأسة *yaʼsat*, (v. n. of يأس) Despairing. Despair, desperation.

P ياستن *yāstan*, Power, strength.

P ياسج *yāsij*, (or ياسچ *yāsuch*) A pointed arrow. An arrow with the king's name on it.

A ياسر *yāsir*, Soft, easy, smooth. Kind, humane. Any thing that may be easily accomplished. Unfortunate. The left side. One who games with cards, dice, or the arrows called ازلام *azlām*. (pl. ايسار *aysār*) One who presides and distributes the joints of a slaughtered camel, according to the lots. A camel-butcher.

A P ياسم ياسمن *yāsim*, *yāsam*, *yāsaman*, ياسمون *yāsamūn*, or ياسمين *yāsamīn*) Jasmine or jessamine.

P ياسمن بو *yāsaman-bo* (or *bū*) Scented like jasmine. ياسمن بوئي *yāsaman-boī* (or *būī*) Jasmine-fragrance.

P ياسہ *yāsa*, Law, regulation. Way, manner, custom. Will, wish, desire.

A ياسين *yāsīn*, Pharaoh.

P ياش *yāsh*, A kind of jasper.

P ياشداش *yāshdāsh*, Cotemporary, of same age.

P ياشق *yāshuk*, Name of a tree.

P ياشہ *yāsha*, A foolish, useless fellow.

A ياصول *yāsūl*, Root, foundation.

A ياعاط *yā'āt*, Used in crying to horses or wolves. An alarm given by a sentinel on the approach of an enemy.

P ياغمہ *yāghma*, Prey, plunder.

A ياغوز *yāghūz*, Name of a place.

P ياغي *yāghī*, The ground, earth. An enemy.

P ياغي گري *yāghīgarī*, Enmity, hostility.

P ياف *yāf*, Vain, foolish, futile.

P يافا *yāfā*, Jaffa (Joppa).

P يافت *yāft*, He found. Discoverable, to be

found. نا يافت شدن yāft shudan, To be found. نا يافت nā yāft, Not to be found.

T يافت yāfit, Japhet, son of Noah.

P يافتن yāftan, To find, discover. To obtain, acquire, get, meet with, experience. اتّصال يافتن ittisāl yāftan, To be joined, united. امتياز يافتن imtiyāz yāftan, To obtain distinction, get promotion. جراحت يافتن jarāhat yāftan, To be wounded. دست يافتن dast yāftan, To prevail. در يافتن dar yāftan, To understand, comprehend.

P يافته yāfta, Found, discovered. A finder. Arrival. Attainment. A receipt. A diploma or privilege of immunity from taxes. Name of an herb, رغبت يافتهٔ كبار raghbat-yāfta-i kibār, Esteemed by the great. بار يافته bār-yāfta, (pl. بار يافتگان bār-yāftagān) A courtier; admitted at court. ستم يافته sitam-yāfta, Oppressed.

P يافته يزد yāfta yazd, Name of a city in Persia celebrated for its college, the manufacture of aprons and rose-water.

A يافث yāfis, Japhet.

P يافر yāfar or yāfir, A dancer, mountebank.

A يافع yāfiʻ, (pl. يفعة yafaʻat and يفعان yufʻān) Tall. A young man about twenty years of age.

A يافعات yāfiʻat, Arduous (affairs): high (hills).

A يافوخ yāfūkh, (pl. يوافيخ yawāfīkh) The middle or fore part of the head; the membraneous part found in new-born infants at the coronal and sagittal commissures, which, in time, hardens into bone. The middle, also the greater part of the night.

A يافوف yāfūf, Timid, fearful, cowardly. Weak, tired. A stammerer. Brisk, active, quick. Bitter food. The young of the Asiatic woodcock.

P يافه yāfa, Vain, futile, frivolous, absurd. A foolish speech. Ribaldry, obscenity. One who speaks ridiculously or ludicrously. A joke, jest, drollery, witticism, humour. Scattered, dissipated, lost, missing. Absent, invisible. Thus, in this manner.

P يافه داري yāfa-dārī, Idle talk.

P يافه دراي yāfa-darāy, An idle talker.

A P ياقوت yākūt, (pl. يواقيت yawākīt) A ruby. A sapphire. A precious stone. ياقوت احمر yākūti ahmar, A red gem, ruby. ياقوت خام yākūti khām, Lip of a mistress. ياقوت رمّاني yākūti rummānī, (or ياقوت ناروان yākūti nārwān) A precious kind of ruby. ياقوت روان yākūti rawān, Tears of blood. Red wine. ياقوت زرد yākūti zard, The sun. ياقوت سربسته yākūti sar basta, Mouth of a mistress. Lips closed in silence. ياقوت كبود yākūti kabūd, A blue gem, sapphire. ياقوت مذاب yākūti muzāb, Red wine. Tears of blood. Blood.

A ياقوتة yākūtat, A single ruby.

T ياقي yākī, (Tartaric) Burning; cautery.

T ياقيجي yākīchī, A burner.

P ياك yāk, Name of a king.

P ياكند yākand, Ruby-coloured. A ruby.

P يال yāl, A horse's mane. A bird's comb or crest. Lust, rut. Stature, shape, posture. The neck. The root of the neck. The arm from the shoulder to the elbow. The hand, both hands. Corpulent, big, strong. Power, strength. A hero, an athletic man. Drunk. Hurtful. Servants, household, family. Face, cheek. The vault of heaven. One who plans any thing. يال بال yāl bāl, (or يال و بال yāl u bāl) Crest and wing. بيال آمدن ba yāl āmadan, To be in rut.

T P يالغ yāligh, (or يالغي yālighī) A cup made of rhinoceros-horn. A wooden drinking-cup.

P يالمند yālmand, The master of a family.

P يالوانه yālwāna, A swallow; small water-fowl.

P يالود yālūd, The sea-shore.

P يالوغ yālūgh, A cup of a rhinoceros' horn.

P يالونيك yālūnīk, A hero, Hercules, giant, renowned warrior. Gestures or behaviour of lovers.

P ياله yāla, A cow's horn.

A يا ليت yā layt, I wish, would that!

A ياليل yālīl, Name of an idol.

P يام yām, A post-horse.

A يام yām, Ham, the son of Noah.

A يامن yāmin, Happy, fortunate, prosperous.

A يأمور yaʼmūr, A certain animal living in the desert. A species of mountain-goat.

A يامور yāmūr, A male camel.

P يان yān, Incoherent, unintelligible language. The reverie of a fanatic, or raving of one in a delirium. A trance.

A يانع yāniʻ, Ripe (fruit). Red, scarlet-coloured.

P يانه yāna, A mortar. Lint-seed. Yā nih, If not, otherwise.

A ياني yānī, (or يانو yānū) John.

P يانيچ yānīch, A grave.

A يانيسون yānīsūn, Anise.

P ياود yāvad, (for يابد yābad) He may find.

P ياور yāwar, An assistant, coadjutor. A friend, companion. Assistance. A pestle. The tenth day of every solar month.

P ياوري yāwarī, Assistance. Victory. Boldness, audacity: power, strength. Society, company. A wound. ياوري كردن yāvari kardan, To favour.

P ياوگي yāwagī, Loss, ruin. Absurdity, vain talk.

P ياوند yāwand, A king. An obtainer, finder.

P ياوه yāva, Lost, ruined. Vain, foolish, futile, absurd, stupid. Men or things whose origin is not known. Fictions, foolish expressions. ياوه كردن yāva kardan, To lose.

P ياوه تاز yāva-tāz, An idle, worthless fellow.

P ياوه دراي yāva-darāy, A vain, prating babbler.

A ياويّ yāwiy, (fem. ياويّة yāwiyat) Belonging to the letter ي yā; verses rhyming in it.

A ياه yāh yāh or yāhi yāhi, Used by a shepherd in calling to his companion, or to his camels.

P ياهو yāhū, Jehovah. Adieu. ياهو كردن yāhū kardan, To bid farewell.

A ياهياه yā hayāh, (dual masc. يا هياهان yā hayāhāni, fem. يا هياهتان yā hayāhatāni, pl. masc. يا هياهون yā hayāhūna, fem. يا هياهات yā hayāhāt) Welcome.

P ياي yāy, Sick, indisposed, unwell, unsound.

A يايا yāyā, Courage!

A يأيأ yaʼyāʼ, The cry of the sparrow-hawk. Yaʼyāʼ, (and يأيأة yaʼyaʼat) (v. n. of يأيأ Q) Receiving kindly, soothing, treating with humanity. Calling to one repeatedly with the particle يا yā, Ho! Calling to people, assembling them together by crying out يا يا yā yā. Making (camels) quiet by crying اي اي ay ay.

A يائس yāʼis, Despondent, despairing, hopeless.

A يائسة yāʼisat, Barren, despairing (woman).

P يايه yāya, Silly, stupid.

A يايه yāyah, Courage!

A يآئئ yaʼāʼiʼ, (pl. of يؤيؤ yuʼyuʼ) Kestrel-hawks.

P يايي yāyī, Sick, unwell, miserable, unsound.

A يائيّ yāʼiy, Containing the letter ي yā.

P يب yab, A pointed arrow. (Samarcand dialect) Also, likewise. So much the worse.

P يباب yabāb, A desert.

P يبابگر yabābgar, A destroyer, spoiler.

P يبات yabāt, Waste, desolate, uncultivated.

A P يباس yabās, Pudendum, pubes. Shame, ignominy, dishonour. A bad-tempered woman.

P يبروج yabrūj, The mandrake.

A يبروح yabrūh, The mandrake.

A يبرين yabrīn, Name of a sandy tract in Arabia: also of a village near Aleppo.

A يبس yabs, (v. n. of يبس) Being or becoming dry. Withered, dry. (A sheep) without milk. (pl. of يابس yābis) Dry. Yubs, (v. n. of يبس) Becoming dry. Dryness. Stiffness. Yabas, Dry (woman) producing nothing. (A sheep) without milk. Yabas or yabs, Naturally dry, that has never become wet. A wet place becoming dry. Yabis, Dry.

P يبست yabast, A herb like spinage.

A يبوسة yubūsat, Dryness, aridity, siccity.

P يبه yaba, Injury, mischief. Spoil, damage.

A يبيس yabīs, Dry, withered (vegetable). Sweat.

P يت yat, is written for ات at, after nouns ending in ا or و: as, عصايت ʻasāyat, Thy staff; گيسويت gīsūyat, Thy ringlets.

A يتاجر yatājara, (a strange kind of verb) He turned away.

P يتاق yatāk or yutāk, Guard, care, watch. يتاق كردن yatāk kardan, To guard, preserve.

P يتاق دار yatāk-dār, A guard, watchman.

P يتاقي yatākī or yutākī, A guard, watchman.

A يتامى yatāmaʼ, (pl. of يتيم yatīm) Orphans.

A يتم yatm, Solicitude, grief. Yatm or yutm, (v. n. of يتم) (A child) being deprived of a father, (or a young animal) of its dam. Being solitary, alone, unique, or incomparable. Yutm, Separation. Solitude. Orphanage. Yatam, (v. n. of يتم) Becoming torpid, lazy, indolent, fatigued. Slowness (in travelling). Loss of a father, orphanage.

A يتمان *yatmān*, Under age, pupil, ward, minor.

A يتمة *yatamat*, (pl. of يتيم *yatīm*) Orphans.

A يتن *yatn*, (v. n. of يتن) Coming forth with the feet foremost (a child).

A يتوع *yatūʿ*, (يتّوع *yattūʿ* or يتوّع *yatūwuʿ*) Any plant yielding a milky juice, such as شبرم *shubrum*, لاعية *lāʿiyat*, ماهودانه *māhūdāna*, عرطنيثا *ʿartanīsā*, mezereon, and agnus castus.

A يتيم *yatīm*, (pl. ايتام *aytām*, يتامى *yatāma'*, يتمة *yatamat*, and ميتمة *maytamat*) An orphan, pupil, ward. An animal that has lost its dam. Singular, unique, uncommon, rare, incomparable. A servant. A robber, cut-throat, assassin. درّ يتيم *durri yatīm*, (or P يتيم دريا) A precious pearl.

A يتيمة *yatīmat*, An orphan-girl. A fine pearl.

P يتيم خانه *yatīm-khāna*, Assassins' rendezvous.

P يتيم دار *yatīm-dār*, (A woman, a mother) having fatherless children.

A يثرب *yasrib*, Name of the city of Madīna.

A يثربيّ *yasribīy*, Of the city of Madīna.

A يثريط *yusrīt*, (A camel) shooting liquid dung.

A يثلث *yaslas* and *yaslis*, Firm, fixed, solid.

A يثموم *yasmūm*, The plant ثمام *sumām*.

P يج *yaj*, The interior part of the cheek.

A يحابر *yahābir*, (and يحابير *yahābīr*) (pl. of يحبور *yahbūr*) Young bustards.

A يحبور *yahbūr*, Glad, smiling, happy. A kind of bird. A male bustard.

A P يحتمل كه *yahtamil ki*, It is suspected that; it may be; it is possible.

P يحكم *yahkam*, A summer-house.

A يحمور *yahmūr*, Red. Name of a beast; also of a bird. A wild ass.

A يحموم *yahmūm*, Black. Smoke. A black mountain. A kind of bird. Name of a horse.

A يحيا *yahya'*, St. John the Baptist. John.

A يحيط *yahīt*, A barren year.

A (ابو) يحيى *(abū) yahya'*, Death.

P يخ *yakh*, Ice. يخ بستن *yakh bastan*, To freeze. يخ در بهشت *yakh dar bihisht*, A kind of sweetmeat. بر يخ نوشتن *bar yakh navishtan*, (To write upon the ice) To labour in vain.

A يخاضير *yakhāzīr*, (pl. of يخضور) Verdant spots.

P يخاو *yakhāv*, Ice-water, *i.e.* cooled with ice.

P يخاور *yakhāwar*, Congealed, frozen.

P يخ بسته *yakh-basta*, Frozen, ice-bound.

P يخچال *yakh-chāl*, An ice-house. Any place or vessel in which ice is kept.

P يخچه *yakhcha*, Hail. A hailstone.

P يخدان *yakhdān*, A place for keeping ice, an icehouse. A travelling-portmanteau or trunk.

P يخشودن *yakhshūdan*, To curry (a horse).

P يخصص *yakhsis*, A larger kind of parsley.

A يخضود *yakhzūd*, A branch fresh cut.

A يخضور *yakhzūr*, (pl. يخاضير) A verdant spot.

A يخمور *yakhmūr*, Hollow and unsteady. A kind of white sea-shell.

P يخني *yakhnī*, Cooked, dressed. A store of food. Hot and cold. يخني نهادن *yakhnī nihādan*, To lay up a store.

P يخني نهاده *yakhnī-nihāda*, Stored, laid by.

P يخور *yakhwar*, Frozen. Icy.

P يخ يخ *yakh yakh*, A word used in making camels lie down.

A يد *yad*, (originally يدي *yady*) (pl. ايدي *aydī* and يديّ *yudīy*) The hand. The arm from the shoulder to the tips of the fingers. Fore-foot in animals. Wing of a bird. A handle. Horn of a bow. A branch, portion (of a tribe). End (of a piece of cloth), extremity (of a garment) hanging down. A sleeve. (pl. يديّ *yadīy*, *yidīy*, *yudīy*, and ايدي *aydī*) Assistance, aid, succour, protection, benefit, favour, service. A cry for help. A crowd, troop, body. Power, vigour, strength. Force (of the wind). Prevention of injury and oppression. The keeping of any one from his rights. Authority, dignity, grandeur, rank, office, sovereignty. Sedateness, gravity. Possession. Riches, wealth, affluence. Surrender, submission. Baseness, meanness of spirit. A promise, pledge, engagement. Length, extension of time. Eating. Repentance. A way, road. Yaman. يد بيضا *yadi bayzā*, A miracle (in allusion to the white hand of Moses). يد الدهر *yadu'd dahr*, Ever. تقبيل اليد *takbīlu'l yad*, Kissing hands. اعطاه عن ظهر يد *aʿtāhu ʿan zahri yadin*, He gave it gratis.

A يدّ *yadd*, The hand.

A يداء *yudāʿ*, A pain in the hand.

A يدان *yadāni*, (dual) The two hands. مالك يدان به *mā laka yadāni bihi*, You have not the power of doing that. باليدين *bi'l yadayn*, (I bought it) at two different prices, sometimes at one, sometimes at another. بين يديه *bayn yadayhi*, Between his hands, *i. e.* before him, in his presence. ذو اليدين *zū'l yadayn*, Ambidexter, using both hands. على يديه *ʿala' yadayhi*, By his assistance, under his auspices. هذا ما قدّمت يداك *hāzā mā kaddamat yadāk*, That is what you deserved (what your hands have sent on before). اوّل ذات يدين *awwala zāti yadayni*, The first thing. سقط في يديه *sukita* (or اسقط *ushkita*) *fī yadayhi*, He repented.

A يدة *yadat*, The hand.

P يدره *yadra*, (Hedera) Ivy.

A يد طولائى *yad tūlāʾī*, Power, strength. Skill.

P يدقه *yadaka*, The dwarf-elder.

P يدك *yadak*, A led horse. يدكچي *yadakchī*, One that leads a horse of state; a groom.

P يدمن *yadmin*, (in zand and Pāz.) The hand.

A يدويّ *yadawīy*, Manual, handy. Possessive.

P يده *yada*, The production of an appearance of snow or rain by magic.

A يدي *yady*, (v. n. of يدي) Hurting in the hand; amputating or lopping it off. Catching (a wild beast) by the fore-foot. Receiving a benefit. Conferring a favour. Despairing; desperation. *Yada'*, (v. n. of يدي) Losing the hand, having a withered hand. The hand. Wide (garment).

A يديّ *yadīy*, Possessing, possessive, possessory. Ready, manual, handy, nimble-handed. Large; also narrow-sleeved (garment). عيش يدي *ʿīshi yadī*, An easy, agreeable life; also distress, narrow circumstances. *Yadīy*, *yidīy*, or *yudīy*, (pl. of يد *yad*) Hands. Fore-feet. Benefits.

A يدياء *yadyāʿ*, Nimble-handed (woman).

A يديان *yadayāni*, (dual of يدي) Both hands.

A يديّة *yadīyat*, Dexterous, handy (woman). *Yudayyat*, (dim. of يدي *yada'*) A little hand.

A يرّ *yarr*, (or الشرّ و اليرّ *ash'sharr wa'l yarr*, Evil, an evil. *Yurr*, Hard and smooth (stones).

P يرا *yarā*, Because. A fold, wrinkle. يرا گرفتن *yarā giriftan*, To shrivel, shrink, wither, contract, pucker, be wrinkled.

A يرّاء *yarrāʿ*, fem. of ايرّ, Hard and smooth (stone).

A يرابيع *yarābīʿ*, (pl. of يربوع *yarbūʿ*) Fleshy parts of the back and loins. Male jerboas.

P يراسه *yarāsa*, A bat, rere-mouse.

A يراع *yarāʿ*, A fire-fly. A reed, cane. A coward. A kind of gnat which infests the face.

A يراعة *yarāʿat*, A single fire-fly. A plantation of reeds. A single reed. A cowardly man. Foolish, stupid. A she-ostrich.

P يراغ *yarāgh*, A well-trained saddle-horse. A meeting, assembly, consultation.

P يراغه *yarāgha*, A reed prepared for writing.

T يراق *yarāk*, Arms, accoutrements, weapons.

P يرا گرفته *yarā girifta*, Shrunk, shrivelled.

A يرامع *yarāmiʿ*, Small shining white stones.

A يراميع *yarāmīʿ*, Asparagus.

A يربغ *yarbagh*, Name of a place between Omān and Bahrayn.

A يربوع *yarbūʿ*, (pl. يرابيع *yarābīʿ*) The flesh of the back or loins; an oblique descending muscle. The jerboa, an animal much resembling the dormouse, which makes prodigious bounds by means of its long hind legs. Name of the father of a branch of the tribe of Tamīm.

A يرّة *yarrat*, Fire.

P يرتش *yartish*, A fellow-citizen.

P يرتقچي *yartakchī*, Merciful, co[...]ionate.

P يرتقن *yartakan*, The Creator.

A يرحمك الله *yarhamuka'llāh*, God have mercy on you! (said to a person sneezing).

A يرخفج *yarkhafj*, The night-mare.

A يرخم *yarkhum*, *yarkham*, (or يرخوم *yarkhūm*) The male رخم *rakhm*, or pelican.

A يرد *yard*, Name of the father of ادريس *idrīs*.

A يرر *yarar*, (v. n. of يرّ) Being hard (a stone). Hardness and smoothness of a stone.

P يرسقى *yarsakī*, A bat.

A يرع *yarʿ*, A calf. *Yaraʿ*, Cowardice. A gnat.

P يرغ *yaragh*, A well-trained horse. A meeting.

P يرغمال *yarghamāl*, Hostage, security, bail.

P يرغو *yarghū*, A sergeant, bailiff. Contention, dispute, litigation, quarrel. Forbidden.

P يرغه *yargha*, A swift horse.

A يرفئي *yarfaïy*, Downcast, quaking with fear. Timid, fleeing (male-ostrich). Jumping, leaping (deer). One who turns his back. A shepherd.

A يرقان *yarhān* or *yarakān*, Blight, smut, mildew. Yellow jaundice. Paleness. King's evil.

P يرقاني *yarkānī*, Yellow, mildewed, withered.

A يرقود *yarkūd*, (A man) sleeping much.

A يرقوع *yarkūʻ*, Excessive (hunger).

P يرلغ *yarlagh*, (or يرليغ *yarlīgh*) A diploma, letter patent or royal mandate, especially of the khān of the Tartars. Hopeless.

P يرم *yarm*, A musical instrument, a species of lute with a large belly, strung with brass wires, and struck with a bow. A player on this instrument.

P يرمر *yarmar*, Expectation, hope.

A يرمع *yarmaʻ*, Small shining white stones, soft and broken. Any thing fastened to the end of a string and which makes a whizzing noise when whirled round with velocity. تركته يفتّ اليرمع *taraktuhu yafuttu'l yarmaʻ*, I left him breaking stones (a phrase applied to any one sad and melancholy).

P يرمغان *yarmaghān*, A curiosity or rarity brought from afar as a present to a great man.

P يرمق *yarmak*, Money.

A يرموق *yarmūk*, Weak-sighted (man).

A يرمول *yarmūl*, (A palm-leaf) covered with sand.

A يرمىّ *yaramīy*, A stone or post erected in the desert to guide travellers.

A يرنأ *ya, yurannaʼ*, or يرنّاء *yurannāʼ*) Privet.

A يرنب *yarnab*, A species of field-mouse with a short tail.

P يرنداق *yarandāk*, A kind of white buck or doeskin, of which they make gloves. Intestines.

P يرندج *yarandaj*, A kind of black skin. Blacking for boots and shoes.

A يرنّؤ *yarannuʼ*, A dyeing with privet.

A يروع *yarūʻ*, Fear, trepidation.

A يرون *yarūn*, Brain of an elephant. Perspiration of beasts of burden. Sperma admissarii.

P يريان *yaryān*, The city of Samarcand.

P يز *yaz*, A thorny plant set round tents as a fence. The plant ثمام *sumām*.

A يزأنى *yazʼanīy*, A kind of spear so named from يزن *yazan*, a certain valley or tribe of Himyar.

A يزانىّ *yazānīy*, A kind of spear named after ذو يزن *zū yazan*.

P يزبهانتن *yazbahānitan*, (in zand and Pāzand) To mutter as the Pārsīs do at their meals.

P يزد *yazd*, A city in the most eastern part of Fārs or Persia Proper, famous for a manufacture of cloth called yazdī. God.

P يزدادي *yazdādī*, Hashed meat dressed with yolk of egg.

P يزدان *yazdān*, God. Omnipotence. Name of a good angel, from whom no evil proceeds.

P يزدان بخش *yazdān-bakhsh*, Gift of God. Name of the vazir of هرمز *hurmuz*, son of Noshiravān.

P يزدان پرست *yazdān-parast*, A worshipper of God. A name assumed by some fire-worshippers.

P يزداني *yazdānī*, Divine.

P يزد پرست *yazd-parast*, A worshipper of God.

A يزدجرد *yazdajird*, (P يزدگرد *yazdagird*) Name of several kings of Persia of the Sassanian race, especially the grandson of Noshiravān, and last of the kings of Persia.

P يزش خوان *yazish-khwān*, An intercessor. A high priest of the Magi.

P يزشگاه *yazish-gāh*, Place of prayer, oratory.

P يزشني *yazishnī*, Divine. Name of the 17th book of the Zand.

P يزغند *yazghand*, Name of a tree. A hunting-dog. The cry of the lynx.

P يزك *yazak*, Commander of the night-guard or watch. The advanced guard. A spy.

P يزله *yazla*, Hurt, detriment.

A يزليّ *yazalīy*, Eternal.

A ذو يزن *zū yazan*, Name of a king of Yaman to whom is ascribed a kind of spear called يزنيّ.

P يزنه *yazna*, A sister's husband.

A يزيد *yazīd*, Name of three caliphs of the house of Umayya. Name of an arch-heretic among the Muhammadans. Wicked, cruel, cursed, execrable.

P يزيدي *yazīdī*, One of the sect of Yazīd.

A يسّ *yass*, (v. n. of يسّ) Walking, proceeding.

P يسار *yasār*, One of a sinister aspect.

A يسار *yasār*, Plenty, affluence, opulence. Ease. *Yasār*, *yisār*, or *yassār*, (pl. يسر *yusr* and *yusur*) Left. The left side. P دست يسار *dasti yasār*, Left hand. توانگران صاحب يسار *tuwāngarāni sāhib-yasār*, Wealthy nobles. درجناح يسار *dar janāhi yasār*, In the left wing. A *Yasāri*, A little. انظرني حتّى يسار *unzurnī hatta' yasāri*, Wait for me a little. *Yisār*, (v. n. 3 of يسر) Being mild and gentle.

A يسارا *yasāran*, Towards the left.

A يسارة *yasārat*, Prosperity, affluence. Ease.

P يسال *yasāl*, A garland of flowers, a chaplet worn on festal days. A crowd, procession.

P يساول *yasāwal*, Horsemen, attendant upon a man of rank. A state-messenger. A servant of parade carrying a silver or gold staff. يساول صحبت *yasāwali suhbat*, Master of the ceremonies.

P يسب *yasb*, Jasper. (See يشب *yashb*.)

A يستعور *yastaʻūr*, Any thing vain, fruitless, trifling. A cloth which they throw over a camel's crupper. A tree of which they make elegant tooth-picks. Name of a place.

A يستوي *yastawī*, (the aorist of the 8th conj. of سوي *sawa'*, "It was equal," used as a substantive) Equality.

A يسر *yasr*, (v. n. of يسر) Playing at dice, or with the gaming arrows called ازلام *azlām*. Bringing forth with ease (a woman). Approaching from the left side. Distributing the limbs of a slaughtered camel. Pulling or twisting a cord towards one's self. Digging or stabbing opposite to one's face. Facility, lenity. Softness. *Yasr* or *yasar*, (v. n. of يسر) Being easy, soft, submissive, and obedient. Softness. Submission, obedience. *Yusr*, (v. n. of يسر) Being easy. Being, or becoming rich, abounding in wealth. Playing at dice, or with the gaming arrows ازلام *azlām*. Ease. Prosperity. Opulence. (pl. of يسار *yasār*) Left. *Yasar*, Facility, lenity, softness. (pl. ايسار *aysār*) Easy, soft, gentle, humane. Ready, prepared. A gaming-party, a meeting to play at dice or arrows. The third gaming arrow; also he who draws it. اعسر يسر *aʻsaru yasarun*, Ambidexter; one who uses both hands alike. *Yusur*, Facility. Opulence. Prosperity. (pl. of يسار *yasār*) Left. P درحالت يسر *dar hālati yusur*, In times of prosperity or affluence.

A يسرا *yasaran*, (She brought forth) with ease.

A يسرات *yasarāt*, Nimble hands and feet.

A يسرة *yasrat*, The left side. *Yusrat*, Ease. Prosperity. *Yasarat*, (pl. ايسار *aysār*) The lines on the palms of the hands when distant one from another. A mark burnt on the thigh.

A يسرةً *yasratan*, To the left.

A يسروع *yasrūʻ* or *yusrūʻ*, A worm found among pot-herbs; also one amongst sand, having a white body and a red head (to this they often compare the fingers of a woman).

A يسري *yusra'*, (pl. يسريات *yusrayāt*) The left hand, side, or part. اليسري *al yusra'*, To the left.

A يسريّ *yasrīy*, Prosperous, successful in one's undertakings. *Yasarīy*, Easy, facile.

A يسف *yasaf*, A fly.

T A يسق *yasak*, Law, regulation.

A يسن *yasan*, The putrid, noisome, or narcotic effluvia of a well; fainting occasioned by it.

A يسور *yasūr*, A gamester.

A يسول *yasūl*, Moss.

A يسير *yasīr*, Small, little. Easy. A gamester.

P درزمان يسير *dar zamāni yasīr*, In a little time.

A يسيرا *yasīran*, By little, by degrees.

P يش *yash*, is written for اش *ash* after nouns in ا or و; as, عصايش *ʻasāyash*, His staff; گيسويش *gīsūyash*, Her ringlets; خويش *khoyash*, His temper.

A يشّ *yashsh*, (v. n. of يشّ) Being glad, rejoicing.

A يشب *yashb*, (P يشپ *yashp*) Jasper, especially a whitish kind found on Mount Imaus.

P يشت *yasht*, Name of a chapter of the Zand.

P يشترم *yashtaram*, Pimple, pustule, small-pox.

P يشتن *yashtan*, (in zand and Pāzand) To pray in a low murmuring tone as the fire-worshippers do at meal-time. To beg, supplicate. To celebrate.

P يشته كردن *yashta kardan*, To pray.

A يشجب yashjub, Name of the son of يعرب yaʿrab, son of قحطان kahtān.

P يشف yashf, Jasper.

P يشك yashk, A lancet or similar instrument. The projecting tusks of a wild beast. Dew. Pure, unadulterated.

P يشكرده yashkarda, A long-necked lute played with a long plectrum or bow.

P يشم yashm, A sort of jasper or agate; one particularly which, according to Castellus, comes from China or India, and has the quality of diverting lightning from any place where it is laid, or any person who wears it.

A يشمذة yashmazat, (A bird) swift of flight.

P يشمه yashma, Raw white leather.

A يشهبور yashhabūr, An old woman with some remains of strength.

A يصب yasb, (or يصف yasf) Jasper.

A يع yaʿ, Used in checking one who is about to take any thing.

A يعار yuʿār, (v. n. of يعر) Bleating (a goat or sheep), especially loud. Loud bleating.

A يعارة yaʿārat, When a stallion camel is brought to try the female; especially if, from her high blood, she refuses him.

A يعاسيب yaʿāsīb, (pl. of يعسوب yaʿsūb) King-bees. Princes, chiefs of a nation.

A يعاط yaʿāti, yiʿāti, or yuʿāti, An alarm given by a sentinel on the approach of an enemy. Used in crying to horses or wolves.

A يعافير yaʿāfīr, (pl. of يعفور) Young deer.

A يعاقبة yaʿākibat, (pl. of يعقوبيّ) Jacobites.

A يعاقيب yaʿākīb, (pl. of يعقوب yaʿkūb) Male partridges. Jacobs.

A يعاليل yaʿālīl, (pl. of يعلول) Floating bubbles.

A يعامير yaʿāmīr, (pl. of يعمور yaʿmūr) Kids. (pl. of يعمورة yaʿmūrat) Certain kinds of trees.

A يعبوب yaʿbūb, A rapid river; also overflowing. A cloud. A swift and long horse. A locust springing a great distance.

A يعر yaʿr, A kid; especially one fastened in a ditch to catch a lion; any bait for entrapping wild beasts. Name of a tree. اذلّ من اليعر azall mini'l yaʿr, More mean (or more helpless) than a kid placed to decoy a lion.

A يعرب yaʿrab, Yareb the son of قحطان kahtān.

A يعرة yaʿrat, A kid, as mentioned above.

A يعزي yaʿzī, By my life!

A يعسوب yaʿsūb, (pl. يعاسيب yaʿāsīb) The king of the bees. A prince or chief of a nation. A sort of partridge. A kind of insect larger or smaller than a locust. A star on a horse's face. A circle on that part which the spur touches. Name of a horse which belonged to Muhammad.

A يعضيد yaʿzīd, A sort of pot-herb. Succory.

A يعفور yaʿfūr, A young deer, a fawn. A division or hour of the night. Noise, motion, agitation. Name of an ass on which Muhammad used to ride. Yaʿfūr or yuʿfūr, A deer of an ash-colour.

A يعقوب yaʿkūb, (pl. يعاقيب yaʿākīb) A male partridge. James, Jacob. P يعقوب پيغمبر yaʿkūb paygham-bar, The prophet (patriarch) Jacob.

A يعقوبيّ yaʿkūbīy, A jacobite, a Eutychian.

A يعقيد yaʿkīd, Honey concreted by the fire. Victuals thickened with honey.

A يعلم الله yaʿlamu'llāh, God knoweth.

A يعلول yaʿlūl, (pl. يعاليل yaʿālīl) A bubble floating on water. Clouds piled upon clouds, especially white. Shower following shower. A camel with two bunches. Colour imbibed time after time, twice-dyed. A ditch of pure water. Dew.

A يعملة yaʿmalat, A she-camel, patient, tractable, and fit for labour.

A يعمور yaʿmūr, (pl. يعامير) A kid. A lamb.

A يعمورة yaʿmūrat, (pl. يعامير) Name of a tree.

A يعموم yaʿmūm, Tall (plant).

A يعني yaʿnī, That is to say, viz., to wit, namely.

A يعور yaʿūr, Bleating much (sheep or goat). A sheep staling when milked and spoiling the milk.

A يعوق yaʿūk, Name of an idol supposed to have been worshipped in the time of Noah.

A يعياع yaʿyāʿ, A sort of game in which boys throw something to and fro at one another.

P يغام yaghām, A sylvan demon.

P يغتج yaghtaj, (or يغتنج yaghtanj) A beautiful harmless serpent found in gardens.

P يغر yaghir, Name of one of the Chinese emperors. A name for the Emperor of China.

P يغرب yaghrab, Sour, coagulated milk.

P يغروش yaghrūsh, Name of a king of Persia.

A يغفر الله لي ولكم yaghfuru'llāh lī wa lakum, God forgive me and you (uttered in return to a congratulation when sneezing).

P يغلا yughlā or yaghlā, (or يغلاوي yaghlāwī) A frying-pan.

P يغلغ yaghligh, A pointed arrow.

P يغلو yaghlav, (or يغلوي yaghlavī) A frying-pan.

P يغما yaghmā, Prey, plunder, booty, spoil, pillage, sacking, ravishment. Name of a city in Turkistān celebrated for the beauty of its inhabitants. يغما كردن yaghmā kardan, (or يغما گرفتن yaghmā giriftan) To spoil or carry off plunder. يغماي اوّل yaghmāyi awwal, Name of a city in Turkistān.

P يغماناز yaghmānāz, Name of the Emperor of China's daughter married to بهرام گور bahrām-gūr.

P يغميصا yaghmīsā, Sorrel.

P يغناغ yaghnāgh, An embroidered cap.

P يغني yaghnī, Boiled meat.

A يغوث yaghūs, Name of an old Arabian idol.

A يفاع yafāʿ, (or yaffāʿ) A hill, high ground.

P يفت yaft, A decrepit old man.

P يفتج yaftaj, (or يفتنج yaftanj) A large harmless black snake found in vineyards.

P يفج yafj, Spittle.

A يفخ yafkh, A striking on the يافوخ yāfūkh.

P يفر yafir, Emperor, monarch, Chinese emperor.

A يفع yafʿ, (v. n. of يفع) Ascending (a mountain). Approaching twenty years of age (a youth). Yafaʿ, A hill. (pl. ايفاع) Tall, well-grown (youth).

A يفعان yufʿān, (pl. of يافع yāfiʿ) Young men approaching twenty years of age.

A يفعة yafaʿat, Tall, well-grown (youth). (pl. of يافع yāfiʿ) (Young men) approaching to twenty years of age.

A يفن yufn, Old men. Aged (bulls). Yafan, (pl. يفن yufn) A very old man, a decrepit old dotard. A bullock four years old. Also منفنّ munfaʿinn.

A يفنة yafanat, A cow. Pregnant.

A يفوع yufūʿ, High places.

A يقاظة yakāzat, Wakefulness, vigilance.

A يقاظى yakāza', (pl. of يقظي yakza') Vigilant, watchful, circumspect (women).

A بيض يقائق bīz yakāʾik, (pl. of ابيض يقق abyazu yakak) Pure white.

A يقدميّة yakdumīyat, A going before, a leading of the van.

A يقطين yaktīn, A gourd or similar creeper.

A يقطينة yaktīnat, One gourd.

A يقظ yakaz, (v. n. of يقظ) Waking, being watchful. Yakiz or yakuz, (pl. ايقاظ aykāz) Vigilant, wakeful, provident, circumspect.

A يقظان yakzān, Vigilant, provident, awake. ابو اليقظان abū'lyakzān, Father Vigilant, i. e. the cock.

A يقظة yakazat, Night-watch, sentry. Vigils. Watching, being awake. A watch of the night.

A يقظي yakza', Vigilant, watchful (woman).

A يقق yakak, Cotton. Pith of the palm-tree. ابيض يقق abyaz yakak, (or yakik) Very white.

A يققة yakakat, Part of the pith of a palm.

A يقن yakn or yakan, (v. n. of يقن) Knowing (any thing) for certain. Yakan, Certainty, the absence or removal of all doubt. Any thing certain. Yakan, yakin, and yakun, One who knows any thing certainly, sure of. Yakin, Greedy, addicted.

A يقنة yakanat, One who firmly believes what he hears; credulous.

A يقوقة yakūkat, (v. n. of يقّ) Being intensely white. Whiteness.

P يقّه yakka, The collar of a garment. A seizure of any one by the collar.

A يقين yakīn, Certainty, assurance, sure knowledge, true faith, truth, infallibility, evidence: opinion, belief. Death. True, sure. P يقين داشتن yakīn dāshtan, To hold true, to feel assured. يقين درست yakīni durust, True belief. A انا على يقين منه ana ʿala' yakīn minhu, I am certain of it. علم اليقين ʿilmu'l yakīn, Inferential knowledge, or that acquired by the exercise of reason (as when the presence of fire is inferred from the sight of smoke). عين اليقين ʿaynu'l yakīn, (also حقّ اليقين hakku'l yakīn) Experimental knowledge (as of the presence of fire from seeing it or falling into it). بعض اصحاب يقين *bazi as-hābi yakīn*, Some learned doctors.

A يقيناً *yakīnan*, Certainly, truly, surely.

A يقينيّ *yakīnīy*, Scientific, certain, sure, infallible, belonging to truth or faith.

A يقينيّات *yakīnīyāt*, Certainties, as articles of religion, demonstrations in geometry, truths.

P يك *yak*, One, every one. Once. An ace. Custom, habit. Law, canon. Noble. A frog. A flea. يك دفعه *yak dafa*, At once, at one blow. يك ذرّه *yak zarra*, One atom, the least part. يك رنگان *yak rangān*, Of one colour. Simple, sincere. يك يك *yak yak*, (or يكي يكي *yakī yakī*) One by one, singly. Placed after the denominative, a fraction is formed: as, چهاريك *chahār yak*, A fourth; ده يك *dah yak*, A tenth; صد يك *sad yak*, A hundredth. سه يك كردن *sih yak kardan*, To divide into three (parts).

A يكُ (لم) *(lam) yaku*, Was not, existed not.

A يكّ *yakk*, (from P يك *yak*), من يكّ الى يكّ *min yakkin ila' yakkin*, From one to another.

P يك اسبه *yak-asba*, Possessed of one horse. One who rides alone. The sun.

P يك انداز *yak-andāz*, A small arrow flying far. An arrow which, when discharged, is never sought for. A double-headed arrow. A perpendicular precipice or river's bank. Equal, even.

P يك آويز *yak-āwez*, A short, broad sword.

P يكايك *yak-ā-yak*, One by one. Suddenly, all at once. One opposed to another.

P يكبار *yak-bār*, Once, one time.

P يكبارگي *yak-bāragī*, One time or turn. At once, all at once. Wholly, universally.

P يكباسرك *yak-bāsarak*, At once, all together.

P يك بدو *yak badu*, All at once, unexpectedly.

P يك بريك *yar bar yak*, (or يك بيك *yak ba yak*) One by one, successively.

P يك بسي *yak basī*, One time or turn. At once.

P يكبن *yak-bun*, (Single-rooted) Sweet basil.

P يك بيك *yak ba yak*, One by one. Suddenly, all at once. Like. Sure.

P يكپاره *yak-pāra*, Solid, massive, all of a piece. One part or segment. At one stroke, at once. One piece.

P يك پهن كشتي *yak pahni kashtī*, The Muhammadan faith.

P يكتا *yak-tā*, Single, simple. Unique, incomparable. A garment without a lining. God.

P يكتا دلي *yaktā dilī*, Amity, union of hearts.

P يك تاز *yak-tāz*, Who charges the foe alone.

P يكتاش *yak-tāsh*, A fellow-servant.

P يكتركرد *yaktarkard*, One basket, especially a large one in which they carry grapes.

P يكتمل *yaktamal*, A place of worship.

P يك تنه *yak-tana*, Alone.

P يك تهي *yak-tahī*, A shirt, a shift.

P يك تيغ كردن *yak tegh kardan*, To make level, to smooth.

P يكجا *yak-jā*, In one place, at the same time, together, equally.

P يكجان *yak-jān*, One soul, a friend.

P يكجانب *yak-jānib*, Of one side, a partisan.

P يك جدّي *yak-jaddī*, Of the same stock, descended from a common ancestor.

P يك جهت *yak-jihat*, Of one accord, unanimous. Determined, resolved. A friend.

P يكجهتي *yak-jihatī*, Concord, friendship.

P يكچبه *yak-chaba*, (for يكشبه *yak-shaba*) Lasting one night, sufficient for one night. A little, a little while.

P يكچشم *yak-chashm*, (or يكچشمه *yak-chashma*) One-eyed. Single-eyed. Purblind. Who looks on, or only considers, the exterior. A hypocrite. One who professes to believe in one God.

P يك چشمي *yak-chashmī*, One-eyedness.

P يكچنبه *yak-chambih*, (for يكشنبه *yak-shambih*) Sunday, the first day of the week.

P يكچند *yak-chand*, Somewhat; a little. يكچند بار *yak-chand bār*, Sometimes, often. Many burdens. A string of horses.

P يكچندي *yak-chande*, A little time, a while.

P يك چوبه *yak-choba*, One-poled (tent).

P يكدانه *yak-dāna*, An incomparable gem. A string of pearls. A necklace.

P يكدست *yak-dast*, Entire. Whatever can be lifted with one hand. Even (cloth). Homogeneous. يكدست جامه *yak-dast jāma*, A kind of garment reaching from the head to the heels.

P يكدش *yahdish*, The rational soul. Mixture. Union. A horse of a mixed breed. A beloved object.

P يكدك *yakdah*, Milk and water. Any thing lukewarm.

P يكدگر *yak-digar*, One another. از يكدگر *az yak digar*, From each other. در يكدگر *dar yak-digar*, In one another.

P يكدل *yak-dil*, Unanimous; one-hearted. Uniform. Unanimously, with one accord. يكدل و يكجهت شدن *yak-dil u yak-jihat shudan*, To agree in all things to unite, consent, conspire.

P يكدله *yak-dila*, Single-hearted. Uniform, consonant to. Sincere.

P يكدلي *yak-dilī*, Concord, unanimity.

P يكدم *yak-dam*, One moment; one breath.

P يكدمه *yak-dama*, Momentary. مقارنت يكدمه *muhāranati yak-dama*, The society of a moment, a transient acquaintance.

P يك دو *yak du*, One or two.

P يكديگر *yak dīgar*, One another.

P يكران *yakrān*, A light bay, dun, chesnut, or flea-bitten horse. A chesnut-coloured horse with a white mane and tail. The colour of myrtle and of the pistachio-nut; likewise yellow and grey. A fine, full-grown, high-bred horse. A horse which takes a shorter step with one hind-foot than the other (one-thighed).

P يك راه *yak-rāh*, Going on (the same road).

P يك رخي *yak rukhī*, A kind of bow.

P يكرسيدن *yak rasīdan*, To arrive singly; to meet together.

P يكرشته *yak-rishta*, Consenting, agreeing.

P يكرك *yakrak*, Better, best.

P يك ركابي *yak-rikābī*, A led horse of state. A being prepared.

P يكرنگ *yak-rang*, Of one colour. Sincere, faithful, true. يك رنگي *yak-rangī*, Sincerity, friendship.

P يكرو *yak-rū*, Unanimous. Sincere, pure. يكرو كردن *yak rū kardan*, To give up an acquaintance.

P يكروزه *yak roza*, Of one day. يكروزه راه *yak-roza rāh*, A day's journey.

P يكروي *yak-rūy*, Unanimously. Of one face. Single, simple, sincere. يك روي كردن *yak-rūy kardan*, To pacify, to make of one accord.

P يكرويه *yak-rūya*, Single-faced. Clear, open, manifest. Consenting, agreeing. Pacificatory.

P يكروئي *yak-rūī*, Unanimity. Friendship. Sincerity.

P يكره *yak-rah*, In one way; by one road. At once, at one glance, at first look. Sincere, pure.

P يكزبان *yak-zabān*, With one voice; unanimous. يكزبان شدن *yak-zabān shudan*, To agree nem. con.

P يك زخم *yak-zakhm*, Sām Narīmān (because he killed a dragon at a single blow).

P يكزده *yak-zada*, By one rule; in one line.

P يكزمان *yak-zamān*, Cotemporary.

P يكساعت *yak-sāat*, Of an hour's duration, momentary, transitory. صحبت يكساعت *suhbati yak-sāa*, An hour's conversation. يكساعت پرداختن *yak-sāat pardākhtan*, To devote an hour.

P يكساله *yak-sāla*, Of one year, yearling.

P يكسان *yaksān*, The same, ditto, equal to, conformable, all one, uniform, similar. Plain, level, parallel, of equal sides, of the same order, in the same series or manner, equally. Always, for ever. يكسان كردن *yaksān kardan*, To make equal, level.

P يكساني *yaksānī*, Uniformity, parity, identity.

P يكسانيدن *yaksānīdan*, To be or make equal.

P يكسر *yak-sar*, Under one head. Subject to one chief. Together in one body, at one stroke. From beginning to end. Suddenly. Alone.

P يكسره *yak-sara*, Solitary. A friend, having the same sentiments. At one time, all at once.

P يكسريدن *yaksarīdan*, To meet in one place.

P يكسو *yak-sū*, On one side, one side. يكسوشدن *yak-sū shudan*, To go aside, to stray.

P يكسوار *yak-suwār*, A single horseman, one who rides along fearing nothing; knight-errant.

P يكسواره *yak-suwāra*, The sun.

A يكسوم *yaksūm*, (A garden) full of herbs. ابو يكسوم *abū yaksūm*, Name of the صاحب الفيل *sāhibu'l fīl*, Lord of the elephant, mentioned in the Kur'ān.

P يكسون *yaksūn*, (or يكسونه *yaksūna*) Plain, level, equal. Always, for ever.

P يكسونيدن *yaksūnīdan*, To level, make plain.

P يكشبه *yak-shaba*, A thing one night old. A sort of fine white linen embroidered with gold thread.

P يك شست *yak-shist*, One who sits or converses with another. Two companions.

P يكشنبه *yak-shambih*, Sunday.

P يكقلم *yak-kalam*, Consistent (writer). Together, at one stroke, at once, all, total.

P يكك *yakak*, A lake, a pool.

P يك گره *yak-girih*, Like, resembling.

P يكگونه *yak-gūna*, Of one colour, sort, kind.

P يكلخت *yak-lakht*, Single-leathered (shoe). Of one key, *i.e.* most powerful, an emperor, commander-in-chief. All at once.

P يكلو *yaklū*, Simple, single (thread).

P يكم *yakum*, The first.

P يكماهه *yak-māha*, Of a month, a month old.

P يكمصلّب *yak musallab*, A sort of coin stampt with a cross.

P يك نشست *yak-nishast*, Who sits or converses with another.

P يكنفر *yak-nafar*, One man, a certain person.

P يك نورد *yak-naward*, One way, road, manner.

P يك نه يك *yak na yak*, One or other.

P يكون *yakūn*, Of one kind. A kind of silk stuff.

A يكون *yakūn*, It will be. Sum total.

P يك و نيم ساز *yak u nīm sāz*, A term or property of musical instruments. A kind of music.

P يكه *yaka*, One, singular, unique, At once, together. The first, former. Every one, somebody.

P يكّه *yakka*, Some one. A one-horse chaise.

P يكه جوان *yaka-jawān*, A single youth.

P يكه سوار *yaka-suwār*, A single cavalier, one unequalled in the army, a hero.

P يكه شبان روز *yaka shabān roz*, A day and night.

P يكي *yake*, One, somebody, a certain one. The one. يكي از ملوك *yake az mulūk*, One of the kings; a certain king. يكي در چند *yake dar chand*, How many folds or sorts. يكي در ده *yake dar dah*, Ten-fold, ten times so much. يكي سرخ *yake surkh*, One piece of gold. يكي يكي *yake yake*, One with another; singly. يكي از يكي *yake az yake*, One with another. *Yakī*, Unity, oneness. Concord, unanimity. يكي بودن *yakī būdan*, To consent, to be of one mind.

P يكيتا *yakītā*, A master, a teacher.

P يكيدن *yakīdan*, To be or become one.

P يكين *yakīn*, Name of a sweet and branchy herb.

P يگان *yagān*, One, single, alone, only. Singular. Incomparable, peerless. Orthodox, unitarians. يگان يگان *yagān yagān*, Singly, one by one.

P يگانگت *yagānagat* (or يگانگيت) Unity.

P يگانگي *yagānagī* (or يگاني *yagānī*) Singularity, unity. Excellence, any thing incomparable. Union, conjunction. Solitude. Victory. Concord, unanimity. يگانگي داشتن *yagānagī dāshtan*, To be unparalleled, inimitable.

P يگانه *yagāna*, (originally يك گانه *yak gāna*) One, single, sole, unique, singular, incomparable. Alone. A person unequalled in any thing. A conqueror. A brother, a friend. A pearl. يگانۀ اعصار *yagānaï aʿṣār*, The phœnix, ornament of the age. يگانه شدن *yagāna shudan*, To be united. To be alone. يگانه شدن براي *yagāna shudan ba raʾy*, To be of one opinion.

P يگانه گوي *yagāna-gūy* or *goy*, One who professes faith in one God.

P يگونه *yagūna*, Of one kind, same, equal to.

P يل *yal*, A hero, a brave athletic warrior. A horse pasturing at large. Corpulent, strong, robust. Utility, profit. A heart free from sorrow. Released, liberated, allowed to have one's own way.

A يلّاء *yallāʾ*, (fem. of ايلّ *ayall*) (A woman) with short teeth bent inwardly, and not placed regularly in the gums. (A horn) bent backward.

P يلابستان *yilābistān*, Name of a certain village.

A يلاغ *yalāgh*, Any thing white.

A يلاق *yalāk*, A broken pan in which they feed dogs and cats. *Yilāk*, Name of a king.

A يلامع *yalāmiʿ*, (pl. of يلمع *yalmaʿ*) Shining, glittering things (as armour or a helmet).

A يلامق *yalāmik*, (pl. of يلمق) Tartar garments.

P يلان *yalān*, Name of a champion of Tūrān. (pl. of يل *yal*) Heroes.

P يلا يلا *yalā yalā*, Come along, come along.

A يلب *yalab*, (noun of unity يلبة *yalabat*) The skin of the back of a wild beast, of which they make shields, helmets, and other armour for the body, without iron. A shield or any defensive armour made of felt, stuffed with honey and sand. Any thing of great bulk or weight. Good iron, steel.

P يلچي *yilchī*, An ambassador, an envoy. A guide, conductor.

P يلدا *yaldā*, The longest night of winter. Name of one of the attendants upon Jesus Christ.

P يلدك *yaldak*, Milk-warm water.

P يلغران *yalgharān*, Dressed food for a journey.

P يلغز *yalghaz*, Alone. A horse.

P يلغزه *yalghaza*, The rind of a poppy.

P يلفچي *yalfchī*, A shepherd, pastor.

A يلق *yalak*, White, clear.

A يلقة *yalakat*, White, glossy-haired (she-goat).

P يلك *yalak*, A sort of crown worn by kings.

P يلكن *yalkan*, A machine used in fortified places for throwing stones and dirt.

A يلل *yalal*, Shortness of the fore-teeth, especially bent inwardly; inequality of the teeth in shape and situation. Smoothness of a rock.

P يلم *yalam*, Isinglass, glue.

P يلما *yalmā*, A thing of great bulk, but light.

A يلمع *yalmaʿ*, Lightning when followed by rain (proverbially, a vain promiser). A kind of vapour called سراب *sarāb*. اكذب من يلمع *akzab min yalmaʿ*, More deceitful than the vapour سراب *sarāb* (mirage), or than this kind of lightning.

A يلمعيّ *yalmaʿiy*, Ingenious, keen, shrewd, quick, clever, witty. A liar.

AP يلمق *yalmak*, (pl. يلامق *yalāmik*) A Tartar garment quilted with cotton, which opens at the side from the arm-pits to the lower extremity; a kind of four-square cloak or mantle.

A يلمك *yalmak*, A strong, able-bodied youth.

P يلمه *yalma*, A coat of mail made with rings of iron. A kind of garment.

P يلمه ريش *yalma-rish*, A large or long beard.

A يلنجج *yalanjaj*, (يلنجوج *yalanjūj*, or يلنجوجيّ *yalanjūjiy*) The wood of aloes.

A يلندد *yalandad*, A formidable adversary.

P يلوك *yalūk*, Corpulent, strong, robust. *Yalūk*, (يلوليك *yalūlīk*, or يلولنگ *yalūlang*) An athletic man, warrior, hero, champion.

P يلوه *yalwa*, (or يلوي) A woodcock: a rail.

P يله *yala*, Deliverance, escape, release. Turned loose, allowed to pasture at liberty. Crooked. A whore. Foolish, false, vain, trifling. Alone, solitary. Running, rushing, making an assault.

P يله دار *yala-dār*, A scout, plunderer.

P يله يشم *yala yasham*, Name of a mountain near Kazwin, where petrified animals may be seen.

P يلي آمدن *yalī āmadan*, To descend.

P يلي زن *yalī-zan*, A musician, a singer.

P يليله *yalyala*, Corpulent, strong. A hero.

P يليم *yilīm*, Glue, isinglass.

P يم *yam*, is put for ام *am* after nouns in ا or و; as, عصا *ʿasā*, A staff; عصايم *ʿasāyam*, My staff; گيسو *gīsū*, A ringlet; گيسويم *gīsūyam*, My ringlet.

A يمّ *yamm*, The ocean, mighty deep; a sea with no shore in sight. A great river. A wood-pigeon. سلاطين يمّ كرم *salātīni yamm*, or *yam-karam*, Princes bounteous as the sea. P شاه كرم يم شيم *shāhi karīmi yam-shiyam*, A sovereign bountiful as the ocean.

P يماك *yamāk*, Name of an ancient king.

A يمام *yamām*, A turtle-dove, a wood-pigeon; also a domestic pigeon. Intention, purpose, design. Before, in front of.

A يمامة *yamāmat*, A single pigeon. Intention, design. Name of a blue-eyed maiden who could see a person mounted at a distance of three days' journey. Name of a large district in Arabia very fruitful in palm-trees, and which comprehends Najd, Tihāmah, Bahrayn, and Omān. Before, in front of.

A يمامي *yamāmī*, Before me.

A يماميّ *yamāmiy*, Of the province of Yamāmah.

P يمان *yamān*, Light, splendour.

A يمانون *yamānūna*, Natives of Yaman.

A يماني *yamānī*, (fem. يمانية *yamāniyat*) A native of, or any thing belonging to, Yaman. The Yaman side (of Sanaa), opposed to شامي *shiām*, q.v.

A يمانيّ *yamāniy*, Belonging to Yaman.

A يمانيّة *yamāniyat*, A species of red barley.

A يمجوج *yamjūj*, Magog.

P يمخور *yamkhūr*, A horse or dog-flea.

A يمخور *yam* or *yumkhūr*, Tall. Long (neck).

P يمرده *yam rada*, The mandrake.

P يمرود *yamrūd*, A man of a delicate constitution. Tender shoot of a tree; an offset. Name of a place.

P يمسو *yamsū*, Gunpowder.

P يمشن *yamshan*, The Egyptian lote-fruit.

A يمقور *yamkūr*, Bitter.

P يمك *yamak*, Name of a city and country. Name of the kings of ايغور *ighūr* (oriental Tartary).

A يمكن *yumkinu*, It is possible; possibly, perhaps.

P يمگان *yumgān*, A town in Badakhshān.

A يمم *yamam*, A wood-pigeon.

A يمن *yamn*, (v. n. of يمن) Taking (one) to the right. Approaching on the right side. Being fortunate and happy. Death. *Yumn*, Felicity, prosperity. A token for good. *Yaman*, The right hand or side. The south country. Arabia Felix, Yaman.

A يمناء *yamnā*, Right-handed (woman). Happy, fortunate (woman).

A يمنة *yamnat*, The right hand or side. Any thing stretched or held out in the right hand. يمنة من طعام *yamnatun min taꜥām*, Victuals presented with the right hand. *Yumnat*, Happiness, prosperity. A kind of Arabian striped cloth.

A يمنةً *yamnatan*, On, or toward the right.

A يمنى *yumna'*, (pl. يمنيات) The right hand.

A يمنيّ *yamanīy*, Belonging to Arabia Felix. A kind of flowered or painted stuff made in that country, used as covers for bedsteads or footstools.

A يموم *yumūm*, (pl. of يمّ *yamm*) Shoreless seas, boundless oceans, vasty deeps, mighty waters.

A يمؤود *yamꜥūd*, (fem. of يمؤودة *yamꜥūdat*) Soft (thing); delicate (youth); tender (branch).

A يمين *yamīn*, (pl. ايمن *aymun* and ايمان *aymān*) An oath. (pl. ايمن *aymun*, ايمان *aymān*, ايامن *ayāmin*, and ايامين *ayāmīn*) The right hand, side, or part. Strength, power. Blessing, felicity, plenty. Happy, prosperous, fortunate. Beginning of the day. P يمين كردن *yamīn kardan*, To take an oath, to swear. يمين بالله كردن *yamīni bi'llāh kardan*, To swear by God. A يمين لغو *yamīni laghw*, An oath taken concerning an incident already past, when the swearer believes that the matter to which he thus bears testimony accords with what he swears, and it should happen to be actually otherwise. يمين منعقد *yamīni munꜥakid*, An oath concerning a matter yet to come. يمين ويسار *yamīn u yasār*, Right and left. The two wings of an army. ذو يمين ويسار *zū yamīn u yasār*, Ambidexter. اليمين *al yamīna*, Towards the right. عن اليمين *ꜥani'l yamīn*, (Assistance came to us) from the right, or from an auspicious quarter. هو عندنا باليمين *huwa ꜥindanā bi'l yamīn*, He is with us in excellent condition, or in a good situation. كف يمين *kafi yamīn*, The right hand.

A يميناً *yamīnan*, To the right. Southward.

A يميّن *yumayyin*, (dim.) A small right hand.

P يمينه *yamīna*, The stomach.

A ين *ayni*, (an affix to form the oblique case dual of Arabic nouns); as, بحر *bahr*, A sea; بحرين *bahrayni*, Of, from, by, in two seas. *Īna*, (used to form the oblique case in the regular plural); as, فرحين *farihīna*, (oblique of فرحون *farihūna*) (pl. of فرح *farih*) Gladsome, joyous, blithe.

P ين *īn*, (for اين) This. برين *barīn*, On this; درين *darīn*, In this. واز ينجاست *wa az īn jā'st*, And hence it is. *Īn* is an affix to form adjectives of relation; as, سيمين *sīmīn*, Made of silver, silvery; آهنين *āhanīn*, Made of iron, &c.

A ينابيع *yanābīꜥ*, (pl. of ينبوع) Fountains.

A ينبع *yambuꜥ*, Yembo, a sea-port in Hijāz.

A ينبغي *yambaghī*, It is proper, it behoveth.

A ينبوت *yambūt*, A kind of Arabian or Nabathæan pulse: fenugreek, poppy. The carob-tree.

A ينبوع *yambūꜥ*, (pl. ينابيع *yanābīꜥ*) A spring, source, fountain. A rivulet with plenty of water.

P ينپلو *yampalū*, A market-place. A weekly market; a market-town. A caravan. Goods, wares.

A ينتوح *yantūh*, A kind of bird.

A ينتون *yantūn*, Thapsia, toothpick-fennel. Gum of mountain-rue.

A ينجلب *yanjalib*, Shells used as amulets, whether for counteracting the influence of evil eyes, bringing back a fugitive, or securing a husband's affections.

A ينخوب *yankhūb*, Cowardly, timid, timorous.

P يند *yand*, for اند *and*, Are; as, خدم اويند *khadami u yand*, (They) are his servants.

A يندد *yandad*, Name of Madīna.

P يندو *yandū*, Light, the rays of the sun.

A ينص *yans*, A porcupine.

A ينع *yanꜥ*, (pl. of يانع *yāniꜥ*) Ripe (fruits). *Yanꜥ* or *yunꜥ*, (v. n. of ينع) Coming to maturity, being ripe. Maturity, ripeness. *Yunꜥ*, A large tree. *Yanaꜥ*, A species of cornelian stone.

A ينعة *yanaꜥat*, A species of red shell.

A ينفور *yanfūr*, Flying in terror, timid.

A ينفوز *yanfūz*, Bounding (doe).

A ينق *yank*, Rennet for curdling milk.

P ينقون *yankūn*, The herb Noli me tangere.

A ينكف *yankaf*, Name of a king of Himyar.

A ينكور *yankūr*, Uncertain (road).

P ينگ *yang*, Name of a yellow-coloured animal found amongst grass and corn. Like, resembling. A rule, law, habit, or custom. Power, grandeur. Gravity.

A ينم *yanam*, A species of vulnerary herb. Seed of fleawort.

P ينمه *yanma*, Name of a healing plant.

A ينوع *yunūꜥ*, A coming to maturity, a being ripe.

A ينيع *yanīꜥ*, Ripe (fruit).

P يو *yo*, One. *Yū*, A yoke.

P يوا *yawā*, The loss of any thing which cannot again be found (as strayed cattle). One who loses his way. يوا شدن *yawā shudan*, To be lost. يوا كردن *yawā kardan*, To lose.

P يواشه *yawāsha*, Lost.

A يوافيخ *yawāfīkh*, (pl. of يافوخ *yāfūkh*) Middles and fore parts of heads, which in infants are soft.

A يواقيت *yawākīt*, (pl. of ياقوت) Rubies.

A يوام *yiwām*, Bargaining by the day (يوم *yawm*, as شهار *shihār* means by the month, شهر *shahr*).

P يوب *yūb*, A rich carpet.

P يوبب *yawbab* or *yūbab*, Jobab, father of Jethro, by the Arabians called شعيب *shuꜥayb*.

P يوبره *yūbra*, Desirous, covetous, wishful.

P يوبه *yoba* or *yūba*, Desire, wish, longing.

P يوبيدن *yo* or *yūbīdan*, To desire, will, wish.

P يوت *yūt*, A murrain amongst cattle.

P يوج *yūj*, A sort of creeping animalcule.

P يوجه *yūja*, A drop of water or blood.

A يوح *yūh*, (and يوحىٰ *yūha'*) The sun.

A يوخ *yawkh*, The day.

P يوخه *yokha*, The height of sensual enjoyment, the moment of fruition.

P يودك *yūdak*, (يوذك *yūzak*, يوذل *yūzal*, and يوزل *yūzal*), A little dog, a whelp.

P يوده *yoda*, A unit.

P يورد *yūrd*, (يورده *yūrda*, or يوردي *yūrdi*) A chamber, room, apartment.

A يوردان *yūrdān*, The Jordan.

P يورش *yūrish*, An assault, attack, storm.

P يوز *yūz*, A small panther or ounce, especially that used in hunting deer, a cheeta. A hunter, seeker, searcher. Inquiry, search. A dog which hunts by the scent. Jump, leap.

P يوزان *yūzān*, (pl. of يوز *yūz*) Pards, panthers, cheetas, ounces, hunting-leopards.

P يوزانيدن *yūzānīdan*, To cause to leap.

P يوزبان *yūzbān*, (يوزبنده *yūz-banda*, or يوزدار *yūz-dār*) A keeper of hunting-panthers.

P يوزبك *yūzbak*, Kingdom of Samarcand. Uzbek Tartary.

P يوزغند *yūzghand*, The voice of a man. The cry of a panther.

P يوزك *yūzak*, A young panther, a cheeta. Rolling, wallowing in the dirt, as horses. A hunting-dog.

P يوزه *yūza*, The trunk of a tree. A young panther. A hunting-dog. Wallowing in the dirt. Name of an importunate beggar.

P يوزيدن *yūzīdan*, To leap, spring, jump. To clean a well.

A يؤوس *yaꜥus*, Despondent, despairing.

A يوسف *yūsuf*, Joseph, the patriarch. Groaning, sighing. A groan, a sigh. يوسف ثاني *yūsufi sānī*, A second Joseph, *i.e.* extremely beautiful. (Joseph is the Adonis of the East, A handsome young man being often compared to him. See زليخا *zulaykhā*.) P يوسف روز *yūsufi roz* (or يوسف زرّين رسن *yūsufi zarrīn-rasan*) The world-illuminating sun. يوسف زيبق نقاب *yūsufi zībak-nikāb*) The sun veiled by a cloud. يوسف گرگ مست *yūsufi gurgi mast*, A beloved object. يوسفي كردن *yūsufī kardan*, To reign.

T يوسون *yūsūn*, Custom, use, manner.

P يوسه *yosa*, A saw. A carpenter.

P يوش *yosh*, Seeking, hunting for. *Yūsh*, Dark.

A يوشع *yūshaʻ*, Joshua, the son of Nun.

P يوشيدن *yūshīdan*, To hear, to listen.

A يوصيّ *yawassīy*, (or يوصى *yūsa'*) A kind of hawk.

A يوطة *yūtat*, An iota, a jot.

P يوغ *yūgh* or *yogh*, A yoke for oxen.

P يوغيدن *yūghīdan*, To yoke oxen.

P يوك *yūk*, A roasting-spit. Old clothes or rags sewed together whereon bread is laid to be baked.

P يوگان *yūgān*, The womb. The membrane which enwraps the fœtus in the womb. Sheeps' chitterlings not cleaned.

P يولاخ *yūlākh*, A sterile country without water.

P يولچي *yūlchī*, A road-guide.

A يوم *yawm*, (pl. ايّام *ayyām*) A day, or twenty-four hours; (day in contradistinction to night being called نهار *nahār*). Time. A battle, especially one that makes a day celebrated. يوم بدر *yawmi badr*, (The day of Badr) A battle, famous in Arabia, gained by Muhammad. يوم الاحد *yawmu'l ahad*, First day, Sunday. يوم الاثنين *yawmu'l isnayn*, Second day, Monday. يوم الثلثاء *yawmu's salāsāʻ*, Third day, Tuesday. يوم الاربعاء *yawmu'l arbaʻāʻ*, Fourth day, Wednesday. يوم الخميس *yawmu'l khamīs*, Fifth day, Thursday. يوم الجمعة *yawmu'l jumʻat*, Day of meeting, Friday (the principal day of religious worship among the Muhammadans). يوم السبت *yawmu's sabt*, Sabbath-day, Saturday. يوم العاشوراء *yawmu'l ʻāshūrāʻ*, The tenth day of the month محرّم *muharram*. يوم التورية *yawmu't tawriyat*, The eighth day of the month ذي الحجة *zi'l hijja*. يوم عرفة *yawmi ʻarafat*, The ninth day of that month. يوم النحر *yawmu'n nahr*, (and يوم الاضحى *yawmu'l azha'*) The tenth day of that month. يوم القرّ *yawmu'l karr*, The eleventh day of the same month. يوم النفر *yawmu'n nafr*, (or يوم النفور *yawmu'n nufūr*) The twelfth day. يوم ايوم *yawmun aywamu*, A disastrous day. The last day of the month. The following words, preceded by يوم *yawm*, signify the day of judgment: القيام *al kiyām*, (القيمة or القيامة *al kiyāmat*) البعث *al baʻs*, الحشر *al hashr*, الميزان *al mīzān*, الدين *ad dīn*, الجواب *al jawāb*, السؤال *as suʻāl*, قرار *karār*, وعد *waʻd*, جزاء *jazāʻ*, حساب *hisāb*, ميثاق *mīsāk*, واقعة *wākiʻat*, قارعة *kāriʻa*, عهد *ʻahd*, عوض *ʻiwaz*, جمع *jamʻ*, فصل *fasl*, موعود *mawʻūd*, ميعاد *mīʻād*, and فزع الاكبر *fazaʻi'l akbar*. يوم حصاد *yawmi hasād*, Harvest-time. يوم العسر *yawmu'l ʻusr*, Day of affliction. يوم عيد *yawmi ʻīd*, A festival; Easter. يوماً واحداً *yawman wāhidan*, One day, *i.e.* never. يوما من الايّام *yawman mini'l ayyām*, One day amongst others. يوما فيوما *yawman fa yawman*, (or فيوما *fa yawman*) From day to day, de die in diem, without intermission, daily. *Yawma*, Then when. اليوم *al yawm*, To-day. اوّل يوم *awwal yawmin*, The first day. يوم يوم *yawma yawma*, Each day. كلّ يوم *kull yawm*, Every day. *Yawam*, (v. n. of يوم) Being disastrous (a day).

A يوما *yawman*, On a certain day.

A يوميّ *yawmīy*, (fem. يوميّة *yawmīyat*) Daily, diurnal; every day's, for one day. Daily pay, provisions, or any other allowance per day. اخراجات يوميّه *ikhrājāti yawmīya*, Daily expenses.

A يومئذ *yawmaʻizin*, Then, on that day.

A باب اليون *bābu'l yūn*, Babylon of Egypt, on the site of which Cairo is now built. (See قاهرة *kāhirat*.)

P يون *yūn*, A felt or woollen saddle-cloth. Colour. A shell. An obolus, small coin. Name of a river.

A يونان *yūnān*, Ionia. Greece; the Greek nation, from يون *yūn* or *yavan*, Son of Japhet. حكماي يونان *hukamāyi yūnān*, The sages of Greece.

A يونانيّ *yūnānīy*, One Grecian. Any thing Greek, Grecian. Hellenist.

P يونانيان *yūnāniyān*, The Grecians, Greeks.

A يونانيّة *yūnānīyat*, A Greek word, a Grecism, Hellenism.

P يونس *yūnas*, The prophet Jonah. شدن يونس در دهان ماهي *shudani yūnas dar dahāni māhī*, The descending of Jonah into the fish's belly, (metaphorically) sun-set.

P يونغار *yūnghār*, A three-stringed Turkish lute.

T يونيوس *yūniyūs*, June.

A يؤوس *yaʻūs*, Despondent, despairing, desperate.

P يوه *yūh*, (يوهر *yūhar*, or يوهه *yūha*) A kestrel, an inferior kind of hawk that cannot be trained.

A يؤيؤ *yuʻyuʻ*, (pl. يآئي *yaʻāʻī*) A kind of sparrow-hawk, a merlin.

P يهان *yahān*, (in zand and Pazand) God.

A يهديك الله *yahdīk'allāh*, God direct you! (said in answer to one who congratulates another when sneezing).

A يهر *yahr* or *yahar*, A large place. Litigation, importunity.

P يهر *yuhr*, Desire, eagerness.

P يهره *yuhra*, Desirous.

A يهفوف *yahfūf*, Timid, cowardly. Bold, intrepid. Foolish, stupid. Desert, uncultivated.

A يهكوك *yahkūk*, A foolish man.

A يهم *yaham*, Insanity, madness.

A يهماء *yahmāʻ*, (fem. of ايهم *ayham*) Foolish, stupid. Deaf. A trackless waste. A severe season.

A يهمور *yahmūr*, Verbose, prating, idly talkative. Much sand.

A يهود *yahūd*, (pl. يهدان *yuhdān*) A Jew. شرب اليهود *shurbu'l yahūd*, Drinking clandestinely (as the Jews are obliged to do their wine).

A يهودا *yahūdā*, Judah, Jacob's fourth son.

P يهودانه *yahūdāna*, Judaical. A strip of yellow cloth which the Jews are obliged to wear in some Muhammadan countries.

A يهوديّ *yahūdīy*, (fem. يهوديّة *yahūdīyat*) Hebrew, Jewish, Judaical. A Jew. A kind of sea-fish. P يهودي شدن *yahūdī shudan*, To play the Jew, to be avaricious, to cheat.

P يهوديان *yahūdiyān*, (pl. of يهودي *yahūdī*) Jews.

A يهوديّة *yahūdīyat*, Judea. Judaism.

A يهوديث *yahūdīs*, Judith.

A يهوذيّ *yahūzīy*, Judaical. A Jew.

P يهه *yuha*, A kestrel-hawk.

A يهيا *yahyā*, Used by a shepherd in calling to his companion at a distance, or to his camels.

P يهيدن *yahīdan*, To ruin, corrupt, destroy, demolish, erase.

A يهيرّ *yahyarr*, Hard (stone). A hard stone, one especially which resembles the hand. The gum of a tree called طلح *talh*, as being hard. A lump of gum. Any thing ludicrous or trifling. The vapour called سراب *sarāb*. A lie. Contention, litigation, dispute. The colocynth or wild gourd. Venom, poison. Name of an animal resembling a rat, but larger. اكذب من اليهيرّ *akzab mini'l yahyarr*, More fallacious than the mirage.

A يهيرّة *yahyarrat*, A camel whose milk flows spontaneously by reason of its abundance.

A يهيرّي *yahyarra'*, A hard stone. Much water. A foolish, trifling thing. A kind of plant.

A يهيهة *yahyahat*, (v. n. of يهيه Q) Calling to camels ياه ياه *yāh yāh*.

A يئس *yaʻis*, Despondent, despairing.

A ييعث *yayʻus*, A district of moving sands in Arabia Felix dangerous to travel through.

T ييلاق *yaylāk*, (or ييلا *yaylā*) Summer-quarters.

A يين *yayan*, The time between the first dawn and sun-rise. Name of a place in Arabia Felix, and of a district near Madina; also of a valley, a river, and a fountain.

ADDITIONAL.

ا

A اجامرة *ajāmirat*, Turbulent fellows.

A اجزل *ajzal*, More or most copious or eloquent.

A اختاجيّة *akhtājīyat*, Equerries, grooms.

T اختجي *akhtajī*, An equerry, groom.

T اخته بيگي *akhta-begī*, Grand equerry, master of the horse.

P اخته خانه *akhta-khāna*, A stable.

A ادرار *idrār*, (add) A scholarship, fellowship: exhibition, bursary.

P استخوان *ustukhwān*, (add) A race, nation.

P اولجه *ūlja*, (or اولجا *ūljā*) A prisoner.

A اهل اختيار *ahli ikhtiyār*, A patrician, one of the upper class.

ب

P باز *bāz*, (add) From, since.

P بازي *bāzī*, (add) The condition of, or pretensions to, the rank of a falcon.

A باشورة *bāshūrat*, (pl. بواشير *bawāshīr*) A bastion.

P بتا *butā*, (add) O idol (of my affections).

P بخشي *bakhshī*, (add) A writer, scribe, secretary. A surgeon. A vicegerent. An inspector. A grand falconer.

P بخشي گري *bakhshīgarī*, The office of secretary.

A بدري *badrī*, Plenilunar.

P بدمست *bad-mast*, (add) Ruttish.

P بدمستي *bad-mastī*, (add) Ruttishness.

A بدنة *badanat*, (add) Curtain (in fortification).

P برات ذمت *barātizimmat*, Innocence. Fidelity.

P برگردانيدن *bar gardānīdan*, To reverse, invert.

A بزاق *buzāk*, (add) A snail.

A بساطة *basātat*, (add) The state of a simple, uncompounded substance.

P بسيار بوده *bisyār būda*, It has often happened.

A بصاق *busāk*, (add) A snail.

A بعيد *baɛīd*, (add) Strange.

A بندقي *bunduḳīy*, (add) A fusileer.

A بندقية *bunduḳīyat*, A pistol.

A بياض *bayāz*, (add) A fair copy, any thing written out fair. P درېياض افتادن *dar bayāz uftādan*, To be written out.

P بي ثباتي *bī sabātī*, Instability. Fickleness.

P بي عاقبت *bī ɛāḳibat*, Lost, unhappy.

P بيناك *bīnāk*, Eye, vision.

پ

P پارس *pārs*, (add) A panther, ounce, cheeta.

P پارسجي *pārsjī*, One who has charge of panthers or cheetas.

P پدر فرزندي *pidar-farzandī*, Relationship of father and son. The paternal relationship.

P پرداختن *pardākhtan*, (add) To attend to, mind. To employ, devote.

P پناه آوردن *panāh āwardan*, To take refuge or shelter.

P پنجره *panjara*, (add) A lattice.

ت

A تحريص *tahrīs*, (add) Instigating, exciting, stimulating. Encouraging, animating.

P ترسائي *tarsāī*, Christianity.

P ترغو *turghū*, Meat and drink, provisions.

A تشريف *tashrīf*, (pl. تشاريف *tashārīf*) (add) A robe of honour.

A تفوق *tafawwuk*, (add) Superiority, ascendancy.

ج

P جادووش *jādūvash*, Like magic, bewitching.

P جاهي *jāhī*, Connected with rank or station.

P از جزئي وكلي *az juzī u kullī*, In whole and in part.

P جگردار *jigar-dār*, Bold, brave.

P جگرداري *jigar-dārī*, Boldness, bravery.

P جمازگان *jammāzagān*, (pl. of جمازه *jammāza*) Camels, dromedaries.

A جناية *jināyat*, (add) Remorse for sin.

چ

P چاره *chāra*, (add) Business, affairs. Power to dispense with, ability to do without.

P چاه *chāh*, (add) A prison, dungeon.

P چرخ *charkh*, (add) An arbalist.

P چرخي *charkhī*, (add) An arbalister.

P چشم زخم *chashm-zakhm*, (add) An eye-sore.

ح

A حجار *hajjār*, (add) A slinger of stones.

A حسودي *hasūdī*, Envy.

A حشاش *hashshāsh*, Addicted to the use of the inebriating electuary حشيش *hashīsh*.

A حشر *hashar*, (add) A troop, corps. Militia.

A حشري *hasharī*, A militiaman.

A حشيشي *hashīshīy*, An eater of the inebriating electuary حشيش *hashīsh*. An assassin.

P حقاني *hakkānī*, God-like, spiritual.

P حكيمانه *hakīmāna*, Wisely, judiciously.

A حمل *haml*, (pl. حمول *humūl*) (add) Revenue.

A حيوانية *haywānīyat*, Condition of an animal.

خ

P خامه راني *khāma-rānī*, Quill-driving, writing.

A خانية *khānīyat*, The rank of خان *khān*.

P خجل زده *khajal-zada*, Shame-stricken.

A خطاب *khitāb*, (add) A voice from heaven.

A خليطة *khalītat*, (add) A bag, a purse.

A خمر و زمر *khamr u zamr*, Wine and music.

A خمودة *khumūdat*, Stillness (of the eye).

P خندناك *khandnāk*, A laugher. Merry.

د

P داراد *dārād*, May he keep or maintain.

P دانستن *dānistan*, (add) To command, govern, fill a place.

A داوية *dāwiyat*, Knights Templars.

A دراسة *dirāsat*, (add) Instructing, lecturing.

P دست تهي *dast-tihī*, Empty-handed.

A دسومة *dusūmat*, (add) Greasiness.

A دواعي *dawāɛī*, (add) Calls, clamours, importunings, desires, hankerings.

P دوانيدن *dawānīdan*, (add) To send, despatch. To pursue.

ر

A رخوت *rukhūt*, (Ar. pl. of P رخت *rakht*) Baggages, traps. Goods, wares.

P رنجه كردن *ranja kardan*, To toil, labour.

A رنود *runūd*, (Ar. pl. of P رند *rind*) Knaves, ruffians.

ز

A زراق *zarrāk*, (add) An artificer.

P زناربند *zunnār-band*, Girt with a zone or girdle. An idolater.

P زنجير *zinjīr*, (add) Rippling surface of water.

P زود نويس *zūd-navīs*, A short-hand writer.

A زيادة *ziyādat*, (add) Extortion, oppression.

س

P ساختن *sākhtan*, (add) To suit, agree.

P سبقت گرفتن *sabahat giriftan*, To take the lead, to get precedence, to anticipate.

P ستم كاره *sitam-kāra*, An oppressor.

P سفلگي *siflagī*, Stinginess, meanness.

P سمجور *samjūr* or *sumjūr*, Poor, houseless.

A سمير *samīr*, (add) The inmost recess.

A سياق *siyāk*, (add) Arithmetic. Subject, topic. Manner, custom, way, mode, means.

A سياقة *siyāḳat*, (add) A subject.

P سيهي *siyahī*, Blackness.

ش

A شامل *shāmil*, (add) Comprehensive.

P شكنج *shikanj*, A wrinkle, crease.

P شوهركش *shawhar-kush*, Murderer of a husband.

ض

A ضعيف تركيب *zaɛīf-tarkīb*, Weak of structure.

ع

A عاقبة *ɛāḳibat*, (add) At least.

A عامر *ɛāmir*, (add) A builder.

A عوارف *ɛawārif*, (add) Acknowledgments.

غ

P غرض جوي *gharaz-joy* or *jūy*, Selfish, interested.

A غيرتي *ghayratī*, Jealous.

ف

A فتح الباب *fathu'l bāb*, Good result, success.

A فداوي *fidāwīy*, (add) A bravo, assassin.

A فداوية *fidāwīyat*, Self-sacrifice.

P فرزندي *farzandī*, The properties or qualities, state, nature, or condition of a child.

A فضول *fazūl*, Busy, meddling, officious.

A فوائت *fawāit*, Losses, things or opportunities that have escaped, missed, or been lost.

A فيض *fayz*, (add) Emanation.

ق

P قلبه *kalba*, (or قلبي *kalbī*) Bad money.

ك

P كاهانيدن *kāhānīdan*, To diminish.

P كشت ورزي *kisht-warzī*, Agriculture.

P كفايت شدن *kifāyat shudan*, To be accomplished or successful. كفايت كردن *kifāyat kardan*, To accomplish, prosper, render successful.

P كوتاه دستي *kotāh-dastī*, Moderation, honesty.

گ

P گرگاني *gurgānī*, Wolfish.

P گرم *garm*, Closely, strictly. Warmly, ardently. Anxiously. Kindly.

P گشتن *gashtan*, To saunter.

م

A ماجرائي *mā jarāī*, Relating to what had occurred or passed.

P مالش *mālish*, (add) Chastisement.

P مالي *mālī*, (add) Connected with wealth.

P مچلكاجي *muchalkājī*, One who writes out a مچلكا *muchalkā*.

A محمول *mahmūl*, (add) Laid, charged, imputed.

A مدابير *madābīr*, (pl. of مدبور *madbūr*) Sore-backed, wounded or galled in the back: (hence) unsound, unsafe, not trustworthy.

A مغتنمات *mughtanamāt*, Privileges.

A ملتمس *multamas*, Requested, begged. A request.

A ملهومون *malhūmūn*, (pl.) Inspired.